CW00704519

# Raceform

## FLAT ANNUAL FOR 1997

All The 1996 Returns

### The BHB's Official Form Book

Complete record of all Flat Racing in Great Britain from November 8th, 1995 to November 11th, 1996

Published by Raceform Ltd,
Compton, Newbury, Berkshire, RG20 6NL
Tel: 01635-578080
Fax: 01635-578101
Editorial: 01635-578643

Printed by BPC Wheatons, Hennock Road,
Exeter, DEVON EX2 8RP
01392-420222

Typeset by Raceform

Edited by Graham Wheldon



ISBN 1 901100 00 6

**£22.00**

# CONTENTS



As a result of the ever-increasing number of races within each season, and the larger number of British-trained horses racing abroad, the number of pages was getting close to the maximum number able to bind at the old size. Therefore, it has become necessary to change the format of the Raceform Annual to the A5 size already employed in the loose-leaf Form Book, and thus include the exclusive Note Book comments.

Raceform, The Official Form Book, is updated weekly. Subscribers receive a binder including a front section, which contains the Index to Performances and many other features, together with all the early racing. Weekly sections and a new index are threaded into the binder to keep it up to date.

The data contained in Raceform Annual for 1997 is available in paper form or on computer disk. The disk service contains the same data as Raceform, The Form Book, and operates on any PC within a 'Windows' environment. The database is designed to allow you to access the information in a number of different ways, and is extremely quick and easy to use.

Full details of all Raceform services and publications are available from Raceform, Compton, Newbury, Berkshire RG20 6NL.
Tel: 01635 578080 Fax: 01635 578101.

Cover Photo: Alan Johnson
Pentire wins the King George VI and Queen Elizabeth Diamond Stakes

RACE TITLE

RACE DISTANCE

RACE CONDITIONS

VALUE TO FIRST SIX

STALLS PER RACE

RACEFORM GOING ALLOWANCE PER RACE

RACE TIME AND OFF TIME

STARTING PRICE AND FAVOURITE INDICATOR

RACE NUMBER TO WHICH THE INDEX WILL REFER

RACEFORM RATING AWARDED FOR THIS PERFORMANCE

OFFICIAL HANDICAP RATING

SPEED FIGURE AWARDED FOR THIS PERFORMANCE

TIME TAKEN 0.08 QUICKER THAN RACEFORM STANDARD TIME

TRAINER/AGE/WEIGHT/HEADGEAR/JOCKEY/ALLOWANCE/OVERWEIGHT/DRAW

LONG HANDICAP WEIGHT

TOTAL STARTING PRICE PERCENTAGE

OFFICIAL WEIGHT-FOR-AGE

LAST RACE IN WHICH HORSE WARRANTED A NOTE-BOOK COMMENT

IN-FOCUS COMMENT HIGHLIGHTS FACTORS AFFECTING THE RACE

STARTING PRICE AND RELEVANT MARKET MOVES

EXCLUSIVE NOTE-BOOK COMMENT

TOTE DIVIDENDS

OWNER/TRAINER LOCATION/BREEDER

1148-**NEWMARKET** **(R-H) (Good to firm)**

**Saturday June 1st**

WEATHER: overcast; WIND: fresh half bhd

**1630** NGK SPARK PLUGS H'CAP (0-100) (3-Y-O +) (Class C)
4-45 (4-46) **5f (Rowley)** £5,848.00 (£1,744.00: £832.00: £376.00) Stalls: Centre GOING minus 0.40 sec per fur (F)

| | | | | SP | RR | SF |
|---|---|---|---|---|---|---|
| 1107[3] | **Top Banana (91)** (HCandy) **5-9-5** CRutter(4) (lw: hdwy over 1f out: qcknd to ld wl ins fnl f: rdn out) | — | **1** | 3/1[1] | 101 | 70 |
| 1178[4] | **Bowden Rose (83)** (MBlanshard) **4-8-11b** JQuinn(9) (chsd ldrs: led ins fnl f: sn hdd & unable qckn) | ½ | **2** | 7/1[3] | 91 | 60 |
| 13217 | **Croft Pool (100)** (JAGlover) **5-10-0** SDWilliams(10) (a.p: led 1f out: sn hdd & no ex) | ½ | **3** | 25/1 | 107 | 76 |
| 1178[10] | **Tart and a Half (79)** (BJMeehan) **4-8-7b** LDettori(12) (chsd ldrs: ev ch over 1f out: no ex ins fnl f) | hd | **4** | 6/1[2] | 86 | 55 |
| 1113[4] | **Sweet Magic (84)** (PHowling) **5-8-12** FNorton(2) (chsd ldrs: rdn & no ex appr fnl f) | ¾ | **5** | 6/1[2] | 88 | 57 |
| 1149[4] | **Cyrano's Lad (IRE) (89)** (CADwyer) **7-9-3** CDwyer(1) (led 4f: one pce) | s.h | **6** | 12/1 | 93 | 62 |
| 1113[13] | **Pride of Brixton (88)** (GLewis) **3-8-9** PatEddery(3) (dwlt: nvr nrr) | nk | **7** | 8/1 | 91 | 53 |
| 1321[3] | **Takadou (IRE) (95)**(MissLCSiddall) **5-9-9** JWeaver(6) (lw: nvr trbld ldrs) | ¾ | **8** | 12/1 | 96 | 65 |
| 1113[8] | **Laurel Delight (83)** (JBerry) **6-8-11** JCarroll(7) (b. nr fore: chsd ldrs over 3f) | 2 | **9** | 20/1 | 77 | 46 |
| 1446[9] | **Ashtina (68)** (BAPearce) **11-7-5**[(5)] MartinDwyer(8) (lw: outpcd) | 5 | **10** | 50/1 | 46 | 15 |
| 1186[7] | **Master of Passion (83)** (JMPEustace) **7-8-11** MTebbutt(5) (b: prom: stumbled after 2f: no ch after) | 2½ | **11** | 9/1 | 53++ | 22 |
| 1430* | **Sailormaite (85)** (SRBowring) **5-8-13b** DeanMcKeown (11) (ref to r. t.n.p.) | | **R** | 7/1[3] | — | — |
| | | | | (SP 125.6%) | **12 Rn** | |

**58.62 secs** (-0.08) CSF £24.45 CT £428.80 TOTE £3.40: £1.60 £2.30 £7.50 (£25.50) Trio £205.90 OWNER Major M. G. Wyatt (WANTAGE)
BRED Dunchurch Lodge Stud Co.
LONG HANDICAP Ashtina 7-8
WEIGHT FOR AGE 3yo-7lb

IN-FOCUS: **The stalls were placed in the centre for both sprints on the card, but were dominated by horses racing closer to either rail.**

**1107 Top Banana** found a fine turn of speed to pass the field in the last couple of furlongs and goes to Royal Ascot with every chance, although it must be remembered that he finished second in last year's Stewards' Cup off just 79. (3/1)

**1178 Bowden Rose**, who ran a cracker from a bad draw last time, went to post really well. Racing wide apart from the winner, she is having no luck and must surely win soon. (7/1: op 11/1)

**Croft Pool**, off a 12lb higher mark than he has ever won, ran a terrific race and would have prospects in listed company over this trip. (25/1)

**1064 Tart and a Half** is in good form at present but does not exactly make a habit of winning. (6/1)

**1113 Sweet Magic**, lightly-raced for a five-year-old, ran well and should soon find an opportunity. (6/1)

**1149 Cyrano's Lad (IRE)** ran well but found this trip too short. (12/1)

**1186 Master of Passion** lost all chance when clipping the heels of a rival and pulling off a front shoe. (9/1)

# RACEFORM
## The Official Form Book

**RACEFORM, THE OFFICIAL FORM BOOK,** records comprehensive race details of every domestic race, every French and Irish Group 1 and 2 race and every foreign event in which a British-trained runner participated. Extended notes are given to runners worthy of a mention, including all placed horses and all favourites. Generally speaking, the higher the class of race, the greater the number of runners noted.

**MEETING BACK REFERENCE NUMBER** is the Raceform number of the last meeting run at the track and is shown to the left of the course name. Abandoned meetings are signified by a †.

**THE OFFICIAL GOING**, shown at the head of each meeting, is recorded as follows:

| | |
|---|---|
| Turf: | Hard; Firm; Good to firm; Good; Good to soft; Soft; Heavy. |
| All-Weather: | Fast; Standard; Slow. |

**THE WEATHER** is shown below to the date.

**THE WIND** is given as a strength and direction, classified as follows:

| | |
|---|---|
| Strength: | gale; v.str; str; fresh; mod; slt; almost nil; nil. |
| Direction: | (half) against; (half) bhd; (half) across. |

**VISIBILITY** is good unless otherwise stated.

**RACEFORM GOING**, which may differ from the Official Going, now appears against each race to allow for changing conditions of the ground. It takes into account the race times compared with the Raceform Standard Times, the wind and other elements, and is recorded in the following stages:

| | |
|---|---|
| Turf: | **HD** (Hard); **F** (Firm); **GF** (Good to firm); **G** (Good); **GS** (Good to soft); **S** (Soft); **HY** (Heavy). |
| All-Weather: | **FST** (Fast); **STD** (Standard); **SLW** (Slow). |

**THE POSITION OF THE STARTING STALLS** is shown against each race, in the form of: High (H), Centre (C) or Low (L). The actual position of the stalls can make a vital difference to a runner's chances and reference should be made to the *Effect of the Draw* summary when assessing a horse's performance.

**THE RACE DISTANCE** is given for all races, and is accompanied by the suffix (st) for all races run on straight courses at those tracks where there is a round course of comparable distance. **(AWT)** after the distance signifies that such races were run on a Fibresand (Southwell or Wolverhampton) or Equitrack (Lingfield) surface.

**PRIZE MONEY** shows penalty values down to sixth place (where applicable).

**Competitive Racing Classifications** are shown on a scale from Class A to Class G. All Pattern races are Class A.

**Weight-For-Age** allowances are given where applicable for mixed-age races.

**Race Numbers** for Foreign races carry the suffix 'a'.

**In The Race Result,** the figures to the left of each horse show the race number of its most recent listing in Raceform. A figure in *italics* indicates the previous performance was recorded on an All-Weather course. The superscript figures indicate its finishing position in that race and are coded as follows:

> ***** - winner;
> **2..40** - finishing positions second to ninth;
> **b** - brought down; **c** - carried out; **f** - fell; **p** - pulled up;
> **r** - refused (to race); **ro** - ran out; **s** - slipped up; **u** - unseated rider;
> **v** - void race; **w** - withdrawn.

A figure to the left of the *Raceform Note-Book* comment is the last race in which the horse warranted an extended comment.

**The Adjusted Official Rating** is the figure in **bold type** directly after the horse's name in the race result. This figure indicates the Official BHB rating, at entry, after the following adjustments had been made:

(i) Overweight carried by the rider.
(ii) The number of pounds out of the handicap (if applicable).
(iii) Penalties incurred after the publication of the weights.

However, **no** adjustments have been made for:

(i) Weight-for-age.
(ii) Rider's claims.

**The Trainer** is shown in brackets for every runner.

**The Horse's age** is shown immediately before the weight carried.

**Weights** shown are actual weights carried. A figure next to the weight with ow is the amount of overweight put up by the jockey, e.g. ow4.
Allowances are shown between the weight and the jockey name, e.g. **8-10** (3) S. Copp

**Long Handicap Weights** for runners allotted a lower-than-minimum weight at entry **(handicaps only)** are shown directly under the commentary of the last horse in each race, and above the *Note-Book* comments.

**Apprentice Allowances** The holders of apprentice jockeys' licences under the provisions of Rule 60(iii) are permitted to claim the following allowances in Flat races:

7lb until they have won 20 Flat races run under the Rules of any recognised Turf Authority; thereafter 5lb until they have won 50 such Flat races; thereafter 3lb until they have won 95 such Flat races.
These allowances can be claimed in the Flat races set out below, with the exception of races confined to apprentice jockeys:

(a) All handicap and all selling races.
(b) All other races with guaranteed prize money of not more than £8000.

**HEADGEAR** is shown after the actual weight carried and expressed as: **b** (blinkers); **v** (visor); **h** (hood); **e** (eyeshield); **c** (eyecover).

**THE DRAW** for places at the start is shown after each jockey's name in brackets.

**THE OFFICIAL DISTANCES** between the first six horses are shown on the right-hand side immediately preceding their position at the finish. Distances beyond sixth place may be shown after inspection of race-finish photographs. Unknown positions are shown in saddle-cloth number order.

**STARTING PRICES (SP)** appear to the right of the finishing position in the race result. The favourite indicator appears to the right of the Starting Price, 1 for the favourite, 2 for the second-favourite and 3 for third-favourite.

**RACEFORM RATINGS (RR)**, which record the level of performance attained in this race for each horse, are given to the right of the starting price. Reference to the *Raceform Ratings* page should be made for a full description of this feature.

**SPEED FIGURES (SF)** now appear for every horse that clocks a sufficiently fast time, and appear in the column to the right of the *Raceform Ratings*. The figures are adjusted to 9st, and calculations made for going, wind, and distance behind the winner. To apply Speed Figures to future races, add 1 point for each 1lb below 9st, and deduct 1 point for each 1lb above 9st. The highest resultant figure is best.

**WITHDRAWN** horses that fail to come under orders after the jockey has weighed out, are included in the index to past racing (with W after the race number); side reference, odds at the time of withdrawal and the reason for withdrawal (if known) are shown in the race comment for that horse.

**RULE 4C TATTERSALL'S COMMITTEE RULES ON BETTING STATES:**

In the case of bets made at a price on the day of the race before it has been officially notified that a horse has been withdrawn before coming under Starter's Orders or has been declared "not to have started", the liability of a layer against any horse remaining in the race, win or place, will be reduced in accordance with the following scale depending on the odds current against the withdrawn horse at the time of such official notification:

(a) if the current odds are 30/100 or longer odds on by 75p in the £
(b) if shorter odds on than 30/100 up to and including 2/5 by 70p in £
(c) if shorter odds on than 2/5 up to and including 8/15 by 65p in the £

(d) if shorter odds on than 8/15 up to and including 8/13 by 60p in the £
(e) if shorter odds on than 8/13 up to and including 4/5 by 55p in the £
(f) if shorter odds on than 4/5 up to and including 20/21 by 50p in the £
(g) if shorter odds on than 20/21 up to and including 6/5 by 45p in the £
(h) if over 6/5 up to and including 6/4 by 40p in the £
(i) if over 6/4 up to and including 7/4 by 35p in the £
(j) if over 7/4 up to and including 9/4 by 30p in the £
(k) if over 9/4 up to and including 3/1 by 25p in the £
(l) if over 3/1 up to and including 4/1 by 20p in the £
(m) if over 4/1 up to and including 11/2 by 15p in the £
(n) if over 11/2 up to and including 9/1 by 10p in the £
(o) if over 9/1 up to and including 14/1 by 5p in the £
(p) if over 14/1 the liability would be unchanged
(q) in the case of two or more horses being withdrawn, the total deduction shall not exceed 75p in the £

Ante-post bets are not affected and SP bets are also not affected, except in cases where insufficient time arises for a fresh market to be formed, when the above named scale reductions will apply.

**STEWARDS' ENQUIRY**, except in special circumstances, is included only if it concerns a prize winner. Objections by jockeys and Officials are always included.

**OFFICIAL EXPLANATIONS** are included where the horse is deemed to have run well above or below expectation, unless the explanation is covered by the in-running comment.

**RACE TIMES** in Great Britain, (except official times which are electronically recorded and shown to 100th of a second), are clocked by Raceform's own watch-holders. Figures in parentheses following the time show the number of seconds slower than the Raceform Standard Time for the course and distance.

**RACEFORM STANDARD AND RECORD TIMES** were originally compiled from times recorded on good to firm going after adjustments had been made for weights carried above or below a norm of 9st. Times equal to the standard are shown as (equals standard). Times under the standard are preceded by -, for instance, 1.8 seconds under the standard would be shown (-1.8). Record times are displayed either referring to the juvenile record (1.2 under 2y best) or to the overall record (1.2 under best).

**STARTING PRICE PERCENTAGE** is ranged right below the final finisher and gives the total SP percentage of all runners that competed.

**TOTE** prices include £1 stake. Dual Forecast dividends are shown in parentheses. The Tote Trio dividend is preceded by the word Trio. Jackpot, Placepot and Quadpot details appear at the end of the meeting to which they refer.

**THE OWNER** of the winner is shown immediately below the Tote returns together with the breeder, result of the auction for sellers, and details regarding any claimed horse. Friendly claims are not detailed.

# Abbreviations and their meanings

## Paddock comments

| | |
|---|---|
| gd sort | - well made, above average on looks |
| h.d.w | - has done well, improved in looks |
| wl grwn | - well grown, has filled to its frame |
| lengthy | - longer than average for its height |
| tall | - tall |
| rangy | - lengthy and tall but in proportion, covers a deal of ground |
| scope | - scope for physical development |
| str | - strong, powerful looking |
| w'like | - workmanlike, ordinary in looks |
| lt-f | - light-framed, not much substance |
| neat | - smallish, well put together |
| leggy | - long legs compared to body |
| angular | - unfurnished behind the saddle, not filled to frame |
| unf | - unfurnished in the midriff, not filled to frame |
| narrow | - not as wide as side appearance would suggest |
| small | - lacks any physical scope |
| nt grwn | - not grown |
| lw | - looked fit and well |
| bkwd | - backward in condition |
| t | - tubed |
| swtg | - sweating |
| b.(off fore or nr fore) | - bandaged in front |
| b.hind (off or nr) | - bandaged behind |

## At the start

| | |
|---|---|
| stdd s | - jockey purposely reins back the horse |
| dwlt | - missed the break and left for a short time |
| s.s | - slow to start, left longer than a horse that dwelt |
| s.i.s | - started on terms but took time to get going |
| ref to r | - either does not jump off, or travels a few yards and then stops |
| rel to r | - tries to pull itself up in mid-race |

## Position in the race

| | |
|---|---|
| led | - in lead on its own |
| disp ld | - upsides the leader |
| w ldr | - almost upsides the leader |
| w ldrs | - in a line of three or more disputing the lead |
| prom | - on the heels of the leaders, in the front third of the field |
| trckd ldr(s) | - just in behind the leaders giving impression that it could lead if asked |
| chsd ldr | - horse in second place |
| chsd clr ldrs | - horse heads main body of field behind two clear leaders |
| chsd ldrs | - horse is in the first four or five but making more of an effort to stay close to the pace than if it were tracking the leaders. |
| in tch | - close enough to have a chance |
| hdwy | - making ground on the leader |
| gd hdwy | - making ground quickly on the leader, could be a deliberate move |

| | |
|---|---|
| sme hdwy | - making some ground but no real impact on the race |
| stdy hdwy | - gradually making ground |
| ev ch | - upsides the leaders when the race starts in earnest |
| rr | - last of main group but not detached |
| bhd | - detached from the main body of runners |
| hld up | - restrained as a deliberate tactical move |
| nt rcvr | - lost all chance after interference, mistake etc. |
| wknd | - stride shortened as it began to tire |
| lost tch | - had been in the main body but a gap appeared as it tired |
| lost pl | - remains in main body of runners but lost several positions quickly |

## *Riding*

| | |
|---|---|
| effrt | - short-lived effort |
| pushed along | - received urgings with hands only, jockey not using legs |
| rdn | - received forceful urgings without use of whip, or jockey waving whip without making contact |
| drvn | - received forceful urgings, jockey putting in a lot of effort and using whip |
| hrd drvn | - jockey very animated, plenty of kicking, pushing and reminders |

## *Finishing Comments*

| | |
|---|---|
| jst failed | - closing rapidly on the winner and probably would have led a stride after the line |
| r.o | - jockey's efforts usually involved to produce an increase in pace without finding an appreciable turn of speed |
| r.o wl | - jockey's efforts usually involved to produce an obvious increase in pace without finding an appreciable turn of speed |
| unable qckn | - not visibly tiring but does not possess a sufficient change of pace |
| one pce | - not tiring but does not find a turn of speed, from a position further out than unable qckn |
| nt r.o | - did not consent to respond to pressure |
| styd on | - going on well towards the end, utilising stamina |
| nvr plcd to chal | - never apparently given the chance to make a challenge |
| nvr able to chal | - unable to produce a challenge without a specific reason |
| nvr nr to chal | - unable to produce a challenge, normally due to a slow start, stumbling etc. |
| nrst fin | - nearer to the winner in distance beaten than at any time since the race had begun in earnest |
| nvr nrr | - nearer to the winner position wise than at any time since the race had begun in earnest |
| rallied | - responded to pressure to come back with a chance having lost its place |
| no ex | - unable to sustain its run due to lack of strength or effort from the saddle, enthusiasm etc. |
| bttr for r | - likely to improve for the run and experience |
| rn green | - inclined to wander and falter through inexperience |
| too much to do | - left with too much leeway to make up |

## *Winning Comments*

| | |
|---|---|
| v.easily | - a great deal in hand |
| easily | - plenty in hand |
| comf | - something in hand, always holding the others |

| | |
|---|---|
| pushed out | - kept up to its work with hands and heels without jockey resorting to whip or kicking along and wins fairly comfortably |
| rdn out | - pushed and kicked out to the line |
| drvn out | - pushed and kicked out to the line, with the whip employed |
| all out | - nothing to spare, could not have found any more |
| jst hld on | - holding on to a rapidly diminishing lead, could not have found any more if passed |
| unchal | - must either make all or a majority of the running and not be challenged from an early stage |

# *Complete list of abbreviations*

a - always
a.p - always prominent
abt - about
appr - approaching
awrdd - awarded
b.b.v - broke blood-vessel
b.d - brought down
bdly - badly
bef - before
bhd - behind
bk - back
blkd - baulked
bmpd - bumped
bnd - bend
btn - beaten
bttr - better
c - came
ch - chance
chal - challenged
chsd - chased
circ - circuit
cl - close
clr - clear
comf - comfortably
cpld - coupled
crse - course
ct - caught
dismntd - dismounted
disp - disputed
dist - distance
div - division
drvn - driven
dwlt - dwelt
edgd - edged
effrt - effort
ent - entering
ev ch - every chance
ex - extra
f - furlong
fin - finished
fnd - found
fnl - final
fr - from
gd - good
gng - going
grad - gradually
grnd - ground
hd - head
hdd - headed
hdwy - headway
hld - held
hmpd - hampered
hrd rdn - hard ridden
imp - impression
ins - inside
j.b - jumped badly
jnd - joined
jst - just
kpt - kept
l - length
ld - lead
ldr - leader
lft - left
m - mile
m.n.s - made no show
mde - made
mid div - mid division
n.d - never dangerous
n.g.t - not go through
n.m.r - not much room
nk - neck
no ex - no extra
nr - near
nrr - nearer
nrst fin - nearest finish
nt - not
nvr - never
one pce - one pace
out - from finish
outpcd - outpaced
p.u - pulled up
pce - pace
pl - place
plcd - placed
plld - pulled
press - pressure
prog - progress
prom - prominent
qckly - quickly
qckn - quicken
r - race
racd - raced
rch - reach
rcvr - recover
rdn - ridden
rdr - rider
reard - reared
ref - refused
rn - ran
rnd - round
r.o - ran on
rr - rear
rspnse - response
rt - right
s - start
slt - slight
sme - some
sn - soon
spd - speed
st - straight
stdd - steadied
stdy - steady
styd - stayed
swtchd - switched
swvd - swerved
t.o - tailed off
tch - touch
thrght - throughout
trckd - tracked
u.p - under pressure
w - with
w.r.s - whipped round start
wd - wide
whn - when
wknd - weakened
wl - well
wnr - winner
wnt - went
½-wy - halfway

## RACEFORM TOP RATED THREE-YEAR-OLDS AND UPWARDS OF 1996

| | |
|---|---|
| Mark of Esteem (IRE) | 138 |
| Helissio | 136 |
| Bosra Sham (USA) | 134 |
| Halling (USA) | 134 |
| Ashkalani (IRE) | 132 |
| Spinning World (USA) | 132 |
| Pilsudski (IRE) | 132 |
| Pentire (GB) | 132 |
| Singspiel (IRE) | 131 |
| Even Top (IRE) | 131 |
| Oscar Schindler (IRE) | 130 |
| Classic Cliche (IRE) | 130 |
| First Island (IRE) | 129 |
| Valanour (IRE) | 129 |
| Gabr | 129 |
| Anabaa (USA) | 129 |
| Swain (IRE) | 129 |
| Bijou d'Inde | 129 |
| Vetheuil (USA) | 129 |
| Posidonas (GB) | 129 |
| Shaamit (IRE) | 129 |
| Soviet Line (IRE) | 128 |
| Luso (GB) | 128 |

## RACEFORM TOP RATED TWO-YEAR-OLDS OF 1996

| | |
|---|---|
| Revoque (IRE) | 114 |
| Putra (USA) | 113 |
| Abou Zouz (USA) | 112 |
| Sahm (USA) | 112 |
| Easycall | 112 |
| Dazzle | 112 |
| Compton Place | 111 |
| Red Camellia | 111 |
| Medaaly | 111 |
| Bahhare (USA) | 111 |
| Bahamian Bounty | 110 |
| Reams of Verse (USA) | 110 |
| Zamindar (USA) | 110 |
| Poteen (USA) | 110 |
| Muchea | 109 |
| Tipsy Creek (USA) | 109 |
| Benny The Dip (USA) | 109 |
| Indian Rocket | 108 |
| Khassah | 108 |
| Elegant Warning (IRE) | 108 |
| Desert Story (IRE) | 108 |
| Falkenham | 107 |

# RACEFORM RATINGS

**Raceform Ratings for each horse are listed after the Starting Price and indicate the actual level of performance attained in that race. The figure in the back index represents the BEST public form that our Handicappers still believe each horse is capable of reproducing.**

To use the ratings constructively in determining those horses best-in in future events, the following procedure should be followed:

(i) In races where all runners are the same age and are set to carry the same weight, no calculations are necessary. The horse with the highest rating is the horse best in.

(ii) In races where all runners are the same age but are set to carry different weights, add one point to the Raceform rating for every pound less than 10 stone to be carried, deduct one point for every pound more than 10 stone.

For example

| Horse | Age & weight | Adjustment from 10 stone | RR base Rating | Adjusted Rating |
|---|---|---|---|---|
| Chiffchaff | 3-10-1 | -1 | 78 | 77 |
| Fulmar | 3-9-13 | +1 | 80 | 81 |
| Willow Warbler | 3-9-7 | +7 | 71 | 78 |
| Dunnock | 3-8-11 | +17 | 60 | 77 |

***Therefore Fulmar is top-rated (best-in)***

(iii) In races concerning horses of different ages the procedure in example (ii) should again be followed, but reference must also be made to the Official Scale of Weight-For-Age (see page facing).

For example

12 furlongs July 20th

| Horse | Age & weight | Adjust fr 10 st | RPH Rating | Adjust Rating | W-F-A deduct | Final Rating |
|---|---|---|---|---|---|---|
| Treecreeper | 5-10-0 | 0 | 90 | 90 | Nil | 90 |
| Siskin | 4-9-9 | +5 | 83 | 88 | Nil | 88 |
| Ringed Plover | 3-9-4 | +10 | 85 | 95 | -12 | 83 |
| Gadwall | 4-8-7 | +21 | 73 | 94 | Nil | 94 |

***Therefore Gadwall is top-rated (best-in)***

(A 3-y.o is deemed 12lb less mature than a 4-y.o or older horse on 20th July over 12f. Therefore, the deduction of 12 points is necessary).

The following symbols are used in conjunction with the ratings:

++ almost certain to prove better
\+ likely to prove better
**d** disappointing (has run well below best recently)
**?** form hard to evaluate - rating may prove unreliable
**t** tentative rating based on race-time

**Weight adjusted ratings for every race are published daily in Raceform Private Handicap. For subscription terms please contact the Subscription Department on 01635-578080.**

# THE OFFICIAL SCALE OF WEIGHT, AGE & DISTANCE (Flat)

**The following scale of weight-for-age should be used only in conjunction with the Official ratings published in this book. Use of any other scale will introduce errors into calculations. The allowances are expressed as the number of pounds that is deemed the average horse in each group falls short of maturity at different dates and distances.**

| Distance Furlongs | Age | JAN 1/15 | JAN 16/31 | FEB 1/14 | FEB 15/28 | MARCH 1/15 | MARCH 16/31 | APRIL 1/15 | APRIL 16/30 | MAY 1/15 | MAY 16/31 | JUNE 1/15 | JUNE 16/30 | JULY 1/15 | JULY 16/31 | AUGUST 1/15 | AUGUST 16/31 | SEPT 1/15 | SEPT 16/30 | OCT 1/15 | OCT 16/31 | NOV 1/15 | NOV 16/30 | DEC 1/15 | DEC 16/31 |
|---|---|---|---|---|---|---|---|---|---|---|---|---|---|---|---|---|---|---|---|---|---|---|---|---|---|
| 5 | 2 | – | – | – | – | – | 47 | 44 | 41 | 38 | 36 | 34 | 32 | 30 | 28 | 26 | 24 | 22 | 20 | 19 | 18 | 17 | 17 | 16 | 16 |
| | 3 | 15 | 15 | 14 | 14 | 13 | 12 | 11 | 10 | 9 | 8 | 7 | 6 | 5 | 4 | 3 | 2 | 1 | 1 | – | – | – | – | – | – |
| 6 | 2 | – | – | – | – | – | – | – | – | 44 | 41 | 38 | 36 | 33 | 31 | 28 | 26 | 24 | 22 | 21 | 20 | 19 | 18 | 17 | 17 |
| | 3 | 16 | 16 | 15 | 15 | 14 | 13 | 12 | 11 | 10 | 9 | 8 | 7 | 6 | 5 | 4 | 3 | 2 | 2 | 1 | 1 | – | – | – | – |
| 7 | 2 | – | – | – | – | – | – | – | – | – | – | – | – | 38 | 35 | 32 | 30 | 27 | 25 | 23 | 22 | 21 | 20 | 19 | 19 |
| | 3 | 18 | 18 | 17 | 17 | 16 | 15 | 14 | 13 | 12 | 11 | 10 | 9 | 8 | 7 | 6 | 5 | 4 | 3 | 2 | 2 | 1 | 1 | – | – |
| 8 | 2 | – | – | – | – | – | – | – | – | – | – | – | – | – | – | 37 | 34 | 31 | 28 | 26 | 24 | 23 | 22 | 21 | 20 |
| | 3 | 20 | 20 | 19 | 19 | 18 | 17 | 15 | 14 | 13 | 12 | 11 | 10 | 9 | 8 | 7 | 6 | 5 | 4 | 3 | 3 | 2 | 2 | 1 | 1 |
| 9 | 3 | 22 | 22 | 21 | 21 | 20 | 19 | 17 | 15 | 14 | 13 | 12 | 11 | 10 | 9 | 8 | 7 | 6 | 5 | 4 | 4 | 3 | 3 | 2 | 2 |
| | 4 | 1 | 1 | – | – | – | – | – | – | – | – | – | – | – | – | – | – | – | – | – | – | – | – | – | – |
| 10 | 3 | 23 | 23 | 22 | 22 | 21 | 20 | 19 | 17 | 15 | 14 | 13 | 12 | 11 | 10 | 9 | 8 | 7 | 6 | 5 | 5 | 4 | 4 | 3 | 3 |
| | 4 | 2 | 2 | 1 | 1 | – | – | – | – | – | – | – | – | – | – | – | – | – | – | – | – | – | – | – | – |
| 11 | 3 | 24 | 24 | 23 | 23 | 22 | 21 | 20 | 19 | 17 | 15 | 14 | 13 | 12 | 11 | 10 | 9 | 8 | 7 | 6 | 6 | 5 | 5 | 4 | 4 |
| | 4 | 3 | 3 | 2 | 2 | 1 | 1 | – | – | – | – | – | – | – | – | – | – | – | – | – | – | – | – | – | – |
| 12 | 3 | 25 | 25 | 24 | 24 | 23 | 22 | 21 | 20 | 19 | 17 | 15 | 14 | 13 | 12 | 11 | 10 | 9 | 8 | 7 | 7 | 6 | 6 | 5 | 5 |
| | 4 | 4 | 4 | 3 | 3 | 2 | 2 | 1 | 1 | – | – | – | – | – | – | – | – | – | – | – | – | – | – | – | – |
| 13 | 3 | 26 | 26 | 25 | 25 | 24 | 23 | 22 | 21 | 20 | 19 | 17 | 15 | 14 | 13 | 12 | 11 | 10 | 9 | 8 | 8 | 7 | 7 | 6 | 6 |
| | 4 | 5 | 5 | 4 | 4 | 3 | 3 | 2 | 1 | – | – | – | – | – | – | – | – | – | – | – | – | – | – | – | – |
| 14 | 3 | 27 | 27 | 26 | 26 | 25 | 24 | 23 | 22 | 21 | 20 | 19 | 17 | 15 | 14 | 13 | 12 | 11 | 10 | 9 | 9 | 8 | 8 | 7 | 7 |
| | 4 | 6 | 6 | 5 | 5 | 4 | 4 | 3 | 2 | 1 | – | – | – | – | – | – | – | – | – | – | – | – | – | – | – |
| 15 | 3 | 28 | 28 | 27 | 27 | 26 | 25 | 24 | 23 | 22 | 21 | 20 | 19 | 17 | 15 | 14 | 13 | 12 | 11 | 10 | 9 | 8 | 8 | 7 | 7 |
| | 4 | 6 | 6 | 5 | 5 | 4 | 4 | 3 | 3 | 2 | 1 | – | – | – | – | – | – | – | – | – | – | – | – | – | – |
| 16 | 3 | 29 | 29 | 28 | 28 | 27 | 26 | 25 | 24 | 23 | 22 | 21 | 20 | 19 | 17 | 15 | 14 | 13 | 12 | 11 | 10 | 9 | 9 | 8 | 8 |
| | 4 | 7 | 7 | 6 | 6 | 5 | 5 | 4 | 4 | 3 | 2 | 1 | – | – | – | – | – | – | – | – | – | – | – | – | – |
| 18 | 3 | 31 | 31 | 30 | 30 | 29 | 28 | 27 | 26 | 25 | 24 | 23 | 22 | 21 | 20 | 18 | 16 | 14 | 13 | 12 | 11 | 10 | 10 | 9 | 9 |
| | 4 | 8 | 8 | 7 | 7 | 6 | 6 | 5 | 5 | 4 | 3 | 2 | 1 | – | – | – | – | – | – | – | – | – | – | – | – |
| 20 | 3 | 33 | 33 | 32 | 32 | 31 | 30 | 29 | 28 | 27 | 26 | 25 | 24 | 23 | 22 | 20 | 18 | 16 | 14 | 13 | 12 | 11 | 11 | 10 | 10 |
| | 4 | 9 | 9 | 8 | 8 | 7 | 7 | 6 | 6 | 5 | 4 | 3 | 2 | 1 | – | – | – | – | – | – | – | – | – | – | – |

# *Raceform*

## WINTER
## RACING 1995

Complete record of Foreign Turf Racing and All-Weather from November 8th to December 31st, 1995

# 4293-LINGFIELD (L-H) (Standard)
## Wednesday November 8th
WEATHER: fair WIND: almost nil

## 4350 ROTHER APPRENTICE H'CAP (0-70) (I) (3-Y.O+) (Class F)
12-40 (12-43) **7f (Equitrack)** £2,266.50 (£644.00: £319.50) Stalls: Low GOING minus 0.43 sec per fur (FST)

| Form | Horse | Dist | Pos | SP | RR | SF |
|---|---|---|---|---|---|---|
| 3455[16] | **Fort Knox (IRE) (50)** (RMFlower) **4-8-8**ow1 CScudder(8) (hld up in rr: hdwy over 1f out: str run fnl f: led nr fin) | — | 1 | 10/1 | 53 | 26 |
| *3950[9]* | **Milos (65)** (TJNaughton) **4-9-9** TAshley(2) (mid div: hdwy over 3f out: led wl ins fnl f: hdd nr fin) | ½ | 2 | 100/30[2] | 68 | 41 |
| *3319[7]* | **Mr Frosty (64)** (WJarvis) **3-9-7** ElizabethTurner(6) (b.off hind: mid div: hdwy over 1f out: r.o strly fnl f) | s.h | 3 | 10/1 | 68 | 39 |
| *4297[10]* | **Invocation (70)** (AMoore) **8-10-0** ALakeman(10) (chsd ldr after 1f: rdn over 1f out: one pce) | 1½ | 4 | 25/1 | 69 | 42 |
| 4280[3] | **Slivovitz (54)** (MJHeaton-Ellis) **5-8-7v**(5) JFowle(11) (led after 1f: clr over 1f out: hdd wl ins fnl f: no ex) | hd | 5 | 9/1 | 53 | 26 |
| 4057[13] | **Pharaoh's Dancer (60)** (PBurgoyne) **8-9-4** DSweeney(5) (led 1f: chsd ldrs: rdn over 1f out: wknd ins fnl f) | ½ | 6 | 8/1[3] | 58 | 31 |
| 4138[4] | **Benjamins Law (47)** (JAPickering) **4-8-0**(5)ow3 JoanneWebster(1) (mid div whn hmpd on ins 5f out: sme hdwy over 2f out: rdn over 1f out: one pce) | 3½ | 7 | 20/1 | 34 | 7 |
| 3844[7] | **Astrojoy (IRE) (43)** (SGKnight) **3-8-0**ow1 MNutter(12) (b: s.i.s: sn rcvrd to chse ldrs: rdn 3f out: sn wknd) | s.h | 8 | 25/1 | 33 | 4 |
| 4157[21] | **Mutinique (40)** (BAPearce) **4-7-12**ow5 CLowther(13) (b.hind: reard s: sn rcvrd to chse ldrs: wknd over 2f out) | 1½ | 9 | 50/1 | 21 | — |
| 662[11] | **Miss Mercy (IRE) (64)** (CNAllen) **3-9-7** JoHunnam(7) (b.hind: bhd fnl 4f) | 8 | 10 | 20/1 | 33 | 4 |
| 1255[12] | **Pair of Jacks (IRE) (38)** (DAWilson) **5-7-5**(5)ow3 RachaelMoody(4) (dwlt: a bhd) | nk | 11 | 16/1 | 2 | — |
| *4297** | **Set the Fashion (73)** (DLWilliams) **6-10-3v** 7x RStudholme(3) (a bhd) | hd | 12 | 13/8[1] | 40 | 13 |
| 4225[17] | **Anjomajasa (41)** (JFfitch-Heyes) **3-7-7**(5)ow2 TField(9) (a bhd) | ¾ | 13 | 50/1 | 6 | — |

(SP 127.5%) **13 Rn**

**1m 25.62** (1.62) CSF £43.02 CT £325.05 TOTE £14.70: £3.90 £2.10 £2.20 (£52.20) Trio £133.80 OWNER Miss C. Markowiak (JEVINGTON) BRED Leo Collins
LONG HANDICAP Pair of Jacks (IRE) 7-5 Mutinique 7-6
WEIGHT FOR AGE 3yo-1lb

## 4351 ROTHER APPRENTICE H'CAP (0-70) (II) (3-Y.O+) (Class F)
1-10 (1-13) **7f (Equitrack)** £2,263.00 (£643.00: £319.00) Stalls: Low GOING minus 0.43 sec per fur (FST)

| Form | Horse | Dist | Pos | SP | RR | SF |
|---|---|---|---|---|---|---|
| *4297[4]* | **Dancing Heart (66)** (BJMeehan) **3-9-4b**(5) GHannon(10) (mde all: sn clr: unchal) | — | 1 | 5/1[2] | 84 | 49 |
| *4297[2]* | **Present Situation (68)** (LordHuntingdon) **4-9-7**(5) RFfrench(1) (mid div: hdwy 2f out: rdn over 1f out: chsd wnr ins fnl f: kpt on: no ch w wnr) | 4 | 2 | 5/6[1] | 76 | 43 |
| *4298[4]* | **Montone (IRE) (50)** (JRJenkins) **5-8-3**(5) SallyWall(6) (mid div whn rdn 4f out: r.o one pce fnl 2f) | 1½ | 3 | 12/1 | 54 | 21 |
| | **Old Hook (IRE) (71)** (PaulSmith,Belgium) **4-10-1** ALakeman(7) (prom: chsd wnr over 2f out tl ins fnl f: one pce) | 1¾ | 4 | 9/1[3] | 71 | 38 |
| *2600[5]* | **Woolverstone Hall (IRE) (44)** (DJGMurraySmith) **3-8-1** DSweeney(2) (chsd ldrs: hrd rdn over 1f out: one pce) | 1¼ | 5 | 12/1 | 43 | 8 |
| 4194[8] | **Blasted (59)** (RHannon) **3-9-2** EGreehy(8) (nvr nrr) | 4 | 6 | 9/1[3] | 48 | 13 |
| 4049[7] | **Barbrallen (41)** (DJSffrenchDavis) **3-7-12**ow3 RStudholme(9) (chsd wnr over 4f: wknd over 1f out) | hd | 7 | 33/1 | 27 | — |
| 3501[8] | **Myjinka (41)** (JO'Donoghue) **5-7-13b** GayeHarwood(11) (chsd ldrs: rdn 3f out: wknd 2f out) | 1½ | 8 | 16/1 | 26 | — |
| 4060[16] | **Green Golightly (USA) (46)** (DAWilson) **4-7-13**(5) RachaelMoody(12) (a bhd) | s.h | 9 | 20/1 | 31 | — |
| 3874[11] | **Face the Future (56)** (SDow) **6-8-9**(5) PBrookwood(5) (dwlt: a bhd) | 1½ | 10 | 16/1 | 37 | 4 |
| 4054[18] | **Air of Mystery (36)** (NEBerry) **3-7-7** JoHunnam(4) (a bhd) | ¾ | 11 | 50/1 | 17 | — |

(SP 128.0%) **11 Rn**

**1m 24.81** (0.81) CSF £9.88 CT £49.67 TOTE £7.40: £2.20 £1.30 £3.00 (£3.50) Trio £9.80 OWNER Vintage Services Ltd (UPPER LAMBOURN) BRED Vintage Services Ltd
WEIGHT FOR AGE 3yo-1lb

## 4352 E.B.F. WYE MAIDEN STKS (2-Y.O) (Class D)
1-40 (1-41) **1m (Equitrack)** £3,566.25 (£1,080.00: £527.50: £251.25) Stalls: High GOING minus 0.43 sec per fur (FST)

| Form | Horse | Dist | Pos | SP | RR | SF |
|---|---|---|---|---|---|---|
| 3752[2] | **Roman Gold (IRE) (78)** (RHannon) **2-9-0** RPerham(7) (lw: sn prom: rdn along: chsd ldr 5f out: led wl over 2f out: sn clr: v.easily) | — | 1 | 13/8[1] | 73+ | 44 |
| 4262[9] | **Fran Godfrey** (PTWalwyn) **2-8-9** DHarrison(3) (rr: hdwy 4f out: rdn 3f out: chsd wnr wl over 1f out: no imp) | 4 | 2 | 8/1 | 60 | 31 |
| 3873[9] | **Steamroller Stanly** (CACyzer) **2-9-0** GDuffield(6) (bit bkwd: sn rdn along in rr: hdwy 4f out: kpt on one pce fnl 2f) | 2½ | 3 | 16/1 | 60 | 31 |
| 4208[5] | **Laughing Buccaneer (63)** (BJMeehan) **2-9-0b** JFEgan(10) (lw: led: hdd wl over 2f out: wknd over 1f out) | 6 | 4 | 11/2[3] | 48 | 19 |
| 3917[9] | **Mountain Dream** (PFICole) **2-9-0** CRutter(9) (chsd ldrs: rdn 3f out: wknd 2f out) | 2½ | 5 | 8/1 | 43 | 14 |
| 4148[4] | **Reploy** (LordHuntingdon) **2-8-9** SSanders(1) (lw: rr & outpcd: rdn 4f out: nvr nrr) | 1¼ | 6 | 5/2[2] | 36 | 7 |
| 4107[8] | **Makaskamina (53)** (PhilipMitchell) **2-8-9**(5) CAdamson(4) (nvr nrr) | nk | 7 | 33/1 | 40 | 11 |
| 4129[12] | **Lord Ellangowan (IRE)** (RIngram) **2-9-0** WNewnes(8) (rdn after 2f: sn bhd: t.o) | 25 | 8 | 33/1 | — | — |
| | **Be Satisfied** (AMoore) **2-9-0** RCochrane(5) (unf: bit bkwd: bhd fnl 6f: t.o) | 6 | 9 | 33/1 | — | — |
| | **General Henry** (AMoore) **2-9-0** CandyMorris(11) (w'like: bkwd: s.s: a bhd: t.o) | 1¼ | 10 | 33/1 | — | — |
| | **Sakeen** (PaulSmith,Belgium) **2-9-0v** TIves(12) (chsd ldrs 3f: sn wknd: t.o) | 6 | 11 | 20/1 | — | — |

(SP 126.7%) **11 Rn**

**1m 38.24** (0.84) CSF £15.46 TOTE £2.60: £1.30 £2.20 £3.40 (£11.60) Trio £47.30 OWNER Mr George Teo (MARLBOROUGH) BRED Saffron Breeders Club

## 4353 MEDWAY CLAIMING STKS (2-Y.O) (Class E)
2-10 (2-11) **6f (Equitrack)** £3,066.80 (£928.40: £453.20: £215.60) Stalls: Low GOING minus 0.43 sec per fur (FST)

| Form | Horse | Dist | Pos | SP | RR | SF |
|---|---|---|---|---|---|---|
| 3895[5] | **Moi Canard (61)** (JBerry) **2-8-2**(5) PFessey(6) (hld up: hdwy over 2f out: hrd rdn over 1f out: led wl ins fnl f: r.o) | — | 1 | 4/1[3] | 66 | 23 |
| *4273[2]* | **Red Acuisle (IRE) (57)** (GLewis) **2-8-12**(5) AWhelan(3) (prom: chsd ldr 4f out: c sltly wd home turn: led over 1f out: hdd wl ins fnl f: unable qckn) | ½ | 2 | 3/1[2] | 75 | 32 |

| | Horse | Details | Dist | Pos | SP | RR | SF |
|---|---|---|---|---|---|---|---|
| 4219[5] | **Goldsearch (IRE) (74)** | (WAO'Gorman) **2-8-10** EmmaO'Gorman(1) (led: wnt sltly wd home turn: hdd over 1f out: one pce) | 1¾ | **3** | 9/4[1] | 63 | 20 |
| 3953[8] | **Wingnut (IRE) (48)** | (GLewis) **2-7-11**(5) MBaird(5) (chsd ldrs: rdn 3f out: one pce fnl 2f) | 3 | **4** | 8/1 | 47 | 4 |
| 4218[12] | **Rising Stream** | (SirMarkPrescott) **2-8-1**ow1 GDuffield(7) (dwlt: sn rdn along: nvr nrr) | 2½ | **5** | 12/1 | 38 | — |
| 4273[11] | **Jemsilverthorn (IRE) (49)** | (JJBridger) **2-7-12v**(7) ADaly(4) (chsd ldr 2f: hrd rdn over 2f out: sn wknd) | 1 | **6** | 25/1 | 41 | — |
| 4222[9] | **Casino Chip** | (TTClement) **2-8-0**(7) RMullen(8) (dwlt: a bhd) | 6 | **7** | 33/1 | 27 | — |
| 1938[13] | **Riviere Rouge** | (SGKnight) **2-8-1**(3) NVarley(2) (sn rdn along: a bhd) | 3 | **8** | 33/1 | 16 | — |
| 4144[19] | **Saint Rosalina (59)** | (CJHill) **2-8-0c** GBardwell(9) (bhd fnl 4f: t.o) | 30 | **9** | 13/2 | — | — |
| | | | | | (SP 117.6%) | **9 Rn** | |

**1m 12.9** (2.30) CSF £15.78 TOTE £4.10: £1.40 £1.60 £1.20 (£11.00) Trio £8.90 OWNER Bloy & Hughes (COCKERHAM) BRED Llety Stud
Moi Canard clmd by RJG Racing £5,000

## 4354 HOBSONS PUBLISHING PLC RATING RELATED MAIDEN STKS (0-65) (3-Y.O+) (Class F)

2-40 (2-41) **6f (Equitrack)** £2,713.40 (£762.40: £372.20) Stalls: Low GOING minus 0.43 sec per fur (FST)

| | Horse | Details | Dist | Pos | SP | RR | SF |
|---|---|---|---|---|---|---|---|
| 4150[6] | **Duke Valentino (64)** | (RHollinshead) **3-9-0** TIves(11) (rr: hdwy 3f out: led wl over 1f out: sn clr: r.o wl) | — | **1** | 9/4[2] | 64+ | 40 |
| 4071[13] | **Sadly Sober (IRE) (64)** | (PFICole) **3-8-9b** CRutter(6) (mid div: rdn 4f out: r.o one pce fnl 2f) | 8 | **2** | 13/8[1] | 38 | 14 |
| 4152[10] | **Vladivostok (37)** | (BdeHaan) **5-8-10**(5) MHenry(2) (chsd ldrs: hrd rdn over 1f out: one pce) | 1½ | **3** | 33/1 | 39 | 16 |
| 3800[9] | **Northern Grey (45)** | (JBerry) **3-8-7v**(7) PRoberts(10) (rr: rdn 3f out: nvr nrr) | nk | **4** | 15/2[3] | 38 | 14 |
| 4280[11] | **Fallal (IRE) (46)** | (KMcAuliffe) **3-8-9** GDuffield(5) (chsd ldrs: rdn 4f out: n.m.r 2f out: hrd rdn over 1f out: one pce) | s.h | **5** | 9/1 | 33 | 9 |
| 3980[24] | **Sound Trick (USA) (41)** | (GCBravery) **3-8-9v** SWhitworth(7) (outpcd & wl bhd: styd on fnl f: nvr nrr) | 5 | **6** | 25/1 | 19 | — |
| 3055[7] | **Il Furetto (22)** | (JSKing) **3-8-11**(3) NVarley(3) (led after 1f: hdd wl over 1f out: sn wknd) | 1½ | **7** | 66/1 | 20 | — |
| 4060[19] | **Sharp Holly (IRE) (50)** | (JABennett) **3-8-9** WNewnes(4) (prom over 2f) | nk | **8** | 14/1 | 15 | — |
| 4194[14] | **Risky Royal (55)** | (TJNaughton) **3-8-9**(5) JDSmith(8) (mid div: sn rdn along: wknd whn n.m.r 2f out) | 2½ | **9** | 10/1 | 13 | — |
| | **Diamond Bangle (30)** | (CCElsey) **3-8-9** RCochrane(9) (a bhd) | ¾ | **10** | 50/1 | 6 | — |
| | **Chocolate Chip (40)** | (BAPearce) **3-9-0** SSanders(1) (led 1f: wknd over 3f out: t.o) | dist | **11** | 66/1 | — | — |
| | | | | | (SP 118.1%) | **11 Rn** | |

**1m 12.13** (1.53) CSF £5.99 TOTE £3.30: £1.60 £1.10 £8.50 (£2.60) Trio £56.40 OWNER Mr J. E. Bigg (UPPER LONGDON) BRED Shadwell Estate Company Limited

## 4355 SALAMANDER BOOKS H'CAP (0-65) (3-Y.O+) (Class F)

3-10 (3-10) **2m (Equitrack)** £2,877.20 (£809.20: £395.60) Stalls: Low GOING minus 0.76 sec per fur (FST)

| | Horse | Details | Dist | Pos | SP | RR | SF |
|---|---|---|---|---|---|---|---|
| 4126[3] | **Jaraab (58)** | (GLewis) **4-9-10v** SWhitworth(9) (chsd ldrs: hrd rdn 5f out: led 3f out: drvn clr over 1f out: r.o) | — | **1** | 6/1[3] | 67 | 52 |
| 4289* | **La Brief (46)** | (MJRyan) **3-8-3** 5x GBardwell(10) (rdn virtually thrght: rr: hdwy 5f out: hrd rdn fnl 2f: styd on strly fnl f) | ½ | **2** | 5/1[2] | 56 | 31 |
| 4326[8] | **Coleridge (37)** | (JJSheehan) **7-8-0b**(3) NVarley(13) (rr: hdwy over 4f out: hrd rdn fnl 2f: r.o) | 2 | **3** | 9/2[1] | 44 | 29 |
| 4223[5] | **Exhibit Air (IRE) (57)** | (RAkehurst) **5-9-9b** SSanders(6) (led: hdd 3f out: wknd fnl f) | 4 | **4** | 5/1[2] | 60 | 45 |
| 3682[2] | **Upper Mount Clair (48)** | (CEBrittain) **5-8-9**(5) MHenry(8) (chsd ldrs: rdn & outpcd 4f out: styd on again fnl f) | ¾ | **5** | 9/2[1] | 50 | 35 |
| 3318[2] | **Endless Fantasy (47)** | (CACyzer) **3-8-4** WWoods(3) (chsd ldr over 12f: hrd rdn 2f out: sn wknd) | 2½ | **6** | 20/1 | 47 | 22 |
| 4315[3] | **Doddington Flyer (51)** | (RHollinshead) **3-8-8** RCochrane(11) (hld up: sme hdwy 4f out: sn hrd rdn: no imp) | 11 | **7** | 9/1 | 40 | 15 |
| 3318[6] | **Hever Golf Lady (51)** | (TJNaughton) **3-8-8** DHarrison(5) (mid div: rdn 5f out: sn bhd) | nk | **8** | 9/1 | 40 | 15 |
| 3544[7] | **Kentavrus Way (IRE) (32)** | (AMoore) **4-7-12** NAdams(14) (rr: sme hdwy 4f out: sn rdn & btn) | 3½ | **9** | 50/1 | 16 | 1 |
| 4293[3] | **What's Secreto (USA) (49)** | (PAKelleway) **3-8-1v**(5) AWhelan(2) (dwlt: sn rcvrd into mid div: wknd over 4f out) | ½ | **10** | 20/1 | 34 | 9 |
| 2359[3] | **Ismeno (55)** | (SDow) **4-9-0**(7) ADaly(4) (bhd fnl 5f) | 1¾ | **11** | 25/1 | 37 | 22 |
| 4193[14] | **Access Carnival (IRE) (48)** | (RBoss) **4-9-0** GDuffield(12) (unf: rdn 5f out: sn wknd) | 8 | **12** | 40/1 | 22 | 7 |
| 3778[9] | **Docklands Courier (50)** | (BJMcMath) **3-8-7** MRimmer(1) (prom 9f) | 3½ | **13** | 25/1 | 22 | — |
| 4293[5] | **Don't Give Up (33)** | (PBurgoyne) **7-7-13b** JQuinn(7) (sn rdn along: a bhd) | 3 | **14** | 25/1 | 1 | — |
| | | | | | (SP 129.4%) | **14 Rn** | |

**3m 22.76** (0.76) CSF £36.01 CT £140.64 TOTE £9.00: £1.80 £3.10 £2.50 (£19.30) Trio £57.60 OWNER Mr S. I. Ross (EPSOM) BRED Shadwell Estate Company Limited
WEIGHT FOR AGE 3yo-9lb

## 4356 THAMES H'CAP (0-85) (3-Y.O+) (Class D)

3-40 (3-42) **1m 2f (Equitrack)** £3,724.50 (£1,128.00: £551.00: £262.50) Stalls: Low GOING minus 0.43 sec per fur (FST)

| | Horse | Details | Dist | Pos | SP | RR | SF |
|---|---|---|---|---|---|---|---|
| 4149[17] | **River Keen (IRE) (73)** | (RWArmstrong) **3-9-3** WWoods(3) (hld up: hdwy over 3f out: led & edgd lft over 2f out: hrd rdn ins fnl f: r.o) | — | **1** | 10/1 | 80 | 55 |
| 4138[11] | **South Eastern Fred (79)** | (HJCollingridge) **4-9-13** MRimmer(5) (mid div: hdwy gng wl 3f out: ev ch whn hmpd over 2f out: rdn over 1f out: r.o) | 1 | **2** | 9/2[2] | 83 | 63 |
| 4149[5] | **Dance So Suite (61)** | (PFICole) **3-8-5** CRutter(4) (rr: rdn 5f out: hdwy over 3f out: drvn over 1f out: one pce) | 5 | **3** | 2/1[1] | 58 | 33 |
| 4205[2] | **Magic Junction (USA) (80)** | (LordHuntingdon) **4-10-0** DHarrison(9) (mid div: hdwy u.p 5f out: rdn over 2f out: one pce) | 6 | **4** | 6/1[3] | 67 | 47 |
| 3769[12] | **One Off the Rail (USA) (70)** | (AMoore) **5-9-4** CandyMorris(1) (chsd ldrs tl wknd over 2f out) | ½ | **5** | 14/1 | 56 | 36 |
| 3840[7] | **Talented Ting (IRE) (57)** | (PHaslam) **6-8-5** DeanMcKeown(6) (led over 6f: wknd over 2f out) | 1¾ | **6** | 8/1 | 40 | 20 |
| 4229[8] | **Kintwyn (74)** | (CCElsey) **5-9-8** RCochrane(2) (dwlt: a bhd) | 13 | **7** | 16/1 | 36 | 16 |
| 3859[2] | **Balasara (IRE) (73)** | (DRCElsworth) **5-9-2b**(5) AProcter(11) (chsd ldrs tl wknd over 2f out) | 2½ | **8** | 12/1 | 31 | 11 |
| 3898[14] | **Able Choice (IRE) (77)** | (RWArmstrong) **5-9-11** RPrice(7) (mid div: hdwy 5f out: led over 3f out: wkng whn bdly hmpd over 2f out) | 2½ | **9** | 14/1 | 31 | 11 |
| 4217[7] | **Scissor Ridge (51)** | (JJBridger) **3-7-4**(5)ow1 MBaird(12) (prom over 6f) | ¾ | **10** | 20/1 | 4 | — |
| 4297[9] | **Scharnhorst (65)** | (SDow) **3-8-2**(7) ADaly(8) (prom tl wknd qckly over 2f out: p.u & dsmntd ins fnl f) | | **P** | 25/1 | — | — |
| | | | | | (SP 121.5%) | **11 Rn** | |

**2m 4.38** (0.08) CSF £52.15 CT £117.16 TOTE £12.20: £4.80 £2.70 £1.50 (£38.20) Trio £78.90 OWNER Dr Meou Tsen Geoffrey Yeh (NEWMARKET) BRED Ballylinch Stud Ltd
WEIGHT FOR AGE 3yo-4lb

T/Jkpt: Not won; £2,664.40 to Kelso 9/11/95. T/Plpt: £49.00 (245.52 Tckts). T/Qdpt: £10.50 (7.9 Tckts). SM

# 4350-LINGFIELD (L-H) (Standard)
## Friday November 10th

## 4357 LEVIATHAN CLAIMING STKS (I) (3-Y.O+) (Class F)
12-10 (12-17) **7f (Equitrack)** £1,771.00 (£496.00: £241.00) Stalls: High GOING minus 0.09 sec per fur (STD)

| Form | Horse | Dist | Pos | SP | RR | SF |
|---|---|---|---|---|---|---|
| *4298*[3] | **Masnun (USA) (62)** (RJO'Sullivan) **10-8-11** AClark(2) (hld up in tch: chsd ldr over 2f out: led over 1f out: rdn ins fnl f: r.o) | — | 1 | 5/2[1] | 62 | 13 |
| *4350*[2] | **Milos (65)** (TJNaughton) **4-9-0**(7) TAshley(8) (lw: chsd ldrs: rdn over 1f out: r.o ins fnl f) | ½ | 2 | 7/2[3] | 71 | 22 |
| 1785[10] | **Apollo Red (50)** (AMoore) **6-8-11** CandyMorris(14) (led: hdd over 1f out: one pce) | ¾ | 3 | 25/1 | 59 | 10 |
| 4240[6] | **Our Shadee (USA) (58)** (KTIvory) **5-8-13v** DBiggs(16) (mid div: hdwy over 2f out: rdn over 1f out: one pce) | 1¾ | 4 | 9/1 | 57 | 8 |
| 2134[6] | **Perilous Plight (75)** (WRMuir) **4-9-7** DHarrison(12) (hld up: hmpd 5f out: rdn & hdwy over 2f out: r.o one pce) | 2½ | 5 | 3/1[2] | 59 | 10 |
| 3800[12] | **Random (58)** (CJames) **4-8-4** AMcGlone(7) (hld up: hdwy over 2f out: rdn over 1f out: one pce) | 2½ | 6 | 15/2 | 37 | — |
| 4240[9] | **Zuno Flyer (USA) (34)** (GLewis) **3-8-0**(5) AWhelan(15) (nvr nrr) | 2½ | 7 | 33/1 | 34 | — |
| *2963*[4] | **Jersey Belle (48)** (PJMakin) **3-8-2** GDuffield(5) (nvr nrr) | 3½ | 8 | 14/1 | 23 | — |
| 2661[9] | **Scboo** (REPeacock) **6-8-11** WNewnes(13) (s.i.s: hdwy on outside ½-wy: wknd 3f out) | 3½ | 9 | 66/1 | 22 | — |
| *4350*[9] | **Mutinique (34)** (BAPearce) **4-7-11**(7) CLowther(6) (bhd fnl 5f) | 2½ | 10 | 66/1 | 9 | — |
| 503[16] | **Supercool (43)** (DWChapman) **4-8-5** ACulhane(3) (bhd fnl 3f) | nk | 11 | 33/1 | 10 | — |
| *394*[9] | **Pretty Scarce** (BPreece) **4-8-0** NAdams(11) (dwlt: a bhd) | 2 | 12 | 66/1 | — | — |
| 4053[12] | **Try-Haitai (IRE) (49)** (RAkehurst) **4-8-9** SSanders(4) (prom: chsd ldr over 3f out tl over 2f out: sn rdn & wknd) | 4 | 13 | 16/1 | — | — |
| 3859[7] | **Wendals Touch (38)** (RMFlower) **4-8-4** JFEgan(9) (chsd ldrs 2f) | 5 | 14 | 50/1 | — | — |
| *2141*[8] | **Night Excellence** (CWeedon) **3-8-13** RHughes(1) (bit bkwd: chsd ldrs 2f: sn wknd) | 3 | 15 | 33/1 | — | — |

(SP 129.2%) **15 Rn**

**1m 29.29** (5.29) CSF £11.89 TOTE £4.40: £2.90 £1.00 £10.20 (£8.30) Trio £57.10 OWNER Mr I. W. Page (WHITCOMBE) BRED Glencrest Farm
WEIGHT FOR AGE 3yo-1lb

## 4358 EAGLE H'CAP (0-70) (I) (3-Y.O+) (Class E)
12-40 (12-47) **5f (Equitrack)** £1,882.00 (£527.00: £256.00) Stalls: High GOING minus 0.09 sec per fur (STD)

| Form | Horse | Dist | Pos | SP | RR | SF |
|---|---|---|---|---|---|---|
| 3878[19] | **Anytime Baby (46)** (PTDalton) **3-8-10** JFEgan(3) (in rr & rdn along: hdwy 2f out: hrd rdn over 1f out: led wl ins fnl f: r.o) | — | 1 | 20/1 | 53 | 21 |
| 4268[13] | **Spectacle Jim (47)** (JO'Donoghue) **6-8-8b**(3) PMcCabe(1) (outpcd & bhd: hdwy over 1f out: swtchd rt ins fnl f: sn ev ch: unable qckn) | ½ | 2 | 12/1 | 52 | 20 |
| 3961[11] | **Rocky Two (53)** (PHowling) **4-9-3b** JQuinn(6) (a.p: chsd ldr over 2f out: led ins fnl f: sn hdd: one pce) | 1¼ | 3 | 14/1 | 54 | 22 |
| *4295*[7] | **Halliard (58)** (TMJones) **4-9-8** MRimmer(8) (chsd ldrs: hrd rdn over 2f out: one pce) | 3 | 4 | 9/2[3] | 50 | 18 |
| *3524*[6] | **Daaniera (IRE) (50)** (PHowling) **5-8-11b**(3) DWright(5) (led tl hdd & wknd ins fnl f) | 1½ | 5 | 7/2[2] | 37 | 5 |
| 3919[12] | **Bonny Melody (40)** (PDEvans) **4-7-11**(7) AmandaSanders(10) (chsd ldrs: rdn 3f out: one pce fnl 2f) | ½ | 6 | 12/1 | 25 | — |
| *4274** | **Another Batchworth (60)** (SMellor) **3-9-10** CRutter(7) (chsd ldrs: rdn 2f out: 5th whn bdly hmpd ins fnl f: nt rcvr) | s.h | 7 | 5/2[1] | 45 | 13 |
| 4278[7] | **Bajan Frontier (IRE) (43)** (FHLee) **3-8-7** AMcGlone(9) (prom tl wknd over 1f out: btn whn n.m.r ins fnl f) | ½ | 8 | 8/1 | 27 | — |
| 4280[9] | **Light Movement (IRE) (44)** (WSCunningham) **5-8-8** DaleGibson(4) (a bhd) | 15 | 9 | 20/1 | — | — |
| *4272*[11] | **Newbury Coat (60)** (BPreece) **5-9-10b** NAdams(2) (sn outpcd) | 1½ | 10 | 16/1 | — | — |

(SP 117.5%) **10 Rn**

**62.07 secs** (4.07) CSF £205.38 CT £3,089.61 TOTE £29.80: £4.60 £2.00 £3.10 (£127.50) Trio £200.10 OWNER Messinger Stud Ltd (BURTON-ON-TRENT) BRED Messinger Stud Ltd

## 4359 EAGLE H'CAP (0-70) (II) (3-Y.O+) (Class E)
1-10 (1-14) **5f (Equitrack)** £1,871.50 (£524.00: £254.50) Stalls: High GOING minus 0.09 sec per fur (STD)

| Form | Horse | Dist | Pos | SP | RR | SF |
|---|---|---|---|---|---|---|
| *4295** | **Friendly Brave (USA) (67)** (MissGayKelleway) **5-9-6**(5) 7x AWhelan(4) (a.p: c wd over 1f out: led ins fnl f: r.o) | — | 1 | 11/4[2] | 73 | 49 |
| *4295*[5] | **Kalar (69)** (DWChapman) **6-9-13b** RHughes(2) (lw: led: hdd over 2f out: rn wd over 1f out: rdn ins fnl f: one pce) | 2½ | 2 | 13/2 | 67 | 43 |
| 1975[10] | **Perfect Brave (60)** (DRCElsworth) **4-8-13**(5) AProcter(5) (outpcd & bhd: gd hdwy fnl f: r.o) | ½ | 3 | 12/1 | 56 | 32 |
| *4295*[3] | **Tee-Emm (56)** (PHowling) **5-9-0** JQuinn(1) (lw: a.p: led over 2f out: hdd & wknd ins fnl f) | ¾ | 4 | 5/1[3] | 50 | 26 |
| 4322[14] | **Pearl Dawn (IRE) (51)** (GLMoore) **5-8-9** SWhitworth(8) (sn rdn along: chsd ldrs: hrd rdn 2f out: one pce) | 3 | 5 | 5/2[1] | 35 | 11 |
| 3874[5] | **Fascination Waltz (58)** (JJSheehan) **8-9-2** GDuffield(7) (rr: rdn 2f out: one pce) | ¾ | 6 | 16/1 | 40 | 16 |
| *2402*[5] | **Little Saboteur (67)** (PJMakin) **6-9-11** AClark(10) (in tch: rdn 3f out: wknd over 1f out) | 6 | 7 | 12/1 | 30 | 6 |
| *4128*[10] | **Hong Kong Dollar (56)** (BAPearce) **3-9-0** TIves(9) (sn outpcd: bhd fnl 3f) | 1½ | 8 | 25/1 | 14 | — |
| 3177[8] | **La Bossette (IRE) (40)** (RIngram) **3-7-12** AMackay(6) (s.s: a bhd) | 3 | 9 | 25/1 | — | — |
| 4194[20] | **It Is Now (37)** (SGollings) **3-7-9** GBardwell(3) (a bhd) | hd | 10 | 50/1 | — | — |

(SP 116.2%) **10 Rn**

**61.23 secs** (3.23) CSF £19.42 CT £166.11 TOTE £4.50: £1.80 £1.50 £2.60 (£9.70) Trio £17.70 OWNER Grid Thoroughbred Racing Partnership (WHITCOMBE) BRED Foxfield

## 4360 ALBION (S) STKS (2-Y.O) (Class G)
1-40 (1-43) **7f (Equitrack)** £1,683.00 (£473.00: £231.00) Stalls: High GOING minus 0.09 sec per fur (STD)

| Form | Horse | Dist | Pos | SP | RR | SF |
|---|---|---|---|---|---|---|
| 4243[5] | **Vera's First (IRE) (68)** (GLewis) **2-8-1b**(5) AWhelan(9) (lw: hld up in tch: led 2f out: hdd ins fnl f: hrd rdn: led again cl home) | — | 1 | 9/4[1] | 72 | — |
| 3623[12] | **Crimson And Clover (56)** (RAkehurst) **2-8-6** SSanders(11) (lw: a.p: led over 3f out: hdd 2f out: led again ins fnl f: hdd cl home) | s.h | 2 | 5/1[3] | 72 | — |
| 3988[6] | **Miss Pickpocket (IRE) (64)** (PAKelleway) **2-8-3**(3) JStack(13) (lw: hld up: hdwy over 3f out: ev ch over 2f out: sn rdn: one pce) | 4 | 3 | 4/1[2] | 63 | — |
| *4339*[6] | **Shanoora (IRE) (54)** (BPalling) **2-8-6** GCarter(6) (a.p: rdn over 1f out: one pce) | 1¼ | 4 | 14/1 | 60 | — |
| 3533[2] | **Bath Knight (47)** (DJSffrenchDavis) **2-8-11** RHughes(4) (mid div: rdn over 3f out: no hdwy) | 8 | 5 | 6/1 | 47 | — |
| 4130[9] | **Rowlandsons Charm (IRE) (60)** (GLMoore) **2-8-6v** MFenton(5) (nvr nrr) | 1¾ | 6 | 10/1 | 38 | — |

3856[8] **Phoenix House (60)** (GLMoore) **2-8-11** SWhitworth(3) (led over 3f)..........2 **7** 14/1 38 —
4133[12] **Boston Tea Party (40)** (AMoore) **2-8-6** CandyMorris(7) (nvr nrr)..........¾ **8** 25/1 31 —
2526[15] **Nottonitejosephine** (RBoss) **2-8-6** GDuffield(2) (bhd fnl 3f)..........s.h **9** 20/1 31 —
644[W] **Deaken Dancer** (KTIvory) **2-8-6** DBiggs(10) (chsd ldrs 4f)..........1½ **10** 20/1 28 —
*4339*[5] **Hurricane Horn (IRE) (50)** (WRMuir) **2-8-11b** DHarrison(8) (bhd: rdn & hdwy over 3f out: wknd over 2f out) 2½ **11** 14/1 27 —
*4269*[12] **Clint (45)** (JFfitch-Heyes) **2-8-11** AClark(12) (bhd fnl 4f)..........12 **12** 50/1 — —
1336[6] **Digwana (IRE)** (TMJones) **2-8-11** MRimmer(14) (stumbled & uns rdr leaving stalls).......... **U** 50/1 — —
(SP 128.1%) **13 Rn**

**1m 30.72** (6.72) CSF £14.40 TOTE £2.50: £1.70 £1.10 £2.20 (£9.60) Trio £9.70 OWNER Mrs Vera Mason (EPSOM) BRED Ridgecourt Stud

## 4361 BULWARK NURSERY H'CAP (0-85) (2-Y.O) (Class D)

2-10 (2-16) **1m** **(Equitrack)** £3,550.00 (£1,075.00: £525.00: £250.00) Stalls: High GOING minus 0.09 sec per fur (STD)

SP RR SF

4321[8] **Quality (IRE) (75)** (WAO'Gorman) **2-9-2v** 6x EmmaO'Gorman(10) (hld up: hdwy over 3f out: rdn over 1f out: led & edgd lft ins fnl f)..........— **1** 11/2[2] 78 36
4279[2] **Oblomov (80)** (GLewis) **2-9-7b** SWhitworth(8) (lw: a.p: led 4f out: hrd rdn over 1f out: hdd & n.m.r ins fnl f: one pce)..........3 **2** 7/1[3] 77 35
4327* **Jerry Cutrona (IRE) (66)** (NACallaghan) **2-8-2**(5) 6x AWhelan(3) (hld up in tch: hdwy over 2f out: n.m.r & hit rail over 1f out: ev ch & n.m.r ins fnl f: one pce)..........½ **3** 15/8[1] 62 20
3713[5] **Love Bird (IRE) (78)** (MJohnston) **2-9-5** WWoods(12) (chsd ldrs: rdn over 3f out: r.o one pce fnl f)..........3 **4** 16/1 68 26
4206[10] **Supreme Power (75)** (WRMuir) **2-9-2** DHarrison(11) (hdwy over 3f out: rdn 2f out: one pce)..........1¾ **5** 12/1 62 20
4001[5] **Nose No Bounds (IRE) (70)** (MJohnston) **2-8-11** DeanMcKeown(5) (s.i.s: sn chsng ldrs: lost pl 4f out: hrd rdn over 2f out: one pce)..........3½ **6** 11/2[2] 50 8
4045[6] **Velvet Jones (58)** (GFHCharles-Jones) **2-7-13** AMackay(7) (prom: rdn 3f out: sn wknd)..........3 **7** 25/1 32 —
3397[8] **High Desire (IRE) (54)** (JRArnold) **2-7-9** JQuinn(2) (prom tl wknd over 2f out)..........2 **8** 33/1 24 —
3893[5] **Meranti (66)** (SDow) **2-8-0**(7) ADaly(4) (led: hdd 4f out: sn wknd)..........7 **9** 16/1 22 —
4208[12] **Nikita's Star (IRE) (66)** (DJGMurraySmith) **2-8-7b** GDuffield(6) (sn rdn & outpcd)..........nk **10** 11/1 21 —
3858[6] **Mystery Matthias (55)** (MissBSanders) **2-7-7**(3)ow3 NVarley(9) (bhd fr ½-wy)..........2 **11** 14/1 3 —
3985[16] **Arch Angel (IRE) (60)** (DJSffrenchDavis) **2-8-1** NAdams(1) (dwlt: sn chsng ldr: wknd 3f out)..........½ **12** 25/1 10 —
(SP 123.1%) **12 Rn**

**1m 41.88** (4.48) CSF £41.75 CT £91.05 TOTE £4.90: £1.70 £2.30 £1.50 (£14.80) Trio £15.10 OWNER Mr N. S. Yong (NEWMARKET) BRED Major C.R. Philipson
LONG HANDICAP Mystery Matthias 7-6

## 4362 LEVIATHAN CLAIMING STKS (II) (3-Y.O+) (Class F)

2-45 (2-48) **7f** **(Equitrack)** £1,761.20 (£493.20: £239.60) Stalls: High GOING minus 0.09 sec per fur (STD)

SP RR SF

*4272*[10] **Superoo (62)** (MrsPSly) **9-8-11** ACulhane(8) (hld up: hdwy over 2f out: led 1f out: rdn out)..........— **1** 14/1 62 29
4157[11] **Mr Nevermind (IRE) (75)** (GLMoore) **5-9-5** SWhitworth(10) (hld up: hdwy 4f out: rdn & ev ch 1f out: nt qckn)..1 **2** 9/4[1] 68 35
*4217*[9] **Dusk in Daytona (58)** (CJames) **3-7-13**(5) AWhelan(9) (a.p: led 3f out: hdd 1f out: one pce)..........2½ **3** 8/1 49 14
3677[14] **Robo Magic (USA) (67)** (LMontagueHall) **3-9-5** RCochrane(13) (mid div: hdwy 2f out: hrd rdn over 1f out: one pce)..........2½ **4** 6/1[3] 58 23
1659[8] **Dragon Green** (JWhite) **4-9-1** DaleGibson(12) (a.p: hrd rdn 2f out: one pce)..........¾ **5** 20/1 51 18
3844[17] **Pacific Girl (IRE) (42)** (BPalling) **3-8-3**ow1 GCarter(2) (in tch: rdn 2f out: one pce)..........3 **6** 20/1 33 —
*4217*[5] **African Chimes (63)** (WAO'Gorman) **8-9-1b** EmmaO'Gorman(15) (hld up: hdwy over 2f out: rdn & wknd over 1f out)..........nk **7** 5/2[2] 43 10
2719[8] **Mary Macblain (32)** (JLHarris) **6-8-2** SSanders(14) (a mid div)..........2½ **8** 33/1 24 —
4209[4] **Anotherone to Note (42)** (NPLittmoden) **4-8-9b** MFenton(16) (nvr nrr)..........hd **9** 25/1 31 —
3629[15] **Bon Secret (IRE) (70)** (TJNaughton) **3-9-0**(5) JDSmith(4) (a bhd)..........2 **10** 7/1 39 4
*4350*[8] **Astrojoy (IRE) (43)** (SGKnight) **3-7-13**(3) NVarley(5) (a bhd)..........6 **11** 33/1 8 —
3704[18] **Dragonflight (35)** (DHaydnJones) **4-9-1** AMackay(1) (led over 2f)..........2½ **12** 50/1 13 —
**Just a Single (IRE)** (JFfitch-Heyes) **4-8-6**(3) DWright(11) (a bhd)..........1 **13** 33/1 5 —
**Ilyazia** (DMorris) **4-8-2** JTate(6) (a bhd)..........1¾ **14** 14/1 — —
3678[7] **Last World (39)** (JAPickering) **3-8-2** JQuinn(7) (chsd ldr: led over 4f out: hdd 3f out: wknd qckly)..........s.h **15** 33/1 — —
(SP 137.7%) **15 Rn**

**1m 27.92** (3.92) CSF £48.04 TOTE £17.70: £3.00 £1.60 £2.50 (£21.90) Trio £102.50 OWNER Mrs P. Sly (PETERBOROUGH) BRED Irish Thoroughbred Holdings Ltd
WEIGHT FOR AGE 3yo-1lb

## 4363 ARK ROYAL MEDIAN AUCTION MAIDEN STKS (3-Y.O) (Class E)

3-20 (3-21) **1m 2f** **(Equitrack)** £2,316.00 (£651.00: £318.00) Stalls: Low GOING minus 0.09 sec per fur (STD)

SP RR SF

4071[5] **Heboob Alshemaal (IRE) (74)** (JHMGosden) **3-8-9v** GHind(4) (a.p: led gng wl 3f out: sn clr: v.easily)..........— **1** 4/5[1] 81++ 24
4072[16] **Silver Singer (65)** (DRLoder) **3-8-10**ow1 RHughes(14) (a.p: chsd wnr 3f out: sn rdn: no imp)..........13 **2** 3/1[2] 60 3
*4296*[4] **Crystal Gift (56)** (DWPArbuthnot) **3-8-9**(5) PPMurphy(1) (outpcd & bhd: hdwy over 2f out: nrst fin)..........3½ **3** 10/1 60 3
3676[17] **Toat Chieftain (40)** (DMorris) **3-9-0** JTate(8) (hdwy over 4f out: hrd rdn fnl 3f: one pce)..........½ **4** 50/1 59 2
4232[8] **Adaloaldo (USA) (55)** (PAKelleway) **3-8-9v**(5) AWhelan(13) (s.i.s: nvr nrr)..........11 **5** 16/1 41 —
*4271*[9] **Halfabob (IRE) (40)** (DHaydnJones) **3-9-0** AMackay(6) (a mid div)..........2½ **6** 50/1 37 —
4242[9] **Hylters Girl (30)** (MJRyan) **3-8-9** GBardwell(11) (nvr nrr)..........2½ **7** 33/1 28 —
4162[9] **Justforthererecord** (BRMillman) **3-8-9** CNutter(10) (nvr nrr)..........s.h **8** 16/1 28 —
*4296*[11] **Chapel Annie** (CPWildman) **3-8-9** StephenDavies(9) (a bhd)..........3 **9** 20/1 23 —
4220[6] **Zadok** (RTPhillips) **3-9-0** GCarter(3) (a bhd)..........hd **10** 33/1 28 —
4225[14] **Begger's Opera** (PatMitchell) **3-9-0** TIves(12) (sn outpcd)..........1½ **11** 50/1 26 —
4332[13] **Nivasha (37)** (RPCHoad) **3-8-9** WNewnes(2) (led 7f)..........½ **12** 25/1 20 —
4214[4] **Miss Ticklepenny** (MajorDNChappell) **3-8-9** WWoods(5) (bhd fnl 5f)..........5 **13** 15/2[3] 12 —
3980[19] **Chalky Dancer (42)** (HJCollingridge) **3-9-0** JQuinn(7) (chsd ldrs 7f)..........¾ **14** 9/1 16 —
(SP 143.5%) **14 Rn**

**2m 10.77** (6.47) CSF £4.82 TOTE £1.90: £1.10 £1.90 £2.40 (£3.10) Trio £7.60 OWNER Sheikh Ahmed Al Maktoum (NEWMARKET) BRED Lady Richard Wellesley and Grange Nominees

## 4364 KRITER H'CAP (0-70) (3-Y.O+) (Class E)

3-50 (3-51) **1m 4f (Equitrack)** £2,274.00 (£639.00: £312.00) Stalls: Low GOING minus 0.09 sec per fur (STD)

| | | | | SP | RR | SF |
|---|---|---|---|---|---|---|
| *4223[2]* | **Loki (IRE) (64)** (GLewis) **7-9-7**(5) AWhelan(10) (lw: hld up: hdwy 3f out: rdn to ld ins fnl f: r.o) | — | 1 | 15/8[1] | 79 | 41 |
| *4335** | **Father Dan (IRE) (55)** (MissGayKelleway) **6-9-3** 5x RCochrane(5) (lw: hld up: hdwy over 3f out: ev ch ins fnl f: one pce) | 2 | 2 | 5/1[2] | 67 | 29 |
| 2842[3] | **Ikhtiraa (USA) (50)** (RJO'Sullivan) **5-8-12** DBiggs(8) (a.p: led over 2f out: hdd ins fnl f: one pce) | ½ | 3 | 9/1 | 62 | 24 |
| 4135[10] | **Strat's Legacy (43)** (DWPArbuthnot) **8-8-5** RPrice(4) (hld up: hdwy 3f out: rdn over 1f out: r.o one pce) | ½ | 4 | 14/1 | 54 | 16 |
| 3710[11] | **Outstayed Welcome (48)** (MJHaynes) **3-7-13**(5) MBaird(12) (chsd ldr: led over 3f out tl over 2f out: one pce) | 3 | 5 | 16/1 | 56 | 11 |
| *4270[9]* | **Awestruck (40)** (BPreece) **5-8-2b** NAdams(3) (wl bhd tl rdn & hdwy fnl 2f: nrst fin) | 2 | 6 | 33/1 | 44 | 6 |
| 4205[7] | **Witney-de-Bergerac (IRE) (47)** (JSMoore) **3-8-3** JFEgan(11) (a mid div) | 3½ | 7 | 12/1 | 48 | 3 |
| 4261[6] | **Harvey White (IRE) (55)** (JPearce) **3-8-11** GBardwell(16) (prom over 10f) | 2 | 8 | 16/1 | 53 | 8 |
| 3958[3] | **Guest Alliance (IRE) (49)** (AMoore) **3-8-5** CandyMorris(15) (nvr nrr) | 1 | 9 | 25/1 | 46 | 1 |
| 3959[2] | **Water Hazard (IRE) (55)** (SDow) **3-8-11** GDuffield(6) (nvr nrr) | hd | 10 | 12/1 | 52 | 7 |
| 4259[22] | **Pat's Splendour (43)** (HJCollingridge) **4-8-5** JQuinn(14) (chsd ldrs tl wknd over 2f out) | ¾ | 11 | 14/1 | 38 | — |
| 3808[15] | **Don't Drop Bombs (USA) (32)** (DTThom) **6-7-8v** NCarlisle(7) (led over 8f) | ¾ | 12 | 6/1[3] | 26 | — |
| *4271[3]* | **Persian Flower (49)** (GCBravery) **3-8-5** MFenton(2) (bhd fnl 3f) | 1½ | 13 | 12/1 | 42 | — |
| *4128[2]* | **Landlord (59)** (JARToller) **3-9-1b** WNewnes(13) (bhd fnl 3f) | 10 | 14 | 16/1 | 38 | — |
| 817[18] | **Telephus (45)** (BJMcMath) **6-8-7** SSanders(9) (a bhd) | 9 | 15 | 20/1 | 11 | — |
| 3875[11] | **Shining Dancer (54)** (SDow) **3-8-3**(7) ADaly(1) (bhd fnl 6f) | 15 | 16 | 33/1 | 1 | — |

(SP 144.3%) **16 Rn**

**2m 38.57** (8.57) CSF £13.82 CT £74.42 TOTE £3.00: £1.10 £1.10 £1.20 £6.00 (£6.90) Trio £30.70 OWNER Mr Michael Watt (EPSOM) BRED Abbey Lodge Stud

WEIGHT FOR AGE 3yo-6lb

T/Plpt: £259.40 (30.02 Tckts). T/Qdpt: £4.20 (6.1 Tckts). SM

# 4269-WOLVERHAMPTON (L-H) (Standard)

## Saturday November 11th

WEATHER: raining WIND: slt half against

## 4365 ASH MAIDEN STKS (2-Y.O) (Class D)

7-00 (7-01) **7f (Fibresand)** £2,775.00 (£840.00: £410.00: £195.00) Stalls: High GOING: 0.01 sec per fur (STD)

| | | | | SP | RR | SF |
|---|---|---|---|---|---|---|
| 4218[9] | **Sweet Wilhelmina** (LordHuntingdon) **2-8-9** DHarrison(9) (hld up & bhd: hdwy over 3f out: 4th st: led ins fnl f: pushed out) | — | 1 | 3/1[2] | 73 | 26 |
| 4313[7] | **Distinct Beauty (IRE)** (WAO'Gorman) **2-8-9b** EmmaO'Gorman(7) (hld up & bhd: hdwy over 3f out: 3rd st: ev ch over 1f out: nt qckn) | 1 | 2 | 100/30[3] | 71 | 24 |
| *4269[3]* | **Honestly (64)** (BSmart) **2-8-9** SSanders(3) (a.p: led over 2f out tl ins fnl f) | ¾ | 3 | 9/1 | 69 | 22 |
| 3982[5] | **Angus McCoatup (IRE) (66)** (BAMcMahon) **2-9-0** GCarter(4) (a.p: led over 3f out tl over 2f out: 2nd st: ev ch over 1f out: wknd fnl f) | 3½ | 4 | 12/1 | 66 | 19 |
| 4282[5] | **Patrio (IRE)** (MJohnston) **2-8-9** DeanMcKeown(5) (prom tl 6th & wkng st) | 3 | 5 | 9/1 | 54 | 7 |
| 4277[3] | **Arcady** (PTWalwyn) **2-8-9** RHughes(1) (lw: led over 3f: 5th & wkng st) | 5 | 6 | 11/4[1] | 43 | — |
| | **Allstars Dancer** (TJNaughton) **2-8-4**(5) JDSmith(10) (unf: outpcd) | 7 | 7 | 20/1 | 27 | — |
| 4148[15] | **Dangerous Waters** (PGMurphy) **2-8-2**(7) RWaterfield(6) (b.nr hind: wl bhd fnl 3f) | 4 | 8 | 50/1 | 18 | — |
| | **Balmoral Princess** (JHPeacock) **2-8-9** DaleGibson(8) (lengthy: dwlt: sn t.o) | 15 | 9 | 50/1 | — | — |
| 3765[8] | **Flagstaff (USA)** (GLMoore) **2-9-0** SWhitworth(2) (lw: prom over 3f: t.o) | hd | 10 | 25/1 | — | — |

(SP 115.0%) **10 Rn**

**1m 29.8** (3.40 under 2y best) (5.10) CSF £12.47 TOTE £4.50: £1.40 £1.60 £1.80 (£11.80) Trio £42.50 OWNER Mr Chris van Hoorn (WEST ILSLEY) BRED D. Walker

## 4366 C. BEECH & SONS STEEL LIMITED STKS (0-65) (3-Y.O+) (Class F)

7-30 (7-30) **1m 4f (Fibresand)** £2,085.00 (£585.00: £285.00) Stalls: Low GOING: 0.01 sec per fur (STD)

| | | | | SP | RR | SF |
|---|---|---|---|---|---|---|
| 4283[6] | **Kalamata (62)** (JAGlover) **3-8-12** SDWilliams(9) (lw: a.p: 2nd st: hung lft & led over 1f out: r.o) | — | 1 | 10/1 | 81 | 39 |
| 4205[3] | **Knotally Wood (USA) (62)** (JWHills) **3-8-2**(5) MHenry(12) (led tl hdd over 1f out: edgd lft & wknd fnl f) | 4 | 2 | 4/1[2] | 71 | 29 |
| 4233[2] | **Domitia (USA) (65)** (MBell) **3-8-10**ow1 MFenton(8) (hld up & bhd: hdwy over 5f out: outpcd over 3f out: poor 3rd st) | 13 | 3 | 7/2[1] | 56 | 13 |
| *4270[5]* | **Rousitto (57)** (RHollinshead) **7-9-5** TIves(10) (s.s: hdwy over 3f out: poor 6th st: nvr nr ldrs) | 1 | 4 | 12/1 | 57 | 22 |
| 1635[3] | **Mr Bean (60)** (KRBurke) **5-9-7** JTate(2) (b: chsd ldr tl wknd over 3f out: poor 4th st) | 3 | 5 | 8/1 | 55 | 20 |
| 3970[15] | **Colosse (46)** (JLEyre) **3-8-7** RLappin(5) (lw: hdwy over 5f out: wknd over 3f out: poor 5th st) | ¾ | 6 | 20/1 | 47 | 5 |
| 4229[3] | **Ducking (65)** (JRFanshawe) **3-8-7** DHarrison(6) (hld up: hrd rdn 5f out: bhd fnl 3f) | 3 | 7 | 5/1 | 43 | 1 |
| 1987[7] | **Claque (65)** (DWChapman) **3-8-12** ACulhane(7) (lw: a bhd) | 3 | 8 | 20/1 | 44 | 2 |
| 4229[14] | **Bold Acre (45)** (DavidBurchell) **5-9-5** RPrice(11) (sn rdn along: prom tl wknd 4f out) | 5 | 9 | 33/1 | 37 | 2 |
| 2522[6] | **Pharly Reef (56)** (DBurchell) **3-8-12** JQuinn(3) (prom 7f: t.o) | 20 | 10 | 33/1 | 11 | — |
| 1984[4] | **Elly Fleetfoot (IRE) (63)** (BJMeehan) **3-8-9** RHughes(4) (hdwy over 5f out: wknd 4f out: t.o) | 14 | 11 | 9/2[3] | — | — |
| 4229[13] | **Dvorak (IRE) (65)** (RHarris) **4-9-5** AMackay(1) (lw: bhd most of wy: t.o) | 1 | 12 | 12/1 | — | — |

(SP 128.1%) **12 Rn**

**2m 39.9** (7.40) CSF £49.89 TOTE £15.90: £4.10 £2.00 £1.50 (£39.20) Trio £61.60 OWNER Mr B. H. Farr (WORKSOP) BRED Worksop Manor Stud Farm

WEIGHT FOR AGE 3yo-6lb

**OFFICIAL EXPLANATION Elly Fleetfoot (IRE): could have been in season.**

## 4367 KB (WESTERN) H'CAP (0-85) (3-Y.O+) (Class D)

8-00 (8-01) **1m 100y (Fibresand)** £2,905.00 (£880.00: £430.00: £205.00) Stalls: Low GOING: 0.01 sec per fur (STD)

| | | | | SP | RR | SF |
|---|---|---|---|---|---|---|
| 1778[4] | **Lyford Law (IRE) (80)** (JHMGosden) **3-9-8** TIves(11) (led 6f out: rdn over 1f out: qcknd clr) | — | 1 | 3/1[1] | 89 | 68 |

4267[9] **Celestial Choir (76)** (JLEyre) **5-9-6** KFallon(10) (lw: rdn 5f out: hdwy & 6th st: edgd rt ins fnl f: no ch w wnr) ...6 **2** 3/1[1] 73 55
3984[8] **Sandmoor Denim (66)** (SRBowring) **8-8-10** SWebster(8) (b: a.p: 3rd st: one pce)..........nk **3** 14/1 62 44
3241[3] **Rambo Waltzer (76)** (SGNorton) **3-9-4** GCarter(3) (led over 2f: 2nd st: sn outpcd)..........s.h **4** 14/1 73 52
4272* **Heathyards Lady (USA) (72)** (RHollinshead) **4-8-9**(7) FLynch(6) (hld up & bhd: hdwy 3f out: 5th st: one pce)1½ **5** 5/1[2] 65 47
4236[8] **Far Ahead (76)** (JLEyre) **3-9-4** RLappin(7) (prom: rdn over 4f out: wknd over 2f out)..........3½ **6** 16/1 64 43
4319[12] **Q Factor (72)** (DHaydnJones) **3-9-0** AMackay(12) (hdwy 4f out: 4th st: 4th & btn whn hmpd ins fnl f)..........1¼ **7** 25/1 57 36
2330[6] **Tatika (68)** (GWragg) **5-8-5**(7) GMilligan(2) (bkwd: a bhd)..........1½ **8** 14/1 49 31
4272[4] **Desert Invader (IRE) (67)** (DWChapman) **4-8-11** ACulhane(4) (hld up: bhd fnl 3f)..........nk **9** 14/1 48 30
4249[8] **Risky Romeo (85)** (GCBravery) **3-9-13** MFenton(9) (lw: s.s: a bhd)..........5 **10** 14/1 57 36
4325[12] **Wentbridge Lad (IRE) (81)** (PDEvans) **5-9-11v** RHughes(1) (hld up: rdn & hdwy over 2f out: sn wknd)..........9 **11** 11/1[3] 35 17
2746[11] **Pengamon (83)** (HJCollingridge) **3-9-11** JQuinn(13) (prom 5f: t.o)..........10 **12** 14/1 19 —
(SP 124.7%) **12 Rn**

**1m 48.0** (3.00) CSF £12.44 CT £103.43 TOTE £5.40: £2.30 £1.60 £3.90 (£8.40) Trio £136.20 OWNER Sheikh Mohammed (NEWMARKET) BRED T. A. Ryan
WEIGHT FOR AGE 3yo-2lb

## 4368 DAILY STAR TOP TIPSTER H'CAP (0-90) (3-Y.O+) (Class C)

8-30 (8-30) **6f (Fibresand)** £5,654.00 (£1,712.00: £836.00: £398.00) Stalls: Low GOING: 0.01 sec per fur (STD)

SP RR SF

4119[6] **Mr Bergerac (IRE) (85)** (BPalling) **4-9-9** TSprake(5) (lw: hld up: hdwy over 2f out: 6th st: led ins fnl f: r.o wl).— **1** 12/1 92 64
4337[4] **Leigh Crofter (76)** (PDCundell) **6-8-9b**(5) DGriffiths(11) (hdwy over 2f out: 3rd st: led over 1f out tl ins fnl f)..1¼ **2** 12/1 80 52
4322[9] **Little Ibnr (85)** (PDEvans) **4-9-9** KFallon(7) (lw: a.p: led over 2f out tl over 1f out: nt qckn ins fnl f)..........hd **3** 7/1[2] 88 60
3717[22] **Sailormaite (89)** (SRBowring) **4-9-13** SWebster(4) (a.p: 5th st: r.o one pce)..........1½ **4** 9/1[3] 88 60
4033[19] **Inherent Magic (IRE) (85)** (WRMuir) **6-9-9** SSanders(6) (a.p: 2nd st: wknd over 1f out)..........1¾ **5** 12/1 80 52
4193[3] **Loveyoumillions (IRE) (83)** (MJohnston) **3-9-7b** DeanMcKeown(8) (s.i.s: hdwy over 3f out: 7th st: one pce) hd **6** 10/1 79 50
4134[2] **Stoppes Brow (86)** (GLMoore) **3-9-10v** SWhitworth(9) (lw: hdwy over 3f out: one pce fnl 2f)..........2 **7** 9/1[3] 76 47
3717[26] **Ashgore (85)** (MJohnston) **5-9-9** JFanning(1) (lw: bhd fnl 3f)..........nk **8** 25/1 73 45
3830[W] **Nordan Raider (77)** (MJCamacho) **7-9-1** LCharnock(2) (s.i.s: hdwy 3f out: wknd 2f out)..........¾ **9** 25/1 63 35
4324[4] **Croft Pool (90)** (JAGlover) **4-10-0** SDWilliams(10) (lw: a bhd)..........1½ **10** 13/8[1] 72 44
3905[13] **Crystal Loop (78)** (ABailey) **3-9-2** GBardwell(12) (led over 3f: 4th st: wknd qckly: wl over 1f out)..........1¾ **11** 16/1 57 28
1626[10] **Castel Rosselo (87)** (RHarris) **5-9-11** AMackay(13) (a bhd)..........5 **12** 14/1 51 23
(SP 123.0%) **12 Rn**

**1m 14.3** (2.90) CSF £134.27 CT £986.33 TOTE £19.90: £3.90 £3.50 £1.40 (£128.10) Trio £156.00 OWNER Mr P. R. John (COWBRIDGE) BRED Red House Stud

## 4369 SILVER BIRCH (S) STKS (2-Y.O) (Class G)

9-00 (9-03) **5f (Fibresand)** £2,085.00 (£585.00: £285.00) Stalls: Low GOING: 0.01 sec per fur (STD)

SP RR SF

4243[4] **Mullagh Hill Lad (IRE) (45)** (BAMcMahon) **2-8-11** GCarter(8) (a.p: led over 2f out: clr over 1f out: r.o wl) .....— **1** 5/2[1] 65 12
4287[2] **Frances Mary (63)** (CWFairhurst) **2-8-6b** JTate(2) (hdwy & 4th st: chsd wnr over 1f out: no imp)..........4 **2** 9/2[3] 47 —
4329[10] **Learning Curve (IRE)** (SirMarkPrescott) **2-8-6** CNutter(10) (hdwy over 1f out: r.o ins fnl f)..........1¾ **3** 14/1 42 —
3740[8] **Monkey Zanty (IRE) (46)** (JBerry) **2-7-13**(7) CLowther(12) (hld up: 7th st: r.o one pce fnl f)..........hd **4** 16/1 41 —
3953[4] **Touch of Fantasy (47)** (CADwyer) **2-8-3**(3) NVarley(11) (prom: 3rd st: one pce)..........hd **5** 14/1 41 —
4132[10] **Poppy My Love (40)** (RHarris) **2-8-6** DBatteate(4) (5th st: no hdwy)..........1¼ **6** 33/1 37 —
4287[7] **Finisterre (IRE) (62)** (JJO'Neill) **2-8-11** DeanMcKeown(3) (led over 3f: 2nd st: wknd fnl f)..........s.h **7** 16/1 42 —
4243[14] **Don't Tell Anyone (56)** (JBerry) **2-8-11**(5) PFessey(1) (sme late hdwy: n.d)..........¾ **8** 8/1 44 —
2146[6] **Abbott of Whalley (60)** (MartynWane) **2-9-2** LCharnock(9) (bhd fnl 2f)..........2 **9** 16/1 38 —
4231[9] **Poly By Staufan (IRE) (60)** (MRChannon) **2-8-6** CandyMorris(7) (prom: 6th st: wknd wl over 1f out)..........nk **10** 3/1[2] 27 —
3760[P] **Deedeejay (45)** (JMBradley) **2-8-6v** AMackay(6) (sn wl bhd)..........2 **11** 16/1 21 —
1448[7] **Madam Pigtails** (PJMcBride) **2-8-6** JQuinn(13) (bhd fnl 2f)..........3 **12** 25/1 11 —
*4155[11] **Static Love (40)** (TTClement) **2-8-6** JFanning(5) (Withdrawn not under Starter's orders: uns rdr & bolted bef s)* **W** 40/1 — —
(SP 129.0%) **12 Rn**

**63.0 secs** (0.60 under 2y best) (4.30) CSF £14.51 TOTE £4.60: £2.10 £1.60 £3.60 (£7.20) Trio £100.10 OWNER The Bramble Partnership (TAMWORTH) BRED T. Connolly
Bt in 5,600 gns

## 4370 VACUUM FURNACE ENGINEERING H'CAP (0-65) (3-Y.O+) (Class F)

9-30 (9-31) **1m 6f 166y (Fibresand)** £2,085.00 (£585.00: £285.00) Stalls: High GOING: 0.01 sec per fur (STD)

SP RR SF

4288[8] **Ballymac Girl (46)** (JMBradley) **7-8-12** LCharnock(4) (chsd ldr: led over 3f out: sn rdn clr: styd on fnl f)........— **1** 9/1 64 39
4288[7] **Cuango (IRE) (55)** (RHollinshead) **4-9-7** KFallon(8) (hld up & bhd: rdn 8f out: hdwy 4f out: 3rd st: hrd rdn: styd on fnl f)..........¾ **2** 4/1[2] 72 47
4336[3] **Greek Night Out (IRE) (33)** (JLEyre) **4-7-10**(3) NVarley(2) (led tl hdd over 3f out: 2nd st: one pce)..........6 **3** 9/2[3] 44 19
4288[2] **Tremendisto (45)** (CaptJWilson) **5-8-6**(5) PFessey(9) (hld up: hdwy over 1f out: nvr nrr)..........nk **4** 3/1[1] 55 30
4331[4] **Environmentalist (IRE) (53)** (RHarris) **4-9-5** AMackay(5) (prom: hrd rdn 5f out: outpcd over 3f out: 5th st: no hdwy)..........hd **5** 6/1 63 38
3724[11] **Jarrow (29)** (MrsAMNaughton) **4-7-9** JQuinn(10) (hld up & plld hrd: outpcd over 3f out: 7th st: no hdwy)..........3 **6** 25/1 36 11
4126[6] **Premier Dance (60)** (DHaydnJones) **8-9-9**(3) DWright(3) (hld up & bhd: nvr trbld ldrs)..........3 **7** 13/2 64 39
3875[5] **Nautical Jewel (55)** (MDIUsher) **3-8-13** RPrice(1) (b: hld up: drvn 5f out: outpcd over 3f out: 6th & wkng st).2½ **8** 16/1 57 23
4298[11] **Mowlaie (62)** (DWChapman) **4-10-0** ACulhane(11) (hld up & bhd: hdwy 6f out: outpcd over 3f out: 4th st: wknd over 1f out)..........3½ **9** 33/1 59 34
4364[6] **Awestruck (41)** (BPreece) **5-8-7b**ow1 VSlattery(6) (sn rdn along: a in rr)..........7 **10** 20/1 30 5
4248[4] **Harry Welsh (IRE) (54)** (KMcAuliffe) **3-8-12b** JTate(7) (prom tl wknd 4f out: t.o)..........20 **11** 12/1 23 —
(SP 125.9%) **11 Rn**

**3m 18.4** (11.00) CSF £44.67 CT £173.43 TOTE £8.70: £2.70 £1.80 £1.50 (£27.80) Trio £40.40 OWNER Mr Lee Bowles (CHEPSTOW) BRED Miss K. Rausing and Mrs S.M. Rogers
WEIGHT FOR AGE 3yo-8lb

T/Plpt: £193.60 (62.97 Tckts). T/Qdpt: £53.00 (2.5 Tckts). KH

# 4365-WOLVERHAMPTON (L-H) (Standard)

## Monday November 13th

WEATHER: cloudy WIND: nil

## 4371 PORPOISE LIMITED STKS (0-60) (I) (3-Y.O+) (Class F)

1-50 (1-51) **7f (Fibresand)** £2,187.00 (£612.00: £297.00) Stalls: High GOING minus 0.06 sec per fur (STD)

| | Runner | Dist | Pos | SP | RR | SF |
|---|---|---|---|---|---|---|
| 4337* | **La Petite Fusee (60)** (RJO'Sullivan) **4-9-1** RHughes(3) (b.hind: mde all: c wd ent st: sn clr: unchal) | — | 1 | 1/2[1] | 65+ | 32 |
| 4292[14] | **Bogart (56)** (CWFairhurst) **4-9-0** WWoods(4) (a.p: rdn 3f out: r.o one pce) | 4 | 2 | 20/1 | 55 | 22 |
| 1209[8] | **Sand Star (52)** (DHaydnJones) **3-8-7** AMackay(9) (swtg: bit bkwd: hdwy 3f out: rdn over 1f out: one pce) | ¾ | 3 | 20/1 | 48 | 13 |
| 3751[7] | **Superbit (44)** (BAMcMahon) **3-9-1** SSanders(5) (hdwy 3f out: kpt on u.p fnl f) | hd | 4 | 33/1 | 56 | 21 |
| 4280[12] | **Murray's Mazda (IRE) (41)** (JLEyre) **6-9-0** RLappin(10) (b: lw: chsd wnr over 4f: rdn & wknd fnl 2f) | 1¼ | 5 | 20/1 | 50 | 17 |
| 3750[5] | **Bold Aristocrat (IRE) (50)** (RHollinshead) **4-8-10**(7) FLynch(12) (lw: s.i.s: effrt & rdn over 2f out: nvr plcd to chal) | 3½ | 6 | 25/1 | 45 | 12 |
| 4274[5] | **Secret Miss (51)** (APJarvis) **3-8-10** JTate(2) (chsd ldrs over 4f) | ½ | 7 | 16/1[3] | 39 | 4 |
| 3621[10] | **River Wye (IRE) (41)** (JMCarr) **3-8-12** SMorris(8) (nvr trbld ldrs) | 1¼ | 8 | 33/1 | 38 | 3 |
| 3719[5] | **My Gallery (IRE) (60)** (ABailey) **4-8-12**(3) DWright(6) (a bhd & outpcd) | s.h | 9 | 7/1[2] | 39 | 6 |
| 4217[3] | **Maid Welcome (59)** (MrsNMacauley) **8-8-2v**(7) AmandaSanders(11) (b.hind: rdn along ½-wy: no imp) | nk | 10 | 7/1[2] | 32 | — |
| 4280[17] | **Always Grace (57)** (MissGayKelleway) **3-8-5**(5) AWhelan(1) (hdwy 3f out: wknd over 2f out) | ½ | 11 | 20/1 | 34 | — |
| 4193[15] | **Red Five (45)** (DMoffatt) **4-8-11**(3) DarrenMoffatt(7) (hld up in tch: effrt over 3f out: no imp: t.o) | 5 | 12 | 33/1 | 25 | — |

(SP 129.3%) **12 Rn**

**1m 29.2** (4.50) CSF £14.24 TOTE £1.20: £1.10 £6.90 £3.30 (£16.20) Trio £119.00 OWNER Skampcargo Racing Partnership (WHITCOMBE) BRED H. Powis

WEIGHT FOR AGE 3yo-1lb

STEWARDS' ENQUIRY Sanders, Lappin & Whelan fined £100 each for being late into the parade ring.

## 4372 MANATEE MEDIAN AUCTION MAIDEN STKS (3-Y.O) (Class E)

2-20 (2-21) **1m 100y (Fibresand)** £3,081.10 (£932.80: £455.40: £216.70) Stalls: Low GOING minus 0.06 sec per fur (STD)

| | Runner | Dist | Pos | SP | RR | SF |
|---|---|---|---|---|---|---|
| 3974[3] | **Cashmere Lady** (JLEyre) **3-8-9** RLappin(3) (swtg: mde all: clr over 2f out: unchal) | — | 1 | 5/2[1] | 70 | 32 |
| 4271[5] | **Dannistar** (PDEvans) **3-8-9** SSanders(6) (lw: hld up: hdwy on ins 3f out: kpt on: no ch w wnr) | 4 | 2 | 25/1 | 62 | 24 |
| 4335[7] | **Diamond Market (49)** (RHollinshead) **3-9-0** MHills(7) (chsd wnr: pushed along 4f out: one pce fnl 2f) | 2½ | 3 | 14/1 | 63 | 25 |
| 3885[3] | **Arcatura (64)** (CJames) **3-9-0** JWilliams(5) (swtg: hld up: hdwy 3f out: sn rdn: r.o one pce) | 1 | 4 | 5/1[2] | 61 | 23 |
| 4051[4] | **Nessun Doro (76)** (SMellor) **3-9-0v** MWigham(8) (in tch: effrt & rdn over 2f out: nt pce to chal) | 1¾ | 5 | 5/1[2] | 58 | 20 |
| 4049[3] | **Prudent Princess (60)** (AHide) **3-8-9** WWoods(10) (s.s: bhd tl sme late hdwy) | 7 | 6 | 6/1[3] | 39 | 1 |
| 3778[11] | **Homecrest (33)** (MrsAMNaughton) **3-9-0v** JQuinn(4) (chsd ldrs: rdn over 2f out: sn lost tch) | 2 | 7 | 33/1 | 41 | 3 |
| 4060[20] | **See You Again (49)** (MABrittain) **3-9-0** MFenton(9) (lw: in tch: drvn along over 3f out: sn wknd) | nk | 8 | 16/1 | 40 | 2 |
| 3745[8] | **Percy Parrot (37)** (RMWhitaker) **3-9-0** ACulhane(2) (a rr div) | nk | 9 | 33/1 | 39 | 1 |
| 4271[4] | **Adamton** (MrsJCecil) **3-9-0** TIves(13) (chsd ldrs: rdn 3f out: sn wknd) | ½ | 10 | 12/1 | 38 | — |
| 3704[16] | **Walk In The Wild** (ABailey) **3-8-6**(3) DWright(1) (a wl bhd & outpcd: t.o) | 10 | 11 | 33/1 | 15 | — |
| 3725[10] | **Petrico** (JBerry) **3-9-0** SDWilliams(11) (rdn along ½-wy: a in rr: t.o) | 8 | 12 | 33/1 | 4 | — |
| 4049[17] | **Axed Again** (NBycroft) **3-8-9** LCharnock(12) (swtg: a bhd: t.o) | 6 | 13 | 33/1 | — | — |

(SP 115.0%) **13 Rn**

**1m 50.1** (5.10) CSF £49.26 TOTE £2.50: £1.20 £3.30 £2.80 (£33.00) Trio £118.20 OWNER Mrs Sybil Howe (HAMBLETON) BRED J. L. Eyre

## 4373 NARWHAL NURSERY H'CAP (0-75) (2-Y.O) (Class E)

2-50 (2-52) **1m 100y (Fibresand)** £3,023.90 (£915.20: £446.60: £212.30) Stalls: Low GOING minus 0.06 sec per fur (STD)

| | Runner | Dist | Pos | SP | RR | SF |
|---|---|---|---|---|---|---|
| 4327[2] | **Worldwide Elsie (USA) (70)** (RHarris) **2-9-7** AMackay(4) (hld up: hdwy to ld over 4f out: clr fnl 2f: v.easily) | — | 1 | 6/4[1] | 82 | 42 |
| 4263* | **Polar Spirit (61)** (WJHaggas) **2-8-12** MHills(6) (hld up: jnd ldrs 4f out: rdn ent st: sn outpcd) | 12 | 2 | 13/8[2] | 50 | 10 |
| 4192[7] | **Homeland (68)** (TJNaughton) **2-9-0**(5) JDSmith(1) (lw: led over 2f: rdn & one pce fnl 2f) | 6 | 3 | 11/2[3] | 46 | 6 |
| 4273[4] | **Image Maker (IRE) (59)** (BPreece) **2-8-10** NAdams(2) (b.nr hind: led 6f out tl over 4f out: sn rdn & outpcd) | 7 | 4 | 12/1 | 24 | — |
| 4050[18] | **Alistover (46)** (RDickin) **2-7-11**ow1 DaleGibson(3) (prom tl wknd over 3f out) | s.h | 5 | 33/1 | 10 | — |
| 1646[9] | **Abduction (55)** (EWeymes) **2-8-6** WWoods(5) (swtg: a wl bhd & outpcd: t.o) | 25 | 6 | 33/1 | — | — |

(SP 107.1%) **6 Rn**

**1m 50.1** (5.10) CSF £3.91 TOTE £2.30: £1.80 £1.10 (£1.80) OWNER Mr T. J. Dawson (NEWMARKET) BRED Lantern Hill Farm and Dr. M. G. Marenchic

## 4374 H & V NEWS H'CAP (0-70) (I) (3-Y.O+) (Class E)

3-20 (3-21) **1m 1f 79y (Fibresand)** £2,756.10 (£832.80: £405.40: £191.70) Stalls: Low GOING minus 0.06 sec per fur (STD)

| | Runner | Dist | Pos | SP | RR | SF |
|---|---|---|---|---|---|---|
| 3719[9] | **Chairmans Choice (65)** (APJarvis) **5-9-11** JTate(1) (a.p: led 7f out: clr ent st: hld on wl) | — | 1 | 10/1 | 83 | 64 |
| 4233[3] | **Ocean Park (68)** (LadyHerries) **4-10-0** DeanMcKeown(10) (lw: hld up: hdwy 4f out: effrt & rdn appr fnl f: kpt on) | ¾ | 2 | 13/2[3] | 85 | 66 |
| 3952* | **Sudden Spin (63)** (SGNorton) **5-9-9** TIves(3) (chsd ldrs: sn pushed along: rdn 3f out: one pce) | 7 | 3 | 7/2[1] | 68 | 49 |
| 4298[7] | **Maple Bay (IRE) (58)** (ABailey) **6-9-1**(3) DWright(8) (hld up: hdwy on ins over 3f out: nt trble ldrs) | ¾ | 4 | 5/1[2] | 62 | 43 |
| 4194[4] | **Evan 'elp Us (59)** (JLEyre) **3-8-13b**(3) NVarley(6) (swtg: chsd ldrs: rdn over 2f out: sn wknd) | 10 | 5 | 16/1 | 46 | 23 |
| 4296[3] | **Dancing Sioux (59)** (RGuest) **3-9-2e** WWoods(4) (lw: rdn & effrt over 3f out: nvr nr to chal) | 3 | 6 | 11/1 | 41 | 18 |
| 4249[16] | **Farmer's Tern (IRE) (56)** (WJarvis) **3-8-13** MTebbutt(7) (b.nr hind: a rr div) | 1¼ | 7 | 16/1 | 36 | 13 |
| 4227[13] | **Rock Oyster (45)** (BJMeehan) **3-8-2b** GBardwell(13) (led over 2f: wknd 3f out) | 3½ | 8 | 33/1 | 19 | — |
| 4242[4] | **Love Legend (55)** (DWPArbuthnot) **10-9-1** SWhitworth(11) (b: chsd ldrs 5f: sn rdn & wknd) | 3½ | 9 | 16/1 | 22 | 3 |
| 4293[10] | **Good so Fa (IRE) (47)** (CNAllen) **3-8-4** NAdams(12) (a bhd: t.o) | 12 | 10 | 33/1 | — | — |
| 4275[2] | **Mbulwa (57)** (RAFahey) **9-9-3** LCharnock(5) (w ldrs to ½-wy: sn lost tch & eased: t.o) | nk | 11 | 7/1 | 3 | — |
| 4229[11] | **Queenbird (57)** (MJRyan) **4-9-3** AClark(2) (a bhd: t.o) | ½ | 12 | 33/1 | 2 | — |

(SP 108.6%) **12 Rn**

**2m 0.7** (4.70) CSF £61.75 CT £221.42 TOTE £14.90: £3.70 £2.50 £2.40 (£32.10) Trio £37.20 OWNER Mrs D. B. Brazier (ASTON UPTHORPE) BRED D. V. Wakefield

WEIGHT FOR AGE 3yo-3lb

## 4375 SIRENIAN (S) STKS (2-Y.O F) (Class F)
3-50 (3-51) **6f (Fibresand)** £2,537.00 (£712.00: £347.00) Stalls: Low GOING minus 0.06 sec per fur (STD)

| | | | | SP | RR | SF |
|---|---|---|---|---|---|---|
| *4369[2]* | **Frances Mary (53)** (CWFairhurst) **2-8-9b** JTate(8) (chsd ldrs: led 2f out: drvn clr fnl f) | — | **1** | 7/2[1] | 67 | 13 |
| 4133[15] | **Trickledown (52)** (MartynWane) **2-8-9** LCharnock(13) (led to 2f out: rdn & no ex fnl f) | 2½ | **2** | 14/1 | 60 | 6 |
| 4231[14] | **Efipetite (47)** (NBycroft) **2-8-9** JQuinn(6) (hld up: hdwy 2f out: fin wl) | ½ | **3** | 33/1 | 59 | 5 |
| *4353[5]* | **Rising Stream** (SirMarkPrescott) **2-8-9** GDuffield(9) (b.hind: b: a.p: ev ch wl over 1f out: unable qckn) | 1 | **4** | 10/1[3] | 56 | 2 |
| *4127[9]* | **Welsh Melody (49)** (KRBurke) **2-9-0v** AClark(7) (chsd ldrs: gd hdwy 2f out: nvr nrr) | ½ | **5** | 14/1 | 60 | 6 |
| 4287[3] | **Amoeba (IRE) (54)** (JBerry) **2-8-4**(5) PFessey(12) (lw: prom: rdn over 2f out: kpt on one pce) | s.h | **6** | 5/1[2] | 55 | 1 |
| 4290[7] | **Classic Daisy (53)** (MissGayKelleway) **2-8-4b**(5) AWhelan(11) (b.hind: lw: prom tl rdn & wknd wl over 1f out) | ½ | **7** | 12/1 | 54 | — |
| *4339[4]* | **Orange And Blue (43)** (MissJFCraze) **2-9-0c** SWebster(3) (lw: chsd ldrs: hmpd & checked over 3f out: sn bhd) | 2½ | **8** | 14/1 | 52 | — |
| 3858[8] | **Takapuna (IRE) (54)** (TJNaughton) **2-9-0** DHarrison(1) (lw: sn drvn along: a bhd) | hd | **9** | 7/2[1] | 52 | — |
| *4294[8]* | **Simply Miss Chief (IRE) (55)** (DWPArbuthnot) **2-8-9** SSanders(10) (a outpcd & bhd) | 2½ | **10** | 25/1 | 40 | — |
| 3937[9] | **Spanish Luck (47)** (JWHills) **2-9-0b** MHills(4) (hdwy after 2f: ev ch bel dist: wknd & eased fnl f) | nk | **11** | 14/1 | 44 | — |
| 3900[18] | **Tina Katerina** (RChampion) **2-8-2**(7) SGaillard(2) (sn wl bhd & t.o) | 2½ | **12** | 16/1 | 33 | — |
| 4276[10] | **Chamber Music (40)** (JBerry) **2-8-2**(7) PRoberts(5) (b.nr hind: chsd ldrs: sn drvn along: outpcd fr ½-wy) | hd | **13** | 20/1 | 32 | — |
| | | | | (SP 122.0%) | **13 Rn** | |

**1m 16.7** (5.30) CSF £47.62 TOTE £2.90: £2.20 £4.50 £5.60 (£52.30) Trio £248.80; £245.31 to Newton Abbot 14/11/95. OWNER Mr Des Redhead (MIDDLEHAM) BRED A. D. Redhead
Bt in 3,200 gns

## 4376 DOLPHIN APPRENTICE H'CAP (0-65) (3-Y.O+) (Class G)
4-20 (4-21) **1m 4f (Fibresand)** £2,259.00 (£634.00: £309.00) Stalls: Low GOING minus 0.06 sec per fur (STD)

| | | | | SP | RR | SF |
|---|---|---|---|---|---|---|
| 4288[4] | **Opera Buff (IRE) (50)** (MissGayKelleway) **4-9-1** AWhelan(11) (hld up: hdwy 7f out: led 2f out: sn clr: readily) | — | **1** | 3/1[1] | 68+ | 39 |
| 1971[6] | **Heighth of Fame (45)** (DBurchell) **4-8-5**(5) KSked(10) (bit bkwd: a.p: ev ch 2f out: rdn & outpcd appr fnl f) | 10 | **2** | 20/1 | 50 | 21 |
| 3059[3] | **Hill Farm Dancer (48)** (WMBrisbourne) **4-8-10**(3) MartinDwyer(9) (s.s: bhd tl r.o appr fnl f) | hd | **3** | 16/1 | 53 | 24 |
| *4335[3]* | **Our Main Man (53)** (RMWhitaker) **5-9-1**(3) GParkin(5) (chsd ldrs: led 3f out to 2f out: sn rdn & btn) | 1¼ | **4** | 14/1[3] | 56 | 27 |
| *4298[2]* | **Tadellal (IRE) (59)** (WGMTurner) **4-9-5**(5) JWilkinson(4) (mid div: effrt 3f out: outpcd over 2f out) | 2½ | **5** | 12/1[2] | 59 | 30 |
| 4248[8] | **Fabulous Mtoto (43)** (MSSaunders) **5-8-8** DGriffiths(7) (prom tl ½-wy: sn rdn along & wknd) | 1½ | **6** | 16/1 | 41 | 12 |
| 3987[2] | **Golden Torque (47)** (RBastiman) **8-8-12** HBastiman(12) (s.s: hdwy over 3f out: sn rdn: no imp) | ½ | **7** | 3/1[1] | 44 | 15 |
| *4335[2]* | **Instantaneous (54)** (MHEasterby) **3-8-13** LNewton(8) (led after 2f: sn wl clr: wknd & hdd 3f out: t.o) | 10 | **8** | 3/1[1] | 39 | 3 |
| 4259[13] | **Hattaafeh (IRE) (56)** (MAJarvis) **4-9-7** PFessey(3) (prom: rdn 4f out: sn lost tch: t.o) | s.h | **9** | 12/1[2] | 40 | 11 |
| *4126[9]* | **Sommersby (IRE) (63)** (MrsNMacauley) **4-9-11**(3) AmandaSanders(2) (b: a bhd: t.o) | 2 | **10** | 12/1[2] | 44 | 15 |
| 4043[19] | **Mazilla (52)** (AStreeter) **3-8-11** CTeague(6) (b: led 2f: wknd 3f out: t.o) | 25 | **11** | 20/1 | — | — |
| *3076[4]* | **Rosevear (IRE) (46)** (SMellor) **3-8-2v**(3) ADaly(1) (a bhd: t.o) | 12 | **12** | 16/1 | — | — |
| | | | | (SP 131.9%) | **12 Rn** | |

**2m 39.3** (6.80) CSF £59.67 CT £787.67 TOTE £3.40: £2.50 £8.30 £3.20 (£125.90) Trio £396.10; £16.74 to Newton Abbot 14/11/95. OWNER Mr D. C. Toogood (WHITCOMBE) BRED Juddmonte Farms
WEIGHT FOR AGE 3yo-6lb

## 4377 PORPOISE LIMITED STKS (0-60) (II) (3-Y.O+) (Class F)
4-50 (4-50) **7f (Fibresand)** £2,187.00 (£612.00: £297.00) Stalls: High GOING minus 0.06 sec per fur (STD)

| | | | | SP | RR | SF |
|---|---|---|---|---|---|---|
| *4128[7]* | **Certain Way (IRE) (50)** (NPLittmoden) **5-9-0** TIves(8) (hld up: hdwy over 2f out: shkn up to ld wl ins fnl f) | — | **1** | 12/1 | 68 | 24 |
| *4337[11]* | **Jigsaw Boy (59)** (PGMurphy) **6-9-0** JWilliams(12) (hld up & bhd: hdwy 2f out: led ins fnl f: hdd & no ex cl home) | nk | **2** | 9/2[2] | 67 | 23 |
| *4340[10]* | **Exclusive Assembly (57)** (APJames) **3-8-12** JQuinn(6) (lw: led after 2f tl hdd & no ex ins fnl f) | 2 | **3** | 5/1[3] | 63 | 17 |
| 4275[5] | **Dr Caligari (IRE) (54)** (JBerry) **3-8-7v**(5) PFessey(11) (s.i.s: bhd: gd hdwy bel dist: nvr nrr) | 1 | **4** | 8/1 | 61 | 15 |
| *4272[5]* | **Bold Gem (60)** (BJMeehan) **4-8-12b** RHughes(4) (hld up: hdwy over 2f out: rdn & one pce appr fnl f) | nk | **5** | 7/1 | 58 | 14 |
| 3879[15] | **Langtonian (46)** (JLEyre) **6-9-0v** NCarlisle(7) (s.s: nvr nr ldrs) | 2½ | **6** | 20/1 | 54 | 10 |
| 3534[14] | **Jon's Choice (50)** (BPreece) **7-9-0** NAdams(9) (hdwy ½-wy: rdn & wknd wl over 1f out) | 13 | **7** | 14/1 | 24 | — |
| 450[12] | **Newington Butts (IRE) (45)** (KMcAuliffe) **5-8-9** GDuffield(1) (bit bkwd: led 2f: rdn & wknd 2f out: t.o) | 3 | **8** | 16/1 | 13 | — |
| *4217[11]* | **Distant Princess (60)** (BWHills) **3-8-13** MHills(2) (mid div: rdn along ½-wy: no rspnse: t.o) | ¾ | **9** | 11/4[1] | 17 | — |
| *3529[15]* | **Green's Bid (57)** (DWChapman) **5-9-3** ACulhane(5) (bit bkwd: prom over 4f: t.o) | ½ | **10** | 16/1 | 18 | — |
| 3204[7] | **Trioming (42)** (APJones) **9-9-0** DaleGibson(10) (spd 4f: sn lost tch: t.o) | 2½ | **11** | 20/1 | 9 | — |
| *2290[8]* | **Quinzii Martin (53)** (DHaydnJones) **7-9-0** AMackay(3) (bkwd: a bhd & outpcd: t.o) | 1¾ | **12** | 20/1 | 5 | — |
| | | | | (SP 125.5%) | **12 Rn** | |

**1m 30.0** (5.30) CSF £63.78 TOTE £13.50: £3.20 £1.50 £3.10 (£52.80) Trio £81.40 OWNER R A M Racecourses Ltd (WOLVERHAMPTON) BRED Alan Dargan
WEIGHT FOR AGE 3yo-1lb

## 4378 H & V NEWS H'CAP (0-70) (II) (3-Y.O+) (Class E)
5-20 (5-25) **1m 1f 79y (Fibresand)** £2,756.10 (£832.80: £405.40: £191.70) Stalls: Low GOING minus 0.06 sec per fur (STD)

| | | | | SP | RR | SF |
|---|---|---|---|---|---|---|
| *4350[7]* | **Benjamins Law (45)** (JAPickering) **4-8-5** RLappin(10) (led over 2f: jnd ldr 2f out: led wl ins fnl f) | — | **1** | 16/1 | 66 | 48 |
| *4340** | **Rood Music (61)** (MGMeagher) **4-9-7** 5x KFallon(5) (lw: led 7f out: hrd rdn fnl f: ct cl home) | hd | **2** | 13/8[1] | 82 | 64 |
| 4292[8] | **Calder King (64)** (JLEyre) **4-9-7b**(3) OPears(12) (hdwy ½-wy: rdn 2f out: nt rch ldrs) | 12 | **3** | 8/1[3] | 64 | 46 |
| 4234[11] | **Dally Boy (56)** (MHEasterby) **3-8-13** LCharnock(11) (bhd tl styd on fnl 2f) | 6 | **4** | 33/1 | 47 | 25 |
| *4297[6]* | **Brave Princess (67)** (MAJarvis) **3-9-10** WWoods(7) (hdwy 4f out: rdn & outpcd fnl 3f) | s.h | **5** | 9/2[2] | 58 | 36 |
| 4209* | **Cicerone (48)** (JLHarris) **5-8-8** SSanders(9) (chsd ldrs: rdn along 5f out: grad wknd) | 2½ | **6** | 9/1 | 34 | 16 |
| *4357[11]* | **Supercool (44)** (DWChapman) **4-7-13**(5) PFessey(8) (in tch over 6f) | 5 | **7** | 33/1 | 21 | 3 |
| *4340[6]* | **Eastleigh (56)** (RHollinshead) **6-9-2** TIves(13) (a in rr) | 1½ | **8** | 20/1 | 31 | 13 |
| 4261[18] | **Our Tom (65)** (JWharton) **3-9-8** JQuinn(6) (lw: lost pl 4f out: t.o) | 13 | **9** | 20/1 | 18 | — |

| | | | | SP | RR | SF |
|---|---|---|---|---|---|---|
| *628** | **Little Scarlett (48)** (PJMakin) **3-8-5** AClark(3) (swtg: a bhd: t.o) | 4 | **10** | 20/1 | — | — |
| *4128[5]* | **Latin Leader (58)** (CREgerton) **5-9-4b** RHughes(1) (lw: a bhd: t.o) | 8 | **11** | 16/1 | — | — |
| *4271[7]* | **Unforeseen (60)** (SirMarkPrescott) **3-9-3** GDuffield(2) (lw: sn rdn along: a bhd: t.o) | 3 | **12** | 14/1 | — | — |
| 4171[18] | **Prudent Pet (61)** (CWFairhurst) **3-9-4** JTate(4) (lw: chsd ldrs over 5f: t.o) | dist | **13** | 16/1 | — | — |

(SP 121.9%) **13 Rn**

**2m 0.3** (4.30) CSF £40.40 CT £216.37 TOTE £11.20: £2.40 £1.60 £2.40 (£12.60) Trio £138.60 OWNER Mr D. Lowe (HINCKLEY) BRED Dunchurch Lodge Stud
WEIGHT FOR AGE 3yo-3lb

T/Jkpt: £5,911.40 (5.32 Tckts). T/Plpt: £49.00 (318.24 Tckts). T/Qdpt: £48.30 (0.4 Tckts); £39.24 to Newton Abbot 14/11/95. IM

# 4357-LINGFIELD (L-H) (Standard)
## Tuesday November 14th
WEATHER: cloudy WIND: almost nil

## 4379 MIDDLEHAM LIMITED STKS (0-55) (I) (3-Y.O+) (Class F)
12-20 (12-22) **1m 2f (Equitrack)** £2,388.60 (£669.60: £325.80) Stalls: Low

| | | | | SP | RR | SF |
|---|---|---|---|---|---|---|
| 3987[3] | **Spitfire Bridge (IRE) (48)** (MMcCormack) **3-8-13** RCochrane(14) (hld up: led over 2f out: rdn out) | — | **1** | 6/1[3] | 62 | 29 |
| 4249* | **Bellateena (52)** (HJCollingridge) **3-8-10** JQuinn(5) (a.p: rdn over 4f out: unable qckn) | 6 | **2** | 15/8[1] | 49 | 16 |
| *4298[12]* | **Total Rach (IRE) (51)** (RIngram) **3-8-8b** WWoods(9) (rdn 5f out: hdwy over 1f out: r.o) | nk | **3** | 9/2[2] | 47 | 14 |
| 4229[10] | **Yo Kiri-B (42)** (JFfitch-Heyes) **4-8-13** GDuffield(12) (lw: hdwy over 4f out: rdn over 3f out: one pce) | hd | **4** | 12/1 | 47 | 19 |
| 4136[9] | **Fastini Gold (51)** (MDIUsher) **3-8-11** AMackay(13) (hdwy over 4f out: rdn over 3f out: r.o one pce fnl f) | 1½ | **5** | 10/1 | 47 | 14 |
| *4223[11]* | **Studio Thirty (44)** (DMorris) **3-8-13v** JTate(2) (chsd ldr: led over 5f out tl over 2f out: wknd fnl f) | hd | **6** | 16/1 | 49 | 16 |
| *4351[9]* | **Green Golightly (USA) (46)** (DAWilson) **4-8-11**(5) AWhelan(4) (a mid div) | 1½ | **7** | 25/1 | 45 | 17 |
| *4355[9]* | **Kentavrus Way (IRE) (32)** (AMoore) **4-9-2v** CandyMorris(10) (b.hind: nvr nr to chal) | 7 | **8** | 33/1 | 34 | 6 |
| 4131[13] | **Morning Master (23)** (RMFlower) **3-8-11b** AMorris(11) (swtg: nvr nrr) | ½ | **9** | 33/1 | 33 | — |
| 4193[13] | **Cyprus Point (40)** (SWCampion) **4-8-11** DeanMcKeown(8) (bhd fnl 4f) | 5 | **10** | 20/1 | 20 | — |
| | **Sir Oliver (IRE) (42)** (BAPearce) **6-9-2** TIves(6) (bit bkwd: bhd fnl 6f) | 8 | **11** | 20/1 | 12 | — |
| 3920[13] | **Lees Please (IRE) (45)** (KOCunningham-Brown) **3-8-11** DBiggs(7) (a bhd) | 1 | **12** | 20/1 | 10 | — |
| 4054[4] | **Pash (42)** (CWFairhurst) **3-8-6v** SWebster(3) (a bhd) | nk | **13** | 12/1 | 5 | — |
| 4170[7] | **Doodies Pool (IRE) (40)** (PBurgoyne) **5-9-2b** MWigham(1) (led over 4f) | s.h | **14** | 7/1 | 10 | — |

(SP 134.1%) **14 Rn**

**2m 10.42** (6.12) CSF £18.44 TOTE £5.70: £1.30 £1.10 £2.50 (£6.00) Trio £9.20 OWNER East Manton Racing Stables Ltd (WANTAGE) BRED John Harrington
WEIGHT FOR AGE 3yo-4lb

## 4380 NEWMARKET MAIDEN STKS (I) (2-Y.O) (Class D)
12-50 (12-52) **1m (Equitrack)** £3,111.25 (£940.00: £457.50: £216.25) Stalls: High

| | | | | SP | RR | SF |
|---|---|---|---|---|---|---|
| 4161[6] | **Catch The Lights** (RHannon) **2-8-9** RPerham(8) (hld up: shkn up over 2f out: swtchd rt over 1f out: led ins fnl f: r.o wl) | — | **1** | 5/2[2] | 75+ | 32 |
| 3968[5] | **Tissue of Lies (USA)** (MJohnston) **2-9-0** WWoods(7) (led 3f: rdn over 4f out: ev ch ins fnl f: unable qckn) | 2 | **2** | 13/2 | 76 | 33 |
| *4334[2]* | **Milton** (PFICole) **2-9-0** TQuinn(6) (lw: rdn thrght: a.p: led over 1f out tl ins fnl f: one pce) | 1¾ | **3** | 5/4[1] | 73 | 30 |
| 4262[18] | **Victim of Love** (RCharlton) **2-8-9** DHarrison(4) (a.p: led over 3f out tl over 1f out: wknd fnl f) | 3½ | **4** | 12/1 | 61 | 18 |
| 4247[2] | **Bullpen Belle** (PTWalwyn) **2-8-9** RCochrane(9) (hld up: rdn over 4f out: wknd over 3f out) | 4 | **5** | 6/1[3] | 53 | 10 |
| 4314[13] | **Extremely Friendly** (CEBrittain) **2-9-0** JQuinn(5) (lw: outpcd: nvr nrr) | nk | **6** | 16/1 | 57 | 14 |
| *4339[10]* | **Richard House Lad (56)** (RHollinshead) **2-9-0** TIves(3) (lw: a bhd) | 13 | **7** | 20/1 | 31 | — |
| 3673[11] | **Henry Cooper** (DrJDScargill) **2-9-0** MFenton(1) (led 5f out tl over 3f out: sn wknd) | 14 | **8** | 66/1 | 3 | — |
| *4334[13]* | **Gold Kicker** (MJRyan) **2-9-0** AClark(2) (prom over 3f) | 5 | **9** | 25/1 | — | — |

(SP 124.3%) **9 Rn**

**1m 41.55** (4.15) CSF £19.30 TOTE £4.50: £1.60 £2.80 £1.00 (£16.70) Trio £7.20 OWNER Mr T. A. Johnsey (MARLBOROUGH) BRED T. A. Johnsey

## 4381 NEWMARKET MAIDEN STKS (II) (2-Y.O) (Class D)
1-20 (1-21) **1m (Equitrack)** £3,095.00 (£935.00: £455.00: £215.00) Stalls: High

| | | | | SP | RR | SF |
|---|---|---|---|---|---|---|
| 4313[13] | **Charlie Chang (IRE)** (RHannon) **2-9-0** RPerham(8) (hld up: led 2f out: r.o wl) | — | **1** | 8/1[3] | 73 | 35 |
| 4262[13] | **Tart** (RFJohnsonHoughton) **2-8-9** AMcGlone(2) (a.p: rdn 4f out: unable qckn fnl 2f) | 4 | **2** | 100/30[2] | 60 | 22 |
| 4188[9] | **Tintara (IRE)** (BWHills) **2-8-9** MHills(6) (lw: a.p: rdn over 3f out: eased whn btn ins fnl f) | 4 | **3** | Evens[1] | 52 | 14 |
| 4190[8] | **Shirley Sue** (MJohnston) **2-8-9** DeanMcKeown(3) (lost pl over 6f out: rallied fnl f: r.o) | 1¾ | **4** | 8/1[3] | 49 | 11 |
| *4361[11]* | **Mystery Matthias (51)** (MissBSanders) **2-8-9b** SSanders(1) (led 6f) | ¾ | **5** | 20/1 | 47 | 9 |
| 3709[7] | **Sovereign Prince (IRE)** (NACallaghan) **2-9-0** AMackay(4) (b.hind: s.i.s: a bhd) | 7 | **6** | 12/1 | 38 | — |
| | **Presuming Ed (IRE)** (NJHWalker) **2-8-11**(3) JStack(5) (unf: s.s: a bhd) | 7 | **7** | 25/1 | — | — |
| 4320[20] | **Stunning Prospect (USA)** (PFICole) **2-9-0b** TQuinn(7) (chsd ldr 4f) | 13 | **8** | 12/1 | — | — |

(SP 119.3%) **8 Rn**

**1m 41.72** (4.32) CSF £33.79 TOTE £13.10: £2.70 £2.30 £1.10 (£25.00) OWNER Mr Jim Horgan (MARLBOROUGH) BRED Jim Horgan

## 4382 EPSOM MAIDEN STKS (3-Y.O) (Class D)
1-50 (1-55) **7f (Equitrack)** £3,712.50 (£1,125.00: £550.00: £262.50) Stalls: Low

| | | | | SP | RR | SF |
|---|---|---|---|---|---|---|
| *4296[2]* | **Sombreffe (70)** (DRLoder) **3-8-9** LDettori(8) (led 6f out: hrd rdn over 1f out: edgd lft: r.o wl) | — | **1** | 2/5[1] | 72 | 29 |
| 3685[6] | **Takeshi (IRE) (58)** (WRMuir) **3-8-9** DHarrison(9) (hld up: rdn 3f out: r.o one pce fnl f) | 2½ | **2** | 10/1 | 66 | 23 |
| | **Don't Get Caught (IRE)** (NSMcGrath,Ireland) **3-8-9** AClark(3) (unf: a.p: ev ch 2f out: one pce) | s.h | **3** | 9/1[3] | 66 | 23 |
| 4150[8] | **Errant** (DJSCosgrove) **3-9-0** JQuinn(11) (b: outpcd: hdwy over 1f out: r.o) | 2 | **4** | 50/1 | 67 | 24 |
| | **Juba** (DrJDScargill) **3-8-9** MFenton(2) (str: bit bkwd: nvr nr to chal) | ½ | **5** | 66/1 | 61 | 18 |
| | **Big Bands Are Back (USA) (80)** (BWHills) **3-9-0** MHills(1) (bit bkwd: stumbled s: hdwy 4f out: wknd over 1f out) | 1½ | **6** | 9/1[3] | 62 | 19 |

| Form | Horse | Dist | Pos | SP | RR | SF |
|---|---|---|---|---|---|---|
| 1445[U] | **Warm Hearted (USA)** (RIngram) **3-9-0** NGwilliams(6) (hld up: rdn over 2f out: wknd over 1f out) | 1¼ | **7** | 33/1 | 59 | 16 |
| 4266[5] | **Monty** (MajorDNChappell) **3-9-0** WWoods(5) (lw: led 1f: wknd over 3f out) | 1¾ | **8** | 8/1[2] | 55 | 12 |
| *4271[6]* | **Geolly (IRE)** (DrJDScargill) **3-9-0** RPerham(10) (lw: prom over 4f) | 6 | **9** | 16/1 | 42 | — |
| 4205[16] | **Lady Kate (USA) (30)** (KOCunningham-Brown) **3-8-9** DBiggs(4) (swtg: a wl bhd) | 7 | **10** | 66/1 | 21 | — |
| | **Rocky Melody** (PCRitchens) **3-9-0** NAdams(7) (a bhd) | 9 | **11** | 66/1 | 5 | — |
| | | | | (SP 126.9%) | **11 Rn** | |

**1m 27.64** (3.64) CSF £6.59 TOTE £1.10: £1.10 £1.60 £2.50 (£4.60) Trio £8.20 OWNER Sheikh Mohammed (NEWMARKET) BRED Sheikh Mohammed bin Rashid al Maktoum

## 4383 WANTAGE NURSERY H'CAP (0-85) (2-Y.O) (Class E)

2-20 (2-23) **6f (Equitrack)** £3,052.50 (£924.00: £451.00: £214.50) Stalls: Low

| Form | Horse | Dist | Pos | SP | RR | SF |
|---|---|---|---|---|---|---|
| 4144[2] | **Itsinthepost (64)** (MJohnston) **2-8-10** DeanMcKeown(1) (lw: a.p: led over 3f out: hrd rdn over 1f out: r.o wl) | — | **1** | 6/1 | 73 | 35 |
| 4328[4] | **Arctic Romancer (IRE) (70)** (GLewis) **2-8-11**(5) AWhelan(2) (lw: hld up: rdn over 2f out: unable qckn wl ins fnl f) | 1½ | **2** | 5/1[2] | 75 | 37 |
| 4317[7] | **Amber Fort (70)** (PFICole) **2-9-2b** TQuinn(6) (led over 2f: ev ch over 1f out: one pce) | 3½ | **3** | 11/2[3] | 66 | 28 |
| *4353** | **Moi Canard (68)** (BAPearce) **2-8-9**(5) 7x PFessey(12) (lw: outpcd: hdwy over 1f out: r.o) | nk | **4** | 12/1 | 63 | 25 |
| *4294[2]* | **Time For Tea (IRE) (73)** (CACyzer) **2-9-2**(3) PMcCabe(8) (no hdwy fnl 2f) | 4 | **5** | 8/1 | 57 | 19 |
| *4361[5]* | **Supreme Power (75)** (WRMuir) **2-9-7b** DHarrison(7) (lw: outpcd: nvr nrr) | s.h | **6** | 14/1 | 59 | 21 |
| 4263[4] | **Balpare (56)** (NACallaghan) **2-8-2** AMackay(3) (dwlt: outpcd: nvr nrr) | 2½ | **7** | 20/1 | 33 | — |
| *4294[3]* | **Foreman (60)** (WAO'Gorman) **2-8-6v**ow1 RCochrane(4) (lw: n.m.r on ins over 2f out: nvr nr to chal) | 1¼ | **8** | 7/2[1] | 33 | — |
| *4294[4]* | **Dancing Jack (52)** (JJBridger) **2-7-12** JQuinn(10) (prom 4f) | ¾ | **9** | 20/1 | 24 | — |
| 4212[14] | **Frog (61)** (SirMarkPrescott) **2-8-7** GDuffield(9) (a bhd) | ¾ | **10** | 14/1 | 31 | — |
| 4330* | **Village Native (FR) (74)** (KOCunningham-Brown) **2-9-6** 7x DBiggs(13) (prom over 3f) | 1¼ | **11** | 14/1 | 41 | 3 |
| *4294** | **Beeny (67)** (APJarvis) **2-8-13** JTate(11) (prom over 3f) | 1¼ | **12** | 6/1 | 30 | — |
| 4328[6] | **Times of Times (IRE) (70)** (MJRyan) **2-9-2** CRutter(14) (prom over 3f) | nk | **13** | 10/1 | 33 | — |
| 4321[9] | **Capture The Moment (70)** (RJRWilliams) **2-9-2** MHills(5) (b.nr hind: bhd fnl 5f) | 12 | **14** | 16/1 | — | — |
| | | | | (SP 146.1%) | **14 Rn** | |

**1m 14.18** (3.58) CSF £40.80 CT £172.36 TOTE £6.60: £2.10 £2.40 £3.20 (£30.70) Trio £212.60 OWNER FirstClass-FourSeasons (MIDDLEHAM) BRED Roldvale Ltd

## 4384 LAMBOURN H'CAP (0-80) (3-Y.O+) (Class D)

2-50 (2-53) **2m (Equitrack)** £3,517.50 (£1,065.00: £520.00: £247.50) Stalls: Low GOING minus 0.43 sec per fur (FST)

| Form | Horse | Dist | Pos | SP | RR | SF |
|---|---|---|---|---|---|---|
| *4355** | **Jaraab (62)** (GLewis) **4-8-13v** 4x SWhitworth(1) (lw: chsd ldr: led 4f out: sn clr: unchal) | — | **1** | 6/4[1] | 79+ | 39 |
| 4326[3] | **Sea Victor (75)** (JLHarris) **3-9-3** KFallon(6) (hld up: chsd wnr over 3f out: no imp) | 6 | **2** | 2/1[2] | 87 | 37 |
| 3957[11] | **Lear Dancer (USA) (67)** (PhilipMitchell) **4-9-4v** GDuffield(2) (hld up: rdn 5f out: one pce fnl 3f) | 1¾ | **3** | 12/1 | 76 | 36 |
| *346** | **Princely Gait (77)** (CACyzer) **4-10-0** DBiggs(4) (bit bkwd: hld up: rdn 4f out: wknd over 2f out) | 6 | **4** | 11/2[3] | 80 | 40 |
| 4099[4] | **Yougo (69)** (MJohnston) **3-8-11** JFanning(3) (led 12f) | 6 | **5** | 14/1 | 67 | 17 |
| *4223[6]* | **Global Dancer (64)** (SDow) **4-8-8**(7) ADaly(5) (b: b.hind: hld up: rdn over 4f out: wknd over 3f out) | 3 | **6** | 8/1 | 58 | 18 |
| | | | | (SP 114.2%) | **6 Rn** | |

**3m 28.42** (6.42) CSF £4.85 TOTE £2.20: £1.90 £1.90 (£2.40) OWNER Mr S. I. Ross (EPSOM) BRED Shadwell Estate Company Limited
WEIGHT FOR AGE 3yo-9lb

## 4385 MIDDLEHAM LIMITED STKS (0-55) (II) (3-Y.O+) (Class F)

3-20 (3-22) **1m 2f (Equitrack)** £2,401.20 (£673.20: £327.60) Stalls: Low

| Form | Horse | Dist | Pos | SP | RR | SF |
|---|---|---|---|---|---|---|
| 3757[2] | **Double Rush (IRE) (50)** (TGMills) **3-8-11** KFallon(4) (b.hind: hld up: led wl over 1f out: rdn out) | — | **1** | 2/1[1] | 65 | 36 |
| 4232[5] | **Manful (54)** (JHetherton) **3-8-11** SWebster(8) (b: gd hdwy over 1f out: str run fnl f: r.o wl) | ¾ | **2** | 11/1 | 64 | 35 |
| 3770[12] | **Never So Rite (IRE) (48)** (DWPArbuthnot) **3-8-8** TQuinn(13) (hdwy over 4f out: rdn over 2f out: unable qckn) | 4 | **3** | 8/1 | 54 | 25 |
| 3897[15] | **By The Bay (54)** (CCElsey) **3-8-6** DHarrison(11) (hld up: led over 2f out tl wl over 1f out: wknd fnl f) | 2½ | **4** | 20/1 | 48 | 19 |
| *4350** | **Fort Knox (IRE) (49)** (RMFlower) **4-9-4** AMorris(12) (lw: nvr nr to chal) | 3 | **5** | 6/1[3] | 51 | 27 |
| 3259* | **Coven Moon (25)** (DMorris) **5-8-13v** JTate(10) (a.p: led 4f out tl over 2f out: sn wknd) | 4 | **6** | 20/1 | 39 | 15 |
| *4336[6]* | **Stalled (IRE) (48)** (PTWalwyn) **5-9-4** RCochrane(9) (s.s: nvr nrr) | nk | **7** | 4/1[2] | 44 | 20 |
| *4335[5]* | **Lady Highfield (50)** (MJRyan) **4-9-1** AClark(5) (hdwy over 2f out: wknd over 1f out) | 1¾ | **8** | 7/1 | 38 | 14 |
| 3455[9] | **Bakers Daughter (54)** (JRArnold) **3-8-8** CRutter(6) (prom over 6f) | 1½ | **9** | 6/1[3] | 34 | 5 |
| 3248[7] | **Tuigamala (41)** (RIngram) **4-9-4** WWoods(7) (lw: led over 2f: wknd over 3f out) | 15 | **10** | 10/1 | 15 | — |
| 4225[11] | **Arnie (IRE) (39)** (GLMoore) **3-8-6**(5) AWhelan(1) (bhd fnl 4f) | 1½ | **11** | 50/1 | 10 | — |
| *4340[12]* | **Dia Georgy (51)** (MrsNMacauley) **4-9-4** MFenton(2) (b: prom over 5f) | ½ | **12** | 7/1 | 11 | — |
| 4156[15] | **Dalcross (41)** (HJCollingridge) **4-8-11** JQuinn(3) (led over 8f out to 4f out: sn wknd) | 2 | **13** | 50/1 | 1 | — |
| | | | | (SP 148.9%) | **13 Rn** | |

**2m 9.36** (5.06) CSF £29.66 TOTE £3.00: £1.10 £4.60 £2.30 (£24.10) Trio £134.30 OWNER Mr Tony Murray (EPSOM) BRED Dermot Finnegan
WEIGHT FOR AGE 3yo-4lb

## 4386 MALTON H'CAP (0-70) (3-Y.O+) (Class E)

3-50 (3-53) **1m (Equitrack)** £3,166.90 (£959.20: £468.60: £223.30) Stalls: High

| Form | Horse | Dist | Pos | SP | RR | SF |
|---|---|---|---|---|---|---|
| *4354** | **Duke Valentino (68)** (RHollinshead) **3-9-13** 5x TIves(5) (hld up: led 4f out: rdn out) | — | **1** | 3/1[1] | 77 | 56 |
| 4340[15] | **Hawaii Storm (FR) (56)** (DJSffrenchDavis) **7-9-3** JWilliams(9) (hdwy 3f out: ev ch 1f out: unable qckn) | 1¼ | **2** | 33/1 | 62 | 44 |
| 4350[3] | **Mr Frosty (64)** (WJarvis) **3-9-9** SSanders(8) (b.off hind: a.p: n.m.r over 1f out: one pce fnl f) | ½ | **3** | 3/1[1] | 70 | 49 |
| *4272[7]* | **Live Project (IRE) (64)** (MJohnston) **3-9-9** DeanMcKeown(6) (led 2f: led 3f out to 1f out: one pce) | nk | **4** | 10/1 | 69 | 48 |
| *395[2]* | **Renown (64)** (LordHuntingdon) **3-9-9** DHarrison(7) (lw: hld up: rdn over 4f out: one pce fnl f) | 1¼ | **5** | 8/1 | 66 | 45 |
| *4354[2]* | **Sadly Sober (IRE) (63)** (PFICole) **3-9-8b** TQuinn(10) (led 6f out to 3f out: wknd over 1f out) | nk | **6** | 10/1 | 65 | 44 |
| *4297[5]* | **Digpast (IRE) (67)** (RJO'Sullivan) **5-10-0b** DBiggs(3) (s.s: nvr nr to chal) | s.h | **7** | 5/1[2] | 68 | 50 |
| *4340[8]* | **North Esk (USA) (53)** (CADwyer) **6-9-0** CDwyer(2) (nvr nrr) | ½ | **8** | 16/1 | 53 | 35 |
| *4363[3]* | **Crystal Gift (55)** (DWPArbuthnot) **3-8-9b**(5) PPMurphy(12) (b.hind: hdwy 6f out: wknd 3f out) | 20 | **9** | 14/1 | 16 | — |
| 4249[7] | **Hatta Breeze (65)** (MAJarvis) **3-9-7b**(3) DRMcCabe(1) (bhd fnl 4f) | nk | **10** | 11/2[3] | 25 | 4 |
| 3268[6] | **The Little Ferret (55)** (AMoore) **5-9-2** RCochrane(4) (b.hind: lw: prom 5f) | 2 | **11** | 25/1 | 10 | — |

*4296[6]* **Komodo (USA) (61)** (KOCunningham-Brown) **3-9-6** WWoods(11) (b.hind: lw: bhd fnl 3f)........8 **12** 12/1 1 —

(SP 138.4%) **12 Rn**

**1m 40.84** (3.44) CSF £90.74 CT £319.66 TOTE £4.50: £2.30 £5.90 £1.80 (£119.70) Trio £110.80 OWNER Mr J. E. Bigg (UPPER LONGDON) BRED Shadwell Estate Company Limited
WEIGHT FOR AGE 3yo-2lb

T/Plpt: £6.40 (1,146.02 Tckts). T/Qdpt: £7.40 (6.4 Tckts). AK

# 4334-SOUTHWELL (L-H) (Standard)
## Thursday November 16th
WEATHER: overcast WIND: fresh half behind

## 4387 NOTTINGHAM LIFE MANAGERS CIRCLE H'CAP (0-65) (I) (3-Y.O+) (Class F)
12-20 (12-20) **1m 6f (Fibresand)** £2,789.00 (£784.00: £383.00) Stalls: High GOING minus 0.09 sec per fur (STD)

SP RR SF

*2919[9]* **Drimard (IRE) (28)** (KMcAuliffe) **4-7-8b** NAdams(6) (in tch: led over 3f out: styd on strly)........— **1** 20/1 40 27
*4336** **Fair and Fancy (FR) (39)** (DNicholls) **4-7-12**(7) 5x JoHunnam(8) (lw: hld up: stdy hdwy over 4f out: kpt on fnl 2f: nvr able to chal)........2½ **2** 3/1[1] 48 35
*4336[7]* **Philmist (50)** (CWCElsey) **3-8-8b** SWebster(3) (s.i.s: sn bhd & drvn along: hdwy 4f out: hung rt & styd on wl u.p appr fnl f)........4 **3** 16/1 54 34
2439[13] **Wildfire (SWI) (42)** (RAkehurst) **4-8-8** AMcGlone(13) (chsd ldr: led 8f out tl over 3f out: grad wknd)........1¼ **4** 10/1 45 32
*4370[7]* **Premier Dance (60)** (DHaydnJones) **8-9-12** AMackay(5) (s.i.s: bhd: hdwy 6f out: kpt on fnl 2f: nvr rchd ldrs)...5 **5** 12/1 57 44
*4336[5]* **Five to Seven (USA) (54)** (CWThornton) **6-9-3**(3)ow1 OPears(11) (b: trckd ldrs: drvn along & outpcd over 4f out: kpt on fnl 2f)........6 **6** 6/1[3] 45 31
4331[8] **Rose of Glenn (45)** (BPalling) **4-8-11** RPerham(9) (lw: led 6f: chsd ldrs tl outpcd fnl 4f)........1¾ **7** 16/1 34 21
4196[12] **Le Temeraire (27)** (DonEnricoIncisa) **9-7-7** KimTinkler(10) (prom early: sn bhd: hrd rdn & sme hdwy 2f out: n.d)........5 **8** 33/1 10 —
*4370** **Ballymac Girl (51)** (JMBradley) **7-9-3** 5x LCharnock(2) (b: lw: chsd ldrs: sn pushed along: lost pl over 2f out)..7 **9** 9/2[2] 26 13
3153[6] **Black Ice Boy (IRE) (30)** (RBastiman) **4-7-10**ow3 JQuinn(7) (s.i.s: hdwy to chse ldrs 8f out: sn rdn: lost pl over 4f out)........2½ **10** 33/1 2 —
4168[2] **Pampas Breeze (IRE) (63)** (WJarvis) **3-9-7** SSanders(4) (lw: prom: effrt over 3f out: sn wknd)........4 **11** 13/2 29 9
4331[3] **Maronetta (36)** (MJRyan) **3-7-8** GBardwell(1) (in tch: rdn, hung rt & rn v.wd ent st: sn bhd)........1¼ **12** 6/1[3] 1 —
**Dispol Dancer (28)** (MrsVAAconley) **4-7-3**(5)ow1 PFessey(12) (chsd ldrs 5f: sn wl bhd)........12 **13** 33/1 — —
1625[8] **Indian Treasure (IRE) (36)** (DJSCosgrove) **3-7-3**(5)ow1 CAdamson(14) (sn wl bhd)........15 **14** 33/1 — —

(SP 130.2%) **14 Rn**

**3m 7.9** (8.90) CSF £78.67 CT £927.78 TOTE £23.90: £4.10 £1.60 £2.90 (£57.60) Trio £136.40; £46.13 to Ascot 17/11/95 OWNER Mr K. W. J. McAuliffe (LAMBOURN) BRED Airlie Stud
LONG HANDICAP Black Ice Boy (IRE) 7-5 Le Temeraire 7-5 Dispol Dancer 7-5 Indian Treasure (IRE) 7-2
WEIGHT FOR AGE 3yo-8lb

## 4388 RIVER IDLE CLAIMING STKS (I) (3-Y.O+) (Class F)
12-50 (12-51) **1m (Fibresand)** £2,187.00 (£612.00: £297.00) Stalls: High GOING minus 0.09 sec per fur (STD)

SP RR SF

4292[5] **Pine Ridge Lad (IRE) (70)** (JLEyre) **5-8-11** SDWilliams(12) (lw: chsd ldrs: sn drvn along: styd on over 1f out: led wl ins fnl f)........— **1** 3/1[2] 67 47
4044[7] **Hawwam (72)** (EJAlston) **9-8-11** KFallon(2) (sn chsng ldrs: edgd rt & ev ch over 1f out: nt qckn nr fin)........¾ **2** 11/4[1] 66 46
3943[10] **Mislemani (IRE) (47)** (AGNewcombe) **5-8-4**(5)ow2 DGriffiths(13) (chsd ldrs: rdn & outpcd over 2f out: kpt on wl fnl f)........2 **3** 10/1 60 38
3825[15] **No Submission (USA) (68)** (DWChapman) **9-8-4** JQuinn(14) (mde most tl wl ins fnl f: no ex)........s.h **4** 13/2[3] 54 34
4225[8] **Dowdency (40)** (JAPickering) **3-8-1**ow1 RLappin(8) (sn chsng ldr: kpt on fnl 2f: nvr able to chal)........2½ **5** 16/1 48 25
3447[11] **Sarasi (65)** (MJCamacho) **3-8-9** LCharnock(16) (chsd ldrs tl wknd over 1f out)........¾ **6** 14/1 55 33
4060[12] **Frans Lad (59)** (JBerry) **3-7-8**(5) PFessey(6) (w ldrs tl wknd over 1f out)........1½ **7** 11/1 42 20
4170[10] **Swynford Flyer (28)** (JAHarris) **6-8-0**(3)ow7 AWhelan(4) (nvr nr to chal)........3 **8** 20/1 38 11
*4371[6]* **Bold Aristocrat (IRE) (50)** (RHollinshead) **4-7-12**(7) FLynch(3) (chsd ldrs: rdn ½-wy: wknd fnl 2f)........2 **9** 16/1 36 16
*4340[7]* **Vocal Command (56)** (WWHaigh) **3-8-3** DaleGibson(11) (nvr nr ldrs)........3 **10** 14/1 30 8
4152[9] **Just Lucky (IRE) (60)** (MrsNMacauley) **3-8-3** JTate(1) (lw: sn drvn along: sme hdwy over 2f out: sn wknd).....5 **11** 12/1 20 —
**Awfully Risky (35)** (PDEvans) **4-7-10v** NAdams(5) (chsd ldrs: sn drvn along: lost pl 3f out)........3 **12** 20/1 5 —
*4350[10]* **Miss Mercy (IRE) (65)** (CNAllen) **3-7-13**(7) JoHunnam(7) (bhd fr ½-wy)........1½ **13** 20/1 14 —
2278[6] **Amnesty Bay (57)** (MDIUsher) **3-7-13**(5) CAdamson(9) (dwlt: a in rr)........12 **14** 12/1 — —
4232[10] **Handsome Squaw (37)** (BWMurray) **3-8-1**ow1 AMackay(15) (b.hind: a in rr)........2½ **15** 33/1 — —
**Mystictich** (GBarnett) **3-8-0** GBardwell(10) (s.i.s: a bhd)........¾ **16** 33/1 — —

(SP 143.1%) **16 Rn**

**1m 43.4** (3.40) CSF £13.12 TOTE £4.10: £1.80 £2.00 £4.20 (£6.30) Trio £9.70 OWNER Whitestonecliffe Racing Partnership (HAMBLETON) BRED Whitechurch Stud in Ireland
WEIGHT FOR AGE 3yo-2lb

## 4389 GRAND UNION NURSERY H'CAP (2-Y.O) (Class D)
1-20 (1-23) **7f (Fibresand)** £3,615.00 (£1,095.00: £535.00: £255.00) Stalls: High GOING minus 0.09 sec per fur (STD)

SP RR SF

4321[2] **Double Diamond (IRE) (84)** (MJohnston) **2-9-7** DeanMcKeown(4) (lw: chsd ldrs: effrt & hung lft over 1f out: styd on wl to ld ins fnl f)........— **1** 2/1[1] 84 44
*4353[2]* **Red Acuisle (IRE) (58)** (GLewis) **2-7-9**ow1 AMackay(14) (a.p: led over 1f out tl ins fnl f)........2 **2** 7/2[2] 52 12
4327[6] **Knave (68)** (RHannon) **2-8-0v**(5)ow1 AWhelan(1) (a chsng ldrs: chal over 1f out: kpt on same pce ins fnl f)........2 **3** 9/1 58 18
3985[18] **Rawi (65)** (WRMuir) **2-8-2**ow1 SSanders(5) (lw: a chsng ldrs: styd on one pce fnl 2f)........s.h **4** 20/1 55 15
*4361[12]* **Arch Angel (IRE) (60)** (DJSffrenchDavis) **2-7-11v** NAdams(8) (b.hind: chsd ldrs tl wknd over 1f out)........2½ **5** 20/1 45 5
3740[2] **Gracious Gretclo (57)** (CJHill) **2-7-3**(5)ow1 PFessey(3) (mde most tl over 1f out: wknd ins fnl f)........1½ **6** 10/1 38 —
3779[11] **One Life To Live (IRE) (57)** (AHarrison) **2-7-3**(5)ow1 CAdamson(2) (bhd tl styd on fnl 2f)........nk **7** 25/1 37 —

| | | | | SP | RR | SF |
|---|---|---|---|---|---|---|
| 4313[16] | **Dancing Cavalier (56)** (RHollinshead) **2-7-7** NCarlisle(7) (sn wl bhd: hdwy over 2f out: nvr nr ldrs) | 1½ | **8** | 33/1 | 34 | — |
| 4221[6] | **Lagan (67)** (CEBrittain) **2-8-4** JQuinn(11) (s.i.s: bhd tl sme hdwy 2f out: n.d) | 1 | **9** | 20/1 | 42 | 2 |
| *3953[5]* | **Doubleyoubeay (62)** (JBerry) **2-7-13** LCharnock(10) (prom tl lost pl 3f out) | 4 | **10** | 16/1 | 28 | — |
| 4321[3] | **Proud Monk (76)** (GLMoore) **2-8-13** SWhitworth(13) (b.nr hind: mid div: drvn along ½-wy: n.d) | ¾ | **11** | 11/2[3] | 40 | — |
| 4231[10] | **Oriole (56)** (NTinkler) **2-7-7** KimTinkler(6) (sn wl bhd) | 1¼ | **12** | 20/1 | 18 | — |
| *4124[8]* | **China Castle (60)** (PHaslam) **2-7-11** DaleGibson(9) (sn wl bhd) | hd | **13** | 7/1 | 21 | — |
| 4059[4] | **Mulhollande Lad (IRE) (60)** (MCChapman) **2-7-4**(7)ow4 MartinDwyer(15) (sn outpcd & bhd) | 9 | **14** | 33/1 | — | — |
| | | | | (SP 137.2%) | **14 Rn** | |

**1m 31.4** (4.60) CSF £10.60 CT £53.53 TOTE £2.90: £1.70 £1.60 £2.90 (£4.90) Trio £20.20 OWNER The 2nd Middleham Partnership (MIDDLEHAM) BRED Dene Investments N V

LONG HANDICAP One Life To Live (IRE) 7-6 Dancing Cavalier 7-6 Oriole 7-4 Gracious Gretclo 7-3 Mulhollande Lad (IRE) 6-10

## 4390 RIVER IDLE CLAIMING STKS (II) (3-Y.O+) (Class F)

1-50 (1-55) **1m (Fibresand)** £2,187.00 (£612.00: £297.00) Stalls: Low GOING minus 0.09 sec per fur (STD)

| | | | | SP | RR | SF |
|---|---|---|---|---|---|---|
| 3757[15] | **Anistop (43)** (RAkehurst) **3-8-9** SSanders(2) (chsd ldrs: led 1f out: styd on wl u.p) | — | **1** | 16/1 | 72 | 44 |
| *4367[3]* | **Sandmoor Denim (65)** (SRBowring) **8-8-7** SWebster(3) (b: trckd ldrs: chal 3f out: rdn over 1f out: unable qckn) | 2½ | **2** | 11/4[1] | 63 | 37 |
| 4275[10] | **Dante's Rubicon (IRE) (45)** (JDBethell) **4-8-0**(5)ow4 AWhelan(7) (w ldrs: led 3f out to 1f out: one pce) | 1¼ | **3** | 14/1 | 59 | 29 |
| 4138[15] | **Beaumont (IRE) (57)** (JEBanks) **5-8-9** JQuinn(5) (lw: bhd: hdwy 2f out: kpt on u.p fnl f) | 2½ | **4** | 10/1 | 58 | 32 |
| *4335[8]* | **Just Flamenco (50)** (MJRyan) **4-8-7** DBiggs(15) (a chsng ldrs: kpt on sme pce fnl 2f) | 1½ | **5** | 16/1 | 53 | 27 |
| *4335[10]* | **Greek Gold (IRE) (54)** (DNicholls) **6-7-10**(7) MartinDwyer(13) (chsd ldr tl wknd over 2f out) | 5 | **6** | 14/1 | 39 | 13 |
| *3950[7]* | **Sweet Supposin (IRE) (87)** (CADwyer) **4-9-5b** TIves(9) (sn bhd: sme hdwy 2f out: n.d) | 3 | **7** | 100/30[2] | 49 | 23 |
| 4053[5] | **First Gold (59)** (JWharton) **6-8-8b** KFallon(6) (nvr bttr than mid div) | 2 | **8** | 6/1[3] | 34 | 8 |
| *4377** | **Certain Way (IRE) (50)** (NPLittmoden) **5-8-4**ow1 TGMcLaughlin(10) (sn bhd & drvn along: n.d) | 7 | **9** | 8/1 | 16 | — |
| *4377[6]* | **Langtonian (46)** (JLEyre) **6-8-0v**(3) NVarley(8) (s.i.s: sn drvn along & chsng ldrs: led 5f out: hdd & wknd 3f out) | 1 | **10** | 20/1 | 13 | — |
| 2306[6] | **Rose Chime (IRE) (39)** (JLHarris) **3-7-9**(5) PFessey(1) (sn drvn along: sme hdwy ½-wy: sn wknd) | ¾ | **11** | 25/1 | 10 | — |
| *4377[10]* | **Green's Bid (57)** (DWChapman) **5-8-2** LCharnock(4) (led 1f: chsd ldrs tl lost pl 3f out) | ½ | **12** | 20/1 | 9 | — |
| 4209[15] | **Legend Dulac (IRE) (39)** (JAHarris) **6-8-1** DaleGibson(14) (b.off fore: hld up & a bhd) | 3½ | **13** | 33/1 | 1 | — |
| 4079[11] | **Benjarong (40)** (RMMcKellar) **3-8-5**ow1 DHarrison(12) (sn bhd) | 8 | **14** | 16/1 | — | — |
| *4362[12]* | **Dragonflight (35)** (DHaydnJones) **4-8-7v** AMackay(16) (led after 1f to 5f out: wknd 3f out) | ½ | **15** | 33/1 | — | — |
| 1639[12] | **Cabcharge Blue (69)** (TJNaughton) **3-8-5**(7) TAshley(11) (b: a bhd) | 2½ | **16** | 11/1 | — | — |
| | | | | (SP 142.8%) | **16 Rn** | |

**1m 43.5** (3.50) CSF £64.44 TOTE £54.90: £14.00 £1.80 £5.60 (£69.30) Trio £203.10 OWNER Mrs A. Valentine (EPSOM) BRED P. Valentine

WEIGHT FOR AGE 3yo-2lb

## 4391 NOTTINGHAM LIFE MANAGERS CIRCLE H'CAP (0-65) (II) (3-Y.O+) (Class F)

2-20 (2-22) **1m 6f (Fibresand)** £2,789.00 (£784.00: £383.00) Stalls: High GOING minus 0.09 sec per fur (STD)

| | | | | SP | RR | SF |
|---|---|---|---|---|---|---|
| *4355[2]* | **La Brief (58)** (MJRyan) **3-9-2** GBardwell(4) (lw: a.p: led 2f out: hld on wl) | — | **1** | 5/2[1] | 77 | 49 |
| *4336[2]* | **Ijab (CAN) (42)** (JParkes) **5-8-8b** KFallon(1) (trckd ldrs: chal over 1f out: r.o) | hd | **2** | 7/2[2] | 62 | 41 |
| *3076[7]* | **Risky Tu (46)** (PAKelleway) **4-8-12** MWigham(10) (prom: led & qcknd 6f out: hdd 2f out: sn outpcd) | 15 | **3** | 9/1 | 49 | 28 |
| *1210[9]* | **El Nido (57)** (MJCamacho) **7-9-9** LCharnock(2) (led tl hdd 6f out: ev ch tl wknd appr fnl f) | 3½ | **4** | 6/1 | 56 | 35 |
| 3259[4] | **Cashmirie (44)** (JLEyre) **3-8-2** RLappin(9) (a chsng ldrs: nt qckn fnl 2f) | 7 | **5** | 9/1 | 34 | 6 |
| *4366[4]* | **Rousitto (57)** (RHollinshead) **7-9-9** TIves(11) (hld up & bhd: hdwy fnl 4f: nrst fin) | 3½ | **6** | 8/1 | 44 | 23 |
| 4114[3] | **Never Time (IRE) (43)** (MrsVAAconley) **3-8-1** MDeering(5) (hld up: hdwy 5f out: sn prom: rdn & btn over 2f out) | ¾ | **7** | 16/1 | 28 | — |
| 3722[8] | **Victor Laszlo (38)** (JDBethell) **3-7-10**ow1 JQuinn(6) (in tch: hrd rdn 6f out: no imp after) | ¾ | **8** | 20/1 | 21 | — |
| 3705[10] | **Who's the Best (IRE) (48)** (APJarvis) **5-9-0** JTate(8) (prom tl lost pl 4f out) | s.h | **9** | 5/1[3] | 33 | 12 |
| 3876[4] | **Sharazi (USA) (58)** (DJSCosgrove) **4-9-5b**(5) AWhelan(3) (hrd drvn 6f out: n.d) | ¾ | **10** | 14/1 | 42 | 21 |
| *4336[15]* | **Crowther Homes (30)** (EJAlston) **5-7-7**(3) NVarley(13) (bhd fr ½-wy) | 13 | **11** | 33/1 | — | — |
| 4205[14] | **K :stal Diva (50)** (AGNewcombe) **4-8-11**(5) DGriffiths(7) (outpcd & bhd after 5f) | 2½ | **12** | 14/1 | 16 | — |
| | **Mister Lawson (36)** (BSmart) **9-8-2**ow8 SSanders(12) (a bhd) | 7 | **13** | 33/1 | — | — |
| | | | | (SP 142.7%) | **13 Rn** | |

**3m 7.6** (8.60) CSF £13.69 CT £71.77 TOTE £3.90: £2.20 £2.10 £3.00 (£7.00) Trio £21.80 OWNER Four Jays Racing Partnership (NEWMARKET) BRED Stud-On-The-Chart

LONG HANDICAP Victor Laszlo 7-8

WEIGHT FOR AGE 3yo-8lb

## 4392 HUMBER H'CAP (0-90) (3-Y.O+) (Class C)

2-50 (2-52) **7f (Fibresand)** £5,680.00 (£1,720.00: £840.00: £400.00) Stalls: Low GOING minus 0.09 sec per fur (STD)

| | | | | SP | RR | SF |
|---|---|---|---|---|---|---|
| 4068[2] | **Be Warned (75)** (NACallaghan) **4-9-0b** DHarrison(1) (trckd ldrs: stdy hdwy to ld ins fnl f: r.o) | — | **1** | 3/1[1] | 82 | 58 |
| *4368[4]* | **Sailormaite (89)** (SRBowring) **4-10-0** SWebster(2) (trckd ldrs: chal 2f out: hrd drvn & one pce fnl f) | 1¼ | **2** | 7/1[3] | 93 | 69 |
| *4368** | **Mr Bergerac (IRE) (91)** (BPalling) **4-9-11**(5) 6x PFessey(3) (bhd: gd hdwy on ins to ld 3f out: hdd & no ex ins fnl f) | 1¾ | **3** | 12/1 | 91 | 67 |
| *4368[6]* | **Loveyoumillions (IRE) (83)** (MJohnston) **3-9-7b** GDuffield(9) (lw: led 4f: rdn & styd on one pce) | ½ | **4** | 14/1 | 83 | 57 |
| *4297[3]* | **Bentico (72)** (MrsNMacauley) **6-8-4v**(7) AmandaSanders(7) (lw: outpcd tl styd on fnl 2f) | 2 | **5** | 10/1 | 66 | 42 |
| 4233[7] | **Johnnie the Joker (80)** (JPLeigh) **4-9-5b** DeanMcKeown(5) (prom: effrt appr st: no imp) | ½ | **6** | 16/1 | 73 | 49 |
| 4268[7] | **Cretan Gift (73)** (NPLittmoden) **4-8-12v** TGMcLaughlin(12) (s.i.s: hdwy appr st: nvr rchd ldrs) | 2½ | **7** | 12/1 | 61 | 37 |
| *4351[2]* | **Present Situation (70)** (LordHuntingdon) **4-8-4**(5) AWhelan(11) (sn pushed along: nvr able rch ldrs) | 2½ | **8** | 5/1[2] | 52 | 28 |
| *4368[3]* | **Little Ibnr (85)** (PDEvans) **4-9-10** KFallon(15) (lw: chsd ldrs tl wknd fnl 3f) | 6 | **9** | 7/1[3] | 53 | 29 |
| 4319[6] | **Somerton Boy (IRE) (77)** (PCalver) **5-9-2** TIves(8) (b.hind: chsd ldrs tl wknd over 2f out) | ¾ | **10** | 12/1 | 43 | 19 |
| *4367[7]* | **Q Factor (71)** (DHaydnJones) **3-8-9** AMackay(10) (nvr trbld ldrs) | 9 | **11** | 20/1 | 18 | — |
| 4040[23] | **Master Millfield (IRE) (75)** (CJHill) **3-8-8**(5) DGriffiths(13) (drvn along thrght: a rr div) | nk | **12** | 14/1 | 21 | — |
| 4035[12] | **Sharp Rebuff (75)** (PJMakin) **4-9-0** RCochrane(4) (outpcd fr ½-wy) | 7 | **13** | 14/1 | 4 | — |
| 3924[13] | **Bernard Seven (IRE) (85)** (CEBrittain) **3-9-9** JQuinn(6) (lw: outpcd & bhd fnl 3f) | 3 | **14** | 12/1 | 8 | — |
| 4160[13] | **Orange Place (IRE) (84)** (TJNaughton) **4-9-4**(5) JDSmith(14) (mid div & hrd drvn ½-wy: sn bhd) | nk | **15** | 16/1 | 6 | — |

| Form | Horse / details | Dist | Pos | SP | RR | SF |
|---|---|---|---|---|---|---|
| 4147[3] | **Wigberto (IRE) (89)** (JLEyre) **3-9-10**(3) OPears(16) (s.i.s: a bhd) | 9 | **16** | 14/1 | — | — |

**1m 29.6** (2.80) CSF £28.63 CT £233.45 TOTE £3.70: £1.70 £1.10 £3.90 £3.80 (£27.20) Trio £69.20 OWNER Midcourts (NEWMARKET) BRED Patrick Eddery Ltd (SP 149.7%) **16 Rn**
WEIGHT FOR AGE 3yo-1lb

## 4393 BRITISH GYPSUM CLUB 2000 (S) STKS (2-Y.O F) (Class G)

3-20 (3-22) **7f** **(Fibresand)** £2,259.00 (£634.00: £309.00) Stalls: Low GOING minus 0.09 sec per fur (STD)

| Form | Horse / details | Dist | Pos | SP | RR | SF |
|---|---|---|---|---|---|---|
| | **Kind of Light** (RGuest) **2-8-9** DHarrison(2) (cmpt: led after 2f: r.o wl fnl 2f) | — | **1** | 10/1 | 70? | 41 |
| *4360** | **Vera's First (IRE) (68)** (GLewis) **2-8-9b**(5) AWhelan(16) (a chsng ldrs: nt qckn fnl 2f) | 7 | **2** | 5/2[2] | 59 | 30 |
| 4285[5] | **La Finale (57)** (MHEasterby) **2-8-9** KFallon(1) (a.p: effrt appr st: one pce fnl 2f) | 2½ | **3** | 2/1[1] | 48 | 19 |
| *4269[6]* | **People Direct (53)** (KMcAuliffe) **2-8-9** GDuffield(9) (hdwy u.p 3f out: nrst fin) | ¾ | **4** | 16/1 | 47 | 18 |
| *4360[4]* | **Shanoora (IRE) (54)** (BPalling) **2-9-0** RPerham(10) (led 2f: chsd ldrs tl wknd fnl 3f) | ½ | **5** | 16/1 | 50 | 21 |
| 4169[14] | **Holloway Melody (59)** (BAMcMahon) **2-8-9** GCarter(3) (chsd ldrs tl wknd u.p fnl 3f) | 1½ | **6** | 14/1 | 42 | 13 |
| 4239[8] | **Petite Juliette** (WJarvis) **2-8-6**(3) JStack(12) (nvr trbld ldrs) | 12 | **7** | 7/1 | 15 | — |
| 819[13] | **Shepherds Dean (IRE)** (PHaslam) **2-8-9** VHalliday(7) (in tch tl outpcd ½-wy: hung rt & n.d after) | ½ | **8** | 16/1 | 13 | — |
| *4269[8]* | **Magical Mill (50)** (RGuest) **2-8-9** GHind(14) (sn pushed along: in tch to ½-wy) | 2½ | **9** | 20/1 | 8 | — |
| 4216[13] | **Diasafina** (SCWilliams) **2-8-9** JQuinn(5) (sn outpcd & wl bhd) | 5 | **10** | 20/1 | — | — |
| *4339[12]* | **Nutcracker (65)** (CBBBooth) **2-8-9b** ACulhane(15) (prom to ½-wy: sn rdn & wknd) | hd | **11** | 16/1 | — | — |
| *2625[5]* | **Let's Hang On (IRE)** (WWHaigh) **2-8-9b** DaleGibson(13) (bit bkwd: sn outpcd & bhd) | 1½ | **12** | 20/1 | — | — |
| 4137[15] | **Laid Back Lucy** (JAHarris) **2-8-4**(5) PFessey(6) (n.d) | hd | **13** | 33/1 | — | — |
| *4338[7]* | **Contrarie** (MJRyan) **2-8-4**(5) DGibbs(11) (a outpcd & bhd) | s.h | **14** | 25/1 | — | — |
| 4151[14] | **Addie Pray (IRE) (70)** (MAJarvis) **2-8-9** JTate(8) (cl up tl p.u lame ½-wy) | | **P** | 9/2[3] | — | — |

**1m 30.7** (3.90) CSF £41.27 TOTE £82.30: £13.10 £1.70 £1.70 (£74.00) Trio £31.50 OWNER Mrs B. Mills (NEWMARKET) BRED Theakston Stud (SP 152.9%) **15 Rn**
Bt in 8,800 gns

## 4394 TRENT APPRENTICE H'CAP (0-85) (3-Y.O+) (Class E)

3-50 (4-02) **5f** **(Fibresand)** £3,209.80 (£972.40: £475.20: £226.60) Stalls: High GOING minus 0.37 sec per fur (FST)

| Form | Horse / details | Dist | Pos | SP | RR | SF |
|---|---|---|---|---|---|---|
| *4337[13]* | **Broadstairs Beauty (IRE) (75)** (SRBowring) **5-9-4b** CTeague(2) (b: b.hind: chsd ldrs: r.o fnl f to ld cl home) | — | **1** | 9/1 | 83 | 59 |
| 3554[4] | **Hever Golf Star (69)** (TJNaughton) **3-8-7**(5) TAshley(8) (lw: led: rdn over 1f out: ct cl home) | ½ | **2** | 12/1 | 75 | 51 |
| 4322[6] | **Shadow Jury (70)** (DWChapman) **5-8-13b** DRMcCabe(11) (a cl up: hrd rdn over 1f out: kpt on) | 1½ | **3** | 10/1 | 72 | 48 |
| 3777[12] | **Lord Sky (75)** (ABailey) **4-8-13**(5) AngelaGallimore(3) (unruly gng to s: chsd ldrs: nt qckn fnl f) | 1¼ | **4** | 25/1 | 73 | 49 |
| 4322[4] | **Lady Sheriff (61)** (MWEasterby) **4-8-4b** PFessey(14) (lw: pushed along thrght: a chsng ldrs: kpt on fnl f) | 1 | **5** | 4/1[2] | 55 | 31 |
| *4368[2]* | **Leigh Crofter (76)** (PDCundell) **6-9-5b** DGriffiths(7) (nrst fin) | ½ | **6** | 10/1 | 69 | 45 |
| 4322[3] | **I'm Your Lady (67)** (BAMcMahon) **4-8-7**(3) MartinDwyer(5) (a in tch: one pce fnl 2f) | s.h | **7** | 16/1 | 60 | 36 |
| *4359[2]* | **Kalar (69)** (DWChapman) **6-8-12b** MBaird(16) (a chsng ldrs: rdn & btn appr fnl f) | nk | **8** | 14/1 | 61 | 37 |
| *4371** | **La Petite Fusee (67)** (RJO'Sullivan) **4-8-10** 7x SSanders(15) (chsd ldrs: sn drvn along: btn appr fnl f) | s.h | **9** | 2/1[1] | 59 | 35 |
| 4197[5] | **Name the Tune (76)** (PHowling) **4-9-5** AWhelan(12) (b.hind: nvr trbld ldrs) | hd | **10** | 6/1[3] | 67 | 43 |
| 4322[12] | **Insider Trader (71)** (RGuest) **4-9-0b** JStack(6) (chsd ldrs tl wknd over 1f out) | nk | **11** | 14/1 | 61 | 37 |
| 4142[7] | **Bells of Longwick (55)** (WWHaigh) **6-7-7v**(5) JoHunnam(10) (v.unruly & led to s: nvr wnt pce) | ¾ | **12** | 20/1 | 43 | 19 |
| 3964[22] | **Four of Spades (71)** (PDEvans) **4-8-11v**(3) AmandaSanders(1) (s.i.s: a bhd) | s.h | **13** | 25/1 | 59 | 35 |
| *4337[6]* | **Sir Tasker (77)** (JLHarris) **7-9-1**(5) DSweeney(9) (a outpcd & bhd) | ¾ | **14** | 25/1 | 62 | 38 |
| 3972[17] | **Thick as Thieves (62)** (RonaldThompson) **3-8-2**(3) ADaly(17) (n.d) | 1¾ | **15** | 33/1 | 42 | 18 |
| 3905[14] | **Ultra Beet (83)** (PHaslam) **3-9-7**(5) CarolDavison(4) (bhd fr ½-wy) | 3 | **16** | 20/1 | 53 | 29 |
| 3750[19] | **Great Bear (80)** (DWChapman) **3-9-9** OPears(13) (dwlt: a wl bhd) | 5 | **17** | 33/1 | 34 | 10 |

**58.6 secs** (1.60) CSF £121.87 CT £1,047.30 TOTE £11.20: £2.80 £5.80 £3.50 £4.30 (£128.70) Trio £582.10; £245.97 to Ascot 17/11/95. OWNER Mrs Judy Hunt (EDWINSTOWE) BRED Patrick Murnaghan (SP 149.7%) **17 Rn**

T/Plpt: £24.70 (338.63 Tckts). T/Qdpt: £8.80 (3.7 Tckts). AA

# 4173a-CURRAGH (Newbridge, Ireland) (R-H) (Yielding)

## Tuesday November 7th

## 4395a HOPEFUL E.B.F. MAIDEN STKS (2-Y.O F)

3-10 (3-14) **7f** £4,069.00 (£921.00: £386.00)

| Form | Horse / details | Dist | Pos | SP | RR | SF |
|---|---|---|---|---|---|---|
| | **Sommar (IRE)** (JOxx,Ireland) **2-9-0** JPMurtagh | — | **1** | 2/1 | — | — |
| 4262[6] | **Lady Joshua (IRE)** (JLDunlop) **2-9-0** RHughes | s.h | **2** | 4/1 | — | — |
| | **Friendly Bird (IRE)** (Ireland) **2-9-0** WJSupple | 6 | **3** | 10/1 | — | — |

**1m 26.7** (3.70) Tote £2.30: £1.80 £2.00 £2.20 (£6.90) OWNER Mr T. Wada (CURRABEG) **30 Rn**

**Sommar (IRE)** showed the utmost gameness for a newcomer. She took the lead inside the last, and gave her all right to the line. (2/1)
**4262 Lady Joshua (IRE)** was always in the front rank, and held a slight advantage two furlongs out. She was headed inside the last, but produced a renewed effort and was just foiled. The pair finished clear. (4/1)

# 4299a-EVRY (France) (R-H) (Good)

## Tuesday November 7th

## 4396a CRITERIUM DES 2 ANS (Gp 2) (2-Y.O)

1-50 (1-50) **6f 110y** £41,916.00 (£16,766.00: £8,383.00: £4,192.00)

| Form | Horse / details | Dist | Pos | SP | RR | SF |
|---|---|---|---|---|---|---|
| 4250a* | **Titus Livius (FR)** (JEPease,France) **2-9-2** CAsmussen (hld up: rdn 2f out: qcknd over 1f out: led post) | — | **1** | | 111 | — |
| 4250a[2] | **Starmaniac (USA)** (CLaffon-Parias,France) **2-8-11** GMosse (3rd early: prog to ld ins fnl f: hdd post) | s.nk | **2** | | 106 | — |

| | Horse | | Dist | Pos | SP | RR | SF |
|---|---|---|---|---|---|---|---|
| 4250a[3] | **Seattle Special (USA)** | (MmeCHead,France) **2-8-8** ODoleuze (led tl hdd ins fnl f: no ex) | 1 | **3** | | 100 | — |
| | **Jasminola (FR)** | (NClement,France) **2-8-8b** OPeslier (2nd early: rdn 2f out: one pce) | 3 | **4** | | 93 | — |
| 4310a[3] | **Oliviero (FR)** | (France) **2-8-11b** ABadel (outpcd early: nvr nr to chal) | ½ | **5** | | 94 | — |

**5 Rn**

**1m 19.07** (3.37) P-M 1.90F: 1.10F 1.10F (SF 3.10F) OWNER Mr S. S. Niarchos BRED S.Niarchos
**4250a* Titus Livius (FR)** is developing into a serious racehorse. He settled well on this occasion, and was brought with a perfectly timed run to gain a narrow victory. Now that he is beginning to settle he should get further. He will next be seen in the Prix Djebel in April, and it will then be decided if he will tackle the Classics or stick to sprinting.
**4250a Starmaniac (USA)** once again found the winner just a shade too good. He was always close to the pace, and looked the winner briefly inside the last. He deserves to win a Group race, but may have to step up in trip.
**4250a Seattle Special (USA)** set a decent gallop, and kept on well once headed. She may have found this trip stretching her stamina, and may be kept to sprints in future.
**Jasminola (FR)** was prominent until the acceleration of the principals proved too much in the final furlong.

## 4347a-SAN SIRO (Milan, Italy) (R-H) (Good)
## Wednesday November 8th

### 4397a PREMIO EUPILL (Listed) (2-Y.O C & F)
1-25 (1-26) **6f** £17,730.00 (£7,801.00: £3,617.00: £2,128.00)

| | Horse | | Dist | Pos | SP | RR | SF |
|---|---|---|---|---|---|---|---|
| 2043a[2] | **Last Hero (FR)** | (BGrizzetti,Italy) **2-8-8** ACarboni | — | **1** | | 87 | — |
| 4032[3] | **The Man** | (MRChannon) **2-8-8** MFenton | s.nk | **2** | | 87 | — |
| | **Golden Turk (IRE)** | (GFratini,Italy) **2-8-8** MEsposito | 1½ | **3** | | 83 | — |
| 4200[3] | **Greek Icon** | (JLDunlop) **2-8-5** JReid | ¾ | **4** | | 78 | — |

**7 Rn**

**1m 11.8** (3.80) Tote 147L: 34L 217L (187L) OWNER Scuderia Jemncha BRED E.Puerari
**4032 The Man** raced in mid division, and made headway to challenge a furlong and a half from home. He took the leas at the furlong marker, but was caught close home.
**4200 Greek Icon** tracked the leader, but was a little short of room just after halfway. She ran on, but could not quite get into contention in the last furlong.

### 4398a PREMIO BAGUTTA-MEMORIAL SERGIO CUMANI (Gp 3) (3-Y.O F)
2-20 (2-35) **1m** £24,657.00 (£11,164.00: £5,182.00)

| | Horse | | Dist | Pos | SP | RR | SF |
|---|---|---|---|---|---|---|---|
| 4093a[5] | **Senebrova** | (VValiani,Italy) **4-8-7** SLandi | — | **1** | | 105 | — |
| 3912a[2] | **Lara (GER)** | (BSchutz,Germany) **3-8-7** ASuborics | ½ | **2** | | 107 | — |
| 4265[6] | **Louis' Queen (IRE)** | (JLDunlop) **3-8-7** JReid | nk | **3** | | 106 | — |

**7 Rn**

**1m 39.1** (9.10) Tote 50L: 17L 14L (41L) OWNER Scuderia Pieffegi
**4265 Louis' Queen (IRE)** was always close up, and chased the winner from over a furlong out. She was run out of second place close home.

### 4399a GRAN CRITERIUM (Gp 1) (2-Y.O C & F)
2-45 (3-05) **1m** £48,739.00 (£23,118.00: £13,101.00: £6,550.00)

| | Horse | | Dist | Pos | SP | RR | SF |
|---|---|---|---|---|---|---|---|
| | **Glory of Dancer** | (FBrogi,Italy) **2-8-11** OPeslier (hld up in rr: hdwy 2f out: ld 1f out: comf) | — | **1** | | 107 | — |
| 3068[3] | **Line Dancer** | (WJarvis) **2-8-11** TQuinn (a cl up: 3rd st: r.o wl) | 2¼ | **2** | | 103 | — |
| 4310a* | **Polaris Flight (USA)** | (PWChapple-Hyam) **2-8-11** JReid (s.i.s: hdwy & 4th st: r.o one pce fnl 2f) | ¾ | **3** | | 101 | — |
| | **Monkey Trouble (USA)** | (MGuarnieri,Italy) **2-8-11** FJovine (led tl hdd by wnr: fdd) | 1 | **4** | | 99 | — |
| 3797a* | **Coral Reef (ITY)** | (Italy) **2-8-11** MLatorre (a.p: 2nd st: no ex fnl 2f) | ½ | **5** | | 98 | — |
| 4084[24] | **Dankeston (USA)** | (MBell) **2-8-11** MFenton (mid div: nvr plcd to chal) | ½ | **6** | | 97 | — |
| | **Blu Taxidoo (USA)** | (AVefdesi,Italy) **2-8-11** MViargu (mid div: nvr plcd to chal) | 2 | **7** | | 93 | — |
| | **Dancer Mitral** | (LBrogi,Italy) **2-8-11** VMezzatesta (chsd ldrs: 5th st: wknd) | 4¾ | **8** | | 84 | — |
| | **Secret Lear (USA)** | (VCaruso,Italy) **2-8-11** MEsposito (a bhd) | nk | **9** | | 83 | — |

**9 Rn**

**1m 39.1** (9.10) Tote 190L: 25L 16L 12L (703L) OWNER Scuderia Gen Horse BRED Cotswold Stud
**Glory of Dancer** was given an excellent ride by his jockey, coming through from the rear to burst clear a furlong out, and win with something in hand. On this form he must be a major contender for the Premio Parioli next Spring.
**3068 Line Dancer** was always prominent, and kept on well in the straight. He had no chance with the winner in the last furlong.
**4310a* Polaris Flight (USA)** had every chance turning in. Once ridden in the straight, he had nothing extra to give, and just stayed on.
**3301* Dankeston (USA)** was always in the middle of the field, and could never get in a blow at the leaders.

## 4396a-EVRY (France) (R-H) (Good)
## Friday November 10th

### 4400a PRIX SARACA (Listed) (2-Y.O F)
1-40 (1-38) **1m** £16,766.00 (£5,748.00: £3,593.00)

| | Horse | | Dist | Pos | SP | RR | SF |
|---|---|---|---|---|---|---|---|
| 4013a[7] | **Wedding Gift (FR)** | (PDemercastel,France) **2-8-11** SGuillot | — | **1** | | 98 | — |
| | **Krissante (USA)** | (MmeCHead,France) **2-8-11** ODoleuze | ½ | **2** | | 97 | — |
| | **Folle Tempete (FR)** | (JEHammond,France) **2-8-11** GMosse | hd | **3** | | 97 | — |
| 4203[2] | **Pacific Grove** | (PFICole) **2-8-11** TQuinn (btn approx 11 3/4l) | | **8** | | — | — |

**8 Rn**

**1m 44.0** (7.00) P-M 10.20F: 2.40F 2.20F 2.00F (30.00F) OWNER Ecurie Fabien Quaki
**3578a Wedding Gift (FR)** finished seventh in the Prix Marcel Boussac, and benefitted from the drop in class to gain a narrow victory.
**4203 Pacific Grove** found this step up in class too much. She did show in front two furlongs out, but weakened in the closing stages to finish last. Connections feel she may have been over the top.

## 4343a-CAPANNELLE (Rome, Italy) (R-H) (Good to firm)
### Sunday November 12th

### 4401a PREMIO ORASTON (3-Y.O)
12-55 (12-58) **1m** £5,910.00 (£2,634.00: £1,418.00)

| | | | | SP | RR | SF |
|---|---|---|---|---|---|---|
| | **Taxi de Nuit (USA)** (AVerdesi,Italy) **3-8-12** MVargiu | — | 1 | | 87 | — |
| 4186a[4] | **Albinor (IRE)** (JLDunlop) **3-9-3** FJovine | 1½ | 2 | | 89 | — |
| 2724a[3] | **Peco's Bill (IRE)** (GBotti,Italy) **3-8-8** GForte | 1½ | 3 | | 77 | — |

**1m 38.2** Tote 102L: 25L 15L 21L (184L) OWNER Gerecon Italia BRED Le Haras Inc **10 Rn**

**4186a Albinor (IRE)** tracked the leader before moving to the front three furlongs out, and stayed there until headed close home. He was trained by John Dunlop, but ran from Luigi Camici's yard on this occasion, and now remains in Italy.

### 4402a PREMIO RIBOT (Gp 2) (3-Y.O+)
1-45 (2-00) **1m** £29,621.00 (£13,666.00: £7,640.00: £3,820.00)

| | | | | SP | RR | SF |
|---|---|---|---|---|---|---|
| 4186a[2] | **Welsh Liberty (IRE)** (DDucci,Italy) **6-8-11** ACorniani (prog 2f out: r.o wl fnl f to ld post) | — | 1 | | 118 | — |
| 1577a[4] | **Lake Storm (IRE)** (GBotti,Italy) **4-8-11** GForte (trckd ldrs: chal over 1f out: led ins fnl f: hdd cl home) | s.h | 2 | | 118 | — |
| 4093a[3] | **Morigi** (ITellini,Italy) **4-8-11** MTellini (3rd st: led 1½f out: hdd ins fnl f: no ex) | ¾ | 3 | | 116 | — |
| 4324[6] | **Mistle Cat (USA)** (SPCWoods) **5-8-11** WWoods (led tl hdd 1½f out: r.o one pce) | 1½ | 4 | | 113 | — |
| 4093a[10] | **Ravier (ITY)** (Italy) **4-8-11** FJovine (mid div: nvr plcd to chal) | 1¾ | 5 | | 110 | — |
| 4093a[6] | **Bartok (IRE)** (Italy) **4-8-11** JacquelineFreda (prom: 2nd st: rdn & wknd 2f out) | 1¾ | 6 | | 106 | — |
| 4186a* | **Bemont Park (ITY)** (Italy) **4-8-8** GBietolini (nvr plcd to chal) | 2½ | 7 | | 98 | — |
| 3814[5] | **Mr Martini (IRE)** (CEBrittain) **5-8-11** LDettori (5th st: rdn 2f out: sn btn) | ¾ | 8 | | 100 | — |
| | **Golden Perform (USA)** (Italy) **3-8-11** VMezzatesta (m.n.s) | 1¼ | 9 | | 100 | — |
| 2439[7] | **Stormaway (ITY)** (Italy) **3-8-11** ASauli (a rr: t.o) | 15 | 10 | | 70 | — |
| | **Lord President (USA)** (Italy) **5-8-13** GPucciatti (a rr: t.o) | ½ | 11 | | 68 | — |

**1m 36.5** Tote 559L: 63L 39L 20L (2576L) OWNER Az Agr Associate SRL **11 Rn**

**Welsh Liberty (IRE)** was a surprise winner, finishing strongly to lead on the line.
**4324 Mistle Cat (USA)** set a fast pace, but was headed and could find nothing extra well over a furlong out.
**3814 Mr Martini (IRE)** was close to the pace, but when asked for an effort over two furlongs out, weakened. He may have been feeling the effects of a long season.

### 4403a PREMIO ROMA (Gp 1) (3-Y.O+)
2-10 (2-33) **1m 2f** £91,497.00 (£47,858.00: £28,333.00: £20,295.00)

| | | | | SP | RR | SF |
|---|---|---|---|---|---|---|
| 4176a[2] | **Slicious** (VCaruso,Italy) **3-8-12** MEsposito (6th st: gd prog to ld ins fnl f: cmftbly) | — | 1 | | 126+ | — |
| 897a* | **Hollywood Dream (GER)** (UOstmann,Germany) **4-8-9** ABest (hld up: gd prog fnl 2f: nt rch wnr) | 1½ | 2 | | 116 | — |
| 4120[3] | **Montjoy (USA)** (PFICole) **3-8-12** TQuinn (cl up: 4th st: led 2f out tl hdd by wnr: r.o one pce) | hd | 3 | | 123 | — |
| 3811[8] | **Prince of Andros (USA)** (DRLoder) **5-8-13** RHughes (a.p: 5th st: chal 2f out: no ex fnl f) | nk | 4 | | 119 | — |
| 4020a[2] | **Olimpia Dukakis (ITY)** (GBotti,Italy) **3-8-8** GForte (hld up: r.o fnl f: nvr plcd to chal) | 2¼ | 5 | | 115 | — |
| 4204[6] | **Alriffa** (RHannon) **4-8-13** TIves (cl up: hdwy & 3rd st: rdn & btn 2f out) | 1½ | 6 | | 113 | — |
| 4007a[5] | **Marildo (FR)** (DSmaga,France) **8-8-13b** GGuignard | 3 | 7 | | 108 | — |
| 4173a[4] | **Richard of York** (JHMGosden) **5-8-13b** LDettori (2nd st: rdn 2f out: wknd) | 4 | 8 | | 102 | — |
| 2388a[2] | **Sugarland Express (IRE)** (OPessi,Italy) **4-8-13** SDettori | 3½ | 9 | | 96 | — |
| 4020a* | **Pourquoi Pas (IRE)** (MGasparini,Italy) **3-8-8** AHerrera | 1½ | 10 | | 94 | — |

**2m 0.8** Tote 49L: 14L 23L 12L (382L) OWNER Laghi SRL BRED F. C. T. Wilson **10 Rn**

**4176a Slicious** has been second in the Prix de Conseil de Paris, and the Gran Premio d'Italia, and so this was a deserved victory. He stays in training next year, and if he maintains this level of form, should win more good races.
**4120 Montjoy (USA)** showed in front until the winner swept by. He is a consistent sort who should win his share of races next year.
**3576a Prince of Andros (USA)** came to dispute the lead with Montjoy two furlongs out, but had nothing left in the last furlong.
**4204 Alriffa** was close up turning for home, but dropped away when ridden in the last quarter mile. The ground was not in his favour.
**4173a Richard of York** was prominent in the early stages, but was ill at ease on the ground, and weakened in the straight.

## 4344a-SAINT-CLOUD (France) (L-H) (Good)
### Sunday November 12th

### 4404a PRIX LE FABULEUX (Listed) (3-Y.O)
1-40 (1-35) **1m 2f** £16,766.00 (£5,748.00: £3,593.00)

| | | | | SP | RR | SF |
|---|---|---|---|---|---|---|
| | **Le Silencieux (IRE)** (AFabre,France) **3-9-2** SGuillot | — | 1 | | 103 | — |
| | **Suresnes (USA)** (AFabre,France) **3-9-2** TJarnet | ¾ | 2 | | 102 | — |
| | **Parfait Glace (FR)** (JEHammond,France) **3-9-2** GMosse | nse | 3 | | 102 | — |
| 4257[4] | **Alkateb** (MissGayKelleway) **3-9-2** PatEddery (btn approx 4¼l) | | 5 | | — | — |

**2m 5.6** (2.10) P-M 8.30F: 3.40F 1.60F (14.00F) OWNER Mr Gary Biszantz (CHANTILLY) BRED Shalden Stud et al **7 Rn**

**4257 Alkateb** never looked like taking a hand in the finish. Although he ran on steadily, he would have preferred softer ground.

### 4405a PRIX PERTH (Gp 3) (3-Y.O+)
2-40 (2-41) **1m** £26,347.00 (£9,581.00: £4,790.00: £2,395.00)

| | | | | SP | RR | SF |
|---|---|---|---|---|---|---|
| 4016a[3] | **Nec Plus Ultra (FR)** (AdeRoyerDupre,France) **4-9-3** GMosse (fin 2nd, hd: awrdd r) | — | 1 | | 124 | — |
| 4178a[5] | **Neverneyev (USA)** (MmeCHead,France) **5-9-0** ODoleuze (fin 1st: disq: plcd 2nd) | | 2 | | 121 | — |

| Form | Horse (Trainer) Age-Wt Jockey | Dist | Pos | SP | RR | SF |
|---|---|---|---|---|---|---|
| 4178a[4] | **Mutakddim (USA)** (JHMGosden) **4-9-0** WCarson | ¾ | **3** | | 119 | — |
| | **Val D'Arbois (FR)** (MDelcher,Spain) **3-8-11** TJarnet | 2 | **4** | | 115 | — |
| 4094a[4] | **Chato (USA)** (HSteinmetz,Germany) **3-9-1** ABest | 2½ | **5** | | 114 | — |
| 4198[4] | **Moon King (IRE)** (RHannon) **3-8-11** RPerham | 1 | **6** | | 108 | — |
| 2897a[5] | **Fairy Path (USA)** (DSmaga,France) **3-8-8** FHead | 1½ | **7** | | 102 | — |
| 4265[3] | **Bin Rosie** (DRLoder) **3-8-11b** PatEddery | 1½ | **8** | | 102 | — |

**10 Rn**

**1m 38.2** (-0.30) P-M 3.70F: 1.30F 1.80F 1.20F (15.40F) OWNER Marquesa de Moratalla BRED Mrs G Forien & Marquise de Moratalla in France

**4016a Nec Plus Ultra (FR)** was awarded the race after a stewards enquiry, and the decision was justified. He was challenging on the rail when hampered by Neverneyev a furlong and a half out. He is a genuine sort who was giving weight all round, and he should continue to make his presence felt next season.

**Neverneyev (USA)** was always in the front rank, but after taking the lead early in the straight, he hung away from the whip and impeded the runner-up. He is a genuine horse who was returning to form after a disappointing Summer campaign. He could be the type to do well in America.

**4178a Mutakddim (USA)** challenged for the lead in the straight. He could not quite get there, and may prefer easier ground

**Val D'Arbois (FR)** was reluctant to go into the stalls. He was held up for a late run, and was putting in his best work at the finish. He may remain in France next season, and should make his mark if doing so.

**4198 Moon King (IRE)** raced in mid division, but was never seen with a real chance. He stayed on at one pace, but looked out of his depth.

**4265 Bin Rosie** was well in touch turning for home, but gradually dropped out of contention. He is not quite up to this class.

## 4387-SOUTHWELL (L-H) (Standard)

## Monday November 20th

WEATHER: fine & sunny WIND: slt half against

### 4406 CHAD LIMITED STKS (0-55) (I) (3-Y.O+) (Class F)

12-30 (12-31) **1m (Fibresand)** £2,187.00 (£612.00: £297.00) Stalls: Low GOING minus 0.03 sec per fur (STD)

| Form | Horse (Trainer) Age-Wt Jockey (comment) | Dist | Pos | SP | RR | SF |
|---|---|---|---|---|---|---|
| 4333[14] | **Saltando (IRE) (47)** (PatMitchell) **4-9-0** RCochrane(4) (s.i.s: sn drvn along & outpcd: hdwy 3f out: styd on wl to ld ins fnl f) | — | **1** | 10/1 | 66 | 35 |
| *4377*[4] | **Dr Caligari (IRE) (54)** (JBerry) **3-8-12v** GCarter(1) (led: clr over 2f out: hdd & no ex ins fnl f) | 2½ | **2** | 4/1[1] | 61 | 28 |
| 4275[7] | **Peacefull Reply (USA) (38)** (FHLee) **5-9-0** AMcGlone(14) (trckd ldrs: kpt on same pce fnl 2f) | 3 | **3** | 20/1 | 55 | 24 |
| *4374*[9] | **Love Legend (55)** (DWPArbuthnot) **10-9-3** SWhitworth(12) (b: mid div: styd on fnl 2f: nvr nr to chal) | s.h | **4** | 12/1 | 58 | 27 |
| *4378*[8] | **Eastleigh (55)** (RHollinshead) **6-9-0** TIves(2) (in tch: drvn along 3f out: kpt on: nvr nr to chal) | ¾ | **5** | 9/1 | 53 | 22 |
| 4275[4] | **Thwaab (44)** (FWatson) **3-8-12** LCharnock(11) (lw: hdwy ½-wy: sn chsng ldrs: outpcd fnl 2f) | 2 | **6** | 14/1 | 49 | 16 |
| *4385*[8] | **Lady Highfield (48)** (MJRyan) **4-9-1** GBardwell(7) (sn bhd: sme hdwy 2f out: n.d) | 1 | **7** | 12/1 | 48 | 17 |
| *4364*[13] | **Persian Flower (46)** (GCBravery) **3-8-7** NCarlisle(15) (mid div: kpt on fnl 2f: n.d) | hd | **8** | 10/1 | 42 | 9 |
| 4283[7] | **Dancing Destiny (50)** (RBastiman) **3-8-7** DeanMcKeown(16) (hld up: stdy hdwy 2f out: styd on ins fnl f: nvr plcd to chal) | s.h | **9** | 8/1[3] | 42 | 9 |
| 4261[12] | **Miss Jemmima (50)** (LordHuntingdon) **3-8-7** DHarrison(5) (nvr bttr than mid div) | 1¼ | **10** | 5/1[2] | 40 | 7 |
| *4362*[6] | **Pacific Girl (IRE) (42)** (BPalling) **3-8-7** RPerham(3) (sn drvn along & chsng ldrs: lost pl over 2f out) | 7 | **11** | 20/1 | 26 | — |
| *222** | **Donia (USA) (52)** (JLHarris) **6-8-9** SSanders(9) (chsd ldrs: drvn along 3f out: sn lost pl) | 3 | **12** | 10/1 | 20 | — |
| *3529*[6] | **Ripsnorter (IRE) (52)** (KBishop) **6-9-0** RPrice(6) (dwlt: a bhd) | ¾ | **13** | 9/1 | 23 | — |
| 4214[6] | **Marjan (IRE) (42)** (THCaldwell) **4-8-9** ACulhane(8) (sn wl bhd) | 6 | **14** | 33/1 | 6 | — |
| 1738[4] | **Bright Paragon (IRE) (36)** (MCChapman) **6-8-7**(7) CMunday(13) (w ldrs tl lost pl 3f out: sn wl bhd: t.o) | 25 | **15** | 33/1 | — | — |

(SP 132.5%) **15 Rn**

**1m 45.3** (5.30) CSF £50.28 TOTE £9.90: £2.80 £1.70 £24.60 (£35.20) Trio not won; £298.66 to Lingfield 21/11/95. OWNER Mrs Sandy Herridge (NEWMARKET) BRED Thoroughbred Trust

WEIGHT FOR AGE 3yo-2lb

### 4407 TOGO H'CAP (0-65) (I) (3-Y.O+ F & M) (Class F)

12-55 (12-58) **6f (Fibresand)** £2,187.00 (£612.00: £297.00) Stalls: Low GOING minus 0.03 sec per fur (STD)

| Form | Horse (Trainer) Age-Wt Jockey (comment) | Dist | Pos | SP | RR | SF |
|---|---|---|---|---|---|---|
| *4274*[3] | **Peggy Spencer (54)** (CWThornton) **3-9-5** DeanMcKeown(10) (trckd ldrs: led over 2f out: clr over 1f out: drvn out) | — | **1** | 5/1[1] | 69 | 50 |
| 4209[10] | **Fiaba (37)** (MrsNMacauley) **7-7-9**(7) AmandaSanders(2) (mid div: hdwy u.p 2f out: chsd wnr over 1f out: no imp) | 3 | **2** | 20/1 | 43 | 25 |
| *4358*[7] | **Another Batchworth (59)** (SMellor) **3-9-10** RPerham(6) (a chsng ldrs: kpt on same pce fnl 2f) | 3 | **3** | 11/2[2] | 58 | 39 |
| 4278* | **Leading Princess (IRE) (51)** (MissLAPerratt) **4-8-11b**(5) PFessey(5) (mde most tl over 2f out: one pce) | 3 | **4** | 13/2[3] | 41 | 23 |
| 4115[17] | **Hello Hobson's (IRE) (51)** (RBastiman) **5-8-11**(5)ow1 HBastiman(8) (chsd ldrs: kpt on same pce fnl 2f) | ¾ | **5** | 12/1 | 38 | 20 |
| *4371*[9] | **My Gallery (IRE) (60)** (ABailey) **4-9-11** SSanders(3) (in tch: effrt over 2f out: no imp) | nk | **6** | 14/1 | 47 | 29 |
| 4280[6] | **Kira (50)** (JLEyre) **5-9-1** RLappin(16) (chsd ldrs: effrt & hung lft 2f out: wknd over 1f out) | 2½ | **7** | 15/2 | 31 | 13 |
| *4371*[7] | **Secret Miss (50)** (APJarvis) **3-9-1** JTate(12) (hdwy on outside 2f out: edgd rt: nvr nr to chal) | ¾ | **8** | 14/1 | 30 | 11 |
| *4274*[11] | **We're Joken (51)** (JBerry) **3-8-9**(7) CLowther(4) (lw: b.nr hind: s.i.s: sn chsng ldrs: wknd 2f out) | 2 | **9** | 16/1 | 25 | 6 |
| *3522*[11] | **Double Glow (39)** (NBycroft) **3-8-4** JQuinn(1) (w ldr tl wknd 2f out) | s.h | **10** | 20/1 | 13 | — |
| *4358** | **Anytime Baby (49)** (PTDalton) **3-9-0** RCochrane(13) (stumbled & lost pl after 100y: n.d) | s.h | **11** | 8/1 | 23 | 4 |
| 3640[9] | **Fiery Footsteps (45)** (SWCampion) **3-8-10** GCarter(11) (chsd ldrs tl wknd over 2f out) | ¾ | **12** | 33/1 | 17 | — |
| *4354*[5] | **Fallal (IRE) (39)** (KMcAuliffe) **3-8-4b** GDuffield(14) (sn bhd) | 5 | **13** | 8/1 | — | — |
| 2858[5] | **Name That Tune (39)** (CJHill) **3-7-13**(5) AWhelan(15) (in tch: drvn along: hung lft & lost pl over 2f out) | 3 | **14** | 9/1 | — | — |
| 3972[14] | **Rotherfield Park (IRE) (42)** (CSmith) **3-8-4**(3) NVarley(7) (s.i.s: a bhd) | 6 | **15** | 25/1 | — | — |
| 3841[7] | **Lorelei Lee (IRE) (58)** (JohnBerry) **3-9-2**(7) GFaulkner(9) (a bhd) | 8 | **16** | 14/1 | — | — |

(SP 139.3%) **16 Rn**

**1m 17.2** (3.70) CSF £101.17 CT £547.32 TOTE £5.40: £1.90 £4.50 £2.00 £2.10 (£85.00) Trio £224.10; £63.15 to Lingfield 21/11/95. OWNER Mr Guy Reed (MIDDLEHAM) BRED Theakston Stud

### 4408 MOZAMBIQUE MAIDEN STKS (2-Y.O) (Class D)

1-20 (1-24) **6f (Fibresand)** £3,631.25 (£1,100.00: £537.50: £256.25) Stalls: Low GOING minus 0.03 sec per fur (STD)

| Form | Horse (Trainer) Age-Wt Jockey (comment) | Dist | Pos | SP | RR | SF |
|---|---|---|---|---|---|---|
| 4330[4] | **Kings Harmony (IRE) (63)** (PJMakin) **2-9-0** RCochrane(1) (sn chsng ldrs: led after 2f: drvn along over 2f out: hld on towards fin) | — | **1** | 7/2[2] | 69 | 44 |

3784[5] **Agent** (JLEyre) **2-9-0** KFallon(15) (lw: a chsng ldrs: styd on u.p appr fnl f: nt rch wnr) ....¾ **2** 4/1[3] 67 42
4255[6] **Ballymoney (IRE)** (WAO'Gorman) **2-9-0** EmmaO'Gorman(7) (trckd ldrs: effrt over 1f out: r.o same pce ins fnl f) ....nk **3** 3/1[1] 66 41
4222[8] **Oberon's Dart (IRE)** (JLDunlop) **2-9-0** GCarter(13) (a chsng ldrs: one pce fnl 2f) ....2½ **4** 7/2[2] 60 35
3763[23] **Napier Star** (MrsNMacauley) **2-8-2**(7) AmandaSanders(4) (in tch: drvn along & outpcd ½-wy: n.d after) ....9 **5** 20/1 31 6
**Loch Style** (RHollinshead) **2-9-0** TIves(3) (bkwd: s.i.s: bhd: kpt on fnl 2f: nvr nrr) ....¾ **6** 20/1 34 9
4130[11] **Young Frederick (IRE)** (KRBurke) **2-9-0** JTate(6) (chsd ldrs tl wknd 2f out) ....s.h **7** 20/1 33 8
4314[9] **Sharp 'n' Shady** (CFWall) **2-8-9** WLord(9) (sn wl bhd: sme hdwy 2f out: n.d) ....2 **8** 12/1 23 —
**Dicentra** (EWeymes) **2-8-9** GHind(11) (bkwd: s.i.s: a bhd) ....1¾ **9** 33/1 18 —
**Silent System (IRE)** (JGFitzGerald) **2-9-0** JQuinn(8) (leggy: scope: s.i.s: a in rr) ....1½ **10** 14/1 19 —
*4338[10]* **Tagatay** (MJCamacho) **2-9-0** SMorris(5) (bit bkwd: s.i.s: a bhd) ....1½ **11** 40/1 15 —
4317[11] **Snitch (48)** (CSmith) **2-9-0v** NCarlisle(10) (led 2f: chsd ldrs tl lost pl over 2f out) ....5 **12** 33/1 2 —
*1090[6]* **Alpheton Prince** (JLHarris) **2-9-0** SSanders(14) (sn bhd & drvn along) ....8 **13** 66/1 — —
**My West End Girl** (AStreeter) **2-8-9** SDWilliams(12) (unf: bkwd: in tch tl lost pl 3f out) ....7 **14** 33/1 — —
*4269[W]* **Gotla Bird** (MJohnston) **2-8-9** DeanMcKeown(2) (bolted going to s: stdd s: swvd lft & fell after 1f: dead) .... **F** 12/1 — —

**1m 17.3** (3.80) CSF £19.44 TOTE £3.90: £1.50 £2.00 £1.50 (£7.60) Trio £8.90 OWNER Ten of Hearts (MARLBOROUGH) BRED Rathasker Stud (SP 138.5%) **15 Rn**

## 4409 CHAD LIMITED STKS (0-55) (II) (3-Y.O+) (Class F)

1-50 (1-51) **1m** **(Fibresand)** £2,187.00 (£612.00: £297.00) Stalls: Low GOING minus 0.03 sec per fur (STD)

SP RR SF

*4274[10]* **Jalmaid (53)** (BAMcMahon) **3-8-10** GCarter(11) (chsd ldrs: outpcd ½-wy: kpt on fnl 2f: led ins fnl f) ....— **1** 13/2 55 25
3974[15] **Lady Nash (50)** (CEBrittain) **3-8-7** JQuinn(16) (trckd ldrs: led over 1f out: hdd ins fnl f) ....1¼ **2** 14/1 50 20
*4340[3]* **Lady Silk (54)** (MissJFCraze) **4-8-9** SWebster(12) (bhd: n.m.r on ins 3f out: swtchd outside: hrd rdn & hung lft over 1f out: kpt on same pce) ....½ **3** 9/2[1] 49 21
*4354[4]* **Northern Grey (45)** (JBerry) **3-8-5**(7) PRoberts(1) (hdwy to chse ldrs ½-wy: kpt on fnl f) ....¾ **4** 12/1 52 22
*4371[8]* **River Wye (IRE) (41)** (JMCarr) **3-8-12** SMorris(8) (b.hind: chsd ldrs: outpcd over 1f out) ....1¾ **5** 33/1 49 19
*4378[6]* **Cicerone (47)** (JLHarris) **5-9-0** SSanders(7) (mde most: hdd over 1f out: edgd rt & sn wknd) ....1 **6** 9/1 47 19
3154[9] **Lilac Rain (41)** (JRArnold) **3-8-7** CRutter(6) (s.i.s: sn wl bhd: sme hdwy 2f out: n.d) ....4 **7** 20/1 34 4
*4340[4]* **Lucky Tucky (50)** (JRJenkins) **4-9-0** AMcGlone(3) (sn chsng ldrs: drvn along over 2f out: grad wknd) ....¾ **8** 11/2[2] 37 9
*4274[8]* **Panther (IRE) (52)** (JHetherton) **5-9-0** DeanMcKeown(14) (chsd ldrs: drvn along & outpcd over 2f out: grad wknd) ....nk **9** 11/1 36 8
*4376[11]* **Mazilla (53)** (AStreeter) **3-8-2**(5) LNewton(10) (b: hdwy 3f out: sn chsng ldrs: edgd lft & wknd over 1f out) ....hd **10** 12/1 31 1
4275[3] **Matisse (39)** (JDBethell) **4-8-4**(5) AWhelan(15) (outpcd after 1f: sme hdwy over 2f out: n.d) ....2½ **11** 6/1[3] 26 —
4157[10] **Sweet Allegiance (50)** (JRPoulton) **5-8-9** GDuffield(13) (sn drvn along & outpcd) ....6 **12** 20/1 14 —
*4379[14]* **Doodies Pool (IRE) (40)** (PBurgoyne) **5-8-11b**(3) DRMcCabe(9) (s.s: a in rr) ....1 **13** 16/1 17 —
*4372[9]* **Percy Parrot (37)** (RMWhitaker) **3-8-12** ACulhane(5) (chsd ldrs: sn drvn along: lost pl 3f out) ....5 **14** 33/1 7 —
3879[16] **My Godson (42)** (FJO'Mahony) **5-8-11b**(3) JStack(4) (w ldrs tl wknd 2f out) ....¾ **15** 20/1 6 —
3977[16] **Gymcrak Hero (IRE) (52)** (GHolmes) **3-8-12** SDWilliams(2) (sn bhd & drvn along) ....5 **16** 7/1 — —

**1m 46.0** (6.00) CSF £96.49 TOTE £8.30: £1.90 £3.40 £2.30 (£60.80) Trio £281.60; £277.70 to Lingfield 21/11/95. OWNER Breeson (TAMWORTH) BRED W. H. F. Carson (SP 140.1%) **16 Rn**

WEIGHT FOR AGE 3yo-2lb

STEWARDS' ENQUIRY Webster susp. 29-30/11/95 (excessive use of whip).

## 4410 IAN LOFTUS PRINTING NURSERY H'CAP (2-Y.O) (Class C)

2-20 (2-20) **1m** **(Fibresand)** £5,150.65 (£1,559.20: £761.10: £362.05) Stalls: Low GOING minus 0.03 sec per fur (STD)

SP RR SF

*4352** **Roman Gold (IRE) (78)** (RHannon) **2-9-1** RPerham(7) (lw: w ldrs going wl: led 4f out: styd on strly ins fnl f: readily) ....— **1** 13/8[1] 84+ 47
*4361** **Quality (IRE) (80)** (WAO'Gorman) **2-9-3v** EmmaO'Gorman(5) (hld up gng wl: smooth hdwy over 3f out: chsd wnr fnl 2f: no imp) ....3 **2** 5/1[3] 80 43
4291[4] **Los Alamos (68)** (CWThornton) **2-8-5** GDuffield(4) (sn outpcd & drvn along: hdwy over 2f out: n.m.r: styd on fnl f) ....3½ **3** 20/1 61 24
*4338[2]* **Alzotic (IRE) (72)** (SGNorton) **2-8-9** GCarter(2) (chsd ldrs: drvn along over 3f out: one pce fnl 2f) ....1½ **4** 6/1 62 25
4001[9] **Six Clerks (IRE) (65)** (JGFitzGerald) **2-8-2** JQuinn(6) (chsd ldrs: outpcd & rdn ½-wy: styd on one pce fnl 2f)...1 **5** 6/1 53 16
*4389** **Double Diamond (IRE) (90)** (MJohnston) **2-9-13** 6x DeanMcKeown(8) (lw: chsd ldrs: effrt 3f out: sn rdn: wknd over 1f out) ....1 **6** 7/2[2] 76 39
4154[10] **Seeking Destiny (IRE) (58)** (MCChapman) **2-7-6**(3)ow2 NVarley(9) (w ldrs: rdn along ½-wy: outpcd fnl 2f) ....¾ **7** 50/1 41? 4
4285[7] **Influence Pedler (56)** (CEBrittain) **2-7-7** GBardwell(3) (sn outpcd & drvn along: a bhd) ....15 **8** 20/1 11 —
3882[5] **Boundary Bird (IRE) (65)** (MJohnston) **2-8-2** JFanning(1) (mde most 4f: wknd 2f out: eased) ....3½ **9** 20/1 13 —

**1m 44.2** (4.20) CSF £10.47 CT £112.55 TOTE £2.70: £1.40 £2.50 £4.20 (£5.40) Trio £32.00 OWNER Mr George Teo (MARLBOROUGH) BRED Saffron Breeders Club (SP 121.8%) **9 Rn**

LONG HANDICAP Seeking Destiny (IRE) 6-5 Influence Pedler 7-5

## 4411 KIM FEARS 39TH BIRTHDAY AGAIN H'CAP (0-75) (3-Y.O+) (Class D)

2-50 (2-50) **2m** **(Fibresand)** £3,775.20 (£1,143.60: £558.80: £266.40) Stalls: High GOING minus 0.03 sec per fur (STD)

SP RR SF

*4391** **La Brief (58)** (MJRyan) **3-8-2** 4x GBardwell(7) (chsd ldrs: rdn along & outpcd over 3f out: styd on to ld over 1f out: drvn out) ....— **1** 3/1[1] 74 6
*4355[3]* **Coleridge (42)** (JJSheehan) **7-7-9b**ow1 JQuinn(5) (mde most tl over 1f out: kpt on same pce) ....2 **2** 7/1[2] 55 —
4326[11] **Supreme Star (USA) (50)** (PRHedger) **4-8-0v**(3) NVarley(12) (lw: chsd ldrs: rdn to chal over 2f out: one pce)..1 **3** 3/1[1] 63 4
4326[2] **Paradise Navy (67)** (CREgerton) **6-9-6** RHughes(1) (hld up: stdy hdwy 6f out: rdn & outpcd over 3f out: eased fnl f) ....10 **4** 7/1[2] 70 11
*4370[2]* **Cuango (IRE) (60)** (RHollinshead) **4-8-13** RCochrane(8) (hld up: hdwy 6f out: sn prom: rdn over 3f out: no imp) ....3 **5** 7/1[2] 60 1
4288[14] **Great Oration (IRE) (43)** (FWatson) **6-7-10v**ow3 LCharnock(10) (b.nr hind: chsd ldrs: drvn along 5f out: sn outpcd) ....13 **6** 16/1 27 —

| | | | | SP | RR | SF |
|---|---|---|---|---|---|---|
| *4126[10]* | **Castle Secret (51)** (DBurchell) **9-7-11**(7)ow1 KSked(3) (racd wd: bhd: sme hdwy 5f out: n.d) | 11 | **7** | 20/1 | 26 | — |
| *4270[2]* | **Pharly Dancer (75)** (WWHaigh) **6-10-0** DaleGibson(6) (plld hrd: w ldrs: drvn along 6f out: wknd over 3f out) | .10 | **8** | 11/1[3] | 41 | — |
| *4366[8]* | **Claque (60)** (DWChapman) **3-7-13**(5) PFessey(2) (wl bhd fnl 6f) | 1 | **9** | 20/1 | 25 | — |
| | **Master Glen (44)** (GROldroyd) **7-7-11**ow4 AMackay(13) (b: a bhd: t.o 4f out) | nk | **10** | 33/1 | 5 | — |
| *4336[4]* | **Kadiri (IRE) (60)** (JRBosley) **4-8-13** RPerham(11) (bhd & drvn along ½-wy: lost tch 6f out) | s.h | **11** | 7/1[2] | 25 | — |
| *4391[9]* | **Who's the Best (IRE) (48)** (APJarvis) **5-8-1** JTate(4) (chsd ldrs tl wknd 4f out: eased) | 7 | **12** | 11/1[3] | 6 | — |
| *2632[3]* | **The Cottonwool Kid (51)** (THCaldwell) **3-7-4**(5)ow2 CAdamson(9) (w ldrs tl wknd qckly 7f out: t.o 4f out) | dist | **13** | 50/1 | — | — |
| | | | | (SP 137.0%) | **13 Rn** | |

**3m 42.4** (16.40) CSF £26.49 CT £68.37 TOTE £4.50: £2.50 £1.80 £2.00 (£18.80) Trio £38.20 OWNER Four Jays Racing Partnership (NEWMARKET) BRED Stud-On-The-Chart
LONG HANDICAP Master Glen 7-6 Great Oration (IRE) 7-5 The Cottonwool Kid 6-7
WEIGHT FOR AGE 3yo-9lb

## 4412 ZAMBIA (S) STKS (3, 4 & 5-Y.O) (Class F)
3-20 (3-20) **1m 3f** **(Fibresand)** £2,537.00 (£712.00: £347.00) Stalls: Low GOING minus 0.03 sec per fur (STD)

| | | | | SP | RR | SF |
|---|---|---|---|---|---|---|
| 4332[10] | **Jemima Puddleduck (45)** (DWPArbuthnot) **4-8-12b** RPrice(3) (mde all: clr 7f out: unchal) | — | **1** | 8/1 | 49 | 37 |
| 3987[P] | **Buckley Boys (40)** (ABailey) **4-8-7**(5) DGriffiths(5) (hld up: hdwy 5f out: chsd wnr 2f out: hung lft u.p: no imp) | .5 | **2** | 5/1[2] | 42 | 30 |
| 4170[12] | **Magication (28)** (CNAllen) **5-8-12** JQuinn(2) (b: hdwy 5f out: sn drvn along: kpt on fnl 2f: nvr nr to chal) | 1¾ | **3** | 20/1 | 39 | 27 |
| *4378[4]* | **Dally Boy (56)** (MHEasterby) **3-8-12** LCharnock(11) (hmpd after 1f: hdwy to chse ldrs 6f out: sn drvn along: one pce fnl 3f) | 1¼ | **4** | 8/1 | 42 | 25 |
| 4332[4] | **Miltak (37)** (PJMakin) **3-8-7** SSanders(8) (hdwy 6f out: rdn over 3f out: n.d) | 5 | **5** | 6/1[3] | 30 | 13 |
| *4363[4]* | **Toat Chieftain (54)** (DMorris) **3-8-12** JTate(1) (a.p: chsd wnr over 3f out: wknd 2f out) | 15 | **6** | 7/1 | 13 | — |
| 4275[14] | **Saint Amigo (40)** (JLEyre) **3-8-12** RLappin(14) (chsd ldrs tl wknd 4f out) | 3½ | **7** | 16/1 | 8 | — |
| 4232[9] | **Newgate Hush (27)** (BWMurray) **3-8-2**(5) CTeague(6) (b.off hind: hung rt thrght: a bhd: t.o 4f out) | 10 | **8** | 33/1 | — | — |
| *4374[7]* | **Farmer's Tern (IRE) (57)** (WJarvis) **3-8-7b** MTebbutt(7) (b.nr hind: hld up: hmpd after 1f: a in rr) | ½ | **9** | 5/1[2] | — | — |
| 4332[16] | **Alioli (40)** (MJRyan) **3-8-7** GBardwell(4) (in tch: drvn along 7f out: sn wl bhd: t.o 4f out) | 20 | **10** | 16/1 | — | — |
| | **Sheecky** (BAMcMahon) **4-9-3** GCarter(13) (hmpd after 1f: a bhd: t.o 4f out) | 3 | **11** | 33/1 | — | — |
| | **Cast the Line (69)** (CREgerton) **5-9-3b** RHughes(10) (chsd ldrs: rdn & wknd 4f out: eased) | 11 | **12** | 3/1[1] | — | — |
| | **Westfield** (WGMTurner) **3-8-5**(7) ALakeman(12) (tall: unf: in tch: drvn along 7f out: wknd 5f out) | 8 | **13** | 20/1 | — | — |
| | **White Lady (51)** (BJLlewellyn) **4-8-12** VSlattery(9) (wl bhd fr ½-wy: wl t.o 4f out) | 10 | **14** | 20/1 | — | — |
| | | | | (SP 139.3%) | **14 Rn** | |

**2m 29.5** (9.50) CSF £51.05 TOTE £6.70: £2.20 £2.10 £10.60 (£19.50) Trio £224.80 OWNER Mrs B. J. Lee (COMPTON) BRED Haresfoot Stud
WEIGHT FOR AGE 3yo-5lb
Bt in 5,200 gns
**OFFICIAL EXPLANATION Cast the Line: had gurgled.**

## 4413 TOGO H'CAP (0-65) (II) (3-Y.O+ F & M) (Class F)
3-50 (4-01) **6f** **(Fibresand)** £2,187.00 (£612.00: £297.00) Stalls: Low GOING minus 0.03 sec per fur (STD)

| | | | | SP | RR | SF |
|---|---|---|---|---|---|---|
| 4057[16] | **My Cherrywell (51)** (LRLloyd-James) **5-8-8b**(7) KimberleyHart(2) (lw: b.hind: trckd ldrs: led over 2f out: rdn clr over 1f out) | — | **1** | 20/1 | 60 | 33 |
| 4215[18] | **Indiahra (49)** (RHollinshead) **4-8-13v** NCarlisle(1) (bhd & pushed along: gd hdwy over 2f out: kpt on same pce fnl f: nvr able to chal) | 3½ | **2** | 16/1 | 49 | 22 |
| *4377[8]* | **Newington Butts (IRE) (46)** (KMcAuliffe) **5-8-10** GDuffield(10) (lw: chsd ldrs: effrt 2f out: styd on same pce) | 1¾ | **3** | 10/1 | 41 | 14 |
| 4131* | **Anita's Contessa (IRE) (64)** (BPalling) **3-10-0** RPerham(9) (sn drvn & outpcd: styd on fnl 2f: nvr nr ldrs) | 3 | **4** | 12/1 | 52 | 24 |
| *4394[12]* | **Bells of Longwick (56)** (WWHaigh) **6-9-6** RCochrane(15) (in tch: outpcd over 2f out: kpt on fnl f) | 1½ | **5** | 14/1 | 39 | 12 |
| 4193[7] | **Never Such Bliss (52)** (JDBethell) **3-9-2** TIves(3) (wl bhd tl styd on u.p appr fnl f: nt rch ldrs) | nk | **6** | 20/1 | 35 | 7 |
| *4272[9]* | **David James' Girl (58)** (ABailey) **3-9-3**(5) DGriffiths(16) (dwlt: bhd tl styd on fnl 2f) | hd | **7** | 12/1 | 41 | 13 |
| *4377[5]* | **Bold Gem (61)** (BJMeehan) **4-9-11b** RHughes(12) (dwlt: bhd & pushed along: sme hdwy over 1f out: n.d) | ½ | **8** | 8/1[3] | 42 | 15 |
| 3624[6] | **Irchester Lass (41)** (SRBowring) **3-8-0**(5)ow1 CTeague(11) (prom: rdn over 2f out: wknd over 1f out) | nk | **9** | 6/1[2] | 21 | — |
| *4359[6]* | **Fascination Waltz (57)** (JJSheehan) **8-9-7** JQuinn(5) (lw: chsd ldrs tl wknd wl over 1f out) | 1½ | **10** | 10/1 | 33 | 6 |
| 4194[19] | **Polli Pui (44)** (PDEvans) **3-8-8** SSanders(6) (sn bhd & drvn along: n.d) | 1¼ | **11** | 33/1 | 18 | — |
| *4123** | **Blue Sioux (60)** (JWharton) **3-9-10b** AMackay(4) (lw: led tl over 2f out: edgd rt & wknd) | hd | **12** | 3/1[1] | 33 | 5 |
| 4215[19] | **Legatee (62)** (AStreeter) **4-9-7**(5) LNewton(7) (in tch: drvn along ½-wy: wknd over 1f out: eased) | 1¼ | **13** | 10/1 | 31 | 4 |
| *1456[13]* | **Fairey Firefly (57)** (MJCamacho) **4-9-7** LCharnock(8) (sltly hmpd s: n.m.r ½-wy: sn chsng ldrs: wknd over 1f out: eased) | 1 | **14** | 8/1[3] | 23 | — |
| *3649[11]* | ***Graceful Lady (41)*** (EJAlston) **5-8-2**(3) NVarley(13) (Withdrawn not under Starter's orders: v.unruly in stalls: reard over bkwds & rn loose) | | **W** | 14/1 | — | — |
| *4113[14]* | ***Nadwaty (IRE) (52)*** (MCChapman) **3-8-9**(7) CMunday(14) (Withdrawn not under Starter's orders: rdr inj in stalls) | | **W** | 20/1 | — | — |
| | | | | (SP 140.6%) | **14 Rn** | |

**1m 18.2** (4.70) CSF £268.30 CT £2,658.96 TOTE £33.40: £7.40 £5.50 £3.20 (£68.10) Trio £1,090.51 OWNER Mrs Cheryl Owen (MALTON) BRED J. C. and Mrs C. L. Owen

T/Jkpt: Not won; £1,845.36 to Lingfield 21/11/95. T/Plpt: £14.00 (682.23 Tckts). T/Qdpt: £24.00 (5.1 Tckts). WG

# 4379-LINGFIELD (L-H) (Standard)
## Tuesday November 21st

## 4414 LIRA MAIDEN STKS (I) (2-Y.O) (Class D)
12-10 (12-14) **7f** **(Equitrack)** £3,030.00 (£915.00: £445.00: £210.00) Stalls: Low GOING minus 0.26 sec per fur (FST)

| | | | | SP | RR | SF |
|---|---|---|---|---|---|---|
| 3766[6] | **Banzhaf (USA)** (GLMoore) **2-9-0** SWhitworth(5) (lw: a.p: led over 3f out: drvn out) | — | **1** | 5/1[3] | 81 | 20 |
| 4313[14] | **Faith Alone** (CFWall) **2-8-9** GDuffield(6) (a.p: chsd wnr over 3f out: ev ch ins fnl f: unable qckn) | 1 | **2** | 20/1 | 74 | 13 |
| 4262[19] | **Antiguan Jane** (RWArmstrong) **2-8-9** RPrice(3) (bit bkwd: rdn thrght: lost pl 3f out: r.o one pce fnl f) | 5 | **3** | 25/1 | 62 | 1 |
| 4148[14] | **Carmosa (USA)** (WJarvis) **2-8-9** SSanders(9) (hld up: rdn over 4f out: one pce fnl 3f) | nk | **4** | 4/1[2] | 62 | 1 |

4255[2] **Ocean Stream (IRE) (78)** (JLEyre) **2-9-0** DeanMcKeown(1) (dwlt: hld up: rdn over 4f out: one pce fnl 3f).......hd **5** 13/8[1] 66 5

**Waft (USA)** (JHMGosden) **2-8-9v** GHind(10) (neat: outpcd: nvr nrr).......5 **6** 5/1[3] 50 —

3870[9] **Matthias Mystique** (MissBSanders) **2-8-4**(5) AWhelan(4) (bhd fnl 4f).......nk **7** 33/1 49 —

4320[16] **Spinning Mouse** (DMorley) **2-8-9** RCochrane(11) (a bhd).......1½ **8** 20/1 46 —

**Sassy Street (IRE)** (RFJohnsonHoughton) **2-9-0** AMcGlone(7) (w'like: bit bkwd: dwlt: a bhd).......3 **9** 20/1 44 —

*4369*[10] **Poly By Staufan (IRE) (52)** (MRChannon) **2-8-9** WNewnes(2) (led over 3f).......13 **10** 20/1 9 —

4216[12] **Eternally Grateful** (MrsNMacauley) **2-8-9** JQuinn(8) (a bhd).......13 **11** 33/1 — —

**1m 27.79** (3.79) CSF £85.40 TOTE £6.10: £3.40 £12.80 £11.90 (£124.20) Trio Not won; £229.12 to Chepstow 22/11/95 OWNER Mr Bryan Pennick (EPSOM) BRED Pope McLean (SP 120.2%) **11 Rn**

## 4415 PESETA H'CAP (0-65) (I) (3-Y.O+) (Class F)

12-40 (12-41) **1m 2f (Equitrack)** £2,426.40 (£680.40: £331.20) Stalls: Low GOING minus 0.26 sec per fur (FST)

SP RR SF

*4379*[6] **Studio Thirty (44)** (DMorris) **3-8-9** JTate(12) (rdn thrght: hdwy over 3f out: led ins fnl f: r.o wl).......— **1** 16/1 60 27

*4298** **No Speeches (IRE) (56)** (SDow) **4-9-4**(7) ADaly(6) (rdn thrght: hdwy over 4f out: led 1f out tl ins fnl f: r.o).......nk **2** 2/1[1] 72 43

*4378** **Benjamins Law (49)** (JAPickering) **4-9-4** 5x RLappin(10) (led 8f out: clr over 3f out: hdd 1f out: sn wknd).......7 **3** 7/2[2] 53 24

4000[7] **Sparkling Roberta (37)** (MDIUsher) **4-8-6**ow2 RPrice(3) (hld up: chsd ldr over 3f out tl over 1f out: sn wknd).......3 **4** 16/1 35 6

*4351*[3] **Montone (IRE) (49)** (JRJenkins) **5-9-4** AMcGlone(11) (nvr nr to chal).......3½ **5** 9/1 43 14

*4355*[12] **Access Carnival (IRE) (43)** (RBoss) **4-8-12** GDuffield(13) (s.s: hdwy over 4f out: wknd over 2f out).......3 **6** 25/1 32 3

3860[3] **Shady Deed (USA) (58)** (JWHills) **3-9-9** AClark(1) (lw: led 2f: wknd 3f out).......11 **7** 8/1 30 —

4233[5] **Zacaroon (59)** (JFfitch-Heyes) **4-10-0** DHarrison(5) (b.hind: bhd fnl 4f).......2½ **8** 10/1 27 —

*4379*[7] **Green Golightly (USA) (43)** (DAWilson) **4-8-7**(5) AWhelan(9) (prom over 7f).......3½ **9** 16/1 5 —

*4363*[2] **Silver Singer (58)** (DRLoder) **3-9-9** RHughes(4) (lw: prom 6f).......2½ **10** 4/1[3] 16 —

4261[4] **Bakheta (45)** (KTIvory) **3-8-10** DBiggs(8) (prom over 5f).......2 **11** 7/1 — —

*4366*[11] **Elly Fleetfoot (IRE) (60)** (BJMeehan) **3-9-11** RCochrane(7) (lw: a bhd).......nk **12** 16/1 14 —

1501[10] **Charlie-Don't Surf (30)** (RGuest) **3-7-9**ow2 NAdams(2) (lw: s.s: a bhd: t.o fnl 5f).......dist **13** 33/1 — —

**2m 8.57** (4.27) CSF £55.75 CT £145.91 TOTE £190.70: £22.70 £1.90 £3.10 (£98.80) Trio £236.50; £233.18 to Chepstow 22/11/95 OWNER Mr Derek Holder (NEWMARKET) BRED A. F. Budge (Equine) Ltd (SP 148.6%) **13 Rn**

WEIGHT FOR AGE 3yo-4lb

## 4416 GUILDER H'CAP (0-70) (3-Y.O+) (Class E)

1-10 (1-11) **1m 4f (Equitrack)** £3,195.50 (£968.00: £473.00: £225.50) Stalls: Low GOING minus 0.26 sec per fur (FST)

SP RR SF

*4376** **Opera Buff (IRE) (50)** (MissGayKelleway) **4-8-9** RCochrane(11) (lw: hdwy over 4f out: chsd ldr over 3f out: led over 1f out: comf).......— **1** 13/8[2] 73 45

*4335*[4] **H'Ani (48)** (WJHaggas) **3-8-1** SSanders(7) (swtg: led 7f out tl over 1f out: unable qckn).......5 **2** 25/1 64 30

*4385*[2] **Manful (54)** (JHetherton) **3-8-7** SWebster(10) (b: gd hdwy over 1f out: str run fnl f: fin wl: too much to do).......9 **3** 9/1[3] 58 24

*4364** **Loki (IRE) (69)** (GLewis) **7-9-9**(5) AWhelan(12) (b: s.s: hdwy over 4f out: rdn over 3f out: 3rd & btn whn eased wl ins fnl f).......½ **4** 11/8[1] 73 45

*4366*[6] **Colosse (46)** (JLEyre) **3-7-13** LCharnock(14) (no hdwy fnl 3f).......½ **5** 33/1 49 15

4333[17] **Anjou (61)** (JPearce) **3-9-0** GBardwell(3) (led 2f: hrd rdn over 3f out: wknd over 2f out).......1¾ **6** 25/1 62 28

4162[12] **Brick Court (IRE) (45)** (RFJohnsonHoughton) **3-7-12** JQuinn(2) (nvr nr to chal).......10 **7** 33/1 32 —

*4379*[5] **Fastini Gold (51)** (MDIUsher) **3-8-4** AMackay(9) (lw: hdwy 6f out: wknd over 4f out).......1 **8** 25/1 37 3

4259[23] **Comtec's Legend (36)** (JFBottomley) **5-7-4**(5)ow2 CAdamson(5) (hld up: rdn over 3f out: sn wknd).......2 **9** 25/1 17 —

4259[20] **Fresh Look (IRE) (45)** (RCSpicer) **3-7-12**ow3 DGibson(13) (lw: prom over 8f).......15 **10** 33/1 5 —

3896[13] **Miss Parkes (38)** (PCClarke) **6-7-11** NAdams(4) (bhd fnl 5f).......hd **11** 50/1 1 —

*4362*[13] **Just a Single (IRE) (42)** (JFfitch-Heyes) **4-7-10b**(5)ow2 PPMurphy(6) (led 10f out to 7f out: wknd over 4f out) 15 **12** 50/1 — —

**Jari (USA) (67)** (MJPolglase) **4-9-12b** GCarter(8) (virtually ref to r: a t.o).......30 **13** 33/1 — —

*4378*[12] **Unforeseen (60)** (SirMarkPrescott) **3-8-13** GDuffield(1) (bhd fnl 7f: t.o).......6 **14** 33/1 — —

**2m 33.53** (3.53) CSF £39.87 CT £277.47 TOTE £2.70: £1.70 £3.10 £1.50 (£18.30) Trio £31.60 OWNER Mr D. C. Toogood (WHITCOMBE) BRED Juddmonte Farms (SP 124.2%) **14 Rn**

WEIGHT FOR AGE 3yo-6lb

STEWARDS' ENQUIRY Whelan susp. 30/11 & 1, 2 & 6/12/95 (failing to secure best possible placing).

## 4417 LIRA MAIDEN STKS (II) (2-Y.O) (Class D)

1-40 (1-47) **7f (Equitrack)** £3,030.00 (£915.00: £445.00: £210.00) Stalls: Low GOING minus 0.26 sec per fur (FST)

SP RR SF

*4269*[5] **Truth** (SirMarkPrescott) **2-8-9** GDuffield(7) (hld up: led over 2f out: all out).......— **1** 6/1 65 —

4314[18] **Autobabble (IRE) (55)** (RHannon) **2-9-0** RPerham(5) (lw: hld up: rdn over 4f out: r.o wl ins fnl f).......hd **2** 5/2[1] 70 5

1361[7] **Uoni** (CEBrittain) **2-8-9** JQuinn(4) (rdn over 4f out: hdwy over 3f out: r.o one pce).......5 **3** 13/2 53 —

*4352*[9] **Be Satisfied** (AMoore) **2-8-7**(7) ALakeman(3) (b.hind: led 1f: ev ch over 2f out: one pce).......½ **4** 33/1 57 —

*4334*[9] **Ivor's Deed** (CFWall) **2-8-9**(5) LNewton(8) (led 6f out tl over 2f out: wknd fnl f).......7 **5** 4/1[2] 41 —

4103[20] **Mr Teddy** (WJarvis) **2-9-0** SSanders(1) (nvr nr to chal).......7 **6** 10/1 25 —

4161[16] **Naked Emperor** (MJFetherston-Godley) **2-9-0** DaleGibson(6) (s.s: a bhd).......3 **7** 16/1 18 —

**Queens Fancy** (SDow) **2-8-9** DHarrison(10) (unf: lw: a bhd).......1 **8** 16/1 11 —

*4353*[8] **Riviere Rouge (40)** (SGKnight) **2-8-9** GBardwell(2) (lw: outpcd).......1 **9** 40/1 9 —

1590[2] **Petite Annie (57)** (TGMills) **2-8-2**(7) JCornally(9) (prom over 3f).......10 **10** 9/2[3] — —

**1m 29.13** (5.13) CSF £20.87 TOTE £8.40: £1.60 £1.80 £3.00 (£16.50) Trio £84.30 OWNER Cheveley Park Stud (NEWMARKET) BRED Cheveley Park Stud Ltd (SP 120.6%) **10 Rn**

## 4418 MARK MAIDEN STKS (3-Y.O) (Class D)

2-15 (2-22) **1m (Equitrack)** £3,589.30 (£1,086.40: £530.20: £252.10) Stalls: High GOING minus 0.26 sec per fur (FST)

SP RR SF

**Easy Choice (USA)** (PhilipMitchell) **3-9-0** AClark(11) (lw: s.s: hdwy over 3f out: chsd ldr over 2f out: led wl ins fnl f: r.o wl).......— **1** 5/2[2] 59 41

| | | | | SP | RR | SF |
|---|---|---|---|---|---|---|
| 4261[10] | **Kellaire Girl (IRE) (47)** (AMoore) **3-8-4**(5) AWhelan(1) (b.hind: led 6f out: clr over 2f out: hdd wl ins fnl f: unable qckn) | 1¾ | **2** | 9/1 | 51 | 33 |
| *4296*[7] | **Desert Water (IRE) (45)** (JJBridger) **3-9-0** JQuinn(5) (hdwy over 3f out: wknd over 1f out) | 13 | **3** | 25/1 | 30 | 12 |
| | **Taniyar (FR)** (RHollinshead) **3-9-0** TIves(12) (w'like: lost pl over 2f out: r.o one pce) | ½ | **4** | 9/1 | 29 | 11 |
| *4340*[5] | **Action Jackson (54)** (BJMcMath) **3-9-0** RHughes(9) (led 2f: wknd 3f out) | 3 | **5** | 11/2[3] | 23 | 5 |
| 4162[7] | **Mr Medley (67)** (RHannon) **3-9-0** RPerham(10) (lost pl over 4f out: one pce fnl 2f) | ¾ | **6** | 5/4[1] | 21 | 3 |
| *4359*[8] | **Hong Kong Dollar (54)** (BAPearce) **3-9-0** DeanMcKeown(3) (prom over 5f) | nk | **7** | 25/1 | 20 | 2 |
| *4363*[11] | **Begger's Opera** (PatMitchell) **3-9-0** GBardwell(4) (a bhd) | 3 | **8** | 50/1 | 14 | — |
| *4363*[13] | **Miss Ticklepenny** (MajorDNChappell) **3-8-9** NAdams(7) (hdwy over 4f out: wknd over 2f out) | 5 | **9** | 33/1 | — | — |
| *4354*[10] | **Diamond Bangle (30)** (CCElsey) **3-8-9** CRutter(2) (b.hind: prom over 4f) | 14 | **10** | 66/1 | — | — |
| 4362[11] | **Astrojoy (IRE) (38)** (SGKnight) **3-8-9b** WNewnes(6) (Withdrawn not under Starter's orders: veterinary advice) | | **W** | 50/1 | — | — |
| *4054*[17] | ***Celestial Waters*** (APJames) **3-8-9** GHind(8) (Withdrawn not under Starter's orders: veterinary advice) | | **W** | 66/1 | — | — |
| | | | | (SP 125.9%) | **10 Rn** | |

**1m 39.86** (2.46) CSF £24.52 TOTE £4.50: £1.50 £2.10 £6.10 (£12.40) Trio £307.60; £151.68 to Chepstow 22/11/95 OWNER Mr J. Morton (EPSOM) BRED Juddmonte Farms

## 4419 FRANC CONDITIONS STKS (3-Y.O+) (Class D)

2-50 (2-51) **1m 2f (Equitrack)** £3,758.60 (£1,137.80: £555.40: £264.20) Stalls: Low GOING minus 0.26 sec per fur (FST)

| | | | | SP | RR | SF |
|---|---|---|---|---|---|---|
| *4367*[6] | **Far Ahead (74)** (JLEyre) **3-9-2** RLappin(1) (lw: hld up: chsd ldr 2f out: led wl ins fnl f: r.o wl) | — | **1** | 25/1 | 83 | 40 |
| 4201[4] | **Benfleet (83)** (RWArmstrong) **4-9-12** RPrice(3) (lw: hdwy over 4f out: rdn over 3f out: r.o wl ins fnl f) | ¾ | **2** | 4/1[2] | 88 | 49 |
| *4363** | **Heboob Alshemaal (IRE) (80)** (JHMGosden) **3-8-9v** GHind(5) (lw: hld up: led over 2f out: hrd rdn over 1f out:hdd wl ins fnl f: unable qckn) | s.h | **3** | 4/6[1] | 75 | 32 |
| 3957[4] | **Prince Danzig (IRE) (77)** (DJGMurraySmith) **4-9-12** RHughes(4) (lw: led over 7f: wknd over 1f out) | 9 | **4** | 12/1 | 73 | 34 |
| 4065[4] | **Dee-Lady (83)** (WGMTurner) **3-8-8** RPerham(6) (lw: a.p: ev ch over 2f out: sn wknd) | 5 | **5** | 9/2[3] | 51 | 8 |
| 4333[12] | **Todd (USA) (57)** (PhilipMitchell) **4-9-0** TIves(2) (prom over 6f) | s.h | **6** | 66/1 | 53 | 14 |
| 4213[6] | **Sparrowhawk (IRE) (72)** (BWHills) **3-8-11** RCochrane(7) (a.p: ev ch 2f out: wkng whn virt p.u over 1f out) | 5 | **7** | 20/1 | 46 | 3 |
| *1049*[11] | **El Atrevido (FR) (67)** (NJHWalker) **5-9-3**(3) JStack(8) (lw: bhd fnl 5f) | 20 | **8** | 33/1 | 19 | — |
| | | | | (SP 118.9%) | **8 Rn** | |

**2m 7.78** (3.48) CSF £115.18 TOTE £43.10: £4.00 £1.30 £1.10 (£18.10) OWNER Sunpak Potatoes (HAMBLETON) BRED Sir John Astor
WEIGHT FOR AGE 3yo-4lb

## 4420 PESETA H'CAP (0-65) (II) (3-Y.O+) (Class F)

3-25 (3-26) **1m 2f (Equitrack)** £2,413.80 (£676.80: £329.40) Stalls: Low GOING minus 0.26 sec per fur (FST)

| | | | | SP | RR | SF |
|---|---|---|---|---|---|---|
| *4379** | **Spitfire Bridge (IRE) (53)** (MMcCormack) **3-9-4** 5x RCochrane(2) (hld up: chsd ldr 3f out: led 1f out: drvn out) | — | **1** | 4/1[2] | 64 | 39 |
| 4284[2] | **Wahem (IRE) (30)** (CEBrittain) **5-7-13** JQuinn(12) (hld up: led over 3f out to 1f out: unable qckn) | 1¾ | **2** | 9/2[3] | 38 | 17 |
| 4205[5] | **Juct-Mana-Mou (IRE) (55)** (GLewis) **3-9-1b**(5) AWhelan(7) (hdwy over 4f out: hrd rdn over 1f out: one pce) | 2½ | **3** | 5/1 | 59 | 34 |
| 4249[9] | **Mnemonic (48)** (HCandy) **3-8-13** WNewnes(9) (hdwy over 3f out: one pce fnl 2f) | 1¼ | **4** | 16/1 | 50 | 25 |
| 4284[6] | **Pine Essence (USA) (47)** (JLEyre) **4-9-2** RLappin(3) (lw: hdwy over 6f out: wknd over 3f out) | 8 | **5** | 12/1 | 36 | 15 |
| 4261[11] | **Alpine Storm (IRE) (29)** (MDIUsher) **3-7-3**(5)ow1 CAdamson(10) (nvr nr to chal) | ¾ | **6** | 50/1 | 16 | — |
| *4385** | **Double Rush (IRE) (55)** (TGMills) **3-9-6** 5x RHughes(8) (b.hind: hld up: rdn over 2f out: wknd over 1f out) | 1¼ | **7** | 3/1[1] | 41 | 16 |
| 4386[2] | **Hawaii Storm (FR) (56)** (DJSffrenchDavis) **7-9-11** JWilliams(5) (hdwy over 3f out: sn wknd) | nk | **8** | 10/1 | 42 | 21 |
| 4385[3] | **Never So Rite (IRE) (48)** (DWPArbuthnot) **3-8-10**(3) DRMcCabe(11) (a.p: led 4f out tl over 3f out: sn wknd) | 4 | **9** | 8/1 | 27 | 2 |
| 4357[10] | **Mutinique (35)** (BAPearce) **4-7-11**(7)ow1 JWilkinson(4) (b.hind: a bhd) | 3½ | **10** | 40/1 | 8 | — |
| 4249[12] | **El Don (45)** (MJRyan) **3-8-10** GCarter(6) (chsd ldr: led 5f out to 4f out: sn wknd) | 1½ | **11** | 33/1 | 16 | — |
| 1645[16] | **Biased View (29)** (RThompson) **3-7-8** GBardwell(1) (lw: led 5f: t.o) | dist | **12** | 40/1 | — | — |
| | | | | (SP 123.4%) | **12 Rn** | |

**2m 8.18** (3.88) CSF £21.82 CT £85.91 TOTE £6.40: £1.80 £1.70 £2.70 (£18.40) Trio £57.20 OWNER East Manton Racing Stables Ltd (WANTAGE) BRED John Harrington
WEIGHT FOR AGE 3yo-4lb

## 4421 LADBROKE ALL-WEATHER TROPHY H'CAP (Qualifier) (0-70) (3-Y.O+) (Class E)

3-55 (3-57) **7f (Equitrack)** £3,224.10 (£976.80: £477.40: £227.70) Stalls: Low GOING minus 0.26 sec per fur (FST)

| | | | | SP | RR | SF |
|---|---|---|---|---|---|---|
| 4281[4] | **Anzio (IRE) (66)** (BAPearce) **4-9-6b**(3) DRMcCabe(9) (b: b.hind: a.p: led over 2f out: rdn out) | — | **1** | 12/1 | 78 | 49 |
| 3960* | **Crystal Heights (FR) (66)** (RJO'Sullivan) **7-9-9** SSanders(15) (b: lw: gd hdwy over 3f out: chsd wnr over 1f out: unable qckn ins fnl f) | 3½ | **2** | 9/1[3] | 70 | 41 |
| 3943[21] | **Whatever's Right (IRE) (64)** (MDIUsher) **6-9-7** RPerham(1) (hdwy over 1f out: r.o ins fnl f) | 2 | **3** | 9/2[2] | 63 | 34 |
| *4350*[4] | **Invocation (69)** (AMoore) **8-9-7**(5) AWhelan(11) (b.hind: lw: hld up: hrd rdn over 2f out: r.o ins fnl f) | 1 | **4** | 12/1 | 66 | 37 |
| *4356*[10] | **Scissor Ridge (48)** (JJBridger) **3-8-4** JQuinn(7) (lw: led 2f: led over 3f out tl over 2f out: wknd 1f out) | nk | **5** | 33/1 | 46 | 15 |
| *4374*[6] | **Dancing Sioux (60)** (RGuest) **3-9-2** LCharnock(14) (a.p: rdn over 4f out: one pce fnl 3f) | s.h | **6** | 25/1 | 57 | 26 |
| *4357*[3] | **Apollo Red (56)** (AMoore) **6-8-13** CandyMorris(6) (b.hind: led 5f out tl over 3f out: wknd over 1f out) | 1½ | **7** | 20/1 | 49 | 20 |
| 4268[4] | **Canary Falcon (66)** (JohnBerry) **4-9-9** MWigham(4) (b: lw: nvr nrr) | 1¾ | **8** | 14/1 | 55 | 26 |
| *2925*[2] | **Grey Charmer (IRE) (53)** (CJames) **6-8-10** AMcGlone(2) (a mid div) | 1½ | **9** | 20/1 | 39 | 10 |
| *4377*[12] | **Quinzii Martin (54)** (DHaydnJones) **7-8-11** AMackay(13) (nvr nrr) | hd | **10** | 33/1 | 39 | 10 |
| 1595[6] | **Eagle Day (USA) (68)** (DRCElsworth) **4-9-11** JWilliams(10) (bhd fnl 5f) | nk | **11** | 14/1 | 53 | 24 |
| *4359*[3] | **Perfect Brave (62)** (DRCElsworth) **4-9-0**(5)ow1 AProcter(16) (hld up: rdn over 2f out: wknd wl over 1f out) | 1 | **12** | 10/1 | 43 | 14 |
| *4386** | **Duke Valentino (71)** (RHollinshead) **3-9-13** 6x TIves(12) (a bhd) | ½ | **13** | 7/4[1] | 53 | 22 |
| *4386*[4] | **Live Project (IRE) (65)** (MJohnston) **3-9-7** DeanMcKeown(3) (a bhd) | ½ | **14** | 14/1 | 46 | 15 |
| 4268[16] | **Jahangir (IRE) (53)** (PatMitchell) **6-8-10** GBardwell(8) (a bhd) | 1 | **15** | 33/1 | 31 | 2 |
| *4371*[10] | **Maid Welcome (60)** (MrsNMacauley) **8-8-10v**(7) AmandaSanders(5) (bhd fnl 2f) | 1¼ | **16** | 14/1 | 35 | 6 |
| | | | | (SP 137.9%) | **16 Rn** | |

**1m 25.98** (1.98) CSF £117.58 CT £523.31 TOTE £16.00: £2.10 £3.00 £2.70 £3.40 (£42.50) Trio £184.60 OWNER Mr Richard Gray (LIMPSFIELD) BRED Rathduff Stud
WEIGHT FOR AGE 3yo-1lb

T/Jkpt: Not won; £4,661.83 to Windsor 22/11/95. T/Plpt: £1,893.50 (4.47 Tckts). T/Qdpt: £16.20 (3.3 Tckts). AK

## 4401a-CAPANNELLE (Rome, Italy) (R-H) (Soft)
### Thursday November 16th

**4422a** PREMIO SAMBA MAIDEN (2-Y.O)
1-45 (1-52) **6f** £4,925.00

| | | | | SP | RR | SF |
|---|---|---|---|---|---|---|
| | **Reddish Creek (USA)** (ARenzoni,Italy) **2-8-10** JacquelineFreda | — | 1 | | — | — |
| 4320[12] | **On the Carpet (IRE)** (JLDunlop) **2-8-10** VMezzatesta | nk | 2 | | — | — |
| | **Berry Bird (IRE)** (LCamici,Italy) **2-9-0** MPasquale | 1¼ | 3 | | — | — |
| | | | | | | **8 Rn** |

**1m 11.4** Tote 38L: 15L 16L 15L (92L) OWNER D. Venturi BRED Wafare Farm
**4004a On the Carpet (IRE)** battled back when headed at the furlong pole. She is capable of winning similar races on this showing.

## 4400a-EVRY (France) (R-H) (Soft)
### Friday November 17th

**4423a** PRIX FILLE DE L'AIR (Gp 3) (3-Y.O+ F & M)
2-30 (2-43) **1m 2f 110y** £26,347.00 (£9,581.00: £4,790.00: £2,395.00)

| | | | | SP | RR | SF |
|---|---|---|---|---|---|---|
| 4015a[7] | **Marie de Ken (FR)** (AdeRoyerDupre,France) **3-8-8** SGuillot | — | 1 | | 114 | — |
| | **Restiv Star (FR)** (AFabre,France) **3-8-8** TJarnet | 1 | 2 | | 113 | — |
| 4176a[8] | **Daraydala (IRE)** (AdeRoyerDupre,France) **3-8-8** GMosse | ¾ | 3 | | 111 | — |
| 4316* | **Sue's Artiste** (BWHills) **4-8-11** MHills (btn 15¼l) | | 9 | | 102 | — |
| 4316[4] | **Mountains of Mist (IRE)** (RCharlton) **3-8-8** ESaint-Martin (btn 16 3/4l) | | 10 | | 97 | — |
| | | | | | | **13 Rn** |

**2m 16.82** (6.82) P-M 10.50F: 3.00F 2.40F 2.00F (42.00F) OWNER Ecurie Bader
**4316* Sue's Artiste** was close up turning in, and had every chance until weakening quickly in the last furlong.
**4316 Mountains of Mist (IRE)** had a difficult task, but ran well until dropping away in the final furlong and a half.

## 4422a-CAPANNELLE (Rome, Italy) (R-H) (Good)
### Sunday November 19th

**4424a** PREMIO GUIDO BERARDELLI (Gp 2) (2-Y.O)
1-20 (1-32) **1m 1f** £29,442.00 (£13,532.00: £7,550.00: £3,775.00)

| | | | | SP | RR | SF |
|---|---|---|---|---|---|---|
| 3797a[2] | **Brave Indigo** (GBotti,Italy) **2-8-11** FJovine (cl up: 5th st: hdwy to ld over 1f out: jst hld on) | — | 1 | | — | — |
| 4146* | **Latin Reign (USA)** (PWChapple-Hyam) **2-8-11** JReid (chsd ldrs: 4th st: chal over 1f out: r.o wl cl hme) | nse | 2 | | — | — |
| | **Kafhar** (LBrogi,Italy) **2-8-11** VMezzatesta (a.p: n.m.r 2f out: plld out & r.o wl ins fnl f: unlucky) | nse | 3 | | — | — |
| | **Konic (ITY)** (LCamici,Italy) **2-8-11** MPasquale (led tl over 1f out: no ex ins fnl f) | 1¼ | 4 | | — | — |
| 4399a[7] | **Blu Taxidoo (USA)** (Italy) **2-8-11** MViargu (mid div: prog 2f out; one pce fnl f) | ¾ | 5 | | — | — |
| | **Bog Wild (USA)** (Italy) **2-8-11** LSorrentino (nvr plcd to chal) | 2¼ | 6 | | — | — |
| | **Fuoco Stellare (ITY)** (Italy) **2-8-11** MEsposito (dwlt: bhd tl r.o fnl 2f) | 2 | 7 | | — | — |
| | **Anticolano (IRE)** (Italy) **2-8-11** GBietolini (a bhd) | 5 | 8 | | — | — |
| | **General Academy (IRE)** (Italy) **2-8-11** GForte (s.i.s: a rr) | 2 | 9 | | — | — |
| 4399a[4] | **Monkey Trouble (USA)** (Italy) **2-8-11** WCarson (prom tl wknd over 2f out) | 1½ | 10 | | — | — |
| 2387a[2] | **Attimo Fuggente (IRE)** (Italy) **2-8-11** ACorniani (a rr) | ½ | 11 | | — | — |
| | | | | | | **11 Rn** |

**1m 51.9** Tote 23L: 14L 15L 34L (50L) OWNER Dr Carlo Vittadini (ITALY)
**4146* Latin Reign (USA)** is on the small side, but looked very fit. He seemed to be in trouble two furlongs out, but battled on gamely all the way.
**Kafhar** would have probably won had he not been so short of racing room at a crucial stage. Once he saw daylight he finished really strongly.

**4425a** PREMIO UMBRIA (Gp 3)
2-10 (2-32) **6f** £25,477.00 (£11,749.00: £6,572.00: £3,286.00)

| | | | | SP | RR | SF |
|---|---|---|---|---|---|---|
| 1397a[2] | **Beat of Drums** (GBotti,Italy) **4-9-6b** FJovine | — | 1 | | 112 | — |
| 3922[12] | **Baaderah (IRE)** (LMCumani) **3-9-3** JReid | 4 | 2 | | 99 | — |
| | **Munaaji (USA)** (AWohler,Germany) **4-9-6b** ABoschert | ¾ | 3 | | 99 | — |
| 4345a* | **Lavinia Fontana (IRE)** (JLDunlop) **6-9-3** GForte (btn approx 8l) | | 6 | | 96 | — |
| | | | | | | **10 Rn** |

**1m 9.6** Tote 55L: 19L 21L 17L (235L) OWNER Dr Carlo Vittadini (ITALY) BRED Dr C. Vittadini
**Beat of Drums** was quite an impressive winner. He was always travelling well behind the leaders, and when given his head a furlong out, he quickened clear. He will remain in training, and could be a major force in similar events next year.
**1488* Baaderah (IRE)** put up a much better effort here. She was in front at halfway, but was unable to match the winner's acceleration.
**4345a* Lavinia Fontana (IRE)** disputed the lead in the early stages, and was still in with a chance over a furlong out. She then dropped away quickly, and was found to have burst a blood vessel.

## 3583a-BORDEAUX (France) (R-H) (Good to soft)
### Sunday November 19th

**4426a** GRAND PRIX DE BORDEAUX (Listed) (3-Y.O+)
2-00 (1-56) **1m 4f** £23,952.00 (£8,623.00: £4,311.00)

| | | | | SP | RR | SF |
|---|---|---|---|---|---|---|
| 4187a[3] | **Perche No (FR)** (BSecly,France) **3-8-7** OPeslier | — | 1 | | 111 | — |
| | **Kassani (IRE)** (AdeRoyerDupre,France) **3-8-11** GMosse | 1 | 2 | | 114 | — |
| 4346a* | **Taufan's Melody** (LadyHerries) **4-9-5** RCochrane | hd | 3 | | 116 | — |

| | | | | SP | RR | SF |
|---|---|---|---|---|---|---|
| $4325^{7}$ | **Royal Scimitar (USA)** (PFICole) **3-8-5b** TQuinn (btn over 7l) | | **14** | | — | — |
| | | | | | | **14 Rn** |

**No Time Taken** P-M 7.00F: 1.70F 1.30F 2.00F (6.60F) OWNER Mr J. Clerico BRED J. Clerico

**Perche No (FR)**, who finished third to Taufan's Melody at Lyon last month, reversed the form on 5lb better terms. He took the lead inside the final furlong and ran on well.

**4346a* Taufan's Melody** took the lead over half a mile out, and made the best of his way home. He could not sustain the effort inside the last furlong, but this was still a brave attempt at recording the hat-trick.

**4325 Royal Scimitar (USA)** was close to the pace from the start, and was in second place turning in, but soon came under pressure and weakened quickly.

## 4406-SOUTHWELL (L-H) (Standard)
## Friday November 24th

### 4427 FARMERS WEEKLY H'CAP (0-80) (I) (3-Y.O+) (Class D)
12-20 (12-21) **7f** **(Fibresand)** £3,185.00 (£962.00: £468.00: £221.00) Stalls: Low GOING: 0.06 sec per fur (STD)

| | | | | SP | RR | SF |
|---|---|---|---|---|---|---|
| 4240* | **Nashaat (USA) (68)** (MCChapman) **7-8-13**(3) DRMcCabe(11) (swtg: unruly in stalls: sn chsng ldrs: led & hung lft over 1f out: styd on wl) | — | **1** | 8/1 | 78 | 60 |
| $4280^{4}$ | **Stand Tall (47)** (CWThornton) **3-7-8**ow1 GBardwell(9) (lw: led tl over 1f out: one pce) | 2 | **2** | 6/1 3 | 52 | 32 |
| $4041^{5}$ | **Ochos Rios (IRE) (60)** (BSRothwell) **4-8-8** JQuinn(4) (in tch: kpt on same pce fnl 2f: nvr able to chal) | 1½ | **3** | 10/1 | 62 | 44 |
| 4238* | **Saseedo (USA) (80)** (WAO'Gorman) **5-10-0** EmmaO'Gorman(3) (s.s: bhd tl styd on fnl 2f) | ¾ | **4** | 6/1 3 | 80 | 62 |
| *$4390^{2}$* | **Sandmoor Denim (65)** (SRBowring) **8-8-13** SWebster(1) (b: lw: mid div: effrt & swtchd outside over 2f out: kpt on: nvr nr to chal) | 4 | **5** | 5/1 2 | 56 | 38 |
| *$4367^{5}$* | **Heathyards Lady (USA) (71)** (RHollinshead) **4-8-12**(7) FLynch(8) (nvr nr ldrs) | 2½ | **6** | 7/1 | 56 | 38 |
| *$4388^{6}$* | **Sarasi (64)** (MJCamacho) **3-8-11v** LCharnock(10) (chsd ldrs tl rdn & wknd 2f out) | nk | **7** | 16/1 | 50 | 30 |
| $4249^{4}$ | **Barrel of Hope (65)** (JLEyre) **3-8-12b** KFallon(5) (sn bhd & drvn along: sme hdwy 2f out: n.d) | 5 | **8** | 9/4 1 | 39 | 19 |
| *$4272^{6}$* | **Dream Carrier (IRE) (58)** (REPeacock) **7-8-6** RPerham(7) (sn bhd & drvn along) | s.h | **9** | 20/1 | 31 | 13 |
| *$93^{4}$* | **Elton Ledger (IRE) (72)** (MrsNMacauley) **6-9-6v** JTate(2) (b: trckd ldrs: effrt 2f out: sn wknd) | 2½ | **10** | 12/1 | 40 | 22 |
| | **Fortis Pavior (IRE) (54)** (CWCElsey) **5-7-11**(5) PFessey(6) (bit bkwd: in tch: drvn along ½-wy: sn lost pl) | 7 | **11** | 33/1 | 6 | — |
| | | | | (SP 130.0%) | | **11 Rn** |

**1m 30.7** (3.90) CSF £56.00 CT £457.83 TOTE £11.80: £2.90 £2.00 £2.10 (£93.50) Trio £239.60 OWNER Mr Tony Satchell (MARKET RASEN) BRED Echo Valley Horse Farm and Swettenham Stud
WEIGHT FOR AGE 3yo-1lb

### 4428 EAST MIDLANDS ELECTRICITY (LINCOLN) CLAIMING STKS (I) (3, 4 & 5-Y.O) (Class F)
12-45 (12-47) **6f** **(Fibresand)** £2,426.40 (£680.40: £331.20) Stalls: Low GOING: 0.06 sec per fur (STD)

| | | | | SP | RR | SF |
|---|---|---|---|---|---|---|
| *$4337^{3}$* | **Berge (IRE) (75)** (WAO'Gorman) **4-9-0b** EmmaO'Gorman(6) (lw: sn trckng ldrs: led over 2f out: rdn clr over 1f out: eased nr fin) | — | **1** | 4/6 1 | 81+ | 57 |
| *$4354^{3}$* | **Vladivostok (45)** (BdeHaan) **5-7-11**(5) PFessey(7) (lw: a chsng ldrs: kpt on u.p fnl 2f: no ch w wnr) | 7 | **2** | 25/1 | 50 | 26 |
| *$4367^{9}$* | **Desert Invader (IRE) (65)** (DWChapman) **4-8-10** ACulhane(8) (chsd ldrs: rdn over 2f out: kpt on) | 1 | **3** | 5/1 2 | 56 | 32 |
| *2925** | **Matthew David (42)** (SRBowring) **5-8-5b** NCarlisle(3) (b: lw: chsd ldrs tl outpcd over 2f out: kpt on fnl f) | ¾ | **4** | 12/1 | 49 | 25 |
| *$4335^{11}$* | **Sea God (44)** (MCChapman) **4-8-6** KFallon(10) (effrt on outside 3f out: kpt on: nvr nr ldrs) | 1¼ | **5** | 33/1 | 46 | 22 |
| *$4371^{4}$* | **Superbit (44)** (BAMcMahon) **3-8-11** SSanders(11) (in tch: effrt on outside 3f out: kpt on: nvr nr to chal) | nk | **6** | 12/1 | 52 | 27 |
| *$4388^{9}$* | **Bold Aristocrat (IRE) (50)** (RHollinshead) **4-8-1**(7) FLynch(12) (sn outpcd & drvn along: hmpd over 1f out: n.d) | 3 | **7** | 12/1 | 40 | 16 |
| *$4274^{9}$* | **Aljaz (49)** (RHarris) **5-8-4b** AMackay(9) (chsd ldrs tl wknd wl over 1f out: eased) | 1¼ | **8** | 10/1 3 | 32 | 8 |
| $4240^{5}$ | **Framed (IRE)** (SCWilliams) **5-9-4** JTate(2) (b: dwlt: a bhd) | 1¼ | **9** | 10/1 3 | 43 | 19 |
| *$4358^{9}$* | **Light Movement (IRE) (40)** (WSCunningham) **5-8-5b**(3) DRMcCabe(5) (led tl over 2f out: hung lft & wknd over 1f out) | 3½ | **10** | 33/1 | 24 | — |
| $715^{22}$ | **Selmeston (IRE)** (PSFelgate) **3-8-9** GDuffield(1) (s.i.s: a bhd & sn drvn along) | nk | **11** | 50/1 | 25 | — |
| $3649^{15}$ | **Dancing Jazztime** (JSWainwright) **4-8-5** DeanMcKeown(4) (sn outpcd & bhd) | 13 | **12** | 33/1 | — | — |
| | | | | (SP 132.6%) | | **12 Rn** |

**1m 16.9** (3.40) CSF £21.71 TOTE £1.70: £1.10 £4.40 £2.10 (£19.40) Trio £22.50 OWNER Mr S. Fustok (NEWMARKET) BRED S. Fustok
Berge (IRE) clmd MissGKelleway £3,000

### 4429 ORCHID MAIDEN STKS (2-Y.O) (Class D)
1-10 (1-14) **5f** **(Fibresand)** £3,680.00 (£1,115.00: £545.00: £260.00) Stalls: High GOING minus 0.22 sec per fur (FST)

| | | | | SP | RR | SF |
|---|---|---|---|---|---|---|
| $3680^{6}$ | **Galine** (WAO'Gorman) **2-8-9** EmmaO'Gorman(12) (trckd ldrs: led over 1f out: shkn up & r.o wl ins fnl f) | — | **1** | 2/1 1 | 78 | 37 |
| $2221^{2}$ | **Mask Flower (USA) (76)** (MJohnston) **2-8-9** DeanMcKeown(11) (chsd ldr: led ½-wy tl over 1f out: nt qckn appr fnl f) | 2 | **2** | 11/4 2 | 72 | 31 |
| | **Frontman (IRE)** (TDBarron) **2-9-0** JQuinn(2) (w'like: a.p: kpt on wl fnl 2f) | 3½ | **3** | 16/1 | 65+ | 24 |
| $4329^{3}$ | **Last But Not Least** (RFJohnsonHoughton) **2-8-9** RPerham(4) (a chsng ldrs: no imp fnl 2f) | nk | **4** | 6/1 | 59 | 18 |
| | **Kingdom Princess** (MJCamacho) **2-8-9** LCharnock(14) (neat: bhd tl hdwy over 2f out: styd on ins fnl f) | 6 | **5** | 16/1 | 40 | — |
| | **Yeoman Oliver** (BAMcMahon) **2-9-0** GCarter(5) (w'like: mid div: kpt on fnl 2f: nvr rchd ldrs) | ½ | **6** | 16/1 | 44 | 3 |
| $3982^{9}$ | **Quinntessa** (BPalling) **2-8-9** SSanders(3) (mid div: kpt on fnl 2f: n.d) | hd | **7** | 25/1 | 38 | — |
| *$4408^{12}$* | **Snitch (48)** (CSmith) **2-9-0v** NCarlisle(8) (led to ½-wy: grad wknd) | 1½ | **8** | 33/1 | 39 | — |
| *$4369^{3}$* | **Learning Curve (IRE)** (SirMarkPrescott) **2-8-9** GDuffield(13) (lw: hld up: nvr plcd to chal) | 2½ | **9** | 12/1 | 26 | — |
| $3892^{10}$ | **Ya Marhaba** (JWPayne) **2-9-0** MTebbutt(1) (lw: hld up: nvr nr ldrs) | nk | **10** | 33/1 | 30 | — |
| *$4334^{3}$* | **Whitley Grange Boy (70)** (JLEyre) **2-9-0** RLappin(10) (s.i.s: a bhd) | 1¼ | **11** | 11/1 | 26 | — |
| $4237^{5}$ | **Governors Dream (48)** (MrsNMacauley) **2-8-9** JTate(7) (b: outpcd fr ½-wy) | nk | **12** | 33/1 | 20 | — |
| $4314^{14}$ | **Hawksley Hill (IRE)** (MrsJRRamsden) **2-9-0** KFallon(15) (lw: sn bhd & drvn along: hung lft ½-wy: n.d) | s.h | **13** | 12/1 | 24 | — |
| $4329^{2}$ | **Blue Adelaide** (PFICole) **2-8-2**(7) DavidO'Neill(16) (in tch: sn drvn along: outpcd fr ½-wy) | s.h | **14** | 3/1 3 | 19 | — |
| | **Ginas Girl** (SRBowring) **2-8-9** SWebster(6) (w'like: leggy: bit bkwd: s.i.s: hld up & a in rr) | 1 | **15** | 20/1 | 16 | — |
| $4244^{10}$ | **Gresham Flyer (43)** (BRichmond) **2-9-0** SDWilliams(9) (sn outpcd: wl bhd fr ½-wy) | 10 | **16** | 50/1 | — | — |
| | | | | (SP 160.0%) | | **16 Rn** |

**60.2 secs** (3.20) CSF £10.50 TOTE £4.40: £1.70 £2.10 £3.90 (£8.30) Trio £90.30 OWNER Mr S. Fustok (NEWMARKET) BRED Deerfield Farm

## 4430 EAST MIDLANDS ELECTRICITY (LINCOLN) CLAIMING STKS (II) (3, 4 & 5-Y.O) (Class F)

1-40 (1-40) **6f (Fibresand)** £2,413.80 (£676.80: £329.40) Stalls: Low GOING: 0.06 sec per fur (STD)

| Form | Horse | Dist | Pos | SP | RR | SF |
|---|---|---|---|---|---|---|
| 3783[18] | **Most Uppitty (54)** (JBerry) **3-8-0**(7)ow5 JoanneWebster(2) (led over 4f out: styd on wl fnl f) | — | 1 | 10/1 | 60 | 32 |
| 4413[9] | **Irchester Lass (40)** (SRBowring) **3-8-0b** NCarlisle(4) (in tch: ev ch over 1f out: kpt on same pce nr fin) | ¾ | 2 | 8/1 | 51 | 28 |
| 4337[8] | **At the Savoy (IRE) (66)** (TDBarron) **4-8-1b**(7) KimberleyHart(6) (lw: a chsng ldrs: ev ch over 1f out: one pce) | 2½ | 3 | 6/4[1] | 51 | 29 |
| 4123[4] | **Montague Dawson (IRE) (59)** (MrsNMacauley) **3-8-13** TIves(5) (b.hind: chsd ldrs: one pce over 1f out) | 2 | 4 | 4/1[3] | 52 | 29 |
| 4194[9] | **Dissentor (IRE) (47)** (JAGlover) **3-8-7** SDWilliams(10) (hdwy on outside over 2f out: nvr nr ldrs) | 2 | 5 | 7/1 | 41 | 18 |
| 4407[10] | **Double Glow (40)** (NBycroft) **3-8-2** GBardwell(8) (in tch: kpt on fnl 2f: n.d) | hd | 6 | 20/1 | 35 | 12 |
| 4394[17] | **Great Bear (80)** (DWChapman) **3-8-1**(5) PFessey(9) (sn outpcd & drvn along: n.d) | 5 | 7 | 10/1 | 26 | 3 |
| 4362[15] | **Last World (39)** (JAPickering) **3-7-11**(3) DWright(1) (hld up: hdwy to chse ldrs ½-wy: lost pl 2f out) | 10 | 8 | 25/1 | — | — |
| 3750[16] | **Young Ben (IRE) (42)** (JSWainwright) **3-8-1** JFanning(7) (b.hind: led over 1f: wknd over 2f out) | 1¼ | 9 | 20/1 | — | — |
| | **Lord Barnard (IRE)** (JEMulhern,Ireland) **5-9-0** JQuinn(11) (sn outpcd & drvn along: n.d) | 2 | 10 | 11/4[2] | — | — |
| 1647[14] | **Rennyholme (17)** (JHetherton) **4-8-6** KFallon(3) (bit bkwd: chsd ldrs tl wknd 2f out: eased) | nk | 11 | 50/1 | — | — |

(SP 143.8%) **11 Rn**

**1m 17.9** (4.40) CSF £94.84 TOTE £14.60: £4.60 £2.30 £1.10 (£21.30) Trio £56.70 OWNER Mr J. Berry (COCKERHAM) BRED The Sussex Stud

OFFICIAL EXPLANATION **Lord Barnard (IRE): the jockey reported that the horse needs further on this surface.**

## 4431 FOY & CO NURSERY H'CAP (0-75) (2-Y.O) (Class E)

2-10 (2-11) **7f (Fibresand)** £3,166.90 (£959.20: £468.60: £223.30) Stalls: Low GOING: 0.06 sec per fur (STD)

| Form | Horse | Dist | Pos | SP | RR | SF |
|---|---|---|---|---|---|---|
| 3642[10] | **Theatre Magic (56)** (SRBowring) **2-8-2b**(5)ow1 CTeague(5) (s.i.s: hdwy over 2f out: r.o to ld wl ins fnl f) | — | 1 | 8/1[3] | — | 20 |
| 4365[4] | **Angus McCoatup (IRE) (64)** (BAMcMahon) **2-9-1** GCarter(15) (in tch: hdwy to ld over 1f out: hdd wl ins fnl f: kpt on) | nk | 2 | 10/1 | — | 28 |
| 4375[5] | **Welsh Melody (49)** (KRBurke) **2-8-0b** CRutter(10) (chsd ldrs: led over 2f out tl over 1f out: no ex) | 1¼ | 3 | 14/1 | — | 11 |
| 4383[8] | **Foreman (59)** (WAO'Gorman) **2-8-10v** EmmaO'Gorman(11) (b.nr hind: hdwy over 2f out: sn chsng ldrs: one pce fnl f) | 1¼ | 4 | 10/1 | — | 18 |
| 4373[3] | **Homeland (68)** (TJNaughton) **2-9-0**(5) AWhelan(7) (lw: sn drvn along: styd on fnl 2f: nvr able to chal) | nk | 5 | 10/1 | — | 26 |
| 3289[11] | **Ebony Boy (66)** (JWharton) **2-9-3** SDWilliams(1) (bit bkwd: led tl hdd & wknd over 2f out) | nk | 6 | 9/1 | — | 23 |
| 4327[14] | **Silent Guest (IRE) (63)** (SirMarkPrescott) **2-9-0** GDuffield(8) (lw: mid div: rdn ½-wy: no imp) | s.h | 7 | 10/1 | — | 20 |
| 3949[8] | **Two Timer (49)** (MJohnston) **2-8-0** JFanning(3) (sn drvn along & bhd: hdwy 2f out: hmpd over 1f out: styd on) | 1½ | 8 | 14/1 | — | 3 |
| 4144[11] | **Time Clash (64)** (BPalling) **2-9-1** RPerham(4) (chsd ldrs tl wknd fnl 2½f) | nk | 9 | 20/1 | — | 17 |
| 4330[7] | **Hadadabble (44)** (PatMitchell) **2-7-9** JQuinn(16) (mid div: effrt over 2f out: no imp) | ½ | 10 | 16/1 | — | — |
| 3994[9] | **Oversman (70)** (JGFitzGerald) **2-9-7** KFallon(6) (bhd & hmpd 5f out: n.d) | 1¼ | 11 | 8/1[3] | — | 19 |
| 4025[6] | **Bold Enough (63)** (BWHills) **2-8-9**(5) JDSmith(12) (chsd ldrs tl wknd fnl 3f) | 2 | 12 | 11/2[2] | — | 7 |
| 4290[10] | **Contract Bridge (IRE) (45)** (CWThornton) **2-7-10** AMackay(9) (s.i.s: a bhd) | 1¼ | 13 | 9/1 | — | — |
| 4389[7] | **One Life To Live (IRE) (55)** (AHarrison) **2-8-3**(3) JStack(2) (outpcd & bhd whn hmpd 5f out: n.d) | 3½ | 14 | 20/1 | — | — |
| 3540[7] | **Hotlips Houlihan (68)** (RJRWilliams) **2-9-5** DBiggs(13) (cl up tl wknd fnl 3f) | 5 | 15 | 11/1 | — | — |
| 4389[4] | **Rawi (64)** (WRMuir) **2-9-1b** SSanders(14) (lw: chsd ldrs: effrt 3f out: sn wknd) | 1¾ | 16 | 5/1[1] | — | — |

(SP 147.7%) **16 Rn**

**1m 33.4** (6.60) CSF £93.27 CT £1,051.24 TOTE £10.00: £1.90 £2.60 £7.70 £2.30 (£51.50) Trio £239.20 OWNER Green Diamond Racing (EDWINSTOWE) BRED N. S. Yong

OFFICIAL EXPLANATION **Rawi: the trainer's representative stated the the horse did not face the blinkers.**

## 4432 FARMERS WEEKLY H'CAP (0-80) (II) (3-Y.O+) (Class D)

2-40 (2-41) **7f (Fibresand)** £3,185.00 (£962.00: £468.00: £221.00) Stalls: Low GOING: 0.06 sec per fur (STD)

| Form | Horse | Dist | Pos | SP | RR | SF |
|---|---|---|---|---|---|---|
| 4322[7] | **Prima Silk (68)** (MJRyan) **4-9-2** TIves(5) (a.p: led ins fnl f: r.o) | — | 1 | 8/1 | 80 | 57 |
| 4415[3] | **Benjamins Law (51)** (JAPickering) **4-7-13** 7x JQuinn(11) (trckd ldrs: led wl over 1f out tl ins fnl f: kpt on) | nk | 2 | 10/1 | 62 | 39 |
| 4388[3] | **Mislemani (IRE) (48)** (AGNewcombe) **5-7-10**ow1 AMackay(1) (cl up: led ½-wy tl wl over 1f out: no ex) | 3½ | 3 | 100/30[2] | 50 | 27 |
| 4392* | **Be Warned (82)** (NACallaghan) **4-9-9b**(7) 7x AEddery(2) (lw: s.i.s: hdwy over 2f out: swtchd over 1f out: nvr able to chal) | s.h | 4 | 2/1[1] | 85 | 62 |
| 4392[6] | **Johnnie the Joker (80)** (JPLeigh) **4-10-0b** DeanMcKeown(3) (a chsng ldrs: one pce fnl 2f) | 2 | 5 | 12/1 | 79 | 56 |
| 2923[11] | **On Y Va (USA) (46)** (RJRWilliams) **8-7-8**ow1 GBardwell(8) (outpcd & bhd tl sme late hdwy) | 10 | 6 | 20/1 | 21 | — |
| 4292[2] | **Penmar (58)** (TJEtherington) **3-8-0b**(5) AWhelan(6) (s.i.s: nvr rchd ldrs) | 2½ | 7 | 10/1 | 29 | 4 |
| 4394[3] | **Shadow Jury (70)** (DWChapman) **5-9-4** LCharnock(10) (sn pushed along: in tch tl wknd fnl 2f) | 1½ | 8 | 12/1 | 37 | 14 |
| 4319[7] | **Cumbrian Waltzer (69)** (MHEasterby) **10-9-3** KFallon(9) (outpcd tl hdwy appr st: sn wknd) | 1½ | 9 | 9/1 | 32 | 9 |
| 4337[15] | **White Sorrel (76)** (AHarrison) **4-9-7**(3) JStack(7) (disp ld to ½-wy: wknd over 2f out) | ½ | 10 | 20/1 | 38 | 15 |
| 4319[3] | **Super Benz (62)** (FJO'Mahony) **9-8-10** SDWilliams(4) (b: disp ld to ½-wy: wknd 2f out) | nk | 11 | 13/2[3] | 23 | — |

(SP 133.9%) **11 Rn**

**1m 30.9** (4.10) CSF £85.62 CT £297.28 TOTE £10.40: £2.50 £3.30 £1.80 (£53.70) Trio £48.60 OWNER Three Ply Racing (NEWMARKET) BRED R. M. Scott

LONG HANDICAP On Y Va (USA) 7-5

WEIGHT FOR AGE 3yo-1lb

## 4433 A C OFFICE SUPPLIES (S) STKS (2-Y.O) (Class F)

3-10 (3-15) **1m (Fibresand)** £2,814.20 (£791.20: £386.60) Stalls: Low GOING: 0.06 sec per fur (STD)

| Form | Horse | Dist | Pos | SP | RR | SF |
|---|---|---|---|---|---|---|
| 4393[P] | **Addie Pray (IRE) (70)** (MAJarvis) **2-8-6** JTate(14) (unruly s: hdwy ½-wy: rdn to ld ins fnl f: styd on wl) | — | 1 | 9/2[3] | — | 23 |
| 4339* | **Dragonjoy (50)** (JWPayne) **2-9-2b** MTebbutt(10) (lw: led after 2f: clr ent st: hdd & no ex ins fnl f) | 6 | 2 | 10/1 | — | 21 |
| 4393[3] | **La Finale (57)** (MHEasterby) **2-8-6b** KFallon(12) (sn chsng ldrs: hrd rdn over 2f out: one pce) | 4 | 3 | 9/4[1] | — | 3 |
| 4393[6] | **Holloway Melody (59)** (BAMcMahon) **2-8-6** GCarter(3) (prom tl outpcd ½-wy: kpt on fnl 2f) | 5 | 4 | 14/1 | — | — |
| 4339[8] | **Righteous Gent (40)** (KMcAuliffe) **2-8-11e** SSanders(8) (a drvn along: in tch: no imp fnl 3f) | 5 | 5 | 12/1 | — | — |
| 4263[12] | **Bumblefoot (IRE) (63)** (MJohnston) **2-8-11** DeanMcKeown(4) (led after 1f tl after 2f: outpcd fnl 2½f) | nk | 6 | 7/2[2] | — | — |
| 4389[14] | **Mulhollande Lad (IRE) (45)** (MCChapman) **2-8-8**(3) DRMcCabe(15) (bhd tl sme late hdwy) | ½ | 7 | 25/1 | — | — |
| 3975[17] | **Kratz (IRE) (52)** (BSRothwell) **2-8-11b** LCharnock(9) (sn outpcd & bhd: sme late hdwy) | 2 | 8 | 16/1 | — | — |
| 4339[11] | **Gunner B Special (40)** (SRBowring) **2-8-6**(5) CTeague(7) (b: sn bhd & drvn along: n.d) | 1½ | 9 | 16/1 | — | — |

| | | | | SP | RR | SF |
|---|---|---|---|---|---|---|
| 4375[3] | **Efipetite (47)** (NBycroft) **2-8-6** JQuinn(13) (nvr bttr than mid div) | 5 | **10** | 14/1 | — | — |
| 4393[14] | **Contrarie** (MJRyan) **2-8-6** GBardwell(16) (dwlt: nvr trbld ldrs) | 2 | **11** | 20/1 | — | — |
| 4389[8] | **Dancing Cavalier (55)** (RHollinshead) **2-8-11** SDWilliams(5) (a outpcd & bhd) | ¾ | **12** | 7/1 | — | — |
| 4369[6] | **Poppy My Love (43)** (RHarris) **2-8-6** DBatteate(11) (led 1f: chsd ldrs to ½-wy) | 8 | **13** | 20/1 | — | — |
| 4375[7] | **Classic Daisy (53)** (MissGayKelleway) **2-8-1b**(5) AWhelan(1) (b.hind: chsd ldrs 5f) | 1¾ | **14** | 16/1 | — | — |
| 4230[8] | **Spring Silhouette (35)** (MrsVAAconley) **2-8-6v** MDeering(2) (sn outpcd & bhd) | 12 | **15** | 33/1 | — | — |
| | **Ms Jones (IRE)** (RBrotherton) **2-8-6** AMackay(6) (small: bkwd: s.s: sn wl t.o) | dist | **16** | 33/1 | — | — |

(SP 150.7%) **16 Rn**

**1m 46.5** (6.50) CSF £55.89 TOTE £4.70: £2.00 £3.10 £1.80 (£55.40) Trio £32.80 OWNER Mr M. Sinclair (NEWMARKET) BRED Mrs C. L. Weld
No bid

## 4434 IRIS AMATEUR H'CAP (0-80) (4-Y.O+) (Class E)

3-40 (3-41) **1m 6f (Fibresand)** £3,052.50 (£924.00: £451.00: £214.50) Stalls: High GOING: 0.06 sec per fur (STD)

| | | | | SP | RR | SF |
|---|---|---|---|---|---|---|
| 4385[7] | **Stalled (IRE) (48)** (PTWalwyn) **5-10-13**(3) MarchionessofBlandford(1) (a.p: chal 4f out: disp ld 1f out: led cl home) | — | **1** | 6/1 | 65 | 38 |
| 4391[2] | **Ijab (CAN) (45)** (JParkes) **5-10-13b** MrMHNaughton(6) (lw: hdwy ½-wy: led over 2f out: wandered u.p: hdd & no ex nr fin) | hd | **2** | 6/4[1] | 62 | 35 |
| 3970[13] | **Modest Hope (USA) (44)** (BRichmond) **8-10-12** MrsLPearce(4) (lw: cl up: led 8f out to 6f out: led over 4f out tl over 2f out: no ex) | 5 | **3** | 9/1 | 55 | 28 |
| 4411[11] | **Kadiri (IRE) (60)** (JRBosley) **4-11-11e**(3) MrsSBosley(12) (bhd tl hdwy 7f out: chsng ldrs 2f out: one pce) | 10 | **4** | 8/1 | 60 | 33 |
| 4370[9] | **Mowlaie (59)** (DWChapman) **4-11-10**(3) MissRClark(7) (in tch tl outpcd 4f out: styd on fnl 2f) | 3 | **5** | 25/1 | 55 | 28 |
| 4336[11] | **Phanan (28)** (REPeacock) **9-9-3**(7) MrsCPeacock(9) (chsd ldrs tl rdn & wknd 6f out) | 2½ | **6** | 33/1 | 22 | — |
| 4336[16] | **Mrs Jawleyford (USA) (49)** (CSmith) **7-11-0**(3) MrsMMorris(10) (b: hdwy to ld 6f out tl over 4f out: grad wknd) | 3 | **7** | 25/1 | 39 | 12 |
| 4370[4] | **Tremendisto (45)** (CaptJWilson) **5-10-13** MissDianaJones(5) (led 4f: chsd ldrs tl outpcd 5f out) | 5 | **8** | 9/2[2] | 29 | 2 |
| 4336[14] | **Handmaiden (42)** (AHarrison) **5-10-7**(3) MrsDKettlewell(8) (outpcd ½-wy: n.d after) | 2½ | **9** | 5/1[3] | 24 | — |
| 3936[12] | **Bresil (USA) (39)** (KRBurke) **6-10-0**(7)ow9 MrsHSweeting(3) (b: s.s: a wl bhd) | 25 | **10** | 14/1 | — | — |
| 3619[12] | **Starlight Flyer (31)** (JELong) **8-9-6b**(7)ow6 MrTWaters(2) (b: b.nr hind: cl up: led after 4f to 8f out: sn wknd) | 14 | **11** | 33/1 | — | — |
| | **Chorus Boy (25)** (MrsSMAustin) **10-9-0**(7) MrsDWilkinson(11) (b: bhd fr ½-wy) | 1¼ | **12** | 33/1 | — | — |

(SP 133.4%) **12 Rn**

**3m 16.6** (17.60) CSF £16.41 CT £80.31 TOTE £7.30: £2.40 £1.40 £3.00 (£8.30) Trio £36.00 OWNER Mrs P. T. Walwyn (LAMBOURN) BRED D. Aykroyd
STEWARDS' ENQUIRY Naughton susp. 4-5/12/95 (careless riding).

T/Plpt: £674.90 (13.28 Tckts). T/Qdpt: £16.40 (2 Tckts). WG/AA

# 4414-LINGFIELD (L-H) (Standard)

## Saturday November 25th

Race 6: hand timed
WEATHER: rain WIND: almost nil

## 4435 SOUTHRIVER TOOLS & FIXINGS H'CAP (0-80) (I) (3-Y.O+) (Class D)

11-50 (11-52) **1m (Equitrack)** £2,806.80 (£848.40: £413.20: £195.60) Stalls: Low GOING minus 0.28 sec per fur (FST)

| | | | | SP | RR | SF |
|---|---|---|---|---|---|---|
| 3629[4] | **Dancing Lawyer (73)** (BJMeehan) **4-9-7** RCochrane(3) (hld up: hdwy 4f out: led 1f out: pushed out) | — | **1** | 7/2[2] | 84 | 49 |
| 4150* | **Neuwest (USA) (78)** (NJHWalker) **3-9-7**(3) JStack(2) (chsd ldr: led over 2f out to 1f out: one pce) | 2½ | **2** | 3/1[1] | 84 | 47 |
| 3706[6] | **Bagshot (76)** (RHannon) **4-9-3**(7) MarkDenaro(5) (chsd ldrs: rdn & outpcd over 3f out: hdwy over 1f out: r.o one pce fnl f) | 2 | **3** | 3/1[1] | 78 | 43 |
| 4367[12] | **Pengamon (80)** (HJCollingridge) **3-9-12** JQuinn(7) (hld up: n.m.r 3f out: hdwy over 4f out: styd on fnl f) | 1¾ | **4** | 14/1 | 79 | 42 |
| 4297[7] | **Waikiki Beach (USA) (64)** (GLMoore) **4-8-12v** SWhitworth(8) (led tl over 2f out: wknd over 1f out) | 7 | **5** | 11/2[3] | 49 | 14 |
| 4379[4] | **Yo Kiri-B (47)** (JFfitch-Heyes) **4-7-6**(3) DWright(1) (hld up: hdwy 4f out: wknd 2f out) | 3½ | **6** | 7/1 | 25 | — |
| 1745[17] | **Remaadi Sun (69)** (MDIUsher) **3-9-1** RStreet(6) (bhd fnl 5f) | 3 | **7** | 20/1 | 41 | 4 |
| 4379[11] | **Sir Oliver (IRE) (45)** (BAPearce) **6-7-7** GBardwell(9) (bhd fnl 4f) | 7 | **8** | 33/1 | 3 | — |
| 1092[19] | **Clarion Call (IRE) (60)** (GThorner) **4-8-3b**(5) AWhelan(4) (prom 3f) | 13 | **9** | 33/1 | — | — |

(SP 117.4%) **9 Rn**

**1m 39.5** (2.10) CSF £13.87 CT £30.68 TOTE £3.40: £1.40 £1.50 £1.30 (£4.90) Trio £3.40 OWNER Vintage Services Ltd (UPPER LAMBOURN) BRED Vintage Services Ltd
LONG HANDICAP Sir Oliver (IRE) 7-0
WEIGHT FOR AGE 3yo-2lb

## 4436 WILLIAM J. TOWNER MEMORIAL (S) STKS (I) (3-Y.O+) (Class G)

12-20 (12-22) **1m 2f (Equitrack)** £1,279.10 (£357.60: £173.30) Stalls: Low GOING minus 0.28 sec per fur (FST)

| | | | | SP | RR | SF |
|---|---|---|---|---|---|---|
| | **Granique (BEL)** (PaulSmith,Belgium) **3-9-5** TIves(6) (chsd ldr: led over 6f out: rdn & r.o wl fnl f) | — | **1** | 10/1 | 63 | 28 |
| 4386[11] | **The Little Ferret (55)** (AMoore) **5-9-4** RCochrane(2) (a.p: chsd wnr over 4f out: ev ch fnl 2f: rdn & one pce fnl f) | ¾ | **2** | 100/30[2] | 57 | 26 |
| 4293[6] | **Shabanaz (55)** (WRMuir) **10-9-9** CRutter(3) (s.i.s: sn pushed along: hrd rdn over 2f out: one pce) | 3 | **3** | Evens[1] | 57 | 26 |
| 4362[8] | **Mary Macblain (35)** (JLHarris) **6-8-13** JKovarik(4) (chsd ldrs: rdn 4f out: r.o one pce fnl f) | 1¾ | **4** | 12/1 | 44 | 13 |
| 4378[10] | **Little Scarlett (48)** (PJMakin) **3-9-0** RPerham(7) (chsd ldrs tl rdn & outpcd over 2f out: wknd ins fnl f) | 5 | **5** | 17/2[3] | 41 | 6 |
| | **Pertemps Flyer (57)** (SEarle) **4-9-4** JWilliams(9) (nvr nrr) | 2½ | **6** | 50/1 | 37 | 6 |
| 4412[6] | **Toat Chieftain (54)** (DMorris) **3-9-0** JTate(5) (hld up: hdwy 4f out: wknd 2f out) | 3 | **7** | 12/1 | 32 | — |
| 4420[10] | **Mutinique (34)** (BAPearce) **4-8-6b**(7) CLowther(8) (hdwy fr rr 4f out: wknd over 2f out) | 9 | **8** | 33/1 | 13 | — |
| 3681[9] | **Sarasonia (20)** (JWPayne) **4-8-6**(7) SGaillard(1) (led over 3f: wknd over 4f out) | 20 | **9** | 33/1 | — | — |

(SP 115.9%) **9 Rn**

**2m 9.52** (5.22) CSF £40.56 TOTE £11.70: £1.70 £1.40 £1.10 (£16.50) Trio £23.40 OWNER Stal de Moeren BRED Mme R. Delanoye
WEIGHT FOR AGE 3yo-4lb
Sold CSparrowhawk 4,000 gns

## 4437 SCENA HOLDINGS NURSERY H'CAP (2-Y.O) (Class E)

12-50 (12-52) **5f (Equitrack)** £2,211.00 (£621.00: £303.00) Stalls: Low GOING minus 0.28 sec per fur (FST)

| Form | Horse / Trainer / Jockey / Comment | Dist | Pos | SP | RR | SF |
|---|---|---|---|---|---|---|
| 4383[9] | **Dancing Jack (49)** (JJBridger) **2-8-0** JQuinn(3) (chsd ldrs: hrd rdn 2f out: r.o fnl f to ld last stride) | — | 1 | 14/1 | 53 | 21 |
| 4328[9] | **Midnight Cookie (48)** (BAPearce) **2-7-13** GBardwell(8) (led: clr over 2f out: hrd rdn ins fnl f: ct last stride) | s.h | 2 | 14/1 | 52 | 20 |
| 4383[12] | **Beeny (64)** (APJarvis) **2-9-1** JTate(10) (outpcd tl styd on strly fnl f: fin wl) | 2 | 3 | 15/2 | 61 | 29 |
| 3949[10] | **Impington (IRE) (59)** (WRMuir) **2-8-10** SSanders(6) (chsd ldrs: rdn over 1f out: wknd ins fnl f) | 1¾ | 4 | 20/1 | 51 | 19 |
| 4353[3] | **Goldsearch (IRE) (55)** (WAO'Gorman) **2-8-6b** EmmaO'Gorman(5) (chsd ldr: rdn over 2f out: one pce) | hd | 5 | 3/1[1] | 47 | 15 |
| 3568[12] | **No Sympathy (53)** (GLMoore) **2-7-13**(5)ow5 AWhelan(2) (dwlt: outpcd tl styd on fnl f: nvr nrr) | nk | 6 | 4/1[3] | 39 | 7 |
| 4352[4] | **Laughing Buccaneer (60)** (BJMeehan) **2-8-11b** RCochrane(9) (outpcd tl styd on fnl f: nvr nrr) | nk | 7 | 7/2[2] | 50 | 18 |
| 3895[8] | **Don't Tell Vicki (56)** (JSMoore) **2-8-2**(5) PPMurphy(1) (chsd ldrs: rdn over 3f out: wknd over 2f out) | 3½ | 8 | 10/1 | 34 | 2 |
| 4369[5] | **Touch of Fantasy (46)** (CADwyer) **2-7-11** NAdams(4) (chsd ldrs: rdn over 3f out: wknd over 2f out) | 2 | 9 | 12/1 | 18 | — |
| 3132[9] | **The Frisky Farmer (70)** (WGMTurner) **2-9-0**(7) ALakeman(7) (a bhd) | ¾ | 10 | 10/1 | 40 | 8 |
| | | | | (SP 123.0%) | **10 Rn** | |

**60.53 secs** (2.53) CSF £170.72 CT £1,440.03 TOTE £9.70: £1.90 £4.10 £2.60 (£60.30) Trio £160.60 OWNER Mrs J. M. Stamp (LIPHOOK) BRED Mrs J. Stamp and Mrs J. Hitchman

## 4438 WILLIAM J. TOWNER MEMORIAL (S) STKS (II) (3-Y.O+) (Class G)

1-20 (1-21) **1m 2f (Equitrack)** £1,271.40 (£355.40: £172.20) Stalls: Low GOING minus 0.28 sec per fur (FST)

| Form | Horse / Trainer / Jockey / Comment | Dist | Pos | SP | RR | SF |
|---|---|---|---|---|---|---|
| 4298[13] | **Awesome Power (55)** (JWHills) **9-9-4** AClark(6) (chsd ldr tl led over 6f out: clr over 1f out: r.o) | — | 1 | 7/4[1] | 53 | 26 |
| 4388[8] | **Swynford Flyer (28)** (JAHarris) **6-8-8**(5) CAdamson(4) (chsd ldrs tl rdn & outpcd 3f out: styd on ins fnl f) | 2 | 2 | 20/1 | 45 | 18 |
| 4242[11] | **Labudd (USA) (56)** (RIngram) **5-9-4** DBiggs(1) (hld up: hdwy 4f out: chsd wnr 2f out tl ins fnl f: one pce) | ½ | 3 | 3/1[2] | 49 | 22 |
| 4374[10] | **Good so Fa (IRE) (44)** (CNAllen) **3-9-5** NAdams(3) (hld up: hdwy to chse wnr over 4f out to 2f out: wknd over 1f out) | 10 | 4 | 12/1 | 38 | 7 |
| 4332[15] | **Kenyatta (USA) (30)** (AMoore) **6-9-4** CandyMorris(8) (led over 3f: wknd over 3f out) | 1¾ | 5 | 12/1 | 30 | 3 |
| | **Absolute Ruler (IRE)** (JLHarris) **4-9-9** 5x KFallon(7) (hld up: rdn 4f out: no hdwy) | 1½ | 6 | 7/2[3] | 33 | 6 |
| | **Saluting Walter (USA)** (RAkehurst) **7-9-4** SSanders(5) (chsd ldrs tl wknd over 4f out) | 1¾ | 7 | 5/1 | 25 | — |
| | | | | (SP 120.4%) | **7 Rn** | |

**2m 9.64** (5.34) CSF £29.38 TOTE £2.80: £1.80 £4.40 (£79.90) OWNER Mr Garrett Freyne (LAMBOURN) BRED G. J. Freyne

WEIGHT FOR AGE 3yo-4lb

No bid

## 4439 CONFERENCE STAGING MEDIAN AUCTION MAIDEN STKS (2-Y.O) (Class E)

1-55 (1-57) **1m 2f (Equitrack)** £2,253.00 (£633.00: £309.00) Stalls: Low GOING minus 0.28 sec per fur (FST)

| Form | Horse / Trainer / Jockey / Comment | Dist | Pos | SP | RR | SF |
|---|---|---|---|---|---|---|
| 4273[3] | **Thorntoun Estate (IRE) (57)** (MJohnston) **2-9-0** DeanMcKeown(2) (chsd ldrs: rdn over 3f out: swtchd rt over 1f out: hrd rdn & styd on fnl f: led last strides) | — | 1 | 11/4[1] | — | 23 |
| 4222[5] | **Sterling Fellow** (RHannon) **2-9-0** RPerham(5) (led: drvn along 3f out: hrd rdn ins fnl f: ct last strides) | hd | 2 | 9/2[2] | — | 23 |
| 4314[10] | **Sahhar** (RWArmstrong) **2-9-0** RPrice(11) (hld up: hdwy 5f out: chsd ldr over 3f out: rdn over 1f out: one pce) | ¾ | 3 | 9/2[2] | — | 22 |
| 4291[7] | **Chauvelin (IRE)** (MJohnston) **2-9-0** JFanning(6) (chsd ldrs over 6f: hrd rdn 2f out: one pce) | 3½ | 4 | 20/1 | — | 16 |
| 4360[11] | **Hurricane Horn (IRE) (43)** (WRMuir) **2-9-0v** RCochrane(9) (hld up: hdwy 4f out: hrd rdn 2f out: wknd over 1f out) | 5 | 5 | 14/1 | — | 8 |
| 4172[10] | **Brighter Byfaah (IRE)** (NAGraham) **2-9-0** TIves(1) (dwlt: nvr nrr) | 5 | 6 | 10/1 | — | — |
| 4353[6] | **Jemsilverthorn (IRE) (45)** (JJBridger) **2-9-0** JQuinn(10) (chsd ldrs tl wknd 4f out) | 2 | 7 | 33/1 | — | — |
| 4352[5] | **Mountain Dream (60)** (PFICole) **2-9-0** CRutter(12) (chsd ldrs tl rdn & wknd over 2f out) | 1½ | 8 | 5/1[3] | — | — |
| 3779[9] | **Sheemore (IRE) (55)** (JDBethell) **2-9-0** JWilliams(4) (bhd fnl 5f) | 12 | 9 | 16/1 | — | — |
| 4285[12] | **Tablets of Stone (IRE) (47)** (JRBosley) **2-9-0** JTate(7) (a bhd) | 2½ | 10 | 33/1 | — | — |
| | **General Haven** (TJNaughton) **2-9-0** SSanders(14) (w'like: bit bkwd: dwlt: carried wd after 1f: a bhd) | 7 | 11 | 25/1 | — | — |
| 4381[7] | **Presuming Ed (IRE)** (NJHWalker) **2-8-11**(3) JStack(13) (bhd fnl 5f) | 11 | 12 | 20/1 | — | — |
| 3760[18] | **Suparoy (60)** (TGMills) **2-9-0** AMackay(8) (bhd whn carried wd after 1f: sn rcvrd & mid div: wknd 5f out) | 25 | 13 | 8/1 | — | — |
| 4360[5] | **Bath Knight (45)** (DJSffrenchDavis) **2-9-0** NAdams(3) (stmbld & uns rdr s) | | U | 14/1 | — | — |
| | | | | (SP 138.4%) | **14 Rn** | |

**2m 9.6** (5.30) CSF £17.25 TOTE £4.10: £1.50 £2.30 £1.60 (£12.80) Trio £12.70 OWNER Mr W. M. Johnstone (MIDDLEHAM) BRED Mrs Agnes Johnstone

## 4440 SOUTHRIVER TOOLS & FIXINGS H'CAP (0-80) (II) (3-Y.O+) (Class D)

2-25 (2-57) **1m (Equitrack)** £2,806.80 (£848.40: £413.20: £195.60) Stalls: Low GOING minus 0.28 sec per fur (FST)

| Form | Horse / Trainer / Jockey / Comment | Dist | Pos | SP | RR | SF |
|---|---|---|---|---|---|---|
| 4351[4] | **Old Hook (IRE) (70)** (PaulSmith,Belgium) **4-9-7** TIves(2) (chsd ldr: led over 2f out: rdn over 1f out: r.o) | — | 1 | 15/2 | 78 | 42 |
| 4292[3] | **Field of Vision (IRE) (63)** (MJohnston) **5-9-0b** DeanMcKeown(3) (led tl over 2f out: rdn over 1f out: one pce) | 2 | 2 | 3/1[2] | 67 | 31 |
| 4420[8] | **Hawaii Storm (FR) (58)** (DJSffrenchDavis) **7-8-9** JWilliams(6) (bhd tl rdn & hdwy 4f out: hrd rdn over 1f out: one pce) | 2 | 3 | 6/1[3] | 58 | 22 |
| 4357[5] | **Perilous Plight (73)** (WRMuir) **4-9-10** RCochrane(8) (dwlt: hdwy 5f out: rdn over 1f out: one pce) | ¾ | 4 | 13/8[1] | 72 | 36 |
| 4406[4] | **Love Legend (55)** (DWPArbuthnot) **10-8-6** SWhitworth(4) (hld up: sme hdwy over 3f out: sn rdn: wknd over 2f out) | 3½ | 5 | 11/1 | 47 | 11 |
| 4356[7] | **Kintwyn (70)** (CCElsey) **5-9-7** CRutter(7) (dwlt: sn rcvrd to chse ldrs: wknd 2f out) | 4 | 6 | 7/1 | 54 | 18 |
| 3497[14] | **Greenwich Again (73)** (TGMills) **3-9-1**(7) DToole(5) (chsd ldrs tl wknd over 3f out) | 1¾ | 7 | 14/1 | 53 | 15 |
| 4406[13] | **Ripsnorter (IRE) (52)** (KBishop) **6-8-3** NAdams(1) (dwlt: a bhd) | 4 | 8 | 20/1 | 24 | — |
| | | | | (SP 121.4%) | **8 Rn** | |

**1m 40.25** (2.85) CSF £30.05 CT £134.79 TOTE £7.80: £1.50 £1.40 £1.70 (£14.20) OWNER R. Van Slemsbrouck BRED C. Farrell

WEIGHT FOR AGE 3yo-2lb

## 4441 CUTTING EDGE H'CAP (0-85) (3-Y.O+) (Class D)

2-55 (2-57) **6f (Equitrack)** £3,203.30 (£970.40: £474.20: £226.10) Stalls: Low GOING minus 0.28 sec per fur (FST)

| Form | Horse / Trainer / Jockey / Comment | Dist | Pos | SP | RR | SF |
|---|---|---|---|---|---|---|
| 4123[3] | **Southern Dominion (52)** (MJohnston) **3-7-9** NAdams(3) (mde all: hrd rdn ins fnl f: r.o wl) | — | 1 | 7/1[3] | 56 | 23 |
| 4319[9] | **Mister Fire Eyes (IRE) (85)** (CEBrittain) **3-10-0b** JQuinn(1) (chsd ldrs gng wl: rdn over 1f out: styd on strly ins fnl f) | nk | 2 | 14/1 | 88 | 55 |

| Form | Horse | Dist | Pos | SP | RR | SF |
|---|---|---|---|---|---|---|
| 4033[11] | **Chewit (80)** (AMoore) **3-9-9** CandyMorris(6) (a.p: rdn & ev ch 1f out: one pce) | 2 | **3** | 12/1 | 78 | 45 |
| *4394[14]* | **Sir Tasker (73)** (JLHarris) **7-9-2** SSanders(7) (a.p: rdn 2f out: one pce) | 1½ | **4** | 25/1 | 66 | 34 |
| *4357[6]* | **Random (57)** (CJames) **4-8-0** CRutter(14) (outpcd & bhd: hdwy over 2f out: rdn over 1f out: one pce fnl f) | nk | **5** | 20/1 | 49 | 17 |
| 3624[5] | **Patsy Grimes (67)** (JSMoore) **5-8-5(5)** PPMurphy(11) (nvr nrr) | 3 | **6** | 16/1 | 51 | 19 |
| *4295[8]* | **Robellion (63)** (DWPArbuthnot) **4-8-6v** SWhitworth(9) (nvr nrr) | hd | **7** | 25/1 | 47 | 15 |
| *4362[4]* | **Robo Magic (USA) (67)** (LMontagueHall) **3-8-10** RCochrane(13) (nvr nrr) | hd | **8** | 10/1 | 52 | 19 |
| 4322[8] | **Agwa (74)** (RJO'Sullivan) **6-9-3** DBiggs(2) (spd 4f) | s.h | **9** | 7/4[1] | 57 | 25 |
| *4351** | **Dancing Heart (75)** (BJMeehan) **3-8-11b(7)** GHannon(12) (mid div: rdn 3f out: wknd over 2f out) | 3½ | **10** | 6/1[2] | 50 | 17 |
| *4350[6]* | **Pharaoh's Dancer (59)** (PBurgoyne) **8-7-9(7)** DSweeney(5) (dwlt: a bhd) | 1½ | **11** | 12/1 | 29 | — |
| *4359[7]* | **Little Saboteur (66)** (PJMakin) **6-8-9** AClark(8) (chsd ldrs over 3f) | nk | **12** | 25/1 | 35 | 3 |
| 4238[2] | **Moujeeb (USA) (59)** (PatMitchell) **5-8-2v** JFanning(10) (dwlt: a bhd) | hd | **13** | 8/1 | 28 | — |
| 4322[22] | **Ashtina (73)** (BAPearce) **10-9-2** MWigham(4) (spd over 3f) | ½ | **14** | 16/1 | 41 | 9 |

(SP 133.5%) **14 Rn**

**1m 12.97** (2.37) CSF £98.94 CT £1,065.50 TOTE £9.80: £2.70 £5.00 £3.50 (£40.90) Trio not won; £408.18 to 27/11/95. OWNER Mr J. S. Morrison (MIDDLEHAM) BRED A. Wilkinson and J. W. Brown

## 4442 SHOWFORCE SERVICES H'CAP (0-70) (3-Y.O+) (Class E)

3-25 (3-26) **1m 5f (Equitrack)** £2,274.00 (£639.00: £312.00) Stalls: Low GOING minus 0.28 sec per fur (FST)

| Form | Horse | Dist | Pos | SP | RR | SF |
|---|---|---|---|---|---|---|
| *4416** | **Opera Buff (IRE) (68)** (MissGayKelleway) **4-9-7(5) 5x** AWhelan(3) (hld up: hdwy 6f out: led gng wl over 3f out: sn clr: pushed out) | — | **1** | 7/4[1] | 84 | 62 |
| 4355[4] | **Exhibit Air (IRE) (57)** (RAkehurst) **5-9-1b** SSanders(9) (a.p: led 5f out tl over 3f out: sn hrd rdn & one pce) | 6 | **2** | 7/2[2] | 66 | 44 |
| 4384[5] | **Yougo (68)** (MJohnston) **3-9-5** DeanMcKeown(11) (led 8f: hrd rdn fnl 3f: one pce) | ½ | **3** | 25/1 | 75 | 47 |
| 4333[8] | **Broughtons Formula (48)** (WJMusson) **5-8-3b(3)** PMcCabe(8) (sn wl bhd: styd on fnl 3f: nvr nrr) | 3 | **4** | 13/2 | 52 | 30 |
| *4384** | **Jaraab (71)** (GLewis) **4-10-1v** SWhitworth(4) (sn rdn along in mid div: outpcd fnl 6f) | 13 | **5** | 5/1[3] | 59 | 37 |
| *4387[5]* | **Premier Dance (57)** (DHaydnJones) **8-9-1** AMackay(1) (mid div: outpcd fnl 6f) | ½ | **6** | 10/1 | 45 | 23 |
| *4356[5]* | **One Off the Rail (USA) (69)** (AMoore) **5-9-13** CandyMorris(7) (prom 8f) | 5 | **7** | 10/1 | 51 | 29 |
| *4293** | **Elementary (70)** (NJHWalker) **12-9-11(3)** JStack(6) (prom 8f) | 15 | **8** | 10/1 | 33 | 11 |
| 4332[7] | **Smocking (35)** (JPearce) **5-7-7** GBardwell(2) (prom 6f: t.o) | dist | **9** | 33/1 | — | — |
| 3565[19] | **Rasmi (CAN) (63)** (PHowling) **4-9-7** JQuinn(10) (a bhd: to) | 20 | **10** | 25/1 | — | — |
| 4259[15] | **Mafuta (IRE) (44)** (JJSheehan) **3-7-9ow1** NAdams(5) (a bhd: virtually p.u over 5f out: t.o) | dist | **11** | 20/1 | — | — |

(SP 131.3%) **11 Rn**

**2m 46.47** (3.27) CSF £9.23 CT £115.85 TOTE £2.40: £1.10 £1.60 £4.30 (£7.30) Trio £92.90 OWNER Mr D. C. Toogood (WHITCOMBE) BRED Juddmonte Farms
LONG HANDICAP Smocking 6-13
WEIGHT FOR AGE 3yo-7lb

T/Plpt: £66.70 (105.27 Tckts). T/Qdpt: Not won; £43.80 to 27/11/95. SM

# 4371-WOLVERHAMPTON (L-H) (Standard)

## Monday November 27th

WEATHER: cloudy, showers after Race 5 WIND: mod across

## 4443 RICOH (UK) LTD. MAIDEN STKS (2-Y.O F) (Class E)

2-10 (2-13) **7f (Fibresand)** £3,023.90 (£915.20: £446.60: £212.30) Stalls: Low GOING: nil sec per fur (STD)

| Form | Horse | Dist | Pos | SP | RR | SF |
|---|---|---|---|---|---|---|
| *4380[4]* | **Victim of Love** (RCharlton) **2-8-5** SSanders(5) (chsd ldr: led 3f out tl over 1f out: rdn to ld again ins fnl f) | — | **1** | 7/2[3] | 68 | 20 |
| 4329[4] | **Lady Dignity (IRE)** (PJMakin) **2-7-12(5)ow3** AWhelan(2) (lw: b.nr hind: a.p: 2nd st: led over 1f out tl ins fnl f: unable qckn) | ½ | **2** | 11/4[2] | 62 | 14 |
| 4290[2] | **Scenicris (IRE) (65)** (RHollinshead) **2-7-12** NCarlisle(6) (a.p: 3rd st: nt qckn appr fnl f) | 4 | **3** | 9/4[1] | 51 | 3 |
| 2717[3] | **Posen Gold (IRE)** (PAKelleway) **2-8-2** JQuinn(3) (hdwy & 5th st: nvr able to chal) | 5 | **4** | 4/1 | 43 | — |
| 1282[6] | **Havana Heights (IRE)** (JLEyre) **2-7-12** NAdams(8) (hdwy & rdn 4f out: nvr rchd ldrs) | 2½ | **5** | 16/1 | 34 | — |
| *4373[5]* | **Alistover (45)** (RDickin) **2-7-12** DaleGibson(7) (nvr nrr) | hd | **6** | 33/1 | 33 | — |
| 3983[9] | **Beverly Hills** (JWHills) **2-8-0(5)** MHenry(9) (chsd ldrs tl 6th & btn st) | 1¾ | **7** | 16/1 | 36 | — |
| *4393[8]* | **Shepherds Dean (IRE)** (PHaslam) **2-8-0** LCharnock(1) (led 4f: 4th & wkng st) | 1½ | **8** | 33/1 | 28 | — |
| | **Roxane (IRE)** (ABailey) **2-8-0(3)ow1** DWright(4) (leggy: unf: s.i.s: sn rcvd: wknd 3f out) | 20 | **9** | 20/1 | — | — |

(SP 122.1%) **9 Rn**

**1m 30.4** (2.80 under 2y best) (5.70) CSF £13.65 TOTE £4.90: £2.10 £2.40 £1.10 (£6.20) Trio £6.00 OWNER Mr N. Bryce-Smith (BECKHAMPTON) BRED Nasrullah Holdings

## 4444 DAVIES ROSE LIFFORD HALL CLAIMING STKS (I) (3, 4 & 5-Y.O) (Class F)

2-40 (2-41) **1m 1f 79y (Fibresand)** £2,187.00 (£612.00: £297.00) Stalls: Low GOING: nil sec per fur (STD)

| Form | Horse | Dist | Pos | SP | RR | SF |
|---|---|---|---|---|---|---|
| *4372[2]* | **Dannistar** (PDEvans) **3-8-3** SSanders(3) (chsd ldrs: 2nd st: led 2f out: rdn out) | — | **1** | 6/1[2] | 63 | 28 |
| *4409[10]* | **Mazilla (51)** (AStreeter) **3-8-1** JQuinn(7) (lw: chsd ldrs: 3rd st: ev ch 1f out: hrd rdn & unable qckn) | 2½ | **2** | 20/1 | 57 | 22 |
| 3704[6] | **Second Colours (USA) (75)** (MrsMReveley) **5-9-0(5)** GParkin(1) (bit bkwd: bhd: rdn over 4f out: hdwy & 5th st: no ex appr fnl f) | nk | **3** | 4/7[1] | 71 | 39 |
| *4388[5]* | **Dowdency (47)** (JAPickering) **3-7-12(3)** NVarley(6) (bhd: pushed along & hdwy over 3f out: no imp ins fnl f) | ¾ | **4** | 14/1 | 55 | 20 |
| *4340[11]* | **Komiamaite (55)** (SRBowring) **3-8-1b(5)ow3** CTeague(5) (led 6f out to 2f out: wknd over 1f out) | ¾ | **5** | 12/1 | 56 | 21 |
| *4406[8]* | **Persian Flower (46)** (GCBravery) **3-8-2(3)** PMcCabe(8) (chsd ldrs: 6th & rdn st: sn btn) | 6 | **6** | 33/1 | 47 | 12 |
| 1518[9] | **Sweet Disorder (IRE) (32)** (BJMeehan) **5-8-2** CRutter(4) (prom tl 4th & wkng st) | 3 | **7** | 16/1 | 36 | 4 |
| *4406[3]* | **Peacefull Reply (USA) (38)** (FHLee) **5-9-3** ACulhane(10) (trckd ldrs 6f: sn wknd) | 3½ | **8** | 12/1 | 45 | 13 |
| 3871[3] | **Equilibrium (47)** (JWHills) **3-7-7(5)ow1** MHenry(2) (lw: led after 2f to 6f out: wknd over 3f out) | 12 | **9** | 15/2[3] | 8 | — |
| *4388[16]* | **Mystictich** (GBarnett) **3-8-1** NCarlisle(9) (led 2f: wknd over 4f out) | 15 | **10** | 40/1 | — | — |

(SP 127.8%) **10 Rn**

**2m 3.6** (7.60) CSF £104.02 TOTE £5.70: £2.30 £4.70 £1.40 (£139.40) Trio £11.80 OWNER Mr John Pugh (WELSHPOOL) BRED D. Newton
WEIGHT FOR AGE 3yo-3lb

## 4445 DAVIES ROSE LIFFORD HALL CLAIMING STKS (II) (3, 4 & 5-Y.O) (Class F)

3-10 (3-11) **1m 1f 79y (Fibresand)** £2,187.00 (£612.00: £297.00) Stalls: Low GOING: nil sec per fur (STD)

| | | | SP | RR | SF |
|---|---|---|---|---|---|
| *4390*[7] | **Sweet Supposin (IRE) (85)** (CADwyer) **4-9-3v** CDwyer(6) (lw: hld up: hdwy over 3f out: 2nd st: led over 1f out: cheekily) .......—- | 1 | 3/1[2] | 65 | 43 |
| *4421*[8] | **Canary Falcon (65)** (JohnBerry) **4-9-3** MWigham(10) (b: lw: sn pushed along: checked 5f out: hdwy & 5th st: kpt on: nt rch wnr) .......½ | 2 | 7/1 | 64 | 42 |
| *4415*[13] | **Charlie-Don't Surf (28)** (RGuest) **3-8-0** LCharnock(4) (led 8f: no ex) .......1¼ | 3 | 33/1 | 48 | 23 |
| 4259[16] | **Queens Stroller (IRE) (65)** (CCElsey) **4-8-2** JQuinn(9) (trckd ldrs: rdn & 3rd st: kpt on same pce) .......3 | 4 | 5/4[1] | 42 | 20 |
| *4390*[5] | **Just Flamenco (45)** (MJRyan) **4-8-9v** DBiggs(1) (prom: 4th st: sn wknd) .......8 | 5 | 9/1 | 35 | 13 |
| 4284[12] | **Hunza Story (30)** (NPLittmoden) **3-7-7**(5) CAdamson(3) (nvr nrr) .......½ | 6 | 14/1 | 26 | 1 |
| *3950*[10] | **Chadleigh Lane (USA) (60)** (RHollinshead) **3-8-10** TIves(2) (chsd ldrs 6f) .......hd | 7 | 12/1 | 38 | 13 |
| | **Ndaba** (NATwiston-Davies) **4-8-9** VSlattery(5) (w ldr tl rdn, wknd & 6th st) .......5 | 8 | 5/1[3] | 26 | 4 |
| *4357*[12] | **Pretty Scarce** (BPreece) **4-7-12** NAdams(8) (a bhd) .......1½ | 9 | 33/1 | 12 | — |
| | | | (SP 128.9%) | | **9 Rn** |

**2m 3.3** (7.30) CSF £25.07 TOTE £5.90: £1.50 £2.70 £7.80 (£18.30) Trio £124.00 OWNER Mrs Christine Rawson (NEWMARKET) BRED Ballylinch Stud Ltd
WEIGHT FOR AGE 3yo-3lb
Queens Stroller (IRE) clmd P Stringer £5,000

## 4446 SAIT ABRASIVES NURSERY H'CAP (0-75) (2-Y.O) (Class E)

3-40 (3-40) **1m 100y (Fibresand)** £2,995.30 (£906.40: £442.20: £210.10) Stalls: Low GOING: nil sec per fur (STD)

| | | | SP | RR | SF |
|---|---|---|---|---|---|
| 3851[2] | **Domoor (52)** (MJohnston) **2-8-5** JFanning(3) (bit bkwd: mde all: rdn out) .......—- | 1 | 4/5[1] | 51 | 6 |
| *4375*[12] | **Tina Katerina (43)** (RChampion) **2-7-5**(5)ow3 CAdamson(4) (plld hrd: trckd ldrs: pushed along & 4th st: swtchd lft over 1f out: kpt on wl) .......nk | 2 | 12/1 | 38 | — |
| *4410*[3] | **Los Alamos (68)** (CWThornton) **2-9-7** DeanMcKeown(2) (trckd ldr: 2nd st: no ex appr fnl f) .......1¾ | 3 | 7/4[2] | 64 | 18 |
| *4373*[4] | **Image Maker (IRE) (59)** (BPreece) **2-8-12** NAdams(1) (hld up: rdn & 3rd st: sn wknd) .......30 | 4 | 5/1[3] | — | — |
| | | | (SP 116.3%) | | **4 Rn** |

**1m 52.4** (7.40) CSF £8.19 TOTE £1.60 (£3.00) OWNER Mark Johnston Racing Ltd (MIDDLEHAM) BRED Greenland Park Stud
LONG HANDICAP Tina Katerina 7-5
STEWARDS' ENQUIRY Adamson susp. 6/12/95 (improper use of whip).

## 4447 LADBROKE SERIES H'CAP (Qualifier) (0-70) (3-Y.O+) (Class E)

4-10 (4-13) **6f (Fibresand)** £3,224.10 (£976.80: £477.40: £227.70) Stalls: Low GOING: nil sec per fur (STD)

| | | | SP | RR | SF |
|---|---|---|---|---|---|
| *4377*[2] | **Jigsaw Boy (59)** (PGMurphy) **6-9-3** SSanders(11) (trckd ldrs: shkn up to ld ins fnl f: pushed out) .......—- | 1 | 4/1[1] | 68 | 50 |
| 4194[7] | **Sweet Mate (51)** (SRBowring) **3-8-4b**(5) CTeague(9) (hdwy 2f out: r.o wl ins fnl f) .......1¼ | 2 | 15/2 | 58 | 39 |
| *4337*[5] | **Bold Street (IRE) (66)** (ABailey) **5-9-7**(3) DWright(8) (trckd ldrs: led 2f out to ins fnl f: no ex) .......¾ | 3 | 4/1[1] | 70 | 52 |
| 4292[4] | **Northern Spark (48)** (MissLAPerratt) **7-8-3**(3) DRMcCabe(1) (led 2f: r.o again appr fnl f) .......2 | 4 | 9/1 | 46+ | 28 |
| *4413*[7] | **David James' Girl (57)** (ABailey) **3-8-8**(7) IonaWands(7) (bhd tl r.o fnl 2f) .......s.h | 5 | 20/1 | 56 | 37 |
| *2383*[5] | **Efficacy (54)** (APJarvis) **4-8-12** JTate(10) (lw: chsd ldrs: no imp fnl f) .......s.h | 6 | 6/1[3] | 52 | 34 |
| *4407*[3] | **Another Batchworth (59)** (SMellor) **3-9-3** RPerham(3) (lw: led after 2f to 2f out: btn appr fnl f) .......s.h | 7 | 9/2[2] | 58 | 39 |
| *4418*[W] | **Astrojoy (IRE) (37)** (SGKnight) **3-7-6b**(3) NVarley(6) (prom over 3f: sn rdn & btn) .......1¼ | 8 | 33/1 | 33 | 14 |
| | **McKellar (IRE) (47)** (TDBarron) **6-8-5** LCharnock(2) (bit bkwd: nvr plcd to chal) .......1¼ | 9 | 16/1 | 38 | 20 |
| *4413*[2] | **Indiahra (48)** (RHollinshead) **4-8-6v** NCarlisle(4) (bhd fnl 3f) .......nk | 10 | 8/1 | 39 | 21 |
| 3678[9] | **Woodlands Electric (38)** (PAPritchard) **5-7-10**ow3 NAdams(5) (chsd ldrs: rdn 3f out: wknd qckly) .......15 | 11 | 50/1 | — | — |
| | | | (SP 120.9%) | | **11 Rn** |

**1m 15.2** (3.80) CSF £32.18 CT £117.62 TOTE £4.00: £2.10 £2.00 £2.00 (£16.00) Trio £38.40 OWNER Mark Holder Bloodstock (BRISTOL) BRED Mrs J. A. Rawding
LONG HANDICAP Woodlands Electric 6-1

## 4448 STEELWAY FENCESECURE (S) STKS (3, 4 & 5-Y.O) (Class G)

4-40 (4-41) **1m 4f (Fibresand)** £2,259.00 (£634.00: £309.00) Stalls: Low GOING: nil sec per fur (STD)

| | | | SP | RR | SF |
|---|---|---|---|---|---|
| 3899[5] | **Old Provence (75)** (RHarris) **5-9-8** AMackay(10) (b: chsd ldrs: 4th st: rdn & styd on wl to ld ins fnl f) .......—- | 1 | Evens[1] | 53 | 38 |
| *2145*[4] | **Pistols At Dawn (USA) (50)** (BJMeehan) **5-9-1**(7) GHannon(3) (a.p: 3rd st: ev ch 1f out: no ex ins fnl f) .......¾ | 2 | 4/1[2] | 52 | 37 |
| 4332[5] | **Sharp Thrill (37)** (BSmart) **4-9-3** SSanders(9) (a.p: 2nd st: led over 1f out: hdd & no ex ins fnl f) .......2 | 3 | 9/1 | 44 | 29 |
| *4388*[11] | **Just Lucky (IRE) (53)** (MrsNMacauley) **3-8-4**(7) AmandaSanders(2) (b: b.hind: led tl hdd over 1f out: sn btn)2½ | 4 | 11/1 | 41 | 20 |
| *4391*[5] | **Cashmirie (42)** (JLEyre) **3-8-11** RLappin(1) (lw: chsd ldrs: rdn 4f out: 5th & btn st) .......4 | 5 | 8/1[3] | 36 | 15 |
| 2662* | **Coast Along (IRE) (36)** (DBurchell) **3-9-2** DeanMcKeown(8) (hdwy over 4f out: nvr rchd ldrs) .......11 | 6 | 14/1 | 26 | 5 |
| *4409*[7] | **Lilac Rain (41)** (JRArnold) **3-8-6** CRutter(4) (hdwy 6f out: 6th & rdn st: sn btn) .......nk | 7 | 8/1[3] | 16 | — |
| 3426[7] | **Ann Hill (IRE) (24)** (RHollinshead) **5-8-5**(7) FLynch(7) (in tch 9f) .......15 | 8 | 25/1 | — | — |
| 818[12] | **Nord Lys (IRE) (28)** (BJLlewellyn) **4-9-3** JQuinn(6) (prom 8f) .......15 | 9 | 33/1 | — | — |
| 4138[17] | **Horsetrader (39)** (BPJBaugh) **3-8-11v** WLord(5) (b.hind: bhd fnl 7f) .......1½ | 10 | 50/1 | — | — |
| 3517[5] | **Just by Chance** (AKBarrow) **3-8-11** NAdams(11) (a bhd) .......10 | 11 | 40/1 | — | — |
| | | | (SP 128.4%) | | **11 Rn** |

**2m 42.0** (9.50) CSF £6.19 TOTE £1.80: £1.40 £2.70 £1.90 (£4.90) Trio £8.30 OWNER Mr T. J. Dawson (NEWMARKET) BRED Stowell Hill Ltd and A. J. Tree
WEIGHT FOR AGE 3yo-6lb
No bid

## 4449 THORPE VERNON H'CAP (0-65) (3-Y.O+ F & M) (Class F)

5-10 (5-10) **1m 6f 166y (Fibresand)** £2,537.00 (£712.00: £347.00) Stalls: Low GOING: nil sec per fur (STD)

| | | | SP | RR | SF |
|---|---|---|---|---|---|
| *4387*[9] | **Ballymac Girl (53)** (JMBradley) **7-9-13** LCharnock(7) (b: a.p: led 3f out: sn clr: v.easily) .......—- | 1 | 10/11[1] | 65+ | 42 |
| *4415*[10] | **Silver Singer (58)** (DRLoder) **3-9-7**(3) DRMcCabe(4) (led over 11f: 2nd str: sn rdn & btn) .......11 | 2 | 9/2[2] | 58 | 27 |
| 3875[9] | **Tap On Tootsie (42)** (ICampbell) **3-8-3**(5) AWhelan(2) (lw: chsd ldrs: rdn over 3f out: 3rd & btn st) .......6 | 3 | 7/1 | 36 | 5 |
| 3971[18] | **Fools of Pride (IRE) (40)** (RHollinshead) **3-7-13**(7) FLynch(5) (rdn 5f out: went poor 4th st: a bhd) .......15 | 4 | 7/1 | 17 | — |

| | | | SP | RR | SF |
|---|---|---|---|---|---|
| 4406[14] | **Marjan (IRE) (42)** (THCaldwell) **4-9-2** ACulhane(3) (in tch 8f: 6th & bhd st) 15 | **5** | 20/1 | 3 | — |
| 1337[9] | **Cafe Glace (45)** (RAkehurst) **3-8-11** SSanders(6) (b.hind: stdd & reard st: plld hrd: sn prom: 5th & bhd st: eased fnl f) 2½ | **6** | 5/1[3] | 3 | — |
| 3137[7] | **Sure Care (54)** (MJRyan) **4-10-0** TIves(1) (drppd rr 8f out: sn t.o) dist | **7** | 10/1 | — | — |

(SP 126.1%) **7 Rn**

**3m 21.3** (13.90) CSF £6.33 TOTE £1.80: £1.50 £4.00 (£5.30) OWNER Mr Lee Bowles (CHEPSTOW) BRED Miss K. Rausing and Mrs S.M. Rogers
WEIGHT FOR AGE 3yo-8lb

T/Plpt: £10.80 (953.17 Tckts). T/Qdpt: £22.00 (1.25 Tckts). Dk

# 4435-**LINGFIELD (L-H) (Standard)**
## Wednesday November 29th

## 4450 WALTON HEATH LIMITED STKS (0-55) (I) (3-Y.O+) (Class F)
12-10 (12-11) **7f (Equitrack)** £2,350.80 (£658.80: £320.40) Stalls: Low GOING minus 0.27 sec per fur (FST)

| | | | SP | RR | SF |
|---|---|---|---|---|---|
| 4407* | **Peggy Spencer (55)** (CWThornton) **3-8-10** DeanMcKeown(7) (lw: a.p: led over 2f out: rdn out) — | **1** | 8/11[1] | 54 | 31 |
| 4421[5] | **Scissor Ridge (48)** (JJBridger) **3-8-12** JQuinn(9) (lw: led 1f: rdn over 3f out: unable qckn) 3½ | **2** | 16/1 | 48 | 25 |
| 4435[6] | **Yo Kiri-B (47)** (JFfitch-Heyes) **4-8-9b**(3) DWright(3) (hdwy over 3f out: hrd rdn over 1f out: one pce) nk | **3** | 33/1 | 45 | 24 |
| 4363[12] | **Nivasha (32)** (RPCHoad) **3-8-7** RCochrane(8) (hld up: rdn over 2f out: one pce) ¾ | **4** | 33/1 | 41 | 18 |
| 4409[9] | **Panther (IRE) (52)** (JHetherton) **5-9-0** NKennedy(2) (lw: lost pl over 4f out: rallied fnl f: r.o) nk | **5** | 25/1 | 45 | 24 |
| 4406[11] | **Pacific Girl (IRE) (42)** (BPalling) **3-8-7** AClark(10) (nvr nr to chal) s.h | **6** | 33/1 | 40 | 17 |
| 4386[8] | **North Esk (USA) (50)** (CADwyer) **6-9-0** CDwyer(4) (lost pl 3f out: r.o one pce fnl 2f) ½ | **7** | 11/4[2] | 44 | 23 |
| 4413[8] | **Bold Gem (55)** (BJMeehan) **4-8-12b** GDuffield(5) (hld up: n.m.r on ins 2f out: wknd fnl f) 1¼ | **8** | 9/1[3] | 39 | 18 |
| 4044[12] | **Best of Bold (55)** (NAGraham) **3-8-12b** TIves(6) (lw: led 6f out tl over 2f out: wknd fnl f) hd | **9** | 12/1 | 41 | 18 |
| 4214[5] | **Cuckmere Venture (21)** (JRPoulton) **5-8-3**(7)ow1 GFaulkner(11) (bhd fnl 3f) 10 | **10** | 100/1 | 14 | — |

(SP 121.8%) **10 Rn**

**1m 26.15** (2.15) CSF £13.81 TOTE £1.90: £1.40 £2.30 £4.60 (£13.30) Trio £26.00 OWNER Mr Guy Reed (MIDDLEHAM) BRED Theakston Stud
WEIGHT FOR AGE 3yo-1lb

## 4451 GLENEAGLES CONDITIONS STKS (I) (3-Y.O+) (Class D)
12-40 (12-41) **1m (Equitrack)** £3,117.40 (£941.20: £457.60: £215.80) Stalls: High GOING minus 0.27 sec per fur (FST)

| | | | SP | RR | SF |
|---|---|---|---|---|---|
| 4418* | **Easy Choice (USA)** (PhilipMitchell) **3-9-3** AClark(5) (lw: hdwy over 3f out: led over 1f out: rdn out) — | **1** | 9/4[1] | 67 | 46 |
| 3769[5] | **Kaafih Homm (IRE) (68)** (NACallaghan) **4-9-11** RCochrane(1) (b.hind: lw: hld up: led over 2f out tl over 1f out: unable qckn) 1½ | **2** | 3/1[3] | 70 | 51 |
| 4296[5] | **Awasha (IRE)** (MissGayKelleway) **3-8-3**(3) AWhelan(2) (hdwy over 3f out: rdn over 2f out: one pce) 1¾ | **3** | 8/1 | 50 | 29 |
| 4419[5] | **Dee-Lady (83)** (WGMTurner) **3-8-9** RPerham(8) (led over 5f) 1¾ | **4** | 9/2 | 49 | 28 |
| 4367[10] | **Risky Romeo (83)** (GCBravery) **3-9-7** TIves(3) (dwlt: hdwy over 3f out: wknd over 2f out) s.h | **5** | 11/4[2] | 61 | 40 |
| 4164[11] | **Calgary Girl** (PCRitchens) **3-8-6** NAdams(4) (bhd fnl 4f) 20 | **6** | 66/1 | 6 | — |
| 1337[12] | **Shoodah (IRE)** (PHayward) **4-8-13** SWhitworth(6) (chsd ldrs 5f) 10 | **7** | 66/1 | — | — |

(SP 114.7%) **7 Rn**

**1m 39.24** (1.84) CSF £9.10 TOTE £3.30: £1.80 £1.80 (£3.40) OWNER Mr J. Morton (EPSOM) BRED Juddmonte Farms
WEIGHT FOR AGE 3yo-2lb

## 4452 ST ANDREW'S APPRENTICE H'CAP (0-65) (3-Y.O+) (Class F)
1-10 (1-13) **1m 4f (Equitrack)** £2,826.80 (£794.80: £388.40) Stalls: Low GOING minus 0.27 sec per fur (FST)

| | | | SP | RR | SF |
|---|---|---|---|---|---|
| 4051[13] | **Ballynakelly (51)** (RAkehurst) **3-8-8**(5) TAshley(4) (lw: a.p: led over 2f out: clr over 1f out: r.o wl) — | **1** | 5/2[1] | 71 | 55 |
| 4420[3] | **Just-Mana-Mou (IRE) (55)** (GLewis) **3-9-3b** AWhelan(9) (a.p: rdn over 4f out: unable qckn fnl 2f) 10 | **2** | 10/1 | 62 | 46 |
| 4416[2] | **H'Ani (48)** (WJHaggas) **3-8-10** SSanders(10) (swtg: a.p: rdn over 4f out: one pce fnl 2f) hd | **3** | 4/1[2] | 55 | 39 |
| 4376[5] | **Tadellal (IRE) (57)** (WGMTurner) **4-9-6**(5) JWilkinson(6) (dwlt: hdwy over 10f out: led 5f out tl over 2f out: hrd rdn: one pce) nk | **4** | 10/1 | 63 | 53 |
| 4332[3] | **Glow Forum (40)** (GLMoore) **4-8-3**(5)ow10 GFaulkner(8) (b: hld up: rdn over 4f out: one pce) 2½ | **5** | 10/1 | 33 | 23 |
| 4420* | **Spitfire Bridge (IRE) (63)** (MMcCormack) **3-9-11** 5x DGriffiths(16) (hdwy over 3f out: wknd over 2f out) 5 | **6** | 4/1[2] | 59 | 43 |
| 4419[6] | **Todd (USA) (57)** (PhilipMitchell) **4-9-11** DRMcCabe(5) (lw: led 7f: wkng whn n.m.r 3f out:) 1 | **7** | 25/1 | 52 | 42 |
| 4442[9] | **Smocking (27)** (JPearce) **5-7-9** NVarley(12) (hdwy 7f out: wknd over 2f out) 2½ | **8** | 33/1 | 19 | 9 |
| 4332[14] | **Night Edition (39)** (SDow) **5-8-4e**(3) ADaly(1) (b.hind: bhd fnl 4f) 1¼ | **9** | 20/1 | 29 | 19 |
| 4355[13] | **Docklands Courier (48)** (BJMcMath) **3-8-10** LNewton(14) (lw: a bhd) ¾ | **10** | 25/1 | 37 | 21 |
| 4416[3] | **Manful (58)** (JHetherton) **3-9-6** JStack(2) (b: prom over 7f) nk | **11** | 5/1[3] | 46 | 30 |
| 4385[9] | **Bakers Daughter (52)** (JRArnold) **3-9-0** PMcCabe(11) (swtg: a bhd) 1¼ | **12** | 20/1 | 39 | 23 |
| 4293[12] | **More Bills (IRE) (31)** (AMoore) **3-7-2**(5) IonaWands(15) (b.hind: lw: bhd fnl 6f) s.h | **13** | 50/1 | 18 | 2 |
| 4379[3] | **Total Rach (IRE) (50)** (RIngram) **3-8-12b** DWright(7) (a bhd) 3½ | **14** | 14/1 | 32 | 16 |

(SP 141.3%) **14 Rn**

**2m 31.97** (1.97) CSF £31.37 CT £101.73 TOTE £6.10: £2.30 £2.50 £1.90 (£56.90) Trio £49.70 OWNER Y M Y Partnership (EPSOM) BRED Crest Stud Ltd
LONG HANDICAP More Bills (IRE) 7-6
WEIGHT FOR AGE 3yo-6lb

## 4453 WENTWORTH NURSERY H'CAP (0-85) (2-Y.O) (Class D)
1-40 (1-41) **6f (Equitrack)** £3,387.50 (£1,025.00: £500.00: £237.50) Stalls: Low GOING minus 0.27 sec per fur (FST)

| | | | SP | RR | SF |
|---|---|---|---|---|---|
| 4383[2] | **Arctic Romancer (IRE) (73)** (GLewis) **2-9-4**(3) AWhelan(7) (lw: hld up: led wl over 1f out: sn clr: rdn out) — | **1** | 4/1[3] | 83 | 32 |
| 4383[4] | **Moi Canard (61)** (BAPearce) **2-8-6**(3) DRMcCabe(4) (lw: outpcd: hdwy fnl f: r.o wl) 2½ | **2** | 15/2 | 64 | 13 |
| 4383* | **Itsinthepost (70)** (MJohnston) **2-9-4** DeanMcKeown(3) (lw: w ldr: rdn over 3f out: ev ch wl over 1f out: unable qckn) 1¼ | **3** | 13/8[1] | 70 | 19 |

| Form | Horse | Dist | Pos | SP | RR | SF |
|---|---|---|---|---|---|---|
| $4437^{7}$ | **Laughing Buccaneer (60)** (BJMeehan) **2-8-8** RCochrane(1) (lw: outpcd: nvr nrr) | 2 | 4 | 8/1 | 55 | 4 |
| $4328^{7}$ | **To The Whire (62)** (GLMoore) **2-8-10** SWhitworth(6) (a.p: rdn over 2f out: wknd over 1f out) | ¾ | 5 | 3/1$^{2}$ | 55 | 4 |
| $4431^{4}$ | **Foreman (57)** (WAO'Gorman) **2-8-5v**$^{ow1}$ EmmaO'Gorman(5) (b.nr hind: hdwy over 3f out: wknd over 2f out) | 1¾ | 6 | 7/1 | 44 | — |
| $4431^{16}$ | **Rawi (65)** (WRMuir) **2-8-13** SSanders(2) (lw: led over 4f) | 1 | 7 | 33/1 | 50 | — |

(SP 121.4%) **7 Rn**

**1m 13.95** (3.35) CSF £31.41 TOTE £6.90: £1.80 £2.50 (£9.60) OWNER Mr Abdulla Al Khalifa (EPSOM) BRED Peter Phelan

## 4454 GLENEAGLES CONDITIONS STKS (II) (3-Y.O+) (Class D)

2-10 (2-11) **1m (Equitrack)** £3,117.40 (£941.20: £457.60: £215.80) Stalls: High GOING minus 0.27 sec per fur (FST)

| Form | Horse | Dist | Pos | SP | RR | SF |
|---|---|---|---|---|---|---|
| $4362^{2}$ | **Mr Nevermind (IRE) (75)** (GLMoore) **5-8-13** SWhitworth(4) (hld up: led over 1f out: r.o wl) | — | 1 | 6/4$^{1}$ | 73+ | 50 |
| $4297^{11}$ | **Nordic Doll (IRE) (66)** (BWHills) **3-8-3**(3) AWhelan(8) (lw: chsd ldr 5f out: ev ch over 1f out: unable qckn) | 5 | 2 | 7/1$^{3}$ | 58 | 33 |
| $4435^{7}$ | **Remaadi Sun (69)** (MDIUsher) **3-8-11** JQuinn(6) (led over 6f) | 6 | 3 | 25/1 | 51 | 26 |
| $4035^{20}$ | **Sharp 'n Smart (70)** (BSmart) **3-9-3** RCochrane(5) (lw: plld hrd: a.p: rdn over 3f out: wknd over 2f out) | hd | 4 | 11/2$^{2}$ | 57 | 32 |
| $1428^{2}$ | **Light Fantastic** (RCharlton) **3-8-6** SSanders(2) (lw: bhd fnl 4f) | 3 | 5 | 6/4$^{1}$ | 40 | 15 |
| $4164^{10}$ | **Sing Up (59)** (MMcCormack) **3-8-11** RPerham(3) (a bhd) | 1¾ | 6 | 33/1 | 41 | 16 |
| $3542^{13}$ | **Dovedon Lad** (GCBravery) **3-8-11** RPrice(7) (lw: bhd fnl 5f) | 10 | 7 | 40/1 | 21 | — |

(SP 117.1%) **7 Rn**

**1m 38.48** (1.08) CSF £11.97 TOTE £1.80: £1.40 £3.30 (£7.10) OWNER Mr K. Higson (EPSOM) BRED Robert Corridan
WEIGHT FOR AGE 3yo-2lb

## 4455 ROYAL ST GEORGE'S H'CAP (0-65) (3-Y.O+) (Class F)

2-40 (2-41) **2m (Equitrack)** £2,738.60 (£769.60: £375.80) Stalls: Low GOING minus 0.60 sec per fur (FST)

| Form | Horse | Dist | Pos | SP | RR | SF |
|---|---|---|---|---|---|---|
| $4411^{2}$ | **Coleridge (41)** (JJSheehan) **7-8-4b** JQuinn(4) (chsd ldr over 15f out: led over 6f out tl over 4f out: rdn: led nr fin) | — | 1 | 2/1$^{1}$ | 57 | 39 |
| $2119^{7}$ | **Miroswaki (USA) (60)** (RAkehurst) **5-9-9** SSanders(1) (b: hld up: led over 4f out: hrd rdn fnl f: hdd nr fin) | ½ | 2 | 100/30$^{3}$ | 76 | 58 |
| $4411^{3}$ | **Supreme Star (USA) (50)** (PRHedger) **4-8-10v**(3) NVarley(2) (b: hld up: rdn over 4f out: one pce) | 11 | 3 | 5/2$^{2}$ | 55 | 37 |
| $4384^{3}$ | **Lear Dancer (USA) (65)** (PhilipMitchell) **4-10-0v** GDuffield(7) (lw: hld up: rdn over 3f out: wknd over 2f out) | 10 | 4 | 9/2 | 60 | 42 |
| $3047^{6}$ | **Duggan (31)** (PDEvans) **8-7-5**(3)$^{ow1}$ DWright(3) (hld up: rdn over 4f out: sn wknd) | ¾ | 5 | 20/1 | 24 | 6 |
| $4370^{10}$ | **Awestruck (37)** (BPreece) **5-8-0** NAdams(6) (dwlt: a wl bhd) | 6 | 6 | 40/1 | 25 | 7 |
| $4336^{17}$ | **Elpida (USA) (60)** (JPearce) **3-9-0** AClark(8) (led over 9f: t.o) | 25 | 7 | 12/1 | 23 | — |
| $259^{10}$ | **Dallai (IRE) (46)** (MrsNMacauley) **4-8-9** DMcKeown(5) (b: lw: bhd fnl 9f: t.o) | dist | 8 | 20/1 | — | — |
| $4416^{11}$ | **Miss Parkes (38)** (PCClarke) **6-7-8**(7) IonaWands(9) (s.s: a bhd: t.o) | 20 | 9 | 66/1 | — | — |

(SP 124.3%) **9 Rn**

**3m 23.29** (1.29) CSF £9.55 CT £16.37 TOTE £2.20: £1.50 £2.90 £1.10 (£5.40) Trio £11.80 OWNER Mr P. J. Sheehan (FINDON) BRED W. and R. Barnett Ltd
LONG HANDICAP Duggan 7-0
WEIGHT FOR AGE 3yo-9lb

## 4456 WALTON HEATH LIMITED STKS (0-55) (II) (3-Y.O+) (Class F)

3-10 (3-10) **7f (Equitrack)** £2,338.20 (£655.20: £318.60) Stalls: Low GOING minus 0.27 sec per fur (FST)

| Form | Horse | Dist | Pos | SP | RR | SF |
|---|---|---|---|---|---|---|
| $4385^{10}$ | **Tuigamala (39)** (RIngram) **4-8-10**(7) TAshley(3) (rdn thrght: hdwy over 3f out: led wl ins fnl f: r.o wl) | — | 1 | 33/1 | 63 | 34 |
| $4421^{7}$ | **Apollo Red (55)** (AMoore) **6-9-0** CandyMorris(2) (b.hind: led 5f out tl wl ins fnl f: r.o one pce) | ½ | 2 | 4/1$^{3}$ | 59 | 30 |
| $4385^{5}$ | **Fort Knox (IRE) (52)** (RMFlower) **4-9-3** DBiggs(4) (hld up: rdn over 3f out: one pce) | 5 | 3 | 7/2$^{2}$ | 50 | 21 |
| $2428^{8}$ | **Respectable Jones (49)** (RHollinshead) **9-9-3b** MWigham(5) (lw: hdwy over 3f out: rdn over 2f out: one pce) | 1 | 4 | 12/1 | 48 | 19 |
| $2885^{5}$ | **Flair Lady (44)** (WGMTurner) **4-8-9** RPerham(8) (a.p: rdn over 2f out: one pce) | nk | 5 | 10/1 | 40 | 11 |
| $4385^{4}$ | **By The Bay (50)** (CCElsey) **3-8-2**(5) JDSmith(7) (nvr nr to chal) | 4 | 6 | 11/4$^{1}$ | 30 | — |
| $4274^{4}$ | **Harvest Reaper (48)** (JLHarris) **3-8-12** SSanders(9) (led 2f: rdn over 2f out: wknd over 1f out) | 1¾ | 7 | 8/1 | 31 | — |
| $4386^{12}$ | **Komodo (USA) (52)** (KOCunningham-Brown) **3-8-12e** RCochrane(10) (b.hind: bhd whn bmpd 5f out) | 1¼ | 8 | 7/1 | 29 | — |
| $4354^{6}$ | **Sound Trick (USA) (40)** (GCBravery) **3-8-7v** SWhitworth(11) (bhd fnl 3f) | 7 | 9 | 20/1 | 8 | — |
| $4418^{7}$ | **Hong Kong Dollar (54)** (BAPearce) **3-8-9**(3) DRMcCabe(6) (bhd whn bmpd 5f out) | nk | 10 | 12/1 | 12 | — |
| $4377^{7}$ | **Jon's Choice (45)** (BPreece) **7-9-0** NAdams(1) (hld up: rdn over 3f out: sn wknd) | 2 | 11 | 20/1 | 7 | — |

(SP 129.4%) **11 Rn**

**1m 26.4** (2.40) CSF £161.08 TOTE £40.30: £6.60 £1.70 £1.70 (£124.60) Trio £83.30 OWNER Mr Roger Ingram (EPSOM) BRED Mrs S. Ingram
WEIGHT FOR AGE 3yo-1lb

## 4457 LADBROKE ALL-WEATHER TROPHY H'CAP (Qualifier) (0-70) (3-Y.O+) (Class E)

3-40 (3-42) **7f (Equitrack)** £3,181.20 (£963.60: £470.80: £224.40) Stalls: Low GOING minus 0.27 sec per fur (FST)

| Form | Horse | Dist | Pos | SP | RR | SF |
|---|---|---|---|---|---|---|
| 4362* | **Superoo (69)** (MrsPSly) **9-10-0** ACulhane(8) (rdn over 4f out: hdwy over 3f out: nt clr run over 1f out: swtchd rt: led wl ins fnl f: r.o wl) | — | 1 | 5/1$^{2}$ | 72 | 36 |
| $4394^{13}$ | **Four of Spades (69)** (PDEvans) **4-9-7**(7) AmandaSanders(15) (rdn over 3f out: hdwy fnl f: r.o wl) | s.h | 2 | 14/1 | 72 | 36 |
| $3455^{10}$ | **Mediate (IRE) (64)** (AHide) **3-9-5**(3) JStack(6) (hdwy over 1f out: r.o wl ins fnl f) | nk | 3 | 16/1 | 67 | 29 |
| $4421^{4}$ | **Invocation (68)** (AMoore) **8-9-10**(3) AWhelan(4) (b.hind: led over 5f out: rdn over 2f out: hdd wl ins fnl f: unable qckn) | ¾ | 4 | 10/1 | 69 | 33 |
| $4377^{3}$ | **Exclusive Assembly (55)** (APJames) **3-8-13** JQuinn(12) (lw: a.p: hrd rdn over 1f out: r.o one pce) | hd | 5 | 14/1 | 56 | 18 |
| $4382^{2}$ | **Takeshi (IRE) (62)** (WRMuir) **3-9-6** SSanders(10) (hld up: rdn over 3f out: r.o one pce fnl f) | ½ | 6 | 6/1 | 62 | 24 |
| $2073^{11}$ | **Pab's Choice (58)** (MMcCormack) **4-9-3v** RCochrane(14) (led over 1f: rdn over 3f out: one pce fnl 2f) | nk | 7 | 11/2$^{3}$ | 56 | 20 |
| $3771^{5}$ | **Sally Weld (55)** (CJBenstead) **3-8-13** MWigham(1) (lost pl over 4f out: rallied over 1f out: running on whn n.m.r wl ins fnl f) | ¾ | 8 | 16/1 | 53 | 15 |
| $4362^{3}$ | **Dusk in Daytona (57)** (CJames) **3-9-1** CRutter(9) (lw: hld up: rdn over 3f out: one pce fnl f) | hd | 9 | 10/1 | 55 | 17 |
| $4440^{2}$ | **Field of Vision (IRE) (63)** (MJohnston) **5-9-8b** DeanMcKeown(5) (a.p: rdn over 4f out: ev ch 1f out: eased whn btn wl ins fnl f) | hd | 10 | 7/2$^{1}$ | 59 | 23 |
| $4406^{5}$ | **Eastleigh (53)** (RHollinshead) **6-8-12** TIves(11) (nvr nrr) | 3 | 11 | 10/1 | 42 | 6 |
| $976^{7}$ | **Export Mondial (37)** (DJSffrenchDavis) **5-7-7**(3) NVarley(3) (bhd fnl 2f) | 2 | 12 | 40/1 | 22 | — |
| $4385^{13}$ | **Dalcross (43)** (HJCollingridge) **4-7-9v**(7)$^{ow7}$ JoHunnam(13) (bhd fnl 2f) | ¾ | 13 | 40/1 | 26 | — |
| $4194^{10}$ | **Saltis (IRE) (56)** (DWPArbuthnot) **3-9-0** RPrice(7) (b.hind: lw: a bhd) | 2½ | 14 | 20/1 | 34 | — |

| | | | | SP | RR | SF |
|---|---|---|---|---|---|---|
| *4382*$^{8}$ | **Monty (59)** (MajorDNChappell) **3-9-3** NAdams(2) (lw: bhd fnl 4f) | 7 | **15** | 16/1 | 21 | — |

(SP 136.5%) **15 Rn**

**1m 27.11** (3.11) CSF £73.98 CT £990.07 TOTE £6.00: £1.30 £7.60 £5.60 (£51.80) Trio £371.70 OWNER Mrs P. Sly (PETERBOROUGH) BRED Irish Thoroughbred Holdings Ltd
WEIGHT FOR AGE 3yo-1lb

T/Plpt: £22.60 (355.22 Tckts). T/Qdpt: £12.40 (4.8 Tckts). AK

# 4450-LINGFIELD (L-H) (Standard)
## Thursday November 30th

## 4458 FAUCETS SOLD A GROHE MILLION H'CAP (0-60) (I) (3-Y.O+) (Class F)
12-15 (12-17) **6f (Equitrack)** £2,413.80 (£676.80: £329.40) Stalls: Low GOING minus 0.27 sec per fur (FST)

| | | | | SP | RR | SF |
|---|---|---|---|---|---|---|
| *4427*$^{2}$ | **Stand Tall (46)** (CWThornton) **3-8-13** DeanMcKeown(4) (a.p: chsd ldr over 2f out: led ins fnl f: rdn out) | — | **1** | 11/2$^{3}$ | 56 | 37 |
| 3439$^{5}$ | **Sharp Imp (48)** (RMFlower) **5-9-1b** DBiggs(9) (a.p: led over 3f out tl ins fnl f: unable qckn) | 2½ | **2** | 9/1 | 50 | 32 |
| *4441** | **Southern Dominion (59)** (MJohnston) **3-9-12** $^{7x}$ LDettori(2) (lw: a.p: rdn over 3f out: one pce) | 3 | **3** | 7/2$^{1}$ | 54 | 35 |
| *4390*$^{12}$ | **Green's Bid (49)** (DWChapman) **5-9-2** ACulhane(3) (rdn 4f out: hdwy over 1f out: r.o one pce) | nk | **4** | 25/1 | 43 | 25 |
| 4278$^{8}$ | **Serious Fact (40)** (SirMarkPrescott) **3-8-7** GDuffield(14) (lw: outpcd: nvr nrr) | 3 | **5** | 7/1 | 27 | 8 |
| 3961$^{7}$ | **Halbert (50)** (PBurgoyne) **6-9-0v**$^{(3)}$ DRMcCabe(1) (7th whn n.m.r 3f out: nvr nr to chal) | ¾ | **6** | 11/1 | 34 | 16 |
| *4441*$^{13}$ | **Moujeeb (USA) (59)** (PatMitchell) **5-9-12v** RCochrane(5) (outpcd: hdwy over 1f out: one pce) | 1¾ | **7** | 13/2 | 38 | 20 |
| *4350*$^{5}$ | **Slivovitz (55)** (MJHeaton-Ellis) **5-9-8v** AClark(6) (led over 2f: wknd wl over 1f out) | ¾ | **8** | 4/1$^{2}$ | 32 | 14 |
| *4390*$^{16}$ | **Cabcharge Blue (60)** (TJNaughton) **3-9-6**$^{(7)}$ TAshley(7) (lw: nvr nrr) | 2½ | **9** | 25/1 | 31 | 12 |
| *4412*$^{7}$ | **Saint Amigo (40)** (JLEyre) **3-8-7v** RLappin(13) (s.s: a bhd) | nk | **10** | 33/1 | 10 | — |
| *4415*$^{9}$ | **Green Golightly (USA) (44)** (DAWilson) **4-8-11** GCarter(10) (bhd fnl 4f) | 1½ | **11** | 14/1 | 9 | — |
| *4359*$^{9}$ | **La Bossette (IRE) (37)** (RIngram) **3-8-4** AMackay(8) (a bhd) | 1 | **12** | 33/1 | 1 | — |
| *4436*$^{9}$ | **Sarasonia (28)** (JWPayne) **4-7-6b**$^{(3)ow2}$ NVarley(12) (prom 3f) | 1 | **13** | 33/1 | — | — |
| 2491$^{14}$ | **Henry Weston (36)** (PHowling) **3-8-0**$^{(3)}$ DWright(11) (dwlt: sme hdwy over 3f out: sn wknd) | 3 | **14** | 33/1 | — | — |

(SP 127.9%) **14 Rn**

**1m 13.24** (2.64) CSF £51.88 CT £180.24 TOTE £4.90: £2.20 £2.60 £1.30 (£18.90) Trio £13.90 OWNER Mr Guy Reed (MIDDLEHAM) BRED Mrs E. Longton
LONG HANDICAP Sarasonia 7-1

## 4459 FAUCETS GROHE RELAXA PLUS ESQUISIT SHOWER FITTINGS H'CAP (0-70) (I) (3-Y.O+) (Class E)
12-45 (12-45) **5f (Equitrack)** £2,656.00 (£802.00: £390.00: £184.00) Stalls: High GOING minus 0.27 sec per fur (FST)

| | | | | SP | RR | SF |
|---|---|---|---|---|---|---|
| 3442$^{6}$ | **Cheeky Chappy (35)** (DWChapman) **4-7-5b**$^{(5)}$ PFessey(8) (dwlt: rapid hdwy 4f out: led 3f out: pushed out) | — | **1** | 6/1 | 45+ | 24 |
| *4295*$^{2}$ | **Speedy Classic (USA) (63)** (MJHeaton-Ellis) **6-9-10** AClark(3) (hld up: hrd rdn over 1f out: unable qckn) | 1 | **2** | 6/4$^{1}$ | 70 | 49 |
| *4359*$^{4}$ | **Tee-Emm (56)** (PHowling) **5-9-3** DMcKeown(2) (b.hind: lw: led 2f: hrd rdn over 1f out: one pce) | 3 | **3** | 5/1 | 53 | 32 |
| *4407*$^{11}$ | **Anytime Baby (50)** (PTDalton) **3-8-11** RCochrane(1) (hld up: rdn over 2f out: one pce) | ¾ | **4** | 9/2$^{3}$ | 45 | 24 |
| *4295*$^{10}$ | **Windrush Boy (60)** (JRBosley) **5-9-0**$^{(7)}$ AimeeCook(4) (swtg: nvr nr to chal) | ¾ | **5** | 16/1 | 52 | 31 |
| *4358*$^{2}$ | **Spectacle Jim (50)** (JO'Donoghue) **6-8-8b**$^{(3)}$ PMcCabe(7) (a bhd) | 1¾ | **6** | 4/1$^{2}$ | 37 | 16 |
| *4354*$^{7}$ | **Il Furetto (34)** (JSKing) **3-7-6**$^{(3)ow2}$ NVarley(5) (prom over 4f) | 2½ | **7** | 50/1 | 11 | — |
| *4142*$^{10}$ | ***Lochon (54)*** (JLEyre) **4-9-1** RLappin(6) (Withdrawn not under Starter's orders: veterinary advice) | | **W** | | — | — |

(SP 117.0%) **7 Rn**

**60.19 secs** (2.19) CSF £15.29 CT £44.46 TOTE £7.70: £3.40 £1.50 (£9.30) OWNER Mrs Jeanne Chapman (YORK) BRED Ian W. Glenton
LONG HANDICAP Il Furetto 7-5

## 4460 FAUCETS GROHE RELAXA PLUS ESQUISIT SHOWER FITTINGS H'CAP (0-70) (II) (3-Y.O+) (Class E)
1-15 (1-15) **5f (Equitrack)** £2,656.00 (£802.00: £390.00: £184.00) Stalls: High GOING minus 0.27 sec per fur (FST)

| | | | | SP | RR | SF |
|---|---|---|---|---|---|---|
| 3919$^{3}$ | **Half Tone (53)** (RMFlower) **3-8-11b** DBiggs(1) (outpcd: swtchd rt over 1f out: gd hdwy fnl f: led wl ins fnl f: r.o wl) | — | **1** | 5/1$^{3}$ | 58 | 34 |
| *4394*$^{8}$ | **Kalar (69)** (DWChapman) **6-9-13b** LDettori(7) (a.p: led wl over 1f out tl wl ins fnl f: unable qckn) | 1¾ | **2** | 9/4$^{1}$ | 68 | 44 |
| *4413*$^{3}$ | **Newington Butts (IRE) (45)** (KMcAuliffe) **5-8-3** GDuffield(4) (a.p: rdn over 2f out: r.o one pce) | ¾ | **3** | 13/2 | 42 | 18 |
| *4337*$^{7}$ | **Nordico Princess (70)** (MABrittain) **4-10-0** RCochrane(2) (led over 1f: rdn over 2f out: one pce) | ¾ | **4** | 7/2$^{2}$ | 65 | 41 |
| *4358*$^{3}$ | **Rocky Two (53)** (PHowling) **4-8-11b** DMcKeown(6) (b: outpcd: bmpd over 1f out: nvr nr to chal) | 2 | **5** | 13/2 | 41 | 17 |
| *4418*$^{10}$ | **Diamond Bangle (36)** (CCElsey) **3-7-8**$^{ow1}$ NAdams(8) (b.hind: a bhd) | 2½ | **6** | 50/1 | 15 | — |
| *4358*$^{5}$ | **Daaniera (IRE) (49)** (PHowling) **5-8-4b**$^{(3)}$ DWright(5) (b.hind: lw: led over 3f out tl wl over 1f out: wknd fnl f) | s.h | **7** | 7/1 | 29 | 5 |
| 3519$^{14}$ | **Tommy Tempest (43)** (REPeacock) **6-8-1v** AMackay(3) (bhd fnl 2f) | 4 | **8** | 12/1 | 10 | — |

(SP 118.5%) **8 Rn**

**60.4 secs** (2.40) CSF £16.39 CT £67.81 TOTE £6.20: £2.20 £1.40 £2.50 (£8.20) OWNER Mrs G. M. Temmerman (JEVINGTON) BRED T. M. Jennings
LONG HANDICAP Diamond Bangle 7-2

## 4461 FAUCETS HOSPITA LEVER TAPS OLD & NEW MAIDEN STKS (2-Y.O) (Class D)
1-45 (1-47) **6f (Equitrack)** £3,403.75 (£1,030.00: £502.50: £238.75) Stalls: Low GOING minus 0.27 sec per fur (FST)

| | | | | SP | RR | SF |
|---|---|---|---|---|---|---|
| *4429*$^{2}$ | **Mask Flower (USA) (76)** (MJohnston) **2-8-9** LDettori(5) (lw: a.p: led over 3f out: drvn out) | — | **1** | 10/11$^{1}$ | 60 | 13 |
| *4408*$^{3}$ | **Ballymoney (IRE)** (WAO'Gorman) **2-9-0** EmmaO'Gorman(9) (lw: dwlt: hdwy over 3f out: ev ch ins fnl f: r.o) | ½ | **2** | 4/1$^{2}$ | 64 | 17 |
| 3893$^{6}$ | **Blue Flyer (IRE)** (RIngram) **2-9-0** DBiggs(7) (outpcd: rapid hdwy fnl f: fin wl) | nk | **3** | 16/1 | 63 | 16 |
| 4282$^{6}$ | **Green Gem (BEL)** (SCWilliams) **2-8-9** JTate(2) (hld up: rdn over 2f out: r.o one pce) | nk | **4** | 33/1 | 57 | 10 |
| | **Marino Street** (PDEvans) **2-8-9** SSanders(8) (hdwy over 3f out: rdn 2f out: r.o one pce) | hd | **5** | 10/1 | 57 | 10 |
| *4389*$^{2}$ | **Red Acuisle (IRE) (64)** (GLewis) **2-9-0** SWhitworth(11) (lw: hdwy over 3f out: rdn 2f out: r.o one pce) | hd | **6** | 5/1$^{3}$ | 62 | 15 |
| 2656$^{8}$ | **Rowlandsons Stud (IRE)** (GLMoore) **2-9-0** RPerham(6) (a.p: ev ch over 1f out: wknd ins fnl f) | 1½ | **7** | 33/1 | 58 | 11 |
| | **La Perruche (IRE)** (LordHuntingdon) **2-8-9** DeanMcKeown(10) (neat: nvr nr to chal) | 1 | **8** | 16/1 | 50 | 3 |
| 3893$^{8}$ | **Unspoken Prayer** (JRArnold) **2-8-9** CRutter(1) (prom over 2f) | 7 | **9** | 50/1 | 31 | — |

I

| | | | | SP | RR | SF |
|---|---|---|---|---|---|---|
| *4124[11]* | **Latzio (40)** (BAPearce) **2-8-6**(3) DRMcCabe(4) (led over 2f: wknd over 2f out) | ½ | **10** | 50/1 | 30 | — |

(SP 119.7%) **10 Rn**

**1m 14.77** (4.17) CSF £5.17 TOTE £1.70: £1.00 £3.10 £7.30 (£3.10) Trio £30.60 OWNER Sheikh Mohammed (MIDDLEHAM) BRED Darley Stud Management Inc

## 4462 FAUCETS GROHE AUTOMATIC 1000 & 2000 THERMOSTATIC SHOWER VALVES NURSERY (0-85) (2-Y.O) (Class D) 2-15 (2-17) **1m (Equitrack)** £3,468.75 (£1,050.00: £512.50: £243.75) Stalls: High GOING minus 0.27 sec per fur (FST)

| | | | | SP | RR | SF |
|---|---|---|---|---|---|---|
| *4365** | **Sweet Wilhelmina (67)** (LordHuntingdon) **2-8-8** LDettori(6) (led 1f: led on bit over 1f out: shkn up & qcknd: easily) | — | **1** | 13/8[1] | 78+ | 36 |
| *4431[5]* | **Homeland (65)** (TJNaughton) **2-8-6** SSanders(4) (lw: hld up: rdn over 4f out: chsd wnr fnl f: no imp) | 2½ | **2** | 14/1 | 71 | 29 |
| *4383[7]* | **Balpare (54)** (NACallaghan) **2-7-9**ow1 AMackay(2) (lw: s.i.s: hdwy over 2f out: rdn over 1f out: one pce) | 1¾ | **3** | 11/4[2] | 56 | 14 |
| *4410[2]* | **Quality (IRE) (80)** (WAO'Gorman) **2-9-7v** EmmaO'Gorman(1) (hdwy 5f out: rdn over 3f out: wknd 1f out) | 4 | **4** | 7/2[3] | 75 | 33 |
| 4208[17] | **Efficacious (IRE) (53)** (CJBenstead) **2-7-8**ow1 NAdams(3) (hdwy over 5f out: wknd 3f out) | 1¼ | **5** | 50/1 | 44 | 2 |
| *4433[2]* | **Dragonjoy (53)** (JWPayne) **2-7-5b**(3)ow1 DWright(7) (lw: led 7f out tl over 1f out: sn wknd) | 1¼ | **6** | 9/2 | 42 | — |
| *4360[10]* | ***Deaken Dancer (52)*** *(KTIvory)* ***2-7-7*** *GBardwell(5) (Withdrawn not under Starter's orders: ref to enter stalls)* | | ***W*** | *66/1* | — | — |

(SP 115.3%) **6 Rn**

**1m 39.7** (2.30) CSF £19.35 TOTE £2.70: £1.50 £2.60 (£11.80) OWNER Mr Chris van Hoorn (WEST ILSLEY) BRED D. Walker
LONG HANDICAP Efficacious (IRE) 7-5 Dragonjoy 7-5 Deaken Dancer 6-9

## 4463 FAUCETS FOR GROHMASTER SHOWERS LIMITED STKS (0-55) (3-Y.O+) (Class F) 2-45 (2-46) **2m (Equitrack)** £2,726.00 (£766.00: £374.00) Stalls: Low GOING minus 0.60 sec per fur (FST)

| | | | | SP | RR | SF |
|---|---|---|---|---|---|---|
| *4364[9]* | **Guest Alliance (IRE) (47)** (AMoore) **3-8-9** AClark(4) (b.hind: hdwy over 3f out: hrd rdn over 1f out: led nr fin) | — | **1** | 14/1 | 68 | 27 |
| *4355[7]* | **Doddington Flyer (50)** (RHollinshead) **3-8-9** RCochrane(2) (hld up: chsd ldr over 3f out: hrd rdn over 2f out: led ins fnl f: hdd nr fin) | hd | **2** | 11/2 | 68 | 27 |
| *4355[6]* | **Endless Fantasy (48)** (CACyzer) **3-8-4** DBiggs(6) (chsd ldr: led 7f out: hrd rdn over 1f out: hdd ins fnl f: unable qckn) | 2 | **3** | 100/30[2] | 61 | 20 |
| *4355[8]* | **Hever Golf Lady (49)** (TJNaughton) **3-8-6** SSanders(8) (b.hind: hdwy 12f out: wknd over 3f out) | 11 | **4** | 3/1[1] | 52 | 11 |
| | **Fleur de Tal (42)** (WGMTurner) **4-8-13** RPerham(7) (hld up: rdn over 4f out: sn wknd) | ¾ | **5** | 20/1 | 49 | 17 |
| *4364[16]* | **Shining Dancer (50)** (SDow) **3-7-11**(7) ADaly(3) (b.hind: bhd fnl 7f) | 11 | **6** | 20/1 | 38 | — |
| 4331[2] | **Chita Rivera (37)** (PJMakin) **4-8-13** LDettori(5) (led 9f: wknd over 3f out) | 5 | **7** | 6/1 | 33 | 1 |
| *4363[10]* | **Zadok (47)** (RTPhillips) **3-8-9** GDuffield(9) (lw: bhd fnl 10f: t.o) | dist | **8** | 25/1 | — | — |
| *4370[5]* | **Environmentalist (IRE) (53)** (RHarris) **4-9-4** AMackay(1) (b.hind: s.s: bhd tl p.u over 13f out: lame) | | **P** | 7/2[3] | — | — |

(SP 120.0%) **9 Rn**

**3m 27.57** (5.57) CSF £83.42 TOTE £26.50: £2.60 £2.30 £1.20 (£24.00) Trio £70.00 OWNER Ballard (1834) Ltd (BRIGHTON) BRED R. Kennedy
WEIGHT FOR AGE 3yo-9lb

## 4464 FAUCETS SOLD A GROHE MILLION H'CAP (0-60) (II) (3-Y.O+) (Class F) 3-15 (3-20) **6f (Equitrack)** £2,413.80 (£676.80: £329.40) Stalls: Low GOING minus 0.27 sec per fur (FST)

| | | | | SP | RR | SF |
|---|---|---|---|---|---|---|
| *4351[8]* | **Myjinka (41)** (JO'Donoghue) **5-8-5b**(3) PMcCabe(9) (hdwy over 1f out: str run fnl f: led wl ins fnl f: r.o wl) | — | **1** | 16/1 | 47 | 20 |
| *4407[7]* | **Kira (51)** (JLEyre) **5-9-4** RLappin(6) (b.off hind: a.p: rdn over 2f out: led ins fnl f: sn hdd: unable qckn) | 1 | **2** | 7/1 | 54 | 27 |
| 3960[10] | **Colston-C (51)** (CJHill) **3-9-4** SWhitworth(10) (led over 3f: nt clr run on ins over 1f out: r.o ins fnl f) | 1¼ | **3** | 9/2[2] | 52 | 24 |
| *4428[2]* | **Vladivostok (46)** (BdeHaan) **5-8-8**(5) PFessey(11) (s.s: hdwy over 3f out: r.o ins fnl f) | s.h | **4** | 5/1[3] | 46 | 19 |
| *4295[6]* | **Lift Boy (USA) (59)** (AMoore) **6-9-5**(7) ALakeman(5) (b.hind: a.p: led over 2f out: hrd rdn & edgd lft over 1f out: hdd ins fnl f: one pce) | hd | **5** | 6/1 | 59 | 32 |
| *4357[4]* | **Our Shadee (USA) (58)** (KTIvory) **5-9-4v**(7) CScally(13) (rdn & hdwy over 1f out: r.o wl ins fnl f) | ¾ | **6** | 4/1[1] | 56 | 29 |
| *2493[4]* | **Assignment (51)** (JELong) **9-9-4** RCochrane(1) (b.off hind: a.p: rdn over 3f out: wknd fnl f) | 3 | **7** | 16/1 | 41 | 14 |
| *4382[3]* | **Don't Get Caught (IRE) (63)** (JLHarris) **3-10-2v** SSanders(7) (a bhd) | ½ | **8** | 13/2 | 52 | 24 |
| *4413[10]* | **Fascination Waltz (57)** (JJSheehan) **8-9-10** GDuffield(8) (hld up: rdn over 2f out: wkng whn hmpd wl over 1f out) | 1½ | **9** | 14/1 | 41 | 14 |
| *4358[6]* | **Bonny Melody (39)** (PDEvans) **4-7-13**(7) AmandaSanders(4) (bhd fnl 2f) | 1¼ | **10** | 16/1 | 20 | — |
| *3319[6]* | **Ring the Chief (55)** (MDIUsher) **3-9-8** MWigham(2) (b.hind: bhd fnl 2f) | 1½ | **11** | 12/1 | 33 | 5 |

(SP 127.0%) **11 Rn**

**1m 14.19** (3.59) CSF £119.60 CT £547.56 TOTE £20.00: £4.60 £2.70 £1.90 (£72.10) Trio £198.00 OWNER Miss P. I. Westbrook (REIGATE) BRED Miss Prue Westbrook and Bob Pettis
STEWARDS' ENQUIRY Lakeman susp. 9/12/95 (careless riding).

## 4465 FAUCETS FOR GROHE ARABESK & CHIARA AMATEUR H'CAP (0-80) (3-Y.O+) (Class G) 3-45 (3-46) **1m 4f (Equitrack)** £2,427.00 (£682.00: £333.00) Stalls: Low GOING minus 0.27 sec per fur (FST)

| | | | | SP | RR | SF |
|---|---|---|---|---|---|---|
| 4289[6] | **Tethys (USA) (75)** (JLEyre) **4-11-7** MissDianaJones(3) (chsd ldr: led 5f out: r.o wl) | — | **1** | 4/1[3] | 86 | 70 |
| *4415[2]* | **No Speeches (IRE) (56)** (SDow) **4-10-2** MrTMcCarthy(6) (b.hind: hdwy 7f out: chsd wnr fnl 4f: unable qckn) | 1¾ | **2** | 2/1[1] | 65 | 49 |
| 4333[9] | **Retender (USA) (53)** (JPearce) **6-9-13** MrsLPearce(4) (hdwy over 3f out: one pce fnl 2f) | 1¾ | **3** | 6/1 | 59 | 43 |
| *4364[4]* | **Strat's Legacy (42)** (DWPArbuthnot) **8-9-2** MrsDArbuthnot(8) (b.hind: hdwy over 3f out: r.o ins fnl f) | 1¼ | **4** | 3/1[2] | 47 | 31 |
| *4415[5]* | **Montone (IRE) (49)** (JRJenkins) **5-9-5**(4) MrVLukaniuk(10) (nvr nr to chal) | s.h | **5** | 14/1 | 54 | 38 |
| *4366[2]* | **Knotally Wood (USA) (64)** (JWHills) **3-10-4** MissEJohnsonHoughton(5) (a.p: rdn over 1f out: one pce) | 1 | **6** | 7/1 | 67 | 45 |
| *4434[6]* | **Phanan (47)** (REPeacock) **9-9-0**(7)ow7 MrsCPeacock(1) (lw: bhd fnl 10f) | 7 | **7** | 33/1 | 41 | 18 |
| *4364[12]* | **Don't Drop Bombs (USA) (40)** (DTThom) **6-9-0v** MissJFeilden(2) (lw: led 7f: wknd 3f out) | hd | **8** | 12/1 | 34 | 18 |
| 4315[6] | **Fighting Times (69)** (CASmith) **3-10-9** MissJWinter(9) (bhd fnl 8f) | 15 | **9** | 12/1 | 43 | 21 |
| *4436[8]* | **Mutinique (40)** (BAPearce) **4-8-7**(7) MrsSColville(7) (b: b.hind: hdwy 10f: wknd 5f out: t.o) | dist | **10** | 33/1 | — | — |

(SP 133.1%) **10 Rn**

**2m 35.21** (5.21) CSF £13.63 CT £47.18 TOTE £5.90: £1.10 £1.70 £3.00 (£9.30) Trio £26.50 OWNER Mr M. Gleason (HAMBLETON) BRED Cherry Valley Farm Inc
WEIGHT FOR AGE 3yo-6lb

T/Plpt: £56.30 (131.29 Tckts). T/Qdpt: £14.40 (1.25 Tckts). AK

# STERREBEEK (Brussels, Belgium) (L-H)
## Sunday November 12th

### 4466a PRIX J. DE HALLOY H'CAP (4-Y.O+)
**1m 1f 65y** £2,008.00

| | | | | SP | RR | SF |
|---|---|---|---|---|---|---|
| | **Diamond Pro** (JimmyNaylor,Belgium) **4-9-13** MissKMarks | — | 1 | | — | — |
| | **Private Despatch (USA)** (Belgium) **5-9-6** PMassage | 2 | 2 | | — | — |
| | **Sanquillo (BEL)** (Belgium) **7-8-6** NMinner | 5 | 3 | | — | — |
| 4157[12] | **Real Madrid** (GPEnright) **4-8-9** CDehens | 1 | 4 | | — | — |
| | | | | | | **9 Rn** |

**1m 54.7** P-M 29BF: 18BF 14BF 25BF (66BF) OWNER Mr J. Lamote BRED Lariston Bloodstock
**Real Madrid** was out of his depth in this company.

# GROENENDAEL (Brussels, Belgium) (L-H) (Heavy)
## Sunday November 19th

### 4467a PRIX LONGCHAMP H'CAP (3-Y.O+)
**1m 1f 55y** £1,205.00

| | | | | SP | RR | SF |
|---|---|---|---|---|---|---|
| 4466a[4] | **Real Madrid** (GPEnright) **4-9-7b** MO'Callaghan | — | 1 | | — | — |
| | **Music of Dance (IRE)** (Belgium) **4-7-0b** MmeBJacques | 3 | 2 | | — | — |
| | **Philip's Glorie (BEL)** (Belgium) **4-8-6** MlleSd'Hert | nk | 3 | | — | — |
| | | | | | | **14 Rn** |

**1m 59.1** P-M 125BF: 53BF 125BF 38BF OWNER Mr Chris Wall (LEWES) BRED Chris Wall
**4466a Real Madrid** found this opposition more to his liking, and came late to record a comfortable victory. His connections report that his present handicap mark makes it difficult to find suitable opportunities in Britain.

# 4423a-EVRY (France) (R-H) (Soft)
## Wednesday November 22nd

### 4468a PRIX SAINT-ROMAN (Gp 3) (2-Y.O)
1-45 (1-42) **1m 1f** £26,347.00 (£9,581.00: £4,790.00)

| | | | | SP | RR | SF |
|---|---|---|---|---|---|---|
| | **Spinning World (USA)** (JEPease,France) **2-8-11** OPeslier | — | 1 | | — | — |
| | **Luna Wells (IRE)** (DSepulchre,France) **2-8-8** ESaint-Martin | s.nk | 2 | | — | — |
| 4010a[3] | **Radevore** (AFabre,France) **2-8-11** TJarnet | 2 | 3 | | — | — |
| | | | | | | **7 Rn** |

**2m 4.45** (14.45) P-M 3.70F: 2.00F 1.90F (SF 13.20) OWNER Mr S. S. Niarchos
**Spinning World (USA)** was prominent throughout, and having gained the advantage a quarter of a mile from home, held on well for a narrow victory. His trainer thinks he will improve on this, and that he should get further. He will be entered in all the top races, and could make up into a classic colt.

# 4468a-EVRY (France) (R-H) (Soft)
## Friday November 24th

### 4469a PRIX CONTESSINA (Listed) (3-Y.O+)
2-05 (2-04) **6f** £16,766.00 (£5,748.00: £3,593.00)

| | | | | SP | RR | SF |
|---|---|---|---|---|---|---|
| 4345a[6] | **Sharp Prod (USA)** (LordHuntingdon) **5-8-11b** OPeslier | — | 1 | | 110 | — |
| 4324[2] | **Branston Abby (IRE)** (MJohnston) **6-8-12** JWeaver | nse | 2 | | 111 | — |
| 4178a[6] | **Anabaa (USA)** (MmeCHead,France) **3-8-11** FHead | nse | 3 | | 111 | — |
| | | | | | | **10 Rn** |

**1m 14.03** (4.03) P-M 6.60F: 2.20F 2.20F 1.60F (19.00F) OWNER The Queen (WEST ILSLEY) BRED The Queen
**4345a Sharp Prod (USA)**, wearing a visor for the first time, made most of the running. He looked beaten when headed by the second inside the last furlong, but rallied to gain the advantage close home. He is due to go to the December sales at Newmarket.
**4324 Branston Abby (IRE)** looked sure to win when going ahead in the last half furlong, but lost out on the nod. She has retained her form remarkably well.
**Anabaa (USA)** came late on the scene, and came out third best in a desperate finish.

# 4424a-CAPANNELLE (Rome, Italy) (R-H) (Soft)
## Sunday November 26th

### 4470a PREMIO ROMA VECCHIA (Gp 3) (3-Y.O+)
2-00 (2-21) **1m 6f** £29,498.00 (£13,573.00: £7,578.00: £3,789.00)

| | | | | SP | RR | SF |
|---|---|---|---|---|---|---|
| 4182a[3] | **Sternkonig (IRE)** (HBlume,Germany) **5-9-3** AStarke | — | 1 | | 114 | — |
| 4204[2] | **Asterita** (RHannon) **3-8-5** GCarter | nse | 2 | | 109 | — |
| 4258[2] | **Kristal's Paradise (IRE)** (JLDunlop) **3-8-5** GForte | 2½ | 3 | | 106 | — |
| 4030[2] | **Saxon Maid** (LMCumani) **4-9-0** LDettori | 4 | 4 | | 104 | — |
| 4342a[3] | **My Irish** (MCiciarelli,Italy) **5-8-13** SLandi | 2¼ | 5 | | 100 | — |
| 4315* | **Chief Bee** (JLDunlop) **4-8-9** WCarson | 1¼ | 6 | | 95 | — |
| | | | | | | **11 Rn** |

**2m 57.3** Tote 14L: 11L 21L 25L (59L) OWNER Gestut Rottgen BRED Gestut Rottgen

**4182a Sternkonig (IRE)** moved up on the outside three furlongs out, and looked set for a comfortable victory when hitting the front with under a furlong to run. This trip is at the limit of his stamina, and he only just lasted home.
**4204 Asterita** moved up to challenge at the quarter mile pole. She took a long time to wear down the leader, and was almost immediately passed by the winner. She rallied really well, and only just failed to get back up.
**4258 Kristal's Paradise (IRE)** ran a blinder on her first attempt in Pattern company. Having led from the start, she resisted a number of challenges before weakening inside the last furlong.
**4030 Saxon Maid** was always handy, and had every chance until weakening a furlong out.
**4315* Chief Bee** ran creditably. She was held up in the rear until coming through to join the leaders a furlong and a half out. She had nothing left to give in the last furlong.

# 1120a-FUCHU (Tokyo, Japan) (L-H) (Firm)
## Sunday November 26th

### 4471a JAPAN CUP (Gp 1) (3-Y.O+)
6-20 (6-20) **1m 4f** £1,101,928.00 (£442,053.00: £275,482.00: £166,571.00)

| Form | Horse | Dist | Pos | SP | RR | SF |
|---|---|---|---|---|---|---|
| 4307a[12] | **Lando (GER)** (HJentzsch,Germany) **5-9-0** MRoberts (hld up: 6th st: prog to ld 1f out: r.o wl) | — | **1** | | 127 | — |
| | **Hishi Amazon (USA)** (TNakano,Japan) **4-8-10** ENakadate (hld up: bhd st: gd prog fnl 3f: nt rch wnr) | 1½ | **2** | | 121 | — |
| 4307a[5] | **Hernando (FR)** (JEHammond,France) **5-9-0** CAsmussen (hld up: bhd st: r.o wl from 3f out) | nk | **3** | | 125 | — |
| 1120a[3] | **Taiki Blizzard (USA)** (KFujisawa,Japan) **4-9-0** YOkabe (led tl hdd 1f out: no ex) | nse | **4** | | 125 | — |
| 4307a[6] | **Awad (USA)** (DDonk,USA) **5-9-0b** EMaple (hld up: bhd st: r.o: nt rch ldrs) | 1¼ | **5** | | 123 | — |
| | **Narita Brian (JPN)** (MOkubo,Japan) **4-9-0** YTake (mid div: nvr plcd to chal) | 1¾ | **6** | | 121 | — |
| | **Royce and Royce (JPN)** (YMatsuyama,Japan) **5-9-0** NYokoyama (hld up: rr st: nvr plcd to chal) | ½ | **7** | | 120 | — |
| 3576a[2] | **Sandpit (BRA)** (RMandella,USA) **6-9-0** CNakatani (prom tl wknd over 1f out) | 2½ | **8** | | 117 | — |
| | **Danewin (AUS)** (RThomsen,Australia) **4-9-0** CKTse (prom tl rdn & wknd over 3f out) | nse | **9** | | 117 | — |
| 4014a[5] | **Pure Grain** (MRStoute) **3-8-5** JReid (mid div: rdn & btn over 3f out) | ½ | **10** | | 113 | — |
| 4014a[9] | **Carling (FR)** (MmePBarbe,France) **3-8-5** TThulliez (prom: 5th st: wknd over 1f out) | ½ | **11** | | 112 | — |
| | **Matikanetannhauser (JPN)** (YIto,Japan) **6-9-0** YShibata (m.n.s) | ½ | **12** | | 115 | — |
| | **Nice Nature (JPN)** (YMatsunaga,Japan) **7-9-0** MMatsunaga (prom tl 4th & wkng st) | nk | **13** | | 114 | — |
| | **Stony Bay (NZ)** (MrsGWaterhouse,Australia) **4-9-0** RSDye (cl up: 3rd st: sn rdn & btn) | hd | **14** | | 114 | — |
| | | | | | | **14 Rn** |

**2m 24.6** Tote 1450Y: 440Y 170Y 380Y (3310Y) OWNER Gestut Haus Ittlingen BRED Gestut Hof Ittlingen
**4307a Lando (GER)** crowned a wonderful career, and proved that he is a world-beater on fast ground. Given an immaculate ride, he hit the front at the furlong marker, and won well. He now retires to stud at Gestut Ittlingen, near Dortmund.
**4307a Hernando (FR)** retired on a high note. He was still at the rear of the field on the home turn, but ran on really well to claim third place on the line. He retires to Lanwades Stud at Newmarket.
**4014a Pure Grain** saved ground on the inside. She was ninth into the straight, but found nothing when asked to quicken. She was later found to have a spiral fracture of her off-hind cannon bone. Her racing days are over, and it is hoped she can be saved for a stud career.

# 4427-SOUTHWELL (L-H) (Standard)
## Friday December 1st
WEATHER: misty and cold WIND: slt half against

### 4472 KUSTOM KIT CLOTHING H'CAP (0-75) (I) (4-Y.O+) (Class D)
12-40 (12-41) **1m 3f (Fibresand)** £3,160.00 (£955.00: £465.00: £220.00) Stalls: Low GOING minus 0.11 sec per fur (FST)

| Form | Horse | Dist | Pos | SP | RR | SF |
|---|---|---|---|---|---|---|
| *4387*[4] | **Wildfire (SWI) (42)** (RAkehurst) **4-7-9** JQuinn(6) (trckd ldrs: led over 5f out: clr 3f out: unchal) | — | **1** | 9/2[2] | 54 | 36 |
| 4284[4] | **Larn Fort (50)** (CWFairhurst) **5-8-3v** JTate(1) (w ldrs: drvn along over 3f out: one pce) | 5 | **2** | 9/1 | 55 | 37 |
| | **Roseberry Topping (58)** (MrsMReveley) **6-8-11** TIves(4) (dwlt: hdwy to chse ldrs ½-wy: one pce fnl 3f) | 4 | **3** | 10/1 | 57 | 39 |
| *4406** | **Saltando (IRE) (52)** (PatMitchell) **4-8-2**(3) 5x DRMcCabe(2) (hld up & bhd: hdwy 3f out: nt rch ldrs) | 2½ | **4** | 10/1 | 47 | 29 |
| *4364*[2] | **Father Dan (IRE) (60)** (MissGayKelleway) **6-8-13** RCochrane(9) (lw: hld up: effrt over 4f out: nvr nr to chal) | 1¾ | **5** | 6/4[1] | 53 | 35 |
| 2064[6] | **Drummer Hicks (44)** (EWeymes) **6-7-11** DaleGibson(5) (led tl over 5f out: sn drvn along: wknd over 2f out) | 10 | **6** | 14/1 | 22 | 4 |
| 4168[6] | **Karttikeya (FR) (72)** (MrsNMacauley) **4-9-11** SDWilliams(8) (b: prom early: drvn along & outpcd ½-wy: n.d) | 7 | **7** | 14/1 | 40 | 22 |
| *4388*[4] | **No Submission (USA) (68)** (DWChapman) **9-9-7** LDettori(10) (hdwy to chse ldrs 7f out: drvn along 4f out: sn wknd: eased) | 1 | **8** | 10/1 | 35 | 17 |
| 4028[3] | **Sharp Falcon (IRE) (72)** (JWharton) **4-9-11** KFallon(11) (bit bkwd: dwlt: bhd: sme hdwy 7f out: wknd 4f out) | 3 | **9** | 6/1[3] | 34 | 16 |
| 3445[11] | **Augustan (53)** (SGollings) **4-8-6v** VHalliday(3) (in tch: drvn along 5f out: sn lost pl) | 6 | **10** | 20/1 | 7 | — |
| | **Dublin Indemnity (USA) (46)** (MPBielby) **6-7-13b** JFanning(7) (w ldrs tl wknd qckly 7f out: t.o 4f out) | dist | **11** | 33/1 | — | — |
| | | | | (SP 130.8%) | | **11 Rn** |

**2m 26.5** (6.50) CSF £45.07 CT £367.07 TOTE £6.20: £2.00 £4.00 £2.60 (£35.20) Trio £130.60 OWNER Mr R. F. Kilby (EPSOM) BRED J. P. Jackson

### 4473 JULIUS CAESAR NURSERY H'CAP (0-75) (2-Y.O) (Class E)
1-10 (1-12) **5f (Fibresand)** £3,038.20 (£919.60: £448.80: £213.40) Stalls: High GOING minus 0.22 sec per fur (FST)

| Form | Horse | Dist | Pos | SP | RR | SF |
|---|---|---|---|---|---|---|
| 3670[6] | **Krystal Max (IRE) (74)** (TDBarron) **2-9-0**(7) KimberleyHart(12) (trckd ldrs: led jst ins fnl f: hld on wl: sddle slipped) | — | **1** | 16/1 | 84 | 36 |
| *4369** | **Mullagh Hill Lad (IRE) (65)** (BAMcMahon) **2-8-12** GCarter(11) (lw: led tl jst ins fnl f: kpt on wl towards fin) | nk | **2** | 3/1[1] | 74 | 26 |
| 4066* | **Charterhouse Xpres (66)** (MMcCormack) **2-8-13v** LDettori(3) (a chsng ldrs: kpt on same pce appr fnl f) | 2 | **3** | 5/1[2] | 69 | 21 |
| *4389*[6] | **Gracious Gretclo (52)** (CJHill) **2-7-13** JQuinn(8) (chsd ldrs: one pce fnl 2f) | 2 | **4** | 5/1[2] | 48 | — |
| *4124*[4] | **Gi La High (59)** (JBerry) **2-8-1v**(5) PFessey(1) (in tch: kpt on fnl 2f: nvr nr to chal) | 1¼ | **5** | 15/2 | 51 | 3 |
| 3940[3] | **Kazimiera (IRE) (73)** (MJohnston) **2-9-6** TWilliams(4) (s.i.s: sn drvn & outpcd: sme hdwy 2f out: n.d) | hd | **6** | 7/1[3] | 65 | 17 |
| 4287[6] | **Principal Boy (IRE) (46)** (TJEtherington) **2-7-7b** GBardwell(5) (chsd ldrs: rdn 2f out: sn wknd) | ¾ | **7** | 25/1 | 36 | — |
| 4231[7] | **The Barnsley Belle (IRE) (58)** (SGNorton) **2-8-5** DeanMcKeown(6) (sn outpcd: sme hdwy over 1f out: n.d) | ½ | **8** | 20/1 | 46 | — |
| 4141[14] | **Briganoone (55)** (SRBowring) **2-8-2b** NKennedy(2) (swvd lft s: sn drvn along: n.d) | nk | **9** | 7/1[3] | 42 | — |
| *4375*[2] | **Trickledown (49)** (MartynWane) **2-7-10**ow1 AMackay(7) (s.i.s: a outpcd) | 2½ | **10** | 14/1 | 27 | — |

4437[3] **Beeny (64)** (APJarvis) **2-8-11** JTate(9) (outpcd & drvn along ½-wy: sn bhd) ....1½ **11** 8/1 38 —
4429[8] **Snitch (48)** (CSmith) **2-7-9v** NCarlisle(10) (chsd ldrs tl lost pl ½-wy) ....2 **12** 33/1 16 —
(SP 130.3%) **12 Rn**

**60.9 secs** (3.90) CSF £65.05 CT £267.20 TOTE £25.70: £5.70 £1.90 £2.60 (£86.50) Trio £83.10 OWNER The Oakfield Nurseries Partnership (THIRSK) BRED Baronrath Stud
LONG HANDICAP Principal Boy (IRE) 7-5

## 4474 KING HENRY VI CLAIMING STKS (3, 4 & 5-Y.O) (Class F)

1-40 (1-40) **1m 6f (Fibresand)** £2,537.00 (£712.00: £347.00) Stalls: High GOING minus 0.11 sec per fur (FST)

SP RR SF

4387[7] **Rose of Glenn (42)** (BPalling) **4-8-9** RPerham(3) (trckd ldrs: led over 6f out: clr 3f out: eased fnl f) ....— **1** 3/1[2] 53 10
3722[3] **Skedaddle (52)** (RonaldThompson) **3-8-2** GBardwell(2) (chsd ldrs: sn pushed along: one pce fnl 3f) ....10 **2** 7/2[3] 42 —
4448[8] **Ann Hill (IRE) (24)** (RHollinshead) **5-7-12**(7) FLynch(4) (hld up & bhd: stdy hdwy 5f out: drvn along over 3f out: one pce) ....1¾ **3** 14/1 36 —
4363[9] **Chapel Annie** (CPWildman) **3-8-6** AMackay(6) (chsd ldr: drvn along 5f out: wknd & eased over 1f out) ....20 **4** 16/1 21 —
4062[19] **Absolute Folly (50)** (JBerry) **3-8-6v**(7) PRoberts(7) (led tl over 6f out: sn lost pl: t.o 4f out) ....25 **5** 11/2 — —
4412[8] **Newgate Hush (27)** (BWMurray) **3-8-1** TWilliams(5) (sn bhd: sme hdwy u.p 7f out: sn wknd: wl t.o fnl 4f) ....dist **6** 40/1 — —
4411[12] **Who's the Best (IRE) (47)** (APJarvis) **5-8-11**(3) DWright(1) (p.u after 2f: dead).... **P** 6/4[1] — —
(SP 117.6%) **7 Rn**

**3m 13.5** (14.50) CSF £13.59 TOTE £4.20: £2.00 £1.90 (£6.40) OWNER Mr K. M. Rideout (COWBRIDGE) BRED Mrs M. J. Dandy
WEIGHT FOR AGE 3yo-7lb

## 4475 KUSTOM KIT CLOTHING H'CAP (0-75) (II) (4-Y.O+) (Class D)

2-10 (2-11) **1m 3f (Fibresand)** £3,143.75 (£950.00: £462.50: £218.75) Stalls: Low GOING minus 0.11 sec per fur (FST)

SP RR SF

4390[4] **Beaumont (IRE) (52)** (JEBanks) **5-8-9** JQuinn(2) (hld up: hdwy over 3f out: led over 1f out: drvn out) ....— **1** 7/2[1] 60 41
4391[3] **Risky Tu (43)** (PAKelleway) **4-8-0** GBardwell(5) (lw: chsd ldrs: drvn along 7f out: ev ch over 1f out: nt qckn) 1¾ **2** 4/1[2] 49 30
4378[3] **Calder King (62)** (JLEyre) **4-9-5v** RLappin(3) (sn outpcd & pushed along: hdwy over 2f out: hrd rdn & kpt on fnl f) ....1 **3** 6/1 66 47
778[11] **Let's Get Lost (55)** (JAHarris) **6-8-12** LDettori(1) (chsd ldrs tl wknd fnl f) ....4 **4** 7/2[1] 53 34
4335[12] **Tempering (52)** (DWChapman) **9-8-9** JFanning(4) (swtg: led: clr 7f out: hdd over 1f out: sn wknd) ....1 **5** 16/1 49 30
4376[4] **Our Main Man (53)** (RMWhitaker) **5-8-10** ACulhane(7) (hld up: stdy hdwy 5f out: rdn & hung lft over 2f out: sn wknd) ....5 **6** 13/2 43 24
4270[4] **Stevie's Wonder (IRE) (67)** (MJRyan) **5-9-10v** GCarter(9) (chsd ldrs: drvn along 6f out: wknd over 4f out) ....3 **7** 9/2[3] 52 33
**Persian Haze (IRE) (50)** (BJMcMath) **6-8-7** TWilliams(6) (lw: sn bhd: t.o 7f out) ....15 **8** 33/1 13 —
(SP 119.1%) **8 Rn**

**2m 27.7** (7.70) CSF £17.45 CT £74.39 TOTE £5.10: £1.70 £1.10 £1.30 (£10.60) Trio £13.60 OWNER Mr P. Cunningham (NEWMARKET) BRED Mount Coote Stud in Ireland

## 4476 SHARPS INTERNATIONAL POLO H'CAP (0-90) (3-Y.O+) (Class C)

2-40 (2-41) **1m (Fibresand)** £5,758.00 (£1,744.00: £852.00: £406.00) Stalls: Low GOING minus 0.11 sec per fur (FST)

SP RR SF

4378[2] **Rood Music (68)** (MGMeagher) **4-8-11** FNorton(3) (chsd ldrs: sn drvn along: styd on to ld ins fnl f: r.o wl) ....— **1** 7/1[2] 78 40
4374* **Chairmans Choice (74)** (APJarvis) **5-9-3** JTate(10) (mde most tl ins fnl f: kpt on wl) ....¾ **2** 10/1 83 45
4435[3] **Bagshot (76)** (RHannon) **4-9-0**(5) DaneO'Neill(11) (trckd ldrs: ev ch over 2f out: nt qckn fnl f) ....hd **3** 8/1[3] 84 46
4227* **Secret Aly (CAN) (82)** (CEBrittain) **5-9-11** JQuinn(2) (lw: s.i.s: bhd: hdwy 2f out: styd on strly towards fin) ....hd **4** 8/1[3] 90 52
4163[10] **Rambo's Hall (83)** (JAGlover) **10-9-12** SDWilliams(7) (swtg: bhd tl styd on fnl 2f) ....2½ **5** 12/1 86 48
4427* **Nashaat (USA) (74)** (MCChapman) **7-8-10**(7) 6x CMunday(5) (s.i.s: bhd: hdwy 3f out: styd on same pce appr fnl f) ....nk **6** 7/1[2] 77 39
4392[5] **Bentico (70)** (MrsNMacauley) **6-8-6v**(7) AmandaSanders(16) (in tch: effrt on outside 2f out: kpt on ins fnl f) ....1 **7** 16/1 71 33
4202[6] **Tribal Peace (IRE) (69)** (BGubby) **3-8-8**(3) JStack(9) (in tch: kpt on same pce fnl 2f) ....1 **8** 16/1 69 29
4367[2] **Celestial Choir (75)** (JLEyre) **5-9-4** LDettori(1) (sn chsng ldrs: sn drvn along: eased whn btn ins fnl f) ....1¼ **9** 5/1[1] 71 33
4432[5] **Johnnie the Joker (76)** (JPLeigh) **4-9-5b** DeanMcKeown(14) (rr div: effrt 2f out: n.d) ....3½ **10** 25/1 65 27
4415[11] **Bakheta (51)** (KTIvory) **3-7-7** GBardwell(4) (a bhd) ....1 **11** 50/1 39 —
4427[3] **Ochos Rios (IRE) (60)** (BSRothwell) **4-8-3** SSanders(13) (a in rr) ....hd **12** 16/1 47 9
4388[2] **Hawwam (72)** (EJAlston) **9-9-1** KFallon(6) (lw: in tch: drvn along ½-wy: sn lost pl) ....2 **13** 9/1 55 17
3973[14] **Nordinex (IRE) (74)** (RWArmstrong) **3-9-2** RPrice(15) (prom tl lost pl 3f out) ....11 **14** 9/1 36 —
4416[13] **Jari (USA) (67)** (MJPolglase) **4-8-10b** GCarter(12) (s.i.s: reluctant to r: a t.o) ....14 **15** 50/1 — —
4368[12] **Castel Rosselo (85)** (RHarris) **5-10-0** AMackay(8) (prom early: racd wd: lost pl & eased over 3f out) ....2 **16** 12/1 14 —
(SP 133.8%) **16 Rn**

**1m 43.9** (3.90) CSF £74.79 CT £537.93 TOTE £6.80: £1.50 £4.00 £3.00 £2.20 (£46.00) Trio £135.80 OWNER Mr M. R. Johnson (ORMSKIRK) BRED T. R. G. Vestey
LONG HANDICAP Bakheta 7-1
WEIGHT FOR AGE 3yo-1lb

## 4477 ANTHONY & CLEOPATRA (S) STKS (2-Y.O F) (Class F)

3-10 (3-10) **1m (Fibresand)** £2,537.00 (£712.00: £347.00) Stalls: Low GOING minus 0.11 sec per fur (FST)

SP RR SF

4393[4] **People Direct (53)** (KMcAuliffe) **2-8-9** JFanning(5) (b.nr hind: mde all: clr 3f out: eased ins fnl f) ....— **1** 5/1[2] 67 13
4375[9] **Takapuna (IRE) (43)** (TJNaughton) **2-9-0** SSanders(2) (s.i.s: hdwy ½-wy: kpt on ins fnl f) ....10 **2** 6/1[3] 52 —
4339[9] **Hannahs Bay (35)** (MGMeagher) **2-8-6b**(3) JStack(1) (s.i.s: bhd & rdn ½-wy: styd on appr fnl f) ....1¾ **3** 16/1 44 —
4446[4] **Image Maker (IRE) (59)** (BPreece) **2-9-0b** TIves(6) (hld up: hdwy ½-wy: sn chsng wnr: wknd fnl f) ....1 **4** 8/1 47 —
4433[6] **Bumblefoot (IRE) (63)** (MJohnston) **2-9-0** TWilliams(7) (chsd wnr: drvn along ½-wy: sn hrd rdn: one pce) ...1¼ **5** 5/1[2] 44 —
4133[2] **Bells of Holland (59)** (WRMuir) **2-8-9** LDettori(3) (chsd ldrs: drvn along over 3f out: wknd 1f out: eased) ....3½ **6** 5/6[1] 32 —
4393[13] **Laid Back Lucy** (JAHarris) **2-8-9** SDWilliams(4) (chsd ldrs: drvn along ½-wy: sn lost pl) ....9 **7** 50/1 14 —
(SP 121.1%) **7 Rn**

**1m 46.5** (6.50) CSF £32.95 TOTE £6.40: £3.00 £3.10 (£18.90) OWNER Mr Peter Barclay (LAMBOURN) BRED James Thom and Sons and Peter Orr
Bt in 4,800 gns

## 4478 HAMLET H'CAP (0-85) (3-Y.O) (Class D)

3-40 (3-40) **6f (Fibresand)** £3,690.70 (£1,117.60: £545.80: £259.90) Stalls: Low GOING minus 0.11 sec per fur (FST)

| Form | Horse / details | Dist | Pos | SP | RR | SF |
|---|---|---|---|---|---|---|
| *4441*[2] | **Mister Fire Eyes (IRE) (85)** (CEBrittain) **3-9-7b** JQuinn(7) (lw: trckd ldrs: led over 1f out: drvn out) | — | 1 | 2/1[1] | 97 | 56 |
| *4450** | **Peggy Spencer (62)** (CWThornton) **3-7-12**[7x] AMackay(6) (chsd ldrs: rdn over 2f out: styd on fnl f) | 3 | 2 | 7/2[2] | 66 | 25 |
| *4447*[2] | **Sweet Mate (58)** (SRBowring) **3-7-3b**[(5)ow1] PFessey(3) (sn bhd: styd on fnl 2f: nvr nr to chal) | 1¼ | 3 | 8/1[3] | 58 | 17 |
| *4382** | **Sombreffe (70)** (DRLoder) **3-8-6v** LDettori(2) (mde most tl over 1f out: kpt on same pce) | 1¼ | 4 | 7/2[2] | 67 | 26 |
| *4430** | **Most Uppitty (61)** (JBerry) **3-7-8**[(3) 7x] DWright(8) (chsd ldrs: edgd lft u.p & wknd over 1f out) | 3 | 5 | 12/1 | 50 | 9 |
| *4430*[4] | **Montague Dawson (IRE) (63)** (MrsNMacauley) **3-7-6**[(7)ow4] AmandaSanders(10) (in tch: outpcd ½-wy: n.d after) | hd | 6 | 16/1 | 48 | 7 |
| *4413*[W] | **Nadwaty (IRE) (59)** (MCChapman) **3-7-6**[(3)ow2] NVarley(9) (chsd ldrs tl wknd 2f out) | 3 | 7 | 33/1 | 38 | — |
| *4392*[12] | **Master Millfield (IRE) (73)** (CJHill) **3-8-9** RPerham(1) (bhd whn hmpd over 4f out: n.d) | 1½ | 8 | 16/1 | 50 | 9 |
| 3316[6] | **Tafahhus (81)** (MJPolglase) **3-9-3** GCarter(4) (unruly in stalls: s.s: a wl bhd) | ½ | 9 | 20/1 | 57 | 16 |
| *4394*[15] | **Thick as Thieves (57)** (RonaldThompson) **3-7-7** GBardwell(5) (chsd ldrs tl wknd over 2f out) | 6 | 10 | 33/1 | 17 | — |
| 1614[14] | **Solo Prize (62)** (PHowling) **3-7-12**[ow2] FNorton(11) (b.hind: reluctant to r: virtually t.n.p) | dist | 11 | 25/1 | — | — |

(SP 122.8%) **11 Rn**

**1m 16.4** (2.90) CSF £9.53 CT £42.36 TOTE £2.80: £1.50 £2.20 £2.00 (£8.10) Trio £22.10 OWNER Mr C. T. Olley (NEWMARKET) BRED Airlie Stud

LONG HANDICAP Nadwaty (IRE) 7-2 Sweet Mate 7-2

T/Plpt: £1,471.30 (6.34 Tckts). T/Qdpt: Not won; £36.00 to Wolverhampton 2/12/95. WG

# 4443-WOLVERHAMPTON (L-H) (Standard)

## Saturday December 2nd

WEATHER: cloudy & rain WIND: nil

## 4479 DESERT ORCHID H'CAP (0-65) (I) (3-Y.O+ F & M) (Class F)

1-50 (1-53) **7f (Fibresand)** £2,187.00 (£612.00: £297.00) Stalls: High GOING: nil sec per fur (STD)

| Form | Horse / details | Dist | Pos | SP | RR | SF |
|---|---|---|---|---|---|---|
| *4372** | **Cashmere Lady (65)** (JLEyre) **3-10-0** RLappin(2) (bhd & outpcd: hdwy 3f out: led appr fnl f: rdn out) | — | 1 | 3/1[1] | 72 | 42 |
| *4430*[2] | **Irchester Lass (40)** (SRBowring) **3-8-3b** NCarlisle(8) (lw: a.p: led over 2f out tl appr fnl f: unable qckn nr fin) | nk | 2 | 6/1[2] | 46 | 16 |
| *2630*[10] | **Tilly Owl (43)** (JAHarris) **4-8-6** SDWilliams(5) (bit bkwd: chsd ldrs: rdn & kpt on ins fnl f) | 1¾ | 3 | 8/1 | 44 | 15 |
| *4407*[2] | **Fiaba (43)** (MrsNMacauley) **7-7-13**[(7)] AmandaSanders(9) (hld up: hdwy over 2f out: fin wl) | 1¼ | 4 | 8/1 | 42 | 13 |
| 4225[4] | **Gentle Irony (58)** (BJMeehan) **3-9-7b** RHughes(7) (hld up: hdwy 4f out: hrd rdn & edgd rt appr fnl f: no ex) | 2½ | 5 | 10/1 | 52 | 22 |
| *4409*[3] | **Lady Silk (52)** (MissJFCraze) **4-9-1** SWebster(3) (lw: chsd ldrs: rdn & no hdwy fnl 2f) | 4 | 6 | 7/1[3] | 36 | 7 |
| *4413*[4] | **Anita's Contessa (IRE) (61)** (BPalling) **3-9-10** RPerham(4) (led after 2f to 4f out: rdn over 2f out: sn btn) | 1 | 7 | 16/1 | 43 | 13 |
| 4242[2] | **Agoer (51)** (CEBrittain) **3-9-0** JQuinn(6) (b.hind: chsd ldrs tl rdn & wknd over 2f out) | 1½ | 8 | 6/1[2] | 30 | — |
| *3737*[8] | **Palacegate Jo (IRE) (51)** (DWChapman) **4-9-0** ACulhane(12) (a bhd & outpcd) | 6 | 9 | 33/1 | 15 | — |
| *4413*[13] | **Legatee (61)** (AStreeter) **4-9-10v** RCochrane(1) (b: led 2f: led 4f out tl over 2f out: sn rdn & wknd) | 2 | 10 | 25/1 | 21 | — |
| *4413*[6] | **Never Such Bliss (48)** (JDBethell) **3-8-11** LDettori(11) (a bhd: t.o) | 13 | 11 | 16/1 | — | — |
| *180*[2] | **Warwick Mist (IRE) (36)** (PHaslam) **3-7-13** DaleGibson(10) (a rr div: t.o) | 5 | 12 | 14/1 | — | — |

(SP 122.6%) **12 Rn**

**1m 30.1** (5.40) CSF £20.76 CT £122.64 TOTE £2.70: £1.60 £1.80 £2.80 (£14.30) Trio £50.50 OWNER Mrs Sybil Howe (HAMBLETON) BRED J. L. Eyre

## 4480 GOODYEAR MAIDEN STKS (I) (2-Y.O) (Class D)

2-20 (2-20) **1m 100y (Fibresand)** £2,965.00 (£895.00: £435.00: £205.00) Stalls: Low GOING: nil sec per fur (STD)

| Form | Horse / details | Dist | Pos | SP | RR | SF |
|---|---|---|---|---|---|---|
| *4334*[8] | **Belle's Boy** (BPalling) **2-9-0** GCarter(9) (swtg: dwlt: hdwy ½-wy: rdn to ld ins fnl f: r.o) | — | 1 | 33/1 | 69 | 20 |
| 4169[19] | **Balios (IRE)** (MJohnston) **2-9-0** TWilliams(7) (bit bkwd: led over 1f: led 4f out tl hdd & no ex ins fnl f) | 1½ | 2 | 14/1 | 66 | 17 |
| *4417*[3] | **Uoni** (CEBrittain) **2-8-9** JQuinn(3) (led 7f out to 4f out: ev ch tl rdn & nt qckn fnl f) | 1¼ | 3 | 11/4[2] | 59 | 10 |
| *4408*[6] | **Loch Style** (RHollinshead) **2-9-0** TIves(1) (bit bkwd: a.p: rdn bel dist: nt pce to chal) | s.h | 4 | 14/1 | 64 | 15 |
| 4064[6] | **Chalcuchima** (RCharlton) **2-9-0** DHarrison(4) (chsd ldrs: sn drvn along: r.o one pce fnl 2f) | hd | 5 | 6/4[1] | 64 | 15 |
| *4338*[11] | **Maestro Time (USA)** (TDBarron) **2-9-0** JFortune(6) (bit bkwd: bhd tl kpt on appr fnl f: nvr nrr) | 1 | 6 | 33/1 | 62 | 13 |
| 4230[5] | **Niteowl Raider (IRE) (55)** (JAHarris) **2-9-0** SDWilliams(8) (nvr trbld ldrs) | 1½ | 7 | 8/1 | 61 | 12 |
| *4339*[2] | **The Fullbangladesh** (JLEyre) **2-8-9** RLappin(2) (swtg: chsd ldrs over 6f: sn wknd) | ¾ | 8 | 6/1[3] | 54 | 5 |
| *4408*[9] | **Dicentra** (EWeymes) **2-8-9** DaleGibson(5) (bit bkwd: mid div tl wknd over 2f out: t.o) | 5 | 9 | 33/1 | 45 | — |
| *4365*[8] | **Dangerous Waters** (PGMurphy) **2-8-2**[(7)] RWaterfield(10) (b.nr hind: a bhd & outpcd: t.o) | 7 | 10 | 33/1 | 32 | — |

(SP 117.2%) **10 Rn**

**1m 52.5** (7.50) CSF £356.91 TOTE £71.50: £9.20 £3.60 £1.70 (£233.30) Trio £151.50 OWNER Mrs M. M. Palling (COWBRIDGE) BRED Mrs M. M. Palling

## 4481 PLYVINE CATERING H'CAP (0-95) (3-Y.O) (Class C)

2-55 (2-55) **1m 4f (Fibresand)** £10,357.50 (£3,135.00: £1,530.00: £727.50) Stalls: Low GOING: nil sec per fur (STD)

| Form | Horse / details | Dist | Pos | SP | RR | SF |
|---|---|---|---|---|---|---|
| *4356** | **River Keen (IRE) (80)** (RWArmstrong) **3-8-6** RPrice(9) (lw: a gng wl: led 3f out: sn clr: unchal) | — | 1 | 8/1[3] | 98 | 59 |
| *4384*[2] | **Sea Victor (76)** (JLHarris) **3-8-2v** SSanders(10) (led 9f: sn rdn & outpcd) | 10 | 2 | 10/1 | 81 | 42 |
| *4419** | **Far Ahead (76)** (JLEyre) **3-8-2** RLappin(11) (chsd ldrs: rdn 4f out & kpt on) | 6 | 3 | 5/1[2] | 73 | 34 |
| 3730[22] | **Lord Jim (IRE) (95)** (MissGayKelleway) **3-9-7** RCochrane(1) (bit bkwd: hld up: hdwy & rdn 4f out: one pce) | 2 | 4 | 33/1 | 89 | 50 |
| 4071[2] | **Mistinguett (IRE) (75)** (DRLoder) **3-7-12**[(3)] DRMcCabe(7) (lw: bhd: rdn ½-wy: no imp tl r.o wl fnl 2f) | 1 | 5 | 100/30[1] | 68 | 29 |
| 4069[5] | **Heathyards Rock (87)** (RHollinshead) **3-8-13v** TIves(8) (bhd: hdwy 4f out: nt rch ldrs) | 1¼ | 6 | 50/1 | 78 | 39 |
| 2691[8] | **At Liberty (IRE) (90)** (RHannon) **3-9-2** RPerham(5) (bkwd: prom tl rdn & wknd over 3f out) | nk | 7 | 12/1 | 81 | 42 |
| 3945[23] | **Bettergeton (90)** (PJBevan) **3-9-2** NCarlisle(2) (bit bkwd: a in rr: t.o) | 13 | 8 | 9/1 | 63 | 24 |
| 4245[5] | **Bint Zamayem (IRE) (84)** (BWHills) **3-8-10** MHills(6) (chsd ldrs: rdn 7f out: wknd over 4f out: t.o) | 10 | 9 | 12/1 | 44 | 5 |
| 4333[2] | **Fairy Knight (81)** (RHannon) **3-8-2**[(5)ow1] DaneO'Neill(3) (prom tl rdn & wknd over 3f out) | hd | 10 | 9/1 | 40 | 1 |
| 711[7] | **Evezio Rufo (89)** (NPLittmoden) **3-9-1** TGMcLaughlin(12) (prom: rdn along ½-wy: sn wknd: t.o) | 8 | 11 | 40/1 | 38 | — |

| | | | | SP | RR | SF |
|---|---|---|---|---|---|---|
| *4419[3]* | **Heboob Alshemaal (IRE) (80)** (JHMGosden) **3-8-6b** LDettori(4) (t.o fr ½-wy: p.u ent st) | | P | 8/1[3] | — | — |

(SP 113.8%) **12 Rn**

**2m 36.1** (3.60) CSF £73.58 CT £396.07 TOTE £12.70: £3.00 £1.50 £2.20 (£37.80) Trio £64.90 OWNER Dr Meou Tsen Geoffrey Yeh (NEWMARKET) BRED Ballylinch Stud Ltd

OFFICIAL EXPLANATION **Heboob Alshemaal (IRE): had become distressed during the race.**
**Mistinguett (IRE): had resented the kick-back and appeared not to handle the track.**

## 4482 BASS WULFRUN STKS (Listed) (3-Y.O+) (Class A)

3-25 (3-35) **1m 1f 79y (Fibresand)** £32,507.00 (£12,113.00: £5,881.50: £2,482.50) Stalls: Low GOING: nil sec per fur (STD)

| | | | | SP | RR | SF |
|---|---|---|---|---|---|---|
| 4403a[4] | **Prince of Andros (USA) (113)** (DRLoder) **5-9-6** RHughes(12) (lw: hld up & bhd: hdwy over 3f out: led bel dist: r.o wl) | — | 1 | 7/2[3] | 111 | 75 |
| 3991[3] | **Verzen (IRE) (96)** (DRLoder) **3-8-11** DRMcCabe(8) (lw: mde most to bel dist: rallied gamely u.p towards fin) | ¾ | 2 | 14/1 | 103 | 65 |
| 4267* | **Tarawa (IRE) (99)** (NACallaghan) **3-8-11** DHarrison(2) (hld up: hdwy over 3f out: hrd rdn & one pce fnl f) | 1½ | 3 | 9/2 | 100 | 62 |
| 4301a[2] | **Maralinga (IRE) (97)** (LadyHerries) **3-8-11** DeanMcKeown(11) (lw: a.p: ev ch 2f out: unable qckn appr fnl f) | hd | 4 | 8/1 | 100 | 62 |
| 4323[2] | **Capias (USA) (108)** (JHMGosden) **4-9-2v** LDettori(6) (chsd ldrs: rdn & effrt 3f out: nt pce to chal) | 4 | 5 | 5/2[1] | 96 | 60 |
| 4281[5] | **King Rat (IRE) (94)** (TJEtherington) **4-9-0b** CRutter(1) (disp ld fr 7f out tl wknd over 2f out) | 7 | 6 | 33/1 | 82 | 46 |
| 4402a[8] | **Mr Martini (IRE) (100)** (CEBrittain) **5-9-4** TIves(9) (lw: bhd: rdn along ½-wy: n.d) | 3½ | 7 | 8/1 | 80 | 44 |
| 4265* | **Celestial Key (USA) (105)** (MJohnston) **5-9-2** MHills(5) (chsd ldrs: rdn over 2f out: sn outpcd) | 5 | 8 | 6/1 | 70 | 34 |
| 4116[20] | **Band on the Run (95)** (BAMcMahon) **8-9-0** GCarter(3) (lw: a in rr) | ¾ | 9 | 20/1 | 66 | 30 |
| 3845[2] | **Desert Green (FR) (96)** (RHannon) **6-9-0** RPerham(4) (bit bkwd: chsd ldrs over 5f: sn rdn & wknd) | 3 | 10 | 10/1 | 61 | 25 |
| 4267[16] | **Night Dance (95)** (GLewis) **3-8-11** SWhitworth(13) (s.i.s: bhd: effrt 3f out: nvr nr ldrs) | ¾ | 11 | 7/1 | 59 | 21 |
| 4267[5] | **Ertlon (95)** (CEBrittain) **5-9-0** JQuinn(10) (lw: prom: rdn along 4f out: sn lost tch: t.o) | 5 | 12 | 20/1 | 51 | 15 |
| *3562[2]* | ***Nijo (109)*** (DRLoder) **4-9-0** RCochrane(7) (Withdrawn not under Starter's orders: broke out of stalls: rdr inj) | | W | 3/1[2] | — | — |

(SP 171.2%) **12 Rn**

**1m 59.7** (3.70) CSF £57.15 TOTE £4.10: £2.40 £6.70 £1.80 (£38.80) Trio £308.30 OWNER Lucayan Stud (NEWMARKET) BRED Spendthrift Farm

WEIGHT FOR AGE 3yo-2lb

## 4483 LIFTING GEAR & TOOL HIRE (S) STKS (2-Y.O F) (Class F)

3-55 (4-06) **6f (Fibresand)** £2,580.00 (£780.00: £380.00: £180.00) Stalls: Low GOING: nil sec per fur (STD)

| | | | | SP | RR | SF |
|---|---|---|---|---|---|---|
| 4230[6] | **Lady Eclat (50)** (JAGlover) **2-8-9v** SDWilliams(13) (mde all: clr 2f out: drvn out) | — | 1 | 14/1 | 64 | 27 |
| *4429[7]* | **Quinntessa** (BPalling) **2-8-9** RPerham(7) (hdwy ½-wy: kpt on ins fnl f: no ch w wnr) | 1¾ | 2 | 33/1 | 59 | 22 |
| *4414[4]* | **Carmosa (USA) (56)** (WJarvis) **2-8-9** LDettori(11) (chsd ldrs: rdn ½-wy: kpt on fnl f) | 1¾ | 3 | 2/1[2] | 55 | 18 |
| *4437[4]* | **Impington (IRE) (59)** (WRMuir) **2-8-9** DHarrison(8) (chsd wnr tl rdn & wknd fnl f) | s.h | 4 | 10/1[3] | 55 | 18 |
| 3714[9] | **Flood's Fancy (60)** (ABailey) **2-8-7b(7)** PRoberts(1) (sddle slipped & bolted bef s: chsd ldrs: no hdwy fnl 2f) | 2 | 5 | 10/1[3] | 54 | 17 |
| *4369[4]* | **Monkey Zanty (IRE) (47)** (JLHarris) **2-8-9** SSanders(4) (chsd ldrs 4f: sn outpcd) | nk | 6 | 16/1 | 48 | 11 |
| *4393[5]* | **Shanoora (IRE) (52)** (MrsNMacauley) **2-8-7b(7)** AmandaSanders(10) (outpcd: a bhd) | 1¼ | 7 | 20/1 | 50 | 13 |
| *4393[2]* | **Vera's First (IRE) (60)** (GLewis) **2-9-0b** SWhitworth(12) (sn rdn along: a outpcd & bhd) | 1 | 8 | 13/8[1] | 47 | 10 |
| *4375[8]* | **Orange And Blue (43)** (MissJFCraze) **2-9-0c** SWebster(6) (chsd ldrs over 3f: sn outpcd) | 2½ | 9 | 25/1 | 41 | 4 |
| *4339[13]* | **Rocket Grounds (IRE)** (JJQuinn) **2-8-9** DaleGibson(2) (prom over 3f) | nk | 10 | 33/1 | 35 | — |
| 4109[9] | **Hi Hoh (IRE) (47)** (NPLittmoden) **2-8-9** TGMcLaughlin(9) (a bhd & outpcd) | nk | 11 | 20/1 | 34 | — |
| *4294[5]* | **Bouton d'Or (45)** (PHowling) **2-8-9** JQuinn(5) (mid div: rdn over 2f out: sn wknd) | 1 | 12 | 25/1 | 32 | — |
| 3975[20] | **Sizzling Serenade** (SGNorton) **2-8-9** JFortune(3) (a bhd & outpcd) | 1¾ | 13 | 33/1 | 27 | — |

(SP 128.2%) **13 Rn**

**1m 16.2** (4.80) CSF £336.35 TOTE £24.60: £3.80 £3.80 £1.30 (£412.00) Trio £285.90; £201.36 to Ludlow 4/12/95 OWNER The Robin Hood Connection (WORKSOP) BRED Colin G. R. Booth

Bt in 5,200 gns

OFFICIAL EXPLANATION **Vera's First (IRE): had lost interest as she prefers to race prominently and could not do so having been drawn on the outside.**

## 4484 BASS NEAL RADFORD BENEFIT H'CAP (0-60) (3, 4 & 5-Y.O) (Class F)

4-25 (4-32) **5f (Fibresand)** £2,537.00 (£712.00: £347.00) Stalls: Low GOING: nil sec per fur (STD)

| | | | | SP | RR | SF |
|---|---|---|---|---|---|---|
| *4358[8]* | **Bajan Frontier (IRE) (41)** (FHLee) **3-8-9** GCarter(2) (b.hind: broke smartly: mde all: unchal) | — | 1 | 16/1 | 52 | 23 |
| *4428[4]* | **Matthew David (45)** (SRBowring) **5-8-13b** SWebster(12) (hdwy 2f out: rdn & r.o wl ins fnl f) | 2½ | 2 | 6/1 | 48 | 19 |
| *4428[6]* | **Superbit (48)** (BAMcMahon) **3-9-2** SSanders(7) (a.p: swtchd rt ent fnl f: r.o) | nk | 3 | 12/1 | 50 | 21 |
| 4278[14] | **Encore M'Lady (IRE) (60)** (FHLee) **4-10-0b** TIves(10) (hdwy ½-wy: chsd wnr appr fnl f: no ex cl home) | ¾ | 4 | 25/1 | 60 | 31 |
| *4413[12]* | **Blue Sioux (59)** (JWharton) **3-9-13b** LDettori(5) (gd spd over 3f) | ¾ | 5 | 5/1[2] | 56 | 27 |
| *4274[12]* | **Al Shaati (FR) (50)** (RJO'Sullivan) **5-9-4** DBiggs(4) (chsd ldrs: rdn over 2f out: nt pce to chal) | 1½ | 6 | 3/1[1] | 42 | 13 |
| *4358[4]* | **Halliard (56)** (TMJones) **4-9-10v** RPerham(8) (b: drvn along ½-wy: nvr nr ldrs) | 2 | 7 | 9/1 | 42 | 13 |
| *4458[4]* | **Green's Bid (48)** (DWChapman) **5-9-2b** ACulhane(6) (spd over 3f) | 1¼ | 8 | 16/1 | 30 | 1 |
| 3139[4] | **Mister Raider (47)** (SMellor) **3-8-12b(3)** DWright(13) (bit bkwd: outpcd) | nk | 9 | 10/1 | 28 | — |
| 3442[13] | **Delrob (60)** (DHaydnJones) **4-10-0** AMackay(3) (outpcd: a bhd) | nk | 10 | 14/1 | 40 | 11 |
| | **Riston Lady (IRE) (48)** (BSRothwell) **5-9-2** JFortune(11) (lw: prom tl rdn & wknd wl over 1f out) | 1½ | 11 | 25/1 | 23 | — |
| 3777[13] | **The Real Whizzbang (IRE) (46)** (PSFelgate) **4-8-11b(3)** PMcCabe(9) (bit bkwd: a bhd) | nk | 12 | 11/2[3] | 20 | — |
| *4358[10]* | **Newbury Coat (60)** (BPreece) **5-9-7v(7)** FLynch(1) (outpcd) | 1½ | 13 | 33/1 | 30 | 1 |

(SP 127.2%) **13 Rn**

**62.3 secs** (3.60) CSF £105.68 CT £1,110.49 TOTE £58.30: £9.10 £2.30 £3.20 (£81.80) Trio £292.90; £123.79 to Ludlow 4/12/95 OWNER Mrs C. E. Collinson (WILMSLOW) BRED Kilnamoragh Stud

## 4485 GOODYEAR MAIDEN STKS (II) (2-Y.O) (Class D)

4-55 (4-57) **1m 100y (Fibresand)** £2,965.00 (£895.00: £435.00: £205.00) Stalls: Low GOING: nil sec per fur (STD)

| | | | | SP | RR | SF |
|---|---|---|---|---|---|---|
| *4381[2]* | **Tart** (RFJohnsonHoughton) **2-8-9** LDettori(8) (chsd ldrs: shkn up 2f out: led 1f out: rdn clr) | — | 1 | 6/5[1] | 66+ | 24 |
| *4439[U]* | **Bath Knight (45)** (DJSffrenchDavis) **2-9-0** DHarrison(4) (b.hind: led tl hdd 1f out: kpt on same pce) | 3½ | 2 | 20/1 | 64 | 22 |
| | **Filmore West** (PFICole) **2-9-0** CRutter(9) (leggy: lt-f: b.hind: hdwy u.p 3f out: kpt on ins fnl f) | ½ | 3 | 6/1[3] | 63+ | 21 |
| *4365[3]* | **Honestly (64)** (BSmart) **2-8-9** SSanders(1) (lw: s.s: sn rcvrd: hrd rdn 2f out: one pce) | 2 | 4 | 3/1[2] | 55 | 13 |

| Form | Entry | Dist | Pos | SP | RR | SF |
|---|---|---|---|---|---|---|
| | **Catherine's Choice** (JDBethell) **2-9-0** JFortune(7) (w'like: leggy: bkwd: effrt & rdn 3f out: no imp: t.o) | 11 | 5 | 20/1 | 39 | — |
| 4408[13] | **Alpheton Prince** (JLHarris) **2-9-0** JKovarik(3) (chsd ldrs over 5f: grad wknd: t.o) | 2½ | 6 | 40/1 | 34 | — |
| 4334[5] | **Snow Domino (IRE)** (JMJefferson) **2-9-0** DeanMcKeown(6) (dwlt: hdwy ½-wy: wknd over 2f out: t.o) | 1 | 7 | 14/1 | 32 | — |
| | **Supergold (IRE)** (WAO'Gorman) **2-9-0** EmmaO'Gorman(2) (w'like: scope: bkwd: prom tl wknd 3f out: t.o) | nk | 8 | 10/1 | 32 | — |
| 4381[6] | **Sovereign Prince (IRE)** (NACallaghan) **2-9-0** AMackay(5) (a bhd: t.o) | ¾ | 9 | 16/1 | 30 | — |

(SP 118.3%) **9 Rn**

**1m 51.6** (6.60) CSF £23.15 TOTE £2.30: £1.60 £3.50 £1.80 (£12.20) Trio £99.20 OWNER Lady Rothschild (DIDCOT) BRED Exors of the late Mrs D. M. de Rothschild

## 4486 DESERT ORCHID H'CAP (0-65) (II) (3-Y.O+ F & M) (Class F)

5-25 (5-28) **7f (Fibresand)** £2,187.00 (£612.00: £297.00) Stalls: High GOING: nil sec per fur (STD)

| Form | Entry | Dist | Pos | SP | RR | SF |
|---|---|---|---|---|---|---|
| 4371[3] | **Sand Star (52)** (DHaydnJones) **3-9-2** AMackay(5) (mde all: clr fnl 2f: unchal) | — | 1 | 5/1[2] | 74 | 59 |
| 4407[12] | **Fiery Footsteps (42)** (SWCampion) **3-8-6** GCarter(12) (hdwy 4f out: r.o ins fnl f: no ch w wnr) | 9 | 2 | 25/1 | 43 | 28 |
| 4447[5] | **David James' Girl (54)** (ABailey) **3-9-4** LDettori(7) (a.p: rdn over 2f out: kpt on same pce) | 2½ | 3 | 2/1[1] | 50 | 35 |
| 4357[8] | **Jersey Belle (47)** (PJMakin) **3-8-11** RPerham(6) (hld up: hdwy 2f out: nvr nr to chal) | 1¼ | 4 | 14/1 | 40 | 25 |
| 4386[6] | **Sadly Sober (IRE) (60)** (PFICole) **3-9-10b** CRutter(10) (s.s: hdwy 3f out: nt rch ldrs) | s.h | 5 | 8/1 | 53 | 38 |
| 4415[4] | **Sparkling Roberta (35)** (MDIUsher) **4-7-8v**(5) CAdamson(11) (s.i.s: hdwy 2f out: nvr nrr) | s.h | 6 | 20/1 | 27 | 13 |
| 3800[24] | **Brookhead Lady (56)** (PDEvans) **4-9-6** SSanders(4) (chsd ldrs 5f: sn wknd) | 7 | 7 | 14/1 | 32 | 18 |
| 3980[9] | **The Mestral (44)** (MJRyan) **3-8-8** GBardwell(9) (prom: rdn along 3f out: grad wknd) | 1½ | 8 | 14/1 | 17 | 2 |
| 4413* | **My Cherrywell (59)** (LRLloyd-James) **5-9-2b**(7) KimberleyHart(3) (b.hind: lw: dwlt: hdwy ½-wy: rdn over 2f out: sn btn) | hd | 9 | 7/1[3] | 31 | 17 |
| 4152[17] | **Okay Baby (IRE) (48)** (JMBradley) **3-8-9**(3) NVarley(8) (chsd wnr over 4f: sn lost pl) | 1 | 10 | 14/1 | 19 | 4 |
| 3704[9] | **Simand (47)** (GMMoore) **3-8-11** DeanMcKeown(1) (a bhd & outpcd) | 3 | 11 | 10/1 | 11 | — |
| 2972[12] | **Summer Villa (47)** (PHaslam) **3-8-11** JFortune(2) (lw: bhd fr ½-wy) | s.h | 12 | 12/1 | 11 | — |

(SP 125.7%) **12 Rn**

**1m 28.7** (4.00) CSF £106.72 CT £305.33 TOTE £8.50: £2.50 £8.80 £1.90 (£185.90) Trio £260.20 OWNER Mrs T. M. Parry (PONTYPRIDD) BRED Mrs M. L. Parry and P. M. Steele-Mortimer

T/Jkpt: Not won; £16,178.99 to Ludlow 4/12/95. T/Plpt: £381.20 (40.52 Tckts). T/Qdpt: £126.70 (1.7 Tckts). IM

# 4458-LINGFIELD (L-H) (Standard)
## Wednesday December 6th

## 4487 EQUITABLE HOLDINGS H'CAP (0-70) (I) (3-Y.O+) (Class E)

12-40 (12-40) **5f (Equitrack)** £2,656.00 (£802.00: £390.00: £184.00) Stalls: High GOING minus 0.46 sec per fur (FST)

| Form | Entry | Dist | Pos | SP | RR | SF |
|---|---|---|---|---|---|---|
| 4460* | **Half Tone (60)** (RMFlower) **3-9-4b** 7x DBiggs(6) (lost pl over 2f out: rallied fnl f: led last strides) | — | 1 | 5/1[3] | 66 | 35 |
| 4441[8] | **Robo Magic (USA) (65)** (LMontagueHall) **3-9-9** SSanders(3) (hld up: rdn over 3f out: led ins fnl f: hrd rdn: hdd last strides) | nk | 2 | 12/1 | 70 | 39 |
| 4460[2] | **Kalar (69)** (DWChapman) **6-9-8b**(5) PFessey(2) (led tl ins fnl f: one pce) | 1¼ | 3 | 3/1[2] | 70 | 39 |
| 4459[4] | **Anytime Baby (49)** (PTDalton) **3-8-7** SDWilliams(1) (rn wd bnd wl over 1f out: hdwy fnl f: r.o wl) | ½ | 4 | 12/1 | 48 | 17 |
| 4459[3] | **Tee-Emm (56)** (PHowling) **5-9-0** JQuinn(4) (b.hind: a.p: rdn over 2f out: one pce) | nk | 5 | 8/1 | 55 | 24 |
| 4460[4] | **Nordico Princess (70)** (MABrittain) **4-10-0** SWebster(7) (a.p: rdn over 2f out: wknd over 1f out) | 1½ | 6 | 13/2 | 64 | 33 |
| 4464[3] | **Colston-C (51)** (CJHill) **3-8-9** SWhitworth(5) (prom over 2f) | 1 | 7 | 11/4[1] | 42 | 11 |
| 4460[3] | **Newington Butts (IRE) (45)** (KMcAuliffe) **5-8-3** GDuffield(9) (a bhd) | 1 | 8 | 8/1 | 32 | 1 |

(SP 119.3%) **8 Rn**

**59.81 secs** (1.81) CSF £54.53 CT £192.09 TOTE £4.60: £3.90 £2.40 £1.00 (£47.90) Trio £28.50 OWNER Mrs G. M. Temmerman (JEVINGTON) BRED T. M. Jennings

## 4488 EQUITABLE HOLDINGS H'CAP (0-70) (II) (3-Y.O+) (Class E)

1-10 (1-10) **5f (Equitrack)** £2,656.00 (£802.00: £390.00: £184.00) Stalls: High GOING minus 0.46 sec per fur (FST)

| Form | Entry | Dist | Pos | SP | RR | SF |
|---|---|---|---|---|---|---|
| 4459* | **Cheeky Chappy (42)** (DWChapman) **4-7-10b**(5) 7x PFessey(2) (mde all: clr over 2f out: pushed out) | — | 1 | 11/4[2] | 50 | 33 |
| 4458[2] | **Sharp Imp (47)** (RMFlower) **5-8-6b** DBiggs(7) (hdwy 2f out: chsd wnr fnl f: hung lft: r.o wl) | ½ | 2 | 5/2[1] | 53 | 36 |
| 4459[W] | **Lochon (54)** (JLEyre) **4-8-13** RLappin(8) (b: chsd wnr over 3f out to 1f out: 3rd & btn whn n.m.r ins fnl f) | 3 | 3 | 6/1 | 51 | 34 |
| 4441[14] | **Ashtina (65)** (BAPearce) **10-9-10** TIves(1) (b: b.hind: hld up: rdn 2f out: one pce) | 2 | 4 | 12/1 | 55 | 38 |
| 4458[3] | **Southern Dominion (59)** (MJohnston) **3-9-4** TWilliams(5) (lw: rdn thrght: chsd wnr over 1f: wknd over 1f out) | ¾ | 5 | 4/1[3] | 47 | 30 |
| 4430[11] | **Rennyholme (35)** (JHetherton) **4-7-8b**ow1 NAdams(3) (lw: dwlt: nvr nrr) | ¾ | 6 | 100/1 | 20 | 3 |
| 4460[5] | **Rocky Two (53)** (PHowling) **4-8-12b** JQuinn(6) (b: bhd fnl 2f) | ½ | 7 | 11/1 | 37 | 20 |
| 3919[21] | **Mazzarello (IRE) (41)** (RogerCurtis) **5-8-0v** GBardwell(4) (outpcd) | 5 | 8 | 14/1 | 9 | — |

(SP 113.2%) **8 Rn**

**59.42 secs** (1.42) CSF £9.44 CT £32.36 TOTE £3.10: £1.70 £1.80 £1.10 (£3.30) OWNER Mrs Jeanne Chapman (YORK) BRED Ian W. Glenton
LONG HANDICAP Rennyholme 6-4

## 4489 ROB ROT H'CAP (0-70) (3-Y.O+) (Class E)

1-40 (1-40) **1m 5f (Equitrack)** £3,124.00 (£946.00: £462.00: £220.00) Stalls: Low GOING minus 0.46 sec per fur (FST)

| Form | Entry | Dist | Pos | SP | RR | SF |
|---|---|---|---|---|---|---|
| 4452* | **Ballynakelly (51)** (RAkehurst) **3-8-1**(7) TAshley(9) (lw: hld up: led over 4f out: clr over 1f out: r.o wl) | — | 1 | 4/7[1] | 71 | 46 |
| 4364[5] | **Outstayed Welcome (47)** (MJHaynes) **3-7-13**(5) MBaird(4) (b: b.hind: led over 8f: eased whn btn ins fnl f) | 7 | 2 | 14/1 | 58 | 33 |
| 4364[11] | **Pat's Splendour (40)** (HJCollingridge) **4-8-3** JQuinn(7) (hld up: rdn 5f out: one pce) | 12 | 3 | 33/1 | 37 | 18 |
| 3934[11] | **Another Monk (IRE) (30)** (RogerCurtis) **4-7-7** GBardwell(2) (a.p: rdn over 4f out: wknd over 2f out) | 2 | 4 | 50/1 | 24 | 5 |
| 4331* | **Milngavie (IRE) (31)** (MJohnston) **5-7-8b**ow1 NAdams(3) (prom over 9f) | 1¾ | 5 | 8/1[2] | 22 | 3 |
| 4149[15] | **Silktail (IRE) (45)** (CADwyer) **3-7-11**(5) PFessey(1) (hdwy over 8f out: wknd over 2f out) | ½ | 6 | 9/1[3] | 36 | 11 |
| 4442[3] | **Yougo (67)** (MJohnston) **3-9-10** TWilliams(11) (prom over 8f) | 7 | 7 | 9/1[3] | 50 | 25 |
| 3889[4] | **Volunteer (IRE) (63)** (RJO'Sullivan) **3-9-6** GDuffield(8) (lw: a bhd) | 7 | 8 | 8/1[2] | 37 | 12 |
| 4442[11] | **Mafuta (IRE) (38)** (JJSheehan) **3-7-9** NCarlisle(6) (lw: s.s: a bhd) | 4 | 9 | 33/1 | 7 | — |

| | | | | SP | RR | SF |
|---|---|---|---|---|---|---|
| | **Native Chieftan (51)** (SDow) **6-8-7**(7) PBrookwood(10) (b.hind: bhd fnl 8f) | 1 | **10** | 33/1 | 19 | — |
| | | | | (SP 123.3%) | **10 Rn** | |

**2m 44.11** (0.91) CSF £10.58 CT £149.98 TOTE £1.70: £1.10 £6.60 £3.00 (£8.90) Trio £42.90 OWNER Y M Y Partnership (EPSOM) BRED Crest Stud Ltd
LONG HANDICAP Another Monk (IRE) 7-5
WEIGHT FOR AGE 3yo-6lb

## 4490 SYRUP OF FIGS LIMITED STKS (0-60) (3-Y.O+) (Class F)

2-10 (2-11) **1m 2f (Equitrack)** £2,763.80 (£776.80: £379.40) Stalls: Low GOING minus 0.46 sec per fur (FST)

| | | | | SP | RR | SF |
|---|---|---|---|---|---|---|
| *4364*[14] | **Landlord (60)** (JARToller) **3-8-10b** WNewnes(7) (hld up: rdn over 3f out: led ins fnl f: r.o wl) | — | **1** | 7/1 | 66 | 28 |
| *4438** | **Awesome Power (55)** (JWHills) **9-9-2** AClark(6) (a.p: led over 2f out: clr over 1f out: hdd ins fnl f: nt qckn) | 1½ | **2** | 6/1 | 66 | 32 |
| *4415** | **Studio Thirty (51)** (DMorris) **3-9-0** JTate(4) (rdn over 6f out: hdwy over 1f out: r.o) | 1 | **3** | 7/2[2] | 66 | 28 |
| *4298*[10] | **Camden's Ransom (USA) (56)** (HGRowsell) **8-8-7**(7) DSweeney(2) (w ldr: led over 5f out tl over 2f out: one pce) | nk | **4** | 5/1[3] | 62 | 28 |
| *4452*[6] | **Spitfire Bridge (IRE) (60)** (MMcCormack) **3-9-2** GDuffield(3) (a.p: rdn over 8f out: wknd wl over 1f out) | 3 | **5** | 13/8[1] | 63 | 25 |
| *4436*[2] | **The Little Ferret (53)** (AMoore) **5-9-0** SWhitworth(1) (b.hind: lw: led over 4f: wknd over 2f out) | 2 | **6** | 8/1 | 54 | 20 |
| *4421*[15] | **Jahangir (IRE) (45)** (PatMitchell) **6-9-0** GBardwell(8) (bhd fnl 5f) | 20 | **7** | 50/1 | 22 | — |
| | **Thunderous (55)** (JJBridger) **4-9-0b** JQuinn(5) (b: a bhd) | 13 | **8** | 66/1 | 1 | — |
| | | | | (SP 118.3%) | **8 Rn** | |

**2m 6.67** (2.37) CSF £44.91 TOTE £7.70: £3.10 £2.00 £2.00 (£10.50) OWNER Mr A. J. Morrison (WHITSBURY) BRED Fonthill Stud and Philip Wroughton
WEIGHT FOR AGE 3yo-3lb

## 4491 PRINCE OF DARKNESS MAIDEN AUCTION STKS (2-Y.O) (Class F)

2-40 (2-42) **7f (Equitrack)** £2,763.80 (£776.80: £379.40) Stalls: Low GOING minus 0.46 sec per fur (FST)

| | | | | SP | RR | SF |
|---|---|---|---|---|---|---|
| *4414*[2] | **Faith Alone (63)** (CFWall) **2-8-2** GDuffield(11) (lw: chsd ldr over 4f out: led 1f out: drvn out) | — | **1** | 6/1 | 74 | 14 |
| *4360*[6] | **Rowlandsons Charm (IRE) (40)** (GLMoore) **2-7-12v** NAdams(8) (led: hrd rdn over 2f out: hdd 1f out: r.o) | nk | **2** | 33/1 | 69 | 9 |
| *4461*[2] | **Ballymoney (IRE)** (WAO'Gorman) **2-8-4**[ow1] EmmaO'Gorman(3) (lw: hdwy over 3f out: hrd rdn over 1f out: edgd lft fnl f: unable qckn) | 2 | **3** | 7/2[3] | 70 | 10 |
| *4443*[2] | **Lady Dignity (IRE)** (PJMakin) **2-7-12** JQuinn(4) (b.nr hind: lw: a.p: rdn over 2f out: one pce) | hd | **4** | 5/1 | 65 | 5 |
| 4312[6] | **Mawingo (IRE)** (GWragg) **2-8-7** MHills(12) (rdn thrght: lost pl wl over 1f out: r.o one pce) | 2 | **5** | 11/4[1] | 69 | 9 |
| *4439*[7] | **Jemsilverthorn (IRE) (40)** (JJBridger) **2-8-7** GBardwell(2) (a.p: rdn over 3f out: one pce) | ½ | **6** | 50/1 | 68 | 8 |
| *4417*[5] | **Ivor's Deed** (CFWall) **2-7-12**(5) LNewton(13) (lw: nvr nrr) | 1½ | **7** | 20/1 | 41 | — |
| *4443*[3] | **Scenicris (IRE) (65)** (RHollinshead) **2-7-12** NCarlisle(7) (a mid div) | nk | **8** | 12/1 | 55 | — |
| *4439*[11] | **General Haven** (TJNaughton) **2-7-11**(7)[ow1] TAshley(9) (lw: nvr nrr) | 6 | **9** | 33/1 | 46 | — |
| 4045[15] | **Illegally Yours (42)** (LMontagueHall) **2-7-11**(5) PFessey(10) (a bhd) | ½ | **10** | 33/1 | 44 | — |
| 4312[13] | **Farfeste** (DMorris) **2-7-9**(3) DWright(14) (a bhd) | 1¾ | **11** | 10/1 | 36 | — |
| *4417*[2] | **Autobabble (IRE) (65)** (RHannon) **2-8-7** RPerham(1) (lw: chsd ldr over 2f) | 1 | **12** | 3/1[2] | 43 | — |
| 4312[9] | **My Mother's Local (USA)** (KOCunningham-Brown) **2-7-7e**(5) MBaird(5) (hmpd on ins 5f out: a bhd) | 2½ | **13** | 20/1 | 28 | — |
| | **Hever Golf Diamond** (TJNaughton) **2-8-7** SSanders(6) (neat: bkwd: outpcd) | 3 | **14** | 25/1 | 30 | — |
| | | | | (SP 145.8%) | **14 Rn** | |

**1m 25.95** (1.95) CSF £179.42 TOTE £9.00: £3.40 £8.90 £2.10 (£189.10) Trio £275.50; £271.68 to Taunton 07/12/95 OWNER Mrs R. M. S. Neave (NEWMARKET) BRED J. R. Mitchell

## 4492 FAIRFAX DATA PROCESSING NURSERY H'CAP (0-75) (2-Y.O) (Class E)

3-10 (3-10) **6f (Equitrack)** £3,052.50 (£924.00: £451.00: £214.50) Stalls: Low GOING minus 0.46 sec per fur (FST)

| | | | | SP | RR | SF |
|---|---|---|---|---|---|---|
| *4431*[9] | **Time Clash (59)** (BPalling) **2-8-10** SDWilliams(3) (chsd ldr over 4f out: led ins fnl f: rdn out) | — | **1** | 25/1 | 63 | 25 |
| *4473*[4] | **Gracious Gretclo (52)** (CJHill) **2-7-12**(5) MBaird(5) (lw: led: hrd rdn over 1f out: hdd ins fnl f: unable qckn) | 3 | **2** | 10/1 | 48 | 10 |
| *4437** | **Dancing Jack (55)** (JJBridger) **2-8-6** JQuinn(1) (lw: hdwy 2f out: hrd rdn over 1f out: one pce) | 3 | **3** | 10/1 | 43 | 5 |
| *4414** | **Banzhaf (USA) (70)** (GLMoore) **2-9-7** SWhitworth(2) (lw: hld up: rdn 4f out: one pce fnl 2f) | nk | **4** | 5/4[1] | 57 | 19 |
| *4453*[2] | **Moi Canard (61)** (BAPearce) **2-8-12** TIves(7) (hld up: rdn 4f out: wknd 2f out) | 5 | **5** | 5/2[2] | 35 | — |
| 4321[12] | **Flahuil (60)** (RHannon) **2-8-11** RPerham(6) (a bhd) | ½ | **6** | 12/1 | 33 | — |
| *4375*[4] | **Rising Stream (45)** (SirMarkPrescott) **2-7-7**(3) DWright(4) (b.hind: bhd fnl 3f) | 15 | **7** | 8/1[3] | — | — |
| | | | | (SP 113.8%) | **7 Rn** | |

**1m 12.85** (2.25) CSF £201.63 TOTE £20.70: £3.10 £4.10 (£188.80) OWNER Mrs D. J. Hughes (COWBRIDGE) BRED Terry Minahan

## 4493 LADBROKE ALL-WEATHER TROPHY H'CAP (Qualifier) (0-70) (3-Y.O+) (Class E)

3-40 (3-41) **1m (Equitrack)** £3,066.80 (£928.40: £453.20: £215.60) Stalls: High GOING minus 0.46 sec per fur (FST)

| | | | | SP | RR | SF |
|---|---|---|---|---|---|---|
| 4038[18] | **Prizefighter (62)** (JLEyre) **4-9-8** RLappin(3) (mde all: hrd rdn over 1f out: r.o wl) | — | **1** | 11/2[3] | 72 | 41 |
| *4421*[3] | **Whatever's Right (IRE) (63)** (MDIUsher) **6-9-9** RPerham(5) (hld up: chsd wnr over 2f out: nt qckn fnl f) | 1½ | **2** | 9/4[1] | 70 | 39 |
| *4367*[8] | **Tatika (65)** (GWragg) **5-9-4**(7) GMilligan(2) (hld up: stdy hdwy over 3f out: nvr plcd to chal) | ¾ | **3** | 11/1 | 71 | 40 |
| *4457*[11] | **Eastleigh (52)** (RHollinshead) **6-8-12**[ow1] TIves(1) (b.off hind: chsd wnr over 5f: one pce) | ½ | **4** | 16/1 | 56 | 25 |
| *4457*[5] | **Exclusive Assembly (55)** (APJames) **3-9-0** JQuinn(4) (lw: a.p: rdn over 3f out: one pce) | nk | **5** | 8/1 | 60 | 27 |
| *4440*[3] | **Hawaii Storm (FR) (59)** (DJSffrenchDavis) **7-9-0**(5) PPMurphy(10) (hld up: hrd rdn over 1f out: one pce) | 1½ | **6** | 8/1 | 60 | 29 |
| *4457*[6] | **Takeshi (IRE) (62)** (WRMuir) **3-9-7** JTate(9) (hld up: rdn over 2f out: one pce) | 1¼ | **7** | 5/1[2] | 61 | 28 |
| 4152[14] | **Jackatack (IRE) (59)** (MRChannon) **3-8-11**(7) JDennis(8) (lw: outpcd: hdwy over 1f out: nvr nrr) | 1½ | **8** | 25/1 | 55 | 22 |
| *4418*[2] | **Kellaire Girl (IRE) (49)** (AMoore) **3-8-8** SSanders(11) (b.hind: prom over 5f) | 1 | **9** | 5/1[2] | 43 | 10 |
| *4430*[3] | **At the Savoy (IRE) (62)** (TDBarron) **4-9-8b** WNewnes(6) (prom over 6f) | 2 | **10** | 14/1 | — | — |
| *4456*[8] | **Komodo (USA) (51)** (KOCunningham-Brown) **3-8-5b**(5) MBaird(7) (a bhd) | 25 | **11** | 25/1 | — | — |
| | | | | (SP 130.3%) | **11 Rn** | |

**1m 39.06** (1.66) CSF £19.19 CT £127.18 TOTE £6.40: £2.40 £1.20 £5.10 (£13.80) Trio £118.90 OWNER Diamond Racing Ltd (HAMBLETON) BRED J. K. Bloodstock Ltd
WEIGHT FOR AGE 3yo-1lb

T/Jkpt: £55,884.20 (0.2 Tckts); £62,968.17 to Taunton 7/12/95. T/Plpt: £711.50 (18.36 Tckts). T/Qdpt: £10.30 (1 Tckt). AK

## 4404a-**SAINT-CLOUD (France)** (L-H) (Good)
### Monday November 27th

**4494a** PRIX PRINCESSE KARA (2-Y.O F)
1-00 (1-02) **7f 110y** £10,180.00

| | Horse | | Dist | Pos | SP | RR | SF |
|---|---|---|---|---|---|---|---|
| | **Amiarma (IRE)** | (EChevalierduFau,France) **2-9-0** WMongil | — | 1 | | — | — |
| | **Moon Is Up (USA)** | (France) **2-9-0** ESaint-Martin | ½ | 2 | | — | — |
| | **Chelsea (USA)** | (France) **2-8-10** TJarnet | ½ | 3 | | — | — |
| 3909a* | **Hever Golf Queen** | (TJNaughton) **2-9-0** MHills (btn approx 7½l) | | 9 | | — | — |

**11 Rn**

**1m 37.2** (5.80) P-M 14.20F: 3.10F 1.60F 2.30F (31.50F) OWNER Marquesa de Moratalla BRED Childwick Bury Stud Management
**3909a* Hever Golf Queen** was badly squeezed over a furlong out when poised to challenge. This run is best ignored.

**4495a** PRIX ISOLA BELLA (Listed) (3-Y.O F)
2-30 (2-30) **1m** £16,766.00 (£5,748.00: £3,593.00)

| | Horse | | Dist | Pos | SP | RR | SF |
|---|---|---|---|---|---|---|---|
| | **Passionnee (USA)** | (MmeCHead,France) **3-9-2** ODoleuze | — | 1 | | 100 | — |
| 1105* | **Ludgate (USA)** | (NClement,France) **3-9-2** ESaint-Martin | nk | 2 | | 99 | — |
| 4019a[2] | **Mandarina (USA)** | (LMCumani) **3-9-2** LDettori | ½ | 3 | | 98 | — |

**13 Rn**

**1m 43.7** (5.20) P-M 23.60F: 9.30F 5.30F 3.20F (265.50F) OWNER Mr J. Wertheimer (CHANTILLY) BRED Alec Head & Wertheimer & Frere
**4019a Mandarina (USA)** attempted to make all the running, but was caught inside the last furlong. Connections believe that this trip was beyond the limit of her stamina.

## 4469a-**EVRY (France)** (R-H) (Soft)
### Friday December 1st

**4496a** PRIX ZEDDAAN (Listed) (2-Y.O)
1-35 (1-40) **6f** £16,766.00 (£5,748.00: £3,593.00)

| | Horse | | Dist | Pos | SP | RR | SF |
|---|---|---|---|---|---|---|---|
| | **Floresta (FR)** | (MRolland,France) **2-8-8** OPeslier | — | 1 | | 100 | — |
| 2726a[6] | **Miss Ebene (FR)** | (DSmaga,France) **2-8-8** GGuignard | 1 | 2 | | 97 | — |
| | **Septieme Brigade (USA)** | (MmeCHead,France) **2-8-11** ODoleuze | ¾ | 3 | | 98 | — |
| 4318[4] | **Henry The Fifth** | (CEBrittain) **2-8-11** FSanchez (btn approx 3 3/4l) | | 5 | | — | — |

**9 Rn**

**1m 14.34** (4.34) P-M 6.20F: 1.70F 2.60F 1.20F (42.00F) OWNER Mr G. Barbarin BRED Olivier Nicol & Horstinvest Corp
**4318 Henry The Fifth** was close up early, but was ridden over two furlongs out, and lacked the pace to go with the principals in the closing stages.

## 4494a-**SAINT-CLOUD (France)** (L-H) (Good to soft)
### Saturday December 2nd

**4497a** PRIX TANTIEME (Listed) (3-Y.O+)
1-05 (1-04) **1m** £16,766.00 (£5,748.00: £3,593.00)

| | Horse | | Dist | Pos | SP | RR | SF |
|---|---|---|---|---|---|---|---|
| 4405a[4] | **Val D'Arbois (FR)** | (MDelcher,Spain) **3-9-0** WMongil | — | 1 | | 120 | — |
| 4015a[6] | **Erin Bird (FR)** | (MmePBarbe,France) **4-8-9** TThulliez | ¾ | 2 | | 112 | — |
| 4021a[2] | **Wizard King** | (SirMarkPrescott) **4-9-1** GDuffield | 1 | 3 | | 116 | — |
| 4345a[5] | **Prince of India** | (LordHuntingdon) **3-8-11** OPeslier (btn approx 16¼l) | | 8 | | 85 | — |

**8 Rn**

**1m 41.4** (2.90) P-M 12.10F: 2.90F 2.60F 1.70F (46.00F) OWNER Marques de San Anton BRED Societe R & M Wattinne
**4021a Wizard King** took the lead at halfway, but perhaps finding the trip a little too far on this ground, was caught inside the last furlong. He remains in training next year, and should once again pay his way.
**4345a Prince of India** was up with the pace until weakening in the last quarter mile.

**4498a** PRIX EDELLIC (Listed) (3-Y.O+)
2-05 (2-01) **1m 2f** £16,766.00 (£5,748.00: £3,593.00)

| | Horse | | Dist | Pos | SP | RR | SF |
|---|---|---|---|---|---|---|---|
| | **Admise (FR)** | (DSmaga,France) **3-8-7**ow1 DBoeuf | — | 1 | | 108 | — |
| 1387a[2] | **Sand Reef** | (MmeCHead,France) **4-9-2** ODoleuze | nk | 2 | | 114 | — |
| | **Zarma (FR)** | (ASpanu,France) **3-8-7** TThulliez | 1½ | 3 | | 106 | — |
| 4017a[3] | **Cedez le Passage (FR)** | (CEBrittain) **4-8-12** FSanchez (btn approx 5l) | | 6 | | — | — |

**8 Rn**

**2m 11.7** (8.20) P-M 11.40F: 2.30F 1.20F 2.30F (17.90F) OWNER A. Lequeux BRED Exors of Comte L. de Keroura
**4017a Cedez le Passage (FR)** was a little out of his depth in this company, but this was a creditable effort.

## **TOULOUSE (France)** (R-H) (Heavy)
### Sunday December 3rd

**4499a** CRITERIUM DE LANGUEDOC (Listed) (2-Y.O)
2-00 (2-00) **1m** £14,371.00 (£4,790.00: £2,395.00)

| | Horse | | Dist | Pos | SP | RR | SF |
|---|---|---|---|---|---|---|---|
| | **Malquet (FR)** | (J-CRouget,France) **2-8-7** J-RDubosc | — | 1 | | 97 | — |
| | **Kalmoss (FR)** | (BRenard,France) **2-9-0** DSicaud | nk | 2 | | 103 | — |
| | **Zalamalec (USA)** | (DSmaga,France) **2-8-4** FSanchez | 2½ | 3 | | 88 | — |

| | | | | | | |
|---|---|---|---|---|---|---|
| 4073* | **Circled (USA)** (BWHills) **2-8-4** WCarson (btn approx 6¼l) | | **5** | | — | — |
| | | | | | | **9 Rn** |

**1m 41.9** P-M 6.10F: 1.60F 2.50F 3.20F (12.30F) OWNER Mr J. F. Gribomont BRED Haras du Bois Roussel
**4073* Circled (USA)** ran a little green, and although making late headway, never really got into the race.

## 4500a PRIX MAX SICARD (Listed) (3-Y.O+)
3-00 (3-00) **1m 4f** £28,742.00 (£10,539.00: £5,269.00)

| | | | | SP | RR | SF |
|---|---|---|---|---|---|---|
| 1709a[9] | **Matarun (IRE)** (HVandePoele,France) **7-9-5** OPeslier | — | **1** | | 117 | — |
| 1709a[6] | **Fanion de Fete (FR)** (JBernard,France) **4-9-5** TThulliez | 4 | **2** | | 112 | — |
| | **Fay Wray (FR)** (PKhozian,France) **5-9-0** GElorriaga-Santos | 2½ | **3** | | 103 | — |
| 4182a[8] | **Close Conflict (USA)** (PWChapple-Hyam) **4-8-10** DHarrison (btn approx 14 3/4l) | | **6** | | 93 | — |
| | | | | | | **13 Rn** |

**2m 36.8** P-M 2.50F: 1.50F 4.00F 2.30F (50.10F) OWNER Mr R. Soula BRED Roland Soula in Ireland
**4182a Close Conflict (USA)** was close up until fading in the straight. He is likely to be fitted with a tongue-strap next time, and may be kept on the go in order to take in similar races at the start of the new French flat season.

# 4479-WOLVERHAMPTON (L-H) (Standard)
## Saturday December 9th
WEATHER: cold WIND: nil

## 4501 MEASURE FOR MEASURE MAIDEN STKS (2-Y.O) (Class D)
7-00 (7-01) **1m 100y (Fibresand)** £2,850.30 (£800.80: £390.90) Stalls: Low GOING: nil sec per fur (STD)

| | | | | SP | RR | SF |
|---|---|---|---|---|---|---|
| *4338[4]* | **Kissing Gate (USA)** (RCharlton) **2-8-9** SSanders(7) (lw: prom: led 5f out to 2f out: 2nd st: led ins fnl f: all out) | — | **1** | 11/8[1] | 65 | 19 |
| *4334[7]* | **Red Rusty (USA)** (DMorris) **2-9-0** JTate(2) (a.p: led 2f out: hrd rdn over 1f out: edgd lft & hdd ins fnl f: r.o) | nk | **2** | 25/1 | 69 | 23 |
| 3339[18] | **Conquistajade (USA)** (SPCWoods) **2-8-2**(7) JMoon(8) (b.hind: lw: a.p: 3rd st: one pce) | 9 | **3** | 8/1[3] | 47 | 1 |
| | **Henry Island (IRE)** (GWragg) **2-9-0** JQuinn(12) (leggy: s.s: hrd rdn over 3f out: hdwy over 1f out: nvr nrr) | 6 | **4** | 7/2[2] | 41+ | — |
| | **Adler (IRE)** (MJCamacho) **2-9-0** SMorris(1) (leggy: unf: prom: 4th & wkng st) | 3½ | **5** | 33/1 | 34 | — |
| | **Skipman (IRE)** (NASmith) **2-9-0** SDWilliams(4) (w'like: prom: rdn & wknd 3f out: 6th & btn st) | nk | **6** | 14/1 | 34 | — |
| | **Bridlington Bay** (JLEyre) **2-9-0** RLappin(3) (lt-f: chsd ldrs: 5th & wkng st) | nk | **7** | 16/1 | 33 | — |
| | **Brume La Voile** (SCWilliams) **2-8-11**(3) DWright(11) (w'like: b.nr hind: dwlt: a bhd) | 1¾ | **8** | 16/1 | 30 | — |
| | **Dhes-C** (RHollinshead) **2-8-2**(7) FLynch(6) (w'like: rdn & swtchd rt over 4f out: a bhd) | 3 | **9** | 14/1 | 19 | — |
| | **Dream of My Life (USA)** (FMurphy) **2-9-0** TWilliams(9) (lt-f: s.i.s: hrd rdn over 3f out: sn bhd) | 5 | **10** | 20/1 | 15 | — |
| *4408[10]* | **Silent System (IRE)** (JGFitzGerald) **2-9-0** ACulhane(13) (lw: a bhd) | 1¾ | **11** | 12/1 | 12 | — |
| 3541[8] | **Martins Folly** (JWhite) **2-8-2**(7) CCarver(5) (led over 4f: wknd 3f out) | ¾ | **12** | 33/1 | 5 | — |
| | **Shoot The Minstrel** (JAPickering) **2-9-0** NCarlisle(10) (leggy: unf: s.s: bhd fnl 4f: t.o) | 20 | **13** | 25/1 | — | — |
| | | | | (SP 126.6%) | | **13 Rn** |

**1m 53.9** (8.90) CSF £35.36 TOTE £2.60: £1.10 £4.70 £3.30 (£18.70) Trio £28.20 OWNER The Queen (BECKHAMPTON) BRED Indian Creek, C. McGaughey III and Hint At Love Pa

## 4502 AS YOU LIKE IT H'CAP (0-70) (3-Y.O+) (Class E)
7-30 (7-30) **6f (Fibresand)** £2,305.50 (£648.00: £316.50) Stalls: Low GOING: nil sec per fur (STD)

| | | | | SP | RR | SF |
|---|---|---|---|---|---|---|
| *4484[4]* | **Encore M'Lady (IRE) (59)** (FHLee) **4-9-3b** RLappin(11) (mde all: rdn 2f out: r.o wl) | — | **1** | 8/1 | 75 | 57 |
| *4337[2]* | **Deeply Vale (IRE) (62)** (GLMoore) **4-9-6** SWhitworth(10) (lw: a.p: rdn & 2nd st: ev ch ins fnl f: nt qckn) | 2 | **2** | 7/1 | 73 | 55 |
| *4457[2]* | **Four of Spades (70)** (PDEvans) **4-9-7**(7) AmandaSanders(12) (lw: sn rdn: hdwy over 1f out: r.o) | 5 | **3** | 11/2[3] | 67 | 49 |
| *4447** | **Jigsaw Boy (65)** (PGMurphy) **6-9-9** SSanders(1) (s.i.s: hdwy on ins & 6th st: nt rch ldrs) | nk | **4** | 9/2[2] | 62 | 44 |
| *4413[14]* | **Fairey Firefly (55)** (MJCamacho) **4-8-13** JQuinn(8) (prom: 3rd st: one pce) | hd | **5** | 16/1 | 51 | 33 |
| 4280[5] | **Hi Rock (48)** (MJCamacho) **3-8-6** JFanning(4) (prom: 4th st: wknd over 1f out) | 1½ | **6** | 20/1 | 40 | 22 |
| *4447[3]* | **Bold Street (IRE) (67)** (ABailey) **5-9-8v**(3) DWright(13) (chsd ldrs: 5th st: wknd over 1f out) | ½ | **7** | 4/1[1] | 58 | 40 |
| *4421[9]* | **Grey Charmer (IRE) (50)** (CJames) **6-8-8** AMcGlone(7) (n.d) | 3 | **8** | 16/1 | 33 | 15 |
| *4484[6]* | **Al Shaati (FR) (48)** (RJO'Sullivan) **5-8-6** DBiggs(6) (lw: bhd fnl 3f) | nk | **9** | 7/1 | 30 | 12 |
| *4484[10]* | **Delrob (57)** (DHaydnJones) **4-8-10**(5) PPMurphy(9) (outpcd) | nk | **10** | 20/1 | 38 | 20 |
| *4479[10]* | **Legatee (58)** (AStreeter) **4-9-2v** SDWilliams(5) (b: rdn over 4f out: bhd fnl 3f) | 4 | **11** | 33/1 | 29 | 11 |
| *4407[5]* | **Hello Hobson's (IRE) (49)** (RBastiman) **5-8-7** ACulhane(3) (lw: hld up: 7th & wkng st: eased whn btn over 1f out) | 1 | **12** | 20/1 | 17 | — |
| *4428[7]* | **Bold Aristocrat (IRE) (46)** (RHollinshead) **4-7-11**(7)ow3 FLynch(2) (lw: s.i.s: a bhd) | 6 | **13** | 20/1 | — | — |
| | | | | (SP 123.4%) | | **13 Rn** |

**1m 15.8** (4.40) CSF £59.54 CT £309.52 TOTE £10.90: £2.80 £1.50 £2.20 (£40.60) Trio £68.10 OWNER Mr F. H. Lee (WILMSLOW) BRED Irish National Stud Co Ltd in Ireland

## 4503 'SOMERFORD CLAIMS' H'CAP (0-75) (3-Y.O+) (Class D)
8-00 (8-02) **1m 1f 79y (Fibresand)** £2,866.00 (£868.00: £424.00: £202.00) Stalls: Low GOING: nil sec per fur (STD)

| | | | | SP | RR | SF |
|---|---|---|---|---|---|---|
| *4432[2]* | **Benjamins Law (56)** (JAPickering) **4-9-0** JQuinn(6) (lw: hdwy over 3f out: led over 2f out: r.o wl) | — | **1** | 4/1[1] | 67 | 44 |
| *4388** | **Pine Ridge Lad (IRE) (70)** (JLEyre) **5-10-0** RLappin(8) (lw: a.p: 3rd st: ev ch ins fnl f: r.o) | ¾ | **2** | 11/1 | 80 | 57 |
| *4409** | **Jalmaid (55)** (BAMcMahon) **3-8-6**(5) LNewton(5) (a.p: led over 3f out tl over 2f out: 2nd st: ev ch 1f out: r.o) | ½ | **3** | 15/2 | 64 | 39 |
| *4378[9]* | **Our Tom (62)** (JWharton) **3-8-13**(5) CTeague(13) (plld hrd: a.p: rdn over 2f out: 4th st: one pce) | 2 | **4** | 25/1 | 67 | 42 |
| *4372[4]* | **Arcatura (60)** (CJames) **3-9-2** AMcGlone(9) (lw: hld up: stdy hdwy 5f out: 5th st: one pce) | nk | **5** | 12/1 | 65 | 40 |
| *4444** | **Dannistar (57)** (PDEvans) **3-8-13** SSanders(1) (hld up: stdy hdwy over 4f out: rdn over 2f out: 7th & btn st) | 5 | **6** | 11/2[2] | 53 | 28 |
| *4476[13]* | **Hawwam (70)** (EJAlston) **9-10-0** SDWilliams(10) (hld up & plld hrd: sme hdwy & 8th st: n.d) | ½ | **7** | 14/1 | 66 | 43 |
| *4445[2]* | **Canary Falcon (60)** (JohnBerry) **4-9-4** MWigham(11) (b: rdn 5f out: bhd fnl 3f) | 1¾ | **8** | 11/2[2] | 53 | 30 |
| *4421[10]* | **Quinzii Martin (48)** (DHaydnJones) **7-8-3**(3) DWright(4) (hdwy 4f out: 6th st: wknd over 1f out) | 4 | **9** | 33/1 | 34 | 11 |
| | **Avenue Foch (IRE) (56)** (FMurphy) **6-9-0** TWilliams(7) (b: b.nr hind: led over 5f) | 1¾ | **10** | 33/1 | 39 | 16 |
| 4061[5] | **Polly Peculiar (48)** (BSmart) **4-8-6** JTate(3) (s.s: a bhd) | 6 | **11** | 6/1[3] | 20 | — |
| *4454[3]* | **Remaadi Sun (60)** (MDIUsher) **3-9-2** RStreet(2) (lw: s.s: a bhd: t.o) | 14 | **12** | 25/1 | 9 | — |

| | | | | SP | RR | SF |
|---|---|---|---|---|---|---|
| 3021$^{3}$ | **Desert Power (65)** (DBurchell) **6-9-4**$^{(5)}$ AProcter(12) (prom 6f: t.o) | nk | **13** | 14/1 | 13 | — |

(SP 119.8%) **13 Rn**

**2m 4.6** (8.60) CSF £43.28 CT £287.79 TOTE £4.60: £1.50 £2.80 £4.10 (£24.40) Trio £28.50 OWNER Mr D. Lowe (HINCKLEY) BRED Dunchurch Lodge Stud
WEIGHT FOR AGE 3yo-2lb

## 4504 'CLAIMS DIRECT' CONDITIONS STKS (2-Y.O) (Class D)

8-30 (8-31) **7f (Fibresand)** £3,452.50 (£1,045.00: £510.00: £242.50) Stalls: High GOING: nil sec per fur (STD)

| | | | | SP | RR | SF |
|---|---|---|---|---|---|---|
| 4320$^{18}$ | **Le Sport** (ABailey) **2-8-8**$^{(3)}$ DWright(8) (hdwy ½-wy: 4th st: hrd rdn over 1f out: str run to ld last strides) | — | **1** | 33/1 | 70? | 26 |
| *4443*$^{*}$ | **Victim of Love** (RCharlton) **2-8-10** SSanders(2) (lw: prom: hrd rdn & 3rd st: led ins fnl f: hdd last strides) | hd | **2** | 9/2$^{3}$ | 69? | 25 |
| *4393*$^{*}$ | **Kind of Light** (RGuest) **2-8-6** JTate(5) (lw: led: rdn over 2f out: hdd ins fnl f) | 4 | **3** | 2/1$^{2}$ | 56? | 12 |
| 3917$^{5}$ | **Double Oscar (IRE) (95)** (MJohnston) **2-9-3** TWilliams(7) (lw: w ldr: rdn & 2nd st: ev ch over 1f out: eased whn btn ins fnl f) | 9 | **4** | 6/4$^{1}$ | 46 | 2 |
| 4494a$^{9}$ | **Hever Golf Queen** (TJNaughton) **2-8-6** AMcGlone(6) (prom: hrd rdn over 3f out: 5th & wkng st) | hd | **5** | 6/1 | 35 | — |
| *4433*$^{12}$ | **Dancing Cavalier (40)** (RHollinshead) **2-8-11** ACulhane(4) (lw: last st: a bhd) | 1¾ | **6** | 40/1 | 36 | — |
| | **Ordained** (TTClement) **2-8-6** JQuinn(1) (b: lengthy: unf: s.s: 6th st: a bhd) | s.h | **7** | 40/1 | 31 | — |

(SP 113.6%) **7 Rn**

**1m 31.6** (1.60 under 2y best) (6.90) CSF £155.36 TOTE £33.60: £4.10 £2.70 (£92.30) OWNER Simple Technology UK Ltd (TARPORLEY) BRED R. G. R. Chapman
STEWARDS' ENQUIRY Wright susp. 30/12/95-9/1/96 (excessive use of whip).

## 4505 KB (NORTHERN) (S) STKS (3, 4 & 5-Y.O) (Class F)

9-00 (9-00) **1m 1f 79y (Fibresand)** £2,433.00 (£683.00: £333.00) Stalls: Low GOING: nil sec per fur (STD)

| | | | | SP | RR | SF |
|---|---|---|---|---|---|---|
| *4427*$^{7}$ | **Sarasi (62)** (MJCamacho) **3-9-2** JQuinn(1) (mde virtually all: rdn 2f out: r.o wl) | — | **1** | 14/1 | 74 | 53 |
| 4163$^{20}$ | **Tartan Gem (IRE) (73)** (MABrittain) **4-8-11**$^{(3)}$ DWright(11) (hdwy over 3f out: 3rd st: r.o fnl f) | 1¾ | **2** | 7/1$^{3}$ | 67 | 48 |
| 4170$^{13}$ | **Sea Spouse (41)** (MTWBlanshard) **4-9-0** NAdams(3) (a.p: 2nd st: wknd fnl f) | 5 | **3** | 25/1 | 59 | 40 |
| 3658$^{2}$ | **Hard Love (62)** (JLEyre) **3-8-11** RLappin(12) (b.off hind: a.p: rdn over 2f out: 6th st: one pce) | 3 | **4** | 9/4$^{1}$ | 52 | 31 |
| 3872$^{7}$ | **Owdbetts (IRE) (56)** (GLMoore) **3-8-11** SWhitworth(2) (lw: bhd: hdwy 5f out: rdn over 3f out: 4th st: one pce) | ¾ | **5** | 8/1 | 51 | 30 |
| *4390*$^{9}$ | **Certain Way (IRE) (55)** (NPLittmoden) **5-9-4** TGMcLaughlin(7) (b: hdwy & 7th st: one pce fnl f) | nk | **6** | 7/1$^{3}$ | 56 | 37 |
| *4444*$^{4}$ | **Dowdency (47)** (JAPickering) **3-8-11** NCarlisle(13) (lw: rdn & hdwy 3f out: 5th st: wknd over 1f out) | ¾ | **7** | 14/1 | 49 | 28 |
| *4448*$^{*}$ | **Old Provence (71)** (RHarris) **5-9-4** DBatteate(9) (b: a bhd) | 8 | **8** | 11/2$^{2}$ | 41 | 22 |
| *4444*$^{2}$ | **Mazilla (49)** (AStreeter) **3-8-11** SDWilliams(4) (b: prom over 6f) | 7 | **9** | 10/1 | 24 | 3 |
| *4456*$^{5}$ | **Flair Lady (43)** (WGMTurner) **4-8-9** RPerham(8) (bhd fnl 4f) | ½ | **10** | 16/1 | 19 | — |
| *4438*$^{6}$ | **Absolute Ruler (IRE) (55)** (JLHarris) **4-8-11**$^{(7)}$ KJaroslav(6) (b.off hind: a bhd) | ½ | **11** | 25/1 | 27 | 8 |
| 3879$^{18}$ | **Passion Sunday (32)** (LRLloyd-James) **4-8-7b**$^{(7)}$ KimberleyHart(10) (b: b.hind: plld hrd: rdn 4f out: sn bhd) | ¾ | **12** | 33/1 | 22 | 3 |
| *4456*$^{7}$ | **Harvest Reaper (48)** (JLHarris) **3-8-12v** SSanders(5) (lw: bhd fnl 4f: t.o) | 20 | **13** | 16/1 | — | — |

(SP 127.1%) **13 Rn**

**2m 3.7** (7.70) CSF £104.77 TOTE £14.90: £3.80 £1.90 £5.20 (£53.10) Trio £94.10; £106.60 to Newton Abbot 11/12/95 OWNER The Blue Chip Group (MALTON) BRED C. J. R. Trotter
WEIGHT FOR AGE 3yo-2lb
No bid

## 4506 COMEDY OF ERRORS H'CAP (0-70) (3-Y.O+) (Class E)

9-30 (9-30) **1m 4f (Fibresand)** £2,295.00 (£645.00: £315.00) Stalls: Low GOING: nil sec per fur (STD)

| | | | | SP | RR | SF |
|---|---|---|---|---|---|---|
| *4442*$^{6}$ | **Premier Dance (56)** (DHaydnJones) **8-8-11**$^{(3)}$ DWright(2) (lw: a gng wl: 2nd st: led 1f out: rdn & r.o wl) | — | **1** | 4/1$^{3}$ | 67 | 37 |
| 4201$^{14}$ | **Shakiyr (FR) (62)** (RHollinshead) **4-9-6** ACulhane(4) (bhd: rdn after 3f: hdwy 5f out: 3rd st: ev ch ins fnl f: nt qckn) | 1¼ | **2** | 3/1$^{1}$ | 71 | 41 |
| 3973$^{13}$ | **Alzoomo (IRE) (63)** (JAGlover) **3-9-2** SDWilliams(11) (hld up: hdwy 5f out: led over 3f out to 1f out: nt qckn) | ½ | **3** | 8/1 | 73 | 37 |
| 4332$^{*}$ | **El Volador (70)** (RJO'Sullivan) **8-9-9**$^{(5)}$ AProcter(9) (lw: hld up & bhd: hdwy 5f out: 4th st: ev ch 1f out: nt qckn) | 1½ | **4** | 5/1 | 77 | 47 |
| *4449*$^{*}$ | **Ballymac Girl (62)** (JMBradley) **7-9-6** SSanders(10) (b: prom: rdn 6f out: 5th st: no hdwy) | 3½ | **5** | 7/2$^{2}$ | 64 | 34 |
| | **Nordic Sun (IRE) (67)** (LRLloyd-James) **7-9-4**$^{(7)}$ KimberleyHart(3) (bit bkwd: prom: led 5f out tl over 3f out: 6th & wkng st) | 1 | **6** | 25/1 | 68 | 38 |
| *4370*$^{6}$ | **Jarrow (38)** (MrsAMNaughton) **4-7-10**$^{ow3}$ JQuinn(5) (hld up: rdn & wknd 2f out: poor 7th st) | 13 | **7** | 33/1 | 18 | — |
| *4366*$^{12}$ | **Dvorak (IRE) (58)** (RHarris) **4-9-2** DBatteate(8) (prom 5f: t.o) | 10 | **8** | 14/1 | 28 | — |
| 4000$^{21}$ | **Zalament (46)** (NPLittmoden) **3-7-13** NCarlisle(7) (hld up & plld hrd: bhd fnl 4f: t.o) | 2 | **9** | 14/1 | 14 | — |
| *4416*$^{10}$ | **Fresh Look (IRE) (42)** (RCSpicer) **3-7-4**$^{(5)ow2}$ MBaird(6) (plld hrd: jnd ldrs after 4f: wknd over 4f out: t.o) | 9 | **10** | 20/1 | — | — |
| *4444*$^{7}$ | **Sweet Disorder (IRE) (35)** (BJMeehan) **5-7-7** GBardwell(1) (led 7f: sn wknd: t.o) | 5 | **11** | 12/1 | — | — |

(SP 127.6%) **11 Rn**

**2m 43.3** (10.80) CSF £16.91 CT £88.39 TOTE £5.80: £1.70 £2.20 £2.70 (£6.60) Trio £47.50 OWNER J S Fox and Sons (PONTYPRIDD) BRED Brick Kiln Stud Farm
LONG HANDICAP Jarrow 6-13 Sweet Disorder (IRE) 7-4
WEIGHT FOR AGE 3yo-5lb

T/Plpt: £1,024.40 (15.04 Tckts). T/Qdpt: £118.10 (0.1 Tckts); £143.64 to Newton Abbot 11/12/95. KH

# 4501-WOLVERHAMPTON (L-H) (Standard)

## Tuesday December 12th

WEATHER: drizzle & foggy WIND: nil

## 4507 IMI AIR CONDITIONING AMATEUR H'CAP (0-60) (I) (3-Y.O+) (Class F)

1-15 (1-15) **1m 4f (Fibresand)** £2,187.00 (£612.00: £297.00) Stalls: Low GOING: 0.47 sec per fur (SLW)

| | | | | SP | RR | SF |
|---|---|---|---|---|---|---|
| *4416*$^{9}$ | **Comtec's Legend (34)** (JFBottomley) **5-10-2** MrsLPearce(7) (hld up: hdwy 6f out: qcknd to ld over 2f out: sn clr) | — | **1** | 10/1 | 45 | 26 |

| | | | | SP | RR | SF |
|---|---|---|---|---|---|---|
| 4452[11] | **Manful (58)** (JHetherton) **3-11-7** MissAElsey(8) (hld up mid div: hdwy over 3f out: 5th st: styd on fnl f: no ch w wnr) | 6 | **2** | 5/1[3] | 62 | 37 |
| 4420[6] | **Alpine Storm (IRE) (27)** (MDIUsher) **3-8-13**(5) MrsAUsher(5) (a.p: jnd ldr 3f out: 2nd st: unable qckn: wknd fnl f) | 2 | **3** | 25/1 | 28 | 3 |
| 4376[3] | **Hill Farm Dancer (49)** (WMBrisbourne) **4-10-12**(5) MrWMcLaughlin(12) (s.s: hdwy 5f out: 4th & rdn st: no imp) | 7 | **4** | 11/4[1] | 40 | 21 |
| 744[10] | **Pigalle Wonder (26)** (NMBabbage) **7-9-3**(5) MissCPegna(9) (led & sn clr: hdd over 2f out: 3rd & btn st) | 1 | **5** | 25/1 | 16 | — |
| 4455[5] | **Duggan (24)** (PDEvans) **8-9-6** MissJAllison(10) (bhd tl styd on fnl 2f) | ¾ | **6** | 4/1[2] | 13 | — |
| 4364[15] | **Telephus (41)** (BJMcMath) **6-10-9** MissPJones(4) (hld up in rr: effrt 3f out: n.d) | 5 | **7** | 33/1 | 23 | 4 |
| 4209[16] | **Forgetful (37)** (DBurchell) **6-10-0**(5) MissEJJones(2) (chsd ldr to ½-wy: wknd over 4f out) | 10 | **8** | 10/1 | 6 | — |
| 153[5] | **Carrolls Marc (IRE) (42)** (CMurray) **7-10-10** MissDianaJones(1) (a bhd) | ¾ | **9** | 10/1 | 10 | — |
| 4412[3] | **Magication (43)** (BRichmond) **5-10-6**(5) MrsMMorris(3) (a rr div: t.o) | 5 | **10** | 12/1 | 4 | — |
| 138[12] | **Media Messenger (41)** (NPLittmoden) **6-10-4**(5) MrOAGunter(6) (chsd ldrs tl wknd 3f out: poor 6th st: t.o) | nk | **11** | 33/1 | 2 | — |
| | **Beau Quest (35)** (BRCambidge) **8-9-12**(5)ow7 MrsHNoonan(11) (a in rr: t.o) | 3½ | **12** | 50/1 | — | — |
| | | | | (SP 113.8%) | **12 Rn** | |

**2m 50.0** (17.50) CSF £52.63 CT £1,093.89 TOTE £8.80: £2.50 £2.50 £5.10 (£23.60) Trio £90.10 OWNER Qualitair Holdings Ltd (MALTON) BRED Qualitair Stud Ltd
WEIGHT FOR AGE 3yo-5lb

## 4508 BAXI HEATING CLAIMING STKS (3, 4 & 5-Y.O) (Class F)
1-45 (1-47) **6f (Fibresand)** £2,537.00 (£712.00: £347.00) Stalls: Low GOING: 0.47 sec per fur (SLW)

| | | | | SP | RR | SF |
|---|---|---|---|---|---|---|
| 4392[9] | **Little Ibnr (86)** (PDEvans) **4-9-0**(7) AmandaSanders(11) (a.p: led bel dist: pushed out) | — | **1** | 9/4[1] | 85 | 63 |
| 4392[7] | **Cretan Gift (71)** (NPLittmoden) **4-9-5** TGMcLaughlin(13) (a.p: rdn & r.o wl ins fnl f) | nk | **2** | 7/1 | 82 | 60 |
| 4125[2] | **Sing With the Band (73)** (BAMcMahon) **4-9-2** SSanders(7) (b: bit bkwd: led to bel dist: sn outpcd) | 5 | **3** | 7/2[2] | 66 | 44 |
| 4125[9] | **Monis (IRE) (51)** (JBalding) **4-8-4**(7) JEdmunds(3) (a.p: rdn & one pce fnl 2f) | 1½ | **4** | 50/1 | 57 | 35 |
| 4479[7] | **Anita's Contessa (IRE) (60)** (BPalling) **3-8-6** RPerham(10) (prom: outpcd after 1f: hdwy ent st: kpt on) | 3½ | **5** | 20/1 | 43 | 21 |
| 4484[2] | **Matthew David (46)** (SRBowring) **5-8-2b** NCarlisle(6) (b: chsd ldrs: rdn over 2f out: no imp) | 3½ | **6** | 8/1 | 29 | 7 |
| | **Recessions Over** (NPLittmoden) **4-8-3**(5) CAdamson(8) (w'like: leggy: bkwd: dwlt: nvr nrr) | s.h | **7** | 50/1 | 35 | 13 |
| 4368[11] | **Crystal Loop (77)** (ABailey) **3-9-2** GBardwell(2) (disp ld: rdn over 3f out: eased whn btn fnl f) | 3 | **8** | 9/1 | 35 | 13 |
| 4430[7] | **Great Bear (70)** (DWChapman) **3-8-1**(5) PFessey(5) (outpcd) | 3½ | **9** | 25/1 | 16 | — |
| 4478[9] | **Tafahhus (80)** (MJPolglase) **3-9-1** MTebbutt(12) (rdn along ½-wy: a bhd) | 1½ | **10** | 6/1[3] | 21 | — |
| 3510[10] | **Bex Hill (42)** (DHaydnJones) **3-7-11**(3) DWright(4) (bit bkwd: s.s: a bhd & outpcd) | ¾ | **11** | 50/1 | 4 | — |
| 4428[11] | **Selmeston (IRE)** (PSFelgate) **3-8-4**(3) PMcCabe(9) (bit bkwd: outpcd: t.o) | 5 | **12** | 50/1 | — | — |
| 4430[8] | **Last World (35)** (JAPickering) **3-7-12** JQuinn(1) (s.s: a outpcd: t.o) | 10 | **13** | 50/1 | — | — |
| | | | | (SP 119.3%) | **13 Rn** | |

**1m 17.0** (5.60) CSF £16.98 TOTE £3.90: £1.50 £2.50 £1.50 (£18.10) Trio £11.10 OWNER Swinnerton Transport Ltd (WELSHPOOL) BRED R. E. Waugh

## 4509 CRANE FLUID SYSTEMS NURSERY H'CAP (0-85) (2-Y.O) (Class E)
2-15 (2-16) **7f (Fibresand)** £3,103.20 (£939.60: £458.80: £218.40) Stalls: High GOING: 0.47 sec per fur (SLW)

| | | | | SP | RR | SF |
|---|---|---|---|---|---|---|
| 4485[4] | **Honestly (64)** (BSmart) **2-8-12** SSanders(10) (a.p: led over 2f out: drvn clr fnl f) | — | **1** | 12/1 | 77 | 17 |
| 3714[17] | **Chilibang Bang (61)** (JBerry) **2-8-2**(7) PRoberts(5) (a.p: led over 2f out: sn hdd: 2nd st: one pce) | 4 | **2** | 10/1 | 65 | 5 |
| 3947[14] | **Myttons Mistake (73)** (ABailey) **2-9-4**(3) DWright(11) (hdwy 3f out: 3rd st: one pce appr fnl f) | 1½ | **3** | 9/1[3] | 73 | 13 |
| 4431[6] | **Ebony Boy (63)** (JWharton) **2-8-11** JQuinn(9) (chsd ldrs: 4th st: rdn & one pce appr fnl f) | ½ | **4** | 12/1 | 62 | 2 |
| 4431[2] | **Angus McCoatup (IRE) (66)** (BAMcMahon) **2-9-0** OUrbina(12) (hld up: hdwy 3f out: 5th st: no imp) | 1 | **5** | 8/1[2] | 63 | 3 |
| 4461[9] | **Unspoken Prayer (46)** (JRArnold) **2-7-3**(5)ow1 CAdamson(7) (sme late hdwy: n.d) | ½ | **6** | 33/1 | 42 | — |
| 4453[3] | **Itsinthepost (70)** (MJohnston) **2-9-4** TWilliams(2) (prom: rdn along ½-wy: wknd over 2f out) | ½ | **7** | 7/2[1] | 65 | 5 |
| 4461[3] | **Blue Flyer (IRE) (68)** (RIngram) **2-8-9**(7) TAshley(8) (nvr trbld ldrs) | hd | **8** | 7/2[1] | 63 | 3 |
| 4389[5] | **Arch Angel (IRE) (56)** (DJSffrenchDavis) **2-8-4v** NAdams(1) (b.hind: sn outpcd: t.o) | 6 | **9** | 25/1 | 37 | — |
| 3915[11] | **Dhulikhel (48)** (DMarks) **2-7-5**(5) PFessey(6) (s.i.s: a in rr: t.o) | 3 | **10** | 10/1 | 22 | — |
| 4453[7] | **Rawi (60)** (WRMuir) **2-8-8** SDWilliams(3) (lw: hrd rdn over 3f out: sn bhd: t.o) | 1 | **11** | 20/1 | 32 | — |
| 4492[2] | **Gracious Gretclo (50)** (CJHill) **2-7-7**(5) MBaird(4) (led over 4f: 6th & wkng st: t.o) | 8 | **12** | 9/1[3] | 3 | — |
| | | | | (SP 120.7%) | **12 Rn** | |

**1m 34.1** (9.40) CSF £114.46 CT £1,031.79 TOTE £21.00: £2.60 £2.30 £4.20 (£38.60) Trio £167.40 OWNER Mr B. Hoggart (LAMBOURN) BRED Aston Park Stud
LONG HANDICAP Unspoken Prayer 7-2

## 4510 AIR MOVEMENT GROUP H'CAP (0-70) (3-Y.O) (Class E)
2-45 (2-45) **1m 100y (Fibresand)** £3,246.20 (£983.60: £480.80: £229.40) Stalls: Low GOING: 0.47 sec per fur (SLW)

| | | | | SP | RR | SF |
|---|---|---|---|---|---|---|
| 4436[5] | **Little Scarlett (45)** (PJMakin) **3-7-10** NCarlisle(6) (hld up: hdwy over 3f out: 4th st: hrd rdn to ld post) | — | **1** | 14/1 | 57 | 5 |
| 4171[11] | **Forzair (65)** (SRBowring) **3-9-2** ACulhane(11) (lw: hdwy 5f out: led over 2f out: sn clr: rdn fnl f: ct last stride) | s.h | **2** | 8/1 | 77 | 25 |
| 4478[8] | **Master Millfield (IRE) (70)** (CJHill) **3-9-7** RPerham(7) (prom: 6th & outpcd ent st: styd on fnl f) | 6 | **3** | 16/1 | 71 | 19 |
| 4406[2] | **Dr Caligari (IRE) (51)** (SGollings) **3-8-2v** JQuinn(5) (lw: led 2f: 2nd st: rdn & one pce appr fnl f) | ¾ | **4** | 7/2[1] | 50 | — |
| 4486[8] | **The Mestral (42)** (MJRyan) **3-7-7b** GBardwell(8) (led after 2f tl over 2f out: 3rd st: sn rdn & outpcd) | nk | **5** | 16/1 | 41 | — |
| 4490[3] | **Studio Thirty (51)** (DMorris) **3-8-2** JTate(9) (rdn 4f out: n.d) | hd | **6** | 4/1[2] | 49 | — |
| 4505[9] | **Mazilla (49)** (AStreeter) **3-8-0** JFanning(3) (chsd ldrs: effrt 4f out: wknd over 2f out) | 2 | **7** | 14/1 | 44 | — |
| 4457[3] | **Mediate (IRE) (66)** (AHide) **3-8-12**(5) MBaird(1) (sn outpcd & bhd: effrt over 3f out: no imp) | 4 | **8** | 6/1[3] | 53 | 1 |
| 4479[5] | **Gentle Irony (56)** (BJMeehan) **3-8-7b** JFEgan(13) (hld up in tch: effrt & 5th st: sn rdn & btn: t.o) | 5 | **9** | 8/1 | 34 | — |
| 3844[8] | **Florismart (59)** (BPJBaugh) **3-8-10** WLord(4) (a bhd: t.o) | 11 | **10** | 33/1 | 16 | — |
| 4194[17] | **Ambidextrous (IRE) (57)** (EJAlston) **3-8-8** SDWilliams(10) (lw: sn drvn along & bhd: t.o) | nk | **11** | 16/1 | 13 | — |
| 4366[10] | **Pharly Reef (53)** (DBurchell) **3-8-4**ow2 SSanders(2) (b.off fore: a towards rr: t.o) | 2 | **12** | 25/1 | 5 | — |
| | | | | (SP 116.5%) | **12 Rn** | |

**1m 56.2** (11.20) CSF £107.76 CT £1,636.21 TOTE £12.40: £3.90 £2.00 £2.70 (£84.40) Trio £187.50; £126.81 to Exeter 13/12/95. OWNER Mrs P. J. Makin (MARLBOROUGH) BRED Mrs J. McColl
STEWARDS' ENQUIRY Culhane susp 30/12/95 & 1-2/1/96 (excessive use of whip).

## 4511 HVCA (S) STKS (2-Y.O) (Class G)

3-15 (3-16) **6f** **(Fibresand)** £2,259.00 (£634.00: £309.00) Stalls: Low GOING: 0.47 sec per fur (SLW)

| | | | | SP | RR | SF |
|---|---|---|---|---|---|---|
| 4483$^{6}$ | **Monkey Zanty (IRE) (47)** (JLHarris) **2-8-3**$^{(3)}$ DWright(7) (a.p: 2nd st: led 1f out: r.o) | — | **1** | 33/1 | 61 | 20 |
| 4461$^{5}$ | **Marino Street** (PDEvans) **2-8-6** SSanders(5) (lw: hdwy over 1f out: r.o wl ins fnl f) | nk | **2** | 7/2$^{1}$ | 60 | 19 |
| 4483* | **Lady Eclat (59)** (JAGlover) **2-8-11v** SDWilliams(4) (led 5f: nt qckn) | 1¾ | **3** | 7/2$^{1}$ | 61 | 20 |
| 4480$^{4}$ | **Loch Style** (RHollinshead) **2-8-4**$^{(7)}$ FLynch(8) (rdn 3f out: hdwy & 5th st: r.o ins fnl f) | hd | **4** | 7/2$^{1}$ | 60 | 19 |
| 4483$^{5}$ | **Flood's Fancy (57)** (ABailey) **2-8-4b**$^{(7)}$ PRoberts(9) (prom: 3rd st: hrd rdn over 1f out: r.o one pce) | s.h | **5** | 7/1$^{2}$ | 60 | 19 |
| 4429$^{6}$ | **Yeoman Oliver** (BAMcMahon) **2-8-6**$^{(5)}$ LNewton(6) (lw: prom: 4th st: wknd over 1f out) | 7 | **6** | 15/2$^{3}$ | 42 | 1 |
| 4477$^{4}$ | **Image Maker (IRE) (56)** (BPreece) **2-8-11b** NAdams(12) (nvr trbld ldrs) | 5 | **7** | 16/1 | 28 | — |
| 3953$^{9}$ | **Sporting Fantasy (54)** (JBalding) **2-8-9**$^{(7)}$ JEdmunds(3) (rdn 3f out: sn bhd) | ¾ | **8** | 25/1 | 31 | — |
| 4483$^{2}$ | **Quinntessa (55)** (BPalling) **2-8-6** RPerham(13) (chsd ldrs: rdn 3f out: 6th st: eased whn btn fnl f) | nk | **9** | 7/1$^{2}$ | 20 | — |
| | **Guy's Gamble** (JWharton) **2-8-11** JFanning(10) (w'like: bit bkwd: outpcd) | 2½ | **10** | 20/1 | 19 | — |
| 4369$^{9}$ | **Abbott of Whalley (55)** (MartynWane) **2-9-2** JFEgan(2) (a bhd) | 1¾ | **11** | 20/1 | 19 | — |
| 4437$^{8}$ | **Don't Tell Vicki (52)** (JSMoore) **2-8-6**$^{(5)}$ PPMurphy(1) (a bhd: t.o) | 14 | **12** | 16/1 | — | — |
| | **Parellie** (CJHill) **2-8-6** JQuinn(11) (w'like: bit bkwd: a bhd: t.o) | 5 | **13** | 20/1 | — | — |

(SP 136.3%) **13 Rn**

**1m 19.1** (7.70) CSF £151.61 TOTE £22.80: £4.30 £2.70 £2.40 (£67.80) Trio £177.90 OWNER Mr J. L. Harris (MELTON MOWBRAY) BRED Stan Policky
No bid

## 4512 RADIAL & AXIAL GROUP H'CAP (0-65) (I) (3-Y.O+) (Class F)

3-45 (3-48) **7f** **(Fibresand)** £2,187.00 (£612.00: £297.00) Stalls: High GOING: 0.47 sec per fur (SLW)

| | | | | SP | RR | SF |
|---|---|---|---|---|---|---|
| 4505$^{6}$ | **Certain Way (IRE) (56)** (NPLittmoden) **5-9-4** TGMcLaughlin(4) (b: lw: hld up: hdwy & 4th st: hrd rdn to ld wl ins fnl f: r.o) | — | **1** | 12/1 | 66 | 26 |
| 4374$^{4}$ | **Maple Bay (IRE) (58)** (ABailey) **6-9-3**$^{(3)}$ DWright(9) (lw: hdwy over 2f out: 6th st: hrd rdn & r.o wl ins fnl f) | nk | **2** | 8/1$^{3}$ | 67 | 27 |
| 4502$^{2}$ | **Deeply Vale (IRE) (63)** (GLMoore) **4-9-11** SWhitworth(2) (dwlt: hdwy over 3f out: led over 2f out: hrd rdn & hdd wl ins fnl f) | 1¼ | **3** | 5/2$^{1}$ | 70 | 30 |
| 4427$^{9}$ | **Dream Carrier (IRE) (55)** (REPeacock) **7-9-0**$^{(3)}$ PMcCabe(8) (wl bhd tl gd hdwy over 1f out: nrst fin) | 3½ | **4** | 20/1 | 54 | 14 |
| 4371$^{2}$ | **Bogart (59)** (CWFairhurst) **4-9-7** JTate(10) (led over 5f out tl over 2f out: 2nd st: wknd fnl f) | ½ | **5** | 10/1 | 56 | 16 |
| 4478$^{3}$ | **Sweet Mate (56)** (SRBowring) **3-9-4b** SDWilliams(11) (chsd ldrs: 6th st: no hdwy) | ½ | **6** | 4/1$^{2}$ | 53 | 12 |
| 4464$^{8}$ | **Don't Get Caught (IRE) (63)** (JLHarris) **3-9-11** JFEgan(5) (chsd ldrs over 3f) | 3½ | **7** | 20/1 | 52 | 11 |
| 4421$^{14}$ | **Live Project (IRE) (63)** (MJohnston) **3-9-11** TWilliams(3) (lw: prom: rdn 4f out: 5th st: wknd over 1f out) | nk | **8** | 16/1 | 52 | 11 |
| 4456$^{11}$ | **Jon's Choice (46)** (BPreece) **7-8-8b** NAdams(12) (prom: 3rd & rdn st: wknd qckly wl over 1f out) | 3 | **9** | 20/1 | 27 | — |
| 4484$^{8}$ | **Green's Bid (47)** (DWChapman) **5-8-4**$^{(5)}$ PFessey(1) (led over 1f: 7th & wkng st) | 1½ | **10** | 20/1 | 24 | — |
| 4456$^{4}$ | **Respectable Jones (50)** (RHollinshead) **9-8-12** MWigham(7) (a bhd) | 2½ | **11** | 16/1 | 22 | — |
| | **Wolver Murphy (IRE) (47)** (KMcAuliffe) **3-8-9** JQuinn(6) (a bhd: t.o) | 8 | **12** | 20/1 | 1 | — |

(SP 112.0%) **12 Rn**

**1m 33.8** (9.10) CSF £83.16 CT £285.32 TOTE £13.90: £3.20 £3.10 £1.70 (£59.40) Trio £54.10 OWNER R A M Racecourses Ltd (WOLVERHAMPTON) BRED Alan Dargan

## 4513 IMI AIR CONDITIONING AMATEUR H'CAP (0-60) (II) (3-Y.O+) (Class F)

4-15 (4-18) **1m 4f** **(Fibresand)** £2,187.00 (£612.00: £297.00) Stalls: Low GOING: 0.47 sec per fur (SLW)

| | | | | SP | RR | SF |
|---|---|---|---|---|---|---|
| 4448$^{2}$ | **Pistols At Dawn (USA) (56)** (BJMeehan) **5-11-7** MissJAllison(9) (lw: hld up & bhd: hdwy over 5f out: 3rd st: led over 1f out: r.o) | — | **1** | 9/2$^{2}$ | 71 | 45 |
| 4391$^{6}$ | **Rousitto (55)** (RHollinshead) **7-11-6** MrMRimell(12) (hld up & bhd: hdwy over 5f out: led 2f out tl over 1f out: r.o) | ½ | **2** | 8/1 | 69 | 43 |
| 4434$^{3}$ | **Modest Hope (USA) (44)** (BRichmond) **8-10-9** MrsLPearce(8) (hld up & bhd: hdwy over 4f out: 4th st: one pce) | 5 | **3** | 6/1 | 52 | 26 |
| 4434* | **Stalled (IRE) (53)** (PTWalwyn) **5-10-13**$^{(5)}$ MarchionessofBlandford(2) (chsd ldr 9f: 6th st: one pce) | nk | **4** | 11/2$^{3}$ | 60 | 34 |
| 820$^{12}$ | **Hill Farm Katie (40)** (WMBrisbourne) **4-10-5** MissDianaJones(10) (bit bkwd: dwlt: hdwy over 3f out: 5th st: one pce) | 1½ | **5** | 16/1 | 45 | 19 |
| 4472$^{2}$ | **Larn Fort (54)** (CWFairhurst) **5-11-5b** MrsSBosley(6) (lw: prom: led over 3f out to 2f out: 2nd st: wknd over 1f out) | 1¾ | **6** | 11/2$^{3}$ | 57 | 31 |
| 4445$^{6}$ | **Hunza Story (31)** (NPLittmoden) **3-9-0**$^{(5)ow2}$ MrMSalaman(7) (b.hind: nvr trbld ldrs) | 5 | **7** | 33/1 | 26 | — |
| 4434$^{5}$ | **Mowlaie (56)** (DWChapman) **4-11-2**$^{(5)}$ MissRClark(5) (chsd ldrs: rdn 6f out: wknd over 2f out) | 6 | **8** | 25/1 | 44 | 18 |
| 4465$^{7}$ | **Phanan (33)** (REPeacock) **9-9-7**$^{(5)}$ MrsCPeacock(1) (led 3f: wknd over 5f out: t.o) | 11 | **9** | 33/1 | 7 | — |
| 4412$^{2}$ | **Buckley Boys (44)** (ABailey) **4-10-9** MissPJones(4) (hld up: rdn 4f out: sn wknd: t.o) | 6 | **10** | 11/4$^{1}$ | 10 | — |
| 389$^{11}$ | **Petitjean (IRE) (37)** (DBurchell) **4-9-11**$^{(5)}$ MissEJJones(11) (bit bkwd: plld hrd: led after 3f tl over 3f out: wknd qckly: t.o) | 1 | **11** | 20/1 | 1 | — |

(SP 121.4%) **11 Rn**

**2m 49.7** (17.20) CSF £38.01 CT £198.53 TOTE £4.70: £1.80 £2.30 £1.80 (£14.70) Trio £24.70 OWNER Mr G. Howard-Spink (UPPER LAMBOURN) BRED North Ridge Farm
WEIGHT FOR AGE 3yo-5lb

## 4514 RADIAL & AXIAL GROUP H'CAP (0-65) (II) (3-Y.O+) (Class F)

4-45 (4-48) **7f** **(Fibresand)** £2,187.00 (£612.00: £297.00) Stalls: High GOING: 0.47 sec per fur (SLW)

| | | | | SP | RR | SF |
|---|---|---|---|---|---|---|
| 3638$^{10}$ | **Rakis (IRE) (57)** (MABrittain) **5-9-3**$^{(3)}$ DWright(6) (mde all: rdn over 1f out: r.o wl) | — | **1** | 33/1 | 71 | 40 |
| 4447$^{4}$ | **Northern Spark (46)** (MissLAPerratt) **7-8-9** JFanning(5) (a.p: 2nd st: rdn & ev ch over 1f out: nt qckn ins fnl f) | 3 | **2** | 7/4$^{1}$ | 53 | 22 |
| 4428$^{3}$ | **Desert Invader (IRE) (61)** (DWChapman) **4-9-10** ACulhane(12) (lw: s.i.s: hdwy over 3f out: 3rd st: one pce) | 1¼ | **3** | 6/1$^{2}$ | 65 | 34 |
| 4390$^{8}$ | **First Gold (55)** (JWharton) **6-9-4** SDWilliams(3) (hdwy over 2f out: hrd rdn & 4th st: r.o one pce fnl f) | nk | **4** | 10/1 | 59 | 28 |
| 3703$^{18}$ | **Snake Plissken (IRE) (48)** (DHaydnJones) **4-8-11** JQuinn(7) (bit bkwd: hdwy & 7th st: nvr nr to chal) | 2½ | **5** | 9/1 | 46 | 15 |
| 4502$^{4}$ | **Jigsaw Boy (65)** (PGMurphy) **6-10-0** SSanders(1) (hdwy on ins 3f out: hrd rdn & 4th st: wknd over 1f out) | nk | **6** | 6/1$^{2}$ | 62 | 31 |
| 4337$^{14}$ | **Young Benson (55)** (BAMcMahon) **3-9-4** OUrbina(10) (prom: rdn 3f out: 6th st: wknd over 1f out) | 2½ | **7** | 16/1 | 48 | 16 |

| Form | Horse / details | Dist | Pos | SP | RR | SF |
|---|---|---|---|---|---|---|
| 4456* | **Tuigamala (59)** (RIngram) **4-9-1**(7) TAshley(8) (lw: a bhd) | 6 | **8** | 8/1[3] | 37 | 6 |
| 2588[7] | **Private Fixture (IRE) (64)** (DMarks) **4-9-13** MTebbutt(4) (bkwd: bhd fnl 3f) | 6 | **9** | 25/1 | 28 | — |
| 5071[4] | **Life's a Breeze (46)** (RLee) **6-8-9** JFEgan(2) (bit bkwd: a bhd: t.o) | 4 | **10** | 33/1 | 1 | — |
| 4487[7] | **Colston-C (49)** (CJHill) **3-8-12** SWhitworth(11) (prom: rdn over 3f out: sn wknd: t.o) | s.h | **11** | 10/1 | 5 | — |
| 2188[5] | **Flamboro (49)** (JDBethell) **3-8-12** TWilliams(9) (bkwd: a bhd: t.o) | dist | **12** | 10/1 | — | — |

(SP 128.9%) **12 Rn**

**1m 32.9** (8.20) CSF £92.13 CT £395.19 TOTE £41.40: £7.10 £1.70 £2.30 (£100.30) Trio £222.60 OWNER Mr P. G. Shorrock (WARTHILL) BRED The Mount Coote Partnership

T/Jkpt: Not won; £10,455.43 to Exeter 13/12/95. T/Plpt: £672.20 (25.4 Tckts). T/Qdpt: £163.10 (0.4 Tckts); £220.52 to Exeter 13/12/95. KH/IM

## 4487-LINGFIELD (L-H) (Standard)
## Thursday December 14th

### 4515 BROMLEY H'CAP (0-60) (I) (3-Y.O+) (Class F)

12-20 (12-22) **7f** **(Equitrack)** £2,476.80 (£694.80: £338.40) Stalls: Low GOING minus 0.19 sec per fur (FST)

| Form | Horse / details | Dist | Pos | SP | RR | SF |
|---|---|---|---|---|---|---|
| 4493[6] | **Hawaii Storm (FR) (59)** (DJSffrenchDavis) **7-9-13** JWilliams(3) (outpcd: gd hdwy over 1f out: led wl ins fnl f: r.o wl) | — | **1** | 8/1 | 64 | 46 |
| 4421[16] | **Maid Welcome (55)** (MrsNMacauley) **8-9-2v**(7) AmandaSanders(1) (led 5f out tl wl ins fnl f: unable qckn) | 1 | **2** | 7/1[2] | 58 | 40 |
| 4464[6] | **Our Shadee (USA) (57)** (KTIvory) **5-9-11v** AClark(4) (hld up: rdn over 4f out: r.o one pce fnl f) | 3½ | **3** | 7/1[2] | 52 | 34 |
| 4488[2] | **Sharp Imp (50)** (RMFlower) **5-9-4b** DBiggs(2) (hld up: rdn over 1f out: one pce) | ¾ | **4** | 7/2[1] | 43 | 25 |
| 4510[5] | **The Mestral (41)** (MJRyan) **3-8-9b** GBardwell(12) (a.p: rdn over 3f out: one pce) | 1¼ | **5** | 12/1 | 32 | 13 |
| 4268[15] | **Racing Telegraph (39)** (JWPayne) **5-8-7** MTebbutt(15) (hdwy over 2f out: drvn over 1f out: one pce) | ½ | **6** | 7/1[2] | 28 | 10 |
| 4479[8] | **Agoer (47)** (CEBrittain) **3-8-10**(5) MBaird(9) (b.hind: nvr nrr) | 2½ | **7** | 15/2[3] | 31 | 12 |
| 4458[9] | **Cabcharge Blue (54)** (TJNaughton) **3-9-1**(7) TAshley(8) (a mid div) | ½ | **8** | 25/1 | 37 | 18 |
| 4493[8] | **Jackatack (IRE) (59)** (MRChannon) **3-9-6v**(7) JDennis(14) (nvr nrr) | 1½ | **9** | 20/1 | 39 | 20 |
| 4486[2] | **Fiery Footsteps (43)** (SWCampion) **3-8-11** SDWilliams(13) (b.nr hind: prom 5f) | s.h | **10** | 16/1 | 23 | 4 |
| 4493[9] | **Kellaire Girl (IRE) (49)** (AMoore) **3-9-3** SSanders(7) (b. hind: led 2f: rdn over 3f out: wknd over 1f out) | nk | **11** | 12/1 | 28 | 9 |
| 4445[3] | **Charlie-Don't Surf (43)** (RGuest) **3-8-11** JTate(5) (s.i.s: a bhd) | nk | **12** | 10/1 | 21 | 2 |
| 4450[4] | **Nivasha (40)** (RPCHoad) **3-8-8**ow2 WNewnes(10) (prom over 5f) | 1¼ | **13** | 12/1 | 13 | — |
| 4447[8] | **Astrojoy (IRE) (36)** (SGKnight) **3-8-4b**ow3 AMcGlone(6) (bhd fnl 4f) | 6 | **14** | 20/1 | — | — |
| 4458[14] | **Henry Weston (30)** (PHowling) **3-7-12** JQuinn(11) (prom over 3f) | 5 | **15** | 33/1 | — | — |
| 4435[8] | **Sir Oliver (IRE) (38)** (BAPearce) **6-8-6** MWigham(16) (a bhd) | 2½ | **16** | 33/1 | — | — |

(SP 139.9%) **16 Rn**

**1m 27.02** (3.02) CSF £66.10 CT £393.36 TOTE £12.50: £1.90 £1.90 £2.50 £1.60 (£26.80) Trio £27.00 OWNER Mr C. C. Capel (UPPER LAMBOURN) BRED Horse France

### 4516 MENDIP APPRENTICE H'CAP (0-65) (3-Y.O+) (Class G)

12-50 (12-51) **1m 5f** **(Equitrack)** £2,322.50 (£660.00: £327.50) Stalls: Low GOING minus 0.19 sec per fur (FST)

| Form | Horse / details | Dist | Pos | SP | RR | SF |
|---|---|---|---|---|---|---|
| 4442[4] | **Broughtons Formula (48)** (WJMusson) **5-8-11b** JWilkinson(3) (lw: gd hdwy over 4f out: led on bit over 1f out: comf) | — | **1** | 7/2[2] | 49 | 32 |
| 4452[5] | **Glow Forum (37)** (GLMoore) **4-7-7**(7)ow3 TField(7) (hdwy over 1f out: r.o) | 2½ | **2** | 7/1[3] | 35 | 15 |
| 4472* | **Wildfire (SWI) (52)** (RAkehurst) **4-8-12**(3) TAshley(9) (a.p: ev ch over 1f out: one pce) | 2 | **3** | 11/4[1] | 48 | 31 |
| 4356[6] | **Talented Ting (IRE) (55)** (PHaslam) **6-8-13v**(5) CarolDavison(11) (led over 11f: one pce) | s.h | **4** | 10/1 | 50 | 33 |
| 4452[2] | **Just-Mana-Mou (IRE) (55)** (JJBridger) **3-8-7**(5) ALakeman(14) (lw: chsd ldr: rdn over 3f out: ev ch over 1f out: one pce) | hd | **5** | 7/1[3] | 50 | 27 |
| 4438[5] | **Kenyatta (USA) (35)** (AMoore) **6-7-12**ow5 AEddery(12) (b: b.hind: a.p: rdn over 3f out: one pce) | 3 | **6** | 20/1 | 27 | 5 |
| 4474[3] | **Ann Hill (IRE) (35)** (RHollinshead) **5-7-12**ow5 FLynch(10) (nvr nrr) | 11 | **7** | 14/1 | 13 | — |
| 4507[7] | **Telephus (40)** (BJMcMath) **6-8-0**(3) DSweeney(8) (nvr nr to chal) | 2½ | **8** | 25/1 | 15 | — |
| 4434[10] | **Bresil (USA) (30)** (KRBurke) **6-7-7** IonaWands(4) (lw: nvr nrr) | ½ | **9** | 20/1 | 4 | — |
| 4449[3] | **Tap On Tootsie (40)** (ICampbell) **3-7-6**(5)ow2 RMullen(1) (bhd fnl 5f) | s.h | **10** | 14/1 | 14 | — |
| | **Sweet Romeo (65)** (AlexVanderhaeghen,Belgium) **5-9-11**(3) JDennis(6) (b: b.hind: bhd fnl 6f) | 1¾ | **11** | 7/1[3] | 37 | 20 |
| 4331[12] | **Fattash (USA) (45)** (RPCHoad) **3-8-2** AimeeCook(2) (lw: a bhd) | 2 | **12** | 16/1 | 15 | — |
| | **Quiet Amusement (USA) (66)** (TTClement) **4-9-8**(7)ow8 RPooles(5) (lw: bhd fnl 3f) | 6 | **13** | 20/1 | 28 | 3 |
| 4474[4] | **Chapel Annie (39)** (CPWildman) **3-7-7**(3)ow3 JoHunnam(13) (bhd fnl 4f) | 5 | **14** | 50/1 | — | — |

(SP 134.8%) **14 Rn**

**2m 50.28** (7.08) CSF £29.74 CT £75.31 TOTE £5.20: £1.80 £2.40 £2.00 (£33.40) Trio £26.60 OWNER Crawford Gray & Aylett (NEWMARKET) BRED The Lavington Stud
LONG HANDICAP Ann Hill (IRE) 7-1 Chapel Annie 6-13
WEIGHT FOR AGE 3yo-6lb

### 4517 COMMERCIAL CEILING FACTORS H'CAP (0-85) (3-Y.O+) (Class D)

1-20 (1-21) **5f** **(Equitrack)** £3,589.30 (£1,086.40: £530.20: £252.10) Stalls: High GOING minus 0.19 sec per fur (FST)

| Form | Horse / details | Dist | Pos | SP | RR | SF |
|---|---|---|---|---|---|---|
| 4197[6] | **Ziggy's Dancer (USA) (80)** (EJAlston) **4-9-10** SDWilliams(1) (a.p: rdn 2f out: led ins fnl f: r.o wl) | — | **1** | 100/30[1] | 82 | 39 |
| 4368[5] | **Inherent Magic (IRE) (84)** (WRMuir) **6-10-0** JTate(3) (b: n.m.r 2f out: hdwy over 1f out: n.m.r & r.o wl fnl f) | ½ | **2** | 9/1 | 84 | 41 |
| 4432[8] | **Shadow Jury (72)** (DWChapman) **5-9-2b** JQuinn(5) (hdwy over 1f out: r.o wl ins fnl f) | 1¼ | **3** | 9/1 | 68 | 25 |
| 4441[3] | **Chewit (82)** (AMoore) **3-9-12** AClark(10) (b.hind: a.p: led wl over 1f out tl ins fnl f: one pce) | 1½ | **4** | 6/1[3] | 74 | 31 |
| 3622[12] | **Hannah's Usher (80)** (CMurray) **3-9-10** MTebbutt(9) (lost pl 2f out: r.o one pce fnl f) | 1½ | **5** | 11/1 | 67 | 24 |
| 4394[4] | **Lord Sky (75)** (ABailey) **4-9-5** SWhitworth(6) (lw: hld up: rdn over 3f out: one pce) | hd | **6** | 7/2[2] | 62 | 19 |
| 4487[3] | **Kalar (69)** (DWChapman) **6-8-13b** ACulhane(8) (led over 3f: wknd fnl f) | 1 | **7** | 7/1 | 52 | 9 |
| 1537[11] | **Myasha (USA) (75)** (AlexVanderhaeghen,Belgium) **6-9-5b** MServranckx(4) (hld up: rdn over 1f out: wknd) | 1¼ | **8** | 6/1[3] | 54 | 11 |
| 4394[16] | **Ultra Beet (80)** (PHaslam) **3-9-10** VHalliday(2) (bhd fnl 3f) | 2 | **9** | 8/1 | 53 | 10 |

(SP 125.8%) **9 Rn**

**61.26 secs** (3.26) CSF £32.60 CT £234.49 TOTE £4.20: £2.30 £3.30 £4.00 (£16.40) Trio £63.60 OWNER Mr John Patrick Barry (PRESTON) BRED Warren W. Rosenthal

## 4518 KENSINGTON CLAIMING STKS (2-Y.O) (Class F)

1-50 (1-54) **7f (Equitrack)** £2,814.20 (£791.20: £386.60) Stalls: Low GOING minus 0.19 sec per fur (FST)

| | | | | SP | RR | SF |
|---|---|---|---|---|---|---|
| *4124** | **Ultra Barley (79)** (PHaslam) **2-8-8**(5) MBaird(7) (hld up: rdn over 3f out: led 1f out: r.o wl) | — | 1 | 5/2[1] | 82+ | 34 |
| | **Plein Gaz (FR)** (AndreHermans,Belgium) **2-9-0** JQuinn(3) (neat: led 6f: unable qckn) | 3½ | 2 | 5/2[1] | 75 | 27 |
| *4491[2]* | **Rowlandsons Charm (IRE) (40)** (GLMoore) **2-8-0v** NAdams(8) (s.i.s: rdn & hdwy over 3f out: one pce fnl f) | ½ | 3 | 6/1[3] | 60 | 12 |
| *4433[5]* | **Righteous Gent (43)** (KMcAuliffe) **2-8-6be** SSanders(5) (chsd ldr 4f out tl over 1f out: one pce) | 1½ | 4 | 50/1 | 62? | 14 |
| *4408[7]* | **Young Frederick (IRE)** (KRBurke) **2-8-8** JFEgan(9) (lw: nvr nr to chal) | 2½ | 5 | 33/1 | 59 | 11 |
| *4383[6]* | **Supreme Power (72)** (WRMuir) **2-8-11b** SDWilliams(4) (lw: chsd ldr 3f: wknd over 2f out) | 3½ | 6 | 4/1[2] | 54 | 6 |
| *4491[6]* | **Jemsilverthorn (IRE) (40)** (JJBridger) **2-8-2** GBardwell(11) (no hdwy fnl 3f) | ¾ | 7 | 33/1 | 43 | — |
| *3675[11]* | **Multi Franchise (59)** (BGubby) **2-8-1** JTate(10) (bit bkwd: nvr nrr) | nk | 8 | 20/1 | 41 | — |
| *4477[2]* | **Takapuna (IRE) (48)** (TJNaughton) **2-7-11**(3) DWright(6) (bhd fnl 4f) | 1½ | 9 | 16/1 | 37 | — |
| *4461[6]* | **Red Acuisle (IRE) (65)** (GLewis) **2-8-8** SWhitworth(12) (sme hdwy over 4f out: wknd over 3f out) | 2½ | 10 | 7/1 | 39 | — |
| 3378[9] | **Peterrex (52)** (MRChannon) **2-7-13**(7) AEddery(1) (a bhd) | 10 | 11 | 20/1 | 14 | — |
| *4352[10]* | **General Henry** (AMoore) **2-8-6**ow2 AClark(2) (b.hind: dwlt: a bhd) | 1¼ | 12 | 50/1 | 10 | — |

(SP 129.1%) **12 Rn**

**1m 26.97** (2.97) CSF £9.64 TOTE £2.60: £1.70 £1.90 £1.90 (£7.70) Trio £12.70 OWNER Pet Express Ltd T/A Nutrimix (MIDDLEHAM) BRED Benham Stud

## 4519 WESTMINSTER MAIDEN STKS (2-Y.O) (Class D)

2-20 (2-21) **6f (Equitrack)** £3,436.25 (£1,040.00: £507.50: £241.25) Stalls: Low GOING minus 0.19 sec per fur (FST)

| | | | | SP | RR | SF |
|---|---|---|---|---|---|---|
| 4244[3] | **Carmarthen Bay (72)** (GLMoore) **2-9-0** JWilliams(2) (lw: chsd ldr: led 3f out: r.o wl) | — | 1 | 9/2[3] | 81 | 29 |
| | **Creeking** (SirMarkPrescott) **2-8-9** CNutter(8) (leggy: unf: dwlt: hdwy 3f out: chsd wnr over 1f out: nt qckn) | 8 | 2 | 11/2 | 55 | 3 |
| 3733[23] | **Darby Flyer** (WRMuir) **2-9-0** SDWilliams(7) (outpcd: hdwy over 1f out: r.o) | 6 | 3 | 12/1 | 44 | — |
| | **Lavender Bloom (IRE)** (MCunningham,Ireland) **2-8-9** JQuinn(5) (lt-f: a.p: rdn over 2f out: wknd over 1f out) | hd | 4 | 100/30[2] | 38 | — |
| *4417[4]* | **Be Satisfied** (AMoore) **2-8-7**(7) ALakeman(3) (b.hind: prom over 3f) | 2½ | 5 | 12/1 | 37 | — |
| | **Common Divine (IRE)** (CMurray) **2-8-9** MTebbutt(6) (lt-f: a.p: rdn over 2f out: wknd over 1f out) | nk | 6 | 25/1 | 31 | — |
| *4461[8]* | **La Perruche (IRE)** (LordHuntingdon) **2-8-9** SSanders(1) (led 3f: wknd over 1f out) | 1¼ | 7 | 5/2[1] | 28 | — |
| 4313[17] | **Irish Kinsman** (PTWalwyn) **2-9-0** AMcGlone(9) (outpcd) | 6 | 8 | 9/1 | 17 | — |
| | **Mutee (IRE)** (MJohnston) **2-8-9** TWilliams(4) (lt-f: dwlt: a wl bhd) | 10 | 9 | 8/1 | — | — |

(SP 125.6%) **9 Rn**

**1m 14.37** (3.77) CSF £29.50 TOTE £5.40: £1.40 £2.00 £6.20 (£57.50)Trio £60.20 OWNER Mr D. R. W. Jones (EPSOM) BRED D.R.Wynn Jones

STEWARDS' ENQUIRY Tebbutt susp. 30/12/95-6/1/96 (careless riding).

## 4520 BEXLEY H'CAP (0-85) (3-Y.O+) (Class D)

2-50 (2-52) **1m (Equitrack)** £3,656.90 (£1,107.20: £540.60: £257.30) Stalls: High GOING minus 0.19 sec per fur (FST)

| | | | | SP | RR | SF |
|---|---|---|---|---|---|---|
| *4451** | **Easy Choice (USA) (66)** (PhilipMitchell) **3-8-9** AClark(3) (lw: rdn & gd hdwy over 2f out: drvn over 1f out: led ins fnl f: r.o wl) | — | 1 | 7/2[2] | 76 | 44 |
| *4421[13]* | **Duke Valentino (70)** (RHollinshead) **3-8-13** MWigham(8) (hld up: chsd ldr over 3f out: led wl over 1f out tl ins fnl f: unable qckn) | 2 | 2 | 6/1 | 76 | 44 |
| 4104[7] | **Toujours Riviera (84)** (JPearce) **5-10-0** GBardwell(1) (led over 6f: one pce) | 3 | 3 | 12/1 | 83 | 53 |
| 433[16] | **Harpoon Louie (USA) (77)** (AlexVanderhaeghen,Belgium) **5-9-7** MServranckx(5) (b: b.hind: a.p: rdn over 2f out: sn wknd) | ¾ | 4 | 10/1 | 75 | 45 |
| *4392[14]* | **Bernard Seven (IRE) (79)** (CEBrittain) **3-9-5b**(3) PMcCabe(4) (chsd ldr over 3f: wknd over 2f out) | 4 | 5 | 8/1 | 70 | 38 |
| *4451[5]* | **Risky Romeo (79)** (GCBravery) **3-9-8** MTebbutt(7) (nvr nr to chal) | ¾ | 6 | 14/1 | 68 | 36 |
| *4435** | **Dancing Lawyer (81)** (BJMeehan) **4-9-11** JFEgan(9) (a bhd) | 13 | 7 | 5/1[3] | 43 | 13 |
| *4356[2]* | **South Eastern Fred (84)** (HJCollingridge) **4-10-0** JQuinn(2) (b.hind: bhd fnl 5f) | 1 | 8 | 11/4[1] | 44 | 14 |
| 4227[12] | **Gulf Shaadi (79)** (EJAlston) **3-9-8** SWhitworth(6) (s.s: a wl bhd) | 12 | 9 | 16/1 | 16 | — |

(SP 120.3%) **9 Rn**

**1m 39.58** (2.18) CSF £23.82 CT £209.08 TOTE £4.30: £1.80 £2.10 £3.10 (£21.60) Trio £59.30 OWNER Mr J. Morton (EPSOM) BRED Juddmonte Farms

WEIGHT FOR AGE 3yo-1lb

**OFFICIAL EXPLANATION South Eastern Fred: was outpaced early and was never able to get into contention.**

## 4521 BROMLEY H'CAP (0-60) (II) (3-Y.O+) (Class F)

3-20 (3-29) **7f (Equitrack)** £2,464.20 (£691.20: £336.60) Stalls: Low GOING minus 0.19 sec per fur (FST)

| | | | | SP | RR | SF |
|---|---|---|---|---|---|---|
| *4450[2]* | **Scissor Ridge (46)** (JJBridger) **3-8-13** JQuinn(9) (led 1f: led 3f out: drvn out) | — | 1 | 9/2[2] | 53 | 28 |
| *4464** | **Myjinka (45)** (JO'Donoghue) **5-8-9b**(3) PMcCabe(1) (outpcd: gd hdwy over 1f out: r.o wl ins fnl f) | nk | 2 | 5/1[3] | 50 | 26 |
| *2963[8]* | **It's So Easy (33)** (APJames) **4-8-0** NAdams(10) (hdwy over 3f out: nt clr run 2f out: unable qckn) | 3 | 3 | 33/1 | 32 | 8 |
| *4457[8]* | **Sally Weld (55)** (CJBenstead) **3-9-8** MWigham(5) (rdn over 4f out: n.m.r 2f out: hdwy over 1f out: n.m.r & swtchd rt 1f out: r.o one pce) | s.h | 4 | 7/2[1] | 54 | 29 |
| *4430[5]* | **Dissentor (IRE) (47)** (JAGlover) **3-9-0v** SDWilliams(11) (a.p: chsd ldr over 2f out tl ins fnl f: sn wknd) | 3½ | 5 | 12/1 | 38 | 13 |
| *4456[6]* | **By The Bay (50)** (CCElsey) **3-9-3** JWilliams(13) (outpcd: nvr nrr) | ½ | 6 | 8/1 | 40 | 15 |
| *4454[6]* | **Sing Up (55)** (MMcCormack) **3-9-8** RPerham(7) (a.p: rdn over 4f out: wknd 1f out) | 1½ | 7 | 12/1 | 42 | 17 |
| 4209[11] | **Shaynes Domain (47)** (RMFlower) **4-9-0b** DBiggs(3) (nvr nr to chal) | 2½ | 8 | 20/1 | 27 | 3 |
| *4351[5]* | **Woolverstone Hall (IRE) (44)** (DJGMurraySmith) **3-8-11** WNewnes(14) (hdwy over 3f out: wkng whn hmpd wl over 1f out) | 1½ | 9 | 11/1 | 22 | — |
| | **Palacegate Gold (IRE) (39)** (RJHodges) **6-8-6** AMcGlone(6) (bit bkwd: bhd fnl 4f) | 2½ | 10 | 33/1 | 10 | — |
| 4240[7] | **Tomal (47)** (RIngram) **3-9-0** SSanders(12) (hld up: rdn over 4f out: wknd wl over 1f out) | 1½ | 11 | 9/1 | 16 | — |
| *4421[6]* | **Dancing Sioux (58)** (RGuest) **3-9-11b** SWhitworth(8) (led 6f out to 3f out: wknd wl over 1f out) | 1¼ | 12 | 6/1 | 24 | — |
| *4464[7]* | **Assignment (49)** (JELong) **9-8-13**(3) DWright(2) (b.off hind: prom over 3f) | 7 | 13 | 25/1 | — | — |

(SP 130.7%) **13 Rn**

**1m 27.43** (3.43) CSF £27.93 CT £627.81 TOTE £5.20: £2.00 £2.50 £22.70 (£7.90) Trio £215.40 OWNER Mr Donald Smith (LIPHOOK) BRED J. K. Keegan

T/Plpt: £15.80 (560.27 Tckts). T/Qdpt: £29.00 (0.38 Tckts); £24.33 to Hereford 15/12/95. AK

# 0606a-SHA TIN (Kowloon, Hong Kong) (R-H) (Firm)
## Sunday December 10th

### 4522a HONG KONG INTERNATIONAL VASE (3-Y.O+)
6-40 (6-42) **1m 4f** £239,699.00 (£90,909.00: £41,322.00: £19,421.00: £13,636.00: £8,264.00)

| | | | | SP | RR | SF |
|---|---|---|---|---|---|---|
| 4252a⁴ | **Partipral (USA)** (ELellouche,France) **6-9-0** OPeslier | — | **1** | | 122 | — |
| 3690a⁵ | **Needle Gun (IRE)** (CEBrittain) **5-9-0** LDettori | nk | **2** | | 122 | — |
| | **Royal Snack (AUS)** (GHanlon,Australia) **6-9-0** PPayne | ¾ | **3** | | 121 | — |
| 4185a⁶ | **Commoner (USA)** (RHannon) **3-8-13** RHughes (btn 5½l) | | **6** | | 115 | — |
| | | | | | | **14 Rn** |

**2m 25.7** Tote £34.50: £16.00 £19.00 £55.00 (£78.00) OWNER Mr Enrique Sarasola BRED Thorpe Investments in USA
**4252a Partipral (USA)** came with a steady run from the rear. Close up entering the straight, he only struck the front in the last thirty yards and may have won with something in hand.
**3690a Needle Gun (IRE)**, always close up, was chasing the leaders entering the straight. Taking the lead two furlongs out, he battled on gamely, but was just run out of it close home. This was a very good effort over a trip at the limit of his stamina.
**4185a Commoner (USA)** ran a highly creditable race given that he had suffered minor back and leg problems. Held up in the early stages, he moved up turning for home, only to stay on at one pace in the straight. He stays in training, and is capable of winning a good prize next year.

### 4523a HONG KONG INTERNATIONAL BOWL (Gp 2) (3-Y.O+)
7-20 (7-20) **7f** £263,636.00 (£100,000.00: £45,456.00)

| | | | | SP | RR | SF |
|---|---|---|---|---|---|---|
| | **Monopolize (AUS)** (GBegg,Australia) **5-9-0** WHarris (bhd tl hdwy over 2f out: r.o wl fnl f to ld cl hme) | — | **1** | | 127 | — |
| 3834⁷ | **Desert Style (IRE)** (JSBolger,Ireland) **3-8-13b** KJManning (a.p: chal to ld wl ins fnl f: hdd last strides) | hd | **2** | | 127 | — |
| | **Finder's Fortune (USA)** (DVienna,USA) **6-9-0b** PValenzuela (a.p: led 4f out: rdn 2f out: hdd wl ins fnl f) | 1 | **3** | | 125 | — |
| 4469a² | **Branston Abby (IRE)** (MJohnston) **6-8-11** MRoberts (a bhd: btn 5¼l) | | **10** | | 114 | — |
| 4178a¹⁰ | **Young Ern** (SDow) **5-9-0** TQuinn (prom early: rdn & wknd 3f out: btn 6½l) | | **12** | | 114 | — |
| 4078⁸ | **Cool Jazz** (CEBrittain) **4-9-0** MJKinane (chsd ldrs tl wknd over 2f out: btn 17l) | | **14** | | 93 | — |
| | | | | | | **14 Rn** |

**1m 21.5** Tote £128.50: £38.00 £24.00 £27.00 (£386.00) OWNER N Begg & Partners Syndicate
**3198a* Desert Style (IRE)**, wearing blinkers for the first time, ran a tremendous race. Always in the firing line, he got his head in front in the final fifty yards, but was caught in the shadow of the post. He is now due to retire to stud.
**4469a Branston Abby (IRE)** was unsettled in the stalls and, on ground which did not suit her, was never able to get into contention.
**4178a Young Ern** was a disappointing favourite. Struggling to maintain a good position in the early stages, and having lost his place on the turn for home, he could never get back into contention.
**4012a Cool Jazz** was in touch in the early stages, but struggled on this firm ground, and was well beaten when eased in the final furlong.

### 4524a HONG KONG INTERNATIONAL CUP (Gp 2) (3-Y.O+)
8-30 (8-30) **1m 1f** £287,603.00 (£109,091.00: £49,587.00)

| | | | | SP | RR | SF |
|---|---|---|---|---|---|---|
| | **Fujiyama Kenzan (JPN)** (HMori,Japan) **7-9-0** MEbina (a.p: 2nd st: r.o to ld wl ins fnl f) | — | **1** | | 125 | — |
| | **Ventiquattrofogli (IRE)** (WDollase,USA) **5-9-0b** PAtkinson (a.p: led 6f out: qcknd clr over 1f out: hdd cl home) | ¾ | **2** | | 124 | — |
| | **Jade Age** (DAOughton,HongKong) **5-9-0** MJKinane (bhd tl r.o wl fnl 2f: nt rch ldrs) | 2¾ | **3** | | 119 | — |
| 4185a⁷ | **Volochine (IRE)** (RCollet,France) **4-9-0** TJarnet (r.o fnl f: nt rch ldrs: btn 5½l) | | **5** | | 114 | — |
| 4305a¹¹ | **Shaanxi (USA)** (ELellouche,France) **3-8-10** OPeslier (alwys abt same plce: btn 11¼l) | | **8** | | 101 | — |
| 4007a³ | **Triarius (USA)** (SbinSuroor) **5-9-0** LDettori (bhd: prog to chs ldrs 6f out: rdn & btn 2f out: btn 27l) | | **10** | | — | — |
| | | | | | | **12 Rn** |

**1m 47.0** Tote £386.50: £91.00 £76.50 £110.00 (£3226.50) OWNER T. Fujimoto BRED Yoshida Bokujo
**4007a Triarius (USA)**, representing Dubai, was disappointing. Having been forced to make a move too early in the race, he had nothing left for the business end and dropped away tamely.

# 4515-LINGFIELD (L-H) (Standard)
## Friday December 15th

### 4525 BROOKNIGHT GUARDING CLAIMING STKS (I) (3-Y.O+) (Class E)
12-30 (12-33) **1m (Equitrack)** £2,827.60 (£854.80: £416.40: £197.20) Stalls: High GOING minus 0.24 sec per fur (FST)

| | | | | SP | RR | SF |
|---|---|---|---|---|---|---|
| 4240² | **Spencer's Revenge (78)** (MJRyan) **6-9-3** GBardwell(3) (rdn thrght: hdwy over 2f out: str run fnl f: led last strides) | — | **1** | 3/1¹ | 81 | 53 |
| *4444*³ | **Second Colours (USA) (73)** (MrsMReveley) **5-8-12**⁽⁵⁾ GParkin(9) (hdwy 3f out: led & edgd lft wl over 1f out: drvn fnl f: hdd last strides) | hd | **2** | 4/1² | 81 | 53 |
| *4357** | **Masnun (USA) (66)** (RJO'Sullivan) **10-8-7** AClark(11) (hdwy 3f out: ev ch whn hmpd wl over 1f out: r.o wl ins fnl f) | ¾ | **3** | 3/1¹ | 69 | 41 |
| *4440*⁷ | **Greenwich Again (69)** (TGMills) **3-8-11** WNewnes(6) (a.p: rdn over 2f out: 4th & btn whn hmpd 2f out) | 3½ | **4** | 12/1 | 68 | 38 |
| *123** | **Everset (FR)** (ABailey) **7-9-4**⁽³⁾ DWright(4) (bit bkwd: led: clr over 4f out: hdd wl over 1f out: wknd fnl f) | 1¼ | **5** | 6/1³ | 74 | 46 |
| *4493*⁴ | **Eastleigh (51)** (RHollinshead) **6-8-0**⁽⁷⁾ FLynch(1) (b.off hind: chsd ldr 7f out tl over 3f out: wknd over 2f out) | 1¾ | **6** | 14/1 | 56 | 28 |
| | **Duveen (IRE)** (JWhite) **5-8-8**⁽⁵⁾ PPMurphy(7) (a bhd) | 3½ | **7** | 14/1 | 55 | 27 |
| 4319¹⁰ | **Euphyllia (66)** (BobJones) **3-7-13** JFanning(5) (b.hind: prom over 3f) | s.h | **8** | 12/1 | 43 | 13 |
| *4490*⁶ | **The Little Ferret (53)** (AMoore) **5-8-7** TWilliams(12) (b.hind: lw: a bhd) | ½ | **9** | 20/1 | 48 | 20 |
| *4418*³ | **Desert Water (IRE) (45)** (JJBridger) **3-8-5** JQuinn(10) (bhd fnl 3f) | 7 | **10** | 33/1 | 34 | 4 |
| 853¹⁹ | **Shedansar (IRE)** (GLMoore) **3-8-1** NAdams(8) (s.s: a bhd) | 2 | **11** | 50/1 | 26 | — |
| *216*² | **Superlao (BEL)** (AndreHermans,Belgium) **3-8-6** JTate(2) (neat: prom 3f: t.o) | dist | **12** | 14/1 | — | — |
| | | | | (SP 129.3%) | | **12 Rn** |

**1m 39.07** (1.67) CSF £16.07 TOTE £2.70: £1.90 £1.30 £1.90 (£9.10) Trio £9.10 OWNER Mr A. S. Reid (NEWMARKET) BRED Lord Crawshaw
WEIGHT FOR AGE 3yo-1lb

## 4526 LONDON CAR HIRE AMATEUR H'CAP (0-75) (3-Y.O+) (Class G)

1-00 (1-01) **1m 2f (Equitrack)** £2,808.00 (£707.60: £345.80) Stalls: Low GOING minus 0.24 sec per fur (FST)

| | | | | SP | RR | SF |
|---|---|---|---|---|---|---|
| 4261[8] | **Almuhtaram (62)** (MissGayKelleway) **3-11-2b** MrMArmytage(2) (stdy hdwy over 3f out: squeezed thro on ins to ld ins fnl f: pushed out) | — | **1** | 9/2[2] | 75 | 53 |
| *4476[8]* | **Tribal Peace (IRE) (68)** (BGubby) **3-11-4**(4) MrsMTingey(14) (a.p: led 4f out tl ins fnl f: pushed out) | 1¾ | **2** | 11/1 | 78 | 56 |
| *4505[5]* | **Owdbetts (IRE) (56)** (GLMoore) **3-10-6**(4) MrKGoble(8) (s.s: hdwy over 3f out: rdn over 2f out: sn wknd) | 1 | **3** | 9/1 | 65 | 43 |
| 4163[16] | **Seventeens Lucky (70)** (BobJones) **3-11-6**(4) MissDJJones(6) (hld up: rdn over 2f out: one pce) | 1¼ | **4** | 15/2 | 77 | 55 |
| *4465[3]* | **Retender (USA) (55)** (JPearce) **6-10-12** MrsLPearce(4) (b.hind: hdwy over 1f out: nvr nrr) | 6 | **5** | 100/30[1] | 51 | 33 |
| *4293[2]* | **Sir Norman Holt (IRE) (66)** (RJO'Sullivan) **6-11-9b** MrsAPerrett(5) (rdn over 4f out: n.m.r & lost pl over 3f out: r.o one pce fnl f) | hd | **6** | 13/2[3] | 62 | 44 |
| *4457[14]* | **Saltis (IRE) (54)** (DWPArbuthnot) **3-10-8** MrsDArbuthnot(1) (b.hind: lw: hld up: rdn over 2f out: sn wknd) | ¾ | **7** | 20/1 | 50 | 28 |
| *4513[9]* | **Phanan (36)** (REPeacock) **9-9-0**(7) MrsCPeacock(7) (nvr nrr) | ½ | **8** | 33/1 | 30 | 12 |
| *4465[5]* | **Montone (IRE) (49)** (JRJenkins) **5-10-2**(4) MrMMannish(9) (hdwy over 7f out: wknd over 2f out) | 2½ | **9** | 8/1 | 39 | 21 |
| 3129[6] | **Take Two (58)** (JWhite) **7-10-8**(7)ow2 MrNMoran(10) (rdn 6f out: hdwy over 3f out: wknd over 2f out) | ½ | **10** | 14/1 | 45 | 27 |
| *4440[8]* | **Ripsnorter (IRE) (43)** (KBishop) **6-9-10**(4) MissAPurdy(13) (lw: s.s: a bhd) | 4 | **11** | 20/1 | 26 | 8 |
| 4149[16] | **Backview (70)** (BJLlewellyn) **3-11-10** MrJLLlewellyn(12) (lw: led over 6f out to 4f out: wknd 3f out) | 1 | **12** | 14/1 | 52 | 30 |
| 2007[10] | **Absolutely Fayre (67)** (RAkehurst) **4-11-10** MrTMcCarthy(3) (lw: led over 3f: wknd over 3f out) | 6 | **13** | 7/1 | 38 | 20 |

(SP 134.1%) **13 Rn**

**2m 9.62** (5.32) CSF £54.29 CT £411.02 TOTE £6.20: £3.40 £7.30 £5.00 (£49.10) Trio £130.10 OWNER Mr A. M. Al-Midani (WHITCOMBE) BRED A. M. Midani

LONG HANDICAP Phanan 9-4

WEIGHT FOR AGE 3yo-3lb

## 4527 BROOKNIGHT GUARDING CLAIMING STKS (II) (3-Y.O+) (Class E)

1-30 (1-32) **1m (Equitrack)** £2,827.60 (£854.80: £416.40: £197.20) Stalls: High GOING minus 0.24 sec per fur (FST)

| | | | | SP | RR | SF |
|---|---|---|---|---|---|---|
| *4454** | **Mr Nevermind (IRE) (76)** (GLMoore) **5-9-1** SWhitworth(4) (hdwy 5f out: chsd ldr over 3f out: led 2f out: clr over 1f out: comf) | — | **1** | 4/5[1] | 82 | 44 |
| *4445** | **Sweet Supposin (IRE) (82)** (CADwyer) **4-9-7v** CDwyer(3) (lw: wl bhd 4f: gd hdwy over 2f out: r.o wl ins fnl f: t.m.t.d) | 2½ | **2** | 5/1[2] | 83 | 45 |
| *4441[10]* | **Dancing Heart (74)** (BJMeehan) **3-9-5b** JFEgan(6) (led 6f: unable qckn) | 5 | **3** | 8/1[3] | 73 | 33 |
| 4209[13] | **Oozlem (IRE) (33)** (JRPoulton) **6-8-10b** GBardwell(7) (b: s.s: t.o over 6f: gd hdwy fnl f: r.o wl) | 3 | **4** | 12/1 | 56 | 18 |
| | **Gallic Victory (IRE)** (JohnBerry) **4-8-13** JQuinn(2) (lost pl over 6f out: one pce fnl 3f) | 1¼ | **5** | 33/1 | 57 | 19 |
| *4454[2]* | **Nordic Doll (IRE) (62)** (BWHills) **3-8-8** AMcGlone(5) (lw: chsd ldr over 4f: wknd 2f out) | hd | **6** | 12/1 | 53 | 13 |
| *4436[6]* | **Pertemps Flyer (52)** (SEarle) **4-8-3b** CRutter(8) (hdwy over 3f out: wknd over 2f out) | 1¾ | **7** | 50/1 | 43 | 5 |
| *4418[6]* | **Mr Medley (60)** (RHannon) **3-8-11** WNewnes(12) (nvr nr to chal) | 1¼ | **8** | 16/1 | 50 | 10 |
| *4458[11]* | **Green Golightly (USA) (40)** (DAWilson) **4-8-3** TWilliams(9) (prom over 3f) | 6 | **9** | 33/1 | 28 | — |
| | **Vintage Red** (NATwiston-Davies) **5-8-9** VSlattery(10) (prom over 3f) | 1 | **10** | 50/1 | 32 | — |
| | **Triple (FR)** (LordHuntingdon) **3-8-2** SSanders(11) (unf: prom over 4f) | ¾ | **11** | 20/1 | 26 | — |
| *4451[6]* | **Calgary Girl** (PCRitchens) **3-9-0** NAdams(1) (a bhd: t.o) | 30 | **12** | 66/1 | — | — |

(SP 120.7%) **12 Rn**

**1m 39.82** (2.42) CSF £5.49 TOTE £1.80: £1.40 £1.10 £3.50 (£3.60) Trio £5.90 OWNER Mr K. Higson (EPSOM) BRED Robert Corridan

WEIGHT FOR AGE 3yo-1lb

## 4528 EASAL NURSERY H'CAP (2-Y.O) (Class D)

2-00 (2-01) **1m (Equitrack)** £3,468.75 (£1,050.00: £512.50: £243.75) Stalls: High GOING minus 0.24 sec per fur (FST)

| | | | | SP | RR | SF |
|---|---|---|---|---|---|---|
| *4453** | **Arctic Romancer (IRE) (81)** (GLewis) **2-8-12** SWhitworth(6) (lw: stdd s: hdwy 5f out: led 1f out: r.o wl) | — | **1** | 4/1[2] | 84 | 32 |
| *4410[5]* | **Six Clerks (IRE) (64)** (JGFitzGerald) **2-7-9**ow2 JQuinn(8) (hld up: led 2f out to 1f out: unable qckn) | 2 | **2** | 8/1 | 61 | 9 |
| *4509[8]* | **Blue Flyer (IRE) (69)** (RIngram) **2-8-0**ow1 DBiggs(5) (rdn over 3f out: hdwy wl over 1f out: one pce) | 3 | **3** | 13/2 | 61 | 9 |
| *4491[12]* | **Autobabble (IRE) (65)** (RHannon) **2-7-10** NCarlisle(7) (lw: rdn over 4f out: hdwy over 1f out: nvr nrr) | ½ | **4** | 7/1 | 57 | 5 |
| *4410[6]* | **Double Diamond (IRE) (90)** (MJohnston) **2-9-7** TWilliams(2) (led over 3f: ev ch over 1f out: wknd fnl f) | 1¾ | **5** | 7/1 | 79 | 27 |
| *4477** | **People Direct (64)** (KMcAuliffe) **2-7-6**(3)ow2 DWright(4) (b.nr hind: lw: prom 5f) | 2½ | **6** | 5/1[3] | 46 | — |
| *4485[2]* | **Bath Knight (63)** (DJSffrenchDavis) **2-7-8** NAdams(1) (b.hind: led over 4f out to 2f out: wknd over 1f out) | nk | **7** | 14/1 | 46 | — |
| *4462[2]* | **Homeland (66)** (TJNaughton) **2-7-11** GBardwell(3) (bhd fnl 5f) | 1¼ | **8** | 7/4[1] | 46 | — |

(SP 129.1%) **8 Rn**

**1m 40.72** (3.32) CSF £35.70 CT £194.69 TOTE £5.10: £2.00 £2.70 £2.10 (£46.70) OWNER Mr Abdulla Al Khalifa (EPSOM) BRED Peter Phelan

LONG HANDICAP People Direct 7-5

## 4529 KERSTEN PROMOTIONS MEDIAN AUCTION MAIDEN STKS (2-Y.O) (Class F)

2-30 (2-31) **7f (Equitrack)** £2,738.60 (£769.60: £375.80) Stalls: Low GOING minus 0.24 sec per fur (FST)

| | | | | SP | RR | SF |
|---|---|---|---|---|---|---|
| | **Accountancy Jewel (IRE)** (KMcAuliffe) **2-8-6**(3) DWright(7) (neat: s.i.s: gd hdwy over 3f out: led over 1f out: drvn out) | — | **1** | 7/1[3] | 78 | 19 |
| 4330W | **Farmost** (SirMarkPrescott) **2-9-0** CNutter(2) (lw: hld up: shkn up over 1f out: r.o wl ins fnl f) | 1 | **2** | 14/1 | 81+ | 22 |
| 4109[10] | **Tahya (USA) (60)** (CCElsey) **2-8-9** CRutter(6) (outpcd: hdwy over 1f out: r.o) | 7 | **3** | 20/1 | 60 | 1 |
| 3441[8] | **Take Note (IRE)** (NAGraham) **2-9-0** AMcGlone(1) (hld up: nt clr run 3f out: rdn over 2f out: one pce) | 3 | **4** | 14/1 | 58 | — |
| | **Happy Traveller (IRE)** (CMurray) **2-9-0** MTebbutt(9) (unf: scope: a.p: led over 3f out to over 1f out: sn wknd) | nk | **5** | 4/1[2] | 57 | — |
| *4461[4]* | **Green Gem (BEL)** (SCWilliams) **2-8-9** JTate(3) (led 3f: wknd over 2f out) | 5 | **6** | 2/1[1] | 41 | — |
| *4429[14]* | **Blue Adelaide (60)** (PFICole) **2-8-9b** JQuinn(8) (hld up: rdn over 3f out: wknd over 2f out) | 6 | **7** | 4/1[2] | 27 | — |
| *4365[10]* | **Flagstaff (USA) (55)** (GLMoore) **2-9-0v** SWhitworth(5) (led 4f out to over 3f out: wknd 2f out) | 4 | **8** | 4/1[2] | 23 | — |
| *4491[13]* | **My Mother's Local (USA)** (KOCunningham-Brown) **2-8-9** SSanders(4) (w ldr 3f: wknd 3f out) | 3½ | **9** | 16/1 | 10 | — |

(SP 129.8%) **9 Rn**

**1m 27.58** (3.58) CSF £91.79 TOTE £18.00: £2.00 £2.00 £16.40 (£22.60) Trio £189.20 OWNER Brennan Accountants (LAMBOURN) BRED Peter Casey

## 4530 BIFFA RE-CYCLING H'CAP (0-65) (3-Y.O+) (Class F)

3-00 (3-02) **2m (Equitrack)** £2,839.40 (£798.40: £390.20) Stalls: Low GOING minus 0.57 sec per fur (FST)

| | | | | SP | RR | SF |
|---|---|---|---|---|---|---|
| 4416[6] | **Anjou (60)** (JPearce) **3-9-11** GBardwell(9) (a.p: led over 3f out: drvn over 1f out: r.o wl) | — | **1** | 20/1 | 75 | 43 |
| 4364[3] | **Ikhtiraa (USA) (50)** (RJO'Sullivan) **5-9-9** WWoods(3) (hdwy over 9f out: rdn over 3f out: r.o one pce fnl f) | 3½ | **2** | 10/1 | 62 | 38 |
| 3569[2] | **Chez Catalan (47)** (RAkehurst) **4-9-6b** SSanders(11) (lw: a.p: rdn over 4f out: ev ch over 1f out: one pce) | ½ | **3** | 3/1[1] | 58 | 34 |
| 3884[11] | **Call Me Albi (IRE) (44)** (GLMoore) **4-9-3** SWhitworth(6) (lw: hld up: rdn over 6f out: one pce fnl f) | nk | **4** | 14/1 | 55 | 31 |
| 4465[4] | **Strat's Legacy (42)** (DWPArbuthnot) **8-9-1** JFEgan(7) (b.hind: hdwy over 3f out: rdn over 2f out: one pce) | ½ | **5** | 8/1 | 52 | 28 |
| 4455* | **Coleridge (51)** (JJSheehan) **7-9-10b** JQuinn(12) (lw: a.p: led 5f out tl over 3f out: ev ch over 1f out: wknd) | 1 | **6** | 4/1[2] | 60 | 36 |
| 4463* | **Guest Alliance (IRE) (55)** (AMoore) **3-9-6** AClark(2) (b.hind: rdn & hdwy 7f out: one pce fnl 3f) | 1 | **7** | 10/1 | 63 | 31 |
| 4463[4] | **Hever Golf Lady (47)** (TJNaughton) **3-8-5**(7) TAshley(14) (b: b.hind: hdwy over 4f out: wknd wl over 1f out) | s.h | **8** | 20/1 | 55 | 23 |
| 4449[4] | **Fools of Pride (IRE) (38)** (RHollinshead) **3-7-10**(7)ow2 FLynch(10) (nvr nrr) | 2 | **9** | 20/1 | 42 | 10 |
| 4489[5] | **Milngavie (IRE) (30)** (MJohnston) **5-8-3b** TWilliams(4) (led 2f: wknd over 4f out) | 2 | **10** | 10/1 | 34 | 10 |
| 4463[3] | **Endless Fantasy (47)** (CACyzer) **3-8-12** DBiggs(13) (a bhd) | 1 | **11** | 7/1[3] | 50 | 18 |
| 3986[13] | **Al Corniche (IRE) (39)** (KOCunningham-Brown) **3-8-1**(3) DWright(5) (a bhd) | 8 | **12** | 20/1 | 34 | 2 |
| 3470[14] | **Mr Copyforce (49)** (MissBSanders) **5-9-8v** WNewnes(8) (led 14f out to 5f out: wknd over 3f out) | 3 | **13** | 16/1 | 41 | 17 |
| 3425[6] | **Chucklestone (36)** (JSKing) **12-8-9** JTate(1) (bhd fnl 7f: t.o) | dist | **14** | 11/1 | — | — |
| | | | | (SP 135.8%) | **14 Rn** | |

**3m 27.77** (5.77) CSF £200.69 CT £705.64 TOTE £27.30: £8.60 £2.40 £1.90 (£58.90) Trio £216.60 OWNER Mr G. H. Tufts (NEWMARKET) BRED Sheikh Mohammed bin Rashid al Maktoum

WEIGHT FOR AGE 3yo-8lb

## 4531 LADBROKE ALL-WEATHER TROPHY H'CAP (Qualifier) (0-70) (3-Y.O+) (Class E)

3-30 (3-35) **7f (Equitrack)** £3,138.30 (£950.40: £464.20: £221.10) Stalls: Low GOING minus 0.24 sec per fur (FST)

| | | | | SP | RR | SF |
|---|---|---|---|---|---|---|
| 4502[3] | **Four of Spades (70)** (PDEvans) **4-9-7b**(7) AmandaSanders(10) (lw: w ldr: led 4f out to over 2f out: led wl over 1f out: edgd rt ins fnl f: all out) | — | **1** | 6/1[2] | 75 | 43 |
| 4503[9] | **Quinzii Martin (48)** (DHaydnJones) **7-8-3v**(3) DWright(6) (hdwy over 3f out: rdn over 1f out: r.o wl ins fnl f) | s.h | **2** | 33/1 | 53 | 21 |
| 4457[10] | **Field of Vision (IRE) (64)** (MJohnston) **5-9-8b** TWilliams(12) (lw: a.p: rdn 2f out: ev ch over 1f out: 3rd & btn whn snatched up nr fin) | 1½ | **3** | 9/1 | 66 | 34 |
| 4441[7] | **Robellion (60)** (DWPArbuthnot) **4-9-4v** SWhitworth(5) (b: hdwy over 3f out: rdn over 2f out: r.o) | 1½ | **4** | 20/1 | 58 | 26 |
| 4456[3] | **Fort Knox (IRE) (52)** (RMFlower) **4-8-10b** DBiggs(7) (lw: a.p: rdn & ev ch 2f out: one pce) | ½ | **5** | 7/1[3] | 49 | 17 |
| 3977[9] | **Intendant (55)** (JGFitzGerald) **3-8-13** MWigham(13) (hdwy over 2f out: one pce) | 2½ | **6** | 9/1 | 47 | 14 |
| 4272[8] | **What a Nightmare (IRE) (67)** (PHowling) **3-9-11** JQuinn(4) (lost pl over 4f out: one pce fnl 2f) | nk | **7** | 12/1 | 59 | 26 |
| 4457[4] | **Invocation (68)** (AMoore) **8-9-5**(7) ALakeman(9) (b.hind: lw: led 3f: led over 2f out tl wl over 1f out: wknd fnl f) | 2 | **8** | 9/1 | 54 | 22 |
| 1797[13] | **Indrapura (IRE) (69)** (PFICole) **3-9-13** CRutter(3) (nvr nrr) | 2½ | **9** | 12/1 | 50 | 17 |
| 4165[17] | **Rockcracker (IRE) (57)** (GGMargarson) **3-9-1** AClark(8) (lw: hdwy over 3f out: wknd over 2f out) | ½ | **10** | 33/1 | 37 | 4 |
| 4421[2] | **Crystal Heights (FR) (68)** (RJO'Sullivan) **7-9-12** SSanders(1) (b: lw: s.s: bhd fnl 4f) | ¾ | **11** | 7/4[1] | 45 | 13 |
| 3874[10] | **Tyrian Purple (IRE) (60)** (TJNaughton) **7-8-11b**(7) TAshley(11) (b: lw: prom over 2f) | ¾ | **12** | 14/1 | 36 | 4 |
| 3715[21] | **Wardara (67)** (CADwyer) **3-9-11v** CDwyer(2) (s.s: a bhd) | 3 | **13** | 20/1 | 37 | 4 |
| | | | | (SP 130.6%) | **13 Rn** | |

**1m 27.04** (3.04) CSF £161.59 CT £1,630.64 TOTE £6.60: £1.50 £5.30 £2.20 (£63.90) Trio £62.60 OWNER Mrs Anna Sanders (WELSHPOOL) BRED Hesmonds Stud Ltd

STEWARDS' ENQUIRY Amanda Sanders susp. 30/12/95-1/1/96 (careless riding).

T/Plpt: £679.60 (13.75 Tckts). T/Qdpt: Not won; £171.20 to Haydock 16/12/95. AK

# 4525-LINGFIELD (L-H) (Standard)
## Monday December 18th

## 4532 ATROPOS H'CAP (0-60) (I) (3-Y.O+) (Class F)

12-00 (12-02) **1m 2f (Equitrack)** £2,439.00 (£684.00: £333.00) Stalls: Low GOING minus 0.34 sec per fur (FST)

| | | | | SP | RR | SF |
|---|---|---|---|---|---|---|
| 4452[14] | **Total Rach (IRE) (48)** (RIngram) **3-9-2b** WWoods(5) (hld up: led over 3f out: clr over 2f out: rdn out) | — | **1** | 7/1 | 55 | 29 |
| 3544* | **Watch Me Go (IRE) (46)** (BobJones) **6-9-3** MWigham(8) (b: hld up: rdn over 6f out: r.o ins fnl f) | 3½ | **2** | 8/1 | 47 | 24 |
| 4452[12] | **Bakers Daughter (49)** (JRArnold) **3-9-3** JQuinn(7) (a.p: swtg: hld up: led over 4f out tl over 3f out: one pce) | nk | **3** | 16/1 | 50 | 24 |
| 4452[8] | **Smocking (25)** (JPearce) **5-7-10** GBardwell(3) (lost pl 5f out: rallied fnl f: r.o) | ½ | **4** | 25/1 | 25 | 2 |
| 4385[12] | **Dia Georgy (47)** (MrsNMacauley) **4-9-4** SSanders(11) (rdn & hdwy over 3f out: one pce) | 1¾ | **5** | 12/1 | 44 | 21 |
| 4420[5] | **Pine Essence (USA) (44)** (JLEyre) **4-9-1** RLappin(13) (lw: a.p: rdn over 4f out: one pce) | ½ | **6** | 4/1[2] | 41 | 18 |
| 4450[7] | **North Esk (USA) (48)** (CADwyer) **6-9-5** CDwyer(1) (nt clr run 5f out: hmpd on ins over 2f out: nvr nr to chal) | 2 | **7** | 11/2[3] | 41 | 18 |
| 4420[2] | **Wahem (IRE) (34)** (CEBrittain) **5-8-5** JFEgan(9) (lost pl over 8f out: no hdwy fnl 2f) | 7 | **8** | 9/4[1] | 16 | — |
| 4415[8] | **Zacaroon (56)** (JFfitch-Heyes) **4-9-10**(3) DWright(2) (b.hind: lw: sme hdwy over 3f out: sn wknd) | nk | **9** | 14/1 | 38 | 15 |
| | **Tudor Flight (38)** (AGNewcombe) **4-8-9** JTate(10) (a bhd) | 2 | **10** | 20/1 | 16 | — |
| 4505[11] | **Absolute Ruler (IRE) (48)** (JLHarris) **4-9-5b** RHughes(6) (b.off hind: led over 6f out tl over 4f out: wknd 3f out) | ¾ | **11** | 33/1 | 25 | 2 |
| 4438[2] | **Swynford Flyer (35)** (JAHarris) **6-8-1**(5) CAdamson(12) (led over 7f out tl over 6f out: wknd over 4f out) | 1 | **12** | 6/1 | 11 | — |
| 4451[7] | **Shoodah (IRE) (32)** (PHayward) **4-7-12**(5) PFessey(4) (lw: led over 2f: wknd 6f out: t.o) | dist | **13** | 33/1 | — | — |
| | | | | (SP 138.8%) | **13 Rn** | |

**2m 8.39** (4.09) CSF £65.48 CT £822.36 TOTE £6.70: £2.30 £4.40 £13.30 (£80.40) Trio £143.30 OWNER Mrs A. V. Cappuccini (EPSOM) BRED Oldtown Stud

WEIGHT FOR AGE 3yo-3lb

## 4533 WITCH OF ENDOR CLAIMING STKS (2-Y.O) (Class F)

12-30 (12-31) **5f (Equitrack)** £2,738.60 (£769.60: £375.80) Stalls: High GOING minus 0.34 sec per fur (FST)

| | | | | SP | RR | SF |
|---|---|---|---|---|---|---|
| 4473[5] | **Gi La High (57)** (JBerry) **2-8-4**ow1 AMcGlone(5) (hdwy over 3f out: hrd rdn over 1f out: led nr fin) | — | **1** | 13/2 | 62 | 16 |

| | | | | SP | RR | SF |
|---|---|---|---|---|---|---|
| *4511[3]* | **Lady Eclat (59)** (JAGlover) **2-7-12v**(3) DWright(2) (outpcd: hrd rdn over 1f out: hdwy fnl f: r.o wl) | 1½ | **2** | 5/2[1] | 55 | 9 |
| *4473[3]* | **Charterhouse Xpres (67)** (MMcCormack) **2-9-2b** ACulhane(9) (b.hind: led 3f out: clr over 1f out: hrd rdn fnl f: hdd nr fin) | s.h | **3** | 9/2[3] | 70 | 24 |
| *4461[7]* | **Rowlandsons Stud (IRE) (63)** (GLMoore) **2-8-7**ow1 SWhitworth(3) (outpcd: hdwy over 1f out: r.o ins fnl f) | ¾ | **4** | 4/1[2] | 58 | 12 |
| *4509[12]* | **Gracious Gretclo (53)** (CJHill) **2-8-3** JQuinn(6) (lw: a.p: hrd rdn over 1f out: one pce) | ½ | **5** | 10/1 | 53 | 7 |
| 3157[12] | **Double Or Bust** (AGNewcombe) **2-7-5**(5)ow1 PFessey(7) (swtg: led 2f: rdn 2f out: wknd ins fnl f) | 1¼ | **6** | 13/2 | 41 | — |
| *4461[10]* | **Latzio (40)** (BAPearce) **2-7-11b** GBardwell(4) (b.hind: rdn thrght: bhd fnl 2f) | 4 | **7** | 20/1 | 30 | — |
| 4045[17] | **Carwyn's Choice (42)** (PCClarke) **2-7-10**ow1 NAdams(8) (s.s: a bhd) | 1¼ | **8** | 50/1 | 24 | — |
| *4124[10]* | **Chemcast (58)** (DNicholls) **2-9-2** AlexGreaves(1) (lw: bhd fnl 2f) | 1¼ | **9** | 8/1 | 41 | — |

(SP 120.3%) **9 Rn**

**60.7 secs** (2.70) CSF £22.75 TOTE £5.60: £1.30 £1.50 £2.00 (£8.50) Trio £7.30 OWNER Mr Basheer Kielany (COCKERHAM) BRED J. H. Heath

## 4534 HOTSPUR AMATEUR LIMITED STKS (0-60) (3-Y.O+) (Class F)

1-00 (1-02) **1m 4f (Equitrack)** £2,801.60 (£787.60: £384.80) Stalls: Low GOING minus 0.34 sec per fur (FST)

| | | | | SP | RR | SF |
|---|---|---|---|---|---|---|
| *4513[4]* | **Stalled (IRE) (53)** (PTWalwyn) **5-10-8**(5) MarchionessofBlandford(8) (lw: stdy hdwy over 3f out: led last strides) | — | **1** | 9/2[3] | 66 | 47 |
| *4507[2]* | **Manful (58)** (JHetherton) **3-10-1**(3) MissAElsey(11) (hdwy over 6f out: led over 2f out: hdd last strides) | hd | **2** | 5/2[1] | 62 | 38 |
| *4516[6]* | **Kenyatta (USA) (30)** (AMoore) **6-10-4**(5) MrsJMoore(5) (led 2f: lost pl over 4f out: rallied over 1f out: r.o one pce) | 6 | **3** | 20/1 | 54 | 35 |
| *4475[2]* | **Risky Tu (45)** (PAKelleway) **4-9-13**(5) MissSKelleway(2) (lw: a.p: ev ch over 1f out: wknd fnl f) | ½ | **4** | 9/2[3] | 48 | 29 |
| 3818[12] | **Streaky Hawk (USA) (53)** (JPearce) **3-10-4** MrsLPearce(6) (b.off fore: a.p: rdn over 3f out: one pce) | 1 | **5** | 8/1 | 52 | 28 |
| 2661[7] | **Sorisky (34)** (BGubby) **3-9-13**(5) MrsMTingey(7) (swtg: bit bkwd: led 10f out tl over 2f out: sn wknd) | 8 | **6** | 66/1 | 41 | 17 |
| 3884[P] | **Quick Million (38)** (JWMullins) **4-9-11**(7) MrsKTierney(10) (nvr nrr) | 2 | **7** | 33/1 | 34 | 15 |
| *4507[11]* | **Media Messenger (40)** (NPLittmoden) **6-10-2**(7) MrOGunter(4) (nvr nrr) | 1¼ | **8** | 33/1 | 37 | 18 |
| 2392[8] | **In the Money (IRE) (57)** (RHollinshead) **6-10-9** MrMRimell(13) (prom 8f) | ¾ | **9** | 9/1 | 36 | 17 |
| *4364[10]* | **Water Hazard (IRE) (53)** (SDow) **3-10-4** MrTMcCarthy(1) (b.hind: bhd fnl 4f) | 5 | **10** | 4/1[2] | 29 | 5 |
| 4205[13] | **Huish Cross (44)** (SGKnight) **3-9-10**(3) MrJCulloty(12) (lw: hdwy 10f out: wknd over 4f) | 2½ | **11** | 33/1 | 21 | — |
| 4135[6] | **Air Command (BAR) (34)** (CTNash) **5-10-4**(5) MrPPhillips(9) (b: bhd fnl 10f) | 5 | **12** | 25/1 | 19 | — |
| 1714[20] | **Bite the Bullet (25)** (AJChamberlain) **4-10-2**(7) MrYMehmet(3) (bhd fnl 10f: t.o) | 30 | **13** | 100/1 | — | — |

(SP 126.0%) **13 Rn**

**2m 36.75** (6.75) CSF £16.02 TOTE £7.00: £1.90 £1.30 £5.50 (£7.60) Trio £31.90 OWNER Mrs P. T. Walwyn (LAMBOURN) BRED D. Aykroyd
WEIGHT FOR AGE 3yo-5lb

## 4535 INVICTA BLOODSTOCK MAIDEN STKS (I) (2-Y.O) (Class D)

1-30 (1-31) **1m (Equitrack)** £2,981.25 (£900.00: £437.50: £206.25) Stalls: High GOING minus 0.34 sec per fur (FST)

| | | | | SP | RR | SF |
|---|---|---|---|---|---|---|
| *4501[2]* | **Red Rusty (USA)** (DMorris) **2-9-0** JTate(2) (lw: mde all: rdn out) | — | **1** | 4/1[3] | 69 | 24 |
| *4439[3]* | **Sahhar** (RWArmstrong) **2-9-0** JWilliams(7) (lw: hdwy 5f out: hrd rdn over 1f out: r.o) | 2 | **2** | 2/1[1] | 65 | 20 |
| 3340[10] | **Well Drawn** (HCandy) **2-9-0** WNewnes(5) (rdn over 4f out: hdwy over 1f out: r.o wl ins fnl f) | s.h | **3** | 9/4[2] | 65 | 20 |
| | **Elegantissima** (SDow) **2-8-9** DBiggs(3) (b.hind: neat: a.p: chsd wnr over 4f out tl ins fnl f: one pce) | 1½ | **4** | 14/1 | 57 | 12 |
| | **Docklands Limo** (BJMcMath) **2-9-0** MWigham(8) (b.hind: neat: bit bkwd: s.s: nvr nr to chal) | 4 | **5** | 10/1 | 54 | 9 |
| | **Only (USA)** (RHannon) **2-9-0** RHughes(1) (str: bkwd: chsd wnr over 3f: wknd over 1f out) | 3 | **6** | 15/2 | 48 | 3 |
| *4408[5]* | **Napier Star** (MrsNMacauley) **2-8-4**(5) AmandaSanders(9) (hdwy over 3f out: sn wknd) | 2½ | **7** | 33/1 | 38 | — |
| | **Hampi (USA)** (SPCWoods) **2-8-9** WWoods(6) (neat: s.i.s: a bhd) | nk | **8** | 16/1 | 37 | — |
| 3427[11] | **Tartan Express (IRE) (50)** (BAPearce) **2-9-0** JFEgan(4) (bit bkwd: prom over 3f) | 11 | **9** | 33/1 | 20 | — |

(SP 123.4%) **9 Rn**

**1m 40.86** (3.46) CSF £12.70 TOTE £4.10: £1.60 £1.40 £1.10 (£6.00) Trio £3.50 OWNER Exors of the Late Mr R E Mason (NEWMARKET) BRED Ron Mason

## 4536 LE REVE H'CAP (0-85) (3-Y.O+) (Class D)

2-00 (2-01) **6f (Equitrack)** £3,656.90 (£1,107.20: £540.60: £257.30) Stalls: Low GOING minus 0.34 sec per fur (FST)

| | | | | SP | RR | SF |
|---|---|---|---|---|---|---|
| *4487[2]* | **Robo Magic (USA) (67)** (LMontagueHall) **3-8-13** JFEgan(8) (chsd ldr: hrd rdn over 1f out: led wl ins fnl f: r.o wl) | — | **1** | 9/2[2] | 72 | 36 |
| *4488[5]* | **Southern Dominion (58)** (MJohnston) **3-8-4b** NAdams(9) (lw: led: hrd rdn over 1f out: hdd wl ins fnl f: unable qckn) | 1¼ | **2** | 8/1 | 60 | 24 |
| *4441[6]* | **Patsy Grimes (64)** (JSMoore) **5-8-10** AMcGlone(6) (hld up: hrd rdn over 1f out: r.o one pce) | 1¼ | **3** | 11/2 | 62 | 26 |
| *4459[2]* | **Speedy Classic (USA) (67)** (MJHeaton-Ellis) **6-8-13** WNewnes(1) (a.p: n.m.r on ins 5f out: rdn 2f out: r.o one pce) | s.h | **4** | 5/1[3] | 65 | 29 |
| *4515[3]* | **Our Shadee (USA) (57)** (KTIvory) **5-8-3v** GBardwell(7) (outpcd: hdwy fnl f: r.o) | 1¼ | **5** | 9/1 | 52 | 16 |
| *4487** | **Half Tone (64)** (RMFlower) **3-8-10b** DBiggs(2) (lw: hdwy over 2f out: hrd rdn over 1f out: one pce) | hd | **6** | 4/1[1] | 59 | 23 |
| *4441[4]* | **Sir Tasker (72)** (JLHarris) **7-9-4** SSanders(3) (prom 4f) | 6 | **7** | 12/1 | 51 | 15 |
| *4508[10]* | **Tafahhus (80)** (MJPolglase) **3-9-12** MTebbutt(4) (dwlt: a bhd) | 7 | **8** | 16/1 | 40 | 4 |
| 2677[4] | **Rockville Pike (IRE) (82)** (SDow) **3-10-0** WWoods(5) (dwlt: a bhd) | 1¾ | **9** | 20/1 | 37 | 1 |
| 4322* | **Elle Shaped (IRE) (82)** (ABailey) **5-9-11**(3) DWright(10) (a bhd) | 5 | **10** | 6/1 | 24 | — |

(SP 124.0%) **10 Rn**

**1m 12.87** (2.27) CSF £38.86 CT £188.56 TOTE £7.80: £2.60 £3.10 £2.80 (£23.60) Trio £92.00 OWNER Mr A D Green and Partners (EPSOM) BRED Curtis C. Green
STEWARDS' ENQUIRY Newnes susp. 30/12/95 & 1/1/96 (excessive use of whip).

## 4537 ATROPOS H'CAP (0-60) (II) (3-Y.O+) (Class F)

2-30 (2-31) **1m 2f (Equitrack)** £2,426.40 (£680.40: £331.20) Stalls: Low GOING minus 0.34 sec per fur (FST)

| | | | | SP | RR | SF |
|---|---|---|---|---|---|---|
| 4261[14] | **Wet Patch (IRE) (60)** (RHannon) **3-10-0** RHughes(1) (lw: stdy hdwy over 3f out: rdn over 2f out: led ins fnl f: r.o wl) | — | **1** | 9/2[2] | 69 | 41 |
| | **Explosive Power (51)** (GCBravery) **4-9-8** SWhitworth(10) (hld up: led over 1f out tl ins fnl f: unable qckn) | 1¼ | **2** | 10/1 | 58 | 33 |
| 4467a* | **Real Madrid (34)** (GPEnright) **4-8-5v** NAdams(8) (dwlt: hdwy over 3f out: rdn over 2f out: r.o ins fnl f) | 3 | **3** | 9/1 | 36 | 11 |

| Form | Horse / details | Dist | Pos | SP | RR | SF |
|---|---|---|---|---|---|---|
| 4335[6] | **Rival Bid (USA) (55)** (MrsNMacauley) **7-9-7**(5) AmandaSanders(2) (dwlt: stdy hdwy over 3f out: nt clr run on ins wl over 1f out: r.o) | hd | **4** | 4/1[1] | 57 | 32 |
| 4420[9] | **Never So Rite (IRE) (48)** (DWPArbuthnot) **3-9-2** JQuinn(3) (a.p: rdn over 3f out: one pce) | 2½ | **5** | 8/1 | 46 | 18 |
| 4514[5] | **Snake Plissken (IRE) (48)** (DHaydnJones) **4-9-2**(3) DWright(9) (lw: led over 8f) | ½ | **6** | 10/1 | 45 | 20 |
| 4416[5] | **Colosse (44)** (JLEyre) **3-8-12** RLappin(12) (a.p: led wl over 1f out: sn hdd: wknd fnl f) | s.h | **7** | 9/2[2] | 41 | 13 |
| 4445[5] | **Just Flamenco (42)** (MJRyan) **4-8-13** DBiggs(4) (prom 5f) | 4 | **8** | 7/1[3] | 33 | 8 |
| 4390[6] | **Greek Gold (IRE) (44)** (DNicholls) **6-9-1** AlexGreaves(11) (prom over 7f) | 2½ | **9** | 10/1 | 31 | 6 |
| 4521[10] | **Palacegate Gold (IRE) (38)** (RJHodges) **6-8-9** AMcGlone(5) (bhd fnl 4f) | 2½ | **10** | 20/1 | 21 | — |
| 4436[4] | **Mary Macblain (39)** (JLHarris) **6-8-10** SSanders(7) (bhd fnl 4f) | ½ | **11** | 9/1 | 21 | — |
| 4458[12] | **La Bossette (IRE) (31)** (RIngram) **3-7-13** GBardwell(6) (prom over 5f) | 3 | **12** | 25/1 | 8 | — |
| 449[6] | **Ketchican (40)** (SGKnight) **3-8-8** JWilliams(13) (s.s: a wl bhd: t.o) | 30 | **13** | 25/1 | — | — |

(SP 139.7%) **13 Rn**

**2m 8.24** (3.94) CSF £52.35 CT £376.17 TOTE £7.10: £2.40 £4.20 £3.80 (£24.30) Trio £38.40 OWNER Mr Peter Hammond (MARLBOROUGH) BRED S. Niarchos

WEIGHT FOR AGE 3yo-3lb

## 4538 INVICTA BLOODSTOCK MAIDEN STKS (II) (2-Y.O) (Class D)

3-00 (3-02) **1m (Equitrack)** £2,981.25 (£900.00: £437.50: £206.25) Stalls: High GOING minus 0.34 sec per fur (FST)

| Form | Horse / details | Dist | Pos | SP | RR | SF |
|---|---|---|---|---|---|---|
| 4075[4] | **Apartments Abroad (54)** (KMcAuliffe) **2-8-9** JFEgan(7) (b.hind: a.p: rdn over 3f out: led ins fnl f: r.o wl) | — | **1** | 3/1[2] | 64 | 3 |
| | **Shenango (IRE)** (GWragg) **2-9-0** AMcGlone(6) (scope: a.p: rdn over 3f out: wandered ins fnl f: r.o) | hd | **2** | 13/8[1] | 69 | 8 |
| | **Note of Caution (USA)** (LordHuntingdon) **2-8-9** SSanders(9) (lt-f: a.p: led 2f out tl ins fnl f: unable qckn) | 2 | **3** | 5/1[3] | 60 | — |
| 4439[13] | **Suparoy (50)** (TGMills) **2-9-0** JQuinn(1) (hdwy over 1f out: r.o) | 3 | **4** | 12/1 | 59 | — |
| 2597[4] | **Straight Thinking (USA)** (PFICole) **2-9-0** CRutter(5) (lw: lost pl over 4f out: r.o one pce fnl 2f) | ¾ | **5** | 5/1[3] | 57 | — |
| | **Native Song** (MJHaynes) **2-8-9** SWhitworth(3) (b.hind: unf: a bhd) | 5 | **6** | 10/1 | 42 | — |
| 4518[7] | **Jemsilverthorn (IRE) (45)** (JJBridger) **2-9-0b** GBardwell(4) (led 6f: wknd over 1f out) | ¾ | **7** | 33/1 | 46 | — |
| | **Eben Naas (USA)** (SCWilliams) **2-9-0** JTate(2) (w'like: bit bkwd: s.s: a bhd) | ¾ | **8** | 10/1 | 44 | — |
| 4365[7] | **Allstars Dancer** (TJNaughton) **2-8-2**(7) TAshley(8) (prom 5f) | 1¾ | **9** | 33/1 | 36 | — |

(SP 128.2%) **9 Rn**

**1m 42.25** (18.25) CSF £8.92 TOTE £4.40: £1.60 £1.30 £1.50 (£8.60) Trio £4.10 OWNER Mr Peter Barclay (LAMBOURN) BRED Fulling Mill Farm and Stud

## 4539 LADBROKE ALL-WEATHER TROPHY H'CAP (Qualifier) (0-80) (3-Y.O+) (Class D)

3-30 (3-33) **7f (Equitrack)** £3,758.30 (£1,138.40: £556.20: £265.10) Stalls: Low GOING minus 0.34 sec per fur (FST)

| Form | Horse / details | Dist | Pos | SP | RR | SF |
|---|---|---|---|---|---|---|
| 4520[2] | **Duke Valentino (71)** (RHollinshead) **3-9-5** MWigham(10) (hdwy over 3f out: rdn over 2f out: led wl ins fnl f: r.o wl) | — | **1** | 5/1[1] | 83 | 50 |
| 4486* | **Sand Star (67)** (DHaydnJones) **3-8-12**(3) DWright(8) (led 1f: led over 1f out: hrd rdn: hdd wl ins fnl f: unable qckn) | ¾ | **2** | 10/1 | 77 | 44 |
| 4392[8] | **Present Situation (69)** (LordHuntingdon) **4-9-3** SSanders(9) (lw: a.p: rdn over 2f out: one pce fnl f) | 1 | **3** | 12/1 | 76 | 44 |
| 4432[11] | **Super Benz (59)** (JLEyre) **9-8-7** RLappin(5) (b: lw: rdn & hdwy over 1f out: r.o) | 1½ | **4** | 20/1 | 63 | 31 |
| 4493[3] | **Tatika (66)** (GWragg) **5-8-7**(7) GMilligan(15) (lw: hdwy over 3f out: rdn over 2f out: one pce) | 1 | **5** | 8/1[3] | 67 | 35 |
| 4476[7] | **Bentico (70)** (MrsNMacauley) **6-8-13v**(5) AmandaSanders(12) (no hdwy fnl 3f) | 2½ | **6** | 20/1 | 66 | 34 |
| 4512[3] | **Deeply Vale (IRE) (69)** (GLMoore) **4-9-3** SWhitworth(7) (nvr nr to chal) | 3 | **7** | 11/1 | 58 | 26 |
| 4386[7] | **Digpast (IRE) (67)** (RJO'Sullivan) **5-9-1b** DBiggs(11) (nvr nrr) | hd | **8** | 16/1 | 56 | 24 |
| 4510[3] | **Master Millfield (IRE) (70)** (CJHill) **3-8-13**(5) PFessey(3) (prom over 2f) | 2½ | **9** | 6/1[2] | 54 | 21 |
| 4527[3] | **Dancing Heart (74)** (BJMeehan) **3-9-8b** JFEgan(13) (led 6f out: clr 5f out: hdd over 1f out: sn wknd) | 1¼ | **10** | 16/1 | 55 | 22 |
| 4357[2] | **Milos (67)** (TJNaughton) **4-8-8**(7) TAshley(6) (lw: a bhd) | ½ | **11** | 12/1 | 46 | 14 |
| 4435[4] | **Pengamon (80)** (HJCollingridge) **3-10-0** JQuinn(1) (b.off hind: prom over 4f) | hd | **12** | 8/1[3] | 60 | 27 |
| 4457* | **Superoo (72)** (MrsPSly) **9-9-6** ACulhane(14) (hdwy over 3f out: sn wknd) | 1¼ | **13** | 10/1 | 48 | 16 |
| 4476[14] | **Nordinex (IRE) (73)** (RWArmstrong) **3-9-7** WWoods(2) (lw: bhd fnl 4f) | nk | **14** | 14/1 | 49 | 16 |
| 4421* | **Anzio (IRE) (76)** (BAPearce) **4-9-10b** RHughes(4) (b: b.hind: prom 4f) | 4 | **15** | 5/1[1] | 42 | 10 |

(SP 139.7%) **15 Rn**

**1m 24.98** (0.98) CSF £57.29 CT £545.94 TOTE £7.40: £2.90 £5.60 £2.90 (£74.40) Trio £452.50 OWNER Mr J. E. Bigg (UPPER LONGDON) BRED Shadwell Estate Company Limited

T/Jkpt: Not won; £6,886.15 to Lingfield 19/12/95. T/Plpt: £175.00 (66.8 Tckts). T/Qdpt: £13.80 (3.65 Tckts). AK

# 4532-LINGFIELD (L-H) (Standard)
## Tuesday December 19th

## 4540 THIN RED LINE MAIDEN STKS (I) (3-Y.O+) (Class D)

12-00 (12-05) **7f (Equitrack)** £3,185.00 (£962.00: £468.00: £221.00) Stalls: Low GOING minus 0.32 sec per fur (FST)

| Form | Horse / details | Dist | Pos | SP | RR | SF |
|---|---|---|---|---|---|---|
| 1168[6] | **Samwar (78)** (MissGayKelleway) **3-8-13** RHughes(5) (hld up: a gng wl: led on bit over 1f out: shkn up: v easily) | — | **1** | Evens[1] | 76+ | 37 |
| 4382[4] | **Errant (64)** (DJSCosgrove) **3-8-13** JQuinn(8) (b: chsd ldr over 4f out: led wl over 1f out: sn hdd: unable qckn) | 6 | **2** | 13/8[2] | 62 | 23 |
| | **Raffles Rooster** (AGNewcombe) **3-8-13** JTate(6) (hdwy over 1f out: r.o) | 2½ | **3** | 25/1 | 57 | 18 |
| 4409[4] | **Northern Grey (50)** (JBerry) **3-8-8**(5) PFessey(7) (lw: led over 5f: wknd fnl f) | 2½ | **4** | 14/1[3] | 51 | 12 |
| 4362[9] | **Anotherone to Note (42)** (NPLittmoden) **4-9-0b** TGMcLaughlin(10) (a.p: rdn over 2f out: sn wknd) | 1½ | **5** | 66/1 | 47 | 9 |
| 2490[11] | **Double Jeopardy (67)** (JWhite) **4-9-0** JWilliams(9) (outpcd: nvr nrr) | 1¼ | **6** | 14/1[3] | 45 | 7 |
| 3844[15] | **Considerable Charm (50)** (LordHuntingdon) **3-8-8** SSanders(3) (lw: prom over 3f) | 1½ | **7** | 14/1[3] | 36 | — |
| | **Trapper Norman** (RIngram) **3-8-13** WNewnes(4) (unf: bit bkwd: dwlt: a bhd) | 7 | **8** | 50/1 | 25 | — |
| 4049[13] | **Crowning Tino (36)** (MrsNMacauley) **3-8-3**(5) AmandaSanders(2) (prom over 3f) | 12 | **9** | 66/1 | — | — |
| | ***La Sorrela (IRE)*** (NACallaghan) **3-8-8** JFEgan(1) (Withdrawn not under Starter's orders: ref to ent stalls) | | **W** | 14/1[3] | — | — |

(SP 123.6%) **9 Rn**

**1m 25.78** (1.78) CSF £2.88 TOTE £2.40: £1.30 £1.10 £2.10 (£1.10) Trio £8.30 OWNER Maygain Ltd (WHITCOMBE) BRED Juddmonte Farms

## 4541 LIGHT BRIGADE MEDIAN AUCTION MAIDEN STKS (2-Y.O) (Class F)
12-30 (12-31) **5f (Equitrack)** £2,637.80 (£740.80: £361.40) Stalls: High GOING minus 0.32 sec per fur (FST)

| | | | | SP | RR | SF |
|---|---|---|---|---|---|---|
| *4360*[3] | **Miss Pickpocket (IRE)** (PAKelleway) **2-8-9** MWigham(1) (rdn thrght: chsd ldrs: led ins fnl f: drvn out) | — | **1** | 6/4[1] | 63 | 7 |
| *4483*[12] | **Bouton d'Or (42)** (PHowling) **2-8-9** JQuinn(4) (b.hind: hld up: rdn 2f out: ev ch ins fnl f: unable qckn) | 1¼ | **2** | 33/1 | 59 | 3 |
| *4483*[4] | **Impington (IRE) (55)** (WRMuir) **2-8-9** SDWilliams(3) (w ldr: led over 1f out tl ins fnl f: one pce) | nk | **3** | 7/4[2] | 58 | 2 |
| *4519*[4] | **Lavender Bloom (IRE)** (MCunningham,Ireland) **2-8-9** JFEgan(2) (led over 3f: wknd fnl f) | 3 | **4** | 4/1[3] | 48 | — |
| | **Blue Duck (IRE)** (TDBarron) **2-9-0** WNewnes(5) (neat: bit bkwd: outpcd) | 10 | **5** | 8/1 | 21 | — |
| | | | | (SP 110.4%) | **5 Rn** | |

**61.73 secs** (3.73) CSF £23.83 TOTE £1.80: £1.30 £2.50 (£23.80) OWNER Mr F. M. Kalla (NEWMARKET) BRED Limestone Stud

## 4542 INKERMAN H'CAP (0-60) (3-Y.O+) (Class F)
1-00 (1-01) **5f (Equitrack)** £2,776.40 (£780.40: £381.20) Stalls: High GOING minus 0.32 sec per fur (FST)

| | | | | SP | RR | SF |
|---|---|---|---|---|---|---|
| 4113[5] | **Super Rocky (58)** (RBastiman) **6-9-9**(5) HBastiman(10) (a.p: rdn 2f out: led wl ins fnl f: r.o wl) | — | **1** | 9/2[3] | 72 | 46 |
| 3139[10] | **Distant Dynasty (52)** (BAPearce) **5-9-8** SSanders(6) (led over 2f: led ins fnl f: sn hdd: unable qckn) | 1 | **2** | 11/1 | 63 | 37 |
| *4488** | **Cheeky Chappy (47)** (DWChapman) **4-8-12b**(5) PFessey(3) (a.p: led over 2f out tl ins fnl f: one pce) | 1½ | **3** | 7/4[1] | 53 | 27 |
| *4478*[10] | **Thick as Thieves (53)** (RonaldThompson) **3-9-9** GBardwell(7) (s.s: outpcd: hdwy over 1f out: r.o) | 1½ | **4** | 33/1 | 54 | 28 |
| *4458*[6] | **Halbert (45)** (PBurgoyne) **6-8-8v**(7) DSweeney(1) (a.p: rdn over 1f out: one pce) | s.h | **5** | 7/2[2] | 46 | 20 |
| *4460*[7] | **Daaniera (IRE) (47)** (PHowling) **5-8-10v**(7) DebbieBiggs(4) (b.hind: lw: a.p: rdn over 1f out: one pce) | hd | **6** | 11/1 | 48 | 22 |
| 3134[10] | **Riskie Things (56)** (JSMoore) **4-9-12** JFEgan(8) (nvr nr to chal) | 1¾ | **7** | 10/1 | 51 | 25 |
| *4484*[9] | **Mister Raider (45)** (SMellor) **3-9-1b** JWilliams(2) (lw: outpcd) | 1¾ | **8** | 9/1 | 35 | 9 |
| | **My Bonus (52)** (DJSCosgrove) **5-9-8** MWigham(5) (outpcd) | 2 | **9** | 50/1 | 35 | 9 |
| *4123*[9] | **Flashing Sabre (57)** (JBerry) **3-9-6**(7) PRoberts(9) (prom over 2f) | 2 | **10** | 14/1 | 34 | 8 |
| | | | | (SP 124.1%) | **10 Rn** | |

**60.41 secs** (2.41) CSF £49.87 CT £109.59 TOTE £4.90: £1.30 £3.00 £1.20 (£32.40) Trio £22.10 OWNER Mr I. B. Barker (WETHERBY) BRED J. Berry

## 4543 THIN RED LINE MAIDEN STKS (II) (3-Y.O+) (Class D)
1-30 (1-31) **7f (Equitrack)** £3,185.00 (£962.00: £468.00: £221.00) Stalls: Low GOING minus 0.32 sec per fur (FST)

| | | | | SP | RR | SF |
|---|---|---|---|---|---|---|
| | **Bubble Wings (FR)** (SPCWoods) **3-8-8** WWoods(3) (w'like: s.s: hdwy & hung lft over 1f out: led & hung lft ins fnl f: r.o wl) | — | **1** | 4/1[2] | 61+ | 15 |
| 4065[8] | **Fresh Fruit Daily (74)** (PAKelleway) **3-8-8** MWigham(2) (a.p: rdn over 3f out: unable qckn ins fnl f) | 3 | **2** | 6/4[1] | 54 | 8 |
| *4451*[3] | **Awasha (IRE) (50)** (MissGayKelleway) **3-8-8** SSanders(4) (led tl ins fnl f: one pce) | ½ | **3** | 6/4[1] | 53 | 7 |
| *4382*[7] | **Warm Hearted (USA)** (RIngram) **3-8-13** NGwilliams(5) (a.p: hrd rdn over 2f out: one pce) | ¾ | **4** | 16/1 | 56 | 10 |
| *4525*[10] | **Desert Water (IRE) (45)** (JJBridger) **3-8-13b** JQuinn(7) (a.p: rdn over 2f out: wknd 1f out) | 6 | **5** | 33/1 | 43 | — |
| | **Red Channel (IRE)** (TCasey) **5-9-0** NAdams(8) (nvr nr to chal) | 1½ | **6** | 33/1 | 39 | — |
| 4249[19] | **Spumante (60)** (MPMuggeridge) **3-8-13** RHughes(6) (hld up: rdn over 3f out: wknd over 2f out) | 2½ | **7** | 12/1[3] | 33 | — |
| *4506*[9] | **Zalament (43)** (NPLittmoden) **3-8-8** TGMcLaughlin(1) (a bhd) | 6 | **8** | 25/1 | 15 | — |
| | **Golden Punch (USA)** (CACyzer) **4-9-0** DBiggs(10) (s.s: a wl bhd) | 1¼ | **9** | 25/1 | 17 | — |
| | **Pushka Fair** (TRWatson) **4-9-0** RCochrane(9) (hld up: rdn over 4f out: wknd over 3f out) | 2½ | **10** | 20/1 | 11 | — |
| | | | | (SP 131.9%) | **10 Rn** | |

**1m 27.26** (3.26) CSF £11.34 TOTE £4.40: £1.20 £1.40 £1.20 (£13.90) Trio £2.90 OWNER Dr Frank Chao (NEWMARKET) BRED H. S. Verrerie, Gue Foulon and Florent Couturier

## 4544 CRIMEA H'CAP (0-70) (3-Y.O+) (Class E)
2-00 (2-01) **1m 2f (Equitrack)** £3,166.90 (£959.20: £468.60: £223.30) Stalls: Low GOING minus 0.32 sec per fur (FST)

| | | | | SP | RR | SF |
|---|---|---|---|---|---|---|
| *4386*[5] | **Renown (65)** (LordHuntingdon) **3-9-6** SSanders(5) (lw: a.p: led over 1f out: drvn out) | — | **1** | 11/4[2] | 71 | 26 |
| *4451*[2] | **Kaafih Homm (IRE) (70)** (NACallaghan) **4-10-0** RCochrane(7) (b.hind: lw: dwlt: hld up: rdn over 1f out: ev ch ins fnl f: r.o) | hd | **2** | 13/8[1] | 76 | 34 |
| *4465*[2] | **No Speeches (IRE) (62)** (SDow) **4-9-6** JWilliams(6) (b.hind: dwlt: hdwy over 2f out: r.o one pce) | 1¾ | **3** | 5/1[3] | 65 | 23 |
| *4532*[12] | **Swynford Flyer (35)** (JAHarris) **6-7-2**(5) CAdamson(1) (no hdwy fnl 2f) | 3½ | **4** | 33/1 | 32 | — |
| *4505*[4] | **Hard Love (60)** (JLEyre) **3-9-1** RLappin(4) (nvr nr to chal) | 2½ | **5** | 12/1 | 53 | 8 |
| 4225[3] | **Burnt Sienna (IRE) (48)** (JSMoore) **3-8-3** JFEgan(3) (led over 8f) | 3½ | **6** | 16/1 | 36 | — |
| 2339[3] | **Pip's Dream (37)** (MJRyan) **4-7-9** GBardwell(2) (chsd ldr over 7f) | 4 | **7** | 6/1 | 18 | — |
| | | | | (SP 112.2%) | **7 Rn** | |

**2m 9.45** (5.15) CSF £7.23 TOTE £4.70: £2.50 £1.80 (£5.00) OWNER The Queen (WEST ILSLEY) BRED The Queen
WEIGHT FOR AGE 3yo-3lb

## 4545 ALMA NURSERY H'CAP (2-Y.O) (Class D)
2-30 (2-30) **6f (Equitrack)** £3,420.00 (£1,035.00: £505.00: £240.00) Stalls: Low GOING minus 0.32 sec per fur (FST)

| | | | | SP | RR | SF |
|---|---|---|---|---|---|---|
| *4473** | **Krystal Max (IRE) (80)** (TDBarron) **2-9-0**(7) KimberleyHart(8) (hld up: rdn over 1f out: led nr fin) | — | **1** | 9/2[2] | 84 | 30 |
| *4492** | **Time Clash (66)** (BPalling) **2-8-7** SDWilliams(7) (rdn over 2f out: hdwy over 1f out: r.o wl ins fnl f) | ½ | **2** | 3/1[1] | 69 | 15 |
| *4492*[3] | **Dancing Jack (55)** (JJBridger) **2-7-10** JQuinn(5) (a.p: led over 1f out tl ins fnl f: unable qckn) | hd | **3** | 6/1[3] | 57 | 3 |
| *4437*[6] | **No Sympathy (52)** (GLMoore) **2-7-2**(5) CAdamson(1) (lw: hld up: rdn over 2f out: one pce) | 1½ | **4** | 13/2 | 50 | — |
| *4511*[2] | **Marino Street (66)** (PDEvans) **2-8-7** SSanders(6) (b.off fore: a.p: rdn 2f out: one pce) | hd | **5** | 8/1 | 64 | 10 |
| *4511** | **Monkey Zanty (IRE) (55)** (JLHarris) **2-7-7**(3)ow1 7x DWright(4) (led over 4f: wknd fnl f) | 2½ | **6** | 9/2[2] | 46 | — |
| *4485*[9] | **Sovereign Prince (IRE) (55)** (NACallaghan) **2-7-5**(5)ow3 PFessey(2) (b.off hind: a bhd) | 1¼ | **7** | 14/1 | 40 | — |
| 4211[9] | **Miss Carottene (52)** (MJRyan) **2-7-7v** GBardwell(3) (outpcd: hdwy 2f out: wknd over 1f out) | 1 | **8** | 12/1 | 38 | — |
| | | | | (SP 114.5%) | **8 Rn** | |

**1m 14.01** (3.41) CSF £17.30 CT £72.58 TOTE £5.40: £1.50 £1.20 £2.10 (£9.40) OWNER The Oakfield Nurseries Partnership (THIRSK) BRED Baronrath Stud
LONG HANDICAP No Sympathy 7-1 Sovereign Prince (IRE) 7-1 Miss Carottene 7-5

## 4546 SEVASTOPOL APPRENTICE H'CAP (0-70) (3-Y.O+) (Class G)
3-00 (3-01) **1m 5f (Equitrack)** £2,471.80 (£694.80: £339.40) Stalls: Low GOING minus 0.32 sec per fur (FST)

| | | | | SP | RR | SF |
|---|---|---|---|---|---|---|
| *4516** | **Broughtons Formula (53)** (WJMusson) **5-8-12b**(5) 5x JWilkinson(11) (wl bhd 7f: gd hdwy over 4f out: rdn over 1f out: led nr fin) | — | 1 | 13/8 1 | 67 | 48 |
| 3676 11 | **Iron N Gold (41)** (AMoore) **3-7-8**(5) DDenby(3) (b.hind: hdwy over 4f out: led over 2f out: rdn: hdd nr fin) | nk | 2 | 12/1 | 54 | 30 |
| *4516 5* | **Just-Mana-Mou (IRE) (56)** (JJBridger) **3-8-7b**(7) TField(10) (a.p: led over 5f out tl over 2f out: one pce) | 7 | 3 | 11/1 | 60 | 36 |
| *4489 2* | **Outstayed Welcome (50)** (MJHaynes) **3-8-8** LNewton(7) (b.hind: led 8f out tl over 5f out: ev ch over 2f out: wknd over 1f out) | 2 | 4 | 9/2 2 | 52 | 28 |
| *4474 2* | **Skedaddle (48)** (RonaldThompson) **3-8-6** PFessey(5) (prom over 8f) | 8 | 5 | 33/1 | 40 | 16 |
| *4474** | **Rose of Glenn (47)** (BPalling) **4-8-8**(3) RHavlin(9) (hld up: rdn over 5f out: sn wknd) | ¾ | 6 | 12/1 | 39 | 20 |
| *4513 7* | **Hunza Story (35)** (NPLittmoden) **3-7-4**(3) CAdamson(1) (b.hind: nvr nr to chal) | 1½ | 7 | 33/1 | 24 | — |
| | **Forest Star (USA) (46)** (RAkehurst) **6-8-5b**(5) TAshley(8) (b: led 10f out to 8f out: wknd over 4f out) | 4 | 8 | 9/1 3 | 31 | 12 |
| 3710 10 | **Missed the Boat (IRE) (39)** (AGNewcombe) **5-7-12**(5) GMilligan(4) (a bhd) | 3 | 9 | 12/1 | 20 | 1 |
| 741 11 | **Sir Thomas Beecham (64)** (SDow) **5-9-7**(7) PBrookwood(12) (b.hind: a bhd) | 6 | 10 | 33/1 | 38 | 19 |
| *4387 12* | **Maronetta (35)** (MJRyan) **3-7-7** MBaird(2) (lw: led 3f: wknd 6f out) | 3½ | 11 | 20/1 | 4 | — |
| | | | | (SP 111.3%) | **11 Rn** | |

**2m 46.85** (3.65) CSF £18.65 CT £139.82 TOTE £2.30: £1.10 £3.20 £2.40 (£19.70) Trio £75.10 OWNER Crawford Gray & Aylett (NEWMARKET)
BRED The Lavington Stud
LONG HANDICAP Hunza Story 7-2 Maronetta 7-4
WEIGHT FOR AGE 3yo-6lb

T/Jkpt: £9,899.20 (0.2 Tckts); £11,154.05 to Ludlow 20/12/95. T/Plpt: £7.00 (1,566.87 Tckts). T/Qdpt: £4.70 (5.8 Tckts). AK

## 4507-WOLVERHAMPTON (L-H) - Saturday December 30th
**4547-4560 Abandoned**-Frost

# ABU DHABI (UAE) (L-H) (Good to firm)
## Sunday December 3rd

## 4561a ABU DHABI NATIONAL OIL CO. NATIONAL DAY CUP (3-Y.O+)
**1m (Turf)** £8,696.00 (£4,348.00: £2,609.00: £1,739.00)

| | | | SP | RR | SF |
|---|---|---|---|---|---|
| **Wafayt (IRE)** (DJSelvaratnam,UAE) **4-8-10** BDoyle | — | 1 | | 100 | — |
| **Ihtiraz** (KPMcLaughlin,UAE) **5-8-10** RHills | 1 | 2 | | 98 | — |
| **Great Lord (IRE)** (ECharpy,UAE) **6-8-10** WJSupple | 2¼ | 3 | | 94 | — |
| **Wathik (USA)** (PLRudkin,UAE) **5-8-11b** PaulEddery | 2¼ | 4 | | 90 | — |
| | | | | | **6 Rn** |

**1m 33.81** OWNER Sheikh Ahmed Al Maktoum BRED T. A. Ryan
**Wafayt (IRE)** tracked the leaders and produced a sustained challenge from two furlongs out to lead near the finish.
**Ihtiraz** came through to join the leaders over two furlongs out, but was headed close home.

# 4496a-EVRY (France) (R-H) (Soft)
## Tuesday December 5th

## 4562a PRIX ISONOMY (Listed) (2-Y.O)
1-10 (1-08) **1m 1f** £16,766.00 (£5,748.00: £3,593.00)

| | | | | SP | RR | SF |
|---|---|---|---|---|---|---|
| | **Supreme Commander (FR)** (AFabre,France) **2-8-11** TJarnet | — | 1 | | — | — |
| | **Le Tourron (FR)** (ELellouche,France) **2-8-11** OPeslier | ½ | 2 | | — | — |
| | **River Bay (USA)** (JEHammond,France) **2-8-11** WMongil | 4 | 3 | | — | — |
| 4264 4 | **Zaforum** (LMontagueHall) **2-8-11** GGuignard (btn approx 11½l) | | 8 | | — | — |
| | | | | | | **9 Rn** |

**2m 1.44** (11.44) P-M 1.80F: 1.10F 1.40F 1.60F (6.90F) OWNER Mr Wafic Said (CHANTILLY) BRED Bruce McNall
**4264 Zaforum** led until ridden and weakened over two furlongs out.

# NAKAYAMA (Tokyo, Japan) (Firm)
## Sunday December 17th

## 4563a SPRINTERS STKS (Gp 1) (3-Y.O+)
6-25 **6f (Turf)** £624,012.00 (£249,676.00: £156,871.00)

| | | | | SP | RR | SF |
|---|---|---|---|---|---|---|
| | **Hishi Akebono (USA)** (MSayama,Japan) **3-8-9** KTsunoda | — | 1 | | 128 | — |
| | **Biko Pegasus (USA)** (TYanagida,Japan) **4-8-13** NYokoyama | 1¼ | 2 | | 129 | — |
| 3187* | **So Factual (USA)** (SbinSuroor) **5-8-13** OPeslier | ¾ | 3 | | 127 | — |
| | | | | | | **16 Rn** |

**1m 8.1** Tote 230Y: 120Y 130Y 210Y (510Y) OWNER M. Abe BRED Swettenham Stud
**3187* So Factual (USA)** was close up turning for home, but could not quicken in the closing stages.

# *Raceform*

## TURF AND ALL-WEATHER FLAT RACING 1996

Complete record of Turf and All-Weather Racing from January 1st to November 11th, 1996

## SOUTHWELL (L-H) - Monday January 1st

**1-8 Abandoned** - Fog

# LINGFIELD (L-H) (Standard)

## Tuesday January 2nd

**9** SHELLEY H'CAP (0-60) (I) (4-Y.O+) (Class F)
12-30 (12-30) **2m (Equitrack)** £2,373.20 (£665.20: £323.60) Stalls: Low GOING minus 0.36 sec per fur (FST)

| | | SP | RR | SF |
|---|---|---|---|---|
| **Wottashambles (33)** (LMontagueHall) **5-8-10** RCochrane(1) (a.p: led over 3f out: clr over 2f out: r.o wl)....... — | 1 | 4/1 2 | 44 | 21 |
| **Captain Marmalade (47)** (DTThom) **7-9-10** JTate(3) (b: lw: hdwy over 6f out: rdn over 4f out: unable qckn) ....5 | 2 | 10/1 | 53 | 30 |
| **Red Spectacle (IRE) (51)** (PCHaslam) **4-9-7** JFortune(4) (chsd ldr 14f out: led 7f out to 4f out: one pce) .......nk | 3 | 2/1 1 | 57 | 27 |
| **Rose of Glenn (44)** (BPalling) **5-9-7** SSanders(8) (hld up: led 4f out tl over 3f out: one pce) ....................nk | 4 | 13/2 3 | 49 | 26 |
| **Oh So Handy (34)** (RCurtis) **8-8-11b** GBardwell(6) (s.s: hdwy over 6f out: wknd over 3f out) ....................9 | 5 | 10/1 | 30 | 7 |
| **Telephus (35)** (BJMcMath) **7-8-12** MWigham(7) (a bhd).....................................2 | 6 | 16/1 | 29 | 6 |
| **Sophie May (40)** (GLMoore) **5-9-3** AClark(9) (hrd rdn over 9f out: bhd fnl 5f) .............................nk | 7 | 8/1 | 34 | 11 |
| **Forest Star (USA) (43)** (RAkehurst) **7-9-6** JWeaver(2) (b: lw: led 9f: wknd over 4f out) .......................3½ | 8 | 10/1 | 34 | 11 |
| **Fattash (USA) (40)** (RPCHoad) **4-8-10b** NAdams(5) (lw: bhd fnl 8f: t.o fnl 6f) .................................dist | 9 | 20/1 | — | — |

(SP 115.7%) **9 Rn**

**3m 31.36** (9.36) CSF £38.38 CT £91.92 TOTE £5.40: £1.60 £3.50 £1.20 (£13.50) Trio £15.90 OWNER Dream On Racing Partnership (EPSOM) BRED Arthur Sims
WEIGHT FOR AGE 4yo-7lb

**10** TENNYSON CLAIMING STKS (3-Y.O) (Class E)
1-00 (1-03) **5f (Equitrack)** £3,074.60 (£930.80: £454.40: £216.20) Stalls: High GOING minus 0.36 sec per fur (FST)

| | | SP | RR | SF |
|---|---|---|---|---|
| **Charterhouse Xpres (67)** (MMcCormack) **3-8-13b** RCochrane(3) (mde virtually all: drvn out) ....................— | 1 | 4/1 3 | 70 | 2 |
| **Jemsilverthorn (IRE) (45)** (JJBridger) **3-8-1v** GBardwell(8) (a.p: rdn over 2f out: r.o wl ins fnl f)....................½ | 2 | 20/1 | 56 | — |
| **Gi La High (59)** (JBerry) **3-8-4** GCarter(6) (lw: a.p: hrd rdn over 1f out: r.o wl ins fnl f) ..............................s.h | 3 | 11/4 2 | 59 | — |
| **Copper Bright (39)** (PCHaslam) **3-7-10v**(5) MBaird(5) (lost pl over 3f out: hdwy fnl f: r.o wl)........................s.h | 4 | 16/1 | 56 | — |
| **Plein Gaz (FR)** (AndreHermans,Belgium) **3-9-7** JQuinn(4) (a.p: hrd rdn over 1f out: unable qckn) ...............1½ | 5 | 15/8 1 | 71 | 3 |
| **Convent Guest (IRE)** (MRChannon) **3-8-1**(5) PPMurphy(7) (neat: s.i.s: a bhd) .......................................½ | 6 | 14/1 | 55 | — |
| **Kind of Light (69)** (RGuest) **3-9-0** JTate(1) (a bhd) ..............................................1¾ | 7 | 5/1 | 57 | — |
| **Zuno Princess (IRE) (40)** (JO'Donoghue) **3-7-7**(3) NVarley(2) (bit bkwd: s.s: a bhd)..................................¾ | 8 | 33/1 | 37 | — |
| ***Hi Hoh (IRE) (42)*** (NPLittmoden) 3-7-6(5) CAdamson(9) (Withdrawn not under Starter's orders: vet's advice) .... | W | 33/1 | — | — |

(SP 121.3%) **8 Rn**

**61.19 secs** (3.19) CSF £62.68 TOTE £6.20: £4.30 £2.90 £1.10 (£81.00) Trio £18.00 OWNER Charterhouse Holdings Plc (WANTAGE) BRED I and F Yorkshire Holdings

**11** WORDSWORTH LIMITED STKS (0-60) (3-Y.O) (Class F)
1-30 (1-32) **1m (Equitrack)** £2,786.20 (£783.20: £382.60) Stalls: High GOING minus 0.36 sec per fur (FST)

| | | SP | RR | SF |
|---|---|---|---|---|
| **Billaddie (56)** (RBoss) **3-8-12** JWeaver(3) (lost pl 6f out: rallied 4f out: str run fnl f: led last strides) ..............— | 1 | 4/1 2 | 59 | 20 |
| **Posen Gold (IRE) (60)** (PAKelleway) **3-8-7** MWigham(1) (a.p: led over 3f out: hrd rdn fnl f: hdd last strides).........................s.h | 2 | 5/1 3 | 54 | 15 |
| **Hotlips Houlihan (50)** (RJRWilliams) **3-8-10** DBiggs(6) (led over 4f: hrd rdn over 1f out: r.o)......................½ | 3 | 9/1 | 56 | 17 |
| **Apartments Abroad (56)** (KMcAuliffe) **3-8-10** RCochrane(5) (b.hind: a.p: rdn over 3f out: wknd fnl f)..............6 | 4 | 7/4 1 | 44 | 5 |
| **Be My Bird (56)** (BJMeehan) **3-8-7** CRutter(10) (no hdwy fnl 3f) .......................................5 | 5 | 14/1 | 31 | — |
| **Suparoy (52)** (TGMills) **3-8-12** JQuinn(9) (bhd fnl 4f)..................................................3 | 6 | 15/2 | 30 | — |
| **Peterrex (47)** (MRChannon) **3-8-5**(7) AEddery(7) (nvr nrr)...............................................7 | 7 | 33/1 | 16 | — |
| **Take Note (IRE) (58)** (NAGraham) **3-8-12** MRimmer(8) (hdwy 7f out: wknd over 3f out)..........................11 | 8 | 12/1 | — | — |
| **Moving Up (IRE) (59)** (GLMoore) **3-8-8**ow1 AClark(4) (lw: a bhd)...........................................8 | 9 | 10/1 | — | — |
| **Wingnut (IRE) (42)** (JJBridger) **3-8-10** GBardwell(2) (lw: a bhd) ..........................................nk | 10 | 25/1 | — | — |

(SP 125.0%) **10 Rn**

**1m 42.04** (4.64) CSF £24.38 TOTE £3.30: £1.10 £1.90 £3.50 (£20.90) Trio £108.70 OWNER Mr Richard Gurr (NEWMARKET) BRED T. M. Jennings

**12** SHELLEY H'CAP (0-60) (II) (4-Y.O+) (Class F)
2-00 (2-00) **2m (Equitrack)** £2,373.20 (£665.20: £323.60) Stalls: Low GOING minus 0.36 sec per fur (FST)

| | | SP | RR | SF |
|---|---|---|---|---|
| **Milngavie (IRE) (29)** (MJohnston) **6-8-1b** TWilliams(4) (chsd ldr: led 8f out: clr over 1f out: r.o wl) ...............— | 1 | 8/1 | 45 | 18 |
| **Coleridge (51)** (JJSheehan) **8-9-9b** GCarter(1) (lost pl 8f out: rallied over 1f out: chsd wnr fnl f: r.o).............3½ | 2 | 4/1 3 | 64 | 37 |
| **Ikhtiraa (USA) (52)** (RJO'Sullivan) **6-9-10** JWeaver(2) (led 8f: rdn over 7f out: ev ch over 2f out: unable qckn) 6 | 3 | 3/1 2 | 59 | 32 |
| **Intention (USA) (46)** (PRHedger) **6-9-4** RCochrane(5) (lw: a.p: rdn over 4f out: one pce) .......................1½ | 4 | 12/1 | 51 | 24 |
| **Dvorak (IRE) (56)** (RHarris) **5-10-0** AMackay(6) (nvr plcd to chal).......................................2 | 5 | 20/1 | 59 | 32 |
| **Iron N Gold (46)** (AMoore) **4-8-4**(7) DDenby(7) (b.hind: no hdwy fnl 4f) ...................................2½ | 6 | 15/8 1 | 47 | 13 |
| **Pat's Splendour (36)** (HJCollingridge) **5-8-8** JQuinn(3) (hdwy over 7f out: wknd over 5f out).......................25 | 7 | 12/1 | 12 | — |
| **Night Edition (37)** (SDow) **6-8-9** DBiggs(8) (b.hind: a bhd: t.o)...........................................dist | 8 | 14/1 | — | — |

(SP 117.7%) **8 Rn**

**3m 30.15** (8.15) CSF £37.90 CT £107.89 TOTE £12.30: £2.20 £1.40 £1.10 (£21.40) OWNER Mr A. S. Robertson (MIDDLEHAM) BRED D. Oldrey and D. P. Aykroyd
WEIGHT FOR AGE 4yo-7lb

**13** KEATS H'CAP (0-80) (4-Y.O+) (Class D)
2-30 (2-31) **1m 2f (Equitrack)** £3,884.05 (£1,176.40: £574.70: £273.85) Stalls: Low GOING minus 0.36 sec per fur (FST)

| | | SP | RR | SF |
|---|---|---|---|---|
| **Celestial Choir (75)** (JLEyre) **6-9-10** RLappin(7) (hdwy over 3f out: led over 1f out: r.o wl) ......................— | 1 | 8/1 | 89 | 53 |
| **Digpast (IRE) (64)** (RJO'Sullivan) **6-8-13b** SSanders(6) (lw: dwlt: hdwy over 3f out: ev ch over 1f out: r.o)....1¾ | 2 | 20/1 | 75 | 39 |

| Horse | Dist | Pos | SP | RR | SF |
|---|---|---|---|---|---|
| **Kaafih Homm (IRE) (72)** (NACallaghan) **5-9-7** RCochrane(9) (b.hind: lw: hdwy 5f out: rdn over 2f out: one pce) | 4 | **3** | 11/4[1] | 77 | 41 |
| **Access Adventurer (IRE) (73)** (RBoss) **5-9-8** JWeaver(3) (led over 10f: wknd fnl f) | 1¾ | **4** | 4/1[2] | 75 | 39 |
| **Anistop (55)** (RAkehurst) **4-8-2** JQuinn(4) (b.hind: lw: hmpd 5f out: rdn over 4f out: hdwy over 1f out: r.o) | nk | **5** | 11/2 | 58 | 19 |
| **Dancing Lawyer (79)** (BJMeehan) **5-9-7**(7) GHannon(5) (nvr nr to chal) | 1¾ | **6** | 14/1 | 78 | 42 |
| **Greenwich Again (66)** (TGMills) **4-8-13** JFortune(2) (lw: hld up: rdn over 4f out: wknd over 3f out) | 1¼ | **7** | 14/1 | 64 | 25 |
| **Tribal Peace (IRE) (68)** (BGubby) **4-8-12**(3) JStack(1) (chsd ldr 7f) | 1¾ | **8** | 9/2[3] | 63 | 24 |
| **No Speeches (IRE) (62)** (SDow) **5-8-11** DBiggs(8) (b.hind: hdwy 5f out: wknd over 3f out) | 6 | **9** | 8/1 | 46 | 10 |
| **Manabar (74)** (MJPolglase) **4-9-7** GCarter(10) (dwlt: hdwy over 8f out: wknd 5f out) | 25 | **10** | 33/1 | 19 | — |

(SP 123.5%) **10 Rn**

**2m 7.55** (3.25) CSF £131.57 CT £504.72 TOTE £8.10: £2.60 £4.30 £2.00 (£44.90) Trio £82.30 OWNER Mrs Carole Sykes (HAMBLETON) BRED J. L. Eyre
WEIGHT FOR AGE 4yo-2lb

## 14 COLERIDGE H'CAP (0-75) (4-Y.O+) (Class D)

3-00 (3-01) **1m (Equitrack)** £3,796.30 (£1,149.40: £561.20: £267.10) Stalls: High GOING minus 0.36 sec per fur (FST)

| Horse | Dist | Pos | SP | RR | SF |
|---|---|---|---|---|---|
| **Labudd (USA) (54)** (RIngram) **6-8-7** DBiggs(1) (b: mde virtually all: drvn out) | — | **1** | 14/1 | 62 | 40 |
| **Bentico (68)** (MrsNMacauley) **7-9-2v**(5) AmandaSanders(12) (hdwy over 4f out: hrd rdn 2f out: unable qckn) | ½ | **2** | 9/1[3] | 75 | 53 |
| **Golden Pound (USA) (71)** (MissGayKelleway) **4-9-10** RCochrane(10) (hdwy 3f out: rdn over 1f out: one pce) | 1¼ | **3** | 7/2[2] | 77 | 54 |
| **Robellion (58)** (DWPArbuthnot) **5-8-11v** SWhitworth(8) (b: hdwy over 2f out: one pce) | ¾ | **4** | 11/1 | 61 | 39 |
| **Queen of All Birds (IRE) (70)** (RBoss) **5-9-9** JWeaver(9) (nvr nr to chal) | 5 | **5** | 20/1 | 63 | 41 |
| **Prizefighter (66)** (JLEyre) **5-9-5** RLappin(6) (prom 5f) | ¾ | **6** | 7/2[2] | 58 | 36 |
| **Duke Valentino (75)** (RHollinshead) **4-10-0** MWigham(11) (hdwy over 3f out: wknd over 1f out) | 1¾ | **7** | 11/4[1] | 64 | 41 |
| **Our Shadee (USA) (55)** (KTIvory) **6-8-1v**(7) MartinDwyer(5) (a mid div) | hd | **8** | 14/1 | 43 | 21 |
| **General Shirley (IRE) (52)** (PRHedger) **5-8-5** AMcGlone(4) (a bhd) | 3½ | **9** | 33/1 | 33 | 11 |
| **Jackatack (IRE) (56)** (MRChannon) **4-8-9** Jean-PierreLopez(7) (hdwy over 4f out: wknd over 2f out) | 2½ | **10** | 20/1 | 33 | 10 |
| **Tafahhus (69)** (MJPolglase) **4-9-8** MRimmer(2) (prom 5f) | 1¼ | **11** | 33/1 | 43 | 20 |
| **Willrack Farrier (62)** (BJMeehan) **4-9-1** AClark(3) (bhd fnl 4f: t.o) | dist | **12** | 33/1 | — | — |

(SP 121.1%) **12 Rn**

**1m 39.55** (2.15) CSF £122.45 CT £488.57 TOTE £9.90: £2.00 £4.40 £1.90 (£60.10) Trio £200.40 OWNER Isaac, Cloutte, Adam Ingram (EPSOM) BRED Winsome Farm Inc. & Star Stable

## 15 SHAKESPEARE AMATEUR H'CAP (0-70) (4-Y.O+) (Class E)

3-30 (3-33) **1m 5f (Equitrack)** £3,217.60 (£974.80: £476.40: £227.20) Stalls: Low GOING minus 0.36 sec per fur (FST)

| Horse | Dist | Pos | SP | RR | SF |
|---|---|---|---|---|---|
| **Cuango (IRE) (57)** (RHollinshead) **5-10-12** MrMRimell(4) (rdn & hdwy over 3f out: str run fnl f: led nr fin) | — | **1** | 6/1 | 68 | 49 |
| **Don't Drop Bombs (USA) (32)** (DTThom) **7-9-1v** MissJFeilden(6) (lw: chsd ldr: led 8f out: clr 4f out: hdd nr fin) | 1 | **2** | 12/1 | 42 | 23 |
| **Stalled (IRE) (58)** (PTWalwyn) **6-10-9**(4) MarchionessofBlandford(5) (lw: s.s: hdwy over 2f out: fin wl) | 2 | **3** | 7/2[1] | 65 | 46 |
| **Royal Circus (39)** (PRWebber) **7-9-8** MrsSBosley(1) (led 5f: rdn over 4f out: one pce) | 6 | **4** | 12/1 | 39 | 20 |
| **Sorisky (39)** (BGubby) **4-8-12**(4) MrsMTingey(13) (hld up: rdn over 3f out: wknd over 1f out) | 4 | **5** | 20/1 | 33 | 9 |
| **Shaarid (USA) (66)** (IABalding) **8-11-7** MrABalding(3) (lost pl 13f out: no hdwy fnl 3f) | nk | **6** | 9/2[2] | 61 | 42 |
| **Strat's Legacy (42)** (DWPArbuthnot) **9-9-11** MrsDArbuthnot(2) (b.hind: nvr nr to chal) | ¾ | **7** | 11/2[3] | 36 | 17 |
| **Pistols At Dawn (USA) (62)** (BJMeehan) **6-11-3** MissJAllison(12) (lw: hdwy 6f out: wknd 4f out) | 5 | **8** | 13/2 | 50 | 31 |
| **Quick Million (38)** (JWMullins) **5-9-0**(7) MrsKTierney(7) (a bhd) | ½ | **9** | 33/1 | 25 | 6 |
| **Hard Love (56)** (JLEyre) **4-10-6** MissDianaJones(10) (bhd fnl 7f) | ½ | **10** | 9/1 | 42 | 18 |
| **Ilandra (IRE) (57)** (SDow) **4-10-7** MrTMcCarthy(11) (b.hind: lw: prom over 9f) | 3 | **11** | 16/1 | 40 | 16 |
| **Persian Haze (IRE) (46)** (BJMcMath) **7-10-1** MissPJones(14) (lw: hdwy 10f out: wknd over 5f out) | 2 | **12** | 33/1 | 26 | 7 |
| **Fourofus (52)** (NBThomson) **7-10-0**(7)ow12 MrSDavis(9) (t.o fnl 7f) | dist | **13** | 50/1 | — | — |

(SP 127.3%) **13 Rn**

**2m 50.58** (7.38) CSF £72.29 CT £270.35 TOTE £7.80: £3.50 £2.70 £3.00 (£24.90) Trio £69.60 OWNER Barouche Stud Ltd (UPPER LONGDON) BRED Citadel Stud Establishment
WEIGHT FOR AGE 4yo-5lb

T/Jkpt: Not won; £47,658.46 to Lingfield 3/1/96. T/Plpt: £181.80 (122.98 Tckts). T/Qdpt: £21.90 (1.9 Tckts). AK

# WOLVERHAMPTON (L-H) (Standard)

## Wednesday January 3rd

WEATHER: overcast WIND: almost nil

## 16 LADBROKE SERIES H'CAP (Qualifier) (0-65) (I) (3-Y.O+) (Class F)

1-05 (1-06) **5f (Fibresand)** £2,385.00 (£720.00: £350.00: £165.00) Stalls: Low GOING: 0.36 sec per fur (SLW)

| Horse | Dist | Pos | SP | RR | SF |
|---|---|---|---|---|---|
| **Super Rocky (64)** (RBastiman) **7-9-8**(5) HBastiman(10) (hld up: rdn & hdwy over 1f out: str run ins fnl f: led last strides) | — | **1** | 2/1[1] | 72 | 46 |
| **Chadwell Hall (65)** (SRBowring) **5-9-9b**(5) CTeague(8) (a.p: led wl ins fnl f: hdd last strides) | nk | **2** | 11/2[3] | 72 | 46 |
| **Featherstone Lane (61)** (MissLCSiddall) **5-9-10v** JWeaver(7) (a.p: ev ch ins fnl f: unable qckn) | hd | **3** | 13/2 | 68 | 42 |
| **Newington Butts (IRE) (43)** (KMcAuliffe) **6-8-6** SSanders(2) (a.p: ev ch ins fnl f: unable qckn) | ½ | **4** | 8/1 | 48 | 22 |
| **Green's Bid (45)** (DWChapman) **6-8-8v**[1] ACulhane(6) (led tl wl ins fnl f: hdd & no ex towards fin) | hd | **5** | 20/1 | 50 | 24 |
| **Dissentor (IRE) (44)** (JAGlover) **4-8-7v** SDWilliams(1) (a.p: chal wl over 1f out: one pce ins fnl f) | nk | **6** | 16/1 | 48 | 22 |
| **Daaniera (IRE) (45)** (PHowling) **6-8-1v**(7) DebbieBiggs(4) (b.hind: lw: hld up: rdn over 1f out: no hdwy) | 1½ | **7** | 16/1 | 44 | 18 |
| **Primula Bairn (58)** (DNicholls) **6-9-7b** AlexGreaves(5) (hld up: rdn over 1f out: a bhd) | ¾ | **8** | 10/1 | 55 | 29 |
| **Lochon (52)** (JLEyre) **5-9-1** RLappin(9) (rdn over 2f out: sn bhd) | 1¾ | **9** | 5/1[2] | 43 | 17 |
| **So Natural (IRE) (60)** (EJAlston) **4-9-2**(7) CHalliwell(3) (outpcd) | 5 | **10** | 20/1 | 35 | 9 |

(SP 120.2%) **10 Rn**

**64.3 secs** (5.60) CSF £13.25 CT £54.10: £2.90: £1.20 £2.60 £2.50 (£6.10) Trio £12.50 OWNER Mr I. B. Barker (WETHERBY) BRED J. Berry

## 17 ROWAN MAIDEN STKS (3-Y.O) (Class D)

1-35 (1-36) **1m 100y (Fibresand)** £3,743.65 (£1,133.20: £553.10: £263.05) Stalls: Low GOING: 0.36 sec per fur (SLW)

| | | | SP | RR | SF |
|---|---|---|---|---|---|
| **Doctor Bravious (IRE)** (MBell) **3-9-0v[1]** MFenton(1) (lw: mde all: clr 2f out: r.o wl) | — | **1** | 7/2[2] | 71 | 33 |
| **Reploy** (LordHuntingdon) **3-8-9** DeanMcKeown(8) (bhd: rdn over 4f out: hdwy 2f out: hung lft over 1f out: styd on: nt rch wnr) | 2 | **2** | 9/2[3] | 62 | 24 |
| **Scenicris (IRE) (55)** (RHollinshead) **3-8-9** NCarlisle(6) (hdwy 4f out: one pce fnl 2f) | 3 | **3** | 9/1 | 57 | 19 |
| **Mister Aspecto (IRE) (67)** (MJohnston) **3-9-0** JWeaver(10) (lw: bhd tl hdwy 4f out: rdn over 2f out: one pce) | 3 | **4** | 11/4[1] | 56 | 18 |
| **Crystal Fast (USA)** (PAKelleway) **3-9-0** MWigham(7) (hld up: rdn & hdwy over 2f out: wknd over 1f out) | 7 | **5** | 25/1 | 43 | 5 |
| **The Wad (55)** (DNicholls) **3-9-0** AlexGreaves(9) (lw: prom tl wknd over 1f out) | 1 | **6** | 10/1 | 41 | 3 |
| **Straight Thinking (USA)** (PFICole) **3-9-0** CRutter(3) (hld up: hdwy on ins 4f out: rdn over 2f out: wknd qckly over 1f out) | 5 | **7** | 7/1 | 31 | — |
| **Dream of My Life (USA)** (FMurphy) **3-9-0** JFanning(5) (rdn over 4f out: a bhd: t.o) | 30 | **8** | 25/1 | — | — |
| **Conquistajade (USA) (52)** (SPCWoods) **3-8-9** RCochrane(2) (prom: rdn 4f out: wknd qckly: t.o) | dist | **9** | 6/1 | — | — |
| **Catherine's Choice** (JDBethell) **3-9-0** TWilliams(4) (bkwd: prom tl rdn & wknd over 3f out: eased whn btn 2f out: p.u ins fnl f) | | **P** | 14/1 | — | — |

(SP 127.3%) **10 Rn**

**1m 55.0** (10.00) CSF £20.27 TOTE £5.30: £1.30 £2.30 £2.90 (£28.10) Trio £33.10 OWNER Mr Luciano Gaucci (NEWMARKET) BRED Tony O'Reilly

## 18 ASH H'CAP (0-75) (4-Y.O+) (Class D)

2-05 (2-06) **1m 1f 79y (Fibresand)** £3,761.20 (£1,138.60: £555.80: £264.40) Stalls: Low GOING: 0.36 sec per fur (SLW)

| | | | SP | RR | SF |
|---|---|---|---|---|---|
| **Maple Bay (IRE) (59)** (ABailey) **7-8-8**(7) PRoberts(11) (mde all: edgd lft ins fnl f: rdn out) | — | **1** | 13/2[3] | 69 | 51 |
| **Beauman (59)** (PDEvans) **6-8-10**(5) AmandaSanders(9) (lw: plld hrd: a.p: chal fnl f: unable qckn) | ½ | **2** | 7/1 | 68 | 50 |
| **Pine Ridge Lad (IRE) (71)** (JLEyre) **6-9-13** RLappin(6) (a.p: rdn over 2f out: ev ch over 1f out: one pce) | 1¾ | **3** | 13/2[3] | 77 | 59 |
| **Almuhtaram (65)** (MissGayKelleway) **4-9-6b** SSanders(10) (hld up: bmpd after 2f: rdn over 2f out: no hdwy) | 2 | **4** | 7/4[1] | 69 | 49 |
| **Benjamins Law (59)** (JAPickering) **5-9-1** JQuinn(3) (prom tl wknd over 1f out) | 7 | **5** | 6/1[2] | 50 | 32 |
| **Avenue Foch (IRE) (51)** (FMurphy) **7-8-7** TWilliams(2) (hld up & bhd: effrt 3f out: no hdwy fnl 2f) | 4 | **6** | 40/1 | 35 | 17 |
| **Arcatura (57)** (CJames) **4-8-12** AMcGlone(5) (bhd fnl 2f) | ¾ | **7** | 12/1 | 41 | 21 |
| **Marowins (67)** (EJAlston) **7-9-9** SDWilliams(7) (bkwd: hld up: rdn over 3f out: wknd over 2f out) | 4 | **8** | 14/1 | 43 | 25 |
| **Life Is Precious (IRE) (56)** (RHollinshead) **4-8-11** MWigham(8) (bit bkwd: hdwy on ins 3f out: wknd 2f out) | 1¾ | **9** | 12/1 | 30 | 10 |
| **Colorful Ambition (72)** (MrsASwinbank) **6-10-0** JWeaver(4) (b.hind: s.s: a bhd) | 5 | **10** | 12/1 | 36 | 18 |
| **Jari (USA) (63)** (MJPolglase) **5-9-5** JMcLaughlin(1) (reluctant to r: a t.o) | dist | **11** | 40/1 | — | — |

(SP 124.4%) **11 Rn**

**2m 5.0** (9.00) CSF £49.65 CT £283.98 TOTE £8.10: £2.00 £3.70 £3.00 (£28.90) Trio £47.50 OWNER Mr Roy Matthews (TARPORLEY) BRED Berkshire Equestrian Services Ltd

WEIGHT FOR AGE 4yo-1lb

## 19 BEECH H'CAP (0-80) (4-Y.O+) (Class D)

2-35 (2-38) **1m 6f 166y (Fibresand)** £3,743.65 (£1,133.20: £553.10: £263.05) Stalls: High GOING: 0.36 sec per fur (SLW)

| | | | SP | RR | SF |
|---|---|---|---|---|---|
| **Lear Dancer (USA) (63)** (PhilipMitchell) **5-8-13b** AClark(6) (b.hind: hld up: hdwy over 4f out: rdn & edgd lft over 1f out: led last strides: all out) | — | **1** | 14/1 | 78 | 43 |
| **High Patriarch (IRE) (80)** (NJHWalker) **4-9-7**(3) JStack(3) (lw: a.p: led 4f out: hdd last strides) | hd | **2** | 12/1 | 95 | 54 |
| **Shakiyr (FR) (65)** (RHollinshead) **5-9-1** RCochrane(9) (lw: hld up: rdn over 3f out: one pce) | 11 | **3** | 100/30[2] | 68 | 33 |
| **Noyan (49)** (DNicholls) **6-7-13** JQuinn(2) (lw: a.p: rdn over 3f out: one pce) | 2 | **4** | 7/4[1] | 50 | 15 |
| **Mizyan (IRE) (69)** (JEBanks) **8-9-0**(5) CTeague(7) (hld up: no hdwy fnl 3f) | 1 | **5** | 13/2[3] | 69 | 34 |
| **Johns Act (USA) (71)** (DHaydnJones) **6-9-7v** AMackay(8) (led after 2f to 4f out: rdn & wknd over 2f out) | 2½ | **6** | 7/1 | 68 | 33 |
| **Ballymac Girl (62)** (JMBradley) **8-8-12** LCharnock(4) (b: led 2f: rdn & wknd over 2f out) | 2½ | **7** | 12/1 | 56 | 21 |
| **Slmaat (68)** (DNicholls) **5-9-4** AlexGreaves(5) (lw: hld up: wl bhd fnl 3f) | 9 | **8** | 14/1 | 53 | 18 |
| **Absolutely Fayre (61)** (RAkehurst) **5-8-11** JWeaver(1) (hld up: wl bhd fnl 3f) | 3½ | **9** | 12/1 | 42 | 7 |
| **Honey Mount (63)** (NJHWalker) **5-8-13** CRutter(10) (dwlt: a bhd) | 1¾ | **10** | 25/1 | 42 | 7 |

(SP 125.5%) **10 Rn**

**3m 22.8** (15.40) CSF £155.34 CT £635.76 TOTE £9.90: £2.60 £3.50 £1.90 (£29.50) Trio £43.80 OWNER Mrs R. A. Johnson (EPSOM) BRED Alan S. Kline

WEIGHT FOR AGE 4yo-6lb

## 20 OAK H'CAP (0-90) (4-Y.O+) (Class C)

3-05 (3-05) **7f (Fibresand)** £5,608.80 (£1,697.40: £828.20: £393.60) Stalls: High GOING: 0.36 sec per fur (SLW)

| | | | SP | RR | SF |
|---|---|---|---|---|---|
| **Ashgore (82)** (MJohnston) **6-9-6** JWeaver(1) (lw: mde all: clr over 1f out: rdn out) | — | **1** | 14/1 | 88 | 64 |
| **High Premium (70)** (RAFahey) **8-8-8** ACulhane(9) (b: hdwy over 3f out: r.o one pce fnl f) | 2½ | **2** | 8/1 | 70 | 46 |
| **Pengamon (77)** (HJCollingridge) **4-9-1** JQuinn(7) (b.hind: bhd tl hdwy 2f out: styd on fnl f) | 1¼ | **3** | 10/1 | 74 | 50 |
| **Cretan Gift (77)** (NPLittmoden) **5-9-1v** TGMcLaughlin(2) (lw: prom: lost pl 4f out: rallied over 2f out: wknd over 1f out) | 2½ | **4** | 5/1[2] | 69 | 45 |
| **Sailormaite (89)** (SRBowring) **5-9-13** SDWilliams(6) (hld up: nt clr run & swtchd lft over 2f out: no hdwy) | hd | **5** | 4/1[1] | 81 | 57 |
| **Neuwest (USA) (80)** (NJHWalker) **4-9-1**(3) JStack(4) (lw: s.i.s: sn rcvrd: rdn over 2f out: sn wknd) | 3 | **6** | 4/1[1] | 65 | 41 |
| **Four of Spades (72)** (PDEvans) **5-8-10** SSanders(5) (prom 3f) | 7 | **7** | 6/1[3] | 41 | 17 |
| **Little Ibnr (85)** (PDEvans) **5-9-4**(5) AmandaSanders(8) (lw: prom over 4f) | nk | **8** | 6/1[3] | 53 | 29 |
| **Everset (FR) (90)** (ABailey) **8-9-7**(7) PRoberts(3) (dwlt: wl bhd fnl 4f: t.o) | 13 | **9** | 5/1[2] | 28 | 4 |

(SP 128.8%) **9 Rn**

**1m 30.7** (6.00) CSF £116.68 CT £1,085.64 TOTE £14.60: £3.20 £1.30 £6.80 (£38.40) Trio £113.10 OWNER Mr Harvey Ashworth (MIDDLEHAM) BRED D. A. and Mrs Hicks

## 21 ACORN (S) STKS (Qualifier) (3-Y.O) (Class E)

3-35 (3-37) **6f (Fibresand)** £3,088.90 (£935.20: £456.60: £217.30) Stalls: Low GOING: 0.36 sec per fur (SLW)

| | | | SP | RR | SF |
|---|---|---|---|---|---|
| **Mystic Tempo (USA) (70)** (DrJDScargill) **3-8-13** RCochrane(1) (b: a.p: led over 3f out: rdn out) | — | **1** | 11/4[2] | 69 | 38 |

**Marino Street (62)** (PDEvans) **3-8-7** SSanders(10) (b.nr hind: lw: led over 1f: rdn over 2f out: kpt on fnl f) ¾ **2** 9/4[1] 61 30
**Miss Pickpocket (IRE) (54)** (PAKelleway) **3-8-13** MWigham(9) (hld up: hdwy over 1f out: kpt on u.p fnl f) ½ **3** 5/1[3] 66 35
**Boffy (IRE) (56)** (BPJBaugh) **3-8-11**(7) IonaWands(4) (b: hdwy 2f out: one pce fnl f) 1½ **4** 10/1 67 36
**Red Acuisle (IRE) (64)** (JBerry) **3-8-7**(5) PFessey(6) (led over 4f out tl over 3f out: wknd fnl f) nk **5** 8/1 60 29
**Dhes-C** (RHollinshead) **3-8-0**(7) FLynch(2) (hdwy on ins 2f out: one pce fnl f) nk **6** 20/1 54 23
**Flood's Fancy (58)** (ABailey) **3-8-6**(7) PRoberts(5) (bhd fnl 3f) 5 **7** 9/1 47 16
**Peters Folly (45)** (JLEyre) **3-8-7** RLappin(8) (prom over 3f) 2½ **8** 14/1 34 3
**Quinntessa (55)** (BPalling) **3-8-7** SDWilliams(3) (prom: rdn over 2f out: sn wknd) ¾ **9** 16/1 32 1
**Shoot The Minstrel** (JAPickering) **3-8-12** NCarlisle(7) (b.nr hind: bit bkwd: s.i.s: bhd fnl 3f) 5 **10** 33/1 24 —
(SP 124.6%) **10 Rn**

**1m 17.8** (6.40) CSF £9.62 TOTE £3.40: £1.40 £1.10 £2.00 (£8.30) Trio £4.60 OWNER Just Passing Through Partnership (NEWMARKET) BRED Swetteham Stud and Ben Sangster
Bt in 3,200 gns

## 22 LADBROKE SERIES H'CAP (Qualifier) (0-65) (II) (3-Y.O+) (Class F)

4-05 (4-06) **5f (Fibresand)** £2,385.00 (£720.00: £350.00: £165.00) Stalls: Low GOING: 0.36 sec per fur (SLW)

SP RR SF
**Cheeky Chappy (47)** (DWChapman) **5-8-5b**(5) PFessey(3) (mde all: clr over 1f out: pushed out) — **1** 6/4[1] 58 39
**The Institute Boy (48)** (MissJFCraze) **6-8-11** NKennedy(4) (a.p: drvn & r.o wl ins fnl f: nt rch wnr) ½ **2** 8/1 57 38
**The Real Whizzbang (IRE) (44)** (PSFelgate) **5-8-4b**(3) PMcCabe(8) (a.p: rdn & chsd wnr 2f out: one pce fnl f) 3 **3** 13/2 44 25
**Rennyholme (33)** (JHetherton) **5-7-10b** NAdams(2) (no hdwy fnl 2f) 2 **4** 50/1 26 7
**Pursuance (IRE) (63)** (JBalding) **4-9-5v**(7) JEdmunds(9) (s.s: hdwy 2f out: nvr nr to chal) nk **5** 9/2[2] 55 36
**Man of May (35)** (NPLittmoden) **4-7-12** AMackay(7) (nvr trbld ldrs) 4 **6** 33/1 15 —
**Tommy Tempest (43)** (REPeacock) **7-8-6v** JQuinn(6) (prom over 3f) 1¼ **7** 14/1 19 —
**Margaretrose Anna (60)** (EJAlston) **4-9-9** SDWilliams(5) (hld up: hmpd over 3f out: sn bhd) 7 **8** 12/1 13 —
**Sigama (USA) (62)** (DNicholls) **10-9-11** AlexGreaves(1) (bhd fnl 3f) 4 **9** 6/1[3] 2 —
(SP 116.2%) **9 Rn**

**63.7 secs** (5.00) CSF £13.25 CT £55.76 TOTE £2.40: £2.50 £1.10 £2.40 (£10.00) Trio £18.80 OWNER Mrs Jeanne Chapman (YORK) BRED Ian W. Glenton
LONG HANDICAP Rennyholme 6-8
STEWARDS' ENQUIRY McCabe susp. 12 & 13/1/96 (careless riding).

T/Plpt: £229.50 (59.75 Tckts). T/Qdpt: £68.90 (0.7 Tckts); £27.96 to Nottingham 4/1/96. KH

# 0009-LINGFIELD (L-H) (Standard)
## Thursday January 4th

## 23 ROLLING STONE H'CAP (0-60) (4-Y.O+) (Class F)

1-00 (1-01) **1m 4f (Equitrack)** £2,874.40 (£808.40: £395.20) Stalls: Low GOING minus 0.19 sec per fur (FST)

SP RR SF
**Erlking (IRE) (35)** (SMellor) **6-8-6b** CRutter(3) (hdwy over 4f out: rdn over 3f out: led ins fnl f: r.o wl) — **1** 10/1 45 27
**Never So Rite (IRE) (45)** (DWPArbuthnot) **4-8-12** RCochrane(5) (hdwy over 6f out: led over 2f out: sn clr: hdd ins fnl f: unable qckn) 2 **2** 8/1 53 30
**Tomal (44)** (RIngram) **4-8-11** WNewnes(12) (b.hind: plld hrd: hdwy over 5f out: swtchd lft over 1f out: one pce) 8 **3** 7/1 42 19
**Dia Georgy (46)** (MrsNMacauley) **5-9-3** SSanders(10) (b: hdwy over 6f out: wknd over 3f out) 5 **4** 13/2 36 18
**Pip's Dream (35)** (MJRyan) **5-8-6**ow3 AClark(13) (hld up: rdn over 5f out: wknd over 3f out) hd **5** 6/1[3] 25 4
**Sweet Disorder (IRE) (30)** (BJMeehan) **6-8-1** JQuinn(4) (led 2f: led 4f out tl over 2f out: sn wknd) nk **6** 20/1 20 2
**Mafuta (IRE) (33)** (JJSheehan) **4-8-0** GBardwell(6) (s.s: nvr nrr) 1 **7** 33/1 22 —
**Missed the Boat (IRE) (37)** (AGNewcombe) **6-8-1**(7) MartinDwyer(7) (nvr nrr) 1 **8** 8/1 24 6
**Chez Catalan (48)** (RAkehurst) **5-8-12b**(7) TAshley(9) (lw: rdn thrght: nvr nrr) 3 **9** 4/1[1] 31 13
**Shedansar (IRE) (33)** (GLMoore) **4-8-0** NAdams(1) (hdwy over 3f out: sn wknd) 1¼ **10** 33/1 15 —
**Water Hazard (IRE) (51)** (SDow) **4-9-4** DBiggs(8) (b.hind: prom 6f) 3½ **11** 12/1 29 6
**Talented Ting (IRE) (55)** (PCHaslam) **7-9-12v** JFortune(11) (led 10f out to 4f out: sn wknd) nk **12** 5/1[2] 31 13
**Tudor Flight (35)** (AGNewcombe) **5-8-6** AMackay(2) (a bhd) 14 **13** 25/1 — —
(SP 130.3%) **13 Rn**

**2m 37.45** (7.45) CSF £86.40 CT £555.28 TOTE £9.80: £1.70 £2.30 £3.00 (£30.90) Trio £146.80; £188.17 to Newcastle 5/1/96 OWNER Mr S. P. Tindall (SWINDON) BRED Mrs P. Grubb
WEIGHT FOR AGE 4yo-4lb

## 24 BAD PENNY MAIDEN STKS (4-Y.O+) (Class D)

1-30 (1-32) **1m 2f (Equitrack)** £3,778.75 (£1,144.00: £558.50: £265.75) Stalls: Low GOING minus 0.19 sec per fur (FST)

SP RR SF
**Rainbow Top** (WJHaggas) **4-8-12** RCochrane(2) (hld up: led 2f out: clr over 1f out: rdn out) — **1** 6/1 81+ 57
**Secret Spring (FR) (73)** (PRHedger) **4-8-12** SRaymont(7) (b.hind: a.p: ev ch over 2f out: unable qckn) 6 **2** 9/4[1] 71 47
**Fresh Fruit Daily (65)** (PAKelleway) **4-8-7** MWigham(10) (chsd ldr over 8f out: led 4f out to 2f out: one pce) 4 **3** 11/4[2] 60 36
**Errant (62)** (DJSCosgrove) **4-8-12** JQuinn(6) (b: hld up: rdn over 4f out: one pce) 3 **4** 7/2[3] 60 36
**Callonescy (IRE) (48)** (DCO'Brien) **4-8-12** GBardwell(8) (rdn over 4f out: hdwy over 3f out: wknd wl over 1f out) 15 **5** 20/1 36 12
**Raffles Rooster** (AGNewcombe) **4-8-12** AMackay(3) (wl bhd 8f: nvr nrr) 3 **6** 9/2 31 7
**Saltis (IRE) (50)** (DWPArbuthnot) **4-8-12b**[1] AClark(4) (lw: led 6f) 4 **7** 33/1 25 1
**Legal Drama (USA)** (PJMcBride) **4-8-0**(7) RMullen(5) (a bhd) ¾ **8** 33/1 19 —
**Golden Punch (USA)** (CACyzer) **5-9-0b**[1] DBiggs(11) (bhd fnl 4f) 8 **9** 33/1 10 —

| Horse | Btn | Pos | SP | RR | SF |
|---|---|---|---|---|---|
| **Northern Trove (USA) (50)** (RonaldThompson) **4-8-12** SSanders(1) (swtg: bhd fnl 5f : t.o) | dist | **10** | 33/1 | — | — |

(SP 128.7%) **10 Rn**

**2m 7.37** (3.07) CSF £20.62 TOTE £4.90: £3.00 £1.10 £2.10 (£14.80) Trio £10.80 OWNER Mr B. Haggas (NEWMARKET) BRED Sir Robin McAlpine
WEIGHT FOR AGE 4yo-2lb
STEWARDS' ENQUIRY Wigham fined £100 (not riding to his draw).

## 25 STITCH IN TIME CLAIMING STKS (3-Y.O) (Class E)

2-00 (2-01) **1m (Equitrack)** £3,060.30 (£926.40: £452.20: £215.10) Stalls: High GOING minus 0.19 sec per fur (FST)

| Horse | Btn | Pos | SP | RR | SF |
|---|---|---|---|---|---|
| **Rowlandsons Charm (IRE) (60)** (GLMoore) **3-7-11v** NAdams(4) (hung rt thrght: led: hrd rdn over 1f out: hdd wl ins fnl f: led last stride) | — | **1** | 6/4[1] | 64 | 15 |
| **Rawi (58)** (WRMuir) **3-7-8**(7) MartinDwyer(3) (lw: chsd wnr 2f: chsd wnr 4f out: led wl ins fnl f: hdd last stride) | s.h | **2** | 10/1 | 68 | 19 |
| **Righteous Gent (50)** (KMcAuliffe) **3-8-8be** RCochrane(6) (rdn 4f out: hdwy over 1f out: one pce) | 8 | **3** | 8/1 | 59 | 10 |
| **Multi Franchise (56)** (BGubby) **3-8-1** JQuinn(7) (hdwy over 6f out: chsd wnr 6f out to 4f out: wknd over 2f out) | 1½ | **4** | 7/1[3] | 49 | — |
| *11[5]* **Be My Bird (56)** (BJMeehan) **3-8-1** CRutter(5) (rdn thrght: nvr nr to chal) | 1½ | **5** | 10/1 | 46 | — |
| **Domettes (IRE) (64)** (RHannon) **3-8-9** GCarter(2) (lw: prom 3f) | 1¾ | **6** | 2/1[2] | 50 | 1 |
| **Naked Emperor** (MJFetherston-Godley) **3-8-10** DaleGibson(1) (s.s: a bhd: t.o) | dist | **7** | 20/1 | — | — |

(SP 119.9%) **7 Rn**

**1m 42.51** (5.11) CSF £16.02 TOTE £2.40: £2.40 £7.20 (£17.00) OWNER Allen & Associates (EPSOM) BRED Mrs Catherine O'Malley

## 26 TOO MANY COOKS H'CAP (0-70) (4-Y.O+) (Class E)

2-30 (2-31) **6f (Equitrack)** £3,103.20 (£939.60: £458.80: £218.40) Stalls: Low GOING minus 0.19 sec per fur (FST)

| Horse | Btn | Pos | SP | RR | SF |
|---|---|---|---|---|---|
| **Pageboy (61)** (PCHaslam) **7-9-5b** JFortune(8) (a.p: rdn over 2f out: led ins fnl f: r.o wl) | — | **1** | 4/1[1] | 69 | 27 |
| **Fort Knox (IRE) (51)** (RMFlower) **5-8-9b** DBiggs(4) (rdn over 3f out: hdwy fnl f: r.o) | 1½ | **2** | 10/1 | 55 | 13 |
| **Rockcracker (IRE) (54)** (GGMargarson) **4-8-12** AClark(10) (hld up: rdn over 3f out: r.o ins fnl f) | 1 | **3** | 16/1 | 55 | 13 |
| **Speedy Classic (USA) (66)** (MJHeaton-Ellis) **7-9-7**(3) SDrowne(9) (a.p: rdn 2f out: unable qckn) | s.h | **4** | 5/1[2] | 67 | 25 |
| **Warm Hearted (USA) (56)** (AGNewcombe) **4-9-0** NGwilliams(5) (hdwy fnl f: r.o) | ¾ | **5** | 9/1 | 55 | 13 |
| **Milos (65)** (TJNaughton) **5-9-2**(7) TAshley(2) (outpcd: hdwy fnl f: r.o) | nk | **6** | 10/1 | 63 | 21 |
| **Distant Dynasty (55)** (BAPearce) **6-8-13** SSanders(1) (led: rdn over 1f out: hdd ins fnl f: sn wknd) | nk | **7** | 4/1[1] | 53 | 11 |
| **Random (56)** (CJames) **5-9-0** CRutter(3) (lw: nvr nr to chal) | 1¾ | **8** | 8/1 | 49 | 7 |
| **Dahiyah (USA) (58)** (GLMoore) **5-9-2** SWhitworth(7) (prom 4f) | 6 | **9** | 12/1 | 35 | — |
| **Montague Dawson (IRE) (54)** (MrsNMacauley) **4-8-12** SDWilliams(6) (b.hind: lw: prom tl hmpd & wknd over 2f out) | hd | **10** | 7/1[3] | 31 | — |

(SP 122.0%) **10 Rn**

**1m 14.93** (4.33) CSF £40.83 CT £534.48 TOTE £3.50: £1.90 £3.10 £2.00 (£20.00) Trio not won; £144.91 to Newcastle 5/1/96 OWNER Lord Scarsdale (MIDDLEHAM) BRED K. T. Ivory and Partners
**OFFICIAL EXPLANATION Warm Hearted (USA): was found to have an irregular heart beat.**

## 27 MANY HANDS LIMITED STKS (0-60) (4-Y.O+) (Class F)

3-00 (3-01) **1m 2f (Equitrack)** £2,748.40 (£772.40: £377.20) Stalls: Low GOING minus 0.19 sec per fur (FST)

| Horse | Btn | Pos | SP | RR | SF |
|---|---|---|---|---|---|
| **Rival Bid (USA) (55)** (MrsNMacauley) **8-9-1**(5) AmandaSanders(6) (stdy hdwy over 2f out: rdn fnl f: led last strides) | — | **1** | 6/1[3] | 67 | 46 |
| **Secretary of State (55)** (DWPArbuthnot) **10-9-0** CRutter(9) (b: hdwy over 4f out: led over 2f out: clr over 1f out: hrd rdn ins fnl f: hdd last strides) | nk | **2** | 13/2 | 61 | 40 |
| **Total Rach (IRE) (54)** (RIngram) **4-8-13b** DBiggs(3) (s.i.s: hdwy on ins 7f out: led over 3f out tl over 2f out: unable qckn) | 4 | **3** | 6/1[3] | 56 | 32 |
| **Risky Tu (45)** (PAKelleway) **5-8-9** MWigham(5) (lost pl over 4f out: r.o one pce fnl f) | ½ | **4** | 8/1 | 48 | 27 |
| **Blasted (58)** (GEThorner) **4-8-12** JWilliams(2) (hld up: rdn over 2f out: wknd over 1f out) | 4 | **5** | 8/1 | 48 | 24 |
| **Awesome Power (56)** (JWHills) **10-9-3** AClark(1) (led over 1f: wknd wl over 1f out) | 1 | **6** | 6/1[3] | 48 | 27 |
| **Tadellal (IRE) (57)** (WGMTurner) **5-8-10**(5) MBaird(8) (s.s: hdwy over 8f out: wknd over 3f out) | 2½ | **7** | 3/1[1] | 42 | 21 |
| **Chancey Fella (47)** (KTIvory) **5-9-0** RCochrane(4) (b: a bhd) | 9 | **8** | 16/1 | 27 | 6 |
| **Landlord (60)** (JARToller) **4-9-1b** WNewnes(10) (plld hrd: led over 8f out tl over 3f out: sn wknd) | 14 | **9** | 9/2[2] | 9 | — |

(SP 127.5%) **9 Rn**

**2m 9.66** (5.36) CSF £44.49 TOTE £7.10: £2.60 £2.30 £2.40 (£17.40) Trio £88.40 OWNER Mr G. Wiltshire (MELTON MOWBRAY) BRED Marvin L. Warner Jnr.
WEIGHT FOR AGE 4yo-2lb
**OFFICIAL EXPLANATION Landlord: ran too freely in the early stages.**

## 28 BIRD IN THE HAND H'CAP (0-80) (3-Y.O) (Class D)

3-30 (3-31) **7f (Equitrack)** £3,673.45 (£1,111.60: £542.30: £257.65) Stalls: Low GOING minus 0.19 sec per fur (FST)

| Horse | Btn | Pos | SP | RR | SF |
|---|---|---|---|---|---|
| **Banzhaf (USA) (70)** (GLMoore) **3-9-2** SWhitworth(4) (lw: mde virtually all: clr over 1f out: r.o wl) | — | **1** | 9/4[1] | 81 | 32 |
| **Bells of Holland (59)** (WRMuir) **3-8-5** Jean-PierreLopez(5) (chsd wnr: rdn 2f out: unable qckn) | 3 | **2** | 10/1 | 63 | 14 |
| **Time Clash (67)** (BPalling) **3-8-13** SDWilliams(3) (rdn 4f out: hdwy 3f out: r.o one pce fnl 2f) | 1½ | **3** | 7/2[3] | 68 | 19 |
| *10[4]* **Copper Bright (50)** (PCHaslam) **3-7-5v**(5) MBaird(2) (nvr nr to chal) | 5 | **4** | 6/1 | 39 | — |
| **Victim of Love (75)** (RCharlton) **3-9-7** SSanders(1) (prom 4f) | 8 | **5** | 5/2[2] | 46 | — |
| **Maple Burl (66)** (SDow) **3-8-12** DBiggs(6) (prom over 3f) | 20 | **6** | 9/1 | — | — |

(SP 114.9%) **6 Rn**

**1m 28.47** (4.47) CSF £20.72 TOTE £2.50: £2.00 £4.00 (£14.10) OWNER Mr Bryan Pennick (EPSOM) BRED Pope McLean
LONG HANDICAP Copper Bright 6-13

T/Plpt: £311.90 (30.1 Tckts). T/Qdpt: Not won; £54.10 to Towcester 5/1/96. AK

# 0001-SOUTHWELL (L-H) (standard)
## Friday January 5th

### 29 LEICESTERSHIRE CLAIMING STKS (I) (4-Y.O+) (Class F)
12-30 (12-33) **1m (Fibresand)** £2,222.00 (£622.00: £302.00) Stalls: Low GOING: 0.02 sec per fur (STD)

| | | | SP | RR | SF |
|---|---|---|---|---|---|
| **Rambo Waltzer (76)** (DNicholls) **4-9-3** AlexGreaves(6) (a gng wl: led 3f out: sn clr) | — | **1** | 11/8[2] | 81+ | 56 |
| **Hawwam (69)** (EJAlston) **10-8-11** SDWilliams(2) (a chsng ldrs: kpt on fnl 2f: no ch w wnr) | 8 | **2** | 5/4[1] | 58 | 34 |
| **Faez (54)** (RSimpson) **6-8-3b** GBardwell(3) (led tl hdd 3f out: sn outpcd) | 1¾ | **3** | 16/1 | 47 | 23 |
| **First Gold (55)** (JWharton) **7-8-13** RCochrane(4) (hdwy ½-wy: sn prom: one pce fnl 2f) | 4 | **4** | 7/1[3] | 49 | 25 |
| **Absolute Ruler (IRE) (43)** (JLHarris) **5-8-7b** SSanders(9) (hdwy to chse ldrs ½-wy: wknd 2f out) | 5 | **5** | 33/1 | 33 | 9 |
| **Lord Barnard (IRE) (30)** (CMurray) **6-8-7** DBiggs(5) (hrd drvn ½-wy: n.d) | 10 | **6** | 20/1 | 13 | — |
| **Recessions Over** (NPLittmoden) **5-8-9** TGMcLaughlin(1) (sn chsng ldrs: rdn & btn 3f out) | s.h | **7** | 33/1 | 14 | — |
| **Bex Hill (38)** (DHaydnJones) **4-8-2** AMackay(7) (prom tl rdn & wknd ½-wy) | 10 | **8** | 50/1 | — | — |
| **Dublin Indemnity (USA) (42)** (MPBielby) **7-8-3b** JFanning(8) (a outpcd & bhd) | 2 | **9** | 50/1 | — | — |
| | | | (SP 119.5%) **9 Rn** | | |

**1m 44.8** (4.80) CSF £3.46 TOTE £2.70: £1.00 £1.10 £4.20 (£1.70) Trio £8.90 OWNER Keystone Racing Club Partnership (THIRSK) BRED Triangle Thoroughbreds Ltd

### 30 LINCOLNSHIRE AMATEUR H'CAP (0-70) (4-Y.O+) (Class F)
1-00 (1-02) **1m (Fibresand)** £2,572.00 (£722.00: £352.00) Stalls: Low GOING: 0.02 sec per fur (STD)

| | | | SP | RR | SF |
|---|---|---|---|---|---|
| **Komiamaite (51)** (SRBowring) **4-10-1**(4) MrsMMorris(13) (hdwy ½-wy: led ins fnl f: hld on wl) | — | **1** | 12/1 | 63 | 41 |
| **Personimus (33)** (CaptJHWilson) **6-9-1** MrsAFarrell(3) (bhd: hdwy 3f out: styd on towards fin) | nk | **2** | 8/1 | 43 | 22 |
| **Karinska (60)** (MCChapman) **6-10-10**(4) MrMMackley(4) (bhd: hdwy appr st: ev ch ins fnl f: nt qckn) | ¾ | **3** | 7/1 | 69 | 48 |
| **Jon's Choice (42)** (BPreece) **8-9-3**(7) MissLBoswell(15) (gd hdwy ½-wy: led 3f out tl ins fnl f: no ex) | 1¾ | **4** | 33/1 | 47 | 26 |
| **Araboybill (62)** (RSimpson) **5-10-12b**(4)ow8 MrEWilliams(1) (mde most tl hdd 3f out: one pce) | 3 | **5** | 12/1 | 61 | 32 |
| **Cicerone (45)** (JLHarris) **6-9-13b** MissPRobson(6) (chsd ldrs tl outpcd fnl 2f) | 4 | **6** | 7/1 | 36 | 15 |
| **Eastleigh (51)** (RHollinshead) **7-10-5** MrMRimell(8) (b.off hind: nvr rchd ldrs) | ¾ | **7** | 13/2[3] | 41 | 20 |
| **Summer Villa (43)** (PCHaslam) **4-9-11** MrsDKettlewell(14) (n.d) | 2 | **8** | 12/1 | 30 | 8 |
| **It's So Easy (34)** (APJames) **5-9-2**ow2 MissAElsey(10) (n.d) | s.h | **9** | 10/1 | 19 | — |
| **Love Legend (50)** (DWPArbuthnot) **11-10-4** MrsDArbuthnot(12) (b: nvr trbld ldrs) | 3 | **10** | 12/1 | 29 | 8 |
| **Shotley Again (34)** (NBycroft) **6-8-9**(7)ow2 MrsCWilliams(11) (sn pushed along: n.d) | s.h | **11** | 25/1 | 12 | — |
| **Whackford Squeers (67)** (DNicholls) **4-11-7** MrsAPerrett(2) (chsd ldrs tl wknd wl over 1f out) | ½ | **12** | 6/1[2] | 45 | 23 |
| **Media Messenger (36)** (NPLittmoden) **7-8-11**(7) MrOGunter(9) (s.s: a bhd) | 6 | **13** | 33/1 | 1 | — |
| **Roar on Tour (64)** (MrsMReveley) **7-11-4** MrMHNaughton(5) (s.i.s: a bhd) | 4 | **14** | 5/1[1] | 21 | — |
| **Le Bal (38)** (MissJFCraze) **4-8-13b**(7) MrWWenyon(7) (w ldr 5f: wknd qckly) | 20 | **15** | 33/1 | — | — |
| | | | (SP 132.9%) **15 Rn** | | |

**1m 47.8** (7.80) CSF £103.84 CT £671.85 TOTE £11.20. £2.40 £2.90 £3.10 (£40.70) Trio £132.00; £37.45 to Sandown 6/1/96 OWNER Mrs Zoe Grant (EDWINSTOWE) BRED Mrs Z. Grant and S. R. Bowring
LONG HANDICAP Le Bal 9-7 Shotley Again 8-12 It's So Easy 8-13

### 31 LEICESTERSHIRE CLAIMING STKS (II) (4-Y.O+) (Class F)
1-30 (1-30) **1m (Fibresand)** £2,222.00 (£622.00: £302.00) Stalls: Low GOING: 0.02 sec per fur (STD)

| | | | SP | RR | SF |
|---|---|---|---|---|---|
| **Spencer's Revenge (78)** (MJRyan) **7-9-1** GBardwell(3) (sn pushed along: hdwy ½-wy: led 2f out: rdn & styd on wl) | — | **1** | Evens[1] | 70 | 40 |
| **Lilac Rain (34)** (JRArnold) **4-7-12b** CRutter(4) (a chsng ldrs: kpt on u.p towards fin) | 1 | **2** | 50/1 | 52 | 21 |
| **No Submission (USA) (68)** (DWChapman) **10-8-1v**(5) PFessey(2) (led tl hdd 2f out: one pce) | 1 | **3** | 4/1[3] | 57 | 27 |
| **Warhurst (IRE) (57)** (DNicholls) **5-8-0**(7) JoHunnam(8) (s.i.s: sn trckng ldrs: outpcd 4f out: styd on fnl 2f) | 5 | **4** | 16/1 | 48 | 18 |
| **Smart Guest (87)** (JAHarris) **4-9-7** JWeaver(7) (chsd ldrs tl wknd fnl 2f) | 9 | **5** | 9/4[2] | 45 | 14 |
| **Shuttlecock (60)** (MrsNMacauley) **5-8-6**(5) AmandaSanders(6) (sn outpcd & bhd: n.d) | 2½ | **6** | 12/1 | 29 | — |
| **Solo Prize (60)** (PHowling) **4-8-11** JQuinn(5) (b.hind: s.i.s: n.d) | 4 | **7** | 50/1 | 22 | — |
| **Prestige Lad** (BSmart) **4-8-9** SSanders(1) (s.i.s: sn prom: wknd over 2f out) | 1 | **8** | 33/1 | 18 | — |
| | | | (SP 121.2%) **8 Rn** | | |

**1m 46.1** (6.10) CSF £36.28 TOTE £1.80: £1.10 £3.40 £1.10 (£36.00) OWNER Mr A. S. Reid (NEWMARKET) BRED Lord Crawshaw

### 32 NOTTINGHAMSHIRE H'CAP (0-75) (3-Y.O) (Class D)
2-00 (2-00) **6f (Fibresand)** £3,726.10 (£1,127.80: £550.40: £261.70) Stalls: Low GOING: 0.02 sec per fur (STD)

| | | | SP | RR | SF |
|---|---|---|---|---|---|
| **Weetman's Weigh (IRE) (64)** (RHollinshead) **3-9-6** MWigham(9) (a chsng ldrs: led wl over 1f out: hld on wl) | — | **1** | 100/30[2] | 71 | 29 |
| **First Maite (65)** (SRBowring) **3-9-2b**(5) CTeague(7) (in tch: hdwy to chall ins fnl f: kpt on) | nk | **2** | 4/1[3] | 71 | 29 |
| **Briganoone (51)** (SRBowring) **3-8-7** NCarlisle(8) (bhd tl hdwy 2f out: kpt on wl) | 4 | **3** | 10/1 | 47 | 5 |
| **Castle Governor (45)** (PCHaslam) **3-7-10**(5) MBaird(4) (a.p: shkn up & one pce fnl 2f) | 3 | **4** | 8/1 | 33 | — |
| **Madam Zando (46)** (JBalding) **3-8-2** ClaireBalding(6) (in tch: outpcd ½-wy: kpt on fnl f) | 1 | **5** | 16/1 | 31 | — |
| **Rothley Imp (IRE) (58)** (JWharton) **3-9-0** JQuinn(5) (outpcd & bhd tl sme late hdwy) | 2 | **6** | 10/1 | 38 | — |
| **Efipetite (47)** (NBycroft) **3-8-3** SMaloney(1) (n.m.r early: outpcd fr ½-wy) | ½ | **7** | 14/1 | 25 | — |
| **Chemcast (58)** (DNicholls) **3-9-0** AlexGreaves(3) (led tl hdd & wknd wl over 1f out) | 3 | **8** | 10/1 | 28 | — |
| **Lady Eclat (59)** (JAGlover) **3-9-1b**1 SDWilliams(2) (lw: sn drvn along: chsd ldr 4f: sn lost pl) | 1¾ | **9** | 3/1[1] | 25 | — |
| | | | (SP 119.0%) **9 Rn** | | |

**1m 19.2** (5.70) CSF £16.56 CT £110.28 TOTE £3.60: £1.60 £1.60 £1.50 (£5.60) Trio £36.30 OWNER Ed Weetman (Haulage & Storage) Ltd (UPPER LONGDON) BRED David Commins
**OFFICIAL EXPLANATION Lady Eclat: was unable to dominate and was never travelling smoothly.**

### 33 DERBYSHIRE MAIDEN H'CAP (0-70) (4-Y.O+) (Class E)
2-30 (2-31) **1m 4f (Fibresand)** £3,274.80 (£992.40: £485.20: £231.60) Stalls: High GOING: 0.02 sec per fur (STD)

| | | | SP | RR | SF |
|---|---|---|---|---|---|
| **Mr Moriarty (IRE) (32)** (SRBowring) **5-7-10** NCarlisle(14) (mde most: kpt on wl fnl 3f) | — | **1** | 9/2[2] | 46 | — |

| Horse | Dist | Pos | SP | RR | SF |
|---|---|---|---|---|---|
| **Alzoomo (IRE) (64)** (JAGlover) **4-9-3**(7) VictoriaAppleby(10) (hdwy 5f out: styd on wl: nvr able to chal) | 4 | **2** | 5/1[3] | 74 | 18 |
| **Thatcher's Era (IRE) (54)** (TDBarron) **4-9-0** JFortune(5) (hdwy u.p 3f out: styd on towards fin) | 1¾ | **3** | 10/1 | 61 | 5 |
| **Parklife (IRE) (38)** (PCHaslam) **4-7-7**(5) MBaird(12) (bhd tl hdwy over 2f out: styd on wl towards fin) | 1 | **4** | 14/1 | 44 | — |
| **Todd (USA) (56)** (PhilipMitchell) **5-9-6** AClark(8) (w wnr tl outpcd fnl 2f) | 1¼ | **5** | 25/1 | 59 | 8 |
| **Tremendisto (43)** (CaptJHWilson) **6-8-7** AMackay(9) (trckd ldrs tl outpcd fnl 3f) | 1¼ | **6** | 14/1 | 45 | — |
| **Roseberry Topping (58)** (MrsMReveley) **7-9-3**(5) GParkin(11) (hdwy ½-wy: chsng ldrs ent st: one pce) | 1¼ | **7** | 4/1[1] | 58 | 7 |
| **Heighth of Fame (45)** (AJWilson) **5-8-2**(7) KSked(3) (chsd ldrs: outpcd 6f out: no imp after) | 1¾ | **8** | 9/1 | 43 | — |
| **Inovar (32)** (CBBBooth) **6-7-10** NKennedy(7) (hld up: hdwy 6f out: nvr nr to chal) | ½ | **9** | 16/1 | 29 | — |
| **Anchorena (59)** (JAHarris) **4-9-5** JWeaver(2) (nvr nr to chal) | 14 | **10** | 7/1 | 38 | — |
| **Buzzards Hall (33)** (MCChapman) **6-7-6**(5)ow1 PFessey(13) (chsd ldrs tl rdn & wknd over 3f out) | 2½ | **11** | 33/1 | 8 | — |
| **Mudlark (41)** (JNorton) **4-8-1** DaleGibson(1) (prom tl wknd 5f out) | nk | **12** | 14/1 | 17 | — |
| **Claque (55)** (DWChapman) **4-9-1** ACulhane(16) (a bhd) | 5 | **13** | 20/1 | 24 | — |
| **Bobby's Dream (40)** (MHTompkins) **4-8-0** GBardwell(15) (a outpcd & bhd) | 15 | **14** | 14/1 | — | — |
| **Nebrangus (IRE) (37)** (NBycroft) **4-7-11**ow1 SMaloney(6) (a outpcd & bhd) | 6 | **15** | 50/1 | — | — |
| **Astrojoy (IRE) (36)** (SGKnight) **4-7-10** JQuinn(4) (chsd ldrs tl outpcd 6f out: sn wknd) | 7 | **16** | 14/1 | — | — |

(SP 139.2%) **16 Rn**

**2m 46.2** (13.70) CSF £29.11 CT £212.66 TOTE £5.80: £1.70 £1.10 £2.20 £2.20 (£27.50) Trio £72.90 OWNER Mr D. H. Bowring (EDWINSTOWE) BRED Joseph Hernon and Partners

LONG HANDICAP Buzzards Hall 7-5 Mr Moriarty (IRE) 7-2 Inovar 7-7 Nebrangus (IRE) 6-10 Astrojoy (IRE) 7-5

WEIGHT FOR AGE 4yo-4lb

## 34 YORKSHIRE (S) STKS (4, 5 & 6-Y.O) (Class F)

3-00 (3-00) **1m 3f (Fibresand)** £2,572.00 (£722.00: £352.00) Stalls: High GOING: 0.02 sec per fur (STD)

| Horse | Dist | Pos | SP | RR | SF |
|---|---|---|---|---|---|
| **Tartan Gem (IRE) (65)** (MBrittain) **5-9-1** RCochrane(15) (lw: racd wd: hdwy on bit 5f out: led over 1f out: r.o wl) | — | **1** | 4/1[2] | 75 | 20 |
| **Troubadour Song (61)** (WWHaigh) **4-8-12** DaleGibson(6) (a.p: kpt on one pce fnl 3f) | 4 | **2** | 12/1 | 70 | 11 |
| **Sarasi (66)** (MJCamacho) **4-9-3** LCharnock(5) (cl up: led 7f out: hdd over 1f out: sn btn) | 3½ | **3** | 6/4[1] | 70 | 11 |
| **Sharp Gazelle (33)** (BSmart) **6-8-10** SSanders(4) (a chsng ldrs: rdn appr st: r.o one pce) | nk | **4** | 20/1 | 59 | 4 |
| **Sea Spouse (48)** (MBlanshard) **5-9-1** NAdams(11) (chsd ldrs tl wknd fnl 3f) | 15 | **5** | 12/1 | 42 | — |
| **Hello Peter (IRE) (48)** (MHTompkins) **4-8-5**(7) JGotobed(14) (bhd tl styd on fnl 3f) | 1½ | **6** | 6/1[3] | 41 | — |
| **Fools of Pride (IRE) (36)** (RHollinshead) **4-8-0**(7) FLynch(13) (bhd: sme hdwy appr st: n.d) | hd | **7** | 16/1 | 36 | — |
| **Arecibo (FR) (50)** (JParkes) **4-8-12** JFortune(1) (prom tl outpcd fnl 5f) | 10 | **8** | 20/1 | 26 | — |
| **Magication (39)** (BRichmond) **6-8-10** JQuinn(2) (nvr trbld ldrs) | ¾ | **9** | 25/1 | 19 | — |
| **Rose Chime (IRE) (39)** (JLHarris) **4-8-7** TWilliams(9) (a rr div) | 5 | **10** | 25/1 | 13 | — |
| **Kindakoola (30)** (MCChapman) **5-8-8**(7) CMunday(8) (chsd ldrs tl rdn & wknd 4f out) | 2 | **11** | 33/1 | 14 | — |
| **Akola Angel (39)** (CREgerton) **4-8-7** AClark(7) (outpcd & bhd fr ½-wy) | 3 | **12** | 12/1 | 5 | — |
| **Rafter-J (54)** (JAHarris) **5-9-1** JWeaver(12) (led 4f: wknd & eased fnl 3f) | 8 | **13** | 11/1 | — | — |
| **Tempting (IRE) (68)** (JNorton) **4-8-7** ACulhane(3) (sn bhd: t.o) | dist | **14** | 12/1 | — | — |

(SP 139.4%) **14 Rn**

**2m 31.4** (11.40) CSF £54.37 TOTE £3.60: £2.10 £8.40 £1.40 (£50.20) Trio £19.70 OWNER Consultco Ltd (WARTHILL) BRED James Hannan

WEIGHT FOR AGE 4yo-3lb

Bt in 4,000 gns

## 35 LADBROKE ALL-WEATHER CHALLENGE SERIES H'CAP (Qualifier) (0-65) (3-Y.O) (Class F)

3-30 (3-31) **7f (Fibresand)** £2,821.20 (£793.20: £387.60) Stalls: Low GOING: 0.02 sec per fur (STD)

| Horse | Dist | Pos | SP | RR | SF |
|---|---|---|---|---|---|
| **China Castle (54)** (PCHaslam) **3-8-12** JWeaver(12) (hld up: stdy hdwy ½-wy: led over 1f out: sn clr) | — | **1** | 9/1 | 78 | 43 |
| **Theatre Magic (59)** (SRBowring) **3-8-12b**(5) CTeague(4) (plld hrd: led after 2f tl over 1f out: no ex) | 12 | **2** | 3/1[1] | 56 | 21 |
| **Seeking Destiny (IRE) (40)** (MCChapman) **3-7-7**(5) PFessey(6) (s.i.s: hdwy ½-wy: kpt on wl: nvr able to chal) | 2½ | **3** | 11/2[2] | 31 | — |
| *17[6]* **The Wad (55)** (DNicholls) **3-8-13** AlexGreaves(10) (cl up: effrt over 2f out: one pce) | 1 | **4** | 8/1 | 44 | 9 |
| **Ebony Boy (61)** (JWharton) **3-9-5** SDWilliams(2) (chsd ldrs: one pce fnl 3f) | 1¼ | **5** | 7/1[3] | 47 | 12 |
| **Lady Dignity (IRE) (63)** (PJMakin) **3-9-7** RCochrane(7) (b.nr hind: a chsng ldrs: one pce fnl 3f) | 3½ | **6** | 11/2[2] | 41 | 6 |
| **Ticka Ticka Timing (51)** (BWMurray) **3-8-2**(7) MartinDwyer(5) (cl up tl wknd over 2f out) | 5 | **7** | 12/1 | 17 | — |
| **Image Maker (IRE) (53)** (BPreece) **3-8-11b** NAdams(1) (sn outpcd) | 2½ | **8** | 20/1 | 14 | — |
| **Bit of Bother (IRE) (63)** (TDBarron) **3-9-7** JFortune(11) (sn pushed along: n.d) | 4 | **9** | 7/1[3] | 14 | — |
| **Shanoora (IRE) (52)** (MrsNMacauley) **3-8-5v**(5) AmandaSanders(9) (hld up: n.d) | ½ | **10** | 20/1 | 2 | — |
| **Fortuitious (IRE) (39)** (JRJenkins) **3-7-11** DaleGibson(13) (s.i.s: n.d) | 8 | **11** | 20/1 | — | — |
| **Gresham Flyer (43)** (BRichmond) **3-8-1** JQuinn(8) (nvr wnt pce) | 4 | **12** | 33/1 | — | — |
| **Derek's Bo (40)** (NBycroft) **3-7-12** SMaloney(3) (led 2f: wknd over 2f out) | 7 | **13** | 33/1 | — | — |

(SP 129.7%) **13 Rn**

**1m 31.7** (4.90) CSF £36.63 CT £155.95 TOTE £7.60: £2.00 £1.50 £1.80 (£18.90) Trio £56.00 OWNER Mr J. M. Davis (MIDDLEHAM) BRED Mrs Frances Cronin

T/Plpt: £46.50 (166.86 Tckts). T/Qdpt: £8.90 (2.95 Tckts). AA

# 0023-LINGFIELD (L-H) (Standard)

## Saturday January 6th

WIND: almost nil

## 36 BLUEBELL H'CAP (0-60) (I) (3-Y.O+) (Class F)

12-15 (12-17) **6f (Equitrack)** £2,436.20 (£683.20: £332.60) Stalls: Low GOING minus 0.36 sec per fur (FST)

| Horse | Dist | Pos | SP | RR | SF |
|---|---|---|---|---|---|
| **Myjinka (46)** (JO'Donoghue) **6-8-12b**(3) PMcCabe(12) (outpcd in rr: gd hdwy over 1f out: str run fnl f: led nr fin) | — | **1** | 11/2[3] | 52 | 16 |
| **Awasha (IRE) (52)** (MissGayKelleway) **4-9-7** RCochrane(7) (hld up: hdwy over 2f out: rdn to ld wl ins fnl f: hdd nr fin) | hd | **2** | 5/1[2] | 58 | 22 |

| | | | | SP | RR | SF |
|---|---|---|---|---|---|---|
| | **Fiery Footsteps (42)** (SWCampion) **4-8-11** SDWilliams(3) (b.nr hind: a.p: led over 2f out: hdd wl ins fnl f: unable qckn) | nk | **3** | 25/1 | 47 | 11 |
| 26[2] | **Fort Knox (IRE) (51)** (RMFlower) **5-9-6b** DBiggs(13) (chsd ldrs: rdn over 1f out: r.o one pce fnl f) | hd | **4** | 6/1 | 56 | 20 |
| | **Thick as Thieves (51)** (RonaldThompson) **4-9-6** JWeaver(6) (b: lw: chsd ldrs: rdn & one pce fnl 2f) | 6 | **5** | 3/1[1] | 40 | 4 |
| | **Classic Pet (IRE) (46)** (CAHorgan) **4-9-1** AClark(8) (b.all rnd: led 5f out: hdd over 2f out: grad wknd) | ½ | **6** | 16/1 | 33 | — |
| | **Mister Raider (42)** (SMellor) **4-8-11** JQuinn(1) (a mid div) | 1½ | **7** | 12/1 | 25 | — |
| | **Riskie Things (55)** (JSMoore) **5-9-5**(5) PPMurphy(2) (led 1f: wknd over 2f out) | ½ | **8** | 16/1 | 37 | 1 |
| | **Vladivostok (45)** (BdeHaan) **6-8-9**(5) PFessey(5) (chsd ldrs tl wknd 2f out) | ½ | **9** | 12/1 | 26 | — |
| | **Slivovitz (53)** (MJHeaton-Ellis) **6-9-3**(5) AmandaSanders(11) (a.p: cl 3rd whn fell 2 out: broke leg: dead) | | **F** | 11/1 | — | — |
| | **Prince Rudolf (IRE) (44)** (MrsNMacauley) **4-8-8v**(5) CTeague(10) (rr tl bdly hmpd & uns rdr 2f out) | | **U** | 16/1 | — | — |
| | **Delrob (55)** (DHaydnJones) **5-9-10** AMackay(9) (in rr tl bdly hmpd & uns rdr 2f out) | | **U** | 25/1 | — | — |
| | | | | (SP 120.4%) | | **12 Rn** |

**1m 14.46** (3.86) CSF £31.23 CT £572.82 TOTE £6.20: £2.20 £1.10 £9.20 (£25.70) Trio £97.20 OWNER Miss P. I. Westbrook (REIGATE) BRED Miss Prue Westbrook and Bob Pettis

## 37 SNOWDROP CLAIMING APPRENTICE STKS (4-Y.O+) (Class F)

12-45 (1-01) **1m 4f (Equitrack)** £2,634.00 (£749.00: £372.00) Stalls: Low GOING minus 0.36 sec per fur (FST)

| | | | | SP | RR | SF |
|---|---|---|---|---|---|---|
| 34* | **Tartan Gem (IRE) (65)** (MBrittain) **5-9-0**(3) JDennis(3) (confidently rdn: hld up in rr: hdwy 3f out: led ins fnl f: comf) | — | **1** | 10/11[1] | 58 | 32 |
| | **Jobber's Fiddle (44)** (DLWilliams) **4-7-13b** AimeeCook(11) (chsd ldr: led 5f out: clr over 1f out: hdd ins fnl f: one pce) | 3½ | **2** | 8/1 | 40 | 9 |
| | **Duveen (IRE) (57)** (JWhite) **6-9-2**(7) CCarver(5) (hld up: hdwy 7f out: rdn over 1f out: one pce) | 2 | **3** | 15/2[3] | 57 | 31 |
| | **Cabcharge Blue (52)** (TJNaughton) **4-8-5**(3) TAshley(10) (a.p: chsd ldr 5f out: rdn 2f out: wknd over 1f out) | 7 | **4** | 33/1 | 37 | 6 |
| | **Tamandu** (CJames) **6-8-12** FLynch(6) (dwlt: rr: hdwy 5f out: sn rdn: one pce fnl 3f) | 1¼ | **5** | 7/1[2] | 35 | 9 |
| | **Elly Fleetfoot (IRE) (57)** (BJMeehan) **4-8-6b**[1](5) GHannon(8) (plld hrd: chsd ldrs: wknd 2f out) | 1¾ | **6** | 8/1 | 36 | 5 |
| | **Voices in the Sky** (AGNewcombe) **5-8-9** IonaWands(9) (a bhd) | 9 | **7** | 33/1 | 17 | — |
| | **Ela-Ment (IRE)** (BAPearce) **4-9-2** JWilkinson(2) (a bhd) | 2½ | **8** | 20/1 | 26 | — |
| | **La Bossette (IRE) (28)** (RIngram) **4-7-13** DDenby(7) (mid div tl wknd 5f out) | ¾ | **9** | 33/1 | 8 | — |
| | **Nahrawali (IRE)** (AndreHermans,Belgium) **5-9-1b**[1](5) ALakeman(1) (led: hdd 5f out: sn wknd) | 8 | **10** | 11/1 | 13 | — |
| | | | | (SP 120.8%) | | **10 Rn** |

**2m 36.16** (6.16) CSF £9.14 TOTE £2.30: £1.50 £1.70 £1.80 (£7.30) Trio £18.90 OWNER Consultco Ltd (WARTHILL) BRED James Hannan
WEIGHT FOR AGE 4yo-4lb

## 38 DAFFODIL H'CAP (0-80) (4-Y.O+) (Class D)

1-15 (1-26) **1m 4f (Equitrack)** £3,761.20 (£1,138.60: £555.80: £264.40) Stalls: Low GOING minus 0.36 sec per fur (FST)

| | | | | SP | RR | SF |
|---|---|---|---|---|---|---|
| | **Ballynakelly (62)** (RAkehurst) **4-7-13**(7) TAshley(9) (lw: a.p: chsd ldr 9f out: led 5f out: rdn 2f out: r.o wl) | — | **1** | 100/30[2] | 77 | 54 |
| | **Opera Buff (IRE) (76)** (MissGayKelleway) **5-9-10** RCochrane(8) (hld up in rr: hdwy 7f out: chsd wnr over 3f out: rdn over 1f out: unable qckn) | 1¾ | **2** | 6/4[1] | 88 | 70 |
| | **Prince Danzig (IRE) (77)** (DJGMurraySmith) **5-9-11** JWeaver(4) (hld up: hdwy 4f out: rdn 3f out: one pce) | 12 | **3** | 20/1 | 73 | 55 |
| | **Sir Norman Holt (IRE) (63)** (RJO'Sullivan) **7-8-11b** DBiggs(7) (led: hdd 5f out: rdn over 3f out: one pce) | 2½ | **4** | 33/1 | 55 | 37 |
| | **Benfleet (80)** (RWArmstrong) **5-10-0** JWilliams(10) (hld up in rr: hdwy 7f out: rdn 3f out: one pce) | 1¾ | **5** | 6/1[3] | 70 | 52 |
| | **Premier Dance (62)** (DHaydnJones) **9-8-10** AMackay(6) (mid div: rdn 4f out: sn outpcd) | 1½ | **6** | 12/1 | 50 | 32 |
| | **Wet Patch (IRE) (64)** (RHannon) **4-8-8** GCarter(2) (bhd fnl 6f) | 7 | **7** | 6/1[3] | 44 | 21 |
| | **Warm Spell (71)** (GLMoore) **6-9-5** MFenton(3) (bit bkwd: bhd fnl 6f) | ½ | **8** | 12/1 | 49 | 31 |
| | **Caspian Beluga (64)** (SGKnight) **8-8-12** SDWilliams(1) (b: chsd ldr 3f: sn wknd) | 14 | **9** | 25/1 | 23 | 5 |
| | **Much Sought After (78)** (KRBurke) **7-9-12** JTate(5) (chsd ldrs tl wknd qckly 5f out) | nk | **10** | 20/1 | 37 | 19 |
| | | | | (SP 123.3%) | | **10 Rn** |

**2m 31.22** (1.22) CSF £8.84 CT £81.31 TOTE £4.70: £2.10 £1.30 £2.80 (£4.50) Trio £59.30 OWNER Y M Y Partnership (EPSOM) BRED Crest Stud Ltd
WEIGHT FOR AGE 4yo-4lb

## 39 VIOLET H'CAP (0-80) (3-Y.O) (Class D)

1-45 (1-48) **5f (Equitrack)** £3,655.90 (£1,106.20: £539.60: £256.30) Stalls: High GOING minus 0.36 sec per fur (FST)

| | | | | SP | RR | SF |
|---|---|---|---|---|---|---|
| | **Krystal Max (IRE) (83)** (TDBarron) **3-9-3**(7) KimberleyHart(2) (chsd ldr: led 3f out: pushed out) | — | **1** | 11/8[1] | 88 | 36 |
| | **Dancing Jack (55)** (JJBridger) **3-7-10** JQuinn(4) (a.p: ev ch 1f out: hrd rdn fnl f: one pce) | 1 | **2** | 7/4[2] | 57 | 5 |
| | **Ghostly Apparition (60)** (JRUpson) **3-7-8**(7)ow3 DSweeney(1) (outpcd tl styd on fnl f: nvr nrr) | 2 | **3** | 14/1 | 55 | — |
| | **Impington (IRE) (56)** (WRMuir) **3-7-4**(7)ow1 MartinDwyer(3) (led 2f: rdn & ev ch 2f out: wknd over 1f out) | 7 | **4** | 3/1[3] | 29 | — |
| | | | | (SP 110.1%) | | **4 Rn** |

**60.42 secs** (2.42) CSF £3.99 TOTE £2.30 (£3.00) OWNER The Oakfield Nurseries Partnership (THIRSK) BRED Baronrath Stud
LONG HANDICAP Impington (IRE) 7-6

## 40 COWSLIP MEDIAN AUCTION MAIDEN STKS (3-Y.O) (Class E)

2-15 (2-15) **1m 2f (Equitrack)** £3,031.70 (£917.60: £447.80: £212.90) Stalls: Low GOING minus 0.36 sec per fur (FST)

| | | | | SP | RR | SF |
|---|---|---|---|---|---|---|
| 11[2] | **Posen Gold (IRE) (60)** (PAKelleway) **3-8-9** RCochrane(2) (lw: hld up in tch: led over 1f out: hrd rdn fnl f: r.o) | — | **1** | 13/8[2] | 62 | 23 |
| | **In The Band** (LordHuntingdon) **3-8-9** JWeaver(3) (lw: a.p: chsd ldr 6f out: led 5f out: hdd over 1f out: hrd rdn fnl f: r.o) | nk | **2** | Evens[1] | 62 | 23 |
| | **Bath Knight (63)** (DJSffrenchDavis) **3-9-0** JWilliams(5) (hld up: hdwy 4f out: rdn over 2f out: one pce) | 5 | **3** | 12/1 | 59 | 20 |
| | **Highlights** (DMorris) **3-8-9** JTate(1) (lt-f: dwlt: sn in tch: chsd ldr 5f out: ev ch 3f out: wknd over 2f out) | 9 | **4** | 7/1[3] | 39 | — |
| 11[7] | **Peterrex (47)** (MRChannon) **3-9-0** CandyMorris(4) (led: hdd 5f out: sn wknd) | 14 | **5** | 50/1 | 22 | — |
| | **Cupla Focail (44)** (WRMuir) **3-8-9** Jean-PierreLopez(6) (chsd ldr 4f: sn wknd) | 25 | **6** | 50/1 | — | — |
| | | | | (SP 112.2%) | | **6 Rn** |

**2m 9.56** (5.26) CSF £3.49 TOTE £2.10: £1.50 £1.10 (£1.40) OWNER Mr F. M. Kalla (NEWMARKET) BRED John O'Connor

## 41 BLUEBELL H'CAP (0-60) (II) (3-Y.O+) (Class F)

2-45 (2-45) **6f (Equitrack)** £2,423.60 (£679.60: £330.80) Stalls: Low GOING minus 0.36 sec per fur (FST)

| Runner | Dist | Pos | SP | RR | SF |
|---|---|---|---|---|---|
| **Sharp Imp (50)** (RMFlower) **6-9-5b** DBiggs(5) (hld up in tch: led over 1f out: rdn & edgd lft ins fnl f: r.o) | — | 1 | 4/1[2] | 60 | 16 |
| **Halbert (43)** (PBurgoyne) **7-8-5v**(7) DSweeney(4) (led: hdd over 1f out: ev ch whn sltly hmpd ins fnl f: unable qckn) | 1 | 2 | 5/1 | 50 | 6 |
| **Nivasha (38)** (RPCHoad) **4-8-7** MFenton(3) (prom: rdn & outpcd over 2f out: styd on fnl f) | 1¾ | 3 | 20/1 | 41 | — |
| **Assignment (45)** (JELong) **10-8-7**(7) TField(8) (b.off hind: hmpd after 1f: rdn over 3f out: swtchd rt over 1f out: styd on fnl f) | 1¾ | 4 | 20/1 | 43 | — |
| **Aston Manor (IRE) (59)** (RHannon) **4-9-7**(7) MarkDenaro(7) (rr: hdwy 2f out: rdn over 1f out: r.o one pce) | nk | 5 | 8/1 | 56 | 12 |
| **Superlao (BEL) (55)** (AndreHermans,Belgium) **4-9-10** RCochrane(10) (b.hind: outpcd in rr: swtchd rt over 1f out: styd on fnl f: nvr nrr) | ½ | 6 | 10/1 | 51 | 7 |
| **Fallal (IRE) (37)** (KMcAuliffe) **4-8-6be** SSanders(1) (sn outpcd & rdn along: nvr nrr) | 2½ | 7 | 16/1 | 26 | — |
| **Al Shaati (FR) (46)** (RJO'Sullivan) **6-9-1b** JWeaver(9) (hld up: hdwy 3f out: rdn 2f out: sn wknd) | 5 | 8 | 7/2[1] | 22 | — |
| **Tyrian Purple (IRE) (57)** (TJNaughton) **8-9-5b**(7) TAshley(11) (b: spd 4f) | ½ | 9 | 8/1 | 32 | — |
| **Apollo Red (53)** (AMoore) **7-9-8** CandyMorris(12) (prom 4f) | ¾ | 10 | 9/2[3] | 26 | — |

(SP 123.8%) **10 Rn**

**1m 14.73** (4.13) CSF £24.12 CT £325.95 TOTE £4.90: £1.60 £7.90 £4.70 (£12.20) Trio £89.20; £87.95 to Southwell 8/1/96. OWNER Mrs G. M. Temmerman (JEVINGTON) BRED James Wigan

## 42 LADBROKE ALL-WEATHER TROPHY H'CAP (Qualifier) (0-70) (4-Y.O+) (Class E)

3-20 (3-21) **7f (Equitrack)** £3,131.80 (£948.40: £463.20: £220.60) Stalls: Low GOING minus 0.36 sec per fur (FST)

| Runner | Dist | Pos | SP | RR | SF |
|---|---|---|---|---|---|
| **Rakis (IRE) (64)** (MBrittain) **6-9-10** RCochrane(13) (hld up in tch: led wl over 1f out: r.o wl) | — | 1 | 8/1 | 64 | 46 |
| **Crystal Heights (FR) (68)** (RJO'Sullivan) **8-10-0** SSanders(7) (dwlt: hdwy 3f out: rdn over 1f out: chsd wnr ins fnl f: r.o) | 3 | 2 | 9/1 | 61 | 43 |
| **Patsy Grimes (63)** (JSMoore) **6-9-9** AMcGlone(15) (hld up in tch: chsd wnr over 1f out tl ins fnl f: one pce) | 1½ | 3 | 10/1 | 53 | 35 |
| **Tuigamala (57)** (RIngram) **5-8-10**(7) TAshley(4) (rr: hdwy over 1f out: nvr nrr) | ¾ | 4 | 12/1 | 45 | 27 |
| **At the Savoy (IRE) (60)** (TDBarron) **5-8-13b**(7) KimberleyHart(11) (b: in rr: hdwy over 2f out: rdn over 1f out: one pce) | 2½ | 5 | 16/1 | 42 | 24 |
| **Hawaii Storm (FR) (65)** (DJSffrenchDavis) **8-9-11** JWilliams(8) (nvr nrr) | ½ | 6 | 15/2 | 46 | 28 |
| **Field of Vision (IRE) (64)** (MJohnston) **6-9-10b** JWeaver(3) (led: hdd wl over 1f out: grad wknd) | 2 | 7 | 4/1[1] | 41 | 23 |
| **Woolverstone Hall (IRE) (41)** (DJGMurraySmith) **4-7-8**(7) DSweeney(12) (chsd ldrs tl rdn over 2f out: wknd over 1f out) | 1¾ | 8 | 25/1 | 14 | — |
| **Quinzii Martin (50)** (DHaydnJones) **8-8-10v** AMackay(2) (nvr nrr) | ½ | 9 | 6/1[2] | 21 | 3 |
| **Shaynes Domain (44)** (RMFlower) **5-8-4b** DBiggs(10) (chsd ldrs over 4f) | 1¼ | 10 | 20/1 | 13 | — |
| 14[8] **Our Shadee (USA) (55)** (KTIvory) **6-9-1v** MWigham(9) (a bhd) | hd | 11 | 12/1 | 23 | 5 |
| **Moody (61)** (MissGayKelleway) **4-9-0**(7) BFord(5) (b.hind: bhd fnl 3f) | 1 | 12 | 14/1 | 27 | 9 |
| **Maid Welcome (59)** (MrsNMacauley) **9-9-0v**(5) CTeague(6) (prom 5f) | ½ | 13 | 13/2[3] | 24 | 6 |
| **Mac's Taxi (56)** (PCHaslam) **4-8-11**(5) MBaird(14) (bhd fnl 3f) | 2½ | 14 | 8/1 | 15 | — |
| **My Bonus (47)** (DJSCosgrove) **6-8-7**ow1 MRimmer(1) (chsd ldrs 4f: sn wknd: t.o) | 25 | 15 | 33/1 | — | — |

(SP 140.2%) **15 Rn**

**1m 26.66** (2.66) CSF £81.77 CT £693.87 TOTE £12.10: £2.90 £4.40 £5.30 (£27.70) Trio £192.40 OWNER Mr P. G. Shorrock (WARTHILL) BRED The Mount Coote Partnership

T/Plpt: £17.90 (367.45 Tckts). T/Qdpt: £5.80 (3.15 Tckts). SM

# 0029-SOUTHWELL (L-H) (Standard)

## Monday January 8th

WEATHER: overcast WIND: fresh half against

## 43 TIPPERARY APPRENTICE H'CAP (0-60) (I) (4-Y.O+) (Class F)

12-25 (12-27) **1m (Fibresand)** £2,235.00 (£635.00: £315.00) Stalls: Low GOING: 0.08 sec per fur (STD)

| Runner | Dist | Pos | SP | RR | SF |
|---|---|---|---|---|---|
| **Ladybower (IRE) (39)** (LordHuntingdon) **4-8-8** AimeeCook(8) (lw: a.p: led over 1f out: r.o) | — | 1 | 12/1 | 46 | 29 |
| **Carol Again (34)** (NBycroft) **4-8-3** FLynch(5) (cl up: led ½-wy: hdd over 1f out: no ex) | 2½ | 2 | 33/1 | 36 | 20 |
| **Anotherone to Note (42)** (NPLittmoden) **5-8-8b**(3) JDennis(4) (stdd s: hdwy over 2f out: styd on wl nr fin) | 1¼ | 3 | 12/1 | 41 | 25 |
| 18[2] **Beauman (59)** (PDEvans) **6-9-9**(5) JEdmunds(9) (lw: in tch: effrt over 2f out: rdn, edgd lft & no ex) | 2 | 4 | 4/6[1] | 54 | 37 |
| **Scent of Power (38)** (NMBabbage) **6-8-7** IonaWands(10) (in tch: outpcd ½-wy: no imp after) | 3 | 5 | 10/1[3] | 27 | 13 |
| **Great Bear (59)** (DWChapman) **4-9-9**(5) KSked(6) (lw: disp ld to ½-wy: lost pl: styd on towards fin) | hd | 6 | 16/1 | 48 | 32 |
| **Broughton's Port (37)** (WJMusson) **6-8-3**(3) TAshley(1) (hld up: effrt over 2f out: n.d) | hd | 7 | 10/1[3] | 25 | 11 |
| **East Barns (IRE) (44)** (SGollings) **8-8-13b** AEddery(2) (prom tl outpcd ½-wy: n.d after) | 11 | 8 | 6/1[2] | 10 | — |
| **Woodlands Lad Too (34)** (PAPritchard) **4-8-0**(3) JoHunnam(3) (outpcd & bhd fr ½-wy) | 9 | 9 | 50/1 | — | — |
| **Green Apache (27)** (KGWingrove) **4-7-3**(7) JBosley(7) (disp ld to ½-wy: sn wknd) | 5 | 10 | 14/1 | — | — |

(SP 125.3%) **10 Rn**

**1m 47.1** (7.10) CSF £263.83 CT £4,327.76 TOTE £11.60: £2.30 £4.70 £1.80 (£116.90) Trio £190.70; £166.50 to Lingfield 9/1/96 OWNER Lord Huntingdon (WEST ILSLEY) BRED James Waldron

STEWARDS' ENQUIRY Cook susp. 17-18/1/96 (excessive use of whip).

## 44 WICKLOW H'CAP (0-70) (I) (4-Y.O+) (Class E)

12-50 (12-54) **7f (Fibresand)** £2,806.80 (£848.40: £413.20: £195.60) Stalls: Low GOING: 0.08 sec per fur (STD)

| Runner | Dist | Pos | SP | RR | SF |
|---|---|---|---|---|---|
| **So Amazing (57)** (MissSEHall) **4-9-3** JWeaver(9) (lw: mde most: kpt on u.p fnl f) | — | 1 | 4/1[2] | 65 | 47 |
| **Peggy Spencer (64)** (CWThornton) **4-9-10** DeanMcKeown(7) (a cl up: disp ld 2f out: no ex towards fin) | hd | 2 | 5/4[1] | 72 | 53 |
| **Hi Rock (45)** (MJCamacho) **4-8-5** LCharnock(4) (s.i.s: sn rdn: hdwy 3f out: one pce appr fnl f) | 6 | 3 | 13/2[3] | 39 | 23 |
| **Legal Issue (IRE) (60)** (WWHaigh) **4-9-6** DaleGibson(8) (lw: a chsng ldrs: nt qckn fnl 2f) | s.h | 4 | 4/1[2] | 54 | 37 |
| **Grey Again (56)** (SRBowring) **4-8-11b**(5) CTeague(5) (s.i.s: hdwy u.p 3f out: n.d) | 4 | 5 | 9/1 | 41 | 25 |

**Daawe (USA) (56)** (MrsVAAconley) **5-9-2v** ACulhane(2) (cl up tl rdn & wknd over 2f out)........9 **6** 14/1 20 7
**Macaroon Lady (37)** (NBycroft) **5-7-11**ow1 SMaloney(10) (in tch tl wl outpcd fr ½-wy)........1½ **7** 33/1 — —
**Crowning Tino (36)** (MrsNMacauley) **4-7-10** JQuinn(6) (sn outpcd & bhd)........13 **8** 40/1 — —
**Woodlands Electric (44)** (PAPritchard) **6-7-11**(7)ow8 JoHunnam(3) (sn outpcd & bhd)........6 **9** 66/1 — —
***Sea God (44)*** (MCChapman) **5-7-11**(7) CMunday(1) (Withdrawn not under Starter's orders: sddle slipped & bolted 2 circuits bef s)........**W** 20/1 — —
(SP 126.1%) **9 Rn**

**1m 32.1** (5.30) CSF £9.46 CT £29.73 TOTE £4.30: £1.60 £1.10 £2.70 (£4.70) Trio £13.30 OWNER Mr C. Platts (MIDDLEHAM) BRED C. Platts and Miss S. E. Hall
LONG HANDICAP Woodlands Electric 6-3 Macaroon Lady 7-7
STEWARDS' ENQUIRY McKeown susp. 17-18/1/96 (excessive use of whip).

## 45 TIPPERARY APPRENTICE H'CAP (0-60) (II) (4-Y.O+) (Class F)

1-15 (1-17) **1m (Fibresand)** £2,235.00 (£635.00: £315.00) Stalls: Low GOING: 0.08 sec per fur (STD)

SP RR SF

*31[4]* **Warhurst (IRE) (57)** (DNicholls) **5-9-9**(3) JoHunnam(8) (lw: hdwy ½-wy: led over 1f out: edgd lft & r.o)........— **1** 5/4[1] 50 41
*30[11]* **Shotley Again (34)** (NBycroft) **6-8-0**(3)ow4 TAshley(7) (outpcd tl hdwy 3f out: styd on wl towards fin)........3 **2** 16/1 21 14
**Lucky Tucky (46)** (JRJenkins) **5-8-8**(7) SallyWall(4) (a chsng ldrs: outpcd over 2f out: no imp after)........3½ **3** 6/1[3] 26 19
**Genesis Four (42)** (SRBowring) **6-8-6b**(5) JEdmunds(2) (lw: chsd ldrs: rdn over 2f out: one pce)........¾ **4** 4/1[2] 21 14
**Selmeston (IRE) (34)** (PSFelgate) **4-8-3** IonaWands(3) (sn outpcd & wl bhd: styd on fnl 2f: n.d)........¾ **5** 33/1 12 6
**Young Benson (52)** (BAMcMahon) **4-9-7** FLynch(6) (chsd ldrs tl wknd over 2f out)........1 **6** 10/1 28 20
*16[5]* **Green's Bid (45)** (DWChapman) **6-8-9**(5) KSked(1) (led & sn clr: hdd & wknd over 1f out)........¾ **7** 6/1[3] 19 13
**Donia (USA) (50)** (JLHarris) **7-9-2b**(3) DSweeney(9) (lw: a outpcd & bhd)........15 **8** 7/1 — —
**Royal Dancer (39)** (RJWeaver) **4-8-8** GFaulkner(5) (s.i.s: a bhd: eased fnl 2f: wl t.o)........dist **9** 33/1 — 24
(SP 126.4%) **9 Rn**

**1m 47.6** (7.60) CSF £21.92 CT £91.30 TOTE £2.20: £1.10 £4.20 £2.40 (£17.30) Trio £47.60 OWNER V.Greaves (THIRSK) BREDMrs G.Lanzara

## 46 LIMERICK CLAIMING STKS (3-Y.O) (Class F)

1-45 (1-46) **1m (Fibresand)** £2,572.00 (£722.00: £352.00) Stalls: Low GOING: 0.08 sec per fur (STD)

SP RR SF

**People Direct (59)** (KMcAuliffe) **3-8-7** JFanning(5) (b.hind: mde most: kpt on wl fnl f)........— **1** 8/15[1] 67 22
**Arch Angel (IRE) (53)** (DJSffrenchDavis) **3-8-2** NAdams(1) (lw: sn chsng ldrs: ev ch 2f out: kpt on)........¾ **2** 5/1[2] 61 16
**Dancing Cavalier (40)** (RHollinshead) **3-7-12**(7) FLynch(3) (sn outpcd & bhd: hdwy u.p over 2f out: r.o towards fin)........1¾ **3** 20/1 60 16
**Bumblefoot (IRE) (56)** (MJohnston) **3-8-5** TWilliams(2) (dlsp ld 5f: one pce)........nk **4** 5/1[2] 59 15
**Hever Golf Diamond** (TJNaughton) **3-8-8**(7) TAshley(8) (in tch: hdwy u.p 3f out: wknd over 1f out)........3 **5** 20/1 63 19
**Havana Heights (IRE) (45)** (JLEyre) **3-8-4** RLappin(7) (chsd ldrs tl rdn & btn over 2f out)........5 **6** 14/1[3] 42 1
**Mulhollande Lad (IRE) (43)** (MCChapman) **3-8-2**(7) CMunday(4) (cl up early: wl outpcd after 3f)........8 **7** 100/1 31 —
**Alpheton Prince (46)** (JLHarris) **3-8-7** JFEgan(6) (a outpcd & bhd)........1¼ **8** 100/1 27 —
(SP 116.7%) **8 Rn**

**1m 47.7** (7.70) CSF £3.93 TOTE £1.70: £1.10 £1.70 £3.30 (£3.30) OWNER Mr Peter Barclay (LAMBOURN) BRED James Thom & Sons & P. Orr

## 47 WATERFORD MEDIAN AUCTION MAIDEN STKS (4, 5 & 6-Y.O) (Class F)

2-15 (2-16) **1m 4f (Fibresand)** £2,572.00 (£722.00: £352.00) Stalls: High GOING: 0.08 sec per fur (STD)

SP RR SF

**Yougo (65)** (MJohnston) **4-8-13** JWeaver(6) (lw: mde most: rdn over 3f out: sn clr: eased towards fin)........— **1** 8/11[1] 77 25
**Zesti (48)** (TTClement) **4-8-10**(3) JStack(7) (b: prom: rdn over 3f out: kpt on fnl f: no ch w wnr)........30 **2** 50/1 37 —
**Nick the Biscuit (69)** (RTPhillips) **5-9-3** AClark(8) (b: chsd ldrs: chal 4f out: one pce fnl 2f)........½ **3** 9/1[3] 35 —
**Bescaby (IRE)** (JWharton) **5-9-3** JQuinn(10) (prom: chal 4f out: outpcd fnl 2f)........1½ **4** 33/1 33 —
**I'll Be Bound** (WJMusson) **5-9-0**(3) PMcCabe(2) (nvr nr to chal)........3½ **5** 33/1 29 —
**Burntwood Melody (36)** (JAHarris) **5-9-3** JFEgan(5) (cl up tl outpcd 7f out: n.d after)........hd **6** 50/1 29 —
**Loch Style** (RHollinshead) **3-8-13** RCochrane(9) (in tch: rdn 5f out: wknd fnl 3f)........4 **7** 5/2[2] 24 —
**Zalament (38)** (NPLittmoden) **4-8-8** TGMcLaughlin(3) (chsd ldrs tl outpcd 4f out: n.d after)........2 **8** 16/1 17 —
**Never Time (IRE) (40)** (MrsVAAconley) **4-8-13** ACulhane(1) (in tch tl outpcd 7f out: t.o)........dist **9** 16/1 — 25
**Burrough Hill Lass** (MrsNMacauley) **6-8-12v**[1] SSanders(4) (t.o fnl 7f)........dist **10** 66/1 — 24
(SP 119.5%) **10 Rn**

**2m 44.6** (12.10) CSF £32.38 TOTE £1.70: £1.20 £11.40 £1.50 (£44.50) Trio £96.70 OWNER Mr C. H. Greensit (MIDDLEHAM) BRED C. H. and W. A. Greensit
WEIGHT FOR AGE 3yo-25lb, 4yo-4lb
**STEWARDS' ENQUIRY Loch Style mistakenly ran in place of Taniyar (FR)**

## 48 KILDARE H'CAP (0-80) (4-Y.O+) (Class D)

2-45 (2-46) **1m 3f (Fibresand)** £3,831.40 (£1,160.20: £566.60: £269.80) Stalls: High GOING: 0.08 sec per fur (STD)

SP RR SF

**Our Tom (59)** (JWharton) **4-8-4** NCarlisle(11) (lw: a.p: led over 2f out: r.o: hung rt towards fin)........— **1** 14/1 71 41
**Rambo's Hall (80)** (JAGlover) **11-10-0** SDWilliams(6) (a.p: rdn over 3f out: hdwy 2f out: nt qckn fnl f)........3 **2** 3/1[1] 87 60
**Wildfire (SWI) (52)** (RAkehurst) **5-8-0** JQuinn(10) (lw: led 7f out tl over 2f out: grad wknd)........4 **3** 7/2[2] 53 29
**Far Ahead (75)** (JLEyre) **4-9-6** RLappin(8) (a chsng ldrs: rdn over 3f out: one pce)........2½ **4** 10/1 73 44
**Sudden Spin (63)** (JNorton) **6-8-11** RCochrane(7) (a chsng ldrs: drvn 5f out: no imp after)........11 **5** 11/2 44 22
**Mr Towser (74)** (WWHaigh) **5-9-8** DaleGibson(5) (a chsng ldrs: one pce fnl 3f)........½ **6** 25/1 55 31
**Manful (57)** (JHetherton) **4-8-2** NKennedy(3) (lw: effrt over 4f out: nvr able rch ldrs)........1¼ **7** 12/1 37 11
**Nashaat (USA) (72)** (MCChapman) **8-8-13**(7) CMunday(1) (hld up: effrt over 3f out: no imp)........4 **8** 12/1 45 23
**Magic Junction (USA) (76)** (LordHuntingdon) **5-9-10** JWeaver(9) (nvr nr ldrs)........12 **9** 9/2[3] 31 11
*19[8]* **Slmaat (68)** (DNicholls) **5-9-2** AlexGreaves(2) (prom tl lost pl 5f out)........1¼ **10** 12/1 22 3
**Elite Justice (61)** (NTinkler) **4-8-6** KimTinkler(4) (led tl hdd 7f out: sn wknd)........5 **11** 33/1 8 —
(SP 126.4%) **11 Rn**

**2m 27.6** (7.60) CSF £55.96 CT £172.40 TOTE £24.80: £5.50 £1.50 £2.10 (£52.00) Trio £292.40 OWNER Mr J. M. Berry (MELTON MOWBRAY) BRED Bylon Farmers Ltd
WEIGHT FOR AGE 4yo-3lb

## 49 KERRY (S) STKS (3-Y.O) (Class F)

3-15 (3-17) **7f (Fibresand)** £2,607.00 (£732.00: £357.00) Stalls: Low GOING: 0.08 sec per fur (STD)

| | Horse | Dist | Pos | SP | RR | SF |
|---|---|---|---|---|---|---|
| | **Guy's Gamble** (JWharton) **3-9-0** JFanning(6) (hdwy ½-wy: led ins fnl f: r.o) | — | 1 | 33/1 | 63 | 31 |
| | **Welsh Melody (49)** (KRBurke) **3-9-0v** CRutter(5) (a.p: hdwy over 2f out: kpt on fnl f) | 1¼ | 2 | 13/2[3] | 60 | 28 |
| | **Dragonjoy (56)** (JWPayne) **3-9-5b** AMcGlone(9) (cl up: led over 3f out tl ins fnl f: sn btn) | 3½ | 3 | 100/30[1] | 57 | 26 |
| 32[7] | **Efipetite (47)** (NBycroft) **3-8-9** SMaloney(12) (hdwy ½-wy: sn in tch: kpt on fnl f) | ¾ | 4 | 16/1 | 45 | 15 |
| | **Stilly Night (IRE)** (JWharton) **3-8-9** JQuinn(3) (bhd: hdwy ½-wy: one pce fnl 2f) | 1½ | 5 | 8/1 | 42 | 12 |
| | **Still Here (IRE) (58)** (MJHeaton-Ellis) **3-9-0** AClark(2) (a in tch: rdn & one pce fnl 3f) | 6 | 6 | 8/1 | 33 | 4 |
| | **Niteowl Raider (IRE) (55)** (JAHarris) **3-8-9**(5) CTeague(4) (led over 3f: cl up tl wknd over 2f out) | ½ | 7 | 6/1[2] | 32 | 3 |
| | **Florrie'm** (JLHarris) **3-8-9** JFEgan(11) (outpcd & bhd tl sme late hdwy) | 5 | 8 | 10/1 | 16 | — |
| | **Radmore Brandy** (NPLittmoden) **3-8-9** TGMcLaughlin(8) (s.i.s: n.d) | 8 | 9 | 6/1[2] | — | — |
| | **Adler (IRE)** (MJCamacho) **3-9-0** LCharnock(1) (s.i.s: a outpcd & bhd) | 1½ | 10 | 7/1 | — | — |
| | **Napier Star (46)** (MrsNMacauley) **3-8-9** SDWilliams(7) (sn outpcd & bhd) | 1½ | 11 | 14/1 | — | — |
| | **Trickledown (48)** (MartynWane) **3-8-9** AMackay(13) (a outpcd & bhd) | 10 | 12 | 9/1 | — | — |

(SP 134.3%) **12 Rn**

**1m 33.3** (6.50) CSF £235.53 TOTE £31.30: £9.00 £2.20 £1.80 (£91.80) Trio £78.30 OWNER Parkers of Peterborough Plc (MELTON MOWBRAY) BRED Highfield Stud Ltd
No bid

## 50 WICKLOW H'CAP (0-70) (II) (4-Y.O+) (Class E)

3-45 (3-46) **7f (Fibresand)** £2,806.80 (£848.40: £413.20: £195.60) Stalls: Low GOING: 0.08 sec per fur (STD)

| | Horse | Dist | Pos | SP | RR | SF |
|---|---|---|---|---|---|---|
| | **White Sorrel (70)** (AHarrison) **5-9-11**(3) JStack(8) (hdwy ½-wy: led wl over 1f out: styd on) | — | 1 | 12/1 | 76 | 44 |
| | **Awesome Venture (55)** (MCChapman) **6-8-6**(7) CMunday(5) (disp ld tl wl over 1f out: rallied towards fin) | ½ | 2 | 12/1 | 60 | 29 |
| | **Monis (IRE) (55)** (JBalding) **5-8-6**(7) JEdmunds(4) (disp ld tl wl over 1f out: one pce) | 1½ | 3 | 6/1[3] | 56 | 26 |
| | **Don't Get Caught (IRE) (60)** (JLHarris) **4-9-4** JFEgan(2) (disp ld 4f: rdn & btn over 1f out) | 2½ | 4 | 10/1 | 56 | 25 |
| | **Aquado (51)** (SRBowring) **7-8-4b**(5) CTeague(6) (lw: hld up: hdwy 3f out: rdn & no ex appr fnl f) | 1 | 5 | 4/1[2] | 44 | 15 |
| | **Geolly (IRE) (55)** (DrJDScargill) **4-8-13b[1]** JFanning(7) (swtg: chsd ldrs tl wknd fnl 2f) | 6 | 6 | 11/1 | 35 | 7 |
| | **Rainbows Rhapsody (40)** (MJCamacho) **5-7-12** LCharnock(3) (b: b.hind: rdn most of wy: in tch tl wknd fnl 3f) | 4 | 7 | 10/1 | 11 | — |
| | **Dr Caligari (IRE) (49)** (SGollings) **4-8-7v** JQuinn(1) (chsd ldrs: rdn ½-wy: wknd fnl 2f) | 5 | 8 | 2/1[1] | 8 | — |
| 30[12] | **Whackford Squeers (68)** (DNicholls) **4-9-12** AlexGreaves(9) (sn bhd) | 8 | 9 | 13/2 | 9 | — |

(SP 122.9%) **9 Rn**

**1m 33.3** (6.50) CSF £129.84 CT £869.12 TOTE £25.40: £6.90 £3.70 £4.00 (£156.40) Trio £71.70 OWNER Mr R. Fenwick-Gibson (MIDDLEHAM) BRED Stud-On-The-Chart

T/Plpt: £344.50 (48.45 Tckts). T/Qdpt: £16.30 (4.8 Tckts). AA

# 0036-LINGFIELD (L-H) (Standard)

## Tuesday January 9th

Racing delayed 35 minutes due to late arrival of doctor

## 51 VICTORY MEDIAN AUCTION MAIDEN STKS (3-Y.O) (Class F)

1-30 (2-05) **5f (Equitrack)** £2,672.80 (£750.80: £366.40) Stalls: High GOING minus 0.46 sec per fur (FST)

| | Horse | Dist | Pos | SP | RR | SF |
|---|---|---|---|---|---|---|
| | **Happy Partner (IRE)** (CMurray) **3-9-0** MTebbutt(3) (hld up: led over 1f out: rdn out) | — | 1 | 11/8[1] | 66 | 17 |
| 28[4] | **Copper Bright (39)** (PCHaslam) **3-9-0b[1]** JFortune(6) (lw: a.p: led over 2f out tl over 1f out: unable qckn) | 1¼ | 2 | 7/2[3] | 62 | 13 |
| | **Bouton d'Or (51)** (PHowling) **3-8-9** JQuinn(1) (plld hrd: hld up: rdn over 1f out: one pce) | nk | 3 | 3/1[2] | 56 | 7 |
| | **Governors Dream (45)** (MrsNMacauley) **3-8-9** DBiggs(5) (b: led over 2f: wknd over 1f out) | 6 | 4 | 10/1 | 37 | — |
| | **Kury Girl** (JAHarris) **3-8-9** SDWilliams(4) (neat: a.p: n.m.r on ins 2f out: wknd over 1f out) | nk | 5 | 20/1 | 36 | — |
| | **Darby Flyer** (WRMuir) **3-9-0** JWeaver(2) (a bhd) | 1¼ | 6 | 5/1 | 37 | — |

(SP 119.8%) **6 Rn**

**60.51 secs** (2.51) CSF £6.92 TOTE £2.30: £1.20 £2.30 (£4.50) OWNER The Happy Partnership (NEWMARKET) BRED Shadwell Estate Company Ltd

## 52 RENOWN CLAIMING STKS (3-Y.O) (Class E)

2-00 (2-26) **7f (Equitrack)** £3,103.20 (£939.60: £458.80: £218.40) Stalls: Low GOING minus 0.46 sec per fur (FST)

| | Horse | Dist | Pos | SP | RR | SF |
|---|---|---|---|---|---|---|
| | **Ultra Barley (80)** (PCHaslam) **3-9-0**(5) MBaird(2) (rdn 2f out: hdwy on ins wl over 1f out: led ins fnl f: r.o wl) | — | 1 | 10/11[1] | 93 | 39 |
| 25* | **Rowlandsons Charm (IRE) (60)** (GLMoore) **3-8-0v** NAdams(4) (lw: hung rt thrght: w ldr: led over 2f out: hrd rdn over 1f out: hdd ins fnl f: unable qckn) | 1¼ | 2 | 4/1[2] | 71 | 17 |
| 21[2] | **Marino Street (62)** (PDEvans) **3-8-0** JQuinn(7) (b.nr fore: rdn 2f out: hdwy on ins wl over 1f out: one pce) | 6 | 3 | 5/1[3] | 57 | 3 |
| 10[5] | **Plein Gaz (FR)** (AndreHermans,Belgium) **3-8-8**(7) ALakeman(6) (b.hind: led over 4f: wknd over 1f out) | 1½ | 4 | 5/1[3] | 69 | 15 |
| | **Music Mistress (IRE) (59)** (JSMoore) **3-8-6** JFEgan(3) (lw: bhd fnl 2f) | 13 | 5 | 16/1 | 30 | — |
| 11[10] | **Wingnut (IRE) (42)** (JJBridger) **3-8-0** GBardwell(8) (lw: bhd fnl 4f) | 12 | 6 | 20/1 | — | — |
| | **Baker (54)** (JAkehurst) **3-8-1** TWilliams(1) (bhd fnl 4f) | 8 | 7 | 20/1 | — | — |

(SP 121.1%) **7 Rn**

**1m 26.2** (2.20) CSF £5.46 TOTE £1.80: £2.40 £1.70 (£3.10) OWNER Pet Express Ltd T/A Nutrimix (MIDDLEHAM) BRED Benham Stud
STEWARDS' ENQUIRY Adams susp. 18-19/1/96 (improper use of whip).

## 53 WARSPITE H'CAP (0-65) (4-Y.O+) (Class F)

2-30 (2-52) **1m (Equitrack)** £2,811.40 (£790.40: £386.20) Stalls: High GOING minus 0.46 sec per fur (FST)

| | Horse | Dist | Pos | SP | RR | SF |
|---|---|---|---|---|---|---|
| 14[4] | **Robellion (58)** (DWPArbuthnot) **5-9-8v** RCochrane(9) (b: hld up: bmpd over 2f out: rdn over 1f out: led wl ins fnl f: r.o wl) | — | 1 | 11/4[1] | 61 | 44 |
| | **Bakers Daughter (49)** (JRArnold) **4-8-13** JQuinn(10) (hdwy over 3f out: led over 2f out: hrd rdn over 1f out: hdd wl ins fnl f: unable qckn) | ½ | 2 | 8/1 | 52 | 34 |

| Form | Horse | Dist | Pos | SP | RR | SF |
|---|---|---|---|---|---|---|
| | **Paronomasia (39)** (MBell) **4-8-3** MFenton(7) (a.p: rdn over 3f out: one pce fnl 2f) | 4 | **3** | 6/1[2] | 34 | 16 |
| | **Racing Telegraph (37)** (JWPayne) **6-7-12**(3) NVarley(6) (hld up: rdn over 3f out: bmpd over 2f out: one pce) | 1 | **4** | 7/1 | 29 | 12 |
| | **Snake Plissken (IRE) (46)** (DHaydnJones) **5-8-10** AMackay(3) (lw: s.i.s: rdn 3f out: hdwy over 1f out: one pce) | nk | **5** | 10/1 | 37 | 20 |
| 14[9] | **General Shirley (IRE) (52)** (PRHedger) **5-9-2** AMcGlone(11) (nvr nr to chal) | ¾ | **6** | 16/1 | 42 | 25 |
| | **Fiaba (41)** (MrsNMacauley) **8-7-12**(7) TAshley(2) (nvr nrr) | 5 | **7** | 13/2[3] | 21 | 4 |
| 42[10] | **Shaynes Domain (44)** (RMFlower) **5-8-8b** DBiggs(1) (hdwy over 5f out: wknd wl over 1f out) | hd | **8** | 16/1 | 24 | 7 |
| | **Mediate (IRE) (64)** (AHide) **4-9-11**(3) JStack(8) (led 3f: led 4f out tl over 2f out: wknd over 1f out) | 1¼ | **9** | 8/1 | 42 | 24 |
| | **Burnt Sienna (IRE) (42)** (JSMoore) **4-8-6** JFEgan(4) (a.p: led 5f out to 4f out: sn wknd) | 8 | **10** | 8/1 | 4 | — |
| | **Ilustre (IRE) (43)** (GFierro) **4-8-7** SDWilliams(5) (lw: bhd fnl 3f) | 2½ | **11** | 20/1 | — | — |
| | **Pacific Girl (IRE) (41)** (BPalling) **4-8-5**ow2 AClark(12) (prom tl hmpd & wknd over 2f out) | nk | **12** | 20/1 | — | — |

(SP 130.5%) **12 Rn**

**1m 39.8** (2.40) CSF £26.01 CT £117.14 TOTE £3.10: £2.00 £1.90 £1.70 (£9.70) Trio £104.50 OWNER Mr George Thompson (COMPTON) BRED Pitts Farm Stud

## 54 HOOD (S) H'CAP (0-60) (4-Y.O+) (Class G)

3-00 (3-20) **1m 5f (Equitrack)** £2,505.40 (£704.40: £344.20) Stalls: Low GOING minus 0.46 sec per fur (FST)

| Form | Horse | Dist | Pos | SP | RR | SF |
|---|---|---|---|---|---|---|
| 15[5] | **Sorisky (38)** (BGubby) **4-9-0** JQuinn(9) (a.p: led over 4f out: hrd rdn over 1f out: r.o wl) | — | **1** | 20/1 | 49 | 25 |
| | **Miltak (37)** (PJMakin) **4-8-13** SSanders(6) (hdwy over 3f out: chsd wnr fnl f: r.o wl) | ¾ | **2** | 13/2[3] | 47 | 23 |
| | **Duggan (23)** (PDEvans) **9-7-11**(7) DSweeney(5) (b.off hind: a.p: rdn over 3f out: r.o wl ins fnl f) | 1½ | **3** | 8/1 | 31 | 12 |
| | **Alpine Storm (IRE) (27)** (MDIUsher) **4-7-12**(5) CAdamson(7) (hdwy 6f out: rdn over 4f out: chsd wnr over 2f out to 1f out: unable qckn) | ½ | **4** | 8/1 | 35 | 11 |
| 23[7] | **Mafuta (IRE) (34)** (JJSheehan) **4-8-10** MFenton(14) (hdwy over 1f out: nvr nrr) | 2½ | **5** | 16/1 | 39 | 15 |
| | **Sharp Thrill (43)** (BSmart) **5-9-10** RCochrane(2) (lw: led over 8f: wknd wl over 1f out) | 3 | **6** | 9/2[2] | 44 | 25 |
| 23[10] | **Shedansar (IRE) (34)** (GLMoore) **4-8-10** NAdams(11) (nvr nrr) | hd | **7** | 16/1 | 35 | 11 |
| | **Kenyatta (USA) (37)** (AMoore) **7-9-4** CandyMorris(1) (b: b.hind: prom over 8f) | s.h | **8** | 11/4[1] | 38 | 19 |
| 9[6] | **Telephus (35)** (BJMcMath) **7-9-2b** MWigham(10) (hdwy 4f out: wknd over 3f out) | ¾ | **9** | 7/1 | 35 | 16 |
| | **Hunza Story (30)** (NPLittmoden) **4-8-6** TGMcLaughlin(12) (b.hind: hdwy over 3f out: wknd over 2f out) | ½ | **10** | 20/1 | 29 | 5 |
| | **Maronetta (30)** (MJRyan) **4-8-1**(5) MBaird(8) (lw: a bhd) | 1½ | **11** | 7/1 | 27 | 3 |
| | **Ballad Ruler (21)** (PAPritchard) **10-7-9**(7)ow1 JoHunnam(3) (b: chsd ldr over 8f: wknd over 3f out) | 1¾ | **12** | 33/1 | 16 | — |
| | **Inishmann (IRE) (35)** (JSMoore) **5-9-2** JFEgan(13) (lw: bhd fnl 4f) | 20 | **13** | 33/1 | 6 | — |
| | **Starlight Flyer (21)** (JELong) **9-7-9b**(7) TField(15) (b: b.hind: virtually ref to r: a t.o) | dist | **14** | 33/1 | — | — |

(SP 135.5%) **14 Rn**

**2m 49.37** (6.17) CSF £146.84 CT £1,051.15 TOTE £18.90: £4.10 £2.90 £7.00 (£27.10) Trio £174.50; £998.32 to Wolverhampton 10/1/96. OWNER Brian Gubby Ltd (BAGSHOT) BRED Roldvale Ltd
WEIGHT FOR AGE 4yo-5lb
No bid

## 55 REPULSE H'CAP (0-80) (4-Y.O+) (Class D)

3-30 (3-47) **6f (Equitrack)** £3,848.95 (£1,165.60: £569.30: £271.15) Stalls: Low GOING minus 0.46 sec per fur (FST)

| Form | Horse | Dist | Pos | SP | RR | SF |
|---|---|---|---|---|---|---|
| | **Chewit (80)** (AMoore) **4-10-0** CandyMorris(9) (stdy hdwy 3f out: led ins fnl f: qcknd: comf) | — | **1** | 12/1 | 94+ | 58 |
| 26* | **Pageboy (68)** (PCHaslam) **7-9-2b** 7x JFortune(13) (rdn thrght: hdwy over 3f out: r.o one pce) | 5 | **2** | 9/2[1] | 69 | 33 |
| | **Robo Magic (USA) (71)** (LMontagueHall) **4-9-5** JFEgan(12) (b.hind: a.p: led over 1f out tl ins fnl f: one pce) | 1 | **3** | 9/2[1] | 69 | 33 |
| 20[7] | **Four of Spades (72)** (PDEvans) **5-9-6v** SSanders(11) (lw: rdn thrght: hdwy over 1f out: nvr nrr) | 3 | **4** | 11/1 | 62 | 26 |
| | **Ultra Beet (75)** (PCHaslam) **4-9-9v** JWeaver(2) (led over 2f: ev ch 1f out: sn wknd) | nk | **5** | 11/2[2] | 64 | 28 |
| | **Hannah's Usher (80)** (CMurray) **4-10-0** MTebbutt(10) (no hdwy fnl 3f) | ¾ | **6** | 14/1 | 67 | 31 |
| | **Spender (79)** (PWHarris) **7-9-10**(3) JStack(6) (led over 3f out tl over 1f out: sn wknd) | ¾ | **7** | 6/1[3] | 64 | 28 |
| | **Q Factor (68)** (DHaydnJones) **4-9-2** AMackay(5) (outpcd: nvr nrr) | 2½ | **8** | 20/1 | 47 | 11 |
| | **Anzio (IRE) (74)** (BAPearce) **5-9-8b** TIves(1) (b: b.hind: prom 2f) | s.h | **9** | 6/1[3] | 52 | 16 |
| | **Squire Corrie (67)** (GHarwood) **4-8-8**(7) GayeHarwood(4) (prom over 3f) | ¾ | **10** | 11/1 | 43 | 7 |
| | **Pab's Choice (57)** (MMcCormack) **5-8-5v** MFenton(8) (bhd fnl 3f) | 1¼ | **11** | 8/1 | 30 | — |
| 14[12] | **Willrack Farrier (63)** (BJMeehan) **4-8-11** AClark(3) (bhd fnl 3f) | 6 | **12** | 33/1 | 20 | — |
| | **Rockville Pike (IRE) (77)** (SDow) **4-9-11** WWoods(7) (a bhd) | 2 | **13** | 25/1 | 29 | — |

(SP 134.0%) **13 Rn**

**1m 11.62** (1.02) CSF £67.43 CT £268.83 TOTE £9.80: £2.60 £3.00 £2.10 (£48.10) Trio £50.70 OWNER Ballard (1834) Ltd (BRIGHTON) BRED B. Minty

## 56 NELSON H'CAP (0-75) (3-Y.O) (Class D)

4-00 (4-12) **1m 2f (Equitrack)** £3,761.20 (£1,138.60: £555.80: £264.40) Stalls: Low GOING minus 0.46 sec per fur (FST)

| Form | Horse | Dist | Pos | SP | RR | SF |
|---|---|---|---|---|---|---|
| 35* | **China Castle (59)** (PCHaslam) **3-8-13** 5x JFortune(10) (hdwy over 3f out: rdn 2f out: led wl ins fnl f: r.o wl) | — | **1** | 7/4[1] | 70 | 32 |
| | **Domoor (54)** (MJohnston) **3-8-8** JWeaver(6) (led: rdn over 3f out: hdd wl ins fnl f: unable qckn) | ¾ | **2** | 7/2[2] | 64 | 26 |
| | **Thorntoun Estate (IRE) (57)** (MJohnston) **3-8-11** DeanMcKeown(11) (a.p: chsd ldr 6f out tl over 1f out: one pce) | 1¾ | **3** | 7/1 | 64 | 26 |
| | **Montecristo (63)** (RGuest) **3-9-3** GBardwell(2) (hld up: rdn over 4f out: one pce) | 4 | **4** | 16/1 | 64 | 26 |
| 11[6] | **Suparoy (52)** (TGMills) **3-8-6** JQuinn(9) (hld up: rdn over 4f out: one pce) | 3 | **5** | 20/1 | 48 | 10 |
| | **Blue Flyer (IRE) (67)** (RIngram) **3-9-7b**1 DBiggs(1) (prom over 4f) | 2 | **6** | 10/1 | 60 | 22 |
| | **Belle's Boy (67)** (BPalling) **3-9-7** AClark(8) (dwlt: nvr nr to chal) | 2½ | **7** | 25/1 | 56 | 18 |
| | **Four Weddings (USA) (55)** (MBell) **3-8-9** MFenton(3) (bhd fnl 8f) | 1 | **8** | 20/1 | 42 | 4 |
| | **Sterling Fellow (57)** (RHannon) **3-8-11** GCarter(7) (prom over 5f) | 7 | **9** | 9/1 | 33 | — |
| | **Kissing Gate (USA) (62)** (RCharlton) **3-9-2** SSanders(5) (lw: a bhd) | 12 | **10** | 5/1[3] | 19 | — |
| | **Tartan Express (IRE) (45)** (BAPearce) **3-7-13**ow1 TWilliams(4) (a bhd) | 8 | **11** | 50/1 | — | — |

(SP 128.1%) **11 Rn**

**2m 7.88** (3.58) CSF £8.93 CT £34.61 TOTE £2.00: £1.10 £1.20 £1.90 (£6.80) Trio £6.90 OWNER Mr J. M. Davis (MIDDLEHAM) BRED Mrs Frances Cronin

T/Jkpt: Not won; £22,914.02 to Wolverhampton 10/1/96. T/Plpt £107.20 (147.82 Tckts). T/Qdpt: Not won; £104.20 to Wolverhampton 10/1/96. AK

# 0016-WOLVERHAMPTON (L-H) (Standard)
## Wednesday January 10th
WEATHER: cloudy WIND: slt bhd

### 57 BASIL (S) STKS (I) (4-Y.O+) (Class E)
1-00 (1-01) **1m 100y (Fibresand)** £2,821.10 (£852.80: £415.40: £196.70) Stalls: Low GOING minus 0.09 sec per fur (STD)

| | Horse / details | Dist | Pos | SP | RR | SF |
|---|---|---|---|---|---|---|
| 18* | **Maple Bay (IRE) (59)** (ABailey) **7-8-12**(7) PRoberts(3) (chsd ldr: led over 2f out: rdn over 1f out: r.o wl) | — | 1 | 11/4 1 | 81 | 65 |
| | **Live Project (IRE) (61)** (MJohnston) **4-9-0** JWeaver(9) (lw: a.p: r.o one pce fnl f) | 4 | 2 | 8/1 | 69 | 52 |
| 34³ | **Sarasi (66)** (MJCamacho) **4-9-5** LCharnock(4) (led 6f: one pce) | 1¼ | 3 | 8/1 | 72 | 55 |
| 45* | **Warhurst (IRE) (57)** (DNicholls) **5-9-0** AlexGreaves(5) (hld up: no hdwy fnl 2f) | 4 | 4 | 3/1 2 | 59 | 43 |
| | **Certain Way (IRE) (58)** (NPLittmoden) **6-9-5** TGMcLaughlin(12) (lw: chsd ldrs: rdn 5f out: wknd over 2f out) | 9 | 5 | 7/1 3 | 47 | 31 |
| | **Northern Grey (50)** (JBerry) **4-8-9**(5) PFessey(7) (prom tl wknd 2f out) | nk | 6 | 20/1 | 42 | 25 |
| 29⁸ | **Bex Hill (38)** (DHaydnJones) **4-8-9v¹** AMackay(6) (a bhd) | 3½ | 7 | 50/1 | 30 | 13 |
| | **Dannistar (55)** (PDEvans) **4-9-0** SSanders(10) (b.hind: hld up: rdn over 3f out: wknd over 2f out) | hd | 8 | 12/1 | 35 | 18 |
| | **Scottish Park (32)** (JLHarris) **7-8-6**(3) DWright(11) (a bhd) | 2½ | 9 | 33/1 | 24 | 8 |
| | **Desert Invader (IRE) (61)** (DWChapman) **5-9-0** ACulhane(2) (swtg: rdn 5f out: sn bhd) | 1 | 10 | 7/1 3 | 28 | 12 |
| | **Dream Carrier (IRE) (52)** (REPeacock) **8-8-11**(3) PMcCabe(8) (a bhd) | s.h | 11 | 16/1 | 27 | 11 |
| | **Sheroot (40)** (DMoffatt) **4-9-0** JQuinn(13) (b.hind: a bhd: t.o) | 13 | 12 | 33/1 | 4 | — |
| | **Nord Lys (IRE) (22)** (BJLlewellyn) **5-9-0** TWilliams(1) (bhd fnl 4f: t.o) | 5 | 13 | 50/1 | — | — |

(SP 127.0%) **13 Rn**

**1m 48.2** (3.20) CSF £25.08 TOTE £3.70: £1.30 £3.80 £2.40 (£25.70) Trio £53.10 OWNER Mr Roy Matthews (TARPORLEY) BRED Berkshire Equestrian Services Ltd
Bt in 3,600 gns

### 58 JAMUNA MAIDEN STKS (3-Y.O) (Class D)
1-30 (1-32) **7f (Fibresand)** £3,884.05 (£1,176.40: £574.70: £273.85) Stalls: High GOING minus 0.09 sec per fur (STD)

| Horse / details | Dist | Pos | SP | RR | SF |
|---|---|---|---|---|---|
| **Coachella** (SirMarkPrescott) **3-8-9** CNutter(10) (leggy: unf: a.p: led 1f out: r.o wl) | — | 1 | 11/2 3 | 62+ | 19 |
| **Yeoman Oliver** (BAMcMahon) **3-9-0** GCarter(2) (lw: prom: rdn over 2f out: nt clr run 1f out: r.o) | 1¾ | 2 | 14/1 | 63 | 20 |
| **Cointosser (IRE)** (SPCWoods) **3-8-9** WWoods(11) (leggy: unf: s.i.s: sn chsg ldrs: hung lft 1f out: one pce) | ¾ | 3 | 9/1 | 56 | 13 |
| **Note of Caution (USA)** (LordHuntingdon) **3-8-9** JWeaver(7) (led: rdn & hdd 1f out: no ex) | ½ | 4 | 10/11 1 | 55 | 12 |
| **Dirab** (TDBarron) **3-9-0** JFortune(3) (prom: outpcd 3f out: styd on fnl 2f) | 3 | 5 | 9/2 2 | 53 | 10 |
| **Kingdom Princess** (MJCamacho) **3-8-9** LCharnock(9) (lw: prom: rdn 4f out: wknd over 2f out) | 1 | 6 | 12/1 | 46 | 3 |
| **Thenorthernplayboy (IRE)** (BPreece) **3-9-0** NAdams(6) (bit bkwd: s.i.s: a bhd) | 7 | 7 | 25/1 | 35 | — |
| **Bluntswood Hall** (RHollinshead) **3-9-0** MWigham(8) (lt-f: unf: s.s: a wl bhd) | 5 | 8 | 25/1 | 24 | — |
| **Skipman (IRE)** (NASmith) **3-9-0** SDWilliams(5) (bhd fnl 3f) | 2 | 9 | 33/1 | 19 | — |
| **Highland Fawn** (BAMcMahon) **3-8-2**(7) FLynch(4) (leggy: lt-f: s.i.s: a bhd: t.o) | 5 | 10 | 20/1 | 3 | — |
| **Roxane (IRE)** (ABailey) **3-8-6**(3) DWright(1) (prom 4f: t.o) | 1½ | 11 | 20/1 | — | — |

(SP 130.5%) **11 Rn**

**1m 30.5** (5.80) CSF £76.52 TOTE £7.20: £1.90 £2.60 £2.10 (£47.70) Trio £109.90; £97.52 to Wincanton 11/1/96 OWNER Lord Derby (NEWMARKET) BRED Stanley Estate and Stud Co

### 59 BAILEY CLAIMING STKS (3-Y.O+) (Class F)
2-00 (2-01) **6f (Fibresand)** £2,838.00 (£858.00: £418.00: £198.00) Stalls: Low GOING minus 0.09 sec per fur (STD)

| | Horse / details | Dist | Pos | SP | RR | SF |
|---|---|---|---|---|---|---|
| | **Sense of Priority (70)** (DNicholls) **7-9-10** AlexGreaves(11) (hld up: hdwy over 2f out: edgd lft & led wl ins fnl f: r.o wl) | — | 1 | 11/2 3 | 71 | 50 |
| | **Sir Tasker (69)** (JLHarris) **8-9-10b¹** JWeaver(12) (lw: led 4f out: clr 2f out: hdd wl ins fnl f) | 1½ | 2 | 7/2 2 | 67 | 46 |
| | **Brookhead Lady (53)** (PDEvans) **5-8-13** SSanders(4) (b.nr fore: a.p: one pce fnl 2f) | 3 | 3 | 9/1 | 48 | 27 |
| | **Best Kept Secret (66)** (PDEvans) **5-9-6** JFortune(3) (led 1f: one pce fnl 2f) | hd | 4 | 8/1 | 55 | 34 |
| | **Promise Fulfilled (USA) (66)** (ABailey) **5-9-2**(3) DWright(13) (hld up: hdwy 3f out: one pce fnl 2f) | 2 | 5 | 6/1 | 48 | 27 |
| | **Jigsaw Boy (64)** (PGMurphy) **7-9-9**(3) SDrowne(8) (sme hdwy 2f out: nvr nr to chal) | 3½ | 6 | 3/1 1 | 46 | 25 |
| 22⁶ | **Man of May (35)** (NPLittmoden) **4-9-8** TGMcLaughlin(10) (chsd ldrs: hrd drvn over 3f out: wknd over 1f out) | nk | 7 | 33/1 | 41 | 20 |
| 21⁵ | **Red Acuisle (IRE) (64)** (JBerry) **3-8-2**(5) PFessey(6) (chsd ldrs 3f) | 4 | 8 | 6/1 | 32 | — |
| | **Bold Aristocrat (IRE) (41)** (RHollinshead) **5-8-13**(7) FLynch(9) (lw: a bhd) | 1½ | 9 | 33/1 | 25 | 4 |
| | **Caherass Court (IRE) (32)** (BPreece) **5-8-11** NAdams(2) (bhd fnl 3f) | 3 | 10 | 33/1 | 8 | — |
| | **Scboo (35)** (REPeacock) **7-9-8** VSlattery(5) (outpcd) | ½ | 11 | 50/1 | 17 | — |
| | **Seenthelight (40)** (DMoffatt) **4-9-5** TWilliams(7) (a bhd: t.o) | 10 | 12 | 25/1 | — | — |
| | **Flashing Sabre (54)** (JBerry) **4-8-11v¹**(7) PRoberts(1) (led 5f out to 4f out: sn wknd: t.o) | 4 | 13 | 20/1 | — | — |

(SP 131.7%) **13 Rn**

**1m 15.0** (3.60) CSF £25.91 TOTE £14.10: £3.40 £1.70 £3.40 (£29.90) Trio £58.20 OWNER Mr S. Schofield (THIRSK) BRED Cheveley Park Stud Ltd
WEIGHT FOR AGE 3yo-16lb

### 60 JERICHO H'CAP (0-75) (4-Y.O+) (Class D)
2-30 (2-30) **1m 6f 166y (Fibresand)** £3,796.30 (£1,149.40: £561.20: £267.10) Stalls: High GOING minus 0.09 sec per fur (STD)

| | Horse / details | Dist | Pos | SP | RR | SF |
|---|---|---|---|---|---|---|
| 19* | **Lear Dancer (USA) (67)** (PhilipMitchell) **5-9-12b** 4x AClark(9) (hld up: hrd drvn over 2f out: edgd lft & led 1f out: r.o) | — | 1 | 15/8 1 | 81 | 41 |
| 19³ | **Shakiyr (FR) (65)** (RHollinshead) **5-9-10** RCochrane(6) (hld up: hmpd & lost pl over 6f out: hdwy 5f out: rdn 4f out: led over 1f out: sn hdd: unable qckn) | 1¼ | 2 | 7/2 2 | 78 | 38 |
| | **Badawi (FR) (37)** (NMBabbage) **6-7-10** JQuinn(2) (led over 7f: ev ch whn sltly hmpd over 1f out: styd on) | 1¼ | 3 | 12/1 | 48 | 8 |
| | **Thrower (39)** (BPreece) **5-7-12** NAdams(3) (a.p: led 7f out tl over 1f out: one pce) | 2½ | 4 | 4/1 3 | 48 | 8 |
| | **Mrs Jawleyford (USA) (46)** (CSmith) **8-8-0**(5) MBaird(7) (b: hld up: jnd ldrs 8f out: wknd over 3f out) | 11 | 5 | 33/1 | 43 | 3 |
| 33⁸ | **Heighth of Fame (45)** (AJWilson) **5-8-4** GBardwell(5) (prom: hrd drvn 4f out: wknd over 2f out) | 1½ | 6 | 12/1 | 40 | — |
| | **Backview (66)** (BJLlewellyn) **4-9-5b¹** TWilliams(4) (wl bhd 5f out: styd on fnl 2f) | 1½ | 7 | 14/1 | 59 | 13 |
| | **Bold Elect (47)** (EJAlston) **8-8-1**(5)ow1 CTeague(10) (drppd rr 5f out: t.o fnl 3f) | 20 | 8 | 16/1 | 19 | — |

**Swordking (IRE) (37)** (JLHarris) **7-7-7**(3) DWright(8) (prom: rdn 6f out: wknd qckly over 4f out: t.o) ................11 **9** 6/1 — —
**Genuine Leader (43)** (PGMurphy) **4-7-7b**(3) NVarley(1) (prom: rdn & wknd qckly over 6f out: t.o fnl 4f)..........20 **10** 33/1 — —
(SP 125.1%) **10 Rn**

**3m 19.0** (11.60) CSF £9.32 CT £57.74 TOTE £3.00: £1.30 £1.70 £3.10 (£4.50) Trio £39.30 OWNER Mrs R. A. Johnson (EPSOM) BRED Alan S. Kline
LONG HANDICAP Badawi (FR) 7-3 Swordking (IRE) 7-8 Genuine Leader 7-4
WEIGHT FOR AGE 4yo-6lb

## 61 JAFFA H'CAP (0-90) (4-Y.O+) (Class C)

3-00 (3-01) **1m 1f 79y (Fibresand)** £5,662.10 (£1,713.80: £836.40: £397.70) Stalls: Low GOING minus 0.09 sec per fur (STD)

SP RR SF

**Bernard Seven (IRE) (76)** (CEBrittain) **4-9-4b** JWeaver(12) (lw: led over 2f: led 5f out: rdn out) ....................— **1** 14/1 81 47
**South Eastern Fred (84)** (HJCollingridge) **5-9-13** MRimmer(5) (a.p: chsd wnr 2f out: unable qckn fnl f)........1¾ **2** 8/1 85 53
**Kintwyn (68)** (CCElsey) **6-8-11** CRutter(6) (b: hld up & bhd: hdwy 3f out: r.o one pce fnl f)............................¾ **3** 20/1 68 36
**Komreyev Dancer (80)** (ABailey) **4-9-5**(3) DWright(10) (hld up & bhd: hdwy over 2f out: styd on fnl f)............1½ **4** 16/1 78 44
29* **Rambo Waltzer (81)** (DNicholls) **4-9-9** 5x AlexGreaves(11) (hld up: hdwy 4f out: wknd over 1f out)...................2 **5** 6/1[3] 76 42
20[2] **High Premium (70)** (RAFahey) **8-8-13** ACulhane(1) (no hdwy fnl 2f)..............................................................1¼ **6** 9/1 62 30
30[5] **Araboybill (54)** (RSimpson) **5-7-11b** GBardwell(9) (prom tl rdn & wknd over 3f out)..........................................4 **7** 20/1 39 7
**Leif the Lucky (USA) (78)** (MissSEHall) **7-9-4**(3) JStack(4) (b.hind: prom tl wknd over 1f out)..........................1 **8** 5/1[2] 61 29
**Nigel's Lad (IRE) (72)** (PCHaslam) **4-9-0** JFortune(13) (rdn & bhd fnl 5f) ..................................................1¾ **9** 3/1[1] 53 19
**Second Colours (USA) (76)** (MrsMReveley) **6-9-5** RCochrane(7) (a bhd)..................................................1¾ **10** 5/1[2] 53 21
**Sweet Supposin (IRE) (82)** (CADwyer) **5-9-4v**(7) TAshley(8) (hld up: hdwy over 4f out: wknd over 2f out)..........................................................................................................................3 **11** 10/1 54 22
**Easy Choice (USA) (74)** (PhilipMitchell) **4-9-2** AClark(3) (lw: chsd ldrs: rdn 6f out: eased whn btn 1f out) ........3 **12** 7/1 42 8
**Make a Note (USA) (85)** (PDEvans) **5-10-0** SSanders(2) (led 7f out to 5f out: rdn over 3f out: wknd over 2f out).......................................................................................................................1¼ **13** 25/1 50 18
(SP 141.2%) **13 Rn**

**2m 1.6** (5.60) CSF £128.08 CT £2,095.70 TOTE £13.90: £2.90 £6.80 £14.20 (£38.70) Trio £367.40; £465.81 to Wincanton 11/1/96 OWNER Mr Bernard Butt (NEWMARKET) BRED Bobby Donworth and Honora Corridan
WEIGHT FOR AGE 4yo-1lb
OFFICIAL EXPLANATION **Nigel's Lad(IRE): was reported to have never been travelling in the race.**

## 62 BASIL (S) STKS (II) (4-Y.O+) (Class E)

3-30 (3-31) **1m 100y (Fibresand)** £2,806.80 (£848.40: £413.20: £195.60) Stalls: Low GOING minus 0.09 sec per fur (STD)

SP RR SF

**Hand of Straw (IRE) (52)** (PGMurphy) **4-8-11v**[1](3) SDrowne(2) (lw: hld up: hdwy on ins 4f out: led over 1f out: all out).............................................................................................................— **1** 16/1 72 36
29[3] **Faez (54)** (RSimpson) **6-9-0b** GBardwell(3) (led over 6f out tl over 5f out: led 4f out tl over 1f out: unable qckn)...........................................................................................................2½ **2** 9/1 66 31
**Miss Zanzibar (60)** (RAFahey) **4-8-9** ACulhane(1) (hld up: hdwy over 3f out: ev ch over 1f out: one pce)......2½ **3** 5/1[2] 58 22
**Little Scarlett (50)** (PJMakin) **4-9-0** NCarlisle(4) (a.p: rdn over 2f out: no hdwy) ...................................2½ **4** 11/2[3] 58 22
30[7] **Eastleigh (51)** (RHollinshead) **7-9-0** TIves(5) (b.off hind: hdwy over 1f out: n.d) ........................................3 **5** 9/1 51 16
**Off the Air (IRE) (45)** (BJLlewellyn) **5-8-9b** TWilliams(9) (rdn thrght: chsd ldrs: no hdwy fnl 3f)......................1¼ **6** 20/1 44 9
31[3] **No Submission (USA) (68)** (DWChapman) **10-8-9v**(5) PFessey(11) (lw: led over 5f out to 4f out: wknd over 2f out)...........................................................................................................................s.h **7** 7/4[1] 48 13
**Peacefull Reply (USA) (45)** (FHLee) **6-9-0** RLappin(6) (hld up: rdn over 3f out: no rspnse) ..........................1½ **8** 16/1 45 10
**Pigalle Wonder (25)** (NMBabbage) **8-9-0** JQuinn(8) (lw: led 2f: wknd 3f out).................................................1 **9** 16/1 43 8
**Vocal Command (50)** (WWHaigh) **4-9-0** DaleGibson(10) (b.off hind: lw: a bhd) .............................................2½ **10** 10/1 39 3
**Timely Example (USA) (64)** (BRCambidge) **5-9-0** NAdams(12) (wl bhd fnl 5f) ...............................................2 **11** 20/1 35 —
**Dance on Sixpence (40)** (JHPeacock) **8-9-0** CRutter(7) (wl bhd fnl 5f)..........................................................4 **12** 25/1 27 —
**Dance of Joy (41)** (JMCarr) **4-8-9** SMorris(13) (bit bkwd: a bhd)...............................................................5 **13** 20/1 14 —
(SP 133.3%) **13 Rn**

**1m 50.8** (5.80) CSF £151.21 TOTE £39.30: £6.20 £2.30 £2.80 (£89.90) Trio £196.40; £193.65 to Wincanton 11/1/96 OWNER Mrs Louise Murphy (BRISTOL) BRED M. J. Dargan
No bid

## 63 LADBROKE SERIES H'CAP (Qualifier) (0-75) (3-Y.O+) (Class D)

4-00 (4-01) **5f (Fibresand)** £3,848.95 (£1,165.60: £569.30: £271.15) Stalls: Low GOING minus 0.09 sec per fur (STD)

SP RR SF

**Shadow Jury (72)** (DWChapman) **6-9-13b** LCharnock(4) (a.p: hrd drvn to ld nr fin) ........................................— **1** 9/1 76 42
22* **Cheeky Chappy (54)** (DWChapman) **5-8-4b**(5) 7x PFessey(1) (a.p: led 3f out: clr over 1f out: hdd nr fin) ........hd **2** 5/1[1] 58 24
16[3] **Featherstone Lane (61)** (MissLCSiddall) **5-9-2v** JWeaver(10) (racd wd: hdwy wl over 1f out: r.o ins fnl f).....1¾ **3** 7/1[3] 59 25
16[2] **Chadwell Hall (65)** (SRBowring) **5-9-1b**(5) CTeague(11) (a.p: r.o one pce fnl f) .............................................¾ **4** 5/1[1] 61 27
36[U] **Delrob (55)** (DHaydnJones) **5-8-10** AMackay(12) (lw: dwlt: swtchd ins after 1f: hdwy over 1f out: nvr nrr) .....1½ **5** 14/1 46 12
**Lord Sky (73)** (ABailey) **5-9-7**(7) AngelaGallimore(6) (prom tl wknd over 1f out).............................................2½ **6** 12/1 56 22
22[3] **The Real Whizzbang (IRE) (44)** (PSFelgate) **5-7-6b**(7) IonaWands(7) (prom tl wknd wl over 1f out) .................½ **7** 12/1 25 —
**Tenor (64)** (DNicholls) **5-9-5** AlexGreaves(13) (bkwd: n.d)...........................................................................3½ **8** 9/1 34 —
**Gagajulu (66)** (PDEvans) **3-8-6** SSanders(3) (lw: outpcd)...........................................................................hd **9** 5/1[1] 36 —
**Bajan Frontier (IRE) (49)** (FHLee) **4-8-4** GCarter(2) (b.hind: led 2f: wknd wl over 1f out) ...............................1¼ **10** 13/2[2] 15 —
**Anytime Baby (48)** (PTDalton) **4-8-3** JFEgan(5) (b.hind: lw: a bhd) ...............................................................4 **11** 14/1 1 —
22[8] **Margaretrose Anna (60)** (EJAlston) **4-9-1** JFortune(9) (bhd fnl 2f).................................................................1¾ **12** 25/1 7 —
**Branston Kristy (41)** (CSmith) **4-7-5v**(5) MBaird(8) (bkwd: dwlt: sn t.o) ...................................................dist **13** 33/1 — —
(SP 131.3%) **13 Rn**

**62.3 secs** (3.60) CSF £54.33 CT £317.56 TOTE £15.10: £3.00 £1.40 £1.90 (£30.00) Trio £89.50 OWNER Mrs Jeanne Chapman (YORK) BRED J. S. Bell
LONG HANDICAP Branston Kristy 7-7
WEIGHT FOR AGE 3yo-15lb

T/Jkpt: Not won; £32,548.41 to Wincanton 11/1/96. T/Plpt: £2,241.70 (6.89 Tckts). T/Qdpt: £241.30 (0.18 Tckts). KH

# 0051-LINGFIELD (L-H) (Standard)
## Thursday January 11th

## 64 GUY MANNERING CLAIMING STKS (4-Y.O+) (Class E)
1-00 (1-01) **5f (Equitrack)** £3,074.60 (£930.80: £454.40: £216.20) Stalls: High GOING minus 0.44 sec per fur (FST)

| | | | | SP | RR | SF |
|---|---|---|---|---|---|---|
| | **Lift Boy (USA) (57)** (AMoore) **7-8-3** CandyMorris(6) (b.hind: hld up: hrd rdn over 1f out: led ins fnl f: r.o wl) | — | 1 | 10/1$^{2}$ | 59 | 20 |
| $26^{7}$ | **Distant Dynasty (55)** (BAPearce) **6-8-11** SSanders(5) (w ldr: led over 1f out tl ins fnl f: unable qckn) | 1½ | 2 | 10/1$^{2}$ | 62 | 23 |
| | **Inherent Magic (IRE) (87)** (WRMuir) **7-9-0** JWeaver(8) (b: s.s: hdwy over 1f out: r.o) | 1 | 3 | 2/5$^{1}$ | 62 | 23 |
| $41^{9}$ | **Tyrian Purple (IRE) (57)** (TJNaughton) **8-7-11b**(7)ow1 TAshley(2) (b: led over 3f: wknd fnl f) | ½ | 4 | 16/1$^{3}$ | 50 | 10 |
| $55^{5}$ | **Ultra Beet (75)** (PCHaslam) **4-9-5b$^{1}$** JFortune(3) (lost pl over 2f out: r.o one pce fnl f) | ½ | 5 | 10/1$^{2}$ | 64 | 25 |
| $41^{6}$ | **Superlao (BEL) (55)** (AndreHermans,Belgium) **4-7-12** JQuinn(4) (b.hind: a.p: rdn over 2f out: wknd over 1f out) | ¾ | 6 | 10/1$^{2}$ | 40 | 1 |
| $41^{5}$ | **Aston Manor (IRE) (59)** (RHannon) **4-8-9**ow2 WNewnes(7) (s.s: a bhd) | 3 | 7 | 10/1$^{2}$ | 42 | 1 |
| $22^{7}$ | **Tommy Tempest (43)** (REPeacock) **7-8-0v**(3) PMcCabe(1) (b: prom 3f) | 7 | 8 | 50/1 | 13 | — |

(SP 124.7%) **8 Rn**

**59.82 secs** (1.82) CSF £95.07 TOTE £35.10: £3.80 £2.80 £1.10 (£29.20) OWNER Mr A. Moore (BRIGHTON) BRED Paul & Arnold Bryant in USA

## 65 REDGAUNTLET (S) STKS (4-Y.O+) (Class G)
1-30 (1-31) **7f (Equitrack)** £2,259.00 (£634.00: £309.00) Stalls: Low GOING minus 0.44 sec per fur (FST)

| | | | | SP | RR | SF |
|---|---|---|---|---|---|---|
| | **Star Talent (USA) (105)** (MissGayKelleway) **5-8-12** RCochrane(10) (b.hind: hld up: led over 1f out: all out) | — | 1 | 10/11$^{1}$ | 75 | 41 |
| | **Perilous Plight (73)** (WRMuir) **5-8-12** JWeaver(3) (hld up: rdn 2f out: r.o wl ins fnl f) | s.h | 2 | 3/1$^{2}$ | 75 | 41 |
| | **Deeply Vale (IRE) (68)** (GLMoore) **5-8-12** AClark(6) (a.p: led over 2f out tl over 1f out: unable qckn) | 3 | 3 | 5/1$^{3}$ | 68 | 34 |
| | **Respectable Jones (47)** (RHollinshead) **10-8-12b** MWigham(5) (lw: nvr nr to chal) | 6 | 4 | 25/1 | 54 | 20 |
| | **Dragon Green** (JWhite) **5-8-9**(3) SDrowne(1) (a.p: rdn over 2f out: sn wknd) | nk | 5 | 33/1 | 54 | 20 |
| | **Thunderous (43)** (JJBridger) **5-8-12b** JQuinn(7) (b: swtg: nvr nrr) | 7 | 6 | 50/1 | 38 | 4 |
| | **Justinianus (IRE)** (AndreHermans,Belgium) **4-8-5b$^{1}$**(7) ALakeman(4) (led over 4f) | 2 | 7 | 14/1 | 33 | — |
| | **Dusk in Daytona (57)** (CJames) **4-8-7** AMcGlone(9) (prom over 4f) | s.h | 8 | 14/1 | 28 | — |
| | **Nordic Colours (IRE)** (CDondi,Belgium) **5-8-13b$^{1}$** NinoMinner(8) (prom over 2f) | 8 | 9 | 16/1 | 16 | — |
| | **Thorny Bishop (53)** (JJBridger) **5-8-12v** GBardwell(2) (a bhd) | 10 | 10 | 25/1 | — | — |

(SP 125.9%) **10 Rn**

**1m 25.57** (1.57) CSF £4.54 TOTE £1.60: £1.60 £1.40 £1.70 (£3.30) Trio £2.10 OWNER Miss Jo Crowley (WHITCOMBE) BRED Mrs Afaf A. Al Essa

Bt in 3,200 gns

## 66 TALISMAN H'CAP (0-65) (4-Y.O+) (Class F)
2-00 (2-04) **1m 2f (Equitrack)** £2,977.00 (£837.00: £409.00) Stalls: Low GOING minus 0.44 sec per fur (FST)

| | | | | SP | RR | SF |
|---|---|---|---|---|---|---|
| | **Explosive Power (54)** (GCBravery) **5-9-5** TIves(7) (hdwy over 3f out: led over 1f out: rdn out) | — | 1 | 5/1$^{2}$ | 61 | 37 |
| | **Real Madrid (34)** (GPEnright) **5-7-13v** NAdams(11) (lw: a.p: led over 3f out tl over 1f out: unable qckn) | 1 | 2 | 11/1 | 39 | 15 |
| 27* | **Rival Bid (USA) (60)** (MrsNMacauley) **8-9-4**(7) 5x TAshley(3) (rdn & hdwy over 3f out: r.o one pce) | 5 | 3 | 11/4$^{1}$ | 57 | 33 |
| | **Swynford Flyer (32)** (JAHarris) **7-7-6**(5) CAdamson(9) (hdwy over 1f out: r.o one pce) | 1¼ | 4 | 16/1 | 27 | 3 |
| | **Oozlem (IRE) (39)** (JRPoulton) **7-8-4b** SSanders(12) (b: hdwy 7f out: wknd over 1f out) | nk | 5 | 10/1 | 34 | 10 |
| | **Your Most Welcome (49)** (DJSffrenchDavis) **5-9-0** GCarter(14) (a.p: led over 4f out tl over 3f out: wknd over 2f out) | hd | 6 | 25/1 | 44 | 20 |
| $15^{11}$ | **Ilandra (IRE) (57)** (SDow) **4-9-6** WWoods(8) (hdwy over 4f out: wknd over 2f out) | 1 | 7 | 20/1 | 51 | 24 |
| | **Queens Stroller (IRE) (60)** (TRWall) **5-9-8**(3) PMcCabe(2) (lw: lost pl 8f out: no hdwy fnl 3f) | 1¼ | 8 | 20/1 | 51 | 27 |
| | **The Mestral (40)** (MJRyan) **4-8-3** GBardwell(6) (prom over 6f) | 3 | 9 | 14/1 | 27 | — |
| | **Agoer (46)** (CEBrittain) **4-8-9** MLarsen(10) (led 2f: wknd over 3f out) | hd | 10 | 16/1 | 33 | 6 |
| $38^{7}$ | **Wet Patch (IRE) (65)** (RHannon) **4-9-7**(7) MarkDenaro(1) (prom 4f) | 1¼ | 11 | 6/1$^{3}$ | 50 | 23 |
| $27^{9}$ | **Landlord (60)** (JARToller) **4-9-9b** JWeaver(5) (a bhd) | 1 | 12 | 12/1 | 44 | 17 |
| $23^{3}$ | **Tomal (47)** (RIngram) **4-8-10**ow2 WNewnes(13) (b.hind: led 8f out tl over 4f out: sn wknd) | 10 | 13 | 6/1$^{3}$ | 15 | — |
| | **Shoodah (IRE) (31)** (PHayward) **5-7-10** JQuinn(4) (lw: bhd fnl 7f: t.o) | dist | 14 | 66/1 | — | — |

(SP 130.3%) **14 Rn**

**2m 8.22** (3.92) CSF £58.01 CT £171.14 TOTE £3.90: £3.20 £3.60 £1.50 (£28.70) Trio £42.30 OWNER Mr H. T. Short (NEWMARKET) BRED Mrs P. Hollingsworth

LONG HANDICAP Shoodah (IRE) 7-4

WEIGHT FOR AGE 4yo-2lb

## 67 QUENTIN DURWARD MAIDEN STKS (3-Y.O) (Class D)
2-30 (2-34) **1m (Equitrack)** £3,866.50 (£1,171.00: £572.00: £272.50) Stalls: High GOING minus 0.44 sec per fur (FST)

| | | | | SP | RR | SF |
|---|---|---|---|---|---|---|
| | **Well Drawn** (HCandy) **3-9-0** WNewnes(2) (led over 3f: hrd rdn fnl f: led last stride) | — | 1 | 7/4$^{1}$ | 70 | 33 |
| $56^{6}$ | **Blue Flyer (IRE) (67)** (RIngram) **3-9-0b** WWoods(12) (a.p: led over 4f out: hrd rdn over 1f out: hdd last stride) | s.h | 2 | 10/1 | 70 | 33 |
| | **Love Bird (IRE) (75)** (MJohnston) **3-9-0** JWeaver(8) (lw: a.p: rdn over 4f out: one pce) | 6 | 3 | 9/4$^{2}$ | 58 | 21 |
| | **Creeking** (SirMarkPrescott) **3-8-9** CNutter(3) (a.p: rdn over 4f out: one pce) | 2½ | 4 | 6/1$^{3}$ | 48 | 11 |
| | **Baranov (IRE)** (DJGMurraySmith) **3-9-0** JFEgan(6) (w'like: bit bkwd: hdwy over 4f out: wknd over 3f out) | 3 | 5 | 16/1 | 47 | 10 |
| | **Anak-Ku** (MissGayKelleway) **3-9-0** RCochrane(5) (neat: nvr nrr) | 13 | 6 | 8/1 | 21 | — |
| | **My Mother's Local (USA) (46)** (KOCunningham-Brown) **3-8-9** GCarter(1) (prom over 2f) | 2½ | 7 | 33/1 | 11 | — |
| | **Tahya (USA) (58)** (CCElsey) **3-8-9** CRutter(7) (prom over 3f) | nk | 8 | 33/1 | 10 | — |
| | **Lord Ellangowan (IRE) (45)** (RIngram) **3-9-0** DBiggs(4) (a bhd) | 4 | 9 | 33/1 | 7 | — |
| | **General Henry** (AMoore) **3-9-0** CandyMorris(9) (b.hind: bhd fnl 5f) | 8 | 10 | 33/1 | — | — |
| | **Freedom Run** (RHarris) **3-9-0** DBatteate(10) (w'like: bkwd: a bhd) | 1 | 11 | 50/1 | — | — |

| | Horse | Dist | Pl | SP | RR | SF |
|---|---|---|---|---|---|---|
| | **Tormount (USA)** (LordHuntingdon) **3-9-0** SSanders(11) (w'like: bit bkwd: hdwy over 4f out: wknd over 2f out) | 8 | **12** | 10/1 | — | — |

(SP 130.3%) **12 Rn**

**1m 40.35** (2.95) CSF £20.95 TOTE £2.20: £1.10 £2.00 £1.30 (£12.30) Trio £10.10 OWNER Mrs David Blackburn (WANTAGE) BRED Mrs R. D. Peacock

## 68 WAVERLEY H'CAP (0-80) (3-Y.O) (Class D)

3-00 (3-01) **6f (Equitrack)** £3,655.90 (£1,106.20: £539.60: £256.30) Stalls: Low GOING minus 0.44 sec per fur (FST)

| | Horse | Dist | Pl | SP | RR | SF |
|---|---|---|---|---|---|---|
| *$32^{4}$* | **Castle Governor (51)** (PCHaslam) **3-7-5**(5) MBaird(2) (lw: w ldr: led over 2f out: r.o wl) | — | **1** | 8/1 | 51 | — |
| | **Rowlandsons Stud (IRE) (61)** (GLMoore) **3-8-6** MFenton(4) (hld up: rdn 2f out: chsd wnr over 1f out: unable qckn) | 1¼ | **2** | 4/1$^{3}$ | 58 | — |
| *$28^{6}$* | **Maple Burl (66)** (SDow) **3-8-11** WWoods(5) (hdwy over 2f out: r.o ins fnl f) | hd | **3** | 16/1 | 62 | — |
| | **Shontaine (76)** (MJohnston) **3-9-7** JWeaver(1) (led over 3f: wknd fnl f) | 4 | **4** | 7/4$^{2}$ | 62 | — |
| *$28^{2}$* | **Bells of Holland (59)** (WRMuir) **3-8-4** Jean-PierreLopez(3) (hld up: rdn over 2f out: 5th & btn whn hmpd on ins 1f out) | 1 | **5** | 6/4$^{1}$ | 42 | — |

(SP 113.4%) **5 Rn**

**1m 14.91** (4.31) CSF £34.64 TOTE £14.10: £1.80 £1.80 (£10.20) OWNER Patrick Haslam Racing Club (MIDDLEHAM) BRED Longdon Stud Ltd
LONG HANDICAP Castle Governor 7-4

## 69 IVANHOE H'CAP (0-60) (4-Y.O+) (Class F)

3-30 (3-30) **1m 5f (Equitrack)** £2,798.80 (£786.80: £384.40) Stalls: Low GOING minus 0.44 sec per fur (FST)

| | Horse | Dist | Pl | SP | RR | SF |
|---|---|---|---|---|---|---|
| *$12^{6}$* | **Iron N Gold (46)** (AMoore) **4-8-9** SSanders(10) (hdwy over 4f out: chsd ldr over 3f out: led ins fnl f: r.o wl) | — | **1** | 8/1 | 56 | 37 |
| *9** | **Wottashambles (38)** (LMontagueHall) **5-8-6** 5x JFEgan(6) (a.p: led over 3f out tl ins fnl f: unable qckn) | 1 | **2** | 11/2$^{2}$ | 47 | 33 |
| | **Doddington Flyer (54)** (RHollinshead) **4-9-3v**$^{1}$ RCochrane(2) (hld up: rdn over 3f out: one pce) | 3 | **3** | 4/1$^{1}$ | 59 | 40 |
| *$9^{3}$* | **Red Spectacle (IRE) (51)** (PCHaslam) **4-8-9**(5) MBaird(4) (led over 9f: one pce) | ½ | **4** | 13/2$^{3}$ | 56 | 37 |
| *23** | **Erlking (IRE) (40)** (SMellor) **6-8-8b** 5x MWigham(9) (no hdwy fnl 3f) | 10 | **5** | 11/2$^{2}$ | 32 | 18 |
| | **Wahem (IRE) (32)** (CEBrittain) **6-8-0** JQuinn(8) (nvr nr to chal) | 3 | **6** | 12/1 | 21 | 7 |
| *$23^{5}$* | **Pip's Dream (32)** (MJRyan) **5-8-0** GBardwell(1) (prom over 8f) | ¾ | **7** | 20/1 | 20 | 6 |
| *$12^{5}$* | **Dvorak (IRE) (56)** (RHarris) **5-9-10** AMackay(7) (a bhd) | ¾ | **8** | 9/1 | 43 | 29 |
| | **Broughtons Formula (60)** (WJMusson) **6-9-11b**(3) PMcCabe(3) (s.s: a t.o) | 13 | **9** | 11/2$^{2}$ | 31 | 17 |
| | **Lunar Risk (33)** (MissBSanders) **6-8-1** NAdams(5) (bhd fnl 4f: t.o) | 7 | **10** | 14/1 | — | — |

(SP 119.7%) **10 Rn**

**2m 46.85** (3.65) CSF £48.51 CT £185.82 TOTE £9.70: £3.30 £2.10 £1.70 (£19.80) Trio £29.60 OWNER A Family Affair Partnership (BRIGHTON) BRED M. F. Kentish
WEIGHT FOR AGE 4yo-5lb

T/Plpt: £26.10 (366.04 Tckts). T/Qdpt: Not won; £23.80 to Ascot 12/1/96. AK

# 0043-SOUTHWELL (L-H) (Standard)
## Friday January 12th

WEATHER: cloudy & rain WIND: fresh half against

## 70 BUTTERCUP AMATEUR H'CAP (0-65) (I) (4-Y.O+) (Class F)

12-30 (12-32) **1m 3f (Fibresand)** £2,222.00 (£622.00: £302.00) Stalls: Low GOING minus 0.03 sec per fur (STD)

| | Horse | Dist | Pl | SP | RR | SF |
|---|---|---|---|---|---|---|
| | **Modest Hope (USA) (44)** (BRichmond) **9-10-3** MrsDKettlewell(2) (lw: trckd ldrs: styd on to ld jst ins fnl f: drvn out) | — | **1** | 10/1 | 54 | 24 |
| *33** | **Mr Moriarty (IRE) (29)** (SRBowring) **5-8-11**(5) 5x MrsMMorris(4) (led 1f: chsd ldr: led 2f out: sn hdd & nt qckn) | 2 | **2** | 5/4$^{1}$ | 36 | 6 |
| *$43^{4}$* | **Beauman (59)** (PDEvans) **6-10-13**(5) MrAEvans(6) (trckd ldrs: led over 1f out: sn hdd & nt qckn) | 2 | **3** | 8/1 | 63 | 33 |
| | **Tempering (52)** (DWChapman) **10-10-6**(5) MissRClark(8) (led after 1f to 2f out: wknd 1f out) | 2 | **4** | 12/1 | 53 | 23 |
| | **Larn Fort (54)** (CWFairhurst) **6-10-13v** MrsSBosley(5) (racd wd: hdwy to chse ldrs 5f out: rdn 2f out: one pce) | ½ | **5** | 10/1 | 55 | 25 |
| | **Beaumont (IRE) (57)** (JEBanks) **6-10-11**(5) MrJGTownson(1) (in tch: outpcd ½-wy: styd on fnl f: nt rch ldrs) | ½ | **6** | 11/4$^{2}$ | 57 | 27 |
| *$15^{8}$* | **Pistols At Dawn (USA) (62)** (BJMeehan) **6-11-7** MissJAllison(9) (sn bhd: styd on fnl 2f: n.d) | ¾ | **7** | 15/2$^{3}$ | 61 | 31 |
| | **Sergio (IRE) (34)** (JPLeigh) **4-8-13**(5)ow4 MrVLukaniuk(7) (w ldrs 3f: lost pl over 6f out: t.o 4f out) | dist | **8** | 40/1 | — | — |
| | **Precious Caroline (IRE) (35)** (PDCundell) **8-9-3**(5) MrRThornton(3) (sn bhd: t.o 4f out) | 5 | **9** | 33/1 | — | — |

(SP 125.2%) **9 Rn**

**2m 32.6** (12.60) CSF £23.74 CT £106.41 TOTE £11.00: £2.10 £1.10 £3.70 (£12.80) Trio £54.80 OWNER Mr J. McManamon (WELLINGORE) BRED Ralph Wilson
WEIGHT FOR AGE 4yo-3lb

## 71 RYEGRASS H'CAP (0-65) (I) (3-Y.O+) (Class F)

12-55 (12-58) **6f (Fibresand)** £2,222.00 (£622.00: £302.00) Stalls: Low GOING minus 0.03 sec per fur (STD)

| | Horse | Dist | Pl | SP | RR | SF |
|---|---|---|---|---|---|---|
| *$16^{6}$* | **Dissentor (IRE) (44)** (JAGlover) **4-8-10v** GCarter(8) (chsd ldrs: styd on to ld ins fnl f: drvn out) | — | **1** | 12/1 | 55 | 39 |
| | **Kira (51)** (JLEyre) **6-9-3** RLappin(6) (b.off hind: chsd ldrs: led over 2f out tl ins fnl f) | 3 | **2** | 8/1 | 54 | 38 |
| | **Stand Tall (55)** (CWThornton) **4-9-7** DeanMcKeown(2) (swtg: sn chsng ldrs: rdn 2f out: kpt on same pce) | 2 | **3** | 2/1$^{1}$ | 53 | 37 |
| *$45^{7}$* | **Green's Bid (45)** (DWChapman) **6-8-11v** ACulhane(7) (led tl over 2f out: wknd over 1f out) | 4 | **4** | 10/1 | 32 | 16 |
| | **Irchester Lass (44)** (SRBowring) **4-8-5b**(5) CTeague(10) (mid div: hrd rdn 2f out: styd on ins fnl f) | s.h | **5** | 5/1$^{2}$ | 31 | 15 |
| | **Matthew David (45)** (SRBowring) **6-8-11b** NCarlisle(4) (b: s.s: bhd: sme hdwy 2f out: nvr nr ldrs) | 3 | **6** | 7/1$^{3}$ | 24 | 8 |
| | **Grey Charmer (IRE) (48)** (CJames) **7-9-0** CRutter(11) (sn bhd: sme hdwy 2f out: n.d) | ½ | **7** | 12/1 | 26 | 10 |
| | **McKellar (IRE) (47)** (TDBarron) **7-8-13** JFortune(9) (bhd: styd on fnl 2f: nvr nr ldrs) | ¾ | **8** | 20/1 | 23 | 7 |
| *$36^{9}$* | **Vladivostok (45)** (BdeHaan) **6-8-6**(5) PFessey(3) (s.s: a bhd) | 2 | **9** | 14/1 | 15 | — |
| *$53^{3}$* | **Paronomasia (40)** (MBell) **4-8-6v** MFenton(12) (s.i.s: a in rr) | 1¼ | **10** | 7/1$^{3}$ | 7 | — |
| *$16^{8}$* | **Primula Bairn (58)** (DNicholls) **6-9-10b** AlexGreaves(1) (chsd ldrs tl lost pl over 2f out: eased) | ½ | **11** | 10/1 | 24 | 8 |

**Double Glow (40)** (NBycroft) **4-8-6** GBardwell(5) (b.nr hind: sn drvn: outpcd ½-wy: sn bhd) ..........2 **12** 33/1 — —
(SP 134.0%) **12 Rn**

**1m 17.4** (3.90) CSF £105.76 CT £255.70 TOTE £14.60: £2.20 £2.40 £1.70 (£110.10) Trio £68.80 OWNER Mr Brian Eastick (WORKSOP) BRED Lynaire Ltd

## 72 BUTTERCUP AMATEUR H'CAP (0-65) (II) (4-Y.O+) (Class F)

1-20 (1-20) **1m 3f (Fibresand)** £2,222.00 (£622.00: £302.00) Stalls: Low GOING minus 0.03 sec per fur (STD)

SP RR SF

**Ajdar (42)** (MissGayKelleway) **5-9-10**(5) MissSKelleway(5) (lw: trckd ldrs: hrd rdn 2f out: hung lft: led post) ..........— **1** 13/2 50 22
**Calder King (62)** (JLEyre) **5-11-7b** MissDianaJones(3) (hdwy to ld 4f out: clr over 2f out: jst ct)..........s.h **2** 2/1[2] 70 42
**Comtec's Legend (42)** (JFBottomley) **6-10-1** MrsLPearce(7) (lw: b: trckd ldrs: effrt over 2f out: kpt on one pce) ..........8 **3** 6/5[1] 38 10
45[2] **Shotley Again (34)** (NBycroft) **6-9-7**ow4 MrsDKettlewell(4) (led 4f: drvn & lost pl 5f out: styd on one pce fnl 2f) ..........2½ **4** 6/1[3] 27 —
**Phanan (33)** (REPeacock) **10-9-1**(5)ow3 MrsCPeacock(8) (w ldrs: chal 4f out: one pce) ..........3 **5** 33/1 21 —
**Spring Sunrise (33)** (BdeHaan) **6-9-6** MrsSBosley(2) (w ldrs: outpcd over 4f out: sn lost pl)..........1 **6** 20/1 20 —
30[13] **Media Messenger (36)** (NPLittmoden) **7-9-4**(5) MrOGunter(1) (dwlt: sn w ldrs: led 7f out to 4f out: sn lost pl)...6 **7** 50/1 14 —
(SP 116.1%) **7 Rn**

**2m 32.6** (12.60) CSF £19.39 CT £23.58 TOTE £6.50: £3.20 £1.00 (£13.40) OWNER Mrs Sue Catt (WHITCOMBE) BRED Floors Farming

## 73 DAISY CLAIMING STKS (4-Y.O+) (Class F)

1-55 (1-55) **2m (Fibresand)** £2,572.00 (£722.00: £352.00) Stalls: Low GOING minus 0.03 sec per fur (STD)

SP RR SF

**Eulogy (FR)** (KRBurke) **9-8-8**(7) TAshley(7) (sn chsng ldrs: rdn 5f out: styd on to ld wl ins fnl f)..........— **1** 12/1 74 —
**Supermodel** (MJohnston) **4-8-5** TWilliams(9) (rangy: w ldrs: led ½-wy tl wl ins fnl f)..........¾ **2** 12/1 70 —
**El Nido (56)** (MJCamacho) **8-9-3** LCharnock(12) (trckd ldrs: drvn 5f out: one pce: eased fnl f)..........20 **3** 7/4[1] 55 —
34[7] **Fools of Pride (IRE) (36)** (RHollinshead) **4-7-13**(7)ow3 FLynch(10) (hdwy ½-wy: one pce fnl 5f)..........15 **4** 16/1 36 —
33[12] **Mudlark (42)** (JNorton) **4-8-8b** DaleGibson(3) (in tch: outpcd 7f out: grad wknd)..........4 **5** 20/1 34 —
**Gunmaker (30)** (BJLlewellyn) **7-8-13** JWeaver(13) (chsd ldrs: rdn 9f out: lost pl 7f out)..........1¾ **6** 7/1 31 —
**Tristan's Comet (45)** (JLHarris) **9-9-1v**[1] AMackay(1) (reluctant to r: a bhd)..........s.h **7** 14/1 32 —
**Acquittal (IRE) (56)** (JMackie) **4-8-5**(3) NVarley(5) (in tch: rdn ½-wy: sn lost pl)..........5 **8** 6/1[3] 27 —
9[4] **Rose of Glenn (44)** (BPalling) **5-8-10** GCarter(6) (led to ½-wy: sn wknd)..........20 **9** 4/1[2] 2 —
**Mister Lawson (28)** (BSmart) **10-9-1** SSanders(4) (swtg: in tch tl lost pl 7f out)..........20 **10** 33/1 — —
29[5] **Absolute Ruler (IRE) (43)** (JLHarris) **5-8-9b** JFEgan(2) (sn bhd)..........4 **11** 20/1 — —
**Tifasi (IRE)** (JohnBerry) **6-8-11** JQuinn(11) (swtg: s.s: a wl bhd)..........5 **12** 25/1 — —
**Fret (USA) (45)** (JSWainwright) **6-9-1b**[1] DeanMcKeown(8) (chsd ldrs tl rdn & lost pl ½-wy)..........½ **13** 16/1 — —
(SP 133.3%) **13 Rn**

**3m 49.0** (23.00) CSF £144.41 TOTE £11.20: £3.20 £4.00 £1.70 (£167.60) Trio £130.50 OWNER Mrs Elaine Burke (WANTAGE) BRED Martine Teyssot
WEIGHT FOR AGE 4yo-7lb

## 74 RYEGRASS H'CAP (0-65) (II) (3-Y.O+) (Class F)

2-25 (2-28) **6f (Fibresand)** £2,222.00 (£622.00: £302.00) Stalls: Low GOING minus 0.03 sec per fur (STD)

SP RR SF

**Fairey Firefly (54)** (MJCamacho) **5-9-5** LCharnock(5) (swtg: b.nr fore: w ldr: led over 2f out: hld on wl)..........— **1** 10/1 60 17
**Serious Fact (36)** (SirMarkPrescott) **4-8-1** GBardwell(9) (chsd ldrs: rdn ½-wy: hung lft: styd on fnl f)..........½ **2** 7/2[1] 41 —
**My Cherrywell (56)** (LRLloyd-James) **6-9-0b**(7) KimberleyHart(8) (b.hind: dwlt: hdwy ½-wy: effrt & hung lft 2f out: nvr nr ldrs)..........1¾ **3** 5/1[2] 56 13
**Indiahra (49)** (RHollinshead) **5-9-0** JWeaver(2) (sn outpcd & drvn: hdwy over 1f out: styng on wl nr fin)..........½ **4** 6/1[3] 48 5
**Brisas (45)** (CWFairhurst) **9-8-10** DMcKeown(7) (bit bkwd: in tch: drvn over 2f out: no imp)..........1¾ **5** 12/1 39 —
22[5] **Pursuance (IRE) (63)** (JBalding) **4-9-7v**(7) JEdmunds(4) (led tl over 2f out: grad wknd)..........¾ **6** 6/1[3] 55 12
**Speedy Snaps Pride (40)** (PDCundell) **4-8-5** GCarter(6) (sn outpcd & bhd: sme hdwy 2f out: n.d)..........1¼ **7** 11/1 29 —
**Chloella (38)** (CBBBooth) **4-8-3** NKennedy(1) (chsd ldrs tl grad wknd fnl 2f)..........½ **8** 20/1 25 —
**Diamond Bangle (31)** (CCElsey) **4-7-10** NAdams(10) (b.hind: racd wd: outpcd fr ½-wy)..........1½ **9** 33/1 14 —
**Most Uppitty (56)** (JBerry) **4-9-0**(7) JoanneWebster(3) (s.s: bhd: sme hdwy 2f out: sn wknd)..........nk **10** 7/1 39 —
**Strip Cartoon (IRE) (47)** (SRBowring) **8-8-7b**(5) CTeague(11) (racd wd: chsd ldrs tl lost pl over 2f out)..........1¼ **11** 10/1 26 —
(SP 121.9%) **11 Rn**

**1m 19.8** (6.30) CSF £43.42 CT £183.67 TOTE £17.20: £3.30 £2.20 £2.20 (£34.90) Trio £75.10 OWNER Mr B. P. Skirton (MALTON) BRED B. P. Skirton and Mrs S. Camacho
LONG HANDICAP Diamond Bangle 7-9

## 75 COWSLIP LIMITED STKS (0-75) (4-Y.O+) (Class D)

2-55 (2-55) **1m 4f (Fibresand)** £3,655.90 (£1,106.20: £539.60: £256.30) Stalls: High GOING minus 0.03 sec per fur (STD)

SP RR SF

13* **Celestial Choir (75)** (JLEyre) **6-9-1** RLappin(4) (lw: trckd ldrs: led 3f out: drvn out)..........— **1** 6/4[1] 89 26
**What's the Verdict (IRE) (74)** (MJohnston) **4-8-12** JWeaver(5) (led to 3f out: kpt on: no ch w wnr)..........13 **2** 6/1[3] 74 6
37* **Tartan Gem (IRE) (65)** (MBrittain) **5-8-11**(7) JDennis(6) (bhd: effrt & rdn 5f out: kpt on fnl 2f: nvr nr ldrs)..........5 **3** 7/1 68 5
**Nijmegen (65)** (JGFitzGerald) **8-9-2** SMorris(2) (b: chsd ldrs: rdn 5f out: sn wl outpcd)..........8 **4** 14/1 55 —
19[6] **Johns Act (USA) (71)** (DHaydnJones) **6-9-2v** AMackay(1) (chsd ldrs: drvn 6f out: sn lost pl)..........5 **5** 6/1[3] 49 —
**Kalamata (73)** (JAGlover) **4-9-0** SDWilliams(3) (trckd ldrs: ev ch tl wknd qckly over 2f out)..........1½ **6** 11/4[2] 50 —
(SP 114.4%) **6 Rn**

**2m 43.4** (10.90) CSF £10.21 TOTE £1.90: £1.30 £2.80 (£4.50) OWNER Mrs Carole Sykes (HAMBLETON) BRED J. L. Eyre
WEIGHT FOR AGE 4yo-4lb

## 76 BLUEBELL (S) STKS (4-Y.O+) (Class F)

3-25 (3-28) **7f (Fibresand)** £2,607.00 (£732.00: £357.00) Stalls: Low GOING minus 0.03 sec per fur (STD)

SP RR SF

29[4] **First Gold (55)** (JWharton) **7-8-12b** SDWilliams(4) (chsd ldrs: sn drvn: styd on to ld ins fnl f)..........— **1** 10/1 57 21

| Form | Horse | Dist | Pos | SP | RR | SF |
|---|---|---|---|---|---|---|
| 42[5] | **At the Savoy (IRE) (60)** (TDBarron) **5-8-12v** JFortune(3) (w ldr: led ½-wy: clr over 1f out: hdd & no ex ins fnl f) | 1¼ | **2** | 11/2[2] | 54 | 18 |
| 59* | **Sense of Priority (70)** (DNicholls) **7-9-4** 6x AlexGreaves(5) (in tch: effrt over 2f out: kpt on: no imp) | 3½ | **3** | 5/4[1] | 52 | 16 |
| 57[10] | **Desert Invader (IRE) (61)** (DWChapman) **5-8-12** ACulhane(1) (led to ½-wy: sn hrd rdn: one pce) | nk | **4** | 10/1 | 46 | 10 |
| 53[12] | **Pacific Girl (IRE) (40)** (BPalling) **4-8-7** Jean-PierreLopez(10) (rn wd ent st: kpt on fnl 2f: nvr nr ldrs) | nk | **5** | 16/1 | 40 | 4 |
| | **Chadleigh Lane (USA) (55)** (RHollinshead) **4-8-12v[1]** NCarlisle(14) (racd wd: nvr nr ldrs) | 1 | **6** | 20/1 | 43 | 7 |
| | **Jersey Belle (46)** (PJMakin) **4-8-7b[1]** SSanders(9) (chsd ldrs tl wknd over 1f out) | hd | **7** | 20/1 | 37 | 1 |
| | **Sea Devil (66)** (MJCamacho) **10-8-12** LCharnock(13) (in tch: drvn 3f out: grad wknd) | 5 | **8** | 7/1[3] | 31 | — |
| | **Fortis Pavior (IRE) (47)** (CWCElsey) **6-8-12** GCarter(2) (chsd ldrs tl lost pl ½-wy) | 7 | **9** | 25/1 | 15 | — |
| | **Mixed Mood (60)** (BJLlewellyn) **4-8-7** TWilliams(8) (sn drvn: outpcd fr ½-wy) | 3½ | **10** | 20/1 | 2 | — |
| | **Monkey's Wedding (78)** (JBerry) **5-8-12v** LeTolboll(6) (b: dwlt: a in rr) | 1¼ | **11** | 12/1 | 4 | — |
| | **Rupert's Princess (IRE) (53)** (MJHeaton-Ellis) **4-8-7b** AClark(7) (chsd ldrs tl wknd 3f out) | s.h | **12** | 14/1 | — | — |
| | **Here's Honour (IRE)** (RBastiman) **4-8-12** DeanMcKeown(12) (leggy: lt-f: unf: s.i.s: a bhd) | 11 | **13** | 16/1 | — | — |
| | **Joyful Times (40)** (MrsNMacauley) **4-8-0(7)** JoHunnam(11) (a wl bhd) | ½ | **14** | 16/1 | — | — |

(SP 140.6%) **14 Rn**

**1m 33.2** (6.40) CSF £68.73 TOTE £8.50: £2.30 £3.00 £1.20 (£12.10) Trio £29.80 OWNER Mr K. D. Standen (MELTON MOWBRAY) BRED Messinger Stud Ltd
No bid

## 77 LADBROKE ALL-WEATHER CHALLENGE SERIES H'CAP (Qualifier) (0-70) (4-Y.O+) (Class E)

3-55 (3-59) **1m (Fibresand)** £3,260.50 (£988.00: £483.00: £230.50) Stalls: Low GOING minus 0.03 sec per fur (STD)

| Form | Horse | Dist | Pos | SP | RR | SF |
|---|---|---|---|---|---|---|
| 57* | **Maple Bay (IRE) (65)** (ABailey) **7-9-4(7)** 6x PRoberts(9) (lw: a chsng ldrs: led over 1f out: rdn clr) | — | **1** | 3/1[1] | 80 | 57 |
| 18[5] | **Benjamins Law (59)** (JAPickering) **5-9-5** JQuinn(13) (trckd ldrs: led 2f out: sn hdd: nt qckn) | 3 | **2** | 6/1[3] | 68 | 45 |
| | **Barrel of Hope (62)** (JLEyre) **4-9-8b** JFortune(12) (hdwy to ld 5f out: hdd 2f out: kpt on one pce) | 6 | **3** | 8/1 | 60 | 36 |
| 55[8] | **Q Factor (67)** (DHaydnJones) **4-9-13** AMackay(6) (s.i.s: hld up: stdy hdwy on outside 2f out: styd on nr fin) | ¾ | **4** | 33/1 | 64 | 40 |
| | **Forzair (68)** (SRBowring) **4-9-9(5)** CTeague(11) (racd wd: in tch: hung rt 2f out: sn wknd) | 3 | **5** | 6/1[3] | 59 | 35 |
| | **Palacegate Jo (IRE) (50)** (DWChapman) **5-8-10** ACulhane(3) (sn bhd: sme hdwy 2f out: n.d) | 4 | **6** | 20/1 | 32 | 9 |
| | **Major Snugfit (42)** (MWEasterby) **4-8-2** SMaloney(8) (dwlt: bhd tl styd on appr fnl f) | 2½ | **7** | 33/1 | 20 | — |
| | **Kingchip Boy (49)** (MJRyan) **7-9-9b** AClark(4) (chsd ldrs tl wknd 2f out) | 4 | **8** | 6/1[3] | 18 | — |
| | **Bogart (56)** (CWFairhurst) **5-9-2** SDWilliams(1) (w ldrs: rdn & hung lft over 1f out: sn wknd) | 4 | **9** | 16/1 | 17 | — |
| | **Red Hot Risk (41)** (SWCampion) **4-8-1** LCharnock(5) (led to 5f out: sn lost pl) | 2 | **10** | 33/1 | — | — |
| | **Samana Cay (49)** (PSFelgate) **4-8-9** JWeaver(10) (racd wd: a bhd) | nk | **11** | 16/1 | 6 | — |
| 44[2] | **Peggy Spencer (63)** (CWThornton) **4-9-9** DeanMcKeown(2) (sltly hmpd s: mid div: sn rdn: n.d) | hd | **12** | 5/1[2] | 20 | — |
| | **Forgotten Empress (59)** (AHarrison) **4-9-2(3)** JStack(7) (sn rdn & outpcd) | hd | **13** | 6/1[3] | 16 | — |

(SP 135.3%) **13 Rn**

**1m 44.9** (4.90) CSF £23.06 CT £127.35 TOTE £3.20: £1.80 £1.90 £2.50 (£18.20) Trio £20.20 OWNER Mr Roy Matthews (TARPORLEY) BRED Berkshire Equestrian Services Ltd

T/Plpt: £45.60 (160.34 Tckts). T/Qdpt: £19.00 (2.2 Tckts). WG

# 0064-LINGFIELD (L-H) (Standard)

## Saturday January 13th

1st race-hand timed
WEATHER: fine WIND: mod half bhd

## 78 ANTRIM LIMITED STKS (0-60) (3-Y.O) (Class F)

12-50 (12-50) **5f (Equitrack)** £2,698.00 (£758.00: £370.00) Stalls: Low GOING minus 0.50 sec per fur (FST)

| Form | Horse | Dist | Pos | SP | RR | SF |
|---|---|---|---|---|---|---|
| | **Last But Not Least (60)** (RFJohnsonHoughton) **3-8-6** JWeaver(2) (mde all: clr over 1f out: drvn out) | — | **1** | 6/4[1] | 68 | 16 |
| 21[3] | **Miss Pickpocket (IRE) (56)** (PAKelleway) **3-8-9** MFenton(3) (lw: s.i.s: sn rdn & outpcd: styd on fnl f) | 3½ | **2** | 11/4[2] | 60 | 8 |
| 51[3] | **Bouton d'Or (51)** (PHowling) **3-8-6** JQuinn(4) (lw: chsd wnr: rdn over 1f out: no ex ins fnl f) | s.h | **3** | 7/1 | 57 | 5 |
| 39[2] | **Dancing Jack (55)** (JJBridger) **3-9-0** GBardwell(1) (chsd ldrs: sn rdn: kpt on one pce fnl f) | 1 | **4** | 7/1 | 61 | 9 |
| 51[2] | **Copper Bright (50)** (PCHaslam) **3-8-11b** JFortune(5) (sn rdn: a outpcd) | 6 | **5** | 9/2[3] | 39 | — |

(SP 109.8%) **5 Rn**

**59.9 secs** (1.90) CSF £5.64 TOTE £2.70: £1.20 £2.60 (£2.70) OWNER Mr Keith Wills (DIDCOT) BRED Keith Wills

## 79 TYRONE MAIDEN STKS (4-Y.O+) (Class D)

1-25 (1-27) **1m 5f (Equitrack)** £3,989.35 (£1,208.80: £590.90: £281.95) Stalls: Low GOING minus 0.50 sec per fur (FST)

| Form | Horse | Dist | Pos | SP | RR | SF |
|---|---|---|---|---|---|---|
| | **Miroswaki (USA) (68)** (RAkehurst) **6-9-5** JWeaver(13) (lw: hld up: hdwy to ld over 7f out: clr 3f out: unchal) | — | **1** | 5/6[1] | 74+ | 51 |
| | **Kymin (IRE)** (DJGMurraySmith) **4-8-9v[1]** JFEgan(7) (lw: mid div: rdn over 5f out: styd on to go 2nd ins fnl f: no imp) | 15 | **2** | 5/1[2] | 51 | 23 |
| | **Royal Legend** (JPearce) **4-9-0** JMcLaughlin(16) (bit bkwd: chsd wnr 5f out tl ins fnl f: one pce) | 1¼ | **3** | 14/1 | 54 | 26 |
| 24[5] | **Callonescy (IRE) (48)** (DCO'Brien) **4-9-0** GBardwell(10) (hdwy 7f out: rdn over 3f out: one pce) | 1¾ | **4** | 20/1 | 52 | 24 |
| | **Miss Cashtal (IRE)** (DTThom) **5-9-0** MFenton(4) (s.i.s: hdwy 7f out: rdn over 3f out: one pce) | 1¼ | **5** | 20/1 | 45 | 22 |
| | **Royal Print (IRE) (45)** (WRMuir) **7-9-5** Jean-PierreLopez(12) (mid div: rdn over 5f out: one pce fnl 3f) | ¾ | **6** | 40/1 | 49 | 26 |
| | **Discorsi (63)** (MissGayKelleway) **4-9-0** AClark(1) (b.hind: hld up: hdwy 7f out: rdn over 3f out: one pce) | 1¼ | **7** | 14/1 | 48 | 20 |
| | **Fraise du Roi (IRE)** (LordHuntingdon) **4-8-2(7)** AimeeCook(8) (nvr nrr) | nk | **8** | 20/1 | 43 | 15 |
| | **Double Jeopardy (62)** (JWhite) **5-9-0(5)** PPMurphy(9) (b.off hind: hld up: rdn 4f out: no hdwy) | 5 | **9** | 16/1 | 41 | 18 |
| | **Valisky** (RLee) **6-9-0** JFortune(17) (b: chsd ldrs tl wknd over 3f out) | 2½ | **10** | 25/1 | 33 | 10 |
| | **Taniyar (FR)** (RHollinshead) **4-9-0** TIves(18) (bhd fnl 5f) | 4 | **11** | 7/1[3] | 33 | 5 |
| | **My Dutch Girl (45)** (MissBSanders) **4-8-9** DBiggs(11) (led: hdd over 7f out: wknd 4f out) | 7 | **12** | 40/1 | 20 | — |
| | **More Bills (IRE) (28)** (AMoore) **4-9-0** CandyMorris(14) (bhd fnl 6f) | 1½ | **13** | 50/1 | 23 | — |
| | **Lady Elizabeth (FR)** (KOCunningham-Brown) **4-8-9** JQuinn(5) (chsd ldrs tl wknd 3f out) | 6 | **14** | 12/1 | 11 | — |
| 29[6] | **Lord Barnard (IRE) (30)** (CMurray) **6-9-5** MTebbutt(15) (a bhd) | 7 | **15** | 50/1 | 7 | — |
| | **Calgary Girl (32)** (PCRitchens) **4-8-9** NAdams(6) (prom 6f) | 3½ | **16** | 40/1 | — | — |

| | Horse | Dist | Pos | SP | RR | SF |
|---|---|---|---|---|---|---|
| | **Shy Mystic** (RJHodges) **6-8-11**(3) SDrowne(3) (bkwd: a bhd) | 14 | **17** | 50/1 | — | — |

(SP 142.0%) **17 Rn**

**2m 45.15** (1.95) CSF £7.01 TOTE £2.00: £1.30 £2.10 £3.40 (£3.70) Trio £28.00 OWNER Mrs A. Naughton (EPSOM) BRED Buckram Oak Farm
WEIGHT FOR AGE 4yo-5lb

## 80 ARMAGH H'CAP (0-70) (4-Y.O+) (Class E)

1-55 (1-56) **1m 4f (Equitrack)** £3,046.00 (£922.00: £450.00: £214.00) Stalls: Low GOING minus 0.50 sec per fur (FST)

| Form | Horse | Dist | Pos | SP | RR | SF |
|---|---|---|---|---|---|---|
| 13[9] | **No Speeches (IRE) (60)** (SDow) **5-9-4** SSanders(4) (hld up: hdwy 6f out: led over 3f out: rdn over 1f out: r.o) | — | **1** | 11/2[3] | 70 | 41 |
| | **Seventeens Lucky (69)** (BobJones) **4-9-9** MWigham(1) (chsd ldrs: rdn 3f out: chsd wnr 2f out: sn rdn: kpt on one pce) | 1 | **2** | 4/1[1] | 79 | 45 |
| | **El Volador (70)** (RJO'Sullivan) **9-9-9**(5) DGriffiths(5) (hld up: hdwy 3f out: rdn over 1f out: one pce) | ½ | **3** | 11/2[3] | 78 | 49 |
| 75[3] | **Tartan Gem (IRE) (67)** (MBrittain) **5-9-8**(3) DWright(2) (hld up: hdwy over 2f out: rdn over 1f out: one pce) | 1½ | **4** | 4/1[1] | 73 | 44 |
| 23[2] | **Never So Rite (IRE) (48)** (DWPArbuthnot) **4-8-2** JQuinn(3) (b: b.off hind: plld hrd: chsd ldrs: wknd over 1f out) | 5 | **5** | 9/2[2] | 48 | 14 |
| | **One Off the Rail (USA) (66)** (AMoore) **6-9-10** CandyMorris(7) (led 10f out: hdd over 3f out: wknd 2f out) | 1 | **6** | 10/1 | 64 | 35 |
| | **Serious Option (IRE) (61)** (PFICole) **5-9-5** CRutter(8) (prom: chsd ldrs 6f out tl over 3f out: sn wknd) | 13 | **7** | 8/1 | 42 | 13 |
| 23[12] | **Talented Ting (IRE) (55)** (PCHaslam) **7-8-13** JFortune(6) (led 2f: wknd 6f out) | 6 | **8** | 10/1 | 28 | — |

(SP 118.2%) **8 Rn**

**2m 33.16** (3.16) CSF £26.57 CT £115.85 TOTE £7.80: £4.80 £1.40 £2.10 (£14.90) OWNER Top Class Racing (EPSOM) BRED Lyonstown Stud and Swettenham Stud
WEIGHT FOR AGE 4yo-4lb
STEWARDS' ENQUIRY Fortune fined £100 (failure to ride to draw).

## 81 LONDONDERRY H'CAP (0-60) (3-Y.O) (Class F)

2-30 (2-30) **7f (Equitrack)** £2,761.00 (£776.00: £379.00) Stalls: Low GOING minus 0.50 sec per fur (FST)

| Form | Horse | Dist | Pos | SP | RR | SF |
|---|---|---|---|---|---|---|
| | **Sovereign Prince (IRE) (46)** (NACallaghan) **3-8-4**(3) SDrowne(7) (bhd: rdn over 4f out: hdwy over 1f out: str run to ld ins fnl f: r.o wl) | — | **1** | 11/4[2] | 53 | 6 |
| 25[2] | **Rawi (60)** (WRMuir) **3-9-7** JWeaver(2) (led: rdn over 1f out: hdd ins fnl f: unable qckn) | 1½ | **2** | 9/2[3] | 64 | 17 |
| | **Young Frederick (IRE) (60)** (KRBurke) **3-9-7** JFEgan(4) (chsd ldrs: rdn & outpcd 2f out: n.m.r over 1f out: swtchd rt: styd on fnl f) | ¾ | **3** | 33/1 | 62 | 15 |
| | **Miss Carottene (47)** (MJRyan) **3-8-3b**(5) MBaird(5) (chsd ldr: ev ch 2f out: rdn over 1f out: wknd ins fnl f) | 3 | **4** | 14/1 | 42 | — |
| 68* | **Castle Governor (48)** (PCHaslam) **3-8-9** 6x JFortune(8) (chsd ldrs: rdn 2f out: one pce) | ½ | **5** | 6/4[1] | 42 | — |
| | **Mystery Matthias (51)** (MissBSanders) **3-8-12b** SSanders(6) (chsd ldrs: rdn 2f out: wknd 1f out) | 1½ | **6** | 10/1 | 41 | — |
| | **Merlin's Honour (40)** (JohnBerry) **3-8-1** JQuinn(1) (dwlt: a bhd) | 2 | **7** | 25/1 | 26 | — |
| 39[3] | **Ghostly Apparition (57)** (JRUpson) **3-8-11**(7) DSweeney(3) (a bhd) | hd | **8** | 9/1 | 43 | — |

(SP 117.4%) **8 Rn**

**1m 27.85** (3.85) CSF £14.95 CT £301.07 TOTE £4.50: £2.00 £1.50 £2.60 (£17.40) OWNER M. Tabor (NEWMARKET) BRED Barronstown Stud

## 82 DOWN CLAIMING STKS (4-Y.O+) (Class E)

3-00 (3-01) **1m 2f (Equitrack)** £3,274.80 (£992.40: £485.20: £231.60) Stalls: Low GOING minus 0.50 sec per fur (FST)

| Form | Horse | Dist | Pos | SP | RR | SF |
|---|---|---|---|---|---|---|
| 13[8] | **Tribal Peace (IRE) (68)** (BGubby) **4-8-7**(3) JStack(10) (hld up in tch: led over 3f out: rdn & edgd lft over 1f out: hdd ins fnl f: rallied to ld last strides: fin 1st: originally disq: plcd 2nd: reinstated after appeal) | — | **1** | 7/2[2] | 73 | 27 |
| | **Masnun (USA) (66)** (RJO'Sullivan) **11-8-9** AClark(5) (mid div: hdwy 4f out: chsd wnr over 2f out: n.m.r over 1f out: led ins fnl f: ct last strides: fin 2nd, s.h: originally awrdd r: later plcd 2nd) | s.h | **2** | 11/10[1] | 69 | 26 |
| | **Gallic Victory (IRE) (60)** (JohnBerry) **5-9-1** MFenton(1) (chsd ldrs: rdn over 2f out: one pce) | 7 | **3** | 33/1 | 64 | 21 |
| 13[7] | **Greenwich Again (65)** (TGMills) **4-9-2** JFortune(3) (chsd ldrs: rdn 3f out: wknd over 1f out) | 2 | **4** | 9/1 | 65 | 19 |
| | **Northern Trial (USA) (41)** (KRBurke) **8-8-6v** JTate(9) (nvr nrr) | 4 | **5** | 25/1 | 45 | 2 |
| 66[4] | **Swynford Flyer (32)** (JAHarris) **7-7-7**(5) CAdamson(11) (s.i.s: nvr nrr) | 4 | **6** | 20/1 | 31 | — |
| | **The Little Ferret (52)** (AMoore) **6-8-9** CandyMorris(6) (dwlt: sn rcvrd: rdn 4f out: no hdwy) | hd | **7** | 20/1 | 42 | — |
| 23[6] | **Sweet Disorder (IRE) (30)** (BJMeehan) **6-7-12** JQuinn(4) (chsd ldr: led 4f out: sn hdd: grad wknd) | s.h | **8** | 25/1 | 31 | — |
| 37[2] | **Jobber's Fiddle (44)** (DLWilliams) **4-7-11b**ow1 AMackay(13) (sn rdn: a bhd) | 2 | **9** | 6/1[3] | 29 | — |
| | **Good so Fa (IRE) (44)** (CNAllen) **4-8-1** NAdams(14) (s.i.s: hdwy 5f out: wknd over 3f out) | 11 | **10** | 20/1 | 16 | — |
| | **Northern Singer** (RJHodges) **6-8-3**(3) SDrowne(7) (dwlt: a bhd) | 5 | **11** | 50/1 | 10 | — |
| | **Thorniwama (35)** (JJBridger) **5-7-12** GBardwell(8) (bhd fnl 5f: t.o) | 20 | **12** | 33/1 | — | — |
| | **Komodo (USA) (47)** (KOCunningham-Brown) **4-9-5** JWeaver(2) (led: hdd 4f out: sn wknd: t.o) | 15 | **13** | 25/1 | — | — |

(SP 127.8%) **13 Rn**

**2m 7.75** (3.45) CSF £5.85 TOTE £2.20: £1.20 £2.70 £4.40 (£2.40) Trio £23.40 OWNER Mr I. W. Page (WHITCOMBE) BRED Glencrest Farm
WEIGHT FOR AGE 4yo-2lb

## 83 FERMANAGH AMATEUR H'CAP (0-70) (4-Y.O+) (Class E)

3-35 (3-36) **2m (Equitrack)** £3,260.50 (£988.00: £483.00: £230.50) Stalls: Low GOING minus 0.50 sec per fur (FST)

| Form | Horse | Dist | Pos | SP | RR | SF |
|---|---|---|---|---|---|---|
| | **Wild Strawberry (57)** (MissBSanders) **7-10-11**(5) MrKGoble(7) (hld up: hdwy 9f out: led 4f out: clr 2f out: easily) | — | **1** | 9/2[2] | 72 | 57 |
| 12[2] | **Coleridge (53)** (JJSheehan) **8-10-5b**(7) MissCHannaford(6) (dwlt: bhd: hdwy over 1f out: styd on to go 2nd wl ins fnl f) | 5 | **2** | 8/1 | 63 | 48 |
| 15* | **Cuango (IRE) (62)** (RHollinshead) **5-11-7** MrMRimell(13) (mid div: rdn over 3f out: r.o one pce fnl 2f) | 1 | **3** | 6/1[3] | 71 | 56 |
| 15[4] | **Royal Circus (39)** (PRWebber) **7-9-9**(3) MrsSBosley(12) (prom: led 5f out: hdd 4f out: one pce) | ¾ | **4** | 20/1 | 47 | 32 |
| 15[3] | **Stalled (IRE) (58)** (PTWalwyn) **6-10-12**(5) MarchionessBlandford(10) (hld up: hdwy 6f out: rdn over 2f out: one pce) | 3½ | **5** | 4/1[1] | 56 | 48 |
| | **Flashman (38)** (BJLlewellyn) **6-9-11** MrJLLlewellyn(11) (mid div: rdn 6f out: one pce fnl 4f) | 3½ | **6** | 12/1 | 32 | 24 |
| 54* | **Sorisky (41)** (BGubby) **4-9-2**(5) 4x MrsMTingey(14) (chsd ldrs: rdn 4f out: wknd 3f out) | 1¼ | **7** | 16/1 | 34 | 19 |
| 9[2] | **Captain Marmalade (47)** (DTThom) **7-10-6** MissDianaJones(8) (nvr nrr) | ½ | **8** | 12/1 | 40 | 32 |
| 15[2] | **Don't Drop Bombs (USA) (34)** (DTThom) **7-9-4v**(3) MissJFeilden(4) (led: hdd 5f out: sn wknd) | 7 | **9** | 11/1 | 20 | 12 |
| | **Retender (USA) (53)** (JPearce) **7-10-12** MrsLPearce(9) (hld up: sme hdwy 8f out: rdn 4f out: sn wknd) | 7 | **10** | 8/1 | 32 | 24 |
| | **Rock Oyster (42)** (BJMeehan) **4-9-8b** MissJAllison(5) (chsd ldrs tl wknd 4f out) | 6 | **11** | 33/1 | 15 | — |

**Sir Thomas Beecham (60)** (SDow) **6-11-5** MrTMcCarthy(2) (prom tl wknd over 4f out) ....12 **12** 8/1 21 13
**Lady Poly (30)** (JRPoulton) **8-8-12**(5)ow3 MrVLukaniuk(1) (a bhd) ....¾ **13** 66/1 — —
15[12] **Persian Haze (IRE) (43)** (BJMcMath) **7-9-11**(5) MrsMMorris(3) (bhd fnl 8f) ....3½ **14** 33/1 — —
(SP 127.5%) **14 Rn**

**3m 28.07** (6.07) CSF £39.49 CT £205.78 TOTE £5.00: £2.40 £3.40 £4.20 (£31.90) Trio £72.10 OWNER Copyforce Ltd (EPSOM) BRED Castle Farm Stud
LONG HANDICAP Lady Poly 8-9
WEIGHT FOR AGE 4yo-7lb

T/Plpt: £33.30 (211 Tckts). T/.Qdpt: £33.80 (7.7 Tckts). SM

# 0070-SOUTHWELL (L-H) (Standard)
## Monday January 15th
WEATHER: sunny WIND: almost nil

## 84 FAIR ISLE H'CAP (0-65) (I) (4-Y.O+) (Class F)
1-05 (1-06) **1m (Fibresand)** £2,222.00 (£622.00: £302.00) Stalls: Low GOING minus 0.07 sec per fur (STD)

SP RR SF
77[2] **Benjamins Law (59)** (JAPickering) **5-9-10** JQuinn(1) (lw: a gng wl: led 2f out: r.o) ....— **1** 7/4[1] 76+ 42
31[2] **Lilac Rain (45)** (JRArnold) **4-8-10b** CRutter(7) (sn outpcd & wl bhd: r.o fnl 2f: no ch w wnr) ....5 **2** 6/1[3] 53 18
66[9] **The Mestral (39)** (MJRyan) **4-8-4b** PBloomfield(5) (led 6f: sn btn) ....3½ **3** 20/1 40 5
50[5] **Aquado (51)** (SRBowring) **7-8-11b**(5) CTeague(8) (hld up: effrt over 3f out: no imp) ....5 **4** 9/2[2] 41 7
**Halfabob (IRE) (38)** (DHaydnJones) **4-8-3** TWilliams(2) (chsd ldrs: rdn 3f out: one pce) ....2 **5** 25/1 25 —
43[5] **Scent of Power (38)** (NMBabbage) **6-8-3** FNorton(10) (b.nr fore: prom tl outpcd fnl 3f) ....1¾ **6** 14/1 21 —
34[13] **Rafter-J (50)** (JAHarris) **5-9-1** JFEgan(3) (a outpcd & bhd) ....¾ **7** 16/1 31 —
27[5] **Blasted (54)** (GEThorner) **4-9-5** AMcGlone(4) (prom 5f: sn outpcd) ....10 **8** 11/1 16 —
**Chalky Dancer (37)** (HJCollingridge) **4-8-2b[1]** DaleGibson(6) (chsd ldrs tl hrd rdn & wknd 3f out) ....11 **9** 7/1 — —
44[7] **Macaroon Lady (34)** (NBycroft) **5-7-13b**ow1 SMaloney(9) (a outpcd & bhd) ....¾ **10** 33/1 — —
(SP 113.8%) **10 Rn**

**1m 46.1** (6.10) CSF £11.69 CT £137.26 TOTE £3.20: £1.20 £3.60 £6.30 (£6.90) Trio £34.30 OWNER Mr D. Lowe (HINCKLEY) BRED Dunchurch Lodge Stud

## 85 BARRA MAIDEN APPRENTICE H'CAP (0-60) (4-Y.O+) (Class F)
1-35 (1-36) **1m 4f (Fibresand)** £2,572.00 (£722.00: £352.00) Stalls: High GOING minus 0.07 sec per fur (STD)

SP RR SF
**Adaloaldo (USA) (47)** (JParkes) **4-9-5** RHavlin(11) (lw: a cl up: led over 2f out: r.o wl) ....— **1** 12/1 55 11
33[4] **Parklife (IRE) (39)** (PCHaslam) **4-8-6**(5) CarolDavison(16) (w ldrs: led 7f out tl over 2f out: no ex) ....2 **2** 9/2[1] 44 —
54[4] **Alpine Storm (IRE) (27)** (MDIUsher) **4-7-13** CAdamson(8) (hdwy ½-wy: chsng ldrs 3f out: one pce after) ....2½ **3** 8/1 29 —
77[7] **Major Snugfit (43)** (MWEasterby) **4-9-1** GParkin(13) (hld up: gd hdwy 6f out: ev ch 2f out: no ex) ....hd **4** 12/1 45 1
33[9] **Inovar (29)** (CBBBooth) **6-8-2**(3) FLynch(6) (a.p: rdn 4f out: one pce) ....2 **5** 16/1 27 —
33[10] **Anchorena (56)** (JAHarris) **4-9-9**(5) DSweeney(9) (sn prom: one pce fnl 3f) ....1¾ **6** 12/1 53 9
45[5] **Selmeston (IRE) (35)** (PSFelgate) **4-8-4**(3) IonaWands(15) (lw: bhd: hdwy 4f out: nvr rchd ldrs) ....¾ **7** 6/1[3] 31 —
33[3] **Thatcher's Era (IRE) (55)** (TDBarron) **4-9-13** KimberleyHart(4) (effrt ½-wy: no imp) ....1¼ **8** 9/2[1] 49 5
**Much Too High (46)** (TJNaughton) **4-9-1**(3) TAshley(2) (nvr trbld ldrs) ....11 **9** 5/1[2] 26 —
**Skedaddle (44)** (RonaldThompson) **4-9-2v[1]** PRoberts(14) (nvr bttr than mid div) ....3½ **10** 14/1 19 —
**Auckland Castle (34)** (SRBowring) **5-8-5**(5) JEdmunds(1) (led tl hdd 7f out: wknd over 3f out) ....7 **11** 12/1 — —
33[15] **Nebrangus (IRE) (24)** (NBycroft) **4-7-7**(3) DDenby(10) (s.s: a bhd) ....4 **12** 33/1 — —
33[11] **Buzzards Hall (27)** (MCChapman) **6-8-3** CMunday(3) (chsd ldrs tl wknd 4f out: t.o) ....dist **13** 33/1 — —
44[8] **Crowning Tino (36)** (MrsNMacauley) **4-8-5**(3) AimeeCook(7) (nvr wnt pce: t.o) ....1¼ **14** 33/1 — —
**Keep Quiet (35)** (WJMusson) **4-8-4**(3)ow1 GFaulkner(12) (sn outpcd & wl bhd: t.o) ....20 **15** 16/1 — —
(SP 136.5%) **15 Rn**

**2m 46.0** (13.50) CSF £67.56 CT £436.03 TOTE £15.10: £3.80 £1.60 £3.80 (£47.70) Trio £120.10 OWNER Mr R. Flegg (MALTON) BRED S.Ross
LONG HANDICAP Nebrangus (IRE) 7-9
WEIGHT FOR AGE 4yo-4lb

## 86 ISLE OF SKYE CLAIMING STKS (4-Y.O+) (Class F)
2-05 (2-05) **7f (Fibresand)** £2,572.00 (£722.00: £352.00) Stalls: Low GOING minus 0.07 sec per fur (STD)

SP RR SF
**Berge (IRE) (75)** (WAO'Gorman) **5-8-11b** EmmaO'Gorman(3) (lw: trckd ldrs: led over 2f out: sn clr) ....— **1** 2/1[2] 77 45
18[3] **Pine Ridge Lad (IRE) (71)** (JLEyre) **6-8-8**(7) SCopp(2) (sn cl up: one pce fnl 2f) ....2½ **2** 5/2[3] 75 43
31* **Spencer's Revenge (78)** (MJRyan) **7-8-13** GBardwell(6) (bhd: effrt ½-wy: nt qckn fnl 2f) ....1 **3** 7/4[1] 71 39
42[12] **Moody (59)** (MissGayKelleway) **4-7-12** JQuinn(1) (b.hind: bhd: hdwy 3f out: no imp) ....5 **4** 10/1 45 13
57[7] **Bex Hill (34)** (DHaydnJones) **4-7-12v** AMackay(8) (cl up tl wknd over 2f out) ....7 **5** 50/1 29 —
**Legatee (56)** (AStreeter) **5-8-0** FNorton(5) (led tl hdd over 2f out: sn btn) ....2½ **6** 25/1 25 —
**Hallstar** (KAMorgan) **4-8-4** DaleGibson(7) (b.hind: carried wd & outpcd appr str: n.d after) ....6 **7** 100/1 15 —
**All Apologies (IRE)** (RHollinshead) **4-8-7** JFEgan(4) (plld hrd: rn v.wd st: sn bhd) ....9 **8** 25/1 — —
(SP 118.0%) **8 Rn**

**1m 30.7** (3.90) CSF £7.40 TOTE £2.40: £1.20 £1.10 £1.10 (£4.30) OWNER Mr S. Fustok (NEWMARKET) BRED S. Fustok
**OFFICIAL EXPLANATION All Apologies (IRE): the jockey reported that the horse had taken a very strong hold causing the saddle to slip forward, making it difficult for him to prevent the horse hanging wide in the home straight.**

## 87 MULL H'CAP (0-70) (4-Y.O+) (Class E)
2-35 (2-35) **1m 3f (Fibresand)** £3,074.60 (£930.80: £454.40: £216.20) Stalls: High GOING minus 0.07 sec per fur (STD)

SP RR SF
44[5] **Grey Again (56)** (SRBowring) **4-9-3b**(5) CTeague(9) (dwlt: hdwy 8f out: led over 2f out: styd on u.p) ....— **1** 10/1 65 19
43[2] **Carol Again (35)** (NBycroft) **4-8-1** JQuinn(8) (trckd ldrs: effrt over 2f out: edgd lft: styd on towards fin) ....½ **2** 7/1[3] 43 —
**Tonka (40)** (PJMakin) **4-8-6** SSanders(7) (hld up: hdwy ½-wy: trckng ldrs 3f out: sn rdn & nt qckn) ....6 **3** 11/2[2] 40 —
**Suivez (56)** (MrsNMacauley) **6-9-11** SDWilliams(2) (b: in tch: rdn 5f out: hdwy 3f out: one pce fnl 2f) ....¾ **4** 6/4[1] 54 12

| | Horse | | | SP | RR | SF |
|---|---|---|---|---|---|---|
| | **Mill Dancer (IRE) (46)** (EJAlston) **4-8-9**(3) DWright(6) (led tl hdd over 2f out: wknd) | 2½ | **5** | 7/1 3 | 41 | — |
| 43[8] | **East Barns (IRE) (44)** (SGollings) **8-8-13b** FNorton(5) (outpcd 6f out: n.d) | 8 | **6** | 8/1 | 26 | — |
| | **Jarrow (29)** (MrsAMNaughton) **5-7-12v**ow2 AMackay(1) (chsd ldrs tl wknd fnl 3f) | 2½ | **7** | 20/1 | 8 | — |
| | **Canary Falcon (59)** (JohnBerry) **5-10-0** VSmith(3) (b: a bhd) | nk | **8** | 8/1 | 37 | — |
| 48[11] | **Elite Justice (62)** (NTinkler) **4-10-0** KimTinkler(4) (outpcd & bhd fnl 6f) | 1¼ | **9** | 16/1 | 39 | — |

(SP 122.3%) **9 Rn**

**2m 31.7** (11.70) CSF £73.48 CT £391.72 TOTE £15.80: £2.90 £1.70 £2.00 (£16.70) Trio £134.90 OWNER Green Diamond Racing (EDWINSTOWE) BRED Mrs K. M. Watts
WEIGHT FOR AGE 4yo-3lb

## 88 LUNDY H'CAP (0-80) (3-Y.O+) (Class D)

3-05 (3-08) **6f (Fibresand)** £3,796.30 (£1,149.40: £561.20: £267.10) Stalls: Low GOING minus 0.07 sec per fur (STD)

| | Horse | | | SP | RR | SF |
|---|---|---|---|---|---|---|
| | **Super Benz (58)** (JLEyre) **10-8-1**(5) CTeague(3) (cl up: led ½-wy: hld on wl) | — | **1** | 8/1 | 63 | 30 |
| 50[2] | **Awesome Venture (55)** (MCChapman) **6-7-10**(7) CMunday(4) (a cl up: kpt on wl towards fin) | nk | **2** | 9/1 | 59 | 26 |
| 20[4] | **Cretan Gift (77)** (NPLittmoden) **5-9-11v** TGMcLaughlin(6) (in tch: hdwy 2f out: styd on towards fin) | hd | **3** | 6/1 3 | 81 | 48 |
| 55[6] | **Hannah's Usher (80)** (CMurray) **4-10-0** MTebbutt(5) (a chsng ldrs: ev ch over 1f out: grad wknd) | 3 | **4** | 20/1 | 76 | 43 |
| 50[3] | **Monis (IRE) (55)** (JBalding) **5-8-3** ClaireBalding(2) (lw: in tch: effrt over 2f out: no imp) | 4 | **5** | 12/1 | 40 | 7 |
| 74[4] | **Indiahra (49)** (RHollinshead) **5-7-11** NCarlisle(7) (outpcd ½-wy: sme late hdwy) | 1¼ | **6** | 9/1 | 31 | — |
| 48[8] | **Nashaat (USA) (72)** (MCChapman) **8-9-3**(3) PMcCabe(10) (racd wd: outpcd ½-wy: n.d) | 2½ | **7** | 11/1 | 47 | 14 |
| | **Elton Ledger (IRE) (70)** (MrsNMacauley) **7-9-4v** SDWilliams(8) (b: racd wd: nvr wnt pce) | hd | **8** | 13/2 | 45 | 12 |
| | **Leigh Crofter (77)** (PDCundell) **7-9-6b**(5) DGriffiths(9) (in tch tl racd wd & lost pl appr st) | 8 | **9** | 8/1 | 31 | — |
| | **Nordan Raider (76)** (MJCamacho) **8-9-10** LCharnock(11) (b: lw: plld hrd: swtchd lft after 1f: hdwy ½-wy: wknd 2f out) | 2½ | **10** | 11/2 2 | 23 | — |
| | **Encore M'Lady (IRE) (69)** (FHLee) **5-9-3b** RLappin(1) (led to ½-wy: sn wknd) | nk | **11** | 5/1 1 | 15 | — |

(SP 122.7%) **11 Rn**

**1m 17.6** (4.10) CSF £72.70 CT £426.03 TOTE £6.60: £2.70 £2.30 £2.50 (£23.60) Trio £86.20 OWNER Whitestonecliffe Racing Partnership (HAMBLETON) BRED Scarteen Stud

## 89 SHETLAND (S) STKS (Qualifier) (3-Y.O) (Class F)

3-35 (3-36) **1m (Fibresand)** £2,607.00 (£732.00: £357.00) Stalls: Low GOING minus 0.07 sec per fur (STD)

| | Horse | | | SP | RR | SF |
|---|---|---|---|---|---|---|
| | **Panama Jive (IRE)** (MJohnston) **3-8-9** TWilliams(5) (chsd ldrs: rdn over 2f out: hmpd & swtchd ins fnl f: r.o wl towards fin: fin 2nd, nk: awrdd r) | — | **1** | 16/1 | 55 | — |
| 46[2] | **Arch Angel (IRE) (53)** (DJSffrenchDavis) **3-9-0** NAdams(8) (sn chsng ldrs: rdn 2f out: edgd lft: styd on to ld cl home: fin 1st: disq: plcd 2nd) | | **2** | 6/4 2 | 61 | 5 |
| 46* | **People Direct (59)** (KMcAuliffe) **3-9-0** JFanning(3) (b: led tl ct cl home) | nk | **3** | 5/4 1 | 60 | 4 |
| 25[5] | **Be My Bird (50)** (WJMusson) **3-8-6**(3) PMcCabe(4) (hld up & wl bhd: hdwy 2f out: r.o wl towards fin) | ¾ | **4** | 14/1 3 | 53 | — |
| | **Kratz (IRE) (43)** (BSRothwell) **3-9-0v** MFenton(2) (outpcd ½-wy: sme hdwy 2f out: n.d) | 3½ | **5** | 20/1 | 51 | — |
| | **Savanna Blue** (JLEyre) **3-8-9** JFortune(1) (s.i.s: a outpcd & bhd) | 14 | **6** | 16/1 | 18 | — |
| | **Bridlington Bay** (JLEyre) **3-9-0** RLappin(6) (prom tl outpcd ½-wy) | 1½ | **7** | 20/1 | 20 | — |
| | **Mutee (IRE)** (MJohnston) **3-8-9** JWeaver(7) (chsd ldrs tl outpcd ½-wy: sn bhd) | 15 | **8** | 14/1 3 | — | — |

(SP 119.1%) **8 Rn**

**1m 49.0** (9.00) CSF £40.07 TOTE £11.40: £2.80 £1.10 £1.10 (£47.80) OWNER Mr J. S. Morrison (MIDDLEHAM) BRED Sheikh Mohammed Bin Rashid Al Maktoum
Bt in 6,000 gns

## 90 FAIR ISLE H'CAP (0-65) (II) (4-Y.O+) (Class F)

4-05 (4-06) **1m (Fibresand)** £2,222.00 (£622.00: £302.00) Stalls: Low GOING minus 0.07 sec per fur (STD)

| | Horse | | | SP | RR | SF |
|---|---|---|---|---|---|---|
| 77[8] | **Kingchip Boy (49)** (MJRyan) **7-9-3v** TIves(4) (led 3f: cl up: led over 2f out: hld on wl) | — | **1** | 5/1 3 | 63 | 48 |
| 53[5] | **Snake Plissken (IRE) (46)** (DHaydnJones) **5-9-0** AMackay(3) (lw: chsd ldrs: rdn 3f out: disp ld ins fnl f: no ex towards fin) | ½ | **2** | 6/1 | 59 | 44 |
| 30* | **Komiamaite (53)** (SRBowring) **4-9-2**(5) CTeague(2) (sn outpcd & bhd: hdwy u.p 2f out: nvr able to chal) | 5 | **3** | 5/2 1 | 57 | 41 |
| 44W | **Sea God (44)** (MCChapman) **5-8-12** JWeaver(8) (hld up & bhd: effrt 3f out: styd on: no imp) | s.h | **4** | 8/1 | 47 | 32 |
| 44[6] | **Daawe (USA) (56)** (MrsVAAconley) **5-9-10v** MDeering(6) (led after 3f tl over 2f out: wknd) | 8 | **5** | 16/1 | 43 | 28 |
| 72[4] | **Shotley Again (30)** (NBycroft) **6-7-12** LCharnock(5) (chsd ldrs: outpcd ½-wy: n.d after) | 3½ | **6** | 8/1 | 10 | — |
| | **Colosse (41)** (JLEyre) **4-8-9b**1 RLappin(7) (chsd ldrs tl wknd over 2f out) | 2 | **7** | 4/1 2 | 18 | 2 |
| | **Mazilla (46)** (AStreeter) **4-9-0** DeanMcKeown(9) (b: cl up 3f: outpcd & bhd fr ½-wy) | 4 | **8** | 12/1 | 15 | — |
| 43[3] | **Anotherone to Note (42)** (NPLittmoden) **5-8-3b**(7) JBramhill(1) (s.i.s: plld hrd: hdwy ½-wy: sn wknd) | hd | **9** | 6/1 | 10 | — |

(SP 129.6%) **9 Rn**

**1m 44.8** (4.80) CSF £35.89 CT £87.72 TOTE £5.90: £2.50 £2.70 £1.60 (£24.80) Trio £21.20 OWNER Four Jays Racing Partnership (NEWMARKET) BRED R. M. Scott

T/Jkpt: Not won; £198,162.83 to Carlisle 16/1/96. T/Plpt: £18.40 (1,111.69 Tckts). T/Qdpt: £23.60 (9.65 Tckts). AA

# 0078-LINGFIELD (L-H) - Tuesday January 16th

**91-96 Abandoned** - Fog

# 0057-WOLVERHAMPTON (L-H) (Standard)

## Wednesday January 17th

WEATHER: drizzle WIND: nil

## 97 DUDLEY H'CAP (0-75) (4-Y.O+) (Class D)

2-00 (2-00) **2m 46y (Fibresand)** £3,691.00 (£1,117.00: £545.00: £259.00) Stalls: Low GOING: 0.20 sec per fur (SLW)

| | Horse | | | SP | RR | SF |
|---|---|---|---|---|---|---|
| 60[2] | **Shakiyr (FR) (65)** (RHollinshead) **5-9-10** RCochrane(1) (hld up: led over 2f out: rdn out) | — | **1** | 5/2 2 | 76 | 50 |

| Form | Horse / details | Dist | Pos | SP | RR | SF |
|---|---|---|---|---|---|---|
| 12* | **Milngavie (IRE) (37)** (MJohnston) **6-7-10b** TWilliams(6) (chsd ldr: led over 3f out tl over 2f out: hrd drvn: one pce) | 4 | 2 | 2/1[1] | 44 | 18 |
| 19[7] | **Ballymac Girl (60)** (JMBradley) **8-9-5** LCharnock(2) (b: led: rdn over 4f out: hdd over 3f out: wknd over 2f out) | 11 | 3 | 10/1 | 56 | 30 |
| | **Anjou (67)** (JPearce) **4-9-5** GBardwell(8) (lw: hld up: hdwy over 5f out: rdn & wknd 3f out) | 7 | 4 | 7/2[3] | 56 | 23 |
| 60[7] | **Backview (66)** (BJLlewellyn) **4-8-13**(5) CTeague(5) (b.nr hind: wl bhd fnl 7f) | hd | 5 | 25/1 | 55 | 22 |
| 69[8] | **Dvorak (IRE) (56)** (RHarris) **5-9-1** AMackay(4) (hld up: rdn 7f out: wknd over 3f out: t.o) | dist | 6 | 11/1 | — | — |
| | **Ranger Sloane (44)** (GFierro) **4-7-10** JQuinn(7) (dropped rr 9f out: hrd drvn 7f out: sn t.o) | 3 | 7 | 40/1 | — | — |
| 18[6] | **Avenue Foch (IRE) (47)** (FMurphy) **7-8-6** JFanning(3) (s.i.s: plld hrd: sn prom: wknd qckly over 6f out: sn t.o) | 5 | 8 | 25/1 | — | — |

(SP 111.7%) **8 Rn**

**3m 42.2** (15.20) CSF £7.34 CT £34.18 TOTE £2.30: £1.10 £1.30 £1.70 (£2.60) OWNER L & R Roadlines (UPPER LONGDON) BRED S. A. Aga Khan in France

LONG HANDICAP Ranger Sloane 7-7 Milngavie (IRE) 7-9

WEIGHT FOR AGE 4yo-7lb

## 98 TIPTON CLAIMING STKS (4-Y.O+) (Class E)

2-30 (2-31) **1m 4f (Fibresand)** £3,189.00 (£966.00: £472.00: £225.00) Stalls: Low GOING: 0.20 sec per fur (SLW)

| Form | Horse / details | Dist | Pos | SP | RR | SF |
|---|---|---|---|---|---|---|
| | **Old Provence (70)** (RHarris) **6-8-12** AMackay(4) (b: a.p: rdn 5f out: led over 3f out: drvn out) | — | 1 | 5/2[2] | 71 | 49 |
| 61[13] | **Make a Note (USA) (85)** (PDEvans) **5-9-10** SSanders(2) (chsd ldr 6f: ev ch 2f out: hrd drvn: r.o one pce) | 1¼ | 2 | 5/1[3] | 81 | 59 |
| | **Pharly Dancer (73)** (WWHaigh) **7-9-6** DaleGibson(5) (swtg: plld hrd: a.p: led over 4f out tl over 3f out: ev ch 2f out: hrd drvn: one pce) | ½ | 3 | 7/4[1] | 77 | 55 |
| 62[11] | **Timely Example (USA) (64)** (BRCambidge) **5-8-8** NAdams(8) (hld up: hrd drvn over 3f out: sn wknd) | 20 | 4 | 20/1 | 38 | 16 |
| | **Tony's Mist (52)** (JMBradley) **6-8-7**(3) SDrowne(7) (lw: hld up: rdn & hdwy 6f out: wknd over 2f out) | 1¾ | 5 | 7/1 | 38 | 16 |
| 62[6] | **Off the Air (IRE) (45)** (BJLlewellyn) **5-8-3** TWilliams(6) (prom: rdn over 6f out: sn lost pl: eased whn no ch 2f out) | 6 | 6 | 20/1 | 23 | 1 |
| | **Kerry Jane** (NMBabbage) **6-8-13** JQuinn(3) (led over 7f: sn wknd: t.o) | 20 | 7 | 50/1 | 6 | — |
| | **Maradata (IRE)** (RHollinshead) **4-8-11** MWigham(1) (s.i.s: hld up: bhd fnl 4f: t.o) | 25 | 8 | 6/1 | — | — |

(SP 119.9%) **8 Rn**

**2m 42.2** (9.70) CSF £15.17 TOTE £2.50: £1.40 £1.30 £1.40 (£7.20) OWNER Mr T. J. Dawson (NEWMARKET) BRED Stowell Hill Ltd and A. J. Tree

WEIGHT FOR AGE 4yo-4lb

STEWARDS' ENQUIRY Mackay susp. 26-27 & 29-30/1/96 (excessive use of whip).

## 99 NETHERTON MAIDEN STKS (4-Y.O+) (Class D)

3-00 (3-01) **1m 100y (Fibresand)** £3,848.95 (£1,165.60: £569.30: £271.15) Stalls: Low GOING: 0.20 sec per fur (SLW)

| Form | Horse / details | Dist | Pos | SP | RR | SF |
|---|---|---|---|---|---|---|
| | **Ocean Park (75)** (LadyHerries) **5-9-0** AClark(6) (a.p: led over 1f out: edgd lft wl ins fnl f: rdn out) | — | 1 | 5/6[1] | 81 | 63 |
| 14[3] | **Golden Pound (USA) (72)** (MissGayKelleway) **4-9-0** RCochrane(7) (lw: a.p: led over 2f out tl over 1f out: unable qckn) | 2 | 2 | 15/8[2] | 77 | 59 |
| | **Restate (IRE)** (FMurphy) **5-8-9** JFanning(3) (led 1f: led over 4f out tl over 2f out: wknd over 1f out) | 8 | 3 | 20/1 | 57 | 39 |
| | **Night Time (58)** (AStreeter) **4-9-0** SDWilliams(8) (lw: hld up: rdn & wknd over 2f out) | 7 | 4 | 16/1 | 49 | 31 |
| 45[6] | **Young Benson (53)** (BAMcMahon) **4-9-0b[1]** GCarter(4) (lw: prom tl wknd over 2f out) | 7 | 5 | 16/1 | 36 | 18 |
| | **Showtime Blues (IRE)** (ABailey) **7-8-11**(3) DWright(1) (led after 1f tl over 4f out: rdn 3f out: sn wknd) | 13 | 6 | 14/1 | 11 | — |
| | **Lovescape** (BJLlewellyn) **5-8-9** TWilliams(5) (bkwd: outpcd: sn t.o) | 30 | 7 | 25/1 | — | — |
| | **Otaru (IRE)** (SirMarkPrescott) **4-8-9** CNutter(2) (prom 8f: t.o) | 2½ | 8 | 11/1[3] | — | — |

(SP 124.7%) **8 Rn**

**1m 50.4** (5.40) CSF £3.13 TOTE £2.40: £1.00 £2.10 £3.40 (£1.20) OWNER Mr E. Reitel (LITTLEHAMPTON) BRED Mrs H. Khan

## 100 CONTROLS CENTER H'CAP (0-90) (4-Y.O+) (Class C)

3-30 (3-30) **1m 4f (Fibresand)** £5,635.45 (£1,705.60: £832.30: £395.65) Stalls: Low GOING: 0.20 sec per fur (SLW)

| Form | Horse / details | Dist | Pos | SP | RR | SF |
|---|---|---|---|---|---|---|
| 48[9] | **Magic Junction (USA) (76)** (LordHuntingdon) **5-9-3v[1]** TIves(9) (lw: a.p: led over 4f out tl over 2f out: rdn to ld nr fin) | — | 1 | 12/1 | 85 | 69 |
| 77* | **Maple Bay (IRE) (67)** (ABailey) **7-8-1**(7) 5x PRoberts(2) (led over 7f: led over 2f out: hdd nr fin) | nk | 2 | 7/2[3] | 76 | 60 |
| 38[2] | **Opera Buff (IRE) (85)** (MissGayKelleway) **5-9-12** RCochrane(6) (hld up: hdwy over 4f out: rdn over 3f out: ev ch ins fnl f: unable qckn) | nk | 3 | 3/1[2] | 93 | 77 |
| 38[3] | **Prince Danzig (IRE) (77)** (DJGMurraySmith) **5-9-4** SSanders(7) (hld up: hdwy 3f out: styd on fnl 2f) | 3 | 4 | 12/1 | 81 | 65 |
| 80[2] | **Seventeens Lucky (69)** (BobJones) **4-8-6** JFanning(1) (prom tl wknd over 2f out) | 9 | 5 | 7/1 | 61 | 41 |
| 61[7] | **Araboybill (57)** (RSimpson) **5-7-12b** GBardwell(5) (hld up: rdn & wknd over 3f out) | ¾ | 6 | 33/1 | 48 | 32 |
| 48[6] | **Mr Towser (74)** (WWHaigh) **5-8-10**(5) CTeague(8) (prom tl wknd over 3f out) | s.h | 7 | 12/1 | 65 | 49 |
| 48* | **Our Tom (65)** (JWharton) **4-8-2** 5x NCarlisle(3) (plld hrd: prom tl wknd over 4f out: t.o) | 20 | 8 | 5/2[1] | 30 | 10 |
| | **Shahik (USA) (75)** (JGMO'Shea) **6-9-2** JQuinn(4) (bhd fnl 6f: t.o) | 3 | 9 | 50/1 | 36 | 20 |

(SP 116.3%) **9 Rn**

**2m 39.8** (7.30) CSF £50.29 CT £146.00 TOTE £10.20: £2.10 £2.60 £1.10 (£99.00) Trio £28.20 OWNER The Queen (WEST ILSLEY) BRED The Queen in USA

WEIGHT FOR AGE 4yo-4lb

**OFFICIAL EXPLANATION Our Tom: the jockey reported that the horse ran too freely and needs a truly run race.**

## 101 BILSTON (S) STKS (Qualifier) (3-Y.O) (Class F)

4-00 (4-01) **5f (Fibresand)** £2,870.50 (£868.00: £423.00: £200.50) Stalls: Low GOING: 0.20 sec per fur (SLW)

| Form | Horse / details | Dist | Pos | SP | RR | SF |
|---|---|---|---|---|---|---|
| 21[4] | **Boffy (IRE) (58)** (BPJBaugh) **3-8-12**(7) IonaWands(5) (b: hdwy over 2f out: led over 1f out: r.o wl) | — | 1 | 100/30[1] | 79 | 34 |
| 52[3] | **Marino Street (62)** (PDEvans) **3-8-7v[1]** SSanders(2) (b.nr fore: a.p: led wl over 1f out: sn hdd: unable qckn) | 2 | 2 | 100/30[1] | 61 | 16 |
| 59[8] | **Red Acuisle (IRE) (62)** (JBerry) **3-8-5b[1]**(7) PRoberts(12) (lw: a.p: led 2f out: sn hdd: unable qckn) | ½ | 3 | 13/2[2] | 64 | 19 |
| 21[6] | **Dhes-C** (RHollinshead) **3-8-0**(7) FLynch(6) (hdwy over 1f out: r.o ins fnl f) | s.h | 4 | 8/1 | 59 | 14 |
| | **Victoria Sioux (52)** (JWharton) **3-8-7** JQuinn(10) (rdn over 2f out: hdwy over 1f out: r.o) | hd | 5 | 7/1[3] | 59 | 14 |
| 39[4] | **Impington (IRE) (51)** (WRMuir) **3-8-7** RCochrane(7) (b.hind: hdwy over 1f out: no ex ins fnl f) | 1¼ | 6 | 10/1 | 55 | 10 |
| | **Monkey Zanty (IRE) (59)** (JLHarris) **3-8-11**(3) DWright(4) (prom 3f) | 2 | 7 | 7/1[3] | 55 | 10 |

| | | | SP | RR | SF |
|---|---|---|---|---|---|
| 46[6] | **Havana Heights (IRE) (45)** (JLEyre) **3-8-7** NAdams(11) (prom: rdn 3f out: sn bhd) ....8 | **8** | 16/1 | 23 | — |
| 21[10] | **Shoot The Minstrel** (JAPickering) **3-8-12** NCarlisle(8) (b.nr hind: a bhd) ....¾ | **9** | 33/1 | 25 | — |
| | **My West End Girl** (AStreeter) **3-8-7** SDWilliams(3) (led 3f: wknd qckly over 1f out) ....nk | **10** | 33/1 | 19 | — |
| | **Common Divine (IRE)** (CMurray) **3-8-7** MTebbutt(1) (prom: rdn over 3f out: wknd over 2f out) ....2½ | **11** | 20/1 | 11 | — |
| | **Touch of Fantasy (46)** (CADwyer) **3-8-0**(7) RMullen(9) (b.hind: prom over 2f) ....s.h | **12** | 20/1 | 11 | — |

(SP 126.0%) **12 Rn**

**63.8 secs** (5.10) CSF £14.99 TOTE £3.70: £2.10 £1.20 £1.70 (£5.50) Trio £21.20 OWNER Mr Stan Baugh (LITTLE HAYWOOD) BRED J. Hayden
No bid

## 102 BIRMINGHAM H'CAP (0-75) (3-Y.O) (Class D)

4-30 (4-31) **7f (Fibresand)** £3,743.65 (£1,133.20: £553.10: £263.05) Stalls: High GOING: 0.20 sec per fur (SLW)

| | | | SP | RR | SF |
|---|---|---|---|---|---|
| 32[3] | **Briganoone (49)** (SRBowring) **3-7-12** NCarlisle(8) (dwlt: hdwy over 4f out: nt clr run over 1f out: r.o wl u.p to ld nr fin) ....— | **1** | 13/2 | 53 | 19 |
| | **Agent (67)** (JLEyre) **3-9-2** RLappin(1) (s.i.s: plld hrd: sn prom: led over 1f out: edgd rt: hdd nr fin) ....nk | **2** | 2/1 [1] | 70 | 36 |
| | **Myttons Mistake (72)** (ABailey) **3-9-4**(3) DWright(6) (led over 5f: unable qckn) ....1¾ | **3** | 9/2 [2] | 71 | 37 |
| | **Honestly (72)** (BSmart) **3-9-7** RCochrane(7) (hdwy 2f out: r.o ins fnl f) ....s.h | **4** | 9/2 [2] | 71 | 37 |
| | **Chilibang Bang (62)** (JBerry) **3-8-4**(7) PRoberts(9) (prom: hrd drvn over 2f out: one pce fnl f) ....nk | **5** | 6/1 [3] | 61 | 27 |
| | **The Frisky Farmer (65)** (WGMTurner) **3-9-0** AClark(5) (prom: rdn over 3f out: wknd over 2f out) ....12 | **6** | 20/1 | 36 | 2 |
| 32[6] | **Rothley Imp (IRE) (54)** (JWharton) **3-8-3** JQuinn(2) (nvr nr ldrs) ....4 | **7** | 11/1 | 16 | — |
| | **Carwyn's Choice (48)** (PCClarke) **3-7-11**ow1 NAdams(3) (lw: bhd fnl 3f) ....nk | **8** | 50/1 | 9 | — |
| | **Touch of Snow (47)** (JABennett) **3-7-5**(5) PFessey(4) (prom tl wknd qckly over 4f out) ....6 | **9** | 33/1 | — | — |

(SP 115.3%) **9 Rn**

**1m 31.6** (6.90) CSF £18.81 CT £58.63 TOTE £9.20: £2.40 £1.70 £1.10 (£7.40) Trio £18.00 OWNER Mr G. E. Griffiths (EDWINSTOWE) BRED Red House Stud
LONG HANDICAP Carwyn's Choice 7-1 Touch of Snow 7-3

T/Plpt: £6.80 (1,786.42 Tckts). T/Qdpt: £5.30 (14.53 Tckts). KH

# 0091-LINGFIELD (L-H) (Standard)
## Thursday January 18th

## 103 MORE HASTE MAIDEN STKS (I) (4-Y.O+) (Class D)

1-00 (1-01) **1m 2f (Equitrack)** £3,236.00 (£977.00: £475.00: £224.00) Stalls: Low GOING minus 0.45 sec per fur (FST)

| | | | SP | RR | SF |
|---|---|---|---|---|---|
| 33[5] | **Todd (USA) (55)** (PhilipMitchell) **5-9-2** AClark(5) (a.p: led 4f out: rdn out) ....— | **1** | 11/4 [2] | 60 | 30 |
| | **Jade Venture** (SPCWoods) **5-8-11** JWeaver(7) (hdwy over 4f out: chsd wnr over 2f out: unable qckn) ....1 | **2** | 8/13 [1] | 53 | 23 |
| 79[4] | **Callonescy (IRE) (48)** (DCO'Brien) **4-9-0** GBardwell(2) (a.p: rdn over 4f out: one pce) ....9 | **3** | 8/1 [3] | 45 | 12 |
| 24[9] | **Golden Punch (USA)** (CACyzer) **5-9-2v[1]** DBiggs(9) (s.i.s: wl bhd 8f: nvr nrr) ....7 | **4** | 33/1 | 33 | 3 |
| 65[6] | **Thunderous (43)** (JJBridger) **5-9-2b** JQuinn(6) (b: hdwy over 4f out: sn wknd) ....2½ | **5** | 33/1 | 29 | — |
| | **Mister** (KMcAuliffe) **4-9-0** JFortune(1) (lw: led 6f: wknd over 2f out) ....7 | **6** | 20/1 | 19 | — |
| | **Red Channel (IRE)** (TCasey) **6-9-2** MFenton(8) (chsd ldr 7f out to 5f out: wknd 4f out) ....½ | **7** | 14/1 | 17 | — |
| | **Emperors Wood** (PHayward) **5-9-2** AMcGlone(4) (chsd ldr 3f: wknd over 4f out) ....3½ | **8** | 33/1 | 11 | — |
| 31[8] | **Prestige Lad** (BSmart) **4-9-0** SSanders(3) (bhd fnl 5f) ....8 | **9** | 33/1 | — | — |

(SP 122.9%) **9 Rn**

**2m 8.62** (4.32) CSF £4.86 TOTE £4.20: £1.10 £1.10 £1.90 (£2.30) Trio £3.00 OWNER Mr J. Morton (EPSOM) BRED Allen E. Paulson
WEIGHT FOR AGE 4yo-2lb

## 104 LITTLE ACORNS (S) H'CAP (0-60) (4-Y.O+) (Class G)

1-30 (1-31) **1m 4f (Equitrack)** £2,505.40 (£704.40: £344.20) Stalls: Low GOING minus 0.45 sec per fur (FST)

| | | | SP | RR | SF |
|---|---|---|---|---|---|
| | **Carrolls Marc (IRE) (40)** (CMurray) **8-9-1** JWeaver(2) (stdd s: hdwy over 3f out: led wl ins fnl f: r.o wl) ....— | **1** | 12/1 | 51 | 36 |
| 54[2] | **Miltak (37)** (PJMakin) **4-8-8** SSanders(15) (hdwy over 6f out: led over 1f out tl wl ins fnl f: unable qckn) ....1 | **2** | 11/4 [1] | 47 | 28 |
| | **Harry (49)** (AJWilson) **6-9-10** JFortune(3) (b: a.p: chsd ldr over 5f out: led 3f out tl over 1f out: one pce) ....2½ | **3** | 14/1 | 55 | 40 |
| 60[6] | **Heighth of Fame (45)** (AJWilson) **5-9-6** GBardwell(13) (lost pl 5f out: rallied fnl f: r.o) ....hd | **4** | 12/1 | 51 | 36 |
| 54[3] | **Duggan (23)** (PDEvans) **9-7-12** JQuinn(10) (b.off hind: hdwy over 4f out: wknd 1f out) ....5 | **5** | 6/1 [3] | 23 | 8 |
| 54[6] | **Sharp Thrill (43)** (BSmart) **5-9-4b[1]** RCochrane(1) (rdn & hdwy over 3f out: sn wknd) ....6 | **6** | 8/1 | 35 | 20 |
| 54[9] | **Telephus (32)** (BJMcMath) **7-8-7** MRimmer(5) (rdn & hdwy over 3f out: sn wknd) ....1 | **7** | 14/1 | 22 | 7 |
| 37[4] | **Cabcharge Blue (50)** (TJNaughton) **4-9-0**(7) TAshley(6) (a mid div) ....2½ | **8** | 16/1 | 37 | 18 |
| | **Surprise Guest (IRE) (40)** (CADwyer) **5-9-1** MWigham(12) (nvr nrr) ....s.h | **9** | 12/1 | 27 | 12 |
| | **Trumble (46)** (CWThornton) **4-9-3** AMackay(4) (led 9f: wknd 2f out) ....½ | **10** | 4/1 [2] | 32 | 13 |
| | **Quadrant (44)** (AMoore) **7-9-5** AClark(9) (b: b.hind: bkwd: bhd fnl 5f) ....9 | **11** | 25/1 | 18 | 3 |
| 54[5] | **Mafuta (IRE) (31)** (JJSheehan) **4-8-2** NCarlisle(7) (b: hdwy over 4f out: wknd over 3f out) ....hd | **12** | 11/1 | 5 | — |
| 82[9] | **Jobber's Fiddle (45)** (DLWilliams) **4-8-11b**(5) DGriffiths(11) (prom over 7f) ....1¼ | **13** | 11/1 | 17 | — |
| 15[9] | **Quick Million (36)** (JWMullins) **5-8-11v** JFEgan(14) (prom over 7f) ....2 | **14** | 33/1 | 6 | — |
| | **Feeling Hope (41)** (MSSaunders) **5-9-2** AMcGlone(8) (chsd ldr 10f out tl over 5f out: sn wknd) ....4 | **15** | 33/1 | 5 | — |

(SP 140.8%) **15 Rn**

**2m 34.16** (4.16) CSF £48.44 CT £465.30 TOTE £13.70: £3.50 £1.10 £11.00 (£21.50) Trio £114.40; £132.20 to Catterick 19/1/96 OWNER P I P Electrics Ltd (NEWMARKET) BRED John Connaughton
WEIGHT FOR AGE 4yo-4lb
No bid

## 105 PENNY WISE CLAIMING STKS (4-Y.O+) (Class E)

2-00 (2-02) **1m (Equitrack)** £3,274.80 (£992.40: £485.20: £231.60) Stalls: Low GOING minus 0.45 sec per fur (FST)

| | | | SP | RR | SF |
|---|---|---|---|---|---|
| 82* | **Masnun (USA) (66)** (RJO'Sullivan) **11-8-6** AClark(11) (hdwy over 3f out: rdn over 2f out: led last strides) ....— | **1** | 9/2 [3] | 69 | 36 |

| | | | | SP | RR | SF |
|---|---|---|---|---|---|---|
| | **Mr Nevermind (IRE) (76)** (GLMoore) **6-8-13**(7) ALakeman(5) (hdwy over 3f out: led 1f out: hrd rdn: hdd last strides) | s.h | **2** | 8/1 | 83 | 50 |
| 62* | **Hand of Straw (IRE) (52)** (PGMurphy) **4-8-9v**(3) SDrowne(12) (lw: hdwy over 3f out: rdn over 2f out: r.o ins fnl f) | 1¾ | **3** | 20/1 | 72 | 38 |
| 65[2] | **Perilous Plight (73)** (WRMuir) **5-8-12** JWeaver(4) (lw: hdwy 2f out: r.o ins fnl f) | nk | **4** | 5/2[1] | 71 | 38 |
| 61[11] | **Sweet Supposin (IRE) (82)** (CADwyer) **5-8-9v**(7) TAshley(2) (lw: hdwy over 1f out: r.o) | ½ | **5** | 5/1 | 74 | 41 |
| 61[5] | **Rambo Waltzer (79)** (DNicholls) **4-9-2** AlexGreaves(8) (lw: a.p: led over 2f out to 1f out: sn wknd) | 1¼ | **6** | 100/30[2] | 72 | 38 |
| 13[10] | **Manabar (70)** (MJPolglase) **4-9-0** MRimmer(9) (a.p: rdn over 2f out: wknd fnl f) | nk | **7** | 100/1 | 70 | 36 |
| 66[5] | **Oozlem (IRE) (39)** (JRPoulton) **7-8-7b**(3) PMcCabe(10) (b: s.s: a bhd) | 3½ | **8** | 20/1 | 58 | 25 |
| | **Zuno Flyer (USA) (34)** (AMoore) **4-8-4** MFenton(1) (b: b.hind: led over 3f: wknd over 3f out) | hd | **9** | 25/1 | 53 | 19 |
| 62[2] | **Faez (54)** (RSimpson) **6-8-2b** GBardwell(6) (w ldr: led over 4f out tl over 2f out: sn wknd) | 10 | **10** | 20/1 | 30 | — |
| | **Flair Lady (40)** (WGMTurner) **5-7-12**(5) CAdamson(3) (prom over 3f) | 4 | **11** | 50/1 | 23 | — |
| | **Percussion Bird** (JRPoulton) **4-7-8**(7)ow4 TField(7) (bhd fnl 6f) | 7 | **12** | 100/1 | 8 | — |
| | | | | (SP 119.7%) | | **12 Rn** |

**1m 39.14** (1.74) CSF £37.32 TOTE £6.50: £2.50 £1.90 £10.40 (£14.20) Trio £32.60 OWNER Mr I. W. Page (WHITCOMBE) BRED Glencrest Farm

## 106 MORE HASTE MAIDEN STKS (II) (4-Y.O+) (Class D)

2-30 (2-32) **1m 2f (Equitrack)** £3,218.45 (£971.60: £472.30: £222.65) Stalls: Low GOING minus 0.45 sec per fur (FST)

| | | | | SP | RR | SF |
|---|---|---|---|---|---|---|
| 66[6] | **Your Most Welcome (49)** (DJSffrenchDavis) **5-8-11** GCarter(4) (w ldr: led over 6f out: edgd rt ins fnl f: all out) | — | **1** | 9/2[3] | 53 | 22 |
| 24[4] | **Errant (62)** (DJSCosgrove) **4-9-0** JQuinn(7) (b: hdwy over 3f out: chsd wnr over 2f out: ev ch fnl f: r.o) | s.h | **2** | Evens[1] | 59 | 25 |
| | **Ganador (47)** (BSmart) **4-8-9** RCochrane(2) (hdwy 3f out: rdn over 1f out: unable qckn) | 3 | **3** | 6/1 | 49 | 15 |
| | **Sweet Allegiance (43)** (JRPoulton) **6-8-8**(3) PMcCabe(5) (b: plld hrd: hld up: rdn over 2f out: one pce) | s.h | **4** | 33/1 | 48 | 17 |
| | **Cultural Icon (USA)** (PhilipMitchell) **4-9-0** AClark(1) (bit bkwd: sme hdwy over 3f out: sn wknd) | 11 | **5** | 4/1[2] | 36 | 2 |
| | **Boost (40)** (MrsNMacauley) **4-8-11v**[1](3) SDrowne(3) (lw: prom over 6f) | 8 | **6** | 12/1 | 24 | — |
| 37[7] | **Voices in the Sky** (AGNewcombe) **5-8-6**(5) DGriffiths(6) (prom over 5f) | nk | **7** | 50/1 | 17 | — |
| | **Bay Bob (IRE)** (TCasey) **7-9-2** AMackay(8) (led over 3f: wknd over 3f out) | 8 | **8** | 50/1 | 9 | — |
| | | | | (SP 117.0%) | | **8 Rn** |

**2m 9.03** (4.73) CSF £9.24 TOTE £5.30: £1.10 £1.10 £1.50 (£3.70) OWNER Mrs J. E. Lambert (UPPER LAMBOURN) BRED Collin Stud
WEIGHT FOR AGE 4yo-2lb

## 107 MANY COOKS H'CAP (0-70) (3-Y.O+) (Class E)

3-00 (3-01) **6f (Equitrack)** £3,217.60 (£974.80: £476.40: £227.20) Stalls: Low GOING minus 0.45 sec per fur (FST)

| | | | | SP | RR | SF |
|---|---|---|---|---|---|---|
| 26[8] | **Random (53)** (CJames) **5-8-12** CRutter(6) (b: lw: hdwy over 2f out: hrd rdn fnl f: led nr fin) | — | **1** | 14/1 | 56 | 14 |
| 36[4] | **Fort Knox (IRE) (53)** (RMFlower) **5-8-12b** DBiggs(13) (outpcd: gd hdwy fnl f: fin wl) | nk | **2** | 8/1[3] | 55 | 13 |
| 16[4] | **Newington Butts (IRE) (43)** (KMcAuliffe) **6-8-2be** SSanders(9) (a.p: led over 1f out: hrd rdn: hdd nr fin) | hd | **3** | 11/1 | 45 | 3 |
| 41[2] | **Halbert (46)** (PBurgoyne) **7-7-12v**(7) DSweeney(1) (led over 4f: ev ch ins fnl f: one pce) | 1¼ | **4** | 8/1[3] | 45 | 3 |
| | **Jaazim (58)** (MMadgwick) **6-8-10**(7) AEddery(10) (hdwy over 3f out: rdn over 2f out: r.o wl ins fnl f) | s.h | **5** | 33/1 | 57 | 15 |
| 55[2] | **Pageboy (67)** (PCHaslam) **7-9-12b** JFortune(4) (rdn thrght: chsd ldrs: one pce fnl 2f) | 1½ | **6** | 15/8[1] | 62 | 20 |
| 26[10] | **Montague Dawson (IRE) (53)** (MrsNMacauley) **4-8-9v**[1](3) SDrowne(11) (b.hind: lw: nvr nr to chal) | 1¾ | **7** | 14/1 | 43 | 1 |
| | **Master Millfield (IRE) (68)** (CJHill) **4-9-13** JWeaver(12) (nvr nrr) | s.h | **8** | 12/1 | 58 | 16 |
| 41[3] | **Nivasha (38)** (RPCHoad) **4-7-11** JQuinn(5) (prom 4f) | 1½ | **9** | 14/1 | 24 | — |
| 36[3] | **Fiery Footsteps (43)** (SWCampion) **4-8-2** TWilliams(2) (w ldr over 3f: wknd over 1f out) | nk | **10** | 8/1[3] | 28 | — |
| 63[8] | **Tenor (64)** (DNicholls) **5-9-9** AlexGreaves(8) (a bhd) | 2 | **11** | 11/1 | 44 | 2 |
| 26[3] | **Rockcracker (IRE) (54)** (GGMargarson) **4-8-13** AClark(7) (lw: bhd fnl 2f) | nk | **12** | 7/1[2] | 33 | — |
| 42[8] | **Woolverstone Hall (IRE) (39)** (DJGMurraySmith) **4-7-12**ow1 AMackay(3) (s.s: a bhd) | 1¾ | **13** | 25/1 | 13 | — |
| | | | | (SP 131.8%) | | **13 Rn** |

**1m 13.82** (3.22) CSF £120.28 CT £1,189.11 TOTE £10.90: £2.20 £2.40 £5.10 (£59.20) Trio £121.40; £87.23 to Catterick 19/1/96 OWNER Mr A. G. Waldie (NEWBURY) BRED Alan Hogan

## 108 CAVEAT EMPTOR H'CAP (0-65) (4-Y.O+) (Class F)

3-30 (3-31) **2m (Equitrack)** £2,824.00 (£794.00: £388.00) Stalls: Low GOING minus 0.45 sec per fur (FST)

| | | | | SP | RR | SF |
|---|---|---|---|---|---|---|
| 38[4] | **Sir Norman Holt (IRE) (63)** (RJO'Sullivan) **7-10-0b** DBiggs(11) (hdwy over 4f out: led over 3f out to 2f out: led over 1f out: hrd rdn: r.o wl: lame) | — | **1** | 20/1 | 79 | 54 |
| 83* | **Wild Strawberry (61)** (MissBSanders) **7-9-12** 4x SSanders(2) (hdwy over 4f out: led 2f out tl over 1f out: ev ch fnl f: r.o wl) | ½ | **2** | 11/8[1] | 77 | 52 |
| | **Hever Golf Lady (47)** (TJNaughton) **4-7-12**(7)ow1 TAshley(8) (b: b.hind: hdwy 4f out: rdn over 3f out: unable qckn) | 3½ | **3** | 10/1[3] | 59 | 26 |
| | **Call Me Albi (IRE) (45)** (GLMoore) **5-8-10** AClark(3) (lw: rdn over 7f out: hdwy 4f out: one pce) | 10 | **4** | 14/1 | 47 | 22 |
| 69[2] | **Wottashambles (40)** (LMontagueHall) **5-8-5** JFEgan(1) (no hdwy fnl 3f) | hd | **5** | 13/2[2] | 42 | 17 |
| | **Sassiver (USA) (33)** (PAKelleway) **6-7-12b** JQuinn(14) (hld up: rdn 4f out: wknd over 2f out) | 2 | **6** | 12/1 | 33 | 8 |
| | **Fabulous Mtoto (40)** (MSSaunders) **6-8-5** AMcGlone(5) (lw: a.p: led over 5f out tl over 3f out: wknd over 2f out) | ½ | **7** | 33/1 | 39 | 14 |
| 69[4] | **Red Spectacle (IRE) (51)** (PCHaslam) **4-8-2b**[1](7) CarolDavison(10) (led over 10f: wknd 4f out) | 2½ | **8** | 10/1[3] | 48 | 16 |
| | **Durham (59)** (RSimpson) **5-9-7b**(3) SDrowne(4) (nvr nrr) | 6 | **9** | 25/1 | 50 | 25 |
| 12[4] | **Intention (USA) (46)** (PRHedger) **6-8-11** CRutter(9) (lw: hld up: rdn over 7f out: wknd 4f out) | 1¾ | **10** | 20/1 | 35 | 10 |
| 23[8] | **Missed the Boat (IRE) (34)** (AGNewcombe) **6-7-6**(7) MartinDwyer(13) (a bhd) | nk | **11** | 10/1[3] | 23 | — |
| 15[7] | **Strat's Legacy (42)** (DWPArbuthnot) **9-8-7**ow1 RCochrane(6) (b: b.hind: bhd fnl 5f) | ½ | **12** | 10/1[3] | 30 | 4 |
| | **Outstayed Welcome (49)** (MJHaynes) **4-8-2**(5) MBaird(7) (b.hind: prom over 11f) | 1 | **13** | 10/1[3] | 36 | 4 |
| 33[14] | **Bobby's Dream (38)** (MHTompkins) **4-7-10** GBardwell(12) (a bhd: t.o) | dist | **14** | 25/1 | — | — |
| | | | | (SP 135.4%) | | **14 Rn** |

**3m 26.39** (4.39) CSF £50.18 CT £311.08 TOTE £31.30: £5.30: £1.20 £9.00 (£28.80) Trio £143.50 OWNER Mr Jack Joseph (WHITCOMBE) BRED Ovidstown Investments Ltd
LONG HANDICAP Bobby's Dream 7-8
WEIGHT FOR AGE 4yo-7lb

## 109 FRIEND IN NEED H'CAP (0-70) (4-Y.O+) (Class E)
4-00 (4-00) **7f (Equitrack)** £3,117.50 (£944.00: £461.00: £219.50) Stalls: Low GOING minus 0.45 sec per fur (FST)

| Form | Horse | Dist | Pos | SP | RR | SF |
|---|---|---|---|---|---|---|
| | **Soaking (63)** (PBurgoyne) **6-9-10** JWeaver(11) (a.p: led 3f out: clr over 1f out: r.o wl) | — | 1 | 4/1[3] | 72 | 40 |
| | **Invocation (67)** (AMoore) **9-10-0** JFEgan(9) (b.hind: lw: hld up: rdn over 2f out: chsd wnr over 1f out: unable qckn) | 3 | 2 | 12/1 | 69 | 37 |
| 53* | **Robellion (63)** (DWPArbuthnot) **5-9-10v** 6x RCochrane(6) (b: hdwy 3f out: rdn over 2f out: r.o one pce) | ½ | 3 | 7/2[2] | 64 | 32 |
| 42[14] | **Mac's Taxi (53)** (PCHaslam) **4-9-0** JFortune(7) (lw: lost pl 3f out: rallied over 1f out: r.o one pce) | ½ | 4 | 10/1 | 53 | 21 |
| 26[6] | **Milos (64)** (TJNaughton) **5-9-4**(7) TAshley(5) (b: lw: a.p: led over 4f out to 3f out: hrd rdn over 2f out: wknd fnl f) | 1¾ | 5 | 5/2[1] | 60 | 28 |
| 59[4] | **Best Kept Secret (66)** (PDEvans) **5-9-6**(7) DSweeney(10) (nvr nr to chal) | 3½ | 6 | 14/1 | 54 | 22 |
| 41* | **Sharp Imp (55)** (RMFlower) **6-9-2b** DBiggs(2) (nvr nrr) | nk | 7 | 5/1 | 42 | 10 |
| 30[9] | **It's So Easy (35)** (APJames) **5-7-5**(5) MBaird(4) (bhd fnl 4f) | 2½ | 8 | 25/1 | 17 | — |
| | **Takeshi (IRE) (61)** (WRMuir) **4-9-8** Jean-PierreLopez(3) (a bhd) | 1½ | 9 | 14/1 | 39 | 7 |
| | **Colston-C (50)** (CJHill) **4-8-11** SSanders(8) (led over 2f: wknd 3f out) | 1½ | 10 | 12/1 | 25 | — |
| 31[7] | **Solo Prize (52)** (PHowling) **4-8-13b** JQuinn(1) (virtually ref to r: a t.o) | dist | 11 | 33/1 | — | — |

(SP 132.1%) **11 Rn**

**1m 26.56** (2.56) CSF £51.29 CT £176.40 TOTE £6.70: £2.20 £2.90 £2.40 (£55.60) Trio £77.00 OWNER Mr Philip Saunders (LAMBOURN) BRED David John Brown
LONG HANDICAP It's So Easy 7-6

T/Plpt: £142.70 (64.71 Tckts). T/Qdpt: £47.20 (2.39 Tckts). AK

# 0084-SOUTHWELL (L-H) (Standard)
## Friday January 19th
WEATHER: misty & drizzle WIND: slt half against

## 110 OYSTER MEDIAN AUCTION MAIDEN STKS (4, 5 & 6-Y.O) (Class F)
1-40 (1-40) **7f (Fibresand)** £2,676.00 (£751.00: £366.00) Stalls: Low GOING: 0.05 sec per fur (STD)

| Form | Horse | Dist | Pos | SP | RR | SF |
|---|---|---|---|---|---|---|
| | **Flirty Gertie (67)** (RBoss) **4-8-9** JWeaver(7) (lw: trckd ldrs: led over 2f out: rdn clr fnl f) | — | 1 | 13/8[1] | 68 | 50 |
| | **Square Deal (FR)** (SRBowring) **5-8-9**(5) CTeague(5) (mde most tl over 2f out: nt qckn fnl f) | 5 | 2 | 2/1[2] | 62 | 44 |
| | **Our Robert (53)** (JGFitzGerald) **4-9-0** MWigham(6) (chsd ldrs: rdn & outpcd ½-wy: kpt on fnl 2f) | 6 | 3 | 10/1 | 48 | 30 |
| | **Tame Deer** (WAO'Gorman) **4-9-0** EmmaO'Gorman(2) (in tch: outpcd ½-wy: kpt on one pce fnl 2f) | 2½ | 4 | 4/1[3] | 42 | 24 |
| | **Maybank (IRE)** (BAMcMahon) **4-9-0** GCarter(8) (bhd tl styd on appr fnl f) | 7 | 5 | 20/1 | 26 | 8 |
| 16[10] | **So Natural (IRE) (60)** (EJAlston) **4-8-9** JFortune(11) (w ldrs: sn drvn: lost pl over 2f out) | 1¾ | 6 | 16/1 | 17 | — |
| | **Lochbuie** (JMPEustace) **4-9-0** RCochrane(4) (sn bhd: sme hdwy 2f out: n.d) | 3 | 7 | 16/1 | 15 | — |
| 57[6] | **Northern Grey (50)** (JBerry) **4-8-7**(7) PRoberts(9) (hdwy to chse ldrs ½-wy: sn wknd) | 1¼ | 8 | 12/1 | 12 | — |
| 59[7] | **Man of May (30)** (NPLittmoden) **4-9-0** TGMcLaughlin(1) (s.i.s: hdwy to chse ldrs ½-wy: sn wknd) | 1¼ | 9 | 33/1 | 10 | — |
| | **Pushka Fair** (TRWatson) **5-9-0** DeanMcKeown(3) (sn drvn & outpcd: bhd fnl 3f) | 20 | 10 | 33/1 | — | — |
| | **Henry Weston (25)** (PHowling) **4-9-0** JQuinn(10) (chsd ldrs tl lost pl over 2f out) | s.h | 11 | 50/1 | — | — |

(SP 132.6%) **11 Rn**

**1m 30.9** (4.10) CSF £5.94 TOTE £2.50: £1.10 £1.80 £2.70 (£3.00) Trio £16.60 OWNER Mrs G. F. R. Boss (NEWMARKET) BRED Mrs K. M. Watts

## 111 HALIBUT CLAIMING APPRENTICE STKS (4-Y.O+) (Class F)
2-10 (2-10) **1m (Fibresand)** £2,572.00 (£722.00: £352.00) Stalls: Low GOING: 0.05 sec per fur (STD)

| Form | Horse | Dist | Pos | SP | RR | SF |
|---|---|---|---|---|---|---|
| 76[6] | **Chadleigh Lane (USA) (55)** (RHollinshead) **4-8-5v**(5) FLynch(5) (hdwy ½-wy: led over 2f out: rdn out) | — | 1 | 10/1 | 63 | 31 |
| 62[7] | **No Submission (USA) (65)** (DWChapman) **10-8-10v** PFessey(6) (lw: mde most tl over 2f out: kpt on fnl f) | 1½ | 2 | 5/1[3] | 59 | 28 |
| 30[8] | **Summer Villa (42)** (PCHaslam) **4-7-13b[1]** MBaird(7) (chsd ldrs: outpcd & drvn along ½-wy: kpt on fnl 2f) | 1 | 3 | 10/1 | 47 | 15 |
| 29[2] | **Hawwam (67)** (EJAlston) **10-8-13** CTeague(4) (lw: dwlt: bhd: effrt on outside 3f out: n.d) | 6 | 4 | 6/4[1] | 48 | 17 |
| 34[8] | **Arecibo (FR) (44)** (JParkes) **4-8-4** RHavlin(2) (w ldrs: sn rdn along: lost pl ½-wy: styd on fnl 2f) | 2 | 5 | 33/1 | 36 | 4 |
| | **Manila Bay (USA) (39)** (JSKing) **6-7-13b[1]**(5) DSweeney(3) (lw: trckd ldrs tl wknd 3f out: sn bhd) | 14 | 6 | 16/1 | 7 | — |
| 62[3] | **Miss Zanzibar (60)** (RAFahey) **4-8-5** LNewton(1) (chsd ldrs 3f: sn lost pl & bhd) | 1½ | 7 | 9/4[2] | 6 | — |

(SP 114.4%) **7 Rn**

**1m 46.8** (6.80) CSF £53.23 TOTE £14.30: £5.30 £2.20 (£35.00) OWNER Mr J. E. Bigg (UPPER LONGDON) BRED Windwoods Farm, Bruce Brown and Connie Brown
STEWARDS' ENQUIRY Fessey susp. 29/1/96 (excessive use of whip).

## 112 SHARK H'CAP (0-70) (3-Y.O) (Class E)
2-40 (2-42) **6f (Fibresand)** £3,131.80 (£948.40: £463.20: £220.60) Stalls: Low GOING: 0.05 sec per fur (STD)

| Form | Horse | Dist | Pos | SP | RR | SF |
|---|---|---|---|---|---|---|
| 35[3] | **Seeking Destiny (IRE) (45)** (MCChapman) **3-7-5**(5) PFessey(5) (mde virtually all: hld on wl nr fin) | — | 1 | 8/1 | 50 | 13 |
| 32* | **Weetman's Weigh (IRE) (70)** (RHollinshead) **3-9-7** MWigham(6) (a in tch: swtchd lft over 1f out: sn ev ch: nt qckn nr fin) | nk | 2 | 9/4[1] | 74 | 37 |
| 10[7] | **Kind of Light (68)** (RGuest) **3-9-5** JTate(10) (prom on outside: ev ch 2f out: nt qckn appr fnl f) | 2½ | 3 | 8/1 | 66 | 29 |
| 35[9] | **Bit of Bother (IRE) (60)** (TDBarron) **3-8-11** JFortune(9) (a chsng ldrs: ev ch 2f out: nt qckn fnl f) | nk | 4 | 12/1 | 57 | 20 |
| 32[2] | **First Maite (70)** (SRBowring) **3-9-2b**(5) CTeague(8) (s.i.s: hdwy on outside to chse ldrs ½-wy: hung rt & lft: styd on ins fnl f) | hd | 5 | 11/4[2] | 67 | 30 |
| | **Down The Yard (46)** (MCChapman) **3-7-4**(7)ow1 MartinDwyer(4) (s.i.s: bhd: hdwy & prom 2f out: sn wl outpcd) | 8 | 6 | 25/1 | 13 | — |
| | **Chillam (55)** (JPLeigh) **3-8-6** DeanMcKeown(7) (plld hrd: w wnr tl wknd wl over 1f out) | 8 | 7 | 16/1 | 1 | — |
| 32[5] | **Madam Zando (45)** (JBalding) **3-7-10** ClaireBalding(11) (dwlt: hdwy on outside 3f out: sn wknd) | ½ | 8 | 25/1 | — | — |
| 49[5] | **Stilly Night (IRE) (67)** (JWharton) **3-9-4** JQuinn(3) (chsd ldrs tl lost pl over 2f out) | 3 | 9 | 16/1 | 4 | — |
| 81[5] | **Castle Governor (49)** (PCHaslam) **3-7-9**(5) 7x MBaird(1) (chsd ldrs: sn drvn along: lost pl 2f out) | 8 | 10 | 6/1[3] | — | — |

| | | | | SP | RR | SF |
|---|---|---|---|---|---|---|
| $35^{12}$ | **Gresham Flyer (46)** (BRichmond) **3-7-11**ow1 AMackay(2) (sn bhd) | 7 | **11** | 50/1 | — | — |

(SP 123.1%) **11 Rn**

**1m 18.9** (5.40) CSF £25.94 CT £142.10 TOTE £10.70: £2.50 £1.10 £2.40 (£23.90) Trio £35.60 OWNER Mr Mattie O'Toole (MARKET RASEN) BRED Major V. McCalmont
LONG HANDICAP Madam Zando 7-7 Down The Yard 7-9 Seeking Destiny (IRE) 7-5 Gresham Flyer 7-1

## 113 OCTOPUS H'CAP (0-70) (4-Y.O+) (Class E)

3-10 (3-10) **1m 4f (Fibresand)** £3,117.50 (£944.00: £461.00: £219.50) Stalls: Low GOING: 0.05 sec per fur (STD)

| | | | | SP | RR | SF |
|---|---|---|---|---|---|---|
| $38^{6}$ | **Premier Dance (62)** (DHaydnJones) **9-9-8** AMackay(7) (bhd & pushed along: hdwy on outside 5f out: led 2f out: rdn out) | — | **1** | 7/1 | 67 | 25 |
| $13^{5}$ | **Anistop (55)** (RAkehurst) **4-8-4**(7) TAshley(3) (chsd ldrs: drvn along & outpcd 5f out: swtchd & rallied fnl f) | ¾ | **2** | 7/2 2 | 59 | 13 |
| | **Record Lover (IRE) (36)** (MCChapman) **6-7-5**(5) PFessey(1) (led to 2f out: one pce fnl f) | ¾ | **3** | 33/1 | 39 | — |
| | **Hullbank (56)** (WWHaigh) **6-9-2** DaleGibson(8) (lw: b.nr fore: hld up & plld hrd: effrt 5f out: hung lft 2f out: kpt on one pce) | 1½ | **4** | 3/1 1 | 57 | 15 |
| $48^{7}$ | **Manful (58)** (JHetherton) **4-9-0** RCochrane(6) (b: in tch: rdn ½-wy: swtchd rt 2f out: kpt on) | 2½ | **5** | 5/1 | 56 | 10 |
| $70^{*}$ | **Modest Hope (USA) (49)** (BRichmond) **9-8-9** 5x JWeaver(4) (lw: trckd ldrs: effrt over 2f out: wknd over 1f out: eased) | 6 | **6** | 4/1 3 | 39 | — |
| | **Museum (IRE) (64)** (DNicholls) **5-9-10** AlexGreaves(5) (trckd ldrs: drvn 5f out: lost pl over 3f out: eased) | 15 | **7** | 10/1 | 34 | — |
| | **Cross Talk (IRE) (66)** (RHollinshead) **4-9-8** TIves(2) (prom tl lost pl 6f out: sn bhd) | s.h | **8** | 12/1 | 36 | — |

(SP 116.1%) **8 Rn**

**2m 45.7** (13.20) CSF £29.91 CT £686.99 TOTE £9.00: £2.50 £1.80 £5.10 (£10.70) OWNER J S Fox and Sons (PONTYPRIDD) BRED Brick Kiln Stud Farm
LONG HANDICAP Record Lover (IRE) 6-11
WEIGHT FOR AGE 4yo-4lb

## 114 LOBSTER (S) STKS (4-Y.O+) (Class F)

3-40 (3-40) **1m 3f (Fibresand)** £2,607.00 (£732.00: £357.00) Stalls: Low GOING: 0.05 sec per fur (STD)

| | | | | SP | RR | SF |
|---|---|---|---|---|---|---|
| $34^{4}$ | **Sharp Gazelle (38)** (BSmart) **6-8-11** RCochrane(4) (trckd ldrs: led 2f out: hrd rdn: all out) | — | **1** | 12/1 | 63 | 19 |
| $57^{3}$ | **Sarasi (66)** (MJCamacho) **4-9-4** LCharnock(8) (lw: led to 2f out: hrd rdn & edgd rt: nt qckn nr fin) | nk | **2** | 3/1 2 | 74 | 26 |
| $15^{10}$ | **Hard Love (54)** (JLEyre) **4-8-8** RLappin(9) (hdwy 5f out: sn drvn: kpt on same pce fnl 2f: nvr able to chal) | 1¾ | **3** | 4/1 3 | 61 | 13 |
| | **Ballyrag (USA)** (RAFahey) **5-9-2** ACulhane(1) (trckd ldrs: effrt 4f out: kpt on one pce fnl 2f) | 8 | **4** | 9/2 | 53 | 9 |
| $62^{5}$ | **Eastleigh (51)** (RHollinshead) **7-9-2** TIves(6) (chsd ldr: drvn along over 4f out: wknd over 2f out) | 5 | **5** | 12/1 | 46 | 2 |
| $57^{4}$ | **Warhurst (IRE) (57)** (DNicholls) **5-9-2** AlexGreaves(2) (hld up: effrt 5f out: drvn along over 2f out: sn lost pl: fin lame) | 9 | **6** | 5/2 1 | 33 | — |
| $76^{10}$ | **Mixed Mood (60)** (BJLlewellyn) **4-8-8** TWilliams(5) (chsd ldrs: drvn along ½-wy: lost pl 5f out: sn wl bhd) | 15 | **7** | 33/1 | 7 | — |
| | **Something Speedy (IRE) (42)** (PJBevan) **4-8-8** NCarlisle(3) (dwlt: a bhd: t.o 5f out) | 10 | **8** | 20/1 | — | — |
| | **Pumpkin Pie (IRE)** (AHarrison) **4-8-8** GCarter(7) (sn bhd: t.o 4f out) | 4 | **9** | 33/1 | — | — |

(SP 117.8%) **9 Rn**

**2m 31.5** (11.50) CSF £45.73 TOTE £12.30: £2.80 £2.00 £1.20 (£9.60) Trio £11.90 OWNER Mr M. J. Samuel (LAMBOURN) BRED Aston Park Stud
WEIGHT FOR AGE 4yo-3lb
No bid
STEWARDS' ENQUIRY Cochrane susp. 29-30/1/96 & Charnock susp. 29-31/1/96 (excessive use of whip).

## 115 LADBROKE ALL-WEATHER CHALLENGE SERIES H'CAP (Qualifier) (0-70) (3-Y.O+) (Class E)

4-10 (4-11) **7f (Fibresand)** £3,160.40 (£957.20: £467.60: £222.80) Stalls: Low GOING: 0.05 sec per fur (STD)

| | | | | SP | RR | SF |
|---|---|---|---|---|---|---|
| $44^{*}$ | **So Amazing (63)** (MissSEHall) **4-9-7** 6x JWeaver(8) (lw: b: mde virtually all: rdn out) | — | **1** | 7/2 2 | 73 | 49 |
| | **Cashmere Lady (70)** (JLEyre) **4-10-0** RLappin(4) (lw: chsd ldrs: chal over 2f out: nt qckn ins fnl f) | ¾ | **2** | 3/1 1 | 78 | 54 |
| $88^{6}$ | **Indiahra (49)** (RHollinshead) **5-8-0v**(7) FLynch(2) (sn bhd: hdwy on outside 2f out: kpt on: nvr nr to chal) | 3 | **3** | 6/1 3 | 50 | 26 |
| $76^{*}$ | **First Gold (61)** (JWharton) **7-9-5b** 6x SDWilliams(7) (hdwy on outside ½-wy: sn drvn along: outpcd fnl 2f) | 2½ | **4** | 7/1 | 57 | 33 |
| $90^{4}$ | **Sea God (44)** (MCChapman) **5-7-9**(7) CMunday(9) (in tch: racd wd: sn drvn along: outpcd fnl 2f) | ¾ | **5** | 12/1 | 38 | 14 |
| | **Zain Dancer (61)** (DNicholls) **4-9-5** AlexGreaves(1) (bit bkwd: hld up & bhd: hdwy over 2f out: nvr nr ldrs) | 2½ | **6** | 12/1 | 49 | 25 |
| $42^{9}$ | **Quinzii Martin (50)** (DHaydnJones) **8-8-8v** TWilliams(5) (w ldrs tl wknd over 1f out) | 1 | **7** | 7/1 | 36 | 12 |
| $50^{4}$ | **Don't Get Caught (IRE) (60)** (JLHarris) **4-9-4b**1 JFEgan(3) (sn rdn along & bhd) | 2½ | **8** | 12/1 | 40 | 16 |
| $84^{4}$ | **Aquado (51)** (SRBowring) **7-8-4b**(5) CTeague(6) (reminders s: chsd ldrs tl wknd 2f out) | 1¼ | **9** | 8/1 | 28 | 4 |

(SP 120.7%) **9 Rn**

**1m 32.0** (5.20) CSF £14.32 CT £56.31 TOTE £3.00: £1.50 £1.60 £1.40 (£8.80) Trio £41.50 OWNER Mr C. Platts (MIDDLEHAM) BRED C. Platts and Miss S. E. Hall

T/Plpt: £128.70 (81.11 Tckts). T/Qdpt: £16.40 (17.81 Tckts). WG

# 0103-LINGFIELD (L-H) (Standard)

## Saturday January 20th

WEATHER: overcast WIND: slt half against

## 116 STUBBS AMATEUR H'CAP (0-65) (4-Y.O+) (Class F)

1-25 (1-25) **1m 4f (Equitrack)** £2,786.20 (£783.20: £382.60) Stalls: Low GOING minus 0.44 sec per fur (FST)

| | | | | SP | RR | SF |
|---|---|---|---|---|---|---|
| $83^{4}$ | **Royal Circus (39)** (PRWebber) **7-10-0** MrsSBosley(14) (lw: w ldr: led 3f out: rdn & edgd lft over 2f out: clr over 1f out: r.o) | — | **1** | 9/1 3 | 50 | 32 |
| | **Gold Blade (60)** (JPearce) **7-11-7** MrsLPearce(9) (hld up: hdwy 5f out: rdn over 2f out: styd on to go 2nd ins fnl f) | 2½ | **2** | 9/1 3 | 68 | 50 |
| $83^{9}$ | **Don't Drop Bombs (USA) (34)** (DTThom) **7-9-9v** MissJFeilden(13) (led: hdd 3f out: sltly hmpd over 2f out: sn rdn: one pce) | 1 | **3** | 4/1 2 | 40 | 22 |
| | **Montone (IRE) (45)** (JRJenkins) **6-10-1**(5) DrMMannish(1) (mid div: rdn 4f out: r.o one pce fnl 2f) | 2 | **4** | 12/1 | 49 | 31 |

| Form | Horse | Dist | Pos | SP | RR | SF |
|---|---|---|---|---|---|---|
| 82[6] | **Swynford Flyer (32)** (JAHarris) **7-9-2**(5) MrVLukaniuk(3) (rr: hdwy 4f out: rdn over 2f out: one pce) | 3½ | **5** | 14/1 | 31 | 13 |
| | **Forgetful (32)** (DBurchell) **7-9-2**(5) MissEJJones(12) (chsd ldrs: sltly hmpd after 1f: rdn over 3f out: one pce) | ½ | **6** | 20/1 | 30 | 12 |
| 85[2] | **Parklife (IRE) (39)** (PCHaslam) **4-9-10** MrsDKettlewell(5) (chsd ldrs: hrd rdn 3f out: wknd over 1f out) | 3 | **7** | 4/1[2] | 33 | 11 |
| | **Father Dan (IRE) (60)** (MissGayKelleway) **7-11-7** MrMArmytage(6) (bit bkwd: mid div whn hmpd 6f out: rdn 3f out: no hdwy) | 7 | **8** | 3/1[1] | 45 | 27 |
| | **Toskano (57)** (DLWilliams) **4-10-9**(5) MissSHiggins(7) (a bhd) | 2 | **9** | 33/1 | 39 | 17 |
| 24[8] | **Legal Drama (USA) (51)** (PJMcBride) **4-10-3**(5)ow3 MrVCoogan(10) (dwlt: sme hdwy 5f out: sn rdn & btn) | 2 | **10** | 33/1 | 31 | 6 |
| 38[9] | **Caspian Beluga (60)** (SGKnight) **8-11-7** MrJDurkan(11) (b: chsd ldrs 7f) | 2½ | **11** | 14/1 | 36 | 18 |
| | **Lady Woodstock (35)** (MissAEEmbiricos) **4-9-1**(5) MrCJMcEntee(4) (bhd fnl 5f) | 3 | **12** | 33/1 | 7 | — |
| | **Verro (USA) (35)** (KBishop) **9-9-5e**(5)ow10 MissAPurdy(2) (bit bkwd: a bhd) | ¾ | **13** | 66/1 | 6 | — |

(SP 121.1%) **13 Rn**

**2m 36.84** (6.84) CSF £80.12 CT £344.13 TOTE £10.20: £2.00 £2.20 £1.80 (£19.10) Trio £18.90 OWNER Mr P. W. Hiatt (BANBURY) BRED Snailwell Stud Co Ltd

LONG HANDICAP Verro (USA) 8-4

WEIGHT FOR AGE 4yo-4lb

STEWARDS' ENQUIRY Bosley susp. 29/1-1/2/96 (careless riding).

## 117 HARRINGTON BIRD CLAIMING STKS (4-Y.O+) (Class E)

1-55 (1-56) **6f (Equitrack)** £3,203.30 (£970.40: £474.20: £226.10) Stalls: Low GOING minus 0.44 sec per fur (FST)

| Form | Horse | Dist | Pos | SP | RR | SF |
|---|---|---|---|---|---|---|
| 109[5] | **Milos (64)** (TJNaughton) **5-8-10**(7) TAshley(10) (b: b.hind: outpcd in rr: gd hdwy over 1f out: led wl ins fnl f: r.o) | — | **1** | 8/1 | 73 | 16 |
| 64[5] | **Ultra Beet (75)** (PCHaslam) **4-9-1v** JWeaver(13) (a.p: led over 2f out tl hdd wl ins fnl f: unable qckn) | 1½ | **2** | 9/1 | 67 | 10 |
| 65[4] | **Respectable Jones (47)** (RHollinshead) **10-8-7b** MWigham(9) (s.i.s: bhd tl gd hdwy fnl f: fin wl) | 1 | **3** | 20/1 | 56 | — |
| | **Sea-Deer (85)** (DWChapman) **7-9-1** ACulhane(2) (hld up: hdwy & nt clr run over 2f out tl ins fnl f: r.o nr fin) | hd | **4** | 5/1[2] | 64 | 7 |
| 107[6] | **Pageboy (67)** (PCHaslam) **7-9-7** JFortune(1) (chsd ldrs: rdn over 1f out: one pce) | 1 | **5** | 9/1 | 67 | 10 |
| 64* | **Lift Boy (USA) (57)** (AMoore) **7-8-7** CandyMorris(3) (b.hind: chsd ldrs: rdn over 1f out: one pce) | hd | **6** | 12/1 | 53 | — |
| 88[4] | **Hannah's Usher (80)** (CMurray) **4-9-7** MTebbutt(7) (b.off hind: chsd ldrs: rdn over 1f out: one pce) | ½ | **7** | 6/1[3] | 66 | 9 |
| 26[4] | **Speedy Classic (USA) (66)** (MJHeaton-Ellis) **7-8-12**(3) SDrowne(8) (rr: sme hdwy & nt clr run 1f out: nt rcvr) | 1 | **8** | 9/1 | 57 | — |
| 64[6] | **Superlao (BEL) (53)** (AndreHermans,Belgium) **4-8-0** FNorton(12) (b.hind: prom: ev ch over 1f out: sn rdn: wknd ins fnl f) | 1¼ | **9** | 20/1 | 39 | — |
| 20[8] | **Little Ibnr (83)** (PDEvans) **5-9-7** RCochrane(6) (led: hdd over 2f out: wknd over 1f out) | nk | **10** | 11/4[1] | 59 | 2 |
| 65[7] | **Justinianus (IRE)** (AndreHermans,Belgium) **4-7-10b**(7) DSweeney(11) (chsd ldrs tl wknd over 1f out) | 1¼ | **11** | 33/1 | 38 | — |
| 41[4] | **Assignment (43)** (JELong) **10-7-10**(7) TField(5) (b.off hind: bhd fnl 3f) | 5 | **12** | 33/1 | 24 | — |
| | **Lonely Vigil (FR)** (KOCunningham-Brown) **4-8-12** GCarter(14) (b: a bhd: t.o) | 15 | **13** | 33/1 | — | — |

(SP 124.8%) **13 Rn**

**1m 14.04** (3.44) CSF £73.69 TOTE £11.10: £2.10 £3.00 £5.40 (£24.60) Trio £241.30; £271.87 to Southwell 22/1/96 OWNER Mr R. A. Popely (EPSOM) BRED R. A. and J. H. Popely

## 118 SNAFFLES MEDIAN AUCTION MAIDEN STKS (3-Y.O) (Class E)

2-25 (2-27) **6f (Equitrack)** £3,117.50 (£944.00: £461.00: £219.50) Stalls: Low GOING minus 0.44 sec per fur (FST)

| Form | Horse | Dist | Pos | SP | RR | SF |
|---|---|---|---|---|---|---|
| | **Princely Sound (64)** (MBell) **3-9-0** MFenton(11) (a.p: led over 1f out: sn clr: pushed out) | — | **1** | 5/2[1] | 79 | 4 |
| 68[3] | **Maple Burl (62)** (SDow) **3-9-0** RCochrane(10) (b.nr hind: hdwy over 3f out: rdn over 1f out: styd on to go 2nd ins fnl f) | 4 | **2** | 4/1[2] | 68 | — |
| 68[2] | **Rowlandsons Stud (IRE) (61)** (GLMoore) **3-9-0** AClark(8) (a.p: led over 2f out: hdd over 1f out: one pce) | 2½ | **3** | 11/2[3] | 62 | — |
| | **Badger Bay (IRE) (75)** (CADwyer) **3-8-6**(3) JStack(6) (chsd ldrs: rdn & outpcd 3f out: r.o one pce fnl f) | 1½ | **4** | 4/1[2] | 53 | — |
| 10[2] | **Jemsilverthorn (IRE) (54)** (JJBridger) **3-9-0v** GBardwell(3) (prom: led over 3f out: hdd over 2f out: wknd over 1f out) | hd | **5** | 12/1 | 57 | — |
| | **Dauphin (IRE)** (WJMusson) **3-8-11**(3) PMcCabe(4) (b: outpcd in rr: sme hdwy fnl f: nvr nrr) | 1½ | **6** | 20/1 | 53 | — |
| | **Mogin** (JFfitch-Heyes) **3-8-9** AMackay(9) (s.s: outpcd & bhd: sme hdwy fnl f: nvr nrr) | 1¼ | **7** | 33/1 | 45 | — |
| | **Ben'a'vachei Boy (60)** (JDBethell) **3-9-0b** JWeaver(2) (led: hdd over 3f out: wknd over 2f out) | 1 | **8** | 11/2[3] | 47 | — |
| | **Cindy Kate (IRE)** (CCElsey) **3-8-9** CRutter(7) (lt-f: b: bhd fnl 4f) | 1¼ | **9** | 33/1 | 39 | — |
| | **Hever Golf Eagle** (TJNaughton) **3-8-7**(7) TAshley(1) (b: a bhd) | nk | **10** | 10/1 | 43 | — |
| 51[4] | **Governors Dream (45)** (MrsNMacauley) **3-8-9v** DBiggs(5) (bhd fnl 3f) | 5 | **11** | 25/1 | 25 | — |

(SP 130.6%) **11 Rn**

**1m 14.85** (4.25) CSF £13.19 TOTE £3.20: £2.00 £2.50 £1.50 (£10.30) Trio £16.30 OWNER Mr G. W. Byrne (NEWMARKET) BRED James William Mitchell and Simon Edward Mitchell

## 119 MUNNINGS LIMITED STKS (0-65) (3-Y.O) (Class F)

2-55 (2-56) **1m 2f (Equitrack)** £2,685.40 (£754.40: £368.20) Stalls: Low GOING minus 0.44 sec per fur (FST)

| Form | Horse | Dist | Pos | SP | RR | SF |
|---|---|---|---|---|---|---|
| | **Distinct Beauty (IRE) (65)** (WAO'Gorman) **3-8-8**ow2 EmmaO'Gorman(5) (hld up: hdwy gng wl 3f out: rdn to ld ins fnl f: pushed clr) | — | **1** | 9/4[2] | 72 | 28 |
| 40[3] | **Bath Knight (63)** (DJSffrenchDavis) **3-8-11** GCarter(4) (a.p: chsd ldr 5f out: led over 2f out: hdd ins fnl f: one pce) | 3 | **2** | 20/1 | 70 | 28 |
| 11* | **Billaddie (62)** (RBoss) **3-8-13** JWeaver(6) (b: b.hind: chsd ldrs: hrd rdn over 2f out: one pce) | 8 | **3** | 11/10[1] | 59 | 17 |
| 11[3] | **Hotlips Houlihan (57)** (RJRWilliams) **3-8-8** DBiggs(3) (led: hdd over 2f out: wknd over 2f out) | 3 | **4** | 6/1[3] | 50 | 8 |
| | **Society Girl (65)** (CWThornton) **3-8-6** DeanMcKeown(8) (b.hind: chsd ldrs tl wknd over 2f out) | 10 | **5** | 13/2 | 32 | — |
| 17[9] | **Conquistajade (USA) (52)** (SPCWoods) **3-7-13**(7) JMoon(2) (chsd ldrs to ½-wy: sn wknd) | nk | **6** | 50/1 | 31 | — |
| 81[7] | **Merlin's Honour (38)** (JohnBerry) **3-7-13**(7) TAshley(7) (a bhd) | 20 | **7** | 50/1 | — | — |

(SP 114.7%) **7 Rn**

**2m 8.05** (3.75) CSF £34.64 TOTE £3.50: £1.40 £3.50 (£24.90) OWNER Mr N. S. Yong (NEWMARKET) BRED Green Ireland Properties Ltd

## 120 SOLID STATE SUPPLIES H'CAP (0-80) (4-Y.O+) (Class D)

3-25 (3-27) **1m (Equitrack)** £3,761.20 (£1,138.60: £410.10: £410.10) Stalls: Low GOING minus 0.44 sec per fur (FST)

| Form | Horse | Dist | Pos | SP | RR | SF |
|---|---|---|---|---|---|---|
| 14[5] | **Queen of All Birds (IRE) (70)** (RBoss) **5-9-9** JWeaver(3) (b: b.hind: hld up in tch: led gng wl over 2f out: clr over 1f out: easily) | — | **1** | 7/2[2] | 86 | 44 |

| Form | Runner | Dist | Pl | SP | RR | SF |
|---|---|---|---|---|---|---|
| | **Master Beveled (68)** (PDEvans) **6-9-7** RCochrane(8) (outpcd in rr: hdwy over 1f out: styd on to go 2nd nr fin) | 6 | **2** | 3/1[1] | 72 | 30 |
| 14[2] | **Bentico (70)** (MrsNMacauley) **7-9-6**(3) SDrowne(2) (b.hind: chsd ldrs: rdn over 3f out: one pce) | nk | **3** | 5/1[3] | 73 | 31 |
| 14* | **Labudd (USA) (57)** (RIngram) **6-8-10** DBiggs(7) (b: lw: a.p: rdn over 1f out: one pce) | d.h | **3** | 3/1[1] | 60 | 18 |
| 53[9] | **Mediate (IRE) (63)** (AHide) **4-8-13b**(3) JStack(1) (hld up: hdwy over 2f out: rdn over 1f out: one pce) | 1 | **5** | 14/1 | 65 | 22 |
| | **Owdbetts (IRE) (56)** (GLMoore) **4-8-9** AClark(9) (hld up: sme hdwy 4f out: rdn 3f out: wknd 2f out) | 7 | **6** | 10/1 | 44 | 1 |
| 48[4] | **Far Ahead (75)** (JLEyre) **4-10-0** RLappin(4) (bhd fnl 5f) | 1 | **7** | 12/1 | 61 | 18 |
| 41[8] | **Al Shaati (FR) (44)** (RJO'Sullivan) **6-7-11** JQuinn(6) (lw: bhd fnl 3f) | nk | **8** | 16/1 | 29 | — |
| 14[11] | **Tafahhus (66)** (MJPolglase) **4-9-5b[1]** MRimmer(5) (led: hdd over 2f out: sn wknd) | 4 | **9** | 16/1 | 44 | 1 |
| | | | | (SP 124.1%) | **9 Rn** | |

**1m 40.03** (2.63) CSF £14.77 CT QB, MB, B £24.71 QB, MB, L £16.48 TOTE £5.50: £1.60 £2.00 B £1.00 L £1.10 (£9.40) Trio QB, MB, L £8.10 QB, MB, L £10.30 OWNER Mr John Arnou (NEWMARKET) BRED Brownstown Stud Farm

## 121 LADBROKE ALL-WEATHER TROPHY H'CAP (Final) (4-Y.O+) (Class B)

4-00 (4-01) **7f (Equitrack)** £9,585.00 (£2,880.00: £1,390.00: £645.00) Stalls: Low GOING minus 0.44 sec per fur (FST)

| Form | Runner | Dist | Pl | SP | RR | SF |
|---|---|---|---|---|---|---|
| 42* | **Rakis (IRE) (72)** (MBrittain) **6-9-10** RCochrane(11) (hld up: hdwy over 1f out: str run to ld wl ins fnl f: r.o) | — | **1** | 3/1[1] | 83 | 47 |
| 42[6] | **Hawaii Storm (FR) (64)** (DJSffrenchDavis) **8-8-11**(5) CAdamson(9) (rr: hdwy 3f out: rdn over 1f out: ev ch wl ins fnl f: unable qckn) | 1½ | **2** | 16/1 | 72 | 36 |
| 107[2] | **Fort Knox (IRE) (53)** (RMFlower) **5-8-5b** DBiggs(15) (hld up: hdwy over 2f out: led over 1f out: hdd wl ins fnl f: one pce) | nk | **3** | 6/1[2] | 60 | 24 |
| 42[4] | **Tuigamala (57)** (RIngram) **5-8-2**(7) TAshley(10) (rr: hdwy over 1f out: r.o fnl f) | 1¾ | **4** | 14/1 | 60 | 24 |
| 88* | **Super Benz (62)** (JLEyre) **10-8-9**(5) 4x CTeague(7) (b: chsd ldrs: nt clr run over 1f out: styd on wl ins fnl f) | 1¼ | **5** | 10/1 | 62 | 26 |
| | **Superoo (71)** (MrsPSly) **10-9-9** ACulhane(13) (nvr nrr) | s.h | **6** | 16/1 | 71 | 35 |
| 14[7] | **Duke Valentino (76)** (RHollinshead) **4-10-0** MWigham(4) (hld up mid div: rdn over 1f out: one pce) | 1 | **7** | 9/1 | 74 | 38 |
| 109[2] | **Invocation (67)** (AMoore) **9-9-5** JFEgan(8) (b.hind: led after 1f: hdd over 1f out: grad wknd) | nk | **8** | 20/1 | 64 | 28 |
| | **Yo Kiri-B (45)** (JFfitch-Heyes) **5-7-11**ow1 AMackay(2) (rr: hdwy over 2f out: nt clr run over 1f out tl ins fnl f: nt rcvr) | 1 | **9** | 25/1 | 40 | 3 |
| 55[9] | **Anzio (IRE) (72)** (BAPearce) **5-9-10b** TIves(12) (b: b.hind: prom tl wknd over 1f out) | ½ | **10** | 14/1 | 66 | 30 |
| 42[2] | **Crystal Heights (FR) (70)** (RJO'Sullivan) **8-9-8** AClark(1) (s.s: a bhd) | nk | **11** | 15/2 | 63 | 27 |
| 42[3] | **Patsy Grimes (63)** (JSMoore) **6-9-1** AMcGlone(5) (in tch to ½-wy) | 1½ | **12** | 14/1 | 52 | 16 |
| 55[4] | **Four of Spades (71)** (PDEvans) **5-9-9v** RLappin(6) (chsd ldrs 5f) | hd | **13** | 14/1 | 60 | 24 |
| 76[2] | **At the Savoy (IRE) (60)** (TDBarron) **5-8-12v** JFortune(14) (prom tl wknd over 1f out) | ½ | **14** | 25/1 | 48 | 12 |
| 57[2] | **Live Project (IRE) (61)** (MJohnston) **4-8-13** JWeaver(3) (chsd ldrs 4f) | 2 | **15** | 7/1[3] | 45 | 9 |
| 109[4] | **Mac's Taxi (53)** (PCHaslam) **4-8-0v[1]**(5) MBaird(16) (led 1f: wknd over 2f out) | 7 | **16** | 16/1 | 21 | — |
| | | | | (SP 139.4%) | **16 Rn** | |

**1m 26.02** (2.02) CSF £53.16 CT £269.44 TOTE £4.30: £2.80 £3.90 £1.80 £4.20 (£113.60) Trio £94.90 OWNER Mr P. G. Shorrock (WARTHILL) BRED The Mount Coote Partnership
LONG HANDICAP Yo Kiri-B 7-9

T/Plpt: £252.00 (43.86 Tckts). T/Qdpt: £19.50 (11.1 Tckts). SM

# 0110-SOUTHWELL (L-H) (Standard)

## Monday January 22nd

WEATHER: overcast WIND: fresh half against

## 122 CHAMPAGNE GOLD H'CAP (0-70) (4-Y.O+) (Class E)

1-40 (1-46) **1m (Fibresand)** £3,189.00 (£966.00: £472.00: £225.00) Stalls: Low GOING: 0.05 sec per fur (STD)

| Form | Runner | Dist | Pl | SP | RR | SF |
|---|---|---|---|---|---|---|
| 90* | **Kingchip Boy (52)** (MJRyan) **7-9-2v** 6x TIves(3) (mde all: qcknd clr over 2f out: styd on wl) | — | **1** | 11/4[1] | 73 | 49 |
| 44[4] | **Legal Issue (IRE) (59)** (WWHaigh) **4-9-9** DaleGibson(13) (lw: s.i.s: hdwy over 3f out: nvr able to chal) | 4 | **2** | 7/1[3] | 73 | 48 |
| | **Mezzoramio (40)** (KAMorgan) **4-8-4v** MFenton(9) (w ldrs: edgd lft over 2f out: one pce) | 3 | **3** | 33/1 | 48 | 23 |
| 84* | **Benjamins Law (69)** (JAPickering) **5-10-5** 6x JQuinn(11) (in tch: hdwy ½-wy: rdn & one pce fnl 2f) | 2½ | **4** | 13/2[2] | 71 | 47 |
| 71[5] | **Irchester Lass (44)** (SRBowring) **4-8-3b**(5) CTeague(6) (cl up tl wknd over 2f out) | 2 | **5** | 10/1 | 43 | 18 |
| 30[3] | **Karinska (60)** (MCChapman) **6-9-3**(7) CMunday(8) (s.i.s: hdwy ½-wy: nvr able to chal) | 2 | **6** | 13/2[2] | 54 | 30 |
| 66[2] | **Real Madrid (39)** (GPEnright) **5-8-3v** NAdams(1) (cl up tl wknd fnl 3f) | 7 | **7** | 8/1 | 19 | — |
| 43[7] | **Broughton's Port (35)** (WJMusson) **6-7-13**ow1 AMackay(10) (s.i.s: bhd tl late hdwy) | 2 | **8** | 14/1 | 11 | — |
| 90[8] | **Mazilla (47)** (AStreeter) **4-8-11** FNorton(7) (prom 5f: eased whn btn fnl 2f) | 1 | **9** | 20/1 | 22 | — |
| | **Twin Creeks (55)** (MDHammond) **5-9-5** RCochrane(12) (sn outpcd & bhd: n.d) | 8 | **10** | 12/1 | 13 | — |
| 50[9] | **Whackford Squeers (64)** (DNicholls) **4-10-0** AlexGreaves(4) (chsd ldrs tl wknd fnl 3f) | 5 | **11** | 12/1 | 13 | — |
| | **Superbit (48)** (BAMcMahon) **4-8-12** JFortune(2) (prom 5f: sn wknd) | hd | **12** | 16/1 | — | — |
| | **Lord Palmerston (USA) (52)** (KAMorgan) **4-8-11**(5) LNewton(14) (b.hind: sn outpcd & bhd) | 9 | **13** | 25/1 | — | — |
| | | | | (SP 125.5%) | **13 Rn** | |

**1m 45.5** (5.50) CSF £22.15 CT £496.23 TOTE £4.50: £2.80 £2.70 (£17.70) Trio Not won; £197.84 to Leicester 23/1/96 OWNER Four Jays Racing Partnership (NEWMARKET) BRED R. M. Scott

## 123 SCARLET FLAME H'CAP (0-60) (3-Y.O) (Class F)

2-10 (2-12) **1m (Fibresand)** £2,572.00 (£722.00: £352.00) Stalls: Low GOING: 0.05 sec per fur (STD)

| Form | Runner | Dist | Pl | SP | RR | SF |
|---|---|---|---|---|---|---|
| 46[3] | **Dancing Cavalier (52)** (RHollinshead) **3-8-6**(7) FLynch(9) (pushed along & bhd: c wd & hdwy over 2f out: led wl ins fnl f: r.o) | — | **1** | 12/1 | 67 | 32 |
| 58[2] | **Yeoman Oliver (60)** (BAMcMahon) **3-9-2**(5) LNewton(10) (lw: cl up: rdn to ld over 1f out: hdd & no ex wl ins fnl f) | 3 | **2** | 7/1 | 69 | 34 |
| 49* | **Guy's Gamble (55)** (JWharton) **3-9-2** JFanning(6) (trckd ldrs: led over 2f out tl ins fnl f: sn btn) | 1½ | **3** | 9/2[1] | 61 | 26 |
| | **Foreman (56)** (WAO'Gorman) **3-9-3** EmmaO'Gorman(14) (lw: in tch: stdy hdwy 3f out: one pce appr fnl f) | 1½ | **4** | 6/1[2] | 59 | 24 |
| 49[4] | **Efipetite (45)** (NBycroft) **3-8-6** JQuinn(12) (in tch: hdwy u.p ½-wy: one pce fnl 2f) | 4 | **5** | 25/1 | 40 | 5 |
| 58[5] | **Dirab (60)** (TDBarron) **3-9-7** JFortune(3) (s.i.s: styd on wl fnl 3f: nrst fin) | ¾ | **6** | 8/1 | 54 | 19 |
| | **Cocoon (IRE) (48)** (CWThornton) **3-8-9** DeanMcKeown(16) (reard s: hdwy ½-wy: no imp) | 7 | **7** | 14/1 | 28 | — |

| | | | | SP | RR | SF |
|---|---|---|---|---|---|---|
| 89[2] | **Arch Angel (IRE) (53)** (DJSffrenchDavis) **3-9-0** NAdams(5) (chsd ldrs tl rdn & wknd over 2f out) | hd | **8** | 10/1 | 32 | — |
| | **Onefourseven (50)** (SRBowring) **3-8-11b** NCarlisle(11) (effrt ½-wy: n.d) | nk | **9** | 20/1 | 29 | — |
| 11[4] | **Apartments Abroad (54)** (KMcAuliffe) **3-9-1be** JFEgan(15) (prom tl wknd fnl 3f) | 12 | **10** | 10/1 | 9 | — |
| | **Tina Katerina (43)** (RChampion) **3-7-13**(5) PFessey(13) (s.i.s: n.d) | 6 | **11** | 14/1 | — | — |
| 67[7] | **My Mother's Local (USA) (42)** (KOCunningham-Brown) **3-8-3**ow2 DBiggs(4) (chsd ldrs 5f) | ¾ | **12** | 33/1 | — | — |
| 35[4] | **The Wad (54)** (DNicholls) **3-9-1b**[1] AlexGreaves(7) (led & sn clr: hdd & wknd over 2f out) | 1¼ | **13** | 8/1 | — | — |
| | **Miss Offset (51)** (MJohnston) **3-8-12b** JWeaver(1) (nvr wnt pce) | ¾ | **14** | 13/2[3] | — | — |
| | **Killatty Lark (IRE) (45)** (WJMusson) **3-8-3**(3) PMcCabe(2) (dwlt: a bhd) | 9 | **15** | 12/1 | — | — |
| | **Victory Commander (55)** (TJNaughton) **3-8-9**(7) TAshley(8) (sn outpcd & bhd) | 1¾ | **16** | 25/1 | — | — |
| | | | | (SP 142.8%) | **16 Rn** | |

**1m 47.0** (7.00) CSF £99.21 CT £417.20 TOTE £19.40: £5.70 £2.80 £1.00 £3.00 (£102.40) Trio £220.10 OWNER The Three R's (UPPER LONGDON) BRED A. P. Hume

## 124 BLUE VELVET H'CAP (0-70) (4-Y.O+) (Class E)

2-40 (2-41) **1m 3f (Fibresand)** £3,189.00 (£966.00: £472.00: £225.00) Stalls: High GOING: 0.05 sec per fur (STD)

| | | | | SP | RR | SF |
|---|---|---|---|---|---|---|
| | **Ashover (64)** (TDBarron) **6-9-5**(7) KimberleyHart(1) (a.p: led over 1f out: r.o wl) | — | **1** | 5/1[2] | 82 | 31 |
| | **Wonderful Day (66)** (TTClement) **5-9-11**(3) JStack(11) (b: hld up: smooth hdwy 4f out: led 2f out & sn rdn: hdd over 1f out: no ex) | 6 | **2** | 10/1 | 75 | 24 |
| 33[2] | **Alzoomo (IRE) (65)** (JAGlover) **4-9-10** SDWilliams(10) (in tch: hdwy 4f out: ev ch over 2f out: nt qckn) | 3 | **3** | 3/1[1] | 71 | 16 |
| 87[2] | **Carol Again (37)** (NBycroft) **4-7-10** JQuinn(4) (cl up: led 3f out tl hdd 2f out: wknd fnl f) | 4 | **4** | 11/2[3] | 37 | — |
| | **Bold Acre (40)** (DBurchell) **6-8-2** AMackay(9) (pushed along & hdwy 4f out: styd on: nvr able to chal) | 3½ | **5** | 25/1 | 34 | — |
| 70[3] | **Beauman (59)** (PDEvans) **6-9-7** JFortune(3) (lw: chsd ldrs: rdn over 3f out: one pce) | 4 | **6** | 8/1 | 47 | — |
| 87[5] | **Mill Dancer (IRE) (46)** (EJAlston) **4-8-2**(3) DWright(6) (led tl hdd & wknd 3f out) | 5 | **7** | 8/1 | 28 | — |
| | **Drummer Hicks (42)** (EWeymes) **7-8-4** DaleGibson(7) (lw: chsd ldrs: rdn 4f out: wknd over 2f out) | ½ | **8** | 14/1 | 22 | — |
| 62[8] | **Peacefull Reply (USA) (45)** (FHLee) **6-8-7** RCochrane(5) (hld up: hdwy 5f out: nvr rchd ldrs) | 11 | **9** | 14/1 | 9 | — |
| | **Darika Lad (34)** (AHarrison) **8-7-10** LCharnock(12) (outpcd fr ½-wy) | 1¼ | **10** | 33/1 | — | — |
| 66[8] | **Queens Stroller (IRE) (58)** (TRWall) **5-9-3**(3) PMcCabe(8) (a bhd) | 3 | **11** | 16/1 | 16 | — |
| 87[9] | **Elite Justice (58)** (NTinkler) **4-9-3** KimTinkler(13) (drvn along & bhd fnl 7f) | 1 | **12** | 20/1 | 16 | — |
| 48[10] | **Slmaat (64)** (DNicholls) **5-9-12b**[1] AlexGreaves(2) (in tch tl rdn & wknd over 3f out) | dist | **13** | 9/1 | — | — |
| | | | | (SP 129.1%) | **13 Rn** | |

**2m 31.7** (11.70) CSF £53.30 CT £165.54 TOTE £2.30: £2.60 £2.10 £2.10 (£36.20) Trio £45.90 OWNER Mr Timothy Cox (THIRSK) BRED Bridge End Bloodstock

LONG HANDICAP Carol Again 7-8 Darika Lad 7-8

WEIGHT FOR AGE 4yo-3lb

## 125 JADE JEWEL MEDIAN AUCTION MAIDEN STKS (4, 5 & 6-Y.O) (Class F)

3-10 (3-10) **1m 4f (Fibresand)** £2,572.00 (£722.00: £352.00) Stalls: High GOING: 0.05 sec per fur (STD)

| | | | | SP | RR | SF |
|---|---|---|---|---|---|---|
| 77[5] | **Forzair (68)** (SRBowring) **4-8-7**(5) CTeague(6) (hld up: stdy hdwy to ld over 4f out: shkn up & r.o wl fnl f) | — | **1** | 11/4[2] | 72+ | 8 |
| | **Katie Oliver (72)** (BSmart) **4-8-7** RCochrane(7) (lw: hld up: stdy hdwy ½-wy: chal 3f out: rdn 2f out: one pce) | 7 | **2** | 4/6[1] | 58 | — |
| 47[2] | **Zesti (48)** (TTClement) **4-8-9**(3) JStack(5) (b: cl up: led 6f out tl over 4f out: sn outpcd) | 20 | **3** | 16/1 | 36 | — |
| 47[5] | **I'll Be Bound** (WJMusson) **5-8-13**(3) PMcCabe(4) (in tch tl wl outpcd fnl 4f) | 3½ | **4** | 16/1 | 31 | — |
| 47[4] | **Bescaby (IRE)** (JWharton) **5-9-2** JQuinn(1) (prom tl outpcd 4f out: n.d after) | 15 | **5** | 14/1[3] | 11 | — |
| 79[14] | **Lady Elizabeth (FR)** (KOCunningham-Brown) **4-8-7** LCharnock(3) (prom tl outpcd & lost tch over 4f out) | 1 | **6** | 20/1 | 5 | — |
| | **Fiorenz (USA)** (KMcAuliffe) **4-8-7** MTebbutt(2) (b: led tl hdd ½-wy: sn rdn & wknd) | 2 | **7** | 14/1[3] | 2 | — |
| | | | | (SP 116.5%) | **7 Rn** | |

**2m 46.9** (14.40) CSF £4.92 TOTE £4.20: £2.50 £1.10 (£2.10) OWNER Charterhouse Holdings Plc (EDWINSTOWE) BRED J. G. Charlton

WEIGHT FOR AGE 4yo-4lb

## 126 SILVER ICE (S) STKS (3-Y.O+) (Class F)

3-40 (3-44) **6f (Fibresand)** £2,607.00 (£732.00: £357.00) Stalls: Low GOING: 0.05 sec per fur (STD)

| | | | | SP | RR | SF |
|---|---|---|---|---|---|---|
| 110[4] | **Tame Deer** (WAO'Gorman) **4-9-7** EmmaO'Gorman(3) (hdwy over 2f out: r.o wl to ld cl home) | — | **1** | 7/1 | 71 | 28 |
| 76[8] | **Sea Devil (65)** (MJCamacho) **10-9-7** LCharnock(6) (a.p: rdn to ld ins fnl f: hdd & no ex towards fin) | ½ | **2** | 6/1[3] | 70 | 27 |
| 59[2] | **Sir Tasker (71)** (JLHarris) **8-9-7** JWeaver(4) (hdwy ½-wy: styd on wl fnl f: nrst fin) | hd | **3** | 5/2[1] | 69 | 26 |
| 65[3] | **Deeply Vale (IRE) (68)** (GLMoore) **5-9-7** AClark(8) (lw: cl up: chal 2f out: one pce fnl f) | 3½ | **4** | 7/2[2] | 60 | 17 |
| 71[11] | **Primula Bairn (55)** (DNicholls) **6-9-2b** AlexGreaves(5) (trckd ldrs: ev ch 2f out: no ex) | s.h | **5** | 10/1 | 55 | 12 |
| | **Nadwaty (IRE) (52)** (MCChapman) **4-8-9**(7) CMunday(1) (b.off hind: mde most tl hdd & wknd ins fnl f) | s.h | **6** | 16/1 | 55 | 12 |
| 88[8] | **Elton Ledger (IRE) (70)** (MrsNMacauley) **7-9-2**(5) CTeague(12) (b: s.i.s: nrst fin) | 3 | **7** | 9/1 | 52 | 9 |
| 59[9] | **Bold Aristocrat (IRE) (41)** (RHollinshead) **5-9-0**(7) FLynch(13) (outpcd & bhd tl styd on fnl 2f) | hd | **8** | 33/1 | 52 | 9 |
| 86[6] | **Legatee (56)** (AStreeter) **5-9-2** FNorton(14) (outpcd ½-wy: n.d) | 3 | **9** | 20/1 | 39 | — |
| 30[15] | **Le Bal (34)** (MissJFCraze) **4-9-2b** RCochrane(9) (prom 4f) | ½ | **10** | 33/1 | 37 | — |
| 76[11] | **Monkey's Wedding (70)** (JBerry) **5-9-7b** LeTolboll(2) (b: s.i.s: a rr div) | 2½ | **11** | 20/1 | 36 | — |
| 76[12] | **Rupert's Princess (IRE) (51)** (MJHeaton-Ellis) **4-8-13b**(3) SDrowne(11) (gd spd over 3f: wknd) | nk | **12** | 25/1 | 30 | — |
| | **First Option (62)** (RBastiman) **6-9-2**(5) HBastiman(7) (n.d) | 4 | **13** | 33/1 | 24 | — |
| 59[13] | **Flashing Sabre (51)** (JBerry) **4-9-7b**[1] SDWilliams(15) (prom: wnt wd ent st: wknd 2f out: t.o) | 14 | **14** | 20/1 | — | — |
| | | | | (SP 129.5%) | **14 Rn** | |

**1m 19.5** (6.00) CSF £48.26 TOTE £10.50: £2.00 £2.60 £1.30 (£22.10) Trio £8.60 OWNER Red Seven Stable (NEWMARKET) BRED Stetchworth Park Stud Ltd

sold MChapman 5,000 gns

STEWARDS' ENQUIRY Charnock susp. 1-3/2/96 (excessive use of whip).

## 127 PURPLE IRIS H'CAP (0-70) (4-Y.O+) (Class E)

4-10 (4-14) **6f (Fibresand)** £3,217.60 (£974.80: £476.40: £227.20) Stalls: Low GOING: 0.05 sec per fur (STD)

| | | | | SP | RR | SF |
|---|---|---|---|---|---|---|
| 90[5] | **Daawe (USA) (52)** (MrsVAAconley) **5-8-10v** MDeering(14) (a.p: led wl over 1f out: kpt on) | — | **1** | 20/1 | 63 | 31 |
| 88[11] | **Encore M'Lady (IRE) (69)** (FHLee) **5-9-13b** RCochrane(15) (a.p: ev ch 2f out: kpt on one pce) | 2 | **2** | 14/1 | 75 | 43 |
| 74[3] | **My Cherrywell (57)** (LRLloyd-James) **6-9-1b** TWilliams(11) (b.hind: led tl hdd wl over 1f out: kpt on) | ½ | **3** | 12/1 | 61 | 29 |

$88^{2}$ **Awesome Venture (57)** (MCChapman) **6-8-8**(7) CMunday(3) (a chsng ldrs: one pce fnl 2f)....¾ **4** 8/1 59 27
$71^{*}$ **Dissentor (IRE) (53)** (JAGlover) **4-8-11v** JWeaver(2) (hdwy over 2f out: nvr able to chal)....½ **5** 2/1 1 54 22
$74^{2}$ **Serious Fact (39)** (SirMarkPrescott) **4-7-11** GBardwell(6) (mid div: hdwy u.p 2f out: nvr rchd ldrs)....4 **6** 9/2 2 29 —
$22^{4}$ **Rennyholme (38)** (JHetherton) **5-7-10b** NAdams(5) (nvr rchd ldrs)....3 **7** 50/1 20 —
$74^{10}$ **Most Uppitty (55)** (JBerry) **4-8-6**(7) JoanneWebster(13) (effrt over 2f out: n.d)....1¾ **8** 20/1 33 1
$107^{11}$ **Tenor (63)** (DNicholls) **5-9-7** AlexGreaves(7) (bhd tl styd on fnl 2f)....s.h **9** 12/1 41 9
$74^{8}$ **Chloella (38)** (CBBBooth) **4-7-10** NKennedy(1) (in tch: rdn ½-wy: sn btn)....½ **10** 40/1 14 —
**Pharaoh's Dancer (53)** (PBurgoyne) **9-8-11** MWigham(12) (outpcd & bhd tl sme late hdwy)....nk **11** 20/1 28 —
$71^{7}$ **Grey Charmer (IRE) (46)** (CJames) **7-8-4** DaleGibson(8) (drvn along ½-wy: n.d)....1 **12** 25/1 19 —
$74^{*}$ **Fairey Firefly (59)** (MJCamacho) **5-9-3** LCharnock(4) (chsd ldrs 4f: wknd qckly fnl f)....1½ **13** 7/1 3 28 —
$71^{12}$ **Double Glow (38)** (NBycroft) **4-7-10b** JQuinn(10) (cl up 4f: wknd qckly)....½ **14** 40/1 5 —
**Cheerful Groom (IRE) (41)** (SRBowring) **5-7-13** NCarlisle(9) (dwlt: a outpcd & bhd)....14 **15** 12/1 — —
(SP 129.8%) **15 Rn**

**1m 18.5** (5.00) CSF £256.16 CT £3,174.61 TOTE £27.40: 33.20 £3.60 £3.50 (£301.10) Trio £292.80; £206.22 to Leicester 23/1/96 OWNER Mrs Andrea M.allinson (WESTOW) BRED Gainsborough Farm W.C.
LONG HANDICAP Rennyholme 6-13 Chloella 7-7 Double Glow 7-8
STEWARDS' ENQUIRY Munday susp. 31/1-3/2/96 (excessive use of whip).

TJkpt: Not won; £70,063.47 to Leicester 23/1/96. T/Plpt: £247.40 (64.17 Tckts). T/Qdpt: £31.10 (13.46 Tckts). AA

## 0116-LINGFIELD (L-H) (Standard)
## Tuesday January 23rd
WEATHER: raining

### 128 WESTMINSTER CLAIMING STKS (4-Y.O+) (Class E)
1-50 (1-50) **1m 4f (Equitrack)** £3,131.80 (£948.40: £463.20: £220.60) Stalls: Low GOING minus 0.37 sec per fur (FST)

SP RR SF
$80^{3}$ **El Volador (71)** (RJO'Sullivan) **9-8-11** DBiggs(3) (hdwy 4f out: led 2f out: pushed out)....— **1** 4/9 1 64 41
$82^{5}$ **Northern Trial (USA) (41)** (KRBurke) **8-8-2v**(7) TAshley(2) (a.p: led over 3f out to 2f out: unable qckn)....2 **2** 20/1 59 36
$80^{4}$ **Tartan Gem (IRE) (67)** (MBrittain) **5-9-7** RCochrane(7) (lw: hdwy over 3f out: rdn over 1f out: one pce)....½ **3** 4/1 2 68 48
$79^{5}$ **Miss Cashtal (IRE)** (DTThom) **5-8-6** MFenton(5) (a.p: rdn over 4f out: wknd over 3f out)....9 **4** 20/1 41 21
$37^{3}$ **Duveen (IRE) (62)** (JWhite) **6-8-13** MTebbutt(6) (hdwy 6f out: wknd over 2f out)....8 **5** 6/1 3 37 17
$34^{10}$ **Rose Chime (IRE) (36)** (JLHarris) **4-8-0** AMackay(4) (w ldr: led over 7f out tl over 3f out: sn wknd)....2½ **6** 50/1 25 1
**Bobby Blue (IRE) (45)** (RonaldThompson) **5-9-7** SDWilliams(1) (b: bit bkwd: led over 4f: wknd 4f out: t.o)...dist **7** 66/1 — —
(SP 116.5%) **7 Rn**

**2m 33.83** (3.83) CSF £10.22 TOTE £1.20: £1.00 £12.20 (£15.30) OWNER Mr R. J. O'Sullivan (WHITCOMBE) BRED L. and Mrs Hutch
WEIGHT FOR AGE 4yo-4lb
El Volador clmd JHanley £5,000

### 129 VAUXHALL (S) STKS (3-Y.O) (Class G)
2-20 (2-21) **1m (Equitrack)** £2,438.20 (£685.20: £334.60) Stalls: High GOING minus 0.37 sec per fur (FST)

SP RR SF
$52^{2}$ **Rowlandsons Charm (IRE) (60)** (GLMoore) **3-8-11v** NAdams(3) (w ldr: led over 4f out: rdn out)....— **1** 5/4 1 70 22
$25^{4}$ **Multi Franchise (52)** (BGubby) **3-8-8**(3) JStack(5) (a.p: rdn over 2f out: r.o one pce)....3½ **2** 10/1 3 63 15
$68^{5}$ **Bells of Holland (60)** (WRMuir) **3-8-6** Jean-PierreLopez(9) (led over 3f: hrd rdn over 1f out: one pce)....1 **3** 7/4 2 56 8
**Illegally Yours (42)** (LMontagueHall) **3-8-6b**1 JFEgan(4) (hld up: rdn over 4f out: one pce)....2 **4** 11/1 52 4
**Ordained** (TTClement) **3-8-6** JQuinn(7) (b.hind: nvr nr to chal)....¾ **5** 16/1 51 3
**Digwana (IRE) (40)** (TMJones) **3-8-11** SRaymont(8) (no hdwy fnl 3f)....3 **6** 33/1 50 2
$21^{9}$ **Quinntessa (52)** (BPalling) **3-8-6** SDWilliams(2) (hdwy over 6f out: 3rd & btn whn n.m.r on ins over 1f out) ...nk **7** 16/1 44 —
$49^{8}$ **Florrie'm (45)** (JLHarris) **3-8-6** AMackay(6) (bhd fnl 3f: t.o)....20 **8** 25/1 4 —
**Diasafina** (SCWilliams) **3-8-1**(5) MBaird(1) (s.s: a wl bhd: t.o)....10 **9** 33/1 — —
(SP 119.7%) **9 Rn**

**1m 41.71** (4.31) CSF £14.11 TOTE £1.80: £1.00 £2.90 £1.10 (£7.00) Trio £2.70 OWNER Allen & Associates (EPSOM) BRED Mrs Catherine O'Malley
No bid

### 130 TOWER H'CAP (0-80) (4-Y.O+) (Class D)
2-50 (2-50) **2m (Equitrack)** £3,743.65 (£1,133.20: £553.10: £263.05) Stalls: Low GOING minus 0.37 sec per fur (FST)

SP RR SF
$12^{3}$ **Ikhtiraa (USA) (52)** (RJO'Sullivan) **6-8-0b** NCarlisle(2) (mde all: rdn out)....— **1** 5/1 3 66 35
$83^{2}$ **Coleridge (54)** (JJSheehan) **8-8-2b** JQuinn(3) (s.s: hdwy over 12f out: chsd wnr 11f out: ev ch wl over 1f out: edgd rt: unable qckn)....1½ **2** 11/4 2 67 36
$38^{5}$ **Benfleet (80)** (RWArmstrong) **5-10-0** JWeaver(1) (lw: stdy hdwy over 3f out: rdn over 2f out: one pce)....10 **3** 15/8 1 83 52
$19^{5}$ **Mizyan (IRE) (69)** (JEBanks) **8-9-0**(3) JStack(8) (lost pl over 3f out: r.o one pce fnl 2f)....hd **4** 6/1 71 40
$79^{2}$ **Kymin (IRE) (69)** (DJGMurraySmith) **4-8-10v** JFEgan(7) (b.off hind: hld up: rdn over 6f out: one pce)....hd **5** 8/1 71 33
$83^{12}$ **Sir Thomas Beecham (57)** (SDow) **6-8-5** FNorton(5) (bhd fnl 4f)....5 **6** 16/1 54 23
$9^{5}$ **Oh So Handy (48)** (RCurtis) **8-7-10b** GBardwell(4) (bhd fnl 7f)....25 **7** 40/1 20 —
$66^{12}$ **Landlord (56)** (JARToller) **4-7-11** DaleGibson(6) (chsd wnr 5f: wknd over 9f out: t.o)....dist **8** 14/1 — —
(SP 118.5%) **8 Rn**

**3m 26.33** (4.33) CSF £18.72 CT £31.73 TOTE £7.40: £1.60 £1.10 £1.10 (£4.60) OWNER Mr I. Kerman (WHITCOMBE) BRED Stuart Ross
LONG HANDICAP Oh So Handy 6-8
WEIGHT FOR AGE 4yo-7lb

### 131 CHELSEA H'CAP (0-60) (3-Y.O) (Class F)
3-20 (3-21) **6f (Equitrack)** £2,786.20 (£783.20: £382.60) Stalls: Low GOING minus 0.37 sec per fur (FST)

SP RR SF
$81^{4}$ **Miss Carottene (44)** (MJRyan) **3-8-0**(5) MBaird(9) (hdwy 3f out: hrd rdn over 1f out: led nr fin)....— **1** 10/1 52 —

| | Horse | Dist | Pos | SP | RR | SF |
|---|---|---|---|---|---|---|
| | **Sunset Harbour (IRE) (56)** (DAWilson) **3-9-3** RCochrane(4) (led over 4f out: hrd rdn fnl f: hdd nr fin) | nk | **2** | 4/1[2] | 63 | 10 |
| 81[6] | **Mystery Matthias (49)** (MissBSanders) **3-8-10b** DBiggs(5) (a.p: rdn over 3f out: r.o one pce fnl f) | 2 | **3** | 12/1 | 51 | — |
| 81[8] | **Ghostly Apparition (55)** (JRUpson) **3-8-9**(7) DSweeney(2) (a.p: rdn over 2f out: r.o one pce fnl f) | ¾ | **4** | 20/1 | 55 | 2 |
| | **Elfin Queen (IRE) (60)** (JLHarris) **3-9-7** JWeaver(6) (swtchd lft & hdwy over 1f out: nvr nrr) | 2½ | **5** | 11/1 | 53 | — |
| 52[6] | **Wingnut (IRE) (40)** (JJBridger) **3-8-1v[1]** GBardwell(3) (lw: nvr nr to chal) | ½ | **6** | 11/1 | 32 | — |
| | **No Sympathy (48)** (GLMoore) **3-8-9** SWhitworth(7) (lw: s.i.s: nvr nrr) | 3 | **7** | 5/1[3] | 32 | — |
| | **Balpare (53)** (NACallaghan) **3-8-11**(3) SDrowne(12) (s.s: nvr nrr) | 1½ | **8** | 11/4[1] | 33 | — |
| | **Petite Annie (57)** (TGMills) **3-9-4** JFortune(10) (prom over 4f) | nk | **9** | 13/2 | 36 | — |
| 52[5] | **Music Mistress (IRE) (55)** (JSMoore) **3-8-11**(5) CAdamson(11) (a bhd) | 5 | **10** | 16/1 | 21 | — |
| | **Gracious Gretclo (52)** (CJHill) **3-8-8**(5) PFessey(8) (prom 4f) | s.h | **11** | 8/1 | 18 | — |
| 51[6] | **Darby Flyer (55)** (WRMuir) **3-9-2** Jean-PierreLopez(1) (led over 1f: wknd over 3f out) | 15 | **12** | 20/1 | — | — |

(SP 136.6%) **12 Rn**

**1m 15.07** (4.47) CSF £53.17 CT £465.82 TOTE £9.30: £1.60 £1.70 £3.20 (£81.30) Trio £138.50; £158.02 to Folkestone 24/1/96 OWNER Mr Faiz Al-Mutawa (NEWMARKET) BRED L. Audus

## 132 ALBERT H'CAP (0-85) (4-Y.O+) (Class D)

3-50 (3-51) **1m 2f (Equitrack)** £3,813.85 (£1,154.80: £563.90: £268.45) Stalls: Low GOING minus 0.37 sec per fur (FST)

| | Horse | Dist | Pos | SP | RR | SF |
|---|---|---|---|---|---|---|
| | **King of Tunes (FR) (68)** (JJSheehan) **4-8-9** JQuinn(7) (hld up: rdn over 3f out: str run to ld wl ins fnl f: r.o wl) | — | **1** | 12/1 | 77 | 52 |
| 18[4] | **Almuhtaram (66)** (MissGayKelleway) **4-8-0b**(7) TAshley(6) (nt clr run wl over 1f out: swtchd rt & hdwy 1f out: r.o wl) | ¾ | **2** | 6/1[2] | 74 | 49 |
| 13[4] | **Access Adventurer (IRE) (72)** (RBoss) **5-9-1** JWeaver(13) (led 8f out: rdn over 2f out: hdd wl ins fnl f: 2nd & btn whn eased last strides) | hd | **3** | 3/1[1] | 79 | 57 |
| 48[3] | **Wildfire (SWI) (53)** (RAkehurst) **5-7-10** NCarlisle(10) (a.p: rdn over 3f out: one pce) | 1 | **4** | 10/1 | 58 | 36 |
| 61[2] | **South Eastern Fred (85)** (HJCollingridge) **5-10-0** MRimmer(4) (hld up: rdn over 4f out: one pce fnl 2f) | nk | **5** | 13/2[3] | 90 | 68 |
| | **Progression (69)** (CMurray) **5-8-12** MTebbutt(3) (s.i.s: nvr plcd to chal) | 4 | **6** | 20/1 | 67 | 45 |
| | **Renown (68)** (LordHuntingdon) **4-8-9** TIves(14) (hdwy over 3f out: wknd fnl f) | ½ | **7** | 7/1 | 66 | 41 |
| 82[2] | **Tribal Peace (IRE) (69)** (BGubby) **4-8-7**(3) JStack(12) (hld up: rdn over 3f out: wknd over 1f out) | 1¼ | **8** | 12/1 | 65 | 40 |
| 61* | **Bernard Seven (IRE) (80)** (CEBrittain) **4-9-7b** MLarsen(11) (hdwy 6f out: wknd over 1f out) | 2½ | **9** | 9/1 | 72 | 47 |
| 61[9] | **Nigel's Lad (IRE) (70)** (PCHaslam) **4-8-11** JFortune(5) (hld up: rdn over 3f out: wknd wl over 1f out) | 2 | **10** | 7/1 | 59 | 34 |
| | **Nordinex (IRE) (69)** (RWArmstrong) **4-8-10** DaleGibson(2) (lw: led 2f: wknd 5f out) | 1¾ | **11** | 25/1 | 55 | 30 |
| | **Noble Neptune (57)** (WJMusson) **4-7-12** AMackay(9) (a bhd) | 15 | **12** | 20/1 | 19 | — |
| | **Toujours Riviera (84)** (JPearce) **6-9-13** GBardwell(8) (lw: a bhd: t.o fnl 4f) | 25 | **13** | 14/1 | 5 | — |
| | **Office Hours (72)** (CACyzer) **4-8-13** DBiggs(1) (prom 6f) | ½ | **14** | 33/1 | — | — |

(SP 135.1%) **14 Rn**

**2m 5.83** (1.53) CSF £84.30 CT £258.35 TOTE £22.70: £5.70 £3.40 £2.60 (£38.70) Trio £251.50 OWNER Mrs Eileen Sheehan (FINDON) BRED Thierry Storme

LONG HANDICAP Wildfire (SWI) 7-8

WEIGHT FOR AGE 4yo-2lb

## 133 HUNGERFORD APPRENTICE H'CAP (0-60) (4-Y.O+) (Class F)

4-20 (4-21) **7f (Equitrack)** £2,824.00 (£794.00: £388.00) Stalls: Low GOING minus 0.37 sec per fur (FST)

| | Horse | Dist | Pos | SP | RR | SF |
|---|---|---|---|---|---|---|
| | **King Parrot (IRE) (51)** (LordHuntingdon) **8-9-1**(5) AimeeCook(9) (hdwy over 1f out: led ins fnl f: r.o wl) | — | **1** | 4/1[2] | 63 | 30 |
| 26[9] | **Dahiyah (USA) (54)** (GLMoore) **5-9-4v**(5) ALakeman(8) (led: clr over 1f out: hdd ins fnl f: unable qckn) | ¾ | **2** | 6/1[3] | 64 | 31 |
| | **Nuthatch (IRE) (34)** (MDIUsher) **4-8-0**(3) CAdamson(6) (b: hdwy over 1f out: r.o wl ins fnl f) | 3 | **3** | 14/1 | 37 | 4 |
| 107[5] | **Jaazim (58)** (MMadgwick) **6-9-8**(5) AEddery(1) (chsd ldr 5f out tl ins fnl f: one pce) | 1¼ | **4** | 11/4[1] | 59 | 26 |
| 65[8] | **Dusk in Daytona (56)** (CJames) **4-9-6**(5) FLynch(11) (hld up: hrd rdn over 1f out: one pce) | ¾ | **5** | 6/1[3] | 55 | 22 |
| 117[12] | **Assignment (43)** (JELong) **10-8-5**(7) TField(2) (prom over 4f) | 3 | **6** | 14/1 | 35 | 2 |
| | **Pair of Jacks (IRE) (33)** (DAWilson) **6-7-9**(7) RachaelMoody(5) (bhd fnl 4f) | ½ | **7** | 14/1 | 24 | — |
| 36[5] | **Thick as Thieves (51)** (RonaldThompson) **4-9-3**(3) PRoberts(10) (bhd fnl 4f) | 3 | **8** | 4/1[2] | 35 | 2 |
| 36[8] | **Riskie Things (53)** (JSMoore) **5-9-3**(5) DSweeney(3) (lw: a bhd) | 4 | **9** | 14/1 | 28 | — |
| | **Formidable Lass (28)** (LGCottrell) **5-7-11** MBaird(7) (a wl bhd) | 4 | **10** | 33/1 | — | — |
| | **Halleluja Time (53)** (PCRitchens) **4-9-8** JStack(4) (a bhd) | 1 | **11** | 33/1 | 16 | — |

(SP 127.8%) **11 Rn**

**1m 27.68** (3.68) CSF £28.60 CT £287.45 TOTE £6.90: £1.70 £2.30 £3.50 (£21.50) Trio £139.70 OWNER Lord Huntingdon (WEST ILSLEY) BRED W. Hastings-Bass in Ireland

T/Plpt: £136.80 (72.93 Tckts). T/Qdpt: £88.40 (5.75 Tckts) AK

# 0097-WOLVERHAMPTON (L-H) (Standard)

## Wednesday January 24th

WEATHER: Overcast

## 134 HADDOCK MAIDEN STKS (3-Y.O+) (Class D)

2-00 (2-02) **6f (Fibresand)** £3,866.50 (£1,171.00: £572.00: £272.50) Stalls: Low GOING: 0.25 sec per fur (SLW)

| | Horse | Dist | Pos | SP | RR | SF |
|---|---|---|---|---|---|---|
| | **Farmost (73)** (SirMarkPrescott) **3-8-8** CNutter(11) (chsd ldr: led 2f out: drvn out) | — | **1** | 4/7[1] | 62 | 37 |
| | **Dummer Golf Time** (LordHuntingdon) **3-8-8** DeanMcKeown(2) (chsd ldrs: hdwy to jn ldr fnl f: no ex cl home) | ½ | **2** | 3/1[2] | 61+ | 36 |
| | **Coastguards Hero** (MDIUsher) **3-8-8** MWigham(1) (bhd & outpcd tl r.o ins fnl f) | 6 | **3** | 50/1 | 45 | 20 |
| | **Call Tophorse (27)** (CMurray) **4-9-10** MTebbutt(9) (mid div: rdn 2f out: edgd lft appr fnl f: one pce) | 4 | **4** | 33/1 | 34 | 25 |
| | **Eben Naas (USA)** (SCWilliams) **3-8-8** JTate(7) (bhd: effrt & rdn 2f out: kpt on) | ½ | **5** | 20/1 | 33 | 8 |
| | **Giftbox (USA)** (SirMarkPrescott) **4-9-10** MRimmer(3) (bhd & outpcd tl styd on ins fnl f) | 1¼ | **6** | 20/1 | 29 | 20 |
| | **Pats Delight (37)** (SCoathup) **4-9-5** TWilliams(8) (led 4f: wknd qckly over 1f out) | 1½ | **7** | 50/1 | 20 | 11 |
| 49[9] | **Radmore Brandy** (NPLittmoden) **3-7-10**(7) JBramhill(5) (in tch: effrt & rdn wl over 1f out: sn btn) | 5 | **8** | 16/1 | 7 | — |

| Form | Horse | Dist | Pos | SP | RR | SF |
|---|---|---|---|---|---|---|
| | **Heathyards Rose (IRE)** (RHollinshead) **3-7-10**(7) FLynch(6) (trckd ldrs over 4f) | 1¼ | **9** | 33/1 | 4 | — |
| | **Oakley Folly** (RHollinshead) **3-8-3** NCarlisle(4) (s.s: a bhd & outpcd) | 5 | **10** | 33/1 | — | — |
| *58$^{11}$* | **Roxane (IRE)** (ABailey) **3-8-0**(3) DWright(12) (trckd ldrs 4f: sn wknd) | 1¼ | **11** | 25/1 | — | — |
| | **Rizal (USA)** (DJGMurraySmith) **4-9-10** JWeaver(13) (dwlt: racd wd: sn pushed along: a bhd) | ¾ | **12** | 10/1$^{3}$ | — | — |
| *58$^{10}$* | **Highland Fawn** (BAMcMahon) **3-7-12**(5) LNewton(10) (spd over 3f: sn lost tch) | ½ | **13** | 33/1 | — | — |

(SP 132.7%) **13 Rn**

**1m 16.9** (5.50) CSF £3.37 TOTE £1.80: £1.10 £1.30 £63.20 (£3.40) Trio £103.30: £7.28 to Huntingdon 25/1/96. OWNER Mr W. E. Sturt (NEWMARKET) BRED Hesmonds Stud Ltd
WEIGHT FOR AGE 3yo-16lb

## 135 MACKEREL CLAIMING STKS (4-Y.O+) (Class F)

2-30 (2-30) **7f (Fibresand)** £2,870.50 (£868.00: £423.00: £200.50) Stalls: High GOING: 0.25 sec per fur (SLW)

| Form | Horse | Dist | Pos | SP | RR | SF |
|---|---|---|---|---|---|---|
| *105$^{6}$* | **Rambo Waltzer (79)** (DNicholls) **4-9-2** AlexGreaves(3) (a.p: chal ent st: styd on wl to ld nr fin) | — | **1** | 5/1$^{3}$ | 84 | 55 |
| *86** | **Berge (IRE) (75)** (WAO'Gorman) **5-9-0b** EmmaO'Gorman(2) (hdwy ½-wy: led wl over 1f out tl ct nr fin) | nk | **2** | 5/4$^{1}$ | 81 | 52 |
| *20$^{9}$* | **Everset (FR) (85)** (ABailey) **8-8-13**(3) DWright(5) (a.p: led 2f out: sn hdd: hrd drvn & no ex ins fnl f) | 1½ | **3** | 3/1$^{2}$ | 80 | 51 |
| *59$^{6}$* | **Jigsaw Boy (63)** (PGMurphy) **7-8-9**(3) SDrowne(4) (trckd ldrs: rdn along over 1f out: one pce) | 5 | **4** | 10/1 | 65 | 36 |
| *59$^{5}$* | **Promise Fulfilled (USA) (64)** (ABailey) **5-7-10**(7) IonaWands(9) (s.s: hdwy on ins 2f out: nt trble ldrs) | nk | **5** | 14/1 | 55 | 26 |
| *109$^{6}$* | **Best Kept Secret (62)** (PDEvans) **5-7-11v**(7) DSweeney(1) (sn pushed along: a bhd & outpcd) | 2 | **6** | 14/1 | 51 | 22 |
| *76$^{3}$* | **Sense of Priority (75)** (DNicholls) **7-8-8** MTebbutt(7) (hdwy on outside ½-wy: rdn over 1f out: nt pce to chal) | 1¾ | **7** | 5/1$^{3}$ | 51 | 22 |
| | **Persian Gusher (IRE)** (NASmith) **6-8-2** NCarlisle(6) (ld 4f: sn rdn & wknd) | 4 | **8** | 25/1 | 36 | 7 |
| *86$^{5}$* | **Bex Hill (34)** (DHaydnJones) **4-7-11v** AMackay(10) (trckd ldrs: drvn over 2f out: sn btn) | ½ | **9** | 20/1 | 30 | 1 |
| *18$^{9}$* | **Life Is Precious (IRE) (55)** (RHollinshead) **4-8-7** MWigham(11) (s.i.s: effrt & faltered 3f out: n.d) | 2 | **10** | 20/1 | 35 | 6 |
| *100$^{9}$* | **Shahik (USA) (75)** (JGMO'Shea) **6-9-2v$^{1}$** JQuinn(8) (trckd ldrs: rdn 3f out: sn lost tch) | 1¼ | **11** | 25/1 | 42 | 13 |

(SP 142.4%) **11 Rn**

**1m 30.3** (5.60) CSF £13.55 TOTE £10.50: £4.10 £1.10 £1.90 (£8.30) Trio £8.80 OWNER Keystone Racing Club Partnership (THIRSK) BRED Triangle Thoroughbreds Ltd

## 136 SALMON H'CAP (0-80) (4-Y.O+) (Class D)

3-00 (3-01) **1m 1f 79y (Fibresand)** £3,813.85 (£1,154.80: £563.90: £268.45) Stalls: Low GOING: 0.25 sec per fur (SLW)

| Form | Horse | Dist | Pos | SP | RR | SF |
|---|---|---|---|---|---|---|
| *42$^{7}$* | **Field of Vision (IRE) (63)** (MJohnston) **6-8-11** JWeaver(4) (hld up in tch: hdwy over 2f out: r.o to ld fnl 50y) | — | **1** | 8/1 | 71 | 33 |
| *100$^{2}$* | **Maple Bay (IRE) (74)** (ABailey) **7-9-1**(7) PRoberts(2) (led 7f out tl hdd wl ins fnl f) | hd | **2** | 5/2$^{1}$ | 82 | 44 |
| *61$^{3}$* | **Kintwyn (68)** (CCElsey) **6-9-2** MTebbutt(1) (hld up: hdwy 4f out: hrd rdn & one pce appr fnl f) | 2½ | **3** | 9/2$^{3}$ | 72 | 34 |
| *61$^{6}$* | **High Premium (70)** (RAFahey) **8-9-4** ACulhane(13) (hdwy over 3f out: sn hrd rdn: kpt on fnl f) | ¾ | **4** | 8/1 | 72 | 34 |
| *98$^{2}$* | **Make a Note (USA) (80)** (PDEvans) **5-10-0** JFortune(9) (trck ldrs: drvn along over 3f out: sn btn) | 5 | **5** | 12/1 | 74 | 36 |
| *90$^{2}$* | **Snake Plissken (IRE) (48)** (DHaydnJones) **5-7-10** AMackay(10) (hdwy 5f out: hrd drvn wl over 1f out: sn btn) | 3 | **6** | 11/4$^{2}$ | 37 | |
| *61$^{4}$* | **Komreyev Dancer (79)** (ABailey) **4-9-9**(3) DWright(7) (swvd lft start: a bhd & outpcd) | 2½ | **7** | 8/1 | 64 | 24 |
| | **Rainbow Walk (IRE) (71)** (JGMO'Shea) **6-9-5v** JQuinn(6) (prom tl wknd 2f out) | 1¾ | **8** | 25/1 | 52 | 14 |
| *105$^{7}$* | **Manabar (70)** (MJPolglase) **4-9-3** MRimmer(12) (prom over 6f) | hd | **9** | 12/1 | 52 | 12 |
| | **Hillzah (USA) (77)** (RBastiman) **8-9-6**(5) HBastiman(11) (dwlt: a bhd: t.o) | 20 | **10** | 14/1 | 24 | — |
| | **Orchestral Designs (IRE) (64)** (GAHam) **5-8-9**(3) SDrowne(8) (rdn over 4f out: sn lost tch) | 6 | **11** | 33/1 | 1 | — |
| | **P G Tips (IRE) (72)** (MrsNMacauley) **5-9-6** SDWilliams(3) (led over 2f: wknd over 4f out: t.o) | dist | **12** | 20/1 | — | — |

(SP 140.4%) **12 Rn**

**2m 5.7** (9.70) CSF £31.50 CT £102.94 TOTE £10.70: £3.20 £1.90 £3.30 (£38.90) Trio £31.30 OWNER Mr R. W. Huggins (MIDDLEHAM) BRED Sean Collins
LONG HANDICAP Snake Plissken (IRE) 7-6
WEIGHT FOR AGE 4yo-1lb

## 137 TROUT H'CAP (0-90) (3-Y.O) (Class C)

3-30 (3-30) **1m 100y (Fibresand)** £5,582.15 (£1,689.20: £824.10: £391.55) Stalls: Low GOING: 0.25 sec per fur (SLW)

| Form | Horse | Dist | Pos | SP | RR | SF |
|---|---|---|---|---|---|---|
| *56** | **China Castle (68)** (PCHaslam) **3-8-12** JFortune(4) (trckd ldrs: rdn & outpcd 3f out: hdwy appr fnl f: str burst to ld cl home) | — | **1** | 9/4$^{2}$ | 78 | 33 |
| *35$^{2}$* | **Theatre Magic (62)** (SRBowring) **3-8-1b**(5)ow2 CTeague(3) (led: clr ent fnl f: wknd & ct nr fin) | 1¼ | **2** | 7/1$^{3}$ | 70 | 23 |
| *35$^{6}$* | **Lady Dignity (IRE) (60)** (PJMakin) **3-8-4** JQuinn(2) (a.p: hrd rdn over 1f out: kpt on) | 1¼ | **3** | 10/1 | 65 | 20 |
| | **Galapino (65)** (CEBrittain) **3-8-9** MLarsen(7) (chsd ldrs: rdn along over 2f out: styd on wl appr fnl f) | hd | **4** | 14/1 | 70 | 25 |
| *56$^{2}$* | **Domoor (56)** (MJohnston) **3-8-0** TWilliams(9) (a.p: effrt & rdn 2f out: nt pce to chal) | ½ | **5** | 7/4$^{1}$ | 60 | 15 |
| *17$^{3}$* | **Scenicris (IRE) (53)** (RHollinshead) **3-7-11** NCarlisle(6) (a in rr: t.o) | 8 | **6** | 12/1 | 42 | — |
| | **Le Sport (77)** (ABailey) **3-9-4**(3) DWright(5) (a in rr: t.o fnl 3f) | ¾ | **7** | 7/1$^{3}$ | 65 | 20 |
| *28$^{5}$* | **Victim of Love (72)** (RCharlton) **3-9-2** JWeaver(1) (rr: drvn along ½-wy: no rspnse: t.o) | 4 | **8** | 8/1 | 52 | 7 |
| | **Autumn (FR) (62)** (CMurray) **3-8-6** MTebbutt(8) (a bhd: t.o fnl 3f) | 2½ | **9** | 16/1 | 37 | — |

(SP 132.6%) **9 Rn**

**1m 53.8** (8.80) CSF £20.03 CT £133.07 TOTE £3.80: £1.40 £3.20 £3.50 (£16.00) Trio £24.60 OWNER Mr J. M. Davis (MIDDLEHAM) BRED Mrs Frances Cronin

## 138 BREAM (S) STKS (4-Y.O+) (Class E)

4-00 (4-01) **1m 6f 166y (Fibresand)** £3,160.40 (£957.20: £467.60: £222.80) Stalls: High GOING: 0.25 sec per fur (SLW)

| Form | Horse | Dist | Pos | SP | RR | SF |
|---|---|---|---|---|---|---|
| | **Stevie's Wonder (IRE) (66)** (MJRyan) **6-9-3v** GBardwell(2) (led after 2f: hrd drvn fnl f: jst hld on) | — | **1** | Evens$^{1}$ | 76 | 28 |
| *79$^{8}$* | **Fraise du Roi (IRE)** (LordHuntingdon) **4-8-0v$^{1}$**(7)ow1 AimeeCook(10) (hdwy over 4f out: chsd wnr 2f: r.o wl fnl f) | hd | **2** | 8/1$^{3}$ | 71 | 17 |
| *73$^{3}$* | **El Nido (56)** (MJCamacho) **8-9-3** LCharnock(1) (a.p: wnt 2nd 5f out tl wknd 2f out) | 20 | **3** | 7/2$^{2}$ | 54 | 6 |
| *73$^{4}$* | **Fools of Pride (IRE) (36)** (RHollinshead) **4-7-13**(7) FLynch(4) (sme hdwy 3f out: nvr nr ldrs) | 15 | **4** | 14/1 | 32 | — |
| *73$^{8}$* | **Acquittal (IRE) (53)** (JMackie) **4-8-11b$^{1}$** JQuinn(12) (in tch tl lost pl 5f out) | 1 | **5** | 12/1 | 36 | — |
| *104$^{5}$* | **Duggan (23)** (PDEvans) **9-8-10**(7) DSweeney(9) (a rr div) | nk | **6** | 16/1 | 37 | — |

| | Horse / details | Dist | Pos | SP | RR | SF |
|---|---|---|---|---|---|---|
| | **Musical Vocation (IRE)** (BPreece) **5-8-12** ACulhane(7) (s.i.s: a bhd: t.o) | 20 | **7** | 33/1 | 10 | — |
| $69^{6}$ | **Wahem (IRE) (31)** (CEBrittain) **6-9-3** MLarsen(8) (w wnr tl wknd over 5f out: t.o) | 15 | **8** | 14/1 | — | — |
| | **Bushehr (IRE) (60)** (SCoathup) **4-8-11** JWeaver(3) (led 2f: lost pl ½-wy: t.o) | 10 | **9** | 8/1$^{3}$ | — | — |
| | **Hill Farm Katie (40)** (WMBrisbourne) **5-8-12** RCochrane(5) (trckd ldrs: rdn ½-wy: sn lost tch: t.o) | 1¾ | **10** | 10/1 | — | — |
| $97^{7}$ | **Ranger Sloane (41)** (GFierro) **4-8-11** MWigham(6) (prom early: sn dropped rr: t.o) | 12 | **11** | 33/1 | — | — |

(SP 136.3%) **11 Rn**

**3m 25.0** (17.60) CSF £11.78 TOTE £2.10: £1.20 £2.20 £1.90 (£12.70) Trio £4.80 OWNER Newmarket Consortium (NEWMARKET) BRED Ovidstown Investments Ltd in Ireland
WEIGHT FOR AGE 4yo-6lb
No bid

## 139 LADBROKE SERIES H'CAP (Qualifier) (0-75) (3-Y.O+) (Class D)

4-30 (4-31) **5f (Fibresand)** £3,743.65 (£1,133.20: £553.10: £263.05) Stalls: Low GOING: 0.25 sec per fur (SLW)

| | Horse / details | Dist | Pos | SP | RR | SF |
|---|---|---|---|---|---|---|
| $63^{4}$ | **Chadwell Hall (66)** (SRBowring) **5-9-2b**(5) CTeague(8) (a.p: qcknd to ld ins fnl f: sn cl) | — | **1** | 5/1 | 79 | 41 |
| | **King Rambo (67)** (RHollinshead) **5-9-1**(7) FLynch(7) (hdwy 2f out: r.o fnl f: no ch w wnr) | 2 | **2** | 10/1 | 74 | 36 |
| $63^{3}$ | **Featherstone Lane (62)** (MissLCSiddall) **5-9-3v** DeanMcKeown(5) (a.p: ev ch over 1f out: unable qckn) | 1¾ | **3** | 8/1 | 63 | 25 |
| | **Southern Dominion (59)** (MJohnston) **4-9-0b** JWeaver(6) (a.p: rdn to ld over 1f out: sn hdd: no ex fnl f) | ½ | **4** | 7/2$^{1}$ | 58 | 20 |
| $63^{2}$ | **Cheeky Chappy (59)** (DWChapman) **5-8-9b**(5) PFessey(2) (trckd ldrs: rdn & one pce appr fnl f) | 1¼ | **5** | 9/2$^{3}$ | 54 | 16 |
| $22^{2}$ | **The Institute Boy (52)** (MissJFCraze) **6-8-7** NKennedy(11) (dwlt: effrt u.p over 1f out: nvr nrr) | 1¾ | **6** | 4/1$^{2}$ | 42 | 4 |
| $64^{2}$ | **Distant Dynasty (59)** (BAPearce) **6-8-7**(7) TAshley(10) (s.i.s: r.o u.p fnl f: nvr nrr) | ¾ | **7** | 10/1 | 46 | 8 |
| $63^{10}$ | **Bajan Frontier (IRE) (49)** (FHLee) **4-8-4** NCarlisle(1) (led tl hdd over 1f out) | nk | **8** | 12/1 | 35 | — |
| $63^{6}$ | **Lord Sky (71)** (ABailey) **5-9-12b** RCochrane(3) (chsd ldrs over 3f: eased whn btn) | 2½ | **9** | 8/1 | 49 | 11 |
| | **Kalar (69)** (DWChapman) **7-9-10b** ACulhane(9) (mid div: hrd drvn ½-wy: wknd fnl 2f) | 4 | **10** | 14/1 | 35 | — |
| | **Crystal Loop (73)** (ABailey) **4-9-11**(3) DWright(4) (trckd ldrs: hrd rdn & lost pl whn broke leg & fell wl over 1f out: dead) | | **F** | 10/1 | — | — |

(SP 140.9%) **11 Rn**

**63.7 secs** (5.00) CSF £58.06 CT £384.36 TOTE £8.40: £2.10 £6.40 £2.30 (£54.40) Trio £73.00 OWNER Mr D. H. Bowring (EDWINSTOWE) BRED J. C. and Mrs C. L. Owen

T/Plpt: £18.50 (624.44 Tckts). T/Qdpt: £14.10 (48.41 Tckts). IM

# 0128-LINGFIELD (L-H) (Standard)

## Thursday January 25th

WEATHER: bitter

## 140 THATCHER LIMITED STKS (0-50) (4-Y.O+) (Class F)

1-40 (1-40) **1m 4f (Equitrack)** £2,836.60 (£797.60: £389.80) Stalls: Low GOING minus 0.31 sec per fur (FST)

| | Horse / details | Dist | Pos | SP | RR | SF |
|---|---|---|---|---|---|---|
| 104* | **Carrolls Marc (IRE) (40)** (CMurray) **8-9-4** JWeaver(6) (hdwy 4f out: led wl over 1f out: rdn out) | — | **1** | 7/2$^{2}$ | 61 | 43 |
| | **Hill Farm Dancer (48)** (WMBrisbourne) **5-8-6**(5) DGriffiths(5) (lw: hdwy over 3f out: rdn over 1f out: r.o wl) | ½ | **2** | 5/1$^{3}$ | 53 | 35 |
| $108^{6}$ | **Sassiver (USA) (33)** (PAKelleway) **6-9-2b** AClark(9) (hld up: led 3f out tl wl over 1f out: one pce) | 5 | **3** | 12/1 | 52 | 34 |
| $79^{6}$ | **Royal Print (IRE) (45)** (WRMuir) **7-9-2** Jean-PierreLopez(10) (rdn & hdwy over 3f out: one pce) | 3 | **4** | 20/1 | 48 | 30 |
| 116* | **Royal Circus (39)** (PRWebber) **7-8-11**(7) FLynch(3) (led 9f: wknd wl over 1f out) | ¾ | **5** | 3/1$^{1}$ | 49 | 31 |
| | **Endless Fantasy (45)** (CACyzer) **4-8-4**(3) JStack(11) (a.p: rdn over 3f out: wknd over 1f out) | 1 | **6** | 5/1$^{3}$ | 40 | 18 |
| | **Kentavrus Way (IRE) (27)** (AMoore) **5-9-2** CandyMorris(13) (b.hind: hdwy over 3f out: wknd over 2f out) | 2½ | **7** | 25/1 | 42 | 24 |
| | **Jady's Dream (IRE) (40)** (BPalling) **5-8-11** SDWilliams(12) (hld up: hrd rdn over 3f out: wknd wl over 1f out) | ¾ | **8** | 33/1 | 36 | 18 |
| | **See You Again (49)** (MBrittain) **4-8-12** RCochrane(8) (bhd fnl 2f) | 1 | **9** | 8/1 | 40 | 18 |
| $45^{8}$ | **Donia (USA) (48)** (JLHarris) **7-8-11v**[1] JFEgan(2) (chsd ldr 8f) | 2½ | **10** | 9/1 | 31 | 13 |
| $72^{7}$ | **Media Messenger (28)** (NPLittmoden) **7-8-9**(7) JBramhill(14) (a bhd) | 5 | **11** | 33/1 | 30 | 12 |
| | **Fair Attraction (31)** (JARToller) **4-8-12** MRimmer(4) (bhd fnl 7f) | 15 | **12** | 12/1 | 10 | — |
| $82^{10}$ | **Good so Fa (IRE) (35)** (CNAllen) **4-8-12v**[1] NAdams(7) (bhd fnl 5f) | 7 | **13** | 12/1 | — | — |
| $103^{5}$ | **Thunderous (43)** (JJBridger) **5-9-2b** JQuinn(1) (prom 7f) | 25 | **14** | 33/1 | — | — |

(SP 142.2%) **14 Rn**

**2m 35.22** (5.22) CSF £24.04 TOTE £4.60: £1.30 £1.80 £6.00 (£17.50) Trio £22.50 OWNER P I P Electrics Ltd (NEWMARKET) BRED John Connaughton
WEIGHT FOR AGE 4yo-4lb
STEWARDS' ENQUIRY Cochrane fined £100 (failure to ride to his draw).

## 141 GLADSTONE CLAIMING STKS (4-Y.O+) (Class E)

2-10 (2-13) **1m (Equitrack)** £3,117.50 (£944.00: £461.00: £219.50) Stalls: High GOING minus 0.31 sec per fur (FST)

| | Horse / details | Dist | Pos | SP | RR | SF |
|---|---|---|---|---|---|---|
| $61^{10}$ | **Second Colours (USA) (75)** (MrsMReveley) **6-9-3** JFortune(8) (hdwy 4f out: rdn 2f out: led nr fin) | — | **1** | 6/1$^{3}$ | 85 | 52 |
| $86^{3}$ | **Spencer's Revenge (78)** (MJRyan) **7-8-13** GBardwell(5) (lost pl over 5f out: rallied over 3f out: led & edged lft over 1f out: hrd rdn: hdd nr fin) | nk | **2** | 8/11$^{1}$ | 80 | 47 |
| $105^{2}$ | **Mr Nevermind (IRE) (76)** (GLMoore) **6-8-12**(7) ALakeman(6) (lw: hld up: shkn up fnl f: one pce) | 1¼ | **3** | 2/1$^{2}$ | 84 | 51 |
| $24^{3}$ | **Fresh Fruit Daily (63)** (PAKelleway) **4-8-12** RCochrane(1) (a.p: led over 3f out tl over 1f out: one pce) | ½ | **4** | 11/1 | 77 | 43 |
| $98^{6}$ | **Off the Air (IRE) (43)** (BJLlewellyn) **5-8-0v** NCarlisle(2) (a bhd) | 11 | **5** | 50/1 | 42 | 9 |
| | **White Heat (47)** (WGMTurner) **4-7-13**(5) CAdamson(3) (outpcd) | s.h | **6** | 50/1 | 47 | 13 |
| $53^{10}$ | **Burnt Sienna (IRE) (39)** (JSMoore) **4-7-9v**(5) MBaird(7) (prom 5f) | 2½ | **7** | 33/1 | 38 | 4 |
| $65^{10}$ | **Thorny Bishop (53)** (JJBridger) **5-8-3b** JQuinn(4) (led over 4f) | 14 | **8** | 50/1 | 12 | — |

(SP 122.7%) **8 Rn**

**1m 39.71** (2.31) CSF £11.16 TOTE £4.40: £1.30 £1.00 £1.60 (£3.70) OWNER Mr P. D. Savill (SALTBURN) BRED Dinnaken Farm in USA

## 142 MACMILLAN H'CAP (0-70) (3-Y.O) (Class E)

2-40 (2-42) **5f (Equitrack)** £3,163.95 (£957.60: £467.30: £222.15) Stalls: High GOING minus 0.31 sec per fur (FST)

| | Horse / details | Dist | Pos | SP | RR | SF |
|---|---|---|---|---|---|---|
| $32^{8}$ | **Chemcast (55)** (DNicholls) **3-8-10** AlexGreaves(1) (a.p: led over 2f out: r.o wl) | — | **1** | 7/2$^{3}$ | 68 | — |

| Form | Horse | Dist | Pos | SP | RR | SF |
|---|---|---|---|---|---|---|
| 78[4] | **Dancing Jack (55)** (JJBridger) **3-8-10** JQuinn(4) (lw: led over 2f: rdn: unable qckn) | 1½ | 2 | 8/1 | 63 | — |
| 131[2] | **Sunset Harbour (IRE) (56)** (DAWilson) **3-8-11** RCochrane(2) (w ldr: ev ch 2f out: one pce) | 1¾ | 3 | 3/1[2] | 59 | — |
| 10[3] | **Gi La High (59)** (JBerry) **3-9-0** AMcGlone(3) (s.i.s: hdwy over 3f out: rdn 2f out: one pce) | 1¾ | 4 | 8/1 | 56 | — |
| 78* | **Last But Not Least (60)** (RFJohnsonHoughton) **3-9-1** JWeaver(6) (prom over 2f) | 1½ | 5 | 6/4[1] | 52 | — |
| 63[9] | **Gagajulu (66)** (PDEvans) **3-9-7** JFortune(5) (bhd fnl 3f) | ½ | 6 | 8/1 | 57 | — |
| | **Double Or Bust (46)** (AGNewcombe) **3-7-10**(5) PFessey(7) (swtg: prom over 2f) | 3½ | 7 | 25/1 | 25 | — |

(SP 124.4%) **7 Rn**

**62.21 secs** (4.21) CSF £29.78 TOTE £3.40: £2.30 £3.40 (£50.80) OWNER Mr B. L. Cassidy (THIRSK) BRED C. R. and V. M. Withers

## 143 DISRAELI MAIDEN STKS (3-Y.O) (Class D)

3-10 (3-11) **7f (Equitrack)** £3,673.45 (£1,111.60: £542.30: £257.65) Stalls: Low GOING minus 0.31 sec per fur (FST)

| Form | Horse | Dist | Pos | SP | RR | SF |
|---|---|---|---|---|---|---|
| | **Double-O-Seven** (MJohnston) **3-9-0** JWeaver(5) (w'like: scope: hld up: rdn 3f out: led 2f out: rn green) | — | 1 | 4/1[3] | 68 | 25 |
| 67[4] | **Creeking** (SirMarkPrescott) **3-8-9** CNutter(2) (chsd ldrs: rdn 6f out: hmpd on ins 5f out: swtchd rt wl over 1f out: r.o wl ins fnl f) | nk | 2 | 11/4[2] | 62 | 19 |
| 81[2] | **Rawi (61)** (WRMuir) **3-9-0** Jean-PierreLopez(4) (led 5f: one pce) | 2½ | 3 | 4/6[1] | 62 | 19 |
| | **Northern Miracle (IRE)** (CFWall) **3-8-9** WLord(3) (bhd fnl 2f) | 10 | 4 | 20/1 | 34 | — |
| | **Allstars Dancer** (TJNaughton) **3-8-2**(7) TAshley(1) (hdwy over 4f out: ev ch 3f out: wknd over 2f out) | 1½ | 5 | 25/1 | 30 | — |

(SP 115.3%) **5 Rn**

**1m 28.11** (4.11) CSF £14.60 TOTE £3.80: £1.20 £1.60 (£5.90) OWNER Mr R. W. Huggins (MIDDLEHAM) BRED N. Abbott
STEWARDS' ENQUIRY Lopez susp. 3 & 5/2/96 (careless riding).

## 144 LLOYD GEORGE H'CAP (0-80) (4-Y.O+) (Class D)

3-40 (3-40) **7f (Equitrack)** £3,708.55 (£1,122.40: £547.70: £260.35) Stalls: Low GOING minus 0.31 sec per fur (FST)

| Form | Horse | Dist | Pos | SP | RR | SF |
|---|---|---|---|---|---|---|
| 121* | **Rakis (IRE) (78)** (MBrittain) **6-10-0** 6x RCochrane(3) (hld up: rdn wl over 1f out: led ins fnl f: r.o wl) | — | 1 | 4/6[1] | 85 | 61 |
| 121[13] | **Four of Spades (71)** (PDEvans) **5-9-7b** JFortune(4) (lw: chsd ldr: led wl over 1f out tl ins fnl f: unable qckn) | 1½ | 2 | 12/1 | 75 | 51 |
| 105[4] | **Perilous Plight (73)** (WRMuir) **5-9-9** JWeaver(6) (lw: hld up: rdn over 2f out: one pce) | 3½ | 3 | 4/1[2] | 69 | 45 |
| 55[3] | **Robo Magic (USA) (71)** (LMontagueHall) **4-9-7** JFEgan(2) (hld up: rdn over 2f out: wknd over 1f out) | 3 | 4 | 9/1[3] | 60 | 36 |
| | **Abtaal (78)** (RJHodges) **6-9-11**(3) SDrowne(1) (led over 5f) | nk | 5 | 20/1 | 66 | 42 |
| | **Prima Silk (74)** (MJRyan) **5-9-10** TIves(5) (bhd fnl 2f) | 1½ | 6 | 4/1[2] | 59 | 35 |

(SP 122.5%) **6 Rn**

**1m 26.11** (2.11) CSF £9.67 TOTE £1.60: £1.10 £3.30 (£8.90) OWNER Mr P. G. Shorrock (WARTHILL) BRED The Mount Coote Partnership

## 145 WILSON H'CAP (0-60) (4-Y.O+) (Class F)

4-10 (4-11) **1m 2f (Equitrack)** £2,977.00 (£837.00: £409.00) Stalls: Low GOING minus 0.31 sec per fur (FST)

| Form | Horse | Dist | Pos | SP | RR | SF |
|---|---|---|---|---|---|---|
| 122[7] | **Real Madrid (39)** (GPEnright) **5-8-8v** NAdams(10) (lw: a.p: led 5f out: clr over 1f out: drvn out) | — | 1 | 11/2 | 48 | 31 |
| | **Ultimate Warrior (55)** (CACyzer) **6-9-10** JWeaver(6) (rdn & hdwy over 3f out: chsd wnr wl over 1f out: r.o wl ins fnl f) | nk | 2 | 4/1[2] | 64 | 47 |
| 105[9] | **Zuno Flyer (USA) (36)** (AMoore) **4-8-3**ow2 MFenton(2) (b: b.hind: lost pl over 3f out: r.o one pce fnl f) | 3½ | 3 | 9/1 | 40 | 18 |
| 45[3] | **Lucky Tucky (44)** (JRJenkins) **5-8-13** JFortune(3) (led 5f: rdn over 3f out: one pce) | 2½ | 4 | 12/1 | 43 | 26 |
| 66[7] | **Ilandra (IRE) (55)** (SDow) **4-9-8** RCochrane(8) (nvr nr to chal) | 1¾ | 5 | 14/1 | 52 | 32 |
| 54[10] | **Hunza Story (29)** (NPLittmoden) **4-7-3**(7) JBramhill(11) (hdwy 5f out: wknd over 2f out) | s.h | 6 | 25/1 | 26 | 6 |
| 87[8] | **Canary Falcon (59)** (JohnBerry) **5-10-0** VSmith(4) (b: lw: hmpd 5f out: nt rcvr) | 1¾ | 7 | 12/1 | 52 | 35 |
| 27[3] | **Total Rach (IRE) (54)** (RIngram) **4-9-0b**(7) TAshley(12) (hdwy 6f out: wknd wl over 1f out) | nk | 8 | 11/4[1] | 48 | 28 |
| 33[13] | **Claque (51)** (DWChapman) **4-9-4** ACulhane(7) (prom tl wknd & hmpd 5f out) | nk | 9 | 33/1 | 44 | 24 |
| 27[6] | **Awesome Power (56)** (JWHills) **10-9-11** AClark(9) (prom 8f) | 1¼ | 10 | 12/1 | 46 | 29 |
| | **Lady Sabina (36)** (WJMusson) **6-8-2**(3) PMcCabe(5) (a bhd) | ½ | 11 | 9/2[3] | 26 | 9 |
| | **Princess Parrot (IRE) (44)** (LordHuntingdon) **5-8-6**(7) AimeeCook(1) (bhd fnl 4f) | 5 | 12 | 16/1 | 26 | 9 |
| 84[6] | **Scent of Power (35)** (NMBabbage) **6-8-4** FNorton(13) (b.nr hind: bhd fnl 5f: to whn virtually p.u fnl 3f) | dist | 13 | 33/1 | — | — |

(SP 135.6%) **13 Rn**

**2m 8.94** (4.64) CSF £29.54 CT £189.42 TOTE £6.30: £1.40 £2.40 £1.80 (£29.70) Trio £90.00 OWNER Mr Chris Wall (LEWES) BRED Chris Wall
LONG HANDICAP Hunza Story 7-8
WEIGHT FOR AGE 4yo-2lb
STEWARDS' ENQUIRY Ashley susp. 3 & 5/2/96 (careless riding).

T/Plpt: £267.30 (45.97 Tckts). T/Qdpt: £83.40 (15.52 Tckts). AK

# CAGNES-SUR-MER (Nice, France) (L-H) (Very Soft)
## Wednesday January 17th

## 146a PRIX DU CANNET (3-Y.O C & G)

2-03 (2-03) **1m 110y** £6,588.00

| Horse | Dist | Pos | SP | RR | SF |
|---|---|---|---|---|---|
| **Megaron (FR)** (MPimbonnet,France) **3-9-2** FBlondel | — | 1 | | 71 | — |
| **Tivolio (FR)** (LBoulard,France) **3-8-7** FSauret | nk | 2 | | 61 | — |
| **Danish Melody (IRE)** (RCollet,France) **3-8-7** WMongil | hd | 3 | | 61 | — |
| **Asking For Kings (IRE)** (SDow) **3-8-7** ESaint-Martin (btn over 10l) | | 13 | | — | — |

**17 Rn**

**1m 52.05** P-M 3.20F: 1.60F 9.50F 1.40F (242.50F) OWNER Mr L. Peyraud BRED Werner Wolf
**Asking For Kings (IRE)** broke well but when asked a question two furlongs from home, was unable to answer. He was not given a hard ride and will improve from the outing.

## 147a PRIX DE JUAN-LES-PINS (4-Y.O+)

2-31 (2-30) **1m** £7,246.00 (£3,623.00)

| Horse | Dist | Pos | SP | RR | SF |
|---|---|---|---|---|---|
| **Roi Ho (FR)** (J-CRouget,France) **5-8-12** PDumortier | — | 1 | | 90 | — |

| | | | SP | RR | SF |
|---|---|---|---|---|---|
| | **Wakeel (USA)** (SDow) **4-8-5** ESaint-Martin | nk **2** | | 82 | — |
| | **Mill Boy (FR)** (PKhozian,France) **7-8-12** GElorriaga-Santos | 3½ **3** | | 82 | — |

**15 Rn**

**1m 43.0** P-M 2.10F: 1.30F 3.90F 2.50F (27.60F) OWNER Mme M. de Chambure (PAU) BRED H. Rouillere & Therese Louveau in France
**Wakeel (USA)** put up a very spirited display on the very soft ground. Breaking well, he raced in mid-division and quickened nicely two furlongs from home. He was just not able to peg back the winner and only lost by a neck. He should be able to pick up a race here before long.

## 0146a-CAGNES-SUR-MER (Nice, France) (L-H) (Very Soft)
### Friday January 19th

### 148a PRIX DE TUNIS H'CAP (4-Y.O+)
2-31 (2-31) **1m** £7,905.00

| | | | SP | RR | SF |
|---|---|---|---|---|---|
| | **Spinario (USA)** (Jean-MarcCapitte,Belgium) **5-8-7** MBoutin | — **1** | | 68 | — |
| | **Cher Laskar (FR)** (MPimbonnet,France) **4-8-11** FBlondel | ½ **2** | | 71 | — |
| | **Master Fontenaille (FR)** (J-PGallorini,France) **6-8-9** TThulliez | 1 **3** | | 67 | — |
| | **Confronter** (SDow) **7-9-13** ESaint-Martin (btn approx. 6¼l) | **7** | | 75 | — |

**20 Rn**

**1m 44.8** P-M 13.90F: 3.80F 2.50F 1.90F (81.70F) OWNER Stal Cardona BRED G A Oldham
**Confronter** put up a fair performance but found the weight too much. Always in a prominent position and sixth into the straight, he was unable to quicken in the soft ground and ran on at one pace.

## 0148a-CAGNES-SUR-MER (Nice, France) (L-H) (Very Soft)
### Sunday January 21st

### 149a PRIX DES CAMELIAS (3-Y.O C & G)
1-22 (1-24) **1m** £5,270.00

| | | | SP | RR | SF |
|---|---|---|---|---|---|
| | **Mongol Warrior (USA)** (LordHuntingdon) **3-8-11** GGuignard | — **1** | | 87 | — |
| | **Fun Harbour (FR)** (J-CRouget,France) **3-8-11** PDumortier | 2½ **2** | | 82 | — |
| 146a[3] | **Danish Melody (IRE)** (RCollet,France) **3-8-11** ESaint-Martin | 2 **3** | | 78 | — |
| | **Daily Risk** (SDow) **3-8-11** CBrechon (btn approx. 8½l) | **6** | | 70 | — |

**19 Rn**

**1m 47.6** P-M 4.20F: 1.50F 1.50F 1.50F (16.60F) OWNER Mr Henryk De Kwiatkowski (WEST ILSLEY) BRED Kennelot Stables Limited
**Mongol Warrior (USA)** put up a very promising display to give Lord Huntingdon his first win of the season at the Riviera track. Racing in third and never far away from the leaders, he made his effort at the two furlong marker and hit the front one and a half furlongs out. He ran on well and never looked like being caught. He is well capable of winning more races.
**Daily Risk** just found the others too good on the day. Racing in fifth and with every chance when fourth turning for home, he was unable to quicken and ran on at one pace from one and a half furlongs out. He should improve on this performance.

### 150a PRIX FIROUZAN (3-Y.O F)
1-50 (1-55) **1m** £5,270.00

| | | | SP | RR | SF |
|---|---|---|---|---|---|
| | **Constance Do** (J-CRouget,France) **3-8-11** PDumortier | — **1** | | 78 | — |
| | **Fine Gachette (FR)** (J-PGauvin,France) **3-8-11** J-PGauvin | ½ **2** | | 77 | — |
| | **La Grande Ourse (FR)** (ASpanu,France) **3-8-11b[1]** MBoutin | 2½ **3** | | 72 | — |
| | **Western Sonata (IRE)** (LordHuntingdon) **3-8-7** GGuignard (btn approx. 9½l) | **6** | | 59 | — |

**20 Rn**

**1m 48.6** P-M 3.30F: 2.40F 4.60F 3.20F (62.30F) OWNER Mme A. Corcoral (PAU) BRED D. Muir
**Western Sonata (IRE)** tracked the leaders for most of the way, but when asked for an effort in the straight, found nothing on the very soft ground and gradually weakened from the furlong marker. She will have come on for the run but may prefer firmer ground.

### 151a PRIX CHARLES DU BREIL GENTLEMENS' (4-Y.O+)
3-14 (3-11) **1m** £3,953.00

| | | | SP | RR | SF |
|---|---|---|---|---|---|
| | **Bybus (FR)** (MmeARossio,France) **5-10-3** MrJ-CMonnin | — **1** | | 89 | — |
| | **Gold Delivery (USA)** (ELellouche,France) **5-10-12** MrHHalfon | 5 **2** | | 88 | — |
| | **Dusty Ocean (USA)** (FChappet,France) **5-10-3** MrRodCollet | hd **3** | | 79 | — |
| | **Country Lover** (LordHuntingdon) **5-10-3** MrTTrapenard (btn 6l) | **5** | | 77 | — |

**11 Rn**

**1m 47.2** P-M 1.60F: 1.40F 3.70F 3.00F (13.40F) OWNER Mme M. de Andreis BRED Herve de la Heronniere in France
**Country Lover** was always prominent in the early stages and was fifth entering the straight. When the pace hotted up, he was unable to respond but stayed on to finish not that far behind the second.

## 0122-SOUTHWELL (L-H) (Standard)
### Friday January 26th
No time taken Race 7 - bad snow storm.
WEATHER: sunny, cold & snow showers WIND: fresh half against

### 152 BALDERTON AMATEUR H'CAP (0-60) (I) (4-Y.O+) (Class F)
12-40 (12-40) **1m 4f (Fibresand)** £2,222.00 (£622.00: £302.00) Stalls: Low GOING: 0.06 sec per fur (STD)

| | | | SP | RR | SF |
|---|---|---|---|---|---|
| *116*[2] | **Gold Blade (60)** (JPearce) **7-12-0** MrsLPearce(9) (hld up: hdwy ½-wy: led over 2f out: pushed clr: eased towards fin) | — **1** | 13/8[1] | 73 | 27 |
| *113*[6] | **Modest Hope (USA) (48)** (BRichmond) **9-11-2** MrsDKettlewell(5) (lw: hld up: stdy hdwy 5f out: effrt over 2f out: kpt on same pce) | 6 **2** | 8/1 | 53 | 7 |

| Form | Horse | Pos | SP | RR | SF |
|---|---|---|---|---|---|
| 70[4] | **Tempering (51)** (DWChapman) **10-11-5** MissRClark(8) (led & sn clr: hdd over 2f out: wknd fnl f) 4 | 3 | 12/1 | 51 | 5 |
| | **Chantry Beath (51)** (CWThornton) **5-11-5** MrSSwiers(7) (trckd ldrs: effrt over 3f out: one pce) ¾ | 4 | 11/2 [2] | 50 | 4 |
| 85[4] | **Major Snugfit (40)** (MWEasterby) **4-10-4b** MrMRimell(4) (stdd s: hdwy ½-wy: sn chsng ldrs: effrt 3f out: sn wknd) 14 | 5 | 7/1 | 20 | — |
| 72[3] | **Comtec's Legend (40)** (JFBottomley) **6-10-8** MrsAFarrell(2) (b: chsd ldrs tl hmpd & lost pl over 5f out: n.d) 1 | 6 | 9/1 | 19 | — |
| 72[5] | **Phanan (27)** (REPeacock) **10-9-4b1(5)** MrsCPeacock(6) (chsd ldrs tl wknd over 4f out) 1¼ | 7 | 25/1 | 4 | — |
| 116[8] | **Father Dan (IRE) (60)** (MissGayKelleway) **7-12-0** MrJDurkan(3) (hmpd & lost pl 6f out: sn hrd rdn: kpt on fnl 3f: n.d) 8 | 8 | 6/1 [3] | 26 | — |
| 85[12] | **Nebrangus (IRE) (29)** (NBycroft) **4-9-2(5)** MrsCWilliams(10) (s.s: a bhd: t.o 5f out) 25 | 9 | 33/1 | — | — |
| | **Junction Twentytwo (41)** (CDBroad) **6-10-9** MrMDaly(1) (w ldrs: reminders after 1f: wknd qckly ½-wy: t.o) 4 | 10 | 20/1 | — | — |

(SP 120.6%) **10 Rn**

**2m 50.5** (18.00) CSF £14.92 CT £111.92 TOTE £2.40: £1.30 £1.40 £4.60 (£7.90) Trio £13.10 OWNER Mr Jeff Pearce (NEWMARKET) BRED Ballymacoll Stud Co

LONG HANDICAP Nebrangus (IRE) 9-1

WEIGHT FOR AGE 4yo-4lb

STEWARDS' ENQUIRY Pearce susp. 5-6/2/96 (careless riding).

## 153 LADBROKE ALL-WEATHER CHALLENGE SERIES H'CAP (Qualifier) (0-65) (I) (4-Y.O+) (Class F)

1-05 (1-07) **1m (Fibresand)** £2,471.20 (£693.20: £337.60) Stalls: Low GOING: 0.06 sec per fur (STD)

| Form | Horse | Pos | SP | RR | SF |
|---|---|---|---|---|---|
| 115* | **So Amazing (66)** (MissSEHall) **4-10-1** 6x JWeaver(7) (lw: w ldrs: led over 2f out: hld on wl towards fin) — | 1 | 9/4 [1] | 81 | 66 |
| 115[5] | **Sea God (44)** (MCChapman) **5-8-0(7)** CMunday(3) (s.i.s: sn drvn along & chsng ldrs: styd on wl appr fnl f: nt qckn nr fin) s.h | 2 | 12/1 | 58 | 44 |
| 115[3] | **Indiahra (48)** (RHollinshead) **5-8-4(7)** FLynch(4) (s.i.s: bhd: hdwy on outside over 2f out: styd on: nvr nr ldrs) 11 | 3 | 17/2 | 40 | 26 |
| | **Jalmaid (55)** (BAMcMahon) **4-8-13(5)** LNewton(8) (lw: trckd ldrs: effrt 3f out: one pce) 2 | 4 | 11/1 | 44 | 29 |
| 90[3] | **Komiamaite (54)** (SRBowring) **4-8-12v1(5)** CTeague(6) (reluctant to r: sn drvn along: bhd tl styd on fnl 2f) ¾ | 5 | 7/1 [3] | 41 | 26 |
| 77[3] | **Barrel of Hope (61)** (JLEyre) **4-9-10b** JFortune(1) (chsd ldrs: sn drvn along: hung rt over 2f out: n.d) 3½ | 6 | 3/1 [2] | 41 | 26 |
| 53[2] | **Bakers Daughter (52)** (JRArnold) **4-9-1** JQuinn(2) (in tch tl rdn & wknd 3f out) 5 | 7 | 7/1 [3] | 22 | 7 |
| 84[3] | **The Mestral (37)** (MJRyan) **4-7-9b(5)** MBaird(5) (led tl over 2f out: sn wknd) 5 | 8 | 20/1 | — | — |
| 77[9] | **Bogart (54)** (CWFairhurst) **5-9-3** RCochrane(10) (hld up & bhd: effrt over 3f out: sn wknd) 1 | 9 | 12/1 | 11 | — |
| | **Leedons Park (33)** (MWEasterby) **4-7-10b1** LCharnock(9) (in tch: rdn ½-wy: lost pl 3f out) 4 | 10 | 33/1 | — | — |

(SP 122.7%) **10 Rn**

**1m 45.1** (5.10) CSF £28.13 CT £185.69 TOTE £3.30: £2.00 £3.40 £1.90 (£53.10) Trio £63.90 OWNER Mr C. Platts (MIDDLEHAM) BRED C. Platts and Miss S. E. Hall

## 154 BALDERTON AMATEUR H'CAP (0-60) (II) (4-Y.O+) (Class F)

1-30 (1-30) **1m 4f (Fibresand)** £2,222.00 (£622.00: £302.00) Stalls: Low GOING: 0.06 sec per fur (STD)

| Form | Horse | Pos | SP | RR | SF |
|---|---|---|---|---|---|
| | **Greek Night Out (IRE) (33)** (JLEyre) **5-11-1** MissDianaJones(4) (in tch: hdwy to ld over 4f out: clr over 2f out: unchal) — | 1 | 8/1 | 52 | 15 |
| 70[2] | **Mr Moriarty (IRE) (36)** (SRBowring) **5-11-4** MrsMMorris(6) (lw: mde most tl over 4f out: kpt on: no ch w wnr) 9 | 2 | 5/2 [1] | 43 | 6 |
| 113[3] | **Record Lover (IRE) (23)** (MCChapman) **6-10-5** MrVLukaniuk(2) (chsd ldrs: rdn & one pce fnl 3f) s.h | 3 | 3/1 [2] | 30 | — |
| 85[3] | **Alpine Storm (IRE) (26)** (MDIUsher) **4-10-4** MrsAUsher(10) (hdwy ½-wy: sn chsng ldrs: wknd over 2f out) 2½ | 4 | 6/1 [3] | 30 | — |
| 90[6] | **Shotley Again (32)** (NBycroft) **6-11-0** MrsDKettlewell(7) (lw: chsd ldrs: hrd rdn & outpcd over 4f out: one pce) nk | 5 | 12/1 | 35 | — |
| 104[6] | **Sharp Thrill (41)** (BSmart) **5-11-9b** MissVMarshall(5) (bhd & pushed along: sme hdwy 4f out: wknd over 2f out: t.o) dist | 6 | 10/1 | — | — |
| | **Pontynyswen (43)** (DBurchell) **8-11-11b** MissEJJones(9) (sn chsng ldrs: drvn along 5f out: sn wknd: t.o) 14 | 7 | 8/1 | — | — |
| | **Pretty Scarce (27)** (BPreece) **5-10-4(5)** MissLBoswell(3) (s.i.s: a bhd: t.o 3f out) dist | 8 | 33/1 | — | — |
| | **Bitch (45)** (GPKelly) **4-11-9** MrMKneafsey(8) (sn bhd: t.o 4f out) dist | 9 | 33/1 | — | — |
| | **Streaky Hawk (USA) (50)** (JPearce) **4-12-0** MrsLPearce(1) (in tch tl wknd qckly 7f out: sn t.o: virtually p.u) dist | 10 | 7/1 | — | — |

(SP 125.2%) **10 Rn**

**2m 50.6** (18.10) CSF £28.66 CT £69.63 TOTE £5.10: £2.10 £1.10 £1.40 (£8.50) Trio £5.80 OWNER Sunpak Potatoes (HAMBLETON) BRED Airlie Stud

WEIGHT FOR AGE 4yo-4lb

STEWARDS' ENQUIRY Lukaniuk susp. 5-6/2/96 (excessive & incorrect use of whip).

**OFFICIAL EXPLANATION Streaky Hawk (USA): the jockey reported that the gelding felt wrong entering the straight and she had eased him.**

## 155 ANNESLEY LIMITED STKS (0-55) (4-Y.O+) (Class F)

2-00 (2-04) **6f (Fibresand)** £2,572.00 (£722.00: £352.00) Stalls: Low GOING: 0.06 sec per fur (STD)

| Form | Horse | Pos | SP | RR | SF |
|---|---|---|---|---|---|
| 71[2] | **Kira (54)** (JLEyre) **6-8-6** RLappin(1) (lw: mde virtually all: clr over 1f out: edgd rt: drvn out) — | 1 | 4/1 [2] | 60 | 23 |
| 88[5] | **Monis (IRE) (55)** (JBalding) **5-8-4v(7)** JEdmunds(15) (chsd ldrs: rdn & hung lft over 1f out: kpt on nr fin) 2½ | 2 | 12/1 | 58 | 21 |
| 36[2] | **Awasha (IRE) (54)** (MissGayKelleway) **4-8-8b1ow2** RCochrane(8) (lw: chsd ldrs: rdn & chsd wnr 2f out: sltly hmpd ins fnl f: kpt on same pce) hd | 3 | 5/2 [1] | 55 | 16 |
| | **Sweet Mate (55)** (SRBowring) **4-8-6b(5)** CTeague(10) (lw: bhd: hdwy on outside 2f out: styd on wl nr fin) ¾ | 4 | 8/1 | 56 | 19 |
| 26[5] | **Warm Hearted (USA) (55)** (AGNewcombe) **4-8-11** NGwilliams(14) (chsd ldrs: kpt on one pce whn sltly hmpd ins fnl f: eased nr fin) ½ | 5 | 10/1 | 55 | 18 |
| 107[10] | **Fiery Footsteps (43)** (SWCampion) **4-8-6** SDWilliams(7) (b.nr hind: nvr nr to chal) 3½ | 6 | 20/1 | 40 | 3 |
| 127[5] | **Dissentor (IRE) (53)** (JAGlover) **4-9-0v** JWeaver(5) (in tch: effrt over 2f out: kpt on: nvr able to chal) ¾ | 7 | 6/1 [3] | 46 | 9 |
| | **Panther (IRE) (48)** (JHetherton) **6-8-11** NKennedy(3) (bhd: styd on fnl 2f: nt rch ldrs) 1¼ | 8 | 14/1 | 40 | 3 |
| 107[7] | **Montague Dawson (IRE) (53)** (MrsNMacauley) **4-8-4(7)** IonaWands(12) (b.hind: in tch: rdn over 2f out: grad wknd) s.h | 9 | 12/1 | 40 | 3 |
| 115[9] | **Aquado (51)** (SRBowring) **7-8-11b** JQuinn(9) (bhd: sme hdwy 2f out: n.d) hd | 10 | 14/1 | 40 | 3 |
| 127[8] | **Most Uppitty (55)** (JBerry) **4-8-9** LeTolboll(4) (chsd ldrs: sn drvn along: lost pl 2f out) ½ | 11 | 16/1 | 36 | — |
| | **Tael of Silver (53)** (KRBurke) **4-8-6** TWilliams(13) (in tch tl lost pl 3f out) nk | 12 | 10/1 | 33 | — |
| 127[12] | **Grey Charmer (IRE) (46)** (CJames) **7-8-11v1** AMcGlone(11) (a bhd) 4 | 13 | 20/1 | 27 | — |
| 76[9] | **Fortis Pavior (IRE) (43)** (CWCElsey) **6-8-11b1** ACulhane(2) (a bhd) 2½ | 14 | 33/1 | 20 | — |
| 116[10] | **Legal Drama (USA) (48)** (PJMcBride) **4-8-4b1(7)ow5** GFaulkner(6) (s.i.s: a wl bhd) 2½ | 15 | 33/1 | 14 | — |

We're Joken (49) (SGollings) 4-8-6v[1] VHalliday(16) (chsd ldrs: c wd & lost pl 3f out: eased)....25 16 25/1 — —
(SP 146.0%) 16 Rn
1m 18.9 (5.40) CSF £56.64 TOTE £6.30: £2.60 £3.90 £1.30 (£56.90) Trio £61.60 OWNER Mr J. E. Wilson (HAMBLETON) BRED J. S. Bell

## 156 DANETHORPE MEDIAN AUCTION MAIDEN STKS (3-Y.O) (Class E)
2-30 (2-35) 1m (Fibresand) £3,074.60 (£930.80: £454.40: £216.20) Stalls: Low GOING: 0.06 sec per fur (STD)

| | Horse | | | SP | RR | SF |
|---|---|---|---|---|---|---|
| 58[6] | **Kingdom Princess** (MJCamacho) **3-8-9** LCharnock(6) (trckd ldrs: led over 2f out: pushed out: readily) | — | 1 | 14/1 | 60 | 19 |
| | **Green Gem (BEL) (58)** (SCWilliams) **3-8-9** JTate(5) (b.hind: hld up: hdwy on outside to chal 2f out: styd on same pce ins fnl f) | 1 | 2 | 9/1 | 58 | 17 |
| 123[2] | **Yeoman Oliver (60)** (BAMcMahon) **3-8-9**(5) LNewton(3) (led 1f: led & sddle slipped over 4f out: hdd over 2f out: nt qckn appr fnl f) | 2½ | 3 | 10/11 1 | 58 | 17 |
| | **Threesocks (74)** (BSmart) **3-8-9** RCochrane(2) (bit bkwd: v.unruly s: w ldrs tl wknd wl over 1f out) | 7 | 4 | 8/1 3 | 39 | — |
| 58[8] | **Bluntswood Hall** (RHollinshead) **3-9-0** MWigham(4) (s.s: outpcd & lost pl 3f out: sn bhd) | 10 | 5 | 14/1 | 24 | — |
| | **Belacqua (USA)** (DWChapman) **3-8-9** ACulhane(7) (s.s: hdwy to ld after 1f: hdd over 4f out: lost pl 3f out) | 4 | 6 | 25/1 | 11 | — |
| | **Mofasa** (WAO'Gorman) **3-9-0** TIves(1) (tall: bit bkwd: s.s: stumbled after 100y: hdwy to chse ldrs over 3f out: sn wl outpcd: wknd 2f out) | 2½ | 7 | 9/4 2 | 11 | — |

(SP 121.4%) 7 Rn
1m 48.1 (8.10) CSF £114.78 TOTE £11.70: £7.30 £4.00 (£52.70) OWNER G B Turnbull Ltd (MALTON) BRED Dr and Mrs St J. Collier

## 157 CARLTON-ON-TRENT H'CAP (0-80) (3-Y.O) (Class D)
3-00 (3-00) 7f (Fibresand) £3,708.55 (£1,122.40: £547.70: £260.35) Stalls: Low GOING: 0.06 sec per fur (STD)

| | Horse | | | SP | RR | SF |
|---|---|---|---|---|---|---|
| 102[5] | **Chilibang Bang (62)** (JBerry) **3-8-4**(7) PRoberts(4) (w ldrs: led over 3f out tl over 2f out: led ins fnl f: rdn out) | — | 1 | 8/1 | 66 | 23 |
| 112[2] | **Weetman's Weigh (IRE) (70)** (RHollinshead) **3-9-5** MWigham(3) (s.s: effrt over 2f out: hung rt: edgd lft & kpt on wl ins fnl f: nt rch wnr) | ½ | 2 | 9/4 1 | 73 | 30 |
| 81[3] | **Young Frederick (IRE) (60)** (KRBurke) **3-8-2**(7) TAshley(6) (a chsng ldrs: led over 2f out tl ins fnl f: one pce) | ¾ | 3 | 11/2 3 | 61 | 18 |
| 123[4] | **Foreman (57)** (WAO'Gorman) **3-8-6b**ow1 EmmaO'Gorman(7) (hld up: hdwy & ev ch 2f out: wknd ins fnl f) | 1¼ | 4 | 11/2 3 | 55 | 11 |
| 102* | **Briganoone (55)** (SRBowring) **3-8-4** 6x NCarlisle(5) (sn pushed along: outpcd 4f out: kpt on fnl 2f: n.d) | 1¼ | 5 | 3/1 2 | 50 | 7 |
| 68[4] | **Shontaine (72)** (MJohnston) **3-9-7** JWeaver(2) (led tl over 4f out: lost pl 3f out) | 6 | 6 | 8/1 | 54 | 11 |
| 131[4] | **Ghostly Apparition (55)** (JRUpson) **3-8-4** MFenton(1) (sn drvn along: sn chsng ldrs: led over 4f out tl over 3f out: wknd over 2f out) | ½ | 7 | 16/1 | 36 | — |

(SP 114.6%) 7 Rn
1m 33.6 (6.80) CSF £25.18 TOTE £13.10: £3.00 £2.40 (£20.00) OWNER Mr Ian Crawford (COCKERHAM) BRED G. W. Hampson

## 158 FACKLEY (S) STKS (3-Y.O) (Class F)
3-30 (3-30) 7f (Fibresand) £2,607.00 (£732.00: £357.00) Stalls: Low GOING: 0.06 sec per fur (STD)

| | Horse | | | SP | RR | SF |
|---|---|---|---|---|---|---|
| 49[3] | **Dragonjoy (56)** (JWPayne) **3-9-4b** AMcGlone(1) (mde virtually all: styd on u.p fnl f) | — | 1 | 11/2 | 60 | — |
| 49[2] | **Welsh Melody (52)** (KRBurke) **3-8-13v** TWilliams(8) (in tch: effrt 3f out: styd on fnl f: no ch w wnr) | 2 | 2 | 6/4 1 | 50 | — |
| 112[6] | **Down The Yard (44)** (MCChapman) **3-8-6**(7) CMunday(4) (a chsng ldrs: one pce fnl 2f) | 5 | 3 | 14/1 | 39 | — |
| 49[11] | **Napier Star (43)** (MrsNMacauley) **3-8-2**(5) CTeague(9) (in tch: styd on fnl f: nvr nr to chal) | s.h | 4 | 25/1 | 33 | — |
| 47[7] | **Loch Style (59)** (RHollinshead) **3-8-12** RCochrane(2) (trckd wnr tl wknd 2f out) | 1¾ | 5 | 7/2 2 | 34 | — |
| 10[6] | **Convent Guest (IRE)** (MRChannon) **3-8-2**(5) PPMurphy(6) (effrt over 2f out: nvr nr ldrs) | 3 | 6 | 5/1 3 | 22 | — |
| 89[5] | **Kratz (IRE) (43)** (BSRothwell) **3-8-12v** MFenton(5) (sn bhd) | 10 | 7 | 16/1 | 4 | — |
| 35[7] | **Ticka Ticka Timing (49)** (BWMurray) **3-9-1**(3) PMcCabe(10) (chsd ldrs tl wknd over 1f out) | ½ | 8 | 12/1 | 9 | — |
| 46[5] | **Hever Golf Diamond** (TJNaughton) **3-8-12** JWeaver(7) (a bhd) | 3 | 9 | 9/1 | — | — |
| 49[10] | **Adler (IRE)** (MJCamacho) **3-8-12b**[1] LCharnock(3) (a bhd) | ½ | 10 | 14/1 | — | — |

(SP 135.0%) 10 Rn
No Time Taken CSF £15.71 TOTE £4.10: £1.10 £2.00 £4.20 (£8.60) Trio £74.30 OWNER Mr T. H. Barma (NEWMARKET) BRED T. H. Barma
No bid

## 159 LADBROKE ALL-WEATHER CHALLENGE SERIES H'CAP (Qualifier) (0-65) (II) (4-Y.O+) (Class F)
4-00 (4-00) 1m (Fibresand) £2,471.20 (£693.20: £337.60) Stalls: Low GOING: 0.06 sec per fur (STD)

| | Horse | | | SP | RR | SF |
|---|---|---|---|---|---|---|
| 122* | **Kingchip Boy (52)** (MJRyan) **7-9-5v** 6x TIves(10) (mde all: pushed clr over 3f out: eased ins fnl f) | — | 1 | 4/5 1 | 72+ | 39 |
| | **Mislemani (IRE) (51)** (AGNewcombe) **6-8-13**(5) DGriffiths(9) (a chsng wnr: kpt on fnl 2f) | 6 | 2 | 11/2 2 | 59 | 26 |
| | **Pc's Cruiser (IRE) (50)** (JLEyre) **4-9-3** RLappin(8) (a chsng ldrs: one pce fnl 3f) | ¾ | 3 | 14/1 | 58 | 24 |
| 110[3] | **Our Robert (53)** (JGFitzGerald) **4-9-6** MWigham(5) (rr div: styd on fnl 2f: nvr nr ldrs) | ½ | 4 | 10/1 | 60 | 26 |
| 45[4] | **Genesis Four (41)** (SRBowring) **6-8-3v**[1](5) CTeague(1) (sltly hmpd & lost pl over 4f out: kpt on fnl 2f) | 1¼ | 5 | 6/1 3 | 44 | 11 |
| 43[6] | **Great Bear (57)** (DWChapman) **4-9-5**(5) PFessey(6) (chsd ldrs: hmpd & lost pl over 4f out: sn bhd) | 15 | 6 | 14/1 | 31 | — |
| 23[4] | **Dia Georgy (44)** (MrsNMacauley) **5-8-11** JQuinn(3) (b: sn bhd & pushed along) | nk | 7 | 12/1 | 16 | — |
| 124[10] | **Darika Lad (32)** (AHarrison) **8-7-13** LCharnock(2) (chsd ldrs tl wknd over 2f out) | 7 | 8 | 33/1 | — | — |
| | **Aconorace (54)** (RAFahey) **4-9-7** ACulhane(7) (trckd ldrs: n.m.r & lost pl over 4f out: sn bhd) | 10 | 9 | 25/1 | — | — |
| | **Lady Silk (50)** (MissJFCraze) **5-9-3** NKennedy(4) (reard & uns rdr s) | | U | 12/1 | — | — |

(SP 129.8%) 10 Rn
1m 46.9 (6.90) CSF £6.86 CT £40.98 TOTE £1.80: £1.10 £1.30 £5.50 (£6.40) Trio £29.50 OWNER Four Jays Racing Partnership (NEWMARKET) BRED R. M. Scott
T/Jkpt: Not won; £4,960.01 to Lingfield 27/1/96. T/Plpt: £385.70 (56.74 Tckts). T/Qdpt: £89.20 (56.2 Tckts). WG

# 0140-LINGFIELD (L-H) (Standard)
## Saturday January 27th

## 160 CRUSADER CLAIMING STKS (3-Y.O) (Class F)
1-40 (1-40) 5f (Equitrack) £2,735.80 (£768.80: £375.40) Stalls: High GOING minus 0.37 sec per fur (FST)

| | Horse | | | SP | RR | SF |
|---|---|---|---|---|---|---|
| 142* | **Chemcast (55)** (DNicholls) **3-9-3** RCochrane(1) (lw: w ldr: led wl over 1f out: hrd rdn: hdd nr fin: fin 2nd, 1l: awrdd r) | — | 1 | Evens 1 | 71 | 11 |

| | | | | SP | RR | SF |
|---|---|---|---|---|---|---|
| 78[3] | **Bouton d'Or (51)** (PHowling) **3-8-6** JQuinn(8) (led over 3f: one pce fnl f: fin 3rd, ½l: plcd 2nd) | | 2 | 14/1 | 58 | — |
| 101[3] | **Red Acuisle (IRE) (60)** (JBerry) **3-8-2b**(7) PRoberts(5) (hld up: bmpd 4f out: rdn over 1f out: one pce: fin 4th, 2½l: plcd 3rd) | | 3 | 7/1 | 53 | — |
| | **Born A Lady (71)** (NPLittmoden) **3-8-10** TGMcLaughlin(10) (lw: s.i.s: rdn thrght: chsd ldrs: one pce fnl 2f: fin 5th, 1l: plcd 4th) | | 4 | 6/1[2] | 51 | — |
| 78[5] | **Copper Bright (55)** (PCHaslam) **3-8-9b** JFortune(4) (lw: bdly hmpd 4f out: nt rcvr: fin 6th, hd: plcd 5th) | | 5 | 20/1 | 50+ | — |
| | **Supreme Illusion (AUS)** (JohnBerry) **3-8-4** MFenton(9) (unf: bit bkwd: hdwy over 3f out: wknd wl over 1f out) | 1¾ | 7 | 33/1 | 39 | — |
| 101[6] | **Impington (IRE) (51)** (WRMuir) **3-7-5v**[1](7) MartinDwyer(3) (b: hld up: bmpd 4f out: rdn 2f out: wknd over 1f out) | s.h | 8 | 6/1[2] | 33 | — |
| 101[7] | **Monkey Zanty (IRE) (59)** (JLHarris) **3-7-7**(5) PFessey(7) (hld up: rdn over 1f out: led nr fin: fin 1st: disq: plcd last) | | D | 13/2[3] | 55 | — |
| | | | | (SP 118.8%) | | **8 Rn** |

**61.48 secs** (3.48) CSF £14.97 TOTE £2.10: £1.10 £2.20 £1.90 (£8.10) Trio £17.40 OWNER Mr B. L. Cassidy (THIRSK) BRED C. R. and V. M. Withers

STEWARDS' ENQUIRY Fessey susp. 5-8/2/96 (careless riding).

## 161 CHIEFTAIN MEDIAN AUCTION MAIDEN STKS (3-Y.O) (Class E)

2-10 (2-13) **1m (Equitrack)** £3,031.70 (£917.60: £447.80: £212.90) Stalls: High GOING minus 0.37 sec per fur (FST)

| | | | | SP | RR | SF |
|---|---|---|---|---|---|---|
| 67[12] | **Tormount (USA)** (LordHuntingdon) **3-9-0** TIves(6) (hld up: chsd ldr 2f out: hrd rdn fnl f: led nr fin) | — | 1 | 9/1 | 68 | 35 |
| 67[6] | **Anak-Ku** (MissGayKelleway) **3-9-0** RCochrane(5) (led: clr over 1f out: hrd rdn: hdd nr fin) | hd | 2 | 6/1[3] | 68 | 35 |
| 102[2] | **Agent (70)** (JLEyre) **3-9-0** DeanMcKeown(2) (lw: plld hrd: hld up: chsd ldr over 4f out to 2f out: one pce) | 5 | 3 | 4/9[1] | 58 | 25 |
| 40[4] | **Highlights** (DMorris) **3-8-9** JTate(4) (lw: hld up: rdn over 3f out: one pce fnl 2f) | 1¼ | 4 | 5/1[2] | 50 | 17 |
| 118[10] | **Hever Golf Eagle** (TJNaughton) **3-8-7**(7) TAshley(1) (bhd fnl 4f) | 1¼ | 5 | 20/1 | 53 | 20 |
| 118[7] | **Mogin** (JFfitch-Heyes) **3-8-9** JFortune(3) (chsd ldr over 3f: wknd over 2f out) | 1¼ | 6 | 33/1 | 45 | 12 |
| | | | | (SP 117.9%) | | **6 Rn** |

**1m 40.62** (3.22) CSF £54.22 TOTE £5.70: £1.90 £3.20 (£21.70) OWNER Coriolan Partnership (WEST ILSLEY) BRED Caper Hill Farm Inc.

## 162 CHURCHILL CLAIMING STKS (4-Y.O+) (Class E)

2-45 (2-46) **1m 2f (Equitrack)** £3,131.80 (£948.40: £463.20: £220.60) Stalls: Low GOING minus 0.37 sec per fur (FST)

| | | | | SP | RR | SF |
|---|---|---|---|---|---|---|
| 105* | **Masnun (USA) (66)** (RJO'Sullivan) **11-8-9** AClark(2) (hld up: chsd ldr over 2f out: led over 1f out: pushed out) | — | 1 | 11/10[1] | 64+ | 38 |
| 105[5] | **Sweet Supposin (IRE) (76)** (CADwyer) **5-9-7v** CDwyer(7) (lw: hdwy over 4f out: led & edgd lft over 3f out: hdd over 1f out: r.o) | ½ | 2 | 9/2[3] | 75 | 49 |
| 57[9] | **Scottish Park (32)** (JLHarris) **7-7-12** JQuinn(5) (hld up: rdn over 4f out: r.o one pce fnl 2f) | 1¾ | 3 | 40/1 | 49 | 23 |
| | **Pine Essence (USA) (43)** (JLEyre) **5-7-10**(5) PFessey(3) (hdwy 8f out: rdn over 2f out: sn wknd) | 8 | 4 | 8/1 | 40 | 14 |
| | **Mandy's Bet (USA)** (NACallaghan) **4-8-2** JFEgan(9) (chsd ldr: rdn over 2f out: sn wknd) | 4 | 5 | 33/1 | 37 | 8 |
| 82[3] | **Gallic Victory (IRE) (60)** (JohnBerry) **5-9-1** MFenton(6) (led over 6f) | 2½ | 6 | 14/1 | 43 | 17 |
| 105[3] | **Hand of Straw (IRE) (64)** (PGMurphy) **4-8-7v**(3) SDrowne(1) (lw: bhd fnl 8f) | 1½ | 7 | 5/2[2] | 39 | 10 |
| | **Laser Light Lady** (NPLittmoden) **4-7-3**(7) JBramhill(4) (bhd fnl 5f) | 5 | 8 | 66/1 | 17 | — |
| | | | | (SP 119.0%) | | **8 Rn** |

**2m 7.6** (hand-timed) (3.30) CSF £6.73 TOTE £2.20: £1.10 £1.10 £3.70 (£5.40) Trio £27.90 OWNER Mr I. W. Page (WHITCOMBE) BRED Glencrest Farm

WEIGHT FOR AGE 4yo-2lb

## 163 COMET H'CAP (0-70) (4-Y.O+) (Class E)

3-20 (3-20) **6f (Equitrack)** £3,253.65 (£985.20: £481.10: £229.05) Stalls: Low GOING minus 0.37 sec per fur (FST)

| | | | | SP | RR | SF |
|---|---|---|---|---|---|---|
| 16[9] | **Lochon (51)** (JLEyre) **5-8-9** RLappin(12) (b: hdwy over 1f out: led wl ins fnl f: r.o wl) | — | 1 | 6/1[3] | 58 | 18 |
| 121[8] | **Invocation (67)** (AMoore) **9-9-11** JFEgan(2) (b.hind: chsd ldr: led over 2f out: edgd rt wl over 1f out: hdd wl ins fnl f: unable qckn) | 2 | 2 | 10/1 | 69 | 29 |
| 117[2] | **Ultra Beet (68)** (PCHaslam) **4-9-12v** JFortune(9) (outpcd: gd hdwy fnl f: fin wl) | nk | 3 | 3/1[1] | 69 | 29 |
| 107[4] | **Halbert (45)** (PBurgoyne) **7-8-0v**(3) PMcCabe(5) (lw: hld up: hrd rdn over 1f out: one pce) | 1½ | 4 | 8/1 | 42 | 2 |
| 53[8] | **Shaynes Domain (39)** (RMFlower) **5-7-6b**(5) CAdamson(8) (hdwy on ins over 1f out: nvr nrr) | 1¼ | 5 | 40/1 | 33 | — |
| | **Agwa (70)** (RJO'Sullivan) **7-10-0** DBiggs(11) (nvr nr to chal) | nk | 6 | 8/1 | 63 | 23 |
| 76[7] | **Jersey Belle (46)** (PJMakin) **4-8-4b** SSanders(10) (prom 4f) | s.h | 7 | 20/1 | 39 | — |
| 121[3] | **Fort Knox (IRE) (56)** (RMFlower) **5-9-0b** MTebbutt(4) (outpcd: nvr nrr) | ¾ | 8 | 3/1[1] | 47 | 7 |
| | **Pearl Dawn (IRE) (49)** (GLMoore) **6-8-7** SWhitworth(1) (led over 3f: 2nd & btn whn hmpd on ins wl over 1f out) | nk | 9 | 11/2[2] | 39 | — |
| | **Desert Water (IRE) (45)** (JJBridger) **4-8-3b** JQuinn(7) (sme hdwy over 2f out: wknd over 1f out) | nk | 10 | 33/1 | 34 | — |
| 55[10] | **Squire Corrie (65)** (GHarwood) **4-9-2b**(7) GayeHarwood(6) (prom 4f) | 6 | 11 | 12/1 | 38 | — |
| | | | | (SP 128.8%) | | **11 Rn** |

**1m 13.83** (3.23) CSF £63.07 CT £201.55 TOTE £11.10: £3.10 £2.50 £1.50 (£41.30) Trio £46.40 OWNER Mr J. Lynam (HAMBLETON) BRED M. and Mrs Young

STEWARDS' ENQUIRY Egan susp. 5-6/2/96 (careless riding).

## 164 CHALLENGER H'CAP (0-80) (3-Y.O) (Class D)

3-50 (3-51) **1m (Equitrack)** £3,673.45 (£1,111.60: £542.30: £257.65) Stalls: High GOING minus 0.37 sec per fur (FST)

| | | | | SP | RR | SF |
|---|---|---|---|---|---|---|
| 28* | **Banzhaf (USA) (77)** (GLMoore) **3-9-7** SWhitworth(4) (lw: mde all: qcknd 3f out: clr over 1f out: r.o wl) | — | 1 | 7/2[2] | 85 | 33 |
| 119* | **Distinct Beauty (IRE) (67)** (WAO'Gorman) **3-8-11** EmmaO'Gorman(1) (lw: chsd wnr: rdn 3f out: unable qckn) | 1¾ | 2 | 4/5[1] | 72 | 20 |
| 81* | **Sovereign Prince (IRE) (52)** (NACallaghan) **3-7-10** JQuinn(3) (hld up: rdn 3f out: one pce) | 3½ | 3 | 4/1[3] | 50 | — |
| | **To The Whire (59)** (GLMoore) **3-8-3** MFenton(2) (hld up: rdn 3f out: one pce) | ½ | 4 | 7/1 | 56 | 4 |
| | | | | (SP 110.3%) | | **4 Rn** |

**1m 41.53** (4.13) CSF £6.57 TOTE £5.30 (£3.40) OWNER Mr Bryan Pennick (EPSOM) BRED Pope McLean

LONG HANDICAP Sovereign Prince (IRE) 7-8

## 165 CENTURION H'CAP (0-70) (4-Y.O+ F & M) (Class E)

4-25 (4-27) **1m 4f (Equitrack)** £3,088.90 (£935.20: £456.60: £217.30) Stalls: Low GOING minus 0.37 sec per fur (FST)

| Form | Horse and details | Dist | Pos | SP | RR | SF |
|---|---|---|---|---|---|---|
| | **Sacred Mirror (IRE) (48)** (CEBrittain) **5-8-11** MLarsen(4) (bit bkwd: led 4f: led over 3f out: pushed out) | — | 1 | 10/1 | 58 | 27 |
| 80[5] | **Never So Rite (IRE) (48)** (DWPArbuthnot) **4-8-7**[ow2] RCochrane(6) (b.hind: hdwy over 4f out: chsd wnr over 2f out: unable qckn) | 1¾ | 2 | 7/2[2] | 56 | 19 |
| 108[2] | **Wild Strawberry (65)** (MissBSanders) **7-10-0** DBiggs(5) (a.p: rdn over 4f out: r.o ins fnl f) | hd | 3 | 10/11[1] | 73 | 42 |
| | **All the Joys (40)** (CACyzer) **5-8-3** JQuinn(2) (hld up: rdn over 3f out: one pce) | 2 | 4 | 6/1[3] | 45 | 14 |
| | **Uncharted Waters (45)** (CACyzer) **5-8-8** JFortune(1) (bit bkwd: bhd fnl 10f) | 5 | 5 | 14/1 | 43 | 12 |
| 37[6] | **Elly Fleetfoot (IRE) (53)** (BJMeehan) **4-8-5**[(7)] GHannon(3) (lw: hdwy over 4f out: rdn over 2f out: sn wknd) | 1¼ | 6 | 16/1 | 50 | 15 |
| 116[5] | **Swynford Flyer (33)** (JAHarris) **7-7-5**[(5)] CAdamson(7) (plld hrd: hdwy 10f out: led 8f out tl over 3f out: wknd over 2f out) | 4 | 7 | 8/1 | 24 | — |

(SP 121.6%) **7 Rn**

**2m 36.0** (6.00) CSF £44.11 TOTE £17.50: £5.20 £1.20 (£17.50) OWNER Mr C. E. Brittain (NEWMARKET) BRED Saeed Manana
LONG HANDICAP Swynford Flyer 7-9
WEIGHT FOR AGE 4yo-4lb

T/Jkpt: Not won; £23,268.19 to Southwell 29/1/96. T/Plpt: £520.20 (80.5 Tckts). T/Qdpt: £65.50 (133.88 Tckts). AK

# 0152-SOUTHWELL (L-H) (Standard)
## Monday January 29th

WEATHER: cloudy WIND: fresh half against

## 166 LONDONDERRY H'CAP (0-65) (I) (4-Y.O+ F & M) (Class F)

1-30 (1-30) **1m (Fibresand)** £2,048.00 (£573.00: £278.00) Stalls: Low

| Form | Horse and details | Dist | Pos | SP | RR | SF |
|---|---|---|---|---|---|---|
| 104[8] | **Cabcharge Blue (48)** (TJNaughton) **4-9-2** JWeaver(5) (lw: led 1f: led over 2f out: drvn out) | — | 1 | 11/1 | 58 | 34 |
| 122[6] | **Karinska (60)** (MCChapman) **6-9-11**[(3)] PMcCabe(2) (unruly: s.s: bhd tl hdwy 2f out: styd on ins fnl f: no ch w wnr) | 2 | 2 | 3/1[1] | 65 | 42 |
| 153[3] | **Indiahra (48)** (RHollinshead) **5-8-9v**[(7)] FLynch(9) (w ldrs: led over 4f out tl over 2f out: one pce) | ½ | 3 | 9/2[3] | 52 | 29 |
| | **David James' Girl (54)** (ABailey) **4-9-1**[(7)] AngelaGallimore(4) (sn chsng ldrs: drvn along ½-wy: sn outpcd: kpt on fnl f) | 1¾ | 4 | 9/1 | 56 | 32 |
| | **Shanghai Lil (44)** (MJFetherston-Godley) **4-8-12** JFortune(1) (chsd ldrs: outpcd 3f out: n.d) | 1½ | 5 | 14/1 | 43 | 19 |
| 66[10] | **Agoer (43)** (CEBrittain) **4-8-11** MLarsen(6) (b.hind: led after 1f tl over 4f out: rdn & lost pl over 2f out) | ½ | 6 | 10/1 | 41 | 17 |
| 62[4] | **Little Scarlett (50)** (PJMakin) **4-9-4** NCarlisle(8) (chsd ldrs: drvn along over 3f out: sn wl outpcd) | ½ | 7 | 9/2[3] | 47 | 23 |
| 84[2] | **Lilac Rain (46)** (JRArnold) **4-9-0b** CRutter(7) (b.nr fore: sn bhd & drvn along) | 6 | 8 | 4/1[2] | 31 | 7 |

(SP 115.5%) **8 Rn**

**1m 47.5** (7.50) CSF £41.48 CT £156.72 TOTE £17.30: £2.00 £1.60 £1.40 (£29.70) Trio £37.70 OWNER Mrs A. Wise (EPSOM) BRED Dullingham House Stud

## 167 FERMANAGH MEDIAN AUCTION MAIDEN STKS (3, 4 & 5-Y.O) (Class F)

2-00 (2-01) **7f (Fibresand)** £2,398.00 (£673.00: £328.00) Stalls: Low

| Form | Horse and details | Dist | Pos | SP | RR | SF |
|---|---|---|---|---|---|---|
| 110[2] | **Square Deal (FR) (67)** (SRBowring) **5-9-5**[(5)] CTeague(8) (a.p: led on bit 2f out: pushed clr ins fnl f) | — | 1 | 1/2[1] | 57 | 33 |
| 63[12] | **Margaretrose Anna (55)** (EJAlston) **4-9-5** JFortune(6) (led after 2f to 2f out: no ch w wnr) | 4 | 2 | 20/1 | 43 | 19 |
| 161[5] | **Hever Golf Eagle (51)** (TJNaughton) **3-7-13**[(7)] TAshley(5) (in tch: effrt over 3f out: kpt on: nvr nr to chal) | 3 | 3 | 12/1 | 41 | — |
| | **Mooncusser (60)** (JGFitzGerald) **3-7-13be**[(7)] FLynch(4) (sn chsng ldrs: one pce fnl 2f) | nk | 4 | 7/1[2] | 40 | — |
| 112[8] | **Madam Zando (38)** (JBalding) **3-8-1** TWilliams(3) (chsd ldrs: chal over 2f out: wknd over 1f out) | 3 | 5 | 20/1 | 29 | — |
| | **Rajah** (CWThornton) **3-8-6** DeanMcKeown(11) (cmpt: bit bkwd: sn drvn along: outpcd over 4f out: sn wknd & eased) | 7 | 6 | 14/1 | 18 | — |
| 50[8] | **Dr Caligari (IRE) (48)** (SGollings) **4-9-5b**[1][(5)] DGriffiths(10) (led 2f: chsd ldrs tl wknd 2f out) | 9 | 7 | 10/1[3] | — | — |
| | **Brafferton Bella** (JMJefferson) **4-9-5** SDWilliams(7) (s.i.s: sn wl bhd) | 3½ | 8 | 33/1 | — | — |
| | **Foothill (IRE)** (RTPhillips) **3-8-6** GCarter(9) (bkwd: b: s.i.s: sn bhd) | 11 | 9 | 14/1 | — | — |
| 45[9] | **Royal Dancer (32)** (RJWeaver) **4-8-12**[(7)] JDennis(1) (s.i.s: sme hdwy ½-wy: sn bhd) | 3 | 10 | 33/1 | — | — |

(SP 124.7%) **10 Rn**

**1m 34.1** (7.30) CSF £13.25 TOTE £1.60: £1.10 £4.50 £1.70 (£7.60) Trio £23.70 OWNER Mr Padraig Flanagan (EDWINSTOWE) BRED Crest Stud Ltd
WEIGHT FOR AGE 3yo-18lb

## 168 DOWN CLAIMING STKS (4-Y.O+) (Class F)

2-30 (2-30) **6f (Fibresand)** £2,398.00 (£673.00: £328.00) Stalls: Low

| Form | Horse and details | Dist | Pos | SP | RR | SF |
|---|---|---|---|---|---|---|
| 126[8] | **Bold Aristocrat (IRE) (41)** (RHollinshead) **5-7-13**[(7)ow1] FLynch(3) (led 3f out: edgd rt 2f out: drvn out) | — | 1 | 7/1[3] | 54 | 22 |
| 127[4] | **Awesome Venture (57)** (MCChapman) **6-8-6**[(3)] PMcCabe(4) (s.s: sn chsg ldrs: ev ch 2f out: styd on nr fin) | ½ | 2 | 7/4[1] | 56 | 25 |
| 126[7] | **Elton Ledger (IRE) (67)** (MrsNMacauley) **7-8-9v** JTate(1) (b: s.i.s: hdwy to chse ldrs ½-wy: sn hrd rdn: nt qckn fnl 2f) | ¾ | 3 | 9/2[2] | 54 | 23 |
| 126[9] | **Legatee (53)** (AStreeter) **5-8-0** FNorton(5) (w ldr tl hung lft & lost pl over 2f out) | 3½ | 4 | 10/1 | 35 | 4 |
| 121[14] | **At the Savoy (IRE) (59)** (TDBarron) **5-8-7b** JFortune(2) (led to 3f out: wknd over 1f out: b.b.v) | 1¾ | 5 | 7/4[1] | 38 | 7 |

(SP 112.5%) **5 Rn**

**1m 19.2** (5.70) CSF £18.77 TOTE £9.20: £2.40 £1.10 (£9.30) OWNER Mrs J. Hughes (UPPER LONGDON) BRED Scarteen Stud
STEWARDS' ENQUIRY Tate susp. 7-8/2/96 (excessive use of whip).

## 169 ANTRIM H'CAP (0-70) (4-Y.O+) (Class E)

3-00 (3-01) **2m (Fibresand)** £2,995.65 (£907.20: £443.10: £211.05) Stalls: Low

| Form | Horse and details | Dist | Pos | SP | RR | SF |
|---|---|---|---|---|---|---|
| 60[3] | **Badawi (FR) (37)** (NMBabbage) **6-7-10** JQuinn(6) (led 10f out: clr 4f out: unchal) | — | 1 | 6/1[3] | 54 | — |
| | **Upper Mount Clair (48)** (CEBrittain) **6-8-7** MLarsen(13) (hld up: hdwy 6f out: chsd wnr fnl 2f: no imp) | 11 | 2 | 11/2[2] | 54 | — |
| 130[4] | **Mizyan (IRE) (69)** (JEBanks) **8-9-11**[(3)] JStack(10) (chsd ldrs: reminders 9f out: one pce) | 4 | 3 | 13/2 | 71 | — |

73* **Eulogy (FR) (64)** (KRBurke) **9-9-2**(7) TAshley(7) (hdwy u.p 6f out: nvr nr ldrs) ....7 **4** 10/1 59 —
33$^{6}$ **Tremendisto (42)** (CaptJHWilson) **6-8-1** CRutter(12) (chsd ldrs: rdn 6f out: wknd over 2f out) ....nk **5** 12/1 37 —
103$^{4}$ **Golden Punch (USA) (39)** (CACyzer) **5-7-12v** NAdams(2) (s.i.s: sn chsng ldrs: rdn ½-wy: wknd 3f out) ....½ **6** 20/1 33 —
**La Menorquina (USA) (43)** (DMarks) **6-8-2** JFanning(4) (sn bhd & pushed along: n.d) ....1¾ **7** 5/1 1 35 —
**Pride of May (IRE) (53)** (CWFairhurst) **5-8-12v** DeanMcKeown(8) (b.nr fore: mid div: drvn 6f out: sn wknd) ....5 **8** 11/1 40 —
97$^{2}$ **Milngavie (IRE) (37)** (MJohnston) **6-7-10b** TWilliams(9) (led 6f: wknd qckly 5f out: eased) ....5 **9** 13/2 19 —
85$^{8}$ **Thatcher's Era (IRE) (55)** (TDBarron) **4-8-7**ow2 JFortune(11) (bhd: hdwy u.p 6f out: sn wknd) ....4 **10** 10/1 33 —
85$^{6}$ **Anchorena (54)** (JAHarris) **4-7-13**(7) DSweeney(5) (trckd ldrs tl lost pl 6f out) ....2 **11** 16/1 30 —
113$^{8}$ **Cross Talk (IRE) (63)** (RHollinshead) **4-9-1** TIves(3) (bhd: hdwy u.p 7f out: sn wknd) ....5 **12** 16/1 34 —
**Nordic Sun (IRE) (67)** (LRLloyd-James) **8-9-12** JWeaver(1) (b.hind: hld up & a bhd) ....nk **13** 16/1 38 —
(SP 129.6%) **13 Rn**

**3m 50.2** (24.20) CSF £39.19 CT £210.51 TOTE £5.90: £2.10 £3.20 £1.70 (£19.80) Trio £43.20 OWNER Mr Glyn Harris (CHELTENHAM) BRED Buckram Oak Holdings
WEIGHT FOR AGE 4yo-7lb

## 170 ARMAGH H'CAP (0-80) (4-Y.O+) (Class D)
3-30 (3-32) **6f (Fibresand)** £3,452.50 (£1,045.00: £510.00: £242.50) Stalls: Low

SP RR SF
71$^{3}$ **Stand Tall (55)** (CWThornton) **4-8-5** DeanMcKeown(2) (trckd ldrs: drvn along ½-wy: led over 1f out: hrd rdn & hld on wl) ....— **1** 3/1 1 60 25
50* **White Sorrel (74)** (AHarrison) **5-9-7**(3) JStack(1) (in tch: effrt 2f out: sn chsng ldrs: nt qckn fnl f) ....¾ **2** 5/1 2 77 42
117* **Milos (71)** (TJNaughton) **5-9-0**(7) TAshley(6) (s.i.s: bhd: hdwy on outside over 2f out: styd on wl fnl f) ....hd **3** 11/2 3 74 39
88$^{3}$ **Cretan Gift (78)** (NPLittmoden) **5-10-0v** TGMcLaughlin(4) (s.i.s: bhd: effrt & hung rt over 2f out: styd on fnl f) ....s.h **4** 6/1 81 46
139$^{4}$ **Southern Dominion (59)** (MJohnston) **4-8-9** JWeaver(9) (led over 1f: chsd ldrs tl wknd over 1f out) ....6 **5** 11/2 3 46 11
120$^{9}$ **Tafahhus (60)** (MJPolglase) **4-8-10v**1 MFenton(5) (led over 4f out tl over 1f out: wknd) ....½ **6** 16/1 45 10
127$^{2}$ **Encore M'Lady (IRE) (69)** (FHLee) **5-9-5b** TIves(8) (chsd ldrs tl wknd qckly wl over 1f out) ....3 **7** 11/2 3 46 11
88$^{9}$ **Leigh Crofter (76)** (PDCundell) **7-9-7b**(5) DGriffiths(3) (chsd ldrs 2f: sn wl outpcd) ....½ **8** 12/1 52 17
155$^{16}$ **We're Joken (49)** (SGollings) **4-7-13b**1 JQuinn(7) (bhd fr ½-wy: t.o) ....30 **9** 33/1 — —
(SP 118.6%) **9 Rn**

**1m 18.9** (5.40) CSF £17.68 CT £71.87 TOTE £4.10: £2.20 £2.80 £2.70 (£12.30) Trio £15.90 OWNER Mr Guy Reed (MIDDLEHAM) BRED Mrs E. Longton
STEWARDS' ENQUIRY McKeown susp. 7-9/2/96 (excessive use of whip).

## 171 TYRONE (S) H'CAP (Qualifier) (0-60) (3-Y.O) (Class F)
4-00 (4-00) **1m (Fibresand)** £2,398.00 (£673.00: £328.00) Stalls: Low

SP RR SF
**Bailiwick (48)** (NAGraham) **3-8-9b**1 MFenton(5) (led after 1f: clr 2f out: jst hld on) ....— **1** 8/1 54 16
46$^{4}$ **Bumblefoot (IRE) (53)** (MJohnston) **3-9-0** JWeaver(2) (trckd ldrs: effrt 2f out: styd on u.p fnl f) ....hd **2** 4/1 1 59 21
123$^{5}$ **Efipetite (45)** (NBycroft) **3-8-6** JQuinn(7) (trckd ldrs: effrt over 2f out: one pce appr fnl f) ....1½ **3** 7/1 3 48 10
**Sporting Fantasy (49)** (JBalding) **3-8-3**(7) JEdmunds(4) (in tch: outpcd ½-wy: hdwy 2f out: hung lft: nvr nr ldrs) ....4 **4** 20/1 44 6
**Snow Domino (IRE) (55)** (JMJefferson) **3-9-2** JFortune(6) (led 1f: chsd ldrs: one pce fnl 2f) ....3 **5** 14/1 44 6
89$^{4}$ **Be My Bird (50)** (WJMusson) **3-8-8**(3) PMcCabe(1) (sn bhd: styd on fnl 2f: nvr nr ldrs) ....½ **6** 9/2 2 38 —
123$^{7}$ **Cocoon (IRE) (48)** (CWThornton) **3-8-9** DeanMcKeown(3) (trckd ldrs: effrt over 2f out: grad wknd) ....10 **7** 9/2 2 16 —
25$^{7}$ **Naked Emperor (45)** (MJFetherston-Godley) **3-8-6v**1 CRutter(9) (chsd ldrs tl lost pl over 2f out) ....d.h **7** 12/1 13 —
25$^{6}$ **Domettes (IRE) (60)** (RHannon) **3-9-0**(7) MarkDenaro(8) (sn bhd & drvn along) ....2½ **9** 4/1 1 23 —
(SP 119.1%) **9 Rn**

**1m 48.7** (8.70) CSF £38.22 CT £216.83 TOTE £11.60: £2.90 £1.40 £1.90 (£20.30) Trio £53.40 OWNER Mrs Lesley Graham (NEWMARKET) BRED Elsdon Farms
No bid

## 172 LONDONDERRY H'CAP (0-65) (II) (4-Y.O+ F & M) (Class F)
4-30 (4-30) **1m (Fibresand)** £2,048.00 (£573.00: £278.00) Stalls: Low

SP RR SF
122$^{5}$ **Irchester Lass (44)** (SRBowring) **4-8-9v**1(5) CTeague(3) (hdwy on outside over 2f out: chal 1f out: wandered: led post) ....— **1** 9/2 2 51 25
153$^{8}$ **The Mestral (37)** (MJRyan) **4-8-7** PBloomfield(2) (chsd ldrs: led 2f out: hdd post) ....s.h **2** 10/1 44 18
86$^{4}$ **Moody (53)** (MissGayKelleway) **4-9-9** MFenton(8) (lw: b.hind: chsd ldrs: effrt 2f out: hung lft: one pce) ....6 **3** 5/1 3 48 22
124$^{7}$ **Mill Dancer (IRE) (43)** (EJAlston) **4-8-13** SDWilliams(7) (chsd ldrs tl lost pl over 2f out: styd on again nr fin) ....5 **4** 7/2 1 28 2
**By The Bay (47)** (CCElsey) **4-9-3** MTebbutt(1) (sn bhd: sme hdwy over 2f out: sn wknd) ....hd **5** 13/2 32 6
127$^{14}$ **Double Glow (36)** (NBycroft) **4-8-6** GBardwell(6) (led to 2f out: sn wknd) ....8 **6** 33/1 5 —
**Me Cherokee (54)** (CWThornton) **4-9-10** DeanMcKeown(4) (bit bkwd: s.i.s: a bhd) ....5 **7** 13/2 13 —
**Gentle Irony (53)** (WJMusson) **4-9-9b** TIves(5) (plld hrd: trckd ldrs: effrt over 2f out: sn wknd) ....11 **8** 5/1 3 — —
77$^{11}$ **Samana Cay (48)** (PSFelgate) **4-9-4** JTate(9) (s.i.s: a bhd & sn drvn along) ....1¼ **9** 20/1 — —
(SP 117.2%) **9 Rn**

**1m 48.23** (8.23) CSF £43.40 CT £211.60 TOTE £6.60: £2.10 £4.30 £3.00 (£21.70) Trio £20.50 OWNER South Forest Racing (EDWINSTOWE) BRED R. Hacker

T/Jkpt: Not won; £39,312.68 to Lingfield 30/01/96. T/Plpt: £62.60 (307.85 Tckts). T/Qdpt: £19.50 (193.83 Tckts) WG

# 0160-LINGFIELD (L-H) (Standard)
## Tuesday January 30th

## 173 LANDAU H'CAP (0-80) (3-Y.O+) (Class D)
1-40 (1-41) **5f (Equitrack)** £3,420.00 (£1,035.00: £505.00: £240.00) Stalls: High GOING minus 0.44 sec per fur (FST)

SP RR SF
**Hever Golf Star (73)** (TJNaughton) **4-9-10** JWeaver(6) (mde virtually all: qcknd over 1f out: all out) ....— **1** 7/4 1 79 28

| | Horse / details | Dist | Pos | SP | RR | SF |
|---|---|---|---|---|---|---|
| 55[7] | **Spender (77)** (PWHarris) **7-9-11**(3) JStack(4) (gd hdwy fnl f: fin wl) | s.h | 2 | 9/2[3] | 83 | 32 |
| | **Half Tone (64)** (RMFlower) **4-9-1b** DBiggs(3) (outpcd: gd hdwy fnl f: fin wl) | hd | 3 | 6/1 | 70 | 19 |
| 16* | **Super Rocky (67)** (RBastiman) **7-8-13**(5) HBastiman(1) (hld up: hrd rdn over 1f out: one pce) | 2 | 4 | 9/4[2] | 66 | 15 |
| 117[7] | **Hannah's Usher (75)** (CMurray) **4-9-12b** MTebbutt(5) (chsd wnr over 3f out: ev ch wl over 1f out: wknd fnl f) | 1½ | 5 | 11/1 | 69 | 18 |
| 139[7] | **Distant Dynasty (59)** (BAPearce) **6-8-10** SSanders(7) (b.hind: prom over 3f) | 1¾ | 6 | 12/1 | 48 | — |

(SP 115.6%) **6 Rn**

**60.47 secs** (2.47) CSF £9.68 TOTE £2.50: £1.10 £3.80 (£9.60) OWNER Hever Racing Club I (EPSOM) BRED Mrs L. Popely

## 174 DOG CART CLAIMING STKS (4-Y.O+) (Class E)

2-10 (2-10) **1m** **(Equitrack)** £2,859.15 (£865.20: £422.10: £200.55) Stalls: High GOING minus 0.44 sec per fur (FST)

| | Horse / details | Dist | Pos | SP | RR | SF |
|---|---|---|---|---|---|---|
| 13[6] | **Dancing Lawyer (78)** (BJMeehan) **5-9-5** JWeaver(1) (a.p: led 3f out: clr over 1f out: drvn out) | — | 1 | 5/2[3] | 87 | 58 |
| 141[2] | **Spencer's Revenge (76)** (MJRyan) **7-9-1** GBardwell(2) (rdn thrght: hdwy over 2f out: chsd wnr over 1f out: r.o wl) | ¾ | 2 | 2/1[2] | 82 | 53 |
| 141[3] | **Mr Nevermind (IRE) (76)** (GLMoore) **6-9-5** SWhitworth(3) (hld up: chsd wnr over 2f out tl over 1f out: one pce) | 3½ | 3 | 13/8[1] | 79 | 50 |
| 114[5] | **Eastleigh (48)** (RHollinshead) **7-8-9v** GCarter(7) (b.off hind: chsd ldr 7f out tl over 3f out: wknd over 2f out) | 7 | 4 | 16/1 | 55 | 26 |
| | **What a Nightmare (IRE) (67)** (PHowling) **4-9-3b** JQuinn(4) (led 5f) | 2½ | 5 | 20/1 | 59 | 29 |
| | **Elusive Star** (JWhite) **6-8-7**(3) SDrowne(6) (s.s: a bhd) | 5 | 6 | 66/1 | 41 | 12 |
| | **Cannizaro (IRE) (59)** (RJRWilliams) **4-8-6** DBiggs(8) (b: bit bkwd: a bhd) | 4 | 7 | 16/1 | 30 | — |
| 117[13] | **Lonely Vigil (FR)** (KOCunningham-Brown) **4-8-10** AClark(5) (Withdrawn not under Starter's orders: lame) | | W | 50/1 | — | — |

(SP 120.0%) **7 Rn**

**1m 38.28** (0.88) CSF £7.97 TOTE £3.30: £1.50 £2.50 (£4.00) OWNER Vintage Services Ltd (UPPER LAMBOURN) BRED Vintage Services Ltd
Spencer's Revenge clmd MHemmings £8,000

## 175 SULKY MAIDEN STKS (3-Y.O+) (Class D)

2-40 (2-40) **1m 2f** **(Equitrack)** £3,598.75 (£1,090.00: £532.50: £253.75) Stalls: Low GOING minus 0.44 sec per fur (FST)

| | Horse / details | Dist | Pos | SP | RR | SF |
|---|---|---|---|---|---|---|
| | **Diego (88)** (CEBrittain) **3-8-4**ow1 MLarsen(6) (hld up: chsd ldr over 2f out: rdn over 1f out: led wl ins fnl f: r.o wl) | — | 1 | 4/5[1] | 71 | 25 |
| 119[2] | **Bath Knight (64)** (DJSffrenchDavis) **3-8-3** GCarter(4) (led over 1f: led 4f out: clr 2f out: hdd wl ins fnl f: unable qckn) | ¾ | 2 | 6/1[3] | 69 | 24 |
| | **Barbason** (AMoore) **4-9-10** CandyMorris(1) (b.hind: bit bkwd: led over 8f out to 4f out: wknd over 2f out) | 14 | 3 | 40/1 | 47 | 22 |
| 79[11] | **Taniyar (FR)** (RHollinshead) **4-9-10** TIves(2) (rdn & no hdwy fnl 4f) | 3 | 4 | 14/1 | 43 | 18 |
| | **Boyfriend** (DRCElsworth) **6-9-9**(3) AProcter(5) (bkwd: nvr nr to chal) | 3 | 5 | 16/1 | 37 | 15 |
| 79[9] | **Double Jeopardy (60)** (JWhite) **5-9-12b**[1] MTebbutt(9) (b.off hind: prom 5f) | 13 | 6 | 20/1 | 16 | — |
| 125[6] | **Lady Elizabeth (FR)** (KOCunningham-Brown) **4-9-5** SWhitworth(7) (hdwy over 4f out: wknd over 3f out) | 10 | 7 | 40/1 | — | — |
| 67[3] | **Love Bird (IRE) (72)** (MJohnston) **3-8-3** TWilliams(3) (s.i.s: a bhd: lame) | 5 | 8 | 9/4[2] | — | — |
| | **Full of Tricks** (JJBridger) **8-9-12** JQuinn(8) (a bhd) | 9 | 9 | 66/1 | — | — |

(SP 124.3%) **9 Rn**

**2m 7.94** (3.64) CSF £6.90 TOTE £2.40: £1.30 £1.10 £7.90 (£4.20) Trio £56.30 OWNER Mr C. E. Brittain (NEWMARKET) BRED T. R. Lock
WEIGHT FOR AGE 3yo-23lb, 4yo-2lb

## 176 CAROLE BLACKBURN H'CAP (0-70) (3-Y.O) (Class E)

3-10 (3-11) **1m 2f** **(Equitrack)** £2,927.40 (£886.20: £432.60: £205.80) Stalls: Low GOING minus 0.44 sec per fur (FST)

| | Horse / details | Dist | Pos | SP | RR | SF |
|---|---|---|---|---|---|---|
| 56[3] | **Thorntoun Estate (IRE) (57)** (MJohnston) **3-8-10** DeanMcKeown(3) (mde all: all out) | — | 1 | 11/4[1] | 64 | 27 |
| 67[9] | **Lord Ellangowan (IRE) (43)** (RIngram) **3-7-5**(5) MBaird(6) (chsd wnr 9f out: ev ch fnl 3f: r.o) | hd | 2 | 50/1 | 50 | 13 |
| 164[3] | **Sovereign Prince (IRE) (50)** (NACallaghan) **3-8-3** JQuinn(4) (a.p: ev ch fnl 3f: r.o) | s.h | 3 | 8/1 | 57 | 20 |
| 137* | **China Castle (73)** (PCHaslam) **3-9-12** 5x JFortune(7) (rdn & hdwy over 3f out: r.o wl ins fnl f) | ½ | 4 | 3/1[2] | 79 | 42 |
| | **Flahuil (53)** (RHannon) **3-8-6** GCarter(9) (nvr nr to chal) | 7 | 5 | 12/1 | 48 | 11 |
| 164[2] | **Distinct Beauty (IRE) (67)** (WAO'Gorman) **3-9-6b** EmmaO'Gorman(2) (lw: hdwy over 3f out: wknd over 2f out) | 3½ | 6 | 3/1[2] | 56 | 19 |
| 119[4] | **Hotlips Houlihan (56)** (RJRWilliams) **3-8-9** DBiggs(5) (plld hrd: hld up: rdn over 4f out: wknd over 2f out) | 3 | 7 | 16/1 | 40 | 3 |
| | **Uoni (57)** (CEBrittain) **3-8-10** MLarsen(10) (prom over 6f) | 1¼ | 8 | 7/1[3] | 39 | 2 |
| | **Signs R Us (IRE) (43)** (DrJDScargill) **3-7-10** NAdams(1) (bhd fnl 5f) | 12 | 9 | 50/1 | 6 | — |
| 56[11] | **Tartan Express (IRE) (43)** (BAPearce) **3-7-10** GBardwell(8) (prom over 4f) | 5 | 10 | 66/1 | — | — |

(SP 119.3%) **10 Rn**

**2m 8.45** (4.15) CSF £90.47 CT £910.38 TOTE £4.20: £1.10 £8.80 £2.40 (£659.80) Trio £324.80; £324.84 to Wolverhampton 31/1/96 OWNER Mr W. M. Johnstone (MIDDLEHAM) BRED Mrs Agnes Johnstone
LONG HANDICAP Lord Ellangowan (IRE) 7-7 Signs R Us (IRE) 7-7 Tartan Express (IRE) 7-3
STEWARDS' ENQUIRY McKeown susp. 10 & 12-13/2/96 (excessive use of whip).

## 177 HANSOM LIMITED STKS (0-70) (3-Y.O+) (Class E)

3-40 (3-41) **7f** **(Equitrack)** £2,900.10 (£877.80: £428.40: £203.70) Stalls: Low GOING minus 0.44 sec per fur (FST)

| | Horse / details | Dist | Pos | SP | RR | SF |
|---|---|---|---|---|---|---|
| | **Present Situation (69)** (LordHuntingdon) **5-9-0**(7) AimeeCook(5) (hld up: led 1f out: rdn out) | — | 1 | 11/2[3] | 75 | 38 |
| 121[2] | **Hawaii Storm (FR) (68)** (DJSffrenchDavis) **8-9-5**(5) CAdamson(2) (s.s: hdwy over 3f out: rdn over 2f out: r.o wl ins fnl f) | 1 | 2 | 9/1 | 76 | 39 |
| 121[11] | **Crystal Heights (FR) (70)** (RJO'Sullivan) **8-9-10** AClark(8) (lw: s.s: hdwy 4f out: ev ch over 1f out: unable qckn) | ¾ | 3 | 4/1[2] | 74 | 37 |
| 136[9] | **Manabar (65)** (MJPolglase) **4-9-7** MFenton(4) (w ldr: led over 1f out: sn hdd & wknd) | 3½ | 4 | 50/1 | 63 | 26 |
| 107[8] | **Master Millfield (IRE) (66)** (CJHill) **4-9-10** JWeaver(9) (a.p: rdn over 4f out: wknd 2f out) | ¾ | 5 | 6/1 | 64 | 27 |
| | **Moi Canard (62)** (BAPearce) **3-8-9** SSanders(7) (led over 5f) | ½ | 6 | 25/1 | 66 | 11 |
| 144[2] | **Four of Spades (70)** (PDEvans) **5-9-8b**(5) AmandaSanders(3) (lw: bhd fnl 3f) | ½ | 7 | 11/1 | 65 | 28 |
| 110* | **Flirty Gertie (70)** (RBoss) **4-9-5** LDettori(6) (prom 5f) | 1 | 8 | 11/10[1] | 55 | 18 |
| 65[5] | **Dragon Green (59)** (JWhite) **5-9-4**(3) SDrowne(10) (prom 4f) | 1¼ | 9 | 50/1 | 54 | 17 |

**Ansal Boy (68)** (MissGayKelleway) **4-9-0**(7) BFord(1) (dwlt: a bhd) ....................3½ **10** 40/1 46 9
(SP 125.8%) **10 Rn**

**1m 26.57** (2.57) CSF £52.15 TOTE £7.40: £1.70 £2.40 £1.30 (£21.60) Trio £23.50 OWNER Mr Chris van Hoorn (WEST ILSLEY) BRED The Queen
WEIGHT FOR AGE 3yo-18lb

## 178 PHAETON H'CAP (0-65) (4-Y.O+) (Class F)

4-10 (4-11) **6f (Equitrack)** £2,540.80 (£713.80: £348.40) Stalls: Low GOING minus 0.44 sec per fur (FST)

SP RR SF

133[2] **Dahiyah (USA) (54)** (GLMoore) **5-9-5v** SWhitworth(6) (lw: chsd ldr: led 2f out: rdn out)....................— **1** 100/30[2] 64 21
121[12] **Patsy Grimes (63)** (JSMoore) **6-9-9**(5) PPMurphy(3) (hld up: rdn over 3f out: r.o ins fnl f)....................1¼ **2** 9/1 70 27
155[3] **Awasha (IRE) (54)** (MissGayKelleway) **4-9-5** LDettori(9) (b: s.s: hdwy 3f out: hrd rdn over 1f out: r.o one pce)....................3 **3** 9/4[1] 53 10
170[6] **Tafahhus (60)** (MJPolglase) **4-9-11v** MFenton(1) (a.p: rdn over 3f out: one pce)....................1¼ **4** 20/1 55 12
107[3] **Newington Butts (IRE) (44)** (KMcAuliffe) **6-8-9be** SSanders(2) (led 4f: wknd fnl f)....................¾ **5** 7/1[3] 37 —
107* **Random (56)** (CJames) **5-9-7** CRutter(10) (b: lw: nvr nr to chal)....................1¾ **6** 8/1 45 2
163[5] **Shaynes Domain (39)** (RMFlower) **5-8-4b** DBiggs(8) (hld up: rdn over 3f out: wknd over 2f out)....................1¼ **7** 16/1 24 —
55[12] **Willrack Farrier (56)** (BJMeehan) **4-9-7** JWeaver(5) (a bhd)....................3 **8** 40/1 33 —
107[12] **Rockcracker (IRE) (54)** (GGMargarson) **4-9-5** AClark(7) (lw: a bhd)....................1¼ **9** 12/1 28 —
63[11] **Anytime Baby (47)** (PTDalton) **4-8-12** SDWilliams(4) (a bhd)....................½ **10** 8/1 20 —
(SP 119.3%) **10 Rn**

**1m 13.87** (3.27) CSF £31.00 CT £73.89 TOTE £2.60: £1.10 £1.40 £1.50 (£17.20) Trio £17.10 OWNER Mr Bryan Pennick (EPSOM) BRED Foxfield

T/Jkpt: £3,491.00 (17.92 Tckts). T/Plpt: £90.70 (270.84 Tckts). T/Qdpt: £14.80 (280.02 Tckts) AK

# 0134-WOLVERHAMPTON (L-H) (Standard)

## Wednesday January 31st

All races were put back by 5 minutes.
WEATHER: overcast & cold WIND: slt against

## 179 CHIVE MAIDEN H'CAP (0-70) (4-Y.O+) (Class E)

2-10 (2-16) **7f (Fibresand)** £2,900.10 (£877.80: £428.40: £203.70) Stalls: High GOING: 0.73 sec per fur (SLW)

SP RR SF

127[6] **Serious Fact (39)** (SirMarkPrescott) **4-8-3** GDuffield(1) (led early: led over 2f out: hrd drvn & kpt on wl)........— **1** 5/1[2] 47 19
107[13] **Woolverstone Hall (IRE) (34)** (DJGMurraySmith) **4-7-12b[1]** NAdams(5) (a.p: led 3f out tl over 2f out: ev ch tl no ex wl ins fnl f)....................¾ **2** 33/1 40 12
**Lady Nash (50)** (CEBrittain) **4-9-0** MLarsen(6) (a.p: rdn along 2f out: kpt on fnl f)....................3½ **3** 9/2[1] 48 20
110[6] **So Natural (IRE) (53)** (EJAlston) **4-9-3** JWeaver(2) (a.p: effrt & drvn ent st: ev ch over 1f out: one pce)..........¾ **4** 12/1 50 22
106[6] **Boost (37)** (MrsNMacauley) **4-7-10v**(5) AmandaSanders(3) (lw: in tch: effrt over 2f out: no imp)....................5 **5** 10/1 22 —
74[7] **Speedy Snaps Pride (39)** (PDCundell) **4-8-3** GCarter(11) (bhd & outpcd tl sme late hdwy)....................1 **6** 12/1 22 —
36[7] **Mister Raider (40)** (SMellor) **4-7-11**(7)ow2 ADaly(10) (in rr & drvn along over 2f out: no imp)....................½ **7** 16/1 22 —
71[10] **Paronomasia (39)** (MBell) **4-8-3**ow1 MFenton(8) (a bhd)....................nk **8** 8/1 20 —
90[9] **Anotherone to Note (41)** (NPLittmoden) **5-8-5b** TGMcLaughlin(12) (hdwy on outside ½-wy: drvn & btn wl over 1f out)....................1¼ **9** 12/1 19 —
106[2] **Errant (60)** (DJSCosgrove) **4-9-10** JQuinn(4) (b: trckd ldrs tl rdn & wknd over 2f out)....................¾ **10** 5/1[2] 37 9
**Considerable Charm (45)** (LordHuntingdon) **4-8-9v[1]** LDettori(9) (led over 5f out to 3f out: wknd & eased appr fnl f)....................3½ **11** 6/1[3] 14 —
**Graceful Lady (40)** (EJAlston) **6-7-11**(7) CHalliwell(7) (bkwd: a bhd: t.o fnl 3f)....................12 **12** 16/1 — —
(SP 123.8%) **12 Rn**

**1m 35.7** (11.00) CSF £128.84 CT £732.85 TOTE £5.10: £2.30 £2.90 £2.40 (£165.60) Trio £254.30; £45.56 to Lingfield 1/2/96. OWNER Mr G. Moore (NEWMARKET) BRED Clanville Lodge Stud

## 180 SAGE CLAIMING STKS (3-Y.O+) (Class F)

2-40 (2-45) **5f (Fibresand)** £2,398.00 (£673.00: £328.00) Stalls: Low GOING: 0.73 sec per fur (SLW)

SP RR SF

126[5] **Primula Bairn (55)** (DNicholls) **6-9-1b** AlexGreaves(8) (hdwy on outside 3f out: led ins fnl f: readily)............— **1** 7/1 70 44
139[2] **King Rambo (67)** (RHollinshead) **5-8-13**(7) FLynch(3) (a.p: led 2f out tl hdd & no ex ins fnl f)....................1½ **2** 15/8[1] 70 44
117[4] **Sea-Deer (80)** (DWChapman) **7-9-11** ACulhane(1) (lw: s.i.s: hdwy & drvn along ½-wy: one pce fnl f)............2½ **3** 9/4[2] 67 41
126[3] **Sir Tasker (71)** (JLHarris) **8-9-8** LDettori(4) (rdn along thrght: prom tl outpcd appr fnl f)....................1¼ **4** 4/1[3] 60 34
**Magic Pearl (68)** (RFMarvin) **6-8-10**(3) SDrowne(7) (bit bkwd: trckd ldrs 3f: sn outpcd)....................1¾ **5** 16/1 46 20
**Montrestar (60)** (PDEvans) **3-8-7** SSanders(5) (bkwd: a bhd & outpcd)....................6 **6** 20/1 35 —
**Bonny Melody (36)** (PDEvans) **5-8-6**(5) AmandaSanders(2) (b: a bhd & outpcd)....................4 **7** 50/1 12 —
126[14] **Flashing Sabre (51)** (JBerry) **4-8-11b**(5) PRoberts(6) (led 3f: wknd over 1f out)....................2½ **8** 33/1 9 —
(SP 113.6%) **8 Rn**

**65.6 secs** (6.90) CSF £19.37 TOTE £7.90: £1.50 £1.10 £1.50 (£12.30) OWNER Mr J. P. Hames (THIRSK) BRED Kavli Ltd
WEIGHT FOR AGE 3yo-15lb

## 181 ROSEMARY H'CAP (0-90) (4-Y.O+) (Class C)

3-10 (3-16) **1m 1f 79y (Fibresand)** £5,329.70 (£1,613.60: £787.80: £374.90) Stalls: Low GOING: 0.73 sec per fur (SLW)

SP RR SF

136* **Field of Vision (IRE) (68)** (MJohnston) **6-8-11** 5x JWeaver(2) (a.p: led over 2f out: r.o wl)....................— **1** 11/2[3] 78 49
136[7] **Komreyev Dancer (79)** (ABailey) **4-9-7** GCarter(8) (hld up: hdwy over 2f out: r.o wl ins fnl f)....................1 **2** 12/1 88 57
132[5] **South Eastern Fred (85)** (HJCollingridge) **5-10-0** MRimmer(6) (in tch: effrt & rdn 2f out: kpt on appr fnl f: nt pce to chal)....................2½ **3** 8/1 89 60
75* **Celestial Choir (82)** (JLEyre) **6-9-8**(3) OPears(3) (a.p: led over 3f out tl over 2f out: hrd drvn & one pce appr fnl f)....................1¼ **4** 9/2[2] 84 55
99* **Ocean Park (76)** (LadyHerries) **5-9-5** DeanMcKeown(7) (trckd ldrs: drvn along over 2f out: nvr nrr)..............1½ **5** 7/2[1] 75 46

| | Horse | | Pos | SP | RR | SF |
|---|---|---|---|---|---|---|
| 87* | **Grey Again (59)** (SRBowring) **4-8-1b** NCarlisle(11) (effrt 3f out: sn drvn along: nvr able to chal) | 1 | **6** | 14/1 | 58 | 27 |
| 120[3] | **Bentico (70)** (MrsNMacauley) **7-8-8v**(5) AmandaSanders(1) (b.hind: led after 3f tl over 5f out: wknd wl over 1f out) | 2½ | **7** | 12/1 | 63 | 34 |
| | **Quivira (74)** (TTClement) **5-9-0**(3) JStack(10) (bit bkwd: prom tl hrd drvn & wknd fnl 2f) | 2½ | **8** | 14/1 | 63 | 34 |
| 132[9] | **Bernard Seven (IRE) (80)** (CEBrittain) **4-9-8b** LDettori(5) (lw: led 3f: led over 5f out tl over 3f out: eased whn btn appr fnl f) | 1½ | **9** | 9/2[2] | 68 | 37 |
| | **Locorotondo (IRE) (64)** (MBell) **5-8-7** MFenton(9) (bit bkwd: a in rr) | ¾ | **10** | 10/1 | 49 | 20 |
| | **Jungle Patrol (IRE) (77)** (CMurray) **4-9-5** MTebbutt(12) (bit bkwd: a bhd: t.o) | 6 | **11** | 25/1 | 53 | 22 |
| | **Gulf Shaadi (75)** (EJAlston) **4-9-3** JFortune(4) (s.s: a bhd: t.o) | 7 | **12** | 20/1 | 39 | 8 |
| | | | | (SP 131.5%) | | **12 Rn** |

**2m 8.2** (12.20) CSF £68.73 CT £496.97 TOTE £7.10: £1.10 £3.10 £4.80 (£77.30) Trio £219.70 OWNER Mr R. W. Huggins (MIDDLEHAM) BRED Sean Collins
WEIGHT FOR AGE 4yo-1lb

## 182 HEADLAM FLOOR COVERING H'CAP (0-90) (3-Y.O) (Class C)

3-40 (3-46) **6f (Fibresand)** £5,255.60 (£1,590.80: £776.40: £369.20) Stalls: Low GOING: 0.73 sec per fur (SLW)

| | Horse | | Pos | SP | RR | SF |
|---|---|---|---|---|---|---|
| 157[2] | **Weetman's Weigh (IRE) (74)** (RHollinshead) **3-8-12** LDettori(4) (rdn & outpcd ½-wy: hdwy to ld jst ins fnl f: wandered: hld on) | — | **1** | 13/2 | 80 | 34 |
| | **Hever Golf Express (75)** (TJNaughton) **3-8-13** JWeaver(1) (b.hind: bhd & outpcd tl r.o strly appr fnl f) | ½ | **2** | 10/1 | 80 | 34 |
| 102[3] | **Myttons Mistake (72)** (ABailey) **3-8-3**(7) IonaWands(5) (bhd & outpcd tl gd hdwy over 1f out: fin wl) | nk | **3** | 7/1 | 76 | 30 |
| 118* | **Princely Sound (72)** (MBell) **3-8-10** MFenton(3) (lw: led 2f: led over 1f out: sn hdd: wknd ins fnl f) | 2½ | **4** | 9/4[1] | 69 | 23 |
| 137[2] | **Theatre Magic (60)** (SRBowring) **3-7-12b** NCarlisle(8) (lw: led after 2f tl hdd & wknd over 1f out) | 1¾ | **5** | 4/1[2] | 53 | 7 |
| | **Celandine (83)** (JLEyre) **3-9-7** RLappin(9) (prom tl rdn & wknd wl over 1f out) | 2½ | **6** | 14/1 | 69 | 23 |
| 102[6] | **The Frisky Farmer (60)** (WGMTurner) **3-7-7**(5) CAdamson(2) (trckd ldrs tl outpcd over 3f out) | 1¾ | **7** | 33/1 | 41 | — |
| 52* | **Ultra Barley (82)** (PCHaslam) **3-9-6** JFortune(7) (trckd ldrs 4f: sn lost tch) | ¾ | **8** | 6/1[3] | 61 | 15 |
| | **Carmarthen Bay (80)** (GLMoore) **3-9-4** AClark(6) (sn pushed along: a bhd: t.o fr ½-wy) | dist | **9** | 13/2 | — | — |
| | | | | (SP 122.9%) | | **9 Rn** |

**1m 20.3** (8.90) CSF £64.03 CT £432.04 TOTE £4.60: £1.40 £4.00 £3.30 (£24.00) Trio £171.60 OWNER Ed Weetman (Haulage & Storage) Ltd (UPPER LONGDON) BRED David Commins
**OFFICIAL EXPLANATION Carmarthen Bay: the colt reportedly felt lame.**

## 183 MARJORAM (S) STKS (3-Y.O) (Class G)

4-10 (4-15) **6f (Fibresand)** £2,224.00 (£624.00: £304.00) Stalls: Low GOING: 0.73 sec per fur (SLW)

| | Horse | | Pos | SP | RR | SF |
|---|---|---|---|---|---|---|
| 21* | **Mystic Tempo (USA) (70)** (DrJDScargill) **3-8-12** RCochrane(1) (a.p: led over 3f out: clr ent st: hrd drvn: hld on) | — | **1** | Evens[1] | 70 | 36 |
| 101* | **Boffy (IRE) (69)** (BPJBaugh) **3-8-10**(7) IonaWands(6) (b: lw: hld up: hdwy 2f out: str run fnl f: jst failed) | ½ | **2** | 4/1[2] | 74 | 40 |
| 101[4] | **Dhes-C (52)** (RHollinshead) **3-8-0**(7) FLynch(10) (prom: drvn along & outpcd over 2f out: r.o wl cl home) | 1 | **3** | 12/1 | 61 | 27 |
| | **Flagstaff (USA) (48)** (GLMoore) **3-8-12v** SWhitworth(4) (bhd & outpcd: hdwy ½-wy: kpt on ins fnl f) | 3 | **4** | 20/1 | 58 | 24 |
| | **Don't Tell Anyone (52)** (PDEvans) **3-9-3** SSanders(7) (bkwd: led over 2f: outpcd wl over 1f out) | 1 | **5** | 16/1 | 60 | 26 |
| 131[5] | **Elfin Queen (IRE) (60)** (JLHarris) **3-8-7** JWeaver(9) (gd spd 4f) | ½ | **6** | 6/1[3] | 49 | 15 |
| 21[7] | **Flood's Fancy (57)** (ABailey) **3-8-5**(7) AngelaGallimore(2) (hdwy over 3f out: outpcd wl over 1f out) | hd | **7** | 16/1 | 54 | 20 |
| | **The Fullbangladesh (50)** (JLEyre) **3-8-7** RLappin(11) (b: nvr nr to chal) | 2 | **8** | 14/1 | 43 | 9 |
| 101[9] | **Shoot The Minstrel (32)** (JAPickering) **3-8-12** NCarlisle(8) (b.nr hind: trckd ldrs over 3f: sn lost tch) | 2 | **9** | 50/1 | 43 | 9 |
| 101[5] | **Victoria Sioux (52)** (JWharton) **3-8-7** JQuinn(5) (sn bhd & outpcd) | nk | **10** | 8/1 | 37 | 3 |
| | **Lila Pedigo (IRE) (58)** (MissJFCraze) **3-8-12** NKennedy(3) (blnd: a bhd & outpcd) | ½ | **11** | 20/1 | 41 | 7 |
| | | | | (SP 133.0%) | | **11 Rn** |

**1m 20.1** (8.70) CSF £6.53 TOTE £1.70: £1.10 £1.80 £2.30 (£4.50) Trio £14.80 OWNER Just Passing Through Partnership (NEWMARKET) BRED Swetteham Stud and Ben Sangster
Bt in 5,600 gns
STEWARDS' ENQUIRY Cochrane fined £200 (failure to ride to the draw).

## 184 THYME H'CAP (0-80) (4-Y.O+) (Class D)

4-40 (4-46) **1m 4f (Fibresand)** £3,468.75 (£1,050.00: £512.50: £243.75) Stalls: Low GOING: 0.73 sec per fur (SLW)

| | Horse | | Pos | SP | RR | SF |
|---|---|---|---|---|---|---|
| 70[6] | **Beaumont (IRE) (56)** (JEBanks) **6-9-0** RCochrane(8) (hld up: hdwy ½-wy: led wl over 2f out: clr appr fnl f) | — | **1** | 4/1[2] | 72 | 48 |
| | **Mentalasanythin (70)** (ABailey) **7-10-0** AMackay(10) (bkwd: trckd ldrs: styd on appr fnl f: no ch w wnr) | 8 | **2** | 5/1[3] | 75 | 51 |
| 124[2] | **Wonderful Day (66)** (TTClement) **5-9-7**(3) JStack(3) (b: a.p: led over 4f out tl wl over 2f out: outpcd appr fnl f) | ½ | **3** | 7/2[1] | 71 | 47 |
| 122[4] | **Benjamins Law (68)** (JAPickering) **5-9-12** JQuinn(5) (hld up: hdwy 5f out: nvr nr to chal) | 5 | **4** | 7/1 | 66 | 42 |
| 66[3] | **Rival Bid (USA) (62)** (MrsNMacauley) **8-9-1**(5) AmandaSanders(9) (lw: racd wd: led after 2f tl over 4f out: wknd fnl 2f) | 3 | **5** | 5/1[3] | 56 | 32 |
| 125* | **Forzair (73)** (SRBowring) **4-9-8**(5) 5x CTeague(4) (lw: wl bhd tl sme hdwy 4f out: nt rch ldrs) | 4 | **6** | 5/1[3] | 62 | 34 |
| | **Drum Battle (68)** (WGMTurner) **4-9-8** SWhitworth(1) (b: prom over 8f: t.o) | 12 | **7** | 14/1 | 41 | 13 |
| | **Desert Power (60)** (DBurchell) **7-9-4** DeanMcKeown(7) (bit bkwd: a bhd: t.o fnl 4f) | dist | **8** | 20/1 | — | — |
| 62[12] | **Dance on Sixpence (40)** (JHPeacock) **8-7-12**ow2 DaleGibson(2) (led 1f: prom tl wknd qckly over 3f out: t.o) | 15 | **9** | 50/1 | — | — |
| | **Endowment (74)** (RMMcKellar) **4-10-0b** TWilliams(6) (b.off hind: bkwd: led after 1f tl after 2f: wknd qckly 5f out: t.o) | 9 | **10** | 10/1 | — | — |
| | | | | (SP 127.2%) | | **10 Rn** |

**2m 49.0** (16.50) CSF £24.84 CT £72.86 TOTE £4.90: £1.70 £1.90 £2.00 (£13.70) Trio £18.60 OWNER Mr P. Cunningham (NEWMARKET) BRED Mount Coote Stud in Ireland
LONG HANDICAP Dance on Sixpence 7-4
WEIGHT FOR AGE 4yo-4lb
**OFFICIAL EXPLANATION Rival Bid (USA): it was reported that the horse does not respond to pressure, preferred the firmer going on the outside and has shown his best form over shorter distances.**

T/Jkpt: Not won; £7,284.80 to Lingfield 1/2/96. T/Plpt: £90.70 (360.74 Tckts). T/Qdpt: £24.80 (269.43 Tckts). IM

# 0173-LINGFIELD (L-H) (Standard)

## Thursday February 1st

WEATHER: sunny WIND: almost nil

## 185 BRITISH COLUMBIA CLAIMING STKS (4-Y.O+) (Class F)

1-50 (1-50) **6f (Equitrack)** £2,576.50 (£724.00: £353.50) Stalls: Low GOING minus 0.47 sec per fur (FST)

| Form | Horse | Dist | Pos | SP | RR | SF |
|---|---|---|---|---|---|---|
| 121$^{10}$ | **Anzio (IRE) (72)** (BAPearce) **5-8-6b**(3) DRMcCabe(3) (b: b.hind: lw: lost pl 2f out: rallied fnl f: led nr fin) | — | **1** | 7/2$^{3}$ | 72 | 6 |
| 64$^{3}$ | **Inherent Magic (IRE) (87)** (WRMuir) **7-9-2** JWeaver(2) (b: led 3f: led over 1f out: hrd rdn: hdd nr fin) | ¾ | **2** | 15/8$^{2}$ | 77 | 11 |
| 117$^{6}$ | **Lift Boy (USA) (57)** (AMoore) **7-8-5** CandyMorris(4) (b.hind: hld up: hrd rdn over 1f out: ev ch ins fnl f: one pce) | nk | **3** | 10/1 | 65 | — |
| 65* | **Star Talent (USA) (80)** (MissGayKelleway) **5-8-12**(7) TAshley(1) (b.hind: w ldr: led 3f out tl over 1f out: ev ch ins fnl f: one pce) | 1½ | **4** | 5/4$^{1}$ | 75 | 9 |
| 141$^{8}$ | **Thorny Bishop (53)** (JJBridger) **5-8-3b** JQuinn(5) (a bhd) | 20 | **5** | 40/1 | 6 | — |

(SP 113.0%) **5 Rn**

**1m 14.1** (3.50) CSF £10.11 TOTE £3.90: £1.50 £1.30 (£4.20) OWNER Mr Richard Gray (LIMPSFIELD) BRED Rathduff Stud
Anzio (IRE) clmd MissGayKelleway £6,000
STEWARDS' ENQUIRY Morris susp.10 & 12/2/96 (excessive use of whip).

## 186 ALBERTA (S) H'CAP (0-60) (4-Y.O+) (Class G)

2-20 (2-21) **1m 5f (Equitrack)** £2,305.50 (£648.00: £316.50) Stalls: Low GOING minus 0.47 sec per fur (FST)

| Form | Horse | Dist | Pos | SP | RR | SF |
|---|---|---|---|---|---|---|
| 104$^{4}$ | **Heighth of Fame (43)** (AJWilson) **5-9-5** JFortune(1) (led over 3f: led over 4f out: all out) | — | **1** | 7/1 | 58 | 37 |
| 104$^{2}$ | **Miltak (37)** (PJMakin) **4-8-9** SSanders(7) (n.m.r on ins over 4f out: hdwy over 3f out: nt clr run & swtchd rt over 1f out: ev ch fnl f: r.o wl) | s.h | **2** | 5/1$^{2}$ | 53 | 27 |
| 128$^{2}$ | **Northern Trial (USA) (41)** (KRBurke) **8-8-10v**(7) TAshley(15) (hdwy over 6f out: hrd rdn over 1f out: ev ch ins fnl f: unable qckn) | 3½ | **3** | 9/2$^{1}$ | 52 | 31 |
| 83$^{8}$ | **Captain Marmalade (46)** (DTThom) **7-9-8v**[1] JTate(11) (b: lw: hdwy over 4f out: one pce fnl 2f) | 3 | **4** | 11/1 | 53 | 32 |
| 83$^{7}$ | **Sorisky (40)** (BGubby) **4-8-12** JQuinn(12) (hld up: rdn over 4f out: wknd over 1f out) | 2 | **5** | 5/1$^{2}$ | 46 | 20 |
| 73$^{10}$ | **Mister Lawson (25)** (BSmart) **10-8-1** AMackay(6) (nvr nr to chal) | s.h | **6** | 25/1 | 29 | 8 |
| 140$^{2}$ | **Hill Farm Dancer (48)** (WMBrisbourne) **5-9-5**(5) DGriffiths(17) (lw: hdwy 7f out: wknd over 1f out) | 1¾ | **7** | 6/1$^{3}$ | 50 | 29 |
| 138$^{6}$ | **Duggan (22)** (PDEvans) **9-7-12** FNorton(9) (b.off hind: nvr nrr) | 6 | **8** | 14/1 | 17 | — |
| 116$^{5}$ | **Swynford Flyer (32)** (JAHarris) **7-8-8** DaleGibson(10) (rdn & hdwy over 3f out: wknd over 2f out) | 1¾ | **9** | 16/1 | 25 | 4 |
| 73$^{9}$ | **Rose of Glenn (44)** (BPalling) **5-9-6** RCochrane(8) (led over 9f out tl over 4f out: wknd over 2f out) | ¾ | **10** | 11/1 | 36 | 15 |
| 104$^{11}$ | **Quadrant (43)** (AMoore) **7-9-5** AClark(4) (b: bkwd: prom over 8f) | ¾ | **11** | 25/1 | 34 | 13 |
| 138$^{4}$ | **Fools of Pride (IRE) (36)** (RHollinshead) **4-8-1**(7) FLynch(16) (nvr nrr) | nk | **12** | 20/1 | 28 | 2 |
| | **Commanchero (37)** (RJHodges) **9-8-10**(3) SDrowne(3) (bhd fnl 10f) | 12 | **13** | 20/1 | 13 | — |
| 116$^{13}$ | **Verro (USA) (20)** (KBishop) **9-7-10e** NCarlisle(13) (lw: a bhd) | 7 | **14** | 50/1 | — | |
| | **Jimbo (42)** (JRJenkins) **5-8-11**(7) SallyWall(5) (bhd fnl 6f) | 2 | **15** | 33/1 | 7 | — |
| 54$^{7}$ | **Shedansar (IRE) (31)** (GLMoore) **4-8-3** NAdams(18) (prom 9f) | 11 | **16** | 9/1 | — | — |
| 105$^{12}$ | **Percussion Bird (28)** (JRPoulton) **4-7-7**(7) TField(14) (a bhd) | 13 | **17** | 33/1 | — | — |
| 141$^{6}$ | **White Heat (47)** (WGMTurner) **4-9-0**(5) CAdamson(2) (bhd fnl 5f) | 9 | **18** | 25/1 | — | — |

(SP 146.4%) **18 Rn**

**2m 47.96** (4.76) CSF £45.76 CT £173.86 TOTE £12.10: £1.70 £1.10 £1.80 £2.60 (£30.40) Trio £38.20 OWNER Mr Simon Lewis (CHELTENHAM) BRED Paul Mellon
LONG HANDICAP Verro (USA) 7-5
WEIGHT FOR AGE 4yo-4lb
No bid

## 187 MANITOBA H'CAP (0-80) (4-Y.O+) (Class D)

2-50 (2-52) **1m 4f (Equitrack)** £3,452.50 (£1,045.00: £510.00: £242.50) Stalls: Low GOING minus 0.47 sec per fur (FST)

| Form | Horse | Dist | Pos | SP | RR | SF |
|---|---|---|---|---|---|---|
| 100$^{4}$ | **Prince Danzig (IRE) (77)** (DJGMurraySmith) **5-9-11** JWeaver(2) (lw: rdn & hdwy 4f out: led 1f out: r.o wl) | — | **1** | 11/4$^{2}$ | 82 | 50 |
| 132$^{6}$ | **Progression (69)** (CMurray) **5-9-3b** MTebbutt(5) (stdy hdwy 6f out: led over 3f out to 1f out: unable qckn) | 1¼ | **2** | 5/6$^{1}$ | 72 | 40 |
| 108$^{8}$ | **Red Spectacle (IRE) (51)** (PCHaslam) **4-7-5**(5) MBaird(7) (led over 8f: rdn: one pce) | 1½ | **3** | 8/1$^{3}$ | 53 | 17 |
| | **Courbaril (58)** (SDow) **4-7-10**(7)ow1 ADaly(3) (chsd ldr 8f: rdn over 3f out: one pce) | nk | **4** | 8/1$^{3}$ | 60 | 23 |
| 169$^{12}$ | **Cross Talk (IRE) (63)** (RHollinshead) **4-8-8** RCochrane(1) (nvr nr to chal) | 1½ | **5** | 33/1 | 63 | 27 |
| | **Conic Hill (IRE) (62)** (JPearce) **5-8-10** GBardwell(6) (bit bkwd: bhd fnl 6f) | 10 | **6** | 33/1 | 48 | 16 |
| | **Let's Get Lost (55)** (JAHarris) **7-8-3** DaleGibson(4) (bhd fnl 6f) | 13 | **7** | 20/1 | 23 | — |

(SP 114.1%) **7 Rn**

**2m 33.18** (3.18) CSF £5.25 TOTE £3.60: £1.30 £1.10 (£2.20) OWNER Mr A. H. Ulrick (LAMBOURN) BRED J. N. McCaffrey in Ireland
WEIGHT FOR AGE 4yo-3lb
No bid

## 188 QUEBEC MAIDEN STKS (3-Y.O) (Class D)

3-20 (3-21) **1m (Equitrack)** £3,517.50 (£1,065.00: £520.00: £247.50) Stalls: High GOING minus 0.47 sec per fur (FST)

| Form | Horse | Dist | Pos | SP | RR | SF |
|---|---|---|---|---|---|---|
| 67$^{2}$ | **Blue Flyer (IRE) (67)** (RIngram) **3-9-0** JWeaver(6) (hdwy over 4f out: led over 1f out: rdn out) | — | **1** | 4/5$^{1}$ | 70 | 31 |
| | **Lancashire Legend (74)** (SDow) **3-9-0** RCochrane(3) (s.s: rdn & hdwy over 2f out: r.o ins fnl f) | 2½ | **2** | 8/1$^{3}$ | 65 | 26 |
| 143$^{3}$ | **Rawi (61)** (WRMuir) **3-9-0v**[1] Jean-PierreLopez(7) (led over 6f out tl over 1f out: unable qckn) | 1¼ | **3** | 8/1$^{3}$ | 63 | 24 |
| | **Blueberry Fields** (CFWall) **3-8-9** NDay(2) (bit bkwd: hdwy over 1f out: nvr nrr) | 1¼ | **4** | 16/1 | 55 | 16 |
| 17$^{5}$ | **Crystal Fast (USA)** (PAKelleway) **3-9-0** AClark(4) (a.p: ev ch 2f out: wknd over 1f out) | 3½ | **5** | 20/1 | 53 | 14 |
| | **Native Song** (MJHaynes) **3-8-9** SWhitworth(1) (led over 1f: wknd over 3f out) | 8 | **6** | 33/1 | 32 | — |
| 58$^{4}$ | **Note of Caution (USA)** (LordHuntingdon) **3-8-9** LDettori(5) (b: bhd fnl 2f) | 3½ | **7** | 3/1$^{2}$ | 25 | — |
| 119$^{6}$ | **Conquistajade (USA) (48)** (SPCWoods) **3-8-9b**[1] JFortune(8) (prom over 5f) | 2 | **8** | 33/1 | 21 | — |

(SP 119.3%) **8 Rn**

**1m 40.28** (2.88) CSF £8.14 TOTE £1.60: £1.10 £2.40 £1.50 (£6.40) OWNER Mrs A. V. Cappuccini (EPSOM) BRED Matt Carr

## 189 NEWFOUNDLAND H'CAP (0-65) (4-Y.O+) (Class F)

3-50 (3-51) **1m 2f (Equitrack)** £2,695.50 (£758.00: £370.50) Stalls: Low GOING minus 0.47 sec per fur (FST)

| | Horse | Dist | Pos | SP | RR | SF |
|---|---|---|---|---|---|---|
| 109[3] | **Robellion (63)** (DWPArbuthnot) **5-10-0v** RCochrane(10) (b: hdwy over 3f out: led 1f out: pushed out) | — | 1 | 4/1[2] | 68 | 51 |
| | **Zahid (USA) (43)** (KRBurke) **5-8-8v** JQuinn(4) (lw: a.p: led over 1f out: sn hdd: unable qckn) | 2½ | 2 | 10/1 | 44 | 27 |
| 66* | **Explosive Power (61)** (GCBravery) **5-9-12** TIves(7) (hdwy over 3f out: ev ch 1f out: one pce) | hd | 3 | 13/8[1] | 62 | 45 |
| 121[16] | **Mac's Taxi (51)** (PCHaslam) **4-9-1** JFortune(8) (lost pl over 3f out: r.o one pce fnl f) | 3½ | 4 | 16/1 | 47 | 28 |
| 103* | **Todd (USA) (58)** (PhilipMitchell) **5-9-9** AClark(11) (hld up: ev ch over 1f out: wknd fnl f) | hd | 5 | 15/2 | 53 | 36 |
| 120[3] | **Labudd (USA) (57)** (RIngram) **6-9-8** DBiggs(6) (b: hdwy over 3f out: wknd over 2f out) | 2½ | 6 | 7/1 | 48 | 31 |
| 106* | **Your Most Welcome (53)** (DJSffrenchDavis) **5-9-4** GCarter(12) (hdwy over 3f out: wknd wl over 1f out) | 1¾ | 7 | 12/1 | 41 | 24 |
| 106[3] | **Ganador (47)** (BSmart) **4-8-11** SSanders(3) (hdwy over 2f out: wknd over 1f out) | nk | 8 | 14/1 | 36 | 17 |
| 145* | **Real Madrid (44)** (GPEnright) **5-8-9v** 5x NAdams(1) (led over 8f) | 2½ | 9 | 13/2[3] | 28 | 11 |
| 138[10] | **Hill Farm Katie (40)** (WMBrisbourne) **5-8-5** AGarth(5) (bhd fnl 4f) | 6 | 10 | 33/1 | 14 | — |
| | **Rubadub (31)** (JMBradley) **5-7-10** GBardwell(13) (prom 6f) | 1½ | 11 | 50/1 | 3 | — |
| | **Smiley Face (47)** (RJHodges) **4-8-8**(3) SDrowne(9) (b.off hind: s.s: a bhd: t.o) | 25 | 12 | 50/1 | — | — |
| | | | | (SP 131.9%) | **12 Rn** | |

**2m 7.21** (2.91) CSF £44.37 CT £85.30 TOTE £6.10: £2.50 £2.70 £1.20 (£33.40) Trio £53.90 OWNER Mr George Thompson (COMPTON) BRED Pitts Farm Stud

LONG HANDICAP Rubadub 7-4

WEIGHT FOR AGE 4yo-1lb

## 190 ONTARIO AMATEUR H'CAP (0-70) (4-Y.O+) (Class E)

4-20 (4-20) **1m (Equitrack)** £2,968.35 (£898.80: £438.90: £208.95) Stalls: High GOING minus 0.47 sec per fur (FST)

| | Horse | Dist | Pos | SP | RR | SF |
|---|---|---|---|---|---|---|
| 13[2] | **Digpast (IRE) (67)** (RJO'Sullivan) **6-10-13b**(5) MrDavyJones(8) (s.s: plld hrd: hdwy 4f out: led over 2f out: sn clr: r.o wl) | — | 1 | 100/30[2] | 80 | 58 |
| 177[7] | **Four of Spades (70)** (PDEvans) **5-11-2b**(5) MrAEvans(5) (lw: hdwy over 2f out: r.o ins fnl f) | 2½ | 2 | 11/2[3] | 78 | 56 |
| 57[11] | **Dream Carrier (IRE) (51)** (REPeacock) **8-9-11**(5) MrsCPeacock(12) (hdwy over 4f out: led over 3f out tl over 2f out: unable qckn) | 4 | 3 | 16/1 | 51 | 29 |
| 30[10] | **Love Legend (47)** (DWPArbuthnot) **11-9-12** MrsDArbuthnot(7) (b: hdwy 3f out: wknd 2f out: fin 5th, 3/4l: plcd 4th) | | 4 | 14/1 | 42 | 20 |
| | **Mr Frosty (65)** (WJarvis) **4-11-2** MrJDurkan(9) (a.p: rdn over 2f out: wknd fnl f: fin 6th, 3l: plcd 5th) | | 5 | 11/8[1] | 55 | 32 |
| | **Royal Acclaim (41)** (JMBradley) **11-9-1v**(5)ow1 MissEDent(11) (nvr nrr) | ¾ | 7 | 20/1 | 29 | 6 |
| 30[4] | **Jon's Choice (42)** (BPreece) **8-9-2**(5) MissLBoswell(4) (hdwy on ins over 4f out: wknd over 3f out: bhd whn hmpd on ins over 2f out) | 3 | 8 | 12/1 | 24 | 2 |
| 135[6] | **Best Kept Secret (62)** (PDEvans) **5-10-13v** MrWMcLaughlin(10) (led 1f: wknd over 2f out) | s.h | 9 | 25/1 | 43 | 21 |
| | **Magic Leader (IRE) (35)** (TTClement) **4-9-0** MrVLukaniuk(2) (b: prom over 4f: bhd whn hmpd over 2f out) | ¾ | 10 | 66/1 | 16 | — |
| | **Southern Ridge (53)** (RJBaker) **5-9-13**(5) MrAHoldsworth(1) (led 7f out tl over 3f out: sn wknd: bhd whn hmpd over 2f out) | 5 | 11 | 33/1 | 23 | 1 |
| | **Holiday Island (44)** (PButler) **7-9-4**(5) MrJGoldstein(3) (s.i.s: a bhd: t.o fnl 5f) | 25 | 12 | 33/1 | — | — |
| 116[4] | **Montone (IRE) (45)** (JRJenkins) **6-9-10** DrMMannish(6) (lost pl over 3f out: edgd lft over 2f out: rallied wl over 1f out: r.o one pce: fin 4th, 1 3/4l: disq: plcd last) | | D | 13/2 | 42 | 20 |
| | | | | (SP 130.1%) | **12 Rn** | |

**1m 40.52** (3.12) CSF £22.85 CT £249.44 TOTE £4.60: £1.40 £2.20 £9.60 (£18.00) Trio £100.00 OWNER Miss Sarah Jones (WHITCOMBE) BRED Somerville Stud

STEWARDS' ENQUIRY Mannish susp.10 & 12-14/2/96 (irresponsible riding).

T/Jkpt: £11,971.40 (0.09 Tckts); £15,343.68 to Southwell 2/2/96. T/Plpt: £14.90 (1,495.8 Tckts). T/Qdpt: £4.40 (1,086 Tckts). AK

# 0149a-CAGNES-SUR-MER (Nice, France) (L-H) (Heavy)

### Friday January 26th

## 191a PRIX DES PEUPLIERS ET DES BOULEAUX H'CAP (4-Y.O+)

2-31 (2-29) **1m** £9,881.00 (£4,941.00: £2,964.00: £2,055.00)

| | Horse | Dist | Pos | SP | RR | SF |
|---|---|---|---|---|---|---|
| | **Countdown (FR)** (AdeMoussac,France) **4-9-0** CTellier | — | 1 | | 79 | — |
| 148a* | **Spinario (USA)** (Jean-MarcCapitte,Belgium) **5-8-7** MBoutin | s.h | 2 | | 72 | — |
| 147a[3] | **Mill Boy (FR)** (PKhozian,France) **7-8-9** GElorriaga-Santos | 1 | 3 | | 72 | — |
| 148a[7] | **Confronter** (SDow) **7-9-5** CBrechon | 8 | 4 | | 66 | — |
| | | | | | | **15 Rn** |

**1m 50.1** P-M 6.70F: 2.00F 2.50F 1.70F (29.70F) OWNER S. Vidal BRED Haras bu Bois Roussel

**148a Confronter** may not have found the going to his liking but, nevertheless, put up a decent performance. He was ridden to dispute the lead three furlongs out, but was unable to quicken with the others and ran on at one pace. If the ground improves, he should be able to pick up a race.

# 0191a-CAGNES-SUR-MER (Nice, France) (L-H) (Heavy)

### Sunday January 28th

## 192a PRIX DE BASTIA (3-Y.O)

1-50 (1-59) **1m 2f** £5,270.00 (£2,635.00: £1,581.00: £1,054.00)

| | Horse | Dist | Pos | SP | RR | SF |
|---|---|---|---|---|---|---|
| | **How Long (FR)** (JVanHandenhove,France) **3-9-2** MBoutin | — | 1 | | 69 | — |
| | **Yamamoto (FR)** (RCollet,France) **3-9-2** CHanotel | 2½ | 2 | | 65 | — |
| | **Tsimtsoum (FR)** (CScandella,France) **3-9-2** CEscuder | 2 | 3 | | 62 | — |
| 146a[13] | **Asking For Kings (IRE)** (SDow) **3-9-2** ESaint-Martin | 1 | 4 | | 60 | — |
| | | | | | | **17 Rn** |

**2m 25.6** P-M 112.80f: 7.40f 3.20f 3.20f (382.00f) OWNER Mr W. Van Handenhove BRED W. Van Handenhove

**146a Asking For Kings (IRE)** put up a much better display than his disappointing run here last time. Racing in fifth, this son of Thatching ran on well down the straight, but was never able to get on terms with the leading pair. He showed a great deal of potential and should be able to pick up a small race.

## 193a PRIX DUFY (4-Y.O+)

3-14 (3-17) **1m 2f** £5,270.00

| Horse | Dist | Pos | SP | RR | SF |
|---|---|---|---|---|---|
| **But Not For Me (IRE)** (JMartens,Belgium) **6-8-8b**(1)(5) NPerret | — | 1 | | — | — |
| **Courroux (FR)** (MmeARossio,France) **5-8-12** DBoeuf | 1 | 2 | | — | — |
| **Frutti Tutti (FR)** (JDelaporte,France) **5-8-12** TThulliez | 2 | 3 | | — | — |
| **Al Widyan (IRE)** (LordHuntingdon) **4-9-1** GGuignard (btn over 10l) | | 12 | | — | — |
| | | | | | **13 Rn** |

**2m 22.5** P-M 8.80f: 2.30f 3.00f 2.60f (54.50f) OWNER B. Lalemant BRED R. M. Fox

**Al Widyan (IRE)** can be excused this performance as he hated the heavy ground. Prominent in the early stages, he began to lose his place turning for home and his jockey went easy on him when he realised that he was not handling the heavy conditions. When the ground gets better, he should improve.

# 0166-SOUTHWELL (L-H) (Standard)

## Friday February 2nd

WEATHER: overcast & misty WIND: mod half bhd

## 194 HALHAM H'CAP (0-70) (3-Y.O) (Class E)

2-00 (2-00) **6f (Fibresand)** £2,780.25 (£852.00: £423.50: £209.25) Stalls: Low GOING: 0.18 sec per fur (SLW)

| | Horse | Dist | Pos | SP | RR | SF |
|---|---|---|---|---|---|---|
| *112** | **Seeking Destiny (IRE) (50)** (MCChapman) **3-8-1**(3) DRMcCabe(6) (w ldrs: led over 1f out: r.o u.p) | — | 1 | $100/30^{1}$ | 54 | 24 |
| *$112^{4}$* | **Bit of Bother (IRE) (58)** (TDBarron) **3-8-12** GCarter(7) (chsd ldrs: ev ch over 1f out: styd on towards fin) | ¾ | 2 | $7/2^{2}$ | 60 | 30 |
| *$112^{3}$* | **Kind of Light (67)** (RGuest) **3-9-0**(7) FLynch(1) (w ldrs: ev ch 1f out: nt qckn) | hd | 3 | 5/1 | 69 | 39 |
| *$157^{4}$* | **Foreman (57)** (WAO'Gorman) **3-8-11v**ow1 EmmaO'Gorman(2) (hld up: hdwy over 2f out: sn chsng ldrs: wknd fnl f) | 2½ | 4 | 5/1 | 52 | 21 |
| *157** | **Chilibang Bang (69)** (JBerry) **3-9-2**(7) 7x CLowther(4) (chsd ldrs: drvn along ½-wy: wknd 2f out) | 2½ | 5 | $9/2^{3}$ | 57 | 27 |
| *$112^{7}$* | **Chillam (52)** (JPLeigh) **3-8-6** DeanMcKeown(5) (led tl over 1f out: sn wknd) | ½ | 6 | 16/1 | 39 | 9 |
| *131** | **Miss Carottene (51)** (MJRyan) **3-8-0**(5) 7x MBaird(3) (s.i.s: n.m.r & outpcd after 2f: sn bhd) | 10 | 7 | 6/1 | 11 | — |
| | | | | (SP 117.0%) | | **7 Rn** |

**1m 19.4** (5.90) CSF £14.91 TOTE £4.40: £2.10 £3.50 (£18.60) OWNER Mr Mattie O'Toole (MARKET RASEN) BRED Major V. McCalmont

## 195 LANGFORD CLAIMING APPRENTICE STKS (4-Y.O+) (Class F)

2-30 (2-30) **7f (Fibresand)** £2,398.00 (£673.00: £328.00) Stalls: Low GOING: 0.18 sec per fur (SLW)

| | Horse | Dist | Pos | SP | RR | SF |
|---|---|---|---|---|---|---|
| *$170^{3}$* | **Milos (71)** (TJNaughton) **5-9-7** TAshley(5) (drvn along & hdwy ½-wy: led wl over 1f out: styd on) | — | 1 | $2/5^{1}$ | 70 | 35 |
| *$110^{8}$* | **Northern Grey (47)** (JBerry) **4-7-12b**(5) JoanneWebster(6) (led: clr over 3f out: hdd wl over 1f out: kpt on) | 3½ | 2 | $10/1^{3}$ | 50 | 9 |
| | **Komlucky (44)** (ABMulholland) **4-8-2b**ow1 GFaulkner(4) (chsd ldr: hung lft 2f out: one pce) | 3 | 3 | 14/1 | 42 | — |
| *$100^{6}$* | **Araboybill (52)** (RSimpson) **5-9-1b** IonaWands(3) (sn drvn along & bhd: styd on fnl 2f: nvr nr ldrs) | 1½ | 4 | $11/2^{2}$ | 52 | 11 |
| *$168^{4}$* | **Legatee (53)** (AStreeter) **5-7-12**(3) DSweeney(2) (chsd ldrs tl wknd over 2f out) | 5 | 5 | $10/1^{3}$ | 26 | — |
| | **Desert Man** (RDEWoodhouse) **5-9-7** FLynch(1) (bkwd: sn drvn along: chsd ldrs tl lost pl over 3f out: sn bhd) | 4 | 6 | 50/1 | 37 | — |
| | | | | (SP 113.6%) | | **6 Rn** |

**1m 34.2** (7.40) CSF £5.20 TOTE £1.90: £1.10 £5.20 (£5.00) OWNER Mr R. A. Popely (EPSOM) BRED R. A. and J. H. Popely

## 196 MANSFIELD H'CAP (0-70) (4-Y.O+) (Class E)

3-00 (3-03) **1m 4f (Fibresand)** £3,022.95 (£915.60: £447.30: £213.15) Stalls: Low GOING: 0.18 sec per fur (SLW)

| | Horse | Dist | Pos | SP | RR | SF |
|---|---|---|---|---|---|---|
| *$154^{2}$* | **Mr Moriarty (IRE) (36)** (SRBowring) **5-7-10** NCarlisle(3) (chsd ldrs: styd on wl to ld ins fnl f: pushed clr) | — | 1 | $9/2^{3}$ | 47 | — |
| *$152^{2}$* | **Modest Hope (USA) (48)** (BRichmond) **9-8-3**(5) CTeague(10) (lw: hld up: smooth hdwy 5f out: chal 2f out: nt qckn ins fnl f) | 2½ | 2 | 12/1 | 56 | 8 |
| | **Exclusion (38)** (JHetherton) **7-7-12** JQuinn(5) (chsd ldrs: led over 3f out tl ins fnl f: one pce) | 2 | 3 | 25/1 | 43 | — |
| *124** | **Ashover (69)** (TDBarron) **6-9-8**(7) 5x KimberleyHart(11) (chsd ldrs: led 5f out tl over 3f out: one pce fnl 2f) | ½ | 4 | $7/4^{1}$ | 73 | 25 |
| | **Noble Canonire (44)** (SRBowring) **4-8-1** NKennedy(1) (s.i.s: bhd & sn drvn along: hdwy 4f out: nvr nr ldrs) | 3½ | 5 | 25/1 | 45 | — |
| | **Bold Pursuit (IRE) (55)** (JGFitzGerald) **7-9-1** JFortune(7) (b: bhd: hdwy u.p 4f out: eased ins fnl f) | 7 | 6 | 16/1 | 45 | — |
| | **Non Vintage (IRE) (55)** (MCChapman) **5-9-1** JWeaver(8) (lw: hld up: effrt 4f out: hung lft & wknd 2f out) | 5 | 7 | $7/2^{2}$ | 39 | — |
| | **New Inn (60)** (SGollings) **5-9-6** VHalliday(6) (prom early: sn drvn along & lost pl) | 14 | 8 | 12/1 | 25 | — |
| *85** | **Adaloaldo (USA) (51)** (JParkes) **4-8-8** GBardwell(4) (plld hrd: w ldrs tl lost pl over 4f out) | 1¾ | 9 | 7/1 | 15 | — |
| | **Just Flamenco (38)** (MJRyan) **5-7-7**(5) MBaird(2) (led to 5f out: sn lost pl & bhd) | 25 | 10 | 14/1 | — | — |
| | **Turgenev (IRE) (67)** (RBastiman) **7-9-8**(5) HBastiman(9) (bkwd: t.o fnl 5f) | dist | 11 | 14/1 | — | — |
| | | | | (SP 131.6%) | | **11 Rn** |

**2m 47.6** (15.10) CSF £56.90 CT £1,137.12 TOTE £4.50: £1.40 £2.40 £8.50 (£13.40) Trio £92.60 OWNER Mr D. H. Bowring (EDWINSTOWE) BRED Joseph Hernon and Partners

WEIGHT FOR AGE 4yo-3lb

## 197 OLD CLIPSTONE MEDIAN AUCTION MAIDEN STKS (3-Y.O) (Class F)

3-30 (3-36) **1m 3f (Fibresand)** £2,398.00 (£673.00: £328.00) Stalls: Low GOING: 0.18 sec per fur (SLW)

| | Horse | Dist | Pos | SP | RR | SF |
|---|---|---|---|---|---|---|
| | **Balios (IRE)** (MJohnston) **3-9-0** JWeaver(2) (h.d.w: mde all: rdn & hung lft over 2f out: hld on wl towards fin) | — | 1 | $7/2^{3}$ | 69 | 17 |
| | **Oversman (65)** (JGFitzGerald) **3-9-0** JFortune(3) (lw: trckd ldrs: ev ch fnl 2f: edgd rt & nt qckn nr fin) | hd | 2 | $3/1^{2}$ | 69 | 17 |
| *$17^{2}$* | **Reploy (59)** (LordHuntingdon) **3-8-9** LDettori(6) (w ldrs: rdn over 4f out: wandered over 1f out: kpt on same pce) | 2 | 3 | $8/11^{1}$ | 61 | 9 |
| *$129^{9}$* | **Diasafina** (SCWilliams) **3-8-9** JQuinn(4) (b.nr fore: in tch: drvn along over 7f out: wknd over 4f out: sn bhd) | 25 | 4 | 100/1 | 25 | — |
| | **Kai's Lady (IRE)** (SWCampion) **3-8-9** DeanMcKeown(1) (unruly s: hld up: drvn along 6f out: sn lost pl) | 30 | 5 | 100/1 | — | — |

| | | | Pos | SP | RR | SF |
|---|---|---|---|---|---|---|
| $58^{9}$ | **Skipman (IRE)** (NASmith) **3-9-0** SDWilliams(5) (chsd ldrs: drvn along ½-wy: wknd over 3f out: collapsed & died after r) | 5 | **6** | 33/1 | — | — |
| $46^{7}$ | ***Mulhollande Lad (IRE) (43)*** *(MCChapman)* ***3-8-11***$^{(3)}$ *DRMcCabe(7) (Withdrawn not under Starter's orders: lame at s)* | | ***W*** | *50/1* | — | — |

(SP 112.0%) **6 Rn**

**2m 33.6** (13.60) CSF £13.14 TOTE £3.50: £1.60 £1.20 (£4.50) OWNER Mr & Mrs A Mordain (MIDDLEHAM) BRED P. Myerscough

## 198 NEW BALDERTON (S) STKS (4-Y.O+) (Class F)

4-00 (4-03) **1m 3f (Fibresand)** £2,398.00 (£673.00: £328.00) Stalls: Low GOING: 0.18 sec per fur (SLW)

| | | | Pos | SP | RR | SF |
|---|---|---|---|---|---|---|
| $111^{2}$ | **No Submission (USA) (60)** (DWChapman) **10-9-0** ACulhane(7) (sn bhd: hdwy on outside 5f out: rdn & edgd lft 2f out: styd on to ld ins fnl f) | — | **1** | 8/1 | 64 | 16 |
| | **Kismetim (46)** (WWHaigh) **6-9-0**$^{(5)}$ DGriffiths(2) (hld up: hdwy to chse ldrs 5f out: edgd lft & led jst ins fnl f: sn hdd & no ex) | 2 | **2** | 14/1 | 66 | 18 |
| $99^{4}$ | **Night Time (57)** (AStreeter) **4-8-7**$^{(5)}$ LNewton(4) (hdwy 5f out: sn chsng ldrs: outpcd 3f out: styd on appr fnl f) | nk | **3** | 11/1 | 62 | 11 |
| $114^{*}$ | **Sharp Gazelle (53)** (BSmart) **6-9-0** RCochrane(8) (hld up: hdwy to chse ldrs 5f out: outpcd 2f out: n.m.r & kpt on ins fnl f) | ¾ | **4** | $4/1^{2}$ | 60 | 12 |
| $104^{10}$ | **Trumble (45)** (CWThornton) **4-8-12** DeanMcKeown(3) (led: clr 3f out: hdd & wknd jst ins fnl f) | 3 | **5** | 11/1 | 56 | 5 |
| $153^{5}$ | **Komiamaite (54)** (SRBowring) **4-8-12**$^{(5)}$ CTeague(12) (hdwy 7f out: sn prom & pushed along: wknd 2f out) | 4 | **6** | 10/1 | 55 | 4 |
| $128^{4}$ | **Miss Cashtal (IRE)** (DTThom) **5-8-9v**$^{1}$ MFenton(9) (dwlt: hdwy to chse ldrs ½-wy: wknd over 2f out) | 1 | **7** | 12/1 | 43 | — |
| $111^{4}$ | **Hawwam (65)** (EJAlston) **10-9-0** JWeaver(1) (hung bdly rt & reluctant to r: t.o 8f out) | 7 | **8** | $11/2^{3}$ | 38 | — |
| $104^{3}$ | **Harry (49)** (AJWilson) **6-9-0** JFortune(11) (b: trckd ldrs tl rdn & wknd qckly over 4f out) | ¾ | **9** | $3/1^{1}$ | 37 | — |
| $128^{5}$ | **Duveen (IRE) (62)** (JWhite) **6-9-0b**$^{1}$ MTebbutt(6) (hdwy & u.p 5f out: wknd over 3f out) | ½ | **10** | $11/2^{3}$ | 36 | — |
| $169^{11}$ | **Anchorena (54)** (JAHarris) **4-8-7** SDWilliams(5) (chsd ldrs tl wknd qckly 6f out: sn bhd: t.o) | 6 | **11** | 12/1 | 23 | — |
| $136^{8}$ | **Rainbow Walk (IRE) (71)** (JGMO'Shea) **6-9-0v** JQuinn(10) (chsd ldrs tl wknd qckly over 5f out: sn bhd: t.o) | 5 | **12** | 12/1 | 20 | — |

(SP 142.4%) **12 Rn**

**2m 33.8** (13.80) CSF £117.81 TOTE £13.70: £3.00 £8.60 £3.80 (£413.50) Trio £251.90 OWNER Mr T. S. Redman (YORK) BRED Mr. Francis X. Weber

WEIGHT FOR AGE 4yo-2lb

No bid

OFFICIAL EXPLANATION **Hawwam: had hung so badly in the early stages that his jockey had been unable to ride him properly.**

## 199 LADBROKE ALL-WEATHER CHALLENGE SERIES H'CAP (Qualifier) (0-70) (3-Y.O+) (Class E)

4-30 (4-32) **1m (Fibresand)** £3,022.95 (£915.60: £447.30: £213.15) Stalls: Low GOING: 0.18 sec per fur (SLW)

| | | | Pos | SP | RR | SF |
|---|---|---|---|---|---|---|
| | **Tatika (65)** (GWragg) **6-9-2**$^{(7)}$ GMilligan(5) (trckd ldrs: led over 1f out: pushed out) | — | **1** | 10/1 | 82 | 56 |
| $159^{*}$ | **Kingchip Boy (61)** (MJRyan) **7-9-5v** 7x TIves(7) (led after 1f tl over 1f out: kpt on same pce) | 2½ | **2** | $9/4^{1}$ | 73 | 47 |
| $34^{5}$ | **Sea Spouse (48)** (MBlanshard) **5-8-6** NAdams(10) (chsd ldrs: kpt on same pce appr fnl f) | 1¾ | **3** | 33/1 | 57 | 31 |
| $153^{2}$ | **Sea God (43)** (MCChapman) **5-8-1** GBardwell(1) (chsd ldrs: rdn & outpcd 3f out: styd on fnl f) | ½ | **4** | $11/4^{2}$ | 51 | 25 |
| $122^{10}$ | **Twin Creeks (55)** (MDHammond) **5-8-13** RCochrane(8) (hld up: hdwy on outside over 2f out: nvr plcd to chal) | 5 | **5** | 20/1 | 53 | 27 |
| $120^{2}$ | **Master Beveled (68)** (PDEvans) **6-9-12** SSanders(4) (sn outpcd & bhd: styd on fnl 2f: nvr nr to chal) | hd | **6** | 11/2 | 65 | 39 |
| $122^{2}$ | **Legal Issue (IRE) (59)** (WWHaigh) **4-9-3** DaleGibson(3) (s.i.s: hdwy u.p ½-wy: n.d) | 4 | **7** | $9/2^{3}$ | 49 | 22 |
| $153^{4}$ | **Jalmaid (55)** (BAMcMahon) **4-8-13** GCarter(9) (led 1f: chsd ldrs tl lost pl over 3f out) | ½ | **8** | 20/1 | 44 | 17 |
| $30^{14}$ | **Roar on Tour (64)** (MrsMReveley) **7-9-8** ACulhane(6) (a in rr) | 5 | **9** | 16/1 | 42 | 16 |
| $127^{15}$ | **Cheerful Groom (IRE) (41)** (SRBowring) **5-7-13** NKennedy(2) (in tch tl rdn & outpcd over 3f out) | ½ | **10** | 50/1 | 18 | — |
| $155^{10}$ | **Aquado (48)** (SRBowring) **7-8-6b** JQuinn(11) (reluctant to r: a t.o) | 20 | **11** | 20/1 | — | — |

(SP 125.2%) **11 Rn**

**1m 46.5** (6.50) CSF £32.81 CT £689.23 TOTE £10.50: £4.10 £2.00 £10.70 (£48.70) Trio £437.00 OWNER Mr G. Wragg (NEWMARKET) BRED D. J. and Mrs Deer

T/Jkpt: £29,790.00 (0.7 Tckts); £12,587.35 to Lingfield 3/2/96. T/Plpt: £397.80 (83.43 Tckts). T/Qdpt: £140.30 (44.16 Tckts). WG

# 0185-LINGFIELD (L-H) (Standard)

## Saturday February 3rd

WEATHER: fair WIND: almost nil

## 200 PELLEW APPRENTICE H'CAP (0-60) (I) (4-Y.O+) (Class G)

1-15 (1-16) **1m (Equitrack)** £1,871.50 (£524.00: £254.50) Stalls: High GOING minus 0.34 sec per fur (FST)

| | | | Pos | SP | RR | SF |
|---|---|---|---|---|---|---|
| $105^{8}$ | **Oozlem (IRE) (39)** (JRPoulton) **7-8-2b**$^{(7)}$ TField(7) (b: racd wd: sn rdn along: hdwy 4f out: hrd rdn over 2f out: led ins fnl f: r.o) | — | **1** | 11/2 | 54 | 37 |
| | **Roman Reel (USA) (57)** (GLMoore) **5-9-10**$^{(3)}$ LSuthern(4) (lw: chsd ldr: led 3f out: hdd ins fnl f: unable qckn) | 2 | **2** | $5/2^{1}$ | 68 | 51 |
| | **Zahran (IRE) (50)** (JMBradley) **5-9-3**$^{(3)}$ FLynch(8) (b: hld up: hdwy 3f out: rdn over 1f out: r.o one pce fnl f) | 3½ | **3** | 7/1 | 54 | 37 |
| $189^{4}$ | **Mac's Taxi (51)** (PCHaslam) **4-9-2**$^{(5)}$ CarolDavison(6) (chsd ldrs tl rdn & wknd over 1f out) | 3 | **4** | $5/1^{3}$ | 50 | 32 |
| $179^{8}$ | **Paronomasia (38)** (MBell) **4-8-5v**$^{(3)}$ GFaulkner(1) (chsd ldrs: rdn over 3f out: wknd 2f out) | 6 | **5** | 12/1 | 25 | 7 |
| $145^{12}$ | **Princess Parrot (IRE) (42)** (LordHuntingdon) **5-8-12v**$^{1}$ AimeeCook(2) (sn outpcd: a bhd) | 3 | **6** | 20/1 | 22 | 5 |
| | **Exclusive Assembly (55)** (APJames) **4-9-11** ADaly(5) (chsd ldrs tl wknd over 2f out) | ¾ | **7** | $5/1^{3}$ | 35 | 17 |
| $42^{13}$ | **Maid Welcome (58)** (MrsNMacauley) **9-10-0v** AmandaSanders(3) (b: led: hdd 3f out: sn wknd) | 2½ | **8** | $9/2^{2}$ | 32 | 15 |

(SP 120.4%) **8 Rn**

**1m 40.26** (2.86) CSF £19.58 CT £90.69 TOTE £5.50: £2.50 £1.10 £1.30 (£26.00) OWNER Brooknight Guarding Ltd (LEWES) BRED J. R. Jameson

## 201 PELLEW APPRENTICE H'CAP (0-60) (II) (4-Y.O+) (Class G)

1-45 (1-45) **1m (Equitrack)** £1,871.50 (£524.00: £254.50) Stalls: High GOING minus 0.34 sec per fur (FST)

| | | | Pos | SP | RR | SF |
|---|---|---|---|---|---|---|
| | **Hatta Sunshine (USA) (49)** (AMoore) **6-9-7**$^{(3)}$ IonaWands(2) (hld up: hdwy gng wl over 3f out: n.m.r over 2f out & over 1f out: swtchd rt: str run to ld wl ins fnl f: r.o) | — | **1** | $5/1^{3}$ | 55 | 33 |

| | Horse / details | Dist | Pos | SP | RR | SF |
|---|---|---|---|---|---|---|
| 43* | **Ladybower (IRE) (45)** (LordHuntingdon) **4-9-6** AimeeCook(1) (a.p: led over 1f out: hdd wl ins fnl f: unable qckn) | 2½ | **2** | 13/8[1] | 47 | 24 |
| | **Palacegate Gold (IRE) (33)** (RJHodges) **7-8-8** ADaly(7) (b.nr hind: led: hdd over 1f out: one pce) | 4 | **3** | 20/1 | 26 | 4 |
| 159[7] | **Dia Georgy (41)** (MrsNMacauley) **5-9-2b[1]** AmandaSanders(8) (prom: jnd ldr 4f out tl over 2f out: wknd over 1f out) | 10 | **4** | 7/1 | 14 | — |
| 133[3] | **Nuthatch (IRE) (34)** (MDIUsher) **4-8-9** CAdamson(6) (b: hld up: hdwy over 3f out: wknd over 2f out) | 3½ | **5** | 4/1[2] | 1 | — |
| | **Bad News (43)** (JMBradley) **4-8-13**(5) DSweeney(5) (chsd ldrs tl wknd over 3f out) | 1½ | **6** | 20/1 | 7 | — |
| 53[4] | **Racing Telegraph (35)** (JWPayne) **6-8-7**(3) FLynch(4) (chsd ldrs tl wknd over 2f out) | s.h | **7** | 5/1[3] | — | — |
| | **Air of Mystery (32)** (NEBerry) **4-8-4**(3) AEddery(3) (s.s: a bhd) | 14 | **8** | 50/1 | — | — |
| | | | | (SP 115.4%) | **8 Rn** | |

**1m 42.03** (4.63) CSF £13.04 CT £133.79 TOTE £5.60: £1.20 £1.20 £5.70 (£5.70) OWNER Mr R. Kiernan (BRIGHTON) BRED Daniel M. Galbreath

## 202 BLACKWOOD CLAIMING STKS (3-Y.O+) (Class E)

2-20 (2-21) **5f (Equitrack)** £2,886.45 (£873.60: £426.30: £202.65) Stalls: High GOING minus 0.34 sec per fur (FST)

| | Horse / details | Dist | Pos | SP | RR | SF |
|---|---|---|---|---|---|---|
| 185[3] | **Lift Boy (USA) (57)** (AMoore) **7-9-1** CandyMorris(5) (a.p: rdn to ld ins fnl f: r.o wl) | — | **1** | 6/1 | 64 | 19 |
| 170[5] | **Southern Dominion (59)** (MJohnston) **4-9-3** NAdams(4) (lw: led: hdd ins fnl f: r.o) | nk | **2** | 12/1 | 65 | 20 |
| 173[5] | **Hannah's Usher (75)** (CMurray) **4-9-11** RCochrane(2) (hld up: hdwy over 1f out: hrd rdn ins fnl f: r.o) | ¾ | **3** | 5/1[3] | 71 | 26 |
| 185[2] | **Inherent Magic (IRE) (87)** (WRMuir) **7-9-8** JWeaver(3) (b: lw: hld up: hdwy 2f out: hrd rdn ins fnl f: one pce) | nk | **4** | 6/5[1] | 67 | 22 |
| 180[3] | **Sea-Deer (80)** (DWChapman) **7-9-9** ACulhane(1) (lw: hld up in tch: rdn & n.m.r over 1f out: kpt on one pce fnl f) | 2½ | **5** | 5/2[2] | 60 | 15 |
| 117[9] | **Superlao (BEL) (48)** (JJBridger) **4-8-10** JQuinn(7) (prom: rdn over 2f out: wknd over 1f out) | 5 | **6** | 50/1 | 31 | — |
| | **Ezekiel (27)** (TTClement) **5-9-1** MTebbutt(6) (dwlt: a outpcd) | 9 | **7** | 150/1 | 7 | — |
| | | | | (SP 115.3%) | **7 Rn** | |

**61.07 secs** (3.07) CSF £60.20 TOTE £7.10: £2.70 £4.20 (£31.90) OWNER Mr A. Moore (BRIGHTON) BRED Paul & Arnold Bryant in USA
Southern Dominion clmd CWoof £5,000

## 203 COCHRANE LIMITED STKS (0-50) (3-Y.O+) (Class F)

2-50 (2-58) **6f (Equitrack)** £2,671.70 (£751.20: £367.10) Stalls: Low GOING minus 0.34 sec per fur (FST)

| | Horse / details | Dist | Pos | SP | RR | SF |
|---|---|---|---|---|---|---|
| 179[7] | **Mister Raider (38)** (SMellor) **4-8-13b**(7) ADaly(14) (mid div: rdn thrght: hdwy over 1f out: str run to ld wl ins fnl f) | — | **1** | 16/1 | 54 | 13 |
| 163[7] | **Jersey Belle (44)** (PJMakin) **4-9-1b** SSanders(4) (chsd ldrs: led 1f out: hdd wl ins fnl f: unable qckn) | nk | **2** | 10/1 | 48 | 7 |
| 107[9] | **Nivasha (37)** (RPCHoad) **4-9-1** MFenton(13) (rr: rdn over 2f out: styd on strly fnl f) | 2½ | **3** | 16/1 | 42 | 1 |
| 161[6] | **Mogin (45)** (JFfitch-Heyes) **3-8-0** AMackay(3) (outpcd in rr: gd hdwy fnl f: nvr nrr) | 1¼ | **4** | 14/1 | 39 | — |
| | **Learning Curve (IRE) (47)** (SirMarkPrescott) **3-8-1**ow1 GDuffield(11) (lw: chsd ldr: led over 3f out: hdd 1f out: no ex) | hd | **5** | 5/2[2] | 40 | — |
| 36[U] | **Prince Rudolf (IRE) (44)** (MrsNMacauley) **4-9-1v**(5) AmandaSanders(7) (outpcd in rr: hdwy fnl f: nvr nrr) | ¾ | **6** | 12/1 | 41 | — |
| 163[9] | **Pearl Dawn (IRE) (46)** (GLMoore) **6-9-7** SWhitworth(10) (chsd ldrs: rdn 2f out: wknd ins fnl f) | ½ | **7** | 7/4[1] | 41 | — |
| 163[10] | **Desert Water (IRE) (42)** (JJBridger) **4-9-6b** JQuinn(9) (rr: hdwy 3f out: rdn 2f out: wknd over 1f out) | ¾ | **8** | 20/1 | 38 | — |
| 36[6] | **Classic Pet (IRE) (43)** (CAHorgan) **4-9-4** AClark(12) (chsd ldrs tl wknd 2f out) | 2½ | **9** | 9/1 | 29 | — |
| 155[6] | **Fiery Footsteps (43)** (SWCampion) **4-9-1** SDWilliams(5) (b.nr hind: led: hdd over 3f out: wknd over 1f out) | nk | **10** | 8/1 | 25 | — |
| | **Blyton Star (IRE) (30)** (MissJFCraze) **8-9-6** NKennedy(2) (bit bkwd: a bhd) | hd | **11** | 50/1 | 30 | — |
| 133[6] | **Assignment (41)** (JELong) **10-8-13**(7) TField(1) (bhd fnl 3f) | hd | **12** | 12/1 | 30 | — |
| 74[9] | **Diamond Bangle (25)** (CCElsey) **4-9-1** NAdams(8) (a bhd) | s.h | **13** | 50/1 | 25 | — |
| *178[10]* | ***Anytime Baby (47)** (PTDalton) **4-9-1**(3) PMcCabe(6) (Withdrawn not under Starter's orders: broke out of stalls)* | | ***W*** | *7/1[3]* | — | — |
| | | | | (SP 150.1%) | **13 Rn** | |

**1m 15.15** (4.55) CSF £168.74 TOTE £30.10: £5.40 £2.90 £4.60 (£81.10) Trio £254.70 OWNER Raiders Partnership (SWINDON) BRED Alan Hogan
WEIGHT FOR AGE 3yo-15lb

## 204 LODESTONE PATIENT CARE MAIDEN STKS (4-Y.O+) (Class D)

3-20 (3-23) **1m (Equitrack)** £3,615.00 (£1,095.00: £535.00: £255.00) Stalls: High GOING minus 0.34 sec per fur (FST)

| | Horse / details | Dist | Pos | SP | RR | SF |
|---|---|---|---|---|---|---|
| 24[2] | **Secret Spring (FR) (73)** (PRHedger) **4-9-0** SRaymont(3) (lw: hld up in tch: led over 3f out: clr over 1f out: pushed out) | — | **1** | 100/30[3] | 87 | 61 |
| 99[2] | **Golden Pound (USA) (72)** (MissGayKelleway) **4-9-0** AClark(2) (lw: hld up in mid div: hdwy to chse wnr over 2f out: rdn over 1f out: no imp) | 5 | **2** | 7/4[1] | 77 | 51 |
| 141[4] | **Fresh Fruit Daily (65)** (PAKelleway) **4-8-9** RCochrane(6) (mid div: hdwy 3f out: rdn over 2f out: one pce) | 3½ | **3** | 11/4[2] | 65 | 39 |
| | **Kellaire Girl (IRE) (47)** (AMoore) **4-8-9** SSanders(9) (prom: led over 4f out tl over 3f out: wknd over 2f out) | 10 | **4** | 16/1 | 45 | 19 |
| 99[3] | **Restate (IRE)** (FMurphy) **5-8-9** JFanning(7) (led 1f: styd prom tl wknd over 2f out) | 1 | **5** | 10/1 | 42 | 17 |
| | **Verde Luna (64)** (DWPArbuthnot) **4-9-0** SWhitworth(8) (mid div: rdn 3f out: wknd over 2f out) | ¾ | **6** | 12/1 | 47 | 21 |
| | **Opening Range** (NEBerry) **5-8-2**(7) AEddery(1) (chsd ldrs tl wknd over 2f out) | ¾ | **7** | 33/1 | 39 | 14 |
| | **Clytha Hill Lad** (JMBradley) **5-8-11**(3) SDrowne(11) (rr: hdwy 4f out: wknd over 2f out) | 1½ | **8** | 50/1 | 41 | 16 |
| 110[7] | **Lochbuie** (JMPEustace) **4-9-0** MTebbutt(10) (a bhd) | 1 | **9** | 33/1 | 40 | 14 |
| | **Trapper Norman** (RIngram) **4-9-0** NAdams(4) (a bhd) | 5 | **10** | 50/1 | 30 | 4 |
| 134[12] | **Rizal (USA)** (DJGMurraySmith) **4-9-0** JWeaver(5) (led after 1f: hdd over 4f out: sn wknd) | 13 | **11** | 16/1 | 4 | — |
| | | | | (SP 124.5%) | **11 Rn** | |

**1m 38.37** (0.97) CSF £9.66 TOTE £4.20: £1.40 £1.10 £1.90 (£5.10) Trio £3.10 OWNER Mr M. K. George (CHICHESTER) BRED T. D. Rootes

## 205 JERVIS H'CAP (0-80) (4-Y.O+) (Class D)

3-55 (3-58) **7f (Equitrack)** £3,566.25 (£1,080.00: £527.50: £251.25) Stalls: Low GOING minus 0.34 sec per fur (FST)

| | Horse / details | Dist | Pos | SP | RR | SF |
|---|---|---|---|---|---|---|
| 144* | **Rakis (IRE) (82)** (MBrittain) **6-10-2** RCochrane(11) (lw: hld up gng wl: hdwy over 1f out: led ins fnl f: r.o wl) | — | **1** | 11/8[1] | 91 | 59 |
| 121[7] | **Duke Valentino (75)** (RHollinshead) **4-9-9** MWigham(10) (hld up: hdwy 2f out: rdn ins fnl f: r.o) | nk | **2** | 5/1[3] | 83 | 51 |
| 121[9] | **Yo Kiri-B (49)** (JFfitch-Heyes) **5-7-11**ow1 AMackay(5) (lw: hld up: hdwy 3f out: n.m.r 2f out: swtchd lft over 1f out: hrd rdn ins fnl f: one pce) | 1½ | **3** | 14/1 | 54 | 21 |

| | | | | SP | RR | SF |
|---|---|---|---|---|---|---|
| 109* | **Soaking (70)** (PBurgoyne) **6-9-4** JWeaver(8) (lw: chsd ldrs: led 2f out: hdd ins fnl f: one pce) | ½ | **4** | 4/1[2] | 74 | 42 |
| 121[4] | **Tuigamala (57)** (RIngram) **5-8-5** NAdams(9) (hld up: hdwy 3f out: rdn over 1f out: one pce) | 2½ | **5** | 12/1 | 55 | 23 |
| 163[2] | **Invocation (68)** (AMoore) **9-9-2** SSanders(6) (hld up: hdwy 3f out: rdn over 1f out: 5th whn hmpd 1f out: nt rcvr) | ½ | **6** | 14/1 | 65 | 33 |
| 144[5] | **Abtaal (78)** (RJHodges) **6-9-9**(3) SDrowne(7) (chsd ldr: ev ch 2f out: wknd over 1f out) | 2½ | **7** | 20/1 | 69 | 37 |
| 163[3] | **Ultra Beet (68)** (PCHaslam) **4-9-2v** JFortune(3) (bhd fnl 4f) | 3 | **8** | 8/1 | 52 | 20 |
| | **Old Hook (IRE) (77)** (PaulSmith,Belgium) **5-9-11** TIves(4) (chsd ldrs tl rdn & wknd over 2f out) | 1 | **9** | 14/1 | 59 | 27 |
| 163[6] | **Agwa (67)** (RJO'Sullivan) **7-9-1** DBiggs(2) (led: hdd 2f out: wkng whn hmpd over 1f out) | 2 | **10** | 14/1 | 45 | 13 |
| | ***Scorpius (58)*** (TTClement) **6-8-3b**(3)ow2 JStack(1) (Withdrawn not under Starter's orders: veterinary advice) | | **W** | 16/1 | — | — |

(SP 134.9%) **10 Rn**

**1m 26.22** (2.22) CSF £9.73 CT £70.53 TOTE £2.10: £1.40 £2.20 £3.50 (£12.10) Trio £25.30 OWNER Mr P. G. Shorrock (WARTHILL) BRED The Mount Coote Partnership
LONG HANDICAP Yo Kiri-B 7-5

## 206 COLLINGWOOD H'CAP (0-70) (4-Y.O+) (Class E)

4-25 (4-29) **1m 5f (Equitrack)** £2,954.70 (£894.60: £436.80: £207.90) Stalls: Low GOING minus 0.34 sec per fur (FST)

| | | | | SP | RR | SF |
|---|---|---|---|---|---|---|
| 145[9] | **Claque (47)** (DWChapman) **4-8-13b**[1] ACulhane(1) (chsd ldrs: rdn over 2f out: led ins fnl f: r.o) | — | **1** | 25/1 | 57 | 33 |
| 169[9] | **Milngavie (IRE) (37)** (MJohnston) **6-8-7b** JWeaver(6) (a.p: led over 3f out to 2f out: ev ch ins fnl f: nt qckn) | 1¼ | **2** | 4/1[2] | 45 | 26 |
| 130* | **Ikhtiraa (USA) (58)** (RJO'Sullivan) **6-10-0b** NCarlisle(8) (led 10f out: hdd over 3f out: led again 2f out: hdd ins fnl f: one pce) | nk | **3** | 9/2[3] | 65 | 46 |
| 108[5] | **Wottashambles (42)** (LMontagueHall) **5-8-12** SSanders(2) (chsd ldrs: pushed along 5f out: hrd rdn over 2f out: one pce) | 5 | **4** | 15/2 | 43 | 24 |
| 140[3] | **Sassiver (USA) (36)** (PAKelleway) **6-8-6b** JQuinn(5) (hld up: hdwy 7f out: ev ch 3f out: sn rdn: one pce) | 1 | **5** | 6/1 | 36 | 17 |
| 165* | **Sacred Mirror (IRE) (53)** (CEBrittain) **5-9-9** MLarsen(12) (lw: chsd ldrs: rdn over 3f out: wknd over 2f out) | 7 | **6** | 3/1[1] | 44 | 25 |
| 84[8] | **Blasted (49)** (GEThorner) **4-9-1** AMcGlone(4) (bhd fnl 5f) | 20 | **7** | 25/1 | 17 | — |
| 23[9] | **Chez Catalan (48)** (RAkehurst) **5-9-4** AClark(9) (a bhd) | 2½ | **8** | 8/1 | 11 | — |
| | **Just Lucky (IRE) (49)** (MrsNMacauley) **4-8-10**(5) AmandaSanders(11) (led 3f: wknd 6f out) | 2½ | **9** | 25/1 | 10 | — |
| | **Md Thompson (51)** (TTClement) **4-9-3** RCochrane(10) (mid div tl rdn & wknd 4f out) | 8 | **10** | 16/1 | 3 | — |
| | ***Brave Spy (57)*** (CACyzer) **5-9-13** DBiggs(3) (Withdrawn not under Starter's orders: veterinary advice) | | **W** | 16/1 | — | — |

(SP 123.6%) **10 Rn**

**2m 49.38** (6.18) CSF £113.75 CT £488.17 TOTE £45.40: £4.40 £1.40 £2.00 (£156.90) Trio £270.60 OWNER Mr Michael Hill (YORK) BRED Lord Howard de Walden
WEIGHT FOR AGE 4yo-4lb

T/Jkpt: Not won; £25,024.54 to Southwell 5/2/96. T/Plpt: £725.90 (24.81 Tckts). T/Qdpt: £122.20 (17.64 Tckts) SM

# 0194-SOUTHWELL (L-H) (Standard)

## Monday February 5th

WEATHER: cold WIND: fresh half against

## 207 MACKENZIE H'CAP (0-60) (I) (4-Y.O+) (Class F)

1-30 (1-32) **7f (Fibresand)** £2,048.00 (£573.00: £278.00) Stalls: Low GOING: 0.25 sec per fur (SLW)

| | | | | SP | RR | SF |
|---|---|---|---|---|---|---|
| 111* | **Chadleigh Lane (USA) (57)** (RHollinshead) **4-9-6v**(7) FLynch(10) (lw: s.i.s: smooth hdwy ½-wy: led over 1f out: r.o) | — | **1** | 4/1[2] | 69 | 41 |
| 127* | **Daawe (USA) (58)** (MrsVAAconley) **5-10-0v** MDeering(5) (trckd ldrs: led over 2f tl over 1f out: no ex) | 4 | **2** | 9/4[1] | 61 | 33 |
| 179* | **Serious Fact (44)** (SirMarkPrescott) **4-9-0** 6x GDuffield(4) (sn drvn: in tch: hdwy & ev ch 2f out: one pce) | 3½ | **3** | 9/4[1] | 39 | 11 |
| 159[5] | **Genesis Four (40)** (SRBowring) **6-8-5**(5) CTeague(1) (sn outpcd & bhd: styd on fnl 3f: nrst fin) | 1¼ | **4** | 8/1[3] | 32 | 4 |
| 172[6] | **Double Glow (32)** (NBycroft) **4-8-2** GBardwell(3) (cl up: led over 3f out tl over 2f out: sn btn) | ½ | **5** | 20/1 | 23 | — |
| | **My Godson (37)** (ABMulholland) **6-8-7b** JTate(8) (sn pushed along: in tch: no imp fnl 3f) | 4 | **6** | 16/1 | 19 | — |
| 134[7] | **Pats Delight (37)** (SCoathup) **4-8-7** TWilliams(7) (chsd ldrs over 4f: sn rdn & btn) | 5 | **7** | 33/1 | 7 | — |
| | **Supercool (38)** (DWChapman) **5-8-8** ACulhane(12) (outpcd fr ½-wy) | 2 | **8** | 33/1 | 4 | — |
| 135[8] | **Persian Gusher (IRE) (50)** (NASmith) **6-8-13**(7) JBramhill(6) (led tl hdd over 3f out: sn wknd) | ½ | **9** | 33/1 | 15 | — |
| | **Seconds Away (27)** (JSGoldie) **5-7-11b** JQuinn(11) (outpcd ½-wy: sn lost tch) | 2½ | **10** | 12/1 | — | — |
| 85[14] | **Crowning Tino (28)** (MrsNMacauley) **4-7-12v**[1] NAdams(9) (sn outpcd & bhd) | 3 | **11** | 33/1 | — | — |
| 57[12] | **Sheroot (40)** (DMoffatt) **4-8-7**(3) DarrenMoffatt(2) (b: a outpcd & bhd) | 6 | **12** | 33/1 | — | — |

(SP 125.7%) **12 Rn**

**1m 34.6** (7.80) CSF £13.15 CT £22.00 TOTE £5.80: £1.90 £1.30 £1.10 (£8.00) Trio £4.70 OWNER Mr J. E. Bigg (UPPER LONGDON) BRED Windwoods Farm, Bruce Brown and Connie Brown

## 208 NILE AMATEUR H'CAP (0-75) (4-Y.O+) (Class F)

2-00 (2-00) **2m (Fibresand)** £2,398.00 (£673.00: £328.00) Stalls: Low GOING: 0.25 sec per fur (SLW)

| | | | | SP | RR | SF |
|---|---|---|---|---|---|---|
| 154[3] | **Record Lover (IRE) (36)** (MCChapman) **6-9-4**(3) MrsSBosley(9) (mde most: kpt on gamely fnl f) | — | **1** | 10/1 | 45 | — |
| 154* | **Greek Night Out (IRE) (39)** (JLEyre) **5-9-10** MissDianaJones(7) (a.p: effrt 4f out: ev ch 2f out: styd on nr fin) | ½ | **2** | 13/8[1] | 48 | — |
| 47* | **Yougo (70)** (MJohnston) **4-11-4**(3) MrsDKettlewell(6) (lw: chsd ldr: disp ld 3f out to 2f out: edgd lft & one pce) | 1¾ | **3** | 9/4[2] | 77 | 14 |
| | **Gentleman Sid (50)** (PGMurphy) **6-10-4**(3) MrPPritchard-Gordon(5) (prom tl outpcd 6f out: n.d after) | 25 | **4** | 13/2[3] | 32 | — |
| | **Moonshine Dancer (37)** (MrsMReveley) **6-9-8** MrMHNaughton(2) (effrt 6f out: no imp) | 2½ | **5** | 7/1 | 16 | — |
| 47[9] | **Never Time (IRE) (35)** (MrsVAAconley) **4-8-7**(7) MrsCWilliams(8) (effrt ½-wy: sn btn) | 7 | **6** | 33/1 | 7 | — |
| 60[5] | **Mrs Jawleyford (USA) (44)** (CSmith) **8-9-12**(3) MrsMMorris(3) (lw: outpcd ½-wy: n.d after) | 20 | **7** | 14/1 | — | — |
| | **Air Command (BAR) (47)** (CTNash) **6-10-1**(3)ow13 MrPPhillips(4) (sn bhd: wl t.o fr ½-wy) | dist | **8** | 20/1 | — | — |
| 138[9] | **Bushehr (IRE) (56)** (SCoathup) **4-10-7b**[1] MrCBonner(1) (rdn & lost pl 8f out: sn wl t.o) | 4 | **9** | 16/1 | — | — |

(SP 124.0%) **9 Rn**

**3m 55.3** (29.30) CSF £27.20 CT £48.49 TOTE £9.80: £2.20 £1.10 £1.60 (£11.70) Trio £8.00 OWNER Mr Alan Mann (MARKET RASEN) BRED P. F. I. Cole
WEIGHT FOR AGE 4yo-6lb

## 209 MISSOURI MEDIAN AUCTION MAIDEN STKS (3-Y.O) (Class F)

2-30 (2-30) **6f (Fibresand)** £2,398.00 (£673.00: £328.00) Stalls: Low GOING: 0.25 sec per fur (SLW)

| | | | | SP | RR | SF |
|---|---|---|---|---|---|---|
| 134[3] | **Coastguards Hero (57)** (MDIUsher) **3-9-0** MWigham(5) (in tch: hdwy ½-wy: led wl over 1f out: pushed out) | — | **1** | 4/1[3] | 51 | 12 |
| | **Principal Boy (IRE) (42)** (TJEtherington) **3-9-0** GCarter(2) (a chsng ldrs: kpt on wl towards fin) | ¾ | **2** | 10/1 | 49 | 10 |
| | **General Haven** (TJNaughton) **3-9-0** JWeaver(6) (rdn ½-wy: styd on wl fnl 2f: nrst fin) | hd | **3** | 7/1 | 49 | 10 |
| 129[7] | **Quinntessa (42)** (BPalling) **3-8-6**(3) SDrowne(9) (a chsng ldrs: one pce fnl 2½f) | 7 | **4** | 12/1 | 25 | — |
| | **Ginas Girl** (SRBowring) **3-8-4**(5) CTeague(4) (s.i.s: c wd st: nvr nrr) | 2 | **5** | 11/1 | 20 | — |
| 160[3] | **Red Acuisle (IRE) (57)** (JBerry) **3-8-9b**(5) PRoberts(3) (w ldr tl rdn & btn over 1f out) | 2½ | **6** | 5/2[1] | 18 | — |
| | **Heathyards Jade** (RHollinshead) **3-8-9** JFortune(7) (outpcd fr ½-wy) | 1¼ | **7** | 20/1 | 10 | — |
| 194[6] | **Chillam (52)** (JPLeigh) **3-9-0** DeanMcKeown(8) (led tl hdd & wknd wl over 1f out) | 2½ | **8** | 3/1[2] | 8 | — |
| 51[5] | **Kury Girl** (JAHarris) **3-8-9** SDWilliams(1) (spd 2f: sn outpcd & wl bhd) | 20 | **9** | 16/1 | — | — |
| | | | | (SP 121.8%) | **9 Rn** | |

**1m 21.5** (8.00) CSF £40.42 TOTE £6.90: £2.10 £3.90 £2.10 (£23.80) Trio £35.40 OWNER Coastguards Estate Agent of Bognor Regis (SWINDON) BRED B. Fry

## 210 AMAZON H'CAP (0-70) (4-Y.O+) (Class E)

3-00 (3-02) **1m 3f (Fibresand)** £3,009.30 (£911.40: £445.20: £212.10) Stalls: Low GOING: 0.25 sec per fur (SLW)

| | | | | SP | RR | SF |
|---|---|---|---|---|---|---|
| 152[3] | **Tempering (50)** (DWChapman) **10-8-8** ACulhane(12) (dwlt: led after 2f: hld on wl) | — | **1** | 7/1 | 55 | 13 |
| 72[2] | **Calder King (66)** (JLEyre) **5-9-10b** JFortune(6) (a.p: nt clr run & swtchd 2f out: r.o towards fin) | nk | **2** | 5/1[2] | 71 | 29 |
| | **Star Performer (IRE) (46)** (MrsMReveley) **5-8-4** GCarter(4) (sn bhd: hdwy 3f out: styd on wl towards fin) | 1 | **3** | 10/1 | 49 | 7 |
| 198[8] | **Hawwam (65)** (EJAlston) **10-9-9** SDWilliams(2) (chsd ldrs tl outpcd & lost pl 5f out: styd on fnl 2f) | nk | **4** | 10/1 | 68 | 26 |
| 100[8] | **Our Tom (65)** (JWharton) **4-9-2**(5) CTeague(5) (lw: hld up: stdy hdwy ½-wy: sn chsng ldrs: rdn & wandered 2f out: nt qckn) | ¾ | **5** | 4/1[1] | 68 | 23 |
| 184[2] | **Mentalasanythin (70)** (ABailey) **7-10-0** AMackay(10) (a.p: effrt over 4f out: r.o one pce) | ½ | **6** | 4/1[1] | 71 | 29 |
| | **Greek Gold (IRE) (39)** (WLBarker) **7-7-4**(7) MartinDwyer(8) (chsd ldrs tl wknd fnl 2f) | 3 | **7** | 25/1 | 36 | — |
| 122[9] | **Mazilla (42)** (AStreeter) **4-7-12** FNorton(9) (hdwy u.p 5f out: wknd 2f out) | 7 | **8** | 25/1 | 29 | — |
| | **Fen Terrier (54)** (WJHaggas) **4-8-10** RMcGhin(3) (outpcd 7f out: n.d after) | 6 | **9** | 6/1[3] | 33 | — |
| 140[8] | **Jady's Dream (IRE) (40)** (BPalling) **5-7-12** NAdams(11) (in tch: outpcd 4f out: sn wknd: t.o) | 20 | **10** | 20/1 | — | — |
| 172[9] | **Samana Cay (48)** (PSFelgate) **4-8-4** JTate(7) (outpcd after 3f: a bhd: t.o) | 13 | **11** | 33/1 | — | — |
| | **Built for Comfort (IRE) (60)** (NMBabbage) **4-9-2** JQuinn(1) (led 2f: chsd ldrs tl wknd over 3f out: t.o) | 3½ | **12** | 12/1 | — | — |
| | | | | (SP 124.7%) | **12 Rn** | |

**2m 34.1** (14.10) CSF £40.83 CT £327.07 TOTE £7.00: £2.00 £2.10 £5.00 (£12.70) Trio £54.20 OWNER Mr Richard Berenson (YORK) BRED Lord Howard de Walden

WEIGHT FOR AGE 4yo-2lb

## 211 ORINOCO H'CAP (0-80) (3-Y.O+) (Class D)

3-30 (3-33) **1m (Fibresand)** £3,631.25 (£1,100.00: £537.50: £266.25) Stalls: Low GOING: 0.25 sec per fur (SLW)

| | | | | SP | RR | SF |
|---|---|---|---|---|---|---|
| 86[2] | **Pine Ridge Lad (IRE) (71)** (JLEyre) **6-9-7** RLappin(12) (mde all: styd on wl fnl 2f) | — | **1** | 13/2[3] | 84 | 69 |
| 136[2] | **Maple Bay (IRE) (78)** (ABailey) **7-9-9**(5) PRoberts(13) (trckd ldrs: effrt over 2f out: nt qckn fnl f) | 3 | **2** | 7/2[1] | 85 | 70 |
| 136[4] | **High Premium (69)** (RAFahey) **8-9-5** ACulhane(14) (lw: hdwy u.p 3f out: kpt on: nvr able to chal) | 6 | **3** | 12/1 | 64 | 49 |
| 88[7] | **Nashaat (USA) (70)** (MCChapman) **8-8-13**(7) CMunday(6) (cl up tl outpcd fnl 2f) | 1 | **4** | 12/1 | 63 | 48 |
| 77[4] | **Q Factor (65)** (DHaydnJones) **4-9-1** AMackay(10) (a chsng ldrs: rdn 3f out: one pce) | s.h | **5** | 10/1 | 59 | 43 |
| 135* | **Rambo Waltzer (78)** (DNicholls) **4-10-0** AlexGreaves(4) (lw: chsd ldrs tl grad wknd fnl 2f) | 5 | **6** | 11/2[2] | 62 | 46 |
| 77[13] | **Forgotten Empress (58)** (AHarrison) **4-8-8** JFanning(5) (lw: prom: rdn 3f out: no imp after) | 5 | **7** | 33/1 | 32 | 16 |
| 144[6] | **Prima Silk (74)** (MJRyan) **5-9-10** TIves(1) (in tch: rdn over 3f out: sn btn) | 2 | **8** | 8/1 | 43 | 28 |
| 159[6] | **Great Bear (54)** (DWChapman) **4-7-11**(7) FLynch(8) (c wd st: n.d) | 7 | **9** | 33/1 | 10 | — |
| 61[8] | **Leif the Lucky (USA) (76)** (MissSEHall) **7-9-12** JWeaver(3) (outpcd ½-wy: n.d after) | ¾ | **10** | 7/2[1] | 29 | 14 |
| 181[12] | **Gulf Shaadi (75)** (EJAlston) **4-9-11v**[1] JFortune(2) (s.s: nt rcvr) | 3 | **11** | 33/1 | 23 | 7 |
| 115[4] | **First Gold (60)** (JWharton) **7-8-10** SDWilliams(9) (bhd: effrt ½-wy: n.d) | 1 | **12** | 14/1 | 5 | — |
| | **Bold Amusement (77)** (WSCunningham) **6-9-13** DeanMcKeown(7) (s.i.s: n.d) | 13 | **13** | 16/1 | — | — |
| | | | | (SP 130.1%) | **13 Rn** | |

**1m 45.6** (5.60) CSF £30.02 CT £210.91 TOTE £6.70: £1.60 £1.90 £3.00 (£14.10) Trio £31.00 OWNER Whitestonecliffe Racing Partnership (HAMBLETON) BRED Whitechurch Stud in Ireland

OFFICIAL EXPLANATION **Leif the Lucky (USA): failed to act on the surface.**

## 212 RIO GRANDE (S) STKS (3-Y.O+) (Class F)

4-00 (4-06) **6f (Fibresand)** £2,398.00 (£673.00: £328.00) Stalls: Low GOING: 0.25 sec per fur (SLW)

| | | | | SP | RR | SF |
|---|---|---|---|---|---|---|
| 126[2] | **Sea Devil (62)** (MJCamacho) **10-9-9** LCharnock(4) (trckd ldr: led over 1f out: shkn up: sn qcknd clr) | — | **1** | 4/5[1] | 74 | 39 |
| 135[7] | **Sense of Priority (73)** (DNicholls) **7-9-13** AlexGreaves(1) (led tl hdd over 1f out: no ch w wnr) | 4 | **2** | 3/1[2] | 67 | 32 |
| | **La Dama (USA) (41)** (ABMulholland) **4-9-4** MMcAndrew(5) (unruly gng to s: sn pushed along: hdwy over 1f out: nvr rchd ldrs) | 1¼ | **3** | 100/1 | 55 | 20 |
| 76[4] | **Desert Invader (IRE) (60)** (DWChapman) **5-9-9** ACulhane(6) (cl up tl outpcd fnl 2f) | ½ | **4** | 4/1[3] | 59 | 24 |
| 42[11] | **Our Shadee (USA) (53)** (KTIvory) **6-9-2v**(7) CScally(2) (b: in tch: outpcd ½-wy: n.d after) | ½ | **5** | 9/1 | 57 | 22 |
| 63[13] | **Branston Kristy (35)** (CSmith) **4-8-13v**(5) MBaird(3) (b.hind: spd 3f: sn bhd) | 25 | **6** | 50/1 | — | — |
| | | | | (SP 113.5%) | **6 Rn** | |

**1m 20.0** (6.50) CSF £3.63 TOTE £1.90: £1.30 £2.50 (£2.30) OWNER Mr A. N. Goacher (MALTON) BRED A. L. Goacher and E. G. Noble

Bt in 3,600 gns

## 213 MACKENZIE H'CAP (0-60) (II) (4-Y.O+) (Class F)

4-30 (4-31) **7f (Fibresand)** £2,048.00 (£573.00: £278.00) Stalls: Low GOING: 0.25 sec per fur (SLW)

| | | | | SP | RR | SF |
|---|---|---|---|---|---|---|
| 155[4] | **Sweet Mate (55)** (SRBowring) **4-9-6b**(5) CTeague(7) (bhd: c wd & hdwy over 2f out: r.o to ld post) | — | **1** | 13/2 | 63 | 40 |
| 44[3] | **Hi Rock (43)** (MJCamacho) **4-8-13** LCharnock(11) (sn cl up: led over 2f out: hrd rdn fnl f: jst ct) | s.h | **2** | 11/2[3] | 51 | 28 |
| 115[7] | **Quinzii Martin (48)** (DHaydnJones) **8-9-4** AMackay(9) (in tch: drvn along 3f out: ev ch over 1f out: no ex) | 1¾ | **3** | 10/1 | 52 | 29 |

| | | | | | |
|---|---|---|---|---|---|
| 122[3] **Mezzoramio (40)** (KAMorgan) **4-8-10v** MFenton(1) (led tl hdd over 2f out: one pce)......1¼ | **4** | 8/1 | 41 | 18 |
| 166[3] **Indiahra (48)** (RHollinshead) **5-8-11v**(7) FLynch(4) (styd on fnl 3f: nvr able to chal)......1 | **5** | 7/1 | 47 | 24 |
| **Pinkerton Polka (47)** (CEBrittain) **4-9-3** MLarsen(8) (effrt over 2f out: styd on: no imp)......3 | **6** | 12/1 | 39 | 16 |
| 179[6] **Speedy Snaps Pride (39)** (PDCundell) **4-8-9** GCarter(5) (outpcd & bhd: sme late hdwy)......2½ | **7** | 16/1 | 25 | 2 |
| 168[2] **Awesome Venture (57)** (MCChapman) **6-9-6**(7) CMunday(2) (s.i.s: sn cl up: wknd fnl 2½f)......3 | **8** | 13/2 | 36 | 13 |
| 172[2] **The Mestral (35)** (MJRyan) **4-8-5** PBloomfield(6) (cl up tl wknd over 2f out)......5 | **9** | 5/1 2 | 3 | — |
| **Ohnonotagain (40)** (BWMurray) **4-8-5**(5) GParkin(10) (chsd ldrs over 4f: wknd)......2 | **10** | 33/1 | 3 | — |
| 166* **Cabcharge Blue (54)** (TJNaughton) **4-9-10** 6x JWeaver(3) (lw: chsd ldr tl wknd over 2f out)......hd | **11** | 7/2 1 | 17 | — |

(SP 130.2%) **11 Rn**

**1m 34.6** (7.80) CSF £43.02 CT £337.02 TOTE £6.50: £2.60 £2.30 £2.80 (£30.40) Trio £123.20 OWNER Mrs P. A. Barratt (EDWINSTOWE) BRED T. Barratt

OFFICIAL EXPLANATION **Cabcharge Blue: had been unable to dominate in the race, and reportedly sulked.**

T/Jkpt: £27,642.20 (1.19 Tckts). T/Plpt: £13.20 (2,109.11 Tckts). T/Qdpt: £12.50 (271 Tckts). AA

# 0200-LINGFIELD (L-H) (Standard)
## Tuesday February 6th

WEATHER: bitter WIND: almost nil

## 214 CHERRY H'CAP (0-70) (4-Y.O+) (Class E)

1-50 (1-52) **1m 4f (Equitrack)** £2,900.10 (£877.80: £428.40: £203.70) Stalls: Low GOING minus 0.50 sec per fur (FST)

| | | SP | RR | SF |
|---|---|---|---|---|
| 80[6] **One Off the Rail (USA) (64)** (AMoore) **6-10-0** CandyMorris(8) (b.hind: a.p: led 6f out: hrd rdn over 1f out: r.o wl)......— | **1** | 11/2 | 73 | 39 |
| 165[2] **Never So Rite (IRE) (48)** (DWPArbuthnot) **4-8-9** RCochrane(3) (b.hind: hdwy over 4f out: chsd wnr 3f out: rdn over 2f out: unable qckn)......1½ | **2** | 7/2 1 | 56 | 18 |
| **Royal Expression (59)** (MrsMReveley) **4-9-6** ACulhane(10) (hdwy 10f out: rdn over 4f out: one pce)......5 | **3** | 11/2 | 60 | 22 |
| **Bag of Tricks (IRE) (60)** (SDow) **6-9-3**(7) ADaly(7) (bit bkwd: a.p: rdn 4f out: one pce)......nk | **4** | 12/1 | 60 | 26 |
| 140[5] **Royal Circus (44)** (PRWebber) **7-8-5**(3) DRMcCabe(4) (led 6f: wknd over 3f out)......8 | **5** | 9/2 3 | 33 | — |
| 184[5] **Rival Bid (USA) (62)** (MrsNMacauley) **8-9-7**(5) AmandaSanders(6) (lw: s.s: hdwy over 5f out: wknd over 2f out)......nk | **6** | 7/1 | 51 | 17 |
| 165[5] **Uncharted Waters (43)** (CACyzer) **5-8-7** DBiggs(5) (rdn thrght: bhd fnl 7f)......9 | **7** | 14/1 | 20 | — |
| 145[5] **Ilandra (IRE) (52)** (SDow) **4-8-13** JWeaver(2) (bhd fnl 4f)......6 | **8** | 4/1 2 | 22 | — |
| **Cheveley Dancer (USA) (33)** (TJNaughton) **8-7-11** JQuinn(9) (b: bit bkwd: bhd fnl 5f)......6 | **9** | 33/1 | — | — |

(SP 121.0%) **9 Rn**

**2m 34.97** (4.97) CSF £24.59 CT £102.88 TOTE £5.40: £1.20 £2.00 £2.00 (£11.90) Trio £25.20 OWNER Mr K. Higson (BRIGHTON) BRED Parrish Hill Farm

WEIGHT FOR AGE 4yo-3lb

## 215 DAMSON (S) STKS (3-Y.O) (Class G)

2-20 (2-20) **6f (Equitrack)** £2,190.00 (£615.00: £300.00) Stalls: Low GOING minus 0.50 sec per fur (FST)

| | | SP | RR | SF |
|---|---|---|---|---|
| 160[5] **Copper Bright (55)** (PCHaslam) **3-8-12b** JWeaver(1) (lw: nt clr run on ins 5f out: hdwy over 2f out: hrd rdn wl over 1f out: led wl ins fnl f: r.o wl)......— | **1** | 7/2 3 | 63 | — |
| 182[7] **The Frisky Farmer (60)** (WGMTurner) **3-9-5** AClark(5) (lw: led: rdn over 3f out: hdd wl ins fnl f: unable qckn) ½ | **2** | 11/2 | 69 | 6 |
| 118[3] **Rowlandsons Stud (IRE) (60)** (GLMoore) **3-8-12** MFenton(3) (a.p: rdn over 2f out: ev ch over 1f out: one pce)......2½ | **3** | 6/4 1 | 55 | — |
| 101[11] **Common Divine (IRE)** (CMurray) **3-8-7** RCochrane(4) (nvr nr to chal)......7 | **4** | 20/1 | 31 | — |
| 131[6] **Wingnut (IRE) (37)** (JJBridger) **3-9-0v** JQuinn(7) (hdwy over 4f out: wknd over 2f out)......hd | **5** | 12/1 | 38 | — |
| 143[4] **Northern Miracle (IRE)** (CFWall) **3-8-7** GDuffield(6) (prom over 3f)......¾ | **6** | 9/4 2 | 29 | — |

(SP 120.8%) **6 Rn**

**1m 14.82** (4.22) CSF £21.67 TOTE £6.00: £2.10 £3.20 (£24.90) OWNER Mr Gerald Selby (MIDDLEHAM) BRED Bearstone Stud

No bid

## 216 PLUM CLAIMING STKS (4-Y.O+) (Class E)

2-50 (2-51) **1m 2f (Equitrack)** £3,022.95 (£915.60: £447.30: £213.15) Stalls: Low GOING minus 0.50 sec per fur (FST)

| | | SP | RR | SF |
|---|---|---|---|---|
| 162[2] **Sweet Supposin (IRE) (76)** (CADwyer) **5-9-0v** LDettori(8) (lw: hdwy over 3f out: led over 1f out: rdn out)......— | **1** | 15/8 2 | 83 | 29 |
| 162* **Masnun (USA) (66)** (RJO'Sullivan) **11-8-6** AClark(1) (plld hrd: hdwy over 3f out: hrd rdn over 1f out: r.o)......1¾ | **2** | 7/4 1 | 72 | 18 |
| **El Atrevido (FR) (65)** (NJHWalker) **6-8-3**(3) JStack(7) (lw: chsd ldr: led over 4f out tl over 1f out: nt qckn)......4 | **3** | 20/1 | 66 | 12 |
| 145[3] **Zuno Flyer (USA) (34)** (AMoore) **4-7-10v**1(5) MBaird(5) (b: b.hind: plld hrd: hld up: rdn over 2f out: one pce) 1¼ | **4** | 20/1 | 61 | 5 |
| **Charm Dancer (52)** (MCPipe) **4-9-0** RCochrane(4) (a.p: ev ch 2f out: wknd over 1f out)......1¾ | **5** | 33/1 | 71 | 15 |
| 144[3] **Perilous Plight (70)** (WRMuir) **5-8-8** JWeaver(6) (dwlt: nvr nr to chal)......1½ | **6** | 5/2 3 | 61 | 7 |
| 162[3] **Scottish Park (39)** (JLHarris) **7-7-11** JQuinn(2) (led over 5f: wknd over 2f out)......4 | **7** | 20/1 | 43 | — |
| **Yubralee (USA) (70)** (MCPipe) **4-9-8**(3) AWhelan(9) (dwlt: bhd fnl 3f)......2½ | **8** | 16/1 | 69 | 13 |
| 165[6] **Elly Fleetfoot (IRE) (50)** (BJMeehan) **4-8-2** CRutter(10) (dwlt: a bhd)......3 | **9** | 33/1 | 41 | — |

(SP 125.8%) **9 Rn**

**2m 8.06** (3.76) CSF £5.94 TOTE £3.40: £1.50 £1.10 £4.20 (£3.60) Trio £73.10 OWNER Mrs Christine Rawson (NEWMARKET) BRED Ballylinch Stud Ltd

WEIGHT FOR AGE 4yo-1lb

## 217 NECTARINE MAIDEN STKS (3-Y.O+) (Class D)

3-20 (3-21) **7f (Equitrack)** £3,615.00 (£1,095.00: £535.00: £255.00) Stalls: Low GOING minus 0.50 sec per fur (FST)

| | | SP | RR | SF |
|---|---|---|---|---|
| **Cornish Snow (USA)** (DRLoder) **3-8-7** LDettori(6) (a.p: chsd ldr over 4f out: led on bit wl over 1f out: hrd hld)......— | **1** | 1/4 1 | 66 | 6 |
| 67[5] **Baranov (IRE)** (DJGMurraySmith) **3-8-7** JWeaver(10) (plld hrd: hld up: rdn over 2f out: chsd wnr fnl f: no imp)......2½ | **2** | 8/1 2 | 60 | — |

115[8] **Don't Get Caught (IRE) (57)** (JLHarris) **4-9-5** TIves(5) (rdn over 3f out: hdwy over 1f out: r.o) ....½ **3** 20/1 53 11
109[9] **Takeshi (IRE) (59)** (WRMuir) **4-9-5v[1]** Jean-PierreLopez(12) (a.p: rdn over 2f out: wknd over 1f out) ....4 **4** 25/1 44 2
203[8] **Desert Water (IRE) (42)** (JJBridger) **4-9-10v[1]** JQuinn(9) (led over 5f out tl wl over 1f out: sn wknd) ....1¼ **5** 66/1 46 4
132[14] **Office Hours (70)** (CACyzer) **4-9-10** DBiggs(3) (a.p: rdn over 2f out: wknd over 1f out) ....4 **6** 14/1 37 —
134[6] **Giftbox (USA)** (SirMarkPrescott) **4-9-10** GDuffield(2) (outpcd: nvr nrr) ....nk **7** 11/1[3] 36 —
134[4] **Call Tophorse (43)** (CMurray) **4-9-10** RCochrane(8) (a bhd) ....1¼ **8** 25/1 34 —
**Mr Streaky** (LMontagueHall) **5-9-10** SSanders(1) (bit bkwd: led over 1f: wknd over 2f out) ....3 **9** 66/1 27 —
**Mystic Legend (IRE)** (TJNaughton) **4-9-3**(7) TAshley(4) (a bhd) ....3½ **10** 66/1 19 —
**Valjess** (DCO'Brien) **3-8-2** GBardwell(11) (a bhd) ....1¼ **11** 66/1 12 —
(SP 124.5%) **11 Rn**

**1m 27.89** (3.89) CSF £3.88 TOTE £1.50: £1.10 £2.00 £2.50 (£3.00) Trio £37.80 OWNER Sheikh Mohammed (NEWMARKET) BRED Hermitage Farm Inc.
WEIGHT FOR AGE 3yo-17lb

## 218 GREENGAGE H'CAP (0-75) (3-Y.O+) (Class D)

3-50 (3-51) **6f (Equitrack)** £3,517.50 (£1,065.00: £520.00: £247.50) Stalls: Low GOING minus 0.50 sec per fur (FST)

SP RR SF

144[4] **Robo Magic (USA) (70)** (LMontagueHall) **4-10-0** SSanders(3) (a.p: rdn over 2f out: led over 1f out: r.o wl) ....— **1** 4/1[2] 75 28
177[6] **Moi Canard (62)** (BAPearce) **3-8-2**(3) DRMcCabe(2) (lw: s.s: rdn over 2f out: hdwy over 1f out: r.o wl ins fnl f) ....1½ **2** 5/1 64 1
163* **Lochon (57)** (JLEyre) **5-9-1** RLappin(6) (b: a.p: led over 2f out tl wl over 1f out: unable qckn) ....2 **3** 5/2[1] 53 6
180[4] **Sir Tasker (70)** (JLHarris) **8-10-0** LDettori(4) (a.p: rdn over 2f out: led wl over 1f out: sn hdd: one pce) ....1¼ **4** 9/2[3] 62 15
142[3] **Sunset Harbour (IRE) (60)** (TJNaughton) **3-8-3** JQuinn(5) (hld up: rdn over 2f out: one pce) ....¾ **5** 10/1 51 —
133[5] **Dusk in Daytona (54)** (CJames) **4-8-5**(7) FLynch(9) (hld up: rdn & bmpd over 2f out: one pce) ....1¼ **6** 14/1 41 —
155[12] **Tael of Silver (49)** (KRBurke) **4-8-7** MFenton(7) (outpcd) ....2 **7** 14/1 31 —
168[3] **Elton Ledger (IRE) (62)** (MrsNMacauley) **7-9-6v** RCochrane(1) (b: s.s: a bhd) ....3½ **8** 10/1 34 —
118[2] **Maple Burl (64)** (SDow) **3-8-0**(7) ADaly(8) (outpcd: sme hdwy over 2f out: sn wknd) ....1¼ **9** 8/1 34 —
133[4] **Jaazim (57)** (MMadgwick) **6-9-1** JWeaver(11) (led over 3f: wknd over 1f out) ....hd **10** 8/1 26 —
(SP 137.2%) **10 Rn**

**1m 13.59** (2.99) CSF £26.91 CT £59.13 TOTE £5.80: £1.30 £2.40 £1.70 (£15.90) Trio £17.20 OWNER Mr A D Green and Partners (EPSOM) BRED Curtis C. Green
WEIGHT FOR AGE 3yo-15lb

## 219 PEACH AMATEUR H'CAP (0-70) (4-Y.O+) (Class E)

4-20 (4-23) **1m (Equitrack)** £2,954.70 (£894.60: £436.80: £207.90) Stalls: High GOING minus 0.50 sec per fur (FST)

SP RR SF

116[3] **Don't Drop Bombs (USA) (34)** (DTThom) **7-9-9v** MissJFeilden(5) (lw: chsd ldr: led over 1f out: r.o wl) ....— **1** 8/1 46 35
200[2] **Roman Reel (USA) (57)** (GLMoore) **5-11-0**(4) MrsJMoore(6) (lw: led: sn clr: hdd over 1f out: unable qckn) ....1¾ **2** 13/2 66 55
145[7] **Canary Falcon (56)** (JohnBerry) **5-11-3v[1]** MrMRimell(8) (b: lw: hld up: rdn over 2f out: r.o one pce) ....2½ **3** 11/1 60 49
190[3] **Dream Carrier (IRE) (51)** (REPeacock) **8-10-6**(6) MrsCPeacock(11) (rdn over 3f out: hdwy over 1f out: nvr nrr)3 **4** 25/1 49 38
190[0] **Montone (IRE) (45)** (JRJenkins) **6-10-2**(4) DrMMannish(4) (rdn over 3f out: hdwy over 1f out: nvr nrr) ....nk **5** 20/1 42 31
190* **Digpast (IRE) (72)** (RJO'Sullivan) **6-12-1b**(4) 5x MrDavyJones(12) (lw: s.s: gd hdwy over 3f out: nvr nrr) ....hd **6** 100/30[2] 69 58
190[8] **Jon's Choice (42)** (BPreece) **8-9-11**(6) MissLBoswell(9) (hdwy over 4f out: wknd wl over 1f out) ....2½ **7** 50/1 34 23
159[3] **Pc's Cruiser (IRE) (50)** (JLEyre) **4-10-11** MissDianaJones(7) (a bhd) ....1 **8** 5/1[3] 41 29
**Tragic Hero (58)** (MCPipe) **4-11-5** MrJDurkan(10) (a bhd) ....3 **9** 11/4[1] 43 31
190[4] **Love Legend (47)** (DWPArbuthnot) **11-10-8b** MrsDArbuthnot(1) (b: bhd fnl 3f) ....1½ **10** 16/1 28 17
120[6] **Owdbetts (IRE) (55)** (GLMoore) **4-10-12**(4) MrKGoble(3) (prom 4f) ....nk **11** 15/2 36 24
**Breezed Well (38)** (BRCambidge) **10-9-9**(4) MrsHNoonan(2) (bhd fnl 5f) ....½ **12** 50/1 17 6
(SP 129.4%) **12 Rn**

**1m 40.5** (3.10) CSF £59.08 CT £536.23 TOTE £9.80: £2.00 £2.10 £2.80 (£26.60) Trio £297.90 OWNER Miss J. Feilden (NEWMARKET) BRED Hurstland Farm Incorporated

T/Jkpt: £7,100.00 (0.18 Tckts); £5,789.71 to Southwell 7/2/96. T/Plpt: £61.80 (447.55 Tckts). T/Qdpt: £9.80 (554.14 Tckts). AK

# 0207-SOUTHWELL (L-H) (Standard)
## Wednesday February 7th
**Meeting transferred from Wolverhampton**
WEATHER: overcast & cold WIND: slt half against

## 220 AVON H'CAP (0-75) (3-Y.O) (Class D)

2-15 (2-20) **7f (Fibresand)** £3,485.00 (£1,055.00: £515.00: £245.00) Stalls: Low GOING: 0.20 sec per fur (SLW)

SP RR SF

156* **Kingdom Princess (61)** (MJCamacho) **3-8-10** LCharnock(1) (led after 2f: qcknd ent st: kpt on strly) ....— **1** 11/2 68 31
182[3] **Myttons Mistake (72)** (ABailey) **3-9-0**(7) IonaWands(6) (hdwy ½-wy: chsd wnr fnl 2f: no imp) ....2½ **2** 5/2[1] 73 36
171* **Bailiwick (54)** (NAGraham) **3-8-3b** 6x MFenton(4) (a.p: effrt 2f out: nt pce to chal) ....2 **3** 9/2[3] 51 14
119[5] **Society Girl (63)** (CWThornton) **3-8-12** JWeaver(3) (b.hind: slt ld 2f: rdn over 2f out: sn btn) ....2½ **4** 4/1[2] 54 17
183[3] **Dhes-C (55)** (RHollinshead) **3-7-11**(7)ow3 FLynch(7) (s.i.s: hdwy over 3f out: sn rdn & wknd) ....3 **5** 5/1 39 —
102[4] **Honestly (72)** (BSmart) **3-9-7** RCochrane(2) (lw: prom: pushed along ent st: sn outpcd) ....1¾ **6** 9/2[3] 52 15
(SP 117.0%) **6 Rn**

**1m 33.8** (7.00) CSF £19.16 TOTE £4.90: £2.60 £1.70 (£19.60) OWNER G B Turnbull Ltd (MALTON) BRED Dr and Mrs St J. Collier

## 221 NENE MEDIAN AUCTION MAIDEN STKS (4, 5 & 6-Y.O) (Class E)

2-45 (2-52) **1m 4f (Fibresand)** £2,831.85 (£856.80: £417.90: £198.45) Stalls: Low GOING: 0.20 sec per fur (SLW)

SP RR SF

**Roufontaine (63)** (WRMuir) **5-8-11** JWeaver(4) (hld up: led ent st: rdn & hung rt: sn clr) ....— **1** 6/5[1] 70 14
**Haya Ya Kefaah** (NMBabbage) **4-8-13** JQuinn(5) (hld up: hdwy 5f out: hrd drvn over 2f out: one pce) ....4 **2** 15/2 71 11
85[7] **Selmeston (IRE) (32)** (PSFelgate) **4-8-10**(3) PMcCabe(3) (sn bhd & outpcd: hdwy 4f out: rdn 2f out: kpt on same pce) ....¾ **3** 20/1 70 10

| | | | Pos | SP | RR | SF |
|---|---|---|---|---|---|---|
| 47[3] | **Nick the Biscuit (66)** (RTPhillips) **5-9-2** AClark(8) (b: trckd ldrs: hrd drvn over 2f out: sn btn) | 7 | 4 | 10/1 | 59 | 3 |
| | **Ambidextrous (IRE) (52)** (EJAlston) **4-8-13v** SDWilliams(6) (led tl hdd wl over 2f out: grad fdd) | 2½ | 5 | 14/1 | 57 | — |
| | **Moonlight Air (21)** (JLSpearing) **5-8-8**(3) SDrowne(1) (sn pushed along: trckd ldrs to ½-wy: lost tch: t.o) | 15 | 6 | 7/1[3] | 31 | — |
| | **Kalisko (FR)** (GFierro) **6-9-2** MWigham(2) (bkwd: a bhd: t.o fnl 5f) | dist | 7 | 14/1 | — | — |
| 175[4] | **Taniyar (FR)** (RHollinshead) **4-8-13** LDettori(7) (a in rr: t.o fnl 3f) | 4 | 8 | 4/1[2] | — | — |
| 103[6] | **Mister (53)** (KMcAuliffe) **4-8-13** JFortune(9) (prom 8f: wknd qckly: t.o) | dist | 9 | 33/1 | — | — |

(SP 119.8%) **9 Rn**

**2m 47.6** (15.10) CSF £10.84 TOTE £2.00: £1.10 £1.90 £3.60 (£8.90) Trio £56.90 OWNER Mr D. J. Deer (LAMBOURN) BRED D. J. & Mrs Deer
WEIGHT FOR AGE 4yo-3lb
**OFFICIAL EXPLANATION Taniyar (FR): lost his action, after which his jockey decided not to persevere with him as a precaution.**

## 222 THAMES H'CAP (0-80) (4-Y.O+) (Class D)

3-15 (3-20) **1m 4f (Fibresand)** £3,436.25 (£1,040.00: £507.50: £241.25) Stalls: Low GOING: 0.20 sec per fur (SLW)

| | | | Pos | SP | RR | SF |
|---|---|---|---|---|---|---|
| 210[6] | **Mentalasanythin (70)** (ABailey) **7-8-11**(7) AngelaGallimore(1) (chsd ldng pair: qcknd to ld 2f out: sn clr) | — | 1 | 6/1[3] | 80 | — |
| 184* | **Beaumont (IRE) (61)** (JEBanks) **6-8-9** 5x RCochrane(5) (hld up: effrt & rdn 4f out: kpt on fnl 2f: no ch w wnr) | 8 | 2 | 4/6[1] | 60 | — |
| 97[5] | **Backview (63)** (BJLlewellyn) **4-8-8** TWilliams(8) (lw: w ldr: shkn up to ld over 2f out: sn hdd: outpcd) | 2 | 3 | 33/1 | 61 | — |
| 187[5] | **Cross Talk (IRE) (63)** (RHollinshead) **4-8-8** MWigham(6) (hld up & bhd: effrt ent st: hung lft: no imp) | 5 | 4 | 14/1 | 54 | — |
| | **Toy Princess (USA) (70)** (CEBrittain) **4-9-1** LDettori(3) (bit bkwd: mde most over 9f: rdn over 2f out: wknd) | 8 | 5 | 4/1[2] | 50 | — |
| 136[10] | **Hillzah (USA) (77)** (RBastiman) **8-9-6**(5) HBastiman(4) (bit bkwd: stdd s: hld up: rdn & outpcd over 2f out: t.o) | 6 | 6 | 14/1 | 48 | — |
| | **Analogue (IRE) (62)** (PhilipMitchell) **4-8-7** AClark(2) (bkwd: trckd ldrs: drvn & lost pl over 4f out: t.o) | dist | 7 | 12/1 | — | — |

(SP 118.3%) **7 Rn**

**2m 44.9** (12.40) CSF £10.57 CT £116.67 TOTE £9.20: £1.40 £1.70 (£5.00) OWNER Mrs M. O'Donnell (TARPORLEY) BRED R. B. Warren
WEIGHT FOR AGE 4yo-3lb

## 223 'NUMBER 1 IN 1996' H'CAP (0-100) (3-Y.O+) (Class C)

3-45 (3-47) **1m (Fibresand)** £5,255.60 (£1,590.80: £776.40: £369.20) Stalls: Low GOING: 0.20 sec per fur (SLW)

| | | | Pos | SP | RR | SF |
|---|---|---|---|---|---|---|
| 114[2] | **Sarasi (63)** (MJCamacho) **4-7-10** LCharnock(10) (lw: mde all: clr ent st: edgd rt fnl f: hld on) | — | 1 | 5/1[3] | 74 | 34 |
| 120* | **Queen of All Birds (IRE) (80)** (RBoss) **5-8-13** JWeaver(9) (b: b.hind: prom tl outpcd & pushed along 3f out: hdwy 2f out: unable qckn towards fin) | 1 | 2 | 9/4[1] | 88 | 49 |
| 177[4] | **Manabar (65)** (MJPolglase) **4-7-12** NCarlisle(8) (hdwy over 4f out: ev ch wl over 1f out: no ex fnl f) | 1¼ | 3 | 16/1 | 72 | 32 |
| | **Bardon Hill Boy (IRE) (84)** (BHanbury) **4-9-0**(3) JStack(3) (hld up & bhd: drvn 4f out: styd on fnl 2f: nvr nrr) | 6 | 4 | 8/1 | 79 | 39 |
| 181[2] | **Komreyev Dancer (77)** (ABailey) **4-8-10b**[1] GCarter(7) (sn chsng wnr: hrd drvn over 2f out: grad fdd) | ¾ | 5 | 3/1[2] | 70 | 30 |
| | **Stinging Reply (71)** (LordHuntingdon) **4-8-1**(3) AWhelan(6) (bkwd: prom tl wknd qckly wl over 1f out) | 5 | 6 | 7/1 | 54 | 14 |
| | **Ertlon (95)** (CEBrittain) **6-10-0** LDettori(2) (bit bkwd: hld up & bhd: effrt over 3f out: sn lost tch: t.o) | 15 | 7 | 7/1 | 47 | 8 |
| 135[3] | **Everset (FR) (78)** (ABailey) **8-8-4**(7) AngelaGallimore(5) (prom over 4f: eased whn btn: t.o) | 8 | 8 | 12/1 | 14 | — |

(SP 122.1%) **8 Rn**

**1m 46.3** (6.30) CSF £16.93 CT £148.42 TOTE £7.50: £1.10 £1.60 £4.40 (£7.40) Trio £96.20 OWNER The Blue Chip Group (MALTON) BRED C. J. R. Trotter

## 224 WELLAND (S) STKS (3-Y.O) (Class E)

4-15 (4-15) **5f (Fibresand)** £2,859.15 (£865.20: £422.10: £200.55) Stalls: High GOING: 0.20 sec per fur (SLW)

| | | | Pos | SP | RR | SF |
|---|---|---|---|---|---|---|
| 183[2] | **Boffy (IRE) (69)** (BPJBaugh) **3-8-12**(7) IonaWands(6) (b: a.p: led over 2f out: hld on wl cl home) | — | 1 | 10/11[1] | 58 | 34 |
| 183[10] | **Victoria Sioux (52)** (JAPickering) **3-8-7** JQuinn(2) (b.off hind: led to ½-wy: rallied u.p cl home) | ¾ | 2 | 9/1[3] | 44 | 20 |
| | **General Equation (47)** (JBalding) **3-8-5**(7) JEdmunds(1) (wl grwn: bkwd: a.p: kpt on one pce appr fnl f) | 2½ | 3 | 16/1 | 41 | 18 |
| 160[8] | **Impington (IRE) (50)** (WRMuir) **3-8-4v**(3) PMcCabe(4) (b.off hind: hld up: hdwy wl over 1f out: hrd drvn: nvr able chal) | s.h | 4 | 12/1 | 35 | 13 |
| 183[9] | **Shoot The Minstrel (32)** (JAPickering) **3-8-12** NCarlisle(3) (trckd ldrs: rdn 2f out: sn outpcd) | 2½ | 5 | 33/1 | 32 | 10 |
| 160[4] | **Born A Lady (65)** (NPLittmoden) **3-8-9**(5) CTeague(7) (prom: rdn along ½-wy: sn lost pl) | 2½ | 6 | 2/1[2] | 26 | 5 |
| 160[7] | **Supreme Illusion (AUS)** (JohnBerry) **3-8-7** MFenton(5) (bit bkwd: prom 3f: sn rdn & outpcd) | 4 | 7 | 20/1 | 7 | — |

(SP 117.0%) **7 Rn**

**62.0 secs** (5.00) CSF £9.51 TOTE £1.80: £1.10 £4.20 (£5.80) OWNER Mr Stan Baugh (LITTLE HAYWOOD) BRED J. Hayden
Bt in 4,400 gns

## 225 LADBROKE SERIES H'CAP (Qualifier) (0-70) (3-Y.O+) (Class E)

4-45 (4-45) **5f (Fibresand)** £2,872.80 (£869.40: £424.20: £201.60) Stalls: High GOING: 0.20 sec per fur (SLW)

| | | | Pos | SP | RR | SF |
|---|---|---|---|---|---|---|
| 155* | **Kira (58)** (JLEyre) **6-9-2** RLappin(8) (b.off hind: mde all: pushed out) | — | 1 | 3/1[2] | 68+ | 51 |
| 139[3] | **Featherstone Lane (62)** (MissLCSiddall) **5-9-6v** JWeaver(7) (w wnr: ev ch tl unable qckn cl home) | ¾ | 2 | 7/2[3] | 70 | 53 |
| 178[4] | **Tafahhus (60)** (MJPolglase) **4-9-4v** MFenton(4) (hdwy 2f out: nt pce of ldrs) | 4 | 3 | 10/1 | 55 | 38 |
| 180[2] | **King Rambo (70)** (RHollinshead) **5-9-7**(7) FLynch(3) (hld up in rr: effrt u.p 2f out: nvr nr to chal) | 1¾ | 4 | 11/2 | 59 | 42 |
| 180* | **Primula Bairn (61)** (DNicholls) **6-9-5b** 7x AlexGreaves(2) (lw: hld up & bhd: drvn over 2f out: no imp) | ½ | 5 | 9/4[1] | 49 | 32 |
| 139[10] | **Kalar (67)** (DWChapman) **7-9-11b** ACulhane(1) (spd over 3f) | 2½ | 6 | 10/1 | 25 | 30 |
| 126[13] | **First Option (57)** (RBastiman) **6-9-1** LCharnock(5) (prom tl rdn & hung rt wl over 1f out: sn outpcd) | 6 | 7 | 33/1 | — | — |

(SP 114.5%) **7 Rn**

**60.8 secs** (3.80) CSF £13.19 CT £81.82 TOTE £3.30: £1.10 £3.30 (£6.70) OWNER Mr J. E. Wilson (HAMBLETON) BRED J. S. Bell

T/Jkpt: £6,800.50 (1.77 Tckts). T/Plpt: £29.00 (1,049.28 Tckts). T/Qdpt: £5.90 (1,006.63 Tckts). IM

# 0192a-CAGNES-SUR-MER (Nice, France) (L-H) (Heavy)
## Wednesday January 31st

## 226a PRIX D'ANTHEOR (3-Y.O C & G)

1-35 (1-37) **1m 2f** £13,834.00 (£6,588.00: £3,294.00: £1,976.00)

| | | | Pos | SP | RR | SF |
|---|---|---|---|---|---|---|
| | **Grenadier (FR)** (GCollet,France) **3-9-2** MBoutin | — | 1 | | 84 | — |

| | | | | SP | RR | SF |
|---|---|---|---|---|---|---|
| | **Fantastic Gold (FR)** (JPiednoel,France) **3-8-8b[1]** ABredillet | 5 | **2** | | 68 | — |
| 149a[3] | **Danish Melody (IRE)** (RCollet,France) **3-8-8** ESaint-Martin | ½ | **3** | | 67 | — |
| 149a[6] | **Daily Risk** (SDow) **3-8-8** CBrechon (btn over 19l) | | **7** | | — | — |
| | | | | | | **10 Rn** |

**2m 24.8** P-M 3.50F: 1.80F 2.50F 1.60F (41.80F) OWNER Mme J. Cygler BRED Olivier Nicol
**149a Daily Risk**, always prominent, took the lead two and a half furlongs out until headed by the winner over one furlong out.

## 227a PRID DE LA MADELEINE (4-Y.O+)
2-03 (2-02) **1m** £13,834.00 (£6,588.00: £3,294.00: £1,976.00)

| | | | | SP | RR | SF |
|---|---|---|---|---|---|---|
| 147a[2] | **Wakeel (USA)** (SDow) **4-8-9** ESaint-Martin | — | **1** | | 83 | — |
| 191a[2] | **Spinario (USA)** (Jean-MarcCapitte,Belgium) **5-9-4** MBoutin | 2 | **2** | | 88 | — |
| 151a[2] | **Gold Delivery (USA)** (ELellouche,France) **5-9-0** DBoeuf | 2½ | **3** | | 79 | — |
| | **Shinkoh Rose (FR)** (TStack,Ireland) **4-8-6** TThulliez (btn over 8l) | | **7** | | — | — |
| 151a[5] | **Country Lover** (LordHuntingdon) **5-8-9** GGuignard (btn over 10l) | | **9** | | — | — |
| | | | | | | **12 Rn** |

**1m 49.5** P-M 3.00F: 1.30F 1.50F 1.30F (10.40F) OWNER Mrs J. Churston (EPSOM) BRED Gainsborough Farm Inc

# 0214-LINGFIELD (L-H) (Standard)
## Thursday February 8th
WEATHER: fine WIND: almost nil

## 228 BUDDLEIA MAIDEN STKS (3-Y.O+) (Class D)
1-50 (1-51) **1m 4f (Equitrack)** £3,485.00 (£1,055.00: £515.00: £245.00) Stalls: Low GOING minus 0.53 sec per fur (FST)

| | | | | SP | RR | SF |
|---|---|---|---|---|---|---|
| | **Seattle Saga (USA)** (DRLoder) **3-8-0(3)** DRMcCabe(3) (leggy: lw: sn led: hdd 8f out: hrd rdn fnl 3f: led wl ins fnl f: r.o) | — | **1** | 10/11[1] | 58 | — |
| *17*[4] | **Mister Aspecto (IRE) (62)** (MJohnston) **3-8-3b[1]** TWilliams(7) (led 8f out: hrd rdn 3f out: clr over 2f out: hdd wl ins fnl f: one pce) | 1 | **2** | 4/1[3] | 57 | — |
| | **Burnt Offering** (CEBrittain) **3-8-3** MLarsen(1) (bit bkwd: chsd ldrs: rdn & lost pl over 4f out: kpt on one pce fnl 2f) | 6 | **3** | 11/4[2] | 49 | — |
| *140*[4] | **Royal Print (IRE) (44)** (WRMuir) **7-9-13** Jean-PierreLopez(5) (mid div: hdwy over 4f out: hrd rdn 3f out: one pce) | 3½ | **4** | 33/1 | 68 | 6 |
| *79*[7] | **Discorsi (60)** (MissGayKelleway) **4-9-10** AClark(4) (lw: mid div: hdwy 4f out: hrd rdn 3f out: wknd over 1f out) | 14 | **5** | 10/1 | 50 | — |
| *37*[5] | **Tamandu** (CJames) **6-9-8** AMcGlone(2) (a bhd) | 5 | **6** | 33/1 | 38 | — |
| *106*[5] | **Cultural Icon (USA)** (PhilipMitchell) **4-9-10** JWeaver(6) (bhd fnl 8f) | 2½ | **7** | 25/1 | 40 | — |
| | | | | (SP 117.9%) | | **7 Rn** |

**2m 36.7** (6.70) CSF £5.22 TOTE £1.50: £1.10 £1.70 (£4.00) OWNER Sheikh Mohammed (NEWMARKET) BRED Needham/Bentz Breeding Partnership Two
WEIGHT FOR AGE 3yo-24lb, 4yo-3lb

## 229 WISTERIA CLAIMING STKS (4-Y.O+) (Class F)
2-20 (2-20) **7f (Equitrack)** £2,612.20 (£734.20: £358.60) Stalls: Low GOING minus 0.53 sec per fur (FST)

| | | | | SP | RR | SF |
|---|---|---|---|---|---|---|
| *117*[8] | **Speedy Classic (USA) (66)** (MJHeaton-Ellis) **7-9-0(3)** SDrowne(3) (hld up: hdwy over 2f out: chsd ldr over 1f out: led ins fnl f: drvn out) | — | **1** | 4/1[3] | 73 | 27 |
| *185*[4] | **Star Talent (USA) (80)** (MissGayKelleway) **5-8-12(3)** AWhelan(5) (b.hind: lw: hld up: hdwy over 2f out: hrd rdn & ev ch ins fnl f: r.o) | nk | **2** | 11/10[1] | 70 | 24 |
| *117*[11] | **Justinianus (IRE)** (JJBridger) **4-8-7** JQuinn(1) (led: hdd ins fnl f. one pce) | 2½ | **3** | 33/1 | 57 | 11 |
| *212*[2] | **Sense of Priority (73)** (DNicholls) **7-8-11** AlexGreaves(4) (plld hrd: sddle slipped shortly after s: chsd ldr over 3f out tl over 1f out: one pce) | ½ | **4** | 7/4[2] | 60 | 14 |
| *59*[11] | **Scboo (35)** (REPeacock) **7-8-9** VSlattery(2) (chsd ldr tl 3f out: sn wknd) | 7 | **5** | 100/1 | 42 | — |
| | | | | (SP 107.9%) | | **5 Rn** |

**1m 26.58** (2.58) CSF £8.30 TOTE £5.40: £1.80 £1.10 (£3.20) OWNER Stainless Design Services (WROUGHTON) BRED Lagrange Chance Partnership & Overbrook Farm

## 230 JAPONICA H'CAP (0-70) (3-Y.O) (Class E)
2-50 (2-55) **7f (Equitrack)** £2,845.50 (£861.00: £420.00: £199.50) Stalls: Low GOING minus 0.53 sec per fur (FST)

| | | | | SP | RR | SF |
|---|---|---|---|---|---|---|
| *218*[2] | **Moi Canard (62)** (BAPearce) **3-9-4(3)** DRMcCabe(3) (lw: confidently rdn: hld up: hdwy 2f out: qcknd to ld ins fnl f: sn clr: comf) | — | **1** | 5/2[2] | 74 | 29 |
| *137*[5] | **Domoor (56)** (MJohnston) **3-9-1** JWeaver(6) (lw: led: hdd ins fnl f: unable qckn) | 3 | **2** | 13/8[1] | 61 | 16 |
| *156*[2] | **Green Gem (BEL) (59)** (SCWilliams) **3-9-4** LDettori(2) (chsd ldr: rdn over 1f out: one pce) | ¾ | **3** | 11/4[3] | 62 | 17 |
| *131*[3] | **Mystery Matthias (49)** (MissBSanders) **3-8-8b** DBiggs(1) (prom over 4f) | 8 | **4** | 12/1 | 34 | — |
| *118*[6] | **Dauphin (IRE) (53)** (WJMusson) **3-8-9(3)** PMcCabe(5) (sn outpcd: a bhd) | 9 | **5** | 14/1 | 18 | — |
| | **Heaven Sent (IRE) (56)** (PhilipMitchell) **3-9-1** AClark(4) (prom tl ½-wy) | 13 | **6** | 33/1 | — | — |
| | | | | (SP 110.6%) | | **6 Rn** |

**1m 26.78** (2.78) CSF £6.60 TOTE £3.90: £1.30 £1.10 (£2.20) OWNER Mr Richard Gray (LIMPSFIELD) BRED Llety Stud

## 231 PRIMROSE H'CAP (0-60) (3-Y.O+) (Class F)
3-20 (3-26) **5f (Equitrack)** £2,600.30 (£730.80: £356.90) Stalls: High GOING minus 0.53 sec per fur (FST)

| | | | | SP | RR | SF |
|---|---|---|---|---|---|---|
| *139*[6] | **The Institute Boy (52)** (MissJFCraze) **6-9-7** JWeaver(5) (keen hold: hld up: hdwy gng wl 2f out: rdn 1f out: led last stride) | — | **1** | 7/1 | 63 | 28 |
| *178*[3] | **Awasha (IRE) (54)** (MissGayKelleway) **4-9-9** LDettori(8) (b: a.p: led 1f out: hdd last stride) | s.h | **2** | 5/2[1] | 65 | 30 |
| *163*[4] | **Halbert (45)** (PBurgoyne) **7-8-11v(3)** DRMcCabe(1) (lw: a.p: led over 1f out: sn hdd: one pce) | 2 | **3** | 9/2[3] | 49 | 14 |
| *16*[7] | **Daaniera (IRE) (43)** (PHowling) **6-8-12v** JQuinn(2) (b.hind: sn led: hdd over 1f out: one pce) | ½ | **4** | 12/1 | 46 | 11 |

**Cedar Girl (42)** (MrsNMacauley) **4-8-6**(5) AmandaSanders(4) (prom: ev ch over 1f out: sn rdn: one pce)........s.h **5** 33/1 45 10
127[9] **Tenor (58)** (DNicholls) **5-9-13** AlexGreaves(7) (sn outpcd & rdn along: hdwy u.p over 1f out: nrst fin)........¾ **6** 11/4[2] 58 23
139[5] **Cheeky Chappy (59)** (DWChapman) **5-10-0b** ACulhane(10) (chsd ldrs: rdn over 1f out: one pce)........s.h **7** 10/1 59 24
173[6] **Distant Dynasty (57)** (BAPearce) **6-9-12** SSanders(3) (b.hind: chsd ldrs: rdn 2f out: wknd ins fnl f)........1 **8** 12/1 54 19
202[6] **Superlao (BEL) (48)** (JJBridger) **4-8-10**(7) ADaly(6) (sn rdn along: a bhd)........½ **9** 33/1 43 8
**Rocky Two (51)** (PHowling) **5-9-6b** RCochrane(9) (b: sn rdn along: a bhd)........1¼ **10** 16/1 42 7
(SP 122.2%) **10 Rn**

**59.9 secs** (1.90) CSF £24.55 CT £82.82 TOTE £7.70: £1.70 £1.70 £1.10 (£9.70) Trio £12.60 OWNER Mrs J. Addleshaw (YORK) BRED M. Yiapatos

## 232 FORSYTHIA CONDITIONS STKS (3-Y.O) (Class D)

3-50 (3-56) **1m (Equitrack)** £3,501.25 (£1,060.00: £517.50: £246.25) Stalls: High GOING minus 0.53 sec per fur (FST)

SP RR SF

188* **Blue Flyer (IRE) (67)** (RIngram) **3-9-2** WWoods(2) (chsd ldr: led 2f out: hrd rdn ins fnl f: r.o)........— **1** 14/1 78 42
143* **Double-O-Seven** (MJohnston) **3-9-2** JWeaver(4) (lw: chsd ldr: outpcd over 4f out: hrd rdn 3f out: styd on strly ins fnl f)........nk **2** 16/1 77 41
**Meldorf** (DRLoder) **3-9-2** LDettori(5) (bit bkwd: chsd ldrs: hrd rdn over 3f out: kpt on one pce fnl f)........4 **3** 1/3[1] 69 33
164* **Banzhaf (USA) (83)** (GLMoore) **3-9-7** SWhitworth(1) (lw: led: hdd 2f out: wknd ins fnl f)........nk **4** 11/2[2] 74 38
**Accountancy Jewel (IRE)** (KMcAuliffe) **3-8-7**ow1 JFortune(3) (bhd fnl 4f)........10 **5** 10/1[3] 40 3
**Hever Golf Queen** (TJNaughton) **3-7-13**(7) TAshley(7) (bit bkwd: a bhd)........20 **6** 50/1 — —
**Lovely Smile (BEL)** (PaulSmith,Belgium) **3-8-3**(3) DRMcCabe(6) (a bhd)........1¼ **7** 50/1 — —
(SP 115.9%) **7 Rn**

**1m 38.89** (1.49) CSF £158.62 TOTE £11.30: £3.20 £2.10 (£21.40) OWNER Mrs A. V. Cappuccini (EPSOM) BRED Matt Carr

## 233 CLEMATIS H'CAP (0-80) (4-Y.O+) (Class D)

4-20 (4-25) **1m 2f (Equitrack)** £3,501.25 (£1,060.00: £517.50: £246.25) Stalls: Low GOING minus 0.53 sec per fur (FST)

SP RR SF

136[3] **Kintwyn (68)** (CCElsey) **6-9-12** DHarrison(5) (chsd ldr: led over 3f out: hrd rdn ins fnl f: r.o wl)........— **1** 9/2[3] 78 42
132[2] **Almuhtaram (67)** (MissGayKelleway) **4-9-7b**(3) AWhelan(1) (hld up: hdwy 3f out: rdn over 2f out: styd on ins fnl f)........¾ **2** 9/4[2] 77 39
189* **Robellion (68)** (DWPArbuthnot) **5-9-12v** 5x RCochrane(4) (hld up: hdwy 3f out: ev ch ins fnl f: one pce)........1 **3** 5/4[1] 75 39
145[8] **Total Rach (IRE) (53)** (RIngram) **4-8-10** WWoods(2) (chsd ldrs: rdn 3f out: wknd 2f out)........5 **4** 8/1 53 15
162[6] **Gallic Victory (IRE) (58)** (JohnBerry) **5-9-2** MFenton(3) (bhd fnl 4f)........11 **5** 33/1 40 4
132[12] **Noble Neptune (55)** (WJMusson) **4-8-9**(3) PMcCabe(6) (led: hdd over 3f out: sn wknd)........3 **6** 33/1 33 —
(SP 110.4%) **6 Rn**

**2m 7.47** (3.17) CSF £13.96 TOTE £4.40: £1.60 £3.00 (£8.60) OWNER Mrs F. E. Bacon (LAMBOURN) BRED A. Baxter
WEIGHT FOR AGE 4yo-1lb

T/Jkpt: Not won; £11,352.42 to Southwell 09/02/96. T/Plpt: £83.60 (289.03 Tckts). T/Qdpt: £24.90 (184.62 Tckts). SM

# 0220-SOUTHWELL (L-H) (Standard)

## Friday February 9th

WEATHER: overcast WIND: mod half against

## 234 FLYING DRAGON MAIDEN STKS (3-Y.O+) (Class D)

2-10 (2-12) **7f (Fibresand)** £3,680.00 (£1,115.00: £545.00: £260.00) Stalls: Low GOING: 0.02 sec per fur (STD)

SP RR SF

**Anastina** (NAGraham) **4-9-5** JWeaver(4) (a.p: hdwy 2f out: r.o to ld nr fin)........— **1** 9/1 61 35
204[2] **Golden Pound (USA) (72)** (MissGayKelleway) **4-9-7**(3) AWhelan(11) (lw: a.p: led 1½f out: hung rt: no ex & hdd towards fin)........hd **2** 4/6[1] 66 40
134[5] **Eben Naas (USA)** (SCWilliams) **3-8-7** JTate(7) (b.hind: cl up: ev ch over 1f out: nt qckn)........5 **3** 14/1 54 11
110[5] **Maybank (IRE) (46)** (BAMcMahon) **4-9-10** GCarter(5) (cl up: led 3f out to 1½f out: one pce)........½ **4** 16/1 53 27
86[8] **All Apologies (IRE)** (RHollinshead) **4-9-10** TIves(8) (led 4f: sn outpcd)........10 **5** 25/1 30 4
217[7] **Giftbox (USA)** (SirMarkPrescott) **4-9-10** GDuffield(12) (s.i.s: nvr nrr)........hd **6** 8/1[3] 30+ 4
167[6] **Rajah** (CWThornton) **3-8-7** AMackay(6) (s.i.s: racd wd: a rr div)........2 **7** 20/1 26 —
**Supergold (IRE)** (WAO'Gorman) **3-8-7b**[1] EmmaO'Gorman(2) (effrt ½-wy: sn rdn & no rspnse)........1½ **8** 16/1 22 —
**Pangeran (USA)** (MrsASwinbank) **4-9-10** JFortune(10) (bit bkwd: outpcd fr ½-wy)........½ **9** 14/1 21 —
**Oxgang (IRE)** (JGFitzGerald) **3-8-7** JQuinn(3) (drvn along ½-wy: sn lost tch)........13 **10** 7/1[2] — —
134[13] **Highland Fawn** (BAMcMahon) **3-7-12**(5)ow1 LNewton(1) (sn outpcd & bhd: t.o)........dist **11** 33/1 — —
(SP 130.3%) **11 Rn**

**1m 32.9** (6.10) CSF £16.21 TOTE £10.10: £2.00 £1.10 £3.20 (£7.80) Trio £45.80 OWNER R and A Craddock (NEWMARKET) BRED R. and A. Craddock
WEIGHT FOR AGE 3yo-17lb
**OFFICIAL EXPLANATION Giftbox (USA): the rider's goggles reportedly became coated with sand, making it impossible to see and therefore he was not able to ride the colt out as vigorously as he would have liked.**

## 235 SEA GOAT CLAIMING STKS (4-Y.O+) (Class F)

2-40 (2-42) **1m 4f (Fibresand)** £2,398.00 (£673.00: £328.00) Stalls: Low GOING: 0.02 sec per fur (STD)

SP RR SF

**Heathyards Rock (85)** (RHollinshead) **4-9-8** TIves(8) (lw: dwlt: wnt prom 7f out: led wl over 1f out: hung lft: styd on)........— **1** 4/1[3] 87 16
138* **Stevie's Wonder (IRE) (66)** (MJRyan) **6-8-12v**(5) MBaird(2) (led tl hdd wl over 1f out: one pce)........1¼ **2** 85/40[2] 77 9
98[3] **Pharly Dancer (75)** (WWHaigh) **7-9-11** DaleGibson(7) (trckd ldr: effrt & chal 2f out: one pce)........2 **3** 2/1[1] 83 15
70[7] **Pistols At Dawn (USA) (60)** (BJMeehan) **6-9-11** RCochrane(1) (chsd ldrs: outpcd over 3f out: sn btn)........15 **4** 11/2 63 —
114[4] **Ballyrag (USA)** (RAFahey) **5-9-11** ACulhane(5) (b: in tch: effrt 4f out: no imp)........5 **5** 25/1 56 —
98[8] **Maradata (IRE)** (RHollinshead) **4-9-3** MWigham(4) (hld up: hdwy 6f out: sn btn)........25 **6** 16/1 18 —
86[7] **Hallstar** (KAMorgan) **4-9-3** NCarlisle(3) (b.off hind: prom 4f: sn rdn & wl bhd)........12 **7** 50/1 2 —

| | | Dist | Pos | SP | RR | SF |
|---|---|---|---|---|---|---|
| 125[5] | **Bescaby (IRE)** (JAHarris) **5-8-5** SDWilliams(6) (chsd ldrs tl rdn & wknd 5f out: t.o) | dist | 8 | 33/1 | — | — |
| | | | | (SP 115.3%) | | **8 Rn** |

**2m 46.7** (14.20) CSF £12.39 TOTE £4.20: £2.20 £1.40 £1.10 (£10.30) OWNER Mr L. A. Morgan (UPPER LONGDON) BRED N. E. and Mrs Poole
WEIGHT FOR AGE 4yo-3lb
Stevie's Wonder (IRE) clmd JLLlewellyn £5,000

## 236 MILKY WAY H'CAP (0-65) (4-Y.O+) (Class F)

3-10 (3-12) **2m (Fibresand)** £2,398.00 (£673.00: £328.00) Stalls: Low GOING: 0.02 sec per fur (STD)

| | | Dist | Pos | SP | RR | SF |
|---|---|---|---|---|---|---|
| 169[2] | **Upper Mount Clair (48)** (CEBrittain) **6-9-6** MLarsen(11) (chsd ldrs tl hmpd & lost pl ½-wy: hdwy 6f out: led 2f out: styd on strly) | — | 1 | 3/1 [1] | 68 | — |
| | **Baher (USA) (28)** (MrsASwinbank) **7-8-0** GBardwell(1) (led tl hdd 2f out: sn btn) | 13 | 2 | 50/1 | 35 | — |
| 60[9] | **Swordking (IRE) (34)** (JLHarris) **7-8-6** JQuinn(7) (trckd ldrs: effrt 4f out: one pce fnl 2½f) | 7 | 3 | 10/1 | 34 | — |
| 206* | **Claque (51)** (DWChapman) **4-9-3b** 4x ACulhane(2) (trckd ldrs: outpcd 4f out: no imp after) | 3½ | 4 | 13/2 | 48 | — |
| | **Jalcanto (52)** (MrsMReveley) **6-9-3**(7) SCopp(10) (bhd: hdwy 7f out: in tch & rdn over 3f out: no imp) | s.h | 5 | 5/1 [3] | 48 | — |
| 196* | **Mr Moriarty (IRE) (40)** (SRBowring) **5-8-7**(5) 4x CTeague(6) (w ldr tl rdn & wknd over 3f out) | 1¾ | 6 | 4/1 [2] | 35 | — |
| | **Romalito (40)** (MBlanshard) **6-8-12** RCochrane(4) (hld up & bhd: effrt 7f out: sn btn) | 9 | 7 | 12/1 | 26 | — |
| | **In a Moment (USA) (52)** (TDBarron) **5-9-10b** JFortune(9) (mid div: effrt ½-wy: sn btn) | 12 | 8 | 20/1 | 26 | — |
| | **Zanzara (IRE) (36)** (MrsVAAconley) **5-8-8** MDeering(5) (outpcd & bhd after 6f: n.d) | 1¼ | 9 | 11/1 | 8 | — |
| 208[7] | **Mrs Jawleyford (USA) (44)** (CSmith) **8-8-11**(5) MBaird(3) (b: dwlt: wnt prom after 5f: wknd 6f out: t.o) | dist | 10 | 25/1 | — | — |
| 125[4] | **I'll Be Bound (44)** (WJMusson) **5-8-13**(3) PMcCabe(12) (outpcd fr ½-wy: t.o) | 30 | 11 | 16/1 | — | — |
| | **Can She Can Can (43)** (CSmith) **4-8-9** JFanning(8) (chsd ldrs to ½-wy: sn rdn & wknd qckly: t.o) | 2½ | 12 | 16/1 | — | — |
| | | | | (SP 122.5%) | | **12 Rn** |

**3m 52.7** (26.70) CSF £108.70 CT £1,245.89 TOTE £3.60: £1.10 £27.30 £3.40 (£586.90) Trio £585.70 OWNER Mr C. E. Brittain (NEWMARKET) BRED J. Ward Hill
WEIGHT FOR AGE 4yo-6lb

## 237 NORTH STAR H'CAP (0-70) (3-Y.O) (Class E)

3-40 (3-41) **6f (Fibresand)** £2,818.20 (£852.60: £415.80: £197.40) Stalls: Low GOING: 0.02 sec per fur (STD)

| | | Dist | Pos | SP | RR | SF |
|---|---|---|---|---|---|---|
| 112[5] | **First Maite (70)** (SRBowring) **3-9-2b**(5) CTeague(5) (w ldrs: led 2½f out: r.o) | — | 1 | 3/1 [3] | 84 | 31 |
| 194[2] | **Bit of Bother (IRE) (58)** (TDBarron) **3-8-9** JFortune(2) (lw: led 1½f: cl up: one pce fnl 2f) | 5 | 2 | 13/8 [1] | 59 | 8 |
| 161[3] | **Agent (69)** (JLEyre) **3-9-6** RLappin(1) (unruly s: dwlt: led after 1½f tl 2½f out: sn btn) | 4 | 3 | 9/4 [2] | 59 | 9 |
| 171[3] | **Efipetite (45)** (NBycroft) **3-7-10** JQuinn(4) (s.i.s: hdwy ½-wy: wknd wl over 1f out) | s.h | 4 | 7/1 | 35 | — |
| 171[7] | **Cocoon (IRE) (46)** (CWThornton) **3-7-11** AMackay(3) (in tch tl wknd fnl 2f) | 20 | 5 | 16/1 | — | — |
| | | | | (SP 112.2%) | | **5 Rn** |

**1m 19.1** (5.60) CSF £8.03 TOTE £4.30: £1.80 £1.10 (£3.90) OWNER Mr S. R. Bowring (EDWINSTOWE) BRED S. R. Bowring
LONG HANDICAP Efipetite 7-7

## 238 PEACOCK (S) STKS (3-Y.O) (Class F)

4-10 (4-12) **7f (Fibresand)** £2,398.00 (£673.00: £328.00) Stalls: Low GOING: 0.02 sec per fur (STD)

| | | Dist | Pos | SP | RR | SF |
|---|---|---|---|---|---|---|
| 158* | **Dragonjoy (61)** (JWPayne) **3-9-3b** AMcGlone(3) (trckd ldr: led over 1f out: rdn & r.o) | — | 1 | 11/8 [1] | 69 | 23 |
| 167[4] | **Mooncusser (60)** (JGFitzGerald) **3-8-11** MWigham(6) (chsd ldrs: hdwy to chal u.p ins fnl f: nt qckn nr fin) | ½ | 2 | 7/1 | 62 | 16 |
| 194[4] | **Foreman (55)** (WAO'Gorman) **3-9-3** EmmaO'Gorman(1) (led tl hdd over 1f out: sn btn) | 3½ | 3 | 11/4 [2] | 60 | 14 |
| 123[13] | **The Wad (52)** (DNicholls) **3-8-11** JWeaver(2) (lw: plld hrd: trckd ldrs tl wknd fnl 2f) | 8 | 4 | 4/1 [3] | 36 | — |
| 158[5] | **Loch Style (58)** (RHollinshead) **3-8-4**(7) FLynch(4) (in tch: rdn 3f out: no imp) | 3 | 5 | 8/1 | 29 | — |
| 158[3] | **Down The Yard (42)** (MCChapman) **3-8-5**(7) CMunday(5) (in tch: effrt 3f out: sn btn) | hd | 6 | 16/1 | 30 | — |
| 156[6] | **Belacqua (USA)** (DWChapman) **3-8-6** ACulhane(7) (unruly s: sn outpcd: t.o) | dist | 7 | 50/1 | — | — |
| | | | | (SP 120.2%) | | **7 Rn** |

**1m 33.8** (7.00) CSF £11.50 TOTE £2.20: £1.40 £2.40 (£11.00) OWNER Mr T. H. Barma (NEWMARKET) BRED T. H. Barma
Bt in 4,400 gns

## 239 GREAT BEAR H'CAP (0-65) (3-Y.O+) (Class F)

4-40 (4-43) **1m (Fibresand)** £2,398.00 (£673.00: £328.00) Stalls: Low GOING: 0.02 sec per fur (STD)

| | | Dist | Pos | SP | RR | SF |
|---|---|---|---|---|---|---|
| 199[3] | **Sea Spouse (48)** (MBlanshard) **5-8-13** NAdams(15) (mde all: qcknd clr 3f out: eased wl ins fnl f) | — | 1 | 6/1 | 65 | 27 |
| | **Nautical Jewel (54)** (MDIUsher) **4-9-5** MWigham(14) (b: bhd: c wd & hdwy over 2f out: nrst fin) | 6 | 2 | 20/1 | 59 | 22 |
| 153[7] | **Bakers Daughter (50)** (JRArnold) **4-9-1** JQuinn(12) (a chsng ldrs: one pce fnl 3f) | 1½ | 3 | 11/1 | 52 | 16 |
| 166[2] | **Karinska (59)** (MCChapman) **6-9-3**(7) CMunday(9) (drvn along after s: sn cl up: chsng wnr over 2f out: sn btn) | nk | 4 | 5/1 [3] | 60 | 23 |
| 219[8] | **Pc's Cruiser (IRE) (50)** (JLEyre) **4-9-1** RLappin(6) (drvn along thrght: a chsng ldrs: no imp fnl 3f) | ½ | 5 | 7/1 | 50 | 14 |
| | **Orchidarma (47)** (JJQuinn) **4-8-12** RCochrane(13) (lw: dwlt: sme hdwy over 2f out: n.d) | 1¼ | 6 | 10/1 | 45 | 9 |
| 198[6] | **Komiamaite (53)** (SRBowring) **4-8-13b**(5) CTeague(5) (sn pushed along: hdwy over 3f out: no imp) | ½ | 7 | 7/1 | 50 | 14 |
| 156[3] | **Yeoman Oliver (62)** (BAMcMahon) **3-8-3**(5) LNewton(7) (lw: cl up tl outpcd fnl 3f) | 8 | 8 | 9/2 [2] | 43 | — |
| 124[4] | **Carol Again (39)** (NBycroft) **4-7-11**(7)ow2 FLynch(1) (lw: chsd ldrs tl wknd over 2f out) | hd | 9 | 4/1 [1] | 20 | — |
| | **Glenvally (45)** (BWMurray) **5-8-5**(5) GParkin(10) (sn outpcd & bhd) | 2½ | 10 | 16/1 | 21 | — |
| 111[5] | **Arecibo (FR) (39)** (JParkes) **4-8-4** NCarlisle(2) (a rr div) | 4 | 11 | 25/1 | 7 | — |
| 213[7] | **Speedy Snaps Pride (39)** (JAHarris) **4-8-4** AMackay(3) (in tch: sn drvn along: wknd over 3f out) | 4 | 12 | 20/1 | — | — |
| 87[6] | **East Barns (IRE) (40)** (SGollings) **8-8-5b** VHalliday(4) (in tch tl rdn & btn wl over 2f out) | 1½ | 13 | 14/1 | — | — |
| 154[9] | **Bitch (43)** (GPKelly) **4-8-3**(5)ow2 PRoberts(11) (spd over 3f: sn wknd) | 8 | 14 | 50/1 | — | — |
| | | | | (SP 139.4%) | | **14 Rn** |

**1m 47.3** (7.30) CSF £118.77 CT £830.65 TOTE £8.20: £3.50 £7.90 £3.00 (£126.40) Trio £1,259.80 OWNER Seven Seas Racing (UPPER LAMBOURN) BRED Cheveley Park Stud Ltd
WEIGHT FOR AGE 3yo-19lb
STEWARDS' ENQUIRY Lappin susp. 19-20/2/96 (incorrect use of whip).

T/Jkpt: £19,567.20 (0.79 Tckts); £5,787.51 to Newbury 10/2/96. T/Plpt: £48.10 (707.19 Tckts). T/Qdpt: £25.30 (154.65 Tckts) AA

# 0228-LINGFIELD (L-H) (Standard)
## Saturday February 10th
WEATHER: unsettled WIND: slt half bhd

## 240 RED ROSE (S) H'CAP (0-60) (4-Y.O+) (Class G)
2-05 (2-05) **1m 5f (Equitrack)** £2,263.50 (£636.00: £310.50) Stalls: Low GOING minus 0.66 sec per fur (FST)

| | | | | SP | RR | SF |
|---|---|---|---|---|---|---|
| 138[8] | **Wahem (IRE) (31)** (CEBrittain) **6-8-6** MLarsen(8) (b: sn led: qcknd clr 2f out: pushed out) | — | 1 | 20/1 | 49 | 14 |
| 140* | **Carrolls Marc (IRE) (48)** (CMurray) **8-9-9** RCochrane(5) (hld up: hdwy 4f out: rdn over 2f out: one pce) | 4 | 2 | 9/4[1] | 61 | 26 |
| 206[2] | **Milngavie (IRE) (40)** (MJohnston) **6-9-1** JWeaver(7) (in tch: rdn & outpcd 4f out: styd on again ins fnl f) | 1¼ | 3 | 7/2[2] | 52 | 17 |
| 186[2] | **Miltak (41)** (PJMakin) **4-8-12** SSanders(2) (b: b.hind: mid div: rdn over 2f out: kpt on one pce fnl f) | ½ | 4 | 7/2[2] | 52 | 14 |
| 186[11] | **Quadrant (42)** (AMoore) **7-9-3** AClark(3) (chsd ldr: rdn over 1f out: one pce) | hd | 5 | 20/1 | 53 | 18 |
| 186[3] | **Northern Trial (USA) (45)** (KRBurke) **8-8-13v**(7) TAshley(11) (chsd ldrs: rdn over 2f out: one pce) | 1¾ | 6 | 8/1[3] | 54 | 19 |
| 186[16] | **Shedansar (IRE) (28)** (GLMoore) **4-7-8**(5) MBaird(4) (dwlt: hdwy 5f out: wknd over 1f out) | 3 | 7 | 25/1 | 33 | — |
| 116[6] | **Forgetful (31)** (DBurchell) **7-7-13**(7) IonaWands(1) (a bhd) | 8 | 8 | 14/1 | 26 | — |
| 198[9] | **Harry (49)** (AJWilson) **6-9-7**(3) DRMcCabe(10) (prom over 9f) | nk | 9 | 10/1 | 44 | 11 |
| 54[12] | **Ballad Ruler (21)** (PAPritchard) **10-7-10** NAdams(6) (bhd fnl 6f: t.o) | 30 | 10 | 50/1 | — | — |
| 66[13] | **Tomal (43)** (RIngram) **4-9-0b** WWoods(9) (bhd fnl 5f: t.o) | ½ | 11 | 14/1 | — | — |

(SP 124.1%) **11 Rn**

**2m 47.38** (4.18) CSF £64.17 CT £189.56 TOTE £25.10: £8.70 £1.30 £1.90 (£85.80) Trio £162.20 OWNER Mr C. E. Brittain (NEWMARKET) BRED E. J. Loder
LONG HANDICAP Ballad Ruler 7-9
WEIGHT FOR AGE 4yo-4lb
No bid

## 241 JULIET MEDIAN AUCTION MAIDEN STKS (3-Y.O) (Class E)
2-35 (2-35) **1m 2f (Equitrack)** £2,859.15 (£865.20: £422.10: £200.55) Stalls: Low GOING minus 0.66 sec per fur (FST)

| | | | | SP | RR | SF |
|---|---|---|---|---|---|---|
| | **Simply Katie** (DRLoder) **3-8-9** LDettori(4) (b.hind: lw: a gng wl: chsd ldr: led 3f out: clr 2f out: hrd hld) | — | 1 | 4/5[1] | 64 | — |
| | **Meltemison** (CEBrittain) **3-9-0** MLarsen(1) (s.i.s: sn in tch: rdn over 3f out: chsd wnr over 2f out: one pce) | 2 | 2 | 5/1[3] | 66 | — |
| 161[2] | **Anak-Ku** (MissGayKelleway) **3-9-0** RCochrane(2) (w'like: bit bkwd: plld hrd: hld up in tch: rdn over 4f out: kpt on one pce fnl 2f) | 1¼ | 3 | 6/1 | 64 | — |
| 175[2] | **Bath Knight (64)** (DJSffrenchDavis) **3-9-0** GCarter(3) (w'like: lw: led: hdd 3f out: wknd 2f out) | 11 | 4 | 5/2[2] | 46 | — |

(SP 115.1%) **4 Rn**

**2m 9.85** (5.55) CSF £4.98 TOTE £1.40 (£4.50) OWNER Lucayan Stud (NEWMARKET) BRED P. D. Player and Mrs J. Shipway-Pratt

## 242 ROMEO CLAIMING STKS (3-Y.O) (Class F)
3-05 (3-05) **7f (Equitrack)** £2,528.90 (£710.40: £346.70) Stalls: Low GOING minus 0.66 sec per fur (FST)

| | | | | SP | RR | SF |
|---|---|---|---|---|---|---|
| 58* | **Coachella** (SirMarkPrescott) **3-9-1** GDuffield(1) (pushed along thrght: chsd ldr 3f out: hrd rdn ins fnl f: led last stride) | — | 1 | 6/4[2] | 69 | 25 |
| 188[3] | **Rawi (61)** (WRMuir) **3-7-9v**(7) MartinDwyer(5) (led: clr 2f out: rdn ins fnl f: hdd last stride) | s.h | 2 | 11/8[1] | 56 | 13 |
| 220[4] | **Society Girl (63)** (CWThornton) **3-8-11** JWeaver(6) (in tch: rdn over 4f out: kpt on one pce fnl 2f) | 5 | 3 | 5/1[3] | 54 | 11 |
| 203[4] | **Mogin (45)** (JFfitch-Heyes) **3-9-1** AMackay(4) (prom: rdn over 3f out: wknd over 2f out) | 6 | 4 | 16/1 | 44 | 3 |
| 131[10] | **Music Mistress (IRE) (52)** (JSMoore) **3-8-1** NAdams(3) (a bhd) | 13 | 5 | 25/1 | — | — |
| 215[5] | **Wingnut (IRE) (37)** (JJBridger) **3-7-13v** JQuinn(2) (prom to ½-wy) | ½ | 6 | 20/1 | — | — |

(SP 113.3%) **6 Rn**

**1m 25.73** (1.73) CSF £3.87 TOTE £2.60: £1.10 £1.30 (£2.00) OWNER Lord Derby (NEWMARKET) BRED Stanley Estate and Stud Co
Coachella clmd AReid £12,000; Rawi clmd Consultco Ltd £3,000

## 243 JACK & GILL COLE H'CAP (0-85) (3-Y.O+) (Class D)
3-35 (3-36) **1m (Equitrack)** £3,647.50 (£1,105.00: £540.00: £257.50) Stalls: High GOING minus 0.66 sec per fur (FST)

| | | | | SP | RR | SF |
|---|---|---|---|---|---|---|
| 204* | **Secret Spring (FR) (82)** (PRHedger) **4-10-0** SRaymont(4) (b.hind: lw: stdd s: hld up in rr: gd hdwy over 3f out: led gng wl over 1f out: comf) | — | 1 | 11/4[1] | 89 | 52 |
| 61[12] | **Easy Choice (USA) (74)** (PhilipMitchell) **4-9-6** AClark(10) (lw: hld up: hdwy 4f out: led over 2f out: hdd over 1f out: unable qckn) | 1¼ | 2 | 7/1 | 79 | 42 |
| 205[2] | **Duke Valentino (78)** (RHollinshead) **4-9-10** LDettori(3) (hld up: hdwy 4f out: rdn over 1f out: one pce) | ½ | 3 | 4/1[3] | 82 | 45 |
| 201* | **Hatta Sunshine (USA) (54)** (AMoore) **6-7-7**(7) IonaWands(7) (hld up: hdwy 3f out: rdn 2f out: one pce) | 7 | 4 | 14/1 | 44 | 10 |
| | **Golden Touch (USA) (58)** (NACallaghan) **4-8-4** GCarter(11) (rr: racd wd: rdn over 2f out: styd on one pce ins fnl f) | 3½ | 5 | 20/1 | 41 | 8 |
| 132[3] | **Access Adventurer (IRE) (73)** (RBoss) **5-9-5** JWeaver(2) (led: hdd over 2f out: grad wknd) | s.h | 6 | 7/2[2] | 55 | 22 |
| 189[6] | **Labudd (USA) (59)** (RIngram) **6-8-5**ow2 WWoods(6) (prom: ev ch over 2f out: sn rdn: wknd over 1f out) | nk | 7 | 14/1 | 41 | 8 |
| 159[2] | **Mislemani (IRE) (52)** (AGNewcombe) **6-7-12** NAdams(9) (bit bkwd: mid div: hrd rdn 4f out: no hdwy) | 2½ | 8 | 14/1 | 29 | — |
| 205[9] | **Old Hook (IRE) (80)** (PaulSmith,Belgium) **5-9-5**(7)ow5 MartinSmith(8) (b: prom over 4f) | 2 | 9 | 20/1 | 53 | 20 |
| | **Helios (66)** (NJHWalker) **8-8-9**(3) JStack(1) (lw: prom over 4f) | hd | 10 | 33/1 | 39 | 7 |
| 205[10] | **Agwa (65)** (RJO'Sullivan) **7-8-11** DBiggs(5) (bhd fnl 5f: t.o: b.b.v) | 25 | 11 | 25/1 | — | — |

(SP 117.7%) **11 Rn**

**1m 37.97** (0.57) CSF £20.82 CT £70.66 TOTE £3.80: £2.50 £2.50 £1.90 (£16.50) Trio £19.30 OWNER Mr M. K. George (CHICHESTER) BRED Timothy D. Rootes

## 244 DEMPSTER'S DIARY H'CAP (0-70) (4-Y.O+) (Class E)
4-05 (4-06) **7f (Equitrack)** £2,927.40 (£886.20: £432.60: £205.80) Stalls: Low GOING minus 0.66 sec per fur (FST)

| | | | | SP | RR | SF |
|---|---|---|---|---|---|---|
| | **Sharp 'n Smart (66)** (BSmart) **4-9-10** RCochrane(2) (chsd ldr: led over 2f out: clr over 1f out: r.o) | — | 1 | 11/1 | 74 | 42 |
| 205[6] | **Invocation (68)** (AMoore) **9-9-12** LDettori(3) (a.p: chsd wnr 2f out: rdn over 1f out: one pce) | 2 | 2 | 6/1 | 71 | 40 |
| 205[3] | **Yo Kiri-B (50)** (JFfitch-Heyes) **5-8-8** AMackay(8) (b.hind: chsd ldrs: rdn over 1f out: one pce) | hd | 3 | 13/2 | 53 | 23 |
| 205[5] | **Tuigamala (57)** (RIngram) **5-9-1** WWoods(9) (in tch: rdn & outpcd 3f out: kpt on one pce fnl 2f) | 5 | 4 | 5/1[3] | 49 | 19 |

177[3] **Crystal Heights (FR) (69)** (RJO'Sullivan) **8-9-13** SSanders(6) (dwlt: rr: rdn over 2f out: kpt on fnl f) ...............¾ **5** 4/1[2] 59 29
177[2] **Hawaii Storm (FR) (69)** (DJSffrenchDavis) **8-9-8**(5) CAdamson(4) (hld up in rr: rdn over 2f out: no hdwy) ........4 **6** 3/1[1] 50 21
179[2] **Woolverstone Hall (IRE) (38)** (DJGMurraySmith) **4-7-10b** NAdams(1) (led: hdd over 2f out: wknd over 1f out: eased ins fnl f) ........................................1½ **7** 12/1 16 —
172[8] **Gentle Irony (48)** (WJMusson) **4-8-6b** GCarter(5) (mid div: rdn 4f out: wknd 3f out) ...........................1½ **8** 16/1 22 —
**The Cape Doctor (IRE) (52)** (AGFoster) **4-8-7**(3) AWhelan(7) (a bhd) ...........................................½ **9** 25/1 25 —
(SP 115.0%) **9 Rn**

**1m 24.94** (0.94) CSF £67.84 CT £424.93 TOTE £14.70: £2.30 £2.00 £2.70 (£21.90) Trio £166.20 OWNER Mr K. H. Burks (LAMBOURN) BRED Aston Park Stud
LONG HANDICAP Woolverstone Hall (IRE) 7-9

## 245 SWEETHEART H'CAP (0-65) (3-Y.O) (Class F)
4-35 (4-36) **1m 2f (Equitrack)** £2,612.20 (£734.20: £358.60) Stalls: Low GOING minus 0.66 sec per fur (FST)

SP RR SF

56[4] **Montecristo (60)** (RGuest) **3-9-2** LDettori(2) (chsd ldrs: led over 2f out: rdn clr over 1f out: eased nr fin).......— **1** 9/2[3] 76 28
230[2] **Domoor (56)** (MJohnston) **3-8-12** JWeaver(6) (chsd ldr: led over 3f out: hdd over 2f out: one pce) ...................5 **2** 5/2[1] 64 18
137[4] **Galapino (65)** (CEBrittain) **3-9-7** MLarsen(4) (dwlt: hdwy 4f out: rdn over 2f out: r.o one pce ins fnl f)............hd **3** 7/2[2] 73 26
176[3] **Sovereign Prince (IRE) (52)** (NACallaghan) **3-8-8b[1]** JQuinn(9) (hld up: hdwy 4f out: rdn over 3f out: wknd over 2f out)........................................11 **4** 5/1 42 —
123[14] **Miss Offset (48)** (MJohnston) **3-8-4b** TWilliams(8) (led: hdd over 3f out: wknd over 2f out)..............................7 **5** 25/1 27 —
129[4] **Illegally Yours (42)** (LMontagueHall) **3-7-12b** NCarlisle(7) (in tch: rdn over 3f out: sn wknd) ..........................1¼ **6** 20/1 19 —
25[3] **Righteous Gent (51)** (KMcAuliffe) **3-8-7be**ow1 RCochrane(5) (bhd fnl 4f) .........................................3½ **7** 12/1 22 —
176[2] **Lord Ellangowan (IRE) (45)** (RIngram) **3-7-10**(5) MBaird(1) (a bhd)...................................................2 **8** 6/1 13 —
137[9] **Autumn (FR) (60)** (CMurray) **3-9-2** DBiggs(3) (bhd fnl 4f) ..........................................................nk **9** 33/1 28 —
(SP 119.2%) **9 Rn**

**2m 6.74** (2.44) CSF £15.81 CT £40.14 TOTE £6.80: £2.00 £1.90 £1.40 (£6.30) Trio £10.40 OWNER Matthews Breeding and Racing (NEWMARKET) BRED Lord Matthews

T/Plpt: £33.40 (316.79 Tckts). T/Qdpt: £13.60 (86.61 Tckts). SM

# 0234-SOUTHWELL (L-H) (Standard)
## Saturday February 10th
WEATHER: cloudy WIND: str across

## 246 VERBIER (S) H'CAP (0-60) (I) (4-Y.O+) (Class F)
1-15 (1-15) **1m 3f (Fibresand)** £2,296.50 (£644.00: £313.50) Stalls: Low GOING minus 0.06 sec per fur (STD)

SP RR SF

196[5] **Noble Canonire (44)** (SRBowring) **4-8-8**(5) CTeague(7) (hld up: drvn 4f out: led over 1f out: sn clr)..............— **1** 9/2[2] 54 —
210[7] **Greek Gold (IRE) (39)** (WLBarker) **7-8-3**(7) FLynch(1) (led: clr 3f out: wknd & hdd appr fnl f) ............................6 **2** 15/2 40 —
198[5] **Trumble (47)** (CWThornton) **4-9-2** JFortune(9) (a in tch: chsd ldr over 3f out: hrd rdn & no imp appr fnl f) .....1¾ **3** 5/1[3] 46 —
179[9] **Anotherone to Note (38)** (NPLittmoden) **5-8-9** TGMcLaughlin(6) (hld up: hdwy 4f out: nt rch ldrs)..................6 **4** 14/1 28 —
**Lawnswood Junior (41)** (JLSpearing) **9-8-9**(3) SDrowne(3) (lost pl 5f out: n.d after).........................................12 **5** 14/1 14 —
186[9] **Swynford Flyer (32)** (JAHarris) **7-8-3** DaleGibson(10) (nvr nr to chal).......................................................hd **6** 10/1 4 —
189[11] **Rubadub (25)** (JMBradley) **5-7-10** GBardwell(11) (hdwy 7f out: wknd over 3f out)........................................nk **7** 33/1 — —
196[3] **Exclusion (39)** (JHetherton) **7-8-10** LCharnock(8) (lw: sn chsd along mid div: effrt whn hmpd over 4f out: t.o)15 **8** 7/2[1] — —
207[8] **Supercool (38)** (DWChapman) **5-8-9** ACulhane(5) (trckd ldrs 8f: eased whn btn wl over 1f out: t.o) ...............¾ **9** 25/1 — —
**Calling Jamaica (55)** (MCPipe) **4-9-10** AMcGlone(4) (bit bkwd: trckd ldrs 7f: sn lost tch: t.o)..........................9 **10** 11/1 — —
206[9] **Just Lucky (IRE) (46)** (MrsNMacauley) **4-8-10**(5) AmandaSanders(2) (b.hind: prom tl wknd over 4f out: t.o) ....8 **11** 16/1 — —
(SP 112.3%) **11 Rn**

**2m 33.7** (13.70) CSF £33.23 CT £155.04 TOTE £5.80: £1.50 £2.20 £1.80 (£26.80) Trio £28.00 OWNER Mr Roland Wheatley (EDWINSTOWE) BRED T. Barratt
WEIGHT FOR AGE 4yo-2lb
Bt in 3,600 gns

## 247 WENGEN H'CAP (0-60) (I) (3-Y.O+) (Class F)
1-45 (1-46) **7f (Fibresand)** £2,278.00 (£638.00: £310.00) Stalls: Low GOING minus 0.06 sec per fur (STD)

SP RR SF

209[2] **Principal Boy (IRE) (44)** (TJEtherington) **3-7-11**ow1 DaleGibson(4) (hld up in tch: drvn along 2f out: r.o to ld fnl 100y)........................................— **1** 9/2[2] 51 —
199[10] **Cheerful Groom (IRE) (38)** (SRBowring) **5-8-3**(5) CTeague(1) (led over 3f out tl over 2f out: ev ch fnl f: r.o).....1 **2** 14/1 43 —
155[2] **Monis (IRE) (57)** (JBalding) **5-9-6v**(7) JEdmunds(5) (lw: a.p: led over 2f out: hrd drvn & hdd wl ins fnl f) ..........½ **3** 5/1[3] 61 13
135[10] **Life Is Precious (IRE) (50)** (RHollinshead) **4-9-6** MWigham(8) (bhd: rdn 4f out: hdwy 2f out: one pce fnl f) ......4 **4** 20/1 44 —
**My Gallery (IRE) (58)** (ABailey) **5-9-7**(7) AngelaGallimore(3) (hdwy on ins ½-wy: ev ch fr 2f out: one pce fnl f) .1 **5** 14/1 50 4
213[9] **The Mestral (39)** (MJRyan) **4-8-9** PBloomfield(6) (led to ½-wy: wknd & eased wl over 1f out) ..........................nk **6** 12/1 31 —
84[7] **Rafter-J (45)** (JAHarris) **5-9-1** DHarrison(7) (sn trckng ldrs: rdn & wknd over 1f out)....................................1½ **7** 20/1 33 —
213[2] **Hi Rock (43)** (MJCamacho) **4-8-13** LCharnock(2) (prom: drvn 3f out: sn wknd & eased: t.o) ...............................20 **8** 11/10[1] — —
**Aggies Dream (29)** (JMBradley) **5-7-13** FNorton(9) (b: bkwd: a bhd: t.o fnl 2f) ...............................................7 **9** 50/1 — —
(SP 115.0%) **9 Rn**

**1m 34.8** (8.00) CSF £54.91 CT £295.57 TOTE £5.90: £1.80 £2.10 £1.60 (£52.10) Trio £35.10 OWNER Mr Chris Moreno (MALTON) BRED Mrs M. Mansergh
LONG HANDICAP Principal Boy (IRE) 7-9
WEIGHT FOR AGE 3yo-17lb
OFFICIAL EXPLANATION **Hi Rock: was reportedly never travelling and so she was eased in the final furlong.**

## 248 ST MORITZ MAIDEN STKS (3-Y.O+) (Class D)
2-15 (2-15) **1m (Fibresand)** £3,641.30 (£1,102.40: £538.20: £256.10) Stalls: Low GOING minus 0.06 sec per fur (STD)

SP RR SF

**Suvalu (USA) (68)** (MGMeagher) **4-9-10** JFortune(1) (a.p: led over 2f out: sn clr: hrd rdn & hld on cl home) .— **1** 8/1[3] 65 11

| Form | Horse | Dist | Pos | SP | RR | SF |
|---|---|---|---|---|---|---|
| | **Six Clerks (IRE) (66)** (JGFitzGerald) **3-8-5** ACulhane(7) (hld up: jnd wnr over 2f out: sn rdn & outpcd: r.o strly towards fin) | ½ | **2** | 7/4[2] | 64 | — |
| 40[2] | **In The Band** (LordHuntingdon) **3-8-0** DaleGibson(4) (in tch: pushed along ½-wy: hdwy appr fnl f: fin wl) | s.h | **3** | 11/8[1] | 59 | — |
| | **Infiraaj (USA)** (MrsDHaine) **4-9-10** AMcGlone(5) (bit bkwd: hdwy 4f out: rdn & rn green appr fnl f: sn btn) | 8 | **4** | 12/1 | 48 | — |
| 204[8] | **Clytha Hill Lad** (JMBradley) **5-9-7**(3) SDrowne(6) (bit bkwd: sn bhd & drvn along: sme late hdwy: n.d) | 13 | **5** | 50/1 | 22 | — |
| | **Bold Joker (25)** (GROldroyd) **5-9-5**(5) CTeague(3) (a bhd: t.o) | 6 | **6** | 50/1 | 10 | — |
| 110[10] | **Pushka Fair** (TRWatson) **5-9-10** SDWilliams(8) (bkwd: led tl hdd & wknd over 2f out: eased whn btn: t.o) | ½ | **7** | 33/1 | 9 | — |
| | **Induna Mkubwa** (CFWall) **3-8-6**ow1 NDay(2) (w'like: bkwd: s.s: a rr div: t.o) | ¾ | **8** | 12/1 | 8 | — |
| 212[6] | **Branston Kristy (35)** (CSmith) **4-9-5b**[1] JFanning(9) (trckd ldr: rdn 3f out: sn lost tch: t.o) | 12 | **9** | 25/1 | — | — |

(SP 115.7%) **9 Rn**

**1m 49.5** (9.50) CSF £21.28 TOTE £8.20: £1.60 £1.50 £1.00 (£6.70) Trio £2.20 OWNER Aim High Partnership (ORMSKIRK) BRED M. Arbib

WEIGHT FOR AGE 3yo-19lb

## 249 ASPEN CLAIMING STKS (4-Y.O+) (Class E)

2-45 (2-45) **1m** **(Fibresand)** £2,900.10 (£877.80: £428.40: £203.70) Stalls: Low GOING minus 0.06 sec per fur (STD)

| Form | Horse | Dist | Pos | SP | RR | SF |
|---|---|---|---|---|---|---|
| 141* | **Second Colours (USA) (78)** (MrsMReveley) **6-9-4** JFortune(3) (hld up & bhd: hdwy on bit to ld wl over 1f out: canter) | — | **1** | 7/2[2] | 81+ | 24 |
| 199[2] | **Kingchip Boy (64)** (MJRyan) **7-8-12v** TIves(6) (led tl hdd wl over 1f out: kpt on u.p: no ch w wnr) | 2 | **2** | 9/4[1] | 71 | 15 |
| 216[5] | **Charm Dancer (52)** (MCPipe) **4-8-1**(3)ow1 PMcCabe(4) (a.p: drvn along & ev ch 2f out: one pce) | ¾ | **3** | 8/1 | 62 | 6 |
| 207* | **Chadleigh Lane (USA) (57)** (RHollinshead) **4-8-7v**(7) FLynch(5) (lw: hld up: effrt u.p over 2f out: sn drvn: nt pce to chal) | 3 | **4** | 5/1 | 66 | 10 |
| 198* | **No Submission (USA) (60)** (DWChapman) **10-8-4v** ACulhane(2) (lw: chsd ldr: rdn over 2f out: one pce) | hd | **5** | 15/2 | 55 | 1 |
| 181[7] | **Bentico (70)** (MrsNMacauley) **7-8-5**(5) CTeague(1) (b: b.hind: lw: prom: rdn after 3f: sn lost pl: t.o) | 10 | **6** | 9/2[3] | 41 | — |

(SP 110.7%) **6 Rn**

**1m 47.5** (7.50) CSF £11.02 TOTE £4.00: £2.00 £1.60 (£5.50) OWNER Mrs Richard Pitman (SALTBURN) BRED Dinnaken Farm in USA

## 250 ZERMATT CLAIMING STKS (3-Y.O+) (Class E)

3-15 (3-15) **6f** **(Fibresand)** £2,845.50 (£861.00: £420.00: £199.50) Stalls: Low GOING minus 0.06 sec per fur (STD)

| Form | Horse | Dist | Pos | SP | RR | SF |
|---|---|---|---|---|---|---|
| 229[4] | **Sense of Priority (73)** (DNicholls) **7-9-7** AlexGreaves(7) (a.p gng wl: led over 1f out: edgd lft fnl f: r.o wl) | — | **1** | 4/1[2] | 74 | 29 |
| 212* | **Sea Devil (62)** (MJCamacho) **10-9-8** LCharnock(6) (hld up: hdwy 2f out: kpt on u.p: nt pce of wnr) | 2½ | **2** | 6/4[1] | 68 | 24 |
| 218[4] | **Sir Tasker (69)** (JLHarris) **8-9-2**(5) PFessey(2) (led: rdn & drifted rt 2f out: sn hdd & no ex) | 1 | **3** | 9/2[3] | 65 | 21 |
| 202[5] | **Sea-Deer (75)** (DWChapman) **7-9-12** ACulhane(5) (prom tl hrd drvn & wknd wl over 1f out) | 9 | **4** | 5/1 | 46 | 4 |
| 74[5] | **Brisas (43)** (CWFairhurst) **9-9-2** MFenton(4) (prom: drvn along over 2f out: sn bhd) | 2½ | **5** | 33/1 | 29 | — |
| 168* | **Bold Aristocrat (IRE) (51)** (RHollinshead) **5-8-10**(7) FLynch(1) (outpcd: a in rr) | s.h | **6** | 8/1 | 30 | — |
| 195[2] | **Northern Grey (47)** (JBerry) **4-9-3b** LeTolboll(3) (outpcd: a bhd) | 2½ | **7** | 25/1 | 23 | — |

(SP 112.7%) **7 Rn**

**1m 18.8** (5.30) CSF £9.94 TOTE £4.80: £4.40 £1.80 (£5.80) OWNER Mr S. Schofield (THIRSK) BRED Cheveley Park Stud Ltd

## 251 VAIL H'CAP (0-75) (4-Y.O+) (Class D)

3-45 (3-47) **1m 4f** **(Fibresand)** £3,692.00 (£1,118.00: £546.00: £260.00) Stalls: Low GOING minus 0.06 sec per fur (STD)

| Form | Horse | Dist | Pos | SP | RR | SF |
|---|---|---|---|---|---|---|
| | **Greenspan (IRE) (73)** (WRMuir) **4-9-13** Jean-PierreLopez(7) (lw: hld up: hdwy ½-wy: styd on to ld wl ins fnl f) | — | **1** | 12/1 | 78 | 17 |
| 222* | **Mentalasanythin (75)** (ABailey) **7-9-11**(7) 5x AngelaGallimore(4) (a.p: led 2f out: sn clr: hdd & no ex wl ins fnl f) | ½ | **2** | 9/4[1] | 79 | 21 |
| 210[4] | **Hawwam (65)** (EJAlston) **10-9-8** SDWilliams(14) (trckd ldrs: rdn & effrt wl over 1f out: no imp) | 3½ | **3** | 12/1 | 65 | 9 |
| | **Antarcticern (USA) (42)** (GROldroyd) **6-7-13** FNorton(3) (bhd & outpcd: hdwy 3f out: nrst fin) | 3 | **4** | 25/1 | 38 | — |
| 210* | **Tempering (55)** (DWChapman) **10-8-12** 5x ACulhane(9) (led after 2f to 2f out: wknd over 1f out) | ¾ | **5** | 7/1[2] | 50 | — |
| 198[3] | **Night Time (53)** (AStreeter) **4-8-2**(5) LNewton(11) (hld up: hdwy 5f out: rdn & wknd wl over 1f out) | 2 | **6** | 11/1 | 45 | — |
| 100[7] | **Mr Towser (71)** (WWHaigh) **5-9-9**(5) CTeague(8) (prom tl wknd fnl 2f) | 4 | **7** | 12/1 | 58 | 3 |
| | **Majboor Yafooz (USA) (65)** (JRBosley) **6-9-8** CRutter(5) (a bhd: t.o) | 14 | **8** | 12/1 | 33 | — |
| 152[4] | **Chantry Beath (49)** (CWThornton) **5-8-6** LCharnock(1) (lw: trckd ldrs over 7f: sn lost pl: t.o) | 2½ | **9** | 17/2[3] | 14 | — |
| | **Sommersby (IRE) (61)** (MrsNMacauley) **5-9-1**(3) SDrowne(13) (b: dwlt: hdwy over 4f out: wknd over 2f out: t.o) | 2½ | **10** | 14/1 | 22 | — |
| | **Vasiliev (48)** (SGollings) **8-8-5b** VHalliday(6) (reluctant to r: a wl bhd: t.o) | 20 | **11** | 20/1 | — | — |
| | **General Jimbo (IRE) (49)** (FMurphy) **4-8-3** JFanning(2) (led 2f: wknd 5f out: t.o) | dist | **12** | 20/1 | — | — |
| | ***Island Jewel (39)*** (JRBosley) **8-7-10** GBardwell(12) (Withdrawn not under Starter's orders: ref to enter stalls) | .. | **W** | 10/1 | — | — |

(SP 122.0%) **12 Rn**

**2m 46.3** (13.80) CSF £33.60 CT £267.31 TOTE £13.70: £5.40 £1.10 £4.00 (£24.20) Trio £148.80 OWNER Camelot Racing (LAMBOURN) BRED Dermot and Meta Cantillon

LONG HANDICAP Island Jewel 7-6

WEIGHT FOR AGE 4yo-3lb

## 252 VERBIER (S) H'CAP (0-60) (II) (4-Y.O+) (Class F)

4-15 (4-16) **1m 3f** **(Fibresand)** £2,284.60 (£640.60: £311.80) Stalls: Low GOING minus 0.06 sec per fur (STD)

| Form | Horse | Dist | Pos | SP | RR | SF |
|---|---|---|---|---|---|---|
| 210[8] | **Mazilla (42)** (AStreeter) **4-8-8v**[1] FNorton(9) (hld up: hdwy 3f out: shkn up to ld 2f out: edgd lft: sn clr) | — | **1** | 16/1 | 51 | 1 |
| 196[9] | **Adaloaldo (USA) (51)** (JParkes) **4-8-12**(5) RHavlin(5) (s.i.s: hld up: hdwy 6f out: slt ld over 2f out: sn hdd: one pce) | 4 | **2** | 5/1[3] | 54 | 5 |
| 207[4] | **Genesis Four (40)** (SRBowring) **6-8-3**(5) CTeague(8) (hld up: hdwy over 3f out: sn ev ch: rdn & hung lft: sn btn) | 4 | **3** | 9/2[2] | 37 | — |
| | **Rainbow Road (60)** (MCPipe) **5-10-0** AMcGlone(10) (mde most tl hdd & wknd over 2f out) | 7 | **4** | 9/1 | 47 | 1 |
| 198[2] | **Kismetim (55)** (WWHaigh) **6-9-4**(5) DGriffiths(7) (hld up: hdwy 5f out: rdn & ev ch 2f out: grad wknd) | 7 | **5** | 5/2[1] | 32 | — |
| 154[5] | **Shotley Again (30)** (NBycroft) **6-7-12** LCharnock(3) (prom tl wknd over 3f out) | 2½ | **6** | 6/1 | 3 | — |
| 128[6] | **Rose Chime (IRE) (36)** (JLHarris) **4-7-11**(5) PFessey(2) (trckd ldrs over 7f: sn wknd) | ¾ | **7** | 16/1 | 8 | — |
| 190[7] | **Royal Acclaim (38)** (JMBradley) **11-8-1v**(5) AmandaSanders(4) (bhd: effrt over 4f out: wknd over 2f out) | ¾ | **8** | 16/1 | 9 | — |
| 167[8] | **Brafferton Bella (35)** (JMJefferson) **4-8-1** NKennedy(1) (sn pushed along: a bhd: t.o) | 25 | **9** | 25/1 | — | — |

| | | | | SP | RR | SF |
|---|---|---|---|---|---|---|
| $141^{5}$ | **Off the Air (IRE) (42)** (BJLlewellyn) **5-8-10v** DHarrison(6) (lw: prom tl rdn & wknd over 4f out: t.o) | ½ | **10** | 12/1 | — | — |

(SP 116.9%) **10 Rn**

**2m 32.5** (12.50) CSF £86.26 CT £386.36 TOTE £13.20: £2.70 £2.40 £1.10 (£31.50) Trio £64.70 OWNER Mr M. Rhodes (UTTOXETER) BRED Mrs H. MacFarlane
WEIGHT FOR AGE 4yo-2lb
No bid

## 253 WENGEN H'CAP (0-60) (II) (3-Y.O+) (Class F)

4-45 (4-46) **7f (Fibresand)** £2,265.40 (£634.40: £308.20) Stalls: Low GOING minus 0.06 sec per fur (STD)

| | | | | SP | RR | SF |
|---|---|---|---|---|---|---|
| | **Dancing Sioux (56)** (RGuest) **4-9-5**$^{(7)}$ FLynch(6) (trckd ldrs: qcknd to ld wl over 1f out: sn clr: v.easily) | — | **1** | 10/1 | 63+ | 44 |
| $213^{*}$ | **Sweet Mate (61)** (SRBowring) **4-9-12b**$^{(5)\ 6x}$ CTeague(4) (hld up: hdwy over 2f out: sn ev ch: outpcd appr fnl f) | 10 | **2** | $3/1^{1}$ | 45 | 28 |
| $200^{3}$ | **Zahran (IRE) (48)** (JMBradley) **5-9-1**$^{(3)}$ SDrowne(8) (b: bhd & sn pushed along: hdwy 2f out: nt rch ldrs) | 3½ | **3** | $5/1^{3}$ | 24 | 9 |
| $71^{4}$ | **Green's Bid (43)** (DWChapman) **6-8-13** ACulhane(7) (prom: ev ch 2f out: sn rdn & outpcd) | 3½ | **4** | 7/1 | 11 | — |
| $203^{*}$ | **Mister Raider (50)** (SMellor) **4-8-13b**$^{(7)}$ ADaly(9) (lw: trckd ldr: drvn over 2f out: sn wknd) | ½ | **5** | 11/2 | 17 | 3 |
| $155^{8}$ | **Panther (IRE) (46)** (JHetherton) **6-9-2** NKennedy(1) (sn drvn along: a in rr) | 3 | **6** | $9/2^{2}$ | 6 | — |
| $207^{5}$ | **Double Glow (31)** (NBycroft) **4-8-1** GBardwell(5) (prom: drvn along 3f out: sn btn) | 4 | **7** | 20/1 | — | — |
| $157^{7}$ | **Ghostly Apparition (54)** (JRUpson) **3-8-0**$^{(7)}$ DSweeney(2) (a bhd & outpcd) | ¾ | **8** | 14/1 | 3 | — |
| $167^{2}$ | **Margaretrose Anna (52)** (EJAlston) **4-9-8** JFortune(3) (led tl hdd wl over 1f out: sn wl outpcd) | nk | **9** | 9/1 | 1 | — |

(SP 118.3%) **9 Rn**

**1m 32.1** (5.30) CSF £38.43 CT £156.87 TOTE £12.30: £2.90 £1.10 £1.70 (£25.00) Trio £54.90 OWNER Ms A. M. Jeffrey (NEWMARKET)
WEIGHT FOR AGE 3yo-17lb

T/Plpt: £30.70 (299.59 Tckts). T/Qdpt: £4.10 (175.33 Tckts). IM

# 0246-SOUTHWELL (L-H) (Standard)

## Monday February 12th

WEATHER: overcast WIND: fresh bhd

## 254 NEVADA LIMITED STKS (0-60) (4-Y.O+) (Class F)

2-10 (2-16) **1m 4f (Fibresand)** £2,398.00 (£673.00: £328.00) Stalls: Low GOING minus 0.46 sec per fur (FST)

| | | | | SP | RR | SF |
|---|---|---|---|---|---|---|
| | **El Bailador (IRE) (60)** (JDBethell) **5-9-0** JWeaver(7) (lw: cl up: led over 4f out: styd on wl) | — | **1** | $3/1^{2}$ | 60 | — |
| $181^{6}$ | **Grey Again (58)** (SRBowring) **4-8-3b**$^{(5)}$ CTeague(9) (hld up: hdwy 7f out: effrt over 3f out: nt qckn fnl 2f) | 2½ | **2** | $2/1^{1}$ | 55 | — |
| $249^{5}$ | **No Submission (USA) (60)** (DWChapman) **10-9-2** ACulhane(1) (hld up: effrt on outside 4f out: one pce fnl 2f) | 2 | **3** | $5/1^{3}$ | 56 | — |
| $196^{8}$ | **New Inn (60)** (SGollings) **5-9-0** VHalliday(2) (led after 2f tl over 4f out: one pce) | 3 | **4** | 12/1 | 50 | — |
| $196^{6}$ | **Bold Pursuit (IRE) (55)** (JGFitzGerald) **7-9-0** JFortune(5) (b: hdwy 6f out: prom & rdn over 2f out: wknd over 1f out) | 1½ | **5** | 7/1 | 48 | — |
| | **Tap On Tootsle (36)** (TRWall) **4-8-6** NAdams(6) (lw: prom tl outpcd over 3f out: no imp after) | 2 | **6** | 33/1 | 41 | — |
| $189^{8}$ | **Ganador (44)** (BSmart) **4-8-7**$^{ow1}$ RCochrane(3) (chsd ldr tl wknd fnl 2½f) | 6 | **7** | 16/1 | 34 | — |
| $206^{6}$ | **Sacred Mirror (IRE) (53)** (CEBrittain) **5-8-11** MLarsen(4) (led 2f: disp ld 7f out to 4f out: sn rdn & btn) | 4 | **8** | 7/1 | 29 | — |
| | **Stylish Gent (35)** (GROldroyd) **9-8-7**$^{(7)}$ AColgan(8) (bit bkwd: chsd ldrs tl rdn & lost tch over 5f out) | 25 | **9** | 33/1 | — | — |

(SP 119.5%) **9 Rn**

**2m 42.2** (9.70) CSF £9.32 TOTE £3.70: £1.40 £1.10 £1.90 (£7.50) Trio £8.20 OWNER Mrs John Lee (MIDDLEHAM) BRED Miss Anne Reid
WEIGHT FOR AGE 4yo-3lb

## 255 SYRIAN DESERT CLAIMING STKS (4-Y.O+) (Class F)

2-40 (2-48) **7f (Fibresand)** £2,398.00 (£673.00: £328.00) Stalls: Low GOING minus 0.46 sec per fur (FST)

| | | | | SP | RR | SF |
|---|---|---|---|---|---|---|
| $135^{2}$ | **Berge (IRE) (75)** (WAO'Gorman) **5-9-3b** EmmaO'Gorman(1) (lw: hld up: hdwy 3f out: led over 1f out: r.o) | — | **1** | $8/13^{1}$ | 77 | 25 |
| $168^{5}$ | **At the Savoy (IRE) (59)** (TDBarron) **5-7-12**$^{(7)}$ KimberleyHart(8) (mde most tl hdd over 1f out: no ex) | 3 | **2** | $7/1^{3}$ | 58? | 6 |
| $211^{4}$ | **Nashaat (USA) (70)** (MCChapman) **8-8-6**$^{(7)}$ CMunday(4) (drvn along after s: sn chsng ldrs: disp ld 3f out tl btn over 1f out) | ½ | **3** | $5/1^{2}$ | 65 | 13 |
| $211^{12}$ | **First Gold (60)** (JWharton) **7-8-8b** SDWilliams(2) (chsd ldrs: ev ch over 2f out: sn btn) | 1¼ | **4** | 8/1 | 57 | 5 |
| | **Ashdren (50)** (AHarrison) **9-8-3b**$^{1}$ JFanning(7) (in tch: effrt over 2f out: no imp) | 10 | **5** | 12/1 | 29 | — |
| $248^{9}$ | **Branston Kristy (35)** (CSmith) **4-7-3b**$^{(7)}$ IonaWands(9) (prom tl outpcd fnl 3f) | 1 | **6** | 33/1 | 20 | — |
| $195^{6}$ | **Desert Man** (RDEWoodhouse) **5-8-6**$^{(7)}$ FLynch(6) (bit bkwd: cl up tl wknd 3f out) | 1 | **7** | 50/1 | 35 | — |
| | **Chief's Lady (48)** (JMBradley) **4-8-0** JQuinn(5) (lw: gd spd 3f: wknd qckly) | 7 | **8** | 33/1 | 6 | — |
| | **Natural Path (47)** (MrsVAAconley) **5-8-2v**$^{1}$ MDeering(3) (spd 3f: sn wknd & wl bhd) | 20 | **9** | 50/1 | — | — |

(SP 119.7%) **9 Rn**

**1m 30.3** (3.50) CSF £5.97 TOTE £1.60: £1.10 £2.20 £1.30 (£4.10) Trio £2.40 OWNER Mr S. Fustok (NEWMARKET) BRED S. Fustok
STEWARDS' ENQUIRY Munday susp. 21-23/2/96 (excessive use of whip).

## 256 KALAHARI H'CAP (0-70) (4-Y.O+) (Class E)

3-10 (3-18) **1m 3f (Fibresand)** £3,077.55 (£932.40: £455.70: £217.35) Stalls: Low GOING minus 0.46 sec per fur (FST)

| | | | | SP | RR | SF |
|---|---|---|---|---|---|---|
| $199^{4}$ | **Sea God (44)** (MCChapman) **5-7-12**$^{(7)}$ CMunday(2) (a.p: led wl over 1f out: styd on) | — | **1** | $5/2^{1}$ | 54 | — |
| $113^{7}$ | **Museum (IRE) (61)** (DNicholls) **5-9-8** AlexGreaves(3) (lw: trckd ldrs: nt clr run & swtchd 2f out: r.o towards fin) | ½ | **2** | 16/1 | 70 | — |
| | **Imperial Bid (FR) (53)** (DenysSmith) **8-8-9**$^{(5)}$ CTeague(6) (in tch: effrt 3f out: chsng ldrs 2f out: one pce) | 1¾ | **3** | 8/1 | 60 | — |
| | **Mowlaie (54)** (DWChapman) **5-9-1** ACulhane(8) (trckd ldrs: disp ld 3f out tl btn appr fnl f) | 1½ | **4** | 25/1 | 59 | — |
| $113^{5}$ | **Manful (56)** (JHetherton) **4-9-1b**$^{1}$ NKennedy(1) (lw: b: led 3f: w ldrs tl rdn & btn over 1f out) | 3½ | **5** | $6/1^{3}$ | 57 | — |
| $246^{8}$ | **Exclusion (39)** (JHetherton) **7-8-0** JQuinn(9) (led after 3f tl wl over 1f out: sn btn) | hd | **6** | 7/1 | 38 | — |
| $222^{4}$ | **Cross Talk (IRE) (62)** (RHollinshead) **4-9-0**$^{(7)}$ FLynch(10) (bhd: hdwy ½-wy: ev ch 3f out: wknd over 2f out) | 2 | **7** | 16/1 | 59 | — |
| $159^{4}$ | **Our Robert (52)** (JGFitzGerald) **4-8-11** MWigham(7) (bhd: hrd drvn 5f out: n.d) | 13 | **8** | $6/1^{3}$ | 31 | — |
| | **Tiger Shoot (63)** (DTThom) **9-9-10** RCochrane(4) (b: lost tch 7f out: n.d after) | 1¼ | **9** | $6/1^{3}$ | 39 | — |

196[2] **Modest Hope (USA) (52)** (BRichmond) **9-8-13** ClaireBalding(5) (a bhd: outpcd fnl 5f)....1¼ **10** 11/2[2] 26 —
(SP 126.0%) **10 Rn**

**2m 30.3** (10.30) CSF £39.79 CT £270.49 TOTE £3.00: £1.30 £5.30 £2.70 (£73.40) Trio £132.30 OWNER Mrs B. Ward (MARKET RASEN)
BRED R. D. Hollingsworth
WEIGHT FOR AGE 4yo-2lb

## 257 GREAT SANDY H'CAP (0-70) (4-Y.O+) (Class E)

3-40 (3-47) **1m (Fibresand)** £2,954.70 (£894.60: £436.80: £207.90) Stalls: Low GOING minus 0.46 sec per fur (FST)

| | | | | SP | RR | SF |
|---|---|---|---|---|---|---|
| 14[6] | **Prizefighter (66)** (JLEyre) **5-9-10**(3) OPears(3) (cl up: led over 3f out: hld on wl) | — | **1** | 9/2[2] | 68 | 30 |
| 167* | **Square Deal (FR) (67)** (SRBowring) **5-9-9**(5) CTeague(7) (lw: trckd ldrs: disp ld over 1f out: hung bdly lft: no ex nr fin) | s.h | **2** | 6/4[1] | 69 | 31 |
| 111[7] | **Miss Zanzibar (47)** (RAFahey) **4-8-8** ACulhane(5) (outpcd & bhd 5f out: hdwy 3f out: styd on) | 2 | **3** | 8/1 | 46 | 7 |
| 218[8] | **Elton Ledger (IRE) (58)** (MrsNMacauley) **7-9-5** RCochrane(8) (b: chsd ldrs: one pce fnl 3f) | 3½ | **4** | 8/1 | 49 | 11 |
| 239[13] | **East Barns (IRE) (40)** (SGollings) **8-7-10b**(5) PFessey(4) (drvn along & bhd: styd on fnl 3f: n.d) | nk | **5** | 16/1 | 30 | — |
| | **Flashfeet (58)** (KBishop) **6-9-5** NAdams(1) (chsd ldrs: rdn over 3f out: grad wknd) | 5 | **6** | 10/1 | 38 | — |
| 166[6] | **Agoer (40)** (CEBrittain) **4-8-1** JQuinn(6) (b.hind: chsd ldrs tl wknd fnl 2½f) | 3 | **7** | 8/1 | 15 | — |
| 199[9] | **Roar on Tour (61)** (MrsMReveley) **7-9-8** JFortune(2) (led tl hdd over 3f out: sn wknd) | 5 | **8** | 6/1[3] | 25 | — |

(SP 120.8%) **8 Rn**

**1m 44.5** (4.50) CSF £11.83 CT £49.22 TOTE £4.60: £1.90 £1.30 £2.30 (£5.00) OWNER Diamond Racing Ltd (HAMBLETON) BRED J. K. Bloodstock Ltd

## 258 NUBIAN (S) STKS (3-Y.O F) (Class G)

4-10 (4-16) **1m (Fibresand)** £2,085.00 (£585.00: £285.00) Stalls: Low GOING minus 0.46 sec per fur (FST)

| | | | | SP | RR | SF |
|---|---|---|---|---|---|---|
| 89[3] | **People Direct (52)** (KMcAuliffe) **3-9-4** RCochrane(3) (b.hind: w ldr: slt ld over 2f out: kpt on) | — | **1** | 15/8[1] | 59 | — |
| 123[8] | **Arch Angel (IRE) (52)** (DJSffrenchDavis) **3-9-4** NAdams(6) (led over 5f: kpt on one pce ins fnl f) | ½ | **2** | 11/4[2] | 58 | — |
| 237[4] | **Efipetite (44)** (NBycroft) **3-8-12** JQuinn(4) (trckd ldrs: effrt & ch over 1f out: no ex) | 2 | **3** | 8/1[3] | 48 | — |
| 171[2] | **Bumblefoot (IRE) (55)** (MJohnston) **3-9-4** JWeaver(2) (a chsng ldrs: effrt over 2f out: nt qckn) | nk | **4** | 15/8[1] | 53 | — |
| 158[4] | **Napier Star (40)** (MrsNMacauley) **3-8-7**(5) CTeague(1) (b.hind: s.i.s: hdwy over 2f out: no imp) | 9 | **5** | 20/1 | 29 | — |
| 89[6] | **Savanna Blue** (JLEyre) **3-8-12** RLappin(7) (cl up tl wknd 3f out) | 10 | **6** | 33/1 | 9 | — |
| 134[10] | **Oakley Folly** (RHollinshead) **3-8-12** NCarlisle(5) (s.s: hdwy after 2f: rdn & wknd over 3f out) | 25 | **7** | 25/1 | — | — |

(SP 118.9%) **7 Rn**

**1m 47.1** (7.10) CSF £7.60 TOTE £2.30: £1.20 £2.10 (£5.40) OWNER Mr Peter Barclay (LAMBOURN) BRED James Thom and Sons and Peter Orr
Bt in 6,800 gns

## 259 SAHARA H'CAP (0-65) (4-Y.O+) (Class F)

4-40 (4-48) **6f (Fibresand)** £2,398.00 (£673.00: £328.00) Stalls: Low GOING minus 0.46 sec per fur (FST)

| | | | | SP | RR | SF |
|---|---|---|---|---|---|---|
| 121[5] | **Super Benz (62)** (JLEyre) **10-10-0** RLappin(8) (w ldrs: disp ld 3f out tl led over 1f out: r.o wl) | — | **1** | 6/1 | 66 | 48 |
| 170* | **Stand Tall (59)** (CWThornton) **4-9-11** JWeaver(2) (bhd: hdwy 2f out: r.o) | 1 | **2** | 5/2[1] | 60 | 42 |
| 127[3] | **My Cherrywell (57)** (LRLloyd-James) **6-9-9b** TWilliams(4) (lw: b.hind: a cl up: nt qckn fnl 2f) | 7 | **3** | 8/1 | 40 | 22 |
| 213[8] | **Awesome Venture (58)** (MCChapman) **6-9-3**(7) CMunday(6) (chsd ldrs over 3f: sn outpcd: styd on again fnl f) | 2½ | **4** | 12/1 | 34 | 16 |
| | **Efficacy (53)** (APJarvis) **5-9-5** JTate(10) (b: racd wd: outpcd ½-wy: styd on fnl f) | s.h | **5** | 12/1 | 29 | 11 |
| 155[7] | **Dissentor (IRE) (51)** (JAGlover) **4-9-3v** GCarter(1) (sn outpcd & bhd: hdwy 2f out: nvr rch ldrs) | ½ | **6** | 4/1[2] | 26 | 8 |
| 207[2] | **Daawe (USA) (58)** (MrsVAAconley) **5-9-10v** MDeering(9) (bhd tl styd on fnl 2f) | ¾ | **7** | 11/2[3] | 31 | 13 |
| 203[11] | **Blyton Star (IRE) (31)** (MissJFCraze) **8-7-11**ow1 DaleGibson(11) (racd wd & rdn ½-wy: n.d) | ¾ | **8** | 33/1 | 2 | — |
| 253[7] | **Double Glow (31)** (NBycroft) **4-7-11b** GBardwell(5) (chsd ldrs 4f: sn wknd) | 1½ | **9** | 25/1 | — | — |
| 127[13] | **Fairey Firefly (58)** (MJCamacho) **5-9-10** LCharnock(3) (lw: led to ½-wy: sn rdn & wknd) | 10 | **10** | 12/1 | — | — |
| | **Bowcliffe Grange (IRE) (30)** (DWChapman) **4-7-5**(5) PFessey(7) (s.i.s: sn cl up: disp ld 3f out tl wl over 1f out: wknd qckly) | 3½ | **11** | 16/1 | — | — |

(SP 125.1%) **11 Rn**

**1m 15.4** (1.90) CSF £21.44 CT £116.91 TOTE £6.30: £1.60 £1.50 £1.90 (£9.40) Trio £22.80 OWNER Whitestonecliffe Racing Partnership (HAMBLETON) BRED Scarteen Stud
LONG HANDICAP Bowcliffe Grange (IRE) 7-6
Bt in 6,800 gns

T/Plpt: £10.90 (1,707.2 Tckts). T/Qdpt: £9.50 (157.41 Tckts) AA

# 0240-LINGFIELD (L-H) (Standard)

## Tuesday February 13th

All races put back 5 minutes
WEATHER: cold WIND: mod half bhd

## 260 SEALED WITH A LOVING KISS H'CAP (0-65) (I) (4-Y.O+) (Class F)

1-50 (1-56) **2m (Equitrack)** £2,202.70 (£617.20: £300.10) Stalls: Low GOING minus 0.43 sec per fur (FST)

| | | | | SP | RR | SF |
|---|---|---|---|---|---|---|
| | **Sheriff (52)** (JWHills) **5-9-10** DHarrison(3) (lw: a.p: led 4f out: clr over 1f out: r.o wl) | — | **1** | 100/30[2] | 62+ | 44 |
| | **Guest Alliance (IRE) (54)** (AMoore) **4-9-6** CandyMorris(6) (b.hind: hdwy over 7f out: chsd wnr over 1f out: no imp) | 7 | **2** | 6/1[3] | 57 | 33 |
| | **Namaste (46)** (RPCHoad) **8-9-4** MFenton(9) (hdwy over 4f out: rdn over 3f out: one pce) | 1¾ | **3** | 8/1 | 47 | 29 |
| 169[5] | **Tremendisto (40)** (CaptJHWilson) **6-8-7**(5) PFessey(1) (nt clr run on ins & lost pl over 7f out: rallied over 3f out: one pce) | nk | **4** | 7/1 | 41 | 23 |
| 165[4] | **All the Joys (40)** (CACyzer) **5-8-12** DBiggs(5) (hld up: rdn over 3f out: sn wknd) | 3½ | **5** | 2/1[1] | 37 | 19 |
| 228[4] | **Royal Print (IRE) (44)** (WRMuir) **7-9-2** Jean-PierreLopez(7) (gd hdwy 7f out: led 5f out to 4f out: wknd over 2f out) | 12 | **6** | 10/1 | 29 | 11 |

| Form | Horse | Dist | Pos | SP | RR | SF |
|---|---|---|---|---|---|---|
| 116[12] | **Lady Woodstock (32)** (MissAEEmbiricos) **4-7-7b**(5) MBaird(8) (chsd ldr: led over 11f out to 5f out: wknd 4f out: t.o) | 20 | 7 | 50/1 | — | — |
| 103[3] | **Callonescy (IRE) (47)** (DCO'Brien) **4-8-13** GBardwell(2) (bhd fnl 8f: t.o) | 15 | 8 | 14/1 | — | — |
| 175[9] | **Full of Tricks (25)** (JJBridger) **8-7-11** JQuinn(4) (led over 4f: wknd over 7f out: t.o fnl 5f) | dist | 9 | 50/1 | — | — |

(SP 114.0%) **9 Rn**

**3m 28.07** (6.07) CSF £21.45 CT £129.96 TOTE £2.80: £1.70 £1.90 £3.30 (£10.90) Trio £27.60 OWNER Mr Christopher Brown (LAMBOURN) BRED Stowell Hill Ltd
WEIGHT FOR AGE 4yo-6lb

## 261 SAY IT WITH ROSES LIMITED STKS (0-65) (4-Y.O+) (Class F)

2-20 (2-28) **1m (Equitrack)** £2,505.10 (£703.60: £343.30) Stalls: High GOING minus 0.43 sec per fur (FST)

| Form | Horse | Dist | Pos | SP | RR | SF |
|---|---|---|---|---|---|---|
| | **Mr Teigh (65)** (BSmart) **4-9-0** RCochrane(8) (hdwy over 3f out: led 2f out: rdn out) | — | 1 | 9/4[1] | 66 | 47 |
| 223[3] | **Manabar (62)** (MJPolglase) **4-8-7**(7) IonaWands(6) (a.p: rdn over 2f out: r.o one pce fnl f) | 3 | 2 | 7/2[2] | 60 | 41 |
| 41[10] | **Apollo Red (53)** (AMoore) **7-9-0** CandyMorris(4) (b.hind: led 6f: one pce fnl f) | ½ | 3 | 12/1 | 58 | 40 |
| 217[3] | **Don't Get Caught (IRE) (57)** (JLHarris) **4-8-9** JWeaver(3) (lw: hdwy over 3f out: rdn over 2f out: one pce) | 1¼ | 4 | 7/2[2] | 52 | 33 |
| 162[7] | **Hand of Straw (IRE) (64)** (PGMurphy) **4-9-0v**(3) SDrowne(2) (lost pl over 4f out: one pce fnl 3f) | 3 | 5 | 7/1[3] | 54 | 35 |
| 177[10] | **Ansal Boy (65)** (MissGayKelleway) **4-9-0** AClark(7) (lw: bhd fnl 4f) | 1¾ | 6 | 20/1 | 47 | 28 |
| 200* | **Oozlem (IRE) (43)** (JRPoulton) **7-8-7b**(7) TField(1) (b: s.i.s: a bhd) | ¾ | 7 | 8/1 | 45 | 27 |
| 31[6] | **Shuttlecock (58)** (MrsNMacauley) **5-9-0b** MFenton(5) (lw: chsd ldr 4f) | 7 | 8 | 25/1 | 31 | 13 |

(SP 115.1%) **8 Rn**

**1m 38.95** (1.55) CSF £10.10 TOTE £2.50: £1.10 £1.60 £2.70 (£7.30) OWNER Mrs Hannah McAuliffe (LAMBOURN) BRED K. G. Bridges

## 262 YOUNG LOVE CLAIMING STKS (3-Y.O) (Class E)

2-50 (2-55) **1m 2f (Equitrack)** £2,831.85 (£856.80: £417.90: £198.45) Stalls: Low GOING minus 0.43 sec per fur (FST)

| Form | Horse | Dist | Pos | SP | RR | SF |
|---|---|---|---|---|---|---|
| 129[2] | **Multi Franchise (52)** (BGubby) **3-8-1** JQuinn(1) (led 9f out tl over 7f out: led over 2f out: hrd rdn over 1f out: r.o wl) | — | 1 | 4/1[2] | 63 | 5 |
| 129* | **Rowlandsons Charm (IRE) (60)** (GLMoore) **3-8-4v** NAdams(4) (lw: led over 7f out tl over 2f out: unable qckn fnl f) | 3 | 2 | 5/6[1] | 61 | 3 |
| 129[5] | **Ordained** (TTClement) **3-7-12** GBardwell(2) (lost pl 8f out: rallied fnl f: r.o) | 2½ | 3 | 5/1[3] | 51 | — |
| 123[10] | **Apartments Abroad (50)** (KMcAuliffe) **3-8-4** SSanders(5) (b.hind: chsd ldr 7f out tl over 3f out: wknd over 2f out) | 7 | 4 | 6/1 | 46 | — |
| 67[10] | **General Henry (35)** (AMoore) **3-8-5** CandyMorris(3) (b.hind: led 1f: wknd 8f out) | 25 | 5 | 33/1 | 7 | — |

(SP 108.4%) **5 Rn**

**2m 10.37** (6.07) CSF £7.38 TOTE £5.50: £1.20 £4.10 (£2.00) OWNER Brian Gubby Ltd (BAGSHOT) BRED B. Gubby
Ordained clmd SAlston £4,000

## 263 CASANOVA CONDITIONS STKS (3-Y.O+) (Class D)

3-20 (3-25) **1m 2f (Equitrack)** £3,485.00 (£1,055.00: £515.00: £245.00) Stalls: Low GOING minus 0.43 sec per fur (FST)

| Form | Horse | Dist | Pos | SP | RR | SF |
|---|---|---|---|---|---|---|
| 24* | **Rainbow Top** (WJHaggas) **4-9-12** RCochrane(2) (hdwy 4f out: led wl over 1f out: r.o wl) | — | 1 | 8/13[1] | 82 | 62 |
| | **Quality (IRE) (80)** (WAO'Gorman) **3-8-10b**ow1 EmmaO'Gorman(7) (led over 6f out tl wl over 1f out: unable qckn) | 5 | 2 | 14/1 | 78 | 37 |
| 243[2] | **Easy Choice (USA) (74)** (PhilipMitchell) **4-10-1** AClark(6) (lw: hdwy over 3f out: ev ch over 2f out: wknd over 1f out) | 5 | 3 | 9/1 | 69 | 49 |
| 187* | **Prince Danzig (IRE) (81)** (DJGMurraySmith) **5-10-1** JWeaver(5) (a.p: rdn over 4f out: wknd over 2f out) | 2 | 4 | 7/1[3] | 64 | 46 |
| 175* | **Diego (88)** (CEBrittain) **3-8-6** MLarsen(1) (prom 5f) | 12 | 5 | 4/1[2] | 44 | 4 |
| | **Orange Place (IRE) (79)** (TJNaughton) **5-9-0**(7) TAshley(4) (lw: led over 3f: wknd over 3f out) | 7 | 6 | 50/1 | 25 | 7 |
| | **Expeditious Way (GR)** (RCharlton) **3-8-6** SSanders(3) (lengthy: a bhd) | 12 | 7 | 20/1 | 13 | — |

(SP 117.8%) **7 Rn**

**2m 5.91** (1.61) CSF £9.99 TOTE £1.60: £1.90 £4.20 (£4.80) OWNER Mr B. Haggas (NEWMARKET) BRED Sir Robin McAlpine
WEIGHT FOR AGE 3yo-22lb, 4yo-1lb

## 264 CUPID MEDIAN AUCTION MAIDEN STKS (3-Y.O) (Class F)

3-50 (3-55) **6f (Equitrack)** £2,493.20 (£700.20: £341.60) Stalls: Low GOING minus 0.43 sec per fur (FST)

| Form | Horse | Dist | Pos | SP | RR | SF |
|---|---|---|---|---|---|---|
| 134[2] | **Dummer Golf Time** (LordHuntingdon) **3-9-0** TIves(1) (b: lw: plld hrd: hld up: rdn over 2f out: str run fnl f: led last stride) | — | 1 | 1/4[1] | 55 | — |
| 209[3] | **General Haven** (TJNaughton) **3-9-0** JWeaver(3) (lw: led: rdn over 2f out: hdd last stride) | s.h | 2 | 9/2[2] | 55 | — |
| 118[9] | **Cindy Kate (IRE)** (CCElsey) **3-8-9** CRutter(4) (b: chsd ldr: ev ch fnl 3f: r.o) | hd | 3 | 50/1 | 50 | — |
| 118[5] | **Jemsilverthorn (IRE) (54)** (JJBridger) **3-9-0v** JQuinn(5) (prom over 3f) | 4 | 4 | 11/1[3] | 44 | — |
| 224[4] | **Impington (IRE) (50)** (WRMuir) **3-8-9** Jean-PierreLopez(2) (b.hind: lost pl over 3f out: rallied over 1f out: sn wknd) | 2½ | 5 | 14/1 | 32 | — |

(SP 115.1%) **5 Rn**

**1m 15.42** (4.82) CSF £2.16 TOTE £1.20: £1.00 £2.10 (£1.50) OWNER Coriolan Partnership (WEST ILSLEY) BRED R. M. Whitaker

## 265 SEALED WITH A LOVING KISS H'CAP (0-65) (II) (4-Y.O+) (Class F)

4-20 (4-27) **2m (Equitrack)** £2,202.70 (£617.20: £300.10) Stalls: Low GOING minus 0.43 sec per fur (FST)

| Form | Horse | Dist | Pos | SP | RR | SF |
|---|---|---|---|---|---|---|
| 130[6] | **Sir Thomas Beecham (54)** (SDow) **6-8-11**(7) ADaly(3) (hdwy 7f out: hrd rdn over 2f out: led wl ins fnl f: r.o wl) | — | 1 | 16/1 | 60 | 40 |
| 206[3] | **Ikhtiraa (USA) (60)** (RJO'Sullivan) **6-9-5b**(5) DGriffiths(8) (a.p: led over 10f out tl over 7f out: led over 2f out tl wl ins fnl f: r.o) | ½ | 2 | 5/2[1] | 66 | 46 |
| 108[4] | **Call Me Albi (IRE) (45)** (GLMoore) **5-8-2v**(7) TAshley(5) (lw: a.p: led over 7f out tl over 2f out: wknd over 1f out) | 6 | 3 | 3/1[2] | 45 | 25 |
| 206[4] | **Wottashambles (42)** (LMontagueHall) **5-8-6** SSanders(7) (b: hld up: rdn over 4f out: wknd over 3f out) | 20 | 4 | 11/2 | 22 | 2 |
| | **Elburg (IRE) (57)** (RPCHoad) **6-9-7v** RCochrane(4) (bhd fnl 6f: t.o) | 13 | 5 | 7/2[3] | 24 | 4 |
| 130[7] | **Oh So Handy (32)** (RCurtis) **8-7-10** GBardwell(6) (led over 5f: wknd over 8f out: t.o fnl 6f) | 5 | 6 | 16/1 | — | — |

| | Horse | Details | Dist | Pos | SP | RR | SF |
|---|---|---|---|---|---|---|---|
| 228[5] | **Discorsi (60)** | (MissGayKelleway) **4-9-4** AClark(1) (lw: a bhd: t.o) | dist | 7 | 20/1 | — | — |
| | **Against The Clock (53)** | (JWMullins) **4-8-11** JQuinn(2) (a bhd: t.o) | 2 | 8 | 25/1 | — | — |

(SP 111.6%) **8 Rn**

**3m 27.78** (5.78) CSF £51.30 CT £138.50 TOTE £19.40: £2.60 £1.40 £1.30 (£12.00) OWNER Mrs Heather Chakko (EPSOM) BRED G. R. Smith (Thriplow) Ltd
WEIGHT FOR AGE 4yo-6lb

## 266 ST. VALENTINE'S H'CAP (0-85) (4-Y.O+) (Class D)

4-50 (4-55) **6f (Equitrack)** £3,468.75 (£1,050.00: £512.50: £243.75) Stalls: Low GOING minus 0.43 sec per fur (FST)

| | Horse | Details | Dist | Pos | SP | RR | SF |
|---|---|---|---|---|---|---|---|
| 218* | **Robo Magic (USA) (77)** | (LMontagueHall) **4-9-13** 7x SSanders(3) (led 1f: rdn 2f out: led 1f out: r.o wl) | — | 1 | 9/2 2 | 80 | 41 |
| 109[7] | **Sharp Imp (54)** | (RMFlower) **6-8-4b** DBiggs(5) (rdn over 2f out: hdwy on ins over 1f out: r.o ins fnl f) | 1½ | 2 | 10/1 | 53 | 14 |
| 178* | **Dahiyah (USA) (61)** | (GLMoore) **5-8-11v** SWhitworth(6) (led 5f out to 1f out: unable qckn) | 1½ | 3 | 8/1 | 56 | 17 |
| | **Friendly Brave (USA) (75)** | (MissGayKelleway) **6-9-8**(3) AWhelan(9) (a.p: rdn over 2f out: one pce) | ½ | 4 | 6/1 3 | 69 | 30 |
| 250[3] | **Sir Tasker (69)** | (JLHarris) **8-9-5** JWeaver(8) (outpcd: hdwy over 2f out: one pce) | 1½ | 5 | 6/1 3 | 59 | 20 |
| 225[3] | **Tafahhus (56)** | (MJPolglase) **4-7-13v**(7) IonaWands(4) (a.p: rdn over 2f out: wknd fnl f) | 2½ | 6 | 9/1 | 39 | — |
| 173[2] | **Spender (78)** | (PWHarris) **7-9-11**(3) JStack(2) (a bhd) | 5 | 7 | 11/4 1 | 48d | 9 |
| 202[2] | **Southern Dominion (61)** | (CNAllen) **4-8-11** NAdams(7) (b.hind: lw: bhd fnl 2f) | 3 | 8 | 10/1 | 23 | — |
| 205[7] | **Abtaal (75)** | (RJHodges) **6-9-11** RCochrane(1) (a bhd) | 2½ | 9 | 16/1 | 30 | — |

(SP 118.6%) **9 Rn**

**1m 13.0** (2.40) CSF £43.90 CT £319.05 TOTE £7.50: £1.70 £2.60 £4.00 (£29.60) Trio £110.80 OWNER Mr A D Green and Partners (EPSOM) BRED Curtis C. Green

T/Plpt: £13.30 (1,003.85 Tckts). T/Qdpt: £2.80 (462.99 Tckts) AK

# 0179-WOLVERHAMPTON (L-H) (Standard)

## Wednesday February 14th

WEATHER: overcast WIND: almost nil

## 267 HEARTS AND ROSES APPRENTICE H'CAP (0-70) (4-Y.O+) (Class E)

2-25 (2-27) **1m 4f (Fibresand)** £2,845.50 (£861.00: £420.00: £199.50) Stalls: Low GOING: 0.29 sec per fur (SLW)

| | Horse | Details | Dist | Pos | SP | RR | SF |
|---|---|---|---|---|---|---|---|
| 113* | **Premier Dance (65)** | (DHaydnJones) **9-9-7**(7) AnthonyBond(4) (b.hind: hld up: lost pl over 5f out: hdwy 3f out: led over 1f out: hung lft: r.o) | — | 1 | 3/1 1 | 70 | 39 |
| 169[13] | **Nordic Sun (IRE) (65)** | (LRLloyd-James) **8-9-11**(3) KimberleyHart(6) (chsd ldr 5f: ev ch over 1f out: carried lft fnl f: r.o) | ¾ | 2 | 16/1 | 69 | 38 |
| 152[6] | **Comtec's Legend (38)** | (JFBottomley) **6-8-1** LNewton(7) (hld up: hdwy 5f out: rdn & ev ch over 1f out: nt clr run & swtchd rt ins fnl f: r.o) | 1½ | 3 | 9/2 2 | 40 | 9 |
| 187[3] | **Red Spectacle (IRE) (51)** | (PCHaslam) **4-8-11** MBaird(3) (led over 8f: rdn over 2f out: ev ch over 1f out: wknd ins fnl f) | 1¾ | 4 | 3/1 1 | 52 | 17 |
| | **Torrey Pines (IRE) (42)** | (MBell) **4-7-11v**1(5) RMullen(5) (a.p: wnt 2nd 7f out: rdn to ld over 3f out: hdd over 1f out: wknd ins fnl f) | 1 | 5 | 11/2 3 | 41 | 6 |
| | **In the Money (IRE) (54)** | (RHollinshead) **7-9-0**(3) FLynch(8) (prom tl wknd over 2f out) | 3½ | 6 | 11/1 | 48 | 17 |
| | **Lady Lacey (44)** | (GBBalding) **9-8-2v**(5) IonaWands(2) (hld up: wl bhd fnl 5f) | 10 | 7 | 6/1 | 24 | — |
| 207[7] | **Pats Delight (40)** | (SCoathup) **4-7-11**(3)ow3 AmandaSanders(1) (plld hrd: bhd fnl 5f: t.o) | 30 | 8 | 33/1 | — | — |

(SP 115.0%) **8 Rn**

**2m 47.2** (14.70) CSF £40.60 CT £192.56 TOTE £2.70: £1.10 £1.90 £1.30 (£42.60) OWNER J S Fox and Sons (PONTYPRIDD) BRED Brick Kiln Stud Farm
WEIGHT FOR AGE 4yo-3lb

## 268 CUPID CLAIMING STKS (4-Y.O+) (Class E)

2-55 (2-56) **1m 6f 166y (Fibresand)** £2,941.05 (£890.40: £434.70: £206.85) Stalls: High GOING: 0.29 sec per fur (SLW)

| | Horse | Details | Dist | Pos | SP | RR | SF |
|---|---|---|---|---|---|---|---|
| 98* | **Old Provence (70)** | (RHarris) **6-9-8** DBatteate(5) (b: b.hind: a.p: led over 7f out: clr over 3f out: styd on wl) | — | 1 | 3/1 2 | 76 | 30 |
| 130[5] | **Kymin (IRE) (65)** | (DJGMurraySmith) **4-8-8v** JWeaver(2) (hld up: hdwy 7f out: chsd wnr over 2f out: one pce) | 3½ | 2 | 9/2 | 64 | 12 |
| | **Fox Chapel (47)** | (RTJuckes) **9-9-2** DaleGibson(1) (bhd tl hdwy 6f out: one pce fnl 3f) | 9 | 3 | 25/1 | 56 | 10 |
| 169[4] | **Eulogy (FR) (62)** | (KRBurke) **9-8-7v**(7) TAshley(8) (plld hrd: led 9f out tl over 7f out: wknd over 3f out) | nk | 4 | 10/1 | 54 | 8 |
| 136[5] | **Make a Note (USA) (80)** | (PDEvans) **5-9-8** SSanders(6) (trckd ldrs: hrd drvn 4f out: sn wknd) | 15 | 5 | 15/8 1 | 46 | — |
| | **Bourdonner** | (WPJenks) **4-9-3** DeanMcKeown(3) (led 3f: wknd qckly 8f out) | 12 | 6 | 25/1 | 34 | — |
| | **Iota (64)** | (JLHarris) **7-8-9** LDettori(7) (led over 11f out to 9f out: wknd qckly over 5f out: t.o) | dist | 7 | 4/1 3 | — | — |
| | **Hong Kong Designer (48)** | (APJames) **4-8-1** NCarlisle(4) (t.o fnl 8f) | 5 | 8 | 20/1 | — | — |

(SP 119.5%) **8 Rn**

**3m 26.0** (18.60) CSF £16.54 TOTE £5.10: £1.20 £1.30 £5.80 (£9.00) OWNER Mr T. J. Dawson (NEWMARKET) BRED Stowell Hill Ltd and A. J. Tree
WEIGHT FOR AGE 4yo-5lb

## 269 SWEET NOTHINGS MAIDEN STKS (3-Y.O) (Class D)

3-30 (3-34) **1m 1f 79y (Fibresand)** £3,452.50 (£1,045.00: £510.00: £242.50) Stalls: Low GOING: 0.29 sec per fur (SLW)

| | Horse | Details | Dist | Pos | SP | RR | SF |
|---|---|---|---|---|---|---|---|
| | **Nikita's Star (IRE) (62)** | (DJGMurraySmith) **3-9-0** JWeaver(6) (chsd ldr: led wl over 2f out: rdn over 1f out: r.o wl) | — | 1 | 14/1 3 | 61 | 22 |
| | **Nanshan (IRE)** | (DRLoder) **3-8-9** LDettori(1) (w'like: scope: hld up: hdwy 5f out: chal over 1f out: rdn & unable qckn) | ½ | 2 | 1/3 1 | 55 | 16 |
| 161[4] | **Highlights** | (DMorris) **3-8-9** RCochrane(7) (hld up: rdn & lost pl over 3f out: styd on appr fnl f) | 5 | 3 | 33/1 | 47 | 8 |
| | **Shenango (IRE)** | (GWragg) **3-9-0** AMcGlone(5) (lw: plld hrd: rdn 5f out: wknd over 2f out) | 7 | 4 | 3/1 2 | 40 | 1 |
| | **Margi Boo** | (RTJuckes) **3-8-9** DaleGibson(3) (led over 6f: sn wknd) | 4 | 5 | 66/1 | 28 | — |
| 134[8] | **Radmore Brandy (35)** | (NPLittmoden) **3-8-9** TGMcLaughlin(2) (prom tl wknd 2f out) | 1¾ | 6 | 50/1 | 25 | — |

| | | | Pos | SP | RR | SF |
|---|---|---|---|---|---|---|
| 156$^{5}$ | **Bluntswood Hall** (RHollinshead) **3-9-0** MWigham(4) (bhd fnl 4f) | 13 | **7** | 66/1 | 8 | — |

(SP 114.6%) **7 Rn**

**2m 7.7** (11.70) CSF £19.00 TOTE £13.90: £4.80 £1.00 (£4.40) OWNER Nikita's Partners (LAMBOURN) BRED D. Twomey

## 270 DIXON'S NO 1 IN '96 H'CAP (0-90) (4-Y.O+) (Class C)

4-00 (4-01) **7f (Fibresand)** £5,305.00 (£1,606.00: £784.00: £373.00) Stalls: High GOING: 0.29 sec per fur (SLW)

| | | | Pos | SP | RR | SF |
|---|---|---|---|---|---|---|
| 77$^{12}$ | **Peggy Spencer (66)** (CWThornton) **4-8-6** DeanMcKeown(9) (a.p: led over 2f out: edgd rt ins fnl f: all out) | — | **1** | 5/1$^{2}$ | 72 | 42 |
| 170$^{4}$ | **Cretan Gift (78)** (NPLittmoden) **5-9-4** TGMcLaughlin(11) (hld up: hdwy 4f out: ev ch fnl f: hrd drvn: r.o) | nk | **2** | 10/1 | 83 | 53 |
| 249$^{4}$ | **Chadleigh Lane (USA) (64)** (RHollinshead) **4-7-11**$^{(7)ow1\ 6x}$ FLynch(8) (hld up: hdwy over 1f out: r.o ins fnl f) | 1¾ | **3** | 10/1 | 65 | 34 |
| 178$^{2}$ | **Patsy Grimes (66)** (JSMoore) **6-8-1v**$^{1(5)}$ PPMurphy(6) (a.p: led 3f out: sn hdd: hrd drvn over 1f out: one pce) | 1½ | **4** | 10/1 | 64 | 34 |
| 223$^{8}$ | **Everset (FR) (78)** (ABailey) **8-9-1**$^{(3)}$ DWright(12) (b: s.s: hdwy over 2f out: nvr nr to chal) | 2½ | **5** | 9/1 | 70 | 40 |
| | **Reverand Thickness (71)** (SCWilliams) **5-8-11** JFortune(2) (lw: chsd ldrs: rdn over 3f out: no hdwy) | 4 | **6** | 10/1 | 54 | 24 |
| 20$^{3}$ | **Pengamon (77)** (HJCollingridge) **4-9-3** JQuinn(10) (hld up: hdwy 3f out: wknd wl over 1f out) | ½ | **7** | 6/1$^{3}$ | 59 | 29 |
| 195* | **Milos (71)** (TJNaughton) **5-8-4**$^{(7)}$ TAshley(1) (b: hrd drvn over 3f out: a bhd) | 2½ | **8** | 8/1 | 47 | 17 |
| 139$^{9}$ | **Lord Sky (68)** (ABailey) **5-8-1**$^{(7)}$ AngelaGallimore(7) (hld up: wknd 2f out) | s.h | **9** | 14/1 | 44 | 14 |
| 211$^{11}$ | **Gulf Shaadi (72)** (EJAlston) **4-8-12** SDWilliams(5) (s.s: rdn over 3f out: sn bhd) | 3½ | **10** | 33/1 | 40 | 10 |
| 20* | **Ashgore (88)** (MJohnston) **6-10-0** JWeaver(3) (prom tl over 2f out) | 1¾ | **11** | 3/1$^{1}$ | 52 | 22 |
| 117$^{10}$ | **Little Ibnr (80)** (PDEvans) **5-9-6** LDettori(4) (led 4f) | 3½ | **12** | 8/1 | 36 | 6 |

(SP 134.1%) **12 Rn**

**1m 30.9** (6.20) CSF £55.45 CT £461.17 TOTE £6.40: £2.90 £4.30 £2.50 (£63.90) Trio £174.30 OWNER Mr Guy Reed (MIDDLEHAM) BRED Theakston Stud

STEWARDS' ENQUIRY McLaughlin susp. 23, 24-26/2/96 (excessive use of whip).

**OFFICIAL EXPLANATION Ashgore: was never travelling according to his jockey.**

## 271 BE MY VALENTINE (S) STKS (3-Y.O) (Class E)

4-30 (4-30) **6f (Fibresand)** £2,954.70 (£894.60: £436.80: £207.90) Stalls: Low GOING: 0.29 sec per fur (SLW)

| | | | Pos | SP | RR | SF |
|---|---|---|---|---|---|---|
| 215* | **Copper Bright (55)** (PCHaslam) **3-9-4b** JFortune(3) (a.p: led over 2f out: drvn out) | — | **1** | 11/1 | 67 | 28 |
| 183* | **Mystic Tempo (USA) (67)** (DrJDScargill) **3-8-13** RCochrane(8) (b: a.p: one pce fnl 2f) | 3½ | **2** | 11/10$^{1}$ | 53 | 14 |
| 220$^{5}$ | **Dhes-C (52)** (RHollinshead) **3-7-13**$^{(7)}$ FLynch(5) (hld up: hdwy over 2f out: c wd st: one pce fnl f) | ¾ | **3** | 9/1 | 44 | 5 |
| 224$^{2}$ | **Victoria Sioux (52)** (JAPickering) **3-8-6** JQuinn(7) (b.off hind: bhd: hrd drvn 4f out: styd on appr fnl f) | 1¼ | **4** | 8/1 | 40 | 1 |
| 101$^{2}$ | **Marino Street (57)** (PDEvans) **3-8-6** SSanders(6) (prom: rdn over 2f out: one pce) | 1 | **5** | 11/2$^{2}$ | 38 | — |
| 112$^{10}$ | **Castle Governor (54)** (PCHaslam) **3-9-4** JWeaver(2) (hld up: sn bhd: sme late hdwy) | 1½ | **6** | 8/1 | 46+ | 7 |
| 215$^{2}$ | **The Frisky Farmer (53)** (WGMTurner) **3-8-11**$^{(7)}$ ADaly(1) (led over 3f: wknd over 1f out) | 1½ | **7** | 13/2$^{3}$ | 42 | 3 |
| 46$^{8}$ | **Alpheton Prince (40)** (JLHarris) **3-8-6**$^{(5)}$ PFessey(4) (lw: outpcd) | 5 | **8** | 50/1 | 21 | — |
| 224$^{5}$ | **Shoot The Minstrel (32)** (JAPickering) **3-8-11** NCarlisle(9) (b.nr hind: bhd fnl 2f) | 3 | **9** | 33/1 | 13 | — |

(SP 121.8%) **9 Rn**

**1m 18.5** (7.10) CSF £23.72 TOTE £20.00: £5.60 £1.10 £2.40 (£11.50) Trio £34.40 OWNER Mr Gerald Selby (MIDDLEHAM) BRED Bearstone Stud

Bt in 5,200 gns

## 272 LADBROKE SERIES H'CAP (Qualifier) (0-80) (3-Y.O) (Class D)

5-00 (5-00) **5f (Fibresand)** £3,452.50 (£1,045.00: £510.00: £242.50) Stalls: Low GOING: 0.29 sec per fur (SLW)

| | | | Pos | SP | RR | SF |
|---|---|---|---|---|---|---|
| 142$^{4}$ | **Gi La High (58)** (JBerry) **3-8-2** NCarlisle(5) (mde all: clr over 1f out: pushed out) | — | **1** | 11/1 | 62+ | 13 |
| 224* | **Boffy (IRE) (76)** (BPJBaugh) **3-8-13**$^{(7)\ 7x}$ IonaWands(3) (b: hld up: hdwy over 2f out: r.o one pce fnl f) | ½ | **2** | 11/4$^{2}$ | 78 | 29 |
| 142$^{6}$ | **Gagajulu (61)** (PDEvans) **3-8-5** SSanders(6) (lw: a.p: one pce fnl 2f) | 3 | **3** | 10/1 | 54 | 5 |
| 183$^{5}$ | **Don't Tell Anyone (52)** (PDEvans) **3-7-10** JQuinn(4) (prom tl wknd wl over 1f out) | 3 | **4** | 7/1$^{3}$ | 35 | — |
| 182$^{2}$ | **Hever Golf Express (77)** (TJNaughton) **3-9-7** JWeaver(2) (rdn over 2f out: no rspnse) | 1¼ | **5** | 4/6$^{1}$ | 56 | 7 |
| 160$^{D}$ | **Monkey Zanty (IRE) (57)** (JLHarris) **3-7-10**$^{(5)}$ PFessey(1) (bhd fnl 3f) | 1½ | **6** | 8/1 | 31 | — |

(SP 127.7%) **6 Rn**

**64.6 secs** (5.90) CSF £42.85 TOTE £9.30: £7.20 £1.20 (£27.70) OWNER Mr Basheer Kielany (COCKERHAM) BRED J. H. Heath

T/Plpt: £125.00 (66.13 Tckts). T/Qdpt: £43.30 (22.38 Tckts) KH

# 0260-LINGFIELD (L-H) (Standard)
## Thursday February 15th

WEATHER: overcast WIND: almost nil

## 273 AXA EQUITY & LAW H'CAP (0-60) (I) (3-Y.O+) (Class F)

1-20 (1-23) **6f (Equitrack)** £2,178.90 (£610.40: £296.70) Stalls: Low GOING minus 0.57 sec per fur (FST)

| | | | Pos | SP | RR | SF |
|---|---|---|---|---|---|---|
| 203$^{2}$ | **Jersey Belle (44)** (PJMakin) **4-9-2b** SSanders(5) (a.p: led over 1f out: drvn out) | — | **1** | 7/2$^{1}$ | 52 | — |
| 212$^{5}$ | **Our Shadee (USA) (53)** (KTIvory) **6-9-4v**$^{(7)}$ CScally(2) (broke wl: sn outpcd: in rr tl hdwy over 1f out: styd on fnl f) | 2 | **2** | 6/1 | 56 | — |
| 117$^{3}$ | **Respectable Jones (52)** (RHollinshead) **10-9-10b** MWigham(7) (outpcd in rr: hdwy over 1f out: styd on fnl f) | ½ | **3** | 9/2$^{2}$ | 53 | — |
| 261$^{3}$ | **Apollo Red (53)** (AMoore) **7-9-11** CandyMorris(6) (led: hdd over 1f out: one pce) | ½ | **4** | 7/2$^{1}$ | 53 | — |
| 217$^{5}$ | **Desert Water (IRE) (40)** (JJBridger) **4-8-12v** JQuinn(8) (chsd ldr 4f: wknd over 1f out) | 2½ | **5** | 12/1 | 33 | — |
| 203$^{6}$ | **Prince Rudolf (IRE) (44)** (MrsNMacauley) **4-8-11v**$^{(5)}$ AmandaSanders(9) (mid div: rdn over 3f out: one pce) | s.h | **6** | 9/1 | 37 | — |
| 202$^{7}$ | **Ezekiel (27)** (TTClement) **5-7-13** GBardwell(10) (sn rdn: bhd fnl 3f) | 8 | **7** | 50/1 | — | — |
| 207$^{9}$ | **Persian Gusher (IRE) (50)** (NASmith) **6-9-1b**$^{1(7)}$ JBramhill(4) (bhd fnl 3f) | 1¾ | **8** | 25/1 | 17 | — |
| 203$^{13}$ | **Diamond Bangle (25)** (CCElsey) **4-7-11** NAdams(3) (chsd ldrs tl wknd 3f out) | ¾ | **9** | 33/1 | — | — |
| 120$^{8}$ | **Al Shaati (FR) (40)** (RJO'Sullivan) **6-8-12b** AClark(1) (mid div: rdn 4f out: wknd 3f out) | 3 | **10** | 5/1$^{3}$ | — | — |

(SP 120.0%) **10 Rn**

**1m 13.97** (3.37) CSF £23.70 CT £90.90 TOTE £4.60: £2.30 £2.10 £1.10 (£17.70) Trio £20.60 OWNER Mr D. A. Poole (MARLBOROUGH) BRED B and Mrs Shelton

## 274 DUNGENESS POINT MAIDEN STKS (3-Y.O+) (Class D)

1-50 (1-51) **1m 4f (Equitrack)** £3,485.00 (£1,055.00: £515.00: £245.00) Stalls: Low GOING minus 0.57 sec per fur (FST)

| | Horse | Dist | Pos | SP | RR | SF |
|---|---|---|---|---|---|---|
| 228[2] | **Mister Aspecto (IRE) (62)** (MJohnston) **3-8-3b** TWilliams(5) (lw: led 1f: led over 3f out: rdn out ins fnl f) | — | 1 | 8/11[1] | 50 | — |
| | **Tondres (USA) (59)** (RIngram) **5-9-13** WWoods(8) (b.hind: hld up: hdwy 4f out: chsd wnr 3f out: rdn over 2f out: r.o ins fnl f) | 1½ | 2 | 10/1 | 72 | — |
| 154[10] | **Streaky Hawk (USA) (50)** (JPearce) **4-9-10** GBardwell(1) (towards rr: rdn 6f out: hdwy over 2f out: kpt on one pce fnl f) | 7 | 3 | 14/1 | 64 | — |
| 216[4] | **Zuno Flyer (USA) (34)** (AMoore) **4-9-10v** MFenton(3) (b.hind: chsd ldrs: rdn 5f out: one pce fnl 3f) | 2 | 4 | 9/1[3] | 61 | — |
| 221[8] | **Taniyar (FR) (48)** (RHollinshead) **4-9-10** TIves(4) (rr: sn rdn along: sme hdwy over 2f out: wknd over 1f out) | 5 | 5 | 20/1 | 54 | — |
| | **Yellow Dragon (IRE) (57)** (BAPearce) **3-8-0**(3) DRMcCabe(6) (sltly hmpd after s: sn outpcd: wl bhd tl sme late hdwy) | 7 | 6 | 4/1[2] | 20 | — |
| 82[12] | **Thorniwama (32)** (JJBridger) **5-9-8** JQuinn(2) (chsd ldrs: rdn 5f out: wknd over 3f out) | hd | 7 | 40/1 | 39 | — |
| 260[8] | **Callonescy (IRE) (47)** (DCO'Brien) **4-9-10b**[1] JWeaver(9) (led after 1f: hdd over 3f out: sn wknd) | 5 | 8 | 11/1 | 38 | — |
| 204[4] | **Kellaire Girl (IRE) (47)** (AMoore) **4-9-5** SSanders(10) (b.hind: lw: chsd ldrs: rdn over 4f out: sn wknd) | d.h | 8 | 11/1 | 33 | — |
| | **Red Adair (IRE) (57)** (BobJones) **4-9-10** MWigham(7) (swtchd lft sn after s: sn outpcd: a bhd: t.o) | dist | 10 | 20/1 | — | — |

(SP 132.3%) **10 Rn**

**2m 35.63** (5.63) CSF £10.72 TOTE £2.30: £1.10 £2.80 £3.10 (£17.50) Trio £20.30 OWNER Aspecto Clothing Co Ltd (MIDDLEHAM) BRED Petra Bloodstock Agency Ltd

WEIGHT FOR AGE 3yo-24lb, 4yo-3lb

STEWARDS' ENQUIRY Wigham susp. 24 & 26/2/96 (careless riding).

## 275 HURST POINT (S) H'CAP (0-60) (4-Y.O+) (Class G)

2-25 (2-27) **2m (Equitrack)** £2,274.00 (£639.00: £312.00) Stalls: Low GOING minus 0.57 sec per fur (FST)

| | Horse | Dist | Pos | SP | RR | SF |
|---|---|---|---|---|---|---|
| | **Juliasdarkinvader (36)** (AMoore) **6-8-10** AClark(9) (b: b.hind: hld up in tch: chsd ldr 10f out: led 5f out: hrd rdn ins fnl f: all out) | — | 1 | 16/1 | 46 | 25 |
| 186* | **Heighth of Fame (48)** (AJWilson) **5-9-8** JFortune(2) (a.p: chsd wnr 4f out: hrd rdn 2f out: styd on strly fnl f: jst failed) | hd | 2 | 5/2[2] | 58 | 37 |
| 240[3] | **Milngavie (IRE) (40)** (MJohnston) **6-9-0** JWeaver(1) (chsd ldrs: outpcd 5f out: hrd rdn over 2f out: one pce) | 9 | 3 | 11/10[1] | 41 | 20 |
| 154[4] | **Alpine Storm (IRE) (28)** (MDIUsher) **4-7-5**(5) CAdamson(3) (in tch: rdn 5f out: sn outpcd) | 11 | 4 | 13/2[3] | 18 | — |
| | **Desert President (29)** (RPCHoad) **5-8-3v** JQuinn(8) (hld up: rdn over 4f out: wknd 3f out) | ½ | 5 | 12/1 | 18 | — |
| 240[7] | **Shedansar (IRE) (28)** (GLMoore) **4-7-10** GBardwell(6) (led: hdd 5f out: wknd over 3f out) | 2½ | 6 | 16/1 | 15 | — |
| 128[7] | **Bobby Blue (IRE) (43)** (RonaldThompson) **5-9-3** SDWilliams(5) (b: bhd fnl 6f) | 25 | 7 | 33/1 | 5 | — |
| | **Omidjoy (IRE) (50)** (JRJenkins) **6-9-3b**(7) SallyWall(4) (a bhd: t.o) | 25 | 8 | 33/1 | — | — |
| | **Wicklow Boy (IRE) (37)** (RJWeaver) **5-8-4b**(7) ADaly(7) (virtually ref to r: a t.o) | dist | 9 | 20/1 | — | — |

(SP 119.6%) **9 Rn**

**3m 27.18** (5.18) CSF £54.39 CT £75.24 TOTE £23.60: £2.30 £1.30 £1.10 (£31.20) Trio £13.40 OWNER Mr A. Moore (BRIGHTON) BRED J. and P. Newton

LONG HANDICAP Alpine Storm (IRE) 7-7

WEIGHT FOR AGE 4yo-6lb

No bid

## 276 DURLSTON HEAD MEDIAN AUCTION MAIDEN STKS (3-Y.O F) (Class F)

3-00 (3-00) **7f (Equitrack)** £2,481.30 (£696.80: £339.90) Stalls: Low GOING minus 0.57 sec per fur (FST)

| | Horse | Dist | Pos | SP | RR | SF |
|---|---|---|---|---|---|---|
| | **Charming Bride** (SCWilliams) **3-8-11** JTate(4) (hld up: hdwy to chse ldr over 2f out: rdn over 1f out: led ins fnl f: drvn out) | — | 1 | 10/11[1] | 55 | — |
| 118[4] | **Badger Bay (IRE) (67)** (CADwyer) **3-8-8**(3) JStack(1) (led: hdd ins fnl f: r.o) | ¾ | 2 | 6/4[2] | 53 | — |
| 67[8] | **Tahya (USA) (55)** (CCElsey) **3-8-11** DHarrison(3) (hld up in tch: hrd rdn over 1f out: r.o one pce ins fnl f) | 1¼ | 3 | 5/1[3] | 50 | — |
| | **Bear To Dance (51)** (JohnBerry) **3-8-11** MFenton(2) (chsd ldr over 4f: rdn 2f out: wknd over 1f out) | 5 | 4 | 14/1 | 39 | — |

(SP 115.7%) **4 Rn**

**1m 30.38** (6.38) CSF £2.79 TOTE £2.00 (£1.50) OWNER Mr D. A. Shekells (NEWMARKET) BRED Old Mill Stud

## 277 EDDYSTONE H'CAP (0-70) (3-Y.O) (Class E)

3-35 (3-35) **1m (Equitrack)** £2,872.80 (£869.40: £424.20: £201.60) Stalls: High GOING minus 0.57 sec per fur (FST)

| | Horse | Dist | Pos | SP | RR | SF |
|---|---|---|---|---|---|---|
| 245[2] | **Domoor (56)** (MJohnston) **3-9-3** JWeaver(2) (lw: a gng wl: hld up in tch: led over 1f out: r.o) | — | 1 | 5/4[1] | 64 | 24 |
| 143[2] | **Creeking (60)** (SirMarkPrescott) **3-9-7** GDuffield(4) (lw: chsd ldr: led over 3f out: hdd over 1f out: nt qckn) | 1 | 2 | 5/2[2] | 66 | 26 |
| | **Willie Rushton (58)** (GLMoore) **3-9-5** SWhitworth(7) (stdd s: hld up: hdwy over 2f out: r.o one pce ins fnl f) | 2½ | 3 | 11/1 | 59+ | 19 |
| 119[3] | **Billaddie (60)** (RBoss) **3-9-7** AClark(3) (chsd ldrs: pushed along over 4f out: hrd rdn over 1f out: one pce) | 1¾ | 4 | 5/1[3] | 58 | 18 |
| 35[10] | **Shanoora (IRE) (50)** (MrsNMacauley) **3-8-6**(5) AmandaSanders(5) (in tch: rdn over 2f out: sn wknd) | 5 | 5 | 25/1 | 38 | — |
| 176[7] | **Hotlips Houlihan (51)** (RJRWilliams) **3-8-12** DBiggs(8) (led: hdd over 3f out: wknd 2f out) | 5 | 6 | 9/1 | 29 | — |
| 188[8] | **Conquistajade (USA) (45)** (SPCWoods) **3-8-6b** WWoods(6) (in tch: rdn over 3f out: sn wknd) | 1¼ | 7 | 25/1 | 20 | — |
| | **Colour Counsellor (54)** (RMFlower) **3-9-1** TIves(1) (a bhd) | 4 | 8 | 33/1 | 21 | — |

(SP 118.6%) **8 Rn**

**1m 40.48** (3.08) CSF £4.90 CT £20.62 TOTE £2.30: £1.10 £1.70 £2.20 (£3.30) OWNER The Braindon Partnership (MIDDLEHAM) BRED Greenland Park Stud

## 278 AXA EQUITY & LAW H'CAP (0-60) (II) (3-Y.O+) (Class F)

4-05 (4-10) **6f (Equitrack)** £2,167.00 (£607.00: £295.00) Stalls: Low GOING minus 0.57 sec per fur (FST)

| | Horse | Dist | Pos | SP | RR | SF |
|---|---|---|---|---|---|---|
| 178[5] | **Newington Butts (IRE) (44)** (KMcAuliffe) **6-9-2e** SSanders(9) (a.p: led 3f out: drvn out ins fnl f) | — | 1 | 10/1 | 52 | 13 |
| 266[2] | **Sharp Imp (54)** (RMFlower) **6-9-12b** DBiggs(2) (lw: hld up: hdwy & n.m.r over 2f out: rdn to chse wnr ins fnl f: r.o) | ¾ | 2 | 11/4[1] | 60 | 21 |
| 231* | **The Institute Boy (59)** (MissJFCraze) **6-10-3** 7x JWeaver(10) (hld up: hdwy over 3f out: chsd wnr over 2f out tl ins fnl f: unable qckn) | s.h | 3 | 6/1[3] | 65 | 26 |
| 36* | **Myjinka (49)** (TEPowell) **6-9-4b**(3) PMcCabe(7) (reard s: sn wl bhd: gd hdwy over 1f out: styd on strly ins fnl f) | 1¾ | 4 | 7/2[2] | 50 | 11 |

203$^{3}$ **Nivasha (39)** (RPCHoad) **4-8-11** MFenton(6) (sn rdn along in rr: bhd tl sme hdwy fnl f: nrst fin)..........5 **5** 12/1 27 —
259$^{11}$ **Bowcliffe Grange (IRE) (26)** (DWChapman) **4-7-7**$^{(5)}$ PFessey(8) (hld up: hdwy over 2f out: rdn over 1f out: sn wknd)..........s.h **6** 20/1 14 —
218$^{6}$ **Dusk in Daytona (54)** (CJames) **4-9-5v**$^{1(7)}$ FLynch(3) (chsd ldr: led over 3f out: sn hdd: wknd 2f out)..........2½ **7** 14/1 35 —
133$^{8}$ **Thick as Thieves (49)** (RonaldThompson) **4-9-7** TWilliams(4) (chsd ldrs: rdn over 3f out: wknd over 2f out)....5 **8** 10/1 17 —
231$^{5}$ **Cedar Girl (42)** (MrsNMacauley) **4-8-9**$^{(5)}$ AmandaSanders(5) (chsd ldrs to ½-wy)..........s.h **9** 15/2 10 —
203$^{7}$ **Pearl Dawn (IRE) (46)** (GLMoore) **6-9-4** SWhitworth(1) (lw: led: hdd over 3f out: sn wknd)..........7 **10** 6/1$^{3}$ — —
(SP 126.5%) **10 Rn**

**1m 13.46** (2.86) CSF £38.36 CT £176.00 TOTE £7.90: £1.50 £1.10 £3.40 (£31.00) Trio £53.60 OWNER Mr D. D. Davies (LAMBOURN) BRED A. F. O. Callaghan

## 279 NEEDLES AMATEUR H'CAP (0-70) (4-Y.O+) (Class E)

4-35 (4-45) **1m 5f (Equitrack)** £2,941.05 (£890.40: £434.70: £206.85) Stalls: Low GOING minus 0.57 sec per fur (FST)

SP RR SF

236$^{4}$ **Claque (52)** (DWChapman) **4-9-9b**$^{(4)}$ MissRClark(6) (chsd ldrs: rn wd ent st: sn rdn: led ins fnl f: r.o wl)........— **1** 8/1 59 36
72* **Ajdar (47)** (MissGayKelleway) **5-9-8**$^{(4)}$ MissSKelleway(8) (hld up: hdwy 4f out: led 1f out: hdd ins fnl f: unable qckn)..........1¾ **2** 13/2$^{3}$ 51 33
219* **Don't Drop Bombs (USA) (39)** (DTThom) **7-9-4v** $^{5x}$ MissJFeilden(5) (prom: led over 2f out to 1f out: one pce)4 **3** 9/2$^{2}$ 38 20
69* **Iron N Gold (52)** (AMoore) **4-9-13** MrTMcCarthy(3) (b.hind: a.p: led 6f out: hdd over 2f out: ev ch 1f out: one pce)..........½ **4** 100/30$^{1}$ 51 28
**Mr Copyforce (47)** (MissBSanders) **6-9-8**$^{(4)}$ MrKGoble(9) (nvr nrr)..........2 **5** 14/1 43 25
152* **Gold Blade (70)** (JPearce) **7-11-7** MrsLPearce(10) (lw: hld up in rr: sme hdwy fnl f: nvr nr to chal)..........2½ **6** 100/30$^{1}$ 63 45
152$^{7}$ **Phanan (42)** (REPeacock) **10-9-0**$^{(7)ow7}$ MrsCPeacock(7) (mid div: rdn 4f out: sn wknd)..........1½ **7** 50/1 33 8
140$^{7}$ **Kentavrus Way (IRE) (35)** (AMoore) **5-8-10**$^{(4)}$ MrsJMoore(2) (b.hind: mid div: rdn 3f out: sn wknd)..........hd **8** 33/1 26 8
219$^{5}$ **Montone (IRE) (46)** (JRJenkins) **6-9-7**$^{(4)ow3}$ DrMMannish(4) (prom: rdn over 4f out: wknd 3f out)..........2 **9** 12/1 34 13
186$^{5}$ **Sorisky (40)** (BGubby) **4-8-11**$^{(4)}$ MrsMTingey(1) (led: hdd 6f out: sn wknd: t.o)..........25 **10** 10/1 — —
(SP 117.1%) **10 Rn**

**2m 48.14** (4.94) CSF £53.98 CT £239.08 TOTE £10.00: £1.50 £3.60 £3.30 (£28.40) Trio £42.30 OWNER Mr Michael Hill (YORK) BRED Lord Howard de Walden
LONG HANDICAP Kentavrus Way (IRE) 8-8 Phanan 8-4
WEIGHT FOR AGE 4yo-4lb
OFFICIAL EXPLANATION **Gold Blade: the jockey reported that the gelding was never travelling and when asked for an effort in the straight, he failed to quicken.**

T/Plpt: £15.50 (665.86 Tckts). T/Qdpt: £7.00 (157.17 Tckts) SM

# 0254-SOUTHWELL (L-H) (Standard)

## Friday February 16th

WEATHER: Unsettled WIND: str bhd

## 280 GIRTON H'CAP (0-60) (3-Y.O) (Class F)

1-50 (1-51) **1m 3f (Fibresand)** £2,398.00 (£673.00: £328.00) Stalls: Low GOING: 0.04 sec per fur (STD)

SP RR SF

123* **Dancing Cavalier (59)** (RHollinshead) **3-8-13**$^{(7)}$ FLynch(9) (lw: sn bhd: hdwy 4f out: r.o to ld wl ins fnl f)........— **1** 5/2$^{1}$ 67 29
56$^{5}$ **Suparoy (48)** (TGMills) **3-8-9** JQuinn(11) (trckd ldrs: led 3f out tl wl ins fnl f: sn btn)..........2 **2** 12/1 53 15
176$^{8}$ **Uoni (53)** (CEBrittain) **3-9-0** JWeaver(4) (styd on wl fnl 3f: nrst fin)..........nk **3** 8/1 58 20
123$^{3}$ **Guy's Gamble (55)** (JWharton) **3-9-2** JFanning(8) (trckd ldrs: effrt over 3f out: ev ch over 1f out: no ex)........1½ **4** 7/1 58 20
197$^{4}$ **Diasafina (35)** (SCWilliams) **3-7-10b**$^{1}$ GBardwell(1) (sn outpcd & bhd: rapid hdwy to ld 5f out: hdd 3f out: btn appr fnl f)..........1½ **5** 50/1 35 —
123$^{9}$ **Onefourseven (44)** (SRBowring) **3-8-5b** NCarlisle(2) (chsd ldrs: effrt over 3f out: one pce appr fnl f)..........1½ **6** 16/1 42 4
176* **Thorntoun Estate (IRE) (60)** (MJohnston) **3-9-7** DeanMcKeown(7) (led 2f: chsd ldrs tl outpcd fnl 3f)..........3 **7** 3/1$^{2}$ 54 16
171$^{6}$ **Be My Bird (46)** (WJMusson) **3-8-7** RCochrane(3) (lw: sn wl bhd: sme hdwy 4f out: n.d)..........6 **8** 6/1$^{3}$ 31 —
35$^{5}$ **Ebony Boy (60)** (JWharton) **3-9-2**$^{(5)}$ CTeague(6) (cl up tl outpcd over 3f out: sn wknd)..........7 **9** 12/1 35 —
171$^{4}$ **Sporting Fantasy (45)** (JBalding) **3-8-6** ClaireBalding(10) (cl up tl outpcd 4f out: sn bhd)..........8 **10** 20/1 8 —
238$^{6}$ **Down The Yard (42)** (MCChapman) **3-7-10**$^{(7)}$ CMunday(12) (led after 2f tl hdd 5f out: wknd qckly)..........s.h **11** 20/1 5 —
(SP 124.2%) **11 Rn**

**2m 31.1** (11.10) CSF £31.46 CT £200.76 TOTE £3.20: £1.20 £2.20 £4.50 (£18.80) Trio £109.00 OWNER The Three R's (UPPER LONGDON) BRED A. P. Hume
LONG HANDICAP Diasafina 7-3

## 281 HARDWICK CLAIMING STKS (3-Y.O) (Class F)

2-25 (2-27) **1m (Fibresand)** £2,398.00 (£673.00: £328.00) Stalls: Low GOING: 0.04 sec per fur (STD)

SP RR SF

258$^{3}$ **Efipetite (44)** (NBycroft) **3-8-0** GBardwell(6) (s.i.s: smooth hdwy ½-wy: led 1f out: r.o u.p)..........— **1** 10/1 50 —
258* **People Direct (52)** (KMcAuliffe) **3-8-6** JFortune(2) (b.hind: led tl hdd 1f out: kpt on)..........1 **2** 2/1$^{1}$ 54 —
238$^{2}$ **Mooncusser (57)** (JGFitzGerald) **3-8-9be** MWigham(7) (w ldrs: rdn over 2f out: r.o one pce)..........2 **3** 5/2$^{2}$ 53 —
118$^{8}$ **Ben'a'vachei Boy (55)** (JDBethell) **3-8-13** JWeaver(5) (trckd ldrs: effrt over 2f out: r.o one pce)..........2 **4** 8/1 53 —
258$^{4}$ **Bumblefoot (IRE) (55)** (MJohnston) **3-8-2** TWilliams(8) (lw: cl up tl outpcd fnl 2f)..........2 **5** 9/2$^{3}$ 38 —
**Spirit of Sport** (AGNewcombe) **3-8-8** NAdams(3) (s.i.s: hdwy ½-wy: outpcd fnl 2½f)..........8 **6** 14/1 28 —
89$^{7}$ **Bridlington Bay** (JLEyre) **3-8-4**$^{(5)}$ PFessey(4) (cl up tl outpcd ½-wy: n.d after)..........4 **7** 50/1 21 —
131$^{9}$ **Petite Annie** (TGMills) **3-8-4** JQuinn(1) (b.off hind: chsd ldrs tl outpcd ½-wy: sn bhd: t.o)..........30 **8** 10/1 — —
(SP 118.0%) **8 Rn**

**1m 49.6** (9.60) CSF £29.67 TOTE £13.80: £2.40 £1.30 £1.10 (£10.90) OWNER Mr T. Umpleby (BRANDSBY) BRED T. Umpleby

## 282 KIRKBY-IN-ASHFIELD H'CAP (0-75) (3-Y.O+) (Class D)

2-55 (2-55) **6f (Fibresand)** £3,517.50 (£1,065.00: £520.00: £247.50) Stalls: Low GOING: 0.04 sec per fur (STD)

SP RR SF

237* **First Maite (77)** (SRBowring) **3-8-10b**$^{(5)}$ $^{7x}$ CTeague(9) (lw: trckd ldrs: effrt ½-wy: r.o u.p to ld nr fin)..........— **1** 5/2$^{1}$ 83 50

| | Horse | Btn | Pos | SP | RR | SF |
|---|---|---|---|---|---|---|
| 225* | **Kira (65)** (JLEyre) **6-9-4** [7x] RLappin(6) (b.off hind: led: qcknd over 2f out: jst ct) | nk | **2** | 11/4[2] | 69 | 52 |
| 170[8] | **Leigh Crofter (72)** (JAHarris) **7-9-11b** JWeaver(4) (bhd: rdn 2f out: r.o wl fnl f) | 1¾ | **3** | 12/1 | 72 | 55 |
| 88[10] | **Nordan Raider (74)** (MJCamacho) **8-9-13** RCochrane(7) (b: trckd ldrs: hmpd ½-wy: styd on appr fnl f) | 2 | **4** | 12/1 | 68 | 51 |
| 250[6] | **Bold Aristocrat (IRE) (51)** (RHollinshead) **5-7-11**(7) FLynch(8) (a chsng ldrs: one pce fnl 2f) | hd | **5** | 16/1 | 45 | 28 |
| | **Allinson's Mate (IRE) (67)** (TDBarron) **8-9-6b** JFortune(5) (s.i.s: hdwy u.p 2f out: nvr rchd ldrs) | nk | **6** | 10/1 | 60 | 43 |
| 259[7] | **Daawe (USA) (58)** (MrsVAAconley) **5-8-11v** MDeering(2) (hld up: hdwy on ins over 2f out: no imp) | 1 | **7** | 10/1 | 49 | 32 |
| | **Johnnie the Joker (75)** (JPLeigh) **5-9-9**(5) PRoberts(10) (bit bkwd: outpcd after 2f: n.d) | 2 | **8** | 25/1 | 60 | 43 |
| 194* | **Seeking Destiny (IRE) (58)** (MCChapman) **3-7-5**(5) PFessey(3) (w ldrs tl outpcd over 2f out: sn wknd) | nk | **9** | 11/2[3] | 43 | 10 |
| 259[5] | **Efficacy (53)** (APJarvis) **5-8-6** JTate(1) (cl up 4f: wknd) | 7 | **10** | 12/1 | 19 | 2 |

(SP 121.6%) **10 Rn**

**1m 17.4** (3.90) CSF £9.81 CT £65.71 TOTE £2.40: £1.40 £1.60 £2.10 (£5.80) Trio £56.00 OWNER Mr S. R. Bowring (EDWINSTOWE) BRED S. R. Bowring
LONG HANDICAP Seeking Destiny (IRE) 7-6
WEIGHT FOR AGE 3yo-15lb

## 283 LAXTON H'CAP (0-70) (4-Y.O+) (Class E)

3-30 (3-30) **2m (Fibresand)** £2,886.45 (£873.60: £426.30: £202.65) Stalls: Low GOING: 0.04 sec per fur (STD)

| | Horse | Btn | Pos | SP | RR | SF |
|---|---|---|---|---|---|---|
| 236* | **Upper Mount Clair (52)** (CEBrittain) **6-9-2** [4x] MLarsen(6) (in tch: hdwy ½-wy: led 1½f out: styd on wl) | — | **1** | 3/1[1] | 61 | — |
| 208[3] | **Yougo (70)** (MJohnston) **4-10-0** JWeaver(5) (lw: cl up: effrt whn hmpd 2f out: hdwy over 1f out: hung lft: styd on wl) | 2½ | **2** | 11/2[3] | 77 | — |
| 236[3] | **Swordking (IRE) (34)** (JLHarris) **7-7-12** NCarlisle(4) (a.p: led 3f out tl 1½f out: one pce) | 5 | **3** | 16/1 | 36 | — |
| 236[2] | **Baher (USA) (32)** (MrsASwinbank) **7-7-10** GBardwell(8) (jnd ldrs ½-wy: led 5f out to 3f out: one pce fnl 2½f) | 4 | **4** | 14/1 | 30 | — |
| | **Simafar (IRE) (58)** (NAGraham) **5-9-8** TIves(2) (lw: sn outpcd & wl bhd: hdwy 5f out: nvr rch ldrs) | 3½ | **5** | 9/2[2] | 52 | — |
| | **Douce Maison (IRE) (63)** (APJarvis) **5-9-13** JTate(10) (hld up: hdwy ½-wy: outpcd over 3f out: sn btn) | 8 | **6** | 14/1 | 49 | — |
| 208* | **Record Lover (IRE) (40)** (MCChapman) **6-7-11**(7) [4x] CMunday(1) (mde most tl hdd 5f out: outpcd over 3f out: sn btn) | 2½ | **7** | 9/1 | 24 | — |
| 210[11] | **Samana Cay (40)** (PSFelgate) **4-7-5b**(7) IonaWands(7) (disp ld after 4f to 8f out: sn wknd) | 25 | **8** | 33/1 | — | — |
| 169* | **Badawi (FR) (46)** (NMBabbage) **6-8-10** JQuinn(3) (sn drvn along & wl bhd: t.o) | dist | **9** | 3/1[1] | — | — |

(SP 115.7%) **9 Rn**

**3m 48.7** (22.70) CSF £18.48 CT £202.87 TOTE £4.20: £1.90 £2.20 £3.00 (£7.90) Trio £63.20 OWNER Mr C. E. Brittain (NEWMARKET) BRED J. Ward Hill
LONG HANDICAP Baher (USA) 7-6
WEIGHT FOR AGE 4yo-6lb
OFFICIAL EXPLANATION **Badawi (FR): The horsebox broke down on the way and was held up for two hours, which affected the horse's run.**

## 284 MAPLEBECK (S) STKS (4-Y.O+) (Class G)

4-05 (4-05) **1m 4f (Fibresand)** £2,085.00 (£585.00: £285.00) Stalls: Low GOING: 0.04 sec per fur (STD)

| | Horse | Btn | Pos | SP | RR | SF |
|---|---|---|---|---|---|---|
| 82[4] | **Greenwich Again (64)** (TGMills) **4-8-11** JFortune(8) (lw: hld up: smooth hdwy 3f out: led wl over 1f out: shkn up & r.o ins fnl f) | — | **1** | 13/2[3] | 70 | 31 |
| 235[3] | **Pharly Dancer (75)** (WWHaigh) **7-9-0** DaleGibson(7) (cl up: rdn to ld over 2f out: sn hdd & one pce) | 3 | **2** | 5/6[1] | 66 | 30 |
| 235[5] | **Ballyrag (USA)** (RAFahey) **5-9-0** ACulhane(6) (lw: led tl hdd over 2f out: sn outpcd) | 6 | **3** | 25/1 | 58 | 22 |
| 138[3] | **El Nido (54)** (MJCamacho) **8-9-0** JWeaver(1) (trckd ldrs: effrt over 3f out: no imp) | 2 | **4** | 7/1 | 55 | 19 |
| 251[3] | **Hawwam (65)** (EJAlston) **10-9-0** SDWilliams(5) (pushed along ½-wy: sn outpcd & no imp) | 9 | **5** | 4/1[2] | 43 | 7 |
| | **Kindred Greeting (33)** (DMorris) **4-8-11b** RCochrane(3) (chsd ldrs tl wknd 4f out) | 15 | **6** | 33/1 | 23 | — |
| | **Senso (IRE)** (JSWainwright) **5-9-0** DeanMcKeown(4) (bit bkwd: outpcd & bhd after 4f) | 13 | **7** | 25/1 | 6 | — |
| 254[9] | **Stylish Gent (35)** (GROldroyd) **9-8-7**(7) AColgan(2) (prom 4f: sn rdn & wl bhd) | 25 | **8** | 50/1 | — | — |

(SP 113.0%) **8 Rn**

**2m 42.9** (10.40) CSF £11.69 TOTE £7.00: £2.90 £1.20 £2.30 (£6.70) OWNER John Humphreys (Turf Accountants) Ltd (EPSOM) BRED T. G. Mills Ltd
WEIGHT FOR AGE 4yo-3lb
Bt in 3,600 gns

## 285 LADBROKE ALL-WEATHER CHALLENGE SERIES H'CAP (Final) (3-Y.O+) (Class D)

4-35 (4-36) **1m (Fibresand)** £4,026.00 (£1,218.00: £594.00: £282.00) Stalls: Low GOING: 0.04 sec per fur (STD)

| | Horse | Btn | Pos | SP | RR | SF |
|---|---|---|---|---|---|---|
| 199* | **Tatika (73)** (GWragg) **6-9-6**(7) GMilligan(4) (lw: a gng wl: led 2f out: comf) | — | **1** | 9/4[1] | 84+ | 57 |
| 249[2] | **Kingchip Boy (64)** (MJRyan) **7-9-4v** TIves(6) (a cl up: led over 2f out: sn hdd & one pce) | 7 | **2** | 4/1 | 61 | 34 |
| 243[8] | **Mislemani (IRE) (52)** (AGNewcombe) **6-8-3**(3) DRMcCabe(2) (lost pl after 3f: rdn 2f out: styd on: no imp) | 2 | **3** | 12/1 | 45 | 18 |
| 176[4] | **China Castle (74)** (PCHaslam) **3-8-9** JFortune(1) (lw: a chsng ldrs: no imp fnl 2f) | 1¾ | **4** | 7/2[3] | 64 | 18 |
| 115[2] | **Cashmere Lady (74)** (JLEyre) **4-10-0** RLappin(3) (lw: led tl hdd over 2f out: sn btn) | nk | **5** | 3/1[2] | 63 | 36 |
| 77[6] | **Palacegate Jo (IRE) (48)** (DWChapman) **5-7-11**(5) PFessey(5) (b: dwlt: sn rcvrd & cl up: outpcd over 3f out: sn wknd) | 20 | **6** | 33/1 | — | — |

(SP 108.6%) **6 Rn**

**1m 45.7** (5.70) CSF £10.38 TOTE £2.90: £2.30 £2.60 (£4.80) OWNER Mr G. Wragg (NEWMARKET) BRED D. J. and Mrs Deer
WEIGHT FOR AGE 3yo-19lb

T/Plpt: £9.20 (1,062.3 Tckts). T/Qdpt: £4.60 (222.21 Tckts) AA

# ABU DHABI (UAE) (L-H) (Good)
## Friday January 26th

## 286a H H THE PRESIDENT'S CUP PREP (3-Y.O+)

**7f (Turf)** £5,263.16 (£2,631.58: £1,578.95: £1,052.63)

| Horse | Btn | Pos | SP | RR | SF |
|---|---|---|---|---|---|
| **Faltaat (USA)** (DJSelvaratnam,UAE) **6-9-1** BDoyle | — | **1** | | 119 | — |
| **Heart Lake** (SbinSuroor,UAE) **5-9-8** JCarroll | 1½ | **2** | | 123 | — |

| | | | | SP | RR | SF |
|---|---|---|---|---|---|---|
| | **Alami (USA)** (KPMcLaughlin,UAE) **4-9-1** RHills | 7½ | **3** | | 98 | — |
| | **Jahid (USA)** (ECharpy,UAE) **4-9-1** WSupple | 2¾ | **4** | | 92 | — |

**4 Rn**

**1m 20.65** OWNER Sheikh Ahmed Al Maktoum BRED Jonalbell Farm Inc , J M Robinson

# 0226a-CAGNES-SUR-MER (Nice, France) (L-H) (Heavy)

## Wednesday February 7th

### 287a PRIX DE LA CALIFORNIE (3-Y.O)

1-20 (1-18) **6f 110y** £6,588.00

| | | | | SP | RR | SF |
|---|---|---|---|---|---|---|
| | **Caltroom (FR)** (MmeARossio,France) **3-8-13** DBoeuf | — | **1** | | 79 | — |
| | **Bal Des Sirenes (IRE)** (RCollet,France) **3-8-9** ESaint-Martin | 2 | **2** | | 70 | — |
| | **Minnehaha (FR)** (JForesi,France) **3-8-9** FPardon | 1½ | **3** | | 66 | — |
| 150a[6] | **Western Sonata (IRE)** (LordHuntingdon) **3-8-6** GGuignard (btn over 6½l) | | **7** | | 59 | — |

**11 Rn**

**1m 31.1** P-M 5.70F: 2.00F 1.60F 1.90F (18.50F) OWNER Mme A. Rossio BRED G. Brochard & Mme M.Brochard

**150a Western Sonata (IRE)** struggled in the heavy going. Reverting to this shorter trip, she raced in fourth until losing her place turning for home. She did run on at the finish and will be worth keeping an eye on when the ground begins to improve.

### 288a PRIX D'AVIGNON H'CAP (4-Y.O+)

1-48 (1-46) **1m** £9,881.00 (£4,940.00: £2,964.00: £1,976.00)

| | | | | SP | RR | SF |
|---|---|---|---|---|---|---|
| 151a[3] | **Dusty Ocean (USA)** (FChappet,France) **5-8-7** FSanchez | — | **1** | | 79 | — |
| 227a[2] | **Spinario (USA)** (Jean-MarcCapitte,Belgium) **5-8-7** MBoutin | 2½ | **2** | | 74 | — |
| 191a[3] | **Mill Boy (FR)** (PKhozian,France) **7-8-7** GElorriaga-Santos | ½ | **3** | | 73 | — |
| 191a[4] | **Confronter** (SDow) **7-9-3** ESaint-Martin | 1½ | **4** | | 80 | — |

**14 Rn**

**1m 50.6** P-M 18.50F: 4.20F 1.50F 1.60F (49.90F) OWNER J Bruneau de la Salle BRED Gainsborough Farm Inc.

**191a Confronter** put up a much improved display to finish fourth. Always prominent, the son of Bluebird ran on well under pressure in the closing stages. Improvement should come from this run.

### 289a PRIX DU TRAYAS (3-Y.O)

2-44 (2-43) **1m 2f** £6,588.00 (£3,294.00: £2,055.00)

| | | | | SP | RR | SF |
|---|---|---|---|---|---|---|
| 146a* | **Megaron (FR)** (MPimbonnet,France) **3-8-2** FBlondel | — | **1** | | 61 | — |
| 192a[2] | **Yamamoto (FR)** (RCollet,France) **3-8-7** CHanotel | ½ | **2** | | 65 | — |
| 192a[4] | **Asking For Kings (IRE)** (SDow) **3-8-7** FSanchez | 2 | **3** | | 62 | — |

**19 Rn**

**1m 42.7** P-M 2.70F: 1.50F 3.60F 4.80F (31.60F) OWNER L. Peyraud BRED Werner Wolf

**192a Asking For Kings (IRE)** is clearly improving with every run. Prominent early, he took up the running after two furlongs, and remained at the head of affairs until collared inside the final furlong.

# 0287a-CAGNES-SUR-MER (Nice, France) (L-H) (Soft)

## Sunday February 11th

### 290a PRIX DE VALLAURIS (4-Y.O+)

2-46 (2-44) **7f 110y** £6,588.00 (£3,294.00)

| | | | | SP | RR | SF |
|---|---|---|---|---|---|---|
| | **Cycladic (USA)** (J-PGallorini,France) **4-8-8** TBalcon | — | **1** | | 77 | — |
| 288a[4] | **Confronter** (SDow) **7-8-12** ESaint-Martin | ½ | **2** | | 80 | — |
| | **Norton Sound (USA)** (JEHammond,France) **5-8-8** WMongil | nk | **3** | | 75 | — |

**19 Rn**

**1m 42.7** P-M 44.30F: 6.70F 2.60F 2.30F (62.70F) OWNER J. P. Senechal BRED Flaxman Holdings Ltd

**288a Confronter** put up another bold display and went down narrowly . As usual, he raced very prominently until hitting the front with two and a half furlongs to run. He ran on well, but was caught inside the final one hundred yards.

# 0273-LINGFIELD (L-H) (Standard)

## Saturday February 17th

Race 1: hand-timed

WEATHER: Overcast WIND: fresh half bhd

### 291 DOROTHY L. SAYERS APPRENTICE H'CAP (0-70) (4-Y.O+) (Class E)

2-20 (2-21) **7f (Equitrack)** £2,913.75 (£882.00: £430.50: £204.75) Stalls: Low GOING minus 0.62 sec per fur (FST)

| | | | | SP | RR | SF |
|---|---|---|---|---|---|---|
| *253** | **Dancing Sioux (69)** (RGuest) **4-9-11**(3) FLynch(3) (hld up in tch: a gng wl: led on bit ins fnl f: easily) | — | **1** | 6/4[1] | 76+ | 39 |
| *247[5]* | **My Gallery (IRE) (56)** (ABailey) **5-8-10**(5) AngelaGallimore(10) (hld up: hdwy 4f out: chsd ldr over 2f out: rdn over 1f out: unable qckn) | ¾ | **2** | 13/2 | 61 | 24 |
| *200[8]* | **Maid Welcome (55)** (MrsNMacauley) **9-8-11v**(3) AmandaSanders(6) (b: chsd ldr: led over 3f out: hdd ins fnl f: one pce) | 2 | **3** | 7/1 | 56 | 19 |
| *126[4]* | **Deeply Vale (IRE) (65)** (GLMoore) **5-9-5**(5) ALakeman(7) (dwlt: in rr tl hdwy over 1f out: nrst fin) | 1¼ | **4** | 12/1 | 63 | 26 |
| *177[5]* | **Master Millfield (IRE) (65)** (CJHill) **4-9-10** CTeague(4) (chsd ldrs: rdn & lost pl over 3f out: kpt on one pce fnl f) | 1 | **5** | 11/2[2] | 61 | 24 |
| *244[6]* | **Hawaii Storm (FR) (68)** (DJSffrenchDavis) **8-9-10**(3) CAdamson(9) (mid div: rdn over 2f out: one pce) | 1¾ | **6** | 6/1[3] | 60 | 23 |
| *253[5]* | **Mister Raider (50)** (SMellor) **4-8-6b**(3) ADaly(8) (sn chsd along in rr: hrd rdn over 2f out: no hdwy) | 3 | **7** | 16/1 | 35 | — |
| *253[6]* | **Panther (IRE) (44)** (JHetherton) **6-8-3b[1]** LNewton(1) (led tl hdd over 3f out: sn wknd) | 10 | **8** | 25/1 | 6 | — |

| | | | | SP | RR | SF |
|---|---|---|---|---|---|---|
| | **Thomas Crown (IRE) (55)** (NJHWalker) **4-9-0** DGriffiths(2) (bhd fnl 5f) | ½ | **9** | 33/1 | 16 | — |
| *175[7]* | **Lady Elizabeth (FR) (37)** (KOCunningham-Brown) **4-7-10b[1]** MBaird(5) (a bhd) | 1¼ | **10** | 40/1 | — | — |
| | | | | (SP 118.3%) | | **10 Rn** |

**1m 25.8** (1.80) CSF £11.45 CT £50.00 TOTE £2.30: £1.40 £1.20 £3.30 (£8.10) Trio £34.00 OWNER Ms A. M. Jeffrey (NEWMARKET)
LONG HANDICAP Lady Elizabeth (FR) 7-3

## 292 HELEN MCINNES MAIDEN STKS (3-Y.O+) (Class D)

2-50 (2-51) **5f (Equitrack)** £3,598.75 (£1,090.00: £532.50: £253.75) Stalls: High GOING minus 0.62 sec per fur (FST)

| | | | | SP | RR | SF |
|---|---|---|---|---|---|---|
| *231[2]* | **Awasha (IRE) (54)** (MissGayKelleway) **4-9-5** LDettori(7) (b: lw: w ldr: led 3f out: shkn up ins fnl f: r.o) | — | **1** | 1/2[1] | 55 | 24 |
| *127[7]* | **Rennyholme (27)** (JHetherton) **5-9-10b** NAdams(5) (chsd ldrs: rdn over 1f out: ev ch ins fnl f: unable qckn) | nk | **2** | 50/1 | 59 | 28 |
| *215[3]* | **Rowlandsons Stud (IRE) (60)** (GLMoore) **3-8-10** MFenton(9) (towards rr: pushed along over 2f out: hdwy over 1f out: styd on ins fnl f) | 1¼ | **3** | 7/1[2] | 56 | 10 |
| *183[6]* | **Elfin Queen (IRE) (54)** (JLHarris) **3-8-5** SSanders(4) (mid div: rdn over 2f out: one pce) | 3½ | **4** | 11/1 | 40 | — |
| *209[8]* | **Chillam (50)** (JPLeigh) **3-8-10** DeanMcKeown(2) (led 2f: wknd over 1f out) | 2 | **5** | 10/1 | 38 | — |
| *160[2]* | **Bouton d'Or (52)** (PHowling) **3-8-5** JQuinn(3) (prom: ev ch 3f out: wknd appr fnl f) | ¾ | **6** | 15/2[3] | 31 | — |
| | **Double Impression (IRE)** (JLHarris) **3-8-2**(3) DRMcCabe(8) (a bhd) | 2½ | **7** | 20/1 | 23 | — |
| | **Taylors Revival** (HJCollingridge) **5-9-5** NCarlisle(6) (bit bkwd: a bhd) | 3½ | **8** | 33/1 | 11 | — |
| | **Lincon Twenty One** (MJHaynes) **3-8-0**(5) MBaird(10) (bit bkwd: a bhd) | s.h | **9** | 33/1 | 12 | — |
| | **Ping-Pong Ball** (TRWatson) **3-8-5** SDWilliams(1) (sn outpcd) | 20 | **10** | 50/1 | — | — |
| | | | | (SP 122.9%) | | **10 Rn** |

**59.57 secs** (1.57) CSF £26.36 TOTE £1.50: £1.10 £9.00 £1.70 (£38.90) Trio £59.60 OWNER Mr H. Al-Mutawa (WHITCOMBE) BRED Barronstown Stud
WEIGHT FOR AGE 3yo-14lb

## 293 GEORGETTE HEYER CLAIMING STKS (3-Y.O) (Class F)

3-20 (3-20) **7f (Equitrack)** £2,517.00 (£707.00: £345.00) Stalls: Low GOING minus 0.62 sec per fur (FST)

| | | | | SP | RR | SF |
|---|---|---|---|---|---|---|
| *39** | **Krystal Max (IRE) (86)** (TDBarron) **3-8-10**(7) KimberleyHart(1) (hld up: gd hdwy to ld over 1f out: pushed out) | — | **1** | 11/8[2] | 88 | 21 |
| *230** | **Moi Canard (69)** (BAPearce) **3-8-8**(3) DRMcCabe(6) (lw: hld up: hdwy 2f out: ev ch over 1f out: nt qckn) | 3½ | **2** | 11/10[1] | 74 | 7 |
| *131[7]* | **No Sympathy (46)** (GLMoore) **3-7-12** NAdams(4) (plld hrd: chsd ldr: led wl over 1f out: sn hdd: one pce) | 3 | **3** | 16/1 | 54 | — |
| | **Trible Pet (46)** (BGubby) **3-8-0** JQuinn(5) (chsd ldrs: rdn 2f out: one pce) | 1 | **4** | 25/1 | 54 | — |
| *129[3]* | **Bells of Holland (59)** (WRMuir) **3-7-5v[1]**(7) MartinDwyer(3) (plld hrd: led: clr 4f out: hdd wl over 1f out: wknd qckly) | 15 | **5** | 11/1[3] | 18 | — |
| | **Vera's First (IRE) (60)** (GLewis) **3-7-13b**(3) AWhelan(2) (a bhd) | 9 | **6** | 11/1[3] | 1 | — |
| | | | | (SP 116.1%) | | **6 Rn** |

**1m 26.51** (2.51) CSF £3.30 TOTE £2.30: £1.10 £1.40 (£1.80) OWNER The Oakfield Nurseries Partnership (THIRSK) BRED Baronrath Stud

## 294 EVELYN ANTHONY H'CAP (0-90) (3-Y.O) (Class C)

3-50 (3-51) **1m 2f (Equitrack)** £5,132.10 (£1,552.80: £757.40: £359.70) Stalls: Low GOING minus 0.62 sec per fur (FST)

| | | | | SP | RR | SF |
|---|---|---|---|---|---|---|
| *245[3]* | **Galapino (65)** (CEBrittain) **3-8-12** MLarsen(6) (mde all: qcknd clr over 1f out: pushed out) | — | **1** | 100/30[2] | 75 | 35 |
| *245** | **Montecristo (69)** (RGuest) **3-9-2** LDettori(5) (chsd wnr: pushed along over 3f out: hrd rdn over 1f out: one pce) | 5 | **2** | Evens[1] | 71 | 31 |
| *280[7]* | **Thorntoun Estate (IRE) (60)** (MJohnston) **3-8-7** DeanMcKeown(3) (chsd ldrs: rdn & lost pl over 3f out: kpt on one pce appr fnl f) | 6 | **3** | 16/1 | 52 | 12 |
| *262[2]* | **Rowlandsons Charm (IRE) (60)** (GLMoore) **3-8-7** NAdams(4) (in tch: sn pushed along: hrd rdn 3f out: one pce) | 1¼ | **4** | 16/1 | 50 | 10 |
| *137[7]* | **Le Sport (74)** (ABailey) **3-9-4**(3) DWright(7) (lw: hld up: rdn 3f out: no hdwy) | 5 | **5** | 25/1 | 56 | 16 |
| *277** | **Domoor (61)** (MJohnston) **3-8-8** 5x JWeaver(2) (lw: hld up: n.m.r over 3f out: sn rdn & btn) | 2½ | **6** | 8/1 | 39 | — |
| *161** | **Tormount (USA) (69)** (LordHuntingdon) **3-9-2** TIves(1) (hld up: hdwy 4f out: wknd over 2f out) | 8 | **7** | 6/1[3] | 35 | — |
| | | | | (SP 114.1%) | | **7 Rn** |

**2m 5.78** (1.48) CSF £6.85 TOTE £5.90: £2.00 £1.40 (£2.90) OWNER The Dayspring Company Ltd (NEWMARKET) BRED Dayspring Co Ltd

## 295 AGATHA CHRISTIE (S) STKS (4-Y.O+) (Class G)

4-20 (4-20) **1m (Equitrack)** £2,221.50 (£624.00: £304.50) Stalls: High GOING minus 0.62 sec per fur (FST)

| | | | | SP | RR | SF |
|---|---|---|---|---|---|---|
| *216[6]* | **Perilous Plight (70)** (WRMuir) **5-9-0** Jean-PierreLopez(4) (chsd ldrs: led over 1f out: rdn ins fnl f: eased nr fin) | — | **1** | Evens[1] | 65 | 29 |
| *219[2]* | **Roman Reel (USA) (57)** (GLMoore) **5-9-0** SWhitworth(2) (chsd ldr: led 5f out: hdd over 1f out: r.o) | nk | **2** | 2/1[2] | 64 | 28 |
| *229[3]* | **Justinianus (IRE) (48)** (JJBridger) **4-9-0** JQuinn(5) (led 3f: chsd ldr: ev ch over 1f out: one pce) | 3½ | **3** | 25/1 | 57 | 21 |
| | **Media Express (59)** (MBrittain) **4-9-6** RCochrane(1) (chsd ldrs: rdn 3f out: r.o one pce fnl f) | s.h | **4** | 5/1[3] | 63 | 27 |
| *166[4]* | **David James' Girl (53)** (ABailey) **4-8-6**(3) DWright(6) (in tch: pushed along over 4f out: hrd rdn over 2f out: one pce) | 1 | **5** | 9/1 | 50 | 14 |
| *76[14]* | **Joyful Times (40)** (MrsNMacauley) **4-8-4**(5) AmandaSanders(3) (a bhd) | 20 | **6** | 50/1 | 10 | — |
| | | | | (SP 115.8%) | | **6 Rn** |

**1m 39.29** (1.89) CSF £3.48 TOTE £2.40: £1.20 £2.40 (£1.90) OWNER Mr R. Haim (LAMBOURN) BRED Crest Stud Ltd
Bt in 5,000 gns

## 296 MARGERY ALLINGHAM H'CAP (0-75) (4-Y.O+) (Class D)

4-50 (4-50) **1m 4f (Equitrack)** £3,452.50 (£1,045.00: £510.00: £242.50) Stalls: Low GOING minus 0.62 sec per fur (FST)

| | | | | SP | RR | SF |
|---|---|---|---|---|---|---|
| *83[3]* | **Cuango (IRE) (62)** (RHollinshead) **5-9-5** JWeaver(7) (hld up: hdwy 5f out: pushed along over 3f out: hrd rdn over 1f out: styd on to ld wl ins fnl f) | — | **1** | 100/30[2] | 71 | 40 |
| *128** | **El Volador (70)** (CNAllen) **9-9-13** LDettori(6) (hld up gng wl: jnd ldr over 3f out: led wl over 1f out: rdn & hdd wl ins fnl f: unable qckn) | ¾ | **2** | 5/2[1] | 78 | 47 |
| *214** | **One Off the Rail (USA) (68)** (AMoore) **6-9-11** CandyMorris(5) (lw: b.hind: a.p: led over 4f out: hdd wl over 1f out: one pce) | 3 | **3** | 7/2[3] | 72 | 41 |

| Form | Horse / details | Dist | Pos | SP | RR | SF |
|---|---|---|---|---|---|---|
| | **Jaraab (71)** (GLewis) **5-10-0v** SWhitworth(2) (bit bkwd: hld up: rdn & outpcd 6f out: styd on one pce u.p appr fnl f) | 6 | **4** | 14/1 | 67 | 36 |
| *$179^{10}$* | **Errant (58)** (DJSCosgrove) **4-8-12** JQuinn(1) (chsd ldrs: rdn over 3f out: wknd 2f out) | hd | **5** | 16/1 | 54 | 20 |
| *$214^{4}$* | **Bag of Tricks (IRE) (60)** (SDow) **6-8-12**$^{(5)}$ ADaly(4) (lw: plld hrd: chsd ldr: led 5f out: sn hdd: wknd over 3f out) | 7 | **6** | 10/1 | 47 | 16 |
| *$204^{6}$* | **Verde Luna (60)** (DWPArbuthnot) **4-9-0** RCochrane(8) (b: in tch: rdn over 3f out: wknd over 2f out) | 5 | **7** | 20/1 | 40 | 6 |
| *$222^{5}$* | **Toy Princess (USA) (70)** (CEBrittain) **4-9-10** MLarsen(3) (led: hdd 5f out: sn wknd) | 15 | **8** | $7/2^{3}$ | 30 | — |

(SP 122.5%) **8 Rn**

**2m 32.08** (2.08) CSF £12.41 CT £28.83 TOTE £4.50: £1.60 £1.50 £1.30 (£5.60) OWNER Barouche Stud Ltd (UPPER LONGDON) BRED Citadel Stud Establishment
WEIGHT FOR AGE 4yo-3lb

T/Plpt: £4.40 (2,446.01 Tckts). T/Qdpt: £2.70 (263.27 Tckts). SM

# 0280-SOUTHWELL (L-H) (Standard)
## Monday February 19th
WEATHER: cold & windy WIND: str half bhd

## 297 BERING H'CAP (0-65) (I) (4-Y.O+) (Class F)
1-50 (1-50) **1m 3f** **(Fibresand)** £2,048.00 (£573.00: £278.00) Stalls: Low GOING minus 0.33 sec per fur (FST)

| Form | Horse / details | Dist | Pos | SP | RR | SF |
|---|---|---|---|---|---|---|
| *252** | **Mazilla (47)** (AStreeter) **4-8-10v** FNorton(4) (lw: trckd ldrs gng wl: led on bit over 2f out: pushed clr: eased towards fin) | — | **1** | $4/1^{2}$ | 57 | 7 |
| *$252^{3}$* | **Genesis Four (39)** (SRBowring) **6-8-4** NCarlisle(7) (lw: bhd: effrt 4f out: styd on wl appr fnl f: no ch w wnr) | 1¾ | **2** | 8/1 | 46 | — |
| *$99^{5}$* | **Young Benson (49)** (BAMcMahon) **4-8-12** SSanders(8) (lw: trckd ldrs: effrt over 2f out: kpt on same pce) | 3 | **3** | 16/1 | 52 | 2 |
| *$114^{3}$* | **Hard Love (51)** (JLEyre) **4-9-0** JFortune(9) (chsd ldrs: drvn along over 3f out: one pce) | nk | **4** | $9/2^{3}$ | 54 | 4 |
| *$256^{7}$* | **Cross Talk (IRE) (62)** (RHollinshead) **4-9-4**$^{(7)}$ FLynch(3) (bhd: hdwy on outside over 2f out: nvr nr ldrs) | 1 | **5** | 14/1 | 63 | 13 |
| *$251^{5}$* | **Tempering (53)** (DWChapman) **10-9-4** ACulhane(5) (led tl over 2f out: wknd fnl f) | 1¼ | **6** | $7/2^{1}$ | 51 | 4 |
| *$257^{5}$* | **East Barns (IRE) (35)** (SGollings) **8-7-9b**$^{(5)}$ PFessey(6) (bhd: hdwy over 3f out: styd on: nvr nr ldrs) | s.h | **7** | 14/1 | 33 | — |
| *$252^{2}$* | **Adaloaldo (USA) (50)** (JParkes) **4-8-8**$^{(5)}$ RHavlin(2) (chsd ldrs: outpcd 4f out: sn lost pl) | 2½ | **8** | 7/1 | 46 | — |
| *$213^{6}$* | **Pinkerton Polka (45)** (CEBrittain) **4-8-8** MLarsen(10) (bit bkwd: chsd ldrs: chal 6f out: wknd over 2f out: eased) | 13 | **9** | 5/1 | 22 | — |
| | **Prince Equiname (59)** (DEddy) **4-9-8** JWeaver(1) (s.i.s: t.o 7f out) | 6 | **10** | 14/1 | 27 | — |

(SP 126.6%) **10 Rn**

**2m 28.9** (8.90) CSF £35.58 CT £436.25 TOTE £5.00: £1.50 £3.10 £7.40 (£35.40) Trio £131.10; £22.16 to Southwell 20/2/96 OWNER Mr M. Rhodes (UTTOXETER) BRED Mrs H. MacFarlane
WEIGHT FOR AGE 4yo-2lb

## 298 HUDSON BAY MEDIAN AUCTION MAIDEN STKS (3, 4 & 5-Y.O) (Class E)
2-20 (2-23) **6f** **(Fibresand)** £2,845.50 (£861.00: £420.00: £199.50) Stalls: Low GOING minus 0.33 sec per fur (FST)

| Form | Horse / details | Dist | Pos | SP | RR | SF |
|---|---|---|---|---|---|---|
| *$234^{4}$* | **Maybank (IRE) (47)** (BAMcMahon) **4-9-10** GCarter(2) (chsd ldrs: led 2f out: drvn out) | — | **1** | $3/1^{2}$ | 52 | 34 |
| *$238^{4}$* | **The Wad (48)** (DNicholls) **3-8-9** RCochrane(4) (trckd ldrs: ev ch 2f out: styd on same pce fnl f) | 1½ | **2** | 12/1 | 49 | 15 |
| *$264^{2}$* | **General Haven (53)** (TJNaughton) **3-8-9** JWeaver(3) (chsd ldrs: effrt on outside 2f out: hung lft: kpt on same pce) | ¾ | **3** | $10/11^{1}$ | 47 | 13 |
| *$234^{7}$* | **Rajah** (CWThornton) **3-8-9** DeanMcKeown(1) (in tch: outpcd ½-wy: kpt on fnl 2f) | 2½ | **4** | 25/1 | 40 | 6 |
| *$250^{7}$* | **Northern Grey (47)** (JBerry) **4-9-5b**$^{(5)}$ PRoberts(6) (sn drvn along: nvr nr ldrs) | 2½ | **5** | 10/1 | 33 | 15 |
| | **Lithe Spirit (IRE)** (JAHarris) **4-9-5** SDWilliams(7) (mde most to 2f out: sn wknd) | 5 | **6** | $9/1^{3}$ | 14 | — |
| *$234^{11}$* | **Highland Fawn (27)** (BAMcMahon) **3-7-13**$^{(5)}$ LNewton(8) (chsd ldrs tl lost pl over 2f out) | 3 | **7** | 50/1 | 7 | — |
| *$209^{5}$* | ***Ginas Girl*** *(SRBowring)* ***3-8-1***$^{(5)ow2}$ *CTeague(5) (Withdrawn not under Starter's orders: ref to ent stalls)* | | **W** | *14/1* | — | — |

(SP 116.6%) **7 Rn**

**1m 17.0** (3.50) CSF £29.09 TOTE £3.70: £1.40 £2.30 (£16.70) OWNER Mr Yuk Chin Soong (TAMWORTH) BRED E. O'Leary
WEIGHT FOR AGE 3yo-15lb

## 299 BALTIC CLAIMING STKS (4-Y.O+) (Class F)
2-50 (2-51) **1m 4f** **(Fibresand)** £2,398.00 (£673.00: £328.00) Stalls: Low GOING minus 0.33 sec per fur (FST)

| Form | Horse / details | Dist | Pos | SP | RR | SF |
|---|---|---|---|---|---|---|
| *235** | **Heathyards Rock (81)** (RHollinshead) **4-9-4** TIves(2) (hld up: hdwy 4f out: led on bit over 1f out: v.easily) | — | **1** | $1/2^{1}$ | 71++ | — |
| *$181^{11}$* | **Jungle Patrol (IRE) (74)** (CMurray) **4-8-8** MTebbutt(3) (plld hrd: led tl over 1f out: hung rt: no ch w wnr) | 2½ | **2** | $7/1^{2}$ | 58 | — |
| *$235^{6}$* | **Maradata (IRE)** (RHollinshead) **4-8-13** MWigham(6) (bhd: sme hdwy over 2f out: nvr nr ldrs) | 12 | **3** | 25/1 | 44 | — |
| *$98^{4}$* | **Timely Example (USA) (52)** (BRCambidge) **5-8-11** NAdams(7) (chsd ldrs: drvn along 7f out: lost pl 3f out) | 2½ | **4** | $16/1^{3}$ | 35 | — |
| *$246^{4}$* | **Anotherone to Note (36)** (NPLittmoden) **5-8-0**$^{(7)}$ JBramhill(5) (w ldrs tl wknd over 2f out) | 4 | **5** | $16/1^{3}$ | 26 | — |
| | **Rival Queen (IRE) (64)** (MDHammond) **4-8-11** RCochrane(8) (unruly s: hdwy to chse ldrs 5f out: lost pl over 3f out) | 4 | **6** | $7/1^{2}$ | 28 | — |
| *$255^{7}$* | **Desert Man** (RDEWoodhouse) **5-9-3** JQuinn(1) (prom early: outpcd & bhd fr ½-wy) | 1¾ | **7** | 50/1 | 28 | — |
| | **Newgate Hush (25)** (BWMurray) **4-7-4**$^{(7)}$ MartinDwyer(4) (chsd ldrs: drvn along over 4f out: sn lost pl) | 14 | **8** | 50/1 | — | — |
| *$275^{9}$* | **Wicklow Boy (IRE) (37)** (RJWeaver) **5-8-4**$^{(5)}$ ADaly(9) (b: ref to r: t.n.p) | | **R** | 33/1 | — | — |

(SP 114.1%) **9 Rn**

**2m 44.6** (12.10) CSF £4.62 TOTE £1.60: £1.10 £1.40 £3.20 (£4.70) Trio £18.30 OWNER Mr L. A. Morgan (UPPER LONGDON) BRED N. E. and Mrs Poole
WEIGHT FOR AGE 4yo-3lb

## 300 ADRIATIC MAIDEN H'CAP (0-60) (3-Y.O) (Class F)
3-20 (3-20) **1m** **(Fibresand)** £2,398.00 (£673.00: £328.00) Stalls: Low GOING minus 0.33 sec per fur (FST)

| Form | Horse / details | Dist | Pos | SP | RR | SF |
|---|---|---|---|---|---|---|
| *$237^{2}$* | **Bit of Bother (IRE) (59)** (TDBarron) **3-9-6** JFortune(4) (chsd ldrs: led over 1f out: r.o wl) | — | **1** | 9/2 | 69 | 23 |
| *$234^{3}$* | **Eben Naas (USA) (48)** (SCWilliams) **3-8-9** JTate(2) (b.hind: mde most tl over 1f out: nt qckn) | 2 | **2** | $4/1^{3}$ | 54 | 8 |
| *$167^{3}$* | **Hever Golf Eagle (51)** (TJNaughton) **3-8-12** JWeaver(6) (chsd ldrs: hrd rdn 2f out: one pce) | 1½ | **3** | $3/1^{2}$ | 54 | 8 |

| Form | Horse / Details | Pos | SP | RR | SF |
|---|---|---|---|---|---|
| 277[2] | **Creeking (60)** (SirMarkPrescott) **3-9-7** GDuffield(3) (chsd ldrs: rdn 3f out: one pce) 1½ | 4 | 9/4[1] | 60 | 14 |
| 137[6] | **Scenicris (IRE) (50)** (RHollinshead) **3-8-11** NCarlisle(5) (bhd: sme hdwy over 2f out: nvr nr ldrs) nk | 5 | 10/1 | 49 | 3 |
| 269[6] | **Radmore Brandy (36)** (NPLittmoden) **3-7-11**ow1 TWilliams(1) (trckd ldrs: effrt over 3f out: wknd over 1f out: eased) 6 | 6 | 10/1 | 23 | — |
| 277[7] | **Conquistajade (USA) (45)** (SPCWoods) **3-8-6** WWoods(7) (chsd ldrs: sn drvn: lost pl over 3f out: eased) 25 | 7 | 25/1 | — | — |

(SP 116.0%) **7 Rn**

**1m 45.6** (5.60) CSF £21.50 TOTE £4.10: £2.40 £2.40 (£17.50) OWNER Mr J. Baggott (THIRSK) BRED Lar Dempsey

## 301 CASPIAN H'CAP (0-70) (3-Y.O+ F & M) (Class E)

3-50 (3-51) **1m (Fibresand)** £2,954.70 (£894.60: £436.80: £207.90) Stalls: Low GOING minus 0.33 sec per fur (FST)

| Form | Horse / Details | Pos | SP | RR | SF |
|---|---|---|---|---|---|
| 162[4] | **Pine Essence (USA) (40)** (JLEyre) **5-8-2** TWilliams(11) (w ldrs: led 4f out: hung lft over 2f out: edgd lft: jst hld on) — | 1 | 10/1 | 48 | 19 |
| 199[8] | **Jalmaid (52)** (BAMcMahon) **4-9-0** SSanders(5) (a in tch: effrt over 3f out: styd on wl ins fnl f) hd | 2 | 7/1[3] | 60 | 31 |
| 211[5] | **Q Factor (63)** (DHaydnJones) **4-9-11** JFortune(12) (lw: hdwy on outside over 2f out: styd on wl ins fnl f) hd | 3 | 8/1 | 71 | 42 |
| 213[11] | **Cabcharge Blue (52)** (TJNaughton) **4-9-0** JWeaver(8) (b.hind: unruly s: chsd ldrs: nt qckn appr fnl f) 2 | 4 | 13/2[2] | 56 | 27 |
| 254[2] | **Grey Again (58)** (SRBowring) **4-9-1b**(5) CTeague(10) (s.i.s: bhd: hdwy 2f out: nvr nr ldrs) 2½ | 5 | 5/1[1] | 57 | 28 |
| 239[4] | **Karinska (59)** (MCChapman) **6-9-0**(7) CMunday(2) (unruly s: chsd ldrs tl wknd over 1f out) 2 | 6 | 13/2[2] | 54 | 25 |
| 213[5] | **Indiahra (46)** (RHollinshead) **5-8-1v**(7) FLynch(4) (mid div: effrt 3f out: n.d) 1 | 7 | 12/1 | 39 | 10 |
| | **Failte Ro (60)** (JEBanks) **4-9-8** JQuinn(13) (in tch: effrt over 3f out: sn lost pl) 12 | 8 | 14/1 | 29 | — |
| 247[6] | **The Mestral (36)** (MJRyan) **4-7-7**(5) MBaird(3) (chsd ldr: led over 5f out: hdd 4f out: hung bdly rt: lost pl over 2f out) 3 | 9 | 16/1 | — | — |
| 189[7] | **Your Most Welcome (50)** (DJSffrenchDavis) **5-8-7**(5) GParkin(7) (nvr nr ldrs) ½ | 10 | 14/1 | 12 | — |
| 239[10] | **Glenvally (43)** (BWMurray) **5-7-12b**(7) MartinDwyer(1) (s.i.s: sn rdn along: a bhd) 1 | 11 | 20/1 | 3 | — |
| 172[3] | **Moody (51)** (MissGayKelleway) **4-8-13v**[1] RCochrane(6) (s.s: hld up: effrt over 3f out: sn wknd) 3½ | 12 | 12/1 | 4 | — |
| 210[12] | **Built for Comfort (IRE) (58)** (NMBabbage) **4-9-6v**[1] MTebbutt(9) (led tl over 5f out: sn lost pl & bhd) 25 | 13 | 20/1 | — | — |

(SP 120.2%) **13 Rn**

**1m 44.3** (4.30) CSF £71.88 CT £549.31 TOTE £12.00: £3.90 £2.90 £1.30 (£47.10) Trio £217.90 OWNER Mr K. Meynell (HAMBLETON) BRED David E. Hager II

## 302 PERSIAN GULF (S) STKS (3-Y.O+) (Class G)

4-20 (4-20) **6f (Fibresand)** £2,085.00 (£585.00: £285.00) Stalls: Low GOING minus 0.33 sec per fur (FST)

| Form | Horse / Details | Pos | SP | RR | SF |
|---|---|---|---|---|---|
| 250* | **Sense of Priority (73)** (DNicholls) **7-9-12** AlexGreaves(3) (lw: trckd ldr: led on bit over 2f out: rdn out fnl f) — | 1 | 4/9[1] | 72 | 42 |
| 259[4] | **Awesome Venture (57)** (MCChapman) **6-9-0**(7) CMunday(2) (led tl over 2f out: kpt on u.p) 1½ | 2 | 8/1[3] | 63 | 33 |
| 250[4] | **Sea-Deer (70)** (DWChapman) **7-9-7** ACulhane(1) (hld up: effrt over 2f out: styd on same pce fnl f) ¾ | 3 | 5/2[2] | 61 | 31 |
| | **Cerbera (35)** (JPSmith) **7-9-2**(5) CTeague(4) (chsd ldrs: sn drvn along: wl outpcd fr ½-wy) 15 | 4 | 50/1 | 21 | — |
| 239[14] | **Bitch (36)** (GPKelly) **4-8-11**(5) PRoberts(5) (chsd ldrs: sn drvn along: lost pl ½-wy: sn bhd) 3 | 5 | 50/1 | 8 | — |

(SP 112.8%) **5 Rn**

**1m 16.5** (3.00) CSF £4.56 TOTE £1.50: £1.10 £1.10 (£2.30) OWNER Mr S. Schofield (THIRSK) BRED Cheveley Park Stud Ltd
No bid

## 303 BERING H'CAP (0-65) (II) (4-Y.O+) (Class F)

4-50 (4-50) **1m 3f (Fibresand)** £2,048.00 (£573.00: £278.00) Stalls: Low GOING minus 0.33 sec per fur (FST)

| Form | Horse / Details | Pos | SP | RR | SF |
|---|---|---|---|---|---|
| 279* | **Claque (57)** (DWChapman) **4-9-6b** 5x ACulhane(4) (mde most: hrd rdn & hung rt over 1f out: jst hld on) — | 1 | 7/1 | 61 | 9 |
| 246* | **Noble Canonire (51)** (SRBowring) **4-8-9**(5) CTeague(1) (lw: hdwy on ins over 2f out: ev ch over 1f out: r.o) s.h | 2 | 11/2[3] | 55+ | 3 |
| 189[3] | **Explosive Power (63)** (GCBravery) **5-10-0** TIves(7) (lw: chsd ldrs: n.m.r over 1f out: nt qckn ins fnl f) 2 | 3 | 8/1 | 63 | 14 |
| 244[9] | **The Cape Doctor (IRE) (45)** (AGFoster) **4-8-5**(3) AWhelan(6) (chsd ldrs: edgd lft & styd on one pce fnl 2f) 1 | 4 | 33/1 | 45 | — |
| 279[2] | **Ajdar (47)** (MissGayKelleway) **5-8-12** RCochrane(10) (dwlt s: hld up & bhd: effrt 4f out: styd on fnl 2f: nvr rchd ldrs) 1½ | 5 | 3/1[2] | 43 | — |
| 256* | **Sea God (49)** (MCChapman) **5-8-7**(7) 5x CMunday(9) (trckd ldrs: outpcd over 2f out: n.d after) 3 | 6 | 6/1 | 41 | — |
| 172[7] | **Me Cherokee (50)** (CWThornton) **4-8-13** DeanMcKeown(2) (chsd ldrs tl outpcd fnl 2f) hd | 7 | 16/1 | 43 | — |
| 256[2] | **Museum (IRE) (61)** (DNicholls) **5-9-12** AlexGreaves(3) (chsd ldrs tl lost pl over 3f out) 5 | 8 | 2/1[1] | 46 | — |
| | **Master Ofthe House (59)** (MDHammond) **10-9-10** JWeaver(5) (hld up & a bhd) 11 | 9 | 20/1 | 28 | — |
| 239[6] | **Orchidarma (46)** (JJQuinn) **4-8-9** JFortune(8) (lw: a outpcd & bhd) 1½ | 10 | 14/1 | 13 | — |

(SP 131.9%) **10 Rn**

**2m 30.0** (10.00) CSF £46.93 CT £300.18 TOTE £17.10: £5.80 £2.20 £2.10 (£49.40) Trio £108.30 OWNER Mr Michael Hill (YORK) BRED Lord Howard de Walden
WEIGHT FOR AGE 4yo-2lb

T/Jkpt: £7,120.60 (0.7 Tckts); £3,008.74 to Lingfield 20/2/96. T/Plpt: £520.60 (21.81 Tckts). T/Qdpt: £20.20 (51.3 Tckts). WG

# 0291-LINGFIELD (L-H) (Standard)

## Tuesday February 20th

WEATHER: freezing WIND: v.str half against

## 304 DORDOGNE MEDIAN AUCTION MAIDEN STKS (3-Y.O) (Class F)

2-20 (2-22) **1m (Equitrack)** £2,528.90 (£710.40: £346.70) Stalls: High GOING minus 0.38 sec per fur (FST)

| Form | Horse / Details | Pos | SP | RR | SF |
|---|---|---|---|---|---|
| | **Docklands Limo** (BJMcMath) **3-9-0** VSmith(1) (led over 4f: led over 1f out: pushed out) — | 1 | 14/1[3] | 65 | 23 |
| | **Be Satisfied (55)** (AMoore) **3-9-0** AClark(4) (b.hind: hld up: rdn over 3f out: r.o one pce fnl f) 7 | 2 | 50/1 | 51 | 9 |
| 188[2] | **Lancashire Legend (68)** (SDow) **3-9-0** RCochrane(3) (lw: s.s: hdwy over 4f out: led over 2f out tl over 1f out: wknd ins fnl f) 1 | 3 | 5/2[2] | 49 | 7 |
| | **Shanghai Girl** (DRLoder) **3-8-9** LDettori(2) (neat: lw: chsd ldr: led over 3f out tl over 2f out: wknd over 1f out) 8 | 4 | 2/5[1] | 28d | — |

(SP 108.6%) **4 Rn**

**1m 41.8** (4.40) CSF £119.43 TOTE £13.50 (£37.70) OWNER Mrs Lisa Olley (NEWMARKET) BRED Majors Racing International Ltd

## 305 SEINE CLAIMING STKS (4-Y.O+) (Class E)

2-50 (2-52) **1m 2f (Equitrack)** £2,859.15 (£865.20: £422.10: £200.55) Stalls: Low GOING minus 0.38 sec per fur (FST)

| | | | | SP | RR | SF |
|---|---|---|---|---|---|---|
| 216* | **Sweet Supposin (IRE) (76)** (CADwyer) **5-9-6v** LDettori(3) (lw: hdwy over 3f out: rdn over 1f out: led ins fnl f: r.o wl) | — | **1** | 8/11[1] | 83 | 42 |
| 189[2] | **Zahid (USA) (45)** (KRBurke) **5-8-12** JQuinn(4) (hld up: led over 2f out tl ins fnl f: unable qckn) | 1 | **2** | 8/1[3] | 73 | 32 |
| 216[2] | **Masnun (USA) (65)** (RJO'Sullivan) **11-8-10** AClark(5) (lw: hdwy over 4f out: ev ch over 2f out: one pce) | 7 | **3** | 7/4[2] | 60 | 19 |
| 195[4] | **Araboybill (52)** (RSimpson) **5-9-0b** JWeaver(2) (led over 7f) | 9 | **4** | 14/1 | 50 | 9 |
| 246[7] | **Rubadub (22)** (JMBradley) **5-7-12**(3) DWright(1) (chsd ldr 8f out to 4f out: sn wknd: t.o) | 25 | **5** | 50/1 | — | — |
| 247[9] | **Aggies Dream (22)** (JMBradley) **5-8-3v[1]**(3) SDrowne(7) (chsd ldr 2f: wknd 5f out: t.o fnl 4f) | dist | **6** | 50/1 | — | — |
| | | | | (SP 116.0%) | **6 Rn** | |

**2m 8.26** (3.96) CSF £7.08 TOTE £1.60: £1.10 £2.10 (£8.20) OWNER Mrs Christine Rawson (NEWMARKET) BRED Ballylinch Stud Ltd

## 306 AISNE H'CAP (0-85) (4-Y.O+) (Class D)

3-20 (3-22) **1m 2f (Equitrack)** £3,550.00 (£1,075.00: £525.00: £250.00) Stalls: Low GOING minus 0.38 sec per fur (FST)

| | | | | SP | RR | SF |
|---|---|---|---|---|---|---|
| 181[5] | **Ocean Park (76)** (LadyHerries) **5-9-6** AClark(3) (hld up: rdn over 4f out: nt clr run over 2f out & over 1f out: swtchd rt: led wl ins fnl f: r.o wl) | — | **1** | 10/1 | 83 | 58 |
| 132* | **King of Tunes (FR) (72)** (JJSheehan) **4-9-1** JQuinn(8) (rdn over 4f out: hdwy over 1f out: r.o) | 1 | **2** | 5/2[1] | 78 | 51 |
| 223[4] | **Bardon Hill Boy (IRE) (82)** (BHanbury) **4-9-8**(3) JStack(2) (a.p: rdn over 2f out: r.o ins fnl f) | s.h | **3** | 10/1 | 88 | 61 |
| 181* | **Field of Vision (IRE) (73)** (MJohnston) **6-9-3** JWeaver(11) (a.p: rdn over 3f out: led wl over 1f out tl wl ins fnl f: unable qckn) | s.h | **4** | 4/1[2] | 78 | 53 |
| 233[2] | **Almuhtaram (69)** (MissGayKelleway) **4-8-5b**(7) TAshley(9) (hld up: rdn over 2f out: one pce fnl f) | ½ | **5** | 7/1 | 74 | 47 |
| 219[6] | **Digpast (IRE) (72)** (RJO'Sullivan) **6-9-2b** DBiggs(6) (dwlt: hdwy over 4f out: hrd rdn over 1f out: one pce) | 1¾ | **6** | 12/1 | 74 | 49 |
| | **Secret Aly (CAN) (83)** (CEBrittain) **6-9-13** MLarsen(1) (lw: nvr nr to chal) | 1 | **7** | 10/1 | 83 | 58 |
| 219[3] | **Canary Falcon (55)** (JohnBerry) **5-7-8v**(5) CAdamson(10) (b: lw: led: sn clr: hdd wl over 1f out: wknd fnl f) | 3½ | **8** | 10/1 | 49 | 24 |
| | **Able Choice (IRE) (75)** (RWArmstrong) **6-9-5** LDettori(4) (chsd ldr over 6f: wknd wl over 1f out) | 4 | **9** | 12/1 | 63 | 38 |
| 233[3] | **Robellion (69)** (DWPArbuthnot) **5-8-13v** RCochrane(7) (hdwy over 3f out: wknd over 2f out) | 2½ | **10** | 5/1[3] | 53 | 28 |
| | | | | (SP 129.5%) | **10 Rn** | |

**2m 6.18** (1.88) CSF £36.80 CT £251.02 TOTE £12.80: £4.80 £1.10 £8.00 (£40.90) Trio £132.30 OWNER Mr E. Reitel (LITTLEHAMPTON) BRED Mrs H. Khan
WEIGHT FOR AGE 4yo-1lb

## 307 LOIRE H'CAP (0-70) (3-Y.O) (Class E)

3-50 (3-52) **6f (Equitrack)** £2,818.20 (£852.60: £415.80: £197.40) Stalls: Low GOING minus 0.38 sec per fur (FST)

| | | | | SP | RR | SF |
|---|---|---|---|---|---|---|
| 218[9] | **Maple Burl (62)** (SDow) **3-9-2**(5) ADaly(6) (hld up: rdn over 1f out: led ins fnl f: r.o) | — | **1** | 7/1 | 67 | — |
| 292[3] | **Rowlandsons Stud (IRE) (58)** (GLMoore) **3-9-3** MFenton(3) (a.p: led 2f out tl ins fnl f: r.o) | hd | **2** | 4/1[3] | 63 | — |
| 218[5] | **Sunset Harbour (IRE) (58)** (TJNaughton) **3-9-3** RCochrane(5) (hld up: rdn over 1f out: unable qckn) | 1¾ | **3** | 7/4[1] | 58 | — |
| 143[5] | **Allstars Dancer (40)** (TJNaughton) **3-7-13** FNorton(4) (a.p: rdn over 1f out: one pce) | 1¼ | **4** | 8/1 | 37 | — |
| 10[8] | **Zuno Princess (IRE) (40)** (TEPowell) **3-7-8**(5) MBaird(1) (bhd fnl 4f) | 7 | **5** | 14/1 | 18 | — |
| 203[5] | **Learning Curve (IRE) (44)** (SirMarkPrescott) **3-8-3** GDuffield(2) (lw: led 4f: wknd over 1f out) | 1 | **6** | 2/1[2] | 19 | — |
| | | | | (SP 120.0%) | **6 Rn** | |

**1m 16.21** (5.61) CSF £33.33 TOTE £3.50: £7.80 £1.20 (£15.20) OWNER Mr G. Steinberg (EPSOM) BRED Giles W. Pritchard-Gordon

## 308 RHONE H'CAP (0-70) (4-Y.O+) (Class E)

4-20 (4-21) **1m (Equitrack)** £2,941.05 (£890.40: £434.70: £206.85) Stalls: High GOING minus 0.38 sec per fur (FST)

| | | | | SP | RR | SF |
|---|---|---|---|---|---|---|
| 132[11] | **Nordinex (IRE) (65)** (RWArmstrong) **4-9-12** WWoods(9) (lw: hld up: rdn over 3f out: led over 1f out: r.o wl) | — | **1** | 10/1 | 73 | 55 |
| | **New Albion (USA) (67)** (NJHenderson) **5-10-0** RCochrane(2) (a.p: rdn over 3f out: r.o) | 1 | **2** | 8/1 | 73 | 55 |
| 239[3] | **Bakers Daughter (50)** (JRArnold) **4-8-11** JQuinn(8) (b.off hind: a.p: rdn over 2f out: ev ch 1f out: unable qckn) | ¾ | **3** | 6/1[3] | 55 | 37 |
| 278[4] | **Myjinka (49)** (TEPowell) **6-8-5b**(5) MBaird(4) (rdn over 3f out: hdwy over 1f out: r.o) | ½ | **4** | 7/2[1] | 53 | 35 |
| 261[7] | **Oozlem (IRE) (43)** (JRPoulton) **7-7-11b**(7) TField(6) (b: dwlt: rdn over 3f out: hdwy fnl f: nvr nrr) | 1½ | **5** | 5/1[2] | 44 | 26 |
| | **Halliard (54)** (TMJones) **5-9-1** SRaymont(1) (b: bit bkwd: nvr nr to chal) | s.h | **6** | 20/1 | 54 | 36 |
| 243[5] | **Golden Touch (USA) (56)** (NACallaghan) **4-9-3** GCarter(10) (lw: s.s: a bhd) | 1¾ | **7** | 8/1 | 53 | 35 |
| 253[3] | **Zahran (IRE) (45)** (JMBradley) **5-8-3**(3) SDrowne(7) (b: lw: s.s: bhd fnl 3f) | 4 | **8** | 6/1[3] | 34 | 16 |
| 261[6] | **Ansal Boy (65)** (MissGayKelleway) **4-9-12** AClark(5) (chsd ldr: led 2f out tl over 1f out: sn wknd) | nk | **9** | 25/1 | 53 | 35 |
| 291[5] | **Master Millfield (IRE) (65)** (CJHill) **4-9-12v[1]** JWeaver(3) (led 6f: wknd fnl f) | 1 | **10** | 7/2[1] | 51 | 33 |
| | | | | (SP 129.6%) | **10 Rn** | |

**1m 39.68** (2.28) CSF £86.05 CT £496.68 TOTE £13.30: £3.90 £2.30 £2.70 (£17.70) Trio £138.30 OWNER Mr R. J. Arculli (NEWMARKET) BRED Howard Kaskel in Ireland

## 309 GIRONDE H'CAP (0-60) (4-Y.O+) (Class F)

4-50 (4-51) **1m 4f (Equitrack)** £2,600.30 (£730.80: £356.90) Stalls: Low GOING minus 0.38 sec per fur (FST)

| | | | | SP | RR | SF |
|---|---|---|---|---|---|---|
| 90[7] | **Colosse (37)** (JLEyre) **4-8-2** JQuinn(4) (hdwy over 3f out: rdn 2f out: led ins fnl f: r.o wl) | — | **1** | 12/1 | 45 | 19 |
| 189[9] | **Real Madrid (43)** (GPEnright) **5-8-11v** NAdams(3) (hld up: rdn over 4f out: r.o wl ins fnl f) | ¾ | **2** | 11/1 | 50 | 27 |
| | **Silktail (IRE) (45)** (MissGayKelleway) **4-8-10** RCochrane(9) (a.p: led over 2f out tl ins fnl f: unable qckn) | hd | **3** | 2/1[1] | 52 | 26 |
| | **The Lad (29)** (LMontagueHall) **7-7-4**(7)ow1 MartinDwyer(2) (a.p: rdn over 4f out: one pce fnl 2f) | 2½ | **4** | 16/1 | 33 | 9 |
| 240[2] | **Carrolls Marc (IRE) (49)** (CMurray) **8-9-3** JWeaver(8) (b.hind: nvr nr to chal) | 1¼ | **5** | 6/1 | 51 | 28 |
| 240* | **Wahem (IRE) (38)** (CEBrittain) **6-8-6** MLarsen(10) (b.hind: led over 9f) | 3½ | **6** | 11/2[3] | 35 | 12 |
| 187[4] | **Courbaril (58)** (SDow) **4-9-4**(5) ADaly(1) (hld up: rdn over 4f out: wknd over 3f out) | nk | **7** | 4/1[2] | 55 | 29 |
| 83[10] | **Retender (USA) (53)** (JPearce) **7-9-7** JMcLaughlin(7) (b.nr fore: a bhd) | 1¾ | **8** | 14/1 | 48 | 25 |
| 187[6] | **Conic Hill (IRE) (60)** (JPearce) **5-10-0** GBardwell(5) (lw: prom 7f) | 2½ | **9** | 33/1 | 51 | 28 |
| | **Ginger Jim (52)** (PRHedger) **5-9-3**(3) SDrowne(12) (lw: hdwy over 4f out: wknd 3f out) | ½ | **10** | 12/1 | 43 | 20 |

| | | | | SP | RR | SF |
|---|---|---|---|---|---|---|
| | **Children's Choice (IRE) (56)** (CNAllen) **5-9-10** GCarter(11) (b.hind: a bhd) | 5 | **11** | 14/1 | 40 | 17 |

(SP 128.9%) **11 Rn**

**2m 35.72** (5.72) CSF £130.18 CT £346.28 TOTE £11.80: £2.80 £3.90 £1.60 (£116.10) Trio £159.80 OWNER Diamond Racing Ltd (HAMBLETON) BRED Lariston Bloodstock
LONG HANDICAP The Lad 7-9
WEIGHT FOR AGE 4yo-3lb

T/Jkpt: Not won; £11,757.40 to Wolverhampton 21/2/96. T/Plpt: £20,071.20 (1.28 Tckts). T/Qdpt: £139.90 (41.73 Tckts). AK

# 0267-WOLVERHAMPTON (L-H) (Standard)
## Wednesday February 21st
WEATHER: fine

### 310 JORDAN MEDIAN AUCTION MAIDEN STKS (3, 4 & 5-Y.O) (Class E)
2-00 (2-01) **7f (Fibresand)** £2,845.50 (£861.00: £420.00: £199.50) Stalls: High GOING: 0.16 sec per fur (SLW)

| | | | | SP | RR | SF |
|---|---|---|---|---|---|---|
| $234^{5}$ | **All Apologies (IRE)** (RHollinshead) **4-9-3**(7) FLynch(1) (mde all: clr over 2f out: pushed out) | — | **1** | 33/1 | 53 | 27 |
| $271^{5}$ | **Marino Street (57)** (PDEvans) **3-8-3v**ow1 SSanders(3) (a.p: rdn over 2f out: r.o one pce fnl f) | 5 | **2** | 7/1$^{3}$ | 38 | — |
| $179^{4}$ | **So Natural (IRE) (52)** (EJAlston) **4-9-5** SDWilliams(4) (chsd wnr: rdn over 2f out: no imp) | 1¼ | **3** | 14/1 | 34 | 8 |
| $293^{5}$ | **Bells of Holland (59)** (WRMuir) **3-8-4**ow2 Jean-PierreLopez(2) (prom over 5f) | 6 | **4** | 8/1 | 22 | — |
| $217^{2}$ | **Baranov (IRE)** (DJGMurraySmith) **3-8-7** JWeaver(5) (lw: nvr gng wl: rdn over 3f out: no rspnse) | ¾ | **5** | 4/9$^{1}$ | 23 | — |
| | **Tirra-Lirra (IRE)** (CEBrittain) **4-9-5** MLarsen(6) (w'like: bkwd: s.i.s: bhd fnl 3f) | 2 | **6** | 6/1$^{2}$ | 14 | — |

(SP 116.7%) **6 Rn**

**1m 32.8** (8.10) CSF £202.84 TOTE £28.00: £7.70 £2.40 (£34.70) OWNER Mr Gabriel Mulholland (UPPER LONGDON) BRED Mrs R. Eastwood
WEIGHT FOR AGE 3yo-17lb

### 311 CLASSIC CLAROL CLAIMING STKS (4-Y.O+) (Class E)
2-30 (2-30) **7f (Fibresand)** £2,886.45 (£873.60: £426.30: £202.65) Stalls: High GOING: 0.16 sec per fur (SLW)

| | | | | SP | RR | SF |
|---|---|---|---|---|---|---|
| $135^{4}$ | **Jigsaw Boy (63)** (PGMurphy) **7-8-6**(3) SDrowne(3) (hdwy 2f out: rdn to ld last stride) | — | **1** | 6/1 | 71 | 28 |
| $270^{11}$ | **Ashgore (88)** (MJohnston) **6-9-4** JWeaver(2) (led: hrd rdn ins fnl f: hdd last stride) | hd | **2** | 5/6$^{1}$ | 80 | 37 |
| $270^{8}$ | **Milos (71)** (TJNaughton) **5-8-5**(7) TAshley(5) (a.p: ev ch 2f out: wknd fnl f) | 5 | **3** | 5/1$^{3}$ | 62 | 19 |
| $295^{*}$ | **Perilous Plight (68)** (WRMuir) **5-8-9** Jean-PierreLopez(1) (hld up: rdn over 2f out: eased whn btn fnl f) | 5 | **4** | 4/1$^{2}$ | 48 | 5 |
| $247^{4}$ | **Life Is Precious (IRE) (47)** (RHollinshead) **4-7-13**(7) FLynch(4) (prom: rdn over 2f out: wknd wl over 1f out) | ½ | **5** | 14/1 | 44 | 1 |
| $247^{7}$ | **Rafter-J (40)** (JAHarris) **5-8-8**ow1 DHarrison(6) (hld up: rdn 4f out: wknd over 2f out) | 8 | **6** | 50/1 | 28 | — |

(SP 114.1%) **6 Rn**

**1m 31.4** (6.70) CSF £11.35 TOTE £8.30: £3.10 £1.30 (£6.50) OWNER The Jigsaw Connection (BRISTOL) BRED Mrs J. A. Rawding

### 312 NORTHERN TOWN H'CAP (0-90) (4-Y.O+) (Class C)
3-00 (3-03) **1m 4f (Fibresand)** £5,329.70 (£1,613.60: £787.80: £374.90) Stalls: Low GOING: 0.16 sec per fur (SLW)

| | | | | SP | RR | SF |
|---|---|---|---|---|---|---|
| | **Northern Union (CAN) (81)** (MAJarvis) **5-9-11** WWoods(3) (hld up: rdn over 3f out: hdwy over 2f out: led ins fnl f: r.o wl) | — | **1** | 5/1$^{3}$ | 89 | 58 |
| $75^{5}$ | **Johns Act (USA) (69)** (DHaydnJones) **6-8-13** DHarrison(6) (a.p: led over 3f out tl ins fnl f) | 3½ | **2** | 12/1 | 72 | 41 |
| $181^{3}$ | **South Eastern Fred (84)** (HJCollingridge) **5-10-0** MRimmer(1) (plld hrd: a.p: ev ch 2f out: wknd ins fnl f) | 1¾ | **3** | 13/2 | 85 | 54 |
| $187^{2}$ | **Progression (71)** (CMurray) **5-9-1b** JFortune(11) (lw: hld up: hdwy 5f out: rdn 3f out: one pce fnl 2f) | 8 | **4** | 9/2$^{2}$ | 61 | 30 |
| $206^{W}$ | **Brave Spy (57)** (CACyzer) **5-8-1** DBiggs(5) (prom tl wknd 2f out) | 6 | **5** | 20/1 | 39 | 8 |
| $97^{*}$ | **Shakiyr (FR) (72)** (RHollinshead) **5-9-2** RCochrane(7) (bhd: rdn over 4f out: styd on over 1f out: n.d) | nk | **6** | 5/1$^{3}$ | 54 | 23 |
| $181^{9}$ | **Bernard Seven (IRE) (79)** (CEBrittain) **4-9-3b**(3) DRMcCabe(4) (lw: led over 8f: wknd 2f out) | ¾ | **7** | 9/1 | 60 | 26 |
| $221^{*}$ | **Roufontaine (61)** (WRMuir) **5-8-5**ow1 Jean-PierreLopez(9) (hld up: hdwy 5f out: eased whn btn over 1f out) | 10 | **8** | 12/1 | 29 | — |
| $222^{6}$ | **Hillzah (USA) (75)** (RBastiman) **8-9-0**(5) HBastiman(8) (hld up: wl bhd fnl 3f) | 7 | **9** | 20/1 | 33 | 2 |
| $263^{4}$ | **Prince Danzig (IRE) (81)** (DJGMurraySmith) **5-9-11** JWeaver(2) (hld up: wnt 2nd over 6f out: eased whn btn over 2f out) | 1½ | **10** | 4/1$^{1}$ | 37 | 6 |
| | **Taahhub (IRE) (52)** (RJPrice) **6-7-5**(5) PFessey(10) (prom 7f: t.o) | 10 | **11** | 20/1 | — | — |

(SP 124.5%) **11 Rn**

**2m 41.9** (9.40) CSF £59.45 CT £354.29 TOTE £6.10: £3.00 £4.00 £1.20 (£25.20) Trio £193.10 OWNER Mrs Anita Green (NEWMARKET) BRED Kinghaven Farms Ltd in Canada
LONG HANDICAP Taahhub (IRE) 7-9
WEIGHT FOR AGE 4yo-3lb

### 313 SHAKA'S CRACKERS H'CAP (0-80) (3-Y.O) (Class D)
3-30 (3-30) **1m 1f 79y (Fibresand)** £3,468.75 (£1,050.00: £512.50: £243.75) Stalls: Low GOING: 0.16 sec per fur (SLW)

| | | | | SP | RR | SF |
|---|---|---|---|---|---|---|
| $294^{*}$ | **Galapino (70)** (CEBrittain) **3-9-5** 5x MLarsen(6) (lw: mde all: clr wl over 1f out: easily) | — | **1** | 10/11$^{1}$ | 82+ | 38 |
| $269^{*}$ | **Nikita's Star (IRE) (67)** (DJGMurraySmith) **3-9-2** 5x JWeaver(1) (chsd wnr: rdn over 2f out: no imp) | 6 | **2** | 100/30$^{2}$ | 69 | 25 |
| $157^{5}$ | **Briganoone (53)** (SRBowring) **3-8-2** NCarlisle(2) (hdwy over 3f out: one pce fnl 2f) | 6 | **3** | 7/1$^{3}$ | 45 | 1 |
| $137^{8}$ | **Victim of Love (68)** (RCharlton) **3-9-3** SSanders(3) (prom: rdn over 2f out: wknd wl over 1f out) | 1¾ | **4** | 7/1$^{3}$ | 57 | 13 |
| $247^{*}$ | **Principal Boy (IRE) (50)** (TJEtherington) **3-7-13** DaleGibson(4) (plld hrd: sn prom: rdn & wknd 3f out) | 1 | **5** | 8/1 | 37 | — |
| | **Oriel Lad (72)** (PDEvans) **3-9-7** JFortune(5) (bhd fnl 3f: t.o) | 30 | **6** | 14/1 | 8 | — |

(SP 118.2%) **6 Rn**

**2m 5.1** (9.10) CSF £4.64 TOTE £2.50: £1.80 £1.70 (£2.20) OWNER The Dayspring Company Ltd (NEWMARKET) BRED Dayspring Co Ltd

### 314 BARMBY ARMY (S) STKS (3-Y.O) (Class E)
4-00 (4-00) **1m 100y (Fibresand)** £2,790.90 (£844.20: £411.60: £195.30) Stalls: Low GOING: 0.16 sec per fur (SLW)

| | | | | SP | RR | SF |
|---|---|---|---|---|---|---|
| | **Chauvelin (IRE)** (MJohnston) **3-8-12** DeanMcKeown(1) (lw: hdwy 4f out: led over 2f out: all out) | — | **1** | 7/2$^{3}$ | 55 | 11 |
| $281^{5}$ | **Bumblefoot (IRE) (55)** (MJohnston) **3-8-12** JWeaver(3) (chsd ldr: led over 5f out tl over 2f out: no ex fnl f) | ¾ | **2** | 11/8$^{1}$ | 54 | 10 |
| $220^{3}$ | **Bailiwick (51)** (NAGraham) **3-9-3b** MFenton(4) (b: a.p: rdn & ev ch over 2f out: one pce) | 5 | **3** | 5/2$^{2}$ | 49 | 7 |

| | | | | SP | RR | SF |
|---|---|---|---|---|---|---|
| *280$^{10}$* | **Sporting Fantasy (45)** (JBalding) **3-8-10v**$^{1(7)}$ JEdmunds(6) (hld up & plld hrd: no hdwy fnl 2f) | 3½ | **4** | 12/1 | 43 | 1 |
| *209$^{7}$* | **Heathyards Jade** (RHollinshead) **3-8-7** JFortune(5) (rdn 6f out: sn wl bhd) | 14 | **5** | 8/1 | 6 | — |
| *269$^{5}$* | **Margi Boo (40)** (RTJuckes) **3-8-7** DaleGibson(2) (b: led 3f: hrd drvn & wknd over 3f out: t.o) | 11 | **6** | 25/1 | — | — |
| | | | | (SP 115.5%) | **6 Rn** | |

**1m 55.5** (10.50) CSF £8.70 TOTE £4.40: £2.00 £1.20 (£3.10) OWNER Mr W. M. Johnstone (MIDDLEHAM) BRED William Johnstone
No bid

## 315 LADBROKE SERIES H'CAP (Qualifier) (0-80) (3-Y.O+) (Class D)

4-30 (4-31) **5f (Fibresand)** £3,517.50 (£1,065.00: £520.00: £247.50) Stalls: Low GOING: 0.16 sec per fur (SLW)

| | | | | SP | RR | SF |
|---|---|---|---|---|---|---|
| *225$^{2}$* | **Featherstone Lane (64)** (MissLCSiddall) **5-8-12v** JWeaver(8) (racd wd: a.p: led ins fnl f: all out) | — | **1** | 2/1$^{1}$ | 71 | 32 |
| *139** | **Chadwell Hall (74)** (SRBowring) **5-9-3b**$^{(5)}$ CTeague(2) (b.off hind: led tl ins fnl f: r.o wl) | s.h | **2** | 7/2$^{2}$ | 81 | 42 |
| *282$^{3}$* | **Leigh Crofter (72)** (PDCundell) **7-9-1b**$^{(5)}$ DGriffiths(7) (a.p: one pce fnl 2f) | 3½ | **3** | 11/2 | 68 | 29 |
| *266$^{4}$* | **Friendly Brave (USA) (75)** (MissGayKelleway) **6-9-6**$^{(3)}$ AWhelan(6) (lw: a.p: one pce fnl 2f) | s.h | **4** | 5/1$^{3}$ | 71 | 32 |
| *190$^{9}$* | **Best Kept Secret (59)** (PDEvans) **5-8-7v** JFortune(4) (b.nr fore: outpcd: nvr nr to chal) | 5 | **5** | 14/1 | 39 | — |
| *231$^{7}$* | **Cheeky Chappy (57)** (DWChapman) **5-8-0b**$^{(5)}$ PFessey(3) (outpcd: nvr trbld ldrs) | 2 | **6** | 7/1 | 30 | — |
| *270$^{12}$* | **Little Ibnr (80)** (PDEvans) **5-10-0** SSanders(5) (chsd ldr tl wknd wl over 1f out) | 1¼ | **7** | 11/1 | 49 | 10 |
| *63$^{5}$* | **Delrob (53)** (DHaydnJones) **5-8-1** TWilliams(1) (lw: prom tl wknd wl over 1f out) | 1¾ | **8** | 12/1 | 17 | — |
| *180$^{5}$* | ***Magic Pearl (63)*** *(RFMarvin)* ***6-8-8***$^{(3)}$ *SDrowne(9) (Withdrawn not under Starter's orders: veterinary advice)* | | **W** | *16/1* | — | — |
| | | | | (SP 128.7%) | **8 Rn** | |

**63.3 secs** (4.60) CSF £9.83 CT £31.62 TOTE £3.00: £1.40 £1.60 £2.50 (£7.40) Trio £12.00 OWNER Mr D. Parker (TADCASTER) BRED Qualitair Stud Ltd

T/Jkpt: Not won; £31,137.92 to Lingfield 22/2/96. T/Plpt: £176.00 (156.74 Tckts). T/Qdpt: £10.00 (571.69 Tckts). KH

# 0304-LINGFIELD (L-H) (Standard)

## Thursday February 22nd

Race 1: hand-timed
WEATHER: overcast WIND: almost nil

## 316 GREAT EXPECTATIONS H'CAP (0-70) (4-Y.O+) (Class E)

2-10 (2-21) **5f (Equitrack)** £2,900.10 (£877.80: £428.40: £203.70) Stalls: High GOING minus 0.57 sec per fur (FST)

| | | | | SP | RR | SF |
|---|---|---|---|---|---|---|
| *231$^{6}$* | **Tenor (56)** (DNicholls) **5-9-3** AlexGreaves(3) (hld up in tch: rdn over 1f out: styd on to ld wl ins fnl f) | — | **1** | 9/2$^{2}$ | 64 | 51 |
| *278$^{3}$* | **The Institute Boy (56)** (MissJFCraze) **6-9-3** JWeaver(5) (a.p: ev ch wl ins fnl f: r.o) | hd | **2** | 9/2$^{2}$ | 64 | 51 |
| *225$^{6}$* | **Kalar (65)** (DWChapman) **7-9-7b**$^{(5)}$ PFessey(1) (led: hdd wl ins fnl f: one pce) | 1¼ | **3** | 14/1 | 69 | 56 |
| *173$^{3}$* | **Half Tone (64)** (RMFlower) **4-9-11b** DBiggs(4) (sn outpcd in rr: bhd tl styd on ins fnl f: nrst fin) | 1¼ | **4** | 4/1$^{1}$ | 64 | 51 |
| *202** | **Lift Boy (USA) (61)** (AMoore) **7-9-8** CandyMorris(10) (b.hind: in tch: rdn & outpcd 2f out: kpt on one pce ins fnl f) | nk | **5** | 11/1 | 60 | 47 |
| *266$^{3}$* | **Dahiyah (USA) (61)** (GLMoore) **5-9-8v** SWhitworth(2) (chsd ldrs: sn rdn along: ev ch 1f out: wknd ins fnl f) | nk | **6** | 4/1$^{1}$ | 59 | 46 |
| *173$^{4}$* | **Super Rocky (67)** (RBastiman) **7-9-9**$^{(5)}$ HBastiman(9) (in tch: sn chsd along: kpt on one pce ins fnl f) | hd | **7** | 7/1$^{3}$ | 64 | 51 |
| | **Serious Hurry (54)** (RMMcKellar) **8-8-8b**$^{(7)}$ KSked(6) (prom over 3f) | 2 | **8** | 12/1 | 45 | 32 |
| *218$^{10}$* | **Jaazim (55)** (MMadgwick) **6-9-2** AClark(7) (a outpcd) | 1 | **9** | 33/1 | 43 | 30 |
| *231$^{8}$* | **Distant Dynasty (53)** (BAPearce) **6-9-0** SSanders(8) (b.nr fore: b.hind: chsd ldrs: rdn over 2f out: sn wknd) | 3½ | **10** | 16/1 | 30 | 17 |
| | | | | (SP 120.4%) | **10 Rn** | |

**58.8 secs** (0.80) CSF £24.14 CT £241.72 TOTE £7.90: £2.50 £1.60 £4.40 (£11.50) Trio £36.40 OWNER Mr Geoffrey Thompson (THIRSK) BRED Lord Victor Matthews

## 317 BLEAK HOUSE (S) STKS (3-Y.O+) (Class G)

2-45 (2-50) **6f (Equitrack)** £2,221.50 (£624.00: £304.50) Stalls: Low GOING minus 0.57 sec per fur (FST)

| | | | | SP | RR | SF |
|---|---|---|---|---|---|---|
| *238$^{3}$* | **Foreman (54)** (WAO'Gorman) **3-8-6** EmmaO'Gorman(3) (a.p: chsd ldr over 3f out: led over 2f out: hrd rdn over 1f out: r.o) | — | **1** | 9/1$^{3}$ | 62 | 8 |
| *271$^{7}$* | **The Frisky Farmer (60)** (WGMTurner) **3-8-6** AClark(2) (led: hdd over 2f out: rdn over 1f out: unable qckn) | 2 | **2** | 7/1$^{2}$ | 57 | 3 |
| *273$^{2}$* | **Our Shadee (USA) (51)** (KTIvory) **6-9-0v**$^{(7)}$ CScally(9) (hld up: hdwy over 2f out: rdn over 1f out: styd on ins fnl f) | ¾ | **3** | 14/1 | 54 | 16 |
| *266$^{5}$* | **Sir Tasker (66)** (JLHarris) **8-9-7** SSanders(1) (chsd ldrs: n.m.r over 4f out: rdn over 2f out: one pce) | 1¼ | **4** | 7/1$^{2}$ | 50 | 12 |
| *229$^{2}$* | **Star Talent (USA) (72)** (MissGayKelleway) **5-9-12v**$^{1}$ RCochrane(6) (hld up: hdwy over 2f out: rdn over 1f out: grad wknd) | 2½ | **5** | 9/4$^{1}$ | 49 | 11 |
| *302** | **Sense of Priority (73)** (DNicholls) **7-9-12** AlexGreaves(4) (hld up: rdn over 2f out: no hdwy) | nk | **6** | 9/4$^{1}$ | 48d | 10 |
| *273$^{3}$* | **Respectable Jones (52)** (RHollinshead) **10-9-7b** MWigham(5) (a bhd) | 3 | **7** | 16/1 | 35 | — |
| | **Latzio (40)** (BAPearce) **3-8-1** GBardwell(8) (b.hind: bhd fnl 3f) | 15 | **8** | 100/1 | — | — |
| *174$^{W}$* | **Lonely Vigil (FR)** (KOCunningham-Brown) **4-9-2** DBiggs(7) (b: chsd ldr over 2f: sn wknd) | 12 | **9** | 100/1 | — | — |
| | | | | (SP 111.1%) | **9 Rn** | |

**1m 13.17** (2.57) CSF £60.75 TOTE £9.80: £2.20 £1.30 £2.20 (£22.80) Trio £63.10 OWNER Times of Wigan (NEWMARKET) BRED J. R. Wills
WEIGHT FOR AGE 3yo-15lb
No bid

## 318 BARNABY RUDGE CLAIMING STKS (4-Y.O+) (Class F)

3-15 (3-21) **1m 4f (Equitrack)** £2,588.40 (£727.40: £355.20) Stalls: Low GOING minus 0.57 sec per fur (FST)

| | | | | SP | RR | SF |
|---|---|---|---|---|---|---|
| | **Harlequin Walk (IRE) (53)** (RJO'Sullivan) **5-8-10**$^{ow1}$ DBiggs(2) (chsd ldr: led over 2f out: hdd ins fnl f: unable qckn: fin 2nd, 11/4L: awrdd r) | — | **1** | 5/2$^{2}$ | 58 | 28 |
| *145$^{10}$* | **Awesome Power (53)** (JWHills) **10-8-6** AClark(5) (hld up: hdwy over 4f out: pushed along over 2f out: hrd rdn over 1f out: kpt on ins fnl f: fin 3rd, 3/4l: plcd 2nd) | | **2** | 8/1 | 54 | 24 |
| *299$^{2}$* | **Jungle Patrol (IRE) (74)** (CMurray) **4-8-7** MTebbutt(1) (led: hdd over 2f out: wknd over 1f out: fin 4th, 4l: plcd 3rd) | | **3** | 9/4$^{1}$ | 53 | 20 |

| | | | | SP | RR | SF |
|---|---|---|---|---|---|---|
| 274[4] | **Zuno Flyer (USA) (39)** (AMoore) **4-8-3v** MFenton(8) (b: b.hind: chsd ldrs: rdn 4f out: wknd over 2f out: fin 5th, 10l: plcd 4th) | | **4** | 12/1 | 36 | 3 |
| | **Bel Promise (IRE)** (PRWebber) **7-8-3** NAdams(3) (b: a bhd) | | **5** | 50/1 | 14 | — |
| 216[3] | **El Atrevido (FR) (63)** (NJHWalker) **6-8-9**(3) JStack(6) (in tch: rdn over 5f out: wknd 4f out) | s.h | **7** | 7/2[3] | 23 | — |
| 229[5] | **Scboo (35)** (REPeacock) **7-8-10** VSlattery(7) (bhd fnl 4f) | 1 | **8** | 100/1 | — | — |
| 186[6] | **Mister Lawson (25)** (BSmart) **10-8-7v**[1ow1] RCochrane(9) (mid div: rdn over 4f out: sn wknd) | 5 | **9** | 12/1 | 17 | — |
| 240[6] | **Northern Trial (USA) (43)** (KRBurke) **8-8-1**(7) TAshley(4) (b.hind: hld up: hdwy 5f out: rdn over 1f out: led ins fnl f: r.o: fin 1st: disq: plcd last) | | **D** | 10/1 | 59 | 29 |
| | | | | (SP 120.1%) | | **9 Rn** |

**2m 32.79** (2.79) CSF £34.49 TOTE £10.50: £3.50 £1.10 £2.50 (£24.10) Trio £20.20 OWNER Mr D. A. Johnson (WHITCOMBE) BRED Ronnie Boland in Ireland
WEIGHT FOR AGE 4yo-3lb

## 319 CONOCO CENTRAL EUROPEAN H'CAP (0-70) (4-Y.O+ F & M) (Class E)

3-45 (3-51) **1m 2f (Equitrack)** £2,913.75 (£882.00: £430.50: £204.75) Stalls: Low GOING minus 0.57 sec per fur (FST)

| | | | | SP | RR | SF |
|---|---|---|---|---|---|---|
| 301[10] | **Your Most Welcome (50)** (DJSffrenchDavis) **5-9-4** JWeaver(1) (chsd ldr: led over 2f out: sn clr: easily) | — | **1** | 7/1[3] | 63+ | 40 |
| 233[4] | **Total Rach (IRE) (52)** (RIngram) **4-9-5b** WWoods(6) (hld up: rdn over 3f out: styd on ins fnl f: no ch w wnr) | 15 | **2** | 13/8[1] | 42 | 17 |
| 274[8] | **Kellaire Girl (IRE) (47)** (AMoore) **4-9-0v**[1] SSanders(8) (b.hind: led: hdd over 2f out: wknd ins fnl f) | ½ | **3** | 12/1 | 36 | 11 |
| 216[9] | **Elly Fleetfoot (IRE) (46)** (BJMeehan) **4-8-13** RCochrane(4) (chsd ldrs: rdn 4f out: sn wknd) | 8 | **4** | 20/1 | 22 | — |
| 27[7] | **Tadellal (IRE) (57)** (WGMTurner) **5-9-4**(7) MCotton(3) (dwlt: in tch after 2f: wknd over 4f out) | 2½ | **5** | 11/4[2] | 28 | 5 |
| 244[8] | **Gentle Irony (44)** (WJMusson) **4-8-11b** GCarter(2) (chsd ldrs: rdn 4f out: wknd 3f out) | 2 | **6** | 16/1 | 13 | — |
| | **Benjarong (35)** (RMMcKellar) **4-8-2** TWilliams(7) (bhd fnl 4f: t.o) | dist | **7** | 10/1 | — | — |
| | | | | (SP 104.7%) | | **7 Rn** |

**2m 6.31** (2.01) CSF £16.55 CT £91.28 TOTE £9.10: £2.80 £1.20 (£6.40) OWNER Mrs J. E. Lambert (UPPER LAMBOURN) BRED Collin Stud
WEIGHT FOR AGE 4yo-1lb

## 320 HARD TIMES MAIDEN STKS (3-Y.O+) (Class D)

4-15 (4-21) **7f (Equitrack)** £3,468.75 (£1,050.00: £512.50: £243.75) Stalls: Low GOING minus 0.57 sec per fur (FST)

| | | | | SP | RR | SF |
|---|---|---|---|---|---|---|
| 175[3] | **Barbason (50)** (AMoore) **4-9-10** CandyMorris(6) (b.hind: hld up: hdwy to chse ldr over 2f out: led wl over 1f out: pushed clr: comf) | — | **1** | 8/1 | 58+ | 29 |
| | **Rubbiyati** (CEBrittain) **4-9-5** MLarsen(1) (w' like: dwlt: sn rcvrd: led over 5f out: hdd wl over 1f out: one pce) | 3 | **2** | 8/1 | 46 | 17 |
| | **La Perruche (IRE)** (LordHuntingdon) **3-8-2** SSanders(4) (bit bkwd: hld up: hdwy ½-wy: rdn over 1f out: styd on ins fnl f) | 2 | **3** | 6/1 | 43 | — |
| 261[4] | **Don't Get Caught (IRE) (57)** (JLHarris) **4-9-5** TIves(7) (chsd ldrs: rdn over 2f out: one pce) | ¾ | **4** | 4/1[3] | 40 | 11 |
| | **Elegantissima** (SDow) **3-8-2** JQuinn(5) (chsd ldr ½-wy tl over 2f out: wknd over 1f out) | 6 | **5** | 9/4[1] | 27 | — |
| | **Jebi (USA)** (CMurray) **6-9-10** MTebbutt(3) (in tch: rdn over 2f out: sn wknd) | 1¾ | **6** | 12/1 | 27 | — |
| | **Georgie Boy (USA)** (CADwyer) **3-8-7** WWoods(2) (w'like: led over 1f: chsd ldr to ½-wy: sn wknd) | 5 | **7** | 100/30[2] | 17 | — |
| | | | | (SP 118.0%) | | **7 Rn** |

**1m 26.73** (2.73) CSF £61.17 TOTE £8.70: £2.30 £3.00 (£28.90) OWNER Mr F. L. Hill (BRIGHTON) BRED Sheikh Mohammed bin Rashid al Maktoum
WEIGHT FOR AGE 3yo-17lb

## 321 NICHOLAS NICKLEBY H'CAP (0-80) (3-Y.O) (Class D)

4-45 (4-51) **7f (Equitrack)** £3,667.50 (£1,030.00: £502.50) Stalls: Low GOING minus 0.57 sec per fur (FST)

| | | | | SP | RR | SF |
|---|---|---|---|---|---|---|
| 217* | **Cornish Snow (USA) (80)** (DRLoder) **3-9-7** LDettori(3) (lw: mde all: clr over 1f out: canter) | — | **1** | 4/11[1] | 85+ | 28 |
| 182[9] | **Carmarthen Bay (77)** (GLMoore) **3-9-1**(3) AWhelan(1) (a 2nd: rdn 2f out: kpt on one pce fnl f: no ch w wnr) | 1½ | **2** | 13/2[3] | 79 | 22 |
| 293[2] | **Moi Canard (69)** (BAPearce) **3-8-7**(3) DRMcCabe(2) (disp 2nd: rdn over 2f out: one pce) | 1¾ | **3** | 100/30[2] | 67 | 10 |
| | | | | (SP 109.7%) | | **3 Rn** |

**1m 26.59** (2.59) CSF £2.74 TOTE £1.20 (£2.10) OWNER Sheikh Mohammed (NEWMARKET) BRED Hermitage Farm Inc.

T/Jkpt: £52,763.40 (0.2 Tckts); £59,451.78 to Kempton 23/2/96. T/Plpt: £642.20 (53.87 Tckts). T/Qdpt: £45.60 (107.08 Tckts). SM

# 0290a-CAGNES-SUR-MER (Nice, France) (L-H) (Holding)
## Sunday February 18th

## 322a PRIX D'EZE CLAIMING (3-Y.O)

1-50 (1-48) **1m 2f** £5,270.00 (£1,976.00: £1,186.00)

| | | | | SP | RR | SF |
|---|---|---|---|---|---|---|
| | **Duc De Zoz (FR)** (MmeARossio,France) **3-8-11b**[1] DBoeuf | — | **1** | | — | — |
| | **L'Imperialis (FR)** (ELellouche,France) **3-8-7**(5) TCastanheire | ½ | **2** | | — | — |
| | **Landsome Dove (FR)** (JPiednoel,France) **3-9-2** ABredillet | nk | **3** | | — | — |
| 289a[3] | **Asking For Kings (IRE)** (SDow) **3-9-2** JReid (btn over 3l) | | **8** | | — | — |
| | | | | | | **16 Rn** |

**2m 12.2** P-M 8.50F: 2.60F 11.40F 14.10F (60.20F) OWNER G. Duca BRED G. Duca
**289a Asking For Kings (IRE)** was always prominent and was running in fifth place entering the straight. He kept on at one pace at the finish.

## 323a PRIX POLICEMAN (3-Y.O)

2-55 (2-56) **1m 2f** £13,175.00 (£6,588.00: £3,953.00)

| | | | | SP | RR | SF |
|---|---|---|---|---|---|---|
| | **Top Glory (FR)** (FDoumen,France) **3-8-13** GGuignard | — | **1** | | 92 | — |
| 149a* | **Mongol Warrior (USA)** (LordHuntingdon) **3-8-10** JReid | 1½ | **2** | | 87 | — |
| 226a* | **Grenadier (FR)** (GCollet,France) **3-8-13** MBoutin | nk | **3** | | 89 | — |
| | | | | | | **8 Rn** |

**2m 9.4** P-M 13.20F: 1.90F 1.70F 1.10F (27.70F) OWNER H de Pracomtal (LAMORLAYE) BRED Mme A. G. Lhote & Mme R. Destombes

**149a* Mongol Warrior (USA)** was held up in fifth early on and moved up to be fourth turning into the straight. He kept on to the line but could not match the pace of the winner.

## 324a PRIX DE PASSAU H'CAP (4-Y.O+)

3-25 (3-23) **1m** £7,905.00 (£3,953.00: £2,372.00: £1,581.00: £791.00)

| | | | | SP | RR | SF |
|---|---|---|---|---|---|---|
| $148a^{3}$ | **Master Fontenaille (FR)** (J-PGallorini,France) **6-8-5** TThulliez | — | 1 | | 67 | — |
| 151a* | **Bybus (FR)** (MmeARossio,France) **5-10-0** DBoeuf | 1 | 2 | | 88 | — |
| | **Star Parade (FR)** (FDoumen,France) **4-8-7** GGuignard | 1 | 3 | | 65 | — |
| $290a^{2}$ | **Confronter** (SDow) **7-9-7** OPeslier (btn over 4½l) | | 5 | | 74 | — |
| | | | | | | **18 Rn** |

**1m 42.4** P-M 6.20F: 2.40F 2.10F 5.40F (21.60) OWNER Mme H. Devin BRED R. Jarrossay

**290a Confronter** raced in mid division and began to close up two furlongs out. He ran on at one pace and was nearest at the finish.

## 325a PRIX GENERAL DE SAINT-DIDDIER AMATEUR (4-Y.O+)

3-55 (3-53) **1m** £4,611.00 (£2,306.00: £1,383.00: £922.00: £461.00)

| | | | | SP | RR | SF |
|---|---|---|---|---|---|---|
| | **Hunter Field (FR)** (JRossi,France) **4-10-8** MrsJRossi | — | 1 | | 86 | — |
| | **Tycoon King (IRE)** (RCollet,France) **4-10-0** MrRCollet | nk | 2 | | 77 | — |
| | **Soy Soy (FR)** (FDoumen,France) **4-10-0** MrTDoumen | 1½ | 3 | | 74 | — |
| 227a* | **Wakeel (USA)** (SDow) **4-10-8** MrCMosse | nk | 4 | | 82 | — |
| $227a^{9}$ | **Country Lover** (LordHuntingdon) **5-10-0** MrTTrapenard | s.h | 5 | | 74 | — |
| | | | | | | **13 Rn** |

**1m 45.4** P-M 6.80F: 2.00F 2.00F 1.50F (30.20F) OWNER No Owner BRED Haras de Preaux

**227a* Wakeel (USA)** was always prominent and moved into fifth place in the closing stages, but kept on at one pace.

**227a Country Lover**, held up early on, began to make progress from two furlongs out and kept on well to the line.

## 326a PRIX DE SAINT-BLAISE (3-Y.O)

4-25 (4-23) **1m** £5,270.00 (£2,635.00: £1,581.00)

| | | | | SP | RR | SF |
|---|---|---|---|---|---|---|
| $226a^{3}$ | **Danish Melody (IRE)** (RCollet,France) **3-9-2** CHanotel | — | 1 | | 67 | — |
| | **Alleged Challenge (USA)** (RCollet,France) **3-8-12** ESaint-Martin | nk | 2 | | 62 | — |
| | **Acier Bleu (FR)** (PKhozian,France) **3-8-12** GElorriaga-Santos | 2½ | 3 | | 57 | — |
| $226a^{7}$ | **Daily Risk** (SDow) **3-8-12** JReid (btn over 7l) | | 12 | | — | — |
| | | | | | | **17 Rn** |

**1m 46.1** P-M 3.40F: 3.30F 2.30F 2.90F (17.00F) OWNER R. Collet (CHANTILLY) BRED K. E. Moeran & Mme K. E. Moeran

**226a Daily Risk** led the field with one and a half furlongs to race, but weakened quickly.

# SAINT-MORITZ (Switzerland) (R-H) (Good)

## Sunday February 18th

## 327a FELDSCHLOSSCHEN GROSSER PREIS VON ST. MORITZ (Listed) (4-Y.O+)

2-45 (2-55) **1m 2f** £29,484.00 (£11,794.00: £8,845.00: £5,897.00)

| | | | | SP | RR | SF |
|---|---|---|---|---|---|---|
| | **Galtee (IRE)** (UweStoltefuss,Germany) **4-9-6** PSchiergen | — | 1 | | — | — |
| | **Roditano (USA)** (RStadelmann,Switzerland) **6-9-6** OSchick | 7½ | 2 | | — | — |
| | **Muskat (GER)** (MHofer,Germany) **5-9-5** NGrant | 1¼ | 3 | | — | — |
| | **Bartok (IRE)** (PAKelleway) **5-9-10** JacquelineFreda (btn over 17l) | | 11 | | — | — |
| | | | | | | **18 Rn** |

**2m 12.3** TOTE 7.10SF: 3.50SF 3.50SF 3.30SF (169.60SF) OWNER A. Pereira BRED Gestut Romerhof

**Bartok (IRE)** led after two furlongs to three furlongs out, but gradually weakened.

# 0297-SOUTHWELL (L-H) (Standard)

## Friday February 23rd

## 328 FARNSFIELD MAIDEN APPRENTICE H'CAP (0-60) (4-Y.O+) (Class G)

2-10 (2-10) **1m (Fibresand)** £2,095.00 (£595.00: £295.00) Stalls: Low

| | | | | SP | RR | SF |
|---|---|---|---|---|---|---|
| *$213^{4}$* | **Mezzoramio (39)** (KAMorgan) **4-8-6v**(5) CScudder(2) (mde most: clr 2f out: styd on) | — | 1 | 5/1$^{2}$ | 50 | 30 |
| *$239^{9}$* | **Carol Again (36)** (NBycroft) **4-8-8** TAshley(11) (racd wd: hdwy 3f out: sn prom: styd on one pce appr fnl f) | 8 | 2 | 6/1$^{3}$ | 31 | 11 |
| *$116^{7}$* | **Parklife (IRE) (40)** (PCHaslam) **4-8-7**(5) RMullen(6) (lw: s.i.s: pushed along thrght: styd on strly towards fin) | s.h | 3 | 5/1$^{2}$ | 35 | 15 |
| *$239^{11}$* | **Arecibo (FR) (34)** (JParkes) **4-8-6** GFaulkner(14) (swtg: led early: cl up tl outpcd fnl 2f) | s.h | 4 | 25/1 | 29 | 9 |
| *$255^{6}$* | **Branston Kristy (30)** (CSmith) **4-7-11b**(5) AngelaGallimore(8) (chsd ldrs: one pce fnl 3f) | 9 | 5 | 33/1 | 7 | — |
| *$246^{9}$* | **Supercool (34)** (DWChapman) **5-8-6** JoHunnam(5) (a chsng ldrs: one pce fnl 3f) | nk | 6 | 25/1 | 10 | — |
| | **Most Welcome News (45)** (JRJenkins) **4-8-10b**(7) SallyWall(10) (sme hdwy over 2f out: nvr rchd ldrs) | nk | 7 | 16/1 | 21 | 1 |
| | **Harry's Treat (55)** (JLEyre) **4-9-10**(3) DSweeney(3) (chsd ldrs: outpcd ½-wy: sn btn) | ¾ | 8 | 11/4$^{1}$ | 29 | 9 |
| | **Backhander (IRE) (55)** (MartynWane) **4-9-8**(5) JEdmunds(13) (chsd ldr tl wknd over 2f out) | ½ | 9 | 14/1 | 28 | 8 |
| *$217^{4}$* | **Takeshi (IRE) (56)** (WRMuir) **4-9-7**(7) RPooles(7) (broke wl: outpcd after 2f) | 2½ | 10 | 8/1 | 24 | 4 |
| | **Carmenoura (IRE) (30)** (EJAlston) **4-8-2** IonaWands(12) (nvr trbld ldrs) | 3½ | 11 | 14/1 | — | — |
| *$204^{7}$* | **Opening Range (45)** (NEBerry) **5-8-12**(5) RStudholme(9) (chsd ldrs tl wknd over 2f out) | 3 | 12 | 20/1 | — | — |
| *$201^{8}$* | **Air of Mystery (24)** (NEBerry) **4-7-5b1**(5) AdelleGibbons(1) (s.i.s: a outpcd & bhd: t.o) | 25 | 13 | 33/1 | — | — |
| *$53^{11}$* | **Ilustre (IRE) (39)** (GFierro) **4-8-11** JWilkinson(15) (pushed along thrght: sn bhd: t.o) | 8 | 14 | 20/1 | — | — |
| *$85^{11}$* | **Auckland Castle (31)** (SRBowring) **5-8-3** JDennis(4) (outpcd & bhd after 3f: t.o: dead) | dist | 15 | 10/1 | — | — |
| | | | | (SP 136.8%) | | **15 Rn** |

**1m 45.8** (5.80) CSF £36.84 CT £155.31 TOTE £6.30: £1.20 £3.00 £2.00 (£15.20) Trio £14.90 OWNER Mr T. R. Pryke (MELTON MOWBRAY) BRED Saeed Manana

OFFICIAL EXPLANATION **Auckland Castle: the rider stated the gelding lost his action and appeared to go lame.**

## 329 BEESTHORPE CLAIMING STKS (3-Y.O) (Class F)
2-40 (2-42) **1m 3f (Fibresand)** £2,398.00 (£673.00: £328.00) Stalls: Low

| | | | | SP | RR | SF |
|---|---|---|---|---|---|---|
| *285⁴* | **China Castle (74)** (PCHaslam) **3-9-3** JFortune(1) (hdwy 6f out: led 2f out: sn clr: eased towards fin) | — | **1** | 2/1 2 | 73+ | 20 |
| *280** | **Dancing Cavalier (59)** (RHollinshead) **3-8-6**(7) FLynch(8) (lw: sn wl bhd: hdwy 4f out: styd on wl towards fin: no ch w wnr) | 1 | **2** | 5/4 1 | 68+ | 15 |
| *314²* | **Bumblefoot (IRE) (55)** (MJohnston) **3-8-1** TWilliams(7) (led after 3f tl hdd 2f out: sn outpcd) | 4 | **3** | 9/1 | 50 | — |
| *156⁴* | **Threesocks (58)** (BSmart) **3-8-6** SSanders(3) (lw: chsd ldrs: outpcd 3f out: no imp after) | 6 | **4** | 9/1 | 46 | — |
| *258²* | **Arch Angel (IRE) (52)** (DJSffrenchDavis) **3-8-1** NAdams(5) (hdwy ½-wy: ev ch 2f out: sn rdn & btn) | 1¼ | **5** | 7/1 3 | 39 | — |
| *101⁸* | **Havana Heights (IRE) (40)** (JLEyre) **3-8-1** JQuinn(9) (b.nr hind: chsd ldrs: ev ch 3f out: sn btn) | 1 | **6** | 50/1 | 38 | — |
| *197⁵* | **Kai's Lady (IRE)** (SWCampion) **3-7-7**(5) PFessey(2) (a bhd: t.o) | 25 | **7** | 50/1 | — | — |
| *217¹¹* | **Valjess** (DCO'Brien) **3-7-13** GBardwell(6) (led 3f: lost pl 6f out: t.o) | 14 | **8** | 50/1 | — | — |
| *238⁷* | **Belacqua (USA)** (DWChapman) **3-7-13** LCharnock(4) (prom tl rdn & wknd 6f out: sn t.o) | 11 | **9** | 50/1 | — | — |

(SP 118.1%) **9 Rn**

**2m 30.5** (10.50) CSF £4.77 TOTE £2.40: £1.40 £1.10 £1.50 (£1.80) Trio £6.80 OWNER Mr J. M. Davis (MIDDLEHAM) BRED Mrs F. Cronin

## 330 FARNDON H'CAP (0-70) (3-Y.O+) (Class E)
3-10 (3-10) **6f (Fibresand)** £2,831.85 (£856.80: £417.90: £198.45) Stalls: Low

| | | | | SP | RR | SF |
|---|---|---|---|---|---|---|
| *259²* | **Stand Tall (59)** (CWThornton) **4-9-8** DeanMcKeown(5) (swtg: trckd ldrs: led wl over 1f out: r.o) | — | **1** | 8/11 1 | 70 | 53 |
| *255²* | **At the Savoy (IRE) (59)** (TDBarron) **5-9-1**(7) KimberleyHart(3) (lw: in tch: effrt & c wd over 2f out: styd on: no ch w wnr) | 7 | **2** | 5/1 3 | 51 | 34 |
| *282⁵* | **Bold Aristocrat (IRE) (51)** (RHollinshead) **5-8-7**(7) FLynch(1) (hdwy to ld after 1f: hdd wl over 1f out: sn rdn & btn) | 1 | **3** | 9/1 | 41 | 24 |
| *126** | **Tame Deer (65)** (MCChapman) **4-9-11**(3) DRMcCabe(2) (lw: led 1f: chsd ldrs tl rdn & btn 2f out) | 5 | **4** | 7/2 2 | 41 | 24 |
| *231¹⁰* | **Rocky Two (49)** (PHowling) **5-8-12** JQuinn(4) (b: in tch: rdn ½-wy: no imp) | 2 | **5** | 16/1 | 20 | 3 |

(SP 112.7%) **5 Rn**

**1m 16.8** (3.30) CSF £4.72 TOTE £1.70: £1.20 £1.90 (£2.00) OWNER Mr Guy Reed (MIDDLEHAM) BRED Mrs E. Longton

## 331 RAVENSHEAD H'CAP (0-80) (3-Y.O+) (Class D)
3-40 (3-41) **7f (Fibresand)** £3,485.00 (£1,055.00: £515.00: £245.00) Stalls: Low

| | | | | SP | RR | SF |
|---|---|---|---|---|---|---|
| *255³* | **Nashaat (USA) (68)** (MCChapman) **8-9-0**(3) DRMcCabe(4) (chsd ldrs: pushed thro to ld over 1f out: edgd lft & r.o) | — | **1** | 8/1 | 77 | 56 |
| *211** | **Pine Ridge Lad (IRE) (79)** (JLEyre) **6-10-0** RLappin(7) (led 2½f: a.p: one pce appr fnl f) | 6 | **2** | 5/2 1 | 74 | 53 |
| *270⁹* | **Lord Sky (68)** (ABailey) **5-8-10**(7) AngelaGallimore(1) (lw: led after 2½f: clr over 2f out: hdd over 1f out: sn btn) | 1¼ | **3** | 14/1 | 60 | 39 |
| *282⁶* | **Allinson's Mate (IRE) (67)** (TDBarron) **8-9-2b** JFortune(5) (sn pushed along: hdwy ½-wy: nvr rchd ldrs) | 2 | **4** | 3/1 2 | 55 | 34 |
| *174⁵* | **What a Nightmare (IRE) (64)** (PHowling) **4-8-13** JQuinn(6) (sn outpcd & bhd: sme hdwy 2f out: n.d) | ½ | **5** | 16/1 | 51 | 30 |
| *247⁸* | **Hi Rock (47)** (MJCamacho) **4-7-10** LCharnock(8) (chsd ldrs tl wknd fnl 2½f) | 1¼ | **6** | 7/1 | 31 | 10 |
| *261²* | **Manabar (65)** (MJPolglase) **4-9-0** MLarsen(3) (cl up tl hmpd & wknd 1f out) | 5 | **7** | 5/1 3 | 37 | 16 |
| *301⁷* | **Indiahra (47)** (RHollinshead) **5-7-5v**(5) PFessey(2) (dwlt: a outpcd & bhd) | 7 | **8** | 11/1 | 3 | — |

(SP 114.7%) **8 Rn**

**1m 30.0** (3.20) CSF £26.76 CT £253.22 TOTE £7.30: £2.00 £1.60 £2.70 (£9.50) OWNER Mr Tony Satchell (MARKET RASEN) BRED Echo Valley Horse Farm and Swettenham Stud
LONG HANDICAP Hi Rock 7-9 Indiahra 7-9

## 332 WELLOW (S) STKS (3-Y.O) (Class G)
4-10 (4-12) **7f (Fibresand)** £2,085.00 (£585.00: £285.00) Stalls: Low

| | | | | SP | RR | SF |
|---|---|---|---|---|---|---|
| *194⁵* | **Chilibang Bang (65)** (JBerry) **3-8-8**(5) PRoberts(4) (cl up: led 2½f out: r.o) | — | **1** | 8/13 1 | 56 | 19 |
| *281** | **Efipetite (43)** (NBycroft) **3-8-6**(7) FLynch(2) (hld up: stdy hdwy over 2f out: ev ch over 1f out: no ex fnl f) | 1¼ | **2** | 4/1 3 | 53 | 16 |
| *271⁴* | **Victoria Sioux (52)** (JAPickering) **3-8-6** JQuinn(1) (b.off hind: lw: led tl hdd over 2f out: sn rdn & btn) | 13 | **3** | 100/30 2 | 16 | — |
| | **Brockville Bairn (44)** (MrsASwinbank) **3-8-11** JFortune(3) (bit bkwd: chsd ldrs tl outpcd fnl 2f) | nk | **4** | 14/1 | 21 | — |

(SP 111.6%) **4 Rn**

**1m 33.0** (6.20) CSF £3.41 TOTE £1.40 (£1.80) OWNER Mr Ian Crawford (COCKERHAM) BRED G. W. Hampson
No bid

## 333 THORGATON H'CAP (0-70) (4-Y.O+) (Class E)
4-40 (4-42) **1m 4f (Fibresand)** £2,900.10 (£877.80: £428.40: £203.70) Stalls: Low

| | | | | SP | RR | SF |
|---|---|---|---|---|---|---|
| *222³* | **Backview (60)** (BJLlewellyn) **4-9-5** TWilliams(9) (cl up: led over 6½f out: rdn & r.o wl fnl 2f) | — | **1** | 12/1 | 73 | 29 |
| *236⁶* | **Mr Moriarty (IRE) (44)** (SRBowring) **5-8-1**(5) CTeague(5) (led tl hdd over 6½f out: sltly hmpd 5f out: one pce) | 8 | **2** | 5/1 2 | 46 | 5 |
| | **Philmist (49)** (CWCElsey) **4-8-8b** NKennedy(3) (bhd: hdwy 6f out: ev ch 3f out: one pce) | s.h | **3** | 12/1 | 51 | 7 |
| *124³* | **Alzoomo (IRE) (65)** (JAGlover) **4-9-3**(7) VictoriaAppleby(1) (chsd ldrs: outpcd over 4f out: styd on one pce fnl 2f) | 3½ | **4** | 10/1 | 63 | 19 |
| *113²* | **Anistop (56)** (RAkehurst) **4-8-8**(7) TAshley(4) (prom: n.m.r appr st & lost pl: n.d after) | 3½ | **5** | 7/2 1 | 49 | 5 |
| *254⁵* | **Bold Pursuit (IRE) (55)** (JGFitzGerald) **7-8-10**(7) FLynch(8) (b: trckd ldrs: effrt 6f out: ev ch tl outpcd fnl 2f) | 2½ | **6** | 12/1 | 45 | 4 |
| *248** | **Suvalu (USA) (69)** (MGMeagher) **4-10-0** JFortune(7) (in tch tl outpcd fnl 3f) | ¾ | **7** | 11/2 3 | 58 | 14 |
| *254³* | **No Submission (USA) (60)** (DWChapman) **10-9-8** ACulhane(10) (lw: trckd ldrs: chal 6f out: rdn & wknd over 3f out) | hd | **8** | 10/1 | 49 | 8 |
| *297** | **Mazilla (52)** (AStreeter) **4-8-11v** 5x FNorton(2) (hld up: effrt & nt clr run 5f out & 3f out: nt rcvr) | 8 | **9** | 7/2 1 | 30 | — |
| | ***Heathyards Boy (50)*** (RHollinshead) **6-8-12** JQuinn(6) (Withdrawn not under Starter's orders: ref to ent stalls) | | **W** | 33/1 | — | — |

(SP 120.7%) **9 Rn**

**2m 42.7** (10.20) CSF £65.87 CT £674.36 TOTE £26.30: £7.10 £2.70 £2.70 (£45.40) Trio £220.20 OWNER Mr Eamonn O'Malley (BARGOED) BRED G. D. Dalrymple
WEIGHT FOR AGE 4yo-3lb

T/Plpt: £44.30 (272.23 Tckts). T/Qdpt: £29.10 (33.39 Tckts). AA

# 0316-LINGFIELD (L-H) (Standard)

## Saturday February 24th

WEATHER: rain WIND: fresh half bhd

### 334 MERLIN (S) H'CAP (0-60) (I) (4-Y.O+) (Class F)

1-50 (1-50) **1m (Equitrack)** £2,262.20 (£634.20: £308.60) Stalls: High GOING minus 0.55 sec per fur (FST)

| Form | Horse / details | Dist | Pos | SP | RR | SF |
|---|---|---|---|---|---|---|
| 217$^{8}$ | **Call Tophorse (43)** (CMurray) **4-8-13b$^{1}$** MTebbutt(8) (chsd ldrs: rdn to go 2nd over 2f out: led over 1f out: drvn out) | — | 1 | 8/1$^{3}$ | 48 | 18 |
| 278$^{5}$ | **Nivasha (39)** (RPCHoad) **4-8-9** MFenton(1) (mid div: rdn & outpcd over 4f out: styd on again fr over 1f out: wnt 2nd wl ins fnl f) | 1 | 2 | 14/1 | 42 | 12 |
| | **North Esk (USA) (45)** (CADwyer) **7-8-12**$^{(3)}$ DRMcCabe(7) (hld up: hdwy over 2f out: rdn over 1f out: styd on ins fnl f) | ¾ | 3 | 5/1$^{2}$ | 47 | 17 |
| 295$^{3}$ | **Justinianus (IRE) (50)** (JJBridger) **4-9-6** JQuinn(3) (led tl hdd over 1f out: one pce) | 1 | 4 | 5/1$^{2}$ | 50 | 20 |
| 249$^{3}$ | **Charm Dancer (54)** (MCPipe) **4-9-10** AMcGlone(5) (chsd ldr over 5f: rdn over 1f out: one pce) | 1¼ | 5 | 3/1$^{1}$ | 51 | 21 |
| 53$^{7}$ | **Fiaba (40)** (MrsNMacauley) **8-8-5**$^{(5)}$ AmandaSanders(9) (in tch tl rdn & wknd over 2f out) | 6 | 6 | 12/1 | 25 | — |
| 201$^{5}$ | **Nuthatch (IRE) (34)** (MDIUsher) **4-7-13**$^{(5)}$ CAdamson(2) (a bhd) | 7 | 7 | 10/1 | 5 | — |
| 240$^{11}$ | **Tomal (40)** (RIngram) **4-8-10** JWeaver(6) (b.hind: a bhd) | 5 | 8 | 10/1 | 1 | — |
| 233$^{5}$ | **Gallic Victory (IRE) (52)** (JohnBerry) **5-9-8** TWilliams(4) (a.p: cl 3rd whn broke down & p.u over 1f out: dead) | | P | 16/1 | — | — |

(SP 107.9%) **9 Rn**

**1m 40.92** (3.52) CSF £88.93 CT £490.35 TOTE £8.40: £1.50 £3.50 £2.00 (£63.50) Trio Not won; £123.23 to Southwell 26/2/96 OWNER Mr Darren Croft (NEWMARKET) BRED Mrs V. O'Brien

No bid

### 335 BUZZARD H'CAP (0-80) (3-Y.O) (Class D)

2-20 (2-20) **5f (Equitrack)** £3,452.50 (£1,045.00: £510.00: £242.50) Stalls: High GOING minus 0.55 sec per fur (FST)

| Form | Horse / details | Dist | Pos | SP | RR | SF |
|---|---|---|---|---|---|---|
| 182$^{4}$ | **Princely Sound (70)** (MBell) **3-8-11** MFenton(1) (lw: mde all: pushed out ins fnl f) | — | 1 | 11/8$^{1}$ | 78 | 38 |
| 307$^{3}$ | **Sunset Harbour (IRE) (61)** (TJNaughton) **3-7-13b$^{1}$**$^{(3)ow3}$ DRMcCabe(2) (chsd wnr: rdn over 1f out: one pce) | 2 | 2 | 13/2$^{2}$ | 63 | 20 |
| 220$^{2}$ | **Myttons Mistake (73)** (ABailey) **3-8-11**$^{(3)}$ DWright(4) (lw: hld up: hdwy 2f out: rdn over 1f out: styd on ins fnl f) | ½ | 3 | 13/2$^{2}$ | 73 | 33 |
| | **Johayro (78)** (WGMTurner) **3-9-0**$^{(5)}$ CAdamson(7) (chsd ldrs: rdn 2f out: one pce) | 3 | 4 | 11/1 | 68 | 28 |
| 142$^{5}$ | **Last But Not Least (60)** (RFJohnsonHoughton) **3-8-1** JQuinn(6) (prom tl rdn & wknd 2f out) | s.h | 5 | 7/1$^{3}$ | 50 | 10 |
| 182$^{6}$ | **Celandine (80)** (JLEyre) **3-9-7** RLappin(5) (a bhd) | 3 | 6 | 7/1$^{3}$ | 61 | 21 |
| 272* | **Gi La High (62)** (JBerry) **3-8-3** NCarlisle(3) (sn rdn along: in tch tl wknd 2f out) | 1¼ | 7 | 7/1$^{3}$ | 39 | — |

(SP 114.6%) **7 Rn**

**58.59 secs** (0.59) CSF £10.21 TOTE £2.00: £1.40 £2.50 (£13.60) OWNER Mr G. W. Byrne (NEWMARKET) BRED James William Mitchell and Simon Edward Mitchell

### 336 MERLIN (S) H'CAP (0-60) (II) (4-Y.O+) (Class F)

2-50 (2-50) **1m (Equitrack)** £2,250.30 (£630.80: £306.90) Stalls: High GOING minus 0.55 sec per fur (FST)

| Form | Horse / details | Dist | Pos | SP | RR | SF |
|---|---|---|---|---|---|---|
| 166$^{8}$ | **Lilac Rain (45)** (JRArnold) **4-9-3** JQuinn(2) (in tch: sn rdn along: led over 1f out: drvn out) | — | 1 | 7/1 | 53 | 25 |
| 201$^{2}$ | **Ladybower (IRE) (45)** (LordHuntingdon) **4-8-10**$^{(7)}$ JWilkinson(3) (lw: chsd ldr: led over 2f out: hdd over 1f out: unable qckn) | 1 | 2 | 3/1$^{1}$ | 51 | 23 |
| 166$^{7}$ | **Little Scarlett (48)** (PJMakin) **4-9-6** SSanders(4) (hld up: hdwy 2f out: rdn over 1f out: one pce) | 2½ | 3 | 8/1 | 49 | 21 |
| 301$^{4}$ | **Cabcharge Blue (52)** (TJNaughton) **4-9-10** JWeaver(5) (b.hind: lw: chsd ldrs: rdn over 2f out: one pce) | 2½ | 4 | 5/1$^{3}$ | 48 | 20 |
| 207$^{3}$ | **Serious Fact (43)** (SirMarkPrescott) **4-9-1** GDuffield(7) (chsd ldrs: rdn over 3f out: one pce fnl 2f) | ½ | 5 | 7/2$^{2}$ | 38 | 10 |
| 301* | **Pine Essence (USA) (45)** (JLEyre) **5-9-3** 5x TWilliams(1) (led: hdd over 2f out: sn wknd) | 2½ | 6 | 7/2$^{2}$ | 35 | 7 |
| 273$^{6}$ | **Prince Rudolf (IRE) (42)** (MrsNMacauley) **4-8-9v**$^{(5)}$ AmandaSanders(6) (dwlt: a bhd) | 15 | 7 | 14/1 | 2 | — |

(SP 116.4%) **7 Rn**

**1m 40.5** (3.10) CSF £27.05 CT £156.73 TOTE £14.00: £2.80 £1.60 (£20.70) OWNER Mr J. R. Arnold (UPPER LAMBOURN) BRED R. G. Percival

No bid

### 337 LYNN SPAULDING MEMORIAL MAIDEN STKS (4-Y.O+) (Class D)

3-25 (3-25) **1m (Equitrack)** £3,582.50 (£1,085.00: £530.00: £252.50) Stalls: High GOING minus 0.55 sec per fur (FST)

| Form | Horse / details | Dist | Pos | SP | RR | SF |
|---|---|---|---|---|---|---|
| 296$^{5}$ | **Errant (58)** (DJSCosgrove) **4-9-0** JQuinn(6) (a.p: chsd ldr over 3f out: rdn over 1f out: styd on ins fnl f to ld last stride) | — | 1 | 2/1$^{1}$ | 62 | 32 |
| | **French Ginger (58)** (RIngram) **5-8-9** WWoods(7) (bit bkwd: chsd ldr: led wl over 3f out: hrd rdn ins fnl f: ct last stride) | s.h | 2 | 2/1$^{1}$ | 57 | 27 |
| | **Dantean (47)** (RJO'Sullivan) **4-9-0** AClark(10) (hld up: pushed along over 4f out: hdwy over 3f out: kpt on one pce fnl 2f) | 4 | 3 | 16/1 | 54 | 24 |
| 172$^{5}$ | **By The Bay (44)** (CCElsey) **4-8-9** JWeaver(4) (hld up in rr: styd on fnl 3f: nvr plcd to chal) | 5 | 4 | 9/2$^{2}$ | 39+ | 9 |
| 274$^{7}$ | **Thorniwama (32)** (JJBridger) **5-8-4v$^{1}$**$^{(5)}$ ADaly(11) (chsd ldrs: rdn 5f out: wknd over 3f out) | 2½ | 5 | 40/1 | 34 | 4 |
| | **Black And Amber** (PRWebber) **4-8-9** NAdams(9) (w'like: plld hrd: chsd ldrs: rdn over 3f out: wknd over 2f out) | nk | 6 | 8/1$^{3}$ | 33 | 3 |
| 99$^{6}$ | **Showtime Blues (IRE)** (ABailey) **7-8-11**$^{(3)}$ DWright(3) (led: hdd wl over 3f out: sn wknd) | 2½ | 7 | 20/1 | 33 | 3 |
| 292$^{8}$ | **Taylors Revival** (HJCollingridge) **5-8-9** NCarlisle(1) (bhd fnl 4f) | 3½ | 8 | 33/1 | 21 | — |
| 204$^{11}$ | **Rizal (USA)** (DJGMurraySmith) **4-8-10**$^{(5)ow1}$ RPainter(5) (chsd ldrs to ½-wy) | 2 | 9 | 33/1 | 23 | — |
| | **The Substitute** (RCurtis) **4-8-9** GBardwell(2) (a bhd) | 15 | 10 | 40/1 | — | — |
| | **Sussex Gorse** (BAPearce) **5-8-11**$^{(3)}$ DRMcCabe(8) (bit bkwd: dwlt: a bhd) | 12 | 11 | 33/1 | — | — |

(SP 120.3%) **11 Rn**

**1m 39.55** (2.15) CSF £6.27 TOTE £3.70: £1.70 £2.00 £3.20 (£3.60) Trio £9.60 OWNER Mr Alex Gorrie (NEWMARKET) BRED Sheikh Mohammed bin Rashid al Maktoum

## 338 CHARLIE SPARROWHAWK H'CAP (0-90) (3-Y.O+) (Class C)

3-55 (3-55) **6f (Equitrack)** £5,329.70 (£1,613.60: £787.80: £374.90) Stalls: Low GOING minus 0.55 sec per fur (FST)

| Form | Horse / details | Dist | Pos | SP | RR | SF |
|---|---|---|---|---|---|---|
| 55* | **Chewit (90)** (AMoore) **4-10-0** CandyMorris(1) (hld up: hdwy 2f out: led 1f out: pushed out) | — | 1 | 6/4[1] | 94 | 54 |
| | **Loveyoumillions (IRE) (82)** (MJohnston) **4-9-6** JWeaver(2) (led 1f: styd prom: rdn over 1f out: r.o ins fnl f) | nk | 2 | 6/1 | 85 | 45 |
| 255* | **Berge (IRE) (76)** (WAO'Gorman) **5-9-0b** EmmaO'Gorman(6) (hld up: hdwy to chse ldr over 3f out: rdn & ev ch over 1f out: one pce) | ½ | 3 | 5/1[3] | 78 | 38 |
| 270[4] | **Patsy Grimes (66)** (JSMoore) **6-7-13v**(5) PPMurphy(7) (led after 1f: hdd 1f out: one pce) | ¾ | 4 | 8/1 | 66 | 26 |
| 266* | **Robo Magic (USA) (83)** (LMontagueHall) **4-9-7** SSanders(5) (chsd ldrs: rdn over 1f out: sn wknd) | 4 | 5 | 7/2[2] | 72 | 32 |
| | **Samsolom (78)** (PHowling) **8-9-2** JQuinn(3) (b.hind: bit bkwd: chsd ldrs tl wknd over 2f out) | 2½ | 6 | 20/1 | 61 | 21 |
| | **Stoppes Brow (87)** (GLMoore) **4-9-11b[1]** SWhitworth(4) (bit bkwd: sn pushed along: chsd ldrs tl wknd over 2f out) | 3½ | 7 | 16/1 | 60 | 20 |

(SP 114.9%) **7 Rn**

**1m 11.35** (0.75) CSF £10.42 TOTE £2.50: £1.10 £4.00 (£5.70) OWNER Ballard (1834) Ltd (BRIGHTON) BRED B. Minty

## 339 OSPREY H'CAP (0-75) (4-Y.O+) (Class D)

4-30 (4-32) **2m (Equitrack)** £3,550.00 (£1,075.00: £525.00: £250.00) Stalls: Low GOING minus 0.55 sec per fur (FST)

| Form | Horse / details | Dist | Pos | SP | RR | SF |
|---|---|---|---|---|---|---|
| 296[4] | **Jaraab (70)** (GLewis) **5-10-0v** SWhitworth(8) (lw: chsd ldrs: led 4f out: clr 3f out: easily) | — | 1 | 7/4[1] | 79 | 58 |
| 130[2] | **Coleridge (57)** (JJSheehan) **8-9-1b** JQuinn(7) (reluctant to r: s.s: hdwy 5f out: chsd wnr over 1f out: one pce) | 2½ | 2 | 11/1 | 64 | 43 |
| 283[2] | **Yougo (72)** (MJohnston) **4-9-10** JWeaver(2) (lw: led 1f: styd prom: n.m.r over 3f out tl over 2f out: kpt on one pce fnl 2f) | 2½ | 3 | 9/2[2] | 76 | 49 |
| 165[3] | **Wild Strawberry (65)** (MissBSanders) **7-9-9** SSanders(3) (mid div: pushed along 5f out: hdwy to chse wnr over 3f out tl over 1f out: one pce) | 1½ | 4 | 8/1[3] | 68 | 47 |
| 97[4] | **Anjou (67)** (JPearce) **4-9-5** GBardwell(6) (chsd ldrs: rdn 5f out: wknd 3f out) | 9 | 5 | 10/1 | 61 | 34 |
| 265[2] | **Ikhtiraa (USA) (62)** (RJO'Sullivan) **6-9-1b**(5) DGriffiths(10) (led after 1f: hdd 4f out: grad wknd) | 3½ | 6 | 10/1 | 52 | 31 |
| 260[2] | **Guest Alliance (IRE) (54)** (AMoore) **4-8-6** CandyMorris(9) (b.hind: mid div: rdn 6f out: wknd 4f out) | 5 | 7 | 16/1 | 39 | 12 |
| 265* | **Sir Thomas Beecham (57)** (SDow) **6-8-10**(5) ADaly(1) (prom tl wknd over 3f out) | 2½ | 8 | 11/1 | 40 | 19 |
| 268[2] | **Kymin (IRE) (64)** (DJGMurraySmith) **4-9-2** MLarsen(4) (b.hind: lw: mid div: rdn 6f out: sn btn) | 11 | 9 | 20/1 | 36 | 9 |
| | **Peep O Day (41)** (JLEyre) **5-7-13** NAdams(5) (a bhd) | 15 | 10 | 33/1 | — | — |

(SP 114.1%) **10 Rn**

**3m 23.35** (1.35) CSF £19.20 CT £67.67 TOTE £2.90: £1.90 £2.30 £1.80 (£26.50) Trio £53.80 OWNER Mr S. I. Ross (EPSOM) BRED Shadwell Estate Company Limited

WEIGHT FOR AGE 4yo-6lb

## 340 HARRIER LIMITED STKS (0-65) (3-Y.O+) (Class F)

5-00 (5-01) **7f (Equitrack)** £2,540.80 (£713.80: £348.40) Stalls: Low GOING minus 0.55 sec per fur (FST)

| Form | Horse / details | Dist | Pos | SP | RR | SF |
|---|---|---|---|---|---|---|
| 259* | **Super Benz (70)** (JLEyre) **10-9-12** RLappin(6) (b: chsd ldrs: sn pushed along: rdn to ld over 1f out: r.o wl) | — | 1 | 85/40[2] | 76 | 55 |
| | **Mask Flower (USA) (65)** (MJohnston) **3-8-2** TWilliams(2) (w ldr: led 3f out: hdd over 1f out: unable qckn) | 2 | 2 | 7/4[1] | 65 | 26 |
| 273[4] | **Apollo Red (53)** (AMoore) **7-9-8** CandyMorris(7) (b.hind: a.p: ev ch 2f out: rdn over 1f out: one pce) | 2½ | 3 | 16/1 | 62 | 41 |
| 317* | **Foreman (54)** (WAO'Gorman) **3-8-7** 2x EmmaO'Gorman(4) (lw: hld up: hdwy 3f out: rdn over 1f out: one pce) | 5 | 4 | 5/1[3] | 53 | 14 |
| | **Dance King (58)** (RHarris) **4-9-8** VSmith(1) (a bhd) | 2 | 5 | 20/1 | 46 | 25 |
| 291[3] | **Maid Welcome (55)** (MrsNMacauley) **9-8-12v**(5) AmandaSanders(5) (b.hind: led: hdd 3f out: wknd over 2f out) | nk | 6 | 11/2 | 40 | 19 |
| 293[6] | **Vera's First (IRE) (57)** (GLewis) **3-7-13**(3) AWhelan(3) (bhd fnl 5f) | 5 | 7 | 12/1 | 32 | — |

(SP 118.8%) **7 Rn**

**1m 24.72** (0.72) CSF £6.38 TOTE £2.90: £1.90 £1.80 (£2.90) OWNER Whitestonecliffe Racing Partnership (HAMBLETON) BRED Scarteen Stud

WEIGHT FOR AGE 3yo-17lb

T/Plpt: £200.20 (50.57 Tckts). T/Qdpt: £9.00 (92.53 Tckts). SM

# 0328-SOUTHWELL (L-H) (Standard)

## Monday February 26th

WEATHER: sunny periods WIND: slt half bhd

## 341 CAUCASUS AMATEUR H'CAP (0-60) (I) (4-Y.O+) (Class F)

1-20 (1-21) **7f (Fibresand)** £2,048.00 (£573.00: £278.00) Stalls: Low GOING minus 0.36 sec per fur (FST)

| Form | Horse / details | Dist | Pos | SP | RR | SF |
|---|---|---|---|---|---|---|
| 212[4] | **Desert Invader (IRE) (57)** (DWChapman) **5-11-5** MissRClark(5) (a cl up: led wl over 1f out: hung lft: r.o wl) | — | 1 | 7/1[3] | 67 | 45 |
| 219[10] | **Love Legend (44)** (DWPArbuthnot) **11-10-6** MrsDArbuthnot(7) (b: a.p: rdn over 2f out: styd on: nt pce to chal) | 5 | 2 | 9/1 | 43 | 21 |
| 301[6] | **Karinska (59)** (MCChapman) **6-11-3**(4) MrMMackley(2) (lw: s.i.s: wnt prom ½-wy: kpt on towards fin) | 1¼ | 3 | 9/2[1] | 55 | 33 |
| | **Sporting Risk (48)** (PRWebber) **4-10-6**(4) MrPScott(1) (a chsng ldrs: one pce fnl 2f) | 1¼ | 4 | 7/1[3] | 41 | 19 |
| 219[4] | **Dream Carrier (IRE) (49)** (REPeacock) **8-10-4**(7) MrsCPeacock(6) (bhd: c wd appr st: styd on towards fin) | nk | 5 | 6/1[2] | 41 | 19 |
| 259[8] | **Blyton Star (IRE) (27)** (MissJFCraze) **8-8-10**(7) MrWWenyon(4) (led tl hdd wl over 1f out: hung rt & grad wknd) | 1¼ | 6 | 25/1 | 16 | — |
| | **My Handy Man (55)** (RAllan) **5-10-13**(4) MrARobson(11) (s.i.s: nvr rchd ldrs) | ¾ | 7 | 10/1 | 43 | 21 |
| | **Langtonian (46)** (JLEyre) **7-10-8v** MissDianaJones(9) (b.nr hind: s.i.s: nvr rchd ldrs) | 1½ | 8 | 7/1[3] | 30 | 8 |
| 257[6] | **Flashfeet (55)** (KBishop) **6-10-13**(4) MissAPurdy(10) (sn bhd) | 1½ | 9 | 10/1 | 36 | 14 |
| 219[12] | **Breezed Well (36)** (BRCambidge) **10-9-8**(4)ow2 MrsHNoonan(8) (outpcd fr ½-wy) | 10 | 10 | 50/1 | — | — |
| | **Highspeed (IRE) (49)** (SEKettlewell) **4-10-11** MrsDKettlewell(3) (prom tl wknd fnl 2f) | ½ | 11 | 10/1 | 6 | — |

(SP 113.0%) **11 Rn**

**1m 31.7** (4.90) CSF £59.17 CT £287.26 TOTE £5.40: £2.50 £2.60 £1.40 (£27.60) Trio £37.00 OWNER Mr Michael Hill (YORK) BRED Gainsborough Stud Management Ltd

## 342 APENNINES (S) H'CAP (0-60) (I) (3-Y.O+) (Class F)

1-50 (1-50) **6f (Fibresand)** £2,048.00 (£573.00: £278.00) Stalls: Low GOING minus 0.36 sec per fur (FST)

| Form | Horse and details | Dist | Pos | SP | RR | SF |
|---|---|---|---|---|---|---|
| $330^{3}$ | **Bold Aristocrat (IRE) (50)** (RHollinshead) **5-9-0**(7) FLynch(11) (lw: hld up & bhd: hdwy 2f out: str run to ld cl home) | — | 1 | 2/1 [1] | 52 | 20 |
| $59^{3}$ | **Brookhead Lady (53)** (PDEvans) **5-9-10** SSanders(7) (b: chsd ldrs: chal over 1f out: led wl ins fnl f: hdd & no ex nr fin) | nk | 2 | 3/1 [2] | 54 | 22 |
| $49^{7}$ | **Niteowl Raider (IRE) (53)** (JAHarris) **3-8-9** JO'Reilly(6) (led tl hdd wl ins fnl f) | nk | 3 | 13/2 [3] | 54 | 6 |
| $127^{10}$ | **Chloella (32)** (CBBBooth) **4-8-3** NKennedy(5) (chsd ldrs: one pce appr fnl f) | 2½ | 4 | 20/1 | 26 | — |
| | **Flamboro (46)** (JDBethell) **4-9-3** JFortune(8) (a chsng ldrs: sn drvn along: no hdwy fnl 2f) | ¾ | 5 | 10/1 | 38 | 6 |
| $212^{3}$ | **La Dama (USA) (45)** (ABMulholland) **4-9-2** MMcAndrew(9) (sn outpcd: styd on fnl 2f: n.d) | 5 | 6 | 13/2 [3] | 23 | — |
| $259^{9}$ | **Double Glow (25)** (NBycroft) **4-7-10** ClaireBalding(3) (b.hind: cl up tl grad wknd fnl 2f) | ¾ | 7 | 20/1 | 1 | — |
| | **Secret Miss (48)** (APJones) **4-9-5** JQuinn(4) (in tch tl outpcd fnl 2½f) | ¾ | 8 | 12/1 | 22 | — |
| $295^{6}$ | **Joyful Times (35)** (MrsNMacauley) **4-8-1**(5) AmandaSanders(1) (s.i.s: n.d) | 2½ | 9 | 16/1 | 3 | — |
| $273^{7}$ | **Ezekiel (25)** (TTClement) **5-7-10** GBardwell(2) (drvn along thrght: bhd fnl 3f) | 5 | 10 | 50/1 | — | — |
| | **High Romance (40)** (JSWainwright) **6-8-8**(3) DRMcCabe(10) (p.u lame over 4f out: dead) | | P | 25/1 | — | — |

(SP 123.0%) **11 Rn**

**1m 17.7** (4.20) CSF £8.53 CT £31.62 TOTE £3.20: £1.10 £1.50 £1.80 (£4.60) Trio £17.30 OWNER Mrs J. Hughes (UPPER LONGDON) BRED Scarteen Stud

LONG HANDICAP Ezekiel 7-7

WEIGHT FOR AGE 3yo-15lb

No bid

## 343 CAUCASUS AMATEUR H'CAP (0-60) (II) (4-Y.O+) (Class F)

2-20 (2-20) **7f (Fibresand)** £2,048.00 (£573.00: £278.00) Stalls: Low GOING minus 0.36 sec per fur (FST)

| Form | Horse and details | Dist | Pos | SP | RR | SF |
|---|---|---|---|---|---|---|
| $291^{2}$ | **My Gallery (IRE) (58)** (ABailey) **5-11-3**(4) MissBridgetGatehouse(5) (hdwy 3f out: led over 1f out: r.o wl) | — | 1 | 2/1 [1] | 64 | 46 |
| $302^{2}$ | **Awesome Venture (56)** (MCChapman) **6-11-1**(4) MrMMackley(4) (lw: cl up: rdn to ld 1½f out: sn hdd: one pce) | 3 | 2 | 4/1 [2] | 55 | 37 |
| $239^{7}$ | **Komiamaite (51)** (SRBowring) **4-10-10b**(4) MrsMMorris(8) (bhd: hdwy 2f out: hung lft: nrst fin) | 2 | 3 | 5/1 [3] | 46 | 28 |
| $190^{10}$ | **Magic Leader (IRE) (29)** (TTClement) **4-9-2**(4) MrVLukaniuk(6) (b: bhd tl styd on fnl 2f) | 2½ | 4 | 50/1 | 18 | — |
| $253^{4}$ | **Green's Bid (40)** (DWChapman) **6-10-3** MissRClark(1) (chsd ldrs: disp ld 2½f out tl over 1f out: wknd) | nk | 5 | 7/1 | 28 | 10 |
| $253^{9}$ | **Margaretrose Anna (49)** (EJAlston) **4-10-12** MissDianaJones(7) (mde most tl hdd & wknd 1½f out) | ½ | 6 | 10/1 | 36 | 18 |
| $219^{7}$ | **Jon's Choice (39)** (BPreece) **8-9-9**(7) MissLBoswell(3) (lw: in tch: no imp fnl 3f) | 1¾ | 7 | 10/1 | 22 | 4 |
| $301^{12}$ | **Moody (51)** (MissGayKelleway) **4-10-10b**[1](4) MissSKelleway(9) (chsd ldrs: rdn 3f out: sn wknd) | 2½ | 8 | 8/1 | 28 | 10 |
| $260^{7}$ | **Lady Woodstock (29)** (MissAEEmbiricos) **4-8-13b**(7) MrCJMcEntee(2) (s.i.s: a bhd) | 8 | 9 | 50/1 | — | — |
| | **Shu Fly (NZ) (50)** (HJOliver) **12-10-9**(4) MrNHOliver(10) (s.i.s: a wl bhd) | 2½ | 10 | 20/1 | 3 | — |

(SP 120.5%) **10 Rn**

**1m 31.7** (4.90) CSF £10.39 CT £32.02 TOTE £3.40: £1.10 £2.20 £1.70 (£6.60) Trio £6.20 OWNER Mr Robert Cox (TARPORLEY) BRED East Riding Sack and Paper Co

STEWARDS' ENQUIRY Mackley susp. 6-8/3/96 (excessive use of whip).

## 344 ROCKY CLAIMING STKS (3-Y.O) (Class F)

2-50 (2-52) **1m (Fibresand)** £2,398.00 (£673.00: £328.00) Stalls: Low GOING minus 0.36 sec per fur (FST)

| Form | Horse and details | Dist | Pos | SP | RR | SF |
|---|---|---|---|---|---|---|
| 300* | **Bit of Bother (IRE) (59)** (TDBarron) **3-8-13** JFortune(6) (chsd ldrs: led 1½f out: rdn & styd on wl) | — | 1 | 13/8 [1] | 64 | 15 |
| $242^{3}$ | **Society Girl (61)** (CWThornton) **3-8-10** DeanMcKeown(9) (b.nr hind: w ldr: led over 2f out tl 1½f out: no ex) | 2½ | 2 | 10/1 | 56 | 7 |
| $332^{2}$ | **Efipetite (51)** (NBycroft) **3-8-2** GBardwell(7) (hld up: nt clr run & swtchd 2f out: styd on: nvr able to chal) | nk | 3 | 11/2 [3] | 47 | — |
| $209^{4}$ | **Quinntessa (40)** (BPalling) **3-8-3**(3)ow6 SDrowne(12) (a chsng ldrs: one pce fnl 2f) | 2½ | 4 | 20/1 | 46 | — |
| $329^{5}$ | **Arch Angel (IRE) (54)** (DJSffrenchDavis) **3-7-12v** NAdams(8) (mde most tl hdd over 2f out: one pce) | nk | 5 | 5/1 [2] | 38 | — |
| $262^{4}$ | **Apartments Abroad (47)** (KMcAuliffe) **3-8-4** JTate(3) (b.hind: effrt over 3f out: styd on: no imp) | ¾ | 6 | 16/1 | 42 | — |
| $280^{11}$ | **Down The Yard (38)** (MCChapman) **3-7-9**(7) CMunday(13) (hld up: effrt 3f out: no imp) | 1¼ | 7 | 25/1 | 38 | — |
| $313^{6}$ | **Oriel Lad (72)** (PDEvans) **3-9-1b** SSanders(10) (a.p: effrt 3f out: wknd fnl 2f) | 3½ | 8 | 9/1 | 44 | — |
| $300^{5}$ | **Scenicris (IRE) (50)** (RHollinshead) **3-8-0** NCarlisle(5) (s.i.s: effrt ½-wy: n.d) | 5 | 9 | 10/1 | 19 | — |
| $183^{8}$ | **The Fullbangladesh (48)** (JLEyre) **3-8-4** RLappin(2) (lw: spd over 3f: sn bhd) | 1½ | 10 | 12/1 | 20 | — |
| | **King of Peace (IRE)** (MWEasterby) **3-9-5** LCharnock(1) (cl up tl wknd fnl 2½f) | ¾ | 11 | 14/1 | 33 | — |
| | **Blondane** (SRBowring) **3-8-2**(5) CTeague(11) (bit bkwd: s.i.s: rn green & a bhd) | 5 | 12 | 7/1 | 11 | — |
| | **Topanoora Bay (IRE)** (MrsVAAconley) **3-8-0**(7) FLynch(4) (unf: s.i.s: sn chsng ldrs: wknd qckly ½-wy: t.o) | dist | 13 | 33/1 | — | — |

(SP 142.6%) **13 Rn**

**1m 45.5** (5.50) CSF £21.93 TOTE £2.50: £1.30 £2.40 £3.20 (£9.30) Trio £17.10 OWNER Mr J. Baggott (THIRSK) BRED Lar Dempsey

## 345 ALPS H'CAP (0-70) (3-Y.O+) (Class E)

3-20 (3-21) **1m (Fibresand)** £2,982.00 (£903.00: £441.00: £210.00) Stalls: Low GOING minus 0.36 sec per fur (FST)

| Form | Horse and details | Dist | Pos | SP | RR | SF |
|---|---|---|---|---|---|---|
| $199^{5}$ | **Twin Creeks (52)** (MDHammond) **5-8-10** RCochrane(7) (lw: trckd ldr: brought wd st: led 1f out: r.o) | — | 1 | 4/1 [2] | 60 | 32 |
| $210^{2}$ | **Calder King (68)** (JLEyre) **5-9-12v** RLappin(2) (sn pushed along: hdwy 3f out: styd on wl towards fin) | 2½ | 2 | 11/2 [3] | 71 | 43 |
| 239* | **Sea Spouse (58)** (MBlanshard) **5-9-2** NAdams(4) (lw: led tl hdd 1f out: no ex u.p) | 1¼ | 3 | 7/2 [1] | 59 | 31 |
| $301^{3}$ | **Q Factor (63)** (DHaydnJones) **4-9-7** JFortune(1) (lw: hld up & bhd: effrt 3f out: sn chsng ldrs: nt qckn fnl f) | 2 | 4 | 4/1 [2] | 60 | 32 |
| | **Domino Flyer (57)** (MrsASwinbank) **3-7-10** GBardwell(5) (prom: effrt ½-wy: no imp) | 8 | 5 | 16/1 | 38 | — |
| | **Tilly Owl (43)** (JAHarris) **5-8-1** JO'Reilly(8) (in tch: outpcd 3f out: n.d after) | 2 | 6 | 14/1 | 20 | — |
| $257^{2}$ | **Square Deal (FR) (70)** (SRBowring) **5-9-9**(5) CTeague(9) (hld up: effrt on ins whn hmpd 4f out & 3f out: n.d) | 2½ | 7 | 4/1 [2] | 42 | 14 |
| | **Swandale Flyer (42)** (NBycroft) **4-8-0** JQuinn(6) (chsd ldr 5f: sn wknd) | 1 | 8 | 50/1 | 12 | — |
| $297^{9}$ | **Pinkerton Polka (45)** (CEBrittain) **4-8-0b**[1](3) DRMcCabe(3) (chsd ldrs to ½-wy: sn btn) | 11 | 9 | 9/1 | — | — |

(SP 122.1%) **9 Rn**

**1m 43.4** (3.40) CSF £25.66 CT £78.45 TOTE £3.70: £1.80 £2.70 £2.00 (£16.30) Trio £15.90 OWNER The Armchair Jockeys-Four Seasons Racing (MIDDLEHAM) BRED Crest Stud Ltd

LONG HANDICAP Domino Flyer 7-5

WEIGHT FOR AGE 3yo-19lb

STEWARDS' ENQUIRY Lappin susp. 6 & 9/3/96 (careless riding).

## 346 SIERRA MADRE MEDIAN AUCTION MAIDEN STKS (3,4,5 & 6-Y.O) (Class E)

3-50 (3-50) **1m 4f (Fibresand)** £2,900.10 (£877.80: £428.40: £203.70) Stalls: Low GOING minus 0.36 sec per fur (FST)

| | | | | SP | RR | SF |
|---|---|---|---|---|---|---|
| 197[2] | **Oversman (68)** (JGFitzGerald) **3-8-3** TWilliams(6) (lw: trckd ldrs: led wl over 2f out: shkn up & sn clr) | — | **1** | 15/8[1] | 52+ | — |
| | **Los Alamos (65)** (CWThornton) **3-7-12** LCharnock(7) (w ldr: effrt 3f out: nt qckn) | 6 | **2** | 7/2[3] | 39 | — |
| 241[2] | **Meltemison** (CEBrittain) **3-8-0**(3) DRMcCabe(8) (led tl hdd wl over 2f out: one pce) | 1¼ | **3** | 2/1[2] | 42 | — |
| 254[6] | **Tap On Tootsie (38)** (TRWall) **4-9-5** NAdams(1) (lw: chsd ldrs: pushed along 7f out: wl outpcd fnl 4f) | 8 | **4** | 33/1 | 51 | — |
| 221[3] | **Selmeston (IRE) (32)** (PSFelgate) **4-9-10** TIves(3) (bhd: sme hdwy 4f out: n.d) | 3 | **5** | 20/1 | 52 | — |
| 239[2] | **Nautical Jewel (54)** (MDIUsher) **4-9-10** RCochrane(5) (lw: hung rt most of wy: sn bhd) | 1¼ | **6** | 8/1 | 50 | — |
| | **Bowland Park** (EJAlston) **5-9-8** SDWilliams(2) (a bhd: t.o) | dist | **7** | 33/1 | — | — |
| | **Meadow Foods** (MWEasterby) **4-9-10** MBirch(4) (chsd ldrs after 2f tl p.u lame over 4f out: dead) | | **P** | 33/1 | — | — |
| | | | | (SP 115.0%) | **8 Rn** | |

**2m 42.9** (10.40) CSF £8.53 TOTE £2.90: £2.40 £1.10 £1.40 (£3.60) OWNER Marquesa de Moratalla (MALTON) BRED Addison Racing and Peter V. McCalmont
WEIGHT FOR AGE 3yo-24lb, 4yo-3lb

## 347 APENNINES (S) H'CAP (0-60) (II) (3-Y.O+) (Class F)

4-20 (4-22) **6f (Fibresand)** £2,048.00 (£573.00: £278.00) Stalls: Low GOING minus 0.36 sec per fur (FST)

| | | | | SP | RR | SF |
|---|---|---|---|---|---|---|
| 245[5] | **Miss Offset (45)** (MJohnston) **3-7-13b** TWilliams(9) (mde most: rdn clr over 2f out: styd on wl) | — | **1** | 6/1[3] | 57 | 10 |
| 259[6] | **Dissentor (IRE) (50)** (JAGlover) **4-9-5v** GCarter(8) (a chsng ldrs: drvn along 3f out: r.o one pce) | 5 | **2** | 9/4[1] | 48 | 17 |
| 201[3] | **Palacegate Gold (IRE) (32)** (RJHodges) **7-7-10**(5)ow1 ADaly(10) (outpcd over 3f out: styd on u.p fnl 2f: n.d) | 2 | **3** | 8/1 | 24 | — |
| 126[10] | **Le Bal (34)** (MissJFCraze) **4-8-3** DaleGibson(2) (bhd: hdwy over 2f out: nvr rchd ldrs) | 1¼ | **4** | 14/1 | 23 | — |
| 203[10] | **Fiery Footsteps (42)** (SWCampion) **4-8-11** SDWilliams(7) (chsd ldrs tl outpcd fnl 2½f) | hd | **5** | 9/1 | 31 | — |
| | **Young Ben (IRE) (37)** (JSWainwright) **4-8-6** DeanMcKeown(4) (sn outpcd & bhd: sme hdwy 2f out: n.d) | ½ | **6** | 20/1 | 24 | — |
| 126[12] | **Rupert's Princess (IRE) (47)** (MJHeaton-Ellis) **4-8-13b**(3) SDrowne(1) (lw: outpcd & bhd: sme hdwy 2f out: n.d) | s.h | **7** | 10/1 | 34 | 3 |
| 330[2] | **At the Savoy (IRE) (59)** (TDBarron) **5-9-7**(7) KimberleyHart(3) (effrt 3f out: nvr rchd ldrs) | 2½ | **8** | 4/1[2] | 40 | 9 |
| 59[10] | **Caherass Court (IRE) (36)** (BPreece) **5-7-12**(7)ow4 FLynch(6) (outpcd & bhd: sme hdwy 3f out: sn btn) | ¾ | **9** | 33/1 | 15 | — |
| 221[9] | **Mister (48)** (KMcAuliffe) **4-9-3** JFortune(11) (lw: prom: hdwy u.p 3f out: wknd wl over 1f out) | 2½ | **10** | 20/1 | 20 | — |
| 225[7] | **First Option (50)** (RBastiman) **6-9-0**(5) HBastiman(5) (w wnr after 1f: wknd qckly over 2f out) | 9 | **11** | 16/1 | — | — |
| | | | | (SP 120.3%) | **11 Rn** | |

**1m 16.9** (3.40) CSF £19.15 CT £97.94 TOTE £6.40: £2.50 £1.10 £2.40 (£9.70) Trio £32.20 OWNER Hertford Offset Ltd (MIDDLEHAM) BRED J. Coombes and E. Henshaw
WEIGHT FOR AGE 3yo-15lb
No bid

## 348 PYRENEES H'CAP (0-70) (3-Y.O) (Class E)

4-50 (4-50) **1m 3f (Fibresand)** £2,859.15 (£865.20: £422.10: £200.55) Stalls: Low GOING minus 0.36 sec per fur (FST)

| | | | | SP | RR | SF |
|---|---|---|---|---|---|---|
| 123[6] | **Dirab (59)** (TDBarron) **3-8-11** JFortune(7) (in tch: effrt over 2f out: led 1f out: hrd rdn & hld on wl) | — | **1** | 13/8[1] | 63 | 23 |
| 329[2] | **Dancing Cavalier (65)** (RHollinshead) **3-8-10**(7) FLynch(2) (lw: sn wl bhd: hdwy 3f out: chal over 1f out: nt qckn towards fin) | nk | **2** | 11/4[2] | 69 | 29 |
| 197* | **Balios (IRE) (69)** (MJohnston) **3-9-7** TWilliams(9) (led tl hdd & outpcd 1f out) | 4 | **3** | 9/2[3] | 67 | 27 |
| | **Contract Bridge (IRE) (44)** (CWThornton) **3-7-10** LCharnock(8) (chsd ldrs: effrt 3f out: one pce fnl 2f) | 9 | **4** | 14/1 | 29 | — |
| 280[6] | **Onefourseven (44)** (SRBowring) **3-7-10b** NCarlisle(6) (cl up: rdn over 2f out: sn btn) | 7 | **5** | 25/1 | 19 | — |
| 281[3] | **Mooncusser (54)** (JGFitzGerald) **3-8-6be** DeanMcKeown(5) (lw: chsd ldrs tl outpcd fnl 2½f) | 13 | **6** | 11/1 | 10 | — |
| | **Influence Pedler (50)** (CEBrittain) **3-7-13**(3) DRMcCabe(3) (swtg: chsd ldrs tl outpcd fnl 4f) | 4 | **7** | 20/1 | — | — |
| 280[2] | **Suparoy (50)** (TGMills) **3-8-2** JQuinn(4) (b.nr fore: in tch tl wknd 3f out) | 5 | **8** | 6/1 | — | — |
| 56[7] | **Belle's Boy (63)** (BPalling) **3-9-1** GCarter(1) (lw: a bhd) | 8 | **9** | 16/1 | — | — |
| | | | | (SP 126.7%) | **9 Rn** | |

**2m 26.4** (6.40) CSF £7.11 CT £16.66 TOTE £2.90: £1.40 £1.40 £2.50 (£3.00) Trio £7.70 OWNER Mr Alex Gorrie (THIRSK) BRED Nawara Stud Co Ltd
LONG HANDICAP Onefourseven 7-7 Contract Bridge (IRE) 7-6
STEWARDS' ENQUIRY Fortune susp. 6, 9, 14-16 & 18/3/96 (excessive & improper use of whip).

T/Jkpt: £7,100.00 (0.1 Tckts); £8,510.04 to Catterick 27/2/96. T/Plpt: £5.70 (2,362.99 Tckts). T/Qdpt: £2.60 (674.5 Tckts). AA

# 0334-LINGFIELD (L-H) (Standard)

## Tuesday February 27th

WEATHER: fine WIND: almost nil

## 349 MARCO POLO APPRENTICE H'CAP (0-70) (4-Y.O+) (Class F)

2-00 (2-00) **1m 4f (Equitrack)** £2,459.00 (£699.00: £347.00) Stalls: Low GOING minus 0.49 sec per fur (FST)

| | | | | SP | RR | SF |
|---|---|---|---|---|---|---|
| 296[3] | **One Off the Rail (USA) (68)** (AMoore) **6-9-9**(5) TField(8) (b.hind: w ldr: led 7f out: r.o wl) | — | **1** | 9/2[3] | 76 | 49 |
| 275[2] | **Heighth of Fame (51)** (AJWilson) **5-8-11** GFaulkner(4) (led 5f: rdn over 2f out: r.o ins fnl f) | 1 | **2** | 10/1 | 58 | 31 |
| 309* | **Colosse (42)** (JLEyre) **4-7-13** 5x DDenby(7) (hdwy over 3f out: rdn over 2f out: r.o ins fnl f) | 1¼ | **3** | 4/1[2] | 47 | 17 |
| 284* | **Greenwich Again (65)** (TGMills) **4-9-1**(7) JConnally(2) (hld up: rdn over 3f out: unable qckn) | 8 | **4** | 3/1[1] | 59 | 29 |
| 309[2] | **Real Madrid (43)** (GPEnright) **5-8-3v** OliverCasey(3) (lw: rdn over 4f out: no hdwy fnl 3f) | s.h | **5** | 5/1 | 37 | 10 |
| 309[5] | **Carrolls Marc (IRE) (49)** (CMurray) **8-8-4**(5) RMullen(1) (b.hind: nvr nr to chal) | 5 | **6** | 8/1 | 37 | 10 |
| 274[2] | **Tondres (USA) (59)** (RIngram) **5-9-5** TAshley(6) (b: a bhd) | s.h | **7** | 7/1 | 47 | 20 |
| | **Script (46)** (JRJenkins) **5-7-13**(7)ow9 SallyWall(5) (bhd fnl 4f) | 9 | **8** | 66/1 | 22 | — |
| | | | | (SP 114.0%) | **8 Rn** | |

**2m 33.53** (3.53) CSF £41.60 CT £174.01 TOTE £5.20: £1.10 £2.40 £2.40 (£20.20) OWNER Mr K. Higson (BRIGHTON) BRED Parrish Hill Farm
WEIGHT FOR AGE 4yo-3lb

## 350 COLUMBUS CLAIMING STKS (4-Y.O+) (Class F)

2-30 (2-30) **7f (Equitrack)** £2,540.80 (£713.80: £348.40) Stalls: Low GOING minus 0.49 sec per fur (FST)

| | Horse | Dist | Pos | SP | RR | SF |
|---|---|---|---|---|---|---|
| $305^{3}$ | **Masnun (USA) (65)** (RJO'Sullivan) **11-8-8** AClark(4) (hdwy 4f out: rdn over 3f out: nt clr run & swtchd rt over 1f out: str run fnl f: led nr fin) | — | **1** | $7/2^{2}$ | 60 | 31 |
| $174^{3}$ | **Mr Nevermind (IRE) (76)** (GLMoore) **6-9-4** SWhitworth(6) (hdwy 4f out: chsd ldr over 3f out: led ins fnl f: hdd nr fin) | 1½ | **2** | $11/10^{1}$ | 67 | 38 |
| $317^{5}$ | **Star Talent (USA) (72)** (MissGayKelleway) **5-9-0** RCochrane(1) (b.hind: hdwy over 3f out: led 1f out to ins fnl f: one pce) | ½ | **3** | 7/1 | 61 | 32 |
| $263^{6}$ | **Orange Place (IRE) (75)** (TJNaughton) **5-9-4** JFortune(2) (b: lw: led to 1f out: one pce) | 2 | **4** | 10/1 | 61 | 32 |
| $311^{3}$ | **Milos (71)** (TJNaughton) **5-8-9**(7) TAshley(7) (b.hind: outpcd) | 3 | **5** | $4/1^{3}$ | 52 | 23 |
| | **Rustic League (IRE) (33)** (AJWilson) **5-8-2** JQuinn(3) (chsd ldr over 3f: t.o) | dist | **6** | 66/1 | — | — |

(SP 112.9%) **6 Rn**

**1m 25.77** (1.77) CSF £7.57 TOTE £3.40: £1.60 £1.30 (£3.10) OWNER Mr I. W. Page (WHITCOMBE) BRED Glencrest Farm

## 351 VASCO DA GAMA MAIDEN STKS (3-Y.O+) (Class D)

3-00 (3-01) **1m 2f (Equitrack)** £3,566.25 (£1,080.00: £527.50: £251.25) Stalls: Low GOING minus 0.49 sec per fur (FST)

| | Horse | Dist | Pos | SP | RR | SF |
|---|---|---|---|---|---|---|
| $228^{3}$ | **Burnt Offering (60)** (CEBrittain) **3-8-3** MLarsen(7) (dwlt: rdn 9f out: hdwy over 7f out: chsd ldr over 3f out: hung lft & led over 1f out: r.o wl) | — | **1** | $4/5^{1}$ | 59 | 10 |
| $318^{4}$ | **Zuno Flyer (USA) (40)** (AMoore) **4-9-3v**(7) FLynch(5) (b: b.hind: hld up: chsd ldr over 5f out to over 3f out: r.o one pce fnl f) | 4 | **2** | 10/1 | 54 | 25 |
| $320^{6}$ | **Jebi (USA)** (CMurray) **6-9-11** MTebbutt(1) (hld up: rdn over 6f out: r.o one pce fnl 2f) | 2 | **3** | 10/1 | 49 | 22 |
| $245^{8}$ | **Lord Ellangowan (IRE) (43)** (RIngram) **3-8-4**ow1 WWoods(4) (rdn over 7f out: no hdwy fnl 3f) | 1¼ | **4** | $6/1^{3}$ | 48 | — |
| | **Esta Maria (IRE)** (PaulSmith,Belgium) **3-7-12** JQuinn(6) (neat: bit bkwd: s.s: wl bhd 7f: nvr nrr) | hd | **5** | 10/1 | 42 | — |
| $254^{7}$ | **Ganador (44)** (BSmart) **4-9-5** RCochrane(3) (chsd ldr: led 6f out to over 1f out: wknd qckly fnl f) | 1¼ | **6** | $9/2^{2}$ | 41 | 12 |
| | **Gabriel's Lady (36)** (HGRowsell) **5-9-6** DeanMcKeown(2) (led 4f: t.o) | dist | **7** | 40/1 | — | — |

(SP 117.7%) **7 Rn**

**2m 9.3** (5.00) CSF £9.41 TOTE £1.40: £1.30 £3.80 (£4.20) OWNER Mr A. J. Richards (NEWMARKET) BRED Alan Gibson

WEIGHT FOR AGE 3yo-22lb, 4yo-1lb

## 352 LIVINGSTONE H'CAP (0-80) (3-Y.O) (Class D)

3-30 (3-30) **1m (Equitrack)** £3,420.00 (£1,035.00: £505.00: £240.00) Stalls: High GOING minus 0.49 sec per fur (FST)

| | Horse | Dist | Pos | SP | RR | SF |
|---|---|---|---|---|---|---|
| $321^{2}$ | **Carmarthen Bay (77)** (GLMoore) **3-9-2**(3) AWhelan(4) (lw: chsd ldr 7f out: led over 1f out: rdn out) | — | **1** | $3/1^{2}$ | 80 | 14 |
| 232* | **Blue Flyer (IRE) (79)** (RIngram) **3-9-7** WWoods(2) (led over 6f: unable qckn) | 3 | **2** | $6/4^{1}$ | 76 | 10 |
| $304^{3}$ | **Lancashire Legend (68)** (SDow) **3-8-10** RCochrane(3) (lw: plld hrd: hld up: rdn over 1f out: one pce) | ¾ | **3** | 5/1 | 64 | — |
| $232^{5}$ | **Accountancy Jewel (IRE) (69)** (KMcAuliffe) **3-8-11** JFortune(1) (b.hind: chsd ldr 1f: wknd 2f out) | 7 | **4** | $7/2^{3}$ | 51 | — |

(SP 103.9%) **4 Rn**

**1m 42.32** (4.92) CSF £7.01 TOTE £3.90: (£2.40) OWNER Mr D. R. W. Jones (EPSOM) BRED D. R. Wynne Jones

STEWARDS' ENQUIRY Whelan fined £100 & Fortune fined £200 (failure to ride to draw).

## 353 COOK LIMITED STKS (0-50) (4-Y.O+) (Class F)

4-00 (4-03) **1m 2f (Equitrack)** £2,683.60 (£754.60: £368.80) Stalls: Low GOING minus 0.49 sec per fur (FST)

| | Horse | Dist | Pos | SP | RR | SF |
|---|---|---|---|---|---|---|
| $305^{2}$ | **Zahid (USA) (45)** (KRBurke) **5-9-0** JQuinn(10) (lw: hdwy over 3f out: rdn over 2f out: led last strides) | — | **1** | $3/1^{2}$ | 57 | 39 |
| $309^{3}$ | **Silktail (IRE) (45)** (MissGayKelleway) **4-8-8** RCochrane(2) (hld up: led on bit over 2f out: rdn over 1f out: hdd last strides) | nk | **2** | $9/4^{1}$ | 53 | 33 |
| $279^{9}$ | **Montone (IRE) (42)** (JRJenkins) **6-9-0** JFortune(5) (gd hdwy to ld 3f out tl over 2f out: hrd rdn: r.o wl ins fnl f) | ½ | **3** | 20/1 | 56 | 38 |
| $53^{6}$ | **General Shirley (IRE) (49)** (PRHedger) **5-9-0** AMcGlone(14) (hdwy 5f out: rdn over 2f out: wknd over 1f out) | 5 | **4** | $7/1^{3}$ | 48 | 30 |
| $27^{4}$ | **Risky Tu (45)** (PAKelleway) **5-8-9** GBardwell(3) (prom over 6f) | 9 | **5** | 12/1 | 28 | 10 |
| | **Samaka Hara (IRE) (44)** (WSCunningham) **4-8-13** DeanMcKeown(4) (prom over 7f) | hd | **6** | 16/1 | 34 | 14 |
| $279^{8}$ | **Kentavrus Way (IRE) (29)** (AMoore) **5-9-0v** CandyMorris(11) (b.hind: nvr nr to chal) | hd | **7** | 50/1 | 33 | 15 |
| $214^{8}$ | **Ilandra (IRE) (50)** (SDow) **4-8-3be**(5) ADaly(12) (w ldr: led over 4f out to 3f out: sn wknd) | 3 | **8** | 8/1 | 24 | 4 |
| $239^{5}$ | **Pc's Cruiser (IRE) (49)** (JLEyre) **4-8-13** RLappin(6) (nvr nrr) | hd | **9** | 11/1 | 29 | 9 |
| | **Comedy River (44)** (NEBerry) **9-8-7**(7) AEddery(8) (bkwd: s.s: a bhd) | 3½ | **10** | 66/1 | — | 4 |
| $201^{4}$ | **Dia Georgy (37)** (MrsNMacauley) **5-9-0b** SSanders(9) (b: led over 5f) | 15 | **11** | 20/1 | — | — |
| $291^{9}$ | **Thomas Crown (IRE) (48)** (NJHWalker) **4-8-10**(3) JStack(7) (a bhd) | 3 | **12** | 40/1 | — | — |
| | **Littlemissmischief (IRE) (37)** (PaulSmith,Belgium) **5-8-9** AClark(13) (bhd fnl 4f) | 15 | **13** | 40/1 | — | — |
| | **Lunar Prince (28)** (TTClement) **6-9-0** CHodgson(1) (b: a bhd) | ½ | **14** | 66/1 | — | — |

(SP 120.6%) **14 Rn**

**2m 6.85** (2.55) CSF £9.54 TOTE £3.80: £1.10 £2.30 £3.20 (£3.50) Trio £19.70 OWNER Mr Keith Booth (WANTAGE) BRED Dr. Murray West, Nicholas Lotz & Overbrook Farm

WEIGHT FOR AGE 4yo-1lb

## 354 WALTER RALEIGH H'CAP (0-70) (3-Y.O+) (Class E)

4-30 (4-31) **6f (Equitrack)** £2,818.20 (£852.60: £415.80: £197.40) Stalls: Low GOING minus 0.49 sec per fur (FST)

| | Horse | Dist | Pos | SP | RR | SF |
|---|---|---|---|---|---|---|
| $317^{3}$ | **Our Shadee (USA) (54)** (KTIvory) **6-8-5v**(7) CScally(7) (hdwy over 2f out: led over 1f out: rdn out) | — | **1** | 8/1 | 61 | 17 |
| $278^{2}$ | **Sharp Imp (56)** (RMFlower) **6-9-0b** DBiggs(4) (hdwy over 2f out: hrd rdn & ev ch ins fnl f: unable qckn) | 1½ | **2** | $9/2^{3}$ | 59 | 15 |
| $178^{6}$ | **Random (56)** (CJames) **5-9-0** CRutter(5) (outpcd: hdwy over 1f out: r.o one pce) | 3½ | **3** | 16/1 | 50 | 6 |
| $282^{2}$ | **Kira (67)** (JLEyre) **6-9-11** RLappin(2) (b.off hind: led 5f out to over 1f out: sn wknd) | 1¼ | **4** | $5/2^{2}$ | 57 | 13 |
| $142^{2}$ | **Dancing Jack (57)** (JJBridger) **3-8-0** JQuinn(3) (lw: a.p: rdn over 2f out: wknd over 1f out) | 1½ | **5** | 9/1 | 44 | — |
| 244* | **Sharp 'n Smart (70)** (BSmart) **4-10-0** RCochrane(1) (lw: hld up: rdn over 2f out: wknd over 1f out) | s.h | **6** | $9/4^{1}$ | 56 | 12 |
| $266^{8}$ | **Southern Dominion (61)** (CNAllen) **4-9-5** NAdams(6) (lw: b.hind: led 1f: wknd over 2f out) | 6 | **7** | 16/1 | 31 | — |

(SP 110.4%) **7 Rn**

**1m 13.34** (2.74) CSF £38.59 TOTE £9.90: £2.50 £2.90 (£12.20) OWNER Mr K. T. Ivory (RADLETT) BRED Overbury Stud

WEIGHT FOR AGE 3yo-15lb

T/Plpt: £66.20 (187.67 Tckts). T/Qdpt: £19.40 (46.83 Tckts). AK

# 0310-WOLVERHAMPTON (L-H) (Standard)

## Wednesday February 28th

WEATHER: sunny WIND: almost nil

### 355 CAPRICORN MAIDEN STKS (3-Y.O) (Class D)

2-10 (2-11) **1m 100y (Fibresand)** £3,517.50 (£1,065.00: £520.00: £247.50) Stalls: Low GOING: 0.42 sec per fur (SLW)

| | Horse | Dist | Pos | SP | RR | SF |
|---|---|---|---|---|---|---|
| 239[8] | **Yeoman Oliver (60)** (BAMcMahon) **3-8-9**(5) LNewton(3) (lw: rdn & hdwy over 4f out: led ins fnl f: drvn out) | — | 1 | 5/1[3] | 64 | 17 |
| | **Fairy Highlands (IRE)** (SCWilliams) **3-8-9** JQuinn(6) (a.p: led 3f out tl wandered & hdd ins fnl f: r.o) | 1 | 2 | 9/1 | 57 | 10 |
| 287a[7] | **Western Sonata (IRE)** (LordHuntingdon) **3-8-9** DHarrison(1) (a.p: led over 3f out: sn hdd: r.o one pce fnl f) | ½ | 3 | 7/2[1] | 56 | 9 |
| | **Law Dancer (IRE)** (TGMills) **3-9-0** JFortune(11) (bit bkwd: racd wd: hdwy 6f out: one pce fnl 3f) | 5 | 4 | 7/2[1] | 52 | 5 |
| | **Snow Falcon (70)** (MBell) **3-9-0v[1]** MFenton(9) (prom: rdn & no hdwy fnl 3f) | 3 | 5 | 4/1[2] | 46 | — |
| 238[5] | **Loch Style (58)** (RHollinshead) **3-8-7**(7) FLynch(2) (dwlt: nvr nr to chal) | 1½ | 6 | 25/1 | 43 | — |
| 241[4] | **Bath Knight (66)** (DJSffrenchDavis) **3-9-0** GCarter(5) (led 5f: wknd over 2f out) | 4 | 7 | 9/1 | 36 | — |
| | **Sheemore (IRE) (40)** (JDBethell) **3-9-0** TWilliams(8) (prom: hrd rdn 4f out: wknd 3f out) | 3 | 8 | 33/1 | 30 | — |
| | **Yezza (IRE)** (APJarvis) **3-8-9** JTate(4) (bhd fnl 3f) | 1¼ | 9 | 9/1 | 23 | — |
| 281[6] | **Spirit of Sport** (AGNewcombe) **3-8-9** NAdams(7) (a bhd) | 8 | 10 | 33/1 | 7 | — |
| | **Two Socks (60)** (MMcCormack) **3-9-0** AClark(10) (prom: rdn over 5f out: sn wknd) | ½ | 11 | 14/1 | 12 | — |

(SP 127.5%) **11 Rn**

**1m 57.3** (12.30) CSF £48.46 TOTE £8.50: £4.20 £2.10 £2.30 (£82.60) Trio £127.50 OWNER Mr Michael Stokes (TAMWORTH) BRED M. G. T. Stokes

### 356 ARIES CLAIMING STKS (4-Y.O+) (Class F)

2-40 (2-40) **7f (Fibresand)** £2,398.00 (£673.00: £328.00) Stalls: High GOING: 0.42 sec per fur (SLW)

| | Horse | Dist | Pos | SP | RR | SF |
|---|---|---|---|---|---|---|
| | **Allez Cyrano (IRE) (77)** (MBell) **5-9-3** MFenton(4) (mde virtually all: rdn & r.o wl ins fnl f) | — | 1 | 4/1[2] | 65 | 35 |
| 282[10] | **Efficacy (50)** (APJarvis) **5-8-3**(7) CCarver(9) (b.hind: plld hrd: hdwy over 5f out: ev ch over 1f out: unable qckn ins fnl f) | 1 | 2 | 16/1 | 56 | 26 |
| 311* | **Jigsaw Boy (63)** (PGMurphy) **7-8-8**(3) SDrowne(7) (hld up: hdwy over 3f out: r.o one pce fnl f) | ½ | 3 | 11/4[1] | 56 | 26 |
| 270[3] | **Chadleigh Lane (USA) (66)** (RHollinshead) **4-8-8v**(7) FLynch(1) (hld up: hdwy over 2f out: swtchd lft over 1f out: unable qckn) | hd | 4 | 11/4[1] | 59 | 29 |
| 295[5] | **David James' Girl (51)** (ABailey) **4-7-9**(7) IonaWands(8) (hld up: hdwy over 2f out: one pce fnl f) | ½ | 5 | 7/1 | 45 | 15 |
| 248[4] | **Infiraaj (USA)** (MrsDHaine) **4-8-11** AMcGlone(3) (prom: rdn & ev ch wl over 1f out: eased whn btn ins fnl f) | 9 | 6 | 10/1 | 34 | 4 |
| 282[4] | **Nordan Raider (72)** (MJCamacho) **8-9-0** LCharnock(5) (b: lw: plld hrd: prom tl wknd over 1f out: eased whn btn ins fnl f) | 3 | 7 | 5/1[3] | 30 | — |
| 317[9] | **Lonely Vigil (FR)** (KOCunningham-Brown) **4-8-6** JQuinn(6) (b: chsd wnr over 3f: sn wknd: t.o) | 25 | 8 | 50/1 | — | — |

(SP 119.4%) **8 Rn**

**1m 33.3** (8.60) CSF £54.41 TOTE £4.00: £2.70 £1.80 £1.30 (£69.90) Trio £30.10 OWNER Mr Stephen Carter (NEWMARKET) BRED J. L. C. Pearce

### 357 TAURUS H'CAP (0-90) (3-Y.O+) (Class C)

3-10 (3-11) **7f (Fibresand)** £5,379.10 (£1,628.80: £795.40: £378.70) Stalls: High GOING: 0.42 sec per fur (SLW)

| | Horse | Dist | Pos | SP | RR | SF |
|---|---|---|---|---|---|---|
| 331[2] | **Pine Ridge Lad (IRE) (79)** (JLEyre) **6-9-3** RLappin(9) (a.p: swtchd lft & led ins fnl f: r.o wl) | — | 1 | 10/1 | 85 | 53 |
| 270[2] | **Cretan Gift (82)** (NPLittmoden) **5-9-6v** TGMcLaughlin(2) (a.p: led over 2f out tl over 1f out: unable qckn) | 1¾ | 2 | 10/1 | 84 | 52 |
| | **Shinerolla (83)** (CParker) **4-9-7** WWoods(10) (hld up: hdwy 3f out: led over 1f out tl ins fnl f) | ½ | 3 | 12/1 | 84 | 52 |
| 270* | **Peggy Spencer (71)** (CWThornton) **4-8-9** DeanMcKeown(4) (led 1f: rdn over 3f out: wknd ins fnl f) | 3 | 4 | 6/1[3] | 65 | 33 |
| 270[5] | **Everset (FR) (75)** (ABailey) **8-8-10**(3) DWright(3) (bhd tl hdwy 2f out: r.o ins fnl f) | s.h | 5 | 14/1 | 69 | 37 |
| 282* | **First Maite (80)** (SRBowring) **3-8-1b** NCarlisle(12) (s.i.s: sn prom: wknd over 1f out) | 4 | 6 | 7/1 | 66 | 16 |
| 331[4] | **Allinson's Mate (IRE) (65)** (TDBarron) **8-8-3v[1]** GCarter(7) (s.i.s: nvr trbld ldrs) | 2½ | 7 | 14/1 | 44 | 12 |
| 338[2] | **Loveyoumillions (IRE) (82)** (MJohnston) **4-9-6** TWilliams(11) (prom: hrd drvn & ev ch 2f out: sn wknd) | 2½ | 8 | 7/2[2] | 55 | 23 |
| 291* | **Dancing Sioux (76)** (RGuest) **4-8-7**(7) FLynch(1) (a bhd) | ½ | 9 | 100/30[1] | 48 | 16 |
| 170[2] | **White Sorrel (75)** (AHarrison) **5-8-10**(3) JStack(5) (led after 1f tl over 2f out: sn wknd) | nk | 10 | 10/1 | 47 | 15 |
| 223[7] | **Ertlon (90)** (CEBrittain) **6-10-0** MLarsen(8) (lw: prom tl wknd over 2f out) | ½ | 11 | 16/1 | 60 | 28 |
| | **Amahsan (IRE) (76)** (CDBroad) **4-9-0** MFenton(6) (bhd fnl 4f: t.o) | dist | 12 | 33/1 | — | — |

(SP 129.2%) **12 Rn**

**1m 31.7** (7.00) CSF £102.46 CT £1,134.04 TOTE £10.80: £2.80 £3.10 £2.70 (£28.50) Trio £177.80 OWNER Whitestonecliffe Racing Partnership (HAMBLETON) BRED Whitechurch Stud in Ireland

WEIGHT FOR AGE 3yo-17lb

### 358 BRITISH GAS TRANSCO H'CAP (0-100) (4-Y.O+) (Class C)

3-40 (3-40) **1m 1f 79y (Fibresand)** £5,329.70 (£1,613.60: £787.80: £374.90) Stalls: Low GOING: 0.42 sec per fur (SLW)

| | Horse | Dist | Pos | SP | RR | SF |
|---|---|---|---|---|---|---|
| 211[2] | **Maple Bay (IRE) (80)** (ABailey) **7-8-11**(5) PRoberts(8) (a.p: led over 1f out: rdn out) | — | 1 | 11/2[3] | 86 | 51 |
| | **Mister Fire Eyes (IRE) (92)** (CEBrittain) **4-10-0b** MLarsen(3) (lw: a.p: led 4f out tl over 1f out: r.o) | ½ | 2 | 9/1 | 98 | 62 |
| 233* | **Kintwyn (72)** (CCElsey) **6-8-8** DHarrison(2) (hld up & bhd: hdwy over 4f out: one pce fnl f) | 3½ | 3 | 7/1 | 71 | 36 |
| | **Grand Selection (IRE) (80)** (MBell) **4-9-2** MFenton(9) (hld up: hdwy over 5f out: rdn & wknd over 2f out) | 5 | 4 | 3/1[1] | 72 | 36 |
| 312[3] | **South Eastern Fred (84)** (HJCollingridge) **5-9-6** JQuinn(7) (hld up: rdn over 3f out: wknd over 2f out) | ½ | 5 | 6/1 | 74 | 39 |
| 306[4] | **Field of Vision (IRE) (73)** (MJohnston) **6-8-2**(7) OliverCasey(6) (lw: prom tl wknd over 2f out) | 2½ | 6 | 7/2[2] | 59 | 24 |
| | **Chairmans Choice (76)** (APJarvis) **6-8-12** JTate(4) (led over 5f: wknd over 2f out) | 3 | 7 | 9/1 | 56 | 21 |
| | **Evezio Rufo (85)** (NPLittmoden) **4-9-0v[1]**(7) JBramhill(1) (prom: rdn over 4f out: wknd over 3f out) | 12 | 8 | 33/1 | 46 | 10 |
| | **Castel Rosselo (82)** (RHarris) **6-9-4** DBatteate(5) (a bhd: t.o) | 20 | 9 | 16/1 | 8 | — |

(SP 118.2%) **9 Rn**

**2m 5.7** (9.70) CSF £48.76 CT £319.22 TOTE £6.10: £1.90 £2.60 £1.90 (£16.50) Trio £58.20 OWNER Mr Roy Matthews (TARPORLEY) BRED Berkshire Equestrian Services Ltd

OFFICIAL EXPLANATION **Kintwyn: the gelding slightly missed the break and, as he resents the kick-back, had to race on the outside as he needs to see daylight.**

## 359 AQUARIUS (S) STKS (3-Y.O) (Class F)

4-10 (4-11) **5f (Fibresand)** £2,398.00 (£673.00: £328.00) Stalls: Low GOING: 0.42 sec per fur (SLW)

| Form | Horse | Dist | Pos | SP | RR | SF |
|---|---|---|---|---|---|---|
| 298[7] | **Highland Fawn (27)** (BAMcMahon) **3-8-7** GCarter(4) (led: hrd rdn & hdd over 1f out: led last strides) | — | 1 | 10/1 | 38 | 5 |
| 310[2] | **Marino Street (54)** (PDEvans) **3-8-7** SSanders(7) (a.p: rdn & c wd wl over 1f out: r.o wl ins fnl f) | hd | 2 | 2/1[1] | 38 | 5 |
| 271[3] | **Dhes-C (51)** (RHollinshead) **3-8-0**(7) FLynch(1) (s.i.s: sn prom: led ins fnl f: hdd last strides) | s.h | 3 | 5/1[3] | 38 | 5 |
| 224[3] | **General Equation (51)** (JBalding) **3-8-5**(7) JEdmunds(6) (a.p: led over 1f out tl ins fnl f) | ½ | 4 | 8/1 | 41 | 8 |
| 209[6] | **Red Acuisle (IRE) (54)** (JBerry) **3-8-7b**(5) PRoberts(3) (a.p: rdn & ev ch 2f out: wknd over 1f out) | 7 | 5 | 7/1 | 19 | — |
| 292[4] | **Elfin Queen (IRE) (52)** (JLHarris) **3-8-7** MFenton(2) (bhd fnl 2f) | 1 | 6 | 7/1 | 10 | — |
| | **Nameless (59)** (DJSCosgrove) **3-9-0** JFortune(5) (b.hind: dwlt: a bhd) | 5 | 7 | 11/4[2] | 1 | — |

(SP 121.9%) **7 Rn**

**66.0 secs** (7.30) CSF £30.90 TOTE £13.50: £3.40 £1.90 (£21.50) OWNER Mr Tommy Staunton (TAMWORTH) BRED Rowcliffe Stud
No bid

## 360 GEMINI H'CAP (0-70) (4-Y.O+ F & M) (Class E)

4-40 (4-40) **1m 4f (Fibresand)** £2,913.75 (£882.00: £430.50: £204.75) Stalls: Low GOING: 0.42 sec per fur (SLW)

| Form | Horse | Dist | Pos | SP | RR | SF |
|---|---|---|---|---|---|---|
| 186[7] | **Hill Farm Dancer (47)** (WMBrisbourne) **5-8-9**(5) DGriffiths(2) (hld up: hdwy over 3f out: led over 1f out: edgd lft: r.o wl) | — | 1 | 9/2[3] | 59 | 27 |
| | **Pedaltothemetal (IRE) (43)** (PhilipMitchell) **4-8-7** AClark(9) (lw: a.p: led 3f out tl over 1f out: unable qckn ins fnl f) | 3 | 2 | 7/1 | 51 | 16 |
| 208[2] | **Greek Night Out (IRE) (43)** (JLEyre) **5-8-10** RLappin(3) (led after 1f: hdd 3f out: r.o one pce fnl f) | 1 | 3 | 4/1[2] | 50 | 18 |
| 303[2] | **Noble Canonire (51)** (SRBowring) **4-8-10**(5) CTeague(1) (hld up: hmpd & lost pl over 6f out: hdwy over 5f out: ev ch 2f out: wknd over 1f out) | 3½ | 4 | 3/1[1] | 53 | 18 |
| 268[7] | **Iota (60)** (JLHarris) **7-9-8**(5) PFessey(11) (s.s: hdwy after 3f: wknd 3f out) | 8 | 5 | 12/1 | 51 | 19 |
| 333[9] | **Mazilla (52)** (AStreeter) **4-9-2v** 5x FNorton(8) (lw: prom tl wknd over 2f out) | 2½ | 6 | 9/2[3] | 40 | 5 |
| 283[8] | **Samana Cay (36)** (PSFelgate) **4-8-0b**ow1 JTate(7) (hld up: wl bhd fnl 4f) | 15 | 7 | 100/1 | 4 | — |
| 291[10] | **Lady Elizabeth (FR) (32)** (KOCunningham-Brown) **4-7-10** JQuinn(10) (hld up: hdwy over 6f out: wknd over 3f out: t.o) | 30 | 8 | 33/1 | — | — |
| | **Buckley Boys (41)** (ABailey) **5-8-1**(7) AngelaGallimore(4) (hld up & bhd: lost tch 4f out: t.o) | hd | 9 | 10/1 | — | — |
| 99[7] | **Lovescape (50)** (BJLlewellyn) **5-9-3v**[1] TWilliams(6) (led 1f: wknd over 6f out: sn t.o) | dist | 10 | 25/1 | — | — |

(SP 118.4%) **10 Rn**

**2m 48.5** (16.00) CSF £33.39 CT £124.12 TOTE £6.40: £1.90 £1.90 £1.20 (£19.90) Trio £18.20 OWNER Mr Dennis Newton (NESSCLIFFE) BRED D. Newton
LONG HANDICAP Lady Elizabeth (FR) 7-8
WEIGHT FOR AGE 4yo-3lb

T/Plpt: £165.70 (66.34 Tckts). T/Qdpt: £19.30 (57.49 Tckts). KH

# 0349-LINGFIELD (L-H) (Standard)
## Thursday February 29th

WEATHER: sunny WIND: almost nil

## 361 SUMTER CLAIMING APPRENTICE STKS (3-Y.O) (Class E)

2-10 (2-10) **1m 4f (Equitrack)** £2,763.60 (£835.80: £407.40: £193.20) Stalls: Low GOING minus 0.71 sec per fur (FST)

| Form | Horse | Dist | Pos | SP | RR | SF |
|---|---|---|---|---|---|---|
| 294[2] | **Montecristo (73)** (RGuest) **3-9-3** FLynch(4) (chsd ldr 10f out: led 4f out: clr over 1f out: easily) | — | 1 | 1/9[1] | 60 | — |
| 351[4] | **Lord Ellangowan (IRE) (43)** (RIngram) **3-8-10b**[1](3) TAshley(2) (lw: led 8f: rdn over 3f out: unable qckn) | 5 | 2 | 8/1[2] | 49 | — |
| 317[8] | **Latzio (40)** (BAPearce) **3-7-10**(5)ow3 DSweeney(3) (b.hind: hld up: rdn over 3f out: sn wknd) | 20 | 3 | 16/1[3] | 11 | — |
| 176[10] | **Tartan Express (IRE) (32)** (BAPearce) **3-8-2**(3) JWilkinson(1) (b.hind: chsd ldr 2f: wknd over 5f out) | 15 | 4 | 50/1 | — | — |

(SP 109.0%) **4 Rn**

**2m 39.78** (9.78) CSF £1.73 TOTE £1.10 (£1.10) OWNER Matthews Breeding and Racing (NEWMARKET) BRED Lord Matthews

## 362 CHATTANOOGA H'CAP (0-80) (3-Y.O+) (Class D)

2-40 (2-41) **5f (Equitrack)** £3,485.00 (£1,055.00: £515.00: £245.00) Stalls: High GOING minus 0.71 sec per fur (FST)

| Form | Horse | Dist | Pos | SP | RR | SF |
|---|---|---|---|---|---|---|
| 316[4] | **Half Tone (64)** (RMFlower) **4-9-9b** DBiggs(7) (lw: hdwy over 1f out: led wl ins fnl f: rdn out) | — | 1 | 3/1[1] | 71 | 11 |
| 315* | **Featherstone Lane (71)** (MissLCSiddall) **5-10-2v** 7x RCochrane(5) (hld up: rdn over 2f out: led ins fnl f: sn hdd: unable qckn) | 1¼ | 2 | 8/1 | 74 | 14 |
| 316* | **Tenor (63)** (DNicholls) **5-9-8** 7x AlexGreaves(2) (rdn & hdwy over 2f out: ev ch ins fnl f: one pce) | 1¼ | 3 | 100/30[2] | 62 | 2 |
| 316[2] | **The Institute Boy (61)** (MissJFCraze) **6-9-6** GCarter(4) (hld up: rdn 2f out: swtchd rt over 1f out: one pce) | ½ | 4 | 9/2 | 58 | — |
| 316[3] | **Kalar (65)** (DWChapman) **7-9-5b**(5) PFessey(3) (led tl ins fnl f: sn wknd) | 1½ | 5 | 7/2[3] | 58 | — |
| 316[10] | **Distant Dynasty (53)** (BAPearce) **6-8-9**(3) DRMcCabe(6) (b.hind: bhd fnl 3f) | 1½ | 6 | 25/1 | 41 | — |
| 231[4] | **Daaniera (IRE) (41)** (PHowling) **6-8-0v** JQuinn(1) (b.hind: lw: chsd ldr over 1f: wknd over 2f out) | 4 | 7 | 8/1 | 16 | — |

(SP 114.5%) **7 Rn**

**60.14 secs** (2.14) CSF £23.86 TOTE £3.70: £2.10 £4.30 (£26.90) OWNER Mrs G. M. Temmerman (JEVINGTON) BRED T. M. Jennings

## 363 H.E.A.T. H'CAP (0-70) (3-Y.O+) (Class E)

3-10 (3-12) **7f (Equitrack)** £2,927.40 (£886.20: £432.60: £205.80) Stalls: Low GOING minus 0.71 sec per fur (FST)

| Form | Horse | Dist | Pos | SP | RR | SF |
|---|---|---|---|---|---|---|
| 244[5] | **Crystal Heights (FR) (68)** (RJO'Sullivan) **8-9-12** SSanders(8) (b.hind: hdwy over 3f out: led over 1f out: drvn out) | — | 1 | 11/2 | 75 | 26 |
| 177* | **Present Situation (69)** (LordHuntingdon) **5-9-10**(3) AWhelan(4) (lw: rdn over 3f out: hdwy on ins over 1f out: r.o wl ins fnl f) | s.h | 2 | 3/1[2] | 75 | 26 |
| 213[3] | **Quinzii Martin (48)** (DHaydnJones) **8-8-3**(3) DWright(9) (a.p: nt clr run wl over 1f out: r.o ins fnl f) | 1 | 3 | 8/1 | 52 | 3 |
| 243[7] | **Labudd (USA) (56)** (RIngram) **6-9-0b**[1] WWoods(1) (b: hdwy over 4f out: rdn over 3f out: lost pl wl over 1f out: r.o ins fnl f) | 1 | 4 | 10/1 | 57 | 8 |

| | | | Pos | SP | RR | SF |
|---|---|---|---|---|---|---|
| 205[4] | **Soaking (70)** (PBurgoyne) **6-9-11**(3) DRMcCabe(3) (a.p: ev ch over 1f out: unable qckn) | hd | **5** | 5/1[3] | 71 | 22 |
| | **Friar Street (IRE) (39)** (CJMann) **6-7-11** JQuinn(7) (b: b.hind: led: sn clr: hdd over 1f out: sn wknd) | 1¾ | **6** | 9/1 | 36 | — |
| 320* | **Barbason (56)** (AMoore) **4-9-0** 6x CandyMorris(5) (b.hind: sme hdwy over 2f out: sn wknd) | ¾ | **7** | 5/2[1] | 51 | 2 |
| 330[5] | **Rocky Two (50)** (PHowling) **5-8-8**ow1 RCochrane(6) (b: prom over 4f) | 4 | **8** | 25/1 | 36 | — |
| 217[9] | **Mr Streaky (40)** (LMontagueHall) **5-7-12** GBardwell(2) (swtg: bit bkwd: a bhd) | 7 | **9** | 33/1 | 10 | — |
| | | | | (SP 122.6%) | | **9 Rn** |

**1m 26.21** (2.21) CSF £22.37 CT £124.37 TOTE £6.90: £2.40 £1.30 £2.90 (£10.20) Trio £30.30 OWNER Mr Jack Joseph (WHITCOMBE) BRED Ahmad Fustok

## 364 OIP AND FRAMEWORK MAIDEN STKS (3-Y.O) (Class D)

3-40 (3-41) **1m 2f (Equitrack)** £3,501.25 (£1,060.00: £517.50: £246.25) Stalls: Low GOING minus 0.71 sec per fur (FST)

| | | | Pos | SP | RR | SF |
|---|---|---|---|---|---|---|
| | **Punkah (USA)** (LordHuntingdon) **3-9-0** DHarrison(7) (hdwy over 4f out: hrd rdn over 1f out: led wl ins fnl f: r.o wl) | — | **1** | 5/2[1] | 53 | 13 |
| | **Mattimeo (IRE)** (APJarvis) **3-9-0** JTate(5) (hdwy over 4f out: hrd rdn over 1f out: led ins fnl f: sn hdd: unable qckn) | 1¼ | **2** | 11/4[2] | 51 | 11 |
| | **Classic Beauty (IRE)** (RHarris) **3-8-9** DBatteate(2) (led over 8f out tl ins fnl f: one pce) | 3 | **3** | 7/1 | 41 | 1 |
| 245[7] | **Righteous Gent (49)** (KMcAuliffe) **3-9-0** SSanders(8) (a.p: rdn over 3f out: wknd 2f out) | 11 | **4** | 20/1 | 29 | — |
| | **Eagle Canyon (IRE) (75)** (BHanbury) **3-8-11**(3) JStack(4) (bit bkwd: hld up: rdn over 3f out: wknd over 2f out) | ½ | **5** | 3/1[3] | 28 | — |
| 351[5] | **Esta Maria (IRE)** (PaulSmith,Belgium) **3-8-9** JQuinn(1) (bit bkwd: led over 1f: wknd over 3f out) | 13 | **6** | 6/1 | 2 | — |
| 277[8] | **Colour Counsellor (45)** (RMFlower) **3-9-0** DBiggs(3) (s.s: a bhd) | 6 | **7** | 25/1 | — | — |
| 188[6] | **Native Song** (MJHaynes) **3-8-4**(5) MBaird(6) (a bhd) | 3½ | **8** | 33/1 | — | — |
| | | | | (SP 118.6%) | | **8 Rn** |

**2m 8.04** (3.74) CSF £9.75 TOTE £3.70: £1.60 £1.70 £1.80 (£7.10) OWNER The Queen (WEST ILSLEY) BRED The Queen

## 365 H.E.A.T. CONTRACTORS H'CAP (0-60) (4-Y.O+) (Class F)

4-10 (4-10) **2m (Equitrack)** £2,624.10 (£737.60: £360.30) Stalls: Low GOING minus 0.71 sec per fur (FST)

| | | | Pos | SP | RR | SF |
|---|---|---|---|---|---|---|
| 309[4] | **The Lad (27)** (LMontagueHall) **7-7-4**(7) MartinDwyer(4) (a.p: led over 3f out: clr over 1f out: r.o wl) | — | **1** | 10/1 | 38 | 11 |
| 339[8] | **Sir Thomas Beecham (57)** (SDow) **6-9-8**(5) ADaly(5) (rdn over 7f out: hdwy over 4f out: r.o one pce fnl 2f) | 7 | **2** | 7/1[3] | 61 | 34 |
| 279[5] | **Mr Copyforce (45)** (MissBSanders) **6-9-1** SSanders(7) (hld up: led over 4f out tl over 3f out: unable qckn) | ¾ | **3** | 12/1 | 48 | 21 |
| 169[6] | **Golden Punch (USA) (37)** (CACyzer) **5-8-7v** DBiggs(2) (s.s: hdwy over 4f out: wknd over 2f out) | 8 | **4** | 33/1 | 32 | 5 |
| 265[3] | **Call Me Albi (IRE) (44)** (GLMoore) **5-8-7v**(7) TAshley(6) (rdn & lost pl over 8f out: r.o one pce fnl 2f) | 4 | **5** | 7/1[3] | 35 | 8 |
| 275* | **Juliasdarkinvader (41)** (AMoore) **6-8-11** AClark(12) (b: b.hind: hdwy over 8f out: wknd over 2f out) | s.h | **6** | 15/2 | 32 | 5 |
| | **Arian Spirit (IRE) (37)** (JLEyre) **5-8-7** RLappin(10) (hdwy over 3f out: wknd over 2f out) | 1 | **7** | 9/2[2] | 27 | — |
| 214[5] | **Royal Circus (44)** (PRWebber) **7-8-9**(5) AmandaSanders(11) (lw: prom over 10f) | 2 | **8** | 10/1 | 32 | 5 |
| 186[12] | **Fools of Pride (IRE) (41)** (RHollinshead) **4-7-12**(7)ow6 FLynch(1) (bhd fnl 5f) | 8 | **9** | 33/1 | 21 | — |
| 97[6] | **Dvorak (IRE) (52)** (RHarris) **5-9-8** DBatteate(9) (hdwy over 4f out: wknd over 3f out) | 3½ | **10** | 12/1 | 29 | 2 |
| 254[8] | **Sacred Mirror (IRE) (52)** (CEBrittain) **5-9-8** MLarsen(8) (prom 11f: t.o) | 25 | **11** | 8/1 | 4 | — |
| 349[2] | **Heighth of Fame (51)** (AJWilson) **5-9-0**(7) GFaulkner(3) (led over 11f: t.o) | 9 | **12** | 3/1[1] | — | — |
| | | | | (SP 130.5%) | | **12 Rn** |

**3m 25.21** (3.21) CSF £78.14 CT £790.95 TOTE £10.70: £2.60 £3.30 £3.60 (£203.90) Trio £232.80 OWNER Treberth Partnership (EPSOM) BRED W. R. and M. E. Scale

WEIGHT FOR AGE 4yo-6lb

OFFICIAL EXPLANATION **Heighth of Fame: the trainer reported that the gelding may have been feeling the effects of racing twice in a week.**

## 366 VICKSBURGH H'CAP (0-65) (3-Y.O+) (Class F)

4-40 (4-41) **1m (Equitrack)** £2,683.60 (£754.60: £368.80) Stalls: High GOING minus 0.71 sec per fur (FST)

| | | | Pos | SP | RR | SF |
|---|---|---|---|---|---|---|
| 244[4] | **Tuigamala (55)** (RIngram) **5-9-9** WWoods(11) (hdwy over 3f out: led over 1f out tl wl ins fnl f: led last strides) | — | **1** | 9/1 | 64 | 39 |
| | **Victory Team (IRE) (60)** (GBBalding) **4-10-0** RCochrane(9) (hdwy 4f out: led wl over 1f out: sn hdd: led wl ins fnl f: hdd last strides) | s.h | **2** | 10/1 | 69 | 44 |
| 243[4] | **Hatta Sunshine (USA) (53)** (AMoore) **6-9-0**(7) IonaWands(1) (b: b.hind: hdwy over 4f out: rdn over 1f out: r.o one pce) | 4 | **3** | 7/1 | 54 | 29 |
| 295[2] | **Roman Reel (USA) (58)** (GLMoore) **5-9-12** SWhitworth(5) (lw: led: clr 5f out: hdd wl over 1f out: sn wknd) | 2½ | **4** | 5/1[2] | 54 | 29 |
| | **Sarum (51)** (CPWildman) **10-9-5** CRutter(3) (bit bkwd: lost pl 5f out: r.o one pce fnl 2f) | nk | **5** | 33/1 | 46 | 21 |
| 306[8] | **Canary Falcon (55)** (JohnBerry) **5-9-9v** VSmith(8) (b: lw: hld up: rdn over 3f out: wknd over 1f out) | 5 | **6** | 12/1 | 40 | 15 |
| 308[4] | **Myjinka (49)** (TEPowell) **6-8-12b**(5) MBaird(10) (s.s: hdwy over 4f out: wknd over 1f out) | s.h | **7** | 11/2[3] | 34 | 9 |
| 211[9] | **Great Bear (51)** (DWChapman) **4-9-0**(5) PFessey(7) (bhd fnl 4f) | 3 | **8** | 33/1 | 30 | 5 |
| 337[3] | **Dantean (45)** (RJO'Sullivan) **4-8-13** AClark(6) (prom over 5f) | 2½ | **9** | 5/2[1] | 19 | — |
| 308[3] | **Bakers Daughter (50)** (JRArnold) **4-9-4** JQuinn(4) (prom over 6f) | 1¾ | **10** | 15/2 | 21 | — |
| | **Top Pet (IRE) (49)** (RAkehurst) **6-9-3** SSanders(2) (a bhd) | ½ | **11** | 14/1 | 19 | — |
| | | | | (SP 124.2%) | | **11 Rn** |

**1m 38.4** (1.00) CSF £89.29 CT £622.33 TOTE £9.20: £1.90 £2.90 £2.10 (£57.40) Trio £92.50 OWNER Mr Roger Ingram (EPSOM) BRED Mrs S. Ingram

T/Plpt: £285.60 (39.1 Tckts). T/Qdpt: £115.00 (10.35 Tckts). AK

# 0341-SOUTHWELL (L-H) (Standard)

## Friday March 1st

WEATHER: Overcast WIND: fresh half behind

## 367 TUXFORD H'CAP (0-60) (I) (4-Y.O+) (Class F)

1-40 (1-43) **1m 4f (Fibresand)** £2,048.00 (£573.00: £278.00) Stalls: Low GOING minus 0.15 sec per fur (FST)

| | | | Pos | SP | RR | SF |
|---|---|---|---|---|---|---|
| 85[5] | **Inovar (27)** (CBBBooth) **6-7-10**(7) FLynch(8) (lw: trckd ldr: led over 7f out: clr over 4f out: unchal) | — | **1** | 10/1 | 35 | 5 |

$333^{3}$ **Philmist (49)** (CWCElsey) **4-9-9b** NKennedy(3) (bhd: hdwy to chse wnr over 3f out: one pce)......3 **2** 5/2[1] 54 21
$328^{2}$ **Carol Again (36)** (NBycroft) **4-8-10** GDuffield(5) (trckd ldrs: effrt over 2f out: one pce)......2 **3** 4/1[3] 38 5
$303^{7}$ **Me Cherokee (50)** (CWThornton) **4-9-10** DeanMcKeown(9) (chsd ldrs: effrt over 2f out: one pce)......2½ **4** 11/2 49 16
$333^{2}$ **Mr Moriarty (IRE) (44)** (SRBowring) **5-9-1**(5) CTeague(4) (sn outpcd: pushed along 8f out: styd on towards fin)......1 **5** 3/1[2] 41 11
$283^{3}$ **Swordking (IRE) (32)** (JLHarris) **7-8-8** JQuinn(7) (chsd ldrs: drvn along 6f out: outpcd fnl 4f)......¾ **6** 9/2 28 —
**Runforaction (IRE) (39)** (BSRothwell) **4-8-13** JFortune(2) (led tl over 7f out: sn drvn along: wknd 4f out)......10 **7** 14/1 22 —
*$346^{5}$ **Selmeston (IRE) (32)** (PSFelgate) **4-8-3**(3) PMcCabe(6) (Withdrawn not under Starters' orders: lame at s)......* **W** *8/1* — —
(SP 134.0%) **7 Rn**

**2m 43.6** (11.10) CSF £36.15 CT £112.46 TOTE £13.10: £4.40 £2.00 (£63.90) Trio £48.10 OWNER Mr J. Porteous (FLAXTON) BRED Hyde Stud
WEIGHT FOR AGE 4yo-2lb

## 368 MARKHAM MOOR H'CAP (0-65) (3-Y.O+) (Class F)
2-10 (2-12) **6f (Fibresand)** £2,398.00 (£673.00: £328.00) Stalls: Low GOING minus 0.15 sec per fur (FST)

SP RR SF

$282^{7}$ **Daawe (USA) (58)** (MrsVAAconley) **5-9-0v**(7) FLynch(7) (trckd ldrs: qcknd to ld over 4f out: sn clr: jst hld on)— **1** 7/2[1] 63 45
$343^{2}$ **Awesome Venture (56)** (MCChapman) **6-9-2**(3) DRMcCabe(8) (nt clr run & swtchd rt 2f out: hrd rdn & styd on wl)......hd **2** 9/2[3] 61 43
341* **Desert Invader (IRE) (64)** (DWChapman) **5-9-13** 7x ACulhane(5) (s.i.s: hdwy on outside over 2f out: hung lft: nt qckn ins fnl f)......nk **3** 4/1[2] 68 50
$328^{5}$ **Branston Kristy (33)** (CSmith) **4-7-3b**(7) IonaWands(4) (bhd tl hdwy on outside 2f out: nvr nr ldrs)......5 **4** 25/1 24 6
$247^{3}$ **Monis (IRE) (58)** (JBalding) **5-9-0v**(7) JEdmunds(2) (bhd tl styd on on outside fnl 2f)......½ **5** 11/2 47 29
**Always Grace (52)** (MissGayKelleway) **4-9-1** GDuffield(9) (in tch: effrt ½-wy: sn wknd)......¾ **6** 9/2[3] 39 21
$259^{10}$ **Fairey Firefly (56)** (MJCamacho) **5-9-5** LCharnock(3) (chsd ldrs tl wknd over 1f out)......1¾ **7** 14/1 39 21
$330^{4}$ **Tame Deer (65)** (MCChapman) **4-9-7**(7) CMunday(10) (s.i.s: a in rr)......½ **8** 10/1 46 28
$342^{7}$ **Double Glow (33)** (NBycroft) **4-7-10v**1 GBardwell(1) (w ldrs 2f: wknd over 3f out)......10 **9** 25/1 — —
$167^{10}$ **Royal Dancer (38)** (RJWeaver) **4-7-10b**1(5)ow5 ADaly(6) (mde most tl over 4f out: sn wknd)......10 **10** 50/1 — —
(SP 119.4%) **10 Rn**

**1m 17.0** (3.50) CSF £19.07 CT £60.62 TOTE £5.50: £1.40 £1.50 £2.00 (£7.90) Trio £8.60 OWNER Mrs Andrea Mallinson (WESTOW) BRED Gainsborough Farm W.C.
LONG HANDICAP Branston Kristy 7-7 Double Glow 7-2 Royal Dancer 7-4

## 369 NORMANTON CLAIMING STKS (4-Y.O+) (Class F)
2-40 (2-40) **1m 6f (Fibresand)** £2,398.00 (£673.00: £328.00) Stalls: High GOING minus 0.15 sec per fur (FST)

SP RR SF

$268^{4}$ **Eulogy (FR) (60)** (KRBurke) **9-8-6**(7) TAshley(7) (in tch: led over 5f out: styd on wl over 1f out: sn clr)......— **1** 7/2[2] 60 22
$284^{4}$ **El Nido (52)** (MJCamacho) **8-8-11** LCharnock(8) (trckd ldrs: chal over 3f out: nt qckn over 1f out)......8 **2** 4/1[3] 49 11
$283^{4}$ **Baher (USA) (28)** (MrsASwinbank) **7-9-1** GBardwell(6) (chsd ldrs: drvn along 8f out: outpcd over 3f out: styd on ins fnl f)......2½ **3** 8/1 50 12
$108^{9}$ **Durham (57)** (RSimpson) **5-8-4b**(3)ow2 SDrowne(4) (mde most tl hdd over 5f out: hung rt: one pce fnl 3f)......2½ **4** 20/1 39 —
$128^{3}$ **Tartan Gem (IRE) (67)** (MissGayKelleway) **5-9-0**(7) FLynch(1) (hld up & bhd: hdwy 7f out: chsd ldrs 4f out: rdn & wknd over 2f out)......1½ **5** 10/11[1] 51 13
$260^{3}$ **Namaste (46)** (RPCHoad) **8-9-7** MFenton(2) (in tch tl lost pl over 3f out)......10 **6** 20/1 40 2
**Alkarine** (MPBielby) **4-8-2v**(3) DRMcCabe(5) (bit bkwd: chsd ldrs tl lost pl over 5f out: sn wl bhd)......30 **7** 50/1 — —
$299^{4}$ **Timely Example (USA) (52)** (BRCambidge) **5-8-11b** NAdams(3) (dwlt s: reminders: hdwy to disp ld 9f out: sn wknd: t.o 5f out)......dist **8** 50/1 — —
(SP 119.2%) **8 Rn**

**3m 10.7** (11.70) CSF £17.65 TOTE £6.20: £1.40 £1.70 £1.10 (£13.10) OWNER Cragside Construction (WANTAGE) BRED Martine Teyssot
WEIGHT FOR AGE 4yo-4lb
OFFICIAL EXPLANATION **Tartan Gem (IRE): the trainer stated that the horse was ridden to get the trip and failed to stay in this fast-run race.**

## 370 SKEGBY MAIDEN STKS (3-Y.O) (Class D)
3-10 (3-11) **1m 4f (Fibresand)** £3,452.50 (£1,045.00: £510.00: £242.50) Stalls: Low GOING minus 0.15 sec per fur (FST)

SP RR SF

**Disc of Gold (USA)** (MJohnston) **3-8-9** TWilliams(4) (mde all: pushed clr over 3f out: eased towards fin)......— **1** 6/5[1] 68+ 3
$234^{10}$ **Oxgang (IRE) (55)** (JGFitzGerald) **3-9-0** RCochrane(2) (trckd ldrs: outpcd over 5f out: kpt on fnl 2f: no ch w wnr)......20 **2** 6/4[2] 46 —
$329^{6}$ **Havana Heights (IRE) (40)** (JLEyre) **3-8-9** RLappin(1) (hld up: effrt 6f out: kpt on fnl 2f)......6 **3** 8/1[3] 33 —
**Further Future (IRE) (40)** (JohnBerry) **3-9-0** MFenton(5) (chsd wnr: rdn over 4f out: wknd over 1f out)......nk **4** 33/1 38 —
**Kenilworth Dancer (45)** (RDEWoodhouse) **3-9-0** GDuffield(3) (bit bkwd: drvn along 7f out: sn lost tch)......25 **5** 10/1 5 —
**My Archie** (RDEWoodhouse) **3-9-0** JQuinn(6) (lost tch 5f out: sn t.o)......dist **6** 20/1 — —
(SP 113.4%) **6 Rn**

**2m 44.9** (12.40) CSF £3.36 TOTE £2.40: £1.10 £1.80 (£1.80) OWNER Sheikh Mohammed (MIDDLEHAM) BRED Darley Stud Management Inc

## 371 RETFORD H'CAP (0-80) (3-Y.O+) (Class D)
3-40 (3-40) **1m (Fibresand)** £3,468.75 (£1,050.00: £512.50: £243.75) Stalls: Low GOING minus 0.15 sec per fur (FST)

SP RR SF

$211^{3}$ **High Premium (69)** (RAFahey) **8-9-3** ACulhane(2) (chsd ldrs: led wl over 1f out: hrd rdn & edgd rt: all out)...— **1** 9/1 77 41
234* **Anastina (67)** (NAGraham) **4-9-1** DHarrison(3) (chsd ldrs: ev ch over 1f out: r.o)......s.h **2** 4/1[3] 75 39
249* **Second Colours (USA) (79)** (MrsMReveley) **6-9-13** RCochrane(7) (lw: hld up: hdwy on outside over 2f out: styd on fnl f: nt rch ldrs)......2 **3** 3/1[1] 83 47
$345^{7}$ **Square Deal (FR) (70)** (SRBowring) **5-9-4** SDWilliams(6) (chsd ldrs: rdn & hung lft over 2f out: kpt on same pce)......1¾ **4** 8/1 70 34
$282^{8}$ **Johnnie the Joker (72)** (JPLeigh) **5-8-13**(7) FLynch(8) (w ldr: kpt on one pce over 1f out)......nk **5** 20/1 72 36
358* **Maple Bay (IRE) (86)** (ABailey) **7-10-1**(5) 6x PRoberts(1) (lw: chsd ldrs: drvn along ½-wy: wknd over 1f out)...nk **6** 9/2 85 49
331* **Nashaat (USA) (73)** (MCChapman) **8-9-4**(3) 6x DRMcCabe(4) (led tl wl over 1f out: sn wknd)......6 **7** 7/2[2] 60 24
$331^{5}$ **What a Nightmare (IRE) (64)** (PHowling) **4-8-12** JQuinn(5) (bhd fr ½-wy)......6 **8** 25/1 39 3
(SP 115.1%) **8 Rn**

**1m 44.8** (4.80) CSF £42.03 CT £123.65 TOTE £11.50: £2.10 £1.10 £1.20 (£18.50) OWNER Mr J. C. Parsons (MALTON) BRED M.E Wates

## 372 RUFFORD (S) STKS (4-Y.O+) (Class F)

4-10 (4-11) **1m (Fibresand)** £2,398.00 (£673.00: £328.00) Stalls: Low GOING minus 0.15 sec per fur (FST)

| | | | | SP | RR | SF |
|---|---|---|---|---|---|---|
| 356[5] | **David James' Girl (51)** (ABailey) **4-8-0**(7) IonaWands(3) (sn pushed along: hdwy on outside over 2f out: r.o u.p to ld nr fin) | — | 1 | 11/4[1] | 56 | 23 |
| 333[8] | **No Submission (USA) (60)** (DWChapman) **10-9-4v** ACulhane(7) (led after 2f: clr over 2f out: jst ct) | nk | 2 | 5/1[3] | 66 | 33 |
| 255[4] | **First Gold (58)** (JWharton) **7-9-4b** SDWilliams(2) (bhd: hdwy on outside ½-wy: one pce fnl 2f) | 6 | 3 | 6/1 | 54 | 21 |
| | **Desert Lore** (MrsJRRamsden) **5-8-12** JFortune(5) (b.nr fore: dwlt: hdwy to chse ldrs ½-wy: one pce fnl 2f) | 4 | 4 | 13/2 | 40 | 7 |
| 299[7] | **Desert Man** (RDEWoodhouse) **5-8-12** JQuinn(6) (led 2f: chsd ldrs & sn drvn along: outpcd fnl 2f) | 2 | 5 | 33/1 | 36 | 3 |
| 255[5] | **Ashdren (47)** (AHarrison) **9-8-9**(3) JStack(4) (chsd ldrs tl wknd 2f out) | 2 | 6 | 11/1 | 32 | — |
| 124[13] | **Slmaat (58)** (RDEWoodhouse) **5-8-7** GDuffield(9) (sn chsng ldrs: rdn 2f out: sn wknd) | ¾ | 7 | 14/1 | 26 | — |
| 295[4] | **Media Express (59)** (MBrittain) **4-9-4** RCochrane(1) (lw: chsd ldrs tl wknd wl over 1f out: eased) | 4 | 8 | 3/1[2] | 29 | — |
| | **Call Me Flash (44)** (MrsPSly) **4-8-12** MBirch(8) (outpcd after 3f: sn bhd) | 2½ | 9 | 33/1 | 18 | — |
| | | | | (SP 116.8%) | **9 Rn** | |

**1m 45.8** (5.80) CSF £16.20 TOTE £3.40: £1.10 £1.70 £4.10 (£14.20) Trio £10.80 OWNER One In Ten Racing Club (TARPORLEY) BRED Miss P. E. Decker
No bid

## 373 TUXFORD H'CAP (0-60) (II) (4-Y.O+) (Class F)

4-40 (4-40) **1m 4f (Fibresand)** £2,048.00 (£573.00: £278.00) Stalls: Low GOING minus 0.15 sec per fur (FST)

| | | | | SP | RR | SF |
|---|---|---|---|---|---|---|
| 297[6] | **Tempering (53)** (DWChapman) **10-9-12** ACulhane(6) (mde all: clr over 3f out: unchal) | — | 1 | 9/1 | 64 | 18 |
| 318[0] | **Northern Trial (USA) (48)** (KRBurke) **8-9-0**(7) 5x TAshley(8) (b.hind: effrt 4f out: styd on fnl 2f: no imp) | 3½ | 2 | 7/4[1] | 54 | 8 |
| | **Charlie Bigtime (48)** (RHarris) **6-9-7** DBatteate(3) (hld up & bhd: stdy hdwy on outside over 2f out: r.o: nvr plcd to chal) | 1¼ | 3 | 8/1 | 53 | 7 |
| 360[3] | **Greek Night Out (IRE) (43)** (JLEyre) **5-9-2** RLappin(9) (chsd ldrs: drvn along ½-wy: sn outpcd: kpt on fnl 2f) | 1¾ | 4 | 11/2[2] | 45 | — |
| 251[6] | **Night Time (51)** (AStreeter) **4-9-3**(5) LNewton(1) (bhd: effrt u.p over 4f out: kpt on: nvr nr ldrs) | 1½ | 5 | 14/1 | 52 | 3 |
| 267[5] | **Torrey Pines (IRE) (42)** (MBell) **4-8-13v** MFenton(4) (in tch: effrt 4f out: sn chsng wnr: wknd over 1f out) | 5 | 6 | 7/1[3] | 37 | — |
| 297[2] | **Genesis Four (39)** (SRBowring) **6-8-7**(5) CTeague(2) (lw: bhd: effrt 5f out: n.d) | 2 | 7 | 11/2[2] | 30 | — |
| 346[4] | **Tap On Tootsie (38)** (TRWall) **4-8-9** NAdams(7) (chsd ldrs: drvn along 7f out: wknd 5f out) | 8 | 8 | 12/1 | 19 | — |
| 303[4] | **The Cape Doctor (IRE) (45)** (AGFoster) **4-8-13**(3) AWhelan(5) (b.hind: chsd ldrs: effrt over 3f out: hung rt & wknd qckly over 1f out) | 13 | 9 | 10/1 | 9 | — |
| | | | | (SP 124.2%) | **9 Rn** | |

**2m 45.0** (12.50) CSF £25.97 CT £129.72 TOTE £9.80: £3.20 £1.80 £3.00 (£32.40) Trio £52.70 OWNER Mr Richard Berenson (YORK) BRED Lord Howard de Walden
WEIGHT FOR AGE 4yo-2lb

T/Plpt: £32.10 (309.57 Tckts). T/Qdpt: £4.90 (134.88 Tckts). WG

# 0286a-ABU DHABI (UAE) (L-H) (Good to firm)

## Friday February 9th

## 374a H. H. THE PRESIDENTS CUP (3-Y.O+)

**7f (Turf)** £15,789.47 (£7,894.74: £4,736.84: £3,157.89)

| | | | | SP | RR | SF |
|---|---|---|---|---|---|---|
| | **Diffident (FR)** (SbinSuroor,UAE) **4-9-4** SGuillot | — | 1 | | — | — |
| 286a[2] | **Heart Lake** (SbinSuroor,UAE) **5-9-8** JCarroll | s.h | 2 | | — | — |
| 286a* | **Faltaat (USA)** (DJSelvaratnam,UAE) **6-9-2** BDoyle | 2 | 3 | | — | — |
| | **Ihtiraz** (KPMcLaughlin,UAE) **6-9-2** RHills | 2¼ | 4 | | — | — |
| | **Darbonne (USA)** (ECharpy,UAE) **6-9-2** WJSupple | nk | 5 | | — | — |
| | **Gulf of Gdansk (USA)** (MusabahAlMuhairi,UAE) **6-9-2** PaulEddery | 9 | 6 | | — | — |
| | | | | | | **6 Rn** |

**1m 23.49** OWNER Sheikh Rashid bin Mohammed Al Maktoum BRED Haras d'Etreham & R Ades in France

**Diffident (FR)** stepped up on his second place effort at Nad Al Sheba last time, to beat some useful opponents here. He was always in a prominent position and, with the advantage entering the final furlong, held on well to the line.

**Heart Lake** is in good heart at present, but once again, met one too good. He did, however, reverse the form of his last outing when placed second to Faltaat, so he seems to be improving.

**Faltaat (USA)** was the early leader. Leading the field in the straight, he was headed in the final furlong and could find nothing to cope with the challengers at the finish..

# NAD AL SHEBA (Dubai, UAE) (L-H) (Good)

## Sunday February 11th

## 375a NAT. BANK OF DUBAI H. H. SHEIKH MAKTOUM BIN RASHID AL MAKTOUM CHALLENGE (RND 1) (Listed)

(4-Y.O+) **1m (Dirt)** £8,771.93 (£4,385.96: £2,631.56: £1,754.39)

| | | | | SP | RR | SF |
|---|---|---|---|---|---|---|
| | **Tamayaz (CAN)** (SbinSuroor,UAE) **4-8-11** JCarroll | — | 1 | | — | — |
| | **Wathik (USA)** (PLRudkin,UAE) **6-8-11b** PaulEddery | 3 | 2 | | — | — |
| | **Dover Straits (USA)** (KPMcLaughlin,UAE) **5-8-11** WRyan | nk | 3 | | — | — |
| | **Cezanne** (SbinSuroor,UAE) **7-8-11** JPMurtagh | s.h | 4 | | — | — |
| 286a[3] | **Alami (USA)** (KPMcLaughlin,UAE) **4-8-11** RHills | ¾ | 5 | | — | — |
| | **Wafayt (IRE)** (DJSelvaratnam,UAE) **5-8-11** BDoyle | 2¼ | 6 | | — | — |
| | **Ihtiram (IRE)** (KPMcLaughlin,UAE) **4-8-11** JCArias | ½ | 7 | | — | — |
| | | | | | | **9 Rn** |

**1m 37.18** OWNER Maktoum Al Maktoum BRED Windfields Farm

**Tamayaz (CAN)** was in behind the leaders until ridden to challenge three furlongs from home. Taking it up with two furlongs to go, he was pushed out to go clear and won comfortably. There is more success in the tank.
**Wathik (USA)** has now been placed on his last four outings. With every chance over a furlong out, he could not summon the necessary speed to take the honours. He may be better over a shorter distance.
**Wafayt (IRE)**, after a decent victory last time, could not repeat that performance. He has beaten the runner-up twice in their last two encounters, so there might have been something amiss on this occasion.

# 0361-LINGFIELD (L-H) (Standard)
## Saturday March 2nd
WEATHER: Overcast WIND: almost nil

### 376 TAURUS CLAIMING STKS (3-Y.O) (Class F)
2-10 (2-10) **1m (Equitrack)** £2,540.80 (£713.80: £348.40) Stalls: High GOING minus 0.51 sec per fur (FST)

| | | | | SP | RR | SF |
|---|---|---|---|---|---|---|
| 294[4] | **Rowlandsons Charm (IRE) (58)** (GLMoore) **3-8-2v** NAdams(4) (led over 6f out: rn wd bnd wl over 1f out: edgd rt: drvn out) | — | 1 | 10/11 [1] | 52 | 7 |
| 188[5] | **Crystal Fast (USA) (55)** (PAKelleway) **3-8-6**(7) CDomergue(5) (a.p: carried wd bnd wl over 1f out: n.m.r & ev ch ins fnl f: unable qckn) | ½ | 2 | 8/1 [3] | 62 | 17 |
| 344[6] | **Apartments Abroad (47)** (KMcAuliffe) **3-8-3** SSanders(3) (b.hind: a.p: carried wd bnd wl over 1f out: ev ch ins fnl f: one pce) | hd | 3 | 10/1 | 52 | 7 |
| 293[4] | **Trible Pet (46)** (BGubby) **3-7-12** JQuinn(7) (rdn over 4f out: hdwy over 3f out: wknd over 2f out) | 11 | 4 | 5/1 [2] | 25 | — |
| 171[9] | **Domettes (IRE) (54)** (RHannon) **3-8-0** TWilliams(1) (lw: led over 1f: wknd 4f out) | 3 | 5 | 5/1 [2] | 21 | — |
| | **Old Gold N Tan** (JRPoulton) **3-8-2**(3) PMcCabe(2) (neat: s.s: bhd fnl 5f) | 1 | 6 | 33/1 | 24 | — |
| | **P Grayco Choice** (PCClarke) **3-8-4**ow8 MFenton(6) (w'like: bkwd: bhd fnl 6f) | 1¾ | 7 | 33/1 | 19 | — |

(SP 111.8%) **7 Rn**

**1m 41.26** (3.86) CSF £8.18 TOTE £1.70: £1.10 £4.30 (£3.90) OWNER Allen & Associates (EPSOM) BRED Mrs Catherine O'Malley

### 377 PISCES MEDIAN AUCTION MAIDEN STKS (3-Y.O) (Class F)
2-40 (2-41) **7f (Equitrack)** £2,540.80 (£713.80: £348.40) Stalls: Low GOING minus 0.51 sec per fur (FST)

| | | | | SP | RR | SF |
|---|---|---|---|---|---|---|
| 298[3] | **General Haven (53)** (TJNaughton) **3-9-0** JFortune(8) (a.p: led over 1f out: rdn out) | — | 1 | 3/1 [3] | 62 | 13 |
| 310[5] | **Baranov (IRE) (56)** (DJGMurraySmith) **3-9-0** RCochrane(3) (plld hrd: hld up: nt clr run 2f out: chsd wnr fnl f: r.o wl) | ½ | 2 | 9/4 [1] | 61 | 12 |
| 276[3] | **Tahya (USA) (55)** (CCElsey) **3-8-9** DHarrison(7) (hld up: rdn over 1f out: r.o one pce) | 3 | 3 | 13/2 | 49 | — |
| 276[2] | **Badger Bay (IRE) (60)** (CADwyer) **3-8-6**(3) JStack(2) (w ldr: led over 3f out tl over 1f out: sn wknd) | 2½ | 4 | 5/2 [2] | 43 | — |
| | **Isitoff** (CADwyer) **3-8-11**(3) DRMcCabe(5) (bit bkwd: s.s: outpcd: nvr nrr) | 1½ | 5 | 20/1 | 45 | — |
| | **Spiral Flyer (IRE) (58)** (MDIUsher) **3-8-9** MWigham(4) (bhd fnl 5f) | ¾ | 6 | 20/1 | 38 | — |
| 253[8] | **Ghostly Apparition (50)** (JRUpson) **3-8-7**(7) DSweeney(1) (led over 3f: wknd wl over 1f out) | 1½ | 7 | 20/1 | 40 | — |
| | **Into Debt** (JRPoulton) **3-8-6**(3) PMcCabe(6) (neat: bkwd: s.s: hdwy over 5f out: wknd 2f out) | 3½ | 8 | 33/1 | 27 | — |

(SP 114.9%) **8 Rn**

**1m 27.78** (3.78) CSF £9.84 TOTE £4.30: £1.30 £1.40 £2.40 (£5.50) OWNER Mr A. Callard (EPSOM) BRED Stetchworth Park Stud Ltd

### 378 CLASSIC PROMOTIONS RAPPORTEUR CONDITIONS STKS (3-Y.O+) (Class C)
3-10 (3-10) **1m 2f (Equitrack)** £4,869.54 (£1,822.86: £891.93: £384.15) Stalls: Low GOING minus 0.51 sec per fur (FST)

| | | | | SP | RR | SF |
|---|---|---|---|---|---|---|
| 263[2] | **Quality (IRE) (84)** (WAO'Gorman) **3-8-3b**ow2 EmmaO'Gorman(5) (lw: chsd ldr: led 5f out: clr over 3f out: comf) | — | 1 | 6/4 [1] | 85+ | 20 |
| 327a[11] | **Bartok (IRE)** (PAKelleway) **5-10-3** RCochrane(3) (lw: led 5f: shkn up 2f out: r.o one pce) | 5 | 2 | 9/4 [2] | 84 | 42 |
| | **Statajack (IRE) (86)** (DRCElsworth) **8-9-7b** AProcter(6) (rdn 4f out: hdwy fnl f: r.o one pce) | nk | 3 | 5/1 [3] | 74 | 32 |
| | **Kirov Lady (IRE) (90)** (RHannon) **3-7-10** GBardwell(4) (plld hrd: rdn 4f out: no hdwy fnl 3f) | ½ | 4 | 9/1 | 69 | 6 |
| 263[7] | **Expeditious Way (GR)** (RCharlton) **3-8-4** SSanders(2) (hld up: chsd wnr over 3f out tl ins fnl f: sn wknd) | 1½ | 5 | 25/1 | 74 | 11 |
| | **No Pattern (82)** (GLMoore) **4-9-7** SWhitworth(1) (lw: bhd fnl 3f) | 1¼ | 6 | 9/1 | 69 | 26 |

(SP 111.3%) **6 Rn**

**2m 7.77** (3.47) CSF £5.09 TOTE £2.10: £1.10 £2.60 (£3.30) OWNER Mr N. S. Yong (NEWMARKET) BRED Major C.R. Philipson
WEIGHT FOR AGE 3yo-21lb

### 379 JULIA GARNER H'CAP (0-95) (4-Y.O+) (Class C)
3-45 (3-46) **1m (Equitrack)** £5,403.80 (£1,636.40: £799.20: £380.60) Stalls: High GOING minus 0.51 sec per fur (FST)

| | | | | SP | RR | SF |
|---|---|---|---|---|---|---|
| 270[7] | **Pengamon (74)** (HJCollingridge) **4-8-7** JQuinn(9) (b.hind: hdwy over 3f out: led over 1f out: r.o wl) | — | 1 | 16/1 | 85 | 54 |
| 223[2] | **Queen of All Birds (IRE) (82)** (RBoss) **5-9-1** AClark(11) (b.hind: a.p: rdn over 2f out: r.o one pce) | 2½ | 2 | 10/1 | 88 | 57 |
| | **Sand Star (70)** (DHaydnJones) **4-8-0**(3) DWright(7) (led over 6f: one pce) | nk | 3 | 12/1 | 75 | 44 |
| 20[6] | **Neuwest (USA) (78)** (NJHWalker) **4-8-8**(3) JStack(3) (lw: stdy hdwy over 2f out: rdn over 1f out: one pce) | 1¼ | 4 | 20/1 | 81 | 50 |
| 243* | **Secret Spring (FR) (90)** (PRHedger) **4-9-9** SRaymont(8) (b.hind: s.s: gd hdwy over 3f out: one pce fnl 2f) | 2½ | 5 | 13/8 [1] | 88 | 57 |
| 305* | **Sweet Supposin (IRE) (77)** (CADwyer) **5-8-10v**ow1 CDwyer(5) (lw: nvr nr to chal) | 2 | 6 | 12/1 | 71 | 39 |
| | **Petoskin (78)** (JPearce) **4-8-11** GBardwell(6) (bhd fnl 2f) | hd | 7 | 20/1 | 72 | 41 |
| 308* | **Nordinex (IRE) (70)** (RWArmstrong) **4-8-3**ow1 MFenton(4) (prom over 5f) | 1¼ | 8 | 5/1 [2] | 61 | 29 |
| 306[7] | **Secret Aly (CAN) (82)** (CEBrittain) **6-9-1** MLarsen(2) (lw: s.i.s: hdwy 7f out: wknd 2f out) | nk | 9 | 5/1 [2] | 73 | 42 |
| 174* | **Dancing Lawyer (78)** (BJMeehan) **5-8-11** MTebbutt(1) (hdwy 7f out: wknd over 2f out) | 3½ | 10 | 7/1 [3] | 62 | 31 |

(SP 123.8%) **10 Rn**

**1m 36.98** (-0.42) CSF £154.00 CT £1,208.92 TOTE £23.00: £6.20 £2.70 £2.80 (£65.80) Trio £244.80; £313.78 to Doncaster 4/3/96 OWNER Miss Arabella Smallman (NEWMARKET) BRED John Smallman

### 380 GEMINI H'CAP (0-80) (4-Y.O+) (Class D)
4-15 (4-15) **6f (Equitrack)** £3,485.00 (£1,055.00: £515.00: £245.00) Stalls: Low GOING minus 0.51 sec per fur (FST)

| | | | | SP | RR | SF |
|---|---|---|---|---|---|---|
| 330* | **Stand Tall (69)** (CWThornton) **4-9-5** DeanMcKeown(8) (hdwy over 3f out: rdn over 1f out: led ins fnl f: r.o wl) | — | 1 | 3/1 [1] | 82 | 37 |

| | | | Pos | SP | RR | SF |
|---|---|---|---|---|---|---|
| *354** | **Our Shadee (USA) (60)** (KTIvory) **6-8-3v**(7) 6x CScally(6) (lost pl over 3f out: rallied 1f out: r.o) | 3 | **2** | 7/1 | 65 | 20 |
| *266[7]* | **Spender (78)** (PWHarris) **7-9-11**(3) JStack(4) (led over 1f: led over 2f out tl ins fnl f: unable qckn) | nk | **3** | 10/1 | 82 | 37 |
| *354[2]* | **Sharp Imp (56)** (RMFlower) **6-8-6b** WWoods(9) (hdwy over 1f out: r.o) | nk | **4** | 7/2[2] | 59 | 14 |
| *316[6]* | **Dahiyah (USA) (60)** (GLMoore) **5-8-7v**(3) AWhelan(2) (lw: led over 4f out tl over 2f out: wknd over 1f out) | 3 | **5** | 7/1 | 55 | 10 |
| *244[2]* | **Invocation (68)** (AMoore) **9-9-4** AClark(1) (b.hind: prom 4f) | 1¼ | **6** | 8/1 | 60 | 15 |
| *217[6]* | **Office Hours (60)** (CACyzer) **4-8-10** DBiggs(5) (lw: prom 4f) | 1 | **7** | 14/1 | 49 | 4 |
| *338[6]* | **Samsolom (74)** (PHowling) **8-9-10** JQuinn(7) (lw: hld up: rdn over 2f out: sn wknd) | ¾ | **8** | 20/1 | 61 | 16 |
| *315[4]* | **Friendly Brave (USA) (74)** (MissGayKelleway) **6-9-5**(5) DGriffiths(3) (b.hind: s.s: sme hdwy on ins over 1f out: sn wknd) | ¾ | **9** | 5/1[3] | 59 | 14 |

(SP 120.5%) **9 Rn**

**1m 12.26** (1.66) CSF £23.56 CT £175.41 TOTE £2.90: £1.20 £2.70 £4.60 (£33.20) Trio £35.60 OWNER Mr Guy Reed (MIDDLEHAM) BRED Mrs E. Longton

## 381 LEO H'CAP (0-70) (3-Y.O) (Class E)

4-45 (4-45) **1m 2f (Equitrack)** £2,818.20 (£852.60: £415.80: £197.40) Stalls: Low GOING minus 0.51 sec per fur (FST)

| | | | Pos | SP | RR | SF |
|---|---|---|---|---|---|---|
| *274** | **Mister Aspecto (IRE) (62)** (MJohnston) **3-9-6v**[1] TWilliams(4) (lw: a.p: led over 3f out: hrd rdn & hung lft over 2f out: sn hdd: hung lft 1f out: led ins fnl f: r.o wl) | — | **1** | 6/1[3] | 72 | 33 |
| *300[3]* | **Hever Golf Eagle (51)** (TJNaughton) **3-8-9** DHarrison(8) (hld up: led 2f out: clr over 1f out: hdd ins fnl f: unable qckn) | 1¾ | **2** | 8/1 | 58 | 19 |
| *280[3]* | **Uoni (55)** (CEBrittain) **3-8-13** MLarsen(5) (led over 6f: one pce) | 3 | **3** | 9/1 | 57 | 18 |
| *49[6]* | **Still Here (IRE) (55)** (MJHeaton-Ellis) **3-8-13** AClark(6) (rdn 5f out: hdwy over 3f out: one pce) | 3½ | **4** | 16/1 | 52 | 13 |
| *277[3]* | **Willie Rushton (58)** (GLMoore) **3-9-2** SWhitworth(2) (b.hind: hdwy over 4f out: rdn over 3f out: wknd fnl f) | 1¾ | **5** | 2/1[1] | 52 | 13 |
| | **Sahhar (62)** (RWArmstrong) **3-9-6** WWoods(1) (lw: hdwy over 4f out: wknd over 3f out) | hd | **6** | 11/4[2] | 56 | 17 |
| | **Autobabble (IRE) (63)** (RHannon) **3-9-7** RHughes(7) (prom 5f: t.o) | 25 | **7** | 7/1 | 17 | — |
| *276[4]* | **Bear To Dance (45)** (JohnBerry) **3-8-3** MFenton(3) (prom 5f: t.o) | 20 | **8** | 33/1 | — | — |

(SP 116.7%) **8 Rn**

**2m 8.11** (3.81) CSF £47.82 CT £392.97 TOTE £5.20: £2.10 £1.70 £3.70 (£24.50) OWNER Aspecto Clothing Co Ltd (MIDDLEHAM) BRED Petra Bloodstock Agency Ltd

T/Plpt: £144.60 (72.94 Tckts). T/Qdpt: £32.90 (22.55 Tckts) AK

# 0355-WOLVERHAMPTON (L-H) (Standard)

## Saturday March 2nd

WEATHER: Light Drizzle WIND: almost nil

## 382 BLACKSMITH LIMITED STKS (0-60) (3-Y.O) (Class F)

7-00 (7-01) **1m 100y (Fibresand)** £2,085.00 (£585.00: £285.00) Stalls: Low GOING: 0.22 sec per fur (SLW)

| | | | Pos | SP | RR | SF |
|---|---|---|---|---|---|---|
| *137[3]* | **Lady Dignity (IRE) (60)** (PJMakin) **3-8-7** SSanders(3) (a.p: led wl over 2f out: sn clr: drvn out) | — | **1** | 11/4[2] | 69 | 14 |
| *355** | **Yeoman Oliver (60)** (BAMcMahon) **3-8-10**(5) 3x LNewton(5) (lw: hld up: effrt over 3f out: chsd wnr fnl 2f: no imp) | 4 | **2** | 7/2[3] | 69 | 14 |
| *344** | **Bit of Bother (IRE) (66)** (TDBarron) **3-9-4** 3x JFortune(4) (bhd: pushed along ½-wy: kpt on appr fnl f: nvr nrr) | 2½ | **3** | 7/4[1] | 68 | 13 |
| *230[3]* | **Green Gem (BEL) (58)** (SCWilliams) **3-8-7** JTate(2) (chsd ldr: led 3f out: sn hdd: wknd over 1f out) | 3 | **4** | 11/2 | 51 | — |
| *280[9]* | **Ebony Boy (58)** (JWharton) **3-8-12b**[1] SDWilliams(1) (lw: led & sn clr: wknd & hdd 3f out: grad wknd) | 5 | **5** | 9/1 | 47 | — |

(SP 110.6%) **5 Rn**

**1m 55.2** (10.20) CSF £11.59 TOTE £3.10: £1.20 £2.90 (£5.60) OWNER Mr J. Gamsey (MARLBOROUGH) BRED Mount Coote Stud
STEWARDS' ENQUIRY Newton susp. 14-15/3/96 (careless riding).

## 383 BAKER H'CAP (0-70) (3-Y.O) (Class E)

7-30 (7-30) **6f (Fibresand)** £2,749.00 (£832.00: £406.00: £193.00) Stalls: Low GOING: 0.22 sec per fur (SLW)

| | | | Pos | SP | RR | SF |
|---|---|---|---|---|---|---|
| *294[5]* | **Le Sport (68)** (ABailey) **3-9-4**(3) DWright(5) (bhd & outpcd: hdwy u.p 2f out: r.o to ld fnl 100y) | — | **1** | 10/1 | 75 | 43 |
| *332** | **Chilibang Bang (65)** (JBerry) **3-8-13**(5) PRoberts(6) (lw: trckd ldrs: led wl over 1f out tl hdd & outpcd ins fnl f) | 4 | **2** | 6/1[3] | 61 | 29 |
| *271[2]* | **Mystic Tempo (USA) (63)** (DrJDScargill) **3-8-13**(3) SDrowne(8) (a.p: drvn along fnl 2f: nvr able to chal) | 2 | **3** | 6/1[3] | 54 | 22 |
| | **Lia Fail (IRE) (56)** (RHollinshead) **3-8-2**(7) FLynch(7) (racd wd: r.o fnl 2f: nvr nrr) | nk | **4** | 14/1 | 46 | 14 |
| *347** | **Miss Offset (51)** (MJohnston) **3-8-4b** 6x TWilliams(1) (lw: led 4f out tl hdd wl over 1f out: eased whn btn) | 2 | **5** | 2/1[1] | 36 | 4 |
| *271** | **Copper Bright (68)** (PCHaslam) **3-9-7b** JFortune(3) (hld up in rr: drvn along ½-wy: nt pce to chal) | 4 | **6** | 5/1[2] | 42 | 10 |
| *298[2]* | **The Wad (53)** (DNicholls) **3-7-13**(7) MartinDwyer(2) (led after 1f to 4f out: wknd wl over 1f out) | 1¼ | **7** | 6/1[3] | 24 | — |
| | **Classic Victory (65)** (RHarris) **3-9-4** DBatteate(4) (bkwd: led 1f: wknd wl over 1f out) | 2½ | **8** | 12/1 | 29 | — |
| *307[6]* | **Learning Curve (IRE) (43)** (SirMarkPrescott) **3-7-10** GBardwell(9) (dwlt: a outpcd & bhd: t.o fnl 2f) | 15 | **9** | 14/1 | — | — |

(SP 123.0%) **9 Rn**

**1m 17.2** (5.80) CSF £66.57 CT £367.25 TOTE £12.30: £2.60 £1.90 £2.40 (£55.10) Trio £92.80; £26.17 to Wolverhampton 4/3/96 OWNER Simple Technology UK Ltd (TARPORLEY) BRED R. G. R. Chapman
LONG HANDICAP Learning Curve (IRE) 7-7

## 384 BENTLEY JENNISON H'CAP (0-70) (4-Y.O+) (Class E)

8-00 (8-00) **1m 1f 79y (Fibresand)** £2,775.00 (£840.00: £410.00: £195.00) Stalls: Low GOING: 0.22 sec per fur (SLW)

| | | | Pos | SP | RR | SF |
|---|---|---|---|---|---|---|
| *353** | **Zahid (USA) (52)** (KRBurke) **5-8-10** 5x JQuinn(13) (lw: hld up: hdwy over 4f out: led ent fnl f: sn clr) | — | **1** | 9/2[3] | 66 | 16 |
| *261[5]* | **Hand of Straw (IRE) (62)** (PGMurphy) **4-9-3v**(3) SDrowne(7) (hld up: hdwy over 3f out: kpt on ins fnl f: no ch w wnr) | 5 | **2** | 14/1 | 69 | 18 |
| *285[3]* | **Mislemani (IRE) (51)** (AGNewcombe) **6-8-6**(3) DRMcCabe(1) (trckd ldrs: outpcd 3f out: styd on again appr fnl f) | 2½ | **3** | 8/1 | 52 | 2 |
| *246[3]* | **Trumble (45)** (CWThornton) **4-8-3** LCharnock(5) (lw: led: clr 2f out: wknd & hdd ent fnl f) | ½ | **4** | 10/1 | 46 | — |
| *252[8]* | **Royal Acclaim (38)** (JMBradley) **11-7-7v**(3) DarrenMoffatt(12) (wl bhd tl styd on strly fnl 2f) | ¾ | **5** | 33/1 | 37 | — |

210[5] **Our Tom (65)** (JWharton) **4-9-4b**[1(5)] CTeague(9) (lw: chsd ldr 6f out tl wknd wl over 1f out)....3 **6** 4/1[2] 60 9
270[6] **Reverand Thickness (70)** (SCWilliams) **5-10-0** JFortune(6) (hdwy 5f out: sn hrd drvn: nt rch ldrs)....4 **7** 4/1[2] 57 7
299[3] **Maradata (IRE) (55)** (RHollinshead) **4-8-13** MWigham(3) (dwlt: bhd tl sme late hdwy)....¾ **8** 20/1 42 —
297[7] **East Barns (IRE) (38)** (SGollings) **8-7-5b**[(5)] PFessey(4) (a in rr)....¾ **9** 25/1 23 —
**Whitelock Quest (39)** (NEBerry) **8-7-4**[(7)ow1] AdelleGibbons(8) (a bhd)....hd **10** 10/1 23 —
284[3] **Ballyrag (USA) (55)** (RAFahey) **5-8-13** ACulhane(11) (prom: drvn along 5f out: sn lost tch: t.o)....20 **11** 20/1 5 —
301[2] **Jalmaid (55)** (BAMcMahon) **4-8-13** SSanders(2) (in tch: rdn 6f out: wknd over 3f out: sn t.o)....2½ **12** 3/1[1] 2 —
(SP 135.5%) **12 Rn**

**2m 7.3** (11.30) CSF £67.21 CT £476.42 TOTE £4.60: £2.10 £5.80 £3.10 (£42.00) Trio £146.70; £20.67 Doncaster 4/3/96 OWNER Mr Keith Booth (WANTAGE) BRED Dr. Murray West, Nicholas Lotz & Overbrook Farm
LONG HANDICAP East Barns (IRE) 7-4 Whitelock Quest 7-5 Royal Acclaim 7-7
**OFFICIAL EXPLANATION Jalmaid: connections considered the filly had not recovered from her previous run.**

## 385 ELITE RACING CLUB H'CAP (0-80) (3-Y.O) (Class D)
8-30 (8-30) **1m 4f (Fibresand)** £3,436.25 (£1,040.00: £507.50: £241.25) Stalls: Low GOING: 0.22 sec per fur (SLW)

SP RR SF

313[2] **Nikita's Star (IRE) (66)** (DJGMurraySmith) **3-9-0** MLarsen(7) (hld up gng wl: led on bit over 2f out: readily)....— **1** 6/1 75+ 19
294[3] **Thorntoun Estate (IRE) (58)** (MJohnston) **3-8-6** DeanMcKeown(4) (lw: a.p: hrd drvn 3f out: styd on one pce)....3 **2** 10/1 63 7
329* **China Castle (73)** (PCHaslam) **3-9-7** JFortune(3) (lw: hld up: hdwy 3f out: hrd drvn over 1f out: one pce)....1¼ **3** 5/2[1] 76 20
348[2] **Dancing Cavalier (65)** (RHollinshead) **3-8-6**[(7)] FLynch(1) (hld up & wl bhd: gd hdwy over 3f out: no ex appr fnl f)....1¼ **4** 9/2 67 11
35[8] **Image Maker (IRE) (50)** (BPreece) **3-7-7**[(5)] PFessey(5) (hld up in rr: rdn & outpcd over 2f out: sn bhd)....13 **5** 40/1 34 —
361* **Montecristo (73)** (RGuest) **3-9-4**[(3)] DRMcCabe(6) (led tl over 2f out: sn wknd)....3½ **6** 7/2[2] 53 —
248[3] **In The Band (63)** (LordHuntingdon) **3-8-8**[(3)] PMcCabe(2) (trckd ldrs tl wknd qckly over 4f out: sn t.o)....dist **7** 4/1[3] — —
(SP 114.8%) **7 Rn**

**2m 47.4** (14.90) CSF £53.68 TOTE £6.50: £2.80 £2.90 (£38.00) OWNER Nikita's Partners (LAMBOURN) BRED D. Twomey
**OFFICIAL EXPLANATION In The Band: was in season.**

## 386 SKY ROOFING (S) STKS (4-Y.O+) (Class G)
9-00 (9-00) **5f (Fibresand)** £2,085.00 (£585.00: £285.00) Stalls: Low GOING: 0.22 sec per fur (SLW)

SP RR SF

225[5] **Primula Bairn (61)** (DNicholls) **6-8-13b** AlexGreaves(5) (hdwy over 2f out: led ins fnl f: r.o wl)....— **1** 11/4[3] 64 17
292[2] **Rennyholme (39)** (JHetherton) **5-8-11b** NAdams(7) (lw: a.p: led 2f out tl ins fnl f: kpt on)....¾ **2** 10/1 60 13
202[3] **Hannah's Usher (70)** (CMurray) **4-8-11** MFenton(3) (hdwy 2f out: r.o strly nr fin)....hd **3** 2/1[2] 59 12
63* **Shadow Jury (78)** (DWChapman) **6-9-4b** LCharnock(6) (w ldrs: disp ld over 1f out tl ins fnl f)....1¾ **4** 7/4[1] 61 14
302[4] **Cerbera (30)** (JPSmith) **7-8-6**[(5)] CTeague(8) (effrt 2f out: nt pce to chal)....3½ **5** 50/1 43 —
347[5] **Fiery Footsteps (42)** (SWCampion) **4-7-13**[(7)] FLynch(4) (slt ld 3f: shkn up & outpcd appr fnl f)....2 **6** 33/1 31 —
267[8] **Pats Delight (31)** (SCoathup) **4-8-1**[(5)] AmandaSanders(1) (w ldrs over 2f: sn drvn & outpcd)....4 **7** 50/1 18 —
64[8] **Tommy Tempest (40)** (REPeacock) **7-8-8v**[(3)] PMcCabe(2) (spd 2f: sn lost pl: t.o)....20 **8** 33/1 — —
(SP 115.3%) **8 Rn**

**64.6 secs** (5.90) CSF £26.99 TOTE £4.10: £1.50 £1.90 £1.30 (£18.60) OWNER Mr J. P. Hames (THIRSK) BRED Kavli Ltd
No bid
STEWARDS' ENQUIRY Greaves susp. 14-15/3/96 (excessive use of whip).

## 387 PLYVINE CATERING MAIDEN H'CAP (0-65) (3-Y.O+) (Class F)
9-30 (9-32) **7f (Fibresand)** £2,433.00 (£683.00: £333.00) Stalls: High GOING: 0.22 sec per fur (SLW)

SP RR SF

71[8] **McKellar (IRE) (47)** (TDBarron) **7-9-6** JFortune(11) (hld up: hdwy over 3f out: shkn up to ld wl over 1f out: sn clr)....— **1** 4/1[2] 70 16
244[7] **Woolverstone Hall (IRE) (35)** (DJGMurraySmith) **4-8-8b** NAdams(8) (trckd ldrs: kpt on appr fnl f: no ch w wnr)....9 **2** 11/2[3] 37 —
**Duralock Fencer (54)** (PGMurphy) **3-8-8**[(3)] SDrowne(3) (b.hind: outpcd tl kpt on fnl 2f: nvr nrr)....2½ **3** 12/1 52 —
274[5] **Taniyar (FR) (43)** (RHollinshead) **4-9-2v**[1] MWigham(9) (hdwy over 2f out: nvr nrr)....nk **4** 10/1 39 —
157[3] **Young Frederick (IRE) (60)** (KRBurke) **3-8-10**[(7)] TAshley(6) (lw: hdwy u.p fnl 2f: nvr nrr)....2 **5** 2/1[1] 53 —
239[12] **Speedy Snaps Pride (34)** (PDCundell) **4-8-7b** MLarsen(1) (prom tl wknd u.p 3f out)....2½ **6** 20/1 20 —
310[3] **So Natural (IRE) (52)** (EJAlston) **4-9-11** SDWilliams(4) (nvr bttr than mid div)....6 **7** 9/1 24 —
347[6] **Young Ben (IRE) (37)** (JSWainwright) **4-8-10** DeanMcKeown(12) (outpcd: a bhd)....hd **8** 25/1 9 —
**Ho Mei Surprise (37)** (BPreece) **4-8-3**[(7)] FLynch(5) (bit bkwd: led: clr ½-wy: wknd & hdd wl over 1f out)....1¼ **9** 14/1 6 —
**Classic Delight (USA) (57)** (RHarris) **3-9-0** DBatteate(2) (prom over 4f: t.o)....6 **10** 12/1 13 —
255[8] **Chief's Lady (44)** (JMBradley) **4-9-3** JQuinn(7) (trckd ldrs over 3f: sn outpcd: t.o)....1¼ **11** 25/1 — —
**Malzoom (35)** (SEKettlewell) **4-8-8** LCharnock(10) (s.s: sn bhd & outpcd: t.o)....7 **12** 20/1 — —
(SP 127.1%) **12 Rn**

**1m 33.9** (9.20) CSF £26.66 CT £232.91 TOTE £6.50: £1.50 £2.00 £2.80 (£36.90) Trio £144.40; £101.75 to Doncaster 4/3/96 OWNER M P Burke Developments Ltd (THIRSK) BRED Ardenode Stud Ltd
WEIGHT FOR AGE 3yo-16lb

T/Plpt: £847.20 (14.92 Tckts). T/Qdpt: £75.20 (8.81 Tckts) IM

# 0382-WOLVERHAMPTON (L-H) (Standard)
## Wednesday March 6th
WEATHER: fine WIND: almost nil

## 388 SANDSTORM AMATEUR H'CAP (0-70) (I) (4-Y.O+) (Class E)
1-40 (1-41) **6f (Fibresand)** £2,534.15 (£765.20: £372.10: £175.55) Stalls: Low GOING: 0.23 sec per fur (SLW)

SP RR SF

291[4] **Deeply Vale (IRE) (65)** (GLMoore) **5-11-3**[(4)] MrKGoble(7) (lw: s.i.s: hdwy 4f out: led over 1f out: r.o wl)....— **1** 6/1 72 54

368[3] **Desert Invader (IRE) (64)** (DWChapman) **5-11-6** 7x MissRClark(3) (lw: a.p: ev ch over 1f out: unable qckn) .......1¾ **2** 100/30[2] 66 48
**The Fed (44)** (JAPickering) **6-9-7**(7) MissEGeorge(8) (a.p: rdn & ev ch 2f out: one pce) .......3 **3** 25/1 38 20
218[3] **Lochon (57)** (JLEyre) **5-10-13** MissDianaJones(1) (b: hdwy & c wd 2f out: r.o one pce fnl f) .......s.h **4** 3/1[1] 51 33
**Nomadic Dancer (IRE) (43)** (MSSaunders) **4-9-6**(7) MrsCWilliams(5) (prom: rdn over 3f out: ev ch 2f out: sn wknd) .......7 **5** 33/1 19 1
278* **Newington Butts (IRE) (49)** (KMcAuliffe) **6-10-5e** MrTMcCarthy(4) (led over 4f out tl over 1f out: sn wknd) .....2 **6** 4/1[3] 19 1
386[6] **Fiery Footsteps (42)** (SWCampion) **4-9-5**(7) MrsSJCampion(9) (b.nr hind: hld up: rdn 3f out: bhd whn hung lft fnl 2f) .......3 **7** 20/1 4 —
342[2] **Brookhead Lady (53)** (PDEvans) **5-10-2**(7) MrAEvans(2) (b: led over 1f: rdn & wknd 2f out) .......1½ **8** 9/2 11 —
**Miss Kive (50)** (AJChamberlain) **10-9-13**(7)ow20 MrSHowe(10) (b: sn bhd: t.o) .......25 **9** 100/1 — —
**Bold Time Monkey (40)** (MTate) **5-9-3**(7) MissSTalbot(6) (bkwd: s.s: a t.o) .......10 **10** 100/1 — —
(SP 114.1%) **10 Rn**

**1m 18.3** (6.90) CSF £24.33 CT £427.10 TOTE £6.50: £1.40 £2.30 £5.80 (£8.50) Trio £160.90; £136.00 to Wincanton 7/3/96 OWNER Mr K. Higson (EPSOM)
LONG HANDICAP Miss Kive 8-11

## 389 SANDSTORM AMATEUR H'CAP (0-70) (II) (4-Y.O+) (Class E)

2-10 (2-10) **6f (Fibresand)** £2,520.50 (£761.00: £370.00: £174.50) Stalls: Low GOING: 0.23 sec per fur (SLW)

SP RR SF

316[5] **Lift Boy (USA) (61)** (AMoore) **7-10-13**(4) MrsJMoore(5) (led 1f: led wl over 1f out: r.o wl) .......— **1** 11/8[1] 72 41
302[3] **Sea-Deer (65)** (DWChapman) **7-11-7** MissRClark(3) (a.p: chsd wnr over 1f out: no imp) .......3½ **2** 7/2[2] 67 36
315[5] **Best Kept Secret (56)** (PDEvans) **5-10-5v**(7) MrAEvans(6) (a.p: hrd rdn over 2f out: r.o one pce fnl f) .......1½ **3** 8/1 54 23
**Fighter Squadron (40)** (REPeacock) **7-9-3b**(7) MrsCPeacock(9) (carried wd over 3f out: hdwy 2f out: nt rch ldrs) .......4 **4** 33/1 27 —
387[9] **Ho Mei Surprise (37)** (BPreece) **4-9-0**(7) MissLBoswell(2) (led over 4f out tl wl over 1f out: sn wknd) .......½ **5** 10/1 23 —
311[5] **Life Is Precious (IRE) (47)** (RHollinshead) **4-10-3** MrsSBosley(4) (prom 4f) .......2½ **6** 10/1 26 —
341[6] **Blyton Star (IRE) (32)** (MissJFCraze) **8-8-9**(7)ow2 MrWWenyon(1) (led 5f out: sn hdd: hung rt & wknd 2f out) .......2½ **7** 33/1 4 —
**Prince Rooney (IRE) (50)** (PButler) **8-9-13**(7) MrJGoldstein(8) (carried wd over 3f out: nt rcvr) .......¾ **8** 20/1 20 —
105[10] **Faez (52)** (RSimpson) **6-10-1b**(7) MissLPope(7) (b: lw: prom over 2f: p.u lame 3f out: dead) ....... **P** 6/1[3] — —
(SP 118.6%) **9 Rn**

**1m 19.0** (7.60) CSF £6.73 CT £24.68 TOTE £2.20: £1.10 £1.50 £3.10 (£4.00) Trio £12.90 OWNER Mr A. Moore (BRIGHTON) BRED Paul & Arnold Bryant in USA
LONG HANDICAP Blyton Star (IRE) 8-11

## 390 TEMPEST MAIDEN STKS (3-Y.O+) (Class D)

2-40 (2-41) **1m 100y (Fibresand)** £3,582.50 (£1,085.00: £530.00: £252.50) Stalls: Low GOING: 0.23 sec per fur (SLW)

SP RR SF

**Chief Mouse** (RCharlton) **3-8-6** SSanders(7) (a.p: rdn 4f out: led over 1f out: drvn out) .......— **1** 5/1[2] 77 12
**State Circus** (LordHuntingdon) **3-8-1** DaleGibson(5) (rangy: dwlt: rdn & hdwy over 4f out: r.o wl ins fnl f) .......nk **2** 6/1[3] 71 6
310[6] **Tirra-Lirra (IRE)** (CEBrittain) **4-9-2**(3) DRMcCabe(13) (lw: a.p: r.o one pce fnl f) .......2½ **3** 25/1 67 20
364[3] **Classic Beauty (IRE)** (RHarris) **3-8-1** DBatteate(10) (led over 1f: led over 5f out tl over 1f out: one pce) .......nk **4** 3/1[1] 66 1
**Whitley Grange Boy (67)** (JLEyre) **3-8-6** TWilliams(9) (bit bkwd: prom: rdn 3f out: wknd over 1f out) .......3½ **5** 10/1 65 —
320[2] **Rubbiyati** (CEBrittain) **4-9-5** MLarsen(1) (led 7f out tl over 5f out: rdn over 3f out: sn wknd) .......6 **6** 5/1[2] 48 1
**Lucitino** (SCWilliams) **3-8-1** JTate(4) (leggy: unf: dwlt: nvr nr ldrs) .......6 **7** 16/1 37 —
337[6] **Black And Amber** (PRWebber) **4-9-5** NAdams(8) (hdwy over 5f out: wknd over 2f out) .......4 **8** 20/1 29 —
**Red Time** (MSSaunders) **3-8-6** AMcGlone(2) (rdn 5f out: sn bhd) .......2 **9** 33/1 30 —
**Tirols Tyrant (IRE)** (MrsASwinbank) **3-8-6** GBardwell(12) (a bhd) .......hd **10** 10/1 30 —
344[12] **Blondane** (SRBowring) **3-8-2**(5)ow1 CTeague(3) (a bhd) .......8 **11** 20/1 16 —
**Dosses Dan (IRE)** (BPreece) **4-9-3b[1]**(7) FLynch(11) (bhd fnl 4f: t.o) .......9 **12** 20/1 — —
337[7] **Showtime Blues (IRE)** (ABailey) **7-9-10** LCharnock(6) (rdn over 5f out: sn bhd: t.o) .......3 **13** 25/1 — —
(SP 121.6%) **13 Rn**

**1m 55.4** (10.40) CSF £33.40 TOTE £5.00: £1.70 £2.90 £10.80 (£13.20) Trio £161.60; £207.18 to Wincanton 7/3/96 OWNER Lady Vestey (BECKHAMPTON) BRED Lady Vestey
WEIGHT FOR AGE 3yo-18lb
STEWARDS' ENQUIRY Batteate susp. 15-16/3/96 (excessive use of whip).

## 391 CYCLONE H'CAP (0-90) (3-Y.O) (Class C)

3-10 (3-10) **1m 100y (Fibresand)** £5,181.50 (£1,568.00: £765.00: £363.50) Stalls: Low GOING: 0.23 sec per fur (SLW)

SP RR SF

383* **Le Sport (73)** (ABailey) **3-8-3**(3) 5x DWright(6) (stdy hdwy over 4f out: led over 2f out: clr over 1f out: easily) .......— **1** 5/1[2] 82+ 15
313* **Galapino (80)** (CEBrittain) **3-8-13** MLarsen(7) (lw: w ldr: led over 5f out tl over 3f out: rdn over 2f out: no ch w wnr) .......8 **2** 4/5[1] 74 7
313[4] **Victim of Love (65)** (RCharlton) **3-7-12** GBardwell(5) (prom: rdn over 3f out: wknd over 2f out) .......4 **3** 14/1 51 —
**Double Diamond (IRE) (88)** (MJohnston) **3-9-7** TWilliams(4) (led 3f: wknd 3f out) .......1¾ **4** 10/1 71 4
352* **Carmarthen Bay (82)** (GLMoore) **3-8-12**(3) 5x AWhelan(1) (a.p: led over 3f out tl over 2f out: wknd over 50y out) .......nk **5** 7/1 64 —
220* **Kingdom Princess (67)** (MJCamacho) **3-8-0** LCharnock(3) (lw: hld up: rdn over 3f out: eased whn btn over 1f out) .......30 **6** 6/1[3] — —
**Sualtach (IRE) (80)** (RHollinshead) **3-8-6**(7) FLynch(2) (hld up: rdn 5f out: bhd fnl 4f) .......7 **7** 25/1 — —
(SP 118.6%) **7 Rn**

**1m 55.0** (10.00) CSF £9.67 TOTE £8.50: £1.60 £1.50 (£2.30) OWNER Simple Technology UK Ltd (TARPORLEY) BRED R. G. R. Chapman
**OFFICIAL EXPLANATION Carmarthen Bay: the rider reported the colt changed his legs and gurgled 50 yards before the line, he therefore thought it in the horse's best interest to ease up.**
**Galapino: the rider reported that the horse was not striding out as he usually does.**

## 392 HURRICANE H'CAP (0-100) (4-Y.O+) (Class C)

3-40 (3-40) **1m 4f (Fibresand)** £5,255.60 (£1,590.80: £776.40: £369.20) Stalls: Low GOING: 0.23 sec per fur (SLW)

| Form | Horse | Dist | Pos | SP | RR | SF |
|---|---|---|---|---|---|---|
| | **River Keen (IRE) (92)** (RWArmstrong) **4-10-0** WWoods(1) (hld up & bhd: hdwy over 4f out: led wl ins fnl f: drvn out) | — | **1** | 11/2$^{2}$ | 100 | 54 |
| *312** | **Northern Union (CAN) (88)** (MAJarvis) **5-9-12** PRobinson(9) (b: lw: hld up: hdwy 5f out: nt clr run over 3f out: sn rdn: rallied over 2f out: r.o wl ins fnl f) | hd | **2** | 9/4$^{1}$ | 95 | 52 |
| *345$^{2}$* | **Calder King (68)** (JLEyre) **5-8-1v**(5) PFessey(2) (a.p: led over 3f out: edgd rt & hdd wl ins fnl f) | ¾ | **3** | 16/1 | 74 | 31 |
| *181$^{4}$* | **Celestial Choir (82)** (JLEyre) **6-9-3**(3) OPears(11) (hld up: hdwy over 5f out: one pce fnl 2f) | 6 | **4** | 8/1$^{3}$ | 80 | 37 |
| *296** | **Cuango (IRE) (67)** (RHollinshead) **5-7-12**(7) FLynch(7) (lw: a.p: led over 4f out tl over 3f out: wknd 2f out) | 3 | **5** | 14/1 | 61 | 18 |
| | **Chatham Island (90)** (CEBrittain) **8-10-0** MLarsen(6) (bkwd: prom: rdn over 5f out: wknd 3f out) | 8 | **6** | 12/1 | 73 | 30 |
| *333** | **Backview (70)** (BJLlewellyn) **4-7-13**(7)ow1 JWilkinson(4) (sn w ldr: wknd over 2f out) | 2½ | **7** | 10/1 | 51 | 4 |
| *358$^{6}$* | **Field of Vision (IRE) (74)** (MJohnston) **6-8-12** TWilliams(10) (hld up & bhd: hdwy over 5f out: wknd 3f out) | 5 | **8** | 20/1 | 47 | 4 |
| *251$^{2}$* | **Mentalasanythin (79)** (ABailey) **7-8-10**(7) AngelaGallimore(5) (bhd fnl 3f) | 6 | **9** | 14/1 | 44 | 1 |
| *303** | **Claque (60)** (DWChapman) **4-7-10b** LCharnock(8) (led over 7f: sn wknd) | 5 | **10** | 14/1 | 20 | — |
| *312$^{2}$* | **Johns Act (USA) (71)** (DHaydnJones) **6-8-9** DHarrison(3) (prom tl rdn & wknd over 4f out: t.o) | 12 | **11** | 8/1$^{3}$ | 14 | — |

(SP 115.8%) **11 Rn**

**2m 44.1** (11.60) CSF £17.08 CT £170.34 TOTE £6.50: £2.00 £1.70 £3.20 (£6.50) Trio £78.80 OWNER Dr Meou Tsen Geoffrey Yeh (NEWMARKET) BRED Ballylinch Stud Ltd

WEIGHT FOR AGE 4yo-2lb

## 393 BLIZZARD (S) STKS (4-Y.O+) (Class E)

4-10 (4-11) **1m 1f 79y (Fibresand)** £3,022.95 (£915.60: £447.30: £213.15) Stalls: Low GOING: 0.23 sec per fur (SLW)

| Form | Horse | Dist | Pos | SP | RR | SF |
|---|---|---|---|---|---|---|
| *372$^{2}$* | **No Submission (USA) (58)** (DWChapman) **10-9-4v** ACulhane(9) (lw: hld up & bhd: hdwy 5f out: led over 2f out: sn clr: easily) | — | **1** | 3/1$^{2}$ | 67 | 17 |
| *318$^{3}$* | **Jungle Patrol (IRE) (63)** (CMurray) **4-8-12** MTebbutt(6) (lw: chsd ldr: led over 3f out: hrd rdn & hdd over 2f out: no ch w wnr) | 6 | **2** | 9/4$^{1}$ | 51 | 1 |
| *366$^{11}$* | **Top Pet (IRE) (49)** (RAkehurst) **6-8-12** SSanders(12) (a.p: one pce fnl 2f) | 6 | **3** | 9/1 | 41 | — |
| *366$^{5}$* | **Sarum (51)** (CPWildman) **10-8-12** CRutter(8) (chsd ldrs: hrd rdn 3f out: wknd over 1f out) | 5 | **4** | 6/1$^{3}$ | 32 | — |
| *353$^{12}$* | **Thomas Crown (IRE) (48)** (NJHWalker) **4-8-9b1**(3) JStack(5) (led: rdn & hdd over 3f out: wknd over 2f out) | 3½ | **5** | 33/1 | 26 | — |
| | **Highland Spin** (MrsMReveley) **5-8-5**(7) SCopp(2) (nvr nr ldrs) | 6 | **6** | 12/1 | 16 | — |
| *351$^{2}$* | **Zuno Flyer (USA) (40)** (AMoore) **4-8-5v**(7) FLynch(11) (prom tl wknd 2f out) | 1 | **7** | 7/1 | 14 | — |
| *174$^{7}$* | **Cannizaro (IRE) (54)** (RJRWilliams) **4-8-7** DBiggs(13) (b: prom over 4f) | 5 | **8** | 16/1 | — | — |
| *343$^{7}$* | **Jon's Choice (39)** (BPreece) **8-8-12** NAdams(3) (bhd tl hdwy 4f out: wknd 2f out) | 3½ | **9** | 20/1 | — | — |
| | **Chastleton (47)** (MRChannon) **4-8-7** CandyMorris(4) (wl bhd fnl 4f) | 5 | **10** | 12/1 | — | — |
| *360$^{8}$* | **Lady Elizabeth (FR) (30)** (KOCunningham-Brown) **4-8-7b** MLarsen(10) (a bhd) | 1½ | **11** | 33/1 | — | — |
| *337$^{8}$* | **Taylors Revival** (HJCollingridge) **5-8-7** DaleGibson(1) (wl bhd fnl 4f: t.o) | dist | **12** | 33/1 | — | — |

(SP 127.4%) **12 Rn**

**2m 8.2** (12.20) CSF £10.55 TOTE £3.50: £1.60 £1.10 £5.20 (£4.00) Trio £25.70 OWNER Mr T. S. Redman (YORK) BRED Mr. Francis X. Weber

No bid

## 394 LADBROKE SERIES H'CAP (Final) (3-Y.O+) (Class C)

4-40 (4-40) **5f (Fibresand)** £5,576.00 (£1,688.00: £824.00: £392.00) Stalls: Low GOING: 0.23 sec per fur (SLW)

| Form | Horse | Dist | Pos | SP | RR | SF |
|---|---|---|---|---|---|---|
| *354$^{4}$* | **Kira (67)** (JLEyre) **6-9-0**(3) OPears(9) (b.off hind: hdwy over 1f out: r.o to ld last strides) | — | **1** | 5/1$^{2}$ | 79 | 25 |
| *315$^{6}$* | **Cheeky Chappy (55)** (DWChapman) **5-8-0b**(5) PFessey(1) (w ldr: led over 2f out: hdd last strides) | hd | **2** | 14/1 | 67 | 13 |
| *386$^{2}$* | **Rennyholme (46)** (JHetherton) **5-7-10b** NAdams(6) (led over 2f: one pce fnl f) | 3½ | **3** | 7/1$^{3}$ | 47 | — |
| *331$^{3}$* | **Lord Sky (66)** (ABailey) **5-8-9**(7) AngelaGallimore(7) (a.p: r.o one pce fnl f) | nk | **4** | 4/1$^{1}$ | 66 | 12 |
| *272$^{2}$* | **Boffy (IRE) (77)** (BPJBaugh) **3-8-7**(7) IonaWands(10) (b: a.p: no hdwy fnl 2f) | hd | **5** | 9/1 | 77 | 9 |
| *272$^{3}$* | **Gagajulu (59)** (PDEvans) **3-7-10** LCharnock(8) (hdwy over 2f out: nvr nr to chal) | hd | **6** | 12/1 | 59 | — |
| *315$^{2}$* | **Chadwell Hall (78)** (SRBowring) **5-9-9b**(5) CTeague(4) (b.off hind: lw: prom tl wknd over 1f out) | 1¾ | **7** | 5/1$^{2}$ | 71 | 17 |
| *315$^{7}$* | **Little Ibnr (76)** (PDEvans) **5-9-7v**(5) AmandaSanders(5) (rdn over 3f out: bhd fnl 2f) | ½ | **8** | 20/1 | 68 | 14 |
| *315$^{3}$* | **Leigh Crofter (70)** (PDCundell) **7-9-1b**(5) DGriffiths(2) (n.d) | 1¾ | **9** | 7/1$^{3}$ | 56 | 2 |
| *362$^{2}$* | **Featherstone Lane (69)** (MissLCSiddall) **5-9-5v** DHarrison(3) (stmbld s: a bhd) | 1¾ | **10** | 5/1$^{2}$ | 50 | — |

(SP 124.1%) **10 Rn**

**64.4 secs** (5.70) CSF £66.87 CT £467.81 TOTE £7.40: £4.10 £4.80 £1.60 (£28.20) Trio £339.30 OWNER Mr J. E. Wilson (HAMBLETON) BRED J. S. Bell

LONG HANDICAP Rennyholme 7-3 Gagajulu 7-9

WEIGHT FOR AGE 3yo-13lb

OFFICIAL EXPLANATION **Featherstone Lane: the rider reported the gelding stumbled leaving the stalls and was never giong properly after.**

T/Plpt: £38.70 (239.55 Tckts). T/Qdpt: £13.50 (53.56 Tckts) KH

# 0375a-NAD AL SHEBA (Dubai, UAE) (L-H) (Good)

## Thursday February 15th

## 395a RACE 5 (4-Y.O+)

**1m 2f (Dirt)** £5,263.00 (£2,632.00: £1,579.00)

| Horse | Dist | Pos | SP | RR | SF |
|---|---|---|---|---|---|
| **Valley of Gold (FR)** (SbinSuroor,UAE) **4-9-0**ow1 JPMurtagh | — | **1** | | — | — |
| **Russian Snows (IRE)** (SbinSuroor,UAE) **4-8-2**ow1 JCarroll | ½ | **2** | | — | — |
| **Najm Almaydaan (USA)** (DJSelvaratnam,UAE) **5-8-7** BDoyle | 1½ | **3** | | — | — |

**7 Rn**

**2m 4.17** OWNER Godolphin BRED Darley Stud Management (France)

**Valley of Gold (FR)** was held up in the rear, and despite running wide entering the straight, made good headway in the last two and a half furlongs to lead near the finish. This was a good performance giving 12lb to the second.

**Russian Snows (IRE)** was hampered before the straight, but still came through on the inside to show in front a furlong and a half from home. She ran on well, but was just caught close home.
**Najm Almaydaan (USA)** was always prominent, but could make no impression in the last quarter mile.

# 0395a-NAD AL SHEBA (Dubai, UAE) (L-H) (Fast)
## Sunday February 25th

### 396a CENTRAL TRADING COMPANY MILE (4-Y.O+)
**1m (Dirt)** £5,263.00 (£2,632.00: £1,579.00: £1,053.00)

| Horse | Dist | Pos | SP | RR | SF |
|---|---|---|---|---|---|
| **Airport (USA)** (DJSelvaratnam,UAE) **5-8-12** BDoyle | — | 1 | | — | — |
| **Dancing Beggar (USA)** (SbinSuroor,UAE) **4-8-9** JCarroll | ½ | 2 | | — | — |
| **Moonshell (IRE)** (SbinSuroor,UAE) **4-9-3** LDettori | 15 | 3 | | — | — |
| **Jumilla (USA)** (SbinSuroor,UAE) **4-8-6b** BCrossley | | 4 | | — | — |
| | | | | | **4 Rn** |

**1m 37.34** OWNER Sheikh Ahmed Al Maktoum BRED E. A. Seltzer Irrevocable Trust in USA
**Airport (USA)** tracked the leader until challenging over two furlongs out. He kept on to lead near the finish.
**Dancing Beggar (USA)** set a steady pace until quickening half a mile from home. He ran on well but could not resist the winner's challenge in the closing stages.
**Moonshell (IRE)** was a major disappointment. She was settled in the rear until making a short-lived effort turning for home. She was soon beaten, and was eased in the final furlong. However, this was her first run since last June, the distance may have been on the short side, and it is possible she does not act as well on the dirt.

### 397a SHEIKH MAKTOUM AL MAKTOUM CHALLENGE (RND II) (Listed) (4-Y.O+)
**1m 4f (Dirt)** £13,158.00 (£6,579.00: £3,947.00: £2,632.00)

| Horse | Dist | Pos | SP | RR | SF |
|---|---|---|---|---|---|
| **Larrocha (IRE)** (SbinSuroor,UAE) **4-8-8** LDettori | — | 1 | | — | — |
| **Learmont (USA)** (ECharpy,UAE) **6-9-0** WJSupple | 8 | 2 | | — | — |
| **Cayumanque (CHI)** (SbinSuroor,UAE) **6-9-0** BCrossley | nk | 3 | | — | — |
| | | | | | **10 Rn** |

**2m 30.75** OWNER Sheik Maktoum bin Mohammed Al Maktoum BRED K. and Mrs Prendergast
**Larrocha (IRE)** made virtually all the running, and in a performance reminiscent of her victories at Newbury and York last year, had all her rivals in trouble a quarter of a mile from home, and won unchallenged. She could be a force to be reckoned with in the big races in Europe this year.
**Learmont (USA)** has been running well this winter, and although no match for the winner, came through gamely in the closing stages to be second.

# 0367-SOUTHWELL (L-H) (Standard)
## Saturday March 9th
WEATHER: fine WIND: almost nil

### 398 MARBLES H'CAP (0-65) (I) (4-Y.O+) (Class F)
1-10 (1-10) **2m (Fibresand)** £3,103.00 (£943.00: £463.00: £223.00) Stalls: Low GOING minus 0.05 sec per fur (STD)

| Form | Horse | Dist | Pos | SP | RR | SF |
|---|---|---|---|---|---|---|
| $367^{W}$ | **Selmeston (IRE) (35)** (PSFelgate) **4-7-10**(3) DWright(9) (bhd: gd hdwy 6f out: rdn to ld 2f out: sn clr: eased towards fin) | — | 1 | $5/1^{2}$ | 52 | — |
| 373* | **Tempering (59)** (DWChapman) **10-10-0** ACulhane(7) (led: clr 5f out: hdd 2f out: no ch w wnr) | 9 | 2 | $5/1^{2}$ | 67 | — |
| $268^{3}$ | **Fox Chapel (59)** (RTJuckes) **9-10-0** DaleGibson(2) (bhd & drvn along: styd on fnl 3f: nvr nr ldrs) | 4 | 3 | $12/1^{3}$ | 63 | — |
| $369^{3}$ | **Baher (USA) (38)** (MrsASwinbank) **7-8-7** GDuffield(3) (chsd ldrs: drvn along 7f out: one pce) | 3 | 4 | $5/1^{2}$ | 39 | — |
| 365* | **The Lad (36)** (LMontagueHall) **7-7-12**(7) MartinDwyer(1) (chsd ldrs: drvn along & lost pl 6f out: sme hdwy 2f out: n.d) | 8 | 5 | $7/4^{1}$ | 29 | — |
| $275^{7}$ | **Bobby Blue (IRE) (40)** (RonaldThompson) **5-8-9** SDWilliams(6) (bhd: hdwy u.p 6f out: hung lft & wknd over 3f out) | 1 | 6 | 33/1 | 32 | — |
| $373^{8}$ | **Tap On Tootsie (38)** (TRWall) **4-8-2** NAdams(8) (chsd ldrs tl rdn & wknd over 4f out) | 1¼ | 7 | 16/1 | 29 | — |
| | **Inteabadun (35)** (ABailey) **4-7-13** FNorton(5) (bhd: drvn along 9f out: sn chsng ldrs: wknd over 3f out) | 3 | 8 | 20/1 | 23 | — |
| $186^{10}$ | **Rose of Glenn (44)** (BPalling) **5-8-13** SSanders(4) (chsd ldrs tl lost pl over 5f out) | 7 | 9 | $12/1^{3}$ | 25 | — |
| | | | | (SP 115.3%) | | **9 Rn** |

**3m 51.2** (25.20) CSF £28.08 CT £258.76 TOTE £6.20: £2.10 £3.80 £5.30 (£11.80) Trio £96.30 OWNER Mr Chris Wright (MELTON MOWBRAY) BRED St Simon Foundation
WEIGHT FOR AGE 4yo-5lb
**OFFICIAL EXPLANATION The Lad: was reportedly unsuited by the Fibresand and was never travelling throughout the final circuit.**

### 399 NOTTINGHAM PRINT FINISHERS H'CAP (0-70) (I) (3-Y.O+) (Class E)
1-40 (1-40) **7f (Fibresand)** £3,587.80 (£1,089.40: £534.20: £256.60) Stalls: Low GOING minus 0.05 sec per fur (STD)

| Form | Horse | Dist | Pos | SP | RR | SF |
|---|---|---|---|---|---|---|
| $244^{3}$ | **Yo Kiri-B (50)** (JFfitch-Heyes) **5-8-9** GDuffield(4) (hld up: effrt & nt clr run over 2f out: r.o wl to ld wl ins fnl f) | — | 1 | 6/1 | 58 | 27 |
| $368^{2}$ | **Awesome Venture (58)** (MCChapman) **6-9-0**(3) DRMcCabe(7) (trckd ldrs: nt clr run over 2f out: led over 1f out tl nr fin) | 1¼ | 2 | $4/1^{1}$ | 63 | 32 |
| $363^{3}$ | **Quinzii Martin (50)** (DHaydnJones) **8-8-6**(3) DWright(6) (drvn along & hdwy over 2f out: edgd lft: kpt on one pce) | 6 | 3 | $4/1^{1}$ | 41 | 10 |
| | **Yuppy Girl (IRE) (60)** (CaptJHWilson) **3-8-3**ow1 GCarter(1) (lw: led over 4f out: hung lft & hdd over 1f out: sn wknd) | 1 | 4 | 10/1 | 50 | 1 |
| $371^{4}$ | **Square Deal (FR) (69)** (SRBowring) **5-10-0** SDWilliams(3) (sn chsng ldrs: effrt over 2f out: wknd over 1f out) | 5 | 5 | $5/1^{2}$ | 47 | 16 |
| $345^{8}$ | **Swandale Flyer (37)** (NBycroft) **4-7-10** GBardwell(8) (sn bhd & drvn along: sme hdwy over 1f out: n.d) | 2 | 6 | 33/1 | 10 | — |
| $368^{4}$ | **Branston Kristy (37)** (CSmith) **4-7-3b**(7) IonaWands(9) (chsd ldrs tl lost pl over 2f out) | nk | 7 | 16/1 | 10 | — |

| | | | Pos | SP | RR | SF |
|---|---|---|---|---|---|---|
| 310* | **All Apologies (IRE) (69)** (RHollinshead) **4-9-7**(7) FLynch(5) (led tl over 4f out: wknd over 2f out) | 1 | **8** | 11/2 3 | 39 | 8 |
| | **Cee-Jay-Ay (58)** (JBerry) **9-9-3** LeTolboll(2) (dwlt: a in rr) | 4 | **9** | 9/1 | 19 | — |
| | | | | (SP 114.3%) | | **9 Rn** |

**1m 32.3** (5.50) CSF £28.07 CT £97.49 TOTE £6.90: £2.30 £1.20 £1.60 (£19.80) Trio £8.40 OWNER Miss L. A. Elliott (LEWES) BRED Crescent (UK) Ltd
LONG HANDICAP Branston Kristy 7-0
WEIGHT FOR AGE 3yo-16lb

## 400 MARBLES H'CAP (0-65) (II) (4-Y.O+) (Class F)

2-10 (2-10) **2m (Fibresand)** £3,103.00 (£943.00: £463.00: £223.00) Stalls: Low GOING minus 0.05 sec per fur (STD)

| | | | Pos | SP | RR | SF |
|---|---|---|---|---|---|---|
| | **Ijab (CAN) (49)** (JParkes) **6-9-4b** GBardwell(5) (lw: dwlt: hdwy to trck ldrs ½-wy: hrd rdn & led jst ins fnl f: hld on wl) | — | **1** | 2/1 1 | 62 | — |
| 297[4] | **Hard Love (49)** (JLEyre) **4-8-13** TWilliams(6) (trckd ldr: led 5f out tl jst ins fnl f: r.o) | ¾ | **2** | 5/1 2 | 61 | — |
| 367[6] | **Swordking (IRE) (31)** (JLHarris) **7-8-0** NCarlisle(1) (a chsng ldrs: rdn & edgd lft over 2f out: kpt on one pce) | 4 | **3** | 5/1 2 | 39 | — |
| 297[5] | **Cross Talk (IRE) (60)** (RHollinshead) **4-9-3**(7) FLynch(7) (hld up: hdwy 5f out: effrt over 2f out: no imp) | 1½ | **4** | 7/1 | 67 | — |
| | **Howqua River (54)** (PWChapple-Hyam) **4-8-11**(7) RCody-Boutcher(8) (b.hind: hld up: hdwy ½-wy: drvn along & wknd 2f out) | 15 | **5** | 9/1 | 46 | — |
| 186[4] | **Captain Marmalade (46)** (DTThom) **7-9-1** JTate(4) (b: bit bkwd: hdwy 6f out: wknd over 2f out: sn hmpd & eased) | 7 | **6** | 11/2 3 | 31 | — |
| 236[12] | **Can She Can Can (41)** (CSmith) **4-8-5** JFanning(2) (led to 5f out: sn wknd) | 25 | **7** | 16/1 | 1 | — |
| | **Princess Tallulah (36)** (WGMTurner) **5-8-0**(5) ADaly(3) (in tch: drvn along 7f out: sn bhd) | 11 | **8** | 33/1 | — | — |
| | | | | (SP 113.4%) | | **8 Rn** |

**3m 51.4** (25.40) CSF £11.69 CT £38.78 TOTE £3.20: £1.10 £2.40 £1.70 (£5.80) OWNER Mrs Lynn Parkes (MALTON) BRED R. M. Anderson
WEIGHT FOR AGE 4yo-5lb

## 401 CONKERS CLAIMING STKS (4-Y.O+) (Class F)

2-45 (2-45) **1m 4f (Fibresand)** £2,583.00 (£783.00: £383.00: £183.00) Stalls: Low GOING minus 0.05 sec per fur (STD)

| | | | Pos | SP | RR | SF |
|---|---|---|---|---|---|---|
| 299* | **Heathyards Rock (81)** (RHollinshead) **4-9-7** TIves(2) (hld up: hdwy 6f out: chal over 1f out: edgd lft: styd on to ld nr fin) | — | **1** | 6/4 1 | 87 | 26 |
| 333[5] | **Anistop (56)** (RAkehurst) **4-8-3** SSanders(1) (chsd ldr: led over 4f out tl hdd nr fin) | hd | **2** | 7/2 3 | 69 | 8 |
| 284[2] | **Pharly Dancer (68)** (WWHaigh) **7-8-8**(3) DRMcCabe(6) (led tl over 4f out: kpt on same pce appr fnl f) | 2½ | **3** | 7/4 2 | 72 | 13 |
| 297[8] | **Adaloaldo (USA) (50)** (JParkes) **4-8-2**(3) PMcCabe(4) (plld hrd: chsd ldrs tl lost pl over 3f out) | 15 | **4** | 14/1 | 48 | — |
| 252[5] | **Kismetim (54)** (DWChapman) **6-8-5** LCharnock(3) (hdwy 6f out: sn in tch: outpcd over 3f out) | 6 | **5** | 12/1 | 38 | — |
| | **Beauchief (46)** (RFMarvin) **4-8-3**(3)ow1 SDrowne(9) (b: chsd ldrs tl lost pl over 3f out) | 15 | **6** | 33/1 | 21 | — |
| 372[9] | **Call Me Flash (40)** (MrsPSly) **4-8-5** GDuffield(5) (chsd ldrs tl lost pl over 5f out: sn bhd) | 13 | **7** | 33/1 | 2 | — |
| | **Red O'Reilly** (JLEyre) **4-8-7v** TWilliams(8) (plld v.hrd: trckd ldrs: rdn & wknd 6f out: wl t.o 3f out) | dist | **8** | 25/1 | — | — |
| | | | | (SP 122.7%) | | **8 Rn** |

**2m 44.2** (11.70) CSF £7.70 TOTE £2.30: £1.10 £1.40 £1.10 (£5.40) Trio £2.10 OWNER Mr L. A. Morgan (UPPER LONGDON) BRED N. E. and Mrs Poole
WEIGHT FOR AGE 4yo-2lb
Anistop clmd B Waldron £3,000

## 402 EAST MIDLANDS ELECTRICITY (LINCOLN) MAIDEN STKS (3 & 4-Y.O) (Class D)

3-15 (3-20) **1m 3f (Fibresand)** £5,467.50 (£1,665.00: £820.00: £397.50) Stalls: Low GOING minus 0.05 sec per fur (STD)

| | | | Pos | SP | RR | SF |
|---|---|---|---|---|---|---|
| | **Munaadee (USA)** (BobJones) **4-9-12** MWigham(9) (b: chsd ldrs: led ins fnl f: drvn out: fin lame) | — | **1** | 4/1 1 | 77 | 29 |
| | **Chevalier (USA)** (ICampbell) **4-9-5**(7) GFaulkner(2) (mde most: hung rt over 2f out: hrd rdn: hdd ins fnl f) | ½ | **2** | 11/2 3 | 76 | 28 |
| 346[2] | **Los Alamos (65)** (CWThornton) **3-8-0** LCharnock(8) (b.hind: w ldr: drvn along over 3f out: one pce fnl 2f) | 5 | **3** | 5/1 2 | 64 | — |
| 333[4] | **Alzoomo (IRE) (64)** (JAGlover) **4-9-12** SDWilliams(4) (chsd ldrs: rdn & outpcd over 4f out: wknd over 2f out) | 9 | **4** | 7/1 | 56 | 8 |
| 346[3] | **Meltemison** (CEBrittain) **3-8-5** MLarsen(13) (swtg: chsd ldrs: rdn & outpcd over 3f out: wknd 2f out) | 1 | **5** | 15/2 | 55 | — |
| | **Cuban Nights (USA)** (BJLlewellyn) **4-9-12** SWhitworth(14) (in tch: hdwy 5f out: lost pl over 3f out) | 2½ | **6** | 33/1 | 51 | 3 |
| | **Exactly (IRE) (70)** (JLEyre) **3-7-9**(5) PFessey(1) (bhd fr ½-wy: sme hdwy 3f out: n.d) | 3½ | **7** | 9/1 | 41 | — |
| 314[6] | **Margi Boo (35)** (RTJuckes) **3-7-11b**1(7)ow4 FLynch(6) (hld up & bhd: hdwy 5f out: sn wknd) | 1½ | **8** | 50/1 | 43 | — |
| 370[4] | **Further Future (IRE) (40)** (JohnBerry) **3-8-5** MFenton(5) (chsd ldrs tl wknd 5f out) | 1½ | **9** | 33/1 | 41 | — |
| 297[3] | **Young Benson (47)** (BAMcMahon) **4-9-7**(5) LNewton(3) (lw: sn drvn along: hdwy 5f out: nvr nr ldrs) | ¾ | **10** | 8/1 | 40 | — |
| 228[7] | **Cultural Icon (USA) (37)** (PhilipMitchell) **4-9-12** AClark(12) (b: dwlt: sn drvn along: sme hdwy 6f out: sn wknd: eased) | 15 | **11** | 33/1 | 19 | — |
| | **Metal Badge (IRE)** (MJohnston) **3-8-5** TWilliams(15) (rangy: unf: chsd ldrs: drvn along 6f out: sn lost pl) | 12 | **12** | 9/1 | 1 | — |
| 198[11] | **Anchorena (50)** (JAHarris) **4-9-7** SSanders(11) (chsd ldrs tl lost place over 5f out) | 5 | **13** | 33/1 | — | — |
| 368[10] | **Royal Dancer (27)** (RJWeaver) **4-9-2**(5) ADaly(10) (a bhd: wl t.o fnl 3f) | dist | **14** | 50/1 | — | — |
| 234[9] | **Pangeran (USA)** (MrsASwinbank) **4-9-12** GDuffield(7) (Withdrawn not Starter's orders: v.unruly s: ref to enter stalls) | | **W** | 33/1 | — | — |
| | | | | (SP 126.1%) | | **14 Rn** |

**2m 30.9** (10.90) CSF £25.32 TOTE £4.20: £2.00 £3.60 £1.20 (£11.30) Trio £15.00 OWNER Mrs S. Osborne (NEWMARKET) BRED Gainsborough Farm Inc.
WEIGHT FOR AGE 3yo-22lb, 4yo-1lb
STEWARDS' ENQUIRY Faulkner susp. 18 & 21/3/96 (excessive use of whip).

## 403 NOTTINGHAM PRINT FINISHERS H'CAP (0-70) (II) (3-Y.O+) (Class E)

3-45 (3-45) **7f (Fibresand)** £3,574.15 (£1,085.20: £532.10: £255.55) Stalls: Low GOING minus 0.05 sec per fur (STD)

| | | | Pos | SP | RR | SF |
|---|---|---|---|---|---|---|
| 343* | **My Gallery (IRE) (65)** (ABailey) **5-9-3**(7) AngelaGallimore(2) (chsd ldrs: styd on u.p appr fnl f: led post) | — | **1** | 100/30 2 | 67 | 30 |
| 347[2] | **Dissentor (IRE) (50)** (JAGlover) **4-8-9v** GCarter(8) (chsd ldr: led 3f out: sn clr: hdd last stride) | s.h | **2** | 7/1 | 52 | 15 |
| 387* | **McKellar (IRE) (60)** (TDBarron) **7-9-5** RCochrane(5) (hld up: effrt over 3f out: kpt on appr fnl f: nt rch ldrs) | 1 | **3** | 2/1 1 | 60 | 23 |
| 253[2] | **Sweet Mate (59)** (SRBowring) **4-8-13b**(5) CTeague(6) (sn bhd: hdwy on outside over 2f out: styd on ins fnl f) | 1¼ | **4** | 9/2 3 | 56 | 19 |

| | | | | SP | RR | SF |
|---|---|---|---|---|---|---|
| 344[2] | **Society Girl (61)** (CWThornton) **3-8-4** DeanMcKeown(3) (led 2f: hung lft & outpcd over 2f out: kpt on) | ¾ | 5 | 7/1 | 57 | 3 |
| | **Fairelaine (50)** (APJarvis) **4-8-9** JTate(7) (nvr nr ldrs) | 10 | 6 | 15/2 | 22 | — |
| 383[8] | **Classic Victory (60)** (RHarris) **3-8-3** DBatteate(1) (dwlt: hdwy to ld after 2f: hdd 3f out: sn wknd) | 1¼ | 7 | 14/1 | 30 | — |
| | **Madonna da Rossi (55)** (MDods) **3-7-12** LCharnock(4) (bit bkwd: in tch: sn drvn along: lost pl over 2f out) | 13 | 8 | 16/1 | — | — |

(SP 123.9%) **8 Rn**

**1m 33.3** (6.50) CSF £26.58 CT £55.31 TOTE £7.20: £2.50 £1.70 £1.80 (£15.90) OWNER Mr Robert Cox (TARPORLEY) BRED East Riding Sack and Paper Co

WEIGHT FOR AGE 3yo-16lb

## 404 SOUTHWELL SERIES (S) H'CAP (Final) (3-Y.O) (Class E)

4-20 (4-21) **1m (Fibresand)** £4,026.00 (£1,218.00: £594.00: £282.00) Stalls: Low GOING minus 0.05 sec per fur (STD)

| | | | | SP | RR | SF |
|---|---|---|---|---|---|---|
| 281[2] | **People Direct (55)** (KMcAuliffe) **3-9-1** SSanders(6) (b.hind: chsd ldrs: led 3f out: hld on wl) | — | 1 | 4/1 [1] | 66 | 30 |
| 238* | **Dragonjoy (61)** (JWPayne) **3-9-7b** AMcGlone(2) (hdwy ½-wy: sn chsng wnr: styd on fnl f: nvr able to chal) | 1¼ | 2 | 9/2 [2] | 70 | 34 |
| 344[7] | **Down The Yard (38)** (MCChapman) **3-7-7**(5) PFessey(5) (chsd ldrs: outpcd over 3f out: hrd rdn & kpt on fnl 2f) | 4 | 3 | 7/1 [3] | 39 | 3 |
| 344[3] | **Efipetite (53)** (NBycroft) **3-8-8**(5) CTeague(3) (s.i.s: hdwy on outside over 4f out: one pce) | 8 | 4 | 7/1 [3] | 38 | 2 |
| 158[2] | **Welsh Melody (52)** (KRBurke) **3-8-5b**(7) TAshley(8) (in tch: drvn along & lost pl over 4f out) | 2½ | 5 | 9/2 [2] | 32 | — |
| 314[4] | **Sporting Fantasy (41)** (JBalding) **3-8-1v** NAdams(4) (led to 3f out: sn wknd) | 1¾ | 6 | 14/1 | 17 | — |
| 329[3] | **Bumblefoot (IRE) (53)** (JAHarris) **3-8-6**(7) FLynch(7) (chsd ldrs: drvn along & lost pl over 3f out) | 5 | 7 | 7/1 [3] | 19 | — |
| 344[5] | **Arch Angel (IRE) (48)** (GFHCharles-Jones) **3-8-5**(3) PMcCabe(1) (dwlt: a bhd: sn drvn along) | 3½ | 8 | 8/1 | 7 | — |

(SP 111.6%) **8 Rn**

**1m 46.6** (6.60) CSF £20.33 CT £107.69 TOTE £3.90: £1.90 £1.50 £2.70 (£5.90) OWNER Mr Peter Barclay (LAMBOURN) BRED James Thom and Sons and Peter Orr

No bid

STEWARDS' ENQUIRY Fessey susp. 18 & 21-23/3/96 (excessive use of whip).

## 405 SKITTLES H'CAP (0-60) (3-Y.O) (Class F)

4-50 (4-52) **6f (Fibresand)** £2,713.00 (£823.00: £403.00: £193.00) Stalls: Low GOING minus 0.05 sec per fur (STD)

| | | | | SP | RR | SF |
|---|---|---|---|---|---|---|
| | **Maiteamia (50)** (SRBowring) **3-8-6b**(5) CTeague(14) (chsd ldr: led over 2f out: hld on wl towards fin) | — | 1 | 10/1 [3] | 57 | 22 |
| 313[5] | **Principal Boy (IRE) (48)** (TJEtherington) **3-8-9** GCarter(6) (mid div: effrt u.p over 2f out: styd on wl fnl f) | hd | 2 | 6/1 [2] | 55 | 20 |
| 377* | **General Haven (65)** (TJNaughton) **3-9-5**(7) TAshley(15) (lw: in tch: sn pushed along: hdwy over 2f out: styd on same pce) | 3 | 3 | 10/1 [3] | 64 | 29 |
| 383[5] | **Miss Offset (53)** (MJohnston) **3-9-0b** TWilliams(13) (mde most tl over 2f out: kpt on same pce appr fnl f) | nk | 4 | 5/1 [1] | 51 | 16 |
| 209* | **Coastguards Hero (57)** (MDIUsher) **3-9-4** MWigham(7) (b.hind: chsd ldrs tl outpcd fnl 3f) | 2½ | 5 | 5/1 [1] | 48 | 13 |
| 332[3] | **Victoria Sioux (50)** (JAPickering) **3-8-4**(7) FLynch(9) (b.off hind: s.i.s: bhd tl sme hdwy fnl 2f) | 3 | 6 | 16/1 | 33 | — |
| 282[9] | **Seeking Destiny (IRE) (54)** (MCChapman) **3-8-8**(7) CMunday(11) (chsd ldrs: one pce fnl 3f) | 1¼ | 7 | 6/1 [2] | 34 | — |
| 242[4] | **Mogin (45)** (JFfitch-Heyes) **3-8-6** GDuffield(3) (chsd ldrs: drvn along over 2f out: sn outpcd) | ½ | 8 | 12/1 | 24 | — |
| 344[11] | **King of Peace (IRE) (60)** (MWEasterby) **3-9-2b**[1](5) GParkin(1) (dwlt: bhd tl sme hdwy 2f out: n.d) | 1¼ | 9 | 20/1 | 35 | — |
| 158[8] | **Ticka Ticka Timing (49)** (BWMurray) **3-8-7b**(3) PMcCabe(2) (s.i.s: hdwy after 2f: lost pl 3f out) | 1½ | 10 | 20/1 | 20 | — |
| | **Fergal (USA) (50)** (RonaldThompson) **3-8-6**(5) ADaly(4) (sn drvn along & bhd) | ¾ | 11 | 20/1 | 19 | — |
| 183[11] | **Lila Pedigo (IRE) (55)** (MissJFCraze) **3-9-2** DaleGibson(12) (a in rr) | 5 | 12 | 25/1 | 11 | — |
| 359[6] | **Elfin Queen (IRE) (50)** (JLHarris) **3-8-11b**[1] MFenton(8) (in tch tl lost pl 3f out) | 1 | 13 | 14/1 | 3 | — |
| 258[5] | **Napier Star (36)** (MrsNMacauley) **3-7-11** NAdams(10) (sn bhd: t.o 3f out) | 25 | 14 | 25/1 | — | — |

(SP 122.3%) **14 Rn**

**1m 18.7** (5.20) CSF £64.97 CT £583.70 TOTE £12.60: £2.80 £1.90 £2.60 (£51.00) Trio £198.10 OWNER Mrs Zoe Grant (EDWINSTOWE) BRED Mrs Z. Grant and S. R. Bowring

T/Plpt: £12.40 (895.81 Tckts). T/Qdpt: £3.50 (246.04 Tckts) WG

# 0376-LINGFIELD (L-H) (Standard)
## Thursday March 14th

WEATHER: cold WIND: almost nil

## 406 REID MINTY LITIGATORS AMATEUR H'CAP (0-60) (I) (4-Y.O+) (Class F)

1-55 (1-57) **1m (Equitrack)** £2,214.60 (£620.60: £301.80) Stalls: High GOING minus 0.64 sec per fur (FST)

| | | | | SP | RR | SF |
|---|---|---|---|---|---|---|
| 163[8] | **Fort Knox (IRE) (56)** (RMFlower) **5-11-3b** MrTMcCarthy(6) (gd hdwy 4f out: led 3f out: clr over 1f out: r.o wl) | — | 1 | 4/1 [2] | 63 | 38 |
| 279[3] | **Don't Drop Bombs (USA) (39)** (DTThom) **7-10-0v** MissJFeilden(12) (lw: hld up: chsd wnr over 2f out: r.o wl ins fnl f) | nk | 2 | 3/1 [1] | 45 | 20 |
| 341[2] | **Love Legend (42)** (DWPArbuthnot) **11-10-3** MrsDArbuthnot(9) (hdwy over 3f out: rdn over 2f out: unable qckn) | 1¾ | 3 | 6/1 | 45 | 20 |
| 366* | **Tuigamala (60)** (RIngram) **5-11-7** MissYHaynes(11) (hdwy over 3f out: one pce fnl 2f) | nk | 4 | 9/2 [3] | 62 | 37 |
| 341[4] | **Sporting Risk (44)** (PWHarris) **4-10-2**(3) MissAElsey(5) (lost pl 6f out: r.o one pce fnl 2f) | 4 | 5 | 10/1 | 38 | 13 |
| 316[9] | **Jaazim (53)** (MMadgwick) **6-10-7**(7)ow1 MrPMiddleton(4) (prom 6f) | 2½ | 6 | 16/1 | 42 | 16 |
| | **Scharnhorst (60)** (SDow) **4-11-0**(7) MrSFetherstonhaugh(1) (prom 4f) | 2 | 7 | 20/1 | 45 | 20 |
| 366[7] | **Myjinka (48)** (TEPowell) **6-10-6b**(3) MrsSBosley(2) (nvr plcd to chal) | ½ | 8 | 7/1 | 32 | 7 |
| 133[7] | **Pair of Jacks (IRE) (32)** (TJNaughton) **6-9-2**(5)ow1 MrsJNaughton(7) (prom over 4f) | 1¾ | 9 | 16/1 | 13 | — |
| 334[4] | **Justinianus (IRE) (48)** (JJBridger) **4-10-2**(7) MrDBridger(8) (lw: led 5f: wkng whn n.m.r over 2f out) | ½ | 10 | 16/1 | 28 | 3 |
| 334[2] | **Nivasha (39)** (RPCHoad) **4-10-0** MissJAllison(3) (a bhd) | ¾ | 11 | 9/1 | 17 | — |
| | **Zeliba (32)** (CEBrittain) **4-9-7** MrsLPearce(10) (a bhd) | 7 | 12 | 10/1 | — | — |

(SP 140.6%) **12 Rn**

**1m 41.1** (3.70) CSF £18.82 CT £75.02 TOTE £5.60: £2.50 £1.00 £3.20 (£10.10) Trio £13.10 OWNER Miss C. Markowiak (JEVINGTON) BRED Leo Collins

## 407 REID MINTY SOLICITORS H'CAP (0-85) (3-Y.O+) (Class D)

2-30 (2-31) **5f (Equitrack)** £3,485.00 (£1,055.00: £515.00: £245.00) Stalls: High GOING minus 0.64 sec per fur (FST)

| | Horse | Details | Dist | Pos | SP | RR | SF |
|---|---|---|---|---|---|---|---|
| 380[3] | **Spender (82)** | (PWHarris) **7-9-8**(3) JStack(2) (a.p: chsd ldr over 2f out: led ins fnl f: drvn out) | — | 1 | 8/1 | 93 | 21 |
| 338[7] | **Stoppes Brow (85)** | (GLMoore) **4-10-0v** SWhitworth(3) (hdwy over 2f out: ev ch ins fnl f: r.o wl) | hd | 2 | 14/1 | 96 | 24 |
| 173* | **Hever Golf Star (74)** | (TJNaughton) **4-9-3** JWeaver(4) (b.hind: led tl ins fnl f: sn wknd) | 4 | 3 | 6/4 1 | 72 | — |
| 380[9] | **Friendly Brave (USA) (70)** | (MissGayKelleway) **6-8-10**(3) AWhelan(6) (a.p: rdn over 2f out: one pce) | 1 | 4 | 8/1 | 65 | — |
| 394[10] | **Featherstone Lane (74)** | (MissLCSiddall) **5-9-3v** RCochrane(7) (a.p: rdn over 2f out: one pce) | nk | 5 | 10/1 | 68 | — |
| 389* | **Lift Boy (USA) (68)** | (AMoore) **7-8-11** 7x CandyMorris(5) (b.hind: hld up: rdn over 2f out: one pce) | ½ | 6 | 7/1 3 | 60 | — |
| 394[2] | **Cheeky Chappy (55)** | (DWChapman) **5-7-7b**(5) PFessey(8) (prom over 2f) | 1¾ | 7 | 4/1 2 | 42 | — |
| | **Allwight Then (IRE) (69)** | (REPeacock) **5-8-12** VSlattery(1) (prom over 3f) | 2½ | 8 | 25/1 | 48 | — |
| 335[4] | **Johayro (75)** | (WGMTurner) **3-8-0b**(5) CAdamson(10) (spd over 2f) | nk | 9 | 8/1 | 54 | — |
| | **Baileys Sunset (IRE) (63)** | (JMBradley) **4-7-13**(7)ow3 FLynch(9) (bit bkwd: bhd fnl 2f) | nk | 10 | 20/1 | 40 | — |

(SP 130.2%) **10 Rn**

**60.0 secs** (2.00) CSF £107.65 CT £237.49 TOTE £8.60: £3.00 £9.90 £1.00 (£57.10) Trio £15.60 OWNER The Entrepreneurs (BERKHAMSTED) BRED The Mount Coote Partnership
WEIGHT FOR AGE 3yo-13lb

## 408 REID MINTY 16TH ANNIVERSARY CLAIMING STKS (3-Y.O+) (Class F)

3-05 (3-07) **6f (Equitrack)** £2,600.30 (£730.80: £356.90) Stalls: Low GOING minus 0.64 sec per fur (FST)

| | Horse | Details | Dist | Pos | SP | RR | SF |
|---|---|---|---|---|---|---|---|
| 380[2] | **Our Shadee (USA) (65)** | (KTIvory) **6-9-2v**(7) CScally(1) (outpcd: hdwy over 2f out: rdn over 1f out: led nr fin) | — | 1 | 3/1 1 | 75 | — |
| | **Young Mazaad (IRE)** | (DCO'Brien) **3-8-6** GBardwell(5) (outpcd: hdwy over 3f out: led over 1f out: hrd rdn: hdd nr fin) | ½ | 2 | 33/1 | 72 | — |
| 229* | **Speedy Classic (USA) (66)** | (MJHeaton-Ellis) **7-9-11b**(3) SDrowne(2) (outpcd: hdwy over 1f out: r.o) | 3 | 3 | 9/2 3 | 71 | — |
| 387[11] | **Chief's Lady (40)** | (JMBradley) **4-8-4**(7) FLynch(3) (reard s: outpcd: hdwy over 1f out: r.o) | hd | 4 | 33/1 | 53 | — |
| 317[2] | **The Frisky Farmer (56)** | (WGMTurner) **3-8-10** AClark(4) (prom over 2f) | 1¾ | 5 | 9/2 3 | 63 | — |
| 307[2] | **Rowlandsons Stud (IRE) (61)** | (GLMoore) **3-8-4** MFenton(9) (a.p: led 2f out tl over 1f out: wknd fnl f) | 1 | 6 | 5/1 | 54 | — |
| 354[7] | **Southern Dominion (58)** | (CNAllen) **4-9-6v**[1] NAdams(6) (b.off hind: lw: led 4f) | ¾ | 7 | 10/1 | 53 | — |
| 317[4] | **Sir Tasker (64)** | (JLHarris) **8-9-6** SSanders(8) (a.p: ev ch 2f out: wknd over 1f out) | 1 | 8 | 7/2 2 | 50 | — |
| 340[3] | **Apollo Red (55)** | (AMoore) **7-9-4** CandyMorris(10) (b.hind: prom over 3f) | 7 | 9 | 7/1 | 30 | — |
| | **Iron And Steel (42)** | (AMoore) **3-8-1** FNorton(7) (b.hind: a bhd) | 1 | 10 | 25/1 | 25 | — |

(SP 131.6%) **10 Rn**

**1m 14.8** (4.20) CSF £82.15 TOTE £3.30: £1.80 £22.20 £1.10 (£427.10; £252.68 to Lingfield 15/3/96). Trio Not won; £228.73 to Folkestone 15/3/96. OWNER Mr K. T. Ivory (RADLETT) BRED Overbury Stud
WEIGHT FOR AGE 3yo-14lb

## 409 FLAT SEASON 1996 WALLPLANNER CLAIMING STKS (3-Y.O+) (Class E)

3-45 (3-45) **7f (Equitrack)** £2,968.35 (£898.80: £438.90: £208.95) Stalls: Low GOING minus 0.64 sec per fur (FST)

| | Horse | Details | Dist | Pos | SP | RR | SF |
|---|---|---|---|---|---|---|---|
| 350[2] | **Mr Nevermind (IRE) (73)** | (GLMoore) **6-9-2**(7) FLynch(1) (hdwy over 3f out: led over 1f out: pushed out) | — | 1 | 4/1 3 | 81 | 36 |
| 243[3] | **Duke Valentino (79)** | (RHollinshead) **4-10-0** LDettori(8) (a.p: led wl over 1f out: sn hdd: unable qckn) | 3 | 2 | 9/4 1 | 79 | 34 |
| 311[2] | **Ashgore (85)** | (MJohnston) **6-10-0** JWeaver(10) (led 1f: led 4f out tl wl over 1f out: one pce) | 1¼ | 3 | 7/2 2 | 76 | 31 |
| 356* | **Allez Cyrano (IRE) (72)** | (MBell) **5-9-11** MFenton(9) (b.nr fore: led 6f out to 4f out: wknd 2f out) | 7 | 4 | 7/2 2 | 57 | 12 |
| 363[8] | **Rocky Two (40)** | (PHowling) **5-9-5** RCochrane(11) (b: hdwy 3f out: wknd 2f out) | 1¼ | 5 | 33/1 | 48 | 3 |
| 179[11] | **Considerable Charm (41)** | (AMoore) **4-8-13** CandyMorris(12) (b.hind: hdwy 3f out: wknd over 2f out) | 5 | 6 | 33/1 | 31 | — |
| 337[2] | **French Ginger (55)** | (RIngram) **5-9-1** WWoods(5) (prom over 4f) | 2 | 7 | 15/2 | 28 | — |
| | **Tandridge (IRE)** | (JRJenkins) **4-8-6**(7) SallyWall(3) (a bhd) | 5 | 8 | 33/1 | 15 | — |
| 217[10] | **Mystic Legend (IRE)** | (TJNaughton) **4-9-10** DHarrison(4) (lw: bhd fnl 5f) | 8 | 9 | 33/1 | 8 | — |
| 376[7] | **P Grayco Choice** | (PCClarke) **3-7-10** NAdams(2) (a bhd) | 10 | 10 | 33/1 | — | — |
| 337[11] | **Sussex Gorse** | (BAPearce) **5-9-3**(3) DRMcCabe(7) (lw: a bhd) | 17 | 11 | 33/1 | — | — |

(SP 124.6%) **11 Rn**

**1m 25.5** (1.50) CSF £13.16 TOTE £4.10: £1.60 £1.00 £2.00 (£4.20) Trio £3.30 OWNER Mr K. Higson (EPSOM) BRED Robert Corridan
WEIGHT FOR AGE 3yo-16lb

## 410 REID MINTY LIBEL AND SLANDER H'CAP (0-95) (4-Y.O+) (Class C)

4-20 (4-20) **1m 2f (Equitrack)** £5,230.90 (£1,583.20: £772.60: £367.30) Stalls: Low GOING minus 0.64 sec per fur (FST)

| | Horse | Details | Dist | Pos | SP | RR | SF |
|---|---|---|---|---|---|---|---|
| 306* | **Ocean Park (80)** | (LadyHerries) **5-9-8** AClark(8) (lw: hld up: led 1f out: r.o wl) | — | 1 | 11/4 1 | 90 | 38 |
| 306[9] | **Able Choice (IRE) (71)** | (RWArmstrong) **6-8-13** LDettori(4) (hdwy 2f out: hrd rdn over 1f out: r.o ins fnl f) | 1½ | 2 | 8/1 | 79 | 27 |
| 306[10] | **Robellion (68)** | (DWPArbuthnot) **5-8-10v** RCochrane(7) (hdwy over 4f out: ev ch over 1f out: unable qckn) | ½ | 3 | 12/1 | 75 | 23 |
| 358[3] | **Kintwyn (72)** | (CCElsey) **6-9-0** DHarrison(9) (b.hind: lw: hld up: led over 2f out to 1f out: sn wknd) | 1¾ | 4 | 4/1 2 | 76 | 24 |
| 392[8] | **Field of Vision (IRE) (73)** | (MJohnston) **6-9-1** JWeaver(5) (a.p: ev ch wl over 1f out: wknd fnl f) | 1 | 5 | 11/2 | 75 | 23 |
| 306[3] | **Bardon Hill Boy (IRE) (83)** | (BHanbury) **4-9-8**(3) JStack(6) (prom over 7f) | 7 | 6 | 9/2 3 | 75 | 22 |
| 312[7] | **Bernard Seven (IRE) (77)** | (CEBrittain) **4-9-2b**(3) DRMcCabe(2) (lw: led over 7f: wknd over 1f out) | 3½ | 7 | 10/1 | 64 | 11 |
| | **Hardy Dancer (86)** | (GLMoore) **4-10-0** SWhitworth(3) (lw: bhd fnl 4f) | 17 | 8 | 10/1 | 45 | — |
| 378[3] | **Statajack (IRE) (84)** | (DRCElsworth) **8-9-12b** AProcter(1) (prom over 5f) | 2½ | 9 | 10/1 | 38 | — |

(SP 126.3%) **9 Rn**

**2m 6.38** (2.08) CSF £25.41 CT £220.55 TOTE £3.10: £1.80 £2.60 £3.80 (£13.30) Trio £28.70 OWNER Mr E. Reitel (LITTLEHAMPTON) BRED Mrs H. Khan

## 411 REID MINTY COMMERCIAL SOLUTIONS H'CAP (0-80) (4-Y.O+) (Class D)

4-55 (4-56) **1m 4f (Equitrack)** £3,517.50 (£1,065.00: £520.00: £247.50) Stalls: Low GOING minus 0.64 sec per fur (FST)

| | Horse | Details | Dist | Pos | SP | RR | SF |
|---|---|---|---|---|---|---|---|
| 296[2] | **El Volador (75)** | (CNAllen) **9-9-9** LDettori(7) (hdwy over 3f out: led ins fnl f: r.o wl) | — | 1 | 7/2 2 | 80 | 26 |
| 392[5] | **Cuango (IRE) (70)** | (RHollinshead) **5-8-11**(7) FLynch(5) (s.s: hdwy over 3f out: rdn over 1f out: r.o wl) | hd | 2 | 7/1 | 75 | 21 |
| 312[4] | **Progression (70)** | (CMurray) **5-9-4b** DeanMcKeown(10) (s.s: nt clr run on ins over 3f out, 2f out & wl over 1f out: hdwy fnl f: fin wl) | s.h | 3 | 6/1 | 75 | 21 |

| | | | Pos | SP | RR | SF |
|---|---|---|---|---|---|---|
| 353[2] | **Silktail (IRE) (50)** (MissGayKelleway) **4-7-10** JQuinn(9) (hld up: led 1f out tl ins fnl f: unable qckn) | 1½ | **4** | 3/1[1] | 54 | — |
| 312[10] | **Prince Danzig (IRE) (80)** (DJGMurraySmith) **5-10-0** JWeaver(8) (lw: led 4f: led 4f out to 1f out: one pce) | ¾ | **5** | 8/1 | 82 | 28 |
| 358[5] | **South Eastern Fred (80)** (HJCollingridge) **5-10-0** MTebbutt(4) (plld hrd: no hdwy fnl 3f) | 3½ | **6** | 4/1[3] | 77 | 23 |
| 378[6] | **No Pattern (80)** (GLMoore) **4-9-12v** SWhitworth(1) (lw: hld up: rdn 4f out: wknd fnl f) | nk | **7** | 8/1 | 78 | 21 |
| 279[4] | **Iron N Gold (54)** (AMoore) **4-7-7**(7)ow2 TField(2) (b.hind: led 8f out to 4f out: wknd over 1f out) | 5 | **8** | 12/1 | 45 | — |
| | **Ketabi (USA) (63)** (RAkehurst) **5-8-4**(7) TAshley(3) (prom over 9f) | 3½ | **9** | 20/1 | 48 | — |

(SP 128.7%) **9 Rn**

**2m 34.57** (4.57) CSF £29.12 CT £138.44 TOTE £4.30: £2.00 £2.40 £2.20 (£8.70) Trio £40.50 OWNER British Racing Heritage (NEWMARKET) BRED L. and Mrs Hutch

LONG HANDICAP Silktail (IRE) 7-7

WEIGHT FOR AGE 4yo-2lb

STEWARDS' ENQUIRY McKeown susp. 23 & 25/3/96 (improper use of whip) & fined £100 (failure to ride to draw).

## 412 REID MINTY LITIGATORS AMATEUR H'CAP (0-60) (II) (4-Y.O+) (Class F)

5-25 (5-26) **1m (Equitrack)** £2,214.60 (£620.60: £301.80) Stalls: High GOING minus 0.64 sec per fur (FST)

| | | | Pos | SP | RR | SF |
|---|---|---|---|---|---|---|
| 393[4] | **Sarum (50)** (CPWildman) **10-10-8**(5) MrKGoble(10) (hdwy over 3f out: led ins fnl f: r.o wl) | — | **1** | 10/1 | 55 | 37 |
| 366[3] | **Hatta Sunshine (USA) (52)** (AMoore) **6-10-10**(5) MrsJMoore(1) (b: b.hind: hdwy over 1f out: r.o wl ins fnl f: too much to do) | 1¼ | **2** | 11/4[1] | 55 | 37 |
| 341[5] | **Dream Carrier (IRE) (49)** (REPeacock) **8-10-5**(7) MrsCPeacock(11) (hdwy over 1f out: r.o wl ins fnl f) | ½ | **3** | 10/1 | 51 | 33 |
| 174[4] | **Eastleigh (48)** (RHollinshead) **7-10-11** MrTMcCarthy(3) (b.off hind: w ldr: ev ch ins fnl f: unable qckn) | 1¾ | **4** | 13/2 | 46 | 28 |
| 353[3] | **Montone (IRE) (48)** (JRJenkins) **6-10-6**(5) DrMMannish(5) (lost pl 4f out: rallied over 1f out: r.o) | ¾ | **5** | 6/1[3] | 45 | 27 |
| 351[6] | **Ganador (44)** (BSmart) **4-10-2**(5) MissVMarshall(6) (hdwy 6f out: one pce fnl 2f) | nk | **6** | 20/1 | 40 | 22 |
| | **Timeless (58)** (CADwyer) **4-11-0**(7) MrsSDwyer(9) (lw: a.p: rdn over 1f out: wknd ins fnl f) | ¾ | **7** | 7/2[2] | 52 | 34 |
| 343[5] | **Green's Bid (37)** (DWChapman) **6-9-11**(3) MissRClark(4) (led tl ins fnl f: sn wknd) | 1¼ | **8** | 12/1 | 29 | 11 |
| 328[12] | **Opening Range (40)** (NEBerry) **5-9-12**(5) MissTSpearing(12) (a bhd) | 4 | **9** | 33/1 | 24 | 6 |
| 347[3] | **Palacegate Gold (IRE) (31)** (RJHodges) **7-9-3**(5) MrVLukaniuk(8) (bhd fnl 5f) | ¾ | **10** | 10/1 | 13 | — |
| 308[8] | **Zahran (IRE) (42)** (JMBradley) **5-10-0**(5) MissEJJones(2) (b: lw: prom over 5f) | hd | **11** | 10/1 | 24 | 6 |
| 200[5] | **Paronomasia (36)** (JLHarris) **4-9-13** MrsLPearce(7) (bhd fnl 5f) | 6 | **12** | 12/1 | 6 | — |

(SP 136.0%) **12 Rn**

**1m 40.82** (3.42) CSF £40.84 CT £286.41 TOTE £13.80: £2.40 £2.20 £2.30 (£35.20) Trio £67.00 OWNER Mrs E. M. Wildman (SALISBURY) BRED Miss Suzannah Armstrong

T/Plpt: £10.00 (1,216.68 Tckts). T/Qdpt: £5.30 (190.21 Tckts) AK

# 0388-WOLVERHAMPTON (L-H) (Standard)

## Friday March 15th

WEATHER: overcast & misty WIND: slt half against

## 413 PHOENIX LIMITED STKS (0-65) (4-Y.O+) (Class F)

2-20 (2-21) **7f (Fibresand)** £2,398.00 (£673.00: £328.00) Stalls: High GOING: 0.33 sec per fur (SLW)

| | | | Pos | SP | RR | SF |
|---|---|---|---|---|---|---|
| 403* | **My Gallery (IRE) (65)** (ABailey) **5-8-8**(7) 3x AngelaGallimore(6) (outpcd: hdwy 3 out: chal ent fnl f: kpt on u.p to ld cl home) | — | **1** | 2/1[1] | 74 | 41 |
| 350[5] | **Milos (65)** (TJNaughton) **5-9-3** DHarrison(4) (chsd ldr: led 4f out tl wl ins fnl f) | nk | **2** | 9/1 | 75 | 42 |
| 356[2] | **Efficacy (62)** (APJarvis) **5-8-2**(7) KHopkins(7) (lw: b.hind: hdwy 3f out: rdn wl over 1f out: one pce) | 3 | **3** | 11/1 | 61 | 28 |
| 403[4] | **Sweet Mate (59)** (SRBowring) **4-8-12b**(5) CTeague(3) (outpcd: drvn along 3f out: nt rch ldrs) | 1½ | **4** | 9/1 | 65 | 32 |
| 357[7] | **Allinson's Mate (IRE) (65)** (TDBarron) **8-8-7**(7) KimberleyHart(1) (trckd ldrs: drvn 2f out: sn btn) | 1¾ | **5** | 7/1[3] | 58 | 25 |
| | **Irie Mon (IRE) (62)** (MPBielby) **4-8-11**(3) DRMcCabe(5) (bkwd: prom to ½-wy: sn rdn & lost tch) | 4 | **6** | 20/1 | 49 | 16 |
| 345[6] | **Tilly Owl (42)** (JAHarris) **5-8-9** JO'Reilly(2) (lw: s.i.s: sn drvn along: a bhd) | ½ | **7** | 12/1 | 43 | 10 |
| 388* | **Deeply Vale (IRE) (65)** (GLMoore) **5-9-3** SWhitworth(8) (dwlt: outpcd & bhd: effrt u.p 2f out: eased whn btn) | 7 | **8** | 5/2[2] | 35 | 2 |
| 308[9] | **Ansal Boy (60)** (MissGayKelleway) **4-9-0b**[1] AClark(9) (slt ld 3f: rdn & wknd over 2f out: t.o) | 7 | **9** | 16/1 | 16 | — |

(SP 121.1%) **9 Rn**

**1m 32.0** (7.30) CSF £19.98 TOTE £3.20: £1.80 £4.00 £2.00 (£11.70) Trio £171.10; £147.08 to Wolverhampton 16/3/96 OWNER Mr Robert Cox (TARPORLEY) BRED East Riding Sack and Paper Co

**OFFICIAL EXPLANATION Deeply Vale (IRE): was slightly lame on his near-fore.**

## 414 STARBUCK MAIDEN STKS (3-Y.O+) (Class D)

2-50 (2-50) **6f (Fibresand)** £3,566.25 (£1,080.00: £527.50: £251.25) Stalls: Low GOING: 0.33 sec per fur (SLW)

| | | | Pos | SP | RR | SF |
|---|---|---|---|---|---|---|
| 342[3] | **Niteowl Raider (IRE) (55)** (JAHarris) **3-8-12** JO'Reilly(7) (mde all: clr ent st: hld on wl) | — | **1** | 6/1[3] | 70 | 23 |
| | **School Boy (75)** (TJNaughton) **3-8-12** DHarrison(6) (bit bkwd: a.p: chsd wnr fnl 2f: no ex nr fin) | 1½ | **2** | 9/4[1] | 66 | 19 |
| 390[8] | **Black And Amber** (PRWebber) **4-9-7** NAdams(2) (dwlt: hdwy 3f out: rdn & one pce appr fnl f) | 6 | **3** | 16/1 | 44 | 12 |
| | **Ocean Stream (IRE) (70)** (JLEyre) **3-8-12** DeanMcKeown(4) (lt-f: pushed along & outpcd tl styd on ins fnl f) | nk | **4** | 9/4[1] | 49 | 2 |
| 359[2] | **Marino Street (54)** (PDEvans) **3-8-7v** SSanders(5) (prom: drvn & outpcd over 2f out) | nk | **5** | 9/2[2] | 43 | — |
| 298[6] | **Lithe Spirit (IRE)** (JAHarris) **4-9-7** TGMcLaughlin(8) (bhd: sn rdn: no imp) | 7 | **6** | 10/1 | 24 | — |
| 390[13] | **Showtime Blues (IRE)** (ABailey) **7-9-9b**[1](3) DWright(9) (spd over 3f: sn lost tch) | hd | **7** | 10/1 | 29 | — |
| 389[5] | **Ho Mei Surprise (35)** (BPreece) **4-9-5**(7) FLynch(3) (s.i.s: bhd & outpcd: effrt 3f out: nt rch ldrs) | ¾ | **8** | 33/1 | 27 | — |
| 386[5] | **Cerbera (40)** (JPSmith) **7-9-7**(5) CTeague(1) (s.i.s: a bhd: t.o fr ½-wy: p.u & dismntd fnl f) | | **P** | 50/1 | — | — |

(SP 123.0%) **9 Rn**

**1m 18.7** (7.30) CSF £20.32 TOTE £10.10: £2.30 £1.10 £5.00 (£37.30) Trio £61.60 OWNER Burntwood Sports Ltd (EDINGLEY) BRED Airlie Stud

WEIGHT FOR AGE 3yo-14lb

STEWARDS' ENQUIRY O'Reilly susp. 25-26/3/96 (excessive use of whip).

## 415 CANTON APPRENTICE H'CAP (0-70) (3-Y.O) (Class F)

3-20 (3-20) **1m 1f 79y (Fibresand)** £2,433.00 (£683.00: £333.00) Stalls: Low GOING: 0.33 sec per fur (SLW)

| | | | Pos | SP | RR | SF |
|---|---|---|---|---|---|---|
| 381[4] | **Still Here (IRE) (53)** (MJHeaton-Ellis) **3-7-13**(7) JFowle(5) (racd wd: a.p: styd on to ld fnl stride) | — | **1** | 7/1[3] | 60 | 7 |

| Form | Horse / details | Dist | Pos | SP | RR | SF |
|---|---|---|---|---|---|---|
| 382$^3$ | **Bit of Bother (IRE) (68)** (TDBarron) **3-9-7** GFaulkner(6) (hld up: hdwy to chse ldr over 3f out: led wl over 1f out: ct post) | hd | **2** | 5/4$^1$ | 75 | 22 |
| 348$^5$ | **Onefourseven (43)** (SRBowring) **3-7-5b**(5) PDoe(3) (prom: rdn 3f out: kpt on one pce fnl 2f) | 6 | **3** | 7/1$^3$ | 40 | — |
| 390$^4$ | **Classic Beauty (IRE) (65)** (RHarris) **3-9-4** OliverCasey(1) (led: rdn over 2f out: hdd & wknd wl over 1f out) | 7 | **4** | 11/8$^2$ | 50 | — |
| 385$^5$ | **Image Maker (IRE) (48)** (BPreece) **3-8-1** IonaWands(4) (a bhd: t.o fnl 3f) | 6 | **5** | 20/1 | 22 | — |
| | **Rivercare (IRE) (61)** (MJPolglase) **3-8-9**(5) RMullen(2) (neat: cmpt: s.i.s: sn chsng ldrs: wknd over 4f out: t.o) | hd | **6** | 16/1 | 35 | — |
| | | | | (SP 122.2%) | | **6 Rn** |

**2m 9.1** (13.10) CSF £17.23 TOTE £6.70: £3.60 £1.10 (£7.20) OWNER Mr A. K. Collins (WROUGHTON) BRED John Hennessy
LONG HANDICAP Onefourseven 7-7
STEWARDS' ENQUIRY Faulkner susp. 25-26/3/96 (excessive use of whip).

## 416 JOHNSTON H'CAP (0-80) (3-Y.O+) (Class D)

3-50 (3-50) **1m 100y (Fibresand)** £3,485.00 (£1,055.00: £515.00: £245.00) Stalls: Low GOING: 0.33 sec per fur (SLW)

| Form | Horse / details | Dist | Pos | SP | RR | SF |
|---|---|---|---|---|---|---|
| 285$^5$ | **Cashmere Lady (72)** (JLEyre) **4-9-13** RLappin(1) (trckd ldrs: rdn over 3f out: hdwy to ld over 2f out: sn clr: eased nr fin) | — | **1** | 9/2$^2$ | 83+ | 55 |
| 391* | **Le Sport (80)** (ABailey) **3-9-0**(3) 5x DWright(3) (lw: sn bhd & pushed along: gd hdwy over 2f out: nt rch wnr) | 3 | **2** | 11/10$^1$ | 85 | 39 |
| 345$^3$ | **Sea Spouse (57)** (MBlanshard) **5-8-12** NAdams(4) (led tl over 2f out: rdn & one pce appr fnl f) | 2 | **3** | 12/1 | 59 | 31 |
| | **Sooty Tern (53)** (JMBradley) **9-8-5**(3) SDrowne(5) (b.off fore: prom: drvn 3f out: outpcd over 2f out) | 6 | **4** | 20/1 | 43 | 15 |
| 336* | **Lilac Rain (47)** (JRArnold) **4-8-2** JQuinn(6) (lw: bhd: effrt & rdn 3f out: nvr nrr) | 1 | **5** | 12/1 | 35 | 7 |
| 399$^5$ | **Square Deal (FR) (69)** (SRBowring) **5-9-10** SDWilliams(8) (hld up: hdwy 3f out: rdn 2f out: sn outpcd) | 1 | **6** | 14/1 | 55 | 27 |
| 333$^7$ | **Suvalu (USA) (69)** (MGMeagher) **4-9-10** KFallon(2) (hdwy 4f out: rdn & wknd over 2f out) | 1 | **7** | 6/1 | 54 | 26 |
| 223* | **Sarasi (67)** (MJCamacho) **4-9-8** LCharnock(7) (b.nr fore: prom tl wknd over 2f out) | 1 | **8** | 11/2$^3$ | 50 | 22 |
| | | | | (SP 122.3%) | | **8 Rn** |

**1m 53.6** (8.60) CSF £10.28 CT £53.72 TOTE £5.90: £1.10 £1.30 £4.00 (£4.60) OWNER Mrs Sybil Howe (HAMBLETON) BRED J. L. Eyre
WEIGHT FOR AGE 3yo-18lb

## 417 MARIANA (S) STKS (3-Y.O+) (Class F)

4-20 (4-20) **1m 100y (Fibresand)** £2,398.00 (£673.00: £328.00) Stalls: Low GOING: 0.33 sec per fur (SLW)

| Form | Horse / details | Dist | Pos | SP | RR | SF |
|---|---|---|---|---|---|---|
| 356$^4$ | **Chadleigh Lane (USA) (66)** (RHollinshead) **4-9-7**(7) FLynch(8) (hld up & bhd: hdwy over 4f out: led on bit 3f out: sn clr: v.easily) | — | **1** | 7/4$^1$ | 70+ | 44 |
| 393* | **No Submission (USA) (62)** (DWChapman) **10-10-0v** ACulhane(2) (s.s: sn wl bhd: hdwy over 3f out: wnt 2nd cl home) | 4 | **2** | 5/2$^2$ | 62 | 36 |
| 372* | **David James' Girl (52)** (ABailey) **4-9-2**(7) IonaWands(1) (trckd ldrs: rdn 4f out: kpt on fnl 2f: nt pce to chal) | ¾ | **3** | 4/1$^3$ | 56 | 30 |
| 393$^3$ | **Top Pet (IRE) (45)** (RAkehurst) **6-9-9** SSanders(5) (sn pushed along: in tch: styd on appr fnl f: nvr nrr) | 2 | **4** | 9/1 | 52 | 26 |
| | **Pointer** (MrsPNDutfield) **4-9-6**(3) SDrowne(4) (prom tl rdn & outpcd over 2f out) | 6 | **5** | 14/1 | 41 | 15 |
| 336$^4$ | **Cabcharge Blue (50)** (TJNaughton) **4-9-9** DHarrison(6) (b.hind: chsd ldr: hrd drvn & wknd over 1f out) | 4 | **6** | 10/1 | 33 | 7 |
| 393$^5$ | **Thomas Crown (IRE) (40)** (NJHWalker) **4-9-6b**(3) JStack(3) (lw: led over 6f: sn rdn & wknd) | 4 | **7** | 33/1 | 26 | — |
| | **Moscow Dynamo** (NMBabbage) **9-9-9** JQuinn(7) (trckd ldrs over 5f: sn wknd: t.o) | 18 | **8** | 9/1 | — | — |
| | | | | (SP 123.6%) | | **8 Rn** |

**1m 54.9** (9.90) CSF £7.05 TOTE £3.00: £1.10 £1.10 £4.50 (£3.10) OWNER Mr J. E. Bigg (UPPER LONGDON) BRED Windwoods Farm, Bruce Brown and Connie Brown
Bt in 11,600 gns

## 418 HOWLAND H'CAP (0-70) (3-Y.O+) (Class E)

4-50 (4-50) **6f (Fibresand)** £2,995.65 (£907.20: £443.10: £211.05) Stalls: Low GOING: 0.33 sec per fur (SLW)

| Form | Horse / details | Dist | Pos | SP | RR | SF |
|---|---|---|---|---|---|---|
| | **So Intrepid (IRE) (58)** (JMBradley) **6-8-13**(3) SDrowne(9) (a.p: led wl over 1f out: r.o wl) | — | **1** | 16/1 | 64 | 47 |
| 394$^4$ | **Lord Sky (66)** (ABailey) **5-9-3**(7) AngelaGallimore(12) (a.p: r.o u.p fnl f: nt pce of wnr) | 1½ | **2** | 3/1$^1$ | 68 | 51 |
| 393$^9$ | **Jon's Choice (38)** (BPreece) **8-7-7**(3) DWright(11) (bhd & outpcd: gd hdwy 2f out: fin wl) | 1 | **3** | 20/1 | 37 | 20 |
| 394$^9$ | **Leigh Crofter (70)** (PDCundell) **7-10-0b** TIves(3) (a.p: led over 2f out tl wl over 1f out: one pce fnl f) | s.h | **4** | 9/2$^2$ | 69 | 52 |
| 368$^6$ | **Always Grace (52)** (MissGayKelleway) **4-8-10** KFallon(6) (trckd ldrs: effrt & swtchd rt over 1f out: kpt on u.p fnl f) | ½ | **5** | 8/1$^3$ | 50 | 33 |
| 394* | **Kira (74)** (JLEyre) **6-10-1**(3) 7x OPears(8) (b.off hind: hld up: effrt wl over 1f out: nt pce to chal) | 1¼ | **6** | 9/2$^2$ | 69 | 52 |
| | **Perfect Brave (60)** (JBalding) **5-8-11**(7) JEdmunds(13) (bkwd: outpcd: hdwy 3f out: one pce appr fnl f) | 1¼ | **7** | 16/1 | 51 | 34 |
| 341$^8$ | **Langtonian (41)** (JLEyre) **7-7-13v** NCarlisle(4) (b.nr hind: s.s: a outpcd) | 3½ | **8** | 20/1 | 23 | 6 |
| 388$^3$ | **The Fed (44)** (JAPickering) **6-8-2** JQuinn(1) (spd over 4f) | 3 | **9** | 8/1$^3$ | 18 | 1 |
| 399$^8$ | **All Apologies (IRE) (69)** (RHollinshead) **4-9-6**(7) FLynch(7) (led over 3f: rdn & wknd appr fnl f) | 1 | **10** | 12/1 | 40 | 23 |
| | **Arc Lamp (45)** (JAGlover) **10-7-12**(5) PFessey(2) (bkwd: a in rr: rdn 2f out: no imp) | 1 | **11** | 16/1 | 14 | — |
| | **Stephensons Rocket (66)** (DNicholls) **5-9-10** EmmaO'Gorman(10) (bkwd: dwlt: a bhd) | 3½ | **12** | 14/1 | 25 | 8 |
| 403$^7$ | **Classic Victory (60)** (RHarris) **3-8-4b$^1$** JTate(5) (outpcd: t.o) | 6 | **13** | 16/1 | 4 | — |
| | | | | (SP 131.0%) | | **13 Rn** |

**1m 17.2** (5.80) CSF £65.50 CT £713.70 TOTE £21.90: £4.70 £2.80 £3.50 (£95.40) Trio £259.80; £36.59 to Wolverhampton 16/3/96 OWNER Mr E. A. Hayward (CHEPSTOW) BRED Crest Stud Ltd
LONG HANDICAP Jon's Choice 7-8
WEIGHT FOR AGE 3yo-14lb

T/Plpt: £90.70 (132.87 Tckts). T/Qdpt: £10.40 (110.97 Tckts). IM

# 0413-WOLVERHAMPTON (L-H) (Standard)

## Saturday March 16th

WEATHER: fine

## 419 CORNWALL-LEGH MEDIAN AUCTION MAIDEN STKS (3, 4 & 5-Y.O) (Class E)

7-00 (7-00) **1m 1f 79y (Fibresand)** £2,710.00 (£820.00: £400.00: £190.00) Stalls: Low GOING: 0.33 sec per fur (SLW)

| Form | Horse / details | Dist | Pos | SP | RR | SF |
|---|---|---|---|---|---|---|
| | **Dombey** (RCharlton) **3-8-5** SSanders(8) (lw: hld up: hdwy 4f out: led over 1f out: qcknd clr) | — | **1** | 4/5$^1$ | 83 | 36 |

| | | | | SP | RR | SF |
|---|---|---|---|---|---|---|
| 402[6] | **Cuban Nights (USA)** (BJLlewellyn) **4-9-10** AClark(4) (lw: chsd ldrs: led 3f out tl over 1f out: no ch w wnr) | 10 | **2** | 10/1 | 66 | 38 |
| | **Rostaq** (DJGMurraySmith) **3-8-5** KFallon(1) (led over 6f: rdn & btn over 1f out) | 2½ | **3** | 7/1[3] | 62 | 15 |
| | **Nelly's Cousin** (NACallaghan) **3-8-1**ow1 GCarter(9) (b: b.hind: w'like: racd wd: hld up: hdwy 4f out: nvr trbld ldrs) | 4 | **4** | 14/1 | 51 | 3 |
| | **Letterluna** (DRGandolfo) **4-9-5** AMcGlone(2) (in tch 6f) | 11 | **5** | 50/1 | 31 | 3 |
| 390[3] | **Tirra-Lirra (IRE)** (CEBrittain) **4-9-2**(3) DRMcCabe(6) (w ldrs tl wknd over 2f out) | 16 | **6** | 3/1[2] | 4 | — |
| 402[12] | **Metal Badge (IRE)** (MJohnston) **3-8-5** TWilliams(7) (prom 5f: sn rdn & wknd: virtually p.u fnl f) | dist | **7** | 25/1 | — | — |

(SP 114.6%) **7 Rn**

**2m 5.4** (9.40) CSF £9.12 TOTE £2.00: £1.20 £4.30 (£20.90) Trio £17.00 OWNER Lady Rothschild (BECKHAMPTON) BRED Exors of the late Mrs D. M. de Rothschild
WEIGHT FOR AGE 3yo-19lb

## 420 HARKNESS CLAIMING STKS (4-Y.O+) (Class F)

7-30 (7-30) **1m 4f (Fibresand)** £2,085.00 (£585.00: £285.00) Stalls: Low GOING: 0.33 sec per fur (SLW)

| | | | | SP | RR | SF |
|---|---|---|---|---|---|---|
| 360* | **Hill Farm Dancer (54)** (WMBrisbourne) **5-7-12**(7) IonaWands(2) (lw: trckd ldrs: squeezed thro to ld 1f out: pushed out) | — | **1** | 3/1[2] | 63 | 15 |
| 401* | **Heathyards Rock (81)** (RHollinshead) **4-9-6** TIves(3) (lw: hld up: hdwy over 3f out: chal 1f out: unable qckn nr fin) | ¾ | **2** | 11/8[1] | 79 | 29 |
| 369[5] | **Tartan Gem (IRE) (67)** (MissGayKelleway) **5-9-4** RCochrane(7) (lw: dwlt: hdwy 4f out: led 2f out tl edgd rt 1f out: no ex) | 3½ | **3** | 7/1 | 70 | 22 |
| 235[4] | **Pistols At Dawn (USA) (60)** (BJMeehan) **6-8-5**(7) CRafter(1) (plld hrd: set stdy pce: sddle slipped after 3f: hdd 4f out: ev ch over 1f out: sn btn) | 2 | **4** | 10/1 | 62 | 14 |
| 373[2] | **Northern Trial (USA) (50)** (KRBurke) **8-8-1v**(7) TAshley(4) (b.hind: in tch tl outpcd 4f out) | 5 | **5** | 13/2[3] | 51 | 3 |
| 401[5] | **Kismetim (54)** (DWChapman) **6-8-4** LCharnock(5) (chsd ldrs: qcknd & led 4f out: hdd 2f out: sn wknd) | ¾ | **6** | 14/1 | 46 | — |
| | **Florismart (54)** (BPJBaugh) **4-8-8** WLord(6) (chsd ldrs 8f: sn outpcd & bhd) | dist | **7** | 50/1 | — | — |

(SP 110.7%) **7 Rn**

**2m 48.1** (15.60) CSF £7.11 TOTE £4.30: £2.00 £1.60 (£2.90) OWNER Mr Dennis Newton (NESSCLIFFE) BRED D. Newton
WEIGHT FOR AGE 4yo-2lb

## 421 SULTAN OF ISLAMABAD H'CAP (0-70) (3-Y.O) (Class E)

8-00 (8-00) **7f (Fibresand)** £2,587.70 (£727.20: £355.10) Stalls: High GOING: 0.33 sec per fur (SLW)

| | | | | SP | RR | SF |
|---|---|---|---|---|---|---|
| 405[4] | **Miss Offset (52)** (MJohnston) **3-8-8b** TWilliams(6) (mde all: rdn 3f out: hld on wl ins fnl f) | — | **1** | 7/1 | 58 | 28 |
| 405* | **Maiteamia (57)** (SRBowring) **3-8-8b**(5) CTeague(7) (lw: hdwy 3f out: rdn over 1f out: ev ch ins fnl f: no ex nr fin) | nk | **2** | 4/1[2] | 62 | 32 |
| 391[3] | **Victim of Love (64)** (RCharlton) **3-9-6** SSanders(3) (sn chsng wnr: ev ch over 1f out: unable qckn ins fnl f) | 2 | **3** | 13/2[3] | 65 | 35 |
| 320[3] | **La Perruche (IRE) (52)** (LordHuntingdon) **3-8-1**(7) AimeeCook(8) (hdwy 3f out: nvr trbld ldrs) | 3 | **4** | 7/1 | 46 | 16 |
| 405[5] | **Coastguards Hero (54)** (MDIUsher) **3-8-10** MWigham(4) (b.hind: chsd ldrs: no hdwy fnl 3f) | 3½ | **5** | 8/1 | 40 | 10 |
| | **Katie Komaite (48)** (CaptJHWilson) **3-7-13**(5) PFessey(9) (rdn 3f out: nvr nr ldrs) | 2½ | **6** | 12/1 | 28 | — |
| 383[2] | **Chilibang Bang (65)** (JBerry) **3-9-2**(5) PRoberts(1) (lw: chsd ldrs over 4f) | 1½ | **7** | 4/1[2] | 42 | 12 |
| 405[2] | **Principal Boy (IRE) (54)** (TJEtherington) **3-8-10** GCarter(2) (bhd fnl 3f) | ¾ | **8** | 3/1[1] | 29 | — |
| 344[8] | **Oriel Lad (62)** (PDEvans) **3-9-4b** KFallon(5) (a bhd) | 7 | **9** | 10/1 | 21 | — |

(SP 131.2%) **9 Rn**

**1m 32.5** (7.80) CSF £37.42 CT £186.20 TOTE £9.80: £3.00 £2.50 £1.90 (£55.60) Trio £79.30 OWNER Hertford Offset Ltd (MIDDLEHAM) BRED J. Coombes and E. Henshaw
STEWARDS' ENQUIRY Williams susp. 25-27/3/96 (incorrect use of whip).

## 422 MILES PLATT H'CAP (0-70) (4-Y.O+) (Class E)

8-30 (8-30) **1m 6f 166y (Fibresand)** £2,814.00 (£852.00: £416.00: £198.00) Stalls: High GOING: 0.33 sec per fur (SLW)

| | | | | SP | RR | SF |
|---|---|---|---|---|---|---|
| 392[7] | **Backview (69)** (BJLlewellyn) **4-9-9** TWilliams(12) (a.p: led over 4f out tl over 1f out: rdn & r.o wl to ld ins fnl f) | — | **1** | 9/1 | 78 | 40 |
| 267[3] | **Comtec's Legend (38)** (JFBottomley) **6-7-10** LCharnock(11) (b: hdwy 5f out: led over 1f out tl ins fnl f: unable qckn) | ½ | **2** | 12/1 | 48 | 13 |
| 400[3] | **Swordking (IRE) (38)** (JLHarris) **7-7-10v** JQuinn(4) (chsd ldrs: rdn 2f out: r.o wl fnl f) | 1½ | **3** | 14/1 | 46 | 11 |
| 400* | **Ijab (CAN) (53)** (JParkes) **6-8-11b** GBardwell(10) (trckd ldrs: rdn 3f out: no imp appr fnl f) | 2 | **4** | 11/2[3] | 59 | 24 |
| 373[3] | **Charlie Bigtime (52)** (RHarris) **6-8-3**(7) OliverCasey(6) (b.hind: chsd ldr 11f: sn rdn & outpcd: n.d after) | 5 | **5** | 9/2[2] | 52 | 17 |
| 296[8] | **Toy Princess (USA) (66)** (CEBrittain) **4-9-3**(3) DRMcCabe(1) (lw: led 10f: rdn 2f out: eased whn btn) | 3 | **6** | 14/1 | 62 | 24 |
| 312[5] | **Brave Spy (55)** (CACyzer) **5-8-13** DBiggs(5) (prom 10f) | 7 | **7** | 9/1 | 44 | 9 |
| 367[2] | **Philmist (49)** (CWCElsey) **4-8-3b** NKennedy(8) (in tch 10f) | ½ | **8** | 9/1 | 37 | — |
| 360[5] | **Iota (56)** (JLHarris) **7-8-9**(5) PFessey(7) (dwlt: nvr nr to chal) | 1½ | **9** | 9/1 | 43 | 8 |
| 339[9] | **Kymin (IRE) (61)** (DJGMurraySmith) **4-8-10v**(5) RPainter(3) (hdwy 6f out: wknd 4f out) | 9 | **10** | 20/1 | 38 | — |
| 60* | **Lear Dancer (USA) (70)** (PhilipMitchell) **5-10-0b** AClark(9) (lw: effrt 6f out: a bhd) | 1 | **11** | 9/4[1] | 46 | 11 |
| 398[3] | **Fox Chapel (58)** (RTJuckes) **9-9-2v** DaleGibson(2) (rdn 5f out: sn bhd) | 16 | **12** | 20/1 | 17 | — |

(SP 134.9%) **12 Rn**

**3m 24.8** (17.40) CSF £112.49 CT £1,403.85 TOTE £25.50: £4.80 £3.00 £3.30 (£94.80) Trio £327.30; £299.66 to 18/3/96. OWNER Mr Eamonn O'Malley (BARGOED) BRED G. D. Dalrymple
LONG HANDICAP Swordking (IRE) 7-3
WEIGHT FOR AGE 4yo-4lb
**OFFICIAL EXPLANATION Toy Princess (USA): the filly seemed to lose her action turning into the straight, so the jockey did not persevere.**

## 423 RICHARD WOLVERHAMPTON SPRINT SERIES FINAL (S) H'CAP (3-Y.O) (Class E)

9-00 (9-01) **6f (Fibresand)** £4,006.50 (£1,212.00: £591.00: £280.50) Stalls: Low GOING: 0.33 sec per fur (SLW)

| | | | | SP | RR | SF |
|---|---|---|---|---|---|---|
| 359[3] | **Dhes-C (54)** (RHollinshead) **3-8-8**(7) FLynch(3) (in tch: hdwy 2f out: r.o wl to ld nr fin) | — | **1** | 11/4[2] | 48 | 22 |
| 383[3] | **Mystic Tempo (USA) (60)** (DrJDScargill) **3-9-4**(3) SDrowne(6) (b: a.p: ev ch ins fnl f: unable qckn nr fin) | hd | **2** | 2/1[1] | 54 | 28 |
| 414[5] | **Marino Street (54)** (PDEvans) **3-9-1v** SSanders(1) (chsd ldrs: led over 2f out: rdn fnl f: ct nr fin) | s.h | **3** | 12/1 | 48 | 22 |

| | | | | SP | RR | SF |
|---|---|---|---|---|---|---|
| 272[4] | **Don't Tell Anyone (50)** (PDEvans) **3-8-11** KFallon(5) (w ldr: led over 3f out tl over 2f out: sn rdn & btn) | 6 | **4** | 12/1 | 28 | 2 |
| 78[2] | **Miss Pickpocket (IRE) (55)** (PAKelleway) **3-9-2** MWigham(2) (b.hind: dwlt: sn rdn along: nvr nr ldrs) | 7 | **5** | 3/1[3] | 14 | — |
| 405[6] | **Victoria Sioux (47)** (JAPickering) **3-8-8b[1]** JQuinn(4) (b.off hind: led over 2f: wknd 2f out) | 6 | **6** | 8/1 | — | — |
| | | | | (SP 111.5%) | **6 Rn** | |

**1m 19.0** (7.60) CSF £8.32 TOTE £4.00: £2.40 £1.80 (£6.70) OWNER Dhes-C Partnership (UPPER LONGDON) BRED Longdon Stud Ltd
No bid

## 424 RIDGEMOUNT H'CAP (0-70) (4-Y.O+) (Class E)

9-30 (9-30) **1m 1f 79y (Fibresand)** £2,827.00 (£856.00: £418.00: £199.00) Stalls: Low GOING: 0.33 sec per fur (SLW)

| | | | | SP | RR | SF |
|---|---|---|---|---|---|---|
| 303[3] | **Explosive Power (63)** (GCBravery) **5-9-7**(3) DRMcCabe(5) (lw: mde all: drew clr over 1f out: comf) | — | **1** | 4/1[2] | 81 | 60 |
| 308[7] | **Golden Touch (USA) (54)** (NACallaghan) **4-8-8**(7) FLynch(7) (hld up: hdwy over 3f out: ev ch over 1f out: sn outpcd) | 3½ | **2** | 3/1[1] | 66 | 45 |
| 384* | **Zahid (USA) (59)** (KRBurke) **5-9-6** JQuinn(8) (hdwy 4f out: r.o fnl f) | 5 | **3** | 11/2[3] | 63 | 42 |
| 189[5] | **Todd (USA) (56)** (PhilipMitchell) **5-9-3** AClark(4) (chsd ldrs: one pce fnl 3f) | 2½ | **4** | 14/1 | 55 | 34 |
| 373[7] | **Genesis Four (40)** (SRBowring) **6-8-1** NCarlisle(2) (prom: lost pl 4f out: n.d after) | 8 | **5** | 20/1 | 26 | 5 |
| 384[8] | **Maradata (IRE) (50)** (RHollinshead) **4-8-11** MWigham(11) (bhd tl r.o fnl 3f) | 2½ | **6** | 25/1 | 31 | 10 |
| 285[6] | **Palacegate Jo (IRE) (44)** (DWChapman) **5-8-5** LCharnock(12) (prom over 5f) | ½ | **7** | 25/1 | 24 | 3 |
| 343[3] | **Komiamaite (51)** (SRBowring) **4-8-7**(5) CTeague(10) (chsd wnr tl rdn & wknd 3f out) | hd | **8** | 7/1 | 31 | 10 |
| 345* | **Twin Creeks (57)** (MDHammond) **5-9-4** RCochrane(1) (in tch: rdn 4f out: sn btn) | ¾ | **9** | 11/2[3] | 36 | 15 |
| 384[2] | **Hand of Straw (IRE) (62)** (PGMurphy) **4-9-6v**(3) SDrowne(9) (prom 6f: sn wknd) | 6 | **10** | 12/1 | 31 | 10 |
| | **Brown Eyed Girl (54)** (BJMeehan) **4-8-8**(7) GHannon(3) (bit bkwd: dwlt: a bhd) | 15 | **11** | 25/1 | — | — |
| | **She Said No (56)** (LordHuntingdon) **4-9-3** DHarrison(13) (bhd fnl 5f) | 7 | **12** | 12/1 | — | — |
| 380[7] | **Office Hours (59)** (CACyzer) **4-9-6** DBiggs(6) (hld up: hdwy 5f out: wknd over 3f out: eased) | 8 | **13** | 25/1 | — | — |
| | | | | (SP 130.5%) | **13 Rn** | |

**2m 4.6** (8.60) CSF £16.80 CT £61.16 TOTE £6.30: £1.60 £1.90 £2.40 (£49.00) Trio £30.20 OWNER Mr H. T. Short (NEWMARKET) BRED Mrs P. Hollingsworth

T/Plpt: £261.60 (50.69 Tckts). T/Qdpt: £80.60 (6.51 Tckts). Dk

# 0398-SOUTHWELL (L-H) (Standard)

## Monday March 18th

WEATHER: cloudy

## 425 ST. ANDREWS H'CAP (0-65) (I) (3-Y.O+) (Class F)

2-00 (2-00) **6f (Fibresand)** £2,048.00 (£573.00: £278.00) Stalls: Low GOING minus 0.05 sec per fur (STD)

| | | | | SP | RR | SF |
|---|---|---|---|---|---|---|
| 257[4] | **Elton Ledger (IRE) (55)** (MrsNMacauley) **7-9-4b** JTate(5) (lw: b: in tch: hdwy to ld 1f out: styd on) | — | **1** | 10/1 | 62 | 37 |
| 388[2] | **Desert Invader (IRE) (69)** (DWChapman) **5-10-4** ACulhane(7) (lw: a.p: ev ch 2f out: kpt on) | 1¼ | **2** | 3/1[2] | 73 | 48 |
| 403[2] | **Dissentor (IRE) (53)** (JAGlover) **4-9-2v** GCarter(4) (chsd ldrs: led 2f out tl hdd 1f out: one pce) | 1¾ | **3** | 2/1[1] | 52 | 27 |
| 388[4] | **Lochon (57)** (JLEyre) **5-9-6** RLappin(1) (b: trckd ldrs: chal 2f out: sn rdn & no ex) | 3 | **4** | 4/1[3] | 48 | 23 |
| 368[8] | **Tame Deer (60)** (MCChapman) **4-9-2**(7) CMunday(8) (sn outpcd & bhd: styd on fnl 2f: no imp) | 1½ | **5** | 10/1 | 47 | 22 |
| 418[9] | **The Fed (44)** (JAPickering) **6-8-7** JQuinn(2) (led tl hdd & wknd 2f out) | 4 | **6** | 12/1 | 20 | — |
| | **Blue Lugana (40)** (NBycroft) **4-8-3** LCharnock(9) (outpcd & bhd fr ½-wy) | ¾ | **7** | 33/1 | 14 | — |
| 342[4] | **Chloella (33)** (CBBBooth) **4-7-10** NKennedy(6) (cl up: chal 3f out: wknd 2f out) | ¾ | **8** | 20/1 | 5 | — |
| | **Prime Property (IRE) (36)** (MWEasterby) **4-7-6b**(7)ow3 MartinDwyer(3) (dwlt: a outpcd & bhd) | 1½ | **9** | 14/1 | 4 | — |
| | | | | (SP 118.6%) | **9 Rn** | |

**1m 18.0** (4.50) CSF £38.96 CT £79.01 TOTE £8.60: £2.80 £1.10 £1.20 (£19.20) Trio £16.00 OWNER The Posse (MELTON MOWBRAY) BRED Thomas Doherty
LONG HANDICAP Chloella 7-6 Prime Property (IRE) 7-5

## 426 TROON APPRENTICE H'CAP (0-60) (4-Y.O+) (Class F)

2-30 (2-31) **1m (Fibresand)** £2,410.00 (£685.00: £340.00) Stalls: Low GOING minus 0.05 sec per fur (STD)

| | | | | SP | RR | SF |
|---|---|---|---|---|---|---|
| 336[6] | **Pine Essence (USA) (44)** (JLEyre) **5-9-0** PDoe(5) (s.i.s: hdwy ½-wy: led over 1f out: r.o) | — | **1** | 5/1[2] | 59 | 31 |
| | **Thaleros (55)** (GMMoore) **6-9-11** CLowther(12) (hdwy ½-wy: styd on wl fnl 2f: nrst fin) | 5 | **2** | 14/1 | 60 | 32 |
| 133* | **King Parrot (IRE) (55)** (LordHuntingdon) **8-9-6**(5) CCogan(11) (lw: disp ld 4f: led over 2f out tl over 1f out: one pce) | 1¾ | **3** | 5/1[2] | 57 | 29 |
| 384[4] | **Trumble (44)** (CWThornton) **4-8-9**(5) GMills(10) (w ldrs: one pce fnl 3f) | 1½ | **4** | 8/1[3] | 43 | 15 |
| 367[3] | **Carol Again (35)** (NBycroft) **4-8-5** DSweeney(4) (in tch: rdn over 3f out: styd on: no imp) | 1½ | **5** | 10/1 | 31 | 3 |
| 424[5] | **Genesis Four (40)** (SRBowring) **6-8-10** TField(7) (gd spd 5f: grad wknd) | 4 | **6** | 10/1 | 28 | — |
| 328[4] | **Arecibo (FR) (34)** (JParkes) **4-8-4** RMullen(13) (chsd ldrs over 5f) | 3½ | **7** | 14/1 | 15 | — |
| | **Fred's Delight (IRE) (27)** (MrsVAAconley) **5-7-11v** TFinn(6) (sn pushed along: nvr trbld ldrs) | 1 | **8** | 33/1 | 6 | — |
| 195[3] | **Komlucky (44)** (ABMulholland) **4-9-0b** KSked(3) (disp ld tl over 4f out: hdd & wknd over 2f out) | 6 | **9** | 10/1 | 11 | — |
| 328* | **Mezzoramio (46)** (KAMorgan) **4-9-2v** CScudder(1) (prom tl wknd fnl 3f) | 1¼ | **10** | 4/1[1] | 10 | — |
| 420[6] | **Kismetim (52)** (DWChapman) **6-9-8** AngelaGallimore(2) (a outpcd & bhd) | ¾ | **11** | 16/1 | 15 | — |
| 343[8] | **Moody (47)** (JAGlover) **4-9-3v** VictoriaAppleby(8) (chsd ldrs 5f: wknd) | 1 | **12** | 14/1 | 8 | — |
| 401[6] | **Beauchief (44)** (RFMarvin) **4-9-0b[1]** JEdmunds(9) (b: a bhd) | 3 | **13** | 33/1 | — | — |
| | | | | (SP 123.5%) | **13 Rn** | |

**1m 46.4** (6.40) CSF £67.85 CT £350.51 TOTE £5.80: £3.30 £4.80 £2.30 (£74.40) Trio £163.40 OWNER Mr K. Meynell (HAMBLETON) BRED David E. Hager II

## 427 CARNOUSTIE CLAIMING STKS (3-Y.O+) (Class F)

3-00 (3-04) **7f (Fibresand)** £2,398.00 (£673.00: £328.00) Stalls: Low GOING minus 0.05 sec per fur (STD)

| | | | | SP | RR | SF |
|---|---|---|---|---|---|---|
| 153* | **So Amazing (75)** (MissSEHall) **4-9-7** KFallon(10) (b: mde most: drvn clr fnl 2f) | — | **1** | 5/4[1] | 84 | 52 |
| 409[3] | **Ashgore (85)** (MJohnston) **6-9-12** JWeaver(11) (lw: disp ld tl rdn & btn wl over 1f out) | 5 | **2** | 9/4[2] | 78 | 46 |
| 174[2] | **Spencer's Revenge (73)** (NTinkler) **7-9-12** GCarter(1) (hdwy over 2f out: styd on wl: nrst fin) | s.h | **3** | 5/1[3] | 78 | 46 |

347[8] **At the Savoy (IRE) (58)** (TDBarron) **5-8-10b**(7) KimberleyHart(4) (a chsng ldrs: effrt 3f out: one pce) ..............8 **4** 12/1 50 18
342[6] **La Dama (USA) (40)** (ABMulholland) **4-8-12** MMcAndrew(7) (unruly gng to s: a chsng ldrs: no imp fnl 3f) .....1¾ **5** 33/1 41 9
344[4] **Quinntessa (40)** (BPalling) **3-8-1**ow1 TSprake(8) (cl up tl wknd over 2f out) ..........1¼ **6** 20/1 43 —
**Classic Daisy (35)** (RCSpicer) **3-8-0** NKennedy(6) (in tch: rdn ½-wy: sn btn) ..........2 **7** 50/1 38 —
**Harsh Times (55)** (TDEasterby) **3-7-13** JQuinn(9) (prom tl outpcd fr ½-wy) ..........8 **8** 16/1 19 —
372[5] **Desert Man (44)** (RDEWoodhouse) **5-9-6b**[1] NConnorton(5) (sn outpcd & bhd) ..........6 **9** 50/1 10 —
344[13] **Topanoora Bay (IRE)** (MrsVAAconley) **3-7-13**(5) FLynch(2) (sn outpcd: wl bhd fr ½-wy) ..........18 **10** 50/1 — —
*Cavendish Rose* (JBerry) **5-8-11**(5) PRoberts(3) (Withdrawn not under Starter's orders: ref to enter stalls) ....... **W** 33/1 — —
(SP 122.0%) **10 Rn**

**1m 31.1** (4.30) CSF £4.49 TOTE £2.40: £1.10 £1.50 £1.10 (£2.90) Trio £1.50 OWNER Mr C. Platts (MIDDLEHAM) BRED C. Platts and Miss S. E. Hall
WEIGHT FOR AGE 3yo-15lb
So Amazing clmd BWaldron £12,000

## 428 MUIRFIELD MAIDEN STKS (3-Y.O) (Class D)
3-30 (3-31) **1m (Fibresand)** £3,582.50 (£1,085.00: £530.00: £252.50) Stalls: Low GOING minus 0.05 sec per fur (STD)

SP RR SF

**Naval Hunter (USA)** (PWHarris) **3-9-0** GHind(11) (in tch: stdy hdwy over 2f out: hung lft: r.o to ld wl ins fnl f) ..........— **1** 25/1 73 38
**Hamlet (IRE) (78)** (MBell) **3-9-0** MFenton(1) (led tl hdd & no ex wl ins fnl f) ..........1¼ **2** 10/11 1 71 36
355[2] **Fairy Highlands (IRE)** (SCWilliams) **3-8-9** JTate(5) (chsd ldrs: ev ch over 2f out: one pce appr fnl f) ..........3½ **3** 4/1 2 59 24
**Falcon's Flame (USA)** (MrsJRRamsden) **3-9-0** KFallon(10) (w'like: scope: bit bkwd: stdy hdwy over 2f out: r.o towards fin) ..........7 **4** 7/1 3 50 15
**Winston** (JDBethell) **3-9-0** JWeaver(3) (w ldrs tl wknd 2f out) ..........2 **5** 25/1 46 11
381[6] **Sahhar (62)** (RWArmstrong) **3-9-0** WWoods(4) (chsd ldrs tl outpcd fnl 3f) ..........1¼ **6** 4/1 2 43 8
**Welcome Lu** (PSFelgate) **3-8-6**(3) PMcCabe(8) (nvr nr ldrs) ..........15 **7** 50/1 8 —
**Sweet Seranade (IRE)** (NPLittmoden) **3-8-9** TGMcLaughlin(7) (prom 4f: sn rdn & wknd) ..........3½ **8** 33/1 1 —
**All In Good Time** (CWThornton) **3-9-0** DeanMcKeown(2) (sn outpcd & bhd) ..........5 **9** 33/1 — —
370[5] **Kenilworth Dancer (40)** (RDEWoodhouse) **3-9-0b**[1] NConnorton(6) (s.i.s: a bhd: t.o) ..........25 **10** 33/1 — —
370[6] **My Archie (35)** (RDEWoodhouse) **3-9-0** JQuinn(9) (sn bhd: t.o) ..........1¾ **11** 50/1 — —
(SP 125.3%) **11 Rn**

**1m 45.7** (5.70) CSF £49.27 TOTE £41.30: £4.90 £1.30 £1.20 (£9.10) Trio £20.70 OWNER Mr L. A. Hooper (BERKHAMSTED) BRED Joe Arriola and Pegasus Stud

## 429 FARMERS WEEKLY H'CAP (0-70) (4-Y.O+) (Class E)
4-00 (4-02) **1m 3f (Fibresand)** £2,872.80 (£869.40: £424.20: £201.60) Stalls: Low GOING minus 0.05 sec per fur (STD)

SP RR SF

401[4] **Adaloaldo (USA) (50)** (JParkes) **4-8-7**(5) RHavlin(8) (hdwy 5f out: sn chsng ldrs: styd on to ld wl ins fnl f) .....— **1** 12/1 58 8
369* **Eulogy (FR) (64)** (KRBurke) **9-9-10**(3) DRMcCabe(10) (lw: hdwy ½-wy: led over 2f out: hdd, hrd rdn & no ex wl ins fnl f) ..........½ **2** 8/1 3 71 22
398[2] **Tempering (59)** (DWChapman) **10-9-8** ACulhane(5) (swtg: led tl hdd over 2f out: one pce) ..........4 **3** 6/1 2 61 12
254* **El Bailador (IRE) (65)** (JDBethell) **5-10-0** JWeaver(9) (in tch: effrt 3f out: no imp) ..........5 **4** 11/4 1 59 10
303[6] **Sea God (48)** (MCChapman) **5-8-4**(7) CMunday(6) (prom tl outpcd 5f out: no imp after) ..........5 **5** 6/1 2 35 —
256[6] **Exclusion (37)** (JHetherton) **7-8-0** JQuinn(3) (chsd ldrs tl rdn over 3f out: sn wknd) ..........¾ **6** 14/1 23 —
301[5] **Grey Again (57)** (SRBowring) **4-9-0b**(5) CTeague(4) (hld up: hdwy 7f out: rdn & btn over 2f out) ..........2½ **7** 6/1 2 39 —
367* **Inovar (41)** (CBBBooth) **6-7-13**(5)ow8 FLynch(2) (hdwy 6f out: rdn & outpcd fnl 4f) ..........1¾ **8** 6/1 2 21 —
372[7] **Slmaat (50)** (RDEWoodhouse) **5-8-13** NConnorton(7) (bhd fr ½-wy) ..........9 **9** 25/1 17 —
**Dance Motion (39)** (ABMulholland) **4-8-1b**[1] TWilliams(1) (cl up tl rdn & wknd 6f out: t.o) ..........dist **10** 33/1 — —
(SP 116.1%) **10 Rn**

**2m 32.2** (12.20) CSF £93.68 CT £581.61 TOTE £14.70: £3.30 £3.80 £2.20 (£102.80) Trio £247.40; £38.34 to Uttoxeter 19/3/96 OWNER Mr R. Flegg (MALTON) BRED Stuart Ross
WEIGHT FOR AGE 4yo-1lb
STEWARDS' ENQUIRY McCabe susp. 27-30/3/96 (excessive use of whip).

## 430 SANDWICH (S) STKS (3-Y.O) (Class F)
4-30 (4-31) **5f (Fibresand)** £2,398.00 (£673.00: £328.00) Stalls: High GOING minus 0.05 sec per fur (STD)

SP RR SF

359[4] **General Equation (58)** (JBalding) **3-8-5**(7) JEdmunds(8) (b: hung lft most of wy: mde most: r.o wl fnl f) .........— **1** 5/1 2 73 15
335[7] **Gi La High (62)** (JBerry) **3-8-8**(5) PRoberts(4) (w ldrs: nt qckn appr fnl f) ..........6 **2** 7/4 1 55 —
264[5] **Impington (IRE) (47)** (WRMuir) **3-8-7v** Jean-PierreLopez(2) (w ldrs tl rdn & btn appr fnl f) ..........½ **3** 9/1 3 47 —
383[6] **Copper Bright (65)** (PCHaslam) **3-9-4b** JWeaver(5) (lw: chsd ldrs: outpcd 2f out: no imp after) ..........1 **4** 7/4 1 55 —
101[12] **Touch of Fantasy (41)** (CADwyer) **3-8-4**(3) SDrowne(3) (sme hdwy ½-wy: no imp) ..........7 **5** 16/1 22 —
258[6] **Savanna Blue** (JLEyre) **3-8-7** RLappin(1) (hung lft most of wy: sn bhd) ..........2½ **6** 33/1 14 —
**Musical Heights (IRE)** (CADwyer) **3-8-7** KRutter(7) (hmpd s: a bhd) ..........3 **7** 20/1 4 —
292[10] **Ping-Pong Ball** (TRWatson) **3-8-7** DeanMcKeown(6) (bmpd s: spd to ½-wy) ..........9 **8** 50/1 — —
(SP 114.9%) **8 Rn**

**61.5 secs** (4.50) CSF £13.72 TOTE £7.60: £2.20 £1.10 £3.80 (£6.30) OWNER Make Our Day (DONCASTER) BRED Miss C. Balding
No bid

## 431 ST ANDREWS H'CAP (0-65) (II) (3-Y.O+) (Class F)
5-00 (5-01) **6f (Fibresand)** £2,048.00 (£573.00: £278.00) Stalls: Low GOING minus 0.05 sec per fur (STD)

SP RR SF

**Foist (33)** (MWEasterby) **4-7-10** JQuinn(1) (chsd ldrs: rdn to ld wl over 1f out: edgd rt: styd on wl) ..........— **1** 9/2 2 42 18
298* **Maybank (IRE) (57)** (BAMcMahon) **4-9-6** GCarter(7) (lw: trckd ldrs: chal 2f out: nt qckn ins fnl f) ..........1½ **2** 7/2 1 62 38
399[2] **Awesome Venture (62)** (MCChapman) **6-9-8**(3) DRMcCabe(6) (b.nr hind: hld up: effrt 2f out: styd on: nt pce to chal) ..........6 **3** 11/2 3 51 27
347[4] **Le Bal (34)** (MissJFCraze) **4-7-11**ow1 DaleGibson(2) (cl up: one pce fnl 2f) ..........1½ **4** 12/1 19 —
**Sound the Trumpet (IRE) (56)** (RCSpicer) **4-9-5** DeanMcKeown(5) (disp ld over 4f: grad wknd) ..........¾ **5** 40/1 39 15
247[2] **Cheerful Groom (IRE) (40)** (SRBowring) **5-8-3** NKennedy(8) (outpcd ½-wy: nvr nr ldrs) ..........2 **6** 7/1 18 —

| | | | | | | |
|---|---|---|---|---|---|---|
| 368* | **Daawe (USA) (65)** (MrsVAAconley) **5-10-0v** MDeering(3) (disp ld over 4f: sn wknd) | 2½ | **7** | 7/1 | 36 | 12 |
| 418[8] | **Langtonian (41)** (JLEyre) **7-8-4** NCarlisle(4) (s.i.s: n.d) | 1½ | **8** | 14/1 | 8 | — |
| 342* | **Bold Aristocrat (IRE) (54)** (RHollinshead) **5-8-12**(5) FLynch(9) (racd wd: outpcd & bhd fr ½-wy) | 1¼ | **9** | 6/1 | 18 | — |
| | | | | (SP 111.9%) | | **9 Rn** |

**1m 17.9** (4.40) CSF £18.86 CT £78.38 TOTE £3.90: £1.10 £1.40 £2.40 (£14.80) Trio £21.50 OWNER Mr D. F. Spence (SHERIFF HUTTON) BRED W. Cormack
LONG HANDICAP Foist 7-7 Le Bal 7-7

T/Plpt: £18.30 (633.55 Tckts). T/Qdpt: £6.40 (120.28 Tckts). AA

# JEBEL ALI (Dubai, UAE) (L-H) (Good to soft)
## Friday March 1st

### 432a THE GROSVENOR JEBEL ALI SPRINT (Listed) (4-Y.O+)
**6f (Dirt)** £12,280.70 (£6,140.35: £3,684.21: £2,456.14)

| | | | | SP | RR | SF |
|---|---|---|---|---|---|---|
| | **Try Prospect (USA)** (DJSelvaratnam,UAE) **4-8-9** BDoyle | — | **1** | | 106 | — |
| 375a[5] | **Alami (USA)** (KPMcLaughlin,UAE) **4-8-9** RHills | 5 | **2** | | 93 | — |
| | **Tamim (USA)** (ECharpy,UAE) **7-8-9** WSupple | 7 | **3** | | 74 | — |
| 374a[6] | **Gulf of Gdansk (USA)** (MusabahAlMuhairi,UAE) **6-8-9** JCarroll | 7 | **4** | | 55 | — |
| | | | | | | **4 Rn** |

**1m 12.77** OWNER Sheikh Ahmed Al Maktoum BRED Fourbros Stable,USA
**Try Prospect (USA)** broke well and soon led the way. Clear at halfway, he was driven out entering the final furlong and came home unchallenged.
**Alami (USA)**, twice a winner over six furlongs at Pontefract in 1994, has been tried at three different distances since December '95. Tracking the leader, he stayed on under pressure from two out but could not live with the winner. It is difficult to pin-point his favoured trip.

### 433a GROSVENOR CLUBS - THE CLERMONT CLASSIC (4-Y.O+)
**7f (Dirt)** £7,017.54 (£3,508.77: £2,105.26: £1,403.51)

| | | | SP | RR | SF |
|---|---|---|---|---|---|
| **Darnay** (DJSelvaratnam,UAE) **5-8-12** BDoyle | — | **1** | | 113 | — |
| **Dance Band (USA)** (WDMather,UAE) **4-8-9** PBrette | 3 | **2** | | 103 | — |
| **Shahid** (KPMcLaughlin,UAE) **4-8-12** RHills | ½ | **3** | | 105 | — |
| **Vinza (USA)** (ECharpy,UAE) **4-8-6** WSupple | 4 | **4** | | 90 | — |
| | | | | | **4 Rn** |

**1m 26.01** OWNER Sheikh Mohammed Obaid Al Maktoum BRED Sheikh Mohammed bin Rashid al Maktoum
**Darnay** certainly appreciated this drop in distance, after disappointing on his last two efforts over a mile. Disputing the lead to the straight, he took the initiative four furlongs from home and, turning on the pace approaching the final furlong, was ridden out to take the honours.
**Dance Band (USA)**, continuing the trend of placed efforts this season, once again met one too good. Disputing the lead, he was ridden with every chance two furlongs out, but, running on, could not muster the pace to challenge the winner inside the final furlong.
**Shahid** would have appreciated the outing and will come on a lot for this.

# 0396a-NAD AL SHEBA (Dubai, UAE) (L-H) (Good)
## Sunday March 3rd

### 434a AL-FUTTAIM TROPHY (4-Y.O+)
**1m 2f (Dirt)** £5,263.16 (£2,631.58: £1,578.95: £1,052.63)

| | | | SP | RR | SF |
|---|---|---|---|---|---|
| **Halling (USA)** (SbinSuroor,UAE) **5-9-7** LDettori | — | **1** | | 130+ | — |
| **Torrential (USA)** (SbinSuroor,UAE) **4-9-6** JCarroll | 8 | **2** | | 116 | — |
| **Jandeel (IRE)** (DJSelvaratnam,UAE) **4-8-9** BDoyle | 11 | **3** | | 88 | — |
| | | | | | **5 Rn** |

**2m 5.53** OWNER S. M. R. M BRED Cyril Humphries
**Halling (USA)**, a winner of two Group 1 races at Sandown and York last season, had no trouble in asserting his authority here. Taking an early lead, he quickened clear two furlongs from home and, pushed out inside the final furlong, came home at his leisure. This will leave him in good stead for the Dubai World Cup where the opposition will be somewhat elite.
**Torrential (USA)** had a busy international campaign last season and proved quite useful on his day. He put up another decent show here and had every chance with two and a half furlongs to travel. Despite running on, he was always going to be second best, and was eased down near the finish.
**Jandeel (IRE)**, who ran in fairly useful handicap company in Britain last season, was given a tough task on this occasion, but was by no means disgraced. Close up and ridden in the straight, he was staying on at the same pace inside the final two furlongs, and was eased close home.

# 0434a-NAD AL SHEBA (Dubai, UAE) (L-H) (Heavy)
## Sunday March 10th

### 435a THE KEENELAND MILE (4-Y.O+)
**1m (Dirt)** £8,771.93 (£4,385.97: £2,631.58: £1,754.39)

| | | | | SP | RR | SF |
|---|---|---|---|---|---|---|
| | **Istinsaar (USA)** (ECharpy,UAE) **5-8-4** RHills | — | **1** | | 105 | — |
| | **Dancing Zena (IRE)** (PLRudkin,UAE) **6-8-4** PaulEddery | 2¼ | **2** | | 101 | — |
| 396a* | **Airport (USA)** (DJSelvaratnam,UAE) **5-8-11** BDoyle | nk | **3** | | 107 | — |
| | **Annus Mirabilis (FR)** (SbinSuroor) **4-8-11** LDettori | 10 | **4** | | 87 | — |
| | | | | | | **6 Rn** |

**1m 39.95** OWNER Mr Hamdan Al Maktoum BRED Foxfield

**Istinsaar (USA)** is proving better for the step up to a mile. Tracking the leaders, he took the lead one and a half furlongs out and ran on well in the final furlong.
**Annus Mirabilis (FR)**, who was third in the Irish Derby last year, did not run to form here but may well come on for the run.

## 436a H. H. SHEIKH MAKTOUM BIN RASHID AL MAKTOUM CHALLENGE-ROUND III (Listed) (4-Y.O+)
**1m 2f (Dirt)** £17,543.86 (£8,771.93: £5,263.16: £3,508.77)

| | | | Pos | SP | RR | SF |
|---|---|---|---|---|---|---|
| 375a* | **Tamayaz (CAN)** (SbinSuroor,UAE) **4-8-11** LDettori | — | 1 | | 119 | — |
| 375a[4] | **Cezanne** (SbinSuroor,UAE) **7-8-12** JCarroll | 5 | 2 | | 112 | — |
| | **Esbooain (FR)** (DJSelvaratnam,UAE) **7-8-12** BDoyle | 10 | 3 | | 96 | — |
| 375a[2] | **Wathik (USA)** (PLRudkin,UAE) **6-8-12** PaulEddery | 4 | 4 | | 90 | — |
| | | | | | | **5 Rn** |

**2m 8.41** OWNER Maktoum Al Maktoum BRED Windfields Farm
**375a* Tamayaz (CAN)** is lightly raced, but asserted his authority to make it two wins from two starts so far this season. Breaking well, he soon led, and quickening to go clear two furlongs out, he had the race in hand and was eased down inside the final furlong. He is sure to put in a decent effort if he goes for the Dubai World Cup.
**Cezanne** once again finished behind this impressive winner. He had every chance two and a half furlongs out but could not match the winner in the last quarter mile.

# SAN SIRO (Milan, Italy) (R-H) (Good)
## Wednesday March 13th

## 437a PREMIO MONTELEONE AMATEUR (4-Y.O+)
2-50 (2-50) **1m 1f** £3,691.00 (£1,624.00: £886.00)

| | | Pos | SP | RR | SF |
|---|---|---|---|---|---|
| **Salvatore Grillo (IRE)** (FTrappolini,Italy) **7-11-5** MrACavalli | — | 1 | | — | — |
| **Okeedokee (FR)** (JWHills) **6-11-5** MrFGrasso-Caprioli | ¾ | 2 | | — | — |
| **Mr Dominie (ITY)** (MMarcialis,Italy) **7-11-1** MrGViti | 3¼ | 3 | | — | — |
| | | | | | **9 Rn** |

**1m 52.8** (10.60) TOTE 85L: 20L 18L 28L (202L) OWNER R. Rossi BRED Barronstown
**Okeedokee (FR)** is a former Criquette Head charge having his first run for John Hills, and returning from a near eighteen-month lay-off. Never far off the pace, he moved into second at the distance, but could never peg back the winner. Twice second in French Listed races, he should soon return to winning ways.

# SAINT-CLOUD (France) (L-H) (Good to soft)
## Saturday March 16th

## 438a PRIX EXBURY (Gp 3) (4-Y.O+)
3-15 (3-21) **1m 2f** £28,986.00 (£10,540.00: £5,270.00: £2,635.00)

| | | Pos | SP | RR | SF |
|---|---|---|---|---|---|
| **Gunboat Diplomacy (FR)** (ELellouche,France) **5-9-2** OPeslier | — | 1 | | 119 | — |
| **Red Roses Story** (MmePBarbe,France) **4-8-6** TThulliez | 1½ | 2 | | 107 | — |
| **Tot Ou Tard (IRE)** (JForesi,France) **6-9-4** FPardon | hd | 3 | | 118 | — |
| **Diamond Mix (IRE)** (AFabre,France) **4-9-4** TJarnet | s.h | 4 | | 118 | — |
| **Pater Noster (USA)** (MrsJCecil) **7-8-9** PaulEddery (btn over 14l) | | 9 | | — | — |
| | | | | | **9 Rn** |

**2m 8.6** (5.10) P-M 2.80F: 1.40F 1.40F 2.80F (5.50F) OWNER Mr D. Wildenstein BRED London T'bred Serv. & George Strawbridge in France
**Gunboat Diplomacy (FR)**, this lightly raced individual, was held up throughout. He began to get serious two furlongs out and, taking control with a furlong left to travel, came home to comfortably see off his rivals. He will run next in the Prix d' Harcourt.
**Red Roses Story** put up a good show here. In the rear for most of the way, she picked up ground two furlongs from home and, although running on well, found the winner had her measure inside the final furlong.
**Tot Ou Tard (IRE)** was in last place and had everything to do in the straight, but picking up ground two furlongs from home, stayed on well to suggest a return to a longer distance may be in his favour.
**Diamond Mix (IRE)**, who was four and a half lengths sixth to Celtic Swing in last year's French Derby, was found to be slightly one paced when challenging over a furlong out.
**Pater Noster (USA)**, the early leader, was headed when the race began in earnest two furlongs out, and could not go with the pace from that point. He would have been preferred softer ground.

# DONCASTER (L-H) (Good becoming Good to soft)
## Thursday March 21st
WEATHER: misty & raining WIND: mod half bhd

## 439 RACING CHANNEL APPRENTICE H'CAP (0-80) (4-Y.O+) (Class E)
1-35 (1-37) **1m 4f** £3,027.00 (£921.00: £453.00: £219.00) Stalls: Low GOING: 0.13 sec per fur (G)

| | | | Pos | SP | RR | SF |
|---|---|---|---|---|---|---|
| 221[2] | **Haya Ya Kefaah (48)** (NMBabbage) **4-7-3**(7) RFfrench(7) (chsd ldrs: led over 2f out: edgd lft: styd on) | — | 1 | 33/1 | 61+ | 41 |
| 108[13] | **Outstayed Welcome (49)** (MJHaynes) **4-7-11** DWright(12) (b.off hind: led tl over 2f out: styd on fnl 2f) | 1¼ | 2 | 20/1 | 60 | 40 |
| | **Golden Arrow (IRE) (75)** (IABalding) **5-9-6**(5) CScudder(3) (bhd: hdwy over 2f out: styd on wl fnl f) | 6 | 3 | 25/1 | 78 | 60 |
| 306[5] | **Almuhtaram (64)** (MissGayKelleway) **4-8-12b** AWhelan(2) (a chsng ldrs: one pce fnl 3f) | ½ | 4 | 8/1[2] | 67 | 47 |
| | **Artic Courier (78)** (DJSCosgrove) **5-10-0b** DRMcCabe(5) (in tch: kpt on one pce fnl 3f) | 1½ | 5 | 16/1 | 79 | 61 |
| 411[2] | **Cuango (IRE) (55)** (RHollinshead) **5-8-0**(5) FLynch(6) (hld up: hdwy over 4f out: rdn over 2f out: sn wknd) | 2 | 6 | 6/1[1] | 53 | 35 |
| | **Rock Group (55)** (JPearce) **4-8-3** SDrowne(4) (styd on fnl 2f: nvr nr ldrs) | hd | 7 | 20/1 | 53 | 33 |
| | **Vaugrenier (IRE) (78)** (RHannon) **4-9-9**(3) DaneO'Neill(20) (lw: hdwy & rdn 5f out: hung lft over 2f out: sn wknd) | 1¾ | 8 | 12/1 | 74 | 54 |
| | **Edan Heights (72)** (SDow) **4-9-1**(5) ADaly(9) (chsd ldrs tl lost pl over 2f out) | 2½ | 9 | 12/1 | 64 | 44 |

| Form | Horse | Dist | Pos | SP | RR | SF |
|---|---|---|---|---|---|---|
| 392[9] | **Mentalasanythin (64)** (ABailey) **7-8-9**(5) AngelaGallimore(10) (in tch: effrt & n.m.r over 3f out: no imp) | 1 | **10** | 9/1[3] | 55 | 37 |
| 420[3] | **Tartan Gem (IRE) (73)** (MissGayKelleway) **5-9-4**(5) JDennis(14) (lw: n.d) | 1 | **11** | 20/1 | 63 | 45 |
| 267* | **Premier Dance (54)** (DHaydnJones) **9-7-13**(5)ow6 AnthonyBond(17) (swtg: hld up & bhd: n.d) | 5 | **12** | 11/1 | 37 | 13 |
| | **Sarawat (60)** (DNicholls) **8-8-5**(5) OliverCasey(1) (s.s: bhd: sme hdwy over 3f out: sn wknd) | hd | **13** | 12/1 | 43 | 25 |
| | **Oakbury (IRE) (65)** (MissLCSiddall) **4-8-6**(7)ow3 TSiddall(8) (in tch: effrt over 3f out: sn wknd) | 12 | **14** | 20/1 | 32 | 9 |
| 392[6] | **Chatham Island (70)** (CEBrittain) **8-9-3**(3) MHenry(13) (chsd ldrs: wkng whn hmpd over 2f out) | ½ | **15** | 9/1[3] | 36 | 18 |
| | **Sian Wyn (52)** (KRBurke) **6-7-9**(7)ow6 LauraParkinson(15) (a in rr) | 1 | **16** | 100/1 | 17 | — |
| 303[9] | **Master Ofthe House (59)** (MDHammond) **10-8-2**(7) DHayden(11) (hld up: hdwy 7f out: wknd 3f out) | ½ | **17** | 25/1 | 23 | 5 |
| 38[10] | **Much Sought After (76)** (KRBurke) **7-9-7**(5) TAshley(19) (nvr nr ldrs) | ½ | **18** | 50/1 | 39 | 21 |
| | **Advance East (70)** (MrsJRRamsden) **4-8-11**(7) ClaireWest(16) (bit bkwd: n.d) | 2 | **19** | 14/1 | 31 | 11 |
| | **Curtelace (56)** (MrsMReveley) **6-8-1**(5) GParkin(18) (hld up: gd hdwy 7f out: sn chsng ldrs: wknd & eased fnl 3f) | 10 | **20** | 9/1[3] | 3 | — |
| | **Eight Sharp (IRE) (75)** (MDHammond) **4-9-6**(3) LNewton(21) (a bhd) | 1½ | **21** | 20/1 | 20 | — |

(SP 136.8%) **21 Rn**

**2m 37.57** (7.57) CSF £548.83 CT £14,087.14 TOTE £72.70: £12.60 £4.10 £8.50 £2.10 (£734.30) Trio Not won; £1,045.38 to Doncaster 22/3/96 OWNER Mr Alan Craddock (CHELTENHAM) BRED Sheikh Ahmed bin Rashid al Maktoum

LONG HANDICAP Haya Ya Kefaah 6-9 Sian Wyn 6-6

WEIGHT FOR AGE 4yo-2lb

**Haya Ya Kefaah**, fit after one outing on the All-Weather, raced up with the pace throughout. It was significant that the first and second were always in the first three. (33/1)

**Outstayed Welcome** set out to make this a stamina test and, to his credit, kept on all the way to the line. (20/1)

**Golden Arrow (IRE)**, an in and out performer over hurdles, took it into his head to stay on strongly late in the day. (25/1)

**Almuhtaram** had much more use made of him than usual. Hard at work once in line for home, he could do no more than stick on at the same pace. (8/1)

**Artic Courier**, under topweight, travelled strongly just off the pace but, in the final three furlongs, he could do no more than stick on at the one speed. (16/1)

**Cuango (IRE)**, a stone better in than he is on the All-Weather tracks, was given plenty to do. Picking up ground early in the straight, his run had come to a halt with two furlongs left to run. (6/1)

## 440 FAUCETS FOR MIRA/RADA DOMESTIC & COMMERCIAL SHOWER EQUIPMENT LADIES' H'CAP (0-80) (4-Y.O+) (Class E) 2-05 (2-11) 1m 2f 60y £3,964.00 (£1,192.00: £576.00: £268.00) Stalls: Low GOING: 0.13 sec per fur (G)

| Form | Horse | Dist | Pos | SP | RR | SF |
|---|---|---|---|---|---|---|
| 256[5] | **Manful (54)** (CWCElsey) **4-9-9b** MissAElsey(7) (trckd ldrs gng wl: led over 1f out: pushed out) | — | **1** | 20/1 | 69 | 50 |
| | **Hazard a Guess (IRE) (73)** (DNicholls) **6-11-0** MissEJohnsonHoughton(16) (a.p: led over 3f out tl over 1f out: nt qckn) | 3½ | **2** | 8/1[2] | 82 | 64 |
| | **Princess Danielle (57)** (CCElsey) **4-9-12** MrsSBosley(10) (a in tch: kpt on fnl 2f) | 4 | **3** | 20/1 | 60 | 41 |
| | **Gallardini (IRE) (52)** (BSRothwell) **7-9-7** MissJAllison(5) (bhd tl styd on wl fnl 3f) | 7 | **4** | 33/1 | 43 | 25 |
| | **Witney-de-Bergerac (IRE) (62)** (JSMoore) **4-9-12**(5) MrsSMoore(8) (a in tch: kpt on fnl 3f) | 1½ | **5** | 25/1 | 52 | 33 |
| 100[5] | **Seventeens Lucky (70)** (BobJones) **4-10-6**(5) MissDJJones(26) (a in tch: kpt on one pce fnl 3f) | nk | **6** | 11/1 | 60 | 41 |
| | **Bali Tender (51)** (MWEasterby) **5-9-1**(5)ow6 MrsSHardy(3) (prom early: styd on fnl 2f: n.d) | s.h | **7** | 66/1 | 40 | 16 |
| 83[5] | **Stalled (IRE) (58)** (PTWalwyn) **6-9-8**(5)ow4 MarchionessBlandford(23) (bhd: hdwy over 3f out: nvr nr ldrs) | 1¼ | **8** | 11/1 | 45 | 23 |
| 400[6] | **Captain Marmalade (45)** (DTThom) **7-8-9v**(5) MissEJoyce(25) (wl bhd tl styd on fnl 3f) | 1¾ | **9** | 25/1 | 29 | 11 |
| | **Carlito Brigante (66)** (MrsJRRamsden) **4-10-2**(5) MissERamsden(15) (bit bkwd: hld up & bhd: sme hdwy over 3f out: n.d) | 1½ | **10** | 13/2[1] | 49 | 30 |
| | **Coureur (65)** (MDHammond) **7-10-6** MissPRobson(24) (in tch: styd on one pce fnl 3f: no imp) | ½ | **11** | 16/1 | 46 | 28 |
| | **Western General (76)** (MissMKMilligan) **5-11-3** MissYHaynes(17) (a rr div) | ½ | **12** | 16/1 | 56 | 38 |
| 392[3] | **Calder King (58)** (JLEyre) **5-9-13v** MissDianaJones(19) (nvr nr ldrs) | 5 | **13** | 13/2[1] | 30 | 12 |
| 411[4] | **Silktail (IRE) (69)** (MissGayKelleway) **4-10-5**(5) MissSKelleway(9) (prom: rdn 5f out: wknd over 3f out) | nk | **14** | 10/1[3] | 42 | 23 |
| | **Roseate Lodge (60)** (SEKettlewell) **10-9-10**(5)ow6 MissElizabethDoyle(1) (mid div: sme hdwy over 4f out: sn wknd) | ½ | **15** | 33/1 | 31 | 7 |
| | **Fairy Knight (80)** (RHannon) **4-11-2**(5) MrsKTierney(21) (lw: a in rr) | hd | **16** | 14/1 | 52 | 33 |
| | **Silver Samurai (55)** (MrsVAAconley) **7-9-5**(5) MrsCWilliams(18) (s.s: a bhd) | ½ | **17** | 50/1 | 25 | 7 |
| 384[11] | **Ballyrag (USA) (50)** (RAFahey) **5-9-0**(5) MissAlexMcCabe(13) (a rr div) | s.h | **18** | 50/1 | 20 | 2 |
| 384[9] | **East Barns (IRE) (55)** (SGollings) **8-9-5b**(5)ow9 MrsJMGollings(2) (led tl over 3f out: sn wknd) | 1½ | **19** | 50/1 | 23 | — |
| 412[3] | **Dream Carrier (IRE) (50)** (REPeacock) **8-9-0**(5) MrsCPeacock(20) (a bhd) | ½ | **20** | 25/1 | 17 | — |
| 145[11] | **Lady Sabina (45)** (WJMusson) **6-8-9**(5) MissKWright(11) (a bhd) | ½ | **21** | 16/1 | 11 | — |
| 406[2] | **Don't Drop Bombs (USA) (45)** (DTThom) **7-9-0v** MissJFeilden(12) (lw: chsd ldr tl wknd over 3f out) | 3 | **22** | 20/1 | 6 | — |
| 392[10] | **Claque (60)** (DWChapman) **4-10-1b** MissRClark(28) (a bhd) | 3 | **23** | 20/1 | 18 | — |
| 299[6] | **Rival Queen (IRE) (60)** (MDHammond) **4-9-10**(5) MissMCarson(27) (a in rr) | 1½ | **24** | 33/1 | 15 | — |
| | **Grooms Gold (IRE) (60)** (PJHobbs) **4-10-1** MrsSHobbs(6) (a bhd) | hd | **25** | 14/1 | 15 | — |
| | **King Curan (USA) (61)** (ABailey) **5-9-11b**(5) MissBridgetGatehouse(22) (chsd ldrs: ev ch over 3f out: wknd qckly over 3f out) | 7 | **26** | 16/1 | 4 | — |
| 80[8] | **Talented Ting (IRE) (66)** (PCHaslam) **7-10-7** MrsDKettlewell(14) (prom early: bhd fnl 7f) | ½ | **27** | 20/1 | 9 | — |
| 429[5] | **Sea God (54)** (MCChapman) **5-9-4**(5)ow6 MrsDMcHale(4) (Withdrawn not under Starter's orders: uns rdr at s: jockey inj) | | **W** | 20/1 | — | — |

(SP 156.7%) **27 Rn**

**2m 15.54** (8.54) CSF £180.77 CT £3,063.86 TOTE £29.60: £5.50 £2.80 £7.20 £12.80 (£206.80) Trio £1,660.20 OWNER Mr C. D. Barber-Lomax (MALTON) BRED John Rose

LONG HANDICAP Bali Tender 8-0 Don't Drop Bombs (USA) 8-6 Captain Marmalade 8-11 Lady Sabina 8-12

OFFICIAL EXPLANATION **Claque: the colt's trainer later reported that the horse was found to have a back problem, which was subsequently treated.**

**Manful** is an ideal ride for an inexperienced pilot because he likes to make his own mind up. Often he takes a lot of pushing and shoving, but on this occasion, he tracked the leaders and, simply running away under a most competent ride, had only to be pushed out. (20/1)

**Hazard a Guess (IRE)**, having his first outing for his new trainer, took it up just under half a mile from home, but had no answer when the winner swept past. (8/1)

**Princess Danielle**, never far away, could only keep on at the same pace from halfway up the straight. (20/1)

**Gallardini (IRE)**, fit from hurdling, came from a long way off the pace to make up ground in the final three furlongs. (33/1)

**Witney-de-Bergerac (IRE)**, winner of a similar event at Newbury last autumn, ran creditably. (25/1)

**Seventeens Lucky** (11/1: 10/1-16/1)
**Carlito Brigante** looked and ran as if needing the outing. (13/2)
**Calder King**, 12lb better in on turf than on the All-Weather, was never a factor. (13/2)

## 441 CONSTANT SECURITY BROCKLESBY CONDITIONS STKS (2-Y.O) (Class C)

2-35 (2-37) **5f** £4,710.00 (£1,740.00: £832.50: £337.50: £131.25: £48.75) Stalls: High GOING: 0.13 sec per fur (G)

| | Horse | Dist | Pos | SP | RR | SF |
|---|---|---|---|---|---|---|
| | **Indian Spark** (WGMTurner) **2-8-11** TSprake(7) (w'like: mde all: edgd lft 1f out: r.o wl: readily) | — | 1 | 100/30[2] | 85+ | 44 |
| | **Joint Venture (IRE)** (BJMeehan) **2-8-11** MTebbutt(3) (cmpt: trckd ldrs: chal 1f out: unable qckn) | 4 | 2 | 5/1 | 72 | 31 |
| | **Muchea** (MRChannon) **2-8-11** RHughes(1) (leggy: unf: dwlt: sn trckng ldrs: effrt on ins & ev ch 1f out: sn wknd) | 3½ | 3 | 100/30[2] | 61 | 20 |
| | **Fredrik The Fierce (IRE)** (JBerry) **2-8-11** JCarroll(4) (leggy: scope: sn w ldrs: rdn 2f out: sn wknd) | 5 | 4 | 5/2[1] | 45 | 4 |
| | **Mr Fortywinks (IRE)** (JLEyre) **2-8-11** RLappin(5) (lt-f: unf: b.hind: sn rdn & outpcd) | s.h | 5 | 14/1 | 45 | 4 |
| | **Mujova (IRE)** (RHollinshead) **2-8-11** KDarley(2) (w'like: bit bkwd: s.i.s: a outpcd) | ½ | 6 | 9/1 | 43 | 2 |
| | **M T Vessel** (JRJenkins) **2-8-11** LDettori(6) (leggy: scope: w ldrs to ½-wy: sn wl outpcd & bhd) | 10 | 7 | 9/2[3] | 11 | — |
| | | | | (SP 126.2%) | | **7 Rn** |

**62.03 secs** (3.63) CSF £20.98 TOTE £3.70: £2.20 £2.00 (£21.40) OWNER Mr Frank Brady (SHERBORNE) BRED H. Young
**Indian Spark** certainly knew his job. He won going away and looks an above-average early-season juvenile. (100/30: 2/1-7/2)
**Joint Venture (IRE)** looked to be travelling better than the winner for a long way but had to admit defeat inside the last furlong. He will soon go one better. (5/1)
**Muchea**, restless in the stalls, lost ground at the start. Switched to the stands' side, he stopped quickly in this ground over a furlong out. (100/30)
**Fredrik The Fierce (IRE)** was hard at work two furlongs from home and soon faded. (5/2: 6/4-11/4)
**Mr Fortywinks (IRE)**, completely taken off his legs, will be suited by a stiff five. (14/1)
**Mujova (IRE)** did not look ready and, after missing the break, never threatened to take a hand. (9/1)

## 442 STONES BITTER DONCASTER MILE STKS (Listed) (4-Y.O+) (Class A)

3-05 (3-05) **1m (round)** £12,206.00 (£3,638.00: £1,734.00: £782.00) Stalls: High GOING: 0.13 sec per fur (G)

| | Horse | Dist | Pos | SP | RR | SF |
|---|---|---|---|---|---|---|
| | **First Island (IRE) (107)** (GWragg) **4-8-12** MHills(7) (hld up: gd hdwy on outside over 2f out: edgd lft & led over 1f out: r.o wl) | — | 1 | 9/2[2] | 116 | 55 |
| | **Wijara (IRE) (103)** (RHannon) **4-8-12** JReid(4) (lw: led tl over 1f out: kpt on u.p) | 1½ | 2 | 6/1 | 113 | 52 |
| | **Nwaamis (USA)** (JLDunlop) **4-8-12** WCarson(1) (lw: sn trckng ldrs: n.m.r on ins over 2f out: sn outpcd: kpt on fnl f) | 2½ | 3 | 11/10[1] | 108 | 47 |
| | **Penny Drops (106)** (LordHuntingdon) **7-8-12** DHarrison(2) (chsd ldr: ev ch 2f out: styd on one pce) | ¾ | 4 | 5/1[3] | 107 | 46 |
| | **Cadeaux Tryst (103)** (EALDunlop) **4-8-12** PatEddery(6) (b: trckd ldrs: rdn & ev ch 2f out: wkng whn sltly hmpd over 1f out) | 5 | 5 | 8/1 | 97 | 36 |
| | **Band on the Run (95)** (BAMcMahon) **9-8-12** LDettori(5) (chsd ldrs: drvn along 3f out: no imp) | 2½ | 6 | 20/1 | 92 | 31 |
| *350[3]* | **Star Talent (USA)** (MissGayKelleway) **5-8-12** RCochrane(3) (lw: hld up: effrt 2f out: rdn & wknd 1f out) | 3 | 7 | 50/1 | 86 | 25 |
| | | | | (SP 114.6%) | | **7 Rn** |

**1m 41.54** (5.04) CSF £28.61 TOTE £4.40: £2.40 £2.90 (£9.90) OWNER Mollers Racing (NEWMARKET) BRED Citadel Stud
**First Island (IRE)**, ridden for speed, showed a good turn of foot, despite edging left. Still on the upgrade, he will have one more outing before the Queen Anne at Royal Ascot. (9/2)
**Wijara (IRE)**, turned out in splendid shape, set out to make all and, to his credit, kept on all the way to the line. (6/1)
**Nwaamis (USA)**, absent since the Irish 2000 Guineas apparently with a pelvic problem, took a keen grip. Short of room on the inside halfway up the straight, he then went flat, but kept on again inside the last. He might be worth a try over seven, letting him get on with it. (11/10: Evens-10/11)
**Penny Drops**, a much-travelled mare, ran her usual genuine race. (5/1)
**Cadeaux Tryst** was weakening when the winner went across him over a furlong out. Seven furlongs seems to be his best trip. (8/1)
**Band on the Run** was faced with a stiff task on this reappearance. (20/1)

## 443 MITSUBISHI DIAMOND VISION H'CAP (0-90) (3-Y.O) (Class C)

3-40 (3-42) **5f** £6,108.00 (£1,824.00: £872.00: £396.00) Stalls: High GOING: 0.13 sec per fur (G)

| | Horse | Dist | Pos | SP | RR | SF |
|---|---|---|---|---|---|---|
| | **Little Noggins (IRE) (72)** (CADwyer) **3-8-5**(3) JStack(3) (chsd ldrs: r.o u.p to ld ins fnl f) | — | 1 | 16/1 | 83 | 46 |
| | **Lady Caroline Lamb (IRE) (60)** (MRChannon) **3-7-10** AGorman(8) (chsd ldrs: led ½-wy tl ins fnl f) | ½ | 2 | 20/1 | 69 | 32 |
| | **Passion For Life (85)** (GLewis) **3-9-7** PatEddery(17) (lw: w ldrs stands' side: edgd lft 2f out: r.o wl ins fnl f) | nk | 3 | 4/1[1] | 93 | 56 |
| | **Secret Voucher (67)** (BAMcMahon) **3-7-12**(5)ow1 LNewton(5) (hmpd & swtchd lft after 1f: hdwy & nt clr run over 1f out: swtchd rt: styd on wl towards fin) | 1 | 4 | 16/1 | 72 | 34 |
| | **Amy Leigh (IRE) (66)** (CaptJHWilson) **3-8-2** GCarter(4) (chsd ldrs: edgd lft over 1f out: no ex) | 1¾ | 5 | 12/1 | 66 | 29 |
| *293** | **Krystal Max (IRE) (80)** (TDBarron) **3-8-9**(7) KimberleyHart(14) (sn outpcd & bhd: styd on fnl f: nt rch ldrs) | 1½ | 6 | 9/1[3] | 75 | 38 |
| | **Polly Golightly (82)** (MBlanshard) **3-9-4b** KDarley(10) (led to ½-wy: wknd over 1f out) | nk | 7 | 16/1 | 76 | 39 |
| *335** | **Princely Sound (70)** (MBell) **3-8-6** MFenton(16) (chsd ldrs tl wknd 2f out) | 1½ | 8 | 5/1[2] | 59 | 22 |
| | **Ed's Folly (IRE) (67)** (SDow) **3-7-12**(5) ADaly(6) (sme hdwy 2f out: nvr nr ldrs) | nk | 9 | 25/1 | 55 | 18 |
| | **Welsh Mountain (76)** (MJHeaton-Ellis) **3-8-9**(3) SDrowne(13) (a in rr) | 2 | 10 | 20/1 | 58 | 21 |
| | **U-No-Harry (IRE) (70)** (RHollinshead) **3-8-1**(5) FLynch(9) (lw: in tch: outpcd fr ½-wy) | nk | 11 | 33/1 | 51 | 14 |
| | **Opening Chorus (60)** (MrsMReveley) **3-7-10** LCharnock(7) (sn rdn: nvr wnt pce) | 1 | 12 | 10/1 | 38 | 1 |
| | **Ramsey Hope (78)** (CWFairhurst) **3-9-0** NKennedy(15) (a bhd) | ¾ | 13 | 33/1 | 53 | 16 |
| | **Marjorie Rose (IRE) (75)** (ABailey) **3-8-8**(3) DWright(12) (s.i.s: a bhd) | ¾ | 14 | 25/1 | 48 | 11 |
| | **Miss Bigwig (78)** (JBerry) **3-8-9**(5) PRoberts(18) (in tch tl lost pl ½-wy) | ½ | 15 | 12/1 | 49 | 12 |
| *407[9]* | **Johayro (75)** (WGMTurner) **3-8-6b**(5) CAdamson(2) (in tch: wknd 2f out) | nk | 16 | 25/1 | 45 | 8 |
| *160** | **Chemcast (67)** (DNicholls) **3-8-3** JQuinn(11) (in tch: lost pl 2f out) | 5 | 17 | 10/1 | 21 | — |
| | **Imp Express (IRE) (77)** (GMMoore) **3-8-13** JWeaver(1) (unruly & swvd lft s: wl bhd fr ½-wy) | 20 | 18 | 20/1 | — | — |
| | | | | (SP 129.6%) | | **18 Rn** |

**61.78 secs** (3.38) CSF £278.01 CT £1,443.57 TOTE £18.00: £2.70 £4.30 £1.50 £3.90 (£148.60) Trio £636.10 OWNER Mr M. E. Hall (NEWMARKET) BRED A. M. F. Persse
**Little Noggins (IRE)**, who likes to race up with the pace, stuck her head in front inside the last 100 yards. (16/1)
**Lady Caroline Lamb (IRE)**, a speedy type, was only worn down in the closing stages. (20/1)

**Passion For Life** is a grand type and has been gelded. Taken to post early, he made the running on the stands'-side rail. Edging left towards the first two up the centre, he stuck on in most determined fashion towards the finish. Had he been drawn with them, he would have beaten the first two. (4/1)
**Secret Voucher**, a progressive two-year-old, did not have the run of the race. Hampered twice and forced to switch, he finished best of all. With better luck in running, he might well have prevailed. (16/1)
**Amy Leigh (IRE)**, who has plummeted down in the weights, showed plenty of speed but, edging left over a furlong out, hampered the fourth. (12/1)
**Krystal Max (IRE)**, who came here off the back of four All-Weather wins, struggled to go the pace. Staying on when it was all over, he will be much better suited by six or even seven. (9/1)
**Opening Chorus** (10/1: 8/1-12/1)

## 444 TRANSPENNINE EXPRESS H'CAP (0-85) (3-Y.O) (Class D)

4-10 (4-15) **1m 2f 60y** £4,175.00 (£1,250.00: £600.00: £275.00) Stalls: Low GOING: 0.40 sec per fur (GS)

| | | | | SP | RR | SF |
|---|---|---|---|---|---|---|
| | **Jackson Hill (82)** (RCharlton) **3-9-4** PatEddery(12) (lw: w ldrs: led 3f out: all out) | — | **1** | 6/4$^{1}$ | 95 | 48 |
| | **Deadline Time (IRE) (74)** (MrsMReveley) **3-8-10** KDarley(7) (lw: in tch: pushed along 6f out: ev ch fnl f: r.o u.p) | hd | **2** | 12/1 | 87 | 40 |
| *385$^{4}$* | **Dancing Cavalier (67)** (RHollinshead) **3-7-12**$^{(5)ow2}$ FLynch(5) (bhd: gd hdwy over 2f out: fin wl) | 1¾ | **3** | 16/1 | 77 | 28 |
| *304** | **Docklands Limo (70)** (BJMcMath) **3-8-6** RCochrane(15) (a in tch: one pce fnl 3f) | 6 | **4** | 14/1 | 71 | 24 |
| *248$^{2}$* | **Six Clerks (IRE) (65)** (JGFitzGerald) **3-8-1** JQuinn(14) (a chsng ldrs: rdn 4f out: one pce) | 2½ | **5** | 16/1 | 62 | 15 |
| *402$^{7}$* | **Exactly (IRE) (70)** (JLEyre) **3-8-6** TWilliams(17) (chsd ldrs: rdn 5f out: outpcd fnl 3f) | 1 | **6** | 33/1 | 65 | 18 |
| *351** | **Burnt Offering (67)** (CEBrittain) **3-7-12**$^{(5)}$ MHenry(8) (lw: bhd: hdwy u.p 4f out: nvr nr ldrs) | 3 | **7** | 16/1 | 58 | 11 |
| | **Northern Motto (60)** (MrsJRRamsden) **3-7-10** NKennedy(10) (bhd: sme hdwy 2f out: nvr nr ldrs) | 4 | **8** | 20/1 | 44 | — |
| *378** | **Quality (IRE) (85)** (WAO'Gorman) **3-9-7b** EmmaO'Gorman(6) (lw: chsd ldrs: rdn 5f out: ev ch 3f out: sn wknd) | 7 | **9** | 12/1 | 59 | 12 |
| | **Strategic Ploy (64)** (MrsJRRamsden) **3-8-0** JFEgan(16) (s.i.s: a bhd) | nk | **10** | 12/1 | 37 | — |
| | **Samim (USA) (80)** (JLDunlop) **3-9-2** WCarson(1) (lw: bhd & rdn 7f out: n.d) | 1½ | **11** | 8/1$^{3}$ | 51 | 4 |
| | **Rose of Siberia (USA) (72)** (MBell) **3-8-8** MFenton(3) (prom early: bhd fnl 7f) | 2 | **12** | 16/1 | 40 | — |
| | **Welcome Royale (IRE) (67)** (MHTompkins) **3-8-3**$^{ow1}$ PRobinson(2) (mde most to 3f out: sn wknd) | 15 | **13** | 20/1 | 11 | — |
| *364$^{5}$* | **Eagle Canyon (IRE) (75)** (BHanbury) **3-8-8**$^{(3)}$ JStack(18) (hld up & bhd: effrt over 3f out: sn wknd) | 4 | **14** | 25/1 | 13 | — |
| | **Sedbergh (USA) (65)** (MrsMReveley) **3-8-1** LCharnock(13) (hld up & a bhd) | 5 | **15** | 25/1 | — | — |
| *385$^{3}$* | **China Castle (63)** (PCHaslam) **3-7-8**$^{(5)}$ MBaird(11) (s.i.s: a in rr) | 3½ | **16** | 15/2$^{2}$ | — | — |
| | **Worldwide Elsie (USA) (75)** (RHarris) **3-8-11** AMackay(19) (hdwy to chse ldrs 8f out: wknd over 3f out) | 3 | **17** | 14/1 | — | — |
| *263$^{5}$* | **Diego (85)** (CEBrittain) **3-9-7** LDettori(4) (chsd ldrs tl lost pl over 5f out: sn bhd) | 13 | **18** | 16/1 | — | — |
| | | | | (SP 148.9%) | **18 Rn** | |

**2m 17.97** (10.97) CSF £24.87 CT £249.54 TOTE £2.50: £1.30 £2.60 £3.70 £4.00 (£15.30) Trio £161.80 OWNER Mr James Wolfensohn (BECKHAMPTON) BRED S. Tindall and Stowell Hill Ltd
OFFICIAL EXPLANATION **Worldwide Elsie (USA): the trainer stated that the horse was lame after the race and appeared to have pulled a muscle.**
**Jackson Hill**, who shows plenty of knee-action, took it up travelling strongly but, in the end, he had nothing to spare. He looks a stayer. (6/4)
**Deadline Time (IRE)**, who wore a visor on his final two outings as a juvenile, was pushed along to improve going into the home turn. Moving almost upsides entering the final furlong, he was just held at bay. Sure to take a rise in the weights after this, he will no doubt be out soon and should go one better. (12/1)
**Dancing Cavalier** likes to come from off the pace but rather over-did it here. Only picking up ground two furlongs from home, he finished in tremendous style. (16/1)
**Docklands Limo** looked to have been given plenty to do at the weights and ran like it. (14/1)
**Six Clerks (IRE)** seems to lack anything in the way of finishing speed. (16/1)
**Northern Motto**, who looked in need of the outing, hinted at better things to come in time. (20/1)

## 445 MELTON WOOD MAIDEN STKS (3-Y.O) (Class D)

4-40 (4-44) **1m (straight)** £4,077.50 (£1,220.00: £585.00: £267.50) Stalls: High GOING: 0.40 sec per fur (GS)

| | | | | SP | RR | SF |
|---|---|---|---|---|---|---|
| | **Insiyabi (USA)** (JLDunlop) **3-9-0** WCarson(4) (lw: trckd ldrs: led 1f out: hung rt: r.o wl) | — | **1** | 5/1$^{3}$ | 91+ | 54 |
| | **Polinesso** (BWHills) **3-9-0** MHills(2) (w'like: leggy: bhd: rdn & hdwy 5f out: led briefly over 1f out: r.o) | 2 | **2** | 2/1$^{1}$ | 87+ | 50 |
| | **Courting Danger** (DRGandolfo) **3-9-0** MFenton(12) (unruly s: mde most tl over 1f out: sn wl outpcd) | 7 | **3** | 20/1 | 73 | 36 |
| *17$^{P}$* | **Catherine's Choice** (JDBethell) **3-9-0** JFortune(9) (in tch: rdn & outpcd over 2f out: styd on) | 1½ | **4** | 20/1 | 70 | 33 |
| | **Aerleon Jane** (JHMGosden) **3-8-9** LDettori(8) (bhd: hdwy ½-wy: sn pushed along: styd on one pce fnl 2f) | ¾ | **5** | 4/1$^{2}$ | 64 | 27 |
| | **Lucky Archer** (CEBrittain) **3-8-9**$^{(5)}$ MHenry(10) (w'like: in tch: rdn ½-wy: styd on same pce) | 2½ | **6** | 4/1$^{2}$ | 64 | 27 |
| | **Florentino (IRE)** (BWHills) **3-9-0** GCarter(7) (bhd: rdn ½-wy: styd on fnl f) | 2 | **7** | 16/1 | 60 | 23 |
| | **Village King (IRE)** (RHannon) **3-8-9**$^{(5)}$ DaneO'Neill(1) (nvr rchd ldrs) | nk | **8** | 10/1 | 59 | 22 |
| | **Polish Lady (IRE)** (WLBarker) **3-8-9** LCharnock(16) (w ldr tl wknd over 2f out) | 8 | **9** | 50/1 | 38 | 1 |
| | **Shouldbegrey** (WRMuir) **3-9-0** JReid(15) (leggy: scope: prom to ½-wy) | nk | **10** | 20/1 | 42 | 5 |
| | **Crystal Warrior** (DNicholls) **3-8-9** AlexGreaves(14) (hld up: bhd fr ½-wy) | 7 | **11** | 20/1 | 23 | — |
| *320$^{7}$* | **Georgie Boy (USA)** (CADwyer) **3-9-0** WWoods(6) (nvr wnt pce) | ¾ | **12** | 20/1 | 27 | — |
| | **Dungeon Princess (IRE)** (MRChannon) **3-8-9** CandyMorris(11) (a bhd) | 6 | **13** | 20/1 | 10 | — |
| *390$^{10}$* | **Tirols Tyrant (IRE)** (MrsASwinbank) **3-9-0** NConnorton(5) (chsd ldrs tl lost pl over 2f out) | 1¼ | **14** | 33/1 | 12 | — |
| | **Boozeroo** (MRChannon) **3-9-0** RHughes(3) (w'like: s.s: sn wl bhd) | 22 | **15** | 16/1 | — | — |
| | | | | (SP 144.3%) | **15 Rn** | |

**1m 44.5** (7.50) CSF £17.47 TOTE £5.60: £1.80 £2.00 £5.20 (£9.10) Trio £102.90 OWNER Mr Hamdan Al Maktoum (ARUNDEL) BRED Shadwell Farm Inc
OFFICIAL EXPLANATION **Crystal Warrior: the jockey reported that the filly had run green, hung left-handed and had to be held together in the closing stages as she had blown up and become tired in the ground.**
**Insiyabi (USA)**, easily the pick of the paddock, took it up on the bridle a furlong out. Inexperienced and hanging right, he was right on top at the line. He will go on from here. (5/1: 7/2-6/1)
**Polinesso** looked green beforehand and in the race. After having to be pushed along to make ground, he went on over a furlong out but, in the end, the winner proved much too good. This will bring him on considerably. (2/1: op 5/4)
**Courting Danger**, who misbehaved at the start, was allowed to make the running but, when the chips were down, the first two left him for dead. (20/1)

**Catherine's Choice**, thanks to the modest pace, was able to stay in touch. Left behind when the pace quickened, he was staying on again under strong driving towards the finish. It remains to be seen whether he is flattered by this. (20/1)
**Aerleon Jane**, pushed along to improve from the rear at halfway, kept on in her own time. She might be better suited by a sound surface. (4/1: op 2/1)
**Lucky Archer**, struggling to go the pace from halfway, will come on for the outing and will be suited by further. (4/1)
**Florentino (IRE)** was staying on when it was all over and looks a stayer in the making. (16/1)

T/Jkpt: Not won; £59,279.90 to Doncaster 22/3/96. T/Plpt: £7,481.10 (4.04 Tckts). T/Qdpt: £78.60 (39.64 Tckts). WG

# 0439-DONCASTER (L-H) (Good to soft, Soft patches)
## Friday March 22nd
WEATHER: overcast, misty WIND: almost nil

## 446 CYSTIC FIBROSIS (S) MAIDEN STKS (2-Y.O) (Class F)
1-30 (1-35) **5f** £2,560.00 (£760.00: £360.00: £160.00) Stalls: High GOING: 0.50 sec per fur (GS)

| | | | SP | RR | SF |
|---|---|---|---|---|---|
| **Hit Or Miss** (MRChannon) **2-8-9** TQuinn(5) (neat: chsd ldrs: led 2f out: rdn out) | — | 1 | 11/4 1 | 58 | 12 |
| **Hello Dolly (IRE)** (KTIvory) **2-8-2**(7) CScally(6) (cmpt: unf: hdwy ½-wy: rdn & r.o wl ins fnl f) | ¾ | 2 | 8/1 | 56 | 10 |
| **Rahona (IRE)** (BSRothwell) **2-8-9** MFenton(2) (cmpt: w ldr tl wknd ins fnl f) | 5 | 3 | 6/1 3 | 40 | — |
| **Contravene (IRE)** (JBerry) **2-8-9** JCarroll(3) (leggy: lt-f: unf: led 3f: sn drvn along: wknd over 1f out) | 2 | 4 | 4/1 2 | 33 | — |
| **Don't Forget Shoka (IRE)** (JSMoore) **2-8-9** JFEgan(7) (leggy: unf: s.s: hdwy ½-wy: wknd wl over 1f out) | ¾ | 5 | 6/1 3 | 31 | — |
| **Skyers Flyer (IRE)** (RonaldThompson) **2-8-9** TWilliams(4) (unf: s.s: rn green: a bhd) | ½ | 6 | 10/1 | 29 | — |
| **Nattie** (AGNewcombe) **2-9-0** LDettori(1) (unf: bkwd: racd alone centre: sn drvn along: eased whn btn wl over 1f out) | 6 | 7 | 4/1 2 | 15 | — |

(SP 115.4%) **7 Rn**

**65.74 secs** (7.34) CSF £22.47 TOTE £2.60: £1.70 £3.60 (£13.50) OWNER Mr Brian Lovrey (UPPER LAMBOURN) BRED B. Lovrey
Bt in 4,400 gns
OFFICIAL EXPLANATION **Lalindi: the jockey stated that his instructions were to ride the filly to get the trip but, having got behind early on, she ran lazily.**
**Hit Or Miss**, a very uneasy favourite, nosed ahead on the stands' side entering the final quarter-mile, and though she was being reeled in nearing the finish, found the line arriving just in time. (11/4: op 7/4)
**Hello Dolly (IRE)**, a half-sister to two winners over seven furlongs and a mile, was in top gear inside the distance, but was never going to quite make it. A lightly-made filly, she looked well forward in condition and should be able to get off the mark in the early weeks. (8/1)
**Rahona (IRE)**, who can be made fitter, shared the lead until feeling the strain inside the last 200 yards. (6/1: op 10/1)
**Contravene (IRE)**, a fit-looking, sparely-made filly who played up and got loose in the paddock, broke smartly and held the call for three furlongs before gradually dropping away. She should be able to win a race but will definitely need a sounder surface. (4/1)
**Don't Forget Shoka (IRE)**, still two months off her second birthday, lost ground at the start, and though she did latch on to the tail end of the leaders below the distance, she had soon had enough. (6/1)

## 447 P & J FOODS MAIDEN STKS (3-Y.O) (Class D)
2-05 (2-08) **1m 2f 60y** £3,785.00 (£1,130.00: £540.00: £245.00) Stalls: Low GOING: 0.50 sec per fur (GS)

| | | | | SP | RR | SF |
|---|---|---|---|---|---|---|
| | **Summer Spell (USA)** (RCharlton) **3-9-0** SSanders(1) (w'like: leggy: unf: a.p: shkn up to ld wl over 1f out: drew clr fnl f) | — | 1 | 13/2 2 | 98 | 44 |
| | **Arnhem** (CEBrittain) **3-9-0** BDoyle(2) (rangy: dwlt: sn chsng ldrs: led over 4f out tl wl over 1f out: one pce) | 8 | 2 | 13/2 2 | 86 | 32 |
| | **Ledgendry Line** (MrsMReveley) **3-9-0** KDarley(5) (w'like: leggy: bit bkwd: hld up: hdwy over 3f out: styd on fnl f) | 5 | 3 | 20/1 | 78 | 24 |
| | **Classic Lover (IRE) (75)** (RHarris) **3-8-9** AMackay(3) (outpcd over 3f out: styd on again appr fnl f) | s.h | 4 | 10/1 3 | 73 | 19 |
| | **Three Hills** (BWHills) **3-9-0** PatEddery(11) (h.d.w: bkwd: led tl over 3f out: sn rdn: wknd fnl 2f) | 1 | 5 | 4/5 1 | 76 | 22 |
| | **Al's Alibi (74)** (WRMuir) **3-9-0** Jean-PierreLopez(10) (plld hrd: trckd ldrs tl rdn & wknd over 3f out) | 2½ | 6 | 16/1 | 72 | 18 |
| | **Scandator (IRE)** (PWHarris) **3-9-0** GHind(4) (lengthy: unf: sn bhd & drvn along: nvr nr ldrs: t.o) | 12 | 7 | 14/1 | 54 | — |
| | **Sister Kit (IRE) (70)** (BPalling) **3-8-9** TSprake(7) (w'like: bit bkwd: plld hrd: w ldrs: rdn ent st: wknd 3fout: t.o) | 15 | 8 | 25/1 | 25 | — |
| *376*2 | **Crystal Fast (USA)** (PAKelleway) **3-9-0** LDettori(9) (prom: drvn along over 4f out: sn wknd: t.o) | 11 | 9 | 12/1 | 13 | — |
| | **Poly My Son (IRE)** (MRChannon) **3-9-0** RHughes(6) (w'like: str: bkwd: sn rdn & prom: wknd 5f out: t.o) | 1¼ | 10 | 14/1 | 11 | — |
| | **Zimmy** (TTClement) **3-9-0** JQuinn(8) (tall: unf: b: s.s: a bhd: t.o) | dist | 11 | 33/1 | — | — |

(SP 129.8%) **11 Rn**

**2m 19.01** (12.01) CSF £49.38 TOTE £7.80: £1.70 £1.80 £4.20 (£18.70) Trio £138.30 OWNER E S & W V Robins (BECKHAMPTON) BRED Jim Robinson, Pam Robinson and Walmac Internationa
**Summer Spell (USA)**, an unfurnished colt very much on the leg at present, picked up well when asked to quicken and, staying on strongly, soon put the issue beyond doubt. (13/2: op 10/1)
**Arnhem**, who holds a Derby engagement, kicked on before reaching the straight and, with the winner, came right away from his rivals, but lack of peak-fitness caught up with him and, forced to give best, he could only plug on at the one pace. (13/2)
**Ledgendry Line**, a brother to useful stayer Foundry Lane, made progress from off the pace inside the last half-mile, and will be all the wiser for the experience. (20/1)
**Classic Lover (IRE)** lost her place when the leading pair stepped up the tempo early in the straight, but she was coming back for more after getting her second wind, and her turn will come. (10/1)
**Three Hills** is a half-brother to Irish Oaks winner Bolas. Carrying a summer-bloom on his coat, he was also carrying plenty of surplus condition, and his forceful front-running tactics had come to an end three furlongs out. He was brushed aside with ease but could be a different proposition next time. (4/5)
**Al's Alibi**, needing this, was pushing the pace until beginning to struggle on the home turn after running too freely. (16/1)
**Crystal Fast (USA)** (12/1: 7/1-14/1)

## 448 GLOBAL SHOPFITTERS MAIDEN STKS (3-Y.O) (Class D)
2-35 (2-37) **7f** £4,077.50 (£1,220.00: £585.00: £267.50) Stalls: High GOING: 0.50 sec per fur (GS)

| | | | SP | RR | SF |
|---|---|---|---|---|---|
| **Sorbie Tower (IRE)** (MissGayKelleway) **3-9-0** RCochrane(11) (b: trckd ldrs: led 3f out: edgd lft fnl f: styd on strly) | — | 1 | 6/1 3 | 85 | 41 |

| Form | Horse | Dist | Pos | SP | RR | SF |
|---|---|---|---|---|---|---|
| | **Mansab (USA)** (JLDunlop) **3-9-0** WCarson(5) (b.hind: a chsng ldrs: effrt & drvn ent fnl f: nt pce of wnr) | 3½ | **2** | 3/1 [1] | 77 | 33 |
| | **Depiction** (RGuest) **3-9-0** WWoods(14) (cmpt: bit bkwd: hld up: hdwy 3f out: styd on ins fnl f) | 2 | **3** | 16/1 | 72 | 28 |
| | **Welliran** (AGFoster) **3-9-0** TSprake(12) (b: lengthy: unf: w ldrs: one pce fnl 2f) | 2 | **4** | 10/1 | 68 | 24 |
| | **Ambassador (USA)** (BWHills) **3-9-0** MHills(3) (gd sort: bit bkwd: chsd ldrs: rdn & wandered 2f out: one pce) | 4 | **5** | 5/1 [2] | 59 | 15 |
| | **Alpine Panther (IRE)** (WJarvis) **3-9-0** KDarley(16) (w'like: leggy: hld up & bhd: sme hdwy 2f out: nt rch ldrs) | 4 | **6** | 12/1 | 50 | 6 |
| | **Only (USA)** (RHannon) **3-8-9**(5) DaneO'Neill(4) (hdwy over 2f out: edgd lft appr fnl f: n.d) | 2 | **7** | 14/1 | 45 | 1 |
| | **Sandicliffe (USA)** (BWHills) **3-8-4**(5) JDSmith(15) (chsd ldrs over 4f) | ¾ | **8** | 20/1 | 38 | — |
| | **Sunley Secure** (MRChannon) **3-9-1**ow1 RHughes(10) (led to 3f out: sn rdn & wknd) | 1¾ | **9** | 10/1 | 40 | — |
| | **Mock Trial (IRE)** (MrsJRRamsden) **3-9-0** KFallon(1) (w'like: str: scope: bkwd: a in rr) | nk | **10** | 14/1 | 39 | — |
| | **Sistar Act** (MRChannon) **3-8-9** CandyMorris(6) (s.i.s: a bhd) | 2½ | **11** | 20/1 | 28 | — |
| 414[4] | **Ocean Stream (IRE) (73)** (JLEyre) **3-9-0** DeanMcKeown(8) (stumbled s: bhd fnl 3f) | nk | **12** | 13/2 | 32 | — |
| | **Miletrian City (62)** (JBerry) **3-9-0** JCarroll(13) (chsd ldrs tl rdn & lost pl 3f out: t.o) | 10 | **13** | 25/1 | 9 | — |
| | **Angus McCoatup (IRE) (66)** (BAMcMahon) **3-9-0** TQuinn(7) (chsd ldrs over 4f: sn wknd: t.o) | 3 | **14** | 16/1 | 3 | — |

(SP 133.6%) **14 Rn**

**1m 31.95** (8.35) CSF £25.56 TOTE £9.30: £2.20 £1.60 £7.80 (£11.00) Trio £442.80 OWNER P. D. Q (WHITCOMBE) BRED B. Kennedy

**Sorbie Tower (IRE)**, never too far away, gained a slight lead three furlongs out and, though he veered over towards the far rail when shaken up, proved far too good for the favourite. (6/1)

**Mansab (USA)** delivered a determined challenge approaching the final furlong, but the winner kept pulling out more, and he lacked the speed to go through with his effort. (3/1)

**Depiction**, quite an attractive newcomer who will strip fitter for the run, was doing all his best work in the latter stages, and he should not be too difficult to place. (16/1)

**Welliran** went with the pace and only began to fade below the distance. He did finish clear of the rest, and does look capable of winning races. (10/1: 8/1-12/1)

**Ambassador (USA)**, a fine-looking colt, ran about a bit when shaken up entering the last quarter-mile, and had to admit his measure had been taken. He did look to be travelling strongly for most of the way, and this experience will not be lost. (5/1: op 5/2)

**Alpine Panther (IRE)**, a half-brother to two winning sprinters, made steady progress from off the pace inside the last couple of furlongs, and can soon leave this form behind. (12/1)

## 449 CYSTIC FIBROSIS RESEARCH CUP H'CAP (0-90) (4-Y.O+) (Class C)

3-05 (3-07) **2m 2f** £5,120.00 (£1,520.00: £720.00: £320.00) Stalls: Low GOING: 0.50 sec per fur (GS)

| Form | Horse | Dist | Pos | SP | RR | SF |
|---|---|---|---|---|---|---|
| | **Shadirwan (IRE) (70)** (RAkehurst) **5-9-4** TQuinn(4) (lw: a.p: led on bit 1f out: sn clr) | — | **1** | 10/1 | 89 | 43 |
| 19[4] | **Noyan (49)** (DNicholls) **6-7-11** LCharnock(6) (led: rdn over 2f out: hdd ent fnl f: no ch w wnr) | 5 | **2** | 10/1 | 64 | 18 |
| | **Blaze Away (USA) (79)** (IABalding) **5-9-13** LDettori(7) (lw: hld up: gd hdwy 6f out: styd on fnl 3f) | 5 | **3** | 12/1 | 89 | 43 |
| 283* | **Upper Mount Clair (57)** (CEBrittain) **6-8-5** BDoyle(9) (hld up in tch: effrt over 3f out: one pce fnl 2f) | 3½ | **4** | 6/1 [1] | 64 | 18 |
| | **Sea Freedom (64)** (GBBalding) **5-8-9**(3) SDrowne(18) (hld up: hdwy ½-wy: one pce fnl 3f) | 10 | **5** | 16/1 | 62 | 16 |
| 400[2] | **Hard Love (62)** (JLEyre) **4-8-4** RLappin(8) (chsd ldrs: outpcd fnl 3f) | 6 | **6** | 33/1 | 55 | 3 |
| | **Lalindi (IRE) (68)** (DRCElsworth) **5-9-2** PatEddery(21) (bhd: hdwy 5f out: nt rch ldrs) | 4 | **7** | 11/1 | 57 | 11 |
| 358[8] | **Evezio Rufo (85)** (NPLittmoden) **4-9-13** TGMcLaughlin(10) (in rr tl sme hdwy fnl 3f: nvr nrr) | ½ | **8** | 66/1 | 74 | 22 |
| | **En Vacances (IRE) (73)** (AGFoster) **4-9-1** TSprake(5) (in tch: pushed along ½-wy: wknd over 4f out) | ½ | **9** | 17/2 [2] | 61 | 9 |
| | **Tip the Dove (48)** (RJPrice) **7-7-10** NCarlisle(20) (trckd ldrs tl wknd over 4f out) | 2½ | **10** | 50/1 | 34 | — |
| 339[2] | **Coleridge (48)** (JJSheehan) **8-7-10b** JQuinn(12) (s.s: n.d) | ½ | **11** | 14/1 | 34 | — |
| 312[6] | **Shakiyr (FR) (56)** (RHollinshead) **5-7-13**(5) FLynch(2) (bhd: hdwy 7f out: wknd over 3f out) | 1 | **12** | 14/1 | 41 | — |
| | **Mondragon (70)** (MrsMReveley) **6-9-4** KDarley(11) (hld up & bhd: hdwy 5f out: wknd over 3f out) | 2½ | **13** | 20/1 | 53 | 7 |
| | **Salaman (FR) (82)** (JLDunlop) **4-9-10** WCarson(1) (a bhd) | 5 | **14** | 10/1 | 60 | 8 |
| 208[4] | **Gentleman Sid (50)** (PGMurphy) **6-7-12** NAdams(3) (b.nr fore: in tch 13f: sn wknd) | 5 | **15** | 25/1 | 24 | — |
| 265[5] | **Elburg (IRE) (64)** (RPCHoad) **6-8-12** KFallon(13) (a bhd) | 1¼ | **16** | 25/1 | 37 | — |
| | **Satin Lover (74)** (MrsMReveley) **8-9-8** ACulhane(14) (bhd: sme hdwy 6f out: sn wknd: t.o) | 2 | **17** | 33/1 | 45 | — |
| | **Torch Vert (IRE) (77)** (NJHWalker) **4-9-2**(3) JStack(19) (prom: pushed along ½-wy: lost pl 6f out: t.o) | dist | **18** | 14/1 | — | — |
| | **Meant to Be (79)** (LadyHerries) **6-9-13** JReid(17) (prom tl lost pl 7f out: t.o) | 7 | **19** | 9/1 [3] | — | — |
| 268* | **Old Provence (75)** (RHarris) **6-9-9** AMackay(15) (b: b.hind: lw: t.o fnl 6f) | dist | **20** | 16/1 | — | — |

(SP 131.7%) **20 Rn**

**4m 14.8** (22.80) CSF £102.20 CT £1,140.96 TOTE £16.50: £3.90 £2.90 £2.80 £2.00 (£68.50) Trio £891.10 OWNER Mr Clive Batt (EPSOM) BRED His Highness The Aga Khans Studs S.C.

LONG HANDICAP Coleridge 7-9 Tip the Dove 7-6

WEIGHT FOR AGE 4yo-6lb

OFFICIAL EXPLANATION **Salaman (FR): the trainer later reported that the gelding was not suited by the going.**

**Shadirwan (IRE)**, well behind when falling on his debut over hurdles in January, has turned in his best performances on the Flat on a sound surface, but he was always running away here. Still full of running when leading into the final furlong, he seemed to find this extended trip tailor-made for him. (10/1)

**Noyan**, unplaced over hurdles at Cheltenham last week, tried to put his fitness to good use by setting a telling gallop but, like the winner, he has shown his best form on a faster surface and, though he never stopped trying, he was a sitting duck from some way out. This was a good effort and he will make amends. (10/1: 8/1-12/1)

**Blaze Away (USA)** took closer order before reaching the home straight and kept staying on, but the leading pair were not stopping and he could never get on terms. (12/1)

**Upper Mount Clair**, winner of this event twelve months ago, tried to mount a challenge early in the straight, but on ground more testing than she really cared for, could not summon up the required speed. (6/1)

**Sea Freedom**, poised to challenge turning in, did not find a lot when the pressure was applied and was labouring from some way out. (16/1)

**Hard Love** had the edge in fitness and pushed the pace until finding the demands too great once the battle to the line got under way. (33/1)

## 450 WILLIAM HILL SPRING MILE H'CAP (4-Y.O+) (Class B)

3-40 (3-46) **1m (straight)** £15,920.00 (£4,760.00: £2,280.00: £1,040.00) Stalls: High GOING: 0.50 sec per fur (GS)

| Form | Horse | Dist | Pos | SP | RR | SF |
|---|---|---|---|---|---|---|
| | **Cool Edge (IRE) (80)** (MHTompkins) **5-9-9** PRobinson(2) (a.p far side: led over 1f out: drvn out) | — | **1** | 20/1 | 92 | 75 |
| | **Lynton Lad (72)** (CPEBrooks) **4-9-1b** JReid(1) (led far side tl hdd over 1f out: unable qckn) | 1¾ | **2** | 25/1 | 81 | 64 |
| | **Dances With Hooves (72)** (DJSffrenchDavis) **4-9-1** JWeaver(7) (in tch stands' side: edgd lft 2f out: r.o wl fnl f) | 1 | **3** | 33/1 | 79 | 62 |

| | | | | SP | RR | SF |
|---|---|---|---|---|---|---|
| 234[2] | **Golden Pound (USA) (72)** (MissGayKelleway) **4-9-1** RCochrane(3) (prom far side: effort wl over 1f out: kpt on one pce) | 1½ | **4** | 25/1 | 76 | 59 |
| 392[4] | **Celestial Choir (80)** (JLEyre) **6-9-9** RLappin(12) (chsd ldrs stands' side: led 3f out tl over 1f out: no ex) | 3 | **5** | 12/1 | 78 | 61 |
| | **New Century (USA) (81)** (DNicholls) **4-9-10** WRyan(22) (a.p stands' side: one pce appr fnl f) | 1½ | **6** | 25/1 | 76 | 59 |
| | **Knobbleeneeze (73)** (MRChannon) **6-8-11v**(5) PPMurphy(5) (chsd ldrs far side: rdn & one pce fnl 2f) | ½ | **7** | 20/1 | 67 | 50 |
| 358[2] | **Mister Fire Eyes (IRE) (75)** (CEBrittain) **4-9-4b** BDoyle(17) (chsd ldrs stands' side: ev ch tl wknd over 1f out) | ¾ | **8** | 7/2 [1] | 67 | 50 |
| 325a[5] | **Country Lover (77)** (LordHuntingdon) **5-9-6v** DHarrison(14) (effrt u.p over 2f out: nvr nrr) | 3 | **9** | 16/1 | 63 | 46 |
| | **Tulu (73)** (MrsJRRamsden) **5-9-2** KFallon(20) (bhd & outpcd tl styd on fnl 2f) | 1½ | **10** | 14/1 | 56 | 39 |
| | **Bagshot (76)** (RHannon) **5-9-5** PatEddery(18) (in tch stands' side over 6f) | 3 | **11** | 10/1 [3] | 53 | 36 |
| 409[2] | **Duke Valentino (71)** (RHollinshead) **4-9-0** LDettori(6) (prom far side tl wknd & eased fnl 2f) | 2½ | **12** | 12/1 | 43 | 26 |
| | **Night Wink (USA) (80)** (DNicholls) **4-9-9** AlexGreaves(11) (chsd ldrs stands' side over 5f) | 1¾ | **13** | 20/1 | 49 | 32 |
| 153[6] | **Barrel of Hope (74)** (JLEyre) **4-9-3b** JFortune(19) (in tch stands' side: drvn along ½-wy: sn wknd) | hd | **14** | 20/1 | 42 | 25 |
| | **Mihriz (IRE) (78)** (RAkehurst) **4-9-7** TQuinn(13) (trckd ldrs stands' side tl wknd 2f out) | s.h | **15** | 7/1 [2] | 46 | 29 |
| | **Aeroking (USA) (79)** (GHarwood) **5-9-8** AClark(16) (led stands' side 5f: sn lost tch) | 2 | **16** | 20/1 | 43 | 26 |
| 379[7] | **Petoskin (78)** (JPearce) **4-9-7v[1]** GBardwell(10) (outpcd: t.o) | 12 | **17** | 20/1 | 18 | 1 |
| 379[4] | **Neuwest (USA) (78)** (NJHWalker) **4-9-4**(3) JStack(24) (trckd ldrs stands' side 5f: wknd qckly: t.o) | 2½ | **18** | 25/1 | 13 | — |
| | **Best of All (IRE) (73)** (JBerry) **4-9-2** JCarroll(15) (cl up stands' side over 4f: wknd qckly: t.o) | 9 | **19** | 14/1 | — | — |
| | **Ham N'Eggs (80)** (MDHammond) **5-9-9** KDarley(8) (a bhd: t.o) | 6 | **20** | 14/1 | — | — |
| 31[5] | **Smart Guest (80)** (JAHarris) **4-9-9** DaleGibson(4) (racd far side: spd to ½-wy: sn wknd: t.o) | dist | **21** | 50/1 | — | — |
| | ***Sotoboy (IRE) (80)*** (PWHarris) **4-9-9** GHind(21) (Withdrawn not under Starter's orders: bolted bef s) | | **W** | 14/1 | — | — |
| | | | | (SP 140.6%) | **21 Rn** | |

**1m 44.1** (7.10) CSF £412.92 CT £13,827.88 TOTE £34.80: £7.10 £5.30 £5.60 £5.40 (£215.60) Trio £4,548.30 OWNER Mr Henry Chan (NEWMARKET) BRED Hollybank Breeders

**Cool Edge (IRE)** does run best when fresh, but he had more use made of him on this occasion and, getting his head in front approaching the final furlong, kept on bravely to the post. This was his first success at the trip. (20/1)

**Lynton Lad**, a winner of a couple of sprints two years ago, led the way on the favoured far side and rallied gamely after being collared to go down fighting. (25/1)

**Dances With Hooves**, closely related to two useful middle-distance winners, ran by far his best race yet in this first handicap, and this lightly-raced colt could be just about ready to get it together. (33/1)

**Golden Pound (USA)**, fit from the All-Weather, waited on the leaders on the far side and tried to mount a challenge at the distance, but the pace never relented and he was unable to land a blow. (25/1)

**Celestial Choir** came out best of those racing towards the unfavoured stands' side, and looked the likely winner until getting outpaced inside the last furlong. (12/1)

**New Century (USA)** changed hands for 23,000 guineas at Newmarket's September Sales, and had more than his fair share of weight in this competitive event. With something left to work on, he ran a race full of promise under the stands' rail having every chance until outpaced in the dash to the line, but he will soon be winning. (25/1)

**Mister Fire Eyes (IRE)** pressed the leaders on the stands' side and was travelling as well as any until fading inside the last furlong. He has won over further but seven furlongs is probably his ideal trip. (7/2)

## 451 HOLROYD CONSTRUCTION GROUP H'CAP (0-90) (3-Y.O+) (Class C)

4-10 (4-16) **6f** £4,897.50 (£1,455.00: £690.00: £307.50) Stalls: High GOING: 0.50 sec per fur (GS)

| | | | | SP | RR | SF |
|---|---|---|---|---|---|---|
| 185* | **Anzio (IRE) (76)** (MissGayKelleway) **5-9-0b** PatEddery(17) (a.p centre: led over 1f out: drvn clr) | — | **1** | 11/1 | 92 | 57 |
| | **Sycamore Lodge (IRE) (67)** (MrsJRRamsden) **5-8-5** KFallon(19) (sn wl bhd & outpcd: gd hdwy over 1f out: fin wl) | 4 | **2** | 10/1 [3] | 72 | 37 |
| | **Montserrat (70)** (LGCottrell) **4-8-8v** MFenton(9) (a.p: rdn & one pce appr fnl f) | nk | **3** | 12/1 | 75 | 40 |
| | **Castlerea Lad (83)** (RHollinshead) **7-9-7** LDettori(11) (hld up & bhd: hdwy over 1f out: nrst fin) | 1¾ | **4** | 12/1 | 83 | 48 |
| | **Tiler (IRE) (81)** (MJohnston) **4-9-5** JWeaver(5) (lw: led far side: rdn ½-wy: kpt on) | ¾ | **5** | 8/1 [1] | 79 | 44 |
| | **To the Roof (IRE) (67)** (PWHarris) **4-8-5** GHind(22) (in tch stands side: rdn ½-wy: styd on ins fnl f) | d.h | **5** | 16/1 | 65 | 30 |
| | **Lord High Admiral (CAN) (87)** (MJHeaton-Ellis) **8-9-11** AClark(10) (led centre tl hdd over 1f out: sn btn) | ½ | **7** | 25/1 | 84 | 49 |
| | **Bolshoi (IRE) (70)** (JBerry) **4-8-8** JCarroll(20) (trckd ldrs: drvn along ½-wy: sn outpcd) | 2 | **8** | 20/1 | 61 | 26 |
| | **Sir Joey (USA) (80)** (PGMurphy) **7-9-1**(3) SDrowne(8) (styd on fnl 2f: nvr nrr) | ½ | **9** | 12/1 | 70 | 35 |
| | **Portend (82)** (SRBowring) **4-9-1**(5) CTeague(13) (lw: mid div: rdn 3f out: no imp) | 2½ | **10** | 10/1 [3] | 65 | 30 |
| | **Brecongill Lad (77)** (MissSEHall) **4-9-1** BDoyle(1) (lw: chsd ldr far side tl wknd over 2f out) | ½ | **11** | 8/1 [1] | 59 | 24 |
| | **Fantasy Racing (IRE) (82)** (MRChannon) **4-9-6** RHughes(16) (in tch over 3f) | nk | **12** | 14/1 | 63 | 28 |
| | **Mister Jolson (72)** (RJHodges) **7-8-10** RCochrane(21) (b.nr fore: bit bkwd: hld up: a bhd stands' side) | 2½ | **13** | 16/1 | 46 | 11 |
| 266[6] | **Tafahhus (77)** (MJPolglase) **4-9-1** WRyan(15) (a in rr) | 3½ | **14** | 50/1 | 42 | 7 |
| | **Anonym (IRE) (70)** (DNicholls) **4-8-8** AlexGreaves(2) (n.d) | nk | **15** | 16/1 | 34 | — |
| | **Wigberto (IRE) (90)** (JLEyre) **4-9-11**(3) OPears(6) (hld up: a bhd) | ¾ | **16** | 25/1 | 52 | 17 |
| | **The Happy Fox (IRE) (84)** (BAMcMahon) **4-9-3**(5) LNewton(7) (in tch to ½-wy: sn lost pl) | hd | **17** | 20/1 | 46 | 11 |
| | **Remaadi Sun (69)** (MDIUsher) **4-8-7** RStreet(12) (bit bkwd: dwlt: a bhd) | ½ | **18** | 50/1 | 30 | — |
| | **Highborn (IRE) (83)** (PSFelgate) **7-9-7** KDarley(4) (lw: a rr div) | 1½ | **19** | 9/1 [2] | 40 | 5 |
| 380[8] | **Samsolom (70)** (PHowling) **8-8-8** PaulEddery(14) (s.s: a wl bhd: t.o) | 4 | **20** | 25/1 | 16 | — |
| 55[13] | **Rockville Pike (IRE) (82)** (SDow) **4-9-6** TQuinn(3) (prom to ½-wy: sn wknd: t.o) | 21 | **21** | 20/1 | — | — |
| | | | | (SP 135.9%) | **21 Rn** | |

**1m 16.97** (5.97) CSF £114.66 CT £1,283.07 TOTE £10.80: £2.90 £3.70 £1.90 £3.00 (£48.30) Trio £523.30 OWNER Mr Tommy Staunton (WHITCOMBE) BRED Rathduff Stud

**Anzio (IRE)**, successful on the All-Weather last month, delivered his challenge over a furlong out, and running on strongly after striking the front, won very easily indeed. (11/1)

**Sycamore Lodge (IRE)**, brought back to sprinting for the first time since he left Ireland, was taken off his legs in the early stages. Picking up approaching the final furlong, he finished like a train, and that initial success can not be far away. (10/1)

**Montserrat** acts well when the ground is testing and, in the firing-line from the start, battled on willingly right to the finish. (12/1)

**Castlerea Lad** won this race on much faster ground last year and, judging by the way he finished here, he would have taken all the beating had the conditions been in his favour. (12/1)

**Tiler (IRE)** held the call on the far rail, but he was being led by the centre group and, though he stuck on gamely, was being held inside the distance. (8/1)

**To the Roof (IRE)** has still to get off the mark but, if this promising effort is anything to go by, his turn is near at hand. (16/1)

**Lord High Admiral (CAN)** barely lasts home over this trip, but does pile on the pressure and, forced to give best approaching the final furlong, gave notice he will be the one to beat over the minimum trip. (25/1)

**Brecongill Lad** tracked the leader on the far side, but was being made to work two furlongs out and his measure had been taken. (8/1)

T/Jkpt: Not won; £71,788.08 to Doncaster 23/3/96. T/Plpt: £2,814.10 (10.96 Tckts). T/Qdpt: £134.40 (31.72 Tckts). IM

# 0446-**DONCASTER (L-H) (Soft)**

## Saturday March 23rd

WEATHER: overcast WIND: almost nil

## 452 GREY FRIARS MAIDEN AUCTION STKS (2-Y.O) (Class D)

2-00 (2-02) **5f** £3,526.75 (£1,054.00: £504.50: £229.75) Stalls: High GOING: 0.82 sec per fur (S)

| | | | SP | RR | SF |
|---|---|---|---|---|---|
| **Kingsinger (IRE)** (MRChannon) **2-8-6** TQuinn(12) (neat: trckd ldrs: carried lft over 1f out: led ins fnl f: r.o) | — | 1 | 9/2[2] | 65 | 32 |
| **Magical Times** (RBoss) **2-8-4** AClark(11) (cmpt: sn trckng ldrs: led over 2f out: hung bdly lft: hdd & no ex ins fnl f) | 1¼ | 2 | 7/1 | 59 | 26 |
| **Spondulicks (IRE)** (RHannon) **2-8-0**(5)ow1 DaneO'Neill(2) (leggy: scope: cl up tl outpcd appr fnl f) | 2½ | 3 | 6/1 | 52 | 18 |
| **Fan of Vent-Axia** (CNAllen) **2-8-5** CHodgson(7) (cmpt: unf: sn pushed along: hdwy 2f out: styd on wl towards fin) | hd | 4 | 20/1 | 52 | 19 |
| **Classic Partygoer** (MWEasterby) **2-8-4** MBirch(10) (str: cmpt: led tl hdd over 2f out: styd on one pce) | s.h | 5 | 20/1 | 51 | 18 |
| **Nervous Rex** (WRMuir) **2-8-9** JReid(1) (w'like: scope: cl up tl appr fnl f) | 5 | 6 | 4/1[1] | 40 | 7 |
| **Highland Pass (IRE)** (MMcCormack) **2-8-6**ow1 RCochrane(3) (cmpt: gd spd 3f: wknd) | ½ | 7 | 5/1[3] | 35 | 1 |
| **Majaro** (JBerry) **2-8-4** LeTolboll(6) (lt-f: unf: spd to ½-wy: sn wknd) | 5 | 8 | 10/1 | 17 | — |
| **Lucybod** (NTinkler) **2-8-2** GCarter(8) (cmpt: bkwd: dwlt: a outpcd & bhd) | 8 | 9 | 12/1 | — | — |
| **Magic Blue (IRE)** (RHollinshead) **2-8-8** KDarley(9) (lengthy: dwlt: a bhd) | 3½ | 10 | 11/1 | — | — |
| **Seamus** (AGNewcombe) **2-8-3** JQuinn(4) (cmpt: bit bkwd: s.i.s: sn trckng ldrs: wknd over 2f out) | 3 | 11 | 33/1 | — | — |
| **Risky Flight** (AlfredSmith) **2-8-5**ow2 DHarrison(5) (lt-f: unf: sn outpcd & bhd) | 1¾ | 12 | 20/1 | — | — |
| | | | (SP 124.0%) | **12 Rn** | |

**65.94 secs** (7.54) CSF £35.16 TOTE £5.20: £2.10 £2.70 £1.80 (£19.60) Trio £40.20 OWNER Maygain Ltd (UPPER LAMBOURN) BRED Bernard Eivers

OFFICIAL EXPLANATION **Seamus: got struck into and lost his action.**

**Kingsinger (IRE)** is certainly nothing special to look at but was fit and knew his job, and that won him the day. (9/2: 3/1-5/1)

**Magical Times**, a sturdy colt who threw this away by running green, will surely have learnt plenty from the experience. (7/1)

**Spondulicks (IRE)** ran well and looks the sort to improve as the season progresses. (6/1)

**Fan of Vent-Axia** looks the type who will improve with time and, after getting outpaced here, was getting the hang of things at the end. (20/1)

**Classic Partygoer** needed this and showed plenty of speed. Better looks likely. (20/1)

**Nervous Rex** has plenty of scope for improvement and looked as though he blew up here. (4/1)

**Highland Pass (IRE)** (5/1: 8/1-9/2)

**Majaro** (10/1: 8/1-12/1)

**Magic Blue (IRE)** (11/1: 8/1-12/1)

## 453 MARK THOMAS CHUM SPECIAL H'CAP (0-85) (3-Y.O) (Class D)

2-30 (2-32) **7f** £4,854.00 (£1,452.00: £696.00: £318.00) Stalls: High GOING: 0.82 sec per fur (S)

| | | | | SP | RR | SF |
|---|---|---|---|---|---|---|
| 391[7] | **Sualtach (IRE) (75)** (RHollinshead) **3-9-1** LDettori(2) (lw: cl up far side: led over 1f out: styd on strly) | — | 1 | 16/1 | 89 | 39 |
| 357[6] | **First Maite (72)** (SRBowring) **3-8-7b**(5) CTeague(11) (led tl hdd over 1f out: kpt on one pce) | 5 | 2 | 13/2[3] | 75 | 25 |
| | **Silverdale Knight (56)** (KWHogg) **3-7-5**(5) MBaird(7) (lw: prom: effrt ½-wy: styd on one pce) | nk | 3 | 25/1 | 58 | 8 |
| 182[5] | **Theatre Magic (60)** (SRBowring) **3-8-0** NCarlisle(9) (chsd ldr: ch & rdn 2f out: nt qckn) | ¾ | 4 | 10/1 | 60 | 10 |
| | **Knave (67)** (RHannon) **3-8-2**(5) DaneO'Neill(14) (prom tl ½-wy: sn outpcd: styd on again fnl f) | 6 | 5 | 14/1 | 54 | 4 |
| | **Nilgiri Hills (IRE) (81)** (JLDunlop) **3-9-7** WCarson(13) (prom stands' side 4f: sn outpcd) | ½ | 6 | 9/4[1] | 66 | 16 |
| | **Oriole (57)** (NTinkler) **3-7-11**ow1 KimTinkler(10) (swtg: nvr wnt pce) | ½ | 7 | 33/1 | 41 | — |
| | **Beas River (IRE) (70)** (WRMuir) **3-8-10** JReid(12) (hld up: effrt 3f out: no imp) | 4 | 8 | 10/1 | 45 | — |
| | **Seattle Alley (USA) (65)** (MrsJRRamsden) **3-8-5** KFallon(8) (bit bkwd: hld up & bhd: nvr plcd to chal) | 1¼ | 9 | 8/1 | 37 | — |
| 416[2] | **Le Sport (80)** (ABailey) **3-9-3**(3) DWright(5) (lw: dwlt: a outpcd & wl bhd) | 5 | 10 | 7/1 | 41 | — |
| | **Rebel County (IRE) (70)** (DJSCosgrove) **3-8-3**(7) MNutter(1) (prom far side 4f) | 15 | 11 | 6/1[2] | — | — |
| | **Carmosa (USA) (61)** (DNicholls) **3-8-1** JQuinn(3) (chsd ldrs far side over 4f) | 5 | 12 | 16/1 | — | — |
| | **Craignairn (71)** (JBerry) **3-8-11** JCarroll(6) (spd to ½-wy) | nk | 13 | 12/1 | — | — |
| | **Islay Brown (IRE) (66)** (CWCElsey) **3-8-6** KDarley(4) (chsd ldrs far side 4f: sn rdn & btn) | 3 | 14 | 25/1 | — | — |
| | | | | (SP 136.9%) | **14 Rn** | |

**1m 34.34** (10.74) CSF £121.11 CT £2495.59 TOTE £17.90: £4.60 £2.50 £4.40 (£119.70) Trio £697.80; £688.06 to 25/3/96 OWNER Mr Noel Sweeney (UPPER LONGDON) BRED Brownstown Stud

LONG HANDICAP Oriole 7-7

OFFICIAL EXPLANATION **Islay Brown (IRE): was unable to act on the ground.**

**Sualtach (IRE): the improvement on his previous run at Wolverhampton was put down to the colt running too free and too fresh, then blowing up on that run. It was also his first run following a lay off and an operation.**

**Sualtach (IRE)**, well-drawn, came back to form with a vengeance here but has apparently had problems and valid excuses for his last four disappointing runs. (16/1)

**First Maite** tried hard to make all up the centre of the track, but the winner found the better ground on the far side and that made all the difference. (13/2)

**Silverdale Knight** ran well at his first attempt on ground as soft as this and was keeping on at the finish. (25/1)

**Theatre Magic** improved no end on the All-Weather this winter and looks to have carried that on to the turf. (10/1)

**Knave** ran as though this trip is on the short side. (14/1)

**Nilgiri Hills (IRE)** had a bad draw and was fighting a lost cause from halfway. (9/4)

**Beas River (IRE)**, poorly drawn, raced too freely and should do better in due course. (10/1)

**Seattle Alley (USA)** needed this and never showed in the race, but left the impression that, in time and over further, better will be seen. (8/1: 6/1-9/1)

**Rebel County (IRE)** looked to have been well backed, but it is worth bearing in mind that over £8,000 of the bets struck came from the comedian who sponsored the race. (6/1: op 14/1)

## 454 DONCASTER SPRING CONDITIONS STKS (3-Y.O) (Class C)

3-00 (3-00) **1m (straight)** £6,379.80 (£2,314.80: £1,122.40: £472.00: £201.00) Stalls: High GOING: 0.82 sec per fur (S)

| | | | SP | RR | SF |
|---|---|---|---|---|---|
| **Acharne (98)** (CEBrittain) **3-8-11** BDoyle(2) (hung lft & racd alone far side: led over 4f out: sn clr: styd on wl) | — | **1** | 7/2 3 | 100 | 61 |
| **Mironov** (MRChannon) **3-8-13** RHughes(5) (w'like: leggy: scope: cl up stands' side: chsd wnr fnl 3f: no imp) | 10 | **2** | 7/1 | 82 | 43 |
| **Mushahid (USA) (104)** (JLDunlop) **3-9-3** WCarson(4) (swtg: disp ld stands' side 5f: sn outpcd) | 4 | **3** | 5/2 2 | 78 | 39 |
| **Wight** (RHannon) **3-8-8** TQuinn(3) (unf: disp ld stands' side 5f: sn outpcd) | 9 | **4** | 15/2 | 51 | 12 |
| **Projection (USA)** (BWHills) **3-8-13** PatEddery(1) (b.off fore: hld up: effrt stands' side 3f out: btn 2f out) | 7 | **5** | 7/4 1 | 42 | 3 |

(SP 111.4%) **5 Rn**

**1m 46.86** (9.86) CSF £22.36 TOTE £5.10: £2.20 £2.20 (£21.10) OWNER Parrot Racing (NEWMARKET) BRED M. J. Simmonds

**Acharne** tends to hang left so his rider let him go over to the far rail which proved to be a wise move. In front from halfway, there were soon no challengers. (7/2)

**Mironov** won the main race on the stands' side but had no chance with the sole runner on the favoured far rail. (7/1)

**Mushahid (USA)** got very warm beforehand and this soft ground proved too much for him in the final three furlongs. (5/2)

**Wight** has not wintered well and showed little here once the race began soon after halfway. (15/2)

**Projection (USA)** won on fast ground last year. This soft surface and longer trip really found him out and he stopped dead two furlongs out. (7/4)

## 455 WILLIAM HILL LINCOLN H'CAP (4-Y.O+) (Class B)

3-40 (3-41) **1m (straight)** £47,372.50 (£14,230.00: £6,865.00: £3,182.50) Stalls: High GOING: 0.82 sec per fur (S)

| | | | | SP | RR | SF |
|---|---|---|---|---|---|---|
| | **Stone Ridge (IRE) (87)** (RHannon) **4-8-7**(5) DaneO'Neill(6) (lw: trckd ldrs: hdwy over 3f out: led wl over 1f out: hld on wl) | — | **1** | 33/1 | 103 | 85 |
| | **Roving Minstrel (89)** (BAMcMahon) **5-9-0** GCarter(7) (lw: trckd ldrs: effrt over 2f out: ev ch ins fnl f: r.o) | 1¼ | **2** | 14/1 | 103 | 85 |
| | **Barbaroja (86)** (JGFitzGerald) **5-8-11** JCarroll(15) (a.p: drvn along over 3f out: kpt on wl) | 6 | **3** | 16/1 | 88+ | 70 |
| 357 3 | **Shinerolla (83)** (CParker) **4-8-5**(3) DRMcCabe(1) (in tch: n.m.r over 3f out: hdwy 2f out: styd on wl) | 2½ | **4** | 11/1 | 80 | 62 |
| | **Delta Soleil (USA) (91)** (PWHarris) **4-9-2** GHind(10) (lw: plld hrd: led over 4f out tl wl over 1f out: grad wknd) | 4 | **5** | 14/1 | 80 | 62 |
| | **Beauchamp Jazz (99)** (JLDunlop) **4-9-10** JReid(2) (chsd ldrs: rdn 3f out: one pce) | ½ | **6** | 11/1 | 87 | 69 |
| | **Al Reet (IRE) (90)** (MDHammond) **5-9-1** RCochrane(16) (hdwy 2f out: styd on wl towards fin) | 1¼ | **7** | 25/1 | 75 | 57 |
| | **Cedez le Passage (FR) (89)** (KOCunningham-Brown) **5-9-0** JFEgan(13) (styd on fnl 2f: nvr rchd ldrs) | ½ | **8** | 50/1 | 73 | 55 |
| | **Welton Arsenal (95)** (MRChannon) **4-9-6** RHughes(8) (hld up: n.m.r & effrt 3f out: no imp) | s.h | **9** | 40/1 | 79 | 61 |
| | **Moving Arrow (93)** (MissSEHall) **5-9-4** JWeaver(4) (bit bkwd: led over 3f: wknd over 1f out) | nk | **10** | 8/1 2 | 76 | 58 |
| | **Night Dance (95)** (GLewis) **4-9-3**(3) AWhelan(18) (bhd: sme hdwy fnl 3f: n.d) | 3½ | **11** | 12/1 | 71 | 53 |
| | **Fame Again (82)** (MrsJRRamsden) **4-8-7** KFallon(9) (lw: bhd: hdwy u.p 3f out: sn btn) | 4 | **12** | 10/1 3 | 50 | 32 |
| | **Beyond Doubt (84)** (LordHuntingdon) **4-8-9** DHarrison(11) (lw: prom: rdn over 3f out: sn lost pl) | 6 | **13** | 14/1 | 40 | 22 |
| | **Hoh Express (99)** (IABalding) **4-9-10** LDettori(12) (in tch 5f) | ½ | **14** | 20/1 | 54 | 36 |
| | **Show Faith (IRE) (86)** (RHannon) **6-8-11** SSanders(5) (sn drvn along: n.d) | 5 | **15** | 14/1 | 31 | 13 |
| 379* | **Pengamon (87)** (HJCollingridge) **4-8-12** 5x JQuinn(24) (hld up: effrt 3f out: n.d) | nk | **16** | 33/1 | 32 | 14 |
| | **Kayvee (99)** (GHarwood) **7-9-10** AClark(19) (a bhd) | 5 | **17** | 40/1 | 34 | 16 |
| 132 10 | **Nigel's Lad (IRE) (87)** (PCHaslam) **4-8-12** JFortune(17) (racd centre: no ch fr ½-wy) | 1¾ | **18** | 50/1 | 18 | — |
| 358 9 | **Castel Rosselo (83)** (RHarris) **6-8-8** AMackay(22) (swtg: n.d) | hd | **19** | 40/1 | 14 | — |
| | **Autumn Affair (96)** (CEBrittain) **4-9-7** BDoyle(23) (nvr trbld ldrs) | 2 | **20** | 40/1 | 23 | 5 |
| | **Pearl Venture (87)** (SPCWoods) **4-8-12** WWoods(21) (a bhd) | s.h | **21** | 50/1 | 14 | — |
| | **Billy Bushwacker (88)** (MrsMReveley) **5-8-13b** KDarley(20) (dwlt: n.d) | ¾ | **22** | 16/1 | 13 | — |
| | **Comanche Companion (83)** (TJNaughton) **6-8-8** PatEddery(3) (swtg: cl up 5f: sn wknd & eased) | 8 | **23** | 10/1 3 | — | — |
| | **Sharp Prospect (82)** (RAkehurst) **6-8-7** TQuinn(14) (lw: prom 5f: virtually p.u fnl 2f: lame) | dist | **24** | 7/1 1 | — | — |

(SP 134.7%) **24 Rn**

**1m 44.67** (7.67) CSF £413.08 CT £6,909.57 TOTE £32.00: £5.90 £6.50 £3.90 £2.20 (£320.70) Trio £5782.70 OWNER Mrs Chris Harrington (MARLBOROUGH) BRED Mrs Chris Harrington

OFFICIAL EXPLANATION **Comanche Companion: the mare was completely unsuited by the soft ground.**

**Sharp Prospect: pulled up lame before the finish.**

**Stone Ridge (IRE)**, untried on such a soft surface previously, handled this well and proved to be a game performer when challenged. (33/1)

**Roving Minstrel**, trying to win this for the second year running, put up a terrific effort and looked likely to make it entering the final furlong, but just found the winner too tough. (14/1)

**Barbaroja**, from a moderate draw, never looked to be going that well but he did keep battling on well, suggesting that longer trips should help. (16/1)

**Shinerolla** was a bit short a room just after halfway, but then stayed on well to show that he is in particularly good heart this season. (11/1)

**Delta Soleil (USA)** raced far too freely for his own good and a drop back in distance and a strongly-run event should suit. (14/1)

**Beauchamp Jazz** does not seem to know how to run a bad race, but he was tapped for toe here in the last three furlongs. (11/1)

**Al Reet (IRE)**, an Irish import, ran well from a moderate draw and was finishing in useful style. (25/1)

**Cedez le Passage (FR)** has changed stables and ran well here over a trip that would seem too short. (50/1)

**Welton Arsenal** did his usual and travelled well, but flattered only to deceive. (40/1)

**Moving Arrow** looked as though he would be all the better for this and is happier on faster ground and a turning track. (8/1)

**Night Dance** tried the impossible and crossed over behind the others, attempting to come up the far side, but was never any closer than his final eleventh placing. (12/1)

**Pengamon** ran well from an impossible draw and is in good form at present. (33/1)

**Comanche Companion** showed up well but things seemed to go wrong for her from halfway. Losing her action, she was then eased considerably. (10/1)

## 456 MIDLAND COPYING DONCASTER SHIELD STKS (4-Y.O+) (Class B)

4-15 (4-15) **1m 4f** £7,553.40 (£2,790.60: £1,335.30: £541.50: £210.75: £78.45) Stalls: Low GOING: 0.82 sec per fur (S)

| | | | SP | RR | SF |
|---|---|---|---|---|---|
| **Juyush (USA) (106)** (BWHills) **4-9-4** WCarson(1) (led tl hdd 6f out: disp ld over 3f out: styd on wl fnl f) | — | **1** | 5/1 3 | 119 | 49 |
| **Daraydan (IRE) (102)** (LadyHerries) **4-9-2** KDarley(7) (trckd ldrs: disp ld over 3f out: no ex fnl f) | 3½ | **2** | 7/1 | 112 | 42 |
| **Penny a Day (IRE) (94)** (MrsMReveley) **6-9-2** ACulhane(2) (lw: hld up: effrt over 3f out: styd on: no imp) | 6 | **3** | 4/1 2 | 102 | 34 |
| **Ionio (USA) (107)** (CEBrittain) **5-8-12** BDoyle(3) (prom tl outpcd over 4f out: no imp after) | 1¼ | **4** | 6/1 | 97 | 29 |

| | | | SP | RR | SF |
|---|---|---|---|---|---|
| **Right Win (IRE) (111)** (RHannon) **6-8-12b** RHughes(4) (chsd ldrs: drvn along 4f out: sn btn) | 4 | **5** | 6/4 1 | 91 | 23 |
| **Linpac West (89)** (DNicholls) **10-8-12** AlexGreaves(6) (lw: cl up: led 6f out tl over 3f out: sn wknd) | 15 | **6** | 11/1 | 71 | 3 |
| | | | (SP 111.8%) | **6 Rn** | |

**2m 47.78** (17.78) CSF £33.30 TOTE £4.40: £2.10 £3.00 (£10.50) OWNER Mr Hamdan Al Maktoum (LAMBOURN) BRED Corbin J. Robertson
WEIGHT FOR AGE 4yo-2lb

**Juyush (USA)** always looked to be going best and, in the end, he put it beyond doubt in a most authoritative manner. It looked as though the further he went, the better he got. (5/1)

**Daraydan (IRE)**, dropped back in distance, was upsides the winner going equally as well early in the straight, but was then tapped for toe in the closing stages. (7/1)

**Penny a Day (IRE)**, returning from hurdling, could never get into this and was not over-punished. He basically ran as well as could be expected. (4/1: op 6/1)

**Ionio (USA)** looked short of speed here. Outpaced early in the straight, he had no further chance and is probably better on a faster surface. (6/1)

**Right Win (IRE)** has lost his way of late over hurdles and disappointed again here. (6/4)

**Linpac West** loves this ground and has changed stables, but showed little here. (11/1)

## 457 CAMMIDGE TROPHY STKS (Listed) (3-Y.O+) (Class A)

4-45 (4-46) **6f** £12,648.00 (£3,774.00: £1,802.00: £816.00) Stalls: High GOING: 0.82 sec per fur (S)

| | | | SP | RR | SF |
|---|---|---|---|---|---|
| **Fire Dome (IRE) (99)** (RHannon) **4-9-2** RHughes(7) (bhd: hdwy u.p over 2f out: led ins fnl f: r.o) | — | **1** | 11/1 | 113 | 65 |
| **The Puzzler (IRE)** (BWHills) **5-9-2** WCarson(4) (b: led tl hdd ins fnl f: kpt on) | 1¼ | **2** | 8/1 | 110 | 62 |
| **Cool Jazz (113)** (CEBrittain) **5-9-7** BDoyle(1) (lw: cl up tl outpcd ½-wy: styd on & ev ch ins fnl f: nt qckn) | 5 | **3** | 9/2 2 | 101 | 53 |
| **Hard to Figure (108)** (RJHodges) **10-9-5** RCochrane(2) (lw: chsd ldrs: rdn ½-wy: r.o one pce) | 1 | **4** | 15/2 | 97 | 49 |
| **Montendre (108)** (MMcCormack) **9-9-5** JReid(8) (lw: sn pushed along: nvr trbld ldrs) | 1½ | **5** | 5/1 3 | 93 | 45 |
| **Iktamal (USA) (100)** (EALDunlop) **4-9-2** PaulEddery(10) (bit bkwd: hld up: effrt 2f out: sn rdn & btn) | s.h | **6** | 11/2 | 90 | 42 |
| **Daring Destiny (99)** (KRBurke) **5-9-0** LDettori(9) (trckd ldrs: effrt 2f out: sn btn) | 1¾ | **7** | 13/2 | 83 | 35 |
| **Domulla (102)** (RAkehurst) **6-9-2** TQuinn(6) (prom tl outpcd & wknd fr ½-wy) | 24 | **8** | 100/30 1 | 21 | — |
| | | | (SP 117.9%) | **8 Rn** | |

**1m 18.4** (7.40) CSF £85.72 TOTE £13.90: £2.70 £2.70 £2.20 (£46.00) Trio £75.50 OWNER Mr Mahmood Al-Shuaibi (MARLBOROUGH) BRED Airlie Stud

**Fire Dome (IRE)** won this well but there may be excuses aplenty for his opponents, and he could be flattered. (11/1)

**The Puzzler (IRE)** likes the soft and has plenty of speed but just failed to last this trip out. (8/1)

**Cool Jazz** looked particularly well, but was always struggling with the pace and was short of a real turn of foot in the last furlong and a half. (9/2)

**Hard to Figure** looked and ran well enough, but he usually saves his best for later in the season. (15/2)

**Montendre**, who won this last year, was never happy this time and failed to get into it, despite staying on. (5/1)

**Iktamal (USA)**, who needed this, is happier on faster ground, and he blew up in the last couple of furlongs. (11/2)

**Daring Destiny** looked likely to benefit a great deal from this and failed to make any impression from halfway. (13/2)

## 458 SOUTH YORKSHIRE MAIDEN STKS (3-Y.O) (Class D)

5-15 (5-20) **6f** £3,882.50 (£1,160.00: £555.00: £252.50) Stalls: High GOING: 0.82 sec per fur (S)

| | | | SP | RR | SF |
|---|---|---|---|---|---|
| **Green Barries (80)** (MJohnston) **3-9-0** JWeaver(11) (lw: a.p: led over 1f out: rn green: r.o) | — | **1** | 4/1 1 | 84 | 51 |
| **Proud Look** (BWHills) **3-9-0** LDettori(4) (w'like: str: scope: prom: led over 1f out: sn hdd & one pce) | 5 | **2** | 7/1 | 71 | 38 |
| **Frontman (IRE)** (TDBarron) **3-9-0** JFortune(10) (led tl over 1f out: sn outpcd) | 3½ | **3** | 11/2 3 | 61 | 28 |
| **Sihafi (USA)** (EALDunlop) **3-9-0** WCarson(1) (stdd s: styd hdwy 2f out: r.o: nvr plcd to chal) | ¾ | **4** | 5/1 2 | 59 | 26 |
| **Riverbourne (USA)** (MRChannon) **3-9-0** RHughes(2) (cmpt: lw: stdd s: shkn up over 2f out: styd on towards fin) | 1¼ | **5** | 5/1 2 | 56 | 23 |
| **Loose Talk** (WJarvis) **3-8-9** TQuinn(8) (w'like: bit bkwd: chsd ldrs: rdn 3f out: wknd wl over 1f out) | 2½ | **6** | 9/1 | 44 | 11 |
| **Forest Boy (60)** (KWMcAuliffe) **3-9-0** SSanders(9) (chsd ldrs: rdn 3f out: sn btn) | 1 | **7** | 20/1 | 47 | 14 |
| **Magic Mail** (JMPEustace) **3-9-0** RCochrane(15) (chsd ldrs tl rdn & btn over 1f out) | 1 | **8** | 8/1 | 44 | 11 |
| **Arabian Heights** (MrsJRRamsden) **3-9-0** KFallon(5) (bit bkwd: nvr trbld ldrs) | 6 | **9** | 20/1 | 28 | — |
| **Danamich (IRE)** (JBerry) **3-9-0** JCarroll(16) (a outpcd & bhd) | 1¼ | **10** | 20/1 | 25 | — |
| **Sharp Monty** (RHollinshead) **3-9-0** KDarley(6) (prom 4f) | 4 | **11** | 20/1 | 14 | — |
| 428 4 **Falcon's Flame (USA)** (MrsJRRamsden) **3-9-0** MDeering(7) (bit bkwd: hld up & bhd: n.d) | ½ | **12** | 20/1 | 13 | — |
| 224 7 **Supreme Illusion (AUS)** (JohnBerry) **3-8-4**(7)ow2 AmyQuirk(12) (nvr wnt pce) | 3½ | **13** | 50/1 | — | — |
| **Spotted Eagle** (RHannon) **3-8-9**(5) DaneO'Neill(14) (sn bhd) | 7 | **14** | 12/1 | — | — |
| **Sharvic (IRE)** (MissMKMilligan) **3-9-0** JQuinn(3) (unf: bkwd: dwlt: a outpcd & bhd) | 2½ | **15** | 33/1 | — | — |
| ***Autoberry*** (CWFairhurst) **3-9-0** WWoods(17) (Withdrawn not under Starter's orders: Broke out of stalls) | | **W** | | — | — |
| | | | (SP 138.7%) | **15 Rn** | |

**1m 19.26** (8.26) CSF £34.83 TOTE £4.20: £2.00 £2.40 £3.60 (£7.80) Trio £85.20 OWNER Maktoum Al Maktoum (MIDDLEHAM) BRED Gainsborough Stud Management Ltd

OFFICIAL EXPLANATION **Sihafi (USA): the jockey stated that his main objective had been to teach the colt to settle and to do his best without resorting to too much pressure, due to the horse's tendency to bolt. Sihafi pulled hard in the early stages, blew up and tired two furlongs out. At this point his pilot did not consider that the colt's temperament at this stage would withstand any harder riding.**

**Green Barries** was inclined to wander about last year and has retained the habit, but still won well and there is obviously plenty more ability there. (4/1: op 9/4)

**Proud Look**, a good-looking newcomer, showed plenty of ability and will no doubt do better, especially over further. (7/1: 4/1-8/1)

**Frontman (IRE)** ran well until blowing up approaching the final furlong, and should improve. (11/2)

**Sihafi (USA)** was handled with kid-gloves in the paddock and Carson was certainly wearing them in the race, as he just had a nice quiet run and finished strongly without being asked a serious question. Obviously much better will be seen in due course. (5/1: 4/1-6/1)

**Riverbourne (USA)** decided to give most of the field a start and then picked up when it was all over. He should improve a fair deal for this. (5/1)

**Loose Talk** showed plenty of speed until blowing up in the closing stages. (9/1)

**Magic Mail** ran well from a poor draw and should now do better. (8/1)

**Arabian Heights**, a backward sort, looks likely to improve over further. (20/1)

**Falcon's Flame (USA)**, having his second run in a week, found this trip far too sharp. (20/1)

T/Jkpt: Not won; £97,753.89 to 25/3/96. T/Plpt: £6,617.70 (6.9 Tckts). T/Qdpt: £341.00 (11.12 Tckts). AA

# 0406-LINGFIELD (L-H) (Standard)
## Saturday March 23rd
WEATHER: overcast WIND: almost nil

### 459 CAMDEN ROAD (S) H'CAP (0-60) (3-Y.O) (Class G)
2-25 (2-27) **1m 4f (Equitrack)** £2,259.00 (£624.00: £297.00) Stalls: Low GOING minus 0.62 sec per fur (FST)

| Form | Runner | Dist | Pos | SP | RR | SF |
|---|---|---|---|---|---|---|
| 402[9] | **Further Future (IRE) (45)** (JohnBerry) **3-9-2b[1]** MFenton(5) (a.p: led over 4f out: clr over 3f out: r.o wl) | — | 1 | 9/1[3] | 59 | 12 |
| 348[8] | **Suparoy (50)** (TGMills) **3-9-7** WRyan(2) (led over 2f: led 5f out to over 4f out: unable qckn) | 11 | 2 | 6/5[1] | 49 | 2 |
| | **Driftholme (28)** (GLMoore) **3-7-13** NAdams(3) (rdn over 7f out: hdwy 5f out: chsd wnr over 3f out: one pce) | s.h | 3 | 6/1[2] | 27 | — |
| 329[9] | **Belacqua (USA) (25)** (DWChapman) **3-7-7b[1](3)** DarrenMoffatt(6) (hld up: rdn over 3f out: one pce) | 3 | 4 | 20/1 | 20 | — |
| 277[5] | **Shanoora (IRE) (46)** (MrsNMacauley) **3-8-12v(5)** AmandaSanders(7) (rn wd bnd over 8f out: led over 7f out to 5f out: wknd over 3f out) | 10 | 5 | 6/1[2] | 28 | — |
| 402[8] | **Margi Boo (35)** (RTJuckes) **3-8-1v[1](5)** FLynch(4) (led over 9f out to over 7f out: wknd over 4f out) | 20 | 6 | 16/1 | — | — |
| 361[3] | **Latzio (36)** (BAPearce) **3-8-7** WHollick(1) (b.hind: bhd fnl 8f) | 6 | 7 | 6/1[2] | — | — |

(SP 109.0%) **7 Rn**

**2m 36.19** (6.19) CSF £18.95 TOTE £13.60: £3.60 £1.30 (£6.80) OWNER Mr A. K. Collins (NEWMARKET) BRED Denis Mahony
LONG HANDICAP Belacqua (USA) 7-7
No bid

**Further Future (IRE)**, fitted with blinkers for the first time, moved to the front over half a mile from home, and soon forged clear to win a dreadful race. (9/1: 5/1-10/1)
**Suparoy**, the early leader, managed to get in front again five furlongs out, but he only remained there for a short time and was then totally tapped for toe. (6/5: 6/4-Evens)
**Driftholme** off the course for nearly five months, drifted badly in the market and looked far from enthusiastic about the job in hand, her first run on the sand. Nevertheless, her jockey managed to get her into second over three furlongs out, but she had no hope of reeling in the winner and was caught for the runner-up berth right on the line. (6/1: 5/2-7/1)
**Shanoora (IRE)** (6/1: op 4/1)

### 460 SAINT PIERS MEDIAN AUCTION MAIDEN STKS (3-Y.O) (Class F)
2-55 (2-55) **1m (Equitrack)** £2,642.80 (£730.80: £348.40) Stalls: High GOING minus 0.62 sec per fur (FST)

| Form | Runner | Dist | Pos | SP | RR | SF |
|---|---|---|---|---|---|---|
| | **Cool Fire** (SPCWoods) **3-9-0** WRyan(2) (led 5f out: rn wd bnd wl over 1f out: r.o wl) | — | 1 | 100/30[2] | 62 | 39 |
| 364[2] | **Mattimeo (IRE)** (APJarvis) **3-9-0** JTate(6) (hld up: rdn 3f out: unable qckn) | 5 | 2 | 10/11[1] | 52 | 29 |
| | **Safecracker** (JWHills) **3-8-9(5)** MHenry(7) (a.p: rdn 3f out: one pce) | d.h | 2 | 25/1 | 52 | 29 |
| | **Cherry Garden (IRE) (66)** (TJNaughton) **3-8-7(7)** TAshley(1) (swtg: rdn over 4f out: nvr nr to chal) | 11 | 4 | 11/1 | 30 | 7 |
| 304[2] | **Be Satisfied (55)** (AMoore) **3-9-0** MFenton(5) (b.hind: led 3f: wknd over 3f out) | 3½ | 5 | 11/1 | 23 | — |
| | **Danico** (SCWilliams) **3-8-11(3)** SDrowne(8) (lw: a bhd) | 3½ | 6 | 6/1[3] | 16 | — |
| | **Casino Chip** (TTClement) **3-9-0b[1]** MTebbutt(4) (prom over 3f) | 3 | 7 | 33/1 | 10 | — |

(SP 113.2%) **7 Rn**

**1m 38.26** (0.86) CSF £3.29 £27.79 TOTE £4.80: £1.60 £0.80 £2.90 ( £1.60 £17.50) OWNER Mr D. Sullivan (NEWMARKET) BRED Major R. P. Thorman and P. P. Thorman

**Cool Fire**, who fractured a cannon-bone during his final outing last year, was well supported in the market for this return. Going on five furlongs out, he failed to handle the tight home bend, but nevertheless forged clear for a decisive victory. (100/30: 5/1-3/1)
**Mattimeo (IRE)** chased the leaders. He had no chance with the winner in the straight and, having a tremendous battle for second place, in the end dead-heated for that prize. (10/11: 4/6-Evens)
**Safecracker**, off the course for over six months, had a tremendous battle for second place, and in the end had to share the spoils. (25/1)
**Cherry Garden (IRE)** (11/1: op 5/1)
**Be Satisfied** (11/1: 6/1-12/1)
**Danico** (6/1: op 4/1)

### 461 VINES OF SEVENOAKS BMW H'CAP (0-75) (3-Y.O+) (Class D)
3-30 (3-31) **6f (Equitrack)** £3,694.95 (£1,101.60: £525.30: £237.15) Stalls: Low GOING minus 0.62 sec per fur (FST)

| Form | Runner | Dist | Pos | SP | RR | SF |
|---|---|---|---|---|---|---|
| 362[4] | **The Institute Boy (60)** (MissJFCraze) **6-9-2** AMcGlone(2) (chsd ldr: rdn over 1f out: led wl ins fnl f: r.o wl) | — | 1 | 7/1[3] | 70 | 20 |
| 418[2] | **Lord Sky (68)** (ABailey) **5-9-3(7)** AngelaGallimore(1) (led: rdn over 1f out: hdd wl ins fnl f: unable qckn) | ¾ | 2 | 11/4[1] | 76 | 26 |
| 408* | **Our Shadee (USA) (65)** (KTIvory) **6-9-0v(7)** CScally(4) (lw: rdn over 3f out: hdwy over 1f out: r.o wl ins fnl f) | nk | 3 | 7/2[2] | 72 | 22 |
| 380[6] | **Invocation (68)** (AMoore) **9-9-10** MFenton(5) (b.hind: lw: dwlt: hdwy over 1f out: r.o) | 2½ | 4 | 14/1 | 69 | 19 |
| | **Beeny (65)** (APJarvis) **3-8-8** JTate(8) (a.p: rdn 3f out: one pce) | nk | 5 | 8/1 | 66 | 2 |
| 354[3] | **Random (54)** (CJames) **5-8-10** CRutter(6) (no hdwy fnl 2f) | 4 | 6 | 7/1[3] | 43 | — |
| | **Napoleon Star (IRE) (66)** (MSSaunders) **5-9-8** NAdams(9) (a bhd) | 1½ | 7 | 25/1 | 51 | 1 |
| 388[6] | **Newington Butts (IRE) (49)** (KWMcAuliffe) **6-8-5e** GDuffield(7) (sme hdwy over 3f out: wknd over 2f out) | ½ | 8 | 11/1 | 33 | — |
| 408[4] | **Chief's Lady (46)** (JMBradley) **4-8-2** LCharnock(3) (bhd fnl 2f) | hd | 9 | 14/1 | 30 | — |
| | **Little Saboteur (61)** (PJMakin) **7-9-3** WRyan(10) (b.nr hind: hld up: rdn over 1f out: sn wknd) | 3 | 10 | 16/1 | 37 | — |

(SP 116.4%) **10 Rn**

**1m 12.66** (2.06) CSF £25.19 CT £72.74 TOTE £6.80: £1.50 £1.60 £1.60 (£18.20) Trio £12.70 OWNER Mrs J. Addleshaw (YORK) BRED M. Yiapatos
WEIGHT FOR AGE 3yo-13lb

**The Institute Boy** chased the leader. Asked for his effort below the distance, he came through to gain the upper-hand in the closing stages. (7/1)
**Lord Sky** attempted to make all the running but was worried out of it inside the last 75 yards. (11/4)
**Our Shadee (USA)** continues in good form. At last finding his feet below the distance, he ran on strongly inside the final furlong, but found the line always coming too soon. (7/2)
**Invocation**, sluggish leaving the stalls, was doing some good work in the last furlong and a half, but found it all over bar the shouting. A return to seven furlongs would probably be a help. (14/1)
**Beeny**, given a four-month break, was never far away but was made to look very pedestrian in last three furlongs. (8/1)
**Newington Butts (IRE)** (11/1: 8/1-12/1)
**Chief's Lady** (14/1: 10/1-16/1)

## 462 BLACKBERRY LANE H'CAP (0-80) (3-Y.O+) (Class D)

4-00 (4-00) **1m 2f (Equitrack)** £3,628.65 (£1,081.20: £515.10: £232.05) Stalls: Low GOING minus 0.62 sec per fur (FST)

| Form | Horse | Dist | Pos | SP | RR | SF |
|---|---|---|---|---|---|---|
| 132[7] | **Renown (67)** (LordHuntingdon) **4-8-10**(5) MHenry(5) (lw: chsd ldr 2f: chsd ldr over 4f out: led over 3f out: clr over 1f out: r.o wl) | — | 1 | 10/1 | 79 | 39 |
| | **Herr Trigger (75)** (DrJDScargill) **5-9-9b** MFenton(7) (hdwy 4f out: rdn over 2f out: r.o one pce) | 1¾ | 2 | 9/2[2] | 83 | 44 |
| 424[2] | **Golden Touch (USA) (56)** (NACallaghan) **4-8-1**(3) PMcCabe(1) (lw: plld hrd: rdn & hdwy over 2f out: r.o one pce) | ½ | 3 | 7/2[1] | 64 | 24 |
| 223[5] | **Komreyev Dancer (80)** (ABailey) **4-9-7**(7) AngelaGallimore(2) (hdwy over 1f out: r.o ins fnl f) | 1½ | 4 | 13/2 | 86 | 46 |
| | **Wild Palm (68)** (WAO'Gorman) **4-9-2** EmmaO'Gorman(3) (lw: dwlt: hdwy 4f out: wknd 2f out) | 1¾ | 5 | 7/2[1] | 71 | 31 |
| 409* | **Mr Nevermind (IRE) (73)** (GLMoore) **6-9-2**(5) FLynch(4) (lw: bhd fnl 3f) | 5 | 6 | 13/2 | 67 | 28 |
| 411[6] | **South Eastern Fred (79)** (HJCollingridge) **5-9-13** VSmith(6) (led over 6f) | 2½ | 7 | 5/1[3] | 69 | 30 |
| 409[7] | **French Ginger (55)** (RIngram) **5-8-3** GDuffield(8) (chsd ldr 8f out tl over 4f out: sn wknd) | 17 | 8 | 16/1 | 18 | — |
| | | | | (SP 120.9%) | **8 Rn** | |

**2m 5.59** (1.29) CSF £53.00 CT £177.33 TOTE £10.30: £2.90 £2.00 £1.80 (£17.20) Trio £23.60 OWNER The Queen (WEST ILSLEY) BRED The Queen

**Renown** moved to the front over three furlongs from home and forged clear in the straight. Given a couple of reminders inside the final furlong, he idled badly in the closing stages, and had to be given another crack of the whip to keep him going. (10/1)

**Herr Trigger** moved right up to the leader half a mile from home. Ridden along over a quarter of a mile out as the winner began to assert, he stayed on but was unable to peg back that rival. Winner of three races on turf last year, this was a nice introduction after an absence of seven months, and an early success on grass could well be on the cards if the ground is fast. (9/2)

**Golden Touch (USA)** took a very keen hold in the early stages. Picking up ground over a quarter of a mile out, he stayed on, but was unable to get to the winner in time. (7/2)

**Komreyev Dancer** was out with the washing until staying on from below the distance. (13/2: 5/1-10/1)

**Wild Palm**, off the course for six months, moved up half a mile from home, but had shot his bolt turning into the straight. (7/2)

**Mr Nevermind (IRE)**, held up at the back of the field, made a brief effort over three furlongs from home but it came to little. A return to seven furlongs or a mile in claimer company is required. (13/2: 4/1-7/1)

## 463 LINCOLNS MEAD H'CAP (0-70) (3-Y.O) (Class E)

4-35 (4-36) **1m (Equitrack)** £3,015.60 (£898.80: £428.40: £193.20) Stalls: High GOING minus 0.62 sec per fur (FST)

| Form | Horse | Dist | Pos | SP | RR | SF |
|---|---|---|---|---|---|---|
| 382* | **Lady Dignity (IRE) (64)** (PJMakin) **3-9-7** WRyan(2) (hld up: rdn over 2f out: led ins fnl f: r.o wl) | — | 1 | 4/1[3] | 73 | 30 |
| 294[6] | **Domoor (60)** (MJohnston) **3-9-3** TWilliams(3) (a.p: led over 3f out to ins fnl f: unable qckn) | 1½ | 2 | 3/1[2] | 66 | 23 |
| 376* | **Rowlandsons Charm (IRE) (57)** (GLMoore) **3-8-9v**(5) FLynch(1) (lw: reard s: led 6f out to over 3f out: hrd rdn 2f out: ev ch 1f out: one pce) | 1 | 3 | 11/2 | 61 | 18 |
| | **Sphinx Levelv (IRE) (40)** (APJarvis) **3-7-11** NAdams(5) (lw: rdn & hdwy over 2f out: one pce) | 5 | 4 | 16/1 | 34 | — |
| 281[4] | **Ben'a'vachei Boy (55)** (JDBethell) **3-8-12** MFenton(4) (hld up: rdn 3f out: sn wknd) | 5 | 5 | 7/1 | 39 | — |
| 381[2] | **Hever Golf Eagle (54)** (TJNaughton) **3-8-11** GDuffield(6) (lw: led 2f: wknd over 3f out) | 1 | 6 | 9/4[1] | 36 | — |
| 377[3] | **Tahya (USA) (54)** (CCElsey) **3-8-11** CRutter(7) (bhd fnl 3f) | 5 | 7 | 10/1 | 26 | — |
| | | | | (SP 118.6%) | **7 Rn** | |

**1m 39.82** (2.42) CSF £16.35 TOTE £5.40: £2.70 £1.60 (£7.40) OWNER Mr J. Garnsey (MARLBOROUGH) BRED Mount Coote Stud

**Lady Dignity (IRE)** chased the leaders. Mounting her challenge in the short home straight, she got on top inside the final furlong. (4/1: 3/1-9/2)

**Domoor** moved to the front over three furlongs from home. Collared inside the final furlong, his experienced rider then got in a terrible muddle with his reins, and slightly tightened up the third. However, it made little difference to the result, and the placings remained unaltered after a stewards' enquiry. (3/1)

**Rowlandsons Charm (IRE)** can be a very tricky customer but she was quite well behaved on this occasion. Soon at the head of affairs, she was collared over three furlongs from home, but still had every chance entering the last 200 yards before tapped for toe. This was a good effort considering claiming company is really her level. (11/2: 3/1-6/1)

**Sphinx Levelv (IRE)** moved up over a quarter of a mile from home but could then make no further impression. (16/1)

**Ben'a'vachei Boy** (7/1: 5/1-8/1)

**Tahya (USA)** (10/1: op 6/1)

## 464 HARE LANE LIMITED STKS (0-60) (3-Y.O+) (Class F)

5-10 (5-11) **7f (Equitrack)** £2,619.00 (£724.00: £345.00) Stalls: Low GOING minus 0.62 sec per fur (FST)

| Form | Horse | Dist | Pos | SP | RR | SF |
|---|---|---|---|---|---|---|
| 406* | **Fort Knox (IRE) (59)** (RMFlower) **5-9-8b** DBiggs(5) (hdwy 2f out: led ins fnl f: r.o wl) | — | 1 | 100/30[2] | 72 | 36 |
| | **Again Together (60)** (GLMoore) **3-7-11**(5) FLynch(3) (led: hrd rdn over 1f out: hdd ins fnl f: unable qckn) | 3 | 2 | 5/1 | 61 | 9 |
| 418* | **So Intrepid (IRE) (64)** (JMBradley) **6-9-5**(3) SDrowne(2) (lw: a.p: rdn over 2f out: wknd over 1f out) | 6 | 3 | 9/4[1] | 51 | 15 |
| 337[5] | **Thorniwama (32)** (JJBridger) **5-8-12b**(5) ADaly(4) (outpcd: hdwy fnl f: r.o wl) | nk | 4 | 66/1 | 46 | 10 |
| 363[7] | **Barbason (58)** (AMoore) **4-9-8** CandyMorris(7) (b.hind: lw: nvr nr to chal) | s.h | 5 | 10/1 | 51 | 15 |
| | **Morning Surprise (58)** (APJarvis) **3-8-2** JTate(8) (dwlt: hdwy over 3f out: wknd wl over 1f out) | nk | 6 | 10/1 | 46 | — |
| 403[5] | **Society Girl (61)** (CWThornton) **3-8-2** GDuffield(6) (lost pl over 4f out: rallied 3f out: wknd 2f out) | 3 | 7 | 9/2[3] | 39 | — |
| 362[6] | **Distant Dynasty (49)** (BAPearce) **6-9-6** WHollick(1) (b.hind: plld hrd: prom 4f) | 5 | 8 | 33/1 | 30 | — |
| | | | | (SP 111.3%) | **8 Rn** | |

**1m 25.57** (1.57) CSF £18.42 TOTE £4.60: £1.50 £1.50 £1.50 (£26.40) OWNER Miss C. Markowiak (JEVINGTON) BRED Leo Collins

WEIGHT FOR AGE 3yo-15lb

**Fort Knox (IRE)** began a forward move turning for home and came storming through to grab the initiative inside the final furlong. (100/30)

**Again Together**, off the course for five and a half months, attempted to make all the running. Collared inside the final furlong, she failed to find another gear. (5/1: op 3/1)

**So Intrepid (IRE)** found this trip beyond him. Always close up, he had run out of gas approaching the final furlong. A return to six furlongs is required. (9/4: op 6/4)

**Thorniwama**, last of all approaching the final furlong, put in quite a late flourish and only just failed to take third prize. (66/1)

**Barbason** (10/1: 7/1-12/1)

**Morning Surprise** (10/1: 6/1-12/1)

T/Plpt: £27.60 (382.36 Tckts). T/Qdpt: £13.90 (62.9 Tckts) AK

# FOLKESTONE (R-H) (Good to soft)

## Monday March 25th

WEATHER: overcast

## 465 HEADCORN MAIDEN AUCTION STKS (2-Y.O F) (Class F)

1-50 (1-55) **5f** £2,381.00 (£656.00: £311.00) Stalls: Low GOING: 0.75 sec per fur (S)

| | Horse | Dist | Pos | SP | RR | SF |
|---|---|---|---|---|---|---|
| | **Jennelle** (CADwyer) **2-7-13** JQuinn(9) (neat: a.p: led over 2f out: clr over 1f out: r.o wl) | — | 1 | 5/2[1] | 72 | — |
| | **Swift Refusal** (MJHaynes) **2-8-0** CRutter(7) (unf: rdn over 2f out: hdwy over 1f out: r.o one pce) | 6 | 2 | 11/4[2] | 54 | — |
| | **Caviar And Candy** (DJSCosgrove) **2-7-12**(5)ow4 FLynch(3) (small: led over 2f: one pce) | ¾ | 3 | 25/1 | 54 | — |
| | **Molly Music** (GGMargarson) **2-7-10**(5) MBaird(4) (neat: bkwd: a.p: ev ch 2f out: wknd fnl f) | 1½ | 4 | 25/1 | 48 | — |
| | **Summer Risotto** (DJSffrenchDavis) **2-7-8**(5) CAdamson(5) (neat: a.p: rdn over 2f out: sn wknd) | ½ | 5 | 25/1 | 44 | — |
| | **Face It** (WGMTurner) **2-7-10**(5)ow3 ADaly(11) (neat: a.p: hrd rdn over 2f out: sn wknd) | 5 | 6 | 100/30[3] | 30 | — |
| | **Dozen Roses** (TMJones) **2-7-13**(3)ow3 AWhelan(8) (neat: bkwd: a bhd) | 2 | 7 | 20/1 | 25 | — |
| | **Burberry Quest** (BRMillman) **2-7-12** JFanning(6) (small: a.p: rdn over 2f out: sn wknd) | 4 | 8 | 25/1 | 8 | — |
| | **Anatomic** (MRChannon) **2-7-12** AGorman(10) (small: bhd fnl 3f: t.o: sddle slipped) | dist | 9 | 11/2 | — | — |
| | ***Sylvania Lights*** (WRMuir) **2-7-12**(5) MHenry(2) (Withdrawn not under Starter's orders: uns rdr & bolted bef s) | | W | 12/1 | — | — |

(SP 121.5%) **9 Rn**

**66.7 secs** (9.10) CSF £8.71 TOTE £2.40: £1.10 £1.40 £4.80 (£4.70) Trio £107.90 OWNER Mrs J. A. Cornwell (NEWMARKET) BRED Mrs A. J. Owen

**Jennelle** hardly took the eye in the paddock. Nevertheless, there was plenty of market confidence behind her. Easing her way to the front at halfway, she stormed clear below the distance to win in decisive style. (5/2)

**Swift Refusal**, a weak-looking filly, nevertheless looked fit. Pumped along from halfway, she stayed on in the last furlong and a half but never looked like getting within a stone's throw of the winner. (11/4: op 5/1)

**Caviar And Candy** is only small. In front to halfway, she could then only keep on in her own time. (25/1)

**Molly Music** is not very big and looked far from fit. Nevertheless, she raced up with the pace and had every chance two furlongs from home before tiring inside the last 200 yards. (25/1)

**Summer Risotto**, a neatly-made filly, was always close up but, rousted along from halfway, was soon in trouble. (25/1)

**Face It** is not very big but certainly had a bit more strength than her rivals. Close up on the outside of the field, she had given her all soon after halfway. (100/30: 9/4-7/2)

**Anatomic** (11/2: 7/4-6/1)

**Sylvania Lights** (12/1: op 4/1)

## 466 ROCHESTER H'CAP (0-70) (3-Y.O+) (Class E)

2-20 (2-21) **5f** £3,343.20 (£999.60: £478.80: £218.40) Stalls: Low GOING: 0.75 sec per fur (S)

| | Horse | Dist | Pos | SP | RR | SF |
|---|---|---|---|---|---|---|
| | **Lloc (49)** (CADwyer) **4-8-4**(3) JStack(16) (racd alone far side: mde all: clr over 1f out: r.o wl) | — | 1 | 10/1 | 59 | 42 |
| | **Malibu Man (59)** (SMellor) **4-9-3** TSprake(1) (lw: led stands' side: rdn over 1f out: unable qckn) | 5 | 2 | 10/1 | 53 | 36 |
| 180[7] | **Bonny Melody (45)** (PDEvans) **5-7-12**(5)ow6 AmandaSanders(2) (a.p: rdn over 1f out: one pce) | ¾ | 3 | 33/1 | 37 | 14 |
| | **Sonderise (45)** (NTinkler) **7-8-3** GCarter(6) (rdn over 2f out: hdwy over 1f out: r.o) | 1¼ | 4 | 13/2[3] | 33 | 16 |
| 178[9] | **Rockcracker (IRE) (58)** (GGMargarson) **4-9-2** PRobinson(9) (lw: rdn over 2f out: hdwy over 1f out: one pce) | 1¾ | 5 | 20/1 | 40 | 23 |
| | **Domicksky (53)** (MRChannon) **8-8-4**(7) DSweeney(3) (b.nr hind: bit bkwd: hld up: rdn over 2f out: one pce) | nk | 6 | 10/1 | 34 | 17 |
| | **Followmegirls (50)** (MrsALMKing) **7-8-8b** AGarth(11) (bit bkwd: rdn & hdwy 2f out: one pce) | hd | 7 | 11/2[2] | 31 | 14 |
| 388[5] | **Nomadic Dancer (IRE) (43)** (MSSaunders) **4-8-1** NAdams(8) (s.s: nvr nrr) | 1¾ | 8 | 33/1 | 18 | 1 |
| | **Tauber (45)** (PatMitchell) **12-8-3**ow3 MFenton(4) (bit bkwd: prom 3f) | 4 | 9 | 33/1 | 7 | — |
| | **Wardara (67)** (CADwyer) **4-9-11v** MWigham(7) (s.s: a bhd) | 5 | 10 | 16/1 | 13 | — |
| | **Thai Morning (68)** (PWHarris) **3-9-0** GHind(14) (bit bkwd: hld up: rdn over 2f out: sn wknd) | nk | 11 | 9/2[1] | 14 | — |
| 231[3] | **Halbert (65)** (PBurgoyne) **7-9-6v**(3) DRMcCabe(15) (a bhd) | 5 | 12 | 12/1 | — | — |
| 418[4] | **Leigh Crofter (68)** (PDCundell) **7-9-12b** SWhitworth(5) (a bhd) | hd | 13 | 10/1 | — | — |
| | **La Belle Dominique (55)** (SGKnight) **4-8-13** VSlattery(10) (prom 3f) | ¾ | 14 | 20/1 | — | — |
| 342[8] | **Secret Miss (55)** (APJones) **4-8-13** JQuinn(12) (bhd fnl 2f) | nk | 15 | 20/1 | — | — |
| | **Mazzarello (IRE) (41)** (RCurtis) **6-7-13** JFEgan(13) (bhd fnl 2f) | 1¾ | 16 | 20/1 | — | — |

(SP 124.7%) **16 Rn**

**64.2 secs** (6.60) CSF £99.17 CT £2,983.76 TOTE £14.90: £4.70 £2.90 £8.50 £1.30 (£93.70) Trio £348.00; £196.08 to Huntingdon 26/3/96. OWNER Mrs Christine Rawson (NEWMARKET) BRED Summertree Stud

WEIGHT FOR AGE 3yo-12lb

**Lloc** was given a very enterprising ride. Making a bee-line for the far side in search of the better ground, she certainly found it and, making all the running, had a useful advantage below the distance. (10/1: 6/1-11/1)

**Malibu Man**, looking in good shape for this reappearance, made it all on the stands' side but was unable to catch the winner racing on the opposite side of the track. (10/1: 8/1-12/1)

**Bonny Melody** failed to quicken in the final quarter-mile. (33/1)

**Sonderise**, making the long journey down from North Yorkshire, ran on in the last furlong and a half, only to find it all over bar the shouting. He has not won for nearly three years. (13/2)

**Rockcracker (IRE)** made a forward move below the distance but could then make no further impression. (20/1)

**Domicksky**, not looking fully wound up for this reappearance, is on a long losing run and never looked like quickening up in the last two furlongs. (10/1: 6/1-12/1)

**Leigh Crofter** (10/1: op 6/1)

## 467 SHORNECLIFFE MEDIAN AUCTION MAIDEN STKS (3-Y.O) (Class F)

2-50 (2-52) **6f** £2,381.00 (£656.00: £311.00) Stalls: Low GOING: 0.75 sec per fur (S)

| | Horse | Dist | Pos | SP | RR | SF |
|---|---|---|---|---|---|---|
| | **Beldray Park (IRE) (56)** (MrsALMKing) **3-9-0** JQuinn(13) (hld up: rdn over 2f out: led ins fnl f: r.o wl) | — | 1 | 25/1 | 77 | 47 |
| | **Blessed Spirit** (CFWall) **3-8-9** WWoods(8) (hld up: rdn over 2f out: r.o) | ¾ | 2 | 5/1[2] | 70 | 40 |
| | **Pride of Brixton** (GLewis) **3-9-0** SWhitworth(2) (racd stands' side: led: hrd rdn over 1f out: hdd ins fnl f: unable qckn) | 1¾ | 3 | 13/8[1] | 70 | 40 |
| 408[2] | **Young Mazaad (IRE)** (DCO'Brien) **3-9-0** GBardwell(10) (a.p: rdn over 2f out: one pce) | 1 | 4 | 14/1 | 68 | 38 |

**Mrs McBadger (69)** (BSmart) **3-8-9** RCochrane(7) (a.p: rdn over 2f out: wknd over 1f out) ....13 **5** 13/2 28 —
**Trianna** (LordHuntingdon) **3-8-9** DHarrison(9) (unf: outpcd: nvr nrr) ....3½ **6** 10/1 19 —
**Realms of Glory (IRE)** (PhilipMitchell) **3-9-0** AClark(12) (bit bkwd: outpcd: nvr nrr) ....1¾ **7** 10/1 19 —
376[6] **Old Gold N Tan** (JRPoulton) **3-8-11(3)** PMcCabe(11) (a mid div) ....hd **8** 50/1 19 —
352[3] **Lancashire Legend (75)** (SDow) **3-9-0** TQuinn(4) (racd stands' side: bhd fnl 2f) ....3½ **9** 14/1 9 —
**Will Do** (MartynMeade) **3-9-0** VSlattery(5) (w'like: bit bkwd: racd stands' side: a bhd) ....6 **10** 16/1 — —
**Mister Woodstick (IRE)** (MAJarvis) **3-9-0** PRobinson(3) (bkwd: racd stands' side: a bhd) ....2 **11** 12/1 — —
**Peace House (IRE)** (JLSpearing) **3-8-6(3)** SDrowne(1) (w'like: bit bkwd: racd stands' side: a bhd) ....7 **12** 50/1 — —
**Sharp Stock** (BJMeehan) **3-9-0** RHughes(14) (spd 4f) ....½ **13** 6/1[3] — —
**Mindrace (71)** (KTIvory) **3-9-0** DBiggs(6) (bit bkwd: bhd fnl 3f) ....1¾ **14** 14/1 — —
(SP 141.9%) **14 Rn**

**1m 18.3** (8.10) CSF £156.88 TOTE £55.10: £11.40 £2.30 £1.20 (£198.90) Trio £132.80 OWNER Stainless Threaded Fasteners Ltd (STRATFORD-UPON-AVON) BRED A. J. Poulton (Epping) Ltd

OFFICIAL EXPLANATION **Sharp Stock: could not handle the ground or undulating track.**

**Beldray Park (IRE)** tacked over to the far side in search of the better ground. Asked for his effort soon after halfway, he eventually managed to get on top on the far side approaching the final furlong and, with overall control inside the last 100 yards, kept on well. (25/1)

**Blessed Spirit**, racing on the far side, chased the leaders. Moving to the front a quarter of a mile out but not with overall control, she was collared by the winner on that side approaching the final furlong, but kept on well to the line. (5/1: 4/1-6/1)

**Pride of Brixton**, racing right up the stands' rail, was one of only five who decided to stay on that side of the track. Setting the pace, he came under pressure approaching the final furlong and had little left in the locker when collared by the winner, who was racing on the opposite side of the track. He should soon find a race. (13/8)

**Young Mazaad (IRE)**, always close up on the far side, failed to find another gear in the last two furlongs. (14/1)

**Mrs McBadger**, in the firing-line on the far side, had given her all below the distance. (13/2)

**Trianna**, a narrow, light-framed filly, was completely taken off her feet until staying on past beaten horses in the closing stages. (10/1: 6/1-12/1)

**Realms of Glory (IRE)** (10/1: 5/1-12/1)

**Lancashire Legend** (14/1: op 8/1)

**Sharp Stock** (6/1: op 3/1)

## 468 ALDINGTON RATING RELATED MAIDEN STKS (0-65) (3-Y.O) (Class F)

3-20 (3-21) **6f 189y** £2,381.00 (£656.00: £311.00) Stalls: Low GOING: 0.75 sec per fur (S)

SP RR SF

382[4] **Green Gem (BEL) (57)** (SCWilliams) **3-8-11** KDarley(9) (a.p: rdn over 3f out: led 1f out: r.o wl) ....— **1** 7/1 71 16
**Basood (USA) (65)** (EALDunlop) **3-8-11** JTate(8) (rdn 3f out: hdwy over 1f out: r.o ins fnl f) ....2½ **2** 11/2 65 10
**Nakhal (65)** (DJGMurraySmith) **3-9-0** JWeaver(1) (chsd ldr: led over 2f out to 1f out: unable qckn) ....2½ **3** 100/30[2] 62 7
**Get Tough (57)** (SDow) **3-8-9(5)** ADaly(4) (led over 4f: one pce) ....nk **4** 11/1 62 7
**Ivory's Grab Hire (54)** (KTIvory) **3-8-7(7)** CScally(3) (no hdwy fnl 2f) ....3½ **5** 16/1 54 —
**May Queen Megan (59)** (MrsALMKing) **3-8-11** AGarth(7) (bit bkwd: hdwy & hung bdly lft over 1f out: nt rcvr) ....hd **6** 9/2[3] 50 —
329[8] **Valjess (25)** (DCO'Brien) **3-8-11** GBardwell(5) (bhd fnl 5f) ....7 **7** 33/1 34 —
**Ciserano (IRE) (58)** (MRChannon) **3-8-11** TQuinn(6) (b.nr hind: prom over 5f) ....3 **8** 3/1[1] 27 —
**Longhill Boy (63)** (BJMeehan) **3-9-0** MTebbutt(2) (bit bkwd: plld hrd: prom over 3f: t.o) ....dist **9** 16/1 — —
(SP 117.2%) **9 Rn**

**1m 33.3** (11.70) CSF £42.33 TOTE £7.40: £2.60 £2.40 £2.00 (£11.00) Trio £25.80 OWNER Mr Patrick Madelein (NEWMARKET) BRED Patrick Madelein

**Green Gem (BEL)**, never far away, was being pumped along over three furlongs from home and the signs did not look particularly good. She came through to lead a furlong out however, and proved too strong for her rivals. (7/1: 5/1-8/1)

**Basood (USA)**, a light-framed individual, was going nowhere at the back of the field three furlongs from home. She at last picked up ground below the distance but, despite running on to take second place, never looked like getting to the winner. (11/2: 4/1-6/1)

**Nakhal** moved to the front over a quarter of a mile from home but, headed entering the final furlong, failed to find another gear. (100/30)

**Get Tough** took the field along but, once collared over two furlongs out, was soon tapped for toe. (11/1)

**Ivory's Grab Hire**, who got a little warm beforehand, was making little impression on the principals in the short home straight. (16/1)

**May Queen Megan**, not looking fully wound up, was desperately trying to pick up ground when hanging badly left under pressure below the distance, which effectively ended all hopes. (9/2: 3/1-5/1)

**Ciserano (IRE)** (3/1: op 6/4)

## 469 ALKHAM H'CAP (0-70) (4-Y.O+) (Class E)

3-50 (3-52) **1m 1f 149y** £3,397.80 (£1,016.40: £487.20: £222.60) Stalls: Low GOING: 0.75 sec per fur (S)

SP RR SF

**Swinging Sixties (IRE) (60)** (GLMoore) **5-9-6** SWhitworth(3) (b.nr fore: dwlt: hdwy over 1f out: hrd rdn fnl f: led last stride) ....— **1** 6/1[1] 73 14
**Bellas Gate Boy (60)** (JPearce) **4-9-6** JMcLaughlin(8) (hdwy over 2f out: led ins fnl f: hrd rdn: hdd last stride) ....s.h **2** 25/1 73 14
66[11] **Wet Patch (IRE) (60)** (RHannon) **4-9-6** RHughes(14) (rdn over 2f out: hdwy over 1f out: r.o) ....5 **3** 6/1[1] 66 6
**Harvey White (IRE) (55)** (JPearce) **4-9-1** GBardwell(10) (a.p: led over 2f out tl ins fnl f: unable qckn) ....½ **4** 20/1 60 —
**Kelly Mac (58)** (DCO'Brien) **6-9-4** KDarley(13) (hld up: rdn over 2f out: one pce) ....2 **5** 6/1[1] 59 —
424[4] **Todd (USA) (55)** (PhilipMitchell) **5-9-1** AClark(15) (chsd ldr over 2f: rdn over 2f out: eased whn btn ins fnl f) ....8 **6** 16/1 42 —
**Warning Shot (54)** (MartynMeade) **4-9-0** JReid(7) (no hdwy fnl 3f) ....2½ **7** 14/1 38 —
**Aude la Belle (FR) (60)** (SGKnight) **8-9-6** AMcGlone(9) (bit bkwd: nvr nrr) ....1 **8** 50/1 42 —
**Noeprob (USA) (45)** (RJHodges) **6-8-2(3)ow2** SDrowne(5) (hdwy over 2f out: wknd over 1f out) ....3 **9** 12/1 32 —
384[6] **Our Tom (58)** (JWharton) **4-9-4** JQuinn(4) (lw: bhd fnl 3f) ....6 **10** 10/1[3] 26 —
424* **Explosive Power (68)** (GCBravery) **5-9-11(3)** DRMcCabe(12) (led 7f: eased whn btn over 1f out) ....7 **11** 6/1[1] 23 —
**Pistol (IRE) (61)** (CAHorgan) **6-9-7** JWeaver(11) (b.hind: a bhd) ....8 **12** 8/1[2] 3 —
424[11] **Brown Eyed Girl (54)** (BJMeehan) **4-9-0** MTebbutt(2) (prom 6f) ....2 **13** 20/1 — —
411[9] **Ketabi (USA) (61)** (RAkehurst) **5-9-7** TQuinn(6) (bhd fnl 3f) ....¾ **14** 11/1 — —
366[6] **Canary Falcon (58)** (JohnBerry) **5-9-4** VSmith(1) (b: lw: a bhd) ....3 **15** 25/1 — —
(SP 125.1%) **15 Rn**

**2m 15.7** (18.00) CSF £130.55 CT £874.19 TOTE £10.30: £2.70 £9.80 £3.00 (£129.90) Trio £302.00; £106.34 to Huntingdon 26/3/96. OWNER Mr K. Higson (EPSOM) BRED Ron Con Ltd and Swettenham Stud

**Swinging Sixties (IRE)**, still out with the washing running down the hill, made significant strides in the straight. Throwing down a determined challenge, he managed to get up right on the line to the amazement of many onlookers. (6/1)
**Bellas Gate Boy**, looking big and well for this reappearance, made smooth headway from the back of the field over a quarter of a mile from home. Coming through to lead just inside the final furlong, he did little wrong and was caught right on the line. (25/1)
**Wet Patch (IRE)**, held up at the back of the field, at last began to pick up ground below the distance and ran on to snatch third prize without troubling the front two. (6/1)
**Harvey White (IRE)** went on over quarter of a mile from home but, collared inside the final furlong, was swamped for speed. (20/1)
**Kelly Mac**, the winner of a handicap hurdle at Windsor in January, chased the leaders but failed to quicken in the straight. (6/1)
**Todd (USA)**, a leading light from the off, was being bustled along entering the straight but, when held inside the final furlong, was eased down. (16/1)
**Our Tom** (10/1: 8/1-12/1)
**Ketabi (USA)** (11/1: 8/1-12/1)

## 470 LEVY BOARD H'CAP (0-70) (3-Y.O+) (Class E)

4-20 (4-22) **6f 189y** £3,288.60 (£982.80: £470.40: £214.20) Stalls: Low GOING: 0.75 sec per fur (S)

| | | | | SP | RR | SF |
|---|---|---|---|---|---|---|
| 416[3] | **Sea Spouse (41)** (MBlanshard) **5-7-13** NAdams(2) (lw: mde all: rdn over 1f out: hung lft fnl f: all out) | — | **1** | 6/1[2] | 51 | 12 |
| | **Pride of Kashmir (56)** (PWHarris) **3-7-13** FNorton(6) (a.p: rdn over 2f out: ev ch ins fnl f: r.o) | hd | **2** | 13/2[3] | 67 | 12 |
| | **Zatopek (61)** (JCullinan) **4-9-5** TQuinn(4) (b: rdn over 2f out: hdwy over 1f out: r.o wl ins fnl f) | ½ | **3** | 16/1 | 70 | 31 |
| | **Battleship Bruce (64)** (NACallaghan) **4-9-8** JReid(15) (b.hind: hdwy 5f out: rdn over 2f out: r.o) | nk | **4** | 13/2[3] | 72 | 33 |
| 308[6] | **Halliard (55)** (TMJones) **5-8-13** AMcGlone(3) (a.p: rdn over 2f out: r.o) | ½ | **5** | 14/1 | 62 | 23 |
| | **Almapa (50)** (RJHodges) **4-8-5**(3) SDrowne(9) (rdn over 2f out: hdwy over 1f out: nvr nrr) | 1¾ | **6** | 25/1 | 53 | 14 |
| | **Sharp 'n' Shady (57)** (CFWall) **3-8-0**[ow3] WLord(7) (bit bkwd: nvr plcd to chal) | 1¼ | **7** | 16/1 | 58 | — |
| 412[10] | **Palacegate Gold (IRE) (38)** (RJHodges) **7-7-10b** NCarlisle(8) (a.p: rdn over 2f out: wknd fnl f) | ½ | **8** | 16/1 | 37 | — |
| | **Gee Gee Tee (55)** (JAkehurst) **3-7-12** DaleGibson(1) (b: nvr nrr) | 6 | **9** | 33/1 | 41 | — |
| 387[6] | **Speedy Snaps Pride (44)** (PDCundell) **4-8-2** JQuinn(11) (nt clr run on ins over 2f out: nvr nrr) | 2 | **10** | 25/1 | 24 | — |
| | **Orthorhombus (55)** (DJSCosgrove) **7-8-13b** MWigham(13) (s.i.s: a bhd) | 7 | **11** | 10/1 | 19 | — |
| 409[5] | **Rocky Two (48)** (PHowling) **5-8-6** RCochrane(5) (a bhd) | 2½ | **12** | 20/1 | 6 | — |
| | **Secret Pleasure (IRE) (69)** (RHannon) **3-8-7**(5) DaneO'Neill(14) (bhd fnl 2f) | 4 | **13** | 12/1 | 18 | — |
| 384[7] | **Reverand Thickness (70)** (SCWilliams) **5-10-0b** RHughes(12) (hld up: rdn over 2f out: sn wknd) | 1¼ | **14** | 5/1[1] | 16 | — |
| | **Titanium Honda (IRE) (38)** (DCO'Brien) **5-7-10** GBardwell(10) (b: bit bkwd: bhd fnl 3f) | 9 | **15** | 33/1 | — | — |
| 363[5] | **Soaking (62)** (PBurgoyne) **6-9-3**(3) DRMcCabe(16) (s.i.s: a bhd) | 16 | **16** | 6/1[2] | — | — |

(SP 131.3%) **16 Rn**

**1m 32.7** (11.10) CSF £44.92 CT £412.20 TOTE £7.10: £1.40 £1.60 £2.80 £2.60 (£21.70) Trio £284.00 OWNER Seven Seas Racing (UPPER LAMBOURN) BRED Cheveley Park Stud Ltd
LONG HANDICAP Titanium Honda (IRE) 6-13
WEIGHT FOR AGE 3yo-15lb
**OFFICIAL EXPLANATION Sharp 'n' Shady: the trainer reported that the filly is stuffy and may have needed the race, and that she had just run through beaten horses, despite gurgling.**
**Sea Spouse** made all the running but, tying up and drifting left in the final furlong, held on with not an ounce to spare. (6/1: op 4/1)
**Pride of Kashmir**, always close up, threw down a determined challenge and would probably have prevailed in a few more strides. (13/2)
**Zatopek**, who has changed stables since last year, really found his stride from below the distance. Despite running on strongly inside the final furlong, he found the line always coming just a little bit too soon. (16/1)
**Battleship Bruce**, fit from hurdling, moved up at the top of the hill. Rousted along turning into the straight, he kept on well but just failed to get there. (13/2)
**Halliard**, always close up, kept on in the straight to finish close up in fifth place. (14/1)
**Almapa** stayed on in the last furlong and a half to be nearest at the line. (25/1)
**Sharp 'n' Shady** was given an extremely quiet ride. She will come on for this and looks one to keep an eye on. (16/1)
**Orthorhombus** (10/1: 7/1-11/1)

## 471 KINGSNORTH H'CAP (0-70) (3-Y.O) (Class E)

4-50 (4-51) **1m 4f** £3,370.50 (£1,008.00: £483.00: £220.50) Stalls: Low GOING: 0.75 sec per fur (S)

| | | | | SP | RR | SF |
|---|---|---|---|---|---|---|
| | **Siege Perilous (IRE) (50)** (SCWilliams) **3-8-1** JTate(1) (hdwy on ins over 2f out: nt clr run & swtchd lft over 1f out: led ins fnl f: r.o wl) | — | **1** | 14/1 | 58 | — |
| | **Minnisam (60)** (JLDunlop) **3-8-11** TQuinn(15) (lw: a.p: led over 2f out tl ins fnl f: unable qckn) | 1½ | **2** | 7/1 | 66 | 6 |
| 385[6] | **Montecristo (68)** (RGuest) **3-9-0**(5) FLynch(10) (gd hdwy over 4f out: led 3f out tl over 2f out: ev ch over 1f out: one pce) | 5 | **3** | 8/1 | 67 | 7 |
| | **Atlantic Mist (55)** (BRMillman) **3-8-3**(3) SDrowne(4) (rdn & hdwy over 1f out: one pce) | 6 | **4** | 16/1 | 46 | — |
| 381[7] | **Autobabble (IRE) (58)** (RHannon) **3-8-9b**[1] JReid(8) (nvr nr to chal) | nk | **5** | 9/1 | 49 | — |
| | **Jump The Lights (65)** (SPCWoods) **3-9-2** WWoods(16) (hld up: rdn over 3f out: wknd wl over 1f out) | 3 | **6** | 12/1 | 52 | — |
| 322a[8] | **Asking For Kings (IRE) (68)** (SDow) **3-9-0**(5) ADaly(17) (lw: led 5f: led 5f out to 3f out: sn wknd) | 3½ | **7** | 9/1 | 50 | — |
| 348[7] | **Influence Pedler (54)** (CEBrittain) **3-8-5** KDarley(11) (prom over 9f) | 3 | **8** | 14/1 | 32 | — |
| 269[3] | **Highlights (55)** (DMorris) **3-8-6**[ow2] RCochrane(13) (hld up: rdn over 5f out: wknd over 2f out) | ½ | **9** | 6/1[3] | 33 | — |
| 415[6] | **Rivercare (IRE) (60)** (MJPolglase) **3-8-11** MTebbutt(2) (nvr nrr) | nk | **10** | 25/1 | 37 | — |
| 385[*] | **Nikita's Star (IRE) (70)** (DJGMurraySmith) **3-9-7** JWeaver(6) (a mid div) | 6 | **11** | 5/1[2] | 39 | — |
| 364[8] | **Native Song (45)** (MJHaynes) **3-7-5b**[1](5) MBaird(14) (chsd ldr: led 7f out to 5f out: wknd over 2f out) | 5 | **12** | 20/1 | 8 | — |
| 56[10] | **Kissing Gate (USA) (59)** (RCharlton) **3-8-10** SSanders(12) (hld up: rdn 3f out: sn wknd) | 1 | **13** | 7/2[1] | 20 | — |
| 361[4] | **Tartan Express (IRE) (45)** (BAPearce) **3-7-10** GBardwell(5) (bhd fnl 9f) | 15 | **14** | 33/1 | — | — |
| | **Forliando (47)** (MSSaunders) **3-7-12** FNorton(3) (bit bkwd: bhd fnl 4f) | s.h | **15** | 33/1 | — | — |
| | **Hadadabble (45)** (PatMitchell) **3-7-10** JQuinn(7) (a bhd) | 2 | **16** | 33/1 | — | — |
| | **Shamand (USA) (50)** (BJMeehan) **3-8-1** JFEgan(9) (bhd fnl 4f) | 1½ | **17** | 25/1 | — | — |

(SP 145.0%) **17 Rn**

**2m 54.0** (22.80) CSF £117.13 CT £802.88 TOTE £25.70: £4.20 £1.80 £2.70 £2.90 (£311.80) Trio £781.30 OWNER Mr S. Demanuele (NEWMARKET) BRED Miss Honora Corridan
LONG HANDICAP Tartan Express (IRE) 6-13 Hadadabble 7-9 Native Song 7-4
**OFFICIAL EXPLANATION Nikita's Star (IRE): was unsuited by the ground.**
**Siege Perilous (IRE)** began to pick up ground along the inside rail turning for home. Having to switch left after becoming the meat in the sandwich below the distance, he came through to lead inside the final furlong, and quickly had it sewn up. (14/1)

**Minnisam** went to the front over a quarter of a mile from home but, when passed by the winner inside the final furlong, it was all over. (7/1: 9/2-8/1)
**Montecristo** made giant strides on the outside of the field beginning the downhill run, and poked a nostril in front three furlongs out. Soon collared, he still had every chance below the distance, before tapped for toe. (8/1: op 5/1)
**Atlantic Mist**, rousted along to pick up ground below the distance, could then make no further impression. (16/1)
**Autobabble (IRE)** struggled on but never looked like posing a threat. (9/1: 6/1-10/1)
**Jump The Lights** chased the leaders until calling it a day early in the straight. (12/1)
**Highlights** (6/1: 4/1-13/2)
**Kissing Gate (USA)** (7/2: op 6/1)

T/Jkpt: Not won; £124,991.56 to Huntingdon 26/3/96. T/Plpt: £299.60 (70.25 Tckts). T/Qdpt: £31.30 (32.86 Tckts). AK

# NEWCASTLE (L-H) (Good to soft, Soft st)

## Tuesday March 26th

Race 1: hand-timed
WEATHER: overcast WIND: fresh across

## 472 HOLYSTONE MAIDEN STKS (3-Y.O+) (Class D)

2-30 (2-30) **1m** £3,468.75 (£1,050.00: £512.50: £243.75) Stalls: Low GOING: 0.96 sec per fur (S)

| Horse | Dist | Pos | SP | RR | SF |
|---|---|---|---|---|---|
| **Yeast (78)** (WJHaggas) **4-9-12** RCochrane(7) (lw: mde all: all out) | — | 1 | 5/2[2] | 89 | 30 |
| **Wixim (USA)** (RCharlton) **3-8-9** KDarley(5) (w'like: bit bkwd: trckd ldrs: effrt & ev ch 2f out: styd on towards fin) | ¾ | 2 | 8/15[1] | 88+ | 12 |
| **Green Bopper (USA)** (MBell) **3-8-9** MFenton(2) (lw: a.p: effrt over 3f out: outpcd fnl 2f) | 6 | 3 | 11/2[3] | 76 | — |
| **Batoutoftheblue** (WWHaigh) **3-8-9** DaleGibson(1) (sn pushed along & bhd: styd on fnl 3f: n.d) | 12 | 4 | 50/1 | 52 | — |
| **Known Secret (USA)** (MrsJRRamsden) **3-8-9** KFallon(3) (bit bkwd: stdd s: n.d) | 30 | 5 | 14/1 | — | — |
| **Sheraz (IRE) (75)** (NTinkler) **4-9-12** GCarter(4) (bit bkwd: cl up 3f: sn bhd) | 4 | 6 | 12/1 | — | — |
| **Kashana (IRE)** (WStorey) **4-9-7** JFanning(6) (chsd ldrs tl wknd wl over 3f out) | 13 | 7 | 25/1 | — | — |

(SP 129.3%) **7 Rn**

**1m 54.6** (15.60) CSF £4.78 TOTE £3.30: £1.70 £1.20 (£1.80) OWNER Mr B. Haggas (NEWMARKET) BRED R. T. and Mrs Watson
WEIGHT FOR AGE 3yo-17lb

**Yeast** confirmed his promise of last season, winning here in determined fashion in this very testing ground. (5/2)
**Wixim (USA)** looked as though he would be all the better for this but did try extremely hard and was gradually getting there. His turn should not be long in coming and he will stay further. (8/15)
**Green Bopper (USA)** was turned out in good trim and ran quite well, but found the first two far too good in the last two furlongs. He was not given too hard a time. (11/2)
**Batoutoftheblue** was never on the bridle at any stage but he was keeping on at the finish, suggesting that further should bring improvement. (50/1)
**Known Secret (USA)** needed this and, after taking quite a hold early on, was done with by the home turn. (14/1)

## 473 KILLINGWORTH (S) STKS (3-Y.O) (Class G)

3-05 (3-06) **6f** £2,274.00 (£639.00: £312.00) Stalls: High GOING: 0.96 sec per fur (S)

| | Horse | Dist | Pos | SP | RR | SF |
|---|---|---|---|---|---|---|
| | **Miletrian Refurb (IRE) (60)** (MRChannon) **3-9-0** RHughes(12) (mde all: styd on wl fnl 2f) | — | 1 | 6/4[1] | 68 | 38 |
| | **Polar Refrain (53)** (MrsJRRamsden) **3-8-9** KFallon(4) (lw: pushed along & bhd fr ½-wy: styd on wl fnl 2f: nrst fin) | 2½ | 2 | 8/1[3] | 56 | 26 |
| | **Lucky Bea (45)** (MWEasterby) **3-9-0**(3)ow3 OPears(2) (bit bkwd: chsd ldrs: effrt 2f out: wknd fnl f) | 1 | 3 | 20/1 | 62 | 29 |
| 421[7] | **Chilibang Bang (61)** (JBerry) **3-8-8**(5) PRoberts(6) (cl up tl wknd appr fnl f) | 2½ | 4 | 3/1[2] | 51 | 21 |
| | **Rattle (52)** (JJO'Neill) **3-9-0** SDWilliams(7) (outpcd & bhd tl styd on fnl 2f: n.d) | 2 | 5 | 10/1 | 47 | 17 |
| | **Hobbs Choice (47)** (GMMoore) **3-8-9** DaleGibson(3) (lw: sn pushed along: a in tch: no imp fr ½-wy) | s.h | 6 | 20/1 | 42 | 12 |
| | **Aye Ready** (MissLAPerratt) **3-9-0** GDuffield(9) (s.i.s: hdwy on bit to jn wnr ½-wy: hung lft & sn wknd) | 15 | 7 | 25/1 | 7 | — |
| | **Pearls of Thought (IRE) (55)** (JSHaldane) **3-8-9** KDarley(10) (early spd: sn bhd) | ½ | 8 | 33/1 | — | — |
| | **Tiny Astro** (TDEasterby) **3-9-0** MBirch(11) (outpcd fr ½-wy) | nk | 9 | 20/1 | 4 | — |
| | **Ragtime Cowgirl** (CWThornton) **3-8-9** DeanMcKeown(1) (unf: bkwd: dwlt: a bhd) | 1¼ | 10 | 12/1 | — | — |
| | **Darerock (35)** (MDods) **3-9-0** LCharnock(5) (sn outpcd & bhd) | 9 | 11 | 25/1 | — | — |
| | **Supreme Scholar** (BWMurray) **3-8-4b**1(5) GParkin(8) (b.off hind: sn drvn along: wl bhd fr ½-wy) | 14 | 12 | 50/1 | — | — |

(SP 119.8%) **12 Rn**

**1m 21.6** (10.10) CSF £13.77 TOTE £2.60: £1.20 £2.00 £2.90 (£7.60) Trio £46.50 OWNER Miletrian Plc (UPPER LAMBOURN) BRED Rosebank Stud
No bid; Polar Refrain clmd BParker £6,000

**Miletrian Refurb (IRE)**, like all runners from this yard, was very fit. Leaving nothing to chance, he quickened the pace from halfway and the race was always his. (6/4)
**Polar Refrain** took the eye, responding to pressure in the latter half of the race to finish best of all, suggesting that longer trips will see a deal better. (8/1: op 4/1)
**Lucky Bea** had never run on ground as soft as this before and put up a good performance until blowing up approaching the last furlong. (20/1)
**Chilibang Bang** has been doing well on the All-Weather, but she has not got much of an engine and ran out of petrol approaching the final furlong. (3/1)
**Rattle** failed to impress on looks but was noted picking up ground when the race was over. (10/1)
**Hobbs Choice** looked particularly well but was short of speed and was only holding her position throughout. Further might help. (20/1)
**Aye Ready** has bags of speed but just wants to hang left and there would seem to be plenty of improvement when he can be straightened out. (25/1)
**Ragtime Cowgirl** (12/1: op 6/1)

## 474 EARSDON H'CAP (0-70) (4-Y.O+) (Class E)

3-35 (3-35) **2m 19y** £2,918.00 (£884.00: £432.00: £206.00) Stalls: High GOING: 0.96 sec per fur (S)

| | Horse | Dist | Pos | SP | RR | SF |
|---|---|---|---|---|---|---|
| 365[7] | **Arian Spirit (IRE) (37)** (JLEyre) **5-8-0** LCharnock(6) (sn prom: led wl over 2f out: sn drvn clr: eased towards fin) | — | 1 | 8/1 | 52 | 7 |

Top Prize (38) (MBrittain) 8-8-1v GBardwell(7) (a chsng ldrs: kpt on one pce fnl 3f) ....2 **2** 14/1 51 6
**Hotspur Street (60)** (MWEasterby) **4-9-4** JWeaver(5) (hdwy over 3f out: styd on: nvr able to chal)....2 **3** 7/1[3] 71 21
**White Willow (65)** (MrsMReveley) **7-10-0** KDarley(2) (led tl hdd wl over 2f out: one pce)....3 **4** 7/1[3] 73 28
*48[5]* **Sudden Spin (44)** (JNorton) **6-8-7**ow2 KFallon(8) (bhd tl styd on fnl 3f: nrst fin)....3 **5** 12/1 49 2
**Palace of Gold (39)** (LLungo) **6-8-2** JFanning(3) (effrt 4f out: no imp)....4 **6** 33/1 40 —
*398** **Selmeston (IRE) (45)** (PSFelgate) **4-8-0**(3) DWright(1) (mid div: effrt over 3f out: no imp)....13 **7** 9/1 33 —
**Dally Boy (40)** (TDEasterby) **4-7-12** JQuinn(9) (lw: cl up tl rdn & wknd over 2f out)....6 **8** 9/2[2] 22 —
*339** **Jaraab (46)** (GLewis) **5-8-9v** SWhitworth(10) (a.p: pushed along over 4f out: ev ch over 3f out: sn wknd)....1¾ **9** 11/4[1] 26 —
**Charmed Life (33)** (MrsALMKing) **7-7-5**(5) PFessey(11) (racd wd: drvn along appr st: sn btn)....s.h **10** 50/1 13 —
*429[2]* **Eulogy (FR) (64)** (KRBurke) **9-9-8**(5) RHavlin(4) (w ldrs tl rdn & fnd nil 3f out)....½ **11** 9/1 44 —
(SP 120.2%) **11 Rn**

**3m 57.16** (31.66) CSF £101.79 CT £757.22 TOTE £7.60: £2.60 £7.90 £2.10 (£62.70) Trio £246.90; £173.89 to Catterick 27/3/96 OWNER Mr Martin West (HAMBLETON) BRED M. Ervine in Ireland
LONG HANDICAP Charmed Life 7-2
WEIGHT FOR AGE 4yo-5lb
**OFFICIAL EXPLANATION Palace of Gold: hung in the final stages of the race according to his jockey.**
**Jaraab: had gurgled.**
**Arian Spirit (IRE)** was always going well. Once she saw the front early in the straight, she quickened and the race was always hers. (8/1)
**Top Prize** has previously done all his winning on fast ground but did handle these testing conditions well and was keeping on at the finish. (14/1)
**Hotspur Street** came from off the pace in the straight but always had too much on. He is in particularly good heart at present. (7/1)
**White Willow** is more than a shade unpredictable and, once passed early in the straight, looked very one-paced. (7/1)
**Sudden Spin** is best on the All-Weather and was taking a big step up in distance. He tried to come from behind but failed to make the slightest impression. (12/1)
**Dally Boy** has improved no end over hurdles but this step up in distance on soft ground found him out early in the straight. (9/2)
**Jaraab** is different class on the All-Weather and, never happy here, dropped away once the pace was on turning for home. (11/4)

## 475 MONKSEATON SPRINT H'CAP (0-85) (3-Y.O+) (Class D)

4-10 (4-12) **5f** £3,615.00 (£1,095.00: £535.00: £255.00) Stalls: High GOING: 0.96 sec per fur (S)

SP RR SF

**Stolen Kiss (IRE) (71)** (MWEasterby) **4-9-1b** KDarley(14) (b.nr hind: a gng wl: led appr fnl f: r.o)....— **1** 12/1 80 56
**Bollin Harry (66)** (TDEasterby) **4-8-10** MBirch(5) (a chsng ldrs: kpt on fnl f)....1 **2** 6/1[1] 72 48
**Barato (66)** (MrsJRRamsden) **5-8-3**(7) TFinn(9) (b.nr hind: trckd ldrs: effrt over 1f out: kpt on one pce)....1½ **3** 16/1 67 43
**Captain Carat (61)** (MrsJRRamsden) **5-8-5** NKennedy(8) (b.nr fore: hld up: effrt whn bdly hmpd over 1f out & ins fnl f: nt rcvr: fin 5th, 2l: plcd 4th).... **4** 11/1 55++ 31
**Broadstairs Beauty (IRE) (72)** (SRBowring) **6-9-2b** SDWilliams(6) (b: b.hind: lw: sn led: hdd wl over 1f out: edgd rt: styd on same pce: fin 4th, hd: disq: plcd 5th).... **5** 6/1[1] 73 49
**Just Bob (65)** (SEKettlewell) **7-8-6**(3) JStack(13) (bhd: hdwy & swtchd 2f out: nt clr run: nrst fin)....1¾ **6** 16/1 54 30
**Ansellman (73)** (JBerry) **6-8-12**(5) PRoberts(2) (rdn ½-wy: nvr rchd ldrs)....3 **7** 10/1 52 28
**Rich Glow (64)** (NBycroft) **5-8-8** JWeaver(12) (bhd tl styd on fnl 2f)....s.h **8** 16/1 43 19
**Sue Me (IRE) (69)** (WRMuir) **4-8-13** Jean-PierreLopez(11) (lw: bhd: hdwy 2f out: n.d)....hd **9** 14/1 48 24
**Benzoe (IRE) (76)** (MrsJRRamsden) **6-9-6** KFallon(4) (mid div & drvn along ½-wy: no imp)....¾ **10** 7/1[3] 52 28
**Saddlehome (USA) (80)** (TDBarron) **7-9-10** JFortune(1) (lost tch fr ½-wy)....½ **11** 13/2[2] 55 31
**La Suquet (72)** (NTinkler) **4-9-2** GCarter(10) (led early: w ldr: led wl over 1f out: sn hdd & wknd)....¾ **12** 25/1 44 20
*386[4]* **Shadow Jury (70)** (DWChapman) **6-9-0b** LCharnock(7) (chsd ldrs tl wknd over 1f out)....hd **13** 7/1[3] 42 18
*418[12]* **Stephensons Rocket (66)** (DNicholls) **5-8-10** AlexGreaves(3) (bolted bef s: bhd fr ½-wy)....13 **14** 16/1 — —
(SP 126.1%) **14 Rn**

**65.73 secs** (7.33) CSF £79.80 CT £1,112.80 TOTE £16.30: £3.80 £2.50 £6.80 (£58.80) Trio £537.90; £45.46 to Catterick 27/3/96. OWNER R O M Racing (SHERIFF HUTTON) BRED Rathbarry Stud
**Stolen Kiss (IRE)** did this in tremendous style, travelling on the bridle, and looks to have really improved. (12/1)
**Bollin Harry** handled these testing conditions well and kept staying on but was always second best. Another furlong should suit. (6/1)
**Barato** ran well and kept staying on in the final furlong, but just found this trip a shade shorter than he really prefers. (16/1)
**Captain Carat** got into a lot of trouble and, with any luck at all, would have been shaking up the front two. (11/1)
**Broadstairs Beauty (IRE)** could never get away from his field this time and, inclined to wander about approaching the final furlong, caused some trouble. He was put back a place in the Stewards' Room (6/1)
**Just Bob** did his usual and tried to come from way behind, but he ran into all sorts of trouble and his rider just had to sit and suffer. He is off a good mark now after failing to score last season. (16/1)
**Rich Glow** looked likely to benefit from this run and was noted staying on well at the end. (16/1)

## 476 E.B.F. BACKWORTH MAIDEN STKS (2-Y.O) (Class D)

4-40 (4-40) **5f** £3,176.25 (£960.00: £467.50: £221.25) Stalls: High GOING: 0.96 sec per fur (S)

SP RR SF

**Blue Movie** (MBell) **2-9-0** MFenton(3) (cmpt: trckd ldrs: led wl over 1f out: r.o)....— **1** 1/2[1] 70 18
**I'm Still Here** (JBerry) **2-8-9**(5) PFessey(1) (leggy: cl up: disp ld over 1f out: nt qckn towards fin)....½ **2** 5/1[3] 68 16
**Wagga Moon (IRE)** (JJO'Neill) **2-9-0** SDWilliams(4) (unf: hld up: effrt 2f out: sn btn)....9 **3** 9/2[2] 40 —
**C-Harry (IRE)** (RHollinshead) **2-9-0** KDarley(2) (str: cmpt: led over 3f: sn wknd)....9 **4** 10/1 11 —
(SP 110.6%) **4 Rn**

**67.96 secs** (9.56) CSF £3.35 TOTE £1.40 (£1.90) OWNER Mr C. J. Wates (NEWMARKET) BRED Lowquest Ltd
**Blue Movie**, a handy type, had to struggle to score here, but did it well in the end and further successes should be found. (1/2)
**I'm Still Here**, from a stable that has yet to hit form, ran a fine race and should not be long in going one better. (5/1)
**Wagga Moon (IRE)**, a rather weak individual, looked to be going quite well until hanging when asked a question. (9/2)
**C-Harry (IRE)**, a sturdy sort, set the pace until blowing up over a furlong out. (10/1)

## 477 CULLERCOATS H'CAP (0-70) (3-Y.O+) (Class E)

5-10 (5-12) **1m 2f 32y** £2,957.00 (£896.00: £438.00: £209.00) Stalls: High GOING: 0.96 sec per fur (S)

SP RR SF

**Astral Weeks (IRE) (55)** (LLungo) **5-8-13** KFallon(8) (bhd: hdwy 3f out: styd on u.p to ld post)....— **1** 20/1 64 32
**Steadfast Elite (IRE) (38)** (JJO'Neill) **5-7-5**(5) PFessey(10) (in tch: c wd st: ev ch ins fnl f: styd on)....s.h **2** 10/1 47 15
*124[8]* **Drummer Hicks (44)** (EWeymes) **7-8-2** JQuinn(5) (trckd ldrs: led 3f out tl wl over 1f out: led ins fnl f: jst ct)....s.h **3** 16/1 53 21

424[6] **Maradata (IRE) (46)** (RHollinshead) **4-7-13**(5) FLynch(6) (hld up & bhd: gd hdwy to ld wl over 1f out: hdd & no ex ins fnl f)........¾ **4** 12/1 54 22
184[6] **Forzair (62)** (SRBowring) **4-9-1**(5) CTeague(15) (chsd ldrs: chal over 3f out: wknd over 1f out)........3 **5** 7/1[2] 65 33
**Dana Point (IRE) (62)** (TDBarron) **4-9-6** JFortune(2) (plld hrd: in tch: effrt & ev ch over 2f out: wknd appr fnl f)........2 **6** 7/1[2] 62 30
**Go-Go-Power-Ranger (58)** (BEllison) **3-7-10** NKennedy(9) (slt ld to ½-wy: chsd ldr tl outpcd fnl 2f)........1½ **7** 25/1 55 3
417[2] **No Submission (USA) (38)** (DWChapman) **10-7-10v** LCharnock(14) (lw: nvr bttr than mid div)........2 **8** 7/1[2] 32 —
341[7] **My Handy Man (50)** (RAllan) **5-8-8** JWeaver(13) (dwlt: hld up: hdwy u.p 3f out: no imp)........3 **9** 16/1 40 8
**Kristal Breeze (39)** (WRMuir) **4-7-11** NCarlisle(7) (effrt & hmpd ent st: n.d after)........11 **10** 20/1 11 —
**Gold Desire (38)** (MBrittain) **6-7-10** GBardwell(3) (plld hrd: trckd ldr: chal 3f out: wknd wl over 1f out)........1½ **11** 13/2[1] 8 —
**Roussi (USA) (66)** (DNicholls) **4-9-10** AlexGreaves(1) (bhd fr ½-wy)........hd **12** 9/1[3] 36 4
**Spanish Steps (IRE) (55)** (MWEasterby) **4-8-13** KDarley(11) (hld up: effrt over 3f out: sn wknd)........3 **13** 7/1[2] 20 —
**Mr Slick (51)** (WStorey) **4-8-9** DMcKeown(12) (lost tch fr ½-wy)........3 **14** 16/1 11 —
**Sallyoreally (IRE) (39)** (WStorey) **5-7-11**ow1 JFanning(4) (cl up: slt ld ½-wy: hdd & wknd 3f out)........24 **15** 16/1 — —
(SP 127.0%) **15 Rn**

**2m 24.8** (18.10) CSF £195.57 CT £3,010.09 TOTE £19.90: £5.50 £3.60 £3.20 (£172.10) Trio £417.20; £235.04 to Catterick 27/3/96. OWNER Kenmore Estates Ltd (CARRUTHERSTOWN) BRED J. C. Fagan in Ireland
LONG HANDICAP Gold Desire 7-3 Steadfast Elite (IRE) 7-8 Go-Go-Power-Ranger 7-7 Sallyoreally (IRE) 7-0
WEIGHT FOR AGE 3yo-20lb

**Astral Weeks (IRE)**, who lost his form last season, has been sharpened up by hurdling and showed fine courage under a strong ride to get up close home. (20/1)
**Steadfast Elite (IRE)** has done quite well over hurdles this winter and showed up here but, despite keeping on well in the final furlong, just failed. (10/1)
**Drummer Hicks** looked in good condition and ran his best race for some time, but just failed to last out. His last victory was two and a half years ago and he has subsequently dropped right down the handicap. (16/1)
**Maradata (IRE)** showed a particularly good turn of foot in the straight but he then stopped when in front. More patient tactics are needed. (12/1)
**Forzair** raced with every chance, but was done for speed in the last two furlongs and may need a bit further or certainly a stronger gallop. (7/1)
**Dana Point (IRE)**, who won on much faster ground last season, was stepping up in distance here. In the circumstances, he ran quite well. (7/1)
**Gold Desire** raced too freely and needs a stronger pace than was set here. (13/2)

T/Plpt: £1,211.90 (8.99 Tckts). T/Qdpt: £812.90 (0.09 Tckts); £999.68 to Catterick 27/3/96. AA

# CATTERICK (L-H) (Good to soft, Good patches, Soft patches home bnd)
## Wednesday March 27th
WEATHER: cloudy WIND: fresh across

## 478 SPRINGTIME LIMITED STKS (0-60) (3-Y.O) (Class F)
2-20 (2-20) **5f** £2,679.00 (£744.00: £357.00) Stalls: Low GOING: 0.73 sec per fur (S)

SP RR SF
443[2] **Lady Caroline Lamb (IRE) (60)** (MRChannon) **3-8-8** TQuinn(4) (cl up: led ½-wy: swtchd stands' side: r.o)...— **1** 11/10[1] 70 38
180[6] **Montrestar (60)** (PDEvans) **3-8-11** SSanders(2) (chsd ldrs: kpt on fnl f)........2½ **2** 11/1 65 33
430* **General Equation (55)** (JBalding) **3-8-7**(7) JEdmunds(1) (lw: a chsng ldrs: kpt on same pce fnl f)........1 **3** 11/2[2] 65 33
**April's Joy (50)** (JNorton) **3-8-8** DaleGibson(9) (racd stands' side: a chsng ldrs: kpt on appr fnl f)........½ **4** 14/1 57 25
430[2] **Gi La High (60)** (JBerry) **3-8-9**(5) PRoberts(8) (sn outpcd: sme late hdwy)........3½ **5** 9/1 52 20
**Queens Check (53)** (MissJFCraze) **3-8-11b** AMcGlone(3) (chsd ldrs tl rdn & btn over 1f out)........1¾ **6** 6/1[3] 43 11
414* **Niteowl Raider (IRE) (51)** (JAHarris) **3-9-0** JO'Reilly(7) (outpcd & bhd after 2f)........4 **7** 13/2 34 2
**Finisterre (IRE) (40)** (JJO'Neill) **3-8-11** SDWilliams(6) (a outpcd & bhd)........1½ **8** 66/1 26 —
292[5] **Chillam (50)** (JPLeigh) **3-8-11b**[1] DeanMcKeown(5) (led to ½-wy: wknd qckly)........6 **9** 50/1 7 —
(SP 119.1%) **9 Rn**

**64.2 secs** (6.70) CSF £13.73 CT £22.70 TOTE £1.60: £1.30 £2.00 £2.20 (£8.40) Trio £22.70 OWNER Mr W. H. Ponsonby (UPPER LAMBOURN) BRED Tally-Ho Stud

**Lady Caroline Lamb (IRE)** is not much to look at, but she was always too good for this lot once she crossed over to the stands' side at halfway. (11/10)
**Montrestar** won on faster ground last season and this was not a bad effort on what appeared a very soft surface. (11/1)
**General Equation**, on a day when the faster ground was on the stands' side, had the worst draw but still ran well enough to suggest that a race on turf can be found. (11/2)
**April's Joy** failed to impress on looks and raced up the stands' rail throughout, but she was never doing enough. (14/1)
**Gi La High** is an All-Weather specialist and was never going the pace here. (9/1: op 6/1)
**Niteowl Raider (IRE)** (13/2: 5/1-8/1)

## 479 FORCETT PARK (S) STKS (3-Y.O+) (Class G)
2-50 (2-52) **7f** £2,553.00 (£708.00: £339.00) Stalls: Low GOING: 0.73 sec per fur (S)

SP RR SF
**Bargash (63)** (PDEvans) **4-9-10** SSanders(1) (hld up: stdy hdwy over 2f out: led ins fnl f: r.o)........— **1** 10/1 69 50
**Mustn't Grumble (IRE) (61)** (DNicholls) **6-9-6** AlexGreaves(9) (mde most tl hdd ins fnl f: rallied towards fin)........½ **2** 11/2 64 45
**Larrylukeathugh (45)** (JJO'Neill) **3-8-6**ow1 SDWilliams(2) (chsd ldrs: disp ld over 2f out: no ex ins fnl f)........¾ **3** 50/1 63 28
431[3] **Awesome Venture (48)** (MCChapman) **6-8-13**(7) CMunday(12) (trckd ldrs: effrt over 1f out: styd on towards fin)........s.h **4** 12/1 62 43
413[5] **Allinson's Mate (IRE) (75)** (TDBarron) **8-9-10b** JFortune(11) (lw: chsd ldrs tl n.m.r & wknd fnl 2f)........2 **5** 4/1[2] 62 43
427[3] **Spencer's Revenge (72)** (NTinkler) **7-9-10** GCarter(13) (hld up: effrt appr st: rdn & nvr able to chal)........½ **6** 6/4[1] 60 41
250[2] **Sea Devil (62)** (MJCamacho) **10-9-6** LCharnock(6) (a.p: effrt & ch over 2f out: wknd over 1f out)........2½ **7** 5/1[3] 51 32
**Nukud (USA)** (DNicholls) **4-9-6** MRichardson(5) (s.i.s: sn rcvrd: no imp fnl 2½f)........hd **8** 50/1 50 31
**Framed (IRE)** (SCWilliams) **6-9-6** MBirch(4) (b: bhd: effrt over 2f out: no imp)........3 **9** 25/1 44 25
**Brambles Way** (WLBarker) **7-9-1**(5) FLynch(7) (bhd most of wy)........3 **10** 50/1 37 18

| | | | | SP | RR | SF |
|---|---|---|---|---|---|---|
| | **Reed My Lips (IRE) (32)** (BPJBaugh) **5-8-13**(7) IonaWands(8) (hdwy appr st: wknd 2f out) | hd | **11** | 200/1 | 36 | 17 |
| | **Heathyards Magic (IRE) (67)** (MDods) **4-9-10** DaleGibson(10) (disp ld 3f: chsd ldrs tl n.m.r & outpcd fnl 2f) | d.h | **11** | 25/1 | 41 | 22 |
| *366*[8] | **Great Bear (72)** (DWChapman) **4-9-6** ACulhane(14) (cl up tl lost pl ½-wy) | ½ | **13** | 20/1 | 35 | 16 |
| | **Party Poser** (BWMurray) **3-8-0** FNorton(15) (small: lt-f: unf: dwlt: a bhd) | 15 | **14** | 100/1 | — | — |

(SP 128.7%) **14 Rn**

**1m 33.4** (9.80) CSF £63.72 TOTE £14.90: £2.40 £2.10 £20.10 (£27.50) Trio £250.20; £285.49 to Aintree 28/3/96 OWNER Mr John Pugh (WELSHPOOL) BRED Trafalgar Bloodstock and R. West
WEIGHT FOR AGE 3yo-15lb
No bid
OFFICIAL EXPLANATION **Great Bear: had gurgled during the race.**
**Bargash** travelled well for much of the trip but, when in front in the final furlong, he did not find a lot and needed to be driven out. (10/1)
**Mustn't Grumble (IRE)** tried to make all and looks likely to return to something like his old form this season. (11/2)
**Larrylukeathugh**, from a yard whose runners are going well, held every chance in the straight, but just lacked a turn of foot to take it. (50/1)
**Awesome Venture** has more ability than he cares to show and has been frustrating on the All-Weather, but he was keeping on well here. (12/1)
**Allinson's Mate (IRE)**, dropped in class, showed enough to suggest that he has not finished winning. (4/1)
**Spencer's Revenge**, held up in this moderately-run race, had no chance of getting there. (6/4)

## 480 GODS SOLUTION H'CAP (0-80) (3-Y.O+) (Class D)

3-25 (3-26) **7f** £3,980.00 (£1,190.00: £570.00: £260.00) Stalls: Low GOING: 0.73 sec per fur (S)

| | | | | SP | RR | SF |
|---|---|---|---|---|---|---|
| *340** | **Super Benz (62)** (JLEyre) **10-9-3** RLappin(11) (b: a.p: led 1½f out: sn clr & eased) | — | **1** | 7/1 3 | 77 | 59 |
| | **Evan 'elp Us (60)** (JLEyre) **4-9-1b** KDarley(17) (trckd ldrs: effrt 2f out: nt pce of wnr) | 5 | **2** | 16/1 | 64 | 46 |
| *350*[4] | **Orange Place (IRE) (70)** (TJNaughton) **5-9-11** SSanders(2) (led after 2½f tl hdd 1½f out: one pce) | hd | **3** | 7/1 3 | 73 | 55 |
| *357*[4] | **Peggy Spencer (58)** (CWThornton) **4-8-13** DeanMcKeown(3) (a cl up: rdn 2f out: r.o one pce) | nk | **4** | 9/2 1 | 61 | 43 |
| *371*[5] | **Johnnie the Joker (47)** (JPLeigh) **5-7-11v**(5) FLynch(12) (hdwy 2f out: styd on: nrst fin) | 2½ | **5** | 10/1 | 44 | 26 |
| *371*[7] | **Nashaat (USA) (65)** (MCChapman) **8-9-3**(3) PMcCabe(4) (effrt over 2f out: nvr able to chal) | 3 | **6** | 8/1 | 55 | 37 |
| 450[7] | **Knobbleeneeze (73)** (MRChannon) **6-10-0v** RHughes(6) (chsd ldrs tl rdn & wknd fnl 2f) | hd | **7** | 11/2 2 | 63 | 45 |
| | **Northern Spark (48)** (MissLAPerratt) **8-8-3** JFanning(7) (bhd: styd on fnl 2f: nrst fin) | hd | **8** | 25/1 | 38 | 20 |
| | **Almasi (IRE) (55)** (CFWall) **4-8-10** GDuffield(1) (s.i.s: hdwy & prom ent st: wknd wl over 1f out) | nk | **9** | 12/1 | 44 | 26 |
| *357*[5] | **Everset (FR) (62)** (ABailey) **8-9-0b**[1](3) DWright(8) (b: s.i.s: hdwy on ins 2f out: no imp) | 1¾ | **10** | 14/1 | 47 | 29 |
| | **Spanish Verdict (67)** (DenysSmith) **9-9-3**(5) CTeague(10) (bhd tl sme late hdwy) | ½ | **11** | 20/1 | 51 | 33 |
| | **Maid O'Cannie (57)** (MWEasterby) **5-8-12b** DaleGibson(14) (nvr wnt pce) | 2 | **12** | 12/1 | 36 | 18 |
| | **Commander Glen (IRE) (56)** (MrsJRRamsden) **4-8-11** KFallon(9) (s.i.s: nvr nr to chal) | 1½ | **13** | 25/1 | 32 | 14 |
| *115*[6] | **Zain Dancer (60)** (DNicholls) **4-9-1** AlexGreaves(13) (nvr trbld ldrs) | s.h | **14** | 10/1 | 36 | 18 |
| | **Kid Ory (67)** (PCalver) **5-9-8** MBirch(5) (led 2½f: outpcd ent st: sn wknd) | 5 | **15** | 14/1 | 31 | 13 |
| | **Penny's Wishing (51)** (NBycroft) **4-8-6** LCharnock(15) (prom: hmpd appr st: sn wknd) | 20 | **16** | 50/1 | — | — |

(SP 136.9%) **16 Rn**

**1m 32.1** (8.50) CSF £114.07 CT £800.11 TOTE £6.50: £2.60 £4.50 £1.30 £1.60 (£87.90) Trio £326.80 OWNER Whitestonecliffe Racing Partnership (HAMBLETON) BRED Scarteen Stud
**Super Benz** has come good since changing stables this winter and continued that improvement here, winning with a deal of ease. (7/1)
**Evan 'elp Us**, a stable-companion of the winner, disappointed last year, but he ran well enough here to suggest that he is on his way back. (16/1)
**Orange Place (IRE)**, out in front as usual, had no answer once the winner pressed the button approaching the final furlong. (7/1)
**Peggy Spencer** has improved on the All-Weather this winter but was made to look very one-paced in these soft conditions. (9/2)
**Johnnie the Joker** took time to get going and, when he finally did, it was all over. He is much better on the All-Weather and probably needs better ground on turf. (10/1)
**Nashaat (USA)** seems better on the All-Weather but ran reasonably well here, staying on at the finish. (8/1)
**Northern Spark** is doing particularly well physically, and looks one to keep an eye on, despite his years. (25/1)

## 481 TOYTOP CONDITIONS STKS (2-Y.O) (Class D)

4-00 (4-02) **5f** £3,125.50 (£934.00: £447.00: £203.50) Stalls: Low GOING: 0.73 sec per fur (S)

| | | | | SP | RR | SF |
|---|---|---|---|---|---|---|
| 441[3] | **Muchea** (MRChannon) **2-8-11** RHughes(5) (lw: led after 1½f: qcknd clr over 1f out: easily) | — | **1** | 4/9 1 | 93 | 33 |
| | **Red Garter (IRE)** (KWMcAuliffe) **2-8-6** KDarley(3) (neat: unf: chsd ldrs: rdn ½-wy: styd on: no ch w wnr) | 10 | **2** | 3/1 2 | 56 | — |
| | **Perfect Bliss** (PDEvans) **2-8-6** SSanders(2) (lt-f: unf: led 1½f: outpcd fr ½-wy) | 1 | **3** | 7/1 3 | 53 | — |
| | **Silver Raj** (WTKemp) **2-8-11** KFallon(4) (lt-f: unf: s.s: a wl bhd) | 10 | **4** | 33/1 | 26 | — |
| | **Chilled Wine** (NBycroft) **2-8-6** LCharnock(1) (neat: bkwd: prom to ½-wy: wknd qckly) | 5 | **5** | 66/1 | 5 | — |

(SP 111.2%) **5 Rn**

**64.7 secs** (7.20) CSF £2.22 TOTE £1.50: £1.10 £1.50 (£1.70) OWNER Albion Investments (UPPER LAMBOURN) BRED Lady Richard Wellesley
**Muchea** took up the initiative early on and quickly strode clear just after halfway. This wiry sort is just the type for this time of year. (4/9)
**Red Garter (IRE)** probably needed the experience and was never doing things quickly enough, but she was keeping on at the end. (3/1)
**Perfect Bliss** led the winner early on but this lightly-made sort was quickly put in her place soon after halfway. (7/1)
**Silver Raj** did not look up to much and, after a slow start, showed nothing. (33/1)
**Chilled Wine** badly needed this and blew up by halfway. (66/1)

## 482 YARM H'CAP (0-80) (4-Y.O+) (Class D)

4-30 (4-31) **1m 5f 175y** £3,720.00 (£1,110.00: £530.00: £240.00) Stalls: Low GOING: 0.73 sec per fur (S)

| | | | | SP | RR | SF |
|---|---|---|---|---|---|---|
| *400*[4] | **Cross Talk (IRE) (65)** (RHollinshead) **4-8-8**(5) FLynch(6) (hld up: hdwy 5f out: led over 1f out: hld on wl) | — | **1** | 14/1 | 77 | 45 |
| *312*[9] | **Hillzah (USA) (76)** (RBastiman) **8-9-9**(5) HBastiman(5) (in tch: effrt 3f out: chal over 1f out: hrd rdn & kpt on) | ¾ | **2** | 8/1 3 | 87 | 59 |
| | **Admirals Secret (USA) (63)** (CFWall) **7-9-1** WLord(9) (hdwy 7f out: sn prom: kpt on u.p fnl 2f) | 2 | **3** | 11/2 1 | 72 | 44 |
| *373*[4] | **Greek Night Out (IRE) (44)** (JLEyre) **5-7-5**(5) PFessey(7) (cl up: led 3f out tl over 1f out: one pce) | 1¼ | **4** | 8/1 3 | 51 | 23 |
| 439[13] | **Sarawat (60)** (DNicholls) **8-8-12** AlexGreaves(11) (in tch: one pce fnl 3f) | 3 | **5** | 11/2 1 | 64 | 36 |
| | **House of Dreams (62)** (GMMoore) **4-8-10** JFortune(4) (chsd ldrs tl outpcd fnl 2½f) | 2 | **6** | 16/1 | 64 | 32 |
| *113*[4] | **Hullbank (56)** (WWHaigh) **6-8-8** DaleGibson(13) (lw: b: hld up: effrt 5f out: no imp) | ½ | **7** | 6/1 2 | 57 | 29 |
| | **Desert Fighter (76)** (MrsMReveley) **5-10-0** KDarley(1) (lw: nvr nr to chal) | hd | **8** | 12/1 | 77 | 49 |
| | **Marco Magnifico (USA) (48)** (TDyer) **6-8-0** JFanning(8) (t: led tl hdd 6½f out: wknd 4f out) | 2 | **9** | 12/1 | 47 | 19 |
| | **Muzrak (CAN) (56)** (MDHammond) **5-8-8** GDuffield(2) (cl up: led 6½f out to 3f out: sn wknd) | 3½ | **10** | 10/1 | 51 | 23 |

| | | | Pos | SP | RR | SF |
|---|---|---|---|---|---|---|
| | **Windward Ariom (45)** (KRBurke) **10-7-8**(3)ow1 DWright(10) (a bhd) | 1¾ | **11** | 11/1 | 38 | 9 |
| *236*[8] | **In a Moment (USA) (44)** (TDBarron) **5-7-10b** NCarlisle(3) (prom to ½-wy: sn bhd) | 1½ | **12** | 25/1 | 35 | 7 |
| 439[10] | **Mentalasanythin (64)** (ABailey) **7-8-9**(7) AngelaGallimore(12) (prom to ½-wy) | 4 | **13** | 6/1[2] | 50 | 22 |

(SP 130.8%) **13 Rn**

**3m 14.6** (19.10) CSF £120.78 CT £652.50 TOTE £19.40: £5.00 £2.20 £3.40 (£89.60) Trio £86.30 OWNER Mr J. E. Bigg (UPPER LONGDON) BRED Juddmonte Farms
LONG HANDICAP Windward Ariom 6-7 In a Moment (USA) 7-8 Greek Night Out (IRE) 7-4
WEIGHT FOR AGE 4yo-4lb
STEWARDS' ENQUIRY Bastiman susp. 6 & 8-11/4/96 (excessive use of whip).

**Cross Talk (IRE)** had his only previous win over this course and distance and obviously enjoyed these bends and undulations. (14/1)
**Hilizah (USA)** is obviously on his way back to form and put up a decent show here, but was just outbattled, despite trying hard. (8/1)
**Admirals Secret (USA)** loves this track and ran well again, but lack of a run probably just made the difference. (11/2: 4/1-6/1)
**Greek Night Out (IRE)**, fit from the All-Weather, ran a sound race from 6lb out of the handicap and that probably made the difference. (8/1)
**Sarawat** is certainly nothing like the force he was, but he did show something here and may be coming back to some sort of form. (11/2)
**House of Dreams** has been failing to get home over hurdles and ran similarly here. (16/1)
**Desert Fighter** (12/1: op 8/1)

## 483 WHORLTON H'CAP (0-75) (3-Y.O) (Class D)

5-00 (5-00) **1m 3f 214y** £3,720.00 (£1,110.00: £530.00: £240.00) Stalls: Low GOING: 0.73 sec per fur (S)

| | | | Pos | SP | RR | SF |
|---|---|---|---|---|---|---|
| | **Jackson Park (58)** (TDEasterby) **3-8-5** MBirch(9) (disp ld tl slt ld 3f out: edgd lft fnl f: hld on wl) | — | **1** | 8/1 | 71 | 18 |
| 444[2] | **Deadline Time (IRE) (74)** (MrsMReveley) **3-9-7** KDarley(4) (hld up: hdwy 5f out: disp ld on bit 2f out: sn rdn: edgd lft & no ex towards fin) | nk | **2** | Evens[1] | 87 | 34 |
| 444[3] | **Dancing Cavalier (65)** (RHollinshead) **3-8-7**(5) FLynch(6) (bhd: hdwy appr st: styd on: nvr able to chal) | 2½ | **3** | 4/1[2] | 74 | 21 |
| *385*[2] | **Thorntoun Estate (IRE) (58)** (MJohnston) **3-8-5** DeanMcKeown(3) (lw: disp ld tl hdd 3f out: one pce) | 1½ | **4** | 11/2[3] | 65 | 12 |
| *56*[8] | **Four Weddings (USA) (50)** (MBell) **3-7-4v**[1](7) RMullen(2) (chsd ldrs: rdn over 3f out: no imp after) | nk | **5** | 12/1 | 57 | 4 |
| *370*[2] | **Oxgang (IRE) (55)** (JGFitzGerald) **3-8-2** JFEgan(1) (pushed along ½-wy: sn outpcd & n.d after) | 16 | **6** | 9/1 | 41 | — |
| *405*[11] | **Fergal (USA) (49)** (RonaldThompson) **3-7-5**(5) PFessey(5) (prom tl wknd over 4f out) | 2½ | **7** | 33/1 | 31 | — |
| | **General Glow (55)** (NBycroft) **3-8-2** LCharnock(7) (prom tl wknd 4f out) | 3 | **8** | 50/1 | 33 | — |
| *300*[7] | **Conquistajade (USA) (49)** (SPCWoods) **3-7-10** NCarlisle(8) (nvr trbld ldrs) | 2½ | **9** | 50/1 | 24 | — |

(SP 121.1%) **9 Rn**

**2m 51.0** (19.60) CSF £16.65 CT £36.15 TOTE £8.60: £2.70 £1.10 £1.10 (£8.30) Trio £10.60 OWNER Mr C. H. Stevens (MALTON) BRED M. H. Easterby
LONG HANDICAP Fergal (USA) 7-1 Conquistajade (USA) 7-6

**Jackson Park** proved to be a real battler and, having looked second best in the home straight, it was his courage which won him the day. (8/1)
**Deadline Time (IRE)** ran well and looked odds-on entering the last two furlongs, but he just failed to produce the goods in a driving finish. He is the sort to do much better later on. (Evens)
**Dancing Cavalier** did his usual and came from way behind, but the early pace was not really strong enough and he failed to make any impression. (4/1)
**Thorntoun Estate (IRE)** has been running well on the All-Weather and put up another decent performance, but was tapped for toe in the straight. (11/2)
**Four Weddings (USA)**, in a visor for the first time, ran his best race to date. (12/1)

T/Jkpt: Not won; £5,519.13 to Aintree 28/3/96. T/Plpt: £189.30 (76.62 Tckts). T/Qdpt: £12.70 (257.32 Tckts). AA

# 0459-LINGFIELD (L-H) (Standard)
## Wednesday March 27th

WEATHER: sunny WIND: almost nil

## 484 SAN SEBASTIAN MAIDEN STKS (3-Y.O) (Class D)

2-10 (2-11) **7f (Equitrack)** £3,728.10 (£1,111.80: £530.40: £239.70) Stalls: Low GOING minus 0.49 sec per fur (FST)

| | | | Pos | SP | RR | SF |
|---|---|---|---|---|---|---|
| | **Waypoint** (RCharlton) **3-8-9** TSprake(6) (chsd ldr: led wl over 1f out: pushed out) | — | **1** | 10/1[3] | 67 | 11 |
| | **Domak Amaam (IRE)** (JHMGosden) **3-9-0** GHind(5) (led over 5f: unable qckn) | 1¾ | **2** | 2/7[1] | 68 | 12 |
| | **Victory Bound (USA)** (MJohnston) **3-9-0** JWeaver(3) (scope: dwlt: hdwy over 4f out: rdn over 3f out: one pce) | 5 | **3** | 5/1[2] | 57 | 1 |
| | **Go With The Wind** (MBell) **3-9-0** MFenton(1) (bit bkwd: bhd fnl 5f) | 3½ | **4** | 12/1 | 49 | — |
| *390*[7] | **Lucitino** (SCWilliams) **3-8-9** JTate(4) (b: dwlt: bhd fnl 4f) | 4 | **5** | 33/1 | 34 | — |
| | **Sheilas Dream** (RSimpson) **3-8-6**(3) SDrowne(2) (bkwd: bhd fnl 4f) | s.h | **6** | 66/1 | 34 | — |

(SP 115.7%) **6 Rn**

**1m 27.61** (3.61) CSF £13.75 TOTE £15.10: £4.00 £1.10 (£2.40) OWNER Mr Ray Richards (BECKHAMPTON) BRED Berkshire Equestrian Services Ltd

**Waypoint**, without a run in nearly six months, was settled in second place. In front entering the straight, she needed only to be nudged along to dispose of the very hot favourite inside the final furlong. (10/1: 7/1-11/1)
**Domak Amaam (IRE)**, whose two good efforts last October resulted in him starting extremely short in the betting, was brushed aside inside the final furlong. (2/7)
**Victory Bound (USA)**, slightly on the leg, but with quite a bit of scope, raced with his tongue tied down. Moving up to take third place over half a mile from home, he could make no impression on the front two. (5/1: op 3/1)
**Go With The Wind** (12/1: op 6/1)

## 485 VIGO CLAIMING STKS (4-Y.O+) (Class F)

2-45 (2-45) **2m (Equitrack)** £2,595.20 (£717.20: £341.60) Stalls: Low GOING minus 0.49 sec per fur (FST)

| | | | Pos | SP | RR | SF |
|---|---|---|---|---|---|---|
| 440[9] | **Captain Marmalade (43)** (DTThom) **7-8-12v** JTate(2) (b: hdwy over 7f out: rdn over 5f out: led over 2f out: r.o wl) | — | **1** | 11/2 | 54 | 27 |
| *369*[4] | **Durham (53)** (RSimpson) **5-8-3v**[1](3) SDrowne(1) (led over 1f: lost pl 8f out: rallied over 3f out: r.o wl ins fnl f) | 1 | **2** | 9/1 | 47 | 20 |

| Form | Horse | Btn | Pos | SP | RR | SF |
|---|---|---|---|---|---|---|
| 365[6] | **Juliasdarkinvader (41)** (AMoore) **6-8-8** AClark(6) (b: b.hind: a.p: led 5f out tl over 2f out: ev ch over 1f out: unable qckn) | 2½ | **3** | 5/1[3] | 47 | 20 |
| 318* | **Harlequin Walk (IRE) (51)** (RJO'Sullivan) **5-8-11** DBiggs(3) (a.p: ev ch over 1f out: one pce) | hd | **4** | 11/4[2] | 49 | 22 |
| 393[7] | **Zuno Flyer (USA) (35)** (AMoore) **4-8-0v**(3) AWhelan(4) (b: b.hind: hdwy 8f out: wknd over 3f out) | 12 | **5** | 11/1 | 34 | 2 |
| 409[4] | **Allez Cyrano (IRE) (71)** (MBell) **5-9-6** MFenton(8) (led over 13f out to 5f out: sn wknd) | 14 | **6** | 9/4[1] | 32 | 5 |
| | **Well Suited (34)** (THind) **6-8-12** DHarrison(7) (b: bhd fnl 8f: t.o) | dist | **7** | 33/1 | — | — |
| 409[11] | **Sussex Gorse** (BAPearce) **5-8-7b**[1](5) ADaly(5) (b.nr hind: led over 14f out tl over 13f out: wknd 11f out: t.o whn p.u over 8f out) | | **P** | 100/1 | — | — |
| | | | | (SP 111.8%) | **8 Rn** | |

**3m 28.27** (6.27) CSF £46.11 TOTE £7.60: £1.10 £2.30 £2.20 (£27.40) OWNER Mrs Alison Thom (NEWMARKET) BRED Mrs C. Whitwood and N. E. C Sherwood
WEIGHT FOR AGE 4yo-5lb
**OFFICIAL EXPLANATION Well Suited: following his jockey's comment that the gelding felt lame, a vet subsequently confirmed that the horse had put out vertebrae down his spine.**
**Captain Marmalade** is not easy to win with and this was only his fourth victory from seventy-eight starts. (11/2: 7/2-6/1)
**Durham** really found his feet inside the last 200 yards, and ran on strongly, but found the line always coming too soon. (9/1)
**Juliasdarkinvader** was only brushed aside in the last 200 yards. (5/1)
**Harlequin Walk (IRE)** was only tapped for toe in the last 100 yards. A return to a mile and a half or a mile and three-quarters may be in her favour. (11/4: 6/4-3/1)
**Zuno Flyer (USA)** failed to see out this longer trip. (11/1)
**Allez Cyrano (IRE)** failed to see out this huge step up in distance, his three victories have come over seven and a return to this trip should see him winning. (9/4)

## 486 BILBAO LIMITED STKS (0-65) (4-Y.O+) (Class F)

3-20 (3-20) **1m 2f (Equitrack)** £2,666.60 (£737.60: £351.80) Stalls: Low GOING minus 0.49 sec per fur (FST)

| Form | Horse | Btn | Pos | SP | RR | SF |
|---|---|---|---|---|---|---|
| 337* | **Errant (60)** (DJSCosgrove) **4-9-2** JQuinn(4) (b: hld up: led 1f out: rdn out) | — | **1** | 8/1 | 71 | 40 |
| 349[4] | **Greenwich Again (65)** (TGMills) **4-9-2** JWeaver(1) (led to 1f out: unable qckn) | 1 | **2** | 7/2[2] | 69 | 38 |
| 80* | **No Speeches (IRE) (64)** (SDow) **5-8-13**(5) ADaly(5) (a.p: rdn over 3f out: one pce fnl 2f) | 3½ | **3** | 7/2[2] | 66 | 35 |
| 406[4] | **Tuigamala (60)** (RIngram) **5-9-4** WWoods(2) (lw: rdn & hdwy over 3f out: one pce fnl 2f) | 1½ | **4** | 9/2[3] | 63 | 32 |
| | **Spitfire Bridge (IRE) (60)** (MMcCormack) **4-9-4** RCochrane(6) (hld up: rdn over 3f out: wknd over 1f out) | 3½ | **5** | 8/1 | 58 | 27 |
| 181[10] | **Locorotondo (IRE) (64)** (MBell) **5-8-11** MFenton(3) (a.p: rdn over 2f out: wknd over 1f out) | 21 | **6** | 3/1[1] | 17 | — |
| | | | | (SP 109.8%) | **6 Rn** | |

**2m 6.91** (2.61) CSF £32.39 TOTE £7.30: £4.00 £1.80 (£18.50) OWNER Mr Alex Gorrie (NEWMARKET) BRED Sheikh Mohammed bin Rashid al Maktoum
**Errant**, held up travelling well, was asked for his effort below the distance and, striking the front a furlong out, soon asserted. (8/1: 5/1-9/1)
**Greenwich Again** again attempted to make all the running. Collared a furlong out, he found the winner a little too strong. (7/2)
**No Speeches (IRE)** was always close up but failed to quicken in the home straight. (7/2)
**Spitfire Bridge (IRE)** (8/1: op 5/1)
**Locorotondo (IRE)**, with 4lb or more to spare over her rivals on adjusted official ratings, raced up with the pace, but punters knew their fate early in the straight. (3/1)

## 487 LIMA H'CAP (0-70) (4-Y.O+) (Class E)

3-50 (3-51) **1m (Equitrack)** £3,179.40 (£949.20: £453.60: £205.80) Stalls: High GOING minus 0.49 sec per fur (FST)

| Form | Horse | Btn | Pos | SP | RR | SF |
|---|---|---|---|---|---|---|
| 366[2] | **Victory Team (IRE) (64)** (GBBalding) **4-9-10** RCochrane(2) (hld up: rdn wl over 1f out: led wl ins fnl f: r.o wl) | — | **1** | 4/1[1] | 69 | 46 |
| | **Waikiki Beach (USA) (60)** (GLMoore) **5-9-6** SWhitworth(8) (b: b.hind: a.p: led over 1f out tl wl ins fnl f: unable qckn) | 1 | **2** | 14/1 | 63 | 40 |
| | **Autumn Cover (43)** (RMFlower) **4-8-3** GHind(10) (b: bit bkwd: led 7f out tl over 5f out: led over 3f out tl over 1f out: one pce) | 3 | **3** | 14/1 | 40 | 17 |
| 416[4] | **Sooty Tern (51)** (JMBradley) **9-8-8**(3) SDrowne(5) (b.off fore: led 1f: rdn over 2f out: one pce) | 2½ | **4** | 5/1[3] | 43 | 20 |
| 412* | **Sarum (53)** (CPWildman) **10-8-13** CRutter(4) (hdwy over 3f out: lost pl over 2f out: one pce) | 1¾ | **5** | 15/2 | 42 | 19 |
| 464* | **Fort Knox (IRE) (64)** (RMFlower) **5-9-10b** 5x DBiggs(9) (hdwy over 3f out: lost pl over 2f out: one pce) | hd | **6** | 9/2[2] | 52 | 29 |
| 387[2] | **Woolverstone Hall (IRE) (36)** (DJGMurraySmith) **4-7-10b** NAdams(6) (hdwy over 3f out: wknd over 2f out) | 4 | **7** | 12/1 | 16 | — |
| 363[4] | **Labudd (USA) (54)** (RIngram) **6-9-0b** WWoods(1) (b: lw: led over 5f out tl over 3f out: sn wknd) | 1¾ | **8** | 6/1 | 31 | 8 |
| 366[9] | **Dantean (45)** (RJO'Sullivan) **4-8-5** JQuinn(3) (hld up: rdn over 3f out: wknd over 2f out) | nk | **9** | 9/2[2] | 21 | — |
| 343[4] | **Magic Leader (IRE) (36)** (TTClement) **4-7-10** GBardwell(7) (b: lost pl 5f out: rallied over 3f out: wknd over 2f out) | 2 | **10** | 33/1 | 8 | — |
| | | | | (SP 123.0%) | **10 Rn** | |

**1m 39.43** (2.03) CSF £54.04 CT £683.18 TOTE £3.50: £1.20 £4.50 £4.50 (£68.20) Trio £239.40; £273.22 to Aintree 28/3/96 OWNER Mr R. J. Lavelle (ANDOVER) BRED Barronstown and Swettenham Studs and Ron Con Ltd
LONG HANDICAP Woolverstone Hall (IRE) 7-8 Magic Leader (IRE) 7-3
**Victory Team (IRE)** confirmed the promise shown on his All-Weather debut recently. Asked for his effort early in the straight, he came through to grab the spoils in the closing stages. (4/1)
**Waikiki Beach (USA)**, who was very disappointing last year, ran well here after a four-month rest, but was worried out of it in the closing stages. (14/1)
**Autumn Cover** looked as though this first run in nearly five months would do him good. (14/1)
**Sooty Tern** was never far away but failed to quicken in the last three furlongs. (5/1: op 8/1)
**Woolverstone Hall (IRE)** (12/1: op 7/1)

## 488 SANTANDER H'CAP (0-65) (3-Y.O) (Class F)

4-20 (4-21) **6f (Equitrack)** £2,595.20 (£717.20: £341.60) Stalls: Low GOING minus 0.49 sec per fur (FST)

| Form | Horse | Btn | Pos | SP | RR | SF |
|---|---|---|---|---|---|---|
| 408[6] | **Rowlandsons Stud (IRE) (55)** (GLMoore) **3-8-10**(5) DaneO'Neill(4) (hld up: rdn to ld ins fnl f: r.o wl) | — | **1** | 8/1 | 67 | — |
| 354[5] | **Dancing Jack (57)** (JJBridger) **3-9-3** JQuinn(3) (lw: a.p: led over 2f out tl ins fnl f: unable qckn) | 2½ | **2** | 11/1 | 62 | — |
| | **Arlington Lady (40)** (NACallaghan) **3-7-9**(5) MHenry(1) (hld up: rdn over 2f out: one pce) | ½ | **3** | Evens[1] | 44 | — |
| 467[4] | **Young Mazaad (IRE) (61)** (DCO'Brien) **3-9-7** GBardwell(2) (led 2f: rdn over 3f out: one pce) | nk | **4** | 5/1[2] | 64 | — |

335[2] **Sunset Harbour (IRE) (60)** (TJNaughton) **3-9-6b** RCochrane(6) (led 4f out tl over 2f out: hrd rdn over 1f out: one pce)........1¾ **5** 6/1[3] 59 —
377[4] **Badger Bay (IRE) (54)** (CADwyer) **3-8-11**(3) JStack(7) (hdwy over 3f out: wknd over 2f out)........2½ **6** 10/1 46 —
**Burj (45)** (NAGraham) **3-8-5** DHarrison(5) (hdwy over 3f out: wknd over 2f out)........2½ **7** 20/1 30 —
307[5] **Zuno Princess (IRE) (36)** (TEPowell) **3-7-5**(5) MBaird(8) (hdwy over 3f out: wknd over 2f out)........s.h **8** 33/1 21 —
(SP 117.2%) **8 Rn**

**1m 14.87** (4.27) CSF £79.14 CT £148.34 TOTE £10.20: £2.60 £2.70 £1.10 (£29.60) OWNER Allen & Associates (EPSOM) BRED P. Henley
LONG HANDICAP Zuno Princess (IRE) 7-9

**Rowlandsons Stud (IRE)**, held up travelling well, was woken up to lead inside the final furlong and ran on for a cosy success. (8/1: op 5/1)
**Dancing Jack** went on soon after halfway but was firmly put in his place by the winner inside the final furlong. (11/1: 6/1-12/1)
**Arlington Lady**, well supported, was making her All-Weather debut. Chasing the leaders, she was being bustled along over a quarter of a mile from home and, although just sneaking third place, never looked like posing a real threat. (Evens)
**467 Young Mazaad (IRE)**, making a quick reappearance, showed in front early on and remained close up until tapped for toe in the last two furlongs. (5/1)
**Sunset Harbour (IRE)** (6/1: op 7/2)
**Badger Bay (IRE)** (10/1: op 6/1)

## 489 SANTIAGO H'CAP (0-70) (4-Y.O+) (Class E)

4-50 (4-50) **1m 4f (Equitrack)** £3,070.20 (£915.60: £436.80: £197.40) Stalls: Low GOING minus 0.49 sec per fur (FST)

SP RR SF

349[3] **Colosse (44)** (JLEyre) **4-8-8** JQuinn(1) (lw: hdwy over 4f out: led over 1f out: r.o wl)........— **1** 4/6[1] 49 11
**Ready to Draw (IRE) (45)** (RJO'Sullivan) **7-8-11** DBiggs(4) (b: lw: hld up: rdn over 4f out: led over 2f out tl over 1f out: unable qckn)........2½ **2** 8/1[3] 47 11
296[6] **Bag of Tricks (IRE) (58)** (SDow) **6-9-5**(5) ADaly(2) (plld hrd: w ldr over 10f out: led 7f out tl over 2f out: one pce)........s.h **3** 9/4[2] 60 24
104[7] **Telephus (30)** (BJMcMath) **7-7-10b** NAdams(3) (a bhd)........16 **4** 14/1 10 —
83[14] **Persian Haze (IRE) (39)** (BJMcMath) **7-8-5b** GBardwell(5) (led 5f: wknd 5f out: t.o)........23 **5** 33/1 — —
(SP 111.5%) **5 Rn**

**2m 36.53** (6.53) CSF £6.06 TOTE £1.30: £1.10 £2.10 (£4.80) OWNER Diamond Racing Ltd (HAMBLETON) BRED Lariston Bloodstock
WEIGHT FOR AGE 4yo-2lb

**Colosse** moved up over quarter of a mile from home. Striking the front below the distance, she soon had the race in the bag. (4/6: op Evens)
**Ready to Draw (IRE)**, fit from hurdling, looked well beforehand but drifted badly in the market. (8/1: op 7/2)
**Bag of Tricks (IRE)** is no easy ride and had pulled his way to the front seven furlongs from home. Collared over a quarter of a mile out, he had a real duel for second place and only just lost out. (9/4)
**Telephus** (14/1: op 8/1)

T/Plpt: £219.50 (35.63 Tckts). T/Qdpt: £51.70 (12.46 Tckts). AK

# LEICESTER (R-H) (Soft, Heavy patches)

## Thursday March 28th

WEATHER: overcast & cold, hail-storm race 1 WIND: mod against

## 490 KNIGHTON MEDIAN AUCTION MAIDEN STKS (2-Y.O) (Class F)

2-25 (2-27) **5f 2y** £2,642.80 (£730.80: £348.40) Stalls: High GOING: 0.56 sec per fur (GS)

SP RR SF

**Iechyd-Da (IRE)** (MBell) **2-9-0** MFenton(3) (leggy: unf: outpcd & pushed along: str run fnl f: led nr fin)........— **1** 5/1[2] 62 —
**Irish Fiction (IRE)** (MRChannon) **2-9-0** RHughes(5) (leggy: sn pushed along: hdwy over 1f out: kpt on nr fin)........¾ **2** 6/4[1] 60 —
**Swino** (PDEvans) **2-9-0** SSanders(6) (leggy: lt-f: w ldr: led ins fnl f: hdd & no ex nr fin)........s.h **3** 12/1 59 —
**Foot Battalion (IRE)** (RHollinshead) **2-9-0** LDettori(2) (lt-f: unf: chsd ldrs: no ex appr fnl f)........2½ **4** 10/1 52 —
**Corinchili** (GGMargarson) **2-8-9** PRobinson(7) (cmpt: bit bkwd: led tl ins fnl f: wknd)........1¼ **5** 7/1[3] 43 —
**Gresatre** (CADwyer) **2-9-0** CDwyer(1) (w'like: bkwd: bhd: hdwy & nt clr run ins fnl f: nvr nrr)........½ **6** 5/1[2] 46 —
**Tinker's Surprise (IRE)** (BJMeehan) **2-9-0** MTebbutt(4) (unf: trckd ldrs: rdn over 2f out: wknd over 1f out)..1¼ **7** 5/1[2] 42 —
(SP 119.3%) **7 Rn**

**67.3 secs** (8.80) CSF £13.24 TOTE £6.80: £3.60 £1.20 (£17.20) OWNER Mr & Mrs K Mercer, Mr & Mrs H Ceredig (NEWMARKET) BRED W. Powell-Harris

**Iechyd-Da (IRE)**, from a stable that likes to field a decent juvenile in this race having run Dankeston and Princely Hush in the last two years, looked fit but backward in his coat. Unseating his rider on the way to post, he did not overexert himself and was allowed to take his chance. Stamina not speed won him this race and, as the ground dries up, he will surely need further. (5/1: 2/1-11/2)
**Irish Fiction (IRE)** looked ready and moved well to post but only made his presence felt as his fitness came into play. (6/4: Evens-13/8)
**Swino** did not impress on the way to post but broke fast and battled for the lead throughout. Just getting on top inside the final furlong, the fast finisher in the centre of the track swamped him. (12/1)
**Foot Battalion (IRE)** kept plugging away but made little impact. (10/1: op 5/1)
**Corinchili**, drawn next to the rail, broke fast and looked to have all bar Swino in trouble by halfway. Her stride shortened inside the final furlong as lack of fitness found her out. (7/1: 16/1-5/1)
**Gresatre**, green going to post, looked the least forward of these but would have got closer but for being forced to switch around the weakening Corinchili in the final 100 yards. (5/1: 2/1-11/2)
**Tinker's Surprise (IRE)** (5/1: op 8/1)

## 491 HARBOROUGH H'CAP (0-80) (4-Y.O+ F & M) (Class D)

2-55 (2-56) **1m 8y** £3,794.40 (£1,132.20: £540.60: £244.80) Stalls: High GOING: 0.56 sec per fur (GS)

SP RR SF

371[2] **Anastina (70)** (NAGraham) **4-9-4** JWeaver(1) (a.p: led over 2f out: clr over 1f out: rdn out)........— **1** 9/4[2] 86 31
**It's Academic (69)** (MrsJRRamsden) **4-9-3** KFallon(4) (hld up: rdn & chsd wnr over 1f out: no imp)........7 **2** 100/30[3] 71 16
**Ballard Lady (IRE) (48)** (JSWainwright) **4-7-10** JQuinn(2) (hdwy over 3f out: one pce fnl 2f)........3½ **3** 20/1 43 —
**Victoria's Secret (IRE) (57)** (MRChannon) **4-8-5** TQuinn(3) (bit bkwd: bhd: hdwy over 2f out: nt rch ldrs).....2½ **4** 8/1 47 —
**Queens Consul (IRE) (80)** (BSRothwell) **6-10-0** MFenton(7) (led 3f: wknd over 2f out)........¾ **5** 8/1 69 14
379[2] **Queen of All Birds (IRE) (78)** (RBoss) **5-9-12** AClark(5) (led after 3f tl over 2f out: sn wknd)........1 **6** 15/8[1] 65 10

402[14] **Royal Dancer (53)** (RJWeaver) **4-7-10v[1]**(5)ow5 ADaly(6) (w ldr 4f: wknd qckly)....dist **7** 25/1 — —
(SP 119.5%) **7 Rn**

**1m 46.3** (11.30) CSF £10.39 TOTE £2.60: £1.70 £1.60 (£6.90) OWNER R and A Craddock (NEWMARKET) BRED R. and A. Craddock
LONG HANDICAP Ballard Lady (IRE) 7-5 Royal Dancer 5-10

**OFFICIAL EXPLANATION Queens Consul (IRE): explaining the mare's apparent tender handling, the jockey reported that she likes to race prominently. Having jumped off well, the mare then began to hang on the soft ground and, thereafter, tried to hang left throughout. Only when she became clear of other runners in the final two furlongs was the rider able to ask her to make progress. The mare then ran on past tired horses.**

**Anastina** continues on the upgrade on, judging by her knee-ation, this surface suited. Drawing away with authority, she can make hay until the ground dries up. (9/4)
**It's Academic** looked fit for this and ran well but is always vulnerable to a well-handicapped rival. (100/30)
**Ballard Lady (IRE)**, back on ground softer than Good for the first time since winning at Haydock last June, was hard at work and no match for the winner in the final quarter-mile. (20/1)
**Victoria's Secret (IRE)** does not act on such a soft surface and was not persevered with. (8/1)
**Queens Consul (IRE)**, in form on the All-Weather since coming over from Ireland, is not very robust and the big weight in testing ground probably found her out. (8/1: op 5/1)
**Queen of All Birds (IRE)** (15/8: 5/4-2/1)

## 492 BURTON OVERY (S) STKS (3-Y.O) (Class G)
3-30 (3-30) **5f 218y** £2,238.00 (£618.00: £294.00) Stalls: High GOING: 0.56 sec per fur (GS)

| | | | | SP | RR | SF |
|---|---|---|---|---|---|---|
| 408[5] | **The Frisky Farmer (60)** (WGMTurner) **3-9-5** AClark(3) (lw: mde virtually all: rdn out) | — | **1** | 2/1 1 | 73 | 17 |
| 445[13] | **Dungeon Princess (IRE)** (MRChannon) **3-8-9** TQuinn(1) (hld up: rdn & hdwy fnl 2f: nt trble wnr) | 1½ | **2** | 2/1 1 | 59 | 3 |
| 427[6] | **Quinntessa** (BPalling) **3-8-9** TSprake(2) (w ldrs: outpcd 2f out: styd on ins fnl f) | ¾ | **3** | 11/2 2 | 57 | 1 |
| 458[11] | **Sharp Monty** (RHollinshead) **3-9-0** KDarley(4) (disp ld after 1f: rdn over 1f out: wknd fnl f) | ½ | **4** | 2/1 1 | 61 | 5 |

(SP 115.4%) **4 Rn**

**1m 19.5** (9.50) CSF £6.35 TOTE £2.10 (£1.90) OWNER Mr G. J. Bush (SHERBORNE) BRED Miss Claire Farrow, Dame Elizabeth & Alexander C
No bid

**The Frisky Farmer**, who won on his debut almost a year ago, was scoring for the first time since and proved tenacious in the closing stages. (2/1)
**Dungeon Princess (IRE)** shaped as if she can win over further. (2/1)
**Quinntessa** is only a pony but appeared to stay a mile on the All-Weather. (11/2)
**Sharp Monty** took the winner on and may have nosed ahead at the halfway stage, only to crack in the final furlong. He is sure to do better when his rivals allow him to dictate. (2/1)

## 493 GADSBY H'CAP (0-90) (3-Y.O) (Class C)
4-05 (4-05) **5f 218y** £5,341.10 (£1,590.80: £757.40: £340.70) Stalls: High GOING: 0.56 sec per fur (GS)

| | | | | SP | RR | SF |
|---|---|---|---|---|---|---|
| 182* | **Weetman's Weigh (IRE) (68)** (RHollinshead) **3-8-9** LDettori(3) (lw: hld up: hdwy over 2f out: rdn 1f out: led ins fnl f) | — | **1** | 5/2 1 | 81 | 30 |
| | **Golden Pond (IRE) (68)** (RFJohnsonHoughton) **3-8-9** JReid(2) (led tl hdd & unable qckn ins fnl f) | nk | **2** | 7/2 3 | 80 | 29 |
| | **White Plains (IRE) (65)** (MBell) **3-8-6** MFenton(5) (lw: hld up: styd on fnl 2f: nt trble ldrs) | 6 | **3** | 3/1 2 | 61 | 10 |
| | **Therhea (IRE) (80)** (BRMillman) **3-9-4**(3) SDrowne(4) (bit bkwd: w ldr over 3f: sn rdn & one pce) | hd | **4** | 9/2 | 76 | 25 |
| 307* | **Maple Burl (66)** (SDow) **3-8-2**(5) ADaly(1) (prom 4f: sn btn) | 2½ | **5** | 9/2 | 55 | 4 |

(SP 112.2%) **5 Rn**

**1m 17.8** (7.80) CSF £10.78 TOTE £2.70: £1.70 £1.20 (£3.90) OWNER Ed Weetman (Haulage & Storage) Ltd (UPPER LONGDON) BRED David Commins

**Weetman's Weigh (IRE)**, 6lb lower than for his recent All-Weather win, made hard work of getting to the front but Dettori then stuck to hands and heels once there to win a shade cheekily. (5/2)
**Golden Pond (IRE)**, on her toes beforehand, was happy to dictate and did not give up without a fight. (7/2)
**White Plains (IRE)** is a good mover and a longer trip on faster ground will bring out the best in him. (3/1: op 13/8)
**Therhea (IRE)** looked well in his coat but in need of this. He ran respectably given that he was a maiden in eight races last year, and was forced to concede 12lb and more to four previous winners. (9/2)
**Maple Burl**, in form on the All-Weather, did have one decent run on turf with cut in the ground to his credit, but failed to reproduce it. (9/2)

## 494 LANGHAM MAIDEN STKS (3-Y.O) (Class D)
4-40 (4-41) **1m 3f 183y** £3,595.50 (£1,071.00: £510.00: £229.50) Stalls: High GOING: 0.56 sec per fur (GS)

| | | | | SP | RR | SF |
|---|---|---|---|---|---|---|
| | **Infamous (USA)** (PFICole) **3-9-0** TQuinn(5) (trckd ldrs: plld out 3f out: rdn over 1f out: r.o to ld wl ins fnl f) | — | **1** | 11/4 2 | 85 | 22 |
| | **Sharaf (IRE) (80)** (JLDunlop) **3-9-0** WCarson(2) (led after 1f: hdd & unable qckn wl ins fnl f) | ½ | **2** | 6/5 1 | 84 | 21 |
| | **A Likely Tale (USA)** (MBell) **3-9-0** MFenton(1) (lw: led 1f: ev ch 4f out tl no ex ins fnl f) | 3 | **3** | 3/1 3 | 80 | 17 |
| | **Kathryn's Pet** (MrsMReveley) **3-8-9** KDarley(4) (scope: dwlt: hld up: hdwy 4f out: ev ch 3f out: edgd rt & btn 1f out) | 7 | **4** | 20/1 | 66+ | 3 |
| 17[8] | **Dream of My Life (USA)** (PGMurphy) **3-8-11**(3) SDrowne(3) (in tch 8f: sn rdn & bhd) | dist | **5** | 33/1 | — | — |

(SP 104.8%) **5 Rn**

**2m 47.1** (18.10) CSF £5.90 TOTE £3.80: £2.90 £1.60 (£2.40) OWNER H. R. H. Prince Fahd Salman (WHATCOMBE) BRED George Waggoner Stables Inc

**Infamous (USA)** has a long, raking stride but is by a sire whose stock excel with a little cut in the ground. Running green when initially pulled out, he took time to get going but finished strongly. He should continue to go the right way. (11/4)
**Sharaf (IRE)** does not move like a soft-ground horse, but again went well on the surface and should not remain a maiden for too long.(6/5: 4/5-5/4)
**A Likely Tale (USA)**, who was very fit, has an action suited to the surface, and only gave way inside the final furlong. (3/1: op 7/4)
**Kathryn's Pet** ran green in the final three furlongs after appearing to travel as well as anything. (20/1)
**Dream of My Life (USA)**, as with his two efforts on the All-Weather, showed precious little. (33/1)

## 495 SIMON DE MONTFORT MAIDEN STKS (3-Y.O+) (Class D)
5-10 (5-13) **1m 1f 218y** £4,059.60 (£1,213.80: £581.40: £265.20) Stalls: High GOING: 0.56 sec per fur (GS)

| | | | | SP | RR | SF |
|---|---|---|---|---|---|---|
| | **Maiden Castle** (JHMGosden) **3-8-7** LDettori(8) (b: str: scope: bit bkwd: led 2f: c centre 4f out: led over 1f out: qcknd clr: easily) | — | **1** | 8/11 1 | 96+ | 38 |

| | Horse | Dist | Pos | SP | RR | SF |
|---|---|---|---|---|---|---|
| | **Orchestra Stall** (JLDunlop) **4-9-13** WCarson(4) (lw: led after 2f: hdd over 1f out: r.o) | 10 | **2** | 4/1[2] | 80 | 42 |
| | **Hanbitooh (USA)** (EALDunlop) **3-8-7** TQuinn(5) (lw: plld hrd: w ldrs 7f: outpcd fnl 2f) | 12 | **3** | 10/1 | 61 | 3 |
| | **Frankly Fran** (DWPArbuthnot) **4-9-8** SWhitworth(3) (b: chsd ldrs: one pce fnl 4f) | hd | **4** | 33/1 | 56 | 18 |
| | **Talathath (FR)** (CADwyer) **4-9-13** CDwyer(7) (bit bkwd: hld up: stdy hdwy 4f out: nt rch ldrs) | 13 | **5** | 7/1[3] | 40 | 2 |
| | **Sayitagain** (JRJenkins) **4-9-13** CRutter(2) (in tch: rdn 3f out: sn btn) | hd | **6** | 20/1 | 40 | 2 |
| | **Aim For Stardom** (MJAhern) **4-9-13** RHughes(1) (hdwy 4f out: wknd over 2f out) | ¾ | **7** | 50/1 | 38 | — |
| | **Tarian (USA)** (GBBalding) **4-9-10**(3) SDrowne(9) (bkwd: bhd fnl 4f) | 23 | **8** | 33/1 | 2 | — |
| | **Captive Song (IRE)** (PWHarris) **4-9-13** GHind(6) (bkwd: dwlt: rdn 4f out: a bhd) | 15 | **9** | 16/1 | — | — |
| | | | | (SP 118.0%) | **9 Rn** | |

**2m 15.9** (12.20) CSF £4.30 TOTE £1.70: £1.10 £1.60 £5.00 (£2.10) Trio £6.30 OWNER Sheikh Mohammed (NEWMARKET) BRED Cheveley Park Stud Ltd

WEIGHT FOR AGE 3yo-20lb

**Maiden Castle** looked to need this, but fairly bolted up in style of a useful horse. Despite the bandages, his action suggests he will appreciate better ground. (8/11)

**Orchestra Stall**, third to two Gosden horses in this race last year, has been absent since, but found it was business as usual on his return. Not likely to be well handicapped now he is eligible for a mark, he may prove tricky to place. (4/1)

**Hanbitooh (USA)**, who was noisy and keen in the paddock, looks a real handful. (10/1)

**Frankly Fran**, having only her third race, never really got into the action. (33/1)

**Talathath (FR)**, formerly with Michael Stoute and off since September 1994, had a considerate reintroduction to action and is worth keeping an eye on. (7/1: op 4/1)

**Sayitagain** ran respectably for a long way but has yet to threaten to live up to a decent pedigree. (20/1)

## 496 KIBWORTH H'CAP (0-85) (3-Y.O+) (Class D)

5-40 (5-43) **7f 9y** £3,993.30 (£1,193.40: £571.20: £260.10) Stalls: High GOING: 0.56 sec per fur (GS)

| | Horse | Dist | Pos | SP | RR | SF |
|---|---|---|---|---|---|---|
| 406[7] | **Scharnhorst (66)** (SDow) **4-8-5**(5) ADaly(1) (mde all: edgd rt & hung on wl fnl f) | — | **1** | 20/1 | 76 | 58 |
| | **Duello (59)** (MBlanshard) **5-8-3** NAdams(5) (hdwy over 3f out: ev ch ins fnl f: unable qckn) | ½ | **2** | 12/1 | 68 | 50 |
| 451[2] | **Sycamore Lodge (IRE) (67)** (MrsJRRamsden) **5-8-11** KFallon(10) (sn pushed along: hdwy 2f out: r.o fnl f) | 1½ | **3** | 6/4[1] | 73 | 55 |
| | **Denbrae (IRE) (70)** (DJGMurraySmith) **4-8-9**(5) RPainter(11) (in tch: rdn over 2f out: kpt on one pce) | 7 | **4** | 14/1 | 60 | 42 |
| | **Bon Luck (IRE) (70)** (JRFanshawe) **4-9-0** DHarrison(9) (lw: in tch: rdn & no imp fnl 2f) | 2½ | **5** | 11/1 | 54 | 36 |
| 357[8] | **Loveyoumillions (IRE) (84)** (MJohnston) **4-10-0** JWeaver(3) (w wnr over 4f: wknd over 1f out) | ½ | **6** | 11/1 | 67 | 49 |
| 440[19] | **East Barns (IRE) (52)** (SGollings) **8-7-5b**(5) PFessey(8) (chsd ldrs 5f) | nk | **7** | 12/1 | 34 | 16 |
| | **Great Hall (55)** (PDCundell) **7-7-6**(7) MartinDwyer(7) (sn pushed along & bhd: nvr trbld ldrs) | 2½ | **8** | 12/1 | 31 | 13 |
| | **Sheilana (IRE) (74)** (TGMills) **3-8-3** TWilliams(4) (lw: rdn after 2f: sn bhd) | 5 | **9** | 12/1 | 39 | 6 |
| 357[12] | **Amahsan (IRE) (75)** (CDBroad) **4-9-5** MFenton(6) (plld hrd: prom over 3f: sn wknd) | 16 | **10** | 33/1 | 4 | — |
| | **Hawa Al Nasamaat (USA) (81)** (EALDunlop) **4-9-11** WCarson(12) (chsd ldrs 5f: sn wknd & eased) | 4 | **11** | 10/1[3] | 1 | — |
| | **Duffertoes (73)** (MJRyan) **4-9-3** AClark(2) (plld hrd: chsd ldrs 4f: sn wknd) | 1¼ | **12** | 7/1[2] | — | — |
| | | | | (SP 123.4%) | **12 Rn** | |

**1m 29.9** (6.90) CSF £219.56 CT £541.35 TOTE £33.30: £6.10 £1.60 £1.10 (£80.40) Trio £77.00 OWNER Mackenzie Print (EPSOM) BRED M. F. Kentish

LONG HANDICAP East Barns (IRE) 7-4

WEIGHT FOR AGE 3yo-15lb

**Scharnhorst** seemed to like this ground and bounced back to form, dictating the running. (20/1)

**Duello** has won only once in thirty two outings and was worried out of this where it matters. (12/1: op 7/1)

**451 Sycamore Lodge (IRE)** gave the leaders plenty of rope and could never claw them back. His record of no wins but thirteen places in twenty three outings, suggests he is not one to trust. (6/4)

**Denbrae (IRE)**, taken to post before the others, was never travelling well but kept doing his best. (14/1)

**Bon Luck (IRE)** found precious little when let down, and may have needed this more than it appeared. (11/1: 8/1-12/1)

**Loveyoumillions (IRE)** seems to have forgotten how to win but this trip in such testing conditions is beyond him. (11/1)

**East Barns (IRE)** (12/1: op 33/1)

**Great Hall** (12/1: op 8/1)

**Duffertoes** (7/1: op 4/1)

T/Plpt: £14.20 (553 Tckts). T/Qdpt: £5.50 (109.88 Tckts). Dk

# HANOVER (Germany) (L-H) (Good)

## Sunday March 24th

## 497a TOTO-LOTTO-SPRINTPREIS (Listed) (4-Y.O+)

3-10 **6f 110y** £10,811.00

| Horse | Dist | Pos | SP | RR | SF |
|---|---|---|---|---|---|
| **Walking Possession** (MKahn,Sweden) **7-8-9b** JohnFortune | — | **1** | | 104 | — |
| **Takaddum (USA)** (FrauJSchultheis,Germany) **8-9-2** PVandekeere | 3 | **2** | | 104 | — |
| **Novize** (EGroschel,Germany) **5-8-9b[1]** LPyritz | 3½ | **3** | | 88 | — |
| **Champagne Grandy** (MRChannon) **6-8-7** AGorman (btn over 10l) | | **0** | | — | — |
| | | | | | **13 Rn** |

**1m 20.8** TOTE 147Dm: 43Dm 39Dm 55Dm (1228Dm) OWNER Stall Lambada BRED Downclose Stud

**Champagne Grandy** never looked like posing a threat and appears not to be up to listed class.

# 0484-LINGFIELD (L-H) (Standard)

## Friday March 29th

WEATHER: Fine

## 498 COLD AS CHARITY CLAIMING STKS (4-Y.O+) (Class F)

2-20 (2-25) **1m 4f (Equitrack)** £2,690.40 (£744.40: £355.20) Stalls: Low GOING minus 0.49 sec per fur (FST)

| | Horse | Dist | Pos | SP | RR | SF |
|---|---|---|---|---|---|---|
| 379[6] | **Sweet Supposin (IRE) (75)** (CADwyer) **5-9-6v** LDettori(2) (lw: hld up: led over 2f out: pushed out) | — | **1** | 2/1[2] | 83 | 10 |

| | | | | | |
|---|---|---|---|---|---|
| 339[7] **Guest Alliance (IRE) (53)** (AMoore) **4-8-8** CandyMorris(1) (b.hind: led over 9f: unable qckn) | 4 | **2** | 25/1 | 68 | — |
| 411* **El Volador (76)** (CNAllen) **9-9-1**(5) MHenry(4) (hdwy over 3f out: rdn over 2f out: one pce) | ½ | **3** | 5/4[1] | 77 | 4 |
| 350* **Masnun (USA) (66)** (RJO'Sullivan) **11-8-10** AClark(5) (plld hrd: hdwy over 3f out: wknd over 2f out) | 12 | **4** | 7/2[3] | 51 | — |
| 409[9] **Mystic Legend (IRE)** (TJNaughton) **4-9-4** DHarrison(3) (b: lw: chsd ldr 9f) | 20 | **5** | 100/1 | 34 | — |
| | | | (SP 104.8%) | | **5 Rn** |

**2m 38.58** (8.58) CSF £25.92 TOTE £2.50: £1.10 £5.10 (£15.40) OWNER Binding Matters Ltd (NEWMARKET) BRED Ballylinch Stud Ltd
WEIGHT FOR AGE 4yo-2lb

**Sweet Supposin (IRE)**, back in his own class, was given a lovely ride by Dettori to get this longer trip. Held up in third place in a slowly-run race, he went on over a quarter of a mile out and needed only to be nudged along to secure his sixth win on the Equitrack. (2/1)

**Guest Alliance (IRE)**, 20lb or more behind his three main rivals on Adjusted Official Ratings, ran a fine race in the circumstances. Setting little more than a crawl in the first half of the race, he then quickened things up and, although collared over a quarter of a mile from home, just managed to hold on for second prize. (25/1)

**El Volador**, a real course specialist who is well suited by this trip, was held up off the pace. Moving up over three furlongs from home, he had a real battle for second prize in the straight and just lost out. (5/4)

**Masnun (USA)** has been in great heart this winter but quite simply failed to see out this longer trip. Taking a keen hold in the early stages in this slowly-run race, he made an effort over three furlongs from home, but the writing was on the wall turning into the straight. (7/2: op 9/4)

## 499 APPLE A DAY (S) STKS (4-Y.O+) (Class G)

2-55 (3-00) **1m 2f (Equitrack)** £2,364.00 (£654.00: £312.00) Stalls: Low GOING minus 0.49 sec per fur (FST)

| | | | SP | RR | SF |
|---|---|---|---|---|---|
| 318[2] **Awesome Power (47)** (JWHills) **10-9-4** AClark(6) (chsd ldr over 7f out: led 4f out: clr over 1f out: rdn out) | — | **1** | 11/1 | 61 | 23 |
| 420[5] **Northern Trial (USA) (50)** (KRBurke) **8-8-5v**(7) TAshley(10) (b.hind: a.p: chsd wnr over 2f out: hrd rdn over 1f out: r.o wl) | s.h | **2** | 4/1[1] | 55 | 17 |
| 464[4] **Thorniwama (32)** (JJBridger) **5-8-2b**(5) ADaly(11) (rdn over 4f out: hdwy over 1f out: str run fnl f: fin wl) | 2 | **3** | 20/1 | 47 | 9 |
| 353[7] **Kentavrus Way (IRE) (29)** (AMoore) **5-8-12** CandyMorris(12) (b.hind: stdy hdwy over 7f out: rdn over 3f out: r.o one pce fnl 2f) | 1¼ | **4** | 33/1 | 50 | 12 |
| 406[11] **Nivasha (38)** (RPCHoad) **4-8-7** MFenton(4) (a.p: rdn over 4f out: one pce) | 2 | **5** | 14/1 | 42 | 4 |
| **Our Eddie (64)** (BGubby) **7-8-12v** JQuinn(5) (bit bkwd: hld up: rdn over 4f out: wknd fnl f) | 1 | **6** | 6/1[3] | 45 | 7 |
| 477[8] **No Submission (USA) (62)** (DWChapman) **10-9-4v** ACulhane(9) (stdy hdwy over 6f out: wknd over 2f out) | ¾ | **7** | 4/1[1] | 50 | 12 |
| 373[9] **The Cape Doctor (IRE) (43)** (AGFoster) **4-8-9**(3) AWhelan(1) (b: bhd fnl 4f) | 5 | **8** | 25/1 | 36 | — |
| 319[2] **Total Rach (IRE) (51)** (RIngram) **4-8-13b** WWoods(7) (b: rdn over 4f out: sme hdwy over 3f out: wknd over 2f out) | 2½ | **9** | 5/1[2] | 33 | — |
| 351[3] **Jebi (USA)** (CMurray) **6-8-12** MTebbutt(8) (a bhd) | 4 | **10** | 11/1 | 25 | — |
| 409[8] **Tandridge (IRE) (45)** (JRJenkins) **4-8-7** JFortune(2) (bhd fnl 4f) | 3½ | **11** | 25/1 | 15 | — |
| 451[21] **Rockville Pike (IRE) (72)** (SDow) **4-8-12** TQuinn(3) (led 6f: wknd over 2f out) | nk | **12** | 12/1 | 19 | — |
| | | | (SP 117.4%) | | **12 Rn** |

**2m 9.39** (5.09) CSF £50.77 TOTE £11.50: £1.90 £2.10 £9.50 (£16.60) Trio £283.90; £200.00 to Aintree 30/3/96 OWNER Mr Garrett Freyne (LAMBOURN) BRED G. J. Freyne
No bid

**Awesome Power** may not be as good as he was, but this race was still within his compass. Moving to the front half a mile out, he forged clear in the straight but, with the runner-up finishing really fast, he found the line only coming just in time. This was his eighth course victory. (11/1)

**Northern Trial (USA)** moved into second place over a quarter of a mile out and, running on really strongly inside the final furlong, may well have prevailed in a few more strides. When stepped back up to a mile and a half, he can find a claimer or a seller. (4/1)

**464 Thorniwama** at last found her feet from below the distance and finished in tremendous style, although finding the line always coming too soon. Nevertheless, she remains a maiden after twenty attempts. (20/1)

**Kentavrus Way (IRE)** was soon in a handy position but failed to quicken in the last three furlongs. (33/1)

**Nivasha** is very pedestrian and remains a maiden after nineteen attempts. (14/1)

**Our Eddie**, not looking fully wound up for this first run in a year, chased the leaders. Battling for minor honours in the straight, he eventually tired in the final furlong. (6/1)

**No Submission (USA)** (4/1: op 5/2)

**Jebi (USA)** (11/1: 7/1-12/1)

**Rockville Pike (IRE)** (12/1: 10/1-16/1)

## 500 SPINAL INJURIES ASSOCIATION H'CAP (0-90) (3-Y.O+) (Class C)

3-30 (3-35) **5f (Equitrack)** £5,341.10 (£1,590.80: £757.40: £340.70) Stalls: High GOING minus 0.49 sec per fur (FST)

| | | | SP | RR | SF |
|---|---|---|---|---|---|
| 338[3] **Berge (IRE) (76)** (WAO'Gorman) **5-9-1b** EmmaO'Gorman(4) (lw: hdwy over 3f out: led 1f out: pushed out) | — | **1** | 9/2[3] | 85 | 26 |
| 380* **Stand Tall (80)** (CWThornton) **4-9-5** DeanMcKeown(5) (b.hind: hld up: nt clr run wl over 1f out: rdn & r.o) | ½ | **2** | 5/2[1] | 87 | 28 |
| 362[3] **Tenor (63)** (DNicholls) **5-8-2** FNorton(2) (a.p: led over 1f out: sn hdd: unable qckn) | 3 | **3** | 11/2 | 61 | 2 |
| 461[2] **Lord Sky (68)** (ABailey) **5-8-0**(7) AngelaGallimore(3) (lw: a.p: led over 2f out tl over 1f out: wknd fnl f) | 3 | **4** | 100/30[2] | 56 | — |
| 362[5] **Kalar (65)** (DWChapman) **7-7-13b**(5) PFessey(6) (led over 2f: wknd over 1f out) | 1¼ | **5** | 8/1 | 49 | — |
| 407* **Spender (89)** (PWHarris) **7-9-11**(3) JStack(1) (bhd fnl 4f) | 7 | **6** | 11/2 | 51 | — |
| | | | (SP 111.7%) | | **6 Rn** |

**59.81 secs** (1.81) CSF £15.26 TOTE £5.10: £3.00 £2.00 (£8.70) OWNER Mr S. Fustok (NEWMARKET) BRED S. Fustok
OFFICIAL EXPLANATION **Call Tophorse: swallowed his tongue and finished distressed.**

**Berge (IRE)** moved up on the outside of the field over three furlongs from home and, striking the front entering the last 200 yards, needed only to be nudged along to score. (9/2)

**Stand Tall**, 11lb higher than when winning here at the beginning of the month, found himself with a wall of horses in front of him entering the straight. Nevertheless, an opening soon appeared but, despite running on, he was not going to overhaul the winner. All four of his victories have come over six furlongs and a return to that trip would be in his favour. (5/2)

**Tenor** poked a whisker in front over a furlong out but he was soon headed and failed to quicken. (11/2: 4/1-6/1)

**461 Lord Sky** went on at halfway but, headed below the distance, had little more to give inside the last 200 yards. (100/30)

**Spender** (11/2: 4/1-6/1)

## 501 LIGHTWEIGHT PLASTERING H'CAP (0-65) (3-Y.O+) (Class F)

4-05 (4-11) **1m (Equitrack)** £2,880.80 (£798.80: £382.40) Stalls: High GOING minus 0.49 sec per fur (FST)

| | | | SP | RR | SF |
|---|---|---|---|---|---|
| 487* **Victory Team (IRE) (69)** (GBBalding) **4-10-5** 5x AClark(11) (hdwy over 4f out: led ins fnl f: pushed out) | — | **1** | 5/2[1] | 78 | 59 |

| | | | | SP | RR | SF |
|---|---|---|---|---|---|---|
| $412^{5}$ | **Montone (IRE) (46)** (JRJenkins) **6-8-10b** JFortune(2) (chsd ldr: led over 2f out tl ins fnl f: r.o) | ½ | **2** | $7/1^{3}$ | 54 | 35 |
| $412^{11}$ | **Zahran (IRE) (41)** (JMBradley) **5-8-2**$^{(3)ow1}$ SDrowne(6) (lw: lost pl over 2f out: rallied fnl f: fin wl) | nk | **3** | 16/1 | 48 | 28 |
| $412^{4}$ | **Eastleigh (46)** (RHollinshead) **7-8-10b**$^{1}$ LDettori(7) (b.off hind: led: clr 6f out: hdd over 2f out: unable qckn) | 3 | **4** | $7/1^{3}$ | 47 | 28 |
| $412^{2}$ | **Hatta Sunshine (USA) (53)** (AMoore) **6-8-10**$^{(7)}$ IonaWands(5) (lw: b: b.hind: a.p: rdn over 2f out: one pce) | ¾ | **5** | 9/1 | 53 | 34 |
| $487^{5}$ | **Sarum (53)** (CPWildman) **10-9-3** CRutter(9) (b.nr fore: nvr nr to chal) | 1¼ | **6** | 12/1 | 50 | 31 |
| $487^{8}$ | **Labudd (USA) (54)** (RIngram) **6-9-4** WWoods(10) (b: lw: hdwy over 3f out: wknd over 2f out) | 3 | **7** | 20/1 | 45 | 26 |
| $417^{4}$ | **Top Pet (IRE) (45)** (RAkehurst) **6-8-9** TQuinn(3) (bhd fnl 6f) | 1½ | **8** | 8/1 | 33 | 14 |
| $336^{3}$ | **Little Scarlett (46)** (PJMakin) **4-8-10** SSanders(12) (hdwy over 3f out: wknd over 2f out) | 1¼ | **9** | 12/1 | 32 | 13 |
| $416^{5}$ | **Lilac Rain (46)** (JRArnold) **4-8-10** JQuinn(8) (a bhd) | 8 | **10** | 14/1 | 16 | — |
| $11^{9}$ | **Moving Up (IRE) (54)** (GLMoore) **3-8-1** NAdams(1) (b.nr hind: bhd fnl 5f) | 20 | **11** | 25/1 | — | — |
| 334* | **Call Tophorse (45)** (CMurray) **4-8-9b** MTebbutt(4) (bhd fnl 4f) | 14 | **12** | $13/2^{2}$ | — | — |
| | | | | (SP 124.6%) | **12 Rn** | |

**1m 39.03** (1.63) CSF £20.49 CT £226.17 TOTE £2.60: £1.70 £2.10 £3.90 (£12.50) Trio £42.60 OWNER Mr R. J. Lavelle (ANDOVER) BRED Barronstown and Swettenham Studs and Ron Con Ltd

WEIGHT FOR AGE 3yo-17lb

**OFFICIAL EXPLANATION Call Tophorse: swallowed his tongue and finished distressed.**

**487* Victory Team (IRE)** followed up Wednesday's success here in good style. Moving up just before halfway, he travelled sweetly and needed only to be woken up to lead inside the final furlong. He will step down to seven furlongs or even six for a turf campaign and that should not pose a problem at all. (5/2)

**Montone (IRE)** certainly had his chances, but was just touched off. He went on over a quarter of a mile out, but was put in his place by the winner in the final furlong. (7/1)

**Zahran (IRE)** chased the leaders but got outpaced over a quarter of a mile from home. Getting a second wind in the final furlong to some effect, he was never going to get there in time. (16/1)

**Eastleigh** attempted to make all the running. Eventually overhauled over a quarter of a mile from home, he could only keep on in his own time. (7/1)

**Top Pet (IRE)** (8/1: op 5/1)

## 502 SPINAL INJURIES ASSOCIATION MAIDEN STKS (3-Y.O+) (Class D)

4-40 (4-46) **1m 2f (Equitrack)** £3,794.40 (£1,132.20: £540.60: £244.80) Stalls: Low GOING minus 0.49 sec per fur (FST)

| | | | | SP | RR | SF |
|---|---|---|---|---|---|---|
| | **Carol's Dream (USA) (72)** (JWHills) **4-9-10** TQuinn(6) (lw: led over 8f out: clr over 2f out: hrd rdn over 1f out: eased ins fnl f) | — | **1** | $15/2^{3}$ | 80+ | 46 |
| | **Soviet Shore** (DRLoder) **4-9-10** LDettori(7) (hld up: rdn over 3f out: chsd wnr over 2f out: eased whn btn ins fnl f) | 6 | **2** | $4/7^{1}$ | 70 | 36 |
| $390^{2}$ | **State Circus** (LordHuntingdon) **3-7-8**$^{(5)}$ MHenry(2) (lw: hld up: rdn 4f out: r.o ins fnl f) | 3 | **3** | $3/1^{2}$ | 61 | 7 |
| $319^{3}$ | **Kellaire Girl (IRE) (45)** (AMoore) **4-9-2v**$^{(3)}$ AWhelan(1) (b.hind: lw: led over 1f: 3rd & wkng whn bmpd over 2f out) | 3½ | **4** | 50/1 | 55 | 21 |
| $419^{4}$ | **Nelly's Cousin** (NACallaghan) **3-7-8**$^{(5)}$ PFessey(5) (nvr nr to chal) | nk | **5** | 40/1 | 55 | 1 |
| $355^{11}$ | **Two Socks (55)** (MMcCormack) **3-8-4** AClark(9) (a.p: rdn over 4f out: wknd over 3f out) | 2½ | **6** | 50/1 | 56 | 2 |
| $390^{6}$ | **Rubbiyati** (CEBrittain) **4-9-5** DHarrison(8) (hdwy over 3f out: sn wknd) | 1¾ | **7** | 16/1 | 48 | 14 |
| | **Denomination (USA)** (IABalding) **4-9-10** JWeaver(4) (bhd fnl 4f) | nk | **8** | 25/1 | 52 | 18 |
| $361^{2}$ | **Lord Ellangowan (IRE) (45)** (RIngram) **3-8-4b** WWoods(3) (b: lw: prom 6f) | 2½ | **9** | 66/1 | 48 | — |
| $409^{10}$ | **P Grayco Choice** (PCClarke) **3-7-13** NAdams(10) (a bhd: t.o) | dist | **10** | 100/1 | — | — |
| | | | | (SP 119.0%) | **10 Rn** | |

**2m 7.04** (2.74) CSF £11.95 TOTE £6.20: £1.30 £1.10 £2.60 (£3.70) Trio £2.30 OWNER Mrs Carol Lane (LAMBOURN) BRED North Highland Farm and Louie Roussel III

WEIGHT FOR AGE 3yo-20lb

**Carol's Dream (USA)**, who has had a soft-palate operation since last season, gained a decisive victory on this All-Weather debut. Soon at the head of affairs, he forged clear over a quarter of a mile out, but his jockey was going to take no chances and administered several blows of the whip below the distance. However, he was never going to be caught and was eased down inside the final furlong with the race safely in the bag. (15/2)

**Soviet Shore**, a brother to Soviet Line, made a very promising debut at Yarmouth back in September 1994, but missed last year after fracturing his knee on the gallops. Looking big and well for this reappearance, he was all the rage in the market and moved into second place over a quarter of a mile from home. However, he never looked like reeling in the winner and the situation was accepted inside the last 200 yards. (4/7)

**State Circus** looked really well beforehand but, when the tempo increased from halfway, she was caught rather flat-footed. Bustled along and not making a great deal of impression, she at last ran on from below the distance but, by then, it was all too late. (3/1)

**Kellaire Girl (IRE)** raced up with the pace but was tiring in third place when given a bump by Soviet Shore over two furlongs from home. She remains a maiden after eighteen attempts. (50/1)

## 503 BALD COOT H'CAP (0-75) (3-Y.O) (Class D)

5-10 (5-15) **7f (Equitrack)** £3,529.20 (£1,050.60: £499.80: £224.40) Stalls: Low GOING minus 0.49 sec per fur (FST)

| | | | | SP | RR | SF |
|---|---|---|---|---|---|---|
| $321^{3}$ | **Moi Canard (69)** (BAPearce) **3-9-4** LDettori(2) (lw: hld up: swtchd rt over 1f out: led wl ins fnl f: r.o wl) | — | **1** | $11/4^{1}$ | 76 | 23 |
| $463^{2}$ | **Domoor (60)** (MJohnston) **3-8-9** JWeaver(3) (lw: hld up: led over 1f out tl wl ins fnl f: unable qckn) | 1½ | **2** | $11/4^{1}$ | 64 | 11 |
| $335^{3}$ | **Myttons Mistake (72)** (ABailey) **3-9-4**$^{(3)}$ DWright(4) (b: hld up: rdn over 1f out: ev ch ins fnl f: one pce) | hd | **3** | $4/1^{2}$ | 75 | 22 |
| $468^{5}$ | **Ivory's Grab Hire (54)** (KTIvory) **3-8-0**$^{(3)}$ JStack(5) (hdwy 6f out: led over 3f out tl over 1f out: one pce) | 1¼ | **4** | 16/1 | 55 | 2 |
| $377^{2}$ | **Baranov (IRE) (65)** (DJGMurraySmith) **3-9-0** TQuinn(6) (b.off hind: led 2f: ev ch 2f out: wknd over 1f out) | 7 | **5** | $9/2^{3}$ | 50 | — |
| $488^{3}$ | **Arlington Lady (47)** (NACallaghan) **3-7-5**$^{(5)}$ PFessey(1) (w ldr: led 5f out tl over 3f out: ev ch 2f out: wknd over 1f out) | 2½ | **6** | 5/1 | 26 | — |
| | | | | (SP 114.1%) | **6 Rn** | |

**1m 27.29** (3.29) CSF £10.42 TOTE £2.90: £1.40 £1.70 (£3.70) OWNER Mr Richard Gray (LINGFIELD) BRED Llety Stud

LONG HANDICAP Arlington Lady 7-3

**Moi Canard,** switched right to get a run below the distance, came with a useful rattle to snatch the spoils in the closing stages. (11/4)

**463 Domoor** came through to lead below the distance, but was unable to prevent the winner going by in the closing stages. (11/4)

**Myttons Mistake** chased the leaders. One of three battling for the lead inside the final furlong, he was then tapped for toe. (4/1)

**468 Ivory's Grab Hire,** making a quick reappearance, went on at halfway. Collared below the distance, he was then tapped for toe. (16/1)

**Baranov (IRE)** (9/2: op 5/2)

**488 Arlington Lady** (5/1: 3/1-11/2)

T/Plpt: £112.50 (71.23 Tckts). T/Qdpt: £8.20 (102.51 Tckts). AK

# BEVERLEY (R-H) (Good)
## Saturday March 30th
WEATHER: Cloudy

## 504 VALENTINES (S) STKS (4-Y.O+) (Class G)
2-00 (2-00) **1m 3f 216y** £2,337.50 (£650.00: £312.50) Stalls: High GOING: 0.10 sec per fur (G)

| | Horse / Details | Dist | Pos | SP | RR | SF |
|---|---|---|---|---|---|---|
| 333[6] | **Bold Pursuit (IRE)** (JGFitzGerald) **7-8-13** KFallon(7) (b: pushed along ½-wy: hdwy over 3f out: led over 1f out: drvn out) | — | 1 | 5/2 [1] | 47 | 27 |
| 208[6] | **Never Time (IRE) (40)** (MrsVAAconley) **4-8-11** MDeering(5) (hld up: hdwy over 2f out: ev ch 1f out: edgd lft: kpt on) | 2½ | 2 | 16/1 | 44 | 22 |
| | **Bold Top (40)** (BSRothwell) **4-8-11b** MFenton(4) (chsd ldrs: led over 3f out tl over 1f out: one pce) | 1¼ | 3 | 10/1 | 42 | 20 |
| | **Desert Force (IRE) (35)** (GFierro) **7-8-13** MWigham(12) (bit bkwd: b: chsd ldrs: drvn along 4f out: one pce) | 3½ | 4 | 16/1 | 37 | 17 |
| 400[7] | **Can She Can Can (43)** (CSmith) **4-8-11** JFanning(11) (w ldr: led ½-wy tl over 3f out: one pce) | nk | 5 | 12/1 | 37 | 15 |
| | **Park Ridge (50)** (TGMills) **4-8-11** JFortune(10) (hdwy u.p over 3f out: wknd over 2f out) | 4 | 6 | 10/1 | 32 | 10 |
| 401[2] | **Anistop (50)** (JLEyre) **4-9-2** RLappin(1) (effrt over 3f out: sn rdn: wknd 2f out) | 2 | 7 | 3/1 [2] | 34 | 12 |
| 251[4] | **Antartictern (USA) (42)** (GROldroyd) **6-8-13v[1]** LCharnock(6) (lw: bhd: hdwy ½-wy: wknd 3f out) | 3½ | 8 | 9/1 | 24 | 4 |
| 429* | **Adaloaldo (USA) (55)** (JParkes) **4-8-11**(5) RHavlin(8) (hdwy & swtchd outside ½-wy: sn chsng ldrs: wknd over 1f out) | 6 | 9 | 6/1 [3] | 21 | — |
| | **Hatta River (USA) (48)** (JAHarris) **6-8-13** JWeaver(9) (lw: dwlt s: bhd: hdwy on outside 3f out: wknd over 1f out) | 1¼ | 10 | 8/1 | 15 | — |
| 284[8] | **Stylish Gent** (GROldroyd) **9-8-6v**(7) AColgan(3) (led to ½-wy: lost pl 4f out) | 10 | 11 | 33/1 | 1 | — |
| | **Taufeliane** (JLHarris) **5-8-8** JQuinn(2) (chsd ldrs tl lost pl over 4f out: sn bhd) | ½ | 12 | 33/1 | — | — |

(SP 132.5%) **12 Rn**

**2m 44.4** (12.00) CSF £43.26 TOTE £3.90: £1.50 £5.00 £2.60 (£47.80) Trio £79.80 OWNER Mr R. J. Wragg (MALTON) BRED A. Tarry
WEIGHT FOR AGE 4yo-2lb
No bid

**Bold Pursuit (IRE)** made hard work of this. Pushed along at halfway, in the end, he won going away. (5/2)
**Never Time (IRE)**, still a maiden on this his twenty-sixth outing, wandered and edged left under pressure, and was well beaten in the end. (16/1)
**Bold Top** has run over a variety of distances and made the best of his way home, but tired entering the final furlong. (10/1)
**Desert Force (IRE)**, driven along some way out, proved woefully one-paced. (16/1)
**Can She Can Can** could only keep on in her own time and will be suited by further. (12/1)
**Adaloaldo (USA)** (6/1: 7/2-7/1)

## 505 RACING CHANNEL H'CAP (0-70) (3-Y.O+) (Class E)
2-35 (2-38) **7f 100y** £3,286.50 (£987.00: £476.00: £220.50) Stalls: High GOING: 0.10 sec per fur (G)

| | Horse / Details | Dist | Pos | SP | RR | SF |
|---|---|---|---|---|---|---|
| 357* | **Pine Ridge Lad (IRE) (54)** (JLEyre) **6-8-12** RLappin(7) (mde virtually all: styd on wl towards fin) | — | 1 | 3/1 [1] | 69 | 58 |
| 211[6] | **Rambo Waltzer (50)** (DNicholls) **4-8-8** AlexGreaves(3) (lw: a chsng wnr: chal over 1f out: nt qckn ins fnl f) | ½ | 2 | 8/1 | 64 | 53 |
| | **Primo Lara (65)** (PWHarris) **4-9-9** GHind(1) (trckd ldrs: kpt on same pce fnl 2f) | 3 | 3 | 9/2 [2] | 73 | 62 |
| 199[7] | **Legal Issue (IRE) (65)** (WWHaigh) **4-9-6**(3) PMcCabe(16) (lw: a.p: rdn & hung rt over 1f out: grad wknd) | 7 | 4 | 9/1 | 58 | 47 |
| 205[W] | **Scorpius (54)** (TTClement) **6-8-9**(3) JStack(9) (t: sn chsng ldrs: hung lft & wknd over 1f out) | ¾ | 5 | 16/1 | 45 | 34 |
| 399[9] | **Cee-Jay-Ay (59)** (JBerry) **9-8-12**(5) PRoberts(4) (dwlt s: bhd: hdwy on outside 2f out: nvr nr ldrs) | 1½ | 6 | 16/1 | 47 | 36 |
| | **Sea-Ayr (IRE) (49)** (MrsSMAustin) **6-8-4**(3) DarrenMoffatt(11) (bit bkwd: b: sn trckng ldrs: wknd over 1f out) | hd | 7 | 10/1 | 36 | 25 |
| | **Ochos Rios (IRE) (59)** (BSRothwell) **5-9-3** MFenton(6) (in tch: effrt over 2f out: grad wknd) | nk | 8 | 14/1 | 46 | 35 |
| | **Self Expression (53)** (MrsJRRamsden) **8-8-11** KFallon(15) (bhd: hdwy on ins over 2f out: nvr nr ldrs) | 4 | 9 | 10/1 | 31 | 20 |
| | **Craigie Boy (51)** (NBycroft) **6-8-9** JQuinn(17) (bit bkwd: plld hrd: trckd ldrs: n.m.r on ins 4f out: sn lost pl) | 1 | 10 | 16/1 | 27 | 16 |
| 341[3] | **Karinska (66)** (MCChapman) **6-9-10** JWeaver(5) (a in rr) | 1 | 11 | 7/1 [3] | 40 | 29 |
| 159[U] | **Lady Silk (55)** (MissJFCraze) **5-8-13** JMcLaughlin(12) (bit bkwd: a bhd) | 3 | 12 | 25/1 | 23 | 12 |
| | **Murphy's Gold (IRE) (55)** (RAFahey) **5-8-13** ACulhane(13) (bit bkwd: hld up & plld hrd: hmpd 6f out: n.d) | 1 | 13 | 11/1 | 20 | 9 |
| | **Nizaal (USA) (67)** (DNicholls) **5-9-11** MRichardson(14) (bit bkwd: mid div: rdn ½-wy: n.d) | ¾ | 14 | 25/1 | 31 | 20 |
| | **Desert Calm (IRE) (62)** (MrsPNDutfield) **7-9-3**(3) SDrowne(10) (a bhd) | 3½ | 15 | 16/1 | 18 | 7 |
| | **Birchwood Sun (66)** (MDods) **6-9-10** DaleGibson(2) (bit bkwd: sn bhd: t.o 2f out) | 21 | 16 | 16/1 | — | — |

(SP 147.1%) **16 Rn**

**1m 36.1** (4.10) CSF £31.71 CT £111.17 TOTE £2.90: £1.50 £2.60 £1.20 £2.90 (£10.70) Trio £54.70 OWNER Whitestonecliffe Racing Partnership (HAMBLETON) BRED Whitechurch Stud in Ireland

**Pine Ridge Lad (IRE)**, on a 25lb lower mark than when winning on the All-Weather last time, showed what a tough sort he is, sticking his head out when challenged, and getting on top towards the line. (3/1)
**Rambo Waltzer**, 28lb better handicapped on turf than on the All-Weather, looked to be going slightly better when moving upsides over a furlong out but, in the dash to the line, the winner proved slightly more determined. (8/1)
**Primo Lara**, a keen-going sort, ran well from the worst draw. (9/2)
**Legal Issue (IRE)**, who tends to miss the break, broke on terms this time. Hanging right under pressure over a furlong out, he soon faded. (9/1)
**Scorpius**, who changed hands cheaply, has been tubed. (16/1)

## 506 CHAIR MAIDEN AUCTION STKS (2-Y.O F) (Class F)
3-35 (3-36) **5f** £2,693.00 (£748.00: £359.00) Stalls: Low GOING: 0.10 sec per fur (G)

| Horse / Details | Dist | Pos | SP | RR | SF |
|---|---|---|---|---|---|
| **Enchanting Eve** (CNAllen) **2-7-8**(5) MHenry(1) (leggy: mde all: pushed out) | — | 1 | 3/1 [2] | 66 | 12 |
| **Full Traceability (IRE)** (JBerry) **2-7-9**(5) PFessey(6) (neat: chsd ldrs: hung rt ½-wy: kpt on fnl f) | 3 | 2 | 9/2 [3] | 57 | 3 |
| **Small Risk** (CADwyer) **2-7-13** JQuinn(3) (cmpt: trckd ldrs: rn green & edgd rt ½-wy: wknd appr fnl f) | 5 | 3 | 13/8 [1] | 40 | — |
| **Run For Us (IRE)** (CADwyer) **2-7-6**(7) RMullen(2) (leggy: unf: unruly s: sn outpcd & bhd: kpt on fnl f) | 1 | 4 | 8/1 | 37 | — |

**Ramsey Pride** (CWFairhurst) **2-8-3** NKennedy(5) (w ldrs to ½-wy: sn wknd) ....................2 **5** 13/2 35 —
**Morritt Magic** (CWThornton) **2-8-0** LCharnock(4) (cmpt: unf: s.s: bhd tl sme late hdwy)....................hd **6** 12/1 32 —
446[3] **Rahona (IRE)** (BSRothwell) **2-8-2** MFenton(7) (chsd ldrs: drvn along & wl outpcd ½-wy: sn bhd)....................18 **7** 9/2[3] — —
(SP 131.6%) **7 Rn**

**66.5 secs** (5.00) CSF £18.50 TOTE £4.50: £2.00 £1.90 (£13.80) OWNER Mr Alexander MacGillivray (NEWMARKET) BRED P. Young
**Enchanting Eve** looked as if she can run and proved so in the race. Making all the running up the stands' side, she was pushed clear in the final furlong. She looks a good buy. (3/1)
**Full Traceability (IRE)** hung right from halfway. She kept on to finish a clear second best. (9/2)
**Small Risk**, a poor walker, is a keen-going type. Running green and edging out towards the middle at halfway, she tired over a furlong out. (13/8)
**Run For Us (IRE)** played up in the stalls. Taken off her legs, she was staying on towards the finish. (8/1)
**Ramsey Pride** showed a modest action going down. After sitting upsides travelling strongly, she went out like a light at halfway. (13/2)
**Morritt Magic** (12/1: op 8/1)

## 507 EAST RIDING STKS (Listed) (3-Y.O+) (Class A)

4-05 (4-05) **5f** £11,462.25 (£3,468.00: £1,691.50: £803.25) Stalls: Low GOING: 0.10 sec per fur (G)

SP RR SF

**Carranita (IRE) (107)** (BPalling) **6-9-2** TSprake(5) (sn pushed along: hdwy ½-wy: led over 1f out: jst hld on)....................— **1** 4/1 99 38
**Plum First (58)** (LRLloyd-James) **6-9-3** KimberleyHart(2) (sn outpcd & bhd: gd hdwy u.p over 1f out: swtchd rt & styd on strly towards fin)....................s.h **2** 50/1 100 39
**Venture Capitalist (107)** (DNicholls) **7-9-3** AlexGreaves(6) (hdwy ½-wy: ev ch fnl f: r.o)....................hd **3** 5/1 100 39
**Ziggy's Dancer (USA) (85)** (EJAlston) **5-9-3** KFallon(1) (led over 1f: chsd ldrs tl wknd ins fnl f)....................2½ **4** 7/2[3] 92 31
**Ya Malak (113)** (JWPayne) **5-9-7** AMcGlone(3) (w ldr: led over 3f out tl over 1f out: wknd ins fnl f)....................2½ **5** 5/2[1] 88 27
**Lucky Parkes (99)** (JBerry) **6-8-12** JCarroll(4) (chsd ldrs to ½-wy: sn wknd)....................8 **6** 11/4[2] 53 —
(SP 116.1%) **6 Rn**

**65.8 secs** (4.30) CSF £77.14 TOTE £5.20: £2.90 £6.30 (£49.10) OWNER Lamb Lane Associates (COWBRIDGE) BRED Mrs Anita Quinn
**Carranita (IRE)**, better over six furlongs, found this stiff five on ground considerably softer than the official Good ideal. Making ground to show ahead over a furlong out, the post came just in time. (4/1)
**Plum First**, who would have been meeting the winner on an incredible 50lb better terms in a handicap, was soon struggling badly to go the pace. Really woken up by his rider, he picked up ground over a furlong out and, switched wide inside the last, would have pulled off a shock in one more stride. This form must be taken with a large pinch of salt. (50/1)
**Venture Capitalist** ran really well and is even better suited by fast ground. (5/1)
**Ziggy's Dancer (USA)** helped set a strong pace but it was no surprise to see his stride shorten inside the last. (7/2)
**Ya Malak**, who is better covered up, raced keenly and, seeing far too much daylight, tired entering the final furlong. (5/2)
**Lucky Parkes**, put into the stalls last, ran poorly just as she had done in this race a year ago. (11/4: 2/1-3/1)

## 508 MELLING ROAD H'CAP (0-60) (3-Y.O+) (Class F)

4-40 (4-42) **1m 1f 207y** £3,071.00 (£856.00: £413.00) Stalls: High GOING: 0.10 sec per fur (G)

SP RR SF

**Eskimo Nel (IRE) (40)** (JLSpearing) **5-8-9** KFallon(2) (hdwy over 3f out: led over 1f out: rdn clr ins fnl f)....................— **1** 11/4[1] 55 21
402[13] **Anchorena (58)** (JAHarris) **4-9-13v[1]** JWeaver(19) (swtg: bhd: gd hdwy on outside over 2f out: styd on fnl f: no ch w wnr)....................4 **2** 33/1 67 33
**Chilly Lad (53)** (MJRyan) **5-9-8b** DBiggs(15) (bhd: hdwy over 2f out: kpt on fnl f)....................nk **3** 14/1 61 27
360[4] **Noble Canonire (44)** (SRBowring) **4-8-8(5)** CTeague(6) (a chsng ldrs: one pce fnl 2f)....................1¾ **4** 8/1[3] 49 15
**Lord Hastie (USA) (59)** (CWThornton) **8-9-11(3)** OPears(4) (bhd: gd hdwy on outside 2f out: one pce fnl f) .....2 **5** 11/1 61 27
**Broughton's Pride (IRE) (49)** (JAGlover) **5-8-11(7)** VictoriaAppleby(5) (hld up & bhd: styd on fnl 2f: nvr nr ldrs)....................3 **6** 14/1 46 12
70[5] **Larn Fort (54)** (CWFairhurst) **6-9-9v** LCharnock(8) (in tch: effrt & n.m.r 2f out: sn wknd)....................6 **7** 8/1[3] 42 8
440[W] **Sea God (48)** (MCChapman) **5-8-10(7)** CMunday(14) (s.i.s: a in rr)....................6 **8** 14/1 26 —
**Phase One (IRE) (53)** (JLEyre) **6-9-8** KDarley(17) (chsd ldrs tl wknd 2f out)....................½ **9** 20/1 30 —
410[2] **Able Choice (IRE) (43)** (RWArmstrong) **6-8-12** LDettori(9) (in tch: effrt over 2f out: sn wknd & eased)..........1¼ **10** 11/4[1] 18 —
440[23] **Claque (58)** (DWChapman) **4-9-13b** ACulhane(18) (in tch: drvn along & outpcd 5f out: sn lost pl)....................nk **11** 16/1 33 —
**Joli's Great (43)** (MJRyan) **8-8-12** PBloomfield(11) (bit bkwd: sn bhd)....................hd **12** 16/1 17 —
426[7] **Arecibo (FR) (47)** (JParkes) **4-8-11(5)** RHavlin(1) (swtg: sn prom: drvn along 4f out: sn wknd)....................1½ **13** 25/1 19 —
440[4] **Gallardini (IRE) (51)** (BSRothwell) **7-9-6** MFenton(10) (chsd ldrs tl wknd over 2f out)....................1 **14** 11/1 21 —
417[5] **Pointer (43)** (MrsPNDutfield) **4-8-9(3)** SDrowne(16) (chsd ldrs tl wknd over 2f out)....................½ **15** 25/1 13 —
**Latch Key Lady (USA) (48)** (RDEWoodhouse) **4-9-3** JQuinn(13) (swtg: s.i.s: sn in tch: lost pl over 3f out) ....hd **16** 20/1 18 —
**Carlton Express (IRE) (42)** (JLEyre) **6-8-11** RLappin(7) (b.off hind: prom tl wknd over 2f out)....................¾ **17** 25/1 10 —
**College Night (IRE) (45)** (CADwyer) **4-8-11(3)** JStack(3) (racd v.wd: led tl hdd & wknd over 1f out: eased)......4 **18** 7/1[2] 7 —
(SP 160.5%) **18 Rn**

**2m 12.5** (10.00) CSF £104.97 CT £1,173.99 TOTE £4.50: £1.40 £11.70 £7.40 £1.70 (£83.40) Trio Not won; £497.76 to Exeter 1/4/96 OWNER First Chance Racing (ALCESTER) BRED Leo Collins
**Eskimo Nel (IRE)**, better known as a hurdler, took advantage of her Flat rating, winning in good style in the end. (11/4: 5/1-5/2)
**Anchorena**, tried in a visor, made up a lot of ground on the wide outside in the final quarter-mile, but had no chance with the winner. (33/1)
**Chilly Lad** stuck on up the hill and will be better suited by further. (14/1)
**Noble Canonire**, racing from a 7lb lower mark than the All-Weather, could do no more than plug away at the same pace in the final quarter-mile. (8/1)
**Lord Hastie (USA)** ran well under topweight, tiring slightly in the final furlong. He will do better over further soon. (11/1: 8/1-12/1)
**Broughton's Pride (IRE)**, still a maiden after nineteen starts, did not shape too badly and is no forlorn hope. (14/1)
**Larn Fort** (8/1: op 5/1)
**Able Choice (IRE)** was 8lb lower here than when a runner-up on the All-Weather at Lingfield last time. Clearly he is not as effective on grass and, when all hope had gone, Dettori allowed him to come home in his own time. (11/4)

## 509 GRAND NATIONAL DAY H'CAP (0-85) (3-Y.O) (Class D)

5-15 (5-18) **1m 100y** £3,639.00 (£1,092.00: £526.00: £243.00) Stalls: High GOING: 0.10 sec per fur (G)

SP RR SF

**Tabriz (70)** (JDBethell) **3-8-8** JWeaver(5) (led tl over 1f out: rallied to ld towards fin)....................— **1** 5/1[2] 75 30

| | | | | | | |
|---|---|---|---|---|---|---|
| 453[4] | **Theatre Magic (60)** (SRBowring) **3-7-12** NCarlisle(3) (tckd ldr: led over 1f out tl nr fin) ½ | **2** | 8/1 | 64 | 19 |
| *391[6]* | **Kingdom Princess (66)** (MJCamacho) **3-8-4** LCharnock(8) (a chsng ldrs: rdn ½-wy: styd on fnl f) nk | **3** | 9/1 | 70 | 25 |
| | **Spillo (83)** (LMCumani) **3-9-7** LDettori(4) (bit bkwd: hld up: effrt 3f out: styd on fnl f) ½ | **4** | 5/1 2 | 86 | 41 |
| 453[3] | **Silverdale Knight (58)** (KWHogg) **3-7-5**(5) MBaird(2) (a chsng ldrs: one pce fnl 2f) ¾ | **5** | 6/1 3 | 59 | 14 |
| | **Give Me A Ring (IRE) (70)** (CWThornton) **3-8-8** DeanMcKeown(9) (nvr nr ldrs) 5 | **6** | 5/1 2 | 62 | 17 |
| | **Fly Fishing (USA) (70)** (MrsJCecil) **3-8-3**(5) MHenry(1) (chsd ldrs: rdn & edgd lft 2f out: sn wknd) ½ | **7** | 11/4 1 | 61 | 16 |
| *390[5]* | **Whitley Grange Boy (66)** (JLEyre) **3-8-4** RLappin(7) (in tch tl wknd over 2f out) 1½ | **8** | 14/1 | 54 | 9 |
| | **Appeal Again (IRE) (58)** (MrsJRRamsden) **3-7-10** NKennedy(6) (bkwd: hld up & plld hrd: bhd fr ½-wy) 5 | **9** | 14/1 | 36 | — |
| | **Cumbrian Maestro (65)** (TDEasterby) **3-8-3** JQuinn(10) (a in rr) ½ | **10** | 9/1 | 43 | — |

(SP 135.4%) **10 Rn**

**1m 51.4** (7.40) CSF £47.31 CT £347.41 TOTE £8.60: £2.30 £1.90 £5.40 (£41.40) Trio £44.70 OWNER The Pheasant Partnership (MIDDLEHAM) BRED Al Dahlawi Stud Co Ltd
LONG HANDICAP Appeal Again (IRE) 7-7 Silverdale Knight 7-9
**Tabriz**, given a good chance at the weights, fought back bravely to regain the advantage near the line. (5/1)
**453 Theatre Magic**, with two handlers in the paddock, looked to have it in the bag when going half a length up over a furlong out but, with his stamina stretched, he was edged out near the line. (8/1)
**Kingdom Princess**, hard at work at halfway, to her credit was staying on all the way to the line. (9/1)
**Spillo**, done no favours by the Handicapper, looked as if the outing would do him good. Taking time to find his stride, he was putting in some pleasing work towards the finish. He looks capable of better over further. (5/1: op 3/1)
**453 Silverdale Knight**, who lost his way at two, was reluctant to go down to the start. Up there all the way, he was being driven along at halfway and could do no more than stay on in his own time. (6/1: op 4/1)
**Fly Fishing (USA)**, taken quietly to post, had the worst of the draw. Seeming to find difficulty handling the bend, he edged out towards the centre and dropped away beaten with two furlongs left to run. He is worth another chance on a more orthodox course. (11/4)

T/Plpt: £2,934.70 (3.55 Tckts). T/Qdpt: £312.80 (2.7 Tckts). WG

# 0419-WOLVERHAMPTON (L-H) (Standard)
## Saturday March 30th
WEATHER: Fine

## 510 CODSALL MAIDEN H'CAP (0-70) (3-Y.O+) (Class E)
7-00 (7-00) **1m 1f 79y (Fibresand)** £3,002.00 (£896.00: £428.00: £194.00) GOING: 0.25 sec per fur (SLW)

| | | | SP | RR | SF |
|---|---|---|---|---|---|
| *355[4]* | **Law Dancer (IRE) (60)** (TGMills) **3-8-2** TWilliams(3) (plld hrd: trckd ldrs: chal over 2f out: led 1f out: rdn clr) — | **1** | 2/1 1 | 72 | 25 |
| *414[2]* | **School Boy (68)** (TJNaughton) **3-8-10** DHarrison(2) (hld up: hdwy to ld over 2f out: hdd 1f out: no ex) 4 | **2** | 7/2 3 | 73 | 26 |
| | **Houghton Venture (USA) (67)** (SPCWoods) **4-10-0** WWoods(1) (bit bkwd: hld up: ev ch over 2f out: one pce) 1¼ | **3** | 11/4 2 | 70 | 42 |
| *346[6]* | **Nautical Jewel (53)** (MDIUsher) **4-9-0** MWigham(4) (b: b.hind: plld hrd: trckd ldr: led 4f out: hdd over 2f out: sn btn) 11 | **4** | 7/1 | 37 | 9 |
| | **Pharly Reef (45)** (DBurchell) **4-8-6** SSanders(5) (led over 5f: wknd 3f out) 5 | **5** | 5/1 | 21 | — |

(SP 111.4%) **5 Rn**

**2m 5.5** (9.50) CSF £8.75 TOTE £2.20: £1.10 £2.10 (£3.10) OWNER Mr T. G. Mills (EPSOM) BRED M. Duffy
WEIGHT FOR AGE 3yo-19lb
**Law Dancer (IRE)**, fitter this time, confirmed the ability he had previously shown on turf. (2/1)
**School Boy** moved up on the wide outside to forge ahead as the field were line abreast across the home turn. He was labouring towards the finish but did appear to stay this longer trip. (7/2: 5/2-4/1)
**Houghton Venture (USA)** looked to need this but shaped well on his All-Weather debut. (11/4)
**Nautical Jewel** failed to handle the early tight turn at all and is proving hard to place. (7/1)
**Pharly Reef**, who showed improved form over hurdles recently, failed to last long once headed. (5/1)

## 511 OAKEN CLAIMING STKS (4-Y.O+) (Class F)
7-30 (7-32) **6f (Fibresand)** £2,070.00 (£570.00: £270.00) GOING: 0.25 sec per fur (SLW)

| | | | SP | RR | SF |
|---|---|---|---|---|---|
| *386[3]* | **Hannah's Usher (68)** (CMurray) **4-8-11** MTebbutt(3) (chsd ldrs: led over 1f out: drvn out) — | **1** | 4/1 3 | 72 | 49 |
| 479[2] | **Mustn't Grumble (IRE) (70)** (DNicholls) **6-8-9** AlexGreaves(2) (hld up: nt clr run 3f out: drvn & ev ch 1f out: edgd rt & unable qckn) ½ | **2** | 5/2 1 | 69 | 46 |
| *356[7]* | **Nordan Raider (70)** (MJCamacho) **8-8-7**(5) GParkin(7) (stdd s: hdwy 2f out: styng on whn snatched up ins fnl f) 1¾ | **3** | 7/2 2 | 67 | 44 |
| *413[2]* | **Milos (73)** (TJNaughton) **5-9-5** JFortune(9) (a.p: ev ch over 1f out: sn btn) ¾ | **4** | 9/2 | 72 | 49 |
| *394[8]* | **Little Ibnr (70)** (PDEvans) **5-9-1** KFallon(4) (led over 4f) 1½ | **5** | 8/1 | 64 | 41 |
| *388[8]* | **Brookhead Lady (56)** (PDEvans) **5-8-1**ow1 SSanders(5) (b.nr fore: prom over 2f) 10 | **6** | 9/1 | 23 | — |
| *414[P]* | **Cerbera (40)** (JPSmith) **7-8-9** VSlattery(8) (outpcd after 2f) ¾ | **7** | 50/1 | 29 | 6 |
| *406[10]* | **Justinianus (IRE) (45)** (JJBridger) **4-8-2**(5) ADaly(1) (a bhd) 1¾ | **8** | 50/1 | 23 | — |

(SP 114.0%) **8 Rn**

**1m 16.2** (4.80) CSF £13.75 TOTE £4.30: £1.80 £1.50 £1.50 (£4.40) Trio £9.00 OWNER Mr Bill Fitzgerald (NEWMARKET) BRED P. Dowson
Mustn't Grumble (IRE) clmd MissSWilton £5,000
STEWARDS' ENQUIRY Greaves susp. 8-10/4/96 (careless riding).
**Hannah's Usher**, taken down early, finally got off the mark over the extra furlong - all his previous successes had come over five. He edged slightly right in the final furlong but Tebbutt did his best to keep him straight. (4/1)
**479 Mustn't Grumble (IRE)**, probably better over further, was prevented from moving wide on the track when his pilot wished leaving the back straight. Forced to challenge on the inside, Greaves persisted in using her whip in her left (incorrect) hand and hampered the horse that denied her the space in the first place. (5/2)
**Nordan Raider** was given very little room by the runner-up in the home straight. Forced to snatch up near the finish, he must be considered unlucky. (7/2)
**Milos** moved down keenly and was in the firing-line until outpaced entering the final furlong. (9/2: 4/1-13/2)
**Little Ibnr**, on the go since October, has not run well since Christmas. (8/1)
**Brookhead Lady** was soon being scrubbed along and outpaced. (9/1: 6/1-10/1)

## 512 ANGLO-HOLT 25TH ANNIVERSARY H'CAP (0-70) (3-Y.O+) (Class E)

8-00 (8-01) **1m 4f (Fibresand)** £2,872.00 (£856.00: £408.00: £184.00) GOING: 0.25 sec per fur (SLW)

| | | | | SP | RR | SF |
|---|---|---|---|---|---|---|
| $419^{2}$ | **Cuban Nights (USA) (56)** (BJLlewellyn) **4-9-10** TWilliams(8) (lw: trckd ldrs: led over 4f out: sn clr: jst hld on) | — | 1 | 7/2$^{3}$ | 70 | 49 |
| $267^{6}$ | **In the Money (IRE) (52)** (RHollinshead) **7-9-3**(5) FLynch(4) (lw: hld up: hdwy 5f out: r.o fnl 2f: nt rch wnr) | nk | 2 | 6/1 | 66 | 47 |
| $189^{10}$ | **Hill Farm Katie (35)** (WMBrisbourne) **5-7-12**(7) IonaWands(2) (plld hrd: a.p: eased whn btn wl ins fnl f) | 8 | 3 | 25/1 | 38 | 19 |
| $154^{7}$ | **Pontynyswen (39)** (DBurchell) **8-8-9b** RPrice(6) (b: led over 7f: kpt on again fnl 2f) | hd | 4 | 10/1 | 42 | 23 |
| $422^{2}$ | **Comtec's Legend (40)** (JFBottomley) **6-8-10** LCharnock(5) (b: chsd ldrs: no hdwy fnl 4f) | 5 | 5 | 3/1$^{2}$ | 36 | 17 |
| | **Slapy Dam (54)** (JMackie) **4-9-8** SSanders(1) (bit bkwd: in tch: rdn & no imp 5f out) | 10 | 6 | 2/1$^{1}$ | 37 | 16 |
| $124^{11}$ | **Queens Stroller (IRE) (54)** (TRWall) **5-9-7**(3) PMcCabe(3) (chsd ldrs 7f: sn wknd) | 1¾ | 7 | 16/1 | 35 | 16 |
| $398^{8}$ | **Inteabadun (33)** (ABailey) **4-7-12**(3) DWright(7) (rdn after 5f: sn bhd) | 19 | 8 | 33/1 | — | — |

(SP 116.6%) **8 Rn**

**2m 44.4** (11.90) CSF £23.25 CT £413.66 TOTE £7.30: £1.90 £1.90 £2.40 (£18.70) OWNER Mr Eamonn O'Malley (BARGOED) BRED T. F. Van Meter II

WEIGHT FOR AGE 4yo-2lb

OFFICIAL EXPLANATION **Slapy Dam: his jockey reported that the horse blew up in the back straight.**

**Cuban Nights (USA)** broke his duck under a most enterprising ride, but was tiring on the home turn and the post came just in time. (7/2)

**In the Money (IRE)** bounced back to form and, had he not edged in behind the winner for a few strides when closing, might well have won. (6/1)

**Hill Farm Katie** raced keenly until outpaced by the winner leaving the back straight. (25/1)

**Pontynyswen**, brought to the stands' rail in the straight, stayed on strongly after looking well beaten. (10/1)

**Comtec's Legend** tried to close around the outside on the home turn but achieved little. (3/1)

**Slapy Dam** looked just in need of this and was one of the first beaten. (2/1)

## 513 FOLEY STEELSTOCK H'CAP (0-85) (3-Y.O+) (Class D)

8-30 (8-32) **7f (Fibresand)** £3,694.95 (£1,101.60: £525.30: £237.15) GOING: 0.25 sec per fur (SLW)

| | | | | SP | RR | SF |
|---|---|---|---|---|---|---|
| 371* | **High Premium (73)** (RAFahey) **8-9-3** ACulhane(9) (a.p: led 2f out: drvn out) | — | 1 | 11/2 | 81 | 53 |
| $427^{2}$ | **Ashgore (73)** (MJohnston) **6-9-3** JWeaver(3) (led 2f: ev ch over 1f out: unable qckn nr fin) | hd | 2 | 2/1$^{1}$ | 81 | 53 |
| $480^{10}$ | **Everset (FR) (74)** (ABailey) **8-9-1**(3) DWright(7) (b: hdwy 3f out: no ex fnl f) | 3 | 3 | 4/1$^{2}$ | 75 | 47 |
| $363^{2}$ | **Present Situation (71)** (LordHuntingdon) **5-8-8**(7) AimeeCook(4) (hdwy 4f out: no imp fnl 2f) | 2½ | 4 | 9/2$^{3}$ | 66 | 38 |
| 417* | **Chadleigh Lane (USA) (67)** (RHollinshead) **4-8-6**(5) FLynch(5) (prom: lost pl over 2f out: styd on fnl ) | s.h | 5 | 6/1 | 62 | 34 |
| | **Intiaash (IRE) (75)** (DHaydnJones) **4-8-12**(7) AnthonyBond(8) (bit bkwd: led after 2f to 2f out: wknd over 1f out) | 2 | 6 | 20/1 | 66 | 38 |
| $205^{8}$ | **Ultra Beet (68)** (PCHaslam) **4-8-12** JFortune(6) (bhd fnl 3f) | ½ | 7 | 10/1 | 57 | 29 |
| | **Wentbridge Lad (IRE) (78)** (PDEvans) **6-9-1v**(7) HayleyWilliams(2) (bit bkwd: prom 4f: sn wknd) | 15 | 8 | 25/1 | 33 | 5 |

(SP 115.7%) **8 Rn**

**1m 30.5** (5.80) CSF £16.44 CT £44.76 TOTE £7.30: £1.60 £1.60 £1.60 (£4.50) Trio £15.50 OWNER Mr J. C. Parsons (MALTON) BRED M.E Wates

**High Premium**, dropped back to seven furlongs, proved as tough as old boots once in front. (11/2: op 3/1)

**Ashgore**, worried out of it near the finish, failed to confirm January course and distance placings with the winner, despite meeting that rival on 12lb better terms. (2/1)

**Everset (FR)** is a scratchy mover these days but does still run the occasional good race here. (4/1: op 6/1)

**Present Situation** stuck to the inside throughout, but for which he might have finished closer. (9/2: op 3/1)

**Chadleigh Lane (USA)** was doing good work at the finish and seems to need further here. (6/1: op 7/2)

**Intiaash (IRE)**, who looked well in his coat but just in need of the run, shaped with some promise. (20/1)

## 514 BOWMER AND KIRKLAND (LONDON) (S) STKS (3,4,5 & 6-Y.O) (Class G)

9-00 (9-02) **5f (Fibresand)** £2,070.00 (£570.00: £270.00) GOING: 0.25 sec per fur (SLW)

| | | | | SP | RR | SF |
|---|---|---|---|---|---|---|
| $394^{3}$ | **Rennyholme (52)** (JHetherton) **5-9-5b** NAdams(10) (hdwy over 2f out: led over 1f out: rdn out) | — | 1 | 11/2$^{2}$ | 64 | 42 |
| $431^{5}$ | **Sound the Trumpet (IRE) (53)** (RCSpicer) **4-9-5** DeanMcKeown(8) (lw: a.p: ev ch over 1f out: r.o) | 1½ | 2 | 16/1 | 59 | 37 |
| 386* | **Primula Bairn (61)** (DNicholls) **6-9-6b** AlexGreaves(7) (chsd ldrs: styd on one pce appr fnl f) | 3½ | 3 | 4/5$^{1}$ | 49 | 27 |
| | **Swan At Whalley (62)** (MartynWane) **4-9-0**(5) DaneO'Neill(4) (led wl over 3f: wknd) | 1¼ | 4 | 7/1$^{3}$ | 44 | 22 |
| $414^{8}$ | **Ho Mei Surprise (34)** (BPreece) **4-9-0**(5) FLynch(6) (outpcd: c wd st: nvr nrr) | 2 | 5 | 33/1 | 38 | 16 |
| | **Honey Trader (56)** (JBerry) **4-9-0**(5) PRoberts(2) (bit bkwd: prom over 3f) | 1½ | 6 | 12/1 | 33 | 11 |
| $425^{6}$ | **The Fed (42)** (JAPickering) **6-9-2**(3) DWright(3) (in tch: no hdwy fnl 2f) | 3½ | 7 | 9/1 | 22 | — |
| $231^{9}$ | **Superlao (BEL) (44)** (JJBridger) **4-9-1**(5) ADaly(5) (sn pushed along: hmpd & lost tch after 2f) | ½ | 8 | 50/1 | 21 | — |
| $134^{11}$ | **Roxane (IRE) (30)** (ABailey) **3-7-9**(7) IonaWands(9) (sn outpcd) | 1¼ | 9 | 40/1 | 11 | — |
| | **Ivy Lilian (IRE) (41)** (WMBrisbourne) **4-8-9**(5) DGriffiths(1) (bdly hmpd after 1f: nt rcvr) | 6 | 10 | 50/1 | — | — |

(SP 116.3%) **10 Rn**

**63.5 secs** (4.80) CSF £76.12 TOTE £6.10: £1.70 £2.20 £1.10 (£30.10) Trio £8.40 OWNER Mr G. Cosburn (MALTON) BRED Ravenstonedale Fold and Bloodstock

WEIGHT FOR AGE 3yo-12lb

No bid

**Rennyholme** was getting off the mark after missing what appeared, on paper, to be an easy chance in a handicap last time. He is a big gelding, unlikely to be inconvenienced by high weights or assisted by low ones. (11/2)

**Sound the Trumpet (IRE)** ran much his best race since leaving Jack Berry, but may need to strike quickly before he is re-handicapped. (16/1)

**Primula Bairn** was involved in the scrimmaging on the first bend but this hardly looked an excuse. (4/5)

**Swan At Whalley** broke fast but tied up once headed. Off for six months, he may have needed this more than it appeared and this course and distance are what he needs, having won over Chester's five-furlong track. (7/1)

**Ho Mei Surprise**, taken wide after bunching on the first bend, was already being outpaced and could never get into contention (33/1)

**Honey Trader** cut little ice on his first All-Weather run but had been out since July. (12/1: 7/1-14/1)

## 515 BLAKENHALL H'CAP (0-65) (3-Y.O) (Class F)

9-30 (9-32) **1m 100y (Fibresand)** £2,070.00 (£570.00: £270.00) GOING: 0.25 sec per fur (SLW)

| | | | | SP | RR | SF |
|---|---|---|---|---|---|---|
| $298^{4}$ | **Rajah (45)** (CWThornton) **3-8-1** LCharnock(6) (chsd ldrs: rdn over 2f out: styd on wl to ld ins fnl f) | — | 1 | 11/4$^{1}$ | 52 | 20 |

| | | | | SP | RR | SF |
|---|---|---|---|---|---|---|
| 314[3] | **Bailiwick (51)** (NAGraham) **3-8-7b** MFenton(8) (led: hdd over 2f out: lft in ld ins fnl f: sn hdd & one pce) | 1 | **2** | 7/1[3] | 56 | 24 |
| | **Scathebury (65)** (SPCWoods) **3-9-7** WWoods(1) (trckd ldrs: led over 2f out: rel to r, wnt rt & hdd ins fnl f) | 3 | **3** | 7/1[3] | 64 | 32 |
| 314* | **Chauvelin (IRE) (54)** (MJohnston) **3-8-10c** DeanMcKeown(5) (rdn & dropped rr after 3f: r.o fnl 2f) | 2½ | **4** | 7/2[2] | 49 | 17 |
| 423[3] | **Marino Street (54)** (PDEvans) **3-8-10v** KFallon(4) (stdd s: hdwy 3f out: nvr able to chal) | 1 | **5** | 10/1 | 47 | 15 |
| 423* | **Dhes-C (55)** (RHollinshead) **3-8-6**(5) FLynch(7) (lw: hdwy 3f out: nvr rchd ldrs) | 1 | **6** | 8/1 | 46 | 14 |
| | **Home Cookin' (62)** (DrJDScargill) **3-9-4** JWeaver(3) (nvr trbld ldrs) | 7 | **7** | 7/1[3] | 40 | 8 |
| 387[3] | **Duralock Fencer (54)** (PGMurphy) **3-8-7**(3) SDrowne(2) (lw: chsd ldrs 5f) | 6 | **8** | 12/1 | 20 | — |
| | | | | (SP 114.3%) | **8 Rn** | |

**1m 54.1** (9.10) CSF £20.42 CT £110.89 TOTE £5.10: £1.80 £1.60 £2.70 (£13.10) OWNER Mr Guy Reed (MIDDLEHAM) BRED Catridge Farm Stud Ltd
STEWARDS' ENQUIRY Fenton fined £200 (failure to ride to his draw).
OFFICIAL EXPLANATION **Duralock Fencer: his jockey reported that the horse was not moving well in the back straight and was hanging.**
**Rajah**, having got his mark over a totally inadequate trip, looks like coming into his own over middle-distances. Never travelling well to the home turn, he was at his most impressive in the last half-furlong. (11/4: 7/2-9/4)
**Bailiwick** tried to make all but was brushed aside by first Scathebury and then the winner. (7/1)
**Scathebury** travelled supremely well through the race but, not for the first time, misbehaved and rescued defeat from the jaws of certain victory. It is hard to imagine that backing him will ever make you rich. (7/1)
**Chauvelin (IRE)** looked to be going nowhere in the back straight but ran on strongly in the end. He looks to need further. (7/2)
**Marino Street**, slightly hampered as he was steadied at the start, was never going well enough to take a hand. (10/1)
**Dhes-C** looked a momentary danger on the home turn but the effort soon flaked out. (8/1)
**Home Cookin'** (7/1: op 4/1)
**Duralock Fencer** (12/1: 8/1-14/1)

T/Plpt: £73.80 (156.38 Tckts). T/Qdpt: £29.00 (18.84 Tckts). Dk

## 0425-SOUTHWELL (L-H) (Standard)
## Monday April 1st
WEATHER: fine but cloudy

## 516 KING ARTHUR MEDIAN AUCTION MAIDEN STKS (3-Y.O) (Class F)
2-20 (2-21) **7f (Fibresand)** £2,381.00 (£656.00: £311.00) Stalls: Low GOING: 0.02 sec per fur (STD)

| | | | | SP | RR | SF |
|---|---|---|---|---|---|---|
| | **Call Me** (CWThornton) **3-8-9** DeanMcKeown(3) (w'like: leggy: scope: dwlt s: sn pushed along: hdwy ½-wy: led over 1f out: drew clr) | — | **1** | 4/1[3] | 55 | 19 |
| | **Mels Baby (IRE) (55)** (JLEyre) **3-9-0** RLappin(5) (led 1f: ev ch over 1f out: unable qckn) | 6 | **2** | 4/1[3] | 46 | 10 |
| 460[4] | **Cherry Garden (IRE) (58)** (TJNaughton) **3-9-0** JWeaver(7) (a chsng ldrs: drvn along ½-wy: one pce fnl 2f) | 1¼ | **3** | 5/2[2] | 43 | 7 |
| 428[7] | **Welcome Lu (40)** (PSFelgate) **3-8-6**(3) PMcCabe(2) (in tch: effrt ½-wy: kpt on fnl f) | 1¼ | **4** | 20/1 | 36 | — |
| | **Shermood** (MBell) **3-8-9** MFenton(4) (trckd ldrs: pushed along ½-wy: wknd 2f out) | 6 | **5** | 9/4[1] | 22 | — |
| | **Tagatay** (MJCamacho) **3-9-0** LCharnock(1) (s.i.s: bhd & drvn along: n.d) | ½ | **6** | 20/1 | 26 | — |
| 134[9] | **Heathyards Rose (IRE)** (RHollinshead) **3-8-4**(5) FLynch(6) (led after 1f: hdd over 1f out: wknd) | 2½ | **7** | 7/1 | 15 | — |
| | | | | (SP 121.4%) | **7 Rn** | |

**1m 33.5** (6.70) CSF £20.39 TOTE £4.10: £1.70 £3.50 (£9.60) OWNER Mr Guy Reed (MIDDLEHAM) BRED J. M. Greetham
**Call Me**, who had more size and substance about her than the others in the field, missed the break slightly. Pushed along, she got the hang of things as the race developed and drew clear of a poor lot in the final furlong. There will not be many worse races than this on the Flat all year. (4/1)
**Mels Baby (IRE)**, with the blinkers left off, was the only one to make something of a race of it. (4/1: op 6/1)
**Cherry Garden (IRE)**, on his toes in the paddock, was driven along at halfway. (5/2)
**Welcome Lu**, tailed off on her previous three outings, was not disgraced, which about sums this race up. (20/1)
**Shermood**, who had shown a glimmer of ability in two outings last year, took a keen grip. Pushed along at halfway, she dropped right out with two furlongs left to run. (9/4: 6/4-5/2)

## 517 GALAHAD CLAIMING MAIDEN STKS (3-Y.O+) (Class F)
2-50 (2-51) **6f (Fibresand)** £2,381.00 (£656.00: £311.00) Stalls: Low GOING: 0.02 sec per fur (STD)

| | | | | SP | RR | SF |
|---|---|---|---|---|---|---|
| | **Amoeba (IRE) (47)** (JBerry) **3-7-11**(5) PFessey(3) (mde virtually all: rdn clr over 1f out: unchal) | — | **1** | 7/2[2] | 62 | 17 |
| 328[9] | **Backhander (IRE) (52)** (MartynWane) **4-8-10**(7) JEdmunds(7) (lw: a chsng ldrs: one pce fnl 2f) | 9 | **2** | 10/1 | 41 | 8 |
| | **Jolly Hokey** (JWharton) **4-9-3** KFallon(8) (hdwy ½-wy: one pce fnl 2f) | 1½ | **3** | 33/1 | 37 | 4 |
| | **Melody Wheel** (AHide) **4-9-4** JQuinn(1) (bit bkwd: s.i.s: effrt ½-wy: sn rdn: one pce) | 1 | **4** | 9/4[1] | 35 | 2 |
| 425[8] | **Chloella (29)** (CBBBooth) **4-8-8** NKennedy(5) (trckd ldrs: rdn over 2f out: no imp) | ½ | **5** | 6/1[3] | 24 | — |
| 356[6] | **Infiraaj (USA)** (MrsDHaine) **4-9-5b[1]** AMcGlone(2) (s.i.s: rdn ½-wy: a in rr) | 1 | **6** | 7/2[2] | 32 | — |
| 414[6] | **Lithe Spirit (IRE)** (JAHarris) **4-8-8b[1]** SDWilliams(6) (w wnr: rdn over 2f out: sn wknd) | 2 | **7** | 9/1 | 16 | — |
| | | | | (SP 111.5%) | **7 Rn** | |

**1m 18.8** (5.30) CSF £31.72 TOTE £3.80: £2.10 £1.70 (£17.00) Trio £39.50 OWNER Mr Sam Berry (COCKERHAM) BRED Eddie Fitzpatrick
WEIGHT FOR AGE 3yo-12lb
**Amoeba (IRE)**, who is only small, proved much too good for this lot. Her rider left nothing to chance and kept her going all the way to the line. (7/2: 6/4-4/1)
**Backhander (IRE)** stuck on at the one pace but, like the rest, had no chance with the winner. (10/1)
**Jolly Hokey**, an excitable sort, stuck on under pressure in the final quarter-mile. (33/1)
**Melody Wheel**, on the leg and looking in need of the outing, moved up under pressure once in line for home, but she was never doing anything like enough. (9/4)
**Chloella**, taken to post early and mounted on the track, was hard at work and getting nowhere once in line for home. (6/1)

## 518 LANCELOT LIMITED STKS (0-55) (3-Y.O+) (Class F)
3-20 (3-21) **7f (Fibresand)** £2,381.00 (£656.00: £311.00) Stalls: Low GOING: 0.02 sec per fur (STD)

| | | | | SP | RR | SF |
|---|---|---|---|---|---|---|
| 425* | **Elton Ledger (IRE) (63)** (MrsNMacauley) **7-9-9b** JTate(7) (lw: hld up: stdy hdwy 2f out: led ins fnl f: jst hld on) | — | **1** | 7/4[1] | 51 | 28 |
| 124[9] | **Peacefull Reply (USA) (41)** (FHLee) **6-9-7** AMcGlone(1) (hdwy on ins to ld 3f out: hdd ins fnl f: r.o) | hd | **2** | 25/1 | 49 | 26 |

413$^{7}$ **Tilly Owl (42)** (JAHarris) **5-9-4** JO'Reilly(4) (chsd ldrs: rdn ½-wy: styd on ins fnl f).........1¼ **3** 12/1 43 20
372$^{4}$ **Desert Lore (52)** (MrsJRRamsden) **5-9-7** KFallon(11) (b: hdwy ½-wy: sn rdn: styd on fnl 2f: nvr able to chal).........2½ **4** 6/1$^{3}$ 40 17
405$^{7}$ **Seeking Destiny (IRE) (50)** (MCChapman) **3-8-4**(7) CMunday(5) (mde most to 3f out: one pce).........1 **5** 8/1 42 5
172* **Irchester Lass (47)** (SRBowring) **4-9-1b**(5) CTeague(8) (chsd ldrs: outpcd over 2f out: kpt on fnl f).........¾ **6** 11/2$^{2}$ 35 12
**Battle Colours (IRE) (55)** (DonEnricoIncisa) **7-9-7** KimTinkler(9) (bit bkwd: in tch: rdn & outpcd over 2f out: n.d after).........1¾ **7** 14/1 32 9
389$^{6}$ **Life Is Precious (IRE) (43)** (RHollinshead) **4-8-13**(5) FLynch(6) (s.i.s: bhd tl styd on appr fnl f).........nk **8** 14/1 29 6
**Thwaab (44)** (FWatson) **4-9-7** MFenton(10) (chsd ldrs tl lost pl over 2f out).........3½ **9** 20/1 24 1
**Ring the Chief (54)** (MDIUsher) **4-9-7** MWigham(3) (b.hind: sn bhd & pushed along).........4 **10** 14/1 14 —
417$^{6}$ **Cabcharge Blue (48)** (TJNaughton) **4-9-6** JWeaver(2) (w ldrs tl wknd over 2f out: eased).........2½ **11** 7/1 8 —
(SP 125.9%) **11 Rn**

**1m 33.8** (7.00) CSF £42.44 TOTE £2.80: £1.20 £7.90 £3.60 (£51.40) Trio £223.70; £220.61 to 3.30 Nottingham 2/4/96. OWNER The Posse (MELTON MOWBRAY) BRED Thomas Doherty
WEIGHT FOR AGE 3yo-14lb
**Elton Ledger (IRE)**, taken to post quietly, moved up on the bridle once in line for home. After looking likely to win in comfortable fashion, his stamina was giving out near the line and the post came just in time. (7/4)
**Peacefull Reply (USA)** took it up on the inner turning for home. He battled back when headed and was just held. (25/1)
**Tilly Owl**, under pressure some way from home, was pulling back the first two near the line. (12/1)
**Desert Lore**, taken to post early, struggled to go the pace. Sticking on under firm handling, he would have finished a couple of lengths closer but for being eased near the line. A mile might suit him better nowadays. (6/1: op 4/1)
**Seeking Destiny (IRE)** put two poor efforts behind him and seemed to run up to his best. (8/1: op 5/1)

## 519 PERCEVAL H'CAP (0-70) (3-Y.O) (Class E)
3-50 (3-50) **1m 3f (Fibresand)** £2,906.40 (£865.20: £411.60: £184.80) Stalls: Low GOING: 0.02 sec per fur (STD)
SP RR SF
381* **Mister Aspecto (IRE) (68)** (MJohnston) **3-9-6v** JWeaver(1) (lw: mde all: drvn out).........— **1** 100/30$^{3}$ 75 14
483$^{3}$ **Dancing Cavalier (69)** (RHollinshead) **3-9-2**(5) FLynch(2) (lw: bhd: hdwy 5f out: styd on fnl 2f: r.o nr fin).........1¼ **2** 11/4$^{2}$ 74 13
471* **Siege Perilous (IRE) (55)** (SCWilliams) **3-8-7** 5x JTate(4) (drvn along 5f out: sn chsng ldrs: nt qckn fnl 2f)....1½ **3** 15/8$^{1}$ 58 —
419$^{3}$ **Rostaq (56)** (DJGMurraySmith) **3-8-8** KFallon(3) (lw: chsd ldr: rdn 4f out: wknd over 1f out).........12 **4** 11/2 42 —
**Young Butt (59)** (JFfitch-Heyes) **3-8-6**(5) MHenry(5) (chsd ldrs tl wknd over 2f out).........12 **5** 8/1 27 —
(SP 111.0%) **5 Rn**

**2m 33.1** (13.10) CSF £11.99 TOTE £2.80: £1.30 £1.70 (£3.90) OWNER Aspecto Clothing Co Ltd (MIDDLEHAM) BRED Petra Bloodstock Agency Ltd
**Mister Aspecto (IRE)**, much improved since the headgear was fitted, was given a forceful ride. Tending to look about, he had to be kept right up to his work. He could be an interesting proposition when he returns to turf. (100/30)
**483 Dancing Cavalier** seemed to be kept wide to avoid the kick-back. Running his usual sort of race, he stayed on in determined fashion near the line but too late to trouble the winner. (11/4)
**471* Siege Perilous (IRE)**, carrying a 5lb penalty for his turf success, had every chance but, flat out once in line for home, lacked the pace to get in a serious blow at the winner. (15/8)

## 520 HOLY GRAIL (S) APPRENTICE STKS (4, 5 & 6-Y.O) (Class G)
4-20 (4-21) **1m 4f (Fibresand)** £2,095.00 (£595.00: £295.00) Stalls: Low GOING: 0.02 sec per fur (STD)
SP RR SF
477$^{5}$ **Forzair (68)** (SRBowring) **4-9-1**(3) JEdmunds(6) (b: jnd ldrs ½-wy: led on bit over 1f out: easily).........— **1** 4/6$^{1}$ 73+ 5
504$^{7}$ **Anistop (60)** (JLEyre) **4-8-13**(5) PDoe(7) (w ldrs: led 8f out tl over 1f out: no ch w wnr).........3 **2** 5/2$^{2}$ 69 1
440$^{24}$ **Rival Queen (IRE) (53)** (MDHammond) **4-7-11**(10) DHayden(3) (drvn along ½-wy: wnt prom 4f out: one pce) 13 **3** 12/1$^{3}$ 41 —
246$^{11}$ **Just Lucky (IRE) (44)** (MrsPSly) **4-8-9**(3) CScudder(4) (prom: drvn along 4f out: hung rt & oupcd 2f out) ......1¾ **4** 25/1 43 —
**Laal (USA)** (MFBarraclough) **4-8-12** GFaulkner(5) (wnt prom ½-wy: rdn & lost pl over 3f out).........15 **5** 33/1 23 —
**Milltown Classic (IRE)** (JParkes) **4-8-2**(5) RMullen(8) (unruly in stalls: reard s: sn prom: lost pl 4f out).........nk **6** 25/1 18 —
**Ever Friends (42)** (RHarris) **4-8-12** OliverCasey(1) (chsd ldrs tl wknd ½-wy: sn bhd).........12 **7** 25/1 7 —
**Becky Boo (31)** (DBurchell) **6-8-3**(5) KSked(2) (led 4f: lost pl ½-wy: sn wl bhd).........5 **8** 16/1 — —
(SP 116.6%) **8 Rn**

**2m 47.9** (15.40) CSF £2.83 TOTE £1.70: £1.60 £1.10 £2.50 (£1.70) OWNER Charterhouse Holdings Plc (EDWINSTOWE) BRED J. G. Charlton
WEIGHT FOR AGE 4yo-1lb
Sold PHunt 8,000 gns
**477 Forzair** looked a good thing in this company, especially after his effort on grass at Newcastle, and he scored with the minimum of fuss. (4/6)
**Anistop**, having his second outing in three days, was the only one to make even a token race of it. (5/2)
**Rival Queen (IRE)**, like the rest, was left behind by the first two once in line for home. (12/1)

## 521 EXCALIBUR H'CAP (0-65) (3-Y.O+) (Class F)
4-50 (4-51) **1m (Fibresand)** £2,381.00 (£656.00: £311.00) Stalls: Low GOING: 0.02 sec per fur (STD)
SP RR SF
479$^{4}$ **Awesome Venture (62)** (MCChapman) **6-9-7**(7) CMunday(13) (sn trckng ldrs: shkn up to ld ins fnl f: hld on towards fin).........— **1** 15/2 69 50
426$^{2}$ **Thaleros (56)** (GMMoore) **6-9-8** DeanMcKeown(7) (lw: sn chsng ldrs: led over 2f out: sn rdn: hdd ins fnl f: nt qckn nr fin).........hd **2** 7/2$^{1}$ 63 44
417$^{3}$ **David James' Girl (52)** (ABailey) **4-8-11**(7) IonaWands(14) (lw: bhd: hdwy 2f out: styd on wl ins fnl f).........2½ **3** 8/1 54 35
353$^{9}$ **Pc's Cruiser (IRE) (48)** (JLEyre) **4-9-0b** RLappin(2) (led after 1f: hdd over 2f out: wknd over 1f out).........3 **4** 7/1$^{3}$ 44 25
261$^{8}$ **Shuttlecock (53)** (MrsNMacauley) **5-9-0**(5) CTeague(8) (led 1f: sn outpcd & bhd: hdwy over 1f out: kpt on towards fin).........½ **5** 14/1 48 29
257$^{3}$ **Miss Zanzibar (46)** (RAFahey) **4-8-12** ACulhane(6) (in tch: rdn ½-wy: no imp).........¾ **6** 5/1$^{2}$ 39 20
426$^{8}$ **Fred's Delight (IRE) (30)** (MrsVAAconley) **5-7-10v** NCarlisle(12) (chsd ldrs: rdn ½-wy: wknd 2f out).........¾ **7** 33/1 22 3
413$^{6}$ **Irie Mon (IRE) (62)** (MPBielby) **4-9-11**(3) DRMcCabe(10) (sn bhd: styd on fnl 2f: n.d).........1¾ **8** 16/1 50 31
431$^{6}$ **Cheerful Groom (IRE) (40)** (SRBowring) **5-8-6** NKennedy(5) (in tch: effrt 3f out: sn lost pl).........½ **9** 12/1 27 8
**Hornpipe (57)** (JWharton) **4-9-9** SDWilliams(9) (b: bhd: sme hdwy on outside 2f out: sn wknd).........½ **10** 16/1 43 24
334$^{6}$ **Fiaba (38)** (MrsNMacauley) **8-7-13**(5) AmandaSanders(4) (bhd fr ½-wy).........1 **11** 20/1 22 3
**Zacaroon (52)** (JFfitch-Heyes) **5-9-4** SSanders(11) (sn rr div).........6 **12** 10/1 24 5

$328^{7}$ **Most Welcome News (42)** (JRJenkins) **4-8-8b** JFortune(1) (chsd ldrs: rdn ½-wy: sn wknd)....3 **13** 16/1 8 —
**Nobby Barnes (47)** (DonEnricoIncisa) **7-8-13** KimTinkler(3) (bkwd: dwlt: bhd: sme hdwy over 2f out: sn wknd)....3½ **14** 16/1 6 —
(SP 128:9%) **14 Rn**

**1m 46.3** (6.30) CSF £34.18 CT £215.16 TOTE £8.70: £3.50 £1.80 £2.10 (£22.20) Trio £18.10 OWNER Market Rasen Racing Club (MARKET RASEN) BRED The Lavington Stud
LONG HANDICAP Fred's Delight (IRE) 7-4
**479 Awesome Venture**, who has been hard to win with, was ridden to perfection by the boy. Looking to score in tidy fashion, in the end there was not an ounce to spare. (15/2)
**Thaleros**, over a trip shorter than his best, made the best of his way home. He battled back when headed and had the winner scrambling to hold on at the line. (7/2)
**David James' Girl** came from off the pace and finished in good style. (8/1)
**Pc's Cruiser (IRE)**, with the blinkers left on, was rousted along to take a useful lead. Collared turning in, he weakened over a furlong out. (7/1)
**Shuttlecock**, who has run well here in the past, stayed on late in the day after being badly outpaced. (14/1)

T/Plpt: £168.10 (51.07 Tckts). T/Qdpt: £4.00 (227.31 Tckts). WG

# NOTTINGHAM (L-H) (Good, Good to soft patches)
## Tuesday April 2nd
WEATHER: cloudy WIND: almost nil

## 522 LANGWITH (S) H'CAP (0-60) (3-Y.O) (Class G)
2-00 (2-04) **1m 1f 213y** £2,070.00 (£570.00: £270.00) Stalls: Low GOING: 0.32 sec per fur (G)

SP RR SF

**Esperto (40)** (JPearce) **3-8-1** GBardwell(4) (plld hrd: mid div: hmpd 4f out: effrt & swtchd over 2f out: hdwy over 1f out: styd on u.p to ld wl ins fnl f)....— **1** 7/1 50 14
$348^{9}$ **Belle's Boy (60)** (BPalling) **3-9-7** TSprake(12) (led: rdn 3f out: chal 2f out: hdd & no ex wl ins fnl f)....¾ **2** 14/1 69 33
$300^{6}$ **Radmore Brandy (36)** (NPLittmoden) **3-7-4**(7)ow1 JBramhill(14) (mid div: effrt & hdwy 3f out: chal 2f out tl no ex ins fnl f)....2½ **3** 8/1 41 4
$459^{4}$ **Belacqua (USA) (37)** (DWChapman) **3-7-9b**(3)ow2 DarrenMoffatt(10) (hdwy & rn wd st: in tch wl over 2f out: styd on one pce u.p)....3½ **4** 25/1 36 —
**Sweet Amoret (50)** (PHowling) **3-8-11** RCochrane(1) (hld up & racd keenly: stdy hdwy over 2f out: nvr trbld ldrs)....1½ **5** 33/1 47 11
$415^{3}$ **Onefourseven (39)** (SRBowring) **3-8-0b** NCarlisle(7) (chsd ldrs: drvn along wl over 2f out: btn wl over 1f out)....½ **6** 6/1 3 35 —
$129^{6}$ **Digwana (IRE) (40)** (TMJones) **3-7-12**(3) AWhelan(2) (stumbled in rr after 1f: hdwy over 4f out: edgd lft u.p 2f out: no imp)....6 **7** 33/1 26 —
**Dispol Conqueror (IRE) (40)** (GROldroyd) **3-8-1** LCharnock(11) (chsd ldrs tl rdn & wknd fr over 2f out)....5 **8** 33/1 18 —
**Eskimo Kiss (IRE) (35)** (MJFetherston-Godley) **3-7-10** JQuinn(5) (hld up in tch: effrt & hdwy 3f out: sn rdn: btn 2f out)....nk **9** 4/1 1 13 —
**La Haye Sainte (47)** (DJSCosgrove) **3-8-3**(5) CTeague(6) (rr div: effrt appr st: no imp)....5 **10** 14/1 17 —
$329^{7}$ **Kai's Lady (IRE) (35)** (SWCampion) **3-7-5**(5) PFessey(9) (effrt & hdwy fr rr whn rn wd appr st: rdn & btn 2f out)....½ **11** 50/1 4 —
$176^{5}$ **Flahuil (55)** (RHannon) **3-8-11**(5) DaneO'Neill(13) (prom tl rdn & wknd over 3f out)....1¼ **12** 11/2 2 22 —
**Royal Rapport (41)** (BAMcMahon) **3-8-2**ow1 GCarter(3) (rdn along & outpcd 5f out: sn btn)....3½ **13** 10/1 2 —
$415^{*}$ **Still Here (IRE) (52)** (MJHeaton-Ellis) **3-8-13** AClark(15) (prom tl rdn & wknd 3f out)....2 **14** 6/1 3 10 —
**Reef Raider (40)** (NTinkler) **3-8-1b** FNorton(8) (sn prom: pushed along appr st: wknd qckly 3f out)....7 **15** 14/1 — —
(SP 131.3%) **15 Rn**

**2m 14.6** (12.10) CSF £98.45 CT £756.22 TOTE £8.20: £3.10 £2.80 £1.60 (£61.90) Trio £227.70; £288.64 to Ascot 3/4/96 OWNER Mrs Anne Holman-Chappell (NEWMARKET) BRED Roldvale Ltd
LONG HANDICAP Belacqua (USA) 6-11 Radmore Brandy 7-6 Kai's Lady (IRE) 7-0
No bid
**Esperto** did well to win after taking a fierce hold going down and in the first half of the race. Hampered early in the straight, he stayed on dourly under pressure to take the honours well inside the final furlong. (7/1)
**Belle's Boy** put up a good performance under topweight but, having beaten off one challenger, could not repel the winner's late thrust well inside the final furlong. (14/1)
**Radmore Brandy**, fit from the All-Weather, threw down a determined challenge in the final quarter-mile, but came to the end of her tether inside the final furlong. (8/1: op 20/1)
**Belacqua (USA)**, who picked up ground off the home turn, could find only one speed under pressure inside the final quarter-mile. (25/1)
**Sweet Amoret**, a headstrong individual, was anchored at the back of the field before staying on in the final two furlongs without ever looking likely to trouble the leaders. (33/1)
**Onefourseven** forced the pace until coming under pressure well over two furlongs out, at which stage he could find only one pace. (6/1)
**Eskimo Kiss (IRE)** raced in touch with the leaders and made a short-lived effort once in line for home. Soon driven along, he was going up and down in the same place in the final quarter-mile. (4/1: op 7/1)
**Flahuil** (11/2: op 3/1)
**Royal Rapport** (10/1: 8/1-12/1)
**Still Here (IRE)** (6/1: op 3/1)

## 523 E.B.F. CINDERHILL MAIDEN STKS (2-Y.O) (Class D)
2-30 (2-35) **5f 13y** £3,175.75 (£946.00: £450.50: £202.75) Stalls: High GOING: 0.32 sec per fur (G)

SP RR SF

**Weet Ees Girl (IRE)** (PDEvans) **2-8-9** LDettori(3) (chsd ldrs: rdn 2f out: chal fnl f: styd on to ld wl ins fnl f)....— **1** 14/1 3 60 —
$452^{6}$ **Nervous Rex** (WRMuir) **2-9-0** JReid(5) (led: rdn over 1f out: chal fnl f: edgd lft & hdd wl ins fnl: no ex)....½ **2** 4/1 2 63 —
$441^{6}$ **Mujova (IRE)** (RHollinshead) **2-9-0** KDarley(4) (w ldr: rdn 2f out: no ex ins fnl f)....3½ **3** 16/1 52 —
$441^{2}$ **Joint Venture (IRE)** (BJMeehan) **2-9-0** BDoyle(1) (swvd bdly lft s: sn pushed along: hdwy ½-wy: prom 2f out: btn over 1f out: eased)....10 **4** 4/11 1 21 —

| | | | | SP | RR | SF |
|---|---|---|---|---|---|---|
| | **Bold Welcome** (JWharton) **2-9-0** JQuinn(2) (s.i.s & wnt lft s: hdwy & in tch ½-wy: sn outpcd: wknd qckly appr fnl f) | 12 | **5** | 14/1$^{3}$ | — | — |
| | | | | (SP 112.5%) | | **5 Rn** |

**66.1 secs** (7.50) CSF £59.53 TOTE £10.50: £3.50 £1.50 (£21.00) OWNER Ed Weetman (Haulage & Storage) Ltd (WELSHPOOL) BRED Mrs Catherine Flanagan

**Weet Ees Girl (IRE)** chased the leaders. Ridden along two furlongs out, she threw down a strong challenge inside the final furlong and stayed on dourly to gain the upper hand towards the finish. (14/1: 6/1-16/1)

**452 Nervous Rex** bounced out of the stalls and attempted to make all the running. Having beaten off the challenge of Mujova, he edged left inside the final furlong and was just outpointed by the winner inside the final 75 yards. (4/1)

**441 Mujova (IRE)** raced upsides the leader but, rousted along inside the last two furlongs, was tapped for toe in the final 200 yards. (16/1)

**441 Joint Venture (IRE)** lost several lengths when diving badly left out of the stalls. Soon pushed along, he made good headway to chase the leaders after halfway, but dropped out tamely more than a furlong out and was then eased. This was not his true running. (4/11)

**Bold Welcome** (14/1: op 7/1)

## 524 FLYING HORSE MAIDEN STKS (3-Y.O F) (Class D)

3-00 (3-03) **5f 13y** £3,720.00 (£1,110.00: £530.00: £240.00) Stalls: High GOING: 0.32 sec per fur (G)

| | | | | SP | RR | SF |
|---|---|---|---|---|---|---|
| | **Splicing (70)** (WJHaggas) **3-8-11** MHills(3) (a.p: rdn to ld 1f out: kpt on u.p towards fin) | — | **1** | 3/1$^{2}$ | 61+ | 29 |
| 458$^{6}$ | **Loose Talk** (WJarvis) **3-8-11** TQuinn(10) (led: rdn & hdd over 1f out: rallied u.p ins fnl f: kpt on) | ½ | **2** | 5/2$^{1}$ | 59 | 27 |
| | **Solo Symphony (IRE)** (PWChapple-Hyam) **3-8-11** JReid(8) (w ldr: rdn & slt ld over 1f out: sn hdd: rdn & unable qckn ins fnl f) | nk | **3** | 3/1$^{2}$ | 59 | 27 |
| 443$^{14}$ | **Marjorie Rose (IRE) (73)** (ABailey) **3-8-8**$^{(3)}$ DWright(6) (in tch: effrt over 2f out: kpt on wl ins fnl f) | 1 | **4** | 6/1$^{3}$ | 55 | 23 |
| | **Nicola's Princess** (BAMcMahon) **3-8-11** GCarter(12) (s.i.s: bhd & rn green: effrt & hdwy over 1f out: nrst fin) | 4 | **5** | 20/1 | 43 | 11 |
| | **Madrina** (JBerry) **3-8-11** JCarroll(4) (dwlt: hdwy ½-wy: in tch wl over 1f out: sn outpcd) | 2½ | **6** | 14/1 | 35 | 3 |
| | **Eleanor May** (TDBarron) **3-8-11** JFortune(7) (sn chsng ldrs: rdn & wknd wl over 1f out) | 1 | **7** | 25/1 | 32 | — |
| *405*$^{14}$ | **Napier Star** (MrsNMacauley) **3-8-6**$^{(5)}$ CTeague(9) (drvn along & edgd lft ½-wy: a outpcd) | 2½ | **8** | 50/1 | 24 | — |
| | **Bag And A Bit** (BJMeehan) **3-8-11** MTebbutt(5) (trckd ldrs tl rdn & wknd wl over 1f out) | 1½ | **9** | 25/1 | 19 | — |
| | **Wyse Folly** (RBastiman) **3-8-11** ACulhane(11) (s.i.s: a outpcd & bhd) | 2½ | **10** | 33/1 | 11 | — |
| 118$^{11}$ | **Governors Dream (41)** (MrsNMacauley) **3-8-11** DBiggs(2) (Withdrawn not under Starter's orders: lame at s) ... | | **W** | 50/1 | — | — |
| | | | | (SP 118.8%) | | **10 Rn** |

**64.1 secs** (5.50) CSF £10.49 TOTE £3.40: £1.30 £1.20 £1.30 (£6.30) Trio £5.90 OWNER Mr Tony Hirschfeld (NEWMARKET) BRED Cheveley Park Stud Ltd

**Splicing** changed hands for 12,000 guineas at the end of last season and is a sister to Splice. She was always in the front rank and, strongly ridden to gain the upper hand inside the final furlong, kept on well towards the finish. (3/1)

**458 Loose Talk** raced in the firing-line throughout. Slightly tapped for toe entering the final furlong, she stayed on stoutly to the finish. (5/2)

**Solo Symphony (IRE)**, an unlucky loser of her only juvenile start, moved moderately. Always in the firing-line, she took a slight lead entering the final furlong but, soon headed, was unable to quicken when the chips were down towards the finish. (3/1: op 2/1)

**Marjorie Rose (IRE)**, who raced in touch with the leaders, stayed on particularly well inside the final furlong. (6/1: 7/2-7/1)

**Nicola's Princess** missed the break and ran green on this debut. Picking up ground more than a furlong out, she did some sterling work and is open to plenty of improvement. (20/1)

**Eleanor May** showed plenty of dash on this debut, chasing the leaders until weakening in the final quarter-mile. She is open to improvement. (25/1)

## 525 BAGTHORPE H'CAP (0-70) (3-Y.O) (Class E)

3-30 (3-32) **6f 15y** £3,548.00 (£1,064.00: £512.00: £236.00) Stalls: High GOING: 0.32 sec per fur (G)

| | | | | SP | RR | SF |
|---|---|---|---|---|---|---|
| | **Tymeera (57)** (BPalling) **3-8-13** TSprake(11) (prom far side: led over 2f out: rdn wl over 1f out: jst hld on) | — | **1** | 14/1 | 69 | 38 |
| | **Sea Danzig (65)** (PHowling) **3-9-7** RCochrane(12) (hld up far side: shkn up & hdwy over 1f out: edgd lft ins fnl f: kpt on wl: jst failed) | s.h | **2** | 7/1$^{2}$ | 77 | 46 |
| | **Night Harmony (IRE) (56)** (RHannon) **3-8-7**$^{(5)}$ DaneO'Neill(7) (chsd ldrs far side: effrt & ev ch over 1f out: nt qckn ins fnl f) | ¾ | **3** | 12/1 | 66 | 35 |
| | **Sweet Nature (IRE) (65)** (WJarvis) **3-9-7** JReid(8) (in tch far side: effrt over 2f out: kpt on wl ins fnl f) | 1 | **4** | 9/1$^{3}$ | 72 | 41 |
| | **Meranti (58)** (SDow) **3-9-0** TQuinn(10) (racd far side: drvn along over 2f out: hdwy over 1f out: kpt on wl towards fin) | nk | **5** | 9/1$^{3}$ | 65 | 34 |
| | **Gwespyr (65)** (JBerry) **3-9-7** JCarroll(9) (a.p far side: rdn 2f out: nt qckn ins fnl f) | ¾ | **6** | 12/1 | 70 | 39 |
| | **The Butterwick Kid (52)** (RAFahey) **3-8-8** ACulhane(3) (hdwy far side 2f out: kpt on: nt rch ldrs) | 3 | **7** | 10/1 | 49 | 18 |
| *394*$^{5}$ | **Boffy (IRE) (64)** (BPJBaugh) **3-9-6** WLord(5) (in tch far side: hdwy 2f out: no imp fnl f) | 1½ | **8** | 11/1 | 57 | 26 |
| *272*$^{6}$ | **Monkey Zanty (IRE) (54)** (JLHarris) **3-8-10** KDarley(4) (chsd ldrs far side tl rdn & one pce over 1f out) | 1 | **9** | 20/1 | 44 | 13 |
| *313*$^{3}$ | **Briganoone (46)** (SRBowring) **3-8-2** NCarlisle(13) (swtchd lft s: racd far side: nvr nr to chal) | hd | **10** | 20/1 | 36 | 5 |
| *421*$^{2}$ | **Maiteamia (50)** (SRBowring) **3-8-1b**$^{(5)}$ CTeague(20) (led stands' side: clr ½-wy: btn wl over 1f out) | 1¼ | **11** | 7/2$^{1}$ | 36++ | 5 |
| | **Cinnamon Stick (IRE) (41)** (PSFelgate) **3-7-8**$^{(3)ow1}$ DWright(6) (racd far side: rdn along ½-wy: nvr rchd ldrs) | ½ | **12** | 33/1 | — | — |
| | **Northern Clan (46)** (MWEasterby) **3-8-2** DaleGibson(2) (racd far side: nt pce of ldrs fr ½-wy) | 1¾ | **13** | 20/1 | 1 | — |
| | **Harriet's Beau (54)** (MWEasterby) **3-8-10b** MBirch(1) (led far side tl hdd over 2f out: sn wknd) | 2½ | **14** | 25/1 | 2 | — |
| *102*$^{7}$ | **Rothley Imp (IRE) (53)** (JWharton) **3-8-9** PRobinson(18) (chsd ldrs stands' side tl wknd over 2f out) | 7 | **15** | 16/1 | — | — |
| | **Veesey (55)** (JohnBerry) **3-8-11** MFenton(15) (chsd ldr stands' side tl rdn & btn 2f out) | ½ | **16** | 20/1 | — | — |
| 468$^{6}$ | **May Queen Megan (59)** (MrsALMKing) **3-9-1** AGarth(14) (racd stands' side: in tch 3f) | 1¼ | **17** | 16/1 | — | — |
| | **Magical Midnight (40)** (NTinkler) **3-7-10** KimTinkler(21) (prom stands' side 3f) | hd | **18** | 25/1 | — | — |
| | **Mullagh Hill Lad (IRE) (65)** (BAMcMahon) **3-9-7** GCarter(22) (in tch stands' side tl wknd over 2f out) | 2½ | **19** | 10/1 | — | — |
| | **Rustic Song (IRE) (52)** (JWharton) **3-8-8** AMackay(19) (chsd ldrs stands' side tl rdn & btn over 2f out) | 4 | **20** | 20/1 | — | — |
| | **Pharaoh's Joy (65)** (JWPayne) **3-9-7** MTebbutt(17) (racd stands' side: rdn along ½-wy: sn outpcd & bhd) | 5 | **21** | 16/1 | — | — |
| 468$^{9}$ | **Longhill Boy (63)** (BJMeehan) **3-9-5b**$^{1}$ BDoyle(16) (racd stands' side: bhd ½-wy: t.o) | 21 | **22** | 33/1 | — | — |
| | | | | (SP 158.3%) | | **22 Rn** |

**1m 16.6** (6.10) CSF £123.16 CT £1,181.16 TOTE £17.80: £6.00 £2.20 £3.90 £2.00 (£145.30) Trio £1,547.40 OWNER Glenbrook Associates (COWBRIDGE) BRED R. T. Lingwood

**Tymeera**, in a race dominated by those on the far side of the course, went to the front more than two furlongs out and just held on in a driving finish. (14/1)

**Sea Danzig** was given a patient ride and made steady headway inside the last quarter-mile. Edging left entering the final furlong, he kept on strongly but just failed to catch the winner in time. (7/1)
**Night Harmony (IRE)**, always prominent, threw down a strong challenge more than a furlong out, but was unable to quicken in the final 150 yards. (12/1)
**Sweet Nature (IRE)**, who raced in touch with the leaders, was slightly tapped for toe two furlongs out but kept on particularly well inside the final furlong. (9/1)
**Meranti**, rousted along, picked up ground two furlongs out and stayed on well to be nearest at the finish. (9/1)
**Gwespyr**, always prominent, came under pressure inside the final quarter-mile but was unable to do any more when it mattered. (12/1)
**The Butterwick Kid** picked up ground from the two-furlong marker and kept on without troubling the leaders. He will not be hard to place. (10/1)
**Maiteamia** dominated the stands'-side group and was clear on that side of the course at halfway, but he had no chance with those drawn on the far side. He is worth another chance. (7/2: op 6/1)
**Mullagh Hill Lad (IRE)** (10/1: 7/1-12/1)

## 526 DENNIS FIDLER MAIDEN STKS (I) (3-Y.O) (Class D)

4-00 (4-03) **1m 54y** £3,460.00 (£1,030.00: £490.00: £220.00) Stalls: Low GOING: 0.32 sec per fur (G)

| Horse | Dist | Pos | SP | RR | SF |
|---|---|---|---|---|---|
| **High Baroque (IRE)** (PWChapple-Hyam) **3-9-0** JReid(1) (trckd ldrs: effrt & ev ch 2f out: edgd rt & outpcd over 1f out: rallied & qcknd to ld wl ins fnl f) | — | 1 | $7/1^{3}$ | 88 | 45 |
| **Iamus (108)** (PTWalwyn) **3-9-0** PatEddery(7) (led: edgd rt over 2f out: sn jnd: rdn clr ent fnl f: edgd lft & hdd wl ins fnl f) | 1 | 2 | $4/5^{1}$ | 86 | 43 |
| **Henry Island (IRE)** (GWragg) **3-9-0** MHills(6) (unruly s: s.i.s: hld up & bhd: stdy hdwy over 2f out: r.o fnl f: nrst fin) | 2½ | 3 | $7/1^{3}$ | 81 | 38 |
| **Decision Maker (IRE) (82)** (RHannon) **3-8-9**(5) DaneO'Neill(10) (chsd ldrs: rdn over 2f out: hung lft & outpcd over 1f out) | 1½ | 4 | $6/1^{2}$ | 78 | 35 |
| **Absolute Utopia (USA)** (EALDunlop) **3-9-0** KDarley(8) (hld up & bhd: stdy hdwy fnl 2f: n.d) | 9 | 5 | 14/1 | 61 | 18 |
| **Young Annabel (USA)** (CADwyer) **3-8-9** TQuinn(12) (chsd ldrs tl rdn & outpcd fr 3f out) | 2½ | 6 | 25/1 | 51 | 8 |
| **Threadneedle (USA)** (LordHuntingdon) **3-9-0** DHarrison(4) (prom: effrt 3f out: btn 2f out) | 3 | 7 | 16/1 | 50 | 7 |
| **Daring Venture** (TJNaughton) **3-8-2**(7) TAshley(5) (trckd ldrs: effrt 3f out: wknd over 2f out) | 1¼ | 8 | 33/1 | 43 | — |
| **He's Got Wings (IRE)** (CDBroad) **3-9-0** MFenton(2) (chsd ldrs to st: sn outpcd) | 3½ | 9 | 50/1 | 41 | — |
| **D J Cat** (WRMuir) **3-9-0** RCochrane(3) (dwlt: hdwy ½-wy: btn wl over 2f out) | ¾ | 10 | 25/1 | 40 | — |
| **Alwarqa** (RWArmstrong) **3-8-9** WCarson(11) (hld up in rr: rdn along 3f out: no imp) | hd | 11 | 12/1 | 34 | — |
| **Breydon** (MHTompkins) **3-9-0** PRobinson(9) (a in rr) | 7 | 12 | 25/1 | 26 | — |

(SP 131.5%) **12 Rn**

**1m 49.3** (8.00) CSF £13.77 TOTE £8.90: £2.60 £1.10 £2.00 (£4.00) Trio £21.10 OWNER Mr M. Tabor (MARLBOROUGH) BRED Barronstown Bloodstock Ltd

**High Baroque (IRE)**, unraced last year, held a prominent position from the start. He threw down a challenge to the runner-up from the two-furlong marker but edged right and ran green over a furlong out. His jockey seemed to accept capitulation for a few strides, but the horse responded gamely and produced a decisive late surge to settle the issue close home. (7/1: 3/1-8/1)
**Iamus** is proving hard to win with. He looked to have the measure of the winner when driven clear entering the final furlong but, drifting left, having drifted to his right early in the straight, was run out of it close home. (4/5)
**Henry Island (IRE)** showed temperament and ability. Having taken a deal of persuasion to enter the stalls, he missed the break and was given time to find his stride. Picking up ground in the straight, he stayed on well in the final two furlongs to show promise for the future. (7/1)
**Decision Maker (IRE)** held a prominent position but, asked a question more than two furlongs out, hung to his left and was soon outpaced. (6/1: 4/1-13/2)
**Absolute Utopia (USA)**, a newcomer, raced at the rear of the field until making steady headway in the final two furlongs without ever looking likely to trouble the winner. (14/1: op 7/1)

## 527 LANGWORTH APPRENTICE H'CAP (0-70) (3-Y.O+) (Class G)

4-30 (4-33) **1m 54y** £2,095.00 (£595.00: £295.00) Stalls: Low GOING: 0.32 sec per fur (G)

| Form | Horse | Dist | Pos | SP | RR | SF |
|---|---|---|---|---|---|---|
| *$371^{6}$* | **Maple Bay (IRE) (62)** (ABailey) **7-9-8** AngelaGallimore(10) (rr div: effrt & hdwy 3f out: led over 1f out: hld on wl cl home) | — | 1 | $4/1^{2}$ | 78 | 55 |
| $470^{4}$ | **Battleship Bruce (64)** (NACallaghan) **4-9-10** RSmith(8) (hld up: hdwy over 2f out: sn rdn: kpt on wl ins fnl f: nrst fin) | ½ | 2 | $3/1^{1}$ | 79 | 56 |
| *$426^{*}$* | **Pine Essence (USA) (50)** (JLEyre) **5-8-10** PDoe(2) (dwlt: sn chsng ldrs: rdn wl over 2f out: r.o same pce) | 6 | 3 | $5/1^{3}$ | 53 | 30 |
| $477^{6}$ | **Dana Point (IRE) (62)** (TDBarron) **4-9-8** JEdmunds(5) (w ldrs: rdn along & outpcd 3f out: kpt on over 1f out) | 1 | 4 | 8/1 | 63 | 40 |
| *$30^{6}$* | **Cicerone (45)** (JLHarris) **6-8-5** DSweeney(4) (chsd ldrs: led 3f out: hdd over 1f out: one pce) | ½ | 5 | 12/1 | 46 | 23 |
| | **Glowing Jade (66)** (JAGlover) **6-9-12** VictoriaAppleby(1) (s.i.s: rr div: hmpd & hit rail after 3f: kpt on fnl 2f: n.d) | ½ | 6 | 14/1 | 66 | 43 |
| *$412^{12}$* | **Paronomasia (36)** (JLHarris) **4-7-10v** RMullen(11) (chsd ldrs tl rdn & one pce over 2f out) | 1½ | 7 | 33/1 | 33 | 10 |
| *$384^{12}$* | **Jalmaid (46)** (BAMcMahon) **4-8-6** TField(3) (chsd ldrs tl led appr st: hdd 3f out: btn 2f out) | 2½ | 8 | 11/1 | 38 | 15 |
| $496^{7}$ | **East Barns (IRE) (46)** (SGollings) **8-8-6b** CScudder(13) (effrt appr st: a in rr) | 1¾ | 9 | 14/1 | 34 | 11 |
| *$386^{7}$* | **Pats Delight (37)** (SCoathup) **4-7-6**(5)ow1 RBrisland(6) (slt ld tl hdd appr st: sn rdn & btn) | 6 | 10 | 33/1 | 14 | — |
| | **Artful Dane (IRE) (68)** (MJHeaton-Ellis) **4-10-0** JFowle(7) (chsd ldrs: rn wd appr st: sn lost pl) | 3½ | 11 | 14/1 | 38 | 15 |
| | **Little Pilgrim (51)** (TMJones) **3-7-10** PClarke(12) (bhd: rn wd st: hung lft & btn 3f out) | 1 | 12 | 33/1 | 19 | — |
| *$257^{8}$* | **Roar on Tour (47)** (MrsMReveley) **7-8-7b** CLowther(9) (hld up: effrt 4f out: sn wknd) | 1¾ | 13 | 16/1 | 12 | — |

(SP 123.5%) **13 Rn**

**1m 49.1** (7.80) CSF £16.12 CT £57.78 TOTE £5.00: £2.80 £1.40 £1.40 (£5.30) Trio £6.20 OWNER Mr Roy Matthews (TARPORLEY) BRED Berkshire Equestrian Services Ltd

LONG HANDICAP Paronomasia 7-6 Little Pilgrim 7-4 Pats Delight 7-4

WEIGHT FOR AGE 3yo-15lb

**Maple Bay (IRE)**, fit from the All-Weather, struck the front over a furlong out and, vigorously ridden, held on well to the advantage close home. (4/1)
**470 Battleship Bruce** picked up ground over two furlongs out and was soon driven along. He stayed on well inside the final furlong but found the post coming just too soon. (3/1)
**Pine Essence (USA)** soon recovered from a tardy start to chase the leaders, but came under pressure more than two furlongs out and could not find any more. (5/1)

**477 Dana Point (IRE)**, up with the leaders from the outset, became outpaced three furlongs out and lost his place before staying on again from the distance. (8/1)
**Cicerone** took up the running from three furlongs out but, headed by the winner, could then find only one pace. (12/1)
**Glowing Jade** did well to finish so close. A slow starter, she was hampered and hit the rail leaving the back straight before staying on in the final furlong. (14/1)
**Artful Dane (IRE)** (14/1: op 8/1)

## 528 DENNIS FIDLER MAIDEN STKS (II) (3-Y.O) (Class D)

5-00 (5-05) **1m 54y** £3,460.00 (£1,030.00: £490.00: £220.00) Stalls: Low GOING: 0.32 sec per fur (G)

| | | | | SP | RR | SF |
|---|---|---|---|---|---|---|
| | **Shu Gaa (IRE)** (WJHaggas) **3-9-0** RCochrane(2) (cl up: led over 2f out: rdn over 1f out: kpt on wl) | — | **1** | 3/1[1] | 67 | 30 |
| | **Bowled Over** (CACyzer) **3-9-0** DBiggs(7) (chsd ldrs: effrt over 2f out: hdwy over 1f out: chal wl ins fnl f: nt qckn towards fin) | ½ | **2** | 3/1[1] | 66 | 29 |
| | **Fursan (USA)** (NAGraham) **3-9-0** WCarson(1) (trckd ldrs gng wl: n.m.r 2f out & over 1f out: kpt on ins fnl f: bttr for r) | 2½ | **3** | 7/2[2] | 61 | 24 |
| | **Classic Colours (USA)** (SCWilliams) **3-9-0** AMackay(10) (chsd ldrs: hdwy & ev ch 2f out: hung lft & no ex fnl f) | 2½ | **4** | 9/1 | 56 | 19 |
| | **Needle Match** (CFWall) **3-9-0** WLord(8) (hld up in tch: effrt & hdwy 3f out: one pce fnl 2f) | nk | **5** | 33/1 | 56 | 19 |
| | **Sharp Command** (RWArmstrong) **3-9-0** JReid(3) (hdwy fr rr & in tch appr st: nt pce of ldrs fnl 2f) | 3 | **6** | 5/1[3] | 50 | 13 |
| | **Richard House Lad (46)** (RHollinshead) **3-9-0** WRyan(5) (bhd: effrt 3f out: no imp fnl 2f) | 4 | **7** | 33/1 | 42 | 5 |
| | **Antarctic Storm** (EALDunlop) **3-9-0** TQuinn(11) (unruly bef s: led tl hdd over 2f out: hung rt: eased whn btn fnl f) | 3½ | **8** | 13/2 | 35 | — |
| | **Fro** (TJNaughton) **3-8-9** JFortune(9) (bhd: outpcd & rdn along appr st: no imp after) | 3 | **9** | 33/1 | 25 | — |
| | **Followthe Allstars** (TJNaughton) **3-9-0** DHarrison(6) (s.i.s: hdwy ½-wy: outpcd fnl 3f) | s.h | **10** | 33/1 | 30 | — |
| | **Lahik (IRE)** (KTIvory) **3-8-7**(7) CScally(4) (rdn along appr st: sn bhd) | 8 | **11** | 33/1 | 14 | — |

(SP 126.9%) **11 Rn**

**1m 50.9** (9.60) CSF £12.64 TOTE £4.90: £2.20 £1.90 £1.20 (£9.10) Trio £11.10 OWNER Mr Ali K Al Jafleh (NEWMARKET) BRED Ali K. Al Jafleh
**Shu Gaa (IRE)** took up the running more than two furlongs out and stayed on gamely under pressure to keep his pursuers at bay. (3/1)
**Bowled Over** travelled comfortably throughout the race and threw down a challenge inside the final furlong, but was unable to quicken towards the finish. (3/1)
**Fursan (USA)** is one to note. Short of room on the inside from the two-furlong pole, his rider seemed to accept the situation and treated his mount to a very sympathetic ride. Now qualified for handicaps, this gelding is open to significant improvement. (7/2)
**Classic Colours (USA)** chased the leaders and had every chance two furlongs from home, but did not help his cause by hanging left under pressure. (9/1)
**Needle Match**, who raced in touch with the leaders, made a forward move three furlongs out but could find only one speed in the final quarter-mile. (33/1)
**Sharp Command** was not able to muster the speed to throw down a challenge in the final two furlongs. (5/1: op 3/1)
**Antarctic Storm** was very unruly before the start, bolting back from the stalls towards the paddock. He made the running, but went out tamely when headed by the winner and, hanging right, was eased in the final furlong. He is one to treat with caution. (13/2: op 3/1)

T/Jkpt: Not won; £3,543.44 to Ascot 3/4/96. T/Plpt: £261.60 (55.95 Tckts). T/Qdpt: £8.10 (179 Tckts) O'R

# 0510-WOLVERHAMPTON (L-H) (Standard)
## Tuesday April 2nd

WEATHER: overcast WIND: almost nil

## 529 CHAMBER OF COMMERCE MEDIAN AUCTION MAIDEN STKS (3-Y.O) (Class F)

2-20 (2-20) **6f (Fibresand)** £2,381.00 (£656.00: £311.00) Stalls: Low GOING: 0.23 sec per fur (SLW)

| | | | | SP | RR | SF |
|---|---|---|---|---|---|---|
| | **Sondos** (JWHills) **3-8-4**(5) MHenry(4) (a.p: led ½-wy: drvn clr ent st: unchal) | — | **1** | 2/1[1] | 65 | 40 |
| *383[4]* | **Lia Fail (IRE) (53)** (RHollinshead) **3-8-4**(5) FLynch(3) (trckd ldrs: hdwy to chse wnr wl over 1f out: no imp) | 7 | **2** | 7/2[2] | 46 | 21 |
| *405[8]* | **Mogin (41)** (JFfitch-Heyes) **3-8-9** GDuffield(5) (led 3f: rdn & wknd wl over 1f out) | 1½ | **3** | 20/1 | 42 | 17 |
| 458[9] | **Arabian Heights** (MrsJRRamsden) **3-9-0** KFallon(6) (racd wd: bhd & outpcd tl r.o appr fnl f) | hd | **4** | 14/1 | 47 | 22 |
| | **Golden Tyke (IRE)** (MJohnston) **3-9-0** JWeaver(1) (bit bkwd: prom: hrd drvn ent st: sn lost tch) | 1½ | **5** | 2/1[1] | 43 | 18 |
| | **Golborne Lad** (JBalding) **3-8-7**(7) JEdmunds(8) (w'like: bit bkwd: s.i.s: effort over 3f out: sn drvn along & outpcd) | 4 | **6** | 50/1 | 32 | 7 |
| | **Tallulah Belle (58)** (NPLittmoden) **3-8-9** TGMcLaughlin(2) (chsd ldrs over 3f: sn hrd rdn & wknd) | 3½ | **7** | 10/1[3] | 18 | — |

(SP 111.4%) **7 Rn**

**1m 16.6** (5.20) CSF £8.84 TOTE £3.50: £1.20 £2.20 (£2.50) OWNER Mr Ziad Galadari (LAMBOURN) BRED Maristow Farms Partnership
**Sondos** did not look fully wound up for this seasonal debut, but she quite simply outclassed the opposition on this All-Weather debut. (2/1: op 5/4)
**Lia Fail (IRE)**, still looking to get off the mark, kept on willingly approaching the final furlong but found the winner in a class of her own. (7/2: 9/4-4/1)
**Mogin** adopted forceful tactics on this occasion, but she was hard at work turning in and had to admit her measure taken. (20/1)
**458 Arabian Heights** was taken off his legs from the break but, with stamina coming into play, was doing all his best work when the race was as good as over. (14/1: 6/1-16/1)
**Tallulah Belle** (10/1: op 6/1)

## 530 AVALON ASSOCIATES LIMITED STKS (0-60) (3-Y.O+) (Class F)

2-50 (2-51) **1m 100y (Fibresand)** £2,381.00 (£656.00: £311.00) Stalls: Low GOING: 0.23 sec per fur (SLW)

| | | | | SP | RR | SF |
|---|---|---|---|---|---|---|
| *487[2]* | **Waikiki Beach (USA) (60)** (GLMoore) **5-9-7** SWhitworth(7) (b: b.hind: swtg: hld up gng wl: led over 3f out: clr ent fnl f: easily) | — | **1** | 100/30[2] | 71 | 49 |
| *399** | **Yo Kiri-B (57)** (JFfitch-Heyes) **5-9-6** GDuffield(5) (hld up in tch: effrt 2f out: nt pce of wnr) | 6 | **2** | 8/1 | 59 | 37 |
| *399[4]* | **Yuppy Girl (IRE) (59)** (CaptJHWilson) **3-7-13**(5)ow1 FLynch(2) (hld up & bhd: hdwy over 3f out: rdn & edgd rt appr fnl f: no imp) | 1 | **3** | 12/1 | 56 | 18 |
| | **Last Roundup (60)** (CWThornton) **4-9-7** DeanMcKeown(6) (w'like: cmpt: bkwd: led tl hdd over 3f out: sn rdn along & btn) | 1½ | **4** | 15/2 | 55 | 33 |

| | Horse | Pos | SP | RR | SF |
|---|---|---|---|---|---|
| | **Bubble Wings (FR) (60)** (SPCWoods) **4-9-6** WWoods(1) (hld up & bhd: hdwy 4f out: drvn along over 2f out: grad wknd) ....1 | 5 | 15/8 1 | 52 | 30 |
| 89* | **Panama Jive (IRE) (60)** (MJohnston) **3-8-5** TWilliams(3) (prom: rdn 3f out: wknd over 2f out) ....s.h | 6 | 6/1 3 | 52 | 15 |
| | **Kinnescash (IRE) (58)** (MSSaunders) **3-8-6** AMcGlone(4) (b: unf: trckd ldrs 5f: sn rdn & wknd) ....2½ | 7 | 10/1 | 48 | 11 |

(SP 111.8%) **7 Rn**

**1m 52.8** (7.80) CSF £25.93 TOTE £4.20: £2.20 £4.10 (£7.40) OWNER Mr K. Higson (EPSOM) BRED Dan C. Pitts & Frank Ramos
WEIGHT FOR AGE 3yo-15lb

**487 Waikiki Beach (USA)**, making a quick reappearance, won this in the easiest possible fashion and this winner of a listed event in Germany at the back-end of last year is obviously useful on his day. (100/30)

**Yo Kiri-B** had more on her plate here and, although staying on, could not get within striking range of the winner. (8/1: 6/1-9/1)

**Yuppy Girl (IRE)**, ridden with more restraint, began to stay on from the turn into the straight, but she hung off a true line and could not muster the speed to reach the winner. (12/1: op 7/1)

**Last Roundup**, carrying plenty of surplus condition for this first outing in six months, took a keen pull and made the running for five months before lack of peak-fitness caught him out. (15/2)

**Bubble Wings (FR)** won on her racecourse debut in December and she looked well forward in condition. She was in trouble from a long way out though, and just could not handle the pace. (15/8)

**Panama Jive (IRE)** had a much stiffer test here than she did on her debut. Driven along for all she was worth three furlongs out, she found the principals running all over her. (6/1)

**Kinnescash (IRE)** (10/1: 8/1-12/1)

## 531 FREEDOM FORGE H'CAP (0-70) (3-Y.O F) (Class E)

3-20 (3-20) **7f (Fibresand)** £3,260.25 (£972.00: £463.50: £209.25) Stalls: High GOING: 0.23 sec per fur (SLW)

| | Horse | Pos | SP | RR | SF |
|---|---|---|---|---|---|
| 421[3] | **Victim of Love (64)** (RCharlton) **3-9-7** SSanders(5) (hdwy to ld over 3f out: rdn & r.o gamely fnl f) ....— | 1 | 5/2 1 | 73 | 36 |
| 463[3] | **Rowlandsons Charm (IRE) (57)** (GLMoore) **3-8-11v**(3) SDrowne(8) (a.p: brought wd ent st: ev ch 1f out: unable qckn) ....1½ | 2 | 11/2 3 | 63 | 26 |
| 404[4] | **Efipetite (51)** (NBycroft) **3-8-3**(5) FLynch(9) (s.i.s: hdwy 3f out: c wd & ev ch ent fnl f: no ex) ....1 | 3 | 14/1 | 54 | 17 |
| 421* | **Miss Offset (57)** (MJohnston) **3-9-0b** TWilliams(1) (lw: set str pce: rdn & hdd over 3f out: wknd wl over 1f out) ....6 | 4 | 5/1 2 | 47 | 10 |
| | **Oatey (55)** (MrsJRRamsden) **3-8-12** KFallon(4) (bit bkwd: outpcd in rr: drvn ½-wy: nvr able to chal) ....3 | 5 | 5/1 2 | 38 | 1 |
| 183[7] | **Flood's Fancy (54)** (LJBarratt) **3-8-4**(7) IonaWands(7) (outpcd: a bhd) ....5 | 6 | 16/1 | 25 | — |
| 428[3] | **Fairy Highlands (IRE) (60)** (SCWilliams) **3-9-3** JTate(6) (trckd ldrs: hrd rdn over 2f out: sn wknd) ....2½ | 7 | 5/1 2 | 26 | — |
| 515[5] | **Marino Street (54)** (PDEvans) **3-8-6b**1(5) AmandaSanders(3) (a bhd & outpcd) ....nk | 8 | 12/1 | 19 | — |
| | **Subtle One (IRE) (45)** (TTClement) **3-8-2** GDuffield(2) (nt grwn: trckd ldrs 4f: sn outpcd) ....½ | 9 | 20/1 | 9 | — |

(SP 119.0%) **9 Rn**

**1m 32.2** (7.50) CSF £16.30 CT £149.95 TOTE £3.50: £1.50 £1.70 £2.90 (£9.60) Trio £36.10 OWNER Mr N. Bryce-Smith (BECKHAMPTON) BRED Nasrullah Holdings

**Victim of Love**, having her sixth outing since the turn of the year, is still hanging on to her winter coat. She landed the gamble readily and should improve further with a bit of sun on her back. (5/2)

**463 Rowlandsons Charm (IRE)** broke on level terms this time and looked a live threat when mounting a determined challenge under the stands' rail a furlong out, but the winner found extra and she had to admit she had met her match. (11/2)

**Efipetite** recovered from a slow start and put herself in with every chance into the final furlong, but could not sustain the effort close home. This was possibly her best run yet. (14/1: 10/1-16/1)

**Miss Offset** set off at break-neck speed and quickly opened up a sizeable lead. Her jockey picked up his stick when she was being challenged soon after halfway, and she had run herself into the ground on reaching the straight. (5/1: 3/1-11/2)

**Oatey**, taken off her legs by the hectic early pace, did try to get herself into it on the home turn but lacked the speed to do so. (5/1: 3/1-11/2)

## 532 THORPE VERNON H'CAP (0-85) (3-Y.O+) (Class D)

3-50 (3-50) **1m 4f (Fibresand)** £3,590.00 (£1,070.00: £510.00: £230.00) Stalls: Low GOING: 0.23 sec per fur (SLW)

| | Horse | Pos | SP | RR | SF |
|---|---|---|---|---|---|
| 512[2] | **In the Money (IRE) (53)** (RHollinshead) **7-7-13**(5)ow1 FLynch(3) (led after 3f tl over 3f out: ev ch ins fnl f: r.o: fin 2nd, ½l: awrdd r) ....— | 1 | 3/1 1 | 58 | 28 |
| 420* | **Hill Farm Dancer (59)** (WMBrisbourne) **5-8-5**(5) DGriffiths(6) (hld up & bhd: hdwy 5f out: chsd wnr & carried wd ent st: swtchd lft & r.o fnl f: unlucky: fin 3rd, 1l: plcd 2nd) .... | 2 | 5/1 | 63+ | 34 |
| 422* | **Backview (72)** (BJLlewellyn) **4-9-8** TWilliams(4) (a.p: led over 3f out: rdn & c v.wd ent st: hld on cl home: fin 1st: disq: plcd 3rd) .... | 3 | 7/2 2 | 78 | 48 |
| 251* | **Greenspan (IRE) (78)** (WRMuir) **4-10-0** Jean-PierreLopez(7) (lw: lost pl 7f out: n.d after) ....10 | 4 | 7/1 | 69 | 39 |
| | **Secret Service (IRE) (73)** (CWThornton) **4-9-9** DeanMcKeown(2) (w'like: str: bit bkwd: a in rr: lost tch over 4f out) ....3½ | 5 | 4/1 3 | 59 | 29 |
| 402[2] | **Chevalier (USA) (77)** (ICampbell) **4-9-6**(7) GFaulkner(1) (trckd ldrs over 6f: sn dropped rr: t.o) ....7 | 6 | 6/1 | 54 | 24 |
| | **Racing Hawk (USA) (64)** (MSSaunders) **4-9-0** AMcGlone(5) (bkwd: led 3f: wknd over 4f out: t.o) ....7 | 7 | 25/1 | 31 | 1 |

(SP 114.5%) **7 Rn**

**2m 44.1** (11.60) CSF £17.18 TOTE £3.60: £3.40 £2.90 (£5.60) OWNER Mr J. E. Bigg (UPPER LONGDON) BRED Cheveley Park Stud Ltd
WEIGHT FOR AGE 4yo-1lb
STEWARDS' ENQUIRY Williams susp. 11-13 & 15-16/4/96 (irresponsible riding).
OFFICIAL EXPLANATION **Backview: had lost his near-fore shoe on return.**

**512 In the Money (IRE)** should have finished third but he benefited from the erratic course steered by the original winner, and was promoted to first place in the Stewards' Room. (3/1)

**Hill Farm Dancer** was almost put over the rail entering the straight, but kept on gamely once switched when the damage had already been done. (5/1)

**Backview** took over turning into the back straight, but ran very wide under a left-handed ride off the home turn. Carrying the strong-challenging Hill Farm Dancer with him, he stayed on strongly to the finish. (7/2)

**Secret Service (IRE)**, very much in need of the run, was always struggling in the rear. (4/1)

## 533 OAKLEY-JONES (S) STKS (2-Y.O) (Class F)

4-20 (4-22) **5f (Fibresand)** £2,553.00 (£703.00: £333.00) Stalls: Low GOING: 0.23 sec per fur (SLW)

| | Horse | Pos | SP | RR | SF |
|---|---|---|---|---|---|
| | **Lawful Find (IRE)** (RHollinshead) **2-8-6**(5) FLynch(3) (scope: bit bkwd: mde all: clr fr ½-wy: wknd fnl f) ....— | 1 | 5/1 3 | 57 | 5 |

| | | | | SP | RR | SF |
|---|---|---|---|---|---|---|
| $446^{4}$ | **Contravene (IRE)** (JBerry) **2-8-1**$^{(5)}$ PFessey(5) (dwlt: bhd & outpcd tl gd hdwy appr fnl f: nt rch wnr) | 1¼ | **2** | Evens$^{1}$ | 48 | — |
| | **Abstone Queen** (PDEvans) **2-8-6** KFallon(6) (leggy: lt-f: trckd ldrs: hrd drvn ½-wy: one pce fnl 2f) | 5 | **3** | 13/2 | 32 | — |
| | **Dancing Star (IRE)** (PDEvans) **2-8-6** SSanders(2) (neat: prom over 3f: sn rdn & wknd) | 3½ | **4** | 9/2$^{2}$ | 21 | — |
| | **D-Day-Smoke** (NPLittmoden) **2-8-4**$^{(7)}$ JBramhill(4) (w'like: leggy: bkwd: prom 3f: sn outpcd) | 3½ | **5** | 10/1 | 15 | — |
| $481^{5}$ | **Chilled Wine** (NBycroft) **2-8-6** GDuffield(1) (bkwd: dwlt: outpcd & a bhd) | ½ | **6** | 14/1 | 8 | — |

(SP 113.9%) **6 Rn**

**65.3 secs** (6.60) CSF £10.41 TOTE £8.20: £3.20 £1.10 (£3.60) OWNER Mr J. Doxey (UPPER LONGDON) BRED Joseph O'Callaghan
Bt in 4,000 gns

**Lawful Find (IRE)**, a scopey colt, did not have much trouble in showing these rivals a clean pair of heels but the strength of the opposition could be suspect and only time will tell. (5/1: op 3/1)

**446 Contravene (IRE)** did not get the best start and was soon well adrift and outpaced. Switched towards the outside turning in, she was reeling the tiring winner in inside the last 100 yards, but was never going to make it. (Evens)

**Abstone Queen**, in the chasing group from the start, was always flat to the boards and failed to make any impression inside the distance. (13/2: 9/2-7/1)

**Dancing Star (IRE)** showed speed until past halfway, but she was being scrubbed along for all she was worth and had shot her bolt on reaching the straight. (9/2: op 2/1)

**481 Chilled Wine** (14/1: 10/1-16/1)

## 534 SHERWOOD STAINLESS H'CAP (0-65) (3-Y.O+) (Class F)

4-50 (4-50) **6f (Fibresand)** £2,381.00 (£656.00: £311.00) Stalls: Low GOING: 0.23 sec per fur (SLW)

| | | | | SP | RR | SF |
|---|---|---|---|---|---|---|
| *431** | **Foist (40)** (MWEasterby) **4-8-13** JQuinn(4) (s.i.s: hdwy 3f out: led over 1f out: sn clr: easily) | — | **1** | Evens$^{1}$ | 57+ | 34 |
| | **Disco Boy (55)** (PDEvans) **6-10-0** SSanders(7) (bkwd: led 1f: rdn 2f out: kpt on same pce) | 5 | **2** | 14/1 | 59 | 36 |
| *$408^{8}$* | **Sir Tasker (51)** (JLHarris) **8-9-10v** JWeaver(6) (led after 1f tl hdd over 1f out: sn btn) | 1¼ | **3** | 3/1$^{2}$ | 51 | 28 |
| *$425^{7}$* | **Blue Lugana (35)** (NBycroft) **4-8-8** GDuffield(5) (prom 3f: sn rdn & outpcd) | 5 | **4** | 20/1 | 22 | — |
| *$418^{11}$* | **Arc Lamp (40)** (JAGlover) **10-8-13** SDWilliams(3) (bit bkwd: prom: pushed along & outpcd fnl 2f) | 2 | **5** | 6/1$^{3}$ | 22 | — |
| *$166^{5}$* | **Shanghai Lil (42)** (MJFetherston-Godley) **4-9-1** DeanMcKeown(2) (bkwd: s.i.s: a bhd & outpcd) | 1 | **6** | 12/1 | 21 | — |
| $466^{8}$ | **Nomadic Dancer (IRE) (43)** (MSSaunders) **4-9-2** NAdams(1) (trckd ldrs 3f: sn rdn & wknd) | 6 | **7** | 20/1 | 6 | — |

(SP 113.2%) **7 Rn**

**1m 17.3** (5.90) CSF £13.78 TOTE £2.10: £1.10 £7.70 (£14.30) OWNER Mr D. F. Spence (SHERIFF HUTTON) BRED W. Cormack

**Foist**, sluggish leaving the stalls and soon bustled along, came back on the bridle after striking the front and was able to take things easy close home. He is at the peak of his form just now. (Evens)

**Disco Boy**, off the track for eight months and understandably looking burly, ran extremely well all the way and he will be a force to be reckoned with from now on. (14/1: 8/1-16/1)

**Sir Tasker** has had plenty of chances but has not won a race since the late summer and it could be that he requires a holiday. (3/1)

**Arc Lamp** still needed this to put an edge on him. (6/1)

**Shanghai Lil** missed the kick on this return to sprinting and was out with the washing all the way. (12/1: op 8/1)

T/Plpt: £23.30 (373.73 Tckts). T/Qdpt: £5.10 (163.5 Tckts). IM

# 0435a-NAD AL SHEBA (Dubai, UAE) (L-H) (Good)

## Wednesday March 27th

Floodlit

## 535a DUBAI DUTY FREE (3-Y.O+)

2-15 (2-17) **1m 2f (Dirt)** £193,548.00 (£64,516.00: £32,258.00: £16,129.00: £9,677.00: £6,452.00)

| | | | | SP | RR | SF |
|---|---|---|---|---|---|---|
| | **Key of Luck (USA)** (KPMcLaughlin,UAE) **5-8-12** GStevens | — | **1** | | 131 | — |
| *$436a^{2}$* | **Cezanne** (SbinSuroor,UAE) **7-8-12** PatEddery | 20 | **2** | | 99 | — |
| *395a** | **Valley of Gold (FR)** (SbinSuroor,UAE) **4-8-8** LDettori | 2 | **3** | | 92 | — |
| | **Jural** (SbinSuroor,UAE) **4-8-8** CMcCarron | 10 | **4** | | 76 | — |
| *$395a^{3}$* | **Najm Almaydaan (USA)** (DJSelvaratnam,UAE) **5-8-12** BDoyle | 1 | **5** | | 78 | — |
| | **Triarius (USA)** (SbinSuroor,UAE) **6-8-12** OPeslier | nk | **6** | | 78 | — |
| *$375a^{7}$* | **Ihtiram (IRE)** (KPMcLaughlin,UAE) **4-8-11** RHills | 3 | **7** | | 72 | — |
| | **Motakabber (IRE)** (DJSelvaratnam,UAE) **4-8-11** DOliver | s.h | **8** | | 72 | — |
| | **Regal Discovery (CAN)** (RAttfield,Canada) **4-8-11** JBailey | 6 | **9** | | 62 | — |
| | **Rehlat Farah (USA)** (DJSelvaratnam,UAE) **5-8-12** JChavez | 1 | **10** | | 62 | — |
| | **Volochine (IRE)** (RCollet,France) **5-8-12** TJarnet | 6 | **11** | | 52 | — |
| *$375a^{3}$* | **Dover Straits (USA)** (KPMcLaughlin,UAE) **5-8-12** CArias | 1½ | **12** | | 50 | — |
| | **Waterperry (USA)** (ECharpy,UAE) **4-8-11** WSupple | 4 | **13** | | 42 | — |
| | **Young Buster (IRE)** (GWragg) **8-8-12** MHills | 17 | **14** | | 16 | — |

**14 Rn**

**2m 3.77** OWNER Sheikh Saeed bin Maktoum al Maktoum BRED Gainsborough Farm

**Key of Luck (USA)** slaughtered a good-class field with an all the way success that would not have looked out of place in the World Cup itself. Coming home unchallenged, his time was better than that of Cigar. He will now travel to America with his trainer, where we may see some interesting confrontations.

**436a Cezanne**, an Irish Champion Stakes winner, was having his third race after a fourteen-month lay-off. Giving chase in the last three furlongs, he never looked like catching the impressive winner.

**395a* Valley of Gold (FR)**, a top-class filly for Andre Fabre last season, would ideally prefer a longer trip.

**Jural**, who has not been seen since finishing last in the St Leger, put in a better effort here.

**Triarius (USA)** is useful but finished a distant last on his first start here in Dubai, so this was a better effort.

**Young Buster (IRE)** was disappointing last year, and showed a dislike for the dirt, finishing a tailed-off last.

## 536a DUBAI WORLD CUP (4-Y.O+)

3-00 (3-00) **1m 2f (Dirt)** £1,548,387.00 (£516,129.00: £258,065.00: £129,032.00: £77,419.00: £51,613.00)

| | | | | SP | RR | SF |
|---|---|---|---|---|---|---|
| | **Cigar (USA)** (WMott,USA) **6-8-12** JBailey (a.p: led over 2f out: jnd 1f out: r.o gamely u.p) | — | **1** | | 138 | — |

| | | | | | |
|---|---|---|---|---|---|
| | **Soul of the Matter (USA)** (RMandella,USA) **5-8-12** GStevens (hld up in rr: gd hdwy from 3f out to ld 1f out: no ex u.p ins fnl f) ........½ | **2** | | 137 | — |
| | **L'Carriere (USA)** (HJBond,USA) **5-8-12b** JChavez (disp ld tl led over 3f out: hdd over 2f out: r.o one pce) .....8 | **3** | | 124 | — |
| | **Pentire** (GWragg) **4-8-11** MHills (hld up on outside: hdwy to chal u.p 2f out: wknd over 1f out) ........¾ | **4** | | 122 | — |
| *436a** | **Tamayaz (CAN)** (SbinSuroor,UAE) **4-8-12** CMcCarron (trckd ldrs: rdn & outpcd 4f out: styd on fnl f) ........3½ | **5** | | 118 | — |
| | **Lively Mount (JPN)** (FShibata,Japan) **5-8-12** MIshibashi (disp ld tl rdn & outpcd over 4f out: styd on fnl 2f) ....6 | **6** | | 108 | — |
| | **Needle Gun (IRE)** (CEBrittain) **6-8-12** BDoyle (in tch: rdn 5f out: nt pce to chal) ........1 | **7** | | 106 | — |
| *434a²* | **Torrential (USA)** (SbinSuroor,UAE) **4-8-11** OPeslier (nvr trbld ldrs) ........¾ | **8** | | 104 | — |
| *397a** | **Larrocha (IRE)** (SbinSuroor,UAE) **4-8-8** PatEddery (outpcd early: a bhd) ........3 | **9** | | 96 | — |
| | **Danewin (AUS)** (RThomsen,Australia) **5-8-8** DOliver (prom tl wknd 2f out) ........¾ | **10** | | 95 | — |
| *434a** | **Halling (USA)** (SbinSuroor,UAE) **5-8-12** LDettori (trckd ldrs: rdn 3f out: sn wknd: eased fnl f) ........12 | **11** | | 80 | — |
| | | | | | **11 Rn** |

**2m 3.84** OWNER Mr Allen Paulson BRED A. E. Paulson

**Cigar (USA)** produced a wonderfully game display to confirm his status as the best horse in the world. Close to the pace as usual, he kicked for home soon after entering the straight. He looked sure to be beaten when the runner-up swooped below the distance, but simply refused to be beaten and was comfortably on top at the line. He will now have a break, but will be aimed at the Hollywood Gold Cup and the Breeders' Cup again.

**Soul of the Matter (USA)** was held up well off the pace, and was still at the back turning for home. He then produced a terrific burst of acceleration to cut through the field and looked sure to win at the distance, but could not resist the renewed effort of the winner.

**L'Carriere (USA)** produced another good performance and, although no match for the first two, this consistent performer battled on to regain third place inside the last furlong.

**Pentire** proved best of the non-Americans. He was ridden with restraint and, creeping closer on the home turn, looked sure to be involved in the finish. Despite running on bravely, he was left behind by the first two in the last furlong and a half. On this form, he will be hard to beat in the top European races this year.

**436a* Tamayaz (CAN)** looked beaten when losing his pitch on the home turn, but ran on again in the closing stages. He is finding his feet at the top level.

**Lively Mount (JPN)** seemed well beaten before the bend, but stayed on through beaten horses in the last quarter-mile.

**Needle Gun (IRE)**, despite being out of his depth at this level, was not disgraced.

**434a Torrential (USA)** was soon struggling to hold his place, and was never able to get in a blow.

**397a* Larrocha (IRE)** was soon outpaced, and never in the hunt.

**Danewin (AUS)** ran prominently until stopping quickly in the last quarter-mile. He may have had a problem.

**434a* Halling (USA)** once again proved a disappointment on the big occasion. Well enough placed just behind the leaders, he dropped away tamely in the last two and a half furlongs.

# HAMILTON (R-H) (Good to soft)
## Wednesday April 3rd
WEATHER: overcast WIND: almost nil

## 537 SOUTH LANARKSHIRE CLAIMING STKS (3-Y.O+) (Class F)
2-25 (2-26) **1m 1f 36y** £2,675.00 (£750.00: £365.00) Stalls: Low GOING: 0.02 sec per fur (G)

| | | | SP | RR | SF |
|---|---|---|---|---|---|
| *410⁵* | **Field of Vision (IRE) (70)** (MJohnston) **6-9-9** JWeaver(9) (lw: bhd: hdwy ½-wy: rdn to ld 1½f out: styd on wl) ........— | **1** | 7/2 ² | 70 | 58 |
| 479¹¹ | **Heathyards Magic (IRE) (67)** (MDods) **4-9-6** JCarroll(12) (bhd: hdwy 4f out: ch over 1f out: nt qckn) ........6 | **2** | 50/1 | 57 | 45 |
| | **Flag Fen (USA) (68)** (MartynMeade) **5-9-11** VSlattery(13) (sn chsng clr ldr: ev ch over 1f out: one pce) ........1½ | **3** | 16/1 | 59 | 47 |
| | **Break the Rules (75)** (MrsMReveley) **4-10-0** KDarley(3) (lw: bhd & rdn ½-wy: styd on fnl 2f: nrst fin) ........nk | **4** | 9/4 ¹ | 61 | 49 |
| 455¹⁹ | **Castel Rosselo (80)** (RHarris) **6-10-0b¹** AMackay(6) (b: led: clr 6f out: hdd & wknd 1½f out) ........6 | **5** | 7/1 | 51 | 39 |
| | **Funny Rose (28)** (PMonteith) **6-8-8(5)** PFessey(10) (lw: bhd: effrt ½-wy: nvr rchd ldrs) ........½ | **6** | 50/1 | 35 | 23 |
| 440²⁷ | **Talented Ting (IRE) (64)** (PCHaslam) **7-9-10** JFortune(8) (in tch tl wknd fnl 2f) ........hd | **7** | 14/1 | 46 | 34 |
| | **Fasih (78)** (SEKettlewell) **4-9-10(3)** JStack(4) (b: sn chsng ldrs: effrt ½-wy: wknd fnl 2f) ........1½ | **8** | 9/2 ³ | 46 | 34 |
| | **Jabaroot (IRE) (75)** (DANolan) **5-9-6** JQuinn(7) (lw: outpcd fr ½-wy) ........7 | **9** | 25/1 | 27 | 15 |
| | **Brogans Brush** (JSHaldane) **3-8-1** LCharnock(2) (swtg: prom 4f: sn wknd) ........8 | **10** | 500/1 | 11 | — |
| *428⁹* | **All In Good Time** (CWThornton) **3-8-8** DeanMcKeown(5) (a rr div) ........1¼ | **11** | 50/1 | 16 | — |
| *59¹²* | **Seenthelight (40)** (DMoffatt) **4-8-10v(3)** DarrenMoffatt(11) (prom tl wknd fnl 3f) ........½ | **12** | 66/1 | 3 | — |
| | **To Prove a Point** (JJO'Neill) **4-9-5** SDWilliams(1) (c wd st: bhd fnl 5f) ........5 | **13** | 40/1 | — | — |
| | | | (SP 110.1%) | **13 Rn** | |

**2m** (5.70) CSF £117.96 TOTE £4.10: £1.50 £19.20 £5.50 (£87.10) Trio £112.10; £83.72 to Leicester 4/4/96 OWNER Mr R. W. Huggins (MIDDLEHAM) BRED Sean Collins

WEIGHT FOR AGE 3yo-17lb

Field of Vision (IRE) clmd PByrne £8,000

**Field of Vision (IRE)** has come back to form on the All-Weather this winter and gained his first win on turf for almost three years. He was given a particularly good ride, picking the best ground up the straight. (7/2: 5/2-4/1)

**Heathyards Magic (IRE)** has never won on turf but there was nothing wrong with this effort and a similar race should be within his grasp. (50/1)

**Flag Fen (USA)** showed his first signs of form for a long time. (16/1)

**Break the Rules** ran as though he is crying out for further and was certainly putting in all his best work at the end. (9/4)

**Castel Rosselo**, with blinkers on for the first time, was given a most aggressive ride but had run himself out approaching the final furlong. (7/1: 4/1-8/1)

**Funny Rose** looked really well but, never really happy in the race, failed to make any impression. (50/1)

**Talented Ting (IRE)** loves this track but not softish ground. (14/1: 10/1-16/1)

**Fasih** was always racing on the slower ground on the outside and that found him out in the last two furlongs. (9/2)

## 538 RUTHERGLEN MEDIAN AUCTION MAIDEN STKS (2-Y.O F) (Class E)
2-55 (2-57) **5f 4y** £2,831.85 (£856.80: £417.90: £198.45) Stalls: High GOING: 0.02 sec per fur (G)

| | | | SP | RR | SF |
|---|---|---|---|---|---|
| | **Northern Sal** (JBerry) **2-8-11** JCarroll(3) (unf: cl up: led 2f out: rn green: hld on wl) ........— | **1** | Evens ¹ | 55 | — |
| | **Tazibari** (DMoffatt) **2-8-8(3)** DarrenMoffatt(5) (cmpt: a.p: disp ld over 1f out: no ex towards fin) ........nk | **2** | 5/2 ² | 54 | — |
| 465⁶ | **Face It** (WGMTurner) **2-8-11** TSprake(2) (led 3f: sn outpcd) ........3 | **3** | 14/1 | 45 | — |

| | Horse | | Pos | SP | RR | SF |
|---|---|---|---|---|---|---|
| | **Mill End Girl** (MWEasterby) **2-8-11** DaleGibson(4) (neat: bit bkwd: nvr wnt pce) | 5 | **4** | 20/1 | 29 | — |
| | **Epaulette** (MRChannon) **2-8-11** KDarley(1) (neat: sn drvn along & bhd) | s.h | **5** | 4/1$^{3}$ | 28 | — |
| | | | | (SP 110.0%) | | **5 Rn** |

**64.7 secs** (6.40) CSF £2.36 TOTE £1.70: £1.10 £1.70 (£1.60) OWNER Mr A. R. Breeze (COCKERHAM) BRED Mrs V. E. Hughes

**Northern Sal** raced freely and then ran green when in front, but she did battle on well at the end. (Evens)
**Tazibari** knew her job and made a real fight of it but was just outstayed in the closing stages. (5/2: op 4/1)
**465 Face It** tried to make her experience tell but she was left struggling entering the last quarter-mile. (14/1: 4/1-16/1)
**Mill End Girl** needed this and could never lay up with the pace. (20/1)
**Epaulette** was outpaced throughout and will need further. (4/1: 5/2-9/2)

## 539 HAMILTON H'CAP (0-60) (3-Y.O) (Class F)

3-30 (3-32) **6f 5y** £2,948.00 (£828.00: £404.00) Stalls: High GOING: 0.02 sec per fur (G)

| | Horse | | Pos | SP | RR | SF |
|---|---|---|---|---|---|---|
| 473$^{6}$ | **Hobbs Choice (47)** (GMMoore) **3-8-12** DaleGibson(13) (lw: racd far side: a cl up: styd on to ld cl home) | — | **1** | 8/1 | 63 | 26 |
| | **Goretski (IRE) (54)** (NTinkler) **3-9-5** KDarley(2) (cl up: led ½-wy: hung rt: wknd & ct cl home) | ½ | **2** | 12/1 | 69+ | 32 |
| 473$^{3}$ | **Lucky Bea (45)** (MWEasterby) **3-8-10** JFortune(4) (a chsng ldrs: sn drvn along: kpt on towards fin) | 2 | **3** | 9/2$^{2}$ | 54+ | 17 |
| | **Afisiak (50)** (ABMulholland) **3-9-1** JWeaver(10) (a chsng ldrs: rdn ½-wy: one pce) | 3 | **4** | 5/1$^{3}$ | 51 | 14 |
| | **Toe Tappin Music (USA) (45)** (MartynMeade) **3-8-10** VSlattery(7) (chsd ldrs: outpcd ½-wy: styd on towards fin) | s.h | **5** | 12/1 | 46 | 9 |
| 467* | **Beldray Park (IRE) (63)** (MrsALMKing) **3-10-0** $^{7x}$ JQuinn(8) (outpcd & bhd: sme hdwy 2f out: n.d) | ¾ | **6** | 7/2$^{1}$ | 62 | 25 |
| | **Monsieur Culsyth (52)** (JBerry) **3-9-3** JCarroll(11) (lw: prom: outpcd ½-wy: no imp after) | 3 | **7** | 20/1 | 43 | 6 |
| | **Ya Marhaba (45)** (JWPayne) **3-8-10** AMcGlone(1) (nvr trbld ldrs) | hd | **8** | 15/2 | 36 | — |
| | **Autofyr (35)** (JSWainwright) **3-8-0** LCharnock(9) (bit bkwd: outpcd fr ½-wy) | nk | **9** | 66/1 | 25 | — |
| 479$^{3}$ | **Larrylukeathugh (45)** (JJO'Neill) **3-8-10b** SDWilliams(3) (led to ½-wy: sn wknd) | 1¼ | **10** | 6/1 | 32 | — |
| | **Ready Teddy (IRE) (50)** (MissLAPerratt) **3-9-1** JFanning(12) (spd to ½-wy: sn wknd) | 1¼ | **11** | 20/1 | 34 | — |
| | **Vales Ales (40)** (RMMcKellar) **3-8-5** TSprake(5) (bhd fr ½-wy) | 3½ | **12** | 66/1 | 14 | — |
| 473$^{8}$ | **Pearls of Thought (IRE) (55)** (JSHaldane) **3-9-6** AMackay(6) (sn wl bhd) | 22 | **13** | 100/1 | — | — |
| | | | | (SP 123.1%) | | **13 Rn** |

**1m 15.1** (5.10) CSF £92.82 CT £464.68 TOTE £18.20: £4.70 £2.60 £2.80 (£116.60) Trio £221.60 OWNER Miss Liz Hobbs (MIDDLEHAM) BRED F. Hines

**473 Hobbs Choice** made full use of the best draw and got the favoured far rail and that was what won her the day. She should stay further. (8/1)
**Goretski (IRE)** put up a valiant effort from a bad draw, but had so much running to do to get across to the far side that it sapped all reserves at the finish. (12/1: 8/1-14/1)
**473 Lucky Bea**, poorly drawn, could never find the speed to overcome it. He is well worth another chance. (9/2: op 3/1)
**Afisiak**, edgy and sweaty beforehand, had a good draw but was fighting a lost cause soon after halfway. (5/1)
**Toe Tappin Music (USA)** showed next to nothing in three runs last season, but did give a glimmer of hope here, staying on in the closing stages. (12/1)
**467* Beldray Park (IRE)** was very disappointing, getting left behind early on and never looking likely to get into it. (7/2)

## 540 LANARK (S) STKS (3-Y.O) (Class G)

4-00 (4-01) **1m 65y** £2,234.00 (£624.00: £302.00) Stalls: Low GOING: 0.02 sec per fur (G)

| | Horse | | Pos | SP | RR | SF |
|---|---|---|---|---|---|---|
| | **She's A Winner (IRE)** (SCWilliams) **3-8-6** KDarley(7) (unf: dwlt: hdwy 4f out: hmpd over 3f out: styd on strly fnl f to ld nr fin) | — | **1** | 4/1$^{2}$ | 49 | 11 |
| *418*$^{13}$ | **Classic Victory (65)** (RHarris) **3-9-2hb** AMackay(6) (lw: led: rdn 2f out: jst ct) | hd | **2** | 8/1 | 59 | 21 |
| 473$^{5}$ | **Rattle (52)** (JJO'Neill) **3-8-11** SDWilliams(2) (outpcd & bhd: styd on wl fnl f) | 6 | **3** | 9/2$^{3}$ | 42 | 4 |
| 468$^{8}$ | **Ciserano (IRE) (58)** (MRChannon) **3-8-6** AGorman(5) (a chsng ldrs: ev ch 2f out: edgd lft & sn btn) | 2½ | **4** | 9/2$^{3}$ | 32 | — |
| *404*$^{2}$ | **Dragonjoy (56)** (JWPayne) **3-9-2b** AMcGlone(3) (lw: chsd ldrs: effrt ½-wy: btn 2f out) | 3 | **5** | 2/1$^{1}$ | 37 | — |
| 473$^{11}$ | **Darerock (35)** (MDods) **3-8-11** LCharnock(4) (prom tl wknd 4f out) | 20 | **6** | 100/1 | — | — |
| | **Phantom Dancer (IRE) (49)** (JBerry) **3-8-11** JCarroll(1) (chsd ldr tl hung rt & wknd over 3f out) | 4 | **7** | 5/1 | — | — |
| | | | | (SP 118.5%) | | **7 Rn** |

**1m 52.7** (8.60) CSF £32.47 TOTE £5.00: £1.90 £3.30 (£25.80) OWNER Miss L. J. Ward (NEWMARKET) BRED Grangemore Stud
Sold DPetrie 6,600 gns
STEWARDS' ENQUIRY Darley susp. 12-13 & 15/4/96 (excessive use of whip).

**She's A Winner (IRE)** had plenty of running to do after a slow start and then got messed about twice in the straight, but her capable jockey forced her head in front where it matters. There would seem to be improvement to come, but she did have a very hard introduction. (4/1: 3/1-9/2)
**Classic Victory** made all here last season and tried that again, which almost paid off. (8/1)
**473 Rattle**, struggling in behind, raced in the slowest ground up the straight and only stayed on when switching in the closing stages. (9/2)
**Ciserano (IRE)** had every chance until her stamina gave out in the last furlong and a half. (9/2: op 3/1)
**Dragonjoy** found this much more of a struggle than the All-Weather and was back-pedalling entering the final two furlongs. (2/1)
**Phantom Dancer (IRE)** gave up the ghost over three furlongs from home. (5/1)

## 541 EAST KILBRIDE H'CAP (0-75) (3-Y.O+) (Class D)

4-30 (4-30) **1m 3f 16y** £3,793.70 (£1,148.60: £560.80: £266.90) Stalls: High GOING: 0.02 sec per fur (G)

| | Horse | | Pos | SP | RR | SF |
|---|---|---|---|---|---|---|
| 440$^{13}$ | **Calder King (57)** (JLEyre) **5-9-1v** RLappin(6) (in tch: hdwy 4f out: led 1½f out: styd on) | — | **1** | 5/1$^{3}$ | 66 | 38 |
| 477* | **Astral Weeks (IRE) (61)** (LLungo) **5-9-5** $^{6x}$ KFallon(4) (bhd: hdwy 4f out: styd on u.p fnl 2f: nrst fin) | hd | **2** | 9/2$^{2}$ | 70 | 42 |
| 440* | **Manful (62)** (CWCElsey) **4-9-6b** NKennedy(3) (a.p: effrt over 2f out: r.o one pce) | ¾ | **3** | 3/1$^{1}$ | 70 | 42 |
| 477$^{2}$ | **Steadfast Elite (IRE) (38)** (JJO'Neill) **5-7-5**$^{(5)}$ PFessey(1) (hdwy 6f out: ev ch over 2f out: one pce fnl f) | 1 | **4** | 9/2$^{2}$ | 44 | 16 |
| | **Cutthroat Kid (IRE) (62)** (MrsMReveley) **6-9-6v** KDarley(2) (chsd ldrs: led wl over 2f out to 1½f out: one pce) | hd | **5** | 5/1$^{3}$ | 68 | 40 |
| | **Dont Forget Curtis (IRE) (66)** (GMMoore) **4-9-10** JFortune(8) (chsd ldrs tl wknd fnl 2½f) | 3 | **6** | 12/1 | 68 | 40 |
| | **Rapid Mover (38)** (DANolan) **9-7-10b** JQuinn(5) (led tl hdd wl over 2f out: grad wknd) | 1 | **7** | 100/1 | 38 | 10 |
| 447$^{4}$ | **Classic Lover (IRE) (75)** (RHarris) **3-8-13** AMackay(7) (bhd fnl 4f) | 11 | **8** | 7/1 | 60 | 12 |
| | | | | (SP 115.9%) | | **8 Rn** |

**2m 28.2** (8.80) CSF £26.16 CT £71.90 TOTE £5.00: £1.10 £2.60 £1.90 (£45.80) OWNER Mr D. Clarkson (HAMBLETON) BRED Bellmor Stud
LONG HANDICAP Steadfast Elite (IRE) 7-8 Rapid Mover 6-12
WEIGHT FOR AGE 3yo-20lb

**440 Calder King** last won eighteen months ago but has been running well on the All-Weather. His stable is flying at present, and he scored in most determined style. (5/1)
**477* Astral Weeks (IRE)** was again given plenty to do, but tried hard and the effort was only just too late. (9/2)
**440* Manful**, in a messy race, was always short of toe in the closing stages. A stronger pace would help. (3/1)
**477 Steadfast Elite (IRE)**, who spent most of the race going wide, was always on the slower ground and, in the circumstances, did well. (9/2)
**Cutthroat Kid (IRE)** had his chances but was always tapped for toe over this shorter trip. (5/1)

## 542 CAMBUSLANG H'CAP (0-60) (3-Y.O+) (Class F)
5-00 (5-04) **1m 4f 17y** £2,962.00 (£832.00: £406.00) Stalls: High GOING: 0.02 sec per fur (G)

| | | | | SP | RR | SF |
|---|---|---|---|---|---|---|
| | **Eurotwist (40)** (SEKettlewell) **7-9-1** JFortune(7) (drvn along 7f out: hdwy 6f out: styd on to ld wl ins fnl f) | — | 1 | 8/1 | 52 | 29 |
| $367^{4}$ | **Me Cherokee (46)** (CWThornton) **4-9-6** DeanMcKeown(4) (chsd ldrs: led 2f out: wandered u.p: hdd & no ex wl ins fnl f) | ½ | 2 | 33/1 | 57 | 33 |
| $474^{6}$ | **Palace of Gold (39)** (LLungo) **6-9-0** JFanning(8) (swtg: a in tch: ev ch 2f out: wandered u.p: nt qckn towards fin) | hd | 3 | $5/1^{2}$ | 50 | 27 |
| $483^{4}$ | **Thorntoun Estate (IRE) (58)** (MJohnston) **3-8-12** JWeaver(2) (rr div: hdwy on outside over 2f out: kpt on towards fin) | 2 | 4 | $11/4^{1}$ | 67 | 23 |
| $422^{8}$ | **Philmist (35)** (CWCElsey) **4-8-9b** NKennedy(13) (in tch: effrt & nt clr run 2f out tl ins fnl f: nt rcvr) | nk | 5 | 8/1 | 43 | 19 |
| | **What Jim Wants (IRE) (43)** (JJO'Neill) **3-7-11**$^{ow1}$ FNorton(1) (in tch: effrt on outside 2f out: nt pce to chal) | 1¼ | 6 | 33/1 | 50 | 5 |
| | **Sylvan Celebration (21)** (JSGoldie) **5-7-5**$^{(5)}$ PFessey(12) (cl up: slt ld 8f out to 5f out: sn wknd) | 4 | 7 | 20/1 | 22 | — |
| | **Bark'n'bite (50)** (MrsMReveley) **4-9-10v**$^{1}$ KDarley(6) (lw: cl up tl wknd fnl 3f: eased whn btn) | 15 | 8 | 13/2 | 31 | 7 |
| | **Lord Advocate (33)** (DANolan) **8-8-8b** JQuinn(5) (mde most tl hdd 2f out: wknd) | 1 | 9 | 25/1 | 13 | — |
| | **Sharmoor (27)** (MissLCSiddall) **4-8-1** LCharnock(9) (bhd fnl 4f) | 9 | 10 | 33/1 | — | — |
| $422^{5}$ | **Charlie Bigtime (48)** (RHarris) **6-9-9** AMackay(10) (b.hind: pushed along most of wy: a bhd) | hd | 11 | $11/2^{3}$ | 16 | — |
| | **Doctor's Remedy (27)** (MrsJJordan) **10-7-9**$^{(7)}$ JoHunnam(3) (wl bhd fnl 6f) | 1 | 12 | 33/1 | — | — |
| $429^{6}$ | **Exclusion (38)** (JHetherton) **7-8-13** KFallon(11) (lw: Withdrawn not under Starter's orders: ref to ent stalls) | | W | 12/1 | — | — |
| | | | | (SP 122.3%) | **12 Rn** | |

**2m 43.0** (11.00) CSF £183.30 CT £1,127.54 TOTE £8.60: £2.10 £8.20 £1.30 (£88.50) Trio £209.50 OWNER Mr S. E. Kettlewell (MIDDLEHAM) BRED Waresley Park Stud Ltd
LONG HANDICAP Sylvan Celebration 7-0 What Jim Wants (IRE) 7-8
WEIGHT FOR AGE 3yo-21lb, 4yo-1lb

**Eurotwist** has always loved this easy ground. A real battler, he was given a most determined ride and got there late on. (8/1: op 5/1)
**Me Cherokee** has plenty of ability but needs to concentrate for a race to be found. (33/1)
**Palace of Gold**, an edgy individual, was sweating quite badly before the race and looked to be going quite well in it, but was found wanting when it came down to an effort. (5/1)
**483 Thorntoun Estate (IRE)**, racing on the worst ground in the straight, was staying on to show he is still on good terms with himself. (11/4)
**Philmist** had no luck at all in running and would have been in the shake up. (8/1)
**What Jim Wants (IRE)** was staying on here, suggesting that even stiffer tests of stamina will suit. (33/1)
**Bark'n'bite** needs a much firmer surface than this. (13/2: 9/2-7/1)
**Charlie Bigtime** (11/2: 4/1-6/1)

T/Plpt: £2,099.40 (4.34 Tckts). T/Qdpt: £484.90 (2.04 Tckts). AA

# SAN ROSSORE (Pisa, Italy) (R-H) (Good)
## Sunday March 31st

## 543a PREMIO GOLDONE MAIDEN (3-Y.O)
3-00 (3-13) **7f 110y** £6,090.00 (£2,436.00: £1,461.00: £730.00)

| | | | SP | RR | SF |
|---|---|---|---|---|---|
| **Magic Rama (ITY)** (GGiusti,Italy) **3-9-2** CColombi | — | 1 | | — | — |
| **Nimble (IRE)** (JWHills) **3-8-13** MHills | s.h | 2 | | — | — |
| **Cousin Bull (USA)** (MGuarnieri,Italy) **3-9-2** MTellini | 4¾ | 3 | | — | — |
| | | | | | **8 Rn** |

**1m 32.3** TOTE 80L: 14L 13L 11L (201L) OWNER G. Guisti BRED Lordship and Egerton Studs
**Nimble (IRE)** is an unraced daughter of Danehill who has been housed in Pisa over the winter. She was always close up but just lost out after a terrific duel in the final furlong. With the advantage of the Italian sun on her back, she should pick up a race on her return to Britain.

# 0490-LEICESTER (R-H) (Good, Good to soft patches)
## Thursday April 4th
WEATHER: Fine WIND: almost nil

## 544 BESCABY MAIDEN STKS (3-Y.O) (Class D)
2-10 (2-12) **1m 8y** £4,159.05 (£1,244.40: £596.70: £272.85) Stalls: High GOING: 0.01 sec per fur (G)

| | | | SP | RR | SF |
|---|---|---|---|---|---|
| **Royal Canaska** (DRLoder) **3-9-0** RHughes(12) (still unf: lw: led over 6f out: qcknd clr 2f out: jst hld on) | — | 1 | $10/11^{1}$ | 81 | 27 |
| **North Song** (JHMGosden) **3-9-0** LDettori(10) (b: unf: scope: bit bkwd: hdwy 2f out: str run fnl f: jst failed) | hd | 2 | $9/2^{2}$ | 81 | 27 |
| **Reinhardt (IRE) (97)** (PWChapple-Hyam) **3-9-0** JReid(13) (a.p: styd on fnl f) | 1¼ | 3 | 13/2 | 78 | 24 |
| **Murheb** (RWArmstrong) **3-9-0** RPrice(6) (w ldrs: one pce appr fnl f) | s.h | 4 | $6/1^{3}$ | 78 | 24 |
| **Chinensis (IRE)** (LMCumani) **3-9-0** OUrbina(3) (leggy: scope: bit bkwd: in tch: no imp fnl 2f) | 5 | 5 | 25/1 | 68 | 14 |
| **Family Man** (JRFanshawe) **3-9-0** DHarrison(9) (w'like: leggy: s.i.s: hdwy 3f out: rn green appr fnl f: eased whn btn) | s.h | 6 | 25/1 | 68 | 14 |
| **Tawafek (USA)** (DMorley) **3-9-0** WCarson(1) (bit bkwd: n.d) | ½ | 7 | 10/1 | 67 | 13 |

**Polish Widow** (GWragg) **3-8-9** MHills(7) (hld up: pushed along 4f out: hdwy over 1f out: nvr nrr)....................nk **8** 7/1 62 8
**Quiet Arch (IRE)** (CACyzer) **3-9-0** DBiggs(2) (w'like: leggy: chsd ldrs: rdn 4f out: sn btn)..............................½ **9** 33/1 66 12
**John-T** (JLDunlop) **3-9-0** SWhitworth(4) (nt grwn: bit bkwd: led over 1f: wknd over 3f out)..............................3 **10** 33/1 60 6
**Lazali (USA)** (EALDunlop) **3-9-0** RHills(8) (leggy: unf: bit bkwd: plld hrd: effrt 3f out: wknd 2f out) ................1¾ **11** 25/1 56 2
448[7] **Only (USA)** (RHannon) **3-9-0** RPerham(5) (bhd fnl 3f)..................................................................................5 **12** 33/1 46 —
(SP 140.1%) **12 Rn**

**1m 41.9** (6.90) CSF £7.19 TOTE £1.80: £1.30 £2.10 £1.60 (£8.60) Trio £15.80 OWNER Mrs June Sifton (NEWMARKET) BRED M. L. Page

**Royal Canaska**, a half-brother to the useful Canaska Star, seemed in total charge below the distance, but only scrambled home in the end. The slow early pace may have made him idle but a drop in trip may be beneficial. (10/11: op 6/4)

**North Song**, who looked well in his coat, is a good mover, although rather keen. Picking up ground in the final quarter-mile, he stuck on to the bitter end. (9/2)

**Reinhardt (IRE)**, who rather lost his way last year, stuck on to the bitter end to snatch third right on the line. He has a pedigree which suggests that his trip may be hard to find. (13/2: 3/1-7/1)

**Murheb** raced too keenly to be a factor in the closing stages. (6/1: op 5/2)

**Chinensis (IRE)**, green in the preliminaries, made a satisfactory debut. (25/1)

**Family Man**, a poor mover, missed the break but looked to be travelling as well as anything in the race with three furlongs left. Once let down, he hung and the situation was accepted. (25/1)

**Tawafek (USA)** was given a negative ride in a slowly-run race for a horse racing over what is likely to prove some way short of his optimum trip. He would be an interesting proposition in an ordinary middle-distance handicap. (10/1: 6/1-11/1)

**Polish Widow** (7/1: 3/1-8/1)

## 545 BILLESDON (S) STKS (I) (3-Y.O+) (Class G)

2-40 (2-41) **7f 9y** £2,077.00 (£572.00: £271.00) Stalls: High GOING: 0.01 sec per fur (G)

SP RR SF

527[5] **Cicerone (45)** (JLHarris) **6-9-7** GDuffield(3) (chsd ldrs: hung rt: rdn to ld 1f out: drvn out)..............................— **1** 6/1[2] 62 44
**Proud Image (68)** (APJarvis) **4-9-7** JTate(7) (led 5f out to 1f out: one pce)..........................................................2½ **2** 5/1[1] 56 38
**Cool Caper** (AGFoster) **3-8-0**(7) RWaterfield(1) (bhd: rdn 4f out: r.o appr fnl f)...............................................2½ **3** 25/1 51 19
**Cedar Dancer (43)** (RJHodges) **4-8-13**(3) SDrowne(5) (bkwd: hld up: nt clr run 3f out: rdn 2f out: kpt on)...............................................................................................................................................½ **4** 12/1 45 27
376[5] **Domettes (IRE) (64)** (RHannon) **3-8-7** RPerham(2) (bhd: rdn 3f out: nvr nrr)...................................................¾ **5** 5/1[1] 48 16
372[3] **First Gold (58)** (JWharton) **7-9-12b** JReid(10) (hdwy & edgd rt 3f out: nvr able to chal)...................................1 **6** 5/1[1] 51 33
**Cledeschamps** (MWEllerby) **7-8-11**(5) CTeague(8) (bkwd: chsd ldrs: rdn & btn over 2f out).................................5 **7** 25/1 29 11
427[5] **La Dama (USA) (40)** (ABMulholland) **4-9-2** MMcAndrew(4) (w ldrs 4f)......................................................nk **8** 11/1[3] 29 11
501[4] **Eastleigh (42)** (RHollinshead) **7-9-7b** LDettori(11) (chsd ldrs 4f).............................................................8 **9** 6/1[2] 15 —
**Silver Harrow (60)** (AGNewcombe) **3-8-4**(3) DRMcCabe(6) (bit bkwd: plld hrd: led 2f: wknd 3f out)....................4 **10** 5/1[1] 6 —
**Lizapet (IRE)** (PAPritchard) **4-9-2** CRutter(9) (s.i.s: a bhd).......................................................................5 **11** 33/1 — —
(SP 121.9%) **11 Rn**

**1m 28.1** (5.10) CSF £35.03 TOTE £6.30: £1.90 £1.80 £11.20 (£9.60) Trio £246.50; £180.54 to 6/4/96 OWNER Dr C. W. Ashpole (MELTON MOWBRAY) BRED Aldershawe Stud Farm

WEIGHT FOR AGE 3yo-14lb

No bid

**527 Cicerone** edged towards his rivals throughout but that failed to stop him. He won here over a mile on faster ground last October and the course clearly suits him. (6/1)

**Proud Image** looked well in himself, but likely to improve for the run. Taken down early, he had no more to offer when the winner went by. He is capable of winning similar races. (5/1)

**Cool Caper**, a poor mover, looked likely to finish out with the washing but stayed on under pressure from the distance. (25/1)

**Cedar Dancer**, still a maiden, seems to go well when fresh and may have missed her chance here, for her ground was taken when she was looking dangerous. (12/1)

**Domettes (IRE)**, back on turf, was a little more like her old self, plugging on to the end. (5/1)

**First Gold** does win the occasional race but, when his chance appeared here, all he did was hang. (5/1: op 5/2)

**Silver Harrow** (5/1: 3/1-11/2)

## 546 KINGFISHER H'CAP (0-70) (4-Y.O+) (Class E)

3-10 (3-13) **1m 3f 183y** £3,397.80 (£1,016.40: £487.20: £222.60) Stalls: High GOING: 0.01 sec per fur (G)

SP RR SF

69[7] **Pip's Dream (40)** (MJRyan) **5-8-3** WCarson(16) (a.p: rdn to ld over 1f out: sn clr)........................................— **1** 16/1 53 33
**Cliburnel News (IRE) (57)** (AStreeter) **6-9-1**(5) CTeague(22) (chsd ldrs: led wl over 2f out: hdd over 1f out: unable qckn)..................................................................................................................................4 **2** 12/1 65 45
439[7] **Rock Group (55)** (JPearce) **4-9-3** GBardwell(9) (chsd ldrs: rdn & ev ch over 3f out: no ex appr fnl f)...............1 **3** 7/1[2] 61 40
**Bella Sedona (54)** (LadyHerries) **4-9-2** AClark(2) (hld up: hdwy 2f out: fin wl)................................................1¼ **4** 11/1 59 38
**Fabillion (62)** (CASmith) **4-9-10** CRutter(6) (bit bkwd: r.o fnl 4f: nvr able to chal)..............................................½ **5** 14/1 66 45
**Royrace (48)** (WMBrisbourne) **4-8-5**(5)ow3 DGriffiths(17) (plld hrd: chsd ldrs 6f: styd on again u.p fnl 3f)........................................................................................................................................s.h **6** 33/1 52 28
439[6] **Cuango (IRE) (55)** (RHollinshead) **5-9-4** LDettori(12) (chsd ldrs: rdn & ev ch over 3f out: sn btn)......................½ **7** 5/1[1] 58 38
491[4] **Victoria's Secret (IRE) (57)** (MRChannon) **4-9-5** RHughes(5) (hdwy 6f out: rdn 4f out: sn btn).........................s.h **8** 11/1 60 39
**Full Quiver (42)** (MrsBarbaraWaring) **11-8-5v** JFEgan(18) (b: b.off hind: hdwy 6f out: wknd 2f out)....................½ **9** 20/1 44 24
439* **Haya Ya Kefaah (56)** (NMBabbage) **4-8-11**(7) RFfrench(20) (led 9f out tl wl over 2f out: sn wknd)....................1¼ **10** 7/1[2] 57 36
**Shy Paddy (IRE) (41)** (KOCunningham-Brown) **4-8-3**ow1 RHills(19) (prom tl rdn & btn 5f out).............................5 **11** 20/1 35 13
**Imlak (IRE) (63)** (JLHarris) **4-9-11** GDuffield(13) (swtg: bkwd: hld up: nvr trbld ldrs).........................................4 **12** 20/1 52 31
**World Express (IRE) (56)** (BRMillman) **6-9-2b**(3) SDrowne(10) (lw: nvr nr to chal)................................................¾ **13** 15/2[3] 44 24
**Western Dynasty (58)** (SMellor) **10-9-7** RPerham(11) (bkwd: dropped rr after 4f: n.d after).................................3 **14** 33/1 42 22
196[11] **Turgenev (IRE) (65)** (RBastiman) **7-9-9b**1(5) HBastiman(15) (swtg: bkwd: dwlt: hld up: hdwy over 4f out: wknd 3f out).......................................................................................................................................6 **15** 25/1 40 20
422[7] **Brave Spy (50)** (CACyzer) **5-8-13** DBiggs(21) (led 3f: eased whn btn appr fnl f)...............................................1 **16** 16/1 24 4
**Pennine Wind (IRE) (65)** (SDow) **4-9-13** TQuinn(8) (bkwd: chsd ldrs 6f).......................................................1¼ **17** 33/1 37 16
486[2] **Greenwich Again (60)** (TGMills) **4-9-8** JReid(4) (prom 8f)..........................................................................¾ **18** 12/1 31 10
**Braydon Forest (61)** (CJDrewe) **4-9-9v**1 WRyan(1) (in tch 6f)......................................................................1¼ **19** 14/1 31 10
**James Is Special (IRE) (34)** (RMStronge) **8-7-6**(5) CAdamson(3) (bit bkwd: chsd ldrs: pushed along 6f out: sn wknd)...................................................................................................................................15 **20** 50/1 — —

256[9] **Tiger Shoot (54)** (DTThom) **9-9-3** JTate(14) (b: bkwd: prom 7f: sn rdn & wknd) ....½ **21** 14/1 3 —
(SP 146.2%) **21 Rn**

**2m 37.2** (8.20) CSF £202.97 CT £1,387.89 TOTE £19.40: £3.10 £2.60 £2.20 £3.40 (£168.10) Trio £707.70; £418.68 to 6/4/96 OWNER Mr P. E. Axon (NEWMARKET) BRED Stud-On-The-Chart

WEIGHT FOR AGE 4yo-1lb

OFFICIAL EXPLANATION **Imlak (IRE): the jockey stated that, as this was the gelding's first run since collapsing at Newcastle last October, his instructions were to treat him as sympathetically as possible.**

**Pip's Dream**, second to the runner-up over course and distance last May, is improving and ought to find another race off this lowly mark. (16/1)

**Cliburnel News (IRE)**, sticking to the far rail as the majority headed for the middle of the course, ran her heart out on this her favourite track, but proved no match for the winner. (12/1: op 7/1)

**Rock Group** flashed his tail in the preliminaries but did little wrong in the race, although one-paced. (7/1)

**Bella Sedona** has shown stamina over hurdles but was trying this trip for the first time on the level. (11/1: 8/1-12/1)

**Fabillion** probably needs further to get off the mark. (14/1)

**Royrace** lost his early pace on the home turn, only to rally under pressure near the finish. (33/1)

**491 Victoria's Secret (IRE)** (11/1: 7/1-12/1)

**439* Haya Ya Kefaah** raced too freely and was a spent force once headed. He is much better than this. (7/1)

**486 Greenwich Again** (12/1: op 7/1)

## 547 GREYHOUND H'CAP (0-80) (4-Y.O+) (Class D)

3-40 (3-42) **1m 1f 218y** £4,225.35 (£1,264.80: £606.90: £277.95) Stalls: High GOING: 0.01 sec per fur (G)

| | | | | SP | RR | SF |
|---|---|---|---|---|---|---|
| 410* | **Ocean Park (65)** (LadyHerries) **5-8-13** AClark(14) (in tch: hdwy to ld over 2f out: edgd rt fnl f: drvn out) | — | 1 | 4/1 2 | 72 | 37 |
| | **Lookingforarainbow (IRE) (72)** (BobJones) **8-9-6** MWigham(4) (bit bkwd: chsd ldrs: rdn & edgd lft over 1f out: r.o wl fnl f) | s.h | 2 | 16/1 | 79 | 44 |
| 451[18] | **Remaadi Sun (65)** (MDIUsher) **4-8-13** RStreet(11) (plld hrd: trckd ldrs: n.m.r fr over 1f out: r.o wl nr fin) | hd | 3 | 25/1 | 72+ | 37 |
| 477[4] | **Maradata (IRE) (48)** (RHollinshead) **4-7-10** NCarlisle(10) (hdwy 2f out: edgd rt over 1f out: no ex ins fnl f) | 1¾ | 4 | 14/1 | 52 | 17 |
| 508* | **Eskimo Nel (IRE) (48)** (JLSpearing) **5-7-7**(3) 5x DWright(1) (hld up: hdwy & n.m.r 3f out: swtchd lft over 1f out: fin wl) | ½ | 5 | 2/1 1 | 51 | 16 |
| 221[5] | **Ambidextrous (IRE) (55)** (EJAlston) **4-8-3v** JFEgan(6) (dwlt: rdn 3f out: hung lft & no imp) | 2½ | 6 | 25/1 | 54 | 19 |
| | **Quillwork (USA) (65)** (MrsJCecil) **4-8-8**(5) MHenry(5) (led: clr 5f out: hdd over 2f out: sn btn) | nk | 7 | 12/1 | 64 | 29 |
| | **Clifton Fox (80)** (JAGlover) **4-10-0** SDWilliams(8) (bit bkwd: hld up & plld hrd: nvr trbld ldrs) | ¾ | 8 | 14/1 | 78 | 43 |
| 214[6] | **Rival Bid (USA) (66)** (MrsNMacauley) **8-9-0** JReid(7) (chsd ldrs: rdn 5f out: no imp) | 3 | 9 | 8/1 3 | 59 | 24 |
| 469* | **Swinging Sixties (IRE) (65)** (GLMoore) **5-8-13** 5x SWhitworth(9) (b.nr fore: hld up: rdn over 2f out: no imp) | ¾ | 10 | 8/1 3 | 57 | 22 |
| | **Touch a Million (USA) (76)** (EALDunlop) **4-9-10** WCarson(3) (bit bkwd: chsd ldr 6f) | 5 | 11 | 12/1 | 60 | 25 |
| 393[11] | **Lady Elizabeth (FR) (48)** (KOCunningham-Brown) **4-7-10** GBardwell(12) (plld hrd: chsd ldrs over 6f) | 8 | 12 | 100/1 | 19 | — |
| | **Oneoftheoldones (65)** (JNorton) **4-8-13** KFallon(2) (nvr trbld ldrs) | 2½ | 13 | 25/1 | 32 | — |

(SP 122.7%) **13 Rn**

**2m 11.2** (7.50) CSF £61.14 CT £1,319.19 TOTE £3.70: £1.50 £4.00 £20.40 (£38.60) Trio £238.50; £302.44 to 6/4/96 OWNER Mr E. Reitel (LITTLEHAMPTON) BRED Mrs H. Khan

LONG HANDICAP Eskimo Nel (IRE) 7-2 Maradata (IRE) 7-8 Lady Elizabeth (FR) 6-0

**Ocean Park**, not the force on the Turf that he is on the All-Weather, just managed to take advantage of some lenient handicapping. (4/1)

**Lookingforarainbow (IRE)** normally needs a race or two to come to hand, but ran a cracker and would have prevailed in another couple of strides. His chance should not be long in coming. (16/1)

**Remaadi Sun**, stepping up in trip, pulled his rider's arms out and looked likely to clip something's heels early in the straight. Hampered when sandwiched between two horses at the distance, the winner hung towards him near the finish, and he must be considered unlucky. (25/1)

**477 Maradata (IRE)** came later this time, but tended to hang in toward her rivals and her effort petered out near the finish. (14/1)

**508* Eskimo Nel (IRE)** still looks well handicapped off this mark, for she did not get the run of the race and lost nothing in defeat. (2/1: 6/4-9/4)

**Ambidextrous (IRE)** would have got a great deal closer but for hanging to the centre of the track. (25/1)

## 548 LODDINGTON CONDITIONS STKS (3-Y.O) (Class C)

4-10 (4-12) **5f 218y** £5,066.28 (£1,874.52: £899.26: £367.30: £145.65: £56.99) Stalls: High GOING: 0.01 sec per fur (G)

| | | | | SP | RR | SF |
|---|---|---|---|---|---|---|
| | **Atraf (90)** (DMorley) **3-9-0** RHills(6) (mde all: clr over 1f out: easily) | — | 1 | 16/1 | 104 | 46 |
| | **Marl (90)** (RAkehurst) **3-8-11** TQuinn(2) (outpcd: hdwy 2f out: rdn & edgd rt fnl f: no imp) | 5 | 2 | 3/1 3 | 88 | 30 |
| | **Wisam (105)** (RHannon) **3-9-0** JReid(5) (b: bit bkwd: in tch: rdn 3f out: styd on fnl f) | 1¼ | 3 | 9/4 1 | 87 | 29 |
| | **L'Ami Louis (USA)** (JHMGosden) **3-9-6** LDettori(4) (bit bkwd: chsd ldrs: one pce fnl 2f) | 1 | 4 | 11/4 2 | 91 | 33 |
| 458[4] | **Sihafi (USA)** (EALDunlop) **3-8-10** WCarson(7) (plld hrd: hld up: shkn up & no imp fnl 2f) | 1½ | 5 | 8/1 | 77 | 19 |
| | **Beautiful Ballad (IRE) (95)** (ACStewart) **3-8-9** SWhitworth(3) (b. off hind: dwlt: hdwy 3f out: ev ch 2f out: sn wknd) | s.h | 6 | 16/1 | 76 | 18 |
| | **Whittle Rock (78)** (EJAlston) **3-8-9** KFallon(1) (swtg: bit bkwd: w wnr 3f) | 6 | 7 | 20/1 | 60 | 2 |

(SP 110.1%) **7 Rn**

**1m 13.7** (3.70) CSF £57.97 TOTE £24.10: £5.50 £3.00 (£43.30) OWNER Mr Hamdan Al Maktoum (NEWMARKET) BRED R. T. and Mrs Watson

**Atraf** is clearly still on the up and won this with the minimum of fuss. The race may prove not to be as good as it appeared on paper. (16/1)

**Marl** is not over-big but moved to post well. Having her first run beyond the minimum trip, she appeared to stay. (3/1: 9/4-7/2)

**Wisam** was quite a disappointment, not getting going until the race was over. (9/4: op 6/4)

**L'Ami Louis (USA)** proved a real handful once installed. (11/4)

**458 Sihafi (USA)** pulled too hard early on and failed to find anything once let down. (8/1)

**Beautiful Ballad (IRE)**, who has not yet come in her coat, was loaded last and proved difficult, missing the break in the process. (16/1)

**Whittle Rock** pulled hard on the way to post and in the early stages. Five furlongs on a sharp track must be her trip. (20/1)

## 549 BILLESDON (S) STKS (II) (3-Y.O+) (Class G)

4-40 (4-41) **7f 9y** £2,077.00 (£572.00: £271.00) Stalls: High GOING: 0.01 sec per fur (G)

| | | | | SP | RR | SF |
|---|---|---|---|---|---|---|
| 499[12] | **Rockville Pike (IRE) (80)** (SDow) **4-9-7v1** TQuinn(2) (mde all: rdn out) | — | 1 | 13/2 | 62 | 44 |
| 469[9] | **Noeprob (USA) (43)** (RJHodges) **6-8-13**(3) SDrowne(3) (hld up: hdwy over 2f out: unable qckn ins fnl f) | 1¾ | 2 | 7/1 | 53 | 35 |
| 331[7] | **Manabar (72)** (MJPolglase) **4-9-7** WCarson(4) (b: bit bkwd: chsd ldrs: no ex appr fnl f) | nk | 3 | 3/1 1 | 57 | 39 |
| 216[7] | **Scottish Park (35)** (JLHarris) **7-9-2b** JFEgan(1) (chsd ldrs: one pce fnl 2f) | ¾ | 4 | 14/1 | 51 | 33 |

| | | | | SP | RR | SF |
|---|---|---|---|---|---|---|
| | **Dazzling Star** (RHannon) **3-8-3**[ow1] RHills(11) (hld up: swtchd & stumbled 2f out: styd on fnl f) | 3½ | **5** | 11/2[3] | 44 | 11 |
| 470[8] | **Palacegate Gold (IRE) (38)** (RJHodges) **7-9-7** RHughes(9) (in tch over 4f) | 8 | **6** | 14/1 | 30 | 12 |
| | **Kummel King (59)** (EJAlston) **8-9-7** KFallon(6) (plld hrd: w ldrs 4f: eased whn btn) | 14 | **7** | 5/1[2] | — | — |
| | **Bold Revival (48)** (MrsPSly) **4-9-2** ACulhane(7) (swtg: bit bkwd: hld up: hdwy after 2f: wknd 3f out) | 4 | **8** | 9/1 | — | — |
| | **Super Hero** (AGNewcombe) **4-9-2**(5) DGriffiths(8) (b. off hind: sn outpcd) | 12 | **9** | 14/1 | — | — |
| *413[8]* | ***Deeply Vale (IRE) (60)*** *(GLMoore)* ***5-9-12*** *SWhitworth(5) (bit bkwd: Withdrawn not under Starter's orders)* | | **W** | | — | — |
| | | | | (SP 112.9%) | **9 Rn** | |

**1m 28.1** (5.10) CSF £45.62 TOTE £5.70: £2.30 £2.00 £1.30 (£19.50) Trio £27.80 OWNER Mr Harold Nass (EPSOM) BRED Hans Hintermuller in Ireland

WEIGHT FOR AGE 3yo-14lb

No bid

**OFFICIAL EXPLANATION Rockville Pike (IRE): the jockey reported that the gelding had failed to stay ten furlongs when making the running at Lingfield, and was suited by the first-time visor.**

**Rockville Pike (IRE)**, visored for the first time and taken down very early, won but was hardly impressive. (13/2)

**Noeprob (USA)**, dropping in trip, ran up to her best but is equally effective over a mile. (7/1)

**Manabar** did not impress with his attitude once the chips were down. (3/1)

**Scottish Park**, a poor mover, would be better suited by some cut but is well handicapped at present. (14/1: 10/1-16/1)

**Dazzling Star**, but for stumbling and losing momentum when beginning her run, would have got closer. (11/2: 3/1-6/1)

**Palacegate Gold (IRE)** has not won for a long time but could find a poor race, probably over shorter. (14/1)

**Kummel King** looked in need of the run, virtually bolted the first couple of furlongs to the start, and ran accordingly. (5/1: op 3/1)

**Bold Revival** (9/1: op 16/1)

## 550 KEYTHORPE MAIDEN STKS (3-Y.O F) (Class D)

5-10 (5-13) **7f 9y** £4,159.05 (£1,244.40: £596.70: £272.85) Stalls: High GOING: 0.01 sec per fur (G)

| | | | | SP | RR | SF |
|---|---|---|---|---|---|---|
| | **Inner Circle (USA)** (PWChapple-Hyam) **3-8-11** JReid(9) (mde all: clr 2f out: rdn out) | — | **1** | 4/1[2] | 92 | 50 |
| | **Papaha (FR) (107)** (HRACecil) **3-8-11** WRyan(8) (b: nt grwn: a.p: styd on fnl 2f: nt rch wnr) | 1 | **2** | 2/1[1] | 90 | 48 |
| | **Royal Diversion (IRE)** (JLDunlop) **3-8-11** TQuinn(16) (in tch: styd on fnl 2f: nt trble ldrs) | 4 | **3** | 10/1 | 81 | 39 |
| | **Premier Censure** (JRFanshawe) **3-8-11** DHarrison(6) (b.hind: leggy: scope: bit bkwd: chsd ldrs: no imp fnl 2f) | 4 | **4** | 33/1 | 72 | 30 |
| | **Ewar Sunrise (78)** (CEBrittain) **3-8-6**(5) MHenry(12) (blwd: prom tl wknd over 2f out) | nk | **5** | 33/1 | 71 | 29 |
| | **Charlton Imp (USA)** (RJHodges) **3-8-8**(3) SDrowne(4) (bit bkwd: prom: no hdwy fnl 3f) | hd | **6** | 66/1 | 71 | 29 |
| *355[9]* | **Yezza (IRE)** (APJarvis) **3-8-11** JTate(1) (nvr nrr) | hd | **7** | 25/1 | 70 | 28 |
| | **Dawawin (USA)** (EALDunlop) **3-8-11** WCarson(18) (plld hrd: chsd ldrs over 4f: eased whn btn fnl f) | 3 | **8** | 4/1[2] | 64 | 22 |
| | **Little Black Dress (USA)** (RCharlton) **3-8-11** MHills(2) (lost pl 4f out: n.d after) | s.h | **9** | 12/1 | 64 | 22 |
| | **Mimosa (78)** (SDow) **3-8-11** KFallon(5) (nvr trbld ldrs) | 1¼ | **10** | 25/1 | 61 | 19 |
| | **Cd Super Targeting (IRE)** (MRChannon) **3-8-11** RHughes(15) (bit bkwd: bhd fnl 3f) | ½ | **11** | 20/1 | 60 | 18 |
| | **Zilclare (IRE)** (EALDunlop) **3-8-11** RHills(14) (w'like: leggy: dwlt: nvr trbld ldrs) | 1¾ | **12** | 20/1 | 56 | 14 |
| | **Enchanted Guest (IRE)** (PWHarris) **3-8-11** GDuffield(10) (w'like: bkwd: in tch 4f: sn rdn & btn) | nk | **13** | 33/1 | 55 | 13 |
| | **Remember Star** (AGNewcombe) **3-8-8**(3) DRMcCabe(7) (b: lt-f: unf: nvr nr ldrs) | nk | **14** | 66/1 | 54 | 12 |
| *320[5]* | **Elegantissima** (SDow) **3-8-11** SWhitworth(3) (bhd fnl 3f) | 15 | **15** | 33/1 | 20 | — |
| | **Besweetome** (JHMGosden) **3-8-11** LDettori(17) (unf: scope: bit bkwd: in tch 5f: eased whn btn) | nk | **16** | 7/1[3] | 19 | — |
| | **Domusky** (ABMulholland) **3-8-11** ACulhane(13) (a bhd) | 8 | **17** | 50/1 | 1 | — |
| | | | | (SP 136.5%) | **17 Rn** | |

**1m 26.8** (3.80) CSF £13.04 TOTE £4.80: £2.90 £2.00 £2.90 (£6.40) Trio £26.50 OWNER Mr M. Tabor (MARLBOROUGH) BRED Viking Farm

**OFFICIAL EXPLANATION Besweetome: the trainer later reported that the filly had lost her action on the false ground and the jockey had eased her down.**

**Inner Circle (USA)** looks to have gone the right way over the winter and was never in much danger. (4/1)

**Papaha (FR)** looked bright in her coat but moved poorly to post, and was given a hard race to get so close. (2/1: 5/4-5/2)

**Royal Diversion (IRE)** is not over-big but came home strongly and will come into her own when set a test of stamina. (10/1)

**Premier Censure** showed some promise for the future. (33/1)

**Ewar Sunrise**, rather keen on the way to post, was a spent force by the distance. (33/1)

**Charlton Imp (USA)** showed definite ability and time should see improvement. (66/1)

**Dawawin (USA)**, rather too keen for her own good, ran herself out by the distance and was not persevered with. (4/1: op 6/1)

**Little Black Dress (USA)** (12/1: op 8/1)

**Besweetome**, a big, strong newcomer, is the type to improve and will need middle-distances. (7/1)

T/Jkpt: Not won; £3,369.09 to 6/4/96. T/Plpt: £404.80 (45.19 Tckts). T/Qdpt: £100.40 (16.75 Tckts). IM

# 0498-LINGFIELD (L-H) (Turf Good to soft, Soft patches, AWT Standard)

## Thursday April 4th

WEATHER: sunny WIND: almost nil

## 551 E.B.F. TANDRIDGE MAIDEN STKS (2-Y.O) (Class D)

2-00 (2-00) **5f** £3,146.50 (£937.00: £446.00: £200.50) Stalls: High GOING: 0.29 sec per fur (G)

| | | | | SP | RR | SF |
|---|---|---|---|---|---|---|
| | **Bilko** (GLewis) **2-9-0** PatEddery(5) (str: w ldr: led over 1f out: rdn out) | — | **1** | 4/6[1] | 64 | 8 |
| 490[2] | **Irish Fiction (IRE)** (MRChannon) **2-9-0** JWeaver(4) (hld up: swtchd lft over 1f out: ev ch ins fnl f: r.o) | 1¼ | **2** | 9/4[2] | 60 | 4 |
| 465[4] | **Molly Music** (GGMargarson) **2-8-9** PBloomfield(1) (led over 3f: wknd fnl f) | 5 | **3** | 20/1 | 39 | — |
| | **Salome** (NAGraham) **2-8-9** AMcGlone(2) (small: bhd fnl 3f) | 9 | **4** | 25/1 | 10 | — |
| | **Impulsion (IRE)** (RHannon) **2-8-9**(5) DaneO'Neill(3) (cmpt: bit bkwd: s.s: a bhd) | 13 | **5** | 6/1[3] | — | — |
| | | | | (SP 113.7%) | **5 Rn** | |

**63.71 secs** (6.71) CSF £2.66 TOTE £1.40: £1.10 £2.10 (£1.10) OWNER Mr John Manley (EPSOM) BRED Roldvale Ltd

**Bilko** was far more physically developed than his rivals and made that tell. All the rage in the market, he disputed the lead from the off and, rousted into the lead over a furlong from home, held off the challenge of the runner-up. (4/6)

**490 Irish Fiction (IRE)**, switched left to mount a challenge below the distance, was certainly close enough if good enough inside the final furlong and, although unable to master the winner, kept on well for second prize. (9/4: 6/4-5/2)

**465 Molly Music** attempted to make all the running. Collared below the distance, she was soon put in her place. (20/1)

**Salome** is very small. She was soon in trouble and has no scope at all. (25/1)
**Impulsion (IRE)**, a small, woolly, close-coupled colt with little to like about him, lost ground at the start and was always struggling. (6/1: 4/1-13/2)

## 552 BAKERS LANE CONDITIONS STKS (2-Y.O) (Class D)
2-30 (2-30) **5f** £3,297.50 (£910.00: £432.50) Stalls: High GOING: 0.29 sec per fur (G)

| | | | | SP | RR | SF |
|---|---|---|---|---|---|---|
| 490* | **Iechyd-Da (IRE)** (MBell) **2-8-11** MFenton(2) (hld up: rdn over 2f out: str run to ld wl ins fnl f: r.o wl) | — | 1 | 5/2$^{2}$ | 84 | 18 |
| 452* | **Kingsinger (IRE)** (MRChannon) **2-9-2** JWeaver(3) (led: edgd lft wl over 1f out: sn hdd: ev ch wl ins fnl f: unable qckn) | 2½ | 2 | 11/10$^{1}$ | 81 | 15 |
| | **Salty Behaviour (IRE)** (RHannon) **2-8-6**(5) DaneO'Neill(1) (leggy: chsd ldr: led over 1f out: hung lft ins fnl f: sn hdd: one pce) | ¾ | 3 | 5/2$^{2}$ | 74 | 8 |
| | | | | (SP 104.8%) | | **3 Rn** |

**62.93 secs** (5.93) CSF £5.00 TOTE £3.30 (£2.90) OWNER Mr & Mrs K Mercer, Mr & Mrs H Ceredig (NEWMARKET) BRED W. Powell-Harris
**490* Iechyd-Da (IRE)**, a woolly-looking gelding who is not yet two, produced a fine run in the final furlong to swoop into the lead in the last 50 yards, and win in a time nearly a second faster than the first race. He already needs further. (5/2)
**452* Kingsinger (IRE)**, a woolly, rather dipped-backed individual, attempted to make all the running. Drifting left in the final quarter-mile, he was soon headed but, keeping on well, still had every chance inside the last 100 yards before tapped for toe. (11/10: 4/6-5/4)
**Salty Behaviour (IRE)**, quite a scopey newcomer, was certainly the pick of the paddock. Racing in second place, he gained a narrow lead approaching the final furlong but he drifted left into the centre of the course inside the last 200 yards, and was collared in the closing stages. He will have learnt from this and can find a race before long. (5/2)

## 553 WEATHERBYS BULLETIN MAGAZINE H'CAP (0-70) (3-Y.O+) (Class E)
3-00 (3-01) **1m 2f (Equitrack)** £3,315.90 (£991.20: £474.60: £216.30) Stalls: Low GOING minus 0.35 sec per fur (FST)

| | | | | SP | RR | SF |
|---|---|---|---|---|---|---|
| *499$^{3}$* | **Thorniwama (37)** (JJBridger) **5-7-5b**(5) MBaird(10) (hdwy 5f out: led over 3f out: hrd rdn 1f out: r.o wl) | — | 1 | 14/1 | 48 | 18 |
| *424$^{3}$* | **Zahid (USA) (59)** (KRBurke) **5-8-11**(7) TAshley(14) (lw: rdn & hdwy over 3f out: r.o wl ins fnl f) | 1¾ | 2 | 7/1$^{3}$ | 67 | 37 |
| | **Polly Peculiar (45)** (BSmart) **5-8-1**(3) JStack(13) (b.hind: hdwy over 4f out: ev ch over 1f out: unable qckn) | ¾ | 3 | 7/1$^{3}$ | 52 | 22 |
| 469$^{3}$ | **Wet Patch (IRE) (63)** (RHannon) **4-9-3**(5) DaneO'Neill(3) (a.p: rdn over 3f out: one pce fnl f) | hd | 4 | 7/1$^{3}$ | 70 | 40 |
| *410$^{3}$* | **Robellion (69)** (DWPArbuthnot) **5-10-0v** RCochrane(7) (hdwy over 3f out: rdn 2f out: one pce) | 3 | 5 | 13/2$^{2}$ | 71 | 41 |
| *486** | **Errant (65)** (DJSCosgrove) **4-9-10** 5x JQuinn(6) (b: hld up: rdn over 3f out: one pce) | nk | 6 | 100/30$^{1}$ | 67 | 37 |
| *501$^{5}$* | **Hatta Sunshine (USA) (53)** (AMoore) **6-8-9**(3) AWhelan(4) (b: b.hind: nvr nr to chal) | ½ | 7 | 12/1 | 54 | 24 |
| *340$^{5}$* | **Dance King (56)** (RHarris) **4-9-1** VSmith(5) (prom over 4f) | 7 | 8 | 16/1 | 46 | 16 |
| | **King of Babylon (IRE) (60)** (LadyHerries) **4-9-5** AMcGlone(11) (lw: hld up: rdn over 4f out: wknd over 3f out) | 2 | 9 | 14/1 | 46 | 16 |
| *501$^{6}$* | **Sarum (53)** (CPWildman) **10-8-7**(5) FLynch(12) (b.nr fore: hdwy 7f out: led over 4f out tl over 3f out: sn wknd) | 1¼ | 10 | 16/1 | 37 | 7 |
| | **Premier League (IRE) (58)** (JELong) **6-8-10**(7) TField(2) (bit bkwd: led over 5f) | ¾ | 11 | 33/1 | 41 | 11 |
| | **Jarvey (IRE) (54)** (PEccles) **4-8-13** NAdams(1) (lw: prom over 5f) | 18 | 12 | 33/1 | 8 | — |
| *424$^{12}$* | **She Said No (53)** (LordHuntingdon) **4-8-12** JWeaver(9) (lw: prom over 6f) | 3 | 13 | 11/1 | 3 | — |
| *9$^{8}$* | **Forest Star (USA) (40)** (RAkehurst) **7-7-13b** SSanders(8) (b: rdn thrght: a bhd) | nk | 14 | 16/1 | — | — |
| | | | | (SP 126.8%) | | **14 Rn** |

**2m 8.83** (4.53) CSF £105.20 CT £696.20 TOTE £15.50: £2.60 £3.00 £4.50 (£95.30) Trio £277.40 OWNER Mr J. J. Bridger (LIPHOOK) BRED Fulling Mill Farm and Stud
LONG HANDICAP Thorniwama 7-5
**499 Thorniwama** caused an upset here to lose her maiden tag at the twenty-first attempt. Coming through to lead over three furlongs from home, she responded to pressure a furlong out and kept on well. (14/1)
**Zahid (USA)** continues in fine form. Ridden up to the leaders over three furlongs out, he then made no further progress until storming through inside the final furlong to take second place in the closing stages. (7/1)
**Polly Peculiar**, without a run in four months, moved up soon after halfway. With every chance below the distance, she was then tapped for toe. (7/1)
**469 Wet Patch (IRE)** was always close up. On the heels of the winner a furlong out, he was then tapped for foot. (7/1)
**Robellion** moved up over three furlongs from home but could then only keep on at one pace. (13/2)
**486* Errant** chased the leaders but was tapped for toe in the last three furlongs. (100/30)

## 554 FELCOURT H'CAP (0-95) (3-Y.O+) (Class C)
3-30 (3-35) **7f** £6,032.70 (£1,803.60: £863.80: £393.90) Stalls: High GOING: 0.29 sec per fur (G)

| | | | | SP | RR | SF |
|---|---|---|---|---|---|---|
| | **Champagne Grandy (79)** (MRChannon) **6-8-12**(5) PPMurphy(9) (hld up: led over 1f out: r.o wl) | — | 1 | 12/1 | 92 | 36 |
| | **Proud Monk (75)** (GLMoore) **3-7-13** JQuinn(10) (hdwy over 2f out: chsd wnr over 1f out: r.o one pce) | 2½ | 2 | 6/1$^{2}$ | 82 | 12 |
| 451$^{5}$ | **Tiler (IRE) (81)** (MJohnston) **4-9-5** JWeaver(8) (a.p: rdn over 2f out: one pce) | 4 | 3 | 5/1$^{1}$ | 79 | 23 |
| 450$^{4}$ | **Golden Pound (USA) (72)** (MissGayKelleway) **4-8-5b**1(5) FLynch(6) (swtg: hld up: hrd rdn over 1f out: one pce) | nk | 4 | 13/2$^{3}$ | 70 | 14 |
| | **Mokuti (70)** (GWragg) **4-8-8** WWoods(5) (bit bkwd: rdn over 4f out: hdwy over 1f out: r.o) | 1½ | 5 | 9/1 | 64 | 8 |
| | **Jibereen (71)** (GLewis) **4-8-6**(3) AWhelan(13) (w ldr: led over 3f out tl over 1f out: sn wknd) | 6 | 6 | 8/1 | 51 | — |
| | **Christmas Kiss (84)** (RHannon) **4-9-3**(5) DaneO'Neill(15) (nvr nr to chal) | 1¼ | 7 | 16/1 | 62 | 6 |
| 496* | **Scharnhorst (72)** (SDow) **4-8-5**(5) 6x ADaly(3) (racd far side: prom over 5f) | 2 | 8 | 8/1 | 45 | — |
| *354$^{6}$* | **Sharp 'n Smart (70)** (BSmart) **4-8-8** RCochrane(2) (lw: racd far side: prom over 5f) | 1¾ | 9 | 9/1 | 39 | — |
| *243$^{10}$* | **Helios (65)** (NJHWalker) **8-8-3** GCarter(7) (bhd fnl 3f) | 5 | 10 | 33/1 | 23 | — |
| *357$^{11}$* | **Ertlon (82)** (CEBrittain) **6-9-3**(3) PMcCabe(1) (racd far side: prom over 5f) | 6 | 11 | 16/1 | 26 | — |
| | **Stolen Melody (69)** (SDow) **4-8-7** SSanders(11) (a bhd) | ¾ | 12 | 20/1 | 11 | — |
| | **Be Warned (75)** (NACallaghan) **5-8-6**(7) AEddery(16) (bit bkwd: a bhd) | 1½ | 13 | 11/1 | 14 | — |
| | **Storm Bid (USA) (90)** (EALDunlop) **4-9-11**(3) JStack(4) (bhd fnl 2f) | 2 | 14 | 12/1 | 24 | — |
| | **Dawalib (USA) (67)** (DHaydnJones) **6-8-5** AMackay(12) (led over 3f: wknd over 1f out) | 1¾ | 15 | 12/1 | — | — |
| 475$^{9}$ | **Sue Me (IRE) (69)** (WRMuir) **4-8-7** Jean-PierreLopez(14) (b: bhd fnl 5f) | nk | 16 | 20/1 | — | — |
| | | | | (SP 142.1%) | | **16 Rn** |

**1m 29.02** (7.42) CSF £88.31 CT £396.41 TOTE £19.20: £4.10 £2.10 £2.50 £2.60 (£133.70) Trio £338.00 OWNER Grandy Girls (UPPER LAMBOURN) BRED J. B. and Mrs N. G. Stafford
WEIGHT FOR AGE 3yo-14lb

**497a Champagne Grandy** chased the leaders. Showing in front below the distance, she stormed clear for a decisive victory. (12/1)
**Proud Monk** moved up over a quarter of a mile from home. Struggling into second place below the distance, he finished well clear of the remainder but was unable to peg back the winner. (6/1)
**451 Tiler (IRE)** was always close up but failed to find another gear in the last two furlongs. (5/1)
**450 Golden Pound (USA)**, fitted with blinkers for the first time, chased the leaders. Coming under pressure below the distance, he did not seem terribly enthusiastic and was unable to get past Tiler in a final-furlong scrap. Still a maiden after eleven attempts, he has had enough chances and looks one to avoid from now on. (13/2)
**Mokuti**, not looking fully wound up for this return to action, was doing all his best work in the last furlong and a half, only to find it all over bar the shouting. (9/1)
**Jibereen**, who has been gelded since last season, disputed the lead until going on at halfway. Collared below the distance, he soon capitulated. (8/1)
**Sharp 'n Smart** (9/1: 12/1-8/1)
**Be Warned** (11/1: 8/1-12/1)
**Dawalib (USA)** (12/1: op 8/1)

## 555 HEVER MEDIAN AUCTION MAIDEN STKS (3-Y.O) (Class E)

4-00 (4-00) **1m 2f (Equitrack)** £3,015.60 (£898.80: £428.40: £193.20) Stalls: Low GOING minus 0.35 sec per fur (FST)

| | Horse | Dist | Pos | SP | RR | SF |
|---|---|---|---|---|---|---|
| | **Prince Kinsky** (LordHuntingdon) **3-9-0** JWeaver(2) (lw: hld up: rdn to ld 2f out: r.o wl) | — | **1** | 4/5[1] | 67 | 20 |
| *188*[4] | **Blueberry Fields** (CFWall) **3-8-9** WWoods(8) (a.p: led over 3f out to 2f out: unable qckn) | 5 | **2** | 4/1[2] | 54 | 7 |
| | **Bright Eclipse (USA)** (JWHills) **3-9-0** RCochrane(1) (bit bkwd: hdwy over 4f out: ev ch over 2f out: sn wknd) | 7 | **3** | 6/1[3] | 48 | 1 |
| | **Prompt** (RCharlton) **3-8-9** SSanders(5) (unf: s.s: hdwy over 3f out: wknd over 2f out) | ¾ | **4** | 4/1[2] | 42 | — |
| 471[5] | **Autobabble (IRE) (60)** (RHannon) **3-8-9b**(5) DaneO'Neill(4) (lw: w ldr: led over 4f out tl over 3f out: wknd over 2f out) | 5 | **5** | 16/1 | 39 | — |
| *274*[6] | **Yellow Dragon (IRE) (50)** (BAPearce) **3-9-0** JQuinn(6) (led over 5f: wknd over 3f out) | 5 | **6** | 20/1 | 31 | — |
| 467[8] | **Old Gold N Tan** (JRPoulton) **3-8-11**(3) PMcCabe(7) (hdwy over 7f out: wknd over 3f out) | 9 | **7** | 50/1 | 16 | — |
| | | | | (SP 122.4%) | **7 Rn** | |

**2m 10.65** (6.35) CSF £5.08 TOTE £2.10: £1.30 £1.60 (£4.60) OWNER Mrs J. L. Hislop (WEST ILSLEY) BRED J. L. and Mrs Hislop
**Prince Kinsky** looked in tremendous shape for this reappearance and had little problem. Ridden to lead a quarter of a mile from home, he soon asserted his authority for a decisive victory. (4/5: op 1/2)
**Blueberry Fields** moved to the front over three furlongs from home but was firmly put in her place when collared a quarter of a mile out. (4/1)
**Bright Eclipse (USA)**, carrying condition for this first run in six months, appeared to be travelling well over a quarter of a mile from home, before lack of peak-fitness then took its toll. (6/1)
**Prompt**, quite a lightly-made filly, moved up over three furlongs from home but was a spent force turning in. (4/1: 2/1-9/2)

## 556 LINGFIELD APRIL SPRINT H'CAP (0-80) (3-Y.O+) (Class D)

4-30 (4-30) **6f (Equitrack)** £3,661.80 (£1,091.40: £520.20: £234.60) Stalls: Low GOING minus 0.35 sec per fur (FST)

| | Horse | Dist | Pos | SP | RR | SF |
|---|---|---|---|---|---|---|
| *461*[3] | **Our Shadee (USA) (66)** (KTIvory) **6-9-3v**(7) CScally(5) (lw: a.p: led 3f out: r.o wl) | — | **1** | 3/1[1] | 75 | 14 |
| *461*[4] | **Invocation (66)** (AMoore) **9-9-7**(3) AWhelan(2) (b.hind: hdwy over 2f out: rdn wl over 1f out: unable qckn) | 1½ | **2** | 9/2[2] | 71 | 10 |
| 493[5] | **Maple Burl (66)** (SDow) **3-8-7**(5) ADaly(6) (hdwy over 2f out: rdn wl over 1f out: one pce) | s.h | **3** | 6/1 | 71 | — |
| *461** | **The Institute Boy (64)** (MissJFCraze) **6-9-8** AMcGlone(1) (a.p: ev ch over 1f out: one pce) | nk | **4** | 3/1[1] | 68 | 7 |
| | **Scissor Ridge (49)** (JJBridger) **4-8-7b** JQuinn(3) (led 3f: wknd 2f out) | 7 | **5** | 5/1[3] | 34 | — |
| 470[15] | **Titanium Honda (IRE) (49)** (DCO'Brien) **5-8-2**(5)ow3 DaneO'Neill(4) (b: lw: bhd fnl 4f) | 8 | **6** | 10/1 | 13 | — |
| | | | | (SP 108.2%) | **6 Rn** | |

**1m 15.27** (4.67) CSF £14.82 TOTE £3.60: £1.60 £1.70 (£7.90) OWNER Mr K. T. Ivory (RADLETT) BRED Overbury Stud
WEIGHT FOR AGE 3yo-12lb
**461 Our Shadee (USA)** loves it round here and gained his fifth All-Weather victory. Racing up with the pace on this occasion, he went on at halfway and kept on well under hands and heels riding in the straight. Six furlongs is his ideal trip. (3/1)
**461 Invocation** took closer order turning for home and, in a scrap for the minor placings, just prevailed. (9/2)
**493 Maple Burl** moved up over a quarter of a mile from home but lacked the necessary turn of foot in the straight. (6/1: op 7/2)
**461* The Institute Boy**, always close up, had every chance below the distance before tapped for toe. (3/1)
**Scissor Ridge** (5/1: 7/2-6/1)

T/Plpt: £61.50 (162.12 Tckts). T/Qdpt: £11.30 (123.96 Tckts). AK

# MUSSELBURGH (R-H) (Good)

## Thursday April 4th

WEATHER: sunny WIND: almost nil

## 557 CARLYLE PLACE MAIDEN AUCTION STKS (2-Y.O) (Class F)

2-20 (2-20) **5f** £2,540.80 (£713.80: £348.40) Stalls: High GOING minus 0.05 sec per fur (G)

| | Horse | Dist | Pos | SP | RR | SF |
|---|---|---|---|---|---|---|
| | **Sweet Emmaline** (WGMTurner) **2-8-0** TSprake(4) (w'like: scope: lw: mde most: shkn up & qcknd 2f out: eased fnl f) | — | **1** | 4/1[2] | 76+ | 22 |
| 490[3] | **Swino** (PDEvans) **2-8-7** RLappin(6) (lw: chsd ldrs: hung rt fr ½-wy: styd on one pce) | 5 | **2** | 3/1[1] | 67 | 13 |
| | **Tribal Mischief** (DMoffatt) **2-7-13**(3) DarrenMoffatt(3) (unf: scope: in tch: styd on fnl 2f: nvr able to chal) | ¾ | **3** | 7/1 | 60 | 6 |
| 465[3] | **Caviar And Candy** (DJSCosgrove) **2-7-7**(5) PFessey(7) (chsd ldrs: nt clr run & swtchd 2f out: styd on towards fin) | ½ | **4** | 8/1 | 54 | — |
| | **Bolero Boy** (MWEasterby) **2-8-7** KDarley(9) (cmpt: scope: bit bkwd: disp ld to ½-wy: grad wknd) | 3 | **5** | 3/1[1] | 53 | — |
| | **Super Saint** (TDBarron) **2-8-7** JFortune(8) (leggy: unf: chsd ldrs to ½-wy: sn btn) | 4 | **6** | 5/1[3] | 41 | — |
| 506[5] | **Ramsey Pride** (CWFairhurst) **2-8-2** NKennedy(1) (racd centre: in tch: effrt ½-wy: no imp) | s.h | **7** | 14/1 | 35 | — |
| | **Midyans Song** (JJO'Neill) **2-8-0** DaleGibson(2) (lt-f: dwlt: a bhd) | ¾ | **8** | 10/1 | 31 | — |
| 481[4] | **Silver Raj** (WTKemp) **2-8-3** JCarroll(5) (sn outpcd & wl bhd) | 9 | **9** | 50/1 | 5 | — |
| | | | | (SP 128.0%) | **9 Rn** | |

**61.1 secs** (3.40) CSF £17.52 TOTE £6.80: £2.20 £1.10 £5.80 (£7.90) Trio £36.90 OWNER Mr G. L. Barker (SHERBORNE) BRED Mrs P. J. McCreery

**Sweet Emmaline** was the pick of the bunch on looks and proved far too superior in the latter half of the race. She looks likely to follow this up. (4/1)
**490 Swino** was always struggling to get to the front this time and, tending to hang right, could never match the winner. (3/1: op 7/4)
**Tribal Mischief** was the second two-year-old from this yard to run well in consecutive days and, judged by the way she was staying on, she should pick up a race. (7/1)
**465 Caviar And Candy**, a little filly, was cramped for room at halfway and lacked the pace to get out of trouble, despite staying on. (8/1: op 9/2)
**Bolero Boy** needed this and showed plenty of toe. He will do better in due course. (3/1)
**Super Saint** should be better for the experience but he does look as though plenty of time is needed. (5/1)
**506 Ramsey Pride**, who only ran the previous Saturday, moved very poorly to post here and was obviously feeling that outing. (14/1: op 8/1)

## 558 PINKIE H'CAP (0-60) (4-Y.O+) (Class F)

2-50 (2-51) **1m 4f 31y** £2,719.30 (£764.80: £373.90) Stalls: High GOING minus 0.05 sec per fur (G)

| | | | | SP | RR | SF |
|---|---|---|---|---|---|---|
| | **Kilernan (42)** (TDBarron) **5-9-3** JFortune(2) (a.p: led wl over 2f out: styd on u.p) | — | 1 | 6/1[2] | 56 | 38 |
| 477[11] | **Gold Desire (31)** (MBrittain) **6-8-6** PRobinson(6) (lw: a.p: effrt over 2f out: kpt on: nt pce to chal) | 1 | 2 | 7/1[3] | 44 | 26 |
| | **Keep Battling (39)** (JSGoldie) **6-9-0** JCarroll(10) (hld up: hdwy on bit to disp ld wl over 1f out: sn rdn & no ex) | ¾ | 3 | 14/1 | 51 | 33 |
| | **Tancred Mischief (27)** (WLBarker) **5-8-2** LCharnock(11) (disp ld tl wknd fnl 3f) | 4 | 4 | 16/1 | 33 | 15 |
| 477[3] | **Drummer Hicks (44)** (EWeymes) **7-9-5** KDarley(1) (lw: bhd: effrt appr st: styd on fnl 2f: nrst fin) | hd | 5 | 3/1[1] | 50 | 32 |
| 542[9] | **Lord Advocate (33)** (DANolan) **8-8-8b** VHalliday(9) (mde most tl hdd wl over 2f out: grad wknd) | 2 | 6 | 25/1 | 37 | 19 |
| 541[7] | **Rapid Mover (26)** (DANolan) **9-8-1b** FNorton(8) (lw: cl up: chal over 3f out: wknd over 2f out) | 1¼ | 7 | 16/1 | 28 | 10 |
| 440[7] | **Bali Tender (40)** (MWEasterby) **5-9-1** DaleGibson(12) (plld hrd: trckd ldrs: effrt ent st: one pce) | s.h | 8 | 10/1 | 42 | 24 |
| | **Goodbye Millie (49)** (JLEyre) **6-9-10v** RLappin(4) (sn pushed along & bhd: n.d) | 6 | 9 | 14/1 | 43 | 25 |
| *426*[11] | **Kismetim (39)** (DWChapman) **6-9-0** DeanMcKeown(3) (a bhd) | 1¾ | 10 | 12/1 | 31 | 13 |
| *400*[8] | **Princess Tallulah (34)** (WGMTurner) **5-8-9** TSprake(7) (a rr div) | 3½ | 11 | 14/1 | 21 | 3 |
| | **School of Science (32)** (RMMcKellar) **6-8-0**(7)ow2 DMcGaffin(13) (b: prom tl lost pl appr st) | 8 | 12 | 50/1 | 9 | — |
| *429*[8] | **Inovar (29)** (CBBBooth) **6-8-4** NKennedy(5) (wnt prom 8f out: wknd ent st) | 1 | 13 | 11/1 | 4 | — |
| | | | | (SP 114.5%) | **13 Rn** | |

**2m 42.1** (9.10) CSF £42.29 CT £511.30 TOTE £7.70: £1.90 £2.60 £2.50 (£30.90) Trio £30.90 OWNER Mr J. O. Hall (THIRSK) BRED James Hall
STEWARDS' ENQUIRY Fortune susp. 13 & 15/4/96 (excessive use of whip).
**Kilernan** certainly did not impress on looks as usual, but his performance did all the talking. Given a particularly good ride, he held on well. (6/1)
**477 Gold Desire** looked well and tried hard, but just lacked the turn of foot to get there. (7/1)
**Keep Battling** is in good form and came there swinging off the bit halfway up the straight but, when it came down to a struggle, he declined. This trip might just be stretching things. (14/1)
**Tancred Mischief** is still a maiden but she does stay and, over further, may find a modest event in due course. (16/1)
**477 Drummer Hicks** found this trip too sharp and never got going until it was all over. He looks well and should be given another chance. (3/1)
**Lord Advocate**, having his second run in two days, showed he still retains his ability and can pick up a race or two again this year. (25/1)
**Rapid Mover** raced freely but, once off the bit, looked very slow. (16/1)
**Goodbye Millie** (14/1: op 8/1)

## 559 BRUNTON HALL H'CAP (0-70) (3-Y.O+) (Class E)

3-20 (3-25) **5f** £3,077.55 (£932.40: £455.70: £217.35) Stalls: High GOING minus 0.05 sec per fur (G)

| | | | | SP | RR | SF |
|---|---|---|---|---|---|---|
| 451[5] | **To the Roof (IRE) (67)** (PWHarris) **4-10-0** GHind(3) (racd stands' side: hdwy to ld ½-wy: r.o wl) | — | 1 | 5/1[1] | 75 | 55 |
| 466[6] | **Domicksky (53)** (MRChannon) **8-9-0** KDarley(2) (racd stands' side: in tch: kpt on fnl 2f: no ch w wnr) | 3 | 2 | 11/1 | 51 | 31 |
| *500*[3] | **Tenor (56)** (DNicholls) **5-9-3** AlexGreaves(11) (hdwy far side 2f out: styd on u.p: nrst fin) | hd | 3 | 6/1[2] | 54 | 34 |
| 466[4] | **Sonderise (45)** (NTinkler) **7-8-6** JFortune(14) (racd far side: hdwy & prom ½-wy: rdn & no imp appr fnl f) | 1¼ | 4 | 8/1 | 39 | 19 |
| | **Kenesha (IRE) (45)** (DANolan) **6-8-6b** LCharnock(6) (racd stands' side: w ldrs: nt qckn fnl 2f) | hd | 5 | 25/1 | 39 | 19 |
| *407*[5] | **Featherstone Lane (52)** (MissLCSiddall) **5-8-13v** DeanMcKeown(4) (led stands' side to ½-wy: hrd drvn & grad wknd) | ½ | 6 | 8/1 | 44 | 24 |
| | **Six for Luck (57)** (DANolan) **4-9-4** TSprake(9) (racd centre: a chsng ldrs: kpt on one pce fnl f) | 1¼ | 7 | 50/1 | 45 | 25 |
| *500*[5] | **Kalar (52)** (DWChapman) **7-8-13b** DaleGibson(16) (lw: led far side over 3f: wknd) | ¾ | 8 | 12/1 | 38 | 18 |
| 443[5] | **Amy Leigh (IRE) (66)** (CaptJHWilson) **3-9-2** PRobinson(10) (racd stands' side: nvr trbld ldrs) | 1¼ | 9 | 8/1 | 48 | 17 |
| | **China Hand (IRE) (44)** (MartynWane) **4-8-5** FNorton(15) (racd far side: prom ½-wy: sn btn) | nk | 10 | 33/1 | 25 | 5 |
| | **Leading Princess (IRE) (51)** (MissLAPerratt) **5-8-12b** JCarroll(5) (w ldrs stands' side 3f) | nk | 11 | 20/1 | 31 | 11 |
| | **Coolowen Flash (IRE) (50)** (JLEyre) **5-8-11** RLappin(13) (racd far side: outpcd fr ½-wy) | hd | 12 | 7/1[3] | 30 | 10 |
| | **Bella Coola (46)** (MartynMeade) **4-8-7** VSlattery(8) (racd stands' side: n.d) | nk | 13 | 25/1 | 25 | 5 |
| *408*[7] | **Southern Dominion (61)** (CNAllen) **4-9-1v**(7) CWebb(12) (lw: racd far side: outpcd & bhd fr ½-wy) | nk | 14 | 25/1 | 39 | 19 |
| *316*[8] | **Serious Hurry (53)** (RMMcKellar) **8-8-7b**(7) DMcGaffin(7) (racd stands' side: sn bhd) | 2½ | 15 | 25/1 | 23 | 3 |
| | **River Garnock (65)** (DNicholls) **4-9-12** MRichardson(1) (gd spd stands' side to ½-wy: sn bhd) | ½ | 16 | 66/1 | 33 | 13 |
| | | | | (SP 119.4%) | **16 Rn** | |

**60.7 secs** (3.00) CSF £53.11 CT £323.03 TOTE £4.30: £1.40 £2.00 £2.20 £1.30 (£18.30) Trio £42.30 OWNER Mrs P. W. Harris (BERKHAMSTED) BRED Pendley Farm
WEIGHT FOR AGE 3yo-11lb
**451 To the Roof (IRE)** raced on the favoured stands' side and won this in tremendous style. He should follow up. (5/1)
**466 Domicksky** has only won once in the last two seasons and has dropped way down the handicap. He did show something here, staying on well at the finish. (11/1)
**500 Tenor** proved the best of the bunch on the far side and, had he been drawn low, he might well have given the winner a fright. (6/1)
**466 Sonderise** last won three years ago but he showed he still retains ability, running particularly well from a poor draw. (8/1)
**Kenesha (IRE)**, after twenty-eight runs without a win, ran a reasonable race. (25/1)
**Featherstone Lane** is difficult to win with and things proved too tough from halfway. (8/1)
**443 Amy Leigh (IRE)** (8/1: op 5/1)

## 560 STONEYBANK MEDIAN AUCTION MAIDEN STKS (3-Y.O+) (Class F)

3-50 (3-51) **1m 3f 32y** £2,493.20 (£700.20: £341.60) Stalls: High GOING minus 0.05 sec per fur (G)

| | | | | SP | RR | SF |
|---|---|---|---|---|---|---|
| | **Swan Hunter** (DJSCosgrove) **3-9-0** JFortune(3) (cmpt: lw: trckd ldrs: led over 2f out: r.o) | — | 1 | 7/4[2] | 69 | 17 |

| | Horse | Pos | SP | RR | SF |
|---|---|---|---|---|---|
| | **Anna Soleil (IRE)** (MRChannon) **3-9-0** AGorman(6) (trckd ldrs tl lost pl appr st: hdwy & swtchd over 2f out: styd on wl) ....2½ | 2 | 33/1 | 65 | 13 |
| 444[15] | **Sedbergh (USA) (64)** (MrsMReveley) **3-9-0** KDarley(1) (hld up: hdwy 5f out: ev ch over 2f out: r.o one pce).1¾ | 3 | 5/1 [3] | 63 | 11 |
| | **Poetry (IRE)** (MHTompkins) **3-8-9** PRobinson(2) (carried wd bnd after 1½f: sn led: hdd over 2f out: sn outpcd) ....1¾ | 4 | 5/4 [1] | 55 | 3 |
| | **Sylvan Princess** (CNAllen) **3-8-9** CHodgson(4) (hld up: effrt over 3f out: sn btn)....8 | 5 | 50/1 | 44 | — |
| | **Brighter Byfaah (IRE)** (NAGraham) **3-9-0** JCarroll(5) (led tl rn wd bnd after 1½f: rn wd ent st: sn bhd) ....10 | 6 | 10/1 | 35 | — |
| | | | (SP 111.5%) | | **6 Rn** |

**2m 30.7** (11.00) CSF £32.96 TOTE £2.50: £1.10 £4.90 (£68.30) OWNER Mr Derrick Yarwood (NEWMARKET) BRED The Arrow Farm and Stud
**Swan Hunter**, well touted, looked fit and won in good style. (7/4)
**Anna Soleil (IRE)** put up a decent first effort and was keeping on well at the end, despite showing signs of greenness. (33/1)
**Sedbergh (USA)**, a sturdy sort, should improve for this but his real future looks to be at the jumping game. (5/1)
**Poetry (IRE)** is nothing to look at and put up little fight once in the straight. (5/4)
**Sylvan Princess** has shown little in the past and gave little encouragement here. (50/1)
**Brighter Byfaah (IRE)** gave all sorts of problems, running wide on the bends, and this is best ignored. (10/1)

## 561 MAYFIELD (S) H'CAP (0-60) (3-Y.O+) (Class G)

4-20 (4-20) **1m 16y** £2,326.50 (£654.00: £319.50) Stalls: High GOING minus 0.05 sec per fur (G)

| | Horse | Pos | SP | RR | SF |
|---|---|---|---|---|---|
| | **Bedazzle (34)** (MBrittain) **5-8-7** PRobinson(7) (in tch: hdwy 2f out: styd on to ld wl ins fnl f)....— | 1 | 5/1 [1] | 44 | 19 |
| | **Spirito Libro (USA) (54)** (CNAllen) **3-8-12** CHodgson(8) (lw: a.p: rdn to ld ins fnl f: hdd & nt qckn nr fin)....nk | 2 | 11/2 [2] | 63 | 23 |
| 480[8] | **Northern Spark (48)** (MissLAPerratt) **8-9-7** JFanning(14) (bit bkwd: a chsng ldrs: rdn over 2f out: kpt on).....2½ | 3 | 11/2 [2] | 53 | 28 |
| | **Raindeer Quest (40)** (JLEyre) **4-8-13** RLappin(13) (in tch: effrt & nt clr run 2f out: swtchd & styd on nr fin) .....½ | 4 | 8/1 [3] | 44 | 19 |
| | **Diet (51)** (MissLAPerratt) **10-9-10v** JCarroll(1) (bit bkwd: cl up: led over 2f out tl ins fnl f: wknd)....hd | 5 | 20/1 | 54 | 29 |
| *499[7]* | **No Submission (USA) (38)** (DWChapman) **10-8-11v** KDarley(12) (bhd tl styd on fnl 3f)....hd | 6 | 8/1 [3] | 41 | 16 |
| *319[7]* | **Benjarong (42)** (RMMcKellar) **4-9-1** TSprake(6) (hld up & bhd: hdwy over 2f out: nvr nr to chal) ....2 | 7 | 16/1 | 41 | 16 |
| *207[12]* | **Sheroot (33)** (DMoffatt) **4-8-3(3)** DarrenMoffatt(2) (hdwy 3f out: nvr rchd ldrs)....1¼ | 8 | 25/1 | 30 | 5 |
| 477[9] | **My Handy Man (50)** (RAllan) **5-9-9** DeanMcKeown(9) (sn chsng ldrs: effrt over 2f out: sn wknd)....¾ | 9 | 8/1 [3] | 45 | 20 |
| | **Thisonesforalice (36)** (JSGoldie) **8-8-4(5)** PFessey(5) (hld up & bhd: n.d)....2 | 10 | 14/1 | 27 | 2 |
| 469[7] | **Warning Shot (54)** (MartynMeade) **4-9-13** VSlattery(10) (mid div & rdn ½-wy: n.d)....¾ | 11 | 8/1 [3] | 44 | 19 |
| 470[11] | **Orthorhombus (55)** (DJSCosgrove) **7-10-0b** JFortune(3) (s.i.s: drvn along after s: n.d)....5 | 12 | 16/1 | 35 | 10 |
| | **Pash (42)** (CWFairhurst) **4-9-1v** NKennedy(11) (a bhd)....½ | 13 | 16/1 | 21 | — |
| 445[9] | **Polish Lady (IRE) (52)** (WLBarker) **3-8-10** LCharnock(4) (led tl hdd & wknd over 2f out) ....2 | 14 | 16/1 | 27 | — |
| | | | (SP 130.7%) | | **14 Rn** |

**1m 45.4** (6.80) CSF £33.36 CT £155.80 TOTE £5.90: £1.90 £2.60 £2.10 (£19.70) Trio £45.80 OWNER Mr Mel Brittain (WARTHILL) BRED Bloomsbury Stud
WEIGHT FOR AGE 3yo-15lb
Bt in 4,100 gns
**Bedazzle** gained his first win here at his twenty-sixth attempt and did it in determined style. (5/1: op 8/1)
**Spirito Libro (USA)** looked really well. Stepping up in distance, he tried hard but just failed to last home. (11/2)
**480 Northern Spark** looked as though he would be better for this and ran a sound race, despite being off the bit some way out. (11/2)
**Raindeer Quest** had no luck at all in running and was finishing in useful style. (8/1)
**Diet** looks as good as ever this year and should benefit from this. (20/1)
**Benjarong** looks as though she is coming to hand. (16/1)

## 562 STONEYHILL MAIDEN H'CAP (0-70) (3-Y.O+) (Class E)

4-50 (4-51) **7f 15y** £3,036.60 (£919.80: £449.40: £214.20) Stalls: High GOING minus 0.05 sec per fur (G)

| | Horse | Pos | SP | RR | SF |
|---|---|---|---|---|---|
| *300[2]* | **Eben Naas (USA) (50)** (SCWilliams) **3-8-7** KDarley(1) (lw: b.hind: a.p: led ins fnl f: eased towards fin)....— | 1 | 3/1 [2] | 58 | 11 |
| *517[2]* | **Backhander (IRE) (52)** (MartynWane) **4-9-9** JCarroll(10) (chsd ldrs: led 2f out: hrd drvn: hdd ins fnl f: kpt on) ....nk | 2 | 16/1 | 59 | 26 |
| | **Nkapen Rocks (SPA) (65)** (CaptJHWilson) **3-9-8** JFortune(2) (in tch: rdn 3f out: styd on strly towards fin)......½ | 3 | 25/1 | 71 | 24 |
| 492[2] | **Dungeon Princess (IRE) (60)** (MRChannon) **3-9-3** AGorman(13) (chsd ldrs: rdn over 2f out: r.o one pce).....nk | 4 | 11/1 | 66 | 19 |
| 453[12] | **Carmosa (USA) (57)** (DNicholls) **3-9-0** AlexGreaves(11) (led tl hdd 2f out: r.o one pce) ....½ | 5 | 10/1 | 61 | 14 |
| | **Teejay'n'aitch (IRE) (43)** (JSGoldie) **4-8-9(5)** PFessey(12) (hdwy 3f out: sn chsng ldrs: one pce fnl f) ....hd | 6 | 16/1 | 47 | 14 |
| 470[2] | **Pride of Kashmir (56)** (PWHarris) **3-8-13** GHind(7) (mid div: outpcd ent st: styd on towards fin)....nk | 7 | 9/4 [1] | 60 | 13 |
| | **Generous Present (55)** (JWPayne) **3-8-12** MTebbutt(14) (effrt whn hmpd 3f out: hdwy 2f out: eased whn no ch fnl f) ....5 | 8 | 33/1 | 47 | — |
| | **Monte Cavo (45)** (MBrittain) **5-9-2** PRobinson(4) (chsd ldrs tl grad wknd fnl 2f)....1 | 9 | 33/1 | 35 | 2 |
| | **Miss Iron Heart (USA) (41)** (DJSCosgrove) **4-8-7(5)** LNewton(6) (hmpd appr st: n.d after)....s.h | 10 | 33/1 | 31 | — |
| | **Wire Act (USA) (61)** (MartynMeade) **3-9-4** VSlattery(5) (bhd: hdwy 3f out: nvr trbld ldrs)....s.h | 11 | 20/1 | 51 | 4 |
| *328[8]* | **Harry's Treat (53)** (JLEyre) **4-9-7(3)** OPears(8) (sn outpcd & bhd)....½ | 12 | 7/1 [3] | 42 | 9 |
| | **Samsung Lovelylady (IRE) (46)** (EWeymes) **4-9-3** DeanMcKeown(3) (prom tl rn wd & lost pl appr st: n.d after)....3 | 13 | 25/1 | 28 | — |
| | **Mill End Lady (54)** (MWEasterby) **3-8-11** DaleGibson(9) (a bhd) ....9 | 14 | 33/1 | 15 | — |
| | | | (SP 121.7%) | | **14 Rn** |

**1m 32.2** (6.70) CSF £45.47 CT £931.92 TOTE £4.60: £1.50 £3.30 £11.80 (£36.30) Trio £322.10 OWNER Mr J. W. Lovitt (NEWMARKET) BRED Clovelly Farms
WEIGHT FOR AGE 3yo-14lb
**Eben Naas (USA)**, always in the right place, scored a shade more comfortably than the winning margin would suggest. (3/1)
**517 Backhander (IRE)** was always in the thick of things and, although well held in the final furlong, kept plugging away and should stay a bit further. (16/1)
**Nkapen Rocks (SPA)** was really getting going as the race progressed, but was short of that vital turn of foot to take it. (25/1)
**492 Dungeon Princess (IRE)** had her chances but lacked the turn of foot to take them. (11/1)
**Carmosa (USA)**, having her second run for her new stable, showed signs of ability and seems to be improving. (10/1)
**470 Pride of Kashmir** should be suited by further. (9/4)
**Harry's Treat** (7/1: 6/1-10/1)

T/Plpt: £445.20 (25.75 Tckts). T/Qdpt: £57.90 (28 Tckts). AA

# HAYDOCK (L-H) (Good)

## Saturday April 6th

WEATHER: fine WIND: slt half bhd

## 563

BNFL INSIDE STORIES CONDITIONS STKS (4-Y.O+) (Class B)
1-30 (1-30) **2m 45y** £7,404.60 (£2,771.40: £1,355.70: £583.50) Stalls: Low GOING minus 0.04 sec per fur (G)

| | Horse | Dist | Pos | SP | RR | SF |
|---|---|---|---|---|---|---|
| | **Double Eclipse (IRE) (113)** (MJohnston) **4-9-4** LDettori(6) (bit bkwd: mde all: rdn & drifted lft fnl f: all out) | — | 1 | 4/5[1] | 106 | 64 |
| | **Old Rouvel (USA) (103)** (DJGMurraySmith) **5-9-4** KDarley(4) (s.i.s: hld up: hdwy 3f out: sn chsng wnr: styd on u.p ins fnl f) | ¾ | 2 | 3/1[2] | 101 | 63 |
| | **Noufari (FR) (71)** (RHollinshead) **5-9-0** TIves(2) (bit bkwd: hld up & bhd: hdwy over 3f out: nt rch ldrs) | 6 | 3 | 40/1 | 91 | 53 |
| | **Kristal's Paradise (IRE) (102)** (JLDunlop) **4-8-11** PaulEddery(1) (chsd wnr: pushed along over 3f out: sn wknd) | 14 | 4 | 4/1[3] | 79 | 37 |
| 449[8] | **Evezio Rufo (83)** (NPLittmoden) **4-8-10** TGMcLaughlin(5) (lw: chsd ldng pair tl outpcd ent st: sn btn) | 3½ | 5 | 100/1 | 74 | 32 |
| | **Anglesey Sea View (70)** (ABailey) **7-8-11** DWright(3) (hld up & bhd: effrt 5f out: wknd wl over 2f out) | 5 | 6 | 33/1 | 66 | 28 |

(SP 106.9%) **6 Rn**

**3m 34.33** (7.13) CSF £3.28 TOTE £1.50: £1.20 £1.60 (£2.00) OWNER The Middleham Partnership (MIDDLEHAM) BRED Dene Investments N V in Ireland

WEIGHT FOR AGE 4yo-4lb

**Double Eclipse (IRE)**, sure to strip fitter with this outing under his belt, let his class do the talking but his superior stamina also played a part nearing the finish. (4/5)

**Old Rouvel (USA)**, narrowly beaten in this event last year, was supported to go one better but, after recovering from a tardy start, found the winner just too strong for him in a thrilling duel to the line. (3/1)

**Noufari (FR)**, who has done all his winning on the All-Weather, tried to make his presence felt approaching the last quarter-mile, but the winner kept the pressure on and he was soon fighting a lost cause. (40/1)

**Kristal's Paradise (IRE)**, badly in need of some sun on her back, tracked the winner but she was in trouble halfway up the straight and had to accept it. (4/1: op 5/2)

## 564

BNFL MEDLOCK LINKS H'CAP (0-95) (4-Y.O+) (Class C)
2-00 (2-02) **1m 3f 200y** £3,364.25 (£3,364.25: £761.00: £360.50) Stalls: High GOING minus 0.04 sec per fur (G)

| | Horse | Dist | Pos | SP | RR | SF |
|---|---|---|---|---|---|---|
| | **Lombardic (USA) (89)** (MrsJCecil) **5-9-9** TIves(7) (led tl ins fnl f: rallied u.p cl home: gamely) | — | 1 | 9/2[3] | 101 | 47 |
| | **Taipan (IRE) (90)** (JLDunlop) **4-9-9** LDettori(6) (chsd ldr: shkn up to ld jst ins fnl f: jnd post) | — | 1 | 4/1[2] | 102 | 47 |
| 439[8] | **Vaugrenier (IRE) (78)** (RHannon) **4-8-11** RHughes(3) (hld up & bhd: hdwy 3f out: sn rdn: no imp) | 6 | 3 | 6/1 | 82 | 27 |
| 456[3] | **Penny a Day (IRE) (94)** (MrsMReveley) **6-10-0** KDarley(5) (trckd ldrs: effrt over 2f out: rdn & one pce appr fnl f) | 3 | 4 | 5/2[1] | 94 | 40 |
| | **Thaljanah (IRE) (85)** (DLWilliams) **4-8-13**(5) DGriffiths(1) (bkwd: trckd ldrs tl wknd over 2f out) | 6 | 5 | 12/1 | 77 | 22 |
| | **Tessajoe (71)** (MJCamacho) **4-8-4** LCharnock(2) (bit bkwd: plld hrd: hld up in rr: effrt over 3f out: no imp) | hd | 6 | 13/2 | 63 | 8 |
| | **Out on a Promise (IRE) (85)** (NJHWalker) **4-9-4** CRutter(4) (bkwd: hld up in rr: drvn along & outpcd 3f out: sn lost tch) | 6 | 7 | 11/1 | 69 | 14 |

(SP 110.4%) **7 Rn**

**2m 37.75** (8.35) CSF T & L £10.03, L & T £10.33 TOTE T £2.30 £2.00, L £2.70 £2.60 (£9.80) OWNER Bonusprint (NEWMARKET)/Lord Swaythling (ARUNDEL) BRED Juddmonte Farms/C. H. Wacker III

WEIGHT FOR AGE 4yo-1lb

**Lombardic (USA)** usually needs a run to put an edge on him and he looked to have shot his bolt when collared inside the final furlong but, with the rail to help, he battled to get up and share the spoils right on the line. (9/2)

**Taipan (IRE)**, very impressive to post, pushed the pace from the break. Poking his nose in front 200 yards out, he gave of his all but found the post arriving only just in time. (4/1)

**Vaugrenier (IRE)** had the edge in fitness but he was not quite up to this class and, though he stayed on, he was never a serious factor. (6/1)

**456 Penny a Day (IRE)**, waiting on the leaders, tried to mount a challenge entering the final quarter-mile, but topweight took its toll and he was brushed aside with ease. (5/2)

**Tessajoe**, still to come in his coat, took a keen hold under restraint but did not have anything to give when an effort was called for, and was one of the backmarkers throughout. (13/2)

## 565

BNFL 25TH ANNIVERSARY FIELD MARSHAL STKS (Listed) (3-Y.O) (Class A)
2-30 (2-31) **5f** £12,136.50 (£3,672.00: £1,791.00: £850.50) Stalls: High GOING minus 0.04 sec per fur (G)

| Horse | Dist | Pos | SP | RR | SF |
|---|---|---|---|---|---|
| **Westcourt Magic (104)** (MWEasterby) **3-9-1** LDettori(5) (mde all: clr over 1f out: unchal) | — | 1 | 5/2[1] | 109 | 74 |
| **Repertory** (MRChannon) **3-8-11** RHughes(6) (dwlt: hdwy 2f out: sn hrd rdn: nt pce of wnr) | 3½ | 2 | 100/30[2] | 94 | 59 |
| **Kunucu (IRE)** (TDBarron) **3-8-6** KDarley(4) (bit bkwd: hld up: pushed along ½-wy: hdwy & swtchd appr fnl f: r.o) | ¾ | 3 | 100/30[2] | 86 | 51 |
| **Music Gold (IRE) (89)** (WAO'Gorman) **3-8-11** EmmaO'Gorman(2) (lw: a.p: reminders 2f out: outpcd appr fnl f) | s.h | 4 | 8/1 | 91 | 56 |
| **Eastern Prophets (104)** (TJNaughton) **3-8-11** PaulEddery(3) (bit bkwd: trckd ldrs: outpcd wl over 1f out) | 4 | 5 | 5/1 | 78 | 43 |
| **Prince Aslia (95)** (MJohnston) **3-8-11** JCarroll(1) (bit bkwd: spd 3f: sn wknd) | 3½ | 6 | 9/2[3] | 67 | 32 |

(SP 120.7%) **6 Rn**

**60.49 secs** (1.29) CSF £11.54 TOTE £3.10: £2.20 £2.20 (£7.30) OWNER Mr K. Hodgson (SHERIFF HUTTON) BRED C. R. and V. M. Withers

**Westcourt Magic** got the best of the break and, without having to get serious, stormed clear inside the distance for a runaway success. This was a fine start to his season. (5/2)

**Repertory**, stepping up in class for this first outing in close on twelve months, was getting up to some serious work in the latter stages without having a hope of reaching the winner. (100/30)

**Kunucu (IRE)** finished behind the winner on both occasions when they clashed last year and, even on these better terms, could not gain his revenge. (100/30)

**Music Gold (IRE)**, turned out looking a picture, pressed the winner, but he was struggling to hang on from below the distance and had to admit his measure taken. (8/1)

**Eastern Prophets**, not as far forward as some, kept tabs on the principals until feeling the strain below the distance. (5/1)

## 566 BNFL CRIME CONQUEST MAIDEN STKS (3-Y.O) (Class D)

3-00 (3-02) **7f 30y** £3,647.50 (£1,105.00: £540.00: £257.50) Stalls: Low GOING minus 0.04 sec per fur (G)

| | Horse | Dist | Pos | SP | RR | SF |
|---|---|---|---|---|---|---|
| | **Herodian (USA)** (JHMGosden) **3-9-0** LDettori(7) (a.p: led over 1f out: v.easily) | — | **1** | 4/7[1] | 81+ | 47 |
| | **Alpine Hideaway (IRE)** (BHanbury) **3-9-0** RHills(6) (w'like: scope: chsd ldr: led over 2f out tl over 1f out: one pce) | 3 | **2** | 12/1 | 74 | 40 |
| | **Philosopher (IRE)** (RHannon) **3-9-0** RHughes(2) (unf: hld up: hdwy over 3f out: styd on u.p appr fnl f) | 4 | **3** | 9/2[2] | 65 | 31 |
| | **Crabbie's Pride** (ABailey) **3-8-11**(3) DWright(11) (w'like: bit bkwd: hld up: hdwy 3f out: hung lft & rn green over 1f out: kpt on) | ¾ | **4** | 16/1 | 64 | 30 |
| | **Airborne Harris (IRE)** (ABailey) **3-8-7**(7) AngelaGallimore(3) (neat: bit bkwd: trckd ldrs: rdn over 2f out: sn btn) | ½ | **5** | 25/1 | 63 | 29 |
| | **Kazimiera (IRE) (69)** (CWCElsey) **3-8-4**(5) PFessey(9) (hld up in rr: effrt & hung lft 2f out: nvr nr ldrs) | 3 | **6** | 14/1 | 51 | 17 |
| | **Haute Cuisine** (JBerry) **3-9-0** JCarroll(1) (bkwd: bhd: rdn 3f out: no imp) | ¾ | **7** | 11/1[3] | 54 | 20 |
| | **Backwoods** (WMBrisbourne) **3-9-0** PaulEddery(5) (bit bkwd: a in rr) | 2½ | **8** | 40/1 | 49 | 15 |
| | **Mustang** (CWThornton) **3-9-0** DeanMcKeown(10) (bkwd: a bhd) | hd | **9** | 33/1 | 48 | 14 |
| | **Ashik (IRE)** (LJBarratt) **3-9-0b[1]** LCharnock(12) (bkwd: led & sn clr: wknd & hdd over 2f out: t.o) | 18 | **10** | 40/1 | 8 | — |
| | | | | (SP 122.1%) | | **10 Rn** |

**1m 31.66** (4.16) CSF £9.23 TOTE £1.70: £1.20 £2.60 £1.60 (£5.30) Trio £8.90 OWNER Hesmonds Stud (NEWMARKET) BRED Hesmonds Stud Limited

**Herodian (USA)** did not see a racecourse until the late autumn and he showed signs of his greenness when asked to go and win his race, but he did respond when made to go through with his effort and, in the end, won very cosily indeed. He can certainly improve on this. (4/7)

**Alpine Hideaway (IRE)**, very keen in the early stages, struck the front over two furlongs out and, with the winner, drew away. When the sprint to the post really got underway, he was a bit out of his depth, but there should be more opportunities for him. (12/1: op 8/1)

**Philosopher (IRE)**, who will need much further to show his true worth, stayed on steadily in the final quarter-mile and he could well need more time. (9/2)

**Crabbie's Pride** showed signs of greenness when making progress in the closing stages, but he did stay on and will be all the wiser next time. (16/1)

**Airborne Harris (IRE)** performed with credit but blew up. He does possess ability. (25/1)

## 567 BNFL SUCCEEDING THROUGH SCIENCE RATED STKS H'CAP (0-95) (3-Y.O) (Class C)

3-30 (3-31) **1m 2f 120y** £5,156.10 (£1,558.80: £759.40: £359.70) Stalls: High GOING minus 0.04 sec per fur (G)

| | Horse | Dist | Pos | SP | RR | SF |
|---|---|---|---|---|---|---|
| | **Roman Gold (IRE) (80)** (RHannon) **3-9-2** JCarroll(2) (h.d.w: a.p: shkn up 3f out: r.o to ld wl ins fnl f) | — | **1** | 15/8[1] | 86 | 52 |
| | **House of Riches (84)** (LMCumani) **3-9-6** LDettori(4) (led over 3f: led over 2f out tl wl ins fnl f: rallied u.p) | hd | **2** | 15/8[1] | 90 | 56 |
| 444[9] | **Quality (IRE) (82)** (WAO'Gorman) **3-9-4b** EmmaO'Gorman(1) (lw: led 7f out tl over 2f out: one pce) | 3 | **3** | 8/1 | 83 | 49 |
| | **Warning Reef (85)** (MRChannon) **3-9-7** RHughes(6) (swtg: hld up & bhd: effrt 3f out: kpt on one pce) | 1½ | **4** | 15/2[3] | 84 | 50 |
| 444[11] | **Samim (USA) (80)** (JLDunlop) **3-9-2** RHills(3) (hld up in rr: no imp fnl 2f) | nk | **5** | 9/2[2] | 79 | 45 |
| | | | | (SP 110.6%) | | **5 Rn** |

**2m 17.33** (5.83) CSF £5.59 TOTE £2.70: £1.40 £1.40 (£2.20) OWNER Mr George Teo (MARLBOROUGH) BRED Saffron Breeders Club
STEWARDS' ENQUIRY Carroll susp. 15-16/4/96 (excessive use of whip).

**Roman Gold (IRE)**, who has improved physically since last year, got the better of his market rival in the closing stages, and it would seem that he could be even better when faced with an even stiffer test of stamina. (15/8)

**House of Riches** kicked for home over two furlongs out and briefly looked to have control, but the winner was only getting into his stride by then, and proved the master in an all-out battle to the post. (15/8)

**Quality (IRE)** did his best to make this a true test of stamina, but he could not ward off the runner-up and was at the end of his tether approaching the final furlong. (8/1)

**Warning Reef**, a poor mover who was edgy in the paddock, tried to get into the action three furlongs out, but he lacked the speed to do so, despite staying on. (15/2)

**Samim (USA)** appeared to be tenderly handled and was staying on towards the finish. (9/2)

## 568 BNFL BRASS AND MALE VOICE MAIDEN AUCTION STKS (2-Y.O) (Class E)

4-00 (4-02) **5f** £2,932.50 (£885.00: £430.00: £202.50) Stalls: High GOING minus 0.04 sec per fur (G)

| | Horse | Dist | Pos | SP | RR | SF |
|---|---|---|---|---|---|---|
| | **Aztec Traveller** (JBerry) **2-8-5** JCarroll(8) (lt-f: mde all: drew clr fnl f) | — | **1** | 5/1[3] | 69 | 24 |
| 452[3] | **Spondulicks (IRE)** (RHannon) **2-8-3** RHills(3) (sn bhd & drvn along: swtchd lft over 1f out: fin wl) | 2 | **2** | 9/4[1] | 61 | 16 |
| 476[4] | **C-Harry (IRE)** (RHollinshead) **2-7-12**(5) FLynch(4) (a.p: jnd wnr ½-wy: rdn & wknd appr fnl f) | 3 | **3** | 25/1 | 51 | 6 |
| | **Absolutely Abstone** (PDEvans) **2-7-12** NAdams(1) (lt-f: unf: prom centre: rdn & one pce appr fnl f) | s.h | **4** | 8/1 | 46 | 1 |
| 452[5] | **Classic Partygoer** (MWEasterby) **2-8-4**ow1 MBirch(5) (hdwy 2f out: nt rch ldrs) | nk | **5** | 100/30[2] | 51 | 5 |
| | **Senate Swings** (WRMuir) **2-8-7** KDarley(6) (small: cmpt: bkwd: dwlt: hdwy 2f out: nvr nr to chal) | 3 | **6** | 6/1 | 44 | — |
| | **Weet A Bit (IRE)** (RHollinshead) **2-8-7** LDettori(9) (leggy: bit bkwd: s.i.s: a bhd & outpcd) | s.h | **7** | 6/1 | 44 | — |
| 452[9] | **Lucybod** (NTinkler) **2-8-2** LCharnock(2) (bkwd: a outpcd) | ½ | **8** | 33/1 | 38 | — |
| | **Champagne On Ice** (PDEvans) **2-8-0** CRutter(7) (lt-f: unf: bit bkwd: gd spd over 3f) | nk | **9** | 14/1 | 35 | — |
| | | | | (SP 123.6%) | | **9 Rn** |

**62.92 secs** (3.72) CSF £17.16 TOTE £7.40: £2.10 £1.30 £3.70 (£8.60) Trio £47.40 OWNER Mr J. K. Brown (COCKERHAM) BRED J. R. Thompson

**Aztec Traveller**, a lightly-made debutant hanging onto his winter coat, was smartly into his stride and proceeded to make all and win going away. He will improve on this when the weather gets warmer. (5/1)

**452 Spondulicks (IRE)**, off the bridle and flat to the boards before halfway, picked up well when switched towards the centre of the track below the distance, and finished best of all. (9/4)

**476 C-Harry (IRE)** looked sure to make a race of it when joining issue over two furlongs out, but the winner kept galloping, and he decided enough was enough approaching the final furlong. (25/1)

**Absolutely Abstone** showed up with the pace in the centre of the track until calling enough on the approach to the final furlong. (8/1)

**452 Classic Partygoer** did not run as freely as he did on his debut, and was only getting into top gear when it was too late. (100/30)

**Senate Swings** was sluggish leaving the stalls. Weaving his way through inside the last quarter-mile, he could not get close enough to cause concern. (6/1: 4/1-13/2)

**Weet A Bit (IRE)** (6/1: op 4/1)

T/Plpt: £10.40 (1,785.24 Tckts). T/Qdpt: £2.10 (512.93 Tckts). IM

# KEMPTON (R-H) (Good)
## Saturday April 6th
WEATHER: overcast WIND: almost nil

## 569 E.B.F. REDFERN MAIDEN STKS (2-Y.O) (Class D)
1-45 (1-46) **5f** £3,473.50 (£1,048.00: £509.00: £239.50) Stalls: High GOING: 0.16 sec per fur (G)

| | Horse / details | Dist | Pos | SP | RR | SF |
|---|---|---|---|---|---|---|
| | **Herecomestheknight** (MartynMeade) **2-8-9**(5) RHavlin(7) (unf: bit bkwd: s.s: hdwy over 2f out: led ins fnl f: pushed out) | — | **1** | 25/1 | 73 | 11 |
| | **Rude Awakening** (GLewis) **2-9-0** PatEddery(6) (str: scope: lw: led 1f: led wl over 1f out tl ins fnl f: r.o) | ½ | **2** | 4/6 1 | 71 | 9 |
| | **Masterstroke** (BJMeehan) **2-9-0** BDoyle(3) (neat: bit bkwd: lost pl 3f out: rallied 2f out: unable qckn fnl f) | 2 | **3** | 6/1 2 | 65 | 3 |
| | **Dowry** (RHannon) **2-8-4**(5) DaneO'Neill(4) (neat: a.p: rdn 2f out: one pce) | 2½ | **4** | 9/1 3 | 52 | — |
| 446 5 | **Don't Forget Shoka (IRE)** (JSMoore) **2-8-9** JFEgan(8) (led 4f out tl wl over 1f out: sn wknd) | 2½ | **5** | 33/1 | 44 | — |
| | **Bapsford** (GLMoore) **2-9-0** SWhitworth(5) (neat: nvr nr to chal) | 1¾ | **6** | 16/1 | 43 | — |
| | **Rebuke** (RFJohnsonHoughton) **2-9-0** JReid(2) (neat: a bhd) | s.h | **7** | 10/1 | 43 | — |
| | **Countless Times** (WRMuir) **2-9-0** Jean-PierreLopez(1) (neat: bit bkwd: bhd fnl 3f) | 2½ | **8** | 12/1 | 35 | — |
| | | | | (SP 113.7%) | **8 Rn** | |

**64.15 secs** (5.95) CSF £41.14 TOTE £21.00: £2.90 £1.10 £1.70 (£14.40) OWNER Mr Derek Clee (MALMESBURY) BRED Derek D. Clee

**Herecomestheknight** hardly took the eye in the paddock but was certainly up to the job. Moving up in the second half of the race, he loomed up very dangerously to the odds-on favourite below the distance and, cruising into the lead inside the final furlong, needed only to be nudged along for success. (25/1)

**Rude Awakening**, the second highest lot at the Doncaster Leger Yearling Sales at 42,000 guineas, looked in a different league to his rivals. With far more strength and substance about him, he was all the rage in the market and he cruised to the front early in the final quarter-mile. The winner soon loomed up though and he was worried out of it inside the last 100 yards. He should make no mistake next time. (4/6)

**Masterstroke**, quite a leggy gelding with not much about him, recovered to get back into it a quarter of a mile out but failed to find another gear in the last 200 yards. (6/1: 2/1-7/1)

**Dowry**, quite a leggy individual with very little substance, was never far away but failed to quicken in the last two furlongs. (9/1: 6/1-10/1)

**446 Don't Forget Shoka (IRE)**, the only runner with experience on her side, was soon in front but, when collared early in the final quarter-mile, was soon beaten. (33/1)

**Countless Times** (12/1: 4/1-14/1)

## 570 DURANTE CONDITIONS STKS (3-Y.O) (Class C)
2-15 (2-16) **1m 2f (Jubilee)** £4,582.60 (£1,713.40: £836.70: £358.50) Stalls: High GOING: 0.16 sec per fur (G)

| | Horse / details | Dist | Pos | SP | RR | SF |
|---|---|---|---|---|---|---|
| | **Prospector's Cove** (JPearce) **3-8-10** GBardwell(3) (s.s: hdwy over 4f out: rdn over 3f out: bmpd 1f out: led ins fnl f: r.o wl) | — | **1** | 9/1 | 92 | 55 |
| | **Prince of My Heart (90)** (BWHills) **3-8-10** MHills(7) (lw: hld up: chsd ldr 5f out: led over 2f out: swvd lft over 1f out: hdd ins fnl f: r.o) | ½ | **2** | 7/2 2 | 91 | 54 |
| | **Madame Steinlen (84)** (BWHills) **3-8-5** WCarson(4) (bit bkwd: rdn 5f out: hdwy over 1f out: r.o one pce) | 9 | **3** | 5/1 | 72 | 35 |
| | **Tria Kemata (104)** (JLDunlop) **3-9-1** PatEddery(2) (b.off fore: lw: plld hrd: led over 7f) | 2½ | **4** | 11/4 1 | 78 | 41 |
| | **Ewar Bold** (CEBrittain) **3-8-7** BDoyle(5) (leggy: bit bkwd: s.s: a bhd) | 9 | **5** | 16/1 | 55 | 18 |
| | **Nador** (DRLoder) **3-8-13** TQuinn(6) (lw: a.p: rdn over 3f out: wknd over 2f out) | s.h | **6** | 4/1 3 | 61 | 24 |
| *378 5* | **Expeditious Way (GR)** (RCharlton) **3-8-13** SSanders(1) (prom 5f: t.o) | dist | **7** | 20/1 | — | — |
| | | | | (SP 106.2%) | **7 Rn** | |

**2m 9.98** (6.48) CSF £35.43 TOTE £9.30: £2.00 £2.70 (£27.60) OWNER Saracen Racing (NEWMARKET) BRED Southcourt Stud

**Prospector's Cove**, gelded since winning his only start as a two-year-old last November at Edinburgh, was certainly upped in class but proved up to the task. Moving up in the second half of the race, he was delivering his challenge when interfered with by the leader a furlong out. He got to the front inside the final 100 yards and kept on well. (9/1)

**Prince of My Heart** moved into second place at halfway and took control early in the straight. He swerved violently left a furlong from home, interfering with the winner, and was soon headed. (7/2)

**Madame Steinlen** was carrying condition for this reappearance. Pushed along and going nowhere at the back of the field at halfway, she stayed on in the final furlong and a half but found it all over bar the shouting. (5/1)

**Tria Kemata** has not learnt to settle from last year and raced far too freely in front, so it came as no surprise that he had little in the tank when headed over two furlongs from home. (11/4: op 6/4)

**Nador** looked in very good shape for this reappearance and showed up well until tiring over two furlongs from home. (4/1)

## 571 QUEEN ELIZABETH H'CAP (0-90) (3-Y.O) (Class C)
2-45 (2-46) **6f** £5,426.50 (£1,642.00: £801.00: £380.50) Stalls: High GOING: 0.16 sec per fur (G)

| | Horse / details | Dist | Pos | SP | RR | SF |
|---|---|---|---|---|---|---|
| 443 3 | **Passion For Life (86)** (GLewis) **3-9-5** PatEddery(10) (lw: mde all: clr over 1f out: easily) | — | **1** | 11/4 1 | 109+ | 68 |
| | **Norwegian Blue (IRE) (88)** (APJarvis) **3-9-7** JTate(11) (a.p: chsd wnr over 1f out: no imp) | 8 | **2** | 20/1 | 90 | 49 |
| 493 2 | **Golden Pond (IRE) (71)** (RFJohnsonHoughton) **3-8-4** AMcGlone(9) (a.p: hrd rdn over 1f out: one pce) | 1½ | **3** | 9/1 3 | 69 | 28 |
| | **Erupt (76)** (GBBalding) **3-8-9v** AClark(5) (s.i.s: hdwy over 2f out: one pce) | ½ | **4** | 16/1 | 72 | 31 |
| | **Mallia (77)** (TDBarron) **3-8-10** JFortune(8) (hld up: rdn over 2f out: one pce) | ½ | **5** | 20/1 | 72 | 31 |
| *264** | **Dummer Golf Time (65)** (LordHuntingdon) **3-7-7**(5) MHenry(2) (hdwy 3f out: rdn over 2f out: one pce) | ½ | **6** | 8/1 2 | 59 | 18 |
| 458* | **Green Barries (80)** (MJohnston) **3-8-13** JWeaver(13) (chsd wnr over 4f) | 5 | **7** | 11/4 1 | 60 | 19 |
| 443 9 | **Ed's Folly (IRE) (64)** (SDow) **3-7-11** JQuinn(12) (lw: hld up: rdn over 2f out: sn wknd) | ½ | **8** | 8/1 2 | 43 | 2 |
| | **Dil Dil (68)** (RHannon) **3-8-1** JFEgan(3) (a bhd) | 1¼ | **9** | 33/1 | 44 | 3 |
| | **Missile Toe (IRE) (72)** (JEBanks) **3-8-2**(3) AWhelan(7) (a bhd) | 3½ | **10** | 20/1 | 38 | — |
| 443* | **Little Noggins (IRE) (76)** (CADwyer) **3-8-6**(3) JStack(4) (a bhd) | 6 | **11** | 9/1 3 | 26 | — |
| | **White Emir (87)** (BJMeehan) **3-9-6** BDoyle(1) (a bhd) | 5 | **12** | 25/1 | 24 | — |
| 443 10 | **Welsh Mountain (76)** (MJHeaton-Ellis) **3-8-6**(3) SDrowne(6) (a bhd) | 1¼ | **13** | 33/1 | 10 | — |
| | | | | (SP 125.5%) | **13 Rn** | |

**1m 14.77** (3.47) CSF £53.44 CT £341.87 TOTE £3.10: £2.40 £5.30 £2.80 (£29.20) Trio £77.50 OWNER Mr David Waters (EPSOM) BRED G. R. Smith (Thriplow) Ltd

**443 Passion For Life** was hugely impressive following his unlucky defeat at Doncaster. Making all the running, he forged clear below the distance and, with Eddery having a strong hold of the gelding in the final furlong, won with a ton in hand. He will get clobbered by the Handicapper for this performance and connections must now think about Conditions and Listed races, which he would be more than capable of winning. (11/4)

**Norwegian Blue (IRE)** was never far away. Struggling into second place approaching the final furlong, he had no hope of catching the winner. (20/1)
**493 Golden Pond (IRE)** was always close up but failed to find another gear in the final two furlongs. (9/1)
**Erupt** moved up soon after halfway but then could make no further impression. (16/1)
**Mallia**, off the track for eleven months, chased the leaders but failed to find another gear in the last two furlongs. (20/1)
**Dummer Golf Time**, having his first run on Turf, moved up at halfway but then could only go up and down in the same place. (8/1)
**458* Green Barries** chased the winner. With every chance a quarter of a mile from home, he was collared for the runner-up berth just before the furlong pole and tamely dropped away. (11/4: op 7/4)

## 572 MASAKA STKS (Listed) (3-Y.O F) (Class A)

3-15 (3-17) **1m (Jubilee)** £12,387.50 (£3,725.00: £1,800.00: £837.50) Stalls: High GOING: 0.16 sec per fur (G)

| | | | | SP | RR | SF |
|---|---|---|---|---|---|---|
| | **Sea Spray (IRE)** (PWChapple-Hyam) **3-8-8** JReid(8) (a.p: led over 1f out: all out) | — | **1** | 4/1[2] | 102 | 47 |
| | **Parrot Jungle (IRE) (108)** (JLDunlop) **3-8-8** PatEddery(13) (hdwy & nt clr run on ins over 2f out: swtchd lft over 1f out: hrd rdn: r.o wl ins fnl f) | nk | **2** | 9/2[3] | 101 | 46 |
| | **Miss Universal (IRE)** (CEBrittain) **3-8-8** BDoyle(2) (led over 6f: hrd rdn: r.o) | hd | **3** | 25/1 | 101 | 46 |
| | **Paloma Bay (IRE) (102)** (MBell) **3-8-8** MFenton(12) (rdn & hdwy 2f out: r.o one pce) | 2½ | **4** | 14/1 | 96 | 41 |
| | **Letluce** (JRArnold) **3-8-8** JWeaver(7) (a.p: ev ch over 1f out: one pce) | s.h | **5** | 33/1 | 96 | 41 |
| | **Cyrillic (85)** (PAKelleway) **3-8-8** JFEgan(5) (plld hrd: hld up: nt clr run over 2f out: one pce) | 2 | **6** | 50/1 | 92 | 37 |
| | **Sil Sila (IRE)** (BSmart) **3-8-11** RCochrane(3) (bit bkwd: hld up: rdn over 2f out: wknd over 1f out) | nk | **7** | 13/2 | 95 | 40 |
| *242** | **Coachella** (MJRyan) **3-8-8** GBardwell(1) (bhd fnl 3f) | 3½ | **8** | 25/1 | 85 | 30 |
| | **Anthelia (105)** (GWragg) **3-8-8** MHills(6) (bhd fnl 2f) | ½ | **9** | 7/2[1] | 84 | 29 |
| | **Myrtle (106)** (RHannon) **3-8-8** TQuinn(11) (rdn & hdwy 2f out: eased whn btn over 1f out) | nk | **10** | 10/1 | 83 | 28 |
| | **Willow Dale (IRE) (82)** (DRCElsworth) **3-8-8** WWoods(10) (a bhd) | 2½ | **11** | 33/1 | 78 | 23 |
| | **Tamnia (107)** (JLDunlop) **3-8-11** WCarson(9) (hdwy on ins over 2f out: eased whn btn fnl f) | 1 | **12** | 6/1 | 79 | 24 |
| | **Lilli Claire (74)** (AGFoster) **3-8-8** TSprake(4) (chsd ldr over 4f) | 1¾ | **13** | 33/1 | 72 | 17 |
| | | | | (SP 122.3%) | **13 Rn** | |

**1m 42.88** (5.68) CSF £21.63 TOTE £3.80: £1.90 £2.30 £9.90 (£10.50) Trio £84.50 OWNER Lord Weinstock & The Hon Simon Weinstock (MARLBOROUGH) BRED Ballymacoll Stud Farm Ltd
OFFICIAL EXPLANATION **Anthelia: the trainer reported that the filly blew up.**
**Sea Spray (IRE)** made a winning return to action. Striking the front below the distance, she kept on well but, with the runner-up really flying, found the line coming not a stride too soon. She has not filled out much since last year but should come into her own when tackling further. (4/1: 3/1-9/2)
**Parrot Jungle (IRE)** was an unlucky loser. With nowhere to go on the inside rail as she picked up ground early in the straight, she was switched left below the distance and, running on really strongly inside the final furlong, would surely have prevailed in a few more strides. She showed useful form at two and an early success looks on the cards. (9/2)
**Miss Universal (IRE)** left last season's form well behind. Bowling along in front, she was collared below the distance but, refusing to give way, battled her heart out. A race should soon come her way. (25/1)
**Paloma Bay (IRE)**, who cracked her shoulder and had to be pulled up on her final start last year, was pushed along to take closer order a quarter of a mile out, and struggled on for fourth prize. (14/1)
**Letluce** had every chance over a furlong out before left standing by her rivals. (33/1)
**Cyrillic** took a very keen hold in the early stages. She failed to get a clear run in midfield over a quarter of a mile out but, when a gap did appear, she failed to quicken anyway. (50/1)

## 573 QUEEN'S PRIZE H'CAP (0-95) (4-Y.O+) (Class C)

3-45 (3-46) **2m** £8,559.00 (£2,592.00: £1,266.00: £603.00) Stalls: High GOING: 0.16 sec per fur (G)

| | | | | SP | RR | SF |
|---|---|---|---|---|---|---|
| | **Wannaplantatree (60)** (NMBabbage) **5-8-3**[ow1] AClark(6) (hdwy over 3f out: led over 1f out: rdn out) | — | **1** | 25/1 | 72 | 50 |
| 440[5] | **Witney-de-Bergerac (IRE) (61)** (JSMoore) **4-8-0** JFEgan(7) (lw: rdn & hdwy over 2f out: r.o) | 1¼ | **2** | 33/1 | 72 | 47 |
| 449[4] | **Upper Mount Clair (57)** (CEBrittain) **6-8-0** BDoyle(9) (gd hdwy over 1f out: r.o wl ins fnl f) | hd | **3** | 8/1 | 68 | 47 |
| 439[3] | **Golden Arrow (IRE) (75)** (IABalding) **5-8-11**(7) CScudder(13) (lw: gd hdwy over 1f out: r.o wl) | 3½ | **4** | 16/1 | 82 | 61 |
| 440[8] | **Stalled (IRE) (54)** (PTWalwyn) **6-7-6**(5) MHenry(11) (lw: hld up: chsd ldr over 4f out: ev ch over 1f out: unable qckn) | ½ | **5** | 11/2[1] | 61 | 40 |
| | **Seasonal Splendour (IRE) (85)** (MCPipe) **6-10-0** JWeaver(8) (lw: hdwy 4f out: rdn over 3f out: one pce) | 1¼ | **6** | 10/1 | 90 | 69 |
| *485[2]* | **Durham (53)** (RSimpson) **5-7-10v** FNorton(18) (lw: led 5f: led 6f out tl over 1f out: wknd fnl f) | 3 | **7** | 33/1 | 55 | 34 |
| 449[14] | **Salaman (FR) (82)** (JLDunlop) **4-9-7** WCarson(5) (b.off fore: bmpd over 2f out: nvr nr to chal) | 1½ | **8** | 15/2[3] | 73 | 58 |
| | **Typhoon Eight (IRE) (75)** (BWHills) **4-9-0** MHills(3) (swtg: hdwy 4f out: rdn over 3f out: wknd wl over 1f out) | 3½ | **9** | 8/1 | 62 | 47 |
| 449[5] | **Sea Freedom (63)** (GBBalding) **5-8-3v[1]**(3) SDrowne(10) (prom over 13f) | 1¾ | **10** | 16/1 | 49 | 38 |
| 469[8] | **Aude la Belle (FR) (60)** (SGKnight) **8-8-3** AMcGlone(14) (a mid div) | 5 | **11** | 66/1 | 41 | 30 |
| *38[8]* | **Warm Spell (71)** (GLMoore) **6-9-0** SWhitworth(2) (hld up: rdn over 4f out: wkng whn bmpd over 2f out) | 10 | **12** | 16/1 | 42 | 31 |
| | **Cypress Avenue (IRE) (81)** (RHannon) **4-9-6** RPerham(1) (bit bkwd: a bhd) | 2½ | **13** | 20/1 | 49 | 34 |
| 449[18] | **Torch Vert (IRE) (77)** (NJHWalker) **4-8-13**(3) JStack(17) (a bhd) | s.h | **14** | 25/1 | 45 | 30 |
| 449[7] | **Lalindi (IRE) (68)** (DRCElsworth) **5-8-11** PatEddery(4) (lw: prom 11f) | 4 | **15** | 10/1 | 32 | 21 |
| *392** | **River Keen (IRE) (86)** (RWArmstrong) **4-9-11** WWoods(16) (hld up: rdn 4f out: wkng whn bmpd over 2f out) | 5 | **16** | 12/1 | 45 | 30 |
| | **Proton (78)** (RAkehurst) **6-9-7** SSanders(12) (prom 12f) | ½ | **17** | 12/1 | 37 | 26 |
| | **Chief's Song (54)** (SDow) **6-7-11v[1]** JQuinn(15) (chsd ldr: led 11f out to 6f out: wknd 5f out) | 1¾ | **18** | 7/1[2] | 11 | — |
| | | | | (SP 132.9%) | **18 Rn** | |

**3m 34.72** (10.12) CSF £600.04 CT £6,401.55 TOTE £39.00: £4.40 £6.50 £2.00 £2.80 (£720.40) Trio £2,644.60 OWNER Mr A. M. Tombs (CHELTENHAM) BRED Stetchworth Park Stud Ltd
WEIGHT FOR AGE 4yo-4lb
**Wannaplantatree** caused an upset on this seasonal debut. Moving up smoothly on the home turn, she struck the front below the distance and was ridden along to score. (25/1)
**440 Witney-de-Bergerac (IRE)** began to pick up ground turning into the straight and kept up well, if unable to peg back the winner in time. (33/1)
**449 Upper Mount Clair** raced well off the pace. However, she really motored in the final quarter-mile, but found the line always coming too soon. (8/1)
**439 Golden Arrow (IRE)**, out with the washing in the back straight, ate up the ground in the last two furlongs but was never going to get there in time. (16/1)

**Stalled (IRE)** moved into second place over half a mile from home, and may well have got his head in front for a few strides approaching the final furlong before being tapped for toe. (11/2)
**Seasonal Splendour (IRE)**, fit from hurdling, moved up on the home turn but failed to find another gear in the final two furlongs. (10/1)

## 574 EASTER STKS (Listed) (3-Y.O C & G) (Class A)

4-15 (4-18) **1m (Jubilee)** £11,981.25 (£3,600.00: £1,737.50: £806.25) Stalls: Low GOING: 0.16 sec per fur (G)

| Horse | Dist | Pos | SP | RR | SF |
|---|---|---|---|---|---|
| **Regiment (IRE)** (RHannon) **3-8-8** TQuinn(2) (hdwy 2f out: led 1f out: hrd rdn: r.o wl) | — | **1** | 9/1 | 101+ | 46 |
| **Centre Stalls (IRE)** (RFJohnsonHoughton) **3-8-8** JReid(8) (bit bkwd: hld up: nt clr run over 2f out tl over 1f out: r.o wl ins fnl f) | 1 | **2** | 16/1 | 99+ | 44 |
| **Elshabiba (USA)** (JLDunlop) **3-8-8** WCarson(5) (h.d.w: hld up: ev ch 1f out: unable qckn) | 1 | **3** | 3/1[2] | 97 | 42 |
| **Henry The Fifth (105)** (CEBrittain) **3-8-8** BDoyle(3) (led to 1f out: one pce) | ½ | **4** | 20/1 | 96 | 41 |
| **Dankeston (USA) (90)** (MBell) **3-8-8v** MFenton(6) (swtg: a.p: ev ch wl over 1f out: wknd fnl f) | 3½ | **5** | 20/1 | 89 | 34 |
| **Line Dancer (107)** (WJarvis) **3-8-8** PatEddery(7) (lw: hld up: rdn over 2f out: wknd fnl f) | 1½ | **6** | 9/2[3] | 86 | 31 |
| **Wood Magic (107)** (DRLoder) **3-8-8** DRMcCabe(9) (bit bkwd: a bhd) | ½ | **7** | 5/2[1] | 85 | 30 |
| **Gothenberg (IRE) (105)** (MJohnston) **3-8-11** JWeaver(10) (lw: a bhd) | ½ | **8** | 11/1 | 87 | 32 |
| **Believe Me (102)** (RHannon) **3-8-8** RPerham(4) (chsd ldr 6f) | 1¾ | **9** | 9/1 | 81 | 26 |
| **Bullfinch (94)** (PTWalwyn) **3-8-8** DHarrison(1) (bhd fnl 3f) | 8 | **10** | 20/1 | 65 | 10 |

(SP 120.3%) **10 Rn**

**1m 42.95** (5.75) CSF £123.83 TOTE £11.90: £2.10 £4.60 £1.80 (£74.10) Trio £210.90 OWNER Highclere Thoroughbred Racing Ltd (MARLBOROUGH) BRED N. Browne
**Regiment (IRE)**, reported to have done plenty of work at home, made a winning return to action. Picking up ground a quarter of a mile out, he struck the front a furlong from home but with the unlucky runner-up really finding his feet in the closing stages, he found the line only just coming in time. More winning opportunities await him as long as he is not aimed too high. (9/1)
**Centre Stalls (IRE)** can be considered very unlucky indeed. Boxed in with nowhere to go over a quarter of a mile out, he only found a gap entering the final furlong but, running on really strongly, would surely have succeeded with a clear passage. He will come on a lot for this and an early success looks on the cards. (16/1)
**Elshabiba (USA)** has done really well over the winter and is now an imposing individual. Chasing the leaders, he threw down a challenge in the straight and may well have got his head in front for a few strides approaching the final furlong before being tapped for toe. There are races to be won with him this year. (3/1)
**Henry The Fifth** looked dreadful in the paddock but was certainly fit and ran a much-improved race to lead as far as the furlong pole. (20/1)
**Dankeston (USA)** had every chance early in the final quarter-mile but had come to the end of his tether entering the last 200 yards. (20/1)
**Line Dancer** chased the leaders until calling it a day inside the distance. (9/2: 3/1-5/1)

## 575 MIDDLESEX H'CAP (0-90) (3-Y.O) (Class C)

4-45 (4-47) **1m 1f (round)** £5,784.00 (£1,752.00: £856.00: £408.00) Stalls: High GOING: 0.16 sec per fur (G)

| Form | Horse | Dist | Pos | SP | RR | SF |
|---|---|---|---|---|---|---|
| *419** | **Dombey (79)** (RCharlton) **3-8-10** PatEddery(7) (a.p: led over 2f out: pushed out) | — | **1** | 7/4[1] | 92 | 63 |
| | **Bellator (68)** (GBBalding) **3-7-8**(5) MHenry(2) (hdwy over 3f out: chsd wnr over 2f out: ev ch over 1f out: unable qckn) | 2 | **2** | 33/1 | 77 | 48 |
| | **Clemente (76)** (RHannon) **3-8-2**(5) DaneO'Neill(11) (a.p: rdn over 2f out: one pce) | 2½ | **3** | 20/1 | 81 | 52 |
| | **Classic Ballet (FR) (69)** (SCWilliams) **3-8-0** AMackay(3) (a.p: led 3f out tl over 2f out: wknd over 1f out) | 3½ | **4** | 10/1[3] | 68 | 39 |
| | **Urgent Swift (65)** (APJarvis) **3-7-10** FNorton(6) (lw: nvr nr to chal) | 2 | **5** | 20/1 | 60 | 31 |
| | **Kilvine (90)** (LMCumani) **3-9-7** JWeaver(4) (lw: rdn & no hdwy fnl 2f) | ½ | **6** | 10/1[3] | 84 | 55 |
| | **Al Shafa (84)** (JLDunlop) **3-9-1** TQuinn(10) (lw: nvr nrr) | 1¼ | **7** | 14/1 | 76 | 47 |
| 471[7] | **Asking For Kings (IRE) (65)** (SDow) **3-7-10** JQuinn(5) (lw: hdwy over 3f out: wknd wl over 1f out) | 2 | **8** | 20/1 | 54 | 25 |
| | **Trojan Risk (73)** (GLewis) **3-8-1**(3) AWhelan(9) (lw: s.s: nvr nrr) | 3 | **9** | 20/1 | 56 | 27 |
| *519** | **Mister Aspecto (IRE) (70)** (MJohnston) **3-8-1v** 5x TWilliams(1) (lw: prom over 6f) | 3 | **10** | 12/1 | 48 | 19 |
| | **D'naan (IRE) (80)** (WJHaggas) **3-8-11** MHills(13) (lw: bhd fnl 5f) | 12 | **11** | 20/1 | 37 | 8 |
| | **Albaha (USA) (90)** (RWArmstrong) **3-9-7** WCarson(8) (lw: prom over 4f) | s.h | **12** | 20/1 | — | 18 |
| | **Goodwood Rocket (71)** (JLDunlop) **3-8-2** GCarter(12) (lw: bhd fnl 4f) | 1 | **13** | 8/1[2] | — | — |
| 444[14] | **Eagle Canyon (IRE) (72)** (BHanbury) **3-8-0b1**(3) JStack(14) (led 6f) | 2½ | **14** | 33/1 | — | — |
| *428** | **Naval Hunter (USA) (75)** (PWHarris) **3-8-6** GHind(15) (lw: a bhd: t.o) | dist | **15** | 8/1[2] | — | — |

(SP 125.6%) **15 Rn**

**1m 55.45** (4.85) CSF £54.95 CT £870.49 TOTE £2.30: £1.70 £7.30 £4.20 (£80.60) Trio £722.00 OWNER Lady Rothschild (BECKHAMPTON) BRED Exors of the late Mrs D. M. de Rothschild
OFFICIAL EXPLANATION **Naval Hunter (USA): a subsequent blood test showed the presence of a bacterial infection.**
**Dombey** moved to the front over a quarter of a mile from home and needed only to be nudged along to have the measure of the runner-up. (7/4)
**Bellator** moved into second place over a quarter of a mile from home. With every chance below the distance, he then found the winner simply too good. (33/1)
**Clemente** was always close up but never looked like finding that necessary turn of foot in the last two furlongs. (20/1)
**Classic Ballet (FR)** poked a whisker in front turning into the straight, but she was soon collared and had given her all approaching the final furlong. (10/1: 8/1-12/1)
**Urgent Swift** struggled on in the final two furlongs without posing a threat. (20/1)
**Kilvine**, looking in good shape for this reappearance, closed up entering the straight but could then make no further impression. (10/1)
**519* Mister Aspecto (IRE)** (12/1: op 6/1)

T/Jkpt: Not won; £12,528.73 to Kempton 8/4/96. T/Plpt: £658.60 (51.39 Tckts). T/Qdpt: £50.20 (61.67 Tckts). AK

# 0569-KEMPTON (R-H) (Good)
## Monday April 8th

Race 7: hand-timed
WEATHER: fine WIND: almost nil

## 576 CITY INDUSTRIAL SUPPLIES MAIDEN STKS (I) (3-Y.O) (Class D)

1-40 (1-42) **1m 2f (Jubilee)** £3,161.50 (£952.00: £461.00: £215.50) Stalls: High GOING: 0.06 sec per fur (G)

| Horse | Dist | Pos | SP | RR | SF |
|---|---|---|---|---|---|
| **Magnificient Style (USA)** (HRACecil) **3-8-9** WRyan(8) (unf: hld up: led over 2f out: clr over 1f out: r.o wl) ... | — | **1** | 6/1[2] | 87+ | 55 |

| | Horse | Dist | Pos | SP | RR | SF |
|---|---|---|---|---|---|---|
| | **Migwar** (LMCumani) **3-9-0** OUrbina(10) (bit bkwd: hld up: rdn over 2f out: r.o one pce) | 6 | **2** | 20/1 | 82 | 50 |
| 447[2] | **Arnhem** (CEBrittain) **3-9-0** BDoyle(3) (swtg: a.p: rdn over 3f out: r.o one pce) | nk | **3** | 13/2[3] | 82 | 50 |
| | **Renzo (IRE)** (GHarwood) **3-9-0** AClark(12) (leggy: scope: s.s: hdwy 5f out: ev ch over 2f out: wknd 1f out) | 5 | **4** | 14/1 | 74 | 42 |
| | **Stately Dancer** (GWragg) **3-8-9** MHills(15) (lw: hdwy 2f out: nvr nrr) | 1½ | **5** | 10/1 | 67 | 35 |
| | **Tassili (IRE)** (GWragg) **3-8-7**(7) GMilligan(13) (cmpt: bit bkwd: nvr nr to chal) | 2½ | **6** | 20/1 | 68 | 36 |
| | **Private Song (USA)** (RCharlton) **3-9-0** PatEddery(7) (a.p: rdn over 4f out: eased whn btn fnl 2f) | nk | **7** | 11/10[1] | 67 | 35 |
| | **Desert Dunes** (NAGraham) **3-9-0** DHarrison(4) (leggy: led over 7f) | 1¼ | **8** | 50/1 | 65 | 33 |
| | **Charming Admiral (IRE)** (CFWall) **3-9-0** WWoods(11) (bkwd: nvr nrr) | 4 | **9** | 50/1 | 59 | 27 |
| 447[7] | **Scandator (IRE)** (PWHarris) **3-9-0** GHind(1) (bit bkwd: bhd fnl 3f) | ¾ | **10** | 33/1 | 57 | 25 |
| | **Nereus** (BWHills) **3-8-7**(7) GBrace(2) (prom over 7f) | 1¼ | **11** | 33/1 | 55 | 23 |
| | **Major Dundee (IRE)** (RHannon) **3-9-0** JReid(14) (a bhd) | 3 | **12** | 8/1 | 51 | 19 |
| | **Suitor** (WJarvis) **3-9-0** PaulEddery(9) (a bhd) | ¾ | **13** | 33/1 | 49 | 17 |
| | **Harbet House (FR)** (CACyzer) **3-9-0** DBiggs(5) (w'like: bkwd: s.s: a bhd) | 5 | **14** | 50/1 | 41 | 9 |
| | **Hencarlam (IRE)** (MRChannon) **3-9-0** JFEgan(6) (bhd fnl 4f) | 5 | **15** | 50/1 | 33 | 1 |

(SP 128.3%) **15 Rn**

**2m 8.76** (5.26) CSF £110.21 TOTE £7.20: £2.40 £3.40 £1.80 (£68.90) Trio £70.90 OWNER Buckram Oak Holdings (NEWMARKET) BRED Buckram Oak Farm

**Magnificient Style (USA)**, a plain, weak-looking filly, was sent to the front over a quarter of a mile out and soon stormed clear for a decisive victory. (6/1: 3/1-13/2)

**Migwar** looked as though this reappearance was just needed. Chasing the leaders, he struggled on in the final quarter-mile for second place but had no hope of getting within a stone's throw of the winner. (20/1)

**447 Arnhem** was never far away but was made to look very pedestrian by the winner in the final quarter-mile. (13/2)

**Renzo (IRE)**, a tall colt with plenty of scope, moved up at halfway. With every chance over a quarter of a mile from home, he tired entering the last 200 yards as lack of a previous run took its toll. He should not take long in finding a race. (14/1)

**Stately Dancer** was certainly not given a hard time but was noted staying on in the straight to be nearest at the line. Improvement should be forthcoming. (10/1)

**Tassili (IRE)**, a half-brother to Most Welcome, stayed on from the back of the field in the last two furlongs without posing a threat. (20/1)

**Private Song (USA)**, who showed plenty of promise on his only run last year, was very disappointing on this return. Always close up, he was being pushed along soon after halfway, and Eddery was certainly not hard on him in the final quarter-mile when the writing was on the wall. He should come on for this and a step up to a mile and a half may help him get off the mark. (11/10)

**Major Dundee (IRE)** (8/1: op 5/1)

## 577 STARK MAIDEN STKS (I) (3-Y.O+) (Class D)

2-10 (2-12) **7f (Jubilee)** £3,298.00 (£994.00: £482.00: £226.00) Stalls: High GOING: 0.06 sec per fur (G)

| | Horse | Dist | Pos | SP | RR | SF |
|---|---|---|---|---|---|---|
| | **Regal Archive (IRE)** (PWChapple-Hyam) **3-8-12** JReid(9) (b.hind: unf: scope: a.p: rdn 4f out: swtchd lft over 1f out: led ins fnl f: r.o wl) | — | **1** | 9/4[1] | 93 | 43 |
| | **State of Caution** (JLDunlop) **3-8-12** PatEddery(10) (led 2f: rdn 3f out: led over 1f out tl ins fnl f: unable qckn) | 1¾ | **2** | 7/1 | 89 | 39 |
| | **Zygo (USA)** (WJarvis) **4-9-12** WRyan(6) (lw: a.p: led over 2f out tl over 1f out: one pce) | 1¼ | **3** | 16/1 | 86 | 50 |
| | **Menoo Hal Batal (USA)** (MRStoute) **3-8-12** KBradshaw(15) (hld up: nt clr run 2f out: rdn over 1f out: one pce fnl f) | 2½ | **4** | 16/1 | 80 | 30 |
| | **Crazy Chief (88)** (PFICole) **3-8-12** TQuinn(14) (bit bkwd: a.p: ev ch over 1f out: wknd fnl f) | 2½ | **5** | 5/1[3] | 75 | 25 |
| | **Warren Knight** (CAHorgan) **3-8-12** AClark(17) (lw: rdn & hdwy over 2f out: wknd over 1f out) | 3½ | **6** | 66/1 | 67 | 17 |
| | **Atlantic Storm** (JHMGosden) **3-8-12** LDettori(8) (w'like: bit bkwd: rdn & hdwy over 2f out: wknd over 1f out) | 1¾ | **7** | 11/4[2] | 63 | 13 |
| | **Forest Robin (85)** (RFJohnsonHoughton) **3-8-12** RCochrane(16) (lw: led 5f out tl over 2f out: wknd over 1f out) | nk | **8** | 12/1 | 62 | 12 |
| 445[7] | **Florentino (IRE)** (BWHills) **3-8-12** MHills(12) (nvr nrr) | ¾ | **9** | 20/1 | 60 | 10 |
| | **Allstars Express** (TJNaughton) **3-8-12** PaulEddery(13) (unf: bit bkwd: s.s: nvr nrr) | hd | **10** | 50/1 | 60 | 10 |
| 495[8] | **Tarian (USA)** (GBBalding) **4-9-12** MWigham(11) (a bhd) | 2½ | **11** | 66/1 | 54 | 18 |
| | **Condor Ridge** (BJMeehan) **3-8-12** JFEgan(3) (nvr nrr) | nk | **12** | 50/1 | 54 | 4 |
| 448[10] | **Mock Trial (IRE)** (MrsJRRamsden) **3-8-12** GHind(1) (dwlt: a bhd) | 2 | **13** | 50/1 | 49 | — |
| | **Zaaleff (USA)** (BHanbury) **4-9-12** PBloomfield(5) (bit bkwd: s.s: bhd fnl 3f) | ¾ | **14** | 50/1 | 47 | 11 |
| | **On The Nose** (SCWilliams) **3-8-7** JTate(2) (leggy: unf: scope: lw: a bhd) | 10 | **15** | 66/1 | 20 | — |
| | **Traci's Castle (IRE)** (RAkehurst) **3-8-0**(7) DDenby(4) (bit bkwd: bhd fnl 5f) | 5 | **16** | 66/1 | 8 | — |
| | **Multan** (GLMoore) **4-9-12** SWhitworth(7) (b: bit bkwd: prom 3f) | 1½ | **17** | 50/1 | 10 | — |

(SP 126.6%) **17 Rn**

**1m 29.45** (4.95) CSF £18.19 TOTE £3.00: £1.90 £2.70 £3.40 (£15.90) Trio £222.90 OWNER Mrs B. V. Sangster (MARLBOROUGH) BRED Studcrown Ltd

WEIGHT FOR AGE 3yo-14lb

**Regal Archive (IRE)** has plenty of scope to develop. Never far away, he was being pushed along half a mile from home and it took a long time for him to get going. Pulled to the outside below the distance, he came with a good run to snatch the spoils inside the last 100 yards. He will be much better suited by further. (9/4)

**State of Caution**, the early leader, regained the advantage below the distance. Collared inside the final furlong, he failed to contain the winner. (7/1)

**Zygo (USA)**, a half-brother to Grand Lodge, has not raced for eleven months but looked extremely well in the paddock. Always close up, he went on over a quarter of a mile from home but, collared below the distance, failed to find another gear. A trip to the winner's enclosure is awaiting him. (16/1)

**Menoo Hal Batal (USA)** chased the leaders but failed to get a clear run a quarter of a mile from home. Galvanized into action, he was on the heels of the leaders entering the final furlong before tapped for toe. (16/1)

**Crazy Chief**, always close up, may well have poked his head in front for a few strides around the quarter-mile marker, before lack of race fitness took its toll in the last 200 yards. Placed on all three of his starts last season, he should find the winner's enclosure before long. (5/1)

**Warren Knight** made an effort early in the straight but was a spent force below the distance. (66/1)

**Atlantic Storm** (11/4: 2/1-3/1)

## 578 CITY INDUSTRIAL SUPPLIES MAIDEN STKS (II) (3-Y.O) (Class D)

2-40 (2-42) **1m 2f (Jubilee)** £3,142.00 (£946.00: £458.00: £214.00) Stalls: High GOING: 0.06 sec per fur (G)

| | Horse | Dist | Pos | SP | RR | SF |
|---|---|---|---|---|---|---|
| | **Samraan (USA)** (JLDunlop) **3-9-0** WCarson(1) (lw: a.p: chsd ldr over 3f out: led wl over 1f out: pushed out) | — | **1** | 8/1 | 91+ | 50 |
| | **Clerkenwell (USA)** (MRStoute) **3-9-0** JTate(13) (lw: led over 8f: unable qckn ins fnl f) | 1½ | **2** | 6/1 [2] | 89 | 48 |
| | **Berenice** (GWragg) **3-8-9** MHills(2) (unf: bit bkwd: rdn & hdwy over 2f out: r.o one pce) | 2½ | **3** | 14/1 | 80 | 39 |
| | **Generosa** (HCandy) **3-8-9** RCochrane(12) (a.p: rdn over 3f out: one pce) | 2½ | **4** | 13/2 [3] | 76 | 35 |
| | **Lead Him On (USA)** (PWHarris) **3-9-0** GHind(5) (w'like: scope: rdn & hdwy over 3f out: wknd 2f out) | 4 | **5** | 10/1 | 74 | 33 |
| | **Steamroller Stanly** (CACyzer) **3-9-0** DBiggs(6) (prom over 6f) | 6 | **6** | 33/1 | 65 | 24 |
| | **Brentability (IRE)** (GLewis) **3-9-0** SWhitworth(3) (w'like: bit bkwd: s.s: nvr nrr) | 2 | **7** | 25/1 | 61 | 20 |
| | **Code Red** (JWHills) **3-9-0** PatEddery(9) (leggy: unf: nvr nrr) | 1½ | **8** | 12/1 | 59 | 18 |
| | **Orinoco River (USA)** (PWChapple-Hyam) **3-9-0** JReid(7) (bhd fnl 4f) | 1¼ | **9** | 6/1 [2] | 57 | 16 |
| | **Clouds Hill (FR)** (RHannon) **3-8-9**(5) DaneO'Neill(4) (prom over 6f) | ¾ | **10** | 6/1 [2] | 56 | 15 |
| | **Macmorris (USA)** (PFICole) **3-9-0** TQuinn(11) (bhd fnl 4f) | s.h | **11** | 20/1 | 56 | 15 |
| | **River Captain (USA)** (JHMGosden) **3-9-0** LDettori(10) (lw: s.s: hdwy 7f out: wknd 4f out) | 1 | **12** | 5/1 [1] | 54 | 13 |
| | **Dashing Invader (USA)** (PWHarris) **3-9-0** DHarrison(8) (a bhd) | 1 | **13** | 50/1 | 53 | 12 |
| | **Polonaise Prince (USA)** (RAkehurst) **3-9-0** SSanders(14) (w'like: bit bkwd: chsd ldr over 6f) | 1¼ | **14** | 13/2 [3] | 51 | 10 |

(SP 134.3%) **14 Rn**

**2m 9.97** (6.47) CSF £57.47 TOTE £8.90: £2.80 £2.60 £6.50 (£22.10) Trio £585.60; £453.67 to Uttoxeter 9/4/96 OWNER Mr K. M. Al-Mudhaf (ARUNDEL) BRED Mrs Afaf A. Al Essa

**Samraan (USA)** moved into second place turning for home and, sent on early in the final quarter-mile, needed only to be nudged along to score. However, the time of this race was over a second slower than the first division. (8/1)
**Clerkenwell (USA)** looked really well for this return to action and made a bold attempt to make all. Collared early inside the final quarter-mile, he held on grimly until brushed aside inside the last 200 yards. He should soon go one better. (6/1)
**Berenice** stayed on in the straight to take third prize but had no hope of getting near the front two. (14/1)
**Generosa** was always close up but failed to find another gear in the straight. (13/2)
**Lead Him On (USA)** moved up turning for home but had run his race two furlongs out. (10/1)
**River Captain (USA)** (5/1: op 3/1)

## 579 QUAIL CONDITIONS STKS (3-Y.O+) (Class C)

3-10 (3-11) **6f** £4,971.20 (£1,860.80: £910.40: £392.00: £176.00: £89.60) Stalls: High GOING: 0.06 sec per fur (G)

| | Horse | Dist | Pos | SP | RR | SF |
|---|---|---|---|---|---|---|
| 457[4] | **Hard to Figure (107)** (RJHodges) **10-9-9** RCochrane(1) (outpcd: hdwy on ins over 1f out: str run fnl f: led last strides) | — | **1** | 11/2 | 113 | 59 |
| | **Easy Dollar (107)** (BGubby) **4-9-5b** PatEddery(4) (chsd ldr: rdn over 2f out: led ins fnl f: hdd last strides) | hd | **2** | 5/1 [3] | 109 | 55 |
| 457[2] | **The Puzzler (IRE) (105)** (BWHills) **5-9-2** WCarson(3) (b: led tl ins fnl f: one pce) | 1½ | **3** | 11/4 [1] | 102 | 48 |
| | **Wavian (96)** (RHannon) **4-9-2** JReid(6) (no hdwy fnl 2f) | 5 | **4** | 11/2 | 88 | 34 |
| | **High Priority (IRE) (103)** (MRChannon) **3-8-7** TQuinn(5) (bkwd: a bhd) | 3 | **5** | 9/2 [2] | 83 | 17 |
| | **King of Peru (100)** (APJarvis) **3-8-7** JTate(2) (prom over 4f) | 1¾ | **6** | 13/2 | 79 | 13 |

(SP 105.6%) **6 Rn**

**1m 15.01** (3.71) CSF £27.61 TOTE £6.90: £2.30 £2.10 (£14.50) OWNER Mr J. W. Mursell (SOMERTON) BRED J. W. Mursell
WEIGHT FOR AGE 3yo-12lb

**457 Hard to Figure** was totally taken off his feet for much of the race. He got into top gear though from below the distance, and came storming through to snatch the spoils in the last couple of strides. He obviously still retains all his old ability despite his advancing years but, because of his high rating, is going to be hard to place. (11/2)
**Easy Dollar** chased the leader. Eventually mastering that rival early inside the final furlong, he looked likely to prevail until the strong late burst of the winner caught him out in the last couple of strides. This was a very pleasing reappearance but, like the winner, he will also have problems when it comes to finding suitable opportunities. (5/1)
**457 The Puzzler (IRE)** was certainly not going to hang around and set a very brisk pace. Eventually overhauled inside the final furlong, he failed to find another gear. (11/4)
**Wavian**, sold out of Roger Charlton's stable for 25,000 guineas at the Newmarket Autumn sales, raced in fourth place and was making little impression in the final quarter-mile. (11/2)
**High Priority (IRE)**, who showed useful form last season, was carrying a lot of surplus flesh for this reappearance and was always struggling. (9/2)
**King of Peru** raced in third place until calling it a day inside the distance. (13/2)

## 580 WESTMINSTER TAXI INSURANCE ROSEBERY H'CAP (0-95) (4-Y.O+) (Class C)

3-40 (3-41) **1m 2f** £12,892.00 (£4,828.00: £2,364.00: £1,020.00: £460.00: £236.00) Stalls: High GOING: 0.06 sec per fur (G)

| | Horse | Dist | Pos | SP | RR | SF |
|---|---|---|---|---|---|---|
| 440[2] | **Hazard a Guess (IRE) (76)** (DNicholls) **6-8-11** RCochrane(11) (hdwy & nt clr run over 1f out: led wl ins fnl f: r.o wl) | — | **1** | 10/1 [3] | 87 | 47 |
| | **Special Dawn (IRE) (88)** (JLDunlop) **6-9-9** PatEddery(20) (lw: swtchd lft & hdwy 2f out: led 1f out tl wl ins fnl f: unable qckn) | ¾ | **2** | 7/1 [1] | 98 | 58 |
| *410[8]* | **Hardy Dancer (86)** (GLMoore) **4-9-7** SWhitworth(18) (lw: hld up: nt clr run on ins over 2f out tl over 1f out: r.o ins fnl f) | ½ | **3** | 25/1 | 95 | 55 |
| | **Beauchamp Jade (79)** (HCandy) **4-9-0** JReid(4) (hdwy 5f out: led over 1f out: sn hdd: one pce) | ¾ | **4** | 16/1 | 87 | 47 |
| | **Kings Assembly (76)** (PWHarris) **4-8-11** GHind(8) (a.p: ev ch over 1f out: wknd ins fnl f) | 2½ | **5** | 12/1 | 80 | 40 |
| | **Menas Gold (85)** (SDow) **4-9-6** WRyan(15) (rdn & hdwy 2f out: r.o wl ins fnl f) | hd | **6** | 33/1 | 89 | 49 |
| *379[9]* | **Secret Aly (CAN) (83)** (CEBrittain) **6-9-4** BDoyle(1) (lw: led over 8f: wknd fnl f) | 2½ | **7** | 20/1 | 83 | 43 |
| | **Sheer Danzig (IRE) (88)** (RWArmstrong) **4-9-9** LDettori(9) (hld up: rdn over 2f out: one pce fnl f) | nk | **8** | 7/1 [1] | 87 | 47 |
| | **Noble Sprinter (IRE) (80)** (RHannon) **4-9-1b** RPerham(14) (a.p: rdn over 2f out: wknd 1f out) | ½ | **9** | 16/1 | 78 | 38 |
| | **Burning (USA) (92)** (GHarwood) **4-9-13** AClark(10) (nt clr run & swtchd rt over 1f out: hdwy fnl f: nvr nrr) | nk | **10** | 10/1 [3] | 90 | 50 |
| | **Te Amo (IRE) (78)** (RAkehurst) **4-8-13** DHarrison(6) (nvr nrr) | 3 | **11** | 16/1 | 71 | 31 |
| | **Romios (IRE) (90)** (PFICole) **4-9-11** TQuinn(13) (lw: plld hrd: hdwy over 3f out: wknd 2f out) | 1 | **12** | 16/1 | 82 | 42 |
| | **At Liberty (IRE) (90)** (RHannon) **4-9-6**(5) DaneO'Neill(3) (lw: a.p: rdn over 2f out: wknd over 1f out) | 2½ | **13** | 20/1 | 78 | 38 |
| | **Behaviour (93)** (MrsJCecil) **4-10-0** PaulEddery(7) (lw: s.s: a bhd) | 1 | **14** | 12/1 | 79 | 39 |

| | | | | SP | RR | SF |
|---|---|---|---|---|---|---|
| $455^{8}$ | **Cedez le Passage (FR) (89)** (KOCunningham-Brown) **5-9-10** JFEgan(19) (bhd fnl 4f) | 4 | **15** | 20/1 | 69 | 29 |
| | **Glide Path (USA) (92)** (JWHills) **7-9-13** MHills(5) (lw: hdwy over 3f out: wknd over 2f out) | nk | **16** | 20/1 | 71 | 31 |
| $455^{3}$ | **Barbaroja (86)** (JGFitzGerald) **5-9-7** SSanders(17) (prom tl wknd & hmpd on ins over 3f out) | 1½ | **17** | $8/1^{2}$ | 63 | 23 |
| | **Percy Braithwaite (IRE) (82)** (MJohnston) **4-9-3b** WWoods(16) (bhd fnl 3f) | ½ | **18** | 20/1 | 58 | 18 |
| | **Eurolink the Rebel (USA) (77)** (MDHammond) **4-8-12b** WCarson(2) (chsd ldr over 5f) | 15 | **19** | 14/1 | 29 | — |
| | | | | (SP 130.5%) | **19 Rn** | |

**2m 8.97** (6.47) CSF £75.73 CT £1,601.52 TOTE £12.20: £2.60 £2.20 £4.40 £4.70 (£44.60) Trio £402.70 OWNER Consultco Ltd (THIRSK) BRED A. F. O'Callaghan in Ireland

OFFICIAL EXPLANATION **Eurolink the Rebel (USA): was later found to have pulled a muscle in his hind-quarters.**

**440 Hazard a Guess (IRE)** certainly gave his supporters some worrying moments. Out the back entering the straight, he began to weave his way through the pack but failed to get the best of runs below the distance. Nevertheless, he continued to thread his way through and got on top in the closing stages. (10/1)

**Special Dawn (IRE)**, 10lb higher than when winning this race last year, came with a good run to snatch the lead a furlong out. Grimly trying to hold on, he was worried out of it in the closing stages. A mile and a quarter on fast ground is ideal but he has yet to win after July. (7/1)

**Hardy Dancer** had no luck in running and was trapped against the rail for much of the straight. Eventually finding an opening approaching the final furlong, he ran on for third prize. (25/1)

**Beauchamp Jade** moved up at halfway. Gaining a narrow advantage below the distance, she was soon collared and tapped for toe. A mile and a half is really her trip. (16/1)

**Kings Assembly** was never far away. With every chance below the distance, he tired inside the last 150 yards. (12/1)

**Menas Gold** saw out this longer trip and weaved her way through the field in the final quarter-mile to be nearest at the line. She should come on for this. (33/1)

**Burning (USA)** encountered traffic problems in this fiercely competitive handicap. However, he did make slight headway in the final furlong, but his jockey was not hard on him at all. He ran some good races last season and no doubt connections have handicaps over a mile and a half in mind this time. (10/1)

## 581 MAGNOLIA STKS (Listed) (4-Y.O+) (Class A)

4-15 (4-21) **1m 2f (Jubilee)** £11,981.25 (£3,600.00: £1,737.50: £806.25) Stalls: High GOING: 0.06 sec per fur (G)

| | | | | SP | RR | SF |
|---|---|---|---|---|---|---|
| | **Lucky Di (USA)** (LMCumani) **4-8-11** MHills(2) (hdwy over 3f out: led over 2f out: clr over 1f out: comf) | — | **1** | $11/2^{3}$ | 118+ | 78 |
| | **Star Selection** (JMackie) **5-8-11** AClark(1) (hdwy over 4f out: chsd wnr fnl 2f: no imp) | 3 | **2** | 66/1 | 113 | 73 |
| | **Captain Horatius (IRE) (110)** (JLDunlop) **7-9-0** PatEddery(6) (in rr over 7f: gd hdwy over 1f out: one pce) | 5 | **3** | $5/1^{2}$ | 108 | 68 |
| | **Florid (USA) (104)** (HRACecil) **5-8-11** WRyan(12) (bit bkwd: swtchd lft over 2f out: hdwy over 1f out: one pce) | ¾ | **4** | 9/1 | 104 | 64 |
| | **Poppy Carew (IRE) (106)** (PWHarris) **4-8-9** GHind(4) (lw: hld up: rdn over 2f out: wknd over 1f out) | 1¾ | **5** | 8/1 | 99 | 59 |
| | **Inquisitor (USA) (107)** (JHMGosden) **4-8-11** LDettori(10) (b.hind: a.p: ev ch over 2f out: wknd over 1f out) | 5 | **6** | 6/1 | 93 | 53 |
| | **Fire on Ice (IRE) (103)** (MRStoute) **4-8-11** JReid(8) (bit bkwd: hld up: rdn over 2f out: sn wknd) | ½ | **7** | 16/1 | 92 | 52 |
| | **Lear White (USA)** (PAKelleway) **5-9-2** RCochrane(11) (hld up: rdn over 3f out: wkng whn slipped on ins over 2f out) | 1½ | **8** | 20/1 | 95 | 55 |
| $442^{2}$ | **Wijara (IRE) (103)** (RHannon) **4-8-11** RPerham(7) (lw: prom over 7f) | ¾ | **9** | 15/2 | 89 | 49 |
| | **Musetta (IRE) (110)** (CEBrittain) **4-8-9** BDoyle(3) (swtg: prom 9f) | 7 | **10** | 20/1 | 76 | 36 |
| | **Easy Listening (USA)** (RCharlton) **4-8-11** SSanders(5) (a bhd) | 2 | **11** | 12/1 | 74 | 34 |
| | **Medaille Militaire (104)** (JLDunlop) **4-8-11** TQuinn(9) (led over 7f) | 8 | **12** | $9/2^{1}$ | 62 | 22 |
| | | | | (SP 122.0%) | **12 Rn** | |

**2m 6.24** (2.74) CSF £217.79 TOTE £7.80: £2.50 £9.50 £2.10 (£410.70) Trio £1,048.90 OWNER Mrs Virginia Knott Bender (NEWMARKET) BRED Mrs Virginia K. Bender

**Lucky Di (USA)** put up a highly impressive display in by far the fastest time of the afternoon over this distance. Sent on over a quarter of a mile out, he shot clear to win with plenty in hand. He looks a really exciting prospect and a Group race looks well within his capabilities. A mile and a half should hold no terrors. (11/2)

**Star Selection** moved up soon after halfway. Taking second place a quarter of a mile out, he had absolutely no hope of reeling in the winner. (66/1)

**Captain Horatius (IRE)**, winner of this race in 1993 and 1995, and runner-up in 1994, was well adrift of his rivals until the straight. Picking up ground to go third below the distance, he found the effort of getting there taking its toll and could make no further impression. (5/1: 7/2-11/2)

**Florid (USA)**, looking big and well for his return to action, moved up below the distance but then failed to make any further impression. (9/1)

**Poppy Carew (IRE)** proved very unruly beforehand and delayed the start for quite some time. Chasing the leaders, she had given her all below the distance. (8/1)

**Inquisitor (USA)**, always close up, had every chance early in the straight before tiring below the distance. (6/1)

**442 Wijara (IRE)** (15/2: 5/1-8/1)

**Medaille Militaire** was very disappointing and, after taking the field along, tamely dropped away when collared approaching the final quarter-mile. (9/2)

## 582 TEAL H'CAP (0-85) (4-Y.O+) (Class D)

4-45 (4-52) **6f** £2,558.25 (£2,558.25: £579.00: £274.50) Stalls: High GOING: 0.06 sec per fur (G)

| | | | | SP | RR | SF |
|---|---|---|---|---|---|---|
| | **Latching (IRE) (72)** (RFJohnsonHoughton) **4-9-1** JReid(22) (w ldr: led over 3f out: all out) | — | **1** | 12/1 | 79 | 61 |
| | **Seigneurial (82)** (GHarwood) **4-9-11** AClark(24) (a.p: ev ch fnl 2f: jnd ldr post) | — | **1** | 12/1 | 89 | 71 |
| | **Face the Future (56)** (SDow) **7-7-13** WCarson(21) (a.p: rdn over 2f out: unable qckn) | 4 | **3** | $9/1^{2}$ | 52 | 34 |
| $451^{13}$ | **Mister Jolson (70)** (RJHodges) **7-8-13** RCochrane(3) (b.nr fore: racd stands' side: hdwy over 1f out: r.o) | ½ | **4** | 20/1 | 65 | 47 |
| $451^{3}$ | **Montserrat (71)** (LGCottrell) **4-9-0v** LDettori(1) (racd stands' side: a.p: one pce fnl 2f) | 1 | **5** | $11/1^{3}$ | 63 | 45 |
| | **Spectacle Jim (53)** (MJHaynes) **7-7-10b** FNorton(25) (hld up: rdn over 2f out: r.o one pce) | ¾ | **6** | 20/1 | 43 | 25 |
| | **Bryan Robson (USA) (59)** (GBBalding) **5-8-2** SSanders(23) (bit bkwd: led over 2f: wknd 2f out) | 1¼ | **7** | 12/1 | 46 | 28 |
| $475^{3}$ | **Barato (66)** (MrsJRRamsden) **5-8-9** TQuinn(20) (b.nr hind: nvr nr to chal) | nk | **8** | $6/1^{1}$ | 52 | 34 |
| $451^{*}$ | **Anzio (IRE) (85)** (MissGayKelleway) **5-10-0b** PatEddery(16) (hdwy over 1f out: nvr nrr) | 1¼ | **9** | $6/1^{1}$ | 68 | 50 |
| | **Rocky Waters (USA) (60)** (PBurgoyne) **7-8-0(3)** DRMcCabe(19) (b.hind: swtg: nvr nrr) | 3 | **10** | 25/1 | 35 | 17 |
| $451^{9}$ | **Sir Joey (USA) (80)** (PGMurphy) **7-9-9** DHarrison(8) (racd stands' side: outpcd: nvr nrr) | s.h | **11** | 25/1 | 55 | 37 |
| | **Tinker Osmaston (73)** (MSSaunders) **5-9-2** JFEgan(17) (a.p: stumbled over 3f out: wknd over 2f out) | nk | **12** | 20/1 | 47 | 29 |
| | **Roka (59)** (RHannon) **4-7-9(7)ow6** KSalt(18) (lw: nvr nrr) | nk | **13** | 20/1 | 32 | 8 |

| Form | Horse / details | Dist | Pos | SP | RR | SF |
|---|---|---|---|---|---|---|
| 451[20] | **Samsolom (70)** (PHowling) **8-8-13** PaulEddery(6) (b.hind: racd stands' side: outpcd) | 3½ | **14** | 33/1 | 34 | 16 |
| *338** | **Chewit (81)** (AMoore) **4-9-10** CandyMorris(15) (a mid div) | 3½ | **15** | 9/1[2] | 36 | 18 |
| 451[12] | **Fantasy Racing (IRE) (82)** (MRChannon) **4-9-4**(7) AEddery(4) (racd stands' side: prom 3f) | ½ | **16** | 20/1 | 35 | 17 |
| *513[6]* | **Intiaash (IRE) (75)** (DHaydnJones) **4-9-4** BDoyle(13) (prom over 3f) | nk | **17** | 20/1 | 27 | 9 |
| | **Sally Slade (78)** (CACyzer) **4-9-7** DBiggs(5) (racd stands' side: bhd fnl 3f) | 1¼ | **18** | 25/1 | 27 | 9 |
| | **Macfarlane (71)** (MJFetherston-Godley) **8-8-9**(5) DaneO'Neill(11) (b: bit bkwd: racd stands' side: prom 3f) | nk | **19** | 25/1 | 19 | 1 |
| 496[4] | **Denbrae (IRE) (70)** (DJGMurraySmith) **4-8-13** MHills(14) (bhd fnl 3f) | 2½ | **20** | 14/1 | 12 | — |
| | **Astral Invader (IRE) (57)** (MSSaunders) **4-8-0**[ow2] JTate(9) (b: hdwy over 3f out: wknd over 2f out) | 5 | **21** | 33/1 | — | — |
| 466[9] | **Tauber (59)** (PatMitchell) **12-7-11**(5)[ow6] AmandaSanders(10) (hdwy over 3f out: wknd over 2f out) | hd | **22** | 66/1 | — | — |
| *407[2]* | **Stoppes Brow (70)** (GLMoore) **4-8-13** SWhitworth(7) (racd stands' side: bhd fnl 3f) | 1¼ | **23** | 16/1 | — | — |
| | **Ahjay (54)** (TJNaughton) **6-7-11** AMackay(2) (bit bkwd: s.s: racd stands' side: a bhd) | nk | **24** | 25/1 | — | — |
| 496[10] | **Amahsan (IRE) (70)** (CDBroad) **4-8-13** GHind(12) (bhd fnl 3f) | 18 | **25** | 50/1 | — | — |

(SP 149.7%) **25 Rn**

**1m 14.3** (3.00) CSF £77.65 CT £410.65 TOTE £12.80 S £6.60 L: £4.40 S £3.70 L £2.40 £4.20 (£98.40) Trio £92.90 OWNER Mr R. F. JohnsonHoughton (DIDCOT)/The PBT Group (PULBOROUGH) BRED Tullamaine Castle Stud/Richard M. Whitaker

LONG HANDICAP Spectacle Jim 7-4 Tauber 6-10

**Latching (IRE)** disputed the lead before going on just before halfway. Engaged in a tremendous tussle with her rival, she was forced to share the spoils on the line. (12/1)

**Seigneurial** had a tremendous battle with Latching in the final quarter-mile and, in the end, shared the spoils. (12/1)

**Face the Future**, never far away on the far side, failed to quicken up in the last two furlongs. (9/1)

**Mister Jolson** was one of nine who elected to race on the stands' side, which was not the place to be, so in the circumstances, he did well to finish so close. (20/1)

**451 Montserrat**, racing on the unfavoured stands' side, was never far away, but could only plod on at the one pace in the last two furlongs. (11/1)

**Spectacle Jim** chased the leaders on the far side but could never get in a serious blow. (20/1)

**475 Barato** (6/1: 4/1-13/2)

## 583 STARK MAIDEN STKS (II) (3-Y.O+) (Class D)

5-15 (5-20) **7f** **(Jubilee)** £3,298.00 (£994.00: £482.00: £226.00) Stalls: High GOING: 0.06 sec per fur (G)

| Form | Horse / details | Dist | Pos | SP | RR | SF |
|---|---|---|---|---|---|---|
| | **Thea (USA)** (JRFanshawe) **3-8-7** DHarrison(1) (hdwy over 2f out: led over 1f out: comf) | — | 1 | 7/2[2] | 88+ | 55 |
| | **Civil Liberty** (GLewis) **3-8-12** PatEddery(3) (h.d.w: chsd ldr: led 2f out tl over 1f out: unable qckn) | 4 | 2 | 7/4[1] | 84 | 51 |
| | **Freequent** (LMCumani) **3-8-12** OUrbina(6) (w'like: scope: bit bkwd: hdwy over 1f out: r.o ins fnl f) | 5 | 3 | 10/1 | 72 | 39 |
| | **Reveuse de Jour (IRE)** (RCharlton) **3-8-7** TQuinn(15) (hld up: nt clr run over 2f out: one pce) | ½ | 4 | 8/1 | 66 | 33 |
| | **Arterxerxes** (MJHeaton-Ellis) **3-8-12** AClark(7) (lw: led 5f) | ¾ | 5 | 25/1 | 70 | 37 |
| | **In Tune** (PHowling) **3-8-12** FNorton(12) (w'like: nvr nr to chal) | 3 | 6 | 33/1 | 63 | 30 |
| | **Promissory** (CEBrittain) **3-8-7** BDoyle(11) (a.p: rdn over 2f out: wknd over 1f out) | nk | 7 | 10/1 | 57 | 24 |
| | **Royal Result (USA)** (MRStoute) **3-8-12** KBradshaw(10) (w'like: bit bkwd: nvr plcd to chal) | 1 | 8 | 20/1 | 60 | 27 |
| | **Voodoo Rocket** (JHMGosden) **3-8-7** LDettori(8) (unf: nvr nrr) | 2 | 9 | 11/2[3] | 50 | 17 |
| | **Ameer Alfayaafi (IRE)** (RAkehurst) **3-8-12** SSanders(13) (bkwd: prom over 3f) | 1¼ | 10 | 20/1 | 52 | 19 |
| 448[6] | **Alpine Panther (IRE)** (WJarvis) **3-8-12** GHind(9) (s.s: a bhd) | 1½ | 11 | 14/1 | 49 | 16 |
| | **Sam Rockett** (CAHorgan) **3-8-12** PaulEddery(14) (w'like: bit bkwd: prom over 4f) | 1 | 12 | 33/1 | 47 | 14 |
| | **Superior Force** (MissBSanders) **3-8-12** DBiggs(4) (lw: hld up: rdn over 3f out: sn wknd) | 4 | 13 | 25/1 | 38 | 5 |
| *24[6]* | **Raffles Rooster** (AGNewcombe) **4-9-12** RCochrane(16) (swtg: s.s: a bhd) | hd | 14 | 50/1 | 37 | 18 |
| | **Merrie le Bow (42)** (PatMitchell) **4-9-2**(5) AmandaSanders(5) (bit bkwd: bhd fnl 2f) | 2½ | 15 | 50/1 | 27 | 8 |
| | **Challenger (IRE)** (TJNaughton) **3-8-12** MHills(2) (leggy: unf: scope: s.s: a bhd) | 1¼ | 16 | 20/1 | 29 | — |

(SP 141.7%) **16 Rn**

**1m 28.0** (3.50) CSF £11.15 TOTE £5.40: £1.70 £1.50 £2.90 (£6.10) Trio £13.70 OWNER T & J Vestey (NEWMARKET) BRED Cambremont Ltd Partnership

WEIGHT FOR AGE 3yo-14lb

**Thea (USA)** made an impressive return. Swooping into the lead below the distance, she stormed clear to win with plenty in hand. (7/2)

**Civil Liberty** is an imposing three-year-old. Racing in second place, he gained the upper hand a quarter of a mile out but was easily brushed aside when collared below the distance. He should make no mistake next time out. (7/4: 5/4-Evens)

**Freequent** did not look fully wound up and was out with the washing until staying on in the final furlong and a half to be nearest at the line. He ought to come on a lot for this and should soon be winning, possibly over further. (10/1: op 5/1)

**Reveuse de Jour (IRE)** chased the leaders. Although failing to get a clear run early in the straight, when a gap did appear, she could only go up and down in the one place. (8/1)

**Arterxerxes** set the pace but, once collared two furlongs out, had little left to offer. (25/1)

**In Tune** struggled on without posing a threat. (33/1)

**Royal Result (USA)**, not fully tuned up for this debut, was given a nice educational ride and should soon step up on this. (20/1)

**Voodoo Rocket** (11/2: 4/1-6/1)

T/Jkpt: Not won; £19,705.02 to Uttoxeter 9/4/96. T/Plpt: £730.40 (43.19 Tckts). T/Qdpt: £107.60 (23.64 Tckts). AK

# 0472-NEWCASTLE (L-H) (Good, Good to firm patches)

## Monday April 8th

Race 1: hand-timed

WEATHER: overcast WIND: slt half against

## 584 NATIONAL FIRE SERVICE BENEVOLENT FUND MAIDEN STKS (3-Y.O) (Class D)

2-25 (2-27) **1m (round)** £3,566.25 (£1,080.00: £527.50: £251.25) Stalls: Low GOING: 0.07 sec per fur (G)

| Form | Horse / details | Dist | Pos | SP | RR | SF |
|---|---|---|---|---|---|---|
| 472[3] | **Green Bopper (USA)** (MBell) **3-8-7**(7) GFaulkner(3) (lw: trckd ldrs: led over 2f out: r.o u.p) | — | 1 | 13/2[3] | 86 | 45 |
| | **Terdad (USA)** (MRStoute) **3-9-0** MBirch(6) (lw: swtg: trckd ldrs: hdwy 3f out: ev ch over 1f out: nt qckn) | 2 | 2 | 9/2[2] | 82 | 41 |
| | **Elite Force (IRE)** (PWChapple-Hyam) **3-9-0** GBardwell(1) (plld hrd: trckd ldrs: hdwy over 2f out: kpt on fnl f) | 2 | 3 | 7/1 | 78 | 37 |
| *484[3]* | **Victory Bound (USA)** (MJohnston) **3-9-0** TWilliams(9) (led tl hdd over 2f out: rdn & one pce) | ½ | 4 | 14/1 | 77 | 36 |
| | **Manoy (45)** (JHetherton) **3-9-0** NKennedy(2) (chsd ldrs tl outpcd fnl 2f) | 2 | 5 | 50/1 | 73 | 32 |
| | **Sinking Sun** (BWHills) **3-8-9v**[1] KFallon(10) (plld hrd: in tch: effrt over 2f out: no imp) | hd | 6 | 10/1 | 68 | 27 |

| | Horse | Dist | Pos | SP | RR | SF |
|---|---|---|---|---|---|---|
| | **Misky Bay** (JHMGosden) **3-9-0** DaleGibson(4) (bit bkwd: hld up & bhd: hdwy 3f out: nvr rchd ldrs) | ½ | **7** | 12/1 | 72 | 31 |
| 448[12] | **Ocean Stream (IRE) (73)** (JLEyre) **3-9-0** DeanMcKeown(5) (lw: bhd: sme hdwy over 2f out: n.d) | 2 | **8** | 20/1 | 68 | 27 |
| | **Dispol Gem** (GROldroyd) **3-8-9** ACulhane(12) (neat: bit bkwd: s.s: a bhd) | 6 | **9** | 50/1 | 51 | 10 |
| | **Serendipity (FR)** (JLDunlop) **3-9-0** TIves(11) (lw: prom: c wd st: sn rdn & btn) | ½ | **10** | Evens[1] | 55 | 14 |
| | **Troika (IRE)** (JBerry) **3-8-4**(5) PRoberts(7) (bit bkwd: s.i.s: a bhd) | hd | **11** | 33/1 | 50 | 9 |
| | **Duo Master** (MrsMReveley) **3-9-0** KDarley(8) (bit bkwd: s.i.s: hld up: a rr div) | 1¾ | **12** | 14/1 | 51 | 10 |
| | | | | (SP 135.8%) | **12 Rn** | |

**1m 44.8** (5.80) CSF £38.66 TOTE £12.90: £2.90 £1.70 £2.10 (£22.20) Trio £61.90 OWNER Mr T. F. Harris (NEWMARKET) BRED Lucy G. Bassett

**472 Green Bopper (USA)**, who looked superb, has obviously improved from his previous run and won this in good style. (13/2)
**Tcrdad (USA)**, an excitable sort, got pretty warm beforehand but did settle quite well in the race, only to be outbattled in the closing stages. (9/2)
**Elite Force (IRE)**, who looks the type to improve with time, spoiled his chances by pulling too hard early on, but he was staying on at the finish, suggesting that longer trips should suit. (7/1)
**484 Victory Bound (USA)** went off in front this time, but he was never racing on an even keel when the pressure was on, and was outpaced approaching the final furlong. (14/1: op 8/1)
**Manoy** showed some ability but was well short of speed when the pace was really on in the final three furlongs. (50/1)
**Sinking Sun**, wearing a visor for the first time, raced far too freely and was left struggling some way out. (10/1)
**Misky Bay**, a barrel of a horse, needed this and never got into it, but does look likely to improve. (12/1: op 7/1)
**Serendipity (FR)** looked pretty straight but, after racing up with the pace, he came round the outside on the turn and seemed to lose his action once in line for home. Something was obviously wrong with him this time. (Evens)

## 585 E.B.F. CAP HEATON MAIDEN STKS (2-Y.O F) (Class D)

2-55 (2-56) **5f** £3,420.00 (£1,035.00: £505.00: £240.00) Stalls: High GOING: 0.07 sec per fur (G)

| | Horse | Dist | Pos | SP | RR | SF |
|---|---|---|---|---|---|---|
| | **Marathon Maid** (RAFahey) **2-8-11** ACulhane(3) (leggy: unf: lw: hld up: qcknd to ld over 1f out: r.o) | — | **1** | 16/1 | 67 | 9 |
| | **Top of The Wind (IRE)** (JJO'Neill) **2-8-11** SDWilliams(5) (leggy: unf: outpcd ½-wy: hdwy & n.m.r over 1f out: swtchd & r.o wl towards fin) | 1¼ | **2** | 10/1 | 63 | 5 |
| | **Antonia's Choice** (JBerry) **2-8-11** KDarley(1) (cl up: led ½-wy tl appr fnl f: no ex) | 1¾ | **3** | 13/8[1] | 57 | — |
| | **Trading Aces** (MBell) **2-8-11** KFallon(7) (w'like: b.hind: s.s: outpcd & bhd tl styd on fnl f) | 1½ | **4** | 7/4[2] | 53 | — |
| | **Molly Drummond** (CWCElsey) **2-8-11** MBirch(4) (unf: lw: led to ½-wy: btn whn sltly hmpd ins fnl f) | hd | **5** | 12/1 | 52 | — |
| | **Lycius Touch** (MJohnston) **2-8-11** TWilliams(8) (neat: bit bkwd: spd to ½-wy: sn outpcd) | 4 | **6** | 9/2[3] | 40 | — |
| | **Nostalgic Air (USA)** (EWeymes) **2-8-11** DeanMcKeown(6) (w'like: bit bkwd: dwlt: hdwy to chal ½-wy: wknd over 1f out) | 16 | **7** | 5/1 | — | — |
| | **Hiltons Executive (IRE)** (EJAlston) **2-8-11** TIves(2) (leggy: unf: unruly s: rn green & wl bhd fr ½-wy) | 17 | **8** | 14/1 | — | — |
| | | | | (SP 138.6%) | **8 Rn** | |

**63.9 secs** (5.50) CSF £161.81 TOTE £40.90: £5.20 £2.70 £1.50 (£101.80) OWNER Marathon Thoroughbred Racing (MALTON) BRED Shadwell Estate Company Limited

**Marathon Maid** had nothing much to recommend her on looks, but she was very fit and knew her job, and that was enough in the closing stages. (16/1)
**Top of The Wind (IRE)** is nothing much to look at. Very green and short of room from halfway, she did really get into her stride in the closing stages and flew at the death. She should be a different proposition next time. (10/1)
**Antonia's Choice** looked the pick of the bunch but had plenty to do from an outside draw and just ran out of petrol late on. She will improve for this. (13/8)
**Trading Aces**, a decent type, looked likely to benefit from the run and was gradually getting the hang of things as the race progressed. (7/4)
**Molly Drummond**, a real sharp early-season sort, had plenty of speed and an easier track would probably help. (12/1)
**Lycius Touch** needed this and found things happening far too quickly from halfway. (9/2)
**Nostalgic Air (USA)** looked likely to benefit a good deal from this. (5/1)

## 586 ANGERTON (S) APPRENTICE H'CAP (0-60) (3-Y.O+) (Class G)

3-25 (3-29) **1m (round)** £2,189.50 (£622.00: £308.50) Stalls: Low GOING: 0.07 sec per fur (G)

| | Horse | Dist | Pos | SP | RR | SF |
|---|---|---|---|---|---|---|
| *62*[13] | **Dance of Joy (42)** (JMCarr) **4-8-4**(7)ow2 AColgan(4) (hdwy 3f out: hmpd over 1f out: r.o to ld wl ins fnl f) | — | **1** | 33/1 | 58 | 30 |
| 561[6] | **No Submission (USA) (35)** (DWChapman) **10-8-4v** JoHunnam(6) (lw: chsd ldrs: hung lft over 1f out: led ins fnl f: hdd & nt qckn towards fin) | ½ | **2** | 8/1[2] | 50 | 24 |
| *431*[8] | **Langtonian (28)** (JLEyre) **7-7-8b**(3) AngelaGallimore(19) (b.nr hind: dwlt: sn in tch: led over 1f out tl ins fnl f: no ex) | 4 | **3** | 20/1 | 35 | 9 |
| | **Shareoftheaction (45)** (MrsAMNaughton) **5-9-0** JDennis(7) (in tch: hdwy to chal 1f out: nt qckn) | 1 | **4** | 33/1 | 50 | 24 |
| 491[3] | **Ballard Lady (IRE) (43)** (JSWainwright) **4-8-9**(3) JEdmunds(17) (bhd: c wd st: styd on: nrst fin) | 1¼ | **5** | 7/2[1] | 46 | 20 |
| 439[17] | **Master Ofthe House (59)** (MDHammond) **10-9-4**(10) DHayden(9) (s.s: r.o fnl 3f: nrst fin) | ¾ | **6** | 10/1[3] | 60 | 34 |
| 522[8] | **Dispol Conqueror (IRE) (42)** (GROldroyd) **3-7-3**(7) RFfrench(10) (a.p: one pce fnl 3f) | 1 | **7** | 33/1 | 41 | — |
| | **Move Smartly (IRE) (50)** (FHLee) **6-9-5** GFaulkner(16) (lw: cl up: led over 2f tl over 1f out: wknd) | 3 | **8** | 10/1[3] | 43 | 17 |
| *301*[11] | **Glenvally (40)** (BWMurray) **5-8-6v**(3) CScudder(5) (hdwy 3f out: nt rch ldrs) | ½ | **9** | 16/1 | 32 | 6 |
| 561[13] | **Pash (42)** (CWFairhurst) **4-8-6v**(5) PDoe(2) (hdwy on ins 3f out: hmpd over 1f out: n.d) | 1¼ | **10** | 20/1 | 32 | 6 |
| | **Here Comes Herbie (30)** (WStorey) **4-7-6**(7) CCogan(13) (in tch: c wd st: sn rdn & btn) | 1¾ | **11** | 12/1 | 16 | — |
| 505[9] | **Self Expression (51)** (MrsJRRamsden) **8-9-6** OliverCasey(11) (bhd: c wd st: n.d) | hd | **12** | 7/2[1] | 37 | 11 |
| | **Hats of to Hilda (45)** (MrsMReveley) **4-8-9**(5) RSmith(15) (lw: n.d) | hd | **13** | 12/1 | 31 | 5 |
| 477[15] | **Sallyoreally (IRE) (28)** (WStorey) **5-7-6**(5) RMullen(18) (led tl hdd & wknd over 2f out) | 1 | **14** | 14/1 | 12 | — |
| 540[7] | **Phantom Dancer (IRE) (52)** (JBerry) **3-7-12**(8)ow3 JoanneWebster(8) (cl up tl wknd over 2f out) | hd | **15** | 20/1 | 35 | — |
| *145*[6] | **Hunza Story (43)** (NPLittmoden) **4-8-4**(8) JBramhill(14) (b.hind: nvr bttr than mid div) | nk | **16** | 16/1 | 26 | — |
| | **Four Lane Flyer (47)** (EJAlston) **4-8-6**(10) CHalliwell(3) (dwlt: plld hrd: a bhd) | 7 | **17** | 25/1 | 16 | — |
| | **Napoleon's Return (55)** (AHarrison) **3-7-13**(10) JennyBenson(12) (in tch 5f: wknd) | 3½ | **18** | 12/1 | 17 | — |
| | | | | (SP 142.2%) | **18 Rn** | |

**1m 46.1** (7.10) CSF £286.28 CT £5,097.22 TOTE £53.10: £8.40 £1.80 £3.70 £9.90 (£312.10) Trio £270.30; £342.74 to Uttoxeter 9/3/96
OWNER Mrs Tina Carr (MALTON) BRED Sir Gordon Brunton
LONG HANDICAP Dispol Conqueror (IRE) 7-8
WEIGHT FOR AGE 3yo-15lb
No bid

**Dance of Joy**, despite getting into a bumping match entering the final two furlongs, made up a lot of ground and kept up the gallop to settle it late on. (33/1)
**No Submission (USA)** almost got it right on turf for once, but was inclined to hang when the pressure was on, and was then just worried out of it. (8/1: 6/1-9/1)
**Langtonian** is a law unto himself. He ran his best race for some time and obviously has to be considered when in this mood, but he is certainly not one to trust. (20/1)
**Shareoftheaction** put in his best effort first time out last season and should be treated with caution until he shows some consistency this time. (33/1)
**491 Ballard Lady (IRE)** had an impossible task in trying to come from last approaching the turn, and did remarkably well to finish so close. Easier ground or a bit further would probably help. (7/2: op 8/1)
**Master Ofthe House** fell out of the stalls and did pretty well to finish so close. (10/1)
**Move Smartly (IRE)** travelled well for much of the trip but just failed to get home. He should be better for the run. (10/1: op 6/1)
**Sallyoreally (IRE)** (14/1: op 8/1)

## 587 NEWCASTLE RACES FREE HOPPER H'CAP (0-80) (3-Y.O+) (Class D)

3-55 (4-01) **5f** £3,680.00 (£1,115.00: £545.00: £260.00) Stalls: High GOING: 0.07 sec per fur (G)

| | | | | SP | RR | SF |
|---|---|---|---|---|---|---|
| *418[6]* | **Kira (52)** (JLEyre) **6-7-11**(3) NVarley(1) (b.off hind: racd far side: led after 2f: clr over 1f out: drvn out) | — | **1** | 13/2 | 63 | 38 |
| 507[2] | **Plum First (62)** (LRLloyd-James) **6-8-3**(7) KimberleyHart(4) (b.hind: bhd far side: hdwy over 1f out: r.o wl) | ¾ | **2** | 8/1 | 71 | 46 |
| 475[12] | **La Suquet (72)** (NTinkler) **4-9-6** TIves(3) (cl up far side: nt qckn appr fnl f) | 2 | **3** | 20/1 | 74 | 49 |
| 475[4] | **Captain Carat (61)** (MrsJRRamsden) **5-8-9** KFallon(15) (b.nr fore: racd stands' side: hdwy 2f out: r.o u.p: nrst fin) | nk | **4** | 6/1[3] | 62 | 37 |
| 475[2] | **Bollin Harry (68)** (TDEasterby) **4-9-2** MBirch(13) (lw: cl up stands' side: kpt on fnl 2f: nvr able to chal) | 1 | **5** | 5/1[2] | 66 | 41 |
| | **Beau Venture (USA) (69)** (FHLee) **8-9-3** RLappin(2) (prom far side: hdwy 2f out: sn btn) | ½ | **6** | 16/1 | 65 | 40 |
| | **Stuffed (60)** (MWEasterby) **4-8-8** KDarley(10) (lw: racd stands' side: chsd ldrs: effrt ½-wy: r.o one pce) | nk | **7** | 4/1[1] | 56 | 31 |
| | **Colway Rake (71)** (JWWatts) **5-9-5b** NConnorton(17) (bhd stands' side: hdwy 2f out: no imp) | ½ | **8** | 12/1 | 65 | 40 |
| | **Belinda Blue (50)** (RAFahey) **4-7-5**(7)ow2 MartinDwyer(12) (cl up stands' side tl wknd fnl 1½f) | 1 | **9** | 20/1 | 41 | 14 |
| 475[13] | **Shadow Jury (67)** (DWChapman) **6-9-1b** LCharnock(6) (chsd ldrs far side tl btn wl over 1f out) | 1½ | **10** | 16/1 | 53 | 28 |
| 475[11] | **Saddlehome (USA) (80)** (TDBarron) **7-10-0** JFanning(5) (racd far side: nvr trbld ldrs) | 1¾ | **11** | 10/1 | 60 | 35 |
| 505[10] | **Craigie Boy (49)** (NBycroft) **6-7-11** TWilliams(16) (bhd stands' side: hdwy 2f out: n.d) | 1½ | **12** | 20/1 | 25 | — |
| *357[10]* | **White Sorrel (63)** (AHarrison) **5-8-4**(7) GFaulkner(14) (racd stands' side: spd 3f) | 1¼ | **13** | 16/1 | 35 | 10 |
| 443[13] | **Ramsey Hope (76)** (CWFairhurst) **3-8-13** NKennedy(19) (racd stands' side: n.d) | nk | **14** | 33/1 | 47 | 11 |
| 475[7] | **Ansellman (72)** (JBerry) **6-9-1b**(5) PRoberts(9) (cl up stands' side tl outpcd fnl 2f) | 1½ | **15** | 14/1 | 38 | 13 |
| *343[6]* | **Margaretrose Anna (50)** (EJAlston) **4-7-12** NCarlisle(18) (led stands' side to ½-wy: grad wknd) | 2 | **16** | 25/1 | 9 | — |
| 443[18] | **Imp Express (IRE) (75)** (GMMoore) **3-8-12** DaleGibson(8) (racd far side: n.d) | 1½ | **17** | 33/1 | 30 | — |
| | **Insider Trader (77)** (MrsJRRamsden) **5-9-4v**(7) TFinn(7) (led far side 2f: sn wknd) | 4 | **18** | 20/1 | 19 | — |
| *139[8]* | **Bajan Frontier (IRE) (48)** (FHLee) **4-7-3**(7) RMullen(11) (dwlt: racd stands' side: a bhd) | 1¾ | **19** | 33/1 | — | — |

(SP 148.2%) **19 Rn**

**61.5 secs** (3.10) CSF £63.62 CT £648.33 TOTE £9.70: £1.80 £2.30 £6.90 £2.30 (£33.20) Trio £196.50 OWNER Mr J. E. Wilson (HAMBLETON) BRED J. S. Bell
LONG HANDICAP Belinda Blue 7-7 Bajan Frontier (IRE) 7-3
WEIGHT FOR AGE 3yo-11lb

**Kira**, on the favoured far side, went for home a long way out and, although never looking likely to be caught, she was fast coming to the end of her tether. (13/2)
**507 Plum First** could have done with another furlong as he made up heaps of ground in the last quarter-mile but too late to make it. (8/1)
**La Suquet** had her chances throughout but lacked the speed to take them. (20/1)
**475 Captain Carat** ran a cracker up the stands' side but, despite some strong assistance, could never get into it. With a better draw, he probably would have won this, despite this trip being short of his best. (6/1)
**475 Bollin Harry** ran really well up the stands' side but the draw was always too big a disadvantage. (5/1)
**Beau Venture (USA)**, having his first run of the season, was always in the right place but never really firing. (16/1)
**Stuffed** (4/1: op 6/1)

## 588 BELSAY MEDIAN AUCTION MAIDEN STKS (3-Y.O) (Class E)

4-25 (4-27) **1m 4f 93y** £2,853.00 (£864.00: £422.00: £201.00) Stalls: Low GOING: 0.07 sec per fur (G)

| | | | | SP | RR | SF |
|---|---|---|---|---|---|---|
| | **Athenry** (JPearce) **3-9-0** GBardwell(3) (lw: chal 7f out: sn rdn: led over 2f out: drvn clr: eased towards fin) | — | **1** | 1/2[1] | 95+ | 44 |
| | **Disallowed (IRE) (74)** (MBell) **3-8-4**(7)ow2 GFaulkner(5) (led tl hdd over 2f out: rdn & no ex) | 10 | **2** | 3/1[2] | 79 | 26 |
| | **Phar Closer** (WTKemp) **3-8-9** KFallon(1) (outpcd ½-wy: no imp after) | 25 | **3** | 33/1 | 45 | — |
| | **Comic's Future (USA)** (PWChapple-Hyam) **3-9-0** KDarley(4) (w'like: scope: bit bkwd: cl up tl rdn & wknd over 6f out) | dist | **4** | 4/1[3] | — | — |
| *427[10]* | **Topanoora Bay (IRE)** (MrsVAAconley) **3-9-0** TIves(2) (plld hrd: sn cl up: wknd 6f out) | 14 | **5** | 33/1 | — | — |

(SP 117.5%) **5 Rn**

**2m 46.8** (9.30) CSF £2.75 TOTE £1.70: £1.10 £2.30 (£2.20) OWNER Mr A. J. Thompson (NEWMARKET) BRED Jeff Pearce

**Athenry** was flat out by halfway, but all he does is stay and, once he got his head in front over two furlongs out, he forged clear to win pulling up. (1/2)
**Disallowed (IRE)** looked to be going better than the winner for much of the trip until completely outstayed in the last two furlongs. (3/1)
**Phar Closer**, feeling the pace by halfway, was soon well outclassed. (33/1)
**Comic's Future (USA)**, a reasonable-looking sort, needed this and showed nothing. (4/1: op 9/4)

## 589 BYWELL H'CAP (0-85) (3-Y.O+) (Class D)

4-55 (4-59) **7f** £3,696.25 (£1,120.00: £547.50: £261.25) Stalls: High GOING: 0.07 sec per fur (G)

| | | | | SP | RR | SF |
|---|---|---|---|---|---|---|
| | **Master Charter (58)** (MrsJRRamsden) **4-8-5** KFallon(9) (racd far side: hdwy ½-wy: led appr fnl f: sn pushed clr) | — | **1** | 6/1[2] | 71 | 55 |
| 450[14] | **Barrel of Hope (73)** (JLEyre) **4-9-6b** RLappin(7) (led far side: hdd appr fnl f: no ex) | 3½ | **2** | 14/1 | 78 | 62 |
| | **Sagebrush Roller (77)** (JWWatts) **8-9-10** NConnorton(3) (racd far side: hdwy 3f out: styd on nr fin) | 1 | **3** | 8/1 | 80 | 64 |
| *513** | **High Premium (70)** (RAFahey) **8-9-3** ACulhane(12) (lw: racd far side: a chsng ldrs: rdn over 2f out: one pce) | 2 | **4** | 6/1[2] | 68 | 52 |
| 450[13] | **Night Wink (USA) (80)** (DNicholls) **4-9-6**(7) MartinDwyer(19) (led stands' side: kpt on fnl 2f: no ch w ldrs) | 2 | **5** | 10/1 | 74 | 58 |
| | **Halmanerror (70)** (MrsJRRamsden) **6-9-3** NKennedy(20) (racd stands' side: prom: kpt on wl fnl 2f: no imp) | s.h | **6** | 14/1 | 64 | 48 |

| | | | | SP | RR | SF |
|---|---|---|---|---|---|---|
| | **Crystal Falls (IRE) (80)** (JJO'Neill) **3-8-13** SDWilliams(2) (racd far side: chsd ldrs tl rdn & btn 2f out) | 1¼ | **7** | 12/1 | 71 | 41 |
| | **Scaraben (74)** (SEKettlewell) **8-9-7** GBardwell(1) (racd far side: hdwy ½-wy: one pce fnl 2f) | 2 | **8** | 5/1 [1] | 60 | 44 |
| *153[9]* | **Bogart (55)** (CWFairhurst) **5-8-2v[1]** TWilliams(15) (lw: racd stands' side: nvr rchd ldrs) | ½ | **9** | 33/1 | 40 | 24 |
| | **Flyaway Blues (56)** (MrsMReveley) **4-8-3** DeanMcKeown(17) (lw: racd stands' side: n.d) | nk | **10** | 25/1 | 40 | 24 |
| | **Parliament Piece (69)** (DNicholls) **10-8-9**(7) OliverCasey(4) (racd far side: nvr trbld ldrs) | 4 | **11** | 20/1 | 44 | 28 |
| | **Too Hasty (80)** (TDEasterby) **3-8-13** MBirch(10) (racd far side: outpcd & bhd fr ½-wy) | 1 | **12** | 16/1 | 53 | 23 |
| | **Blue Bomber (73)** (TDBarron) **5-9-6** KDarley(11) (racd far side: cl up tl wknd fnl 2f) | 3 | **13** | 7/1 [3] | 39 | 23 |
| | **Amron (70)** (JBerry) **9-9-3** NCarlisle(8) (racd far side: dwlt: hdwy ½-wy: wknd 2f out) | hd | **14** | 20/1 | 36 | 20 |
| | **Rymer's Rascal (62)** (EJAlston) **4-8-9** LCharnock(14) (bit bkwd: racd stands' side: hld up: n.d) | nk | **15** | 33/1 | 27 | 11 |
| 505[16] | **Birchwood Sun (63)** (MDods) **6-8-10** VHalliday(13) (racd far side: sme hdwy 2f out: n.d) | 1 | **16** | 33/1 | 26 | 10 |
| | **Tawafij (USA) (80)** (TDyer) **7-9-6**(7) GFaulkner(6) (s.s: hdwy ½-wy: wknd fnl 2f) | ¾ | **17** | 14/1 | 41 | 25 |
| 439[21] | **Eight Sharp (IRE) (75)** (MDHammond) **4-9-8** JFanning(5) (racd far side: bhd fr ½-wy) | ½ | **18** | 25/1 | 35 | 19 |
| | **Somerton Boy (IRE) (77)** (PCalver) **6-9-10** DaleGibson(16) (prom stands' side 4f) | 4 | **19** | 16/1 | 28 | 12 |
| | **Call Me I'm Blue (IRE) (81)** (NTinkler) **6-10-0** TIves(18) (bit bkwd: racd stands' side: cl up 4f: wknd) | 2 | **20** | 20/1 | 27 | 11 |
| | | | | (SP 148.2%) | **20 Rn** | |

**1m 27.9** (3.40) CSF £94.19 CT £657.11 TOTE £8.10: £1.80 £2.70 £3.10 £2.70 (£64.30) Trio £225.70 OWNER Mr Jonathan Ramsden (THIRSK) BRED Carlton Consultants Ltd

WEIGHT FOR AGE 3yo-14lb

**Master Charter** had the draw that mattered and produced a run from halfway to win in tremendous style. He looks likely to go on from here. (6/1: op 3/1)

**Barrel of Hope** attempted to make all up the favoured far side, and had the field spread-eagled by halfway, but he was well outclassed in the final furlong. (14/1)

**Sagebrush Roller** ran pretty well but was never quite sharp enough to make his presence felt. This run should improve him. (8/1)

**513* High Premium** looked a picture and ran pretty well, but lacked the pace to make any real impression. (6/1)

**Night Wink (USA)** was the winner on the unfavoured stands' side and was probably second best on merit. (10/1)

**Halmanerror** ran a super race on the stands' side and is one to keep in mind. (14/1)

**Crystal Falls (IRE)** had the right draw but, over this shorter trip, was always struggling with the pace. (12/1)

**Scaraben**, in the form of his life last season, showed here he is again in good heart. He will probably need further than this. (5/1: op 12/1)

T/Plpt: £108.30 (74.78 Tckts). T/Qdpt: £24.50 (19.32 Tckts). AA

## 0522-NOTTINGHAM (L-H) (Good to firm, Good patches)

## Monday April 8th

WEATHER: overcast WIND: slt against

### 590 EASTER EGG (S) STKS (2-Y.O) (Class G)

2-20 (2-20) **5f 13y** £1,932.00 (£532.00: £252.00) Stalls: High GOING: 0.22 sec per fur (G)

| | | | | SP | RR | SF |
|---|---|---|---|---|---|---|
| | **Folly Foot Fred** (BRMillman) **2-8-8**(3) SDrowne(8) (leggy: lt-f: bhd & outpcd: hdwy & wnt lft 2f out: rdn & veered rt ent fnl f: str run to ld cl home) | — | **1** | 8/1 | 50 | — |
| *533[4]* | **Dancing Star (IRE)** (PDEvans) **2-8-6** JFortune(1) (a.p: led 2f out tl wl ins fnl f) | 1 | **2** | 9/1 | 42 | — |
| *533[6]* | **Chilled Wine** (NBycroft) **2-8-6** PRobinson(2) (prom: ev ch 1f out: one pce ins fnl f) | 1¾ | **3** | 33/1 | 36 | — |
| 446[7] | **Nattie** (AGNewcombe) **2-8-11** JQuinn(6) (lw: hdwy 2f out: nvr nr to chal) | ¾ | **4** | 8/1 | 39 | — |
| | **I Can't Remember** (JBerry) **2-8-11** JWeaver(5) (neat: swvd lft s: w ldrs: rdn 2f out: btn whn hmpd appr fnl f) | 2½ | **5** | 7/4 [1] | 31 | — |
| | **Emmas Breeze** (CADwyer) **2-8-6** KRutter(7) (lt-f: wl bhd tl sme late hdwy) | hd | **6** | 7/2 [3] | 26 | — |
| *533** | **Lawful Find (IRE)** (RHollinshead) **2-8-11**(5) FLynch(3) (prom: ev ch 2f out: sn rdn & wknd) | 1¼ | **7** | 3/1 [2] | 32 | — |
| 465[7] | **Dozen Roses** (TMJones) **2-8-3**(3) AWhelan(9) (b: led 3f: sn rdn & outpcd) | 4 | **8** | 16/1 | 9 | — |
| | | | | (SP 124.6%) | **8 Rn** | |

**66.2 secs** (7.60) CSF £72.36 TOTE £12.40: £1.90 £1.90 £3.90 (£80.40) Trio £64.00; £72.21 to Uttoxeter 9/4/96 OWNER Mr Derek Dymond (CULLOMPTON) BRED B. Byford

Bt in 6,200 gns

**Folly Foot Fred**, a half-brother to a couple of winners, was very skittish when mounted in the paddock. He ran very green inside the final quarter-mile, but he still had the ability to put his stamp on proceedings nearing the line. (8/1)

**533 Dancing Star (IRE)**, making a quick reappearance, was in the firing-line all the way and was a shade unfortunate to get touched off close home. She is a very lightly-made filly who will need to strike early. (9/1: op 6/1)

**481 Chilled Wine**, the most experienced in the field, pushed the pace and had every chance until tapped for speed inside the final 50 yards. (33/1)

**Nattie** was again only getting into top gear in the latter stages, and he will come into his own when tackling a longer trip. (8/1)

**I Can't Remember**, a neatly-turned colt who came out of the traps sideways, showed up well but was in trouble and beaten when his ground was taken approaching the final furlong. (7/4)

**Emmas Breeze** was taken off her legs for most of the way, but she kept persevering and was pegging them back inside the distance. (7/2: op 2/1)

**533* Lawful Find (IRE)** (3/1: 2/1-100/30)

### 591 ROBIN HOOD MEDIAN AUCTION MAIDEN STKS (3-Y.O) (Class E)

2-50 (2-55) **5f 13y** £3,106.00 (£861.00: £412.00) Stalls: High GOING: 0.22 sec per fur (G)

| | | | | SP | RR | SF |
|---|---|---|---|---|---|---|
| | **Fond Embrace (74)** (HCandy) **3-8-9** JWeaver(3) (mde virtually all: shkn up appr fnl f: r.o wl) | — | **1** | 11/2 | 76 | 47 |
| 467[3] | **Pride of Brixton (76)** (GLewis) **3-9-0** GDuffield(13) (lw: w ldrs: ev ch tl rdn & unable qckn fnl f) | ¾ | **2** | Evens [1] | 79 | 50 |
| | **Watch The Fire** (JEBanks) **3-8-9** JQuinn(10) (w'like: bit bkwd: hdwy ½-wy: rdn & kpt on fnl f) | 1½ | **3** | 7/2 [2] | 69 | 40 |
| 524[3] | **Solo Symphony (IRE)** (PWChapple-Hyam) **3-8-9** RHills(8) (prom: rdn 2f out: one pce) | 4 | **4** | 4/1 [3] | 56 | 27 |
| 458[3] | **Frontman (IRE)** (TDBarron) **3-9-0** JFortune(9) (prom: rdn over 1f out: eased whn btn fnl f) | s.h | **5** | 6/1 | 61 | 32 |
| | **Princess Efisio** (BAMcMahon) **3-8-4**(5) LNewton(7) (nt grwn: bit bkwd: outpcd: nvr nr ldrs) | 6 | **6** | 20/1 | 37 | 8 |
| 524[9] | **Bag And A Bit** (BJMeehan) **3-8-9** MTebbutt(4) (chsd ldrs: rdn along ½-wy: sn wknd) | 7 | **7** | 25/1 | 15 | — |
| | **Summer Princess** (GFierro) **3-8-9** PRobinson(11) (leggy: scope: bit bkwd: outpcd: a bhd) | 2 | **8** | 20/1 | 9 | — |
| | **Feet On Fire** (WMBrisbourne) **3-8-6**(3) PMcCabe(1) (small: unf: bkwd: carried lft s: a bhd) | nk | **9** | 33/1 | 8 | — |
| | **Gloria Imperator (IRE)** (ABMulholland) **3-9-0** MMcAndrew(2) (w'like: scope: swvd bdly lft s: a bhd & outpcd) | 3½ | **10** | 33/1 | 2 | — |
| | **Quinta Boy** (JBerry) **3-8-9**(5) PFessey(12) (unf: trckd ldrs to ½-wy: sn lost tch: t.o) | 5 | **11** | 20/1 | — | — |

| Form | Horse | Dist | Pos | SP | RR | SF |
|---|---|---|---|---|---|---|
| *355[10]* | *Spirit of Sport (AGNewcombe) 3-8-6(3) SDrowne(5) (Withdrawn not under Starter's orders: unruly at s)* | | **W** | *33/1* | — | — |

(SP 148.8%) **11 Rn**

**62.4 secs** (3.80) CSF £13.72 TOTE £5.80: £1.30 £1.10 £2.30 (£4.90) Trio £10.10 OWNER Cmdr Marten (WANTAGE) BRED Lt-Comdr G. G. Marten

**Fond Embrace**, who will be all the sharper for the run, battled on grimly when strongly pressed throughout the final furlong and deservedly held on. (11/2)

**467 Pride of Brixton**, having his first try at the minimum trip, disputed the lead and had every chance until worried out of it nearing the finish. He is consistent and his turn will come. (Evens)

**Watch The Fire**, who comes from a winning family, was staying on strongly in the closing stages and will be all the wiser next time. (7/2)

**524 Solo Symphony (IRE)** found this race coming too soon and she was flat to the boards and in trouble before reaching the final furlong. (4/1)

**458 Frontman (IRE)**, brought back to the minimum trip, pressed the leaders but was unable to cope when the chips were down. (6/1: op 3/1)

## 592 'FAMILY DAY OUT' H'CAP (0-70) (3-Y.O+) (Class E)

3-20 (3-24) **6f 15y** £3,598.10 (£1,001.60: £482.30) Stalls: High GOING: 0.22 sec per fur (G)

| Form | Horse | Dist | Pos | SP | RR | SF |
|---|---|---|---|---|---|---|
| | **Double Splendour (IRE) (70)** (PSFelgate) **6-10-0** GDuffield(9) (hld up centre: shkn up to ld wl over 1f out: drvn clr) | — | **1** | 9/2[1] | 89+ | 45 |
| *357[2]* | **Cretan Gift (60)** (NPLittmoden) **5-9-4v** TGMcLaughlin(17) (hdwy stands' side over 1f out: fin wl) | 4 | **2** | 5/1[2] | 69 | 25 |
| 479* | **Bargash (66)** (PDEvans) **4-9-10** JFortune(15) (swtg: hdwy stands' side wl over 1f out: nrst fin) | hd | **3** | 7/1 | 74 | 30 |
| *511[2]* | **Mustn't Grumble (IRE) (61)** (MissSJWilton) **6-9-5** MTebbutt(16) (led stands' side: unable qckn fnl f) | 3 | **4** | 10/1 | 61 | 17 |
| *418[5]* | **Always Grace (64)** (MissGayKelleway) **4-9-5**(3) AWhelan(13) (racd stands' side: hdwy fnl 2f: nvr nrr) | 2 | **5** | 14/1 | 59 | 15 |
| | **Giggleswick Girl (59)** (MRChannon) **5-8-12**(5) PPMurphy(18) (spd stands' side over 4f) | s.h | **6** | 10/1 | 54 | 10 |
| *425[3]* | **Dissentor (IRE) (47)** (JAGlover) **4-8-5v** PRobinson(8) (prom: ev ch 2f out: sn rdn & btn) | nk | **7** | 14/1 | 41 | — |
| *534[5]* | **Arc Lamp (45)** (JAGlover) **10-8-3** CRutter(4) (hdwy wl over 1f out: nrst fin) | 3 | **8** | 16/1 | 31 | — |
| *431[2]* | **Maybank (IRE) (58)** (BAMcMahon) **4-8-11**(5) LNewton(11) (w ldrs stands' side 4f) | 5 | **9** | 11/2[3] | 31 | — |
| | **Oggi (66)** (PJMakin) **5-9-10** JWeaver(7) (bkwd: led tl hdd & wknd wl over 1f out) | ¾ | **10** | 16/1 | 37 | — |
| 480[16] | **Penny's Wishing (47)** (NBycroft) **4-8-2**(3) PMcCabe(5) (nvr trbld ldrs) | ½ | **11** | 25/1 | 17 | — |
| *416[6]* | **Square Deal (FR) (65)** (SRBowring) **5-9-4**(5) CTeague(1) (swtg: sn pushed along: a bhd) | 1¼ | **12** | 11/1 | 31 | — |
| | **Mousehole (67)** (RGuest) **4-9-8**(3) SDrowne(6) (bit bkwd: outpcd: a bhd) | 1 | **13** | 14/1 | 31 | — |
| *500** | **Berge (IRE) (64)** (WAO'Gorman) **5-9-8b** EmmaO'Gorman(2) (lw: chsd ldrs 4f: sn wknd) | 2 | **14** | 5/1[2] | 23 | — |
| *273[9]* | **Diamond Bangle (38)** (CCElsey) **4-7-5**(5) MBaird(14) (prom to ½-wy: sn lost tch) | 2½ | **15** | 33/1 | — | — |
| *278[8]* | **Thick as Thieves (60)** (RonaldThompson) **4-8-13**(5) PFessey(3) (outpcd: a in rr) | ¾ | **16** | 20/1 | 10 | — |
| *414[3]* | **Black And Amber (54)** (PRWebber) **4-8-7**(5) FLynch(10) (swtg: racd centre: a in rr) | 1¾ | **17** | 16/1 | — | — |

(SP 155.1%) **17 Rn**

**1m 16.5** (6.00) CSF £32.74 CT £169.00 TOTE £5.30: £1.40 £1.60 £3.10 £2.70 (£25.90) Trio £208.10 OWNER Yorkshire Racing Club Owners Group 1990 (MELTON MOWBRAY) BRED R. McQuillan

LONG HANDICAP Diamond Bangle 6-6

**Double Splendour (IRE)** carried two stone more than when successful in this event last year, but he comprehensively outpointed the opposition for a very easy win on his seasonal debut. (9/2)

**Cretan Gift**, yet to succeed on this surface, was doing all his best work inside the distance, but the winner had taken first run and was not for catching. (5/1)

**479* Bargash** came out of the pack under the stands' rail approaching the final furlong and finished best of all but, on ground plenty fast enough, he could not get in a blow against the winner. (7/1)

**511 Mustn't Grumble (IRE)** made the majority of the running on the stands' side until getting outpaced inside the final furlong. He does look to need all of seven furlongs when the ground is so lively. (10/1)

**Always Grace** could not muster the speed to land a blow, but she did stay on and another success is way overdue. (14/1)

**Giggleswick Girl**, runner-up in this race last year, did look well wound up for this seasonal debut and showed with the pace on the stands' side until feeling the strain approaching the final furlong. (10/1)

**Dissentor (IRE)**, fighting for supremacy two furlongs out, could not lift his pace when the final battle developed but showed enough to suggest there is more success to come. (14/1)

**Maybank (IRE)** (11/2: op 10/1)

## 593 EASTER BONNET H'CAP (0-80) (3-Y.O) (Class D)

3-50 (3-51) **1m 1f 213y** £3,817.50 (£1,140.00: £545.00: £247.50) Stalls: Low GOING minus 0.04 sec per fur (G)

| Form | Horse | Dist | Pos | SP | RR | SF |
|---|---|---|---|---|---|---|
| | **General Macarthur (75)** (JLDunlop) **3-9-2** GDuffield(5) (h.d.w: hmpd & snatched up sn after s: hdwy over 2f out: led wl ins fnl f: all out) | — | **1** | 6/1[3] | 85 | 26 |
| | **Nabhaan (IRE) (74)** (DMorley) **3-9-1** RHills(7) (bit bkwd: hld up: hdwy 2f out: ev ch ins fnl f: r.o) | nk | **2** | 8/1 | 84 | 25 |
| 471[3] | **Montecristo (68)** (RGuest) **3-8-4**(5) FLynch(1) (hld up: hdwy to ld 1f out: sn hdd: no ex) | 1¾ | **3** | 6/1[3] | 75 | 16 |
| 444[8] | **Northern Motto (58)** (MrsJRRamsden) **3-7-8**(5) PFessey(2) (hdwy 3f out: styd on u.p appr fnl f) | 2½ | **4** | 10/1 | 61 | 2 |
| 447[6] | **Al's Alibi (74)** (WRMuir) **3-9-1** Jean-PierreLopez(11) (lw: prom: rdn over 1f out: one pce) | 2½ | **5** | 16/1 | 73 | 14 |
| *510** | **Law Dancer (IRE) (75)** (TGMills) **3-9-2** JFortune(9) (chsd ldrs: ev ch 2f out: unable qckn) | 1¾ | **6** | 6/1[3] | 71 | 12 |
| | **Navigate (USA) (80)** (RHannon) **3-9-4**(3) AWhelan(4) (trckd ldrs: led 2f out to 1f out: sn rdn: one pce) | nk | **7** | 8/1 | 75 | 16 |
| | **Ailesbury Hill (USA) (76)** (PWChapple-Hyam) **3-8-12**(5) LNewton(8) (trckd ldrs: rdn over 2f out: sn btn) | 3½ | **8** | 9/1 | 66 | 7 |
| | **No Cliches (80)** (GLewis) **3-9-7** PRobinson(6) (hld up: effrt & n.m.r over 2f out: no imp) | 1¼ | **9** | 9/4[1] | 68 | 9 |
| *390** | **Chief Mouse (73)** (RCharlton) **3-9-0** JWeaver(12) (in tch: effrt ent st: sn drvn along & wknd) | nk | **10** | 4/1[2] | 60 | 1 |
| *402[5]* | **Meltemison (72)** (CEBrittain) **3-8-10**(3) PMcCabe(10) (swtg: led after 1f to 2f out: sn rdn & wknd) | hd | **11** | 16/1 | 59 | — |
| | **Compass Pointer (64)** (JMPEustace) **3-8-5** CRutter(3) (bit bkwd: led 1f: prom tl rdn & wknd over 2f out) | 1¼ | **12** | 8/1 | 49 | — |

(SP 157.8%) **12 Rn**

**2m 11.2** (8.70) CSF £65.06 CT £305.64 TOTE £9.30: £2.70 £1.80 £2.00 (£36.60) Trio £105.30 OWNER Mr Ian Cameron (ARUNDEL) BRED Lady Richard Wellesley and Grange Nominees

**General Macarthur** has developed into a fine-looking colt and this hard-fought first success could be the first of many. (6/1)

**Nabhaan (IRE)** did not look quite as forward as the winner but he ran a race full of promise, only just failing to collect. He will stay further and could be very much on the upgrade. (8/1)

**471 Montecristo**, looking very lean, definitely had the edge in fitness. However, he was caught out by this step back to ten furlongs, and was tapped for toe in an all-out battle to the line. (6/1)

**444 Northern Motto** turned in his best display yet, staying on strongly after looking to have shot his bolt entering the final quarter-mile. (10/1)

**447 Al's Alibi** should have no trouble staying this trip, but his two runs to date would suggest that he does lack stamina. (16/1)

**510* Law Dancer (IRE)**, in with every chance two furlongs out, looked to be travelling as well as any but, once the pressure was on, he was unable to respond, and was easily brushed aside. (6/1)
**Navigate (USA)**, who will strip fitter for the spin, was only outpointed in the latter stages and that initial success should not be long in coming. (8/1)
**Compass Pointer** (8/1: op 12/1)

## 594 EASTER BUNNY H'CAP (0-70) (3-Y.O) (Class E)

4-20 (4-22) **1m 6f 15y** £2,950.60 (£816.60: £389.80) Stalls: Low GOING minus 0.04 sec per fur (G)

| | | | | SP | RR | SF |
|---|---|---|---|---|---|---|
| *519[3]* | **Siege Perilous (IRE) (58)** (SCWilliams) **3-8-7**(3) AWhelan(3) (hld up in rr: hdwy ent st: led 2f out: hrd drvn: hld on gamely) | — | 1 | 4/1 | 65 | 25 |
| *519[2]* | **Dancing Cavalier (69)** (RHollinshead) **3-9-2**(5) FLynch(1) (lw: hld up in rr: gd hdwy 3f out: str run fnl f: nt rch wnr: fin 3rd, 1¼l: plcd 2nd) | | 2 | 3/1[2] | 73 | 33 |
| 471[8] | **Influence Pedler (51)** (CEBrittain) **3-8-3** GDuffield(4) (swtg: prom: pushed along 3f out: no imp fnl 2f: fin 4th, 5l: plcd 3rd) | | 3 | 11/1 | 49 | 9 |
| 471[2] | **Minnisam (65)** (JLDunlop) **3-9-3** RHills(7) (trckd ldrs: led over 3f out tl over 2f out: kpt on one pce: fin 5th, s.h: plcd 4th) | | 4 | 7/2[3] | 63 | 23 |
| 471[10] | **Rivercare (IRE) (58)** (MJPolglase) **3-8-10** MTebbutt(10) (chsd ldrs: led 6f out to 3f out: sn lost tch: fin 6th, 2½l: plcd 5th) | | 5 | 20/1 | 53 | 13 |
| 483[8] | **General Glow (51)** (NBycroft) **3-8-3**ow2 PRobinson(2) (bit bkwd: a in rr: rdn over 3f out: no imp) | 10 | 7 | 20/1 | 34 | — |
| 483[7] | **Fergal (USA) (44)** (RonaldThompson) **3-7-5**(5) PFessey(8) (prom tl wknd over 3f out: t.o) | 4 | 8 | 33/1 | 23 | — |
| *348[3]* | **Balios (IRE) (69)** (MJohnston) **3-9-7** JWeaver(5) (led 8f: sn rdn along & grad wknd: t.o) | nk | 9 | 5/2[1] | 48 | — |
| 522[15] | **Reef Raider (44)** (NTinkler) **3-7-10** KimTinkler(9) (a bhd: t.o fnl 6f) | dist | 10 | 33/1 | — | — |
| 471[4] | **Atlantic Mist (55)** (BRMillman) **3-8-4**(3) SDrowne(6) (lw: hld up: hdwy over 2f out: styd on u.p ins fnl f: fin 2nd, 1½l: disq: plcd last) | | D | 10/1 | 60 | 20 |

(SP 128.6%) **10 Rn**

**3m 10.4** (11.90) CSF £43.53 CT £129.31 TOTE £7.70: £1.90 £1.70 £2.30 (£15.70) Trio £83.30 OWNER Mr S. Demanuele (NEWMARKET) BRED Miss Honora Corridan
LONG HANDICAP Reef Raider 7-6 Fergal (USA) 7-6
STEWARDS' ENQUIRY Drowne susp. 17-20/4/96 (irresponsible riding).
**519 Siege Perilous (IRE)**, patiently ridden over this extended trip, needed to work hard after striking the front, but he answered his jockey's every call and proved too strong for his pursuers. (4/1)
**519 Dancing Cavalier** produced a determined last-furlong challenge and briefly looked to hold the edge, but he was up against a rival who just would not concede defeat. (3/1)
**Influence Pedler**, a strong, deep-girthed individual, was struggling to hold on two furlongs out and it could be that this lively ground is not for him. (11/1)
**471 Minnisam**, ill at ease cantering to post and troublesome being loaded into the stalls, did poke his nose in front in the straight but the trip seemed to find him out and he had been shaken off below the distance. (7/2: op 9/4)
**471 Atlantic Mist** improved from off the pace over two furlongs out, and stuck on willingly nearing the finish, only to find the winner in no mood to give best. After finishing second, he was disqualified and placed last for causing interference inside the final three furlongs. He stayed on really well and this looks to be his game. (10/1)

## 595 EASTER MONDAY H'CAP (0-70) (3-Y.O) (Class E)

4-50 (4-58) **1m 54y** £3,805.30 (£1,060.80: £511.90) Stalls: Low GOING minus 0.04 sec per fur (G)

| | | | | SP | RR | SF |
|---|---|---|---|---|---|---|
| *428[5]* | **Winston (56)** (JDBethell) **3-8-7**(3) SDrowne(3) (hld up: hdwy over 2f out: swtchd rt: hung lft & r.o to ld wl ins fnl f) | — | 1 | 25/1 | 58 | 31 |
| | **Cerise (IRE) (50)** (CWCElsey) **3-7-13b**(5) FLynch(16) (a.p: ev ch 1f out: kpt on u.p cl home) | ¾ | 2 | 16/1 | 51 | 24 |
| | **Whispering Dawn (62)** (MRChannon) **3-8-11**(5) PPMurphy(12) (hld up: hdwy on ins over 2f out: ev ch ins fnl f: r.o) | hd | 3 | 7/2[1] | 62 | 35 |
| | **Fiona Shann (USA) (53)** (JLDunlop) **3-8-7** GDuffield(6) (trckd ldrs: led wl over 1f out tl wl ins fnl f) | ½ | 4 | 15/2[3] | 52 | 25 |
| 326a[12] | **Daily Risk (66)** (SDow) **3-9-3**(3) AWhelan(17) (swtg: hld up: hdwy over 2f out: no ex wl ins fnl f) | hd | 5 | 14/1 | 65 | 38 |
| *382[2]* | **Yeoman Oliver (66)** (BAMcMahon) **3-9-1**(5) LNewton(8) (lw: trckd ldrs: effrt over 2f out: nt pce to chal) | 1½ | 6 | 9/1 | 62 | 35 |
| | **Ret Frem (IRE) (60)** (MAJarvis) **3-9-0** PRobinson(18) (chsd ldr over 5f: hrd drvn & one pce appr fnl f) | 1¾ | 7 | 10/1 | 53 | 26 |
| | **Farfeste (50)** (DMorris) **3-8-1**(3) PMcCabe(2) (still unf: swtg: hld up & bhd: hdwy 2f out: nvr nrr) | s.h | 8 | 5/1[2] | 43 | 16 |
| | **Petite Heritiere (56)** (MJRyan) **3-8-5**(5) MBaird(10) (in rr tl styd on fnl 2f: nvr nrr) | hd | 9 | 33/1 | 49 | 22 |
| *415[2]* | **Bit of Bother (IRE) (65)** (TDBarron) **3-9-5** JFortune(5) (in tch: effrt 2f out: wknd appr fnl f) | nk | 10 | 5/1[2] | 57 | 30 |
| | **Bright Diamond (58)** (JRArnold) **3-8-12** RHills(4) (b.off fore: b.nr hind: hld up: hdwy on outside 2f out: nt rch ldrs) | hd | 11 | 16/1 | 50 | 23 |
| | **Laughing Buccaneer (57)** (AGFoster) **3-8-4**(7) DLynch(14) (a bhd) | 1 | 12 | 12/1 | 47 | 20 |
| 453[5] | **Knave (65)** (RHannon) **3-8-12**(7) EGreehy(20) (rn v.wd ent st: a bhd) | ½ | 13 | 8/1 | 54 | 27 |
| *421[6]* | **Katie Komaite (67)** (CaptJHWilson) **3-9-7** CRutter(13) (lw: a bhd) | nk | 14 | 20/1 | 55 | 28 |
| | **Mellors (IRE) (65)** (JARToller) **3-9-5** JWeaver(19) (bit bkwd: led tl over 1f out: wknd qckly) | hd | 15 | 12/1 | 53 | 26 |
| | **One Shot (IRE) (60)** (WRMuir) **3-9-0** Jean-PierreLopez(11) (bkwd: nvr nr ldrs) | ½ | 16 | 20/1 | 47 | 20 |
| | **Pleasureland (IRE) (67)** (PJMakin) **3-9-2**(5) RHavlin(9) (mid div tl wknd over 2f out) | 2½ | 17 | 14/1 | 49 | 22 |
| | **Eccentric Dancer (50)** (MPBielby) **3-7-11**(7) TField(7) (bit bkwd: trckd ldrs: rdn 3f out: sn btn) | 1 | 18 | 20/1 | 30 | 3 |
| | **Melos (56)** (RonaldThompson) **3-8-5**(5) PFessey(1) (bit bkwd: a bhd: t.o) | dist | 19 | 33/1 | — | — |

(SP 162.0%) **19 Rn**

**1m 47.4** (6.10) CSF £417.08 CT £1,670.13 TOTE £46.80: £6.30 £6.00 £1.40 £2.50 (£244.90) Trio Not won; £265.39 to Uttoxeter 9/4/96
OWNER Mr John Galvanoni (MIDDLEHAM) BRED Benson Stud
**Winston** produced a sustained challenge down the centre of the track inside the distance, but he hung badly to the left. His jockey did extremely well to keep him straight and balanced, enabling him to forge ahead nearing the post. (25/1)
**Cerise (IRE)** raced at this trip in her first season and showed plenty of promise, but this was possibly her best effort yet, and she would seem to have trained on. (16/1)
**Whispering Dawn** needed to weave her way through a tightly-packed field inside the last quarter-mile and, just when she looked to have struck the front, the relentless surge of the winner proved the last straw. She did try her luck over ten furlongs at the end of last season and it is possible she may need further this term. (7/2)
**Fiona Shann (USA)**, lightly-raced in her first season, appreciated this step up to a mile and produced her best performance yet. She was only worn down inside the last 100 yards and looks a ready-made winner. (15/2: 4/1-8/1)

**326a Daily Risk**, who has enjoyed the warmer climate in the South of France since the turn of the year, delivered his sustained late challenge on the outside throughout the final furlong, but could not quite get to the front. He should not be hard to place. (14/1)
**Yeoman Oliver** has been showing up well on the All-Weather and he was always poised to challenge here but, when it came to the crunch, he was unable to go through with his effort. (9/1)
**Ret Frem (IRE)** needed this but ran much better than his final placing would suggest. He would seem to be getting his act together. (10/1)
**Farfeste** (5/1: op 20/1)
**Bit of Bother (IRE)** lacked the speed to deliver a challenge on this faster ground after being well to the fore throughout. (5/1)
**453 Knave** (8/1: op 5/1)

T/Plpt: £809.90 (8.85 Tckts). T/Qdpt: £42.60 (11.36 Tckts). IM

# WARWICK (L-H) (Good)
## Monday April 8th
WEATHER: cloudy WIND: mod half bhd

## 596 LIONS CLUB INTERNATIONAL MEDIAN AUCTION MAIDEN STKS (2-Y.O F) (Class E)
2-35 (2-37) **5f** £3,015.60 (£898.80: £428.40: £193.20) Stalls: Low GOING minus 0.40 sec per fur (F)

| | | | | SP | RR | SF |
|---|---|---|---|---|---|---|
| | **Connemara (IRE)** (CADwyer) **2-8-8**(3) JStack(10) (leggy: a.p: led over 1f out: easily) | — | **1** | 7/4[1] | 85+ | 30 |
| | **Wait For Rosie** (MRChannon) **2-8-11** RHughes(1) (leggy: a.p: led over 2f out tl over 1f out: no ch w wnr) | 6 | **2** | 7/2[2] | 66 | 11 |
| 446[2] | **Hello Dolly (IRE)** (KTIvory) **2-8-4**(7) CScally(4) (reard s: hdwy over 1f out: rn green: r.o one pce fnl f) | 3 | **3** | 15/2 | 56 | 1 |
| | **Enchantica** (JBerry) **2-8-11** JCarroll(3) (w'like: a.p: edgd rt over 1f out: one pce) | ¾ | **4** | 4/1[3] | 54 | — |
| | **Will To Win** (PGMurphy) **2-8-11** MFenton(6) (lt-f: led over 2f: wknd over 1f out) | s.h | **5** | 33/1 | 54 | — |
| | **Windborn** (KWMcAuliffe) **2-8-6**(5) MHenry(5) (unf: s.s: hdwy over 1f out: nrst fin) | 2 | **6** | 33/1 | 47 | — |
| | **Heavenly Miss (IRE)** (BPalling) **2-8-11** TSprake(8) (unf: chsd ldrs over 3f: btn whn edgd lft ins fnl f) | ½ | **7** | 16/1 | 46 | — |
| | **Northern Girl (IRE)** (BJMeehan) **2-8-11** DeclanO'Shea(7) (bit bkwd: bhd fnl 2f) | 2 | **8** | 12/1 | 39 | — |
| | **Sea Mist (IRE)** (PWChapple-Hyam) **2-8-4**(7) RCody-Boutcher(9) (cmpt: outpcd: t.o) | 15 | **9** | 13/2 | — | — |
| | **Belle Dancer** (TRWall) **2-8-11** NAdams(2) (wl grwn: bit bkwd: s.s: a bhd: t.o) | 2½ | **10** | 20/1 | — | — |

(SP 127.9%) **10 Rn**

**59.8 secs** (1.80) CSF £9.12 TOTE £4.40: £1.80 £1.80 £1.50 (£10.60) Trio £20.90 OWNER Dr A. Haloute (NEWMARKET) BRED Rathasker Stud
**Connemara (IRE)** came from a stable that had a well-backed juvenile winner at Folkestone. Well fancied, having been working well at home, she did her job in fine style and can score again. (7/4: op 3/1)
**Wait For Rosie** found the winner much too smart in the last furlong and a half. (7/2)
**446 Hello Dolly (IRE)** looked inexperienced, despite having had a run, and will probably need a return to selling company. (15/2)
**Enchantica** is out of a half-sister to Lochnager. (4/1)
**Windborn** should be better for the experience. (33/1)
**Northern Girl (IRE)** (12/1: op 5/1)
**Sea Mist (IRE)** (13/2: 4/1-7/1)

## 597 B.B.C. C.W.R. H'CAP (0-70) (3-Y.O) (Class E)
3-05 (3-07) **1m 2f 169y** £3,070.20 (£915.60: £436.80: £197.40) Stalls: Low GOING minus 0.11 sec per fur (G)

| | | | | SP | RR | SF |
|---|---|---|---|---|---|---|
| | **Dhulikhel (50)** (DMarks) **3-7-13**(5) ADaly(3) (a.p: led over 1f out: easily) | — | **1** | 20/1 | 61+ | 31 |
| *381*[3] | **Uoni (54)** (CEBrittain) **3-8-3**(5) MHenry(6) (w ldr: led over 3f out tl over 1f out: no ch w wnr) | 7 | **2** | 4/1[2] | 55 | 25 |
| | **Tintara (IRE) (66)** (BWHills) **3-9-1**(5) JDSmith(4) (hld up & bhd: nt clr run over 3f out: hdwy 2f out: edgd lft over 1f out: r.o one pce) | 2½ | **3** | 4/1[2] | 63 | 33 |
| *503*[4] | **Ivory's Grab Hire (52)** (KTIvory) **3-8-3**(3) JStack(10) (reard s: hdwy 4f out: wknd 2f out) | 6 | **4** | 7/1[3] | 40 | 10 |
| | **Efficacious (IRE) (50)** (CJBenstead) **3-8-4** AMcGlone(1) (bit bkwd: hld up: stdy hdwy on ins 5f out: wknd 2f out) | 1¾ | **5** | 20/1 | 35 | 5 |
| | **Cry Baby (55)** (NTinkler) **3-8-9** JCarroll(11) (bit bkwd: hld up: lost pl over 4f out: n.d after) | nk | **6** | 20/1 | 40 | 10 |
| | **Princely Affair (53)** (MBell) **3-8-7** MFenton(12) (bit bkwd: prom tl rdn & wknd over 3f out) | 1½ | **7** | 14/1 | 36 | 6 |
| | **Quiet Moments (IRE) (49)** (PGMurphy) **3-8-3** NAdams(9) (bkwd: hld up: a bhd) | 2½ | **8** | 25/1 | 28 | — |
| *230*[5] | **Dauphin (IRE) (48)** (WJMusson) **3-8-2** RPrice(2) (b: prom tl wknd over 2f out) | 5 | **9** | 20/1 | 20 | — |
| 447[8] | **Sister Kit (IRE) (67)** (BPalling) **3-9-7** TSprake(8) (prom tl wknd 2f out) | ¾ | **10** | 14/1 | 37 | 7 |
| | **Ship's Dancer (55)** (JLDunlop) **3-8-9** GCarter(7) (bit bkwd: rdn over 6f out: bhd fnl 3f: eased whn btn fnl f) | ¾ | **11** | 11/10[1] | 24 | — |
| *123*[12] | **My Mother's Local (USA) (43)** (KOCunningham-Brown) **3-7-8**(3)ow1 DWright(5) (plld hrd: led 7f: wknd 2f out) | 1½ | **12** | 33/1 | 10 | — |

(SP 139.3%) **12 Rn**

**2m 20.1** (6.60) CSF £106.87 CT £378.64 TOTE £23.20: £4.60 £1.70 £2.10 (£45.90) Trio £57.80 OWNER Mr G. J. King (UPPER LAMBOURN) BRED M. H. D. Madden and Partners
LONG HANDICAP My Mother's Local (USA) 7-3
OFFICIAL EXPLANATION **Ship's Dancer: the jockey reported that the filly was never going.**
**Dhulikhel** won a seven-furlong seller at Brighton last August and relished this first attempt at a longer trip. (20/1)
**Uoni** had finished third on four out of five attempts on the All-Weather during the winter. (4/1)
**Tintara (IRE)**, stepping up in distance, had to be checked briefly when still in last place at the end of the back straight, but should not be considered unlucky. (4/1)
**503 Ivory's Grab Hire**, trying a longer trip, found his stamina limitations exposed in the short home straight. (7/1: op 14/1)
**Efficacious (IRE)** appeared not to stay. (20/1)
**Ship's Dancer** was not fit enough to warrant such a short starting price. (11/10: 5/4-Evens)

## 598 HIGH TENSILE BOLTS H'CAP (0-80) (4-Y.O+) (Class D)
3-35 (3-36) **1m 2f 169y** £4,059.60 (£1,213.80: £581.40: £265.20) Stalls: Low GOING minus 0.11 sec per fur (G)

| | | | | SP | RR | SF |
|---|---|---|---|---|---|---|
| *424*[10] | **Hand of Straw (IRE) (55)** (PGMurphy) **4-8-5v** NAdams(8) (swtg: hld up: reminders 5f out: hdwy 2f out: r.o wl to ld last strides) | — | **1** | 10/1 | 59 | 32 |
| *502*[8] | **Denomination (USA) (58)** (IABalding) **4-8-3**(5) DGriffiths(3) (lw: hld up: hdwy over 3f out: led 1f out: hdd last strides) | ½ | **2** | 16/1 | 61 | 34 |

| Form | Horse | Dist | Pos | SP | RR | SF |
|---|---|---|---|---|---|---|
| 486[6] | **Locorotondo (IRE) (65)** (MBell) **5-9-1** MFenton(10) (a.p: ev ch fnl f: r.o) | hd | **3** | 10/1 | 68 | 41 |
| | **Contrafire (IRE) (70)** (WJarvis) **4-9-1**(5) MHenry(11) (led over 7f out: hdd 1f out: one pce) | 1½ | **4** | 6/1[3] | 71 | 44 |
| | **Domappel (67)** (MrsJCecil) **4-9-0**(3) JStack(7) (hld up: hdwy 6f out: rdn over 3f out: r.o one pce fnl f) | ½ | **5** | 3/1[1] | 67 | 40 |
| 440[16] | **Fairy Knight (78)** (RHannon) **4-10-0** RHughes(6) (hld up: hdwy 3f out: ev ch 1f out: one pce) | s.h | **6** | 7/1 | 78 | 51 |
| 469[13] | **Brown Eyed Girl (49)** (BJMeehan) **4-7-13** DeclanO'Shea(4) (nvr nr to chal) | 2½ | **7** | 12/1 | 45 | 18 |
| 505[6] | **Cee-Jay-Ay (57)** (JBerry) **9-8-7** JCarroll(12) (s.s: hld up: bhd fnl 3f) | 2 | **8** | 7/1 | 50 | 23 |
| *27*[2] | **Secretary of State (53)** (DWPArbuthnot) **10-8-0**(3) DarrenMoffatt(2) (hld up: bhd fnl 3f) | s.h | **9** | 5/1[2] | 46 | 19 |
| *402*[10] | **Young Benson (58)** (BAMcMahon) **4-8-8** GCarter(5) (prom: lost pl 5f out: n.d after) | 5 | **10** | 16/1 | 44 | 17 |
| *553*[8] | **Dance King (67)** (RHarris) **4-8-12**(5) ADaly(1) (led 3f: ev ch 2f out: wknd qckly over 1f out) | 1¼ | **11** | 20/1 | 51 | 24 |
| *512*[3] | **Hill Farm Katie (46)** (WMBrisbourne) **5-7-3**(7) IonaWands(9) (hld up: rdn over 3f out: sn bhd) | 5 | **12** | 20/1 | 23 | — |
| | | | | (SP 128.1%) | | **12 Rn** |

**2m 20.0** (6.50) CSF £147.93 CT £1,510.89 TOTE £13.70: £3.60 £3.30 £3.20 (£924.50) Trio Not won; £217.93 to Uttoxeter 9/4/96 OWNER Mrs Louise Murphy (BRISTOL) BRED M. J. Dargan

LONG HANDICAP Hill Farm Katie 6-13

**Hand of Straw (IRE)** made a successful debut on the sand in a first-time visor, and repeated the trick in the headgear on the turf. (10/1)
**Denomination (USA)** was apparently well fancied by connections and there were some glum faces later on. (16/1)
**486 Locorotondo (IRE)** did not seem to handle the surface on two runs on the sand but bounced back to form with a gallant effort. (10/1)
**Contrafire (IRE)**, a consistent sort, was running off a mark 7lb higher than when he won at Lingfield last August. (6/1)
**Domappel**, who scraped home over hurdles at Haydock in December, may need a shade further. (3/1)
**Fairy Knight** ran well off a mark 7lb higher than his two wins last season. (7/1)

## 599 WARWICK CARNIVAL CLAIMING STKS (3-Y.O) (Class E)

4-05 (4-06) **1m 4f 115y** £2,933.70 (£873.60: £415.80: £186.90) Stalls: Low GOING minus 0.11 sec per fur (G)

| Form | Horse | Dist | Pos | SP | RR | SF |
|---|---|---|---|---|---|---|
| 522[2] | **Belle's Boy (60)** (BPalling) **3-8-12** TSprake(4) (plld hrd: mde all: clr over 1f out: easily) | — | **1** | Evens[1] | 69+ | 27 |
| 483[5] | **Four Weddings (USA) (49)** (MBell) **3-8-8v** MFenton(7) (chsd wnr: no imp fnl 2f) | 6 | **2** | 11/4[2] | 57 | 15 |
| 471[17] | **Shamand (USA) (46)** (BJMeehan) **3-8-10** GCarter(3) (a.p: rdn over 3f out: outpcd over 2f out: styd on fnl f) | 2½ | **3** | 12/1 | 56 | 14 |
| 447[10] | **Poly My Son (IRE)** (MRChannon) **3-9-2** RHughes(6) (prom: rdn over 2f out: wknd over 1f out) | 1¾ | **4** | 7/2[3] | 60 | 18 |
| 494[5] | **Dream of My Life (USA) (39)** (PGMurphy) **3-8-6** NAdams(1) (s.i.s: rdn over 5f out: t.o fnl 4f) | 21 | **5** | 16/1 | 23 | — |
| | **Chillington** (WMBrisbourne) **3-8-5**(5) DGriffiths(5) (bkwd: dropped rr 8f out: t.o fnl 4f) | 5 | **6** | 33/1 | 21 | — |
| | **Scene Stealer** (AKBarrow) **3-8-7** JCarroll(2) (lt-f: unf: a bhd: t.o fnl 4f) | 2½ | **7** | 14/1 | 15 | — |
| | | | | (SP 122.1%) | | **7 Rn** |

**2m 48.2** (9.70) CSF £4.63 TOTE £2.30: £1.60 £2.00 (£2.80) OWNER Mrs M. M. Palling (COWBRIDGE) BRED Mrs M. M. Palling

**522 Belle's Boy** found this a lot less competitive than last week's selling handicap at Nottingham. (Evens)
**483 Four Weddings (USA)** could find no more in the final quarter-mile. (11/4)
**Shamand (USA)** looked a stayer but a poor one at that. (12/1)
**Poly My Son (IRE)**, tailed off on his Doncaster debut, could not take advantage of a big drop in class, but this was a longer trip. (7/2)

## 600 WEST MIDLANDS CONDITIONS STKS (4-Y.O+) (Class C)

4-35 (4-36) **7f** £4,934.04 (£1,824.36: £874.18: £355.90: £139.95: £53.57) Stalls: Low GOING minus 0.11 sec per fur (G)

| Form | Horse | Dist | Pos | SP | RR | SF |
|---|---|---|---|---|---|---|
| 455[9] | **Welton Arsenal (95)** (MRChannon) **4-8-12** RHughes(4) (hld up: hdwy over 3f out: led on bit ins fnl f: shkn up: r.o wl) | — | **1** | 5/1[3] | 97 | 71 |
| 455[16] | **Pengamon (80)** (HJCollingridge) **4-8-12** JQuinn(5) (hld up: hdwy over 3f out: rdn & ev ch ins fnl f: r.o) | nk | **2** | 7/1 | 96 | 70 |
| | **Decorated Hero (105)** (JHMGosden) **4-9-8** JCarroll(1) (lw: a.p: led over 1f out tl ins fnl f) | 3 | **3** | 3/1[2] | 100 | 74 |
| | **Chickawicka (IRE) (83)** (BPalling) **5-9-2** TSprake(3) (bit bkwd: led: rdn over 3f out: hdd over 1f out: one pce) | ½ | **4** | 33/1 | 92 | 66 |
| | **Hoh Magic (109)** (MBell) **4-8-7** MFenton(2) (a.p: rdn & ev ch 2f out: one pce) | s.h | **5** | Evens[1] | 83 | 57 |
| | **Prince Babar** (JEBanks) **5-8-9**(3) JStack(7) (bkwd: lost pl over 3f out: hung lft & styd on fnl f) | s.h | **6** | 33/1 | 88 | 62 |
| | **Ki Chi Saga (USA)** (JLDunlop) **4-8-12** GCarter(8) (hld up: bhd fnl 2f) | 12 | **7** | 12/1 | 61 | 35 |
| | **Lago Di Varano (85)** (JBerry) **4-8-12** AMcGlone(6) (prom over 3f) | 2½ | **8** | 14/1 | 55 | 29 |
| | | | | (SP 124.4%) | | **8 Rn** |

**1m 26.0** (1.40) CSF £38.81 TOTE £7.40: £1.50 £1.70 £1.50 (£21.60) OWNER Business Forms Express (UPPER LAMBOURN) BRED Ian H. Wills

**455 Welton Arsenal**, by no means disgraced in the Lincoln, appreciated this better ground. Never one to find too much off the bridle, his challenge was delayed as long as possible and he may now go for the Victoria Cup. (5/1)
**455 Pengamon**, badly drawn in the Lincoln, finished a lot closer to the winner over a trip which may well be short of his best. (7/1)
**Decorated Hero** found the weight concession too much in the final furlong. (3/1)
**Chickawicka (IRE)** adopted his usual front-running tactics but would have been better off at the weights in a handicap. (33/1)
**Hoh Magic** was well suited by race conditions, so this has to be considered a disappointing performance. (Evens)
**Prince Babar**, off the course since the '94 Jersey Stakes at Royal Ascot, will come on considerably for the outing. (33/1)
**Lago Di Varano** (14/1: op 8/1)

## 601 EASTER H'CAP (0-70) (3-Y.O+) (Class E)

5-05 (5-08) **5f** £3,397.80 (£1,016.40: £487.20: £222.60) Stalls: Low GOING minus 0.40 sec per fur (F)

| Form | Horse | Dist | Pos | SP | RR | SF |
|---|---|---|---|---|---|---|
| | **Canovas Heart (60)** (BobJones) **7-8-13**(5) ADaly(8) (led over 2f: led wl ins fnl f: r.o) | — | **1** | 9/1 | 72 | 50 |
| *394*[7] | **Chadwell Hall (60)** (SRBowring) **5-8-13b**(5) CTeague(5) (lw: w wnr: led over 2f out tl wl ins fnl f) | ½ | **2** | 8/1[3] | 70 | 48 |
| | **Petraco (IRE) (63)** (NASmith) **8-9-0**(7) IonaWands(20) (hdwy whn nt clr run 1f out: swtchd rt: r.o) | 2 | **3** | 33/1 | 67 | 45 |
| 466[15] | **Secret Miss (53)** (APJones) **4-8-11** RPrice(19) (a.p: hung lft fnl f: one pce) | 2 | **4** | 33/1 | 51 | 29 |
| *218*[7] | **Tael of Silver (63)** (KRBurke) **4-9-0**(7) TAshley(14) (hdwy over 1f out: one pce fnl f) | hd | **5** | 33/1 | 60 | 38 |
| *556** | **Our Shadee (USA) (53)** (KTIvory) **6-8-4v**(7) 7x CScally(4) (chsd ldrs: one pce fnl 2f) | s.h | **6** | 10/1 | 50 | 28 |
| 466[2] | **Malibu Man (62)** (SMellor) **4-9-6** TSprake(15) (lw: a.p: one pce fnl 2f) | s.h | **7** | 13/2[2] | 59 | 37 |
| *407*[4] | **Friendly Brave (USA) (62)** (MissGayKelleway) **6-9-6** MFenton(12) (a.p: one pce fnl 2f) | d.h | **7** | 10/1 | 59 | 37 |
| 475[6] | **Just Bob (65)** (SEKettlewell) **7-9-9** JCarroll(13) (nvr nrr) | ½ | **9** | 8/1[3] | 60 | 38 |
| *315*[8] | **Delrob (48)** (DHaydnJones) **5-8-3**(3) DWright(10) (hdwy 2f out: wknd over 1f out) | ½ | **10** | 20/1 | 42 | 20 |
| 466* | **Lloc (56)** (CADwyer) **4-8-11**(3) JStack(1) (prom over 3f) | nk | **11** | 11/2[1] | 49 | 27 |
| | **Jucea (62)** (JLSpearing) **7-9-6** JQuinn(7) (mid div: no hdwy fnl 2f) | 2 | **12** | 9/1 | 48 | 26 |
| | **Sing With the Band (57)** (BAMcMahon) **5-9-1** GCarter(17) (bit bkwd: prom tl rdn & wknd 2f out) | s.h | **13** | 8/1[3] | 43 | 21 |

| | | | | SP | RR | SF |
|---|---|---|---|---|---|---|
| 466[7] | **Followmegirls (50)** (MrsALMKing) **7-8-8** AGarth(18) (wnt lft s: a bhd) | hd | **14** | 16/1 | 36 | 14 |
| *407[8]* | **Allwight Then (IRE) (69)** (REPeacock) **5-9-8**(5) JDSmith(11) (b: prom over 3f) | ½ | **15** | 33/1 | 53 | 31 |
| 559[2] | **Domicksky (52)** (MRChannon) **8-8-10** RHughes(6) (bhd fnl 2f) | ½ | **16** | 8/1 [3] | 35 | 13 |
| *514** | **Rennyholme (45)** (JHetherton) **5-8-3b** NAdams(9) (a bhd) | hd | **17** | 10/1 | 27 | 5 |
| *461[8]* | **Newington Butts (IRE) (46)** (KWMcAuliffe) **6-7-13e**(5) MHenry(3) (prom over 2f) | 1 | **18** | 33/1 | 25 | 3 |
| | **John O'Dreams (48)** (MrsALMKing) **11-8-6** AMcGlone(2) (a bhd) | 2½ | **19** | 16/1 | 19 | — |
| 466[16] | **Mazzarello (IRE) (41)** (RCurtis) **6-7-8v**(5) CAdamson(16) (outpcd) | 5 | **20** | 25/1 | — | — |

(SP 155.5%) **20 Rn**

**59.0 secs** (1.00) CSF £88.23 CT £2,215.37 TOTE £10.40: £2.80 £2.00 £13.20 £21.80 (£65.80) Trio Not won; £629.99 to Uttoxeter 9/4/96
OWNER Mr M J Osborne and Mrs J Woods (NEWMARKET) BRED M. J. Hall

**Canovas Heart** scored first time out here last season and registered his third course and distance win. (9/1)
**Chadwell Hall**, well handicapped compared with the All-Weather, got edged out in a race which only really concerned the leading pair in the last quarter-mile. (8/1)
**Petraco (IRE)** would have finished a bit closer with a trouble-free run. (33/1)
**Secret Miss** did not help her cause by drifting left. (33/1)
**Tael of Silver** could not sustain her run from the furlong pole. (33/1)
**556* Our Shadee (USA)** has never won over the minimum trip. (10/1)
**Friendly Brave (USA)** (10/1: 7/1-12/1)
**466* Lloc** showed speed on the inside but everybody was on a level playing field this time. (11/2)

T/Plpt: £701.80 (9.98 Tckts). T/Qdpt: £127.10 (2.68 Tckts). KH

# 0516-**SOUTHWELL (L-H) (Standard)**
## Tuesday April 9th
WEATHER: cloudy WIND: slt half bhd

## 602 STARLING APPRENTICE H'CAP (0-65) (4-Y.O+) (Class F)
2-00 (2-00) **1m 6f (Fibresand)** £2,410.00 (£685.00: £340.00) Stalls: High GOING: 0.02 sec per fur (STD)

| | | | | SP | RR | SF |
|---|---|---|---|---|---|---|
| 482[4] | **Greek Night Out (IRE) (43)** (JLEyre) **5-8-4**(4) DSweeney(6) (hld up: smooth hdwy to chal over 4f out: led on bit over 2f out: pushed along & hung lft: sn clr) | — | **1** | 5/2 [1] | 59 | 13 |
| *422[3]* | **Swordking (IRE) (38)** (JLHarris) **7-8-3v** DDenby(2) (rel to r: sn wl bhd & pushed along: hdwy 4f out: styd on wl fnl f) | 10 | **2** | 7/2 [2] | 43 | — |
| *429[3]* | **Tempering (59)** (DWChapman) **10-9-10** GFaulkner(4) (swtg: led tl over 2f out: wknd fnl f: eased last strides) | ½ | **3** | 5/1 [3] | 63 | 17 |
| *283[7]* | **Record Lover (IRE) (41)** (MCChapman) **6-8-2**(4) RFfrench(3) (chsd ldrs: pushed along ½-wy: outpcd fnl 4f) | 7 | **4** | 13/2 | 37 | — |
| *198[4]* | **Sharp Gazelle (53)** (BSmart) **6-9-0**(4) MSemple(5) (plld hrd: trckd ldrs: effrt over 4f out: wknd over 2f out) | 7 | **5** | 6/1 | 41 | — |
| 508[13] | **Arecibo (FR) (34)** (JParkes) **4-7-6**(4) RMullen(8) (chsd ldrs: pushed along 6f out: lost pl over 4f out) | 11 | **6** | 25/1 | 9 | — |
| 474[10] | **Charmed Life (31)** (MrsALMKing) **7-7-6b**(4) JBramhill(1) (sn drvn along: bhd fr ½-wy) | 24 | **7** | 33/1 | — | — |
| 504[6] | **Park Ridge (47)** (TGMills) **4-8-9** DToole(7) (chsd ldrs: pushed along ½-wy: lost pl over 4f out: sn bhd) | nk | **8** | 16/1 | — | — |

(SP 107.7%) **8 Rn**

**3m 13.7** (14.70) CSF £10.37 CT £29.74 TOTE £3.10: £1.10 £1.20 £1.20 (£5.30) OWNER Sunpak Potatoes (HAMBLETON) BRED Airlie Stud
LONG HANDICAP Arecibo (FR) 7-7 Charmed Life 7-4
WEIGHT FOR AGE 4yo-3lb

**482 Greek Night Out (IRE)** wanted nothing to do with the strong early pace. Moving up on the bridle out of the back stretch, she looked likely to win very easily when running away turning in, but she hung when in front and had to be pushed out. (5/2)
**Swordking (IRE)**, with the visor back on, was most reluctant to race. Soon virtually tailed off, he began to stay on once in line for home. (7/2)
**Tempering**, awash with sweat at the start, set a strong pace. Swept aside by the winner once in line for home, his stride shortened in the final furlong and, legless near the line, he was not driven right out. (5/1)
**Sharp Gazelle** (6/1: 4/1-13/2)

## 603 SWAN CLAIMING STKS (4-Y.O+) (Class F)
2-30 (2-30) **2m (Fibresand)** £2,381.00 (£656.00: £311.00) Stalls: Low GOING: 0.02 sec per fur (STD)

| | | | | SP | RR | SF |
|---|---|---|---|---|---|---|
| 474[9] | **Jaraab (78)** (GLewis) **5-9-0v** SWhitworth(7) (lw: chsd ldrs: led 4f out: sn wl clr: eased towards fin) | — | **1** | 5/4 [1] | 85 | 13 |
| *420[2]* | **Heathyards Rock (80)** (RHollinshead) **4-9-4** TIves(3) (hld up: hdwy ½-wy: rdn 4f out: no ch w wnr) | 20 | **2** | 7/2 [3] | 73 | — |
| 474[11] | **Eulogy (FR) (68)** (KRBurke) **9-8-11**(3) DRMcCabe(6) (trckd ldrs: led 7f out to 4f out: one pce) | 6 | **3** | 3/1 [2] | 59 | — |
| | **Ciracusa (IRE)** (JMackie) **4-8-8**(3) NVarley(1) (hdwy 6f out: sn chsng ldrs: outpcd fnl 4f) | 6 | **4** | 11/2 | 54 | — |
| *398[4]* | **Baher (USA) (36)** (MrsASwinbank) **7-8-12** JFortune(5) (swtg: led to 7f out: sn drvn along: wknd over 4f out) | 26 | **5** | 16/1 | 25 | — |
| *398[6]* | **Bobby Blue (IRE) (38)** (RonaldThompson) **5-8-9**(5) PFessey(4) (in tch to ½-wy: sn bhd: t.o 4f out) | 19 | **6** | 50/1 | 8 | — |
| | **Le Temeraire (22)** (DonEnricoIncisa) **10-8-6** KimTinkler(2) (lw: bhd fr ½-wy: t.o 4f out) | dist | **7** | 50/1 | — | — |

(SP 116.9%) **7 Rn**

**3m 44.2** (18.20) CSF £6.20 TOTE £2.20: £1.20 £1.50 (£2.60) OWNER Mr S. I. Ross (EPSOM) BRED Shadwell Estate Company Limited
WEIGHT FOR AGE 4yo-4lb
Jaraab clmd MissSWilton £6,000

**474 Jaraab** had his tongue tied down after reportedly gurgling on the turf last time. But for being eased up, he would have won by an even wider margin. (5/4)
**Heathyards Rock**, patiently ridden in an attempt to get him to stay the trip, went in vain pursuit once in line for home. (7/2: 2/1-4/1)
**Eulogy (FR)** looked to be travelling as well as the winner when going on soon after halfway but, when the race began in earnest, he proved woefully one-paced. (3/1: op 5/1)

## 604 HERON MAIDEN H'CAP (0-70) (3-Y.O+) (Class E)
3-00 (3-00) **1m 3f (Fibresand)** £3,234.00 (£966.00: £462.00: £210.00) Stalls: Low GOING: 0.02 sec per fur (STD)

| | | | | SP | RR | SF |
|---|---|---|---|---|---|---|
| *426[5]* | **Carol Again (33)** (NBycroft) **4-7-11** JQuinn(10) (jnd ldrs 6f out: led 3f out: rdn clr over 1f out) | — | **1** | 9/2 [2] | 45 | 19 |
| | **Zidac (64)** (PJMakin) **4-10-0** SSanders(6) (trckd ldr: led over 4f out to 3f out: no ch w wnr) | 9 | **2** | 8/1 | 63 | 37 |
| *520[6]* | **Milltown Classic (IRE) (32)** (JParkes) **4-7-10** NCarlisle(8) (a chsng ldrs: one pce fnl 3f) | 1 | **3** | 25/1 | 30 | 4 |
| | **Jean de Florette (USA) (32)** (RCSpicer) **5-7-10** NKennedy(2) (chsd ldrs: drvn along 8f out: styd on fnl 2f) | 1 | **4** | 20/1 | 28 | 2 |

| | Horse | Dist | Pos | SP | RR | SF |
|---|---|---|---|---|---|---|
| 510[4] | **Nautical Jewel (50)** (MDIUsher) **4-9-0** MWigham(12) (bhd & rel to r: sme hdwy 3f out: nvr nr ldrs) | 16 | **5** | 8/1 | 23 | — |
| 87[7] | **Jarrow (32)** (MrsAMNaughton) **5-7-5v**(5) PFessey(4) (dwlt: a in rr) | 2½ | **6** | 20/1 | 1 | — |
| 527[7] | **Paronomasia (32)** (JLHarris) **4-7-10v** FNorton(1) (trckd ldrs: effrt over 4f out: sn wknd) | 5 | **7** | 20/1 | — | — |
| 495[4] | **Frankly Fran (52)** (DWPArbuthnot) **4-9-2** SWhitworth(3) (b: in tch: rdn 5f out: sn wknd) | 2½ | **8** | 11/2[3] | 10 | — |
| 328[3] | **Parklife (IRE) (41)** (PCHaslam) **4-8-5v[1]**ow1 JFortune(9) (s.s: hdwy to chse ldrs ½-wy: lost pl over 4f out) | ¾ | **9** | 7/2[1] | — | — |
| 516[4] | **Welcome Lu (52)** (PSFelgate) **3-7-3**(7) IonaWands(7) (mid div: effrt over 4f out: hung lft & sn lost pl) | 1 | **10** | 14/1 | 8 | — |
| 360[9] | **Buckley Boys (38)** (ABailey) **5-7-13b**(3) DWright(11) (sn drvn along: bhd fnl 6f) | 6 | **11** | 6/1 | — | — |
| | **Grey Kingdom (32)** (MBrittain) **5-7-10** GBardwell(5) (led tl over 4f out: wknd qckly: t.o) | dist | **12** | 20/1 | — | — |

(SP 121.9%) **12 Rn**

**2m 29.1** (9.10) CSF £38.46 CT £754.11 TOTE £4.50: £1.80 £3.00 £13.00 (£23.40) Trio £210.90; £267.41 to Ripon 10/4/96 OWNER Mr J. G. Lumsden (BRANDSBY)

LONG HANDICAP Milltown Classic (IRE) 7-6 Paronomasia 7-6 Jarrow 7-0 Welcome Lu 6-12 Jean de Florette (USA) 7-7

WEIGHT FOR AGE 3yo-20lb

**Carol Again** finally broke her duck on her sixteenth attempt in this desperate handicap, with her rider leaving nothing to chance. She is certainly genuine. (9/2)

**Zidac**, who starts this year from a 5lb lower mark, looked to be travelling comfortably when taking it up but was soon left for dead by the winner. (8/1)

**Milltown Classic (IRE)** behaved himself at the start this time but possesses limited ability. (25/1)

**Jean de Florette (USA)** decided to stay on when it was all over. (20/1)

**495 Frankly Fran** (11/2: 4/1-6/1)

**Parklife (IRE)**, who was tried in a visor, was reluctant to come out of the stalls. After moving up at halfway, he soon called it a day, and was found to be lame behind afterwards. (7/2)

## 605 PEACOCK H'CAP (0-65) (3-Y.O) (Class F)

3-30 (3-31) **7f (Fibresand)** £2,381.00 (£656.00: £311.00) Stalls: Low GOING: 0.02 sec per fur (STD)

| | Horse | Dist | Pos | SP | RR | SF |
|---|---|---|---|---|---|---|
| | **Hawksley Hill (IRE) (45)** (MrsJRRamsden) **3-8-5** KFallon(4) (lw: mid div: effrt ½-wy: styd on to ld ins fnl f: r.o) | — | **1** | 3/1[2] | 57 | 22 |
| 404[3] | **Down The Yard (38)** (MCChapman) **3-7-7**(5) PFessey(7) (chsd ldrs: led 2f out: hdd & nt qckn ins fnl f) | 1¼ | **2** | 12/1 | 47 | 12 |
| 531[3] | **Efipetite (51)** (NBycroft) **3-8-11** GBardwell(10) (sn trckng ldrs: effrt 2f out: kpt on same pce) | 3½ | **3** | 6/1 | 52 | 17 |
| | **Holloway Melody (43)** (BAMcMahon) **3-7-12**(5) LNewton(6) (led to 2f out: edgd rt: one pce) | ¾ | **4** | 16/1 | 42 | 7 |
| 518[5] | **Seeking Destiny (IRE) (50)** (MCChapman) **3-8-3**(7) CMunday(12) (chsd ldrs: rdn & n.m.r 2f out: kpt on) | 1½ | **5** | 8/1 | 46 | 11 |
| 344[10] | **The Fullbangladesh (45)** (JLEyre) **3-8-5** RLappin(8) (in tch: rdn & outpcd ½-wy: kpt on) | 1¾ | **6** | 20/1 | 37 | 2 |
| 503[2] | **Domoor (61)** (MJohnston) **3-9-7** JWeaver(2) (chsd ldrs: effrt over 2f out: n.m.r: styd on same pce) | ¾ | **7** | 2/1[1] | 51 | 16 |
| 344[9] | **Scenicris (IRE) (46)** (RHollinshead) **3-8-6** NCarlisle(9) (hld up: hdwy ½-wy: wknd over 2f out) | 1½ | **8** | 10/1 | 33 | — |
| | **Hank-a-chief (60)** (BSmart) **3-9-6** RCochrane(3) (trckd ldrs: rdn over 2f out: sn wknd) | 5 | **9** | 5/1[3] | 35 | — |
| | **Tropical Beach (60)** (JBerry) **3-9-1**(5) PRoberts(5) (s.i.s: a in rr) | 1½ | **10** | 12/1 | 32 | — |
| 525[18] | **Magical Midnight (40)** (NTinkler) **3-8-0** KimTinkler(11) (chsd ldrs tl lost pl ½-wy) | 6 | **11** | 25/1 | — | — |
| 539[9] | **Autofyr (36)** (JSWainwright) **3-7-10** LCharnock(1) (hdwy on ins ½-wy: sn lost pl) | ¾ | **12** | 33/1 | — | — |

(SP 142.3%) **12 Rn**

**1m 32.9** (6.10) CSF £43.41 CT £211.82 TOTE £3.90: £1.50 £2.80 £1.50 (£36.40) Trio £280.60 OWNER Mr Hamish Alexander (THIRSK) BRED The Wickfield Stud Ltd

LONG HANDICAP Autofyr 7-9

**Hawksley Hill (IRE)**, a flashy-looking chestnut, is obviously something of a playboy. Showing a modest action going down, he had to work hard but was right on top at the finish. This was his first outing in handicap company and he looks capable of even better, especially over further. (3/1)

**Down The Yard**, running from a plater's mark, was the only one to give the winner serious worries. (12/1)

**531 Efipetite** pulled hard on the wide outside and, in the circumstances, kept on in creditable fashion. (6/1: op 7/2)

**Holloway Melody** made the running, but came off a straight line as she tired, causing problems for Domoor and Seeking Destiny. (16/1)

**Scenicris (IRE)** (10/1: 8/1-12/1)

## 606 JAY (S) STKS (3-Y.O) (Class G)

4-00 (4-01) **6f (Fibresand)** £2,070.00 (£570.00: £270.00) Stalls: Low GOING: 0.02 sec per fur (STD)

| | Horse | Dist | Pos | SP | RR | SF |
|---|---|---|---|---|---|---|
| 478[7] | **Niteowl Raider (IRE) (70)** (JAHarris) **3-9-2** JO'Reilly(8) (led tl over 2f out: styd on u.p to ld wl ins fnl f) | — | **1** | 4/1[2] | 70 | 34 |
| 492* | **The Frisky Farmer (53)** (WGMTurner) **3-9-2** AClark(15) (lw: chsd ldr: led over 2f out tl wl ins fnl f: kpt on wl) | nk | **2** | 13/2[3] | 69 | 33 |
| 224[6] | **Born A Lady (59)** (SRBowring) **3-8-6b[1]**(5) CTeague(1) (a chsng ldrs: one pce fnl 2f) | 4 | **3** | 8/1 | 54 | 18 |
| 525[9] | **Monkey Zanty (IRE) (54)** (JLHarris) **3-8-11** SSanders(3) (a chsng ldrs: rdn over 2f out: one pce) | 2 | **4** | 12/1 | 48 | 12 |
| 517* | **Amoeba (IRE) (47)** (JBerry) **3-8-6**(5) PFessey(14) (chsd ldrs: effrt over 2f out: kpt on same pce) | s.h | **5** | 5/2[1] | 48 | 12 |
| 459[5] | **Shanoora (IRE) (43)** (MrsNMacauley) **3-8-6v**(5) AmandaSanders(11) (styd on fnl 2f: edgd rt: nvr rchd ldrs) | 7 | **6** | 16/1 | 29 | — |
| 492[4] | **Sharp Monty** (RHollinshead) **3-8-11** WRyan(4) (prom: rdn ½-wy: wknd over 2f out) | s.h | **7** | 8/1 | 29 | — |
| | **Forecast** (JWharton) **3-8-11** JQuinn(12) (b: in tch: effrt over 2f out: nvr rchd ldrs) | ½ | **8** | 25/1 | 28 | — |
| | **Inca Bird** (BAMcMahon) **3-8-1**(5) LNewton(2) (sn drvn along: nvr nr ldrs) | 1½ | **9** | 20/1 | 19 | — |
| 529[6] | **Golborne Lad** (JBalding) **3-8-4**(7) JEdmunds(13) (a in rr) | nk | **10** | 33/1 | 23 | — |
| 478[4] | **April's Joy (48)** (JNorton) **3-8-11** DaleGibson(10) (sn drvn along & outpcd) | ½ | **11** | 11/1 | — | — |
| 473[10] | **Ragtime Cowgirl** (CWThornton) **3-8-6** DeanMcKeown(7) (s.i.s: a bhd) | 7 | **12** | 20/1 | — | — |
| | **Thorntoun Jewel (IRE) (45)** (JBalding) **3-8-11b[1]** NAdams(6) (sn bhd) | 5 | **13** | 20/1 | — | — |
| 458[15] | **Sharvic (IRE)** (MissMKMilligan) **3-8-11** JFanning(9) (hld up & plld hrd: stumbled over 4f out: a bhd) | 7 | **14** | 20/1 | — | — |
| 473[7] | **Aye Ready** (MissLAPerratt) **3-8-11** GDuffield(5) (plld hrd: bhd fr ½-wy) | 1¾ | **15** | 16/1 | — | — |

(SP 137.8%) **15 Rn**

**1m 18.5** (5.00) CSF £32.53 TOTE £7.60: £2.10 £1.50 £2.80 (£37.80) Trio £44.80 OWNER Burntwood Sports Ltd (EDINGLEY) BRED Airlie Stud No bid

STEWARDS' ENQUIRY O'Reilly susp. 18-19/4/96 (excessive use of whip).

**Niteowl Raider (IRE)**, who likes to dominate, fought back bravely and regained the advantage near the line. The Stewards took a dim view of his rider's use of the whip and banned him for two days. (4/1)

**492* The Frisky Farmer**, worst drawn, tacked across and, after taking a narrow advantage, he was worried out of it near the line. (13/2)

**Born A Lady** had the blinkers on and they seemed to wake her up. (8/1)

**Monkey Zanty (IRE)** was one of just five to get in the race with a serious chance. (12/1: op 8/1)

**517* Amoeba (IRE)** raced wide and was struggling to get in a blow from halfway. (5/2: 7/4-3/1)

## 607 PUFFIN H'CAP (0-65) (4-Y.O+) (Class F)

4-30 (4-32) **6f (Fibresand)** £2,381.00 (£656.00: £311.00) Stalls: Low GOING: 0.02 sec per fur (STD)

| | | | SP | RR | SF |
|---|---|---|---|---|---|
| 534* | **Foist (47)** (MWEasterby) **4-8-12** 7x JQuinn(6) (trckd ldrs: effrt 2f out: r.o wl u.p to ld wl ins fnl f)......................— | **1** | 11/8[1] | 64 | 50 |
| 418[7] | **Perfect Brave (60)** (JBalding) **5-9-4**(7) JEdmunds(14) (led: clr 2f out: hdd & no ex wl ins fnl f)........................1¼ | **2** | 20/1 | 74 | 60 |
| 521* | **Awesome Venture (69)** (MCChapman) **6-9-13**(7) 7x CMunday(10) (trckd ldrs: hmpd over 2f out: styd on ins fnl f) ........................................6 | **3** | 10/1[3] | 67 | 53 |
| 518* | **Elton Ledger (IRE) (70)** (MrsNMacauley) **7-10-7b** 7x JTate(11) (b: hld up & bhd: hdwy 2f out: r.o ins fnl f) .....nk | **4** | 10/1[3] | 67 | 53 |
| 431[9] | **Bold Aristocrat (IRE) (54)** (RHollinshead) **5-9-0**(5) FLynch(8) (hld up & bhd: hdwy 2f out: styd on nr fin).........½ | **5** | 12/1 | 50 | 36 |
| | **Adamton (45)** (MrsJCecil) **4-8-10** TIves(1) (hld up & bhd: stdy hdwy & swtchd rt wl over 1f out: nvr plcd to chal) ........................................¾ | **6** | 10/1[3] | 39 | 25 |
| 518[3] | **Tilly Owl (42)** (JAHarris) **5-8-7** JO'Reilly(15) (prom: hmpd & lost pl over 2f out: kpt on fnl f) ............................¾ | **7** | 3/1[2] | 34 | 20 |
| | **Strathtore Dream (IRE) (32)** (MissLAPerratt) **5-7-6**(5) PFessey(7) (lw: bhd tl styd on fnl 2f) ............................½ | **8** | 33/1 | 22 | 8 |
| 413[4] | **Sweet Mate (60)** (SRBowring) **4-9-6b**(5) CTeague(12) (sn drvn along: in tch: hmpd over 2f out: sn lost pl) ....3½ | **9** | 10/1[3] | 41 | 27 |
| | **Sunday Mail Too (IRE) (33)** (MissLAPerratt) **4-7-12** JFanning(2) (plld hrd: lost pl ½-wy: n.d)...........................5 | **10** | 25/1 | 1 | — |
| | **Rankaidade (31)** (DonEnricoIncisa) **5-7-10** KimTinkler(4) (chsd ldrs tl lost pl over 2f out) ...............................nk | **11** | 50/1 | — | — |
| 514[2] | **Sound the Trumpet (IRE) (54)** (RCSpicer) **4-9-5** DeanMcKeown(3) (unruly in stalls: s.s: a wl bhd)................11 | **12** | 14/1 | — | — |
| 387[8] | **Young Ben (IRE) (35)** (JSWainwright) **4-8-0** AMackay(9) (a in rr) ..........................................½ | **13** | 33/1 | — | — |
| 534[4] | **Blue Lugana (35)** (NBycroft) **4-8-0** GBardwell(5) (a bhd)..........................................½ | **14** | 25/1 | — | — |
| 412[8] | **Green's Bid (35)** (DWChapman) **6-8-0** LCharnock(13) (chsd ldrs tl p.u over 2f out: dead) ................................ | **P** | 14/1 | — | — |
| | | | (SP 144.8%) | **15 Rn** | |

**1m 17.0** (3.50) CSF £35.25 CT £244.17 TOTE £2.30: £1.50 £3.20 £5.10 (£42.20) Trio £111.50 OWNER Mr D. F. Spence (SHERIFF HUTTON) BRED W. Cormack

LONG HANDICAP Rankaidade 7-9

OFFICIAL EXPLANATION **Adamton: upon returning to the yard he was found to have pulled muscles behind the saddle.**

**534* Foist**, under a 7lb penalty, showed real determination to gain the upper hand in the closing stages. (11/8: Evens-6/4)

**Perfect Brave** had all but the winner shaken off with two furlongs left to run. His stride shortened noticeably in the closing stages, and he might be worth a try over the minimum trip. (20/1)

**521* Awesome Venture** was one of those hampered when Green's Bid had to be pulled up. (10/1: 8/1-12/1)

**518* Elton Ledger (IRE)**, under a 7lb penalty, was ridden off the pace and given a fair bit to do. (10/1: 7/1-12/1)

**Adamton**, who showed little in three outings last year, was anchored in the rear. Switched right over a furlong out, he seemed to finish full of running. His rider's explanation that he pulled hard, hung badly round the bend, and again in the home straight, was accepted. From this low rating, he looks one to keep an eye on. (10/1)

**518 Tilly Owl**, backed from 10/1 to 3/1, was slightly hampered by the injured Green's Bid and could never get back on terms. (3/1: op 10/1)

T/Plpt: £56.20 (194.17 Tckts). T/Qdpt: £35.50 (22.55 Tckts). WG

# RIPON (R-H) (Good)

## Wednesday April 10th

WEATHER: raining WIND: almost nil

## 608 E.B.F. SPA WELTER MAIDEN STKS (2-Y.O) (Class D)

2-10 (2-10) **5f** £3,452.50 (£1,045.00: £510.00: £242.50) Stalls: Low GOING minus 0.28 sec per fur (GF)

| | | | SP | RR | SF |
|---|---|---|---|---|---|
| | **Proud Native (IRE)** (APJarvis) **2-9-0** JTate(1) (cmpt: cl up: led over 1f out: styd on wl) ...............................— | **1** | 8/1 | 78 | 30 |
| | **Double Park (FR)** (MJohnston) **2-8-9** JWeaver(4) (leggy: scope: led tl hdd over 1f out: no ex)......................1½ | **2** | 3/1[2] | 68 | 20 |
| | **The Gay Fox** (BAMcMahon) **2-9-0** GCarter(6) (w'like: unf: chsd ldrs: rn green appr fnl f: nt qckn) .................1¾ | **3** | 10/1 | 68 | 20 |
| | **Danehill Princess (IRE)** (RHollinshead) **2-8-9** WRyan(2) (neat: chsd ldrs: n.m.r over 1f out: kpt on) ..............2 | **4** | 7/1 | 56 | 8 |
| | **Bold African** (PDEvans) **2-9-0v[1]** KFallon(5) (cmpt: chsd ldrs: hmpd over 1f out: styd on one pce) ...............hd | **5** | 9/2[3] | 61 | 13 |
| | **The Bee Man** (MWEasterby) **2-9-0** DaleGibson(8) (leggy: spd to ½-wy)..........................................6 | **6** | 16/1 | 42 | — |
| | **Foolish Flutter (IRE)** (GROldroyd) **2-8-5**(7)ow3 AColgan(7) (neat: unf: dwlt: a bhd) ..........................................¾ | **7** | 66/1 | 37 | — |
| | **Prince of Parkes** (JBerry) **2-9-0** JCarroll(3) (cmpt: scope: s.s: a bhd) ..........................................1 | **8** | 13/8[1] | 36 | — |
| | | | (SP 121.4%) | **8 Rn** | |

**61.0 secs** (2.60) CSF £32.32 TOTE £16.90: £4.00 £1.50 £1.90 (£32.30) OWNER Mr L. Fust (ASTON UPTHORPE) BRED Mrs B. A. Headon

**Proud Native (IRE)** showed a moderate action going down but there was nothing wrong on the way back and he scored most authoritatively. (8/1)

**Double Park (FR)** looks likely to be all the better for this and showed speed aplenty, suggesting that her turn is not far away. (3/1: op 2/1)

**The Gay Fox**, a decent type, looks likely to benefit from the outing and got unbalanced on the downhill section approaching the final furlong. Improvement is on the cards. (10/1)

**Danehill Princess (IRE)**, a handy sort, was always chasing the leaders but she got messed about approaching the final furlong and lacked the pace to get out of trouble. She should find a race at this trip but, if she tries further, better will be seen. (7/1)

**Bold African**, a sharp sort, looked fit and chased the leaders but he got hampered when struggling approaching the final furlong and that was it. (9/2)

**The Bee Man** needed this and got pretty warm beforehand. (16/1)

**Prince of Parkes** missed the break by a good few lengths and never looked likely to recover, but is a useful-looking type who will no doubt do better in time. (13/8)

## 609 MARKINGTON (S) H'CAP (0-60) (4-Y.O+) (Class F)

2-40 (2-41) **1m 4f 60y** £2,742.40 (£771.40: £377.20) Stalls: High GOING: 0.02 sec per fur (G)

| | | | SP | RR | SF |
|---|---|---|---|---|---|
| 512[5] | **Comtec's Legend (27)** (JFBottomley) **6-8-0** LCharnock(8) (hld up: stdy hdwy 4f out: effrt over 2f out: r.o u.p fnl f to ld nr fin)..........................................— | **1** | 7/1[3] | 34 | 21 |
| | **Watch Me Go (IRE) (39)** (BobJones) **7-8-12**ow2 MWigham(14) (b: a chsng ldrs: ev ch ins fnl f: kpt on) ...........nk | **2** | 8/1 | 46 | 31 |
| | **Dots Dee (27)** (JMBradley) **7-7-9**(5) MHenry(15) (b.nr fore: a.p: led & qcknd over 2f out: hdd & no ex nr fin)..s.h | **3** | 20/1 | 34 | 21 |
| 504* | **Bold Pursuit (IRE) (49)** (JGFitzGerald) **7-9-8** KFallon(5) (b: bhd: drvn along over 4f out: hdwy 2f out: nt qckn fnl f)..........................................2½ | **4** | 3/1[1] | 52 | 39 |
| | **Walworth Lady (51)** (MDods) **5-9-10** JCarroll(16) (b: bolted 5f gng to s: stdd s: sn prom: effrt over 2f out: kpt on) ..........................................nk | **5** | 33/1 | 54 | 41 |

| | | | | SP | RR | SF |
|---|---|---|---|---|---|---|
| | **Portite Sophie (33)** (MBrittain) **5-8-6** PRobinson(4) (in tch: effrt 3f out: btn appr fnl f) | 1½ | **6** | 16/1 | 34 | 21 |
| | **Remontant (IRE) (35)** (RHollinshead) **4-8-2**(5) FLynch(9) (bhd: hdwy 4f out: nt rch ldrs) | ½ | **7** | 16/1 | 35 | 21 |
| 504[3] | **Bold Top (40)** (BSRothwell) **4-8-12b** MFenton(1) (hdwy 7f out: sn in tch: one pce fnl 2f) | 1¼ | **8** | 7/1 [3] | 39 | 25 |
| 542[7] | **Sylvan Celebration (23)** (JSGoldie) **5-7-10** DGibson(3) (hld up & bhd: hdwy 4f out: n.d) | 7 | **9** | 33/1 | 13 | — |
| 558[9] | **Goodbye Millie (49)** (JLEyre) **6-9-5v**(3) OPears(10) (s.i.s: nvr rchd ldrs) | hd | **10** | 12/1 | 38 | 25 |
| | **Lexus (IRE) (27)** (RJRWilliams) **8-8-0** GBardwell(12) (nvr rchd ldrs) | 1¼ | **11** | 12/1 | 15 | 2 |
| | **Kierchem (IRE) (48)** (RFFisher) **5-9-7** KDarley(13) (b: led 3f: cl up: chal 3f out: wknd fnl 2f) | 1½ | **12** | 5/1 [2] | 34 | 21 |
| 504[5] | **Can She Can Can (40)** (CSmith) **4-8-12** JFanning(11) (chsd ldrs tl wknd fnl 3f) | 2 | **13** | 14/1 | 23 | 9 |
| | **Don't Cry (23)** (DonEnricoIncisa) **8-7-10** KimTinkler(7) (bkwd: chsd ldrs tl wknd 4f out) | ½ | **14** | 20/1 | 6 | — |
| | **High Flown (USA) (45)** (RonaldThompson) **4-8-12**(5) PFessey(18) (lw: lost tch fnl 4f) | 1½ | **15** | 20/1 | 26 | 12 |
| 504[9] | **Adaloaldo (USA) (50)** (JParkes) **4-9-8** JTate(6) (drvn along after s: n.d) | 7 | **16** | 25/1 | 22 | 8 |
| | **I'm a Nut Man (37)** (CASmith) **5-8-10** ACulhane(2) (led after 3f tl over 2f out: wknd) | hd | **17** | 20/1 | 8 | — |
| | **Gymcrak Hero (IRE) (50)** (GHolmes) **4-9-8b**[1] JWeaver(17) (t: s.i.s: a bhd) | 1 | **18** | 25/1 | 20 | 6 |
| | | | | (SP 144.2%) | **18 Rn** | |

**2m 44.1** (10.10) CSF £66.84 CT £1,037.84 TOTE £10.00: £2.60 £2.10 £4.60 £1.80 (£37.10) Trio £337.30; £247.10 to Hamilton 11/4/96
OWNER Qualitair Holdings Ltd (MALTON) BRED Qualitair Stud Ltd
LONG HANDICAP Don't Cry 7-5 Sylvan Celebration 6-12
WEIGHT FOR AGE 4yo-1lb
No bid

**512 Comtec's Legend** won her first race on turf here for four years and, battling on well to do so, should stay a bit further. (7/1)
**Watch Me Go (IRE)** has improved on the All-Weather and ran off his old mark here but, despite trying hard, he just failed to hang on and this trip may just be at the limits of his stamina. (8/1)
**Dots Dee** finished third in this same race two years ago and, although she was a good deal closer this time, she gives the impression that the trip is just beyond her best. (20/1)
**504* Bold Pursuit (IRE)** is certainly a hard ride and had a lot of running to do in the straight but, just when he looked likely to get there, he ran out of steam. (3/1)
**Walworth Lady**, very fresh after her long lay-off, ran a decent race and should improve as a result. (33/1)
**Portite Sophie** is still a maiden after thirty attempts and was never doing enough in the closing stages. (16/1)
**Remontant (IRE)** stayed on well in the last half-mile, suggesting that further should suit. (16/1)

## 610 FOUNTAINS H'CAP (0-95) (3-Y.O+) (Class C)

3-10 (3-10) **6f** £5,715.80 (£1,732.40: £847.20: £404.60) Stalls: Low GOING: 0.02 sec per fur (G)

| | | | | SP | RR | SF |
|---|---|---|---|---|---|---|
| 480* | **Super Benz (71)** (JLEyre) **10-8-6** RLappin(21) (chsd ldrs far side: sn pushed along: led over 1f out: r.o wl) | — | **1** | 6/1 [1] | 82 | 62 |
| 559* | **To the Roof (IRE) (73)** (PWHarris) **4-8-8** [6x] GHind(1) (trckd ldrs stands' side: chal 2f out: kpt on: nt pce of wnr) | 3 | **2** | 6/1 [1] | 76 | 56 |
| 451[19] | **Highborn (IRE) (83)** (PSFelgate) **7-9-4** WRyan(24) (lw: racd far side: a.p: kpt on fnl f) | ¾ | **3** | 25/1 | 84 | 64 |
| 554[3] | **Tiler (IRE) (81)** (MJohnston) **4-9-2** JWeaver(11) (led stands' side: rdn over 2f out: nt qckn fnl f) | 1 | **4** | 12/1 | 79 | 59 |
| 451[4] | **Castlerea Lad (83)** (RHollinshead) **7-9-4** TIves(18) (racd far side: bhd tl styd on wl fnl 2f) | nk | **5** | 9/1 [3] | 81 | 61 |
| | **French Grit (IRE) (80)** (MDods) **4-9-1** JFortune(9) (jnd ldrs ½-wy stands' side: wknd appr fnl f) | 1 | **6** | 25/1 | 75 | 55 |
| *464*[3] | **So Intrepid (IRE) (70)** (JMBradley) **6-8-2**(3) SDrowne(4) (hdwy stands' side 2f out: nvr able to chal) | 2 | **7** | 25/1 | 60 | 40 |
| | **Blessingindisguise (85)** (MWEasterby) **3-8-8** MBirch(19) (chsd ldrs far side tl outpcd fnl 2f) | 2 | **8** | 20/1 | 69 | 37 |
| | **Lennox Lewis (93)** (APJarvis) **4-9-7**(7) KHopkins(20) (racd far side: led tl hdd over 1f out: sn btn) | ½ | **9** | 50/1 | 76 | 56 |
| | **Just Dissident (IRE) (62)** (RMWhitaker) **4-7-11**[ow1] DaleGibson(3) (gd spd stands' side to ½-wy) | 1½ | **10** | 50/1 | 41 | 20 |
| | **I'm Your Lady (67)** (BAMcMahon) **5-8-2** GCarter(17) (nvr trbld ldrs) | ¾ | **11** | 12/1 | 44 | 24 |
| 475[14] | **Stephensons Rocket (62)** (DNicholls) **5-7-11** FNorton(12) (chsd ldrs far side: carried lft ½-wy: sn lost pl) | ½ | **12** | 66/1 | 38 | 18 |
| | **The Scythian (74)** (BobJones) **4-8-9** MHills(23) (chsd ldrs far side tl wknd over 1f out) | ½ | **13** | 10/1 | 48 | 28 |
| 480[12] | **Maid O'Cannie (61)** (MWEasterby) **5-7-10b** JQuinn(10) (lw: nvr trbld ldrs) | ½ | **14** | 33/1 | 34 | 14 |
| 451[11] | **Brecongill Lad (76)** (MissSEHall) **4-8-11b** WWoods(2) (nvr trbld ldrs) | ½ | **15** | 12/1 | 48 | 28 |
| | **Palacegate Touch (78)** (JBerry) **6-8-13b** JCarroll(22) (chsd ldrs far side: hung lft ½-wy: sn wknd) | s.h | **16** | 13/2 [2] | 49 | 29 |
| *511*[3] | **Nordan Raider (62)** (MJCamacho) **8-7-11** LCharnock(14) (n.d) | nk | **17** | 16/1 | 33 | 13 |
| 455[7] | **Al Reet (IRE) (90)** (MDHammond) **5-9-11** RCochrane(8) (sn outpcd) | s.h | **18** | 16/1 | 61 | 41 |
| 451[10] | **Portend (80)** (SRBowring) **4-8-10**(5) CTeague(5) (nvr wnt pce) | ¾ | **19** | 12/1 | 49 | 29 |
| 505[14] | **Nizaal (USA) (64)** (DNicholls) **5-7-13** JFanning(13) (n.d) | 1 | **20** | 33/1 | 30 | 10 |
| 451[15] | **Anonym (IRE) (70)** (DNicholls) **4-8-5** NConnorton(16) (a rr div far side) | ½ | **21** | 66/1 | 35 | 15 |
| 475[10] | **Benzoe (IRE) (74)** (MrsJRRamsden) **6-8-9** KFallon(6) (sn bhd) | nk | **22** | 14/1 | 38 | 18 |
| 475[8] | **Rich Glow (62)** (NBycroft) **5-7-11** GBardwell(15) (sn bhd) | 1½ | **23** | 20/1 | 22 | 2 |
| | **Musical Season (90)** (TDBarron) **4-9-11** KDarley(7) (sn bhd) | 1½ | **24** | 25/1 | 46 | 26 |
| | | | | (SP 147.9%) | **24 Rn** | |

**1m 12.6** (2.10) CSF £44.71 CT £845.33 TOTE £7.20: £2.10 £2.10 £5.40 £3.30 (£22.10) Trio £776.60 OWNER Whitestonecliffe Racing Partnership (HAMBLETON) BRED Scarteen Stud
LONG HANDICAP Just Dissident (IRE) 7-9 Maid O'Cannie 7-6
WEIGHT FOR AGE 3yo-12lb

**480* Super Benz** has been put up 9lb and was dropping back in distance, but this proved no problem. Once he gained the initiative approaching the final furlong, he again won with plenty to spare. (6/1)
**559* To the Roof (IRE)** looked likely to follow up his easy win of last week for much of the trip but, despite trying hard, he was no match for the winner on the opposite side of the course in the final furlong. (6/1)
**Highborn (IRE)** took the eye in the paddock and ran a sound race up the far rail, but was always short of speed in the last furlong and a half. (25/1)
**554 Tiler (IRE)** is in good form at present and a race should be found in due course. (12/1)
**451 Castlerea Lad** is happier on a faster surface but keeps running well and was never any nearer than at the finish. (9/1)
**French Grit (IRE)** is now slipping down the handicap and ran well enough here to suggest that he is coming back to form. (25/1)
**464 So Intrepid (IRE)** ran pretty well, staying on at the end, and remains in good heart. (25/1)

## 611 GALPHAY CONDITIONS STKS (3-Y.O) (Class C)

3-40 (3-40) **1m 1f** £5,002.60 (£1,750.60: £856.30: £368.50) Stalls: High GOING: 0.02 sec per fur (G)

| | | | | SP | RR | SF |
|---|---|---|---|---|---|---|
| | **Santillana (USA)** (JHMGosden) **3-9-2** GHind(1) (lw: hld up: smooth hdwy to ld wl over 2f out: pushed along & r.o wl fnl f) | — | **1** | 4/6 [1] | 101+ | 50 |

| | | | | SP | RR | SF |
|---|---|---|---|---|---|---|
| *391*[4] | **Double Diamond (IRE) (89)** (MJohnston) **3-9-2** JWeaver(2) (led tl hdd over 3f out: sn outpcd: r.o wl u.p appr fnl f) | nk | 2 | 9/1[3] | 101 | 50 |
| | **Coyote Bluff (IRE)** (PWChapple-Hyam) **3-8-13**(5) RHavlin(4) (bit bkwd: cl up: slt ld over 3f out: hdd wl over 2f out: sn outpcd) | 7 | 3 | 20/1 | 90 | 39 |
| | **Salmis** (JRFanshawe) **3-8-7** DHarrison(3) (hld up: effrt over 3f out: sn btn) | 5 | 4 | 2/1[2] | 70 | 19 |
| | | | | (SP 108.1%) | **4 Rn** | |

**1m 55.9** (5.70) CSF £5.72 TOTE £1.60: (£2.80) OWNER Sheikh Mohammed (NEWMARKET) BRED Mr David Caldwell
**Santillana (USA)** looked likely to score with ease for much of the trip but his rider spent most of the last three furlongs looking round and, in the end, had to pull out most of the stops to hold a very persistent runner-up. He should have learnt plenty from this. (4/6)
**Double Diamond (IRE)** was in trouble a long way out but he does stay and battled on most determinedly in the closing stages. Longer trips are going to see plenty of improvement. (9/1)
**Coyote Bluff (IRE)** needed this and, once the race began in earnest in the last two and a half furlongs, he was soon put in his place. (20/1)
**Salmis** has not progressed since last year and was well outpointed in the final two and a half furlongs. (2/1: op 3/1)

## 612 STUDLEY ROYAL H'CAP (0-70) (3-Y.O+) (Class E)

4-10 (4-10) **1m 4f 60y** £3,096.40 (£938.20: £458.60: £218.80) Stalls: High GOING: 0.02 sec per fur (G)

| | | | | SP | RR | SF |
|---|---|---|---|---|---|---|
| 546* | **Pip's Dream (45)** (MJRyan) **5-8-8** 5x WCarson(12) (chsd ldrs: led wl over 2f out: r.o) | — | 1 | 13/8[1] | 57 | 34 |
| 439[2] | **Outstayed Welcome (55)** (MJHaynes) **4-8-12**(5) MBaird(11) (s.i.s: hdwy to ld after 3f: hdd wl over 2f out: r.o) | 1 | 2 | 6/1[3] | 66 | 42 |
| 558[3] | **Keep Battling (39)** (JSGoldie) **6-8-2** JQuinn(1) (hld up: smooth hdwy over 3f out: n.m.r over 1f out: rdn & nt qckn ins fnl f) | 1 | 3 | 10/1 | 48 | 25 |
| | **Hasta la Vista (50)** (MWEasterby) **6-8-13b** DaleGibson(9) (lw: cl up: effrt 3f out: r.o one pce) | 3½ | 4 | 14/1 | 55 | 32 |
| *520** | **Forzair (61)** (JJO'Neill) **4-9-9** SDWilliams(6) (sn chsng ldrs: chal 4f out: sn rdn: outpcd fnl 2f) | 2 | 5 | 12/1 | 63 | 39 |
| | **Lostris (IRE) (35)** (MDods) **5-7-12** LCharnock(10) (hdwy 3f out: styd on: no imp) | 1 | 6 | 50/1 | 36 | 13 |
| 508[4] | **Noble Canonire (43)** (SRBowring) **4-8-5** NCarlisle(4) (prom: effrt & ev ch over 4f out: wknd over 2f out) | 8 | 7 | 15/2 | 34 | 10 |
| 439[14] | **Oakbury (IRE) (62)** (MissLCSiddall) **4-9-10** JWeaver(8) (led 3f: cl up tl wknd over 3f out) | 1½ | 8 | 25/1 | 51 | 27 |
| *196*[4] | **Ashover (59)** (TDBarron) **6-9-8** JFortune(3) (lw: hld up: effrt 4f out: no imp) | 3½ | 9 | 9/2[2] | 43 | 20 |
| | **Specialize (39)** (KRBurke) **4-8-1** JTate(2) (lw: hld up: effrt 4f out: sn btn) | 14 | 10 | 40/1 | 5 | — |
| | **Bowcliffe (52)** (MrsAMNaughton) **5-9-1v**[1] JCarroll(5) (hld up: hdwy 4f out: wknd wl over 2f out) | 1 | 11 | 25/1 | 16 | — |
| | | | | (SP 117.9%) | **11 Rn** | |

**2m 43.2** (9.20) CSF £11.51 CT £69.15 TOTE £2.60: £1.60 £1.70 £1.60 (£5.30) Trio £18.10 OWNER Mr P. E. Axon (NEWMARKET) BRED Stud-On-The-Chart
WEIGHT FOR AGE 4yo-1lb
**546* Pip's Dream** has really come into her own of late and again won well. She is not all that big though and the Handicapper will no doubt punish her. (13/8)
**439 Outstayed Welcome** stays well and likes to be out in front but just missing the kick made a lot of difference here. Had luck been on his side, he may well have won. (6/1)
**558 Keep Battling** again loomed up behind the leaders in the straight going well, but he then never got a run when it mattered. (10/1)
**Hasta la Vista**, from a stable that is flying at present, ran a sound race and should now improve. (14/1)
**520* Forzair** was in the thick of things from a long way out, but was short of a turn of foot in the closing stages. (12/1: op 8/1)
**Lostris (IRE)** has missed a season but did run reasonably here and was keeping on at the end. (50/1)

## 613 GRANTLEY MAIDEN STKS (3-Y.O+) (Class D)

4-40 (4-42) **1m** £3,793.75 (£1,150.00: £562.50: £268.75) Stalls: High GOING: 0.02 sec per fur (G)

| | | | | SP | RR | SF |
|---|---|---|---|---|---|---|
| 445[2] | **Polinesso** (BWHills) **3-8-12** MHills(6) (lw: trckd ldrs: led over 3f out: qcknd 2f out: easily) | — | 1 | 2/1[2] | 89+ | 52 |
| | **Lost Lagoon (USA)** (HRACecil) **4-9-13** PatEddery(4) (lw: b: trckd ldrs: chal over 3f out: sn rdn: no ch w wnr) | 2½ | 2 | 10/11[1] | 84 | 62 |
| | **Tilaal (USA) (70)** (MDHammond) **4-9-13** WRyan(16) (a chsng ldrs: kpt on strly fnl f) | ½ | 3 | 100/1 | 83 | 61 |
| | **Le Khoumf (FR)** (JMBradley) **5-9-10**(3) SDrowne(2) (chsd ldrs: rdn ½-wy: no imp) | 6 | 4 | 20/1 | 71 | 49 |
| | **Angus-G** (MrsMReveley) **4-9-13** KDarley(9) (bit bkwd: hld up: stdy hdwy over 2f out: nvr plcd to chal) | nk | 5 | 20/1 | 70 | 48 |
| | **Boston Rock (IRE)** (PWHarris) **4-9-13** GHind(12) (bit bkwd: in tch: styd on one pce fnl 3f: nvr plcd to chal) | 3 | 6 | 14/1 | 64 | 42 |
| | **Lady of Leisure (USA)** (MrsJCecil) **4-9-8** TIves(11) (unf: bhd tl sme late hdwy) | 1½ | 7 | 20/1 | 56 | 34 |
| | **Bakers' Gate (USA)** (JHMGosden) **4-9-13** JCarroll(7) (hld up: shkn up over 3f out: nvr nr to chal) | nk | 8 | 9/1[3] | 61 | 39 |
| 477[12] | **Roussi (USA) (64)** (DNicholls) **4-9-13** SMason(10) (nvr nr ldrs) | nk | 9 | 100/1 | 60 | 38 |
| | **Captain Tandy (IRE)** (CSmith) **7-9-13** KRutter(13) (bit bkwd: nvr nr ldrs) | 6 | 10 | 500/1 | 48 | 26 |
| | **Fairywings** (MrsJRRamsden) **3-8-7** KFallon(1) (unruly s: a rr div) | 1 | 11 | 33/1 | 41 | 4 |
| | **Squared Away** (JWPayne) **4-9-13** RCochrane(8) (w'like: bit bkwd: hld up & bhd: shkn up 4f out: n.d) | ¾ | 12 | 50/1 | 45 | 23 |
| | **Riccarton** (PCalver) **3-8-12** MBirch(3) (leggy: scope: dwlt: a bhd) | s.h | 13 | 33/1 | 45 | 8 |
| | **Any Colour** (MJCamacho) **3-8-7** LCharnock(14) (in tch tl wknd fnl 3f) | 3½ | 14 | 100/1 | 33 | — |
| | **Nordisk Legend** (MrsDThomson) **4-9-10**(3) OPears(15) (led tl hdd & wknd over 3f out) | 6 | 15 | 300/1 | 26 | 4 |
| *248*[5] | **Clytha Hill Lad** (JMBradley) **5-9-13** TWilliams(5) (a rr div) | hd | 16 | 300/1 | 25 | 3 |
| | | | | (SP 128.3%) | **16 Rn** | |

**1m 42.2** (4.50) CSF £4.14 TOTE £3.40: £1.20 £1.10 £7.30 (£2.10) Trio £36.20 OWNER Sheikh Mohammed (LAMBOURN) BRED Sheikh Mohammed bin Rashid al Maktoum
WEIGHT FOR AGE 3yo-15lb
**445 Polinesso** has come on a ton for his Doncaster run and won this in tremendous style. There is certainly more to be seen of him. (2/1)
**Lost Lagoon (USA)** raced too freely for his own good and was then well outclassed by the winner. Improvement should come with experience but he does not seem anything special. (10/11)
**Tilaal (USA)** started last season with an eyecatching run on this track and then disappointed, so it will be interesting to see what he does from here. (100/1)
**Le Khoumf (FR)** has been winning over hurdles. Although looking short of pace, he did keep on well. (20/1)
**Angus-G** continued the promise of last year and this good-looking sort will improve no end once connections decide he has learnt his job. (20/1)
**Boston Rock (IRE)** needed this and was given a very kind ride which will no doubt improve him. (14/1)
**Lady of Leisure (USA)** had a nice introduction here and, staying on at the end, showed that improvement is likely. (20/1)
**Bakers' Gate (USA)** (9/1: 5/1-10/1)

## 614 SAWLEY H'CAP (0-70) (3-Y.O) (Class E)

5-10 (5-11) **1m 2f** £3,137.35 (£950.80: £464.90: £221.95) Stalls: High GOING: 0.02 sec per fur (G)

| | | | | SP | RR | SF |
|---|---|---|---|---|---|---|
| | **Muhtadi (IRE) (70)** (JLDunlop) **3-9-7** WCarson(4) (b: sn chsng ldrs: led appr fnl f: drvn out) | — | **1** | 3/1[1] | 77 | 29 |
| | **Nose No Bounds (IRE) (70)** (MJohnston) **3-9-7** JWeaver(9) (lw: cl up: disp ld over 3f out tl hdd over 1f out: hung lft & rallied towards fin) | s.h | **2** | 9/2[2] | 77 | 29 |
| | **Phantom Haze (61)** (MissSEHall) **3-8-12** KDarley(14) (hdwy ½-wy: swtchd rt over 2f out: sn ev ch: kpt on fnl f) | 2½ | **3** | 6/1[3] | 64 | 16 |
| | **One Life To Live (IRE) (50)** (AHarrison) **3-8-1** JFanning(11) (bit bkwd: a cl up: effrt 3f out: nt qckn fnl f) | s.h | **4** | 25/1 | 53 | 5 |
| 355[8] | **Sheemore (IRE) (47)** (JDBethell) **3-7-12**ow2 TWilliams(5) (hdwy ent st: disp ld over 3f out tl hdd appr fnl f: nt qckn) | ¾ | **5** | 20/1 | 49 | — |
| 262[3] | **Ordained (46)** (EJAlston) **3-7-11** JQuinn(6) (a.p: n.m.r over 2f out: kpt on) | s.h | **6** | 9/1 | 48 | — |
| | **Champagne Warrior (IRE) (45)** (MJCamacho) **3-7-10** LCharnock(12) (bit bkwd: jnd ldrs over 4f out: n.m.r whn one pce fnl 2f) | d.h | **6** | 20/1 | 47 | — |
| | **Etterby Park (USA) (45)** (MrsJRRamsden) **3-7-10** NKennedy(15) (lw: hdwy on ins over 2f out: nvr able to chal) | ¾ | **8** | 8/1 | 45 | — |
| | **Marsayas (IRE) (55)** (MJCamacho) **3-8-6** DeanMcKeown(2) (bhd tl styd on fnl 2f: hmpd ins fnl f) | 1¼ | **9** | 25/1 | 53 | 5 |
| | **Forgie (IRE) (53)** (PCalver) **3-8-4** MBirch(1) (bit bkwd: dwlt: sme late hdwy) | 1½ | **10** | 14/1 | 49 | 1 |
| | **Ivor's Deed (52)** (CFWall) **3-8-3** GDuffield(8) (n.d) | 6 | **11** | 14/1 | 19 | — |
| 444[10] | **Strategic Ploy (62)** (MrsJRRamsden) **3-8-13** KFallon(10) (a in rr) | hd | **12** | 8/1 | 48 | — |
| | **Sassetta (IRE) (45)** (NTinkler) **3-7-10** KimTinkler(3) (bit bkwd: swtg: a bhd) | 6 | **13** | 33/1 | 22 | — |
| | **Energy Man (70)** (MDods) **3-9-7** JCarroll(13) (a bhd) | 3½ | **14** | 14/1 | 41 | — |
| 463[4] | **Sphinx Levelv (IRE) (52)** (APJarvis) **3-8-3** JTate(7) (led tl hdd & wknd over 3f out) | nk | **15** | 12/1 | 23 | — |
| | | | | (SP 137.5%) | **15 Rn** | |

**2m 13.2** (9.70) CSF £18.55 CT £78.64 TOTE £2.40: £1.80 £2.00 £1.80 (£5.50) Trio £11.80 OWNER Mr Hamdan Al Maktoum (ARUNDEL) BRED Ash Hill Stud

LONG HANDICAP Sassetta (IRE) 7-0

**Muhtadi (IRE),** given a fine ride, won without being given too hard a time and should improve as a result. (3/1)
**Nose No Bounds (IRE)** appreciated this extra trip and kept fighting back when looking well beaten. Improvement now looks likely. (9/2)
**Phantom Haze** looks to be getting it together this year and kept on well in the final three furlongs, despite being a bit short of room at times. (6/1)
**One Life To Live (IRE)** showed his first signs of form here and looked likely to benefit from the outing. (25/1)
**Sheemore (IRE)** had shown nothing previously but did run quite well here, and would seem to be learning. (20/1)
**Ordained** ran a decent race, despite being messed about, and should improve as a result. (9/1)
**Etterby Park (USA)** did not do anything quickly, but did show something, despite always being a bit short of room in the final three furlongs. (8/1)
**Marsayas (IRE)** only got going when the race was over and then had to be snatched up inside the final furlong, but for which he would have been a deal closer. (25/1)

T/Jkpt: £27,878.50 (0.09 Tckts); £35,731.69 to Hamilton 11/4/96. T/Plpt: £22.40 (728.32 Tckts). T/Qdpt: £6.40 (214.39 Tckts). AA

# 0537-HAMILTON (R-H) (Good to soft, Good patches)

## Thursday April 11th

WEATHER: cloudy WIND: almost nil

## 615 CALDER APPRENTICE H'CAP (0-70) (3-Y.O+) (Class E)

2-20 (2-23) **1m 65y** £2,790.00 (£855.00: £425.00: £210.00) Stalls: High GOING: 0.06 sec per fur (G)

| | | | | SP | RR | SF |
|---|---|---|---|---|---|---|
| 505[2] | **Rambo Waltzer (55)** (DNicholls) **4-9-1** JoHunnam(7) (lw: a.p: led 2f out: r.o wl) | — | **1** | 9/4[1] | 64 | 30 |
| 136[6] | **Snake Plissken (IRE) (44)** (DHaydnJones) **5-8-1**(3) AnthonyBond(8) (lw: a chsng ldrs: kpt on fnl f) | 1¼ | **2** | 9/1[2] | 51 | 17 |
| 586[6] | **Master Ofthe House (59)** (MDHammond) **10-9-0**(5) DHayden(6) (lw: a.p: effrt 2f out: kpt on towards fin) | 1 | **3** | 9/1[2] | 64 | 30 |
| | **Tinklers Folly (46)** (DenysSmith) **4-8-3**(3) RFfrench(4) (chsd ldrs: led 3f out to 2f out: r.o one pce) | 1 | **4** | 25/1 | 49 | 15 |
| 561[9] | **My Handy Man (47)** (RAllan) **5-8-7** JDennis(11) (bhd: hdwy on ins 3f out: rdn & no imp fnl 2f) | nk | **5** | 25/1 | 49 | 15 |
| 558[7] | **Rapid Mover (40)** (DANolan) **9-7-11b**(3)ow4 JoanneWebster(9) (styd on fr ½-wy: nvr rchd ldrs) | 2 | **6** | 66/1 | 38 | — |
| 527* | **Maple Bay (IRE) (67)** (ABailey) **7-9-10**(3) 5x AngelaGallimore(10) (lw: nvr trbld ldrs) | 1¾ | **7** | 9/4[1] | 62 | 28 |
| | **Hey Up Dolly (IRE) (58)** (JJO'Neill) **4-9-4** OliverCasey(12) (bhd: effrt ½-wy: no imp) | 4 | **8** | 50/1 | 45 | 11 |
| 172[4] | **Mill Dancer (IRE) (46)** (EJAlston) **4-8-1**(5) CHalliwell(2) (racd wd: led tl hdd & wknd 3f out) | 6 | **9** | 14/1 | 22 | — |
| 537[7] | **Talented Ting (IRE) (64)** (PCHaslam) **7-9-7v**(3) CarolDavison(5) (in tch: wknd fr ½-wy) | 1 | **10** | 14/1 | 38 | 4 |
| | **Waterlord (IRE) (40)** (DNicholls) **6-7-11**(3) JBramhill(3) (in tch tl ½-wy) | 2½ | **11** | 11/1[3] | 9 | — |
| | **Lancashire Life (IRE) (48)** (EJAlston) **5-8-5**(3) RMullen(1) (racd wd: outpcd & bhd fnl 5f) | 6 | **12** | 25/1 | 5 | — |
| | | | | (SP 118.2%) | **12 Rn** | |

**1m 51.8** (7.70) CSF £21.49 CT £143.23 TOTE £3.40: £1.50 £3.30 £2.20 (£20.10) Trio £69.10 OWNER Keystone Racing Club Partnership (THIRSK) BRED Triangle Thoroughbreds Ltd

LONG HANDICAP Rapid Mover 7-0

STEWARDS' ENQUIRY Gallimore susp. 20 & 22/4/96 (excessive use of whip).

**505 Rambo Waltzer** was turned out looking a credit to all concerned and won in great style. Off a useful mark, he should now be able to find further success. (9/4)
**Snake Plissken (IRE)** has yet to win a race but there was nothing wrong with this effort, and he may at last be getting the right idea. (9/1)
**586 Master Ofthe House** is coming to form just now and is worth keeping in mind. (9/1)
**Tinklers Folly** ran well after a lengthy lay-off and should do better as a result. (25/1)
**My Handy Man** always had the best ground but was never going well enough to take the opportunity. (25/1)
**558 Rapid Mover,** from 10lb out of the handicap and putting up another 4lb overweight on top, was also over a trip shorter than his best, but ran reasonably well. (66/1)
**537 Talented Ting (IRE)** (14/1: op 8/1)

## 616 SPRINGFIELD RATING RELATED MAIDEN STKS (0-60) (3-Y.O) (Class F)

2-55 (2-55) **1m 65y** £2,549.00 (£714.00: £347.00) Stalls: High GOING: 0.06 sec per fur (G)

| | | | | SP | RR | SF |
|---|---|---|---|---|---|---|
| 458[7] | **Forest Boy (60)** (KWMcAuliffe) **3-9-0v** JFEgan(2) (hld up: hdwy to ld 2f out: rdn & r.o wl) | — | **1** | 11/2 | 66 | 33 |

| | | | | SP | RR | SF |
|---|---|---|---|---|---|---|
| 468[4] | **Get Tough (57)** (SDow) **3-8-9**(5) ADaly(8) (a chsng ldrs: effrt 2f out: kpt on) | 1¼ | **2** | 7/2 [2] | 64 | 31 |
| *345[5]* | **Domino Flyer (52)** (MrsASwinbank) **3-9-0** JFortune(1) (a.p: brought wd st: one pce fnl 2f) | 3½ | **3** | 16/1 | 57 | 24 |
| | **Soviet King (IRE) (60)** (PhilipMitchell) **3-8-7**(7) JoHunnam(6) (hdwy & c wd st: ev ch over 2f out: r.o one pce) | hd | **4** | 10/1 | 57 | 24 |
| 540[3] | **Rattle (50)** (JJO'Neill) **3-9-0** SDWilliams(7) (sn pushed along: bhd tl hdwy 3f out: one pce fnl f) | s.h | **5** | 16/1 | 57 | 24 |
| 562[4] | **Dungeon Princess (IRE) (55)** (MRChannon) **3-8-11** RHughes(4) (cl up: led after 2f to 2f out: wknd appr fnl f) | 1 | **6** | 5/2 [1] | 52 | 19 |
| 467[11] | **Mister Woodstick (IRE) (50)** (MAJarvis) **3-9-0** PRobinson(5) (effrt ½-wy: no imp) | 1 | **7** | 9/2 [3] | 53 | 20 |
| | **Boundary Bird (IRE) (60)** (MJohnston) **3-9-0** JWeaver(3) (slt ld 2f: cl up tl rdn & wknd 3f out) | 15 | **8** | 8/1 | 24 | — |
| | | | | (SP 116.3%) | **8 Rn** | |

**1m 51.4** (7.30) CSF £24.02 TOTE £6.60: £1.90 £1.50 £3.40 (£11.80) OWNER Highgrove Developments Ltd (LAMBOURN) BRED J. B. H. Stevens
**Forest Boy** appreciated this longer trip and won really well, suggesting that there is more to come. (11/2)
**468 Get Tough** did not do anything quickly but he did keep staying on and should even stay a bit further. (7/2)
**Domino Flyer** ran a fair race on the worst ground and should pick up a modest event in due course. (16/1)
**Soviet King (IRE)** was always racing in the slower ground towards the centre of the track and was tapped for toe in the closing stages. He can do better. (10/1: op 6/1)
**540 Rattle**, who failed to impress on looks, certainly takes a long time to get going and failed to make any impression. (16/1)
**562 Dungeon Princess (IRE)** failed to get home over this longer trip. (5/2)
**Boundary Bird (IRE)** (8/1: 6/1-10/1)

## 617 DAVIE COOPER MEMORIAL H'CAP (0-75) (3-Y.O+) (Class D)
3-30 (3-31) **6f 5y** £3,934.10 (£1,191.80: £582.40: £277.70) Stalls: Low GOING: 0.06 sec per fur (G)

| | | | | SP | RR | SF |
|---|---|---|---|---|---|---|
| *413** | **My Gallery (IRE) (48)** (ABailey) **5-7-13**(7) AngelaGallimore(3) (drvn along stands' side: hdwy over 1f out: hung rt: styd on to ld wl ins fnl f) | — | **1** | 3/1 [1] | 59+ | 26 |
| | **Mister Westsound (61)** (MissLAPerratt) **4-9-5b** JWeaver(15) (bit bkwd: hdwy ½-wy: sn chsng ldrs: ev ch ins fnl f: kpt on wl) | nk | **2** | 9/1 [3] | 71 | 38 |
| | **Garnock Valley (63)** (JBerry) **6-9-7** JCarroll(14) (chsd ldrs: led over 2f out tl wl ins fnl f) | 1 | **3** | 10/1 | 71 | 38 |
| *291[8]* | **Panther (IRE) (51)** (JHetherton) **6-8-9** KDarley(8) (cl up tl rdn & btn appr fnl f) | 3 | **4** | 12/1 | 51 | 18 |
| 562[13] | **Samsung Lovelylady (IRE) (46)** (EWeymes) **4-8-4** JFanning(17) (disp ld over 3f: grad wknd) | ½ | **5** | 25/1 | 44 | 11 |
| 587[12] | **Craigie Boy (49)** (NBycroft) **6-8-7b** PRobinson(5) (hdwy ½-wy: styd on: no imp) | 2½ | **6** | 7/1 [2] | 41 | 8 |
| 561[5] | **Diet (51)** (MissLAPerratt) **10-8-9v** NConnorton(6) (in tch: rdn ½-wy: no imp) | 4 | **7** | 12/1 | 32 | — |
| | **Rinus Manor (IRE) (40)** (EJAlston) **5-7-12** LCharnock(16) (sn drvn along: nvr trbld ldrs) | 5 | **8** | 7/1 [2] | 8 | — |
| *513[7]* | **Ultra Beet (70)** (PCHaslam) **4-10-0v** JFortune(12) (nvr trbld ldrs) | 2 | **9** | 14/1 | 32 | — |
| | **Another Nightmare (IRE) (41)** (TDyer) **4-7-6**(7) RMullen(11) (no imp fr ½-wy) | 1½ | **10** | 33/1 | — | — |
| | **Mu-Arrik (44)** (GROldroyd) **8-8-2v** JFEgan(9) (nvr trbld ldrs) | 5 | **11** | 25/1 | — | — |
| 554[16] | **Sue Me (IRE) (67)** (WRMuir) **4-9-11** RHughes(13) (lw: in tch: rdn ½-wy: sn btn) | 5 | **12** | 10/1 | — | — |
| 559[11] | **Leading Princess (IRE) (51)** (MissLAPerratt) **5-8-9b** RLappin(7) (disp ld over 3f: grad wknd) | ¾ | **13** | 25/1 | — | — |
| | **Densben (53)** (DenysSmith) **12-8-11** KFallon(4) (nvr wnt pce) | 4 | **14** | 20/1 | — | — |
| | **Cymbalo (39)** (MissLAPerratt) **5-7-8**(3)ow1 DWright(10) (s.i.s: a bhd) | 1¼ | **15** | 50/1 | — | — |
| | **Suedoro (48)** (RMMcKellar) **6-8-1**(5) PFessey(2) (spd to ½-wy: wknd qckly) | 3½ | **16** | 33/1 | — | — |
| | **Natural Key (70)** (DHaydnJones) **3-9-2** AMackay(1) (spd stands' side to ½-wy: wknd qckly) | 1¼ | **17** | 14/1 | — | — |
| | | | | (SP 131.0%) | **17 Rn** | |

**1m 14.9** (4.90) CSF £30.55 CT £243.65 TOTE £5.10: £2.10 £2.30 £2.60 £3.20 (£28.40) Trio £98.60 OWNER Mr Robert Cox (TARPORLEY) BRED East Riding Sack and Paper Co
LONG HANDICAP Cymbalo 7-2
WEIGHT FOR AGE 3yo-12lb
**My Gallery (IRE)** did what appeared impossible and won from a low draw, making up a lot of ground to do so. (3/1: op 9/2)
**Mister Westsound** needed this and ran a cracker. If he really decides to get it together this year, he certainly has the ability to leave this form well behind. (9/1)
**Garnock Valley** last won three seasons ago but he does always seem to put in his best effort first time out, and was only just touched off here. (10/1)
**Panther (IRE)** likes this track and ran a fine race, but was just short of a real turn of foot. (12/1)
**Samsung Lovelylady (IRE)** had trouble with the bend at Musselburgh last time, but appreciated this straight track and ran her best race for a while. (25/1)
**Craigie Boy** ran really well from a poor draw and would seem to be coming to hand. (7/1)
**Rinus Manor (IRE)**, well drawn and well supported at morning prices, never went the pace at any stage. (7/1)

## 618 DUNWAN MEDIAN AUCTION MAIDEN STKS (2-Y.O) (Class F)
4-05 (4-05) **5f 4y** £2,507.00 (£702.00: £341.00) Stalls: Low GOING: 0.06 sec per fur (G)

| | | | | SP | RR | SF |
|---|---|---|---|---|---|---|
| | **Express Girl** (DMoffatt) **2-8-6**(3) DarrenMoffatt(2) (neat: lw: unruly in paddock: mde all: kpt on wl fnl f) | — | **1** | 25/1 | 69 | — |
| 476[2] | **I'm Still Here** (JBerry) **2-9-0** JCarroll(4) (lw: trckd ldrs: hdwy to chal over 1f out: rdn & nt qckn) | 1¾ | **2** | 11/10 [1] | 68 | — |
| 551[2] | **Irish Fiction (IRE)** (MRChannon) **2-9-0** RHughes(1) (lw: s.s: hdwy over 1f out: nvr nr to chal) | 2½ | **3** | 6/4 [2] | 60 | — |
| | **Our Future (IRE)** (MJohnston) **2-9-0** JWeaver(3) (w'like: str: bit bkwd: gd spd over 3f: sn btn) | 5 | **4** | 4/1 [3] | 45 | — |
| | | | | (SP 111.5%) | **4 Rn** | |

**64.6 secs** (6.30) CSF £50.96 TOTE £12.20 (£8.80) OWNER Mr P. G. Airey (CARTMEL) BRED P. G. Airey and R. R. Whitton
**Express Girl** proved to be very unruly in the paddock, but this sharp sort was very fit indeed and proved far too strong for the opposition in the closing stages. (25/1)
**476 I'm Still Here** travelled as though the race was his for the taking for most of the trip but, when it came down to it approaching the final furlong, he proved a shade disappointing. (11/10)
**551 Irish Fiction (IRE)** threw his chances away by starting slowly, and was then not over-punished. (6/4)
**Our Future (IRE)**, a big, strong sort, needed this and certainly did not look the type for this time of year, but he did show plenty of toe until blowing up well over a furlong out. (4/1: 3/1-9/2)

## 619 GLEN LIMITED STKS (0-65) (4-Y.O+) (Class F)
4-40 (4-40) **1m 4f 17y** £2,591.00 (£726.00: £353.00) Stalls: High GOING: 0.06 sec per fur (G)

| | | | | SP | RR | SF |
|---|---|---|---|---|---|---|
| | **Eau de Cologne (62)** (CWThornton) **4-8-12** DeanMcKeown(1) (cl up: led over 2f out: styd on strly) | — | **1** | 4/1 [2] | 69 | 44 |

482[13] **Mentalasanythin (62)** (ABailey) **7-9-1** AMackay(6) (a chsng ldrs: ev ch 2f out: kpt on)....1½ **2** 6/1[3] 69 45
541[2] **Astral Weeks (IRE) (57)** (LLungo) **5-9-1** KFallon(9) (lw: sn bhd & pushed along: hdwy 4f out: chsng ldrs 2f out: one pce after)....11 **3** 7/2[1] 54 30
541* **Calder King (57)** (JLEyre) **5-9-1v** RLappin(5) (hld up: effrt over 3f out: no imp fnl 2f)....½ **4** 4/1[2] 54 30
546[15] **Turgenev (IRE) (65)** (RBastiman) **7-8-13b** ACulhane(3) (s.s: hdwy 3f out: nvr plcd to chal)....nk **5** 14/1 51 27
482[6] **House of Dreams (60)** (GMMoore) **4-8-12** JFortune(2) (led tl hdd & wknd over 2f out)....¾ **6** 16/1 50 25
440[26] **King Curan (USA) (60)** (ABailey) **5-8-13** LCharnock(4) (in tch tl outpcd fnl 2½f)....3½ **7** 25/1 46 22
**Fassan (IRE) (61)** (MDHammond) **4-8-12** JCarroll(7) (trckd ldrs: effrt 4f out: sn btn)....8 **8** 4/1[2] 35 10
*328*[11] **Carmenoura (IRE) (30)** (EJAlston) **4-8-9** SDWilliams(8) (a bhd: eased fnl 2f)....dist **9** 100/1 — —
(SP 113.9%) **9 Rn**

**2m 40.7** (8.70) CSF £25.74 TOTE £5.50: £1.50 £1.90 £1.70 (£16.60) Trio £25.60 OWNER Mr Guy Reed (MIDDLEHAM) BRED G. Reed
WEIGHT FOR AGE 4yo-1lb
**Eau de Cologne** stays a good deal further but these testing conditions suited him well and he was nicely on top at the finish. (4/1)
**Mentalasanythin** has five wins to his credit at this track and ran another useful race, but found the winner too good. (6/1)
**541 Astral Weeks (IRE)**, despite stepping up in distance, got completely outpaced early on and then, after almost getting into it, found the last two furlongs beyond him. (7/2)
**541* Calder King** tried to improve halfway up the straight but was always finding the struggle too much. (4/1: 3/1-9/2)
**Turgenev (IRE)** again missed the break, but he showed enough afterwards to suggest that he is well worth keeping on the right side. (14/1)
**482 House of Dreams**, dropped back in distance, was still done with quite a way from home. (16/1)
**Fassan (IRE)** did not give anything like his true running here. (4/1: 5/2-9/2)

## 620 JOSEPH BODWICK 80TH BIRTHDAY H'CAP (0-70) (4-Y.O+) (Class E)
5-15 (5-15) **1m 5f 9y** £3,439.20 (£1,041.60: £508.80: £242.40) Stalls: High GOING: 0.06 sec per fur (G)

SP RR SF

508[5] **Lord Hastie (USA) (59)** (CWThornton) **8-9-6**(3) OPears(5) (lw: hld up: hdwy to ld over 1f out: r.o u.p)....— **1** 13/2[3] 71 40
482[5] **Sarawat (59)** (DNicholls) **8-9-9** AlexGreaves(2) (lw: trckd ldrs: led over 3f out tl over 1f out: rallied u.p)....½ **2** 5/2[1] 70 39
542[3] **Palace of Gold (37)** (LLungo) **6-8-1** JFanning(14) (mde most tl hdd over 3f out: kpt on u.p fr 2f out)....1¼ **3** 10/1 47 16
542[5] **Philmist (35)** (CWCElsey) **4-7-11b** NKennedy(10) (rr div: effrt 3f out: styd on towards fin)....nk **4** 6/1[2] 45 12
558[6] **Lord Advocate (33)** (DANolan) **8-7-8b**(3) NVarley(9) (hdwy 7f out: chsng ldrs 4f out: ev ch 2f out: grad wknd).2 **5** 66/1 40 9
542[2] **Me Cherokee (46)** (CWThornton) **4-8-8** DeanMcKeown(8) (chsd ldrs: ev ch 3f out: one pce fnl 2f)....2½ **6** 10/1 50 17
439[12] **Premier Dance (48)** (DHaydnJones) **9-8-12** AMackay(6) (bhd: effrt 4f out: no imp)....7 **7** 14/1 43 12
542* **Eurotwist (44)** (SEKettlewell) **7-8-8** 4x JFortune(15) (bhd: hdwy ½-wy: one pce fnl 2f)....½ **8** 8/1 39 8
**Keen To The Last (FR) (60)** (MDHammond) **4-9-8** KFallon(1) (hdwy 6f out: sn prom: wknd fnl 2f)....1 **9** 9/1 54 21
**Vintage Taittinger (IRE) (37)** (TDyer) **4-7-6**(7) RMullen(13) (bhd: hdwy 4f out: sn wknd)....3 **10** 16/1 27 —
541[5] **Cutthroat Kid (IRE) (62)** (MrsMReveley) **6-9-12v** KDarley(7) (nvr rchd ldrs)....1½ **11** 10/1 50 19
**Fanadiyr (IRE) (55)** (WStorey) **4-8-12**(5) PFessey(3) (a rr div)....8 **12** 66/1 33 —
**Friendly Knight (32)** (JSHaldane) **6-7-10** LCharnock(12) (b.nr hind: disp ld 4f: wknd 5f out)....1½ **13** 100/1 8 —
*489** **Colosse (51)** (JLEyre) **4-8-13** RLappin(4) (hld up: smooth hdwy 6f out: rdn & wknd 3f out)....nk **14** 11/1 27 —
**Recluse (47)** (MissLAPerratt) **5-8-11b** JCarroll(11) (cl up tl wknd qckly 6f out)....dist **15** 100/1 — —
(SP 130.4%) **15 Rn**

**2m 57.5** (11.80) CSF £23.40 CT £159.28 TOTE £7.70: £3.80 £2.30 £3.40 (£15.80) Trio £86.80 OWNER Mrs Joy Bendall (MIDDLEHAM) BRED Upland Park Stud
LONG HANDICAP Friendly Knight 7-6
WEIGHT FOR AGE 4yo-2lb
**508 Lord Hastie (USA)** appreciated this step back up in distance, and won really well, despite not doing a lot in front. He should find further success. (13/2)
**482 Sarawat** took the eye in the paddock and is obviously coming back to form. He is very well handicapped. (5/2)
**542 Palace of Gold** ran a decent race, but again left the impression that should he ever decide to there is better to come. (10/1: 8/1-12/1)
**542 Philmist** was again in behind a wall of horses for much of the trip, but he did stay on at the end. He could well be a funny customer. (6/1)
**558 Lord Advocate** ran pretty well but was not made enough use of early on. (66/1)
**542 Me Cherokee**, a stable-companion of the winner, ran a fair race but was tapped for toe in the last quarter-mile. (10/1)
**541 Cutthroat Kid (IRE)** (10/1: op 6/1)

T/Jkpt: Not won; £53,147.21 to Nottingham 12/4/96. T/Plpt: £1,069.10 (15.44 Tckts). T/Qdpt: £124.80 (9.43 Tckts). AA

# LONGCHAMP (Paris, France) (R-H) (Firm)
## Sunday April 7th

## 621a PRIX NOAILLES (Gp 2) (3-Y.O C & F)
2-40 (2-39) **1m 3f** £37,819.00 (£15,053.00: £7,339.00: £3,294.00)

SP RR SF

**Helissio (FR)** (ELellouche,France) **3-9-2** DBoeuf (chsd ldr tl led ent st: rdn clr over 1f out: impressive)....— **1** 109++ 72
**Arbatax (IRE)** (PBary,France) **3-9-2** CAsmussen (chsd ldrs: rdn over 2f out: wnt 2nd over 1f out: styd on one pce ins fnl f)....4 **2** 103 66
**Oliviero (FR)** (AMauchamp,France) **3-9-2** ABadel (rdn & last early: hdwy ent st: chal ins fnl f: no ex)....hd **3** 103 66
**Supreme Commander (FR)** (AFabre,France) **3-9-2** TJarnet (a abt same pl: rdn & one pce fnl 2f)....2½ **4** 99 62
**Go Between (FR)** (GDoleuze,France) **3-9-2** ODoleuze (led tl over 2f out: wknd qckly)....5 **5** 92 55
**5 Rn**

**2m 14.5** (0.50) P-M 2.10F: 1.90F 2.20F (SF 9.60F) OWNER E. Sarasola BRED Ecurie Skymarc Farm
**Helissio (FR)**, an exciting, good-looking individual, spreadeagled this field on only his second racecourse appearance. He has enormous scope for improvement, and broke the track-record with this victory. Apparently an easy horse to ride, he is learning all the time and will now be aimed at the Prix Lupin, which will hopefully be followed by the Prix du Jockey-Club.
**Arbatax (IRE)** never looked like catching the winner but stayed on gamely to hold second place. He is decent but one-paced, so he will do better over a longer distance, but it is unlikely that he is up to Group standard.
**Oliviero (FR)**, held up in last place until making his effort halfway up the straight, was putting in his best work at the finish.. He is consistent, but only listed standard in France.
**Supreme Commander (FR)** looked one-paced, but did stay on in the straight. He ran well below his two-year-old form, but his stable has yet to hit top form.

## 622a PRIX D'HARCOURT (Gp 2) (4-Y.O+ C & F)
4-05 (4-10) **1m 2f** £36,526.00 (£15,810.00: £7,905.00: £3,953.00)

| | Horse | Details | Dist | Pos | SP | RR | SF |
|---|---|---|---|---|---|---|---|
| | **Valanour (IRE)** | (AdeRoyerDupre,France) **4-9-4** GMosse (a.p: 3rd st: gd hdwy to ld over 1f out: r.o wl) | — | **1** | | 126 | 56 |
| | **Carling (FR)** | (MmePBarbe,France) **4-9-1** TThulliez (hld up in rr: rdn 2f out: qcknd wl ins fnl f: r.o) | 1½ | **2** | | 121 | 51 |
| | **Housamix (FR)** | (AFabre,France) **4-9-1** TJarnet (plld hrd: 5th ent st: rdn 2f out: kpt on wl cl home) | nk | **3** | | 120 | 50 |
| | **Marildo (FR)** | (DSmaga,France) **9-8-12b** FHead (led: rdn over 2f out: hdd over 1f out: one pce) | 1½ | **4** | | 115 | 45 |
| 438a[3] | **Tot Ou Tard (IRE)** | (JForesi,France) **6-9-1** FPardon (hld up: 4th st: outpcd 2f out: sme late hdwy) | s.h | **5** | | 118 | 48 |
| 438a* | **Gunboat Diplomacy (FR)** | (ELellouche,France) **5-8-12** OPeslier (a cl up: 2nd st: rdn over 2f out: outpcd cl home) | ½ | **6** | | 114 | 44 |

**6 Rn**

**2m 2.6** (2.60) P-M 3.90F: 2.90F 3.90F (SF 27.90F) OWNER Aga Khan (CHANTILLY) BRED H.H.Aga Khan Farms S.C.

**Valanour (IRE)** carries his head a little high, but is completely genuine and was produced in splendid condition by his trainer. Cruising throughout before taking a decisive lead halfway up the straight, he is a top-class individual when the ground is good or faster, and he also needs a decent pace. Providing the ground is to his advantage, he looks set for a highly successful year and goes next for the Prix Ganay.
**Carling (FR)** looked fairly well forward in the paddock and put up a faultless performance. Held up early on before being brought with a run in the straight, she never looked like catching the winner. She has certainly trained on and will take on Valanour again in the Prix Ganay.
**Housamix (FR)** was always thereabouts, but was outpaced in the straight. He looks as if he might need a little further.
**Marildo (FR)** took up the running after two furlongs and battled all the way to the line. Even at the age of nine, he still runs well in top-class company, and more cut in the ground would have been to his advantage. He will go onto the Ganay, a race he won back in 1994.
DS

# 0437a-SAN SIRO (Milan, Italy) (R-H) (Good to soft)
## Sunday April 7th

## 623a PREMIO D'APRILE (Listed) (4-Y.O+)
3-40 (3-54) **1m 2f** £20,300.00 (£8,932.00: £4,872.00: £2,436.00)

| | Horse | Details | Dist | Pos | SP | RR | SF |
|---|---|---|---|---|---|---|---|
| | **Slicious** | (VCaruso,Italy) **4-9-2** MEsposito | — | **1** | | 117+ | — |
| | **Tarhelm (IRE)** | (GColleo,Italy) **4-8-9** MLatorre | 2¾ | **2** | | 106 | — |
| | **New Herald (IRE)** | (MCiciarelli,Italy) **7-8-13** AParravani | 1½ | **3** | | 107 | — |
| 442[4] | **Penny Drops** | (LordHuntingdon) **7-8-6** DHarrison | 1½ | **4** | | 98 | — |

**7 Rn**

**2m 7.1** (13.10) TOTE 16L: 13L 18L (37L) OWNER Laghi Stable BRED F. C. T. Wilson

**Slicious**, the one obvious hope of a top-class horse in Italy this season, had no trouble in giving weight away all round. The only one of the seven not to have had a race this year, he took over approaching the final furlong, and went clear without being put under serious pressure. He will not be without a chance in the Prix Ganay.
**442 Penny Drops** set off in front but was being pressed by a couple of rivals all the way. Once headed by the winner, she weakened steadily. By the time that she next races, she should be in foal to Barathea.

# 0504-BEVERLEY (R-H) (Good to firm)
## Friday April 12th
WEATHER: overcast WIND: str bhd

## 624 SCARBOROUGH (S) STKS (2-Y.O) (Class F)
2-20 (2-32) **5f** £2,616.00 (£726.00: £348.00) Stalls: Low GOING minus 0.44 sec per fur (F)

| | Horse | Details | Dist | Pos | SP | RR | SF |
|---|---|---|---|---|---|---|---|
| *533*[2] | **Contravene (IRE)** | (JBerry) **2-8-6** JCarroll(6) (trckd ldrs: led ins fnl f: r.o) | — | **1** | 6/4[1] | 47 | 12 |
| 506[3] | **Small Risk** | (CADwyer) **2-8-6** JTate(3) (lw: led tl hdd & no ex ins fnl f) | 1½ | **2** | 13/8[2] | 42 | 7 |
| *533*[3] | **Abstone Queen** | (PDEvans) **2-8-6** KFallon(4) (a chsng ldrs: hdwy over 1f out: no imp) | 1¼ | **3** | 6/1[3] | 38 | 3 |
| 590[3] | **Chilled Wine** | (NBycroft) **2-8-6** GBardwell(2) (chsd ldrs: rdn ½-wy: nvr able to chal) | ¾ | **4** | 10/1 | 36 | 1 |
| 538[4] | **Mill End Girl** | (MWEasterby) **2-8-6** MBirch(1) (unruly leaving paddock & led to s: cl up tl rdn & btn 1f out) | 1½ | **5** | 10/1 | 31 | — |
| | **Flood's Flyer (IRE)** | (NTinkler) **2-8-6** LCharnock(5) (small: str: bkwd: sn outpcd & bhd) | 13 | **6** | 14/1 | — | — |

(SP 117.2%) **6 Rn**

**64.2 secs** (2.70) CSF £4.50 TOTE £2.30: £1.30 £1.60 (£1.90) OWNER Mr William Burns (COCKERHAM) BRED E. O'Leary
No bid

**533 Contravene (IRE)** behaved herself well this time and, in the race, always held a good position and saw this stiff five furlongs out in good style. (6/4: tchd Evens)
**506 Small Risk** looked particularly fit, but was worried out of it in the final furlong and may need a bit of cut in the ground. (13/8)
**533 Abstone Queen** always had the leaders within sight, but lacked the pace to really trouble them, despite keeping on. (6/1: op 7/2)
**590 Chilled Wine**, already having her fourth run here, was off the bit by halfway and could never offer a real threat. (10/1: op 6/1)
**538 Mill End Girl** gave no end of problems before the start, but did show some useful speed to show that if she settles down, there should be a similar event to be picked up. (10/1)
**Flood's Flyer (IRE)** badly needed this and was soon left way behind. (14/1: 10/1-16/1)

## 625 BRIDLINGTON BAY H'CAP (0-70) (4-Y.O+) (Class E)
2-50 (2-56) **2m 35y** £3,286.50 (£987.00: £476.00: £220.50) Stalls: Low GOING minus 0.44 sec per fur (F)

| | Horse | Details | Dist | Pos | SP | RR | SF |
|---|---|---|---|---|---|---|---|
| 474[5] | **Sudden Spin (42)** | (JNorton) **6-8-0** JFanning(15) (in tch: hdwy to ld appr fnl f: r.o) | — | **1** | 15/2[3] | 56 | 28 |
| 474* | **Arian Spirit (IRE) (43)** | (JLEyre) **5-8-1** LCharnock(13) (a.p: effrt 3f out: ev ch 2f out: r.o one pce) | 1¼ | **2** | 9/2[1] | 56 | 28 |
| 482[7] | **Hullbank (54)** | (WWHaigh) **6-8-12** JTate(4) (b: trckd ldrs: led wl over 1f out: hdd appr fnl f: one pce) | 1¼ | **3** | 8/1 | 66 | 38 |
| 449[13] | **Mondragon (70)** | (MrsMReveley) **6-9-7**(7) SCopp(7) (lw: bhd: hdwy on outside 3f out: hung rt: nvr able to chal) | 1¾ | **4** | 10/1 | 80 | 52 |
| | **True Bird (IRE) (60)** | (JDBethell) **4-9-0** JWeaver(2) (b.nr hind: rr div tl styd on fnl 2f) | 1¼ | **5** | 10/1 | 69 | 37 |
| 449[12] | **Shakiyr (FR) (56)** | (RHollinshead) **5-9-0** KFallon(10) (mid div: shkn up 5f out: styd on: n.d) | hd | **6** | 9/1 | 65 | 37 |

| | | | | SP | RR | SF |
|---|---|---|---|---|---|---|
| | **Great Oration (IRE) (38)** (FWatson) **7-7-5**(5) PFessey(11) (bit bkwd: dwlt: hdwy 2f out: nvr nr to chal) | 1½ | **7** | 16/1 | 45 | 17 |
| *60*[8] | **Bold Elect (46)** (EJAlston) **8-8-4** SDWilliams(3) (hld up: hdwy ½-wy: led wl over 2f out tl wl over 1f out: sn btn) | 7 | **8** | 16/1 | 46 | 18 |
| *297*[10] | **Prince Equiname (50)** (DEddy) **4-8-4** NConnorton(12) (nvr bttr than mid div) | ½ | **9** | 25/1 | 50 | 18 |
| 609[8] | **Bold Top (42)** (BSRothwell) **4-7-10b** NKennedy(17) (chsd ldrs tl wknd 3f out) | nk | **10** | 25/1 | 41 | 9 |
| | **Judicial Field (IRE) (69)** (NTinkler) **7-9-13** MBirch(9) (bhd tl sme late hdwy) | hd | **11** | 33/1 | 68 | 40 |
| 474[3] | **Hotspur Street (60)** (MWEasterby) **4-8-11**(3) DRMcCabe(5) (chsd ldrs: outpcd 3f out: sn wknd) | 1 | **12** | 6/1[2] | 58 | 26 |
| 474[7] | **Selmeston (IRE) (43)** (PSFelgate) **4-7-8**(3) DWright(6) (bhd: effrt ent st: n.d) | ¾ | **13** | 14/1 | 40 | 8 |
| 541[6] | **Dont Forget Curtis (IRE) (66)** (GMMoore) **4-9-6** JCarroll(16) (chsd ldrs: rdn 5f out: wknd fnl 3f) | 5 | **14** | 16/1 | 59 | 27 |
| 504[4] | **Desert Force (IRE) (38)** (GFierro) **7-7-10** AMackay(14) (b: prom: rdn over 3f out: sn wknd) | 6 | **15** | 25/1 | 25 | — |
| | **Penbola (IRE) (42)** (TDEasterby) **4-7-10** NCarlisle(18) (led tl hdd & wknd qckly wl over 2f out) | 2½ | **16** | 33/1 | 26 | — |
| *283*[5] | **Simafar (IRE) (57)** (NAGraham) **5-9-1v**[1] MHills(8) (a bhd) | 9 | **17** | 8/1 | 32 | 4 |
| 474[2] | **Top Prize (40)** (MBrittain) **8-7-12v** GBardwell(1) (sn pushed along: bhd fr ½-wy) | 4 | **18** | 6/1[2] | 11 | — |
| | | | | (SP 150.7%) | **18 Rn** | |

**3m 35.5** (5.00) CSF £46.78 CT £280.49 TOTE £8.60: £1.60 £1.50 £2.20 £2.70 (£21.30) Trio £253.50 OWNER Mr Billy Parker (BARNSLEY) BRED The Arrow Farm and Stud

LONG HANDICAP Bold Top 7-8 Desert Force (IRE) 7-7

WEIGHT FOR AGE 4yo-4lb

**474 Sudden Spin** dispelled any doubts about his ability to act on grass by winning this in good style. (15/2)

**474* Arian Spirit (IRE)** ran a sound race, but just found the winner too strong in the final furlong. (9/2)

**Hullbank** travelled well for much of the trip, but found little when in front in the straight. Perhaps more patient tactics are needed at this trip. (8/1)

**Mondragon** has not won for almost two years, but he did show ability here, staying on in the straight, despite hanging right. (10/1)

**True Bird (IRE)** has yet to win a race, but was keeping on well at the finish to suggest that she is in good heart. (10/1)

**Shakiyr (FR)**, off the bit some way out, stayed on, albeit without offering a threat. (9/1)

**Great Oration (IRE)** needed this and ran particularly well, being noted making steady late headway. (16/1)

**Bold Elect** raced too freely and then ran out of petrol in the last quarter-mile. (16/1)

## 626 HUTTON CRANSWICK MAIDEN STKS (3-Y.O+) (Class D)

3-20 (3-25) **5f** £3,691.00 (£1,108.00: £534.00: £247.00) Stalls: Low GOING minus 0.44 sec per fur (F)

| | | | | SP | RR | SF |
|---|---|---|---|---|---|---|
| | **Total Aloof** (WJHaggas) **3-8-7** MHills(8) (cl up: led over 1f out: styd on) | — | **1** | 9/4[2] | 72 | 43 |
| | **Divine Miss-P** (APJarvis) **3-8-7** JTate(5) (neat: in tch: hdwy 2f out: hung rt: styd on towards fin) | 1½ | **2** | 10/1 | 67 | 38 |
| | **Bowlers Boy** (JJQuinn) **3-8-12** MBirch(3) (bit bkwd: chsd ldrs tl n.m.r & lost pl 2f out: styd on towards fin) | 4 | **3** | 25/1 | 59 | 30 |
| 524[2] | **Loose Talk** (WJarvis) **3-8-7** JWeaver(2) (sn led: hung rt ½-wy: hdd over 1f out: sn btn) | nk | **4** | 8/11[1] | 53 | 24 |
| | **Lapu-Lapu** (MJCamacho) **3-8-7** LCharnock(4) (s.i.s: sme late hdwy) | 2½ | **5** | 20/1 | 45 | 16 |
| 591[8] | **Summer Princess** (GFierro) **3-8-7** AMackay(9) (in tch: no hdwy fnl 2f) | 2½ | **6** | 25/1 | 37 | 8 |
| 524[7] | **Eleanor May** (TDBarron) **3-8-7** JFortune(7) (in tch: no imp fr ½-wy) | 1 | **7** | 20/1 | 34 | 5 |
| | **Le Bam Bam** (HAkbary) **4-9-9** GHind(1) (cmpt: led early: outpcd fr ½ wy) | 1¼ | **8** | 8/1[3] | 35 | 17 |
| | **Dispol Duchess** (GROldroyd) **3-8-7** KFallon(10) (lt-f: sn outpcd & bhd) | hd | **9** | 14/1 | 30 | 1 |
| | **Old Hush Wing (IRE)** (PCHaslam) **3-8-5**(7) CarolDavison(6) (w'like: sn outpcd & bhd) | ½ | **10** | 25/1 | 33 | 4 |
| | | | | (SP 136.6%) | **10 Rn** | |

**62.3 secs** (0.80) CSF £27.76 TOTE £3.10: £1.10 £2.80 £4.20 (£21.20) Trio £120.20 OWNER Total (Bloodstock) Ltd (NEWMARKET) BRED Gainsborough Stud Management Ltd

WEIGHT FOR AGE 3yo-11lb

**Total Aloof** is certainly nothing special to look at, and won a modest event here. (9/4)

**Divine Miss-P** was staying on well, despite hanging right, and should have learnt something. (10/1)

**Bowlers Boy** ran well and, once he is fully fit, he should be the pick of this bunch. (25/1)

**524 Loose Talk** attempted to gallop her rivals into the ground, but spoilt her chances by hanging right and was beaten approaching the last furlong. (8/11: Evens-4/6)

**Lapu-Lapu** was slow to realise what was required, but she was keeping on at the finish to suggest that in time she will do better. (20/1)

**Le Bam Bam** (8/1: 6/1-9/1)

**Dispol Duchess** (14/1: op 8/1)

## 627 LECONFIELD CONDITIONS STKS (3-Y.O F) (Class C)

3-50 (3-50) **1m 1f 207y** £5,217.90 (£1,676.40: £810.70) Stalls: High GOING minus 0.44 sec per fur (F)

| | | | | SP | RR | SF |
|---|---|---|---|---|---|---|
| *241** | **Simply Katie** (DRLoder) **3-8-9**(3) DRMcCabe(1) (lw: mde all: shkn up 2f out: r.o wl: eased ins fnl f) | — | **1** | 2/1[2] | 90+ | 25 |
| | **Miss Riviera** (GWragg) **3-9-0** MHills(3) (stdd s: hdwy 3f out: sn chsng wnr: rdn & wknd fnl 2f) | 8 | **2** | 4/7[1] | 79 | 14 |
| | **Silver Wing (USA) (75)** (MBell) **3-8-4**(7)ow1 GFaulkner(2) (b.hind: cl up tl outpcd 3f out: sn btn) | ¾ | **3** | 6/1[3] | 75 | 9 |
| | | | | (SP 111.3%) | **3 Rn** | |

**2m 6.9** (4.40) CSF £3.52 TOTE £2.60 (£1.10) OWNER Lucayan Stud (NEWMARKET) BRED P. D. Player and Mrs J. Shipway-Pratt

**Simply Katie** looked a different class in the paddock, and proved to be so in the race. She should go on from here. (2/1)

**Miss Riviera** was fit but there is not a lot of her and, once off the bit approaching the last two furlongs, she soon cried enough. (4/7)

**Silver Wing (USA)** got pretty warm beforehand and was made to look very slow once the pace increased coming off the home turn. (6/1: 4/1-13/2)

## 628 HORNSEA MERE H'CAP (0-85) (4-Y.O+) (Class D)

4-20 (4-22) **1m 1f 207y** £3,665.00 (£1,100.00: £530.00: £245.00) Stalls: High GOING minus 0.44 sec per fur (F)

| | | | | SP | RR | SF |
|---|---|---|---|---|---|---|
| *462*[4] | **Komreyev Dancer (65)** (ABailey) **4-8-8** JCarroll(3) (lw: in tch: hdwy to ld 1½f out: r.o wl) | — | **1** | 11/2[3] | 76 | 36 |
| 440[10] | **Carlito Brigante (66)** (MrsJRRamsden) **4-8-9** KFallon(9) (hld up: hdwy over 2f out: chsd wnr fnl f: nt pce to chal) | 1½ | **2** | 5/2[2] | 75 | 35 |
| 580* | **Hazard a Guess (IRE) (81)** (DNicholls) **6-9-10** 5x AlexGreaves(6) (lw: hld up: n.m.r 2f out: styd on fnl f: too much to do) | 4 | **3** | 9/4[1] | 83 | 43 |
| | **Westcourt Princess (53)** (MWEasterby) **4-7-10** GBardwell(5) (led: qcknd ent st: hdd 1½f out: sn btn) | 3 | **4** | 12/1 | 50 | 10 |
| 455[18] | **Nigel's Lad (IRE) (85)** (PCHaslam) **4-10-0** JWeaver(4) (chsd ldr tl wknd over 2f out) | ½ | **5** | 12/1 | 82 | 42 |
| | **Wafir (IRE) (82)** (PCalver) **4-9-11** MBirch(1) (hld up & bhd: stdy hdwy 2f out: nvr plcd to chal) | ½ | **6** | 12/1 | 78 | 38 |
| 537[3] | **Flag Fen (USA) (68)** (MartynMeade) **5-8-11** JFortune(8) (chsd ldr tl wknd fnl 2f) | 5 | **7** | 12/1 | 56 | 16 |

| | Horse | Dist | Pos | SP | RR | SF |
|---|---|---|---|---|---|---|
| | **Bobanlyn (IRE) (54)** (JSWainwright) **4-7-11** LCharnock(2) (hld up & bhd: n.d) | nk | **8** | 25/1 | 41 | 1 |
| | **Brave Patriarch (IRE) (77)** (JLDunlop) **5-9-6** MHills(7) (in tch tl wknd fnl 3f) | 3½ | **9** | 8/1 | 59 | 19 |
| | | | | (SP 120.5%) | **9 Rn** | |

**2m 5.0** (2.50) CSF £19.60 CT £37.27 TOTE £6.70: £1.50 £1.50 £1.50 (£12.00) Trio £11.10 OWNER Mr Denis Gallagher (TARPORLEY) BRED G. and Mrs Whittaker

LONG HANDICAP Westcourt Princess 7-9

**462 Komreyev Dancer** has drawn a blank on the All-Weather this year but, fit from that, he gained his first victory on turf here and did it in really useful style. (11/2: 5/1-9/1)

**440 Carlito Brigante** ran well, chasing the winner throughout the final furlong, but was never good enough to peg him back. He did give the impression that he would be all the better for this. (5/2)

**580* Hazard a Guess (IRE)** was given an impossible task and found trouble in running, so did well to finish so close. (9/4: tchd 6/4)

**Westcourt Princess**, from a yard that is going well, likes this track and put up a decent first outing until running out of steam approaching the last furlong. (12/1)

**Nigel's Lad (IRE)** is off a mark 4lb higher than he has previously won off, and ran as well as could be expected. (12/1)

**Wafir (IRE)**, having his first run in this country, certainly caught the eye, making steady late progress without being knocked about. He looks one to bear in mind. (12/1)

**537 Flag Fen (USA)** found this ground too quick. (12/1)

## 629 WITHERNSEA H'CAP (0-80) (3-Y.O+) (Class D)

4-50 (4-51) **7f 100y** £4,029.00 (£1,212.00: £586.00: £273.00) Stalls: High GOING minus 0.44 sec per fur (F)

| | Horse | Dist | Pos | SP | RR | SF |
|---|---|---|---|---|---|---|
| 505[3] | **Primo Lara (65)** (PWHarris) **4-8-13** GHind(11) (mde all: clr over 2f out: eased towards fin) | — | **1** | 6/1[3] | 76+ | 58 |
| 450[3] | **Dances With Hooves (74)** (DJSffrenchDavis) **4-9-8** MTebbutt(7) (bhd: hdwy 3f out: styd on wl: nrst fin) | 1½ | **2** | 4/1[1] | 82 | 64 |
| 496[3] | **Sycamore Lodge (IRE) (68)** (MrsJRRamsden) **5-9-2** KFallon(17) (in tch: hdwy u.p 2f out: hung rt ins fnl f: nvr able to chal) | 1½ | **3** | 9/2[2] | 73 | 55 |
| *513*[2] | **Ashgore (80)** (MJohnston) **6-10-0** JWeaver(9) (chsd ldrs tl outpcd fnl 2f out: btn whn sltly hmpd cl home) | 1½ | **4** | 12/1 | 81 | 63 |
| 491[5] | **Queens Consul (IRE) (80)** (BSRothwell) **6-9-7**(7) OliverCasey(13) (a.p: effrt over 3f out: r.o one pce) | nk | **5** | 14/1 | 81 | 63 |
| 505[8] | **Ochos Rios (IRE) (57)** (BSRothwell) **5-8-5** LCharnock(4) (hdwy 3f out: styd on: no imp) | 2 | **6** | 25/1 | 53 | 35 |
| 480[15] | **Kid Ory (66)** (PCalver) **5-9-0** MBirch(16) (chsd ldrs tl grad wknd fnl 2f) | nk | **7** | 16/1 | 62 | 44 |
| *521*[8] | **Irie Mon (IRE) (56)** (MPBielby) **4-8-1**(3) DRMcCabe(12) (dwlt: bhd tl styd on fnl 2f) | 2½ | **8** | 33/1 | 46 | 28 |
| | **Prudent Pet (60)** (CWFairhurst) **4-8-8** JTate(14) (hdwy over 2f out: nvr rchd ldrs) | hd | **9** | 33/1 | 50 | 32 |
| | **Elpidos (70)** (MDHammond) **4-9-4** JFanning(8) (bhd tl sme late hdwy) | nk | **10** | 12/1 | 60 | 42 |
| *427** | **So Amazing (67)** (JLEyre) **4-9-1** RLappin(10) (chsd ldrs: rdn 3f out: sn btn) | hd | **11** | 4/1[1] | 56 | 38 |
| | **Souperficial (58)** (JAGlover) **5-8-6** SDWilliams(15) (nvr nr ldrs) | s.h | **12** | 25/1 | 47 | 29 |
| 479[5] | **Allinson's Mate (IRE) (72)** (TDBarron) **8-9-6** JFortune(1) (in tch: effrt appr st: sn btn) | 4 | **13** | 16/1 | 53 | 35 |
| | **Up in Flames (IRE) (78)** (MDHammond) **5-9-12** JCarroll(6) (a bhd) | nk | **14** | 12/1 | 58 | 40 |
| *429*[7] | **Grey Again (56)** (SRBowring) **4-8-4b** NCarlisle(2) (lw: hdwy over 2f out: wknd over 1f out) | 1¼ | **15** | 20/1 | 33 | 15 |
| 450[12] | **Duke Valentino (69)** (RHollinshead) **4-9-3** MHills(5) (chsd ldrs 4f: sn wknd) | 2½ | **16** | 16/1 | 41 | 23 |
| | **Elite Racing (57)** (NTinkler) **4-7-12**(7)ow1 AimeeCook(3) (t.o fnl 3f) | dist | **17** | 33/1 | — | — |
| | | | | (SP 141.1%) | **17 Rn** | |

**1m 32.3** (0.30) CSF £32.59 CT £121.03 TOTE £6.30: £1.60 £1.90 £1.40 £2.60 (£11.40) Trio £23.40 OWNER Thanet Leasing Ltd (BERKHAMSTED) BRED Pendley Farm

**505 Primo Lara** left nothing to chance here. Galloping his rivals into the ground, the race was his fully two furlongs out. (6/1)

**450 Dances With Hooves** made up an amazing amount of ground in the straight but had no chance of getting to the winner. Either some cut in the ground or a bit further could be the answer. (4/1)

**496 Sycamore Lodge (IRE)** has plenty of ability but may just have his own ideas and was hanging in the closing stages. (9/2)

**513 Ashgore** could never gain the initiative and was fighting a lost cause up the straight. (12/1)

**491 Queens Consul (IRE)** found things happening too quickly even for her and failed to make any impression. (14/1)

**Ochos Rios (IRE)** ran quite well, staying on when it was all over. (25/1)

T/Plpt: £56.50 (230 Tckts). T/Qdpt: £14.20 (70.47 Tckts). AA

# BRIGHTON (L-H) (Firm)

## Friday April 12th

WEATHER: very cold WIND: str half bhd

## 630 E.B.F. SOUTHWICK MEDIAN AUCTION MAIDEN STKS (2-Y.O) (Class F)

2-10 (2-10) **5f 59y** £2,761.80 (£764.80: £365.40) Stalls: Low GOING minus 0.45 sec per fur (F)

| | Horse | Dist | Pos | SP | RR | SF |
|---|---|---|---|---|---|---|
| 569[3] | **Masterstroke** (BJMeehan) **2-9-0** BDoyle(1) (mde all: pushed out) | — | **1** | 4/6[1] | 65 | 24 |
| | **Royal Emblem** (AGFoster) **2-8-2**(7) RWaterfield(2) (b: neat: chsd wnr: rdn over 2f out: no imp) | 2 | **2** | 8/1[3] | 54 | 13 |
| | **Nightingale Song** (MartynMeade) **2-8-9** JReid(5) (neat: bit bkwd: a.p: rdn over 2f out: one pce) | s.h | **3** | 4/1[2] | 54 | 13 |
| | **Our Kevin** (KWMcAuliffe) **2-9-0** SSanders(3) (neat: no hdwy fnl 2f) | 1½ | **4** | 10/1 | 54 | 13 |
| 506[4] | **Run For Us (IRE)** (CADwyer) **2-8-2**(7) RMullen(7) (s.s: hdwy on ins over 3f out: wknd fnl f) | 2 | **5** | 8/1[3] | 43 | 2 |
| | **Singforyoursupper** (GGMargarson) **2-8-9** PBloomfield(6) (str: scope: bit bkwd: no hdwy fnl 2f) | hd | **6** | 16/1 | 43 | 2 |
| | **Mollily** (MRChannon) **2-8-9** CandyMorris(8) (cmpt: a bhd) | 10 | **7** | 8/1[3] | 13 | — |
| | | | | (SP 128.3%) | **7 Rn** | |

**62.1 secs** (2.10) CSF £8.05 TOTE £1.60: £1.10 £3.30 (£7.70) OWNER Mr N. B. Attenborough (UPPER LAMBOURN) BRED G. C. Morley

**569 Masterstroke** made his experience tell on this very tricky course with an all the way success, needing only to be shaken up in the final quarter-mile to win with something to spare. (4/6)

**Royal Emblem** chased the winner throughout but could make no impression on him in the last two furlongs. (8/1)

**Nightingale Song** raced in third place but failed to increase her work rate in the last two furlongs. (4/1)

**Our Kevin** was carrying a lot of surplus flesh for this racecourse debut. Racing in fourth place, he was making no impression on the principals in the last two furlongs. (10/1: 6/1-12/1)

**506 Run For Us (IRE)** soon recovered from a tardy start but had given her all in the final furlong. (8/1: 6/1-10/1)

**Singforyoursupper**, with far more substance than the rest of the field, will come on for the run. Chasing the leaders, she was making no inroads on them in the final quarter-mile. (16/1)

**Mollily** (8/1: 6/1-10/1)

## 631 ELM GROVE CLAIMING STKS (4-Y.O+) (Class F)

2-40 (2-41) **5f 213y** £2,381.00 (£656.00: £311.00) Stalls: Low GOING minus 0.45 sec per fur (F)

| | Horse | Dist | Pos | SP | RR | SF |
|---|---|---|---|---|---|---|
| *$243^{11}$* | **Agwa (68)** (RJO'Sullivan) **7-8-12** SSanders(3) (mde all: r.o) | — | **1** | 9/1 | 70 | 52 |
| *$407^{10}$* | **Baileys Sunset (IRE) (57)** (JMBradley) **4-8-5**(3) SDrowne(9) (hld up: rdn over 2f out: chsd wnr ins fnl f: r.o) | 2 | **2** | 25/1 | 61 | 43 |
| *$408^{9}$* | **Apollo Red (49)** (AMoore) **7-8-10** CandyMorris(6) (a.p: hrd rdn over 2f out: chsd wnr over 1f out tl ins fnl f: unable qckn) | 1¾ | **3** | 8/1 | 58 | 40 |
| $545^{4}$ | **Cedar Dancer (43)** (RJHodges) **4-8-0**(3) AWhelan(1) (rdn over 2f out: hdwy over 1f out: r.o one pce) | 2½ | **4** | 16/1 | 44 | 26 |
| *$380^{5}$* | **Dahiyah (USA) (61)** (GLMoore) **5-8-12v** SWhitworth(10) (lw: chsd wnr over 4f: wknd fnl f) | s.h | **5** | 13/2[3] | 53 | 35 |
| | **Shikari's Son (95)** (JCullinan) **9-9-12** JReid(2) (hdwy over 2f out: one pce) | ¾ | **6** | 10/11[1] | 65 | 47 |
| *$461^{9}$* | **Chief's Lady (43)** (JMBradley) **4-7-12**(5) PPMurphy(4) (hld up: rdn over 2f out: wknd fnl f) | 1½ | **7** | 33/1 | 38 | 20 |
| *$399^{7}$* | **Branston Kristy** (CSmith) **4-7-10b**(5) MHenry(7) (a bhd) | 1½ | **8** | 33/1 | 32 | 14 |
| 549* | **Rockville Pike (IRE) (80)** (SDow) **4-9-0v** GDuffield(5) (bhd fnl 3f) | 2 | **9** | 6/1[2] | 40 | 22 |
| $559^{14}$ | **Southern Dominion (61)** (CNAllen) **4-8-12** NAdams(8) (lw: s.s: a bhd) | 1½ | **10** | 14/1 | 34 | 16 |
| | | | | (SP 123.4%) | **10 Rn** | |

**1m 7.5** (0.30 under best) (0.30) CSF £172.07 TOTE £9.50: £1.90 £3.60 £2.20 (£84.50) Trio £159.00 OWNER Mr I. A. Baker (WHITCOMBE) BRED Gainsborough Stud Management Ltd

**Agwa**, who was treated with snake venom after he broke a blood-vessel last time out, bounced back to form here. Making it all, he was ridden along in the final quarter-mile to break the course record set by Dahiyah last year. (9/1)

**Baileys Sunset (IRE)** ran his best race for a while. Chasing the leaders, he struggled into second place inside the final furlong but, despite running on, never looked like pegging back the winner. (25/1)

**Apollo Red**, winner of this race in 1994 and second last year, was in the firing-line throughout. Poking a nostril into second place below the distance, he was collared for that position inside the final furlong and failed to quicken. (8/1)

**545 Cedar Dancer** stayed on in the last furlong and a half without ever posing a threat. She remains a maiden after nineteen attempts. (16/1)

**Dahiyah (USA)** raced in second place, but was collared for that position below the distance, and soon capitulated. (13/2)

**Shikari's Son** really loves it round here, and has won nine times on this switch-back course. With his trainer very bullish about his chances, it was a very lack-lustre performance however. Trying to get into it over a quarter of a mile from home, he could then make no further impression. (10/11)

**549* Rockville Pike (IRE)** (6/1: 4/1-13/2)

## 632 BRIGHTON SPRING H'CAP (0-80) (3-Y.O+) (Class D)

3-10 (3-10) **5f 213y** £3,860.70 (£1,152.60: £550.80: £249.90) Stalls: Low GOING minus 0.45 sec per fur (F)

| | Horse | Dist | Pos | SP | RR | SF |
|---|---|---|---|---|---|---|
| | **Bashful Brave (70)** (JWPayne) **5-9-6** RCochrane(5) (lw: led 1f: rdn over 2f out: led ins fnl f: r.o wl) | — | **1** | 8/1[3] | 77 | 52 |
| *$408^{3}$* | **Speedy Classic (USA) (57)** (MJHeaton-Ellis) **7-8-4**(3) SDrowne(8) (a.p: rdn over 2f out: ev ch fnl f: r.o wl) | hd | **2** | 6/1[2] | 64 | 39 |
| $451^{14}$ | **Tafahhus (73)** (MJPolglase) **4-9-9** DHarrison(13) (led 5f out: rdn over 2f out: hdd ins fnl f: r.o) | hd | **3** | 16/1 | 80 | 55 |
| $466^{5}$ | **Rockcracker (IRE) (56)** (GGMargarson) **4-8-6b** PBloomfield(7) (lw: a.p: rdn 2f out: unable qckn) | 2 | **4** | 16/1 | 57 | 32 |
| *503** | **Moi Canard (64)** (BAPearce) **3-8-2** SSanders(12) (lw: hld up: rdn over 2f out: one pce) | 3½ | **5** | 4/1[1] | 56 | 19 |
| *$556^{2}$* | **Invocation (54)** (AMoore) **9-8-1**(3) AWhelan(10) (b.nr hind: lw: no hdwy fnl 2f) | 2 | **6** | 6/1[2] | 40 | 15 |
| | **Tart and a Half (78)** (BJMeehan) **4-9-7**(7) GHannon(2) (nvr nr to chal) | 2½ | **7** | 11/1 | 58 | 33 |
| $466^{14}$ | **La Belle Dominique (55)** (SGKnight) **4-8-5** BDoyle(3) (prom over 4f) | ½ | **8** | 20/1 | 33 | 8 |
| $466^{12}$ | **Halbert (65)** (PBurgoyne) **7-8-12v**(3) PMcCabe(1) (nvr nrr) | ½ | **9** | 14/1 | 42 | 17 |
| | **Dry Point (71)** (JARToller) **10-9-7** GDuffield(6) (a bhd) | s.h | **10** | 14/1 | 48 | 23 |
| | **Martinosky (50)** (GCBravery) **10-8-0** DeclanO'Shea(11) (bit bkwd: a bhd) | ½ | **11** | 14/1 | 26 | 1 |
| *$211^{8}$* | **Prima Silk (65)** (MJRyan) **5-9-1** AClark(9) (hld up: rdn over 3f out: eased whn btn fnl f) | 3 | **12** | 6/1[2] | 33 | 8 |
| | **Asterix (49)** (JMBradley) **8-7-8v**(5) MHenry(4) (bit bkwd: a bhd) | 1¼ | **13** | 14/1 | 13 | — |
| | | | | (SP 125.5%) | **13 Rn** | |

**1m 8.0** (0.80) CSF £54.11 CT £726.98 TOTE £9.40: £2.70 £3.00 £2.70 (£134.50) Trio £314.40; £177.18 to Ascot 13/4/96 OWNER Mrs G. M. Hay (NEWMARKET) BRED Mrs G. M. Hay

WEIGHT FOR AGE 3yo-12lb

**Bashful Brave** loves the firm ground but connections were a bit worried after three hours of rain in the morning. In the front line throughout, he had a tremendous tussle in the final furlong but got on top in the closing stages to win his first race over six furlongs. (8/1)

**Speedy Classic (USA)**, always close up, had a tremendous battle with the winner and third in the final furlong and only just failed. (6/1)

**Tafahhus** was soon at the head of affairs but, despite grimly trying to hold on, was just worried out of it in the closing stages. This was his best run for some time. (16/1)

**466 Rockcracker (IRE)**, always close up, failed to find the necessary turn of foot in the last two furlongs. (16/1)

**503* Moi Canard** chased the leaders but, rousted along over a quarter of a mile from home, could only go up and down in the same place. Seven furlongs is more his trip. (4/1)

**556 Invocation** was making little impression on the principals in the final quarter-mile. (6/1)

## 633 HOLLINGBURY LIMITED STKS (0-80) (3-Y.O+) (Class D)

3-40 (3-40) **6f 209y** £3,728.10 (£1,111.80: £530.40: £239.70) Stalls: Low GOING minus 0.45 sec per fur (F)

| | Horse | Dist | Pos | SP | RR | SF |
|---|---|---|---|---|---|---|
| $442^{7}$ | **Star Talent (USA) (80)** (MissGayKelleway) **5-9-9** RCochrane(2) (lw: stdd s: nt clr run & swtchd rt wl over 1f out: gd hdwy 1f out: str run to ld wl ins fnl f: r.o wl) | — | **1** | 10/1 | 88 | 65 |
| | **Apollono (78)** (JRFanshawe) **4-9-7** DHarrison(8) (hld up: chsd ldr over 2f out: ev ch ins fnl f: unable qckn) | 1 | **2** | 3/1[2] | 84 | 61 |
| | **Jo Maximus (75)** (SDow) **4-9-2**(5) ADaly(6) (bit bkwd: led: clr over 4f out: hdd wl ins fnl f: one pce) | 1 | **3** | 12/1 | 81 | 58 |
| $450^{18}$ | **Neuwest (USA) (76)** (NJHWalker) **4-9-6**(3) JStack(9) (lw: a.p: rdn over 2f out: wknd fnl f) | 3½ | **4** | 6/1[3] | 75 | 52 |
| $450^{11}$ | **Bagshot (75)** (RHannon) **5-9-2**(5) DaneO'Neill(1) (hld up: rdn over 2f out: one pce) | nk | **5** | 13/2 | 73 | 50 |
| *363** | **Crystal Heights (FR) (64)** (RJO'Sullivan) **8-9-9** SSanders(5) (lw: dwlt: rdn & hdwy over 3f out: one pce fnl 2f) | 1¾ | **6** | 10/1 | 71 | 48 |
| | **Delight of Dawn (72)** (KTIvory) **4-8-11**(7) CScally(7) (b: a bhd) | nk | **7** | 14/1 | 65 | 42 |
| *$266^{9}$* | **Abtaal (70)** (RJHodges) **6-9-4**(3) SDrowne(4) (lw: prom over 5f) | 8 | **8** | 33/1 | 50 | 27 |
| 554* | **Champagne Grandy (79)** (MRChannon) **6-9-1**(5) PPMurphy(3) (bhd fnl 4f) | 1¼ | **9** | 2/1[1] | 46 | 23 |
| | | | | (SP 121.4%) | **9 Rn** | |

**1m 20.2** (0.20) CSF £39.88 TOTE £9.00: £1.70 £1.70 £1.60 (£19.00) Trio £63.10 OWNER Miss Jo Crowley (WHITCOMBE) BRED Mrs Afaf A. Al Essa

**Star Talent (USA)**, still in last place a quarter of a mile from home, failed to get a clear passage and his prospects did not look good. However, he came with a tremendous run from below the distance to swoop into the lead in the closing stages. (10/1: 8/1-12/1)
**Apollono**, looking pretty straight for this first run of the season, moved into second place over a quarter of a mile from home. He had just poked a whisker in front inside the final furlong when the winner came storming by. (3/1)
**Jo Maximus**, not looking fully wound up for this seasonal bow, ran a race full of promise. Setting off in front, he had a clear advantage at the top of the hill but was eventually overhauled inside the final furlong. Both his wins to date have come on this course and if the ground remains fast he may well be adding to that tally round here. (12/1: 8/1-14/1)
**Neuwest (USA)** was always close up but had run out of gas in the final furlong. (6/1)
**Bagshot** chased the leaders but failed to find the necessary turn of foot in the final quarter-mile. (13/2)
**Crystal Heights (FR)** made an effort on the outside of the field at halfway but was making little impression from that point. (10/1)
**554* Champagne Grandy** was very disappointing and punters already knew their fate by halfway. Connections reported that the firm ground and tricky course were not in her favour. (2/1: 6/4-9/4)

## 634 VARNDEAN MEDIAN AUCTION MAIDEN STKS (3-Y.O) (Class F)

4-10 (4-10) **1m 1f 209y** £2,381.00 (£656.00: £311.00) Stalls: High GOING minus 0.45 sec per fur (F)

| | | | | SP | RR | SF |
|---|---|---|---|---|---|---|
| 509[4] | **Spillo (83)** (LMCumani) **3-9-0** JReid(5) (a.p: led 3f out: clr over 1f out: r.o wl) | — | **1** | 1/3[1] | 74 | 25 |
| 448[9] | **Sunley Secure (66)** (MRChannon) **3-8-9**(5) PPMurphy(2) (a.p: rdn over 3f out: chsd wnr fnl f: no imp) | 11 | **2** | 11/2[2] | 56 | 7 |
| *377[5]* | **Isitoff** (CADwyer) **3-9-0** KRutter(1) (lw: hld up: rdn over 3f out: one pce) | hd | **3** | 11/1[3] | 56 | 7 |
| | **My Beautiful Dream** (AGNewcombe) **3-8-9** RCochrane(4) (leggy: unf: led 7f: wknd 1f out) | 1¼ | **4** | 20/1 | 49 | — |
| 562[11] | **Wire Act (USA) (61)** (MartynMeade) **3-8-9**(5) RHavlin(3) (hld up: rdn over 3f out: wknd over 2f out) | 3 | **5** | 12/1 | 49 | — |
| 528[10] | **Followthe Allstars** (TJNaughton) **3-9-0** DHarrison(6) (lw: hld up: rdn 4f out: wknd 2f out) | hd | **6** | 33/1 | 49 | — |

(SP 114.1%) **6 Rn**

**2m 2.5** (4.20) CSF £2.96 TOTE £1.60: £1.10 £2.00 (£2.20) OWNER Teknagro L (NEWMARKET) BRED Limestone Stud
**509 Spillo** had a simple task here. Poking a nostril in front three furlongs out, he was ridden clear below the distance to win with plenty in hand. (1/3)
**Sunley Secure** was never far away. He eventually struggled into second place entering the final furlong but had no hope with the winner. (11/2: op 7/2)
**Isitoff** chased the leaders but was made to look very pedestrian in the last three furlongs. (11/1)
**My Beautiful Dream** took the field along. Collared three furlongs from home, she grimly tried to hang on but had nothing in reserve entering the final furlong. (20/1)
**Wire Act (USA)** (12/1: 8/1-14/1)

## 635 SHEEPCOTE VALLEY H'CAP (0-60) (3-Y.O+) (Class F)

4-40 (4-42) **1m 3f 196y** £2,381.00 (£656.00: £311.00) Stalls: High GOING minus 0.45 sec per fur (F)

| | | | | SP | RR | SF |
|---|---|---|---|---|---|---|
| *214[7]* | **Uncharted Waters (45)** (CACyzer) **5-9-0** GDuffield(4) (hdwy 6f out: led over 1f out: drvn out) | — | **1** | 20/1 | 62 | 44 |
| *303[5]* | **Ajdar (49)** (MissGayKelleway) **5-9-4** RCochrane(2) (hld up: rdn over 3f out: r.o ins fnl f) | ½ | **2** | 9/1 | 65 | 47 |
| *309[7]* | **Courbaril (58)** (SDow) **4-9-7**(5) ADaly(6) (a.p: ev ch over 1f out: unable qckn) | 2½ | **3** | 7/1 | 71 | 52 |
| | **Paradise Waters (56)** (RFJohnsonHoughton) **4-9-10** JReid(1) (led over 10f: one pce) | 1 | **4** | 5/1[2] | 68 | 49 |
| *353[5]* | **Risky Tu (46)** (PAKelleway) **5-8-8**(7) CDomergue(14) (hdwy 5f out: wknd over 1f out) | 6 | **5** | 25/1 | 50 | 32 |
| *498[2]* | **Guest Alliance (IRE) (50)** (AMoore) **4-9-4** CandyMorris(5) (lw: nvr nr to chal) | 1¾ | **6** | 9/2[1] | 51 | 32 |
| *339[6]* | **Ikhtiraa (USA) (36)** (RJO'Sullivan) **6-8-5b** SSanders(3) (prom over 9f) | 8 | **7** | 13/2[3] | 26 | 8 |
| *69[10]* | **Lunar Risk (33)** (MissBSanders) **6-7-13v**(3) AWhelan(9) (nvr nrr) | 20 | **8** | 20/1 | — | — |
| | **Double Rush (IRE) (50)** (TGMills) **4-9-4** SWhitworth(7) (bit bkwd: nvr nrr) | ½ | **9** | 9/2[1] | 13 | — |
| | **Bronze Maquette (IRE) (34)** (THind) **6-7-12**(5) MHenry(18) (prom over 8f) | nk | **10** | 16/1 | — | — |
| | **Shahrani (52)** (BJMeehan) **4-9-6** BDoyle(17) (bit bkwd: prom 5f) | s.h | **11** | 16/1 | 14 | — |
| *499[8]* | **The Cape Doctor (IRE) (41)** (AGFoster) **4-8-9** DHarrison(12) (bhd fnl 3f) | ½ | **12** | 20/1 | 3 | — |
| | **Spumante (60)** (MPMuggeridge) **4-9-9**(5) DaneO'Neill(10) (lw: prom 9f) | hd | **13** | 14/1 | 22 | 3 |
| 471[14] | **Tartan Express (IRE) (48)** (BAPearce) **3-7-3**(7) RMullen(13) (bhd fnl 6f) | 1¾ | **14** | 50/1 | 7 | — |
| *520[7]* | **Ever Friends (42)** (RHarris) **4-8-10b1** DBatteate(16) (a bhd) | 5 | **15** | 33/1 | — | — |
| *502[10]* | **P Grayco Choice (48)** (PCClarke) **3-7-10** NAdams(15) (a bhd: t.o) | 30 | **16** | 66/1 | — | — |
| | ***Set-Em-Alight (27)*** (BSmart) **6-7-7**(3) DarrenMoffatt(11) (Withdrawn not under Starter's orders: veterinary advice: bolted bef s) | | **W** | 50/1 | — | — |

(SP 133.8%) **16 Rn**

**2m 30.2** (2.60) CSF £185.26 CT £1,298.79 TOTE £15.40: £1.30 £2.80 £2.10 £1.70 (£58.10) Trio £255.90 OWNER Mr R. M. Cyzer (HORSHAM) BRED Sexton Enterprises and M and M Bloodstock
LONG HANDICAP Tartan Express (IRE) 6-10 P Grayco Choice 6-8 Set-Em-Alight 7-8
WEIGHT FOR AGE 3yo-21lb, 4yo-1lb
**Uncharted Waters** moved up at halfway. Grabbing the initiative below the distance, she responded to pressure and kept on well. (20/1)
**Ajdar** chased the leaders but was being bustled along over three furlongs from home. He did run on inside the final furlong but never looked like overhauling the winner. (9/1)
**Courbaril**, a leading light from the off, had every chance below the distance before tapped for toe. (7/1: 5/1-8/1)
**Paradise Waters** attempted to make all the running. Eventually collared below the distance, she could only keep on in her own time. This was a pleasing reappearance. (5/1: 7/2-11/2)
**Risky Tu** moved up at the top of the hill but was a spent force below the distance. (25/1)
**Double Rush (IRE)** (9/2: 7/1-4/1)

## 636 CHURCHILL SQUARE H'CAP (0-70) (3-Y.O+) (Class E)

5-10 (5-11) **7f 214y** £3,315.90 (£991.20: £474.60: £216.30) Stalls: Low GOING minus 0.45 sec per fur (F)

| | | | | SP | RR | SF |
|---|---|---|---|---|---|---|
| *487[3]* | **Autumn Cover (44)** (RMFlower) **4-8-4**ow1 DHarrison(15) (b: mde all: all out) | — | **1** | 5/1[1] | 57 | 37 |
| 508[18] | **College Night (IRE) (43)** (CADwyer) **4-7-12**(5) MHenry(10) (chsd wnr: ev ch fnl 3f: hrd rdn: r.o wl) | s.h | **2** | 15/2[3] | 56 | 37 |
| *345[9]* | **Pinkerton Polka (47)** (CEBrittain) **4-8-7** BDoyle(2) (lw: a.p: rdn over 3f out: unable qckn) | 3 | **3** | 25/1 | 54 | 35 |
| *462[6]* | **Mr Nevermind (IRE) (64)** (GLMoore) **6-9-3**(7) ALakeman(1) (hdwy over 4f out: rdn over 2f out: one pce) | 1½ | **4** | 10/1 | 68 | 49 |
| | **It'sthebusiness (55)** (SDow) **4-9-1** JReid(13) (hld up: rdn over 2f out: one pce) | 3 | **5** | 11/1 | 53 | 34 |
| | **Mr Rough (63)** (DMorris) **5-9-9** RCochrane(6) (bit bkwd: hld up: rdn over 2f out: one pce) | ½ | **6** | 5/1[1] | 60 | 41 |
| 469[11] | **Explosive Power (62)** (GCBravery) **5-9-8** SWhitworth(3) (hdwy over 4f out: rdn over 2f out: eased whn btn ins fnl f) | ½ | **7** | 10/1 | 58 | 39 |

| | | | | SP | RR | SF |
|---|---|---|---|---|---|---|
| 406[6] | **Jaazim (54)** (MMadgwick) **6-9-0** AClark(14) (hdwy over 2f out: wknd over 1f out) | s.h | **8** | 25/1 | 50 | 31 |
| 501[3] | **Zahran (IRE) (46)** (JMBradley) **5-8-3**(3) SDrowne(12) (lw: nvr nr to chal) | ¾ | **9** | 14/1 | 40 | 21 |
| 470[16] | **Soaking (58)** (PBurgoyne) **6-9-1**(3) PMcCabe(7) (a bhd) | nk | **10** | 10/1 | 52 | 33 |
| 470[5] | **Halliard (54)** (TMJones) **5-9-0** RPerham(4) (b: hld up: rdn over 2f out: sn wknd) | 1 | **11** | 6/1 2 | 46 | 27 |
| | **Crested Knight (IRE) (61)** (CAHorgan) **4-9-2**(5) ADaly(8) (bit bkwd: a bhd) | 3 | **12** | 14/1 | 47 | 28 |
| 120[5] | **Mediate (IRE) (55)** (AHide) **4-8-10b**(5) DaneO'Neill(5) (a bhd) | 2½ | **13** | 16/1 | 36 | 17 |
| 487[9] | **Dantean (42)** (RJO'Sullivan) **4-8-2b** GDuffield(11) (bhd fnl 3f) | 6 | **14** | 16/1 | 11 | — |
| 470[6] | **Almapa (49)** (RJHodges) **4-8-6**(3) JStack(9) (prom over 5f) | 1¾ | **15** | 14/1 | 14 | — |
| | | | | (SP 134.4%) | **15 Rn** | |

**1m 33.4** (1.20) CSF £43.89 CT £836.46 TOTE £7.40: £2.80 £5.60 £9.40 (£41.00) Trio £547.30 OWNER Mr G. A. Alexander (JEVINGTON) BRED P. and Mrs Venner

**487 Autumn Cover** made every post a winning one. Engaged in a tremendous battle with the runner-up in the last three furlongs, he prevailed with not an ounce to spare. (5/1)

**College Night (IRE)**, racing in second place, had a tremendous tussle with the winner in the last three furlongs and failed by only a whisker. She is a winner without a penalty. (15/2: 5/1-8/1)

**Pinkerton Polka**, always close up, never looked like finding the necessary turn of foot in the last two furlongs. (25/1)

**462 Mr Nevermind (IRE)** moved up at halfway but failed to find another gear in the final quarter-mile. (10/1)

**It'sthebusiness** chased the leaders but could only struggle on in his own time in the last two furlongs. (11/1)

**Mr Rough**, who looked as though the run would do him good, chased the leaders but, rousted along over a quarter of a mile from home, could only go up and down in the same place. (5/1)

**Explosive Power** (10/1: op 6/1)

T/Plpt: £191.70 (58.66 Tckts). T/Qdpt: £26.90 (40.64 Tckts) AK

# 0590-NOTTINGHAM (L-H) (Good, Good to soft patches becoming Good to soft)
## Friday April 12th

WEATHER: raining WIND: fresh across

## 637 WATNALL (S) STKS (3-Y.O) (Class G)

2-00 (2-02) **1m 54y** £2,070.00 (£570.00: £270.00) Stalls: Low GOING: 0.69 sec per fur (GS)

| | | | | SP | RR | SF |
|---|---|---|---|---|---|---|
| 448[11] | **Sistar Act (55)** (MRChannon) **3-8-7** TQuinn(5) (hld up: jnd ldrs 3f out: sn led: edgd rt & drew clr fnl f) | — | **1** | 9/2 2 | 61+ | 28 |
| 522[13] | **Royal Rapport (40)** (BAMcMahon) **3-8-12** GCarter(12) (b: hld up: hdwy ent st: ev ch 2f out: sn rdn: one pce) | 4 | **2** | 14/1 | 58 | 25 |
| 549[5] | **Dazzling Star** (RHannon) **3-8-7** PatEddery(13) (a.p: ev ch 2f out: sn rdn: one pce appr fnl f) | 3½ | **3** | 6/5 1 | 46 | 13 |
| 403[8] | **Madonna da Rossi (47)** (MDods) **3-8-7** DeanMcKeown(9) (plld hrd: sn prom: rdn 2f out: one pce) | 1½ | **4** | 8/1 3 | 44 | 11 |
| 271[8] | **Alpheton Prince (40)** (JLHarris) **3-8-12** JQuinn(4) (in tch: rdn 3f out: kpt on same pce) | 1¾ | **5** | 50/1 | 45 | 12 |
| 112[11] | **Gresham Flyer (40)** (BRichmond) **3-8-7**(5) CTeague(2) (hld up: hdwy u.p 3f out: nvr nr ldrs) | 8 | **6** | 50/1 | 30 | — |
| | **Song Song Blue (IRE)** (NTinkler) **3-8-12** TIves(7) (led tl hdd over 2f out: grad wknd) | 1¾ | **7** | 50/1 | 26 | — |
| | **Chipalata** (TWDonnelly) **3-8-12** CRutter(3) (unf: bkwd: s.s: wl bhd tl sme late hdwy) | hd | **8** | 33/1 | 26 | — |
| 242[5] | **Music Mistress (IRE) (55)** (JSMoore) **3-8-11** JFEgan(6) (trckd ldrs tl wknd over 3f out) | 3 | **9** | 10/1 | 19 | — |
| 447[9] | **Crystal Fast (USA) (55)** (PAKelleway) **3-8-12** MWigham(11) (sn pushed along: a in rr) | 1 | **10** | 8/1 3 | 18 | — |
| 52[7] | **Baker (54)** (JAkehurst) **3-8-12** DaleGibson(10) (b.nr hind: sn rdn along: a bhd) | 1 | **11** | 12/1 | 16 | — |
| 11[8] | **Take Note (IRE)** (NAGraham) **3-8-12** WRyan(14) (bit bkwd: plld hrd: chsd ldrs: drvn 4f out: wknd 3f out) | 2 | **12** | 14/1 | 12 | — |
| | **Louisiana Purchase (50)** (MrsBarbaraWaring) **3-8-12** RHughes(8) (lw: chsd ldr: rdn 4f out: sn wknd) | s.h | **13** | 33/1 | 12 | — |
| | **John's Law (IRE)** (MJHeaton-Ellis) **3-8-7**(5) AmandaSanders(15) (in tch tl rn wd ent st: sn bhd: t.o) | 18 | **14** | 20/1 | — | — |
| | | | | (SP 132.5%) | **14 Rn** | |

**1m 53.5** (12.20) CSF £66.03 TOTE £6.60: £2.10 £5.10 £1.10 (£46.50) Trio £42.10 OWNER Mr Tim Corby (UPPER LAMBOURN) BRED D. S. Rigby

Bt in 4,000 gns

**Sistar Act**, stepping down in class on this first attempt at the trip, gradually forged clear and, despite drifting right inside the distance, won very much as she pleased. (9/2)

**Royal Rapport** looked a live threat two furlongs out but the winner found more when set alight and he had to settle for second best. (14/1)

**549 Dazzling Star**, very much in need of some sun on her back, was one of several in with every chance entering the final quarter-mile but, once the tempo increased, was found wanting. (6/5)

**Madonna da Rossi** refused to settle and kept tabs on the leaders but was a spent force when a final effort was called for. (8/1: 6/1-9/1)

**Alpheton Prince** is still not getting his act together but he does look to have some ability and should not be written off yet. (50/1)

**Baker** (12/1: op 8/1)

## 638 NEW BASFORD H'CAP (0-70) (3-Y.O) (Class E)

2-30 (2-33) **6f 15y** £3,343.20 (£999.60: £478.80: £218.40) Stalls: High GOING: 0.69 sec per fur (GS)

| | | | | SP | RR | SF |
|---|---|---|---|---|---|---|
| | **Farhana (69)** (WJarvis) **3-9-7** TQuinn(10) (hld up: hdwy on bit to ld over 1f out: qcknd clr: impressive) | — | **1** | 7/4 1 | 97+ | 51 |
| | **Polish Saga (50)** (MDods) **3-8-2** JFEgan(17) (hdwy over 1f out: r.o: no ch w wnr) | 8 | **2** | 20/1 | 57 | 11 |
| | **Mybotye (67)** (GROldroyd) **3-9-5** WRyan(12) (bit bkwd: hdwy over 2f out: ev ch over 1f out: one pce) | ½ | **3** | 7/1 2 | 73 | 27 |
| 473* | **Miletrian Refurb (IRE) (62)** (MRChannon) **3-9-0** RHughes(4) (lw: a.p: rdn & ev ch over 1f out: no ex fnl f) | ¾ | **4** | 8/1 3 | 66 | 20 |
| 539* | **Hobbs Choice (50)** (GMMoore) **3-8-2** 7x DaleGibson(5) (lw: chsd ldrs: rdn & no hdwy fnl 2f) | hd | **5** | 12/1 | 53 | 7 |
| | **Kings Harmony (IRE) (63)** (PJMakin) **3-9-1** PatEddery(7) (lw: disp ld: ev ch over 1f out: outpcd fnl f) | 1¼ | **6** | 10/1 | 63 | 17 |
| 443[11] | **U-No-Harry (IRE) (67)** (RHollinshead) **3-9-0**(5) FLynch(2) (prom far side: rdn 2f out: one pce) | 3 | **7** | 20/1 | 59 | 13 |
| | **Rhythmic Ball (52)** (TRWatson) **3-8-4** DeanMcKeown(13) (prom 4f) | 1¾ | **8** | 25/1 | 40 | — |
| 525[20] | **Rustic Song (IRE) (52)** (JWharton) **3-8-4** PRobinson(14) (trckd ldrs over 4f) | 1¼ | **9** | 33/1 | 36 | — |
| | **Credite Risque (60)** (JRFanshawe) **3-8-9**(3) NVarley(11) (bit bkwd: chsd ldrs 4f) | nk | **10** | 14/1 | 43 | — |
| 539[2] | **Goretski (IRE) (54)** (NTinkler) **3-8-6** KimTinkler(15) (gd spd over 4f) | ½ | **11** | 11/1 | 36 | — |
| 525[6] | **Gwespyr (65)** (JBerry) **3-8-12**(5) PRoberts(9) (led tl hdd & wknd over 1f out) | 1½ | **12** | 12/1 | 43 | — |
| 525[19] | **Mullagh Hill Lad (IRE) (65)** (BAMcMahon) **3-9-3** GCarter(3) (lw: in tch to ½-wy: sn wknd) | nk | **13** | 20/1 | 42 | — |
| 539[4] | **Afisiak (50)** (ABMulholland) **3-8-2** CRutter(18) (a in rr) | 3 | **14** | 12/1 | 20 | — |
| | **Fairy Prince (IRE) (61)** (MrsALMKing) **3-8-13** AMcGlone(6) (bit bkwd: a bhd: t.o) | 5 | **15** | 33/1 | 17 | — |
| | **Percy Park (USA) (50)** (MWEasterby) **3-8-2** JQuinn(1) (lw: s.s: a bhd: t.o) | 12 | **16** | 10/1 | — | — |

| Form | Horse | Dist | Pos | SP | RR | SF |
|---|---|---|---|---|---|---|
| | **Rapid Liner (56)** (HJOliver) **3-8-8** VSlattery(8) (s.s: a bhd & outpcd: t.o) | 12 | **17** | 16/1 | — | — |
| | | | | (SP 146.1%) | | **17 Rn** |

**1m 18.5** (8.00) CSF £43.12 CT £223.32 TOTE £2.90: £2.10 £6.40 £2.20 £2.20 (£61.90) Trio £661.80 OWNER Mr A. Foustok (NEWMARKET) BRED Ahmed M. Foustok

**Farhana**, a very progressive filly still to come in her coat, turned in a first class display to slaughter these rivals and she has certainly trained on. (7/4: 5/4-9/4)

**Polish Saga**, who is a half-sister to Be Warned amongst others, was doing all her best work in the closing stages and will come into her own when tackling a longer trip. (20/1)

**Mybotye** ended last season in fine style and was far from disgraced on this seasonal debut after getting a sluggish start. He is open to improvement. (7/1)

**473* Miletrian Refurb (IRE)** found these rivals much better than those he beat in a seller on his previous appearance but he was far from disgraced in defeat and there are more prizes to be picked up. (8/1)

**539* Hobbs Choice**, never far away, could not quicken when popped the question two furlongs out as her 7lb penalty took its toll. (12/1)

**Kings Harmony (IRE)**, sure to be much sharper for the run, shared the lead and had every chance until getting tapped for toe inside the final furlong. (10/1)

**Percy Park (USA)** (10/1: op 33/1)

## 639 TROWELL MAIDEN AUCTION STKS (2-Y.O) (Class F)

3-00 (3-02) **5f 13y** £2,381.00 (£656.00: £311.00) Stalls: High GOING: 0.69 sec per fur (GS)

| Form | Horse | Dist | Pos | SP | RR | SF |
|---|---|---|---|---|---|---|
| | **Superior Premium** (RAFahey) **2-8-5** ACulhane(8) (unf: scope: lw: dwlt: led after 2f: qcknd clr fnl f) | — | **1** | 4/1[1] | 79 | 27 |
| | **Castle House** (JAkehurst) **2-8-5** TQuinn(7) (leggy: unf: bit bkwd: plld hrd: chsd ldrs: kpt on one pce fnl f) | 5 | **2** | 11/2[2] | 63 | 11 |
| 557[4] | **Caviar And Candy** (DJSCosgrove) **2-7-12** JQuinn(9) (led 2f: kpt on ins fnl f) | ¾ | **3** | 6/1[3] | 54 | 2 |
| | **Legend of Aragon** (JAGlover) **2-8-3**[ow1] PRobinson(5) (w'like: unf: a.p: rdn & one pce fnl 2f) | ½ | **4** | 12/1 | 57 | 4 |
| | **Chopin (IRE)** (RFJohnsonHoughton) **2-8-7** AMcGlone(1) (narrow: bit bkwd: mid div: effrt & wnt rt over 2f out: no imp) | 5 | **5** | 10/1 | 45 | — |
| | **Hever Golf Lily** (TJNaughton) **2-8-5** PatEddery(3) (w'like: lengthy: bkwd: s.i.s: nvr gng pce of ldrs) | ½ | **6** | 6/1[3] | 42 | — |
| 490[6] | **Gresatre** (CADwyer) **2-8-10** CDwyer(2) (chsd ldrs 3f: sn outpcd) | nk | **7** | 6/1[3] | 46 | — |
| | **Scarrots** (SCWilliams) **2-8-10** RHughes(10) (cmpt: bkwd: dwlt: a bhd & outpcd) | 1 | **8** | 4/1[1] | 43 | — |
| | **Radar O'Reilly** (RJRWilliams) **2-8-7** DBiggs(4) (leggy: unf: bit bkwd: spd centre 3f) | 1¼ | **9** | 14/1 | 36 | — |
| 568[3] | **C-Harry (IRE)** (RHollinshead) **2-8-0**(5) FLynch(6) (spd 3f: sn wknd) | 5 | **10** | 7/1 | 18 | — |
| | | | | (SP 134.2%) | | **10 Rn** |

**65.8 secs** (7.20) CSF £28.60 TOTE £6.00: £1.30 £1.90 £2.20 (£9.90) Trio £32.20 OWNER Mr J. C. Parsons (MALTON) BRED Giles W. Pritchard-Gordon

**Superior Premium**, a lightly-made colt who did not impress to post, came back in fine style and galloped the opposition into submission. (4/1: op 6/1)

**Castle House**, bred to need much further and looking far from fully wound up, showed plenty of promise to stay on to gain the runner-up prize without having any chance of all with the runaway winner. (11/2: op 16/1)

**557 Caviar And Candy**, in the firing line all the way, kept staying on but had to admit the winner in a class of his own. (6/1: op 4/1)

**Legend of Aragon** ran a promising first race, showing plenty of speed and only getting outpointed inside the distance. (12/1)

**Hever Golf Lily**, a workmanlike debutante who is closely related to a couple of winners, was badly in need of this pipe-opener and she did her cause no good at all by missing the break. (6/1: op 3/1)

**490 Gresatre** (6/1: op 3/1)

**Scarrots** missed the beat at the start and was never able to recover. (4/1)

## 640 BASSINGFIELD MAIDEN STKS (3-Y.O) (Class D)

3-30 (3-31) **1m 54y** £4,391.10 (£1,315.80: £632.40: £290.70) Stalls: Low GOING: 0.82 sec per fur (S)

| Form | Horse | Dist | Pos | SP | RR | SF |
|---|---|---|---|---|---|---|
| | **Clever Cliche** (HRACecil) **3-9-0** PatEddery(18) (scope: hld up: hdwy & nt clr run 3f out: rdn over 1f out: str run to ld last stride) | — | **1** | 1/2[1] | 90++ | 66 |
| | **Hal's Pal** (DRLoder) **3-9-0** RHughes(17) (lw: hld up: hdwy over 4f out: led over 2f out: shkn up fnl f: ct post) | hd | **2** | 9/4[2] | 90 | 66 |
| | **Sandy Floss (IRE)** (HRACecil) **3-9-0** WRyan(13) (h.d.w: a.p: outpcd fnl 2f) | 6 | **3** | 12/1[3] | 78+ | 54 |
| | **Tart (FR)** (JRFanshawe) **3-8-6**(3) NVarley(1) (neat: unf: sn trckng ldrs: rdn 2f out: one pce) | 1½ | **4** | 20/1 | 70 | 46 |
| | **Royal Action** (JEBanks) **3-9-0** JQuinn(14) (leggy: unf: hld up: hdwy over 4f out: one pce fnl 2f) | ½ | **5** | 16/1 | 74 | 50 |
| | **Look Who's Calling (IRE)** (BAMcMahon) **3-9-0** GCarter(11) (lengthy: scope: bit bkwd: trckd ldrs: kpt on one pce fnl 2f) | 1¾ | **6** | 33/1 | 71 | 47 |
| 544[5] | **Chinensis (IRE)** (LMCumani) **3-9-0** OUrbina(2) (trckd ldrs: no hdwy fnl 2f: improve) | nk | **7** | 20/1 | 70+ | 46 |
| | **Chocolate Ice** (CACyzer) **3-9-0** DBiggs(16) (neat: dwlt: sn pushed along: n.d) | 6 | **8** | 33/1 | 59 | 35 |
| | **Flame of Hope** (JLDunlop) **3-8-9** TSprake(7) (bit bkwd: hld up & bhd: effrt 3f out: nt trble ldrs) | ½ | **9** | 20/1 | 53 | 29 |
| | **Devil's Dance (FR)** (MRStoute) **3-9-0** KBradshaw(9) (w'like: scope: trckd ldrs 5f: sn lost tch) | nk | **10** | 14/1 | 57 | 33 |
| | **Khabar (75)** (RBastiman) **3-8-10**(5)[ow1] HBastiman(10) (bit bkwd: prom tl wknd qckly wl over 1f out) | 4 | **11** | 16/1 | 50 | 25 |
| | **Flying Pennant (IRE)** (RHannon) **3-9-0** TQuinn(8) (bit bkwd: effrt & rdn 4f out: no imp) | 6 | **12** | 20/1 | 38 | 14 |
| | **Washington Reef (USA)** (JHMGosden) **3-9-0** DaleGibson(5) (b.hind: bit bkwd: sn pushed along: a bhd: t.o) | 10 | **13** | 25/1 | 18 | — |
| | **Star of Ring (IRE)** (MJHeaton-Ellis) **3-9-0** MFenton(4) (led over 5f: wknd qckly) | 2 | **14** | 20/1 | 14 | — |
| 526[12] | **Breydon** (MHTompkins) **3-9-0** PRobinson(6) (bit bkwd: a in rr) | ½ | **15** | 33/1 | 13 | — |
| 526[10] | **D J Cat** (WRMuir) **3-9-0** Jean-PierreLopez(15) (bit bkwd: a bhd: t.o) | 7 | **16** | 33/1 | — | — |
| | | | | (SP 163.0%) | | **16 Rn** |

**1m 51.3** (10.00) CSF £3.47 TOTE £1.60: £1.10 £1.60 £2.40 (£2.40) Trio £6.30 OWNER Mr Ivan Allan (NEWMARKET) BRED Cheveley Park Stud Ltd

**Clever Cliche**, a colt with plenty of scope and thought likely to stay at least a mile and a half, needed to do it the hard way to succeed at the first time of asking, and his courage under a forceful ride from Eddery was proof that he has what it takes. (1/2)

**Hal's Pal**, produced in tip-top condition, looked to have stolen a march when holding a decisive advantage into the final furlong, but his tail went round when he was shown the whip and he was pipped on the post. He should not be long in finding an opening. (9/4: 3/1-2/1)

**Sandy Floss (IRE)**, a high-class colt who has done extremely well physically since last season, pushed the pace until having to admit the leading pair too strong for him inside the final quarter-mile. He was tenderly handled once his measure had been taken and should be more the finished article next time. (12/1: 8/1-14/1)

**Tart (FR)**, who is sure to need a longer trip, showed plenty of promise on this debut and will hardly need to improve to win a race. (20/1)

**Royal Action** has still got plenty of filling out to do, but he ran extremely well on this racecourse debut, and is certainly one for the notebook. (16/1)

**Look Who's Calling (IRE)**, a half-brother to two winning sprinters who has plenty of scope for improvement, was feeling the strain below the distance, but the experience will not be lost. (33/1)
**544 Chinensis (IRE)**, gaining experience all the time, should now be ready to make it third time lucky. (20/1)
**Devil's Dance (FR)** (14/1: 8/1-16/1)

## 641 CARRINGTON H'CAP (0-80) (3-Y.O+) (Class D)

4-00 (4-04) **1m 1f 213y** £4,125.90 (£1,234.20: £591.60: £270.30) Stalls: Low GOING: 0.82 sec per fur (S)

| | | | | SP | RR | SF |
|---|---|---|---|---|---|---|
| 547[5] | **Eskimo Nel (IRE) (48)** (JLSpearing) **5-8-0** JFEgan(12) (hld up: hdwy over 4f out: led over 2f out: clr whn edgd rt fnl f) | — | **1** | 100/30[1] | 62 | 28 |
| 440[3] | **Princess Danielle (57)** (CCElsey) **4-8-9** CRutter(10) (hld up: hdwy 4f out: styd on strly ins fnl f) | 1¼ | **2** | 12/1 | 68 | 34 |
| | **Obelos (USA) (69)** (MrsJCecil) **5-9-7** TIves(2) (prom: outpcd 4f out: kpt on u.p appr fnl f) | 2½ | **3** | 11/1 | 76 | 42 |
| 547[2] | **Lookingforarainbow (IRE) (72)** (BobJones) **8-9-10** MWigham(15) (dwlt: hdwy 4f out: styd on ins fnl f) | 3 | **4** | 5/1[2] | 74 | 40 |
| 469[4] | **Harvey White (IRE) (55)** (JPearce) **4-8-0**(7) SGaillard(6) (trckd ldrs: kpt on same pce fnl 2f) | 1¼ | **5** | 12/1 | 55 | 21 |
| 547[3] | **Remaadi Sun (65)** (MDIUsher) **4-9-3** RStreet(18) (lw: hld up: hdwy ent st: ev ch over 2f out: sn rdn: wknd appr fnl f) | 1¼ | **6** | 9/1[3] | 63 | 29 |
| | **Leading Spirit (IRE) (72)** (CFWall) **4-9-10** WLord(11) (hld up: hdwy wl over 1f out: nrst fin) | 3 | **7** | 16/1 | 66 | 32 |
| | **Another Time (69)** (SPCWoods) **4-9-7** WWoods(13) (wl bhd tl styd on fnl 3f) | 4 | **8** | 12/1 | 56 | 22 |
| | **Sarasota Storm (54)** (MBell) **4-8-6** MFenton(9) (led after 2f to 6f out: led over 3f out tl over 2f out: sn wknd) | 4 | **9** | 16/1 | 35 | 1 |
| | **Dr Edgar (69)** (MDods) **4-9-7** FNorton(17) (bit bkwd: dwlt: sn chsng ldrs: rdn & wknd over 2f out) | 4 | **10** | 12/1 | 43 | 9 |
| | **Westminster (IRE) (63)** (MHTompkins) **4-9-1** PRobinson(3) (led 2f: led 6f tl over 3f out: sn wknd) | ½ | **11** | 20/1 | 37 | 3 |
| | **Ever so Lyrical (66)** (PWHarris) **6-9-4** TQuinn(1) (lw: trckd ldrs: drvn along 3f out: eased whn btn) | ½ | **12** | 14/1 | 39 | 5 |
| 495[5] | **Talathath (FR) (65)** (CADwyer) **4-9-3** CDwyer(5) (lw: trckd ldrs over 6f) | nk | **13** | 10/1 | 37 | 3 |
| | **Just Millie (USA) (75)** (JEBanks) **3-8-8** JQuinn(8) (a bhd) | nk | **14** | 20/1 | 47 | — |
| *498** | **Sweet Supposin (IRE) (58)** (CADwyer) **5-8-10v** GCarter(16) (swtg: chsd ldrs 6f: wknd qckly: t.o) | 25 | **15** | 11/1 | — | — |
| | | | | (SP 134.2%) | **15 Rn** | |

**2m 17.7** (15.20) CSF £44.63 CT £384.63 TOTE £4.00: £2.00 £2.50 £5.10 (£20.80) Trio £215.30 OWNER First Chance Racing (ALCESTER) BRED Leo Collins
WEIGHT FOR AGE 3yo-19lb
OFFICIAL EXPLANATION **Another Time: the trainer reported that the gelding's bridle had broken leaving the parade ring and he would not face up to the steel bit he was forced to wear in place of his rubber one.**
**Ever so Lyrical: was unable to handle the rain-softened ground.**
**547 Eskimo Nel (IRE)** gained her revenge over a couple of rivals with the help of the continuous rain. Despite giving away ground by veering right inside the distance, she was never in any danger of defeat. (100/30)
**440 Princess Danielle** made relentless progress in the latter stages but she was rather flattered to run the winner so close. (12/1)
**Obelos (USA)** made a promising return to action after being sidelined for almost twelve months and an early success will come as no surprise. (11/1: 8/1-12/1)
**547 Lookingforarainbow (IRE)** was done no favours by the easing of the ground but he did stay on towards the finish and will find his way when given a stiffer test of stamina. (5/1)
**469 Harvey White (IRE)** was not disgraced on this step up in class and should be able to pay his way in the coming weeks. (12/1)
**547 Remaadi Sun** saw too much daylight here and failed to maintain his progress when the whips were cracking. (9/1: op 5/1)
**498* Sweet Supposin (IRE)** (11/1: 8/1-12/1)

## 642 SHIPLEY COMMON H'CAP (0-70) (4-Y.O+) (Class E)

4-30 (4-33) **1m 6f 15y** £3,152.10 (£940.80: £449.40: £203.70) Stalls: Low GOING: 0.82 sec per fur (S)

| | | | | SP | RR | SF |
|---|---|---|---|---|---|---|
| | **Bellara (48)** (NMBabbage) **4-8-10** WRyan(12) (lw: trckd ldrs: led 4f out: clr appr fnl f) | — | **1** | 6/1[3] | 65 | 34 |
| | **Love The Blues (66)** (DNicholson) **4-10-0** PatEddery(4) (trckd ldrs: outpcd 3f out: styd on again ins fnl f) | 9 | **2** | 6/1[3] | 73 | 42 |
| 546[7] | **Cuango (IRE) (55)** (RHollinshead) **5-9-1**(5) FLynch(13) (hld up: hdwy 3f out: nvr nrr) | 1 | **3** | 5/1[2] | 61 | 33 |
| | **Bresil (USA) (31)** (KRBurke) **7-7-7**(3) NVarley(5) (lw: plld hrd: chsd ldrs: ev ch over 3f out: one pce fnl 2f) | 2½ | **4** | 50/1 | 34 | 6 |
| | **Tiaphena (45)** (JMackie) **5-8-10** GCarter(9) (bit bkwd: chsd ldr 11f: rdn over 2f out: sn btn) | 4 | **5** | 33/1 | 43 | 15 |
| 546[12] | **Imlak (IRE) (63)** (JLHarris) **4-9-11** JFEgan(3) (wl bhd: hdwy 4f out: no ex appr fnl f) | s.h | **6** | 14/1 | 61 | 30 |
| | **Brick Court (IRE) (45)** (RFJohnsonHoughton) **4-8-0**(7) BarrySmith(8) (a rr div: t.o) | 18 | **7** | 14/1 | 23 | — |
| | **Reaganesque (USA) (58)** (PGMurphy) **4-9-6** MFenton(2) (lw: trckd ldrs tl rdn & outpcd 3f out: t.o) | 2½ | **8** | 13/2 | 33 | 2 |
| 482[3] | **Admirals Secret (USA) (63)** (CFWall) **7-10-0** WWoods(11) (hld up: effrt 4f out: nvr nr to chal: t.o) | s.h | **9** | 7/2[1] | 38 | 10 |
| *108[14]* | **Bobby's Dream (41)** (MHTompkins) **4-8-3** PRobinson(10) (a in rr: t.o) | 2 | **10** | 20/1 | 14 | — |
| | **Firefighter (56)** (BPJBaugh) **7-9-7** WLord(14) (b: bit bkwd: trckd ldrs over 9f: sn lost tch: t.o) | 25 | **11** | 20/1 | — | — |
| 542[10] | **Sharmoor (34)** (MissLCSiddall) **4-7-10** FNorton(6) (led 10f: sn rdn & wknd: t.o) | 2 | **12** | 33/1 | — | — |
| 546[8] | **Victoria's Secret (IRE) (57)** (MRChannon) **4-9-5** RHughes(1) (chsd ldrs 10f: sn wknd: t.o) | 10 | **13** | 5/1[2] | — | — |
| | | | | (SP 128.2%) | **13 Rn** | |

**3m 20.9** (22.40) CSF £41.97 CT £184.57 TOTE £7.40: £2.40 £1.90 £2.30 (£25.60) Trio £24.90 OWNER Mr Gary Leigh (CHELTENHAM) BRED John White
LONG HANDICAP Bresil (USA) 7-9 Sharmoor 7-3
WEIGHT FOR AGE 4yo-3lb
OFFICIAL EXPLANATION **Admirals Secret (USA): the trainer reported that the gelding could not handle the rain-softened ground.**
**Bellara**, a winner over course and distance in the Autumn, came back fresh and well after a six month break and drew right away in the final quarter-mile to win unchallenged. (6/1)
**Love The Blues**, fit from hurdling, lost her pitch early in the straight but stayed on again in the closing stages without getting close enough to cause concern. (6/1)
**439 Cuango (IRE)** began to stay on three furlongs out but the winner had taken first run and he was unable to land a blow. (5/1)
**Bresil (USA)** raced freely and pressed the leaders until lack of a recent outing began to tell entering the last quarter-mile. (50/1)
**Tiaphena**, who has no form to her name, raced in second place until fading early in the straight. (33/1)
**Imlak (IRE)** was a long way adrift until staying on past beaten rivals to reach his final placing. (14/1)
**Reaganesque (USA)** (13/2: 4/1-7/1)
**482 Admirals Secret (USA)** has won on the All-Weather, but he did not seem at all happy on this rain-softened ground and was always nearer last than first. (7/2)

T/Jkpt: £47,215.00 (0.1 Tckts); £59,850.05 to Ascot 13/4/96. T/Plpt: £101.30 (172.28 Tckts). T/Qdpt: £24.40 (42.92 Tckts) IM

# 0596-WARWICK (L-H) (Good to soft)

## Saturday April 13th

WEATHER: fine WIND: slt across

### 643 HATTON MAIDEN STKS (2-Y.O F) (Class D)

1-50 (1-56) **5f** £3,333.50 (£998.00: £479.00: £219.50) Stalls: Low GOING: 0.38 sec per fur (GS)

| | | | | SP | RR | SF |
|---|---|---|---|---|---|---|
| | **Bettynouche** (RHannon) **2-8-11** RHughes(6) (lt-f: unf: a.p: c wd over 2f out: rdn over 1f out: led ins fnl f. r.o wl) | — | **1** | 9/4 [2] | 58 | — |
| | **Woman of Wit (IRE)** (APJarvis) **2-8-11** JTate(1) (unf: scope: bit bkwd: chsd ldr: led over 2f out tl ins fnl f) | 2½ | **2** | 2/1 [1] | 50 | — |
| 551[3] | **Molly Music** (GGMargarson) **2-8-11** PBloomfield(3) (led over 2f: rdn & hung rt wl over 1f out: r.o one pce) | ½ | **3** | 11/2 | 48 | — |
| | **Muppet** (MissGayKelleway) **2-8-11** KFallon(5) (leggy: unf: bkwd: s.s: rdn 3f out: nvr trbld ldrs) | 4 | **4** | 7/2 [3] | 36 | — |
| | **Emilyjill** (JGMO'Shea) **2-8-11** JQuinn(2) (leggy: unf: s.i.s: no hdwy fnl 2f) | 1 | **5** | 8/1 | 32 | — |

(SP 112.8%) **5 Rn**

**66.5 secs** (8.50) CSF £7.02 TOTE £2.40: £1.60 £1.60 (£4.10) OWNER Mr Hubert Honore (MARLBOROUGH) BRED The Sussex Stud

**Bettynouche**, a half-sister to Bookcase and Ikteshaf, seemed to be racing on the slightly faster ground after coming wide off the elbow. (9/4)

**Woman of Wit (IRE)**, a half-sister to a couple of winners in France, looks capable of finding a small race before things get too competitive. (2/1)

**551 Molly Music** again tried to make all but her advantage of previous experience did not prove enough. (11/2)

**Muppet**, out of a full sister to Pebbles, should at least come of for the run. (7/2)

**Emilyjill** is a half-sister to the sprinters Arabellajill and Petonellajill. (8/1: 7/2-10/1)

### 644 WARWICK SPRING H'CAP (0-70) (3-Y.O) (Class E)

2-20 (2-28) **5f** £3,392.00 (£1,016.00: £488.00: £224.00) Stalls: Low GOING: 0.38 sec per fur (GS)

| | | | | SP | RR | SF |
|---|---|---|---|---|---|---|
| 443[4] | **Secret Voucher (66)** (BAMcMahon) **3-8-12**(5) LNewton(14) (lw: a.p: led ins fnl f: all out) | — | **1** | 11/4 [1] | 77 | 52 |
| 478[2] | **Montrestar (58)** (PDEvans) **3-8-9** SSanders(12) (a.p: ev ch fnl f: r.o wl) | hd | **2** | 12/1 | 69 | 44 |
| 478* | **Lady Caroline Lamb (IRE) (62)** (MRChannon) **3-8-13** RHughes(11) (lw: led tl ins fnl f: r.o) | hd | **3** | 11/2 [3] | 72 | 47 |
| 525* | **Tymeera (61)** (BPalling) **3-8-12** TSprake(16) (a.p: one pce fnl 2f) | 4 | **4** | 10/1 | 59 | 34 |
| | **Amber Fort (70)** (PFICole) **3-9-7** TQuinn(2) (bit bkwd: chsd ldrs: rdn over 2f out: wknd wl over 1f out) | ½ | **5** | 5/1 [2] | 66 | 41 |
| 466[11] | **Thai Morning (68)** (PWHarris) **3-9-5** GHind(15) (hdwy 2f out: n.m.r 1f out: nvr nr to chal) | 2 | **6** | 14/1 | 58 | 33 |
| *488[5]* | **Sunset Harbour (IRE) (56)** (TJNaughton) **3-8-7** RCochrane(3) (lw: stdd s: swtchd rt: hdwy over 1f out: r.o) | 2 | **7** | 20/1 | 39 | 14 |
| | **Mystique Smile (50)** (SCWilliams) **3-8-1** GCarter(4) (b.nr hind: bit bkwd: rdn over 1f out: nvr nr to chal) | 3 | **8** | 12/1 | 24 | — |
| 478[3] | **General Equation (58)** (JBalding) **3-8-2**(7) JEdmunds(7) (spd 3f) | 2½ | **9** | 16/1 | 24 | — |
| | **Vax New Way (64)** (JLSpearing) **3-8-12**(3) SDrowne(9) (bit bkwd: chsd ldrs over 2f) | 2 | **10** | 25/1 | 23 | — |
| 525[8] | **Boffy (IRE) (62)** (BPJBaugh) **3-8-6**(7) IonaWands(5) (a bhd) | nk | **11** | 20/1 | 20 | — |
| | **Alakhluki (53)** (GLewis) **3-8-1**(3) AWhelan(17) (hung lft over 1f out: a bhd) | 1½ | **12** | 14/1 | 6 | — |
| *292[6]* | **Bouton d'Or (50)** (PHowling) **3-8-1** FNorton(10) (n.d) | 3 | **13** | 25/1 | — | — |
| | **Never Think Twice (61)** (KTIvory) **3-8-5**(7) CScally(6) (lw: s.s: a wl bhd) | 3 | **14** | 33/1 | — | — |
| | **Kiwud (55)** (TWDonnelly) **3-8-6** CRutter(1) (spd over 2f) | 3 | **15** | 66/1 | — | — |
| | **Incapol (60)** (MJRyan) **3-8-11** AClark(13) (bit bkwd: dwlt: bhd whn p.u lame over 1f out) | | **P** | 25/1 | — | — |

(SP 127.9%) **16 Rn**

**62.7 secs** (4.70) CSF £35.36 CT £166.81 TOTE £3.80: £1.70 £2.30 £1.50 £2.80 (£42.60) Trio £27.50 OWNER Mr Ian Guise (TAMWORTH) BRED R. R. Evans

STEWARDS' ENQUIRY Newton susp. 22-25/4/96 (excessive & improper use of whip).

**443 Secret Voucher** made amends for his unlucky run on the first day of the season but had to give everything and his rider picked up a four day whip ban. (11/4)

**478 Montrestar** seemed to handle the cut in the ground well enough and went down with all guns blazing. (12/1: op 8/1)

**478* Lady Caroline Lamb (IRE)**, 7lb worse off with the runner-up than when successful at Catterick, seemed to just about have matters under control until edged out in the last two hundred yards. (11/2)

**525* Tymeera**, back to the minimum trip, had been raised 4lb for her Nottingham win. (10/1)

**Amber Fort**, in a race where the principals came wide off the elbow, did best of those drawn low. (5/1)

**Thai Morning** can step up on this on better ground. (14/1: op 8/1)

**Mystique Smile** (12/1: 7/1-14/1)

**Alakhluki** (14/1: op 6/1)

### 645 DUNSMORE CLAIMING STKS (I) (4-Y.O+) (Class F)

2-50 (2-57) **1m** £2,539.00 (£704.00: £337.00) Stalls: Low GOING: 0.48 sec per fur (GS)

| | | | | SP | RR | SF |
|---|---|---|---|---|---|---|
| | **Northern Celadon (IRE) (72)** (MJHeaton-Ellis) **5-8-13** AClark(13) (chsd ldr: chal 2f out: led ins fnl f: all out) | — | **1** | 7/2 [1] | 75 | 33 |
| *285[2]* | **Kingchip Boy (63)** (MJRyan) **7-8-13v** RHughes(9) (bit bkwd: led tl ins fnl f: r.o) | 1 | **2** | 9/2 [2] | 73 | 31 |
| *201[6]* | **Bad News (43)** (JMBradley) **4-7-12** LCharnock(12) (hdwy over 4f out: r.o one pce fnl f) | 2 | **3** | 33/1 | 54 | 12 |
| 495[7] | **Aim For Stardom** (MJAhern) **4-9-2**(5) RPainter(5) (lw: a.p: one pce fnl 2f) | ¾ | **4** | 50/1 | 76 | 34 |
| | **High Commotion (IRE)** (DRCElsworth) **4-9-2** AProcter(10) (hld up: stdy hdwy fnl 2f: nvr plcd to chal) | ½ | **5** | 7/1 | 70+ | 28 |
| *513[3]* | **Everset (FR) (59)** (ABailey) **8-8-10b**(3) DWright(14) (prom tl wknd over 1f out) | nk | **6** | 10/1 | 66 | 24 |
| 479[11] | **Reed My Lips (IRE) (32)** (BPJBaugh) **5-7-10**(7) IonaWands(1) (no hdwy fnl 2f) | ¾ | **7** | 50/1 | 54 | 12 |
| | **Cape Pigeon (USA) (63)** (LGCottrell) **11-8-7** GDuffield(2) (prom over 4f) | 2 | **8** | 13/2 | 54 | 12 |
| *291[6]* | **Hawaii Storm (FR) (50)** (DJSffrenchDavis) **8-8-4**(5) CAdamson(4) (nvr nr ldrs) | s.h | **9** | 12/1 | 56 | 14 |
| | **Irish Wildcard (NZ)** (HJOliver) **8-9-3** VSlattery(11) (b: bit bkwd: rdn 3f out: sn bhd) | 1 | **10** | 25/1 | 62 | 20 |
| | **Private Fixture (IRE)** (DMarks) **5-8-6**(5) ADaly(8) (bit bkwd: chsd ldrs: rdn 4f out: wknd 2f out) | 1½ | **11** | 25/1 | 53 | 11 |
| | **Buddy's Friend (IRE)** (RJRWilliams) **8-8-9** DBiggs(7) (n.d) | 3½ | **12** | 20/1 | 44 | 2 |
| | **Finjan (44)** (AGFoster) **9-7-10**(7) DLynch(6) (bkwd: sn wl bhd) | 1½ | **13** | 33/1 | 35 | — |
| 545[2] | **Proud Image (65)** (APJarvis) **4-8-13v** JTate(3) (a bhd: t.o) | 27 | **14** | 5/1 [3] | — | — |

(SP 121.9%) **14 Rn**

**1m 46.5** (10.10) CSF £18.82 TOTE £4.50: £2.00 £1.80 £13.30 (£6.50) Trio £368.10; £279.97 to Musselburgh 15/4/96 OWNER The Over The Bridge Partnership (WROUGHTON) BRED A. F. O'Callaghan

STEWARDS' ENQUIRY Procter susp. 22-27 & 29/4/96 (failure to obtain best possible placing).

**OFFICIAL EXPLANATION Proud Image: pulled a muscle in his near hind and finished lame.**

**Northern Celadon (IRE)** loves soft ground and would have been campaigned on the All-Weather had he not had problems since winning here back in October. (7/2)
**Kingchip Boy** does not seem to know how to run a bad race at the moment and picked up where he left off on the All-Weather in mid-February. (9/2)
**Bad News** kept on in the closing stages and probably ran her best race since her two year old days. (33/1)
**Aim For Stardom**, a half-brother to Dance To The Top, had been well beaten in two bumpers prior to making his Flat race debut at Leicester. He did best of the five who elected to stay on the inside in the back straight. (50/1)
**High Commotion (IRE)** was never put into the race at any stage and his rider took the rap with a seven-day ban. (7/1)
**513 Everset (FR)** has scored eleven times in all, but never beyond seven furlongs. (10/1: op 6/1)

## 646 WELLESBOURNE H'CAP (0-95) (3-Y.O) (Class C)

3-20 (3-30) **1m** £8,832.00 (£2,676.00: £1,308.00: £624.00) Stalls: Low GOING: 0.48 sec per fur (GS)

| | Horse | Dist | Pos | SP | RR | SF |
|---|---|---|---|---|---|---|
| 448* | **Sorbie Tower (IRE) (80)** (MissGayKelleway) **3-8-11** RCochrane(16) (lw: b.hind: swvd rt s: hdwy 4f out: nt clr run 3f out: led over 1f out: qcknd clr: easily) | — | **1** | 7/2[1] | 104+ | 72 |
| 554[2] | **Proud Monk (76)** (GLMoore) **3-8-7** SWhitworth(14) (chsd ldrs: c wd over 2f out: ev ch over 1f out: no ch w wnr) | 8 | **2** | 5/1[3] | 84 | 52 |
| 567[3] | **Quality (IRE) (80)** (WAO'Gorman) **3-8-11v** EmmaO'Gorman(13) (lw: a.p: led over 2f out tl over 1f out: sn btn) | 1½ | **3** | 11/1 | 85 | 53 |
| *17** | **Doctor Bravious (IRE) (71)** (MBell) **3-8-2v**[ow1] MFenton(11) (hld up: r.o fnl 2f: nvr nr to chal) | 2 | **4** | 11/1 | 72 | 39 |
| 453[6] | **Nilgiri Hills (IRE) (81)** (JLDunlop) **3-8-12** WCarson(8) (lw: chsd ldr: led 4f out tl over 2f out: eased whn btn fnl f) | 3 | **5** | 9/2[2] | 76 | 44 |
| | **Capture The Moment (66)** (RJRWilliams) **3-7-11**[ow1] DaleGibson(6) (bit bkwd: mid div: c wd ent st: no hdwy fnl 2f) | s.h | **6** | 33/1 | 60 | 28 |
| | **Prends Ca (IRE) (90)** (RHannon) **3-9-2**[(5)] DaneO'Neill(9) (prom tl wknd 2f out) | nk | **7** | 16/1 | 84 | 52 |
| | **Caricature (IRE) (87)** (GLewis) **3-9-4** PatEddery(10) (led 4f: wknd over 2f out) | 3½ | **8** | 8/1 | 74 | 42 |
| | **Vola Via (USA) (88)** (IABalding) **3-9-5** WRyan(3) (n.d) | 3½ | **9** | 20/1 | 68 | 36 |
| | **Time of Night (USA) (74)** (RGuest) **3-8-5** GHind(15) (s.s: a bhd) | ½ | **10** | 20/1 | 53 | 21 |
| 453[9] | **Seattle Alley (USA) (65)** (MrsJRRamsden) **3-7-10** NKennedy(4) (a bhd) | 3 | **11** | 12/1 | 38 | 6 |
| | **Brighton Road (IRE) (78)** (GBBalding) **3-8-9** AClark(12) (lw: a bhd) | 1¼ | **12** | 25/1 | 49 | 17 |
| | **Lionel Edwards (IRE) (70)** (PFICole) **3-8-1** CRutter(2) (bit bkwd: a bhd) | 13 | **13** | 16/1 | 15 | — |
| | **Sylva Paradise (IRE) (80)** (CEBrittain) **3-8-11** BDoyle(7) (bit bkwd: prom over 4f) | 1¼ | **14** | 20/1 | 22 | — |
| | **Fran Godfrey (67)** (PTWalwyn) **3-7-7**[(5)ow2] MHenry(1) (bit bkwd: wnt lft s: a bhd: t.o) | 19 | **15** | 16/1 | — | — |

(SP 131.3%) **15 Rn**

**1m 42.5** (6.10) CSF £22.04 CT £150.22 TOTE £4.50: £1.80 £1.60 £3.70 (£14.90) Trio £40.30 OWNER P. D. Q (WHITCOMBE) BRED B. Kennedy
**448* Sorbie Tower (IRE)**, described by his trainer as a real racehorse, does look to have a bright future but the Handicapper seems likely to take a dim view of this performance. (7/2)
**554 Proud Monk** raced under the stands' rail in the home straight, the opposite side to the winner, but his rival was so superior he could have won from anywhere. (5/1)
**567 Quality (IRE)** could not live with the winner over this shorter trip. (11/1: 8/1-12/1)
**Doctor Bravious (IRE)**, successful at Wolverhampton at the beginning of the year, did enough to suggest improvement can be expected. (11/1: 6/1-12/1)
**453 Nilgiri Hills (IRE)** was apparently interfered with by Quality after being headed and was allowed to come home in his own time when all chance had gone. (9/2)
**453 Seattle Alley (USA)** (12/1: op 6/1)

## 647 MARTON H'CAP (0-95) (4-Y.O+) (Class C)

3-50 (3-57) **1m 6f 194y** £5,540.00 (£1,670.00: £810.00: £380.00) Stalls: Low GOING: 0.48 sec per fur (GS)

| | Horse | Dist | Pos | SP | RR | SF |
|---|---|---|---|---|---|---|
| | **Purple Splash (80)** (PJMakin) **6-9-2v** PatEddery(2) (b: hdwy & nt clr run over 3f out: rdn over 2f out: r.o wl to ld nr fin) | — | **1** | 4/1[1] | 95 | 64 |
| | **Kadastrof (FR) (75)** (RDickin) **6-8-11** TQuinn(4) (led: clr & c wd over 2f out: sn rdn: ct nr fin) | hd | **2** | 8/1 | 90 | 59 |
| 573[10] | **Sea Freedom (61)** (GBBalding) **5-7-8v**[(3)] NVarley(10) (chsd ldrs: rdn & lost pl 5f out: styd on wl appr fnl f) | ½ | **3** | 12/1 | 75 | 44 |
| | **Brandon Prince (IRE) (63)** (IABalding) **8-7-6b**[(7)] MartinDwyer(7) (bit bkwd: hdwy over 3f out: nvr rchd ldrs) | 3 | **4** | 14/1 | 74 | 43 |
| *532[3]* | **Backview (65)** (BJLlewellyn) **4-7-12** JQuinn(12) (chsd ldrs: no hdwy fnl 4f) | 10 | **5** | 6/1[2] | 65 | 31 |
| 573[15] | **Lalindi (IRE) (66)** (DRCElsworth) **5-8-2** WCarson(6) (lw: prom: hmpd & lost pl 8f out: rallied 5f out: rdn & btn 3f out) | 6 | **6** | 7/1[3] | 60 | 29 |
| *392[11]* | **Johns Act (USA) (71)** (DHaydnJones) **6-8-7** RCochrane(9) (lw: chsd ldrs tl wknd 3f out) | 3 | **7** | 16/1 | 62 | 31 |
| 563[6] | **Anglesey Sea View (70)** (ABailey) **7-8-6** GCarter(8) (prom tl wknd over 2f out) | 4 | **8** | 8/1 | 56 | 25 |
| 439[5] | **Artic Courier (77)** (DJSCosgrove) **5-8-13b** JReid(3) (trckd ldrs: rdn over 2f out: sn wknd) | 1 | **9** | 7/1[3] | 62 | 31 |
| 449[9] | **En Vacances (IRE) (73)** (AGFoster) **4-8-6** TSprake(1) (hmpd & lost pl 8f out: n.d after) | 9 | **10** | 8/1 | 49 | 15 |
| | **English Invader (92)** (RAkehurst) **5-9-7**[(7)] TAshley(5) (bhd fnl 4f) | 10 | **11** | 11/1 | 57 | 26 |
| | **Astrolabe (78)** (JMBradley) **4-8-8**[(3)] SDrowne(11) (rdn 6f out: sn wl bhd) | 16 | **12** | 33/1 | 26 | — |

(SP 124.1%) **12 Rn**

**3m 23.9** (13.90) CSF £35.12 CT £334.13 TOTE £4.60: £1.70 £2.70 £3.30 (£12.70) Trio £85.50 OWNER Sir Christopher Walford (MARLBOROUGH) BRED W. and R. Barnett Ltd
WEIGHT FOR AGE 4yo-3lb
**Purple Splash**, third in this race last year and an easy winner over hurdles at the track last month, moved poorly to post. Sticking to the inside in the home straight, he raced wide apart from the runner-up which did not help his cause and he did well to win. (4/1: 3/1-9/2)
**Kadastrof (FR)**, a decent hurdler who did not run on the Flat last year but won at the 1994 Craven meeting, did his usual front running and looked to have the race won when kicking clear on the home turn and coming over to the stands' rails. However, soon hard at work, his stride shortened in the final furlong. (8/1)
**449 Sea Freedom** is a frustrating maiden, staying on strongly towards the stands' side in the last furlong after looking well held. (12/1)
**Brandon Prince (IRE)**, off since last May, is an out and out stayer and was doing all his best work in the last half mile. He ran well over two miles and five furlongs at Pontefract last year, a race he was recently awarded, and a return there should be noted. (14/1)
**532 Backview**, well handicapped on recent All-Weather form, has shown his best turf form to date on faster ground. (6/1)
**Lalindi (IRE)**, last year's winner, raced more towards the inside than most going out into the country but was cut off and lost her place as the rest of the field cut the corner. She briefly rallied but the damage was done. (7/1)

## 648 OLD MILVERTON MAIDEN STKS (3-Y.O+) (Class D)

4-30 (4-39) **5f** £4,077.50 (£1,220.00: £585.00: £267.50) Stalls: Low GOING: 0.38 sec per fur (GS)

| Form | Horse | Dist | Pos | SP | RR | SF |
|---|---|---|---|---|---|---|
| | **Alpine Twist (USA)** (PWChapple-Hyam) **3-8-3**$^{(5)ow3}$ RHavlin(15) (chsd ldrs: ev ch over 1f out: rdn to ld wl ins fnl f) | — | 1 | 9/1$^{3}$ | 97 | 58 |
| | **Speed On** (HCandy) **3-8-10** CRutter(7) (w'like: neat: hdwy over 2f out: led over 1f out: edgd lft wl ins fnl f) | nk | 2 | 9/2$^{2}$ | 98 | 62 |
| | **Smithereens** (PTWalwyn) **3-8-5** PatEddery(6) (chsd ldrs: led wl over 1f out: sn hdd & btn) | 8 | 3 | 11/8$^{1}$ | 67 | 31 |
| | **Persian Butterfly** (ICampbell) **4-9-2** AClark(1) (gd hdwy over 1f out: fin wl) | 1¾ | 4 | 25/1 | 62+ | 37 |
| | **Lillibella** (IABalding) **3-7-12**$^{(7)}$ MartinDwyer(11) (chsd ldrs: one pce fnl 2f) | 1¼ | 5 | 25/1 | 58 | 22 |
| | **Man of Wit (IRE) (76)** (APJarvis) **3-8-10** JTate(4) (bkwd: in tch: no hdwy appr fnl f) | 2 | 6 | 12/1 | 56 | 20 |
| | **Natal Ridge** (DHaydnJones) **3-8-10** JReid(10) (bkwd: nvr trbld ldrs) | s.h | 7 | 20/1 | 56 | 20 |
| | **Midnight Cookie (48)** (BAPearce) **3-8-10** SWhitworth(16) (lw: led over 3f) | s.h | 8 | 33/1 | 56 | 20 |
| | **Ameliajill** (JGMO'Shea) **3-8-5** JQuinn(8) (neat: unf: bit bkwd: squeezed out s: nvr nr) | ¾ | 9 | 33/1 | 49+ | 13 |
| | **Ca'd'oro** (GBBalding) **3-8-7**$^{(3)}$ SDrowne(9) (nvr trbld ldrs) | 1 | 10 | 16/1 | 51 | 15 |
| | **Smarter Charter** (MrsJRRamsden) **3-8-10** KFallon(12) (hmpd s: nvr nr ldrs) | ½ | 11 | 14/1 | 49+ | 13 |
| | **Red Leo (USA)** (PFICole) **3-8-3**$^{(7)}$ DavidO'Neill(14) (w'like: a bhd) | 6 | 12 | 25/1 | 30 | — |
| 566$^{10}$ | **Ashik (IRE)** (LJBarratt) **3-8-10b** LCharnock(13) (spd 3f) | 3½ | 13 | 50/1 | 19 | — |
| | **Play The Tune** (KRBurke) **3-8-10** TQuinn(3) (unf: swtg: bkwd: a bhd) | ¾ | 14 | 14/1 | 16 | — |
| *514*$^{9}$ | **Roxane (IRE)** (ABailey) **3-8-5b**$^{1}$ SSanders(5) (in tch 3f) | 2½ | 15 | 66/1 | 3 | — |
| 467$^{12}$ | **Peace House (IRE)** (JLSpearing) **3-7-12**$^{(7)}$ SRighton(2) (s.i.s: a bhd) | 2½ | 16 | 66/1 | — | — |
| | | | | (SP 124.3%) | **16 Rn** | |

**61.9 secs** (3.90) CSF £46.75 TOTE £7.10: £2.60 £2.20 £1.50 (£18.60) Trio £7.30 OWNER Mr R. E. Sangster (MARLBOROUGH) BRED Swettenham Stud

WEIGHT FOR AGE 3yo-11lb

OFFICIAL EXPLANATION **Man of Wit (IRE): the jockey stated that the colt tried to hang right all the way, and that he had concentrated on holding him together. The trainer added that the colt has shown a tendency to bolt since incurring a leg injury.**

**Alpine Twist (USA)**, looking well in her coat although as if she should come on for the run, made good use of her high draw and sticking to the stands' rail proved decisive in the dying strides. (9/1: 7/2-10/1)

**Speed On**, already a gelding, moved well to post. Making progress towards the centre of the track, he looked like making a winning debut when going on but could not sustain the effort and wandered off a true line near the finish. (9/2: 6/1-4/1)

**Smithereens** had to do her running to beat a bad draw, virtually the entire field sticking to the outside rail. Once in front, there was little left in the tank. (11/8)

**Persian Butterfly** ran a fine race from the worst draw, finishing best of all. She has the ability to find a race, but is unlikely to be well treated now she is eligible for handicaps given her proximity to Warning Shadows at last year's Craven meeting. (25/1)

**Lillibella**, not keen to post, was never travelling well enough to take a hand. (25/1)

**Man of Wit (IRE)** refused to be ridden past the stables on the way to post and had to be led down the rest of the way. Not knocked about in the last couple of furlongs, his temperament is suspect. (12/1)

**Smarter Charter** (14/1: 7/1-16/1)

## 649 DUNSMORE CLAIMING STKS (II) (4-Y.O+) (Class F)

5-05 (5-08) **1m** £2,518.00 (£698.00: £334.00) Stalls: Low GOING: 0.48 sec per fur (GS)

| Form | Horse | Dist | Pos | SP | RR | SF |
|---|---|---|---|---|---|---|
| 470$^{14}$ | **Reverand Thickness (68)** (SCWilliams) **5-8-11** RHughes(10) (led 2f: led over 3f out tl ins fnl f: led nr fin) | — | 1 | 9/2$^{1}$ | 76 | 52 |
| *485*$^{6}$ | **Allez Cyrano (IRE) (75)** (MBell) **5-8-11** MFenton(12) (dwlt: led after 2f tl over 3f out: led ins fnl f: ct nr fin) | 1¼ | 2 | 13/2$^{3}$ | 74 | 50 |
| *345*$^{4}$ | **Q Factor (68)** (DHaydnJones) **4-8-6** AMackay(2) (hdwy 3f out: ev ch 1f out: unable qckn) | 1½ | 3 | 7/1 | 66 | 42 |
| | **Roi de la Mer (IRE) (63)** (JAkehurst) **5-8-11** SWhitworth(13) (stumbled s: hdwy 3f out: no ex fnl f) | 6 | 4 | 10/1 | 59 | 35 |
| 479$^{6}$ | **Spencer's Revenge (71)** (NTinkler) **7-8-13** GCarter(6) (hmpd s: hdwy over 3f out: nvr rchd ldrs) | 10 | 5 | 5/1$^{2}$ | 41 | 17 |
| | **Cyclone (IRE)** (BRMillman) **5-8-4**$^{(3)}$ SDrowne(14) (nvr nrr) | 3 | 6 | 50/1 | 29 | 5 |
| | **Northern Spruce (IRE) (27)** (AGFoster) **4-8-13** TSprake(5) (hmpd s: nvr trbld ldrs) | 1½ | 7 | 50/1 | 32 | 8 |
| 470$^{3}$ | **Zatopek (62)** (JCullinan) **4-9-7** TQuinn(7) (chsd ldrs: rdn 4f out: wknd 2f out) | 9 | 8 | 8/1 | 22 | — |
| | **Blushing Grenadier (IRE) (52)** (MJFetherston-Godley) **4-8-8**$^{(5)}$ DaneO'Neill(11) (swtg: bkwd: chsd ldrs 6f) | ½ | 9 | 14/1 | 13 | — |
| *517*$^{4}$ | **Melody Wheel** (AHide) **4-8-2** JQuinn(1) (nvr trbld ldrs) | 1 | 10 | 12/1 | — | — |
| | **Indonesian (IRE) (72)** (CPEBrooks) **4-8-13b** JReid(4) (lw: bhd fnl 3f) | ½ | 11 | 7/1 | 10 | — |
| | **Courting Newmarket (42)** (NMBabbage) **8-8-0**$^{(7)}$ RFfrench(8) (bhd fnl 4f) | 1¾ | 12 | 10/1 | — | — |
| | **Simply a Sequel (IRE)** (CFCJackson) **5-8-7** AMcGlone(3) (b: a bhd) | 12 | 13 | 50/1 | — | — |
| 545$^{11}$ | **Lizapet (IRE) (37)** (PAPritchard) **4-7-7v**$^{1(7)}$ JoHunnam(9) (a bhd) | ¾ | 14 | 66/1 | — | — |
| | | | | (SP 124.2%) | **14 Rn** | |

**1m 44.4** (8.00) CSF £32.73 TOTE £8.10: £2.30 £2.60 £3.00 (£16.50) Trio £55.30 OWNER The Waresley Partnership (NEWMARKET) BRED S. J. Mear

OFFICIAL EXPLANATION **Reverand Thickness: the trainer stated that the gelding benefited by finding the better ground on the outside, and having the blinkers left off.**

**Reverand Thickness** took a race which was largely decided in the first couple of furlongs. Strange tactics were used by the majority of the riders, not following the outside route that had been so successful earlier in the day. As a result, the race was a match between winner and second which Reverand Thickness sealed close home despite looking none too keen. (9/2)

**485 Allez Cyrano (IRE)** disputed the issue with the winner throughout and might well have won had he been able to keep the stands' rail approaching the final furlong. (13/2)

**Q Factor** did much the best of those racing on the inside, following the two principals to the stands' side in the straight. In a fair race she would probably have won. (7/1)

**Roi de la Mer (IRE)** stumbled as the stalls opened, but did launch a bid on the home turn. (10/1)

**479 Spencer's Revenge** lost all realistic chance at the start. (5/1)

**Cyclone (IRE)** raced wide but was never going the pace of the front two. (50/1)

**470 Zatopek** (8/1: op 5/1)

## 650 KINETON H'CAP (0-85) (4-Y.O+) (Class D)

5-35 (5-36) **1m 2f 169y** £4,337.50 (£1,300.00: £625.00: £287.50) Stalls: Low GOING: 0.48 sec per fur (GS)

| Form | Horse | Dist | Pos | SP | RR | SF |
|---|---|---|---|---|---|---|
| | **Bit on the Side (IRE) (76)** (NEBerry) **7-9-1**$^{(7)}$ AEddery(20) (a gng wl: led on bit over 1f out: easily) | — | 1 | 20/1 | 85+ | 64 |

| | Horse | Dist | Pos | SP | RR | SF |
|---|---|---|---|---|---|---|
| | **Swallows Dream (IRE) (75)** (JLDunlop) **5-9-7** WCarson(18) (prom: ev ch over 1f out: kpt on) | 1¼ | **2** | 8/1 | 82 | 61 |
| | **Myfontaine (63)** (KTIvory) **9-8-6**(3) JStack(19) (hdwy 4f out: rdn 2f out: one pce fnl f) | 1½ | **3** | 13/2 $^{2}$ | 68 | 47 |
| *199$^{6}$* | **Master Beveled (73)** (PDEvans) **6-9-5** KFallon(9) (in tch: hdwy over 3f out: rdn 2f out: no imp) | nk | **4** | 9/2 $^{1}$ | 78 | 57 |
| | **Zermatt (IRE) (65)** (MDIUsher) **6-8-11** NAdams(7) (led tl hdd over 1f out: sn btn) | 7 | **5** | 33/1 | 59 | 38 |
| | **Silently (78)** (IABalding) **4-9-10** WRyan(15) (hdwy 4f out: rdn & edgd lft over 1f out: eased whn btn) | 2½ | **6** | 12/1 | 68 | 47 |
| 450$^{17}$ | **Petoskin (75)** (JPearce) **4-9-7** GBardwell(8) (lw: bhd tl r.o fnl 3f) | 2 | **7** | 11/1 | 62 | 41 |
| 469$^{14}$ | **Ketabi (USA) (55)** (RAkehurst) **5-8-1b$^{1}$** SSanders(14) (swtg: chsd ldr tl wknd 2f out) | 1¼ | **8** | 14/1 | 41 | 20 |
| *462$^{5}$* | **Wild Palm (68)** (WAO'Gorman) **4-9-0** EmmaO'Gorman(2) (lw: dwlt: nvr nr to chal) | 6 | **9** | 12/1 | 45 | 24 |
| | **Captain's Day (75)** (TGMills) **4-9-7** AMackay(11) (bit bkwd: nvr trbld ldrs) | 1½ | **10** | 25/1 | 49 | 28 |
| 450$^{2}$ | **Lynton Lad (75)** (CPEBrooks) **4-9-7b** JReid(6) (prom over 7f) | 5 | **11** | 7/1 $^{3}$ | 42 | 21 |
| 450$^{10}$ | **Tulu (73)** (MrsJRRamsden) **5-9-0**(5) DaneO'Neill(10) (b.off fore: blt bkwd: bhd fnl 2f) | s.h | **12** | 13/2 $^{2}$ | 40 | 19 |
| | **Blaze of Oak (USA) (62)** (JMBradley) **5-8-5**(3) SDrowne(4) (bit bkwd: chsd ldrs tl wknd 4f out) | 9 | **13** | 20/1 | 16 | — |
| | **Tappeto (73)** (HCandy) **4-9-5** CRutter(1) (bkwd: chsd ldrs tl rdn & wknd 6f out) | 3 | **14** | 14/1 | 22 | 1 |
| *532$^{6}$* | **Chevalier (USA) (75)** (ICampbell) **4-9-7** AClark(12) (s.i.s: a bhd: t.o fnl 4f) | dist | **15** | 25/1 | — | — |

(SP 125.7%) **15 Rn**

**2m 24.2** (10.70) CSF £162.43 CT £1,078.10 TOTE £23.00: £4.50 £2.50 £2.00 (£70.80) Trio £251.90 OWNER Mr Mike Hawkett (UPPER LAMBOURN) BRED Stallion Development Group in Ireland

**Bit on the Side (IRE)**, having her first run for the yard and with the cut in the ground she loves, bounced back to her very best to win with embarrassing ease. She did follow the favoured outside line throughout and could therefore be slightly flattered. (20/1)

**Swallows Dream (IRE)** continues to pay the penalty for consistency, extending his losing sequence to eleven, having risen 3lb in the handicap in the process. (8/1)

**Myfontaine,** bidding for an eighth course and distance victory, did not go down without a fight and should soon be winning. (13/2)

**Master Beveled,** successful over hurdles during the winter, had been considered best on a straight course when winning over shorter trips and is likely to be at his best on more galloping tracks. (9/2)

**Zermatt (IRE)** did his best to dictate matters but had nothing left once headed. (33/1)

**Silently** hung onto the slower ground when asked to make his run in the straight and the situation was quickly accepted. (12/1)

**462 Wild Palm** looked the part but, although he tried to close on the home turn, could never make up for a slow start. (12/1)

T/Plpt: £14.80 (858.8 Tckts). T/Qdpt: £10.00 (75.38 Tckts). KH

## 0529-**WOLVERHAMPTON (L-H) (Standard)**

## Saturday April 13th

WEATHER: fine WIND: nil

### 651 TRESCOTT MEDIAN AUCTION MAIDEN STKS (3-Y.O) (Class E)

7-00 (7-02) **1m 4f (Fibresand)** £2,709.00 (£749.00: £357.00) Stalls: Low GOING: 0.01 sec per fur (STD)

| | Horse | Dist | Pos | SP | RR | SF |
|---|---|---|---|---|---|---|
| 471$^{6}$ | **Jump The Lights (63)** (SPCWoods) **3-9-0** WWoods(7) (trckd ldrs: led 3f out: rdn & r.o wl) | — | **1** | 4/1 $^{2}$ | 60 | 19 |
| 560$^{3}$ | **Sedbergh (USA) (64)** (MrsMReveley) **3-9-0** ACulhane(2) (lw: hld up: hdwy to chse wnr over 2f out: hrd rdn & unable qckn nr fin) | ¾ | **2** | 8/11 $^{1}$ | 59 | 18 |
| | **Nordic Hero (IRE)** (APJarvis) **3-9-0** JTate(3) (w'like: scope: bkwd: hld up in tch: effrt over 3f out: rdn & outpcd fnl 2f) | 14 | **3** | 10/1 | 40 | — |
| 522$^{3}$ | **Radmore Brandy (31)** (NPLittmoden) **3-8-9** MFenton(8) (hld up in rr: effrt 3f out: no imp fnl 2f) | 2 | **4** | 9/1 $^{3}$ | 33 | — |
| | **Cashaplenty** (NPLittmoden) **3-9-0** TGMcLaughlin(1) (leggy: bit bkwd: chsd ldr: led over 4f out to 3f out: sn rdn & outpcd) | 2½ | **5** | 16/1 | 34 | — |
| 528$^{7}$ | **Richard House Lad (40)** (RHollinshead) **3-8-9**(5) FLynch(6) (bit bkwd: a in rr) | 2 | **6** | 10/1 | 32 | — |
| 599$^{6}$ | **Chillington** (WMBrisbourne) **3-9-0** AMcGlone(4) (led over 7f: wknd qckly over 2f out) | 1¾ | **7** | 33/1 | 29 | — |
| *58$^{7}$* | **Thenorthernplayboy (IRE)** (BPreece) **3-9-0** NAdams(5) (bit bkwd: dwlt: sn chsng ldrs: reminders 8f out: wknd 4f out: t.o) | 19 | **8** | 40/1 | 4 | — |

(SP 117.3%) **8 Rn**

**2m 44.8** (12.30) CSF £7.27 TOTE £4.80: £1.30 £1.30 £2.00 (£2.20) OWNER Mr R. A. Crawley (NEWMARKET) BRED High Point Bloodstock Ltd

**471 Jump The Lights,** much sharper after his pipe-opener last month, kicked on at the end of the back straight and, staying on strongly, proved too tough for the hard ridden favourite. (4/1)

**560 Sedbergh (USA),** continuing his step up in distance, looked to have the edge when moving into a challenging position turning in but he had met a rival who was in no mood to give best. (8/11)

**Nordic Hero (IRE),** quite an attractive colt who should be able to improve a lot on this, could not match the extra pace of the principals from the turn into the straight and easily got brushed aside. (10/1: op 5/1)

**522 Radmore Brandy** (9/1: 6/1-10/1)

**Richard House Lad** (10/1: op 6/1)

### 652 PERTON CLAIMING STKS (3-Y.O+) (Class F)

7-30 (7-32) **5f (Fibresand)** £2,070.00 (£570.00: £270.00) Stalls: Low GOING: 0.01 sec per fur (STD)

| | Horse | Dist | Pos | SP | RR | SF |
|---|---|---|---|---|---|---|
| | **Standown (70)** (JBerry) **3-8-10**(5) PRoberts(8) (bit bkwd: hdwy 2f out: c stands' side: str run to ld post) | — | **1** | 9/2 $^{2}$ | 75 | 29 |
| *511** | **Hannah's Usher (70)** (CMurray) **4-9-4** MTebbutt(5) (hdwy & nt clr run wl over 1f out: str burst fnl f: jst failed) | s.h | **2** | 6/4 $^{1}$ | 67 | 32 |
| *461$^{10}$* | **Little Saboteur (57)** (PJMakin) **7-8-9b** AClark(7) (b.nr hind: a.p: rdn to ld 1f out: ct cl home) | nk | **3** | 9/1 | 57 | 22 |
| | **Subfusk (57)** (WGMTurner) **3-8-4** TSprake(9) (bkwd: led after 1f to 1f out: hrd rdn & hmpd nr fin) | ¾ | **4** | 8/1 $^{3}$ | 61 | 15 |
| | **Tee-Emm (55)** (PHowling) **6-8-12** JQuinn(3) (b.hind: bkwd: led 1f: rdn over 1f out: one pce) | 3 | **5** | 11/1 | 48 | 13 |
| *423$^{4}$* | **Don't Tell Anyone (44)** (PDEvans) **3-8-1** SSanders(4) (outpcd tl r.o appr fnl f) | s.h | **6** | 14/1 | 48 | 2 |
| *534$^{7}$* | **Nomadic Dancer (IRE) (41)** (MSSaunders) **4-8-13** JFEgan(10) (trckd ldrs: hrd rdn wl over 1f out: sn btn) | 1 | **7** | 40/1 | 46 | 11 |
| *514$^{4}$* | **Swan At Whalley (57)** (MartynWane) **4-8-11**(5) DaneO'Neill(6) (bit bkwd: prom: ev ch whn n.m.r fnl f: nt rcvr) | 2½ | **8** | 8/1 $^{3}$ | 41 | 6 |
| *362$^{7}$* | **Daaniera (IRE) (41)** (PHowling) **6-9-0b** FNorton(2) (b.hind: prom on ins over 3f) | ¾ | **9** | 25/1 | 36 | 1 |
| *418$^{10}$* | **All Apologies (IRE) (60)** (RHollinshead) **4-8-11**(5) FLynch(1) (outpcd: sn bhd) | ½ | **10** | 9/1 | 37 | 2 |

(SP 121.7%) **10 Rn**

**62.9 secs** (4.20) CSF £11.71 TOTE £7.10: £2.00 £1.40 £2.20 (£5.50) Trio £17.60 OWNER Mrs Chris Deuters (COCKERHAM) BRED Alan Gibson

WEIGHT FOR AGE 3yo-11lb

**Standown** was able to make his first appearance on the All-Weather a successful one. It was a close run affair and a lot of credit must go to his jockey for a tactical manoeuvre that proved spot on. (9/2)
**511* Hannah's Usher** did not enjoy the smoothest of passages when delivering his challenge below the distance but he sprouted wings in the final fifty yards and failed by the width of a cigarette paper. (6/4)
**Little Saboteur**, back over her favourite trip, won a hard fought battle to strike the front passing the furlong marker but just failed to last home in a spirited battle to the line. She can soon make amends. (9/1)
**Subfusk**, twice a winner here over six furlongs, was in the firing line all the way but was getting the worst of the argument when squeezed for room and forced to check inside the last fifty yards. This was a decent initial outing of the season and she should be able to gain reward. (8/1)
**Tee-Emm**, very much in need of this first run since December, was in the thick of the action until feeling the strain approaching the final furlong. (11/1: 8/1-12/1)
**Don't Tell Anyone**, struggling with the pace from the start, did make some late progress but was never able to get himself into contention. (14/1)
**514 Swan At Whalley** pressed the leaders and was not done with when squeezed out entering the final furlong and having no chance of recovering. He can pick up a similar event in the near future. (8/1)

## 653 PORTOBELLO H'CAP (0-70) (3-Y.O+) (Class E)

8-00 (8-01) **6f (Fibresand)** £2,768.00 (£824.00: £392.00: £176.00) Stalls: Low GOING: 0.01 sec per fur (STD)

| | | | | SP | RR | SF |
|---|---|---|---|---|---|---|
| 511[5] | **Little Ibnr (68)** (PDEvans) **5-10-0** KFallon(7) (a.p: shkn up to ld 1f out: r.o strly) | — | **1** | 7/2[1] | 72 | 45 |
| | **Lady Sheriff (60)** (RHollinshead) **5-9-1**(5) FLynch(4) (hld up & bhd: gd hdwy 2f out: fin wl) | 1¼ | **2** | 7/2[1] | 61 | 34 |
| 534[2] | **Disco Boy (56)** (PDEvans) **6-9-2** SSanders(6) (hld up: hdwy wl over 1f out: nrst fin) | 1¾ | **3** | 4/1[2] | 52 | 25 |
| 413[3] | **Efficacy (61)** (APJarvis) **5-9-0**(7) KHopkins(2) (a.p: led 2f out to 1f out: no ex fnl f) | hd | **4** | 4/1[2] | 57 | 30 |
| 418[3] | **Jon's Choice (38)** (BPreece) **8-7-9**(3) DWright(3) (slt ld 4f: rdn & one pce appr fnl f) | 1½ | **5** | 9/2[3] | 30 | 3 |
| 389[4] | **Fighter Squadron (38)** (REPeacock) **7-7-12b** JQuinn(5) (s.i.s: hdwy over 2f out: nvr nr to chal) | 1½ | **6** | 16/1 | 26 | — |
| 514[6] | **Honey Trader (53)** (JBerry) **4-8-8**(5) PRoberts(1) (lw: gd spd 4f) | 7 | **7** | 12/1 | 22 | — |
| | | | | (SP 116.2%) | **7 Rn** | |

**1m 16.2** (4.80) CSF £15.66 TOTE £5.30: £3.10 £1.60 (£7.10) OWNER Swinnerton Transport Ltd (WELSHPOOL) BRED R. E. Waugh
**511 Little Ibnr**, always on the heels of the leaders, quickened up to gain a narrow lead into the final furlong and, running on strongly, won a shade comfortably. (7/2)
**Lady Sheriff**, who has changed stables since she last ran, came from off the pace with a sustained last furlong challenge but, over a trip possibly just beyond her best, could not reel in the winner. She is useful at her best and an early success should follow. (7/2)
**534 Disco Boy**, restrained just behind the leaders, ran on promisingly inside the distance and he is going the right way. (4/1)
**Efficacy**, stepping back to sprinting, shared the lead and had every chance until tapped for toe in the dash to the line. (4/1)
**Jon's Choice** is possibly better coming from behind for he showed in the leading quartet until fading approaching the final furlong. (9/2)
**Fighter Squadron**, sluggish as the stalls opened, could not recover the lost ground but he did keep persevering and all is not lost yet. (16/1)

## 654 PLYVINE CATERING H'CAP (0-70) (3-Y.O+) (Class E)

8-30 (8-32) **1m 100y (Fibresand)** £3,152.10 (£940.80: £449.40: £203.70) Stalls: Low GOING: 0.01 sec per fur (STD)

| | | | | SP | RR | SF |
|---|---|---|---|---|---|---|
| 462[3] | **Golden Touch (USA) (56)** (NACallaghan) **4-9-0**(5) DaneO'Neill(10) (lw: hdwy 6f out: led wl over 2f out tl over 1f out: rallied u.p to ld last stride) | — | **1** | 3/1[1] | 67 | 47 |
| 399[3] | **Quinzii Martin (48)** (DHaydnJones) **8-8-11** AMackay(12) (trckd ldrs: led over 1f out tl ct nr fin) | s.h | **2** | 8/1 | 59 | 39 |
| 513[5] | **Chadleigh Lane (USA) (65)** (RHollinshead) **4-9-9**(5) FLynch(9) (hld up: hdwy on outside over 3f out: kpt on: nt rch ldrs) | 6 | **3** | 6/1[2] | 65 | 45 |
| 487[4] | **Sooty Tern (49)** (JMBradley) **9-8-9**(3) SDrowne(6) (b.off fore: prom: rdn & outpcd 2f out: sn btn) | 3 | **4** | 7/1[3] | 43 | 23 |
| 518[10] | **Ring the Chief (49)** (MDIUsher) **4-8-12** MWigham(5) (lw: hld up & bhd: sme hdwy fnl 2f: nvr nrr) | 1¾ | **5** | 33/1 | 40 | 20 |
| 404* | **People Direct (61)** (KWMcAuliffe) **3-8-9** JFEgan(3) (b.hind: slt ld over 5f: rdn & outpcd ent st) | nk | **6** | 7/1[3] | 51 | 16 |
| 521[3] | **David James' Girl (51)** (ABailey) **4-8-7**(7) AngelaGallimore(4) (rdn 4f out: a in rr) | 1¼ | **7** | 7/1[3] | 39 | 19 |
| 461[7] | **Napoleon Star (IRE) (60)** (MSSaunders) **5-9-9** VSlattery(7) (sn drvn along: a bhd) | 5 | **8** | 33/1 | 38 | 18 |
| | **Great Tern (46)** (NMBabbage) **4-8-9** JQuinn(1) (bit bkwd: mid div: hrd drvn over 4f out: no imp) | 1¾ | **9** | 8/1 | 21 | 1 |
| 530[4] | **Last Roundup (58)** (CWThornton) **4-9-7** DeanMcKeown(11) (trckd ldrs: hrd drvn ½-wy: sn wknd: t.o) | 6 | **10** | 15/2 | 22 | 2 |
| | **Sungrove's Best (33)** (PEccles) **9-7-10** NAdams(8) (dwlt: a bhd: t.o) | 1¾ | **11** | 40/1 | — | — |
| | **Art Tatum (48)** (GMMcCourt) **5-8-11b** KFallon(2) (lost pl over 3f out: sn bhd: t.o) | 2½ | **12** | 14/1 | 4 | — |
| | | | | (SP 125.8%) | **12 Rn** | |

**1m 50.9** (5.90) CSF £27.29 CT £119.09 TOTE £5.00: £1.90 £2.50 £3.40 (£15.80) Trio £19.40 OWNER Mrs Rita Godfrey (NEWMARKET) BRED Woodcote Stud Ltd
LONG HANDICAP Sungrove's Best 7-7
WEIGHT FOR AGE 3yo-15lb
**462 Golden Touch (USA)** got off the mark with a hard fought success but he showed the right commitment and is capable of winning again. (3/1)
**Quinzii Martin**, very free to post, got to the front a shade too soon and, with his stamina giving out, was worried out of it in the dying strides. (8/1)
**513 Chadleigh Lane (USA)** always had too much to do and, though he did stay on in the latter stages, was never a problem. (6/1)
**487 Sooty Tern** continues to run well and he will be worth remembering when switched back to the turf. (7/1)
**Ring the Chief** was unable to get himself into the race but he did stay on and he could well find his way over a longer trip. (33/1)
**People Direct** found this step up in class just too much and her front running tactics had come to an end before reaching the straight. (7/1)
**Great Tern** (8/1: 6/1-10/1)

## 655 PEVERIL INTERIORS (S) STKS (3-Y.O) (Class G)

9-00 (9-00) **1m 1f 79y (Fibresand)** £2,070.00 (£570.00: £270.00) Stalls: Low GOING: 0.01 sec per fur (STD)

| | | | | SP | RR | SF |
|---|---|---|---|---|---|---|
| 522[5] | **Sweet Amoret (50)** (PHowling) **3-8-6** FNorton(1) (b.off hind: mde all: drvn & edgd lft fnl f: comf) | — | **1** | 8/1 | 50+ | 16 |
| 484[6] | **Sheilas Dream** (RSimpson) **3-8-3**(3) SDrowne(4) (chsd wnr most of wy: kpt on u.p ins fnl f) | 2½ | **2** | 25/1 | 46 | 12 |
| 355[6] | **Loch Style (55)** (RHollinshead) **3-8-6**(5) FLynch(7) (hld up: hdwy over 4f out: chsd wnr 2f out tl wknd appr fnl f) | 3 | **3** | 9/2[3] | 46 | 12 |
| 467[6] | **Trianna** (LordHuntingdon) **3-8-6** DHarrison(8) (trckd ldrs: pushed along & outpcd over 2f out: n.d after) | 1¼ | **4** | 4/1[2] | 39 | 5 |
| | **Eurobox Boy (70)** (APJarvis) **3-8-11** JTate(10) (b.nr hind: bit bkwd: in tch: effrt & hrd drvn over 3f out: hung lft & nt qckn appr fnl f) | 2 | **5** | 5/4[1] | 40 | 6 |

| | | | | SP | RR | SF |
|---|---|---|---|---|---|---|
| 471$^{15}$ | **Forliando (45)** (MSSaunders) **3-8-11v$^{1}$** JFEgan(6) (bit bkwd: trckd ldrs: hrd drvn 4f out: sn btn) | 4 | **6** | 25/1 | 33 | — |
| | **Balmoral Princess** (JHPeacock) **3-8-6** CRutter(9) (bkwd: a in rr) | 7 | **7** | 25/1 | 16 | — |
| *529$^{7}$* | **Tallulah Belle (58)** (NPLittmoden) **3-8-6** TGMcLaughlin(2) (b: plld hrd: hld up: a in rr) | 1½ | **8** | 10/1 | 14 | — |
| 522$^{10}$ | **La Haye Sainte (52)** (DJSCosgrove) **3-8-6** JQuinn(3) (a bhd) | 3 | **9** | 16/1 | 9 | — |
| *428$^{8}$* | **Sweet Seranade (IRE)** (NPLittmoden) **3-8-6** MFenton(11) (prom: rdn 4f out: sn wknd) | 1 | **10** | 33/1 | 7 | — |
| *488$^{7}$* | **Burj (39)** (NAGraham) **3-8-11b** AMcGlone(5) (lw: trckd ldrs: drvn along 4f out: sn lost tch: t.o) | 9 | **11** | 10/1 | — | — |

(SP 132.3%) **11 Rn**

**2m 4.9** (8.90) CSF £168.11 TOTE £9.50: £1.60 £2.70 £2.00 (£156.00) Trio £45.50 OWNER Mr Robert Baker (NEWMARKET) BRED J. G. Charlton
No bid

**522 Sweet Amoret**, having her first run on this surface, decided on forceful tactics and they paid off a treat. She is just coming to herself and there could be more success to follow. (8/1)
**Sheilas Dream** was never too far away and stuck to her task inside the distance without threatening the winner. (25/1)
**Loch Style** looked to be going best when mounting a challenge soon after turning in but his stride shortened approaching the final furlong and lack of stamina could be a problem. (9/2: op 10/1)
**467 Trianna**, who is nothing to look at, showed up over this longer trip but she was only there on sufferance in the last quarter-mile and still looks to need time. (4/1: 3/1-9/2)
**Eurobox Boy** looked far from fully wound up for this seasonal debut and, off the bridle a long way out, was never going to trouble the principals. (5/4)
**Tallulah Belle** (10/1: 8/1-12/1)
**Burj** (10/1: 8/1-12/1)

## 656 BUSHBURY H'CAP (0-65) (4-Y.O+) (Class F)

9-30 (9-30) **2m 46y (Fibresand)** £2,070.00 (£570.00: £270.00) Stalls: High GOING: 0.01 sec per fur (STD)

| | | | | SP | RR | SF |
|---|---|---|---|---|---|---|
| *422$^{9}$* | **Iota (53)** (JLHarris) **7-9-7** SSanders(4) (dwlt: sn chsng ldrs: led on bit over 1f out: v.easily) | — | **1** | 8/1$^{3}$ | 65+ | 39 |
| *602$^{2}$* | **Swordking (IRE) (38)** (JLHarris) **7-8-6** JQuinn(9) (hld up: stdy hdwy to ld over 4f out: hdd over 1f out: one pce) | 7 | **2** | 9/4$^{1}$ | 43 | 17 |
| 573$^{7}$ | **Durham (49)** (RSimpson) **5-9-0v$^{(3)}$** SDrowne(7) (lw: a.p: led 5f out tl over 4f out: rdn & one pce fnl 2f) | 4 | **3** | 3/1$^{2}$ | 50 | 24 |
| *83$^{6}$* | **Flashman (38)** (BJLlewellyn) **6-8-6** TSprake(2) (bit bkwd: led 10f out to 5f out: sn pushed along & outpcd) | nk | **4** | 3/1$^{2}$ | 39 | 13 |
| | **Call My Guest (IRE) (60)** (REPeacock) **6-9-9$^{(5)}$** RHavlin(8) (chsd ldrs over 11f: sn lost tch: t.o) | 19 | **5** | 8/1$^{3}$ | 42 | 16 |
| *221$^{4}$* | **Nick the Biscuit (60)** (RTPhillips) **5-10-0b$^{1}$** AClark(3) (swtg: b: hld up in rr: effrt & rdn over 6f out: wknd 4f out: t.o) | 26 | **6** | 12/1 | 16 | — |
| | **Twice the Groom (IRE) (60)** (RLee) **6-9-11$^{(3)}$** OPears(1) (b: hld up: rdn & wknd 7f out: t.o) | 12 | **7** | 14/1 | 5 | — |
| *520$^{4}$* | **Just Lucky (IRE) (44)** (MrsPSly) **4-8-8** JTate(5) (led over 6f: wknd 5f out: t.o) | 4 | **8** | 25/1 | — | — |
| | **She Knew the Rules (IRE) (42)** (FJordan) **6-8-5$^{(5)}$** PPMurphy(6) (lw: sn wl bhd: a t.o) | 23 | **9** | 20/1 | — | — |

(SP 126.0%) **9 Rn**

**3m 40.9** (13.90) CSF £27.49 CT £64.79 TOTE £8.00: £1.80 £1.50 £1.90 (£7.80) Trio £28.60 OWNER Lavender Hill Leisure Ltd (MELTON MOWBRAY) BRED Sheikh Mohammed bin Rashid al Maktoum
WEIGHT FOR AGE 4yo-4lb

**Iota**, given a very competent ride on her favourite track, brushed aside her stable companion with the minimum of fuss below the distance and strode clear on the bridle for a runaway success. (8/1)
**602 Swordking (IRE)** did not see the trip out as well as the winner and he was left for dead approaching the final furlong. (9/4)
**485 Durham** remained in with a shout until finding the tempo too strong for him from the turn into the straight. (3/1)
**Flashman**, who had enjoyed a three month break, helped share the pacemaking and then stayed on again towards the finish but the leading pair had got away and there was only the minor prize at stake. (3/1)

T/Plpt: £111.90 (107.79 Tckts). T/Qdpt: £41.20 (10.48 Tckts). IM

# 0557-MUSSELBURGH (R-H) (Good, Good to firm patches)

## Monday April 15th

WEATHER: overcast WIND: almost nil

## 657 BELFRY MAIDEN AUCTION STKS (2-Y.O) (Class F)

2-00 (2-00) **5f** £2,528.90 (£710.40: £346.70) Stalls: High GOING minus 0.11 sec per fur (G)

| | | | | SP | RR | SF |
|---|---|---|---|---|---|---|
| 506$^{2}$ | **Full Traceability (IRE)** (JBerry) **2-8-0** NCarlisle(5) (mde all far side: kpt on wl) | — | **1** | 11/8$^{2}$ | 58 | 14 |
| | **Docklands Carriage (IRE)** (NTinkler) **2-8-7** RCochrane(4) (leggy: chsd wnr far side: kpt on fnl f: nrst fin) | 1¾ | **2** | 12/1 | 59 | 15 |
| 568$^{4}$ | **Absolutely Abstone** (PDEvans) **2-8-2$^{ow2}$** SSanders(1) (led stands' side: rdn 2f out: nt qckn) | 2½ | **3** | 13/2$^{3}$ | 46 | — |
| | **Neon Deion (IRE)** (SCWilliams) **2-8-7** KFallon(2) (chsd ldr stands' side: hrd drvn ½-wy: no imp) | 5 | **4** | 5/4$^{1}$ | 35 | — |

(SP 107.6%) **4 Rn**

**61.3 secs** (3.60) CSF £11.35 TOTE £1.70: (£4.00) OWNER Mr J. Clayton (COCKERHAM) BRED J. S. A. and Mrs Shorthouse and New England Stud

**506 Full Traceability (IRE)** has obviously learnt plenty from her first run and won this in determined style. (11/8)
**Docklands Carriage (IRE)** is nothing special to look at but seemed to run better than expected and was gradually pegging back the winner as the line approached. (12/1: op 6/1)
**568 Absolutely Abstone**, with the stalls on the far side, crossed over to the stands' rail, which is normally faster but it was a long way to come in such a small field and she was fighting a lost cause from two furlongs out. (13/2: 4/1-7/1)
**Neon Deion (IRE)**, the pick of the bunch, probably just needed it. Crossing over to the stands' side, he was never going the pace but will do better in due course. (5/4)

## 658 PINKIE PILLARS H'CAP (0-70) (3-Y.O) (Class E)

2-30 (2-30) **1m 3f 32y** £2,872.80 (£869.40: £424.20: £201.60) Stalls: High GOING minus 0.11 sec per fur (G)

| | | | | SP | RR | SF |
|---|---|---|---|---|---|---|
| *605** | **Hawksley Hill (IRE) (50)** (MrsJRRamsden) **3-9-2** $^{5x}$ KFallon(4) (lw: hld up: effrt appr st: hung rt 2f out: rdn to ld ins fnl f: r.o) | — | **1** | 5/4$^{1}$ | 57 | 23 |
| 477$^{7}$ | **Go-Go-Power-Ranger (55)** (BEllison) **3-9-7** NKennedy(5) (led: rdn over 2f out: hdd ins fnl f: kpt on) | 1¼ | **2** | 10/1 | 60 | 26 |

| | | | | SP | RR | SF |
|---|---|---|---|---|---|---|
| *$515^{*}$* | **Rajah (49)** (CWThornton) **3-9-1** DeanMcKeown(3) (cl up: chal over 2f out: sn hrd drvn & r.o one pce) | 1½ | **3** | $6/4^{2}$ | 52 | 18 |
| *$530^{6}$* | **Panama Jive (IRE) (52)** (MJohnston) **3-9-4** JWeaver(2) (chsd ldrs: rdn 4f out: outpcd fnl 3f) | 8 | **4** | $5/1^{3}$ | 44 | 10 |
| *$605^{6}$* | **The Fullbangladesh (52)** (JLEyre) **3-9-4** RLappin(1) (outpcd & lost tch ent st: n.d after) | 4 | **5** | 33/1 | 38 | 4 |
| | | | | (SP 113.1%) | | **5 Rn** |

**2m 29.3** (9.60) CSF £11.67 TOTE £2.10: £1.50 £3.00 (£10.20) OWNER Mr Hamish Alexander (THIRSK) BRED The Wickfield Stud Ltd

**605* Hawksley Hill (IRE),** not a good mover, needed all of this extra half-mile to gain the initiative and was continually hanging right. (5/4)

**Go-Go-Power-Ranger** ran quite well, attempting to make all, but did not have a change of gear when it mattered. (10/1)

**515* Rajah**, stepping up in trip, did have his chances but was well tapped for toe approaching the last furlong. (6/4)

**530 Panama Jive (IRE)**, who got a bit warm beforehand, failed to handle the home turn and had no chance thereafter. (5/1)

**The Fullbangladesh** lost it altogether on the sharp turn into the straight, and is basically not very good. (33/1)

## 659 TOLBOOTH LIMITED STKS (0-65) (3-Y.O+) (Class F)

3-00 (3-00) **5f** £2,552.70 (£717.20: £350.10) Stalls: High GOING minus 0.11 sec per fur (G)

| | | | | SP | RR | SF |
|---|---|---|---|---|---|---|
| $617^{3}$ | **Garnock Valley (63)** (JBerry) **6-9-4** RCochrane(7) (cl up: led ½-wy: r.o: comf) | — | **1** | $3/1^{1}$ | 68 | 51 |
| $559^{3}$ | **Tenor (56)** (DNicholls) **5-9-7** AlexGreaves(2) (swtchd rt after s: hdwy ½-wy: kpt on: nvr able to chal) | 2½ | **2** | $4/1^{3}$ | 63 | 46 |
| $601^{9}$ | **Just Bob (65)** (SEKettlewell) **7-9-1**(3) JStack(1) (in tch: hdwy ½-wy: nt qckn fnl f) | nk | **3** | $3/1^{1}$ | 59 | 42 |
| $587^{2}$ | **Plum First (62)** (LRLloyd-James) **6-8-11**(7) KimberleyHart(6) (b.hind: lw: in tch: effrt ½-wy: no imp) | ½ | **4** | $7/2^{2}$ | 57 | 40 |
| $559^{7}$ | **Six for Luck (54)** (DANolan) **4-9-1**(3) NVarley(4) (led to ½-wy: wknd over 1f out) | hd | **5** | 25/1 | 57 | 40 |
| *$516^{*}$* | **Call Me (65)** (CWThornton) **3-8-7** DeanMcKeown(8) (s.i.s: nvr nr to chal) | 1¼ | **6** | 8/1 | 53 | 25 |
| $617^{13}$ | **Leading Princess (IRE) (51)** (MissLAPerratt) **5-8-11b**(7) AngelaGallimore(3) (spd 2f: sn bhd) | 5 | **7** | 25/1 | 37 | 20 |
| $559^{15}$ | **Serious Hurry (52)** (RMMcKellar) **8-8-11b**(7) DMcGaffin(5) (spd to ½-wy: sn wknd) | 9 | **8** | 33/1 | 8 | — |
| | | | | (SP 114.0%) | | **8 Rn** |

**60.1 secs** (2.40) CSF £14.53 TOTE £3.40: £1.70 £1.40 £1.30 (£8.20) OWNER Mr Robert Aird (COCKERHAM) BRED Sunley Stud

WEIGHT FOR AGE 3yo-11lb

OFFICIAL EXPLANATION **Serious Hurry: finished in a distressed state.**

**617 Garnock Valley** made no mistakes this time and won a shade cosily. (3/1)

**559 Tenor**, switched right at the start when his best chance would have been to cross over to the stands' side, did then keep on well at the end, albeit in vain. (4/1)

**475 Just Bob** did not give too much ground away at the start for once, but his final dash was never forthcoming and he just held his own in the final furlong. (3/1)

**587 Plum First** was always finding this track too sharp for his liking but did stay on at the end. He looks particularly well just now. (7/2)

**Six for Luck** showed plenty of early speed and would seem to be improving. (25/1)

**516* Call Me** found this trip too sharp and, after missing the break, was certainly not overpunished. She is one to keep in mind for slightly longer distances. (8/1: op 5/1)

## 660 INVERESK RATING RELATED MAIDEN STKS (0-60) (3-Y.O) (Class F)

3-30 (3-30) **1m 16y** £2,576.50 (£724.00: £353.50) Stalls: High GOING minus 0.11 sec per fur (G)

| | | | | SP | RR | SF |
|---|---|---|---|---|---|---|
| | **Classic Defence (IRE) (60)** (JWHills) **3-8-9**(5) MHenry(2) (lw: mde most: shkn up over 2f out: r.o: eased towards fin) | — | **1** | $9/4^{1}$ | 68+ | 27 |
| $562^{5}$ | **Carmosa (USA) (57)** (DNicholls) **3-8-11** AlexGreaves(6) (cl up: effrt & ev ch 2f out: nt qckn fnl f) | 2½ | **2** | $3/1^{2}$ | 60 | 19 |
| | **Alpine Joker (60)** (MrsJRRamsden) **3-9-0** KFallon(5) (hdwy appr st: rdn 2f out: styd on: nvr able to chal) | 2½ | **3** | 8/1 | 58 | 17 |
| *$460^{6}$* | **Danico (60)** (SCWilliams) **3-9-0** JTate(4) (a.p: effrt 3f out: r.o one pce) | ½ | **4** | $11/2^{3}$ | 57 | 16 |
| *$530^{3}$* | **Yuppy Girl (IRE) (59)** (CaptJHWilson) **3-8-11** SDWilliams(8) (outpcd appr st: styd on fnl 2f: n.d) | 2½ | **5** | 13/2 | 49 | 8 |
| *$516^{2}$* | **Mels Baby (IRE) (55)** (JLEyre) **3-9-0v** RLappin(1) (led early: cl up tl wknd fnl 2f) | 1¼ | **6** | 12/1 | 50 | 9 |
| | **Shirley Sue (56)** (MJohnston) **3-8-11** JWeaver(7) (lost pl appr st: n.d after) | 4 | **7** | 9/1 | 39 | — |
| | **Turbo North (59)** (MDods) **3-9-0** NConnorton(3) (lost pl appr st: n.d after) | 10 | **8** | 25/1 | 22 | — |
| | | | | (SP 117.1%) | | **8 Rn** |

**1m 44.8** (6.20) CSF £9.35 TOTE £2.60: £1.00 £2.40 £4.30 (£4.80) OWNER Mr J. W. Robb (LAMBOURN) BRED James Hennessy

**Classic Defence (IRE)** stood out in the paddock and left nothing to chance. The further they went, the better he got. (9/4)

**562 Carmosa (USA)** ran a fine race only to find the winner far too good. She will not always come across such a useful opponent. (3/1)

**Alpine Joker** enjoyed this step up in distance and, judging by the way he finished, will need further yet. (8/1: op 3/1)

**Danico** looked very fit and had his chances, but was well short of speed in the final quarter-mile. (11/2)

**530 Yuppy Girl (IRE)** took time to get going and, by the time she did, the race was over. A more galloping track should help. (13/2: 9/2-7/1)

**516 Mels Baby (IRE)** (12/1: tchd 20/1)

## 661 ESKMILL (S) H'CAP (0-60) (3-Y.O+) (Class G)

4-00 (4-00) **7f 15y** £2,263.50 (£636.00: £310.50) Stalls: High GOING minus 0.11 sec per fur (G)

| | | | | SP | RR | SF |
|---|---|---|---|---|---|---|
| $617^{7}$ | **Diet (51)** (MissLAPerratt) **10-9-6v** NConnorton(9) (chsd ldrs: led wl over 1f out: r.o) | — | **1** | 8/1 | 63 | 22 |
| $645^{6}$ | **Everset (FR) (59)** (ABailey) **8-9-11b**(3) DWright(5) (a.p: hdwy u.p 2f out: nt qckn ins fnl f) | 3½ | **2** | $7/2^{1}$ | 63 | 22 |
| *$531^{4}$* | **Miss Offset (48)** (MJohnston) **3-8-0b**(3) JStack(3) (sn led: hdd wl over 1f out: no ex) | 1 | **3** | $5/1^{3}$ | 50 | — |
| $545^{8}$ | **La Dama (USA) (38)** (ABMulholland) **4-8-7** MMcAndrew(10) (in tch: n.m.r over 1f out: swtchd & styd on wl) | s.h | **4** | 33/1 | 40 | — |
| *$389^{3}$* | **Best Kept Secret (54)** (PDEvans) **5-9-9** SSanders(14) (hdwy u.p 2f out: nvr able to chal) | 1¾ | **5** | 12/1 | 52 | 11 |
| $537^{6}$ | **Funny Rose (32)** (PMonteith) **6-8-1** LCharnock(1) (hdwy on ins 2f out: nvr rchd ldrs) | s.h | **6** | 14/1 | 30 | — |
| *$342^{5}$* | **Flamboro (50)** (JDBethell) **4-9-5** JWeaver(6) (lw: led early: chsd ldrs: effrt & ev ch 2f out: sn btn) | hd | **7** | 10/1 | 47 | 6 |
| $561^{3}$ | **Northern Spark (48)** (MissLAPerratt) **8-9-3** JFanning(13) (chsd ldrs tl hmpd & lost pl appr st: no imp after) | s.h | **8** | $4/1^{2}$ | 45 | 4 |
| *$140^{13}$* | **Good so Fa (IRE) (35)** (CNAllen) **4-8-4h** CHodgson(8) (s.i.s: drvn along & bhd tl sme late hdwy) | nk | **9** | 16/1 | 32 | — |
| | **Care And Comfort (57)** (NTinkler) **4-9-12** RCochrane(2) (s.i.s: sme hdwy 2f out: nvr rchd ldrs) | nk | **10** | 20/1 | 53 | 12 |
| *$426^{9}$* | **Komlucky (42)** (ABMulholland) **4-8-6b**(5) FLynch(11) (outpcd & bhd ½-wy: n.d) | ¾ | **11** | 20/1 | 36 | — |
| $539^{10}$ | **Larrylukeathugh (51)** (JJO'Neill) **3-8-6** SDWilliams(12) (nvr wnt pce) | 1¾ | **12** | 12/1 | 41 | — |
| *$607^{8}$* | **Strathtore Dream (IRE) (32)** (MissLAPerratt) **5-8-1** NCarlisle(4) (effrt appr st: sn wknd) | 2½ | **13** | 16/1 | 17 | — |
| | **Cacharro (54)** (MissZAGreen) **5-9-6**(3) DarrenMoffatt(7) (prom to st: wknd qckly) | 20 | **14** | 33/1 | — | — |
| | | | | (SP 128.3%) | | **14 Rn** |

**1m 31.8** (6.30) CSF £36.19 CT £151.18 TOTE £9.70: £3.30 £2.80 £2.20 (£22.40) Trio £98.90 OWNER Miss L. A. Perratt (AYR) BRED Rowcliffe Stud

WEIGHT FOR AGE 3yo-14lb

No bid

**561 Diet** appreciates further as he loses his pace, and he got this really well. (8/1)
**645 Everset (FR)** rarely wins on turf but did put up a decent performance, only to find the winner too strong in the closing stages. (7/2)
**531 Miss Offset** was soon out in front where she likes to be but, once collared in the straight, her one pace was never good enough. (5/1)
**La Dama (USA)** gave problems and was again taken to post early. Then she ran quite well, staying on after not having a deal of room. She ought to stay further. (33/1)
**Best Kept Secret**, who failed to win last season, had to really struggle to improve here and was never any nearer at the finish. (12/1)
**537 Funny Rose** needs further than this and did well to finish so close. (14/1: 10/1-16/1)
**Flamboro** found the struggle too much in the last couple of furlongs. (10/1)
**561 Northern Spark** got messed about on the home turn and this run is best forgotten. (4/1)
**479 Larrylukeathugh** (12/1: op 8/1)

## 662 MUSSELBURGH SPRING H'CAP (0-70) (3-Y.O+) (Class E)

4-30 (4-30) **7f 15y** £2,995.65 (£907.20: £443.10: £211.05) Stalls: High GOING minus 0.11 sec per fur (G)

| | | | | SP | RR | SF |
|---|---|---|---|---|---|---|
| $615^{4}$ | **Tinklers Folly (46)** (DenysSmith) **4-8-6** LCharnock(7) (cl up: led wl over 2f out: r.o) | — | **1** | 9/1 | 58 | 25 |
| *$521^{4}$* | **Pc's Cruiser (IRE) (46)** (JLEyre) **4-8-6b** RLappin(12) (a chsng ldrs: kpt on u.p fnl f) | 2½ | **2** | 12/1 | 52 | 19 |
| 617* | **My Gallery (IRE) (54)** (ABailey) **5-8-7**(7) 6x AngelaGallimore(11) (a.p: hdwy over 1f out: nt qckn ins fnl f) | nk | **3** | 3/1 [2] | 60 | 27 |
| $561^{2}$ | **Spirito Libro (USA) (59)** (CNAllen) **3-8-5** CHodgson(3) (lw: a.p: effrt 3f out: one pce appr fnl f) | 1½ | **4** | 14/1 | 61 | 14 |
| *$357^{9}$* | **Dancing Sioux (68)** (RGuest) **4-9-9**(5) FLynch(8) (chsd ldrs: one pce fnl 2f) | ¾ | **5** | 7/1 | 69 | 36 |
| 561* | **Bedazzle (40)** (MBrittain) **5-7-9**(5) MHenry(5) (hdwy 3f out: styd on: no imp) | ½ | **6** | 14/1 | 39 | 6 |
| $592^{3}$ | **Bargash (66)** (PDEvans) **4-9-12** SSanders(6) (nvr bttr than mid div) | 1½ | **7** | 13/2 [3] | 62 | 29 |
| | **Blue Grit (51)** (MDods) **10-8-11** DeanMcKeown(4) (in tch: outpcd over 2f out: sn btn) | ½ | **8** | 40/1 | 46 | 13 |
| $480^{13}$ | **Commander Glen (IRE) (55)** (MrsJRRamsden) **4-9-1v[1]** KFallon(10) (hld up & bhd: shkn up over 2f out: n.d) | 4 | **9** | 20/1 | 41 | 8 |
| *$529^{4}$* | **Arabian Heights (52)** (MrsJRRamsden) **3-7-12** NKennedy(2) (hld up & bhd: shkn up 3f out: nvr nr to chal) | ¾ | **10** | 20/1 | 36 | — |
| *$518^{4}$* | **Desert Lore (60)** (DANolan) **5-9-6** AlexGreaves(1) (hld up & bhd: effrt 3f out: n.d) | s.h | **11** | 66/1 | 44 | 11 |
| | **Don Pepe (65)** (RBoss) **5-9-11** RCochrane(9) (lw: led tl hdd wl over 2f out: sn wknd) | 2 | **12** | 2/1 [1] | 45 | 12 |
| | | | | (SP 128.6%) | | **12 Rn** |

**1m 30.4** (4.90) CSF £107.81 CT £380.58 TOTE £11.30: £2.60 £2.40 £2.80 (£64.10) Trio £95.70 OWNER Mr R. O. Manners (BISHOP AUCKLAND) BRED Qualitair Stud Ltd
WEIGHT FOR AGE 3yo-14lb
**615 Tinklers Folly** likes this track and has won over further. Once in front early in the straight, he was not going to stop. (9/1)
**521 Pc's Cruiser (IRE)**, always in the firing-line, just lacked a turn of foot to do anything serious about it, but was certainly not stopping. (12/1)
**617* My Gallery (IRE)** would have preferred a bit more give in the ground and could never quicken enough at the business end of the race. (3/1: op 2/1)
**561 Spirito Libro (USA)** had her chances, but lacked a turn of foot. (14/1)
**Dancing Sioux** has been in good form on the All-Weather, but found this a different game, and was short of speed in the straight. (7/1)
**561* Bedazzle**, upped 6lb for his win last week and over a shorter distance, was never able to get going until too late. (14/1)
**592 Bargash** (13/2: 10/1-6/1)
**529 Arabian Heights**, dropped out early on, never got into it, but does take the eye in the paddock, and will do a deal better in time. (20/1)

T/Plpt: £61.30 (165.38 Tckts). T/Qdpt: £16.30 (64.17 Tckts). AA

# 0465-FOLKESTONE (R-H) (Good to firm, Firm patches)

## Tuesday April 16th

WEATHER: fine WIND: almost nil

## 663 'PRIVY COUNCILLOR' MAIDEN STKS (I) (3-Y.O) (Class D)

1-20 (1-20) **6f 189y** £3,372.55 (£1,002.40: £475.70: £212.35) Stalls: High GOING minus 0.16 sec per fur (GF)

| | | | | SP | RR | SF |
|---|---|---|---|---|---|---|
| $445^{5}$ | **Aerleon Jane** (JHMGosden) **3-8-9** AMcGlone(4) (lw: a.p: rdn 3f out: led 1f out: r.o wl) | — | **1** | 7/4 [1] | 74 | 42 |
| $560^{4}$ | **Poetry (IRE)** (MHTompkins) **3-8-9** NDay(12) (led to 1f out: r.o) | nk | **2** | 10/1 [3] | 73 | 41 |
| $458^{2}$ | **Proud Look** (BWHills) **3-9-0** RCochrane(8) (chsd ldr over 5f: unable qckn) | 4 | **3** | 9/4 [2] | 69 | 37 |
| | **Dubai College (IRE)** (CEBrittain) **3-9-0** GDuffield(11) (bit bkwd: a.p: rdn over 2f out: r.o one pce fnl f) | nk | **4** | 16/1 | 68 | 36 |
| | **Bold Patriot (IRE)** (JWHills) **3-8-9**(5) MHenry(3) (lw: no hdwy fnl 3f) | 3 | **5** | 25/1 | 61 | 29 |
| | **Mawingo (IRE)** (GWragg) **3-8-7**(7) GMilligan(1) (nvr nr to chal) | 1½ | **6** | 14/1 | 58 | 26 |
| $528^{6}$ | **Sharp Command** (RWArmstrong) **3-9-0** RPrice(9) (lw: nvr nrr) | 4 | **7** | 14/1 | 48 | 16 |
| | **Rossel (USA)** (MRStoute) **3-9-0** KBradshaw(5) (s.s: a bhd) | nk | **8** | 11/1 | 48 | 16 |
| $550^{13}$ | **Enchanted Guest (IRE)** (PWHarris) **3-8-9** GHind(2) (lw: hld up: rdn over 3f out: eased whn btn over 1f out) | 1½ | **9** | 20/1 | 39 | 7 |
| | **Ood Dancer (USA)** (LMCumani) **3-9-0** OUrbina(10) (str: scope: bkwd: s.s: a bhd) | ½ | **10** | 14/1 | 43 | 11 |
| *$460^{5}$* | **Be Satisfied (55)** (AMoore) **3-8-11**(3) AWhelan(13) (hld up: rdn over 2f out: sn wknd) | 4 | **11** | 50/1 | 34 | 2 |
| | **Cane Them** (TJNaughton) **3-8-7**(7) TAshley(7) (w'like: bit bkwd: a bhd) | 2½ | **12** | 50/1 | 28 | — |
| | | | | (SP 123.0%) | | **12 Rn** |

**1m 24.7** (3.10) CSF £19.68 TOTE £2.30: £1.10 £2.50 £1.30 (£18.30) Trio £6.40 OWNER Mr Paul Locke (NEWMARKET) BRED P. Locke
OFFICIAL EXPLANATION **Enchanted Guest (IRE): the jockey reported that the filly, when asked to quicken turning for home, made a respiratory noise and lost her action on the ground. He felt it prudent to hold the filly together in the final stages.**
**445 Aerleon Jane** looked in good shape in the paddock. Always close up, she was being bustled along running down the hill, but eventually managed to poke a nostril in front a furlong out. Her jockey continued to beaver away on her and she just managed to hold the persistent runner-up. (7/4)
**560 Poetry (IRE)**, taking a drop in distance, attempted to make all the running. Collared a furlong out, she refused to give way and kept on well to the line. She should find a race soon. (10/1)
**458 Proud Look**, in second place until below the distance, could then only keep on in his own time. (9/4)
**Dubai College (IRE)**, looking as though the run would do him good, was never far away but was being bustled along turning for home. He did stay on in the final furlong and only just failed to take third prize. (16/1)
**Bold Patriot (IRE)** chased the leaders, but was making little impression in the second half of the race. (25/1)
**Mawingo (IRE)** (14/1: 10/1-20/1)
**528 Sharp Command** (14/1: op 8/1)
**Rossel (USA)** (11/1: 8/1-12/1)
**Ood Dancer (USA)** (14/1: op 8/1)

## 664 LEVY BOARD APPRENTICE H'CAP (0-60) (3-Y.O+) (Class G)

1-50 (1-53) **6f** £2,189.50 (£622.00: £308.50) Stalls: Low GOING minus 0.16 sec per fur (GF)

| | Horse | Dist | Pos | SP | RR | SF |
|---|---|---|---|---|---|---|
| 549[W] | **Deeply Vale (IRE) (60)** (GLMoore) **5-9-11**(3) ALakeman(5) (a.p: led 2f out: r.o wl) | — | 1 | 11/2[2] | 71 | 48 |
| *556[5]* | **Scissor Ridge (45)** (JJBridger) **4-8-13** TField(7) (hld up: rdn over 2f out: unable qckn) | 2½ | 2 | 15/2[3] | 49 | 26 |
| 601[20] | **Mazzarello (IRE) (41)** (RCurtis) **6-8-9v** JBramhill(4) (led 4f: one pce) | s.h | 3 | 14/1 | 45 | 22 |
| 508[15] | **Pointer (39)** (MrsPNDutfield) **4-8-7** JFowle(8) (hdwy over 1f out: r.o) | ½ | 4 | 33/1 | 42 | 19 |
| 592[6] | **Giggleswick Girl (59)** (MRChannon) **5-9-10**(3) DSweeney(13) (a.p: rdn over 2f out: one pce) | nk | 5 | 5/1[1] | 61 | 38 |
| 496[8] | **Great Hall (53)** (PDCundell) **7-8-13**(8) NLovelock(1) (hdwy over 1f out: r.o) | 1¼ | 6 | 8/1 | 52 | 29 |
| | **Waders Dream (IRE) (43)** (PatMitchell) **7-8-11v** VictoriaAppleby(11) (bit bkwd: swtchd lft over 3f out: hdwy over 1f out: nvr nrr) | nk | 7 | 12/1 | 41 | 18 |
| *178[7]* | **Shaynes Domain (42)** (RMFlower) **5-8-10b** CScudder(6) (nvr nr to chal) | hd | 8 | 14/1 | 40 | 17 |
| | **Barranak (IRE) (60)** (GMMcCourt) **4-10-0** RSmith(14) (bit bkwd: prom over 4f) | 2 | 9 | 10/1 | 52 | 29 |
| | **Forgotten Dancer (IRE) (50)** (RIngram) **5-9-4** RFfrench(3) (prom 3f) | nk | 10 | 16/1 | 42 | 19 |
| *464[5]* | **Barbason (56)** (AMoore) **4-9-10** PDoe(10) (outpcd) | hd | 11 | 14/1 | 47 | 24 |
| | **Velvet Jones (55)** (GFHCharles-Jones) **3-8-12** JEdmunds(16) (bit bkwd: prom over 3f) | 3 | 12 | 12/1 | 38 | 4 |
| *514[8]* | **Superlao (BEL) (41)** (JJBridger) **4-8-4**(5) RBrisland(12) (prom over 4f) | ¾ | 13 | 33/1 | 22 | — |
| *521[13]* | **Most Welcome News (42)** (JRJenkins) **4-8-2b**(8)ow5 SallyWall(15) (hld up: rdn over 2f out: sn wknd) | 1½ | 14 | 33/1 | 19 | — |
| *464[8]* | **Distant Dynasty (40)** (BAPearce) **6-8-8** PClarke(2) (bhd fnl 3f) | 1¼ | 15 | 25/1 | 14 | — |
| 525[16] | **Veesey (55)** (JohnBerry) **3-8-4**(8) AmyQuirk(9) (a bhd) | 1¾ | 16 | 10/1 | 24 | — |
| | | | | (SP 127.0%) | **16 Rn** | |

**1m 13.7** (3.50) CSF £44.96 CT £509.62 TOTE £7.40: £1.70 £1.70 £3.30 £10.30 (£15.70) Trio £262.90 OWNER Mr K. Higson (EPSOM)
WEIGHT FOR AGE 3yo-11lb

**Deeply Vale (IRE)**, never far away, gained control a quarter of a mile from home and kept on too well for his rivals. (11/2)
**Scissor Ridge** chased the leaders but, despite staying on for second place, failed to find the necessary turn of foot. (15/2: 9/2-8/1)
**Mazzarello (IRE)** attempted to make all the running towards the stands' side. Collared a quarter of a mile out, he failed to find another turn of foot. Both his wins have come over five furlongs. (14/1)
**Pointer** was doing all his best work in the final furlong and a half but was not going to get there in time. (33/1)
**592 Giggleswick Girl** was always close up but could only keep on in her own time in the last two furlongs. (5/1)
**Great Hall** had his ideal requirements here, six furlongs on a sound surface, and was doing all his best work in the last furlong and a half. (8/1)
**Velvet Jones** (12/1: 8/1-14/1)

## 665 CHATHAM CLAIMING STKS (3-Y.O) (Class F)

2-20 (2-20) **5f** £2,381.00 (£656.00: £311.00) Stalls: Low GOING minus 0.16 sec per fur (GF)

| | Horse | Dist | Pos | SP | RR | SF |
|---|---|---|---|---|---|---|
| 644[3] | **Lady Caroline Lamb (IRE) (62)** (MRChannon) **3-8-10** TQuinn(4) (mde all: qcknd over 1f out: eased ins fnl f) | — | 1 | 8/13[1] | 72+ | 30 |
| | **Primo Lad** (WGMTurner) **3-8-11** AClark(1) (hld up: rdn over 2f out: unable qckn) | 2½ | 2 | 6/1[3] | 65 | 23 |
| *335[5]* | **Last But Not Least (56)** (RFJohnsonHoughton) **3-8-4** KDarley(5) (b.off fore: w wnr over 3f: one pce) | s.h | 3 | 11/4[2] | 58 | 16 |
| *292[9]* | **Lincon Twenty One** (MJHaynes) **3-7-11**(5) MBaird(3) (hld up: rdn over 2f out: sn wknd) | 3 | 4 | 33/1 | 46 | 4 |
| 591[7] | **Bag And A Bit** (BJMeehan) **3-8-8** MTebbutt(2) (hld up: rdn over 2f out: sn wknd) | ½ | 5 | 20/1 | 51 | 9 |
| | | | | (SP 110.6%) | **5 Rn** | |

**60.5 secs** (2.90) CSF £4.60 TOTE £1.30: £1.10 £1.80 (£3.00) OWNER Mr W. H. Ponsonby (UPPER LAMBOURN) BRED Tally-Ho Stud
Lady Caroline Lamb (IRE) clmd TSmith £9,000

**644 Lady Caroline Lamb (IRE)**, making a quick reappearance, had a nice little spin round in this bad race. Making all the running, she quickened away from below the distance to win with a ton in hand. (8/13)
**Primo Lad**, off the track for almost a year, chased the leaders but, although struggling into second place, had no hope with the winner. (6/1)
**Last But Not Least** raced with the winner until left for dead by that rival from below the distance. (11/4)

## 666 GRAVESEND H'CAP (0-70) (4-Y.O+) (Class E)

2-55 (2-55) **1m 7f 92y** £3,370.50 (£1,008.00: £483.00: £220.50) Stalls: Low GOING minus 0.16 sec per fur (GF)

| | Horse | Dist | Pos | SP | RR | SF |
|---|---|---|---|---|---|---|
| *422[6]* | **Toy Princess (USA) (69)** (CEBrittain) **4-10-0** KDarley(16) (lw: chsd ldr: led over 2f out: r.o wl) | — | 1 | 16/1 | 81 | 59 |
| | **Hattaafeh (IRE) (52)** (MissBSanders) **5-9-0** GHind(15) (lw: hld up: chsd wnr over 1f out: r.o) | ¾ | 2 | 20/1 | 63 | 44 |
| 573[5] | **Stalled (IRE) (54)** (PTWalwyn) **6-9-2** RCochrane(11) (lw: hld up: rdn over 2f out: unable qckn) | 5 | 3 | 4/1[1] | 60 | 41 |
| *485[3]* | **Juliasdarkinvader (42)** (AMoore) **6-8-4**ow2 AClark(14) (b: led 13f: wknd over 1f out) | 2½ | 4 | 20/1 | 45 | 24 |
| 635* | **Uncharted Waters (49)** (CACyzer) **5-8-11** 4x GDuffield(8) (hdwy on ins 2f out: one pce) | 1 | 5 | 8/1 | 51 | 32 |
| 546[3] | **Rock Group (55)** (JPearce) **4-9-0** GBardwell(7) (a.p: rdn over 5f out: wknd over 2f out) | nk | 6 | 6/1[3] | 57 | 35 |
| | **Chakalak (46)** (SDow) **8-8-8** TQuinn(9) (nvr nrr) | 2½ | 7 | 14/1 | 46 | 27 |
| *365[2]* | **Sir Thomas Beecham (57)** (SDow) **6-9-0**(5) ADaly(5) (hld up: rdn over 5f out: wknd 4f out) | hd | 8 | 14/1 | 56 | 37 |
| | **Soojama (IRE) (44)** (RMFlower) **6-8-6** WWoods(12) (nvr nrr) | s.h | 9 | 11/2[2] | 43 | 24 |
| *489[2]* | **Ready to Draw (IRE) (35)** (RJO'Sullivan) **7-7-11** NCarlisle(1) (b: lw: nvr nrr) | 3 | 10 | 8/1 | 31 | 12 |
| 573[11] | **Aude la Belle (FR) (57)** (SGKnight) **8-9-5** AMcGlone(4) (hdwy over 7f out: wknd 5f out) | 6 | 11 | 33/1 | 47 | 28 |
| *485** | **Captain Marmalade (42)** (DTThom) **7-8-4v** JTate(13) (b: a bhd: lame) | 16 | 12 | 14/1 | 15 | — |
| 505[15] | **Desert Calm (IRE) (59)** (MrsPNDutfield) **7-9-4**(3) SDrowne(6) (a bhd) | 5 | 13 | 33/1 | 27 | 8 |
| | **Kayartis (43)** (CADwyer) **7-8-2**(3) JStack(2) (hdwy over 9f out: wknd 3f out) | 1¾ | 14 | 11/1 | 9 | — |
| *54[11]* | **Maronetta (39)** (MJRyan) **4-7-7**(5) MBaird(3) (prom 11f) | 1¼ | 15 | 33/1 | 4 | — |
| *222[7]* | **Analogue (IRE) (60)** (PhilipMitchell) **4-8-12b**(7) IonaWands(10) (lw: a bhd) | ¾ | 16 | 33/1 | 24 | 2 |
| | | | | (SP 127.4%) | **16 Rn** | |

**3m 25.8** (7.80) CSF £268.95 CT £1395.71 TOTE £21.30: £4.70 £6.90 £1.40 £5.10 (£99.50) Trio £319.50 OWNER Mr C. E. Brittain (NEWMARKET) BRED Northmore Stud
WEIGHT FOR AGE 4yo-3lb

**Toy Princess (USA)** raced in second place. Gaining control over a quarter of a mile from home, she kept up the gallop in good style. (16/1)
**Hattaafeh (IRE)**, who has changed stables since last season, chased the leaders. Moving into second place below the distance, she ran on but was unable to overhaul the winner in time. (20/1)
**573 Stalled (IRE)**, held up off the pace, was asked for his effort over a quarter of a mile from home but never looked like picking up sufficiently. He is costing punters dear at present. (4/1: 3/1-9/2)

**485 Juliasdarkinvader** attempted to make all the running. Collared over a quarter of a mile from home, he had run out of gas early in the straight. (20/1)
**635* Uncharted Waters**, making a quick reappearance, moved up along the inside rail turning into the straight, but failed to find much more as the step up in distance took its toll. (8/1)
**546 Rock Group** found this longer trip beyond him. Always close up, he had run out of steam turning into the straight. (6/1)
**Sir Thomas Beecham** (14/1: op 8/1)

## 667 GILLINGHAM LIMITED STKS (0-65) (4-Y.O+) (Class F)

3-25 (3-25) **5f** £2,381.00 (£656.00: £311.00) Stalls: Low GOING minus 0.16 sec per fur (GF)

| | Horse | Dist | Pos | SP | RR | SF |
|---|---|---|---|---|---|---|
| $601^{7}$ | **Friendly Brave (USA) (62)** (MissGayKelleway) **6-9-0**(3) AWhelan(8) (b: lw: a.p: led wl over 1f out: edgd lft: r.o) | — | **1** | $11/4^{2}$ | 72 | 40 |
| | **Moujeeb (USA) (62)** (PatMitchell) **6-8-11v** JQuinn(3) (lw: nt clr run over 2f out: hdwy & nt clr run over 1f out: r.o wl ins fnl f) | ¾ | **2** | $5/1^{3}$ | 64 | 32 |
| $601^{3}$ | **Petraco (IRE) (63)** (NASmith) **8-8-4**(7) IonaWands(7) (a.p: ev ch wl over 1f out: bmpd: unable qckn) | nk | **3** | $2/1^{1}$ | 63 | 31 |
| $632^{8}$ | **La Belle Dominique (55)** (SGKnight) **4-8-8** VSlattery(6) (a.p: ev ch ins fnl f: one pce) | ¾ | **4** | 12/1 | 57 | 25 |
| $601^{4}$ | **Secret Miss (53)** (APJones) **4-8-3**(5) CAdamson(5) (lw: nt clr run over 2f out: swtchd rt & hdwy over 1f out: one pce) | hd | **5** | 10/1 | 57 | 25 |
| *$407^{6}$* | **Lift Boy (USA) (45)** (AMoore) **7-9-6** CandyMorris(4) (a.p: ev ch wl over 1f out: wknd fnl f) | 1½ | **6** | 14/1 | 64 | 32 |
| $601^{16}$ | **Domicksky (53)** (MRChannon) **8-8-11** KDarley(1) (led over 3f) | 3 | **7** | 13/2 | 46 | 14 |

(SP 113.4%) **7 Rn**

**60.3 secs** (2.70) CSF £15.68 TOTE £4.10: £1.90 £2.70 (£10.30) OWNER Grid Thoroughbred Racing Partnership (WHITCOMBE) BRED Foxfield
STEWARDS' ENQUIRY Whelan susp. 25-27/4/96 (careless riding).
**Friendly Brave (USA)**, in the firing-line throughout, gained control early in the final quarter mile but, with his jockey having his whip in the wrong hand, the gelding drifted left and bumped Petraco. Nevertheless, he was the best horse on the day and quite rightly was allowed to keep the race. (11/4)
**Moujeeb (USA)**, who failed to get a clear run at the back of the field at halfway, was beginning to pick up ground when again finding his passage blocked below the distance. Despite this, he ran on strongly in the closing stages for second prize, but found the line always coming too soon. (5/1)
**601 Petraco (IRE)** certainly met with interference and was the meat in the sandwich below the distance. He failed to find another gear from that point and just lost out in the battle for second prize. (2/1)
**La Belle Dominique** was always close up. Still in with every chance early inside the final furlong, she was then tapped for toe. (12/1)
**601 Secret Miss**, switched to the outside below the distance, picked up ground but was making no further impression in the final furlong. (10/1: op 6/1)
**Lift Boy (USA)** (14/1: op 8/1)
**559 Domicksky** (13/2: 5/1-15/2)

## 668 DARTFORD MAIDEN STKS (3-Y.O+) (Class D)

4-00 (4-01) **1m 4f** £4,026.45 (£1,203.60: £576.30: £262.65) Stalls: High GOING minus 0.16 sec per fur (GF)

| | Horse | Dist | Pos | SP | RR | SF |
|---|---|---|---|---|---|---|
| $494^{2}$ | **Sharaf (IRE) (80)** (JLDunlop) **3-8-7** KDarley(13) (mde virtually all: clr over 1f out: comf) | — | **1** | $15/8^{1}$ | 86+ | 30 |
| | **Northern Fleet** (GHarwood) **3-8-7** AClark(8) (a.p: ev ch over 2f out: unable qckn) | 6 | **2** | $5/2^{2}$ | 78 | 22 |
| | **Horesti** (CEBrittain) **4-9-12** GDuffield(10) (a.p: rdn over 3f out: one pce) | 1¼ | **3** | $11/2^{3}$ | 76 | 39 |
| $495^{3}$ | **Hanbitooh (USA)** (EALDunlop) **3-8-7** RCochrane(9) (lw: a.p: rdn over 3f out: one pce) | 1½ | **4** | 10/1 | 74 | 18 |
| $578^{11}$ | **Macmorris (USA)** (PFICole) **3-8-7** TQuinn(2) (a.p: rn v.wd bnd over 9f out: rdn over 3f out: one pce) | nk | **5** | 20/1 | 74 | 18 |
| $526^{11}$ | **Alwarqa** (RWArmstrong) **3-8-2** RPrice(4) (nvr plcd to chal) | 1½ | **6** | 14/1 | 67 | 11 |
| | **Opaque** (LMCumani) **4-9-12** OUrbina(7) (bit bkwd: nvr plcd to chal) | 1¾ | **7** | 14/1 | 70 | 33 |
| | **Candle Smoke (USA)** (GHarwood) **3-8-0**(7) GayeHarwood(15) (nvr nrr) | ½ | **8** | 20/1 | 69 | 13 |
| | **Krasnik (IRE)** (MrsDHaine) **3-8-7** GHind(11) (w'like: hdwy 9f out: wknd 5f out) | 8 | **9** | 33/1 | 58 | 2 |
| | **Topanga** (JABennett) **4-9-12** AMcGlone(3) (bhd fnl 4f) | 15 | **10** | 20/1 | 38 | 1 |
| | **Le Teteu (FR)** (BobJones) **3-8-7** NDay(6) (bit bkwd: a bhd) | nk | **11** | 25/1 | 38 | — |
| *$364^{6}$* | **Esta Maria (IRE)** (PaulSmith) **3-8-2** JQuinn(5) (a bhd) | 13 | **12** | 50/1 | 16 | — |
| | **Golden Filigree** (DTThom) **4-9-7** JTate(12) (a bhd) | ¾ | **13** | 66/1 | 15 | — |
| *$485^{P}$* | **Sussex Gorse** (BAPearce) **5-9-13** SWhitworth(1) (lw: s.s: a bhd) | 2½ | **14** | 100/1 | 16 | — |

(SP 126.7%) **14 Rn**

**2m 38.6** (7.40) CSF £7.15 TOTE £2.60: £1.40 £1.70 £1.80 (£2.90) Trio £4.90 OWNER Mr Hamdan Al Maktoum (ARUNDEL) BRED London Thoroughbred Services Ltd and Roncon Ltd
WEIGHT FOR AGE 3yo-20lb, 4yo-1lb
OFFICIAL EXPLANATION **Alwarqa: the jockey reported that the filly had been difficult at home and his instructions were not to be too hard on her during the race. He added that she ran in snatches then ran on up the straight before starting to hang to the left.**
**494 Sharaf (IRE)** had no problems here. Making virtually all the running, he forged clear in the straight to win with plenty in hand. Having said that, he did look uncomfortable on this fast ground and a few drops of rain are sure to be in his favour. (15/8: 5/4-9/4)
**Northern Fleet**, always close up, had every chance entering the home straight before tapped for toe. He should soon go one better. (5/2)
**Horesti**, always close up, failed to find the necessary turn of foot in the straight. (11/2: op 10/1)
**495 Hanbitooh (USA)** was always close up but failed to increase his work-rate in the last three furlongs. (10/1: 7/1-11/1)
**Macmorris (USA)** was a leading light from the off but failed to quicken in the last three furlongs. (20/1)
**Alwarqa** was given a very tender ride which did not go unnoticed by the Stewards, as she crept closer in the straight to finish sixth. She looks one to keep an eye on. (14/1: 10/1-16/1)
**Opaque** did not look straight for this reappearance and was given a considerate ride to finish seventh. He is sure to come on for this and should be suited by further. (14/1)

## 669 'PRIVY COUNCILLOR' MAIDEN STKS (II) (3-Y.O) (Class D)

4-35 (4-36) **6f 189y** £3,339.40 (£992.20: £470.60: £209.80) Stalls: High GOING minus 0.16 sec per fur (GF)

| | Horse | Dist | Pos | SP | RR | SF |
|---|---|---|---|---|---|---|
| | **Sandabar** (MRStoute) **3-9-0** KBradshaw(10) (hdwy over 1f out: str run fnl f: led nr fin) | — | **1** | $5/1^{3}$ | 81 | 50 |
| | **Consort** (GHarwood) **3-9-0** AClark(8) (w'like: a.p: led over 2f out: rdn over 1f out: hdd nr fin) | ¾ | **2** | $5/2^{2}$ | 79 | 48 |
| $577^{5}$ | **Crazy Chief (88)** (PFICole) **3-9-0** TQuinn(6) (a.p: rdn over 2f out: r.o ins fnl f) | nk | **3** | $2/1^{1}$ | 79 | 48 |
| *$488^{4}$* | **Young Mazaad (IRE) (68)** (DCO'Brien) **3-9-0** RCochrane(1) (a.p: ev ch over 1f out: wknd fnl f) | 2½ | **4** | 33/1 | 73 | 42 |
| | **Diminutive (USA) (88)** (JWHills) **3-8-9**(5) MHenry(9) (a.p: ev ch over 2f out: wknd fnl f) | ¾ | **5** | 7/1 | 71 | 40 |

| | | | | SP | RR | SF |
|---|---|---|---|---|---|---|
| | **Classic Leader** (SCWilliams) **3-9-0** AMackay(3) (bit bkwd: nvr nr to chal) | 1½ | **6** | 13/2 | 68 | 37 |
| 583[11] | **Alpine Panther (IRE)** (WJarvis) **3-9-0** KDarley(7) (nvr nrr) | hd | **7** | 16/1 | 67 | 36 |
| | **Crimson Rosella** (WJHaggas) **3-8-9** RMcGhin(11) (nvr nrr) | 4 | **8** | 33/1 | 53 | 22 |
| | **Jona Holley** (IABalding) **3-9-0** GHind(2) (b: a bhd) | 2 | **9** | 20/1 | 53 | 22 |
| 445[10] | **Shouldbegrey** (WRMuir) **3-9-0** Jean-PierreLopez(5) (bhd fnl 4f) | 2½ | **10** | 33/1 | 47 | 16 |
| 597[12] | **My Mother's Local (USA) (35)** (KOCunningham-Brown) **3-8-4b1**(5) MBaird(12) (led: clr over 5f out: hdd over 2f out: wknd qckly) | 15 | **11** | 66/1 | 7 | — |
| | **Governance (IRE)** (KWMcAuliffe) **3-8-9** GDuffield(4) (neat: lw: a wl bhd) | 16 | **12** | 33/1 | — | — |

(SP 128.3%) **12 Rn**

**1m 24.4** (2.80) CSF £18.49 TOTE £4.50: £2.40 £1.70 £1.10 (£10.10) Trio £29.50 OWNER Sheikh Mohammed (NEWMARKET) BRED Sheikh Mohammed bin Rashid al Maktoum

**Sandabar**, who picked up ground from below the distance, came with a storming run to grab the initiative near the line, giving his jockey his first winner in seven years. (5/1)

**Consort**, a newcomer with a bit left to work on, took control over a quarter of a mile from home. Having just got the better of Young Mazaad entering the final furlong, he was unable to withstand the late burst of the winner. (5/2)

**577 Crazy Chief**, always close up, was rousted along turning into the straight. For a long time there was little response, but he did run on inside the final furlong and he just failed to take second prize. (2/1)

**488 Young Mazaad (IRE)**, always close up, had a tremendous battle for the lead in the straight until forced to concede defeat in the final furlong. (33/1)

**Diminutive (USA)**, always close up, had every chance entering the straight before tiring in the last 200 yards. (7/1: op 4/1)

## 670 BOLLINGER CHAMPAGNE CHALLENGE SERIES GENTLEMAN AMATEUR H'CAP (0-70) (4-Y.O+) (Class E)

5-10 (5-11) **1m 1f 149y** £3,315.90 (£991.20: £474.60: £216.30) Stalls: High GOING minus 0.16 sec per fur (GF)

| | | | | SP | RR | SF |
|---|---|---|---|---|---|---|
| | **Scottish Bambi (56)** (PRWebber) **8-10-10**(4) MrPScott(11) (lw: hld up: led over 1f out: r.o wl) | — | **1** | 5/1 3 | 72 | 44 |
| 645[2] | **Kingchip Boy (63)** (MJRyan) **7-11-3v**(4) MrSLavallin(15) (led 8f: hung lft ins fnl f: unable qckn) | 4 | **2** | 9/1 | 72 | 44 |
| 549[3] | **Manabar (65)** (MJPolglase) **4-11-5**(4) MrKSantana(10) (swtchd rt & hdwy over 1f out: r.o one pce) | 1½ | **3** | 12/1 | 72 | 44 |
| *501[2]* | **Montone (IRE) (48)** (JRJenkins) **6-10-2**(4) DrMMannish(1) (a.p: ev ch over 1f out: one pce) | ½ | **4** | 11/1 | 54 | 26 |
| 469[6] | **Todd (USA) (52)** (PhilipMitchell) **5-10-10** MrTMcCarthy(5) (b.nr hind: hld up: rdn over 2f out: one pce) | hd | **5** | 11/1 | 58 | 30 |
| 470[10] | **Speedy Snaps Pride (42)** (PDCundell) **4-10-0** MrJRees(6) (lw: nvr nr to chal) | 3 | **6** | 33/1 | 43 | 15 |
| *306[6]* | **Digpast (IRE) (57)** (RJO'Sullivan) **6-10-11b**(4) MrDavyJones(9) (s.s: nvr nrr) | 2½ | **7** | 8/1 | 54 | 26 |
| | **Rising Dough (IRE) (70)** (GLMoore) **4-11-10**(4) MrKGoble(13) (a.p: rdn over 3f out: wknd over 1f out) | hd | **8** | 4/1 2 | 67 | 39 |
| | **Kevasingo (58)** (BWHills) **4-10-12**(4) MrCBHills(7) (prom over 3f) | 1¼ | **9** | 12/1 | 53 | 25 |
| *553[11]* | **Premier League (IRE) (54)** (JELong) **6-10-8**(4) MrJRyan(4) (bit bkwd: bhd fnl 7f) | 8 | **10** | 33/1 | 35 | 7 |
| *498[5]* | **Mystic Legend (IRE) (37)** (TJNaughton) **4-9-5**(4) MrVLukaniuk(2) (s.s: a bhd) | 6 | **11** | 25/1 | 8 | — |
| *553** | **Thorniwama (44)** (JJBridger) **5-9-12b**(4)ow6 MrDBridger(8) (bhd fnl 6f) | ½ | **12** | 12/1 | 15 | — |
| *553[2]* | **Zahid (USA) (43)** (KRBurke) **5-9-11**(4) MrNMoran(3) (lw: prom 7f) | 5 | **13** | 7/2 1 | 5 | — |
| *155[15]* | **Legal Drama (USA) (53)** (JohnBerry) **4-10-7**(4)ow5 MrVCoogan(12) (prom over 6f) | 6 | **14** | 33/1 | 5 | — |

(SP 132.4%) **14 Rn**

**2m 5.7** (8.00) CSF £50.51 CT £485.22 TOTE £8.90: £2.20 £1.70 £3.00 (£105.30) Trio £344.80; £242.84 to Newmarket 17/4/96 OWNER Mr William Kelly (BANBURY) BRED Cheveley Park Stud Ltd

**Scottish Bambi** chased the leaders. Moving to the front below the distance, he soon pulled away. (5/1: op 8/1)

**645 Kingchip Boy** attempted to make all the running. Collared below the distance, he hung left inside the final furlong and failed to quicken. He has never won beyond a mile. (9/1)

**549 Manabar**, switched over towards the rail as he picked up ground below the distance, struggled on for third prize. (12/1)

**501 Montone (IRE)**, always close up, had every chance below the distance before tapped for toe. (11/1: 7/1-12/1)

**469 Todd (USA)** chased the leaders but failed to quicken in the straight. (11/1)

**Digpast (IRE)** (8/1: 6/1-10/1)

**Kevasingo** (12/1: op 8/1)

**553* Thorniwama** (12/1: op 8/1)

T/Plpt: £57.10 (141.51 Tckts). T/Qdpt: £21.70 (27.37 Tckts). AK

# NEWMARKET (R-H) (Good to firm)

## Tuesday April 16th

WEATHER: overcast WIND: fresh half against

## 671 CONSTANT SECURITY MAIDEN STKS (3-Y.O) (Class D)

2-00 (2-02) **1m 4f (Rowley)** £4,269.00 (£1,272.00: £606.00: £273.00) Stalls: High GOING minus 0.26 sec per fur (GF)

| | | | SP | RR | SF |
|---|---|---|---|---|---|
| **Sherpas (IRE)** (HRACecil) **3-9-0** PatEddery(11) (gd sort: wl grwn: led after 2f: shkn up over 2f out: r.o gamely) | — | **1** | 7/2 1 | 94+ | 61 |
| **Sasuru (106)** (GWragg) **3-9-0** PaulEddery(3) (b: lw: trckd ldrs: stdy hdwy to disp ld 1f out: r.o) | hd | **2** | 9/2 2 | 94 | 61 |
| **Valedictory** (HRACecil) **3-9-0** WRyan(2) (gd sort: bit bkwd: hld up: stdy hdwy to chal 2½f out: outpcd appr fnl f: kpt on wl towards fin) | 1 | **3** | 9/1 3 | 93+ | 60 |
| **Wilawander (99)** (BWHills) **3-9-0** MHills(1) (hld up: smooth hdwy to chal 2f out: sn rdn & nt qckn) | ½ | **4** | 9/2 2 | 92 | 59 |
| **Highland Gift (IRE)** (RCharlton) **3-8-9** RHughes(9) (w'like: leggy: s.i.s: sn trckng ldrs: rdn 3f out: kpt on same pce) | 1¾ | **5** | 10/1 | 85 | 52 |
| **Zaforum (95)** (LMontagueHall) **3-9-0** LDettori(4) (in tch: drvn along over 3f out: r.o one pce) | s.h | **6** | 33/1 | 90 | 57 |
| **Qasida (IRE)** (CEBrittain) **3-9-0** MJKinane(5) (w'like: leggy: trckd ldrs tl wknd fnl 2½f) | 1½ | **7** | 25/1 | 88 | 55 |
| **Lakeline Legend (IRE)** (MAJarvis) **3-9-0** EmmaO'Gorman(7) (hld up: effrt over 3f out: no imp) | 1¼ | **8** | 14/1 | 86 | 53 |
| **Chief Contender (IRE)** (PWChapple-Hyam) **3-9-0** JReid(10) (gd sort: str: led 2f: w wnr tl rdn & wknd 2f out) | nk | **9** | 9/2 2 | 85 | 52 |
| **Glowing Reeds** (CNAllen) **3-8-2**(7) CWebb(6) (outpcd & hung lft 5f out: sn bhd) | 26 | **10** | 100/1 | 52 | 19 |
| ***Petrolio (IRE)*** (LMCumani) **3-9-0** JWeaver(8) (Withdrawn not under Starter's orders: lame at s) | | **W** | 25/1 | — | — |

(SP 114.1%) **10 Rn**

**2m 32.88** (2.38) CSF £17.42 TOTE £3.30: £1.50 £1.50 £3.20 (£6.80) Trio £8.70 OWNER Mr K. Abdulla (NEWMARKET) BRED Juddmonte Farms

**Sherpas (IRE)** is a particularly nice colt but his action on this fast ground left something to be desired. However, his attitude was right and he should improve with the experience. (7/2)
**Sasuru** is a consistent performer but seems to keep finding one too tough. He travels so well in his races that opportunities should be found before long. (9/2: 3/1-5/1)
**Valedictory**, a good staying type, got outpaced at a vital stage on the downhill section approaching the final furlong. By the way he finished, it will not be long before better is seen, especially over further. (9/1)
**Wilawander**, an eyecatching colt, looked very dangerous approaching the last two furlongs, but this trip, at the moment, just proved beyond him. He will do better in time. (9/2)
**Highland Gift (IRE)**, a leggy newcomer, needed the experience and ran well until getting tapped for toe in the closing stages. (10/1: 7/1-12/1)
**Zaforum** looks the type to gallop through anything but is short of a turn of speed. Opportunities will be found though, probably on easier ground. (33/1)
**Qasida (IRE)** looked likely to benefit from this and ran pretty well until blowing up in the last couple of furlongs. (25/1)
**Lakeline Legend (IRE)** (14/1: 12/1-20/1)
**Chief Contender (IRE)** (9/2: op 5/2)

## 672 STETCHWORTH MAIDEN STKS (3-Y.O) (Class D)

2-35 (2-38) **6f (Rowley)** £4,425.00 (£1,320.00: £630.00: £285.00) Stalls: Centre GOING minus 0.26 sec per fur (GF)

| | | | | SP | RR | SF |
|---|---|---|---|---|---|---|
| | **Elsaleet (USA)** (JHMGosden) **3-9-0** LDettori(9) (str: cmpt: cl up: led ½-wy & qcknd: pushed out) | — | **1** | 7/2[2] | 95 | 60 |
| | **Watch Me (IRE) (80)** (RHannon) **3-8-4**(5) DaneO'Neill(8) (led to ½-wy: sn outpcd: r.o appr fnl f) | hd | **2** | 15/2 | 90 | 55 |
| | **Omara (USA)** (HRACecil) **3-8-9** PatEddery(12) (chsd ldrs: effrt ½-wy: nt qckn appr fnl f) | 5 | **3** | 3/1[1] | 76 | 41 |
| | **Mutamanni (USA)** (HThomsonJones) **3-9-0** RHills(1) (in tch: outpcd ½-wy: styd on appr fnl f) | 1½ | **4** | 4/1[3] | 77 | 42 |
| | **Statoyork** (BWHills) **3-9-0** MHills(2) (lw: hld up: effrt ½-wy: nvr rchd ldrs) | nk | **5** | 12/1 | 77 | 42 |
| | **Hoh Returns (IRE) (85)** (MBell) **3-9-0** MFenton(10) (b.nr hind: chsd ldrs over 4f) | 3½ | **6** | 14/1 | 67 | 32 |
| | **Woodbury Lad (USA)** (WRMuir) **3-9-0** JReid(4) (spd 4f) | 2½ | **7** | 4/1[3] | 61 | 26 |
| | **Literary Society (USA)** (JARToller) **3-9-0** JWeaver(5) (w'like: bit bkwd: chsd ldrs 4f: wknd) | 3 | **8** | 14/1 | 53 | 18 |
| 544[9] | **Quiet Arch (IRE)** (CACyzer) **3-9-0** DBiggs(11) (s.s: a outpcd & bhd) | 3 | **9** | 33/1 | 45 | 10 |
| 445[12] | **Georgie Boy (USA)** (CADwyer) **3-9-0** DHarrison(6) (s.i.s: outpcd & bhd fr ½-wy) | 5 | **10** | 100/1 | 31 | — |
| | **Cadeau Elegant** (NACallaghan) **3-8-9** PaulEddery(3) (neat: plld hrd: jnd ldrs after 2f: wknd & eased wl over 1f out) | ¾ | **11** | 25/1 | 24 | — |
| | ***Intisab*** (RWArmstrong) **3-8-9** WCarson(7) (Withdrawn not under Starter's orders: lame at s) | | **W** | 6/1 | — | — |

(SP 142.1%) **11 Rn**

**1m 12.97** (1.17) CSF £30.50 TOTE £5.10: £2.20 £2.80 £1.60 (£35.10) Trio £16.00 OWNER Sheikh Ahmed Al Maktoum (NEWMARKET) BRED David's Farm
**Elsaleet (USA)**, a useful sort, showed a decent turn of foot halfway through the race and just needed hands and heels riding to hold on. Improvement looks likely. (7/2: 2/1-4/1)
**Watch Me (IRE)** looks to have got it together this season but did get chopped for speed at halfway here until finishing well. Longer trips should suit. (15/2)
**Omara (USA)** ran well and was not given too hard a time when obviously beaten in the last furlong. (3/1)
**Mutamanni (USA)** got outpaced halfway through the race but then picked up again in the closing stages to suggest that better is in the pipe-line. (4/1)
**Statoyork**, given plenty to do, ran well but could never get into it seriously and should benefit from the run. (12/1)
**Hoh Returns (IRE)** showed his usual speed but was left struggling some way out. (14/1: 8/1-16/1)
**Woodbury Lad (USA)** went far too freely to post and then, not surprisingly, ran out of petrol a good way from home on the way back. (4/1)
**Literary Society (USA)** needed this and blew up in the last couple of furlongs. (14/1: 10/1-16/1)

## 673 ABERNANT STKS (Listed) (3-Y.O+) (Class A)

3-05 (3-07) **6f (Rowley)** £11,662.00 (£4,318.00: £2,074.00: £850.00: £340.00: £136.00) Stalls: Centre GOING minus 0.26 sec per fur (GF)

| | | | | SP | RR | SF |
|---|---|---|---|---|---|---|
| 571* | **Passion For Life (105)** (GLewis) **3-8-5** PatEddery(9) (lw: mde all far side: qcknd over 1f out: r.o wl) | — | **1** | 11/4[1] | 121+ | 72 |
| 457[6] | **Iktamal (USA) (100)** (EALDunlop) **4-9-2** PaulEddery(2) (hld up & bhd centre: hdwy on bit wl over 1f out: shkn up ins fnl f: nt pce of wnr) | 1¼ | **2** | 15/2 | 118 | 80 |
| | **Struggler** (DRLoder) **4-9-8** LDettori(8) (h.d.w: racd far side: chsd ldrs: effrt u.p 2f out: kpt on one pce) | 2 | **3** | 11/2[2] | 118 | 80 |
| 579[2] | **Easy Dollar (107)** (BGubby) **4-9-2v** MHills(6) (w ldr centre: rdn 2f out: kpt on) | hd | **4** | 12/1 | 112 | 74 |
| 457[3] | **Cool Jazz (113)** (CEBrittain) **5-9-8** MJKinane(7) (lw: racd centre: hdwy 2f out: styd on: nvr able to chal) | s.h | **5** | 12/1 | 118 | 80 |
| | **Welsh Mist (100)** (RBoss) **5-8-11** WRyan(5) (led centre tl rdn & btn appr fnl f) | 1¾ | **6** | 25/1 | 102 | 64 |
| | **Soviet Line (IRE) (120)** (MRStoute) **6-9-12** KFallon(13) (h.d.w: cl up far side tl outpcd fnl 2f) | ½ | **7** | 6/1[3] | 116 | 78 |
| | **Branston Abby (IRE) (113)** (MJohnston) **7-9-1** JWeaver(4) (chsd ldr centre: rdn 2f out: sn outpcd) | s.h | **8** | 8/1 | 105 | 67 |
| | **General Monash (USA)** (PWChapple-Hyam) **4-9-2** JReid(12) (hmpd after s: racd far side: hdwy ½-wy: wknd over 1f out) | ¾ | **9** | 16/1 | 104 | 66 |
| 579[4] | **Wavian (96)** (RHannon) **4-9-2** RHughes(3) (lw: chsd ldr centre tl rdn & btn over 1f out) | ¾ | **10** | 33/1 | 102 | 64 |
| | **Warning Time (106)** (BJMeehan) **3-8-5** BDoyle(1) (lw: racd centre: outpcd fnl 2f) | nk | **11** | 25/1 | 101 | 52 |
| | **Baize (100)** (RFJohnsonHoughton) **3-8-0** WCarson(11) (racd far side: prom 4f) | 2 | **12** | 14/1 | 91 | 42 |
| 582[5] | **Montserrat (71)** (LGCottrell) **4-8-11v** MFenton(10) (racd far side: outpcd fnl 2½f) | hd | **13** | 100/1 | 90? | 52 |

(SP 118.8%) **13 Rn**

**1m 11.49** (-0.31) CSF £22.21 TOTE £3.50: £1.70 £1.90 £2.30 (£13.40) Trio £43.10 OWNER Mr David Waters (EPSOM) BRED G. R. Smith (Thriplow) Ltd
WEIGHT FOR AGE 3yo-11lb
**571* Passion For Life** is in superb form and, once he quickened approaching the final furlong, he had then stolen it. (11/4: op 7/4)
**457 Iktamal (USA)** loves this fast ground and was swinging off the bit for much of the trip, but the winner just got first run and he was then not over-punished. (15/2)
**Struggler** is said to be best on a fast surface but his action does not really confirm that and, although he had every chance, he could never quicken enough. Perhaps this was needed to put him right. (11/2)
**579 Easy Dollar** is in the form of his life just now and he battled all the way to the line. (12/1)
**457 Cool Jazz**, on ground faster than he really prefers, ran pretty well, staying on in the closing stages. (12/1)
**Welsh Mist** last won almost two years ago but she did show plenty of speed here only to find this company too hot in the final furlong and a half. (25/1)

**Soviet Line (IRE)** looked and moved well but his performance was disappointing. (6/1)
**Branston Abby (IRE)** can win on fast ground but is certainly much better with some give and was left struggling here from two furlongs out. (8/1)

## 674 SHADWELL STUD NELL GWYN STKS (Gp 3) (3-Y.O F) (Class A)

3-40 (3-40) **7f (Rowley)** £19,362.00 (£7,158.00: £3,429.00: £1,395.00: £547.50: £208.50) Stalls: Centre GOING minus 0.26 sec per fur (GF)

| Form | Horse / details | Dist | Pos | SP | RR | SF |
|---|---|---|---|---|---|---|
| | **Thrilling Day (104)** (NAGraham) **3-8-9** DHarrison(9) (hld up & bhd: hdwy u.p 2f out: r.o wl fnl f to ld cl home) | — | 1 | 20/1 | 108 | 62 |
| | **Bint Salsabil (USA) (113)** (JLDunlop) **3-8-12** WCarson(6) (lw: led: qcknd over 2f out: hdd cl home: rallied) | s.h | 2 | 7/2 1 | 111 | 65 |
| | **Honest Guest (IRE) (108)** (MHTompkins) **3-8-9** PRobinson(1) (bhd: rdn & hdwy over 2f out: styd on wl fnl f) | 2½ | 3 | 16/1 | 102 | 56 |
| | **My Melody Parkes (108)** (JBerry) **3-8-9** GCarter(4) (a chsng ldrs: hdwy u.p 2f out: ev ch 1f out: nt qckn) | hd | 4 | 12/1 | 102 | 56 |
| | **Maid For The Hills** (DRLoder) **3-8-9** RHughes(3) (trckd ldr: outpcd over 2f out: hdwy u.p over 1f out: no ex ins fnl f) | 1¼ | 5 | 7/2 1 | 99 | 53 |
| | **Darling Flame (USA) (109)** (JHMGosden) **3-8-9** LDettori(7) (lw: in tch: effrt over 2f out: r.o one pce) | ½ | 6 | 15/2 | 98 | 52 |
| | **Mezzogiorno (112)** (GWragg) **3-8-9** MHills(2) (lw: hld up & bhd: effrt over 2f out: btn & eased appr fnl f) | 11 | 7 | 9/2 2 | 73 | 27 |
| | **Wild Rumour (IRE)** (PWChapple-Hyam) **3-8-9** JReid(11) (prom tl outpcd fnl 2f) | 2 | 8 | 7/1 3 | 68 | 22 |
| 572[6] | **Cyrillic (92)** (PAKelleway) **3-8-9** JFEgan(10) (lw: outpcd ½-wy: n.d after) | ½ | 9 | 50/1 | 67 | 21 |
| 548[2] | **Marl (90)** (RAkehurst) **3-8-9** SSanders(5) (chsd ldr tl wknd wl over 1f out) | hd | 10 | 16/1 | 67 | 21 |
| 572[8] | **Coachella (85)** (MJRyan) **3-8-9** MJKinane(8) (in tch tl rdn & wknd 3f out) | 4 | 11 | 50/1 | 58 | 12 |

(SP 115.0%) **11 Rn**

**1m 25.31** (0.81) CSF £81.73 TOTE £26.50: £5.20 £1.70 £3.40 (£44.50) Trio £228.30 OWNER Bloomsbury Stud (NEWMARKET) BRED Bloomsbury Stud

**Thrilling Day,** held up to get the trip, produced a run in the last two furlongs and showed courage aplenty to snatch the verdict. (20/1)
**Bint Salsabil (USA)** had plenty of use made of her stamina and she had most of her rivals in trouble approaching the final furlong, but Carson seemed reluctant to go for everything and, when challenged, she just failed to respond in time. She will improve no end as she tries further. (7/2)
**Honest Guest (IRE)** showed a good action and ran a super race, and will certainly improve when tried over longer distances. (16/1)
**My Melody Parkes** put up a game performance but, in the end, was well held. The stable is not as far forward as previous seasons and she may have some improvement in her. (12/1)
**Maid For The Hills** got caught flat-footed when the tempo increased two furlongs out and, although rallying for a few strides soon afterwards, she was well held at the finish. (7/2)
**Darling Flame (USA)** ran quite well without getting into it, and was not given a hard time. (15/2)
**Mezzogiorno** seemed to lose her action on the downhill section approaching the final furlong and was then eased a fair deal. (9/2)
**Wild Rumour (IRE)** disappointed here, getting well outpaced when the pace was on in the last two and a half furlongs. (7/1)

## 675 NGK SPARK PLUGS SWAFFHAM H'CAP (0-100) (4-Y.O+) (Class C)

4-15 (4-15) **1m 6f (Rowley)** £5,692.00 (£1,696.00: £808.00: £364.00) Stalls: High GOING minus 0.26 sec per fur (GF)

| Form | Horse / details | Dist | Pos | SP | RR | SF |
|---|---|---|---|---|---|---|
| | **Sanmartino (IRE) (97)** (BWHills) **4-10-0** PatEddery(1) (lw: plld hrd: trckd ldrs tl led 6f out: qcknd 2f out: comf) | — | 1 | Evens 1 | 112+ | 66 |
| | **Unchanged (72)** (CEBrittain) **4-8-3** BDoyle(4) (led tl hdd 6f out: outpcd 3f out: kpt on wl fnl f) | 2½ | 2 | 7/2 2 | 84 | 38 |
| 564[5] | **Thaljanah (IRE) (84)** (DLWilliams) **4-9-1** TIves(3) (trckd ldrs: chal 3f out: rdn & wknd wl over 1f out) | 6 | 3 | 6/1 | 89 | 43 |
| 439[19] | **Advance East (70)** (MrsJRRamsden) **4-8-1** JFEgan(2) (hld up: stdy hdwy over 3f out: shkn up 2f out: sn wknd) | 10 | 4 | 9/2 3 | 64 | 18 |

(SP 104.7%) **4 Rn**

**3m 0.32** (4.32) CSF £4.24 TOTE £1.40: (£1.80) OWNER Mr K. Abdulla (LAMBOURN) BRED Juddmonte Farms

**Sanmartino (IRE),** very free early on, left nothing to chance and kicked on some way out to win with a good deal of authority. He looks better than ever this year. (Evens)
**Unchanged** found this trip too sharp and only stayed on when it was too late. (7/2)
**Thaljanah (IRE)** put in a bid with three furlongs to go, only to have his limitations exposed approaching the final furlong. (6/1: 9/2-7/1)
**Advance East** travelled really well for much of the trip but then stopped so quickly in the last two furlongs that he must have seriously blown up. (9/2: op 5/2)

## 676 EQUITY FINANCIAL COLLECTIONS H'CAP (0-95) (3-Y.O) (Class C)

4-45 (4-45) **7f (Rowley)** £6,212.00 (£1,856.00: £888.00: £404.00) Stalls: Centre GOING minus 0.26 sec per fur (GF)

| Form | Horse / details | Dist | Pos | SP | RR | SF |
|---|---|---|---|---|---|---|
| | **Sky Dome (IRE) (75)** (MHTompkins) **3-8-4** PRobinson(9) (hdwy over 2f out: swtchd & r.o u.p to ld cl home) | — | 1 | 14/1 | 86 | 28 |
| | **Welville (89)** (PJMakin) **3-9-4** JWeaver(10) (lw: led after 2f: clr over 1f out: sn rdn: jst ct) | hd | 2 | 11/2 2 | 100 | 42 |
| 493[3] | **White Plains (IRE) (67)** (MBell) **3-7-3**(7) RMullen(5) (hdwy 3f out: chsng wnr over 1f out: nt qckn ins fnl f) | 2 | 3 | 7/1 3 | 73 | 15 |
| *484** | **Waypoint (73)** (RCharlton) **3-8-2** TSprake(11) (a chsng ldrs: rdn 2f out: kpt on fnl f) | s.h | 4 | 9/2 1 | 79 | 21 |
| | **Jerry Cutrona (IRE) (69)** (NACallaghan) **3-7-12** JFEgan(2) (hld up & bhd: hdwy 2f out: r.o: nvr plcd to chal) | 1½ | 5 | 14/1 | 72 | 14 |
| 453[11] | **Rebel County (IRE) (68)** (DJSCosgrove) **3-7-11** NAdams(7) (hld up: hdwy over 2f out: shkn up over 1f out: eased whn btn) | hd | 6 | 25/1 | 70 | 12 |
| 453[8] | **Beas River (IRE) (72)** (WRMuir) **3-7-12**(3)ow2 DRMcCabe(14) (effrt 3f out: nvr trbld ldrs) | 3½ | 7 | 16/1 | 66 | 6 |
| 453* | **Sualtach (IRE) (81)** (RHollinshead) **3-8-10** LDettori(4) (w ldrs tl wknd wl over 1f out) | 1¾ | 8 | 9/2 1 | 71 | 13 |
| | **Consordino (87)** (LMCumani) **3-9-2** MJKinane(13) (lw: hld up: stdy hdwy over 2f out: nvr rchd ldrs) | s.h | 9 | 10/1 | 77 | 19 |
| | **Lyzia (IRE) (80)** (CEBrittain) **3-8-9** BDoyle(1) (bhd: rdn ½-wy: no imp) | s.h | 10 | 16/1 | 70 | 12 |
| | **Ocean Grove (IRE) (92)** (PWChapple-Hyam) **3-9-7** JReid(12) (unf: led 2f: cl up tl wknd 2f out) | 1½ | 11 | 14/1 | 79 | 21 |
| | **Red Rusty (USA) (67)** (DMorris) **3-7-10** LCharnock(8) (lw: prom 5f) | 1½ | 12 | 16/1 | 50 | — |
| 571[10] | **Missile Toe (IRE) (72)** (JEBanks) **3-7-10b1**(5) FLynch(3) (gd spd 5f) | ½ | 13 | 16/1 | 54 | — |

(SP 120.7%) **13 Rn**

**1m 27.8** (3.30) CSF £83.57 CT £546.68 TOTE £16.40: £3.00 £2.20 £2.50 (£88.10) Trio £208.70 OWNER Miss D. J. Merson (NEWMARKET) BRED Andrew Bradley

LONG HANDICAP Red Rusty (USA) 7-9 White Plains (IRE) 7-8

**OFFICIAL EXPLANATION Jerry Cutrona (IRE): has a tendecy to run free and therefore needs to be settled in order to produce his true form.**

**Sky Dome (IRE)** obviously had a problem last year as he never ran after June, but he is certainly back to his best now and had to really battle to score here. (14/1)

**Welville** is a free-runner and, after looking the likely winner, just failed to last home. He will be better for the run. (11/2)
**493 White Plains (IRE)** looked a big danger approaching the final furlong, but then failed to maintain the effort and may still just have needed this. (7/1)
**484* Waypoint**, an All-Weather winner last time, put up a good performance here, keeping on at the end to suggest that further should suit. (9/2: op 3/1)
**Jerry Cutrona (IRE)** had only what can be described as a pipe-opener here and made up a good deal of ground without being knocked about. Better is certainly on the cards. (14/1: 10/1-16/1)
**453 Rebel County (IRE)** ran well and looks to be coming to hand. (25/1)
**453 Beas River (IRE)** ran far too freely early on and failed to get into it. (16/1)
**Consordino** should do better in due course. (10/1: 7/1-12/1)
**Ocean Grove (IRE)** (14/1: op 8/1)

## 677 MUSEUM MAIDEN STKS (3-Y.O) (Class D)

5-20 (5-21) **1m 2f (Rowley)** £4,971.00 (£1,488.00: £714.00: £327.00) Stalls: Centre GOING minus 0.26 sec per fur (GF)

| | | | | SP | RR | SF |
|---|---|---|---|---|---|---|
| | **Dovaly** (HRACecil) **3-9-0** PatEddery(15) (gd sort: bkwd: chsd ldrs: rdn wl over 2f out: r.o wl fnl f to ld cl home) | — | **1** | 8/1[3] | 83+ | 54 |
| | **Sacho (IRE)** (JHMGosden) **3-9-0** LDettori(6) (h.d.w: led: qcknd 3f out: rdn ins fnl f: r.o: jst ct) | ½ | **2** | Evens[1] | 82+ | 53 |
| | **Generosus (FR)** (HRACecil) **3-9-0** WRyan(5) (w'like: scope: bkwd: hld up & bhd: shkn up & gd hdwy over 2f out: ev ch & rn green ins fnl f: r.o) | ½ | **3** | 14/1 | 81+ | 52 |
| 448[5] | **Ambassador (USA)** (BWHills) **3-9-0** JWeaver(13) (trckd ldrs: effrt over 2f out: kpt on) | 1½ | **4** | 25/1 | 79 | 50 |
| | **Robamaset (IRE)** (LMCumani) **3-9-0** RHughes(4) (a chsng ldrs: one pce fnl 2f) | 3 | **5** | 14/1 | 74 | 45 |
| | **Rusk** (JPearce) **3-9-0** MWigham(7) (bkwd: in tch: outpcd 2f out: kpt on fnl f) | 1½ | **6** | 50/1 | 72 | 43 |
| | **Radiant Star** (GWragg) **3-9-0** MHills(9) (lw: hld up: swtchd & hdwy 3f out: nt qckn appr fnl f) | ½ | **7** | 5/1[2] | 71 | 42 |
| | **Mohannad (IRE)** (JWHills) **3-9-0** RHills(8) (lw: trckd ldrs: outpcd over 2f out: no imp after) | nk | **8** | 33/1 | 71 | 42 |
| | **Mazurek** (PWChapple-Hyam) **3-9-0** JReid(3) (cmpt: chsd ldrs: outpcd 3f out: sn no ch) | 6 | **9** | 16/1 | 61 | 32 |
| 528[2] | **Bowled Over** (CACyzer) **3-9-0** DBiggs(10) (hld up & bhd: nvr nr to chal) | nk | **10** | 20/1 | 60 | 31 |
| | **He's My Love (IRE)** (JEBanks) **3-9-0** BDoyle(16) (leggy: prom tl wknd fnl 2½f) | 2½ | **11** | 50/1 | 56 | 27 |
| | **Ajaad Aljaree (IRE)** (ACStewart) **3-9-0** MJKinane(11) (str: cmpt: bkwd: a bhd) | 1¼ | **12** | 16/1 | 54 | 25 |
| | **Get Away With It (IRE)** (MRStoute) **3-9-0** KFallon(1) (leggy: scope: bhd: drvn along over 3f out: n.d) | s.h | **13** | 25/1 | 54 | 25 |
| | **Apicella** (JPearce) **3-9-0** GBardwell(14) (b: hld up & bhd: n.d) | s.h | **14** | 50/1 | 54 | 25 |
| | **Safa (USA)** (ACStewart) **3-8-9** WCarson(2) (leggy: scope: dwlt: a bhd) | ¾ | **15** | 20/1 | 48 | 19 |
| | **Royal Expose (USA)** (RHannon) **3-8-9**(5) DaneO'Neill(12) (prom tl wknd 3f out) | 2 | **16** | 50/1 | 50 | 21 |
| | | | | (SP 130.9%) | **16 Rn** | |

**2m 6.45** (2.85) CSF £16.44 TOTE £8.40: £2.40 £1.40 £2.60 (£6.30) Trio £15.00 OWNER Mr K. Abdulla (NEWMARKET) BRED Juddmonte Farms

**Dovaly**, a decent type, just needed this, but he was given a most positive ride and answered in good style to snatch it late on. He should go on from here. (8/1: 5/1-9/1)
**Sacho (IRE)** both looked and moved well but, despite a valiant effort, just failed to last out. The experience can only improve him. (Evens)
**Generosus (FR)**, given plenty to do, then hung when challenging entering the final furlong and only realised what was required when it was too late. There should be plenty of improvement in him. (14/1: 10/1-16/1)
**448 Ambassador (USA)**, whose action suggests that easier ground should suit, ran well but was tapped for toe in the closing stages. (25/1)
**Robamaset (IRE)** ran a useful race and was not over-punished. (14/1)
**Rusk**, from a stable that is going well, ran promisingly. (50/1)
**Radiant Star** ran as though he still has plenty to learn and there is ability there. (5/1)
**528 Bowled Over** never got into the race but left the impression that this should help put him right. (20/1)

T/Jkpt: Not won; £6,125.78 to Newmarket 17/4/96. T/Plpt: £53.40 (601.13 Tckts). T/Qdpt: £29.80 (55.95 Tckts). AA

# 0671-NEWMARKET (R-H) (Good to firm)
## Wednesday April 17th

WEATHER: bright & sunny WIND: fresh half bhd

## 678 GEOFFREY BARLING MAIDEN STKS (3-Y.O F) (Class D)

2-00 (2-00) **7f (Rowley)** £4,815.00 (£1,440.00: £690.00: £315.00) Stalls: High GOING minus 0.48 sec per fur (F)

| | | | | SP | RR | SF |
|---|---|---|---|---|---|---|
| | **Tawaaded (IRE)** (PTWalwyn) **3-8-11** RHills(6) (mde all: hung rt appr fnl f: hld on wl) | — | **1** | 33/1 | 84 | 61 |
| | **Really A Dream (IRE)** (MRStoute) **3-8-11** MJKinane(15) (a chsng ldrs: hdwy to chal 1f out: nt qckn nr fin) | 1 | **2** | 11/2[2] | 82 | 59 |
| | **Charlotte Corday** (GWragg) **3-8-4**(7) GMilligan(11) (a chsng ldrs: outpcd 2f out: styd on fnl f) | 3½ | **3** | 50/1 | 74 | 51 |
| | **Kerry Ring** (JHMGosden) **3-8-11** LDettori(12) (a chsng ldrs: outpcd 2f out: kpt on fnl f) | 1½ | **4** | 5/4[1] | 70 | 47 |
| | **Nunsharpa** (JRFanshawe) **3-8-11** DHarrison(14) (chsd ldrs: outpcd 2f out: no imp) | 1½ | **5** | 25/1 | 67 | 44 |
| | **Saleemah (USA)** (JLDunlop) **3-8-11** WCarson(4) (leggy: unf: s.i.s: sn pushed along: hdwy 2f out: eased wl ins fnl f) | nk | **6** | 11/2[2] | 66 | 43 |
| | **Singapore Sting (USA)** (HRACecil) **3-8-11** WRyan(8) (cmpt: scope: s.i.s: hdwy ½-wy: styd on: no imp) | hd | **7** | 15/2[3] | 66 | 43 |
| | **La Pellegrina (IRE)** (PWChapple-Hyam) **3-8-11** JReid(7) (w'like: chsd ldrs: rdn over 2f out: one pce) | hd | **8** | 10/1 | 66 | 43 |
| | **Baloustar (USA)** (SPCWoods) **3-8-11** WWoods(3) (chsd ldrs: effrt 2½f out: nt qckn) | 1¼ | **9** | 66/1 | 63 | 40 |
| | **Classic Royale (USA)** (SCWilliams) **3-8-11** AMackay(9) (w'like: outpcd & bhd tl sme late hdwy) | 1 | **10** | 33/1 | 61 | 38 |
| 544[8] | **Polish Widow** (GWragg) **3-8-11** MHills(2) (effrt 3f out: nvr rchd ldrs) | ½ | **11** | 16/1 | 59 | 36 |
| | **Hippy** (CEBrittain) **3-8-11** BDoyle(5) (lw: mid div: rdn ½-wy: no imp after) | ¾ | **12** | 16/1 | 58 | 35 |
| 526[6] | **Young Annabel (USA)** (CADwyer) **3-8-11** CDwyer(13) (lost pl after 2f: nvr plcd to chal after) | s.h | **13** | 66/1 | 58 | 35 |
| | **Petit Point (IRE)** (RHannon) **3-8-11** PatEddery(10) (lw: chsd ldrs tl grad wknd fnl 2½f) | d.h | **13** | 25/1 | 58 | 35 |
| 550[11] | **Cd Super Targeting (IRE)** (MRChannon) **3-8-11** RHughes(1) (s.i.s: a bhd) | 5 | **15** | 66/1 | 46 | — |
| | **Giddy** (DMorley) **3-8-11** RCochrane(16) (in tch 4f) | 4 | **16** | 33/1 | 37 | 14 |
| | | | | (SP 130.8%) | **16 Rn** | |

**1m 23.98** (-0.52) CSF £201.98 TOTE £48.10: £8.00 £2.10 £5.40 (£167.80) Trio Not won; £590.22 to Newmarket 18/4/96 OWNER Mr Hamdan Al Maktoum (LAMBOURN) BRED Shadwell Estate Company Limited

**OFFICIAL EXPLANATION Young Annabel (USA): the trainer reported that the filly tends to hang right and has to be settled in behind, and that she was not suited by the fast ground.**

**Tawaaded (IRE)** has a really good action and put it to some use. She also showed she possesses fine battling qualities, despite signs of greenness. (33/1)
**Really A Dream (IRE)**, one of the best lookers in the race, is sure to improve as a result of this and is one to keep in mind. (11/2: 4/1-6/1)
**Charlotte Corday** ran really well and, judging by the way she finished, looks likely to do better over further. (50/1)
**Kerry Ring**, a sturdy filly, got outpaced on the downhill run to the final furlong and was getting it together again at the finish. She will obviously stay further and should appreciate a bit of cut. (5/4)
**Nunsharpa** looked pretty straight and ran well, but this firm ground just found her out approaching the final furlong. (25/1)
**Saleemah (USA)** is not the best of movers and took time to get going but, had her rider really persevered, she would have been a bit closer. The experience should stand her in good stead. (11/2: 4/1-6/1)
**Singapore Sting (USA)**, a sharp-actioned sort, needed this and took an age to get going, but she was learning as the race progressed. (15/2)
**La Pellegrina (IRE)** is on the weak side as yet and probably needs time. (10/1: op 5/1)
**Young Annabel (USA)** raced far too freely and, when her rider finally got her settled out the back, the race was over. There is obviously more ability there. (66/1)

## 679 RACING & FOOTBALL OUTLOOK RATED STKS H'CAP (0-105) (4-Y.O+) (Class B)

2-35 (2-36) **7f (Rowley)** £8,604.00 (£3,186.00: £1,530.50: £627.50: £251.25: £100.75) Stalls: High GOING minus 0.48 sec per fur (F)

| | | | | SP | RR | SF |
|---|---|---|---|---|---|---|
| | **Tarawa (IRE) (99)** (NACallaghan) **4-9-7** RHughes(10) (trckd ldrs: hdwy 2f out: led ins fnl f: jst hld on) | — | 1 | 10/1 | 113 | 88 |
| | **Monaassib (IRE) (98)** (EALDunlop) **5-9-6** RHills(8) (h.d.w: w ldrs: led over 2f out tl hdd & hung lft ins fnl f: rallied) | s.h | 2 | 8/1 3 | 112 | 87 |
| 455[2] | **Roving Minstrel (93)** (BAMcMahon) **5-9-1** GCarter(6) (lw: chsd ldrs: effrt over 2f out: ev ch over 1f out: nt qckn) | 2½ | 3 | 6/1 2 | 101 | 76 |
| | **Emerging Market (91)** (JLDunlop) **4-8-13** PatEddery(2) (in tch: drvn along 3f out: hdwy 2f out: ev ch & hung rt over 1f out: nt qckn) | nk | 4 | 6/1 2 | 99 | 74 |
| | **Blomberg (IRE) (95)** (JRFanshawe) **4-9-3** DHarrison(3) (chsd ldrs: drvn along 3f out: swtchd & hdwy over 1f out: nvr able to chal) | 1½ | 5 | 9/2 1 | 99 | 74 |
| | **Astrac (IRE) (95)** (RAkehurst) **5-8-10**(7) TAshley(9) (in tch: effrt 3f out: nt rch ldrs) | 3 | 6 | 20/1 | 92 | 67 |
| 554[7] | **Christmas Kiss (83)** (RHannon) **4-8-0**(5) DaneO'Neill(5) (shkn up ½-wy: nvr bttr than mid div) | ½ | 7 | 16/1 | 79 | 54 |
| 455[17] | **Kayvee (99)** (GHarwood) **7-9-7** AClark(1) (w ldrs: effrt over 2f out: btn whn hmpd appr fnl f) | ½ | 8 | 10/1 | 94 | 69 |
| 537[5] | **Castel Rosselo (82)** (RHarris) **6-8-4b** AMackay(4) (led tl hdd over 2f out: wknd over 1f out) | 1¼ | 9 | 33/1 | 74 | 49 |
| | **Prima Cominna (82)** (SPCWoods) **4-8-4** WWoods(11) (nvr trbld ldrs) | 1½ | 10 | 33/1 | 71 | 46 |
| | **Saseedo (USA) (89)** (WAO'Gorman) **6-8-11** EmmaO'Gorman(14) (bkwd: s.i.s: a outpcd & bhd) | ½ | 11 | 16/1 | 77 | 52 |
| | **Pinkerton's Pal (93)** (CEBrittain) **5-9-1** BDoyle(13) (sn outpcd) | 3½ | 12 | 20/1 | 73 | 48 |
| 561[12] | **Orthorhombus (82)** (DJSCosgrove) **7-7-13b**(5) MBaird(7) (a outpcd & bhd) | 1¾ | 13 | 100/1 | 58 | 33 |
| | **Amrak Ajeeb (IRE) (88)** (BHanbury) **4-8-10** WRyan(12) (sn outpcd & wl bhd) | 5 | 14 | 20/1 | 52 | 27 |

(SP 109.0%) **14 Rn**

**1m 22.6** (-1.90) CSF £73.23 CT £432.89 TOTE £10.00: £3.10 £2.70 £1.80 (£30.90) Trio £42.40 OWNER Mrs J. Callaghan (NEWMARKET) BRED Patrick Eddery Ltd
LONG HANDICAP Prima Cominna 8-2 Castel Rosselo 7-8 Orthorhombus 6-0

**Tarawa (IRE)** showed a moderate action on the way down, but battled well in the race over a trip just short of his best and held on most determinedly. (10/1: op 6/1)
**Monaassib (IRE)**, in a race run at a cracking pace, was always in the firing-line and, battling back in the closing stages, almost made it. He is in tremendous form just now. (8/1)
**455 Roving Minstrel** goes in any ground and really battles, but this shorter trip in these faster conditions just found him out. (6/1)
**Emerging Market** had to really struggle to improve and then got unbalanced under pressure approaching the final furlong, which put paid to his chance. (6/1: op 4/1)
**Blomberg (IRE)** was taken off his legs at halfway and, although short of room when responding to pressure, this fast pace was always too much for him. (9/2)
**Astrac (IRE)** won on fast ground last year, but always found things happening too quickly here and never got in a blow. He is definitely better with plenty of cut. (20/1)

## 680 EARL OF SEFTON STKS (Gp 3) (4-Y.O+) (Class A)

3-05 (3-06) **1m 1f (Rowley)** £19,188.00 (£7,092.00: £3,396.00: £1,380.00: £540.00: £204.00) Stalls: High GOING minus 0.48 sec per fur (F)

| | | | | SP | RR | SF |
|---|---|---|---|---|---|---|
| | **Luso (120)** (CEBrittain) **4-9-4** MJKinane(1) (cl up: led 2f out: sn hdd: led ins fnl f: r.o) | — | 1 | 14/1 | 129 | 91 |
| | **Smart Alec** (LMCumani) **4-8-10** LDettori(5) (bit bkwd: trckd ldrs: hdwy to ld over 1f out: hdd ins fnl f: r.o towards fin) | hd | 2 | 6/4 1 | 121 | 83 |
| 442* | **First Island (IRE) (107)** (GWragg) **4-8-10** MHills(9) (hld up: swtchd lft fr 3 out: chsng ldrs & rdn over 1f out: kpt on) | 1½ | 3 | 4/1 2 | 118 | 80 |
| | **Gabr** (RWArmstrong) **6-8-10** WCarson(3) (a chsng ldrs: ev ch 2f out: wknd ins fnl f) | ¾ | 4 | 10/1 | 117 | 79 |
| | **Restructure (IRE) (106)** (MrsJCecil) **4-8-10** PaulEddery(6) (h.d.w: a.p: effrt & ev ch 2f out: btn appr fnl f) | 2 | 5 | 7/1 | 113 | 75 |
| | **Desert Shot (115)** (MRStoute) **6-8-13** PatEddery(8) (lw: bhd: effrt over 2f out: styd on: n.d) | ¾ | 6 | 11/2 3 | 115 | 77 |
| | **Sacrament (108)** (MRStoute) **5-8-10** TQuinn(2) (bhd: pushed along 3f out: n.d) | 1¼ | 7 | 20/1 | 110 | 72 |
| 455[6] | **Beauchamp Jazz (99)** (JLDunlop) **4-8-10** JReid(4) (lw: led tl hdd 2f out: wknd appr fnl f) | 1 | 8 | 20/1 | 108 | 70 |
| 581[8] | **Lear White (USA)** (PAKelleway) **5-8-13** RCochrane(7) (a bhd) | ½ | 9 | 50/1 | 110 | 72 |

(SP 115.1%) **9 Rn**

**1m 47.96** (-3.04) CSF £33.92 TOTE £15.70: £2.40 £1.50 £1.50 (£17.80) Trio £25.00 OWNER Mr Saeed Manana (NEWMARKET) BRED Saeed Manana

**Luso**, over a trip short of his best, won this race of ifs and buts in good style and, considering his 8lb penalty for his Italian Derby win last year, it was a useful performance. (14/1)
**Smart Alec** missed all last season and looked as though he would be all the better for this, but he still ran his heart out and this good-looking colt should improve a lot. (6/4)
**442* First Island (IRE)** has only ever won over a mile but was short of both room and pace at a vital stage here and, despite keeping on at the end, could never get into it. This is probably as good as he is. (4/1: 3/1-9/2)
**Gabr** got a bit warm beforehand but still ran reasonably well until running out of steam in the closing stages. (10/1)

**Restructure (IRE)** was getting a bit warm as he left the paddock, and his performance lacked a bit of spark as he ran into a wall approaching the final furlong. Connections seemed to think he needs easier ground. (7/1)
**Desert Shot**, who won this last year, looked and moved well here, but he never gave any hopes of getting into it, despite staying on. He is much better than this when things go his way. (11/2: op 7/2)
**Sacrament** ran only once last year and that was over an inadequate trip here, but showed enough to suggest that he will do a deal better in due course. (20/1)

## 681 NGK SPARK PLUGS EUROPEAN FREE H'CAP (Listed) (3-Y.O) (Class A)

3-40 (3-40) **7f (Rowley)** £16,570.00 (£6,130.00: £2,940.00: £1,200.00: £475.00: £185.00) Stalls: High GOING minus 0.48 sec per fur (F)

| | Horse | Dist | Pos | SP | RR | SF |
|---|---|---|---|---|---|---|
| | **Cayman Kai (IRE) (113)** (RHannon) **3-9-7** PatEddery(4) (trckd ldrs fr ½-wy: qcknd to ld ins fnl f: r.o) | — | 1 | 7/2 1 | 112 | 83 |
| 454 5 | **Projection (USA) (104)** (BWHills) **3-8-12** MHills(5) (lw: b.hind: a cl up: led 2f out tl ins fnl f: nt qckn) | 1¾ | 2 | 8/1 3 | 99 | 70 |
| | **World Premier (112)** (CEBrittain) **3-9-6** BDoyle(2) (a cl up: disp ld 3f out to 2f out: kpt on u.p) | nk | 3 | 9/1 | 106 | 77 |
| 574 8 | **Gothenberg (IRE) (105)** (MJohnston) **3-8-13** JWeaver(3) (lw: led tl hdd 2f out: sn wl outpcd: kpt on towards fin) | 1 | 4 | 16/1 | 97 | 68 |
| | **Tumbleweed Ridge (113)** (BJMeehan) **3-9-7** MJKinane(8) (lw: hld up: hdwy over 2f out: ch & hrd rdn appr fnl f: sn btn) | 1 | 5 | 7/2 1 | 103 | 74 |
| | **Desert Boy (IRE) (105)** (PWChapple-Hyam) **3-8-13** JReid(7) (h.d.w: prom tl outpcd over 2f out: kpt on fnl f) | nk | 6 | 5/1 2 | 94 | 65 |
| | **Lucky Lionel (USA) (112)** (RHannon) **3-9-6** LDettori(6) (hld up & bhd: effrt over 2f out: btn appr fnl f) | 1¼ | 7 | 5/1 2 | 98 | 69 |
| | **Yarob (IRE) (108)** (HThomsonJones) **3-9-2** RHills(1) (prom tl wknd over 2f out) | 13 | 8 | 16/1 | 65 | 36 |

(SP 110.7%) **8 Rn**

**1m 22.98** (-1.52) CSF £27.31 CT £198.33 TOTE £3.70: £1.60 £2.10 £2.20 (£19.20) OWNER Mr I. A. N. Wight (MARLBOROUGH) BRED Tommy Burns

**Cayman Kai (IRE)**, stepping up in distance again here, won this in great style and further success looks likely. (7/2)
**454 Projection (USA)**, who disappointed last time on soft ground, was back to his best here but found the winner too good in the closing stages. (8/1)
**World Premier**, trying his longest trip to date, ran well, forcing the pace, and kept staying on, but was just short of toe at the finish. (9/1)
**Gothenberg (IRE)**, who ran poorly last time, showed he is on his way back here and was rallying at the end to suggest that longer trips might help. (16/1)
**Tumbleweed Ridge**, although he looked pretty straight, still ran as though he would be all the better for this. (7/2)
**Desert Boy (IRE)**, who looked likely to benefit from this, got left behind entering the final two furlongs, but he was picking up again at the finish and ought to appreciate further. (5/1)

## 682 BABRAHAM H'CAP (0-90) (4-Y.O+) (Class C)

4-15 (4-18) **1m 4f (Rowley)** £6,108.00 (£1,824.00: £872.00: £396.00) Stalls: High GOING minus 0.48 sec per fur (F)

| | Horse | Dist | Pos | SP | RR | SF |
|---|---|---|---|---|---|---|
| *411 3* | **Progression (73)** (CMurray) **5-8-7b**(5) MBaird(13) (hld up & bhd: hdwy over 2f out: qcknd to ld 1½f out: r.o wl) | — | 1 | 9/1 | 89 | 69 |
| | **Speed to Lead (IRE) (76)** (HRACecil) **4-9-0** PatEddery(7) (cl up: rdn 4f out: led 3f out to 1½f out: kpt on wl) | 2 | 2 | 5/1 1 | 89 | 68 |
| *100 3* | **Opera Buff (IRE) (70)** (MissGayKelleway) **5-8-9** RCochrane(6) (hld up on ins: nt clr run & swtchd over 2f out: hung lft: r.o towards fin) | 1¼ | 3 | 11/2 2 | 82 | 62 |
| | **Fahs (USA) (65)** (RAkehurst) **4-8-3** SSanders(10) (trckd ldrs gng wl: disp ld on bit 2f out: rdn & no ex appr fnl f) | 1½ | 4 | 11/2 2 | 75 | 54 |
| | **Dont Shoot Fairies (74)** (CEBrittain) **4-8-12** BDoyle(8) (lw: led tl hdd 3f out: kpt on one pce) | 1¼ | 5 | 25/1 | 82 | 61 |
| *410 9* | **Statajack (IRE) (86)** (DRCElsworth) **8-9-11b** TQuinn(5) (hdwy 3f out: chsng ldrs 2f out: nt qckn) | ¾ | 6 | 25/1 | 93 | 73 |
| | **Meghdoot (71)** (HJCollingridge) **4-8-9** JQuinn(14) (prom: effrt 3f out: one pce) | 3½ | 7 | 16/1 | 73 | 52 |
| 580 13 | **At Liberty (IRE) (90)** (RHannon) **4-9-9**(5) DaneO'Neill(3) (sme hdwy over 2f out: nvr nr to chal) | 1¼ | 8 | 12/1 | 91 | 70 |
| | **Jermyn Street (USA) (75)** (MrsJCecil) **5-9-0** JReid(4) (prom: outpcd whn hmpd over 2f out) | hd | 9 | 12/1 | 76 | 56 |
| | **Pickens (USA) (77)** (NTinkler) **4-9-1** MJKinane(1) (swtg: bhd most of wy) | 5 | 10 | 20/1 | 71 | 50 |
| 564 7 | **Out on a Promise (IRE) (83)** (NJHWalker) **4-9-7** CRutter(11) (bit bkwd: a rr div) | hd | 11 | 33/1 | 77 | 56 |
| *130 3* | **Benfleet (84)** (RWArmstrong) **5-9-9** LDettori(15) (in tch tl outpcd fnl 2f) | ½ | 12 | 13/2 3 | 77 | 57 |
| 449 20 | **Old Provence (75)** (RHarris) **6-9-0** AMackay(16) (b: chsd ldrs tl wknd 4f out) | 3 | 13 | 33/1 | 64 | 44 |
| | **Bob's Ploy (90)** (MHTompkins) **4-10-0** PRobinson(2) (in tch tl wknd fnl 4f) | 2½ | 14 | 14/1 | 76 | 55 |
| | **Saltando (IRE) (57)** (PatMitchell) **5-7-7**(3) NVarley(9) (in tch tl wknd 3f out) | 5 | 15 | 66/1 | 36 | 16 |

(SP 118.5%) **15 Rn**

**2m 28.8** (-1.70) CSF £48.81 CT £251.59 TOTE £9.90: £2.50 £2.40 £2.00 (£23.80) Trio £33.50 OWNER Mr Alex Gorrie (NEWMARKET)
LONG HANDICAP Saltando (IRE) 7-0
WEIGHT FOR AGE 4yo-1lb

**Progression**, fit from All-Weather racing, won this in most emphatic style to show that, when caught in the mood, he is quite useful. (9/1)
**Speed to Lead (IRE)** gave the impression that he would be all the better for this and looked in trouble some way out, but he did battle, and is off a mark that should bring him success before long. (5/1)
**Opera Buff (IRE)** looked a hard ride here, getting short of room and then hanging, but he was finishing well, albeit too late. Longer distances are needed. (11/2)
**Fahs (USA)** travelled like a dream for much of the trip but just failed to see it out. To give him the benefit, he probably needed this, and decent handicaps should be found. (11/2)
**Dont Shoot Fairies** ran a useful race and should be all the better for it. (25/1)
**Statajack (IRE)** was always having to work hard to improve and failed to make any impression, but this was still a big improvement on his last All-Weather effort. (25/1)
**Bob's Ploy** (14/1: 12/1-20/1)

## 683 NGK SPARK PLUGS BARTLOW MAIDEN STKS (2-Y.O F) (Class D)

4-45 (4-48) **5f (Rowley)** £4,113.00 (£1,224.00: £582.00: £261.00) Stalls: High GOING minus 0.48 sec per fur (F)

| | Horse | Dist | Pos | SP | RR | SF |
|---|---|---|---|---|---|---|
| | **Carmine Lake (IRE)** (PWChapple-Hyam) **2-8-11** JReid(3) (leggy: unf: a gng wl: led wl over 1f out: qcknd: rn green ins fnl f) | — | 1 | 1/2 1 | 79 | 43 |

| | Horse | | SP | RR | SF |
|---|---|---|---|---|---|
| | **Dame Laura (IRE)** (PFICole) **2-8-11** TQuinn(5) (leggy: dwlt: hdwy u.p ½-wy: hung lft & styd on fnl f: no ch w wnr)....2½ | **2** | 20/1 | 71 | 35 |
| | **Silca Key Silca** (MRChannon) **2-8-11** RHughes(2) (lt-f: scope: cl up: led after 2f out tl wl over 1f out: sn btn)....2½ | **3** | 25/1 | 63 | 27 |
| 569[4] | **Dowry** (RHannon) **2-8-11** PatEddery(6) (led 2f: sn outpcd)....3½ | **4** | 9/1[3] | 52 | 16 |
| | **Wooderine (USA)** (MBell) **2-8-11** MFenton(4) (neat: outpcd & bhd fr ½-wy)....3 | **5** | 6/1[2] | 42 | 6 |
| | **Simply Times (USA)** (WAO'Gorman) **2-8-11** EmmaO'Gorman(1) (cmpt: s.s: gd hdwy to chse ldrs ½-wy: hung lft & sn wknd: fell fnl 50y).... | **F** | 10/1 | — | — |
| | | | (SP 108.7%) | **6 Rn** | |

**59.35 secs** (0.65) CSF £9.37 TOTE £1.50: £1.20 £2.30 (£6.20) OWNER Mr R. E. Sangster (MARLBOROUGH) BRED Swettenham Stud

**Carmine Lake (IRE)**, backed as though this was a foregone conclusion, never looked in danger, despite running green late on. There is obviously better to come. (1/2)

**Dame Laura (IRE)**, very fit, was clueless early on but did respond to pressure, albeit in vain as far as winning was concerned. (20/1)

**Silca Key Silca** showed plenty of early toe but was left struggling once the favourite pressed the button approaching the final furlong. Her action suggests that easier ground might help. (25/1)

**569 Dowry**, outpaced by halfway, was then not given a hard time and should appreciate the kindness. (9/1: 5/1-10/1)

**Wooderine (USA)** needed this and was soon left behind. (6/1: 5/2-13/2)

**Simply Times (USA)** has an awful action but, after a very slow start, still showed a terrific turn of foot to get into it halfway, only then to tire badly and fall in the closing stages. (10/1: 8/1-16/1)

## 684 WOOD DITTON MAIDEN STKS (3-Y.O) (Class D)

5-20 (5-22) **1m (Rowley)** £5,799.50 (£1,736.00: £833.00: £381.50) Stalls: High GOING minus 0.48 sec per fur (F)

| Horse | | SP | RR | SF |
|---|---|---|---|---|
| **Farasan (IRE)** (HRACecil) **3-9-0** GCarter(18) (trckd ldrs: qcknd to chal ins fnl f: rdn to ld last stride)....— | **1** | 16/1 | 99 | 66 |
| **Whitewater Affair** (MRStoute) **3-8-9** TQuinn(8) (w'like: leggy: sn cl up: led 2f out: hrd rdn ins fnl f: r.o: jst ct)....s.h | **2** | 14/1 | 94 | 61 |
| **Shantou (USA)** (JHMGosden) **3-9-0** LDettori(2) (neat: chsd ldrs: hdwy over 1f out: kpt on wl)....2½ | **3** | 9/1[3] | 94 | 61 |
| **Hismagicmoment (USA)** (PWChapple-Hyam) **3-9-0** JReid(9) (w'like: leggy: a chsng ldrs: nt qckn appr fnl f)..2 | **4** | 13/2[2] | 90 | 57 |
| **Hareb (USA)** (JWHills) **3-9-0** JWeaver(15) (w'like: a cl up: chal 2f out: one pce appr fnl f)....1 | **5** | 33/1 | 88 | 55 |
| **Chabrol (CAN)** (HRACecil) **3-9-0** WRyan(16) (gd sort: led 6f: styd on one pce)....hd | **6** | 10/1 | 88 | 55 |
| **Amfortas (IRE)** (CEBrittain) **3-9-0** BDoyle(5) (cmpt: bit bkwd: in tch: effrt 3f out: hdwy 2f out: nt qckn fnl f)....1 | **7** | 16/1 | 86 | 53 |
| **Master Boots** (DRLoder) **3-9-0** RHughes(19) (wl grwn: chsd ldrs tl outpcd fnl 2f)....1½ | **8** | 7/2[1] | 83 | 50 |
| **Robusta (IRE)** (ACStewart) **3-8-9** SWhitworth(6) (cmpt: scope: hdwy ½-wy: sn rdn: no imp)....1½ | **9** | 33/1 | 75 | 42 |
| **Yom Jameel (IRE)** (MRStoute) **3-9-0** KBradshaw(12) (w'like: mid div: rdn 3f out: no imp)....2 | **10** | 33/1 | 76 | 43 |
| **Lepikha (USA)** (BWHills) **3-8-9** BThomson(11) (chsd ldrs 6f)....s.h | **11** | 25/1 | 71 | 38 |
| **Mubarhin (USA)** (JLDunlop) **3-9-0** WCarson(13) (cmpt: lw: hld up & bhd: n.d)....2½ | **12** | 7/2[1] | 71 | 38 |
| **Gulliver** (BWHills) **3-9-0** PatEddery(4) (gd sort: leggy: hld up & bhd: n.d)....hd | **13** | 10/1 | 70 | 37 |
| **Manaloj (USA)** (PTWalwyn) **3-9-0** RHills(3) (leggy: scope: lw: in tch tl rdn & wknd fnl 3f)....½ | **14** | 25/1 | 69 | 36 |
| **Charnwood Jack (USA)** (RHarris) **3-9-0** AMackay(14) (gd sort: outpcd ½-wy: sn bhd)....1¾ | **15** | 50/1 | 66 | 33 |
| **Nuzu (IRE)** (BWHills) **3-9-0** MHills(10) (w'like: outpcd ½-wy: n.d after)....s.h | **16** | 25/1 | 66 | 33 |
| **Shavinsky** (PHowling) **3-9-0** RCochrane(7) (w'like: scope: s.s: a bhd)....3 | **17** | 50/1 | 60 | 27 |
| **Slievenamon** (JEBanks) **3-9-0** JQuinn(20) (mid div & drvn along ½-wy: n.d)....2 | **18** | 50/1 | 56 | 23 |
| **Shahrur (USA)** (ACStewart) **3-9-0** DHarrison(21) (wl grwn: bkwd: a outpcd & bhd)....s.h | **19** | 33/1 | 56 | 23 |
| **Areed Al Ola (USA)** (ACStewart) **3-9-0** MJKinane(17) (w'like: scope: a bhd)....7 | **20** | 16/1 | 42 | 9 |
| | | (SP 139.5%) | **20 Rn** | |

**1m 36.62** (-0.68) CSF £221.70 TOTE £27.00: £5.60 £6.80 £3.50 (£492.00) Trio £375.50; £476.00 to Newmarket 18/4/96 OWNER Prince A A Faisal (NEWMARKET) BRED Yeomanstown Lodge Stud

STEWARDS' ENQUIRY T.Quinn susp. 26-27/4/96 (excessive use of whip). Cecil fined £50 (declaring incorrect jockey).

**Farasan (IRE)** looks the type to improve with time and he travelled well in the race. Quickening in good style when a gap appeared, he certainly knew his job. (16/1)

**Whitewater Affair** has a lot to like about her and ran a super race, but was just caught, despite keeping on well. Her turn should come. (14/1)

**Shantou (USA)** put in a useful effort and was given a kind introduction when obviously beaten, but still finished quite well. (9/1: 5/1-10/1)

**Hismagicmoment (USA)** ran a useful race and was certainly not knocked about in the closing stages. He should be kept in mind for a similar event. (13/2: 4/1-7/1)

**Hareb (USA)** has a decent look about him and ran well but, judging from his action, he might well apppreciate some give in the ground. (33/1)

**Chabrol (CAN)** will be all the better for this. (10/1: 8/1-12/1)

**Amfortas (IRE)**, a useful sort, needed this but showed fair ability. (16/1)

**Master Boots** took the eye in the paddock but his action to post left a lot to be desired, and he was left struggling in the last couple of furlongs. Perhaps easier ground will see improvement. (7/2: 3/1-2/1)

**Mubarhin (USA)** seemed none too happy on the ground and was allowed to come home in his own time. (7/2: op 9/4)

**Gulliver** took a strong hold on the way down. His rider seemed intent on settling him and he failed to get anywhere near. (10/1: 6/1-12/1)

T/Jkpt: Not won; £14,279.51 to Newmarket 18/4/96. T/Plpt: £216.10 (134.61 Tckts). T/Qdpt: £10.60 (225.66 Tckts). AA

# PONTEFRACT (L-H) (Good)

## Wednesday April 17th

WEATHER: overcast

## 685 STRAWBERRY HILL MEDIAN AUCTION MAIDEN STKS (2-Y.O) (Class E)

2-45 (2-46) **5f** £2,996.00 (£908.00: £444.00: £212.00) Stalls: Low GOING minus 0.16 sec per fur (GF)

| | Horse | | SP | RR | SF |
|---|---|---|---|---|---|
| 490[4] | **Foot Battalion (IRE)** (RHollinshead) **2-8-9**(5) FLynch(2) (lw: outpcd ½-wy: gd hdwy over 1f out: styd on wl to ld nr fin)....— | **1** | 14/1 | 73 | 26 |
| 557[2] | **Swino** (PDEvans) **2-9-0** KFallon(7) (lw: a chsng ldrs: led wl ins fnl f: jst ct)....s.h | **2** | 13/2 | 73 | 26 |
| 596[2] | **Wait For Rosie** (MRChannon) **2-8-9** KDarley(11) (w ldr: led over 1f out tl wl ins fnl f)....1 | **3** | 100/30[1] | 65 | 18 |
| 523[2] | **Nervous Rex** (WRMuir) **2-9-0** Jean-PierreLopez(5) (lw: led tl over 1f out: wknd towards fin)....1½ | **4** | 5/1[3] | 65 | 18 |

452[7] **Highland Pass (IRE)** (MMcCormack) **2-9-0** JFortune(6) (chsd ldrs: rdn ½-wy: kpt on same pce appr fnl f)...1¼ **5** 8/1 61 14
596[3] **Hello Dolly (IRE)** (KTIvory) **2-8-2**(7) CScally(12) (racd wd: chsd ldrs: rdn ½-wy: kpt on)....hd **6** 16/1 56 9
**Pandiculation** (EWeymes) **2-8-11**(3) DRMcCabe(8) (str: cmpt: bit bkwd: mid div: hdwy over 1f out: styd on towards fin)....1½ **7** 12/1 56 · 9
452[4] **Fan of Vent-Axia** (CNAllen) **2-9-0** CHodgson(1) (lw: in tch: drvn along ½-wy: no imp) ....¾ **8** 9/2[2] 53 6
569[7] **Rebuke** (RFJohnsonHoughton) **2-9-0** ACulhane(3) (hld up: stdy hdwy over 1f out: nvr nr to chal)....2 **9** 12/1 47 —
**For Old Times Sake** (JBerry) **2-9-0** JCarroll(10) (unf: s.s: a bhd) ....s.h **10** 15/2 47 —
618[4] **Our Future (IRE)** (MJohnston) **2-9-0** TWilliams(4) (bit bkwd: s.i.s: a outpcd & sn drvn along)....7 **11** 16/1 24 —
568[5] **Classic Partygoer** (MWEasterby) **2-9-0** MBirch(9) (outpcd fr ½-wy: virtually p.u fnl f)....dist **12** 14/1 — —
(SP 134.6%) **12 Rn**

**64.4 secs** (3.00) CSF £105.80 TOTE £20.70. £6.00 £2.50 £1.40 (£105.80) Trio £50.10 OWNER Mr A. S. Hill (UPPER LONGDON) BRED Ennistown Stud

STEWARDS' ENQUIRY Lopez susp. 26-27/4/96 (incorrect use of whip).

**490 Foot Battalion (IRE)**, who is crying out for six furlongs, found this stiff uphill finish ideal. Finishing with a flourish, he led in the last stride. (14/1)

**557 Swino** forced his head in front in the final 50 yards, only to have the prize whipped from under him on the line. (13/2)

**596 Wait For Rosie**, a keen type, looked sure to win when taking it up once in line for home but, with the pace having been fast, her legs turned to jelly near the line. She is sure to find an opening. (100/30)

**523 Nervous Rex** seemed to set a strong pace with his rider free with his use of the stick. His stride shortened considerably near the line. (5/1)

**Highland Pass (IRE)**, who looked very fit, seemed to appreciate the better ground. (8/1: op 16/1)

**Pandiculation**, a burly newcomer, shaped by no means badly and there is better to come in time. (12/1)

**Rebuke** is not without some ability. (12/1)

## 686 RACING CHANNEL H'CAP (0-80) (3-Y.O F) (Class D)

3-20 (3-20) **6f** £5,754.00 (£1,722.00: £826.00: £378.00) Stalls: Low GOING minus 0.16 sec per fur (GF)

SP RR SF

524* **Splicing (70)** (WJHaggas) **3-8-13** KFallon(8) (lw: chsd ldrs: led over 1f out: r.o wl) ....— **1** 6/1[3] 81 48
548[7] **Whittle Rock (78)** (EJAlston) **3-9-7** SDWilliams(4) (in tch: hdwy over 1f out: styd on ins fnl f) ....2½ **2** 16/1 82 49
**Royal Ceilidh (IRE) (69)** (DenysSmith) **3-8-12** JFortune(1) (bit bkwd: mde most tl over 1f out: no ex ins fnl f) ....¾ **3** 8/1 71 38
525[17] **May Queen Megan (55)** (MrsALMKing) **3-7-12** AGarth(12) (a chsng ldrs: styd on one pce fnl 2f)....1¼ **4** 25/1 54 21
*529** **Sondos (67)** (JWHills) **3-8-5**(5) MHenry(13) (a chsng ldrs: rdn 2f out: styd on same pce)....½ **5** 4/1[1] 65 32
**Antonias Melody (69)** (SRBowring) **3-8-7**(5) CTeague(14) (bit bkwd: trckd ldrs: effrt 2f out: kpt on one pce) .1¼ **6** 14/1 63 30
525[4] **Sweet Nature (IRE) (64)** (WJarvis) **3-8-4**(3) DRMcCabe(2) (lw: hld up & bhd: swtchd rt over 1f out: swtchd lft & stdy hdwy: nvr plcd to chal) ....½ **7** 9/2[2] 57 24
*276** **Charming Bride (62)** (SCWilliams) **3-8-5** KDarley(3) (hld up & bhd: stdy hdwy 2f out: nvr plcd to chal) ....1¼ **8** 9/1 52 19
**Lawn Order (53)** (MrsJRRamsden) **3-7-10** NKennedy(6) (bit bkwd: outpcd: sme hdwy over 1f out: nvr nr ldrs) ....s.h **9** 25/1 43 10
**Miss Waterline (75)** (PDEvans) **3-8-11**(7) HayleyWilliams(16) (mid div: effrt on outside over 2f out: sn wknd)....hd **10** 33/1 64 31
**Daffodil Express (IRE) (53)** (MJRyan) **3-7-7**(3) DWright(7) (bit bkwd: swtg: w ldrs tl wknd 2f out) ....3½ **11** 33/1 33 —
595[18] **Eccentric Dancer (53)** (MPBielby) **3-7-10** NCarlisle(10) (s.i.s: a in rr) ....½ **12** 50/1 32 —
**Gladys Althorpe (IRE) (59)** (JLEyre) **3-8-2** RLappin(9) (bit bkwd: a outpcd & bhd)....2 **13** 17/2 32 —
525[21] **Pharaoh's Joy (63)** (JWPayne) **3-8-6**ow1 MTebbutt(11) (a outpcd: bhd fnl 2f)....10 **14** 20/1 10 —
550[5] **Ewar Sunrise (77)** (CEBrittain) **3-9-6** GDuffield(5) (disp ld to ½-wy: sn wknd)....2 **15** 14/1 18 —
(SP 123.6%) **15 Rn**

**1m 17.0** (2.70) CSF £89.85 CT £732.46 TOTE £5.80: £2.50 £4.00 £2.90 (£101.60) Trio £88.50 OWNER Mr Tony Hirschfeld (NEWMARKET) BRED Cheveley Park Stud Ltd

LONG HANDICAP Lawn Order 7-9 Daffodil Express (IRE) 7-8 Eccentric Dancer 7-7

**524* Splicing**, who looked in tremendous condition, was well suited by the step up to six and scored in most decisive fashion. (6/1)

**548 Whittle Rock** ran well under topweight, sticking on gamely inside the last. (16/1)

**Royal Ceilidh (IRE)**, who looked in need of the outing, showed bags of toe. This is surprising as she won over seven last year. (8/1)

**468 May Queen Megan**, badly drawn last time, ran right up to her best. (25/1)

**529* Sondos**, who won on the All-Weather last time, was made to look very one-paced. (4/1)

**Antonias Melody**, who looked in need of the outing, took a keen grip. (14/1: op 7/1)

**525 Sweet Nature (IRE)** was given a strange ride. Well drawn in two, she was dropped right out but switched to the outside over a furlong out when she saw daylight and, for some reason, her rider then decided to go inside. She is a good deal better than her finishing position suggests. (9/2)

**Charming Bride**, absent since winning at Lingfield in February, was dropped right out. Picking up ground on the bridle once in line for home, she appeared to finish full of running and is definitely one to keep an eye on. (9/1: 7/1-12/1)

**Lawn Order** showed a glimmer of ability and there might be better to come. (25/1)

## 687 LADY BALK MAIDEN STKS (I) (3-Y.O+) (Class D)

3-50 (3-51) **1m 2f 6y** £3,176.25 (£960.00: £467.50: £221.25) Stalls: Low GOING minus 0.16 sec per fur (GF)

SP RR SF

**Election Day (IRE)** (MRStoute) **4-9-13** KDarley(7) (lw: dwlt s: sn chsng ldrs: rdn over 3f out: rn green & wandered over 1f out: styd on wl to ld nr fin)....— **1** 7/4[2] 92 54
**Axford (USA)** (PWChapple-Hyam) **3-8-5**(5) RHavlin(5) (trckd ldr: led 2f out: sn qcknd: hdd & bmpd nr fin).....nk **2** 13/8[1] 92 37
**Sweetness Herself** (MJRyan) **3-8-5** PBloomfield(3) (a chsng ldrs: one pce fnl 3f)....9 **3** 9/1[3] 72 17
**Hugwity (75)** (BHanbury) **4-9-10**(3) JStack(2) (b: b.nr hind: bit bkwd: led to 2f out: one pce)....1 **4** 12/1 76 38
**Flocheck (USA)** (JLDunlop) **3-8-10** TSprake(4) (hld up & bhd: styd on fnl 2f: nt rch ldrs) ....2½ **5** 16/1 72 17
494[4] **Kathryn's Pet** (MrsMReveley) **3-8-5** ACulhane(10) (hld up: swtchd outside & stdy hdwy over 1f out: nvr plcd to chal)....2 **6** 33/1 63 8
**Capstone** (WJarvis) **3-8-6**ow1 MTebbutt(8) (b.hind: hld up: effrt over 3f out: n.d)....3½ **7** 33/1 59 3
528[5] **Needle Match** (CFWall) **3-8-10** GDuffield(1) (swtg: trckd ldrs: effrt over 3f out: wknd over 2f out)....5 **8** 33/1 55 —
**Liberatrice (FR)** (EALDunlop) **3-8-5** KFallon(6) (sn outpcd & pushed along: bhd fnl 4f)....2½ **9** 16/1 46 —
**Elashath (USA)** (JHMGosden) **3-8-10** JCarroll(12) (bit bkwd: sn prom: pushed along over 3f out: sn outpcd) ....5 **10** 12/1 43 —
**South Sea Bubble (IRE)** (LMCumani) **4-9-8** OUrbina(11) (bit bkwd: hld up: pushed along 4f out: n.d)....¾ **11** 16/1 37 —

| | | | | SP | RR | SF |
|---|---|---|---|---|---|---|
| 613[15] | **Nordisk Legend** (MrsDThomson) **4-9-10**(3) OPears(9) (prom: rdn 4f out: sn wl bhd: t.o) | dist | **12** | 500/1 | — | — |

(SP 126.5%) **12 Rn**

**2m 13.9** (5.60) CSF £5.20 TOTE £3.00: £1.70 £1.20 £2.60 (£2.60) Trio £18.90 OWNER Lord Weinstock & The Hon Simon Weinstock (NEWMARKET) BRED Ballymacoll Stud Farm Ltd
WEIGHT FOR AGE 3yo-17lb
OFFICIAL EXPLANATION **Kathryn's Pet: the jockey stated that his instructions were to settle the filly as she she had run too free last time, and was a doubtful stayer.**
**Election Day (IRE)**, a typical looking son of Sadler's Wells, is out of a Yorkshire Oaks winner. With just one outing last year behind him, he still has plenty to learn but, proving willing under pressure, he forced his head in front near the line. He is capable of a good deal better, especially over further. (7/4)
**Axford (USA)**, a very narrow type, showed plenty of knee-action going to post. He looked sure to win when quickening three or four lengths clear off the bend, but was worn down near the finish. A drop back to a mile will be no problem. (13/8: Evens-7/4)
**Sweetness Herself** was left well behind in the home straight. (9/1)
**Hugwity**, stepping up in distance, made the running but was left for dead on the bend. (12/1)
**Flocheck (USA)**, coltish in the paddock, was staying on when it was all over. Now qualified for handicaps, he is capable of better over further. (16/1)
**494 Kathryn's Pet** was settled right off the pace. Running on in smooth style when it was all over, she is definitely capable of better and might be suited by a drop back in distance. (33/1)

## 688 OSSETT (S) H'CAP (0-60) (3-Y.O+) (Class G)

4-25 (4-25) **1m 4y** £2,763.00 (£768.00: £369.00) Stalls: Low GOING minus 0.16 sec per fur (GF)

| | | | | SP | RR | SF |
|---|---|---|---|---|---|---|
| 561[4] | **Raindeer Quest (40)** (JLEyre) **4-8-5**(5) MHenry(10) (a in tch: hdwy to ld over 2f out: sn clr: pushed out) | — | **1** | 6/1[2] | 54 | 35 |
| | **My Handsome Prince (40)** (PJBevan) **4-8-10v**[1] NCarlisle(4) (s.i.s: gd hdwy on outside 2f out: hung lft & kpt on ins fnl: nt rch ldrs) | 2½ | **2** | 33/1 | 49 | 30 |
| 615[11] | **Waterlord (IRE) (40)** (DNicholls) **6-8-10** AlexGreaves(2) (a in tch: styd on same pce appr fnl f) | 1¼ | **3** | 8/1 | 47 | 28 |
| 479[9] | **Framed (IRE) (53)** (SCWilliams) **6-9-9** KDarley(6) (b: in tch: effrt & n.m.r over 2f out: kpt on same pce) | 1¾ | **4** | 7/2[1] | 56 | 37 |
| *73*[11] | **Absolute Ruler (IRE) (41)** (JLHarris) **5-8-8v**[1](3) PMcCabe(16) (bhd tl styd on fnl 2f) | ¾ | **5** | 25/1 | 43 | 24 |
| 586[12] | **Self Expression (51)** (MrsJRRamsden) **8-9-7** KFallon(9) (hld up & bhd: hdwy on ins over 2f out: kpt on: nvr nr ldrs) | 2 | **6** | 7/1[3] | 49 | 30 |
| 509[9] | **Appeal Again (IRE) (55)** (MrsJRRamsden) **3-8-11** DeanMcKeown(7) (stdd s: hld up & bhd: gd hdwy 2f out: nvr nr ldrs) | 3 | **7** | 25/1 | 47 | 14 |
| *373*[5] | **Night Time (58)** (AStreeter) **4-9-9**(5) CTeague(8) (lw: sn bhd & drvn along: sme hdwy 2f out: n.d) | 4 | **8** | 33/1 | 42 | 23 |
| 549[2] | **Noeprob (USA) (43)** (RJHodges) **6-8-10**(3) DRMcCabe(11) (lw: nvr bttr than mid div) | nk | **9** | 6/1[2] | 26 | 7 |
| *196*[10] | **Just Flamenco (50)** (MJRyan) **5-9-6** PBloomfield(3) (trckd ldrs: effrt over 2f out: wknd over 1f out) | 1 | **10** | 12/1 | 31 | 12 |
| *284*[5] | **Hawwam (52)** (EJAlston) **10-9-8** SDWilliams(20) (lw: chsd ldrs: led over 3f out tl over 2f out: sn wknd) | 5 | **11** | 12/1 | 23 | 4 |
| 527[9] | **East Barns (IRE) (43)** (SGollings) **8-8-13b** VHalliday(1) (mid div & sn drvn along: n.d) | nk | **12** | 20/1 | 13 | — |
| 527[3] | **Pine Essence (USA) (50)** (JLEyre) **5-9-6** RLappin(5) (mid div: effrt over 3f out: wkng whn n.m.r over 1f out) | ½ | **13** | 6/1[2] | 19 | — |
| *518*[7] | **Battle Colours (IRE) (43)** (DonEnricoIncisa) **7-8-13** KimTinkler(14) (chsd ldrs tl wknd 3f out) | 4 | **14** | 20/1 | 4 | — |
| *499*[9] | **Total Rach (IRE) (54)** (RIngram) **4-9-10b** DeclanO'Shea(15) (a bhd) | 3 | **15** | 20/1 | 9 | — |
| *369*[8] | **Timely Example (USA) (49)** (BRCambidge) **5-9-5** NAdams(17) (a bhd & sn drvn along) | 5 | **16** | 50/1 | — | — |
| *336*[7] | **Prince Rudolf (IRE) (41)** (MrsNMacauley) **4-8-6v**(5) AmandaSanders(13) (led tl over 3f out: sn lost pl) | 5 | **17** | 33/1 | — | — |
| | **My Brave Girl (51)** (BRichmond) **4-9-7** JCarroll(12) (bit bkwd: bhd fnl 3f) | 1¼ | **18** | 33/1 | — | — |

(SP 139.8%) **18 Rn**

**1m 46.2** (4.70) CSF £181.43 CT £1559.55 TOTE £7.90: £1.70 £8.20 £3.50 £1.90 (£79.40) Trio £267.90; £301.97 to Newmarket 18/4/96 OWNER Mr Steve Macdonald (HAMBLETON) BRED Stetchworth Park Stud Ltd
WEIGHT FOR AGE 3yo-14lb
No bid
**561 Raindeer Quest**, who had no luck in running first time, took this in most decisive fashion. (6/1)
**My Handsome Prince**, still a maiden after twelve previous outings, was tried in a visor. Giving his rider problems, he might have troubled the winner had he shown more co-operation. (33/1)
**Waterlord (IRE)** is suited by more give. (8/1)
**Framed (IRE)**, having his first run in a handicap, came in for plenty of market support. Tightened up going into the bend, when he saw daylight, he could do no more than keep on at the same pace. (7/2: op 6/1)
**Absolute Ruler (IRE)**, who showed bits and pieces of form in Ireland last year, was tried in a visor and was staying on late in the day. (25/1)
**Self Expression** is now on a long losing sequence. (7/1)
**Appeal Again (IRE)** again showed ability. A keen-going type, he was dropped right out at the start. Picking up ground in good style on the home turn, he would be very interesting if dropped back in distance, as he looks a sprinter. (25/1)

## 689 WEFT GATE LIMITED STKS (0-80) (3-Y.O) (Class D)

5-00 (5-00) **1m 4y** £3,468.75 (£1,050.00: £512.50: £243.75) Stalls: Low GOING minus 0.16 sec per fur (GF)

| | | | | SP | RR | SF |
|---|---|---|---|---|---|---|
| | **Cheerful Aspect (IRE) (80)** (EALDunlop) **3-8-11** KFallon(7) (bit bkwd: sn drvn along: hdwy over 2f out: styd on wl u.p. to ld nr fin) | — | **1** | 13/2[3] | 88 | 49 |
| | **Arabian Story (80)** (LordHuntingdon) **3-8-11** TIves(2) (lw: b: led: qcknd clr 2f out: edgd rt 1f out: jst ct) | nk | **2** | 15/8[1] | 87 | 48 |
| | **Flying North (IRE) (80)** (MrsMReveley) **3-8-11** ACulhane(5) (bit bkwd: stdd s: hld up & bhd: gd hdwy & nt clr run over 1f out: swtchd ins: r.o strly nr fin) | hd | **3** | 20/1 | 87 | 48 |
| | **Lovely Prospect (75)** (RGuest) **3-8-8** JCarroll(1) (chsd ldrs tl wknd over 1f out) | 13 | **4** | 8/1 | 58 | 19 |
| | **Tasliya (USA) (78)** (JLDunlop) **3-8-8** KDarley(4) (chsd ldrs: drvn along over 3f out: wknd over 2f out) | 7 | **5** | 7/2[2] | 44 | 5 |
| | **Threesome (USA) (80)** (LMCumani) **3-8-8** OUrbina(3) (chsd ldr: rdn over 3f out: lost pl over 2f out) | 2½ | **6** | 7/2[2] | 39 | — |
| 589[12] | **Too Hasty (80)** (TDEasterby) **3-8-11** MBirch(6) (bit bkwd: chsd ldrs tl lost pl over 2f out) | 10 | **7** | 14/1 | 22 | — |

(SP 115.1%) **7 Rn**

**1m 44.9** (3.40) CSF £18.69 TOTE £7.50: £3.20 £1.70 (£13.70) OWNER Maktoum Al Maktoum (NEWMARKET) BRED Gainsborough Stud Management Ltd
**Cheerful Aspect (IRE)**, who looked in need of the outing, made his rider earn his fee. Responding to pressure, he got up near the line and will be suited by a step up in distance. (13/2)
**Arabian Story**, winner of his only outing at two, stands over plenty of ground but he is leggy and unfurnished. Setting his own pace, he looked to have it in the bag when quickening four lengths clear off the bend. Edging right a furlong out, letting the third up his inner, he was just caught. The experience will have done him a power of good and he must be counted a shade unlucky. (15/8)

**Flying North (IRE)**, a light-mouthed individual, races keenly. Dropped right out at the start, he met trouble once in line for home. When switched inside of the runner-up, he stayed on in tremendous style near the line. He looked in need of the outing and, if he goes on the right way, there are more races to be won with him. (20/1)
**Lovely Prospect**, a half-sister to Vindaloo, tired noticeably coming to the final furlong. (8/1)
**Tasliya (USA)**, struggling to keep up at halfway, dropped right out on the home turn. (7/2)
**Threesome (USA)**, a fluent mover, looked in need of the outing. Driven along to keep tabs on the favourite soon after halfway, she dropped right out turning in. Her two-year-old form was solid and she can surely do much better than this. (7/2)
**Too Hasty** (14/1: 16/1-25/1)

## 690 GARFORTH H'CAP (0-70) (3-Y.O+) (Class E)

5-30 (5-39) **1m 2f 6y** £3,470.00 (£1,040.00: £500.00: £230.00) Stalls: Low GOING minus 0.16 sec per fur (GF)

| | | | | SP | RR | SF |
|---|---|---|---|---|---|---|
| 628[2] | **Carlito Brigante (66)** (MrsJRRamsden) **4-9-10** KFallon(1) (lw: hld up: hdwy & swtchd over 2f out: qckned to ld over 1f out: sn clr: eased nr fin) | — | **1** | 11/4[1] | 81+ | 49 |
| 439[20] | **Curtelace (56)** (MrsMReveley) **6-9-0** KDarley(10) (hld up: hdwy 5f out: sn prom: n.m.r over 2f out: kpt on fnl f: no ch w wnr) | 2½ | **2** | 14/1 | 67 | 35 |
| 598[3] | **Locorotondo (IRE) (65)** (MBell) **5-9-2**(7) GFaulkner(3) (lw: trckd ldrs: effrt 2f out: kpt on same pce) | ¾ | **3** | 8/1[3] | 75 | 43 |
| | **Fighting Times (65)** (CASmith) **4-9-9** ACulhane(2) (b.hind: bhd: hdwy 3f out: styd on: nt rch ldrs) | 3½ | **4** | 50/1 | 69 | 37 |
| 508[2] | **Anchorena (58)** (JAHarris) **4-9-2v** JFEgan(13) (bhd tl styd on fnl 3f) | 1 | **5** | 14/1 | 61 | 29 |
| 546[2] | **Cliburnel News (IRE) (58)** (AStreeter) **6-8-11**(5) CTeague(4) (lw: chsd ldr: led over 3f out tl over 1f out: sn wknd) | ½ | **6** | 10/1 | — | — |
| 508[3] | **Chilly Lad (53)** (MJRyan) **5-8-11b** DBiggs(6) (chsd ldrs: effrt over 3f out: wknd over 1f out) | 2½ | **7** | 14/1 | 51 | 19 |
| 527[4] | **Dana Point (IRE) (61)** (TDBarron) **4-9-5** JFortune(17) (hld up & bhd: hdwy 2f out: nvr nr ldrs) | 1 | **8** | 12/1 | 57 | 25 |
| *372*[8] | **Media Express (66)** (MBrittain) **4-9-10** MWigham(12) (b: bhd: hdwy over 3f out: nvr nr ldrs) | 2½ | **9** | 50/1 | 58 | 26 |
| 589[10] | **Flyaway Blues (56)** (MrsMReveley) **4-9-0** DeanMcKeown(18) (bhd tl sme hdwy fnl 2f: n.d) | s.h | **10** | 33/1 | 48 | 16 |
| | **Askern (66)** (DHaydnJones) **5-9-10** LCharnock(9) (mid div: effrt over 2f out: sn wknd) | 1¼ | **11** | 25/1 | 56 | 24 |
| 598[2] | **Denomination (USA) (58)** (IABalding) **4-9-2** GDuffield(8) (lw: prom: sn rdn along: lost pl 3f out) | ½ | **12** | 6/1[2] | 47 | 15 |
| *486*[5] | **Spitfire Bridge (IRE) (51)** (MMcCormack) **4-8-9** MBirch(11) (chsd ldrs tl rdn & wknd over 3f out) | 10 | **13** | 16/1 | 24 | — |
| *501*[7] | **Labudd (USA) (54)** (RIngram) **6-8-12** DeclanO'Shea(14) (b: led tl over 3f out: sn wknd) | 1¼ | **14** | 33/1 | 25 | — |
| | **Segala (IRE) (70)** (JJO'Neill) **5-10-0** SDWilliams(7) (b: in tch tl lost pl 3f out) | 2½ | **15** | 33/1 | 37 | 5 |
| 547[7] | **Quillwork (USA) (63)** (MrsJCecil) **4-9-7** TIves(15) (rel to go to s: prom early: sn drvn along: wl bhd fnl 5f) | ½ | **16** | 20/1 | 30 | — |
| | **Our Main Man (53)** (RMWhitaker) **6-8-11** DaleGibson(19) (bkwd: a bhd & sn rdn along) | 4 | **17** | 16/1 | 13 | — |
| 612[8] | **Oakbury (IRE) (62)** (MissLCSiddall) **4-9-6b**[1] JCarroll(16) (chsd ldrs: drvn along over 4f out: lost pl 3f out) | 4 | **18** | 33/1 | 16 | — |
| | | | | (SP 124.9%) | **18 Rn** | |

**2m 14.2** (5.90) CSF £38.89 CT £262.65 TOTE £3.50: £1.30 £3.00 £1.80 £15.60 (£28.30) Trio £148.30 OWNER Mr Bernard Hathaway (THIRSK) BRED Whitsbury Manor Stud

**628 Carlito Brigante**, turned out in the pink, came in for substantial market support and justified it in style. Showing a good turn of foot to take charge and racing with tremendous enthusiasm, he would have won by five or six lengths but for being eased right up near the finish. (11/4: 7/2-9/4)
**Curtelace**, a frustrating individual, has been tried in blinkers in the past. Tightened up by the winner on the home turn, he did just enough to secure second spot. (14/1)
**598 Locorotondo (IRE)**, who travelled strongly, ran a sound race. (8/1)
**Fighting Times**, who is hard to assess, was staying on when it was all over. (50/1)
**508 Anchorena**, with the visor on again, was putting in all her best work at the finish. She is worth a try over further. (14/1)
**546 Cliburnel News (IRE)**, racing over an inadequate trip, made the best of her way home. Still in need of the outing, she tired in the final furlong. (10/1: 8/1-12/1)
**527 Dana Point (IRE)**, a keen-going type, was settled in the rear. Putting in some pleasing work once in line for home, he looks capable of better. (12/1)

## 691 LADY BALK MAIDEN STKS (II) (3-Y.O+) (Class D)

6-00 (6-07) **1m 2f 6y** £3,176.25 (£960.00: £467.50: £221.25) Stalls: Low GOING minus 0.16 sec per fur (GF)

| | | | | SP | RR | SF |
|---|---|---|---|---|---|---|
| | **Don Vito** (RCharlton) **3-8-10** TSprake(10) (cmpt: sn trckng ldrs: led 2f out: cleverly) | — | **1** | 9/4[2] | 78+ | 25 |
| | **Kass Alhawa** (MRStoute) **3-8-10** DeanMcKeown(8) (trckd ldr: led over 2f out: sn hdd: no ch w wnr) | nk | **2** | 6/4[1] | 78 | 25 |
| | **Blurred (IRE)** (MHTompkins) **3-8-10** NDay(2) (lengthy: scope: bit bkwd: led tl over 2f out: one pce) | 6 | **3** | 25/1 | 68 | 15 |
| | **Velmez** (RGuest) **3-8-10** LCharnock(4) (bit bkwd: sn prom: effrt 3f out: styd on one pce fnl 2f) | hd | **4** | 20/1 | 68 | 15 |
| | **Veronica Franco** (JLDunlop) **3-8-5** GDuffield(9) (in tch: rdn & outpcd 4f out: styd on appr fnl f) | 1¾ | **5** | 20/1 | 60 | 7 |
| | **Old Irish** (LMCumani) **3-8-10** OUrbina(7) (bit bkwd: chsd ldrs tl rdn & wknd 2f out) | ½ | **6** | 14/1 | 64 | 11 |
| | **Doctor Green (FR)** (LordHuntingdon) **3-8-10** TIves(5) (sn bhd: rdn 4f out: styd on appr fnl f) | 2 | **7** | 8/1 | 61 | 8 |
| 472[7] | **Kashana (IRE)** (WStorey) **4-9-8** JFanning(1) (in tch: rdn & outpcd over 3f out: n.d after) | ¾ | **8** | 100/1 | 55 | 19 |
| 447[3] | **Ledgendry Line** (MrsMReveley) **3-8-10** KDarley(11) (hld up: effrt over 3f out: outpcd over 2f out: grad wknd) | ¾ | **9** | 7/1[3] | 59 | 6 |
| | **Rex Mundi** (PDEvans) **4-9-10**(3) PMcCabe(3) (bkwd: hld up: a in rr) | nk | **10** | 50/1 | 58 | 22 |
| 583[14] | **Raffles Rooster** (AGNewcombe) **4-9-10**(3) DRMcCabe(6) (dwlt s: rdn 5f out: sn lost tch) | 19 | **11** | 33/1 | 28 | — |
| | | | | (SP 120.3%) | **11 Rn** | |

**2m 15.6** (7.30) CSF £5.92 TOTE £3.10: £1.80 £1.30 £3.10 (£3.00) Trio £59.20 OWNER Mr Wafic Said (BECKHAMPTON) BRED Ridgecourt Stud

WEIGHT FOR AGE 3yo-17lb

**Don Vito**, a neat son of Generous, wore a tongue-strap on his debut. Travelling smoothly throughout, he won in very cheeky fashion. (9/4: 3/1-2/1)
**Kass Alhawa**, who had only one run at two, is a keen type. Making the best of his way home, it was soon obvious that the winner was simply toying with him. (6/4)
**Blurred (IRE)**, who has plenty of size and scope, is not the best of movers. After making the running, like the rest, he was swept aside once the race began in earnest. (25/1)
**Velmez** ran creditably considering he looked in need of the outing. (20/1)
**Veronica Franco**, an unfurnished, backward-looking type, shapes like a stayer. (20/1)
**Old Irish** still needs time but it remains to be seen whether he is any good or not. (14/1: op 7/1)

T/Plpt: £279.50 (47.14 Tckts). T/Qdpt: £12.10 (76.85 Tckts). WG

# 0678-NEWMARKET (R-H) (Good to firm)

## Thursday April 18th

WEATHER: overcast WIND: str across

## 692 EQUITY FINANCIAL COLLECTIONS H'CAP (0-90) (3-Y.O) (Class C)

2-00 (2-01) **6f (Rowley)** £6,420.00 (£1,920.00: £920.00: £420.00) Stalls: Centre GOING minus 0.38 sec per fur (F)

| | | | | SP | RR | SF |
|---|---|---|---|---|---|---|
| | **Galine (70)** (WAO'Gorman) **3-8-1** SSanders(2) (hld up: hdwy to ld 1f out: rdn out) | — | 1 | 8/1 | 83 | 51 |
| | **Wildwood Flower (75)** (RHannon) **3-8-1**(5) DaneO'Neill(14) (a.p: led over 3f out to 1f out: rallied u.p nr fin) | ½ | 2 | 7/1[3] | 87 | 55 |
| 493* | **Weetman's Weigh (IRE) (73)** (RHollinshead) **3-8-4** KFallon(1) (bhd: hdwy 2f out: swtchd lft appr fnl f: fin wl) | nk | 3 | 9/1 | 84 | 52 |
| *484[2]* | **Domak Amaam (IRE) (75)** (JHMGosden) **3-8-6** LDettori(10) (a.p: chal wl over 1f out: unable qckn fnl f) | ½ | 4 | 5/1[1] | 85 | 53 |
| *352[2]* | **Blue Flyer (IRE) (74)** (RIngram) **3-8-5** WWoods(4) (hld up: hdwy 2f out: n.m.r ent fnl f: kpt on) | 2 | 5 | 20/1 | 78 | 46 |
| 443[8] | **Princely Sound (66)** (MBell) **3-7-11** JQuinn(3) (in tch stands' side: effrt & ev ch 2f out: one pce fnl f) | ¾ | 6 | 6/1[2] | 68 | 36 |
| | **Night Parade (USA) (90)** (PWChapple-Hyam) **3-9-7** JReid(11) (bit bkwd: w ldrs centre tl rdn & wknd over 1f out) | 1½ | 7 | 20/1 | 88 | 56 |
| | **Akalim (80)** (DMorley) **3-8-11** WCarson(13) (bkwd: slt ld over 2f: drvn & ev ch 2f out: eased whn btn fnl f) | 6 | 8 | 10/1 | 62 | 30 |
| *232[4]* | **Banzhaf (USA) (80)** (GLMoore) **3-8-11** SWhitworth(15) (in tch far side: drvn along 3f out: no imp) | 1¼ | 9 | 33/1 | 59 | 27 |
| 525[2] | **Sea Danzig (70)** (PHowling) **3-8-1**ow2 PaulEddery(5) (bhd: hrd rdn ½-wy: no imp) | ½ | 10 | 6/1[2] | 48 | 14 |
| | **Xenophon of Cunaxa (IRE) (75)** (MJFetherston-Godley) **3-8-6** PatEddery(9) (in tch tl outpcd fnl 3f) | s.h | 11 | 8/1 | 52 | 20 |
| *531** | **Victim of Love (68)** (RCharlton) **3-7-8**(5) MHenry(12) (in tch centre: rdn & outpcd over 2f out) | ¾ | 12 | 14/1 | 43 | 11 |
| | **Blue Suede Hoofs (72)** (BJMeehan) **3-8-3** BDoyle(16) (bkwd: disp ld over 3f: sn lost tch) | s.h | 13 | 25/1 | 47 | 15 |
| *488[6]* | **Badger Bay (IRE) (70)** (CADwyer) **3-7-12**(3) NVarley(6) (lw: outpcd & bhd fr ½-wy) | 4 | 14 | 33/1 | 35 | 3 |
| | **Sonic Mail (78)** (KWMcAuliffe) **3-8-9** JFEgan(7) (b.hind: outpcd: a bhd) | 1 | 15 | 33/1 | 40 | 8 |

(SP 127.9%) **15 Rn**

**1m 11.98** (0.18) CSF £61.59 CT £488.40 TOTE £12.40: £4.10 £2.60 £2.50 (£37.80) Trio £194.50 OWNER Mr S. Fustok (NEWMARKET) BRED Deerfield Farm

OFFICIAL EXPLANATION **Xenophon of Cunaxa (IRE): hung badly right and was diffcult to ride.**

**Galine** did not impress to post but she showed the right vibes on the return journey, swooping to lead entering the final furlong and galloping on strongly to the line. (8/1)

**Wildwood Flower** showed plenty of speed to share the lead to the furlong marker and even then did not accept defeat until the post had been reached. (7/1)

**493* Weetman's Weigh (IRE)** needs far more cut in the ground than he had here, but he had the edge in fitness and stayed on strongly up the hill to be nearest at the finish. (9/1)

**484 Domak Amaam (IRE)**, who had a pipe-opener on the All-Weather last month, went with the pace and had every chance until getting tapped for toe in the final 100 yards. An initial success is long overdue. (5/1)

**Blue Flyer (IRE)**, returning to sprinting, could be said to have run extremely well in this company but he does need further, especially when the ground rides so fast. (20/1)

**Princely Sound**, in behind the leaders on the stands' side, put in his bid to join issue two furlongs out, but the pace did not drop and he was hard at work and feeling the strain in the Dip. (6/1: 4/1-13/2)

**Xenophon of Cunaxa (IRE)** (8/1: 5/1-9/1)

## 693 NGK SPARK PLUGS H'CAP (0-95) (3-Y.O) (Class C)

2-35 (2-36) **1m 2f (Rowley)** £5,952.00 (£1,776.00: £848.00: £384.00) Stalls: Centre GOING minus 0.38 sec per fur (F)

| | | | | SP | RR | SF |
|---|---|---|---|---|---|---|
| | **Prize Giving (87)** (GWragg) **3-9-6** MHills(2) (h.d.w: hld up: hdwy to ld over 3f out: sn clr: eased fnl f) | — | 1 | 9/1 | 104 | 64 |
| 447[5] | **Three Hills (82)** (BWHills) **3-9-1** WCarson(3) (trckd ldrs: rdn wl over 2f out: kpt on ins fnl f: no ch w wnr) | 3 | 2 | 6/1[3] | 94 | 54 |
| | **Select Few (80)** (LMCumani) **3-8-13** LDettori(9) (b.hind: w ldrs: rdn along 3f out: sn outpcd) | 1¼ | 3 | 11/4[2] | 90 | 50 |
| | **Daunting Destiny (BEL) (77)** (RHannon) **3-8-5**(5) DaneO'Neill(8) (bit bkwd: trckd ldrs: pushed along 3f out: kpt on same pce) | 2 | 4 | 25/1 | 84 | 44 |
| 444* | **Jackson Hill (88)** (RCharlton) **3-9-7** PatEddery(10) (led over 6f: sn rdn & outpcd: btn whn hmpd ins fnl f) | 1½ | 5 | 9/4[1] | 93 | 53 |
| | **Dance On A Cloud (USA) (85)** (MRStoute) **3-9-4** TQuinn(6) (hld up: effrt 4f out: no imp) | 5 | 6 | 16/1 | 82 | 42 |
| *428[2]* | **Hamlet (IRE) (75)** (MBell) **3-8-8** MFenton(1) (chsd ldrs: pushed along 4f out: sn btn: b.b.v) | 6 | 7 | 14/1 | 62 | 22 |
| 509* | **Tabriz (72)** (JDBethell) **3-8-5** SSanders(7) (plld hrd: prom tl rdn & wknd 4f out) | 6 | 8 | 14/1 | 49 | 9 |
| | **Jean Pierre (63)** (JPearce) **3-7-10** GBardwell(5) (bhd: effrt u.p 4f out: nvr nr ldrs) | nk | 9 | 100/1 | 40 | — |
| *391[2]* | **Galapino (75)** (CEBrittain) **3-8-8** BDoyle(4) (lw: w ldrs: drvn along 3f out: sn wknd) | ½ | 10 | 16/1 | 51 | 11 |

(SP 111.7%) **10 Rn**

**2m 4.71** (1.11) CSF £54.88 CT £168.52 TOTE £10.90: £2.60 £2.10 £1.60 (£44.70) Trio £36.30 OWNER Lady Oppenheimer (NEWMARKET) BRED Hascombe and Valiant Studs

LONG HANDICAP Jean Pierre 7-4

OFFICIAL EXPLANATION **Jackson Hill: the jockey reported that the colt hung and was uncomfortable on the ground, so he was not able to ride him more vigorously.**

**Prize Giving** has strengthened up into a very attractive colt and the way he spreadeagled the field in this competitive handicap would suggest that we have not seen the best of him yet. (9/1: 12/1-8/1)

**447 Three Hills,** who has not raced on ground as lively as this, was throwing out distress signals passing the Bushes. He is flattered to finish so close. (6/1: 4/1-7/1)

**Select Few** ran up to his mark considering he needed the outing, and the way he stayed on in the latter stages suggested another couple of furlongs would not come amiss. (11/4)

**Daunting Destiny (BEL)**, strugggling with the pace from some way out, is certainly not short on stamina. (25/1)

**444* Jackson Hill**, a heavy-topped colt who will always perform better when he can get his toe in, got left behind running into the Dip and the fact that he was impeded inside the final furlong, had little bearing on his finishing position. (9/4)

**Galapino** was meeting better company here than he has met on the All-Weather and was shaken off with ease well over two furlongs out. (16/1)

## 694 FEILDEN STKS (Listed) (3-Y.O) (Class A)

3-05 (3-08) **1m 1f (Rowley)** £11,267.60 (£4,168.40: £1,999.20: £816.00: £323.00: £125.80) Stalls: Centre GOING minus 0.38 sec per fur (F)

| | | | SP | RR | SF |
|---|---|---|---|---|---|
| **Storm Trooper (USA) (112)** (HRACecil) **3-8-11** PatEddery(2) (a gng wl: led over 2f out: sn clr: v.easily) | — | 1 | 2/1[1] | 114+ | 78 |
| **St Mawes (FR)** (JLDunlop) **3-8-11** TQuinn(5) (trckd ldrs: kpt on u.p fnl 2f: no ch w wnr) | 4 | 2 | 14/1 | 107 | 71 |

**Jack Jennings (107)** (BAMcMahon) **3-8-11** GCarter(3) (disp ld: led over 3f out tl over 2f out: kpt on one pce) .1 **3** 14/1 105 69
**Weet-A-Minute (IRE) (100)** (RHollinshead) **3-9-0** KFallon(10) (lw: hld up: effrt u.p 2f out: styd on fnl f) ...........nk **4** 33/1 108 72
**Tawkil (USA)** (BWHills) **3-8-11** WCarson(9) (lw: hld up & bhd: hdwy 2f out: edgd lft: nvr able to chal) .............2 **5** 7/1 101 65
**Heron Island (IRE)** (PWChapple-Hyam) **3-8-11** JReid(7) (lw: led over 5f: wknd appr fnl f) ..............................¾ **6** 6/1 3 100 64
**Mawwal (USA) (113)** (RWArmstrong) **3-8-11** RHills(6) (plld hrd: chsd ldrs over 6f) ...........................................7 **7** 11/1 87 51
574[2] **Centre Stalls (IRE) (107)** (RFJohnsonHoughton) **3-8-11** BThomson(12) (hld up: hdwy over 4f out: sn rdn along & wknd: t.o) ....................................................13 **8** 9/1 64 28
**Bonarelli (IRE) (104)** (MRStoute) **3-9-0** MJKinane(8) (h.d.w: prom: drvn along 4f out: sn lost tch: t.o) ............nk **9** 5/1 2 67 31
570* **Prospector's Cove** (JPearce) **3-8-11** GBardwell(13) (a rr div: t.o)................................................1¼ **10** 14/1 61 25
574[9] **Believe Me (102)** (RHannon) **3-8-11** RHughes(11) (lw: trckd ldrs tl wknd qckly 3f out: t.o)............................22 **11** 33/1 22 —
(SP 121.0%) **11 Rn**

**1m 49.48** (-1.52) CSF £28.69 TOTE £3.10: £1.50 £3.80 £5.20 (£32.10) Trio £249.20 OWNER H R H Prince Fahd Salman (NEWMARKET) BRED Robert N. Clay and Airlie Stud

**Storm Trooper (USA)**, from a stable in cracking form, looked trained to the minute and, though he may prefer easier gorund, did not need to be let down to slaughter this opposition. (2/1)
**St Mawes (FR)** is not the most impressive of movers at the best of times and he looked far from fully wound up here. He gave of his best though and would seem to be a very progressive colt. (14/1)
**Jack Jennings** ran well all the way and stuck to his task up the hill to show a degree of promise for the future. (14/1)
**Weet-A-Minute (IRE)**, very free to post, did not begin to stay on until reaching the closing stages, and the longer trip looks a must. (33/1)
**Tawkil (USA)**, restrained in the rear, took closer order inside the last quarter-mile, but he was inclined to edge left towards the stands' rail, and was never able to land a blow. (7/1: 9/2-15/2)
**Heron Island (IRE)**, a still unfurnished colt, set a good pace for over five furlongs and did not fade until meeting the rising ground. These were new tactics for him and, on the evidence of this, more patient tactics seem to suit him best. (6/1: 7/2-13/2)
**Bonarelli (IRE)** has really developed since his two-year-old days and looked tremendous, but he turned in a most disappointing performance and it is to be hoped that this is a one-off. (5/1)

## 695 CRAVEN STKS (Gp 3) (3-Y.O C & G) (Class A)

3-40 (3-40) **1m (Rowley)** £19,692.00 (£7,092.00: £3,396.00: £1,380.00: £540.00) Stalls: Centre GOING minus 0.38 sec per fur (F) SP RR SF

**Beauchamp King (115)** (JLDunlop) **3-9-0** JReid(2) (lw: hld up & bhd: stdy hdwy 2f out: led ins fnl f: r.o strly)....................................................— **1** 9/2 2 122 61
**Alhaarth (IRE) (120)** (MajorWRHern) **3-9-0** WCarson(4) (h.d.w: bit bkwd: plld hrd: a.p: led over 1f out tl ins fnl f: r.o wl)....................................................nk **2** 1/2 1 121 60
**Polaris Flight (USA) (112)** (PWChapple-Hyam) **3-9-0** PatEddery(5) (h.d.w: chsd ldr: led 3f out: drifted lft: hdd & rdn over 1f out: sn btn)....................................................3½ **3** 25/1 114 53
**Pommard (IRE)** (JHMGosden) **3-8-9** LDettori(1) (bkwd: stdd s: racd alone stands' side over 5f: n.m.r, rdn & btn over 1f out)....................................................8 **4** 11/1 93 32
**Rio Duvida (119)** (DRLoder) **3-8-9** RHughes(3) (led 5f: sn drvn along: outpcd fnl 2f) ...............................nk **5** 10/1 3 93 32
(SP 106.1%) **5 Rn**

**1m 37.82** (0.52) CSF £6.80 TOTE £4.60: £1.50 £1.10 (£2.10) OWNER Mr E. Penser (ARUNDEL) BRED E. Penser

**Beauchamp King**, keen to post but content to settle once in action, produced a well-timed challenge to get the better of the favourite 200 yards out, and only needed to be kept up to his work to win a shade easier than the margin might suggest. His price has been slashed for a rematch in the 2000 Guineas and, as he is still to come in his coat, there could be more improvement to follow. (9/2)
**Alhaarth (IRE)** has thickened out since last year and is a very classy-looking individual, but he did look a gallop short of condition. Taking a strong hold under restraint, he did appear to hold the aces when nosing ahead in the Dip but, once the winner came on the scene, he always looked second best. The race was run slower than Standard which would not be in his favour and he will be relying on a true-run race in the 2000 Guineas if he is to gain his revenge. (1/2)
**Polaris Flight (USA)**, successful over ten furlongs on much softer ground in France in the autumn, did help share the pacemaking but, when the big two delivered their challenge, he had to admit the quickening tempo too much for him. He has done well physically since his two-year-old days and is not far behind the best. (25/1)
**Pommard (IRE)**, short on experience, did not impress to post. Steadied leaving the stalls and brought to race along under the stands' rail, he was found wanting when the field drifted over to join him at the Bushes and was already hard at work when a rival took his ground. (11/1: 5/1-12/1)
**Rio Duvida**, half a length behind Alhaarth in the Laurent-Perrier Champagne Stakes at Doncaster in the autumn, led on sufferance for five furlongs, but got left behind when the pace lifted into the Dip. He was the first beaten, but was turned out in peak-condition and can only improve on this when things are in his favour. (10/1: 6/1-11/1)

## 696 ALEX SCOTT MAIDEN STKS (3-Y.O C & G) (Class D)

4-10 (4-11) **7f (Rowley)** £5,026.00 (£1,498.00: £714.00: £322.00) Stalls: Centre GOING minus 0.38 sec per fur (F) SP RR SF

**Lionize (USA)** (PWChapple-Hyam) **3-8-11** JReid(2) (w'like: scope: a.p: led 1f out: shkn up & r.o wl) ............— **1** Evens 1 82 33
**Mutadarra (IRE)** (RWArmstrong) **3-8-11** WCarson(7) (led to 1f out: rallied & rdn ins fnl f: no ex nr fin)..........1¼ **2** 2/1 2 79 30
**Prime Light** (GWragg) **3-8-11** MHills(1) (neat: scope: prom: rdn over 3f out: nt qckn appr fnl f).....................3½ **3** 10/1 71 22
**Pegram (IRE)** (LMCumani) **3-8-11** LDettori(5) (w'like: scope: bkwd: s.s: sn rcvrd: effrt over 2f out: no imp) ..1¼ **4** 15/2 3 68 19
**Roushan** (JGMO'Shea) **3-8-11** JQuinn(8) (trckd ldrs tl drvn along & outpcd 2f out) .........................................¾ **5** 50/1 67 18
(SP 106.1%) **5 Rn**

**1m 27.09** (2.59) CSF £3.09 TOTE £1.90: £1.50 £1.30 (£1.80) OWNER Mr M. Tabor (MARLBOROUGH) BRED Bloomsbury Stud

**Lionize (USA)**, a newcomer with plenty of scope for improvement, did not need to be put to his best to score, and this highly-regarded colt will win again while fitness is at a premium. (Evens)
**Mutadarra (IRE)**, beaten a short-head at this track in the autumn, set out to make this a true test of stamina, but the winner was always stalking him and had the legs when it mattered. (2/1: 6/4-9/4)
**Prime Light**, who will benefit from easier ground, was off the bridle soon after halfway but he responded to firm driving and was only shaken off in the Dip. He should be able to win his share of races. (10/1: 6/1-12/1)
**Pegram (IRE)**, a strongly-made, good-looking colt carrying plenty of surplus condition, recovered from a tardy start to chase the leaders but earlier exertions took their toll and he was in trouble before reaching the final furlong. (15/2: 6/1-10/1)

## 697 E.B.F. STUNTNEY MAIDEN STKS (2-Y.O C & G) (Class D)

4-45 (4-47) **5f (Rowley)** £4,230.00 (£1,260.00: £600.00: £270.00) Stalls: Centre GOING minus 0.38 sec per fur (F) SP RR SF

**Fletcher** (PFICole) **2-8-11** TQuinn(6) (w'like: a.p: qcknd to ld wl ins fnl f: readily) .............................................— **1** 13/8 2 83+ 26

| | | | Pos | SP | RR | SF |
|---|---|---|---|---|---|---|
| 569[2] | **Rude Awakening** (GLewis) **2-8-11** PatEddery(5) (led: shkn up over 1f out: hdd & nt qckn wl ins fnl f) | ¾ | **2** | Evens[1] | 81 | 24 |
| 441[7] | **M T Vessel** (JRJenkins) **2-8-11** SWhitworth(1) (chsd ldrs 3f: outpcd over 1f out) | 9 | **3** | 40/1 | 52 | — |
| | **Dalmeny Dancer** (BJMeehan) **2-8-11** MTebbutt(3) (small: unf: dwlt: a bhd: outpcd fr ½-wy) | 2 | **4** | 16/1 | 45 | — |
| | **But Why** (CMurray) **2-8-11** MFenton(2) (cmpt: a in rr: lost tch fnl 2f) | 1½ | **5** | 25/1 | 41 | — |
| | **Maraud** (RWArmstrong) **2-8-11** MHills(4) (neat: unf: s.i.s: a outpcd) | s.h | **6** | 12/1[3] | 40 | — |
| | | | | (SP 108.0%) | | **6 Rn** |

**60.91 secs** (2.21) CSF £3.34 TOTE £2.40: £1.30 £1.10 (£1.40) OWNER H R H Prince Fahd Salman (WHATCOMBE) BRED Carroll Bloodstock Ltd

**Fletcher** looks the sort to improve with racing, but he took this without needing to get serious and he could have a bright future. (13/8)

**569 Rude Awakening** attempted to make every post a winning one and was in no mood to give best, but the winner proved to be much too good and he could not do much about it. (Evens)

**M T Vessel** did not impress on the way to the start, but he did show speed until past halfway, before having to admit his measure taken. (40/1)

**Maraud** (12/1: 6/1-14/1)

## 698 THETFORD CONDITIONS STKS (2-Y.O) (Class C)

5-20 (5-21) **5f (Rowley)** £5,524.80 (£1,908.80: £914.40: £372.00) Stalls: Centre GOING minus 0.38 sec per fur (F)

| | | | Pos | SP | RR | SF |
|---|---|---|---|---|---|---|
| 481* | **Muchea** (MRChannon) **2-9-4** RHughes(1) (broke wl: mde all: sn clr: canter) | — | **1** | 8/11[1] | 84+ | 39 |
| 569* | **Herecomestheknight** (MartynMeade) **2-8-13**(5) RHavlin(4) (lw: prom: shkn up 2f out: sn outpcd) | 3½ | **2** | 3/1[2] | 73 | 28 |
| | **Exit To Rio (CAN)** (MrsJRRamsden) **2-8-9** KFallon(2) (neat: s.s: bhd & outpcd tl r.o wl fnl f) | ½ | **3** | 7/1 | 62 | 17 |
| 476* | **Blue Movie** (MBell) **2-8-11**(7) GFaulkner(3) (chsd wnr: rdn 2f out: wknd ins fnl f) | ¾ | **4** | 5/1[3] | 69 | 24 |
| | | | | (SP 112.1%) | | **4 Rn** |

**60.47 secs** (1.77) CSF £3.31 TOTE £1.90 (£1.90) OWNER Albion Investments (UPPER LAMBOURN) BRED Lady Richard Wellesley

**481* Muchea** flew from the traps and made it all to win without a challenger in sight. He is one of the sharpest two-year-olds we have seen this term and it could take something useful to lower his colours. (8/11)

**569* Herecomestheknight** got off on terms this time, but he was under pressure and struggling two furlongs out and backers soon knew their fate. (3/1: 7/4-100/30)

**Exit To Rio (CAN)**, a chunky debutant, stood still as the stalls opened and was taken off his legs until past hallfway. Persevering, he was finding his stride up the hill and will be all the wiser next time. (7/1: 5/1-10/1)

**476* Blue Movie** could not cope with this fast ground, but he showed up in pursuit of the winner until fading going to the furlong pole.(5/1: 3/1-11/2)

T/Jkpt: Not won; £32,600.71 to Newbury 19/4/96. T/Plpt: £37.50 (897.59 Tckts). T/Qdpt: £2.20 (968.92 Tckts). IM/AA

# 0608-RIPON (R-H) (Good to firm)
## Thursday April 18th

WEATHER: cloudy WIND: almost nil

## 699 E.B.F. SHAROW MAIDEN STKS (2-Y.O) (Class D)

2-30 (2-31) **5f** £3,420.00 (£1,035.00: £505.00: £240.00) Stalls: Low GOING minus 0.38 sec per fur (F)

| | | | Pos | SP | RR | SF |
|---|---|---|---|---|---|---|
| | **Statesman** (MRChannon) **2-9-0** KDarley(2) (cmpt: mde virtually all: r.o wl) | — | **1** | 9/2[3] | 69 | 32 |
| | **Roman Imp (IRE)** (APJarvis) **2-9-0** JTate(10) (cmpt: sn chsng ldrs: ev ch over 1f out: wandered: nt qckn towards fin) | nk | **2** | 4/1[2] | 68 | 31 |
| | **Double Action** (TDEasterby) **2-9-0** MBirch(4) (w'like: scope: s.i.s: hdwy ½-wy: kpt on wl fnl f: fin 4th, 1¼l: plcd 3rd) | | **3** | 11/2 | — | 17 |
| | **Young Bigwig (IRE)** (JBerry) **2-9-0** JCarroll(7) (neat: sn chsng ldrs: rdn ½-wy: wknd over 1f out: fin 5th: 13/4l: plcd 4th) | | **4** | 8/1 | — | 12 |
| | **Plan For Profit (IRE)** (MJohnston) **2-9-0** JWeaver(1) (w'like: scope: leggy: s.s: rn green: sme hdwy ½-wy: nvr nr ldrs: fin 6th, nk: plcd 5th) | | **5** | 7/4[1] | — | 11 |
| | **Bold Brief** (DenysSmith) **2-9-0** LCharnock(6) (leggy: scope: s.i.s: sme hdwy ½-wy: wknd over 1f out) | 1 | **7** | 20/1 | — | 8 |
| 608[6] | **The Bee Man** (MWEasterby) **2-9-0** TIves(8) (spd 3f: sn wknd) | 1 | **8** | 20/1 | — | 5 |
| | **Ben's Ridge** (PCHaslam) **2-9-0** JFortune(9) (neat: unf: bit bkwd: sn rdn along: hdwy ½wy: sn chsng ldrs: wknd over 1f out) | nk | **9** | 16/1 | — | 4 |
| 441[5] | **Mr Fortywinks (IRE)** (JLEyre) **2-9-0** RLappin(5) (prom early: outpcd ½-wy: sn lost pl) | 1¾ | **10** | 12/1 | — | — |
| 557[5] | **Bolero Boy** (MWEasterby) **2-9-0** DaleGibson(3) (w ldrs: rdn 2f out: outpcd appr fnl f: fin 3rd, 3l: disq: plcd last) | | **D** | 12/1 | — | 21 |
| | | | | (SP 131.8%) | | **10 Rn** |

**60.4 secs** (2.00) CSF £24.63 TOTE £5.20: £2.00 £1.80 £1.70 (£27.00) Trio £28.50 OWNER Mr Stephen Crown (UPPER LAMBOURN) BRED S. Crown

STEWARDS' ENQUIRY Gibson susp. 27 & 29-30/4/96 (failure to weigh-in).

**Statesman**, who showed a fluent action going down, had certainly been taught his job. Breaking smartly, he had only to be pushed out to make sure. (9/2: op 5/2)

**Roman Imp (IRE)** did not impress with his action going down. Drawn on the wide outside, he wandered under pressure but, to his credit, kept going all the way to the line. (4/1: op 5/2)

**Double Action**, a fair sort, shaped in promising fashion and can do much better. (11/2)

**Young Bigwig (IRE)** showed plenty of speed but was throwing out distress signals at halfway. (8/1)

**Plan For Profit (IRE)**, who has plenty of size and bags of scope, was very green going to post. Falling out of the traps, he showed definite signs of greenness but this will have opened his eyes and, by reputation, he is capable of a great deal better. (7/4)

**557 Bolero Boy**, a keen-going type, showed plenty of toe but was left behind coming to the final furlong. Unfortunately for his supporters, his jockey forgot to weigh in. (12/1: op 8/1)

## 700 COPT HEWICK CLAIMING STKS (3-Y.O+) (Class F)

3-00 (3-00) **5f** £2,599.60 (£730.60: £169.90: £169.90) Stalls: Low GOING minus 0.38 sec per fur (F)

| | | | Pos | SP | RR | SF |
|---|---|---|---|---|---|---|
| 600[8] | **Lago Di Varano (85)** (JBerry) **4-9-7b** JCarroll(6) (mde all: rdn & styd on wl fnl f) | — | **1** | 7/2[2] | 79 | 62 |
| 587[3] | **La Suquet (72)** (NTinkler) **4-9-4** TIves(7) (lw: trckd wnr: effrt over 1f out: unable qckn) | 1¾ | **2** | 100/30[1] | 70 | 53 |
| 601[19] | **John O'Dreams (48)** (MrsALMKing) **11-9-0** AGarth(5) (bkwd: reard s: hdwy ½-wy: n.m.r & swtchd rt over 1f out: kpt on) | 1¼ | **3** | 20/1 | 62 | 45 |

| | | | | SP | RR | SF |
|---|---|---|---|---|---|---|
| $389^{2}$ | **Sea-Deer (82)** (DWChapman) **7-9-5** ACulhane(2) (lw: a.p: effrt 2f out: kpt on same pce) | d.h | **3** | 9/2 | 67 | 50 |
| $316^{7}$ | **Super Rocky (73)** (RBastiman) **7-9-1**(5) HBastiman(8) (trckd ldrs: effrt & n.m.r over 1f out: sn wknd) | 2½ | **5** | 4/1 $^{3}$ | 60 | 43 |
| | **Comic Fantasy (AUS) (83)** (MartynWane) **3-8-11b** KDarley(10) (chsd ldrs: edgd lft & wknd over 1f out) | 2½ | **6** | 4/1 $^{3}$ | 53 | 26 |
| $607^{11}$ | **Rankaidade (30)** (DonEnricoIncisa) **5-8-9** KimTinkler(9) (chsd ldrs: wkng whn sltly hmpd over 1f out) | hd | **7** | 50/1 | 41 | 24 |
| $626^{10}$ | **Old Hush Wing (IRE)** (PCHaslam) **3-8-10** JFortune(3) (s.i.s: a outpcd) | 1¾ | **8** | 20/1 | 47 | 20 |
| $213^{10}$ | **Ohnonotagain** (BWMurray) **4-8-10** TWilliams(4) (sn drvn along & outpcd) | 1½ | **9** | 50/1 | 32 | 15 |
| $302^{5}$ | **Bitch (37)** (GPKelly) **4-8-4b**(5) PRoberts(1) (s.i.s: a bhd) | 3 | **10** | 50/1 | 21 | 4 |
| | | | | (SP 118.9%) | **10 Rn** | |

**59.0 secs** (0.60) CSF £15.18 TOTE £4.90: £1.60 £1.40 SD £0.80 JO £1.70 (£7.90) Trio LG LS SD £4.50, LG LS JO £24.70 OWNER Mr Norman Jackson (COCKERHAM) BRED Miss S. E. Hall

WEIGHT FOR AGE 3yo-10lb

Lago Di Varano clmd RWhitaker £10,000

**Lago Di Varano**, dropped in distance and with the blinkers back on, broke smartly to get the favoured stands' side and he only had to be kept up to his work. He was a useful two-year-old but whether he is capable of running to his present handicap mark remains to be seen. (7/2)

**587 La Suquet**, in pursuit of the winner throughout, looked a serious threat at halfway but, when the cards were played, she was unable to get in a real blow. (100/30)

**John O'Dreams** reared up leaving the stalls. Forced to switch to get a run, he was sticking on in solid fashion at the line. He seemed to run a lot better here than he was entitled to at the weights. (20/1)

**Sea-Deer** stuck on strongly, and connections must be hoping he will be better suited by turf than the All-Weather. (9/2)

**Super Rocky** was starting to struggle when forced to check over a furlong out. He is a real summer firm ground specialist. (4/1)

**Comic Fantasy (AUS)**, having her first run for her new yard, came off a straight line as she tired. (4/1)

## 701 COCKED HAT 'COCK O'THE NORTH' H'CAP (0-90) (3-Y.O) (Class C)

3-30 (3-31) **1m** £5,493.50 (£1,664.00: £813.00: £387.50) Stalls: High GOING minus 0.15 sec per fur (GF)

| | | | | SP | RR | SF |
|---|---|---|---|---|---|---|
| $575^{7}$ | **Al Shafa (84)** (JLDunlop) **3-9-6** KDarley(1) (lw: hld up: effrt 3f out: led over 1f out: edgd lft: r.o u.p) | — | **1** | 9/2 $^{2}$ | 94 | 55 |
| $566^{6}$ | **Kazimiera (IRE) (69)** (CWCElsey) **3-8-0**(5) PFessey(3) (chsd ldrs: led over 2f out tl over 1f out: hung rt & styd on) | nk | **2** | 33/1 | 78 | 39 |
| | **Taufan Boy (75)** (PWHarris) **3-8-11** GHind(8) (trckd ldrs: effrt & n.m.r over 2f out: styd on wl ins fnl f) | 2½ | **3** | 6/1 | 79 | 40 |
| $528^{3}$ | **Fursan (USA) (72)** (NAGraham) **3-8-8** DHarrison(2) (lw: outpcd & drvn along over 3f out: styd on wl ins fnl f) | nk | **4** | 9/4 $^{1}$ | 76 | 37 |
| $509^{2}$ | **Theatre Magic (61)** (SRBowring) **3-7-11** NCarlisle(5) (lw: a chsng ldrs: rdn & n.m.r over 1f out: one pce) | 1 | **5** | 11/2 $^{3}$ | 63 | 24 |
| $445^{4}$ | **Catherine's Choice (70)** (JDBethell) **3-8-6** JFortune(9) (chsd ldr: lft in ld appr st: hdd over 2f out: hung rt: wknd appr fnl f) | 1½ | **6** | 12/1 | 69 | 30 |
| $550^{7}$ | **Yezza (IRE) (70)** (APJarvis) **3-8-6** JTate(7) (s.i.s: a in rr) | 3½ | **7** | 16/1 | 62 | 23 |
| $595^{3}$ | **Whispering Dawn (62)** (MRChannon) **3-7-12** FNorton(4) (s.i.s: hdwy u.p 3f out: sn wl outpcd) | 1 | **8** | 9/2 $^{2}$ | 52 | 13 |
| | **Jo Mell (85)** (TDEasterby) **3-9-7** MBirch(6) (h.d.w: bit bkwd: plld hrd: led tl rn v.wd ent st: hung bdly lft: lost pl over 2f out: eased) | 19 | **9** | 9/1 | 37 | — |
| | | | | (SP 123.3%) | **9 Rn** | |

**1m 41.2** (3.50) CSF £105.15 CT £842.77 TOTE £6.40: £2.00 £6.10 £1.60 (£191.00) Trio £315.30; £359.77 to Newbury 19/4/96. OWNER Prince A A Faisal (ARUNDEL) BRED Fonthill Stud

**Al Shafa**, who came in for plenty of market support, had to wait for an opening. (9/2)

**Kazimiera (IRE)**, upped in distance, again gave her rider problems but, to her credit, stuck on all the way to the line. (33/1)

**Taufan Boy**, who did not have much luck in running halfway up the straight, was staying on in most determined fashion at the finish under a considerate ride. He was clearly well suited by the step up to a mile. (6/1)

**528 Fursan (USA)** only got going late in the day and will be suited by further. (9/4)

**509 Theatre Magic** ran his usual game race but the Handicapper looks to have his measure at present. (11/2)

**Jo Mell**, who has done well over the winter, looked on the burly side. Still a very keen sort, he ran very wide off the bend and, having got his tongue over the bit, his rider had no option but to ease him up in the final quarter-mile. When everything goes right, he looks an interesting sort. (9/1)

## 702 FARM FED CHICKEN H'CAP (0-80) (3-Y.O) (Class D)

4-00 (4-01) **1m 4f 60y** £3,623.10 (£1,096.80: £535.40: £254.70) Stalls: High GOING minus 0.15 sec per fur (GF)

| | | | | SP | RR | SF |
|---|---|---|---|---|---|---|
| $593^{2}$ | **Nabhaan (IRE) (74)** (DMorley) **3-9-3** RCochrane(6) (lw: chsd ldrs: effrt 4f out: led over 1f out: hung rt & sn clr: comf) | — | **1** | 11/8 $^{1}$ | 85+ | 22 |
| 483* | **Jackson Park (64)** (TDEasterby) **3-8-7** MBirch(7) (led tl over 1f out: kpt on: no ch w wnr) | 3 | **2** | 9/2 $^{3}$ | 71 | 8 |
| $444^{7}$ | **Burnt Offering (65)** (CEBrittain) **3-8-8** GDuffield(4) (hld up: effrt over 3f out: styd on fnl f) | nk | **3** | 9/1 | 72 | 9 |
| $567^{5}$ | **Samim (USA) (78)** (JLDunlop) **3-9-7b**1 KDarley(5) (trckd ldrs: rdn over 2f out: n.m.r: no imp over 1f out) | 1 | **4** | 11/2 | 83 | 20 |
| $541^{8}$ | **Classic Lover (IRE) (71)** (RHarris) **3-9-0** AMackay(2) (chsd ldrs: effrt & ev ch over 3f out: edgd rt & wknd over 1f out) | 7 | **5** | 14/1 | 67 | 4 |
| $614^{2}$ | **Nose No Bounds (IRE) (70)** (MJohnston) **3-8-13** JWeaver(3) (lw: hld up: effrt & outpcd over 4f out: rdn 2f out: no imp) | nk | **6** | 4/1 $^{2}$ | 66 | 3 |
| | **Hal Hoo Yaroom (70)** (MajorWRHern) **3-8-13** WRyan(1) (sn trckng ldrs: pushed along 4f out: lost pl over 2f out: eased) | 20 | **7** | 7/1 | 40 | — |
| | | | | (SP 124.8%) | **7 Rn** | |

**2m 44.4** (10.40) CSF £8.83 TOTE £2.50: £1.80 £2.40 (£7.00) OWNER Mr Hamdan Al Maktoum (NEWMARKET) BRED Shadwell Estate Company Limited

**593 Nabhaan (IRE)**, caught flat-footed early in the straight, won in very comfortable fashion in the end, despite a tendency to hang right when he was in front. Though he has had plenty of experience, he still gives the impression that he is something of a baby, and he has the potential to prove a good deal better than his current mark. (11/8: op 9/4)

**483* Jackson Park**, raised 6lb, set a modest pace. Quickening off the bend, he soon had them in trouble but, in the end, the winner proved much too good. (9/2: op 3/1)

**Burnt Offering** went flat early in the straight. Staying on in the final furlong, he might be suited by further. (9/1)

**567 Samim (USA)** went sweetly to post in the blinkers for the first time. Keen early on due to the modest pace, he had little room to work on the inner halfway up the straight but, when daylight came, he was not doing much. (11/2)

**614 Nose No Bounds (IRE)**, held up to get the trip in a slowly-run race, was caught badly flat-footed early in the straight. Under pressure two furlongs out, he found nothing. (4/1: op 5/2)

## 703 PAUL RHODES AND HIS MAIDEN STKS (I) (3-Y.O) (Class D)

4-30 (4-31) **1m** £3,192.50 (£965.00: £470.00: £222.50) Stalls: High GOING minus 0.15 sec per fur (GF)

| | | | | SP | RR | SF |
|---|---|---|---|---|---|---|
| | **Unreal City (IRE)** (HRACecil) **3-9-0** WRyan(8) (lw: mde all: styd on wl u.p) | — | 1 | 5/2[2] | 84+ | 36 |
| 526[3] | **Henry Island (IRE)** (GWragg) **3-9-0** AClark(15) (chsd ldrs: ev ch 1f out: nt qckn) | 1¾ | 2 | 11/2 | 81 | 33 |
| | **Catumbella (USA)** (JHMGosden) **3-8-9** JCarroll(14) (prom: effrt over 2f out: styd on same pce fnl f) | ¾ | 3 | 4/1[3] | 74 | 26 |
| | **Raheen (USA) (103)** (MRStoute) **3-9-0** DeanMcKeown(6) (lw: trckd ldrs: effrt & n.m.r 2f out: wknd fnl f) | ¾ | 4 | 2/1[1] | 78 | 30 |
| 584[9] | **Dispol Gem** (GROldroyd) **3-8-9** RCochrane(13) (a chsng ldrs: kpt on wl fnl 2f) | nk | 5 | 50/1 | 72 | 24 |
| 526[5] | **Absolute Utopia (USA)** (EALDunlop) **3-9-0** JTate(4) (trckd ldrs: chal over 2f out: wknd over 1f out) | 3 | 6 | 14/1 | 71 | 23 |
| | **No-Aman** (MajorWRHern) **3-9-0** TSprake(11) (rangy: bkwd: s.i.s: hdwy over 3f out: styd on fnl f) | 2½ | 7 | 14/1 | 66 | 18 |
| | **Penygarn Guv'nor** (JAGlover) **3-9-0** SDWilliams(12) (w'like: bkwd: mid div: effrt over 3f out: nvr nr ldrs) | 4 | 8 | 33/1 | 58 | 10 |
| | **Gulf of Siam (62)** (MissSEHall) **3-9-0** KDarley(5) (bit bkwd: unruly s: s.i.s: sme hdwy over 2f out: n.d) | ½ | 9 | 16/1 | 57 | 9 |
| 613[13] | **Riccarton** (PCalver) **3-9-0** MBirch(9) (nvr bttr than mid div) | 1¾ | 10 | 33/1 | 53 | 5 |
| | **Bright Pet** (MrsSJSmith) **3-8-9** NConnorton(10) (unf: bit bkwd: s.i.s: a in rr) | 5 | 11 | 50/1 | 38 | — |
| | **Miss Pravda** (PTWalwyn) **3-8-9** DHarrison(2) (in tch tl lost pl over 3f out) | 1¾ | 12 | 16/1 | 35 | — |
| | **Miss Prism** (JLDunlop) **3-8-9** GDuffield(1) (a rr div) | 1 | 13 | 16/1 | 33 | — |
| | **Nordic Gift (DEN)** (MrsDThomson) **3-9-0**(3)ow3 OPears(7) (unf: bhd fnl 3f) | 6 | 14 | 50/1 | 29 | — |
| | **Kudos Blue** (JDBethell) **3-8-9** TWilliams(3) (bit bkwd: hld up & plld hrd: jnd ldrs 6f out: lost pl over 3f out: sn bhd) | 10 | 15 | 50/1 | 1 | — |
| | | | | (SP 142.0%) | | **15 Rn** |

**1m 42.6** (4.90) CSF £19.10 TOTE £3.10: £1.30 £1.40 £1.90 (£5.50) Trio £12.50 OWNER Mr L. Marinopoulos (NEWMARKET) BRED Stilvi Compania Financiera S A

OFFICIAL EXPLANATION **Gulf of Siam: lost his action on the home turn.**

**Unreal City (IRE)**, a likable sort who was beaten only a neck by Prize Giving at Yarmouth on his only outing at two, was turned out in tremendous shape. He stuck on really strongly under pressure to get right on top in the closing stages and, likely to be suited by further, should enjoy further success. (5/2)

**526 Henry Island (IRE)** behaved himself at the stalls this time and, after being upsides coming to the final furlong, found the winner too strong in the closing stages. (11/2)

**Catumbella (USA)** was putting in some solid work near the line and is open to further improvement. (4/1)

**Raheen (USA)**, a keen type, was short of room halfway up the straight but faded coming to the final furlong. He undoubtedly has plenty of ability and might be worth a try over seven. (2/1: 6/4-9/4)

**Dispol Gem** belied her odds. Chasing the leaders throughout and keeping on in solid fashion, in the long run connections might regret this. The Handicapper will take no chances with her. (50/1)

**526 Absolute Utopia (USA)**, who showed plenty of knee-action, faded over a furlong out after having every chance. (14/1)

**No-Aman**, a backward type, showed plenty of knee-action going down. Staying on when it was all over, he looks capable of better over further, probably later on. (14/1)

## 704 NEWBY APPRENTICE H'CAP (0-70) (4-Y.O+) (Class E)

5-05 (5-06) **5f** £2,871.25 (£880.00: £437.50: £216.25) Stalls: Low GOING minus 0.38 sec per fur (F)

| | | | | SP | RR | SF |
|---|---|---|---|---|---|---|
| 601[2] | **Chadwell Hall (60)** (SRBowring) **5-9-7b**(3) JEdmunds(3) (lw: w ldr: led ins fnl f: all out) | — | 1 | 5/1[2] | 69 | 46 |
| | **Able Sheriff (44)** (MWEasterby) **4-8-8b** OliverCasey(1) (mde most: stmbld ½-wy: hdd ins fnl f: edgd rt & r.o) | hd | 2 | 12/1 | 53 | 30 |
| 592[11] | **Penny's Wishing (47)** (NBycroft) **4-8-11** JoHunnam(10) (mid div: hdwy ½-wy: styd on fnl f) | 2½ | 3 | 20/1 | 48 | 25 |
| *500*[2] | **Stand Tall (57)** (CWThornton) **4-8-11**(10) GMills(7) (lw: hld up: effrt ½-wy: styd on wl fnl f: nt rch ldrs) | 1 | 4 | 2/1[1] | 55 | 32 |
| 610[14] | **Maid O'Cannie (57)** (MWEasterby) **5-9-4b**(3) DSweeney(12) (s.i.s: stdy hdwy fnl f: nvr nr to chal) | hd | 5 | 14/1 | 54 | 31 |
| *407*[7] | **Cheeky Chappy (40)** (DWChapman) **5-7-13b**(5) RMullen(2) (chsd ldrs: hmpd ½-wy: wknd over 1f out) | nk | 6 | 7/1[3] | 36 | 13 |
| *207*[6] | **My Godson (38)** (JLEyre) **6-7-11b**(5) PDoe(9) (s.s: bhd tl hdwy over 1f out: nvr nr ldrs) | 2½ | 7 | 14/1 | 26 | 3 |
| *607*[14] | **Blue Lugana (40)** (NBycroft) **4-8-4** JWilkinson(6) (s.i.s: hdwy over 1f out: edgd rt: n.d) | s.h | 8 | 25/1 | 28 | 5 |
| 559[8] | **Kalar (51)** (DWChapman) **7-8-10b**(5) KSked(8) (chsd ldrs tl wknd over 1f out) | 2½ | 9 | 11/1 | 31 | 8 |
| 559[10] | **China Hand (IRE) (42)** (MartynWane) **4-8-6** JDennis(13) (in tch: rdn ½-wy: sn wknd) | nk | 10 | 20/1 | 21 | — |
| 559[6] | **Featherstone Lane (50)** (MissLCSiddall) **5-8-4v**(10) TSiddall(5) (outpcd & rdn ½-wy. n.d) | nk | 11 | 10/1 | 28 | 5 |
| 592[8] | **Arc Lamp (46)** (JAGlover) **10-8-4**(6)ow1 VictoriaAppleby(11) (bit bkwd: nvr wnt pce) | ½ | 12 | 12/1 | 23 | — |
| 587[19] | **Bajan Frontier (IRE) (41)** (FHLee) **4-8-0**(5) TField(4) (b.hind: chsd ldrs 3f: wknd qckly) | 10 | 13 | 25/1 | — | — |
| | | | | (SP 125.9%) | | **13 Rn** |

**60.1 secs** (1.70) CSF £60.97 CT £1,060.68 TOTE £6.10: £2.40 £3.00 £3.90 (£21.90) Trio £280.80 OWNER Mr D. H. Bowring (EDWINSTOWE) BRED J. C. and Mrs C. L. Owen

**601 Chadwell Hall**, racing wide of the runner-up, had nothing at all to spare at the line. His young rider continues to impress. (5/1)

**Able Sheriff**, who looked wintry, showed all his old speed. Stumbling at halfway, he battled on all the way to the line. (12/1)

**Penny's Wishing** came from a spell in the wilderness, staying on when it was all over for her promising young rider. (20/1)

**500 Stand Tall**, racing off a mark 23lb lower than on the All-Weather, was happy to sit off the pace. Picking up ground at halfway, he finished with a determined effort. Likely to be better suited by six, he probably needs a man on his back. There are handicaps to be won with him on turf. (2/1)

**Maid O'Cannie** was staying on in pleasing fashion near the line and will be suited by a step up to six. (14/1)

**Cheeky Chappy**, 15lb lower than on the All-Weather, was hampered by the stumbler. (7/1)

**Kalar** (11/1: 8/1-12/1)

## 705 PAUL RHODES AND HIS MAIDEN STKS (II) (3-Y.O) (Class D)

5-35 (5-36) **1m** £3,192.50 (£965.00: £470.00: £222.50) Stalls: High GOING minus 0.15 sec per fur (GF)

| | | | | SP | RR | SF |
|---|---|---|---|---|---|---|
| 472[2] | **Wixim (USA)** (RCharlton) **3-9-0** KDarley(13) (lw: chsd ldrs: hmpd on ins over 3f out: swtchd outside & qcknd to ld over 1f out: r.o wl) | — | 1 | 6/5[1] | 89+ | 24 |
| | **Fourdaned (IRE)** (PWHarris) **3-9-0** GHind(10) (lw: in tch: effrt over 2f out: kpt on fnl f: no ch w wnr) | 1¾ | 2 | 4/1[2] | 86 | 21 |
| 544[11] | **Lazali (USA)** (EALDunlop) **3-9-0** JTate(14) (led: clr over 3f out: hdd & wknd over 1f out) | 7 | 3 | 20/1 | 72 | 7 |
| 526[2] | **Iamus (100)** (PTWalwyn) **3-9-0** DHarrison(1) (lw: chsd ldrs: rdn & edgd rt over 2f out: wknd over 1f out) | 1 | 4 | 4/1[2] | 70 | 5 |
| 583[8] | **Royal Result (USA)** (MRStoute) **3-9-0** DeanMcKeown(11) (bhd tl styd on fnl 2f: nvr nr ldrs) | ½ | 5 | 10/1 | 69 | 4 |
| | **Perpetual Light** (JJQuinn) **3-8-9** DaleGibson(3) (bit bkwd: plld hrd: trckd ldr tl wknd over 2f out) | 1½ | 6 | 25/1 | 61 | — |
| 544[7] | **Tawafek (USA) (75)** (DMorley) **3-9-0** RCochrane(9) (s.i.s: bhd tl styd on appr fnl f) | 1¾ | 7 | 10/1 | 62 | — |
| | **Bollin Jacob** (TDEasterby) **3-9-0** MBirch(4) (cmpt: bit bkwd: in tch: grad wknd fnl 2f) | s.h | 8 | 25/1 | 62 | — |

| Horse | Dist | Pos | SP | RR | SF |
|---|---|---|---|---|---|
| **Raise A Ripple** (MrsDThomson) **3-9-0**[(3)ow3] OPears(8) (leggy: unf: nvr bttr than mid div) | 10 | **9** | 100/1 | 45 | — |
| **Indiphar** (FHLee) **3-8-9** JWeaver(12) (leggy: unf: s.i.s: a bhd) | 1¼ | **10** | 50/1 | 34 | — |
| **Salsian** (SCWilliams) **3-8-9** ACulhane(5) (hmpd s: a in rr) | 3 | **11** | 33/1 | 28 | — |
| **Celia's Rainbow** (MPBielby) **3-8-9** JFortune(7) (unf: a in rr) | nk | **12** | 100/1 | 28 | — |
| **Esquiline (USA)** (JHMGosden) **3-8-9** JCarroll(6) (lengthy: in tch: effrt over 3f out: sn wknd) | 2½ | **13** | 8/1[3] | 23 | — |
| **Latin Lover (GER)** (MJCamacho) **3-9-0** LCharnock(2) (w'like: scope: bit bkwd: s.s: a bhd) | 8 | **14** | 25/1 | 12 | — |

(SP 137.9%) **14 Rn**

**1m 43.8** (6.10) CSF £7.78 TOTE £2.10: £1.10 £1.90 £6.70 (£5.90) Trio £106.00 OWNER Mr K. Abdulla (BECKHAMPTON) BRED Juddmonte Farms

**472 Wixim (USA)**, who looked exceptionally well, overcame a bad bump just under half a mile from home. Switched outside to get a run, he showed a smart turn of foot and scored in most decisive fashion. Likely to be suited by further, he will be a very interesting proposition in handicap company. (6/5)

**Fourdaned (IRE)** has an awkward head carriage and, in the end, the winner proved far too good. Finishing clear second best, the Handicapper will take no chances with him. (4/1: 3/1-9/2)

**Lazali (USA)** stepped up considerably on his first effort. Sent clear early in the straight, he tired when headed. (20/1)

**526 Iamus**, who showed plenty of knee-action, gave the winner problems. He is obviously highly flattered by his fourth to Beauchamp King at Doncaster last back-end. (4/1: op 5/2)

**583 Royal Result (USA)**, staying on when it was all over, is open to further improvement. (10/1: 6/1-20/1)

**544 Tawafek (USA)**, staying on late in the day, is now qualified for a handicap mark and is likely to do better in that company. (10/1)

**Bollin Jacob** shaped by no means badly on his racecourse debut and should do better with another couple of runs under his belt, probably in handicap company. (25/1)

T/Plpt: £160.70 (76.12 Tckts). T/Qdpt: £42.80 (22.01 Tckts). WG

# NEWBURY (L-H) (Good becoming Good to soft)

## Friday April 19th

WEATHER: overcast WIND: mod against

## 706 BECKHAMPTON MAIDEN STKS (2-Y.O) (Class D)

2-10 (2-11) **5f 34y** £3,752.50 (£1,120.00: £535.00: £242.50) Stalls: Centre GOING: 0.49 sec per fur (GS)

| Horse | Dist | Pos | SP | RR | SF |
|---|---|---|---|---|---|
| **Daylight In Dubai (USA)** (PWChapple-Hyam) **2-9-0** KDarley(6) (neat: led over 3f: led ins fnl f: rdn out) | — | **1** | Evens[1] | 90+ | 34 |
| **Granny's Pet** (PFICole) **2-9-0** TQuinn(8) (scope: lw: a.p: led over 1f out tl ins fnl f: unable qckn) | 2 | **2** | 7/4[2] | 84+ | 28 |
| **Referendum (IRE)** (GLewis) **2-9-0** PaulEddery(1) (str: scope: bkwd: hld up: rdn over 2f out: one pce) | 3 | **3** | 14/1[3] | 75 | 19 |
| **Lucayan Beach** (BGubby) **2-9-0** LDettori(9) (w'like: bkwd: s.s: rdn over 2f out: hdwy over 1f out: one pce) | 2 | **4** | 33/1 | 68 | 12 |
| **Hangover Square (IRE)** (RHannon) **2-9-0** RHughes(13) (neat: lw: a.p: ev ch 2f out: wknd over 1f out) | 1¼ | **5** | 25/1 | 64 | 8 |
| **Petula Boy** (MMcCormack) **2-9-0** RCochrane(7) (neat: bit bkwd: outpcd: nvr nr to chal) | 3½ | **6** | 50/1 | 54 | — |
| **Eager To Please** (JBerry) **2-9-0** JCarroll(12) (lt-f: lw: hld up: rdn over 2f out: sn wknd) | nk | **7** | 16/1 | 53 | — |
| **Grovefair Flyer (IRE)** (BJMeehan) **2-9-0** MTebbutt(5) (neat: outpcd) | 2½ | **8** | 50/1 | 45 | — |
| **Pelham (IRE)** (RHannon) **2-9-0** PatEddery(3) (cmpt: bit bkwd: s.s: outpcd) | hd | **9** | 14/1[3] | 45 | — |
| **Dr Woodstock** (MartynMeade) **2-9-0** RPerham(4) (leggy: bhd fnl 2f) | 1¾ | **10** | 50/1 | 39 | — |
| **Rake Hey** (RFJohnsonHoughton) **2-9-0** JReid(10) (lt-f: s.s: a bhd) | hd | **11** | 50/1 | 39 | — |
| **Classic Mystery (IRE)** (BJMeehan) **2-9-0** BDoyle(2) (w'like: bhd fnl 2f) | 3½ | **12** | 50/1 | 28 | — |
| **Yanavanavano (IRE)** (GLewis) **2-8-11**(3) AWhelan(11) (w'like: bkwd: s.s: a bhd) | 1¼ | **13** | 50/1 | 24 | — |

(SP 124.1%) **13 Rn**

**66.21 secs** (6.01) CSF £3.14 TOTE £2.10: £1.40 £1.10 £2.10 (£2.20) Trio £7.60 OWNER Mr P. D. Savill (MARLBOROUGH) BRED Hargus Sexton & Sandra Ellsworth

**Daylight In Dubai (USA)**, a speedy sort who is a half-brother to high-class juvenile Sri Pekan, had burnt the runner-up off inside the final furlong. The first three could be quite useful, and he can score again. (Evens)

**Granny's Pet**, a scopey sort about whom there is plenty to like, looked in very good shape for this debut. He cruised into a slender lead below the distance and looked to have the winner's measure, but did not find what was required when let down. He should have no problems next time. (7/4)

**Referendum (IRE)** looked further forward physically than his rivals and could have been mistaken for a three-year-old. Despite looking far from fully wound up, he showed a lot of promise and, as he should come on a lot for this, should soon find a race. (14/1: 6/1-16/1)

**Lucayan Beach**, who carried plenty of condition for this debut and lost ground at the start, moved up encouragingly below the distance, only to then fail to make an impression. (33/1)

**Hangover Square (IRE)**, fit enough for this debut, raced up with the front two until tiring below the distance. (25/1)

**Pelham (IRE)** (14/1: 5/1-16/1)

## 707 PETER SMITH MEMORIAL MAIDEN STKS (3-Y.O) (Class D)

2-40 (2-41) **1m 3f 5y** £3,785.00 (£1,130.00: £540.00: £245.00) Stalls: Low GOING: 0.49 sec per fur (GS)

| Form | Horse | Dist | Pos | SP | RR | SF |
|---|---|---|---|---|---|---|
| | **Air Quest** (RCharlton) **3-9-0** PatEddery(7) (leggy: scope: a.p: led over 2f out: r.o wl) | — | **1** | 100/30[2] | 98+ | 65 |
| | **Set Adrift** (HRACecil) **3-9-0** WRyan(2) (w'like: scope: lw: led over 8f: unable qckn) | 5 | **2** | 15/8[1] | 91+ | 58 |
| | **Smilin N Wishin (USA)** (PWChapple-Hyam) **3-8-9** JReid(4) (b.hind: lost pl 7f out: r.o one pce fnl 3f) | hd | **3** | 100/30[2] | 86 | 53 |
| | **Mohawk River (IRE)** (MRStoute) **3-9-0** MHills(5) (w'like: scope: hdwy 5f out: rdn over 3f out: one pce) | 1¾ | **4** | 16/1 | 88 | 55 |
| | **Smart Play (USA)** (MrsJCecil) **3-9-0** TIves(11) (w'like: scope: bkwd: nvr nr to chal) | 10 | **5** | 33/1 | 74 | 41 |
| 570[5] | **Ewar Bold** (CEBrittain) **3-9-0** BDoyle(9) (chsd ldr over 9f out tl over 4f out: sn wknd) | 1½ | **6** | 66/1 | 71 | 38 |
| | **Enriched (IRE)** (JHMGosden) **3-8-9** LDettori(1) (wl grwn: a.p: rdn over 3f out: wknd over 2f out) | 3 | **7** | 12/1[3] | 62 | 29 |
| | **Age of Reality (USA)** (HCandy) **3-8-9** TQuinn(10) (a bhd) | 8 | **8** | 25/1 | 50 | 17 |
| | **Tribal Moon (IRE)** (LadyHerries) **3-9-0** KDarley(8) (w'like: bit bkwd: hdwy over 8f out: wknd over 3f out) | ½ | **9** | 33/1 | 55 | 22 |
| | **Santella Cape** (RHannon) **3-9-0** RPerham(3) (w'like: bit bkwd: s.s: a bhd) | 24 | **10** | 33/1 | 20 | — |
| 550[14] | **Remember Star** (AGNewcombe) **3-8-9** JCarroll(6) (b: bhd fnl 5f) | 10 | **11** | 100/1 | — | — |

(SP 109.7%) **11 Rn**

**2m 27.11** (9.91) CSF £8.77 TOTE £3.80: £1.80 £1.40 £1.30 (£3.50) Trio £3.60 OWNER Mr K. Abdulla (BECKHAMPTON) BRED Juddmonte Farms

**Air Quest**, quite a tall brother to Derby winner Quest for Fame, knew what was required. Sent on over two furlongs out, he lengthened in good style for a decisive victory. He can go on from here and will now be aimed at the Dee Stakes. (100/30: 2/1-7/2)

**Set Adrift**, quite a tall, well-muscled individual, looked in good shape in the paddock. Bowling along in front, he was headed over two furlongs out and then unable to cope with the useful winner. He looks a ready-made winner. (15/8)
**Smilin N Wishin (USA)** has not really filled out since last year, but was fit. Losing her pitch turning out of the back straight, she stayed on in the last three furlongs. (100/30: 9/4-7/2)
**Mohawk River (IRE)**, a good-sized if rather plain sort, moved up entering the straight, but could do no more in the final three furlongs. (16/1)
**Smart Play (USA)**, far from fit, was out with the washing until staying on past beaten horses. (33/1)
**Enriched (IRE)** (12/1: 4/1-14/1)

## 708 DUBAI DUTY FREE FRED DARLING STKS (Gp 3) (3-Y.O F) (Class A)

3-10 (3-11) **7f 64y (round)** £20,400.00 (£7,635.00: £3,667.50: £1,597.50) Stalls: Low GOING: 0.49 sec per fur (GS)

| | | | | SP | RR | SF |
|---|---|---|---|---|---|---|
| | **Bosra Sham (USA)** (HRACecil) **3-9-0** PatEddery(2) (h.d.w: lw: led 2f: led 3f out: impressive) | — | 1 | 2/9[1] | 115+ | 78 |
| | **Keepers Dawn (IRE) (90)** (RFJohnsonHoughton) **3-9-0** KDarley(5) (h.d.w: hld up: ev ch over 2f out: unable qckn) | 6 | 2 | 66/1 | 102 | 65 |
| 572[7] | **Sil Sila (IRE) (102)** (BSmart) **3-9-0** RCochrane(1) (rdn & hdwy on ins 2f out: one pce) | 2 | 3 | 33/1 | 97 | 60 |
| 572[3] | **Miss Universal (IRE) (105)** (CEBrittain) **3-9-0** BDoyle(8) (a.p: rdn 3f out: wknd over 2f out) | 1¾ | 4 | 25/1 | 94 | 57 |
| 572[4] | **Paloma Bay (IRE) (102)** (MBell) **3-9-0** MFenton(9) (s.s: nvr nr to chal) | 1½ | 5 | 25/1 | 90 | 53 |
| | **Silk Masque (USA)** (PWChapple-Hyam) **3-9-0** JReid(6) (hld up: rdn over 2f out: sn wknd) | s.h | 6 | 10/1[2] | 90 | 53 |
| | **Najiya (106)** (JLDunlop) **3-9-0** WCarson(4) (led over 5f out to 3f out: wknd over 1f out) | 5 | 7 | 14/1[3] | 79 | 42 |
| | **Please Suzanne (100)** (RHannon) **3-9-0** LDettori(7) (lost pl over 4f out: rallied over 1f out: eased whn btn fnl f) | 3½ | 8 | 16/1 | 72 | 35 |
| | **Flying Squaw (106)** (MRChannon) **3-9-0** RHughes(3) (hld up: rdn over 3f out: wknd over 2f out) | 10 | 9 | 20/1 | 50 | 13 |

(SP 120.3%) **9 Rn**

**1m 33.46** (5.36) CSF £19.37 TOTE £1.20: £1.00 £22.70 £3.60 (£70.30) Trio £517.70 OWNER Mr Wafic Said (NEWMARKET) BRED Gerald W. Leigh
OFFICIAL EXPLANATION **Flying Squaw: finished distressed.**
**Bosra Sham (USA)** has developed extremely well over the winter and, although still showing signs of holding onto her coat, looked in a different league to her rivals in the paddock. It was the same story in the race as she only needed to be shaken up to pull well clear in the final 200 yards for a highly impressive victory. Described as a lazy filly at home, she is sure to come on for this and there can be no doubting that she is an exceptionally high-class individual. The 1000 Guineas is at her mercy and it is going to take an extremely talented horse to lower her colours this season. (2/9)
**Keepers Dawn (IRE)** has really strengthened up during the winter. She looked out of her depth but ran really well and there are races to be won this term. (66/1)
**Sil Sila (IRE)**, rousted along to pick up along the rail two furlongs out, could then only find one pace. (33/1)
**572 Miss Universal (IRE)** was done with over two furlongs out. (25/1)
**572 Paloma Bay (IRE)** made a little late headway from the rear. (25/1)
**Silk Masque (USA)** has not really developed from last year and is still rather weak. (10/1: op 6/1)
**Najiya** (14/1: op 8/1)
**Flying Squaw** ran no race at all, and was later reported to have finished distressed. She may prove better at sprint distances. (20/1)

## 709 SCOTTISH EQUITABLE RATED STKS H'CAP (0-95) (3-Y.O) (Class C)

3-40 (3-40) **1m (straight)** £5,379.68 (£1,997.12: £963.56: £399.80: £164.90: £70.94) Stalls: Low GOING: 0.49 sec per fur (GS)

| | | | | SP | RR | SF |
|---|---|---|---|---|---|---|
| 493[4] | **Therhea (IRE) (77)** (BRMillman) **3-8-8** TQuinn(6) (lw: hld up: swtchd rt wl over 1f out: led ins fnl f: eased nr fin) | — | 1 | 9/2[3] | 87+ | 32 |
| | **Polar Prince (IRE) (90)** (MAJarvis) **3-9-7** PRobinson(2) (bit bkwd: led 1f: led over 1f out tl ins fnl f: unable qckn) | 5 | 2 | 8/1 | 90 | 35 |
| | **Carburton (88)** (JAGlover) **3-9-5** PaulEddery(4) (a.p: led over 2f out tl over 1f out: sn wknd) | 3½ | 3 | 2/1[1] | 81 | 26 |
| | **Ashjar (USA) (77)** (HThomsonJones) **3-8-8** RHills(5) (swtg: led 7f out tl over 2f out: wknd over 1f out) | 7 | 4 | 4/1[2] | 56 | 1 |
| 526[4] | **Decision Maker (IRE) (82)** (RHannon) **3-8-8**(5) DaneO'Neill(3) (nvr nr to chal) | 1¾ | 5 | 4/1[2] | 58 | 3 |
| | **Tsarnista (90)** (JLDunlop) **3-9-7** JReid(1) (swtg: a bhd) | 3 | 6 | 12/1 | 60 | 5 |
| | **Little Millie (76)** (PHayward) **3-8-2**(5) FLynch(7) (b.hind: hld up: rdn over 2f out: sn wknd) | 2 | 7 | 66/1 | 42 | — |

(SP 111.8%) **7 Rn**

**1m 46.79** (9.79) CSF £34.30 TOTE £5.70: £3.00 £2.70 (£38.20) OWNER Ray Gudge, Colin Lew Calvert (CULLOMPTON) BRED Mrs W. Hanson
LONG HANDICAP Little Millie 7-7
**493 Therhea (IRE)**, the paddock pick, lost his maiden tag at the tenth attempt. Switched right to get a clear passage entering the final two furlongs, he was given a few reminders to wake him up but, once he hit the front, he was eased down to make sure he did not win by too far. (9/2: 6/1-4/1)
**Polar Prince (IRE)** looked as though this run would do him good, and was firmly put in his place inside the final furlong. (8/1: 5/1-9/1)
**Carburton** went on over two furlongs out, but had little left once headed. (2/1)
**Ashjar (USA)** looked fit enough for this reappearance. (4/1)
**Tsarnista** (12/1: op 8/1)

## 710 BRIDGET MAIDEN STKS (3-Y.O F) (Class D)

4-15 (4-17) **7f** £4,012.50 (£1,200.00: £575.00: £262.50) Stalls: Centre GOING: 0.49 sec per fur (GS)

| | | | SP | RR | SF |
|---|---|---|---|---|---|
| **Satin Bell** (JLDunlop) **3-8-11** RHughes(10) (w'like: stdy hdwy over 1f out: led ins fnl f: comf) | — | 1 | 14/1 | 85 | 54 |
| **Aunty Jane** (BWHills) **3-8-11** MHills(12) (w'like: a.p: led 2f out tl ins fnl f: unable qckn) | 3½ | 2 | 11/2[2] | 77 | 46 |
| **Divine Quest** (HRACecil) **3-8-11** PatEddery(1) (w'like: scope: led 2f: ev ch wl over 1f out: one pce) | 6 | 3 | 7/2[1] | 63 | 32 |
| **Sandhill (IRE)** (JHMGosden) **3-8-11** LDettori(4) (w'like: s.s: rdn & hdwy over 2f out: one pce) | ¾ | 4 | 11/2[2] | 62 | 31 |
| **Whispered Melody** (PWHarris) **3-8-11** GHind(6) (unf: led 5f out to 2f out: wknd over 1f out) | 1½ | 5 | 33/1 | 58 | 27 |
| **Taking Liberties (IRE)** (PWChapple-Hyam) **3-8-11** JReid(15) (leggy: scope: no hdwy fnl 3f) | 1¼ | 6 | 7/2[1] | 55 | 24 |
| **Shalateeno** (MRChannon) **3-8-11** AGorman(9) (leggy: s.s: nvr nr to chal) | 1 | 7 | 33/1 | 53 | 22 |
| **Lunda (IRE)** (CEBrittain) **3-8-11** BDoyle(14) (str: scope: bit bkwd: s.s: nvr nrr) | hd | 8 | 16/1 | 53 | 22 |
| **Covered Girl (IRE)** (BWHills) **3-8-11** BThomson(17) (str: scope: bit bkwd: prom over 5f) | ½ | 9 | 16/1 | 52 | 21 |
| **Emy Coasting (USA)** (PFICole) **3-8-11** TQuinn(3) (w'like: bkwd: prom over 4f) | ¾ | 10 | 16/1 | 50 | 19 |
| **Desert Skimmer (USA)** (MBell) **3-8-11** MFenton(5) (unf: scope: nvr nrr) | 3 | 11 | 16/1 | 43 | 12 |
| **Larissa (IRE)** (GWragg) **3-8-11** PRobinson(16) (w'like: s.s: a bhd) | nk | 12 | 14/1 | 42 | 11 |
| **Shine** (IABalding) **3-8-11** KDarley(11) (leggy: prom over 3f) | 8 | 13 | 16/1 | 24 | — |

| | | | | SP | RR | SF |
|---|---|---|---|---|---|---|
| | **Bombay Sapphire** (RHannon) **3-8-11** RPerham(13) (w'like: bit bkwd: bhd fnl 3f) | ¾ | **14** | 33/1 | 22 | — |
| | **Pomona** (PJMakin) **3-8-11** WRyan(8) (w'like: bit bkwd: bhd fnl 3f) | nk | **15** | 33/1 | 22 | — |
| | **Kowtow** (MDIUsher) **3-8-11** RStreet(2) (str: scope: bkwd: a bhd) | 4 | **16** | 66/1 | 13 | — |
| | **Alajyal (IRE)** (PTWalwyn) **3-8-11** WCarson(7) (w'like: scope: bhd fnl 3f) | 4 | **17** | $9/1^{3}$ | 3 | — |
| | | | | (SP 141.2%) | | **17 Rn** |

**1m 31.4** (6.90) CSF £94.35 TOTE £21.90: £3.80 £2.00 £2.10 (£63.00) Trio £121.80 OWNER Mr Nicholas Jones (ARUNDEL) BRED Nicholas M. H. Jones

**Satin Bell** made a good impression on this debut. Swooping into the lead inside the final furlong, she won with plenty in hand. (14/1: 8/1-16/1)

**Aunty Jane**, reported to have been working well, showed in front two furlongs out, but was firmly put in her place in the final 200 yards. She should soon go one better. (11/2)

**Divine Quest**, a scopey half-sister to Pursuit of Love, should soon find a race. (7/2: 9/4-4/1)

**Sandhill (IRE)** could do no more in the final quarter-mile. (11/2: 4/1-13/2)

**Whispered Melody** is a half-sister to Chester Cup winner Top Cees. (33/1)

**Taking Liberties (IRE)**, a tall, scopey filly, was making little impression in the last three furlongs. (7/2: 3/1-9/2)

**Larissa (IRE)** (14/1: op 6/1)

## 711 NEWBURY RACECOURSE SHOPPING ARCADE RATED STKS H'CAP (0-100) (4-Y.O+) (Class B)

4-45 (4-54) **5f 34y** £8,507.20 (£3,164.80: £1,532.40: £642.00: £271.00: £122.60) Stalls: Centre GOING: 0.49 sec per fur (GS)

| | | | | SP | RR | SF |
|---|---|---|---|---|---|---|
| $582^{9}$ | **Anzio (IRE) (85)** (MissGayKelleway) **5-8-7b** RCochrane(7) (a.p: led over 1f out: r.o wl) | — | **1** | $6/1^{2}$ | 100 | 47 |
| | **Top Banana (86)** (HCandy) **5-8-8** CRutter(1) (hld up: rdn over 2f out: r.o ins fnl f) | ¾ | **2** | $6/1^{2}$ | 99 | 46 |
| $457^{7}$ | **Daring Destiny (99)** (KRBurke) **5-9-7v1** RHughes(3) (dwlt: hdwy 2f out: rdn over 1f out: unable qckn) | 3½ | **3** | 10/1 | 101 | 48 |
| *$20^{5}$* | **Sailormaite (83)** (SRBowring) **5-8-5** RPrice(6) (hld up: rdn over 2f out: one pce) | 1¼ | **4** | 12/1 | 81 | 28 |
| | **Brave Edge (98)** (RHannon) **5-9-1**(5) DaneO'Neill(4) (dwlt: hdwy over 1f out: one pce) | 1 | **5** | $8/1^{3}$ | 93 | 40 |
| $507^{4}$ | **Ziggy's Dancer (USA) (85)** (EJAlston) **5-8-7** SDWilliams(14) (lw: a.p: rdn over 2f out: wknd over 1f out) | ½ | **6** | $8/1^{3}$ | 78 | 25 |
| $610^{9}$ | **Lennox Lewis (93)** (APJarvis) **4-8-8**(7) KHopkins(10) (hld up: rdn over 2f out: wknd over 1f out) | ½ | **7** | 16/1 | 85 | 32 |
| | **Jayannpee (92)** (IABalding) **5-9-0** LDettori(9) (nvr nrr) | hd | **8** | $8/1^{3}$ | 83 | 30 |
| | **Lord Olivier (IRE) (86)** (WJarvis) **6-8-8** JReid(13) (bhd fnl 2f) | ½ | **9** | 16/1 | 76 | 23 |
| $451^{7}$ | **Lord High Admiral (CAN) (86)** (MJHeaton-Ellis) **8-8-8v** AClark(15) (led over 3f) | ½ | **10** | $9/2^{1}$ | 74 | 21 |
| | **How's Yer Father (82)** (RJHodges) **10-8-4** BDoyle(2) (bhd fnl 2f) | nk | **11** | 33/1 | 69 | 16 |
| $632^{3}$ | **Tafahhus (82)** (MJPolglase) **4-7-13**(5) FLynch(5) (bhd fnl 2f) | ½ | **12** | 33/1 | 68 | 15 |
| | **Bowden Rose (86)** (MBlanshard) **4-8-3b**(5) CAdamson(11) (lw: spd over 3f) | 2 | **13** | 16/1 | 66 | 13 |
| *$582^{19}$* | ***Macfarlane (82)*** (MJFetherston-Godley) **8-7-11**(7) MartinDwyer(8) (Withdrawn not under Starter's orders: broke out of stalls & bolted: jockey inj.) | | **W** | 33/1 | — | — |
| | | | | (SP 123.3%) | | **13 Rn** |

**65.37 secs** (5.17) CSF £39.35 CT £336.35 TOTE £8.30: £2.30 £1.80 £4.50 (£29.30) Trio £138.00 OWNER Mr Tommy Staunton (WHITCOMBE) BRED Rathduff Stud

LONG HANDICAP How's Yer Father 7-13 Tafahhus 7-9 Macfarlane 7-7

**451* Anzio (IRE)**, backed last time at Kempton, went on below the distance and proved too strong for these. (6/1)

**Top Banana** made a pleasing return to action and kept on well at the end to finish well clear of the rest. Only 2lb higher than when winning here last July, he looks set for another good season. (6/1)

**457 Daring Destiny** was making no impression from below the distance and a step up to six or seven furlongs would be in her favour. (10/1)

**Sailormaite** could not find another gear in the final two furlongs. (12/1)

**Brave Edge** could do no more having picked up below the distance. (8/1)

**507 Ziggy's Dancer (USA)** chased the stands'-side leader until calling it a day below the distance. (8/1)

## 712 THATCHAM H'CAP (0-100) (4-Y.O+) (Class C)

5-15 (5-16) **2m** £5,247.50 (£1,580.00: £765.00: £357.50) Stalls: High GOING: 0.49 sec per fur (GS)

| | | | | SP | RR | SF |
|---|---|---|---|---|---|---|
| $647^{2}$ | **Kadastrof (FR) (75)** (RDickin) **6-8-8**(5) DaneO'Neill(6) (lw: mde all: rdn over 2f out: r.o wl) | — | **1** | $5/1^{3}$ | 91 | 62 |
| | **Kamikaze (64)** (JWhite) **6-8-2**ow2 BDoyle(1) (hdwy over 4f out: chsd wnr over 2f out: unable qckn) | 6 | **2** | 33/1 | 74 | 43 |
| | **Corradini (94)** (HRACecil) **4-10-0** PatEddery(5) (lw: a.p: chsd wnr 7f out tl over 2f out: wknd over 1f out) | 11 | **3** | $2/1^{1}$ | 93 | 60 |
| $573^{2}$ | **Witney-de-Bergerac (IRE) (65)** (JSMoore) **4-7-13** JFEgan(2) (lw: hdwy over 4f out: wknd over 1f out) | 2½ | **4** | 8/1 | 62 | 29 |
| $647^{7}$ | **Johns Act (USA) (71)** (DHaydnJones) **6-8-9v** JReid(4) (lw: bhd fnl 4f) | 22 | **5** | 33/1 | 46 | 17 |
| $573^{4}$ | **Golden Arrow (IRE) (75)** (IABalding) **5-8-13** LDettori(8) (lw: a bhd) | 12 | **6** | 6/1 | 38 | 9 |
| $573^{13}$ | **Cypress Avenue (IRE) (79)** (RHannon) **4-8-13** RPerham(3) (racd wd bk st: chsd wnr 9f) | 1¾ | **7** | 33/1 | 40 | 7 |
| 449* | **Shadirwan (IRE) (81)** (RAkehurst) **5-9-5** TQuinn(7) (bhd fnl 8f: t.o) | 24 | **8** | $9/4^{2}$ | 18 | — |
| | | | | (SP 115.0%) | | **8 Rn** |

**3m 40.04** (15.04) CSF £102.35 CT £390.56 TOTE £7.40: £1.70 £2.30 £1.30 (£32.70) OWNER Mr A. P. Paton (STRATFORD) BRED Roland Lepeau in France

WEIGHT FOR AGE 4yo-4lb

**647 Kadastrof (FR)** was given a lovely ride. Coming to the stands' side in the straight in search of the better ground, he kept up the gallop in relentless style. (5/1)

**Kamikaze** struggled into second over two furlongs out but never got to the winner. (33/1)

**Corradini** really took the eye in the paddock. (2/1)

**573 Witney-de-Bergerac (IRE)** moved up entering the straight, but tired below the distance. (8/1)

T/Jkpt: £40,421.50 (0.9 Tckts); £5,693.17 to Newbury 20/4/96. T/Plpt: £64.80 (422.03 Tckts). T/Qdpt: £53.60 (24.56 Tckts). AK

# THIRSK (L-H) (Good to firm)

## Friday April 19th

WEATHER: cloudy WIND: mod half bhd

## 713 OAKSTRIPE H'CAP (0-65) (3-Y.O+) (Class F)

2-15 (2-15) **1m** £3,344.00 (£934.00: £452.00) Stalls: Low GOING minus 0.23 sec per fur (GF)

| | | | | SP | RR | SF |
|---|---|---|---|---|---|---|
| 615* | **Rambo Waltzer (55)** (DNicholls) **4-9-6** AlexGreaves(1) (lw: chsd ldrs: n.m.r over 2f out: edgd rt & led wl ins fnl f: jst hld on) | — | **1** | $3/1^{1}$ | 70 | 45 |

| | | | | SP | RR | SF |
|---|---|---|---|---|---|---|
| *513*[8] | **Wentbridge Lad (IRE) (60)** (PDEvans) **6-9-11v** SSanders(6) (sn rdn along: hdwy ½-wy: effrt over 2f out: edgd lft u.p fnl f: bmpd & nt qckn nr fin) | hd | **2** | 20/1 | 75 | 50 |
| *358*[7] | **Chairmans Choice (55)** (APJarvis) **6-9-6** JTate(8) (a chsng ldrs: led over 1f out tl wl ins fnl f) | nk | **3** | 8/1 [3] | 69 | 44 |
| | **Edgar Kirby (53)** (PWHarris) **5-8-13**(5) MHenry(9) (chsd ldrs: effrt 2f out: hung rt: kpt on same pce) | 1¼ | **4** | 8/1 [3] | 65 | 40 |
| | **Bollin Frank (57)** (TDEasterby) **4-9-8** MBirch(4) (led after 2f tl over 1f out: grad wknd) | 1¼ | **5** | 12/1 | 66 | 41 |
| 505[13] | **Murphy's Gold (IRE) (53)** (RAFahey) **5-9-4** ACulhane(18) (hld up: hdwy on outside 3f out: styd on: nt rch ldrs) | ¾ | **6** | 16/1 | 61 | 36 |
| 505* | **Pine Ridge Lad (IRE) (60)** (JLEyre) **6-9-11** RLappin(17) (chsd ldrs: sn rdn along: outpcd appr fnl f) | 1½ | **7** | 7/2 [2] | 65 | 40 |
| *607*[3] | **Awesome Venture (54)** (MCChapman) **6-8-12**(7) CMunday(10) (sn trckng ldrs: effrt over 1f out: sn wl outpcd) | 1½ | **8** | 14/1 | 56 | 31 |
| 505[4] | **Legal Issue (IRE) (63)** (WWHaigh) **4-9-11**(3) PMcCabe(15) (lw: styd on fnl 3f: nvr nr ldrs) | nk | **9** | 14/1 | 64 | 39 |
| *424*[9] | **Twin Creeks (52)** (MDHammond) **5-9-3** GDuffield(11) (led 2f: chsd ldrs tl wknd 2f out) | 3 | **10** | 20/1 | 47 | 22 |
| | **Thatched (IRE) (53)** (REBarr) **6-8-13**(5) PFessey(3) (hld up: hdwy ½-wy: rdn & wknd 2f out) | 1½ | **11** | 14/1 | 45 | 20 |
| 477[13] | **Spanish Steps (IRE) (55)** (MWEasterby) **4-9-6** JWeaver(14) (lw: hld up: a in rr) | 1 | **12** | 14/1 | 45 | 20 |
| *233*[6] | **Noble Neptune (57)** (WJMusson) **4-9-8** GCarter(12) (a bhd) | ¾ | **13** | 14/1 | 46 | 21 |
| 547[13] | **Oneoftheoldones (60)** (JNorton) **4-9-11** JFortune(2) (a bhd) | 3½ | **14** | 33/1 | 42 | 17 |
| | **Tee Tee Too (IRE) (50)** (AHarrison) **4-9-1** WWoods(5) (hld up: a bhd) | 13 | **15** | 25/1 | 6 | — |
| 609[18] | **Gymcrak Hero (IRE) (50)** (GHolmes) **4-9-1v**[1] AMcGlone(16) (t: bhd fnl 3f) | 5 | **16** | 33/1 | — | — |
| | | | | (SP 135.6%) | **16 Rn** | |

**1m 40.3** (3.80) CSF £63.01 CT £432.12 TOTE £4.20: £1.50 £5.00 £1.80 £1.70 (£67.80) Trio £172.40 OWNER Keystone Racing Club Partnership (THIRSK) BRED Triangle Thoroughbreds Ltd

**615* Rambo Waltzer**, who escaped a penalty for his Hamilton success, came out just best in what was undoubtedly a rough race. (3/1)

**Wentbridge Lad (IRE)**, who lost his form in the second half of last season and who was tailed off on his reappearance, went under narrowly after he and the winner had got in each others' way. (20/1)

**Chairmans Choice**, reappearing after a seven-week absence and on a mark 21lb lower than on the All-Weather, was only edged out near the line. (8/1)

**Edgar Kirby**, who had only one outing last season, was a springer on the morning line. Tending to hang out towards the centre, he could find no more in the final furlong, but had presumably been showing ability at home. (8/1)

**Bollin Frank**, a confirmed front-runner, was having his first run for six months and shaped promisingly. (12/1)

**Murphy's Gold (IRE)** found himself marooned on the outside. Sticking on at the finish, he is better coming between horses and Beverley suits him ideally. (16/1)

**505* Pine Ridge Lad (IRE)**, badly drawn, had plenty of running to do early. Soon driven along, he could not match his rivals for speed coming to the final furlong. (7/2)

**607 Awesome Venture** travelled strongly as usual but, when called on for an effort over a furlong out, the others ran away from him. The Stewards enquired into his running, but this is the way he runs, and he is never going as easily as it seems. (14/1)

## 714 BRITON RATING RELATED MAIDEN STKS (0-75) (3-Y.O+) (Class D)

2-50 (2-50) **6f** £3,509.00 (£1,052.00: £506.00: £233.00) Stalls: High GOING minus 0.23 sec per fur (GF)

| | | | | SP | RR | SF |
|---|---|---|---|---|---|---|
| 554[4] | **Golden Pound (USA) (71)** (MissGayKelleway) **4-9-10b** KFallon(1) (mde all: pushed clr over 1f out: eased towards fin) | — | **1** | 9/2 [2] | 81 | 59 |
| | **Baileys First (IRE) (75)** (MJohnston) **3-8-10** JWeaver(6) (in tch: rdn & outpcd ½-wy: styd on fnl f) | 3 | **2** | 5/1 [3] | 70 | 37 |
| | **Alamein (USA) (74)** (WJHaggas) **3-8-13** WWoods(5) (a chsng ldrs: rdn over 2f out: one pce) | hd | **3** | 11/10 [1] | 73 | 40 |
| | **Shady Girl (IRE) (70)** (BWHills) **3-8-5**(5) JDSmith(3) (bit bkwd: chsd wnr: rdn over 2f out: no imp) | 1½ | **4** | 9/2 [2] | 66 | 33 |
| | **Brandonville (74)** (NTinkler) **3-8-13** KimTinkler(4) (dwlt: sme hdwy over 2f out: n.d) | 3½ | **5** | 11/1 | 59 | 26 |
| | **Chalice (72)** (JBalding) **3-8-3**(7) JEdmunds(2) (sltly hmpd s: bhd & outpcd: sme hdwy over 2f out: sn wknd) | 3 | **6** | 11/1 | 48 | 15 |
| | | | | (SP 117.3%) | **6 Rn** | |

**1m 11.7** (2.00) CSF £25.21 TOTE £4.50: £1.50 £2.70 (£7.60) OWNER Bellcoil Ltd (WHITCOMBE) BRED Builder's Mart Inc
WEIGHT FOR AGE 3yo-11lb

**554 Golden Pound (USA)**, a frustrating individual, was dropped back in distance here and fitted with a tongue-strap. Drawn one, his rider took a chance, diving across to the stands' rail. Five lengths clear over a furlong out, he won easing up. (9/2)

**Baileys First (IRE)**, placed three times from four outings at two, was badly tapped for toe at halfway. Staying on when it was all over, she is worth a chance over a mile. (5/1)

**Alamein (USA)**, a heavy-topped individual, is a poor mover. He never looked like producing the pace to get near the winner and will be suited by seven furlongs or a mile. (11/10: 5/4-Evens)

**Shady Girl (IRE)** looked backward and was hard at work soon after halfway. (9/2: op 7/1)

**Brandonville**, who gave away ground at the start, will be better suited by seven. (11/1)

## 715 CLIFTON CONDITIONS STKS (2-Y.O F) (Class C)

3-20 (3-20) **5f** £4,691.80 (£1,736.20: £833.10: £340.50: £135.25: £53.15) Stalls: High GOING minus 0.23 sec per fur (GF)

| | | | | SP | RR | SF |
|---|---|---|---|---|---|---|
| 465* | **Jennelle** (CADwyer) **2-8-5**(3) JStack(2) (mde virtually all: shkn up over 1f out: r.o wl) | — | **1** | 13/8 [1] | 73 | 41 |
| 608[2] | **Double Park (FR)** (MJohnston) **2-8-8** JWeaver(5) (w ldrs: rdn ½-wy: hung lft & wandered: nt qckn ins fnl f) | 1½ | **2** | 4/1 [3] | 68 | 36 |
| 446* | **Hit Or Miss** (MRChannon) **2-8-8** DHarrison(3) (a chsng ldrs: kpt on same pce fnl 2f) | 2½ | **3** | 7/1 | 60 | 28 |
| 538* | **Northern Sal** (JBerry) **2-8-10** GCarter(1) (unruly s: s.s: sn chsng ldrs: rdn & hung bdly lft 2f out: kpt on fnl f) | 2½ | **4** | 15/2 | 54 | 22 |
| 630[3] | **Nightingale Song** (MartynMeade) **2-8-3**(5) RHavlin(6) (chsd ldrs: outpcd ½-wy: grad wknd) | 5 | **5** | 14/1 | 36 | 4 |
| 506* | **Enchanting Eve** (CNAllen) **2-8-3**(5) MHenry(4) (chsd ldrs to ½-wy: sn lost pl & bhd: eased) | 12 | **6** | 11/4 [2] | — | — |
| | | | | (SP 115.7%) | **6 Rn** | |

**59.8 secs** (1.80) CSF £8.46 TOTE £3.00: £1.40 £1.80 (£5.10) OWNER Mrs J. A. Cornwell (NEWMARKET) BRED Mrs A. J. Owen
OFFICIAL EXPLANATION **Enchanting Eve: the jockey stated that the filly had not acted on the fast ground.**

**465* Jennelle**, a sharp sort, was always travelling best and had only to be kept up to her work. She would not appreciate the ground any faster. (13/8)

**608 Double Park (FR)** hung away from the rail and gave her rider problems, but she stuck to her task and will be better suited by either six furlongs, or a flatter, more galloping track. (4/1)

**446* Hit Or Miss** is a poor walker and a poor mover. (7/1)

**538* Northern Sal** gave problems at the gates and gave her rivals a headstart. Hanging badly left out towards the centre, she kept on in the final furlong and, considering the ground she forfeited, she was not beaten all that far. (15/2)

**630 Nightingale Song** looks moderate. (14/1)

**506* Enchanting Eve** did not impress with her action going to post. Dropping right out at halfway, her rider told the Stewards she did not appreciate the fast ground, and her trainer said she would not run on anything faster than good in the future. (11/4)

## 716 HAMBLETON LIMITED STKS (0-80) (3-Y.O+) (Class D)

3-50 (3-57) **5f** £4,045.00 (£1,210.00: £580.00: £265.00) Stalls: High GOING minus 0.23 sec per fur (GF)

| | | | | SP | RR | SF |
|---|---|---|---|---|---|---|
| | **Angaar (IRE) (80)** (ACStewart) **3-8-8** DHarrison(3) (s.i.s: hdwy u.p 2f out: r.o to ld ins fnl f: jst hld on) | — | **1** | 6/1 | 83 | 55 |
| $610^{6}$ | **French Grit (IRE) (80)** (MDods) **4-9-4** WWoods(7) (in tch: outpcd ½-wy: rapid hdwy ins fnl f: fin wl) | hd | **2** | 9/1 | 83 | 65 |
| | **Here Comes a Star (74)** (JMCarr) **8-9-4** ACulhane(8) (hld up & bhd: hdwy over 1f out: r.o wl towards fin) | nk | **3** | 16/1 | 82 | 64 |
| $610^{19}$ | **Portend (80)** (SRBowring) **4-8-13**(5) CTeague(4) (chsd ldrs: ev ch ins fnl f: kpt on) | s.h | **4** | 20/1 | 82 | 64 |
| 475* | **Stolen Kiss (IRE) (76)** (MWEasterby) **4-9-4b** JWeaver(6) (trckd ldrs: effrt 2f out: styd on ins fnl f) | hd | **5** | $7/2^{2}$ | 81 | 63 |
| | **Splinter (IRE) (80)** (RCharlton) **3-8-8** SSanders(1) (lw: sn chsng ldrs: effrt 2f out: wknd jst ins fnl f) | ¾ | **6** | $7/4^{1}$ | 79 | 51 |
| $591^{2}$ | **Pride of Brixton (76)** (GLewis) **3-8-8** SWhitworth(5) (led: clr 2f out: hrd rdn & hdd ins fnl f: wknd) | hd | **7** | $4/1^{3}$ | 79 | 51 |
| | **Shashi (IRE) (73)** (WWHaigh) **4-9-1** DaleGibson(2) (bit bkwd: chsd ldrs 3f: sn outpcd) | 4 | **8** | 14/1 | 63 | 45 |
| | | | | (SP 120.2%) | | **8 Rn** |

**59.0 secs** (1.00) CSF £53.51 TOTE £7.00: £2.40 £1.70 £3.40 (£44.10) OWNER Sheikh Ahmed Al Maktoum (NEWMARKET) BRED Ron Con Ltd
WEIGHT FOR AGE 3yo-10lb

**Angaar (IRE)**, who won his only outing at two, did not impress in the paddock or with his action going to the start. After missing the break, he just scraped home. He might be better suited by six. (6/1: op 3/1)
**610 French Grit (IRE)**, a confirmed six-furlong performer, finished with a wet sail. (9/1)
**Here Comes a Star**, who ran no less than eighteen times last year, finished with a flourish. (16/1)
**Portend**, the winner of six last year, ran his best race for some time. But for giving his rider a problem or two, he would have finished even closer. (20/1)
**475* Stolen Kiss (IRE)** tanked along but probably saw too much daylight for her own good. After looking half-hearted at one stage, she consented to stay on again near the finish. She undoubtedly has more ability than her current handicap mark. (7/2)
**Splinter (IRE)**, who looked to have had his shins treated, won his only outing at two. For one so inexperienced, the number-one draw would not have helped, and he faded entering the final furlong. (7/4)
**591 Pride of Brixton**, taken to post early, showed bags of toe and was three lengths clear soon after halfway. Under maximum pressure, his stride shortened in the final 200 yards. (4/1)

## 717 SOWERBY MAIDEN STKS (3-Y.O) (Class D)

4-25 (4-25) **1m 4f** £3,743.00 (£1,124.00: £542.00: £251.00) Stalls: High GOING minus 0.23 sec per fur (GF)

| | | | | SP | RR | SF |
|---|---|---|---|---|---|---|
| | **Benatom (USA)** (HRACecil) **3-9-0** AMcGlone(6) (mde all: styd on strly u.p fnl f: jst hld on) | — | **1** | $11/8^{2}$ | 82 | 27 |
| | **Nayib** (DMorley) **3-9-0** GCarter(7) (rangy: bit bkwd: dwlt: sn chsng ldrs: bmpd 2f out: wknd over 1f out: fin 3rd, 11l: plcd 2nd) | | **2** | $8/1^{3}$ | 67 | 12 |
| $578^{2}$ | **Clerkenwell (USA)** (MRStoute) **3-9-0** KFallon(4) (trckd ldrs: effrt & barged thro 2f out: r.o u.p fnl f: jst failed: fin 2nd, nk: disq: plcd 3rd) | | **3** | $8/11^{1}$ | 82 | 27 |
| | **Anchor Venture** (SPCWoods) **3-9-0** WWoods(2) (hld up & plld hrd: dropped bk 3f out: stdy hdwy fnl f: nvr plcd to chal) | 2 | **4** | 20/1 | 64 | 9 |
| $576^{9}$ | **Charming Admiral (IRE)** (CFWall) **3-9-0** GDuffield(1) (sn bhd & pushed along: styd on appr fnl f) | hd | **5** | 33/1 | 64 | 9 |
| | **Gool Lee Shay (USA)** (RMWhitaker) **3-9-0** ACulhane(5) (lengthy: bit bkwd: prom tl lost pl over 3f out: sn bhd) | 23 | **6** | 100/1 | 34 | — |
| | **Dispol Agenda** (GROldroyd) **3-8-9** MBirch(3) (leggy: unf: in tch tl lost pl 4f out: sn bhd) | 20 | **7** | 100/1 | 2 | — |
| | | | | (SP 120.8%) | | **7 Rn** |

**2m 38.0** (8.00) CSF £12.91 TOTE £2.20: £1.20 £2.70 (£9.40) OWNER Mr T. F. Harris (NEWMARKET) BRED J. S. Meredith
STEWARDS' ENQUIRY Fallon susp. 29/4-4/5/96 (irresponsible riding).

**Benatom (USA)**, a likeable type, was given a good ride. With the role of pacemaker thrust upon him, he stepped up the gallop once in line for home and, really stretching out in the final furlong, the post came just in time. (11/8)
**Nayib**, a brother to Terimon, looked backward. Three-quarters of a length down on the winner two furlongs out, he was then knocked right out of his stride. He should come on for the outing, but looks to need more time yet. (8/1)
**578 Clerkenwell (USA)**, a good mover, was given a poor ride. Finding himself on the heels of the winner and with Nayib on his outside two furlongs out, his hot-headed jockey decided the way to the outside was to barge his way out. He stuck on in the final furlong but, with the winner also running all the way to the line, he could not quite get there. His disqualification and his rider's suspension were a mere formality. (8/11)
**Anchor Venture**, a Slip Anchor colt who showed a glimmer of ability in two outings at two, was clearly ridden with another day in view. Letting the three leaders slip him early in the straight, he was putting in some promising work in the final furlong. Significantly this qualifies him for a handicap mark and he looks the type to appreciate a longer trip. (20/1)
**Charming Admiral (IRE)** is still learning the ropes. After being pushed along a long way from home, he was staying on at the finish. (33/1)

## 718 BIRDFORTH H'CAP (0-70) (3-Y.O+) (Class E)

4-55 (4-57) **7f** £3,361.25 (£1,010.00: £487.50: £226.25) Stalls: Low GOING minus 0.23 sec per fur (GF)

| | | | | SP | RR | SF |
|---|---|---|---|---|---|---|
| 629* | **Primo Lara (71)** (PWHarris) **4-9-10**(5) 6x MHenry(4) (lw: chsd ldrs: led 3f out: sn rdn clr: eased ins fnl f) | — | **1** | $5/4^{1}$ | 88+ | 67 |
| $629^{6}$ | **Ochos Rios (IRE) (57)** (BSRothwell) **5-9-1** LCharnock(10) (mid div: hdwy 2f out: styd on ins fnl f) | 3½ | **2** | 16/1 | 66 | 45 |
| $480^{6}$ | **Nashaat (USA) (63)** (MCChapman) **8-9-7** KFallon(15) (swtchd lft after 1f: hld up: hdwy 2f out: styd on ins fnl f) | 1 | **3** | 14/1 | 70 | 49 |
| | **Selhurstpark Flyer (IRE) (70)** (JBerry) **5-9-9**(5) PRoberts(9) (b: led to 3f out: wknd ins fnl f) | hd | **4** | 14/1 | 77 | 56 |
| $662^{7}$ | **Bargash (66)** (PDEvans) **4-9-10** SSanders(12) (in tch: kpt on one pce fnl 3f) | 1¼ | **5** | 14/1 | 70 | 49 |
| $587^{13}$ | **White Sorrel (63)** (AHarrison) **5-9-0**(7) GFaulkner(6) (bhd: hdwy 2f out: kpt on fnl f) | ¾ | **6** | 25/1 | 65 | 44 |
| *$425^{5}$* | **Tame Deer (57)** (MCChapman) **4-8-8**(7) CMunday(2) (chsd ldrs: hrd rdn 2f out: wknd over 1f out) | ½ | **7** | 25/1 | 58 | 37 |
| $592^{2}$ | **Cretan Gift (60)** (NPLittmoden) **5-9-4v** TGMcLaughlin(1) (chsd ldrs tl wknd over 1f out) | 1¼ | **8** | $6/1^{2}$ | 58 | 37 |
| *$368^{5}$* | **Monis (IRE) (53)** (JBalding) **5-8-4v**(7) JEdmunds(5) (bhd tl sme late hdwy) | ¾ | **9** | 16/1 | 49 | 28 |
| $480^{14}$ | **Zain Dancer (57)** (DNicholls) **4-9-1** AlexGreaves(11) (hld up: nvr plcd to chal) | ¾ | **10** | 16/1 | 52 | 31 |
| $610^{21}$ | **Anonym (IRE) (70)** (DNicholls) **4-10-0** SMason(3) (sn pushed along: nvr nr ldrs) | nk | **11** | 25/1 | 64 | 43 |
| $505^{7}$ | **Sea-Ayr (IRE) (47)** (MrsSMAustin) **6-8-5** GDuffield(16) (b: racd wd: a rr div) | 7 | **12** | 20/1 | 25 | 4 |
| | **Sizzling Symphony (65)** (RAFahey) **3-8-10** ACulhane(7) (a bhd) | 1½ | **13** | 14/1 | 39 | 5 |
| $629^{12}$ | **Souperficial (58)** (JAGlover) **5-9-2v** JFortune(8) (s.s: a bhd) | 1 | **14** | $10/1^{3}$ | 30 | 9 |
| *$425^{2}$* | **Desert Invader (IRE) (55)** (DWChapman) **5-8-13** DeanMcKeown(14) (chsd ldrs tl lost pl 3f out) | 1 | **15** | 14/1 | 25 | 4 |

480[2] **Evan 'elp Us (60)** (JLEyre) **4-9-1b**(3) OPears(13) (reminders after s: sn bhd: t.o whn p.u ½-wy) ........................ **P** 10/1 3 — —
(SP 144.2%) **16 Rn**

**1m 26.4** (2.20) CSF £26.82 CT £229.36 TOTE £2.20: £1.10 £3.50 £3.10 £3.00 (£27.40) Trio £169.50 OWNER Thanet Leasing Ltd (BERKHAMSTED) BRED Pendley Farm
WEIGHT FOR AGE 3yo-13lb

**629* Primo Lara**, under a 6lb penalty, has already been raised 9lb for his runaway Beverley success. Pushed clear early in the straight, he was able to ease right up. He will have much stiffer tasks after the Handicapper has had a chance to look at this effort. (5/4)
**629 Ochos Rios (IRE)**, on a losing run of sixteen, again ran well and finished in pleasing style to snatch second. (16/1)
**480 Nashaat (USA)**, drawn on the wide outside, was switched right, behind the field after a furlong. Staying on inside the last, he is a 10lb better horse on the All-Weather. (14/1)
**Selhurstpark Flyer (IRE)**, who lost his way at four having won four times as a juvenile, was soon setting a strong pace and had shaken off all but the winner turning in. Still second inside the last, his stride then shortened. (14/1)
**592 Bargash**, who never runs two races alike, was having his second outing in four days. (14/1)
**White Sorrel** is a stone better on the All-Weather. (25/1)
**Zain Dancer**, a winner over seven furlongs in the Czech Republic last year, had a quiet run round in midfield. Slipping down the weights, he will no doubt be found an opportunity in due course. (16/1)

T/Plpt: £108.90 (103.43 Tckts). T/Qdpt: £61.20 (15.14 Tckts). WG

# CAPANNELLE (Rome, Italy) (R-H) (Good)
## Monday April 8th

## 719a PREMIO ORTIS MAIDEN (3-Y.O F)
4-30 (4-45) **1m 2f** £6,090.00 (£2,436.00: £1,461.00)

| | | | SP | RR | SF |
|---|---|---|---|---|---|
| **Bellflower (FR)** (LBrogi,Italy) **3-9-2** VMezzatesta | — | **1** | | — | — |
| **Silver Irene** (FCiabattoni,Italy) **3-9-2** DZarroli | 4½ | **2** | | — | — |
| **Alzabella (IRE)** (JWHills) **3-9-2** BCook | 2 | **3** | | — | — |
| | | | | | **12 Rn** |

**2m 13.8** TOTE 49L: 19L 15L 27L (68L) OWNER Scuderia Colle Papa
**Alzabella (IRE)** was held up at the back of the field until staying on well from three furlongs out. She took third close home and will be better for the run.

# EVRY (France) (R-H) (Good)
## Friday April 12th

## 720a PRIX IMPRUDENCE (Listed) (3-Y.O F)
1-50 (1-58) **6f 110y** £18,445.00 (£6,324.00: £3,953.00: £1,107.00)

| | | | SP | RR | SF |
|---|---|---|---|---|---|
| **Mahalia (IRE)** (MmeCHead,France) **3-9-0** FHead | — | **1** | | — | 29 |
| **Rose Bourbon (USA)** (AFabre,France) **3-9-0** TJarnet | 1½ | **2** | | — | 26 |
| **Blushing Gleam** (MmeCHead,France) **3-9-0** ODoleuze | 1½ | **3** | | — | 22 |
| **Floresta (FR)** (MRolland,France) **3-9-0** OPeslier | 3 | **4** | | — | 16 |
| | | | | | **8 Rn** |

**1m 17.96** (2.26) P-M 14.40F: 3.40F 1.60F 2.30F (17.10F) OWNER Mr G. A. Oldham (CHANTILLY) BRED Citadel Stud
**Mahalia (IRE)** won this Classic Trial with something in hand. Always well up, she had taken a clear advantage by the furlong marker and, from then on, was not hard pressed to hold off her rivals. She impressed when making a winning debut at Deauville before disappointing in two subsequent races as a juvenile, and her connections are convinced that she must have good or firmer ground and a straight track to show her best. She displays a lot of speed, so is likely to be kept at distances of under a mile, and a perfect long-term target would be the Prix Maurice de Gheest at Deauville, but it would be no surprise if she crossed the Channel in the meantime. She looks a decent filly when things are in her favour.
**Rose Bourbon (USA)**, always well up, was outpaced in the final furlong before keeping on near the finish. A progressive sort whose stable have yet to really hit top form, she will be much more effective over a longer distance, and will almost certainly now be aimed at a maiden, rather than come over to England for the 1000 Guineas. She will improve a lot for the outing and should be up to Group calibre.
**Blushing Gleam**, who looked fit and well in the paddock, was always well up but made little progress when things warmed up at the furlong marker and just stayed on towards the end. She has won over a longer distance, which she might need in the future to show her best.
**Floresta (FR)**, held up for a late challenge, never really looked like catching the first three. She could do with further and possibly prefer a little cut in the ground.

## 721a PRIX DJEBEL (Listed) (3-Y.O C & G)
2-15 (2-27) **6f 110y** £18,445.00 (£6,324.00: £2,055.00: £1,107.00)

| | | | SP | RR | SF |
|---|---|---|---|---|---|
| **Byzantium (USA)** (JEHammond,France) **3-9-2** GMosse | — | **1** | | — | 19 |
| **Delegate** (AFabre,France) **3-9-2** TJarnet | ½ | **2** | | — | 18 |
| **Titus Livius (FR)** (JEPease,France) **3-9-2** CAsmussen | s.h | **3** | | — | 18 |
| **Starmaniac (USA)** (CLaffon-Parias,France) **3-9-2** FSanchez | 1½ | **4** | | — | 15 |
| | | | | | **6 Rn** |

**1m 18.93** (3.23) P-M 1.80F: 4.10F 2.50F sf 53.90F OWNER Mr S. S. Niarchos (CHANTILLY) BRED Flaxman Holdings Ltd
**Byzantium (USA)**, taking a big step up in class, is a really decent horse in the making with enormous scope for improvement, and he should be followed this season. Held up at the tail of the field before producing a run on the far side, he led over a furlong out and ran on well, despite looking a little green. There are no plans at the moment for this son of Gulch, whose dam is a sister to Miesque, but he holds engagements in both the French and Irish 2000 Guineas, with the latter his likely target.
**Delegate** did absolutely nothing wrong and battled on gamely for second place, which he looked like losing at the furlong marker. Definitely likely to be suited by a longer distance, he will have benefited considerably for the outing and, while there are no plans for this colt at the present, he looks to have a promising future.
**Titus Livius (FR)**, who sweated up badly before the race, shed little light on his stamina on this occasion and no decision has yet been made as to whether he will be sent to Newmarket for the 2000 Guineas. There must be some doubt that the colt will stay the stiff mile there, and it was a shame he was not made more use of on this occasion.

**Starmaniac (USA)** did not have the luckiest of runs before going on well in the latter stages, and ran almost pound for pound with Titus Livius. He is a genuine and consistent colt, but is just below Group standard.

## 0719a-CAPANNELLE (Rome, Italy) (R-H) (Heavy)
### Sunday April 14th

**722a** PREMIO DAUMIER (Listed) (3-Y.O)
3-30 (3-37) **1m** £20,300.00

| | | | | SP | RR | SF |
|---|---|---|---|---|---|---|
| | **Blu Taxidoo (USA)** (AVerdesi,Italy) **3-8-11** MVargiu | — | **1** | | — | — |
| | **Alabastro (IRE)** (LCamici,Italy) **3-8-11** MPasquale | 1¼ | **2** | | — | — |
| | **Dancer Mitral** (LBrogi,Italy) **3-8-11** VMezzatesta | ¾ | **3** | | — | — |
| | **April The Eighth** (BWHills) **3-8-11** WCarson (btn over 7l) | | **5** | | — | — |
| | | | | | | **9 Rn** |

**1m 40.2** TOTE 23L: 13L 13L 18L (60L) OWNER Scuderia Blu Horse BRED G. Redmond
**April The Eighth** was never far off the pace and took up the running five furlongs from home. Collared well over a furlong out, he was soon back-pedalling. A son of Statoblest, this trip stretched his stamina, especially on testing ground.

## 0623a-SAN SIRO (Milan, Italy) (R-H) (Good)
### Sunday April 14th

**723a** PREMIO ALBERTO ZANOLETTI DI ROZZANO (Listed) (3-Y.O F)
3-40 (4-00) **1m 1f** £24,360.00 (£10,718.00: £5,846.00: £2,923.00)

| | | | | SP | RR | SF |
|---|---|---|---|---|---|---|
| | **Robereva (IRE)** (APecoraro,Italy) **3-8-11** SDettori | — | **1** | | — | — |
| | **Grey Way (USA)** (GBotti,Italy) **3-8-11** EBotti | ½ | **2** | | — | — |
| | **Karla Wyller (ITY)** (MLivraghi,Italy) **3-8-11** FJovine | ¾ | **3** | | — | — |
| | **Moody's Cat (IRE)** (BWHills) **3-8-11** MHills | 3½ | **4** | | — | — |
| | | | | | | **8 Rn** |

**1m 51.4** (9.20) TOTE 227L: 37L 20L 19L (442L) OWNER Scuderia Flery BRED R. O'Reilly
**Moody's Cat (IRE)** tracked the leader until hitting the front at the three-furlong marker. When challenged at the quarter-mile pole, her response was disappointing. Like April the Eighth, she has spent the past few months enjoying the winter sun in Pisa, and it will be interesting to see how they fare when they get back to Britain.

## SHA TIN (Kowloon, Hong Kong) (R-H) (Good)
### Sunday April 14th

**724a** QUEEN ELIZABETH II CUP (Gp 1) (3-Y.O+)
8-10 (8-10) **1m 3f** £217,500.00 (£82,500.00: £37,500.00: £17,625.00)

| | | | | SP | RR | SF |
|---|---|---|---|---|---|---|
| | **Overbury (IRE)** (SbinSuroor,UAE) **5-9-0** LDettori | — | **1** | | — | — |
| | **Sapio (NZ)** (MrsSLKay,NewZealand) **5-9-0** BHibberd | 3¾ | **2** | | — | — |
| | **Privilege (IRE)** (IAllan,HongKong) **5-9-0** BMarcus | ¾ | **3** | | — | — |
| *397a*[2] | **Learmont (USA)** (ECharpy,UAE) **6-9-0** PaulEddery | ¾ | **4** | | — | — |
| | | | | | | **14 Rn** |

**2m 14.5** TOTE £26.50: £14.50 £16.50 £34.50 (£59.50) OWNER Godolphin BRED E. J. Loder
**Overbury (IRE)** won this with great authority. Held up in touch, he found himself behind a wall of horses at the top of the straight but, after a brief wait, a gap appeared and he put the issue beyond doubt in a matter of strides. Unsuited by the Sand in Dubai, he will shortly return to Newmarket and, if he fails to make the grade in the very best company, further globe-trotting is expected.

## 0706-NEWBURY (L-H) (Good to soft)
### Saturday April 20th
WEATHER: fine WIND: slt across

**725** ARLINGTON INTERNATIONAL RACECOURSE CONDITIONS STKS (3-Y.O) (Class B)
2-00 (2-00) **1m 3f 5y** £7,724.25 (£2,793.00: £1,346.50: £557.50) Stalls: Low GOING: 0.27 sec per fur (G)

| | | | | SP | RR | SF |
|---|---|---|---|---|---|---|
| 526* | **High Baroque (IRE)** (PWChapple-Hyam) **3-8-13** JReid(1) (w'like: scope: lw: hld up: swtchd lft 2f out: led over 1f out: rdn out) | — | **1** | 9/1 | 100 | 58 |
| | **Flyfisher (IRE) (104)** (GLewis) **3-9-1** PaulEddery(4) (led over 9f: unable qckn) | 3½ | **2** | 20/1 | 97 | 55 |
| | **Mystic Knight (95)** (RCharlton) **3-8-13** TSprake(5) (lw: hld up: rdn over 3f out: wknd 2f out) | 3½ | **3** | 7/1 3 | 90 | 48 |
| | **Bright Water** (HRACecil) **3-8-13** PatEddery(2) (lw: chsd ldr: rdn over 3f out: ev ch 2f out: wknd 1f out) | 1¾ | **4** | 5/6 1 | 87 | 45 |
| 495* | **Maiden Castle** (JHMGosden) **3-8-13** LDettori(3) (b: hld up: rdn over 3f out: eased whn btn over 1f out) | 12 | **5** | 9/4 2 | 70 | 28 |
| | | | | (SP 112.6%) | | **5 Rn** |

**2m 25.53** (8.33) CSF £90.10 TOTE £7.10: £2.90 £3.60 (£35.20) OWNER Mr M. Tabor (MARLBOROUGH) BRED Barronstown Bloodstock Ltd
**OFFICIAL EXPLANATION Bright Water: finished distressed and was unsuited by the soft ground.**
**526* High Baroque (IRE)**, the only one of these not in the Derby, instead has the Italian version as his objective. (9/1: op 5/1)
**Flyfisher (IRE)** made a very pleasing return and should soon be winning, probably over a bit further. (20/1)
**Mystic Knight**, racing with his tongue tied down, called it a day two furlongs out. (7/1)
**Bright Water**, a brother to Tenby, looked in good shape for this return. Still with every chance two furlongs out, he rather worryingly flashed his tail on the two occasions he was hit, and he had been seen off passing the furlong pole. His trainer later reported that the colt had not liked the soft ground and had finished distressed. (5/6)
**495* Maiden Castle** could not cope with the step up in class, and was allowed to come home in his own time. (9/4)

## 726 LANES END JOHN PORTER STKS (Gp 3) (4-Y.O+) (Class A)

2-30 (2-31) **1m 4f 5y** £20,580.00 (£7,704.00: £3,702.00: £1,614.00) Stalls: Low GOING: 0.27 sec per fur (G)

| | Horse | Dist | Pos | SP | RR | SF |
|---|---|---|---|---|---|---|
| | **Spout (109)** (RCharlton) **4-8-8** TSprake(4) (nt clr run over 2f out: hdwy over 1f out: str run fnl f: led last stride) | — | **1** | 6/1[3] | 115 | 60 |
| | **Wayne County (IRE) (109)** (RAkehurst) **6-8-12** TQuinn(9) (lw: plld hrd: chsd ldr 8f out: led over 3f out: hrd rdn over 1f out: hdd last stride) | s.h | **2** | 11/1 | 118 | 64 |
| | **Moonax (IRE) (119)** (BWHills) **5-9-3** PatEddery(8) (bit bkwd: rdn over 8f out: hdwy over 3f out: hrd rdn over 1f out: r.o wl ins fnl f) | ¾ | **3** | 7/4[1] | 122 | 68 |
| 581[4] | **Florid (USA) (104)** (HRACecil) **5-8-12** AMcGlone(3) (lw: a.p: ev ch over 2f out: unable qckn) | 1½ | **4** | 8/1 | 115 | 61 |
| | **Commoner (USA) (112)** (RHannon) **4-8-11** RHughes(5) (lw: hdwy over 3f out: rdn over 2f out: wknd over 1f out) | 7 | **5** | 11/2[2] | 106 | 51 |
| | **Blushing Flame (USA) (103)** (MRStoute) **5-8-12** JReid(6) (lw: nvr nr to chal) | 2½ | **6** | 6/1[3] | 102 | 48 |
| | **Murajja (USA) (104)** (PTWalwyn) **4-8-11** WCarson(1) (bit bkwd: led 2f: wknd over 2f out) | 1¾ | **7** | 14/1 | 100 | 45 |
| | **Zabadi (IRE)** (DNicholson) **4-8-11** MHills(7) (lw: a bhd) | 8 | **8** | 11/1 | 89 | 34 |
| | **Hagwah (USA) (101)** (BHanbury) **4-8-8** KDarley(10) (bit bkwd: plld hrd: led 10f out tl over 3f out: sn wknd: t.o) | dist | **9** | 20/1 | — | — |

(SP 119.5%) **9 Rn**

**2m 38.08** (8.08) CSF £62.86 TOTE £7.60: £2.00 £2.80 £1.30 (£58.30) Trio £37.40 OWNER Lady Rothschild (BECKHAMPTON) BRED Exors of the late Mrs D. M. de Rothschild

WEIGHT FOR AGE 4yo-1lb

**Spout** looked anything but the winner as she failed to get a clear run when in rear going to the two-furlong pole, but a storming run saw her get up in the last stride. (6/1)

**Wayne County (IRE)** made an excellent return, and did nothing wrong, but was caught right on the line. There are again races to be won. (11/1: 8/1-12/1)

**Moonax (IRE)** made a pleasing return, considering the trip was too short and the race was needed. Nearest at the end as his stamina came into play, he looks as good as ever and should again win his share over longer distances, although life will be tough in the Cup races against the Double brothers. (7/4)

**581 Florid (USA)** had every chance over two furlongs out before failing to find another gear. (8/1)

**Commoner (USA)** had cooked his goose below the distance. (11/2)

**Blushing Flame (USA)** (6/1: 4/1-7/1)

**Murajja (USA)** (14/1: 12/1-20/1)

## 727 TRIPLEPRINT GREENHAM STKS (Gp 3) (3-Y.O C & G) (Class A)

3-00 (3-01) **7f** £19,860.00 (£7,428.00: £3,564.00: £1,548.00) Stalls: Centre GOING: 0.49 sec per fur (GS)

| | Horse | Dist | Pos | SP | RR | SF |
|---|---|---|---|---|---|---|
| | **Danehill Dancer (IRE)** (NACallaghan) **3-9-0** PatEddery(8) (lw: stdy hdwy over 2f out: led over 1f out: rdn out) | — | **1** | Evens[1] | 117 | 72 |
| | **Kahir Almaydan (IRE) (115)** (JLDunlop) **3-9-0** WCarson(1) (lw: led over 5f: rdn & r.o ins fnl f) | 1½ | **2** | 11/2[3] | 114 | 69 |
| | **Tagula (IRE) (117)** (IABalding) **3-9-0** LDettori(3) (lw: a.p: chsd ldr over 3f out: ev ch over 1f out: unable qckn) | 1¼ | **3** | 6/1 | 111 | 66 |
| 574[4] | **Henry The Fifth (104)** (CEBrittain) **3-9-0** BDoyle(2) (chsd ldr over 3f: rdn over 2f out: one pce) | 4 | **4** | 25/1 | 102 | 57 |
| | **Woodborough (USA) (116)** (PWChapple-Hyam) **3-9-0** JReid(5) (b.hind: hld up: rdn over 2f out: one pce) | hd | **5** | 5/1[2] | 101 | 56 |
| | **Lucayan Prince (USA)** (DRLoder) **3-9-0** RHughes(6) (bit bkwd: a bhd) | 5 | **6** | 16/1 | 90 | 45 |
| | **Lomberto (107)** (RHannon) **3-9-0** TQuinn(7) (bit bkwd: bhd fnl 4f) | 12 | **7** | 16/1 | 63 | 18 |
| | **Sea Dane (103)** (PWHarris) **3-9-0** GHind(4) (bhd fnl 3f) | 17 | **8** | 40/1 | 24 | — |

(SP 114.4%) **8 Rn**

**1m 30.18** (5.68) CSF £6.88 TOTE £2.00: £1.30 £1.30 £1.80 (£6.20) OWNER Mr M. Tabor (NEWMARKET) BRED L. K. and K. McCreery

**Danehill Dancer (IRE)**, a high-class juvenile, did just what was required on this return. There can be no doubting that he is an extremely useful performer, and connections are quite rightly very excited at the prospect of running him in the 2000 Guineas, but the Greenham has hardly been a good advert for the race in recent years, and life will be very tough for him against Alhaarth and Beauchamp King. (Evens)

**Kahir Almaydan (IRE)** ran a race full of promise. Storming off in front as usual, he was headed going to the final furlong, but kept on well to win the battle for second. At his best when employing forcing tactics, he looks set for a very successful season, but probably at no further than seven furlongs, and more likely short of it. (11/2)

**Tagula (IRE)** may have led for a few strides going to the final furlong before left standing. (6/1: op 4/1)

**574 Henry The Fifth**, second to halfway, was made to look very pedestrian in this company in the final quarter-mile. (25/1)

**Woodborough (USA)** made no impression in the final quarter-mile. (5/1)

## 728 LADBROKES SPRING CUP H'CAP (0-105) (4-Y.O+) (Class B)

3-30 (3-32) **1m 7y (round)** £18,156.25 (£5,500.00: £2,687.50: £1,281.25) Stalls: Low GOING: 0.27 sec per fur (G)

| | Horse | Dist | Pos | SP | RR | SF |
|---|---|---|---|---|---|---|
| | **Royal Philosopher (88)** (JWHills) **4-8-13** MHills(12) (lw: mde virtually all: rdn out) | — | **1** | 25/1 | 106 | 84 |
| 450* | **Cool Edge (IRE) (86)** (MHTompkins) **5-8-11** PRobinson(18) (lw: hld up: chsd wnr over 1f out: r.o) | 2 | **2** | 14/1 | 100 | 78 |
| 442[5] | **Cadeaux Tryst (103)** (EALDunlop) **4-10-0** PaulEddery(2) (b: lw: hld up: swtchd rt wl over 1f out: unable qckn) | 4 | **3** | 12/1 | 109 | 87 |
| 600* | **Welton Arsenal (95)** (MRChannon) **4-9-6** RHughes(19) (stdy hdwy over 1f out: r.o one pce) | 2 | **4** | 16/1 | 97 | 75 |
| 633* | **Star Talent (USA) (82)** (MissGayKelleway) **5-8-7** RCochrane(7) (stdd s: rdn & hdwy over 1f out: one pce) | ½ | **5** | 16/1 | 83 | 61 |
| 442[6] | **Band on the Run (95)** (BAMcMahon) **9-9-1**(5) LNewton(14) (hld up: rdn over 2f out: one pce) | 2½ | **6** | 25/1 | 91 | 69 |
| 455[11] | **Night Dance (95)** (GLewis) **4-9-3**(3) AWhelan(16) (s.s: rdn over 2f out: hdwy over 1f out: nvr nrr) | 1¾ | **7** | 12/1 | 88 | 66 |
| | **Jawaal (99)** (LadyHerries) **6-9-10** JReid(5) (bkwd: a.p: rdn over 1f out: sn wknd) | hd | **8** | 14/1 | 91 | 69 |
| | **Wilcuma (90)** (PJMakin) **5-9-1** SSanders(1) (bit bkwd: a mid div) | 1 | **9** | 14/1 | 80 | 58 |
| 455[4] | **Shinerolla (83)** (CParker) **4-8-8** WWoods(9) (s.s: nvr nrr) | ¾ | **10** | 8/1[2] | 72 | 50 |
| | **Clan Ben (IRE) (96)** (HRACecil) **4-9-7** PatEddery(6) (lw: nt clr run 3f out: nvr nrr) | 1¼ | **11** | 7/1[1] | 82 | 60 |
| 491* | **Anastina (80)** (NAGraham) **4-8-5** DHarrison(13) (prom over 6f) | 1¼ | **12** | 10/1[3] | 64 | 42 |
| | **Embankment (IRE) (83)** (RHannon) **6-8-8** BThomson(17) (bit bkwd: prom over 5f) | 1 | **13** | 33/1 | 65 | 43 |
| 580[12] | **Romios (IRE) (90)** (PFICole) **4-9-1** TQuinn(4) (prom over 6f) | 1¼ | **14** | 14/1 | 70 | 48 |
| 455[14] | **Hoh Express (99)** (IABalding) **4-9-10** KDarley(11) (bhd fnl 2f) | 1½ | **15** | 25/1 | 76 | 54 |
| 455* | **Stone Ridge (IRE) (94)** (RHannon) **4-9-0**(5) DaneO'Neill(20) (lw: bhd fnl 2f) | 4 | **16** | 14/1 | 63 | 41 |

**Akil (IRE) (90)** (RWArmstrong) **4-9-1** WCarson(8) (lw: bhd fnl 2f) ....3 **17** 16/1 53 31
**Czarna (IRE) (83)** (CEBrittain) **5-8-8** BDoyle(3) (bkwd: prom over 5f) ....2½ **18** 12/1 41 19
**Cim Bom Bom (IRE) (93)** (MBell) **4-9-4** MFenton(10) (bit bkwd: bhd fnl 2f) ....6 **19** 50/1 39 17
**Daunt (93)** (JHMGosden) **4-9-4** LDettori(15) (bkwd: a bhd) ....5 **20** 12/1 29 7
(SP 130.9%) **20 Rn**

**1m 39.51** (3.51) CSF £317.23 CT £4,088.36 TOTE £24.80: £4.20 £3.40 £4.40 £3.00 (£144.00) Trio £2,290.70; £2,936.05 to 2.40 Nottingham 22/4/96. OWNER Mr A. N. Miller (LAMBOURN) BRED A. N. Miller

**Royal Philosopher** made a winning start for his new stable and did it the hard way in an ultra-competitive event. (25/1)
**450* Cool Edge (IRE)**, who went down early, chased the leaders. He took second place below the distance and pulled well clear of the rest, but could not get to the winner. (14/1)
**442 Cadeaux Tryst** failed to pick up after being switched, but this was a good effort under topweight. (12/1)
**600* Welton Arsenal** picked up on the bridle as usual below the distance but, once let down, then found little. (16/1)
**633* Star Talent (USA)**, pushed along to pick up below the distance, could make no further impression. (16/1)
**442 Band on the Run** could only keep on in his own time in the final two furlongs. (25/1)
**Jawaal**, who looked far from fit, still showed plenty of promise. Lack of a run told below the distance, but he is sure to come on a lot for this and should not take long to regain the winning thread. (14/1)

## 729 NETHERAVON MEDIAN AUCTION MAIDEN STKS (2-Y.O F) (Class D)

4-00 (4-00) **5f 34y** £3,687.50 (£1,100.00: £525.00: £237.50) Stalls: Centre GOING: 0.49 sec per fur (GS)

SP RR SF

**Cherry Blossom (IRE)** (RHannon) **2-8-11** PatEddery(1) (leggy: mde all: rdn over 1f out: r.o wl) ....— **1** 6/5[1] 79+ 31
**Copperbeech (IRE)** (PWChapple-Hyam) **2-8-11** JReid(2) (leggy: lt-f: a.p: chsd wnr over 1f out: no imp) ....3½ **2** 4/1[2] 68 20
**March Star (IRE)** (JARToller) **2-8-11** WCarson(7) (w'like: bit bkwd: hdwy over 2f out: r.o one pce fnl f) ....s.h **3** 7/1 68 20
**Poly Moon** (MRChannon) **2-8-11** RHughes(4) (neat: rdn over 2f out: no hdwy) ....7 **4** 6/1[3] 46 —
**Life On The Street** (RHannon) **2-8-11** KDarley(5) (scope: bit bkwd: chsd wnr tl wknd over 1f out) ....¾ **5** 6/1[3] 44 —
**Clara Bliss (IRE)** (BJMeehan) **2-8-11** BDoyle(3) (neat: bit bkwd: hld up: rdn over 2f out: sn bhd) ....4 **6** 16/1 32 —
**Zanabay** (MartynMeade) **2-8-6**(5) RHavlin(8) (neat: bkwd: swvd rt s: racd alone stands' side: a bhd) ....5 **7** 25/1 16 —
(SP 116.3%) **7 Rn**

**66.6 secs** (6.40) CSF £6.53 TOTE £2.40: £1.70 £1.70 (£2.80) OWNER Highclere Thoroughbred Racing Ltd (MARLBOROUGH) BRED Arthur Robinson

**Cherry Blossom (IRE)** had been reported to have been working well at home. Smartly away to make the running, she had polished off these rivals in the final furlong. (6/5: 5/2-11/10)
**Copperbeech (IRE)**, a half-sister to Blair Castle, is out of a mare who is related to Mahogany. Unseating her rider when mounted in the paddock, she proved friendless in the market and could not cope with the winner. (4/1: op 6/4)
**March Star (IRE)**, whose dam won over a mile, will be sharper for the outing and should stay further. (7/1)
**Poly Moon**, a half-sister to three winners including Misterioso, may need better ground. (6/1: 4/1-7/1)
**Life On The Street**, a sister to Cross the Border and a half-sister to Venture Capitalist, has more scope than most of these and improvement can be expected. (6/1: 4/1-7/1)

## 730 BURGHCLERE MAIDEN STKS (I) (3-Y.O) (Class D)

4-30 (4-31) **1m** £3,492.50 (£1,040.00: £495.00: £222.50) Stalls: Centre GOING: 0.49 sec per fur (GS)

SP RR SF

**Nash House (IRE)** (PWChapple-Hyam) **3-9-0** JReid(9) (w'like: scope: lw: a gng wl: stdy hdwy over 2f out: led over 1f out: qcknd clr ins fnl f) ....— **1** 4/9[1] 92+ 61
**The Dilettanti (USA)** (JARToller) **3-9-0** SSanders(10) (bkwd: led over 6f: one pce) ....5 **2** 50/1 82 51
**Mukhlles (USA)** (MajorWRHern) **3-9-0** WCarson(12) (h.d.w: lw: hld up: hdwy over 2f out: swtchd lft wl over 1f out: one pce) ....2 **3** 6/1[2] 78 47
**Raise A Prince (FR)** (RWArmstrong) **3-9-0** WWoods(8) (a.p: one pce fnl 2f) ....3 **4** 10/1[3] 72 41
445[6] **Lucky Archer** (CEBrittain) **3-9-0** BDoyle(2) (lw: plld hrd: prom tl wknd over 1f out) ....5 **5** 25/1 62 31
**Bechstein** (JLDunlop) **3-9-0** TQuinn(1) (w'like: bit bkwd: s.i.s: hdwy over 3f out: wknd over 2f out) ....2 **6** 10/1[3] 58 27
**Banneret (USA)** (LordHuntingdon) **3-9-0** DHarrison(6) (w'like: bit bkwd: prom: pushed along over 4f out: wknd over 2f out) ....½ **7** 40/1 57 26
**Waft (USA)** (BWHills) **3-8-9** MHills(4) (bit bkwd: hdwy over 3f out: wknd over 2f out) ....1¼ **8** 33/1 50 19
640[12] **Flying Pennant (IRE)** (RHannon) **3-8-9**(5) DaneO'Neill(14) (prom over 5f) ....5 **9** 50/1 45 14
578[7] **Brentability (IRE)** (GLewis) **3-9-0** SWhitworth(13) (bit bkwd: s.s: rdn 3f out: a bhd) ....1 **10** 50/1 43 12
**Hever Golf Classic** (TJNaughton) **3-9-0** PaulEddery(5) (leggy: scope: s.s: a bhd) ....4 **11** 25/1 35 4
**Battle Spark (USA)** (CACyzer) **3-9-0** DBiggs(3) (wl grwn: dwlt: sn prom: wknd over 2f out) ....4 **12** 50/1 27 —
583[12] **Sam Rockett** (CAHorgan) **3-9-0** AClark(11) (a bhd) ....1¼ **13** 50/1 24 —
**Stoney End (USA)** (MRChannon) **3-9-0** RHughes(7) (bit bkwd: prom over 5f: t.o) ....18 **14** 33/1 — —
(SP 127.5%) **14 Rn**

**1m 44.53** (7.53) CSF £34.84 TOTE £1.40: £1.10 £13.40 £1.60 (£70.40) Trio £118.30 OWNER Lord Weinstock & The Hon Simon Weinstock (MARLBOROUGH) BRED Ballymacoll Stud Farm Ltd

**Nash House (IRE)**, highly regarded at home, lived up to his reputation and showed a nice turn of foot to score impressively in a time two seconds quicker than the other division. He will follow the same route as his three-parts brother Spectrum by taking in the Irish 2000 Guineas before the Derby, and the sky's the limit at this stage. (4/9)
**The Dilettanti (USA)**, although no match for the winner, did not cave in when headed and, given the fact that he looked distinctly burly beforehand, he should soon go one better. (50/1)
**Mukhlles (USA)** has strengthened during the winter and will soon start repaying some of his $275,000 purchase price on this evidence. (6/1: tchd 10/1)
**Raise A Prince (FR)**, a 90,000 guineas half-brother to a listed winner in France, confirmed the promise of his Newmarket debut last September, and seems to be going the right way. (10/1: 6/1-11/1)
**445 Lucky Archer** did himself no favours by refusing to settle. (25/1)
**Bechstein**, a 205,000 guineas half-brother to several winners, did enough to suggest he should live up to the family name. (10/1: op 6/1)

## 731 LEVY BOARD SEVENTH RACE H'CAP (0-90) (3-Y.O) (Class C)

5-00 (5-01) **1m 4f 5y** £5,377.50 (£1,620.00: £785.00: £367.50) Stalls: Low GOING: 0.27 sec per fur (G)

SP RR SF

593[5] **Al's Alibi (72)** (WRMuir) **3-8-10** PatEddery(10) (lw: chsd clr ldr: rdn over 3f out: led wl over 1f out: drvn out) ....— **1** 12/1 81 47

| Form | Horse | Dist | Pos | SP | RR | SF |
|---|---|---|---|---|---|---|
| 494* | **Infamous (USA) (82)** (PFICole) **3-9-6** TQuinn(4) (hld up: rdn & chsd wnr over 1f out: no imp) | 3½ | **2** | 2/1[1] | 86 | 52 |
| 594[5] | **Rivercare (IRE) (58)** (MJPolglase) **3-7-10** NCarlisle(11) (lw: led: racd wd 4f: sn clr: hdd wl over 1f out: one pce) | 2 | **3** | 33/1 | 60 | 26 |
| *364** | **Punkah (USA) (77)** (LordHuntingdon) **3-9-1** DHarrison(3) (lw: prom tl wknd over 1f out) | 8 | **4** | 8/1 | 68 | 34 |
| | **Nosey Native (81)** (JPearce) **3-9-5** GBardwell(9) (hdwy over 4f out: rdn over 3f out: wknd over 1f out) | 3 | **5** | 12/1 | 68 | 34 |
| 594[D] | **Atlantic Mist (58)** (BRMillman) **3-7-10** FNorton(12) (lw: plld hrd: hdwy 4f out: wknd over 2f out) | nk | **6** | 12/1 | 45 | 11 |
| | **Ela-Yie-Mou (IRE) (75)** (LMCumani) **3-8-13** LDettori(2) (bit bkwd: nvr nr to chal) | nk | **7** | 8/1 | 61 | 27 |
| 593[8] | **Ailesbury Hill (USA) (74)** (PWChapple-Hyam) **3-8-7**(5) RHavlin(1) (prom: rdn over 4f out: sn wknd) | 8 | **8** | 14/1 | 50 | 16 |
| | **Oliver Rock (65)** (MajorDNChappell) **3-8-3** BThomson(8) (rdn 4f out: a bhd) | 3 | **9** | 6/1[3] | 37 | 3 |
| 567* | **Roman Gold (IRE) (83)** (RHannon) **3-9-2**(5) DaneO'Neill(5) (lw: prom tl wknd over 3f out) | 1 | **10** | 4/1[2] | 53 | 19 |
| *530[7]* | **Kinnescash (IRE) (73)** (MSSaunders) **3-8-11** RHughes(7) (lw: a bhd) | 10 | **11** | 25/1 | 30 | — |
| 634[5] | **Wire Act (USA) (60)** (MartynMeade) **3-7-12** TSprake(6) (rdn over 4f out: sn bhd: t.o fnl 2f) | 17 | **12** | 20/1 | — | — |

(SP 131.1%) **12 Rn**

**2m 40.33** (10.33) CSF £38.05 CT £777.61 TOTE £14.60: £2.40 £1.60 £12.90 (£21.40) Trio £645.40; £272.73 to 2.40 Nottingham 22/4/96.
OWNER The Sussex Stud Ltd (LAMBOURN) BRED The Sussex Stud and Roncon Ltd
LONG HANDICAP Rivercare (IRE) 7-7 Atlantic Mist 7-9

**593 Al's Alibi**, appreciating this longer trip, stayed on well after gaining the upper hand inside the quarter-mile marker. (12/1)
**494* Infamous (USA)** found the winner too strong in the last furlong and a half. (2/1)
**Rivercare (IRE)**, 3lb out of the handicap, headed straight for the far rail leaving the stalls and soon held a clear advantage. It remains to be seen though if this was little more than a flash in the pan. (33/1)
**Punkah (USA)** seemed to have been given plenty of weight after only winning a bad race at Lingfield in February. (8/1)
**Nosey Native**, 7lb higher than when winning at Yarmouth last back-end, did not last the trip in this yielding ground. (12/1)
**594 Atlantic Mist** did not switch off as well as his jockey would have liked. (12/1: op 8/1)
**Ela-Yie-Mou (IRE)** may not have been particularly well handicapped, but gave the impression he can do better than this. (8/1)

## 732 BURGHCLERE MAIDEN STKS (II) (3-Y.O) (Class D)
5-30 (5-31) **1m (straight)** £3,460.00 (£1,030.00: £490.00: £220.00) Stalls: Centre GOING: 0.49 sec per fur (GS)

| Form | Horse | Dist | Pos | SP | RR | SF |
|---|---|---|---|---|---|---|
| | **Golden Ace (IRE)** (RHannon) **3-8-9**(5) DaneO'Neill(3) (str: scope: a.p: led over 3f out: r.o wl) | — | **1** | 33/1 | 91 | 40 |
| | **Forza Figlio** (MissGayKelleway) **3-9-0** RCochrane(1) (str: scope: bit bkwd: sn prom: ev ch ins fnl f: r.o) | ½ | **2** | 25/1 | 90 | 39 |
| | **Musick House (IRE)** (PWChapple-Hyam) **3-9-0** JReid(12) (b.hind: bit bkwd: a.p: ev ch ins fnl f: r.o) | s.h | **3** | 4/1[2] | 90 | 39 |
| | **Phantom Quest** (HRACecil) **3-9-0** PatEddery(2) (gd sort: a.p: ev ch ins fnl f: unable qckn) | ¾ | **4** | 4/6[1] | 88 | 37 |
| | **Kuala Lipis (USA)** (PFICole) **3-9-0** TQuinn(14) (w'like: scope: a.p: r.o one pce fnl 2f) | ¾ | **5** | 14/1 | 87 | 36 |
| | **Double Bluff (IRE)** (IABalding) **3-9-0** KDarley(13) (prom over 5f) | 6 | **6** | 11/1[3] | 75 | 24 |
| | **Mawared (IRE)** (JLDunlop) **3-9-0** WCarson(8) (w'like: scope: s.s: rdn over 3f out: sme hdwy over 2f out: wknd over 1f out) | 4 | **7** | 14/1 | 67 | 16 |
| 583[10] | **Ameer Alfayaafi (IRE)** (RAkehurst) **3-9-0** SSanders(9) (bit bkwd: dwlt: a bhd) | nk | **8** | 50/1 | 66 | 15 |
| | **Formidable Flame** (WJMusson) **3-9-0** OUrbina(6) (w'like: bhd fnl 2f) | 1¼ | **9** | 50/1 | 64 | 13 |
| | **Fasil (IRE)** (CJBenstead) **3-9-0** MWigham(5) (str: bit bkwd: sme hdwy over 2f out: wknd over 1f out) | 1½ | **10** | 50/1 | 61 | 10 |
| | **Scimitar** (PJMakin) **3-9-0** AMcGlone(4) (wl grwn: s.s: a bhd) | nk | **11** | 50/1 | 60 | 9 |
| 550[6] | **Charlton Imp (USA)** (RJHodges) **3-8-9** FNorton(7) (bhd fnl 2f) | nk | **12** | 50/1 | 55 | 4 |
| | **Kutman (USA)** (MRStoute) **3-9-0** LDettori(10) (str: scope: bit bkwd: s.s: hdwy over 2f out: wknd over 1f out) | hd | **13** | 12/1 | 59 | 8 |
| | **Grey Galava** (BWHills) **3-8-2**(7) GBrace(11) (led over 4f: wknd over 2f out: t.o) | 14 | **14** | 50/1 | 26 | — |

(SP 127.9%) **14 Rn**

**1m 46.54** (9.54) CSF £559.49 TOTE £62.80: £8.90 £6.00 £1.40 (£995.50) Trio £466.90; £65.77 to 2.40 Nottingham 22/4/96. OWNER Mr George Teo (MARLBOROUGH) BRED Miss Roseanne Millett and Paul McEnery

**Golden Ace (IRE)**, a half-brother to several winners including Irish Lincoln winner Bolino Star, held on really well under the stands' rail and possesses the physique to progress. (33/1)
**Forza Figlio**, out of a half-sister to Creag-an-Sgor, ran a fine race in defeat and should not be hard to place. (25/1)
**Musick House (IRE)**, a half-brother to Rodrigo de Triano, is described as a lazy worker at home. He kept on willingly to the end and should come on a bit for this. (4/1: tchd 8/1)
**Phantom Quest**, a half-brother to Painted Desert, had been working well with impressive Newmarket winner Storm Trooper. With plenty of big-race entries, this was a shade disappointing, and it could be that he needs better ground. (4/6)
**Kuala Lipis (USA)**, a half-brother to a couple of winners, showed the right sort of attitude in the later stages and should have little difficulty opening his account. (14/1)
**Double Bluff (IRE)** had refused to enter the stalls on his third appearance as a juvenile and is now qualified for handicaps. (11/1: 7/1-14/1)
**Mawared (IRE)** (14/1: 8/1-16/1)

T/Jkpt: Not won; £15,433.72 to Nottingham 22/4/96. T/Plpt: £235.50 (139.43 Tckts). T/Qdpt: £15.10 (117 Tckts). AK/KH

# 0713-THIRSK (L-H) (Good to firm)
## Saturday April 20th
WEATHER: overcast WIND: slt half against

## 733 KNAYTON CLAIMING STKS (2-Y.O) (Class F)
2-15 (2-16) **5f** £2,652.50 (£740.00: £357.50) Stalls: High GOING minus 0.23 sec per fur (GF)

| Form | Horse | Dist | Pos | SP | RR | SF |
|---|---|---|---|---|---|---|
| 624[5] | **Mill End Girl** (MWEasterby) **2-8-2** JFEgan(2) (chsd ldrs: hung lft & led over 1f out: r.o u.p) | — | **1** | 10/1 | 58 | 13 |
| | **Jib Jab** (DNicholls) **2-9-3** AlexGreaves(3) (leggy: scope: bit bkwd: s.s: rn green: hdwy over 1f out: wandered: styd on wl towards fin) | 1¾ | **2** | 12/1 | 67? | 22 |
| | **Cantsaynowt** (RAFahey) **2-8-6** ACulhane(1) (neat: scope: w ldrs: led ½-wy tl over 1f out: styd on same pce) | ½ | **3** | 5/1[3] | 55 | 10 |
| 699[8] | **The Bee Man** (MWEasterby) **2-8-8**(5) GParkin(5) (trckd ldrs: hung lft thrght: wknd over 1f out) | 2 | **4** | 12/1 | 55 | 10 |
| 590[2] | **Dancing Star (IRE)** (PDEvans) **2-8-2** JQuinn(6) (lw: led to ½-wy: wknd over 1f out) | ¾ | **5** | 7/2[2] | 42 | — |
| 639[3] | **Caviar And Candy** (DJSCosgrove) **2-7-13**(5) MHenry(4) (lw: chsd ldrs: outpcd 2f out: sn btn) | hd | **6** | 13/8[1] | 44 | — |
| | **Loxley's Girl (IRE)** (MWEasterby) **2-8-8** DaleGibson(7) (unf: bit bkwd: s.s: a bhd) | 6 | **7** | 12/1 | 29 | — |
| 624[4] | **Chilled Wine** (NBycroft) **2-8-4** GCarter(8) (chsd ldrs tl lost pl ½-wy: sn bhd) | 5 | **8** | 12/1 | 9 | — |

(SP 116.8%) **8 Rn**

**61.2 secs** (3.20) CSF £103.43 TOTE £22.20: £3.20 £2.30 £2.10 (£76.60) OWNER Mr W. T. Allgood (SHERIFF HUTTON) BRED M. W. Easterby

**624 Mill End Girl** behaved herself in the preliminaries this time. Showing a marked tendency to hang left, she took a poor event, even by claiming race standards. (10/1)
**Jib Jab**, who looked burly, showed a nice action going down. Slowly away and green, he finished in pleasing style and will prove different class to this lot in due course. (12/1: op 8/1)
**Cantsaynowt**, who lacks size, drifted badly in the market. (5/1: op 9/4)
**608 The Bee Man**, dropped in class, raced keenly and tended to hang. (12/1)
**590 Dancing Star (IRE)** showed plenty of speed but was going nowhere with over a furlong to run. (7/2)
**639 Caviar And Candy** is only small. (13/8: 9/4-6/4)
**Loxley's Girl (IRE)** (12/1: op 8/1)

## 734 RACING CHANNEL RATING RELATED MAIDEN STKS (0-65) (I) (3-Y.O+) (Class F)
2-50 (2-50) **7f** £2,407.50 (£670.00: £322.50) Stalls: Low GOING minus 0.23 sec per fur (GF)

| | | | | SP | RR | SF |
|---|---|---|---|---|---|---|
| 598[10] | **Young Benson (53)** (BAMcMahon) **4-9-10** GCarter(2) (lw: led 3f: sn drvn along: styd on to ld jst ins fnl f: all out) | — | 1 | 7/1[3] | 67 | 40 |
| | **Soldier Mak (65)** (AHide) **3-8-11** MTebbutt(8) (swtg: hld up: hdwy on ins & nt clr run over 1f out: swtchd rt: fin wl) | nk | 2 | 7/1[3] | 66 | 26 |
| 562[12] | **Harry's Treat (52)** (JLEyre) **4-9-4**(3) OPears(6) (hld up: stdy hdwy on outside 2f out: styd on wl towards fin) | s.h | 3 | 12/1 | 63 | 36 |
| 595[15] | **Mellors (IRE) (65)** (JARToller) **3-8-11** KFallon(4) (led 4f out tl jst ins fnl f: no ex) | ½ | 4 | 15/8[1] | 65 | 25 |
| 468[3] | **Nakhal (63)** (DJGMurraySmith) **3-8-11v[1]** RHills(7) (b.off fore: sn chsng ldrs: ev ch tl one pce fnl f) | 1¾ | 5 | 2/1[2] | 61 | 21 |
| | **Supermister (60)** (TDEasterby) **3-8-11** MBirch(9) (hld up: effrt over 2f out: sn rdn: wknd over 1f out) | 7 | 6 | 8/1 | 45 | 5 |
| 586[17] | **Four Lane Flyer (41)** (EJAlston) **4-9-7** SDWilliams(3) (swtg: dwlt: sn chsng ldrs: rdn & n.m.r over 2f out: sn wknd) | ½ | 7 | 25/1 | 41 | 14 |

(SP 115.8%) **7 Rn**

**1m 28.3** (4.10) CSF £48.88 TOTE £8.30: £2.10 £3.80 (£22.40) Trio £105.90 OWNER Mr Michael Stokes (TAMWORTH) BRED M. G. T. Stokes
WEIGHT FOR AGE 3yo-13lb
**Young Benson**, who has spent much of his life running over further, stuck on under a forceful ride to take a poor-class event. (7/1)
**Soldier Mak**, warm beforehand, was given a lot to do. After taking time to find an opening, he finished to some purpose and would have made it in a couple more strides. (7/1)
**Harry's Treat**, very fit, ran his best race for some time. Patiently ridden, he was putting in his best work at the line. (12/1)
**Mellors (IRE)**, a keen-going type, took it up before halfway but was run out of it inside the last furlong. (15/8)
**468 Nakhal**, tried in a visor, did not look particularly happy in his work. (2/1)

## 735 THOMAS LORD H'CAP (0-90) (3-Y.O+) (Class C)
3-20 (3-21) **5f** £6,368.00 (£1,904.00: £912.00: £416.00) Stalls: High GOING minus 0.23 sec per fur (GF)

| | | | | SP | RR | SF |
|---|---|---|---|---|---|---|
| 587[7] | **Stuffed (60)** (MWEasterby) **4-7-12** JFEgan(15) (chsd ldrs: r.o u.p to ld ins fnl f) | — | 1 | 13/2[2] | 69 | 41 |
| | **Royal Dome (IRE) (72)** (MartynWane) **4-8-10** JCarroll(16) (bit bkwd: mde most tl ins fnl f: kpt on wl) | hd | 2 | 15/2[3] | 81 | 53 |
| *653*[2] | **Lady Sheriff (81)** (RHollinshead) **5-9-0**(5) FLynch(5) (a chsng ldrs: rdn over 1f out: kpt on wl) | ½ | 3 | 12/1 | 88+ | 60 |
| 644[2] | **Montrestar (68)** (PDEvans) **3-7-3v**(7) IonaWands(13) (swtg: a chsng ldrs: nt qckn fnl f) | 1 | 4 | 14/1 | 72 | 34 |
| 610[12] | **Stephensons Rocket (58)** (DNicholls) **5-7-10b[1]** JQuinn(18) (s.i.s: hdwy on ins & n.m.r over 1f out: kpt on towards fin) | nk | 5 | 16/1 | 61 | 33 |
| 582[16] | **Fantasy Racing (IRE) (80)** (MRChannon) **4-9-4** CandyMorris(14) (mid div: rdn ½-wy: styd on ins fnl f) | 1 | 6 | 20/1 | 80 | 52 |
| 659[2] | **Tenor (58)** (DNicholls) **5-7-7**(3) NVarley(17) (lw: dwlt: effrt & n.m.r ½-wy: kpt on fnl f: nt rch ldrs) | nk | 7 | 3/1[1] | 57 | 29 |
| 700[2] | **La Suquet (72)** (NTinkler) **4-8-10** GCarter(1) (chsd ldrs on outside tl wknd over 1f out) | ½ | 8 | 12/1 | 69 | 41 |
| 610[10] | **Just Dissident (IRE) (60)** (RMWhitaker) **4-7-12** DaleGibson(3) (in tch far side: rdn over 1f out: no imp) | hd | 9 | 20/1 | 57 | 29 |
| 587[10] | **Shadow Jury (65)** (DWChapman) **6-8-3b** LCharnock(2) (w ldrs tl wknd over 1f out) | nk | 10 | 20/1 | 61 | 33 |
| 589[20] | **Call Me I'm Blue (IRE) (78)** (NTinkler) **6-9-2** TIves(12) (bhd fr ½-wy) | ½ | 11 | 14/1 | 72 | 44 |
| 582* | **Latching (IRE) (80)** (RFJohnsonHoughton) **4-9-4** RHills(10) (bhd & rdn along ½-wy: n.d) | ½ | 12 | 8/1 | 73 | 45 |
| | **For the Present (87)** (TDBarron) **6-9-11** JFortune(6) (bit bkwd: hld up: effrt over 2f out: sn wknd) | s.h | 13 | 20/1 | 80 | 52 |
| 587[18] | **Insider Trader (76)** (MrsJRRamsden) **5-9-0v** KFallon(7) (w ldrs tl wknd over 1f out) | hd | 14 | 16/1 | 68 | 40 |
| 587[11] | **Saddlehome (USA) (78)** (TDBarron) **7-9-2** JFanning(4) (swtg: nvr nr ldrs) | s.h | 15 | 14/1 | 70 | 42 |
| | **Surprise Mission (75)** (RMWhitaker) **4-8-13** ACulhane(8) (bit bkwd: hld up & plld hrd: nt clr run ½-wy & over 1f out: nt rcvr) | ½ | 16 | 14/1 | 65 | 37 |
| 587[6] | **Beau Venture (USA) (67)** (FHLee) **8-8-5** RLappin(9) (chsd ldrs 3f: sn wknd) | 1¾ | 17 | 10/1 | 52 | 24 |
| | **Laurel Delight (90)** (JBerry) **6-9-9**(5) PRoberts(11) (bit bkwd: s.i.s: a bhd) | nk | 18 | 20/1 | 74 | 46 |

(SP 147.9%) **18 Rn**

**59.3 secs** (1.30) CSF £57.71 CT £555.63 TOTE £9.60: £2.30 £1.80 £2.50 £3.40 (£18.40) Trio £158.00 OWNER Early Morning Breakfast Syndicate (SHERIFF HUTTON) BRED Manor Grange Stud Co Ltd
LONG HANDICAP Tenor 7-8 Montrestar 7-3
WEIGHT FOR AGE 3yo-10lb
**Stuffed**, well drawn this time, scraped home by the skin of his teeth. (13/2)
**Royal Dome (IRE)**, who improved at three, winning three times, showed plenty of toe from a favourable draw and battled back when headed. (15/2)
**653 Lady Sheriff**, back over five, did not have the best draw. (12/1)
**644 Montrestar** ran well considering he was 7lb wrong at the weights. (14/1)
**Stephensons Rocket**, who has been out of sorts since winning four times as a three-year-old, had the blinkers on for the first time and wore a tongue-strap. After missing the break slightly and being forced to check in the first 100 yards, he did not have the luck of the race and, in the circumstances, did well to finish so close. (16/1)
**Fantasy Racing (IRE)**, who won six from twenty-five outings last season, stuck on towards the finish and is on the way back. (20/1)
**659 Tenor**, who took this prize a year ago from a 4lb higher mark, missed the break. With the field bunching on the stands' side, he had little room to work and, in the circumstances, did well to finish so close. (3/1)

## 736 THIRSK CLASSIC TRIAL CONDITIONS STKS (3-Y.O) (Class B)
3-50 (3-51) **1m** £9,470.00 (£3,530.00: £1,715.00: £725.00) Stalls: Low GOING minus 0.23 sec per fur (GF)

| | | | | SP | RR | SF |
|---|---|---|---|---|---|---|
| | **Ramooz (USA) (104)** (BHanbury) **3-8-11** JStack(7) (hld up: stdy hdwy on outside 2f out: r.o to ld ins fnl f: hld on towards fin) | — | 1 | 4/1[2] | 100 | 47 |
| | **Bahamian Knight (CAN) (106)** (DRLoder) **3-9-0** DRMcCabe(4) (lw: w ldr: led 2f out tl ins fnl f: r.o) | hd | 2 | 7/1[3] | 103 | 50 |

| | Horse | Pos | SP | RR | SF |
|---|---|---|---|---|---|
| | **Ali-Royal (IRE)** (HRACecil) **3-9-0** WRyan(1) (swtg: chsd ldrs: rdn & ev ch over 1f out: nt qckn ins fnl f)..........¾ | **3** | 10/11 1 | 101 | 48 |
| | **Tamhid (USA) (100)** (HThomsonJones) **3-9-5** RHills(5) (lw: hld up: nt clr run & swtchd outside over 2f out: styd on wl fnl f: nt rch ldrs)..........½ | **4** | 10/1 | 105 | 52 |
| | **Van Gurp** (BAMcMahon) **3-8-11** GCarter(2) (dwlt: effrt & nt clr run 2f out: shkn up & one pce appr fnl f).......1¼ | **5** | 14/1 | 95 | 42 |
| 548 3 | **Wisam (100)** (RHannon) **3-9-0** RPerham(6) (b: plld hrd early: w ldrs tl wknd over 1f out)..........4 | **6** | 8/1 | 90 | 37 |
| | **Classic Eagle** (SCWilliams) **3-9-0** AMackay(3) (bit bkwd: led to 2f out: hrd rdn & sn wknd)..........2 | **7** | 8/1 | 86 | 33 |
| | | | (SP 122.9%) | | **7 Rn** |

**1m 39.3** (2.80) CSF £30.60 TOTE £5.60: £1.80 £4.10 (£18.70) OWNER Mr Hilal Salem (NEWMARKET) BRED Gainsborough Stud Management Ltd

**Ramooz (USA)** appreciated the fast ground and, well ridden, scraped home in a race that was a Classic Trial in name only. (4/1)
**Bahamian Knight (CAN)**, absent since Royal Ascot, stuck on strongly under severe pressure and, in the end, was just denied. He will be suited by a step up to a mile and a quarter. (7/1)
**Ali-Royal (IRE)**, very fit, was inclined to get warm beforehand. Showing a scratchy action going down, he was driven almost upsides over a furlong out but, in the dash to the line, was never going to find enough. (10/11: 5/4-4/5)
**Tamhid (USA)** showed a fair bit of knee-action going down. He did not have the best of luck in running, but finished in pleasing style. On the evidence of this, he might be suited by a slight step up in distance. (10/1)
**Van Gurp**, nibbled at in the market, looked to be travelling well, but was short of room two furlongs out and, when the gap came, he could not quicken. Still inexperienced, he should be suited by further. (14/1: 20/1-12/1)
**548 Wisam** raced keenly but did not find much at the business end. (8/1)
**Classic Eagle** looked in need of the outing and dropped away over a furlong out. He will need to have his sights set lower, and probably needs some give underfoot. (8/1)

## 737 MICHAEL FOSTER MEMORIAL CONDITIONS STKS (3-Y.O+) (Class C)

4-20 (4-20) **6f** £5,789.60 (£2,146.40: £1,033.20: £426.00) Stalls: High GOING minus 0.23 sec per fur (GF)

| | Horse | Pos | SP | RR | SF |
|---|---|---|---|---|---|
| 507* | **Carranita (IRE) (107)** (BPalling) **6-9-7** JCarroll(6) (lw: rr div: pushed along bef ½-wy: gd hdwy 2f out: led ent fnl f: r.o gamely)..........— | **1** | 11/2 | 106 | 48 |
| 548* | **Atraf (100)** (DMorley) **3-8-11** RHills(1) (led tl jnd 2f out: sn rdn: hdd ent fnl f: kpt on ins fnl f)..........1 | **2** | 3/1 2 | 104 | 35 |
| 507 3 | **Venture Capitalist (107)** (DNicholls) **7-9-12** AlexGreaves(5) (lw: hld up in tch: nt clr run 2f out: swtchd & hdwy appr fnl f: kpt on wl)..........s.h | **3** | 7/4 1 | 108 | 50 |
| | **Double Blue (104)** (MJohnston) **7-9-7** JWeaver(3) (bit bkwd: chsd ldrs: rdn to chal 2f out: no ex appr fnl f)......2 | **4** | 5/1 3 | 98 | 40 |
| 610 5 | **Castlerea Lad (83)** (RHollinshead) **7-9-0** TIves(7) (hld up & bhd: effrt & hdwy on outside 2f out: nt pce of ldrs fnl f)..........nk | **5** | 12/1 | 90 | 32 |
| | **No Monkey Nuts (80)** (JBerry) **3-7-12**(5) PFessey(2) (dwlt: sn prom: rdn & wknd fnl 2f)..........9 | **6** | 20/1 | 66 | — |
| | **Mazeed (IRE) (100)** (HThomsonJones) **3-8-11** GCarter(4) (chsd ldrs: rdn over 2f out: btn over 1f out)...........2½ | **7** | 10/1 | 67 | — |
| | | | (SP 115.0%) | | **7 Rn** |

**1m 12.3** (2.60) CSF £21.42 TOTE £4.80: £2.80 £2.20 (£9.30) OWNER Lamb Lane Associates (COWBRIDGE) BRED Mrs Anita Quinn
WEIGHT FOR AGE 3yo-11lb

**507* Carranita (IRE)** followed up her Beverley success and is in great form at present. (11/2)
**548* Atraf** set out to make it all and battled on gamely towards the finish. He will find other opportunities. (3/1)
**507 Venture Capitalist**, winner of this race twelve months ago, had no luck in running here. Messed about at a crucial stage, he stayed on late, but the damage was done. (7/4: 5/2-11//4)
**Double Blue** looked in need of the race but ran respectably, and will no doubt benefit from the outing. (5/1)
**610 Castlerea Lad** made a forward move on the outer two furlongs out, but the principals always had the legs of him. (12/1)
**Mazeed (IRE)** showed up until fading tamely in the last two furlongs, and was eased when his chance had gone. (10/1)

## 738 BUSINESS FURNITURE CENTRE LIMITED STKS (0-70) (3-Y.O+) (Class E)

4-50 (4-51) **1m 4f** £3,133.75 (£940.00: £452.50: £208.75) Stalls: High GOING minus 0.23 sec per fur (GF)

| | Horse | Pos | SP | RR | SF |
|---|---|---|---|---|---|
| 564 6 | **Tessajoe (70)** (MJCamacho) **4-9-7** LCharnock(4) (lw: hld up: smooth hdwy 3f out: led 2f out: strly chal appr fnl f: drvn out)..........— | **1** | 3/1 2 | 81 | 55 |
| 598 5 | **Domappel (67)** (MrsJCecil) **4-9-7** JWeaver(3) (hld up & bhd: effrt & gd hdwy fr 3f out: chal appr fnl f: edgd lft: no ex towards fin)..........½ | **2** | 9/2 3 | 80 | 54 |
| | **Ceilidh Star (IRE) (68)** (BWHills) **3-7-13** JFEgan(8) (trckd ldrs tl outpcd & lost pl 5f out: hdwy over 2f out: kpt on one pce fnl f)..........3 | **3** | 7/1 | 73 | 28 |
| 598 4 | **Contrafire (IRE) (70)** (WJarvis) **4-9-2**(5) MHenry(2) (rr div: shkn up & hdwy over 3f out: chsd ldrs & edgd lft u.p 2f out: no ex)..........2 | **4** | 9/4 1 | 74 | 48 |
| 472 6 | **Sheraz (IRE) (70)** (NTinkler) **4-9-7** GCarter(7) (lw: led tl rdn & hdd 2f out: kpt on one pce)..........1¾ | **5** | 14/1 | 71 | 45 |
| 594 9 | **Balios (IRE) (66)** (MJohnston) **3-8-4** JFanning(9) (chsd ldrs: rdn 4f out: wknd over 2f out)..........4 | **6** | 11/1 | 68 | 23 |
| 702 6 | **Nose No Bounds (IRE) (74)** (MJohnston) **3-8-2** TWilliams(11) (sn chsng ldr: drvn along appr st: wknd over 2f out)..........7 | **7** | 11/2 | 57 | 12 |
| 612 5 | **Forzair (59)** (JJO'Neill) **4-9-9** SDWilliams(6) (mid div: rdn over 5f out: outpcd fnl 3f)..........3 | **8** | 20/1 | 55 | 29 |
| *365* 10 | **Dvorak (IRE) (64)** (RHarris) **5-9-8** AMackay(5) (chsd ldrs: drvn 6f out: lost pl & bhd fnl 3f)..........7 | **9** | 33/1 | 43 | 18 |
| 546 6 | **Royrace (45)** (WMBrisbourne) **4-9-2**(5) DGriffiths(1) (a bhd: t.o fr ½-wy)..........6 | **10** | 33/1 | 35 | 9 |
| | **Percy Parrot (36)** (RMWhitaker) **4-9-7** ACulhane(10) (b: a in rr: lost tch 6f out: sn t.o)..........dist | **11** | 50/1 | — | — |
| | | | (SP 129.4%) | | **11 Rn** |

**2m 34.7** (4.70) CSF £17.97 TOTE £4.20: £1.50 £1.80 £2.10 (£9.70) Trio £30.40 OWNER Riley Partnership (MALTON) BRED A. and Mrs Rhodes
WEIGHT FOR AGE 3yo-20lb, 4yo-1lb

**564 Tessajoe** settled well in this fast-run race and won without recourse to the whip. A progressive performer, he should go on from here. (3/1: op 5/1)
**598 Domappel**, who was restrained towards the rear in the early stages, had plenty of running to do off the home turn. He got into a challenging position approaching the final furlong, but was always inclined to edge left under pressure, and could never master the winner. His turn will come. (9/2)
**Ceilidh Star (IRE)**, who raced keenly behind the leaders, was outpaced leaving the back straight but did some good work again in the final quarter-mile, despite edging left. A stiffer test of stamina will probably suit. (7/1)
**598 Contrafire (IRE)** made a forward move rounding the home turn and was soon on the heels of the leaders, but was inclined to hang left when pressure was applied, and could do no more in the closing stages. (9/4)
**Sheraz (IRE)** attempted to lead from pillar-to-post, but could find only one pace when collared. (14/1)
**Balios (IRE)**, flat to the boards entering the home straight, was left for dead in the final quarter-mile. (11/1: 8/1-12/1)

## 739 LEVY BOARD H'CAP (0-80) (3-Y.O+ F & M) (Class D)

5-20 (5-21) **1m** £3,925.00 (£1,180.00: £570.00: £265.00) Stalls: Low GOING minus 0.23 sec per fur (GF)

| | | | | SP | RR | SF |
|---|---|---|---|---|---|---|
| 527[6] | **Glowing Jade (66)** (JAGlover) **6-9-0** GCarter(5) (hld up: rdn appr st: stdy hdwy over 2f out: led ins fnl f: kpt on) | — | **1** | 9/1 | 74 | 45 |
| 629[5] | **Queens Consul (IRE) (79)** (BSRothwell) **6-9-13** JFortune(9) (chsd ldrs: led 2f out tl hdd ins fnl f: r.o u.p) | ½ | **2** | 11/2[3] | 86 | 57 |
| | **Gymcrak Flyer (62)** (GHolmes) **5-8-10** KFallon(3) (b.hind: in tch: effrt appr st: hdwy over 2f out: chal over 1f out: nt qckn ins fnl f) | ½ | **3** | 14/1 | 68 | 39 |
| *416** | **Cashmere Lady (75)** (JLEyre) **4-9-9** RLappin(12) (prom: led on bit wl over 2f out: sn hdd & one pce) | 3½ | **4** | 7/4[1] | 74 | 45 |
| 562[10] | **Miss Iron Heart (USA) (48)** (DJSCosgrove) **4-7-5(5)** MBaird(6) (bit bkwd: chsd ldrs: rdn wl over 2f out: r.o same pce) | nk | **5** | 50/1 | 46 | 17 |
| | **Pendley Rose (62)** (PWHarris) **3-7-10** JQuinn(10) (bit bkwd: swtg: chsd ldrs: rdn 3f out: btn wl over 1f out) | 2 | **6** | 9/2[2] | 56 | 13 |
| 586* | **Dance of Joy (48)** (JMCarr) **4-7-10** NKennedy(7) (bhd & sn rdn: outpcd tl styd on fnl 2f) | hd | **7** | 12/1 | 42 | 13 |
| | **Alfayza (62)** (JDBethell) **3-7-7(3)** DWright(11) (trckd ldrs tl lost pl appr st: n.d after) | 3 | **8** | 12/1 | 50 | 7 |
| | **Classic Romance (75)** (RHarris) **3-8-9** AMackay(8) (s.i.s: drvn bef ½-wy: no imp) | 1¼ | **9** | 11/1 | 61 | 18 |
| | **Three Arch Bridge (62)** (MJohnston) **4-8-10b** JWeaver(4) (led tl wl over 2f out: sn btn) | 2½ | **10** | 11/1 | 43 | 14 |
| | **Ma Petite Anglaise (77)** (WJarvis) **4-9-4(7)** TThomas(1) (s.i.s: a in rr) | 1¼ | **11** | 12/1 | 55 | 26 |
| 615[8] | **Hey Up Dolly (IRE) (56)** (JJO'Neill) **4-8-4b** JFEgan(13) (sn rdn along & outpcd: a in rr) | 1½ | **12** | 25/1 | 31 | 2 |

(SP 132.1%) **12 Rn**

**1m 39.8** (3.30) CSF £59.90 CT £667.03 TOTE £9.40: £2.40 £2.10 £2.80 (£16.90) Trio £69.30 OWNER Mr Brian Eastick (WORKSOP) BRED F. C. T. Wilson

LONG HANDICAP Pendley Rose 7-8 Dance of Joy 7-8 Alfayza 7-8 Miss Iron Heart (USA) 7-0

WEIGHT FOR AGE 3yo-14lb

**527 Glowing Jade** fulfilled the promise of her luckless Nottingham debut, getting on top inside the final furlong and seeing it out well. (9/1)

**629 Queens Consul (IRE)**, who goes well here, ran her usual game race and refused to give in without a fight. If there is any justice, her winning turn will not be far away. (11/2)

**Gymcrak Flyer** made a promising start to the campaign. With every chance from over a furlong out, she just failed to quicken when it mattered most. (14/1)

**Miss Iron Heart (USA)**, always chasing the leaders, could find only one speed in the final quarter-mile. (50/1)

**Pendley Rose**, never too far away, came under pressure two furlongs out, but the writing was on the wall well over a furlong out. (9/2: 3/1-5/1)

**586* Dance of Joy**, always flat to the boards, only got going when the race was over. She surely needs a stiffer test of stamina, despite having won over this trip last time. (12/1)

## 740 RACING CHANNEL RATING RELATED MAIDEN STKS (0-65) (II) (3-Y.O+) (Class F)

5-50 (5-51) **7f** £2,407.50 (£670.00: £322.50) Stalls: Low GOING minus 0.23 sec per fur (GF)

| | | | | SP | RR | SF |
|---|---|---|---|---|---|---|
| | **Willisa (65)** (JDBethell) **3-8-8** JWeaver(7) (led 2f: trckd ldr: rdn to ld 2f out: drvn clr ins fnl f) | — | **1** | 5/1[2] | 70 | 23 |
| *415*[4] | **Classic Beauty (IRE) (62)** (RHarris) **3-8-8** AMackay(8) (chsd ldrs: slt ld over 2f out: sn hdd: no ch w wnr ins fnl f) | 4 | **2** | 9/1 | 61 | 14 |
| *605*[8] | **Scenicris (IRE) (65)** (RHollinshead) **3-8-3(5)** FLynch(4) (s.i.s: bhd: hdwy on outside 2f out: edgd lft & kpt on fnl f) | ½ | **3** | 10/1 | 60 | 13 |
| 562[2] | **Backhander (IRE) (54)** (MartynWane) **4-9-10** JCarroll(2) (lw: chsd ldrs: chal over 2f out: styd on one pce fr over 1f out) | ½ | **4** | 13/2[3] | 62 | 28 |
| | **Belzao (65)** (MRChannon) **3-8-6(5)** PPMurphy(6) (lw: hld up: effrt & nt clr run on ins over 2f out: swtchd & kpt on one pce ins fnl f) | s.h | **5** | 4/5[1] | 62 | 15 |
| 478[8] | **Finisterre (IRE) (40)** (JJO'Neill) **3-8-11** JFEgan(9) (plld hrd: trckd ldrs: drvn 3f out: wknd fnl 2f) | ¾ | **6** | 20/1 | 60 | 13 |
| | **Sis Garden (60)** (TDEasterby) **3-8-8** MBirch(1) (hld up: effrt & hdwy to chse ldrs 3f out: wknd fnl 2f) | 8 | **7** | 16/1 | 39 | — |
| 539[5] | **Toe Tappin Music (USA) (43)** (MartynMeade) **3-8-11** VSlattery(5) (cl up: led after 2f tl over 2f out: sn btn) | s.h | **8** | 20/1 | 41 | — |

(SP 120.1%) **8 Rn**

**1m 28.5** (4.30) CSF £45.09 TOTE £5.80: £2.00 £1.10 £3.80 (£22.20) Trio £28.20 OWNER Sheikh Amin Dahlawi (MIDDLEHAM) BRED Al Dahlawi Stud Co Ltd

WEIGHT FOR AGE 3yo-13lb

**Willisa**, always well to the fore, took it up for the second time two furlongs out and was well on top inside the final 200 yards. (5/1: op 3/1)

**Classic Beauty (IRE)** took a slight lead early in the home straight, but was soon headed by the winner, and was no match. (9/1)

**Scenicris (IRE)**, fit from the All-Weather, picked up from off the pace in the last two furlongs, but hung left and could only stay on at the same pace in the final 200 yards. (10/1)

**562 Backhander (IRE)**, who was the pick of the paddock, was in with every chance early in the home straight, but could find only one speed in the final quarter-mile. (13/2: 12/1-6/1)

**Belzao**, held up off the pace, met trouble in running at a crucial stage and, although staying on from over a furlong out, was never able to land a serious blow. (4/5: tchd Evens)

**Finisterre (IRE)** took a strong hold early on just behind the leaders, but held every chance until weakening inside the final two furlongs. (20/1)

T/Plpt: £5,436.00 (2.09 Tckts). T/Qdpt: £32.20 (26.2 Tckts). WG/AA

# 0630-BRIGHTON (L-H) (Firm)

## Monday April 22nd

WEATHER: overcast WIND: slt half bhd

## 741 SIDNEY THOMPSON MEMORIAL MAIDEN AUCTION STKS (2-Y.O) (Class F)

2-00 (2-01) **5f 59y** £2,381.00 (£656.00: £311.00) Stalls: Low GOING minus 0.61 sec per fur (F)

| | | | | SP | RR | SF |
|---|---|---|---|---|---|---|
| 639[2] | **Castle House** (JAkehurst) **2-8-6** TQuinn(1) (lw: wnt rt s: mde all: rdn ins fnl f: r.o) | — | **1** | 2/1[1] | 63 | 7 |
| | **Seaside (IRE)** (JohnBerry) **2-8-2ow2** MFenton(6) (leggy: lw: a.p: rdn & edgd lft ins fnl f: r.o) | nk | **2** | 9/1 | 58 | — |
| | **Ekaterini Paritsi** (WGMTurner) **2-8-0** TSprake(3) (lt-f: lw: dwlt: sn rcvrd: rdn 3f out: r.o one pce ins fnl f) | 2½ | **3** | 3/1[2] | 49 | — |

| Form | Horse | Dist | Pos | SP | RR | SF |
|---|---|---|---|---|---|---|
| 639[5] | **Chopin (IRE)** (RFJohnsonHoughton) **2-8-8** AMcGlone(2) (sltly hmpd s: chsd wnr: rdn over 2f out: one pce) | hd | 4 | 6/1 | 56 | — |
| 569[5] | **Don't Forget Shoka (IRE)** (JSMoore) **2-8-1** JFEgan(5) (lw: chsd ldrs: rdn over 2f out: one pce) | 1 | 5 | 12/1 | 46 | — |
|  | **Caribbee Beach (IRE)** (CADwyer) **2-8-1** JQuinn(4) (cmpt: bkwd: sn outpcd: a bhd) | 12 | 6 | 9/2[3] | 10 | — |

(SP 108.5%) **6 Rn**

**61.9 secs** (1.90) CSF £16.58 TOTE £2.20: £1.10 £4.20 (£15.30) OWNER Mrs Jackie Mullally (LAMBOURN) BRED Roldvale Ltd

**639 Castle House**, who knew his job well, bounced out of the stalls, albeit to his right. Making it all, he saw it out well inside the final furlong when challenged. (2/1)

**Seaside (IRE)**, quite an attractive, leggy filly, looked likely to prevail when challenging inside the final furlong, but she ran green when asked for her final effort and found the post coming a few strides too soon. Her rider's overweight obviously did not help. (9/1: 6/1-12/1)

**Ekaterini Paritsi**, a finely-made filly, looked fit enough but ran very green. She missed the kick and, although recovering, was slow to pick up when asked to challenge in the straight. Late on, she stayed on quite nicely, and she will improve. (3/1)

**Chopin (IRE)**, green in the paddock, is bred to want further. (6/1: 4/1-7/1)

**569 Don't Forget Shoka (IRE)** (12/1: 6/1-14/1)

**Caribbee Beach (IRE)** was too backward to do himself justice. (9/2: op 2/1)

## 742 LEVY BOARD H'CAP (0-70) (3-Y.O+) (Class E)

2-30 (2-30) **5f 59y** £2,933.70 (£873.60: £415.80: £186.90) Stalls: Low GOING minus 0.61 sec per fur (F)

| Form | Horse | Dist | Pos | SP | RR | SF |
|---|---|---|---|---|---|---|
| 631[3] | **Apollo Red (51)** (AMoore) **7-8-13** CandyMorris(3) (a.p: chsd ldr over 2f out: hrd rdn ins fnl f: led cl home) | — | 1 | 5/1[2] | 59 | 35 |
| 601[15] | **Allwight Then (IRE) (66)** (REPeacock) **5-9-9**(5) MHenry(5) (chsd ldr: led over 3f out: rdn over 1f out: hdd cl home) | hd | 2 | 20/1 | 74 | 50 |
| 667* | **Friendly Brave (USA) (67)** (MissGayKelleway) **6-9-12**(3) 7x AWhelan(6) (b: lw: hld up: hdwy 2f out: hrd rdn ins fnl f: r.o) | ½ | 3 | 9/4[1] | 73 | 49 |
| 664[5] | **Giggleswick Girl (57)** (MRChannon) **5-9-5** RHughes(1) (sn rdn towards rr: hrd rdn over 1f out: one pce) | 2½ | 4 | 9/4[1] | 56 | 32 |
|  | **Regal Fanfare (IRE) (64)** (MrsLStubbs) **4-9-12** RCochrane(2) (dwlt: sn rdn: a bhd) | 5 | 5 | 11/2[3] | 47 | 23 |
| 648[8] | **Midnight Cookie (53)** (BAPearce) **3-8-5** SWhitworth(4) (led tl over 3f out: wknd 2f out) | 8 | 6 | 15/2 | 12 | — |

(SP 110.1%) **6 Rn**

**60.5 secs** (0.50) CSF £61.97 TOTE £4.10: £1.70 £6.30 (£26.80) OWNER Mr A. Moore (BRIGHTON) BRED Crest Stud Ltd

WEIGHT FOR AGE 3yo-10lb

**631 Apollo Red** was never far away and, brought with a well-timed challenge, led near the finish. (5/1)

**Allwight Then (IRE)** took it up after two furlongs and looked sure to score until collared close home. (20/1)

**667* Friendly Brave (USA)** seemed to be ridden a shade over-confidently. Creeping closer two furlongs out, his rider did not get serious until inside the final furlong and, although he did not pick up immediately, he was closing at the line. (9/4: 6/4-5/2)

**664 Giggleswick Girl** was never going the pace. (9/4)

**Regal Fanfare (IRE)** (11/2: 3/1-6/1)

## 743 ORLEANS LIMITED STKS (0-65) (3-Y.O) (Class F)

3-00 (3-02) **5f 213y** £2,381.00 (£656.00: £311.00) Stalls: Low GOING minus 0.61 sec per fur (F)

| Form | Horse | Dist | Pos | SP | RR | SF |
|---|---|---|---|---|---|---|
| 638[6] | **Kings Harmony (IRE) (63)** (PJMakin) **3-9-0** PatEddery(4) (lw: sn led: hrd rdn ins fnl f: r.o wl) | — | 1 | Evens[1] | 72 | 24 |
| 540[4] | **Ciserano (IRE) (55)** (MRChannon) **3-8-8** TQuinn(1) (hld up: rdn over 3f out: hdwy to chse wnr over 1f out: hrd rdn ins fnl f: r.o) | ½ | 2 | 5/1[2] | 65 | 17 |
| *488** | **Rowlandsons Stud (IRE) (62)** (GLMoore) **3-9-0** RCochrane(6) (lw: hld up: hdwy over 2f out: rdn over 1f out: one pce) | 2½ | 3 | 11/2[3] | 64 | 16 |
| *488[2]* | **Dancing Jack (52)** (JJBridger) **3-9-0** JQuinn(2) (chsd ldrs: ev ch 2f out: sn rdn: one pce) | ½ | 4 | 14/1 | 63 | 15 |
| *556[3]* | **Maple Burl (63)** (SDow) **3-8-9**(5) ADaly(3) (lw: chsd ldrs: rdn 2f out: wknd 1f out) | 2 | 5 | 11/2[3] | 57 | 9 |
|  | **Jessica's Song (56)** (WGMTurner) **3-8-8** TSprake(5) (w wnr: ev ch 2f out: sn wknd) | 3 | 6 | 8/1 | 43 | — |

(SP 115.2%) **6 Rn**

**1m 8.6** (1.40) CSF £6.49 TOTE £2.10: £1.10 £2.00 (£3.50) OWNER Ten of Hearts (MARLBOROUGH) BRED Rathasker Stud

**638 Kings Harmony (IRE)** made virtually all the running to record his first success on grass. (Evens)

**540 Ciserano (IRE)** ran her best race of the season and obviously relishes this ground. (5/1: op 5/2)

**488* Rowlandsons Stud (IRE)** moved up menacingly over two furlongs out but was unable to quicken once asked. (11/2)

**488 Dancing Jack** had his chance two furlongs out, but could not raise his gallop. (14/1: op 7/1)

**556 Maple Burl** probably found this ground too fast. (11/2: 4/1-6/1)

## 744 A R DENNIS BOOKMAKERS APRIL H'CAP (0-85) (3-Y.O+) (Class D)

3-30 (3-30) **6f 209y** £3,860.70 (£1,152.60: £550.80: £249.90) Stalls: Low GOING minus 0.61 sec per fur (F)

| Form | Horse | Dist | Pos | SP | RR | SF |
|---|---|---|---|---|---|---|
|  | **My Best Valentine (84)** (JWhite) **6-9-11**(3) AWhelan(7) (hld up: hdwy over 2f out: led over 1f out: rdn & edgd lft ins fnl f: sn straightened: r.o) | — | 1 | 14/1 | 93 | 54 |
| 633[3] | **Jo Maximus (75)** (SDow) **4-9-0**(5) ADaly(3) (chsd ldrs: led over 1f out: sn hdd: sltly hmpd ins fnl f: r.o) | nk | 2 | 4/1[1] | 83 | 44 |
| 554[11] | **Ertlon (80)** (CEBrittain) **6-9-10** BDoyle(6) (lw: chsd ldrs: rdn 2f out: r.o ins fnl f) | hd | 3 | 9/2[2] | 88 | 49 |
| 735[6] | **Fantasy Racing (IRE) (80)** (MRChannon) **4-9-10** RHughes(4) (chsd ldr: ev ch over 1f out: sn rdn: one pce) | 2 | 4 | 10/1 | 84 | 45 |
| *205** | **Rakis (IRE) (82)** (MrsLStubbs) **6-9-12** RCochrane(2) (hld up: rdn over 2f out: styd on ins fnl f: nvr nrr) | ¾ | 5 | 5/1[3] | 84 | 45 |
| 480[3] | **Orange Place (IRE) (70)** (TJNaughton) **5-9-0** PatEddery(8) (led tl over 1f out: sn wknd) | 5 | 6 | 9/2[2] | 60 | 21 |
| 633[6] | **Crystal Heights (FR) (64)** (RJO'Sullivan) **8-8-8** JQuinn(1) (hld up: rdn over 2f out: no hdwy) | 4 | 7 | 9/2[2] | 45 | 6 |
| 632[10] | **Dry Point (70)** (JARToller) **10-9-0** GDuffield(5) (b: sn outpcd: a bhd) | 4 | 8 | 16/1 | 42 | 3 |

(SP 112.9%) **8 Rn**

**1m 20.3** (0.30) CSF £63.34 CT £270.75 TOTE £13.30: £1.20 £2.90 £1.40 (£31.20) OWNER The Valentines (ASTON ROWANT) BRED Ridgecourt Stud

**My Best Valentine** produced a good display to win this on his seasonal debut. Produced to lead just below the furlong pole, he nearly threw it away by edging to his left but, soon straightening up, saw it out well. (14/1)

**633 Jo Maximus** was held up this time and the tactics appeared to suit. He was trying to rally when slightly hampered inside the final furlong but was beaten on merit. (4/1: 3/1-9/2)

**Ertlon** raced prominently throughout. He was asked to quicken two furlongs out, but took a while to respond and it was only close home that he really began to close. (9/2)

**735 Fantasy Racing (IRE)** had her chance below the distance, but was soon tapped for toe. (10/1: 7/1-12/1)

**Rakis (IRE)** ran on in eyecatching fashion below the distance under anything but a forceful ride. A winner five times on the All-Weather this season, it will not be long before he scores on the grass. (5/1)

## 745 ROYAL PAVILION CLAIMING STKS (4-Y.O+) (Class F)

4-00 (4-00) **1m 3f 196y** £2,381.00 (£656.00: £311.00) Stalls: High GOING minus 0.61 sec per fur (F)

| | Horse | Dist | Pos | SP | RR | SF |
|---|---|---|---|---|---|---|
| *489[3]* | **Bag of Tricks (IRE) (48)** (SDow) **6-8-10** TQuinn(10) (dwlt: sn rcvrd: hdwy gng wl 6f out: led 3f out: clr over 1f out: easily) | — | **1** | 5/2[1] | 63+ | 8 |
| | **Grandes Oreilles (IRE) (54)** (NJHWalker) **4-7-9**(5) MHenry(1) (prom: led 6f out to 3f out: one pce) | 5 | **2** | 5/2[1] | 47 | — |
| | **Nigels Choice** (AGNewcombe) **4-9-5** JQuinn(3) (w'like: in tch: rdn over 3f out: kpt on one pce fnl 2f) | 1½ | **3** | 7/1[3] | 64 | 8 |
| *602[8]* | **Park Ridge (47)** (TGMills) **4-8-9** WWoods(5) (led 10f out to 6f out: rdn over 3f out: one pce) | 3½ | **4** | 7/1[3] | 50 | — |
| *485[5]* | **Zuno Flyer (USA) (34)** (AMoore) **4-8-2v**(3) AWhelan(9) (b: bhd fnl 5f) | 12 | **5** | 6/1[2] | 29 | — |
| *343[9]* | **Lady Woodstock (30)** (MissAEEmbiricos) **4-7-12b** GBardwell(7) (led 2f: wknd 5f out) | 11 | **6** | 20/1 | 0 | — |
| | **Premazing (25)** (HMStronge) **4-8-5** CandyMorris(6) (bhd fnl 5f) | 3 | **7** | 16/1 | 11 | — |
| *37[8]* | **Ela-Ment (IRE)** (BAPearce) **4-8-11** PatEddery(8) (sn wl bhd: t.o) | dist | **8** | 14/1 | — | — |
| 649[6] | **Cyclone (IRE) (27)** (BRMillman) **5-8-10** RHughes(2) (sn wl bhd: t.o) | 15 | **9** | 7/1[3] | — | — |
| | | | | (SP 126.2%) | **9 Rn** | |

**2m 33.4** (5.80) CSF £9.85 TOTE £2.80: £1.30 £1.50 £1.40 (£4.90) Trio £22.00 OWNER Eurostrait Ltd (EPSOM) BRED Hesmonds Stud Ltd

WEIGHT FOR AGE 4yo-1lb

**489 Bag of Tricks (IRE)** won this very easily, despite missing the kick. Soon recovering the lost ground, he cruised into the lead early in the straight and the race was soon over. This was a very bad event. (5/2: 5/4-11/4)

**Grandes Oreilles (IRE)** took it up six furlongs out, but the winner was soon laughing at her and she is greatly flattered by the winning margin. (5/2)

**Nigels Choice** plugged on to be third. (7/1: 12/1-6/1)

**485 Zuno Flyer (USA)** (6/1: 4/1-13/2)

**Ela-Ment (IRE)** (14/1: 6/1-16/1)

## 746 CONFLANS MAIDEN STKS (3-Y.O+) (Class D)

4-30 (4-33) **7f 214y** £4,026.45 (£1,203.60: £576.30: £262.65) Stalls: Low GOING minus 0.61 sec per fur (F)

| | Horse | Dist | Pos | SP | RR | SF |
|---|---|---|---|---|---|---|
| | **Frezeliere (89)** (JLDunlop) **3-8-6** TQuinn(6) (hld up: hdwy to chse ldr over 2f out: rdn to ld wl ins fnl f: r.o) | — | **1** | 7/4[2] | 75 | 28 |
| 576[12] | **Major Dundee (IRE)** (RHannon) **3-8-11** JFEgan(1) (lw: chsd ldrs: led over 2f out tl wl ins fnl f: unable qckn) | 1 | **2** | 4/1[3] | 78 | 31 |
| | **Forever Noble (IRE)** (MRChannon) **3-8-11** RHughes(5) (bit bkwd: prom: rdn & outpcd over 2f out: kpt on one pce ins fnl f) | 8 | **3** | 10/1 | 62 | 15 |
| | **Stellar Line (USA) (87)** (BWHills) **3-8-11** PatEddery(9) (hld up: hdwy over 2f out: rdn over 1f out: wknd ins fnl f) | ¾ | **4** | 6/4[1] | 60 | 13 |
| 467[9] | **Lancashire Legend (70)** (SDow) **3-8-11** JQuinn(3) (stdd s: plld hrd: hld up in rr: sme hdwy over 2f out: sn rdn: one pce) | s.h | **5** | 16/1 | 60 | 13 |
| *204[10]* | **Trapper Norman** (RIngram) **4-9-11** DBiggs(7) (led tl over 2f out: sn wknd) | 5 | **6** | 50/1 | 50 | 17 |
| *502[4]* | **Kellaire Girl (IRE) (41)** (AMoore) **4-9-3**(3) AWhelan(2) (b: chsd ldr tl rdn & wknd over 2f out) | nk | **7** | 33/1 | 45 | 12 |
| | **Maid of Cadiz** (JWPayne) **6-9-6** RCochrane(8) (bhd fnl 4f) | 12 | **8** | 50/1 | 21 | — |
| | **Shoemaker Levy** (RJO'Sullivan) **3-8-6** GDuffield(4) (unf: sn outpcd: a bhd) | 10 | **9** | 33/1 | 1 | — |
| | | | | (SP 121.1%) | **9 Rn** | |

**1m 33.1** (0.90) CSF £9.48 TOTE £3.20: £1.10 £1.80 £4.50 (£9.20) Trio £29.50 OWNER Lord Chelsea (ARUNDEL) BRED Lord Chelsea

WEIGHT FOR AGE 3yo-14lb

**Frezeliere** was always travelling quite nicely and was brought with a well-timed challenge to win going away. (7/4: 6/4-9/4)

**Major Dundee (IRE)** looked as though he may have stolen this race when shooting clear over two furlongs out, but the winner pegged him back inside the final furlong. He can find a small race, possibly over seven furlongs. (4/1)

**Forever Noble (IRE)** got his second wind to snatch third place at the finish. He looked just in need of this and can improve. (10/1: 7/1-12/1)

**Stellar Line (USA)** was disappointing, being in trouble fully two furlongs out. (6/4)

## 747 TOWN PURSE H'CAP (0-70) (3-Y.O+) (Class E)

5-00 (5-01) **7f 214y** £3,397.80 (£1,016.40: £487.20: £222.60) Stalls: Low GOING minus 0.61 sec per fur (F)

| | Horse | Dist | Pos | SP | RR | SF |
|---|---|---|---|---|---|---|
| 636* | **Autumn Cover (50)** (RMFlower) **4-8-8** DBiggs(11) (b: led over 2f: chsd ldr: rdn over 1f out: led ins fnl f: r.o) | — | **1** | 6/1[3] | 60 | 43 |
| 636[2] | **College Night (IRE) (48)** (CADwyer) **4-8-1**(5) MHenry(9) (lw: led over 5f out: rdn over 1f out: hdd ins fnl f: r.o) | ½ | **2** | 5/1[2] | 57 | 40 |
| *501** | **Victory Team (IRE) (66)** (GBBalding) **4-9-10** RCochrane(10) (hld up: hdwy over 2f out: rdn over 1f out: r.o one pce ins fnl f) | 1¼ | **3** | 2/1[1] | 73 | 56 |
| *515[3]* | **Scathebury (60)** (SPCWoods) **3-8-4** WWoods(4) (hld up: hdwy over 1f out: kpt on one pce ins fnl f) | 1¾ | **4** | 10/1 | 63 | 32 |
| 636[4] | **Mr Nevermind (IRE) (64)** (GLMoore) **6-9-8** SWhitworth(5) (mid div: rdn 6f out: hdwy 2f out: rdn over 1f out: one pce) | nk | **5** | 10/1 | 66 | 49 |
| | **La Tansani (IRE) (70)** (RHannon) **3-9-0** RHughes(7) (bit bkwd: chsd ldrs tl wknd over 2f out) | 8 | **6** | 8/1 | 56 | 25 |
| *379[10]* | **Dancing Lawyer (68)** (BJMeehan) **5-9-12** BDoyle(6) (mid div: sme hdwy 3f out: rdn over 2f out: sn wknd) | 1¼ | **7** | 9/1 | 52 | 35 |
| 554[10] | **Helios (62)** (NJHWalker) **8-9-3**(3) JStack(1) (mid div: stumbled over 4f out: nt rcvr) | 1¾ | **8** | 20/1 | 42 | 25 |
| | **Newlands Corner (52)** (JAkehurst) **3-7-10** JQuinn(2) (lw: mid div tl wknd over 2f out) | 1½ | **9** | 25/1 | 29 | — |
| | **Northern Chief (38)** (JCullinan) **6-7-10** FNorton(8) (mid div tl wknd over 2f out) | hd | **10** | 33/1 | 15 | — |
| | **North to Glory (38)** (RMFlower) **5-7-5**(5) CAdamson(3) (b: bkwd: sn outpcd & a bhd) | 15 | **11** | 66/1 | — | — |
| | | | | (SP 116.6%) | **11 Rn** | |

**1m 31.9** (-0.30) CSF £33.46 CT £73.89 TOTE £6.80: £2.70 £1.80 £1.90 (£19.60) Trio £11.00 OWNER Mr G. A. Alexander (JEVINGTON) BRED P. and Mrs Venner

LONG HANDICAP Newlands Corner 7-8 Northern Chief 7-4 North to Glory 7-3

WEIGHT FOR AGE 3yo-14lb

**636* Autumn Cover** had a ding-dong battle with the runner-up throughout and just proved the stronger. (6/1)

**636 College Night (IRE)** cut out a lot of the running and went down fighting. Still a maiden, she deserves to find a race. (5/1)

**501* Victory Team (IRE)** moved up threateningly below the distance, but found the quickening pace beyond him. (2/1: op 5/4)

**515 Scathebury** moved up smoothly over a furlong out, but did not appear to go through with his effort. The ability is there but he is a bit of a thinker. (10/1)

**636 Mr Nevermind (IRE)** was always slightly struggling with the pace and possibly finds this ground a shade quick nowadays. (10/1: 8/1-12/1)

T/Plpt: £52.30 (183.64 Tckts). T/Qdpt: £10.40 (86.73 Tckts). SM

# 0637-NOTTINGHAM (L-H) (Good to firm, Good patches st becoming Good)
## Monday April 22nd
WEATHER: overcast & rain WIND: slt half against

## 748 OVAL (S) STKS (3-Y.O) (Class G)
2-10 (2-10) **6f 15y** £2,070.00 (£570.00: £270.00) Stalls: High GOING minus 0.11 sec per fur (G)

| | | | | SP | RR | SF |
|---|---|---|---|---|---|---|
| 383$^{7}$ | **The Wad (52)** (DNicholls) **3-8-11** JFortune(3) (lw: mde all far side: drvn clr over 1f out) | — | 1 | 12/1 | 59 | 28 |
| | **Members Welcome (IRE) (57)** (JMBradley) **3-8-8**(3) SDrowne(6) (hld up far side: hdwy over 1f out: r.o wl) | 2½ | 2 | 16/1 | 52 | 21 |
| | **Pride of Whalley (IRE)** (RAFahey) **3-8-6** ACulhane(12) (bit bkwd: chsd wnr far side tl no ex ins fnl f) | 1 | 3 | 7/1$^{3}$ | 45 | 14 |
| 660$^{6}$ | **Mels Baby (IRE) (55)** (JLEyre) **3-8-8**(3) DWright(9) (lw: gd hdwy appr fnl f: fin wl) | ½ | 4 | 14/1 | 49 | 18 |
| 637$^{3}$ | **Dazzling Star (45)** (RHannon) **3-8-7**ow1 JReid(8) (trckd ldrs far side: rdn & one pce fnl 2f) | 1¼ | 5 | 6/1$^{2}$ | 41 | 9 |
| | **Our Worley (IRE)** (APJarvis) **3-8-6** JTate(1) (b.off hind: prom far side tl wknd over 1f out) | 3½ | 6 | 12/1 | 31 | — |
| 606$^{3}$ | **Born A Lady (64)** (SRBowring) **3-8-6b**(5) CTeague(19) (led stands' side 2f out: r.o) | 1 | 7 | 7/1$^{3}$ | 33 | 2 |
| 606$^{12}$ | **Ragtime Cowgirl** (CWThornton) **3-8-6** DeanMcKeown(10) (trckd ldrs: no hdwy fnl 2f) | 1¼ | 8 | 16/1 | 25 | — |
| 242$^{6}$ | **Wingnut (IRE) (48)** (MJHaynes) **3-8-6**(5) MBaird(5) (racd far side: nvr nr ldrs) | 2½ | 9 | 33/1 | 23 | — |
| | **My Kind (55)** (NTinkler) **3-8-11** KimTinkler(18) (bit bkwd: trckd ldrs stands' side 4f) | hd | 10 | 16/1 | 23 | — |
| 606$^{2}$ | **The Frisky Farmer (66)** (WGMTurner) **3-9-2** AClark(14) (racd stands' side: effrt 2f out: n.d) | hd | 11 | 11/2$^{1}$ | 28 | — |
| 606$^{9}$ | **Inca Bird (40)** (BAMcMahon) **3-8-6** GCarter(4) (nvr gng pce of ldrs) | hd | 12 | 33/1 | 18 | — |
| | **Pathaze (55)** (NBycroft) **3-8-11** LCharnock(17) (nvr nr to chal) | nk | 13 | 12/1 | 22 | — |
| 626$^{6}$ | **Summer Princess** (GFierro) **3-8-6** AMackay(15) (s.s: a in rr) | nk | 14 | 50/1 | 16 | — |
| 525$^{15}$ | **Rothley Imp (IRE) (51)** (JWharton) **3-8-6** PRobinson(13) (outpcd) | s.h | 15 | 12/1 | 16 | — |
| 626$^{9}$ | **Dispol Duchess** (GROldroyd) **3-8-6** KFallon(2) (spd to ½-wy) | 3½ | 16 | 33/1 | 7 | — |
| 524$^{10}$ | **Wyse Folly** (RBastiman) **3-8-6** SDWilliams(11) (dwtl: a outpcd) | 1½ | 17 | 50/1 | 3 | — |
| 638$^{7}$ | **U-No-Harry (IRE) (66)** (RHollinshead) **3-8-11**(5) FLynch(20) (lw: prom stands' side 4f) | hd | 18 | 6/1$^{2}$ | 13 | — |
| 525$^{22}$ | **Longhill Boy (48)** (BJMeehan) **3-8-11** MTebbutt(16) (outpcd: t.o) | 14 | 19 | 33/1 | — | — |
| | **Mobile King (40)** (KRBurke) **3-8-11** TIves(7) (bit bkwd: outpcd: t.o) | 5 | 20 | 33/1 | — | — |
| | | | | (SP 142.7%) | **20 Rn** | |

**1m 14.6** (4.10) CSF £193.14 TOTE £17.40: £4.80 £13.70 £4.80 (£398.30) Trio £202.30; £233.70 to 4.10 Chepstow 23/4/96. OWNER Mr W. J. Kelly (THIRSK) BRED C. R. and V. M. Withers
No bid

**The Wad** has taken a long time to get off the mark but, with forceful tactics employed, stole the race by kicking clear below the distance. (12/1)

**Members Welcome (IRE)**, patiently ridden on this first outing in six months, did not get going until far too late, but showed enough to suggest a race of this description is there for the taking. (16/1)

**Pride of Whalley (IRE)**, still with a bit left to work on, was feeling the strain over a furlong out but she was not disgraced by this and there is a race to be won. (7/1)

**516 Mels Baby (IRE)**, returning to sprinting and running without headgear, only found his stride in the closing stages but finished really fast. He is surely a ready-made winner in this class. (14/1)

**637 Dazzling Star**, in the action on the far side, was being made to work some way out and lacked the pace to mount a challenge. (6/1)

**Our Worley (IRE)**, stepping down to selling company, pressed the leaders on the far rail until blowing up over a furlong out. (12/1)

**606 The Frisky Farmer** moved gingerly to post and was never going well enough to get within striking range. (11/2: 4/1-6/1)

**U-No-Harry (IRE)** had the misfortune to be drawn on the slower stands' side. (6/1: op 4/1)

## 749 EDGBASTON H'CAP (0-70) (3-Y.O+) (Class E)
2-40 (2-40) **6f 15y** £3,725.40 (£1,117.20: £537.60: £247.80) Stalls: High GOING minus 0.11 sec per fur (G)

| | | | | SP | RR | SF |
|---|---|---|---|---|---|---|
| 587$^{5}$ | **Bollin Harry (68)** (TDEasterby) **4-10-0** MBirch(2) (lw: stumbled s: sn led: drvn out fnl f) | — | 1 | 13/2$^{2}$ | 77 | 48 |
| 431$^{7}$ | **Daawe (USA) (53)** (MrsVAAconley) **5-8-13v** MDeering(11) (a.p: rdn over 1f out: kpt on) | 1 | 2 | 12/1 | 59 | 30 |
| 582$^{8}$ | **Barato (65)** (MrsJRRamsden) **5-9-11** KFallon(6) (hld up: hdwy 2f out: nrst fin) | 2½ | 3 | 5/1$^{1}$ | 65 | 36 |
| 592$^{4}$ | **Mustn't Grumble (IRE) (60)** (MissSJWilton) **6-9-6** WRyan(12) (hdwy ½-wy: kpt on u.p fnl f) | 2 | 4 | 14/1 | 55 | 26 |
| 607$^{12}$ | **Sound the Trumpet (IRE) (60)** (RCSpicer) **4-9-6** DeanMcKeown(10) (wnt rt s: hdwy over 1f out: nvr nrr) | 2½ | 5 | 33/1 | 48 | 19 |
| 582$^{3}$ | **Face the Future (56)** (SDow) **7-9-2** DHarrison(22) (w ldrs stands' side: hung bdly lft fnl 2f: eased whn btn nr fin) | s.h | 6 | 8/1$^{3}$ | 44 | 15 |
| 480$^{9}$ | **Almasi (IRE) (54)** (CFWall) **4-9-0** WLord(24) (lw: a.p stands' side: one pce appr fnl f) | 1¼ | 7 | 33/1 | 39 | 10 |
| 601$^{13}$ | **Sing With the Band (56)** (BAMcMahon) **5-9-2** GCarter(4) (prom far side: rdn & wknd over 1f out) | 2½ | 8 | 8/1$^{3}$ | 34 | 5 |
| | **Dashing Dancer (IRE) (59)** (RAkehurst) **5-9-5** SSanders(18) (lw: racd stands' side: prom tl no hdwy fnl 2f) | 1½ | 9 | 11/1 | 33 | 4 |
| 632$^{13}$ | **Asterix (48)** (JMBradley) **8-8-5v**(3) SDrowne(15) (bit bkwd: s.s: nvr nrr) | 1¾ | 10 | 25/1 | 17 | — |
| 163$^{11}$ | **Squire Corrie (67)** (GHarwood) **4-9-6**(7) GayeHarwood(9) (trckd ldrs: one pce fnl 2f) | 1 | 11 | 20/1 | 34 | 5 |
| 582$^{10}$ | **Rocky Waters (USA) (56)** (PBurgoyne) **7-8-13**(3) DRMcCabe(8) (swtg: b: nvr trbld ldrs) | 1 | 12 | 16/1 | 20 | — |
| | **Sizzling (62)** (RHannon) **4-9-3**(5) DaneO'Neill(20) (lw: n.d) | ½ | 13 | 10/1 | 25 | — |
| | **Winter Scout (USA) (62)** (CPEBrooks) **8-9-1**(7) SCopp(19) (bit bkwd: led stands' side over 3f) | 1¼ | 14 | 20/1 | 21 | — |
| 461$^{5}$ | **Beeny (60)** (APJarvis) **3-8-9** JTate(7) (a in rr) | 1¼ | 15 | 16/1 | 16 | — |
| 601$^{6}$ | **Our Shadee (USA) (50)** (KTIvory) **6-8-3v**(7) CScally(17) (nvr nr to chal) | s.h | 16 | 12/1 | 6 | — |
| | **Amnesty Bay (56)** (MDIUsher) **4-9-2** NAdams(3) (bit bkwd: n.d) | hd | 17 | 33/1 | 12 | — |
| 653* | **Little Ibnr (63)** (PDEvans) **5-9-9** AClark(13) (b.nr fore: prom far side 4f) | nk | 18 | 10/1 | 18 | — |
| 617$^{17}$ | **Natural Key (68)** (DHaydnJones) **3-9-3** JFortune(23) (bit bkwd: prom stands' side over 3f) | 1 | 19 | 33/1 | 20 | — |
| 466$^{13}$ | **Leigh Crofter (65)** (PDCundell) **7-9-11b** TIves(16) (a in rr) | ½ | 20 | 20/1 | 16 | — |
| 466$^{10}$ | **Wardara (63)** (CADwyer) **4-9-9v** MWigham(21) (swtg: a bhd) | ½ | 21 | 20/1 | 13 | — |
| | **Blow Dry (IRE) (56)** (MartynWane) **6-9-2** AMackay(1) (outpcd) | 1¼ | 22 | 25/1 | 2 | — |
| 155$^{9}$ | **Montague Dawson (IRE) (54)** (MrsNMacauley) **4-8-9**(5) CTeague(14) (b.hind: early spd: sn lost pl: t.o) | 8 | 23 | 20/1 | — | — |
| | | | | (SP 155.8%) | **23 Rn** | |

**1m 14.1** (3.60) CSF £90.96 CT £418.21 TOTE £11.40: £2.40 £3.00 £1.50 £2.70 (£202.60) Trio £273.80 OWNER Sir Neil Westbrook (MALTON) BRED Sir Neil and Lady Westbrook
WEIGHT FOR AGE 3yo-11lb
STEWARDS' ENQUIRY Harrison susp. 1 & 2/5/96 (careless riding).

**587 Bollin Harry**, down on his knees leaving the stalls, soon recovered to show the way and his class saw him through for a success that was gained with more in hand than the margin suggests. (13/2)

**Daawe (USA)** has been in fine form on the All-Weather, but lacks a turn of finishing speed at this trip on the turf. A return to seven could well be the answer. (12/1)
**475 Barato** had little chance of turning the tables on the winner, without the assistance of the jockey's claim he had had at Newcastle, and his finishing position was as close as he could get. (5/1)
**592 Mustn't Grumble (IRE)** again ran a fine race in defeat, but such displays do not pay the bills and, until he tackles a longer trip, his ability is going to waste. (14/1)
**514 Sound the Trumpet (IRE)**, back on turf, could not hold his pitch after swerving on leaving the stalls, but he found his stride just inside the distance and is knocking at the door. (33/1)
**582 Face the Future** ran an extraordinary race and gave away far more ground than he was beaten. Sharing the lead on the stands' side, he drifted left, into the whip, throughout the last quarter-mile, but still closed up on the principals until being eased when held inside the final furlong. He has only ever won one race but the ability is there when he puts it to good use. (8/1)
**Dashing Dancer (IRE)** (11/1: 8/1-12/1)

## 750 LORDS CLAIMING STKS (3-Y.O+) (Class F)

3-10 (3-10) **5f 13y** £2,738.00 (£758.00: £362.00) Stalls: High GOING minus 0.11 sec per fur (G)

| | | | | SP | RR | SF |
|---|---|---|---|---|---|---|
| 631[2] | **Baileys Sunset (IRE) (57)** (JMBradley) **4-8-13**(3) SDrowne(6) (b: trckd ldrs: hdwy u.p over 1f out: str run to ld cl home) | — | **1** | 7/2[2] | 66 | 41 |
| 700[5] | **Super Rocky (73)** (RBastiman) **7-9-7**(5) HBastiman(3) (racd far side: led 1f out tl ct fnl strides) | nk | **2** | 3/1[1] | 75 | 50 |
| 652[8] | **Swan At Whalley (60)** (MartynWane) **4-9-4** ACulhane(12) (racd centre: led: hung rt & hdd 1f out: no ex) | 2½ | **3** | 8/1 | 59 | 34 |
| 534[3] | **Sir Tasker (54)** (JLHarris) **8-9-4** KDarley(2) (lw: prom far side: rdn over 1f out: one pce) | ½ | **4** | 6/1[3] | 58 | 33 |
| 126[6] | **Nadwaty (IRE) (47)** (MCChapman) **4-8-8**(3) DRMcCabe(5) (prom centre: no hdwy fnl 2f) | 1½ | **5** | 12/1 | 46 | 21 |
| 652[6] | **Don't Tell Anyone (50)** (PDEvans) **3-8-2** SSanders(7) (hld up: hdwy 2f out: nt trble ldrs) | ¾ | **6** | 10/1 | 44 | 9 |
| 700[7] | **Rankaidade (26)** (DonEnricoIncisa) **5-8-9** KimTinkler(1) (lw: nvr nr to chal) | ½ | **7** | 25/1 | 40 | 15 |
| 514[7] | **The Fed (42)** (JAPickering) **6-9-2v** KFallon(4) (prom over 3f) | ½ | **8** | 8/1 | 45 | 20 |
| | **Harry's Coming (53)** (RJHodges) **12-8-12** JReid(13) (a in rr) | 2½ | **9** | 6/1[3] | 33 | 8 |
| 478[9] | **Chillam (45)** (JPLeigh) **3-8-1b**(5) FLynch(11) (a bhd: t.o) | 8 | **10** | 25/1 | 12 | — |
| | **Princess Belfort** (GFierro) **3-8-3** AMackay(10) (lt-f: s.s: a bhd & outpcd: t.o) | 1 | **11** | 25/1 | 6 | — |
| 582[25] | **Amahsan (IRE) (63)** (CDBroad) **4-8-13**(5) BFenton(9) (outpcd: t.o) | 1 | **12** | 16/1 | 8 | — |
| | **Static Love (40)** (HAkbary) **3-8-3** GHind(8) (outpcd: a bhd: t.o) | 6 | **13** | 20/1 | — | — |
| | | | | (SP 137.0%) | **13 Rn** | |

**61.5 secs** (2.90) CSF £15.99 TOTE £5.20: £1.40 £2.50 £3.90 (£6.20) Trio £67.10 OWNER The Crown At Hambrook Racing Club (CHEPSTOW) BRED Vincent and Joseph Fitzpatrick in Ireland
WEIGHT FOR AGE 3yo-10lb
**631 Baileys Sunset (IRE)** had to work hard to wear down the runner-up nearing the line, but he is possibly better at six furlongs nowadays and, due to the faster pace, had the race run to suit him. (7/2)
**700 Super Rocky** looked to have stolen a march when going all out for home after leading into the final furlong but, hard as he tried, the winner's storming late rally proved just too much. He deserves a chance to make amends. (3/1: 2/1-7/2)
**652 Swan At Whalley** was the winner on merit and, if he had kept straight entering the final furlong, he would not have been caught. He is a winner without a penalty. (8/1)
**534 Sir Tasker** could have problems winning at this trip on turf now, and his measure had been taken approaching the final furlong. (6/1)
**Nadwaty (IRE)** showed up prominently in the centre of the track, but could not raise her pace, and was fighting a lost cause throughout the last two furlongs. (12/1: op 8/1)
**652 Don't Tell Anyone** sat in behind the leaders and made his effort two furlongs out, but could not muster the speed to get active. (10/1: 8/1-12/1)

## 751 'MICHELOZZO' CONDITIONS STKS (4-Y.O+) (Class C)

3-40 (3-40) **1m 6f 15y** £4,799.25 (£1,743.00: £846.50: £357.50) Stalls: Low GOING minus 0.39 sec per fur (F)

| | | | | SP | RR | SF |
|---|---|---|---|---|---|---|
| | **Further Flight (110)** (BWHills) **10-9-10** MHills(1) (b.hind: hld up: qcknd to ld 2f out: edgd lft: styd on strly) | — | **1** | 2/1[3] | 116 | 28 |
| | **Assessor (IRE) (108)** (RHannon) **7-9-4** JReid(2) (lt-f: led & sn clr: hdd 2f out: rallied fnl f) | 1¾ | **2** | 15/8[2] | 108 | 20 |
| | **Source of Light (102)** (RCharlton) **7-9-10** DHarrison(4) (stdd s: hdwy over 2f out: ev ch over 1f out: one pce) | 3 | **3** | 7/4[1] | 111 | 23 |
| | **Charter** (MajorDNChappell) **5-8-10** BThomson(3) (chsd ldr: ev ch 3f out: outpcd fnl 2f) | 9 | **4** | 33/1 | 86? | — |
| | | | | (SP 107.4%) | **4 Rn** | |

**3m 7.3** (8.80) CSF £5.66 TOTE £2.90 (£3.20) OWNER Mr S. WingfieldDigby (LAMBOURN) BRED S. Wingfield Digby
**Further Flight**, a tremendous campaigner who has won races every year since 1989, seems to get better as he gets older. Producing a good turn of speed to nose ahead passing the quarter-mile pole, he drifted over to the far rail but quickly had the measure of his rivals and won readily. The Group Three Ormonde Stakes at Chester or the Aston Park Stakes at Newbury next month are possible early-season targets. (2/1)
**Assessor (IRE)** had to settle for second best behind the winner at Newmarket in the Autumn and, even on 3lb better terms, could not gain his revenge. To his credit, he produced a promising first performance of the season and is still capable of winning more races than he loses. (15/8)
**Source of Light** made his move and was just about to take over when the winner beat him to the punch, and from then on he was fighting a lost cause. (7/4)
**Charter** has been competing in bumpers in recent months and, although he was able to win one of those, he found these rivals in a different league. (33/1)

## 752 NOTTINGHAM LADIES' H'CAP (0-75) (3-Y.O+) (Class F)

4-10 (4-11) **1m 1f 213y** £2,381.00 (£656.00: £311.00) Stalls: Low GOING minus 0.39 sec per fur (F)

| | | | | SP | RR | SF |
|---|---|---|---|---|---|---|
| 279[6] | **Gold Blade (44)** (JPearce) **7-10-1** MrsLPearce(10) (hld up & bhd: smooth hdwy over 2f out: hmpd & swtchd rt ent fnl f: str run to ld nr fin) | — | **1** | 5/1[1] | 54 | 36 |
| 508[17] | **Carlton Express (IRE) (42)** (JLEyre) **6-9-13** MissDianaJones(11) (hdwy over 4f out: led ins fnl f: hdd cl home) | 1½ | **2** | 14/1 | 50 | 32 |
| 609[17] | **I'm a Nut Man (33)** (CASmith) **5-9-0**(4) MrsDSmith(19) (bit bkwd: s.s: bhd tl rapid hdwy over 1f out: fin fast) | s.h | **3** | 33/1 | 41 | 23 |
| 214[9] | **Cheveley Dancer (USA) (33)** (TJNaughton) **8-9-4** MissPRobson(15) (b: swtg: hld up: hdwy wl over 1f out: fin wl) | nk | **4** | 20/1 | 40 | 22 |

| | | | | | | |
|---|---|---|---|---|---|---|
| *341[10]* | **Breezed Well (42)** (BRCambidge) **10-9-9**(4)ow12 MrsHNoonan(21) (a.p: led over 1f out tl hdd & no ex ins fnl f) | 1¾ | **5** | 50/1 | 46 | 16 |
| 598[7] | **Brown Eyed Girl (46)** (BJMeehan) **4-10-3** MissJAllison(1) (s.s: hdwy 3f out: one pce fnl f) | 1¼ | **6** | 14/1 | 48 | 30 |
| 615[3] | **Master Ofthe House (59)** (MDHammond) **10-10-12**(4) MissMCarson(4) (hld up: hdwy on ins 3f out: one pce appr fnl f) | ½ | **7** | 12/1 | 60 | 42 |
| *553[3]* | **Polly Peculiar (59)** (BSmart) **5-10-12**(4) MissVMarshall(2) (b.hind: s.s: hdwy over 2f out: nrst fin) | 1¾ | **8** | 12/1 | 58 | 40 |
| 593[4] | **Northern Motto (56)** (MrsJRRamsden) **3-9-6**(4) MissERamsden(6) (lw: prom tl wknd over 1f out) | hd | **9** | 6/1[2] | 54 | 19 |
| *158[9]* | **Hever Golf Diamond (53)** (TJNaughton) **3-9-3**(4) MrsJNaughton(20) (nvr nrr) | hd | **10** | 33/1 | 51 | 16 |
| | **I Recall (IRE) (56)** (PHayward) **5-10-13** MrsSBosley(12) (hdwy 4f out: wknd over 2f out) | nk | **11** | 25/1 | 54 | 36 |
| *98[5]* | **Tony's Mist (51)** (JMBradley) **6-10-4**(4) MrsDMcHale(14) (led 6f out tl over 1f out: wknd fnl f) | nk | **12** | 20/1 | 48 | 30 |
| 541[3] | **Manful (62)** (CWCElsey) **4-11-5b** MissAElsey(7) (nvr nr to chal) | 1 | **13** | 7/1[3] | 58 | 40 |
| | **Dodgy Dancer (52)** (MDIUsher) **6-10-5**(4) MrsAUsher(13) (bit bkwd: a bhd) | nk | **14** | 33/1 | 47 | 29 |
| | **Quick Silver Boy (52)** (DBurchell) **6-10-5**(4) MissEJJones(5) (b: bit bkwd: bhd fnl 3f) | 1¾ | **15** | 33/1 | 44 | 26 |
| 628[7] | **Flag Fen (USA) (64)** (MartynMeade) **5-11-0**(7) MissEFolkes(22) (led 4f: wknd qckly wl over 1f out) | 3 | **16** | 20/1 | 52 | 34 |
| 508[11] | **Claque (55)** (DWChapman) **4-10-12b** MissRClark(8) (trckd ldrs 7f: sn wknd) | ½ | **17** | 14/1 | 42 | 24 |
| *384[5]* | **Royal Acclaim (35)** (JMBradley) **11-8-13v**(7) MissLKerr(18) (a bhd) | 2 | **18** | 33/1 | 19 | 1 |
| | **Studio Thirty (38)** (DMorris) **4-9-9** MissJFeilden(23) (hld up: hdwy over 3f out: wknd over 2f out) | 3 | **19** | 16/1 | 17 | — |
| *602[6]* | **Arecibo (FR) (40)** (JParkes) **4-9-11** MrsDKettlewell(9) (a bhd) | hd | **20** | 33/1 | 19 | 1 |
| 598[9] | **Secretary of State (50)** (DWPArbuthnot) **10-10-7** MrsDArbuthnot(17) (bhd fnl 3f) | 1¼ | **21** | 14/1 | 27 | 9 |
| | **Kama Simba (58)** (JWhite) **4-10-8**(7) MissSBrown(16) (prom over 7f: sn wknd) | ¾ | **22** | 16/1 | 33 | 15 |
| 440[17] | **Silver Samurai (48)** (MrsVAAconley) **7-9-12**(7) MrsCWilliams(3) (ref to r: t.n.p) | | **R** | 20/1 | — | — |

(SP 139.8%) **23 Rn**

**2m 8.0** (5.50) CSF £73.96 CT £2,017.42 TOTE £5.70: £1.60 £3.10 £19.10 £7.10 (£60.20) Trio £358.20; £454.18 to 4.10 Chepstow 23/4/96.
OWNER Mr Jeff Pearce (NEWMARKET) BRED Ballymacoll Stud Co
WEIGHT FOR AGE 3yo-17lb

**Gold Blade**, winning at this trip for the first time since the autumn of 1993, did not enjoy the smoothest of passages but he had plenty in hand and, in the end, won comfortably. (5/1)
**Carlton Express (IRE)**, brought with a perfectly-timed challenge to poke his head in front two hundred yards out, failed to quicken with the winner over this shorter trip and was forced to give best. In these races, his pilot and Lydia Pearce are a class above the rest and worth their weight in gold. (14/1)
**I'm a Nut Man** ran exceptionally well after losing ground at the start and, as this was his first glimpse of form, he could at long last be getting the hang of the game. (33/1)
**Cheveley Dancer (USA)** came very late on the scene and, if he had started his run earlier, could have made a race of it. (20/1)
**Breezed Well** took charge below the distance and only got run out of it as his stamina ebbed inside the final furlong. He carried 12lb more than he should have done and that was sure to make a difference. (50/1)
**Brown Eyed Girl** turned in a promising effort on ground that did not suit, and there is a race to be won when she gets the soft ground that she needs. (14/1)
**615 Master Ofthe House** (12/1: op 8/1)
**553 Polly Peculiar** (12/1: op 8/1)
**593 Northern Motto** ran a bit too free. Pushing the pace until calling enough over a furlong out, he should not have too much trouble in finding a suitable opening. (6/1)
**541 Manful** (7/1: 9/2-8/1)

## 753 TRENT BRIDGE H'CAP (0-80) (4-Y.O+) (Class D)

4-40 (4-41) **1m 6f 15y** £4,305.00 (£1,290.00: £620.00: £285.00) Stalls: Low GOING minus 0.39 sec per fur (F)

| | | | | SP | RR | SF |
|---|---|---|---|---|---|---|
| 546[5] | **Fabillion (61)** (CASmith) **4-8-9** CRutter(4) (hld up: hdwy ent st: chal over 1f out: styd on to ld cl home) | — | **1** | 7/1[2] | 76 | 45 |
| *603[4]* | **Ciracusa (IRE) (59)** (JMackie) **4-8-4**(3) NVarley(9) (hld up: hdwy 6f out: led 3f out: hrd drvn & hdd nr fin) | nk | **2** | 20/1 | 74 | 43 |
| | **Embryonic (IRE) (75)** (RFFisher) **4-9-9** KFallon(8) (hld up in tch: effrt & rdn over 2f out: nt rch ldrs) | 8 | **3** | 10/1 | 81 | 50 |
| 642[3] | **Cuango (IRE) (54)** (RHollinshead) **5-7-13**(5)ow1 FLynch(12) (lw: hld up: hdwy 2f out: r.o ins fnl f) | s.h | **4** | 12/1 | 60 | 30 |
| | **Bowcliffe Court (IRE) (59)** (BWHills) **4-8-7** MHills(2) (bit bkwd: hld up & bhd: hdwy on ins over 2f out: nvr nrr) | ½ | **5** | 7/1[2] | 64 | 33 |
| | **Granby Bell (50)** (PHayward) **5-7-9**(5) PFessey(16) (nvr nr to chal) | 1 | **6** | 14/1 | 54 | 25 |
| *656** | **Iota (53)** (JLHarris) **7-8-3** PRobinson(10) (hld up: hdwy 2f out: nvr nr to chal) | s.h | **7** | 15/2[3] | 57 | 28 |
| 482[2] | **Hillzah (USA) (78)** (RBastiman) **8-9-9**(5) HBastiman(17) (dwlt: hld up: hdwy over 4f out: wknd wl over 1f out) | ½ | **8** | 7/1[2] | 81 | 52 |
| | **Well Arranged (IRE) (62)** (RAkehurst) **5-8-12** SSanders(18) (hld up in tch: hdwy to ld over 4f out: hdd 3f out: grad wknd) | 1 | **9** | 10/1 | 64 | 35 |
| | **Uncle Doug (50)** (MrsMReveley) **5-8-0** LCharnock(7) (swtg: nvr bttr than mid div) | 2½ | **10** | 10/1 | 49 | 20 |
| 546[4] | **Bella Sedona (54)** (LadyHerries) **4-8-2** AClark(20) (lw: hld up: effrt & rdn 3f out: no imp) | nk | **11** | 11/2[1] | 53 | 22 |
| | **Flaming Miracle (IRE) (46)** (GBarnett) **6-7-10b** NCarlisle(15) (bit bkwd: plld hrd: led over 9f: wknd fnl 2f) | 7 | **12** | 33/1 | 37 | 8 |
| | **Top Royal (60)** (JPearce) **7-8-10** NDay(11) (b: bkwd: prom tl wknd wl over 2f out) | 8 | **13** | 20/1 | 42 | 13 |
| | **Mutazz (USA) (67)** (MajorWRHern) **4-9-1** PaulEddery(13) (trckd ldrs: rdn 7f out: wknd 3f out) | 2 | **14** | 15/2[3] | 47 | 16 |
| 546[14] | **Western Dynasty (56)** (SMellor) **10-8-6**ow1 RPerham(6) (lw: trckd ldrs tl wknd over 3f out) | ¾ | **15** | 33/1 | 35 | 5 |
| | **Altermeera (46)** (MrsBarbaraWaring) **8-7-10b** NAdams(1) (b: dwlt: a bhd: t.o) | 18 | **16** | 33/1 | 4 | — |
| | **Amercius (48)** (JLHarris) **4-7-10** AMackay(5) (bhd fnl 4f: t.o) | nk | **17** | 50/1 | 6 | — |
| 647[12] | **Astrolabe (78)** (JMBradley) **4-9-9v**(3) SDrowne(19) (chsd ldr 10f: sn lost tch: t.o) | 8 | **18** | 33/1 | 27 | — |
| 577[14] | **Zaaleff (USA) (55)** (BHanbury) **4-8-3**ow1 WRyan(3) (lw: a bhd: t.o) | 10 | **19** | 14/1 | — | — |
| | **Alaraby (IRE) (71)** (MartynWane) **4-9-5** JCarroll(14) (a bhd: t.o) | 1¾ | **20** | 14/1 | 6 | — |

(SP 154.6%) **20 Rn**

**3m 1.6** (3.10) CSF £152.21 CT £1,360.01 TOTE £9.10: £2.00 £51.10 £2.00 £1.70 (£189.30) Trio £412.00; £522.31 to 4.10 Chepstow 23/4/96.
OWNER Mr Bill Horton (HANLEY SWAN) BRED Juddmonte Farms
LONG HANDICAP Flaming Miracle (IRE) 7-5 Altermeera 7-5 Amercius 7-0
WEIGHT FOR AGE 4yo-2lb

**546 Fabillion** has taken time to win a race and it was not certain he was going through with his effort after joining issue over a furlong out. His jockey made his mind up for him though, and he had his head in front at the right time. (7/1)
**Ciracusa (IRE)**, successful over hurdles in the autumn, threw down the gauntlet over three furlongs out and battled on gamely when challenged, but the winner proved the stronger nearing the finish. (20/1)
**Embryonic (IRE)** could have just needed this first outing in over six months, but did his best, which was not quite good enough when the chips were down. (10/1)

**642 Cuango (IRE)** decided to run on when it was far too late and has more ability than he cares to use on occasions. (12/1)
**Bowcliffe Court (IRE)**, settled towards the rear, made relentless progress in the latter stages but found the race over before he could get to terms. He should strip fitter for the run and will not be hard to place. (7/1)
**Granby Bell**, fit from hurdling, came from off the pace to reach his final placing and is handicapped to take advantage in the coming weeks. (14/1)
**546 Bella Sedona** (11/2: 7/2-6/1)
**Mutazz (USA)**, still to break his duck on the Flat, was being bustled along from halfway and finally called enough early in the straight. (15/2: 5/1-8/1)

## 754 HEADINGLEY LIMITED STKS (0-70) (3-Y.O) (Class E)

5-10 (5-10) **1m 1f 213y** £3,206.70 (£957.60: £457.80: £207.90) Stalls: Low GOING minus 0.39 sec per fur (F)

| | | | | SP | RR | SF |
|---|---|---|---|---|---|---|
| 444[4] | **Docklands Limo (70)** (BJMcMath) **3-8-13** KDarley(4) (lw: trckd ldrs: led over 2f out: edgd lft: drvn out) | — | **1** | 6/1 2 | 80 | 43 |
| 444[6] | **Exactly (IRE) (68)** (JLEyre) **3-8-8** TWilliams(7) (a.p: led over 4f out tl over 2f out: kpt on u.p fnl f) | 1¾ | **2** | 16/1 | 72 | 35 |
| 575[4] | **Classic Ballet (FR) (69)** (SCWilliams) **3-8-8** AMackay(11) (lw: hld up: hdwy ½-wy: hrd rdn 2f out: nt pce to chal) | 3 | **3** | 13/2 3 | 67 | 30 |
| | **Ski For Gold (70)** (JLDunlop) **3-8-8** WCarson(2) (prom: rdn 4f out: wknd wl over 1f out) | 3 | **4** | 2/1 1 | 63 | 26 |
| *176*[6] | **Distinct Beauty (IRE) (67)** (WAO'Gorman) **3-8-10** DeanMcKeown(5) (lw: trckd ldrs tl wknd fnl 2f) | 2½ | **5** | 11/1 | 61 | 24 |
| 595[6] | **Yeoman Oliver (64)** (BAMcMahon) **3-8-13** GCarter(9) (trckd ldrs: outpcd ent st: n.d after) | ¾ | **6** | 16/1 | 62 | 25 |
| | **Salty Girl (IRE) (70)** (BWHills) **3-8-8** MHills(1) (bkwd: hld up: rdn 3f out: no imp) | ¾ | **7** | 7/1 | 56 | 19 |
| 575[5] | **Urgent Swift (65)** (APJarvis) **3-8-11** JTate(8) (s.s: a bhd) | 4 | **8** | 10/1 | 53 | 16 |
| | **Not Quite Grey (70)** (KWMcAuliffe) **3-8-11** SSanders(3) (bkwd: a in rr) | 2½ | **9** | 12/1 | 49 | 12 |
| | **Bullpen Belle (70)** (PTWalwyn) **3-8-8** DHarrison(6) (bit bkwd: led over 5f: sn rdn: wknd 3f out) | 4 | **10** | 12/1 | 39 | 2 |
| | **Name of Our Father (USA) (70)** (MJFetherston-Godley) **3-8-11** CRutter(10) (bit bkwd: hld up & bhd: lost tch 3f out: t.o) | 27 | **11** | 12/1 | — | — |
| | | | | (SP 125.7%) | **11 Rn** | |

**2m 5.2** (2.70) CSF £89.78 TOTE £6.50: £1.80 £6.90 £1.60 (£89.90) Trio £168.30 OWNER Mrs Lisa Olley (NEWMARKET) BRED Majors Racing International Ltd
**444 Docklands Limo**, the paddock pick, put his stamina to good use after leading halfway up the straight, and there was only ever going to be one winner. (6/1)
**Exactly (IRE)** tried her best but the winner was always going that bit better, and she was fighting a lost cause from below the distance. Her courage alone will win her races. (16/1)
**575 Classic Ballet (FR)** is not short on stamina, but does lack a turn of pace and, though she did keep battling away, could never get herself into contention. (13/2: op 4/1)
**Ski For Gold** was not so effective on this livelier ground and, nudged along on the home turn, was never finding the foot to get serious. (2/1)
**Distinct Beauty (IRE)**, returning to the turf, kept tabs on the leaders but she was struggling some way out and was not knocked about when her measure had been taken. (11/1: 7/1-12/1)
**575 Urgent Swift** (10/1: op 6/1)
**Name of Our Father (USA)** (12/1: 8/1-14/1)

T/Jkpt: Not won; £20,702.44 to Pontefract 23/4/96. T/Plpt: £1,738.90 (9.16 Tckts). T/Qdpt: £86.80 (13.32 Tckts). IM

# 0663-FOLKESTONE (R-H) (Firm)

## Tuesday April 23rd

WEATHER: fine WIND: fresh across

## 755 WALMER MAIDEN APPRENTICE STKS (3-Y.O) (Class F)

2-00 (2-02) **6f 189y** £2,381.00 (£656.00: £311.00) Stalls: Low GOING minus 0.32 sec per fur (GF)

| | | | | SP | RR | SF |
|---|---|---|---|---|---|---|
| 583[5] | **Arterxerxes** (MJHeaton-Ellis) **3-8-9**(3) SDrowne(3) (lw: mde all: rdn over 1f out: r.o wl) | — | **1** | 9/1 | 77 | 47 |
| 566[2] | **Alpine Hideaway (IRE) (75)** (BHanbury) **3-8-9**(3) JStack(6) (a.p: chsd wnr 5f out: ev ch over 2f out: rdn over 1f out: unable qckn) | 1½ | **2** | 5/2 2 | 74 | 44 |
| 448[2] | **Mansab (USA) (74)** (JLDunlop) **3-8-12** AWhelan(9) (chsd wnr 2f: rdn wl over 1f out: one pce) | 1½ | **3** | 11/8 1 | 70 | 40 |
| | **Lady Bankes (IRE) (70)** (WGMTurner) **3-8-4**(3) CAdamson(8) (bit bkwd: no hdwy fnl 2f) | 3½ | **4** | 16/1 | 57 | 27 |
| | **A Chef Too Far** (RRowe) **3-8-7**(5) RSmith(10) (w'like: bit bkwd: s.s: stumbled over 2f out: hdwy fnl f: nvr nrr) | 1½ | **5** | 16/1 | 58 | 28 |
| | **Mighty Phantom (USA)** (JWHills) **3-8-4**(3) MHenry(5) (bkwd: nvr nr to chal) | ½ | **6** | 14/1 | 52 | 22 |
| | **Rififi** (RIngram) **3-8-12** PMcCabe(2) (b: lw: prom over 5f) | nk | **7** | 7/1 3 | 57 | 27 |
| 634[2] | **Sunley Secure (66)** (MRChannon) **3-8-9**(3) PPMurphy(7) (hld up: rdn 2f out: sn wknd) | s.h | **8** | 20/1 | 56 | 26 |
| | **Mam'selle Bergerac (IRE) (65)** (PhilipMitchell) **3-8-4**(3) FLynch(1) (a bhd) | 5 | **9** | 25/1 | 40 | 10 |
| *459*[7] | **Latzio (40)** (BAPearce) **3-8-2**(5) JWilkinson(4) (a bhd) | 25 | **10** | 100/1 | — | — |
| | | | | (SP 121.2%) | **10 Rn** | |

**1m 23.4** (1.80) CSF £31.43 TOTE £8.90: £2.50 £1.10 £1.20 (£15.20) Trio £5.10 OWNER Mr P G Lowe & Partners (WROUGHTON) BRED S. Tindall and Stowell Hill Ltd
**583 Arterxerxes** made all the running and had the measure nicely of the second and third in the straight. (9/1: 5/1-10/1)
**566 Alpine Hideaway (IRE)** was soon racing in second place. With every chance entering the straight, he then found the winner too good. (5/2: 5/4-11/4)
**448 Mansab (USA)**, in second place early, was then settled in third. Ridden along in the straight, he failed to find the necessary turn of foot. (11/8)
**Lady Bankes (IRE)** was making little impression on the principals in the straight. (16/1)
**A Chef Too Far**, who looked as though the race would do him good, was out with the washing when stumbling turning into the straight. He made good progress in the final furlong to come through for fifth place and should be all the wiser for this. (16/1)
**Mighty Phantom (USA)** (14/1: op 8/1)

## 756 FOLKESTONE TOWN LIMITED STKS (0-70) (3-Y.O+) (Class E)

2-30 (2-32) **6f 189y** £3,206.70 (£957.60: £457.80: £207.90) Stalls: Low GOING minus 0.32 sec per fur (GF)

| | | | | SP | RR | SF |
|---|---|---|---|---|---|---|
| 554[8] | **Scharnhorst (70)** (SDow) **4-9-3**(5) ADaly(8) (lw: mde all: r.o wl) | — | **1** | 10/1 | 80 | 61 |

| | | | | | | |
|---|---|---|---|---|---|---|
| | **The Stager (IRE) (69)** (JRJenkins) **4-9-6** RCochrane(5) (lw: chsd wnr: ev ch over 2f out: hrd rdn over 1f out: r.o wl ins fnl f) | nk | 2 | 8/1 3 | 77 | 58 |
| *424*13 | **Office Hours (69)** (CACyzer) **4-9-6** RHughes(10) (a.p: 4th whn stumbled over 2f out: rdn over 1f out: unable qckn) | 4 | 3 | 25/1 | 68 | 49 |
| *530** | **Waikiki Beach (USA) (69)** (GLMoore) **5-9-8** SWhitworth(3) (a.p: rdn over 1f out: one pce) | s.h | 4 | 4/1 2 | 70 | 51 |
| 6765 | **Jerry Cutrona (IRE) (69)** (NACallaghan) **3-8-4**(5) DaneO'Neill(2) (hdwy over 1f out: nvr nrr) | 3 | 5 | 11/8 1 | 63 | 31 |
| | **Castan (IRE) (70)** (JLDunlop) **3-8-7** TQuinn(6) (bit bkwd: nvr nr to chal) | 1 | 6 | 12/1 | 59 | 27 |
| 55415 | **Dawalib (USA) (66)** (DHaydnJones) **6-9-6** WCarson(7) (a bhd) | nk | 7 | 10/1 | 58 | 39 |
| 6492 | **Allez Cyrano (IRE) (70)** (MBell) **5-9-8** MFenton(1) (b: lw: hdwy 6f out: wknd over 2f out) | 3½ | 8 | 10/1 | 52 | 33 |
| *655*5 | **Eurobox Boy (70)** (APJarvis) **3-8-4**(3) JStack(9) (bhd fnl 2f) | 1 | 9 | 8/1 3 | 47 | 15 |
| 5288 | **Antarctic Storm (70)** (EALDunlop) **3-8-7h** PaulEddery(4) (a bhd) | 2½ | 10 | 14/1 | 42 | 10 |

(SP 129.8%) **10 Rn**

**1m 23.0** (1.40) CSF £87.12 TOTE £12.90: £2.30 £3.10 £4.20 (£40.40) Trio £147.90 OWNER Mackenzie Print (EPSOM) BRED M. F. Kentish
WEIGHT FOR AGE 3yo-13lb
**OFFICIAL EXPLANATION Jerry Cutrona (IRE): had returned with cuts to his near hind hock.**
**496* Scharnhorst** bounced back to form with a pillar-to-post victory and proved just too good for the runner-up. (10/1: 7/1-12/1)
**The Stager (IRE)** looked extremely well in the paddock for this return. Racing in second place, he had every chance entering the straight but tended to carry his head rather high. He did keep on stoutly though inside the final furlong, and only just lost out. (8/1)
**Office Hours**, in fourth place when stumbling entering the straight, failed to find the necessary turn of foot in the last two furlongs. (25/1)
**530* Waikiki Beach (USA)** was never far away but failed to find the necessary in the straight. (4/1: 5/1-3/1)
**676 Jerry Cutrona (IRE)** raced at the back of the field, a long way off the pace. Coming down the centre of the track in the straight, he never looked like getting near the principals. The Vet later found he had cut his hock, so he is worth another chance. (11/8)
**Castan (IRE)** (12/1: 6/1-14/1)
**Dawalib (USA)** (10/1: 8/1-12/1)
**649 Allez Cyrano (IRE)** (10/1: op 6/1)
**528 Antarctic Storm** (14/1: 10/1-16/1)

## 757 SANDLING (S) STKS (2-Y.O) (Class G)

3-00 (3-01) **5f** £2,070.00 (£570.00: £270.00) Stalls: Low GOING minus 0.53 sec per fur (F)

| | | | | SP | RR | SF |
|---|---|---|---|---|---|---|
| | **Without Friends (IRE)** (RHannon) **2-8-6**(5) DaneO'Neill(5) (neat: bit bkwd: hdwy 2f out: led over 1f out: r.o wl) | — | 1 | 5/2 2 | 63 | 21 |
| 6856 | **Hello Dolly (IRE)** (KTIvory) **2-8-0**(7)ow1 CScally(6) (hld up: swtchd rt 2f out: ev ch 1f out: unable qckn) | 1 | 2 | 15/8 1 | 56 | 13 |
| | **Who Told Vicky (IRE)** (JSMoore) **2-8-6** JFEgan(4) (lt-f: led over 3f: one pce) | 3 | 3 | 14/1 | 45 | 3 |
| 6859 | **Rebuke** (RFJohnsonHoughton) **2-8-8b1**(3) DarrenMoffatt(8) (a.p: rdn 2f out: one pce) | ½ | 4 | 15/2 | 49 | 7 |
| | **Run Lucy Run** (RGuest) **2-8-6** WWoods(7) (neat: bit bkwd: a.p: rdn over 2f out: wknd over 1f out) | ¾ | 5 | 12/1 | 41 | — |
| | **Whizz Kid** (JJBridger) **2-8-1**(5) MBaird(1) (leggy: s.s: hdwy 2f out: wknd 1f out) | 2½ | 6 | 25/1 | 33 | — |
| 6434 | **Muppet** (MissGayKelleway) **2-8-6** RCochrane(3) (hld up: rdn over 2f out: sn wknd) | 5 | 7 | 4/1 3 | 17 | — |
| 6307 | **Mollily** (MRChannon) **2-8-6** CandyMorris(2) (a bhd) | 1½ | 8 | 10/1 | 12 | — |

(SP 122.4%) **8 Rn**

**59.3 secs** (1.70) CSF £7.99 TOTE £3.50: £2.00 £1.50 £2.40 (£5.20) OWNER Mr R. Hannon (MARLBOROUGH) BRED Churchtown House Stud
Bt in 5,600 gns; Hello Dolly (IRE) clmd NShields £6,000
**Without Friends (IRE)** moved through to lead below the distance and soon asserted. (5/2: 6/4-11/4)
**596 Hello Dolly (IRE)** produced her effort in the final quarter-mile and had every chance entering the final furlong before tapped for toe. (15/8)
**Who Told Vicky (IRE)**, a sparely-made filly, took the field along but, once collared below the distance, could only keep on in her own time. (14/1)
**685 Rebuke**, fitted with blinkers for the first time, was always close up but failed to quicken in the last two furlongs. (15/2)
**Run Lucy Run** looked far from fit, but raced up with the pace until tiring approaching the final furlong. (12/1: op 7/1)
**643 Muppet** (4/1: 3/1-9/2)
**Mollily** (10/1: 5/1-12/1)

## 758 BARHAM MEDIAN AUCTION MAIDEN STKS (3-Y.O) (Class E)

3-30 (3-32) **6f** £3,288.60 (£982.80: £470.40: £214.20) Stalls: Low GOING minus 0.53 sec per fur (F)

| | | | | SP | RR | SF |
|---|---|---|---|---|---|---|
| 45814 | **Spotted Eagle** (RHannon) **3-8-9**(5) DaneO'Neill(3) (a.p: n.m.r on ins over 2f out: led ins fnl f: r.o wl) | — | 1 | 14/1 | 78 | 50 |
| 5913 | **Watch The Fire** (JEBanks) **3-8-9** JQuinn(6) (a.p: led wl over 1f out tl ins fnl f: unable qckn) | 1¾ | 2 | Evens 1 | 68 | 40 |
| 4672 | **Blessed Spirit (70)** (CFWall) **3-8-9** WWoods(9) (hld up: rdn over 1f out: one pce) | 2½ | 3 | 100/30 2 | 62 | 34 |
| 6486 | **Man of Wit (IRE) (76)** (APJarvis) **3-9-0** TQuinn(8) (led over 4f) | 4 | 4 | 12/1 | 56 | 28 |
| 5268 | **Daring Venture** (TJNaughton) **3-8-2**(7) TAshley(2) (hld up: rdn over 1f out: wknd fnl f) | 2½ | 5 | 12/1 | 44 | 16 |
| 64414 | **Never Think Twice (61)** (KTIvory) **3-8-7v**(7) CScally(7) (s.s: hdwy over 2f out: wknd fnl f) | nk | 6 | 14/1 | 49 | 21 |
| | **Extra Hour (IRE) (71)** (WRMuir) **3-9-0** RCochrane(4) (bhd fnl 2f) | 6 | 7 | 9/1 3 | 33 | 5 |
| | **Governor's Bid** (MrsLCJewell) **3-9-0** RHughes(1) (w'like: bit bkwd: a bhd) | 16 | 8 | 50/1 | — | — |
| | **First Gallery** (RMFlower) **3-8-9** DBiggs(5) (neat: bit bkwd: a bhd) | 3½ | 9 | 33/1 | — | — |

(SP 116.7%) **9 Rn**

**1m 10.4** (0.10 under best) (0.20) CSF £27.81 TOTE £16.60: £2.80 £1.10 £1.70 (£14.00) Trio £13.10 OWNER Lord Carnarvon (MARLBOR-OUGH) BRED Roldvale Ltd
**Spotted Eagle**, never far away, swooped into the lead inside the final furlong and kept on far too well for the runner-up. (14/1: 10/1-16/1)
**591 Watch The Fire** made her bid for glory early in the final quarter-mile, but found the winner too strong inside the last 200 yards. (Evens)
**467 Blessed Spirit** chased the leaders but failed to find the necessary turn of foot below the distance. (100/30: 9/4-7/2)
**648 Man of Wit (IRE)** took the field along but, collared over a furlong out, soon had bellows to mend. (12/1: 6/1-14/1)
**Daring Venture** chased the leaders but called it a day entering the final furlong. (12/1: op 20/1)
**Extra Hour (IRE)** (9/1: 6/1-10/1)

## 759 LEVY BOARD H'CAP (0-70) (4-Y.O+) (Class E)

4-00 (4-00) **1m 7f 92y** £3,261.30 (£974.40: £466.20: £212.10) Stalls: High GOING minus 0.32 sec per fur (GF)

| | | | | SP | RR | SF |
|---|---|---|---|---|---|---|
| *398*5 | **The Lad (40)** (LMontagueHall) **7-7-5**(7)ow2 MartinDwyer(5) (lw: hdwy over 2f out: led over 1f out: r.o wl) | — | 1 | 4/1 2 | 54 | 27 |
| 6353 | **Courbaril (59)** (SDow) **4-9-0** TQuinn(7) (led tl over 1f out: unable qckn) | 3½ | 2 | 9/2 3 | 69 | 41 |
| 6357 | **Ikhtiraa (USA) (38)** (RJO'Sullivan) **6-7-7b**(3) NVarley(8) (chsd ldr: ev ch over 1f out: nt r.o) | 1¾ | 3 | 11/1 | 47 | 22 |
| 6352 | **Ajdar (53)** (MissGayKelleway) **5-8-11** RCochrane(10) (a.p: rdn over 2f out: one pce) | 1½ | 4 | 5/2 1 | 60 | 35 |

| | Horse | Dist | Pos | SP | RR | SF |
|---|---|---|---|---|---|---|
| *$169^{3}$* | **Mizyan (IRE) (62)** (JEBanks) **8-9-6** JQuinn(3) (bhd fnl 4f) | 9 | **5** | 6/1 | 60 | 35 |
| $573^{12}$ | **Warm Spell (68)** (GLMoore) **6-9-12** SWhitworth(1) (a bhd) | 8 | **6** | 12/1 | 57 | 32 |
| $642^{6}$ | **Imlak (IRE) (60)** (JLHarris) **4-9-1** JFEgan(6) (lw: hdwy 5f out: wknd over 2f out) | s.h | **7** | 14/1 | 49 | 21 |
| *$260^{5}$* | **All the Joys (44)** (CACyzer) **5-8-2**$^{ow4}$ MFenton(9) (lw: hdwy 8f out: wknd 3f out) | 4 | **8** | $9/2^{3}$ | 29 | — |

(SP 121.9%) **8 Rn**

**3m 24.1** (6.10) CSF £22.33 CT £172.29 TOTE £5.30: £1.80 £1.10 £2.60 (£14.30) Trio £76.80 OWNER Treberth Partnership (EPSOM) BRED W. R. and M. E. Scale

LONG HANDICAP The Lad 7-8 Ikhtiraa (USA) 7-6

WEIGHT FOR AGE 4yo-3lb

OFFICIAL EXPLANATION **All the Joys: was lame on her near-fore the morning after the race due to a quarter crack that had opened up.**

**The Lad** picked up ground turning into the straight and, storming into the lead below the distance, soon pulled away. (4/1: 3/1-9/2)

**635 Courbaril** attempted to make all but, collared below the distance, was left standing by the winner. (9/2: 3/1-5/1)

**Ikhtiraa (USA)** chased the leader. Throwing down a challenge turning into the straight, he looked far from enthusiastic and failed to put his best foot forward. (11/1: 6/1-12/1)

**635 Ajdar**, always close up, could only keep on in his own time in the straight. (5/2)

**Mizyan (IRE)** (6/1: tchd 10/1)

**Warm Spell** (12/1: 7/1-14/1)

**642 Imlak (IRE)** (14/1: 10/1-16/1)

**All the Joys** (9/2: 3/1-5/1)

## 760 DOVER H'CAP (0-70) (3-Y.O+) (Class E)

4-30 (4-30) **1m 4f** £3,261.30 (£974.40: £466.20: £212.10) Stalls: High GOING minus 0.32 sec per fur (GF)

| | Horse | Dist | Pos | SP | RR | SF |
|---|---|---|---|---|---|---|
| | **Ashby Hill (IRE) (41)** (RRowe) **5-9-1** RCochrane(4) (stdy hdwy over 3f out: led 1f out: r.o wl) | — | **1** | $7/1^{3}$ | 57 | 29 |
| | **Fast Forward Fred (47)** (LMontagueHall) **5-9-7** JFEgan(12) (a.p: ev ch 1f out: unable qckn) | 1 | **2** | 20/1 | 62 | 34 |
| *$604^{4}$* | **Jean de Florette (USA) (32)** (RCSpicer) **5-8-6** NKennedy(3) (a.p: led over 1f out: sn hdd: one pce) | 3½ | **3** | 16/1 | 42 | 14 |
| | **Old School House (45)** (TJNaughton) **3-7-8**$^{(5)}$ MBaird(8) (bit bkwd: hdwy over 1f out: nvr nrr) | 1½ | **4** | 25/1 | 53 | 5 |
| *$555^{6}$* | **Yellow Dragon (IRE) (57)** (BAPearce) **3-8-6**$^{(5)}$ MHenry(7) (hld up: led over 2f out tl over 1f out: sn wknd) | 2½ | **5** | 14/1 | 62 | 14 |
| 612* | **Pip's Dream (51)** (MJRyan) **5-9-11** WCarson(14) (led over 9f: wknd over 1f out) | 5 | **6** | Evens $^{1}$ | 49 | 21 |
| | **Fresh Look (IRE) (42)** (RCSpicer) **4-9-1** JQuinn(1) (nvr nrr) | 1 | **7** | 16/1 | 39 | 10 |
| | **Yet Again (54)** (BHanbury) **4-9-10**$^{(3)}$ JStack(10) (bit bkwd: nvr nrr) | 8 | **8** | $6/1^{2}$ | 40 | 11 |
| | **Fastini Gold (51)** (MDIUsher) **4-9-10** MWigham(11) (a bhd) | 1 | **9** | 25/1 | 36 | 7 |
| *$502^{9}$* | **Lord Ellangowan (IRE) (45)** (RIngram) **3-7-13b** NAdams(6) (chsd ldr 9f) | 1¼ | **10** | 8/1 | 28 | — |
| $649^{7}$ | **Northern Spruce (IRE) (27)** (AGFoster) **4-8-0** TSprake(9) (bhd fnl 4f) | nk | **11** | 20/1 | 10 | — |
| | **Ruth's Gamble (44)** (MrsLCJewell) **8-9-4** CRutter(2) (b: prom 7f) | 15 | **12** | 50/1 | 7 | — |
| | **Trendy Auctioneer (IRE) (23)** (MrsLCJewell) **8-7-6**$^{(5)}$ CAdamson(13) (b: bit bkwd: bhd fnl 4f) | 8 | **13** | 50/1 | — | — |

(SP 127.5%) **13 Rn**

**2m 38.0** (6.80) CSF £126.79 CT £1,995.60 TOTE £9.70: £3.20 £6.70 £2.50 (£128.60) Trio £159.10 OWNER Miss Meriel Tufnell (PULBOROUGH) BRED Patrick Aspell

WEIGHT FOR AGE 3yo-20lb, 4yo-1lb

**Ashby Hill (IRE)**, travelling supremely well for much of the race, cruised into the action running down the hill. Forging her way to the front a furlong out, she quickly had the race in the bag. (7/1)

**Fast Forward Fred**, always close up, had every chance entering the final furlong before the winner proved too strong. (20/1)

**604 Jean de Florette (USA)**, always close up, moved to the front below the distance. Soon headed, he could then only keep on in his own time. (16/1)

**Old School House**, racing well off the pace, stayed on in the last furlong and a half to be nearest at the line. (25/1)

**Yellow Dragon (IRE)** went on over a quarter of a mile from home but, headed below the distance, had soon cooked his goose. (14/1)

**612* Pip's Dream** attempted to make all. Collared over a quarter of a mile out, she had burnt her boats below the distance. (Evens)

**Lord Ellangowan (IRE)** (8/1: op 5/1)

## 761 TIM FREEMAN H'CAP (0-65) (3-Y.O) (Class F)

5-00 (5-02) **1m 1f 149y** £3,261.60 (£907.60: £436.80) Stalls: High GOING minus 0.32 sec per fur (GF)

| | Horse | Dist | Pos | SP | RR | SF |
|---|---|---|---|---|---|---|
| *$460^{2}$* | **Safecracker (58)** (JWHills) **3-8-11**$^{(5)}$ MHenry(11) (lw: chsd ldr: led over 2f out: clr over 1f out: r.o wl) | — | **1** | $5/2^{2}$ | 71 | 8 |
| $597^{5}$ | **Efficacious (IRE) (48)** (CJBenstead) **3-8-6** AMcGlone(8) (hld up: hdwy 5f out: rdn over 2f out: r.o one pce) | 5 | **2** | 14/1 | 53 | — |
| $616^{6}$ | **Dungeon Princess (IRE) (60)** (MRChannon) **3-9-4** RHughes(14) (lw: chsd ldrs: rdn over 2f out: hung lft ins fnl f: one pce) | ½ | **3** | $8/1^{3}$ | 64 | 1 |
| $545^{5}$ | **Domettes (IRE) (60)** (RHannon) **3-8-13**$^{(5)}$ DaneO'Neill(7) (hld up: hdwy 3f out: rdn over 2f out: r.o one pce ins fnl f) | nk | **4** | $8/1^{3}$ | 63 | — |
| $468^{2}$ | **Basood (USA) (63)** (EALDunlop) **3-9-7** PaulEddery(10) (hld up: hdwy over 5f out: rdn over 2f out: one pce) | 1½ | **5** | $2/1^{1}$ | 64 | 1 |
| $597^{4}$ | **Ivory's Grab Hire (50)** (KTIvory) **3-8-5**$^{(3)}$ JStack(15) (nvr plcd to chal) | 2 | **6** | 20/1 | 48 | — |
| $528^{11}$ | **Lahik (IRE) (48)** (KTIvory) **3-8-6** DBiggs(13) (lw: led: hdd over 2f out: grad wknd) | ½ | **7** | 33/1 | 45 | — |
| *$377^{6}$* | **Spiral Flyer (IRE) (58)** (MDIUsher) **3-9-2** MWigham(3) (chsd ldrs tl wknd over 3f out) | 4 | **8** | 33/1 | 48 | — |
| $577^{12}$ | **Condor Ridge (50)** (BJMeehan) **3-8-8** JFEgan(2) (mid div: rdn over 3f out: eased whn btn over 1f out) | ¾ | **9** | 12/1 | 39 | — |
| | **Siberian Mystic (40)** (PGMurphy) **3-7-12** NAdams(9) (a bhd) | 2½ | **10** | 14/1 | 25 | — |
| | **Astra Martin (47)** (PGMurphy) **3-8-2v**$^{1(3)ow2}$ SDrowne(4) (a bhd) | 3½ | **11** | 20/1 | 26 | — |
| | **Madam Marash (IRE) (53)** (AGFoster) **3-8-11** TSprake(1) (chsd ldrs tl wknd 3f out) | 1 | **12** | 20/1 | 30 | — |

(SP 125.3%) **12 Rn**

**2m 5.6** (7.90) CSF £36.51 CT £234.46 TOTE £3.50: £2.40 £2.80 £1.90 (£51.20) Trio £111.00; £140.78 to 5.20 Catterick 24/4/96. OWNER Mrs R. F. Lowe (LAMBOURN) BRED L. H. J. Ward

**460 Safecracker** chased the leader until going on over a quarter of a mile from home. Forging clear below the distance, he was not going to be caught. (5/2: 7/4-3/1)

**597 Efficacious (IRE)** moved up at halfway. Ridden along turning into the straight, he stayed on for second but had no hope of getting to the winner. (14/1)

**616 Dungeon Princess (IRE)** chased the leaders but hung badly left inside the final furlong and failed to find the necessary turn of foot. (8/1)

**545 Domettes (IRE)** moved up three furlongs from home, but then made no further impression until staying on late in the closing stages for fourth place. (8/1)

**468 Basood (USA)**, racing in midfield, took closer order at halfway. Ridden along three furlongs from home, she was made to look very pedestrian. (2/1: 7/2-15/8)

**597 Ivory's Grab Hire** certainly caught the eye under considerate handling. Out with the washing, he was noted making eye-catching late headway below the distance with his jockey doing very little on him. He looks one to keep an eye on. (20/1)
**Siberian Mystic** (14/1: 8/1-16/1)

T/Plpt: £405.90 (25.33 Tckts). T/Qdpt: £45.70 (16.6 Tckts). AK

# 0685-PONTEFRACT (L-H) (Good)
## Tuesday April 23rd
WEATHER: overcast WIND: fresh bhd

## 762 PONTEFRACT SERIES APPRENTICE H'CAP (Rnd 1) (0-70) (3-Y.O+) (Class E)
2-20 (2-24) **5f** £2,819.25 (£864.00: £429.50: £212.25) Stalls: Low GOING: 0.08 sec per fur (G)

| | Horse | Dist | Pos | SP | RR | SF |
|---|---|---|---|---|---|---|
| 587[4] | **Captain Carat (60)** (MrsJRRamsden) **5-9-0**(7) ClaireWest(11) (b.nr fore: unruly stalls: hdwy ½-wy: led ins fnl f: r.o) | — | 1 | 13/2[2] | 67 | 38 |
| 587[9] | **Belinda Blue (45)** (RAFahey) **4-8-1**(5) RFfrench(16) (dwlt: hdwy 2f out: r.o wl towards fin) | 1 | 2 | 9/1[3] | 49 | 20 |
| *259*[3] | **My Cherrywell (52)** (LRLloyd-James) **6-8-13b** CWebb(18) (b.off hind: chsd ldrs on outside: r.o wl towards fin) | s.h | 3 | 16/1 | 56 | 27 |
| 667[3] | **Petraco (IRE) (63)** (NASmith) **8-9-5**(5) JBramhill(2) (chsd ldrs: led wl over 1f out tl ins fnl f: no ex) | s.h | 4 | 4/1[1] | 67 | 38 |
| 587* | **Kira (58)** (JLEyre) **6-9-0**(5) PDoe(3) (b.off hind: cl up: disp ld wl over 1f out: r.o one pce) | s.h | 5 | 4/1[1] | 61 | 32 |
| 667[7] | **Domicksky (52)** (MRChannon) **8-8-13** AEddery(7) (hdwy ½-wy: kpt on one pce fnl f) | ½ | 6 | 14/1 | 54 | 25 |
| | **Bright Paragon (IRE) (40)** (MCChapman) **7-7-10**(5)ow2 MSemple(5) (led over 3f: grad wknd) | 2½ | 7 | 33/1 | 34 | 3 |
| | **Rotherfield Park (IRE) (37)** (CSmith) **4-7-5**(7) CCogan(9) (chsd ldrs tl grad wknd fnl 2f) | ½ | 8 | 33/1 | 29 | — |
| *653*[3] | **Disco Boy (48)** (PDEvans) **6-8-4v**1(5)ow1 HayleyWilliams(17) (prom on outside: no imp fnl 2f) | ¾ | 9 | 16/1 | 38 | 8 |
| | **Call to the Bar (IRE) (54)** (MDods) **7-8-10**(5) KSked(6) (chsd ldr tl wknd over 1f out) | s.h | 10 | 50/1 | 44 | 15 |
| 659[3] | **Just Bob (62)** (SEKettlewell) **7-9-2**(7) JStockton(10) (lw: hdwy 2f out: nvr rchd ldrs) | 1¼ | 11 | 9/1[3] | 48 | 19 |
| *514*[10] | **Ivy Lilian (IRE) (35)** (WMBrisbourne) **4-7-5**(5) RMullen(15) (racd wd: w ldrs over 3f) | s.h | 12 | 100/1 | 20 | — |
| | **Hickleton Miss (52)** (MrsVAAconley) **3-7-12**(5) TFinn(8) (mid div: rdn over 1f out: n.d) | ½ | 13 | 33/1 | 36 | — |
| | **Doug's Folly (54)** (MWEasterby) **3-8-5** OliverCasey(13) (sn bhd) | 3 | 14 | 14/1 | 28 | — |
| 525[14] | **Harriet's Beau (49)** (MWEasterby) **3-7-11b**(3) DSweeney(4) (w ldrs 3f: wknd qckly) | nk | 15 | 33/1 | 22 | — |
| 644[15] | **Kiwud (47)** (TWDonnelly) **3-7-5**(7) CHalliwell(12) (w ldrs on outside tl wknd wl over 1f out) | 3 | 16 | 66/1 | 11 | — |
| *359** | **Highland Fawn (55)** (BAMcMahon) **3-8-6** JDennis(14) (a bhd) | hd | 17 | 16/1 | 18 | — |
| | ***Snitch (46)*** (CSmith) **3-7-11**ow1 AngelaGallimore(1) (Withdrawn not under Starter's orders: bolted circ bef s) | | W | 33/1 | — | — |

(SP 123.5%) **17 Rn**

**65.3 secs** (4.50) CSF £57.80 CT £854.80 TOTE £5.20: £1.30 £1.80 £2.70 £1.70 (£34.90) Trio £476.60; £335.66 to 5.20 Catterick 24/4/96.
OWNER Mr Colin Webster (THIRSK) BRED Lt-Col J. H. Scott
WEIGHT FOR AGE 3yo-10lb

**587 Captain Carat**, given a fine ride, for once had a trouble-free run and scored most decisively. (13/2: 9/2-7/1)
**Belinda Blue** gave away a lot of ground at the start and then had to come round the whole field, so did remarkably well to finish so close. (9/1)
**My Cherrywell** has not been out for over two months and ran really well here from a poor draw, showing she is in really good heart. (16/1)
**667 Petraco (IRE)** was given the lead when the rest fanned out turning for home but, despite trying hard, his weight proved just too much. (4/1)
**587* Kira** had everything in her favour last time but, on this 6lb higher mark here, she could never stamp her authority on the race. (4/1)
**559 Domicksky** failed to win last season and is currently off a useful mark. This was not a bad effort. (14/1)
**Ivy Lilian (IRE)** showed a lot of speed from a bad draw. (100/1)

## 763 BEAST FAIR MEDIAN AUCTION MAIDEN STKS (3-Y.O) (Class E)
2-50 (2-51) **1m 2f 6y** £3,204.00 (£972.00: £476.00: £228.00) Stalls: Low GOING: 0.08 sec per fur (G)

| | Horse | Dist | Pos | SP | RR | SF |
|---|---|---|---|---|---|---|
| | **Backdrop (IRE)** (PWChapple-Hyam) **3-9-0** JReid(1) (in tch: effrt 4f out: styd on to ld ins fnl f: r.o wl) | — | 1 | 5/4[1] | 74 | 40 |
| | **Shooting Light (IRE)** (MAJarvis) **3-9-0** PBloomfield(4) (chsd ldrs: rdn 3f out: led 1½f out tl ins fnl f: r.o) | ¾ | 2 | 20/1 | 73 | 39 |
| 687[6] | **Kathryn's Pet** (MrsMReveley) **3-8-9** ACulhane(8) (hld up: stdy hdwy whn hmpd 2f out: swtchd over 1f out: r.o) | 6 | 3 | 11/1[3] | 58 | 24 |
| 445[11] | **Crystal Warrior** (DNicholls) **3-8-9** AlexGreaves(3) (cl up: led over 2f out to 1½f out: sn outpcd) | 1¼ | 4 | 33/1 | 56 | 22 |
| 472[4] | **Batoutoftheblue (54)** (WWHaigh) **3-9-0** JTate(6) (bit bkwd: bhd: pushed along 4f out: styd on wl fnl 2f) | 1 | 5 | 50/1 | 60 | 26 |
| | **Always Happy** (JRFanshawe) **3-8-9** DHarrison(2) (trckd ldrs: chal over 2f out: rdn & wknd over 1f out) | 7 | 6 | 6/4[2] | 44 | 10 |
| | **Tudor Falcon** (WJHaggas) **3-9-0** RHills(9) (leggy: mid div: effrt 3f out: no imp) | 1¼ | 7 | 14/1 | 47 | 13 |
| *555*[3] | **Bright Eclipse (USA)** (JWHills) **3-9-0** MHills(11) (cl up: led over 3f tl over 2f out: sn wknd) | 6 | 8 | 16/1 | 37 | 3 |
| | **Hallikeld** (TJEtherington) **3-8-9** LCharnock(5) (prom tl wknd 3f out) | 4 | 9 | 33/1 | 26 | — |
| | **Parrot's Hill (IRE)** (MHTompkins) **3-9-0** PRobinson(10) (lengthy: unf: bkwd: s.s: n.d) | hd | 10 | 20/1 | 30 | — |
| *484*[5] | **Lucitino** (SCWilliams) **3-8-9** KFallon(12) (b: drvn along 4f out: sn t.o) | dist | 11 | 20/1 | — | — |
| | **Lady Benson (IRE)** (WMBrisbourne) **3-8-9** SSanders(7) (leggy: bkwd: led tl hdd & wknd qckly over 3f out) | dist | 12 | 66/1 | — | — |

(SP 128.9%) **12 Rn**

**2m 16.6** (8.30) CSF £28.06 TOTE £2.30: £1.40 £9.10 £1.60 (£106.40) Trio £158.10; £77.97 to 5.20 Catterick 24/4/96. OWNER Mr R. E. Sangster (MARLBOROUGH) BRED John Neary

**Backdrop (IRE)** obviously needs further as he took an age to get going here but, in the end, did win really well. (5/4)
**Shooting Light (IRE)** showed nothing in one run last year, but has certainly come into his own now and really made the winner stretch. (20/1)
**687 Kathryn's Pet** put in another eyecatching run and, but for getting messed about, would have been a good deal closer. She is one to keep on the right side of. (11/1)
**Crystal Warrior** ran really well and is now qualified for handicaps, so will no doubt come into her own in due course. (33/1)
**472 Batoutoftheblue** appreciated the longer trip and was keeping on well at the finish. He will need further yet. (50/1)
**Always Happy** travelled quite well for much of the trip but, when an effort was required in the last couple of furlongs, her response was very disappointing. (6/4)

## 764 BENTLEY (S) STKS (3-Y.O+) (Class G)
3-20 (3-23) **6f** £2,343.00 (£648.00: £309.00) Stalls: Low GOING: 0.08 sec per fur (G)

| | Horse | Dist | Pos | SP | RR | SF |
|---|---|---|---|---|---|---|
| 450[21] | **Smart Guest (75)** (JAHarris) **4-9-7** KFallon(5) (b.nr fore: sn pushed along & bhd: hdwy 2f out: qcknd to ld wl ins fnl f) | — | 1 | 7/1 | 68 | 41 |

| Form | Horse | Dist | Pos | SP | RR | SF |
|---|---|---|---|---|---|---|
| 700[3] | **Sea-Deer (82)** (DWChapman) **7-9-7** JFortune(4) (lw: trckd ldrs: slt ld appr fnl f: sn rdn: hdd & nt qckn towards fin) | ½ | **2** | 5/2[1] | 67 | 40 |
| 662[8] | **Blue Grit (51)** (MDods) **10-9-7** JWeaver(7) (hld up: effrt 2f out: ev ch 1f out: edgd lft & no ex) | 1 | **3** | 9/2[3] | 64 | 37 |
| *511*[6] | **Brookhead Lady (56)** (PDEvans) **5-9-2** SSanders(6) (b.nr fore: led tl hdd appr fnl f: one pce) | ¾ | **4** | 9/2[3] | 57 | 30 |
| 661[11] | **Komlucky (42)** (ABMulholland) **4-9-2b** TWilliams(8) (trckd ldrs: effrt 2f out: one pce fnl f) | 2½ | **5** | 50/1 | 50 | 23 |
| 470[12] | **Rocky Two (43)** (PHowling) **5-9-7v** FNorton(3) (chsd ldrs: n.m.r 2f out: one pce after) | 3 | **6** | 33/1 | 47 | 20 |
| 479[7] | **Sea Devil (60)** (MJCamacho) **10-9-12** LCharnock(2) (chsd ldrs over 4f: wknd) | ½ | **7** | 13/2 | 51 | 24 |
| 665[2] | **Primo Lad** (WGMTurner) **3-8-10** GDuffield(1) (s.i.s: outpcd & lost tch ½-wy) | 9 | **8** | 4/1[2] | 22 | — |
| | | | | (SP 115.7%) | | **8 Rn** |

**1m 19.5** (5.20) CSF £23.96 TOTE £8.50: £2.00 £1.50 £1.10 (£11.80) OWNER Mr Paul Murphy (EDINGLEY) BRED Ahmed M. Foustok
WEIGHT FOR AGE 3yo-11lb
No bid

**Smart Guest** had run miserably both on the Flat and over hurdles recently, but he left that behind here and scored in convincing fashion. (7/1)
**700 Sea-Deer** looked to have at last got everything right here but, when that final effort was required, he was again found wanting. (5/2)
**Blue Grit** loves this track and had every chance, but failed to pick up late on. A stronger gallop would have been in his favour. (9/2)
**511 Brookhead Lady** won this race last year, but she has not been firing on the All-Weather of late, and she was run out of this in the final furlong. (9/2: 3/1-5/1)
**Komlucky** had her chances but lacked the final dash. (50/1)

## 765 PONTEFRACT PARK H'CAP (0-90) (3-Y.O+) (Class C)

3-50 (3-52) **1m 4y** £6,472.00 (£1,936.00: £928.00: £424.00) Stalls: Low GOING: 0.08 sec per fur (G)

| Form | Horse | Dist | Pos | SP | RR | SF |
|---|---|---|---|---|---|---|
| 589* | **Master Charter (66)** (MrsJRRamsden) **4-8-10** KFallon(4) (s.i.s: bhd tl hdwy 2f out: qcknd to ld ins fnl f: eased) | — | **1** | 9/4[1] | 78+ | 40 |
| 450[5] | **Celestial Choir (80)** (JLEyre) **6-9-10** RLappin(6) (chsd ldrs: rdn to ld over 1f out: sn hdd: no ch w wnr) | 2 | **2** | 10/1[3] | 88 | 50 |
| 547[8] | **Clifton Fox (78)** (JAGlover) **4-9-8** SDWilliams(8) (bhd: pushed along over 3f out: hdwy 2f out: r.o wl towards fin) | ½ | **3** | 14/1 | 85 | 47 |
| 713[2] | **Wentbridge Lad (IRE) (60)** (PDEvans) **6-8-4v** SSanders(9) (a chsng ldrs: ev ch & rdn over 1f out: kpt on) | nk | **4** | 10/1[3] | 66 | 28 |
| 440[12] | **Western General (74)** (MissMKMilligan) **5-9-4** NConnorton(1) (bhd: styd on fnl 2f: nrst fin) | 2 | **5** | 25/1 | 76 | 38 |
| | **Rory (76)** (MrsJCecil) **5-9-6** JWeaver(12) (lw: bhd: hdwy wl over 1f out: swtchd & r.o towards fin) | ¾ | **6** | 20/1 | 77 | 39 |
| 450[6] | **New Century (USA) (81)** (DNicholls) **4-9-11** AlexGreaves(15) (cl up: led over 4f out tl over 1f out: sn btn) | nk | **7** | 9/1[2] | 81 | 43 |
| 589[8] | **Scaraben (73)** (SEKettlewell) **8-9-3** JFortune(10) (effrt over 3f out: sn chsng ldrs: one pce appr fnl f) | nk | **8** | 14/1 | 73 | 35 |
| | **Hand Craft (IRE) (83)** (WJHaggas) **4-9-13** RHills(5) (h.d.w: hld up: effrt over 1f out: no imp) | 1 | **9** | 10/1[3] | 81 | 43 |
| *393*[2] | **Jungle Patrol (IRE) (63)** (MBrittain) **4-8-7** BThomson(13) (b: chsd ldrs 6f) | 1½ | **10** | 50/1 | 58 | 20 |
| | **Gadge (63)** (DMorris) **5-8-7** DHarrison(7) (bit bkwd: chsd ldrs over 5f) | 2½ | **11** | 14/1 | 53 | 15 |
| 455[15] | **Show Faith (IRE) (84)** (RHannon) **6-10-0** JReid(17) (a rr div) | 3½ | **12** | 20/1 | 67 | 29 |
| 455[12] | **Fame Again (82)** (MrsJRRamsden) **4-9-12** DeanMcKeown(2) (trckd ldrs tl lost pl fnl 2f) | hd | **13** | 20/1 | 65 | 27 |
| | **Samba Sharply (77)** (AHide) **5-9-7** MTebbutt(11) (bit bkwd: effrt over 3f out: n.d) | 2 | **14** | 25/1 | 56 | 18 |
| 496[2] | **Duello (62)** (MBlanshard) **5-8-6** KDarley(19) (chsd ldrs 5f) | 3 | **15** | 14/1 | 35 | — |
| | **Sveltana (78)** (GWragg) **4-9-8** MHills(16) (in tch 6f: sn wknd) | 1¼ | **16** | 9/1[2] | 48 | 10 |
| 547[11] | **Touch a Million (USA) (74)** (EALDunlop) **4-9-4v[1]** WRyan(3) (lw: prom tl n.m.r & lost pl over 2f out: hmpd over 1f out: n.d) | ½ | **17** | 16/1 | 43 | 5 |
| 629[16] | **Duke Valentino (65)** (RHollinshead) **4-8-9** LDettori(18) (swtg: a rr div) | 13 | **18** | 33/1 | 8 | — |
| | **Quilling (81)** (MDods) **4-9-11** JCarroll(14) (led tl hdd over 4f out: wknd over 2f out) | 1 | **19** | 25/1 | 22 | — |
| | | | | (SP 141.3%) | | **19 Rn** |

**1m 47.6** (6.10) CSF £27.82 CT £273.67 TOTE £3.60: £1.50 £1.80 £3.50 £2.10 (£12.30) Trio £205.20 OWNER Mr Jonathan Ramsden (THIRSK) BRED Carlton Consultants Ltd

**589* Master Charter**, despite going up 8lb, won in most impressive style and there would seem to be a decent race to be picked up before the Handicapper gets his measure. (9/4)
**450 Celestial Choir** was always in the firing line but found the winner in a completely different league. (10/1)
**Clifton Fox** was in a messy race last time and he is well suited by a strongly-run mile such as this. He did find some trouble in running and, despite finishing fast, never had a hope. He is in good form. (14/1: 10/1-16/1)
**713 Wentbridge Lad (IRE)** raced with every chance but just failed to quicken in the closing stages. (10/1)
**Western General**, like the winner, tried to come from behind but was never travelling as well and failed to get in a blow. He looks to be off a useful mark should he really get it together. (25/1)
**Rory** had no luck at all in running. He finished fast, albeit too late, and looks one to keep on the right side of. (20/1)

## 766 CORN MARKET LIMITED STKS (0-80) (3-Y.O+) (Class D)

4-20 (4-21) **1m 2f 6y** £3,566.25 (£1,080.00: £527.50: £251.25) Stalls: Low GOING: 0.08 sec per fur (G)

| Form | Horse | Dist | Pos | SP | RR | SF |
|---|---|---|---|---|---|---|
| | **Humourless (80)** (LMCumani) **3-8-5** LDettori(2) (mde all: qcknd 2f out: r.o wl: eased towards fin) | — | **1** | 7/2[2] | 91+ | 29 |
| 580[9] | **Noble Sprinter (IRE) (80)** (RHannon) **4-9-8b** JReid(3) (lw: a chsng wnr: rdn over 2f out: styd on one pce) | 5 | **2** | 5/1[3] | 83 | 38 |
| | **Ladykirk (80)** (JWWatts) **3-8-2** NConnorton(6) (s.i.s: hdwy 5f out: pushed along 3f out: nt pce to chal) | 1½ | **3** | 5/1[3] | 78 | 16 |
| | **Naval Gazer (IRE) (80)** (DRLoder) **3-7-13**(3) DRMcCabe(4) (lw: sn prom: outpcd over 2f out: kpt on fnl f) | s.h | **4** | 11/2 | 78 | 16 |
| | **Efharisto (71)** (JWhite) **7-9-8** DaleGibson(1) (hld up: lost pl over 2f out: kpt on towards fin) | 1¾ | **5** | 40/1 | 78 | 33 |
| | **Tykeyvor (IRE) (77)** (LadyHerries) **6-9-8** GDuffield(5) (b.hind: chsd ldrs tl rdn & btn 2f out) | 1½ | **6** | 12/1 | 75 | 30 |
| | **Sadler's Walk (80)** (GWragg) **5-9-8** MHills(7) (hld up: hdwy over 3f out: rdn over 2f out: fnd nil) | 7 | **7** | 7/4[1] | 64 | 19 |
| | | | | (SP 117.4%) | | **7 Rn** |

**2m 16.9** (8.60) CSF £20.36 TOTE £3.80: £2.00 £2.50 (£17.00) OWNER Sheikh Mohammed (NEWMARKET) BRED John Warren
WEIGHT FOR AGE 3yo-17lb

**Humourless**, in front throughout, got better the further he went, and he was eased a good deal before the finish. Much better looks likely, especially over another couple of furlongs. (7/2)
**Noble Sprinter (IRE)** tried his best, but was in second place throughout and was well outclassed in the last quarter-mile. (5/1)
**Ladykirk** needed this and ran quite well. Over further, improvement looks likely. (5/1)
**Naval Gazer (IRE)** got left struggling when the tempo increased over two furlongs out, but she was keeping on at the end to show that longer trips should bring improvement. (11/2)
**Efharisto** has been racing in the Arab Emirates and, after showing little over hurdles on his return, this effort was a bit better. (40/1)
**Tykeyvor (IRE)** was never really firing here once the pace hotted up in the last three furlongs. (12/1)
**Sadler's Walk** travelled quite well but, once asked for an effort three furlongs out, he soon decided it was not his day. (7/4)

## 767 LEVY BOARD H'CAP (0-80) (4-Y.O+) (Class D)
4-50 (4-53) **2m 1f 22y** £4,012.50 (£1,200.00: £575.00: £262.50) Stalls: Low GOING: 0.08 sec per fur (G)

| | | | | SP | RR | SF |
|---|---|---|---|---|---|---|
| 573[3] | **Upper Mount Clair (61)** (CEBrittain) **6-9-2** BDoyle(3) (lw: in tch: hdwy 7f out: led over 1f out: styd on strly)...— | 1 | | 9/2[2] | 73 | 52 |
| *602** | **Greek Night Out (IRE) (43)** (JLEyre) **5-7-9**(3) DWright(4) (cl up: led wl over 4f out tl over 1f out: one pce).....3½ | 2 | | 8/1 | 52 | 31 |
| | **Sujud (IRE) (52)** (MrsJRRamsden) **4-8-3** KFallon(13) (hld up & bhd: effrt 3f out: nvr rchd ldrs) ........................nk | 3 | | 5/1[3] | 60 | 35 |
| 625[7] | **Great Oration (IRE) (41)** (FWatson) **7-7-10** AMackay(1) (s.i.s: sn in tch: hmpd over 2f out: styd on fnl f: nrst fin) ........3 | 4 | | 12/1 | 47 | 26 |
| 449[2] | **Noyan (53)** (DNicholls) **6-8-8** AlexGreaves(11) (swtg: in tch: hdwy ½-wy: chsng ldrs & rdn over 2f out: no ex) ........nk | 5 | | 4/1[1] | 58 | 37 |
| 625[6] | **Shakiyr (FR) (55)** (RHollinshead) **5-8-10** LDettori(8) (bhd: hdwy 7f out: chsng ldrs over 2f out: one pce after)..5 | 6 | | 8/1 | 56 | 35 |
| 642[5] | **Tiaphena (43)** (JMackie) **5-7-12** FNorton(9) (chsd ldrs: outpcd 4f out: no imp after)........................................3½ | 7 | | 25/1 | 40 | 19 |
| 625[8] | **Bold Elect (44)** (EJAlston) **8-7-13** LCharnock(10) (hld up: hdwy ½-wy: effrt 5f out: no imp)...................................11 | 8 | | 16/1 | 31 | 10 |
| 625[11] | **Judicial Field (IRE) (67)** (NTinkler) **7-9-8b** KimTinkler(2) (lw: a bhd)..................................................7 | 9 | | 33/1 | 48 | 27 |
| | **Imad (USA) (62)** (JWhite) **6-9-3** DaleGibson(5) (rdn & lost tch 6f out)..........................................................9 | 10 | | 10/1 | 34 | 13 |
| *267[2]* | **Nordic Sun (IRE) (65)** (LRLloyd-James) **8-9-6** TWilliams(6) (b.hind: led tl hdd wl over 4f out: sn btn).............13 | 11 | | 20/1 | 25 | 4 |
| | **Punch (49)** (NTinkler) **4-8-0**ow4 GCarter(15) (a bhd) ...........................................................................5 | 12 | | 16/1 | 4 | — |
| | **Livio (USA) (43)** (LLungo) **5-7-12**ow1 JFanning(12) (b: lost tch 7f out) .................................................11 | 13 | | 8/1 | — | — |
| 563[5] | **Evezio Rufo (77)** (NPLittmoden) **4-10-0v** TGMcLaughlin(7) (cl up: rdn 6f out: sn wknd: t.o) .........................dist | 14 | | 33/1 | — | — |
| *260[4]* | **Tremendisto (52)** (CaptJWilson) **6-8-7** JFortune(14) (cl up tl wknd 4f out: virtually p.u)..................................10 | 15 | | 20/1 | — | — |
| | | | | (SP 136.0%) | **15 Rn** | |

**3m 51.3** (11.80) CSF £42.46 CT £181.80 TOTE £4.00: £2.30 £2.50 £2.90 (£11.70) Trio £40.40 OWNER Mr C. E. Brittain (NEWMARKET) BRED J. Ward Hill
LONG HANDICAP Great Oration (IRE) 7-7
WEIGHT FOR AGE 4yo-4lb
**OFFICIAL EXPLANATION All The Joys: was found to be lame the morning after the race.**
**573 Upper Mount Clair** just stays and, once she saw the front over a furlong out, she was not going to stop. (9/2)
**602* Greek Night Out (IRE)** keeps running remarkably well, but was well outpaced in the closing stages here. (8/1)
**Sujud (IRE)** showed here that there are races to be won by keeping on well in the last half-mile, and she will be all the better for this. (5/1)
**625 Great Oration (IRE)** ran well again and was making ground at the finish after finding trouble. He is coming to hand fast. (12/1)
**449 Noyan** had his chances, but failed to respond to pressure sufficiently in the last three furlongs. (4/1)
**625 Shakiyr (FR)** almost got into it three furlongs out but the effort of getting there left nothing in reserve. (8/1)
**642 Tiaphena** does not as yet look quite right but did run reasonably well here. (25/1)

## 768 SPRING MAIDEN STKS (3-Y.O F) (Class D)
5-20 (5-22) **6f** £3,615.00 (£1,095.00: £535.00: £255.00) Stalls: Low GOING: 0.08 sec per fur (G)

| | | | SP | RR | SF |
|---|---|---|---|---|---|
| | **Promptly (IRE)** (MRStoute) **3-8-11** LDettori(1) (lw: trckd ldrs: swtchd & effrt wl over 1f out: r.o wl to ld wl ins fnl f)..........— | 1 | Evens[1] | 81 | 40 |
| | **Bollin Joanne** (TDEasterby) **3-8-11** MBirch(9) (cl up: led 2f out tl wl ins fnl f: r.o) ..........................................1¼ | 2 | 9/2[2] | 78 | 37 |
| | **Budby** (ACStewart) **3-8-11** RHills(12) (plld hrd: bhd tl hdwy 2f out: styd on)..................................................5 | 3 | 7/1[3] | 64 | 23 |
| | **Fyors Gift (IRE)** (BHanbury) **3-8-11** PBloomfield(11) (trckd ldrs: effrt 2f out: hung lft over 1f out: no imp) ........3 | 4 | 33/1 | 56 | 15 |
| | **Mishaweer** (JRFanshawe) **3-8-11** DHarrison(4) (bit bkwd: mid div: styng on whn hmpd over 1f out: nt rcvr)...½ | 5 | 33/1 | 55 | 14 |
| 524[5] | **Nicola's Princess** (BAMcMahon) **3-8-11** GCarter(5) (hld up & bhd: styd on fnl 2f: nrst fin)..............................1 | 6 | 16/1 | 52 | 11 |
| | **Dispol Diamond** (GROldroyd) **3-8-11** KFallon(3) (leggy: unf: sn pushed along & bhd: nvr rchd ldrs) ............2½ | 7 | 50/1 | 46 | 5 |
| | **Pigeon Hole** (RHannon) **3-8-11** JReid(6) (w ldrs: chal 2f out: wkng whn hmpd over 1f out)...........................1¾ | 8 | 9/1 | 41 | — |
| 626[2] | **Divine Miss-P** (APJarvis) **3-8-11** JTate(2) (b.off hind: slt ld 4f: sn wknd) ..................................................2 | 9 | 14/1 | 36 | — |
| | **Mystic Maid (IRE)** (JWWatts) **3-8-11** JCarroll(13) (w'like: scope: bit bkwd: in tch 4f) .......................................½ | 10 | 10/1 | 34 | — |
| | **Rocky Stream** (RMWhitaker) **3-8-11** ACulhane(14) (rangy: s.s: a bhd)..........................................................9 | 11 | 100/1 | 10 | — |
| | **Power Princess (40)** (JAPickering) **3-8-11** MHills(8) (spd 4f: sn wknd) ........................................................1 | 12 | 100/1 | 8 | — |
| 591[9] | **Feet On Fire** (WMBrisbourne) **3-8-11** SSanders(10) (hld up: outpcd & bhd fr ½-wy)...........................................5 | 13 | 100/1 | — | — |
| | **Fruitful Lady** (BPJBaugh) **3-8-11** NCarlisle(7) (unf: a outpcd & bhd).......................................................3 | 14 | 100/1 | — | — |
| | | | (SP 124.1%) | **14 Rn** | |

**1m 18.9** (4.60) CSF £6.28 TOTE £1.70: £1.10 £2.30 £2.00 (£3.90) Trio £10.20 OWNER Mr James Wigan (NEWMARKET) BRED G. Strawbridge & London Thoroughbred Services Ltd
STEWARDS' ENQUIRY Bloomfield susp. 2-3/5/96 (careless riding).
**Promptly (IRE)** needed to really work to score here and, in the end, did it in fine style. There was a lot to like about the way in which she did this and she should stay further. (Evens)
**Bollin Joanne,** from a stable that has been going well, put in a fine performance and will surely not be long in finding races. (9/2)
**Budby,** who showed promise last year, again ran well and, once she learns to settle, much better will be seen. (7/1)
**Fyors Gift (IRE)** travelled quite well but, once off the bit, she hung left approaching the final furlong, causing quite a bit of trouble and was lucky to keep fourth place in the Stewards' Room. (33/1)
**Mishaweer** was just beginning to respond to pressure when she got stopped by the hanging Fyors Gift approaching the final furlong, and that definitely cost her fourth place. She should have learnt plenty here. (33/1)
**524 Nicola's Princess** was again noted finishing well and seems to be learning all the time. (16/1)
**Pigeon Hole** (9/1: 6/1-10/1)

T/Jkpt: £21,868.30 (0.3 Tckts); £21,560.32 to Catterick 24/4/96. T/Plpt: £63.30 (292.28 Tckts). T/Qdpt: £18.50 (60.35 Tckts). AA

# 0478-CATTERICK (L-H) (Good, Good to soft patches)
## Wednesday April 24th
WEATHER: fine WIND: fresh half against

## 769 BELLE ISLE APPRENTICE LIMITED STKS (0-55) (3-Y.O+) (Class F)
2-20 (2-22) **5f 212y** £2,810.00 (£785.00: £380.00) Stalls: High GOING: 0.39 sec per fur (GS)

| | | | SP | RR | SF |
|---|---|---|---|---|---|
| 617[4] | **Panther (IRE) (50)** (JHetherton) **6-9-5** DWright(12) (chsd ldrs: edgd rt & r.o wl to ld ins fnl f: sn clr) ..............— | 1 | 10/1 | 63 | 40 |

| Form | Horse | Dist | Pos | SP | RR | SF |
|---|---|---|---|---|---|---|
| 661[5] | **Best Kept Secret (54)** (PDEvans) **5-9-5v** DGriffiths(1) (a in tch: styd on ins fnl f) | 4 | **2** | 14/1 | 52 | 29 |
| *556[4]* | **The Institute Boy (46)** (MissJFCraze) **6-9-11** PMcCabe(2) (chsd ldrs: led over 1f out tl ins fnl f) | 1½ | **3** | 8/1 | 54 | 31 |
| *653[4]* | **Efficacy (45)** (APJarvis) **5-8-9**(7) CCarver(3) (led: hung rt & hdd over 1f out: kpt on) | 2 | **4** | 13/2 | 40 | 17 |
|  | **Penny Parkes (50)** (JBerry) **3-8-0**(5) JoanneWebster(9) (chsd ldrs: effrt over 2f out: no imp) | nk | **5** | 10/1 | 39 | 5 |
| *425[4]* | **Lochon (54)** (JLEyre) **5-9-8** OPears(8) (b: sn outpcd & pushed along: hdwy to chse ldrs 2f out: sn wknd) | ½ | **6** | 4/1[1] | 44 | 21 |
| *531[5]* | **Oatey (55)** (MrsJRRamsden) **3-8-5** JStack(5) (lw: in tch: rdn & outpcd 2f out) | ½ | **7** | 5/1[2] | 36 | 2 |
| 559[16] | **River Garnock (55)** (DNicholls) **4-9-0**(5) OliverCasey(7) (chsd ldrs tl wknd over 1f out) | 1¼ | **8** | 11/2[3] | 36 | 13 |
| 592[16] | **Thick as Thieves (55)** (RonaldThompson) **4-9-5** RHavlin(13) (prom to ½-wy: sn wknd) | 2 | **9** | 20/1 | 31 | 8 |
|  | **Jimjareer (IRE) (52)** (CaptJWilson) **3-8-8** MHenry(4) (blind off eye: h.d.w: bit bkwd: a bhd) | 1 | **10** | 12/1 | 28 | — |
|  | **Invigilate (51)** (MartynWane) **7-8-12**(7) GWright(6) (bit bkwd: s.i.s: a in rr) | 6 | **11** | 14/1 | 12 | — |
| *652[4]* | **Subfusk (50)** (WGMTurner) **3-8-2**(3) CAdamson(10) (chsd ldr: hung rt & m wd ent st: sn lost pl) | ½ | **12** | 11/2[3] | 8 | — |
| 586[18] | **Napoleon's Return (50)** (AHarrison) **3-8-1**(7) JennyBenson(11) (dwlt: a bhd) | 3 | **13** | 20/1 | 3 | — |
|  |  |  |  | (SP 140.6%) | **13 Rn** |  |

**1m 17.7** (6.80) CSF £145.58 TOTE £10.20: £2.90 £2.00 £2.70 (£36.70) Trio £70.40 OWNER Mr K. C. West (MALTON) BRED My Treasure Ltd
WEIGHT FOR AGE 3yo-11lb

**617 Panther (IRE)** ended a losing sequence of seventeen, but it must be admitted that ending up on the stands' side on the better ground gave him a big advantage. (10/1)
**661 Best Kept Secret** ran his best race for some time. (14/1)
**556 The Institute Boy**, who wore a tongue-strap, has recorded all his four victories on the All-Weather track at Lingfield. (8/1)
**653 Efficacy**, whose three wins so far have been recorded at Wolverhampton, is a keen sort and gave her rider problems. (13/2)
**Lochon**, who looked very wintry, reserves his best these days for turning tracks. (4/1: 3/1-9/2)
**531 Oatey**, who is not very big, might show improvement if stepped up in distance. (5/1)

## 770 JOCKEY CAP (S) STKS (2-Y.O) (Class G)

2-50 (2-52) **5f** £2,343.00 (£648.00: £309.00) Stalls: Low GOING: 0.39 sec per fur (GS)

| Form | Horse | Dist | Pos | SP | RR | SF |
|---|---|---|---|---|---|---|
| 733* | **Mill End Girl** (MWEasterby) **2-8-13** 7x JFEgan(5) (lw: chsd ldrs: led ½-wy: styd on wl u.p) | — | **1** | 7/2[1] | 57 | 14 |
| 639[10] | **C-Harry (IRE)** (RHollinshead) **2-8-11** KDarley(4) (lw: a chsng ldrs: kpt on fnl f: no ch w wnr) | 1¼ | **2** | 7/1 | 51 | 8 |
| 538[3] | **Face It** (WGMTurner) **2-8-6** AClark(3) (led to ½-wy: styd on same pce appr fnl f) | nk | **3** | 4/1[2] | 45 | 2 |
| 446[6] | **Skyers Flyer (IRE)** (RonaldThompson) **2-8-6** NConnorton(1) (sn chsng ldrs: kpt on one pce fnl 2f) | 1¼ | **4** | 20/1 | 41 | — |
|  | **Abstone Again (IRE)** (PDEvans) **2-8-11v[1]** SSanders(9) (unf: chsd ldrs: rdn ½-wy: grad wknd) | 2½ | **5** | 14/1 | 38 | — |
|  | **Classic Services** (BPalling) **2-8-11** TSprake(10) (b: unf: in tch: hmpd & swtchd lft ½-wy: wknd over 1f out) | 2 | **6** | 7/1 | 32 | — |
| 630[5] | **Run For Us (IRE)** (CADwyer) **2-7-13**(7) RMullen(2) (lw: unruly s: dwlt: sn chsng ldrs: wknd over 1f out) | ½ | **7** | 8/1 | 25 | — |
|  | **Kuda** (JNorton) **2-8-6** DaleGibson(8) (lt-f: unf: bit bkwd: s.i.s: nvr wnt pce) | 3 | **8** | 14/1 | 15 | — |
|  | **Lunar Music** (MartynMeade) **2-8-3**(5)ow2 RHavlin(6) (leggy: scope: s.s: a in rr) | 1¼ | **9** | 6/1[3] | 13 | — |
| 590[5] | **I Can't Remember** (JBerry) **2-8-11** JCarroll(7) (unruly s: s.i.s: bhd fr ½-wy) | 11 | **10** | 7/2[1] | — | — |
|  |  |  |  | (SP 132.9%) | **10 Rn** |  |

**65.3 secs** (7.80) CSF £30.18 TOTE £5.40: £1.50 £2.90 £2.00 (£12.40) Trio £11.70 OWNER Mr W. T. Allgood (SHERIFF HUTTON) BRED M. W. Easterby
Bt in 5,200 gns

**733* Mill End Girl** ended up in the plum stands'-side position and was right on top at the line. (7/2: op 9/4)
**568 C-Harry (IRE)**, dropped in class, was never going to reel in the winner. (7/1)
**538 Face It** again showed plenty of toe. (4/1: 5/2-9/2)
**Skyers Flyer (IRE)** has a pronounced knee-action and seemed to appreciate the give underfoot. (20/1)
**Classic Services**, a May foal, was coltish in the paddock and showed a poor action going down, but ran better than could be expected after meeting trouble. (7/1)
**630 Run For Us (IRE)**, a madam leaving the paddock, looked far from happy in the stalls. (8/1)
**590 I Can't Remember** ran badly and showed nothing after missing the break slightly, and his rider gave up soon after halfway. (7/2)

## 771 'WIN WITH THE TOTE' H'CAP (0-85) (4-Y.O+) (Class D)

3-20 (3-21) **1m 3f 214y** £3,752.50 (£1,120.00: £535.00: £242.50) Stalls: Low GOING: 0.39 sec per fur (GS)

| Form | Horse | Dist | Pos | SP | RR | SF |
|---|---|---|---|---|---|---|
| 612[4] | **Hasta la Vista (51)** (MWEasterby) **6-7-3b**(7) RMullen(4) (lw: mde all: styd far side & racd alone ent st: hrd rdn: all out) | — | **1** | 5/1[1] | 60 | 17 |
| 619[6] | **House of Dreams (58)** (GMMoore) **4-8-2** JFEgan(1) (lw: plld hrd: trckd ldrs: outpcd over 3f out: hdwy & n.m.r jst ins fnl f: swtchd & styd on wl) | ½ | **2** | 16/1 | 66 | 22 |
| *411[7]* | **No Pattern (73)** (GLMoore) **4-9-3** SWhitworth(9) (lw: hld up: effrt over 3f out: hdwy 2f out: styd on same pce fnl f) | ¾ | **3** | 8/1[3] | 80 | 36 |
| 642[9] | **Admirals Secret (USA) (63)** (CFWall) **7-8-8** JReid(6) (hld up: effrt & outpcd over 3f out: styd on appr fnl f) | s.h | **4** | 5/1[1] | 70 | 27 |
| 496[6] | **Loveyoumillions (IRE) (83)** (MJohnston) **4-9-13** JWeaver(2) (trckd ldr: rdn 3f out: kpt on same pce appr fnl f) | s.h | **5** | 12/1 | 90 | 46 |
|  | **George Dillingham (83)** (DenysSmith) **6-10-0** JCarroll(3) (lw: plld hrd: trckd ldrs: effrt over 3f out: wknd ins fnl f) | 1¼ | **6** | 5/1[1] | 89 | 46 |
| 482* | **Cross Talk (IRE) (69)** (RHollinshead) **4-8-8**(5) DGriffiths(10) (lw: hld up: effrt over 3f out: nvr rchd ldrs) | 2 | **7** | 11/2[2] | 72 | 28 |
|  | **Majal (IRE) (55)** (JSWainwright) **7-8-0** LCharnock(8) (stdd s: hld up & bhd: effrt over 3f out: sn wknd) | 9 | **8** | 25/1 | 46 | 3 |
| *532[2]* | **Hill Farm Dancer (52)** (WMBrisbourne) **5-7-4**(7) IonaWands(11) (hld up: effrt over 3f out: sn wknd) | 1 | **9** | 5/1[1] | 42 | — |
|  | **Maftun (USA) (65)** (GMMoore) **4-8-9** DaleGibson(5) (bit bkwd: plld hrd: cl up: rdn over 5f out: wknd over 3f out) | 6 | **10** | 10/1 | 47 | 3 |
| 537[8] | **Fasih (78)** (SEKettlewell) **4-9-8** KDarley(7) (b: in tch tl p.u 5f out: broke down) |  | **P** | 14/1 | — | — |
|  |  |  |  | (SP 126.3%) | **11 Rn** |  |

**2m 45.8** (14.40) CSF £76.26 CT £593.95 TOTE £6.70: £1.90 £5.60 £2.00 (£92.00) Trio Not won; £292.59 to Beverley 25/4/96 OWNER Mr K. Hodgson (SHERIFF HUTTON) BRED Clanville Lodge Stud
LONG HANDICAP Hasta la Vista 7-9
WEIGHT FOR AGE 4yo-1lb

**612 Hasta la Vista**, allowed to set his own pace, was the only one to stick to the far rail in the straight and he did just enough, racing out on his own. (5/1)
**619 House of Dreams**, very keen, is not noted as a strong finisher. After meeting trouble and being switched to the stands'-side rail, he finished best of all. (16/1)

**No Pattern**, with his tongue tied down, had run well behind Zabadi at Aintree. Staying on in pleasing fashion at the end, he is better suited by less give underfoot. (8/1)
**642 Admirals Secret (USA)**, who likes turning tracks, stuck on well at the finish after struggling to keep up turning in. (5/1)
**496 Loveyoumillions (IRE)**, taking a big step up in distance, went for home on the stands' side turning in and seemed to stay the trip all right. (12/1)
**George Dillingham**, gelded after injuring himself when third in the Northumberland Plate, goes well fresh and was beaten a short-head in this race a year ago. He took a keen grip and ran well until fading inside the last furlong, but the outing should bring him on. (5/1)
**532 Hill Farm Dancer**, who has been running well on the All-Weather, was racing from a 10lb lower mark then her sand form, but was dropping back on the turn in. (5/1)
**Maftun (USA)** (10/1: op 6/1)

## 772 RICHMOND CONDITIONS STKS (3-Y.O) (Class C)

3-50 (3-50) **1m 3f 214y** £5,177.60 (£1,785.60: £852.80: £344.00) Stalls: Low GOING: 0.39 sec per fur (GS)

| Form | Horse | Dist | Pos | SP | RR | SF |
|---|---|---|---|---|---|---|
| 570$^{2}$ | **Prince of My Heart (93)** (BWHills) **3-9-1** MHills(1) (lw: trckd ldr: led over 5f out: clr 2f out: v.easily) | — | **1** | 7/4$^{2}$ | 93++ | 19 |
| 560* | **Swan Hunter** (DJSCosgrove) **3-8-12** DeanMcKeown(4) (lw: hld up: dropped bk over 4f out: hdwy to chse wnr 2f out: no imp) | 6 | **2** | 10/1 | 82 | 8 |
| 544$^{3}$ | **Reinhardt (IRE) (90)** (PWChapple-Hyam) **3-8-12** JReid(3) (trckd ldrs: effrt over 4f out: one pce) | 2 | **3** | 5/2$^{3}$ | 79 | 5 |
| 567$^{2}$ | **House of Riches (86)** (LMCumani) **3-9-3** LDettori(2) (lw: led tl over 5f out: sn hrd drvn & no rspnse: virtually p.u 3f out) | dist | **4** | 6/4$^{1}$ | — | — |

(SP 114.0%) **4 Rn**

**2m 48.3** (16.90) CSF £13.16 TOTE £2.40: (£5.40) OWNER Mr G. J. Hicks (LAMBOURN) BRED George Joseph Hicks
OFFICIAL EXPLANATION **House of Riches: the jockey reported that he felt the colt, who also had an abnormally high pulse rate, was sickening for something.**
**570 Prince of My Heart** did nothing wrong this time and hardly knew he had had a race. (7/4: 5/4-15/8)
**560* Swan Hunter**, a poor walker, somehow managed to get trapped behind House of Riches turning out of the back straight. Forfeiting many lengths, to his credit he stuck on grimly in pursuit of the winner in the final quarter-mile. (10/1)
**544 Reinhardt (IRE)** did not take the eye in the paddock and proved woefully one-paced. (5/2)
**567 House of Riches** showed a pronounced knee-action going to post and jumped off in front, but did not look happy at all. Reluctant to turn away from the Stands, he found nothing when overtaken and his rider virtually pulled him up on the home turn. Something was obviously amiss here, and his attitude leaves plenty to be desired. (6/4)

## 773 SEDBURY H'CAP (0-80) (3-Y.O) (Class D)

4-20 (4-21) **5f** £3,850.00 (£1,150.00: £550.00: £250.00) Stalls: Low GOING: 0.39 sec per fur (GS)

| Form | Horse | Dist | Pos | SP | RR | SF |
|---|---|---|---|---|---|---|
| 638$^{11}$ | **Goretski (IRE) (58)** (NTinkler) **3-7-13** LCharnock(10) (lw: w ldr: led ½-wy: qcknd clr ins fnl f: eased towards fin) | — | **1** | 5/1$^{2}$ | 63+ | 21 |
| 453$^{2}$ | **First Maite (73)** (SRBowring) **3-9-0b** NCarlisle(2) (lw: hdwy ½-wy: hung rt & hmpd ½-wy: swtchd & styd on wl u.p: no ch w wnr) | 1 | **2** | 11/2$^{3}$ | 75 | 33 |
| | **Pleasure Time (68)** (CSmith) **3-8-2**(7) AngelaGallimore(11) (bit bkwd: swvd rt s: sn chsng ldrs: one pce fnl 2f) | 4 | **3** | 25/1 | 57 | 15 |
| | **Limerick Princess (IRE) (60)** (JBerry) **3-8-1** GCarter(5) (a in tch: kpt on appr fnl f) | nk | **4** | 11/1 | 48 | 6 |
| 571$^{7}$ | **Green Barries (80)** (MJohnston) **3-9-7** JWeaver(12) (lw: led to ½-wy: wknd over 1f out) | 2 | **5** | 9/4$^{1}$ | 62 | 20 |
| | **Hoh Majestic (IRE) (70)** (MartynWane) **3-8-11v** KDarley(8) (a in tch: no hdwy fnl 2f) | 1 | **6** | 16/1 | 48 | 6 |
| 587$^{17}$ | **Imp Express (IRE) (68)** (GMMoore) **3-8-9** DaleGibson(7) (s.s: nvr nr ldrs) | 6 | **7** | 25/1 | 27 | — |
| 443$^{16}$ | **Johayro (75)** (WGMTurner) **3-8-11b**(5) CAdamson(13) (w ldrs: stumbled ½-wy: hung rt & wknd over 1f out: eased) | s.h | **8** | 16/1 | 34 | — |
| 571$^{11}$ | **Little Noggins (IRE) (76)** (CADwyer) **3-9-0**(3) JStack(3) (lw: in tch to ½-wy: sn lost pl) | nk | **9** | 11/2$^{3}$ | 34 | — |
| 559$^{9}$ | **Amy Leigh (IRE) (64)** (CaptJWilson) **3-8-5** AClark(6) (a outpcd & bhd) | s.h | **10** | 10/1 | 22 | — |
| | **Kustom Kit (IRE) (70)** (BAMcMahon) **3-8-11** DeanMcKeown(9) (bit bkwd: sn bhd) | ½ | **11** | 20/1 | 26 | — |
| *394*$^{6}$ | **Gagajulu (72)** (PDEvans) **3-8-13** SSanders(4) (in tch to ½-wy: sn lost pl) | nk | **12** | 14/1 | 27 | — |
| | **Crissem (IRE) (75)** (RHollinshead) **3-9-2** LDettori(1) (a wl outpcd) | 6 | **13** | 10/1 | 11 | — |

(SP 135.6%) **13 Rn**

**63.1 secs** (5.60) CSF £34.96 CT £622.87 TOTE £7.40: £2.20 £2.90 £13.90 (£23.90) Trio £306.20 OWNER Mr P. D. Savill (MALTON) BRED Pierre Brichart
**539 Goretski (IRE)**, who looked particularly well, found the drop back to five no problem. Travelling strongly, he went on at halfway and would have won by three or four lengths but for being eased near the finish. He has bags of early toe and a tight track like Chester might suit him ideally. (5/1)
**453 First Maite** met trouble in running. Sticking on strongly towards the finish, the margin flatters him but there is no doubt that he is better over six. (11/2)
**Pleasure Time**, who looked in need of the outing, ran without his usual blinkers. (25/1)
**Limerick Princess (IRE)** ran a satisfactory first race. (11/1)
**571 Green Barries** is not short of toe but, taken on at halfway, did not look entirely happy. To be fair, the stable is struggling to find form at present. (9/4)

## 774 HURGILL LODGE MAIDEN STKS (3-Y.O) (Class D)

4-50 (4-50) **7f** £3,752.50 (£1,120.00: £535.00: £242.50) Stalls: Low GOING: 0.39 sec per fur (GS)

| Form | Horse | Dist | Pos | SP | RR | SF |
|---|---|---|---|---|---|---|
| 684$^{8}$ | **Master Boots** (DRLoder) **3-9-0** LDettori(1) (lw: trckd ldrs: led on bit over 1f out: readily) | — | **1** | 7/4$^{2}$ | 84+ | 46 |
| 584$^{3}$ | **Elite Force (IRE) (80)** (PWChapple-Hyam) **3-9-0** JReid(4) (lw: trckd ldr: lft in ld ent st: hdd over 1f out: no ch w wnr) | 2½ | **2** | 3/1$^{3}$ | 78 | 40 |
| 577$^{4}$ | **Menoo Hal Batal (USA)** (MRStoute) **3-9-0** KDarley(2) (lw: sn trckng ldrs: effrt over 2f out: one pce u.p) | ½ | **3** | 11/8$^{1}$ | 77 | 39 |
| 705$^{8}$ | **Bollin Jacob** (TDEasterby) **3-9-0** MBirch(5) (bit bkwd: s.i.s: sn in tch: wl outpcd fnl 2f) | 8 | **4** | 33/1 | 59 | 21 |
| | **Surf City** (WWHaigh) **3-9-0** JTate(6) (w'like: bkwd: dwlt: wl outpcd ½-wy: styd on towards fin) | 3½ | **5** | 50/1 | 51 | 13 |
| 640$^{6}$ | **Look Who's Calling (IRE)** (BAMcMahon) **3-9-0** GCarter(3) (lw: led: hung bdly rt & rn v.wd ent st: no ch after) | 3½ | **6** | 12/1 | 43 | 5 |
| 448$^{13}$ | **Miletrian City (58)** (JBerry) **3-9-0** JCarroll(7) (outpcd fr ½-wy) | hd | **7** | 50/1 | 43 | 5 |
| 458$^{12}$ | **Falcon's Flame (USA)** (MrsJRRamsden) **3-9-0** KFallon(8) (trckd ldrs tl lost pl 3f out) | 2 | **8** | 25/1 | 38 | — |

(SP 121.9%) **8 Rn**

**1m 30.7** (7.10) CSF £7.84 TOTE £2.40: £1.10 £1.50 £1.10 (£4.70) OWNER Mr Chris Brasher (NEWMARKET) BRED Hesmonds Stud Ltd

**684 Master Boots**, a scratchy mover, was well suited by the easier ground. He did the job in good style and looks a promising type. (7/4)
**584 Elite Force (IRE)** did nothing wrong but the winner proved a different class. His turn will surely come. (3/1)
**577 Menoo Hal Batal (USA)**, a keen type, shows a fair bit of knee-action. Keeping on under pressure, he was never going to finish anything better than second. (11/8)
**705 Bollin Jacob** needs more time and was by no means knocked about. (33/1)
**Surf City**, a backward-looking type, was staying on when it was all over, and is not without ability. (50/1)
**640 Look Who's Calling (IRE)**, a likeable type, completely failed to handle the home turn. (12/1: op 7/1)

## 775 SPRING H'CAP (0-70) (3-Y.O) (Class E)

5-20 (5-23) **7f** £3,444.00 (£1,032.00: £496.00: £228.00) Stalls: Low GOING: 0.39 sec per fur (GS)

| | | | | SP | RR | SF |
|---|---|---|---|---|---|---|
| 616* | **Forest Boy (62)** (KMcAuliffe) **3-9-2v** JFEgan(7) (lw: chsd ldrs: styd on u.p to ld jst ins fnl f) | — | **1** | 6/1$^{2}$ | 74 | 46 |
| | **Silver Welcome (56)** (TDEasterby) **3-8-10** MBirch(18) (mde most tl jst ins fnl f: kpt on) | 2 | **2** | 20/1 | 63 | 35 |
| $470^{7}$ | **Sharp 'n' Shady (54)** (CFWall) **3-8-8** WLord(17) (in tch: hdwy to chse ldrs 2f out: edgd lft & styd on towards fin) | 1 | **3** | 6/1$^{2}$ | 59 | 31 |
| 468* | **Green Gem (BEL) (65)** (SCWilliams) **3-9-5** KDarley(1) (a chsng ldrs: rdn over 2f out: styd on one pce) | 3 | **4** | 15/2$^{3}$ | 63 | 35 |
| $676^{3}$ | **White Plains (IRE) (65)** (MBell) **3-9-5** MFenton(12) (lw: a in tch: rdn ½-wy: styd on fnl f) | 1¼ | **5** | 3/1$^{1}$ | 60 | 32 |
| | **Sandblaster (48)** (MrsJRRamsden) **3-8-2** GCarter(19) (chsd ldrs tl outpcd fnl 2f) | ½ | **6** | 9/1 | 42 | 14 |
| *$464^{6}$* | **Morning Surprise (58)** (APJarvis) **3-8-12** JTate(20) (hdwy ½-wy: sn chsng ldrs: wknd over 1f out) | 1 | **7** | 14/1 | 50 | 22 |
| *$605^{10}$* | **Tropical Beach (57)** (JBerry) **3-8-11** JCarroll(9) (chsd ldrs: n.m.r over 2f out: sn wknd) | 8 | **8** | 25/1 | 31 | 3 |
| $562^{3}$ | **Nkapen Rocks (SPA) (67)** (CaptJWilson) **3-9-7** AClark(16) (s.i.s: bhd tl sme hdwy fnl 2f) | s.h | **9** | 14/1 | 41 | 13 |
| | **Ned's Contessa (IRE) (48)** (MDods) **3-8-2** LCharnock(10) (mid div whn sltly hmpd appr st: sme hdwy over 1f out: n.d) | s.h | **10** | 16/1 | 22 | — |
| | **Veshca Lady (IRE) (55)** (EWeymes) **3-8-9** RLappin(13) (bit bkwd: nvr bttr than mid div) | 1 | **11** | 25/1 | 26 | — |
| | **Alzotic (IRE) (60)** (JNorton) **3-9-0** KFallon(3) (bit bkwd: bhd: sme hdwy 2f out: n.d) | 8 | **12** | 10/1 | 13 | — |
| *$28^{3}$* | **Time Clash (64)** (BPalling) **3-9-4** TSprake(2) (chsd ldrs to ½-wy: sn wknd) | 2 | **13** | 20/1 | 12 | — |
| $638^{5}$ | **Hobbs Choice (52)** (GMMoore) **3-8-6** DaleGibson(8) (lw: chsd ldrs to ½-wy: sn lost pl) | 2 | **14** | 10/1 | — | — |
| | **Impromptu Melody (IRE) (50)** (BSRothwell) **3-8-1**(3) JStack(11) (s.i.s: bhd tl sme hdwy 2f out: eased ins fnl f) | 2 | **15** | 33/1 | — | — |
| $638^{16}$ | **Percy Park (USA) (46)** (MWEasterby) **3-7-11**(3) DWright(5) (dwlt: a bhd) | ¾ | **16** | 20/1 | — | — |
| | **Escobar (IRE) (51)** (PCalver) **3-8-5** ACulhane(14) (bit bkwd: a bhd) | hd | **17** | 16/1 | — | — |
| | **Ginger Hodgers (50)** (RMWhitaker) **3-8-4** DeanMcKeown(6) (bit bkwd: a wl bhd) | hd | **18** | 33/1 | — | — |
| | **Euro Express (50)** (TDEasterby) **3-8-1b**(3) PMcCabe(15) (bit bkwd: a wl bhd) | 5 | **19** | 14/1 | — | — |
| | **Diminuet (65)** (JWWatts) **3-9-5** NConnorton(4) (bit bkwd: mid div whn eased appr st: sn p.u: b.b.v) | | **P** | 14/1 | — | — |
| | | | | (SP 159.8%) | **20 Rn** | |

**1m 30.8** (7.20) CSF £136.53 CT £757.08 TOTE £8.70: £2.30 £9.00 £2.40 £1.10 (£135.50) Trio £1,354.80 OWNER Highgrove Developments Ltd (LAMBOURN) BRED J. B. H. Stevens
**616* Forest Boy** looked exceptionally well and found the drop back to seven no problem. There is probably further improvement to come. (6/1)
**Silver Welcome**, an edgy type, was taken to post early. Overcoming his high draw, he was soon showing his rivals a clean pair of heels. Hopefully he will hold his form this time. (20/1)
**470 Sharp 'n' Shady**, nibbled at in the market, was staying on at the line and will be suited by a mile. (6/1: 5/1-8/1)
**468* Green Gem (BEL)** might be suited by another furlong or so. (15/2)
**676 White Plains (IRE)** took an age to get going. Sticking on towards the finish, his best form has been shown on faster ground. (3/1)
**Sandblaster**, on her toes beforehand, struggled to keep up in the final quarter-mile and might show improvement when stepped up in distance. (9/1)
**Morning Surprise** (14/1: op 8/1)
**Alzotic (IRE)** (10/1: op 5/1)

T/Jkpt: £22,828.50 (0.5 Tckts); £16,076.44 to Beverley 25/4/96. T/Plpt: £268.50 (60.32 Tckts). T/Qdpt: £50.40 (18.02 Tckts). WG

# 0602-SOUTHWELL (L-H) (Standard)

## Wednesday April 24th

WEATHER: cloudy WIND: mod half bhd

## 776 APHRODITE CLAIMING STKS (I) (3-Y.O+) (Class F)

2-00 (2-00) **1m (Fibresand)** £2,031.00 (£556.00: £261.00) Stalls: Low GOING: 0.14 sec per fur (SLW)

| | | | | SP | RR | SF |
|---|---|---|---|---|---|---|
| $649^{5}$ | **Spencer's Revenge (73)** (NTinkler) **7-9-10b$^{1}$** GBardwell(3) (sn bhd & drvn along: hdwy to ld 2f out: r.o wl) | — | **1** | 7/2$^{2}$ | 74 | 49 |
| $595^{10}$ | **Bit of Bother (IRE) (69)** (TDBarron) **3-8-10** JFortune(4) (lw: hld up in tch: effrt wl over 1f out: nt pce to chal) | 1½ | **2** | 5/2$^{1}$ | 71 | 32 |
| *$501^{10}$* | **Lilac Rain (44)** (JRArnold) **4-8-10** JQuinn(7) (bhd: effrt & rdn over 2f out: ev ch appr fnl f: one pce) | 3½ | **3** | 12/1 | 50 | 25 |
| $688^{14}$ | **Battle Colours (IRE) (50)** (DonEnricoIncisa) **7-9-1** KimTinkler(2) (lw: lost pl 4f out: swtchd outside over 2f out: styd on fnl f) | 3 | **4** | 33/1 | 49 | 24 |
| | **Princess Pamgaddy (40)** (CNAllen) **3-7-5**(7)ow2 MartinDwyer(9) (bit bkwd: hld up: hdwy ent st: kpt on u.p appr fnl f) | s.h | **5** | 12/1 | 46 | 5 |
| $586^{2}$ | **No Submission (USA) (62)** (DWChapman) **10-9-4v** ACulhane(8) (lw: led to 2f out: sn rdn & wknd) | ½ | **6** | 11/2$^{3}$ | 51 | 26 |
| | **Athinar** (CPWildman) **4-8-10** CRutter(5) (bkwd: a in rr) | ½ | **7** | 16/1 | 42 | 17 |
| *$521^{5}$* | **Shuttlecock (51)** (MrsNMacauley) **5-8-13**(5) CTeague(1) (trckd ldrs over 4f: sn lost pl) | 4 | **8** | 7/1 | 42 | 17 |
| *$518^{2}$* | **Peacefull Reply (USA) (46)** (FHLee) **6-9-4** AMcGlone(6) (lw: prom: wkng whn n.m.r 2f out: eased whn btn) | 6 | **9** | 10/1 | 30 | 5 |
| | | | | (SP 112.0%) | **9 Rn** | |

**1m 47.0** (7.00) CSF £11.71 TOTE £3.40: £1.90 £1.50 £2.40 (£4.80) Trio £28.80 OWNER Elite Racing Club (MALTON) BRED Lord Crawshaw
WEIGHT FOR AGE 3yo-14lb
Bit of Bother (IRE) clmd SWilton £8,000
**649 Spencer's Revenge**, winning for the third time over course and distance, was never on the bridle but answered his rider's every call and, in the end, won with a bit to spare. (7/2: op 2/1)
**595 Bit of Bother (IRE)** took time to find top gear and, when he did, the winner was beyond recall. He was claimed for £8,000 and will now be trained in the Midlands. (5/2)

**Lilac Rain** did look a serious threat entering the final furlong, but she could not sustain her run and was soon galloping on the spot. (12/1: op 8/1)
**Battle Colours (IRE)** lost his pitch turning out of the back straight and, though he did rally after being pulled wide in the straight, was never going to get back into it. (33/1)
**Princess Pamgaddy**, who will improve with this outing under her belt, was never going well enough to cause concern, but she did stay on and another small race is well within her grasp. (12/1: op 8/1)
**586 No Submission (USA)** reverted to his original trail-blazing tactics here, but he had kept nothing in reserve and was soon beaten once collared. (11/2)
**518 Peacefull Reply (USA)** (10/1: 8/1-12/1)

## 777 GREEK GOD APPRENTICE H'CAP (0-70) (3-Y.O+) (Class G)

2-30 (2-30) **1m 4f (Fibresand)** £2,364.00 (£654.00: £312.00) Stalls: Low GOING: 0.14 sec per fur (SLW)

| | | | | SP | RR | SF |
|---|---|---|---|---|---|---|
| *604** | **Carol Again (40)** (NBycroft) **4-8-1**(3) FLynch(8) (chsd ldrs: led on bit over 2f out: sn clr: v.easily) | — | 1 | 7/2[2] | 54+ | 20 |
| *602*[3] | **Tempering (59)** (DWChapman) **10-9-10** PFessey(7) (led after 3f: sn clr: wknd & hdd over 2f out: sn btn) | 8 | 2 | 7/1 | 62 | 29 |
| | **Shepherds Rest (IRE) (35)** (SMellor) **4-7-10**(3)ow3 ADaly(2) (hld up: hdwy 5f out: sn rdn: styd on one pce fnl 2f) | 2½ | 3 | 10/1 | 35 | — |
| 609[16] | **Adaloaldo (USA) (55)** (JParkes) **4-9-5** MBaird(5) (dwlt: hdwy 7f out: rdn & wknd over 2f out) | 8 | 4 | 8/1 | 44 | 10 |
| *367*[5] | **Mr Moriarty (IRE) (44)** (SRBowring) **5-8-9** CTeague(1) (trckd ldrs: rdn & lost pl over 4f out: sn bhd) | 4 | 5 | 5/1[3] | 28 | — |
| | **Instantaneous (54)** (TDEasterby) **4-9-4** DaneO'Neill(4) (lw: trckd ldrs: rdn ½-wy: eased whn btn 2f out) | 9 | 6 | 15/8[1] | 26 | — |
| | **Red Indian (43)** (BRichmond) **10-8-3**(5) JDennis(9) (bkwd: led 3f: chsd ldr tl wknd 5f out: t.o) | dist | 7 | 14/1 | — | — |
| | **Billyback (35)** (PRWebber) **6-7-7**(7) JBosley(3) (bkwd: dwlt: a bhd: t.o fr ½-wy) | dist | 8 | 20/1 | — | — |

(SP 117.8%) **8 Rn**

**2m 44.9** (12.40) CSF £26.38 CT £206.03 TOTE £3.70: £1.10 £1.50 £3.60 (£6.20) Trio £37.70 OWNER Mr J. G. Lumsden (BRANDSBY)
LONG HANDICAP Shepherds Rest (IRE) 7-9
WEIGHT FOR AGE 4yo-1lb

**604* Carol Again** has found her form with a vengeance this term and did not need to be asked a serious question to win as she pleased. (7/2)
**602 Tempering** ran another genuine race but had to admit the concession of so much weight way beyond him. (7/1)
**Shepherds Rest (IRE)**, still to win a race, came here fit from hurdling but, despite staying on in the latter stages, was never going to reach the leading pair. (10/1)
**Adaloaldo (USA)** (8/1: 6/1-9/1)
**Instantaneous** looked trained to the minute and was the only one the ring wanted to know, but she was never happy with the strong early pace and was in trouble at halfway. (15/8: op 3/1)
**Red Indian** (14/1: 8/1-16/1)

## 778 APHRODITE CLAIMING STKS (II) (3-Y.O+) (Class F)

3-00 (3-00) **1m (Fibresand)** £2,031.00 (£556.00: £261.00) Stalls: Low GOING: 0.14 sec per fur (SLW)

| | | | | SP | RR | SF |
|---|---|---|---|---|---|---|
| 713[8] | **Awesome Venture (66)** (MCChapman) **6-9-5**(3) DRMcCabe(9) (lw: hld up: hdwy 3f out: r.o strly to ld cl home) | — | 1 | 4/1[2] | 75 | 41 |
| 480[5] | **Johnnie the Joker (70)** (JPLeigh) **5-9-5b**(5) PRoberts(1) (lw: led: clr wl over 1f out: wknd & ct nr fin) | nk | 2 | 8/1 | 76 | 42 |
| 629[4] | **Ashgore (76)** (MJohnston) **6-10-0** TWilliams(4) (lw: a.p: drvn along ½-wy: hrd rdn 2f out: one pce) | 2½ | 3 | 2/1[1] | 75 | 41 |
| | **Sandmoor Denim (64)** (SRBowring) **9-8-13**(7) JEdmunds(6) (trckd ldrs: rdn over 1f out: one pce) | 1½ | 4 | 7/1 | 64 | 30 |
| *654*[3] | **Chadleigh Lane (USA) (64)** (RHollinshead) **4-9-9**(5) FLynch(3) (lw: trckd ldrs: rdn over 2f out: no hdwy) | 4 | 5 | 6/1[3] | 64 | 30 |
| *426*[10] | **Mezzoramio (45)** (KAMorgan) **4-8-9v**(7) CScudder(8) (b: lw: prom tl rdn & wknd wl over 1f out) | 1½ | 6 | 14/1 | 49 | 15 |
| *553*[10] | **Sarum (51)** (CPWildman) **10-9-1** CRutter(7) (b.nr fore: a in rr) | s.h | 7 | 16/1 | 48 | 14 |
| 645[12] | **Buddy's Friend (IRE) (60)** (RJRWilliams) **8-9-4** DBiggs(2) (hld up in rr: bdly hmpd over 3f out: sn lost tch: t.o) | 22 | 8 | 10/1 | 7 | — |
| | **Triple (FR)** (PEccles) **4-8-11** NAdams(5) (bkwd: s.s: a bhd: t.o) | 10 | 9 | 33/1 | — | — |

(SP 115.8%) **9 Rn**

**1m 47.6** (7.60) CSF £32.71 TOTE £3.60: £1.10 £2.10 £1.20 (£20.10) Trio £15.10 OWNER Market Rasen Racing Club (MARKET RASEN) BRED The Lavington Stud

**713 Awesome Venture**, given a patient ride, made relentless progress once in the straight and responded to hard pressure to force his head in front close home. (4/1: 3/1-9/2)
**480 Johnnie the Joker** enjoyed himself bowling along in the lead and looked to have gone beyond recall below the distance. He is hardly bred to get this trip though and his stamina gave out in the final 100 yards. (8/1)
**629 Ashgore** was soon making hard work of it at this first attempt at the trip. Though he did keep battling away, he was only ever competing for places. (2/1)
**Sandmoor Denim**, reappearing after a five-month break, ran a promising race and it should not be long before he strikes form. (7/1: op 7/2)
**654 Chadleigh Lane (USA)**, involved in a barging match on the home turn, was never going well enough to pose a threat. (6/1)
**Mezzoramio** raced prominently but could not get to the front and he gave up the chase below the distance. (14/1: 10/1-16/1)
**Buddy's Friend (IRE)** (10/1: 8/1-12/1)

## 779 HERA MEDIAN AUCTION MAIDEN STKS (3-Y.O) (Class F)

3-30 (3-30) **6f (Fibresand)** £2,381.00 (£656.00: £311.00) Stalls: Low GOING: 0.14 sec per fur (SLW)

| | | | | SP | RR | SF |
|---|---|---|---|---|---|---|
| 524[8] | **Napier Star (30)** (MrsNMacauley) **3-8-4**(5) CTeague(5) (lw: mde all: rdn & hld on gamely fnl f) | — | 1 | 33/1 | 63 | 29 |
| 591[5] | **Frontman (IRE) (67)** (TDBarron) **3-9-0** JFortune(2) (chsd wnr: ev ch appr fnl f: unable qckn) | ¾ | 2 | 11/4[3] | 66 | 32 |
| 448[3] | **Depiction** (RGuest) **3-9-0** WWoods(1) (lw: hld up in tch: effrt 2f out: sn rdn: nt pce to chal) | 2 | 3 | 6/4[1] | 61 | 27 |
| 714[6] | **Chalice (72)** (JBalding) **3-8-2**(7) JEdmunds(6) (trckd ldrs: hdwy 2f out: wknd fnl f) | 3 | 4 | 7/1 | 48 | 14 |
| | **Tashtaiya** (NPLittmoden) **3-8-9** TGMcLaughlin(3) (small: lt-f: a bhd) | 6 | 5 | 33/1 | 32 | — |
| | **No Hiding Place** (BHanbury) **3-9-0** WRyan(7) (bkwd: s.s: sn rdn along: rn v.green ent st: eased fnl 2f: t.o) | 11 | 6 | 5/2[2] | 7 | — |

(SP 113.6%) **6 Rn**

**1m 19.1** (5.60) CSF £113.39 TOTE £57.10: £7.90 £1.80 (£26.70) OWNER Mr P. M. Heaton (MELTON MOWBRAY) BRED P. M. Heaton
**OFFICIAL EXPLANATION No Hiding Place: was awkward in the stalls, jumped sideways when they opened and had hung throughout the race.**

**Napier Star**, turned out in fine fettle, adopted new tactics on this occasion and they paid off handsomely. (33/1)
**591 Frontman (IRE)** does carry a lot of condition. In pursuit of the winner, it looked to be his day when he joined forces approaching the final furlong, but the winner kept pulling out more and worried him out of it. (11/4: op 7/4)

**448 Depiction** sat in behind the leaders travelling well, but was unable to increase his pace when popped the question, and was unable to land a blow. (6/4)
**Chalice** began a threatening move two furlongs out, but could not go through with his effort and gradually faded inside the final furlong. (7/1)
**No Hiding Place** looked far from fully wound up for this seasonal debut and lost all chance with a slow start. He hung badly and ran very green entering the straight, and was eased right down when the task was hopeless. (5/2)

## 780 ACHILLES H'CAP (0-65) (3-Y.O) (Class F)

4-00 (4-00) **6f (Fibresand)** £2,381.00 (£656.00: £311.00) Stalls: Low GOING: 0.14 sec per fur (SLW)

| | | | | SP | RR | SF |
|---|---|---|---|---|---|---|
| 525[11] | **Maiteamia (61)** (SRBowring) **3-9-2b**(5) CTeague(8) (led after 2f: clr whn edgd lft wl over 1f out: unchal) | — | 1 | 9/4[1] | 79+ | 43 |
| | **Awafeh (40)** (SMcIlor) **3-8-0** NAdams(2) (hld up: effrt 2f out: kpt on fnl f: no ch w wnr) | 5 | 2 | 14/1 | 45 | 9 |
| *605*[5] | **Seeking Destiny (IRE) (48)** (MCChapman) **3-8-5**(3) DRMcCabe(9) (trckd ldrs: pushed along & outpcd 2f out: kpt on ins fnl f) | 1 | 3 | 7/1[3] | 50 | 14 |
| *529*[5] | **Golden Tyke (IRE) (50)** (MJohnston) **3-8-10** TWilliams(3) (bit bkwd: hdwy ½-wy: rdn 2f out: no imp) | s.h | 4 | 7/1[3] | 52 | 16 |
| *421*[8] | **Principal Boy (IRE) (54)** (TJEtherington) **3-9-0** JFortune(1) (lw: s.i.s: bhd: effrt u.p over 2f out: nt rch ldrs) | 2 | 5 | 6/1[2] | 51 | 15 |
| *503*[6] | **Arlington Lady (40)** (NACallaghan) **3-8-0b** JQuinn(5) (chsd ldrs over 3f: sn lost tch) | 4 | 6 | 7/1[3] | 26 | — |
| *515*[6] | **Dhes-C (55)** (RHollinshead) **3-8-10**(5) FLynch(4) (s.s: a bhd & outpcd) | 4 | 7 | 7/1[3] | 30 | — |
| 539[7] | **Monsieur Culsyth (52)** (JBerry) **3-8-7**(5) PFessey(7) (dwlt: a bhd & outpcd) | ¾ | 8 | 14/1 | 25 | — |
| | **Bee Health Boy (59)** (MWEasterby) **3-9-0b**(5) GParkin(6) (bit bkwd: led 2f: rdn & wknd over 2f out) | ¾ | 9 | 10/1 | 30 | — |

(SP 117.5%) **9 Rn**

**1m 18.9** (5.40) CSF £30.21 CT £179.24 TOTE £3.10: £1.40 £4.70 £1.20 (£31.70) Trio £28.80 OWNER Mrs Zoe Grant (EDWINSTOWE) BRED Mrs Z. Grant and S. R. Bowring

**525 Maiteamia**, a class act in a poor race, won this turning handsprings. He seems to be thriving. (9/4)
**Awafeh** could not go the pace but he did run on to gain the runner-up prize and is open to improvement. (14/1: 10/1-16/1)
**518 Seeking Destiny (IRE)**, in touch until outpaced soon after turning for home, did rally but was made to look very one-paced. (7/1)
**Golden Tyke (IRE)**, taken to post early, is only just getting to know what is required and must not be written off yet. (7/1)
**Principal Boy (IRE)**, sluggish leaving the stalls, ran most disappointingly and was never in the race with a chance. (6/1)

## 781 APOLLO (S) STKS (3-Y.O) (Class G)

4-30 (4-30) **7f (Fibresand)** £2,070.00 (£570.00: £270.00) Stalls: Low GOING: 0.14 sec per fur (SLW)

| | | | | SP | RR | SF |
|---|---|---|---|---|---|---|
| *654*[6] | **People Direct (61)** (KMcAuliffe) **3-8-7**(5) DaneO'Neill(2) (b.hind: trckd ldrs: effrt & rdn 2f out: r.o to ld fnl 50y) | — | 1 | 15/8[1] | 66 | 35 |
| 661[3] | **Miss Offset (56)** (MJohnston) **3-8-12b** TWilliams(7) (lw: led: clr ent st: rdn 2f out: ct wl ins fnl f) | ½ | 2 | 9/2[2] | 65 | 34 |
| *655*[3] | **Loch Style (53)** (RHollinshead) **3-8-7**(5) FLynch(9) (s.s: hdwy 3f out: hrd drvn & no ex appr fnl f) | 4 | 3 | 7/1 | 56 | 25 |
| *605*[3] | **Efipetite (51)** (NBycroft) **3-8-12** GBardwell(8) (hld up: hdwy over 2f out: rdn & swtchd lft over 1f out: no imp) | 5 | 4 | 15/2 | 44 | 13 |
| *427*[7] | **Classic Daisy (35)** (RCSpicer) **3-8-4**(3) DRMcCabe(5) (s.i.s: nvr nr to chal) | 10 | 5 | 25/1 | 16 | — |
| *606*[5] | **Amoeba (IRE) (52)** (JBerry) **3-8-7**(5) PFessey(4) (lw: chsd ldrs: rdn & outpcd 3f out: sn btn) | 3 | 6 | 6/1[3] | 15 | — |
| *655*[2] | **Sheilas Dream (50)** (RSimpson) **3-8-4**(3) SDrowne(1) (a in rr) | s.h | 7 | 7/1 | 10 | — |
| *606*[6] | **Shanoora (IRE) (43)** (MrsNMacauley) **3-8-7v**(5) AmandaSanders(3) (trckd ldrs: rdn & lost pl ½-wy: sn bhd) | ¾ | 8 | 16/1 | 13 | — |
| *606*[8] | **Forecast** (JWharton) **3-8-12** JQuinn(6) (b: bkwd: a in rr: t.o fnl 3f) | 14 | 9 | 33/1 | — | — |

(SP 116.7%) **9 Rn**

**1m 33.1** (6.30) CSF £10.49 TOTE £2.10: £1.40 £1.50 £2.20 (£4.20) Trio £9.40 OWNER Mr Peter Barclay (LAMBOURN) BRED James Thom and Sons and Peter Orr
Bt in 8,200 gns

**654 People Direct**, back in her own company, looked to be fighting a lost cause entering the final quarter-mile but, with the leader tiring badly, battled on to forge ahead nearing the line. (15/8)
**661 Miss Offset** was able to dictate at her leisure and looked to have complete control for most of the way, but her stride shortened inside the distance and she was touched off late on. (9/2)
**655 Loch Style**, one of the last to leave the stalls, made good headway and promised to get to terms over a furlong out, but he appeared to run out of stamina. (7/1)
**605 Efipetite** closed up early in the straight and was still making progress when forced to switch inside over a furlong out. Failing to maintain the run, she is finding it difficult to get back to winning ways. (15/2)
**606 Amoeba (IRE)**, a drifter in the ring, was struggling to hold on turning into the back straight and was one of the first beaten. (6/1: op 4/1)

## 782 NEPTUNE MAIDEN H'CAP (0-65) (3-Y.O+) (Class F)

5-00 (5-02) **7f (Fibresand)** £2,381.00 (£656.00: £311.00) Stalls: Low GOING: 0.14 sec per fur (SLW)

| | | | | SP | RR | SF |
|---|---|---|---|---|---|---|
| 616[3] | **Domino Flyer (52)** (MrsASwinbank) **3-8-7** JFortune(12) (led 2f: led over 2f out: drew clr fnl f) | — | 1 | 8/1[2] | 65 | 33 |
| 669[4] | **Young Mazaad (IRE) (59)** (DCO'Brien) **3-9-0** GBardwell(6) (lw: drvn along ½-wy: hdwy wl over 1f out: fin wl) | 5 | 2 | 9/2[1] | 61 | 29 |
| *521*[10] | **Hornpipe (55)** (JWharton) **4-9-9** SDWilliams(8) (b: hld up: hdwy on outside over 2f out: nrst fin) | ½ | 3 | 8/1[2] | 55 | 36 |
| | **Miss Tri Colour (32)** (FHLee) **4-8-0** CRutter(13) (bit bkwd: a.p: jnd wnr 2f out: rdn & outpcd fnl f) | 3 | 4 | 20/1 | 26 | 7 |
| *179*[5] | **Boost (34)** (MrsNMacauley) **4-7-11**(5) FLynch(5) (in tch: no hdwy fnl 2f) | 5 | 5 | 14/1 | 16 | — |
| | **Undawaterscubadiva (29)** (MPBielby) **4-7-11**ow1 AMackay(3) (led after 2f tl over 2f out: wknd wl over 1f out) | 4 | 6 | 33/1 | 2 | — |
| | **Ruby Plus (30)** (GROldroyd) **5-7-12** FNorton(16) (lw: nvr nrr) | 2½ | 7 | 33/1 | — | — |
| | **Prudent Princess (60)** (AHide) **4-10-0** WWoods(10) (bit bkwd: hld up mid div: swtchd rt & effrt over 2f out: no imp) | 1¼ | 8 | 9/1[3] | 24 | 5 |
| | **Smile Forever (USA) (64)** (JARToller) **3-9-5** GDuffield(9) (bkwd: sn drvn along: a in rr) | 1¾ | 9 | 8/1[2] | 24 | — |
| 583[15] | **Merrie le Bow (48)** (PatMitchell) **4-8-11**(5) AmandaSanders(15) (prom tl wknd wl over 1f out) | nk | 10 | 14/1 | 8 | — |
| *517*[3] | **Jolly Hokey (35)** (JWharton) **4-8-3** JQuinn(7) (chsd ldrs: rdn & wknd ent st) | ¾ | 11 | 9/1[3] | — | — |
| | **Northern Falcon (51)** (MWEasterby) **3-8-1**(5)ow6 GParkin(14) (s.i.s: a bhd) | 1 | 12 | 20/1 | 7 | — |
| | **Monty (53)** (MajorDNChappell) **4-9-7** NAdams(1) (a in rr) | 1 | 13 | 14/1 | 7 | — |
| | **Prim Lass (42)** (MissJBower) **5-8-10** AMcGlone(2) (a bhd: t.o) | 5 | 14 | 20/1 | — | — |
| *387*[12] | **Malzoom (30)** (SEKettlewell) **4-7-12** JFanning(11) (lw: a rr div: t.o) | 1¼ | 15 | 10/1 | — | — |
| 566[7] | **Haute Cuisine (60)** (JBerry) **3-8-10**(5) PRoberts(4) (prom tl wknd u.p 2f out: t.o) | ½ | 16 | 12/1 | — | — |

(SP 128.5%) **16 Rn**

**1m 32.9** (6.10) CSF £43.10 CT £282.91 TOTE £8.20: £1.70 £2.00 £3.40 £6.70 (£6.40) Trio £107.60 OWNER Mr S. Smith (RICHMOND) BRED Mrs K. Livingstone
WEIGHT FOR AGE 3yo-13lb

**616 Domino Flyer** helped force the pace and, with stamina coming into play in the latter stages, stayed on strongly to draw away. (8/1)

**669 Young Mazaad (IRE)**, towards the rear and hard at work before reaching the straight, only found his stride when switched into the centre of the track but, by then, the winner was home and dried. (9/2)
**Hornpipe**, lightly-raced in the past year, was staying on well when the race was as good as over and, if he can be kept sound, should be able to find a race. (8/1)
**Miss Tri Colour** ran respectably considering she had been out of action for so long. There would seem to be a race in her. (20/1)
**Boost** appears still to be struggling to find the correct trip and, until he does, he could prove costly to follow. (14/1)
**Undawaterscubadiva** showed plenty of toe to share the lead, but found lack of a recent outing taking its toll below the distance. (33/1)
**Prudent Princess** (9/1: op 6/1)
**Smile Forever (USA)** (8/1: op 4/1)
**Malzoom** (10/1: op 20/1)

T/Plpt: £32.20 (318.72 Tckts). T/Qdpt: £18.90 (37.11 Tckts). IM

# 0624-BEVERLEY (R-H) (Good to firm)
## Thursday April 25th
WEATHER: fine WIND: fresh half against

## 783 FULFORD MAIDEN STKS (3-Y.O+) (Class D)
2-10 (2-15) **5f** £3,795.00 (£1,140.00: £550.00: £255.00) Stalls: High GOING minus 0.36 sec per fur (F)

| | Horse | Dist | Pos | SP | RR | SF |
|---|---|---|---|---|---|---|
| | **Major Quality** (JRFanshawe) **3-9-0** DHarrison(1) (lw: w ldr: led on bit ½-wy: clr over 1f out: easily) | — | 1 | 13/8 1 | 83+ | 10 |
| | **Gormire** (JHetherton) **3-8-9** NKennedy(5) (unf: b.hind: unruly & uns rdr gng to s: bhd tl hdwy u.p 2f out: styd on ins fnl f) | 5 | 2 | 33/1 | 62 | — |
| | **Dark Deed (USA) (83)** (BWHills) **3-8-9** PatEddery(12) (nt grwn: a chsng ldrs: rdn 2f out: kpt on one pce) | 1½ | 3 | 2/1 2 | 57 | — |
| 591$^{4}$ | **Solo Symphony (IRE) (64)** (PWChapple-Hyam) **3-8-9** JReid(13) (lw: racd wd: w ldrs: rdn over 1f out: kpt on) | nk | 4 | 8/1 | 56 | — |
| 458$^{8}$ | **Magic Mail** (JMPEustace) **3-9-0** RCochrane(6) (hld up: stdy hdwy over 1f out: nvr plcd to chal) | 1¼ | 5 | 12/1 | 57 | — |
| | **Farida Seconda** (JLSpearing) **3-8-6**(3) SDrowne(8) (outpcd ½-wy: sme hdwy 1f out: n.d) | nk | 6 | 50/1 | 51 | — |
| 591$^{6}$ | **Princess Efisio (47)** (BAMcMahon) **3-8-9** GCarter(10) (s.s: sn wl bhd: sme late hdwy: n.d) | nk | 7 | 33/1 | 50 | — |
| 524$^{6}$ | **Madrina** (JBerry) **3-8-9** JCarroll(4) (led to ½-wy: edgd rt: sn wknd) | 1¼ | 8 | 20/1 | 46 | — |
| | **Wee Hope (USA) (90)** (MRStoute) **3-9-0** DeanMcKeown(11) (chsd ldrs: rdn 2f out: sn wl outpcd) | 1¼ | 9 | 11/2 3 | 47 | — |
| | **Fernway** (RMWhitaker) **3-8-9** ACulhane(2) (uns rdr gng to s: sn wl bhd) | ¾ | 10 | 50/1 | 40 | — |
| *606*$^{10}$ | **Golborne Lad** (JBalding) **3-8-7v**1(7) JEdmunds(9) (sn bhd) | 4 | 11 | 50/1 | 32 | — |
| 591$^{10}$ | **Gloria Imperator (IRE)** (ABMulholland) **3-9-0** MMcAndrew(3) (s.s: a bhd) | nk | 12 | 50/1 | 31 | — |
| *458*$^{W}$ | ***Autoberry*** (CWFairhurst) **3-9-0** LCharnock(7) (Withdrawn not under Starters' orders: lame at s) | | W | 33/1 | — | — |
| | | | | (SP 127.0%) | **12 Rn** | |

**65.3 secs** (3.80) CSF £47.70 TOTE £2.60: £1.30 £24.40 £1.20 (£159.50) Trio £226.80 OWNER Mrs Mary Watt (NEWMARKET) BRED Mrs M. Watt

**Major Quality** looks to have done himself proud over the winter and carried plenty of condition. Every inch a sprinter in appearance, he scored in impressive fashion. A scratchy mover, he would not want the ground any firmer than this and is probably even better over six. (13/8)
**Gormire**, nothing at all to look at, gave all sorts of problems going to the start. Staying on in good style late in the day, she was probably flattered by the draw as, like the winner, she was racing towards the stands' side. (33/1)
**Dark Deed (USA)**, who has not grown at all from two to three, walks very stiffly behind and was flat out from soon after halfway. (2/1)
**591 Solo Symphony (IRE)**, who looked very fit, has a moderate action. Racing virtually alone up the centre, she was going up and down in the same place over a furlong out. (8/1)
**458 Magic Mail**, having his third outing, was given a predictable ride, picking up ground nicely from off the pace. He will no doubt now show his true ability in handicaps. (12/1)
**Wee Hope (USA)**, placed in two of three outings as a juvenile, looked fit and showed a good action but was hopelessly outpaced from halfway. He probably needs seven or even a mile. (11/2)

## 784 PANNELL CLAIMING STKS (3-Y.O) (Class F)
2-40 (2-41) **1m 1f 207y** £2,721.00 (£756.00: £363.00) Stalls: High GOING minus 0.36 sec per fur (F)

| | Horse | Dist | Pos | SP | RR | SF |
|---|---|---|---|---|---|---|
| 593$^{3}$ | **Montecristo (68)** (RGuest) **3-9-2**(5) FLynch(6) (effrt & swtchd outside over 3f out: hung rt & styd on to ld wl ins fnl f) | — | 1 | 2/5 1 | 71 | 25 |
| 586$^{15}$ | **Phantom Dancer (IRE) (40)** (JBerry) **3-8-9** JCarroll(2) (led tl hdd nr fin) | ½ | 2 | 16/1 | 58 | 12 |
| 660$^{4}$ | **Danico (60)** (SCWilliams) **3-8-11** JTate(7) (chsd ldrs: rdn over 3f out: wknd fnl f) | 2 | 3 | 11/2 2 | 57 | 11 |
| 688$^{7}$ | **Appeal Again (IRE) (55)** (MrsJRRamsden) **3-8-11** KFallon(3) (trckd ldrs: rdn along 3f out: kpt on same pce) | 2 | 4 | 7/1 3 | 54 | 8 |
| 525$^{13}$ | **Northern Clan (42)** (MWEasterby) **3-8-8**(5) GParkin(4) (trckd ldrs: effrt over 3f out: one pce) | 3½ | 5 | 16/1 | 50 | 4 |
| 614$^{13}$ | **Sassetta (IRE) (35)** (NTinkler) **3-7-12** KimTinkler(8) (sme hdwy on outside 6f out: lost pl over 3f out) | 11 | 6 | 25/1 | 17 | — |
| 717$^{7}$ | **Dispol Agenda** (GROldroyd) **3-8-6**ow2 RCochrane(1) (swvd lft s: sn w ldrs: lost pl over 2f out) | 1¼ | 7 | 25/1 | 23 | — |
| 637$^{8}$ | **Chipalata** (TWDonnelly) **3-9-1** CRutter(5) (dwlt: a bhd & sn rdn along) | 10 | 8 | 33/1 | 16 | — |
| | | | | (SP 121.7%) | **8 Rn** | |

**2m 8.8** (6.30) CSF £9.07 TOTE £1.50: £1.10 £2.60 £1.10 (£8.30) Trio £6.00 OWNER Matthews Breeding and Racing (NEWMARKET) BRED Lord Matthews

**593 Montecristo**, with a simple task on paper, gave his rider problems. Persisting in hanging right, it took a fair degree of skill to get him to put his head in front near the line. (2/5)
**540 Phantom Dancer (IRE)**, well away, was only worn down near the finish. (16/1)
**660 Danico**, who looked very fit, ran out of stamina entering the final furlong. (11/2)
**688 Appeal Again (IRE)** took a good grip on the heels of the leaders. He seemed to stay the trip all right but what his correct distance is is anyone's guess. (7/1)
**Northern Clan** seemed to stay the trip. (16/1)

## 785 GANTON RATED STKS H'CAP (0-90) (3-Y.O) (Class C)
3-10 (3-11) **7f 100y** £4,671.20 (£1,740.80: £845.40: £357.00) Stalls: High GOING minus 0.36 sec per fur (F)

| | Horse | Dist | Pos | SP | RR | SF |
|---|---|---|---|---|---|---|
| 611$^{3}$ | **Coyote Bluff (IRE) (80)** (PWChapple-Hyam) **3-8-11** JReid(5) (chsd ldr: led over 1f out: n.m.r nr fin: all out) | — | 1 | 13/2 | 91 | 49 |

676$^{8}$ **Sualtach (IRE) (81)** (RHollinshead) **3-8-12** LDettori(4) (lw: trckd ldrs: effrt 2f out: hung rt & ev ch ins fnl f: jst failed) ....s.h **2** 6/1$^{3}$ 92 50
638$^{3}$ **Mybotye (76)** (GROldroyd) **3-8-7** KFallon(1) (lw: swtchd rt s: hld up: nt clr run over 1f out: swtchd & styd on: nvr nr to chal) ....4 **3** 5/1$^{2}$ 78+ 36
577$^{2}$ **State of Caution (82)** (JLDunlop) **3-8-13** PatEddery(3) (lw: drvn along over 3f out: hung rt 1f out: nvr nr to chal) ....½ **4** 5/4$^{1}$ 83 41
**Marjaana (IRE) (76)** (PTWalwyn) **3-8-7** WCarson(7) (trckd ldrs: nt clr run 2f out: nvr able to chal: hmpd ins fnl f) ....1½ **5** 7/1 74 32
**Kala Sunrise (90)** (CSmith) **3-9-7** WWoods(2) (hld up: hdwy on outside over 3f out: wknd 2f out) ....¾ **6** 14/1 86 44
714$^{2}$ **Baileys First (IRE) (76)** (MJohnston) **3-8-7** TWilliams(6) (sn rdn along: led tl over 1f out: wkng whn hmpd ins fnl f) ....1½ **7** 8/1 69 27
(SP 119.0%) **7 Rn**

**1m 33.6** (1.60) CSF £41.95 TOTE £6.80: £2.40 £2.70 (£18.10) OWNER Mr P. W. Chapple-Hyam (MARLBOROUGH)
LONG HANDICAP Marjaana (IRE) 8-6 Mybotye 7-13 Baileys First (IRE) 8-6
STEWARDS' ENQUIRY Dettori susp. 6-7/5/96 (careless riding)

**611 Coyote Bluff (IRE)** showed plenty of grit and determination to hang on by the skin of his teeth. (13/2: 7/2-8/1)
**453* Sualtach (IRE)**, a keen sort, was hanging right even before he delivered his challenge. With Dettori using his whip in his left hand and the winner on his inside on the rail, he just failed to get there. (6/1)
**638 Mybotye**, racing from 8lb out of the weights in this limited handicap, looked in good nick beforehand but his action going to post left a lot to be desired. He had no luck in running and, when it was clear he was not going to trouble the first two a furlong out, his rider asked him to do just enough to secure third. (5/1)
**577 State of Caution**, who wore bandages, showed a very scratchy action going down. Flat out turning in, he persisted in hanging right and was never going to get in a blow. (5/4)
**Marjaana (IRE)**, who looked backward in her coat, did not have a lot of room to work in, but it would be wrong to look for excuses. (7/1)
**Kala Sunrise**, a poor mover, had a lot to do under topweight. (14/1)
**714 Baileys First (IRE)** (8/1: op 5/1)

## 786 MOORTOWN MAIDEN STKS (3-Y.O+) (Class D)

3-40 (3-42) **1m 100y** £3,951.00 (£1,188.00: £574.00: £267.00) Stalls: High GOING minus 0.36 sec per fur (F)

SP RR SF

583$^{3}$ **Freequent** (LMCumani) **3-8-12** OUrbina(5) (in tch: effrt & edgd rt 2f out: led 1f out: readily) ....— **1** 7/4$^{1}$ 45+ 13
**Melt The Clouds (CAN)** (PWHarris) **3-8-12** GHind(7) (lw: trckd ldrs: plld hrd: led over 2f out to 1f out: kpt on wl fnl f: no ch w wnr) ....½ **2** 9/4$^{2}$ 44 12
584$^{7}$ **Misky Bay** (JHMGosden) **3-8-12** LDettori(13) (hld up: stdy hdwy 2f out: nvr plcd to chal) ....3 **3** 7/1$^{3}$ 38 6
703$^{5}$ **Dispol Gem** (GROldroyd) **3-8-7** RCochrane(11) (chsd ldrs: kpt on same pce fnl 2f) ....hd **4** 7/1$^{3}$ 33 1
**Caribbean Dancer** (MRStoute) **3-8-7** DeanMcKeown(2) (hld up: effrt & hmpd 2f out: kpt on fnl f: nvr rchd ldrs) ....1¼ **5** 12/1 31 —
**Legal Brief (21)** (JSWainwright) **4-9-9b$^{1(3)}$** DRMcCabe(12) (led tl over 2f out: wknd over 1f out) ....3½ **6** 100/1 29 11
577$^{13}$ **Mock Trial (IRE)** (MrsJRRamsden) **3-8-12** KFallon(8) (hld up: shkn up & kpt on fnl 2f: nvr rchd ldrs) ....hd **7** 25/1 29 —
613$^{6}$ **Boston Rock (IRE)** (PWHarris) **4-9-12** JQuinn(4) (hld up & bhd: pushed along & sme hdwy 2f out: nvr nr ldrs) ....1¼ **8** 16/1 27 9
**Bright Desert** (EALDunlop) **3-8-12** KDarley(10) (str: bit bkwd: a in rr) ....1¼ **9** 14/1 24 —
613$^{12}$ **Squared Away** (JWPayne) **4-9-12** MTebbutt(6) (plld hrd: w ldrs tl wknd over 2f out) ....hd **10** 50/1 24 6
**Thaki** (EALDunlop) **3-8-12** WCarson(3) (w'like: str: bit bkwd: a bhd) ....13 **11** 10/1 — —
648$^{16}$ **Peace House (IRE)** (JLSpearing) **3-8-0$^{(7)}$** SRighton(1) (unruly in stalls: s.s: sn w ldrs: sltly hmpd 2f out: edgd lft & sn wknd) ....1 **12** 100/1 — —
***Bashtheboards*** (JJQuinn) **3-8-12** SDWilliams(9) (Withdrawn not under Starters' orders: lame at s) .... **W** 50/1 — —
(SP 131.2%) **12 Rn**

**1m 49.8** (5.80) CSF £6.59 TOTE £3.20: £1.20 £1.40 £2.30 (£3.50) Trio £10.00 OWNER Fittocks Stud (NEWMARKET) BRED Fittocks Stud
WEIGHT FOR AGE 3yo-14lb

**583 Freequent** had only to be nudged out. It will be interesting to see what mark the Handicapper eventually gives him. (7/4: 6/4-5/2)
**Melt The Clouds (CAN)**, a good walker, showed promise on his only outing at two. Racing keenly after hitting the front, he was soon flat out and, in the end, was flattered by the winning margin. Still inexperienced, further improvement looks likely. (9/4)
**584 Misky Bay**, who shows plenty of knee-action, ran a promising race and no doubt he will show improvement now he is qualified for handicaps, especially when stepped up in trip. (7/1)
**703 Dispol Gem** showed her Ripon effort was no fluke. (7/1)
**Caribbean Dancer** met trouble in running. She shaped nicely and this significantly qualifies her for a handicap mark. (12/1: op 7/1)
**Legal Brief**, who had shown precious little before both on the Flat and over hurdles, seemed to run well in blinkers for the first time. (100/1)
**Mock Trial (IRE)** is definitely not without ability and will no doubt show considerable improvement over further now he has had his three outings. (25/1)

## 787 ALWOODLEY H'CAP (0-70) (4-Y.O+ F & M) (Class E)

4-10 (4-17) **1m 1f 207y** £3,241.00 (£973.00: £469.00: £217.00) Stalls: Low GOING minus 0.36 sec per fur (F)

SP RR SF

**Darling Clover (53)** (DMorley) **4-9-5** MFenton(19) (s.i.s: sn chsng ldrs: led over 1f out: hld on wl towards fin) ....— **1** 12/1 65 49
641* **Eskimo Nel (IRE) (55)** (JLSpearing) **5-9-7** KFallon(18) (sn trckng ldrs: effrt & ev ch over 1f out: nt qckn ins fnl f) ....½ **2** 11/4$^{1}$ 66 50
547$^{4}$ **Maradata (IRE) (48)** (RHollinshead) **4-9-0** LDettori(16) (mid div: hdwy over 2f out: effrt & hung rt over 1f out: kpt on same pce) ....1¾ **3** 8/1 56 40
690$^{5}$ **Anchorena (58)** (JAHarris) **4-9-10v** JFEgan(8) (hld up & bhd: hdwy fnl 2f: nt rch ldrs) ....1¼ **4** 14/1 64 48
635$^{5}$ **Risky Tu (44)** (PAKelleway) **5-8-10** RCochrane(9) (mid div: hdwy 2f out: hung rt: nt rch ldrs) ....½ **5** 12/1 50 34
440$^{21}$ **Lady Sabina (43)** (WJMusson) **6-8-9** RPrice(17) (hld up & bhd: styd on fnl 2f: nvr nr ldrs) ....1¼ **6** 20/1 47 31
**Biloela (58)** (JGFitzGerald) **6-9-10** KDarley(11) (trckd ldrs: kpt on same pce fnl 2f) ....¾ **7** 12/1 60 44
615$^{9}$ **Mill Dancer (IRE) (43)** (EJAlston) **4-8-9** SDWilliams(14) (w ldr tl wknd 2f out) ....3½ **8** 20/1 40 24
628$^{4}$ **Westcourt Princess (52)** (MWEasterby) **4-9-4** GBardwell(4) (led tl over 1f out: sn wknd) ....nk **9** 5/1$^{2}$ 48 32
636$^{3}$ **Pinkerton Polka (47)** (CEBrittain) **4-8-13** MBirch(3) (bhd: hdwy on ins 2f out: nvr nr ldrs) ....nk **10** 14/1 43 27
*252$^{7}$* **Rose Chime (IRE) (39)** (JLHarris) **4-8-5** JQuinn(2) (in tch: drvn along over 3f out: sn lost pl) ....1 **11** 33/1 33 17

| | Horse | Dist | Pos | SP | RR | SF |
|---|---|---|---|---|---|---|
| $508^{6}$ | **Broughton's Pride (IRE) (49)** (JAGlover) **5-9-1** GCarter(15) (s.i.s: hld up: a bhd) | 2 | **12** | 7/1 $^{3}$ | 40 | 24 |
| | **Western Horizon (USA) (40)** (CEBrittain) **4-8-1**(5) MHenry(5) (s.i.s: sme hdwy 3f out: wandered & wknd over 1f out) | ¾ | **13** | 16/1 | 30 | 14 |
| $628^{8}$ | **Bobanlyn (IRE) (50)** (JSWainwright) **4-8-13**(3) DRMcCabe(13) (chsd ldrs tl wknd 2f out) | 5 | **14** | 25/1 | 32 | 16 |
| $739^{7}$ | **Dance of Joy (46)** (JMCarr) **4-8-5**(7) AColgan(10) (rr div: effrt on wd outside over 3f out: n.d) | 3 | **15** | 20/1 | 23 | 7 |
| $629^{15}$ | **Grey Again (51)** (SRBowring) **4-8-12b**(5) CTeague(6) (prom: pushed along 4f out: lost pl over 2f out: eased) | 1¾ | **16** | 20/1 | 25 | 9 |
| | **Last Spin (51)** (JRJenkins) **4-9-3** NDay(12) (bhd: rdn 3f out: no rspnse) | 3½ | **17** | 33/1 | 19 | 3 |
| | **Appearance Money (IRE) (41)** (FMurphy) **5-8-7** JFanning(1) (racd wd: bhd fnl 3f: t.o) | 25 | **18** | 33/1 | — | — |

(SP 141.0%) **18 Rn**

**2m 5.5** (3.00) CSF £47.70 CT £280.36 TOTE £19.10: £3.70 £1.40 £1.70 £3.30 (£49.60) Trio £144.60 OWNER Mr K. Craddock (NEWMARKET) BRED Astalon Ltd

**Darling Clover**, who looked very fit, always looked to have just the upper hand in the closing stages. (12/1)

**641* Eskimo Nel (IRE)**, 15lb higher in the weights than when winning here first time, had every chance but, in truth, she was always going to come off second best. (11/4)

**547 Maradata (IRE)**, who looked very fit, gave her rider problems, persisting in hanging right. (8/1)

**690 Anchorena**, over a stone better off with Eskimo Nel than when runner-up here, was putting in some solid work late in the day. (14/1)

**635 Risky Tu**, who has slipped down the weights, was staying on at the finish, despite a marked tendency to hang right. (12/1)

**Lady Sabina**, who did not take the eye in the paddock, was putting in some pleasing late work up the hill. (20/1)

**Biloela**, lightly-raced on the Flat since three, has also been in action over hurdles. She showed that she still retains some of her old ability and will be suited by further. (12/1)

**628 Westcourt Princess**, drawn towards the outside, could never dominate her field. (5/1)

## 788 WOODHALL SPA H'CAP (0-85) (3-Y.O) (Class D)

4-40 (4-45) **1m 1f 207y** £3,769.00 (£1,132.00: £546.00: £253.00) Stalls: Low GOING minus 0.36 sec per fur (F)

| | Horse | Dist | Pos | SP | RR | SF |
|---|---|---|---|---|---|---|
| | **Faateq (76)** (JLDunlop) **3-9-1** WCarson(10) (lw: v.unruly s: plld hrd: led after 1f: rn wd appr st: styd on wl fnl 2f) | — | **1** | 11/4 $^{1}$ | 82 | 37 |
| $528^{4}$ | **Classic Colours (USA) (66)** (SCWilliams) **3-8-5** AMackay(9) (lw: chsd ldrs: rdn over 4f out: styd on same pce fnl 3f: no ch w wnr) | 2 | **2** | 7/1 $^{3}$ | 69 | 24 |
| | **Pine Needle (78)** (DMorley) **3-9-3** BThomson(3) (in tch: effrt over 2f out: styd on same pce fnl f) | 1¼ | **3** | 9/2 $^{2}$ | 79 | 34 |
| $614^{12}$ | **Strategic Ploy (59)** (MrsJRRamsden) **3-7-12** NKennedy(8) (hld up: nt clr run & swtchd lft over 1f out: styd on steadily) | s.h | **4** | 14/1 | 60 | 15 |
| $575^{10}$ | **Mister Aspecto (IRE) (67)** (MJohnston) **3-8-6v** LDettori(7) (led 1f: chsd wnr tl outpcd over 1f out) | ½ | **5** | 9/1 | 67 | 22 |
| | **Alambar (IRE) (71)** (PTWalwyn) **3-8-10** RHills(5) (plld hrd: trckd ldrs: hung rt 2f out: one pce) | 1¼ | **6** | 8/1 | 69 | 24 |
| | **Fikra (USA) (67)** (SPCWoods) **3-8-6** WWoods(6) (hld up & bhd: hmpd 4f out: sme hdwy over 1f out: nvr nr ldrs) | 3 | **7** | 12/1 | 60 | 15 |
| $578^{9}$ | **Orinoco River (USA) (76)** (PWChapple-Hyam) **3-9-1** JReid(4) (chsd ldrs: drvn along over 4f out: lost pl 3f out) | 5 | **8** | 9/2 $^{2}$ | 61 | 16 |
| $575^{11}$ | **D'naan (IRE) (78)** (WJHaggas) **3-9-3** RCochrane(2) (s.i.s: hld up: a in rr) | 1¼ | **9** | 10/1 | 61 | 16 |
| $444^{18}$ | **Diego (82)** (CEBrittain) **3-9-2**(5) MHenry(1) (a bhd) | 3 | **10** | 12/1 | 60 | 15 |

(SP 127.8%) **10 Rn**

**2m 6.5** (4.00) CSF £23.23 CT £82.37 TOTE £4.10: £1.50 £2.20 £2.10 (£30.50) Trio £72.30 OWNER Mr Hamdan Al Maktoum (ARUNDEL) BRED Shadwell Estate Company Limited

**Faateq** gave all sorts of problems at the stalls. Refusing to settle, Carson wisely allowed him to stride on. After having difficulty making the turn, he stayed on in most determined fashion and was right on top in the closing stages. (11/4)

**528 Classic Colours (USA)** looked to give a good account of himself but there is a question mark over his attitude. (7/1)

**Pine Needle** was staying on when it was all over and will be suited by a mile and a half. (9/2)

**Strategic Ploy**, travelling nicely with nowhere to go halfway up the straight, eventually pulled to the outside and was staying on in promising fashion at the line. There is no doubt she is capable of better, especially over further. (14/1)

**519* Mister Aspecto (IRE)**, badly drawn at Kempton last time, helped force the pace but was getting nowhere with over a furlong left to run. (9/1: op 6/1)

**Alambar (IRE)** lacks substance and races keenly. (8/1)

**Orinoco River (USA)** (9/2: 3/1-5/1)

T/Jkpt: £8,586.50 (2.25 Tckts). T/Plpt: £28.30 (620.39 Tckts). T/Qdpt: £19.30 (44.31 Tckts). WG

# GELSENKIRCHEN-HORST (Gelsenkirchen, Germany) (R-H) (Good)

## Sunday April 14th

## 789a GROSSER PREIS DER GELSENKIRCHENER WIRTSCHAFT (Gp 3) (4-Y.O+)

3-40 (3-42) **1m 2f** £27,027.00 (£10,811.00: £5,405.00)

| Horse | Dist | Pos | SP | RR | SF |
|---|---|---|---|---|---|
| **Oxalagu (GER)** (BSchutz,Germany) **4-8-13** AStarke | — | **1** | | 122 | — |
| **Sir King (GER)** (RSuerland,Germany) **4-8-13** AHelfenbein | 2 | **2** | | 119 | — |
| **Kornado** (ALowe,Germany) **6-8-13** MRimmer | 2½ | **3** | | 115 | — |

**8 Rn**

**2m 0.4** TOTE 61DM: 18DM 35DM 19DM (SF 620DM) OWNER Gestut Rietberg

**Oxalagu (GER)** took this event comfortably and had the race sewn up from two furlongs out.

# 0720a-EVRY (France) (R-H) (Good)

## Wednesday April 17th

## 790a PRIX SERVANNE (Listed) (3-Y.O+)

2-20 (2-21) **5f 110y** £18,445.00 (£6,324.00: £3,953.00: £2,055.00)

| Horse | Dist | Pos | SP | RR | SF |
|---|---|---|---|---|---|
| **Anabaa (USA)** (MmeCHead,France) **4-9-7** FHead | — | **1** | | 110 | — |

| | | | | SP | RR | SF |
|---|---|---|---|---|---|---|
| | **Sepoy (IRE)** (MmeMBollack-Badel,France) **3-8-8** ABadel | 4 | **2** | | 95 | — |
| $565^{5}$ | **Eastern Prophets** (TJNaughton) **3-8-8** CAsmussen | s.h | **3** | | 95 | — |
| | | | | | | **6 Rn** |

**64.85 secs** (0.45) P-M 1.30F: 1.10F 1.70F (SF 3.30F) OWNER Mme A. Head (CHANTILLY) BRED Gainsborough Farm Inc

**Anabaa (USA)** took this in style. A son of Danzig who is very much on the upgrade, he could prove to be France's top sprinter this season, and now goes for the Group Two Prix de Saint-Georges at Longchamp in early May.

**565 Eastern Prophets** found no response when the winner passed him at the two-furlong pole. Connections felt that he would improve from this and would be spot on next time out. No definite plans have been made, but he could well be campaigned on the continent this summer.

DS

## 0438a-SAINT-CLOUD (France) (L-H) (Good)

### Thursday April 18th

### 791a PRIX PENELOPE (Gp 3) (3-Y.O F)

3-10 (3-12) **1m 2f 110y** £28,986.00 (£10,540.00: £5,270.00)

| | | | | SP | RR | SF |
|---|---|---|---|---|---|---|
| | **Tulipa (USA)** (AFabre,France) **3-9-0** TJarnet | — | **1** | | 100 | — |
| | **Camille** (PDemercastel,France) **3-9-0** WMongil | ¾ | **2** | | 99 | — |
| | **Amiarma (IRE)** (EChevalierduFau,France) **3-9-0** TGillet | nk | **3** | | 98 | — |
| | | | | | | **7 Rn** |

**2m 15.7** (5.70) P-M 1.70F: 3.90F 5.50F (SF 85.20F) OWNER Sheikh Mohammed (CHANTILLY) BRED Fares Farm Inc

**Tulipa (USA)**, settled in fifth, made her effort halfway up the straight and took the lead inside the final furlong. Going away from her rivals at the finish, she is a talented filly and may go now for the Oaks d'Italia.

**Camille** made a courageous effort to make all and stuck gamely to her task, but did not have quite enough speed when tackled by the winner inside the final furlong. She is still a maiden, but looks capable of winning a listed race.

**Amiarma (IRE)**, well backed, proved slightly disappointing. Held up for a late run, she was probably a little out of her ground when the pace was really switched on, and was then unable to find a gap in the last furlong and a half, so can be considered a little unlucky. She may be suited by more cut in the ground, and a decent race should come her way this season.

DS

## 0723a-SAN SIRO (Milan, Italy) (R-H) (Good to firm)

### Saturday April 20th

### 792a PREMIO ASSIANO MAIDEN (3-Y.O F)

4-10 **1m 1f** £8,120.00

| | | | | SP | RR | SF |
|---|---|---|---|---|---|---|
| | **Twist Again (GER)** (MGasparini,Italy) **3-9-2** AHerrera | — | **1** | | — | — |
| | **Lasco With'Em (ITY)** (MTavazzani,Italy) **3-9-2** LManiezzi | s.h | **2** | | — | — |
| | **Histoire D'Amour (ITY)** (GBotti,Italy) **3-9-2** EBotti | 1½ | **3** | | — | — |
| | **Maid To Last** (JWHills) **3-9-2** BCook (btn over 16½l) | | **6** | | — | — |
| | | | | | | **10 Rn** |

**1m 53.4** (11.20) TOTE 43L: 15L 59L 20L (758L) OWNER Signorina Turri BRED Dr S. Kosic et al

**Maid To Last**, a small filly, raced prominently but faded quite quickly entering the straight, and was comprehensively beaten in the end. It is hard to assess this performance against moderate opposition.

## 0722a-CAPANNELLE (Rome, Italy) (R-H) (Good)

### Sunday April 21st

### 793a PREMIO BAHADIR (3-Y.O)

2-00 **1m 2f** £8,120.00

| | | | | SP | RR | SF |
|---|---|---|---|---|---|---|
| | **Pierrot Solaire (FR)** (AColella,Italy) **3-8-11** ACorniani | — | **1** | | 83 | — |
| | **Camp Follower** (JLDunlop) **3-8-11** PatEddery | s.h | **2** | | 83 | — |
| | **Attimo Fuggente (IRE)** (APeraino,Italy) **3-9-4** MJKinane | 2 | **3** | | 87 | — |
| | | | | | | **8 Rn** |

**2m 4.3** TOTE 24L: 12L 15L 14L (47L) OWNER Scuderia Tamara BRED Haras D'Ommeel

**Camp Follower**, on drying ground, put up a gutsy performance. In fifth place entering the straight, he put his best foot forward and battled on gamely with the winner inside the final furlong, but was just unable to get his head in front. A son of Warrshan, he is sure to win soon.

### 794a PREMIO REGINA ELENA (Gp 2) (3-Y.O F)

4-00 (4-18) **1m** £49,259.00 (£24,359.00: £14,074.00: £7,033.00)

| | | | | SP | RR | SF |
|---|---|---|---|---|---|---|
| | **Beauty To Petriolo (IRE)** (LCamici,Italy) **3-8-11** MPasquale | — | **1** | | 105 | — |
| | **Sagar Pride (IRE)** (JGBurns,Ireland) **3-8-11** GForte | nk | **2** | | 104 | — |
| | **Blu Tuama (USA)** (AVerdesi,Italy) **3-8-11** MVargiu | 2 | **3** | | 100 | — |
| | **Ally Camp (USA)** (ALodigiano,Italy) **3-8-11** ACorniani | s.h | **4** | | 100 | — |
| | **Germignana (ITY)** (Italy) **3-8-11** MCangiano | ½ | **5** | | 99 | — |
| | **Pappa Reale** (Italy) **3-8-11** GBietolini | s.h | **6** | | 99 | — |
| $572^{2}$ | **Parrot Jungle (IRE)** (JLDunlop) **3-8-11** PatEddery | nk | **7** | | 99 | — |
| | **Super Gift (IRE)** (DKWeld,Ireland) **3-8-11** MJKinane | 1 | **8** | | 97 | — |
| 550* | **Inner Circle (USA)** (PWChapple-Hyam) **3-8-11** JReid | ½ | **9** | | 96 | — |
| | **Bog Wild (USA)** (Italy) **3-8-11** FJovine | 2½ | **10** | | 91 | — |
| | **Boccadirosa (IRE)** (Italy) **3-8-11** AHerrera | 3 | **11** | | 85 | — |
| | **Naskramar** (Italy) **3-8-11** EBotti | 1½ | **12** | | 82 | — |
| | **Infiel** (Italy) **3-8-11** PPerlanti | 1½ | **13** | | 79 | — |

| | | | | SP | RR | SF |
|---|---|---|---|---|---|---|
| **Bella Michela (IRE)** (Italy) **3-8-11** BJovine | 2 | **14** | | | 75 | — |
| | | | | | | **14 Rn** |

**1m 39.3** TOTE 416L: 89L 70L 35L (3098L) OWNER Scuderia Ri Ma BRED C. J. Haughey

**Sagar Pride (IRE)** put in her best performance to date. In third place entering the straight, she was hard ridden inside the final furlong, but was just unable to catch the winner. She had to survive a lengthy enquiry into possible interference.

**572 Parrot Jungle (IRE)** never really got into this and was unhappy on the drying ground. In rear early, she made some late headway in the final two furlongs, but she was never able to get on terms with the winner. On suitable ground, she should be capable of picking up a decent race.

**550* Inner Circle (USA)** tried to make every post a winning one. She set a decent pace until the furlong marker before weakening quite quickly, but there are definitely doubts about her getting the mile, and she may run over shorter next time.

# KREFELD (Germany) (R-H) (Good)
## Sunday April 21st

## 795a DR BUSCH MEMORIAL (Gp 3) (3-Y.O)
3-30 (3-42) **1m 110y** £27,027.00 (£10,811.00: £5,405.00: £2,703.00)

| Horse | Btn | Pos | SP | RR | SF |
|---|---|---|---|---|---|
| **Surako (GER)** (HJentzsch,Germany) **3-9-0** PSchiergen | — | **1** | | 84 | — |
| **Lavirco (GER)** (PRau,Germany) **3-9-0** TMundry | 1 | **2** | | 82 | — |
| **Catoki (USA)** (BSchutz,Germany) **3-9-0** AStarke | 3 | **3** | | 77 | — |
| | | | | | **7 Rn** |

**1m 46.6** TOTE 44DM: 12DM 11DM 13DM (SF 86DM) OWNER Gestut Fahrhof BRED Gestut Fahrhof Stiftung

# 0621a-LONGCHAMP (Paris, France) (R-H) (Good to firm)
## Sunday April 21st

## 796a PRIX DE LA GROTTE (Gp 3) (3-Y.O F)
2-40 (2-40) **1m** £28,986.00 (£10,540.00: £5,270.00: £2,635.00)

| Horse | Btn | Pos | SP | RR | SF |
|---|---|---|---|---|---|
| **Shake the Yoke** (ELellouche,France) **3-9-0** DBoeuf | — | **1** | | 121+ | 68 |
| **Raisonnable** (DSepulchre,France) **3-9-0** CAsmussen | 10 | **2** | | 101 | 48 |
| **Miss Tahiti (IRE)** (AFabre,France) **3-9-0** OPeslier | 2½ | **3** | | 96 | 43 |
| **Occupandiste (IRE)** (MmeCHead,France) **3-9-0** ODoleuze | 5 | **4** | | 86 | 33 |
| | | | | | **4 Rn** |

**1m 36.7** (1.70) P-M 4.20F: 2.20F 2.10F (SF 18.20F) OWNER S. Brunswick BRED Sussex Stud & Calogo Bloodstock

**Shake the Yoke,** whose jockey blamed himself for the defeat in last October's Prix Marcel Boussac, reversed the form in no uncertain manner and put up a super display to win the second Group race of her career. Hacking around early on, she burst clear soon after entering the straight to beat three useful rivals by upwards of ten lengths in a time under a second outside the course record. She looked pretty fit, having worked brilliantly with Shaanxi earlier in the week, and now heads for the Poule d'Essai des Pouliches where she will be difficult to beat, providing the ground remains good or faster.

**Raisonnable,** close up before taking the advantage early in the straight, was found lacking in speed when the winner swept past her, but was not too pressed to hold second, despite losing a shoe. She had had the advantage of a prep-race this season and is a thoroughly consistent filly, but does not look up to Group One class, although she may still be allowed to take her chance in the Pouliches.

**Miss Tahiti (IRE),** who looked well enough in the paddock, was never going well and was beaten early in the straight, but was later found to have bled. She will now be rested, but it is hoped to get her back for either the Prix de Diane or the Oaks, where she will certainly be aided by softer ground and the longer distance.

**Occupandiste (IRE),** who took the field along at a decent pace until the straight, then looked ready to collapse and just cantered home, and was said not to have been able to catch her breath. She almost certainly needs much softer ground and, if none the worse for the outing and there is some cut for the Pouliches, she will probably be allowed to take her chance. This effort should be completely forgotten, and she could be a very lively outsider in the Pouliches providing things go her way.

## 797a PRIX GREFFULHE (Gp 2) (3-Y.O C & F)
3-05 (3-09) **1m 2f 110y** £46,298.00 (£18,314.00: £8,643.00: £3,294.00)

| | Horse | Btn | Pos | SP | RR | SF |
|---|---|---|---|---|---|---|
| | **Ragmar (FR)** (PBary,France) **3-9-2** GMosse (a.p: rdn 2f out: chal over 1f out: led ins fnl f: kpt on) | — | **1** | | 111 | 68 |
| | **Egeo (FR)** (CLaffon-Parias,France) **3-9-2** FHead (led tl ins fnl f: no imp cl home) | 3 | **2** | | 106 | 63 |
| | **Radevore** (AFabre,France) **3-9-2** TJarnet (hld up & bhd: hdwy ½-wy: rdn over 2f out: unable qckn) | 2 | **3** | | 103 | 60 |
| 621a[3] | **Oliviero (FR)** (AMauchamp,France) **3-9-2** ABadel (mid div early: rdn 3f out: 5th & outpcd st: sme late hdwy) | ½ | **4** | | 103 | 60 |
| | **General Academy (IRE)** (PAKelleway) **3-9-2** RCochrane (a.p: rdn ent st: ev ch 2f out: outpcd cl home) | 1½ | **5** | | 100 | 57 |
| | **Hoist To Heaven (USA)** (MmeCHead,France) **3-9-2** ODoleuze (a in rr) | ¾ | **6** | | 99 | 56 |
| | | | | | | **6 Rn** |

**2m 10.6** (2.60) P-M 3.00F: 1.90F 4.00F (SF 30.10F) OWNER Mr J-L Bouchard (CHANTILLY) BRED Dr G. & Mme J. Sandor

**Ragmar (FR)** won this race in a workmanlike manner. Always prominent, he tackled the long-time leader halfway up the straight before going on to a comfortable victory. He is a thoroughly genuine if rather one-paced horse, who may go directly for the Prix du Jockey-Club. Like Celtic Arms and Sierra Madre, he was bought as a two-year-old and, while he is unlikely to be a Group One horse, he will always find out the faults in his rivals, and should definitely stay further.

**Egeo (FR)** ran a terrific race after winning just a maiden last time out. Setting out to make all the running, he had no answer when tackled by the winner halfway up the straight and, while unlikely to be top-class, he will probably be better suited by a slightly shorter distance.

**Radevore** was yet another disappointing favourite from the powerful Fabre stable which has yet to hit form. Slowly away and fourth for much of the race, he proved one-paced and rather disappointing when asked in the straight. He had shown such great promise when beating Loup Solitaire first time out, but has now been third on his last three outings. He may do better over a longer distance, or when there is more cut in the ground.

**621a Oliviero (FR),** held up, produced a run halfway up the straight but never looked a danger to the leaders, and may be in need of a break having already run four times this season.

**General Academy (IRE),** a tall, fine-looking horse, appeared to be running well within himself on the descent to the straight, but could find no more in the final two furlongs. His trainer was rather disappointed with the performance, and now believes that he needs a shorter distance and more cut in the ground.

## 798a PRIX DE FONTAINEBLEAU (Gp 3) (3-Y.O C)

3-35 (3-39) **1m** £28,986.00 (£10,540.00: £5,270.00: £2,635.00)

| | Horse | Details | Dist | Pos | SP | RR | SF |
|---|---|---|---|---|---|---|---|
| | **Ashkalani (IRE)** | (AdeRoyerDupre,France) **3-9-2** GMosse | — | 1 | | 112 | 52 |
| | **Eternity Range (USA)** | (PBary,France) **3-9-2** FHead | 1½ | 2 | | 109 | 49 |
| | **Spinning World (USA)** | (JEPease,France) **3-9-2** CAsmussen | 2½ | 3 | | 104 | 44 |
| | **Anziyan (USA)** | (AFabre,France) **3-9-2** TJarnet | 1 | 4 | | 102 | 42 |

**6 Rn**

**1m 38.4** (3.40) P-M 3.70F: 2.10F 2.10F (SF 11.00F) OWNER Aga Khan (CHANTILLY) BRED Aga Khan's Studs S.C.

**Ashkalani (IRE)**, produced in superb condition and easily the pick of the paddock, looks a most exciting individual and is certainly out of the top-drawer. Slowly into his stride and inclined to pull a little early on, he still had plenty to do a furlong and a half out, but then launched a challenge which cut down the rest in most impressive style. Despite being eased towards the line, he covered the last 200 metres in a sprint-time of 10.8 seconds and his jockey said afterwards that he is the best he has ridden. Now heading for the Poule d'Essai des Poulains, his devastating turn of foot will make him difficult to beat on top of the ground.

**Eternity Range (USA)** did absolutely nothing wrong, laying close up in second place and taking the advantage a furlong and a half out before having no answer to the winner. Likely to improve for the outing, he also goes for the Poulains, and is a colt with plenty of scope who looks like staying further.

**Spinning World (USA)**, who raced behind the leaders, was short of room halfway up the straight before putting in his best work at the finish. Hailing from a stable which has yet to hit top form, he was supplemented for the Derby recently, having won over ten furlongs at two, and will no doubt leave this form behind when upped in distance. He will now be aimed at either the Poulains, the Prix Lupin or the Prix Jean Prat.

**Anziyan (USA)** raced in fourth place and looked dangerous when starting his challenge in the straight, but his effort petered out in the final furlong.

DS

# 0792a-SAN SIRO (Milan, Italy) (R-H) (Good to firm)

## Sunday April 21st

## 799a PREMIO MURISENGO MAIDEN (3-Y.O)

4-35 **1m 1f** £8,120.00

| | Horse | Details | Dist | Pos | SP | RR | SF |
|---|---|---|---|---|---|---|---|
| | **Dry Rocks (ITY)** | (RRossini,Italy) **3-9-2** AMarcialis | — | 1 | | — | — |
| | **Nabeel Moon (IRE)** | (GBotti,Italy) **3-9-2** ACarboni | 5½ | 2 | | — | — |
| | **Paris Circus (ITY)** | (AAngelelli,Italy) **3-9-2** MLatorre | hd | 3 | | — | — |
| | **Algonquin (IRE)** | (NAGraham) **3-9-2** LSorrentino (btn over 39l) | | 9 | | — | — |

**9 Rn**

**1m 52.7** (10.50) TOTE 20L: 12L 39L 16L (297L) OWNER G. Gariboldi BRED Az. Agr. Pallorsi

**Algonquin (IRE)** was never going well and always in the rear. He picked up an injury during the race and is likely to remain in Italy.

# CARLISLE (R-H) (Good to soft, Soft patches)

## Friday April 26th

WEATHER: overcast WIND: fresh half against

## 800 BUZZARD MAIDEN STKS (2-Y.O) (Class D)

2-10 (2-12) **5f** £3,264.40 (£989.20: £483.60: £230.80) Stalls: High GOING: 0.27 sec per fur (G)

| | Horse | Details | Dist | Pos | SP | RR | SF |
|---|---|---|---|---|---|---|---|
| 698[3] | **Exit To Rio (CAN)** | (MrsJRRamsden) **2-9-0** KFallon(7) (lw: trckd ldrs: effrt ½-wy: r.o on ins to ld wl ins fnl f) | — | 1 | 11/10[1] | 65+ | 22 |
| | **Recondite (IRE)** | (MRChannon) **2-9-0** KDarley(9) (w'like: wl grwn: scope: mde most: rdn ½-wy: kpt on wl whn hdd ins fnl f) | hd | 2 | 15/8[2] | 65+ | 22 |
| | **Blazing Castle** | (WGMTurner) **2-9-0** TSprake(6) (lt-f: unf: disp ld 3f: outpcd fnl f) | 4 | 3 | 16/1 | 52 | 9 |
| | **Grate Times** | (EWeymes) **2-9-0** JFortune(3) (w'like: bit bkwd: in tch: outpcd ½-wy: kpt on wl appr fnl f) | 1¾ | 4 | 33/1 | 46 | 3 |
| 733[2] | **Jib Jab** | (DNicholls) **2-9-0** AlexGreaves(4) (in tch: outpcd ½-wy: kpt on) | 1¼ | 5 | 7/1[3] | 42 | — |
| | **High Spirits (IRE)** | (TDEasterby) **2-9-0** MBirch(1) (leggy: scope: bit bkwd: carried lft s: bhd tl sme hdwy fnl f) | 2½ | 6 | 14/1 | 34 | — |
| 452[10] | **Magic Blue (IRE)** | (RHollinshead) **2-8-9**(5) FLynch(5) (chsd ldrs: rdn & swvd bdly lft 2f out: sn bhd) | 2½ | 7 | 20/1 | 26 | — |
| | **Mill End Boy** | (MWEasterby) **2-8-9**(5) GParkin(2) (lt-f: unf: bit bkwd: swvd lft s: a in rr) | hd | 8 | 25/1 | 26 | — |
| | **Zorba** | (CWThornton) **2-9-0** DeanMcKeown(8) (cmpt: scope: bit bkwd: s.v.s: a wl bhd) | 11 | 9 | 14/1 | — | — |

(SP 125.7%) **9 Rn**

**66.2 secs** (6.00) CSF £3.95 TOTE £2.00: £1.10 £1.10 £1.70 (£1.90) Trio £19.70 OWNER Mr P. A. Leonard (THIRSK) BRED Black Canyon Thoroughbreds Ltd

**698 Exit To Rio (CAN)** was noisy in the paddock. Making his effort on the inside, he stuck on strongly to show ahead near the line, and can do nothing but improve further. (11/10)

**Recondite (IRE)**, a grand sort, was pushed along to make the running. He kept on strongly and was only worn down near the finish. The first two are above-average and they should go on from here. (15/8)

**Blazing Castle**, nothing to look at, ran better than could be expected, disputing the lead and only being left behind entering the final furlong. (16/1)

**Grate Times**, a likeable type, struggled to keep up at halfway, but stayed on in pleasing fashion in the final furlong. (33/1)

**733 Jib Jab**, stepped up in class, was far from disgraced. (7/1)

**High Spirits (IRE)**, an immature type, was carried badly left at the start. He stayed on nicely coming to the final furlong, and can be expected to do better in due course. (14/1)

## 801 KESTREL CLAIMING STKS (I) (4-Y.O+) (Class F)

2-45 (2-45) **6f 206y** £2,283.00 (£638.00: £309.00) Stalls: High GOING: 0.27 sec per fur (G)

| | Horse | Details | Dist | Pos | SP | RR | SF |
|---|---|---|---|---|---|---|---|
| 645[14] | **Proud Image (65)** | (APJarvis) **4-8-13v** JTate(9) (led after 1f: clr over 2f out: rdn out) | — | 1 | 6/1[2] | 69 | 19 |

| | Horse | Dist | Pos | SP | RR | SF |
|---|---|---|---|---|---|---|
| 661[7] | **Flamboro (50)** (JDBethell) **4-8-3** TWilliams(1) (lw: hdwy u.p 3f out: kpt on fnl f: no ch w wnr) | 2½ | **2** | 11/1 | 53 | 3 |
| 589[3] | **Sagebrush Roller (77)** (JWWatts) **8-9-1** NConnorton(2) (b: lw: chsd ldrs: sn rdn: no imp) | hd | **3** | 1/3[1] | 65 | 15 |
| *426[6]* | **Genesis Four (33)** (MrsLStubbs) **6-8-7b** JFortune(5) (in tch: kpt on one pce fnl 3f) | 2½ | **4** | 25/1 | 51 | 1 |
| | **De-Veers Currie (IRE)** (RFFisher) **4-9-2** KFallon(4) (bit bkwd: sn bhd & rdn along) | 9 | **5** | 40/1 | 40 | — |
| 537[13] | **To Prove a Point (30)** (JJO'Neill) **4-8-3b** DeanMcKeown(7) (s.i:s: sn in tch: lost pl ½-wy) | 5 | **6** | 33/1 | 15 | — |
| 586[14] | **Sallyoreally (IRE) (23)** (WStorey) **5-8-2** JFanning(3) (w ldrs: rdn 3f out: sn wknd) | 5 | **7** | 40/1 | 2 | — |
| 549[7] | **Kummel King (56)** (EJAlston) **8-8-5** SDWilliams(8) (led 1f: rdn 3f out: sn wknd) | 7 | **8** | 10/1[3] | — | — |
| | **Thrushwood** (NChamberlain) **4-8-1** NCarlisle(6) (bkwd: hmpd s: a wl bhd) | 10 | **9** | 100/1 | — | — |

(SP 119.4%) **9 Rn**

**1m 34.4** (8.70) CSF £62.78 TOTE £5.10: £1.40 £1.70 £1.10 (£91.10) Trio £6.00 OWNER Mr L. Fust (ASTON UPTHORPE) BRED Miss S. E. Jarvis

STEWARDS' ENQUIRY Connorton susp. 6-7/5/96 (careless riding).

**545 Proud Image**, who apparently finished lame last time, was able to dominate and was in no danger from halfway up the straight. (6/1)

**661 Flamboro** stuck on to snatch second place near the line. (11/1: 9/1-14/1)

**589 Sagebrush Roller** had upwards of 10lb in hand on this lot on Official figures, but he managed to avoid winning all last season and it is not hard to see why. Soon pushed along, he never knuckled down to the task in hand. (1/3)

**Genesis Four**, who was well beaten on his two previous outings, ran better here, sticking on well up the hill. (25/1)

## 802 GOLDEN EAGLE H'CAP (0-85) (3-Y.O+) (Class D)

3-15 (3-15) **7f 214y** £3,712.50 (£1,125.00: £550.00: £262.50) Stalls: High GOING: 0.27 sec per fur (G)

| | Horse | Dist | Pos | SP | RR | SF |
|---|---|---|---|---|---|---|
| 554[5] | **Mokuti (70)** (GWragg) **4-9-1** PRobinson(4) (chsd ldrs: sn rdn: hung lft & led last strides) | — | **1** | 9/2[2] | 83 | 62 |
| 580[18] | **Percy Braithwaite (IRE) (80)** (MJohnston) **4-9-11** JWeaver(3) (lw: w ldrs: led over 1f out tl ct nr fin) | s.h | **2** | 14/1 | 93 | 72 |
| | **Tertium (IRE) (75)** (MartynWane) **4-9-6** JFortune(11) (bit bkwd: hld up: stdy hdwy over 2f out: r.o steadily fnl f: nvr plcd to chal) | 1½ | **3** | 10/1 | 85 | 64 |
| | **Kemo Sabo (78)** (CParker) **4-9-4**(5) FLynch(10) (trckd ldrs: effrt & n.m.r over 2f out: wknd over 1f out) | 9 | **4** | 14/1 | 70 | 49 |
| 589[5] | **Night Wink (USA) (80)** (DNicholls) **4-9-11** AlexGreaves(9) (lw: led tl over 1f out: sn wknd) | 1¾ | **5** | 5/1[3] | 68 | 47 |
| | **Sue's Return (83)** (APJarvis) **4-10-0** JTate(2) (hld up & bhd: sme hdwy 3f out: nvr nr ldrs) | 3½ | **6** | 7/1 | 64 | 43 |
| 450[19] | **Best of All (IRE) (73)** (JBerry) **4-9-4** JCarroll(6) (chsd ldrs: wkng whn n.m.r 2f out) | 6 | **7** | 11/1 | 42 | 21 |
| 480[11] | **Spanish Verdict (67)** (DenysSmith) **9-8-7**(5) CTeague(1) (lw: w ldrs: rdn & hmpd over 2f out: sn wknd) | 2½ | **8** | 14/1 | 31 | 10 |
| 491[2] | **It's Academic (69)** (MrsJRRamsden) **4-9-0** KFallon(7) (lw: hld up: effrt & swtchd over 2f out: sn rdn & wknd: eased) | 2 | **9** | 9/4[1] | 29 | 8 |
| 690[15] | **Segala (IRE) (70)** (JJO'Neill) **5-9-1** KDarley(5) (b: prom early: bhd & rdn ½-wy) | 7 | **10** | 20/1 | 16 | — |
| *211[13]* | **Bold Amusement (76)** (WSCunningham) **6-9-7** DeanMcKeown(8) (bit bkwd: s.i.s: a bhd: t.o) | 16 | **11** | 20/1 | — | — |

(SP 125.1%) **11 Rn**

**1m 44.4** (5.80) CSF £61.82 CT £564.90 TOTE £4.90: £2.30 £2.90 £4.50 (£53.60) Trio £88.50; £24.93 to Sandown 27/4/96 OWNER Baron G Von Ullmann (NEWMARKET) BRED Tsarina Stud

**OFFICIAL EXPLANATION Bold Amusement: had a heart irregularity.**

**Tertium: the jockey reported that his orders had been to ride the gelding with confidence as the trainer wanted him to settle and was concerned about the soft ground over such a stiff mile. In the race, the horse had done everything right but, when asked to quicken at the furlong marker, he blew up and started to hang left. He therefore only rode him out with hands and heels.**

**554 Mokuti**, having his first outing in handicap company, is clearly not a straightforward ride. His jockey was hard at work some way from home, and he hung left and almost threw it away near the finish. (9/2)

**Percy Braithwaite (IRE)**, with the blinkers left off again, was only edged out in the final strides. (14/1)

**Tertium (IRE)**, having his first outing since changing stables, has been gelded and reportedly hobdayed, and was given a strange ride. His jockey sat motionless most of the way and, only offering token assistance, his mount was running on strongly in a straight line in the final furlong. The impression was that, with a more forceful ride, he would have made it. (10/1)

**Kemo Sabo**, a flop over hurdles, was short of room early in the straight, but dropped out tamely over a furlong out. (14/1)

**589 Night Wink (USA)**, who ran well from a poor draw at Nottingham last time, set the pace but dropped out over a furlong out. (5/1)

**491 It's Academic**, who is reported to be in foal, had to look for an opening once in line for home but, once she did get out, she found nothing and her rider soon gave up. She is probably better over seven. (9/4)

## 803 MERLIN H'CAP (0-75) (3-Y.O) (Class D)

3-50 (3-54) **1m 4f** £3,598.75 (£1,090.00: £532.50: £253.75) Stalls: Low GOING: 0.27 sec per fur (G)

| | Horse | Dist | Pos | SP | RR | SF |
|---|---|---|---|---|---|---|
| 658[2] | **Go-Go-Power-Ranger (55)** (BEllison) **3-8-1** NKennedy(1) (lw: chsd ldrs: led over 2f out: sn hdd: styd on wl to ld nr fin) | — | **1** | 10/1 | 63 | 30 |
| 594* | **Siege Perilous (IRE) (63)** (SCWilliams) **3-8-9** JTate(15) (lw: hld up: hdwy 6f out: led 2f out: hrd rdn & hdd nr fin) | hd | **2** | 3/1[1] | 71 | 38 |
| 614[10] | **Forgie (IRE) (53)** (PCalver) **3-7-10**(3) NVarley(11) (chsd ldrs: outpcd 2f out: styd on wl ins fnl f) | 1½ | **3** | 16/1 | 59 | 26 |
| *484[4]* | **Go With The Wind (63)** (MBell) **3-8-9** MFenton(9) (hdwy 6f out: rdn over 2f out: sn outpcd) | 10 | **4** | 12/1 | 56 | 23 |
| | **State Approval (60)** (APJarvis) **3-8-6** JCarroll(2) (bit bkwd: hdwy 5f out: one pce fnl 3f) | s.h | **5** | 16/1 | 53 | 20 |
| 594[7] | **General Glow (51)** (NBycroft) **3-7-8**(3)ow1 DWright(6) (swtg: bhd tl sme hdwy fnl 2f) | 11 | **6** | 40/1 | 29 | — |
| 614[6] | **Ordained (50)** (EJAlston) **3-7-5**(5) PFessey(4) (s.i.s: sn chsng ldrs: led over 4f out tl over 2f out: sn wknd) | 2½ | **7** | 12/1 | 25 | — |
| 444[5] | **Six Clerks (IRE) (65)** (JGFitzGerald) **3-8-11** KFallon(12) (lw: prom tl wknd 2f out) | nk | **8** | 12/1 | 39 | 6 |
| 597[8] | **Quiet Moments (IRE) (50)** (PGMurphy) **3-7-10** NCarlisle(14) (b.hind: bhd tl sme late hdwy) | 3½ | **9** | 33/1 | 19 | — |
| 702[2] | **Jackson Park (64)** (TDEasterby) **3-8-10** MBirch(3) (chsd ldrs: effrt over 3f out: sn lost pl) | 6 | **10** | 5/1[3] | 25 | — |
| 542[4] | **Thorntoun Estate (IRE) (57)** (MJohnston) **3-8-3b**[1] DeanMcKeown(13) (led tl over 4f out: sn wknd) | 9 | **11** | 10/1 | 6 | — |
| 614[9] | **Marsayas (IRE) (55)** (MJCamacho) **3-8-1** LCharnock(5) (bhd & rdn 6f out) | 5 | **12** | 14/1 | — | — |
| | **Daira (58)** (JDBethell) **3-8-4** PRobinson(8) (bit bkwd: hld up: a bhd) | 2½ | **13** | 20/1 | — | — |
| 658[4] | **Panama Jive (IRE) (52)** (MJohnston) **3-7-12** TWilliams(7) (swtg: unruly s: chsd ldrs tl lost pl 6f out) | 7 | **14** | 20/1 | — | — |
| 614* | **Muhtadi (IRE) (75)** (JLDunlop) **3-9-7** KDarley(10) (b: lw: mid div & rdn 8f out: hmpd & lost pl 6f out: no ch after) | ½ | **15** | 7/2[2] | 4 | — |

(SP 138.5%) **15 Rn**

**2m 42.7** (11.70) CSF £42.94 CT £478.19 TOTE £12.70: £2.90 £2.10 £5.70 (£34.20) Trio £236.20; £33.28 to Sandown 27/4/96 OWNER Mr Fred Hayne (LANCHESTER) BRED Leslie R. Smith

LONG HANDICAP General Glow 7-9 Ordained 7-6 Quiet Moments (IRE) 7-6

**658 Go-Go-Power-Ranger** battled back strongly to regain the advantage on the line. (10/1)

**594* Siege Perilous (IRE)**, from a 5lb higher mark, was worried out of it in the closing stages. (3/1: op 9/2)
**Forgie (IRE)** was staying on strongly when it was all over, and will be suited by a stiffer test. (16/1)
**Go With The Wind**, having his first outing in handicap company, was given a patient ride but, after getting onto the heels of the leaders turning in, was soon left behind. (12/1)
**614* Muhtadi (IRE)**, 5lb higher, was soon flat out and still had a lot of work to do when he was hampered and carried towards the rear at halfway. (7/2)

## 804 SPARROW HAWK MAIDEN STKS (3-Y.O) (Class D)

4-20 (4-24) **1m 4f** £3,533.75 (£1,070.00: £522.50: £248.75) Stalls: Low GOING: 0.27 sec per fur (G)

| Form | Horse | Dist | Pos | SP | RR | SF |
|---|---|---|---|---|---|---|
| | **Lallans (IRE)** (MJohnston) **3-9-0** JWeaver(3) (gd sort: scope: dwlt: hld up: smooth hdwy over 4f out: shkn up to ld 2f out: sn pushed wl clr) | — | 1 | 4/1[2] | 86+ | 48 |
| 576[2] | **Migwar (85)** (LMCumani) **3-9-0** KDarley(1) (trckd ldrs: led over 3f out to 2f out: no ch w wnr) | 15 | 2 | 1/2[1] | 66 | 28 |
| 560[2] | **Anna Soleil (IRE)** (MRChannon) **3-9-0** JFortune(4) (lw: led tl over 3f out: one pce) | 2½ | 3 | 11/2[3] | 63 | 25 |
| | **Classic Colleen (IRE)** (SCWilliams) **3-8-9** AMackay(8) (w'like: scope: bit bkwd: s.i.s: drvn & hung lft 8f out: sn chsng ldrs: hung lft & outpcd fnl 2f) | ¾ | 4 | 8/1 | 57 | 19 |
| | **Respecting** (DenysSmith) **3-9-0** KFallon(5) (lengthy: s.i.s: hld up: sme hdwy 6f out: sn lost pl) | 27 | 5 | 25/1 | 26 | — |
| *651[3]* | **Nordic Hero (IRE)** (APJarvis) **3-9-0** JTate(6) (prom early: bhd fnl 6f) | 13 | 6 | 33/1 | 8 | — |
| 584[11] | **Troika (IRE)** (JBerry) **3-8-9** JCarroll(2) (prom tl rdn & wknd over 4f out: sn bhd) | 5 | 7 | 33/1 | — | — |
| | ***Gildoran Sound*** (TDEasterby) **3-8-9** MBirch(7) (Withdrawn not under Starter's orders: failed to rch s) | | W | 25/1 | — | — |

(SP 126.7%) **7 Rn**

**2m 41.8** (10.80) CSF £6.83 TOTE £4.50: £2.10 £1.50 (£2.60) OWNER Sheikh Mohammed (MIDDLEHAM) BRED Sheikh Mohammed Bin Rashid Al Maktoum
**Lallans (IRE)**, a quality colt, took this in runaway style after travelling easily some way from home. He looks a real stayer and will be suited by a step up to a mile and six. (4/1: 3/1-9/2)
**576 Migwar**, very coltish beforehand, carries plenty of condition. He took it up on the bridle but, when the winner played his card, there was no doubting who was going to be second best. (1/2)
**560 Anna Soleil (IRE)** made the running but proved woefully one-paced. (11/2)
**Classic Colleen (IRE)** had trouble handling the bends. Hanging badly left, she was left behind in the final quarter-mile. (8/1)

## 805 KESTREL CLAIMING STKS (II) (4-Y.O+) (Class F)

4-55 (4-56) **6f 206y** £2,283.00 (£638.00: £309.00) Stalls: High GOING: 0.27 sec per fur (G)

| Form | Horse | Dist | Pos | SP | RR | SF |
|---|---|---|---|---|---|---|
| 610[16] | **Palacegate Touch (75)** (JBerry) **6-9-1b** JCarroll(4) (lw: mde all: clr ½-wy: edgd bdly lft over 1f out: unchal) | — | 1 | 9/4[2] | 71 | 46 |
| *518[9]* | **Thwaab (44)** (FWatson) **4-8-9** MFenton(7) (sn rdn: hdwy ½-wy: styd on fnl 2f: no ch w wnr) | 6 | 2 | 10/1 | 51 | 26 |
| *427[4]* | **At the Savoy (IRE) (42)** (MrsLStubbs) **5-8-9b** JFortune(3) (chsd ldrs: rdn ½-wy: one pce) | 6 | 3 | 6/1[3] | 37 | 12 |
| 700[9] | **Ohnonotagain (33)** (BWMurray) **4-8-0** TWilliams(1) (chsd wnr: rdn ½-wy: wknd over 1f out) | 3 | 4 | 25/1 | 21 | — |
| 537[2] | **Heathyards Magic (IRE) (60)** (MDods) **4-8-9b[1]** KDarley(2) (lw: s.i.s: hdwy over 4f out: rdn & edgd rt over 2f out: no imp) | 2½ | 5 | 6/4[1] | 25 | — |
| 691[8] | **Kashana (IRE)** (WStorey) **4-8-6** JFanning(6) (sn bhd & rdn along) | ¾ | 6 | 10/1 | 20 | — |
| 479[10] | **Brambles Way (33)** (WLBarker) **7-8-3v** LCharnock(5) (chsd ldrs: rdn ½-wy: wknd over 2f out) | 1 | 7 | 16/1 | 15 | — |
| 713[15] | **Tee Tee Too (IRE) (50)** (AHarrison) **4-9-7** AMackay(8) (a outpcd & bhd) | 2 | 8 | 14/1 | 28 | 3 |

(SP 119.6%) **8 Rn**

**1m 32.1** (6.40) CSF £23.47 TOTE £2.80: £1.70 £4.70 £1.70 (£32.00) OWNER Laurel (Leisure) Ltd (COCKERHAM) BRED The Woodhaven Stud
**Palacegate Touch** could hardly lose this at his best. Showing his rivals a clean pair of heels, he then did his best to throw it away, edging badly left and ending up under the stands'-side rail. (9/4)
**Thwaab** kept on to finish second best but, in truth, there was no second. (10/1)
**At the Savoy (IRE)** was hard at work and getting nowhere at halfway. (6/1)
**Ohnonotagain** faded over a furlong out. (25/1)
**537 Heathyards Magic (IRE)**, tried in blinkers, dived right under pressure and gave his rider no co-operation whatsoever. (6/4: op 9/4)

## 806 PEREGRINE FALCON H'CAP (0-65) (3-Y.O+) (Class F)

5-25 (5-28) **5f 207y** £2,871.00 (£806.00: £393.00) Stalls: High GOING: 0.27 sec per fur (G)

| Form | Horse | Dist | Pos | SP | RR | SF |
|---|---|---|---|---|---|---|
| | **Henry the Hawk (44)** (MDods) **5-8-2**(5)ow1 CTeague(11) (w ldrs: led over 1f out: hld on wl towards fin) | — | 1 | 25/1 | 53 | 24 |
| 617[11] | **Mu-Arrik (42)** (GROldroyd) **8-8-5v** DeanMcKeown(12) (bhd: hdwy on outside 2f out: edgd rt: styd on ins fnl f) | ½ | 2 | 25/1 | 50 | 22 |
| 559[4] | **Sonderise (44)** (NTinkler) **7-8-7** JFortune(10) (a chsng ldrs: rdn & hung lft 2f out: styd on ins fnl f) | ¾ | 3 | 14/1 | 50 | 22 |
| | **Superpride (65)** (MrsMReveley) **4-10-0** KDarley(6) (chsd ldrs: kpt on wl fnl f) | hd | 4 | 16/1 | 70 | 42 |
| *607** | **Foist (45)** (MWEasterby) **4-8-3**(5) GParkin(13) (lw: hld up: effrt & nt clr run over 2f out: styd on fnl f: n.m.r towards fin) | 1 | 5 | 15/8[1] | 48+ | 20 |
| *356[3]* | **Jigsaw Boy (60)** (PGMurphy) **7-9-9** MFenton(16) (lw: hdwy over 2f out: nvr nr to chal) | 2½ | 6 | 10/1 | 56 | 28 |
| 749[3] | **Barato (65)** (MrsJRRamsden) **5-10-0v** KFallon(15) (b.nr hind: lw: hld up: effrt & n.m.r over 1f out: nvr rchd ldrs) | ½ | 7 | 5/1[2] | 60 | 32 |
| *607[5]* | **Bold Aristocrat (IRE) (40)** (RHollinshead) **5-7-12**(5) FLynch(5) (effrt on outside ½-wy: kpt on: nvr nr ldrs) | 2½ | 8 | 12/1 | 28 | — |
| *278[6]* | **Bowcliffe Grange (IRE) (33)** (DWChapman) **4-7-10** NKennedy(1) (trckd ldrs tl grad wknd over 1f out) | 1¼ | 9 | 50/1 | 18 | — |
| 617[14] | **Densben (51)** (DenysSmith) **12-9-0** JWeaver(7) (nvr bttr than mid div) | hd | 10 | 14/1 | 35 | 7 |
| 586[3] | **Langtonian (33)** (JLEyre) **7-7-7b**(3) DWright(9) (chsd ldrs over 3f: sn lost pl) | s.h | 11 | 14/1 | 17 | — |
| 762[4] | **Petraco (IRE) (63)** (NASmith) **8-9-12** SDWilliams(14) (mde most tl over 1f out: sn wknd) | 1 | 12 | 9/1[3] | 44 | 16 |
| 617[8] | **Rinus Manor (IRE) (40)** (EJAlston) **5-8-3** JFanning(17) (w ldrs over 3f: sn wknd) | ¾ | 13 | 20/1 | 19 | — |
| 610[23] | **Rich Glow (59)** (NBycroft) **5-9-8** PRobinson(4) (s.i.s: a in rr) | ¾ | 14 | 12/1 | 36 | 8 |
| 661[8] | **Northern Spark (48)** (MissLAPerratt) **8-8-11** JCarroll(8) (a bhd) | ¾ | 15 | 14/1 | 23 | — |
| 661[13] | **Strathtore Dream (IRE) (33)** (MissLAPerratt) **5-7-5v[1]**(5) PFessey(3) (lw: s.i.s: wl bhd fr ½-wy) | 8 | 16 | 50/1 | — | — |
| | **Ragazzo (IRE) (33)** (JSWainwright) **6-7-10b** LCharnock(2) (bit bkwd: sn outpcd & bhd) | 1¼ | 17 | 50/1 | — | — |

(SP 136.8%) **17 Rn**

**1m 19.0** (6.50) CSF £505.18 CT £8,001.75 TOTE £53.80: £5.60 £5.00 £4.30 £3.50 (£230.50) Trio Not won; £346.08 to Sandown 27/4/96
OWNER Mr S. Barras (DARLINGTON) BRED Mrs Celia Miller
LONG HANDICAP Langtonian 7-5 Bowcliffe Grange (IRE) 7-0 Strathtore Dream (IRE) 7-5 Ragazzo (IRE) 7-9

**Henry the Hawk** raced on the favoured far side and did just enough. (25/1)
**Mu-Arrik**, making his effort on the wide outside, edged right, causing problems for those on his inner. (25/1)
**559 Sonderise** persisted in hanging, but stayed on towards the finish. (14/1)
**Superpride**, a keen-running sort, stuck on strongly in the closing stages, and is possibly better over seven. (16/1)
**607* Foist**, a three times winner on the All-Weather, had no luck at all in running and will possibly be better suited by seven on turf. (15/8)
**749 Barato** was another to have a poor run. (5/1)

T/Plpt: £52.00 (185.66 Tckts). T/Qdpt: £40.60 (9.58 Tckts). WG

# SANDOWN (R-H) (Good, Rnd crse Good to soft fnl 3f)
## Friday April 26th
WEATHER: fine WIND: almost nil

### 807 ALBERT MEDIAN AUCTION MAIDEN STKS (2-Y.O F) (Class D)
2-00 (2-02) **5f 6y** £3,403.75 (£1,030.00: £502.50: £238.75) Stalls: High GOING minus 0.15 sec per fur (GF)

| | | | | SP | RR | SF |
|---|---|---|---|---|---|---|
| | **Sabotini** (BWHills) **2-8-11** PatEddery(4) (str: mde virtually all: rdn out) | — | 1 | 3/1[2] | 61 | 19 |
| 481[2] | **Red Garter (IRE)** (KMcAuliffe) **2-8-11** SSanders(8) (w ldr: ev ch over 1f out: unable qckn) | 1½ | 2 | 10/1 | 56 | 14 |
| 630[2] | **Royal Emblem** (AGFoster) **2-8-4**(7) RWaterfield(3) (b: a.p: rdn over 3f out: 3rd & btn whn n.m.r on ins wl ins fnl) | nk | 3 | 16/1 | 55 | 13 |
| | **Magnolia** (PFICole) **2-8-11** MHills(5) (leggy: lt-f: lw: outpcd: hdwy over 1f out: r.o one pce) | ¾ | 4 | 9/2[3] | 53 | 11 |
| | **Preskidul (IRE)** (DWPArbuthnot) **2-8-11** SWhitworth(2) (b.hind: unf: hld up: rdn over 2f out: one pce) | 2 | 5 | 10/1 | 47 | 5 |
| | **Show Off** (WJarvis) **2-8-11** LDettori(1) (neat: lw: hld up: rdn over 2f out: wknd fnl f) | 3½ | 6 | 13/8[1] | 35 | — |
| | **Loch Dibidale** (JEBanks) **2-8-8**(3) JStack(7) (w'like: bit bkwd: bhd fnl 2f) | 1½ | 7 | 25/1 | 31 | — |
| | **Alimerjam** (JWhite) **2-8-11** KRutter(6) (str: bkwd: s.s: a wl bhd) | 11 | 8 | 50/1 | — | — |

(SP 111.1%) **8 Rn**

**63.66 secs** (3.86) CSF £28.13 TOTE £4.20: £1.40 £1.90 £2.70 (£11.10) OWNER Mrs E. Roberts (LAMBOURN) BRED Mrs E. Roberts
**Sabotini**, who has a lot of strength for a two-year-old filly, was the pick of a moderate-looking bunch by Sandown's standards and was ridden along to assert her superiority from below the distance. (3/1: op 2/1)
**481 Red Garter (IRE)** disputed the lead from the start until put in her place by the winner from below the distance. (10/1: 6/1-12/1)
**630 Royal Emblem** was held in third place when slightly tightened up for room in the closing stages by the runner-up. (16/1)
**Magnolia**, a sparely-made filly with little scope, was certainly fit for this debut but drifted very badly in the market. Unable to go the early pace, she stayed on from below the distance to be nearest at the line. (9/2: 7/4-5/1)
**Preskidul (IRE)**, whose dam is a half-sister to the top-class Double Schwartz, chased the leaders, but failed to find another gear in the last two furlongs. (10/1: 14/1-33/1)
**Show Off** is not very big, but looked in good heart for this debut. Chasing the leaders, she was at the end of her tether entering the final furlong. (13/8)

### 808 TUDOR CONDITIONS STKS (3-Y.O C & G) (Class C)
2-35 (2-36) **1m 14y** £4,878.40 (£1,825.60: £892.80: £384.00: £172.00: £87.20) Stalls: High GOING minus 0.15 sec per fur (GF)

| | | | | SP | RR | SF |
|---|---|---|---|---|---|---|
| 577* | **Regal Archive (IRE)** (PWChapple-Hyam) **3-9-0** JReid(3) (b.hind: lw: hdwy over 2f out: led wl over 1f out: rdn out) | — | 1 | 3/1[2] | 97 | 70 |
| | **Gold Spats (USA)** (MRStoute) **3-8-7** RCochrane(4) (scope: dwlt: hdwy over 1f out: r.o) | 2½ | 2 | 20/1 | 85 | 58 |
| | **Red Robbo (CAN)** (HRACecil) **3-9-0** PatEddery(2) (bit bkwd: chsd ldr: led 3f out tl wl over 1f out: unable qckn) | ½ | 3 | 9/2[3] | 91 | 64 |
| 544* | **Royal Canaska** (DRLoder) **3-9-0** LDettori(6) (lw: a.p: rdn over 2f out: wknd fnl f) | 2½ | 4 | 5/1 | 86 | 59 |
| | **Censor (83)** (HRACecil) **3-9-0** WRyan(1) (lw: a.p: rdn over 2f out: wknd fnl f) | 1¼ | 5 | 12/1 | 84 | 57 |
| | **Al Abraq (IRE)** (JWHills) **3-8-10** RHills(7) (hld up: n.m.r on ins over 2f out: wknd over 1f out) | 4 | 6 | 9/4[1] | 72 | 45 |
| | **Gold Disc (USA)** (BWHills) **3-9-0** MHills(5) (led 5f: wkng whn n.m.r on ins over 1f out) | 3 | 7 | 14/1 | 70 | 43 |

(SP 109.7%) **7 Rn**

**1m 42.85** (1.65) CSF £43.27 TOTE £3.70: £1.90 £6.80 (£41.70) OWNER Mrs B. V. Sangster (MARLBOROUGH) BRED Studcrown Ltd
**577* Regal Archive (IRE)** is looking a very useful individual. Moving up on the outside of the field to lead early in the final quarter-mile, he was ridden along to assert his authority and win in a time 0.80 seconds faster than the very competitive handicap half an hour later. This race is often won by a very decent performer - Spectrum and Kahyasi are past winners - and this year's renewal looked an extremely hot contest. The Irish 2000 Guineas now looks on the cards and, however he gets on there, some decent races will be won with him this year. (3/1)
**Gold Spats (USA)**, an angular-looking colt, was the least developed in this high-quality field. However, had he been making his debut at a lesser track, one would have been taken by him. Only getting the hang of things from below the distance, he stayed on well to snatch second place near home. He should have no difficulty in finding a race. (20/1)
**Red Robbo (CAN)** looked the most backward of the field, but still showed a lot of promise for the months ahead. Moving to the front three furlongs from home, he was collared early in the final quarter-mile and was worried out of second place near the line. He should have no problems in opening his account for the season, but probably wants a sound surface, as he flopped on easy ground last year. (9/2: op 2/1)
**544* Royal Canaska** looked extremely well in the paddock. Always close up, he did not have a great deal of room over a quarter of a mile from home, but it made no difference to his chances, and he had run out of gas inside the last 200 yards. (5/1: 7/2-6/1)
**Censor** looked in good shape for this reappearance. Never far away, he had given his all entering the final furlong. (12/1: op 6/1)
**Al Abraq (IRE)** chased the leaders. With not a great deal of room in which to manoeuvre against the inside rail in the straight, he had come to the end of his tether below the distance. (9/4: op 7/2)
**Gold Disc (USA)** (14/1: 7/1-16/1)

### 809 ATHLONE RATED STKS H'CAP (0-95) (4-Y.O+) (Class C)
3-05 (3-12) **1m 14y** £8,073.92 (£3,025.28: £1,482.64: £641.20: £290.60: £150.36) Stalls: High GOING minus 0.15 sec per fur (GF)

| | | | | SP | RR | SF |
|---|---|---|---|---|---|---|
| | **Star Manager (USA) (81)** (PFICole) **6-8-7** MHills(9) (swtg: hdwy over 1f out: str run fnl f: led nr fin) | — | 1 | 10/1[2] | 95 | 55 |
| | **Almond Rock (84)** (JRFanshawe) **4-8-10** DHarrison(6) (hdwy over 2f out: hrd rdn over 1f out: led ins fnl f: hdd nr fin) | ½ | 2 | 5/1[1] | 97 | 57 |
| | **Moments of Fortune (USA) (95)** (BHanbury) **4-9-4b**(3) JStack(1) (a.p: led over 2f out tl ins fnl f: one pce) | ½ | 3 | 33/1 | 107 | 67 |
| | **Desert Green (FR) (95)** (RHannon) **7-9-2**(5) DaneO'Neill(10) (hdwy 1f out: r.o wl ins fnl f) | 3 | 4 | 12/1 | 101 | 61 |

| | | | | SP | RR | SF |
|---|---|---|---|---|---|---|
| 600[2] | **Pengamon (83)** (HJCollingridge) **4-8-9** JQuinn(7) (hdwy over 2f out: hrd rdn over 1f out: one pce) | 1¼ | **5** | 10/1[2] | 87 | 47 |
| | **Donna Viola (88)** (CFWall) **4-9-0** JReid(2) (lw: hdwy over 2f out: hrd rdn over 1f out: one pce) | 1 | **6** | 10/1[2] | 90 | 50 |
| 455[21] | **Pearl Venture (85)** (SPCWoods) **4-8-11** WWoods(8) (a.p: ev ch over 2f out: wknd 1f out) | 1¼ | **7** | 20/1 | 84 | 44 |
| 324a[5] | **Confronter (81)** (SDow) **7-8-7** GDuffield(14) (lw: prom over 5f) | nk | **8** | 14/1 | 80 | 40 |
| 450[W] | **Sotoboy (IRE) (81)** (PWHarris) **4-8-7** RHills(13) (nvr nrr) | 1¾ | **9** | 14/1 | 76 | 36 |
| | **Blaze of Song (82)** (RHannon) **4-8-8** PatEddery(11) (b.off fore: bit bkwd: led over 5f: wknd over 1f out) | 1½ | **10** | 11/1[3] | 74 | 34 |
| | **Il Trastevere (FR) (85)** (MissGayKelleway) **4-8-11** RCochrane(4) (swtg: a mid div) | nk | **11** | 20/1 | 77 | 37 |
| | **Saifan (81)** (DMorris) **7-8-7** CHodgson(5) (s.s: nvr nrr) | hd | **12** | 40/1 | 72 | 32 |
| 728[17] | **Akil (IRE) (90)** (RWArmstrong) **4-9-2** WCarson(15) (hdwy over 1f out: eased whn btn fnl f) | ¾ | **13** | 10/1[2] | 80 | 40 |
| | **Above the Cut (USA) (88)** (PWHarris) **4-9-0** GHind(3) (prom over 5f) | 1¼ | **14** | 14/1 | 75 | 35 |
| | **Sejaal (IRE) (81)** (RAkehurst) **4-8-0**(7) TAshley(12) (lw: bhd fnl 2f) | ¾ | **15** | 10/1[2] | 67 | 27 |
| | **Elite Hope (USA) (81)** (CREgerton) **4-8-2**(5) ADaly(18) (bit bkwd: hdwy & n.m.r on ins over 1f out: eased whn btn ins fnl f) | 1½ | **16** | 25/1 | 64 | 24 |
| | **Ron's Secret (84)** (JWPayne) **4-8-10** LDettori(16) (bit bkwd: hld up: rdn over 3f out: wknd over 1f out) | nk | **17** | 11/1[3] | 66 | 26 |
| *263*[3] | **Easy Choice (USA) (81)** (PhilipMitchell) **4-8-7** AClark(17) (lw: a bhd) | 8 | **18** | 33/1 | 47 | 7 |
| | | | | (SP 128.2%) | **18 Rn** | |

**1m 43.65** (2.45) CSF £57.08 CT £1,544.85 TOTE £9.80: £2.30 £1.90 £9.30 £2.30 (£17.50) Trio £175.10 OWNER Mr M. Arbib (WHATCOMBE) BRED Hickory Tree Farm

LONG HANDICAP Saifan 8-0 Star Manager (USA) 8-4 Sotoboy (IRE) 8-6 Sejaal (IRE) 8-4 Elite Hope (USA) 8-6 Confronter 8-6 Easy Choice (USA) 8-1

**Star Manager (USA)**, out with the washing a quarter of a mile from home, came with a tremendous run from below the distance to swoop into the lead near the line. He has never scored more than once a year and is sure to be raised quite a bit for this as he was racing from 3lb out of the handicap, so he looks one to pass over in the future. (10/1)

**Almond Rock** made a very pleasing return and a handicap should soon come his way. (5/1)

**Moments of Fortune (USA)** failed to find another gear when headed inside the final furlong. (33/1)

**Desert Green (FR)**, with apparently no chance at the back of the field below the distance, really found his feet in the final furlong and came storming through to take fourth prize. This was a good eyecatching performance - he was racing off a mark of 95 here and has never won off more than 85. (12/1)

**600 Pengamon** failed to find another gear from below the distance. (10/1: 8/1-12/1)

**Donna Viola** made headway over a quarter of a mile out, but could make no further impression from below the distance. (10/1)

**Blaze of Song** (11/1: 8/1-12/1)

**Akil (IRE)** caught the eye under considerate handling. Noted making headway through the pack below the distance, his rider then put the brakes on inside the final furlong and allowed the colt to come home at his leisure. A winner of three races last season, it would be no surprise to see him pop up at a decent price. (10/1)

**Above the Cut (USA)** (14/1: 10/1-16/1)

**Sejaal (IRE)** (10/1: 7/1-12/1)

**Ron's Secret** (11/1: 8/1-12/1)

## 810 SANDOWN MILE STKS (Gp 2) (4-Y.O+) (Class A)

3-40 (3-44) **1m 14y** £36,605.00 (£13,646.50: £6,510.75: £2,787.75) Stalls: High GOING minus 0.15 sec per fur (GF)

| | | | | SP | RR | SF |
|---|---|---|---|---|---|---|
| 680[4] | **Gabr** (RWArmstrong) **6-9-0** WCarson(2) (a.p: led over 1f out: all out) | — | **1** | 13/2 | 121 | 85 |
| 673[7] | **Soviet Line (IRE) (120)** (MRStoute) **6-9-6** PatEddery(8) (lw: gd hdwy over 1f out: hrd rdn & swtchd rt ins fnl f: fin wl) | s.h | **2** | 6/1[3] | 127 | 91 |
| | **Mistle Cat (USA) (111)** (SPCWoods) **6-9-0** WWoods(11) (bit bkwd: led over 6f: unable qckn ins fnl f) | ½ | **3** | 16/1 | 120 | 84 |
| 442[3] | **Nwaamis (USA) (114)** (JLDunlop) **4-9-0** RHills(5) (hdwy over 2f out: hrd rdn over 1f out: r.o) | ¾ | **4** | 10/1 | 118 | 82 |
| 680[3] | **First Island (IRE) (107)** (GWragg) **4-9-0** MHills(1) (hdwy 2f out: hrd rdn over 1f out: one pce) | 1¾ | **5** | 11/2[2] | 115 | 79 |
| | **Myself (111)** (PWChapple-Hyam) **4-8-11** JReid(3) (lw: hdwy over 2f out: hrd rdn over 1f out: wknd fnl f) | 2½ | **6** | 9/2[1] | 107 | 71 |
| | **Lap of Luxury (107)** (WJarvis) **7-8-11** BThomson(12) (nvr nr to chal) | 6 | **7** | 33/1 | 95 | 59 |
| 455[20] | **Autumn Affair (96)** (CEBrittain) **4-8-11** WRyan(6) (nvr nrr) | ½ | **8** | 40/1 | 94 | 58 |
| | **Bishop of Cashel (112)** (JRFanshawe) **4-9-0** DHarrison(10) (bit bkwd: hdwy 2f out: wknd over 1f out) | ½ | **9** | 7/1 | 96 | 60 |
| | **Nijo (109)** (DRLoder) **5-9-0** RHughes(4) (lw: chsd ldr 6f) | 4 | **10** | 9/1 | 88 | 52 |
| | **Inzar (USA) (112)** (PFICole) **4-9-0** RCochrane(9) (prom over 6f) | 1½ | **11** | 9/1 | 85 | 49 |
| 600[3] | **Decorated Hero (105)** (JHMGosden) **4-9-0** LDettori(7) (hdwy over 2f out: eased whn btn over 1f out) | 28 | **12** | 20/1 | 30 | — |
| | | | | (SP 118.8%) | **12 Rn** | |

**1m 41.34** (0.14) CSF £42.21 TOTE £7.80: £3.20 £2.30 £2.50 (£19.30) Trio £180.90 OWNER Mr Hamdan Al Maktoum (NEWMARKET) BRED Shadwell Estate Company Limited

**680 Gabr** put up a tremendous performance in by far the fastest time of the three races run over a mile. The Lockinge at Newbury is next on the agenda. (13/2)

**673 Soviet Line (IRE)**, unsuited by the sharp six furlongs last time, was back over a more suitable trip and ran a tremendous race under a 6lb penalty for his Group One success last year. Having to weave his way through the pack in the final quarter-mile, he stormed up the hill and would surely have prevailed in another couple of strides. (6/1)

**Mistle Cat (USA)** went off like a scalded cat and set a tremendous pace. He looked sure to fold up quickly when caught below the distance but, to his credit, was only shaken off inside the final furlong. This was a tremendous performance, especially considering that he looked as though he would come on for this, and a first Group success will surely not be long in coming. (16/1)

**442 Nwaamis (USA)** stayed on well under pressure from below the distance. (10/1)

**680 First Island (IRE)** made his effort on the outside a quarter of a mile from home, but then failed to find the necessary turn of foot. (11/2)

**Myself** looked extremely well beforehand, but failed to last home over this stiff mile. Back over seven furlongs, she should be able to open her account for the season. (9/2)

## 811 GUILDFORD H'CAP (0-85) (4-Y.O+) (Class D)

4-10 (4-12) **2m 78y** £4,240.50 (£1,284.00: £627.00: £298.50) Stalls: High GOING minus 0.15 sec per fur (GF)

| | | | | SP | RR | SF |
|---|---|---|---|---|---|---|
| | **Darter (IRE) (67)** (RAkehurst) **4-8-7** SSanders(7) (lw: hdwy over 3f out: led 2f out: rdn & r.o wl) | — | **1** | 9/2[2] | 85 | 51 |
| | **Rocky Forum (56)** (GLMoore) **4-7-10** JQuinn(5) (b: bit bkwd: hdwy over 2f out: hrd rdn over 1f out: r.o one pce) | 5 | **2** | 16/1 | 69 | 35 |
| 682[2] | **Speed to Lead (IRE) (76)** (HRACecil) **4-9-2** PatEddery(14) (led over 13f out to 2f out: one pce) | ½ | **3** | 2/1[1] | 89 | 55 |
| | **Barford Sovereign (67)** (JRFanshawe) **4-8-7** DHarrison(4) (swtg: hdwy over 2f out: hrd rdn over 1f out: one pce) | 2½ | **4** | 8/1[3] | 77 | 43 |

| Form | Horse | Dist | Pos | SP | RR | SF |
|---|---|---|---|---|---|---|
| 666$^{2}$ | **Hattaafeh (IRE) (52)** (MissBSanders) **5-7-10** GBardwell(6) (lw: lost pl 4f out: one pce fnl 2f) | 3 | **5** | 9/1 | 59 | 29 |
| | **Erzadjan (IRE) (84)** (MrsMReveley) **6-10-0** ACulhane(8) (nvr nr to chal) | 3½ | **6** | 8/1$^{3}$ | 88 | 58 |
| 666* | **Toy Princess (USA) (73)** (CEBrittain) **4-8-8**$^{(5)}$ $^{4x}$ MHenry(10) (lw: a.p: chsd ldr over 4f out tl over 2f out: wknd over 1f out) | ¾ | **7** | 9/1 | 76 | 42 |
| | **Paradise Navy (68)** (CREgerton) **7-8-12** RHughes(3) (nvr nrr) | 5 | **8** | 12/1 | 66 | 36 |
| *656*$^{5}$ | **Call My Guest (IRE) (60)** (REPeacock) **6-8-4** WCarson(9) (led 3f: wknd over 4f out) | nk | **9** | 20/1 | 58 | 28 |
| 712$^{7}$ | **Cypress Avenue (IRE) (79)** (RHannon) **4-9-5b$^{1}$** RPerham(13) (a bhd) | 3½ | **10** | 33/1 | 74 | 40 |
| 642$^{8}$ | **Reaganesque (USA) (56)** (PGMurphy) **4-7-10** FNorton(2) (hld up: rdn over 3f out: wknd over 2f out) | ¾ | **11** | 33/1 | 50 | 16 |
| 449$^{15}$ | **Gentleman Sid (52)** (PGMurphy) **6-7-10** NAdams(1) (lw: prom 13f) | ¾ | **12** | 33/1 | 45 | 15 |
| *422*$^{11}$ | **Lear Dancer (USA) (67)** (PhilipMitchell) **5-8-11b** AClark(11) (hdwy 4f out: wknd over 2f out) | 1½ | **13** | 14/1 | 59 | 29 |

(SP 127.6%) **13 Rn**

**3m 38.1** (6.10) CSF £70.84 CT £174.07 TOTE £5.90: £2.30 £4.50 £1.50 (£30.60) Trio £101.70 OWNER Mr A. D. Spence (EPSOM) BRED Sheikh Mohammed bin Rashid al Maktoum

LONG HANDICAP Rocky Forum 7-9 Reaganesque (USA) 7-9 Gentleman Sid 7-8

WEIGHT FOR AGE 4yo-4lb

OFFICIAL EXPLANATION **Paradise Navy: the jockey stated that the gelding was hampered, and gurgled at the two-furlong pole. The trainer added that the horse was inconsistent and needed to be ridden from the rear.**

**Darter (IRE)**, a very useful juvenile hurdler this winter when winning three times, looked in fine shape and put up a useful performance as he got off the mark on the Flat. Hitting the front a quarter of a mile out, he was ridden along to pull clear. (9/2: 5/2-5/1)

**Rocky Forum**, looking as though this reappearance was needed, struggled on under pressure to snatch second place in the closing stages. (16/1)

**682 Speed to Lead (IRE)** was collared a quarter of a mile from home and then could only keep on in her own time. (2/1)

**Barford Sovereign**, a winner of two race over hurdles this winter, moved up over a quarter of a mile from home, but failed to find another gear under pressure from below the distance. (8/1)

**666 Hattaafeh (IRE)**, rather outpaced turning for home, plodded on up the hill in the last two furlongs. (9/1)

**Erzadjan (IRE)**, winner of four races over hurdles this spring, made a little late headway without posing a threat. (8/1)

**Paradise Navy** was given a very quiet ride at the back of the field which did not go unnoticed by the Stewards. However, he is not easy to win with. (12/1)

## 812 SURREY RACING H'CAP (0-90) (3-Y.O+) (Class C)

4-45 (4-47) **5f 6y** £5,784.00 (£1,752.00: £856.00: £408.00) Stalls: High GOING minus 0.15 sec per fur (GF)

| Form | Horse | Dist | Pos | SP | RR | SF |
|---|---|---|---|---|---|---|
| 582$^{4}$ | **Mister Jolson (70)** (RJHodges) **7-8-8** RCochrane(18) (b.nr fore: lw: hdwy 2f out: led 1f out: pushed out) | — | **1** | 100/30$^{1}$ | 79 | 55 |
| 582$^{11}$ | **Sir Joey (USA) (77)** (PGMurphy) **7-8-12**$^{(3)}$ SDrowne(17) (hld up: rdn over 1f out: r.o one pce) | 2 | **2** | 8/1$^{2}$ | 80 | 56 |
| | **Glorious Aragon (80)** (RFJohnsonHoughton) **4-9-4** ACulhane(1) (swtg: rdn & hdwy over 1f out: r.o) | s.h | **3** | 33/1 | 83++ | 59 |
| | **Master of Passion (85)** (JMPEustace) **7-9-9** MTebbutt(15) (bit bkwd: led 3f out tl over 1f out: one pce fnl f) | ½ | **4** | 8/1$^{2}$ | 86 | 62 |
| | **Gone Savage (60)** (WJMusson) **8-7-12** FNorton(13) (bkwd: a.p: led over 1f out: sn hdd: one pce) | s.h | **5** | 9/1$^{3}$ | 61 | 37 |
| | **Rock Symphony (87)** (WJHaggas) **6-9-4**$^{(7)}$ ElizabethTurner(14) (s.s: hdwy over 1f out: nvr nrr) | 1¼ | **6** | 25/1 | 84 | 60 |
| 692* | **Galine (76)** (WAO'Gorman) **3-8-4** $^{6x}$ SSanders(16) (a.p: rdn over 2f out: wknd fnl f) | ¾ | **7** | 100/30$^{1}$ | 70 | 36 |
| 601$^{14}$ | **Followmegirls (58)** (MrsALMKing) **7-7-10** JQuinn(11) (s.s: nvr nr to chal) | 1¾ | **8** | 33/1 | 47 | 23 |
| 749$^{16}$ | **Our Shadee (USA) (58)** (KTIvory) **6-7-10v** NAdams(10) (lw: prom over 3f) | nk | **9** | 33/1 | 46 | 22 |
| 577$^{17}$ | **Multan (61)** (GLMoore) **4-7-13**$^{ow1}$ WCarson(8) (b: nvr nrr) | 1 | **10** | 33/1 | 46 | 21 |
| 582$^{12}$ | **Tinker Osmaston (71)** (MSSaunders) **5-8-9** JFEgan(5) (lw: bhd fnl 2f) | ½ | **11** | 20/1 | 54 | 30 |
| 711$^{7}$ | **Lennox Lewis (90)** (APJarvis) **4-9-7**$^{(7)}$ KHopkins(12) (prom over 3f) | ¾ | **12** | 20/1 | 71 | 47 |
| 582$^{18}$ | **Sally Slade (77)** (CACyzer) **4-9-1** JReid(2) (a bhd) | s.h | **13** | 33/1 | 58 | 34 |
| 632$^{7}$ | **Tart and a Half (77)** (BJMeehan) **4-8-8**$^{(7)}$ GHannon(3) (lw: a bhd) | nk | **14** | 33/1 | 57 | 33 |
| | **Twice as Sharp (84)** (PWHarris) **4-9-8** GHind(6) (prom over 3f) | nk | **15** | 12/1 | 63 | 39 |
| | **Ashtina (72)** (BAPearce) **11-8-10** PatEddery(7) (led 2f: wknd over 2f out) | 2 | **16** | 20/1 | 44 | 20 |
| 632$^{9}$ | **Halbert (65)** (PBurgoyne) **7-8-0v**$^{(3)}$ DRMcCabe(4) (bhd fnl 2f) | hd | **17** | 33/1 | 37 | 13 |

(SP 124.8%) **17 Rn**

**61.3 secs** (1.50) CSF £26.82 CT £682.40 TOTE £3.90: £1.40 £2.50 £5.10 £2.80 (£7.60) Trio £399.60 OWNER Mr Bob Froome (SOMERTON) BRED Mrs D. D. Scott

LONG HANDICAP Our Shadee (USA) 7-2 Followmegirls 7-2

WEIGHT FOR AGE 3yo-10lb

**582 Mister Jolson** had the plum draw here and took full advantage. Beginning his effort a quarter of a mile from home, he swooped into the lead a furlong out and needed only to be nudged along for a decisive victory. (100/30)

**Sir Joey (USA)** chased the leaders and stayed on up the hill to snatch second prize. (8/1)

**Glorious Aragon** ran a tremendous race from her poor draw. Picking up ground from below the distance, she kept on really well up the hill, and only just failed to take second prize. She should be followed. (33/1)

**Master of Passion**, with something left to work on, hit the front three furlongs from home but, headed below the distance, failed to summon up another gear. (8/1: 6/1-9/1)

**Gone Savage**, with plenty left to work on, had just poked a nostril in front below the distance when passed by the winner and tapped for toe. (9/1)

**Rock Symphony**, who lost ground at the start, stayed on in the last furlong and a half without ever looking likely to get to the principals in time. (25/1)

**Twice as Sharp** (12/1: 8/1-14/1)

## 813 APRIL MAIDEN STKS (3-Y.O F) (Class D)

5-20 (5-23) **1m 2f 7y** £4,032.50 (£1,220.00: £595.00: £282.50) Stalls: High GOING minus 0.15 sec per fur (GF)

| Form | Horse | Dist | Pos | SP | RR | SF |
|---|---|---|---|---|---|---|
| | **Quota** (HRACecil) **3-8-7** PatEddery(5) (unf: scope: hld up: rdn over 2f out: led over 1f out: r.o wl) | — | **1** | 11/8$^{1}$ | 96+ | 56 |
| | **Alessandra (92)** (BWHills) **3-8-11** RHughes(4) (hdwy over 2f out: hrd rdn over 1f out: r.o) | 3½ | **2** | 10/1 | 94 | 54 |
| | **Ninotchka (USA)** (JLDunlop) **3-8-11** WCarson(12) (a.p: led over 2f out tl over 1f out: unable qckn) | ¾ | **3** | 8/1$^{3}$ | 93 | 53 |
| | **Flame Valley (USA)** (MRStoute) **3-8-11** RHills(6) (lw: a.p: ev ch over 1f out: one pce) | nk | **4** | 20/1 | 93 | 53 |
| | **Unalloyed (USA)** (DRLoder) **3-8-7** LDettori(11) (leggy: unf: led over 7f: wknd 1f out) | 3 | **5** | 5/1$^{2}$ | 84 | 44 |
| | **Lothlorien (USA)** (PWChapple-Hyam) **3-8-11** JReid(3) (lw: prom over 7f) | 1¼ | **6** | 8/1$^{3}$ | 86 | 46 |
| | **Forest Heights** (MrsJCecil) **3-8-7** BThomson(13) (w'like: scope: prom over 7f) | hd | **7** | 25/1 | 82 | 42 |
| | **Annecy (USA)** (HRACecil) **3-8-11** WRyan(2) (nvr nr to chal) | 1¾ | **8** | 20/1 | 83 | 43 |
| | **Antiguan Jane** (RWArmstrong) **3-8-11** RPrice(9) (bit bkwd: prom over 6f) | 3½ | **9** | 66/1 | 77 | 37 |
| 576$^{5}$ | **Stately Dancer (70)** (GWragg) **3-8-11** MHills(14) (lw: bhd fnl 2f) | 1 | **10** | 10/1 | 76 | 36 |

| | Horse | Dist | Pos | SP | RR | SF |
|---|---|---|---|---|---|---|
| | **Reiterate** (GBBalding) **3-8-8**(3) SDrowne(8) (a bhd) | 5 | **11** | 66/1 | 68 | 28 |
| | **Amber Ring** (MRChannon) **3-8-7** CandyMorris(7) (neat: bhd fnl 3f) | 2 | **12** | 66/1 | 61 | 21 |
| | **Nawaji (USA)** (WRMuir) **3-8-7** RCochrane(1) (str: bit bkwd: dwlt: a bhd) | 3 | **13** | 33/1 | 56 | 16 |
| 550[10] | **Mimosa (72)** (SDow) **3-8-11** GDuffield(10) (bhd fnl 4f) | 10 | **14** | 66/1 | 44 | 4 |

(SP 121.5%) **14 Rn**

**2m 9.72** (3.02) CSF £15.37 TOTE £2.10: £1.20 £2.90 £2.30 (£6.70) Trio £36.30 OWNER Mr K. Abdulla (NEWMARKET) BRED Juddmonte Farms

**Quota**, well regarded at home, has not yet fully developed but certainly has plenty of scope. Chasing the leaders, she was woken up in the straight and, hitting the front below the distance, soon asserted. She will have learnt a lot from this, and can go on from here. Entered in all the big races, she is now as low as 14/1 for the Oaks, and may now go for either the Musidora or Middleton Stakes at York. (11/8)

**Alessandra** took closer order over a quarter of a mile from home, and kept on well for second prize without having a hope with the winner. (10/1: 5/1-11/1)

**Ninotchka (USA)**, sent to the front over a quarter of a mile out, was headed below the distance and failed to find another gear. (8/1: op 12/1)

**Flame Valley (USA)** delivered her challenge in the straight, and still had every chance below the distance before being left standing by the winner. (20/1)

**Unalloyed (USA)**, a tall, unfurnished filly, took the field along. Collared over a quarter of a mile out, she held on until tiring entering the final furlong. (5/1: 5/2-6/1)

**Lothlorien (USA)** played an active role until calling it a day over two furlongs from home. (8/1: 5/1-10/1)

**Annecy (USA)** caught the eye under considerate handling. Noted making headway below the distance, she stayed on without ever looking likely to threaten the principals, and the kindness will no doubt be repaid in due course. (20/1)

**576 Stately Dancer** (10/1: 7/1-11/1)

T/Jkpt: £7,100.00 (0.09 Tckts); £4,430.04 to Sandown 27/4/96. T/Plpt: £189.90 (145.59 Tckts). T/Qdpt: £14.40 (177.16 Tckts). AK

# 0544-LEICESTER (R-H) (Good)

## Saturday April 27th

WEATHER: fine WIND: almost nil

## 814 TOTE PLACEPOT H'CAP (0-85) (3-Y.O+) (Class D)

2-00 (2-01) **5f 218y** £4,225.35 (£1,264.80: £606.90: £277.95) Stalls: High GOING minus 0.31 sec per fur (GF)

| | Horse | Dist | Pos | SP | RR | SF |
|---|---|---|---|---|---|---|
| 610[7] | **So Intrepid (IRE) (68)** (JMBradley) **6-8-8**(3) SDrowne(15) (lw: trckd ldrs: rdn & r.o to ld nr fin) | — | **1** | 16/1 | 78 | 43 |
| 610[2] | **To the Roof (IRE) (75)** (PWHarris) **4-9-4** GHind(2) (lw: plld hrd: hdwy 3f out: led ins fnl f: ct cl home) | nk | **2** | 6/1[2] | 84 | 49 |
| 601* | **Canovas Heart (65)** (BobJones) **7-8-3**(5) ADaly(6) (mde most tl hdd & no ex ins fnl f) | 1½ | **3** | 9/1 | 70 | 35 |
| 592* | **Double Splendour (IRE) (81)** (PSFelgate) **6-9-10** GDuffield(12) (lw: hld up in tch: swtchd lft & effrt 2f out: kpt on u.p fnl f) | ½ | **4** | 7/4[1] | 85 | 50 |
| 610[11] | **I'm Your Lady (66)** (BAMcMahon) **5-8-4**(5) LNewton(5) (bit bkwd: hdwy 2f out: rdn & one pce appr fnl f) | 1¾ | **5** | 14/1 | 65 | 30 |
| 589[14] | **Amron (68)** (JBerry) **9-8-11** NCarlisle(11) (lw: hdwy wl over 1f out: nrst fin) | 1 | **6** | 25/1 | 65 | 30 |
| 554[12] | **Stolen Melody (66)** (SDow) **4-8-9** BThomson(4) (dwlt: hdwy over 1f out: nvr nrr) | 2 | **7** | 33/1 | 57 | 22 |
| 711[6] | **Ziggy's Dancer (USA) (85)** (EJAlston) **5-10-0** SDWilliams(3) (lw: trckd ldrs 4f: sn rdn: no imp) | 2 | **8** | 12/1 | 71 | 36 |
| 592[13] | **Mousehole (64)** (RGuest) **4-8-7** MFenton(7) (wl bhd tl sme late hdwy) | 1½ | **9** | 33/1 | 46 | 11 |
| 749[20] | **Leigh Crofter (65)** (PDCundell) **7-8-8** SWhitworth(8) (nvr plcd to chal) | s.h | **10** | 33/1 | 47 | 12 |
| 711[4] | **Sailormaite (81)** (SRBowring) **5-9-10** RPrice(14) (mid div: effrt u.p 2f out: sn btn) | nk | **11** | 15/2[3] | 62 | 27 |
| 589[16] | **Birchwood Sun (61)** (MDods) **6-8-4** WWoods(13) (lw: s.i.s: a bhd) | 2 | **12** | 33/1 | 37 | 2 |
| 610[22] | **Benzoe (IRE) (71)** (MrsJRRamsden) **6-9-0** JFEgan(16) (s.s: a in rr) | 1 | **13** | 11/1 | 44 | 9 |
| | **Louisville Belle (IRE) (53)** (MDIUsher) **7-7-10** NAdams(9) (b: bkwd: prom: hung rt 2f out: sn btn) | 2 | **14** | 33/1 | 21 | — |
| 629[14] | **Up in Flames (IRE) (75)** (MDHammond) **5-8-11**(7) DHayden(1) (dwlt: a bhd & outpcd: t.o) | 7 | **15** | 25/1 | 24 | — |
| | **Bajan Rose (74)** (MBlanshard) **4-9-3** DeanMcKeown(10) (w ldr 4f: sn wknd: t.o) | 5 | **16** | 12/1 | 10 | — |

(SP 131.1%) **16 Rn**

**1m 11.8** (1.80) CSF £105.48 CT £879.87 TOTE £32.30: £5.10 £2.00 £1.40 £1.10 (£44.20) Trio £222.50 OWNER Mr E. A. Hayward (CHEPSTOW) BRED Crest Stud Ltd

LONG HANDICAP Louisville Belle (IRE) 7-8

**OFFICIAL EXPLANATION Mousehole: was found to have a bruised foot.**

**610 So Intrepid (IRE)**, very much on his toes in the preliminaries, responded to strong pressure to thrust his head in front nearing the line. His stable are flying at the moment. (16/1)

**610 To the Roof (IRE)**, still hanging onto his winter coat, raced freely and kicked for home 200 yards out, but the determined late challenge of the winner proved too much in the dying strides. (6/1: op 4/1)

**601* Canovas Heart** did not impress to post, but held the call until being overhauled inside the final furlong. He still has to succeed beyond the minimum trip. (9/1: 6/1-10/1)

**592* Double Splendour (IRE)**, pulled out for a clear run entering the final quarter-mile, was unable to pick up as he had done at Nottingham. Despite running on, he was never going to finish any closer. (7/4: 5/2-13/8)

**I'm Your Lady**, possibly just needing this outing to put an edge on her, ran well and she will not be long in making it pay. (14/1: 16/1-33/1)

**Amron**, who does prefer easier ground, was doing all his best work late on and could be on the way back. (25/1)

**Stolen Melody**, who has done most of her racing over a slightly longer trip, was only finding her stride when the race was as good as over. (33/1)

**711 Sailormaite** (15/2: 5/1-8/1)

**Benzoe (IRE)** (11/1: 8/1-12/1)

**Bajan Rose** (12/1: op 8/1)

## 815 E.B.F. WILLOUGHBY MEDIAN AUCTION MAIDEN STKS (2-Y.O) (Class F)

2-30 (2-31) **5f 2y** £2,880.80 (£798.80: £382.40) Stalls: High GOING minus 0.31 sec per fur (GF)

| | Horse | Dist | Pos | SP | RR | SF |
|---|---|---|---|---|---|---|
| | **Hil Rhapsody** (BPalling) **2-8-9** TSprake(2) (leggy: unf: w ldrs: led ins fnl f: r.o wl) | — | **1** | 20/1 | 69+ | 23 |
| 706[4] | **Lucayan Beach** (BGubby) **2-8-11**(3) JStack(7) (bit bkwd: stdd s: plld hrd: led over 1f out tl ins fnl f) | 1¾ | **2** | 7/2[1] | 68 | 22 |
| 596[6] | **Windborn** (KMcAuliffe) **2-8-9** JFEgan(9) (b.hind: hdwy 2f out: kpt on u.p nr fin) | nk | **3** | 11/2 | 63 | 17 |
| | **Braveheart (IRE)** (MRChannon) **2-9-0** SSanders(3) (lengthy: unf: led over 3f: kpt on u.p towards fin) | 1 | **4** | 4/1[2] | 64 | 18 |
| | **Petite Danseuse** (SDow) **2-8-9** BThomson(5) (neat: unf: hdwy 2f out: no imp fnl f) | ½ | **5** | 9/1 | 58 | 12 |
| | **Mike's Double (IRE)** (GLewis) **2-9-0** SWhitworth(1) (lt-f: bhd: rdn & hdwy 2f out: nt rch ldrs) | 6 | **6** | 9/1 | 44 | — |
| | **Yangtze (IRE)** (BRMillman) **2-8-11**(3) SDrowne(4) (leggy: scope: sn rdn: a outpcd) | hd | **7** | 20/1 | 43 | — |

| | Horse | Btn | Pos | SP | RR | SF |
|---|---|---|---|---|---|---|
| | **Class Distinction (IRE)** (RHannon) **2-8-9**(5) DaneO'Neill(6) (unf: scope: in tch to ½-wy: hung rt 2f out: sn btn) | 2½ | **8** | 5/1[3] | 35 | — |
| | **Time Can Tell** (CMurray) **2-9-0** MFenton(10) (tall: scope: bkwd: spd to ½-wy) | ½ | **9** | 20/1 | 34 | — |
| | **Remski** (MAJarvis) **2-9-0** PRobinson(11) (w'like: lengthy: bit bkwd: dwlt: a bhd: t.o) | 6 | **10** | 7/2[1] | 14 | — |
| | | | | (SP 130.8%) | **10 Rn** | |

**61.1 secs** (2.60) CSF £92.79 TOTE £36.00: £6.50 £1.40 £2.10 (£66.20) Trio £144.10; £75.14 to 29/4/96 OWNER Mr A. J. Rhead (COWBRIDGE) BRED Tibthorpe Stud

STEWARDS' ENQUIRY Egan susp. 6-7/5/96 (incorrect use of whip).

**Hil Rhapsody**, a sparely-made, early foal, knew her job and, lengthening up to lead inside the final furlong, won with plenty in hand. (20/1)

**706 Lucayan Beach**, with the advantage of a run under his belt, set sail for home below the distance, but the filly had the legs of him in a good race to the line. He should not have much trouble in picking up a small race. (7/2: 9/4-4/1)

**596 Windborn**, a very poor mover in her slower paces, was pegging back the principals in the closing stages and she does look to have ability. (11/2)

**Braveheart (IRE)** is bred to need middle-distances, but he broke well to show the way for over three furlongs before failing to quicken with the principals. (4/1)

**Petite Danseuse**, a neatly-made filly, was grasping what was needed in the latter stages and she will be all the wiser for the run. (9/1)

**Mike's Double (IRE)** (9/1: 5/1-10/1)

**Remski**, an April foal who did not look fully wound up, missed the break and brought up the rear throughout. (7/2)

## 816 TOTE BOOKMAKERS H'CAP (0-80) (3-Y.O+) (Class D)

3-00 (3-01) **1m 3f 183y** £4,192.20 (£1,254.60: £601.80: £275.40) Stalls: High GOING minus 0.31 sec per fur (GF)

| | Horse | Btn | Pos | SP | RR | SF |
|---|---|---|---|---|---|---|
| | **Riparius (USA) (76)** (HCandy) **5-9-12** CRutter(2) (hld up & bhd: hdwy over 2f out: hrd rdn to ld ins fnl f) | — | **1** | 10/1 | 90 | 56 |
| | **Bayrak (USA) (70)** (MJRyan) **6-9-6** DBiggs(1) (lw: led: qcknd clr over 2f out: hdd & no ex ins fnl f) | ½ | **2** | 11/1 | 83 | 49 |
| | **Midyan Blue (IRE) (78)** (JMPEustace) **6-9-11**(3) DRMcCabe(4) (bit bkwd: trckd ldrs: outpcd over 2f out: styd on fnl f) | 3½ | **3** | 8/1[3] | 87 | 53 |
| 650[12] | **Tulu (71)** (MrsJRRamsden) **5-9-0**(7) TFinn(8) (b.off fore: hld up: hdwy on ins & nt clr run over 2f out: styd on wl fnl f) | 1 | **4** | 10/1 | 78 | 44 |
| 628[9] | **Brave Patriarch (IRE) (73)** (JLDunlop) **5-9-9** GCarter(5) (hld up & bhd: hdwy on outside over 3f out: one pce fnl 2f) | 2 | **5** | 14/1 | 78 | 44 |
| 641[10] | **Dr Edgar (69)** (MDods) **4-9-4** FNorton(6) (hld up: effrt over 2f out: no imp appr fnl f) | 5 | **6** | 20/1 | 67 | 32 |
| 439[15] | **Chatham Island (70)** (CEBrittain) **8-9-1**(5) MHenry(11) (trckd ldrs: drvn over 2f out: sn btn) | hd | **7** | 10/1 | 68 | 34 |
| *512[6]* | **Slapy Dam (63)** (JMackie) **4-8-12** SSanders(10) (chsd ldrs 8f: sn wknd) | 1¼ | **8** | 6/1[2] | 59 | 24 |
| | **Sea Victor (76)** (JLHarris) **4-9-11** PRobinson(7) (trckd ldrs: rdn 3f out: sn btn) | 1½ | **9** | 6/1[2] | 70 | 35 |
| 619* | **Eau de Cologne (69)** (CWThornton) **4-9-4** DeanMcKeown(9) (swtg: prom tl rdn & wknd 3f out) | 1¾ | **10** | 2/1[1] | 61 | 26 |
| 495[6] | **Sayitagain (59)** (JRJenkins) **4-8-8** SWhitworth(3) (lw: prom tl wknd 3f out: t.o) | 9 | **11** | 25/1 | 38 | 3 |
| | | | | (SP 123.9%) | **11 Rn** | |

**2m 33.3** (4.30) CSF £107.11 CT £857.01 TOTE £12.30: £4.30 £3.60 £1.50 (£39.20) Trio £144.20; £91.45 to 29/4/96 OWNER Mrs David Blackburn (WANTAGE) BRED Rogers Trust

WEIGHT FOR AGE 4yo-1lb

**Riparius (USA)**, who has been gelded since his last run, began to stay on inside the last three furlongs, but needed to barge his way through before nosing ahead halfway through the final furlong. (10/1: op 6/1)

**Bayrak (USA)** looked extremely well but may be not quite 100% straight. Trying hard to make every post a winning post, he found the winner just too strong for him in an all-out duel to the finish. Compensation awaits. (11/1: 8/1-12/1)

**Midyan Blue (IRE)** needs a much stiffer test of stamina than he had here, but he performed with credit on this seasonal debut, and looks as good as ever. (8/1: 6/1-9/1)

**Tulu**, creeping through on the inside rail, had a very interrupted passage throughout the final quarter-mile. In the circumstances, she looked more than a shade unlucky. (10/1)

**Brave Patriarch (IRE)** tried to make his presence felt early in the straight, but could not muster the pace to get himself into it. (14/1: op 8/1)

**Dr Edgar**, held up to get the trip, did make a forward move over two furlongs out, but it came to little and he was never a factor. (20/1)

**619* Eau de Cologne** did not have the testing ground that he had on his previous successful run earlier in the month, and he was being bustled along and going in reverse three furlongs out. (2/1)

## 817 TOTE TRIO H'CAP (0-70) (3-Y.O+) (Class E)

3-35 (3-36) **1m 1f 218y** £3,616.20 (£1,083.60: £520.80: £239.40) Stalls: High GOING minus 0.31 sec per fur (GF)

| | Horse | Btn | Pos | SP | RR | SF |
|---|---|---|---|---|---|---|
| *604[2]* | **Zidac (64)** (PJMakin) **4-9-9** SSanders(10) (a.p: led over 1f out: rdn & r.o wl) | — | **1** | 16/1 | 78 | 56 |
| 690[4] | **Fighting Times (65)** (CASmith) **4-9-10** DeanMcKeown(14) (b.hind: bhd: hdwy on ins over 3f out: ev ch over 1f out: kpt on fnl f) | nk | **2** | 6/1[3] | 79 | 57 |
| | **Hawkish (USA) (52)** (DMorley) **7-8-11** MFenton(15) (bhd: hdwy 3f out: nt clr run 2f out: no imp fnl f) | 5 | **3** | 6/1[3] | 58 | 36 |
| | **Koathary (USA) (56)** (LGCottrell) **5-9-1** TSprake(16) (hld up: effrt & rdn 4f out: styd on towards fin) | 3½ | **4** | 33/1 | 56 | 34 |
| *18[7]* | **Arcatura (64)** (CJames) **4-9-9** JFEgan(17) (trckd ldrs: n.m.r over 2f out: styd on one pce) | 1¼ | **5** | 33/1 | 62 | 40 |
| 650[5] | **Zermatt (IRE) (65)** (MDIUsher) **6-9-10** NAdams(7) (swtg: trckd ldrs: no hdwy fnl 2f) | 1 | **6** | 14/1 | 61 | 39 |
| 527[2] | **Battleship Bruce (68)** (NACallaghan) **4-9-8**(5) DaneO'Neill(6) (prom: rdn over 2f out: sn btn) | nk | **7** | 5/1[1] | 64 | 42 |
| 650[3] | **Myfontaine (63)** (KTIvory) **9-9-1**(7) CScally(19) (b: lw: hld up: hdwy 4f out: no imp fnl 2f) | ¾ | **8** | 11/1 | 58 | 36 |
| 670* | **Scottish Bambi (64)** (PRWebber) **8-9-9** BThomson(4) (prom: ev ch over 2f out: wknd wl over 1f out) | nk | **9** | 11/2[2] | 58 | 36 |
| | **Reefa's Mill (IRE) (68)** (JNeville) **4-9-13** FNorton(11) (lw: dwlt: nvr nrr) | hd | **10** | 33/1 | 62 | 40 |
| 649[4] | **Roi de la Mer (IRE) (63)** (JAkehurst) **5-9-8** SWhitworth(1) (lw: led: clr 4f out: wknd & hdd over 1f out) | 5 | **11** | 20/1 | 49 | 27 |
| *604[8]* | **Frankly Fran (52)** (DWPArbuthnot) **4-8-8**(3) DarrenMoffatt(18) (b: a in rr) | ¾ | **12** | 33/1 | 37 | 15 |
| *510[3]* | **Houghton Venture (USA) (67)** (SPCWoods) **4-9-12** WWoods(9) (hld up: a in rr) | 5 | **13** | 12/1 | 44 | 22 |
| *132[8]* | **Tribal Peace (IRE) (67)** (BGubby) **4-9-9**(3) JStack(3) (hld up: hdwy 6f out: wknd 3f out) | nk | **14** | 33/1 | 43 | 21 |
| 670[3] | **Manabar (64)** (MJPolglase) **4-9-4**(5) FLynch(12) (s.s: hdwy over 4f out: wknd 2f out) | hd | **15** | 16/1 | 40 | 18 |
| 636[5] | **It'sthebusiness (55)** (SDow) **4-9-0** GDuffield(2) (swtg: trckd ldrs 6f: sn wknd) | ½ | **16** | 14/1 | 30 | 8 |
| 636[7] | **Explosive Power (60)** (GCBravery) **5-9-2**(3) DRMcCabe(13) (in tch 6f: sn lost pl) | ½ | **17** | 12/1 | 35 | 13 |
| 690[9] | **Media Express (63)** (MBrittain) **4-9-8** MWigham(5) (b: mid div tl wknd over 3f out) | hd | **18** | 33/1 | 37 | 15 |
| 619[7] | **King Curan (USA) (58)** (ABailey) **5-9-3** AMackay(8) (bhd fr ½-wy: t.o) | 29 | **19** | 33/1 | — | — |
| | | | | (SP 134.8%) | **19 Rn** | |

**2m 6.8** (3.10) CSF £103.86 CT £594.40 TOTE £20.20: £4.20 £2.10 £1.70 £13.30 (£116.70) Trio £287.10 OWNER Mr Brian Brackpool (MARLBOROUGH) BRED A. J. Struthers

**604 Zidac**, a very scratchy mover, opened his account here. He got his head in front over a furlong out, and proved much too powerful for the persistent runner-up. (16/1)
**690 Fighting Times** stayed on to dispute the lead entering the final furlong, and tried his heart out, but could just not worry the winner out of it. His stable is in fine form and his turn will come. (6/1)
**Hawkish (USA)** threaded his way through inside the last three furlongs, but had to switch several times, and would have finished much closer with a clear run. (6/1)
**Koathary (USA)** lacks pace, but he does stay and may well benefit from a longer trip. (33/1)
**Arcatura** could not hold his pitch after being squeezed for room early in the straight, but he did stay on and is capable of better. (33/1)
**650 Zermatt (IRE)**, ridden with more restraint, tried to improve over two furlongs out, but could not summon the pace to get serious. (14/1)
**527 Battleship Bruce**, ill-at-ease going to the start, went with the pace but was struggling over two furlongs out. (5/1)
**650 Myfontaine** (11/1: 7/1-12/1)

## 818 EQUITY FINANCIAL COLLECTIONS LEICESTERSHIRE STKS (Listed) (4-Y.O+) (Class A)

4-10 (4-10) **7f 9y** £11,070.40 (£4,093.60: £1,961.80: £799.00: £314.50: £120.70) Stalls: High GOING minus 0.31 sec per fur (GF)

| | | | | SP | RR | SF |
|---|---|---|---|---|---|---|
| | **Young Ern (119)** (SDow) **6-9-2** BThomson(1) (bit bkwd: w ldrs: led 3f out: rdn clr fnl f) | — | **1** | 8/11 1 | 124 | 54 |
| 673 4 | **Easy Dollar (105)** (BGubby) **4-8-12b** GDuffield(6) (set stdy pce 4f: ev ch over 1f out: kpt on) | 2 | **2** | 10/1 | 116 | 46 |
| 673 8 | **Branston Abby (IRE) (113)** (MJohnston) **7-8-11** PRobinson(4) (trckd ldrs: rdn & r.o fnl f) | ½ | **3** | 9/2 2 | 113 | 43 |
| | **Bin Rosie (104)** (DRLoder) **4-9-2b** DRMcCabe(5) (lw: dwlt: hdwy over 2f out: rdn & ev ch over 1f out: nt r.o) | 1½ | **4** | 7/1 3 | 115 | 45 |
| 457* | **Fire Dome (IRE) (108)** (RHannon) **4-9-2** RPerham(3) (hld up: rdn & no imp fnl 2f) | 1¾ | **5** | 8/1 | 111 | 41 |
| | **High Shot** (GLewis) **6-8-12** SWhitworth(2) (bit bkwd: plld hrd: in tch over 4f: sn outpcd) | 11 | **6** | 40/1 | 82 | 12 |
| | | | | (SP 111.2%) | | **6 Rn** |

**1m 24.6** (1.60) CSF £7.87 TOTE £1.70: £1.10 £2.50 (£6.50) OWNER Mr M. F. Kentish (EPSOM) BRED M. F. Kentish
**Young Ern** put his two bad runs at the end of last year behind him, returning with an authoritative success, despite looking in need of the run. (8/11)
**673 Easy Dollar** gets this trip well enough, but did not set a searching pace, and was found wanting when the winner quickened. (10/1)
**673 Branston Abby (IRE)** ran her usual sound race, but her late burst was less effective than usual as the whole field were quickening off the steady early pace. (9/2: op 3/1)
**Bin Rosie**, put to sleep at the back of the field, travelled sweetly. Produced below the distance, he looked a big danger to the winner but, once the chips were down, his head went up, he edged right, away from his rivals, and put the brakes on. (7/1)
**457* Fire Dome (IRE)**, content to track the others, found his turn of foot merely enough to maintain his position in the final sprint. (8/1)
**High Shot**, the winner of a French amateurs' race over ten furlongs on his most recent appearance, found stamina about as useful as a string space-suit the way this race developed. (40/1)

## 819 TOTE CREDIT H'CAP (0-80) (3-Y.O) (Class D)

4-45 (4-47) **1m 8y** £4,556.85 (£1,366.80: £657.90: £303.45) Stalls: High GOING minus 0.31 sec per fur (GF)

| | | | | SP | RR | SF |
|---|---|---|---|---|---|---|
| 562* | **Eben Naas (USA) (55)** (SCWilliams) **3-7-12(5)** MHenry(8) (b.hind: lw: mde virtually all: rdn 2f out: hld on wl ins fnl f) | — | **1** | 3/1 1 | 63 | 31 |
| *460** | **Cool Fire (70)** (SPCWoods) **3-9-4** WWoods(12) (lw: chsd ldrs: ev ch fnl f: unable qckn nr fin) | hd | **2** | 5/1 2 | 78 | 46 |
| *510 2* | **School Boy (68)** (TJNaughton) **3-9-2** SWhitworth(2) (hdwy 2f out: r.o fnl f) | 1 | **3** | 8/1 | 74 | 42 |
| | **Forest Fantasy (51)** (JWharton) **3-7-13** FNorton(4) (dwlt: hdwy over 1f out: fin wl) | 2½ | **4** | 25/1 | 52 | 20 |
| | **Ben Bowden (65)** (MBlanshard) **3-8-13** NAdams(6) (w wnr 6f: sn btn) | ½ | **5** | 33/1 | 65 | 33 |
| 575 13 | **Goodwood Rocket (70)** (JLDunlop) **3-9-4** GCarter(5) (chsd ldrs: no imp appr fnl f) | 1½ | **6** | 9/1 | 67 | 35 |
| 646 11 | **Seattle Alley (USA) (62)** (MrsJRRamsden) **3-8-10** JFEgan(9) (trckd ldrs 6f) | ½ | **7** | 10/1 | 58 | 26 |
| | **Tarry (62)** (SESherwood) **3-8-10** TSprake(3) (nvr nrr) | 3 | **8** | 14/1 | 52 | 20 |
| | **Mr Speaker (IRE) (66)** (CFWall) **3-9-0** GDuffield(1) (hld up: nvr nrr) | 1¾ | **9** | 14/1 | 52 | 20 |
| | **Sound Check (57)** (BJMeehan) **3-8-5** NCarlisle(13) (bit bkwd: chsd ldrs 5f) | 4 | **10** | 14/1 | 35 | 3 |
| 595 11 | **Bright Diamond (58)** (JRArnold) **3-8-3(3)** DRMcCabe(10) (prom tl wknd 3f out) | 1¼ | **11** | 20/1 | 34 | 2 |
| 570 7 | **Expeditious Way (GR) (73)** (RCharlton) **3-9-7** SSanders(11) (lw: in tch 5f) | nk | **12** | 16/1 | 48 | 16 |
| 595 5 | **Daily Risk (66)** (SDow) **3-9-0** BThomson(15) (chsd ldrs 5f) | ¾ | **13** | 15/2 3 | 40 | 8 |
| 702 5 | **Classic Lover (IRE) (67)** (RHarris) **3-9-1** AMackay(7) (bhd: rdn over 2f out: no imp) | 1¼ | **14** | 16/1 | 38 | 6 |
| | **Craven Cottage (70)** (CJames) **3-9-4** CRutter(14) (bhd fnl 3f) | s.h | **15** | 20/1 | 41 | 9 |
| | | | | (SP 131.7%) | | **15 Rn** |

**1m 37.9** (2.90) CSF £19.19 CT £111.01 TOTE £5.00: £2.10 £2.20 £3.10 (£10.60) Trio £14.10 OWNER Mr J. W. Lovitt (NEWMARKET) BRED Clovelly Farms
STEWARDS' ENQUIRY Henry susp. 6-8/5/96 (excessive use of whip)
OFFICIAL EXPLANATION **Forest Fantasy: the jockey stated that the filly had become unbalanced coming down the hill, only to find her stride on meeting the rising ground. The trainer added that she probably needed a longer trip.**
**562* Eben Naas (USA)** whipped round coming out onto the course, and Henry showed his rodeo skills in staying in the plate. Doing nothing wrong in the race, he had to pull out all the stops in the last furlong. (3/1)
**460* Cool Fire**, a fine mover, was never far away and did not go down without a real fight. This was only his fourth start and he is still improving. (5/1)
**510 School Boy**, travelling well if some way off the pace, finished strongly. It is only a matter of time before he gets off the mark. (8/1)
**Forest Fantasy**, who went into the notebooks on her two-year-old debut only to disappoint twice subsequently, again made an eyecatching start to the year. Settled at the back, her pilot glanced down a couple of times as if concerned about her action but, on meeting the level ground, she finished to great effect. (25/1)
**Ben Bowden**, making his handicap debut, showed plenty of pace before lack of peak-fitness told. His half-sister Bowden Rose made giant strides as a three-year-old and he has the physique to improve throughout the year. (33/1)
**Goodwood Rocket** has not progressed much in appearance from two and will struggle to win off this mark. (9/1: op 6/1)
**453 Seattle Alley (USA)** (10/1: 7/1-12/1)
**Mr Speaker (IRE)** (14/1: op 8/1)

## 820 REDMILE MAIDEN STKS (I) (3-Y.O+) (Class D)

5-15 (5-21) **1m 1f 218y** £3,704.05 (£1,104.40: £526.70: £237.85) Stalls: High GOING minus 0.31 sec per fur (GF)

| | | | | SP | RR | SF |
|---|---|---|---|---|---|---|
| 687 4 | **Hugwity (75)** (BHanbury) **4-9-7(3)** JStack(15) (b: b.off hind: a.p: led 4f out: rdn over 1f out: r.o wl) | — | **1** | 5/2 1 | 79 | 50 |

| | | | SP | RR | SF |
|---|---|---|---|---|---|
| | **Sunset Wells (USA)** (DRLoder) **3-7-13**(3) DRMcCabe(4) (lengthy: unf: plld hrd: a.p: ev ch over 2f out: no ex ins fnl f)........1¾ | **2** | 6/1[2] | 71 | 25 |
| | **Spartan Heartbeat** (CEBrittain) **3-8-2**(5) MHenry(11) (swtg: hdwy 5f out: r.o wl fnl f)........1½ | **3** | 20/1 | 74 | 28 |
| 613[7] | **Lady of Leisure (USA)** (MrsJCecil) **4-9-5** BThomson(2) (hld up: hdwy 2f out: r.o)........1¾ | **4** | 7/1 | 66 | 37 |
| | **Finlana** (MRStoute) **3-8-3**ow1 DeanMcKeown(1) (unf: scope: in tch: styd on u.p fnl 2f)........1½ | **5** | 13/2[3] | 65 | 18 |
| | **Devon Peasant (72)** (LGCottrell) **4-9-5** GCarter(16) (bit bkwd: hld up: hdwy 6f out: eased whn btn ins fnl f).....2 | **6** | 7/1 | 60 | 31 |
| | **Classic Find (USA)** (SCWilliams) **3-8-7** AMackay(14) (b: b.hind: w'like: hdwy 3f out: nvr rchd ldrs)........½ | **7** | 16/1 | 65 | 19 |
| 668[11] | **Le Teteu (FR)** (BobJones) **3-8-7** NDay(17) (lw: prom 6f: styd on again fnl f)........1¼ | **8** | 40/1 | 63 | 17 |
| | **Arietta's Way (IRE)** (RCharlton) **3-8-2** TSprake(8) (b.nr hind: leggy: unf: prom: rdn over 2f out: no imp)......2½ | **9** | 13/2[3] | 54 | 8 |
| 684[15] | **Charnwood Jack (USA)** (RHarris) **3-8-7** DBatteate(3) (in tch 5f: eased whn btn)........2½ | **10** | 14/1 | 55 | 9 |
| | **Seventh Edition** (DBurchell) **3-8-7** FNorton(18) (unf: led 8f out to 4f out: wknd over 2f out)........3 | **11** | 33/1 | 50 | 4 |
| 640[15] | **Breydon** (MHTompkins) **3-8-7** PRobinson(13) (sn rdn: bhd fnl 5f)........10 | **12** | 50/1 | 34 | — |
| | **Pompier** (JLDunlop) **3-8-7** GDuffield(7) (leggy: scope: sn rdn: a wl bhd)........nk | **13** | 7/1 | 33 | — |
| | **Begger's Opera (45)** (PatMitchell) **4-9-3**(7) VictoriaAppleby(6) (led 2f: wknd 3f out)........5 | **14** | 50/1 | 25 | — |
| | **Formentiere** (JMBradley) **3-8-1**(3)ow2 SDrowne(5) (leggy: unf: in tch: rdn 5f out: sn bhd)........1¾ | **15** | 25/1 | 20 | — |
| | **Nobleata** (SRBowring) **4-9-5** RPrice(12) (neat: unf: a bhd)........2½ | **16** | 50/1 | 14 | — |
| 645[4] | **Aim For Stardom** (MJAhern) **4-9-5**(5) RPainter(10) (lw: chsd ldrs: ev ch over 3f out: wknd 2f out)........2½ | **17** | 50/1 | 15 | — |

(SP 141.4%) **17 Rn**

**2m 7.7** (4.00) CSF £20.05 TOTE £3.40: £1.20 £2.40 £6.70 (£12.90) Trio Not won; £124.93 to 29/4/96 OWNER Mr Abdullah Ali (NEWMARKET) BRED Gainsborough Stud Management Ltd
WEIGHT FOR AGE 3yo-17lb
**OFFICIAL EXPLANATION Charnwood Jack (USA): the saddle slipped after the colt had pulled too hard.**
**687 Hugwity** has found his trip at last and proved plenty good enough to cope with a rather ordinary bunch of maidens. (5/2: op 6/1)
**Sunset Wells (USA)** has a good action, but has yet to come in her coat. She will come on aplenty for this debut. (6/1: op 3/1)
**Spartan Heartbeat** gave trouble at the start and needed to be ridden along to chase the others. Doing his best work at the finish, he will do better over further if he can get over his problems. (20/1)
**613 Lady of Leisure (USA)**, cruising on the home turn, did not find as much as might have been anticipated, but is going the right way. (7/1: 4/1-8/1)
**Finlana** moved down nicely, but failed to pick up to any great extent once pressure was applied. (13/2: 4/1-7/1)
**Devon Peasant**, who twice failed in photos to lose her maiden tag last term, was hard at work to pick up ground on the home turn. She took a couple of runs to get her act together last year. (7/1: op 4/1)
**Arietta's Way (IRE)** (13/2: 3/1-7/1)
**Charnwood Jack (USA)** (14/1: 10/1-16/1)
**Pompier** (7/1: op 4/1)

## 821 REDMILE MAIDEN STKS (II) (3-Y.O+) (Class D)

5-45 (5-52) **1m 1f 218y** £3,704.05 (£1,104.40: £526.70: £237.85) Stalls: High GOING minus 0.31 sec per fur (GF)

| | | | SP | RR | SF |
|---|---|---|---|---|---|
| | **King Alex** (RCharlton) **3-8-7** TSprake(13) (scope: bit bkwd: trckd ldr: led 3f out: shkn up & qcknd clr over 1f out: eased fnl f)........— | **1** | 10/11[1] | 72++ | 28 |
| 677[13] | **Get Away With It (IRE)** (MRStoute) **3-8-7** DeanMcKeown(10) (lw: dwlt: sn chsng ldrs: outpcd 2f out: r.o fnl f: no ch w wnr)........2½ | **2** | 10/1 | 68 | 24 |
| | **St Rita** (JLDunlop) **3-8-2** GDuffield(16) (lengthy: unf: sn rdn: chsd ldrs: styd on same pce fnl 3f)........hd | **3** | 10/1 | 63 | 19 |
| | **King Rufus** (JRArnold) **3-8-4**(3) DRMcCabe(17) (w'like: scope: led 7f: one pce)........½ | **4** | 10/1 | 67 | 23 |
| 613[4] | **Le Khoumf (FR)** (JMBradley) **5-9-7**(3) SDrowne(5) (hld up: hdwy over 1f out: nrst fin)........s.h | **5** | 20/1 | 67 | 40 |
| 578[5] | **Lead Him On (USA)** (PWHarris) **3-8-7** GHind(2) (lw: s.i.s: hdwy after 2f: n.m.r 3f out: eased whn btn fnl f)........4 | **6** | 8/1[3] | 61+ | 17 |
| 566[8] | **Backwoods** (WMBrisbourne) **3-8-7** AGarth(14) (prom tl rdn & wknd over 2f out)........s.h | **7** | 50/1 | 61 | 17 |
| 732[9] | **Formidable Flame** (WJMusson) **3-8-7** RPrice(6) (hdwy & n.m.r over 2f out: nvr rchd ldrs)........1½ | **8** | 20/1 | 58 | 14 |
| | **Future's Trader** (RHannon) **3-8-2**(5) DaneO'Neill(11) (effrt 3f out: nvr nr to chal)........1½ | **9** | 16/1 | 56 | 12 |
| | **Bronhallow** (MrsBarbaraWaring) **3-8-7** JFEgan(3) (nvr trbld ldrs)........hd | **10** | 33/1 | 56 | 12 |
| | **The Boozing Brief (USA)** (MAJarvis) **3-8-7** PRobinson(4) (chsd ldrs 6f)........¾ | **11** | 10/1 | 54 | 10 |
| | **Ghusn** (TThomsonJones) **3-8-7** DBiggs(15) (w'like: unf: trckd ldrs: rdn 4f out: sn btn)........1¼ | **12** | 14/1 | 52 | 8 |
| | **Vitus** (HRACecil) **4-9-10** GCarter(1) (bit bkwd: chsd ldrs: eased whn btn over 1f out)........2½ | **13** | 3/1[2] | 48 | 21 |
| | **Mathon (IRE)** (MRChannon) **3-8-7** AGorman(9) (cmpt: bkwd: in tch 5f)........2½ | **14** | 16/1 | 44 | — |
| 668[13] | **Golden Filigree** (DTThom) **4-9-5** MFenton(8) (a bhd)........1½ | **15** | 50/1 | 37 | 10 |
| | **Miletrian Fit-Out** (CEBrittain) **3-8-7** WHollick(7) (leggy: s.i.s: a t.o)........dist | **16** | 20/1 | — | — |

(SP 164.4%) **16 Rn**

**2m 8.5** (4.80) CSF £16.87 TOTE £2.00: £1.50 £3.40 £3.90 (£22.40) Trio £45.10 OWNER Mr Wafic Said (BECKHAMPTON) BRED Jon Hanson
WEIGHT FOR AGE 3yo-17lb
**King Alex** is impeccably bred, and his Group-winning dam started 11/4 favourite in Sun Princess' Oaks thirteen years ago. Showing a fine action on the way to post, he cruised upsides the leader and could hardly have been more impressive once let down. He looks to have a bright future. (10/11)
**Get Away With It (IRE)**, a brother to Ezzoud and closely related to both Distant Relative and Jundi, showed signs of temperament as well as ability, but would be worth looking at if blinkers or a visor are fitted, as he would not be the first member of the family to improve for their application. (10/1: 8/1-12/1)
**St Rita**, bustled along throughout, tied up in the last quarter-mile, but there was little coming from behind. (10/1: 7/1-14/1)
**King Rufus** set the pace, but was leg-weary once headed. (10/1: 33/1-8/1)
**613 Le Khoumf (FR)**, held up going well, could not help but stay on in the last couple of furlongs as those in front bar the winner stopped to nothing. (20/1)
**578 Lead Him On (USA)**, loaded some time after the others, does seem to have stalls trouble as he got badly left. Failing to get the run of the race at any stage, his pilot gave up, presumably in disgust, in the final furlong. If his temperament allows, he certainly has the ability to win races. (8/1: 6/1-10/1)
**Ghusn** (14/1: 10/1-16/1)
**Vitus** gave an awful lot of trouble before the start, having to be taken out of the stalls after injuring Carter. Given the pilot's obvious discomfort before remounting, it was surprising he was allowed to take his chance, and he is probably worth another chance after a little stalls training. (3/1)

T/Plpt: £416.60 (24.97 Tckts). T/Qdpt: £156.20 (2.76 Tckts). IM/Dk

# 0699-RIPON (R-H) (Good)
## Saturday April 27th
WEATHER: Overcast WIND: mod across

## 822 BANDSTAND INAUGURATION (S) STKS (3-Y.O+) (Class F)
2-05 (2-07) **1m 2f** £2,659.10 (£747.60: £365.30) Stalls: High GOING minus 0.05 sec per fur (G)

| Form | Horse | Dist | Pos | SP | RR | SF |
|---|---|---|---|---|---|---|
| $609^{5}$ | **Walworth Lady (51)** (MDods) **5-9-5** JCarroll(8) (b: lw: trckd ldr: led over 4f out tl ins fnl f: hung lft & rallied to ld cl home) | — | **1** | $3/1^{2}$ | 59 | 33 |
| | **Castletown Count** (KWHogg) **4-9-10** NKennedy(9) (a.p: qcknd to ld ins fnl f: hung lft: ct cl home) | hd | **2** | 66/1 | 64 | 38 |
| $752^{7}$ | **Master Ofthe House (59)** (MDHammond) **10-9-10** JFortune(3) (hld up: nt clr run over 2f out: hdwy over 1f out: no imp) | 6 | **3** | $13/8^{1}$ | 54 | 28 |
| $477^{10}$ | **Kristal Breeze (37)** (WRMuir) **4-9-5** KFallon(7) (a.p: one pce fnl 2f) | s.h | **4** | 25/1 | 49 | 23 |
| *$34^{2}$* | **Troubadour Song (61)** (WWHaigh) **4-9-10** DHarrison(4) (lw: mid div: hdwy 3f out: sn prom: nt qckn & eased appr fnl f) | 8 | **5** | $4/1^{3}$ | 41 | 15 |
| | **Pearl Anniversary (IRE)** (MJohnston) **3-8-7** JFanning(6) (in tch: effrt over 3f out: outpcd fnl 2f) | 3½ | **6** | 10/1 | 36 | — |
| $661^{10}$ | **Care And Comfort (56)** (NTinkler) **4-9-5** LCharnock(11) (plld hrd: led tl over 4f out: sn btn) | 7 | **7** | 9/1 | 20 | — |
| $586^{16}$ | **Hunza Story (36)** (NPLittmoden) **4-9-0**(5) JDSmith(2) (b.hind: hld up & bhd: gd hdwy 4f out: rdn & btn 2f out) | 4 | **8** | 20/1 | 13 | — |
| $479^{13}$ | **Great Bear (65)** (DWChapman) **4-9-10** ACulhane(1) (a bhd) | 15 | **9** | 20/1 | — | — |
| | **Howard the Duck** (RBastiman) **6-9-5**(5) HBastiman(5) (bit bkwd: dwlt: a bhd: t.o) | 23 | **10** | 33/1 | — | — |

(SP 120.0%) **10 Rn**

**2m 11.7** (8.20) CSF £115.34 TOTE £4.80: £1.50 £8.20 £1.10 (£124.30) Trio £39.00 OWNER Mr Vernon Spinks (DARLINGTON) BRED Mrs L. Steele

WEIGHT FOR AGE 3yo-17lb

No bid

**609 Walworth Lady**, after travelling well, looked likely to be beaten when headed inside the final furlong, but the one thing she does is stay, and she fought back to settle it late on. She might well do better over further. (3/1)

**Castletown Count** lost his form altogether last season, but is obviously on his way back and should be all the better for this. (66/1)

**615 Master Ofthe House**, who needs things to go just right, cried enough when they did not. (13/8)

**Kristal Breeze** has yet to finish nearer than fourth, but this was still not a bad effort and she was keeping on at the end. She might find a modest race. (25/1)

**Troubadour Song**, having his first run since January, showed up well in the straight but, when beaten, was given a pretty easy time. (4/1)

**Care And Comfort** went far too freely to post and spoilt any chances by racing in similar fashion. (9/1: 6/1-10/1)

## 823 LISHMAN, SIDWELL, CAMPBELL & PRICE MAIDEN AUCTION STKS (2-Y.O F) (Class E)
2-35 (2-36) **5f** £3,363.50 (£1,019.00: £498.00: £237.50) Stalls: Low GOING minus 0.33 sec per fur (GF)

| Form | Horse | Dist | Pos | SP | RR | SF |
|---|---|---|---|---|---|---|
| | **Daylight Dreams** (CACyzer) **2-8-8** KFallon(7) (unf: s.i.s: hdwy ½-wy: r.o wl to ld wl ins fnl f) | — | **1** | 9/1 | 79 | 24 |
| $596^{4}$ | **Enchantica** (JBerry) **2-8-6** JCarroll(8) (led: hung bdly rt over 1f out: hdd & no ex wl ins fnl f) | 2½ | **2** | $3/1^{2}$ | 69 | 14 |
| $729^{4}$ | **Poly Moon** (MRChannon) **2-8-6** JFortune(4) (cl up: outpcd 2f out: no imp after) | 3½ | **3** | $7/2^{3}$ | 58 | 3 |
| $639^{4}$ | **Legend of Aragon** (JAGlover) **2-8-2** JQuinn(6) (chsd ldrs: effrt 2f out: one pce fnl f) | 2½ | **4** | $5/2^{1}$ | 46 | — |
| $506^{6}$ | **Morritt Magic** (CWThornton) **2-8-0** JFanning(11) (prom tl outpcd fnl 2f) | 4 | **5** | 25/1 | 31 | — |
| $729^{6}$ | **Clara Bliss (IRE)** (BJMeehan) **2-8-3**ow1 DHarrison(9) (lw: gd spd 3f: wknd) | ¾ | **6** | 9/1 | 32 | — |
| | **Clonavon Girl (IRE)** (MJCamacho) **2-8-0** LCharnock(5) (neat: bit bkwd: dwlt: nrst fin) | 1½ | **7** | 33/1 | 24 | — |
| | **Melbourne Princess** (RMWhitaker) **2-8-8** ACulhane(10) (neat: scope: bit bkwd: dwlt: a bhd) | 1¼ | **8** | 7/1 | 28 | — |
| $557^{7}$ | **Ramsey Pride** (CWFairhurst) **2-8-3** NKennedy(3) (outpcd & lost tch fr ½-wy) | ½ | **9** | 25/1 | 21 | — |
| | **Loch-Hurn Lady** (KWHogg) **2-7-10**(3) DWright(1) (neat: s.s: a bhd) | 5 | **10** | 14/1 | 1 | — |
| | **Just Typical** (NTinkler) **2-7-12** KimTinkler(2) (neat: str: bkwd: prom to ½-wy: sn wknd) | 1 | **11** | 25/1 | — | — |

(SP 129.4%) **11 Rn**

**60.8 secs** (2.40) CSF £37.69 TOTE £10.80: £2.40 £1.70 £1.80 (£15.70) Trio £35.60 OWNER Mr R. M. Cyzer (HORSHAM) BRED S. Wingfield Digby

**Daylight Dreams** looked fit and won quite well after a poor start. She will obviously stay further. (9/1)

**596 Enchantica** showed speed aplenty but threw away her chance by hanging badly right approaching the final furlong. Her pace should bring success once she learns to run straight. (3/1)

**729 Poly Moon** had her chances but was short of a change of gear. (7/2: op 9/4)

**639 Legend of Aragon** was never far off the pace, but was short of a turn of foot and may need a bit further. (5/2)

**Morritt Magic** was always off the bit here and looks likely to appreciate at least another furlong. (25/1)

**Clara Bliss (IRE)** looked fit and showed plenty of toe, but she failed to see it out. (9/1: 6/1-10/1)

**Clonavon Girl (IRE)**, slow to realise what was required, only ran on when it was too late. Experience is the key. (33/1)

**Melbourne Princess** (7/1: 4/1-8/1)

## 824 RACING CHANNEL H'CAP (0-80) (3-Y.O) (Class D)
3-05 (3-06) **6f** £3,775.20 (£1,143.60: £558.80: £266.40) Stalls: Low GOING minus 0.33 sec per fur (GF)

| Form | Horse | Dist | Pos | SP | RR | SF |
|---|---|---|---|---|---|---|
| $686^{6}$ | **Antonias Melody (68)** (SRBowring) **3-8-8**(5) CTeague(1) (lw: mde all: shkn up ½-wy: r.o wl) | — | **1** | $6/1^{2}$ | 77 | 22 |
| $735^{4}$ | **Montrestar (67)** (PDEvans) **3-8-12** JFortune(5) (hdwy over 2f out: chsng ldrs 1f out: kpt on) | 1¼ | **2** | 10/1 | 73 | 18 |
| $644^{6}$ | **Thai Morning (65)** (PWHarris) **3-8-10** AMcGlone(2) (lw: in tch: hdwy 2f out: nt qckn ins fnl f) | ½ | **3** | 9/1 | 69 | 14 |
| $571^{6}$ | **Dummer Golf Time (63)** (LordHuntingdon) **3-8-8** DHarrison(6) (mid div: effrt ½-wy: styd on: nvr able to chal) | 2 | **4** | $3/1^{1}$ | 62 | 7 |
| | **Mister Joel (61)** (MWEasterby) **3-8-1**(5)ow1 GParkin(4) (in tch: styd on fnl f) | 1½ | **5** | 14/1 | 56 | — |
| $686^{3}$ | **Royal Ceilidh (IRE) (69)** (DenysSmith) **3-9-0** KFallon(7) (hdwy ½-wy: n.m.r 2f out: r.o fnl f) | 1 | **6** | $7/1^{3}$ | 61 | 6 |
| $626^{3}$ | **Bowlers Boy (65)** (JJQuinn) **3-8-5**(5) PFessey(16) (prom 4f: grad lost pl) | 1 | **7** | 16/1 | 55 | — |
| $525^{7}$ | **The Butterwick Kid (51)** (RAFahey) **3-7-10** JQuinn(14) (nvr plcd to chal) | 2½ | **8** | $7/1^{3}$ | 34 | — |
| | **Safio (75)** (CSmith) **3-9-6** AClark(9) (nvr trbld ldrs) | s.h | **9** | 33/1 | 58 | 3 |
| | **Amanita (76)** (JWWatts) **3-9-7** JCarroll(3) (w wnr over 3f: wknd appr fnl f) | 5 | **10** | 10/1 | 46 | — |
| *$157^{6}$* | **Shontaine (73)** (MJohnston) **3-9-4** TWilliams(12) (lw: nvr nr ldrs) | s.h | **11** | 25/1 | 42 | — |
| $587^{14}$ | **Ramsey Hope (73)** (CWFairhurst) **3-9-4** NKennedy(13) (cl up over 3f) | ¾ | **12** | 33/1 | 40 | — |
| $689^{7}$ | **Too Hasty (73)** (TDEasterby) **3-9-4** MBirch(15) (spd 4f: grad lost pl) | 1¼ | **13** | 20/1 | 37 | — |

| | | | | SP | RR | SF |
|---|---|---|---|---|---|---|
| 652* | **Standown (70)** (JBerry) **3-8-10**(5) PRoberts(11) (gd spd to ½-wy) | nk | **14** | 10/1 | 33 | — |
| | **Camionneur (IRE) (58)** (TDEasterby) **3-8-3** JFanning(10) (spd to ½-wy) | 1¼ | **15** | 20/1 | 18 | — |
| 640[11] | **Khabar (72)** (RBastiman) **3-8-12**(5) HBastiman(8) (s.i.s: a bhd) | 2½ | **16** | 12/1 | 25 | — |
| | | | | (SP 141.1%) | | **16 Rn** |

**1m 13.9** (3.40) CSF £68.95 CT £379.03 TOTE £10.50: £2.20 £2.50 £2.00 £1.90 (£46.40) Trio £25.90 OWNER Mrs B. D. Georgiou (EDWINSTOWE) BRED B. D. Georgiou

LONG HANDICAP The Butterwick Kid 7-9

OFFICIAL EXPLANATION **Bowlers Boy: the jockey reported that his instructions had been to keep the gelding on the bridle as long as possible and not to use the whip but 'to kid' him along. When niggled along in the final furlong, the horse's head came up and the jockey felt he would not have quickened under any further pressure.**

**686 Antonias Melody** had the best draw and made full use of it. Constantly kept up to her work, she never looked likely to stop. (6/1)
**735 Montrestar** has plenty of ability but, when it comes down to it, he just fails to find enough. (10/1)
**644 Thai Morning** looked and ran well, but failed to quicken when it mattered. (9/1)
**571 Dummer Golf Time**, taken to post early, met with trouble in running and could never get in a blow. (3/1)
**Mister Joel**, without the blinkers this time, ran pretty well and is one to watch when they are refitted. (14/1)
**686 Royal Ceilidh (IRE)** had no luck at all in running and should be forgiven this lapse. (7/1)
**626 Bowlers Boy**, having his first run in a handicap, was badly drawn and showed promise again. He is well worth keeping in mind. (16/1)
**525 The Butterwick Kid** had a poor draw and failed to offer a threat, but should not be written off yet. (7/1)
**Khabar** (12/1: 8/1-14/1)

## 825 C. B. HUTCHINSON MEMORIAL CHALLENGE CUP H'CAP (0-90) (4-Y.O+) (Class C)

3-40 (3-40) **2m** £6,937.50 (£2,100.00: £1,025.00: £487.50) Stalls: Low GOING minus 0.05 sec per fur (G)

| | | | | SP | RR | SF |
|---|---|---|---|---|---|---|
| 495[2] | **Orchestra Stall (75)** (JLDunlop) **4-9-1** JCarroll(8) (lw: a.p: led 2f out: r.o u.p) | — | **1** | 5/1[3] | 88 | 52 |
| | **Great Easeby (IRE) (52)** (WStorey) **6-7-10** JQuinn(9) (in tch: effrt over 3f out: ev ch over 1f out: styd on wl) | nk | **2** | 5/1[3] | 65 | 33 |
| | **Fujiyama Crest (IRE) (88)** (MRStoute) **4-10-0** KFallon(7) (b.nr hind: a chsng ldrs: ev ch 2f out: nt qckn fnl f) | 3½ | **3** | 7/2[2] | 97 | 61 |
| 675[2] | **Unchanged (74)** (CEBrittain) **4-9-0** DHarrison(5) (lw: a chsng ldrs: ev ch over 2f out: r.o one pce) | ¾ | **4** | 11/4[1] | 82 | 46 |
| 753[8] | **Hillzah (USA) (78)** (RBastiman) **8-9-3**(5) HBastiman(3) (led to 2f out: one pce) | s.h | **5** | 9/1 | 86 | 54 |
| 625[4] | **Mondragon (70)** (MrsMReveley) **6-8-7**(7) SCopp(2) (bhd: hdwy 4f out: edgd rt & one pce fnl 2f) | 5 | **6** | 5/1[3] | 73 | 41 |
| 682[10] | **Pickens (USA) (74)** (NTinkler) **4-9-0** LCharnock(4) (hdwy appr st: sn rdn & btn) | 23 | **7** | 25/1 | 54 | 18 |
| | **Taroudant (75)** (RDEWoodhouse) **9-9-5** NConnorton(6) (hld up & bhd: wl outpcd fnl 4f) | hd | **8** | 10/1 | 55 | 23 |
| | **Blackpatch Hill (83)** (NTinkler) **7-9-13** KimTinkler(1) (bit bkwd: chsd ldrs to st: sn t.o) | 23 | **9** | 50/1 | 40 | 8 |
| | | | | (SP 123.8%) | | **9 Rn** |

**3m 33.9** (8.90) CSF £30.22 CT £93.19 TOTE £5.10: £1.50 £1.90 £1.80 (£19.70) Trio £17.40 OWNER Mr D. Sieff (ARUNDEL) BRED Alan Gibson

LONG HANDICAP Great Easeby (IRE) 7-7

WEIGHT FOR AGE 4yo-4lb

**495 Orchestra Stall**, taking a big step up in distance, appreciated every yard of it and proved to be most determined in a driving finish. (5/1)
**Great Easeby (IRE)** was off the bit a long way out but kept fighting on, and would have appreciated further and softer ground. He has improved no end over hurdles and it would appear that he is on the upgrade on the level. (5/1)
**Fujiyama Crest (IRE)**, normally a front-runner, was happy to sit just off the pace and was tapped for foot in the final furlong. This should have put him straight and, if his front-running tactics are adopted once more, they would certainly be suited to Chester. (7/2)
**675 Unchanged** had her chances but was tapped for toe in the last three furlongs. (11/4)
**482 Hillzah (USA)** has never won over quite as far as this but, after making it, was outstayed in the final quarter-mile. This was still not a bad effort. (9/1)
**625 Mondragon** last won almost two years ago and, off the bit a long way out here, was never doing enough. (5/1)
**Taroudant** (10/1: 8/1-12/1)

## 826 NORPACK MAIDEN STKS (3-Y.O) (Class D)

4-15 (4-18) **1m 2f** £3,728.75 (£1,130.00: £552.50: £263.75) Stalls: High GOING minus 0.05 sec per fur (G)

| | | | | SP | RR | SF |
|---|---|---|---|---|---|---|
| | **Kinlochewe** (HRACecil) **3-8-9** AMcGlone(3) (unf: lw: a.p: led over 2f out: r.o wl) | — | **1** | 4/1[2] | 77 | 33 |
| | **Dear Life (USA)** (MrsJCecil) **3-8-9** AClark(1) (neat: lw: a.p: disp ld over 3f out: hdd over 2f out: r.o) | 1½ | **2** | 10/1 | 75 | 31 |
| 640[8] | **Chocolate Ice** (CACyzer) **3-9-0** JFortune(7) (a chsng ldrs: hung rt & one pce fnl 2f) | 4 | **3** | 16/1 | 73 | 29 |
| 691[6] | **Old Irish** (LMCumani) **3-9-0** OUrbina(9) (hdwy 4f out: kpt on wl: nvr nr to chal) | ½ | **4** | 14/1 | 72 | 28 |
| | **Karisma (IRE) (75)** (DenysSmith) **3-9-0** KFallon(6) (plld hrd: cl up: led after 3f tl over 3f out: outpcd fnl 2f) | s.h | **5** | 9/1[3] | 72 | 28 |
| | **Amusing Aside (IRE)** (JWWatts) **3-8-9** JCarroll(10) (neat: b: bkwd: hdwy 4f out: nt clr run appr fnl f: nt rcvr) | 1½ | **6** | 10/1 | 65 | 21 |
| 640[5] | **Royal Action** (JEBanks) **3-9-0** JQuinn(5) (a.p: disp ld over 3f out: sn rdn & wknd) | 5 | **7** | Evens[1] | 62 | 18 |
| 691[7] | **Doctor Green (FR)** (LordHuntingdon) **3-9-0** DHarrison(4) (unruly stalls: dwlt: hdwy over 3f out: nvr able to chal) | 1½ | **8** | 12/1 | 60 | 16 |
| 717[6] | **Gool Lee Shay (USA)** (RMWhitaker) **3-9-0** JFanning(15) (led 3f: cl up tl wknd over 2f out) | ½ | **9** | 200/1 | 59 | 15 |
| | **Noir Esprit (56)** (JMCarr) **3-9-0** LCharnock(8) (nvr trbld ldrs) | 6 | **10** | 200/1 | 49 | 5 |
| | **Philgem** (JHetherton) **3-8-9** NKennedy(12) (bit bkwd: n.d) | hd | **11** | 200/1 | 44 | — |
| | **Clash of Swords** (PCalver) **3-9-0** MBirch(2) (w'like: bit bkwd: bhd: shkn up 4f out: n.d) | nk | **12** | 50/1 | 49 | 5 |
| | **Dicentra** (EWeymes) **3-8-9** RLappin(14) (chsd ldrs tl wknd fnl 4f) | ¾ | **13** | 200/1 | 42 | — |
| 576[10] | **Scandator (IRE)** (PWHarris) **3-9-0** NConnorton(13) (a bhd) | 21 | **14** | 20/1 | 14 | — |
| | | | | (SP 127.1%) | | **14 Rn** |

**2m 10.5** (7.00) CSF £42.70 TOTE £4.90: £2.20 £3.10 £6.30 (£21.90) Trio £161.80; £207.38 to 29/4/96 OWNER Sir David Wills (NEWMARKET) BRED Sir David Wills

**Kinlochewe**, who is nothing special to look, was fit and certainly does have an engine, and won in useful style. (4/1)
**Dear Life (USA)**, a handy sort, looked well and ran a sound race. She kept running on and her turn should soon come. (10/1: op 5/1)
**Chocolate Ice** put in a much-improved performance, but did rather spoil his chances by hanging right in the last couple of furlongs. (16/1)
**691 Old Irish** is getting the hang of things as he gains experience and, judging by the way he stayed on in the last half-mile, it will not be long before he finds a suitable race, probably over further. (14/1: op 7/1)
**Karisma (IRE)** spoiled his chances by racing far too freely and was left struggling in the final two furlongs. An imposing sort, he should have learnt from this. (9/1: 6/1-10/1)
**Amusing Aside (IRE)** showed ability and would have been a good deal closer but for running into trouble. (10/1: op 6/1)

**640 Royal Action** was a big disappointment here, dropping out tamely in the last three furlongs, and ran as though something was wrong. (Evens)
**Doctor Green (FR)** (12/1: op 8/1)

## 827 YORKSHIRE-TYNE TEES TELEVISION PRO-AM LADIES' H'CAP (0-70) (3-Y.O+) (Class E)
4-50 (4-52) **1m** £3,132.50 (£950.00: £465.00: £222.50) Stalls: High GOING minus 0.05 sec per fur (G)

| | | | | SP | RR | SF |
|---|---|---|---|---|---|---|
| 713* | **Rambo Waltzer (61)** (DNicholls) **4-10-6** AlexGreaves(14) (lw: a.p: led wl over 2f out: r.o) | — | **1** | 9/4[1] | 74 | 46 |
| *521[14]* | **Nobby Barnes (42)** (DonEnricoIncisa) **7-9-1** KimTinkler(5) (bhd: hdwy 3f out: styd on wl fnl f) | 2½ | **2** | 20/1 | 50 | 22 |
| 688* | **Raindeer Quest (47)** (JLEyre) **4-9-6** MissDianaJones(18) (lw: a.p: effrt 3f out: kpt on fnl f) | 2 | **3** | 5/1[2] | 51 | 23 |
| 629[3] | **Sycamore Lodge (IRE) (68)** (MrsJRRamsden) **5-10-8**(5) MissERamsden(20) (lw: styd on wl fnl 3f: nrst fin) | s.h | **4** | 8/1 | 72 | 44 |
| 539[3] | **Lucky Bea (58)** (MWEasterby) **3-8-12**(5)ow8 MrsSHardy(12) (styd on wl fnl 3f: nrst fin) | 1¾ | **5** | 16/1 | 58 | 8 |
| | **Persian Fayre (61)** (JBerry) **4-10-1**(5) JoanneWebster(4) (cl up: carried wd st: sn led: hdd wl over 2f out: one pce) | ¾ | **6** | 16/1 | 60 | 32 |
| 718[11] | **Anonym (IRE) (66)** (DNicholls) **4-10-6**(5) CarolDavison(16) (lw: chsd ldrs: one pce fnl 3f) | 1¼ | **7** | 20/1 | 62 | 34 |
| 688[3] | **Waterlord (IRE) (40)** (DNicholls) **6-8-13** JoHunnam(2) (lw: a.p: no imp fnl 3f) | ¾ | **8** | 10/1 | 35 | 7 |
| 629[13] | **Allinson's Mate (IRE) (69)** (TDBarron) **8-10-9**(5) ClaireWest(10) (hdwy & swtchd 3f out: nvr rchd ldrs) | nk | **9** | 50/1 | 63 | 35 |
| | **Thunder River (IRE) (61)** (MJHeaton-Ellis) **6-10-6v** AmandaSanders(6) (led: rn wd st: sn hdd: grad wknd) | ½ | **10** | 20/1 | 54 | 26 |
| | **Habeta (USA) (39)** (JWWatts) **10-8-12** AngelaGallimore(17) (hdwy on outside over 3f out: nvr rchd ldrs) | hd | **11** | 16/1 | 32 | 4 |
| 641[12] | **Ever so Lyrical (66)** (PWHarris) **6-10-11** MissAElsey(11) (n.d) | ½ | **12** | 11/2[3] | 58 | 30 |
| 440[11] | **Coureur (63)** (MDHammond) **7-10-3**(5) MissMCarson(1) (nvr nr to chal) | nk | **13** | 14/1 | 55 | 27 |
| 440[15] | **Roseate Lodge (54)** (SEKettlewell) **10-9-13** MrsDKettlewell(15) (n.d) | 1¾ | **14** | 50/1 | 42 | 14 |
| *366[4]* | **Roman Reel (USA) (65)** (GLMoore) **5-10-10** CandyMorris(3) (cl up tl wknd 3f out) | s.h | **15** | 16/1 | 53 | 25 |
| | **Guesstimation (USA) (65)** (JPearce) **7-10-10** MrsLPearce(8) (bhd: effrt over 3f out: n.d) | 1¼ | **16** | 10/1 | 50 | 22 |
| 629[9] | **Prudent Pet (59)** (CWFairhurst) **4-10-4b[1]** MrsSBosley(9) (lw: chsd ldrs tl wknd 3f out) | 1½ | **17** | 20/1 | 41 | 13 |
| | **Kernof (IRE) (62)** (MDHammond) **3-9-7** MissJAllison(13) (n.d) | 6 | **18** | 33/1 | 32 | — |
| 586[10] | **Pash (37)** (CWFairhurst) **4-8-5v**(5) MrsCWilliams(19) (a bhd) | 3 | **19** | 33/1 | 1 | — |
| | **Globe Runner (65)** (JJO'Neill) **3-9-5**(5) MissSKerswell(7) (sn bhd) | 6 | **20** | 33/1 | 17 | — |
| | | | | (SP 154.1%) | **20 Rn** | |

**1m 44.2** (6.50) CSF £55.86 CT £231.80 TOTE £3.40: £1.40 £3.40 £1.70 £2.10 (£41.00) Trio £56.60 OWNER Keystone Racing Club Partnership (THIRSK) BRED Triangle Thoroughbreds Ltd
WEIGHT FOR AGE 3yo-14lb
**713* Rambo Waltzer** was always in the right place and there was only one winner in the last three furlongs. (9/4)
**Nobby Barnes** had a lot of running to do from a bad draw and did well to finish so close. (20/1)
**688* Raindeer Quest** was always in a good position, but lacked a turn of foot to take the opportunity. (5/1)
**629 Sycamore Lodge (IRE)** is becoming most frustrating and finished well here, but is certainly his own worst enemy. (8/1)
**539 Lucky Bea**, stepping up in distance, ran well and kept staying on in most determined style. (16/1)
**Persian Fayre** ran pretty well after getting messed about early on, and seems to be at his best in the early part of the season. (16/1)
**Ever so Lyrical** (11/2: 8/1-5/1)

## 828 LANGTHORPE CONDITIONS STKS (4-Y.O+) (Class C)
5-20 (5-20) **1m 4f 60y** £4,955.48 (£1,733.88: £847.94: £364.70) Stalls: High GOING minus 0.05 sec per fur (G)

| | | | | SP | RR | SF |
|---|---|---|---|---|---|---|
| | **Suplizi (IRE)** (LMCumani) **5-8-12** OUrbina(1) (hld up: stdy hdwy 3f out: led 1f out: r.o) | — | **1** | 2/1[2] | 106 | 30 |
| | **Prussian Blue (USA) (92)** (HRACecil) **4-9-1** AMcGlone(3) (lw: trckd ldr: led wl over 2f out: hdd 1f out: r.o) | 1¼ | **2** | 6/4[1] | 108 | 31 |
| | **Suranom (IRE)** (LMCumani) **4-8-8**(7) JoHunnam(4) (led tl wl over 2f out: kpt on same pce) | 2½ | **3** | 16/1[3] | 105 | 28 |
| 581[2] | **Star Selection (106)** (JMackie) **5-8-12** AClark(2) (lw: hld up: hdwy over 3f out: rdn over 2f out: sn btn) | 6 | **4** | 2/1[2] | 93 | 17 |
| | | | | (SP 112.5%) | **4 Rn** | |

**2m 43.6** (9.60) CSF £5.34 TOTE £2.70: (£4.90) OWNER Scuderia Rencati Srl (NEWMARKET) BRED Swettenham Stud
WEIGHT FOR AGE 4yo-1lb
**Suplizi (IRE)**, given a fine ride, won nicely and looks likely to go on from here. (2/1: 6/4-9/4)
**Prussian Blue (USA)**, like all runners from this yard, is really firing and, although he was always second best here, he refused to give in, and really made a fight of it. (6/4: op 9/4)
**Suranom (IRE)** has done all his racing in Italy previously, but he did run really well here and should benefit from the outing. (16/1)
**581 Star Selection** raced too freely and failed to get the trip. He needs a strongly-run mile and a quarter. (2/1)

T/Plpt: £48.20 (247.17 Tckts). T/Qdpt: £30.50 (18.33 Tckts). AA

# 0807-SANDOWN (R-H) (Good)
## Saturday April 27th
Other races run under Flat Racing Rules
WEATHER: fine & warm WIND: almost nil

## 829 PIZZA HUT MAIDEN STKS (2-Y.O C & G) (Class D)
2-15 (2-17) **5f 6y** £3,434.50 (£1,036.00: £503.00: £236.50) Stalls: High GOING minus 0.18 sec per fur (GF)

| | | | | SP | RR | SF |
|---|---|---|---|---|---|---|
| 699[2] | **Roman Imp (IRE)** (APJarvis) **2-8-11** JTate(6) (lw: a.p: chsd ldr over 2f out: led ins fnl f: rdn out) | — | **1** | 6/1[3] | 81 | 42 |
| | **Vasari (IRE)** (MRChannon) **2-8-11** RHughes(5) (w'like: scope: lw: led: qcknd 2f out: hdd ins fnl f: r.o) | ½ | **2** | 5/4[1] | 79 | 40 |
| | **Burlington House (USA)** (PFICole) **2-8-11** PatEddery(1) (neat: bit bkwd: outpcd: hdwy over 1f out: unable qckn) | 5 | **3** | 9/1 | 64 | 25 |
| 608[5] | **Bold African** (PDEvans) **2-8-11** LDettori(4) (chsd ldr over 2f: wknd over 1f out) | ¾ | **4** | 25/1 | 61 | 22 |
| 706[11] | **Rake Hey** (RFJohnsonHoughton) **2-8-11** JReid(8) (no hdwy fnl 2f) | 1½ | **5** | 50/1 | 56 | 17 |
| | **Spaniards Inn** (BJMeehan) **2-8-11** MTebbutt(2) (neat: bit bkwd: outpcd) | 1 | **6** | 25/1 | 53 | 14 |
| | **Cadeaux Cher** (BWHills) **2-8-11** MHills(9) (scope: hdwy 3f out: wknd over 1f out) | ¾ | **7** | 4/1[2] | 51 | 12 |
| | **Supercharmer** (CEBrittain) **2-8-11** BDoyle(7) (str: scope: hld up: rdn over 2f out: sn wknd) | ¾ | **8** | 7/1 | 48 | 9 |
| | **Streamline (IRE)** (GLewis) **2-8-11** PaulEddery(3) (leggy: s.s: a bhd) | 7 | **9** | 25/1 | 26 | — |
| | | | | (SP 114.7%) | **9 Rn** | |

**62.1 secs** (2.30) CSF £13.30 TOTE £4.40: £1.30 £1.30 £2.20 (£6.70) Trio £10.80 OWNER Mr Ambrose Turnbull (ASTON UPTHORPE) BRED Massimo Marchetti

**699 Roman Imp (IRE)**, who made an encouraging debut at Ripon last week, made his experience tell. Moving into second place at halfway, he wore down the leader to get on top in the last 100 yards. (6/1)
**Vasari (IRE)**, reported to be one of Mick Channon's best two-year-olds, is slightly on the leg but has plenty of scope. Taken down early, he set the pace and showed a nice turn of foot to quicken things up entering the final quarter-mile. He looked likely to succeed but was eventually worn down in the last 100 yards. He looks a ready-made winner. (5/4)
**Burlington House (USA)**, whose sire Housebuster was a leading sprinter in the States, looked as though the run would do him good. (9/1: 4/1-10/1)
**608 Bold African**, in second place to halfway, had burnt his boats below the distance. (25/1)
**Rake Hey** was making no impression on the principals in the last two furlongs. (50/1)
**Cadeaux Cher** (4/1: op 2/1)
**Supercharmer** (7/1: 8/1-12/1)

## 830 THRESHER CLASSIC TRIAL STKS (Gp 3) (3-Y.O) (Class A)

4-05 (4-11) **1m 2f 7y** £42,564.00 (£15,946.20: £7,673.10: £3,356.70) Stalls: High GOING minus 0.18 sec per fur (GF)

| | | | | SP | RR | SF |
|---|---|---|---|---|---|---|
| 611* | **Santillana (USA)** (JHMGosden) **3-8-10** LDettori(3) (lw: hdwy over 2f out: led over 1f out: hrd rdn: r.o wl) .....— | **1** | 6/1 3 | 118 | 81 |
| | **Glory of Dancer** (PAKelleway) **3-9-2** OPeslier(4) (b: w'like: scope: a.p: led 2f out tl over 1f out: r.o wl) .....nk | **2** | 14/1 | 124 | 87 |
| | **Mons (115)** (LMCumani) **3-9-0** JReid(5) (chsd ldr: led over 3f out to 2f out: unable qckn) .....6 | **3** | 4/1 2 | 112 | 75 |
| | **Double Leaf** (MRStoute) **3-8-10** WCarson(9) (lw: hld up: rdn over 2f out: r.o one pce) .....¾ | **4** | 7/2 1 | 107 | 70 |
| | **Silver Dome (USA)** (HRACecil) **3-8-10** PatEddery(6) (bit bkwd: hld up: rdn over 2f out: one pce) .....¾ | **5** | 4/1 2 | 106 | 69 |
| | **Busy Flight (109)** (BWHills) **3-8-10** MHills(1) (bit bkwd: rdn over 2f out: hdwy over 1f out: wknd fnl f) .....3 | **6** | 8/1 | 101 | 64 |
| 684 7 | **Amfortas (IRE)** (CEBrittain) **3-8-10** BDoyle(2) (lw: nvr nr to chal) .....3 | **7** | 25/1 | 96 | 59 |
| | **South Salem (USA) (112)** (DRLoder) **3-8-10** RHughes(7) (bit bkwd: prom over 7f) .....15 | **8** | 9/1 | 72 | 35 |
| | **Brighstone** (HRACecil) **3-8-10** WRyan(8) (led over 6f: wknd wl over 1f out) .....3 | **9** | 12/1 | 67 | 30 |

(SP 115.8%) **9 Rn**

**2m 6.64** (-0.06) CSF £73.02 TOTE £7.20: £1.80 £2.60 £2.00 (£42.70) Trio £40.10 OWNER Sheikh Mohammed (NEWMARKET) BRED Mr David Caldwell
STEWARDS' ENQUIRY Peslier susp. 6-7/5/96 (incorrect use of the whip)
**611* Santillana (USA)** looks a very useful individual judging on this display. Moving up to take the lead below the distance, he was given no peace whatsoever from the runner-up, but the pair drew well clear from the remainder. He is not entered in the Derby, but there are plenty of decent races to be picked up with him. (6/1)
**Glory of Dancer**, an ex-Italian colt who won the Gran Criterium last Autumn, certainly looks useful if this performance is anything to go by. Sent on a quarter of a mile out, he was collared below the distance but was certainly no pushover as the pair drew well clear of the remainder. Giving his all, he only just lost out. He looks to have a very bright future and a decent prize should soon come his way. (14/1)
**Mons**, winner of last year's Royal Lodge, looked fit enough for this seasonal bow. Sent on early in the straight, he was collared a quarter of a mile out and left standing by the front two. (4/1: op 5/2)
**Double Leaf** was a shade disappointing. Chasing the leaders, he was rousted along in the last three furlongs but he made a real meal of it as he struggled on, only just failing to get third prize. (7/2)
**Silver Dome (USA)**, with something left to work on, chased the leaders but was made to look very pedestrian in the last two furlongs. (4/1: op 2/1)
**Busy Flight** did not look wound up for this and so it proved as his effort soon petered out. (8/1)

## 831 T.G.I. FRIDAY'S GORDON RICHARDS STKS (Gp 3) (4-Y.O+) (Class A)

4-40 (4-46) **1m 2f 7y** £19,600.00 (£7,390.00: £3,595.00: £1,615.00) Stalls: High GOING minus 0.18 sec per fur (GF)

| | | | | SP | RR | SF |
|---|---|---|---|---|---|---|
| | **Singspiel (IRE) (120)** (MRStoute) **4-8-10** LDettori(10) (a.p: led over 2f out: rdn out) .....— | **1** | 11/10 1 | 118 | 81 |
| | **Pilsudski (IRE) (98)** (MRStoute) **4-8-10** KDarley(4) (lw: hld up: ev ch over 1f out: unable qckn) .....3 | **2** | 16/1 | 113 | 76 |
| | **Naked Welcome (101)** (MJFetherston-Godley) **4-8-10** WRyan(9) (bit bkwd: hdwy over 1f out: r.o wl ins fnl f) .½ | **3** | 25/1 | 112 | 75 |
| | **Punishment** (CEBrittain) **5-8-10** BDoyle(3) (bit bkwd: rdn & hdwy over 2f out: one pce) .....½ | **4** | 33/1 | 112 | 75 |
| 680 9 | **Lear White (USA)** (PAKelleway) **5-8-13** RCochrane(6) (rdn over 2f out: hdwy over 1f out: r.o) .....½ | **5** | 50/1 | 114 | 77 |
| | **Prince of Andros (USA) (113)** (DRLoder) **6-9-1** RHughes(7) (bkwd: rdn & hdwy over 2f out: wknd fnl f) .....2 | **6** | 9/1 | 113 | 76 |
| 581 5 | **Poppy Carew (IRE) (106)** (PWHarris) **4-8-7** RHills(2) (rdn & hdwy 2f out: wknd fnl f) .....s.h | **7** | 16/1 | 105 | 68 |
| | **Prince Arthur (IRE)** (PWChapple-Hyam) **4-9-3** JReid(11) (b: b.hind: styd centre st: bhd fnl 2f) .....2½ | **8** | 11/2 2 | 111 | 74 |
| | **Maralinga (IRE) (100)** (LadyHerries) **4-8-10** PaulEddery(8) (led: styd far side st: hdd over 2f out: wknd fnl f) .....2½ | **9** | 33/1 | 100 | 63 |
| 581 12 | **Medaille Militaire (104)** (JLDunlop) **4-8-10** PatEddery(1) (prom over 7f) .....1½ | **10** | 13/2 3 | 97 | 60 |
| | **Ela-Aristokrati (IRE) (109)** (MRStoute) **4-8-10** MHills(5) (prom over 7f) .....nk | **11** | 16/1 | 97 | 60 |

(SP 115.7%) **11 Rn**

**2m 6.68** (-0.02) CSF £17.99 TOTE £2.00: £1.30 £3.50 £3.20 (£11.60) Trio £42.40 OWNER Sheikh Mohammed (NEWMARKET) BRED Sheikh Mohammed bin Rashid al Maktoum
**Singspiel (IRE)** gained a richly-deserved first victory in Group class following a string of fine efforts in top company last year. Further Group success should soon come his way. (11/10: 4/6-6/5)
**Pilsudski (IRE)**, the winner of two valuable handicaps last summer, can certainly find a listed race. (16/1)
**Naked Welcome** looked big and well for this return. Out with the washing for much of the trip, he was putting in some good work in the last furlong and a half, only just failing to take second place. (25/1)
**Punishment**, an ex-French individual who raced only once last year, did not look fully tuned up. (33/1)
**Lear White (USA)** stayed on in the last furlong and a half, but never looked like getting to the principals. (50/1)
**Prince of Andros (USA)**, lumbered with a Group Two penalty, looked very fat and ran accordingly. He found lack of a recent run taking its toll in the last 200 yards, but will come on a lot for this. (9/1: 6/1-10/1)
**Prince Arthur (IRE)** failed to stay the trip and a return to a mile is required. (11/2)
**581 Medaille Militaire** again failed to sparkle and connections may be better off trying to find a conditions race for him. (13/2)

## 832 BEEFEATER RESTAURANT RATED STKS H'CAP (0-100) (3-Y.O) (Class B)

5-10 (5-15) **5f 6y** £7,565.84 (£2,832.56: £1,386.28: £597.40: £268.70: £137.22) Stalls: High GOING minus 0.18 sec per fur (GF)

| | | | | SP | RR | SF |
|---|---|---|---|---|---|---|
| | **Dashing Blue (93)** (IABalding) **3-9-1** LDettori(2) (hdwy over 1f out: led ins fnl f: pushed out) .....— | **1** | 11/2 3 | 100 | 49 |
| | **Cross The Border (95)** (RHannon) **3-9-3** KDarley(6) (w ldr: led over 2f out tl ins fnl f: unable qckn) .....1¾ | **2** | 9/1 | 96 | 45 |
| | **Unconditional Love (IRE) (94)** (MJohnston) **3-9-2** JReid(7) (lw: lost pl 3f out: rallied fnl f: r.o wl) .....s.h | **3** | 6/1 | 95 | 44 |

| | Horse | Dist | Pos | SP | RR | SF |
|---|---|---|---|---|---|---|
| 571[2] | **Norwegian Blue (IRE) (91)** (APJarvis) **3-8-13** JTate(5) (hld up: rdn 2f out: one pce fnl f) | nk | **4** | 5/1[2] | 91 | 40 |
| 571[12] | **White Emir (85)** (BJMeehan) **3-8-7** MTebbutt(8) (hdwy over 1f out: one pce) | 2½ | **5** | 8/1 | 77 | 26 |
| 467[14] | **Mindrace (82)** (KTIvory) **3-7-11**(7) MartinDwyer(4) (spd over 3f) | 3½ | **6** | 50/1 | 63 | 12 |
| | **Laafee (99)** (HThomsonJones) **3-9-7** RHills(9) (bit bkwd: prom over 3f) | ½ | **7** | 7/2[1] | 79 | 28 |
| | **Swynford Dream (85)** (JFBottomley) **3-8-7** RCochrane(3) (led over 2f: wknd 1f out) | ½ | **8** | 14/1 | 63 | 12 |
| 565[2] | **Repertory (98)** (MRChannon) **3-9-6** RHughes(1) (bhd fnl 2f) | 3 | **9** | 5/1[2] | 67 | 16 |
| | | | | (SP 115.0%) | | **9 Rn** |

**61.87 secs** (2.07) CSF £47.99 CT £280.40 TOTE £4.90: £1.80 £2.40 £1.60 (£45.70) Trio £44.50 OWNER Mrs Duncan Allen (KINGSCLERE) BRED Mrs I. A. Balding

LONG HANDICAP Mindrace 7-6

OFFICIAL EXPLANATION **Laafee: blew up and spread a plate.**

**Dashing Blue** made a very encouraging reappearance. Moving into top gear below the distance, he swooped into the lead inside the final furlong and needed only to be nudged along to score. (11/2)

**Cross The Border** disputed the lead until going on at halfway. Collared inside the final furlong, he had no chance with the winner. (9/1: 6/1-10/1)

**Unconditional Love (IRE)**, who resented the whip being used last year, obviously still does. Losing her pitch after a couple of furlongs, she got her second wind from below the distance, but when her jockey hit her with the whip, she swished her tail and he quickly had to put it down. Nevertheless, she ran on strongly up the hill and only just failed to take second place. She has plenty of ability but is no easy ride. (6/1)

**571 Norwegian Blue (IRE)** tried to mount a challenge in the final quarter-mile but was tapped for toe in the last 200 yards. (5/1: op 3/1)

**White Emir** moved up below the distance, but could then make no further impression. (8/1)

**Mindrace** showed plenty of speed until tiring approaching the final furlong. (50/1)

## 833 MARRIOTT HOTELS H'CAP (0-105) (3-Y.O) (Class B)

5-40 (5-45) **1m 14y** £12,718.00 (£4,762.00: £2,331.00: £1,005.00: £452.50: £231.50) Stalls: High GOING minus 0.18 sec per fur (GF)

| | Horse | Dist | Pos | SP | RR | SF |
|---|---|---|---|---|---|---|
| 646* | **Sorbie Tower (IRE) (96)** (MissGayKelleway) **3-9-3** RCochrane(8) (b.hind: lw: hdwy over 2f out: edgd lft over 1f out: led ins fnl f: r.o) | — | **1** | 2/1[1] | 107+ | 76 |
| 577[8] | **Forest Robin (82)** (RFJohnsonHoughton) **3-8-3** BDoyle(2) (hdwy 3f out: led wl over 1f out tl ins fnl f: unable qckn) | 2 | **2** | 25/1 | 89 | 58 |
| 567[4] | **Warning Reef (83)** (MRChannon) **3-8-4** KDarley(10) (hdwy over 2f out: hrd rdn over 1f out: one pce) | 1 | **3** | 20/1 | 88 | 57 |
| 454[3] | **Mushahid (USA) (100)** (JLDunlop) **3-9-7** WCarson(4) (nt clr run over 2f out: hdwy over 1f out: one pce) | 2½ | **4** | 9/2[2] | 100 | 69 |
| 574[10] | **Bullfinch (94)** (PTWalwyn) **3-9-1** JReid(5) (hdwy over 3f out: rdn over 2f out: one pce) | 1½ | **5** | 25/1 | 91 | 60 |
| 575[6] | **Kilvine (90)** (LMCumani) **3-8-11** MHills(6) (lw: dwlt: hdwy over 1f out: one pce) | s.h | **6** | 12/1 | 87 | 56 |
| | **Classy Chief (85)** (RBoss) **3-8-6** WRyan(14) (a.p: led over 2f out tl wl over 1f out: wkng whn n.m.r over 1f out) | 6 | **7** | 12/1 | 70 | 39 |
| 646[8] | **Caricature (IRE) (87)** (GLewis) **3-8-8** PatEddery(11) (nvr nrr) | 1¼ | **8** | 7/1 | 70 | 39 |
| | **Half An Inch (IRE) (75)** (BJMeehan) **3-7-10** GBardwell(1) (bkwd: prom over 6f) | 1¾ | **9** | 33/1 | 54 | 23 |
| 709[3] | **Carburton (88)** (JAGlover) **3-8-9** PaulEddery(9) (hld up: rdn over 2f out: sn wknd) | 1 | **10** | 6/1[3] | 65 | 34 |
| *232[3]* | **Meldorf (100)** (DRLoder) **3-9-7** LDettori(13) (lw: dwlt: bhd fnl 2f) | nk | **11** | 12/1 | 77 | 46 |
| | **Baltic Dream (USA) (75)** (KRBurke) **3-7-7**(3) NVarley(7) (hld up: rdn over 2f out: sn wknd) | 1½ | **12** | 33/1 | 49 | 18 |
| 593[9] | **No Cliches (78)** (GLewis) **3-7-13** RStreet(12) (s.s: a wl bhd) | 10 | **13** | 14/1 | 32 | 1 |
| *378[4]* | **Kirov Lady (IRE) (90)** (RHannon) **3-8-11** RHughes(3) (led: styd far side st: hdd over 2f out: sn wknd) | 3 | **14** | 33/1 | 38 | 7 |
| | | | | (SP 129.3%) | | **14 Rn** |

**1m 42.33** (1.13) CSF £50.44 CT £779.53 TOTE £2.60: £1.50 £7.80 £4.70 (£150.40) Trio £278.00 OWNER P. D. Q (WHITCOMBE) BRED B. Kennedy

LONG HANDICAP Half An Inch (IRE) 7-9

OFFICIAL EXPLANATION **No Cliches: gurgled on the run-in.**

**646* Sorbie Tower (IRE)** defied a 16lb rise in the weights to complete the hat-trick. Moving up over a quarter of a mile from home, he drifted left below the distance doing a beaten rival no favours but he got on top inside the final furlong and was certainly the best horse on the day. (2/1)

**Forest Robin** came through to lead early in the final quarter-mile but had no answer to the winner's turn of foot inside the final furlong. (25/1)

**567 Warning Reef** moved up over a quarter of a mile from home, but failed to quicken from below the distance. (20/1)

**454 Mushahid (USA)**, who was the meat in the sandwich over a quarter of a mile from home, picked up ground below the distance but could then only struggle on at one pace. (9/2)

**Bullfinch** took closer order early in the straight but could only go up and down in the same place in the final quarter-mile. (25/1)

**575 Kilvine** tried to get into the action below the distance but then failed to find another gear. (12/1)

T/Jkpt: £10,550.50 (0.1 Tckts); £13,373.96 to 29/4/96. T/Plpt: £147.60 (330.34 Tckts). T/Qdpt: £45.20 (54.45 Tckts). AK

# 0651-WOLVERHAMPTON (L-H) (Standard)

## Saturday April 27th

WEATHER: Fine WIND: slt half across

## 834 SARUMAN MAIDEN H'CAP (0-65) (3-Y.O+) (Class F)

7-00 (7-00) **6f (Fibresand)** £2,381.00 (£656.00: £311.00) Stalls: Low GOING: 0.04 sec per fur (STD)

| | Horse | Dist | Pos | SP | RR | SF |
|---|---|---|---|---|---|---|
| *529[2]* | **Lia Fail (IRE) (51)** (RHollinshead) **3-8-7**(5) FLynch(6) (bhd & outpcd: hdwy & brought stands' side st: str run to ld post) | — | **1** | 5/2[1] | 56 | 23 |
| *183[4]* | **Flagstaff (USA) (48)** (GLMoore) **3-8-9v** SWhitworth(8) (hdwy wl over 1f out: led wl ins fnl f: ct post) | hd | **2** | 6/1[3] | 53 | 20 |
| *605[4]* | **Holloway Melody (43)** (BAMcMahon) **3-7-13**(5) LNewton(5) (outpcd tl rapid hdwy appr fnl f: fin fast) | s.h | **3** | 13/2 | 48 | 15 |
| | **Black Boy (IRE) (37)** (RFMarvin) **7-8-9b** JO'Reilly(9) (hdwy 2f out: swtchd lft & led ins fnl f: sn hdd: unable qckn) | ½ | **4** | 33/1 | 40 | 18 |
| 740[4] | **Backhander (IRE) (52)** (MartynWane) **4-9-10** ACulhane(10) (trckd ldrs: drvn along fr ½-wy: kpt on ins fnl f) | 1¼ | **5** | 3/1[2] | 52 | 30 |
| *387[7]* | **So Natural (IRE) (50)** (EJAlston) **4-9-8** SDWilliams(11) (led 2f: led wl over 1f out tl ins fnl f) | ¾ | **6** | 14/1 | 48 | 26 |
| *514[5]* | **Ho Mei Surprise (34)** (BPreece) **4-8-3**(3) DWright(7) (led after 2f tl wl over 1f out: wknd fnl f) | 2½ | **7** | 12/1 | 25 | 3 |
| *487[7]* | **Woolverstone Hall (IRE) (31)** (DJGMurraySmith) **4-8-3b** NAdams(3) (gd spd over 3f) | 3½ | **8** | 13/2 | 13 | — |

| Form | Horse | Dist | Pos | SP | RR | SF |
|---|---|---|---|---|---|---|
| *655[8]* | **Tallulah Belle (50)** (NPLittmoden) **3-8-6v1**(5) ADaly(2) (sn drvn along: a bhd) | 5 | **9** | 12/1 | 19 | — |
| 638[17] | **Rapid Liner (53)** (HOliver) **3-9-0v1** VSlattery(4) (spd over 3f) | 2 | **10** | 14/1 | 16 | — |
| | **Polli Pui (38)** (WMBrisbourne) **4-8-5**(5) DGriffiths(1) (s.i.s: a bhd & outpcd) | 1 | **11** | 33/1 | — | — |
| | | | | (SP 129.1%) | **11 Rn** | |

**1m 16.9** (5.50) CSF £19.01 CT £85.39 TOTE £3.20: £1.10 £2.20 £3.30 (£13.70) OWNER Mr Noel Sweeney (UPPER LONGDON) BRED Sean Twomey

WEIGHT FOR AGE 3yo-11lb

**529 Lia Fail (IRE)** timed her effort to perfection, sprinting up the stands' rail to poke her nose in front right on the line. (5/2)
**Flagstaff (USA)** is an improving individual. Fresh after almost three months out of action, he worked hard to strike the front 75 yards out, and was a shade unfortunate to be touched off in the dying strides. (6/1)
**605 Holloway Melody**, brought back to sprinting, could not go the early pace, but came between horses with a sustained last-furlong challenge that failed narrowly. She should be able to win races. (13/2)
**Black Boy (IRE)**, who ran with his tongue tied down, looked very burly for this first outing in over six months, but turned in possibly his best effort yet. On this showing he should have little trouble in making his mark. (33/1)
**740 Backhander (IRE)** goes well on this surface, but this step back to six furlongs was not in his favour and he was unable to land a blow. (3/1)
**So Natural (IRE)** made most of the running until worn down and outpaced in the dash to the line. (14/1)
**514 Ho Mei Surprise** (12/1: op 7/1)
**Tallulah Belle** (12/1: op 8/1)

## 835 STRIDER CLAIMING STKS (3-Y.O+) (Class F)

7-30 (7-31) **5f (Fibresand)** £2,381.00 (£656.00: £311.00) Stalls: Low GOING: 0.04 sec per fur (STD)

| Form | Horse | Dist | Pos | SP | RR | SF |
|---|---|---|---|---|---|---|
| 718[8] | **Cretan Gift (87)** (NPLittmoden) **5-9-7b1**(5) DaneO'Neill(7) (hld up: hdwy to ld wl over 1f out: sn clr: v.easily) | — | **1** | 7/2[2] | 88 | 67 |
| 582[17] | **Intiaash (IRE) (72)** (DHaydnJones) **4-9-2**(5) FLynch(2) (outpcd & bhd tl r.o wl ins fnl f) | 6 | **2** | 8/1 | 64 | 43 |
| | **Wasblest (55)** (JBerry) **4-8-12**(5) PRoberts(12) (bit bkwd: a.p: led 2f out: sn hdd: nt pce of wnr) | s.h | **3** | 12/1 | 60 | 39 |
| *652[5]* | **Tee-Emm (55)** (PHowling) **6-8-12** JQuinn(11) (disp ld over 3f: outpcd appr fnl f) | ½ | **4** | 14/1 | 53 | 32 |
| *652[3]* | **Little Saboteur (57)** (PJMakin) **7-8-9b** SSanders(6) (b.nr hind: trckd ldrs on ins: rdn 2f out: one pce) | nk | **5** | 7/1[3] | 49 | 28 |
| *347[10]* | **Mister (44)** (KMcAuliffe) **4-9-2** JFEgan(5) (b.hind: prom: rdn over 2f out: sn btn) | 1¼ | **6** | 50/1 | 52 | 31 |
| 601[17] | **Rennyholme (57)** (JHetherton) **5-9-1b** NAdams(13) (lw: hdwy on outside ½-wy: nt rch ldrs) | s.h | **7** | 12/1 | 51 | 30 |
| *225[4]* | **King Rambo (70)** (RHollinshead) **5-8-6**(5) DGriffiths(4) (bit bkwd: rdn & effrt 2f out: nt pce to chal) | s.h | **8** | 9/4[1] | 47 | 26 |
| 769[12] | **Subfusk (60)** (WGMTurner) **3-8-7** TSprake(1) (lw: chsd ldrs 3f: sn rdn & wknd) | 3½ | **9** | 14/1 | 42 | 11 |
| 762[12] | **Ivy Lilian (IRE) (35)** (WMBrisbourne) **4-8-0**(7) IonaWands(9) (outpcd) | ½ | **10** | 50/1 | 30 | 9 |
| 750[3] | **Swan At Whalley (57)** (MartynWane) **4-9-2b1** ACulhane(3) (led 3f: wknd qckly: t.o) | 10 | **11** | 8/1 | 7 | — |
| *606** | **Niteowl Raider (IRE) (70)** (JAHarris) **3-8-10** JO'Reilly(8) (outpcd: a bhd: t.o) | 2½ | **12** | 8/1 | 3 | — |
| | **Bobaluna** (RFMarvin) **3-8-5**ow1 SDWilliams(10) (lt-f: s.i.s: a bhd & outpcd) | 1½ | **13** | 50/1 | — | — |
| | | | | (SP 133.4%) | **13 Rn** | |

**61.4 secs** (2.70) CSF £33.39 TOTE £4.00: £1.60 £3.30 £3.20 (£53.60) OWNER R A M Racecourses Ltd (WOLVERHAMPTON) BRED Hesmonds Stud Ltd

WEIGHT FOR AGE 3yo-10lb

**592 Cretan Gift**, lowered in class, won his first race at this minimum trip with authority, handing out a thorough thrashing to these rivals. (7/2: op 7/4)
**513 Intiaash (IRE)** was unable to match strides in the early exchanges, but ran on to gain the runner-up prize nearing the finish, without being able to offer a serious threat to the winner. (8/1)
**Wasblest** performed with credit after being so long on the sidelines. There would seem to be another race in the pipe-line. (12/1)
**652 Tee-Emm** is not quite lasting home on this track, but he has reserved his best for Lingfield in past years, and is running well enough to register another success. (14/1)
**652 Little Saboteur** showed plenty of speed racing towards the inside but she was flat out once in line for home, and always finding the task beyond her. (7/1)
**Mister**, still having trouble in finding a correct trip, went with the pace but was struggling to hold on from the turn into the straight. (50/1)
**King Rambo** needed this run after ten weeks out of action and was never going the pace of the leaders. (9/4)

## 836 SERVACRANE H'CAP (0-70) (3-Y.O+) (Class E)

8-00 (8-00) **1m 1f 79y (Fibresand)** £3,234.00 (£966.00: £462.00: £210.00) Stalls: Low GOING: 0.04 sec per fur (STD)

| Form | Horse | Dist | Pos | SP | RR | SF |
|---|---|---|---|---|---|---|
| 593[6] | **Law Dancer (IRE) (68)** (TGMills) **3-9-0** TWilliams(12) (lw: hld up gng wl: led over 1f out: sn clr: drvn out) | — | **1** | 3/1[1] | 80 | 43 |
| 612[7] | **Noble Canonire (53)** (SRBowring) **4-8-9**(5) CTeague(10) (hld up: hdwy ½-wy: hrd rdn & kpt on ins fnl f) | 2½ | **2** | 8/1 | 61 | 39 |
| *521[6]* | **Miss Zanzibar (45)** (RAFahey) **4-8-6** ACulhane(5) (hld up: hdwy over 2f out: swtchd lft & r.o wl fnl f) | 1½ | **3** | 8/1 | 50 | 28 |
| *778[5]* | **Chadleigh Lane (USA) (64)** (RHollinshead) **4-9-6**(5) FLynch(1) (bhd & outpcd tl gd hdwy over 2f out: nrst fin) | ¾ | **4** | 10/1 | 68 | 46 |
| 645* | **Northern Celadon (IRE) (62)** (MJHeaton-Ellis) **5-9-9** AClark(9) (led tl hdd & wknd over 1f out) | 1½ | **5** | 4/1[3] | 63 | 41 |
| 598[12] | **Hill Farm Katie (35)** (WMBrisbourne) **5-7-3v1**(7) IonaWands(11) (prom: rdn over 2f out: grad wknd) | 1½ | **6** | 25/1 | 34 | 12 |
| 676[12] | **Red Rusty (USA) (66)** (DMorris) **3-8-12** JTate(8) (lw: trckd ldrs tl wknd u.p 2f out) | 3½ | **7** | 7/2[2] | 59 | 22 |
| 688[8] | **Night Time (50)** (AStreeter) **4-8-6**(5) LNewton(13) (lw: a bhd: rdn 4f out: no rspnse) | 2½ | **8** | 12/1 | 39 | 17 |
| | **Rasayel (USA) (41)** (PDEvans) **6-8-2** JFanning(2) (bkwd: dwlt: nvr nr to chal) | 1½ | **9** | 7/1 | 27 | 5 |
| 747[10] | **Northern Chief (35)** (JCullinan) **6-7-10** JQuinn(4) (bkwd: hld up: effrt 5f out: sn no imp: t.o) | 16 | **10** | 33/1 | — | — |
| | **Arabian Flight (50)** (TTClement) **4-8-11** AMackay(7) (b: dwlt: a bhd: t.o) | 22 | **11** | 33/1 | — | — |
| *388[10]* | **Bold Time Monkey (36)** (MTate) **5-7-11**ow1 NAdams(6) (trckd ldrs to ½-wy: sn wknd: t.o) | ¾ | **12** | 33/1 | — | — |
| | | | | (SP 131.4%) | **12 Rn** | |

**2m 2.8** (6.80) CSF £28.67 CT £168.06 TOTE £4.30: £1.70 £2.30 £2.50 (£35.50) Trio £95.80 OWNER Mr T. G. Mills (EPSOM) BRED M. Duffy

LONG HANDICAP Hill Farm Katie 7-8 Northern Chief 7-7 Bold Time Monkey 7-5

WEIGHT FOR AGE 3yo-15lb

**593 Law Dancer (IRE)**, always travelling strongly, won this with the minimum amount of fuss. He has found his true mark on the sand. (3/1)
**508 Noble Canonire** finds this trip insufficient, and her determined late challenge was never quite going to get her there. (8/1)
**Miss Zanzibar** always had far too much to do, but she stayed on willingly when switched inside the distance and could be ready to strike. (8/1)
**778 Chadleigh Lane (USA)** made good progress from off the pace straightening up for home, but was never going to get near enough to cause concern. (10/1)

**645* Northern Celadon (IRE)** set a brisk pace, but the winner was always waiting to pounce, and he was brushed aside with ease once the race began in earnest. (4/1)
**512 Hill Farm Katie** kept tabs on the leaders, but she was at full stretch turning in and her measure had been taken. (25/1)

## 837 S. J. DIXONS & SON H'CAP (0-85) (3-Y.O+) (Class D)

8-30 (8-31) **1m 6f 166y (Fibresand)** £4,056.25 (£1,210.00: £577.50: £261.25) Stalls: High GOING: 0.04 sec per fur (STD)

| | Horse | Details | Dist | Pos | SP | RR | SF |
|---|---|---|---|---|---|---|---|
| *603** | **Jaraab (82)** | (MissSJWilton) **5-10-0v** SWhitworth(1) (sn chsng ldrs: led 5f out: clr over 2f out: unchal) | — | **1** | $4/1^{2}$ | 91 | 61 |
| | **Star Rage (IRE) (75)** | (JLHarris) **6-9-7** KFallon(3) (hld up: hdwy ½-wy: chsd wnr fnl 3f: no imp) | 3 | **2** | $9/2^{3}$ | 81 | 51 |
| $563^{3}$ | **Noufari (FR) (80)** | (RHollinshead) **5-9-12** LDettori(2) (trckd ldrs: pushed along 4f out: nvr able to chal) | 6 | **3** | $4/5^{1}$ | 79 | 49 |
| $682^{13}$ | **Old Provence (75)** | (RHarris) **6-9-7** DBatteate(4) (b: lw: trckd ldrs: rdn & outpcd over 3f out: sn btn) | 5 | **4** | 16/1 | 69 | 39 |
| $620^{7}$ | **Premier Dance (68)** | (DHaydnJones) **9-9-0** AMackay(5) (lw: hld up: effrt over 3f out: no imp) | 8 | **5** | 10/1 | 53 | 23 |
| *$235^{2}$* | **Stevie's Wonder (IRE) (70)** | (BJLlewellyn) **6-9-2** TWilliams(7) (bit bkwd: chsd ldr: slt ld 8f out: rdn & hdd 5f out: sn lost tch: t.o) | 18 | **6** | 10/1 | 36 | 6 |
| | **Culrain (50)** | (THCaldwell) **5-7-10** JQuinn(6) (bit bkwd: led over 6f: wknd 5f out: t.o) | 27 | **7** | 66/1 | — | — |
| | | | | | (SP 119.3%) | | **7 Rn** |

**3m 17.4** (10.00) CSF £21.75 TOTE £4.50: £2.30 £2.80 (£10.80) OWNER Gilberts Animal Feed Products (STOKE-ON-TRENT) BRED Shadwell Estate Company Limited
LONG HANDICAP Culrain 6-9
**603* Jaraab**, having his first run since changing stables, showed what a useful animal he is on this surface with another runaway success. There should be plenty more opportunities for him. (4/1: op 9/4)
**Star Rage (IRE)**, who has enjoyed a rewarding season over hurdles, could not muster the pace to get in a blow against the winner, but was far from disgraced and will find easier pickings. (9/2: 11/4-5/1)
**563 Noufari (FR)** was hard at work down the back straight and never held out much hope for his supporters. He may still have needed this run. (4/5: op 9/4)
**Old Provence** was fighting a lost cause from a long way out, and was possibly out of his depth at the weights against the principals. (16/1)
**Premier Dance** (10/1: 6/1-11/1)

## 838 STAR ENGINEERING (S) STKS (Qualifier) (2-Y.O) (Class F)

9-00 (9-00) **5f (Fibresand)** £2,415.00 (£665.00: £315.00) Stalls: Low GOING: 0.04 sec per fur (STD)

| | Horse | Details | Dist | Pos | SP | RR | SF |
|---|---|---|---|---|---|---|---|
| $590^{7}$ | **Lawful Find (IRE)** | (RHollinshead) **$2\text{-}8\text{-}12^{(5)}$** FLynch(5) (hdwy over 2f out: brought wd s: shkn up to ld cl home) | — | **1** | 10/1 | 57 | 17 |
| $706^{8}$ | **Grovefair Flyer (IRE)** | (BJMeehan) **2-8-12** MTebbutt(7) (chsd ldr: led ½-wy: hrd drvn & hdd nr fin) | ½ | **2** | 5/1 | 50 | 10 |
| | **Come Too Mamma's** | (JBerry) **2-8-7** JCarroll(6) (w'like: bit bkwd: s.i.s: bhd & outpcd tl r.o strly appr fnl f) | ¾ | **3** | $7/2^{2}$ | 43 | 3 |
| $770^{5}$ | **Abstone Again (IRE)** | (PDEvans) **2-8-12** SSanders(4) (lw: trckd ldrs: drvn along 2f out: styng on whn n.m.r appr fnl f) | 1 | **4** | 12/1 | 45 | 5 |
| $733^{5}$ | **Dancing Star (IRE)** | (PDEvans) **$2\text{-}8\text{-}7v^{1}$** LDettori(3) (led to ½-wy: sn rdn: kpt on appr fnl f) | hd | **5** | 6/1 | 40 | — |
| | **Tazio Nuvolari** | (WGMTurner) **2-8-7** TSprake(9) (leggy: scope: outpcd tl sme late hdwy) | 2½ | **6** | $9/2^{3}$ | 32 | — |
| $624^{2}$ | **Small Risk** | (CADwyer) **2-8-7** JQuinn(8) (lw: gd spd 3f) | 2 | **7** | $9/2^{3}$ | 25 | — |
| $596^{10}$ | **Belle Dancer** | (TWall) **$2\text{-}8\text{-}2^{(5)}$** LNewton(10) (bit bkwd: outpcd: t.o) | 9 | **8** | 25/1 | — | — |
| $733^{3}$ | **Cantsaynowt** | (RAFahey) **2-8-7** ACulhane(2) (spd to ½-wy: wknd qckly: t.o) | ½ | **9** | $3/1^{1}$ | — | — |
| | **White Nemesis (IRE)** | (MartynMeade) **2-8-7** VSlattery(1) (lt-f: unf: s.s: a bhd & outpcd) | 1½ | **10** | 25/1 | — | — |
| | | | | | (SP 139.0%) | | **10 Rn** |

**63.9 secs** (5.20) CSF £65.22 TOTE £6.80: £1.90 £1.90 £2.40 (£23.60) OWNER Mr J. Doxey (UPPER LONGDON) BRED Joseph O'Callaghan
No bid
OFFICIAL EXPLANATION **Cantsaynowt: failed to act on the surface.**
**533* Lawful Find (IRE)**, pulled wide to deliver his challenge, picked up well when set alight and powered through to take control close home. (10/1: op 6/1)
**Grovefair Flyer (IRE)**, making a quick return to action for this first appearance on the All-Weather, proved a tough nut to crack in the closing stages, and an early success should come as just reward. (5/1)
**Come Too Mamma's**, whose dam was a useful winning sprinter, did well to finish so close after missing the break and will take all the beating next time. (7/2)
**Abstone Again (IRE)**, brought out far too soon after making his racecourse debut four days ago, did not enjoy the run of the race in the closing stages, and a race of this description is there for the taking. (12/1: op 7/1)
**733 Dancing Star (IRE)** was visored for the first time and flew from the stalls to set a very brisk pace. She had been collared on the home turn though, and it is to her credit that she was able to finish so close. (6/1)
**733 Cantsaynowt** found this race coming far too soon, and she had been shaken off soon after halfway. (3/1)

## 839 HARRY'S BIRTHDAY H'CAP (0-60) (3-Y.O+) (Class F)

9-30 (9-30) **7f (Fibresand)** £2,381.00 (£656.00: £311.00) Stalls: High GOING: 0.04 sec per fur (STD)

| | Horse | Details | Dist | Pos | SP | RR | SF |
|---|---|---|---|---|---|---|---|
| 734* | **Young Benson (47)** | (BAMcMahon) **4-9-4** GCarter(7) (lw: mde all: clr 2f out: unchal) | — | **1** | $4/1^{2}$ | 70 | 52 |
| $764^{5}$ | **Komlucky (39)** | (ABMulholland) **4-8-10b** TWilliams(8) (trckd ldrs: wnt 2nd 2f out: no imp) | 10 | **2** | 16/1 | 39 | 21 |
| *$654^{2}$* | **Quinzii Martin (53)** | (DHaydnJones) **8-9-10** AMackay(4) (lw: trckd ldrs: hrd drvn over 2f out: one pce) | 1½ | **3** | $2/1^{1}$ | 50 | 32 |
| *$518^{6}$* | **Irchester Lass (47)** | (SRBowring) **$4\text{-}8\text{-}13b^{(5)}$** CTeague(10) (chsd ldrs: rdn 3f out: kpt on same pce) | 1½ | **4** | 12/1 | 40 | 22 |
| *$521^{9}$* | **Cheerful Groom (IRE) (38)** | (SRBowring) **5-8-9** NKennedy(9) (hdwy over 2f out: nvr nrr) | 2½ | **5** | 12/1 | 26 | 8 |
| $586^{4}$ | **Shareoftheaction (45)** | (MrsAMNaughton) **5-9-2v** VHalliday(3) (rdn ½-wy: nvr nr to chal) | 2½ | **6** | 14/1 | 27 | 9 |
| *$320^{4}$* | **Don't Get Caught (IRE) (48)** | (JLHarris) **4-9-5** JFEgan(5) (a bhd & outpcd) | 2½ | **7** | $10/1^{3}$ | 24 | 6 |
| | **Miss Charlie (38)** | (TWall) **6-8-9** RLappin(11) (b.hind: bkwd: trckd ldrs over 4f) | 1¼ | **8** | 20/1 | 11 | — |
| *$607^{7}$* | **Tilly Owl (42)** | (JAHarris) **5-8-13** JO'Reilly(2) (prom 4f: wknd qckly) | 2½ | **9** | $4/1^{2}$ | 10 | — |
| $661^{4}$ | **La Dama (USA) (40)** | (ABMulholland) **4-8-11** MMcAndrew(12) (racd wd: a bhd: t.o) | 5 | **10** | 14/1 | — | — |
| *$556^{6}$* | **Titanium Honda (IRE) (39)** | (DCO'Brien) **5-8-10** GBardwell(6) (b: bit bkwd: a bhd & outpcd: t.o) | hd | **11** | 25/1 | — | — |
| $540^{2}$ | **Classic Victory (50)** | (RHarris) **3-8-8hb** DBatteate(1) (w wnr 3f: wknd wl over 3f out: t.o) | 4 | **12** | 12/1 | — | — |
| | | | | | (SP 133.3%) | | **12 Rn** |

**1m 29.2** (4.50) CSF £66.11 CT £158.85 TOTE £4.90: £1.60 £5.80 £1.50 (£56.60) OWNER Mr Michael Stokes (TAMWORTH) BRED M. G. T. Stokes
WEIGHT FOR AGE 3yo-13lb

**734* Young Benson**, at the top of his form just now, can obviously handle all types of ground and, in winning this race in a common canter, is only just finding his way. (4/1)
**764 Komlucky** won a separate race for the runner-up prize but could not get within striking range of the winner. (16/1)
**654 Quinzii Martin**, stepping back to his ideal trip, was always flat to the boards in an attempt to keep tabs on the winner and could do little more than gallop on the spot from the turn into the straight. (2/1: op 7/2)
**Irchester Lass**, off the bridle for most of the way, kept plugging on, but failed to make any impression. (12/1)
**247 Cheerful Groom (IRE)** did stay on past beaten rivals in the latter stages, but was never seen in the race at any stage. (12/1)
**586 Shareoftheaction** has shown his best form on this surface in the past, but this step down in distance was certainly not in his favour. (14/1)
**540 Classic Victory** (12/1: op 7/1)

T/Plpt: £265.80 (46.12 Tckts). T/Qdpt: £49.80 (16.58 Tckts). IM

# 0576-KEMPTON (R-H) (Good to firm)
## Monday April 29th

Races 1, 3-6 & 8 hand-timed
WEATHER: fine WIND: fresh half bhd

## 840 KEMPTON ANTIQUES MARKET MAIDEN STKS (I) (3-Y.O+) (Class D)

1-50 (1-52) **7f (Jubilee)** £3,239.50 (£976.00: £473.00: £221.50) Stalls: High GOING minus 0.24 sec per fur (GF)

| | | | | SP | RR | SF |
|---|---|---|---|---|---|---|
| | **Azizzi** (CREgerton) **4-9-10** RHughes(8) (hdwy over 2f out: led wl over 1f out: hrd rdn: r.o wl) | — | **1** | 33/1 | 97 | 67 |
| | **Sabot (102)** (BWHills) **3-8-11** MHills(3) (led over 3f: led over 2f out tl wl over 1f out: unable qckn fnl f) | 2 | **2** | 9/4[2] | 92 | 49 |
| | **Biscay** (RCharlton) **3-8-6** TSprake(5) (w'like: scope: w ldr: led over 3f out tl over 2f out: wknd over 1f out) | 10 | **3** | 12/1 | 65 | 22 |
| | **Smooth Asset (IRE)** (PWChapple-Hyam) **3-8-6** JReid(13) (unf: hmpd on ins & lost pl over 3f out: rallied over 1f out: r.o) | nk | **4** | 11/10[1] | 64 | 21 |
| | **Ironheart** (JHMGosden) **3-8-11** LDettori(11) (a.p: rdn over 2f out: wknd over 1f out) | 1½ | **5** | 6/1[3] | 66 | 23 |
| 626[8] | **Le Bam Bam** (HAkbary) **4-9-10** GHind(9) (nvr nr to chal) | ½ | **6** | 50/1 | 64 | 34 |
| | **Formidable Partner** (RWArmstrong) **3-8-11** RHills(7) (bkwd: nvr nrr) | nk | **7** | 10/1 | 64 | 21 |
| 648[7] | **Natal Ridge (63)** (DHaydnJones) **3-8-11** RCochrane(10) (prom over 4f) | 3 | **8** | 50/1 | 57 | 14 |
| | **Rose Tint (IRE)** (LordHuntingdon) **3-8-7**[ow1] PatEddery(4) (bhd fnl 3f) | 3 | **9** | 14/1 | 46 | 2 |
| | **Spandrel** (HCandy) **4-9-5** CRutter(1) (prom over 4f) | 1¼ | **10** | 33/1 | 42 | 12 |
| | **Tiama (IRE) (60)** (SDow) **3-8-6** WRyan(12) (a bhd) | s.h | **11** | 33/1 | 42 | — |
| | **The Grey Weaver** (RMFlower) **3-8-11** DBiggs(2) (str: v.bkwd: bmpd s: a wl bhd: t.o fnl 4f) | dist | **12** | 50/1 | — | — |
| | **Jades Shadow** (JJBridger) **3-8-8**[(3)] SDrowne(6) (leggy: s.s: a wl bhd: t.o fnl 4f) | 1½ | **13** | 50/1 | — | — |
| | | | | (SP 132.8%) | **13 Rn** | |

**1m 26.2** (1.70) CSF £110.90 TOTE £68.40: £9.30 £1.10 £3.40 (£101.70) Trio £141.50; £121.60 to Bath 30/4/96 OWNER Mr Chris Brasher (CHADDLEWORTH) BRED E. Aldridge
WEIGHT FOR AGE 3yo-13lb

**Azizzi** was making a belated racecourse debut, but was up to the job. Moving through to hit the front early in the final quarter-mile, he was given a few reminders but, in the end, won with a bit to spare. (33/1)
**Sabot** regained the advantage over a quarter of a mile from home. Headed well over a furlong out, he tried to live with the winner, but was tapped for toe in the last 200 yards. (9/4)
**Biscay**, a filly with some scope, disputed the lead until going on at halfway. Collared over a quarter of a mile from home, she was left standing by the front two. (12/1: op 6/1)
**Smooth Asset (IRE)**, quite a sparely-made individual, did not have the happiest of introductions. Almost put over the rail at halfway, she lost quite a bit of ground as a result and her jockey was not hard on her subsequently. However, she was noted staying on from below the distance and would certainly have been at least third but for the incident. She is worth another chance. (11/10: Evens-10/11)
**Ironheart** (6/1: op 5/2)
**Rose Tint (IRE)** (14/1: 6/1-16/1)

## 841 E.B.F. POLYANTHUS MAIDEN STKS (2-Y.O) (Class D)

2-20 (2-23) **5f** £3,551.50 (£1,072.00: £521.00: £245.50) Stalls: Low GOING minus 0.24 sec per fur (GF)

| | | | | SP | RR | SF |
|---|---|---|---|---|---|---|
| | **Arethusa** (RHannon) **2-8-9** LDettori(1) (scope: hld up: led 2f out: pushed out) | — | **1** | 2/1[2] | 75+ | 19 |
| 523[4] | **Joint Venture (IRE)** (BJMeehan) **2-9-0** MTebbutt(3) (led 3f: unable qckn) | 2½ | **2** | 7/1 | 72 | 16 |
| | **Mantles Prince** (GLewis) **2-9-0** SWhitworth(4) (str: scope: lost pl over 2f out: rallied fnl f: r.o) | 1¼ | **3** | 16/1 | 68 | 12 |
| | **Bold Catch (USA)** (RCharlton) **2-9-0** PatEddery(9) (cmpt: a.p: ev ch 2f out: one pce) | 1 | **4** | 15/8[1] | 65 | 9 |
| | **Tough Act** (GHarwood) **2-9-0** AClark(10) (neat: bit bkwd: s.i.s: nvr nr to chal) | nk | **5** | 16/1 | 64 | 8 |
| 685[5] | **Highland Pass (IRE)** (MMcCormack) **2-9-0** RCochrane(6) (spd over 3f) | 1½ | **6** | 14/1 | 59 | 3 |
| | **Kewarra** (BRMillman) **2-8-11**[(3)] SDrowne(5) (leggy: lt-f: bhd fnl 3f) | 1½ | **7** | 33/1 | 54 | — |
| | **Heart Full of Soul** (PFICole) **2-9-0** TQuinn(7) (w'like: scope: bit bkwd: hld up: rdn over 2f out: wknd over 1f out) | 1 | **8** | 6/1[3] | 51 | — |
| | **Speedfit** (GGMargarson) **2-9-0** WCarson(8) (w'like: bkwd: bhd fnl 2f) | 1¼ | **9** | 12/1 | 47 | — |
| | **Zaretski** (CEBrittain) **2-9-0** BDoyle(2) (str: bkwd: s.s: a bhd) | 12 | **10** | 14/1 | 9 | — |
| | | | | (SP 130.6%) | **10 Rn** | |

**61.39 secs** (3.19) CSF £17.96 TOTE £3.30: £1.40 £1.60 £4.50 (£12.60) Trio £45.90 OWNER Lord Carnarvon (MARLBOROUGH) BRED P. and Mrs Venner

**Arethusa**, a scopey newcomer, certainly knew what was required. Cruising into the lead a quarter of a mile out, she needed only to be nudged along for a thoroughly convincing display. (2/1)
**523 Joint Venture (IRE)**, with experience on his side, took the field along but, collared by the winner a quarter of a mile out, was firmly put in his place. (7/1: op 3/1)
**Mantles Prince**, a well-built individual, was outpaced at halfway, but got his second wind in the final furlong and managed to reach third place. He should be a lot wiser for this. (16/1)
**Bold Catch (USA)**, a close-coupled individual, had every chance a quarter of a mile from home before tapped for toe. (15/8)
**Heart Full of Soul** (6/1: op 5/2)
**Zaretski** (14/1: 7/1-16/1)

## 842 KEMPTON ANTIQUES MARKET MAIDEN STKS (II) (3-Y.O+) (Class D)

2-50 (2-51) **7f (Jubilee)** £3,220.00 (£970.00: £470.00: £220.00) Stalls: High GOING minus 0.24 sec per fur (GF)

| | Horse | Dist | Pos | SP | RR | SF |
|---|---|---|---|---|---|---|
| | **West Humble** (LadyHerries) **3-8-6** DeclanO'Shea(13) (hld up: led over 1f out: comf) | — | **1** | 6/1[3] | 79+ | 50 |
| 583[4] | **Reveuse de Jour (IRE)** (RCharlton) **3-8-6** TQuinn(1) (w ldr: led over 2f out: sn hdd: unable qckn) | 4 | **2** | 4/1[2] | 70 | 41 |
| | **Almuhimm (USA) (75)** (EALDunlop) **4-9-10** RHills(10) (s.s: hdwy over 3f out: led 2f out tl over 1f out: one pce) | ¾ | **3** | 12/1 | 73 | 57 |
| 640[3] | **Sandy Floss (IRE)** (HRACecil) **3-8-11** WRyan(8) (lw: a.p: rdn over 2f out: one pce) | 1 | **4** | 7/4[1] | 71 | 42 |
| 575[12] | **Albaha (USA) (88)** (RWArmstrong) **3-8-11** WCarson(5) (led over 4f: wknd over 1f out) | 2 | **5** | 7/1 | 66 | 37 |
| | **Silver Showers (USA)** (MRStoute) **3-8-6** KBradshaw(4) (leggy: nvr nr to chal) | nk | **6** | 16/1 | 61 | 32 |
| | **Soaked** (JRFanshawe) **3-8-11** DHarrison(7) (w'like: scope: bit bkwd: prom over 4f) | hd | **7** | 10/1 | 65 | 36 |
| | **Funny Wave** (HCandy) **3-8-6** CRutter(3) (w'like: a mid div) | 1¾ | **8** | 25/1 | 56 | 27 |
| 663[10] | **Ood Dancer (USA)** (LMCumani) **3-8-11** OUrbina(6) (nvr plcd to chal) | ¾ | **9** | 25/1 | 60++ | 31 |
| 583[6] | **In Tune** (PHowling) **3-8-11** FNorton(9) (nvr nrr) | d.h | **9** | 33/1 | 60 | 31 |
| | **Croagh Patrick** (JCFox) **4-9-5**(5) DaneO'Neill(11) (a bhd) | nk | **11** | 50/1 | 59 | 43 |
| | **Barrack Yard** (ACStewart) **3-8-6**(5) MHumphries(12) (w'like: bit bkwd: mid div over 5f) | 1 | **12** | 16/1 | 57 | 28 |
| | **Pusey Street Girl** (JRBosley) **3-8-6** RCochrane(2) (w'like: bit bkwd: s.s: a bhd) | hd | **13** | 25/1 | 52 | 23 |
| | | | | (SP 128.1%) | | **13 Rn** |

**1m 26.2** (1.70) CSF £30.58 TOTE £9.10: £2.20 £1.50 £3.20 (£31.30) Trio £31.80 OWNER Mrs P. J. Sheen (LITTLEHAMPTON) BRED The Overbury Stud

WEIGHT FOR AGE 3yo-13lb

STEWARDS' ENQUIRY Urbina susp. 8-11 & 13-14/5/96 (failure to ensure best possible placing). Cumani fined £100 (failure to give adequate instructions).

**West Humble** put up a convincing display. Chasing the leaders, she came through to lead below the distance and soon shot clear for a comfortable success. (6/1)

**583 Reveuse de Jour (IRE)** disputed the lead until going on over a quarter of a mile out. Soon headed, she failed to find another gear, but stuck on well for second prize. (4/1)

**Almuhimm (USA)**, who has been gelded since last year, moved up to grab a narrow advantage a quarter of a mile out. Soon headed by the winner, he could only struggle on at one pace. (12/1: op 7/1)

**640 Sandy Floss (IRE)** was made to look very pedestrian in the straight. A step up in trip is definitely required. (7/4: Evens-2/1)

**Albaha (USA)** found the writing on the wall come the distance. (7/1)

**Silver Showers (USA)**, a tall filly, stayed on without over posing a serious threat. (16/1)

**Soaked** (10/1: op 4/1)

**Ood Dancer (USA)** was never allowed to get in the race with his jockey anchoring him at the back of the field. The Stewards were quick to pick up on this and suspended his rider for six days and fined Cumani £100 over his riding instructions. The colt still looked in need of the run and is sure to benefit from this. (25/1)

## 843 FLORENCE NAGLE GIRL APPRENTICE H'CAP (0-80) (3-Y.O+) (Class F)

3-20 (3-23) **1m 1f** £2,710.00 (£760.00: £370.00) Stalls: Low GOING minus 0.24 sec per fur (GF)

| | Horse | Dist | Pos | SP | RR | SF |
|---|---|---|---|---|---|---|
| *654** | **Golden Touch (USA) (60)** (NACallaghan) **4-8-11** AngelaGallimore(1) (lw: hdwy over 2f out: stumbled over 1f out: led last strides) | — | **1** | 9/2[2] | 68 | 38 |
| *654[4]* | **Sooty Tern (69)** (JMBradley) **9-9-6** SophieMitchell(11) (b.off fore: a.p: led over 2f out: hrd rdn fnl f: hdd last strides) | nk | **2** | 11/2[3] | 77 | 47 |
| 752[11] | **I Recall (IRE) (56)** (PHayward) **5-8-7v1** IonaWands(12) (hdwy over 2f out: r.o ins fnl f) | ¾ | **3** | 33/1 | 62 | 32 |
| 752[16] | **Flag Fen (USA) (64)** (MartynMeade) **5-9-1** JoanneWebster(4) (hdwy over 2f out: r.o ins fnl f) | ¾ | **4** | 33/1 | 69 | 39 |
| 650[4] | **Master Beveled (73)** (PDEvans) **6-9-10** HayleyWilliams(7) (lw: a.p: ev ch over 1f out: one pce) | nk | **5** | 7/2[1] | 77 | 47 |
| | **Sharp Consul (IRE) (69)** (HCandy) **4-9-1**(5) SallySandes(9) (hld up: rdn over 2f out: sn wknd) | 3 | **6** | 8/1 | 68 | 38 |
| *353[10]* | **Comedy River (45)** (NEBerry) **9-7-10** JoHunnam(2) (hdwy over 4f out: wknd over 2f out) | nk | **7** | 66/1 | 43 | 13 |
| 450[16] | **Aeroking (USA) (77)** (GHarwood) **5-10-0** GayeHarwood(6) (a.p: led over 4f out tl over 2f out: sn wknd) | 2 | **8** | 9/2[2] | 72 | 42 |
| 547[9] | **Rival Bid (USA) (66)** (MrsNMacauley) **8-9-3** AmandaSanders(5) (s.i.s: a bhd) | 2½ | **9** | 13/2 | 56 | 26 |
| | **Persian Affair (IRE) (59)** (TJNaughton) **5-8-5**(5) RachaelMoody(10) (bit bkwd: s.s: hdwy over 4f out: wknd over 2f out) | 3 | **10** | 10/1 | 44 | 14 |
| 752[12] | **Tony's Mist (51)** (JMBradley) **6-8-2v1** AimeeCook(8) (lw: bhd fnl 3f) | nk | **11** | 20/1 | 36 | 6 |
| | **Clancy's Express (54)** (JCFox) **5-8-0**(5)ow9 HannahFox(3) (lw: led over 4f: wknd over 3f out) | 26 | **12** | 66/1 | — | — |
| | | | | (SP 121.1%) | | **12 Rn** |

**1m 54.8** (4.20) CSF £28.28 CT £683.77 TOTE £4.10: £1.90 £2.70 £5.50 (£14.20) Trio £82.90 OWNER Mrs Rita Godfrey (NEWMARKET) BRED Woodcote Stud Ltd

LONG HANDICAP Comedy River 7-7 Clancy's Express 6-1

**654* Golden Touch (USA)** began to thread his way through the field over a quarter of a mile from home. Soon throwing down his challenge, he stumbled approaching the final furlong but, despite this, managed to get up in the last few strides. (9/2: 3/1-5/1)

**654 Sooty Tern** was given a fine ride by the best jockey by far in the race. Showing in front over a quarter of a mile from home, Mitchell very stylishly got down to work on the horse, only to be worried out of it in the last few strides. (11/2)

**I Recall (IRE)** picked up ground over a quarter of a mile from home and kept on well inside the final furlong. (33/1)

**628 Flag Fen (USA)** made a forward move early in the straight and stuck to his task really well inside the final furlong. (33/1)

**650 Master Beveled** was never far away. Close enough if good enough below the distance, he was then tapped for toe. (7/2)

**Sharp Consul (IRE)** chased the leaders but the writing was on the wall early in the straight. (8/1)

## 844 NORMAN HILL PLANT HIRE H'CAP (0-85) (4-Y.O+) (Class D)

3-50 (3-51) **1m 4f** £3,733.50 (£1,128.00: £549.00: £259.50) Stalls: High GOING minus 0.24 sec per fur (GF)

| | Horse | Dist | Pos | SP | RR | SF |
|---|---|---|---|---|---|---|
| | **Roisin Clover (66)** (SDow) **5-8-11** WRyan(11) (hdwy 2f out: led 1f out: r.o wl) | — | **1** | 6/1[2] | 78 | 60 |
| | **General Mouktar (54)** (BJMeehan) **6-7-13**ow2 WCarson(12) (hdwy over 2f out: ev ch 1f out: unable qckn) | 2½ | **2** | 10/1 | 63 | 43 |
| | **George Bull (63)** (MajorWRHern) **4-8-7** TSprake(2) (lw: a.p: led over 3f out to 1f out: one pce) | 1¼ | **3** | 13/2[3] | 70 | 51 |
| 636[12] | **Crested Knight (IRE) (60)** (CAHorgan) **4-8-4**ow1 DHarrison(3) (hdwy over 2f out: one pce) | 2½ | **4** | 16/1 | 64 | 44 |
| 580[7] | **Secret Aly (CAN) (82)** (CEBrittain) **6-9-13** BDoyle(14) (lw: hld up: rdn over 2f out: one pce) | 5 | **5** | 10/1 | 79 | 61 |
| | **Dormy Three (69)** (RJHodges) **6-9-0** RCochrane(4) (hdwy over 2f out: wknd over 1f out) | 1½ | **6** | 14/1 | 64 | 46 |
| 816[11] | **Sayitagain (59)** (JRJenkins) **4-8-3** FNorton(5) (hdwy over 2f out: wknd over 1f out) | 5 | **7** | 33/1 | 47 | 28 |

| | Horse | Dist | Pos | SP | RR | SF |
|---|---|---|---|---|---|---|
| 650$^{7}$ | **Petoskin (72)** (JPearce) **4-9-2** GBardwell(1) (nvr nrr) | 5 | **8** | 9/1 | 54 | 35 |
| 573$^{9}$ | **Typhoon Eight (IRE) (74)** (BWHills) **4-9-4** MHills(8) (rdn & hdwy over 3f out: wknd over 2f out) | nk | **9** | 9/1 | 55 | 36 |
| 564$^{3}$ | **Vaugrenier (IRE) (77)** (RHannon) **4-9-7** PatEddery(7) (lw: prom 10f) | nk | **10** | 5/1$^{1}$ | 58 | 39 |
| | **Exhibit Air (IRE) (60)** (RAkehurst) **6-8-5** TQuinn(9) (led over 9f out tl over 3f out: wknd over 2f out) | nk | **11** | 8/1 | 41 | 23 |
| 573$^{17}$ | **Proton (76)** (RAkehurst) **6-9-7** SSanders(13) (prom over 8f) | ½ | **12** | 7/1 | 56 | 38 |
| | **Jovie King (IRE) (54)** (PhilipMitchell) **4-7-12**$^{ow2}$ CRutter(10) (lw: bhd fnl 5f) | 1 | **13** | 33/1 | 33 | 12 |
| | **Gloriana (73)** (LadyHerries) **4-9-3** JReid(6) (lw: led over 2f: wknd 3f out) | ¾ | **14** | 10/1 | 51 | 32 |

(SP 133.6%) **14 Rn**

**2m 33.1** (2.40) CSF £65.91 CT £383.56 TOTE £5.60: £2.40 £2.70 £2.20 (£42.00) Trio £124.10 OWNER Brighthelm Racing (EPSOM) BRED D. A. and Mrs Hicks

LONG HANDICAP Jovie King (IRE) 7-8

WEIGHT FOR AGE 4yo-1lb

**Roisin Clover** followed up last year's victory in this race. Picking up ground in the straight, she hit the front a furlong out and soon asserted. (6/1)

**General Mouktar**, who has changed stables since last season, began a forward move early in the straight. With every chance entering the final furlong, he was then tapped for toe. He has slipped down the weights substantially due to a series of poor efforts last year - he was racing off 52 here but has won off 72 - and may now be ready to strike. (10/1)

**George Bull** made his bid for glory turning into the straight and soon had a useful advantage. However, he may have hit the front too soon because, once collared a furlong out, he could only plod on at one pace. (13/2)

**Crested Knight (IRE)** could only go up and down in the same place from below the distance. (16/1)

**Secret Aly (CAN)** was made to look very pedestrian in the straight. (10/1)

**Dormy Three** made an effort early in the straight but was a spent force below the distance. (14/1)

**Petoskin** (9/1: 6/1-10/1)

## 845 HEWITT OF SUNBURY MAIDEN STKS (I) (3-Y.O+) (Class D)

4-20 (4-23) **1m 2f (Jubilee)** £3,239.50 (£976.00: £473.00: £221.50) Stalls: High GOING minus 0.24 sec per fur (GF)

| | Horse | Dist | Pos | SP | RR | SF |
|---|---|---|---|---|---|---|
| 544$^{4}$ | **Murheb (90)** (RWArmstrong) **3-8-9** RPrice(10) (plld hrd: a.p: led over 2f out: r.o wl) | — | **1** | 11/2$^{3}$ | 85 | 47 |
| | **Count Basie** (HRACecil) **3-8-9** PatEddery(4) (w'like: bit bkwd: hld up: ev ch over 2f out: r.o ins fnl f) | ½ | **2** | 5/1$^{2}$ | 84 | 46 |
| | **Jiyush** (HThomsonJones) **3-8-9** RHills(2) (hdwy over 1f out: r.o wl ins fnl f) | s.h | **3** | 10/1 | 84 | 46 |
| 732$^{5}$ | **Kuala Lipis (USA)** (PFICole) **3-8-9** TQuinn(1) (a.p: led 3f out tl over 2f out: wknd fnl f) | 2½ | **4** | 2/1$^{1}$ | 80 | 42 |
| | **Candle Smile (USA)** (MRStoute) **4-9-12** JReid(9) (hdwy over 1f out: r.o one pce) | ¾ | **5** | 10/1 | 79 | 58 |
| | **King of Sparta** (LMCumani) **3-8-9** OUrbina(8) (str: bkwd: nvr nr to chal) | 1¾ | **6** | 12/1 | 76 | 38 |
| | **Naseem Alsahar** (MajorWRHern) **3-8-4** TSprake(11) (prom 7f) | 3 | **7** | 6/1 | 66 | 28 |
| 684$^{13}$ | **Gulliver** (BWHills) **3-8-9** MHills(7) (lw: hdwy over 3f out: wknd 2f out) | s.h | **8** | 12/1 | 71 | 33 |
| | **Alicia (IRE)** (JLDunlop) **3-8-4** SWhitworth(6) (nvr nrr) | s.h | **9** | 25/1 | 66 | 28 |
| 677$^{14}$ | **Apicella** (JPearce) **3-8-9** GBardwell(13) (bhd fnl 3f) | 2½ | **10** | 50/1 | 67 | 29 |
| | **Scottish Hero** (JRFanshawe) **3-8-9** DHarrison(3) (w'like: bit bkwd: hld up: rdn over 2f out: wknd wl over 1f out) | nk | **11** | 14/1 | 67 | 29 |
| | **Lizium** (JCFox) **4-9-2**$^{(5)}$ DaneO'Neill(5) (bkwd: s.s: hdwy 6f out: wknd over 2f out) | 14 | **12** | 50/1 | 39 | 18 |
| *103*$^{8}$ | **Emperors Wood** (PHayward) **5-9-12** RHughes(12) (led 7f: sn wknd: t.o) | dist | **13** | 50/1 | — | — |

(SP 129.6%) **13 Rn**

**2m 6.8** (3.30) CSF £33.85 TOTE £6.60: £1.70 £1.60 £2.70 (£35.90) Trio £55.00 OWNER Mr Ahmed Al Shafar (NEWMARKET) BRED Ahmed Shufaar

WEIGHT FOR AGE 3yo-17lb

**544 Murheb**, who took a keen hold, was never far away. Sent on early in the straight, he kept his rivals at bay. (11/2)

**Count Basie**, a plain half-brother to numerous winners in Ireland, France and Italy, kept on really well to the line. He should be able to find a race. (5/1: op 2/1)

**Jiyush** really found his feet from below the distance and was finishing best of all, only to find the line coming a bit too soon. He should soon open his account. (10/1)

**732 Kuala Lipis (USA)** had run out of gas entering the final furlong. (2/1)

**Candle Smile (USA)** will be better suited by a return to further. (10/1: 6/1-12/1)

**King of Sparta**, a well-made newcomer, looked far from fit but struggled on from the back of the field in the last two furlongs. (12/1: 6/1-14/1)

**Naseem Alsahar** (6/1: op 7/2)

**684 Gulliver** (12/1: 8/1-14/1)

**Scottish Hero** (14/1: 7/1-20/1)

## 846 SYRINGA H'CAP (0-80) (3-Y.O+) (Class D)

4-50 (4-51) **6f** £3,792.00 (£1,146.00: £558.00: £264.00) Stalls: Low GOING minus 0.24 sec per fur (GF)

| | Horse | Dist | Pos | SP | RR | SF |
|---|---|---|---|---|---|---|
| 735$^{12}$ | **Latching (IRE) (80)** (RFJohnsonHoughton) **4-10-0** JReid(4) (lw: hdwy over 1f out: hrd rdn: led last stride) | — | **1** | 10/1 | 85 | 52 |
| | **Efra (64)** (RHannon) **7-8-7**$^{(5)}$ DaneO'Neill(11) (lw: hld up: rdn over 2f out: led wl ins fnl f: hdd last stride) | s.h | **2** | 9/1 | 69 | 36 |
| | **La Petite Fusee (71)** (RJO'Sullivan) **5-9-5** RHughes(10) (chsd ldr: led 2f out tl wl ins fnl f: one pce) | 1¾ | **3** | 12/1 | 71 | 38 |
| 711$^{11}$ | **How's Yer Father (77)** (RJHodges) **10-9-8**$^{(3)}$ SDrowne(3) (outpcd: hdwy over 1f out: r.o wl ins fnl f) | ½ | **4** | 20/1 | 76 | 43 |
| | **Time For Tea (IRE) (70)** (CACyzer) **3-8-7** TQuinn(6) (lw: hld up: hrd rdn over 2f out: wknd ins fnl f) | 2½ | **5** | 16/1 | 62 | 18 |
| 582$^{24}$ | **Ahjay (54)** (TJNaughton) **6-7-13**$^{(3)}$ DRMcCabe(1) (nvr nr to chal) | 3 | **6** | 20/1 | 38 | 5 |
| 667$^{2}$ | **Moujeeb (USA) (62)** (PatMitchell) **6-8-10v** LDettori(13) (lw: hdwy over 2f out: wknd fnl f) | nk | **7** | 9/1 | 45 | 12 |
| 582$^{6}$ | **Spectacle Jim (48)** (MJHaynes) **7-7-5b**$^{(5)}$ MBaird(2) (dwlt: outpcd: nvr nrr) | 1 | **8** | 14/1 | 29 | — |
| | **Dwingeloo (IRE) (66)** (MajorDNChappell) **3-8-3** BThomson(12) (led 4f) | hd | **9** | 3/1$^{1}$ | 47 | 3 |
| | **Judgement Call (48)** (PHowling) **9-7-10** FNorton(9) (prom over 2f) | 2 | **10** | 25/1 | 23 | — |
| | **Allyana (IRE) (68)** (RHannon) **4-9-2** PatEddery(5) (dwlt: a bhd) | 2½ | **11** | 6/1$^{3}$ | 37 | 4 |
| | **Rise Up Singing (58)** (WJMusson) **8-8-6b** OUrbina(8) (lw: bhd fnl 2f) | 3½ | **12** | 25/1 | 17 | — |
| 632* | **Bashful Brave (74)** (JWPayne) **5-9-8** RCochrane(7) (lw: hld up: rdn over 2f out: sn wknd: lame) | ¾ | **13** | 9/2$^{2}$ | 31 | — |

(SP 124.0%) **13 Rn**

**1m 14.1** (2.80) CSF £91.63 CT £1,037.27 TOTE £11.90: £3.30 £4.50 £2.30 (£62.20) Trio £215.00 OWNER Mr R. F. JohnsonHoughton (DIDCOT) BRED Tullamaine Castle Stud

LONG HANDICAP Spectacle Jim 7-9

WEIGHT FOR AGE 3yo-11lb

**582* Latching (IRE)** began to find her feet from below the distance and came with a useful run to snatch the spoils right on the line. (10/1)
**Efra** chased the leaders. Getting down to some good work in the last two furlongs, he got on top in the closing stages only to be caught right on the line. He is a winner without a penalty. (9/1)
**La Petite Fusee** chased the leader until going on a quarter of a mile out. Grimly trying to hold on, she was worried out of it in the closing stages. (12/1)
**How's Yer Father**, unable to lay up with the early pace, stayed on really well from below the distance but was never going to get there in time. (20/1)
**Time For Tea (IRE)** chased the leaders. Almost on terms with the leader below the distance, she tired inside the last 100 yards. (16/1)
**Dwingeloo (IRE)** (3/1: op 7/4)

## 847 HEWITT OF SUNBURY MAIDEN STKS (II) (3-Y.O+) (Class D)

5-20 (5-21) **1m 2f (Jubilee)** £3,220.00 (£970.00: £470.00: £220.00) Stalls: High GOING minus 0.24 sec per fur (GF)

| | | | | SP | RR | SF |
|---|---|---|---|---|---|---|
| 684[10] | **Yom Jameel (IRE)** (MRStoute) **3-8-9** BDoyle(1) (lw: rdn over 2f out: hdwy over 1f out: str run fnl f: led nr fin) | — | **1** | 12/1 | 81 | 51 |
| 687[2] | **Axford (USA) (95)** (PWChapple-Hyam) **3-8-9** JReid(12) (lw: plld hrd: chsd ldr: led wl over 1f out: rdn & hdd nr fin) | ½ | **2** | 4/6[1] | 80 | 50 |
| 578[4] | **Generosa** (HCandy) **3-8-5**[ow1] RCochrane(8) (led over 8f: r.o) | ½ | **3** | 5/1[3] | 75 | 44 |
| | **Raed** (PTWalwyn) **3-8-9** WCarson(11) (a.p: rdn over 2f out: hung rt fnl 2f: nt rcvr) | 8 | **4** | 4/1[2] | 67 | 37 |
| 684[16] | **Nuzu (IRE)** (BWHills) **3-8-9** MHills(5) (nvr nr to chal) | s.h | **5** | [illegible] | 67 | 37 |
| 578[8] | **Code Red** (JWHills) **3-8-9** BThomson(9) (hld up: rdn over 2f out: sn wknd) | nk | **6** | 20/1 | 66 | 36 |
| | **Dolliver (USA) (63)** (SDow) **4-9-12** WRyan(7) (hld up: rdn over 2f out: sn wknd) | 1½ | **7** | 66/1 | 64 | 51 |
| | **Hoofprints (IRE)** (GHarwood) **3-8-9** AClark(3) (bit bkwd: prom over 8f) | 2 | **8** | 20/1 | 60 | 30 |
| | **Dance Model** (JJSheehan) **3-8-2**(3)[ow1] SDrowne(4) (leggy: lt-f: s.s: a bhd) | 4 | **9** | 40/1 | 50 | 19 |
| 707[9] | **Tribal Moon (IRE)** (LadyHerries) **3-8-9** MTebbutt(10) (a bhd) | 6 | **10** | 25/1 | 44 | 14 |
| | **Executive Officer** (RMFlower) **3-8-9** DBiggs(6) (w'like: bit bkwd: s.s: a bhd) | 24 | **11** | 100/1 | 6 | — |
| | | | | (SP 128.5%) | **11 Rn** | |

**2m 6.3** (2.80) CSF £21.43 TOTE £10.90: £2.50 £1.30 £1.20 (£6.10) Trio £7.80 OWNER Sheikh Ahmed Al Maktoum (NEWMARKET) BRED Mitchelstown Stud
WEIGHT FOR AGE 3yo-17lb
**Yom Jameel (IRE)**, scrubbed along and going nowhere in midfield early in the straight, really found his feet from below the distance and, sprouting wings in the final furlong, swooped into the lead near the line. (12/1: 8/1-14/1)
**687 Axford (USA)** once again had to settle for being the bridesmaid. Taking a keen hold as he chased the leader, he moved to the front early in the final quarter-mile and at last looked likely to break his duck. However, the strong burst of the winner caught him out near the line. He richly deserves a change of luck. (4/6)
**578 Generosa** stuck to her task well to the bitter end. (5/1: op 5/2)
**Raed**, never far away, gave his rider real steering problems in the straight and could never recover. (4/1: 5/1-3/1)
**Nuzu (IRE)** stayed on in the closing stages without posing a threat. (16/1)
**Code Red** chased the leaders but was done with early in the home straight. (20/1)

T/Plpt: £267.00 (47.91 Tckts). T/Qdpt: £115.60 (7.63 Tckts). AK

# 0762-PONTEFRACT (L-H) (Good to firm)

## Monday April 29th

WEATHER: cloudy WIND: fresh half bhd

## 848 E.B.F. TOTE MAIDEN STKS (2-Y.O) (Class D)

2-40 (2-41) **5f** £4,221.00 (£1,278.00: £624.00: £297.00) Stalls: Low GOING minus 0.31 sec per fur (GF)

| | | | | SP | RR | SF |
|---|---|---|---|---|---|---|
| 697[2] | **Rude Awakening** (GLewis) **2-9-0** PaulEddery(6) (lw: chsd ldrs: led appr fnl f: r.o) | — | **1** | 4/6[1] | 81 | 23 |
| 685[2] | **Swino** (PDEvans) **2-9-0** KDarley(3) (lw: w ldrs: led wl over 1f out tl appr fnl f: nt qckn) | 3 | **2** | 11/2[2] | 71 | 13 |
| | **For Your Eyes Only** (TDEasterby) **2-9-0** MBirch(4) (b: w'like: scope: s.i.s: sn in tch & pushed along: kpt on fnl f) | ¾ | **3** | 11/2[2] | 69 | 11 |
| | **Ride Sally Ride (IRE)** (JBerry) **2-9-0** JCarroll(2) (w'like: str: w ldrs: led ½-wy tl wl over 1f out: no ex) | 1½ | **4** | 20/1 | 64 | 6 |
| | **Topatori (IRE)** (MHTompkins) **2-8-9** PRobinson(5) (lt-f: unf: in tch: outpcd 2f out: kpt on fnl f) | hd | **5** | 11/1[3] | 59 | 1 |
| | **Fast Spin** (TDBarron) **2-9-0** JFortune(7) (w'like: scope: bit bkwd: sn pushed along: nvr nr ldrs) | 5 | **6** | 33/1 | 48 | — |
| 733[7] | **Loxley's Girl (IRE)** (MWEasterby) **2-8-4**(5) GParkin(8) (s.s: wl bhd tl sme late hdwy) | 4 | **7** | 100/1 | 30 | — |
| | **Antares** (NTinkler) **2-9-0** WWoods(9) (str: scope: bkwd: a outpcd) | s.h | **8** | 25/1 | 35 | — |
| | **Calchou** (CWFairhurst) **2-8-9** DeanMcKeown(1) (unf: bit bkwd: slt ld to ½-wy: btn whn sltly hmpd over 1f out) | 1 | **9** | 33/1 | 27 | — |
| | | | | (SP 114.6%) | **9 Rn** | |

**63.9 secs** (3.10) CSF £4.86 TOTE £1.50: £1.00 £1.80 £2.60 (£2.60) Trio £6.40 OWNER Mr David Barker (EPSOM) BRED Capt A. L. Smith-Maxwell
**697 Rude Awakening** has a laid-back attitude in the paddock, but he got things right in the race this time and won authoritatively. (4/6)
**685 Swino** again had his chances but, when the pace was on, was found wanting. (11/2)
**For Your Eyes Only** is a decent type, but his action left something to be desired. However, he ran well and should have learnt plenty. (11/2: 4/1-6/1)
**Ride Sally Ride (IRE)** looked and moved well, but lack of experience told in the final furlong. Better looks likely. (20/1)
**Topatori (IRE)** is nothing special to look at, but she did show some promise in the race and was picking up at the end. (11/1: 6/1-12/1)
**Fast Spin**, a decent type, needed this but failed to make any impression. Time should see improvement. (33/1)

## 849 TOTE CREDIT (S) STKS (3-Y.O) (Class G)

3-10 (3-14) **1m 4f 8y** £2,469.00 (£684.00: £327.00) Stalls: Low GOING minus 0.31 sec per fur (GF)

| | | | | SP | RR | SF |
|---|---|---|---|---|---|---|
| 599[2] | **Four Weddings (USA) (49)** (MBell) **3-8-12v** MFenton(14) (swtg: hdwy 6f out: led 4f out: hld on wl) | — | **1** | 6/1[3] | 58 | 24 |
| 614[6] | **Champagne Warrior (IRE) (45)** (MJCamacho) **3-8-7** NConnorton(7) (chsd ldrs: outpcd over 3f out: hdwy over 1f out: chal ins fnl f: kpt on) | hd | **2** | 4/1[1] | 53 | 19 |

| | Horse | Dist | Pos | SP | RR | SF |
|---|---|---|---|---|---|---|
| | **Noble Lord** (MrsJRRamsden) **3-8-12** JFortune(5) (w'like: s.i.s: hdwy ½-wy: sn chsng ldrs: ev ch 2f out: r.o one pce) | 4 | **3** | 20/1 | 53 | 19 |
| 542[6] | **What Jim Wants (IRE) (40)** (JJO'Neill) **3-8-12** JQuinn(13) (chsd ldrs tl outpcd over 3f out: styd on wl fnl f) | 3 | **4** | 16/1 | 49 | 15 |
| 599[4] | **Poly My Son (IRE)** (MRChannon) **3-8-12** WWoods(11) (lw: a in tch: chal 4f out: wknd fnl 2f) | 1½ | **5** | 12/1 | 47 | 13 |
| 784[4] | **Appeal Again (IRE) (53)** (MrsJRRamsden) **3-8-12** DeanMcKeown(10) (swtg: hld up: hdwy 4f out: chsng ldrs 2f out: hung lft & nt r.o) | hd | **6** | 7/1 | 46 | 12 |
| 597[6] | **Cry Baby (53)** (NTinkler) **3-8-12** JCarroll(16) (hdwy over 3f out: chsng ldrs 2f out: one pce appr fnl f) | 1¾ | **7** | 10/1 | 44 | 10 |
| 616[5] | **Rattle (50)** (JJO'Neill) **3-8-12** AMackay(15) (bhd: hdwy fnl 3f: nrst fin) | 1¼ | **8** | 7/1 | 42 | 8 |
| *651*[4] | **Radmore Brandy (35)** (NPLittmoden) **3-8-7** TWilliams(6) (hdwy 4f out: n.d) | 9 | **9** | 20/1 | 26 | — |
| 637[6] | **Gresham Flyer (36)** (BRichmond) **3-8-7**(5) CTeague(1) (nvr trbld ldrs) | 2 | **10** | 50/1 | 28 | — |
| 588[3] | **Phar Closer** (WTKemp) **3-8-7** KDarley(9) (rdn 4f out: a bhd) | 18 | **11** | 20/1 | — | — |
| 599[3] | **Shamand (USA) (46)** (BJMeehan) **3-8-12** RPerham(3) (led to 4f out: sn wknd) | s.h | **12** | 10/1 | 4 | — |
| *459*[2] | **Suparoy (53)** (TGMills) **3-8-12** PaulEddery(12) (in tch tl wknd over 3f out) | 15 | **13** | 5/1[2] | — | — |
| | **Friendly Dreams (IRE)** (PTDalton) **3-8-2**(5) RHavlin(4) (bit bkwd: w ldr tl wknd 5f out) | 22 | **14** | 50/1 | — | — |
| | **Blenheim Terrace (58)** (CBBBooth) **3-8-12** MBirch(8) (swtg: bit bkwd: chsd ldrs tl wknd over 4f out) | ¾ | **15** | 20/1 | — | — |
| | **Martins Folly** (JWhite) **3-8-4**(3) DWright(2) (swtg: s.i.s: a bhd: t.o) | dist | **16** | 33/1 | — | — |
| | | | | (SP 133.6%) | | **16 Rn** |

**2m 41.9** (7.60) CSF £31.07 TOTE £8.30: £3.40 £1.20 £9.10 (£18.40) Trio £186.30 OWNER Mr R. P. B. Michaelson (NEWMARKET) BRED James D. Conway

Four Weddings (USA) soldMPipe 6,200gns; Noble Lord clmd JAllison £6,000

**599 Four Weddings (USA)** really had to battle to hold on here and answered in the gamest fashion. (6/1)

**Champagne Warrior (IRE)** has improved each time she has stepped up in distance. Gambled on, it was just lack of battling experience that beat her. (4/1: op 10/1)

**Noble Lord**, very green early on, came there with a serious challenge on the home turn, only to run out of petrol. (20/1)

**542 What Jim Wants (IRE)** was again putting in all his best work when it was too late and would seem to be crying out for longer trips. (16/1)

**599 Poly My Son (IRE)** should have beaten the winner strictly on form on their last run at Warwick, but this stiff finish sapped his stamina. (12/1)

**784 Appeal Again (IRE)** took a big step up in distance, but all he wanted to do was hang when the pressure was on and he is, without doubt, a very hard ride. (7/1)

**Cry Baby** showed some ability here, but failed to see the trip out. (10/1)

## 850 TOTE BOOKMAKERS H'CAP (0-80) (3-Y.O+) (Class D)

3-40 (3-43) **6f** £6,576.00 (£1,968.00: £944.00: £432.00) Stalls: Low GOING minus 0.31 sec per fur (GF)

| | Horse | Dist | Pos | SP | RR | SF |
|---|---|---|---|---|---|---|
| 589[2] | **Barrel of Hope (74)** (JLEyre) **4-9-8b** RLappin(10) (lw: mde most: r.o wl fnl 2f) | — | **1** | 14/1 | 86 | 59 |
| 749* | **Bollin Harry (75)** (TDEasterby) **4-9-9** 7x MBirch(15) (a chsng ldrs: hdwy 2f out: r.o) | 1½ | **2** | 10/1 | 83 | 56 |
| 704[4] | **Stand Tall (55)** (CWThornton) **4-8-3** DeanMcKeown(5) (lw: sn chsng ldrs: effrt 2f out: kpt on: nt pce to chal) | 3½ | **3** | 9/4[1] | 54 | 27 |
| 451[8] | **Bolshoi (IRE) (69)** (JBerry) **4-9-3b** JCarroll(4) (cl up: rdn wl over 1f out: one pce) | 1 | **4** | 16/1 | 65 | 38 |
| 582[14] | **Samsolom (67)** (PHowling) **8-9-1** PaulEddery(2) (b.off hind: lw: outpcd & bhd: hdwy over 1f out: styd on wl towards fin) | s.h | **5** | 25/1 | 63 | 36 |
| 764[3] | **Blue Grit (51)** (MDods) **10-7-13**ow1 AMackay(7) (bhd: styd on fnl f: nrst fin) | nk | **6** | 20/1 | 46 | 18 |
| 762* | **Captain Carat (60)** (MrsJRRamsden) **5-8-8** JFortune(12) (b.nr fore: lw: hdwy ½-wy: sn in tch: rdn & no imp fnl 1½f) | ¾ | **7** | 4/1[2] | 53 | 26 |
| | **Sea Thunder (79)** (IABalding) **4-9-13** KDarley(6) (bit bkwd: hdwy ½-wy: sn rdn & no imp) | 1¼ | **8** | 16/1 | 69 | 42 |
| 589[6] | **Halmanerror (70)** (MrsJRRamsden) **6-9-4** MFenton(13) (dwlt: hdwy 2f out: n.d) | hd | **9** | 9/1[3] | 60 | 33 |
| 659[4] | **Plum First (66)** (LRLloyd-James) **6-9-0** TWilliams(9) (b.hind: lw: in tch: rdn & no imp fnl 2f) | hd | **10** | 9/1[3] | 55 | 28 |
| 592[7] | **Dissentor (IRE) (49)** (JAGlover) **4-7-8v**(3)ow1 DWright(3) (swtg: in tch over 3f: wknd) | nk | **11** | 20/1 | 37 | 9 |
| 633[7] | **Delight of Dawn (72)** (KTIvory) **4-8-13**(7) CScally(16) (b: a bhd) | 2 | **12** | 33/1 | 55 | 28 |
| 716[4] | **Portend (78)** (SRBowring) **4-9-7**(5) CTeague(11) (racd wd: in tch tl wknd fnl 2f) | ¾ | **13** | 14/1 | 59 | 32 |
| 686[10] | **Miss Waterline (73)** (PDEvans) **3-8-5**(5) MHenry(14) (lost tch fr ½-wy) | 4 | **14** | 20/1 | 43 | 5 |
| *425*[9] | **Prime Property (IRE) (50)** (MWEasterby) **4-7-5b**(7)ow2 MartinDwyer(8) (gd spd over 3f: wknd qckly) | 5 | **15** | 33/1 | 7 | — |
| | | | | (SP 129.0%) | | **15 Rn** |

**1m 15.9** (1.60) CSF £141.51 CT £410.84 TOTE £17.40: £3.30 £4.90 £2.10 (£51.50) Trio £115.60 OWNER Mr Peter Watson (HAMBLETON) BRED Bolton Grange

LONG HANDICAP Dissentor (IRE) 7-7 Prime Property (IRE) 7-3

WEIGHT FOR AGE 3yo-11lb

**589 Barrel of Hope**, moderately drawn, stays further than this and, once he turned the heat on and got away from the halfway point, he was not going to stop. (14/1)

**749* Bollin Harry** ran well from a poor draw but, despite responding to pressure, always found the winner too good. (10/1)

**704 Stand Tall** was always struggling to get on terms and, despite staying on, never looked likely to make it. Either some cut in the ground or a bit further might help. (9/4)

**Bolshoi (IRE)** gave the impression that he has more ability than he cares to show but, to give him credit, he was staying on at the end. (16/1)

**Samsolom** had run moderately in two previous races this season, but he showed here that he still has the ability. (25/1)

**764 Blue Grit** likes to come from off a strong pace such as this, but his effort was always too late this time. (20/1)

**762* Captain Carat** was close enough if good enough in the last two furlongs, but that vital spark was never there on this occasion. (4/1)

**589 Halmanerror** likes this course and distance but is not quite firing as yet. (9/1)

**716 Portend** (14/1: 10/1-16/1)

## 851 TOTE DUAL FORECAST LIMITED STKS (0-60) (3-Y.O+) (Class F)

4-10 (4-14) **1m 4y** £2,920.00 (£820.00: £400.00) Stalls: Low GOING minus 0.31 sec per fur (GF)

| | Horse | Dist | Pos | SP | RR | SF |
|---|---|---|---|---|---|---|
| | **Shaffishayes (60)** (MrsMReveley) **4-9-8** DeanMcKeown(1) (bhd: nt clr run over 2f out: hdwy 2f out: led ins fnl f: rdn & r.o) | — | **1** | 11/2[3] | 72 | 33 |
| 713[5] | **Bollin Frank (57)** (TDEasterby) **4-9-8** MBirch(4) (led tl hdd ins fnl f: kpt on wl) | 1½ | **2** | 8/1 | 69 | 30 |
| | **Intendant (55)** (JGFitzGerald) **4-9-8** PaulEddery(10) (bit bkwd: hdwy over 2f out: styd on wl fnl f: nrst fin) | 2 | **3** | 20/1 | 65 | 26 |

| | | | | SP | RR | SF |
|---|---|---|---|---|---|---|
| 648$^{11}$ | **Smarter Charter (60)** (MrsJRRamsden) **3-8-8** JFortune(2) (lw: bhd: sn pushed along: hdwy 3f out: sn chsng ldrs: one pce fnl f) | 1½ | **4** | 5/1$^{2}$ | 62 | 9 |
| 660$^{3}$ | **Alpine Joker (58)** (MrsJRRamsden) **3-8-8** MFenton(14) (bhd: hdwy over 2f out: styd on strly) | 1½ | **5** | 14/1 | 59 | 6 |
| *190$^{2}$* | **Four of Spades (57)** (PDEvans) **5-9-10b** KDarley(3) (a chsng ldrs: effrt 2f out: wknd fnl f) | 1¾ | **6** | 20/1 | 58 | 19 |
| 660* | **Classic Defence (IRE) (68)** (JWHills) **3-8-5**(5) MHenry(5) (lw: cl up: rdn 3f out: wknd wl over 1f out) | ½ | **7** | 2/1$^{1}$ | 57 | 4 |
| 584$^{5}$ | **Manoy (60)** (JHetherton) **3-8-8** NKennedy(7) (prom tl wknd & hmpd over 2f out) | 1¾ | **8** | 10/1 | 51 | — |
| 598$^{8}$ | **Cee-Jay-Ay (54)** (JBerry) **9-9-8** JCarroll(8) (dwlt: hdwy whn hmpd over 2f out: nt rcvr) | 3½ | **9** | 16/1 | 44 | 5 |
| 734$^{3}$ | **Harry's Treat (53)** (JLEyre) **4-9-2**(3) OPears(13) (in tch: effrt 3f out: sn wknd) | 3 | **10** | 16/1 | 35 | — |
| | **Cowboy Dreams (IRE) (54)** (MHTompkins) **3-8-8** PRobinson(6) (n.d) | 4 | **11** | 33/1 | 30 | — |
| 610$^{20}$ | **Nizaal (USA) (60)** (DNicholls) **5-9-8** AlexGreaves(12) (lw: bhd fr ½-wy) | ¾ | **12** | 16/1 | 29 | — |
| | **Mbulwa (57)** (RAFahey) **10-9-8** ACulhane(9) (prom tl wknd fnl 3f) | 21 | **13** | 14/1 | — | — |
| | **Bellateena (52)** (HJCollingridge) **4-9-5** JQuinn(11) (prom 5f) | 13 | **14** | 14/1 | — | — |
| | | | | (SP 135.7%) | **14 Rn** | |

**1m 46.4** (4.90) CSF £51.40 TOTE £8.40: £2.50 £3.10 £7.30 (£29.90) Trio £147.60 OWNER Mr P. Davidson-Brown (SALTBURN) BRED W. G. Barker

WEIGHT FOR AGE 3yo-14lb

STEWARDS' ENQUIRY Eddery susp. 8-9/5/96 (careless riding).

**Shaffishayes** has now won first time out two seasons running and did it this time in most determined style. (11/2)

**713 Bollin Frank** likes to be out in front and tried hard here, but had to admit he had met one too good in the last furlong. (8/1)

**Intendant** needs some strong driving to get him going and, by the time he stayed on, it was all too late. He should be all the better for this. (20/1)

**Smarter Charter**, stepping up in distance, was never on the bridle at any stage and finally ran out of steam with a furlong to go. This should have taught him something. (5/1)

**660 Alpine Joker** again finished in pleasing style and is obviously learning. (14/1: 8/1-16/1)

**660* Classic Defence (IRE)** could never dominate this time. (2/1)

## 852 TOTE MARATHON H'CAP (0-70) (4-Y.O+) (Class E)

4-40 (4-42) **2m 5f 122y** £3,752.50 (£1,120.00: £535.00: £242.50) Stalls: Centre GOING minus 0.31 sec per fur (GF)

| | | | | SP | RR | SF |
|---|---|---|---|---|---|---|
| | **Izza (32)** (WStorey) **5-7-10** JQuinn(8) (hld up: hdwy gng wl 4f out: led 1f out: edgd rt: r.o u.p) | — | **1** | 5/1$^{3}$ | 48 | 25 |
| 666$^{7}$ | **Chakalak (45)** (SDow) **8-8-4**(5) ADaly(5) (drvn 10f out: swtchd & hdwy 4f out: led wl over 1f out: hdd 1f out: kpt on) | 3½ | **2** | 16/1 | 58 | 35 |
| 767$^{4}$ | **Great Oration (IRE) (38)** (FWatson) **7-8-2** AMackay(3) (lw: hdwy ½-wy: sn trckng ldrs: nt clr run over 2f out: swtchd & styd on: nt pce to chal) | 4 | **3** | 7/1 | 48 | 25 |
| 712$^{2}$ | **Kamikaze (64)** (JWhite) **6-10-0** MFenton(1) (bhd: gd hdwy 6f out: sn chsng ldrs: kpt on wl fnl 2f) | 4 | **4** | 8/1 | 72 | 49 |
| 625$^{2}$ | **Arian Spirit (IRE) (46)** (JLEyre) **5-8-10** RLappin(13) (lw: a.p: led 4f out tl wl over 1f out: sn outpcd) | 5 | **5** | 10/1 | 50 | 27 |
| 767$^{3}$ | **Sujud (IRE) (46)** (MrsJRRamsden) **4-8-10** JFortune(12) (lw: in tch: drvn 4f out: one pce) | hd | **6** | 2/1$^{1}$ | 50 | 27 |
| 625$^{18}$ | **Top Prize (40)** (MBrittain) **8-8-4v** PRobinson(11) (in tch tl outpcd fnl 4f) | 10 | **7** | 25/1 | 36 | 13 |
| 647$^{4}$ | **Brandon Prince (IRE) (63)** (IABalding) **8-9-6**(7) MartinDwyer(7) (swtg: bhd: hdwy 8f out: rdn & no imp fnl 4f) | 5 | **8** | 9/2$^{2}$ | 56 | 33 |
| | **Hit the Canvas (USA) (63)** (MrsMReveley) **5-9-13** KDarley(2) (lost pl & bhd after 8f: n.d after) | 1½ | **9** | 14/1 | 54 | 31 |
| 767$^{5}$ | **Noyan (53)** (DNicholls) **6-9-3b** AlexGreaves(14) (swtg: led to 12f out: led 7f out & qcknd: hdd 4f out: wknd qckly) | 25 | **10** | 10/1 | 26 | 3 |
| 625$^{15}$ | **Desert Force (IRE) (35)** (GFierro) **7-7-8**(5) MHenry(15) (b: chsd ldrs tl wknd fnl 6f) | 24 | **11** | 66/1 | — | — |
| 738$^{9}$ | **Dvorak (IRE) (61)** (RHarris) **5-9-11b$^{1}$** JCarroll(6) (chsd ldrs tl wknd 6f out: sn bhd) | ½ | **12** | 66/1 | 16 | — |
| 753$^{12}$ | **Flaming Miracle (IRE) (41)** (GBarnett) **6-8-5b** NCarlisle(10) (plld hrd: led 12f out to 7f out: sn lost pl) | 16 | **13** | 66/1 | — | — |
| 635$^{15}$ | **Ever Friends (35)** (RHarris) **4-7-13**ow3 DBatteate(9) (chsd ldrs tl wknd 7f out: sn wl bhd) | 16 | **14** | 66/1 | — | — |
| | **Sweet Noble (IRE) (37)** (KJDrewry) **7-8-1** TWilliams(4) (bkwd: t.o fnl 8f) | dist | **15** | 66/1 | — | — |
| | | | | (SP 133.8%) | **15 Rn** | |

**4m 51.8** (9.30) CSF £80.50 CT £530.45 TOTE £6.20: £1.90 £3.00 £1.90 (£80.40) Trio £119.10 OWNER Mr D. C. Batey (CONSETT) BRED G.W. Mills & Sons

**Izza** is in terrific form and really travelled on the bridle here and, although this marathon trip was beginning to find her out at the finish, she still stayed on well enough under pressure. (5/1)

**Chakalak** just stays but he certainly makes his rider work for it. (16/1)

**767 Great Oration (IRE)** managed to run into a pocket approaching the straight and, when switched, lacked a change of gear to get back into contention. (7/1)

**712 Kamikaze** had his chances in the last half-mile, but would probably have preferred softer ground. (8/1)

**625 Arian Spirit (IRE)**, racing off her highest mark for some time, ran well until her stamina gave out in the home straight. (10/1)

**767 Sujud (IRE)** was disappointing here and perhaps this came too quick after her efforts last week. (2/1)

**767 Noyan** (10/1: 7/1-11/1)

## 853 TOTE PLACEPOT H'CAP (0-75) (4-Y.O+) (Class D)

5-10 (5-15) **1m 2f 6y** £4,175.00 (£1,250.00: £600.00: £275.00) Stalls: Low GOING minus 0.31 sec per fur (GF)

| | | | | SP | RR | SF |
|---|---|---|---|---|---|---|
| 641$^{6}$ | **Remaadi Sun (68)** (MDIUsher) **4-9-8** RStreet(10) (lw: hld up: hdwy & swtchd wl over 1f out: r.o wl to ld cl home) | — | **1** | 11/1 | 80 | 49 |
| 641$^{8}$ | **Another Time (69)** (SPCWoods) **4-9-9** WWoods(13) (hld up: stdy hdwy 2f out: rdn to ld ins fnl f: nt qckn & hdd towards fin) | ½ | **2** | 11/4$^{2}$ | 80 | 49 |
| *520$^{2}$* | **Anistop (45)** (JLEyre) **4-7-10**(3) DWright(5) (cl up: led over 2f out tl ins fnl f: kpt on u.p) | ½ | **3** | 20/1 | 55 | 24 |
| 690$^{8}$ | **Dana Point (IRE) (60)** (TDBarron) **4-9-0** JFortune(9) (lw: hld up: hdwy on ins 3f out: chal over 1f out: hrd rdn & no ex) | 1¾ | **4** | 10/1 | 68 | 37 |
| 690$^{2}$ | **Curtelace (58)** (MrsMReveley) **6-8-12** KDarley(1) (hld up & bhd: hdwy over 3f out: rdn 2f out: no rspnse) | 1 | **5** | 5/2$^{1}$ | 64 | 33 |
| 558$^{5}$ | **Drummer Hicks (44)** (EWeymes) **7-7-12** JQuinn(6) (lw: in tch: effrt 3f out: outpcd fnl 2f) | 3 | **6** | 12/1 | 45 | 14 |
| | **Beau Matelot (55)** (MissMKMilligan) **4-8-9** NConnorton(2) (lw: trckd ldrs: one pce fnl 2f) | 2 | **7** | 20/1 | 53 | 22 |
| | **Tissisat (USA) (70)** (JohnBerry) **7-9-10** RPerham(4) (b: led tl over 2f out: sn wknd) | 4 | **8** | 16/1 | 62 | 31 |
| 619$^{4}$ | **Calder King (61)** (JLEyre) **5-9-1v** RLappin(3) (nvr trbld ldrs) | 5 | **9** | 9/1$^{3}$ | 45 | 14 |
| | **Fern's Governor (44)** (WJMusson) **4-7-12** AMackay(15) (bit bkwd: s.i.s: n.d) | 11 | **10** | 10/1 | 10 | — |
| *393$^{12}$* | **Taylors Revival (42)** (HJCollingridge) **5-7-10** NKennedy(8) (s.i.s: n.d) | 3½ | **11** | 100/1 | 3 | — |
| | **Java Red (IRE) (56)** (JGFitzGerald) **4-8-10** MBirch(7) (bit bkwd: chsd ldrs tl wknd fnl 3f) | 3½ | **12** | 20/1 | 11 | — |
| 690$^{12}$ | **Denomination (USA) (59)** (IABalding) **4-8-6b$^{1}$**(7) MartinDwyer(14) (plld hrd: sn w ldrs: wknd over 3f out) | 10 | **13** | 12/1 | — | — |

*416*[7] **Suvalu (USA) (68)** (MGMeagher) **4-9-8** JCarroll(12) (lw: trckd ldrs tl wknd 6f out: eased whn btn)....23 **14** 16/1 — —
752[19] **Studio Thirty (45)** (DMorris) **4-7-8**(5)ow3 MHenry(11) (chsd ldrs tl wknd 4f out)....12 **15** 16/1 — —
(SP 140.1%) **15 Rn**

**2m 12.5** (4.20) CSF £44.79 CT £604.65 TOTE £15.00: £4.00 £2.40 £3.50 (£30.50) Trio £166.50 OWNER Mr Trevor Barker (SWINDON) BRED Whitsbury Manor Stud

LONG HANDICAP Taylors Revival 6-5 Studio Thirty 7-6

**OFFICIAL EXPLANATION Suvalu: the jockey reported that the colt was unable to get his wind.**

**641 Remaadi Sun** has been unlucky previously this season but got everything right this time and produced a perfectly-timed run to snatch it. (11/1)

**Another Time** improved no end for his pipe-opener last time but, after travelling in the style of a winner, was just done for speed late on. (11/4)

**520 Anistop** kept responding to pressure in fine style in the last half-mile and it would appear he will appreciate further. (20/1)

**690 Dana Point (IRE)** got a great run up the inner entering the straight but, when the pressure was applied, was then never good enough. (10/1)

**690 Curtelace** has his own ideas about the game and was not giving it his best shot in the closing stages. (5/2)

**558 Drummer Hicks**, better suited by this galloping track, tried hard, but was short of turn of foot in the last two furlongs. (12/1)

**Beau Matelot** again gave the impression that longer distances might help. (20/1)

T/Jkpt: Not won; £18,941.96 to Bath 30/4/96. T/Plpt: £675.30 (24.89 Tckts). T/Qdpt: £215.20 (5.66 Tckts). AA

# 0776-SOUTHWELL (L-H) (Standard)

## Monday April 29th

WEATHER: fine WIND: slt half bhd

## 854 BRIE AMATEUR H'CAP (0-70) (4-Y.O+) (Class G)

2-30 (2-30) **1m (Fibresand)** £2,070.00 (£570.00: £270.00) Stalls: Low GOING: 0.04 sec per fur (STD)

SP RR SF

670[2] **Kingchip Boy (64)** (MJRyan) **7-10-9v**(7) MrSLavallin(8) (led to 2f out: styd on u.p to ld nr fin)....— **1** 6/1[2] 75 56
670[4] **Montone (IRE) (48)** (JRJenkins) **6-9-10v**[1](4)ow1 DrMMannish(3) (w ldrs: led 2f out tl towards fin)....¾ **2** 12/1 58 38
752[18] **Royal Acclaim (35)** (JMBradley) **11-8-8v**(7) MissLKerr(7) (s.i.s: racd wd: hdwy 3f out: styd on appr fnl f)....7 **3** 33/1 31 12
827[4] **Sycamore Lodge (IRE) (68)** (MrsJRRamsden) **5-11-2**(4) MissERamsden(12) (lw: hld up: hdwy 2f out: styd on towards fin)....1¼ **4** 6/1[2] 61 42
*521*[2] **Thaleros (59)** (GMMoore) **6-10-11** MrTMcCarthy(2) (a chsng ldrs: rdn ½-wy: one pce)....hd **5** 3/1[1] 52 33
455[23] **Comanche Companion (69)** (TJNaughton) **6-11-3**(4) MrsJNaughton(11) (effrt ½-wy: rdn over 1f out: no imp)....1¼ **6** 6/1[2] 59 40
*406*[3] **Love Legend (42)** (DWPArbuthnot) **11-9-8** MrsDArbuthnot(10) (sn chsng ldrs: one pce fnl 2f)....1 **7** 12/1 30 11
*487*[10] **Magic Leader (IRE) (36)** (TTClement) **4-8-12**(4)ow2 MrVLukaniuk(4) (b: prom early: sn drvn along & bhd)....1 **8** 50/1 22 1
440[20] **Dream Carrier (IRE) (49)** (REPeacock) **8-9-8**(7) MrsCPeacock(5) (s.i.s: a in rr)....2½ **9** 16/1 30 11
*776*[6] **No Submission (USA) (62)** (DWChapman) **10-11-0v** MissRClark(6) (lw: sn outpcd & bhd: rdn over 3f out: n.d)....¾ **10** 12/1 42 23
713[10] **Twin Creeks (57)** (MDHammond) **5-10-9** MrCBonner(9) (in tch: effrt ½-wy: wknd over 1f out)....hd **11** 7/1[3] 37 18
**Super Park (62)** (JPearce) **4-11-0** MrsLPearce(1) (chsd ldrs: rdn ½-wy: sn wknd & bhd)....27 **12** 14/1 — —
(SP 120.9%) **12 Rn**

**1m 47.3** (7.30) CSF £69.50 CT £2,033.47 TOTE £6.60: £1.70 £2.90 £9.90 (£21.20) Trio £141.70 OWNER Four Jays Racing Partnership (NEWMARKET) BRED R. M. Scott

LONG HANDICAP Magic Leader (IRE) 8-8

**670 Kingchip Boy** set a fierce gallop and, with the rail on his inside to help his inexperienced pilot, he regained the advantage near the line. (6/1)

**670 Montone (IRE)** and Kingchip Boy seemed to set a very strong pace. After going a neck up two furlongs out, the partnership were worried out of it towards the line. (12/1)

**Royal Acclaim** went the longest way round. (33/1)

**827 Sycamore Lodge (IRE)**, happy to sit off the pace, was staying on nicely at the finish. This trip is possibly on the short side for him these days. (6/1)

**521 Thaleros**, with an experienced pilot on his back, chased the leaders but was hard at work and only keeping on at the one pace from soon after halfway. (3/1)

## 855 LEICESTER CLAIMING STKS (4-Y.O+) (Class F)

3-00 (3-01) **1m 4f (Fibresand)** £2,381.00 (£656.00: £311.00) Stalls: Low GOING: 0.04 sec per fur (STD)

SP RR SF

*532*[4] **Greenspan (IRE) (78)** (WRMuir) **4-9-7** Jean-PierreLopez(11) (lw: trckd ldrs: wnt 2nd over 4f out: hrd rdn over 1f out: styd on)....— **1** 11/8[1] 80 22
*777*[2] **Tempering (59)** (DWChapman) **10-8-2**(5) PFessey(1) (swtg: led: clr 9f out: hdd over 1f out: kpt on)....3½ **2** 3/1[2] 60 3
546[16] **Brave Spy (54)** (CACyzer) **5-9-4** GDuffield(8) (lw: sn chsng ldrs: rdn over 4f out: kpt on one pce)....7 **3** 16/1 62 5
771[7] **Cross Talk (IRE) (59)** (RHollinshead) **4-8-13** JWeaver(7) (bhd: hdwy u.p over 4f out: nvr nr ldrs)....9 **4** 5/1[3] 46 —
*604*[3] **Milltown Classic (IRE) (28)** (JParkes) **4-7-12** NCarlisle(4) (bhd: sme hdwy 5f out: nvr nr ldrs)....4 **5** 16/1 26 —
*777*[7] **Red Indian (43)** (BRichmond) **10-8-4** GCarter(5) (bhd: sme hdwy u.p 5f out: wknd over 2f out: eased)....¾ **6** 40/1 30 —
*603*[7] **Le Temeraire (18)** (DonEnricoIncisa) **10-8-2** KimTinkler(10) (sn rdn & bhd: t.o 4f out)....dist **7** 66/1 — —
**Battery Boy (36)** (CWCElsey) **4-8-3b** JFEgan(6) (chsd ldrs tl wknd ½-wy: t.o 4f out)....19 **8** 40/1 — —
*654*[11] **Sungrove's Best (27)** (PEccles) **9-8-4** NAdams(2) (hld up: lost tch 7f out: wl t.o 4f out)....¾ **9** 66/1 — —
688[18] **My Brave Girl (46)** (BRichmond) **4-7-7**(3) NVarley(3) (sn bhd: t.o 4f out)....2 **10** 50/1 — —
609[4] **Bold Pursuit (IRE) (51)** (JGFitzGerald) **7-9-0** LCharnock(9) (b: lw: hld up: p.u lame over 7f out: dead).... **P** 5/1[3] — —
(SP 122.0%) **11 Rn**

**2m 45.7** (13.20) CSF £6.11 TOTE £2.40: £1.10 £1.20 £2.90 (£2.90) Trio £21.10 OWNER Camelot Racing (LAMBOURN) BRED Dermot and Meta Cantillon

WEIGHT FOR AGE 4yo-1lb

**Greenspan (IRE)**, who was apparently hampered when running poorly last time, was given a forceful ride by his jockey, four times Austrian champion. (11/8)

**777 Tempering**, awash with sweat, soon had his rivals strung out but had to give best to the winner coming to the final furlong. (3/1)

**Brave Spy** ran his best race for a while, sticking on at the one pace all the way to the line. (16/1)

**482* Cross Talk (IRE)** came from off the pace and probably found this trip on the sharp side. (5/1)

## 856 CHEDDAR MEDIAN AUCTION MAIDEN STKS (3-Y.O) (Class F)

3-30 (3-31) **1m** **(Fibresand)** £2,381.00 (£656.00: £311.00) Stalls: Low GOING: 0.04 sec per fur (STD)

| Form | Horse | Dist | Pos | SP | RR | SF |
|---|---|---|---|---|---|---|
| $705^{6}$ | **Perpetual Light** (JJQuinn) **3-8-9** AMcGlone(6) (trckd ldrs: led over 2f out: sn rdn: hld on wl towards fin) | — | **1** | $4/1^{3}$ | 65 | 24 |
| *$782^{2}$* | **Young Mazaad (IRE) (59)** (DCO'Brien) **3-9-0** GCarter(3) (lw: led 2f: chal 2f out: nt qckn ins fnl f) | ½ | **2** | $9/4^{1}$ | 69 | 28 |
| $577^{10}$ | **Allstars Express** (TJNaughton) **3-9-0** JWeaver(5) (bit bkwd: s.i.s: hld up: hdwy over 2f out: sn prom: kpt on one pce) | 5 | **3** | $11/4^{2}$ | 59 | 18 |
| $634^{3}$ | **Isitoff (66)** (CADwyer) **3-8-11**(3) PMcCabe(8) (hld up: effrt over 2f out: rdn, wnt lft & no imp) | 1¾ | **4** | 8/1 | 56 | 15 |
| | **Spencer Stallone** (LordHuntingdon) **3-8-11**(3) AWhelan(9) (leggy: unf: trckd ldrs: effrt 2f out: grad wknd) | 5 | **5** | 7/1 | 46 | 5 |
| | **Tonto** (CWThornton) **3-9-0** LCharnock(7) (plld hrd: trckd ldrs: led over 3f out tl over 2f out: sn wknd & eased) | 10 | **6** | 12/1 | 26 | — |
| $576^{14}$ | **Harbet House (FR)** (CACyzer) **3-9-0** GDuffield(4) (s.i.s: sn rdn along: hdwy to ld after 2f: hdd over 3f out: sn wknd) | nk | **7** | 14/1 | 25 | — |
| $545^{3}$ | **Cool Caper (44)** (AGFoster) **3-8-7**(7) RWaterfield(1) (sn pushed along: bhd & rn wd ent st) | ¾ | **8** | 12/1 | 23 | — |
| *$516^{7}$* | **Heathyards Rose (IRE)** (RHollinshead) **3-8-4**(5) FLynch(10) (s.i.s: hld up & plld hrd: rdn over 2f out: no rspnse) | 5 | **9** | 33/1 | 8 | — |
| $761^{9}$ | **Condor Ridge (50)** (BJMeehan) **3-9-0** JFEgan(2) (sn pushed along: outpcd ½-wy: sn bhd) | 16 | **10** | 33/1 | — | — |

(SP 129.0%) **10 Rn**

**1m 47.3** (7.30) CSF £14.37 TOTE £6.30: £1.70 £1.50 £1.40 (£10.00) Trio £17.40 OWNER The Four Point Partnership (MALTON) BRED Lord Matthews

**Perpetual Light**, who has a pronounced knee-action, settled better and showed the right sort of spirit. She will be suited by a step up in distance now she has learnt to relax. (4/1)

**782 Young Mazaad (IRE)** appreciated the mile and, after a good battle, only gave best inside the last. (9/4)

**Allstars Express** is still green and does not look fully fit yet. Further improvement is likely. (11/4)

**634 Isitoff** wanted to do nothing but go left under pressure. (8/1)

**Spencer Stallone** is nothing to look at, but showed a measure of ability, tracking the leaders until tiring in the final quarter-mile. (7/1: op 7/2)

**545 Cool Caper** (12/1: op 8/1)

## 857 WENSLEYDALE H'CAP (0-65) (3-Y.O) (Class F)

4-00 (4-00) **6f** **(Fibresand)** £2,381.00 (£656.00: £311.00) Stalls: Low GOING: 0.04 sec per fur (STD)

| Form | Horse | Dist | Pos | SP | RR | SF |
|---|---|---|---|---|---|---|
| *$340^{2}$* | **Mask Flower (USA) (63)** (MJohnston) **3-9-7** JWeaver(1) (sn led: rdn over 2f out: styd on wl) | — | **1** | $4/6^{1}$ | 68 | 30 |
| $732^{14}$ | **Grey Galava (60)** (BWHills) **3-9-4** JFEgan(7) (chsd ldrs: rdn over 3f out: styd on ins fnl f) | 1½ | **2** | $7/1^{3}$ | 61 | 23 |
| *$780^{5}$* | **Principal Boy (IRE) (54)** (TJEtherington) **3-8-12** GCarter(3) (lw: effrt on outside over 3f out: kpt on same pce fnl 2f: nvr able to chal) | nk | **3** | 8/1 | 54 | 16 |
| $626^{5}$ | **Lapu-Lapu (55)** (MJCamacho) **3-8-13** LCharnock(4) (trckd ldrs: effrt & ev ch over 2f out: wknd towards fin) | ¾ | **4** | $9/2^{2}$ | 53 | 15 |
| *$421^{5}$* | **Coastguards Hero (52)** (MDIUsher) **3-8-10** NAdams(6) (trckd ldrs: effrt over 2f out: wknd fnl f) | 2 | **5** | 10/1 | 45 | 7 |
| | **Ballykissangel (40)** (NBycroft) **3-7-9**(3) NVarley(2) (b.off hind: bit bkwd: dwlt: effrt ½-wy: sn wl outpcd: kpt on towards fin) | 1¼ | **6** | 50/1 | 30 | — |
| *$780^{9}$* | **Bee Health Boy (59)** (MWEasterby) **3-9-3b** GDuffield(5) (led early: chsd ldrs: rdn & wandered over 2f out: sn lost pl) | 12 | **7** | 10/1 | 17 | — |

(SP 121.9%) **7 Rn**

**1m 19.3** (5.80) CSF £6.68 TOTE £1.20: £1.10 £4.60 (£5.60) OWNER Sheikh Mohammed (MIDDLEHAM) BRED Darley Stud Management Inc

**Mask Flower (USA)**, dropping back in distance, made sure there was no hanging about. Flat out turning in, she raced with her ears right back, but she showed courage and determination and was never going to be beaten. (4/6)

**Grey Galava**, tailed off on her reappearance, struggled to keep up at halfway. Despite looking far from happy in her work, she stuck on towards the finish. (7/1: op 4/1)

**780 Principal Boy (IRE)** made his effort on the outside turning in. Soon hard at work, he lacked the pace to get in a telling blow. (8/1)

**626 Lapu-Lapu** showed clear second early in the straight. After having every chance, her stride shortened in the last 150 yards. Perhaps the minimum trip will suit her better. (9/2)

## 858 GLOUCESTER (S) STKS (2-Y.O) (Class G)

4-30 (4-31) **5f** **(Fibresand)** £2,070.00 (£570.00: £270.00) Stalls: High GOING: 0.04 sec per fur (STD)

| Form | Horse | Dist | Pos | SP | RR | SF |
|---|---|---|---|---|---|---|
| $685^{10}$ | **For Old Times Sake** (JBerry) **2-8-11** GCarter(2) (lw: chsd ldr: shkn up to ld over 1f out: qcknd wl clr ins fnl f: eased towards fin) | — | **1** | $3/1^{2}$ | 57+ | 29 |
| $757^{5}$ | **Run Lucy Run** (RGuest) **2-8-6** LCharnock(1) (led tl over 1f out: wknd towards fin) | 4 | **2** | 15/2 | 39 | 11 |
| $685^{8}$ | **Fan of Vent-Axia** (CNAllen) **2-8-11** CHodgson(7) (racd stands' side: chsd ldrs: rdn & edgd lft ½-wy: kpt on) | 3 | **3** | $85/40^{1}$ | 35 | 7 |
| $551^{4}$ | **Salome** (NAGraham) **2-8-6** AMcGlone(3) (stumbled s: chsd ldrs tl lost pl ½-wy) | 7 | **4** | 9/1 | 7 | — |
| | **Silver Jubilee** (BPalling) **2-8-6** SDWilliams(6) (leggy: unf: s.s: racd stands' side: a wl outpcd) | 7 | **5** | 11/2 | — | — |
| | **Nefertiti** (RFMarvin) **2-8-1**(5) LNewton(4) (b: leggy: lt-f: unf: s.s: pushed along & sn chsng ldrs: lost pl ½-wy: sn bhd) | 7 | **6** | $7/2^{3}$ | — | — |
| | **Chloezymp (IRE)** (JBalding) **2-7-13**(7) JEdmunds(5) (leggy: bit bkwd: racd stands' side: sn pushed along: wl outpcd after 2f: sn bhd) | 10 | **7** | 14/1 | — | — |

(SP 123.0%) **7 Rn**

**61.0 secs** (4.00) CSF £24.77 TOTE £4.60: £5.30 £7.90 (£21.60) OWNER Mrs Bridget Blum (COCKERHAM) BRED Shutford Stud
Bt in 5,200 gns

**For Old Times Sake**, badly drawn on his debut, looked in a different class to his rivals both in the paddock and on the way down to the start and so it proved. Quickening well clear inside the last, he looks better than the average selling-race winner. (3/1: 2/1-7/2)

**757 Run Lucy Run**, a keen-going type, made the running but, totally outclassed by the winner, her stride shortened towards the finish. (15/2: 5/1-8/1)

**452 Fan of Vent-Axia**, who looked very fit, was soon driven along to keep up on the stands' side. (85/40)

**551 Salome**, who is only small, stumbled at the start and dropped right out at halfway. (9/1)

**Silver Jubilee** (11/2: op 3/1)

**Nefertiti**, a most unattractive sort, showed plenty of knee-action going to post. Supported in the market, she fell out of the traps and dropped right out at halfway. (7/2)

## 859 MELTON MOWBRAY BUILDING SOCIETY H'CAP (0-65) (3-Y.O F) (Class F)

5-00 (5-05) **7f (Fibresand)** £2,381.00 (£656.00: £311.00) Stalls: Low GOING: 0.04 sec per fur (STD)

| Form | Horse | Dist | Pos | SP | RR | SF |
|---|---|---|---|---|---|---|
| *781[2]* | **Miss Offset (56)** (MJohnston) **3-8-12b** JWeaver(12) (mde all: sn clr: styd on wl) | — | **1** | 3/1[2] | 66 | 31 |
| 659[6] | **Call Me (65)** (CWThornton) **3-9-7** GCarter(7) (lw: trckd ldrs: wnt 2nd over 2f out: kpt on: nt rch wnr) | 2½ | **2** | 13/8[1] | 69 | 34 |
| *781** | **People Direct (67)** (KMcAuliffe) **3-9-4**(5) 6x FLynch(6) (in tch: effrt over 2f out: kpt on same pce) | 3½ | **3** | 10/1 | 63 | 28 |
| 458[13] | **Supreme Illusion (AUS) (40)** (JohnBerry) **3-7-10b[1]** NAdams(13) (chsd ldrs: rdn ½-wy: one pce) | 5 | **4** | 33/1 | 25 | — |
| *421[4]* | **La Perruche (IRE) (51)** (LordHuntingdon) **3-8-4**(3) AWhelan(3) (sme hdwy ½-wy: nvr nr ldrs) | 5 | **5** | 10/1 | 24 | — |
| 686[9] | **Lawn Order (49)** (MrsJRRamsden) **3-7-12**(7) TFinn(8) (s.i.s: bhd tl sme hdwy fnl 2f) | ¾ | **6** | 8/1[3] | 21 | — |
| 739[8] | **Alfayza (60)** (JDBethell) **3-8-9**(7) GFaulkner(10) (chsd ldr tl wknd 2f out) | 2 | **7** | 14/1 | 27 | — |
| | **Natatarl (IRE) (52)** (BPalling) **3-8-8** SDWilliams(5) (in tch: rdn & outpcd ½-wy: n.d after) | nk | **8** | 14/1 | 19 | — |
| 613[14] | **Any Colour (55)** (MJCamacho) **3-8-11** LCharnock(2) (dwlt: a outpcd & sn drvn along: eased whn no ch 2f out) | 7 | **9** | 14/1 | 6 | — |
| 522[4] | **Belacqua (USA) (40)** (DWChapman) **3-7-5b**(5) PFessey(4) (unruly s: a in rr) | nk | **10** | 20/1 | — | — |
| | **La Fandango (IRE) (40)** (MWEasterby) **3-7-3**(7) PDoe(11) (sn bhd) | 7 | **11** | 12/1 | — | — |
| 468[7] | **Valjess (40)** (DCO'Brien) **3-7-3**(7) RMullen(1) (sn bhd) | 4 | **12** | 33/1 | — | — |
| *550[15]* | ***Elegantissima (50)*** (SDow) **3-8-6** GDuffield(9) (Withdrawn not under Starter's orders: lame at s) | | **W** | 14/1 | — | — |

(SP 137.4%) **12 Rn**

**1m 32.8** (6.00) CSF £8.59 CT £38.95 TOTE £2.90: £1.10 £1.20 £3.20 (£3.10) Trio £2.60 OWNER Hertford Offset Ltd (MIDDLEHAM) BRED J. Coombes and E. Henshaw

LONG HANDICAP Supreme Illusion (AUS) 7-7 Valjess 6-9 Belacqua (USA) 6-6

**781 Miss Offset**, meeting People Direct on 11lb better terms for a half-length defeat here five days earlier, made no mistake. Overcoming her high draw, she was soon in a commanding lead and, sticking on strongly, never looked in any danger. (3/1)

**659 Call Me** went in pursuit of the winner once in line for home. Keeping on under pressure, she was never going to get in a blow. (13/8: 5/2-5/4)

**781* People Direct**, who had an impossible task at the weights with the winner, ran as well as could be expected. (10/1: op 6/1)

**Supreme Illusion (AUS)** is only plating class. (33/1)

**686 Lawn Order** (8/1: 6/1-9/1)

**Natatarl (IRE)** (14/1: 10/1-16/1)

T/Plpt: £9.90 (909.95 Tckts). T/Qdpt: £4.60 (165.8 Tckts). WG

# BATH (L-H) (Good, Good to firm patches)

## Tuesday April 30th

WEATHER: unsettled WIND: slt across

## 860 BLATHWAYT MAIDEN STKS (3-Y.O) (Class D)

2-00 (2-02) **1m 2f 46y** £3,848.75 (£1,160.00: £562.50: £263.75) Stalls: Low GOING minus 0.43 sec per fur (F)

| Form | Horse | Dist | Pos | SP | RR | SF |
|---|---|---|---|---|---|---|
| | **Lear Jet (USA)** (PFICole) **3-9-0** TQuinn(10) (lw: mde all: rdn 3f out: jst hld on) | — | **1** | 6/1[3] | 85 | 49 |
| 576[7] | **Private Song (USA)** (RCharlton) **3-9-0** RHughes(5) (lw: chsd wnr: rdn & ev ch 2f out: r.o wl) | s.h | **2** | 4/1[2] | 85 | 49 |
| | **Illuminate** (JARToller) **3-9-0** SSanders(12) (rdn & hdwy over 4f out: r.o wl ins fnl f) | s.h | **3** | 12/1 | 85 | 49 |
| 710[7] | **Shalateeno** (MRChannon) **3-8-9** AGorman(4) (s.s: hdwy 7f out: r.o one pce fnl 2f) | 5 | **4** | 50/1 | 72 | 36 |
| 684[4] | **Hismagicmoment (USA)** (PWChapple-Hyam) **3-9-0** JReid(11) (hld up: hmpd 8f out: hdwy 6f out: wknd over 2f out) | 2½ | **5** | 4/5[1] | 73 | 37 |
| | **Double Up** (LadyHerries) **3-8-9** DeclanO'Shea(14) (prom: rdn over 4f out: wknd 3f out) | 6 | **6** | 66/1 | 59 | 23 |
| | **Sadler's Realm** (MRStoute) **3-9-0** BThomson(13) (lw: a mid div) | ½ | **7** | 16/1 | 63 | 27 |
| 703[6] | **Absolute Utopia (USA)** (EALDunlop) **3-9-0** WCarson(3) (bhd fnl 3f) | 7 | **8** | 16/1 | 52 | 16 |
| | **Windyedge (USA)** (BWHills) **3-9-0** MHills(2) (bit bkwd: dwlt: n.d) | hd | **9** | 20/1 | 52 | 16 |
| | **Northern Ballet (IRE)** (RHannon) **3-8-4**(5) DaneO'Neill(15) (bkwd: a bhd) | 5 | **10** | 25/1 | 39 | 3 |
| | **Ela Agapi Mou (USA)** (GLewis) **3-9-0** PaulEddery(8) (lt-f: bit bkwd: a bhd) | 2½ | **11** | 66/1 | 40 | 4 |
| 672[9] | **Quiet Arch (IRE)** (CACyzer) **3-9-0** JCarroll(6) (bhd fnl 4f) | ¾ | **12** | 66/1 | 39 | 3 |
| | **Absolutelystunning** (MrsBarbaraWaring) **3-8-9** NAdams(1) (b: s.i.s: a bhd) | nk | **13** | 100/1 | 33 | — |
| | **Random Kindness** (PWHarris) **3-9-0** AMcGlone(7) (w'like: bit bkwd: prom early: bhd fnl 4f) | 2½ | **14** | 50/1 | 35 | — |
| | **Indian Wolf** (PGMurphy) **3-8-11**(3) SDrowne(9) (neat: s.s: a bhd: t.o) | 10 | **15** | 100/1 | 19 | — |

(SP 128.3%) **15 Rn**

**2m 9.4** (1.90) CSF £30.04 TOTE £5.60: £1.70 £1.70 £2.80 (£10.70) Trio £43.50 OWNER H R H Prince Fahd Salman (WHATCOMBE) BRED Newgate Stud Farm Inc.

**Lear Jet (USA)**, who subsequently was reported to have wintered well, had to dig deep to hold on. Described as blowing hard after the race, he should come on a bit for this run. (6/1: 3/1-13/2)

**576 Private Song (USA)** fared much better than at Kempton. He seemed to have the winner covered early in the home straight until put to the test at the quarter-mile marker, but he kept on willingly to the end. (4/1)

**Illuminate** stayed on well in the closing stages but could not quite overhaul the first two in time. (12/1: op 8/1)

**Shalateeno**, a Teenoso half-sister to Shalholme, not surprisingly did better over this longer trip. (50/1)

**684 Hismagicmoment (USA)** should have been suited by this step up in distance and perhaps, not for the first time, the Wood Ditton form should be treated with caution at the moment, even though two subsequent winners have come from it. (4/5)

## 861 SPA (S) STKS (3-Y.O) (Class G)

2-30 (2-31) **5f 11y** £2,346.00 (£656.00: £318.00) Stalls: High GOING minus 0.43 sec per fur (F)

| Form | Horse | Dist | Pos | SP | RR | SF |
|---|---|---|---|---|---|---|
| | **Songsheet (77)** (RGuest) **3-8-7** JReid(16) (a.p: led over 2f out: comf) | — | **1** | 7/4[1] | 68+ | 34 |
| 638[4] | **Miletrian Refurb (IRE) (62)** (MRChannon) **3-9-3** RHughes(9) (led over 2f: r.o one pce) | 3 | **2** | 4/1[2] | 69 | 35 |
| 545[10] | **Silver Harrow (58)** (AGNewcombe) **3-8-7**(5) DGriffiths(7) (a.p: rdn 3f out: one pce fnl 2f) | hd | **3** | 11/1 | 63 | 29 |
| 748[2] | **Members Welcome (IRE) (57)** (JMBradley) **3-8-9**(3) SDrowne(2) (b: a.p: one pce fnl 2f) | 1¼ | **4** | 8/1 | 59 | 25 |
| *390[9]* | **Red Time (43)** (MSSaunders) **3-8-12** RPrice(13) (a.p: one pce fnl 2f) | ½ | **5** | 50/1 | 58 | 24 |
| 748[5] | **Dazzling Star (45)** (RHannon) **3-8-2b[1]**(5) DaneO'Neill(8) (rdn & hdwy over 2f out: one pce fnl f) | 1¾ | **6** | 14/1 | 47 | 13 |
| 743[3] | **Rowlandsons Stud (IRE) (62)** (GLMoore) **3-9-3** RCochrane(6) (lw: hld up: no hdwy fnl 2f) | ½ | **7** | 13/2[3] | 56 | 22 |
| 669[11] | **My Mother's Local (USA) (35)** (KOCunningham-Brown) **3-8-7b** BDoyle(5) (nrst fin) | ¾ | **8** | 50/1 | 43 | 9 |

| | Horse | Dist | Pos | SP | RR | SF |
|---|---|---|---|---|---|---|
| 743[5] | **Maple Burl (63)** (SDow) **3-9-3** TQuinn(4) (nvr nr to chal) | ½ | **9** | 14/1 | 52 | 18 |
| 743[6] | **Jessica's Song (56)** (WGMTurner) **3-8-10**(7)ow5 MCotton(10) (prom over 2f) | ¾ | **10** | 9/1 | 49 | 10 |
| 749[15] | **Beeny (60)** (APJarvis) **3-9-3** FNorton(15) (lw: chsd ldrs over 2f) | s.h | **11** | 16/1 | 49 | 15 |
| | **In Cahoots** (AGNewcombe) **3-8-12** JCarroll(11) (lt-f: bkwd: s.s: a bhd) | 3 | **12** | 33/1 | 35 | 1 |
| | **Duet** (JSKing) **3-8-7** PaulEddery(12) (unf: bkwd: a bhd) | 1¼ | **13** | 33/1 | 26 | — |
| 740[8] | **Toe Tappin Music (USA) (43)** (MartynMeade) **3-8-12** RPerham(14) (reard s: a bhd) | ½ | **14** | 33/1 | 29 | — |
| 748[9] | **Wingnut (IRE) (48)** (MJHaynes) **3-8-7b**1(5) MBaird(1) (outpcd) | ½ | **15** | 33/1 | 27 | — |
| 762[W] | **Snitch (45)** (CSmith) **3-8-12** KRutter(3) (a bhd: t.o) | 13 | **16** | 50/1 | — | — |

(SP 136.0%) **16 Rn**

**61.8 secs** (1.30) CSF £10.24 TOTE £3.50: £2.20 £1.90 £4.70 (£8.00) Trio £71.90 OWNER Matthews Breeding and Racing (NEWMARKET) BRED Lord Matthews

Songsheet sold MMeade 10,000gns

**Songsheet**, dropped into selling company, scored with a fair bit in hand. (7/4: 5/4-2/1)

**638 Miletrian Refurb (IRE)** seemed to have come up against an above-average sort for this type of race. (4/1)

**Silver Harrow**, bought out of Sir Mark Prescott's stable for 4,500 guineas, did not progress as a two-year-old and was eventually tried in blinkers. (11/1)

**748 Members Welcome (IRE)** may not have been suited by this shorter trip. (8/1)

**Red Time** may require a shade further. (50/1)

**748 Dazzling Star** was tried in blinkers for this return to the minimum trip. (14/1: 10/1-16/1)

**Jessica's Song** (9/1: op 14/1)

## 862 TRIPLEPRINT H'CAP (0-70) (3-Y.O+) (Class E)

3-00 (3-03) **5f 11y** £3,226.50 (£972.00: £471.00: £220.50) Stalls: High GOING minus 0.43 sec per fur (F)

| | Horse | Dist | Pos | SP | RR | SF |
|---|---|---|---|---|---|---|
| 587[15] | **Ansellman (70)** (JBerry) **6-10-0b** JCarroll(6) (a.p: led ins fnl f: r.o wl) | — | **1** | 20/1 | 84 | 44 |
| 601[12] | **Jucea (62)** (JLSpearing) **7-9-6** JReid(12) (hmpd after 1f: hdwy on ins over 1f out: r.o) | 1½ | **2** | 8/1[3] | 71 | 31 |
| 742[3] | **Friendly Brave (USA) (68)** (MissGayKelleway) **6-9-12** CandyMorris(8) (b: lw: hdwy 2f out: r.o ins fnl f) | hd | **3** | 16/1 | 77 | 37 |
| 773* | **Goretski (IRE) (65)** (NTinkler) **3-8-8**(5) 7x DaneO'Neill(4) (led: rdn 2f out: hdd ins fnl f) | 1¼ | **4** | 9/4[1] | 70 | 20 |
| 700[3] | **John O'Dreams (50)** (MrsALMKing) **11-8-8** AGarth(9) (b: hdwy over 1f out: r.o) | 2 | **5** | 11/1 | 49 | 9 |
| 667[4] | **La Belle Dominique (54)** (SGKnight) **4-8-12** BDoyle(1) (hdwy over 1f out: nt rch ldrs) | 1¼ | **6** | 20/1 | 49 | 9 |
| 632[4] | **Rockcracker (IRE) (55)** (GGMargarson) **4-8-13b** AClark(3) (swtg: s.s: hdwy over 1f out: nvr nrr) | nk | **7** | 16/1 | 49 | 9 |
| 631[4] | **Cedar Dancer (43)** (RJHodges) **4-8-1** DeclanO'Shea(7) (nvr trbld ldrs) | 1 | **8** | 25/1 | 34 | — |
| 750* | **Baileys Sunset (IRE) (64)** (JMBradley) **4-9-5**(3) 7x SDrowne(18) (n.d) | nk | **9** | 16/1 | 54 | 14 |
| 769[4] | **Efficacy (45)** (APJarvis) **5-8-3** FNorton(13) (rdn over 2f out: no hdwy) | hd | **10** | 20/1 | 34 | — |
| | **Miami Banker (63)** (WRMuir) **10-9-0b**(7)ow9 RPooles(2) (bkwd: prom over 2f) | 1½ | **11** | 33/1 | 48 | — |
| 601[7] | **Malibu Man (62)** (SMellor) **4-9-6** RPerham(14) (hmpd after 1f: a bhd) | ½ | **12** | 14/1 | 45 | 5 |
| 638[15] | **Fairy Prince (IRE) (56)** (MrsALMKing) **3-8-4** AMcGlone(17) (a bhd) | s.h | **13** | 66/1 | 39 | — |
| 742[2] | **Allwight Then (IRE) (66)** (REPeacock) **5-9-10** WCarson(10) (spd over 2f) | s.h | **14** | 7/1[2] | 49 | 9 |
| | **Raisa Point (43)** (WRMuir) **5-7-12**(3)ow1 AWhelan(16) (bkwd: chsd ldrs over 2f) | s.h | **15** | 25/1 | 26 | — |
| 644[12] | **Alakhluki (51)** (GLewis) **3-7-13** RStreet(19) (bit bkwd: a bhd) | 4 | **16** | 25/1 | 21 | — |
| 664[3] | **Mazzarello (IRE) (41)** (RCurtis) **6-7-8v**(5) MBaird(5) (prom over 2f) | 2 | **17** | 12/1 | 5 | — |
| 667[5] | **Secret Miss (51)** (APJones) **4-8-9** RPrice(20) (dwlt: a bhd) | 1½ | **18** | 20/1 | 10 | — |
| 742[6] | **Midnight Cookie (53)** (BAPearce) **3-7-10**(5) MHenry(15) (lw: a bhd) | ¾ | **19** | 33/1 | 9 | — |

(SP 132.7%) **19 Rn**

**62.4 secs** (1.90) CSF £167.14 CT £2,444.68 TOTE £20.70: £5.00 £2.00 £3.80 £1.50 (£62.00) Trio £518.60 OWNER Ansells of Watford (COCKERHAM) BRED W. L. Caley

WEIGHT FOR AGE 3yo-10lb

OFFICIAL EXPLANATION **Ansellman: his apparent improvement was accounted for by his trainer who said the horse is an enigmatic character, who appreciated the stronger handling of his jockey and also the stiffer course.**

**Allwight Then (IRE): the gelding was struck into and lost interest thereafter.**

**Ansellman**, who has recently been fitted with blinkers for the first time since 1993, was helped by some heavy showers before racing. (20/1)

**Jucea**, who likes this course, was possibly a shade unlucky and deserves another chance. (8/1)

**742 Friendly Brave (USA)** continues in good form but has gone up 6lb in the ratings this season. (16/1)

**773* Goretski (IRE)** could not make the long journey from Yorkshire pay off under his penalty. (9/4)

**700 John O'Dreams** did his best work in the closing stages and ran another sound race. (11/1: 7/1-12/1)

**667 La Belle Dominique** was never close enough to land a blow. (20/1)

## 863 RACING CHANNEL H'CAP (0-80) (3-Y.O) (Class D)

3-30 (3-31) **1m 2f 46y** £3,803.25 (£1,146.00: £555.50: £260.25) Stalls: Low GOING minus 0.43 sec per fur (F)

| | Horse | Dist | Pos | SP | RR | SF |
|---|---|---|---|---|---|---|
| | **Meg's Memory (IRE) (55)** (JohnBerry) **3-7-7**(3) NVarley(8) (bhd: hdwy over 2f out: r.o to ld last strides) | — | **1** | 40/1 | 65 | 20 |
| 575[9] | **Trojan Risk (72)** (GLewis) **3-8-13** PaulEddery(12) (hld up & plld hrd: hdwy 5f out: led over 1f out: hdd last strides) | hd | **2** | 6/1 | 82 | 37 |
| | **Arcady (65)** (PTWalwyn) **3-8-6** RCochrane(9) (hdwy on ins over 1f out: r.o wl ins fnl f) | ¾ | **3** | 14/1 | 74 | 29 |
| 689* | **Cheerful Aspect (IRE) (80)** (EALDunlop) **3-9-7** JReid(13) (a.p: led over 2f out: sn rdn & edgd rt: hdd over 1f out: one pce) | ¾ | **4** | 7/2[1] | 88 | 43 |
| 597* | **Dhulikhel (62)** (DMarks) **3-8-3** SSanders(7) (a.p: one pce fnl 2f) | 2 | **5** | 7/1 | 66 | 21 |
| 693[4] | **Daunting Destiny (BEL) (76)** (RHannon) **3-8-12**(5) DaneO'Neill(3) (prom: rdn over 2f out: no hdwy) | 2½ | **6** | 9/2[2] | 76 | 31 |
| *381*[5] | **Willie Rushton (58)** (GLMoore) **3-7-13** FNorton(10) (nvr nr to chal) | 1¼ | **7** | 11/1 | 57 | 12 |
| | **Labeed (USA) (66)** (MajorWRHern) **3-8-7** WCarson(14) (led over 7f) | 2 | **8** | 5/1[3] | 61 | 16 |
| 595[12] | **Laughing Buccaneer (57)** (AGFoster) **3-7-7b**(5) MHenry(4) (a bhd) | 1¼ | **9** | 16/1 | 50 | 5 |
| | **One Pound (70)** (BWHills) **3-8-11** MHills(2) (dwlt: hdwy over 7f out: wknd over 3f out) | 2 | **10** | 12/1 | 60 | 15 |
| *519*[4] | **Rostaq (65)** (DJGMurraySmith) **3-8-6** TQuinn(1) (prom tl wknd over 2f out) | 2 | **11** | 16/1 | 52 | 7 |
| *515*[8] | **Duralock Fencer (55)** (PGMurphy) **3-7-10** NAdams(6) (dwlt: a bhd) | 1¼ | **12** | 40/1 | 40 | — |
| 731[11] | **Kinnescash (IRE) (68)** (MSSaunders) **3-8-6**(3) SDrowne(5) (bhd fnl 4f) | ½ | **13** | 25/1 | 52 | 7 |
| | **Petros Pride (60)** (MJBolton) **3-8-1** DeclanO'Shea(11) (a bhd: t.o) | dist | **14** | 40/1 | — | — |

(SP 129.5%) **14 Rn**

**2m 10.9** (3.40) CSF £259.00 CT £3,264.94 TOTE £63.20: £9.90 £2.30 £3.40 (£531.70) Trio £338.50; £433.87 to Ascot 1/5/96 OWNER Mrs Anthony Veale (NEWMARKET) BRED Golden Vale Stud

LONG HANDICAP Duralock Fencer 7-9
**OFFICIAL EXPLANATION Petros Pride: was badly impeded and almost brought down in the early stages.**
**Meg's Memory (IRE)**, a half-sister to Bean King, did well to finish runner-up on her first two starts in sprints here last season but then went the wrong way. (40/1)
**Trojan Risk** seems to stay well enough but did not help his rider by taking such a strong tug. (6/1)
**Arcady** is bred to stay even further and should not be hard to place. (14/1)
**689* Cheerful Aspect (IRE)**, trying a longer trip, did not help Reid by wanting to edge into the centre of the course after taking it up. (7/2)
**597* Dhulikhel** could not overcome a 12lb hike in the ratings. (7/1)
**693 Daunting Destiny (BEL)** had run respectably at Newmarket and should have found this company a little easier. (9/2)
**Willie Rushton** may well have been on a scouting mission after a disappointing effort on the Equitrack at the beginning of March. (11/1: 8/1-12/1)
**Labeed (USA)** was in trouble once headed with over a quarter of a mile to go. (5/1)

## 864 CORSTON CONDITIONS STKS (3-Y.O+) (Class C)

4-00 (4-01) **5f 11y** £4,851.00 (£1,809.00: £879.50: £372.50) Stalls: High GOING minus 0.43 sec per fur (F)

| | Horse / details | Dist | Pos | SP | RR | SF |
|---|---|---|---|---|---|---|
| | **Cape Merino** (MajorDNChappell) **5-8-13** BThomson(8) (mde all: clr over 1f out: r.o wl) | — | **1** | 8/1 | 107 | 51 |
| 673[10] | **Wavian (95)** (RHannon) **4-8-13**(5) DaneO'Neill(5) (lw: rdn over 2f out: hdwy over 1f out: nt trble wnr) | 3½ | **2** | 17/2 | 101 | 45 |
| | **Warning Star (103)** (BWHills) **4-9-5** MHills(9) (rdn over 2f out: hdwy over 1f out: r.o ins fnl f) | ½ | **3** | 7/2 [2] | 100 | 44 |
| | **That Man Again (101)** (GLewis) **4-9-1b**(3) AWhelan(7) (bit bkwd: prom: rdn over 2f out: one pce) | nk | **4** | 3/1 [1] | 98 | 42 |
| 735[18] | **Laurel Delight (85)** (JBerry) **6-8-13** RHughes(3) (prom: rdn over 2f out: wknd fnl f) | 2½ | **5** | 12/1 | 86 | 30 |
| | **Hello Mister (102)** (TEPowell) **5-9-9**(3) PMcCabe(1) (sn outpcd) | 5 | **6** | 9/1 | 83 | 27 |
| 579* | **Hard to Figure (109)** (RJHodges) **10-10-0** RCochrane(2) (outpcd) | 3½ | **7** | 9/2 [3] | 74 | 18 |
| | **Palacegate Jack (IRE) (83)** (JBerry) **5-9-4b** JCarroll(6) (chsd wnr: wknd qckly over 1f out) | 4 | **8** | 10/1 | 51 | — |
| | | | | (SP 113.8%) | **8 Rn** | |

**61.11 secs** (0.61) CSF £64.17 TOTE £9.10: £1.70 £2.10 £1.20 (£30.40) Trio £173.20 OWNER Mrs D. Ellis (WHITSBURY) BRED H. Ellis
**Cape Merino**, a useful performer at her best, was a sick horse last year and spent four months in her box suffering from a temperature. Making quite a comeback, she may now go for a listed race at Kempton. (8/1)
**579 Wavian**, highly tried last time, may have found this trip on the sharp side. (17/2)
**Warning Star** can step up on this when reverting back to six furlongs. (7/2)
**That Man Again** looked as though he would come on for the run. (3/1)
**Laurel Delight** had a foal when missing last season. (12/1)

## 865 PENSFORD MAIDEN AUCTION STKS (2-Y.O) (Class D)

4-30 (4-31) **5f 11y** £3,259.00 (£982.00: £476.00: £223.00) Stalls: High GOING minus 0.43 sec per fur (F)

| | Horse / details | Dist | Pos | SP | RR | SF |
|---|---|---|---|---|---|---|
| 706[9] | **Pelham (IRE)** (RHannon) **2-8-1**(5) DaneO'Neill(1) (mde virtually all: clr 1f out: pushed out) | — | **1** | 9/4 [2] | 73 | 21 |
| 697[4] | **Dalmeny Dancer** (BJMeehan) **2-8-8** BDoyle(7) (lw: rdn & outpcd 3f out: hdwy 2f out: no ch w wnr) | 4 | **2** | 9/1 | 62 | 10 |
| | **Just Nick** (MMcCormack) **2-8-6** JReid(8) (unf: w ldrs: ev ch whn rdn & hung bdly rt over 1f out: nt rcvr) | ½ | **3** | 9/1 | 59 | 7 |
| 441[4] | **Fredrik The Fierce (IRE)** (JBerry) **2-8-8** JCarroll(5) (lw: w wnr: wknd wl over 1f out) | 5 | **4** | 2/1 [1] | 45 | — |
| | **Sun O'Tirol (IRE)** (MRChannon) **2-8-4**ow1 TQuinn(3) (w'like: scope: no hdwy fnl 3f) | ¾ | **5** | 6/1 [3] | 39 | — |
| 643[3] | **Molly Music** (GGMargarson) **2-7-13**ow1 WCarson(6) (bhd fnl 2f) | s.h | **6** | 13/2 | 33 | — |
| | **Candle Light (IRE)** (APJarvis) **2-7-12** FNorton(2) (neat: lw: rdn over 2f out: sn bhd) | 1¾ | **7** | 20/1 | 27 | — |
| 706[13] | **Yanavanavano (IRE)** (GLewis) **2-8-6** PaulEddery(4) (bit bkwd: stdd s: outpcd fnl 3f) | hd | **8** | 25/1 | 35 | — |
| | | | | (SP 120.3%) | **8 Rn** | |

**62.6 secs** (2.10) CSF £21.82 TOTE £3.90: £1.40 £2.60 £2.00 (£20.90) OWNER Mr D. A. Lucie-Smith (MARLBOROUGH) BRED Golden Vale Stud
**Pelham (IRE)**, from a stable that can do little wrong with their two-year-olds this season, was sharper for his Newbury debut earlier in the month. (9/4: 6/4-5/2)
**Dalmeny Dancer**, like his sister Myrtle, seems to require further. (9/1)
**Just Nick** may have been just in front when throwing his chance away by coming over to the stands' rail. He would have given the winner plenty to think about. (9/1)
**441 Fredrik The Fierce (IRE)** is looking something of a short-runner at the moment. (2/1)
**Sun O'Tirol (IRE)**, a half-brother to four winners, had more scope about him than the rest of the field. (6/1: 4/1-13/2)

## 866 EMPIRE H'CAP (0-75) (4-Y.O+ F & M) (Class D)

5-00 (5-03) **1m 3f 144y** £3,735.00 (£1,125.00: £545.00: £255.00) Stalls: Low GOING minus 0.43 sec per fur (F)

| | Horse / details | Dist | Pos | SP | RR | SF |
|---|---|---|---|---|---|---|
| 635[4] | **Paradise Waters (56)** (RFJohnsonHoughton) **4-9-2** JReid(13) (mde all: rdn over 1f out: r.o wl) | — | **1** | 9/2 [2] | 64 | 49 |
| | **Soviet Bride (IRE) (64)** (SDow) **4-9-10** TQuinn(7) (lw: hld up & plld hrd: swtchd rt & hdwy over 2f out: r.o wl ins fnl f) | ½ | **2** | 5/2 [1] | 71 | 56 |
| 635[10] | **Bronze Maquette (IRE) (35)** (THind) **6-7-10** FNorton(3) (hdwy over 3f out: ev ch over 1f out: unable qckn ins fnl f) | hd | **3** | 33/1 | 42 | 28 |
| 771[9] | **Hill Farm Dancer (52)** (WMBrisbourne) **5-8-8**(5) DGriffiths(11) (dwlt: hdwy fnl 2f: nt rch ldrs) | 3 | **4** | 5/1 [3] | 55 | 41 |
| | **Damarita (36)** (LadyHerries) **5-7-11** DeclanO'Shea(2) (s.s: bhd tl styd on fnl 2f: nvr nrr) | 1½ | **5** | 20/1 | 37 | 23 |
| *654*[9] | **Great Tern (44)** (NMBabbage) **4-7-13**(5) MHenry(12) (plld hrd: prom tl wknd over 1f out) | 1 | **6** | 16/1 | 44 | 29 |
| 666[5] | **Uncharted Waters (50)** (CACyzer) **5-8-11** PaulEddery(9) (hdwy over 2f out: wknd over 1f out) | 6 | **7** | 9/1 | 41 | 27 |
| 609[3] | **Dots Dee (35)** (JMBradley) **7-7-3**(7) IonaWands(5) (lw: lost pl 6f out: n.d after) | 2½ | **8** | 20/1 | 23 | 9 |
| 760[6] | **Pip's Dream (51)** (MJRyan) **5-8-12** WCarson(14) (prom tl rdn & wknd over 2f out: eased fnl f) | 1¼ | **9** | 5/1 [3] | 37 | 23 |
| 670[12] | **Thorniwama (38)** (JJBridger) **5-7-8b**(5) MBaird(10) (bit bkwd: dwlt: a bhd: t.o) | 20 | **10** | 20/1 | — | — |
| 666[14] | **Kayartis (40)** (CADwyer) **7-7-12**(3) NVarley(8) (prom tl wknd over 2f out: t.o) | nk | **11** | 16/1 | — | — |
| *104*[12] | **Mafuta (IRE) (42)** (CLPopham) **4-8-2** SSanders(4) (hdwy on ins over 3f out: wknd over 2f out: t.o) | nk | **12** | 33/1 | — | — |
| 752[6] | **Brown Eyed Girl (46)** (BJMeehan) **4-8-6** BDoyle(1) (prom tl wknd over 2f out) | ¾ | **13** | 10/1 | 3 | — |
| | | | | (SP 131.1%) | **13 Rn** | |

**2m 29.2** (2.50) CSF £16.93 CT £324.21 TOTE £4.40: £1.50 £1.60 £13.70 (£10.20) Trio £489.00; £309.98 to Ascot 1/5/96 OWNER Mr R. Crutchley (DIDCOT) BRED R. E. Crutchley
LONG HANDICAP Dots Dee 7-4 Bronze Maquette (IRE) 7-5
WEIGHT FOR AGE 4yo-1lb
**635 Paradise Waters** adopted her usual front-running tactics and held on gamely under a lovely ride. (9/2: 5/2-5/1)

**Soviet Bride (IRE)**, a well-backed favourite, proved difficult to settle and could not peg back the winner in the closing stages. (5/2)
**Bronze Maquette (IRE)**, 5lb out of the handicap, ran her best race for a long time. (33/1)
**771 Hill Farm Dancer** has been in good form on the All-Weather and is rated 7lb lower on the turf. (5/1)
**Damarita** is lightly-raced and at last showed signs of better things to come. (20/1)
**Great Tern** ran too freely and did not give herself a chance of lasting the trip. (16/1)
**666 Uncharted Waters** (9/1: 6/1-10/1)

T/Jkpt: Not won; £27,696.83 to Ascot 1/5/96. T/Plpt: £2,405.70 (6.41 Tckts). T/Qdpt: £194.10 (6.36 Tckts). KH

## 0748-NOTTINGHAM (L-H) (Good to firm, Good patches in st)
## Tuesday April 30th
WEATHER: showers WIND: slt half against

### 867 MEADOWS (S) STKS (3-Y.O) (Class G)
2-15 (2-15) **6f 15y** £2,070.00 (£570.00: £270.00) Stalls: High GOING minus 0.20 sec per fur (GF)

| Form | Horse | Dist | Pos | SP | RR | SF |
|---|---|---|---|---|---|---|
| $781^{9}$ | **Forecast** (JWharton) **3-8-12** PRobinson(6) (bhd: sn pushed along: hdwy over 1f out: r.o strly to ld cl home) | — | **1** | 50/1 | 60 | — |
| $748^{3}$ | **Pride of Whalley (IRE)** (RAFahey) **3-8-7** ACulhane(11) (racd centre: drifted lft & led over 2f out: ct fnl strides) | nk | **2** | 9/4 1 | 54 | — |
| $748^{11}$ | **The Frisky Farmer (66)** (WGMTurner) **3-9-4** TSprake(8) (led far side over 3f: kpt on u.p fnl f) | 1¼ | **3** | 6/1 3 | 62 | 1 |
| $637^{9}$ | **Music Mistress (IRE) (50)** (JSMoore) **3-8-13** WJO'Connor(7) (a.p far side: rdn over 1f out: one pce) | 4 | **4** | 12/1 | 46 | — |
| $423^{6}$ | **Victoria Sioux (52)** (JAPickering) **3-8-7** JQuinn(1) (trckd ldrs far side: rdn & one pce appr fnl f) | hd | **5** | 12/1 | 40 | — |
| $605^{11}$ | **Magical Midnight (35)** (NTinkler) **3-8-7** KimTinkler(9) (s.i.s: hrd rdn over 2f out: no imp fnl f) | 2 | **6** | 25/1 | 35 | — |
| $123^{16}$ | **Victory Commander (46)** (TJNaughton) **3-8-12** JFortune(2) (bit bkwd: bhd fnl 2f far side) | 1¾ | **7** | 16/1 | 35 | — |
| | **Mystic Times (55)** (MissJFCraze) **3-8-13** LDettori(12) (racd stands' side: hdwy ½-wy: no ch fnl 2f) | 1¼ | **8** | 10/1 | 33 | — |
| $748^{16}$ | **Dispol Duchess** (GROldroyd) **3-8-7** GDuffield(5) (s.i.s: a in rr) | 1½ | **9** | 50/1 | 23 | — |
| | **Maysimp (IRE) (40)** (BPJBaugh) **3-8-7** WLord(3) (prom far side 4f) | s.h | **10** | 50/1 | 23 | — |
| $748^{18}$ | **U-No-Harry (IRE) (66)** (RHollinshead) **3-9-4** KDarley(14) (lw: chsd ldr stands' side: rdn 2f out: sn btn) | ½ | **11** | 13/2 | 33 | — |
| $748^{6}$ | **Our Worley (IRE)** (APJarvis) **3-8-7** JTate(4) (b.off hind: spd far side over 3f) | 5 | **12** | 5/1 2 | 8 | — |
| $660^{8}$ | **Turbo North (52)** (MDods) **3-8-12** DeanMcKeown(16) (in tch stands' side 4f) | 1¼ | **13** | 33/1 | 10 | — |
| | **Astral's Chance** (KRBurke) **3-8-12** JFEgan(15) (bkwd: chsd ldrs stands' side over 3f) | ¾ | **14** | 11/1 | 8 | — |
| $775^{15}$ | **Impromptu Melody (IRE) (50)** (BSRothwell) **3-8-7b1** MFenton(17) (led stands' side: no ch fnl 2f) | 2½ | **15** | 14/1 | — | — |
| $638^{14}$ | **Afisiak (47)** (ABMulholland) **3-8-13** JWeaver(10) (racd centre: a in rr: t.o) | 11 | **16** | 14/1 | — | — |
| | | | | (SP 139.7%) | **16 Rn** | |

**1m 16.4** (5.90) CSF £170.13 TOTE £33.50: £5.30 £1.40 £2.40 (£121.20) Trio £157.40; £93.14 to Ascot 1/5/96 OWNER Mr P. W. Lambert (MELTON MOWBRAY) BRED Barrettstown Stud Farms Ltd
No bid

**Forecast** carries a lot of condition but made this first appearance on turf a winning one by running on strongly to catch the favourite in the shadow of the post. (50/1)
**748 Pride of Whalley (IRE)** had to overcome a poor draw before she could get herself into the action and, giving her all, was a shade unfortunate to be worn down in the dying strides. (9/4)
**748 The Frisky Farmer** ran much better than he did eight days ago here, but at least he did race on the favoured far side on this occasion, and he battled on gamely to the finish. (6/1)
**Music Mistress (IRE)**, dropping back to a more suitable trip, pressed the leaders all the way and only dropped away inside the final furlong. (12/1)
**Victoria Sioux** is still having a problem trying to get it together but does seem to be a trier, and her turn will come. (12/1)
**Magical Midnight** could not make her presence felt after missing a beat at the start, but she beat more than beat her, and all is not lost yet. (25/1)

### 868 BRADMORE H'CAP (0-70) (3-Y.O+ F & M) (Class E)
2-45 (2-46) **6f 15y** £3,496.00 (£1,048.00: £504.00: £232.00) Stalls: High GOING minus 0.20 sec per fur (GF)

| Form | Horse | Dist | Pos | SP | RR | SF |
|---|---|---|---|---|---|---|
| $749^{7}$ | **Almasi (IRE) (54)** (CFWall) **4-9-2** GDuffield(3) (hld up: hdwy ½-wy: shkn up to ld cl home) | — | **1** | 10/1 | 62 | 39 |
| $704^{5}$ | **Maid O'Cannie (55)** (MWEasterby) **5-9-3b** KDarley(2) (trckd ldrs: hdwy to ld ins fnl f: hrd rdn & hdd nr fin) | ¾ | **2** | 4/1 1 | 61 | 38 |
| $782^{10}$ | **Merrie le Bow (42)** (PatMitchell) **4-7-13(5)** AmandaSanders(10) (hdwy 2f out: rdn & r.o wl towards fin) | nk | **3** | 33/1 | 47 | 24 |
| | **Faraway Lass (65)** (LordHuntingdon) **3-9-2** DHarrison(12) (bit bkwd: a.p far side: led 2f out tl ins fnl f: no ex) | 1½ | **4** | 14/1 | 66 | 32 |
| $775^{7}$ | **Morning Surprise (58)** (APJarvis) **3-8-9** JTate(11) (a.p: rdn & nt clr run appr fnl f: kpt on) | nk | **5** | 14/1 | 59 | 25 |
| $632^{12}$ | **Prima Silk (64)** (MJRyan) **5-9-12** DBiggs(14) (chsd ldrs far side: rdn 2f out: nvr able to chal) | 3½ | **6** | 16/1 | 55 | 32 |
| | **Premium Gift (64)** (CBBBooth) **4-9-12** MBirch(18) (bit bkwd: trckd ldr far side: ev ch 2f out: one pce fnl f) | ¾ | **7** | 25/1 | 53 | 30 |
| $762^{5}$ | **Kira (58)** (JLEyre) **6-9-6** RLappin(4) (b.off hind: led far side 3f: wknd over 1f out) | ¾ | **8** | 6/1 3 | 45 | 22 |
| $601^{5}$ | **Tael of Silver (61)** (KRBurke) **4-9-2(7)** TAshley(6) (mid div: rdn over 2f out: no imp) | hd | **9** | 8/1 | 48 | 25 |
| $762^{2}$ | **Belinda Blue (45)** (RAFahey) **4-8-7** ACulhane(13) (dwlt: sn trckng ldrs: no hdwy fnl 2f) | s.h | **10** | 9/2 2 | 32 | 9 |
| | **Diebiedale (51)** (RBoss) **4-8-13** PatEddery(16) (bkwd: prom far side: led 3f out to 2f out: eased whn btn) | 2½ | **11** | 12/1 | 31 | 8 |
| $850^{15}$ | **Prime Property (IRE) (44)** (MWEasterby) **4-8-1b(5)ow3** GParkin(1) (prom: drvn along ½-wy: grad wknd) | s.h | **12** | 14/1 | 24 | — |
| $748^{7}$ | **Born A Lady (64)** (SRBowring) **3-8-10b(5)** CTeague(8) (w ldrs far side: nt clr run & wknd 2f out) | 1 | **13** | 10/1 | 42 | 8 |
| $704^{3}$ | **Penny's Wishing (46)** (NBycroft) **4-8-1(7)** JoHunnam(19) (b.off hind: racd stands' side: n.d) | hd | **14** | 14/1 | 23 | — |
| $644^{4}$ | **Tymeera (60)** (BPalling) **3-8-11** TSprake(9) (w ldrs far side: edgd lft over 2f out: sn btn) | hd | **15** | 9/1 | 37 | 3 |
| $571^{9}$ | **Dil Dil (65)** (RHannon) **3-9-2** JQuinn(15) (lw: outpcd) | 2½ | **16** | 16/1 | 35 | 1 |
| $617^{5}$ | **Samsung Lovelylady (IRE) (42)** (EWeymes) **4-8-4** JFanning(5) (bhd fr ½-wy) | 1½ | **17** | 14/1 | 9 | — |
| | **Tutu Sixtysix (36)** (DonEnricoIncisa) **5-7-12** KimTinkler(20) (bkwd: chsd ldr stands' side: bhd fnl 2f) | 3½ | **18** | 25/1 | — | — |
| $762^{16}$ | **Kiwud (48)** (TWDonnelly) **3-7-13ow1** CRutter(21) (led stands' side 4f) | s.h | **19** | 50/1 | 5 | — |
| $207^{11}$ | **Crowning Tino (34)** (MrsNMacauley) **4-7-10** NKennedy(7) (sn outpcd & bhd) | dist | **20** | 33/1 | — | — |
| $518^{8}$ | **Life Is Precious (IRE) (43)** (RHollinshead) **4-8-0(5)** FLynch(17) (bhd whn collapsed & fell 2f out: dead) | | **F** | 16/1 | — | — |
| | | | | (SP 166.0%) | **21 Rn** | |

**1m 13.6** (3.10) CSF £60.34 CT £1,331.99 TOTE £9.10: £3.00 £1.60 £21.80 £6.60 (£24.20) Trio £438.60; £12.36 to Ascot 1/5/96 OWNER The Equema Partnership (NEWMARKET) BRED Newtownbarry House Stud
LONG HANDICAP Crowning Tino 7-6
WEIGHT FOR AGE 3yo-11lb

**Almasi (IRE)** got back to winning ways with a hard-fought success, and showed how unlucky she was to be drawn on the slower stands' side last week. (10/1)
**704 Maid O'Cannie** looked to have timed it just right when taking over 200 yards out, but the strong-finishing winner had the speed to take her measure late on. (4/1: 3/1-9/2)
**Merrie le Bow**, brought back to sprinting, put in a sustained last-furlong challenge and went down fighting. She will not need to improve much to win a small race. (33/1)
**Faraway Lass**, a half-sister to winning sprinter Bangles, ran a fine race on this seasonal debut and, though she has yet to get off the mark, gave notice that she is going the right way. (14/1)
**Morning Surprise**, who had to be mounted on the track, pushed the pace and may well have been concerned in the outcome had she not been squeezed for room approaching the final furlong. She has been competing over a slightly longer trip this term, but she has plenty of speed and could win another race at sprint distances. (14/1)
**Prima Silk** did not impress to post but did keep tabs on the principals until failing to quicken when the sprint to the line developed. (16/1)
**Premium Gift** turned in a pleasing display on this first run since the autumn and she will not have much trouble in finding an opening. (25/1)
**601 Tael of Silver** (8/1: op 4/1)

## 869 PORCHESTER MEDIAN AUCTION MAIDEN STKS (2-Y.O) (Class F)

3-15 (3-18) **5f 13y** £2,385.00 (£660.00: £315.00) Stalls: High GOING minus 0.20 sec per fur (GF)

| | | | | SP | RR | SF |
|---|---|---|---|---|---|---|
| | **Mirror Four Life (IRE)** (MHTompkins) **2-8-9** PRobinson(7) (lt-f: dwlt: sn rcvrd to chse ldrs: led 1f out: r.o wl) | — | 1 | 10/1 | 71 | 21 |
| 523[5] | **Bold Welcome** (JWharton) **2-9-0** JQuinn(2) (s.i.s: hdwy ½-wy: swtchd rt appr fnl f: r.o u.p) | 1 | 2 | 16/1 | 73 | 23 |
| 741[3] | **Ekaterini Paritsi** (WGMTurner) **2-8-9** TSprake(3) (bhd & outpcd: rdn along ½-wy: hdwy appr fnl f: fin wl) | 2½ | 3 | 9/2[3] | 60 | 10 |
| 618[3] | **Irish Fiction (IRE)** (MRChannon) **2-9-0** KDarley(9) (w ldrs: led over 2f out tl over 1f out: one pce) | 1½ | 4 | 5/2[1] | 60 | 10 |
| 697[5] | **But Why** (CMurray) **2-9-0** MTebbutt(4) (trckd ldrs: rdn ½-wy: one pce fnl 2f) | nk | 5 | 14/1 | 59 | 9 |
| 685[7] | **Pandiculation** (EWeymes) **2-9-0** JFortune(8) (bit bkwd: w ldrs tl wknd 1f out) | 1 | 6 | 9/2[3] | 56 | 6 |
| 657[2] | **Docklands Carriage (IRE)** (NTinkler) **2-9-0** LCharnock(6) (led to ½-wy: rdn over 1f out: eased whn btn) | ¾ | 7 | 3/1[2] | 54 | 4 |
| 697[3] | **M T Vessel** (JRJenkins) **2-9-0** LDettori(5) (trckd ldrs: hrd drvn ½-wy: wknd over 1f out) | 3½ | 8 | 6/1 | 43 | — |
| | **Always Alight** (KRBurke) **2-9-0** JFEgan(1) (unf: scope: s.i.s: a outpcd) | 2½ | 9 | 12/1 | 35 | — |

(SP 133.6%) **9 Rn**

**61.9 secs** (3.30) CSF £144.27 TOTE £11.40: £2.60 £2.40 £2.80 (£77.10) Trio £74.50 OWNER Mirror 4 Punters Club (NEWMARKET) BRED Dullingham House Stud

**Mirror Four Life (IRE)**, a fit-looking debutante who was sluggish leaving the stalls, soon held a prominent pitch and, let down to lead entering the final furlong, always had the measure of her rivals. (10/1: op 5/1)
**Bold Welcome** had learned a lot from his debut earlier in the month and, though he could not match strides with the winner, he showed that he is moving in the right direction. (16/1)
**741 Ekaterini Paritsi** could not go the early pace and was struggling in the rear until picking up and fairly sprinting through the final furlong. (9/2: op 3/1)
**618 Irish Fiction (IRE)** shared the lead, but may have dome too much too soon for he was tapped for toe in the dash to the line. (5/2)
**But Why**, off the bridle at halfway, was always being taken along much too fast and could not summon up the pace to deliver a challenge. (14/1)
**685 Pandiculation**, an impressive mover, went with the pace and was a live factor until weakening inside the final furlong. (9/2)
**657 Docklands Carriage (IRE)** had more use made of him this time and had nothing more to give when pressure was applied in the final furlong. (3/1)
**697 M T Vessel** (6/1: op 4/1)
**Always Alight** (12/1: op 8/1)

## 870 RADFORD MAIDEN STKS (3-Y.O F) (Class D)

3-45 (3-48) **1m 54y** £4,077.50 (£1,220.00: £585.00: £267.50) Stalls: Low GOING minus 0.20 sec per fur (GF)

| | | | | SP | RR | SF |
|---|---|---|---|---|---|---|
| | **Abeyr** (MAJarvis) **3-8-11** PRobinson(1) (scope: a.p: rdn 2f out: drifted lft ins fnl f: led nr fin) | — | 1 | 33/1 | 69 | 36 |
| | **Dawna** (HRACecil) **3-8-11** PatEddery(4) (w'like: bit bkwd: chsd ldr: shkn up to ld over 1f out: hdd cl home) | nk | 2 | 4/6[1] | 68 | 35 |
| | **Lubaba (USA)** (HThomsonJones) **3-8-11** RHills(5) (neat: prom: effrt over 2f out: disp ld ins fnl f: r.o) | s.h | 3 | 12/1 | 68 | 35 |
| | **Dimakya (USA) (95)** (DRLoder) **3-8-11** LDettori(3) (led tl over 1f out: eased whn btn fnl f) | 6 | 4 | 11/2[2] | 57 | 24 |
| 710[5] | **Whispered Melody** (PWHarris) **3-8-11** GHind(12) (hld up: hdwy ½-wy: rdn over 2f out: sn btn) | ½ | 5 | 6/1[3] | 56 | 23 |
| | **Skelton Countess (IRE)** (RHollinshead) **3-8-6**(5) FLynch(6) (bkwd: mid div: drvn along 3f out: no imp) | hd | 6 | 33/1 | 56 | 23 |
| | **Indian Relative (74)** (RGuest) **3-8-11** KDarley(13) (a in rr) | 5 | 7 | 9/1 | 46 | 13 |
| | **Another Quarter (IRE)** (SPCWoods) **3-8-11** WWoods(10) (b: bkwd: hld up: rdn whn hmpd 2f out: n.d) | nk | 8 | 33/1 | 45 | 12 |
| | **Gold Lining (IRE)** (CDBroad) **3-8-11** MFenton(2) (w'like: scope: trckd ldrs: wkng whn hmpd 2f out) | ¾ | 9 | 50/1 | 44 | 11 |
| | **The Jolly Barmaid (IRE)** (PCalver) **3-8-11** MBirch(9) (mid div: no ch whn bdly hmpd 2f out) | 5 | 10 | 66/1 | 34 | 1 |
| | **Persephone** (ICampbell) **3-8-11** MTebbutt(8) (bkwd: a bhd) | 4 | 11 | 66/1 | 26 | — |
| | **Mustard** (ABMulholland) **3-8-11** MMcAndrew(7) (w'like: unf: bkwd: s.i.s: sn wnt prom: rdn & wkng whn hung lft 2f out) | 2½ | 12 | 66/1 | 22 | — |
| | **Matam** (MWEasterby) **3-8-6**(5) GParkin(11) (lengthy: s.s: hld up in rr: no ch whn hmpd 2f out) | ½ | 13 | 66/1 | 21 | — |

(SP 124.1%) **13 Rn**

**1m 45.7** (4.40) CSF £55.34 TOTE £27.40: £5.40 £1.10 £2.20 (£13.90) Trio £31.20 OWNER Sheikh Ahmed Al Maktoum (NEWMARKET) BRED W. H. F. Carson

**Abeyr**, a scopey filly bred by Willie Carson, showed the right battling qualities inside the distance and, with the far rail to help, forced her head in front in the dying strides. (33/1)
**Dawna**, very much in need of some sun on her back, looked set to make a winning debut when leading into the final furlong, but she found lack of a previous outing costing her dear in the battle to the line. (4/6)
**Lubaba (USA)**, a choicely-bred filly hanging onto her winter coat and very much in need of the run, turned in an extremely good first effort and only failed on the nod. She should not let the family down. (12/1: op 5/1)
**Dimakya (USA)**, looking very wintry, made the running for over six furlongs but then faded rather quickly, and she could be some way below her peak. (11/2: 3/1-6/1)
**710 Whispered Melody**, a bit of a handful at the start, showed she possesses ability and will continue to improve as she gains experience. (6/1)
**Indian Relative** (9/1: op 7/2)

## 871 COTMANHAY H'CAP (0-80) (4-Y.O+) (Class D)

4-15 (4-16) **1m 1f 213y** £4,337.50 (£1,300.00: £625.00: £287.50) Stalls: Low GOING minus 0.20 sec per fur (GF)

| | | | | SP | RR | SF |
|---|---|---|---|---|---|---|
| 580[5] | **Kings Assembly (76)** (PWHarris) **4-9-10** GHind(5) (lw: a.p: led over 2f out: clr ent fnl f: rdn out) | — | **1** | 7/2[2] | 86 | 45 |
| 641[5] | **Harvey White (IRE) (53)** (JPearce) **4-8-1** GBardwell(12) (hld up in rr: pushed along 6f out: styd on strly towards fin) | 1½ | **2** | 14/1 | 61 | 20 |
| | **Prize Pupil (IRE) (73)** (CFWall) **4-9-7** GDuffield(13) (bit bkwd: hld up in tch: rdn 3f out: r.o strly fnl f) | nk | **3** | 16/1 | 80 | 39 |
| 641[3] | **Obelos (USA) (69)** (MrsJCecil) **5-9-3** LDettori(9) (a.p: rdn to chse wnr 2f out: no ex appr fnl f) | hd | **4** | 3/1[1] | 76 | 35 |
| | **Yaverland (IRE) (60)** (CADwyer) **4-8-8** RHills(6) (b: bkwd: hld up: stdy hdwy over 3f out: swtchd lft over 1f out: r.o) | s.h | **5** | 25/1 | 67 | 26 |
| | **Shining Example (72)** (PJMakin) **4-9-6** PatEddery(11) (swtg: bit bkwd: plld hrd: hld up & bhd: hdwy over 2f out: nt rch ldrs) | 2½ | **6** | 6/1[3] | 75 | 34 |
| 682[11] | **Out on a Promise (IRE) (79)** (NJHWalker) **4-9-13** CRutter(14) (hld up mid div: effrt 3f out: sn drvn: one pce) | 2½ | **7** | 12/1 | 78 | 37 |
| 537[4] | **Break the Rules (73)** (MrsMReveley) **4-9-7** KDarley(3) (lw: hld up: effrt over 3f out: n.d) | 3½ | **8** | 7/1 | 66 | 25 |
| | **Rushen Raider (58)** (KWHogg) **4-8-1**(5) ADaly(1) (bkwd: led over 7f: sn wknd) | hd | **9** | 25/1 | 51 | 10 |
| | **Silver Sleeve (IRE) (55)** (MDHammond) **4-8-3** JFanning(7) (trckd ldrs: rdn 3f out: sn btn) | ¾ | **10** | 25/1 | 47 | 6 |
| | **Mister Rm (77)** (RGuest) **4-9-11** MFenton(8) (bit bkwd: s.s: hld up: drvn along over 3f out: grad wknd) | 2 | **11** | 16/1 | 66 | 25 |
| *462** | **Renown (68)** (LordHuntingdon) **4-9-2** DHarrison(4) (chsd ldr: pushed along 3f out: wknd & eased appr fnl f: t.o) | 6 | **12** | 13/2 | 47 | 6 |
| 598[6] | **Fairy Knight (77)** (RHannon) **4-9-11** JQuinn(10) (hld up: a bhd: t.o) | 1½ | **13** | 10/1 | 54 | 13 |
| | | | | (SP 134.1%) | **13 Rn** | |

**2m 8.2** (5.70) CSF £53.16 CT £661.73 TOTE £4.50: £1.60 £3.20 £2.50 (£73.00) Trio £113.80 OWNER The Everhopefuls I (BERKHAMSTED) BRED Benham Stud

**580 Kings Assembly** has grown into quite an attractive colt and he is certainly going the right way, winning with far more in hand than the verdict would suggest. (7/2)

**641 Harvey White (IRE)**, towards the rear and hard at work at halfway, picked up well when stamina came into play and will be suited by a stiffer test. (14/1)

**Prize Pupil (IRE)** produced his best form in the early part of last season, and this pleasing performance suggests he will not be long in returning to form. (16/1)

**641 Obelos (USA)**, ill-at-ease cantering to post, pressed the leaders but was flat to the boards early in the straight and, in the circumstances, did well to finish so close. (3/1)

**Yaverland (IRE)**, carrying surplus condition and winning no supporters with his action to post, ran by far his best race yet in his first handicap and would seem to be very much on the upgrade. (25/1)

**Shining Example** took a fierce pull but, restrained off the pace, improved up the centre of the track over two furlongs out, but blew up before he could get to terms. Immediate improvement should follow. (6/1)

## 872 ATTENBOROUGH H'CAP (0-70) (4-Y.O+) (Class E)

4-45 (4-45) **1m 6f 15y** £3,704.00 (£1,112.00: £536.00: £248.00) Stalls: Low GOING minus 0.20 sec per fur (GF)

| | | | | SP | RR | SF |
|---|---|---|---|---|---|---|
| 753[4] | **Cuango (IRE) (53)** (RHollinshead) **5-8-8**(5) FLynch(8) (hld up: hdwy 3f out: styd on to ld wl ins fnl f) | — | **1** | 12/1 | 65 | 43 |
| 668[7] | **Opaque (63)** (LMCumani) **4-9-7** LDettori(14) (hld up: hdwy 5f out: rdn ent st: ev ch ins fnl f: r.o) | ¾ | **2** | 11/2[3] | 74 | 50 |
| 753[2] | **Ciracusa (IRE) (59)** (JMackie) **4-9-3** GCarter(3) (lw: hld up: hdwy 6f out: led over 1f out tl ins fnl f: hrd rdn & nt qckn) | 1¼ | **3** | 11/4[1] | 69 | 45 |
| | **Prussia (42)** (WClay) **5-8-2** TSprake(18) (a.p: led over 2f out tl over 1f out: unable qckn fnl f) | ½ | **4** | 50/1 | 51 | 29 |
| 690[6] | **Cliburnel News (IRE) (58)** (AStreeter) **6-9-4** JWeaver(6) (hld up: hdwy over 2f out: rdn & no ex ins fnl f) | 2 | **5** | 10/1 | 65 | 43 |
| 753[10] | **Uncle Doug (50)** (MrsMReveley) **5-8-10** KDarley(7) (lw: hld up: hdwy over 2f out: one pce appr fnl f) | 5 | **6** | 12/1 | 51 | 29 |
| 625[3] | **Hullbank (56)** (WWHaigh) **6-9-2** JTate(17) (b: hld up: hdwy over 4f out: one pce fnl 2f) | nk | **7** | 11/1 | 57 | 35 |
| 767[2] | **Greek Night Out (IRE) (43)** (JLEyre) **5-8-0**(3) DWright(19) (prom: chsd ldr 6f out tl wknd 2f out) | 1¼ | **8** | 7/1 | 42 | 20 |
| 635[11] | **Shahrani (48)** (BJMeehan) **4-8-6** MTebbutt(2) (swtg: led 2f: prom tl wknd 3f out) | ¾ | **9** | 8/1 | 47 | 23 |
| 753[17] | **Amercius (39)** (JLHarris) **4-7-6b**(5)ow1 PFessey(20) (prom tl wknd fnl 3f) | 2½ | **10** | 50/1 | 35 | 10 |
| 753[7] | **Iota (53)** (JLHarris) **7-8-13** PRobinson(5) (a in rr) | 1¼ | **11** | 5/1[2] | 47 | 25 |
| 753[13] | **Top Royal (60)** (JPearce) **7-9-6** NDay(9) (b: s.s: a in rr) | 2 | **12** | 33/1 | 52 | 30 |
| 666[8] | **Sir Thomas Beecham (56)** (SDow) **6-8-11**(5) ADaly(15) (a in rr) | 3½ | **13** | 14/1 | 44 | 22 |
| | **My Rossini (52)** (PJBevan) **7-8-5**(7) DDenby(1) (bhd: drvn along ½-wy: no imp) | 3 | **14** | 12/1 | 37 | 15 |
| 642[11] | **Firefighter (51)** (BPJBaugh) **7-8-11** WLord(13) (b: nvr nr ldrs) | hd | **15** | 50/1 | 36 | 14 |
| 675[4] | **Advance East (66)** (MrsJRRamsden) **4-9-10** JFortune(12) (prom: rdn to ld over 3f out: hdd & wknd over 2f out) | 2½ | **16** | 10/1 | 48 | 24 |
| 690[18] | **Oakbury (IRE) (57)** (MissLCSiddall) **4-9-1** DHarrison(11) (hld up: drvn along over 3f out: no imp) | hd | **17** | 50/1 | 39 | 15 |
| | **Kings Cay (IRE) (55)** (THCaldwell) **5-9-1** ACulhane(10) (prom tl rdn & wknd 4f out) | 1 | **18** | 50/1 | 35 | 13 |
| 625[10] | **Bold Top (38)** (BSRothwell) **4-7-10b** JQuinn(4) (led after 2f tl over 3f out: sn wknd: t.o) | 2½ | **19** | 20/1 | 16 | — |
| | **Rasmi (CAN) (62)** (PHowling) **5-9-8** RHills(16) (bkwd: bhd fnl 5f: t.o) | dist | **20** | 33/1 | — | — |
| | | | | (SP 159.0%) | **20 Rn** | |

**3m 5.4** (6.90) CSF £88.77 CT £231.61 TOTE £8.80: £1.80 £2.10 £1.40 £7.50 (£41.00) Trio £50.00 OWNER Barouche Stud Ltd (UPPER LONGDON) BRED Citadel Stud Establishment

WEIGHT FOR AGE 4yo-2lb

**753 Cuango (IRE)** turned the tables on the favourite on slightly better terms, producing a determined late challenge to nose ahead nearing the finish. (12/1)

**668 Opaque** showed much improved form over this more suitable trip and was only caught close home. He is bred to need a stiff test of stamina and that initial success is just around the corner. (11/2: 7/2-6/1)

**753 Ciracusa (IRE)** gave of his best under a forceful ride but could not withstand the powerful late challenges of the principals. (11/4)

**Prussia**, fit from hurdling, ran by far his best race for quite some time and a repeat could see him back in the winner's enclosure. (50/1)

**690 Cliburnel News (IRE)**, produced from off the pace, could not sustain the run inside the final furlong, but showed enough to suggest another success is near at hand. (10/1)

**Uncle Doug** crept closer in the latter stages but, on ground much faster than he cares for, could not muster the pace to mount a challenge. (12/1)

**Shahrani** (8/1: op 20/1)

**656* Iota** (5/1: 4/1-6/1)

## 873 LEVY BOARD H'CAP (0-70) (3-Y.O) (Class E)

5-15 (5-18) **1m 54y** £3,808.00 (£1,144.00: £552.00: £256.00) Stalls: Low GOING minus 0.20 sec per fur (GF)

| Form | Runner | Dist | Pos | SP | RR | SF |
|---|---|---|---|---|---|---|
| | **Samara (IRE) (70)** (JLDunlop) **3-9-7** PatEddery(12) (hld up: plld hrd: hdwy 4f out: rdn to ld over 1f out: sn clr) | — | 1 | $2/1^{1}$ | 82+ | 50 |
| $509^{5}$ | **Silverdale Knight (57)** (KWHogg) **3-8-8** DHarrison(14) (a.p: led 5f out tl over 1f out: one pce) | 2 | 2 | 20/1 | 65 | 33 |
| | **Mazcobar (62)** (PJMakin) **3-8-13** LDettori(10) (bit bkwd: hld up: hdwy over 2f out: styd on u.p fnl f) | ¾ | 3 | $8/1^{3}$ | 69 | 37 |
| *$405^{3}$* | **General Haven (65)** (TJNaughton) **3-9-2** JFortune(13) (hld up: hdwy over 3f out: nvr nrr) | 1¾ | 4 | 25/1 | 68 | 36 |
| $701^{7}$ | **Yezza (IRE) (65)** (APJarvis) **3-9-2** JTate(11) (hld up & bhd: styd on fnl 2f: nrst fin) | 2½ | 5 | 33/1 | 63+ | 31 |
| | **Alreeh (IRE) (70)** (JHMGosden) **3-9-7** RHills(2) (bit bkwd: hld up & bhd tl styd on fnl 2f: nvr nrr) | ¾ | 6 | 20/1 | 67 | 35 |
| | **Swift Maiden (63)** (JNeville) **3-9-0** DeanMcKeown(16) (bkwd: led over 3f: prom tl wknd 2f out) | s.h | 7 | 33/1 | 60 | 28 |
| | **Windswept (IRE) (65)** (DJSffrenchDavis) **3-8-11**(5) CAdamson(18) (prom: rdn along over 3f out: wknd wl over 1f out) | 2½ | 8 | 33/1 | 57 | 25 |
| $692^{10}$ | **Sea Danzig (67)** (PHowling) **3-9-4** JQuinn(9) (bhd: effrt over 2f out: n.d) | s.h | 9 | 9/1 | 59 | 27 |
| $595^{14}$ | **Katie Komaite (60)** (CaptJWilson) **3-8-11** CRutter(19) (s.s: hdwy over 4f out: wknd fnl 2f) | s.h | 10 | 25/1 | 52 | 20 |
| | **Gilling Dancer (IRE) (60)** (PCalver) **3-8-11** MBirch(15) (bit bkwd: prom: ev ch over 2f out: wknd qckly fnl f) | hd | 11 | 16/1 | 52 | 20 |
| $616^{2}$ | **Get Tough (57)** (SDow) **3-8-8** JWeaver(7) (prom: rdn 3f out: sn lost tch) | 1¼ | 12 | $8/1^{3}$ | 46 | 14 |
| | **Night of Glass (60)** (DMorris) **3-8-11** JHBrown(20) (nvr nr ldrs) | ¾ | 13 | 33/1 | 48 | 16 |
| $562^{7}$ | **Pride of Kashmir (56)** (PWHarris) **3-8-7** GHind(3) (unruly s: prom: rdn along ½-wy: grad wknd) | s.h | 14 | $8/1^{3}$ | 44 | 12 |
| $584^{12}$ | **Duo Master (70)** (MrsMReveley) **3-9-7** KDarley(5) (s.s: a in rr) | 4 | 15 | 20/1 | 50 | 18 |
| $575^{8}$ | **Asking For Kings (IRE) (62)** (SDow) **3-8-8**(5) ADaly(6) (a in rr) | s.h | 16 | 33/1 | 42 | 10 |
| $663^{8}$ | **Rossel (USA) (70)** (MRStoute) **3-9-7** PRobinson(4) (mid div tl lost pl 3f out: t.o) | 11 | 17 | $6/1^{2}$ | 28 | — |
| $718^{13}$ | **Sizzling Symphony (62)** (RAFahey) **3-8-13** ACulhane(8) (mid div: drvn along ½-wy: sn bhd: t.o) | 5 | 18 | 20/1 | 11 | — |
| $646^{10}$ | **Time of Night (USA) (70)** (RGuest) **3-9-7** MFenton(17) (bhd fnl 4f: t.o) | 4 | 19 | 20/1 | 11 | — |
| $472^{5}$ | **Known Secret (USA) (52)** (MrsJRRamsden) **3-8-3** JFEgan(1) (hld up & bhd: t.o) | 8 | 20 | 14/1 | — | — |

(SP 149.7%) **20 Rn**

**1m 45.2** (3.90) CSF £47.41 CT £282.84 TOTE £2.50: £1.20 £4.00 £3.40 £4.20 (£25.20) Trio £117.40 OWNER Aylesfield Farms Stud (ARUNDEL) BRED Mount Coote Stud

OFFICIAL EXPLANATION **Duo Master: the jockey reported that the gelding, who has suffered knee problems, hung on the way down and sweated up at the start. He said his instructions were to settle the horse but, when he let the gelding down, he moved badly.**
**Time of Night: was struck into on her near-hind leg.**

**Samara (IRE)**, looking well forward in condition, opened her account in the easiest possible fashion and this could be the first of many. (2/1: op 5/4)
**509 Silverdale Knight** had the edge in fitness and did not fail for the want of trying, but the winner was a class apart when the chips were down. (20/1)
**Mazcobar** stayed on relentlessly inside the last quarter-mile, but his finishing position was as close as he could get. (8/1)
**General Haven** has been kept busy on the All-Weather but needed to be ridden to get the trip here and, though he did stay on, he could not get within striking range of the winner. (25/1)
**Yezza (IRE)**, attempting the trip for the first time, was doing all her best work late on and there would seem to be a race in mind. (33/1)
**Alreeh (IRE)**, settled in the rear, was really getting into her stride in the closing stages and there would seem to be plenty of improvement to come. (20/1)
**Swift Maiden** ran much better than her finishing position would suggest and, with this run to put an edge on her, should be capable of picking up a small prize. (33/1)
**562 Pride of Kashmir** (8/1: 6/1-9/1)
**Rossel (USA)** (6/1: 8/1-5/1)
**472 Known Secret (USA)** (14/1: 10/1-16/1)

T/Plpt: £764.70 (15.73 Tckts). T/Qdpt: £88.90 (13.49 Tckts). IM

# ASCOT (R-H) (Good to firm)
## Wednesday May 1st

WEATHER: overcast WIND: almost nil

## 874 INSULPAK CONDITIONS STKS (3-Y.O F) (Class B)

2-30 (2-30) **1m (round)** £7,814.30 (£2,923.70: £1,429.35: £614.25: £274.62: £138.78) Stalls: High GOING minus 0.36 sec per fur (F)

| Form | Runner | Dist | Pos | SP | RR | SF |
|---|---|---|---|---|---|---|
| | **Distant Oasis (USA)** (HRACecil) **3-8-8** WRyan(1) (w'like: scope: s.s: hdwy over 2f out: led over 1f out: rdn: r.o wl) | — | 1 | $11/4^{2}$ | 90+ | 41 |
| 678* | **Tawaaded (IRE)** (PTWalwyn) **3-9-0** WCarson(6) (led over 6f: unable qckn) | 2½ | 2 | $7/2^{3}$ | 91 | 42 |
| 710* | **Satin Bell** (JLDunlop) **3-9-0** RHughes(4) (lw: rdn over 2f out: hdwy over 1f out: one pce) | 1 | 3 | $5/2^{1}$ | 89 | 40 |
| $627^{2}$ | **Miss Riviera (80)** (GWragg) **3-9-0** MHills(2) (lw: a.p: rdn over 2f out: one pce) | 1 | 4 | 20/1 | 87 | 38 |
| $678^{2}$ | **Really A Dream (IRE)** (MRStoute) **3-8-11** MJKinane(3) (chsd ldr over 5f: eased whn btn ins fnl f) | 3 | 5 | $7/2^{3}$ | 78 | 29 |
| | **More Than You Know (IRE)** (RHannon) **3-9-0** JReid(5) (hld up: rdn over 2f out: sn wknd) | 1½ | 6 | 12/1 | 78 | 29 |

(SP 112.1%) **6 Rn**

**1m 43.06** (2.26) CSF £11.98 TOTE £3.50: £1.50 £2.20 (£5.80) OWNER H R H Prince Fahd Salman (NEWMARKET) BRED Newgate Stud Co

**Distant Oasis (USA)** was given no easy task on the racecourse debut, but this good-bodied filly proved well up to it, despite giving her rivals a five-length headstart as she remained in the stalls as they opened. She will have one more run before a decision about a return trip for the Coronation Stakes at the Royal meeting. (11/4: op 6/4)
**678* Tawaaded (IRE)** attempted to make all the running. Eventually collared below the distance, she was put in her place by the winner. (7/2)
**710* Satin Bell**, scrubbed along at the back of the field entering the straight, made heavy weather of picking up ground below the distance and could than make no further impression. (5/2)
**627 Miss Riviera** failed to quicken in the home straight. (20/1)
**678 Really A Dream (IRE)** was eased down when all chance had gone inside the final furlong. This was disappointing after a good effort at Newmarket. (7/2)
**More Than You Know (IRE)**, who had to miss the Nell Gwyn as she threw a splint, chased the leaders until calling it a day early in the straight. (12/1: 5/1-14/1)

## 875 INSULPAK SAGARO STKS (Gp 3) (4-Y.O+) (Class A)

3-05 (3-05) **2m 45y** £25,000.00 (£9,460.00: £4,630.00: £2,110.00) Stalls: High GOING minus 0.36 sec per fur (F)

| | Horse | Btn | Pos | SP | RR | SF |
|---|---|---|---|---|---|---|
| | **Double Trigger (IRE) (119)** (MJohnston) **5-9-5** JWeaver(2) (lw: chsd ldr: rdn over 4f out: led ins fnl f: r.o wl) | — | **1** | 11/8 1 | 125 | 73 |
| | **Grey Shot (104)** (IABalding) **4-8-12** LDettori(8) (lw: led: rdn over 2f out: hdd ins fnl f: r.o wl) | hd | **2** | 5/1 3 | 121 | 66 |
| | **Always Aloof (USA) (104)** (MRStoute) **5-8-12** WCarson(3) (hdwy over 4f out: rdn 3f out: wknd over 1f out) | 7 | **3** | 16/1 | 111 | 59 |
| 456 2 | **Daraydan (IRE) (102)** (LadyHerries) **4-8-9** KDarley(9) (rdn & hdwy over 4f out: wknd over 1f out) | 1¼ | **4** | 8/1 | 110 | 55 |
| 563 2 | **Old Rouvel (USA) (103)** (DJGMurraySmith) **5-8-12** MJKinane(4) (lw: hdwy over 4f out: wknd over 3f out) | ½ | **5** | 12/1 | 109 | 57 |
| 675* | **Sanmartino (IRE) (103)** (BWHills) **4-8-9** MHills(6) (lw: rdn & hdwy over 4f out: wknd over 2f out) | 7 | **6** | 7/2 2 | 102 | 47 |
| | **Jellaby Askhir (103)** (RAkehurst) **4-8-9** TQuinn(1) (prom 11f) | 25 | **8** | 33/1 | 78 | 23 |

(SP 108.6%) **7 Rn**

**3m 27.64** (0.44) CSF £7.86 TOTE £2.20: £1.40 £1.80 (£3.50) Trio £16.00 OWNER Mr R. W. Huggins (MIDDLEHAM) BRED Dene Investments N V

WEIGHT FOR AGE 4yo-3lb

**Double Trigger (IRE)**, out to capture the Champion Stayers' Title of Europe, found this return no cake-walk but he showed here just what a battler he is, as well as demonstrating that he stays for ever and a day. The signs looked very bad indeed half a mile out, but he stuck to his task commendably well and eventually managed to get on top inside the final furlong. The Henry II Stakes at Sandown is next on the agenda, for which he looks nailed on. (11/8)

**Grey Shot** ran a tremendous race on this reappearance. Bowling along in front, he appeared to be travelling really well turning for home, but he had not bargained on such a determined opponent as the winner and he was eventually broken inside the final furlong. He is certainly going to be a force to be reckoned with in the staying events this season. (5/1)

**Always Aloof (USA)** moved up over half a mile from home and was in a challenging position entering the straight. However, he failed to contain the front two from below the distance. (16/1)

**456 Daraydan (IRE)**, scrubbed along to pick up ground over half a mile from home, had run out of gas below the distance. (8/1: 6/1-9/1)

**563 Old Rouvel (USA)** moved up over half a mile from home but was a spent force turning into the straight. (12/1)

**675* Sanmartino (IRE)**, scrubbed along to take closer order over half a mile from home, had burnt his boats approaching the last two furlongs. (7/2: 5/2-4/1)

## 876 INSULPAK VICTORIA CUP H'CAP (0-110) (4-Y.O+) (Class B)

3-40 (3-43) **7f** £22,665.00 (£6,870.00: £3,360.00: £1,605.00) Stalls: Low GOING minus 0.36 sec per fur (F)

| | Horse | Btn | Pos | SP | RR | SF |
|---|---|---|---|---|---|---|
| 472* | **Yeast (80)** (WJHaggas) **4-8-9** RCochrane(15) (a.p: led over 2f out: drvn out) | — | **1** | 8/1 3 | 93 | 57 |
| 765* | **Master Charter (72)** (MrsJRRamsden) **4-8-1** 6x JFEgan(3) (lw: rdn & hdwy 2f out: r.o) | 1 | **2** | 13/2 1 | 83 | 47 |
| 600 6 | **Prince Babar (82)** (JEBanks) **5-8-8**(3) JStack(9) (a.p: ev ch over 1f out: unable qckn) | s.h | **3** | 20/1 | 93 | 57 |
| 679 4 | **Emerging Market (91)** (JLDunlop) **4-9-6** KDarley(13) (lw: hdwy 2f out: hrd rdn over 1f out: one pce) | nk | **4** | 20/1 | 101 | 65 |
| | **Sharp Rebuff (75)** (PJMakin) **5-8-4** TQuinn(8) (rdn & hdwy 2f out: one pce) | 2½ | **5** | 40/1 | 79 | 43 |
| | **Samwar (78)** (MissGayKelleway) **4-8-7** LDettori(12) (a.p: rdn over 2f out: one pce) | 2 | **6** | 8/1 3 | 78 | 42 |
| 679 8 | **Kayvee (98)** (GHarwood) **7-9-13** AClark(1) (hdwy over 1f out: r.o) | 1 | **7** | 20/1 | 95 | 59 |
| 455 5 | **Delta Soleil (USA) (91)** (PWHarris) **4-9-6** GHind(21) (hld up: ev ch 2f out: wknd over 1f out) | 1½ | **8** | 15/2 2 | 85 | 49 |
| | **Gymcrak Premiere (90)** (GHolmes) **8-9-5** MJKinane(11) (b.hind: nvr nr to chal) | 2 | **9** | 20/1 | 79 | 43 |
| 744 2 | **Jo Maximus (75)** (SDow) **4-7-13**(5) ADaly(4) (led over 3f) | 1 | **10** | 33/1 | 62 | 26 |
| 679 3 | **Roving Minstrel (93)** (BAMcMahon) **5-9-3**(5) LNewton(2) (lw: prom over 4f) | nk | **11** | 16/1 | 79 | 43 |
| | **Safey Ana (USA) (73)** (BHanbury) **5-8-2** WRyan(6) (b: b.hind: swtg: a.p: rdn over 2f out: eased whn btn fnl f) | hd | **12** | 16/1 | 59 | 23 |
| | **Quintus Decimus (74)** (RAkehurst) **4-8-3** SSanders(5) (hld up: rdn over 2f out: sn wknd) | hd | **13** | 14/1 | 60 | 24 |
| 728 8 | **Jawaal (99)** (LadyHerries) **6-10-0** JReid(10) (lw: hdwy over 2f out: wknd over 1f out) | 1¼ | **14** | 14/1 | 82 | 46 |
| 756 7 | **Dawalib (USA) (67)** (DHaydnJones) **6-7-10** AMackay(14) (swtg: hdwy over 2f out: wknd over 1f out) | hd | **15** | 66/1 | 50 | 14 |
| | **Wild Rice (90)** (GWragg) **4-9-5** MHills(17) (bit bkwd: hld up: rdn over 2f out: sn wknd) | 1¼ | **16** | 20/1 | 70 | 34 |
| | **Roderick Hudson (86)** (JARToller) **4-9-1** RHughes(7) (lw: w ldr: led over 3f out tl over 2f out: sn wknd) | ½ | **17** | 50/1 | 65 | 29 |
| 554 13 | **Be Warned (75)** (NACallaghan) **5-8-4b** PaulEddery(22) (a bhd) | ½ | **18** | 33/1 | 53 | 17 |
| | **Charlie Sillett (82)** (BWHills) **4-8-11** WCarson(23) (swtg: a bhd) | ½ | **19** | 10/1 | 59 | 23 |
| 450 8 | **Mister Fire Eyes (IRE) (75)** (CEBrittain) **4-8-4b** BDoyle(20) (hdwy over 2f out: sn wknd) | 1 | **20** | 16/1 | 49 | 13 |
| | **Whatever's Right (IRE) (69)** (MDIUsher) **7-7-12** JQuinn(24) (bhd fnl 2f) | 1½ | **21** | 33/1 | 40 | 4 |
| | **Bold Effort (FR) (95)** (KOCunningham-Brown) **4-9-10** JWeaver(19) (a.p: ev ch 2f out: wknd over 1f out) | ½ | **22** | 40/1 | 65 | 29 |
| 610 18 | **Al Reet (IRE) (85)** (MDHammond) **5-8-11**(3) SDrowne(16) (bhd fnl 2f) | 7 | **23** | 25/1 | 39 | 3 |
| 744 3 | **Ertlon (80)** (CEBrittain) **6-8-4**(5) MHenry(18) (swtg: prom over 3f) | nk | **24** | 25/1 | 33 | — |

(SP 136.0%) **24 Rn**

**1m 27.86** (0.66) CSF £57.84 CT £976.00 TOTE £9.80: £2.50 £1.90 £4.40 £4.30 (£24.70) Trio £172.10 OWNER Mr B. Haggas (NEWMARKET) BRED R. T. and Mrs Watson

LONG HANDICAP Dawalib (USA) 7-9

**472* Yeast**, a leading light from the off, gained control over a quarter of a mile from home and, responding to pressure, held on well. (8/1)

**765* Master Charter**, ridden along to take closer order a quarter of a mile from home, kept on really well but was unable to overhaul the winner. (13/2)

**600 Prince Babar** had every chance below the distance before tapped for toe. (20/1)

**679 Emerging Market** took closer order a quarter of a mile from home, but failed to find another gear in the final 200 yards. (20/1)

**Sharp Rebuff** made headway a quarter of a mile out, but could then make no further impression. (40/1)

**Samwar**, never far away, failed to quicken in the final two furlongs. (8/1)

**Quintus Decimus** (14/1: 10/1-16/1)

**728 Jawaal**, winner of this race last year, moved up over a quarter of a mile from home, but the writing was on the wall from below the distance, and his jockey was not hard on him. He is gradually coming to hand. (14/1)

## 877 GARTER CONDITIONS STKS (2-Y.O) (Class B)

4-10 (4-12) **5f** £6,354.00 (£2,376.00: £1,160.50: £497.50: £221.25: £110.75) Stalls: Low GOING minus 0.36 sec per fur (F)

| | Horse | Btn | Pos | SP | RR | SF |
|---|---|---|---|---|---|---|
| | **Smokey Pete** (RHannon) **2-8-8** JReid(2) (str: bit bkwd: a.p: rdn over 1f out: led nr fin) | — | **1** | 6/4 1 | 78 | 28 |
| 551* | **Bilko** (GLewis) **2-9-1** PaulEddery(1) (led: rdn over 1f out: hdd nr fin) | nk | **2** | 5/2 2 | 84 | 34 |
| 552 2 | **Kingsinger (IRE)** (MRChannon) **2-9-1** RHughes(3) (a.p: ev ch over 1f out: one pce) | 1 | **3** | 9/2 3 | 81 | 31 |

| | | | | SP | RR | SF |
|---|---|---|---|---|---|---|
| 590* | **Folly Foot Fred** (BRMillman) **2-8-11** SDrowne(7) (outpcd) | 12 | **4** | 33/1 | 38 | — |
| | **Mangus (IRE)** (KOCunningham-Brown) **2-8-8** JWeaver(6) (unf: hdwy over 2f out: wknd over 1f out) | 1½ | **5** | 14/1 | 31 | — |
| | **Battle Ground (IRE)** (NACallaghan) **2-8-8** LDettori(5) (cmpt: bit bkwd: s.s: outpcd) | 7 | **6** | 11/2 | 8 | — |

(SP 111.7%) **6 Rn**

**62.07 secs** (2.07) CSF £5.48 TOTE £2.50: £1.40 £1.30 (£2.80) OWNER Mr J. G. Davis (MARLBOROUGH) BRED Highfield Stud Ltd
**Smokey Pete**, a half-brother to Battleship Bruce, looked as though this run would do him good. Disputing second place, he was rousted along below the distance and eventually managed to get on top near the line. (6/4)
**551* Bilko** attempted to make all the running and looked in command as the runners entered the final furlong. Despite doing little wrong, he was worried out of it near the line. He should soon make amends. (5/2)
**552 Kingsinger (IRE)**, disputing second place from the start, was close enough if good enough below the distance before tapped for toe. (9/2)
**Mangus (IRE)** (14/1: 10/1-16/1)

## 878 CHOBHAM CONDITIONS STKS (4-Y.O+) (Class C)

4-40 (4-42) **1m (round)** £4,832.00 (£1,808.00: £884.00: £380.00: £170.00: £86.00) Stalls: High GOING minus 0.36 sec per fur (F)

| | | | | SP | RR | SF |
|---|---|---|---|---|---|---|
| 679* | **Tarawa (IRE) (106)** (NACallaghan) **4-9-8** RHughes(5) (rdn & hdwy over 2f out: led ins fnl f: drvn out) | — | **1** | 5/4 1 | 105 | 68 |
| 580 14 | **Behaviour (93)** (MrsJCecil) **4-9-1** PaulEddery(2) (hld up: rdn over 2f out: r.o ins fnl f) | ½ | **2** | 12/1 | 97 | 60 |
| | **Green Green Desert (FR) (107)** (LadyHerries) **5-8-12** KDarley(3) (lw: chsd ldr: led over 3f out tl ins fnl f: unable qckn) | nk | **3** | 10/1 | 93 | 56 |
| 581 9 | **Wijara (IRE) (103)** (RHannon) **4-9-3** JReid(6) (lw: hld up: rdn over 2f out: lost pl over 1f out: r.o ins fnl f) | 1¼ | **4** | 7/1 | 96 | 59 |
| | **Grand du Lac (USA)** (DRLoder) **4-9-1** LDettori(4) (lw: hld up: rdn over 2f out: one pce) | ½ | **5** | 13/2 3 | 93 | 56 |
| 600 7 | **Ki Chi Saga (USA)** (JLDunlop) **4-8-12** WCarson(8) (lw: nvr nr to chal) | 1¼ | **6** | 40/1 | 87 | 50 |
| 679 5 | **Blomberg (IRE) (95)** (JRFanshawe) **4-8-12** TQuinn(7) (lw: led over 4f: wknd over 1f out) | 2½ | **7** | 5/1 2 | 82 | 45 |
| 456 4 | **Ionio (USA) (107)** (CEBrittain) **5-8-12** BDoyle(1) (lw: bhd fnl 5f) | 1½ | **8** | 10/1 | 79 | 42 |

(SP 115.3%) **8 Rn**

**1m 42.12** (0.92) CSF £15.49 TOTE £2.30: £1.20 £2.70 £2.00 (£10.10) OWNER Mrs J. Callaghan (NEWMARKET) BRED Patrick Eddery Ltd
**679* Tarawa (IRE)** put up a decent display giving weight all round to some useful rivals. Ridden along to take closer order early in the straight, he managed to get on top early inside the final furlong and, responding to pressure, held on well. (5/4)
**Behaviour** left his previous run well behind. Chasing the leaders, he ran on nicely inside the final furlong but was unable to master the winner. He should soon be winning. (12/1)
**Green Green Desert (FR)**, sold out of Michael Stoute's stable for 36,000 guineas last autumn, chased the leader until going on soon after halfway. Headed early inside the last furlong, he failed to find another gear. (10/1: 7/1-11/1)
**442 Wijara (IRE)** chased the leaders but got rather outpaced below the distance. He did stay on again in the closing stages but, by then, it was too late. (7/1: 9/2-8/1)
**Grand du Lac (USA)** chased the leaders, but failed to find another gear from below the distance. (13/2)
**456 Ionio (USA)** (10/1: 6/1-11/1)

## 879 WHITE ROSE H'CAP (0-80) (3-Y.O+) (Class D)

5-15 (5-18) **1m (straight)** £8,140.00 (£2,470.00: £1,210.00: £580.00) Stalls: Low GOING minus 0.36 sec per fur (F)

| | | | | SP | RR | SF |
|---|---|---|---|---|---|---|
| | **Tregaron (USA) (69)** (RAkehurst) **5-9-3** TQuinn(1) (lw: a.p: led over 1f out: rdn & r.o wl) | — | **1** | 5/1 2 | 85 | 67 |
| 765 14 | **Samba Sharply (77)** (AHide) **5-9-11** WWoods(22) (bit bkwd: rdn & hdwy over 1f out: unable qckn fnl f) | 3½ | **2** | 20/1 | 86 | 68 |
| 613 5 | **Angus-G (69)** (MrsMReveley) **4-9-3** KDarley(26) (lw: a.p: rdn over 2f out: one pce) | ¾ | **3** | 9/2 1 | 77 | 59 |
| 747* | **Autumn Cover (55)** (RMFlower) **4-8-3** 5x DBiggs(6) (b: a.p: led over 2f out tl over 1f out: one pce) | 1½ | **4** | 16/1 | 60 | 42 |
| | **Fakih (USA) (75)** (ACStewart) **4-9-9** WCarson(4) (rdn over 2f out: hdwy over 1f out: nt clr run ins fnl f: r.o) | ¾ | **5** | 10/1 | 78 | 60 |
| 682 15 | **Saltando (IRE) (48)** (PatMitchell) **5-7-10** DeclanO'Shea(32) (hdwy over 2f out: hrd rdn over 1f out: one pce) | nk | **6** | 40/1 | 50 | 32 |
| 766 2 | **Noble Sprinter (IRE) (80)** (RHannon) **4-10-0b** JReid(15) (rdn & hdwy over 2f out: one pce fnl f) | ½ | **7** | 25/1 | 81 | 63 |
| 765 4 | **Wentbridge Lad (IRE) (63)** (PDEvans) **6-8-11v** SSanders(8) (hdwy over 5f out: hrd rdn & ev ch over 1f out: wknd fnl f) | 1¼ | **8** | 16/1 | 62 | 44 |
| 613 3 | **Tilaal (USA) (70)** (MDHammond) **4-9-4** WRyan(11) (hdwy over 1f out: nvr nrr) | 1¼ | **9** | 12/1 | 66 | 48 |
| 547* | **Ocean Park (69)** (LadyHerries) **5-9-3** AClark(27) (hld up: hmpd over 3f out: rdn over 2f out: wknd fnl f) | nk | **10** | 8/1 3 | 65 | 47 |
| | **Mo-Addab (IRE) (80)** (ACStewart) **6-9-9**(5) MHumphries(25) (nvr nrr) | 1½ | **11** | 33/1 | 73 | 55 |
| | **Super High (60)** (PHowling) **4-8-8** RCochrane(3) (a mid div) | ¾ | **12** | 33/1 | 51 | 33 |
| | **Pay Homage (79)** (IABalding) **8-9-13** LDettori(31) (bit bkwd: hld up: rdn over 2f out: sn wknd) | 3 | **13** | 20/1 | 64 | 46 |
| 450 9 | **Country Lover (75)** (LordHuntingdon) **5-9-2v**(7) AimeeCook(5) (lw: a mid div) | s.h | **14** | 20/1 | 60 | 42 |
| 827 12 | **Ever so Lyrical (66)** (PWHarris) **6-9-0** GHind(30) (nvr nrr) | ½ | **15** | 33/1 | 50 | 32 |
| 650 9 | **Wild Palm (66)** (WAO'Gorman) **4-9-0b**1 TIves(14) (lw: nvr nrr) | s.h | **16** | 25/1 | 50 | 32 |
| 633 4 | **Neuwest (USA) (75)** (NJHWalker) **4-9-6**(3) JStack(16) (lw: hld up: rdn over 2f out: wknd over 1f out) | 3 | **17** | 33/1 | 53 | 35 |
| 469 12 | **Pistol (IRE) (61)** (CAHorgan) **6-8-9** PaulEddery(19) (nvr nrr) | 1¼ | **18** | 40/1 | 37 | 19 |
| 650 11 | **Lynton Lad (75)** (CPEBrooks) **4-9-9b** JWeaver(2) (led over 5f) | nk | **19** | 20/1 | 50 | 32 |
| | **Admirals Flame (IRE) (73)** (CFWall) **5-9-7** GDuffield(21) (bit bkwd: nvr nrr) | 1½ | **20** | 16/1 | 48 | 30 |
| 809 12 | **Saifan (74)** (DMorris) **7-9-8b** CHodgson(20) (lw: hdwy over 2f out: wknd wl over 1f out) | d.h | **20** | 20/1 | 46 | 28 |
| | **Balasara (IRE) (73)** (RJO'Sullivan) **6-9-7b** RHughes(12) (s.s: nvr nrr) | 2 | **22** | 40/1 | 41 | 23 |
| 713 6 | **Murphy's Gold (IRE) (51)** (RAFahey) **5-7-13** JQuinn(18) (lw: hdwy over 3f out: wknd over 2f out) | 1 | **23** | 10/1 | 17 | — |
| 688 15 | **Total Rach (IRE) (50)** (RIngram) **4-7-7b**(5) MBaird(10) (hdwy 5f out: wknd over 2f out) | 1 | **24** | 66/1 | 14 | — |
| 739* | **Glowing Jade (68)** (JAGlover) **6-9-2** GCarter(28) (bmpd over 3f out: hdwy over 2f out: eased whn btn over 1f out) | nk | **25** | 20/1 | 31 | 13 |
| *379* 8 | **Nordinex (IRE) (78)** (RWArmstrong) **4-9-12** MHills(7) (lw: bhd fnl 3f) | nk | **26** | 33/1 | 41 | 23 |
| | **Deevee (71)** (CJBenstead) **7-9-5** PRobinson(23) (nt clr run 3f out: a bhd) | 3 | **27** | 16/1 | 28 | 10 |
| | **Cuban Reef (48)** (WJMusson) **4-7-10** AMackay(24) (a bhd) | 1½ | **28** | 25/1 | 2 | — |
| 636 11 | **Halliard (53)** (TMJones) **5-8-1** AMcGlone(29) (swtg: prom over 5f) | 1¼ | **29** | 33/1 | 4 | — |
| *82* 13 | **Komodo (USA) (66)** (KOCunningham-Brown) **4-8-11**(3) DRMcCabe(9) (lw: bhd fnl 4f) | 6 | **30** | 66/1 | 5 | — |
| 631 9 | **Rockville Pike (IRE) (70)** (SDow) **4-9-4v** BThomson(13) (prom over 4f) | 15 | **31** | 66/1 | — | — |

(SP 164.9%) **31 Rn**

**1m 41.36** (0.16) CSF £114.16 CT £491.36 TOTE £6.70: £2.20 £10.80 £1.90 £4.50 (£399.50) Trio £987.70 OWNER Mr Hefin Jones (EPSOM) BRED Stonethorn Stud Farms
LONG HANDICAP Saltando (IRE) 7-9 Cuban Reef 7-9

**Tregaron (USA)** was having his first run for Reg Akehurst, who is certainly the master at knowing how to transform a horse - he had failed to get his head in front before today. Always close up, he breezed into the lead below the distance and, shaken up, soon pulled clear. Better things look on the cards. (5/1)
**Samba Sharply** still looked as though this run would do him good. (20/1)
**613 Angus-G** has been allowed to come on quietly to date and ran a fine race in this competitive race. Always close up, he grimly tried to get on terms below the distance but was tapped for toe. (9/2)
**747* Autumn Cover** moved to the front over a quarter of a mile from home but, headed below the distance, could only keep on in his own time. (16/1)
**Fakih (USA)** made a pleasing return. Picking up ground below the distance, he stayed on to be nearest at the line. (10/1)
**Saltando (IRE)** moved up over a quarter of a mile from home but, under pressure below the distance, failed to find another gear. (40/1)
**713 Murphy's Gold (IRE)** (10/1: op 20/1)

T/Jkpt: £5,278.20 (5.62 Tckts). T/Plpt: £61.00 (543.4 Tckts). T/Qdpt: £15.70 (147.35 Tckts). AK

# 0615-HAMILTON (R-H) (Heavy, Soft Patches)
## Thursday May 2nd
WEATHER: sunny WIND: almost nil

## 880 COATBRIDGE MAIDEN AUCTION STKS (2-Y.O) (Class F)
2-10 (2-12) **5f 4y** £2,675.00 (£750.00: £365.00) Stalls: Low GOING: 0.51 sec per fur (GS)

| | | | | SP | RR | SF |
|---|---|---|---|---|---|---|
| 741$^{2}$ | **Seaside (IRE)** (JohnBerry) **2-8-0** TWilliams(5) (lw: a cl up: led wl over 1f out: r.o) | — | **1** | 11/4$^{2}$ | 64+ | 2 |
| 557$^{3}$ | **Tribal Mischief** (DMoffatt) **2-7-13**(3) DarrenMoffatt(3) (lw: cl up: outpcd: kpt on towards fin) | 2 | **2** | 11/4$^{2}$ | 60 | — |
| 630$^{4}$ | **Our Kevin** (KMcAuliffe) **2-8-5** JFEgan(2) (a chsng ldrs: rdn ½-wy: no imp) | 5 | **3** | 5/2$^{1}$ | 47 | — |
| 618$^{2}$ | **I'm Still Here** (JBerry) **2-8-3** JCarroll(1) (led over 3f: sn wknd) | 8 | **4** | 11/4$^{2}$ | 19 | — |
| | **Apiculate (IRE)** (WTKemp) **2-8-4**ow1 KDarley(4) (leggy: unf: bit bkwd: dwlt: a outpcd & bhd) | 18 | **5** | 50/1$^{3}$ | — | — |
| | | | | (SP 110.5%) | **5 Rn** | |

**65.8 secs** (7.50) CSF £9.98 TOTE £2.70: £1.20 £1.90 (£3.20) OWNER The 1997 Partnership (NEWMARKET) BRED Airlie Stud
**741 Seaside (IRE)** handed this ground well and, always going best, there was never any doubt about the result. (11/4: 2/1-3/1)
**557 Tribal Mischief** got a shade unbalanced when put under pressure, but was sticking on well at the end to suggest that longer trips might suit. (11/4)
**630 Our Kevin** was always struggling in these testing conditions and left the impression that, over further, he should improve a little. (5/2)
**618 I'm Still Here** had difficulty seeing the trip out in these testing conditions. (11/4: 7/4-3/1)

## 881 LEVY BOARD H'CAP (0-70) (3-Y.O) (Class E)
2-40 (2-41) **5f 4y** £2,954.70 (£894.60: £436.80: £207.90) Stalls: Low GOING: 0.51 sec per fur (GS)

| | | | | SP | RR | SF |
|---|---|---|---|---|---|---|
| *780** | **Maiteamia (57)** (SRBowring) **3-8-6b**(5) 7x CTeague(9) (lw: led 1f: led after 2f tl disp ld ins fnl f: kpt on wl u.p) | — | **1** | 6/4$^{1}$ | 74 | 60 |
| 862$^{4}$ | **Goretski (IRE) (65)** (NTinkler) **3-9-5** 7x KDarley(8) (lw: chsd ldrs: disp ld ins fnl f: no ex towards fin) | hd | **2** | 5/2$^{2}$ | 82 | 68 |
| 740$^{6}$ | **Finisterre (IRE) (42)** (JJO'Neill) **3-7-10** GBardwell(3) (styd on u.p fnl 2f: n.d) | 12 | **3** | 9/1 | 20 | 6 |
| *606*$^{15}$ | **Aye Ready (42)** (MissLAPerratt) **3-7-10b**$^{1}$ LCharnock(6) (qcknd to ld after 1f: hdd after 2f: wknd 2f out) | 1½ | **4** | 50/1 | 16 | 2 |
| 638$^{12}$ | **Gwespyr (63)** (JBerry) **3-9-3v**$^{1}$ JCarroll(5) (lw: s.s: gd hdwy to chse ldrs after 1½f: rdn & btn over 1f out) | 7 | **5** | 7/2$^{3}$ | 14 | — |
| 539$^{11}$ | **Ready Teddy (IRE) (43)** (MissLAPerratt) **3-7-11** JFanning(2) (outpcd & bhd fr ½-wy) | 2½ | **6** | 20/1 | — | — |
| | **Swifty Nifty (IRE) (54)** (WWHaigh) **3-8-8** DaleGibson(4) (lw: prom to ½-wy: sn bhd) | 9 | **7** | 20/1 | — | — |
| *780*$^{4}$ | **Golden Tyke (IRE) (50)** (MJohnston) **3-8-4** TWilliams(1) (lw: racd alone stands' side: t.o fnl 2f) | dist | **8** | 16/1 | — | — |
| | | | | (SP 118.2%) | **8 Rn** | |

**62.9 secs** (4.60) CSF £5.78 CT £22.29 TOTE £2.50: £1.20 £1.50 £1.30 (£2.90) Trio £6.60 OWNER Mrs Zoe Grant (EDWINSTOWE) BRED Mrs Z. Grant and S. R. Bowring
LONG HANDICAP Aye Ready 6-12 Finisterre (IRE) 7-8
OFFICIAL EXPLANATION **Golden Tyke (IRE): the jockey reported that the gelding appeared to be lame.**
**780* Maiteamia** did not take full advantage of his draw and crossed all the way over to the far rail, but he proved to be a game individual and just got home. (6/4)
**862 Goretski (IRE)** was given the best ride, but was just not up to the task, despite trying really hard. (5/2)
**740 Finisterre (IRE)** ran reasonably well from a low draw and only got going when the race was over. (9/1)
**473 Aye Ready** again showed he has speed to burn but, as yet, it does not last for more than half the trip. (50/1)
**525 Gwespyr**, wearing a visor for the first time, showed bags of pace to recover from a very slow start but that effort had sapped all reserves soon after halfway. (7/2)

## 882 I.M.I. YORKSHIRE FITTINGS H'CAP (0-75) (3-Y.O+) (Class D)
3-10 (3-12) **6f 5y** £4,056.95 (£1,229.60: £601.30: £287.15) Stalls: Low GOING: 0.51 sec per fur (GS)

| | | | | SP | RR | SF |
|---|---|---|---|---|---|---|
| 617$^{6}$ | **Craigie Boy (46)** (NBycroft) **6-7-13b** TWilliams(13) (cl up: led 2½f out: drvn out) | — | **1** | 4/1$^{1}$ | 51 | 20 |
| 769* | **Panther (IRE) (50)** (JHetherton) **6-8-0**(3) DWright(8) (lw: outpcd tl hdwy 2f out: styd on wl towards fin) | 3½ | **2** | 9/2$^{2}$ | 46 | 15 |
| 718$^{15}$ | **Desert Invader (IRE) (50)** (DWChapman) **5-8-3** DeanMcKeown(15) (chsd ldrs: outpcd 2f out: kpt on fnl f) | ½ | **3** | 12/1 | 44 | 13 |
| | **Millemay (43)** (PMonteith) **6-7-10** LCharnock(16) (cl up: led after 2f to 2½f out: kpt on one pce) | ¾ | **4** | 33/1 | 35 | 4 |
| *607*$^{10}$ | **Sunday Mail Too (IRE) (44)** (MissLAPerratt) **4-7-11**ow1 JFanning(12) (chsd ldrs: rdn ½-wy: one pce) | ½ | **5** | 50/1 | 35 | 3 |
| 749$^{22}$ | **Blow Dry (IRE) (56)** (MartynWane) **6-8-9** JFortune(14) (lw: chsd ldrs: outpcd ½-wy: no imp after) | nk | **6** | 8/1 | 46 | 15 |
| 806$^{2}$ | **Mu-Arrik (43)** (GROldroyd) **8-7-10v** GBardwell(9) (sme hdwy over 1f out: nvr rchd ldrs) | 3 | **7** | 7/1$^{3}$ | 25 | — |
| 704$^{7}$ | **My Godson (43)** (JLEyre) **6-7-10b** NKennedy(4) (nvr trbld ldrs) | 1¾ | **8** | 50/1 | 21 | — |
| 762$^{6}$ | **Domicksky (51)** (MRChannon) **8-8-4**ow1 KDarley(7) (lw: chsd ldrs: rdn 2f out: grad wknd) | 1¾ | **9** | 8/1 | 24 | — |
| 659$^{7}$ | **Leading Princess (IRE) (49)** (MissLAPerratt) **5-7-11b**(5) PFessey(11) (led 2f: hung lft & wknd 2f out) | 1¼ | **10** | 25/1 | 19 | — |
| | **Dictation (USA) (75)** (JJO'Neill) **4-10-0** GDuffield(2) (n.d) | 1½ | **11** | 25/1 | 41 | 10 |
| 617$^{16}$ | **Suedoro (48)** (RMMcKellar) **6-7-10**(5) CAdamson(6) (s.i.s: nvr wnt pce) | ½ | **12** | 50/1 | 12 | — |
| 814$^{12}$ | **Birchwood Sun (61)** (MDods) **6-9-0b** JCarroll(5) (s.s: swtchd rt & n.d) | ¾ | **13** | 8/1 | 23 | — |
| 750$^{7}$ | **Rankaidade (43)** (DonEnricoIncisa) **5-7-10** KimTinkler(10) (prom 4f: sn btn) | hd | **14** | 50/1 | 5 | — |
| 525$^{10}$ | **Briganoone (53)** (SRBowring) **3-7-10b** NCarlisle(1) (racd alone stands' side: sn bhd) | 4 | **15** | 20/1 | 5 | — |

| | | | | SP | RR | SF |
|---|---|---|---|---|---|---|
| *$834^{6}$* | **So Natural (IRE) (55)** (EJAlston) **4-8-8** SDWilliams(3) (sn bhd) | 2½ | **16** | 40/1 | — | — |

(SP 117.4%) **16 Rn**

**1m 17.6** (7.60) CSF £19.95 CT £183.68 TOTE £4.70: £1.40 £1.20 £2.90 £10.30 (£9.60) Trio £32.00 OWNER Mr Bernard Rayner (BRANDSBY) BRED Clive Tomkins

LONG HANDICAP Sunday Mail Too (IRE) 6-10 My Godson 7-4 Millemay 6-11 Rankaidade 6-7 Briganoone 7-1 Mu-Arrik 7-9

WEIGHT FOR AGE 3yo-10lb

**617 Craigie Boy** had the draw that mattered and has only ever won on this track. Although tired, he was well in command throughout the last two furlongs. (4/1)

**769* Panther (IRE)** is in fine form at present and, with a better draw here, would have taken some beating. (9/2)

**Desert Invader (IRE)** had the right draw but was always struggling at this trip, and is also better on the All-Weather. (12/1)

**Millemay**, with the best draw of all, ran well from 13lb out of the handicap and, had she had a previous outing, she might well have done a deal better. (33/1)

**Sunday Mail Too (IRE)** was a stone wrong in the handicap and that was too big a disadvantage, despite her good draw. (50/1)

**Blow Dry (IRE)**, well drawn, ran a decent race and looks to be coming to hand. (8/1)

## 883 EAGLESHAM LIMITED STKS (0-50) (4-Y.O+) (Class F)

3-40 (3-41) **1m 1f 36y** £2,997.00 (£842.00: £411.00) Stalls: High GOING: 0.51 sec per fur (GS)

| | | | | SP | RR | SF |
|---|---|---|---|---|---|---|
| *$234^{6}$* | **Giftbox (USA) (48)** (SirMarkPrescott) **4-8-11** GDuffield(9) (lw: shkn up & hdwy 6f out: sn gng wl: led 3f out: styd on strly) | — | **1** | 15/8 [1] | 65 | 37 |
| $827^{2}$ | **Nobby Barnes (42)** (DonEnricoIncisa) **7-8-11** KimTinkler(2) (bhd: hdwy 4f out: styd on: no ch w wnr) | 8 | **2** | 8/1 | 51 | 23 |
| $609^{12}$ | **Kierchem (IRE) (45)** (RFFisher) **5-8-11** JFortune(8) (cl up: led over 4f out tl hdd 3f out: one pce) | hd | **3** | 16/1 | 51 | 23 |
| $827^{3}$ | **Raindeer Quest (47)** (JLEyre) **4-8-11** RLappin(15) (in tch: effrt 4f out: styd on one pce) | 3 | **4** | 9/2 [2] | 46 | 18 |
| $827^{8}$ | **Waterlord (IRE) (40)** (DNicholls) **6-8-11** AlexGreaves(11) (a.p: effrt 4f out: no imp) | 2 | **5** | 5/1 [3] | 42 | 14 |
| $827^{19}$ | **Pash (37)** (CWFairhurst) **4-8-8v** NKennedy(3) (bhd: sme hdwy 3f out: n.d) | 1¾ | **6** | 50/1 | 36 | 8 |
| $688^{11}$ | **Hawwam (47)** (EJAlston) **10-8-11** SDWilliams(4) (outpcd & lost pl ½-wy: styd on fnl 2f) | ½ | **7** | 16/1 | 38 | 10 |
| *$777^{5}$* | **Mr Moriarty (IRE) (35)** (SRBowring) **5-8-12b**(5) CTeague(10) (bhd: hdwy 3f out: nvr rchd ldrs) | 2½ | **8** | 20/1 | 40 | 12 |
| $787^{14}$ | **Bobanlyn (IRE) (50)** (JSWainwright) **4-8-8** LCharnock(6) (nvr trbld ldrs) | 10 | **9** | 13/2 | 13 | — |
| $805^{8}$ | **Tee Tee Too (IRE) (47)** (AHarrison) **4-8-11** DaleGibson(16) (chsd ldrs to ½-wy) | nk | **10** | 20/1 | 16 | — |
| $738^{11}$ | **Percy Parrot (32)** (RMWhitaker) **4-8-11** ACulhane(7) (b: chsd ldrs tl wknd over 3f out) | s.h | **11** | 66/1 | 16 | — |
| $561^{8}$ | **Sheroot (28)** (DMoffatt) **4-8-8**(3) DarrenMoffatt(5) (a rr div) | 8 | **12** | 33/1 | 2 | — |
| $688^{10}$ | **Just Flamenco (48)** (MJRyan) **5-8-11** DBiggs(13) (a bhd) | hd | **13** | 14/1 | 2 | — |
| | **Balata Bay (43)** (JJBirkett) **5-8-11** JCarroll(1) (led tl hdd over 4f out: sn wknd: t.o) | dist | **14** | 100/1 | — | — |
| *$836^{11}$* | **Arabian Flight (50)** (TTClement) **4-8-8**(3) DWright(14) (b: prom to ½-wy: sn wknd & eased: t.o) | 2½ | **15** | 100/1 | — | — |
| | **Public Way (IRE) (48)** (NChamberlain) **6-8-11** DeanMcKeown(17) (lost tch fr ½-wy: p.u over 1f out) | | **P** | 20/1 | — | — |

(SP 135.2%) **16 Rn**

**2m 5.7** (11.40) CSF £19.01 TOTE £2.30: £1.40 £2.80 £6.60 (£15.60) Trio £224.50; £164.49 to Newmarket 3/5/96 OWNER Mr Charles Walker (NEWMARKET) BRED Juddmonte Farms

**OFFICIAL EXPLANATION Public Way (IRE): lost his action and was subsequently pulled up a furlong out.**

**Giftbox (USA)**, after three runs on the All-Weather, was stepped up in distance here. In this moderate event, the further they went, the better he got. There is certainly more to come. (15/8)

**827 Nobby Barnes**, trying his usual and come from way behind, did well but had no hope with the winner. (8/1: op 5/1)

**Kierchem (IRE)** improved no end from his previous run and would seem to be coming to hand. (16/1)

**827 Raindeer Quest** keeps running well but was short of any turn of foot here to take a serious hand in things. (9/2: op 3/1)

**688 Waterlord (IRE)** looks in pretty good heart and is running well but is, at present, on a long losing run. (5/1)

**Pash** loved this ground but, after a moderate start, had a lot of running to do and never got into it, despite staying on. (50/1)

## 884 DRUMLOCH H'CAP (0-70) (3-Y.O+) (Class E)

4-10 (4-11) **1m 65y** £3,595.20 (£1,089.60: £532.80: £254.40) Stalls: High GOING: 0.51 sec per fur (GS)

| | | | | SP | RR | SF |
|---|---|---|---|---|---|---|
| | **Hutchies Lady (38)** (RMMcKellar) **4-7-5**(5) CAdamson(14) (chsd ldrs: nt clr run 3f: swtchd 1f out: led ins fnl f: hung bdly lft: kpt on) | — | **1** | 33/1 | 47 | 18 |
| *$30^{2}$* | **Personimus (38)** (CaptJWilson) **6-7-5**(5) PFessey(7) (hdwy ½-wy: styd on fnl f: nrst fin) | 1 | **2** | 10/1 | 45 | 16 |
| $739^{10}$ | **Three Arch Bridge (60)** (MJohnston) **4-9-4b** TWilliams(9) (led tl hdd ins fnl f: hung lft towards fin) | ¾ | **3** | 6/1 | 66 | 37 |
| $505^{5}$ | **Scorpius (52)** (TTClement) **6-8-10** KDarley(4) (effrt on outside over 3f out: styd on: nrst fin) | 1¾ | **4** | 9/1 | 54 | 25 |
| $690^{7}$ | **Chilly Lad (52)** (MJRyan) **5-8-10b** DBiggs(11) (in tch: kpt on fnl 2f: nvr able to chal) | 2½ | **5** | 9/2 [2] | 49 | 20 |
| $527^{13}$ | **Roar on Tour (41)** (MrsMReveley) **7-7-13** LCharnock(1) (outpcd & lost pl ½-wy: sme late hdwy) | 7 | **6** | 20/1 | 25 | — |
| $586^{5}$ | **Ballard Lady (IRE) (43)** (JSWainwright) **4-8-1** JFEgan(12) (chsd ldrs tl grad wknd fnl 2½f) | ½ | **7** | 4/1 [1] | 26 | — |
| $806^{16}$ | **Strathtore Dream (IRE) (39)** (MissLAPerratt) **5-7-11**ow1 JFanning(10) (chsd ldrs tl wknd fnl 2f) | ½ | **8** | 40/1 | 21 | — |
| $851^{12}$ | **Nizaal (USA) (60)** (DNicholls) **5-9-4b**[1] AlexGreaves(13) (trckd ldrs gng wl: effrt over 2f out: no rspnse) | ¾ | **9** | 11/2 | 41 | 12 |
| *$778^{4}$* | **Sandmoor Denim (65)** (SRBowring) **9-9-4**(5) CTeague(8) (chsd ldrs: effrt 3f out: wknd fnl 2f) | ¾ | **10** | 5/1 [3] | 44 | 15 |
| $802^{10}$ | **Segala (IRE) (68)** (JJO'Neill) **5-9-12b**[1] GDuffield(5) (hmpd after s: n.d) | ½ | **11** | 16/1 | 46 | 17 |
| *$776^{4}$* | **Battle Colours (IRE) (38)** (DonEnricoIncisa) **7-7-10** KimTinkler(6) (in tch tl wknd fnl 3f) | 3½ | **12** | 14/1 | 9 | — |
| $805^{5}$ | **Heathyards Magic (IRE) (60)** (MDods) **4-9-4** JCarroll(2) (a bhd) | 2½ | **13** | 8/1 | 27 | — |
| | **Amnesia (IRE) (38)** (MrsSCBradburne) **5-7-10v** NCarlisle(3) (a bhd) | 11 | **14** | 33/1 | — | — |

(SP 140.4%) **14 Rn**

**1m 55.0** (10.90) CSF £338.53 CT £2,154.23 TOTE £71.10: £12.20 £1.60 £2.90 (£930.50) Trio Not won; £323.66 to Newmarket 3/5/96 OWNER Mrs Linda Mckellar (LESMAHAGOW) BRED Mrs E. Campbell

LONG HANDICAP Personimus 7-3 Strathtore Dream (IRE) 6-12 Hutchies Lady 7-2 Amnesia (IRE) 7-2

**Hutchies Lady**, a little filly, got herself shut in halfway up the straight and hung left when in front, but still won well. (33/1)

**Personimus** had a lot of running to do but, given an intelligent ride, stuck to the far rail all the way up the straight and finished well. (10/1)

**Three Arch Bridge** loves this track but normally likes faster ground and did well here in the conditions. (6/1: op 4/1)

**505 Scorpius** was always racing in the slower ground off the rail so did quite well, staying on in the last half-mile. (9/1)

**508 Chilly Lad** always had a good enough position but, over this shorter trip, could never summon a turn of foot to really get into it. (9/2)

**Roar on Tour** showed something this time, staying on at the end after getting well outpaced at halfway. (20/1)

## 885 BELLSHILL CLAIMING STKS (3-Y.O) (Class F)
4-40 (4-40) **1m 65y** £2,647.00 (£742.00: £361.00) Stalls: High GOING: 0.51 sec per fur (GS)

| | | | SP | RR | SF |
|---|---|---|---|---|---|
| 755[8] | **Sunley Secure (66)** (MRChannon) **3-8-8**(5) PPMurphy(7) (lw: trckd ldr: led 2f out: hung lft: styd on u.p) ........— | 1 | 4/1 2 | 70 | 20 |
| 784[3] | **Danico (57)** (SCWilliams) **3-8-11** KDarley(1) (lw: led tl hdd 2f out: kpt on one pce) ........7 | 2 | 7/4 1 | 55 | 5 |
| 700[8] | **Old Hush Wing (IRE)** (PCHaslam) **3-9-3** JFortune(3) (outpcd tl styd on wl fnl 2f: nrst fin) ........3 | 3 | 5/1 3 | 55 | 5 |
| 748[10] | **My Kind (55)** (NTinkler) **3-8-4** KimTinkler(8) (bhd: hdwy u.p 3f out: nvr rchd ldrs) ........½ | 4 | 7/1 | 41 | — |
| 540* | **She's A Winner (IRE)** (PMonteith) **3-9-2** LCharnock(5) (in tch tl rdn & btn over 3f out) ........6 | 5 | 5/1 3 | 41 | — |
| 539[13] | **Pearls of Thought (IRE) (41)** (JSHaldane) **3-7-12** DaleGibson(4) (chsd ldrs: sn drvn along: wknd 4f out) ......12 | 6 | 100/1 | — | — |
| *605*[12] | **Autofyr (28)** (JSWainwright) **3-7-13**(3) DWright(9) (a bhd) ........3½ | 7 | 33/1 | — | — |
| 849[11] | **Phar Closer** (WTKemp) **3-7-7**(5) PFessey(2) (in tch to ½-wy: sn bhd) ........nk | 8 | 66/1 | — | — |
| | **Mon Pere (50)** (KMcAuliffe) **3-8-13** JFEgan(6) (lw: chsd ldrs: hrd rdn ½-wy: btn & eased fnl 2f) ........5 | 9 | 11/1 | — | — |

(SP 116.0%) **9 Rn**

**1m 56.5** (12.40) CSF £11.01 TOTE £5.50: £1.90 £1.70 £1.50 (£6.00) Trio £14.80 OWNER Mr Sunley Tice (UPPER LAMBOURN) BRED Sunley Stud

STEWARDS' ENQUIRY Murphy susp. 11 & 13/5/96 (excessive use of whip).

**634 Sunley Secure** was always going best but, when in front two furlongs out, just wanted to hang left, and his young rider certainly sorted him out with the whip. (4/1: 5/2-9/2)

**784 Danico** made this a real test of stamina but was well outpointed in the last two furlongs. (7/4)

**Old Hush Wing (IRE)**, stepped up in trip here, was picking up ground in pleasing style at the end to suggest that, over even further, he should do better. (5/1)

**My Kind** began to respond to pressure halfway through the race but soon came to the end of her tether. (7/1: 5/1-8/1)

**540* She's A Winner (IRE)** failed to impress on looks and, after his hard race last time, ran moderately here. (5/1)

## 886 EAST KILBRIDE H'CAP (0-70) (3-Y.O+) (Class E)
5-10 (5-11) **1m 5f 9y** £3,517.20 (£1,065.60: £520.80: £248.40) Stalls: High GOING: 0.51 sec per fur (GS)

| | | | SP | RR | SF |
|---|---|---|---|---|---|
| 620[2] | **Sarawat (63)** (DNicholls) **8-9-7** AlexGreaves(4) (trckd ldrs: led wl over 3f out: r.o) ........— | 1 | 7/1 3 | 75 | 37 |
| 620* | **Lord Hastie (USA) (65)** (CWThornton) **8-9-6**(3) OPears(11) (lw: sn in tch: effrt over 2f out: styd on u.p: nt pce of wnr) ........3 | 2 | 5/1 1 | 73 | 35 |
| 620[11] | **Cutthroat Kid (IRE) (60)** (MrsMReveley) **6-9-4v** KDarley(2) (prom: ev ch 3f out: one pce fnl 2f) ........1¼ | 3 | 17/2 | 67 | 29 |
| 620[3] | **Palace of Gold (39)** (LLungo) **6-7-11** JFanning(12) (lw: led tl hdd wl over 3f out: grad wknd) ........3 | 4 | 6/1 2 | 42 | 4 |
| 753* | **Fabillion (66)** (CASmith) **4-9-10** 5x DeanMcKeown(10) (hdwy 6f out: sn chsng ldrs: no imp whn sltly hmpd by a dog over 1f out) ........1¾ | 5 | 5/1 1 | 67 | 29 |
| 612[6] | **Lostris (IRE) (38)** (MDods) **5-7-10** NKennedy(3) (in tch tl outpcd fnl 4f) ........27 | 6 | 20/1 | 6 | — |
| 816[2] | **Bayrak (USA) (70)** (MJRyan) **6-10-0** DBiggs(1) (lw: chsd ldrs tl wknd over 3f out) ........½ | 7 | 5/1 1 | 37 | — |
| 619[5] | **Turgenev (IRE) (59)** (RBastiman) **7-8-12b**(5) HBastiman(6) (swrg: bhd: racd wd: no imp) ........1½ | 8 | 17/2 | 24 | — |
| 609[14] | **Don't Cry (38)** (DonEnricoIncisa) **8-7-10** KimTinkler(7) (a bhd) ........2½ | 9 | 100/1 | — | — |
| 666[6] | **Rock Group (55)** (JPearce) **4-8-13** GBardwell(9) (bhd: effrt ½-wy: sn btn) ........1 | 10 | 14/1 | 16 | — |
| 767[8] | **Bold Elect (47)** (EJAlston) **8-8-5**ow3 SDWilliams(5) (lost tch appr st: n.d after) ........1¼ | 11 | 14/1 | 7 | — |
| 558[10] | **Kismetim (38)** (DWChapman) **6-7-10** LCharnock(8) (a bhd: t.o) ........dist | 12 | 33/1 | — | — |
| 803[11] | **Thorntoun Estate (IRE) (59)** (MJohnston) **3-7-11**ow1 TWilliams(13) (chsd ldrs: sn hrd drvn: wknd qckly 6f out: t.o) ........5 | 13 | 14/1 | — | — |

(SP 126.5%) **13 Rn**

**3m 3.7** (18.00) CSF £41.57 CT £287.37 TOTE £7.40: £3.70 £1.10 £3.00 (£7.40) Trio £48.90 OWNER Mr S. Aitken (THIRSK) BRED Nawara Stud Co Ltd

LONG HANDICAP Lostris (IRE) 7-5 Don't Cry 6-4 Kismetim 7-8 Thorntoun Estate (IRE) 7-9

WEIGHT FOR AGE 3yo-20lb

**620 Sarawat**, suited by the strong pace, led a long way from home and was never going to stop. (7/1: 9/2-8/1)

**620* Lord Hastie (USA)** tried hard to follow up his recent victory on this track but, racing in the slower ground away from the fence, the effort was always too much in the last furlong. (5/1)

**541 Cutthroat Kid (IRE)**, given a much more positive ride this time, had every chance but failed to quicken when the pressure was on in the last two and a half furlongs. (17/2)

**620 Palace of Gold** set a breakneck pace and, once headed over three furlongs out, was soon treading water. (6/1)

**753* Fabillion** finished as close as he could, despite being hampered by a dog entering the last two furlongs. (5/1)

**619 Turgenev (IRE)**, who sweated up as he often does, was in an unco-operative mood and, always racing wide, could never get in to it. (17/2)

T/Plpt: £95.20 (116.13 Tckts). T/Qdpt: £29.90 (37.96 Tckts). AA

# SALISBURY (R-H) (Good to firm, Good patches)
## Thursday May 2nd
WEATHER: overcast WIND: str half bhd

## 887 ALMOND APPRENTICE H'CAP (0-70) (3-Y.O+) (Class G)
2-00 (2-04) **6f 212y** £2,224.50 (£632.00: £313.50) Stalls: High GOING minus 0.41 sec per fur (F)

| | | | SP | RR | SF |
|---|---|---|---|---|---|
| *426*[3] | **King Parrot (IRE) (46)** (LordHuntingdon) **8-7-11**(7) CCogan(8) (lw: hld up: rdn over 3f out: led wl ins fnl f: r.o wl) ........— | 1 | 12/1 | 56 | 24 |
| 636[8] | **Jaazim (50)** (MMadgwick) **6-8-8** AEddery(7) (hdwy over 2f out: ev ch ins fnl f: r.o) ........nk | 2 | 20/1 | 59 | 27 |
| 666[13] | **Desert Calm (IRE) (55)** (MrsPNDutfield) **7-8-8b**1(5) MSemple(6) (gd hdwy over 1f out: r.o wl ins fnl f) ........nk | 3 | 40/1 | 64 | 32 |
| 582[23] | **Stoppes Brow (70)** (GLMoore) **4-9-9v**(5) ALakeman(18) (hdwy over 2f out: ev ch ins fnl f: unable qckn) ........¾ | 4 | 16/1 | 77 | 45 |
| 644[5] | **Amber Fort (69)** (PFICole) **3-8-8b**(7) DavidO'Neill(1) (a.p: led over 2f out tl ins fnl f: one pce) ........nk | 5 | 13/2 2 | 75 | 31 |
| 843[10] | **Persian Affair (IRE) (59)** (TJNaughton) **5-8-10**(7) RachaelMoody(3) (bit bkwd: s.s: gd hdwy over 1f out: r.o wl ins fnl f) ........nk | 6 | 20/1 | 65 | 33 |
| 577[11] | **Tarian (USA) (54)** (GBBalding) **4-8-5**(7) RGordon(4) (hdwy over 1f out: r.o ins fnl f) ........hd | 7 | 40/1 | 59 | 27 |
| 664[2] | **Scissor Ridge (45)** (JJBridger) **4-7-12**(5) TField(19) (a.p: rdn over 3f out: led ins fnl f: sn hdd: one pce) ........s.h | 8 | 6/1 1 | 50 | 18 |

| | | | | SP | RR | SF |
|---|---|---|---|---|---|---|
| 641[13] | **Talathath (FR) (62)** (CADwyer) **4-8-13v1**(7) FTynan(11) (hdwy over 1f out: r.o) | nk | **9** | 10/1 | 67 | 35 |
| *80*[7] | **Serious Option (IRE) (61)** (PFICole) **5-8-12**(7) JBosley(16) (bit bkwd: nvr nr to chal) | 3 | **10** | 25/1 | 59 | 27 |
| 470* | **Sea Spouse (45)** (MBlanshard) **5-8-3**ow1 GFaulkner(15) (prom over 5f) | nk | **11** | 7/1[3] | 42 | 9 |
| 632[5] | **Moi Canard (62)** (BAPearce) **3-8-8** JWilkinson(13) (prom 4f) | 1¼ | **12** | 9/1 | 56 | 12 |
| 636[15] | **Almapa (45)** (RJHodges) **4-7-12**(5) PDoe(20) (led over 4f: wknd over 1f out) | s.h | **13** | 14/1 | 39 | 7 |
| 645[9] | **Hawaii Storm (FR) (50)** (DJSffrenchDavis) **8-8-3**(5) GHannon(10) (a bhd) | 4 | **14** | 16/1 | 35 | 3 |
| 496[12] | **Duffertoes (70)** (MJRyan) **4-9-9**(5) RMullen(9) (bhd fnl 3f) | 2½ | **15** | 20/1 | 49 | 17 |
| | **Mr Cube (IRE) (59)** (JMBradley) **6-9-3v** RWaterfield(2) (bkwd: hdwy 3f out: wknd over 1f out) | 4 | **16** | 11/1 | 29 | — |
| 582[13] | **Roka (53)** (RHannon) **4-8-4**(7) KSalt(5) (lw: a bhd) | 5 | **17** | 16/1 | 11 | — |
| 669[9] | **Jona Holley (61)** (IABalding) **3-8-4**(3)ow1 CScudder(14) (a bhd) | ½ | **18** | 20/1 | 18 | — |
| | **Nabjelsedr (46)** (AGNewcombe) **6-7-13**(5) JFowle(17) (reluctant to r: a wl bhd) | 4 | **19** | 33/1 | — | — |
| 709[7] | **Little Millie (62)** (PHayward) **3-8-8** JDennis(12) (b.hind: a bhd) | nk | **20** | 33/1 | 9 | — |
| | | | | (SP 133.2%) | | **20 Rn** |

**1m 28.78** (2.78) CSF £218.24 CT £8,219.54 TOTE £11.60: £2.70 £8.50 £14.20 £2.40 (£178.60) Trio Not won; £531.27 to Newmarket 3/5/96
OWNER Lord Huntingdon (WEST ILSLEY) BRED W. Hastings-Bass in Ireland
WEIGHT FOR AGE 3yo-12lb

**King Parrot (IRE)**, who chased the leaders, was already being nudged along at halfway, but came with a rattle in the final furlong to snatch the spoils in the closing stages. (12/1)
**Jaazim** took closer order over a quarter of a mile from home, and was one of several battling for the lead inside the final furlong, before the winner swooped. (20/1)
**Desert Calm (IRE)**, who raced over two miles last time, was out with the washing until storming through from below the distance, only to find the line coming just a little but too soon. This trip is just too sharp for him. (40/1)
**Stoppes Brow** moved up over two furlongs from home. With every chance inside the last 200 yards, he was just run out of it in the closing stages. (16/1)
**644 Amber Fort** went on over quarter of a mile from home, but failed to find another gear when collared inside the final furlong. (13/2: op 4/1)
**Persian Affair (IRE)** lost ground at the start and was another who was well adrift until running on really strongly from below the distance to be nearest at the line. (20/1)
**Mr Cube (IRE)** (11/1: 7/1-12/1)

## 888 LAUDERDALE H'CAP (0-80) (3-Y.O+ F & M) (Class D)

2-30 (2-31) **1m** £4,077.50 (£1,220.00: £585.00: £267.50) Stalls: High GOING minus 0.41 sec per fur (F)

| | | | | SP | RR | SF |
|---|---|---|---|---|---|---|
| 572[13] | **Lilli Claire (74)** (AGFoster) **3-9-1** TSprake(4) (lw: hdwy over 2f out: led wl over 1f out: r.o wl) | — | **1** | 14/1 | 83 | 47 |
| | **Honorable Estate (IRE) (70)** (RHannon) **3-8-6**(5) DaneO'Neill(2) (lw: hdwy over 1f out: r.o one pce) | 3½ | **2** | 13/2[2] | 72 | 36 |
| | **Zelda Zonk (66)** (BJMeehan) **4-9-6** RHughes(7) (hdwy 2f out: rdn over 1f out: one pce) | 1 | **3** | 10/1 | 66 | 43 |
| | **Mystic Dawn (60)** (SDow) **3-7-10**(5) ADaly(10) (s.s: hdwy over 1f out: r.o) | ½ | **4** | 25/1 | 59 | 23 |
| 550[9] | **Little Black Dress (USA) (72)** (RCharlton) **3-8-13** MHills(8) (a.p: ev ch 2f out: wknd fnl f) | ½ | **5** | 7/1[3] | 70 | 34 |
| 752[8] | **Polly Peculiar (59)** (BSmart) **5-8-13** RCochrane(3) (s.s: hdwy over 2f out: rdn over 1f out: one pce) | ½ | **6** | 9/1 | 56 | 33 |
| | **Miss Laughter (51)** (JWHills) **4-8-5** RHills(5) (led over 6f) | 4 | **7** | 16/1 | 40 | 17 |
| | **Capilano Princess (72)** (DHaydnJones) **3-8-10**(3) DRMcCabe(12) (b: bit bkwd: nvr nr to chal) | ½ | **8** | 10/1 | 60 | 24 |
| 641[2] | **Princess Danielle (60)** (WRMuir) **4-9-0** JReid(1) (bhd fnl 3f) | 1¼ | **9** | 7/2[1] | 46 | 23 |
| | **Aldaneh (74)** (RHannon) **4-10-0** LDettori(6) (bit bkwd: hdwy 2f out: rdn over 1f out: sn wknd) | 2½ | **10** | 13/2[2] | 55 | 32 |
| | **Jubilee Place (IRE) (75)** (TThomsonJones) **3-9-2** WCarson(11) (b: bit bkwd: prom over 4f) | 14 | **11** | 7/1[3] | 28 | — |
| 644[7] | **Sunset Harbour (IRE) (57)** (TJNaughton) **3-7-7**(5)ow2 MHenry(9) (w ldr 6f) | 10 | **12** | 25/1 | — | — |
| | | | | (SP 122.3%) | | **12 Rn** |

**1m 42.32** (1.92) CSF £96.89 CT £891.11 TOTE £18.70: £3.70 £1.90 £2.60 (£133.20) Trio £207.80; £266.41 to Newmarket 3/5/96 OWNER Mr C. Leafe (LAMBOURN) BRED Roger C. Denton
LONG HANDICAP Sunset Harbour (IRE) 7-7
WEIGHT FOR AGE 3yo-13lb
OFFICIAL EXPLANATION **Mystic Dawn: the jockey stated that his instructions were to jump out, get the filly switched off and make a move three furlongs out but, tha when a gap had appeared, she got unbalanced, and he nursed her home.**

**Lilli Claire**, out of her depth in listed company last time out, came through to lead early in the final quarter-mile and kept on far too strongly for her rivals. (14/1)
**Honorable Estate (IRE)** at last picked up ground below the distance and stayed on for second place, if having no chance with the winner. (13/2)
**Zelda Zonk** took closer order a quarter of a mile from home, but then failed to find another turn of foot. (10/1)
**Mystic Dawn**, who lost ground at the start, was noted staying on nicely in the last furlong and a half to be nearest at the line. (25/1)
**Little Black Dress (USA)** had every chance a quarter of a mile from home, before coming to the end of her tether inside the last 200 yards. (7/1)
**553 Polly Peculiar** moved up over a quarter of a mile from home but, despite her rider's efforts, failed to quicken in the last furlong and a half. (9/1: 6/1-12/1)
**641 Princess Danielle** (7/2: 5/2-4/1)

## 889 CHEVIOT CONDITIONS STKS (3-Y.O+) (Class C)

3-00 (3-01) **6f** £4,938.00 (£1,842.00: £896.00: £380.00) Stalls: High GOING minus 0.41 sec per fur (F)

| | | | | SP | RR | SF |
|---|---|---|---|---|---|---|
| 673[2] | **Iktamal (USA) (108)** (EALDunlop) **4-9-11** PaulEddery(10) (swtchd lft 3f out: hdwy 2f out: led ins fnl f: r.o) | — | **1** | 13/8[1] | 117 | 67 |
| | **Everglades (IRE) (96)** (RCharlton) **8-9-3** SSanders(6) (b: bkwd: rdn over 1f out: hdwy fnl f: r.o wl) | 1¼ | **2** | 14/1 | 106 | 56 |
| | **Loch Patrick (104)** (MMadgwick) **6-9-9** AMcGlone(3) (hld up: rdn 2f out: unable qckn) | nk | **3** | 25/1 | 111 | 61 |
| 737* | **Carranita (IRE) (107)** (BPalling) **6-9-8** TSprake(8) (lw: led tl ins fnl f: one pce) | ½ | **4** | 5/1[3] | 109 | 59 |
| 818[3] | **Branston Abby (IRE) (113)** (MJohnston) **7-9-8** LDettori(1) (hld up: rdn 3f out: one pce) | hd | **5** | 7/2[2] | 108 | 58 |
| | **Rambling Bear (104)** (MBlanshard) **3-9-3** RCochrane(2) (plld hrd: a.p: ev ch wl over 1f out: wknd ins fnl f) | 2½ | **6** | 13/2 | 107 | 47 |
| 457[5] | **Montendre (106)** (MMcCormack) **9-9-3** JReid(9) (hld up: rdn 4f out: wknd fnl f) | nk | **7** | 7/1 | 96 | 46 |
| 631[6] | **Shikari's Son (95)** (JCullinan) **9-9-11** TQuinn(4) (a bhd) | 11 | **8** | 33/1 | 75 | 25 |
| | **Queenfisher (95)** (GLMoore) **4-9-4** CandyMorris(5) (lw: spd 3f) | ¾ | **9** | 40/1 | 66 | 16 |
| | | | | (SP 118.7%) | | **9 Rn** |

**1m 13.59** (0.59) CSF £23.01 TOTE £2.70: £1.50 £2.70 £4.20 (£21.80) Trio £204.70 OWNER Maktoum Al Maktoum (NEWMARKET) BRED Green Ireland Properties Ltd
WEIGHT FOR AGE 3yo-10lb

**673 Iktamal (USA)**, pulled to the outside three furlongs from home, made steady headway a quarter of a mile out. Despite carrying his head rather high, he came through to lead inside the final furlong and, ridden along, asserted his authority. (13/8)

**Everglades (IRE)** was still out with the washing entering the final furlong, but he then really found his feet and came storming through for second place. (14/1: 8/1-16/1)
**Loch Patrick** chased the leaders, but failed to find that vital turn of foot in the last two furlongs. (25/1)
**737* Carranita (IRE)** attempted to make all. Still grimly trying to hold off her rivals entering the final furlong, she was soon passed by the winner. (5/1)
**818 Branston Abby (IRE)** chased the leaders but, scrubbed along at halfway, could only go up and down in the same place. (7/2)
**Rambling Bear** took a keen hold and had every chance early in the final quarter-mile before eventually tiring inside the last 200 yards. (13/2)

## 890 GRAMPIAN H'CAP (0-70) (3-Y.O) (Class E)

3-30 (3-30) **1m 4f** £3,418.00 (£1,024.00: £492.00: £226.00) Stalls: High GOING minus 0.41 sec per fur (F)

| | Horse | | Pos | SP | RR | SF |
|---|---|---|---|---|---|---|
| | **Serious Trust (52)** (SirMarkPrescott) **3-8-5** SSanders(8) (hld up: led over 3f out: hrd rdn over 1f out: r.o wl) | — | **1** | 7/2 1 | 61 | 27 |
| 668 5 | **Macmorris (USA) (68)** (PFICole) **3-9-7** TQuinn(10) (led over 6f out tl over 3f out: unable qckn) | 2½ | **2** | 7/1 | 74 | 40 |
| | **High Desire (IRE) (54)** (JRArnold) **3-8-2**(5) MHenry(7) (rdn & hdwy over 2f out: one pce) | ½ | **3** | 33/1 | 59 | 25 |
| 597 11 | **Ship's Dancer (54)** (JLDunlop) **3-8-7**ow1 JReid(9) (rdn & hdwy over 2f out: one pce) | ½ | **4** | 13/2 | 58 | 23 |
| | **Galway Blade (60)** (APJarvis) **3-8-13** RHughes(4) (lw: rdn & hdwy over 2f out: one pce) | 1 | **5** | 12/1 | 63 | 29 |
| *56* 9 | **Sterling Fellow (54)** (RHannon) **3-8-2**(5) DaneO'Neill(2) (lw: prom over 9f) | 11 | **6** | 10/1 | 42 | 8 |
| 599* | **Belle's Boy (65)** (BPalling) **3-9-4** TSprake(6) (led over 5f: wknd over 2f out) | 1 | **7** | 9/2 3 | 52 | 18 |
| 597 7 | **Princely Affair (51)** (MBell) **3-8-4** MFenton(1) (a bhd) | 2½ | **8** | 12/1 | 35 | 1 |
| 560 6 | **Brighter Byfaah (IRE) (49)** (NAGraham) **3-8-2**ow5 PaulEddery(12) (bhd fnl 3f) | nk | **9** | 20/1 | 32 | — |
| 522 9 | **Eskimo Kiss (IRE) (45)** (MJFetherston-Godley) **3-7-5**(7)ow2 MartinDwyer(5) (bhd fnl 4f) | 2½ | **10** | 33/1 | 25 | — |
| 668 4 | **Hanbitooh (USA) (68)** (EALDunlop) **3-9-7** RCochrane(11) (lw: prom over 8f) | 1½ | **11** | 4/1 2 | 46 | 12 |
| 761 11 | **Astra Martin (45)** (PGMurphy) **3-7-12v** NAdams(3) (a bhd) | 19 | **12** | 33/1 | — | — |

(SP 124.3%) **12 Rn**

**2m 37.24** (4.64) CSF £27.87 CT £637.69 TOTE £3.60: £1.10 £3.70 £38.80 (£21.10) Trio £278.70; £90.31 to Newmarket 3/5/96 OWNER Mr G. Moore (NEWMARKET) BRED W. and R. Barnett Ltd
LONG HANDICAP Eskimo Kiss (IRE) 6-13
**Serious Trust**, who showed little last year, was all the rage in the betting on this first run of the season and his first at this much longer trip. Cruising into the lead over three furlongs from home, his jockey was not taking any risks and, bringing the colt under pressure below the distance, the combination kept on well. (7/2: op 8/1)
**668 Macmorris (USA)** went on turning for home but, collared over three furlongs out, failed to cope with the winner. (7/1)
**High Desire (IRE)**, scrubbed along to take closer order over a quarter of a mile from home, was then only treading water. (33/1)
**597 Ship's Dancer**, scrubbed along over two furlongs from home, was then made to look very pedestrian. (13/2)
**Galway Blade**, another who took closer order over two furlongs out, could then only plod on at one insufficient pace. (12/1)
**599* Belle's Boy** (9/2: op 3/1)

## 891 PENTLAND CONDITIONS STKS (3-Y.O) (Class C)

4-00 (4-00) **1m 1f 209y** £5,410.50 (£1,743.00: £846.50) Stalls: Low GOING minus 0.41 sec per fur (F)

| | Horse | | Pos | SP | RR | SF |
|---|---|---|---|---|---|---|
| 694 6 | **Heron Island (IRE) (105)** (PWChapple-Hyam) **3-9-0** JReid(4) (lw: trckd ldr: shkn up over 1f out: led wl ins fnl f: r.o wl) | — | **1** | 4/5 1 | 102 | 12 |
| | **Story Line** (BWHills) **3-8-13** MHills(3) (h.d.w: bkwd: led: rdn over 1f out: hdd wl ins fnl f) | ¾ | **2** | 7/4 2 | 100 | 10 |
| | **Alzanti (88)** (PFICole) **3-9-0** TQuinn(2) (lw: hld up: rdn 3f out: wknd wl over 1f out) | 9 | **3** | 11/2 3 | 86 | — |

(SP 107.3%) **3 Rn**

**2m 12.16** (6.86) CSF £2.36 TOTE £1.40: (£1.50) OWNER Mr R. E. Sangster (MARLBOROUGH) BRED Barronstown Stud and Roncon Ltd
**694 Heron Island (IRE)**, given a good lead this time, ran out a decisive winner. An outsider for Epsom, he will now go for the Lingfield Derby Trial. (4/5)
**Story Line** has wintered well but was the most backward of the three runners. Bred to stay further, she should come on quite a lot for this. (7/4: 5/4-2/1)
**Alzanti** found this company too hot in the last quarter-mile. (11/2: op 3/1)

## 892 MORRISTON MAIDEN STKS (I) (3-Y.O) (Class D)

4-30 (4-32) **1m** £3,622.50 (£1,080.00: £515.00: £232.50) Stalls: High GOING minus 0.41 sec per fur (F)

| | Horse | | Pos | SP | RR | SF |
|---|---|---|---|---|---|---|
| | **Side Note** (HRACecil) **3-9-0** WRyan(5) (cmpt: bit bkwd: a.p: shkn up to ld over 2f out: r.o wl) | — | **1** | 4/1 2 | 86 | 47 |
| | **Alzeus (IRE)** (CAHorgan) **3-9-0** PaulEddery(3) (w'like: hld up & bhd: rdn & hdwy over 2f out: r.o ins fnl f) | 1½ | **2** | 40/1 | 83 | 44 |
| | **Male-Ana-Mou (IRE)** (DRCElsworth) **3-9-0** AProcter(15) (w'like: hdwy 2f out: one pce fnl f) | 3½ | **3** | 33/1 | 76 | 37 |
| 669 3 | **Crazy Chief (80)** (PFICole) **3-9-0** TQuinn(14) (lw: a.p: rdn 3f out: one pce fnl 2f) | 1 | **4** | 4/1 2 | 74 | 35 |
| | **Moon Mischief** (LadyHerries) **3-9-0** MHills(1) (w'like: scope: bit bkwd: hld up: hdwy 3f out: one pce fnl 2f) | 2 | **5** | 8/1 3 | 70 | 31 |
| | **Far Dawn (USA)** (GHarwood) **3-9-0** AClark(12) (w'like: scope: bit bkwd: mid div: rdn over 2f out: hmpd over 1f out: nt rch ldrs) | 1½ | **6** | 20/1 | 67 | 28 |
| | **Effectual** (JARToller) **3-9-0** SSanders(9) (w'like: bkwd: prom over 5f) | nk | **7** | 33/1 | 66 | 27 |
| | **Beauchamp Knight** (HCandy) **3-9-0** CRutter(2) (w'like: scope: bit bkwd: nvr nrr) | ½ | **8** | 33/1 | 65 | 26 |
| | **Premier Generation (IRE)** (DWPArbuthnot) **3-9-0** RCochrane(10) (bit bkwd: nvr plcd to chal) | 1½ | **9** | 33/1 | 62 | 23 |
| | **Alsahib (USA)** (HThomsonJones) **3-9-0** RHills(7) (prom 6f) | nk | **10** | 3/1 1 | 62 | 23 |
| | **Gain Line (USA)** (RCharlton) **3-9-0** TSprake(13) (lengthy: scope: a bhd) | 1½ | **11** | 14/1 | 59 | 20 |
| | **Don Bosio (USA)** (MRStoute) **3-9-0** JReid(6) (w'like: scope: lw: bhd fnl 2f) | s.h | **12** | 10/1 | 59 | 20 |
| | **Firbur** (NAGraham) **3-9-0** RHughes(11) (bit bkwd: prom tl wknd wl over 1f out) | ¾ | **13** | 33/1 | 57 | 18 |
| | **Dramatic Act** (CRBarwell) **3-8-9** NAdams(8) (bit bkwd: led over 5f: wknd qckly) | ¾ | **14** | 8/1 3 | 51 | 12 |
| | **Society Magic (USA)** (IABalding) **3-9-0** LDettori(4) (prom over 5f) | 8 | **15** | 10/1 | 40 | 1 |
| | **Motrib (USA)** (MMadgwick) **3-9-0** MFenton(16) (w'like: bkwd: a bhd: t.o fnl 2f) | 30 | **16** | 40/1 | — | — |

(SP 136.4%) **16 Rn**

**1m 42.23** (1.83) CSF £142.49 TOTE £5.40: £3.00 £7.50 £3.70 (£102.30) Trio Not won; £306.90 to Newmarket 3/5/96 OWNER Mr K. Abdulla (NEWMARKET) BRED Juddmonte Farms
OFFICIAL EXPLANATION **Premier Generation (IRE): the jockey stated that his instructions were to jump out, try to settle the gelding and ride his race from there, but that horses were coming back on him, and he was unable to reach a challenging position.**
**Side Note**, a well-bred colt, did not look fully wound up and took a walk in the market. Proving too good for this field, he should go on from here. (4/1: op 7/4)
**Alzeus (IRE)** did all his best work in the later stages and will not be inconvenienced by further. (40/1)

**Male-Ana-Mou (IRE)** seems sure to prove better than his brother Africannightingale, but that is not saying a lot. (33/1)
**669 Crazy Chief** looked tremendously well for this step up to a mile, but it is beginning to look like he has had plenty of chances. (4/1)
**Moon Mischief**, a half-brother to Sheriff's Star and Moon Madness, looks capable of improvement when trying a longer trip. (8/1)
**Far Dawn (USA)** would probably have finished closer with a trouble-free run. (20/1)
**Premier Generation (IRE)** caught the eye of the Stewards but the explanations were accepted. (33/1)
**Alsahib (USA)** (3/1: op 5/1)
**Gain Line (USA)** (14/1: op 6/1)
**Don Bosio (USA)** (10/1: 8/1-12/1)
**Dramatic Act** (8/1: 4/1-10/1)
**Society Magic (USA)** (10/1: tchd 20/1)

## 893 SUTHERLAND H'CAP (0-70) (3-Y.O+) (Class E)

5-00 (5-03) **6f** £3,548.00 (£1,064.00: £512.00: £236.00) Stalls: High GOING minus 0.41 sec per fur (F)

| | | | | SP | RR | SF |
|---|---|---|---|---|---|---|
| *338$^{4}$* | **Patsy Grimes (64)** (JSMoore) **6-9-10** RHughes(5) (hdwy over 2f out: hrd rdn over 1f out: r.o to ld last strides) | — | 1 | 12/1$^{3}$ | 71 | 51 |
| 525$^{5}$ | **Meranti (57)** (SDow) **3-8-7** TQuinn(16) (lw: w ldr: led 3f out: hrd rdn over 1f out: hdd last strides) | hd | 2 | 4/1$^{1}$ | 64 | 34 |
| 582$^{20}$ | **Denbrae (IRE) (68)** (DJGMurraySmith) **4-9-9**(5) RPainter(2) (hdwy over 2f out: r.o one pce fnl f) | ½ | 3 | 33/1 | 73 | 53 |
| | **Sing Up (51)** (MMcCormack) **4-8-11** JReid(4) (lw: a.p: one pce fnl 2f) | 1¼ | 4 | 10/1$^{2}$ | 53 | 33 |
| 806$^{6}$ | **Jigsaw Boy (60)** (PGMurphy) **7-9-6** MFenton(11) (lw: a.p: one pce fnl 2f) | ¾ | 5 | 10/1$^{2}$ | 60 | 40 |
| 664$^{4}$ | **Pointer (39)** (MrsPNDutfield) **4-7-13** CRutter(6) (lw: hdwy over 1f out: nvr nrr) | s.h | 6 | 20/1 | 39 | 19 |
| | **Lorins Gold (36)** (AndrewTurnell) **6-7-10** NAdams(14) (bit bkwd: led 3f: wknd fnl f) | ¾ | 7 | 33/1 | 34 | 14 |
| 747$^{9}$ | **Newlands Corner (50)** (JAkehurst) **3-8-0** AMcGlone(3) (lw: hdwy over 2f out: nvr trbld ldrs) | ¾ | 8 | 33/1 | 46 | 16 |
| | **Anita's Contessa (IRE) (58)** (BPalling) **4-9-4** TSprake(12) (prom: rdn over 2f out: eased whn btn ins fnl f) | ¾ | 9 | 25/1 | 52 | 32 |
| 592$^{10}$ | **Oggi (66)** (PJMakin) **5-9-12** PaulEddery(13) (nvr nrr) | ¾ | 10 | 20/1 | 58 | 38 |
| 601$^{10}$ | **Delrob (46)** (DHaydnJones) **5-8-3**(3) DRMcCabe(9) (prom over 3f) | ¾ | 11 | 25/1 | 36 | 16 |
| 749$^{13}$ | **Sizzling (62)** (RHannon) **4-9-3**(5) DaneO'Neill(7) (lw: mid div: rdn 3f out: no rspnse) | ½ | 12 | 4/1$^{1}$ | 51 | 31 |
| 648$^{10}$ | **Ca'd'oro (60)** (GBBalding) **3-8-7**(3) SDrowne(17) (lw: bhd fnl 2f) | 1¾ | 13 | 14/1 | 44 | 14 |
| | **Andsome Boy (46)** (CRBarwell) **3-7-7**(3) NVarley(1) (lw: s.s: a bhd) | s.h | 14 | 33/1 | 30 | — |
| 592$^{5}$ | **Always Grace (60)** (MissGayKelleway) **4-8-13**(7) BFord(19) (prom over 3f) | s.h | 15 | 20/1 | 44 | 24 |
| | **Jolis Present (55)** (MJRyan) **3-8-5b** WCarson(15) (prom over 3f) | ½ | 16 | 10/1$^{2}$ | 37 | 7 |
| 582$^{7}$ | **Bryan Robson (USA) (57)** (GBBalding) **5-9-3** SSanders(10) (a bhd) | 1¾ | 17 | 14/1 | 35 | 15 |
| 664$^{6}$ | **Great Hall (51)** (PDCundell) **7-8-4b**(7) MartinDwyer(20) (s.s: a bhd) | ½ | 18 | 10/1$^{2}$ | 27 | 7 |
| 749$^{14}$ | **Winter Scout (USA) (62)** (CPEBrooks) **8-9-8** RCochrane(18) (bhd fnl 2f) | 1½ | 19 | 20/1 | 34 | 14 |
| | **Admirals Realm (48)** (AGNewcombe) **7-8-3**(5) MHenry(8) (prom over 3f) | 2 | 20 | 33/1 | 15 | — |
| | | | | (SP 138.8%) | | **20 Rn** |

**1m 14.64** (1.64) CSF £59.78 CT £1,492.65 TOTE £14.40: £3.30 £1.60 £12.60 £1.40 (£21.10) Trio £990.00 OWNER Mr J. K. Grimes (HUNGERFORD) BRED J. C. Fox
LONG HANDICAP Lorins Gold 7-2 Andsome Boy 7-9
WEIGHT FOR AGE 3yo-10lb
STEWARDS' ENQUIRY Painter susp. 11/5/96 (incorrect use of whip).
**Patsy Grimes**, given a break after an All-Weather campaign, wore down the front-runner near the line. (12/1: op 8/1)
**525 Meranti** got touched off in the shadow of the post and can be considered a winner without a penalty. (4/1)
**496 Denbrae (IRE)**, disappointing when dropped back to six furlongs last time, ran much better here and kept on willingly to the end. (33/1)
**Sing Up** has slipped down the ratings and probably ran his best race since his two-year-old days. (10/1)
**Jigsaw Boy** could never quite make his presence felt. (10/1)
**664 Pointer** dropped back to this distance last time but again seemed to find it inadequate. (20/1)
**Sizzling**, well supported in the offices, was in trouble at halfway. (4/1: 7/1-7/2)
**Ca'd'oro** (14/1: op 6/1)
**Bryan Robson (USA)** (14/1: op 8/1)

## 894 MORRISTON MAIDEN STKS (II) (3-Y.O) (Class D)

5-30 (5-33) **1m** £3,590.00 (£1,070.00: £510.00: £230.00) Stalls: High GOING minus 0.41 sec per fur (F)

| | | | | SP | RR | SF |
|---|---|---|---|---|---|---|
| 684$^{14}$ | **Manaloj (USA)** (PTWalwyn) **3-9-0** RHills(4) (a.p: led over 3f out tl over 2f out: rallied to ld nr fin) | — | 1 | 12/1 | 86 | 47 |
| | **Dilazar (USA)** (JRFanshawe) **3-8-11**(3) NVarley(5) (leggy: scope: hdwy 4f out: led over 2f out: clr over 1f out: wknd & hdd nr fin) | 1 | 2 | 20/1 | 84 | 45 |
| | **Degree** (HRACecil) **3-8-9** WRyan(3) (bit bkwd: a.p: rdn 3f out: one pce fnl 2f) | 5 | 3 | 13/8$^{1}$ | 69 | 30 |
| 732$^{2}$ | **Forza Figlio** (MissGayKelleway) **3-9-0** RCochrane(10) (b.hind: prom: lost pl 4f out: nt clr run on ins over 1f out: swtchd lft: r.o) | 3½ | 4 | 9/4$^{2}$ | 67 | 28 |
| | **Tsarskaya (USA)** (MrsJCecil) **3-8-9** BThomson(11) (prom: no hdwy fnl 3f) | 2½ | 5 | 16/1 | 57 | 18 |
| | **Morning Sir** (CRBarwell) **3-8-11**(3) DRMcCabe(6) (nvr nrr) | 1¼ | 6 | 50/1 | 60 | 21 |
| 703$^{7}$ | **No-Aman** (MajorWRHern) **3-9-0** WCarson(14) (hld up: rdn & wknd over 2f out) | 1¼ | 7 | 12/1 | 57 | 18 |
| 730$^{13}$ | **Sam Rockett** (CAHorgan) **3-9-0** AClark(1) (nvr nr to chal) | ¾ | 8 | 50/1 | 56 | 17 |
| 705$^{3}$ | **Lazali (USA)** (EALDunlop) **3-9-0** MHills(2) (nvr nr ldrs) | nk | 9 | 14/1 | 55 | 16 |
| | **Samuel Scott** (MBell) **3-9-0** MFenton(9) (bit bkwd: a bhd) | 1¼ | 10 | 33/1 | 52 | 13 |
| 640$^{10}$ | **Devil's Dance (FR)** (MRStoute) **3-9-0** JReid(12) (led over 4f: wknd over 2f out) | nk | 11 | 8/1 | 52 | 13 |
| | **Apache Len (USA) (75)** (RHannon) **3-9-0** RHughes(16) (prom 5f) | ½ | 12 | 7/1$^{3}$ | 51 | 12 |
| | **Phonetic** (GBBalding) **3-8-11**(3) SDrowne(13) (leggy: unf: a bhd) | ½ | 13 | 50/1 | 50 | 11 |
| | **Claire's Dancer (IRE)** (AndrewTurnell) **3-9-0** NAdams(15) (w'like: a bhd) | 1¾ | 14 | 50/1 | 46 | 7 |
| | **Jelali (IRE)** (DJGMurraySmith) **3-9-0** PaulEddery(8) (bit bkwd: prom tl rdn & wknd over 3f out) | ¾ | 15 | 25/1 | 45 | 6 |
| | **Utmost Zeal (USA)** (PWHarris) **3-9-0** GHind(7) (prom over 4f) | 7 | 16 | 16/1 | 31 | — |
| | | | | (SP 145.7%) | | **16 Rn** |

**1m 42.19** (1.79) CSF £232.81 TOTE £15.00: £4.40 £3.70 £1.70 (£737.70) Trio £147.60 OWNER Mr Hamdan Al Maktoum (LAMBOURN) BRED Brushwood Stable
**Manaloj (USA)**, a $160,000 colt, stepped up considerably on his debut in the Wood Ditton. Looking well held below the distance, he came with a renewed effort to collar the tiring runner-up. (12/1)
**Dilazar (USA)**, a half-brother to Legal View among others, seemed sure to score when edging over to the far rail in the final quarter-mile. However, his rider became anxious in the last 200 yards and the combination could not quite last home. He will soon make amends. (20/1)

**Degree** looked short of peak-fitness and could not go with the two principals in the last quarter-mile. (13/8)
**732 Forza Figlio** did not seem to get the run of the race and his debut suggests he is better than this. (9/4)
**Tsarskaya (USA)** is a half-sister to Stone Flake. (16/1)
**Morning Sir** gave connections encouragement in the closing stages and seems to have benefited from being gelded. (50/1)
**Devil's Dance (FR)** (8/1: op 12/1)

T/Jkpt: Not won; £3,208.77 to Newmarket 3/5/96. T/Plpt: £2,941.80 (5.02 Tckts). T/Qdpt: £73.30 (16.62 Tckts). AK/KH

# 0834-WOLVERHAMPTON (L-H) (Standard)
## Thursday May 2nd
WEATHER: overcast & cold WIND: mod against

## 895 SLOANE MAIDEN AUCTION STKS (2-Y.O) (Class F)
2-20 (2-23) **5f (Fibresand)** £2,381.00 (£656.00: £311.00) Stalls: Low GOING minus 0.07 sec per fur (STD)

| | Horse | Details | Dist | Pos | SP | RR | SF |
|---|---|---|---|---|---|---|---|
| $699^{4}$ | **Young Bigwig (IRE)** | (JBerry) **2-8-10** GCarter(10) (hdwy 2f out: r.o u.p to ld wl ins fnl f) | — | **1** | $6/4^{1}$ | 65 | 18 |
| $757^{3}$ | **Who Told Vicky (IRE)** | (JSMoore) **2-7-7**$^{(5)}$ MBaird(8) (led 1f: led ½-wy: clr ent fnl f: ct nr fin) | ¾ | **2** | 10/1 | 51 | 4 |
| $770^{2}$ | **C-Harry (IRE)** | (RHollinshead) **2-8-0v**$^{1(5)}$ FLynch(4) (lw: hdwy wl over 1f out: kpt on u.p ins fnl f) | 2 | **3** | $7/1^{3}$ | 51 | 4 |
| $757^{2}$ | **Hello Dolly (IRE)** | (KRBurke) **2-8-2** JTate(5) (in tch: effrt & rdn 2f out: nvr able to chal) | hd | **4** | $5/1^{2}$ | 48 | 1 |
| | **Colins Choice** | (JLSpearing) **2-7-7**$^{(7)}$ IonaWands(6) (leggy: hdwy 2f out: nt rch ldrs) | 2 | **5** | 33/1 | 40 | — |
| | **Jingoist (IRE)** | (MJohnston) **2-8-2** PRobinson(9) (leggy: bit bkwd: sn pushed along: nvr gng pce of ldrs) | hd | **6** | $7/1^{3}$ | 41 | — |
| $733^{6}$ | **Caviar And Candy** | (DJSCosgrove) **2-7-12** JQuinn(7) (prom 3f) | 1¼ | **7** | 14/1 | 33 | — |
| | **Court House** | (BAMcMahon) **2-8-2**$^{(5)}$ LNewton(11) (lt-f: unf: a bhd & outpcd) | ¾ | **8** | 16/1 | 40 | — |
| | **Just Loui** | (WGMTurner) **2-8-7** JWeaver(2) (unf: bkwd: dwlt: a bhd) | 1¼ | **9** | 10/1 | 36 | — |
| *$838^{5}$* | **Dancing Star (IRE)** | (PDEvans) **2-7-12v** AMackay(3) (led after 1f tl over 2f out: rdn & wknd qckly appr fnl f) | 3½ | **10** | 12/1 | 16 | — |
| $465^{8}$ | **Burberry Quest** | (BRMillman) **2-7-12** FNorton(1) (bit bkwd: outpcd: sn bhd & t.o) | 8 | **11** | 33/1 | — | — |

(SP 126.0%) **11 Rn**

**62.9 secs** (0.70 under 2y best) (4.20) CSF £17.83 TOTE £1.90: £1.20 £3.30 £2.10 (£23.50) Trio £110.30; £32.64 to Newmarket 3/5/96
OWNER Mr W. R. Milner (COCKERHAM) BRED Thoroughbred Trust

**699 Young Bigwig (IRE)**, much sharper for his initial outing last month, found all that was needed when shaken up and powered on to gain command nearing the line. (6/4: 5/2-11/8)
**757 Who Told Vicky (IRE)**, beaten in a seller on her debut, looked to have gained a winning lead when entering the final furlong a couple of lengths to the good, but the winner's relentless challenge proved just too much in the closing stages. (10/1: op 6/1)
**770 C-Harry (IRE)**, making progress from off the pace, was doing all his best work inside the distance. (7/1)
**757 Hello Dolly (IRE)**, asked for an effort two furlongs out, did keep staying on, but without having the speed to mount a challenge. (5/1: 3/1-11/2)
**Colins Choice**, a leggy newcomer who did not impress to post, could not muster the pace to reach the leaders, but she did stay on, and the experience will stand her in good stead. (33/1)
**Jingoist (IRE)**, a half-sister to Marchant Ming, was off the bridle all the way, but edged closer in the final stages, if unable to muster the speed to reach the principals. (7/1: op 4/1)
**733 Caviar And Candy** (14/1: 10/1-20/1)
**Just Loui** (10/1: op 4/1)
**838 Dancing Star (IRE)** (12/1: op 8/1)

## 896 GROSVENOR CLAIMING STKS (3-Y.O+) (Class F)
2-50 (2-50) **6f (Fibresand)** £2,381.00 (£656.00: £311.00) Stalls: Low GOING minus 0.07 sec per fur (STD)

| | Horse | Details | Dist | Pos | SP | RR | SF |
|---|---|---|---|---|---|---|---|
| *$835^{2}$* | **Intiaash (IRE) (72)** | (DHaydnJones) **4-8-13**$^{(7)}$ AnthonyBond(10) (hdwy over 2f out: led & edgd lft appr fnl f: drvn clr) | — | **1** | $5/1^{3}$ | 81 | 63 |
| 805* | **Palacegate Touch (90)** | (JBerry) **6-9-11b** GCarter(5) (lw: led 2f: rdn whn n.m.r over 1f out: one pce) | 3½ | **2** | $11/4^{2}$ | 77 | 59 |
| $749^{21}$ | **Wardara (63)** | (CADwyer) **4-8-11b**$^{(3)}$ JStack(2) (led after 2f tl appr fnl f: one pce) | hd | **3** | 25/1 | 65 | 47 |
| $749^{4}$ | **Mustn't Grumble (IRE) (67)** | (MissSJWilton) **6-9-6** FNorton(7) (lw: hdwy ent st: hmpd & swtchd ins appr fnl f: kpt on) | 2½ | **4** | 9/1 | 65 | 47 |
| $749^{18}$ | **Little Ibnr (73)** | (PDEvans) **5-9-2**$^{(5)}$ AmandaSanders(4) (lw: trckd ldrs: r.o one pce appr fnl f) | ¾ | **5** | 8/1 | 64 | 46 |
| *835** | **Cretan Gift (87)** | (NPLittmoden) **5-9-11b** WWoods(1) (s.i.s: sn pushed along: hdwy ½-wy: rdn, wkng & n.m.r appr fnl f) | hd | **6** | $11/8^{1}$ | 68 | 50 |
| $805^{3}$ | **At the Savoy (IRE) (56)** | (MrsLStubbs) **5-9-5b** JWeaver(6) (sn pushed along: a in rr) | 2 | **7** | 16/1 | 56 | 38 |
| $806^{8}$ | **Bold Aristocrat (IRE) (52)** | (RHollinshead) **5-8-12**$^{(5)}$ FLynch(3) (mid div: rdn over 2f out: sn btn) | hd | **8** | 33/1 | 54 | 36 |
| $631^{5}$ | **Dahiyah (USA) (58)** | (GLMoore) **5-9-2v** SWhitworth(8) (lw: disp ld 2f: wknd over 2f out: t.o) | 7 | **9** | 14/1 | 34 | 16 |
| | **Princess Renata (IRE) (45)** | (RHarris) **3-8-10** AMackay(9) (bkwd: sn bhd & outpcd: t.o) | 20 | **10** | 33/1 | — | — |

(SP 128.8%) **10 Rn**

**1m 13.9** (2.50) CSF £20.29 TOTE £5.90: £1.40 £1.50 £9.70 (£14.80) Trio £119.80; £121.50 to Newmarket 3/5/96 OWNER Mr Howard Thomas (PONTYPRIDD) BRED Shadwell Estate Company Limited
WEIGHT FOR AGE 3yo-10lb

**835 Intiaash (IRE)**, back over a more suitable trip, was able to turn the tables on the favourite on these more favourable terms and, in winning going away, should be able to follow up. (5/1: op 12/1)
**805* Palacegate Touch** would only have finished second had he not been hampered over a furlong from the finish. (11/4)
**Wardara**, showing her first glimpse of form since the autumn of '94, proved hard to wear down and she would appear about to get back to winning ways. (25/1)
**749 Mustn't Grumble (IRE)** was unable to improve on his previous outings this term, but once again ran well in defeat. If he does not go over the top, it can only be a matter of time before he does win another race. (9/1)
**653* Little Ibnr** sat in behind the leaders but failed to quicken when set alight, and was always being held. (8/1)
**835* Cretan Gift**, a shade sluggish leaving the stalls, obtained a clear passage down the inside rail to join issue on the home turn, but was struggling to hold his pitch when short of room over a furlong out. (11/8)

## 897 MAYFAIR H'CAP (0-85) (3-Y.O F) (Class D)
3-20 (3-21) **6f (Fibresand)** £3,694.95 (£1,101.60: £525.30: £237.15) Stalls: Low GOING minus 0.07 sec per fur (STD)

| | Horse | Details | Dist | Pos | SP | RR | SF |
|---|---|---|---|---|---|---|---|
| $773^{4}$ | **Limerick Princess (IRE) (60)** | (JBerry) **3-8-1** GCarter(3) (hld up: hdwy over 1f out: led fnl 100y: readily) | — | **1** | 10/1 | 73+ | 34 |

| | | | | SP | RR | SF |
|---|---|---|---|---|---|---|
| 686* | **Splicing (80)** (WJHaggas) **3-9-7** WWoods(1) (lw: a.p: led over 2f out tl hdd & no ex wl ins fnl f) | 1½ | **2** | 2/1 1 | 89 | 50 |
| *859** | **Miss Offset (63)** (MJohnston) **3-8-4b** 7x PRobinson(4) (dwlt: racd wd: hdwy 2f out: r.o wl fnl f) | 1¾ | **3** | 5/1 3 | 67 | 28 |
| 768[4] | **Fyors Gift (IRE) (63)** (BHanbury) **3-8-1**(3) JStack(7) (a.p: ev ch over 1f out: unable qckn) | 1¼ | **4** | 7/1 | 64 | 25 |
| *779** | **Napier Star (55)** (MrsNMacauley) **3-7-3**(7) 7x IonaWands(6) (lw: led over 3f: rdn over 1f out: one pce) | nk | **5** | 14/1 | 55 | 16 |
| *464[2]* | **Again Together (56)** (GLMoore) **3-7-11** JQuinn(2) (reard s: sn chsng ldrs: rdn & one pce appr fnl f) | hd | **6** | 8/1 | 56 | 17 |
| 686[7] | **Sweet Nature (IRE) (70)** (WJarvis) **3-8-11b[1]** JWeaver(5) (sn drvn along: a bhd) | nk | **7** | 9/4 2 | 69 | 30 |

(SP 120.1%) **7 Rn**

**1m 14.7** (3.30) CSF £30.81 TOTE £11.00: £4.70 £3.40 (£8.90) OWNER Mr Thomas Doherty (COCKERHAM) BRED Thomas Doherty
LONG HANDICAP Napier Star 5-13
STEWARDS' ENQUIRY Woods fined £100 (failing to ride to his draw).
**773 Limerick Princess (IRE)**, waiting on the leaders going well, quickened up to lead halfway through the final furlong and soon put the issue beyond doubt. This trip seemed to suit her style of racing. (10/1)
**686* Splicing**, who was onto a hat-trick, did not go down without a fight but was running off a 10lb higher mark this time and could not contain the well-handicapped winner. (2/1)
**859* Miss Offset**, who has been kept very busy, was unfortunate to miss the kick on this return to six furlongs, and was hard at work and struggling until running into the prizes inside the last furlong. (5/1)
**768 Fyors Gift (IRE)** did not fare badly on this first run on the Fibresand, having every chance until tapped for speed inside the final furlong. (7/1: 5/1-8/1)
**779* Napier Star** attempted another all-the-way success, but she had lost that battle on the home turn, and had met her match below the distance. (14/1)
**464 Again Together**, on her hind legs when the stalls were released, did recover some of the lost ground but was flat to the boards and held before reaching the final furlong. (8/1: 12/1-7/1)
**686 Sweet Nature (IRE)**, wearing blinkers for the first time, would not take hold of the bit, and sulked in the rear all the way. This effort must be over-looked. (9/4: 7/2-2/1)

## 898 BERKELEY H'CAP (0-70) (3-Y.O+) (Class E)

3-50 (3-50) **1m 4f (Fibresand)** £3,359.40 (£1,003.20: £479.60: £217.80) Stalls: Low GOING minus 0.07 sec per fur (STD)

| | | | | SP | RR | SF |
|---|---|---|---|---|---|---|
| *532** | **In the Money (IRE) (56)** (RHollinshead) **7-8-9**(5) FLynch(6) (hld up: hdwy over 5f out: led ent fnl f: drvn out) | .— | **1** | 7/1 | 67 | 44 |
| | **Canton Venture (63)** (SPCWoods) **4-9-7** WWoods(2) (bit bkwd: trckd ldrs: led over 2f out tl appr fnl f: one pce) | 3 | **2** | 12/1 | 70 | 47 |
| 542[11] | **Charlie Bigtime (51)** (RHarris) **6-8-9** AMackay(3) (b.hind: mid div: drvn along 7f out: styd on fnl 2f: nrst fin) | nk | **3** | 6/1 3 | 58 | 35 |
| 753[19] | **Zaaleff (USA) (54)** (BHanbury) **4-8-9b[1]**(3) JStack(11) (a.p: led over 4f out tl over 2f out: rdn & btn ent fnl f) | 2½ | **4** | 20/1 | 57 | 34 |
| *512** | **Cuban Nights (USA) (61)** (BJLlewellyn) **4-9-5** JWeaver(4) (led tl over 4f out: hrd rdn & wknd 2f out) | hd | **5** | 9/2 2 | 64 | 41 |
| 666[12] | **Captain Marmalade (47)** (DTThom) **7-8-5v** JTate(8) (b: nvr nr to chal) | 3½ | **6** | 14/1 | 46 | 23 |
| 609* | **Comtec's Legend (38)** (JFBottomley) **6-7-5**(5) MBaird(7) (nvr nrr) | ¾ | **7** | 8/1 | 36 | 13 |
| *777** | **Carol Again (40)** (NBycroft) **4-7-12** JQuinn(10) (hld up: effrt & drvn over 3f out: no imp fnl 2f) | 1¾ | **8** | 13/8 1 | 35 | 12 |
| | **Kutan (IRE) (38)** (MrsBarbaraWaring) **6-7-10b** FNorton(9) (b: b.hind: plld hrd: trckd ldrs tl outpcd 3f out) | 2½ | **9** | 33/1 | 30 | 7 |
| *837[7]* | **Culrain (44)** (THCaldwell) **5-7-9**(7)ow6 AngelaGallimore(1) (bit bkwd: prom over 8f: sn rdn & lost tch) | hd | **10** | 40/1 | 36 | 7 |
| 642[4] | **Bresil (USA) (38)** (KRBurke) **7-7-3**(7) IonaWands(5) (in tch tl wknd over 3f out) | ¾ | **11** | 33/1 | 29 | 6 |
| | **Red Phantom (IRE) (70)** (SMellor) **4-10-0** MWigham(12) (bkwd: s.i.s: a bhd) | 1¼ | **12** | 16/1 | 59 | 36 |

(SP 127.5%) **12 Rn**

**2m 39.9** (7.40) CSF £84.49 CT £501.61 TOTE £7.00: £2.70 £2.70 £1.80 (£106.10) Trio £104.40 OWNER Mr J. E. Bigg (UPPER LONGDON) BRED Cheveley Park Stud Ltd
LONG HANDICAP Culrain 7-7 Bresil (USA) 6-13 Kutan (IRE) 7-2
**532* In the Money (IRE)** looked very wintry on this cold day. Patiently ridden, he was produced with a perfectly-timed challenge to put his stamp on proceeding inside the final furlong. (7/1)
**Canton Venture** looked far from right in himself both in his coat and condition, but ran well and will hardly need to improve to pick up a race. (12/1)
**Charlie Bigtime**, driven along and going nowhere for most of the way, began to stay on approaching the home straight and, in the circumstances, did well to finish so close. He has bags of ability when the urge takes him. (6/1)
**Zaaleff (USA)**, a half-brother to Shadeed, turned in his best effort with the introduction of blinkers and there could be a race in him. (20/1)
**512* Cuban Nights (USA)** had little chance of confirming his form with the winner on these altered terms, but he did cut out the running for almost a mile and only dropped away once in line for home. (9/2)
**777* Carol Again** does her winning at Southwell and failed to fire on this track when the principals stepped on the gas turning for home. (13/8)

## 899 MANCHESTER (S) STKS (3-Y.O) (Class G)

4-20 (4-21) **1m 4f (Fibresand)** £2,070.00 (£570.00: £270.00) Stalls: Low GOING minus 0.07 sec per fur (STD)

| | | | | SP | RR | SF |
|---|---|---|---|---|---|---|
| 822[6] | **Pearl Anniversary (IRE)** (MJohnston) **3-8-11** JWeaver(5) (lw: hld up: hdwy over 3f out: swtchd ins over 1f out: str run to ld fnl strides) | — | **1** | 7/1 3 | 57 | 17 |
| 752[10] | **Hever Golf Diamond (53)** (TJNaughton) **3-8-4**(7) TAshley(11) (hld up & bhd: hdwy 6f out: rdn to ld wl ins fnl f: ct cl home) | hd | **2** | 5/2 2 | 57 | 17 |
| 849[12] | **Shamand (USA) (46)** (BJMeehan) **3-8-11** MTebbutt(8) (hld up: hdwy 4f out: kpt on u.p ins fnl f) | 1 | **3** | 8/1 | 56 | 16 |
| 804[6] | **Nordic Hero (IRE)** (APJarvis) **3-8-11** JTate(4) (a.p: led over 5f out: hrd drvn & hdd wl ins fnl f) | 1¼ | **4** | 12/1 | 54 | 14 |
| *655** | **Sweet Amoret (55)** (PHowling) **3-8-11** FNorton(9) (b.off hind: led after 2f tl over 5f out: hrd drvn & one pce appr fnl f) | ¾ | **5** | 9/4 1 | 53 | 13 |
| 637[10] | **Crystal Fast (USA) (57)** (PAKelleway) **3-8-4**(7) CDomergue(2) (hld up & bhd: hdwy over 3f out: rdn & no imp fnl 2f) | 1 | **6** | 8/1 | 52 | 12 |
| | **Pandora's Gift** (KRBurke) **3-8-6** JQuinn(10) (w'like: bit bkwd: s.s: hdwy 8f out: wknd 4f out: t.o) | 23 | **7** | 12/1 | 16 | — |
| *459[3]* | **Driftholme (28)** (GLMoore) **3-8-6v[1]** SWhitworth(1) (prom tl wknd qckly over 3f out: t.o) | 2½ | **8** | 7/1 3 | 13 | — |
| *651[7]* | **Chillington (35)** (WMBrisbourne) **3-8-6b[1]**(5) DGriffiths(3) (led 2f: wknd ½-wy: t.o) | 17 | **9** | 50/1 | — | — |
| | **Water Chestnut** (MrsNMacauley) **3-8-6**(5) AmandaSanders(7) (b: bit bkwd: trckd ldrs over 6f: sn wknd t.o) | nk | **10** | 33/1 | — | — |
| *655[7]* | **Balmoral Princess** (JHPeacock) **3-8-3**(3) JStack(6) (bit bkwd: in tch tl lost pl 5f out: t.o) | 2½ | **11** | 33/1 | — | — |

(SP 129.8%) **11 Rn**

**2m 43.8** (11.30) CSF £26.14 TOTE £5.20: £2.30 £2.00 £2.10 (£8.60) Trio £78.60 OWNER Mr & Mrs A Mordain (MIDDLEHAM) BRED Ovidstown Investments Ltd
No bid

**Pearl Anniversary (IRE)**, making a quick return to action, found this extra distance made to measure and stuck on grimly to force his head in front a stride from the post. (7/1)
**Hever Golf Diamond** had to work hard to poke his head in front 50 yards out but, just when the prize looked landed, the winner pounced over by the far rail and edged him out of it. Compensation awaits. (5/2)
**599 Shamand (USA)** adopted more patient tactics this time and was clawing back the principals all the way to the line. This would seem the way to ride him, and he would seem to be knocking at the door. (8/1)
**651 Nordic Hero (IRE)** made the principals work hard to wear him down inside the final furlong, and a race of this description could come his way in the near future. (12/1)
**655* Sweet Amoret** helped force the pace, but did not appear to see the trip out. More patient tactics could pay off. (9/4: op 6/4)
**Crystal Fast (USA)** tried to get himself into the action on the home turn, but the pace did not drop and he was unable to stake his bid. (8/1: op 5/1)

## 900 PORTMAN H'CAP (0-70) (3-Y.O+) (Class E)

4-50 (4-51) **5f (Fibresand)** £3,042.90 (£907.20: £432.60: £195.30) Stalls: Low GOING minus 0.07 sec per fur (STD)

| | Horse | | Pos | SP | RR | SF |
|---|---|---|---|---|---|---|
| $735^{3}$ | **Lady Sheriff (62)** (RHollinshead) **5-9-6**(5) FLynch(5) (hdwy on outside ½-wy: str run to ld cl home) | — | **1** | 6/4 1 | 65 | 41 |
| *$607^{2}$* | **Perfect Brave (65)** (JBalding) **5-9-7**(7) JEdmunds(3) (a.p: led wl over 1f out tl ct fnl strides) | hd | **2** | 9/2 2 | 68 | 44 |
| *$835^{7}$* | **Rennyholme (57)** (JHetherton) **5-9-6b** SWhitworth(7) (lw: a.p: ev ch fnl f: unable qckn) | ¾ | **3** | 20/1 | 57 | 33 |
| *$835^{4}$* | **Tee-Emm (55)** (PHowling) **6-9-4** JQuinn(9) (a.p: ev ch 1f out: no ex u.p) | ¾ | **4** | 10/1 | 53 | 29 |
| $750^{4}$ | **Sir Tasker (51)** (JLHarris) **8-9-0v** WWoods(4) (prom tl rdn & one pce appr fnl f) | 1½ | **5** | 7/1 | 44 | 20 |
| *$652^{9}$* | **Daaniera (IRE) (41)** (PHowling) **6-8-4** FNorton(1) (slt ld tl hdd wl over 1f out) | 1½ | **6** | 25/1 | 29 | 5 |
| $762^{9}$ | **Disco Boy (55)** (PDEvans) **6-9-4b** WJO'Connor(8) (trckd ldrs: drvn along fr ½-wy: no imp) | 2½ | **7** | 13/2 | 35 | 11 |
| $769^{3}$ | **The Institute Boy (64)** (MissJFCraze) **6-9-13** JWeaver(2) (hung rt: outpcd: a bhd) | hd | **8** | 6/1 3 | 44 | 20 |
| $762^{17}$ | **Highland Fawn (55)** (BAMcMahon) **3-8-9** GCarter(6) (s.i.s: a outpcd: t.o) | 15 | **9** | 8/1 | — | — |
| | | | | (SP 127.1%) | **9 Rn** | |

**62.3 secs** (3.60) CSF £9.65 CT £98.36 TOTE £2.50: £1.10 £2.50 £4.10 (£5.90) Trio £46.30 OWNER Mr E. J. Mangan (UPPER LONGDON) BRED Jeremy Green and Sons
WEIGHT FOR AGE 3yo-9lb
**735 Lady Sheriff** gave herself plenty to do but, producing her run on the favoured stands' side, had her head in front where it mattered to pull off quite a gamble. (6/4)
**607 Perfect Brave** was hell-bent for home when he struck the front and did nothing at all wrong. The winner beat him to the punch but another success is richly deserved. (9/2: op 3/1)
**514* Rennyholme** sat closer to the pace and turned in his best effort yet, but was outpointed in a spirited battle to the finish. (20/1)
**835 Tee-Emm** matched the leaders for pace and stayed in the thick of the action, but had to admit them too fleet-footed in the sprint to the post. (10/1)
**750 Sir Tasker** pushed the pace and was a live factor until feeling the strain approaching the final furlong. (7/1)
**Daaniera (IRE)** still retains his blistering speed and, with the help of the inside rail, held the call until finding demands too great for him once into the straight. (25/1)
**653 Disco Boy** (13/2: 4/1-7/1)

T/Plpt: £331.00 (31.73 Tckts). T/Qdpt: £92.50 (11.81 Tckts). IM

# 0793a-CAPANNELLE (Rome, Italy) (R-H) (Good)
## Thursday April 25th

## 901a PREMIO DELL'AERONAUTICA (3-Y.O F)

2-30 **1m** £6,090.00

| | Horse | | Pos | SP | RR | SF |
|---|---|---|---|---|---|---|
| 543a2 | **Nimble (IRE)** (JWHills) **3-9-2** MHills | — | **1** | | — | — |
| | **High Tower (ITY)** (LCamici,Italy) **3-9-2** MPasquale | 4½ | **2** | | — | — |
| | **Silvia Carpio (ITY)** (PGuarsegnati,Italy) **3-9-2** GDiChio | 1½ | **3** | | — | — |
| | | | | | | **15 Rn** |

**1m 39.8** TOTE 23L: 14L 15L 19L (50L) OWNER Highclere Thoroughbreds (LAMBOURN)
**543a Nimble (IRE)** turned in a dominant display. Prominent throughout the race, this daughter of Danehill took up the running with three furlongs to go and soon went clear, never looking in any danger. She is sure to win more races.

# 0796a-LONGCHAMP (Paris, France) (R-H) (Good)
## Thursday April 25th

## 902a PRIX DE BARBEVILLE (Gp 3) (4-Y.O+)

3-35 (3-41) **1m 7f** £28,986.00 (£10,540.00: £5,270.00: £2,635.00)

| | Horse | | Pos | SP | RR | SF |
|---|---|---|---|---|---|---|
| 563* | **Double Eclipse (IRE)** (MJohnston) **4-8-11** JWeaver | — | **1** | | 114 | — |
| | **Samiri (FR)** (J-PGallorini,France) **5-8-9** TThulliez | 2½ | **2** | | 106 | — |
| | **Helen Of Spain** (AFabre,France) **4-8-6** OPeslier | s.h | **3** | | 106 | — |
| | **Affidavit (USA)** (AFabre,France) **4-9-2** TJarnet | 1 | **4** | | 115 | — |
| | | | | | | **12 Rn** |

**3m 6.6** (0.60) P-M 3.10F: 1.60F 2.30F 4.30F (26.10F) OWNER The Middleham Partnership (MIDDLEHAM) BRED Dene Investments N V in Ireland
**563* Double Eclipse (IRE)** shattered the track record by a staggering 2.7 seconds in a race run at a true pace all the way thanks to King Cobra taking the field along at a blistering pace from the start. When King Cobra tried to slow things down, he moved up to challenge and the pace increased once more. Shortly after entering the straight, he built up a commanding lead and was never going to be pegged back. A brilliant and game effort by a horse who is maturing all the time, he can only go on to better things and will next be seen out in the Yorkshire Cup.
**Samiri (FR)** was putting in his best work at the finish and took second place shortly before the post. He has plenty of stamina and stays well, and now heads for the Prix Vicomptesse Vigier.
**Helen Of Spain** raced in third place for much of the event. Shortly after entering the straight, she gave chase to the winner, but never looked like getting on terms.

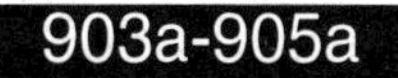


**Affidavit (USA)** put up a splendid performance, considering he was making his seasonal debut and giving 5lb to the winner. By no means given a hard time, he loomed up dangerously halfway up the straight, but did not go through with his challenge. This race will have brought him on tremendously as he was racing for the first time since the St Leger, and he will probably next be seen out in the Prix Vicomtesse Vigier, and then possibly the Ascot Gold Cup.

## 0901a-CAPANNELLE (Rome, Italy) (R-H) (Soft)
### Sunday April 28th

### 903a PREMIO PARIOLI (Gp 2) (3-Y.O C & F)
4-00 (4-08) **1m** £58,157.00 (£27,748.00: £16,117.00: £8,058.00)

| | Horse | Dist | Pos | SP | RR | SF |
|---|---|---|---|---|---|---|
| 722a3 | **Dancer Mitral** (LBrogi,Italy) **3-9-2b1** VMezzatesta | — | 1 | | 102 | — |
| 5745 | **Dankeston (USA)** (MBell) **3-9-2** WCarson | s.h | 2 | | 102 | — |
| | **Dungeon Master (IRE)** (LBrogi,Italy) **3-9-2** CFiocchi | 1¼ | 3 | | 99 | — |
| | **Tuareg Blu (ITY)** (PMazzoni,Italy) **3-9-2** BJovine | s.h | 4 | | 99 | — |
| 454* | **Acharne** (CEBrittain) **3-9-2** BDoyle (btn 3½l) | 1½ | 5 | | 96 | — |
| 722a2 | **Alabastro (IRE)** (LCamici,Italy) **3-9-2** MPasquale | s.h | 6 | | 96 | — |
| 722a* | **Blu Taxidoo (USA)** (AVerdesi,Italy) **3-9-2** MVargiu | ¾ | 7 | | 95 | — |
| 4542 | **Mironov** (MRChannon) **3-9-2** RHughes (btn 3 1/4l) | 1 | 8 | | 93 | — |
| 6953 | **Polaris Flight (USA)** (PWChapple-Hyam) **3-9-2** BThomson (btn 6 3/4l) | 1½ | 9 | | 90 | — |
| | **Smurda (USA)** (ALodigiano,Italy) **3-9-2b1** GLigas | 1 | 10 | | 88 | — |
| | **Try My Segnor** (AVerdesi,Italy) **3-9-2** JacquelineFreda | 5 | 11 | | 78 | — |
| | **Sharp Reproach** (Ld'Auria,Italy) **3-9-2** LDettori | 6 | 12 | | 66 | — |
| | **Golden Quint (ITY)** (GFratini,Italy) **3-9-2** MEsposito | ¾ | 13 | | 64 | — |
| | **Semper (IRE)** (Ld'Auria,Italy) **3-9-2b1** FJovine | 1½ | 14 | | 61 | — |

**14 Rn**

**1m 40.6** TOTE 128L: 64L 41L 158L (1309L) OWNER Allevamento La Nuova Sbarra SRL
**Dancer Mitral** hung on by a neck at the line to keep his closest rival at bay. He had been beaten by three of these rivals when finishing third on two previous appearances, and would have been at longer odds if he had not been one of three representatives of Sergio Scarpellini's Allevamento la Nuova Sbarra.
**574 Dankeston (USA)** lacked the finishing speed to overhaul the winner, but put up a brave display. Always prominent, he made headway two furlongs out and, after having every chance inside the final furlong, was just unable to catch the winner.
**454* Acharne** never really got into the reckoning. Racing in eighth place, he was brought wide three furlongs from home, but was never able to get into a challenging position. He finished sixth but was moved up to fifth after a stewards' enquiry.
**454 Mironov** ran a decent race but was subject to an enquiry and was disqualified from fifth and placed eighth. Fourth into the straight, he made headway two furlongs out, but hung right and caused interference. Once the interference had taken place, he ran on at one pace.
**695 Polaris Flight (USA)** was the big disappointment of the race. Third into the straight, he looked to have every chance but, when asked a question three furlongs from home, he was unable to find anything and weakened from the furlong marker. He is capable of a lot better.

## FRANKFURT (Germany) (L-H) (Good)
### Sunday April 28th

### 904a BMW HANDLER-TROPHY (Gp 3) (3-Y.O)
4-20 (4-26) **1m 2f** £31,531.00 (£12,613.00: £6,306.00: £3,604.00)

| | Horse | Dist | Pos | SP | RR | SF |
|---|---|---|---|---|---|---|
| | **Ardilan (IRE)** (HHorwart,Germany) **3-8-11** TMundry | — | 1 | | 91 | — |
| 323a2 | **Mongol Warrior (USA)** (LordHuntingdon) **3-8-9** DHarrison | 1½ | 2 | | 87 | — |
| | **Sir Warren (IRE)** (HBlume,Germany) **3-8-11** ASuborics | s.h | 3 | | 89 | — |

**12 Rn**

**2m 8.57** TOTE 227DM: 41DM 21DM 16DM (SF 1664DM) OWNER Frau U & A Stettendorf BRED Gestut Zoppenbroich
**Mongol Warrior (USA)** ran another game race to finish second. Always prominent, he came with a run to lead briefly two and a half furlongs out, but wandered off a true line and slightly hampered the winner. Headed a furlong and a half out, he kept on well inside the final furlong, but should be winning soon.

## 0902a-LONGCHAMP (Paris, France) (R-H) (Good to firm)
### Sunday April 28th

### 905a PRIX VANTEAUX (Gp 3) (3-Y.O F)
2-15 (2-21) **1m 1f** £28,986.00 (£10,540.00: £5,270.00: £2,635.00)

| Horse | Dist | Pos | SP | RR | SF |
|---|---|---|---|---|---|
| **Luna Wells (IRE)** (AFabre,France) **3-9-0** TJarnet | — | 1 | | 101+ | 17 |
| **Ecoute (USA)** (MmeCHead,France) **3-9-0** ODoleuze | ¾ | 2 | | 100 | 16 |
| **Wedding Gift (FR)** (PDemercastel,France) **3-9-0** WMongil | 1½ | 3 | | 97 | 13 |
| **Motzki (FR)** (JEPease,France) **3-9-0** GMosse | 1½ | 4 | | 94 | 10 |

**5 Rn**

**1m 56.0** (8.00) P-M 2.00F: 1.30F 1.50F (SF 5.30F) OWNER J-L Lagadere (CHANTILLY) BRED S.N.C. Lagardere Elevage et al
**Luna Wells (IRE)**, who was transferred to Andre Fabre in the winter, has certainly done well and made the grade in this first attempt in a Group race. Despite looking a little backward in the paddock and running a little green when hitting the front halfway up the straight, she possesses a turn of foot and that won the day. Likely to stay even further and sure to improve for the outing, she will probably next be seen in the Prix Saint-Alary, and a tilt at the Epsom Oaks is not out of the question.
**Ecoute (USA)**, who tried to make her superior fitness tell, set a decent gallop from the start and, after being passed in the straight, ran on again in the closing stages. She probably needs softer ground to show her best and will take on the winner again in the Prix Saint-Alary.
**Wedding Gift (FR)** was held up for a late run but, by the time she arrived on the scene, the race was over. She is just short of Group standard, but a decent listed race should come her way this season.
**Motzki (FR)**, always in contention, was outpaced in the straight and lost third place inside the final furlong. She may turn out for the German 1000 Guineas at Dusseldorf next Sunday.

## 906a PRIX GANAY (Gp 1) (4-Y.O+ C & F)
3-20 (3-34) **1m 2f 110y** £65,876.00 (£26,350.00: £13,175.00: £6,588.00)

| | Horse | | Pos | SP | RR | SF |
|---|---|---|---|---|---|---|
| 622a* | **Valanour (IRE)** (AdeRoyerDupre,France) **4-9-2** GMosse (trckd ldrs pllng hrd: 4th st: qckndd 1f out: led ins fnl f: r.o) | — | 1 | | 129 | 70 |
| 680* | **Luso** (CEBrittain) **4-9-2** MJKinane (a.p: led 2f out tl ins fnl f: kpt on wl u.p) | ½ | 2 | | 128 | 69 |
| | **Swain (IRE)** (AFabre,France) **4-9-2** TJarnet (a.p: rdn st: ev ch wl over 1f out: kpt on one pce fnl f) | nk | 3 | | 128 | 69 |
| | **Spectrum (IRE)** (PWChapple-Hyam) **4-9-2** JReid (hld up in rr: smooth hdwy 2f out: rdn & unable qckn fnl f) | 2½ | 4 | | 124 | 65 |
| | **Muncie (IRE)** (AFabre,France) **4-8-13** OPeslier (hld up: rdn 2f out: r.o one pce) | 1 | 5 | | 119 | 60 |
| 438a4 | **Diamond Mix (IRE)** (AFabre,France) **4-9-2** SGuillot (hld up in rr: nvr nr to chal) | s.h | 6 | | 122 | 63 |
| 622a5 | **Tot Ou Tard (IRE)** (JForesi,France) **6-9-2** WMongil (mid div: nt pce to chal) | 1 | 7 | | 121 | 62 |
| 622a4 | **Marildo (FR)** (DSmaga,France) **9-9-2b** FHead (led to 2f out: wknd) | 2½ | 8 | | 117 | 58 |
| 622a2 | **Carling (FR)** (MmePBarbe,France) **4-8-13** TThulliez (hld up: n.m.r in st: nvr able to chal) | hd | 9 | | 114 | 55 |
| 623a* | **Slicious** (VCaruso,Italy) **4-9-2** CAsmussen (prom early: rdn over 2f out: wknd) | ½ | 10 | | 116 | 57 |

**10 Rn**

**2m 10.9** (2.90) P-M 2.20F: 1.20F 3.40F 1.70F (17.80F) OWNER S A Aga Khan (CHANTILLY) BRED H.H.Aga Khan Farms S.C.

**622a* Valanour (IRE)**, once again presented in perfect condition by his trainer, easily justified favouritism and won his second Group One event at Longchamp. Taking a good tug early because of the steady pace in the first few furlongs, he was galloping all over his rivals in the straight and, when asked to go on at the furlong marker, produced an explosive turn of foot. A top-class four-year-old, his stamina was not tested on this occasion as he had his favourite good to firm ground, but he will be very difficult to beat in the Prix D'Ispahan and is then likely to go on for Ascot for possibly the Prince Of Wales's Stakes. He could also have targets such as the Eclipse and the Arlington Million, and he has enough speed to make his presence felt in Group One company over a mile.

**680* Luso** ran a very brave race but had no answer when the winner slipped into overdrive. Always well placed, he joined the battle with Swain two furlongs out but, hard ridden, had given all he had. This was a very different performance to his one in the Arc, but his trainer thinks he was over the top on that occasion. He has filled out during the winter and, probably better suited to a longer distance, will now go for the Coronation Cup at Epsom.

**Swain (IRE)**, a beautifully-balanced individual who has done well during the winter, was racing over a distance short of his best. Sent on early in the straight, he lacked the necessary acceleration and fitness to finish in the first two, but this was a really promising effort and it would be very surprising if he does not win a Group One race in the near future. The long-term target must be the Arc but in the meantime he goes to Epsom for the Coronation Cup, and he is certainly a colt to keep a very close eye on this season.

**Spectrum (IRE)** looked as if he would cruise to victory a furlong and a half out, but his stride began to shorten when put under pressure. Held up in last, he was brought up the centre of the track to make a run, but simply blew up as it was his first run of the season and the ground was probably a little too firm. An exciting prospect, he will have the Eclipse as one of his main targets and is sure to improve for the outing.

## 907a PRIX D'HEDOUVILLE (Gp 3) (4-Y.O+)
4-15 (4-36) **1m 4f** £28,986.00 (£10,540.00: £5,270.00: £2,635.00)

| Horse | | Pos | SP | RR | SF |
|---|---|---|---|---|---|
| **Percutant** (DSmaga,France) **5-8-9** CAsmussen | — | 1 | | 116 | 32 |
| **Rainbow Dancer (FR)** (PBary,France) **5-8-11** DBoeuf | 2 | 2 | | 115 | 31 |
| **Bobinski** (AFabre,France) **4-8-9** TJarnet | 1½ | 3 | | 112 | 27 |
| **De Quest** (AFabre,France) **4-9-4** PatEddery | 3 | | | — | — |

**7 Rn**

**2m 33.9** (7.90) P-M 2.50F: 1.50F 2.50F (SF 7.10F) OWNER Baron T de Zuylen de Nyevelt (LAMORLAYE) BRED Baron T. de Zuylen

**Percutant**, back to the form that made him a Classic prospect two years ago, moved smoothly into the lead a furlong and a half out and had the race sewn up a few strides later. He nearly died over the winter with a hock infection, but that is very much in the past now. Not the easiest of horses, he is going the right way at the moment and now heads for the Prix Jean de Chaudenay at Deauville.

**Rainbow Dancer (FR)** put in a good effort in the final furlong and was running on well at the line. A slightly fragile horse who is not easy to train, he is pretty useful when right and was giving a couple of pounds to the winner. He deserves to pick up a group race this season.

**Bobinski** looked beaten halfway up the straight but then ran on again near the finish. This was his second race since being fired and he certainly seemed to stay twelve furlongs well. He has been extremely unlucky in the past and may be allowed to take his chance in the Jean de Chaudenay.

**De Quest**, giving 9lb to the winner, was not given a hard race when beaten more than a furlong out. Making his seasonal debut here and racing on ground which was probably a little firm for his liking, he will improve enormously for the outing.

# 0799a-SAN SIRO (Milan, Italy) (R-H) (Yielding)
## Sunday April 28th

## 908a PREMIO CESATE MAIDEN (3-Y.O F)
3-15 (3-25) **1m 2f** £8,120.00

| | Horse | | Pos | SP | RR | SF |
|---|---|---|---|---|---|---|
| 719a3 | **Alzabella (IRE)** (JWHills) **3-9-2** TQuinn | — | 1 | | — | — |
| | **Sopran Benda (ITY)** (JHeloury,Italy) **3-9-2** MBotti | 5¼ | 2 | | — | — |
| | **Tancia (ITY)** (AAiello,Italy) **3-9-2** SDettori | 4¼ | 3 | | — | — |

**10 Rn**

**2m 11.0** (17.00) TOTE 23L: 12L 12L 14L (359L) OWNER Mr M. Wauchope (LAMBOURN)

**719a Alzabella (IRE)** gained her first victory in Italy. Travelling well throughout in third, she joined the leader over two furlongs out and hit the front approaching the final furlong. Soon putting daylight between herself and her rivals, she went on to score a comfortable victory.

## 909a PREMIO AMBROSIANO (Listed) (4-Y.O+)
3-40 (3-59) **1m 2f** £24,360.00

| | Horse | | Pos | SP | RR | SF |
|---|---|---|---|---|---|---|
| 623a2 | **Tarhelm (IRE)** (GColleo,Italy) **4-8-11** MLatorre | — | 1 | | 105 | — |
| | **Ice and Glacial (IRE)** (GBotti,Italy) **4-8-11** EBotti | 2 | 2 | | 102 | — |
| 623a3 | **New Herald (IRE)** (MCiciarelli,Italy) **7-9-1b** AParravani | ½ | 3 | | 105 | — |

581³ **Captain Horatius (IRE)** (JLDunlop) **7-8-11** TQuinn (btn 6 3/4l) ........ 5 — —
7 Rn

**2m 6.9** (12.90) TOTE 31L: 16L 22L (71L) OWNER Scuderia Andy Capp BRED Scuderia Andy Capp in Ireland
**581 Captain Horatius (IRE)** put up a fairly lack-lustre display and finished a disappointing fifth. Racing in third, he was rousted along three furlongs from home, but found very little. He is capable of much better.

# 0880-**HAMILTON** (R-H) (Soft, Heavy patches)

## Friday May 3rd

WEATHER: unsettled WIND: almost nil

## 910 E.B.F. LOCH STRIVEN MEDIAN AUCTION MAIDEN STKS (2-Y.O F) (Class F)

2-15 (2-17) **5f 4y** £2,836.00 (£796.00: £388.00) Stalls: Low GOING: 0.51 sec per fur (GS)

| | | | SP | RR | SF |
|---|---|---|---|---|---|
| 538² | **Tazibari** (DMoffatt) **2-8-8**(3) DarrenMoffatt(4) (lw: cl up: led ½-wy tl rdn & hdd over 1f out: kpt on to ld wl ins fnl f) .......— | 1 | 4/1³ | 54 | — |
| | **Bollero (IRE)** (JBerry) **2-8-11** JCarroll(1) (leggy: scope: dwlt: sn prom: rdn & rn green 2f out: led over 1f out: hdd & nt qckn wl ins fnl f) .......½ | 2 | 7/2² | 52 | — |
| 729⁵ | **Life On The Street** (RHannon) **2-8-11** KDarley(5) (prom: effrt & ev ch 2f out: rdn & btn over 1f out) .......15 | 3 | 4/7¹ | 5 | — |
| 807⁸ | **Alimerjam** (JWhite) **2-8-11** DaleGibson(6) (s.i.s: sn outpcd: effrt & hdwy over 1f out: nrst fin) .......nk | 4 | 50/1 | 4 | — |
| 624⁶ | **Flood's Flyer (IRE)** (NTinkler) **2-8-11** LCharnock(3) (chsd ldrs: rdn along bef ½-wy: btn wl over 1f out) .......1½ | 5 | 100/1 | — | — |
| 585⁸ | **Hiltons Executive (IRE)** (EJAlston) **2-8-11** SDWilliams(2) (led tl hdd ½-wy: sn rdn & btn) .......9 | 6 | 33/1 | — | — |

(SP 111.8%) **6 Rn**

**67.2 secs** (8.90) CSF £16.96 TOTE £4.20: £1.80 £2.20 (£9.70) OWNER Cowga Partners (CARTMEL) BRED P. G. Airey and R. R. Whitton
**538 Tazibari** gained compensation for her narrow debut defeat on this course and showed plenty of courage in doing so. (4/1: op 5/2)
**Bollero (IRE)** looked the most likely winner as she struck the front more than a furlong out, but she was unable to repel the winner towards the finish. She should be able to go one better. (7/2: 5/2-4/1)
**729 Life On The Street** proved a disappointment. After showing up in the front rank, she stopped to nothing approaching the final furlong. (4/7)
**Alimerjam**, who missed the break at the start and was badly outpaced, stayed on all too late. She is bred to get further. (50/1)

## 911 LOCH GOIL LIMITED STKS (0-65) (4-Y.O+) (Class F)

2-45 (2-46) **5f 4y** £2,605.00 (£730.00: £355.00) Stalls: Low GOING: 0.51 sec per fur (GS)

| | | | SP | RR | SF |
|---|---|---|---|---|---|
| 762¹¹ | **Just Bob (60)** (SEKettlewell) **7-8-11** JFortune(4) (lw: dwlt: swtchd to far side: trckd ldr: led 2f out: sn clr: easily) .......— | 1 | 6/1³ | 75? | 36 |
| 762³ | **My Cherrywell (52)** (LRLloyd-James) **6-8-11b** TWilliams(3) (b.off hind: chsd ldrs stands' side: rdn 2f out: kpt on: no ch w wnr far side) .......9 | 2 | 8/1 | 46++ | 7 |
| 806¹³ | **Rinus Manor (IRE) (40)** (EJAlston) **5-8-11** SDWilliams(7) (swtchd to far side: led tl hung left & hdd 2f out: wknd over 1f out) .......nk | 3 | 33/1 | 45? | 6 |
| 882⁹ | **Domicksky (50)** (MRChannon) **8-8-6**(5) PPMurphy(5) (sn pushed along & bhd stands' side: styd on same pce fnl 2f: n.d) .......2½ | 4 | 20/1 | 37++ | — |
| 814³ | **Canovas Heart (65)** (BobJones) **7-8-9**(5) ADaly(1) (lw: led stands' side group to ½-wy: sn rdn & no ex) .......4 | 5 | 5/2² | 28++ | — |
| 659* | **Garnock Valley (65)** (JBerry) **6-9-0** JCarroll(6) (lw: a chsng ldrs stands' side: drvn along ½-wy: btn wl over 1f out) .......8 | 6 | 6/5¹ | 2++ | — |
| *835*¹¹ | **Swan At Whalley (60)** (MartynWane) **4-8-11** KDarley(2) (cl up stands' side: led ½-wy: sn hdd & wknd) .......¾ | 7 | 14/1 | —++ | — |

(SP 113.8%) **7 Rn**

**64.3 secs** (6.00) CSF £45.68 TOTE £8.20: £4.90 £4.40 (£46.10) OWNER Mr J. Fotherby (MIDDLEHAM) BRED Mrs D. Whittingham
**IN-FOCUS: It is unlikely that many of the jockeys who chose to race up the stands' rail are going to appear on Mastermind with "the effect of the draw" as their specialist subject.**
**659 Just Bob** was one of two to be switched to race on the far side of the track where the ground was faster. In front two furlongs out, he won easily. (6/1)
**762 My Cherrywell** ran creditably, coming out on top of those on the stands' side, but she had no chance with the winner on the other side of the course. (8/1)
**617 Rinus Manor (IRE)**, another to be switched to the far side, did the donkey work for the winner until hanging left two furlongs out and then being able to find nothing more. (33/1)
**762 Domicksky**, who was making his second appearance in twenty-four hours, last won a race in June 1994. (20/1)
**814 Canovas Heart** blazed a trail down the stands' side to halfway before going out tamely. (5/2: 7/4-11/4)
**659* Garnock Valley**, driven along with the stands'-side group at halfway, was a spent force well over a furlong out. (6/5)
**750 Swan At Whalley** (14/1: 10/1-16/1)

## 912 BOLLINGER CHAMPAGNE CHALLENGE SERIES GENTLEMENS' H'CAP (0-70) (3-Y.O+) (Class F)

3-20 (3-20) **1m 3f 16y** £2,598.00 (£728.00: £354.00) Stalls: High GOING: 0.51 sec per fur (GS)

| | | | SP | RR | SF |
|---|---|---|---|---|---|
| 853⁹ | **Calder King (61)** (JLEyre) **5-11-7v**(4) MrVLukaniuk(6) (cl up: led over 2f out: sn rdn: kpt on fnl f) .......— | 1 | 4/1 | 71 | 9 |
| 547¹⁰ | **Swinging Sixties (IRE) (64)** (GLMoore) **5-11-10**(4) MrKGoble(1) (b: lw: hld up in rr: hdwy to chse ldrs 4f out: rdn along & n.m.r 3f out: wandered u.p over 1f out: styd on ins last) .......1 | 2 | 7/2³ | 73 | 11 |
| 760⁴ | **Old School House (46)** (TJNaughton) **3-9-3**(4) MrKSantana(4) (in tch: hdwy & prom 4f out: rdn over 2f out: kpt on fnl f) .......½ | 3 | 3/1² | 54 | — |
| 620⁶ | **Me Cherokee (45)** (CWThornton) **4-10-9** MrMHNaughton(2) (lw: led: set stdy pce tl strly pressed & qcknd 4f out: hdd over 2f out: sn hrd rdn: kpt on ins fnl f) .......½ | 4 | 7/4¹ | 52 | — |
| 739¹² | **Hey Up Dolly (IRE) (50)** (JJO'Neill) **4-10-10**(4) MrLCorcoran(3) (chsd ldrs: wnt cl up over 5f out: rdn over 3f out: btn 2f out) .......16 | 5 | 16/1 | 34 | — |

(SP 109.5%) **5 Rn**

**2m 43.1** (23.70) CSF £16.25 TOTE £4.90: £2.50 £1.80 (£5.60) OWNER Mr D. Clarkson (HAMBLETON) BRED Bellmor Stud
LONG HANDICAP Old School House 9-6
WEIGHT FOR AGE 3yo-17lb
**619 Calder King**, competently handled, went to the front more than two furlongs out and was kept up to his work to keep his rivals at bay. (4/1)

**469* Swinging Sixties (IRE)**, held up in a slowly-run race, made headway half a mile out but then did not get the run of the race. Slightly short of room and speed, he wandered under pressure before staying on late in the day. (7/2: 5/2-4/1)
**760 Old School House**, in with every chance as the tempo increased half a mile out, then got outpaced before staying on stoutly again inside the final furlong. (3/1)
**620 Me Cherokee**, who made the running, set a modest gallop until quickening the tempo half a mile out. Headed more than two furlongs from the finish, she soon came under strong pressure and was staying on again towards the line. (7/4)
**Hey Up Dolly (IRE)** raced prominently until fading out of the picture in the final quarter-mile. (16/1)

## 913 SCOTTISH EQUITABLE/JOCKEYS ASSOCIATION H'CAP (0-95) (3-Y.O+) (Class C)

3-55 (3-55) **1m 1f 36y** £7,295.00 (£2,210.00: £1,080.00: £515.00) Stalls: High GOING: 0.51 sec per fur (GS)

| | | | | SP | RR | SF |
|---|---|---|---|---|---|---|
| 765[3] | **Clifton Fox (78)** (JAGlover) **4-9-4** SDWilliams(5) (dwlt: hld up: rdn along over 3f out: hung rt u.p: swtchd on outside to ld wl ins fnl f) | — | **1** | 5/2[2] | 90 | 53 |
| | **Ten Past Six (88)** (MartynWane) **4-10-0** DeanMcKeown(2) (bit bkwd: chsd ldrs: rdn along over 3f out: kpt on wl towards fin) | ½ | **2** | 20/1 | 99 | 62 |
| | **Sarmatian (USA) (65)** (MDHammond) **5-8-5** GDuffield(6) (plld hrd: trckd ldr: led over 3f out: sn strly pressed: hdd & no ex wl ins fnl f) | 1 | **3** | 7/2[3] | 74 | 37 |
| 771[5] | **Loveyoumillions (IRE) (83)** (MJohnston) **4-9-9** JWeaver(3) (lw: led: hdd over 3f out: rallied gamely & ev ch tl nt qckn wl ins fnl f) | 1¾ | **4** | 9/4[1] | 89 | 52 |
| 766[5] | **Efharisto (71)** (JWhite) **7-8-11** DaleGibson(1) (hld up: effrt & hdwy over 2f out: nt pce of ldrs fnl 2f) | 2 | **5** | 5/1 | 74 | 37 |
| 628[5] | **Nigel's Lad (IRE) (83)** (PCHaslam) **4-9-9** JFortune(4) (lw: in tch: rdn along 4f out: outpcd fnl 2f) | ½ | **6** | 12/1 | 85 | 48 |

(SP 110.7%) **6 Rn**

**2m 4.5** (10.20) CSF £33.90 TOTE £3.30: £1.50 £3.00 (£20.30) OWNER P and S Partnership (WORKSOP) BRED Crest Stud Ltd
**765 Clifton Fox** owed this to the strength of his jockey. Having missed the break, he persistently hung to his right in behind his rivals and it was not until well inside the final furlong that he gained the day. (5/2: 7/4-11/4)
**Ten Past Six**, a 10,000 guineas purchase out of Barry Hills' stable last Autumn, showed promise for his new connections here. Never far away, he kept on well towards the finish and would probably prefer better ground. (20/1)
**Sarmatian (USA)**, who raced keenly, went to the front more than three furlongs out and gamely kept his rivals at bay until the front two went past him in the final 50 yards. (7/2: op 9/4)
**771 Loveyoumillions (IRE)**, who attempted to make all the running, rallied in great style after being headed more than three furlongs out, but had nothing more to give inside the final furlong. (9/4)
**766 Efharisto** made a short-lived effort three furlongs out, but was just lacking the pace of the leaders in the final quarter-mile. (5/1)
**628 Nigel's Lad (IRE)**, ridden along to hold his place half a mile out, was unable to pose a serious threat in the final two furlongs. (12/1: op 7/1)

## 914 HOLY LOCH RATING RELATED MAIDEN STKS (0-60) (3-Y.O) (Class F)

4-30 (4-36) **1m 65y** £2,675.00 (£750.00: £365.00) Stalls: High GOING: 0.51 sec per fur (GS)

| | | | | SP | RR | SF |
|---|---|---|---|---|---|---|
| 885[2] | **Danico (57)** (SCWilliams) **3-8-9**(5) ADaly(7) (in tch: hdwy 4f out: rdn over 2f out: led 1f out: edgd rt: kpt on) | — | **1** | 14/1 | 66 | 29 |
| 851[5] | **Alpine Joker (58)** (MrsJRRamsden) **3-9-0** JFEgan(2) (lw: hld up: gd hdwy on ins over 2f out: n.m.r over 1f out: kpt on ins fnl f) | 1 | **2** | 4/1[1] | 64 | 27 |
| | **Flash In The Pan (IRE) (55)** (MBell) **3-8-11** JCarroll(8) (b: in tch: rdn along & outpcd 3f out: styd on appr fnl f) | 2½ | **3** | 5/1[3] | 54 | 17 |
| 761[3] | **Dungeon Princess (IRE) (60)** (MRChannon) **3-8-6**(5) PPMurphy(3) (chsd ldr: led 3f out: hrd rdn 2f out: hdd & no ex 1f out) | 1¾ | **4** | 6/1 | 51 | 14 |
| *463*[6] | **Hever Golf Eagle (52)** (TJNaughton) **3-9-0** JWeaver(4) (lw: in tch: rdn along 3f out: one pce fnl 2f) | 2½ | **5** | 7/1 | 51 | 14 |
| 705[11] | **Salsian (56)** (SCWilliams) **3-8-11** KDarley(1) (lw: b.hind: chsd ldrs: effrt 3f out: btn wl over 1f out) | 5 | **6** | 6/1 | 36 | — |
| | **Silent Guest (IRE) (60)** (SirMarkPrescott) **3-9-0** GDuffield(6) (unruly in stalls: hld up in rr: effrt 3f out: no imp) | 1½ | **7** | 9/2[2] | 39 | 2 |
| 595[9] | **Petite Heritiere (56)** (MJRyan) **3-8-6**(5) MBaird(9) (led tl hdd 3f out: sn rdn: wknd 2f out) | nk | **8** | 10/1 | 33 | — |
| 803[7] | **Ordained (46)** (EJAlston) **3-8-11** SDWilliams(5) (in tch tl rdn & wknd fnl 3f) | 6 | **9** | 16/1 | 21 | — |

(SP 117.6%) **9 Rn**

**1m 55.6** (11.50) CSF £65.67 TOTE £10.40: £2.80 £2.20 £1.80 (£11.20) Trio £109.60 OWNER Mr P. Geoghan (NEWMARKET) BRED Coral'S Farm and Stud
**885 Danico**, who ran in a claimer here twenty four hours earlier, was driven into the lead at the furlong pole and, despite showing a tendency to go to his right, kept on well to repel the challenge of the runner-up. (14/1: 10/1-16/1)
**851 Alpine Joker** did not have a lot of room to manoeuvre when launching his challenge more than a furlong out but could find only one speed inside the final furlong. (4/1)
**Flash In The Pan (IRE)** was taken off his legs more than three furlongs out but did some good work in the closing stages. She will probably benefit from a longer distance. (5/1)
**761 Dungeon Princess (IRE)** went for home at the three-furlong marker but soon came under pressure and had nothing more to give from a furlong out. (6/1: op 7/2)
**Hever Golf Eagle** raced in touch with the leaders, but was unable to make any impression in the final quarter-mile. (7/1)
**Salsian** (6/1: 4/1-7/1)
**Silent Guest (IRE)** (9/2: 5/2-5/1)
**Petite Heritiere** (10/1: 7/1-12/1)

## 915 MCKIBBIN GUMMERS H'CAP (0-80) (3-Y.O) (Class D)

5-00 (5-03) **1m 65y** £3,951.65 (£1,197.20: £585.10: £279.05) Stalls: High GOING: 0.51 sec per fur (GS)

| | | | | SP | RR | SF |
|---|---|---|---|---|---|---|
| 775* | **Forest Boy (67)** (KMcAuliffe) **3-8-13b**[1] 5x JFEgan(5) (lw: chsd ldr: led wl over 2f out tl rdn & hdd over 1f out: rallied to ld again towards fin) | — | **1** | 5/2[2] | 76 | 46 |
| 775[4] | **Green Gem (BEL) (65)** (SCWilliams) **3-8-11** KDarley(3) (hld up: hdwy over 3f out: rdn to ld over 1f out: hdd & no ex towards fin) | ¾ | **2** | 12/1 | 73 | 43 |
| 693[8] | **Tabriz (71)** (JDBethell) **3-9-3** JWeaver(1) (led: rdn & hdd wl over 2f out: rallied u.p tl no ex appr fnl f) | 3½ | **3** | 7/1[3] | 72 | 42 |
| 687[3] | **Sweetness Herself (72)** (MJRyan) **3-8-13**(5) MBaird(4) (chsd ldrs tl grad lost pl fr 2f out) | 1¾ | **4** | 12/1 | 69 | 39 |
| | **Pasternak (75)** (SirMarkPrescott) **3-9-7** GDuffield(2) (lw: hld up: effrt & hdwy 4f out: rdn & no imp 2f out: eased fnl f) | 5 | **5** | 8/11[1] | 63 | 33 |

(SP 114.4%) **5 Rn**

**1m 53.6** (9.50) CSF £23.14 TOTE £2.90: £1.30 £3.00 (£8.90) OWNER Highgrove Developments Ltd (LAMBOURN) BRED J. B. H. Stevens

**775* Forest Boy**, blinkered for the first time, duly completed his hat-trick and showed tremendous determination to do so. (5/2)
**775 Green Gem (BEL)** looked to have the measure of the winner when taking the lead more than a furlong out, but was outbattled towards the finish. (12/1)
**509* Tabriz** set a brisk pace until collared more than two furlongs out and had nothing more to give in the closing stages. (7/1: 5/1-8/1)
**687 Sweetness Herself**, who chased the leaders until gradually losing her pitch in the final two furlongs, was not knocked about and is open to improvement. (12/1)
**Pasternak**, who has developed into an eyecatching horse, looked ill at ease on the ground and was allowed to come home more or less in his own time when his chance had gone in the final furlong. He will do better on a sounder surface. (8/11)

T/Plpt: £442.20 (19.06 Tckts). T/Qdpt: £43.50 (19.92 Tckts). O'R

# 0692-NEWMARKET (R-H) (Good to firm, Good patches)

## Friday May 3rd

WEATHER: sunny periods & cool WIND: str half bhd

## 916 NGK SPARK PLUGS ARLINGTON MAIDEN AUCTION STKS (2-Y.O) (Class E)

2-00 (2-01) **5f** **(Rowley)** £5,253.50 (£1,568.00: £749.00: £339.50) Stalls: Centre GOING minus 0.29 sec per fur (GF)

| | | | | SP | RR | SF |
|---|---|---|---|---|---|---|
| 683$^{2}$ | **Dame Laura (IRE)** (PFICole) **2-9-0** TQuinn(6) (lw: a cl up: led over 1f out: r.o wl) | — | 1 | 9/4$^{1}$ | 76 | 43 |
| 452$^{2}$ | **Magical Times** (RBoss) **2-8-11** PatEddery(1) (cl up: effrt over 1f out: kpt on) | 1 | 2 | 9/2$^{3}$ | 70 | 37 |
| 729$^{3}$ | **March Star (IRE)** (JARToller) **2-8-10** WCarson(12) (racd alone far side: a w ldrs: no ex ins fnl f) | nk | 3 | 5/1 | 68 | 35 |
| 706$^{5}$ | **Hangover Square (IRE)** (RHannon) **2-9-1** LDettori(5) (lw: led tl hdd over 1f out: no ex) | 2½ | 4 | 100/30$^{2}$ | 65 | 32 |
| | **Latin Master (IRE)** (RHannon) **2-8-4**(3) DaneO'Neill(3) (w'like: leggy: s.i.s: sn in tch: kpt on wl fnl f) | nk | 5 | 20/1 | 56+ | 23 |
| | **Supercal** (DRCElsworth) **2-8-6** RCochrane(8) (leggy: scope: lw: s.i.s: hdwy 2f out: styd on towards fin) | 2½ | 6 | 20/1 | 47+ | 14 |
| | **Ocker (IRE)** (MHTompkins) **2-8-11** PRobinson(2) (w'like: scope: lw: prom: shkn up over 1f out: sn outpcd) | ¾ | 7 | 8/1 | 50 | 17 |
| 815$^{9}$ | **Time Can Tell** (CMurray) **2-8-11** MTebbutt(9) (prom to ½-wy: sn outpcd) | 3 | 8 | 50/1 | 40 | 7 |
| 639$^{7}$ | **Gresatre** (CADwyer) **2-8-11** CDwyer(10) (sn bhd) | 4 | 9 | 50/1 | 27 | — |
| | **Sandkatoon (IRE)** (JSMoore) **2-7-13**(3) NVarley(13) (lt-f: neat: nvr wnt pce) | ¾ | 10 | 33/1 | 16 | — |
| | **Grovefair Lad (IRE)** (BJMeehan) **2-9-1** BDoyle(7) (cmpt: bkwd: nvr wnt pce) | nk | 11 | 50/1 | 24 | — |
| 657$^{4}$ | **Neon Deion (IRE)** (SCWilliams) **2-8-11** JTate(4) (spd to ½-wy: wknd qckly) | ¾ | 12 | 33/1 | 21 | — |
| | **Miss Barcelona (IRE)** (MJPolglase) **2-8-6** NCarlisle(11) (cmpt: bit bkwd: sn bhd) | 3½ | 13 | 33/1 | 5 | — |
| | | | | (SP 124.0%) | | **13 Rn** |

**60.49 secs** (1.79) CSF £12.87 TOTE £2.70: £1.10 £2.10 £1.80 (£6.40) Trio £7.00 OWNER Mr A. J. Morrison (WHATCOMBE) BRED Mervyn Stewkesbury

**683 Dame Laura (IRE)** learnt from her first run and made no mistake this time, winning convincingly. (9/4: 5/4-5/2)
**452 Magical Times** kept straight this time but his action left a lot to be desired. However, he did run well and will surely find a race or two before long. (9/2: 3/1-5/1)
**729 March Star (IRE)** spent most of the race running on her own towards the far side, which must have been a disadvantage and she kept battling all the way home. She should get further. (5/1)
**706 Hangover Square (IRE)** again showed plenty of speed but his measure had been taken with over a furlong left. (100/30: 9/4-7/2)
**Latin Master (IRE)**, slow to realise what was required, gradually warmed to the task and should have learnt plenty. (20/1)
**Supercal** put in an eyecatching run after a slow start and is one to keep on the right side. (20/1)
**Ocker (IRE)** looked the part but got left behind on the downhill run approaching the final furlong and should now do better as a result. (8/1: tchd 12/1)

## 917 ROYAL MAIL ANGLIA H'CAP (0-100) (3-Y.O) (Class C)

2-35 (2-36) **7f** **(Rowley)** £9,600.00 (£2,850.00: £1,350.00: £600.00) Stalls: High GOING minus 0.29 sec per fur (GF)

| | | | | SP | RR | SF |
|---|---|---|---|---|---|---|
| | **Angel Chimes (75)** (JEBanks) **3-8-0**(3) JStack(5) (hdwy 3f out: chal ins fnl f: led nr fin) | — | 1 | 9/1 | 84 | 41 |
| 571$^{3}$ | **Golden Pond (IRE) (71)** (RFJohnsonHoughton) **3-7-13** AMcGlone(8) (cl up: led ½-wy tl ct cl home) | s.h | 2 | 15/2 | 80 | 37 |
| | **Warming Trends (85)** (SirMarkPrescott) **3-8-13** WWoods(4) (bhd: hdwy 2f out: edged rt: styd on wl towards fin) | 1¼ | 3 | 9/2$^{2}$ | 91 | 48 |
| | **Charlie Chang (IRE) (75)** (RHannon) **3-8-0**(3)ow3 DaneO'Neill(1) (w'like: prom: outpcd 2f out: styd on ins fnl f) | nk | 4 | 5/1$^{3}$ | 80 | 34 |
| 676$^{6}$ | **Rebel County (IRE) (68)** (DJSCosgrove) **3-7-10** NAdams(7) (bhd: effrt over 2f out: hmpd over 1f out: styd on towards fin) | nk | 5 | 8/1 | 73 | 30 |
| 676* | **Sky Dome (IRE) (80)** (MHTompkins) **3-8-8** PRobinson(9) (in tch: n.m.r & lost pl 3f out: styd on again fnl f: no imp) | ½ | 6 | 4/1$^{1}$ | 84 | 41 |
| | **Paint It Black (85)** (RHannon) **3-8-13** RHughes(3) (bhd: effrt over 1f out: sme late hdwy) | 1¼ | 7 | 16/1 | 86 | 43 |
| | **Polish Spring (IRE) (85)** (BWHills) **3-8-13** MHills(11) (lw: led to ½-wy: eased whn btn fnl f) | 1¼ | 8 | 11/1 | 83 | 40 |
| | **Truancy (90)** (MBell) **3-9-4** MFenton(12) (in tch: effrt 3f out: sn outpcd) | ½ | 9 | 14/1 | 87 | 44 |
| | **Expensive Taste (84)** (MRStoute) **3-8-12** JReid(6) (plld hrd: prom over 4f) | 4 | 10 | 9/1 | 72 | 29 |
| 445$^{3}$ | **Courting Danger (72)** (DRGandolfo) **3-8-0** JQuinn(10) (w ldrs to ½-wy: wknd qckly) | 14 | 11 | 16/1 | 28 | — |
| | | | | (SP 124.5%) | | **11 Rn** |

**1m 26.4** (1.90) CSF £72.29 CT £322.36 TOTE £17.80: £4.10 £2.40 £1.90 (£63.80) Trio £75.30 OWNER Mr Giles Pritchard-Gordon (NEWMARKET) BRED Giles W. Pritchard-Gordon

IN-FOCUS: **None of these looked particularly well in, and they finished in a heap, with nothing finishing to real effect.**
**Angel Chimes** just got there after looking likely to make it entering the final furlong, but she is improving and still gives the impression that easier ground would also help. (9/1)
**571 Golden Pond (IRE)** is an honest sort who keeps trying hard but just lacks a turn of foot. Her consistency should bring rewards. (15/2)
**Warming Trends** ran really well but was always feeling this fast ground and, tending to hang right, will do a deal better once he can get his toe in. (9/2)
**Charlie Chang (IRE)** failed to handle the downhill section approaching the final furlong but was keeping on at the end. With a bit easier ground, better should follow. (5/1: 7/2-11/2)
**676 Rebel County (IRE)** again ran well but just got slightly messed about at a vital stage and then finished to some purpose. She will do better soon. (8/1)
**676* Sky Dome (IRE)** was always a bit short of room and was certainly short of the necessary pace to get out of trouble. This effort is best ignored. (4/1)

**Paint It Black** should be all the better for this first effort of the season and was never any nearer than at the finish. (16/1)
**Polish Spring (IRE)** showed bags of speed and was given a sympathetic ride when beaten. (11/1: 8/1-12/1)
**Truancy** (14/1: 10/1-16/1)

## 918 SUNLEY NEWMARKET STKS (Listed) (3-Y.O C) (Class A)

3-05 (3-06) **1m 2f (Rowley)** £12,652.00 (£4,552.00: £2,176.00: £880.00: £340.00) Stalls: Centre GOING minus 0.29 sec per fur (GF)

| | | | | SP | RR | SF |
|---|---|---|---|---|---|---|
| | **Mick's Love (IRE)** (SbinSuroor) **3-8-8** LDettori(3) (w ldr: led over 3f out: rdn appr fnl f: hld on wl) | — | 1 | 3/1[2] | 103 | 53 |
| 736[2] | **Bahamian Knight (CAN) (106)** (DRLoder) **3-8-8** TQuinn(4) (lw: cl up: effrt 2f out: chal ins fnl f: r.o) | s.h | 2 | 10/1 | 103 | 53 |
| 736* | **Ramooz (USA) (104)** (BHanbury) **3-8-8** JStack(2) (lw: hld up: hdwy on bit to chal 2f out: sn rdn: nt qckn ins fnl f) | 2 | 3 | 6/1[3] | 100 | 50 |
| 640* | **Clever Cliche** (HRACecil) **3-8-8** PatEddery(1) (hld up: effrt 2f out: hung rt u.p & nt qckn) | 2½ | 4 | 8/11[1] | 96 | 46 |
| 671[7] | **Qasida (IRE)** (CEBrittain) **3-8-8** BDoyle(5) (led tl hdd over 3f out: wknd wl over 1f out) | 4 | 5 | 50/1 | 89 | 39 |
| | | | | (SP 108.2%) | | **5 Rn** |

**2m 5.5** (1.90) CSF £23.44 TOTE £2.90: £1.50 £2.40 (£5.40) OWNER Godolphin (NEWMARKET) BRED Collinstown Stud Farm Ltd
OFFICIAL EXPLANATION **Clever Cliche: was unable to act on the fast ground and never let himself down.**
IN-FOCUS: **The first Godolphin runner of the season was weak in the market, but that did not seem to be as accurate a guide to their chances as it was last term at this meeting.**
**Mick's Love (IRE)**, on ground faster than he has previously encountered, is obviously still improving and is certainly tough, which is a quality that will bring him further success. (3/1: 7/4-100/30)
**736 Bahamian Knight (CAN)** enjoyed the step up in distance and kept battling all the way to the line. He should get further. (10/1: op 11/2)
**736* Ramooz (USA)** travelled on the bridle and it looked a question of how far two furlongs out, but he failed to see the trip out. Judging by this, he is going to win some top-class mile events. (6/1: 5/1-8/1)
**640* Clever Cliche** failed to handle this fast ground when off the bit and looks likely to be a soft-ground specialist. (8/11)
**671 Qasida (IRE)**, thrown in at the deep-end here, was well outclassed in the final two furlongs but will no doubt have learnt plenty from the experience. (50/1)

## 919 PERTEMPS JOCKEY CLUB STKS (Gp 2) (4-Y.O+) (Class A)

3-40 (3-43) **1m 4f (Rowley)** £33,111.00 (£12,249.00: £5,874.50: £2,397.50: £948.75: £369.25) Stalls: High GOING minus 0.29 sec per fur (GF)

| | | | | SP | RR | SF |
|---|---|---|---|---|---|---|
| | **Riyadian (120)** (PFICole) **4-8-9** TQuinn(2) (lw: a gng wl: chal on bit 2f out: disp ld ins fnl f: shkn up & r.o) | — | 1 | 10/11[1] | 122 | 59 |
| | **Burooj (110)** (DMorley) **6-8-9** WCarson(9) (h.d.w: hld up: hdwy on bit 3f out: nt clr run over 1f out: qcknd to disp ld ins fnl f: no ex towards fin) | nk | 2 | 12/1 | 122 | 59 |
| 680[7] | **Sacrament (108)** (MRStoute) **5-8-9** JReid(3) (lw: a.p: led wl over 2f out tl ins fnl f: kpt on wl) | 1 | 3 | 12/1 | 120 | 57 |
| | **Midnight Legend (114)** (LMCumani) **5-8-9** PatEddery(5) (h.d.w: bkwd: led tl hdd wl over 2f out: hmpd wl over 1f out: sn btn) | 5 | 4 | 10/1[3] | 114 | 51 |
| 726[5] | **Commoner (USA) (112)** (RHannon) **4-8-9** RHughes(8) (a chsng ldrs: effrt over 3f out: one pce fnl 2f) | hd | 5 | 33/1 | 114 | 51 |
| *535a*[3] | **Valley of Gold (FR)** (SbinSuroor) **4-8-11** MJKinane(6) (h.d.w: hld up: effrt 4f out: rdn & no imp fnl 3f) | 6 | 6 | 10/1[3] | 108 | 45 |
| 831[3] | **Naked Welcome (101)** (MJFetherston-Godley) **4-8-9** WRyan(7) (bhd: hdwy over 3f out: rdn & no imp) | s.h | 7 | 12/1 | 105 | 42 |
| 456* | **Juyush (USA) (108)** (BWHills) **4-8-9** RHills(4) (prom tl rdn & wknd over 2f out) | 2½ | 8 | 20/1 | 102 | 39 |
| *396a*[3] | **Moonshell (IRE)** (SbinSuroor) **4-8-11** LDettori(1) (lw: cl up tl wknd qckly over 3f out: sn t.o) | dist | 9 | 6/1[2] | — | — |
| | | | | (SP 115.6%) | | **9 Rn** |

**2m 32.2** (1.70) CSF £12.04 TOTE £2.10: £1.20 £1.90 £2.60 (£7.40) Trio £47.40 OWNER H R H Prince Fahd Salman (WHATCOMBE) BRED Newgate Stud Co.
OFFICIAL EXPLANATION **Moonshell (IRE): never let herself down on the ground.**
IN-FOCUS: **This looked a solid Group two beforehand and the form ought to be pretty reliable.**
**Riyadian**, who improved no end last season, seems to have continued that and won with more in hand than the winning margin suggests. (10/11: op Evens)
**Burooj** is a real character who is still improving. Although meeting trouble here more than once, the winner always had his measure but, when things go his way, he will win decent races. (12/1)
**680 Sacrament** is certainly on his way back and put up a splendid show here and better now looks likely. (12/1)
**Midnight Legend** looked full of condition but certainly needed it and ran well until blowing up in the last quarter-mile. A Group event will come his way this season. (10/1: 7/1-11/1)
**726 Commoner (USA)** keeps running well in this type of event but is just short of a turn of foot to really stake his claim. Perhaps more use should be made of him. (33/1)
**535a Valley of Gold (FR)** looked pretty fit but could never get into this and probably needs easier ground. (10/1: op 6/1)
**831 Naked Welcome**, full of himself beforehand, always found this company too hot. (12/1)
**456* Juyush (USA)** is basically a stayer and was left behind in the last two and a half furlongs. (20/1)
**396a Moonshell (IRE)**, who ran miserably, was virtually pulled up and now retires to stud. (6/1: 4/1-13/2)

## 920 MILCARS LEASING H'CAP (0-85) (3-Y.O+) (Class D)

4-15 (4-16) **1m 2f (Rowley)** £3,890.00 (£1,190.00: £590.00: £290.00) Stalls: Centre GOING minus 0.29 sec per fur (GF)

| | | | | SP | RR | SF |
|---|---|---|---|---|---|---|
| 843* | **Golden Touch (USA) (60)** (NACallaghan) **4-8-3** WCarson(12) (hld up: hdwy 3f out: led ins fnl f: edgd lft: r.o) | — | 1 | 9/2[2] | 74 | 48 |
| 634* | **Spillo (83)** (LMCumani) **3-8-11** LDettori(11) (trckd ldrs: led 2f out tl ins fnl f: r.o) | ½ | 2 | 2/1[1] | 96 | 55 |
| 690[11] | **Askern (66)** (DHaydnJones) **5-8-9** AMackay(2) (lw: hld up: hdwy 3f out: kpt on u.p: nt pce to chal) | 2½ | 3 | 11/1 | 75 | 49 |
| 817[15] | **Manabar (64)** (MJPolglase) **4-8-7** NCarlisle(8) (plld hrd: bhd tl hdwy over 2f out: rdn & nt qckn appr fnl f) | ½ | 4 | 33/1 | 72 | 46 |
| | **Sovereign Page (USA) (77)** (BHanbury) **7-9-3**(3) JStack(5) (b: trckd ldrs: effrt over 2f out: one pce) | 3 | 5 | 11/2[3] | 81 | 55 |
| *553*[6] | **Errant (62)** (DJSCosgrove) **4-8-5** JQuinn(9) (lw: b: trckd ldrs: effrt 3f out: one pce fnl 2f) | ¾ | 6 | 11/1 | 64 | 38 |
| | **Domitia (USA) (65)** (MBell) **4-8-8** MFenton(6) (b: prom: effrt 3f out: outpcd fnl 2f) | 2½ | 7 | 20/1 | 63 | 37 |
| | **Tissue of Lies (USA) (78)** (MJohnston) **3-8-6** JReid(3) (led 3f: wl outpcd & lost pl 3f out: n.d after) | 6 | 8 | 9/1 | 67 | 26 |
| *309*[9] | **Conic Hill (IRE) (62)** (JPearce) **5-8-5** GBardwell(7) (cl up: led after 3f out tl over 3f out: wknd 2f out) | s.h | 9 | 40/1 | 51 | 25 |
| *410*[7] | **Bernard Seven (IRE) (85)** (CEBrittain) **4-10-0b** BDoyle(10) (lw: w ldrs: led over 3f out: hdd 2f out: wknd) | 1 | 10 | 40/1 | 72 | 46 |
| 682[6] | **Statajack (IRE) (84)** (DRCElsworth) **8-9-13b** TQuinn(4) (a bhd: lost tch fnl 3f) | 12 | 11 | 9/1 | 52 | 26 |

778[8] **Buddy's Friend (IRE) (55)** (RJRWilliams) **8-7-7**(5)ow2 MHenry(1) (in tch tl rdn & wknd 3f out)...........................2 **12** 50/1 20 —
(SP 118.1%) **12 Rn**

**2m 5.63** (2.03) CSF £13.14 CT £85.93 TOTE £3.80: £1.20 £1.70 £3.30 (£4.40) Trio £49.50 OWNER Mrs Rita Godfrey (NEWMARKET) BRED Woodcote Stud Ltd
WEIGHT FOR AGE 3yo-15lb
**IN-FOCUS: These looked a fully exposed bunch with three exceptions, and two of those fought out the finish without looking that far ahead of the Handicapper.**
**843* Golden Touch (USA)**, despite showing a tendency to edge left, always looked in command here and won nicely. (9/2)
**634* Spillo** showed a really good action on the way down and ran a game race, but was always second best in the closing stages. He is on the upgrade. (2/1: 6/4-9/4)
**Askern** can be a funny customer, but was certainly in a co-operative mood here and kept staying on, albeit in vain. (11/1)
**670 Manabar** ran too freely for his own good and is probably happier over a slightly shorter trip run at a stronger pace. (33/1)
**Sovereign Page (USA)** has not won for almost two years but did run quite well after a lengthy absence here. (11/2)
**553 Errant** has done most of his running on the All-Weather and was short of toe in the closing stages on this fast ground. (11/1: 7/1-12/1)
**Domitia (USA)** did not show the best of actions for this fast ground and was left struggling once the pace was really on. (20/1)

## 921 EQUITY FINANCIAL COLLECTIONS MAIDEN STKS (3-Y.O F) (Class D)
4-50 (4-51) **7f (Rowley)** £5,481.00 (£1,638.00: £784.00: £357.00) Stalls: Centre GOING minus 0.29 sec per fur (GF)

| | | | SP | RR | SF |
|---|---|---|---|---|---|
| | **Ta Rib (USA)** (EALDunlop) **3-8-11** WCarson(7) (lw: trckd ldrs: led 3f out: rdn & r.o wl fnl f) .....— | **1** | 11/4 2 | 90 | 39 |
| | **Fatefully (USA)** (SbinSuroor) **3-8-11** LDettori(14) (w'like: scope: led tl hdd 3f out: kpt on: no ch w wnr).....5 | **2** | Evens 1 | 79 | 28 |
| | **Seirenes** (PTWalwyn) **3-8-11** PatEddery(3) (prom: effrt over 2f out: hung rt: kpt on).....2½ | **3** | 12/1 | 73 | 22 |
| | **Scarpetta (USA)** (JWHills) **3-8-11** RHills(6) (leggy: scope: hld up: hdwy over 2f out: kpt on: nvr able chal).....nk | **4** | 14/1 | 72 | 21 |
| | **Royal Jade** (BWHills) **3-8-11** MHills(10) (b.off hind: chsd ldrs: rdn over 2f out: r.o one pce).....2½ | **5** | 10/1 3 | 67 | 16 |
| | **Love Bateta (IRE)** (RHannon) **3-8-8**(3) DaneO'Neill(12) (still unf: prom: effrt over 2f out: nt qckn).....nk | **6** | 33/1 | 66 | 15 |
| | **Passage Creeping (IRE)** (LMCumani) **3-8-11** JReid(9) (chsd ldrs tl grad wknd fnl 2f).....½ | **7** | 20/1 | 65 | 14 |
| | **Ember** (LMCumani) **3-8-11** OUrbina(13) (w'like: plld hrd: effrt 3f out: hung rt & btn over 1f out).....3½ | **8** | 33/1 | 57 | 6 |
| | **Hannalou (FR)** (SPCWoods) **3-8-11** WWoods(8) (b.off hind: s.i.s: sn trckng ldrs: wknd fnl 2f).....hd | **9** | 33/1 | 56 | 5 |
| 710[16] | **Kowtow** (MDIUsher) **3-8-11** RStreet(5) (bkwd: w ldrs 4f: sn lost pl).....nk | **10** | 100/1 | 56 | 5 |
| 710[11] | **Desert Skimmer (USA)** (MBell) **3-8-11** MFenton(2) (bhd fnl 3f).....3 | **11** | 50/1 | 49 | — |
| | **Atienza (USA)** (SCWilliams) **3-8-6**(5) MHenry(11) (lw: chsd ldrs tl rdn & wknd 3f out).....nk | **12** | 66/1 | 48 | — |
| | **Mujtahida (IRE)** (RWArmstrong) **3-8-11** RPrice(1) (w'like: lost tch fnl 3f).....8 | **13** | 20/1 | 30 | — |
| | **Amazing Grace (IRE)** (SCWilliams) **3-8-11** JTate(4) (cmpt: dwlt: sn wl t.o).....dist | **14** | 50/1 | — | — |
| | | | (SP 124.9%) | **14 Rn** | |

**1m 27.26** (2.76) CSF £5.75 TOTE £3.70: £1.70 £1.40 £2.70 (£2.80) Trio £8.50 OWNER Mr Hamdan Al Maktoum (NEWMARKET) BRED Shadwell Estate Co., Ltd. and Shadwell Farm, Inc.
**IN-FOCUS: The first two home were the only ones quoted at single-figure prices.**
**Ta Rib (USA)**, on fast ground for the first time, won in tremendous style, going right away in the closing stages. She should certainly get further. (11/4)
**Fatefully (USA)**, a lean type of filly, showed a particularly good action and ran well until finding the winner far too good in the last furlong and a half. (Evens)
**Seirenes** ran pretty well and gave the impression that, with easier ground, she will do better. (12/1: op 7/1)
**Scarpetta (USA)** showed plenty of promise here and, once she is put over further, there should be plenty of improvement in the pipe-line. (14/1)
**Royal Jade** has plenty of speed but was going nowhere when ridden in the last two furlongs. (10/1: op 6/1)
**Love Bateta (IRE)** failed to impress on looks and made little impression in the race. (33/1)
**Passage Creeping (IRE)** was given a good blow out here and should be all the better for it. (20/1)
**Ember**, who needed this, raced too freely and then hung right when tired. (33/1)
**Kowtow** showed plenty of speed this time and, once she was beaten, was given an easy time. Better looks likely as she gets fitter. (100/1)

## 922 NEWMARKET CHALLENGE WHIP MAIDEN STKS (3-Y.O) (Class G)
5-20 (5-20) **1m (Rowley)** Stalls: Centre GOING minus 0.29 sec per fur (GF)

| | | | SP | RR | SF |
|---|---|---|---|---|---|
| 703[12] | **Miss Pravda** (PTWalwyn) **3-8-9** PatEddery(2) (lw: mde all: qcknd over 2f out: easily).....— | **1** | 5/2 2 | 58+ | 7 |
| | **Beau Bruno** (MBell) **3-9-0** MFenton(1) (w'like: leggy: trckd wnr: effrt over 2f out: sn btn).....20 | **2** | 1/3 1 | 23 | — |
| | | | (SP 103.6%) | **2 Rn** | |

**1m 43.55** (6.25) TOTE £2.00: OWNER Lord Howard de Walden (LAMBOURN) BRED Lord Howard de Walden
**Miss Pravda** beat her sole opponent with a deal of ease. (5/2: 6/4-3/1)
**Beau Bruno** showed a very poor action going down and, once the race began in the last three furlongs, he was all at sea. (1/3)

T/Jkpt: £7,770.70 (0.1 Tckts); £9,850.20 to Newmarket 4/5/96. T/Plpt: £33.80 (862.97 Tckts). T/Qdpt: £4.40 (423.32 Tckts). AA

# 0916-NEWMARKET (R-H) (Good to firm, Good fnl 6f)
## Saturday May 4th
WEATHER: overcast & cold WIND: mod half bhd

## 923 MAYER PARRY CONDITIONS STKS (3-Y.O) (Class C)
2-00 (2-01) **1m 4f (Rowley)** £5,548.00 (£1,768.00: £844.00) Stalls: Low GOING minus 0.22 sec per fur (GF)

| | | | SP | RR | SF |
|---|---|---|---|---|---|
| | **Dushyantor (USA)** (HRACecil) **3-9-0** PatEddery(3) (nt grwn: hld up: hdwy 4f out: led over 2f out: qcknd & edgd rt: pushed out).....— | **1** | Evens 1 | 99++ | 19 |
| 804* | **Lallans (IRE)** (MJohnston) **3-9-0** JWeaver(2) (lw: led after 1f: qcknd over 3f out: hdd over 2f out: unable qckn).....2 | **2** | 9/4 2 | 96 | 16 |
| 578* | **Samraan (USA)** (JLDunlop) **3-9-0** WCarson(1) (led 1f: chal 3f out: n.m.r & outpcd wl over 1f out).....3½ | **3** | 7/2 3 | 92 | 12 |
| | | | (SP 103.0%) | **3 Rn** | |

**2m 39.86** (9.36) CSF £3.01 TOTE £1.60: (£1.30) OWNER Mr K. Abdulla (NEWMARKET) BRED Juddmonte Farms
**IN-FOCUS: The winner was amazingly not sent off odds-on, with Bookmakers unusually generous in the over-round percentages.**

**Dushyantor (USA)**, in a race that has been farmed by the master of Warren Place in the nineties, only needed to be pushed out for a comfortable success. He has not grown much since his two-year-old days, but he is highly thought of, and has probably done enough to warrant a run in the Derby. (Evens)
**804* Lallans (IRE)**, a clear-cut winner of his maiden at Carlisle last week, decided that he would have to force the pace with neither of his rivals prepared to do so. Overtaken passing the Bushes, he gave his all but was nowhere near good enough on the day. The German Derby could be his immediate target instead of a rematch with the winner at Epsom. (9/4)
**578* Samraan (USA)**, who walked stiffly behind in the paddock, was happy to accept a lead once in action. Joining issue three furlongs out, he was feeling the strain when squeezed for room in the Dip and his measure had been taken. His trainer was disappointed with this performance. (7/2: 9/4-4/1)

## 924 CITROEN FLEET MAIDEN STKS (2-Y.O) (Class D)

2-35 (2-35) **5f (Rowley)** £4,980.50 (£1,484.00: £707.00: £318.50) Stalls: Low GOING minus 0.22 sec per fur (GF)

| Horse | Btn | Pos | SP | RR | SF |
|---|---|---|---|---|---|
| **Abou Zouz (USA)** (DRLoder) **2-9-0** LDettori(2) (w'like: a w ldrs: led wl over 1f out: r.o wl) | — | 1 | 11/10[1] | 94+ | 51 |
| **Taufan Rookie (IRE)** (RHannon) **2-9-0** RHughes(6) (leggy: scope: s.i.s: hdwy after 2f: kpt on wl ins fnl f) | 1¾ | 2 | 11/1 | 88+ | 45 |
| **Grand Lad (IRE)** (RWArmstrong) **2-9-0** RHills(5) (w'like: scope: led tl hdd wl over 1f out: unable qckn u.p) | 1½ | 3 | 11/2[3] | 78+ | 41 |
| **Hawait (IRE)** (BWHills) **2-9-0** MHills(3) (cmpt: scope: bit bkwd: sn trckng ldrs: outpcd over 1f out: styd on fnl f) | s.h | 4 | 5/2[2] | 77 | 40 |
| **Janie's Boy** (MHTompkins) **2-9-0** PRobinson(4) (neat: unf: gd spd to ½-wy) | 5 | 5 | 25/1 | 61 | 24 |
| **Puzzlement** (CEBrittain) **2-9-0** BDoyle(1) (w'like: scope: sn prom: outpcd fr ½-wy) | ½ | 6 | 16/1 | 60 | 23 |
| **Protaras Bay** (TTClement) **2-8-9**(5) DGibbs(7) (b: b.hind: neat: sn bhd & outpcd) | 3½ | 7 | 66/1 | 49 | 12 |

(SP 111.1%) **7 Rn**

**60.37 secs** (1.67) CSF £12.14 TOTE £2.20: £1.50 £2.50 (£6.20) OWNER Mr Wafic Said (NEWMARKET) BRED G. Watts Humphrey Jnr
IN-FOCUS: **These were a good-looking bunch and the form could turn out to be more than decent.**
**Abou Zouz (USA)**, an attractive colt described his trainer as the best two-year-old he has trained, won this in the style of a very useful individual and either the Coventry or the Norfolk Stakes at Royal Ascot will be his target next month. (11/10: 4/5-5/4)
**Taufan Rookie (IRE)**, a scopey half-brother to three winners, could not match strides with the useful winner, but he was getting down to some serious work up the hill and is considered Royal Ascot material. (11/1: 8/1-14/1)
**Grand Lad (IRE)**, whose dam was a very smart sprinter, did not look fully tuned up for this debut. Setting the pace until the winner decided to go, he has a lot going for him and could clash swords again at the Royal Meeting. (11/2)
**Hawait (IRE)**, poised to challenge until getting outpaced running into the Dip, stayed on again towards the finish and he will be all the wiser for the experience. (5/2: 2/1-7/2)

## 925 TORCH MOTOR POLICIES AT LLOYDS RATED STKS H'CAP (0-100) (4-Y.O+) (Class B)

3-05 (3-06) **1m 2f (Rowley)** £10,081.20 (£3,730.80: £1,790.40: £732.00: £291.00: £114.60) Stalls: Low GOING minus 0.22 sec per fur (GF)

| | Horse | Btn | Pos | SP | RR | SF |
|---|---|---|---|---|---|---|
| | **Ball Gown (84)** (DTThom) **6-8-4**(3) DRMcCabe(13) (lw: hld up: hdwy 3f out: led wl over 1f out: r.o strly) | — | 1 | 12/1 | 100 | 62 |
| 580[3] | **Hardy Dancer (87)** (GLMoore) **4-8-10** SWhitworth(2) (lw: hld up: hdwy over 2f out: qcknd to chal over 1f out: edgd rt: nt pce of wnr) | 1¾ | 2 | 11/2[2] | 100 | 62 |
| | **Major Change (84)** (RHannon) **4-8-4**(3) DaneO'Neill(6) (a.p: ev ch 2f out: kpt on one pce appr fnl f) | 4 | 3 | 20/1 | 91 | 53 |
| | **Polydamas (84)** (MRStoute) **4-8-7** JReid(12) (bit bkwd: trckd ldrs: chal 3f out: one pce fnl 2f) | 1¾ | 4 | 10/1 | 88 | 50 |
| 580[2] | **Special Dawn (IRE) (90)** (JLDunlop) **6-8-13** PatEddery(5) (hld up: pushed along over 3f out: no imp) | s.h | 5 | 4/1[1] | 94 | 56 |
| 682[8] | **At Liberty (IRE) (87)** (RHannon) **4-8-10** TQuinn(9) (lw: bhd tl styd on u.p fnl 2f) | 1¾ | 6 | 16/1 | 88 | 50 |
| 455[13] | **Beyond Doubt (84)** (LordHuntingdon) **4-8-7** DHarrison(11) (sn pushed along: nvr on terms) | nk | 7 | 11/2[2] | 85 | 47 |
| | **Better Offer (IRE) (98)** (GHarwood) **4-9-7** AClark(14) (hld up: hdwy over 4f out: sn w ldrs: wknd fnl 2f) | ½ | 8 | 12/1 | 98 | 60 |
| | **My Learned Friend (84)** (AHide) **5-8-7** WWoods(3) (mid div tl wknd 3f out) | 7 | 9 | 20/1 | 73 | 35 |
| | **Time for Action (IRE) (87)** (MHTompkins) **4-8-10** PRobinson(8) (led tl hdd & wknd wl over 1f out) | 6 | 10 | 33/1 | 66 | 28 |
| 679[14] | **Amrak Ajeeb (IRE) (85)** (BHanbury) **4-8-8** WRyan(7) (sn drvn along: a bhd) | ¾ | 11 | 20/1 | 63 | 25 |
| | **Korambi (91)** (CEBrittain) **4-9-0** BDoyle(1) (prom 7f) | s.h | 12 | 12/1 | 69 | 31 |
| | **Verzen (IRE) (96)** (DRLoder) **4-9-5** LDettori(4) (bit bkwd: prom tl wknd over 2f out: eased whn btn) | 3 | 13 | 6/1[3] | 69 | 31 |

(SP 120.3%) **13 Rn**

**2m 4.97** (1.37) CSF £71.74 CT £1,214.15 TOTE £17.30: £3.50 £2.00 £5.30 (£34.50) Trio £124.60 OWNER Mr C. V. Lines (NEWMARKET) BRED J. M. Greetham
LONG HANDICAP Ball Gown 8-4 Polydamas 8-6 Major Change 8-6
IN-FOCUS: **This looked very competitive beforehand and was run at a fast, true pace.**
**Ball Gown**, well supported in the market despite her starting price, swooped to lead running into the Dip and won readily. She is an ultra-consistent mare and thoroughly deserved to win a decent prize. (12/1)
**580 Hardy Dancer**, produced to win his race approaching the final furlong, found the mare too smart for him in the race to the line. He has not won a race since the spring of last year but he is running up to his mark and deserves to gain reward. (11/2)
**Major Change** has only ever won a maiden race but he ran extremely well here and, sure to strip fitter for the run, will not be long in staking his claim. (20/1)
**Polydamas**, carrying plenty of surplus condition, performed with credit in this competitive handicap. Though he may well need another run, he could be very much on the upgrade this term. (10/1)
**580 Special Dawn (IRE)** could not muster the pace to deliver his challenge but he did keep staying on and he should not be hard pressed to regain losses. (4/1)
**At Liberty (IRE)** struggled with the pace and never going got going until far too late. This trip is hardly far enough for him now. (16/1)
**Beyond Doubt**, nudged along from the start, was always a few lengths off the pace and he could not summon the speed to land a blow. (11/2)
**Korambi** (12/1: op 8/1)

## 926 PERTEMPS 2000 GUINEAS STKS (Gp 1) (3-Y.O C & F) (Class A)

3-45 (3-50) **1m (Rowley)** £122,262.00 (£45,258.00: £21,729.00: £8,895.00: £3,547.50: £1,408.50) Stalls: High GOING minus 0.22 sec per fur (GF)

| Horse | Btn | Pos | SP | RR | SF |
|---|---|---|---|---|---|
| **Mark of Esteem (IRE)** (SbinSuroor) **3-9-0** LDettori(2) (hld up stands' side: hdwy to ld over 1f out: hld on gamely) | — | 1 | 8/1 | 124 | 77 |
| **Even Top (IRE) (113)** (MHTompkins) **3-9-0** PRobinson(5) (h.d.w: trckd ldrs stands' side: chal fnl 2f: hrd rdn fnl f: r.o wl) | s.h | 2 | 40/1 | 124 | 77 |

| | | | | SP | RR | SF |
|---|---|---|---|---|---|---|
| | **Bijou d'Inde (110)** (MJohnston) **3-9-0** JWeaver(4) (h.d.w: a.p stands' side: led over 3f out tl over 1f out: rallied u.p nr fin) | hd | **3** | 14/1 | 124 | 77 |
| 695[2] | **Alhaarth (IRE) (120)** (MajorWRHern) **3-9-0** WCarson(12) (lw: hld up centre: effrt 3f out: sn rdn: nt pce to chal) | 6 | **4** | 2/1 [1] | 112+ | 65 |
| 695* | **Beauchamp King (120)** (JLDunlop) **3-9-0** JReid(6) (lw: swtg: plld hrd: hld up stands' side: effrt u.p 2f out: nvr nr ldrs) | 2 | **5** | 9/2 [2] | 108 | 61 |
| 727* | **Danehill Dancer (IRE) (120)** (NACallaghan) **3-9-0** MJKinane(11) (lw: racd centre: hld up: effrt over 2f out: one pce) | 1 | **6** | 10/1 | 106+ | 59 |
| | **Masehaab (IRE) (104)** (JLDunlop) **3-9-0** RHills(3) (chsd ldrs stands' side: one pce fnl 2f) | 1 | **7** | 200/1 | 104 | 57 |
| 681[3] | **World Premier (112)** (CEBrittain) **3-9-0** BDoyle(1) (led stands' side tl over 3f out: sn rdn along & grad wknd) | 1¼ | **8** | 66/1 | 101 | 54 |
| | **Leonine (IRE)** (PFICole) **3-9-0** TQuinn(9) (trckd ldrs centre over 5f) | ½ | **9** | 50/1 | 100+ | 53 |
| | **Royal Applause (120)** (BWHills) **3-9-0** MHills(8) (lw: b: led & clr centre: wknd & hdd over 2f out: sn btn) | 4 | **10** | 15/2 | 92+ | 45 |
| 694* | **Storm Trooper (USA) (116)** (HRACecil) **3-9-0** PatEddery(10) (lw: chsd ldr centre over 5f: sn rdn & wknd) | 3½ | **11** | 5/1 [3] | 85+ | 38 |
| 681[5] | **Tumbleweed Ridge (113)** (BJMeehan) **3-9-0** RHughes(7) (hld up stands' side: effrt 3f out: n.m.r & wknd 2f out) | ¾ | **12** | 66/1 | 84 | 37 |
| 574* | **Regiment (IRE) (108)** (RHannon) **3-9-0** KDarley(13) (lw: swtg: racd centre: bhd fnl 3f) | 3½ | **13** | 33/1 | 77+ | 30 |

(SP 117.6%) **13 Rn**

**1m 37.59** (0.29) CSF £222.36 TOTE £7.00: £2.60 £8.30 £3.10 (£197.90) Trio £2,013.20 OWNER Godolphin (NEWMARKET) BRED Sheikh Mohammed Bin Rashid Al Maktoum

STEWARDS' ENQUIRY Dettori susp. 13-20/5/96, Robinson susp. 13-16/5/96 & Weaver susp. 13-14/5/96 (excessive use of whip). Dettori fined £500 (dismounting bef ent wnrs enclosure).

IN-FOCUS: **Both rails seemed to be where the best ground was all meeting, which could have had a bearing on the result, and the first three were drawn five and under (along with two outsiders). Alhaarth and Beauchamp King finished together again, albeit the other way round, and would doubtless have been a lot closer had they raced closer to the stands' rail. The Derby will answer a few questions.**

**Mark of Esteem (IRE)**, who had wintered in Dubai, looked trained to the minute. Pushing the pace on the stands' side, he took charge coming to the final furlong and, despite tying up near the line, deservedly held on. Very short on experience, he will improve on this but, whether he has the stamina for the Derby, only time will tell. (8/1)

**Even Top (IRE)** gives the impression that he will need further than a mile this term, but he has the will to win and it was only on the nod that he lost out. This was a very punishing first race of the year and his next race should tell us if he has the constitution to take it. (40/1)

**Bijou d'Inde** ran his best race yet and showed he has what it takes by staying on doggedly up the final climb to fail narrowly. A winner at this trip in his first season, he definitely needs further now and his future looks rosy. (14/1)

**695 Alhaarth (IRE)** gained his revenge on Beauchamp King but could not confirm his superiority over the winner and, though he came out best of those racing in the centre of the track, he was never going well enough to mount a serious challenge. (2/1)

**695* Beauchamp King**, very geed up in the preliminaries, raced keenly under restraint but did not find a lot when asked for his effort, and was always fighting a lost cause. (9/2: 3/1-5/1)

**727* Danehill Dancer (IRE)** is hardly bred to stay further than a mile and he was only finding his stride up the hill. (10/1)

**Masehaab (IRE)** definitely needs more cut in the ground than he had here but he was not disgraced in his biggest test yet, and he has certainly trained on. (200/1)

**Royal Applause** lost his unbeaten record by tearing off like a cat on hot bricks and his forceful tactics had come to an end passing the Bushes. He will soon regain winning ways, but a step down in distance would seem the most obvious solution. (15/2)

## 927 DUBAI RACING CLUB PALACE HOUSE STKS (Gp 3) (3-Y.O+) (Class A)

4-20 (4-21) **5f (Rowley)** £20,467.20 (£7,564.80: £3,622.40: £1,472.00: £576.00: £217.60) Stalls: High GOING minus 0.22 sec per fur (GF)

| | | | | SP | RR | SF |
|---|---|---|---|---|---|---|
| 673[5] | **Cool Jazz (113)** (CEBrittain) **5-9-1** MJKinane(1) (bhd: sn drvn along: hdwy over 1f out: str run fnl f: led cl home) | — | **1** | 16/1 | 115 | 63 |
| 681[7] | **Lucky Lionel (USA) (112)** (RHannon) **3-8-9** PatEddery(7) (bhd: drvn & hdwy over 1f out: ev ch ins fnl f: r.o) | ¾ | **2** | 11/1 | 116 | 55 |
| 565* | **Westcourt Magic (109)** (MWEasterby) **3-8-3** KDarley(4) (lw: a chsng ldrs: ev ch ins fnl f: kpt on) | nk | **3** | 9/2 [2] | 109 | 48 |
| 673[3] | **Struggler** (DRLoder) **4-9-1** RHughes(8) (hdwy 2f out: led ins fnl f: sn hdd: unable qckn) | ¾ | **4** | 13/2 | 109 | 57 |
| 507[5] | **Ya Malak (110)** (JWPayne) **5-8-12** BThomson(5) (s.i.s: sn chsng ldrs: chal ins fnl f: unable qckn) | hd | **5** | 12/1 | 106 | 54 |
| | **Eveningperformance (112)** (HCandy) **5-8-9** JReid(2) (lw: led tl ins fnl f) | 1½ | **6** | 5/1 [3] | 98 | 46 |
| | **Blue Iris (109)** (MAJarvis) **3-8-0** PRobinson(3) (w ldr: rdn over 1f out: no ex fnl f) | 1½ | **7** | 3/1 [1] | 93 | 32 |
| | **Double Quick (IRE) (102)** (MJohnston) **4-8-9** JWeaver(9) (h.d.w: spd centre over 3f) | 1½ | **8** | 14/1 | 89 | 37 |
| 507[6] | **Lucky Parkes (99)** (JBerry) **6-8-9** JCarroll(11) (racd centre: chsd ldrs over 3f) | nk | **9** | 33/1 | 88 | 36 |
| | **Takadou (IRE) (91)** (MissLCSiddall) **5-8-12** RCochrane(12) (h.d.w: outpcd & bhd tl sme late hdwy) | 1¾ | **10** | 100/1 | 85 | 33 |
| | **Hever Golf Rose (119)** (TJNaughton) **5-9-3** PaulEddery(6) (b.hind: chsd ldrs 3f) | ½ | **11** | 11/2 | 88 | 36 |

(SP 121.1%) **11 Rn**

**59.7 secs** (1.00) CSF £163.48 TOTE £19.10: £3.30 £2.30 £2.10 (£84.40) Trio £99.80 OWNER Mr Saeed Manana (NEWMARKET) BRED Saeed Manana

WEIGHT FOR AGE 3yo-9lb

IN-FOCUS: **This was a strong-looking Group three, the complexion of which changed completely in the final furlong. Those drawn high again had little joy.**

**673 Cool Jazz**, winning for the first time at the minimum trip, enjoyed a trouble-free passage up the stands'-side rail but had to work hard to get on top nearing the finish. The Kings' Stand at Royal Ascot could be a future target. (16/1)

**Lucky Lionel (USA)**, brought back to five furlongs, could not go the early pace but he picked up approaching the final furlong and had every chance until the winner's late burst beat him to the punch. (11/1)

**565* Westcourt Magic**, taking on older rivals for the first time, ran a fine race in defeat and is always going to be tough to beat. He was engaged in a barging match with the runner-up inside the last furlong but it is doubtful if it had any bearing on the outcome. (9/2)

**673 Struggler** looked the likely winner when poking his head in front 150 yards out but, on ground still a bit too lively, lacked the extra finishing speed of the principals. He is ready to return to form. (13/2: 9/2-7/1)

**507 Ya Malak** broke well enough but was slow to find his stride. Soon recovering to push the pace, he got himself with a live chance inside the final furlong, but failed to pull out that bit extra that was needed in the sprint to the post. (12/1)

**Eveningperformance** adopted her now familiar trail-blazing tactics and did not go down for the want of trying, but the final climb proved just too much. She would seem as good as ever. (5/1)

**Blue Iris** tried hard to match the very speedy Eveningperformance for pace, but she was getting the worse of that battle in the Dip and had to admit her measure taken. This was her first run against older rivals and she lost no caste in defeat. (3/1)

## 928 LADBROKES H'CAP (0-95) (3-Y.O+) (Class C)

4-50 (5-00) **6f (Rowley)** £24,855.00 (£7,440.00: £3,570.00: £1,635.00) Stalls: Low GOING minus 0.22 sec per fur (GF)

| | | | | SP | RR | SF |
|---|---|---|---|---|---|---|
| 711[8] | **Jayannpee (90)** (IABalding) **5-9-11** LDettori(10) (swtchd rt after s: chsd ldrs: led wl ins fnl f: r.o) | — | **1** | 14/1 | 101 | 76 |
| 812[2] | **Sir Joey (USA) (77)** (PGMurphy) **7-8-9**(3) SDrowne(8) (racd stands' side: hdwy over 1f out: fin wl) | nk | **2** | 16/1 | 87 | 62 |
| | **Perryston View (86)** (PCalver) **4-9-7v** JCarroll(20) (racd far side: led: clr 2f out: wknd & hdd wl ins fnl f) | 1¼ | **3** | 16/1 | 93 | 68 |
| 735* | **Stuffed (64)** (MWEasterby) **4-7-13** JQuinn(4) (racd stands' side: cl up: styd on u.p fnl f) | ¾ | **4** | 12/1 | 69 | 44 |
| 582* | **Seigneurial (90)** (GHarwood) **4-9-11** AClark(24) (hdwy far side over 1f out: nrst fin) | 1½ | **5** | 16/1 | 91 | 66 |
| 673[13] | **Montserrat (70)** (LGCottrell) **4-8-5v** WCarson(5) (led stands' side tl no ex ins fnl f) | hd | **6** | 14/1 | 71 | 46 |
| 679[11] | **Saseedo (USA) (87)** (WAO'Gorman) **6-9-8** EmmaO'Gorman(9) (swtg: racd stands' side: gd hdwy over 1f out: nvr nrr) | d.h | **6** | 20/1 | 88 | 63 |
| 711[13] | **Bowden Rose (86)** (MBlanshard) **4-9-2b**(5) CAdamson(17) (racd far side: hdwy 2f out: kpt on u.p) | hd | **8** | 33/1 | 86 | 61 |
| 806[14] | **Rich Glow (61)** (NBycroft) **5-7-7**(3) NVarley(1) (lw: racd stands' side: rdn ½-wy: nvr nrr) | nk | **9** | 50/1 | 61 | 36 |
| 711[9] | **Lord Olivier (IRE) (85)** (WJarvis) **6-9-6** JReid(22) (trckd ldrs over 4f) | ½ | **10** | 25/1 | 83 | 58 |
| 737[5] | **Castlerea Lad (82)** (RHollinshead) **7-8-12**(5) DGriffiths(21) (nvr nr ldrs) | s.h | **11** | 9/1[3] | 80 | 55 |
| | **Go Hever Golf (90)** (TJNaughton) **4-9-11** PatEddery(23) (b.hind: chsd ldrs far side over 4f) | 1 | **12** | 10/1 | 85 | 60 |
| | **Sweet Magic (84)** (PHowling) **5-9-5** PaulEddery(6) (hld up stands' side: nvr nr to chal) | s.h | **13** | 50/1 | 79 | 54 |
| 610[4] | **Tiler (IRE) (80)** (MJohnston) **4-9-1** JWeaver(12) (chsd ldrs far side over 4f) | 1¼ | **14** | 16/1 | 72 | 47 |
| 812[5] | **Gone Savage (61)** (WJMusson) **8-7-10** FNorton(3) (b: chsd ldrs stands' side over 3f) | ½ | **15** | 14/1 | 52 | 27 |
| 812[6] | **Rock Symphony (87)** (WJHaggas) **6-9-8** MHills(19) (racd far side: n.d) | 1¼ | **16** | 11/1 | 74 | 49 |
| | **Thatcherella (68)** (MajorDNChappell) **5-8-3** BThomson(18) (bkwd: spd 4f) | d.h | **16** | 8/1[2] | 55 | 30 |
| 747[6] | **La Tansani (IRE) (71)** (RHannon) **3-7-10** GBardwell(2) (in tch stands' side over 3f) | 3 | **18** | 33/1 | 50 | 15 |
| 735[15] | **Saddlehome (USA) (77)** (TDBarron) **7-8-12** KDarley(11) (trckd ldrs far side 4f) | 1½ | **19** | 33/1 | 52 | 27 |
| | **Bayin (USA) (73)** (MDIUsher) **7-8-8** RStreet(16) (s.s: a bhd) | ½ | **20** | 33/1 | 47 | 22 |
| 711[12] | **Tafahhus (76)** (MJPolglase) **4-8-11** DHarrison(7) (racd stands' side: bhd fnl 2f) | nk | **21** | 40/1 | 49 | 24 |
| 716[2] | **French Grit (IRE) (78)** (MDods) **4-8-13** WWoods(14) (lw: chsd ldrs far side: rdn & wknd wl over 1f out) | 1¼ | **22** | 10/1 | 48 | 23 |
| 812* | **Mister Jolson (76)** (RJHodges) **7-8-11** RCochrane(13) (b.nr fore: racd far side: n.d) | 1½ | **23** | 5/1[1] | 42 | 17 |
| 735[13] | **For the Present (85)** (TDBarron) **6-9-6** JFortune(15) (outpcd) | s.h | **24** | 14/1 | 51 | 26 |
| | | | | (SP 148.9%) | | **24 Rn** |

**1m 12.83** (1.03) CSF £227.83 CT £3,397.27 TOTE £18.00: £4.50 £3.40 £5.20 £2.80 (£206.90) Trio £2,907.30; £3,685.40 to Newmarket 5/5/96 OWNER Mr J. Paniccia (KINGSCLERE) BRED C. H. Bothway

LONG HANDICAP Gone Savage 7-9 Rich Glow 7-6 La Tansani (IRE) 7-9

WEIGHT FOR AGE 3yo-10lb

OFFICIAL EXPLANATION **For the Present: was found to be slightly lame the following morning, possibly the result of interference leaving the stalls.**

IN-FOCUS: **The field split into two distinct groups and neither rail looked to hold much of an advantage.**

**Jayannpee**, who ran with his tongue tied down, was winning his first race since August 1994. Ploughing a lone furrow up the centre of the track in the early stages, he decided to drift towards the far-side group after a couple of furlongs and, running on strongly on meeting the rising ground, powered through to take control inside the last 100 yards. (14/1)

**812 Sir Joey (USA)** came out of the pack on the stands' side approaching the final furlong and stayed on strongly nearing the finish, but was unfortunate to meet the winner on one of his good days. (16/1)

**Perryston View**, twice successful on the July course, ran a cracker on this seasonal debut. Forcing the pace on the far side and going clear entering the last quarter-mile, his stride shortened up the hill and he was forced to give best. An early return to form is on the cards. (16/1)

**735* Stuffed**, a very progressive individual, went with the pace on the stands' side and had every chance until failing to quicken close home. It was possible the hill caught him out. (12/1)

**582* Seigneurial**, a very poor-actioned individual, produced a determined late challenge up the far rail but found the race over before he could deliver it. (16/1)

**582 Montserrat** dictated the stands'-side group and battled on willingly when headed but, on ground much too lively for him, was found wanting in a good race to the line. (14/1)

**Saseedo (USA)**, winner of this race twelve months ago, was doing all his best work in the latter stages but the effort was always going to be too late. (20/1)

**Go Hever Golf** (10/1: 8/1-12/1)

**812 Gone Savage** (14/1: 16/1-25/1)

**716 French Grit (IRE)** (10/1: 7/1-11/1)

**812* Mister Jolson**, racing on the far side, never got in a blow against the leaders and must have had an off-day. (5/1)

## 929 CHIPPENHAM PARK CONDITIONS STKS (4-Y.O+) (Class C)

5-20 (5-28) **1m 2f (Rowley)** £5,489.20 (£1,979.20: £949.60: £388.00: £154.00) Stalls: Low GOING minus 0.22 sec per fur (GF)

| | | | | SP | RR | SF |
|---|---|---|---|---|---|---|
| 726[4] | **Florid (USA) (106)** (HRACecil) **5-8-10** PatEddery(6) (lw: hld up & prom: hdwy over 1f out: rdn to ld ins fnl f: gamely) | — | **1** | 6/4[1] | 107 | 66 |
| *535a[4]* | **Jural** (SbinSuroor) **4-8-5** LDettori(3) (led tl ins fnl f: rallied gamely u.p) | ¾ | **2** | 13/8[2] | 101 | 60 |
| | **Djais (FR)** (JRJenkins) **7-8-10** JFortune(2) (b.nr fore: bhd & outpcd tl styd on over 1f out) | 4 | **3** | 33/1 | 99 | 58 |
| | **Tinashaan (IRE) (97)** (JRFanshawe) **4-8-13** DHarrison(5) (b: hld up: effrt over 2f out: outpcd appr fnl f) | 1 | **4** | 7/1 | 101 | 60 |
| | **Tremplin (USA)** (NACallaghan) **4-8-10** MJKinane(7) (lw: disp ld over 6f: sn lost tch: t.o) | 15 | **5** | 5/1[3] | 74 | 33 |
| | | | | (SP 110.2%) | | **5 Rn** |

**2m 4.9** (1.30) CSF £4.19 TOTE £2.30: £1.30 £1.40 (£1.70) OWNER Lord Howard de Walden (NEWMARKET) BRED Lord Howard de Walden

**726 Florid (USA)**, delaying his challenge, looked to have taken the leader's measure entering the final furlong but, with that rival refusing to accept defeat, had to get serious to shake her off inside the final 50 yards. (6/4: op 9/4)

**535a Jural**, a recent arrival from the sunshine of Dubai, tried to make every post a winning one but, hard as she tried, she was forced to give best towards the finish. She has not won beyond a mile as yet but she does have the stamina to succeed at this trip. (13/8)

**Djais (FR)**, who ran over hurdles earlier in the week, was taken off his legs in the early stages and, in the circumstances, did well to finish so close. He does need more cut in the ground, but is capable of winning another race over a longer trip. (33/1)

**Tinashaan (IRE)** sat in behind the leaders, but got left behind when the pace lifted running into the Dip and, though she did stay on again, was never a serious factor. (7/1: 5/1-15/2)

**Tremplin (USA)** (5/1: 4/1-6/1)

T/Jkpt: Not won; £21,227.25 to Newmarket 5/5/96. T/Plpt: £1,325.90 (30.27 Tckts). T/Qdpt: £394.50 (6.8 Tckts). IM

# 0733-THIRSK (L-H) (Good to firm)
## Saturday May 4th
WEATHER: fine & cold WIND: mod half against

## 930 E.B.F. MARKET PLACE MEDIAN AUCTION MAIDEN STKS (2-Y.O) (Class F)
2-20 (2-22) **5f** £3,367.75 (£1,012.00: £488.50: £226.75) Stalls: High GOING minus 0.16 sec per fur (GF)

| | Horse | Dist | Pos | SP | RR | SF |
|---|---|---|---|---|---|---|
| 815[4] | **Braveheart (IRE)** (MRChannon) **2-8-9**(5) PPMurphy(4) (trckd ldrs: shkn up to ld over 1f out: styd on wl) | — | 1 | 4/1[2] | 64 | 26 |
| 699[D] | **Bolero Boy** (MWEasterby) **2-9-0** DaleGibson(12) (lw: led tl over 1f out: nt qckn) | 1¾ | 2 | 85/40[1] | 58 | 20 |
| 800[8] | **Mill End Boy** (MWEasterby) **2-8-9**(5) GParkin(2) (s.i.s: hdwy 2f out: r.o wl ins fnl f: bttr for r) | 2 | 3 | 33/1 | 52+ | 14 |
| | **Top of The Form (IRE)** (MJohnston) **2-8-9** TWilliams(9) (unf: bit bkwd: dwlt: sn chsng ldrs: rdn 2f out: grad wknd) | 1¾ | 4 | 6/1[3] | 41 | 3 |
| 800[4] | **Grate Times** (EWeymes) **2-9-0** GHind(5) (in tch: outpcd & rdn after 2f: styd on fnl f) | s.h | 5 | 9/1 | 46 | 8 |
| 706[7] | **Eager To Please** (JBerry) **2-9-0** GCarter(8) (chsd ldrs: edgd lft & wknd over 1f out) | 1¾ | 6 | 8/1 | 41 | 3 |
| | **Smokey From Caplaw** (JJO'Neill) **2-9-0** GDuffield(11) (w'like: unf: scope: s.s: outpcd & bhd tl styd on appr fnl f) | 1¼ | 7 | 33/1 | 37 | — |
| | **Gipsy Princess** (MWEasterby) **2-8-9** JFEgan(1) (leggy: unf: s.s: bhd tl stdy hdwy fnl 2f: nvr plcd to chal) | s.h | 8 | 50/1 | 32 | — |
| 585[5] | **Molly Drummond** (CWCElsey) **2-8-9** MBirch(7) (chsd ldrs: hung lft thrght: lost pl over 1f out) | 2 | 9 | 14/1 | 25 | — |
| | **Thewrightone (IRE)** (GROldroyd) **2-8-9** DMcKeown(6) (unf: bit bkwd: s.s: a bhd) | 5 | 10 | 50/1 | 9 | — |
| | **Tear White (IRE)** (TGMills) **2-9-0** AMackay(3) (w'like: unf: swvd lft s: hung violently lft & rn off crse: crashed through rails & uns rdr after 1½f) | | R | 4/1[2] | — | — |
| | | | | (SP 123.9%) | **11 Rn** | |

**61.4 secs** (3.40) CSF £13.05 TOTE £3.90: £1.90 £1.20 £10.90 (£4.80) Trio £59.20 OWNER Mr W. H. Ponsonby (UPPER LAMBOURN) BRED A. F. O'Callaghan

OFFICIAL EXPLANATION **Mill End Boy: was found to have sore shins after the race.**
**Tear White (IRE): panicked leaving the stalls and ran badly left, giving the rider no chance before crashing through the rail.**

**815 Braveheart (IRE)**, who looked very fit, got right on top in the closing stages and, quite stoutly bred, will be even better suited by six. (4/1)

**699 Bolero Boy**, who showed a good action going down, had the best of the draw but, even so, was decisively beaten in the end. (85/40)

**Mill End Boy**, who lost his chance at the start first time, was again not well away but showed definite promise, staying on strongly under a sympathetic ride inside the last. (33/1)

**Top of The Form (IRE)** is not the best of walkers but showed ability and her trainer's two-year-olds usually improve from their debut. (6/1: op 7/2)

**800 Grate Times** is still backward in his coat and should improve further. (9/1)

**Eager To Please** is an excitable sort. (8/1)

**Gipsy Princess**, a short-backed filly, was cheaply bought but showed definite promise and is a lot better than she was allowed to show here. (50/1)

**585 Molly Drummond** (14/1: 10/1-16/1)

## 931 BALDERSBY H'CAP (0-80) (3-Y.O+) (Class D)
2-50 (2-50) **5f** £4,003.00 (£1,204.00: £582.00: £271.00) Stalls: High GOING: minus 0.16 sec per fur (GF)

| | Horse | Dist | Pos | SP | RR | SF |
|---|---|---|---|---|---|---|
| *292** | **Awasha (IRE) (58)** (MissGayKelleway) **4-8-9** OUrbina(20) (b: b.hind: chsd ldrs stands' side: hrd rdn & styd on to ld ins fnl f) | — | 1 | 7/1[3] | 66 | 38 |
| 749[8] | **Sing With the Band (55)** (BAMcMahon) **5-8-6** GCarter(2) (trckd ldrs far side: nt qckn ins fnl f) | 1 | 2 | 20/1 | 60 | 32 |
| 704[9] | **Kalar (49)** (DWChapman) **7-7-9b**(5) PFessey(14) (led tl ins fnl f) | 1¼ | 3 | 20/1 | 50 | 22 |
| 610[13] | **The Scythian (73)** (BobJones) **4-9-5**(5) ADaly(11) (a chsng ldrs: styd on same pce appr fnl f) | ¾ | 4 | 20/1 | 71 | 43 |
| 812[13] | **Sally Slade (74)** (CACyzer) **4-9-11** GDuffield(21) (bhd: hdwy over 1f out: styd on wl towards fin) | s.h | 5 | 12/1 | 72 | 44 |
| 735[14] | **Insider Trader (74)** (MrsJRRamsden) **5-9-11** MDeering(5) (led far side tl over 1f out: no ex) | nk | 6 | 25/1 | 71 | 43 |
| 735[5] | **Stephensons Rocket (57)** (DNicholls) **5-8-8b** JFEgan(19) (sn chsng ldrs: rdn & hung lft ½-wy: wknd over 1f out) | 1¼ | 7 | 4/1[1] | 50 | 22 |
| 735[7] | **Tenor (58)** (DNicholls) **5-8-9** AlexGreaves(4) (a in tch: styd on same pce fnl 2f) | s.h | 8 | 12/1 | 51 | 23 |
| 735[17] | **Beau Venture (USA) (65)** (FHLee) **8-9-2** RLappin(1) (trckd ldrs: kpt on same pace fnl 2f) | s.h | 9 | 16/1 | 58 | 30 |
| 824[2] | **Montrestar (68)** (PDEvans) **3-8-10b** SSanders(18) (sn chsng ldrs: effrt & hmpd over 1f out: no imp) | s.h | 10 | 5/1[2] | 61 | 24 |
| 716[3] | **Here Comes a Star (77)** (JMCarr) **8-10-0** ACulhane(22) (lw: bhd tl sme hdwy fnl 2f: n.d) | ¾ | 11 | 10/1 | 67 | 39 |
| | **Ned's Bonanza (69)** (MDods) **7-9-6** DeanMcKeown(17) (rr div: hdwy whn n.m.r over 1f out: nvr nr ldrs) | ½ | 12 | 16/1 | 58 | 30 |
| | **Palo Blanco (73)** (TDBarron) **5-9-10** JFanning(8) (s.i.s: bhd: styng on whn hmpd ins fnl f) | ½ | 13 | 25/1 | 60 | 32 |
| | **Dominelle (49)** (TDEasterby) **4-8-0** TWilliams(3) (bhd: sme hdwy 2f out: n.d) | 1¼ | 14 | 33/1 | 32 | 4 |
| 735[11] | **Call Me I'm Blue (IRE) (76)** (NTinkler) **6-9-13** MBirch(16) (in tch: rdn ½-wy: hung lft & sn wknd) | s.h | 15 | 12/1 | 59 | 31 |
| 704[2] | **Able Sheriff (49)** (MWEasterby) **4-7-7b**(7) RMullen(7) (chsd ldrs centre 3f: sn wknd) | ½ | 16 | 10/1 | 30 | 2 |
| 617[9] | **Ultra Beet (68)** (PCHaslam) **4-8-12**(7) CarolDavison(13) (a in rr) | 1¾ | 17 | 25/1 | 44 | 16 |
| 773[12] | **Gagajulu (69)** (PDEvans) **3-8-11** GHind(15) (chsd ldrs to ½-wy: sn lost pl) | 1 | 18 | 33/1 | 42 | 5 |
| | **Silk Cottage (61)** (RMWhitaker) **4-8-12** DaleGibson(10) (sn bhd) | 6 | 19 | 33/1 | 14 | — |
| 749[19] | **Natural Key (63)** (DHaydnJones) **3-8-5** AMackay(12) (nvr wnt pce) | 1 | 20 | 20/1 | 13 | — |
| | | | | (SP 141.6%) | **20 Rn** | |

**60.4 secs** (2.40) CSF £140.46 CT £2,543.33 TOTE £6.20: £1.40 £5.90 £5.10 £4.40 (£224.80) Trio Not won; £995.13 to Newmarket 5/5/96 OWNER Mr H. Al-Mutawa (WHITCOMBE) BRED Barronstown Stud

WEIGHT FOR AGE 3yo-9lb

STEWARDS' ENQUIRY Urbina susp.15-18/5/96 (excessive & incorrect use of whip).

**Awasha (IRE)** is apparently difficult to train and spends most of her time swimming. She enjoyed a good run up the inside rail and, with maximum assistance from the saddle, was right on top at the line. (7/1)

**Sing With the Band**, whose two previous successes have been recorded on the All-weather at Southwell, ran really well from an unfavourable draw. (20/1)

**Kalar** showed all his old speed. (20/1)

**The Scythian**, who still looked as though the outing was needed, is better over six. (20/1)

**Sally Slade**, who looked very fit, had been poorly drawn on her two previous outings. She came from the back to be staying on strongly at the line. (12/1)

**Insider Trader**, poorly drawn, showed that he retains all his old speed. (25/1)

**735 Stephensons Rocket**, as usual taken to post early and fitted with a tongue-strap, wanted to do nothing but hang left. (4/1)

## 932 SPRING MAIDEN STKS (3-Y.O+) (Class D)

3-20 (3-25) **1m 4f** £3,821.00 (£1,148.00: £554.00: £257.00) Stalls: High GOING minus 0.03 sec per fur (G)

| Form | Horse | Dist | Pos | SP | RR | SF |
|---|---|---|---|---|---|---|
| 707[5] | **Smart Play (USA)** (MrsJCecil) **3-8-5** GCarter(9) (trckd ldrs: led over 2f out: hung lft: styd on strly: readily) | — | **1** | 5/2[2] | 82+ | 35 |
| | **Shirley Venture** (SPCWoods) **3-8-0** JTate(2) (w'like: leggy: scope: sn trckng ldrs: kpt on wl fnl 2f: no imp) | 1½ | **2** | 20/1 | 75 | 28 |
| | **Arctic Fancy (USA) (80)** (PWHarris) **3-8-5** GHind(8) (unruly s: sn trckng ldrs: effrt 3f out: styd on one pce) | 1¾ | **3** | 9/2[3] | 78 | 31 |
| 691[4] | **Velmez** (RGuest) **3-8-5** LCharnock(7) (trckd ldrs: kpt on same pce fnl 2f) | 1¾ | **4** | 12/1 | 75 | 28 |
| 691[2] | **Kass Alhawa** (MRStoute) **3-8-5** DeanMcKeown(3) (lft in ld after 2f: hdd over 2f out: wknd over 1f out) | 3½ | **5** | 7/4[1] | 71 | 24 |
| | **Mental Pressure** (MrsMReveley) **3-8-5** ACulhane(6) (bit bkwd: hld up: outpcd over 3f out: hdwy over 1f out: fin wl) | 2½ | **6** | 20/1 | 67 | 20 |
| 663[7] | **Sharp Command** (RWArmstrong) **3-8-5** RPrice(4) (chsd ldrs: pushed along ½-wy: wknd 2f out) | 1½ | **7** | 25/1 | 65 | 18 |
| *248*[8] | **Induna Mkubwa** (CFWall) **3-8-5** GDuffield(10) (trckd ldrs tl outpcd fnl 3f) | 2½ | **8** | 33/1 | 62 | 15 |
| *856*[7] | **Harbet House (FR)** (CACyzer) **3-8-5** SSanders(11) (mid div: effrt over 2f out: sn wknd) | hd | **9** | 50/1 | 62 | 15 |
| 804[W] | **Gildoran Sound** (TDEasterby) **3-8-0** TWilliams(1) (unruly s: led: plld hrd: rn wd & hdd bnd after 2f: lost pl 4f out) | 20 | **10** | 100/1 | 30 | — |
| | **Secondment** (LMCumani) **3-8-5** OUrbina(13) (w'like: unf: scope: s.i.s: sn bhd & drvn along: t.o 4f out) | ½ | **11** | 12/1 | 35 | — |
| | **Michelle's Ella (IRE)** (CDBroad) **4-9-5** MFenton(5) (unruly s: w ldrs: carried wd after 2f: wknd over 4f out) | 2½ | **12** | 100/1 | 26 | — |
| | **Dark Sound (IRE)** (ABMulholland) **3-8-5** MMcAndrew(12) (leggy: unf: bit bkwd: s.s: a bhd: dead) | 6 | **13** | 100/1 | 23 | — |
| | | | | (SP 119.7%) | **13 Rn** | |

**2m 37.8** (7.80) CSF £46.65 TOTE £3.70: £1.60 £4.70 £1.90 (£58.00) Trio £56.90 OWNER Mrs George Ward (NEWMARKET) BRED Joseph Taub & Dennis W. Milne

WEIGHT FOR AGE 3yo-19lb

**707 Smart Play (USA)** stepped up considerably on his first effort. Showing definite signs of greenness, he is still something of a baby and should improve further. (5/2: 7/2-9/4)

**Shirley Venture** ran a pleasing first ever race. (20/1)

**Arctic Fancy (USA)**, a handful at the start, appreciated the step up in distance. (9/2)

**691 Velmez** still does not look 100% fit and better is likely. (12/1)

**691 Kass Alhawa** did not improve for the extra two furlongs and, after being left in front, dropped away with over a furlong left to run. (7/4: Evens-15/8)

**Mental Pressure**, who has not grown from two to three, looked far from fully fit. After taking a keen grip, he dropped right back on the home turn, but really found his stride inside the last and finished full of running. Significantly this qualifies him for handicaps and he will be suited by further. (20/1)

**Secondment** (12/1: op 7/1)

## 933 THIRSK HUNT CUP H'CAP (0-90) (3-Y.O+) (Class C)

3-55 (3-57) **1m** £13,175.00 (£3,950.00: £1,900.00: £875.00) Stalls: Low GOING minus 0.03 sec per fur (G)

| Form | Horse | Dist | Pos | SP | RR | SF |
|---|---|---|---|---|---|---|
| 765[7] | **New Century (USA) (79)** (DNicholls) **4-9-8** WJO'Connor(12) (trckd ldrs: led over 2f out: shkn up over 1f out: r.o wl) | — | **1** | 13/2[2] | 93 | 68 |
| | **Sandmoor Chambray (70)** (TDEasterby) **5-8-13** MBirch(18) (a chsng ldrs: kpt on wl fnl 2f: no ch w wnr) | 2½ | **2** | 33/1 | 79 | 54 |
| 600[4] | **Chickawicka (IRE) (83)** (BPalling) **5-9-12** TSprake(9) (a chsng ldrs: kpt on same pce fnl 2f) | ¾ | **3** | 16/1 | 91 | 66 |
| 589[4] | **High Premium (69)** (RAFahey) **8-8-12** ACulhane(6) (lw: sn prom: styd on wl ins fnl f) | ½ | **4** | 11/1 | 76 | 51 |
| 641[4] | **Lookingforarainbow (IRE) (75)** (BobJones) **8-8-13**(5) ADaly(7) (s.i.s: hdwy over 2f out: hung lft: nvr rchd ldrs) | 2½ | **5** | 20/1 | 77 | 52 |
| 843[2] | **Sooty Tern (69)** (JMBradley) **9-8-7**(5) FLynch(1) (lw: led early: chsd ldrs: kpt on same pce fnl 2f) | 1 | **6** | 9/1 | 69 | 44 |
| 765[13] | **Fame Again (80)** (MrsJRRamsden) **4-9-9** NKennedy(8) (s.i.s: bhd tl styd on fnl 2f) | ¾ | **7** | 16/1 | 78 | 53 |
| 505[11] | **Karinska (64)** (MCChapman) **6-8-4**(3) PMcCabe(3) (s.i.s: hdwy on ins over 2f out: one pce) | nk | **8** | 33/1 | 62 | 37 |
| 765[8] | **Scaraben (71)** (SEKettlewell) **8-9-0** DeanMcKeown(13) (s.i.s: bhd tl styd on fnl 2f) | 2 | **9** | 12/1 | 65 | 40 |
| 814[15] | **Up in Flames (IRE) (75)** (MDHammond) **5-9-4** GDuffield(10) (nvr bttr than mid div) | 3½ | **10** | 20/1 | 62 | 37 |
| 827* | **Rambo Waltzer (70)** (DNicholls) **4-8-13** AlexGreaves(2) (lw: hld up: sme hdwy whn hmpd over 1f out: n.d) | 1¼ | **11** | 9/1 | 54 | 29 |
| 679[9] | **Castel Rosselo (72)** (RHarris) **6-9-1** AMackay(11) (mid div: rdn over 3f out: sn wknd) | ½ | **12** | 16/1 | 55 | 30 |
| 718* | **Primo Lara (84)** (PWHarris) **4-9-13** GHind(5) (lw: sn led: hdd over 2f out: wknd over 1f out: eased towards fin) | ¾ | **13** | 9/2[1] | 66 | 41 |
| 802[8] | **Spanish Verdict (65)** (DenysSmith) **9-8-3**(5) CTeague(4) (mid div: rdn over 2f out: n.d) | 2½ | **14** | 14/1 | 42 | 17 |
| 765[2] | **Celestial Choir (82)** (JLEyre) **6-9-11** RLappin(17) (racd wd: a in rr) | 3 | **15** | 10/1 | 53 | 28 |
| 879[8] | **Wentbridge Lad (IRE) (62)** (PDEvans) **6-8-5b** SSanders(14) (chsd ldrs tl rdn & wknd over 2f out) | 7 | **16** | 14/1 | 19 | — |
| 765[6] | **Rory (76)** (MrsJCecil) **5-9-0**(5) MHenry(16) (racd wd: a bhd) | 10 | **17** | 7/1[3] | 13 | — |
| 802[3] | **Tertium (IRE) (77)** (MartynWane) **4-9-6** SDWilliams(15) (lw: racd wd: a in rr) | 16 | **18** | 8/1 | — | — |
| | | | | (SP 146.6%) | **18 Rn** | |

**1m 39.9** (3.40) CSF £202.79 CT £3,179.19 TOTE £14.60: £3.30 £10.70 £3.20 £2.90 (£320.60) Trio £495.40; £418.72 to Newmarket 5/5/96 OWNER Mr W. J. Kelly (THIRSK) BRED Sterlingbrook Farm

**450 New Century (USA)**, an excitable type, won well in the end. (13/2)

**Sandmoor Chambray**, badly drawn, ran easily his best race for a long time. (33/1)

**600 Chickawicka (IRE)** stuck on strongly, and is at his best when allowed to dominate. (16/1)

**589 High Premium** was putting in some solid work late on. (11/1)

**641 Lookingforarainbow (IRE)**, who looked on the big side, acquitted himself with credit considering his best form has been shown with an extra half-mile. (20/1)

**843 Sooty Tern**, with the plum number-one draw, could never get to the head of affairs. (9/1)

**Fame Again**, dropped 2lb, shaped a bit on the way back. (16/1)

**589 Scaraben**, 2lb lower in the weights, shaped nicely and will soon regain top form. (12/1)

## 934 MILLGATE MAIDEN STKS (3-Y.O) (Class D)

4-25 (4-27) **7f** £4,055.00 (£1,220.00: £590.00: £275.00) Stalls: Low GOING minus 0.03 sec per fur (G)

| Form | Horse | Dist | Pos | SP | RR | SF |
|---|---|---|---|---|---|---|
| | **Hammerstein (103)** (MRStoute) **3-9-0** DeanMcKeown(2) (lw: trckd ldrs: shkn up to ld over 1f out: r.o wl) | — | **1** | 5/6[1] | 84+ | 39 |

663[9] **Enchanted Guest (IRE)** (PWHarris) **3-8-9** GHind(4) (unruly s: mde most tl over 1f out: eased whn no ch w wnr) ....3½ **2** 33/1 71 26
696[2] **Mutadarra (IRE)** (RWArmstrong) **3-9-0** RPrice(5) (a chsng ldrs: rdn & hung lft 2f out: styd on one pce) ....hd **3** 13/8[2] 76 31
730[12] **Battle Spark (USA)** (CACyzer) **3-9-0** ACulhane(10) (hld up: outpcd & pushed along ½-wy: styd on fnl 2f: nt rch ldrs) ....1¾ **4** 33/1 72 27
*779*[3] **Depiction** (RGuest) **3-9-0** LCharnock(11) (a chsng ldrs: one pce fnl 2f) ....½ **5** 12/1[3] 71 26
740[2] **Classic Beauty (IRE) (62)** (RHarris) **3-8-9** AMackay(13) (a in tch: one pce fnl 2f) ....1¾ **6** 20/1 62 17
774[4] **Bollin Jacob** (TDEasterby) **3-9-0** MBirch(12) (sme hdwy 2f out: nvr nr ldrs) ....7 **7** 20/1 51 6
705[9] **Raise A Ripple** (MrsDThomson) **3-9-0**(3)ow3 OPears(8) (w ldrs: n.m.r & wknd over 2f out) ....2 **8** 66/1 49 1
**Alfahaal (IRE)** (HThomsonJones) **3-9-0** GCarter(3) (bit bkwd: stumbled s: nvr nr ldrs) ....½ **9** 20/1 45 —
783[12] **Gloria Imperator (IRE)** (ABMulholland) **3-9-0** TWilliams(1) (hld up & plld hrd: swtchd rt over 2f out: n.d) ....1 **10** 100/1 43 —
**Winn Caley** (CWFairhurst) **3-8-9** JTate(7) (leggy: unf: hmpd s: a bhd) ....½ **11** 100/1 37 —
774[5] **Surf City** (WWHaigh) **3-9-0** DaleGibson(9) (bit bkwd: hld up: a in rr) ....½ **12** 66/1 40 —
768[11] **Rocky Stream** (RMWhitaker) **3-8-9** JFanning(14) (bit bkwd: hld up: hdwy on outside ½-wy: wknd over 2f out) ....2 **13** 200/1 31 —
703[14] **Nordic Gift (DEN)** (MrsDThomson) **3-9-0** RLappin(6) (swvd rt st: a bhd) ....½ **14** 200/1 35 —
(SP 126.5%) **14 Rn**

**1m 29.0** (4.80) CSF £30.49 TOTE £1.90: £1.10 £4.80 £1.50 (£151.60) Trio £19.80 OWNER Sheikh Mohammed (NEWMARKET) BRED Sheikh Mohammed bin Rashid al Maktoum

**Hammerstein** looked the part and moved down well. Runner up to Bijou d'Inde at York in August, he ought to go on to better things. (5/6)
**Enchanted Guest (IRE)**, who carried plenty of condition, proved a handful at the start. After making the running, she was asked to do just enough to secure second as it was clear the winner was in a different league. (33/1)
**696 Mutadarra (IRE)**, very hard, carried no condition. Showing plenty of knee action going down, all he wanted to do was hang left, and he looks one to be wary of. (13/8)
**Battle Spark (USA)**, a tall type, seemed to have trouble handling the track. Sticking on in the final quarter-mile, there should be better to come. (33/1)
**779 Depiction** showed his appreciation of a return to turf. (12/1)
**740 Classic Beauty (IRE)**, who looked lean, lacked anything in the way of speed. (20/1)
**774 Bollin Jacob**, having his third run, shaped by no means badly, and should show his true ability in handicap company. (20/1)

## 935 COXWOLD H'CAP (0-90) (3-Y.O+) (Class C)

4-55 (4-58) **7f** £5,858.00 (£1,754.00: £842.00: £386.00) Stalls: Low GOING minus 0.03 sec per fur (G)

SP RR SF

814[5] **I'm Your Lady (65)** (BAMcMahon) **5-8-6** GCarter(3) (trckd ldr: led over 1f out: sn clr: unchal) ....— **1** 12/1 79 42
728[5] **Star Talent (USA) (82)** (MissGayKelleway) **5-9-9** OUrbina(8) (lw: b.hind: hld up & bhd: hdwy on outside over 2f out: styd on wl u.p ins fnl f: nt rch wnr) ....2½ **2** 4/1[2] 90 53
850* **Barrel of Hope (79)** (JLEyre) **4-9-6b** 5x RLappin(5) (led: clr ½-wy: hdd over 1f out: kpt on) ....2 **3** 9/4[1] 83 46
718[5] **Bargash (66)** (PDEvans) **4-8-7b** SSanders(4) (trckd ldrs: effrt 2f out: rdn & one pce) ....1½ **4** 16/1 66 29
**Pride of Pendle (75)** (DNicholls) **7-9-2** AlexGreaves(10) (hld up: hdwy 2f out: kpt on wl: nt rch ldrs) ....1½ **5** 14/1 72 35
744[5] **Rakis (IRE) (80)** (MrsLStubbs) **6-9-4**(3) DWright(15) (mid div: effrt u.p over 2f out: nvr nr to chal) ....hd **6** 7/1[3] 77 40
718[3] **Nashaat (USA) (63)** (MCChapman) **8-8-1**(3) PMcCabe(9) (wnt lft s: chsd ldrs: one pce fnl 2f) ....1¼ **7** 9/1 57 20
802[9] **It's Academic (67)** (MrsJRRamsden) **4-8-8** MDeering(16) (hld up & bhd: styd on fnl 2f: nvr nr ldrs) ....¾ **8** 20/1 59 22
589[19] **Somerton Boy (IRE) (75)** (PCalver) **6-9-2** GDuffield(14) (chsd ldrs: rdn along & outpcd 4f out: n.d after) ....¾ **9** 20/1 65 28
701[9] **Jo Mell (85)** (TDEasterby) **3-9-0** MBirch(13) (stdd s: hld up & bhd: nvr nr ldrs) ....hd **10** 14/1 75 26
827[9] **Allinson's Mate (IRE) (65)** (TDBarron) **8-8-6** JFanning(11) (a bhd) ....s.h **11** 33/1 55 18
480[7] **Knobbleeneeze (71)** (MRChannon) **6-8-7v**(5) PPMurphy(12) (b.off fore: chsd ldrs: effrt 2f out: grad wknd) ....¾ **12** 14/1 59 22
*379*[3] **Sand Star (70)** (DHaydnJones) **4-8-11** AMackay(6) (reard s: a bhd) ....2½ **13** 12/1 53 16
554[14] **Storm Bid (USA) (87)** (EALDunlop) **4-10-0** JTate(1) (hld up: a in rr) ....1¼ **14** 12/1 67 30
765[19] **Quilling (80)** (MDods) **4-9-7** DeanMcKeown(7) (b: bmpd sn after s: chsd ldrs tl wknd over 2f out) ....½ **15** 20/1 59 22
*718*[6] ***White Sorrel (61)*** (AHarrison) **5-7-13**(3) JStack(2) (Withdrawn not under Starter's orders: lame in paddock) .... **W** 16/1 — —
(SP 145.3%) **15 Rn**

**1m 28.1** (3.90) CSF £63.79 CT £145.47 TOTE £19.50: £4.40 £2.40 £2.10 (£51.80) Trio £65.00 OWNER Mr Michael Stokes (TAMWORTH) BRED M. G. T. Stokes

WEIGHT FOR AGE 3yo-12lb

**814 I'm Your Lady** travelled strongly on the heels of the leader and stayed the seven furlongs well. (12/1)
**728 Star Talent (USA)** was given a lot to do. Making his ground on the wide outside, he stuck on strongly inside the last. His rider's four-day whip ban earlier in the day was possibly at the back of his mind. (4/1)
**850* Barrel of Hope**, under a 5lb penalty and over an extra furlong, set a strong pace and kept on all the way to the line. (9/4: op 7/2)
**718 Bargash**, an in and out performer, ran one of his better races. (16/1)
**Pride of Pendle**, an amazing mare, had won twelve of her previous seventy-five races. Looking on the big side, she kept on nicely and, now the weather has warmed up, she will not be long in adding to her record. (14/1)
**701 Jo Mell**, taken to post quietly, was dropped right in at the start and this will have taught him much. He looks one to keep an eye on. (14/1)

T/Plpt: £1,039.60 (12.61 Tckts). T/Qdpt: £87.30 (7.5 Tckts). WG

# 0923-NEWMARKET (R-H) (Good to firm)

## Sunday May 5th

WEATHER: fine WIND: fresh half bhd, almost nil by Race 4

## 936 LORDS TAVERNERS CONDITIONS STKS (3-Y.O) (Class C)

2-00 (2-00) **7f (Rowley)** £5,720.00 (£2,120.00: £1,020.00: £420.00: £170.00: £70.00) Stalls: Centre GOING minus 0.33 sec per fur (GF)

SP RR SF

681[2] **Projection (USA) (104)** (BWHills) **3-9-1** PatEddery(4) (mde all: qcknd 3f out: r.o wl: comf) ....— **1** 3/1[2] 103+ 45
**Hidden Oasis** (SbinSuroor) **3-9-1** LDettori(5) (lw: trckd wnr: effrt over 2f out: r.o: nt pce to chal) ....1¾ **2** Evens[1] 99 41
730[5] **Lucky Archer** (CEBrittain) **3-8-12** BDoyle(2) (hld up & bhd: styd on fnl 2f: nvr able to chal) ....2½ **3** 50/1 90 32
**Obsessive (USA) (100)** (MRStoute) **3-8-10** JReid(1) (hdw: trckd ldrs: effrt over 2f out: r.o one pce) ....½ **4** 11/2[3] 87 29
**Brandon Magic (108)** (IABalding) **3-9-10** KDarley(7) (lw: chsd ldrs: effrt 3f out: one pce) ....1¼ **5** 16/1 98 40

| | | | Pos | SP | RR | SF |
|---|---|---|---|---|---|---|
| 672* | **Elsaleet (USA)** (JHMGosden) **3-9-1** GHind(3) (stdd s: plld hrd: effrt 3f out: sn btn) | 5 | **6** | 15/2 | 78 | 20 |
| | | | | (SP 110.0%) | | **6 Rn** |

**1m 26.75** (2.25) CSF £6.12 TOTE £3.30: £1.70 £1.50 (£2.70) OWNER Mr K. Abdulla (LAMBOURN) BRED Juddmonte Farms

**681 Projection (USA)** was allowed to dictate things at a very steady pace and, once he turned the tap on in the last three furlongs, he always had more than the edge. There was a lot to like about the way he did this. (3/1: 2/1-100/30)

**Hidden Oasis** sat on the winner's heels, ready to cover any move but, once the pace was on in the last three furlongs, he was never up to the task. Easier ground could be the answer. (Evens)

**730 Lucky Archer** settled better this time, even at this muddling pace and he was staying on at the end, suggesting that he is improving. (50/1)

**Obsessive (USA)** has not grown all that much but she has put on plenty of condition and ran as though she will be all the better for this. (11/2: 7/2-6/1)

**Brandon Magic** showed a preference for softer ground last year and was left behind once the tempo increased on this occasion. (16/1)

**672* Elsaleet (USA)** was the only runner from this stable at the meeting and ran a stinker. (15/2: 9/2-8/1)

## 937 MAIL ON SUNDAY MILE H'CAP (Qualifier) (0-90) (3-Y.O) (Class C)

2-30 (2-31) **1m (Rowley)** £14,720.00 (£4,460.00: £2,180.00: £1,040.00) Stalls: Centre GOING minus 0.33 sec per fur (GF)

| | | | Pos | SP | RR | SF |
|---|---|---|---|---|---|---|
| 662[4] | **Spirito Libro (USA) (67)** (CNAllen) **3-7-5**(7)ow2 MartinDwyer(15) (chsd ldrs far side: led ins fnl f: styd on) | — | **1** | 33/1 | 79 | 46 |
| | **She's My Love (76)** (JEBanks) **3-8-7** JQuinn(3) (mde most stands' side: kpt on fnl f: edgd rt: nrst fin) | 1¼ | **2** | 25/1 | 86 | 55 |
| 709[2] | **Polar Prince (IRE) (90)** (MAJarvis) **3-9-7** PRobinson(12) (lw: chsd ldr far side: ev ch ins fnl f: kpt on) | hd | **3** | 12/1 | 99 | 68 |
| 701* | **Al Shafa (88)** (JLDunlop) **3-9-5** WCarson(9) (racd far side: led tl hdd ins fnl f: nt qckn) | nk | **4** | 8/1[3] | 97 | 66 |
| | **Royal Mark (IRE) (88)** (JWWatts) **3-9-5** PatEddery(8) (h.d.w: racd far side: hld up: hdwy over 2f out: kpt on fnl f) | 1¾ | **5** | 10/1 | 93+ | 62 |
| | **Tarneem (USA) (88)** (MRStoute) **3-9-5** JReid(5) (lw: hdwy stands' side 3f out: styd on: no imp) | nk | **6** | 10/1 | 93 | 62 |
| | **Traceability (80)** (SCWilliams) **3-8-11** GCarter(4) (racd stands' side: hdwy 3f out: styd on: no imp) | nk | **7** | 10/1 | 84 | 53 |
| 640[2] | **Hal's Pal (86)** (DRLoder) **3-9-3** LDettori(13) (lw: chsd ldrs far side: rdn 2f out: sn btn) | hd | **8** | 7/2[1] | 90 | 59 |
| | **Uncle George (72)** (MHTompkins) **3-8-3** RHills(2) (racd stands' side: outpcd fnl 3f) | 5 | **9** | 20/1 | 66 | 35 |
| 689[3] | **Flying North (IRE) (80)** (MrsMReveley) **3-8-11** KDarley(14) (prom far side: hrd drvn over 2f out: sn btn) | s.h | **10** | 11/1 | 74 | 43 |
| 756[5] | **Jerry Cutrona (IRE) (69)** (NACallaghan) **3-8-0** JFEgan(7) (lw: hld up stands' side: effrt 3f out: hrd drvn & no imp) | 1½ | **11** | 7/1[2] | 60 | 29 |
| 740* | **Willisa (70)** (JDBethell) **3-8-1** TWilliams(10) (racd far side: prom tl rdn & wknd fnl 3½f) | 2 | **12** | 20/1 | 57 | 26 |
| 709[6] | **Tsarnista (85)** (JLDunlop) **3-9-2** JCarroll(1) (cl up stands' side over 5f) | s.h | **13** | 25/1 | 72 | 41 |
| 471[16] | **Hadadabble (65)** (PatMitchell) **3-7-10** NCarlisle(11) (racd far side: n.d) | nk | **14** | 100/1 | 51 | 20 |
| 584* | **Green Bopper (USA) (84)** (MBell) **3-9-1** MFenton(6) (hld up stands' side: drvn along 3f out: sn wknd) | 2 | **15** | 7/1[2] | 66 | 35 |
| | | | | (SP 122.8%) | | **15 Rn** |

**1m 38.26** (0.96) CSF £585.70 CT £9,321.37 TOTE £57.10: £9.90 £3.20 £5.70 (£373.10) Trio £1,094.80 OWNER Camelot Racing (NEWMARKET) BRED T. J. Rooney

LONG HANDICAP Hadadabble 6-2 Spirito Libro (USA) 7-3

**662 Spirito Libro (USA)** put up a much-improved performance from 7lb out of the handicap, and did it nicely. (33/1)

**She's My Love** moved moderately to post but ran really well, winning the race on the stands' side and just failing to catch the far-side group, despite hanging right in the closing stages. (25/1)

**709 Polar Prince (IRE)**, a heavy-topped individual, ran a super race and kept battling all the way to the line. He should get further. (12/1: op 8/1)

**701* Al Shafa**, ridden the opposite way to last time when successful, ran a decent race, only to be touched off in the closing stages. (8/1)

**Royal Mark (IRE)** ran a useful race after a lengthy absence and should now do a deal better. (10/1: 8/1-12/1)

**Tarneem (USA)** ran well up the stands' side, but could never get in a blow, and should do better as a result. (10/1: 7/1-12/1)

**Traceability** ran a useful race on the unfancied stands' side. (10/1: op 16/1)

**640 Hal's Pal** had his chances until failing to produce the goods when the pressure was on, and probably found this ground too fast. (7/2: op 6/1)

## 938 R. L. DAVISON PRETTY POLLY STKS (Listed) (3-Y.O F) (Class A)

3-05 (3-05) **1m 2f (Rowley)** £12,524.00 (£4,676.00: £2,278.00: £970.00: £425.00: £207.00) Stalls: Low GOING minus 0.33 sec per fur (GF)

| | | | Pos | SP | RR | SF |
|---|---|---|---|---|---|---|
| | **Pricket (USA)** (SbinSuroor) **3-8-8** LDettori(6) (a gng wl: smooth hdwy to ld over 1f out: pushed along & r.o strly) | — | **1** | 4/1[3] | 108++ | 64 |
| | **Faraway Waters (100)** (DWPArbuthnot) **3-8-8** JReid(7) (b.hind: trckd ldrs: led over 2f out: hdd over 1f out: no ch w wnr) | 5 | **2** | 40/1 | 100 | 56 |
| 576* | **Magnificient Style (USA)** (HRACecil) **3-8-8** PatEddery(5) (lw: plld hrd: trckd ldrs tl outpcd 4f out: styd on u.p fnl 2f: no imp) | ½ | **3** | 6/4[1] | 99 | 55 |
| | **Ruznama (USA) (109)** (BWHills) **3-8-13** WCarson(2) (hld up: effrt & swtchd over 2f out: rdn & no imp) | 1¾ | **4** | 9/4[2] | 101 | 57 |
| | **Classic Flyer (IRE) (80)** (SCWilliams) **3-8-8** AMackay(4) (led after 2f tl over 2f out: sn outpcd) | 6 | **5** | 66/1 | 87 | 43 |
| | **Scarlet Plume (106)** (JLDunlop) **3-9-1** KDarley(1) (led 2f: cl up: chal 3f out: wknd fnl 2f) | 3 | **6** | 7/1 | 89 | 45 |
| 583[7] | **Promissory** (CEBrittain) **3-8-8** BDoyle(3) (hld up: effrt 3f out: sn btn) | 3½ | **7** | 66/1 | 76? | 32 |
| | | | | (SP 108.7%) | | **7 Rn** |

**2m 3.85** (0.25) CSF £80.89 TOTE £3.70: £1.90 £5.00 (£49.30) OWNER Godolphin (NEWMARKET) BRED Mrs.Dillman

**Pricket (USA)**, like most of the runners from this yard, was ultra-fit and proved a class above her rivals. She is obviously a very useful filly. (4/1: op 5/2)

**Faraway Waters** showed a superb action on the way to post and ran a cracking race, but ran out of fuel in the last couple of furlongs. This trip may be a shade too far at present. (40/1)

**576* Magnificient Style (USA)** pulled too hard early on and then got outpaced. She did pick up well at the end, albeit without having a chance and, once she learns to settle and gets some cut in the ground over a bit further, she will come into her own. (6/4)

**Ruznama (USA)** ran reasonably well but failed to get into it seriously. She will do better as a result. (9/4)

**Classic Flyer (IRE)** was quickly put in her place in the last couple of furlongs. (66/1)

**Scarlet Plume** did her winning on easy ground last year and proved disappointing here once the pressure was on. (7/1: 8/1-12/1)

## 939 PERTEMPS 1000 GUINEAS STKS (Gp 1) (3-Y.O F) (Class A)

3-45 (3-47) **1m (Rowley)** £100,525.00 (£37,075.00: £17,687.50: £7,112.50: £2,706.25: £943.75) Stalls: Low GOING minus 0.33 sec per fur (GF)

| | | | Pos | SP | RR | SF |
|---|---|---|---|---|---|---|
| 708* | **Bosra Sham (USA) (118)** (HRACecil) **3-9-0** PatEddery(11) (lw: a.p: hdwy to ld over 1f out: hrd rdn & edgd lft: r.o wl) | — | **1** | 10/11[1] | 115++ | 66 |

Matiya (IRE) (101) (BHanbury) 3-9-0 RHills(4) (h.d.w: trckd ldrs: hdwy over 2f out: swtchd ins fnl f: kpt on wl) ....1½ 2 25/1 112 63
Bint Shadayid (USA) (107) (SbinSuroor) 3-9-0 LDettori(6) (rr div: hdwy 3f out: chsng ldrs appr fnl f: kpt on) ....hd 3 11/2 2 112 63
My Branch (112) (BWHills) 3-9-0 MHills(1) (plld hrd: hld up & bhd: hdwy whn nt clr run over 1f out: r.o towards fin) ....1½ 4 14/1 109+ 60
674[3] Honest Guest (IRE) (108) (MHTompkins) 3-9-0 PRobinson(3) (hld up: hdwy 3f out: sn hrd drvn: n.m.r, swtchd rt & styd on fnl f) ....¾ 5 14/1 107 58
Dance Sequence (USA) (110) (MRStoute) 3-9-0 JReid(2) (hld up: hdwy 3f out: drifted rt & kpt on one pce appr fnl f) ....1 6 12/1 105 56
674[2] Bint Salsabil (USA) (116) (JLDunlop) 3-9-0 WCarson(5) (trckd ldrs: rdn to ld over 2f out: hdd over 1f out: edgd rt: eased whn btn towards fin) ....hd 7 6/1 3 105 56
674[4] My Melody Parkes (108) (JBerry) 3-9-0 JCarroll(8) (chsd ldrs: led wl over 2f out: sn hdd: wknd appr fnl f) ....2 8 66/1 101 52
708[4] Miss Universal (IRE) (100) (CEBrittain) 3-9-0 BDoyle(9) (lw: prom tl rdn & wknd over 3f out) ....6 9 100/1 89 40
Portuguese Lil (60) (DNicholls) 3-9-0 AlexGreaves(12) (h.d.w: a bhd) ....nk 10 500/1 89? 40
Papering (IRE) (100) (LMCumani) 3-9-0 GCarter(10) (h.d.w: led tl hdd wl over 2f out: eased fnl 2f) ....6 11 33/1 77 28
674[5] Maid For The Hills (106) (DRLoder) 3-9-0b[1] DHarrison(7) (plld hrd: rdn 4f out: a bhd) ....7 12 33/1 63 14
708[2] Keepers Dawn (IRE) (106) (RFJohnsonHoughton) 3-9-0 KDarley(13) (in tch: rdn ½-wy: sn btn) ....2 13 50/1 59 10
(SP 117.4%) 13 Rn

**1m 37.75** (0.45) CSF £22.98 TOTE £2.10: £1.40 £4.90 £2.20 (£45.70) Trio £56.50 OWNER Mr Wafic Said (NEWMARKET) BRED Gerald W. Leigh

STEWARDS' ENQUIRY Eddery susp.14-15/05/96 (careless riding)

IN-FOCUS: **As in the 2000 Guineas, those drawn low, with the exception of the winner, dominated the finish, although this time it was probably purely on merit.**

**708* Bosra Sham (USA)** has had plenty of problems with her preparation of late and she was poorly drawn here, as the rail on either side of this well-watered track held an advantage. Nevertheless, she showed great courage under a most determined ride and is obviously going to take a lot of beating in future. (10/11)

**Matiya (IRE)** was the pick of the bunch looks-wise and ran a super race, but was short of speed when the winner crossed her entering the final furlong. She looks likely to improve. (25/1)

**Bint Shadayid (USA)** has an easy action and ran a super race, but was just short of a turn of foot in the last two furlongs. She will find easier opportunities. (11/2)

**My Branch** was unlucky as she found trouble in running but, with her style of racing, that is always a possibility. She might well have been second best had things gone her way here. (14/1)

**674 Honest Guest (IRE)** ran a game race, but was short of a turn of speed to get into it, despite staying on, and probably needs further or some easier ground. (14/1)

**Dance Sequence (USA)** spoilt her chances by getting into a state beforehand, but she did run pretty well, only to lack a real finishing dash. (12/1)

**674 Bint Salsabil (USA)** had the run of the race up the stands' rail but, when it came down to it, she edged right and found little and was then eased late on. (6/1)

**674 My Melody Parkes** ran well until her stamina gave out approaching the final furlong. (66/1)

**Papering (IRE)** acted as pacemaker here and, when headed, was eased a good deal in the final two furlongs. She gave the impression that she will be all the better for a run. (33/1)

**674 Maid For The Hills** had blinkers on for the first time and pulled far too hard. (33/1)

## 940 BRETBY RATED STKS H'CAP (0-110) (4-Y.O+) (Class B)

4-20 (4-22) **6f (Rowley)** £7,607.60 (£2,848.40: £1,394.20: £601.00: £270.50: £138.30) Stalls: Centre GOING minus 0.33 sec per fur (GF)

SP RR SF

Madly Sharp (93) (JWWatts) 5-8-7 PatEddery(8) (lw: a.p: rdn to ld ent fnl f: all out) ....— 1 9/1 106 57
737[3] Venture Capitalist (107) (DNicholls) 7-9-7 AlexGreaves(1) (bhd: hdwy on ins 2f out: ev ch ins fnl f: r.o) ....hd 2 6/1 3 120 71
Espartero (IRE) (101) (SirMarkPrescott) 4-9-1 GDuffield(4) (hmpd s: sn prom: led over 1f out: sn hdd: edgd rt & nt qckn towards fin) ....1¼ 3 3/1 1 110 61
457[8] Domulla (102) (RAkehurst) 6-9-2 SSanders(5) (carried rt s: hdwy ½-wy: n.m.r wl over 1f out: kpt on towards fin) ....nk 4 14/1 111 62
711[5] Brave Edge (97) (RHannon) 5-8-11 RHills(10) (prom: hdwy over 2f out: nt qckn appr fnl f) ....2½ 5 10/1 99 50
Cyrano's Lad (IRE) (93) (CADwyer) 7-8-7 CDwyer(2) (led tl hdd appr fnl f: no ex) ....1¼ 6 12/1 92 43
737[4] Double Blue (102) (MJohnston) 7-9-2 LDettori(7) (lw: spd over 4f: sn btn) ....½ 7 6/1 3 99 50
673[6] Welsh Mist (100) (RBoss) 5-9-0 WCarson(6) (b: effrt ½-wy: sn rdn: wknd wl over 1f out) ....1¾ 8 12/1 93 44
Cheyenne Spirit (105) (BHanbury) 4-9-2(3) JStack(9) (b: chsd ldrs tl rdn & grad wknd fnl 2f) ....½ 9 11/2 2 96 47
Shamanic (93) (RHannon) 4-8-7 JReid(3) (h.d.w: prom tl wknd wl over 1f out) ....1¾ 10 20/1 80 31
864[6] Hello Mister (102) (TEPowell) 5-8-13(3) PMcCabe(11) (bhd: hdwy u.p over 2f out: sn btn) ....7 11 12/1 70 21
(SP 122.6%) 11 Rn

**1m 12.29** (0.49) CSF £59.86 CT £190.37 TOTE £14.90: £3.60 £2.20 £1.90 (£50.50) Trio £74.80 OWNER Lord Swaythling (RICHMOND) BRED A. K. Zivanaris

LONG HANDICAP Cyrano's Lad (IRE) 8-6

STEWARDS' ENQUIRY Greaves susp. 14-16/5/96 (excessive & improper use of whip).

**Madly Sharp** has looked better over further in recent times, but did travel particularly well here at this shorter trip and, when it came down to a battle, he did all that was required and deservedly held on. (9/1)

**737 Venture Capitalist** needs things to go just right and produced a storming late run, but just failed, and is obviously in tremendous heart at present. (6/1)

**Espartero (IRE)** got messed about early on but still had his chances, only to hang under pressure in the closing stages. He will find plenty of other opportunities. (3/1)

**Domulla** is happier on easier ground and did not have the best of luck in running here, but still finished well to show that he is one to keep on the right side. (14/1: 10/1-20/1)

**711 Brave Edge** has only ever won over the minimum trip and he was making no impression in the final furlong here. (10/1)

**Cyrano's Lad (IRE)**, for a horse that wins over seven, has speed to burn. He should be all the better for this. (12/1)

**737 Double Blue** disappointed here and dropped out tamely in the last couple of furlongs. (6/1)

**941** EQUITY FINANCIAL COLLECTIONS H'CAP (0-105) (4-Y.O+) (Class B)
4-50 (4-54) **1m 4f (Rowley)** £9,625.50 (£3,604.50: £1,764.75: £761.25: £343.13: £175.87) Stalls: High GOING minus 0.33 sec per fur (GF)

| | | | | SP | RR | SF |
|---|---|---|---|---|---|---|
| 580[4] | **Beauchamp Jade (79)** (HCandy) **4-8-4** GCarter(10) (lw: hld up: stdy hdwy 5f out: led wl over 1f out: rdn & r.o) | — | 1 | 7/1 | 90 | 59 |
| 564* | **Taipan (IRE) (95)** (JLDunlop) **4-9-6** KDarley(9) (lw: chsd ldrs: led over 3f out tl wl over 1f out: kpt on u.p) | 1 | 2 | 9/1 | 105 | 74 |
| | **Backgammon (84)** (JABOld) **5-8-9** GDuffield(2) (cl up: led wl over 3f out: sn hdd: styd on u.p: nt qckn wl ins fnl f) | ½ | 3 | 10/1 | 93 | 62 |
| | **Mezaan (IRE) (94)** (MRStoute) **4-9-5** JReid(3) (hld up: hdwy 4f out: ch 2f out: nt qckn) | 2½ | 4 | 8/1 | 100 | 69 |
| 682* | **Progression (81)** (CMurray) **5-8-1b**(5) MBaird(7) (hld up & bhd: hdwy 4f out: ev ch over 2f out: no ex) | 1½ | 5 | 11/2 1 | 85 | 54 |
| | **Celeric (90)** (DMorley) **4-9-1** WCarson(5) (bkwd: bhd: hmpd over 2f out: nvr nr to chal: fin 7th, 7l: plcd 6th) | | 6 | 11/2 1 | 81 | 53 |
| | **Son of Sharp Shot (IRE) (98)** (JLDunlop) **6-9-9** PatEddery(11) (hdwy 4f out: sn rdn & outpcd) | 3½ | 8 | 13/2 3 | 84 | 53 |
| 682[14] | **Bob's Ploy (87)** (MHTompkins) **4-8-12** PRobinson(13) (led tl wl over 3f out: sn btn) | 2½ | 9 | 25/1 | 70 | 39 |
| 580[10] | **Burning (USA) (92)** (GHarwood) **4-9-3** AClark(1) (hld up: hdwy 5f out: sn rdn & btn) | 2 | 10 | 8/1 | 72 | 41 |
| 564* | **Lombardic (USA) (94)** (MrsJCecil) **5-9-5** LDettori(6) (chsd ldrs tl wknd over 3f out) | 2½ | 11 | 6/1 2 | 71 | 40 |
| | **Painted Hall (USA) (72)** (JARToller) **4-7-11**ow1 TWilliams(4) (h.d.w: prom: hdwy & ev ch 3f out: sn wknd) | ½ | 12 | 33/1 | 48 | 16 |
| 726[9] | **Hagwah (USA) (101)** (BHanbury) **4-9-12** MHills(12) (lw: bhd: hdwy & swtchd lft over 2f out: nvr rchd ldrs: fin 6th, 2½l: disq: plcd last) | | D | 25/1 | 101 | 61 |

(SP 122.8%) **12 Rn**

**2m 30.97** (0.47) CSF £64.80 CT £585.83 TOTE £7.90: £1.70 £3.70 £4.10 (£40.20) Trio £171.40 OWNER Mr E. Penser (WANTAGE) BRED E. Penser

STEWARDS' ENQUIRY Hills susp.14-17/5/96 (careless riding).

**580 Beauchamp Jade** gained her first ever victory here and did it well. Now she has got the hang of things, more should follow. (7/1)
**564* Taipan (IRE)** likes to be in the thick of things and keeps battling, but he was up against it in the final furlong this time. (9/1)
**Backgammon** has found his form over hurdles recently and ran a sound race, but was just short of a turn of foot, despite battling back in great style. (10/1)
**Mezaan (IRE)** ran a useful race and was certainly not over-punished. Better should soon be forthcoming. (8/1: 6/1-9/1)
**682* Progression**, put up 8lb for his victory last time, just found that too much. (11/2)
**Celeric**, needing this, got virtually knocked over approaching the final quarter-mile and was not given a hard time thereafter. (11/2)

**942** HASTINGS MAIDEN STKS (3-Y.O) (Class D)
5-25 (5-26) **1m (Rowley)** £4,970.00 (£1,505.00: £735.00: £350.00) Stalls: Centre GOING minus 0.33 sec per fur (GF)

| | | | | SP | RR | SF |
|---|---|---|---|---|---|---|
| 732[4] | **Phantom Quest** (HRACecil) **3-9-0** PatEddery(1) (lw: mde most: qcknd over 2f out: kpt on wl) | — | 1 | 11/10 1 | 95+ | 61 |
| | **Kammtarra (USA)** (SbinSuroor) **3-9-0** LDettori(10) (gd sort: lw: trckd ldrs: hdwy 3f out: rdn & edgd lft over 1f out: r.o) | 1¾ | 2 | 11/4 2 | 92+ | 58 |
| | **Marigliano (USA)** (MRStoute) **3-9-0** JReid(3) (h.d.w: a.p: hdwy over 2f out: kpt on wl) | 1½ | 3 | 12/1 | 89 | 55 |
| 730[2] | **The Dilettanti (USA)** (JARToller) **3-9-0** SSanders(4) (lw: cl up: ev ch 3f out: btn whn sltly hmpd ins fnl f) | 2½ | 4 | 11/2 3 | 84 | 50 |
| 696[4] | **Pegram (IRE)** (LMCumani) **3-9-0** KDarley(2) (trckd ldrs: ev ch 3f out: wknd fnl 2f) | 8 | 5 | 14/1 | 68 | 34 |
| | **Crown Court (USA)** (LMCumani) **3-9-0** OUrbina(6) (wl grwn: b: s.s: hdwy 3f out: no imp) | 8 | 6 | 25/1 | 52 | 18 |
| | **Prince Zizim** (CADwyer) **3-9-0** MWigham(9) (a bhd) | 1 | 7 | 50/1 | 50 | 16 |
| | **Lucky Begonia (IRE)** (CNAllen) **3-8-9** CHodgson(7) (w'like: b: a bhd) | 11 | 8 | 50/1 | 23 | — |
| 678[13] | **Young Annabel (USA)** (CADwyer) **3-8-9** JQuinn(8) (w ldr tl wknd 3f out) | 13 | 9 | 50/1 | — | — |

(SP 113.8%) **9 Rn**

**1m 38.28** (0.98) CSF £4.36 TOTE £2.00: £1.30 £1.50 £2.00 (£2.40) Trio £7.40 OWNER Mr K. Abdulla (NEWMARKET) BRED Juddmonte Farms

STEWARDS' ENQUIRY Dettori susp. 21-22/5/96 (careless riding).

**732 Phantom Quest**, happy on this faster ground, got things his own way and did it nicely. (11/10)
**Kammtarra (USA)** is Lammtarra's half-brother and obviously has plenty of ability, but he was slow to realise what was required, and should improve a good deal as a result. (11/4: 6/4-3/1)
**Marigliano (USA)**, a useful sort, was getting the hang of things as the race progressed. He will benefit from the experience. (12/1: 7/1-14/1)
**730 The Dilettanti (USA)** had his chances, but his measure had been taken when he was slightly hampered inside the final furlong. He has taken on some very useful opponents already this year and a drop in class might help his confidence. (11/2)
**696 Pegram (IRE)** showed up well until blowing up in the final two furlongs. (14/1: op 8/1)
**Crown Court (USA)** has a terrible action and looks to need plenty of time. (25/1)

T/Jkpt: Not won; £37,704.04 to Kempton 6/5/96. T/Plpt: £2,598.00 (15.21 Tckts). T/Qdpt: £65.20 (37.58 Tckts). AA

## 0887-SALISBURY (R-H) (Good, Good to firm patches)

### Sunday May 5th

Race 2: Flip start
WEATHER: fine WIND: nil

**943** WOODFORD MAIDEN STKS (I) (3-Y.O+) (Class D)
2-15 (2-17) **6f** £3,078.75 (£930.00: £452.50: £213.75) Stalls: High GOING minus 0.35 sec per fur (F)

| | | | | SP | RR | SF |
|---|---|---|---|---|---|---|
| 672[2] | **Watch Me (IRE) (90)** (RHannon) **3-8-4**(3) DaneO'Neill(9) (lw: w ldr: led 3f out: sn clr: easily) | — | 1 | 9/4 2 | 94+ | 52 |
| | **Saheeel (USA)** (SbinSuroor) **3-8-12** RCochrane(10) (str: scope: bit bkwd: a.p: chsd wnr fnl 2f: no imp) | 12 | 2 | 4/6 1 | 67+ | 25 |
| | **Mellow Master** (NJHWalker) **3-8-12** CRutter(8) (leggy: unf: rdn over 3f out: hdwy over 1f out: r.o one pce fnl f) | 3½ | 3 | 50/1 | 58 | 16 |
| | **Flint And Steel** (RHannon) **3-8-12** TQuinn(5) (bhd: rdn 5f out: styd on fnl f: nvr nrr) | 1¾ | 4 | 16/1 | 53 | 11 |
| | **Cassimere** (MajorDNChappell) **4-9-3** RHughes(3) (dwlt: swtchd lft over 2f out: no hdwy) | ¾ | 5 | 33/1 | 46 | 14 |
| | **Volare** (BJMeehan) **3-8-7** MTebbutt(6) (hld up: wknd over 2f out) | ¾ | 6 | 20/1 | 44 | 2 |
| | **Incatinka** (JLSpearing) **3-8-4**(3) SDrowne(4) (bit bkwd: prom 3f) | 3½ | 7 | 25/1 | 35 | — |

| | | | | SP | RR | SF |
|---|---|---|---|---|---|---|
| 527[12] | **Little Pilgrim (42)** (TMJones) **3-8-12** RPerham(11) (led 3f) | 2½ | **8** | 100/1 | 33 | — |
| | **King of Munster (AUS)** (MrsJCecil) **4-9-8** WRyan(2) (a bhd) | 2 | **9** | 14/1[3] | 28 | — |
| | **Dancing Man (40)** (MrsMELong) **3-8-12** CandyMorris(1) (bhd fnl 3f) | 1 | **10** | 100/1 | 25 | — |
| *779[6]* | **No Hiding Place** (BHanbury) **3-8-12b[1]** JTate(12) (prom over 3f) | 5 | **11** | 40/1 | 12 | — |
| | **Saucy Soul** (SEarle) **3-9-0**ow2 AProcter(7) (a bhd: t.o fnl 3f) | 10 | **12** | 66/1 | — | — |
| | | | | (SP 122.7%) **12 Rn** | | |

**1m 13.75** (0.75) CSF £4.02 TOTE £2.90: £1.20 £1.10 £5.60 (£1.90) Trio £31.20 OWNER Mr Salem Suhail (MARLBOROUGH) BRED London Thoroughbred Services Ltd

WEIGHT FOR AGE 3yo-10lb

**672 Watch Me (IRE)** looked particularly well and turned this into a procession from the quarter-mile marker. (9/4)

**Saheeel (USA)** unseated his rider when apparently spooked by the crowd on the way down. He should come on for the run, but it is hard to imagine him ever turning the tables on the winner. (4/6)

**Mellow Master** will benefit from a longer trip. (50/1)

**Flint And Steel** seemed likely to finish nearer last than first for most of the trip. Both his runs as a two-year-old were over further and he could be an interesting prospect in a handicap over a longer trip. (16/1)

**Volare** showed promise on his only outing for Martin Pipe last year. (20/1)

## 944 SMITH & WILLIAMSON H'CAP (0-90) (4-Y.O+) (Class C)

2-50 (2-51) **1m 6f** £5,550.00 (£1,680.00: £820.00: £390.00) GOING minus 0.35 sec per fur (F)

| | | | | SP | RR | SF |
|---|---|---|---|---|---|---|
| 642* | **Bellara (58)** (NMBabbage) **4-8-11** KFallon(7) (lw: pushed along & hdwy 8f out: rdn 4f out: styd on to ld wl ins fnl f) | — | **1** | 7/2[1] | 68 | 44 |
| 647[6] | **Lalindi (IRE) (65)** (DRCElsworth) **5-9-5b** TQuinn(4) (lw: led 5f: led over 2f out: edgd rt over 1f out: hdd wl ins fnl f) | 1 | **2** | 13/2 | 74 | 51 |
| *656[3]* | **Durham (50)** (RSimpson) **5-8-1b**(3) NVarley(5) (chsd ldr: led 9f out tl over 2f out: ev ch 1f out: unable qckn) | 1¼ | **3** | 12/1 | 57 | 34 |
| | **Kilcoran Bay (69)** (IABalding) **4-9-8b[1]** WRyan(3) (bhd: hrd rdn 6f out: sme hdwy fnl 2f: n.d) | 5 | **4** | 7/1 | 71 | 47 |
| 753[6] | **Granby Bell (50)** (PHayward) **5-8-4** GBardwell(2) (hrd rdn 6f out: no hdwy) | 4 | **5** | 13/2 | 47 | 24 |
| 647[3] | **Sea Freedom (62)** (GBBalding) **5-9-2v** RCochrane(1) (prom tl rn wd bnd 7f out) | 5 | **6** | 4/1[2] | 53 | 30 |
| | **He's a King (USA) (70)** (CLPopham) **6-9-10** RPerham(8) (lw: prom 9f) | 2½ | **7** | 16/1 | 59 | 36 |
| | **Sails Legend (48)** (MrsMELong) **5-7-9**(7)ow6 TField(6) (bit bkwd: bhd: rdn 6f out: t.o fnl 4f) | dist | **8** | 50/1 | — | — |
| 712[4] | **Witney-de-Bergerac (IRE) (63)** (JSMoore) **4-9-2** RHughes(9) (hld up: hdwy 8f out: wknd 4f out: eased whn btn over 2f out: t.o: b.b.v) | 15 | **9** | 5/1[3] | — | — |
| | | | | (SP 113.6%) **9 Rn** | | |

**3m 2.98** (4.28) CSF £24.06 CT £220.44 TOTE £4.30: £1.90 £1.70 £2.40 (£11.90) Trio £54.80 OWNER Mr Gary Leigh (CHELTENHAM) BRED John White

LONG HANDICAP Sails Legend 7-1

WEIGHT FOR AGE 4yo-1lb

STEWARDS' ENQUIRY Varley susp. 14 & 15/5/96 (excessive use of whip).

**642* Bellara** defied a 10lb rise in the weights, despite never looking really happy. His rider reported she hated the fast ground, and her trainer said she will now be put away until the autumn. (7/2)

**647 Lalindi (IRE)** ran much better in the blinkers than when last wearing them back in June '94, but she could not cope with the winner in the final 75 yards. (13/2)

**656 Durham**, dropping back in distance, certainly did not go down without a fight, but his rider picked up a whip ban. (12/1)

**Kilcoran Bay** was tried in blinkers, having twice found the visor doing the trick over hurdles this winter. (7/1)

## 945 GIBBS-MEW RATED STKS H'CAP (0-100) (3-Y.O) (Class B)

3-25 (3-25) **6f** £7,411.56 (£2,774.04: £1,357.02: £584.10: £262.05: £133.23) Stalls: High GOING minus 0.35 sec per fur (F)

| | | | | SP | RR | SF |
|---|---|---|---|---|---|---|
| 638* | **Farhana (85)** (WJarvis) **3-7-13** AMcGlone(5) (b: a.p: led over 3f out: easily) | — | **1** | 5/4[1] | 99+ | 45 |
| 832[3] | **Unconditional Love (IRE) (96)** (MJohnston) **3-8-10** TQuinn(2) (a.p: outpcd 2f out: r.o ins fnl f) | 3½ | **2** | 5/2[2] | 101 | 47 |
| 579[6] | **King of Peru (100)** (APJarvis) **3-9-0** JTate(1) (lw: hdwy to chse wnr over 2f out: rdn & edgd rt over 1f out: no imp) | 1 | **3** | 11/1 | 102 | 48 |
| | **Depreciate (90)** (CJames) **3-8-4** RCochrane(3) (hld up: hmpd 3f out: hdwy fnl f: r.o) | 1 | **4** | 12/1 | 89 | 35 |
| 832[5] | **White Emir (83)** (BJMeehan) **3-7-11** GBardwell(9) (led 1f: rdn over 2f out: one pce) | nk | **5** | 7/1[3] | 82 | 28 |
| | **Prima Volta (83)** (RHannon) **3-7-11** NAdams(6) (a bhd) | 1½ | **6** | 11/1 | 78 | 24 |
| 832[9] | **Repertory (98)** (MRChannon) **3-8-12** RHughes(4) (lw: plld hrd: led after 1f tl over 3f out: wknd 2f out) | 6 | **7** | 9/1 | 77 | 23 |
| | | | | (SP 119.9%) **7 Rn** | | |

**1m 13.7** (0.70) CSF £5.10 CT £21.15 TOTE £1.80: £1.30 £1.90 (£2.50) Trio £8.20 OWNER Mr A. Foustok (NEWMARKET) BRED Ahmed M. Foustok

STEWARDS' ENQUIRY Bardwell susp.14-15/5/96 (careless riding)

**638* Farhana** found no difficulty in defying a 16lb hike in the weights and seems to have a touch of class about her. (5/4)

**832 Unconditional Love (IRE)**, who was not inconvenienced by the extra furlong, came through to take the separate race for runner-up, and probably had a tough task at the weights. (5/2)

**579 King of Peru** had an impossible task in trying to concede weight to the progressive winner. (11/1: 6/1-12/1)

**Depreciate** had to be snatched up at halfway and could well have been second best on merit. (12/1: 8/1-14/1)

**832 White Emir**, dropped 2lb after each of his runs this season, is still 3lb higher than when winning at Sandown as a two-year-old. (7/1)

**Prima Volta** should step up on this when trying further. (11/1: 6/1-12/1)

**565 Repertory** (9/1: 6/1-10/1)

## 946 SALISBURY CONDITIONS STKS (2-Y.O) (Class C)

4-00 (4-01) **5f** £4,561.37 (£1,664.50: £814.75: £351.25: £158.13) Stalls: High GOING minus 0.35 sec per fur (F)

| | | | | SP | RR | SF |
|---|---|---|---|---|---|---|
| 877[3] | **Kingsinger (IRE)** (MRChannon) **2-9-0** RHughes(1) (lw: w ldr: led over 2f out: shkn up over 1f out: r.o wl) | — | **1** | 7/4[1] | 81 | 40 |
| 698[2] | **Herecomestheknight** (MartynMeade) **2-8-9**(5) RHavlin(4) (a.p: chsd wnr fnl f: one pce) | 2½ | **2** | 4/1[3] | 73 | 32 |
| | **Powder River** (RHannon) **2-8-5**(3) DaneO'Neill(5) (w'like: scope: bit bkwd: outpcd: hdwy fnl f: r.o: bttr for r) | hd | **3** | 2/1[2] | 67+ | 26 |
| 741* | **Castle House** (JAkehurst) **2-8-11** RCochrane(2) (a.p: rdn 2f out: one pce) | 1¼ | **4** | 9/1 | 66 | 25 |
| 807[2] | **Red Garter (IRE)** (KMcAuliffe) **2-8-6** TQuinn(3) (led over 2f: wknd 1f out: eased whn btn) | 3½ | **5** | 6/1 | 50 | 9 |
| | | | | (SP 114.0%) **5 Rn** | | |

**61.72 secs** (1.72) CSF £8.69 TOTE £2.30: £1.30 £2.40 (£3.60) OWNER Maygain Ltd (UPPER LAMBOURN) BRED Bernard Eivers

**877 Kingsinger (IRE)** found this a lot easier than what was probably a hot contest at Ascot last week. (7/4)
**698 Herecomestheknight** could make no impression on the winner in the last 200 yards. (4/1)
**Powder River**, out of a half-sister to Sheikh Albadou, ran green and jumped two paths during the race. Grasping what was required in the closing stages, he should not be hard to place. (2/1)
**741* Castle House**, a half-brother to the stayer Lunar Risk, is probably going to require further against this sort of company. (9/1: op 6/1)
**807 Red Garter (IRE)** ran better than his finishing position suggests. (6/1)

## 947 WEATHERBYS BULLETIN MAGAZINE H'CAP (0-100) (3-Y.O) (Class C)

4-35 (4-36) **1m 1f 209y** £5,498.00 (£1,238.00: £1,238.00: £386.00) Stalls: High GOING minus 0.35 sec per fur (F)

| | Horse | Dist | Pos | SP | RR | SF |
|---|---|---|---|---|---|---|
| 093[5] | **Jackson Hill (88)** (RCharlton) **3-9-8** TSprake(4) (lw: plld hrd early: rdn over 3f out: led over 1f out: sn clr: r.o wl) | — | **1** | 15/8[1] | 99 | 57 |
| 746* | **Frezeliere (87)** (JLDunlop) **3-9-5** TQuinn(7) (hld up: hdwy 2f out: r.o one pce fnl f) | 5 | **2** | 4/1[2] | 90 | 48 |
| 575[3] | **Clemente (76)** (RHannon) **3-8-5**(3) DaneO'Neill(8) (a.p: hrd rdn over 3f out: styd on fnl f) | d.h | **2** | 9/2[3] | 79 | 37 |
| 570[6] | **Nador (89)** (DRLoder) **3-9-4**(3) DRMcCabe(5) (lw: bhd: swtchd lft over 3f out: hdwy over 2f out: one pce fnl f) | 1¼ | **4** | 14/1 | 90 | 48 |
| 731[4] | **Punkah (USA) (75)** (LordHuntingdon) **3-8-2**(5) MHenry(1) (led: rn wd bnd over 6f out: rdn over 3f out: hdd over 1f out: wknd fnl f) | 1 | **5** | 9/1 | 74 | 32 |
| 701[4] | **Fursan (USA) (71)** (NAGraham) **3-8-3** AMcGlone(3) (chsd ldr: rn wd bnd over 6f out: ev ch over 1f out: wknd ins fnl f) | s.h | **6** | 5/1 | 70 | 28 |
| | **Villeggiatura (88)** (BWHills) **3-9-6** KFallon(2) (bkwd: hld up: hdwy over 3f out: wknd over 2f out) | 3 | **7** | 7/1 | 82 | 40 |
| | | | | (SP 118.8%) | **7 Rn** | |

**2m 7.6** (2.30) CSF JH & F £4.98 JH & C £5.42 CT JH, F & C £13.71 JH, C & F £14.10 TOTE £2.80: £1.60 F £1.00 C £1.40 ( JH & F £2.70 JH & C £2.90) OWNER Mr James Wolfensohn (BECKHAMPTON) BRED S. Tindall and Stowell Hill Ltd
STEWARDS' ENQUIRY O'Neill susp.14-16/5/96 (excessive use of whip)
**693 Jackson Hill**, whose rider was determined that the colt would not lead this time, drew right away, despite being 6lb higher than when winning at Doncaster. A grand stamp of a horse, he may to go Ascot for the King George V Handicap providing the ground is not too fast. (15/8)
**746* Frezeliere**, raised 5lb for the Brighton maiden win, proved no match for the winner at these weights (4/1)
**575 Clemente** had a hard race and it came as no surprise to find his rider receiving a whip ban. (9/2)
**570 Nador** hails from a stable that has yet to strike form this season. (14/1: op 6/1)
**731 Punkah (USA)**, back to ten furlongs, still needs to come down a few pounds. (9/1)
**701 Fursan (USA)** could not go with the winner in the last furlong and a half. (5/1)

## 948 WINCANTON MAIDEN STKS (3-Y.O) (Class D)

5-10 (5-12) **1m 4f** £3,501.25 (£1,060.00: £517.50: £246.25) Stalls: Low GOING minus 0.35 sec per fur (F)

| | Horse | Dist | Pos | SP | RR | SF |
|---|---|---|---|---|---|---|
| 671[9] | **Chief Contender (IRE)** (PWChapple-Hyam) **3-8-9**(5) RHavlin(3) (lw: mde all: rdn 3f out: clr 1f out: r.o wl) | — | **1** | 10/1 | 102 | 74 |
| 671[4] | **Wilawander (99)** (BWHills) **3-9-0** KFallon(1) (a.p: chsd wnr over 3f out: wknd over 1f out) | 9 | **2** | 9/4[2] | 90 | 62 |
| 668[2] | **Northern Fleet** (GHarwood) **3-9-0** CRutter(7) (lw: hld up: hdwy 5f out: one pce fnl 3f) | 6 | **3** | 9/1[3] | 82 | 54 |
| 576[8] | **Desert Dunes** (NAGraham) **3-9-0** RCochrane(5) (hld up: hdwy 5f out: wknd 3f out) | 1¾ | **4** | 33/1 | 80 | 52 |
| 677[16] | **Royal Expose (USA)** (RHannon) **3-8-11**(3) DaneO'Neill(8) (chsd ldrs tl wknd over 3f out) | 10 | **5** | 33/1 | 66 | 38 |
| 707[2] | **Set Adrift** (HRACecil) **3-9-0** WRyan(6) (lw: hld up: hdwy 5f out: rdn & wknd 3f out) | 4 | **6** | Evens[1] | 61 | 33 |
| 691[5] | **Veronica Franco** (JLDunlop) **3-8-9** TQuinn(4) (a bhd) | 9 | **7** | 20/1 | 44 | 16 |
| 746[3] | **Forever Noble (IRE)** (MRChannon) **3-9-0** RHughes(2) (prom: rdn & wknd 4f out) | nk | **8** | 20/1 | 49 | 21 |
| 821[14] | **Mathon (IRE)** (MRChannon) **3-9-0** CandyMorris(10) (a bhd) | 4 | **9** | 50/1 | 43 | 15 |
| 707[10] | **Santella Cape** (RHannon) **3-9-0** RPerham(9) (hrd rdn over 5f out: a bhd: t.o) | 13 | **10** | 50/1 | 26 | — |
| | | | | (SP 119.2%) | **10 Rn** | |

**2m 32.08** (0.27 under best) (-0.52) CSF £31.94 TOTE £15.90: £2.30 £1.10 £1.90 (£29.80) Trio £22.40 OWNER Mrs John Magnier (MARLBOROUGH) BRED Jayeff 'B' Stables and Calogo Bloodstock A G
**Chief Contender (IRE)**, a $385,000 colt, stepped up considerably on his Newmarket debut and scored by such a wide margin that one had to question the merits of the opposition. (10/1: op 5/1)
**671 Wilawander** finished in front of the winner at Newmarket but does not seem to quite get this trip at the moment. (9/4)
**668 Northern Fleet** was made to look pedestrian from the three-furlong pole. (9/1: op 6/1)
**Desert Dunes** is a half-brother to Endowment. (33/1)
**707 Set Adrift**, a Derby entry, was disappointing to say the least. (Evens)

## 949 WOODFORD MAIDEN STKS (II) (3-Y.O+) (Class D)

5-40 (5-43) **6f** £3,078.75 (£930.00: £452.50: £213.75) Stalls: High GOING minus 0.35 sec per fur (F)

| | Horse | Dist | Pos | SP | RR | SF |
|---|---|---|---|---|---|---|
| | **Pleading** (HCandy) **3-8-12** CRutter(8) (a.p: rdn over 2f out: led ins fnl f: r.o) | — | **1** | 7/2[2] | 83 | 53 |
| 678[13] | **Petit Point (IRE) (70)** (RHannon) **3-8-7** TQuinn(1) (w ldr: hrd rdn over 2f out: ev ch ins fnl f: unable qckn) | 1½ | **2** | 4/1[3] | 74 | 44 |
| 467[10] | **Will Do** (MartynMeade) **3-8-7**(5) RHavlin(5) (led: rdn over 2f out: hdd ins fnl) | ¾ | **3** | 33/1 | 77 | 47 |
| | **Blossom Dearie** (RGFrost) **3-8-7** RStreet(7) (hld up & plld hrd: hdwy fnl 2f: nt rch ldrs) | 3½ | **4** | 66/1 | 63 | 33 |
| *242*[2] | **Rawi (60)** (MissGayKelleway) **3-8-12** KFallon(12) (a.p: no hdwy fnl 2f) | 1½ | **5** | 11/2 | 64 | 34 |
| | **Arch Enemy (IRE)** (MRChannon) **3-8-12** RHughes(9) (w'like: plld hrd: prom over 4f) | ¾ | **6** | 3/1[1] | 62 | 32 |
| | **Sharp Pearl (85)** (JWhite) **3-8-12** JTate(6) (nvr trbld ldrs) | 2 | **7** | 11/1 | 56 | 26 |
| | **Out Line** (MMadgwick) **4-9-3** WRyan(3) (unf: dwlt: a bhd) | 1¾ | **8** | 50/1 | 47 | 27 |
| | **Deardaw (39)** (MDIUsher) **4-9-3** NAdams(10) (hld up & plld hrd: bhd fnl 3f) | 3½ | **9** | 66/1 | 37 | 17 |
| | **Bella's Legacy** (RJHodges) **3-8-4**(3) SDrowne(11) (bhd fnl 3f) | nk | **10** | 50/1 | 37 | 7 |
| | **Corrina Corrina** (RHannon) **3-8-4**(3) DaneO'Neill(2) (neat: prom 3f) | 7 | **11** | 11/2 | 18 | — |
| | **Doth Protest (IRE)** (NoelChance) **4-9-3** WJO'Connor(4) (dwlt: a bhd: t.o) | 15 | **12** | 20/1 | — | — |
| | | | | (SP 120.9%) | **12 Rn** | |

**1m 14.06** (1.06) CSF £17.36 TOTE £3.80: £2.00 £1.40 £6.90 (£9.20) Trio £201.20 OWNER Mr Simon Broke (WANTAGE) BRED Cheveley Park Stud Ltd
WEIGHT FOR AGE 3yo-10lb
**Pleading** showed promise on his second run as a two-year-old and gained the upper hand in the final 150 yards. (7/2: op 6/4)
**Petit Point (IRE)** stepped up on his seasonal debut at Newmarket but could never quite force her head in front. (4/1)
**Will Do** made a bold effort to make all and this was much better than his debut. (33/1)
**Blossom Dearie** had one run over seven last backend and shaped as though she requires further. (66/1)

**Rawi**, who ran well on the All-Weather during the winter without winning, was a springer in the market. (11/2)
**Arch Enemy (IRE)** ran too freely on this debut. (3/1)
**Sharp Pearl** (11/1: 8/1-12/1)
**Corrina Corrina** (11/2: 4/1-6/1)

T/Plpt: £15.40 (885.81 Tckts). T/Qdpt: £5.70 (130.94 Tckts). KH

# 0452-DONCASTER (L-H) (Good to firm)
## Monday May 6th
WEATHER: sunny WIND: almost nil

### 950 WISETON MAIDEN AUCTION STKS (2-Y.O) (Class D)
2-20 (2-22) **5f** £3,439.00 (£1,027.00: £491.00: £223.00) Stalls: High GOING minus 0.47 sec per fur (F)

| | Horse | Dist | Pos | SP | RR | SF |
|---|---|---|---|---|---|---|
| | **Ice Age** (RJRWilliams) **2-7-12**(5) MBaird(8) (cmpt: bit bkwd: mde all: qcknd ½-wy: edgd lft: r.o wl) | — | 1 | 12/1 | 80+ | 10 |
| | **Caviar Royale (IRE)** (RHannon) **2-8-13** RHughes(6) (cmpt: scope: trckd ldrs: chal ½-wy: sn rdn: nt pce of wnr) | 1¾ | 2 | 8/13 1 | 84+ | 14 |
| | **Bailieborough Boy (IRE)** (TDBarron) **2-8-6** JFortune(1) (w'like: leggy: bit bkwd: wnt lft s: sn prom: nt qckn fnl 2f) | 4 | 3 | 25/1 | 65+ | — |
| | **Belle Vue** (SirMarkPrescott) **2-8-5** WWoods(2) (neat: scope: sn pushed along: styd on fnl 2f: nrst fin) | hd | 4 | 10/1 3 | 63 | — |
| 585² | **Top of The Wind (IRE)** (JJO'Neill) **2-8-5** SDWilliams(3) (lw: pushed along thrght: sme hdwy fnl 2f: no imp) | hd | 5 | 100/30 2 | 63 | — |
| | **Fine Times** (CWFairhurst) **2-8-1**(5) LNewton(9) (w'like: leggy: scope: chsd ldrs tl outpcd fr ½-wy) | 3½ | 6 | 20/1 | 53 | — |
| 706⁶ | **Petula Boy** (MMcCormack) **2-8-10** TIves(4) (s.i.s: nvr wnt pce) | 1½ | 7 | 10/1 3 | 52 | — |
| | **Style Dancer (IRE)** (RMWhitaker) **2-8-10** KFallon(5) (leggy: dwlt: nvr nr to chal) | 6 | 8 | 25/1 | 33 | — |

(SP 123.3%) **8 Rn**

**60.65 secs** (2.25) CSF £20.93 TOTE £21.00: £2.40 £1.10 £3.70 (£5.40) Trio £203.20; £148.84 to Chester 7/5/96 OWNER Mr Peter Charter (NEWMARKET) BRED Mrs Mary Taylor
**Ice Age** is obviously pretty useful and, judging from his appearance, there is a fair bit of improvement yet to come. (12/1)
**Caviar Royale (IRE)** came here with a big reputation and this attractive colt had his chances, but always found the winner too much when the pressure was on. His turn will come. (8/13)
**Bailieborough Boy (IRE)** needed this and showed plenty of promise without being given a hard time. He looks one to watch. (25/1)
**Belle Vue** took time to get going but was staying on well at the end and should be all the better for this. He should appreciate further. (10/1)
**585 Top of The Wind (IRE)** showed some signs of temperament in the paddock and was never on the bridle at any stage, but was staying on at the end. (100/30)
**Fine Times** has plenty of early speed but was left struggling soon after halfway. He should improve as a result of this. (20/1)
**Petula Boy** (10/1: op 9/2)

### 951 BAWTRY CLAIMING STKS (4-Y.O+) (Class E)
2-50 (2-51) **5f** £2,976.00 (£888.00: £424.00: £192.00) Stalls: High GOING minus 0.47 sec per fur (F)

| | Horse | Dist | Pos | SP | RR | SF |
|---|---|---|---|---|---|---|
| 850⁴ | **Bolshoi (IRE) (69)** (JBerry) **4-9-0b** SDWilliams(1) (cl up: led after 2f: jst hld on) | — | 1 | 4/1 2 | 74 | 33 |
| 764² | **Sea-Deer (74)** (DWChapman) **7-8-10** JFortune(5) (hdwy ½-wy: r.o u.p fnl f: nrst fin) | nk | 2 | 11/2 3 | 69 | 28 |
| 664⁹ | **Barranak (IRE) (58)** (GMMcCourt) **4-8-10** JWeaver(4) (bhd tl hdwy over 1f out: styd on wl towards fin) | nk | 3 | 12/1 | 68 | 27 |
| 750² | **Super Rocky (72)** (RBastiman) **7-8-13**(5) HBastiman(2) (chsd ldrs: hdwy u.p 2f out: nvr able to chal) | 2 | 4 | 100/30 1 | 70 | 29 |
| 862⁵ | **John O'Dreams (50)** (MrsALMKing) **11-8-2** AGarth(6) (b: s.i.s: rdn ½-wy: sme late hdwy) | nk | 5 | 7/1 | 53 | 12 |
| *652*² | **Hannah's Usher (64)** (CMurray) **4-9-0** MTebbutt(7) (hdwy u.p ½-wy: no imp) | ¾ | 6 | 8/1 | 62 | 21 |
| 735⁸ | **La Suquet (72)** (NTinkler) **4-8-11b¹** RHughes(8) (chsd ldrs: hdwy ½-wy: edgd lft: btn wl over 1f out) | ¾ | 7 | 100/30 1 | 57 | 16 |
| 750⁵ | **Nadwaty (IRE) (47)** (MCChapman) **4-7-8b**(5) MBaird(3) (led 2f: wknd 2f out) | 2½ | 8 | 14/1 | 37 | — |

(SP 119.5%) **8 Rn**

**59.84 secs** (1.44) CSF £25.34 TOTE £4.80: £2.30 £1.60 £2.50 (£11.10) OWNER Mrs David Brown (COCKERHAM) BRED David John Brown
**850 Bolshoi (IRE)** showed just what he can do here and stretched his field at halfway, but the line came just in time. (4/1)
**764 Sea-Deer** is proving extremely difficult to win with, but he was keeping on well at the end, suggesting that he can pick up a race. (11/2)
**Barranak (IRE)** took time to find his stride but did finish well, albeit too late. A stiffer track might help. (12/1)
**750 Super Rocky**, whose stable is right out of form at present, was always struggling and could never offer a serious threat. (100/30)
**862 John O'Dreams** still has the ability but takes time to get going these days, and on this occasion it was always too late. (7/1)
**652 Hannah's Usher**, an All-Weather specialist, ran reasonably well, but always found this trip on turf a bit sharp. (8/1)
**700 La Suquet**, tried in blinkers this time, did not respond. (100/30)

### 952 CARR HILL CONDITIONS STKS (3-Y.O) (Class C)
3-20 (3-20) **1m (round)** £5,551.50 (£1,921.50: £923.25: £378.75) Stalls: High GOING minus 0.47 sec per fur (F)

| | Horse | Dist | Pos | SP | RR | SF |
|---|---|---|---|---|---|---|
| 705* | **Wixim (USA)** (RCharlton) **3-9-1** KFallon(4) (trckd ldrs: led over 1f out: r.o) | — | 1 | Evens 1 | 105+ | 32 |
| 572⁹ | **Anthelia (105)** (GWragg) **3-8-12** WWoods(2) (chsd ldr: led 2f out: sn hdd & one pce) | 2 | 2 | 7/2 3 | 98 | 25 |
| 727⁶ | **Lucayan Prince (USA) (103)** (DRLoder) **3-8-12b¹** RHughes(3) (lw: hld up: qcknd to ld over 3f out: hdd 2f out: sn btn) | 1½ | 3 | 5/1 | 95 | 22 |
| 566* | **Herodian (USA)** (JHMGosden) **3-9-1** JWeaver(1) (led tl hdd over 3f out: eased fnl 2f) | 22 | 4 | 5/2 2 | 54 | — |

(SP 117.5%) **4 Rn**

**1m 39.24** (2.74) CSF £4.97 TOTE £1.70: (£3.70) OWNER Mr K. Abdulla (BECKHAMPTON) BRED Juddmonte Farms
**OFFICIAL EXPLANATION Herodian (USA): finished distressed.**
**705* Wixim (USA)** did the job required well despite idling in front. He has a good attitude and is certainly going the right way. (Evens)
**Anthelia** is coming to hand and this run should have put her right. (7/2)
**Lucayan Prince (USA)**, tried in blinkers, looked a bit of a character and soon gave up when the pressure was on in the last two furlongs. (5/1)
**566* Herodian (USA)** is another from this yard to run badly and seemed to have a problem, as his rider was looking down while easing in the last two furlongs. (5/2)

## 953 MAY DAY H'CAP (0-90) (3-Y.O+) (Class C)

3-55 (3-55) **1m 2f 60y** £5,952.00 (£1,776.00: £848.00: £384.00) Stalls: Low GOING minus 0.47 sec per fur (F)

| | | | | SP | RR | SF |
|---|---|---|---|---|---|---|
| 804[2] | **Migwar (83)** (LMCumani) **3-8-8** RHughes(5) (trckd ldrs: rdn to ld 2f out: styd on wl: comf) | — | **1** | 4/1[3] | 91+ | 35 |
| 455[22] | **Billy Bushwacker (88)** (MrsMReveley) **5-10-0** JFortune(6) (hld up: hdwy 3f out: hung lft: styd on wl nr fin) | 2 | **2** | 5/1 | 93 | 52 |
| 690* | **Carlito Brigante (75)** (MrsJRRamsden) **4-9-1** KFallon(1) (trckd ldr: chal over 2f out: sn rdn & one pce) | ½ | **3** | 5/2[1] | 79 | 38 |
| 628[6] | **Wafir (IRE) (82)** (PCalver) **4-9-8** NCarlisle(4) (lw: hld up: shkn up over 2f out: styd on towards fin) | 1¾ | **4** | 8/1 | 83 | 42 |
| 650[2] | **Swallows Dream (IRE) (78)** (JLDunlop) **5-9-4** JWeaver(3) (chsd ldr tl outpcd fnl 2½f) | 6 | **5** | 3/1[2] | 70 | 29 |
| 809[7] | **Pearl Venture (83)** (SPCWoods) **4-9-9** WWoods(2) (led tl hdd 2f out: sn btn) | 3 | **6** | 15/2 | 70 | 29 |
| 580[19] | **Eurolink the Rebel (USA) (77)** (MDHammond) **4-9-3v[1]** TIves(7) (in tch tl wknd 4f out) | 14 | **7** | 20/1 | 43 | 2 |
| | | | | (SP 117.9%) | **7 Rn** | |

**2m 9.54** (2.54) CSF £23.15 TOTE £4.60: £2.70 £2.50 (£12.70) OWNER Umm Qarn Racing (NEWMARKET) BRED Meon Valley Stud
WEIGHT FOR AGE 3yo-15lb

OFFICIAL EXPLANATION **Eurolink the Rebel (USA): was found to be lame the following morning.**

**804 Migwar** behaved himself this time and did the business in good style. He looks to be getting it together. (4/1)
**Billy Bushwacker** is without doubt a funny customer but he does possess plenty of ability and, although hanging left, was making ground as the line approached. (5/1)
**690* Carlito Brigante**, normally held up, was up with the pace on this occasion and then ran out of petrol late on. His 9lb rise in the weights was probably the cause of this defeat. (5/2)
**628 Wafir (IRE)** looks really well and is improving. Once he tries longer distances, better should be seen. (8/1)
**650 Swallows Dream (IRE)** last won two years ago and was done with approaching the final quarter-mile here. (3/1)
**Pearl Venture** had too much use made of her. (15/2)

## 954 INTAKE H'CAP (0-80) (3-Y.O) (Class D)

4-25 (4-27) **1m 6f 132y** £3,557.50 (£1,060.00: £505.00: £227.50) Stalls: Low GOING minus 0.47 sec per fur (F)

| | | | | SP | RR | SF |
|---|---|---|---|---|---|---|
| 594[3] | **Influence Pedler (49)** (CEBrittain) **3-7-7**(5) MBaird(7) (swtg: chsd ldr: chal appr st: carried rt: led ins fnl f: r.o) | — | **1** | 15/2 | 56 | 23 |
| 687[5] | **Flocheck (USA) (72)** (JLDunlop) **3-9-7** JWeaver(3) (lw: hld up & bhd: effrt 3f out: ev ch over 1f out: nt qckn towards fin) | nk | **2** | 3/1[2] | 79 | 46 |
| 803[2] | **Siege Perilous (IRE) (65)** (SCWilliams) **3-9-0** KFallon(4) (lw: in tch: pushed along appr st: styd on wl fnl 2f: gng on fin) | nk | **3** | 5/2[1] | 71 | 38 |
| 731[3] | **Rivercare (IRE) (58)** (MJPolglase) **3-8-7** NCarlisle(8) (racd wd 3f: led & sn clr: jnd appr st: hung bdly rt fnl 3f: hdd ins fnl f: no ex) | ½ | **4** | 12/1 | 64 | 31 |
| 754[2] | **Exactly (IRE) (68)** (JLEyre) **3-9-0**(3) OPears(2) (chsd ldrs: effrt 3f out: outpcd fnl 2f) | 6 | **5** | 5/1[3] | 67 | 34 |
| *651** | **Jump The Lights (63)** (SPCWoods) **3-8-12** WWoods(6) (lw: in tch: effrt ent st: wknd fnl 2f) | nk | **6** | 8/1 | 62 | 29 |
| 886[13] | **Thorntoun Estate (IRE) (56)** (MJohnston) **3-8-5**[ow1] JFortune(1) (outpcd ½-wy: a bhd) | 26 | **7** | 14/1 | 26 | — |
| 444[12] | **Rose of Siberia (USA) (72)** (MBell) **3-9-7** RHughes(5) (chsd ldrs: rdn over 3f out: sn btn) | 14 | **8** | 6/1 | 27 | — |
| | | | | (SP 121.8%) | **8 Rn** | |

**3m 7.9** (4.30) CSF £30.47 CT £68.27 TOTE £9.80: £2.40 £1.90 £1.40 (£16.80) OWNER Mr C. E. Brittain (NEWMARKET) BRED Stetchworth Park Stud Ltd

**594 Influence Pedler**, who always sweats up, would probably have won this more decisively had he not been carried right across the course in the final three furlongs. (15/2)
**687 Flocheck (USA)**, patiently ridden, carried his head high when asked for an effort and was never doing enough when it mattered. (3/1)
**803 Siege Perilous (IRE)** is having a very busy time but is as game as they come and certainly stays. The further they went, the better he got. (5/2)
**731 Rivercare (IRE)** has plenty more ability if he can be managed, but is a difficult ride. (12/1)
**754 Exactly (IRE)** looked extremely fit, but this trip found her out. (5/1)
**651* Jump The Lights**, a winner on the All-Weather last time, was stepped up in trip here and was left struggling with two furlongs to go. (8/1)

## 955 MAY DAY HOLIDAY LIMITED STKS (0-70) (3-Y.O) (Class E)

4-55 (4-56) **1m 2f 60y** £2,976.00 (£888.00: £424.00: £192.00) Stalls: Low GOING minus 0.47 sec per fur (F)

| | | | | SP | RR | SF |
|---|---|---|---|---|---|---|
| | **Ground Game (65)** (DRLoder) **3-8-10** RHughes(2) (lw: trckd ldrs: smooth hdwy to ld over 3f out: sn clr) | — | **1** | Evens[1] | 76 | 32 |
| 788[2] | **Classic Colours (USA) (68)** (SCWilliams) **3-8-11** AMackay(8) (prom: chal 3f out: hung lft & no ch w wnr) | 5 | **2** | 6/1[3] | 69 | 25 |
| | **Fijon (IRE) (65)** (BWHills) **3-8-8** KFallon(6) (hdwy 3f out: styd on wl: nrst fin) | s.h | **3** | 6/1[3] | 66 | 22 |
| 663[4] | **Dubai College (IRE) (70)** (CEBrittain) **3-8-11** JWeaver(4) (led tl hdd over 3f out: wknd fnl 2f) | 5 | **4** | 4/1[2] | 61 | 17 |
| 788[7] | **Fikra (USA) (65)** (SPCWoods) **3-8-8** WWoods(1) (dwlt: bhd: sme hdwy over 2f out: nvr nr to chal) | 2½ | **5** | 10/1 | 55 | 11 |
| 754[10] | **Bullpen Belle (65)** (PTWalwyn) **3-8-8** TIves(7) (cl up tl wknd 3f out) | 18 | **6** | 10/1 | 26 | — |
| 646[6] | **Capture The Moment (64)** (RJRWilliams) **3-8-3**(5) MBaird(3) (dwlt: rdn & bhd fnl 3f) | 8 | **7** | 12/1 | 14 | — |
| | **Tashjir (USA) (58)** (DMorley) **3-8-8** JFortune(5) (prom tl rdn & wknd 4f out: p.u ins fnl f) | | **P** | 20/1 | — | — |
| | | | | (SP 129.2%) | **8 Rn** | |

**2m 10.13** (3.13) CSF £8.87 TOTE £2.40: £1.30 £1.80 £1.50 (£4.70) OWNER Mrs P. T. Fenwick (NEWMARKET) BRED Michael Watt and Miss Jemima Johnson

OFFICIAL EXPLANATION **Fikra (USA): reared up in the saddling boxes and cut its hock.**
**Tashjir (USA): finished distressed.**

**Ground Game** turned this into a procession in the final three furlongs and should stay further yet. She is obviously pretty useful. (Evens)
**788 Classic Colours (USA)** had her chances but, when the pressure was on, just hung left and was never doing enough. (6/1)
**Fijon (IRE)** had a nice pipe-opener and was keeping on well at the end to suggest that better should soon be seen. (6/1)
**663 Dubai College (IRE)**, stepped up in trip, had his limitations exposed a long way out. (4/1)
**Fikra (USA)** never got into the race but did leave the impression that she is learning. (10/1: 8/1-12/1)
**Bullpen Belle** (10/1: 8/1-12/1)

## 956 COAL MINER H'CAP (0-85) (3-Y.O+) (Class D)

5-25 (5-26) **6f** £4,045.00 (£1,210.00: £580.00: £265.00) Stalls: High GOING minus 0.47 sec per fur (F)

| | | | | SP | RR | SF |
|---|---|---|---|---|---|---|
| 749[2] | **Daawe (USA) (56)** (MrsVAAconley) **5-8-2v** MDeering(6) (lw: mde all: kpt on wl fnl f) | — | **1** | 7/1[3] | 69 | 42 |
| *896[6]* | **Cretan Gift (61)** (NPLittmoden) **5-8-7b** TGMcLaughlin(1) (a chsng ldrs: effrt 2f out: nt qckn ins fnl f) | ½ | **2** | 14/1 | 73 | 46 |

| | Horse | | Pos | SP | RR | SF |
|---|---|---|---|---|---|---|
| $617^{2}$ | **Mister Westsound (65)** (MissLAPerratt) **4-8-11b** MTebbutt(8) (hld up: effrt 2f out: styd on wl: nrst fin) | 2 | **3** | 9/1 | 71 | 44 |
| | **Double Matt (IRE) (77)** (RHannon) **4-9-9** RHughes(10) (hdwy over 2f out: styd on: nrst fin) | 2 | **4** | 9/1 | 78 | 51 |
| $735^{9}$ | **Just Dissident (IRE) (58)** (RMWhitaker) **4-8-4** AMackay(12) (chsd ldrs: rdn over 2f out: nt qckn) | 1¾ | **5** | 14/1 | 54 | 27 |
| $850^{7}$ | **Captain Carat (63)** (MrsJRRamsden) **5-8-9** KFallon(11) (b.nr fore: bhd: shkn up over 2f out: nrst fin) | 1 | **6** | $7/2^{1}$ | 57 | 30 |
| $716^{8}$ | **Shashi (IRE) (71)** (WWHaigh) **4-9-0**(3) OPears(9) (nvr nr to chal) | 2½ | **7** | 20/1 | 58 | 31 |
| $814^{6}$ | **Amron (65)** (JBerry) **9-8-11** NCarlisle(13) (rdn over 3f out: n.d) | ¾ | **8** | $9/2^{2}$ | 50 | 23 |
| $587^{8}$ | **Colway Rake (70)** (JWWatts) **5-9-2b** TIves(2) (lw: shkn up ½-wy: a bhd) | ¾ | **9** | 8/1 | 53 | 26 |
| | **Keston Pond (IRE) (72)** (MrsVAAconley) **6-9-4** WWoods(5) (bit bkwd: chsd ldrs tl wknd appr fnl f) | nk | **10** | 14/1 | 54 | 27 |
| $868^{7}$ | **Premium Gift (64)** (CBBBooth) **4-8-10** JFortune(7) (lw: chsd ldrs tl wknd fnl 2f) | ¾ | **11** | 14/1 | 44 | 17 |
| $778^{3}$ | **Ashgore (79)** (MJohnston) **6-9-11** JWeaver(4) (prom to ½-wy: sn btn & eased) | 4 | **12** | 12/1 | 49 | 22 |
| $935^{3}$ | **Barrel of Hope (81)** (JLEyre) **4-9-13b** 7x SDWilliams(3) (lw: dwlt: a outpcd & bhd) | 5 | **13** | $7/1^{3}$ | 37 | 10 |
| | | | | (SP 135.6%) | **13 Rn** | |

**1m 11.35** (0.35) CSF £101.38 CT £870.34 TOTE £12.40: £3.40 £3.60 £2.40 (£66.30) Trio £184.10 OWNER Mrs Andrea Mallinson (WESTOW) BRED Gainsborough Farm W.C.

**749 Daawe (USA)** is in tremendous form at present and can win more races. (7/1)
**896 Cretan Gift**, like the winner an All-Weather specialist, ran a super race here to suggest that a win on grass is on the cards. (14/1)
**617 Mister Westsound** is going to figure in some good handicaps this year and is now coming to hand. (9/1)
**Double Matt (IRE)** only got going when the race was over and should be all the better for it. (9/1)
**Just Dissident (IRE)** ran reasonably but was fighting a lost cause from halfway. (14/1)
**850 Captain Carat**, who won this last year, never got into it this time, despite staying on well. (7/2)
**Shashi (IRE)** showed enough to suggest that there is something more to come. (20/1)
**Keston Pond (IRE)** needed this and blew up approaching the final furlong after running well. (14/1)

T/Plpt: £87.80 (94.61 Tckts). T/Qdpt: £23.90 (16.54 Tckts). AA

## 0563-HAYDOCK (L-H) (Good to soft)
## Monday May 6th

WEATHER: fine & sunny WIND: almost nil

### 957 TAPSTER'S MOSS MAIDEN STKS (3-Y.O F) (Class D)

2-00 (2-01) **1m 2f 120y** £3,615.00 (£1,095.00: £535.00: £255.00) Stalls: Low GOING: 0.13 sec per fur (G)

| | Horse | | Pos | SP | RR | SF |
|---|---|---|---|---|---|---|
| | **Camporese (IRE)** (PWChapple-Hyam) **3-8-11** JReid(1) (b.nr hind: leggy: lt-f: mde most: drvn clr over 1f out: unchal) | — | **1** | $13/2^{3}$ | 91 | 67 |
| | **Place de L'Opera** (HRACecil) **3-8-11** GCarter(10) (lt-f: unf: bit bkwd: hld up: hdwy & n.m.r over 2f out: nt rch wnr) | 9 | **2** | $11/2^{2}$ | 77 | 53 |
| | **Classic Parisian (IRE)** (SCWilliams) **3-8-11** DHarrison(9) (leggy: lt-f: hld up: effrt & rdn 3f out: styd on: no imp) | 2 | **3** | 25/1 | 74 | 50 |
| | **Mount Row** (LMCumani) **3-8-11** KDarley(7) (w'like: scope: hld up: hdwy over 3f out: one pce fnl 2f) | nk | **4** | $13/2^{3}$ | 74 | 50 |
| | **Aethra (USA)** (LadyHerries) **3-8-11** DeclanO'Shea(11) (lw: hld up: effrt u.p 3f out: nvr able to chal) | 1 | **5** | $7/4^{1}$ | 72 | 48 |
| | **Nanda** (DRLoder) **3-8-8**(3) PMcCabe(2) (lengthy: scope: chsd ldrs 7f: sn wknd) | 1¼ | **6** | 14/1 | 70 | 46 |
| $826^{2}$ | **Dear Life (USA)** (MrsJCecil) **3-8-11** AClark(3) (chsd wnr: disp ld ent st: wknd over 2f out: t.o) | 7 | **7** | 7/1 | 60 | 36 |
| | **Most Wanted (IRE)** (PFICole) **3-8-11** TQuinn(5) (w'like: leggy: lw: trckd ldrs tl wknd 2f out: t.o) | hd | **8** | 11/1 | 60 | 36 |
| | **Alana's Ballad (IRE)** (BPJBaugh) **3-8-11** WLord(8) (w'like: leggy: bkwd: chsd ldrs to ½-wy: sn wknd: t.o fnl 3f) | dist | **9** | 66/1 | — | — |
| | **Badius (IRE)** (JHMGosden) **3-8-11** JCarroll(4) (unf: scope: bit bkwd: s.s: a in rr: t.o fnl 3f) | ½ | **10** | 8/1 | — | — |
| | | | | (SP 122.4%) | **10 Rn** | |

**2m 16.56** (5.06) CSF £41.07 TOTE £5.90: £1.80 £2.10 £6.90 (£9.10) Trio £209.50; £132.79 to Chester 7/5/96 OWNER Mr M. Tabor (MARLBOROUGH) BRED M. Tabor

OFFICIAL EXPLANATION **Badius (IRE): became unsettled in the stalls and missed the break, due to a protective rug slipping.**
**Camporese (IRE)**, a sparely-made filly who looked well prepared, hugged the rail throughout and forged clear inside the distance to score very easily indeed. (13/2)
**Place de L'Opera**, a quick-actioned daughter of Park Hill winner Madame Dubois, made progress from off the pace to reach her final placing and should soon be able to go one better. (11/2: 4/1-6/1)
**Classic Parisian (IRE)** stayed on steadily in the latter stages but was never going well enough to take a hand in the finish. (25/1)
**Mount Row** tried to get herself into the action halfway up the straight, but the effort petered out, and she ran as if she may not have seen the trip out. (13/2: 9/2-7/1)
**Aethra (USA)**, an attractive filly who showed plenty of promise in her only outing last year, could not summon up the pace to mount a challenge, and it is possible that she needs further. (7/4)
**Nanda**, a sister to the useful Myself, looked to have done plenty of work but was feeling the strain entering the final three furlongs and, like her sister, quite possibly needs no further than seven furlongs. (14/1)

### 958 E.B.F. GALLOWS HALL MAIDEN STKS (2-Y.O) (Class D)

2-30 (2-30) **5f** £3,403.75 (£1,030.00: £502.50: £119.38: £119.38) Stalls: High GOING: 0.13 sec per fur (G)

| | Horse | | Pos | SP | RR | SF |
|---|---|---|---|---|---|---|
| | **Bali Paradise (USA)** (PFICole) **2-9-0** TQuinn(8) (sn pushed along: swtchd lft 2f out: ev ch whn snatched up ins fnl f: nt rcvr: fin 2nd, nk: awrdd r) | — | **1** | $6/4^{1}$ | 67 | 27 |
| $608^{3}$ | **The Gay Fox** (BAMcMahon) **2-9-0** GCarter(2) (outpcd & rdn ½-wy: hdwy & drifted rt 2f out: led wl ins fnl f: hld on: fin 1st: disq: plcd 2nd) | | **2** | 11/2 | 68 | 28 |
| | **Rockaroundtheclock** (PDEvans) **2-9-0** KDarley(3) (lt-f: bhd & outpcd tl kpt on wl ins fnl f) | 2 | **3** | 12/1 | 61 | 21 |
| | **Janib (USA)** (HThomsonJones) **2-9-0** RHills(5) (neat: cmpt: bit bkwd: disp ld 4f: rdn & one pce ins fnl f) | hd | **4** | $4/1^{2}$ | 60 | 20 |
| $699^{3}$ | **Double Action** (TDEasterby) **2-9-0** MBirch(6) (disp ld tl hdd & no ex ins fnl f) | d.h | **4** | $5/1^{3}$ | 60 | 20 |
| $800^{7}$ | **Magic Blue (IRE)** (RHollinshead) **2-8-9**(5) FLynch(1) (outpcd: a bhd) | 2½ | **6** | 25/1 | 52 | 12 |
| | **Changed To Baileys (IRE)** (JBerry) **2-9-0** JCarroll(4) (lt-f: s.i.s: sn wnt prom: wknd wl over 1f out) | 7 | **7** | 6/1 | — | — |
| | | | | (SP 117.9%) | **7 Rn** | |

**64.02 secs** (4.82) CSF £10.21 TOTE £2.50: £1.60 £2.10 (£6.30) OWNER Al Muallim Partnership (WHATCOMBE) BRED Galbreath/Phillips Racing Partnership

STEWARDS' ENQUIRY Carter susp. 15-16/5/96 (careless riding).

**Bali Paradise (USA)**, a well-grown colt who is a most impressive mover, struggled to keep tabs on the leaders but he picked up well once switched and, but for being the meat in the sandwich inside the final furlong, would have won quite comfortably. He was rightly promoted a place in the Stewards' Room. (6/4)
**608 The Gay Fox**, one of the first to be ridden, responded and stayed on to take command 200 yards out, but he continually drifted right under a strong ride and disqualification was a formality. He should improve with experience and, with luck, will win races. (11/2)
**Rockaroundtheclock** is bred to need further and was only getting into top gear inside the final furlong. (12/1)
**Janib (USA)**, a compact colt who is a brother to three winners, showed plenty of speed to share the lead until getting outpaced inside the last 100 yards. He can only improve on this. (4/1)
**699 Double Action** got the best of the start this time and held a slight lead until getting done for toe in the sprint to the line. He is going the right way. (5/1)

## 959 LODGE LANE CONDITIONS STKS (3-Y.O) (Class C)

3-00 (3-02) **5f** £4,698.60 (£1,757.40: £858.70: £368.50: £164.25: £82.55) Stalls: High GOING: 0.13 sec per fur (G)

| | Horse / details | | Pos | SP | RR | SF |
|---|---|---|---|---|---|---|
| 591* | **Fond Embrace (75)** (HCandy) **3-8-9** GCarter(6) (mde all: rdn & r.o wl) | — | 1 | 5/1 3 | 93 | 61 |
| 783* | **Major Quality** (JRFanshawe) **3-9-2** DHarrison(7) (hld up: hdwy 2f out: rdn to chal ent fnl f: nt pce of wnr) | 1½ | 2 | 11/8 1 | 95 | 63 |
| 676 11 | **Ocean Grove (IRE) (90)** (PWChapple-Hyam) **3-8-11** JReid(3) (dwlt: bhd & outpcd tl kpt on ins fnl f) | 7 | 3 | 6/1 | 68 | 36 |
| 548 6 | **Beautiful Ballad (IRE) (93)** (ACStewart) **3-8-11** RHills(4) (b.nr hind: sn drvn along: nt pce to chal) | 2 | 4 | 12/1 | 61 | 29 |
| 832 2 | **Cross The Border (96)** (RHannon) **3-9-0** KDarley(2) (chsd wnr tl wknd wl over 1f out) | 5 | 5 | 100/30 2 | 48 | 16 |
| | **Whicksey Perry (85)** (JBerry) **3-9-4** JCarroll(5) (bit bkwd: trckd ldrs: rdn 2f out: sn wknd) | 4 | 6 | 9/1 | 40 | 8 |
| 867 14 | **Astral's Chance** (KRBurke) **3-8-12** AClark(1) (trckd ldrs 3f: sn outpcd) | 1¼ | 7 | 33/1 | 30 | — |

(SP 116.8%) **7 Rn**

**61.75 secs** (2.55) CSF £12.34 TOTE £4.60: £1.80 £1.40 (£4.80) OWNER Cmdr Marten (WANTAGE) BRED Lt-Comdr G. G. Marten
**591* Fond Embrace** is really getting her act together now and, as long as she is not aimed too high, can go on paying her way. (5/1)
**783* Major Quality** delivered his challenge approaching the final furlong, but the winner was not stopping and he lacked the ammunition to do anything about it. (11/8)
**Ocean Grove (IRE)** was certainly not suited by this step down to the minimum trip and a tardy start did nothing to help. (6/1)
**548 Beautiful Ballad (IRE)** again proved difficult to load into the stalls and was never going well enough to get herself into the action. (12/1)

## 960 HAYDOCK PARK SPRING TROPHY RATED STKS H'CAP (0-110) (Listed) (3-Y.O+) (Class A)

3-30 (3-31) **7f 30y** £11,407.20 (£4,264.80: £2,082.40: £892.00: £396.00: £197.60) Stalls: Low GOING: 0.13 sec per fur (G)

| | Horse / details | | Pos | SP | RR | SF |
|---|---|---|---|---|---|---|
| 728 2 | **Cool Edge (IRE) (91)** (MHTompkins) **5-8-10** PRobinson(3) (lw: plld hrd: hld up: led over 1f out: sn clr: eased nr fin) | — | 1 | 4/1 1 | 101 | 59 |
| 673 9 | **General Monash (USA) (103)** (PWChapple-Hyam) **4-9-8** JReid(2) (bit bkwd: hld up: hdwy over 2f out: styd on u.p fnl f: fin 3rd, 2l: plcd 2nd) | | 2 | 15/2 3 | 105 | 63 |
| 728 6 | **Band on the Run (93)** (BAMcMahon) **9-8-12** GCarter(4) (hld up: hdwy over 2f out: styd on ins fnl f: fin 4th, 3l: plcd 3rd) | | 3 | 10/1 | 88 | 46 |
| 681 8 | **Yarob (IRE) (105)** (HThomsonJones) **3-8-12** RHills(9) (lw: hld up: effrt over 2f out: rdn whn hmpd over 1f out: nt rcvr: fin 5th, 3½l: plcd 4th) | | 4 | 20/1 | 93 | 39 |
| 809 3 | **Moments of Fortune (USA) (98)** (BHanbury) **4-9-3b** JStack(6) (prom: led over 2f out tl over 1f out: sn btn: fin 6th, nk: plcd 5th) | | 5 | 7/1 2 | 85 | 43 |
| 711 3 | **Daring Destiny (98)** (KRBurke) **5-9-3** AClark(5) (hld up: plld wd & effrt over 3f out: sn hrd rdn: no imp: fin 7th, 13l: plcd 6th) | | 6 | 9/1 | 56 | 14 |
| | **Tropical Dance (USA) (98)** (MrsJCecil) **3-8-5** DHarrison(11) (still unf: trckd ldrs tl wknd 2f out) | 5 | 8 | 12/1 | 45 | — |
| | **Alessia (90)** (WRMuir) **4-8-9** Jean-PierreLopez(13) (bkwd: a in rr) | 1¾ | 9 | 33/1 | 33 | — |
| 876 11 | **Roving Minstrel (93)** (BAMcMahon) **5-8-12** KDarley(12) (nvr plcd to chal) | nk | 10 | 8/1 | 35 | — |
| 728* | **Royal Philosopher (97)** (JWHills) **4-9-2** TQuinn(10) (led: shkn up 3f out: hdd over 2f out: btn whn hmpd wl over 1f out: eased) | 5 | 11 | 4/1 1 | 28 | — |
| 728 19 | **Cim Bom Bom (IRE) (90)** (MBell) **4-8-9** JCarroll(7) (bit bkwd: trckd ldrs tl wknd wl over 1f out: eased whn btn) | 1¼ | 12 | 16/1 | 18 | — |
| 572 5 | **Letluce (95)** (JRArnold) **3-8-2** FLynch(1) (b.nr hind: hld up: hdwy & swtchd wl over 1f out: r.o fnl f: no ch w wnr: fin 2nd, 1½l: disq: plcd last) | | D | 14/1 | 102 | 48 |

(SP 122.4%) **12 Rn**

**1m 31.46** (3.96) CSF £32.83 CT £215.88 TOTE £4.40: £2.10 £2.30 £2.80 (£29.50) Trio £77.80 OWNER Mr Henry Chan (NEWMARKET) BRED Hollybank Breeders
WEIGHT FOR AGE 3yo-12lb
STEWARDS' ENQUIRY Lynch susp. 15-18 & 20/5/96 (irresponsible riding).
**728 Cool Edge (IRE)** took a keen grip and pressed the leaders. Set alight below the distance, he came clear at will and was eased considerably nearing the finish. (4/1)
**General Monash (USA)**, still not fully wound up, ran well and, though he failed to make much impact inside the final furlong, he did stay on, and success at this trip is certainly possible. (15/2)
**728 Band on the Run** made relentless progress in the last quarter-mile without ever promising to reach the leaders, and age is beginning to catch up with him. (10/1)
**Yarob (IRE)** moved into a challenging position two furlongs out, but was hard at work when squeezed for room entering the final furlong and had little hope of recovery. (20/1)
**809 Moments of Fortune (USA)** battled on to force his head in front entering the last quarter-mile, but was swamped for speed after being collared. This trip is much too sharp for him now. (7/1)
**728* Royal Philosopher** again set out to make it all, but he had already been headed and was struggling to hold his place when forced into the rail by Letluce over a furlong out, and that was the final straw. (4/1)
**572 Letluce** has only won a maiden auction event but has been highly tried since then. Coming from off the pace, she needed to barge a rival out of the way to get a run approaching the final furlong and, though she ran on strongly to gain the runner-up prize, was demoted after a stewards' enquiry. She is a very progressive filly and more will be heard of her. (14/1)

## 961 DEAN MOOR H'CAP (0-85) (4-Y.O+) (Class D)

4-05 (4-07) **1m 6f** £3,566.25 (£1,080.00: £527.50: £251.25) Stalls: Centre GOING: 0.13 sec per fur (G)

| | Horse / details | | Pos | SP | RR | SF |
|---|---|---|---|---|---|---|
| 647* | **Purple Splash (85)** (PJMakin) **6-10-0v** AClark(7) (hld up: hdwy to ld 3f out: sn rdn: drew clr appr fnl f) | — | 1 | 3/1 1 | 100 | 61 |

| | Horse | Details | Dist | Pos | SP | RR | SF |
|---|---|---|---|---|---|---|---|
| | **Robingo (IRE) (75)** | (JNeville) **7-9-4b** JReid(2) (b: a.p: jnd ldrs 3f out: rdn & one pce fnl 2f) | 5 | **2** | 12/1 | 84 | 45 |
| $666^{3}$ | **Stalled (IRE) (53)** | (PTWalwyn) **6-7-10** LCharnock(5) (hld up: hdwy 3f out: kpt on u.p fnl 2f) | 1¼ | **3** | $7/2^{2}$ | 61 | 22 |
| $449^{17}$ | **Satin Lover (72)** | (MrsMReveley) **8-8-8**$^{(7)}$ SCopp(3) (trckd ldrs: hrd rdn over 3f out: one pce) | ¾ | **4** | 14/1 | 79 | 40 |
| $767^{6}$ | **Shakiyr (FR) (58)** | (RHollinshead) **5-7-10**$^{(5)ow5}$ FLynch(1) (trckd ldrs: led 4f out to 3f out: wknd wl over 1f out) | 5 | **5** | $11/2^{3}$ | 59 | 15 |
| $767^{15}$ | **Tremendisto (53)** | (CaptJWilson) **6-7-10** DeclanO'Shea(4) (lw: led: clr 9f out: hdd 4f out: sn btn) | hd | **6** | 20/1 | 54 | 15 |
| | **Executive Design (79)** | (MrsMReveley) **4-9-7** KDarley(8) (hld up: hdwy over 3f out: sn rdn & wknd: t.o) | 7 | **7** | $3/1^{1}$ | 72 | 32 |
| | **Zuboon (USA) (80)** | (JJO'Neill) **5-9-9** JCarroll(6) (bit bkwd: a bhd: t.o fnl 3f) | 2 | **8** | 9/1 | 71 | 32 |

(SP 116.7%) **8 Rn**

**3m 8.98** (10.78) CSF £33.87 CT £120.42 TOTE £3.90: £1.70 £2.30 £1.20 (£18.40) OWNER Sir Christopher Walford (MARLBOROUGH) BRED W. and R. Barnett Ltd

LONG HANDICAP Tremendisto 7-5

WEIGHT FOR AGE 4yo-1lb

**647* Purple Splash** is in the form of his life this year and, completing a hat-trick of wins which includes a success over hurdles, won this running away. (3/1)

**Robingo (IRE)** looked to need this first outing in ten months but turned in a very pleasing performance and he would seem to be on the way back. (12/1)

**666 Stalled (IRE)** had the edge in fitness over most of his rivals but he took a long time to get going and his final placing was as close as he could manage. (7/2)

**Satin Lover** ran much better than he did on his previous outing but he was flat to the boards from some way out and making very little impression. (14/1)

**Executive Design** has been in quite good form over hurdles but he has got two ways of running and, though he was close enough three furlongs out, he did not go through with his effort. (3/1)

## 962 DERBYSHIRE HILL MAIDEN STKS (3-Y.O) (Class D)

4-35 (4-37) **7f 30y** £3,712.50 (£1,125.00: £550.00: £262.50) Stalls: Low GOING: 0.13 sec per fur (G)

| | Horse | Details | Dist | Pos | SP | RR | SF |
|---|---|---|---|---|---|---|---|
| $732^{3}$ | **Musick House (IRE)** | (PWChapple-Hyam) **3-9-0** JReid(9) (b.hind: a.p: led wl over 2f out: qcknd clr fnl f) | — | **1** | $4/5^{1}$ | 94+ | 41 |
| | **Keltoi** | (LMCumani) **3-9-0** KDarley(5) (lengthy: unf: hld up in tch: effrt 2f out: kpt on: no ch w wnr) | 5 | **2** | $4/1^{2}$ | 83 | 30 |
| $696^{5}$ | **Roushan** | (JGMO'Shea) **3-9-0** GCarter(8) (led tl wl over 2f out: sn rdn: one pce) | 2½ | **3** | 16/1 | 77 | 24 |
| | **Azwah (USA)** | (PTWalwyn) **3-8-9** RHills(10) (bit bkwd: a.p: jnd wnr over 2f out: rdn & one pce appr fnl f) | 1¾ | **4** | $9/1^{3}$ | 68 | 15 |
| $774^{6}$ | **Look Who's Calling (IRE)** | (BAMcMahon) **3-8-11**$^{(3)}$ PMcCabe(2) (trckd ldrs: rdn over 2f out: one pce) | 1¼ | **5** | 20/1 | 71 | 18 |
| | **Oberon's Dart (IRE)** | (PJMakin) **3-9-0** AClark(11) (lw: hdwy on ins over 2f out: nt rch ldrs) | 2 | **6** | 25/1 | 66 | 13 |
| | **Northern Judge** | (BHanbury) **3-8-11**$^{(3)}$ JStack(7) (bit bkwd: mid div: rdn over 3f out: no imp) | 5 | **7** | $9/1^{3}$ | 55 | 2 |
| $768^{7}$ | **Dispol Diamond** | (GROldroyd) **3-8-9** JCarroll(3) (nvr nr to chal) | hd | **8** | 33/1 | 50 | — |
| $786^{W}$ | **Bashtheboards** | (JJQuinn) **3-9-0** LCharnock(6) (still unf: dwlt: a bhd) | 1¼ | **9** | 50/1 | 52 | — |
| | **Sabrak (IRE)** | (MAJarvis) **3-9-0** PRobinson(4) (w'like: bit bkwd: a bhd) | 2 | **10** | $9/1^{3}$ | 47 | — |
| | **White Hare** | (MrsMReveley) **3-8-3**$^{(7)ow1}$ SCopp(1) (cmpt: bkwd: s.s: a bhd: t.o) | 23 | **11** | 25/1 | — | — |

(SP 128.8%) **11 Rn**

**1m 33.41** (5.91) CSF £5.27 TOTE £1.50: £1.10 £1.70 £2.50 (£3.10) Trio £19.70 OWNER Mr R. E. Sangster (MARLBOROUGH) BRED Swettenham Stud

**732 Musick House (IRE)** did not have a lot to beat and opened his account with a clear-cut success, but must not be over-rated until he does prove himself in more exposed company. (4/5)

**Keltoi**, a half-brother to high class French winner Cherokee Rose, was unable to match strides with the winner on this occasion but he showed he has ability and will be much sharper next time. (4/1: 5/2-9/2)

**Roushan** appears to be getting the hang of things and a race of this description is well within his reach. (16/1)

**Azwah (USA)** was upsides the winner early in the straight and looked likely to make a race of it but lack of peak-fitness caught her out, and she could only plug on at the pace. She will be all the better for the run. (9/1: 6/1-10/1)

**774 Look Who's Calling (IRE)** did his best to hang on in there when the race began in earnest, but he was labouring over two furlongs out and his measure had been taken. (20/1)

**Northern Judge** (9/1: 6/1-10/1)

**Sabrak (IRE)** (9/1: 6/1-10/1)

## 963 BOTANY BAY H'CAP (0-90) (3-Y.O+) (Class C)

5-05 (5-06) **1m 3f 200y** £5,244.50 (£1,586.00: £773.00: £366.50) Stalls: Low GOING: 0.13 sec per fur (G)

| | Horse | Details | Dist | Pos | SP | RR | SF |
|---|---|---|---|---|---|---|---|
| $787^{2}$ | **Eskimo Nel (IRE) (61)** | (JLSpearing) **5-7-11**$^{(5)ow3}$ FLynch(1) (plld hrd: chsd ldng pair: led over 1f out: all out) | — | **1** | $3/1^{2}$ | 71 | 39 |
| | **Braille (IRE) (70)** | (MGMeagher) **5-8-11** JCarroll(2) (chsd ldr: led over 2f out tl over 1f out: rallied nr fin) | nk | **2** | 8/1 | 80 | 51 |
| | **Monarch (87)** | (PFICole) **4-10-0** TQuinn(5) (b: bit bkwd: hld up & bhd: effrt & rdn 3f out: styd on appr fnl f) | 4 | **3** | $7/2^{3}$ | 91 | 62 |
| 738* | **Tessajoe (75)** | (MJCamacho) **4-9-2** LCharnock(7) (lw: hld up: hdwy 4f out: rdn over 2f out: wknd fnl f) | 1¾ | **4** | $11/4^{1}$ | 77 | 48 |
| *855** | **Greenspan (IRE) (77)** | (WRMuir) **4-9-4** $^{4x}$ Jean-PierreLopez(4) (hld up in tch: rdn wl over 2f out: sn btn) | 3 | **5** | 7/1 | 75 | 46 |
| | **Desert Spring (72)** | (PWHarris) **4-8-13** RHills(6) (bit bkwd: led tl hdd & wknd over 2f out: t.o) | 16 | **6** | 9/1 | 48 | 19 |
| | **Amaze (77)** | (LadyHerries) **7-9-4** DeclanO'Shea(3) (b: dwlt: in rr: rdn 3f out: no imp: t.o) | hd | **7** | 9/1 | 53 | 24 |

(SP 117.5%) **7 Rn**

**2m 38.05** (8.65) CSF £24.76 TOTE £3.00: £1.40 £2.60 (£9.60) OWNER First Chance Racing (ALCESTER) BRED Leo Collins

**787 Eskimo Nel (IRE)**, winning for the first time at the trip, had to work hard in the end to ward off a persistent challenger. (3/1)

**Braille (IRE)** would probably have won this had he had a previous outing this term for he battled on grimly inside the distance and only just failed to get back up. (8/1)

**Monarch** can win after being out of action for some time, but he was carrying surplus condition here and, in the end, did well to finish so close. He will soon pay his way. (7/2)

**738* Tessajoe** is not quite so effective when the ground is anywhere near testing and his run had come to an end entering the final furlong. (11/4)

**855* Greenspan (IRE)** found this company just too good for him at the weights and failed to make his presence felt. (7/1)

**Desert Spring**, short on experience, forced the pace for almost ten furlongs before lack of a recent outing took its toll. (9/1)

T/Plpt: £45.50 (246.6 Tckts). T/Qdpt: £6.10 (99.32 Tckts). IM

# 0840-KEMPTON (R-H) (Good to firm)

## Monday May 6th

WEATHER: sunny WIND: almost nil

### 964 'RACE TO READ' MAIDEN STKS (3-Y.O F) (Class D)

2-10 (2-11) **1m (Jubilee)** £3,694.50 (£1,116.00: £543.00: £256.50) Stalls: High GOING minus 0.38 sec per fur (F)

| | | | | SP | RR | SF |
|---|---|---|---|---|---|---|
| 684[2] | **Whitewater Affair** (MRStoute) **3-8-11** RCochrane(3) (lw: a.p: led over 2f out: pushed out) | — | 1 | 11/8 [1] | 87 | 55 |
| | **My Lewicia (IRE)** (PWHarris) **3-8-11** GHind(2) (b.nr hind: bit bkwd: s.s: rdn over 3f out: hdwy 2f out: r.o one pce) | 1¾ | 2 | 33/1 | 84 | 52 |
| 678[6] | **Saleemah (USA)** (JLDunlop) **3-8-11** WCarson(9) (lw: plld hrd: a.p: rdn over 2f out: one pce) | ¾ | 3 | 5/2 [2] | 82 | 50 |
| | **Premier Night** (SDow) **3-8-11** BThomson(6) (leggy: scope: s.s: hdwy over 3f out: wknd wl over 1f out) | 4 | 4 | 50/1 | 74 | 42 |
| 710[3] | **Divine Quest** (HRACecil) **3-8-11** PatEddery(1) (lw: led over 5f: wknd over 1f out) | 2½ | 5 | 5/1 [3] | 69 | 37 |
| | **Abir** (HThomsonJones) **3-8-11** PaulEddery(5) (plld hrd: hld up: rdn 3f out: wknd over 2f out) | 9 | 6 | 10/1 | 51 | 19 |
| | **Kalao Tua (IRE)** (JRFanshawe) **3-8-8**(3) NVarley(8) (bhd fnl 3f) | nk | 7 | 16/1 | 50 | 18 |
| 813[12] | **Amber Ring** (MRChannon) **3-8-11** BDoyle(7) (a bhd) | 14 | 8 | 50/1 | 22 | — |
| | **In The Highlands** (DJSCosgrove) **3-8-8**(3) AWhelan(4) (b: str: bkwd: prom over 4f) | 11 | 9 | 50/1 | — | — |

(SP 111.1%) **9 Rn**

**1m 38.03** (0.83) CSF £34.98 TOTE £2.30: £1.60 £6.70 £1.20 (£109.20) Trio £77.00 OWNER Mr J. M. Greetham (NEWMARKET) BRED J. M. Greetham

**684 Whitewater Affair** confirmed the promise shown in the Wood Ditton. Moving to the front over a quarter of a mile from home, she needed only to be shaken up to have the situation in hand. (11/8: 5/4-4/5)

**My Lewicia (IRE)** did not look fully wound up and appeared a hopeless cause as she was being pushed along at the back of the field turning for home. Getting her act together in the final two furlongs, she stayed on well to snatch second. (33/1)

**678 Saleemah (USA)** took a very keen hold in the early stages and raced up with the pace. Asked for her effort in the straight, she could only keep on at one pace. (5/2)

**Premier Night**, a tall filly with substance, moved up turning for home, but had shot her bolt early in the final quarter-mile. (50/1)

**710 Divine Quest** took the field along. Collared over a quarter of a mile from home, she disappointingly faded below the distance. (5/1: 3/1-11/2)

**Abir** took a very keen hold in midfield and was hung out to dry early in the straight. (10/1: 7/1-14/1)

### 965 RACECALL CONDITIONS STKS (4-Y.O+) (Class C)

2-40 (2-40) **1m 6f 92y** £6,512.00 (£1,808.00) Stalls: High GOING minus 0.38 sec per fur (F)

| | | | | SP | RR | SF |
|---|---|---|---|---|---|---|
| | **Proposing (IRE)** (JHMGosden) **4-8-9** GHind(2) (lw: mde all: qcknd 4f out: shkn up: r.o wl) | — | 1 | Evens [2] | 96 | — |
| | **Bahamian Sunshine (USA) (102)** (DRLoder) **5-9-2** PatEddery(1) (stdd s: chsd wnr: rdn over 2f out: ev ch over 1f out: unable qckn) | 1¾ | 2 | 4/5 [1] | 100 | — |

(SP 105.6%) **2 Rn**

**3m 30.49** (27.49) TOTE £1.90 OWNER Sheikh Marwan Al Maktoum (NEWMARKET) BRED Sheikh Mohammed bin Rashid al Maktoum

WEIGHT FOR AGE 4yo-1lb

**Proposing (IRE)** looked very well considering he had not raced since finishing second in a valuable All-Weather race at Lingfield thirteen months ago. (Evens)

**Bahamian Sunshine (USA)** looked very nervous in the paddock and was led round by two handlers. Content to sit in behind his rival, he was asked for his effort early in the straight, but failed to find the necessary turn of foot. (4/5)

### 966 BALLYGALLON STUD CONDITIONS STKS (3-Y.O F) (Class C)

3-10 (3-11) **6f** £4,878.40 (£1,825.60: £892.80: £384.00: £172.00: £87.20) Stalls: High GOING minus 0.38 sec per fur (F)

| | | | | SP | RR | SF |
|---|---|---|---|---|---|---|
| 708[8] | **Please Suzanne (97)** (RHannon) **3-8-10**(3) DaneO'Neill(8) (hld up: led 1f out: pushed out) | — | 1 | 4/1 [2] | 100 | 54 |
| 673[12] | **Baize (100)** (RFJohnsonHoughton) **3-9-5** GHind(1) (lw: hld up: ev ch 1f out: unable qckn) | 1¼ | 2 | 8/1 | 103+ | 57 |
| 710[10] | **Emy Coasting (USA)** (PFICole) **3-8-2**(7) DavidO'Neill(9) (hdwy over 1f out: r.o wl ins fnl f) | 2½ | 3 | 20/1 | 86 | 40 |
| | **Babsy Babe (93)** (JJQuinn) **3-8-9** RCochrane(7) (a.p: led over 2f out to 1f out: sn wknd) | 1¼ | 4 | 13/2 [3] | 83 | 37 |
| 572[11] | **Willow Dale (IRE) (82)** (DRCElsworth) **3-8-13** BDoyle(3) (lw: a.p: rdn over 2f out: wknd over 1f out) | 4 | 5 | 25/1 | 76 | 30 |
| | **Amaniy (USA) (100)** (HThomsonJones) **3-9-5** WCarson(4) (nt grwn: spd over 4f) | 1 | 6 | 7/1 | 79 | 33 |
| | **Forentia (98)** (JRFanshawe) **3-8-10**(3) NVarley(2) (bhd fnl 2f) | ½ | 7 | 8/1 | 72 | 26 |
| 565[3] | **Kunucu (IRE)** (TDBarron) **3-9-5** PaulEddery(5) (lw: bhd fnl 2f) | s.h | 8 | 13/2 [3] | 78 | 32 |
| 648* | **Alpine Twist (USA)** (PWChapple-Hyam) **3-8-13** PatEddery(6) (led over 3f) | 5 | 9 | 100/30 [1] | 59 | 13 |

(SP 113.1%) **9 Rn**

**1m 12.1** (0.80) CSF £31.91 TOTE £4.20: £1.90 £2.80 £5.00 (£19.10) Trio £109.10 OWNER Mr Mohamed Suhail (MARLBOROUGH) BRED GAINSBOROUGH STUD MANAGEMENT LTD

OFFICIAL EXPLANATION **Alpine Twist (USA): did not act on the ground.**

**Please Suzanne** appreciated this return to a sprint distance. She moved to the front a furlong out and, shaken up, soon asserted. (4/1)

**Baize** chased the leaders. One of three almost in line a furlong out, she then failed to live with the winner. (8/1: 6/1-9/1)

**Emy Coasting (USA)**, who has not yet come in her summer coat, was going nowhere at halfway. She at last got the hang of things from below the distance and ran on nicely for third prize. (20/1)

**Babsy Babe**, collared by the winner a furlong out, soon had bellows to mend. (13/2)

**Willow Dale (IRE)** had shot her bolt below the distance. (25/1)

**Amaniy (USA)** has not grown since last year and is still a small filly. Life is going to be very tough for her this season. (7/1)

**565 Kunucu (IRE)** (13/2: 9/2-7/1)

**648* Alpine Twist (USA)**, collared a quarter of a mile out after leading, faded on this fast ground. (100/30)

### 967 DYSLEXIA INSTITUTE JUBILEE H'CAP (0-105) (4-Y.O+) (Class B)

3-40 (3-40) **1m (Jubilee)** £21,300.00 (£6,450.00: £3,150.00: £1,500.00) Stalls: High GOING minus 0.38 sec per fur (F)

| | | | | SP | RR | SF |
|---|---|---|---|---|---|---|
| 809[4] | **Desert Green (FR) (95)** (RHannon) **7-9-6**(3) DaneO'Neill(2) (lw: hdwy over 2f out: led over 1f out: r.o wl) | — | 1 | 9/2 [1] | 107 | 67 |
| 728[11] | **Clan Ben (IRE) (96)** (HRACecil) **4-9-10** PatEddery(7) (lw: a.p: led over 2f out tl over 1f out: r.o) | ¾ | 2 | 6/1 [2] | 107 | 67 |
| | **Crumpton Hill (IRE) (82)** (NAGraham) **4-8-10** PaulEddery(4) (bit bkwd: hld up: rdn over 2f out: ev ch over 1f out: unable qckn) | ¾ | 3 | 7/1 [3] | 91 | 51 |

| | | | | SP | RR | SF |
|---|---|---|---|---|---|---|
| 809* | **Star Manager (USA) (86)** (PFICole) **6-9-0** CRutter(10) (hdwy over 1f out: r.o wl) | ¾ | **4** | 15/2 | 94 | 54 |
| 809[13] | **Akil (IRE) (88)** (RWArmstrong) **4-9-2** WCarson(3) (a.p: rdn over 2f out: ev ch over 1f out: one pce) | ½ | **5** | 6/1[2] | 95 | 55 |
| 925[11] | **Amrak Ajeeb (IRE) (85)** (BHanbury) **4-8-13** GHind(6) (lw: hdwy & nt clr run over 1f out: nt clr run ins fnl f: nt rcvr) | nk | **6** | 25/1 | 91 | 51 |
| 325a[4] | **Wakeel (USA) (85)** (SDow) **4-8-13** BThomson(12) (lw: prom 6f) | 1 | **7** | 10/1 | 89 | 49 |
| | **Blue Zulu (IRE) (91)** (JRFanshawe) **4-9-2**(3) NVarley(1) (nvr nr to chal) | 1 | **8** | 12/1 | 93 | 53 |
| 728[13] | **Embankment (IRE) (83)** (RHannon) **6-8-11** SWhitworth(13) (led over 5f: wknd wl over 1f out) | ½ | **9** | 25/1 | 84 | 44 |
| 933[9] | **Scaraben (71)** (SEKettlewell) **8-7-6**(7) MartinDwyer(5) (sme hdwy over 1f out: sn wknd) | 1¾ | **10** | 16/1 | 68 | 28 |
| 809[11] | **Il Trastevere (FR) (83)** (MissGayKelleway) **4-8-11** OUrbina(8) (lw: hld up: rdn over 2f out: sn wknd) | ¾ | **11** | 25/1 | 79 | 39 |
| | **Zajko (USA) (80)** (LadyHerries) **6-8-8** RCochrane(9) (lw: hdwy on ins over 2f out: sn wknd) | s.h | **12** | 8/1 | 76 | 36 |
| 728[7] | **Night Dance (93)** (GLewis) **4-9-4**(3) AWhelan(11) (lw: bhd fnl 2f) | 2½ | **13** | 15/2 | 84 | 44 |

(SP 128.1%) **13 Rn**

**1m 37.99** (0.79) CSF £31.95 CT £173.67 TOTE £5.50: £1.90 £2.40 £3.90 (£10.40) Trio £62.20 OWNER Mrs P. Jubert (MARLBOROUGH) BRED Gainsborough Stud Management

**809 Desert Green (FR)**, who caught the eye at Sandown last time out, won this race for the second year running, despite carrying 10lb more. (9/2)

**Clan Ben (IRE)**, who encountered traffic problems on his reappearance, ran a fine race here under topweight. Sent on over a quarter of a mile out, he was collared by the winner approaching the final furlong but, to his credit, stuck to his task well to the bitter end. (6/1)

**Crumpton Hill (IRE)**, who had been gelded since last year, looked as though the run was needed but still ran very well. He should come on nicely for this. (7/1)

**809* Star Manager (USA)** was doing all his best work in the final furlong and a half, but was unable to get there in time. (15/2)

**809 Akil (IRE)**, another to catch the eye at Sandown last time out, raced up with the pace on this occasion. With every chance below the distance, he was then tapped for toe. (6/1)

**Amrak Ajeeb (IRE)** had no luck in running, but still left his two previous runs this season well behind. Beginning to weave his way through the pack below the distance, he then got stopped in his tracks and again encountered traffic problems inside the final furlong. Not surprisingly, he failed to recover from this but still finished a very creditable sixth. (25/1)

## 968 EUROPEAN HEALTHCARE GROUP H'CAP (0-80) (3-Y.O+) (Class D)

4-10 (4-12) **1m 4f** £3,792.00 (£1,146.00: £558.00: £264.00) Stalls: High GOING minus 0.38 sec per fur (F)

| | | | | SP | RR | SF |
|---|---|---|---|---|---|---|
| 647[9] | **Artic Courier (76)** (DJSCosgrove) **5-9-11**(3) AWhelan(9) (hld up: swtchd lft over 2f out: led over 1f out: hrd rdn: hdd last stride: fin 2nd, s.h: awrdd r) | — | **1** | 10/1 | 86 | 68 |
| | **Nordansk (44)** (MMadgwick) **7-7-7**(3) NVarley(10) (lw: rdn over 3f out: hdwy 2f out: hrd rdn & r.o fnl f: led last stride: fin 1st: disq: plcd 2nd) | | **2** | 33/1 | 55 | 37 |
| 844[2] | **General Mouktar (52)** (BJMeehan) **6-8-4** WCarson(5) (lw: hdwy over 2f out: swtchd rt over 1f out: ev ch ins fnl f: hmpd nr fin) | 2 | **3** | 100/30[1] | 60 | 42 |
| 817[6] | **Zermatt (IRE) (63)** (MDIUsher) **6-9-1** PaulEddery(4) (lw: led 2f: led over 2f out tl over 1f out: sn wknd) | 3½ | **4** | 20/1 | 66 | 48 |
| 682[5] | **Dont Shoot Fairies (74)** (CEBrittain) **4-9-12** BDoyle(1) (hld up: rdn over 2f out: wknd over 1f out) | ¾ | **5** | 8/1 | 76 | 58 |
| 738[2] | **Domappel (73)** (MrsJCecil) **4-9-11** BThomson(14) (stdy hdwy over 4f out: nvr plcd to chal) | 1¼ | **6** | 13/2[3] | 73 | 55 |
| | **Summerhill Special (IRE) (70)** (MrsPNDutfield) **5-9-8** CRutter(13) (bit bkwd: nvr nr to chal) | 1¾ | **7** | 50/1 | 68 | 50 |
| 771[3] | **No Pattern (73)** (GLMoore) **4-9-11v** SWhitworth(11) (lw: hdwy over 4f out: wknd over 2f out) | 1 | **8** | 8/1 | 70 | 52 |
| *181*[8] | **Quivira (74)** (HAkbary) **5-9-12** GHind(7) (hdwy over 4f out: wknd over 2f out) | 4 | **9** | 50/1 | 65 | 47 |
| | **Bolivar (IRE) (63)** (RAkehurst) **4-8-8**(7) TAshley(8) (lw: hdwy 8f out: rdn over 4f out: wknd over 2f out) | 2½ | **10** | 4/1[2] | 51 | 33 |
| 439[9] | **Edan Heights (72)** (SDow) **4-9-10** PatEddery(15) (lw: led 10f out tl over 2f out: sn wknd) | 1¼ | **11** | 8/1 | 58 | 40 |
| 469[5] | **Kelly Mac (56)** (DCO'Brien) **6-8-5**(3) DaneO'Neill(12) (hld up: rdn over 3f out: sn wknd) | 25 | **12** | 20/1 | 9 | — |
| 760[8] | **Yet Again (50)** (BHanbury) **4-7-9**(7) MartinDwyer(16) (lw: bhd fnl 5f) | 2½ | **13** | 25/1 | — | — |
| | **Lucky Coin (66)** (PHowling) **4-9-4** RCochrane(2) (a bhd) | 1¾ | **14** | 20/1 | 13 | — |
| | **Desert Harvest (74)** (GMMcCourt) **4-9-5**(7) RStudholme(6) (lw: prom 7f) | 4 | **15** | 50/1 | 16 | — |

(SP 125.8%) **15 Rn**

**2m 32.69** (1.99) CSF £256.91 CT £1,222.88 TOTE £15.00: £4.10 £4.90 £1.70 (£89.60) Trio £80.30 OWNER Britam Promotions Ltd (NEWMARKET) BRED Stud-On-The-Chart

LONG HANDICAP Nordansk 7-6

**439 Artic Courier** is not easy to win with. He did nothing wrong here though and, with a bit of help from the Stewards, won the second race of his career. Switched left over a quarter of mile from home, he moved to the front below the distance but was immediately challenged by Nordansk. Grimly trying to hold on, he was headed right on the line, but was later awarded the race. (10/1)

**Nordansk**, winner of two handicap hurdles in the mud this winter, was ridden along at the back of the field turning for home. Picking up ground a quarter of a mile out, he threw down his challenge from below the distance and went at it nip and tuck with the winner. He drifted to his right inside the final furlong, but managed to get up right on the line. He was later disqualified, but can soon gain compensation. (33/1)

**844 General Mouktar**, switched onto the rail below the distance, was soon throwing down his challenge. One of three battling for honours inside the final furlong, he was hampered near the finish. (100/30)

**817 Zermatt (IRE)**, the early leader, then raced in second place until going on again over a quarter of a mile from home. Headed below the distance, he had nothing more to give. This trip is just beyond him. (20/1)

**682 Dont Shoot Fairies** chased the leaders but ran out of gas below the distance. (8/1)

**738 Domappel** caught the eye in no uncertain terms. Moving up into midfield turning for home, his rider appeared to have quite a tight rein in one hand whilst administering several cosmetic reminders with the other. Under more vigorous riding, he would surely have been a lot closer. (13/2)

## 969 ROTHMANS ROYALS NORTH SOUTH CHALLENGE SERIES H'CAP (0-90) (3-Y.O) (Class C)

4-40 (4-43) **1m 1f (round)** £7,100.00 (£2,150.00: £1,050.00: £500.00) Stalls: Low GOING minus 0.38 sec per fur (F)

| | | | | SP | RR | SF |
|---|---|---|---|---|---|---|
| 863[2] | **Trojan Risk (72)** (GLewis) **3-8-7** PaulEddery(1) (lw: squeezed out on ins over 4f out: rdn & hdwy 2f out: led wl ins fnl f: r.o wl) | — | **1** | 5/1[1] | 77 | 41 |
| | **Kriscliffe (80)** (MissGayKelleway) **3-9-1** RCochrane(10) (lw: led: qcknd over 2f out: hdd wl ins fnl f: unable qckn) | ¾ | **2** | 16/1 | 84 | 48 |
| 833[2] | **Forest Robin (85)** (RFJohnsonHoughton) **3-9-6** BDoyle(3) (lw: n.m.r 2f out: hdwy over 1f out: r.o wl ins fnl f) | hd | **3** | 5/1[1] | 89 | 53 |
| 663* | **Aerleon Jane (86)** (JHMGosden) **3-9-7** GHind(6) (lw: a.p: rdn over 2f out: eased whn btn ins fnl f) | 5 | **4** | 7/1[2] | 81 | 45 |
| 578[10] | **Clouds Hill (FR) (78)** (RHannon) **3-8-10**(3) DaneO'Neill(2) (b: a.p: rdn over 2f out: one pce) | s.h | **5** | 5/1[1] | 73 | 37 |

| | | | | SP | RR | SF |
|---|---|---|---|---|---|---|
| 754* | **Docklands Limo (78)** (BJMcMath) **3-8-13** EJohnson(9) (a.p: rdn over 2f out: eased whn btn ins fnl f) | 1¾ | **6** | 5/1[1] | 69 | 33 |
| 693[6] | **Dance On A Cloud (USA) (83)** (MRStoute) **3-9-4** BThomson(7) (hld up: rdn over 2f out: wknd over 1f out) | 1½ | **7** | 14/1 | 72 | 36 |
| 550[3] | **Royal Diversion (IRE) (84)** (JLDunlop) **3-9-5** PatEddery(8) (a bhd) | nk | **8** | 5/1[1] | 72 | 36 |
| 705[7] | **Tawafek (USA) (72)** (DMorley) **3-8-7** WCarson(4) (lw: a bhd) | 1 | **9** | 8/1[3] | 58 | 22 |
| 588[2] | **Disallowed (IRE) (74)** (MBell) **3-8-2**(7) GFaulkner(5) (lw: chsd ldr over 6f) | 2½ | **10** | 12/1 | 56 | 20 |
| | | | | (SP 127.2%) | **10 Rn** | |

**1m 52.8** (2.20) CSF £75.55 CT £404.49 TOTE £5.20: £1.60 £4.00 £2.70 (£35.10) Trio £120.80 OWNER Mr Jim McCarthy (EPSOM) BRED Roldvale Ltd

**863 Trojan Risk**, who looked in good heart beforehand, began to get going in the straight and came with a sustained run to get up in the closing stages. (5/1: op 3/1)

**Kriscliffe**, sold out of Peter Walwyn's stable for 10,500 guineas at the Autumn Sales, took the field along. Quickening up in impressive style early in the straight, he poached a good few lengths on his rivals and had them all at it. Grimly trying to hold on, he was worried out of it in the closing stages. His new connections should not have to wait long for victory. (16/1)

**833 Forest Robin**, who did not have a great deal of room a quarter of a mile out, soon began to pick up ground and ran on strongly inside the final furlong, only just failing to take second prize. (5/1)

**663* Aerleon Jane** failed to find the necessary turn of foot, and was eased when beaten inside the final furlong. (7/1)

**Clouds Hill (FR)** never looked like quickening in the last two furlongs. (5/1: op 8/1)

**754* Docklands Limo** was never far away but, when asked for his effort early in the straight, he failed to quicken and was eased thereafter. (5/1)

**705 Tawafek (USA)** (8/1: 6/1-9/1)

## 970 HOME STUD MAIDEN STKS (3-Y.O) (Class D)

5-10 (5-11) **1m (Jubilee)** £3,694.50 (£1,116.00: £543.00: £256.50) Stalls: High GOING minus 0.38 sec per fur (F)

| | | | | SP | RR | SF |
|---|---|---|---|---|---|---|
| | **Dr Massini (IRE)** (MRStoute) **3-8-11** RCochrane(9) (w'like: scope: hld up: rdn over 2f out: led ins fnl f: r.o wl) | — | **1** | 9/4[1] | 102 | 58 |
| | **Wall Street (USA)** (SbinSuroor) **3-8-11** BThomson(1) (leggy: scope: a.p: led over 2f out tl ins fnl f: unable qckn) | 1¼ | **2** | 5/1[3] | 100 | 56 |
| 847[2] | **Axford (USA) (95)** (PWChapple-Hyam) **3-8-8**(3) AWhelan(6) (lw: a.p: ev ch over 1f out: one pce) | 3 | **3** | 4/1[2] | 94 | 50 |
| 566[3] | **Philosopher (IRE)** (RHannon) **3-8-8**(3) DaneO'Neill(3) (rdn over 3f out: hdwy over 1f out: one pce) | 3 | **4** | 14/1 | 88 | 44 |
| | **Lituus (USA)** (JHMGosden) **3-8-11** GHind(8) (bit bkwd: s.s: rdn over 2f out: hdwy over 1f out: wknd fnl f) | 1½ | **5** | 25/1 | 85 | 41 |
| 833[3] | **Warning Reef (84)** (MRChannon) **3-8-11** BDoyle(5) (nvr nr to chal) | hd | **6** | 10/1 | 84 | 40 |
| 732[7] | **Mawared (IRE)** (JLDunlop) **3-8-11** WCarson(7) (s.s: a bhd) | 4 | **7** | 16/1 | 76 | 32 |
| 684[5] | **Hareb (USA)** (JWHills) **3-8-11** PaulEddery(4) (led over 5f: wknd over 1f out) | 3½ | **8** | 6/1 | 69 | 25 |
| | **Serious Account (USA)** (HRACecil) **3-8-11** PatEddery(2) (str: scope: bkwd: a.p: ev ch 2f out: wknd over 1f out) | 2 | **9** | 5/1[3] | 65 | 21 |
| | | | | (SP 123.9%) | **9 Rn** | |

**1m 37.79** (0.59) CSF £14.45 TOTE £4.40: £1.30 £1.80 £1.70 (£7.20) Trio £23.60 OWNER Mr M. Tabor (NEWMARKET) BRED Mount Coote Partnership

**Dr Massini (IRE)** looked as though the run would do him good yet still managed to carry the day. Woken up early in the straight, he came with a useful run from below the distance to snatch the spoils inside the final furlong. (9/4)

**Wall Street (USA)** poked a nostril in front over quarter of a mile from home. Grimly trying to hold on, he was unable to match the winner inside the final furlong. He should soon go one better. (5/1: op 3/1)

**847 Axford (USA)**, always close up, had every chance below the distance before tapped for toe. He is becoming costly to follow. (4/1)

**566 Philosopher (IRE)**, ridden along and going nowhere turning for home, moved up below the distance but could then make no further impression. (14/1)

**Lituus (USA)** moved up through the pack below the distance, but then tired in the final furlong as lack of race fitness took its toll. He should come on a lot for this. (25/1)

**833 Warning Reef** (10/1: 8/1-12/1)

**Serious Account (USA)**, a strongly-made newcomer, looked far from fit but still showed plenty of promise before tiring. Always close up, he was one of four battling for the lead a quarter of a mile from home, before calling it a day. A race can be found for him in due course. (5/1: op 3/1)

T/Jkpt: £19,519.90 (2.59 Tckts). T/Plpt: £128.80 (220.47 Tckts). T/Qdpt: £55.60 (34.23 Tckts). AK

# 0584-NEWCASTLE (L-H) (Good)

## Monday May 6th

Races 2,4 & 6 hand-timed.

WEATHER: fine WIND: almost nil

## 971 CENTENARY OLYMPIC GAMES CLAIMING STKS (3-Y.O+) (Class F)

2-25 (2-28) **7f** £2,703.00 (£758.00: £369.00) Stalls: High GOING minus 0.01 sec per fur (G)

| | | | | SP | RR | SF |
|---|---|---|---|---|---|---|
| 882[8] | **My Godson (37)** (JLEyre) **6-9-3b** RLappin(2) (dwlt: hdwy to ld far side over 2f out: all out) | — | **1** | 25/1 | 55 | 24 |
| | **Broctune Gold (60)** (MrsMReveley) **5-9-7** ACulhane(11) (led stands' side: edgd lft 2f out: kpt on ins fnl f) | 1 | **2** | 11/2[3] | 57 | 26 |
| 801[7] | **Sallyoreally (IRE) (20)** (WStorey) **5-8-10** NKennedy(14) (hdwy over 2f out: edgd lft & styd on same pce fnl f) | hd | **3** | 50/1 | 46 | 15 |
| 801[3] | **Sagebrush Roller (77)** (JWWatts) **8-9-11** GDuffield(16) (chsd ldrs: styd on ins fnl f) | nk | **4** | 7/4[1] | 60 | 29 |
| 545[6] | **First Gold (54)** (JWharton) **7-9-8b** MWigham(9) (hdwy over 1f out: styd on wl ins fnl f) | 1 | **5** | 10/1 | 55 | 24 |
| 586[11] | **Here Comes Herbie (26)** (WStorey) **4-9-1** JFanning(7) (racd far side: styd on fnl 2f: nvr nr ldrs) | 1¾ | **6** | 50/1 | 44 | 13 |
| 756[8] | **Allez Cyrano (IRE) (69)** (MBell) **5-9-4**(7) PTurner(12) (b: chsd ldrs: rdn & hung lft over 2f out: sn wknd) | 3 | **7** | 5/1[2] | 47 | 16 |
| 822[7] | **Care And Comfort (52)** (NTinkler) **4-8-8** KimTinkler(15) (sme hdwy over 2f out: nvr nr ldrs) | 2 | **8** | 20/1 | 25 | — |
| 868[12] | **Prime Property (IRE) (41)** (MWEasterby) **4-9-1b**(5) GParkin(3) (lw: led far side tl over 2f out: sn wknd) | nk | **9** | 33/1 | 36 | 5 |
| 850[6] | **Blue Grit (51)** (MDods) **10-9-9** DeanMcKeown(6) (chsd ldrs far side 4f: sn wknd) | 4 | **10** | 12/1 | 30 | — |
| 805[2] | **Thwaab (48)** (FWatson) **4-9-2**(5) CTeague(5) (chsd ldrs far side: effrt over 2f out: sn wknd) | 6 | **11** | 12/1 | 15 | — |
| | **Steel Sovereign (38)** (MDods) **5-9-0**(5) PFessey(4) (dwlt s: sn chsng ldrs far side: lost pl 3f out) | 3½ | **12** | 50/1 | 5 | — |
| 817[18] | **Media Express (60)** (MBrittain) **4-9-11** WRyan(8) (sn bhd & pushed along) | 5 | **13** | 14/1 | — | — |
| | **Chilly Looks (45)** (WLBarker) **3-8-1**(3) DWright(13) (swtg: chsd ldrs 4f: sn wknd) | 1¼ | **14** | 25/1 | — | — |

| | | | | SP | RR | SF |
|---|---|---|---|---|---|---|
| | **Europex (50)** (TDEasterby) **3-8-5** DaleGibson(10) (bit bkwd: sn outpcd & drvn along) | 1 | **15** | 10/1 | — | — |
| $801^{2}$ | **Flamboro (45)** (JDBethell) **4-9-1** TWilliams(1) (chsd ldrs far side tl virtually p.u over 2f out) | 28 | **16** | 6/1 | — | — |

(SP 144.2%) **16 Rn**

**1m 31.01** (6.51) CSF £169.03 TOTE £27.00: £5.30 £2.70 £25.90 (£67.40) Trio Not won; £339.14 to Chester 7/5/96 OWNER Linkchallenge Ltd (HAMBLETON) BRED Mrs M. Russell

WEIGHT FOR AGE 3yo-12lb

**OFFICIAL EXPLANATION Flamboro: lost his action shortly after the start.**

**My Godson** raced on the favoured far side and recorded his first victory for over two years. There was no doubt that the draw played a major part. (25/1)

**Broctune Gold**, whose four previous victories at two and three have been recorded in May, is an excitable type who is always likely to run his best race in his first couple of outings. Drifting left towards the centre, he kept on under pressure but could not overhaul the winner on the far side. (11/2)

**Sallyoreally (IRE)** seemed to run easily her best ever race, but the form must be taken with a pinch of salt. (50/1)

**801 Sagebrush Roller**, drawn sixteen of sixteen, had no option but to keep to the stands' side. (7/4)

**545 First Gold**, drawn nine, ended up racing bang under the unfavoured stands' side and, in the circumstances, ran creditably. (10/1)

## 972 BANK HOLIDAY H'CAP (0-80) (3-Y.O+) (Class D)

2-55 (2-55) **1m 4f 93y** £3,566.25 (£1,080.00: £527.50: £251.25) Stalls: Low GOING minus 0.01 sec per fur (G)

| | | | | SP | RR | SF |
|---|---|---|---|---|---|---|
| | **Latvian (62)** (RAllan) **9-9-1** ACulhane(2) (chsd ldr: led over 2f out: hld on wl ins fnl f) | — | **1** | 10/1 | 73 | 42 |
| $787^{7}$ | **Biloela (58)** (JGFitzGerald) **6-8-11** MWigham(1) (swtg: trckd ldrs: plld hrd: chal over 1f out: nt qckn ins fnl f) | 1½ | **2** | 5/2 [1] | 67 | 36 |
| *$532^{5}$* | **Secret Service (IRE) (73)** (CWThornton) **4-9-12** DeanMcKeown(7) (hld up: effrt & outpcd over 3f out: styd on fnl f: nt rch ldrs) | ¾ | **3** | 4/1 [3] | 81 | 50 |
| 771* | **Hasta la Vista (54)** (MWEasterby) **6-8-2b**(5) GParkin(6) (lw: led tl over 2f out: one pce) | 2 | **4** | 3/1 [2] | 60 | 29 |
| | **Amiarge (47)** (MBrittain) **6-7-11**(3) DWright(4) (chsd ldrs: pushed along 5f out: outpced fnl 2f) | 1½ | **5** | 12/1 | 51 | 20 |
| | **Mr Christie (44)** (MissLCSiddall) **4-7-11** TWilliams(5) (in tch: pushed along 6f out: lost pl over 3f out) | 14 | **6** | 16/1 | 30 | — |
| $619^{3}$ | **Astral Weeks (IRE) (62)** (LLungo) **5-9-1** WRyan(8) (b: hld up & bhd: effrt 3f out: sn wknd) | 2½ | **7** | 11/2 | 44 | 13 |
| | **Lindisfarne Lady (43)** (MrsMReveley) **4-7-10** DaleGibson(3) (hld up: effrt over 4f out: sn wknd) | 16 | **8** | 14/1 | 5 | — |

(SP 118.3%) **8 Rn**

**2m 46.4** (8.90) CSF £34.66 CT £110.18 TOTE £9.20: £1.60 £1.80 £1.90 (£38.90) OWNER Mr I. Bell (CORNHILL-ON-TWEED) BRED Fittocks Stud Ltd

LONG HANDICAP Lindisfarne Lady 7-7

**Latvian**, looking big and well, has had a wind operation. Though he carries his head high, there is nothing wrong in his resolution. He now heads to Musselburgh where he has already scored three times. (10/1)

**787 Biloela**, awash with sweat at the start, raced keenly and, after looking to be going slightly the better, was outstayed in the end. The mile and a quarter might suit her better. (5/2)

**532 Secret Service (IRE)**, tapped for toe turning in, was staying on when it was all over. He showed a poor action and will be suited by soft ground. (4/1)

**771* Hasta la Vista**, raised 3lb, was never going to shake off his rivals, and the Handicapper probably has his measure for the time being. (3/1)

**Amiarge**, very fit, was under pressure to keep in touch almost three-quarters of a mile from home. Sticking on at the finish, he might be better over two miles. (12/1)

## 973 18.29M TRIPLE JUMP WORLD RECORD H'CAP (0-70) (3-Y.O) (Class E)

3-25 (3-27) **6f** £2,983.00 (£904.00: £442.00: £211.00) Stalls: High GOING minus 0.01 sec per fur (G)

| | | | | SP | RR | SF |
|---|---|---|---|---|---|---|
| | **Desert Lynx (IRE) (60)** (TRWatson) **3-9-2** GDuffield(2) (racd far side: effrt & swtchd rt over 2f out: qcknd to ld 1f out: r.o strly) | — | **1** | 14/1 | 73 | 45 |
| *$167^{5}$* | **Madam Zando (42)** (JBalding) **3-7-12**ow2 JFanning(5) (racd far side: chsd ldrs: led over 1f out: sn hdd & nt qckn) | 3½ | **2** | 33/1 | 46 | 16 |
| $748^{13}$ | **Pathaze (53)** (NBycroft) **3-8-9** NKennedy(4) (racd far side: bhd tl styd on fnl 2f: nvr nr to chal) | 3 | **3** | 20/1 | 49 | 21 |
| $775^{2}$ | **Silver Welcome (63)** (TDEasterby) **3-9-5** TWilliams(7) (led far side tl over 1f out: kpt on one pce) | 1½ | **4** | 6/1 [2] | 55 | 27 |
| $824^{7}$ | **Bowlers Boy (65)** (JJQuinn) **3-9-7** WRyan(11) (lw: chsd ldrs stands' side: kpt on wl fnl f) | 1½ | **5** | 7/1 | 53+ | 25 |
| $762^{14}$ | **Doug's Folly (51)** (MWEasterby) **3-8-2**(5) GParkin(3) (s.i.s: racd far side: hdwy & nt clr run over 2f out: kpt on fnl f) | 1 | **6** | 14/1 | 36 | 8 |
| $453^{7}$ | **Oriole (53)** (NTinkler) **3-8-9** KimTinkler(17) (swtg: racd alone stands' side: a in tch: kpt on wl fnl f) | 1 | **7** | 33/1 | 35 | 7 |
| $861^{2}$ | **Miletrian Refurb (IRE) (62)** (MRChannon) **3-8-13**(5) PPMurphy(9) (led stands' side over 4f: grad wknd) | 1½ | **8** | 11/2 [1] | 40 | 12 |
| $769^{5}$ | **Penny Parkes (50)** (JBerry) **3-8-1**(5) PFessey(6) (dwlt s: racd far side: sn chsng ldrs: wknd over 1f out) | ¾ | **9** | 11/1 | 26 | — |
| $638^{8}$ | **Rhythmic Ball (48)** (TRWatson) **3-8-1**(3) DarrenMoffatt(1) (racd far side: prom over 3f) | 2½ | **10** | 20/1 | 18 | — |
| $638^{2}$ | **Polish Saga (52)** (MDods) **3-8-8** DeanMcKeown(12) (in tch to ½-wy) | 1½ | **11** | 13/2 [3] | 18 | — |
| $701^{5}$ | **Theatre Magic (60)** (SRBowring) **3-8-11**(5) CTeague(10) (chsd ldrs stands' side: tl lost pl over 3f out) | ¾ | **12** | 6/1 [2] | 24 | — |
| *$405^{12}$* | **Lila Pedigo (IRE) (58)** (MissJFCraze) **3-9-0** DaleGibson(14) (a bhd) | 11 | **13** | 33/1 | — | — |
| | **Jambo (55)** (JLEyre) **3-8-11** RLappin(15) (bit bkwd: prom to ½-wy: sn wknd) | 1½ | **14** | 16/1 | — | — |
| $443^{12}$ | **Opening Chorus (58)** (MrsMReveley) **3-9-0** ACulhane(13) (s.i.s: a bhd) | ½ | **15** | 11/1 | — | — |
| 867* | **Forecast (42)** (JWharton) **3-7-9b**1(3) 7x DWright(8) (racd centre: sn bhd & rdn along: hung lft ½-wy: nt r.o) | 4 | **16** | 11/2 [1] | — | — |
| $773^{7}$ | **Imp Express (IRE) (65)** (GMMoore) **3-9-7** MWigham(16) (s.i.s: a bhd) | 3½ | **17** | 20/1 | — | — |

(SP 144.2%) **17 Rn**

**1m 15.36** (3.86) CSF £388.04 CT £4,283.75 TOTE £20.70: £4.30 £6.00 £7.80 £2.30 (£284.10) Trio £271.50 OWNER Mrs R. T. Watson (GAINSBOROUGH) BRED Mr and Mrs Dare Wigan

**IN-FOCUS: Those drawn on the far side held an advantage similar in length to Jonathan Edwards' Triple Jump record.**

**Desert Lynx (IRE)** won this decisively, but the draw was a major factor - the first four home raced on the far side. Even so, she quickened right away inside the last to give her trainer his first ever winner, and a follow up must be on the cards. (14/1: op 8/1)

**Madam Zando**, having her first outing for ninety-eight days, appeared to run very well, but the draw factor should be taken into account. (33/1)

**Pathaze** raced on the favoured far side and this was in her favour. (20/1)

**775 Silver Welcome**, again taken to post early, set the pace but could never dominate. (6/1: op 4/1)

**824 Bowlers Boy** came out best of those racing towards the stands' side. An opening should soon be found for him. (7/1)

**Doug's Folly** has slipped down the weights but did not take the eye in the paddock. She showed ability though after not having the best of runs. (14/1)
**Oriole**, drawn top of the shop in seventeen, raced almost alone up the unfavoured stands' side and, in the circumstances, probably ran a highly creditable race. (33/1)
**861 Miletrian Refurb (IRE)** set the pace on the stands' side, but it was clear over a furlong out that those on the far side were some way ahead. (11/2)
**Penny Parkes** (11/1: 8/1-12/1)
**Opening Chorus** (11/1: 8/1-12/1)
**867* Forecast**, tried in a visor, was warm beforehand and wanted no part of it. His 50/1 Nottingham win was probably a fluke. (11/2)

## 974 1996 ATLANTA OLYMPIC GAMES MAIDEN STKS (3-Y.O+) (Class D)

4-00 (4-00) **1m 2f 32y** £3,566.25 (£1,080.00: £527.50: £251.25) Stalls: Low GOING minus 0.01 sec per fur (G)

| | | | | SP | RR | SF |
|---|---|---|---|---|---|---|
| 677[3] | **Generosus (FR)** (HRACecil) **3-8-9** WRyan(6) (lw: mde most: clr 3f out: pushed out: unchal) | — | 1 | 2/9[1] | 93+ | 25 |
| 845[5] | **Candle Smile (USA)** (MRStoute) **4-9-10** DeanMcKeown(1) (trckd ldrs: effrt on ins & nt clr run over 1f out: swtchd: no ch w wnr) | 4 | 2 | 9/2[2] | 87 | 34 |
| | **Beacontree** (MJohnston) **3-8-9** TWilliams(5) (swtg: chsd wnr: rdn & hung lft 2f out: nt run on) | 2½ | 3 | 14/1 | 83 | 15 |
| 691[9] | **Ledgendry Line** (MrsMReveley) **3-8-9** ACulhane(4) (stdd s: effrt over 3f out: kpt on: nvr nr to chal) | 3½ | 4 | 12/1[3] | 77 | 9 |
| | **Fiasco** (MJCamacho) **3-8-4** DaleGibson(3) (cmpt: bit bkwd: dwlt s: sn chsng ldrs: pushed along 5f out: one pce) | nk | 5 | 50/1 | 36 t | 4 |
| | **Baraqueta** (JLEyre) **4-9-10** RLappin(2) (unf: a in rr: lost tch over 3f out) | 11 | 6 | 33/1 | 23 t | 6 |

(SP 119.3%) **6 Rn**

**2m 15.4** (8.70) CSF £2.23 TOTE £1.10: £1.20 £1.10 (£1.40) OWNER H R H Prince Fahd Salman (NEWMARKET) BRED Societe Aland
WEIGHT FOR AGE 3yo-15lb
**677 Generosus (FR)**, backed as if defeat was out of the question, found this plain sailing. Showing a round action, he had only to be kept to his work after showing in a clear lead once in line for home. He should go on from here. (2/9)
**845 Candle Smile (USA)**, trying to make his effort on the inside of the third, found himself short off room and had to be switched. He stuck on but had no chance with the winner and will be better suited by one and a half miles. (9/2)
**Beacontree**, on edge beforehand, swished his tail in the race. Hanging violently left under pressure, he looked anything but in love with the game. No doubt he will be gelded before long. (14/1: op 8/1)
**447 Ledgendry Line**, a keen-going type, was dropped out at the start. He will have to learn to settle. (12/1)
**Fiasco** was pushed along some way from home. (50/1)

## 975 OLYMPIC SPIRIT MAIDEN AUCTION STKS (2-Y.O) (Class F)

4-30 (4-31) **5f** £2,619.00 (£734.00: £357.00) Stalls: High GOING minus 0.01 sec per fur (G)

| | | | | SP | RR | SF |
|---|---|---|---|---|---|---|
| 823[4] | **Legend of Aragon** (JAGlover) **2-8-2** GDuffield(2) (mde all far side: r.o wl) | — | 1 | 5/1[2] | 62 | 13 |
| | **Bayford Thrust** (JBerry) **2-8-2**(5) PFessey(10) (leggy: b: chsd ldr stands' side: styd on wl ins fnl f: nt rch wnr) | 2 | 2 | 7/1[3] | 61 | 12 |
| 800[6] | **High Spirits (IRE)** (TDEasterby) **2-8-9** MWigham(4) (sltly hmpd s: sn chsng ldrs: kpt on same pce appr fnl f) | nk | 3 | 5/1[2] | 62 | 13 |
| 699[5] | **Plan For Profit (IRE)** (MJohnston) **2-8-9** TWilliams(11) (led stands' side tl outpcd fnl f) | 2 | 4 | 5/4[1] | 55 | 6 |
| 585[7] | **Nostalgic Air (USA)** (EWeymes) **2-8-2** JFanning(3) (bit bkwd: a chsng ldrs: kpt on one pce fnl 2f) | ½ | 5 | 12/1 | 47 | — |
| 699[7] | **Bold Brief** (DenysSmith) **2-8-5** WRyan(7) (hdwy ½-wy: kpt on same pce) | 3 | 6 | 8/1 | 40 | — |
| | **Bellaf** (MWEasterby) **2-8-4**(5) GParkin(12) (unf: bit bkwd: s.i.s: racd stands' side: bhd tl sme hdwy fnl f) | nk | 7 | 25/1 | 43 | — |
| | **Emily-Jayne** (MrsMReveley) **2-8-4** ACulhane(6) (unf: scope: sn outpcd & bhd: sme hdwy over 1f out: n.d) | hd | 8 | 16/1 | 38 | — |
| 823[7] | **Clonavon Girl (IRE)** (MJCamacho) **2-8-0** DaleGibson(1) (chsd ldrs tl wknd over 1f out) | 2 | 9 | 16/1 | 27 | — |
| 848[8] | **Antares** (NTinkler) **2-8-9** KimTinkler(5) (chsd ldrs tl wknd over 1f out) | ½ | 10 | 25/1 | 35 | — |
| 823[10] | **Loch-Hurn Lady** (KWHogg) **2-7-12** NKennedy(9) (sn outpcd: edgd rt ½-wy: n.d) | 2 | 11 | 33/1 | 17 | — |
| | **Soviet Lady (IRE)** (JLEyre) **2-7-13**(3) DWright(8) (lt-f: unf: a outpcd & sn bhd) | 5 | 12 | 10/1 | 5 | — |

(SP 140.6%) **12 Rn**

**62.75 secs** (4.35) CSF £44.19 TOTE £4.40: £2.50 £2.70 £3.80 (£14.00) Trio £78.90 OWNER Mr S. J. Beard (WORKSOP) BRED Limestone Stud
**823 Legend of Aragon** was thought to be unsuited by the undulations at Ripon last time by her trainer. Making a bee-line for the favoured far side, she kept up the gallop in tremendous style and was never in any danger. She will even better suited by six. (5/1)
**Bayford Thrust**, a half-brother to Captain Carat, was one of three to race on the unfavoured stands' side. Putting in some solid work inside the last, connections will have been encouraged by this. (7/1)
**800 High Spirits (IRE)** could only keep on at the same pace in the final furlong and will be better suited by six or seven in due course. (5/1)
**699 Plan For Profit (IRE)**, again made market leader, led his two rivals on the stands' side, but it was clear coming to the final furlong the winner was clear. He is not a five furlong horse and will be suited by seven or a mile later in the season. (5/4: 6/4-Evens)
**585 Nostalgic Air (USA)** still looked burly but there should be better to come. (12/1)
**Bold Brief** (8/1: 6/1-10/1)

## 976 NORTH OF ENGLAND BRITISH OLYMPIC APPEAL H'CAP (0-80) (3-Y.O) (Class D)

5-00 (5-02) **1m** £3,631.25 (£1,100.00: £537.50: £256.25) Stalls: Low GOING minus 0.01 sec per fur (G)

| | | | | SP | RR | SF |
|---|---|---|---|---|---|---|
| 827[5] | **Lucky Bea (54)** (MWEasterby) **3-8-1** DaleGibson(10) (drvn along ½-wy: hdwy over 2f out: styd on to ld wl ins fnl f) | — | 1 | 12/1 | 62 | 15 |
| 873[2] | **Silverdale Knight (57)** (KWHogg) **3-8-4** DeanMcKeown(11) (led tl wl ins fnl f) | nk | 2 | 6/1[3] | 64 | 17 |
| 595* | **Winston (59)** (JDBethell) **3-8-3**(3) DWright(5) (hld up: effrt 3f out: nt clr run over 1f out: swtchd & styd on strly) | nk | 3 | 8/1 | 66 | 19 |
| 786[4] | **Dispol Gem (72)** (GROldroyd) **3-9-5** WRyan(4) (lw: chsd ldrs: kpt on wl fnl f) | nk | 4 | 7/1 | 78 | 31 |
| *134** | **Farmost (63)** (SirMarkPrescott) **3-8-10** GDuffield(8) (trckd ldrs: effrt over 2f out: wl outpcd appr fnl f) | 4 | 5 | 5/4[1] | 61 | 14 |
| 915* | **Forest Boy (78)** (KMcAuliffe) **3-9-6v**(5) 5x CTeague(9) (chsd ldrs: rdn 3f out: hung lft: wknd appr fnl f) | 1½ | 6 | 11/2[2] | 73 | 26 |
| 453[14] | **Islay Brown (IRE) (62)** (CWCElsey) **3-8-4**(5) PFessey(7) (in tch: sn pushed along: hung lft over 2f out: sn wknd) | 3 | 7 | 25/1 | 51 | 4 |
| 714[5] | **Brandonville (74)** (NTinkler) **3-9-7** KimTinkler(1) (dwlt s: hld up & plld hrd: sme hdwy whn nt clr run 2f out: n.d) | ½ | 8 | 20/1 | 62 | 15 |
| 703[9] | **Gulf of Siam (62)** (MissSEHall) **3-8-9** MWigham(6) (swtg: hld up & a in rr) | ½ | 9 | 7/1 | 49 | 2 |

| | | | | | |
|---|---|---|---|---|---|
| 605[7] **Domoor (55)** (MJohnston) **3-8-2** TWilliams(3) (chsd ldrs tl wknd 3f out) ....9 | **10** | 10/1 | 24 | — |
| 509[10] **Cumbrian Maestro (65)** (TDEasterby) **3-8-12** ACulhane(2) (lost pl ½-wy: sn bhd) ....1 | **11** | 14/1 | 32 | — |
| | | (SP 142.3%) | | **11 Rn** |

**1m 46.0** (7.00) CSF £90.70 CT £601.49 TOTE £18.30: £3.60 £2.00 £2.80 (£40.40) Trio £48.30 OWNER Bee Health Ltd (SHERIFF HUTTON) BRED Mrs L. M. Tong

**827 Lucky Bea**, a keen sort, was taken to post early. Under a most capable ride, he stuck on to force his head in front near the line. (12/1)

**873 Silverdale Knight** looked to have stolen a march on his rivals when sent two or three lengths clear early in the straight. Though he did nothing wrong, he was just worn down near the line. (6/1)

**595* Winston** was possibly unlucky. With nowhere to go over a furlong out, when switched, he finished best of all and would have been suited by a more strongly-run race. (8/1)

**786 Dispol Gem** looked and ran well, but the Handicapper seems to have guessed her right. (7/1: op 12/1)

**Farmost**, a grand sort, took a keen grip in the early stages. Making his effort over a quarter of a mile from home, he was soon badly tapped for toe and might be worth a try over further. (5/4)

**915* Forest Boy**, 16lb higher than at Catterick, tended to hang left under pressure and it was no surprise to see him fade approaching the final furlong. (11/2)

T/Plpt: £399.80 (18.19 Tckts). T/Qdpt: £34.80 (13.96 Tckts). WG

# 0643-WARWICK (L-H) (Firm)
## Monday May 6th
WEATHER: fine WIND: almost nil

## 977 E.B.F. PRIMROSE MAIDEN STKS (2-Y.O F) (Class D)
2-15 (2-16) **5f** £3,850.00 (£1,150.00: £550.00: £250.00) Stalls: Low GOING minus 0.41 sec per fur (F)

| | | SP | RR | SF |
|---|---|---|---|---|
| **Nightbird (IRE)** (BWHills) **2-8-11** MHills(4) (w'like: mde all: r.o wl) ....— | **1** | 9/2 3 | 82 | 33 |
| **Open Credit** (HRACecil) **2-8-11** AMcGlone(2) (w'like: scope: hld up: chsd wnr fnl 2f: rdn 1f out: unable qckn) 1 | **2** | 8/15 1 | 79 | 30 |
| **Third Party** (SDow) **2-8-6**(5) ADaly(5) (unf: bkwd: s.i.s: outpcd: hdwy over 1f out: nvr nrr) ....6 | **3** | 50/1 | 60 | 11 |
| **Sharp But Fair** (SirMarkPrescott) **2-8-11** RPerham(7) (neat: bit bkwd: w wnr 3f: sn wknd) ....2 | **4** | 20/1 | 53 | 4 |
| **Bramble Bear** (MBlanshard) **2-8-11** JQuinn(6) (lt-f: prom over 3f) ....s.h | **5** | 33/1 | 53 | 4 |
| 807[4] **Magnolia** (PFICole) **2-8-11** TSprake(3) (rdn over 2f out: sn bhd) ....14 | **6** | 4/1 2 | 8 | — |
| | | (SP 113.1%) | | **6 Rn** |

**59.6 secs** (1.60) CSF £7.27 TOTE £5.60: £2.30 £1.20 (£3.60) OWNER Mr S. P. Tindall (LAMBOURN) BRED S. Tindall and Stowell Hill Ltd

**Nightbird (IRE)**, who became fractious in the paddock, is out of a mare who won over a mile and a half. (9/2)

**Open Credit** looked sure to pick up the winner coming to the final furlong, but did not find the anticipated response when put to the test. (8/15: Evens-1/2)

**Third Party** has yet to come in her coat and improvement can be expected. (50/1)

**Sharp But Fair** should come on a bit for the run (20/1)

## 978 STONELEIGH PARK POLO CLUB H'CAP (0-80) (3-Y.O) (Class D)
2-45 (2-47) **7f** £4,357.95 (£1,305.60: £627.30: £288.15) Stalls: Low GOING minus 0.41 sec per fur (F)

| | | SP | RR | SF |
|---|---|---|---|---|
| 663[6] **Mawingo (IRE) (64)** (GWragg) **3-7-12**(7) GMilligan(8) (lw: dwlt: rdn & hdwy over 1f out: edgd lft & str run to ld nr fin) ....— | **1** | 11/2 1 | 71 | 37 |
| 646[14] **Sylva Paradise (IRE) (80)** (CEBrittain) **3-9-7** JQuinn(10) (a.p: led over 1f out: hdd nr fin) ....¾ | **2** | 16/1 | 85 | 51 |
| 571[8] **Ed's Folly (IRE) (60)** (SDow) **3-7-10**(5) ADaly(14) (lw: led: hdd over 1f out: r.o one pce) ....1½ | **3** | 14/1 | 62 | 28 |
| 887[12] **Moi Canard (62)** (BAPearce) **3-8-0**(3) DRMcCabe(5) (hdwy fnl 2f: nvr nrr) ....s.h | **4** | 14/1 | 64 | 30 |
| **Wilfull Lad (IRE) (60)** (MartynMeade) **3-8-1** FNorton(9) (bit bkwd: prom: rdn & no hdwy fnl 2f) ....¾ | **5** | 16/1 | 60 | 26 |
| 637* **Sistar Act (60)** (MRChannon) **3-8-1** CandyMorris(12) (hdwy over 3f out: one pce fnl f) ....2½ | **6** | 6/1 2 | 54 | 20 |
| 686[8] **Charming Bride (60)** (SCWilliams) **3-8-1** JTate(2) (prom tl rdn & wknd over 1f out) ....3½ | **7** | 6/1 2 | 46 | 12 |
| 444[13] **Welcome Royale (IRE) (66)** (MHTompkins) **3-8-7** NDay(16) (nvr nrr) ....½ | **8** | 9/1 3 | 51 | 17 |
| 833[9] **Half An Inch (IRE) (73)** (BJMeehan) **3-9-0** WJO'Connor(13) (prom tl rdn & wknd wl over 1f out) ....¾ | **9** | 14/1 | 57 | 23 |
| **Bold Enough (67)** (BWHills) **3-8-3**(5)ow2 JDSmith(7) (hmpd & lost pl 4f out: nt rcvr) ....s.h | **10** | 11/1 | 50 | 14 |
| 732[8] **Ameer Alfayaafi (IRE) (65)** (RAkehurst) **3-8-6** SSanders(3) (dwlt: a bhd) ....2½ | **11** | 10/1 | 43 | 9 |
| 834[10] **Rapid Liner (55)** (HOliver) **3-7-10** NAdams(11) (prom 5f) ....hd | **12** | 50/1 | 32 | — |
| **Fervent Fan (IRE) (75)** (MBell) **3-9-2** MFenton(4) (hdwy over 3f out: wknd over 2f out) ....1¾ | **13** | 20/1 | 48 | 14 |
| **Western Venture (IRE) (70)** (JWPayne) **3-8-6**(5) DGriffiths(1) (b: swtg: hdwy over 3f out: wknd 2f out) ....1¾ | **14** | 20/1 | 39 | 5 |
| 689[5] **Tasliya (USA) (76)** (JLDunlop) **3-9-3** AMcGlone(6) (a bhd) ....hd | **15** | 10/1 | 45 | 11 |
| | | (SP 123.7%) | | **15 Rn** |

**1m 26.2** (1.60) CSF £82.90 CT £1,110.33 TOTE £6.30: £2.50 £5.90 £4.30 (£89.80) Trio £266.90 OWNER Mrs Claude Lilley (NEWMARKET) BRED Miss Geraldine Browne

LONG HANDICAP Rapid Liner 7-3

**Mawingo (IRE)** surged through to land the spoils, despite drifting over to the far rail. There seems no reason why he should not stay a mile. (11/2)

**Sylva Paradise (IRE)**, all the better for a run over a mile here last month, could not withstand the winner's late run. (16/1)

**Ed's Folly (IRE)** showed improved form over this longer trip. (14/1)

**632 Moi Canard** is rated 7lb lower on the turf than when winning on the Equitrack at Lingfield at the end of March. (14/1)

**Wilfull Lad (IRE)** has come down a stone in the handicap since being over-rated for winning an auction race over the minimum trip at Hamilton last July. (16/1)

**637* Sistar Act** had to contend with a shorter trip and faster ground than when winning a Nottingham seller last month. (6/1)

**Bold Enough** (11/1: 8/1-12/1)

## 979 WARWICK SPRING H'CAP (0-70) (4-Y.O+) (Class E)
3-15 (3-16) **1m 2f 169y** £3,561.60 (£1,066.80: £512.40: £235.20) Stalls: Low GOING minus 0.41 sec per fur (F)

| | | SP | RR | SF |
|---|---|---|---|---|
| 871[2] **Harvey White (IRE) (53)** (JPearce) **4-8-6**(7) SGaillard(16) (hdwy over 2f out: led over 1f out: r.o wl) ....— | **1** | 8/1 | 68 | 36 |
| 222[2] **Beaumont (IRE) (56)** (JEBanks) **6-9-2** JQuinn(6) (a.p: rdn & ev ch over 1f out: unable qckn) ....1½ | **2** | 5/1 1 | 69 | 37 |
| 598* **Hand of Straw (IRE) (57)** (PGMurphy) **4-9-3v** MHills(2) (bhd tl gd hdwy over 1f out: r.o ins fnl f) ....1½ | **3** | 7/1 3 | 68 | 36 |

| | Horse / details | Dist | Pos | SP | RR | SF |
|---|---|---|---|---|---|---|
| 817[4] | **Koathary (USA) (56)** (LGCottrell) **5-9-2** MFenton(12) (hld up: hdwy 4f out: one pce fnl 2f) | 4 | **4** | 13/2[2] | 61 | 29 |
| *410*[4] | **Kintwyn (48)** (WRMuir) **6-8-8** WJO'Connor(7) (hdwy 3f out: one pce fnl f) | 1 | **5** | 12/1 | 51 | 19 |
| 884[4] | **Scorpius (52)** (TTClement) **6-8-7**(5) DGibbs(18) (b: t: hdwy over 3f out: wkng whn nt clr run ins fnl f) | hd | **6** | 20/1 | 55 | 23 |
| 817[10] | **Reefa's Mill (IRE) (66)** (JNeville) **4-9-12** FNorton(5) (nvr nr to chal) | ¾ | **7** | 25/1 | 68 | 36 |
| 817[8] | **Myfontaine (63)** (KTIvory) **9-9-9** GBardwell(13) (hdwy 2f out: one pce fnl f) | s.h | **8** | 5/1[1] | 65 | 33 |
| 688[4] | **Framed (IRE) (52)** (SCWilliams) **6-8-12** JTate(20) (a.p: led 2f out tl over 1f out: wknd fnl f) | ½ | **9** | 16/1 | 53 | 21 |
| 633[8] | **Abtaal (64)** (RJHodges) **6-9-10** TSprake(17) (hdwy over 3f out: wknd over 1f out) | 1 | **10** | 33/1 | 64 | 32 |
| | **Kirov Protege (IRE) (40)** (HJCollingridge) **4-7-7**(7) PDoe(4) (n.d) | 2 | **11** | 33/1 | 37 | 5 |
| *360*[6] | **Mazilla (47)** (AStreeter) **4-8-2**(5)ow5 RHavlin(3) (prom tl wknd over 2f out) | 2½ | **12** | 16/1 | 40 | 3 |
| 760[9] | **Fastini Gold (47)** (MDIUsher) **4-8-7** NAdams(14) (hld up: hdwy over 4f out: wknd 3f out) | 1¼ | **13** | 33/1 | 38 | 6 |
| 739[5] | **Miss Iron Heart (USA) (41)** (DJSCosgrove) **4-8-1**ow1 AMcGlone(9) (prom: led over 3f out to 2f out: eased whn btn fnl f) | 1¼ | **14** | 33/1 | 30 | — |
| *782*[13] | **Monty (56)** (MajorDNChappell) **4-9-2** SSanders(11) (a bhd) | s.h | **15** | 20/1 | 45 | 13 |
| | **Irish Groom (41)** (AStreeter) **9-7-10**(5)ow1 ADaly(1) (bhd fnl 3f) | 3 | **16** | 33/1 | 26 | — |
| | **African-Pard (IRE) (68)** (DHaydnJones) **4-9-11**(3) DRMcCabe(8) (led tl hdd over 3f out: sn wknd) | 3 | **17** | 25/1 | 48 | 16 |
| 690[14] | **Labudd (USA) (50)** (RIngram) **6-8-10** DBiggs(19) (b: w ldr tl wknd qckly over 3f out) | ½ | **18** | 20/1 | 29 | — |
| 645[3] | **Bad News (44)** (JMBradley) **4-7-11**(7) DSweeney(15) (chsd ldrs tl wknd over 3f out) | 1¼ | **19** | 16/1 | 22 | — |

(SP 132.3%) **19 Rn**

**2m 17.3** (3.80) CSF £46.00 CT £274.31 TOTE £6.70: £1.20 £1.50 £1.90 £2.20 (£13.80) Trio £36.30 OWNER The Harvey White Partnership (NEWMARKET) BRED Mrs C. L. Weld

OFFICIAL EXPLANATION **Myfontaine: finished sore.**

**871 Harvey White (IRE)** likes fast ground and fulfilled the promise shown when runner-up last week. (8/1)

**Beaumont (IRE)** had twice been placed over hurdles. (5/1)

**598* Hand of Straw (IRE)** could not repeat his course and distance win of Easter Monday off a 2lb higher mark on faster ground. (7/1)

**817 Koathary (USA)** lacked the required finishing speed. (13/2)

**Kintwyn** is rated no less than 24lb lower than on the All-Weather, and ran his best race on turf for some time. (12/1)

**884 Scorpius** would probably have preferred more give in the ground. (20/1)

**650 Myfontaine** was reported to have finished sore. (5/1)

## 980 MAY QUEEN H'CAP (0-80) (3-Y.O) (Class D)

3-45 (3-46) **1m 4f 115y** £3,761.25 (£1,122.00: £535.50: £242.25) Stalls: Low GOING minus 0.41 sec per fur (F)

| | Horse / details | Dist | Pos | SP | RR | SF |
|---|---|---|---|---|---|---|
| 597[3] | **Tintara (IRE) (66)** (BWHills) **3-8-12** MHills(1) (hld up: hdwy over 3f out: led on bit wl over 1f out: rdn & edgd lft: r.o wl) | — | **1** | 5/2[1] | 72+ | 34 |
| 597[2] | **Uoni (54)** (CEBrittain) **3-8-0** JQuinn(5) (a.p: led over 2f out tl wl over 1f out: unable qckn) | 1½ | **2** | 9/2[2] | 58 | 20 |
| 594[4] | **Minnisam (65)** (JLDunlop) **3-8-11** TSprake(4) (hdwy 5f out: rdn over 1f out: one pce) | 1½ | **3** | 5/2[1] | 67 | 29 |
| 627[3] | **Silver Wing (USA) (75)** (MBell) **3-9-7** MFenton(2) (hld up: hdwy over 3f out: one pce fnl 2f) | 3 | **4** | 13/2[3] | 73 | 35 |
| 788[5] | **Mister Aspecto (IRE) (67)** (MJohnston) **3-8-13v** JTate(7) (led tl over 2f out: wknd qckly) | 15 | **5** | 10/1 | 46 | 8 |
| 593[10] | **Chief Mouse (70)** (RCharlton) **3-9-2v**[1] SSanders(3) (prom: hrd rdn 6f out: wknd over 3f out) | 4 | **6** | 10/1 | 44 | 6 |
| 687[7] | **Capstone (59)** (WJarvis) **3-8-5b**[1] AMcGlone(6) (chsd ldr over 8f: sn wknd) | 7 | **7** | 10/1 | 24 | — |
| 761[7] | **Lahik (IRE) (50)** (KTIvory) **3-7-10** GBardwell(8) (rdn over 4f out: sn bhd) | 3 | **8** | 50/1 | 11 | — |

(SP 117.9%) **8 Rn**

**2m 43.2** (4.70) CSF £13.91 CT £28.03 TOTE £2.70: £1.10 £1.30 £1.60 (£5.20) OWNER Mr R. E. Sangster (LAMBOURN) BRED Swettenham Stud

LONG HANDICAP Lahik (IRE) 7-5

**597 Tintara (IRE)** may well have been feeling the ground when let down, after leading with the best part of a quarter-mile to go. (5/2)

**597 Uoni** had finished seven lengths in front of the winner here last month on identical terms. (9/2)

**594 Minnisam**, back to a mile and a half, just lacked the required turn of foot on this fast surface. (5/2)

**627 Silver Wing (USA)**, stepping up in distance, could not sustain a promising forward move leaving the back straight. (13/2)

**788 Mister Aspecto (IRE)** (10/1: op 6/1)

**Capstone** (10/1: op 6/1)

## 981 STILL MATERIALS HANDLING LIMITED STKS (0-60) (4-Y.O+) (Class F)

4-15 (4-19) **6f** £3,101.00 (£861.00: £413.00) Stalls: Low GOING minus 0.41 sec per fur (F)

| | Horse / details | Dist | Pos | SP | RR | SF |
|---|---|---|---|---|---|---|
| 862[7] | **Rockcracker (IRE) (55)** (GGMargarson) **4-8-11b** PBloomfield(6) (hld up: bmpd over 2f out: led over 1f out: r.o wl) | — | **1** | 10/1[3] | 60 | 32 |
| 749[9] | **Dashing Dancer (IRE) (59)** (RAkehurst) **5-8-11** SSanders(14) (hdwy over 3f out: bmpd over 2f out: ev ch over 1f out: unable qckn) | 1¾ | **2** | 4/1[1] | 55 | 27 |
| *511*[4] | **Milos (60)** (TJNaughton) **5-9-0** TSprake(18) (gd hdwy over 1f out: r.o wl ins fnl f) | hd | **3** | 10/1[3] | 58 | 30 |
| *653*[5] | **Jon's Choice (40)** (BPreece) **8-8-4**(7) DDenby(8) (a.p: edgd rt over 2f out: r.o one pce) | 3 | **4** | 33/1 | 47 | 19 |
| 879[29] | **Halliard (53)** (TMJones) **5-8-11** AMcGlone(15) (led over 4f: one pce) | s.h | **5** | 16/1 | 47 | 19 |
| 649[12] | **Courting Newmarket (42)** (NMBabbage) **8-8-4**(7) RFfrench(11) (hrd rdn 3f out: no hdwy fnl 2f) | hd | **6** | 33/1 | 47 | 19 |
| 749[5] | **Sound the Trumpet (IRE) (56)** (RCSpicer) **4-8-6**(5) RHavlin(7) (s.s: gd hdwy over 1f out: nt rch ldrs) | ¾ | **7** | 14/1 | 45 | 17 |
| 893[15] | **Always Grace (60)** (MissGayKelleway) **4-8-3**(5) ADaly(13) (nvr nr to chal) | 1 | **8** | 10/1[3] | 39 | 11 |
| 893[5] | **Jigsaw Boy (59)** (PGMurphy) **7-9-3** MFenton(10) (nvr nr to chal) | 1 | **9** | 8/1[2] | 45 | 17 |
| 632[11] | **Martinosky (46)** (GCBravery) **10-8-11b** NDay(12) (lw: prom: wnt 2nd over 3f out: wknd over 1f out) | ½ | **10** | 25/1 | 38 | 10 |
| 632[2] | **Speedy Classic (USA) (60)** (MJHeaton-Ellis) **7-8-11**(3) SDrowne(4) (lw: prom over 4f) | ½ | **11** | 4/1[1] | 40 | 12 |
| 862[8] | **Cedar Dancer (43)** (RJHodges) **4-8-3**(5) AmandaSanders(3) (bhd fnl 2f) | 1¼ | **12** | 33/1 | 30 | 2 |
| | **Cats Bottom (58)** (AGNewcombe) **4-8-3**(5) DGriffiths(16) (bkwd: hdwy over 3f out: wknd over 1f out) | hd | **13** | 8/1[2] | 30 | 2 |
| 527[10] | **Pats Delight (30)** (SCoathup) **4-8-8** JQuinn(2) (prom over 3f) | nk | **14** | 50/1 | 29 | 1 |
| 846[8] | **Spectacle Jim (47)** (MJHaynes) **7-8-8b**(3) DRMcCabe(19) (a bhd) | nk | **15** | 25/1 | 32 | 4 |
| | **High Domain (IRE) (60)** (JLSpearing) **5-8-11** FNorton(1) (bhd fnl 3f) | nk | **16** | 20/1 | 31 | 3 |
| 649[9] | **Blushing Grenadier (IRE) (52)** (MJFetherston-Godley) **4-8-11** WJO'Connor(5) (bit bkwd: bhd fnl 3f) | 1¼ | **17** | 25/1 | 27 | — |
| *836*[12] | **Bold Time Monkey (40)** (MTate) **5-8-8** NAdams(9) (swtg: a bhd) | hd | **18** | 50/1 | 24 | — |
| *203*[12] | **Assignment (42)** (JELong) **10-8-4**(7) TField(17) (prom early: rdn over 3f out: sn bhd) | 8 | **19** | 50/1 | 6 | — |

(SP 133.1%) **19 Rn**

**1m 14.1** (2.10) CSF £49.34 TOTE £13.70: £3.80 £2.10 £3.50 (£56.30) Trio £274.40; £34.78 to Chester 7/5/96 OWNER Mr P. E. Axon (NEWMARKET) BRED Mrs Amanda Skiffington

**632 Rockcracker (IRE)** was his trainer's first winner and landed a gamble in the process. (10/1: op 20/1)
**Dashing Dancer (IRE)**, badly drawn on his seasonal debut, could not cope with the winner in the final furlong and a half. (4/1)
**511 Milos** came from way off the pace to secure the minor berth. (10/1)
**653 Jon's Choice**, an All-Weather specialist, would have been much better off at the weights had this been a handicap. (33/1)
**470 Halliard** has been running over further and set out to make all. (16/1)
**Courting Newmarket**, dropping back in distance, seems to need further nowadays. (33/1)
**749 Sound the Trumpet (IRE)** again did himself no favours at the start. (14/1)
**893 Jigsaw Boy** ran better than his finishing position would suggest. (8/1)
**632 Speedy Classic (USA)** found his measure taken approaching the final furlong. (4/1)

## 982 ALVESTON MAIDEN STKS (3-Y.O+) (Class D)

4-45 (4-49) **1m** £4,623.15 (£1,387.20: £668.10: £308.55) Stalls: Low GOING minus 0.41 sec per fur (F)

| | | | | SP | RR | SF |
|---|---|---|---|---|---|---|
| | **El Penitente (IRE)** (DRLoder) **3-8-8**(3) DRMcCabe(15) (w'like: scope: a gng wl: led over 1f out: shkn up & qcknd clr ins fnl f) | — | **1** | $7/4^{1}$ | 89+ | 40 |
| | **Kamari (USA)** (ACStewart) **3-8-6**(5) MHumphries(5) (hld up & bhd: hdwy over 1f out: r.o ins fnl f: bttr for r) | 4 | **2** | 10/1 | 81 | 32 |
| $842^{9}$ | **Ood Dancer (USA)** (LMCumani) **3-8-4**(7) JoHunnam(12) (hdwy over 3f out: hrd rdn over 1f out: one pce) | nk | **3** | 12/1 | 80 | 31 |
| $786^{2}$ | **Melt The Clouds (CAN)** (PWHarris) **3-8-11** MFenton(14) (led over 2f: one pce fnl 2f) | 1 | **4** | $4/1^{2}$ | 78 | 29 |
| $772^{3}$ | **Reinhardt (IRE) (90)** (PWChapple-Hyam) **3-8-6**(5) RHavlin(3) (led over 5f out tl over 1f out: one pce) | nk | **5** | $13/2^{3}$ | 78 | 29 |
| | **Mountain Dream (72)** (LMCumani) **3-8-4**(7) RFfrench(10) (hdwy over 2f out: rdn over 1f out: one pce) | 1¼ | **6** | 33/1 | 75 | 26 |
| | **Aldevonie** (HRACecil) **4-9-5** AMcGlone(11) (prom tl wknd over 1f out) | 1½ | **7** | $4/1^{2}$ | 67 | 31 |
| $821^{5}$ | **Le Khoumf (FR)** (JMBradley) **5-9-7**(3) SDrowne(4) (nvr nr to chal) | nk | **8** | 20/1 | 72 | 36 |
| $710^{15}$ | **Pomona** (PJMakin) **3-8-6** SSanders(2) (nvr trbld ldrs) | 2½ | **9** | 33/1 | 64 | 15 |
| $842^{13}$ | **Pusey Street Girl** (JRBosley) **3-8-6** RPerham(7) (prom tl wknd wl over 1f out) | 3½ | **10** | 33/1 | 57 | 8 |
| $730^{8}$ | **Waft (USA)** (BWHills) **3-8-6** MHills(9) (a bhd) | 2 | **11** | 25/1 | 53 | 4 |
| $684^{18}$ | **Slievenamon** (JEBanks) **3-8-11** JQuinn(6) (a bhd) | 1¼ | **12** | 33/1 | 55 | 6 |
| | **Budding Annie** (JRBosley) **3-8-6** VSlattery(18) (hdwy 3f out: wknd 2f out) | 1 | **13** | 33/1 | 48 | — |
| $763^{10}$ | **Parrot's Hill (IRE)** (MHTompkins) **3-8-11** NDay(1) (a bhd) | ¾ | **14** | 40/1 | 52 | 3 |
| | **Flow Back** (GPEnright) **4-9-10** NAdams(17) (a bhd) | 4 | **15** | 50/1 | 44 | 8 |
| | **Risky Baby** (THind) **4-9-5** FNorton(13) (chsd ldrs tl wknd 3f out) | 1 | **16** | 50/1 | 37 | 1 |
| | **Beaver Brook** (RIngram) **6-9-10** DBiggs(16) (a bhd) | 8 | **17** | 50/1 | 26 | — |
| $746^{8}$ | **Maid of Cadiz** (JWPayne) **6-9-0**(5) DGriffiths(8) (t.o) | 14 | **18** | 50/1 | — | — |

(SP 140.1%) **18 Rn**

**1m 38.4** (2.00) CSF £22.18 TOTE £2.60: £1.10 £5.30 £3.40 (£27.40) Trio £193.80; £150.19 to Chester 7/5/96 OWNER Mr B. E. Nielsen (NEWMARKET) BRED Airlie Stud
WEIGHT FOR AGE 3yo-13lb

**El Penitente (IRE)** did this well enough but whether he will be up to the St. James's Palace Stakes at Royal Ascot remains to be seen. (7/4: 5/4-2/1)
**Kamari (USA)**, despite little assistance from the saddle, finished in eyecatching style and is one to note. (10/1)
**842 Ood Dancer (USA)** got connections into trouble last time and was probably taking on an above-average type in the winner. (12/1: op 8/1)
**786 Melt The Clouds (CAN)** could not raise his game in the short home straight. (4/1)
**772 Reinhardt (IRE)**, reverting to a mile, could not increase his tempo when taken on by the winner. (13/2)
**Mountain Dream** did not show a lot when trained by Paul Cole last year. (33/1)

## 983 LEVY BOARD APPRENTICE H'CAP (0-70) (3-Y.O+) (Class G)

5-15 (5-22) **1m** £2,214.00 (£629.00: £312.00) Stalls: Low GOING minus 0.41 sec per fur (F)

| | | | | SP | RR | SF |
|---|---|---|---|---|---|---|
| | **Risky Romeo (61)** (GCBravery) **4-9-4**(5) TField(11) (hld up: hdwy over 2f out: rdn 1f out: led ins fnl f: r.o wl) | — | **1** | 16/1 | 73 | 44 |
| | **Runic Symbol (34)** (MBlanshard) **5-7-10** GMilligan(18) (gd hdwy over 1f out: fin wl) | 1½ | **2** | 16/1 | 43 | 14 |
| | **Leguard Express (IRE) (34)** (OO'Neill) **8-7-5b**(5) JBramhill(3) (led: clr 2f out: hdd ins fnl f) | 1½ | **3** | 20/1 | 40 | 11 |
| $636^{9}$ | **Zahran (IRE) (44)** (JMBradley) **5-8-6** AEddery(15) (hdwy over 1f out: r.o ins fnl f) | 1¼ | **4** | $8/1^{3}$ | 48 | 19 |
| $688^{2}$ | **My Handsome Prince (42)** (PJBevan) **4-7-13v**(5) PDoe(2) (a.p: no hdwy fnl 2f) | 1¼ | **5** | 11/1 | 43 | 14 |
| $834^{11}$ | **Polli Pui (47)** (WMBrisbourne) **4-8-4**(5) RMullen(5) (s.s: hdwy fnl 2f: nt rch ldrs) | 1½ | **6** | 50/1 | 45 | 16 |
| $485^{7}$ | **Well Suited (34)** (THind) **6-7-10b** AngelaGallimore(16) (nvr nr to chal) | nk | **7** | 33/1 | 31 | 2 |
| $106^{7}$ | **Voices in the Sky (34)** (AGNewcombe) **5-7-5**(5) JFowle(19) (nvr nrr) | hd | **8** | 14/1 | 31 | 2 |
| $336^{2}$ | **Ladybower (IRE) (40)** (LordHuntingdon) **4-8-2** JWilkinson(7) (prom tl wknd over 1f out) | hd | **9** | $4/1^{1}$ | 37 | 8 |
| $778^{6}$ | **Mezzoramio (47)** (KAMorgan) **4-8-6v**(3)ow2 CScudder(4) (chsd ldr: rdn 2f out: edgd lft & wknd over 1f out) | hd | **10** | 16/1 | 44 | 13 |
| $749^{10}$ | **Asterix (46)** (JMBradley) **8-8-8v** RWaterfield(12) (n.d) | hd | **11** | $8/1^{3}$ | 43 | 14 |
| $747^{8}$ | **Helios (62)** (NJHWalker) **8-9-10** DToole(1) (prom over 5f) | s.h | **12** | 16/1 | 59 | 30 |
| $519^{5}$ | **Young Butt (58)** (JFfitch-Heyes) **3-8-7** JDennis(8) (n.d) | 1¼ | **13** | 20/1 | 52 | 10 |
| $655^{9}$ | **La Haye Sainte (47)** (DJSCosgrove) **3-7-3v**1(7) JMcAuley(21) (bhd fnl 2f) | 1½ | **14** | 33/1 | 38 | — |
| $664^{10}$ | **Forgotten Dancer (IRE) (47)** (RIngram) **5-8-4**(5) RFfrench(14) (prom tl hrd rdn & wknd over 1f out) | ¾ | **15** | 33/1 | 37 | 8 |
| | **Mhemeanles (41)** (CaptJWilson) **6-7-10**(7) AngelaHartley(17) (a bhd) | hd | **16** | 25/1 | 30 | 1 |
| | **Henry Otis (65)** (RAkehurst) **3-9-0** DDenby(20) (a bhd) | ¾ | **17** | 10/1 | 53 | 11 |
| $843^{4}$ | **Flag Fen (USA) (62)** (MartynMeade) **5-9-7**(3) DSweeney(6) (hld up: wknd over 2f out) | s.h | **18** | 12/1 | 50 | 21 |
| | **Little Kenny (50)** (MJFetherston-Godley) **3-7-8**(5) CCogan(13) (hdwy on ins over 2f out: wknd over 1f out) | 1¼ | **19** | 20/1 | 35 | — |
| $138^{11}$ | **Ranger Sloane (34)** (GFierro) **4-7-10** JoHunnam(10) (a bhd) | ½ | **20** | 50/1 | 18 | — |
| | **Delmour (37)** (WMBrisbourne) **5-7-8**(5)ow3 PClarke(9) (prom over 4f) | nk | **21** | 50/1 | 21 | — |
| 545* | ***Cicerone (49)*** (JLHarris) **6-8-6**(5) RSmith(22) (Withdrawn not Starters' orders: unruly in stalls) | | **W** | $15/2^{2}$ | — | — |

(SP 142.1%) **21 Rn**

**1m 39.2** (2.80) CSF £210.05 CT £3,519.21 TOTE £13.40: £4.90 £4.10 £8.30 £1.80 (£157.40) Trio Not won; £356.73 to Chester 7/5/96.
OWNER Miss Sonja Quince (NEWMARKET) BRED Mrs S. Quince
LONG HANDICAP Leguard Express (IRE) 7-6 La Haye Sainte 7-5 Ranger Sloane 7-5 Delmour 6-7 Voices in the Sky 7-4
WEIGHT FOR AGE 3yo-13lb

**Risky Romeo**, 2lb higher than when successful over course and distance last August, again showed his liking for firm ground. (16/1)
**Runic Symbol**, fit from hurdling, finished with a flourish but could not overhaul the winner. (16/1)

**Leguard Express (IRE)** had a handy lead early in the home straight, but it soon became apparent the winner was just waiting to pounce. (20/1)
**501 Zahran (IRE)**, well backed, likes fast ground and kept on in the closing stages without ever looking likely to score. (8/1)
**688 My Handsome Prince** found this a bit more competitive than when runner-up in a seller last time. (11/1)
**Polli Pui** could never recover from a poor start. (50/1)
**Ladybower (IRE)**, a well-supported favourite, had been given a break after being campaigned on the All-Weather. (4/1: op 7/1)

T/Plpt: £137.80 (55.8 Tckts). T/Qdpt: £14.50 (28.97 Tckts). KH

# CHESTER (L-H) (Good)
## Tuesday May 7th
WEATHER: fine WIND: slt half bhd

## 984 LILY AGNES CONDITIONS STKS (2-Y.O) (Class B)
2-10 (2-10) **5f 16y** £7,417.80 (£2,770.20: £1,350.10: £575.50: £252.75: £123.65) Stalls: Low GOING minus 0.03 sec per fur (G)

| | | | | SP | RR | SF |
|---|---|---|---|---|---|---|
| 596* | **Connemara (IRE)** (CADwyer) **2-8-6**[ow1] KFallon(2) (mde all: qcknd over 1f out: r.o wl) | — | **1** | 100/30[2] | 82 | 37 |
| 685* | **Foot Battalion (IRE)** (RHollinshead) **2-8-10** WRyan(6) (hld up: hdwy on ins ent st: r.o fnl f) | 1½ | **2** | 16/1 | 81? | 37 |
| 683* | **Carmine Lake (IRE)** (PWChapple-Hyam) **2-8-8** JReid(4) (hld up: pushed along whn carried wd ent st: kpt on u.p fnl f) | 2 | **3** | 4/9[1] | 73 | 29 |
| 523* | **Weet Ees Girl (IRE)** (PDEvans) **2-8-8** JFortune(1) (prom: drvn along 2f out: one pce) | 1½ | **4** | 16/1 | 68 | 24 |
| 568* | **Aztec Traveller** (JBerry) **2-8-10** JCarroll(3) (prom: rn wd ent s: sn rdn: wknd appr fnl f) | 5 | **5** | 10/1[3] | 55 | 11 |
| | **Amy** (CSmith) **2-8-2** NCarlisle(5) (small: bit bkwd: s.s: a bhd & outpcd) | 8 | **6** | 25/1 | 21 | — |
| | | | | (SP 117.0%) | **6 Rn** | |

**63.06 secs** (3.06) CSF £39.99 TOTE £3.80: £1.60 £4.40 (£39.60) OWNER Dr A. Haloute (NEWMARKET) BRED Rathasker Stud
**596* Connemara (IRE)** got the best of the start and proceeded to gallop her rivals into submission. She is bred to need a longer trip but has made a fine start to her career as a sprinter. (100/30)
**685* Foot Battalion (IRE)** obtained a smooth passage on the inside turning for home and ran on well, but the winner was always holding him. (16/1)
**683* Carmine Lake (IRE)**, restrained off the pace, was being nudged along when carried wide on the home turn. Though she did run on, she could not muster the pace to trouble the winner. (4/9)
**523* Weet Ees Girl (IRE)** has still not got rid of all her winter coat, but she pushed the pace and had every chance until having to admit the principals too smart. (16/1)
**568* Aztec Traveller** tracked the winner, but failed to negotiate the turn into the straight and his chance soon disappeared. (10/1)

## 985 GROSVENOR MAIDEN STKS (3-Y.O) (Class D)
2-40 (2-40) **1m 2f 75y** £8,367.00 (£2,526.00: £1,228.00: £579.00) Stalls: High GOING minus 0.03 sec per fur (G)

| | | | | SP | RR | SF |
|---|---|---|---|---|---|---|
| | **Legal Right (USA)** (PWChapple-Hyam) **3-9-0** JReid(9) (bit bkwd: hld up in tch: hdwy to ld over 3f out: r.o strly fnl f) | — | **1** | 3/1[2] | 88+ | 63 |
| 684[3] | **Shantou (USA)** (JHMGosden) **3-9-0** GHind(2) (hld up: hdwy over 4f out: jnd wnr 3f out: rdn & one pce fnl f) | 1½ | **2** | 13/8[1] | 86 | 61 |
| 677[10] | **Bowled Over (74)** (CACyzer) **3-9-0** KFallon(4) (a.p: outpcd 2f out: kpt on u.p ins fnl f) | 1¼ | **3** | 25/1 | 84 | 59 |
| 576[3] | **Arnhem** (CEBrittain) **3-9-0** BDoyle(5) (lw: trckd ldrs: effrt u.p 3f out: nt pce to chal) | 2½ | **4** | 10/1 | 80 | 55 |
| 684[6] | **Chabrol (CAN)** (HRACecil) **3-9-0** PatEddery(3) (disp ld: drvn along whn hdd over 3f out: wknd 2f out) | 7 | **5** | 11/2[3] | 69 | 44 |
| 677[4] | **Ambassador (USA)** (BWHills) **3-9-0** MHills(6) (lw: disp ld: rdn & hdd over 3f out: sn outpcd) | 2 | **6** | 11/2[3] | 66 | 41 |
| 566[4] | **Crabbie's Pride** (ABailey) **3-8-11**(3) DWright(8) (a in rr: no ch fnl 4f) | 1 | **7** | 33/1 | 64 | 39 |
| | **Ancient Quest** (NACallaghan) **3-9-0** PaulEddery(1) (lt-f: bit bkwd: s.i.s: a bhd: lost tch fnl 4f) | 7 | **8** | 20/1 | 54 | 29 |
| *781*[3] | **Loch Style (50)** (RHollinshead) **3-9-0** WRyan(7) (s.i.s: a bhd: t.o) | 7 | **9** | 50/1 | 43 | 18 |
| | | | | (SP 116.5%) | **9 Rn** | |

**2m 12.88** (4.18) CSF £8.05 TOTE £3.60: £1.40 £1.30 £4.30 (£3.10) Trio £74.40 OWNER Mr R. E. Sangster (MARLBOROUGH) BRED Ron Con 1 and Swettenham Stud
OFFICIAL EXPLANATION **Chabrol (CAN): gurgled in ther closing stages of the race.**
**Legal Right (USA)** struck the front plenty soon enough and had to work hard to shake off the favourite, but he was up to it and was well on top at the end. He saw the trip out without much difficulty and could prove a useful colt. (3/1: op 7/4)
**684 Shantou (USA)** moved upsides the winner two furlongs out and appeared to be going best, but he ran green and was inclined to hang in behind when set alight in the straight. He then had to admit he had met one too good. (13/8)
**677 Bowled Over**, tapped for speed when the leading pair quickened the tempo turning in, was staying on best of all at the finish and stamina could be his strong suit. (25/1)
**576 Arnhem**, never far away, kept staying on under pressure in the latter stages but a turn of finishing speed was the one thing missing. (10/1)
**684 Chabrol (CAN)** had a running battle for the lead, which he eventually won, but it left him with nothing more to offer and he had shot his bolt before reaching the straight. (11/2)
**677 Ambassador (USA)** did not impress even on this extremely good ground but he did help set the pace until left behind on the home turn. (11/2)

## 986 CHESTER VASE STKS (Gp 3) (3-Y.O) (Class A)
3-10 (3-11) **1m 4f 66y** £28,710.00 (£10,728.00: £5,139.00: £2,223.00) Stalls: Low GOING minus 0.03 sec per fur (G)

| | | | | SP | RR | SF |
|---|---|---|---|---|---|---|
| 725* | **High Baroque (IRE)** (PWChapple-Hyam) **3-8-10** JReid(3) (hld up & bhd: pushed along 6f out: gd hdwy to ld ins fnl f: r.o wl) | — | **1** | 11/4[2] | 109 | 69 |
| 694[2] | **St Mawes (FR) (107)** (JLDunlop) **3-8-10** WCarson(6) (lw: trckd ldrs: drvn along & lost pl ½-wy: hdwy over 2f out: led 1f out: sn hdd: nt pce of wnr) | 1¼ | **2** | 11/4[2] | 107 | 67 |
| 772* | **Prince of My Heart (98)** (BWHills) **3-8-10** KFallon(2) (chsd ldr: led over 4f out to 1f out: unable qckn fnl f) | 2½ | **3** | 9/1 | 104 | 64 |
| 671[2] | **Sasuru (106)** (GWragg) **3-8-10** PaulEddery(1) (b: lw: hld up: hdwy & wnt 2nd 4f out: rdn & one pce fnl 2f) | 5 | **4** | 15/2[3] | 98 | 58 |
| 707* | **Air Quest** (RCharlton) **3-8-10** PatEddery(5) (s.i.s: hld up: drvn 4f out: no imp) | 2½ | **5** | 2/1[1] | 94 | 54 |
| 736[7] | **Classic Eagle** (SCWilliams) **3-8-10** AMackay(4) (led tl hdd & wknd over 4f out: sn t.o) | 30 | **6** | 25/1 | 55 | 15 |
| | | | | (SP 112.3%) | **6 Rn** | |

**2m 40.16** (3.56) CSF £10.24 TOTE £4.00: £2.00 £1.60 (£5.50) OWNER Mr M. Tabor (MARLBOROUGH) BRED Barronstown Bloodstock Ltd

**725* High Baroque (IRE)**, one of three off the bridle at halfway, was still the backmarker four furlongs out, but he found stamina coming into play and, staying on stoutly to lead 200 yards out, won cosily in the end. He was the only one in the race not entered for the Derby. (11/4)
**694 St Mawes (FR)** always looks to have plenty left to work on and he dropped towards the rear out in the country. Driven along for all he was worth, he did stay on to poke his nose in front briefly entering the final furlong, but the winner easily had his measure in the run to the line. This was the first time he has raced round bends. (11/4)
**772* Prince of My Heart** appeared to have the situation under control turning in, but his stride shortened and he was forced to give best passing the furlong pole. This was a step up for him and he coped with it adequately. (9/1)
**671 Sasuru** had a trouble-free run up the inside rail and moved into the action half a mile out, but he did not find much when put to the test and was galloping on the spot once in line for home. (15/2)
**707* Air Quest** is inclined to run in snatches and, after taking time to find his stride, did not look happy on this tight track. (2/1)
**736 Classic Eagle** set a telling gallop and had half the field in trouble soon after going out on the final circuit, but he was unable to maintain the pace and stopped to a walk after being headed. (25/1)

## 987 EARL OF CHESTER H'CAP (0-100) (3-Y.O) (Class C)

3-40 (3-48) **7f 122y** £18,050.00 (£5,450.00: £2,650.00: £1,250.00) Stalls: Low GOING minus 0.03 sec per fur (G)

| | | | | SP | RR | SF |
|---|---|---|---|---|---|---|
| 646[7] | **Prends Ca (IRE) (88)** (RHannon) **3-9-5** PatEddery(8) (hld up & bhd: hdwy & n.m.r over 2f out: qcknd to ld ins fnl f: r.o) | — | **1** | 14/1 | 95 | 49 |
| | **React (90)** (WJarvis) **3-9-7** TQuinn(2) (h.d.w: a.p: rdn wl over 1f out: ev ch ins fnl f: unable qckn) | 1¼ | **2** | 16/1 | 94 | 48 |
| | **Pharmacy (77)** (JWWatts) **3-8-8** GDuffield(11) (hld up & bhd: gd hdwy on outside wl over 1f out: fin wl) | hd | **3** | 10/1 | 81 | 35 |
| 785[2] | **Sualtach (IRE) (84)** (RHollinshead) **3-9-1** JWeaver(3) (led tl hdd & no ex ins fnl f) | 1½ | **4** | 9/2[1] | 85 | 39 |
| 701[2] | **Kazimiera (IRE) (72)** (CWCElsey) **3-7-12**(5) PFessey(4) (hld up: effrt & rdn 2f out: kpt on ins fnl f) | nk | **5** | 11/1 | 72 | 26 |
| 453[10] | **Le Sport (77)** (ABailey) **3-8-5**(3) DWright(13) (wl bhd tl gd hdwy appr fnl f: nvr nrr) | 3 | **6** | 33/1 | 71 | 25 |
| 774[3] | **Menoo Hal Batal (USA) (79)** (MRStoute) **3-8-10** WCarson(7) (hung rt thrght: trckd ldrs tl outpcd fnl 2f) | 1¼ | **7** | 5/1[2] | 70 | 24 |
| 646[2] | **Proud Monk (78)** (GLMoore) **3-8-9** SWhitworth(9) (hld up: hdwy on outside 3f out: no imp fnl 2f) | 3½ | **8** | 9/1 | 62 | 16 |
| 755[2] | **Alpine Hideaway (IRE) (77)** (BHanbury) **3-8-5**(3) JStack(10) (chsd ldrs 5f: sn lost tch) | 5 | **9** | 11/1 | 50 | 4 |
| | **Naissant (80)** (CEBrittain) **3-8-11** BDoyle(1) (trckd ldrs: effrt 3f out: sn rdn & btn) | hd | **10** | 16/1 | 53 | 7 |
| 819[3] | **School Boy (70)** (TJNaughton) **3-8-1** JQuinn(6) (lw: nvr nr to chal) | ½ | **11** | 7/1[3] | 42 | — |
| 774[2] | **Elite Force (IRE) (80)** (PWChapple-Hyam) **3-8-11** JReid(5) (lw: prom tl rdn & outpcd fnl 2f) | ½ | **12** | 7/1[3] | 51 | 5 |
| | **Desert Cat (IRE) (75)** (HThomsonJones) **3-8-6** RHills(12) (bkwd: a in rr: t.o) | 6 | **13** | 14/1 | 33 | — |
| | | | | (SP 123.6%) | **13 Rn** | |

**1m 36.7** (4.70) CSF £197.36 CT £2,214.43 TOTE £16.90: £4.60 £4.90 £3.80 (£103.40) Trio £725.00 OWNER Mr P. B. Adams (MARLBOROUGH) BRED Sheikh Mohammed Bin Rashid Al Maktoum

**Prends Ca (IRE)** was fortunate to find a way through when making stealthy progress on the approach to the straight, but she was always travelling strongly and should have no trouble in defying a penalty. (14/1)
**React** has done extremely well since last year and this fine performance matched her looks. Sure to be more at home on a galloping track, she may well stay a mile. (16/1)
**Pharmacy**, turned out in tip-top condition for this seasonal debut and adopting more patient tactics over this longer trip, ran on strongly in the closing stages and looks set for another rewarding season. (10/1)
**785 Sualtach (IRE)** attempted to make all but could not get away from the chasing pack and they did him for toe in the sprint to the post. (9/2)
**701 Kazimiera (IRE)** began to edge closer starting the home turn and battled on well in the closing stages, but could not raise her pace sufficiently to land a blow. Her turn is near. (11/1)
**Le Sport**, who has done all his winning on the All-Weather, trailed the field by quite some way until running on strongly when it was all too late. (33/1)
**774 Menoo Hal Batal (USA)**, taking on handicappers for the first time, hung right throughout and was never galloping on an even keel. (5/1)
**755 Alpine Hideaway (IRE)** (11/1: 8/1-12/1)

## 988 WALKER SMITH & WAY H'CAP (0-90) (4-Y.O+) (Class C)

4-10 (4-13) **1m 2f 75y** £11,022.00 (£3,336.00: £1,628.00: £774.00) Stalls: High GOING minus 0.03 sec per fur (G)

| | | | | SP | RR | SF |
|---|---|---|---|---|---|---|
| 820* | **Hugwity (75)** (BHanbury) **4-8-12**(3) JStack(4) (b: trckd ldrs: led over 2f out: drvn out) | — | **1** | 6/1[2] | 86 | 57 |
| 913[2] | **Ten Past Six (88)** (MartynWane) **4-10-0** MHills(1) (a.p: rdn & n.m.r ent st: r.o wl ins fnl f) | 1 | **2** | 14/1 | 98 | 69 |
| 925[2] | **Hardy Dancer (87)** (GLMoore) **4-9-13** SWhitworth(7) (lw: a.p: hrd drvn over 2f out: kpt on) | nk | **3** | 5/1[1] | 96 | 67 |
| 844[5] | **Secret Aly (CAN) (82)** (CEBrittain) **6-9-8** BDoyle(3) (lw: a.p: led 4f out tl over 2f out: one pce ins fnl f) | ¾ | **4** | 16/1 | 90 | 61 |
| 920* | **Golden Touch (USA) (65)** (NACallaghan) **4-8-5** 5x WCarson(5) (hld up in tch: effrt on ins 2f out: kpt on ins fnl f) | nk | **5** | 5/1[1] | 72 | 43 |
| *358*[4] | **Grand Selection (IRE) (80)** (MBell) **4-9-6** MFenton(11) (hld up & bhd: hdwy over 2f out: nrst fin) | ¾ | **6** | 12/1 | 86 | 57 |
| | **Conspicuous (IRE) (78)** (LGCottrell) **6-9-4** JQuinn(6) (hld up: hdwy 4f out: wknd appr fnl f) | 5 | **7** | 14/1 | 77 | 48 |
| 580[17] | **Barbaroja (86)** (JGFitzGerald) **5-9-12b** KFallon(9) (hld up: effrt & rdn over 3f out: nvr nrr) | 5 | **8** | 12/1 | 77 | 48 |
| 888[10] | **Aldaneh (74)** (RHannon) **4-9-0** JReid(10) (hld up: effrt & n.m.r over 2f out: n.d) | 1¾ | **9** | 20/1 | 62 | 33 |
| *285** | **Tatika (72)** (GWragg) **6-8-5**(7) GMilligan(12) (hld up: hdwy over 3f out: wknd fnl 2f) | 3 | **10** | 13/2[3] | 55 | 26 |
| 580[11] | **Te Amo (IRE) (78)** (RAkehurst) **4-9-4** TQuinn(13) (nvr plcd to chal) | s.h | **11** | 12/1 | 61 | 32 |
| | **Nordic Breeze (IRE) (73)** (ABailey) **4-8-13b1** PaulEddery(14) (bit bkwd: nvr trbld ldrs) | hd | **12** | 20/1 | 56 | 27 |
| 738[5] | **Sheraz (IRE) (68)** (NTinkler) **4-8-8** PatEddery(2) (led over 6f: wknd over 3f out) | 1½ | **13** | 12/1 | 49 | 20 |
| 728[14] | **Romios (IRE) (88)** (PFICole) **4-9-9**(5) DGriffiths(16) (lw: a in rr: t.o) | 7 | **14** | 20/1 | 58 | 29 |
| 628* | **Komreyev Dancer (71)** (ABailey) **4-8-8**(3) DWright(8) (mid div tl wknd over 3f out: t.o) | ¾ | **15** | 13/2[3] | 40 | 11 |
| | | | | (SP 138.6%) | **15 Rn** | |

**2m 13.76** (5.06) CSF £89.81 CT £426.13 TOTE £9.10: £2.70 £4.90 £3.10 (£74.50) Trio £144.30 OWNER Mr Abdullah Ali (NEWMARKET) BRED Gainsborough Stud Management Ltd

**820* Hugwity** had no trouble stepping up into handicap company and he gives every indication that there is more improvement to come. (6/1)
**913 Ten Past Six** could not hold his pitch when the field bunched over two furlongs out, but he did eventually weave his way through again. Running on willingly, he found the concession of 16lb just too much. This was a very encouraging effort. (14/1)
**925 Hardy Dancer**, having his second run in four days, sat close up to the pace on this tight track and stuck on gamely to go down fighting. (5/1)
**844 Secret Aly (CAN)**, in the firing-line all the way, looked sure to make the frame but just could not hold on in a spirited dash to the line. (16/1)
**920* Golden Touch (USA)**, waiting on the leaders, did not enjoy a trouble-free passage when creeping up on the inside rail, but he was into his stride in the final furlong and was still closing at the finish. (5/1)
**Grand Selection (IRE)** took time to find top gear and, when he did, the race was almost over. He will not be long in returning to form. (12/1)

## 989 PRINCE OF WALES H'CAP (0-100) (3-Y.O) (Class C)
4-40 (4-47) **5f 16y** £7,304.00 (£2,192.00: £1,056.00: £488.00) Stalls: Low GOING minus 0.03 sec per fur (G)

| | | | | SP | RR | SF |
|---|---|---|---|---|---|---|
| 716[7] | **Pride of Brixton (78)** (GLewis) **3-8-3** PaulEddery(2) (hld up in tch: qcknd to ld ent fnl f: sn clr) | — | 1 | 4/1[2] | 87 | 43 |
| 692[7] | **Night Parade (USA) (88)** (PWChapple-Hyam) **3-8-13** JReid(5) (trckd ldrs: rdn & r.o appr fnl f: no ch w wnr) | 3½ | 2 | 11/4[1] | 86 | 42 |
| | **Tadeo (96)** (MJohnston) **3-9-7** JWeaver(8) (a.p: rdn & outpcd appr fnl f) | 2 | 3 | 8/1 | 88 | 44 |
| 443[7] | **Polly Golightly (82)** (MBlanshard) **3-8-7b** TQuinn(7) (led tl hdd & outpcd appr fnl f) | ¾ | 4 | 10/1 | 71 | 27 |
| 750[6] | **Don't Tell Anyone (71)** (PDEvans) **3-7-3**(7) IonaWands(1) (hdwy 2f out: swtchd ins & r.o wl fnl f) | ¾ | 5 | 50/1 | 58 | 14 |
| 443[15] | **Miss Bigwig (78)** (JBerry) **3-7-12**(5) PFessey(6) (b.nr fore: prom tl rdn & outpcd appr fnl f) | 2 | 6 | 11/1 | 59 | 15 |
| 644* | **Secret Voucher (71)** (BAMcMahon) **3-7-10** JQuinn(10) (chsd ldrs over 3f) | 1 | 7 | 7/1 | 49 | 5 |
| 773[3] | **Pleasure Time (73)** (CSmith) **3-7-5b**(7)ow2 MartinDwyer(3) (reard s: s.v.s: a bhd & outpcd) | 2½ | 8 | 9/1 | 43 | — |
| 790a[3] | **Eastern Prophets (96)** (TJNaughton) **3-9-7** PatEddery(9) (outpcd: a bhd) | 1 | 9 | 6/1[3] | 62 | 18 |
| | **Dande Flyer (74)** (DWPArbuthnot) **3-7-10**(3) DarrenMoffatt(4) (b: bit bkwd: outpcd) | ½ | 10 | 8/1 | 39 | — |

(SP 125.1%) **10 Rn**

**62.05 secs** (2.05) CSF £15.90 CT £82.75 TOTE £4.30: £2.00 £1.80 £2.90 (£7.00) Trio £15.40 OWNER The Voice Group Ltd (EPSOM) BRED Lady McAlpine

LONG HANDICAP Secret Voucher 7-9 Pleasure Time 7-7 Don't Tell Anyone 6-1

**716 Pride of Brixton,** content to be given a lead, quickened impressively when let loose approaching the final furlong and opened his account with ease. He could run up a sequence. (4/1: 3/1-9/2)

**Night Parade (USA),** a winner over course and distance twelve months ago, still looked to need the run. Unable to respond when the winner stepped on the gas, he did run on towards the finish, but was never going to be better than second best. (11/4)

**Tadeo,** smartly into his stride to press the leaders, had every chance until getting left behind approaching the final furlong. This run will have done him good. (8/1)

**Polly Golightly,** pretty smart on her day, set a brisk pace until put in her place by the winner. She is coming to hand. (10/1)

**750 Don't Tell Anyone** only began to get into the race after being switched over towards the inside rail in the closing stages. (50/1)

**Miss Bigwig** has bags of speed and stalked the leader until they both got taken off their legs by the superior finishing pace of the winner. (11/1)

T/Jkpt: Not won; £8,034.59 to Chester 8/5/96. T/Plpt: £1,595.40 (19.7 Tckts). T/Qdpt: £145.70 (19.9 Tckts). IM

# 0950-DONCASTER (L-H) (Good to firm)
## Tuesday May 7th
WEATHER: overcast WIND: mod half bhd

## 990 CAPRICORN (S) STKS (2-Y.O) (Class F)
6-00 (6-03) **5f** £2,976.00 (£888.00: £424.00: £192.00) Stalls: High GOING minus 0.19 sec per fur (GF)

| | | | | SP | RR | SF |
|---|---|---|---|---|---|---|
| *838*[2] | **Grovefair Flyer (IRE)** (BJMeehan) **2-8-11** MTebbutt(2) (mde most: shkn up over 1f out: r.o strly: comf) | — | 1 | 5/1[3] | 70 | 17 |
| 823[3] | **Poly Moon** (MRChannon) **2-8-6** KDarley(4) (s.s: sn drvn along: hdwy to chse ldrs ½-wy: nt qckn appr fnl f) | 2½ | 2 | 9/4[2] | 57 | 4 |
| 624* | **Contravene (IRE)** (JBerry) **2-8-13** JCarroll(6) (chsd ldrs: rdn, outpcd & hung lft ½-wy: styd on fnl f) | 1¾ | 3 | 6/1 | 58 | 5 |
| 657[3] | **Absolutely Abstone** (PDEvans) **2-8-6v[1]** JFortune(7) (disp ld 2f: wknd over 1f out) | 1¾ | 4 | 7/1 | 46 | — |
| | **Super Sheriff** (MWEasterby) **2-8-6**(5) GParkin(8) (unf: unruly s: chsd ldrs: rdn ½-wy: outpcd over 1f out) | 1½ | 5 | 20/1 | 46 | — |
| 506[7] | **Rahona (IRE)** (BSRothwell) **2-8-6** DHarrison(9) (chsd ldrs 3f: sn wknd) | 1¾ | 6 | 10/1 | 35 | — |
| 770[6] | **Classic Services** (BPalling) **2-8-11** TSprake(1) (b: a wl outpcd: swvd rt over 1f out) | hd | 7 | 14/1 | 40 | — |
| | ***Treasure Touch (IRE)*** (AHarrison) **2-8-11** DeanMcKeown(5) (Withdrawn not under Starter's orders. ref to ent stalls) | | W | 13/8[1] | — | — |

(SP 132.8%) **7 Rn**

**62.07 secs** (3.67) CSF £9.81 TOTE £5.80: £2.10 £1.60 (£5.10) Trio £3.70 OWNER Grovefair plc (UPPER LAMBOURN) BRED Richard Barry Smyth

Bt in 5,800 gns

**838 Grovefair Flyer (IRE),** who is not the best of movers, found this relatively simple and scored with plenty in hand in the end. (5/1)

**823 Poly Moon,** who is only small and not a good mover, was dropped in class here. After forfeiting ground at the start, she always had a struggle on her hands and, in the end, the winner proved much too good. (9/4: op 6/4)

**624* Contravene (IRE),** who looked very fit, did not help her cause by hanging under pressure, but she did stay on in the final furlong. (6/1: op 7/2)

**657 Absolutely Abstone,** tried in a visor, proved very keen. (7/1)

**Super Sheriff,** a backward-looking newcomer, showed a poor action going down. After proving a handful at the start, he was flat out at halfway. (20/1)

**446 Rahona (IRE)** (10/1: 8/1-12/1)

## 991 BEACHCOMBER H'CAP (0-75) (3-Y.O+) (Class D)
6-30 (6-32) **7f** £4,175.00 (£1,250.00: £600.00: £275.00) Stalls: High GOING minus 0.19 sec per fur (GF)

| | | | | SP | RR | SF |
|---|---|---|---|---|---|---|
| *839*[5] | **Cheerful Groom (IRE) (41)** (SRBowring) **5-7-10** NKennedy(12) (hdwy over 2f out: styd on wl to ld ins fnl f) | — | 1 | 20/1 | 48 | 30 |
| *854*[4] | **Sycamore Lodge (IRE) (68)** (MrsJRRamsden) **5-9-9** KFallon(17) (lw: hdwy & swtchd rt over 2f out: styd on wl ins fnl f: nt rch wnr) | 1 | 2 | 11/2[3] | 73 | 55 |
| 629[7] | **Kid Ory (64)** (PCalver) **5-9-5** MBirch(4) (w ldrs far side: led over 2f out tl ins fnl f: r.o same pce) | 1¾ | 3 | 12/1 | 65 | 47 |
| | **Special-K (62)** (EWeymes) **4-9-3** GHind(5) (in tch: styd on wl fnl f: nt rch ldrs) | hd | 4 | 12/1 | 63 | 45 |
| 636[10] | **Soaking (55)** (PBurgoyne) **6-8-7**(3) PMcCabe(6) (s.i.s: hdwy u.p over 2f out: styd on fnl f) | ¾ | 5 | 6/1 | 54 | 36 |
| 718[9] | **Monis (IRE) (52)** (JBalding) **5-8-0v**(7)ow2 JEdmunds(1) (lw: w ldrs: hung rt over 1f out: sn wknd) | ¾ | 6 | 16/1 | 49 | 29 |
| | **Darcey Bussell (55)** (BWHills) **4-8-10** RCochrane(2) (in tch: effrt & swtchd lft over 1f out: sn wknd) | 1¼ | 7 | 5/1[2] | 49 | 31 |
| 814[13] | **Benzoe (IRE) (69)** (MrsJRRamsden) **6-9-10** JFortune(10) (s.s: racd stands' side: bhd tl styd on appr fnl f) | hd | 8 | 16/1 | 63 | 45 |
| 827[10] | **Thunder River (IRE) (61)** (MJHeaton-Ellis) **6-8-11v**(5) AmandaSanders(3) (lw: led far side tl over 2f out: wkng whn sltly hmpd over 1f out) | hd | 9 | 10/1 | 55 | 37 |
| 765[10] | **Jungle Patrol (IRE) (61)** (MBrittain) **4-9-2** BThomson(9) (b: racd far side: nvr nr ldrs) | 1¼ | 10 | 16/1 | 52 | 34 |
| *778** | **Awesome Venture (53)** (MCChapman) **6-8-5**(3) DRMcCabe(13) (sn trckng ldrs: effrt over 2f out: sn wknd) | 1¾ | 11 | 8/1 | 40 | 22 |
| 764[6] | **Rocky Two (43)** (PHowling) **5-7-12b** FNorton(8) (racd far side: a bhd) | 1¼ | 12 | 33/1 | 27 | 9 |
| 806[4] | **Superpride (64)** (MrsMReveley) **4-9-5** KDarley(14) (effrt over 3f out: sltly hmpd over 2f out: sn wknd) | 3½ | 13 | 6/1 | 40 | 22 |

| | Horse | Dist | Pos | SP | RR | SF |
|---|---|---|---|---|---|---|
| | **Alabang (48)** (MJCamacho) **5-8-3** LCharnock(15) (led stands' side to 2f out: eased whn btn) | 3 | **14** | 3/1[1] | 17 | — |
| 820[14] | **Begger's Opera (45)** (PatMitchell) **4-8-0** GBardwell(18) (a in rr) | hd | **15** | 33/1 | 14 | — |
| 806[17] | **Ragazzo (IRE) (41)** (JSWainwright) **6-7-3b**(7) RMullen(7) (sn outpcd & rdn along: a bhd) | 1¼ | **16** | 50/1 | 7 | — |
| 704[12] | **Arc Lamp (43)** (JAGlover) **10-7-12** NCarlisle(11) (chsd ldrs stands' side tl lost pl 2f out) | 7 | **17** | 25/1 | — | — |
| | | | | (SP 155.3%) | **17 Rn** | |

**1m 26.57** (2.97) CSF £145.14 CT £1,379.19 TOTE £60.80: £9.00 £2.10 £3.90 £1.80 (£126.00) Trio £450.60; £387.19 to 9/5/96 OWNER Mr Bill Cahill (EDWINSTOWE) BRED Leo Collins

LONG HANDICAP Cheerful Groom (IRE) 7-5 Ragazzo (IRE) 6-13

**839 Cheerful Groom (IRE)**, who has just won one of forty-three previous outings, was racing from 5lb out of the handicap. In a confusing race, after the far side looked to hold a commanding advantage, in the end the first two raced towards the stands' side. (20/1)

**854 Sycamore Lodge (IRE)**, a frustrating character who is still a maiden, was putting in some solid work when it was all over and will surely be better suited by a step up to a mile. (11/2)

**Kid Ory** ran right up to his best but the Handicapper has him assessed to the pound at present. (12/1)

**Special-K**, winner of three of her last six outings last year, ran a pleasing first race, putting in some solid late work. (12/1)

**Soaking** ran much better than his last two outings on turf. (6/1)

**Benzoe (IRE)** looked in tremendous fettle. As usual put into the stalls late, he gave ground away but stuck on in promising fashion in the closing stages. Seven furlongs seemed to suit him and all he needs now is some give underfoot. (16/1)

## 992 MCGREGOR CORY LIMITED STKS (0-80) (3-Y.O) (Class D)

7-00 (7-05) **6f** £5,162.50 (£1,540.00: £735.00: £332.50) Stalls: High GOING minus 0.19 sec per fur (GF)

| | Horse | Dist | Pos | SP | RR | SF |
|---|---|---|---|---|---|---|
| 672[6] | **Hoh Returns (IRE) (80)** (MBell) **3-8-11** MFenton(3) (trckd ldrs: led over 2f out: shkn up over 1f out: r.o wl) | — | **1** | 7/1[3] | 87 | 47 |
| | **Thordis (75)** (PJMakin) **3-8-11** KDarley(6) (b.nr hind: s.i.s: sn pushed along: hdwy ½-wy: styd on appr fnl f: no ch w wnr) | 5 | **2** | 7/1[3] | 74 | 34 |
| 737[6] | **No Monkey Nuts (80)** (JBerry) **3-8-11** JCarroll(4) (lw: led over 4f out tl over 2f out: hdd & edgd rt: kpt on same pce) | ½ | **3** | 11/2[2] | 72 | 32 |
| 692[13] | **Blue Suede Hoofs (72)** (BJMeehan) **3-8-11** MTebbutt(2) (chsd ldrs: rdn & hung lft ½-wy: wknd over 1f out) | 3½ | **4** | 20/1 | 63 | 23 |
| 448[14] | **Angus McCoatup (IRE) (58)** (BAMcMahon) **3-8-11** GCarter(1) (sn wl outpcd & bhd: sme hdwy over 1f out: n.d) | 1½ | **5** | 50/1 | 59 | 19 |
| 692[8] | **Akalim (80)** (DMorley) **3-8-11** WCarson(5) (led over 1f: rdn & sltly hmpd over 3f out: lost pl over 2f out: eased) | 2 | **6** | 8/15[1] | 54 | 14 |
| 692[15] | **Sonic Mail (75)** (KMcAuliffe) **3-8-11** WJO'Connor(7) (b.nr hind: chsd ldrs: n.m.r over 3f out: wknd over 2f out) | 2½ | **7** | 25/1 | 47 | 7 |
| | | | | (SP 116.2%) | **7 Rn** | |

**1m 13.25** (2.25) CSF £49.03 TOTE £6.30: £2.50 £3.30 (£15.30) OWNER Mr D. F. Allport (NEWMARKET) BRED Airlie Stud

**672 Hoh Returns (IRE)** left his initial effort this year well behind. Travelling smoothly, he won in some style and connections will be hoping that the Handicapper is not too hard on him. (7/1)

**Thordis**, pushed along to go the pace, was staying on when it was all over. He will be suited by a step up to seven. (7/1)

**No Monkey Nuts** edged right before halfway, hampering the favourite who was already in trouble. (11/2)

**Blue Suede Hoofs** showed a marked tendency to hang left under pressure. (20/1)

**Angus McCoatup (IRE)** had an impossible task at the weights and struggled to go the pace, but was staying on when it was all over. Seven furlongs in handicap company will surely suit him better. (50/1)

**Akalim** was backed as if defeat was out of the question, even though on paper he just had an average chance. After breaking first, he was already under pressure when hampered just before halfway. Soon dropping out, Carson soon called it a day, and there was no obvious excuse. (8/15: 4/5-1/2)

## 993 DONCASTER SPONSORSHIP CLUB H'CAP (0-75) (3-Y.O+) (Class D)

7-30 (7-35) **1m 4f** £4,485.25 (£1,342.00: £643.50: £294.25) Stalls: Low GOING minus 0.19 sec per fur (GF)

| | Horse | Dist | Pos | SP | RR | SF |
|---|---|---|---|---|---|---|
| 546[10] | **Haya Ya Kefaah (55)** (NMBabbage) **4-8-9** AClark(5) (chsd ldrs: led over 3f out: sn clr: rdr dropped whip over 1f out: hld on wl towards fin) | — | **1** | 12/1 | 66 | 37 |
| 612[2] | **Outstayed Welcome (57)** (MJHaynes) **4-8-6**(5) MBaird(11) (b.off hind: led tl over 3f out: styd on wl fnl f) | 1 | **2** | 8/1 | 67 | 38 |
| 731[7] | **Ela-Yie-Mou (IRE) (73)** (LMCumani) **3-8-8** RCochrane(10) (lw: in tch: effrt over 3f out: styd on same pce: nvr nr to chal) | 1 | **3** | 5/2[1] | 81 | 33 |
| 817[2] | **Fighting Times (70)** (CASmith) **4-9-10** DeanMcKeown(6) (b.hind: effrt & n.m.r over 3f out: styd on fnl 2f: nt rch ldrs) | 1 | **4** | 7/2[2] | 77 | 48 |
| 872[5] | **Cliburnel News (IRE) (58)** (AStreeter) **6-8-12** JWeaver(7) (lw: effrt & swtchd rt over 2f out: styd on: nt rch ldrs) | ½ | **5** | 9/1 | 64 | 35 |
| 816[4] | **Tulu (71)** (MrsJRRamsden) **5-9-4**(7) ClaireWest(9) (b.off fore: hld up: hdwy & n.m.r over 2f out: grad wknd) | 6 | **6** | 11/1 | 69 | 40 |
| *898** | **In the Money (IRE) (60)** (RHollinshead) **7-8-9**(5) 5x FLynch(2) (chsd ldrs tl wknd over 2f out) | 2 | **7** | 7/1[3] | 56 | 27 |
| | **Tirolette (IRE) (57)** (RJRWilliams) **4-8-4b**(7) AimeeCook(8) (hdwy on ins whn hmpd over 3f out: nvr nr ldrs) | ½ | **8** | 16/1 | 52 | 23 |
| | **Green Land (BEL) (68)** (SCWilliams) **4-9-8** KFallon(1) (b.nr fore: in tch: outpcd 3f out: n.d after) | 5 | **9** | 11/1 | 56 | 27 |
| 771[8] | **Majal (IRE) (53)** (JSWainwright) **7-8-7** LCharnock(12) (hld up & plld hrd: a in rr) | 1½ | **10** | 25/1 | 39 | 10 |
| | **Ring of Vision (IRE) (52)** (MrsMReveley) **4-8-6** KDarley(14) (hld up: sme hdwy over 3f out: hung lft & sn wknd) | 6 | **11** | 10/1 | 30 | 1 |
| 872[4] | **Prussia (42)** (WClay) **5-7-10** NCarlisle(13) (chsd ldrs tl lost pl over 3f out) | 3½ | **12** | 11/1 | 16 | — |
| | **Island Cascade (42)** (DonEnricoIncisa) **4-7-10** KimTinkler(4) (a wl bhd) | 2½ | **13** | 50/1 | 12 | — |
| 825[7] | **Pickens (USA) (70)** (NTinkler) **4-9-10b**[1] JFortune(15) (jnd ldrs 7f out: rdn & swvd rt over 3f out: sn bhd) | 10 | **14** | 33/1 | 27 | — |
| | **Haido'hart (60)** (BSRothwell) **4-9-0** MFenton(3) (chsd ldrs tl lost pl 3f out: sn bhd) | 19 | **15** | 33/1 | — | — |
| | | | | (SP 143.8%) | **15 Rn** | |

**2m 36.13** (6.13) CSF £112.93 CT £306.08 TOTE £19.80: £4.70 £2.50 £1.90 (£72.80) Trio £250.30 OWNER Mr Alan Craddock (CHELTENHAM) BRED Sheikh Ahmed bin Rashid al Maktoum

LONG HANDICAP Island Cascade 7-2

WEIGHT FOR AGE 3yo-19lb

**546 Haya Ya Kefaah** was given an enterprising ride. Stepping up the pace and shooting clear just under half a mile from home, his rider dropped his whip and, slapping down the shoulder with his hand, his mount held on grimly. (12/1)

**612 Outstayed Welcome**, raised 8lb after two good efforts on his last two starts, made the running and stuck on strongly. In the end, he proved the only real threat to the winner. (8/1)

**731 Ela-Yie-Mou (IRE)**, who looked very fit, was flat out halfway up the straight. Sticking on under pressure, he never looked likely to find the pace to trouble the winner and should be suited by further. (5/2)
**817 Fighting Times**, raised 5lb, did not have the best of runs but it was almost certainly his lack of pace to get out of trouble that was his downfall. (7/2)
**872 Cliburnel News (IRE)** looked really well but had to be switched to get a run. Putting in her best work at the finish, she is crying out for a longer trip. (9/1)
**816 Tulu**, ridden by an inexperienced 7lb claimer, met trouble and caused some too halfway up the straight. She is not back to her very best yet. (11/1: 8/1-12/1)

## 994 MAURITIUS' MILE MAIDEN STKS (3-Y.O+) (Class D)

8-00 (8-09) **1m (straight)** £4,370.00 (£1,310.00: £630.00: £290.00) Stalls: High GOING minus 0.19 sec per fur (GF)

| | Horse | Dist | Pos | SP | RR | SF |
|---|---|---|---|---|---|---|
| 678$^{7}$ | **Singapore Sting (USA)** (HRACecil) **3-8-6** WRyan(10) (lw: chsd ldr: led 2f out: hrd drvn: all out) | — | **1** | 11/4$^{2}$ | 78 | 40 |
| 669$^{6}$ | **Classic Leader** (SCWilliams) **3-8-11** AMackay(9) (a.p: chal 2f out: sn rdn & edgd rt: nt qckn fnl f) | 1 | **2** | 5/2$^{1}$ | 81 | 43 |
| 584$^{4}$ | **Victory Bound (USA)** (MJohnston) **3-8-11** JWeaver(3) (swvd lft s: led to 2f out: styd on same pce) | 2 | **3** | 9/1 | 77 | 39 |
| | **Muhassil (IRE)** (MajorWRHern) **3-8-11** WCarson(12) (w'like: chsd ldrs: pushed along over 3f out: rn green: kpt on) | 3 | **4** | 8/1 | 71 | 33 |
| | **Pep Talk (USA)** (HRACecil) **3-8-11** AMcGlone(6) (lt-f: lw: in tch: outpcd ½-wy: kpt on fnl 2f) | 3½ | **5** | 7/1 | 64 | 26 |
| 820$^{4}$ | **Lady of Leisure (USA)** (MrsJCecil) **4-9-5** TIves(14) (lw: in tch: effrt over 3f out: sn btn) | 1½ | **6** | 4/1$^{3}$ | 56 | 31 |
| 826$^{9}$ | **Gool Lee Shay (USA)** (RMWhitaker) **3-8-11** JFanning(4) (bhd: sme hdwy 2f out: n.d) | 3½ | **7** | 66/1 | 54 | 16 |
| 705$^{10}$ | **Indiphar** (FHLee) **3-8-6** KDarley(8) (in tch: pushed along over 3f out: sn wl outpcd) | ¾ | **8** | 50/1 | 48 | 10 |
| 786$^{10}$ | **Squared Away** (JWPayne) **4-9-10** MTebbutt(7) (a in rr) | nk | **9** | 33/1 | 52 | 27 |
| 703$^{11}$ | **Bright Pet** (MrsSJSmith) **3-8-6** NCarlisle(2) (sltly hmpd s: nvr nr ldrs) | 2 | **10** | 66/1 | 43 | 5 |
| | **Newbridge Boy** (MGMeagher) **3-8-11** JFortune(5) (leggy: unf: chsd ldrs tl wknd 3f out) | ½ | **11** | 50/1 | 47 | 9 |
| | **Mr Speculator** (PAKelleway) **3-8-11** MWigham(1) (v.unruly in stalls: s.s: a bhd) | 1½ | **12** | 20/1 | 44 | 6 |
| | **Comedie Arrete (FR)** (MCChapman) **4-9-2**$^{(3)}$ DRMcCabe(13) (leggy: t.o fr ½-wy: virtually p.u) | dist | **13** | 33/1 | — | — |
| | ***Gabrielle Gerard*** (MrsAMNaughton) **4-9-5** VHalliday(11) (Withdrawn not under Starter's orders. v.unruly & ref to ent stalls) | | **W** | 66/1 | — | — |

(SP 127.9%) **13 Rn**

**1m 40.36** (3.36) CSF £10.23 TOTE £3.00: £1.60 £1.90 £2.00 (£10.40) Trio £5.60 OWNER Mr Bernard Gover (NEWMARKET) BRED Crystal Springs Farm and Jayeff B Stables
WEIGHT FOR AGE 3yo-13lb
**OFFICIAL EXPLANATION Comedie Arrete (FR): lost her action early in the race.**
**678 Singapore Sting (USA)** answered her rider's calls willingly but, at the line, there was nothing at all to spare. This looked a very ordinary maiden. (11/4: 5/4-3/1)
**Classic Leader**, heavily backed to step up on her last effort, had every chance but, under pressure, edged right and carried his head high, looking far from enthusiastic. (5/2)
**584 Victory Bound (USA)**, who wore a tongue-strap, recovered from a tardy start to make the running. After hanging left last time out, it was noted that his rider still carried his whip in his left hand. Sticking on when headed, he might be capable of better in handicap company over further. (9/1: op 5/1)
**Muhassil (IRE)**, who is already a gelding, ran green and was not knocked about when it was clear he was booked for fourth. (8/1)
**Pep Talk (USA)**, who lacks substance, was flat out at halfway. Keeping on in his own time, he probably needs a considerable step up in distance. (7/1: op 9/2)
**820 Lady of Leisure (USA)**, dropped back in distance, surprisingly came in for some market support. In trouble soon after halfway, her future surely lies in handicaps over much further. (4/1)

## 995 PORT LOUIS H'CAP (0-70) (3-Y.O+) (Class E)

8-30 (8-40) **1m 2f 60y** £4,337.50 (£1,300.00: £625.00: £287.50) Stalls: Low GOING minus 0.19 sec per fur (GF)

| | Horse | Dist | Pos | SP | RR | SF |
|---|---|---|---|---|---|---|
| *836*$^{9}$ | **Rasayel (USA) (50)** (PDEvans) **6-8-11** JFortune(12) (trckd ldrs: qcknd to ld over 2f out: sn clr: hld on wl) | — | **1** | 11/1 | 63 | 34 |
| 787$^{3}$ | **Maradata (IRE) (48)** (RHollinshead) **4-8-4**$^{(5)}$ FLynch(8) (lw: hld up: gd hdwy on outside over 2f out: edgd lft: nt qckn ins fnl f) | 1½ | **2** | 5/1$^{2}$ | 59 | 30 |
| | **Master M-E-N (IRE) (50)** (NMBabbage) **4-8-11v** AClark(5) (hld up: hdwy & nt clr run over 2f out: styd on one pce appr fnl f) | 1¾ | **3** | 16/1 | 58 | 29 |
| 819$^{7}$ | **Seattle Alley (USA) (59)** (MrsJRRamsden) **3-8-5** KFallon(3) (lw: hld up: gd hdwy on ins to chse ldrs over 2f out: kpt on same pce) | 1¼ | **4** | 7/2$^{1}$ | 65 | 21 |
| 752$^{2}$ | **Carlton Express (IRE) (42)** (JLEyre) **6-8-3** RLappin(4) (hld up: effrt & swtchd rt over 2f out: styd on same pce) | s.h | **5** | 8/1 | 48 | 19 |
| *604*$^{7}$ | **Paronomasia (35)** (JLHarris) **4-7-3b**$^{1(7)}$ RMullen(9) (a chsng ldrs: one pce fnl 3f) | 6 | **6** | 33/1 | 32 | 3 |
| 609$^{2}$ | **Watch Me Go (IRE) (41)** (BobJones) **7-8-2** FNorton(16) (unruly s: styd on fnl 2f: nvr nr ldrs) | ¾ | **7** | 8/1 | 36 | 7 |
| 641$^{9}$ | **Sarasota Storm (52)** (MBell) **4-8-13** MFenton(6) (nvr nrr) | 3 | **8** | 10/1 | 43 | 14 |
| 871$^{9}$ | **Rushen Raider (58)** (KWHogg) **4-9-5** DHarrison(1) (leggy: mid div: effrt & hmpd over 2f out: nvr nr ldrs) | 2 | **9** | 12/1 | 46 | 17 |
| 636$^{6}$ | **Mr Rough (63)** (DMorris) **5-9-10** RCochrane(19) (s.s: bhd tl sme hdwy over 2f out: n.d) | 1½ | **10** | 12/1 | 48 | 19 |
| | **Miswaki Dancer (USA) (58)** (LadyHerries) **6-9-5** DeclanO'Shea(14) (mid div: sme hdwy 4f out: n.d) | 2½ | **11** | 10/1 | 39 | 10 |
| | **Doreen's Delight (35)** (HJCollingridge) **10-7-10** NCarlisle(20) (s.s: wl bhd: sme hdwy on ins whn hmpd 2f out: n.d) | hd | **12** | 33/1 | 16 | — |
| 775$^{12}$ | **Alzotic (IRE) (55)** (JNorton) **3-8-1** JFanning(13) (s.i.s: a bhd) | 1¼ | **13** | 11/1 | 34 | — |
| 752$^{3}$ | **I'm a Nut Man (35)** (CASmith) **5-7-7**$^{(3)}$ NVarley(17) (chsd ldrs: rdn over 3f out: sn wknd) | nk | **14** | 10/1 | 14 | — |
| 718$^{7}$ | **Tame Deer (55)** (MCChapman) **4-8-13**$^{(3)}$ DRMcCabe(11) (mde most tl over 2f out: sn wknd & eased) | 3 | **15** | 20/1 | 29 | — |
| 873$^{7}$ | **Swift Maiden (63)** (JNeville) **3-8-9** DeanMcKeown(10) (trckd ldrs: hmpd over 3f out: sn wknd) | ¾ | **16** | 12/1 | 36 | — |
| 863$^{8}$ | **Labeed (USA) (66)** (MajorWRHern) **3-8-12** WCarson(18) (w'like: hld up: a bhd) | 5 | **17** | 7/1$^{3}$ | 31 | — |
| 872$^{17}$ | **Oakbury (IRE) (57)** (MissLCSiddall) **4-9-4** JWeaver(7) (w ldr: wkng whn hmpd 2f out: eased) | 1 | **18** | 33/1 | 21 | — |
| | **Eden Dancer (55)** (MrsMReveley) **4-9-2** KDarley(15) (lw: hld up: sme hdwy over 3f out: sn wknd) | 2½ | **19** | 10/1 | 15 | — |
| | **Tirlie (IRE) (45)** (JWPayne) **4-8-6** BThomson(2) (chsd ldrs tl lost pl 6f out: t.o fnl 3f) | dist | **20** | 25/1 | — | — |

(SP 173.0%) **20 Rn**

**2m 12.87** (5.87) CSF £82.45 CT £894.00 TOTE £24.60: £4.40 £2.20 £4.00 £2.30 (£93.10) Trio £599.90 OWNER Pentons Haulage and Cold Storage Ltd (WELSHPOOL) BRED Gainsborough Farm
LONG HANDICAP I'm a Nut Man 7-8 Paronomasia 7-7
WEIGHT FOR AGE 3yo-15lb

**Rasayel (USA)** showed the benefit of her initial outing this year on the All-Weather. Given a fine ride, she took the initiative when quickening clear halfway up the straight and, with the runner-up not showing the same resolution, she was firmly in command at the line. (11/1)
**787 Maradata (IRE)** has plenty of ability, more than her handicap mark, but lacks courage. Making ground in smooth style on the outside, she edged left towards the winner and was reluctant to go past. On her previous start at Beverley, she went right, so a rail might help. (5/1)
**Master M-E-N (IRE)**, on his reappearance, met some trouble but, in truth, was never giving his rider 100% co-operation. The stable's horses are running well at present. (16/1)
**453 Seattle Alley (USA)**, dropped 3lb and stepped up two furlongs in distance, proved awkward at the start. Sticking to the inner, he made several lengths to join issue halfway up the straight but, soon flat out, could only stay on at the same pace. A mile and a half looks necessary. (7/2)
**752 Carlton Express (IRE)** met trouble in running, but was never doing enough to take a serious hand. (8/1)
**636 Mr Rough** (12/1: op 8/1)

T/Plpt: £290.80 (53.53 Tckts). T/Qdpt: £60.00 (20.08 Tckts). WG

# AYR (L-H) (Good to soft)
## Wednesday May 8th
WEATHER: sunny WIND: almost nil

## 996 AYR MAY CONDITIONS STKS (2-Y.O) (Class D)
1-50 (1-51) **5f** £3,818.00 (£1,154.00: £562.00: £266.00) Stalls: Low GOING: 0.48 sec per fur (GS)

| | | | | SP | RR | SF |
|---|---|---|---|---|---|---|
| 618* | **Express Girl** (DMoffatt) **2-8-8**(3) DarrenMoffatt(6) (lw: mde most: kpt on wl fnl 2f) | — | 1 | 8/1 | 69 | 22 |
| 639* | **Superior Premium** (RAFahey) **2-9-2** ACulhane(8) (lw: sn cl up: effrt ½-wy: nt qckn appr fnl f) | 2½ | 2 | 6/4 1 | 66 | 19 |
| 699 9 | **Ben's Ridge** (PCHaslam) **2-8-12** JFortune(7) (hdwy 2f out: styd on: nt pce to chal) | 1 | 3 | 12/1 | 59 | 12 |
| | **Osomental** (DHaydnJones) **2-8-12** AMackay(1) (str: s.s: outpcd & bhd: hdwy & rn green 2f out: r.o) | ¾ | 4 | 7/4 2 | 56+ | 9 |
| 715 3 | **Hit Or Miss** (MRChannon) **2-8-6**(5) PPMurphy(5) (in tch: n.m.r ½-wy: no imp) | 6 | 5 | 8/1 | 36 | — |
| 630* | **Masterstroke** (BJMeehan) **2-9-2** MTebbutt(3) (in tch: outpcd ½-wy: no imp after) | hd | 6 | 7/1 3 | 41 | — |
| 715 6 | **Enchanting Eve** (CNAllen) **2-8-6**(5) LNewton(2) (cl up to ½-wy: sn outpcd) | 1 | 7 | 8/1 | 33 | — |
| | **Biff-Em (IRE)** (MissLAPerratt) **2-8-12** GDuffield(4) (scope: w'like: bit bkwd: gd spd to ½-wy: wknd) | 1 | 8 | 100/1 | 31 | — |
| 657* | **Full Traceability (IRE)** (JBerry) **2-8-11** JCarroll(9) (nvr wnt pce) | 6 | 9 | 11/1 | 10 | — |
| | | | | (SP 139.2%) | **9 Rn** | |

**63.62 secs** (6.62) CSF £23.78 TOTE £19.60: £3.10 £1.10 £8.70 (£19.30) Trio £90.40; £103.20 to Chester 9/5/96 OWNER Mr P. G. Airey (CARTMEL) BRED P. G. Airey and R. R. Whitton
**618* Express Girl**, a sharp filly, always had too much speed for the opposition and was going away at the end. (8/1)
**639* Superior Premium**, who again showed a moderate action, could never dictate this time and was well held at the finish. (6/4: 4/5-13/8)
**Ben's Ridge** is learning fast and looks one to keep in mind. (12/1)
**Osomental** was absolutely clueless early on and took a deal of persuading to get going. Although making up an incredible amount of ground, he never had a hope of getting there. If he ever decides to get it together, he could be pretty useful. (7/4)
**715 Hit Or Miss** looks weak as yet and needs time. (8/1)
**630* Masterstroke** did not take to these slightly sticky conditions and was out of it from halfway. (7/1)
**Biff-Em (IRE)** is a decent sort but needed this quite badly and, after showing plenty of toe, he blew up soon after halfway. (100/1)
**657* Full Traceability (IRE)** (11/1: 8/1-12/1)

## 997 BALLANTRAE H'CAP (0-70) (3-Y.O+) (Class E)
2-20 (2-20) **5f** £3,146.10 (£952.80: £465.40: £221.70) Stalls: Low GOING: 0.48 sec per fur (GS)

| | | | | SP | RR | SF |
|---|---|---|---|---|---|---|
| 911* | **Just Bob (67)** (SEKettlewell) **7-9-13**(7) 7x MartinDwyer(2) (lw: s.s: swtchd rt & hdwy 2f out: str run to ld wl ins fnl f) | — | 1 | 4/1 2 | 75 | 57 |
| *207* 10 | **Seconds Away (31)** (JSGoldie) **5-7-12b**ow2 TWilliams(4) (prom: led ins fnl f: hdd & nt qckn towards fin) | 1¼ | 2 | 33/1 | 35 | 15 |
| 868 14 | **Penny's Wishing (46)** (NBycroft) **4-8-13** GDuffield(6) (b.off hind: led tl hdd & no ex ins fnl f) | 3 | 3 | 6/1 | 40 | 22 |
| | **Precious Girl (70)** (DMoffatt) **3-9-11**(3) DarrenMoffatt(3) (lw: effrt & hmpd ½-wy: bmpd over 1f out: styd on) | 1¼ | 4 | 7/2 1 | 60 | 33 |
| 762 10 | **Call to the Bar (IRE) (51)** (MDods) **7-9-4** JCarroll(5) (hdwy ½-wy: styd on: no imp) | 3½ | 5 | 12/1 | 30 | 12 |
| 882 10 | **Leading Princess (IRE) (49)** (MissLAPerratt) **5-8-11b**(5) PFessey(9) (w ldr 3f: sn btn) | ½ | 6 | 33/1 | 27 | 9 |
| *500* 4 | **Lord Sky (54)** (ABailey) **5-9-0**(7) AngelaGallimore(8) (lw: squeezed out s: hdwy ½-wy: no imp) | 1¾ | 7 | 6/1 | 26 | 8 |
| 882 5 | **Sunday Mail Too (IRE) (29)** (MissLAPerratt) **4-7-10b** LCharnock(11) (nvr wnt pce) | 1 | 8 | 12/1 | — | — |
| 617 10 | **Another Nightmare (IRE) (39)** (TDyer) **4-7-13**(7) RMullen(1) (chsd ldrs over 3f: sn btn) | ½ | 9 | 10/1 | 6 | — |
| *779* 2 | **Frontman (IRE) (67)** (TDBarron) **3-9-11** JFortune(7) (in tch: edgd rt ½-wy: grad wknd) | 1½ | 10 | 5/1 3 | 29 | 2 |
| | **Middle East (70)** (TDBarron) **3-10-0** DeanMcKeown(10) (swtg: s.s: a outpcd & bhd) | s.h | 11 | 14/1 | 32 | 5 |
| | | | | (SP 124.5%) | **11 Rn** | |

**62.8 secs** (5.80) CSF £104.53 CT £731.46 TOTE £3.10: £2.10 £15.70 £2.10 (£47.90) Trio Not won; £112.25 to Chester 9/5/96 OWNER Mr J. Fotherby (MIDDLEHAM) BRED Mrs D. Whittingham
LONG HANDICAP Seconds Away 7-8
WEIGHT FOR AGE 3yo-9lb
**911* Just Bob** is in top form just now and, although giving his usual ground away at the start and then having to switch right round the whole field, he produced a turn of foot that left the opposition bewildered. (4/1)
**Seconds Away** looked likely to break his duck at his eighteenth attempt here, but had no answer to the winner's late burst. (33/1)
**704 Penny's Wishing** has bags of speed but, despite trying hard, she failed to get home. (6/1)
**Precious Girl**, always struggling with the pace, subsequently found trouble and may need a bit further. (7/2)
**Call to the Bar (IRE)** has ability but it is a long time since he put it to full use. (12/1)
**Leading Princess (IRE)** needed thirteen runs before she found winning form last season and seems to be taking just as long this time. (33/1)
**500 Lord Sky** got messed about leaving the stalls and his chance had then gone. (6/1)
**Middle East** (14/1: op 7/1)

## 998 FENWICK MAIDEN CLAIMING STKS (3-Y.O+) (Class F)
2-50 (2-50) **1m 2f** £2,696.00 (£756.00: £368.00) Stalls: Low GOING: 0.26 sec per fur (G)

| | | | | SP | RR | SF |
|---|---|---|---|---|---|---|
| 801 5 | **De-Veers Currie (IRE) (44)** (RFFisher) **4-9-9** JFortune(7) (hld up: hdwy 3f out: rdn to ld wl ins fnl f) | — | 1 | 5/1 3 | 59 | 19 |

849[8] **Rattle (50)** (JJO'Neill) **3-8-6b[1]** JCarroll(2) (trckd ldrs: led 2f out: rdn 1f out: hdd wl ins fnl f: nt qckn towards fin)....nk **2** 2/1[2] 57 2
690[10] **Flyaway Blues (53)** (MrsMReveley) **4-10-0** DeanMcKeown(5) (lw: hld up: effrt 3f out: sn rdn: nt pce to chal)...6 **3** 6/4[1] 54 14
**Trumped (IRE) (37)** (PMonteith) **4-8-11** LCharnock(1) (led to 2f out: sn rdn & btn)....¾ **4** 10/1 36 —
883[12] **Sheroot (28)** (DMoffatt) **4-8-12**(3) DarrenMoffatt(6) (cl up tl rdn & wknd over 2f out)....2 **5** 66/1 37 —
826[11] **Philgem** (JHetherton) **3-7-12** NKennedy(3) (s.i.s: hdwy bef ½-wy: rdn & outpcd fnl 3f)....1 **6** 12/1 33 —
560[5] **Sylvan Princess (49)** (CNAllen) **3-7-8**(7) MartinDwyer(4) (prom tl rdn & wknd fnl 3f)....15 **7** 5/1[3] 12 —
(SP 124.9%) **7 Rn**

**2m 18.31** (13.71) CSF £16.45 TOTE £10.10: £3.00 £1.40 (£9.00) OWNER Great Head House Estates Ltd (ULVERSTON) BRED Roland Blennerhassett
WEIGHT FOR AGE 3yo-15lb

**De-Veers Currie (IRE)**, after a pipe-opener at an inadequate trip, won this moderate event in determined style. (5/1: 4/1-6/1)
**616 Rattle**, in blinkers for the first time, did most things right but just failed to last home. (2/1)
**Flyaway Blues** has yet to win a race and, although making some ground under pressure in the closing stages, was never giving it his best shot. (6/4: Evens-13/8)
**Trumped (IRE)**, an Irish import, ran reasonably until blowing up in the last couple of furlongs. (10/1: op 6/1)
**Sheroot** kept his record in this poor event and is yet to reach the first four. (66/1)

## 999 TORRANYARD H'CAP (0-70) (3-Y.O+) (Class E)
3-20 (3-21) **1m 2f 192y** £3,663.75 (£1,110.00: £542.50: £258.75) Stalls: Low GOING: 0.26 sec per fur (G)

SP RR SF
752[13] **Manful (62)** (CWCElsey) **4-9-10b** NKennedy(1) (trckd ldrs: led over 3f out: hld on wl fnl f)....— **1** 12/1 73 59
612[3] **Keep Battling (40)** (JSGoldie) **6-8-2** TWilliams(7) (hld up: hdwy over 2f out: chal ins fnl f: nt qckn towards fin)....½ **2** 10/1 50 36
853[6] **Drummer Hicks (44)** (EWeymes) **7-8-6** DeanMcKeown(8) (rr div: nt clr run over 2f out: swtchd twice: styd on wl appr fnl f)....3½ **3** 14/1 49 35
883* **Giftbox (USA) (53)** (SirMarkPrescott) **4-9-1** 5x GDuffield(5) (lw: trckd ldrs: chal over 3f out: sn rdn & one pce)....7 **4** 4/5[1] 48 34
822* **Walworth Lady (51)** (MDods) **5-8-13** JCarroll(4) (a chsng ldrs: one pce fnl 3f)....1 **5** 12/1 44 30
853[4] **Dana Point (IRE) (60)** (TDBarron) **4-9-8** JFortune(6) (lw: prom: effrt 3f out: one pce)....2 **6** 14/1 50 36
**Achilles Heel (41)** (CNAllen) **5-7-10**(7) MartinDwyer(2) (b: lw: bhd: hdwy on ins 3f out: n.m.r: n.d)....4 **7** 8/1[3] 26 12
*836[3]* **Miss Zanzibar (54)** (RAFahey) **4-9-2** ACulhane(13) (lost tch appr st: n.d after)....7 **8** 25/1 28 14
**Stormless (37)** (PMonteith) **5-7-13** LCharnock(12) (in tch tl wknd wl over 2f out)....nk **9** 20/1 11 —
**Guards Brigade (35)** (JHetherton) **5-7-6**(5) PFessey(3) (led tl hdd & wknd over 3f out)....2½ **10** 20/1 5 —
612[11] **Bowcliffe (48)** (MrsAMNaughton) **5-8-10** MTebbutt(10) (bhd fnl 3½f)....1½ **11** 80/1 16 2
883[11] **Percy Parrot (35)** (RMWhitaker) **4-7-11v[1]**ow1 DaleGibson(9) (chsd ldrs tl wknd 3f out)....5 **12** 100/1 — —
920[3] **Askern (66)** (DHaydnJones) **5-10-0** AMackay(11) (hdwy u.p 7f out: sn wknd: t.o)....dist **13** 6/1[2] — —
(SP 134.4%) **13 Rn**

**2m 25.27** (9.37) CSF £127.48 CT £1,594.68 TOTE £24.60: £8.50 £1.40 £2.70 (£82.10) Trio £106.20 OWNER Mr C. D. Barber-Lomax (MALTON) BRED John Rose
LONG HANDICAP Percy Parrot 7-8
OFFICIAL EXPLANATION **Askern: may have been affected by his overnight stay.**

**541 Manful** got the strong pace he needed here and produced a turn of foot early in the straight that virtually won him the race. (12/1)
**612 Keep Battling** looked to have got it right here when challenging entering the final furlong, but then failed to live up to his name. (10/1)
**853 Drummer Hicks** is short of a turn of foot, and getting messed about here spoilt his chances, but he was keeping on well at the end. (14/1)
**883* Giftbox (USA)** ran inexplicably badly, failing to respond when the pressure was on early in the straight. (4/5)
**822* Walworth Lady**, stepping up in class, ran reasonably but was short of speed in the last three furlongs. (12/1)
**853 Dana Point (IRE)** showed up but, when the pressure was on, was again one-paced. (14/1)

## 1000 CROSSHILL LIMITED STKS (0-70) (3-Y.O) (Class E)
3-50 (3-51) **1m** £3,017.40 (£913.20: £445.60: £211.80) Stalls: Low GOING: 0.26 sec per fur (G)

SP RR SF
663[5] **Bold Patriot (IRE) (69)** (JWHills) **3-8-12** GDuffield(2) (mde all: qcknd over 2f out: r.o wl)....— **1** 7/2[2] 78 35
788[6] **Alambar (IRE) (70)** (PTWalwyn) **3-8-12** JCarroll(4) (trckd ldrs: hdwy 3f out: ev ch over 1f out: no ex)....1¾ **2** 6/4[1] 75 32
873[4] **General Haven (65)** (TJNaughton) **3-9-1** JFortune(5) (cl up: ev ch over 3f out: rdn & one pce)....8 **3** 4/1[3] 62 19
885* **Sunley Secure (66)** (MRChannon) **3-8-10**(5) PPMurphy(3) (hld up: effrt 3f out: hung lft & no imp)....2 **4** 7/2[2] 58 15
851[8] **Manoy (60)** (JHetherton) **3-8-12** NKennedy(1) (chsd ldrs: rdn over 3f out: wknd 2f out)....1½ **5** 20/1 52 9
**Sunday Maelstrom (IRE) (38)** (TDyer) **3-8-2**(7) RMullen(6) (swtg: bolted gng to s: s.s: sn wl t.o)....dist **6** 500/1 — —
(SP 109.4%) **6 Rn**

**1m 45.44** (8.04) CSF £8.67 TOTE £3.60: £2.60 £1.10 (£3.40) OWNER Racegoers Club Owners Group (1995) (LAMBOURN) BRED Adstock Manor Stud

**663 Bold Patriot (IRE)**, stepping up in distance, got it well and was nicely on top by the finish. More success looks likely. (7/2)
**788 Alambar (IRE)**, dropped back in distance, had his chances but always found the winner too tough when the pressure was on. (6/4)
**873 General Haven** had his chances, but was most disappointing when the pressure was applied early in the straight. (4/1)
**885* Sunley Secure** is not the easiest of rides and just wanted to hang left. (7/2)
**584 Manoy** had a chance early in the straight, but soon under pressure, looked very one-paced indeed. (20/1)

## 1001 KILMACOLM H'CAP (0-60) (3-Y.O+) (Class F)
4-20 (4-22) **7f** £3,100.00 (£940.00: £460.00: £220.00) Stalls: Low GOING: 0.26 sec per fur (G)

SP RR SF
*341[11]* **Highspeed (IRE) (49)** (SEKettlewell) **4-9-3** JFortune(8) (lw: mid div: hdwy 3f out: led 1f out: r.o u.p)....— **1** 33/1 64 30
662[3] **My Gallery (IRE) (55)** (ABailey) **5-9-2**(7) AngelaGallimore(15) (lw: hdwy ½-wy: led over 1f out to 1f out: one pce)....1½ **2** 6/1[3] 67 33
**Miss Pigalle (41)** (MissLAPerratt) **5-8-4b**(5) PFessey(13) (sn chsng ldrs: ev ch 2f out: kpt on one pce)....4 **3** 33/1 43 9
*782[15]* **Malzoom (30)** (SEKettlewell) **4-7-12** NKennedy(10) (styd on fnl 3f: nrst fin)....1½ **4** 33/1 29 —
**Taurean Fire (43)** (MrsMReveley) **3-7-6**(7) MartinDwyer(17) (sn cl up: led over 2f out tl over 1f out: btn appr fnl f)....nk **5** 16/1 41 —
882[4] **Millemay (30)** (PMonteith) **6-7-12** LCharnock(11) (sn in tch: one pce fnl 3f)....½ **6** 12/1 27 —

562[6] **Teejay'n'aitch (IRE) (43)** (JSGoldie) **4-8-11b[1]** JCarroll(6) (hdwy appr st: one pce fnl 2f)....1½ **7** 14/1 37 3
662* **Tinklers Folly (52)** (DenysSmith) **4-9-1**(5) CTeague(5) (a chsng ldrs: one pce fnl 2f)....½ **8** 10/1 45 11
615[2] **Snake Plissken (IRE) (46)** (DHaydnJones) **5-9-0** AMackay(4) (effrt ent st: nvr rchd ldrs)....1½ **9** 5/1[2] 35 1
819* **Eben Naas (USA) (60)** (SCWilliams) **3-9-2** JTate(14) (b.hind: lw: led tl hdd over 2f out: grad wknd)....1½ **10** 3/1[1] 46 —
**Morocco (IRE) (56)** (MRChannon) **7-9-5**(5) PPMurphy(16) (nvr trbld ldrs)....8 **11** 20/1 24 —
806[15] **Northern Spark (47)** (MissLAPerratt) **8-9-1** GDuffield(7) (b: sn outpcd & bhd)....hd **12** 25/1 14 —
*839*[6] **Shareoftheaction (40)** (MrsAMNaughton) **5-8-8** VHalliday(3) (n.d)....2 **13** 33/1 3 —
662[6] **Bedazzle (39)** (MBrittain) **5-8-2b[1]**(5) MBaird(12) (hdwy to chse ldrs appr st: wknd 3f out)....1 **14** 33/1 — —
883[10] **Tee Tee Too (IRE) (47)** (AHarrison) **4-9-1b** DaleGibson(18) (prom to ½-wy)....1¾ **15** 33/1 3 —
480[4] **Peggy Spencer (58)** (CWThornton) **4-9-12** DeanMcKeown(2) (lw: chsd ldrs: outpcd ent st: sn wknd)....s.h **16** 8/1 14 —
704[8] **Blue Lugana (37)** (NBycroft) **4-8-5** TWilliams(9) (n.d)....1¼ **17** 25/1 — —
*206*[10] **Md Thompson (51)** (HAkbary) **4-9-5** MTebbutt(1) (lw: bhd fr ½-wy)....1¼ **18** 12/1 2 —
(SP 134.2%) **18 Rn**

**1m 31.83** (7.83) CSF £212.42 CT £6,101.97 TOTE £94.60: £8.10 £2.30 £13.20 £12.20 (£153.20) Trio Not won; £364.88 to Chester 9/5/96
OWNER Mr David Wright (MIDDLEHAM) BRED R.McQuillan
WEIGHT FOR AGE 3yo-12lb
**Highspeed (IRE)** loves this easier ground and showed a fine turn of foot in the straight. Once in front, he won going away. (33/1)
**662 My Gallery (IRE)** keeps running her heart out, but she had no answer when challenged with a furlong left. (6/1)
**Miss Pigalle** has ability and raced with every chance here but was never doing enough when it mattered. (33/1)
**Malzoom** has shown ability before and, should his temperament not get the better of him, he can win a race. (33/1)
**Taurean Fire** was a real handful in the preliminaries but, should he learn to settle, there ought to be some improvement. (16/1)
**882 Millemay** has the ability to pick up a small race. (12/1: op 8/1)
**662* Tinklers Folly** (10/1: op 6/1)
**819* Eben Naas (USA)** presumably went too fast early on and was done with two furlongs out. (3/1)
**Md Thompson** (12/1: 10/1-33/1)

T/Plpt: £1,479.40 (4.94 Tckts). T/Qdpt: £123.10 (3.75 Tckts). AA

# 0984-CHESTER (L-H) (Good)
## Wednesday May 8th
WEATHER: cloudy WIND: mod half bhd

## 1002 CHESHIRE REGIMENT H'CAP (0-95) (3-Y.O) (Class C)
2-10 (2-11) **1m 4f 66y** £8,968.00 (£2,704.00: £1,312.00: £616.00) Stalls: Low GOING minus 0.24 sec per fur (GF)

SP RR SF
763* **Backdrop (IRE) (80)** (PWChapple-Hyam) **3-8-12** JReid(12) (b.off fore: a.p: rdn to ld over 1f out: hdd nr fin: fin 2nd, nk: awrdd r)....— **1** 6/1[2] 87 55
**Pleasant Surprise (89)** (MJohnston) **3-9-7** JWeaver(6) (led 1f: hld up: hdwy over 2f out: effrt & sltly hmpd appr fnl f: r.o wl: fin 3rd, 3/4l: plcd 2nd).... **2** 16/1 95 63
*346** **Oversman (75)** (JGFitzGerald) **3-8-7** KFallon(4) (trckd ldrs: effrt & ev ch over 1f out: kpt on u.p: fin 4th, 2l: plcd 3rd).... **3** 20/1 78 46
575[2] **Bellator (72)** (GBBalding) **3-8-1**(3) NVarley(5) (hld up: hdwy 3f out: kpt on u.p appr fnl f: fin 5th, 1¼l: plcd 4th).... **4** 11/1[3] 73 41
717* **Benatom (USA) (86)** (HRACecil) **3-9-4** PatEddery(10) (lw: chsd ldrs: led over 3f out tl over 1f out: one pce: fin 6th, 3/4l: plcd 5th).... **5** 6/1[2] 86 54
731* **Al's Alibi (79)** (WRMuir) **3-8-11** TQuinn(2) (lw: prom: rdn & btn whn bdly hmpd over 1f out)....8 **7** 12/1 69 37
**Overruled (IRE) (84)** (DRLoder) **3-9-2** MJKinane(8) (lw: led after 1f tl over 3f out: wknd wl over 1f out)....1¼ **8** 11/2[1] 72 40
693[2] **Three Hills (84)** (BWHills) **3-9-2** MHills(1) (lw: hld up: pushed along 4f out: nvr able to chal)....2½ **9** 11/2[1] 69 37
786[3] **Misky Bay (78)** (JHMGosden) **3-8-10** LDettori(9) (hld up mid div: drvn along & effrt 2f out: no imp: t.o)....19 **10** 11/2[1] 38 6
483[2] **Deadline Time (IRE) (79)** (MrsMReveley) **3-8-11v** KDarley(13) (lw: trckd ldrs over 9f: grad wknd: t.o)....3½ **11** 11/1[3] 35 3
788[10] **Diego (78)** (CEBrittain) **3-8-10** BDoyle(11) (a bhd: t.o fnl 3f)....5 **12** 33/1 27 —
821[7] **Backwoods (68)** (WMBrisbourne) **3-8-0** AGarth(7) (a bhd: t.o fr ½-wy)....1 **13** 66/1 16 —
784* **Montecristo (71)** (RGuest) **3-7-12**(5)ow3 FLynch(3) (hld up: gd hdwy on ins over 2f out: swtchd rt over 1f out: r.o to ld wl ins fnl f: fin 1st: disq: plcd last).... **D** 16/1 78 43
(SP 120.0%) **13 Rn**

**2m 40.65** (4.05) CSF £87.23 CT £1,652.48 TOTE £7.00: £2.10 £5.10 £7.20 (£110.50) Trio £893.10 OWNER Mr R. E. Sangster (MARLBOROUGH) BRED John Neary
STEWARDS' ENQUIRY Lynch susp. 21-25 & 27/5/96 (irresponsible riding)
**763* Backdrop (IRE)** got the extra distance he needs in this first clash with handicappers and, after being outpointed in the last 100 yards, was promoted a place after a stewards' enquiry. (6/1)
**Pleasant Surprise**, looking very fit for this first outing since the autumn, ran well all the way and, but for getting impeded approaching the final furlong, would have made a race of it. (16/1)
**Oversman**, fit from the All-Weather, turned in a very promising effort and should be able to win a race on the turf. (20/1)
**575 Bellator**, patiently ridden on this first attempt at the trip, did not pick up until too late and was never a serious factor. (11/1)
**717* Benatom (USA)**, who will be much better with some sunshine on his back, was in the thick of the action until finding his measure taken approaching the last furlong. (6/1)
**Overruled (IRE)**, well forward in condition for this seasonal debut, made the majority of the running until calling enough below the distance. (11/2)
**693 Three Hills**, towards the rear and pushed along four furlongs out, failed to respond and ran a very lack-lustre race. (11/2)
**784* Montecristo**, more experienced than most of his rivals, had to barge his way through when making progress from off the home turn. Though he won cosily, he was relegated to last in the Stewards' Room, and is a winner without a penalty. (16/1)

## 1003 EVELYN DELVES BROUGHTON MAIDEN STKS (2-Y.O C & G) (Class D)
2-40 (2-42) **5f 16y** £7,112.50 (£2,140.00: £1,035.00: £482.50) Stalls: Low GOING minus 0.24 sec per fur (GF)

SP RR SF
829[2] **Vasari (IRE)** (MRChannon) **2-8-11** PatEddery(8) (lw: bhd: rdn 2f out: swtchd ins 1f out: str run to ld nr fin)...— **1** 5/6[1] 83+ 23
**Raven Master (USA)** (PWChapple-Hyam) **2-8-11** JReid(5) (w'like: a.p: led over 1f out: hdd wl ins fnl f)....½ **2** 5/1[2] 81+ 21
523[3] **Mujova (IRE)** (RHollinshead) **2-8-11** GCarter(3) (a.p: led over 1f out: sn hdd: unable qckn fnl f)....1¾ **3** 33/1 76 16
**Rainbow Rain (USA)** (MJohnston) **2-8-11** JWeaver(7) (w'like: lw: s.s: hdwy ½-wy: ev ch appr fnl f: no ex)....2 **4** 5/1[2] 70+ 10

8293 **Burlington House (USA)** (PFICole) **2-8-11** TQuinn(6) (lw: chsd ldrs: rdn ½-wy: swtchd ins over 1f out: kpt on same pce) ....1 **5** 7/1 3 66 6
8482 **Swino** (PDEvans) **2-8-11** KFallon(9) (sn pushed along: nvr gng pce of ldrs) ....1¾ **6** 14/1 61 1
8294 **Bold African** (PDEvans) **2-8-11** LDettori(1) (led over 1f: ev ch tl wknd & eased appr fnl f) ....hd **7** 14/1 61 1
**Nomore Mr Niceguy** (EJAlston) **2-8-11** SDWilliams(2) (str: scope: bit bkwd: s.i.s: led over 3f out tl hdd & wknd over 1f out) ....3½ **8** 25/1 50 —
8295 **Rake Hey** (RFJohnsonHoughton) **2-8-11** KDarley(4) (outpcd & a bhd) ....2 **9** 25/1 43 —
(SP 124.3%) **9 Rn**

**63.15 secs** (3.15) CSF £6.25 TOTE £1.90: £1.20 £2.30 £5.20 (£4.30) Trio £41.80 OWNER Mr Alec Tuckerman (UPPER LAMBOURN) BRED Eamon and Mary Salmon

**829 Vasari (IRE)**, in the rear and going nowhere at halfway, responded to the Eddery treatment when switched to the inside rail entering the final furlong. Quickening up to lead, he was able to take things easy close home. (5/6: Evens-4/5)

**Raven Master (USA)**, a late foal who is only just two, set sail for home approaching the final furlong and was only collared nearing the finish. He could be useful in time. (5/1: 3/1-11/2)

**523 Mujova (IRE)**, very keen to post, pushed the pace and nosed ahead in the straight, but was swamped for speed in the sprint to the post. (33/1)

**Rainbow Rain (USA)** was the unlucky one of the race as he lost more ground at the start than he was eventually beaten by. He should soon make amends. (5/1)

**829 Burlington House (USA)**, off the bridle and hard at work over two furlongs out, did run on towards the finish and the experience will not be lost. (7/1: op 4/1)

## 1004 SHADWELL STUD CHESHIRE OAKS STKS (Listed) (3-Y.O F) (Class A)

3-10 (3-11) **1m 3f 79y** £24,595.00 (£7,360.00: £3,530.00: £1,615.00) Stalls: Low GOING minus 0.24 sec per fur (GF) SP RR SF

**Tout A Coup (IRE)** (GACusack,Ireland) **3-8-9** MJKinane(6) (lw: hld up gng wl: qcknd to ld 1f out: edgd lft & r.o strly) ....— **1** 8/1 103 54
**Solar Crystal (IRE) (112)** (HRACecil) **3-9-0** WRyan(3) (lw: set str pce: rdn & hdd 1f out: no ex) ....2 **2** 5/4 1 105 56
**Shemozzle (IRE)** (JHMGosden) **3-8-9** LDettori(2) (lw: a.p: wnt 2nd 3f out: ev ch over 1f out: swtchd rt & kpt on) ....hd **3** 7/1 3 100 51
8132 **Alessandra (89)** (BWHills) **3-8-9** PatEddery(1) (hld up: hdwy wl over 2f out: nvr able to chal) ....4 **4** 11/2 2 94 45
7073 **Smilin N Wishin (USA)** (PWChapple-Hyam) **3-8-9** JReid(7) (b.hind: trckd ldrs: drvn along over 3f out: wknd 2f out) ....9 **5** 8/1 82 33
5783 **Berenice** (GWragg) **3-8-9** MHills(8) (stdd s: hld up: effrt over 3f out: no imp) ....s.h **6** 7/1 3 82 33
**Gryada (102)** (WJarvis) **3-8-9** TQuinn(4) (lw: chsd ldr to 3f out: sn rdn & wknd) ....10 **7** 12/1 68 19
7108 **Lunda (IRE)** (CEBrittain) **3-8-9** BDoyle(5) (bit bkwd: a in rr) ....1¼ **8** 14/1 66? 17
(SP 121.4%) **8 Rn**

**2m 26.5** (2.90) CSF £18.98 TOTE £7.50: £1.80 £1.40 £1.60 (£5.50) OWNER Mr E. J. Loder (NAAS) BRED E. J. Loder

**Tout A Coup (IRE)**, a very fit-looking challenger from Ireland, travelled smoothly throughout the race. Sent about her business entering the final furlong, she won readily and, though she is not entered for the Oaks, she is likely to be supplemented after this. (8/1)

**Solar Crystal (IRE)**, intent on making this a true test of stamina, had most of her pursuers in trouble half a mile out, but the winner had the race run to suit her, and she was left in her wake when that rival said go. (5/4)

**Shemozzle (IRE)** was forced to forfeit her unbeaten record but she ran by far her best race yet. She will be a force to be reckoned with wherever she appears. (7/1)

**813 Alessandra** was never put in the race over this longer trip, but did stay on well in the latter stages and there is plenty more improvement to come. (11/2)

**707 Smilin N Wishin (USA)**, flat to the boards over three furlongs out, dropped away tamely and would seem to be some way adrift of this class. (8/1)

**Gryada** looked well but the performance would suggest she needed this, judging by the way she faded inside the final quarter-mile. (12/1)

## 1005 TOTE CHESTER CUP H'CAP (4-Y.O+) (Class B)

3-40 (3-42) **2m 2f 147y** £36,328.75 (£11,005.00: £5,377.50: £2,563.75) Stalls: High GOING minus 0.24 sec per fur (GF) SP RR SF

**Merit (IRE) (74)** (PFICole) **4-7-10** JQuinn(12) (lw: hld up: hdwy 6f out: led over 2f out: drvn clr) ....— **1** 11/2 3 90 35
8754 **Daraydan (IRE) (102)** (LadyHerries) **4-9-10** KDarley(6) (lw: hld up: hdwy over 3f out: n.m.r 2f out: styd on fnl f: no ch w wnr) ....6 **2** 14/1 113 58
7123 **Corradini (92)** (HRACecil) **4-9-0** PatEddery(15) (lw: hld up & bhd: hdwy 4f out: styd on u.p appr fnl f) ....1 **3** 12/1 102 47
8254 **Unchanged (74)** (CEBrittain) **4-7-10** GBardwell(2) (hld up: hdwy 4f out: styd on ins fnl f) ....½ **4** 14/1 84 29
8253 **Fujiyama Crest (IRE) (88)** (MRStoute) **4-8-10** LDettori(10) (b.nr hind: led tl hdd over 2f out: sn hrd drvn: wknd fnl f) ....nk **5** 5/1 2 97 42
**Trainglot (78)** (JGFitzGerald) **9-8-4** KFallon(3) (b: hld up & bhd: hdwy 4f out: hrd rdn 2f out: no imp) ....1 **6** 4/1 1 87 36
4493 **Blaze Away (USA) (79)** (IABalding) **5-8-5** WRyan(14) (trckd ldrs: hrd drvn 3f out: sn btn) ....3 **7** 8/1 85 34
*8373* **Noufari (FR) (80)** (RHollinshead) **5-8-1**(5) FLynch(8) (hld up & bhd: hdwy over 4f out: rdn 2f out: nt rch ldrs) .1¼ **8** 16/1 85 34
5736 **Seasonal Splendour (IRE) (84)** (MCPipe) **6-8-10** JWeaver(4) (hld up in rr: sme hdwy fnl 3f: eased whn btn fnl f) ....hd **9** 14/1 89 38
6823 **Opera Buff (IRE) (72)** (MissGayKelleway) **5-7-12** NAdams(1) (lw: trckd ldrs: hrd rdn & wknd over 3f out) ....4 **10** 17/2 73 22
6478 **Anglesey Sea View (70)** (ABailey) **7-7-7**(3) DWright(18) (bhd: effrt 5f out: sn rdn & wknd) ....5 **11** 25/1 67 16
8169 **Sea Victor (76)** (JLHarris) **4-7-12v** JFEgan(13) (lw: chsd ldng pair tl drvn & wknd over 3f out) ....3½ **12** 16/1 70 15
6753 **Thaljanah (IRE) (83)** (DLWilliams) **4-8-5** WCarson(17) (nvr bttr than mid div) ....1¼ **13** 25/1 76 21
4566 **Linpac West (86)** (DNicholls) **10-8-12** AlexGreaves(9) (a in rr: t.o: collapsed after r: dead) ....13 **14** 50/1 68 17
**Nawar (FR) (70)** (JRJenkins) **6-7-10** DeclanO'Shea(16) (trckd ldrs: rdn 7f out: grad lost tch: t.o) ....3 **15** 50/1 49 —
712* **Kadastrof (FR) (82)** (RDickin) **6-8-5**(3) DaneO'Neill(5) (w ldr tl wknd over 3f out: t.o) ....3 **16** 12/1 59 8
8258 **Taroudant (75)** (RDEWoodhouse) **9-8-1b1** NConnorton(11) (a bhd: t.o fnl 4f) ....5 **17** 50/1 47 —
76714 **Evezio Rufo (75)** (NPLittmoden) **4-7-11v** NCarlisle(7) (a in rr: t.o) ....dist **18** 100/1 — —
(SP 135.4%) **18 Rn**

**4m 6.63** (6.63) CSF £80.28 CT £851.64 TOTE £7.40: £2.00 £4.10 £3.30 £2.90 (£77.80) Trio £377.40 OWNER H R H Prince Fahd Salman (WHATCOMBE) BRED Newgate Stud Co

LONG HANDICAP Merit (IRE) 7-6 Nawar (FR) 7-9 Anglesey Sea View 7-9

WEIGHT FOR AGE 4yo-4lb

**Merit (IRE)** found his form at the end of last season and, in this stiffest test yet, showed how much he has progressed. With joint bottom-weight, he may have been thrown in, but could hardly have been more impressive. (11/2)

**875 Daraydan (IRE)**, back in his own class here, had a daunting task with topweight. He is not short on stamina though and stayed on well in the latter stages to finish a worthy runner-up. (14/1)
**712 Corradini** stayed on strongly in the closing stages to run into the prizes nearing the finish. He is comparatively short of experience but showed here that he does stay, although he is badly handicapped with only a maiden success to his name. (12/1)
**825 Unchanged** took a keen tug to post but was able to be settled in such a big field. Making relentless progress inside the final half-mile, she stayed on well toward the finish and there are more prizes to be won. (14/1)
**825 Fujiyama Crest (IRE)** had company for almost fifteen furlongs. In the battle for supremacy, he did emerge the winner in that set-to, but it drained him and he was legless inside the distance. (5/1)
**Trainglot** did a lot of running to get within striking range on the home turn, but the tempo never slackened and he was unable to mount a challenge. (4/1)
**449 Blaze Away (USA)**, in the chasing group from the start, was hard at work three furlongs out and his one pace was just not good enough to enable him to deliver a challenge. (8/1)
**712* Kadastrof (FR)** does his running form the front, but he was unable to gain that pitch and he called enough over three furlongs out. He eventually finished tailed off. (12/1)

## 1006 BOODLE & DUNTHORNE DIAMOND H'CAP (0-90) (3-Y.O) (Class C)

4-10 (4-14) **6f 18y** £10,710.00 (£3,240.00: £1,580.00: £750.00) Stalls: Low GOING minus 0.24 sec per fur (GF)

| | | | | SP | RR | SF |
|---|---|---|---|---|---|---|
| $692^{6}$ | **Princely Sound (64)** (MBell) **3-8-5** MFenton(10) (lw: mde all: hld on gamely fnl f) | — | **1** | 11/1 | 78 | 43 |
| *$503^{3}$* | **Myttons Mistake (70)** (ABailey) **3-8-8**(3) DWright(2) (a.p: jnd wnr appr fnl f: unable qckn nr fin) | ½ | **2** | 11/1 | 83 | 48 |
| $692^{3}$ | **Weetman's Weigh (IRE) (75)** (RHollinshead) **3-9-2** KFallon(4) (hld up: hdwy on ins over 2f out: kpt on ins fnl f) | 1½ | **3** | 9/1 | 84 | 49 |
| $692^{2}$ | **Wildwood Flower (78)** (RHannon) **3-9-5** PatEddery(6) (s.i.s: hld up & bhd: effrt & n.m.r on ins ent st: rdn & r.o wl fnl f) | 1 | **4** | 7/2 2 | 84 | 49 |
| 716* | **Angaar (IRE) (80)** (ACStewart) **3-9-7** LDettori(1) (lw: trckd ldrs: rdn & effrt 2f out: nt pce to chal) | hd | **5** | 5/2 1 | 86 | 51 |
| $773^{6}$ | **Hoh Majestic (IRE) (67)** (MartynWane) **3-8-8v** JFEgan(12) (lw: trckd ldrs: rdn & one pce fnl 2f) | 1¼ | **6** | 25/1 | 70 | 35 |
| 626* | **Total Aloof (72)** (WJHaggas) **3-8-13** MHills(7) (lw: chsd wnr over 4f: r.o one pce) | ½ | **7** | 9/1 | 73 | 38 |
| | **Air Wing (77)** (MHTompkins) **3-9-4** RHills(9) (b: hld up: hdwy & nt clr run 2f out: nt rch ldrs) | s.h | **8** | 8/1 3 | 78 | 43 |
| $686^{2}$ | **Whittle Rock (80)** (EJAlston) **3-9-7** SDWilliams(8) (nvr nr to chal) | 1½ | **9** | 11/1 | 77 | 42 |
| $443^{6}$ | **Krystal Max (IRE) (80)** (TDBarron) **3-9-7** JFanning(5) (in tch: hdwy & hmpd over 2f out: sn bhd) | ¾ | **10** | 14/1 | 75 | 40 |
| $931^{10}$ | **Montrestar (68)** (PDEvans) **3-8-9** GCarter(13) (spd over 3f) | 2½ | **11** | 16/1 | 57 | 22 |
| *$421^{9}$* | **Oriel Lad (72)** (PDEvans) **3-8-8v**(5) FLynch(11) (lw: in tch over 3f: sn wknd: t.o) | 7 | **12** | 25/1 | 42 | 7 |

(SP 127.1%) **12 Rn**

**1m 15.21** (1.91) CSF £120.37 CT £1,065.69 TOTE £18.70: £3.80 £2.80 £2.40 (£117.80) Trio £234.40 OWNER Mr G. W. Byrne (NEWMARKET) BRED James William Mitchell and Simon Edward Mitchell
**692 Princely Sound**, winning for the first time on turf, adopted the ideal tactics for this course and dictated throughout for a much-deserved success. (11/1)
**503 Myttons Mistake** has not won since July but he has made the frame in most of his races. He looked set to score when moving upsides the winner entering the final furlong, but was up against a rival who just would not concede defeat. (11/1)
**692 Weetman's Weigh (IRE)** tried to mount a challenge entering the final furlong, but could not raise his pace and was always being held. (9/1)
**692 Wildwood Flower** did extremely well to finish so close after getting stopped more than once when she was just about to begin a forward move. She should be kept in mind. (7/2)
**716* Angaar (IRE)**, waiting on the leaders, was always close enough if good enough but, when the go button was pressed, he lacked the speed to deliver his challenge. (5/2)
**Hoh Majestic (IRE)** has done most of his racing at the minimum trip and, though he was posed to challenge, he could only run on at the one pace from the turn into the straight. (25/1)

## 1007 SEFTON MAIDEN STKS (3-Y.O F) (Class D)

4-40 (4-42) **7f 2y** £7,067.00 (£2,126.00: £1,028.00: £479.00) Stalls: Low GOING minus 0.24 sec per fur (GF)

| | | | | SP | RR | SF |
|---|---|---|---|---|---|---|
| $710^{2}$ | **Aunty Jane** (BWHills) **3-8-11** PatEddery(4) (mde all: drvn clr over 1f out: v.easily) | — | **1** | 2/1 1 | 83+ | 49 |
| $678^{3}$ | **Charlotte Corday** (GWragg) **3-8-11** MHills(12) (hld up in tch: effrt & rdn ent st: kpt on fnl f) | 4 | **2** | 5/1 3 | 74 | 40 |
| | **Hulm (IRE)** (HThomsonJones) **3-8-11** RHills(2) (a.p: drvn wl over 1f out: one pce) | 1¼ | **3** | 14/1 | 71 | 37 |
| $768^{2}$ | **Bollin Joanne** (TDEasterby) **3-8-11** MBirch(1) (lw: hld up: hdwy on ins 2f out: nvr nrr) | ½ | **4** | 4/1 2 | 70 | 36 |
| | **Iberian Dancer (CAN)** (JWHills) **3-8-11** TQuinn(5) (s.s: hdwy fnl 2f: nvr nrr) | 3½ | **5** | 11/1 | 62 | 28 |
| $710^{4}$ | **Sandhill (IRE)** (JHMGosden) **3-8-11** WCarson(6) (mid div: no hdwy fnl 2f) | s.h | **6** | 11/2 | 62 | 28 |
| | **Tillyard (IRE)** (PWChapple-Hyam) **3-8-11** JReid(10) (b.off hind: w'like: trckd ldrs: wnt 2nd 3f out: wknd wl over 1f out) | 2½ | **7** | 8/1 | 56 | 22 |
| | **Ashanti Dancer (IRE)** (MJHaynes) **3-8-11** RCochrane(11) (swvd rt s: hld up & bhd: nvr nr to chal) | 1¾ | **8** | 20/1 | 52 | 18 |
| $710^{9}$ | **Covered Girl (IRE)** (BWHills) **3-8-11** KFallon(3) (hld up: effrt & nt clr run over 2f out: n.d) | ¾ | **9** | 20/1 | 50 | 16 |
| $524^{4}$ | **Marjorie Rose (IRE) (65)** (ABailey) **3-8-8b**1(3) DWright(8) (lw: plld hrd: hld up: a bhd) | nk | **10** | 33/1 | 50 | 16 |
| $768^{6}$ | **Nicola's Princess** (BAMcMahon) **3-8-11** GCarter(7) (a bhd: outpcd: t.o) | 9 | **11** | 25/1 | 29 | — |
| $710^{14}$ | **Bombay Sapphire** (RHannon) **3-8-8**(3) DaneO'Neill(9) (lw: chsd wnr 4f: sn rdn & wknd: t.o) | 4 | **12** | 25/1 | 20 | — |

(SP 131.7%) **12 Rn**

**1m 27.47** (2.27) CSF £13.70 TOTE £2.70: £1.50 £2.50 £3.80 (£6.30) Trio £61.80 OWNER Mr Paul Locke (LAMBOURN) BRED P. Locke
**710 Aunty Jane**, a very late foal who could just be maturing, won this impressively with an all-the-way success and looks a class act. (2/1)
**678 Charlotte Corday**, who has only raced on straight tracks before, had trouble handling these bends, but did stay on inside the distance and her turn can not be far away. (5/1)
**Hulm (IRE)**, running away on the heels of the winner, found lack of a previous race this term beating her from below the distance. She has trained on and will soon be winning. (14/1)
**768 Bollin Joanne** ran on steadily in the closing stages, but never really promised to take a hand in the outcome. (4/1)
**Iberian Dancer (CAN)**, very free to post, was flat-footed as the stalls opened and never able to get any nearer than at the finish. Capable of better, she is still in the process of learning. (11/1: 8/1-12/1)
**710 Sandhill (IRE)** did not get away on terms but was settled in mid-division, keeping on at the same pace in the final quarter-mile. She can only benefit from the experience. (11/2)
**Tillyard (IRE)** went in pursuit of the winner soon after halfway, but lack of peak-fitness caught up with her and she was tenderly handled when beaten. (8/1)

T/Jkpt: £13,490.80 (0.3 Tckts); £13,300.86 to Chester 9/5/96. T/Plpt: £386.90 (110.17 Tckts). T/Qdpt: £43.60 (62.6 Tckts). IM

# 0741-BRIGHTON (L-H) (Firm)

## Thursday May 9th

WEATHER: unsettled WIND: str bhd

### 1008 E.B.F. ST ANN'S WELLS MAIDEN STKS (2-Y.O) (Class D)

2-20 (2-20) **5f 59y** £3,117.25 (£928.00: £441.50: £198.25) Stalls: Low GOING minus 0.60 sec per fur (F)

| | Horse / Details | Dist | Pos | SP | RR | SF |
|---|---|---|---|---|---|---|
| 685$^{3}$ | **Wait For Rosie** (MRChannon) **2-8-4**$^{(5)}$ PPMurphy(4) (chsd ldr: rdn over 1f out: led last stride) | — | 1 | 6/4$^{2}$ | 67 | 26 |
| 841$^{2}$ | **Joint Venture (IRE)** (BJMeehan) **2-9-0** MTebbutt(3) (led: hrd rdn ins fnl f: hdd last stride) | s.h | 2 | 5/6$^{1}$ | 72 | 31 |
| | **Misty Cay (IRE)** (SDow) **2-8-9** BThomson(1) (unf: s.s: hdwy over 3f out: one pce) | 5 | 3 | 20/1 | 52 | 11 |
| 815$^{6}$ | **Mike's Double (IRE)** (GLewis) **2-9-0** SWhitworth(2) (bit bkwd: outpcd) | 8 | 4 | 14/1$^{3}$ | 32 | — |
| | | | | (SP 106.0%) | | **4 Rn** |

**60.9 secs** (0.90) CSF £2.92 TOTE £2.40 (£1.30) OWNER Four Seasons Racing Ltd (UPPER LAMBOURN) BRED T. Wong and R. G. Percival

**685 Wait For Rosie** stalked her main rival. Shaken up and asked for her effort below the distance, she eventually managed to get up right on the line. (6/4)

**841 Joint Venture (IRE)** attempted to make all the running and had only the winner to worry about. It looked as if he was going to hold on inside the final furlong, but his main rival managed to get up right on the line. He deserves a change of luck. (5/6: Evens-4/5)

**Misty Cay (IRE)**, a dainty filly, lost all chance with a very slow start. She struggled into third place over three furlongs out, but could then make no further impression. (20/1)

**Mike's Double (IRE)** (14/1: op 5/1)

### 1009 HOLLINGBURY CLAIMING STKS (3-Y.O) (Class F)

2-50 (2-50) **6f 209y** £2,381.00 (£656.00: £311.00) Stalls: Low GOING minus 0.60 sec per fur (F)

| | Horse / Details | Dist | Pos | SP | RR | SF |
|---|---|---|---|---|---|---|
| *293*$^{3}$ | **No Sympathy (45)** (GLMoore) **3-8-2**$^{(3)}$ow3 DaneO'Neill(4) (w ldr: led over 3f out: clr over 1f out: pushed out) | — | 1 | 4/1$^{2}$ | 68 | 31 |
| 664$^{12}$ | **Velvet Jones (52)** (GFHCharles-Jones) **3-8-9** SWhitworth(6) (hld up: rdn over 2f out: r.o one pce) | 2½ | 2 | 12/1 | 66 | 32 |
| 861$^{5}$ | **Red Time (43)** (MSSaunders) **3-8-13** RPrice(1) (led over 3f: rdn over 2f out: one pce) | ½ | 3 | 20/1 | 69 | 35 |
| 819$^{13}$ | **Daily Risk (65)** (SDow) **3-8-7** BThomson(2) (lw: a.p: rdn over 2f out: 5th & btn whn n.m.r ins fnl f) | 1¾ | 4 | 13/8$^{1}$ | 59 | 25 |
| *340*$^{4}$ | **Foreman (54)** (RSimpson) **3-8-4b**$^{(3)}$ SDrowne(8) (a.p: rdn over 2f out: wknd fnl f) | 1 | 5 | 5/1$^{3}$ | 57 | 23 |
| 861$^{15}$ | **Wingnut (IRE) (44)** (MJHaynes) **3-7-12** DeclanO'Shea(5) (lw: prom 3f) | 10 | 6 | 16/1 | 25 | — |
| | **May King Mayhem** (MrsALMKing) **3-8-9** AGarth(9) (a bhd) | 2½ | 7 | 33/1 | 30 | — |
| 707$^{11}$ | **Remember Star** (AGNewcombe) **3-8-4** AMcGlone(11) (bhd fnl 3f) | 2 | 8 | 9/1 | 20 | — |
| 637$^{11}$ | **Baker (49)** (JAkehurst) **3-8-2**$^{(5)}$ow2 JDSmith(7) (a bhd) | 1 | 9 | 20/1 | 21 | — |
| | **Simply Seven** (PButler) **3-8-1**$^{(3)}$ow1 PMcCabe(3) (unf: bit bkwd: s.s: a wl bhd) | 13 | 10 | 33/1 | — | — |
| *381*$^{8}$ | **Bear To Dance (45)** (JohnBerry) **3-8-4b**$^{1}$ RPerham(10) (a bhd) | 8 | 11 | 20/1 | — | — |
| | | | | (SP 118.5%) | | **11 Rn** |

**1m 20.5** (0.50) CSF £46.49 TOTE £4.60: £1.10 £4.00 £2.90 (£19.90) Trio £164.80; £162.53 to Lingfield 10/5/96 OWNER Mr K. Higson (EPSOM) BRED Mrs Sara Hood

**No Sympathy**, without a run in twelve weeks, disputed the lead until going on at halfway. Forging clear below the distance, she needed only to be nudged along to maintain her superiority. (4/1)

**Velvet Jones** stayed on to take second place in the closing stages. (12/1: op 5/1)

**861 Red Time**, with a slender advantage to halfway, could then only keep on in his own time. (20/1)

**595 Daily Risk** failed to make the most of this drop in class, and was held when slightly tightened up for room early inside the final furlong. (13/8)

**Foreman**, having his first run for his new stable, played an active role until coming to the end of his tether in the final furlong. (5/1)

### 1010 BRIGHTON FESTIVAL H'CAP (0-70) (3-Y.O+) (Class E)

3-20 (3-21) **6f 209y** £3,397.80 (£1,016.40: £487.20: £222.60) Stalls: Low GOING minus 0.60 sec per fur (F)

| | Horse / Details | Dist | Pos | SP | RR | SF |
|---|---|---|---|---|---|---|
| *311*$^{4}$ | **Perilous Plight (60)** (WRMuir) **5-9-4** Jean-PierreLopez(13) (lw: hdwy over 2f out: hrd rdn over 1f out: led ins fnl f: r.o wl) | — | 1 | 16/1 | 68 | 51 |
| 749$^{12}$ | **Rocky Waters (USA) (53)** (PBurgoyne) **7-8-8**$^{(3)}$ PMcCabe(4) (b.hind: rdn over 3f out: hdwy over 1f out: r.o wl ins fnl f) | nk | 2 | 10/1 | 60 | 43 |
| 747$^{2}$ | **College Night (IRE) (51)** (CADwyer) **4-8-4**$^{(5)}$ MHenry(3) (led 6f out: hrd rdn & edgd lft over 2f out: hdd ins fnl f: r.o) | s.h | 3 | 3/1$^{1}$ | 58 | 41 |
| 887$^{16}$ | **Mr Cube (IRE) (59)** (JMBradley) **6-8-10v**$^{(7)}$ RWaterfield(10) (hdwy over 1f out: unable qckn) | 3 | 4 | 14/1 | 59 | 42 |
| 744$^{6}$ | **Orange Place (IRE) (70)** (TJNaughton) **5-9-11**$^{(3)}$ DaneO'Neill(7) (b: lw: led 1f: rdn over 2f out: wknd over 1f out) | 5 | 5 | 12/1 | 59 | 42 |
| 662$^{12}$ | **Don Pepe (62)** (RBoss) **5-9-6** GDuffield(12) (a.p: rdn over 2f out: wknd over 1f out) | ½ | 6 | 15/2$^{3}$ | 50 | 33 |
| *654*$^{8}$ | **Napoleon Star (IRE) (65)** (MSSaunders) **5-9-9** RPrice(11) (lw: nvr nr to chal) | ½ | 7 | 25/1 | 52 | 35 |
| *605*$^{9}$ | **Hank-a-chief (58)** (BSmart) **3-8-1**$^{(3)}$ AWhelan(8) (nvr nrr) | 1¾ | 8 | 33/1 | 40 | 11 |
| 744$^{7}$ | **Crystal Heights (FR) (64)** (RJO'Sullivan) **8-9-8** DBiggs(14) (hdwy over 3f out: wknd over 1f out) | nk | 9 | 12/1 | 46 | 29 |
| 983* | **Risky Romeo (61)** (GCBravery) **4-8-12**$^{(7)}$ TField(5) (rel to r: a wl bhd) | 4 | 10 | 11/2$^{2}$ | 34 | 17 |
| 756$^{3}$ | **Office Hours (69)** (CACyzer) **4-9-13** WJO'Connor(9) (lw: a.p: n.m.r over 2f out: wknd over 1f out) | s.h | 11 | 12/1 | 41 | 24 |
| 746$^{5}$ | **Lancashire Legend (67)** (SDow) **3-8-13** BThomson(1) (prom tl bdly hmpd over 2f out: nt rcvr) | 1½ | 12 | 14/1 | 36 | 7 |
| 746$^{6}$ | **Trapper Norman (47)** (RIngram) **4-8-5** AMcGlone(6) (lw: bhd fnl 5f) | 12 | 13 | 25/1 | — | — |
| 747$^{7}$ | **Dancing Lawyer (68)** (BJMeehan) **5-9-5**$^{(7)}$ GHannon(2) (hld up: rdn 3f out: b.d over 2f out) | | B | 11/1 | — | — |
| | | | | (SP 122.5%) | | **14 Rn** |

**1m 19.9** (-0.10) CSF £153.80 CT £579.92 TOTE £17.30: £4.70 £2.80 £1.70 (£262.40) Trio £250.40 OWNER The Sun Punters Club (LAMBOURN) BRED Crest Stud Ltd

WEIGHT FOR AGE 3yo-12lb

OFFICIAL EXPLANATION **Office Hours: finished with cuts on his hind legs.**

**Perilous Plight**, off the course since February, gained his first success on grass in this country. Moving up as mayhem took place over a quarter of a mile from home, he responded to pressure below the distance to get up inside the final furlong. (16/1)

**Rocky Waters (USA)** ran his best race for a long time. Ridden along and going nowhere at halfway, he at last found his feet from below the distance and, running on really strongly, only just failed to get there. (10/1: 8/1-12/1)

**747 College Night (IRE)** was soon at the head of affairs. Given a crack of the whip and drifting left over a quarter of a mile from home, she was eventually headed inside the final furlong but, to her credit, kept on well to the line. (3/1)

**Mr Cube (IRE)** picked up ground below the distance but could then make no further impression. (14/1)
**480 Orange Place (IRE)**, the early leader, remained bang in contention until calling it a day below the distance. (12/1: 8/1-14/1)
**Don Pepe** played an active role until coming to the end of his tether below the distance. (15/2)
**756 Office Hours** (12/1: 9/1-14/1)
**Dancing Lawyer** chased the leaders and was only some three lengths off the leader when brought down in the mayhem over a quarter of a mile from home. (11/1: 8/1-12/1)

## 1011 JIM TAYLOR MEMORIAL H'CAP (0-70) (4-Y.O+) (Class E)

3-50 (3-59) **1m 3f 196y** £3,124.80 (£932.40: £445.20: £201.60) Stalls: High GOING minus 0.60 sec per fur (F)

| | | | | SP | RR | SF |
|---|---|---|---|---|---|---|
| *411*$^{5}$ | **Prince Danzig (IRE) (63)** (DJGMurraySmith) **5-9-7**(3) DaneO'Neill(6) (lw: hdwy 5f out: led wl over 1f out: rdn out) | — | **1** | 3/1 $^{1}$ | 70 | 32 |
| 866$^{7}$ | **Uncharted Waters (50)** (CACyzer) **5-8-11** GDuffield(8) (hld up: rdn 4f out: r.o ins fnl f) | ½ | **2** | 6/1 | 56 | 18 |
| 787$^{5}$ | **Risky Tu (43)** (PAKelleway) **5-8-1**(3) PMcCabe(11) (lw: hdwy over 1f out: r.o wl ins fnl f) | hd | **3** | 5/1 $^{3}$ | 49 | 11 |
| | **Prerogative (61)** (RSimpson) **6-9-5**(3) SDrowne(4) (bit bkwd: hdwy 2f out: n.m.r over 1f out: unable qckn) | 2½ | **4** | 33/1 | 64 | 26 |
| | **Scenic Dancer (44)** (AHide) **8-8-2**(3) AWhelan(9) (bkwd: hdwy over 2f out: nt clr run on ins over 1f out: one pce) | 1½ | **5** | 10/1 | 45 | 7 |
| 844$^{11}$ | **Exhibit Air (IRE) (60)** (RAkehurst) **6-9-7** NGwilliams(3) (lw: led over 10f) | 5 | **6** | 7/1 | 54 | 16 |
| *406*$^{12}$ | **Zeliba (37)** (CEBrittain) **4-7-7**(5)ow2 MHenry(2) (chsd ldr 5f: chsd ldr 4f out: ev ch over 2f out: wknd wl over 1f out) | 3½ | **7** | 25/1 | 26 | — |
| 745* | **Bag of Tricks (IRE) (56)** (SDow) **6-9-3** BThomson(1) (hld up: chsd ldr 7f out to 4f out: wkng whn n.m.r over 2f out) | 1¼ | **8** | 4/1 $^{2}$ | 44 | 6 |
| 879$^{24}$ | **Total Rach (IRE) (50)** (RIngram) **4-8-11b** AMcGlone(7) (lw: hdwy 5f out: wknd over 2f out) | 2½ | **9** | 16/1 | 34 | — |
| *532*$^{7}$ | **Racing Hawk (USA) (60)** (MSSaunders) **4-9-7** WJO'Connor(5) (bhd fnl 5f: t.o) | dist | **10** | 33/1 | — | — |
| 747$^{11}$ | **North to Glory (35)** (RMFlower) **5-7-10** DeclanO'Shea(10) (bit bkwd: s.s: a bhd: t.o fnl 5f) | 26 | **11** | 50/1 | — | — |
| | | | | (SP 115.1%) | **11 Rn** | |

**2m 31.7** (4.10) CSF £19.65 CT £78.82 TOTE £4.10: £1.50 £2.50 £1.40 (£10.30) Trio £21.40 OWNER Mr A. H. Ulrick (LAMBOURN) BRED J. N. McCaffrey in Ireland
LONG HANDICAP Zeliba 7-3 North to Glory 7-6
**Prince Danzig (IRE)** always gives a good account of himself and was notching his third victory on this difficult switch-back track. Moving up soon after halfway, he struck the front early inside the final quarter-mile and needed only to be ridden along to secure victory. (3/1: op 9/2)
**666 Uncharted Waters** chased the leaders but her rider was throwing everything at her in the straight. It took her a long time to respond but she eventually ran on inside the final furlong although, by then, it was just too late. (6/1: 3/1-13/2)
**787 Risky Tu** began to find her feet below the distance but, despite motoring inside the final furlong, found the line coming too soon. (5/1)
**Prerogative**, campaigned over hurdles with Martin Pipe, has now changed stables and was having his first run on the Flat since August 1993. Taking closer order over a quarter of a mile from home, he did not have a great deal of room in which to manoeuvre below the distance, but could only struggle on at one pace. (33/1)
**Scenic Dancer** was carrying plenty of condition for this reappearance. Moving up along the rail over a quarter of a mile from home, he found himself boxed in below the distance but, when a gap did appear, he could only keep on at one pace. (10/1: 8/1-12/1)
**Exhibit Air (IRE)** took the field along but, headed well over a furlong out, soon had bellows to mend. (7/1)
**745* Bag of Tricks (IRE)** (4/1: op 9/4)

## 1012 VARNDEAN (S) STKS (3-Y.O+) (Class G)

4-20 (4-26) **1m 1f 209y** £2,070.00 (£570.00: £270.00) Stalls: High GOING minus 0.60 sec per fur (F)

| | | | | SP | RR | SF |
|---|---|---|---|---|---|---|
| 827$^{15}$ | **Roman Reel (USA) (65)** (GLMoore) **5-9-8** SWhitworth(10) (lw: a.p: chsd ldr over 4f out: led over 1f out: all out) | — | **1** | 2/1 $^{1}$ | 67 | 42 |
| *305*$^{4}$ | **Araboybill (54)** (RSimpson) **5-9-5b**(3) SDrowne(6) (b.hind: w ldr: led over 5f out: hrd rdn over 2f out: hdd over 1f out: r.o wl) | s.h | **2** | 12/1 | 67 | 42 |
| | **Hang a Right** (CADwyer) **9-9-8** CDwyer(4) (hld up: unable qckn fnl 3f) | 13 | **3** | 25/1 | 46 | 21 |
| *82*$^{7}$ | **The Little Ferret (50)** (AMoore) **6-9-8** RPerham(9) (lw: hdwy over 3f out: one pce) | ½ | **4** | 16/1 | 45 | 20 |
| *602*$^{5}$ | **Sharp Gazelle (38)** (BSmart) **6-9-0**(7) MSemple(12) (lw: hdwy over 4f out: wknd over 1f out) | 5 | **5** | 12/1 | 36 | 11 |
| | **Boston Tea Party (42)** (AMoore) **3-8-2** CandyMorris(2) (nvr nr to chal) | 3 | **6** | 33/1 | 27 | — |
| *555*$^{5}$ | **Autobabble (IRE) (58)** (RHannon) **3-8-4b**(3) DaneO'Neill(7) (lw: prom 6f) | 4 | **7** | 5/1 $^{3}$ | 26 | — |
| *899*$^{2}$ | **Hever Golf Diamond (51)** (TJNaughton) **3-8-0**(7) TAshley(11) (b: hdwy over 4f out: wknd over 1f out) | ½ | **8** | 9/2 $^{2}$ | 25 | — |
| | **Ginka (28)** (JWMullins) **5-9-3** GDuffield(3) (a bhd) | 5 | **9** | 33/1 | 12 | — |
| *553*$^{12}$ | **Jarvey (IRE) (54)** (PEccles) **4-9-3**(5) BFenton(5) (lw: bhd fnl 5f) | ½ | **10** | 33/1 | 16 | — |
| 634$^{4}$ | **My Beautiful Dream** (AGNewcombe) **3-8-2** AMcGlone(8) (led over 4f: wknd 4f out) | 20 | **11** | 5/1 $^{3}$ | — | — |
| | **Hartfields Boy (57)** (BJMeehan) **3-8-7** MTebbutt(13) (bit bkwd: a bhd) | 17 | **12** | 16/1 | — | — |
| | **Red Sky Delight (IRE) (40)** (PButler) **3-7-11**(5) MHenry(1) (a bhd) | 7 | **13** | 33/1 | — | — |
| | | | | (SP 127.6%) | **13 Rn** | |

**1m 59.9** (1.60) CSF £26.28 TOTE £4.00: £2.50 £3.00 £5.60 (£8.20) Trio £60.40 OWNER Mr K. Higson (EPSOM) BRED Dorothy Price, Jackie W. Ramos & Ken Hickson
WEIGHT FOR AGE 3yo-15lb
No bid
STEWARDS' ENQUIRY Whitworth & Drowne susp. 19-20/5/96 (excessive use of whip).
**Roman Reel (USA)** moved into second place over half a mile from home. Gaining a slender advantage approaching the final furlong, he failed to pull away from the runner-up and his jockey was all out to get him home. (2/1: 6/4-5/2)
**Araboybill** appreciated the return to grass. Disputing the lead until going on just before halfway, he was narrowly headed approaching the final furlong but, refusing to give way and responding to stern pressure, only just failed to get back up. Compensation awaits in similar company. (12/1)
**Hang a Right**, an ex-Irish gelding who had a couple of runs over hurdles for Barry Stevens, has not been seen out since December 1994 and had since changed stables. Given considerate handling, he was in third place in the straight but failed to make any inroads on the front two. Although nine, with a string of duck eggs to his name, he did win three races in 1993 and, with this run under his belt, he is worth noting for a similar event. (25/1)
**The Little Ferret** moved up over three furlongs from home. His rider did give him a crack of the whip but then appeared to give up below the distance, only to push away again in the final furlong. However, the combination never looked like making any impression on the principals. (16/1)
**Sharp Gazelle** moved up over half a mile from home but had shot her bolt below the distance. (12/1: 8/1-14/1)
**471 Autobabble (IRE)** (5/1: 4/1-6/1)

## 1013 COLDEAN MAIDEN H'CAP (0-70) (3-Y.O+) (Class E)

4-50 (4-51) **5f 213y** £3,343.20 (£999.60: £478.80: £218.40) Stalls: Low GOING minus 0.60 sec per fur (F)

| Form | Horse / Trainer / Weight / Jockey (comment) | Dist | Pos | SP | RR | SF |
|---|---|---|---|---|---|---|
| $893^{7}$ | **Lorins Gold (30)** (AndrewTurnell) **6-7-7**(5)ow2 MHenry(7) (mde virtually all: rdn over 2f out: r.o wl) | — | **1** | $4/1^{3}$ | 37 | 6 |
| *$834^{2}$* | **Flagstaff (USA) (55)** (GLMoore) **3-8-13v** SWhitworth(3) (hld up: chsd wnr over 2f out: ev ch wl over 1f out: unable qckn fnl f) | 2 | **2** | $7/2^{2}$ | 57 | 18 |
| $846^{5}$ | **Time For Tea (IRE) (70)** (CACyzer) **3-10-0** GDuffield(4) (lw: hld up: rdn over 2f out: r.o ins fnl f) | s.h | **3** | $5/2^{1}$ | 72 | 33 |
| $631^{7}$ | **Chief's Lady (43)** (JMBradley) **4-8-8**(3) SDrowne(5) (dwlt: hld up: rdn over 2f out: wknd fnl f) | 3 | **4** | 14/1 | 37 | 8 |
| $636^{14}$ | **Dantean (38)** (RJO'Sullivan) **4-8-6** DBiggs(1) (a.p: rdn over 2f out: wknd over 1f out) | 2½ | **5** | 16/1 | 25 | — |
| $686^{4}$ | **May Queen Megan (53)** (MrsALMKing) **3-8-11** AGarth(9) (bhd fnl 3f) | 1¾ | **6** | 9/2 | 35 | — |
| *$052^{7}$* | **Nomadic Dancer (IRE) (41)** (MSSaunders) **4-8-9v**[1] WJO'Connor(8) (lw: dwlt: a bhd) | 2 | **7** | 20/1 | 18 | — |
| *$555^{7}$* | **Old Gold N Tan (38)** (JRPoulton) **3-7-3**(7) RMullen(2) (b: lw: spd over 3f) | ½ | **8** | 25/1 | 13 | — |
| $867^{5}$ | **Victoria Sioux (52)** (JAPickering) **3-8-7**(3) DaneO'Neill(6) (lw: bhd fnl 4f) | 14 | **9** | 14/1 | — | — |

(SP 116.8%) **9 Rn**

**1m 8.9** (1.70) CSF £17.67 CT £38.15 TOTE £5.00: £1.20 £1.20 £1.30 (£12.20) Trio £8.10 OWNER Mrs M. R. Taylor (WANTAGE) BRED E. and G. Bosley

WEIGHT FOR AGE 3yo-10lb

**Lorins Gold** at last came good at the thirty-fourth attempt. Making virtually all the running, he was rousted along in the final quarter-mile and kept on well. (4/1)

**834 Flagstaff (USA)** moved into second place over a quarter of a mile from home. Soon in with every chance, he failed to contain the winner in the final furlong. (7/2)

**846 Time For Tea (IRE)** chased the leaders. Scrubbed along over a quarter of a mile from home, it took her some while to get going, but she did run on inside the final furlong and failed by only a whisker to take second prize. (5/2)

**Chief's Lady** soon recovered from a tardy start to chase the leaders. Pushed along over two furlongs from home, she had nothing more to give in the final furlong. (14/1)

**Dantean** played an active role until coming to the end of tether below the distance. (16/1)

**686 May Queen Megan** (9/2: 100/30-5/1)

T/Plpt: £100.50 (70.26 Tckts). T/Qdpt: £7.20 (113.16 Tckts). AK

# 1002-CHESTER (L-H) (Good)

## Thursday May 9th

WEATHER: cloudy WIND: str half bhd

## 1014 E.B.F. SCEPTRE MAIDEN STKS (2-Y.O F) (Class D)

2-10 (2-11) **5f 16y** £6,976.00 (£2,098.00: £1,014.00: £472.00) Stalls: Low GOING minus 0.10 sec per fur (G)

| Form | Horse / Trainer / Weight / Jockey (comment) | Dist | Pos | SP | RR | SF |
|---|---|---|---|---|---|---|
| $585^{3}$ | **Antonia's Choice** (JBerry) **2-8-11** KDarley(3) (mde all: qckned clr wl over 1f out: pushed out) | — | **1** | $5/2^{2}$ | 72+ | 26 |
| $465^{2}$ | **Swift Refusal** (MJHaynes) **2-8-11** CRutter(4) (lw: chsd wnr: hrd drvn ent st: no imp) | 3 | **2** | 15/2 | 63 | 17 |
| $608^{4}$ | **Danehill Princess (IRE)** (RHollinshead) **2-8-11** LDettori(1) (bit bkwd: trckd ldng pair: rdn 2f out: r.o one pce) | 2 | **3** | $2/1^{1}$ | 56 | 10 |
| | **Ruby Tuesday** (BAMcMahon) **2-8-11** GCarter(5) (lt-f: bkwd: s.s: wl bhd tl r.o ins fnl f) | 2½ | **4** | 11/1 | 48 | 2 |
| | **Dizzy Dancer** (ABailey) **2-8-11** SSanders(2) (leggy: lt-f: unf: sn drvn along: outpcd fnl 2f) | hd | **5** | 7/1 | 48 | 2 |
| | **Manhattan Diamond** (ABailey) **2-8-8**(3) DWright(6) (neat: s.i.s: sn pushed along: outpcd fr ½-wy) | 2½ | **6** | $13/2^{3}$ | 40 | — |
| $568^{9}$ | **Champagne On Ice** (PDEvans) **2-8-11** KFallon(7) (prom 3f: sn rdn & wknd) | 2½ | **7** | 20/1 | 32 | — |

(SP 112.6%) **7 Rn**

**63.71 secs** (3.71) CSF £19.14 TOTE £3.70: £2.20 £2.90 (£9.40) OWNER Mrs Chris Deuters (COCKERHAM) BRED David John Brown

**585 Antonia's Choice** carries condition but made up for the lapse on her debut by showing these rivals a clean pair of heels from the start. (5/2)

**465 Swift Refusal,** always second best, tried hard to deliver a blow once in line for home but lacked the speed to do so. (15/2: 5/1-8/1)

**608 Danehill Princess (IRE)** opened a short price but paddock inspection suggested she still needed this, and she performed likewise. She will come to herself when she tackles a longer trip. (2/1: op 5/4)

**Ruby Tuesday,** a very mediocre mover, was flat-footed as the stalls opened. Taken off her legs, she did run on inside the distance and will know more next time. (11/1: 8/1-12/1)

**Dizzy Dancer** (7/1: 4/1-15/2)

## 1015 BNFL INTERNATIONAL DEE STKS (Listed) (3-Y.O C & G) (Class A)

2-40 (2-41) **1m 2f 75y** £24,010.00 (£7,180.00: £3,440.00: £1,570.00) Stalls: High GOING minus 0.10 sec per fur (G)

| Form | Horse / Trainer / Weight / Jockey (comment) | Dist | Pos | SP | RR | SF |
|---|---|---|---|---|---|---|
| 693* | **Prize Giving (100)** (GWragg) **3-8-8** MHills(2) (a.p: nudged along 3f out: led wl over 1f out: edgd lft: r.o wl) | — | **1** | $9/4^{1}$ | 107 | 58 |
| $681^{6}$ | **Desert Boy (IRE) (103)** (PWChapple-Hyam) **3-8-8** JReid(4) (bit bkwd: hld up: rdn 4f out: gd hdwy appr fnl f: fin wl) | ¾ | **2** | $6/1^{3}$ | 106 | 57 |
| $694^{4}$ | **Weet-A-Minute (IRE) (107)** (RHollinshead) **3-8-11** KFallon(5) (hld up & bhd: hrd drvn 4f out: hdwy over 1f out: styd on towards fin) | 2 | **3** | 8/1 | 106 | 57 |
| | **Babinda** (CEBrittain) **3-8-8** BDoyle(6) (hld up: hdwy 5f out: rdn to chal ent st: one pce appr fnl f) | 1 | **4** | 9/1 | 101 | 52 |
| $694^{9}$ | **Bonarelli (IRE) (102)** (MRStoute) **3-8-11v**[1] LDettori(1) (lw: prom: rdn over 3f out: wknd & eased fnl 2f) | 3½ | **5** | 8/1 | 99 | 50 |
| $694^{5}$ | **Tawkil (USA) (105)** (BWHills) **3-8-8** WCarson(7) (set str pce: rdn & hdd wl over 1f out: sn btn) | 1 | **6** | $11/4^{2}$ | 94 | 45 |
| $808^{3}$ | **Red Robbo (CAN) (98)** (HRACecil) **3-8-8** PatEddery(3) (bit bkwd: unruly s: s.i.s: a bhd) | 3 | **7** | 8/1 | 90 | 41 |

(SP 115.1%) **7 Rn**

**2m 12.11** (3.41) CSF £15.14 TOTE £2.70: £1.70 £3.50 (£14.90) OWNER Lady Oppenheimer (NEWMARKET) BRED Hascombe and Valiant Studs

**693* Prize Giving** was never travelling as smoothly as he was at Newmarket but he was tackling stronger opposition and found all that was necessary to maintain his stable's good record in this listed event. (9/4)

**681 Desert Boy (IRE),** who can still be made fitter, was towards the rear and hard at work half a mile out, but he responded in fine style inside the distance and was gaining hand over fist at the finish. He is bred to need all of this trip and he should not be long in going one better. (6/1)

**694 Weet-A-Minute (IRE),** struggling with the pace out in the country, stayed on strongly in the closing stages and, with stamina the last of his problems, will be placed to advantage before long. (8/1)

**Babinda** looked well tuned up for this first outing of the year and put in a determined challenge turning for home, but the race-fit winner kept the pressure on and he had met his match entering the final furlong. He should not be hard to place. (9/1)
**694 Bonarelli (IRE)**, a grand stamp of a horse who covers a lot of ground, raced freely in his first-time visor but was sending out distress signals before reaching the home straight and was eased when all chance had gone. (8/1)
**694 Tawkil (USA)** reverted to his original tactics and forced the pace, but he had been collared soon after turning in and was a spent force. (11/4)
**808 Red Robbo (CAN)**, a strongly-made colt whose burly looks are often deceiving, was very unruly in the stalls. Missing the break, he was content to bide his time in the rear but failed to respond when set alight and was the backmarker throughout. (8/1)

## 1016 WAYMAN-HALES RATED STKS H'CAP (0-100) (4-Y.O+) (Class B)

3-10 (3-11) **5f 16y** £9,446.80 (£3,521.20: £1,710.60: £723.00: £311.50: £146.90) Stalls: Low GOING minus 0.10 sec per fur (G)

| | | | | SP | RR | SF |
|---|---|---|---|---|---|---|
| 711* | **Anzio (IRE) (92)** (MissGayKelleway) **5-8-13b** RCochrane(3) (lw: hmpd sn after s: sn bhd: rapid hdwy appr fnl f: r.o to ld cl home) | — | **1** | 6/1[3] | 102 | 50 |
| 700* | **Lago Di Varano (83)** (RMWhitaker) **4-8-4v** DaleGibson(1) (trckd ldrs: effrt 2f out: ev ch ins fnl f: r.o wl) | nk | **2** | 10/1 | 92 | 40 |
| 814[8] | **Ziggy's Dancer (USA) (83)** (EJAlston) **5-8-4** SDWilliams(7) (hdwy 2f out: led ins fnl f: hdd nr fin) | nk | **3** | 6/1[3] | 91 | 39 |
| *900** | **Lady Sheriff (86)** (RHollinshead) **5-8-2**(5) 3x FLynch(2) (mid div: hdwy wl over 1f out: r.o wl) | 1 | **4** | 8/1 | 91 | 39 |
| 451[17] | **The Happy Fox (IRE) (84)** (BAMcMahon) **4-8-5** GCarter(11) (bhd & outpcd: swtchd ins appr fnl f: fin fast) | 1¼ | **5** | 16/1 | 85 | 33 |
| 812[3] | **Glorious Aragon (83)** (RFJohnsonHoughton) **4-8-4** ACulhane(5) (hdwy on outside ent st: kpt on u.p: nt pce to chal) | ½ | **6** | 5/1[2] | 82 | 30 |
| | **Mr Oscar (100)** (MJohnston) **4-9-7** JWeaver(4) (led tl hdd & no ex ins fnl f) | ¾ | **7** | 11/4[1] | 97 | 45 |
| | **Crowded Avenue (96)** (PJMakin) **4-9-3** SSanders(9) (swtg: bit bkwd: prom tl wknd over 1f out) | 3 | **8** | 7/1 | 84 | 32 |
| | **Hinton Rock (IRE) (84)** (ABailey) **4-8-5**ow1 LDettori(10) (bkwd: outpcd: a in rr) | ½ | **9** | 10/1 | 70 | 17 |
| 812[16] | **Ashtina (83)** (BAPearce) **11-8-4** JQuinn(8) (lw: prom to ½-wy: sn lost pl) | 2½ | **10** | 33/1 | 61 | 9 |
| 864[8] | **Palacegate Jack (IRE) (83)** (JBerry) **5-8-4b** KDarley(12) (lw: w ldr tl wknd qckly wl over 1f out) | 3 | **11** | 20/1 | 52 | — |

(SP 127.3%) **11 Rn**

**62.3 secs** (2.30) CSF £63.04 CT £360.33 TOTE £5.60: £2.30 £3.20 £1.70 (£27.60) Trio £84.70 OWNER Mr Tommy Staunton (WHITCOMBE) BRED Rathduff Stud
LONG HANDICAP Glorious Aragon 8-2 Lago Di Varano 8-1 Hinton Rock (IRE) 8-1 Ashtina 7-5
**711* Anzio (IRE)** turned in an amazing performance to win from where he was entering the straight, and he is certainly on song this term. (6/1)
**700* Lago Di Varano** looked to have timed his challenge to perfection when moving through to dispute the lead 150 yards out, but the winner, racing wide of him, swooped to conquer nearing the finish. (10/1)
**711 Ziggy's Dancer (USA)**, a previous winner here, showed a return to form with a much-improved performance and, though he was tapped for toe in the final 50 yards, deserves to find reward. (6/1)
**900* Lady Sheriff** turned in another pleasing display and is maintaining her consistency this term. (8/1)
**The Happy Fox (IRE)** could not go the pace and was bringing up the rear and flat to the boards until producing a sustained last-furlong challenge that only just failed to make the frame. He has the ability to win when he wants. (16/1)
**812 Glorious Aragon**, involved in some bunching in the early stages, was pulled wide to make headway on the home turn and, though she gave her best, could not quite get to terms. (5/1)
**Mr Oscar**, a lightly-raced individual, had a tough task from the top of the handicap, but he did force the pace and looked likely to remain there until running out of steam inside the final furlong. (11/4)
**Hinton Rock (IRE)** (10/1: 8/1-12/1)

## 1017 ORMONDE STKS (Gp 3) (4-Y.O+) (Class A)

3-40 (3-40) **1m 5f 89y** £29,520.00 (£11,038.50: £5,294.25: £2,297.25) Stalls: Low GOING minus 0.10 sec per fur (G)

| | | | | SP | RR | SF |
|---|---|---|---|---|---|---|
| | **Oscar Schindler (IRE)** (KPrendergast,Ireland) **4-8-11** MJKinane(2) (gd sort: lw: hld up gng wl: qcknd to ld ins fnl f: readily) | — | **1** | 11/4[2] | 121 | 55 |
| 687* | **Election Day (IRE)** (MRStoute) **4-8-11** WCarson(1) (lw: trckd ldrs: n.m.r 7f out: hdwy on ins over 1f out: fin wl) | 1½ | **2** | 10/1 | 119 | 53 |
| | **Minds Music (USA) (114)** (HRACecil) **4-8-11** PatEddery(3) (lw: chsd ldr: led 7f out tl ins fnl f: r.o) | s.h | **3** | 2/1[1] | 119 | 53 |
| 831[7] | **Poppy Carew (IRE) (104)** (PWHarris) **4-8-8** GHind(4) (hld up & bhd: hdwy ent st: kpt on u.p fnl f) | 2½ | **4** | 20/1 | 113 | 47 |
| | **Dance a Dream (116)** (MRStoute) **4-8-8** LDettori(8) (lw: led over 6f: prom tl rdn & one pce appr fnl f) | nk | **5** | 9/2[3] | 113 | 47 |
| 751* | **Further Flight (110)** (BWHills) **10-9-0** MHills(6) (hld up: effrt & rdn 2f out: nt pce to chal) | ¾ | **6** | 9/1 | 118 | 52 |
| | **Shambo (111)** (CEBrittain) **9-8-11** BDoyle(7) (bkwd: hld up: hdwy 6f out: pushed along 3f out: one pce appr fnl f) | 1 | **7** | 8/1 | 114 | 48 |

(SP 113.1%) **7 Rn**

**2m 55.39** (5.39) CSF £25.82 TOTE £3.10: £1.70 £3.40 (£16.00) OWNER Mr Oliver Lehane BRED Oliver Lehane
**Oscar Schindler (IRE)**, a very attractive high-class colt who is trained in Ireland, sat on the tail of the leading pair running away. Without being asked a serious question, he burst through to lead just inside the last furlong and quickly put the issue beyond doubt. This was one of the easiest winners of such a prestigious event and was a joy to watch. The Hardwicke Stakes at Royal Ascot has been pencilled in as an immediate target. (11/4)
**687* Election Day (IRE)**, continually trying for a run up the rail, got stopped several times and, in the circumstances, showed his true grit to be a fast-finishing runner-up. This was a massive step up from maiden company and a lot more will be heard of him. (10/1)
**Minds Music (USA)** tried to stretch his rivals out in the country but the winner was always cantering in behind him and, once the battle to the line developed, it proved a one-sided contest. There was no disgrace in this defeat and he can go on from here. (2/1)
**581 Poppy Carew (IRE)**, taking a strong hold but restrained in the rear at the first attempt at the trip, did stay on well in the closing stages and it would seem she could win a less hotly-contested race over a distance of ground. (20/1)
**Dance a Dream**, winner of the Cheshire Oaks at this meeting twelve months ago and runner-up in the Epsom Oaks, shared the lead and remained in the thick of the action until feeling the strain approaching the final furlong. (9/2)
**751* Further Flight**, shaken up to mount a challenge entering the straight, never faltered but just could not conjure up the speed to go through with his effort. (9/1)
**Shambo**, twice successful in this race and runner-up last year, was close enough to be a live threat turning in but, unable to respond to pressure, the situation was accepted on the run to the final furlong. Age catches up with us all. (8/1)

## 1018 WYNN H'CAP (0-90) (4-Y.O+) (Class C)

4-10 (4-11) **7f 122y** £9,228.00 (£2,784.00: £1,352.00: £636.00) Stalls: Low GOING minus 0.10 sec per fur (G)

| | | | | SP | RR | SF |
|---|---|---|---|---|---|---|
| 610[3] | **Highborn (IRE) (83)** (PSFelgate) **7-9-7** KDarley(9) (trckd ldrs: drvn along 4f out: styd on to ld wl ins fnl f) | — | **1** | 15/2[2] | 94 | 58 |

| | | | | SP | RR | SF |
|---|---|---|---|---|---|---|
| $827^{6}$ | **Persian Fayre (62)** (JBerry) **4-8-0**ow1 GCarter(17) (a.p: rdn to ld ins fnl f: sn hdd: no ex) | ¾ | **2** | 14/1 | 71 | 34 |
| $933^{16}$ | **Wentbridge Lad (IRE) (63)** (PDEvans) **6-8-1**ow1 GHind(12) (hdwy over 2f out: r.o wl ins fnl f) | 1¼ | **3** | 20/1 | 70 | 33 |
| $933^{3}$ | **Chickawicka (IRE) (83)** (BPalling) **5-9-7v** TSprake(10) (a.p: rdn & nt clr run appr fnl f: kpt on towards fin) | s.h | **4** | 8/1 3 | 90 | 54 |
| 756* | **Scharnhorst (73)** (SDow) **4-8-6**(5) ADaly(8) (led tl rdn & hdd ins fnl f) | s.h | **5** | 12/1 | 80 | 44 |
| $809^{5}$ | **Pengamon (82)** (HJCollingridge) **4-9-6** JQuinn(7) (in tch: effrt u.p 2f out: nt pce to chal) | 1¾ | **6** | 10/1 | 85 | 49 |
| | **Crossillion (82)** (GWragg) **8-8-13**(7) GMilligan(4) (chsd ldrs: effrt u.p over 1f out: unable qckn) | ¾ | **7** | 16/1 | 83 | 47 |
| *$896^{5}$* | **Little Ibnr (62)** (PDEvans) **5-7-7**(7) IonaWands(5) (prom tl rdn & wknd over 1f out) | 1 | **8** | 33/1 | 61 | 25 |
| $589^{11}$ | **Parliament Piece (66)** (DNicholls) **10-7-11**(7) JBramhill(3) (in tch: swtchd ins over 1f out: nt qckn) | nk | **9** | 20/1 | 65 | 29 |
| $633^{2}$ | **Apollono (77)** (JRFanshawe) **4-9-1v**1 DHarrison(15) (hld up: hdwy over 2f out: nt rch ldrs) | 2½ | **10** | 10/1 | 70 | 34 |
| $679^{12}$ | **Pinkerton's Pal (90)** (CEBrittain) **5-10-0** BDoyle(6) (trckd ldrs: rdn ent st: wknd over 1f out) | ½ | **11** | 25/1 | 82 | 46 |
| $933^{7}$ | **Fame Again (80)** (MrsJRRamsden) **4-9-4** KFallon(13) (swtchd ins s: snatched up over 4f out: nt rcvr) | 2½ | **12** | 9/1 | 67 | 31 |
| $809^{16}$ | **Elite Hope (USA) (80)** (CREgerton) **4-9-4** TQuinn(14) (trckd ldrs to ½-wy: sn rdn & wknd: t.o) | 10 | **13** | 25/1 | 46 | 10 |
| $887^{4}$ | **Stoppes Brow (70)** (GLMoore) **4-8-8v** RCochrane(1) (a in rr: t.o) | 1½ | **14** | 14/1 | 33 | — |
| $876^{15}$ | **Dawalib (USA) (64)** (DHaydnJones) **6-8-2** AMackay(2) (nvr trbld ldrs: t.o) | nk | **15** | 9/1 | 26 | — |
| $765^{9}$ | **Hand Craft (IRE) (83)** (WJHaggas) **4-9-7** RHills(16) (a bhd: t.o) | ½ | **16** | 10/1 | 44 | 8 |
| 764* | **Smart Guest (75)** (JAHarris) **4-8-13** JWeaver(11) (a bhd: t.o) | 8 | **17** | 33/1 | 19 | — |
| $876^{6}$ | **Samwar (78)** (MissGayKelleway) **4-9-2** LDettori(18) (a in rr: t.o) | 6 | **18** | 5/1 1 | 9 | — |

(SP 136.8%) **18 Rn**

**1m 35.56** (3.56) CSF £108.25 CT £1,943.45 TOTE £6.40: £2.00 £6.70 £6.10 £2.20 (£142.80) Trio £1,305.20 OWNER Yorkshire Racing Club Owners Group 1990 (MELTON MOWBRAY) BRED Mrs P. F. McQuillan

OFFICIAL EXPLANATION **Samwar: was not suited by the ground and finished sore.**

**610 Highborn (IRE)**, scrubbed along to keep tabs on the leaders at halfway, looked to be fighting a lost cause but, appreciating the step back up to seven furlongs, persevered and kept on to forge ahead nearing the line. (15/2)

**827 Persian Fayre** ran by far his best race yet and obviously needs a strongly-run contest at this trip to bring his stamina to full use. (14/1)

**765 Wentbridge Lad (IRE)** did not get going until far too late, but he did finish strongly and would seem to be approaching his peak. (20/1)

**933 Chickawicka (IRE)**, in the action all the way, was slightly impeded when the leader weakened approaching the final furlong, otherwise he would have taken all the beating. He is high enough in the handicap and may well benefit from easier ground. (8/1)

**756* Scharnhorst** ran a brave race from the front and attempted to burn his rivals off, but the extra 122 yards proved just that bit too far. He will always be the one to beat when adopting forceful tactics. (12/1)

**809 Pengamon** rarely runs a bad race and he had to struggle here to hold his pitch, but he tried his heart out and will find easier opportunities. (10/1)

**Crossillion** ran extremely well after being out of action for eighteen months and, if he remains sound, he should be able to add to his score. (16/1)

**876 Samwar** never fired and it could have been that he found this race coming too soon. His trainer stated that he could not handle the ground and finished sore. (5/1)

## 1019 EATON H'CAP (0-80) (3-Y.O+) (Class D)

4-40 (4-41) **1m 4f 66y** £7,460.00 (£2,240.00: £1,080.00: £500.00) Stalls: Low GOING minus 0.10 sec per fur (G)

| | | | | SP | RR | SF |
|---|---|---|---|---|---|---|
| $788^{8}$ | **Orinoco River (USA) (72)** (PWChapple-Hyam) **3-8-3v1** DHarrison(4) (a.p: drvn along 4f out: led & drifted lft appr fnl f: sn clr) | — | **1** | 9/1 | 86 | 48 |
| $641^{7}$ | **Leading Spirit (IRE) (72)** (CFWall) **4-9-8** PatEddery(2) (led: rdn 2f out: hdd over 1f out: hmpd ins fnl f: kpt on nr fin) | 4 | **2** | 11/2 3 | 81 | 62 |
| $682^{4}$ | **Fahs (USA) (65)** (RAkehurst) **4-9-1** TQuinn(8) (hdwy 4f out: ev ch over 1f out: rdn & one pce fnl f) | s.h | **3** | 5/4 1 | 74 | 55 |
| $759^{4}$ | **Ajdar (52)** (MissGayKelleway) **5-8-2** SSanders(9) (hld up: hdwy over 2f out: nvr nrr) | 8 | **4** | 10/1 | 50 | 31 |
| $547^{6}$ | **Ambidextrous (IRE) (53)** (EJAlston) **4-8-0v**(3) DWright(5) (s.s: effrt & rdn 5f out: no imp) | 1¼ | **5** | 20/1 | 50 | 31 |
| $615^{7}$ | **Maple Bay (IRE) (67)** (ABailey) **7-8-12**(5) PRoberts(1) (chsd ldrs: rdn 4f out: sn outpcd) | 1 | **6** | 9/1 | 62 | 43 |
| | **Ela Man Howa (55)** (NTinkler) **5-8-5** GCarter(6) (hld up: hdwy over 4f out: nt rch ldrs) | 6 | **7** | 16/1 | 43 | 24 |
| $963^{2}$ | **Braille (IRE) (70)** (MGMeagher) **5-8-13**(7) GFaulkner(10) (lw: trckd ldrs: pushed along 6f out: wknd 3f out) | ¾ | **8** | 5/1 2 | 57 | 38 |
| | **Kadari (46)** (WClay) **7-7-10v** NCarlisle(7) (lost pl ½-wy: t.o) | 8 | **9** | 33/1 | 22 | 3 |
| $668^{3}$ | **Horesti (75)** (CEBrittain) **4-9-11** BDoyle(3) (prom: rdn & lost pl 5f out: t.o) | 5 | **10** | 12/1 | 45 | 26 |

(SP 126.9%) **10 Rn**

**2m 41.47** (4.87) CSF £58.08 CT £98.04 TOTE £15.80: £2.90 £2.00 £1.40 (£42.60) Trio £62.20 OWNER Mr R. E. Sangster (MARLBOROUGH) BRED Poole Investments

LONG HANDICAP Kadari 7-9

WEIGHT FOR AGE 3yo-19lb

**Orinoco River (USA)** came good at the first time of asking over this extended trip, possibly helped in no small way by the application of a visor. (9/1: 6/1-10/1)

**Leading Spirit (IRE)** did a good job of pacemaking and had most of his rivals in trouble some way out, but the weight concession took its toll and he was forced to give best. (11/2)

**682 Fahs (USA)** took a lot of settling but looked sure to score when poised to challenge soon after straightening up. However, he went from one extreme to the other, and quite simply failed to quicken. (5/4)

**759 Ajdar** stayed on to reach his finishing position but was never seen in the race at any stage. (10/1)

**527* Maple Bay (IRE)**, trying his luck again at this longer trip, gave the impression that he failed to see it out. (9/1)

**963 Braille (IRE)** was not given enough time to get over him promising run earlier in the week and it came as no surprise to see him back-pedalling some way before reaching the home straight. (5/1)

T/Jkpt: £17,462.20 (0.2 Tckts); £19,675.79 to Lingfield 10/5/96. T/Plpt: £225.00 (173.69 Tckts). T/Qdpt: £44.10 (56.84 Tckts). IM

# 0910-HAMILTON (R-H) (Soft, Good to soft patches)

**Thursday May 9th**

WEATHER: sunny WIND: mod across

## 1020 PIZZA HUT AMATEUR H'CAP (0-65) (3-Y.O+) (Class F)

6-30 (6-30) **5f 4y** £2,640.00 (£740.00: £360.00) Stalls: Low GOING: 0.01 sec per fur (G)

| | | | | SP | RR | SF |
|---|---|---|---|---|---|---|
| 806* | **Henry the Hawk (47)** (MDods) **5-10-4v**(7) MissEMaude(8) (lw: mde all: kpt on wl) | — | **1** | 6/1 3 | 57 | 39 |

| | | | | | | |
|---|---|---|---|---|---|---|
| 769² | **Best Kept Secret (52)** (PDEvans) **5-10-9v**(7) MrAEvans(10) (chsd ldrs far side tl outpcd 2f out: kpt on wl towards fin)......1 | **2** | 4/1 ² | 59 | 41 |
| 882* | **Craigie Boy (53)** (NBycroft) **6-11-3b** 7x MrsDKettlewell(7) (racd far side: sn outpcd: styd on fnl 2f: no imp) ......4 | **3** | 5/2 ¹ | 47 | 29 |
| 882¹² | **Suedoro (48)** (RMMcKellar) **6-10-12** MrRHale(9) (lw: racd far side: outpcd ½-wy: kpt on u.p fnl f) ......hd | **4** | 8/1 | 42 | 24 |
| 704⁶ | **Cheeky Chappy (39)** (DWChapman) **5-10-3b** MissRClark(6) (lw: racd centre: gd spd tl rdn & btn appr fnl f) .1¾ | **5** | 10/1 | 27 | 9 |
| 806⁹ | **Bowcliffe Grange (IRE) (29)** (DWChapman) **4-9-7** MissPRobson(4) (lw: racd centre: gd spd over 3f)......2 | **6** | 10/1 | 11 | — |
| 997⁸ | **Sunday Mail Too (IRE) (29)** (MissLAPerratt) **4-9-7v** MissDianaJones(3) (racd centre: outpcd fr ½-wy) ......¾ | **7** | 20/1 | 8 | — |
| 997⁶ | **Leading Princess (IRE) (53)** (MissLAPerratt) **5-10-10b**(7)ow4 MrJDelahunt(5) (racd centre: n.d)......3½ | **8** | 25/1 | 21 | — |
| 661* | **Diet (58)** (MissLAPerratt) **10-11-4v**(4) MrJWeymes(2) (racd stands' side: outpcd fr ½-wy) ......1½ | **9** | 9/1 | 21 | 3 |
| | **Aljaz (64)** (MissGayKelleway) **6-11-7**(7) MrNMoran(1) (lw: racd stands' side to ½-wy: sn outpcd)......1½ | **10** | 7/1 | 23 | 5 |
| | | | (SP 123.3%) | | **10 Rn** |

**63.2 secs** (4.90) CSF £30.15 CT £71.12 TOTE £6.60: £2.20 £1.20 £1.70 (£17.30) Trio £9.00 OWNER Mr S. Barras (DARLINGTON) BRED Mrs Celia Miller

LONG HANDICAP Bowcliffe Grange (IRE) 9-1

**806* Henry the Hawk**, who has bags of speed, made full use of his draw and never looked likely to be caught. (6/1)

**769 Best Kept Secret** had the best draw and stayed on at the end, but was never quite doing enough. (4/1: op 6/1)

**882* Craigie Boy**, switched over to the far side with the other principals, found this trip a bit too sharp and he failed to offer a real threat. (5/2)

**Suedoro** ran her best race of the season and is coming to hand. (8/1)

**704 Cheeky Chappy** ran well up the middle of the track but the draw made all the difference. (10/1)

**Bowcliffe Grange (IRE)** ran as well as could be expected from his draw. (10/1)

## 1021 ARTHUR GUINNESS MEDIAN AUCTION STKS (2-Y.O) (Class F)

7-00 (7-01) **5f 4y** £2,507.00 (£702.00: £341.00) Stalls: Low GOING: 0.01 sec per fur (G)

| | | | SP | RR | SF |
|---|---|---|---|---|---|
| 585⁶ | **Lycius Touch** (MJohnston) **2-8-4** TWilliams(2) (swtchd rt after s & racd far side: cl up: rdn to ld ins fnl f) ......— **1** | | 15/2 | 68 | 9 |
| 869³ | **Ekaterini Paritsi** (WGMTurner) **2-7-7**(5) CAdamson(5) (racd centre: led tl hdd ins fnl f: kpt on) ......½ **2** | | 11/8 ¹ | 60 | 1 |
| | **Robec Girl (IRE)** (JBerry) **2-7-7**(5) PFessey(1) (cmpt: scope: racd centre: a chsng ldrs: kpt on wl towards fin) ......hd **3** | | 9/4 ² | 60+ | 1 |
| | **Janglynyve** (SPCWoods) **2-8-4** WWoods(3) (leggy: racd centre: sn drvn along: nvr able rch ldrs)......2½ **4** | | 5/2 ³ | 58 | — |
| 757⁷ | **Muppet** (MissGayKelleway) **2-7-12**(3) NVarley(4) (sn drvn along: racd far side: no imp fnl 2f) ......nk **5** | | 50/1 | 54 | — |
| | | | (SP 115.2%) | | **5 Rn** |

**63.1 secs** (4.80) CSF £18.30 TOTE £5.30: £2.00 £1.60 (£4.10) OWNER Mrs Trude Cutler (MIDDLEHAM) BRED Sheikh Mohammed Bin Rashid Al Maktoum

STEWARDS' ENQUIRY Varley susp.18-20/5/96 (excessive use of whip)

**585 Lycius Touch**, given a great ride, switched all the way over to the far rail and that won her the day. (15/2: 5/1-8/1)

**869 Ekaterini Paritsi** failed to take advantage of her draw and that probably cost her the race. (11/8)

**Robec Girl (IRE)** was by far the nicest horse in the race but had the worst draw. If this were run again, she would no doubt come out on top. (9/4)

**Janglynyve** was always being taken off her legs and looks the type to do better on faster ground. (5/2)

**643 Muppet** was flat out the whole way and, inclined to hang under strong pressure, never offered a threat. (50/1)

## 1022 'NOT EVERYTHING IN BLACK AND WHITE MAKES SENSE' H'CAP (0-75) (4-Y.O+) (Class D)

7-30 (7-30) **1m 5f 9y** £3,811.25 (£1,154.00: £563.50: £268.25) Stalls: High GOING: 0.01 sec per fur (G)

| | | | SP | RR | SF |
|---|---|---|---|---|---|
| 620⁵ | **Lord Advocate (40)** (DANolan) **8-7-7b**(3) NVarley(3) (pushed along appr st: hdwy 3f out: led ins fnl f: styd on wl) ......— **1** | | 14/1 | 49 | 16 |
| 620⁴ | **Philmist (40)** (CWCElsey) **4-7-10b** NKennedy(1) (mde most tl hdd ins fnl f: no ex)......3½ **2** | | 4/1 ³ | 45 | 12 |
| 537* | **Field of Vision (IRE) (72)** (MrsASwinbank) **6-10-0** WSupple(4) (chsd ldrs: rdn 3f out: ev ch 2f out: one pce) ...1 **3** | | 8/1 | 76 | 43 |
| 886⁴ | **Palace of Gold (41)** (LLungo) **6-7-11**ow1 JFanning(6) (chsd ldrs tl outpcd appr st: sn lost pl: styd on fnl 2f) ......½ **4** | | 3/1 ¹ | 44 | 10 |
| 816¹⁰ | **Eau de Cologne (69)** (CWThornton) **4-9-11** DeanMcKeown(9) (chsd ldrs: rdn 4f out: wknd fnl 3f) ......6 **5** | | 7/2 ² | 65 | 32 |
| | **Principal Player (USA) (51)** (PMonteith) **6-8-7** SDWilliams(2) (lw: hdwy to trck ldrs 5f out: effrt 3f out: hung rt & no rspnse)......s.h **6** | | 8/1 | 46 | 13 |
| 767⁹ | **Judicial Field (IRE) (63)** (NTinkler) **7-9-5b** KimTinkler(8) (rdn 5f out: n.d) ......nk **7** | | 16/1 | 58 | 25 |
| 752¹⁷ | **Claque (50)** (DWChapman) **4-8-6b** ACulhane(5) (outpcd appr st: sn wknd: t.o) ......25 **8** | | 20/1 | 14 | — |
| 787¹⁰ | **Pinkerton Polka (47)** (CEBrittain) **4-8-3** TWilliams(7) (prom 5f: sn outpcd & bhd: wl t.o)......dist **9** | | 15/2 | — | — |
| | | | (SP 118.5%) | | **9 Rn** |

**2m 56.8** (11.10) CSF £66.17 CT £448.37 TOTE £14.50: £2.30 £1.20 £2.40 (£19.70) Trio £93.60 OWNER Mrs J. McFadyen-Murray (WISHAW) BRED London Thoroughbred Services Ltd

LONG HANDICAP Lord Advocate 7-2 Philmist 7-7 Palace of Gold 7-9

**620 Lord Advocate**, in a strongly-run event, came from off the pace to win decisively but, in doing so, will have done himself no favours from 8lb out of the handicap. (14/1)

**620 Philmist** escaped any trouble this time by making the running but she tired in the closing stages and was easily picked off. (4/1)

**537* Field of Vision (IRE)** ran well over this much longer trip and was certainly not losing ground in the last furlong and a half. (8/1)

**886 Palace of Gold** has more ability than he cares to show. (3/1)

**816 Eau de Cologne** seems to have lost his dash for the time being and was going nowhere in the last half-mile. (7/2)

**Principal Player (USA)** travelled well but, once off the bit in the last three furlongs, just wanted to hang right, and failed to go through with the effort. (8/1)

## 1023 TWO PART POUR PERFECT PINT MEDIAN AUCTION MAIDEN STKS (3-Y.O) (Class E)

8-00 (8-03) **1m 4f 17y** £2,818.20 (£852.60: £415.80: £197.40) Stalls: High GOING: 0.01 sec per fur (G)

| | | | SP | RR | SF |
|---|---|---|---|---|---|
| 763² | **Shooting Light (IRE)** (MAJarvis) **3-9-0** PBloomfield(5) (lw: in tch: pushed along over 5f out: styd on to ld ins fnl f) ......— **1** | | 6/5 ¹ | 72 | 28 |
| *402*³ | **Los Alamos (65)** (CWThornton) **3-8-9** DeanMcKeown(3) (chsd ldr: disp ld 4f out tl led 2f out: hdd ins fnl f: kpt on) ......1¼ **2** | | 14/1 | 65 | 21 |
| 707⁶ | **Ewar Bold** (CEBrittain) **3-9-0** KFallon(1) (led tl disp ld 4f out: hdd 2f out: outpcd fnl f)......2 **3** | | 5/2 ² | 68 | 24 |

*651*[2] **Sedbergh (USA) (64)** (MrsMReveley) **3-9-0** KDarley(4) (chsd ldrs: one pce fnl 3f)....nk **4** 10/1 67 23
763[3] **Kathryn's Pet (67)** (MrsMReveley) **3-8-9** ACulhane(2) (lw: plld hrd: in tch: effrt over 3f out: wknd over 2f out: eased)....dist **5** 3/1[3] — —
**Lord Cornelious** (DANolan) **3-8-11**(3) NVarley(6) (lost tch over 5f out: t.o)....dist **6** 50/1 — —
(SP 116.7%) **6 Rn**

**2m 42.9** (10.90) CSF £15.75 TOTE £2.20: £1.80 £4.10 (£8.60) OWNER Lord Harrington (NEWMARKET) BRED The Earl of Harrington

**763 Shooting Light (IRE)**, a good-looking sort, made heavy weather of this, but enjoyed the longer trip and was nicely on top by the finish. Better ground would probably suit. (6/5: op 4/5)

**Los Alamos** has been running well on the All-Weather and showed here that she can win a race before long. (14/1)

**Ewar Bold** had his sights lowered and ran a fine race, but the testing conditions just found him out. (5/2)

**651 Sedbergh (USA)** is steadily improving. (10/1: 8/1-12/1)

**763 Kathryn's Pet** pulled too hard early on and then ran a stinker. He obviously had a problem. (3/1)

## 1024 WIMPEY HOMES H'CAP (0-70) (4-Y.O+) (Class E)

8-30 (8-31) **1m 65y** £3,361.20 (£1,017.60: £496.80: £236.40) Stalls: High GOING: 0.01 sec per fur (G)

SP RR SF

883[6] **Pash (37)** (CWFairhurst) **4-7-11v** NKennedy(10) (in tch: hmpd 3f out: styd on to ld ins fnl f)....— **1** 16/1 47 25
851[3] **Intendant (55)** (JGFitzGerald) **4-9-1** KFallon(11) (lw: prom: effrt 3f out: ev ch over 1f out: nt qckn)....2 **2** 2/1[1] 61 39
615[6] **Rapid Mover (36)** (DANolan) **9-7-7b**(3) NVarley(4) (pushed along 5f out: hdwy 3f out: chsng ldrs appr fnl f: nt qckn)....1 **3** 20/1 40 18
884* **Hutchies Lady (36)** (RMMcKellar) **4-7-5**(5) 5x CAdamson(6) (a.p: led over 1f out: hung lft: hdd & one pce ins fnl f)....½ **4** 4/1[3] 39 17
884[3] **Three Arch Bridge (60)** (MJohnston) **4-9-6b** TWilliams(5) (lw: chsd ldr: led over 3f out: hung lft & hdd over 1f out: sn btn)....2½ **5** 7/2[2] 58 36
883[2] **Nobby Barnes (46)** (DonEnricoIncisa) **7-8-6** KimTinkler(7) (bhd: effrt 4f out: hrd rdn & no imp)....3½ **6** 12/1 38 16
883[3] **Kierchem (IRE) (45)** (RFFisher) **5-8-5b**[1] NConnorton(8) (led tl hdd over 3f out: eased whn btn)....4 **7** 10/1 29 7
562[9] **Monte Cavo (44)** (MBrittain) **5-8-4v**[1]ow2 KDarley(1) (lw: hdwy 6f out: wknd over 3f out)....½ **8** 25/1 27 3
912* **Calder King (66)** (JLEyre) **5-9-9v**(3) 5x DWright(3) (bhd & drvn along over 5f out: n.d)....½ **9** 9/1 48 26
882[3] **Desert Invader (IRE) (50)** (DWChapman) **5-8-10** ACulhane(9) (lw: bhd: rdn 5f out: n.d)....nk **10** 12/1 32 10
817[13] **Houghton Venture (USA) (64)** (SPCWoods) **4-9-10** WWoods(2) (prom tl wknd fnl 2f)....2½ **11** 10/1 41 19
(SP 133.6%) **11 Rn**

**1m 50.1** (6.00) CSF £51.94 CT £667.73 TOTE £29.90: £5.50 £2.20 £3.00 (£71.60) Trio £297.00; £313.76 to 11/5/96 OWNER Mr C. D. Barber-Lomax (MIDDLEHAM) BRED Mrs M. Morley

LONG HANDICAP Hutchies Lady 7-4 Rapid Mover 7-0

**883 Pash** met with trouble in running but this soft-ground specialist still won well. (16/1)

**851 Intendant** looked in excellent condition and had his chances, but proved too slow under pressure. A bit further might help. (2/1: op 3/1)

**615 Rapid Mover** ran well from 10lb out of the handicap but he had given his all inside the final furlong. (20/1)

**884* Hutchies Lady** is in good form at present and has plenty of ability, but more patient tactics might be the answer. (4/1: op 5/2)

**884 Three Arch Bridge** again hung left under pressure but she will come into her own once the ground dries out. (7/2)

**883 Nobby Barnes** was again given a lot to do and never got into it with a chance. (12/1)

## 1025 UPPER CRUST LIMITED STKS (0-60) (3-Y.O) (Class F)

9-00 (9-00) **1m 1f 36y** £2,577.00 (£722.00: £351.00) Stalls: High GOING: 0.01 sec per fur (G)

SP RR SF

*782** **Domino Flyer (52)** (MrsASwinbank) **3-8-13** WSupple(1) (hld up: qcknd to ld over 2f out: edgd lft & hdd ins fnl f: sn led again: r.o)....— **1** 3/1[3] 69 25
914[4] **Dungeon Princess (IRE) (60)** (MRChannon) **3-8-8** KDarley(3) (trckd ldrs: qcknd 2f out: led ins fnl f: hrd rdn & no ex towards fin)....½ **2** 5/1 63 19
914[2] **Alpine Joker (58)** (MrsJRRamsden) **3-8-11** KFallon(4) (cl up: disp ld 4f out tl over 2f out: one pce)....5 **3** 9/4[2] 57 13
914[3] **Flash In The Pan (IRE) (55)** (MBell) **3-8-1**(7) GFaulkner(5) (b: led tl hdd over 2f out: one pce)....hd **4** 13/8[1] 54 10
*232*[6] **Hever Golf Queen (58)** (TJNaughton) **3-8-8** WWoods(2) (b.hind: lw: in tch tl outpcd fnl 3½f)....15 **5** 14/1 28 —
(SP 117.2%) **5 Rn**

**2m 2.7** (8.40) CSF £16.59 TOTE £4.10: £1.90 £2.00 (£8.80) OWNER Mr S. Smith (RICHMOND) BRED Mrs K. Livingstone

**782* Domino Flyer** is certainly tough and gets the trip really well which made all the difference. (3/1)

**914 Dungeon Princess (IRE)** got a run up the rail and looked likely to run away with it entering the final furlong, but she cried enough once in front. (5/1)

**914 Alpine Joker** raced with every chance but that final dash was never there, and he was well tapped for speed in the last furlong and a half. (9/4: op 6/4)

**914 Flash In The Pan (IRE)** tried different tactics this time but they still came to nothing. (13/8: 5/2-11/8)

**Hever Golf Queen** is a decent type but this ground was probably far too soft. (14/1)

T/Plpt: £172.70 (69.57 Tckts). T/Qdpt: £45.70 (17.69 Tckts). AA

# 0854-SOUTHWELL (L-H) (Standard)

## Thursday May 9th

WEATHER: overcast WIND: str across

## 1026 TULIP MEDIAN AUCTION STKS (2-Y.O) (Class F)

2-00 (2-01) **5f (Fibresand)** £2,381.00 (£656.00: £311.00) Stalls: High GOING: 0.00 sec per fur (STD)

SP RR SF

**Fonzy** (RBoss) **2-8-3** FNorton(2) (small: neat: chsd ldr: led 1f out: drvn out)....— **1** 5/2[2] 54 1
*838*[3] **Come Too Mamma's** (JBerry) **2-8-0** LCharnock(3) (led: hrd rdn & hdd 1f out: r.o)....1¼ **2** 8/13[1] 47 —
**Komasta** (CaptJWilson) **2-8-3** JCarroll(4) (lengthy: bit bkwd: dwlt: sn rcvrd: hrd rdn over 2f out: wknd over 1f out)....6 **3** 7/1[3] 31 —
**Alisadara** (NBycroft) **2-7-12** GBardwell(1) (neat: bit bkwd: dwlt: rdn over 3f out: bhd fnl 2f)....10 **4** 14/1 — —
865[7] **Candle Light (IRE)** (APJarvis) **2-7-13** JTate(5) (lw: bhd fnl 2f)....3 **5** 7/1[3] — —
(SP 122.1%) **5 Rn**

**62.1 secs** (5.10) CSF £4.90 TOTE £4.30: £2.10 £1.10 (£1.80) OWNER Mrs G. F. R. Boss (NEWMARKET) BRED J. and Mrs Rose

**Fonzy**, an 800 guinea yearling, may only have won a poor contest but it was certainly happy days for connections. (5/2: op 5/1)
**838 Come Too Mamma's** could not hold the winner from the furlong pole. (8/13: 4/9-4/6)
**Komasta** had a bit more about him than the others in the paddock, but this was a desperate race. (7/1)

## 1027 CAMELLIA CLAIMING STKS (3-Y.O) (Class F)
2-30 (2-32) **1m (Fibresand)** £2,381.00 (£656.00: £311.00) Stalls: Low GOING: 0.00 sec per fur (STD)

| | | | SP | RR | SF |
|---|---|---|---|---|---|
| 575[14] | **Eagle Canyon (IRE) (67)** (BHanbury) **3-9-4**(3) JStack(10) (lw: a.p: hrd rdn over 1f out: edgd lft & led wl ins fnl f: r.o) —— | **1** | 13/2 [3] | 78 | 45 |
| *859*[3] | **People Direct (61)** (KMcAuliffe) **3-8-10** JFEgan(13) (b.hind: led tl wl ins fnl f) 1 | **2** | 3/1 [2] | 65 | 32 |
| *776*[5] | **Princess Pamgaddy (44)** (CNAllen) **3-7-5**(7) MartinDwyer(2) (hdwy 3f out: r.o one pce fnl f) 4 | **3** | 14/1 | 45 | 12 |
| 763[7] | **Tudor Falcon** (WJHaggas) **3-9-3** DeanMcKeown(11) (prom: lost pl 4f out: styd on fnl f) hd | **4** | 8/1 | 64 | 31 |
| *776*[2] | **Bit of Bother (IRE) (69)** (MissSJWilton) **3-8-13** JFortune(8) (prom tl wknd 2f out) 2½ | **5** | 2/1 [1] | 55 | 22 |
| *781*[4] | **Efipetite (50)** (NBycroft) **3-8-2** GBardwell(5) (hld up & plld hrd: hdwy over 3f out: one pce fnl 2f) 1 | **6** | 7/1 | 42 | 9 |
| *859*[4] | **Supreme Illusion (AUS) (37)** (JohnBerry) **3-8-2b** MFenton(12) (lw: nvr nr to chal) 2 | **7** | 20/1 | 38 | 5 |
| 614[15] | **Sphinx Levelv (IRE) (38)** (APJarvis) **3-8-7** JTate(6) (prom tl wknd over 2f out) 3 | **8** | 25/1 | 37 | 4 |
| 637[2] | **Royal Rapport (46)** (BAMcMahon) **3-8-12**(5) LNewton(1) (b: bhd fnl 4f) 11 | **9** | 10/1 | 25 | — |
| *604*[10] | **Welcome Lu (40)** (PSFelgate) **3-7-12** FNorton(9) (prom: rdn 5f out: wknd over 2f out) ¾ | **10** | 20/1 | 4 | — |
| | **Below The Red Line** (MrsNMacauley) **3-8-8**(5) CTeague(14) (bkwd: prom tl wknd over 2f out) 2½ | **11** | 33/1 | 14 | — |
| | **Raw Deal** (GFierro) **3-7-13**(3) DRMcCabe(7) (lt-f: bit bkwd: dwlt: sn wl bhd) ½ | **12** | 25/1 | 2 | — |
| 761[6] | **Ivory's Grab Hire (50)** (KTIvory) **3-8-4**(7) CScally(4) (lw: rel to r: a wl t.o) 18 | **13** | 10/1 | — | — |
| | | | (SP 140.3%) | **13 Rn** | |

**1m 46.0** (6.00) CSF £29.33 TOTE £12.00: £3.10 £1.20 £2.50 (£28.20) Trio £143.10 OWNER Mr Clinton Lane Jnr (NEWMARKET) BRED Mount Coote Stud
Eagle Canyon (IRE) clmd £9,000
**Eagle Canyon (IRE)** appreciated this drop in class on his return to an artificial surface. (13/2)
**859 People Direct** could not quite manage her sixth course win. (3/1)
**776 Princess Pamgaddy** plugged on without troubling the two principals. (14/1: 10/1-20/1)
**Tudor Falcon** made his debut at Pontefract last month over ten furlongs and probably needs further. (8/1)
**776 Bit of Bother (IRE)** was safely held entering the final quarter-mile. (2/1)
**761 Ivory's Grab Hire** (10/1: op 16/1)

## 1028 FREESIA H'CAP (0-65) (3-Y.O+ F & M) (Class F)
3-00 (3-02) **5f (Fibresand)** £2,381.00 (£656.00: £311.00) Stalls: High GOING: 0.00 sec per fur (STD)

| | | | SP | RR | SF |
|---|---|---|---|---|---|
| 478[6] | **Queens Check (53)** (MissJFCraze) **3-8-11** NConnorton(9) (hdwy 2f out: led ins fnl f: r.o wl) —— | **1** | 12/1 | 59 | 32 |
| 911[2] | **My Cherrywell (56)** (LRLloyd-James) **6-9-9b** JFortune(16) (b.off hind: hdwy over 1f out: r.o ins fnl f) ¾ | **2** | 4/1 [2] | 60 | 42 |
| | **Ninety-Five (61)** (JGFitzGerald) **4-10-0** TIves(7) (lw: a.p: led 2f out tl ins fnl f) 1½ | **3** | 10/1 | 60 | 42 |
| *835*[5] | **Little Saboteur (57)** (PJMakin) **7-9-10b** WRyan(12) (b.nr hind: hdwy 2f out: one pce fnl f) 1 | **4** | 12/1 | 53 | 35 |
| 783[7] | **Princess Efisio (47)** (BAMcMahon) **3-8-0**(5) LNewton(10) (hrd rdn over 2f out: nvr nr to chal) 2½ | **5** | 12/1 | 35 | 8 |
| 951[8] | **Nadwaty (IRE) (50)** (MCChapman) **4-9-0**(3) DRMcCabe(15) (nvr nrr) nk | **6** | 14/1 | 37 | 19 |
| | **Freckles Kelly (48)** (TDEasterby) **4-9-1** MBirch(3) (lw: prom: ev ch over 1f out: wknd ins fnl f) hd | **7** | 10/1 | 34 | 16 |
| *835*[3] | **Wasblest (58)** (JBerry) **4-9-11** JCarroll(5) (prom: led 3f out to 2f out: sn wknd) 2½ | **8** | 7/1 [3] | 36 | 18 |
| 868[3] | **Merrie le Bow (48)** (PatMitchell) **4-8-10**(5) AmandaSanders(4) (dwlt: outpcd) s.h | **9** | 10/1 | 26 | 8 |
| | **Dancing Rainbow (52)** (MJCamacho) **3-8-10** LCharnock(6) (led 2f: wknd over 1f out) 3 | **10** | 12/1 | 21 | — |
| *779*[4] | **Chalice (62)** (JBalding) **3-8-13**(7) JEdmunds(1) (s.s: a bhd) 2 | **11** | 20/1 | 24 | — |
| 868[13] | **Born A Lady (56)** (SRBowring) **3-8-9v**[1](5) CTeague(17) (outpcd) ¾ | **12** | 7/1 [3] | 16 | — |
| 762[13] | **Hickleton Miss (49)** (MrsVAAconley) **3-8-7** MDeering(2) (lw: bhd fnl 2f) s.h | **13** | 20/1 | 9 | — |
| | **Avant Huit (52)** (MrsNMacauley) **4-9-5** JTate(13) (bit bkwd: outpcd) 5 | **14** | 14/1 | — | — |
| *897*[4] | **Fyors Gift (IRE) (63)** (BHanbury) **3-9-4**(3) JStack(14) (chsd ldrs tl eased over 2f out: sddle slipped) 5 | **15** | 3/1 [1] | — | — |
| 704[13] | **Bajan Frontier (IRE) (47)** (FHLee) **4-9-0v**[1] MWigham(11) (a bhd) 1¼ | **16** | 20/1 | — | — |
| | | | (SP 155.7%) | **16 Rn** | |

**60.6 secs** (3.60) CSF £70.36 CT £512.90 TOTE £23.70: £3.50 £1.10 £4.80 £2.80 (£152.40) Trio £109.80 OWNER Mr W. Cooper (YORK) BRED Mrs Sandra Cooper
WEIGHT FOR AGE 3yo-9lb
OFFICIAL EXPLANATION **Fyors Gift (IRE): the saddle had slipped.**
**Queens Check**, considered to have been suffering from a touch of the virus last time, did not need the blinkers to get back into winning ways. (12/1)
**911 My Cherrywell** does not seem to know how to run a bad race. (4/1)
**Ninety-Five** ran well on this seasonal reappearance under a big weight. (10/1)
**835 Little Saboteur** is slipping down the handicap ratings. (12/1)
**Princess Efisio** could never make her presence felt. (12/1)
**750 Nadwaty (IRE)** . making a quick reappearance, did her best work late on. (14/1)
**606 Born A Lady** (7/1: op 12/1)
**897 Fyors Gift (IRE)** had trouble with a slipping saddle and this return to the minimum trip can be safely ignored. (3/1: op 5/1)

## 1029 PETUNIA H'CAP (0-70) (3-Y.O+) (Class E)
3-30 (3-31) **7f (Fibresand)** £3,343.20 (£999.60: £478.80: £218.40) Stalls: Low GOING: 0.00 sec per fur (STD)

| | | | SP | RR | SF |
|---|---|---|---|---|---|
| *857*[3] | **Principal Boy (IRE) (52)** (TJEtherington) **3-7-12** LCharnock(10) (a.p: led wl ins fnl f: r.o) —— | **1** | 7/1 | 58 | 28 |
| *607*[4] | **Elton Ledger (IRE) (63)** (MrsNMacauley) **7-9-7b** JTate(4) (b: hld up: hdwy 2f out: ev ch ins fnl f: r.o) nk | **2** | 7/1 | 68 | 50 |
| 991[11] | **Awesome Venture (69)** (MCChapman) **6-9-10**(3) DRMcCabe(7) (lw: prom: swtchd rt over 1f out: hrd rdn & r.o ins fnl f) hd | **3** | 7/1 | 74 | 56 |
| 592[9] | **Maybank (IRE) (61)** (BAMcMahon) **4-9-0**(5) LNewton(9) (lw: a.p: led on bit 2f out: sn rdn: hdd wl ins fnl f) nk | **4** | 3/1 [1] | 65 | 47 |
| 991[6] | **Monis (IRE) (58)** (JBalding) **5-8-9v**(7) JEdmunds(2) (hdwy over 2f out: one pce appr fnl f) 3½ | **5** | 9/1 | 54 | 36 |
| 887[8] | **Scissor Ridge (49)** (JJBridger) **4-8-2**(5) MBaird(8) (led over 5f out to 2f out: sn wknd) 4 | **6** | 9/2 [2] | 36 | 18 |
| *521*[7] | **Fred's Delight (IRE) (38)** (MrsVAAconley) **5-7-10v** FNorton(3) (prom 4f) nk | **7** | 33/1 | 25 | 7 |
| 748[4] | **Mels Baby (IRE) (57)** (JLEyre) **3-7-10**(7)ow2 DSweeney(6) (prom over 4f) 2½ | **8** | 7/1 | 38 | 6 |
| 887[11] | **Sea Spouse (57)** (MBlanshard) **5-9-1** NAdams(5) (led over 1f: wknd 2f out: t.o) 12 | **9** | 7/1 | 10 | — |

| | | | | SP | RR | SF |
|---|---|---|---|---|---|---|
| *776$^{9}$* | **Peacefull Reply (USA) (46)** (FHLee) **6-8-4** MBirch(1) (bhd fnl 3f: t.o) | 3 | **10** | 6/1$^{3}$ | — | — |

(SP 132.9%) **10 Rn**

**1m 31.6** (4.80) CSF £57.44 CT £348.10 TOTE £6.90: £1.40 £2.10 £2.60 (£31.20) Trio £24.40 OWNER Mr Chris Moreno (MALTON) BRED Mrs M. Mansergh
LONG HANDICAP Fred's Delight (IRE) 6-9
WEIGHT FOR AGE 3yo-12lb
**OFFICIAL EXPLANATION Peacefull Reply (USA): resented the kickback and lost interest.**
**857 Principal Boy (IRE)** was back to his best trip. (7/1)
**607 Elton Ledger (IRE)** ran a fine race, despite being 8lb higher than when successful here at the beginning of last month. (7/1)
**778* Awesome Venture** finds this trip on the sharp side nowadays. (7/1)
**Maybank (IRE)** finds this trip beyond his best. (3/1: 4/1-5/2)
**518 Peacefull Reply (USA)** (6/1: tchd 10/1)

## 1030 BEGONIA (S) STKS (3-Y.O+) (Class G)

4-00 (4-03) **6f (Fibresand)** £2,070.00 (£570.00: £270.00) Stalls: Low GOING: 0.00 sec per fur (STD)

| | | | | SP | RR | SF |
|---|---|---|---|---|---|---|
| | **Klipspinger (46)** (BSRothwell) **3-8-1**$^{(3)}$ JStack(11) (a.p: led over 1f out: rdn & r.o wl) | — | **1** | 20/1 | 66 | 26 |
| 764$^{7}$ | **Sea Devil (67)** (MJCamacho) **10-9-10** LCharnock(10) (chsd ldrs: r.o one pce fnl f) | 3 | **2** | 4/1$^{2}$ | 68 | 38 |
| 812$^{9}$ | **Our Shadee (USA) (69)** (KTIvory) **6-9-3v**$^{(7)}$ CScally(6) (hdwy 2f out: r.o one pce fnl f) | ¾ | **3** | 9/2$^{3}$ | 66 | 36 |
| | **Juba** (DrJDScargill) **4-9-0** MFenton(8) (b: a.p: one pce fnl f) | 4 | **4** | 9/2$^{3}$ | 45 | 15 |
| *782$^{4}$* | **Miss Tri Colour (32)** (FHLee) **4-9-0** MBirch(12) (lw: led over 4f: one pce) | ½ | **5** | 10/1 | 44 | 14 |
| *896$^{7}$* | **At the Savoy (IRE) (56)** (MrsLStubbs) **5-9-5** JFortune(3) (chsd ldrs: no hdwy fnl 2f) | 1¾ | **6** | 8/1 | 44 | 14 |
| *511$^{8}$* | **Justinianus (IRE) (45)** (JJBridger) **4-9-0**$^{(5)}$ MBaird(14) (hmpd & lost pl over 4f out: nvr nrr) | nk | **7** | 25/1 | 44 | 14 |
| *780$^{3}$* | **Seeking Destiny (IRE) (48)** (MCChapman) **3-8-11b**$^{1(3)}$ DRMcCabe(7) (nvr nrr) | ½ | **8** | 10/1 | 47 | 7 |
| 775$^{8}$ | **Tropical Beach (55)** (JBerry) **3-8-9** JCarroll(4) (uns rdr bef s: n.d) | nk | **9** | 20/1 | 41 | 1 |
| *835$^{12}$* | **Niteowl Raider (IRE) (70)** (JAHarris) **3-9-0** JO'Reilly(5) (w ldrs tl wknd over 1f out) | 2 | **10** | 11/4$^{1}$ | 41 | 1 |
| *834$^{4}$* | **Black Boy (IRE) (37)** (RFMarvin) **7-8-12b**$^{(7)}$ JEdmunds(2) (lw: rdn & hdwy on ins over 2f out: wknd wl over 1f out) | nk | **11** | 25/1 | 35 | 5 |
| 750$^{11}$ | **Princess Belfort** (GFierro) **3-8-4** RLappin(13) (bit bkwd: s.i.s: plld hrd: bhd fnl 2f) | 6 | **12** | 25/1 | 14 | — |
| | **Rebounder** (KMcAuliffe) **3-8-9** JFEgan(15) (lt-f: bhd fnl 2f) | 7 | **13** | 10/1 | 1 | — |
| *835$^{13}$* | **Bobaluna** (RFMarvin) **3-8-9** TGMcLaughlin(1) (a bhd) | nk | **14** | 25/1 | — | — |
| 749$^{23}$ | **Montague Dawson (IRE) (49)** (MrsNMacauley) **4-9-5v** JTate(9) (a bhd) | 1¼ | **15** | 25/1 | — | — |

(SP 150.2%) **15 Rn**

**1m 18.1** (4.60) CSF £108.58 TOTE £180.00: £28.10 £2.70 £3.30 (£582.00) Trio Not won; £121.62 to Lingfield 10/5/96 OWNER The Action Racing Club Ltd (MALTON) BRED Carlton Consultants Ltd
WEIGHT FOR AGE 3yo-10lb
No bid
**Klipspinger**, on her first run for a year having thrown a splint, had apparently been working well and was not totally unfancied by her trainer. (20/1)
**Sea Devil** chased the winner through the final furlong without making any impression. (4/1: 5/2-9/2)
**601 Our Shadee (USA)** appreciated the combination of a return to sand and selling company. (9/2: 5/2-5/1)
**Juba** had made her debut over seven furlongs so this could easily have been on the sharp side. (9/2)
**782 Miss Tri Colour**, dropped into a seller, forced the pace over this shorter distance. (10/1: 12/1-8/1)
**805 At the Savoy (IRE)** (8/1: 5/1-10/1)
**606* Niteowl Raider (IRE)** did not live up to the market support. (11/4: 4/1-5/2)
**Rebounder** (10/1: 6/1-12/1)

## 1031 MAGNOLIA H'CAP (0-65) (3-Y.O+) (Class F)

4-30 (4-31) **1m 4f (Fibresand)** £2,381.00 (£656.00: £311.00) Stalls: Low GOING: 0.00 sec per fur (STD)

| | | | | SP | RR | SF |
|---|---|---|---|---|---|---|
| *898$^{5}$* | **Cuban Nights (USA) (61)** (BJLlewellyn) **4-10-0** AClark(12) (lw: hld up: stdy hdwy 7f out: led over 1f out: r.o wl) | — | **1** | 9/1 | 71 | 24 |
| 760$^{3}$ | **Jean de Florette (USA) (29)** (RCSpicer) **5-7-10** FNorton(13) (stdy hdwy 7f out: styd on fnl f) | 3½ | **2** | 10/1 | 34 | — |
| *855$^{2}$* | **Tempering (58)** (DWChapman) **10-9-11** JFortune(2) (lw: led: sn clr: hdd over 1f out: one pce) | ½ | **3** | 5/1$^{2}$ | 63 | 16 |
| 803$^{5}$ | **State Approval (58)** (APJarvis) **3-8-6** JTate(5) (lw: a.p: one pce fnl 2f) | 1¼ | **4** | 6/1$^{3}$ | 61 | — |
| *898$^{4}$* | **Zaaleff (USA) (52)** (BHanbury) **4-9-2b**$^{(3)}$ JStack(8) (lw: a.p: one pce fnl 2f) | nk | **5** | 5/1$^{2}$ | 55 | 8 |
| | **Efaad (IRE) (50)** (JNorton) **5-9-3** JFEgan(10) (nvr nr ldrs) | 18 | **6** | 25/1 | 29 | — |
| | **Mega Tid (50)** (BAPearce) **4-8-10**$^{(7)}$ JWilkinson(4) (b.nr hind: nvr nr ldrs) | 5 | **7** | 20/1 | 22 | — |
| *602$^{4}$* | **Record Lover (IRE) (39)** (MCChapman) **6-8-3**$^{(3)}$ DRMcCabe(9) (prom: wknd 5f out: eased whn btn ove 3f out) | 5 | **8** | 12/1 | 4 | — |
| *836$^{8}$* | **Night Time (48)** (AStreeter) **4-8-10**$^{(5)}$ CTeague(3) (hld up: bhd fnl 5f) | 1¾ | **9** | 20/1 | 11 | — |
| *855$^{6}$* | **Red Indian (39)** (BRichmond) **10-8-6** JCarroll(11) (a bhd) | 2½ | **10** | 14/1 | — | — |
| *251$^{10}$* | **Sommersby (IRE) (60)** (MrsNMacauley) **5-9-13** MBirch(14) (hdwy 6f out: wknd over 4f out) | 2½ | **11** | 11/1 | 16 | — |
| | **Triple Tie (USA) (37)** (MBlanshard) **5-8-4** NAdams(7) (sn bhd) | 1¼ | **12** | 20/1 | — | — |
| 546$^{21}$ | **Tiger Shoot (57)** (DTThom) **9-9-10v** WRyan(1) (prom 6f) | nk | **13** | 7/2$^{1}$ | 11 | — |
| 853$^{3}$ | **Anistop (61)** (JLEyre) **4-10-0** RLappin(6) (lw: nvr gng wl: bhd fnl 6f: virtually p.u fnl f) | dist | **14** | 7/1 | — | — |

(SP 142.3%) **14 Rn**

**2m 46.0** (13.50) CSF £102.34 CT £482.08 TOTE £18.00: £5.50 £3.00 £1.10 (£54.00) Trio £125.40; £141.31 to Lingfield 10/9/96 OWNER Mr Eamonn O'Malley (BARGOED) BRED T. F. Van Meter II
WEIGHT FOR AGE 3yo-19lb
**898 Cuban Nights (USA)** needs a good gallop and had to make his own running last time but, with Tempering in the field, there was no such problem here. (9/1: op 6/1)
**760 Jean de Florette (USA)** does not find stamina a problem, but it still a maiden after twenty-nine attempts. (10/1)
**855 Tempering** staged another of his bold displays of front-running but merely set up the race for the winner. (5/1)
**State Approval** seems to stay a mile and a half well enough. (6/1)
**898 Zaaleff (USA)** lacks finishing pace rather than stamina. (5/1)
**Tiger Shoot** was disappointing on this first run in a visor since 1992. (7/2: 9/2-3/1)

T/Plpt: £33.10 (183.47 Tckts). T/Qdpt: £10.60 (49.74 Tckts). KH

# 0783-BEVERLEY (R-H) (Good to firm)
## Friday May 10th
WEATHER: changeable WIND: str half bhd

### 1032 LUND CLAIMING STKS (2-Y.O) (Class F)
2-30 (2-30) **5f** £2,798.00 (£778.00: £374.00) Stalls: Centre GOING minus 0.35 sec per fur (F)

| Form | Horse / details | Dist | Pos | SP | RR | SF |
|---|---|---|---|---|---|---|
| *858** | **For Old Times Sake** (JBerry) **2-8-10** GCarter(6) (lw: w ldr: led ½-wy: shkn up & wnt clr over 1f out: eased towards fin) | — | 1 | Evens [1] | 78+ | 35 |
| 869[4] | **Irish Fiction (IRE)** (MRChannon) **2-8-8** PaulEddery(4) (chsd ldrs: rdn 2f out: no ch w wnr) | 5 | 2 | 7/4 [2] | 60 | 17 |
| *838** | **Lawful Find (IRE)** (RHollinshead) **2-8-1**(5) FLynch(3) (chsd ldrs: rdn ½-wy: styd on same pce) | 1¾ | 3 | 9/2 [3] | 52 | 9 |
| | **Shandana** (PCHaslam) **2-7-11**(5) PFessey(7) (small: bkwd: dwlt s: sn chsng ldrs: ran green & outpcd ½-wy: kpt on fnl f) | ¾ | 4 | 12/1 | 46 | 3 |
| 590[4] | **Nattie** (AGNewcombe) **2-8-4** WRyan(2) (swrvd lft s: led to ½-wy: wandered & wknd 1f out) | 5 | 5 | 8/1 | 32 | — |
| | | | | (SP 123.3%) | | **5 Rn** |

**63.4 secs** (1.90) CSF £3.63 TOTE £1.70: £1.10 £1.50 (£1.80) OWNER Mrs Bridget Blum (COCKERHAM) BRED Shutford Stud

**858* For Old Times Sake**, who is not very big, can certainly shift and was well clear when eased inside the last. He is bred to appreciate seven. (Evens)

**869 Irish Fiction (IRE)**, who has a round action, was having his first run in a claimer but proved no match for the winner. (7/4)

**838* Lawful Find (IRE)**, a lean sort, has been well beaten in both his outings on turf. Winner of both his All-Weather races, he is clearly better on sand. (9/2: op 3/1)

**Shandana**, a small, backward newcomer, missed the break and ran green. (12/1: 8/1-14/1)

**590 Nattie**, a handful leaving the paddock, raced keenly before dropping away. (8/1)

### 1033 HOUGHTON MAIDEN STKS (3-Y.O) (Class D)
3-00 (3-02) **5f** £3,977.00 (£1,196.00: £578.00: £269.00) Stalls: Centre GOING minus 0.35 sec per fur (F)

| Form | Horse / details | Dist | Pos | SP | RR | SF |
|---|---|---|---|---|---|---|
| 648[2] | **Speed On** (HCandy) **3-9-0** CRutter(13) (chsd ldrs: swtchd lft over 1f out: qcknd to ld jst ins fnl f: edgd rt & rdn clr) | — | 1 | 13/8 [1] | 93 | 55 |
| 548[5] | **Sihafi (USA) (77)** (EALDunlop) **3-9-0** WCarson(9) (chsd ldrs: kpt on fnl f: no ch w wnr) | 5 | 2 | 4/1 [3] | 77 | 39 |
| 768[10] | **Mystic Maid (IRE)** (JWWatts) **3-8-9** LDettori(12) (mde most tl jst ins fnl f: kpt on same pce) | ½ | 3 | 12/1 | 70 | 32 |
| 870[13] | **Matam** (MWEasterby) **3-8-4**(5) GParkin(8) (dwlt s: styd on fnl 2f: nvr nr ldrs) | 2 | 4 | 33/1 | 64 | 26 |
| 672[3] | **Omara (USA) (81)** (HRACecil) **3-8-9** WRyan(4) (reard s: sn chsng ldrs: wknd over 1f out) | ½ | 5 | 2/1 [2] | 62 | 24 |
| | **Nattier** (SirMarkPrescott) **3-8-9** RPerham(11) (cmpt: bit bkwd: chsd ldrs: shkn up 2f out: sn wknd) | 1¾ | 6 | 12/1 | 57 | 19 |
| 768[8] | **Pigeon Hole** (RHannon) **3-8-6**(3) DaneO'Neill(1) (in tch: outpcd ½-wy: n.d after) | ¾ | 7 | 8/1 | 54 | 16 |
| 648[9] | **Ameliajill** (JGMO'Shea) **3-8-4**(5) FLynch(6) (dwlt s: nvr wnt pce) | nk | 8 | 10/1 | 53 | 15 |
| 783[2] | **Gormire** (JHetherton) **3-8-9** NKennedy(7) (cl up: swvd lft & lost pl ½-wy) | 1 | 9 | 16/1 | 50 | 12 |
| | **Goldrill** (MissSEHall) **3-9-0** NConnorton(2) (bit bkwd: s.i.s: a outpcd) | ½ | 10 | 33/1 | 54 | 16 |
| | **Manolo (FR)** (JBerry) **3-9-0** GCarter(5) (prom to ½-wy: sn wknd) | nk | 11 | 16/1 | 53 | 15 |
| 783[10] | **Fernway** (RMWhitaker) **3-8-9** ACulhane(10) (sn wl outpcd: t.o) | 20 | 12 | 50/1 | — | — |
| | | | | (SP 146.6%) | | **12 Rn** |

**62.4 secs** (0.90) CSF £11.05 TOTE £2.70: £1.30 £2.20 £2.80 (£6.10) Trio £46.30 OWNER Mr P. A. Deal (WANTAGE) BRED Wheelersland Stud

OFFICIAL EXPLANATION **Gormire: had just come into season.**

**648 Speed On**, who chipped a bone in a knee as a two-year-old, showed a good action going down. When he saw daylight, he quickened in good style, despite a tendency to edge right. Though not very big, he is clearly useful and is always likely to be best over five. (13/8)

**548 Sihafi (USA)** is settling down with his racing. Dropped back to five, he was made much more use of but, in the end, proved no match for the winner. (4/1)

**Mystic Maid (IRE)**, well drawn, showed plenty of toe to lead for just over four. (12/1)

**Matam** showed promise for the future, staying on late in the day. She needs one more run to qualify for a handicap mark. (33/1)

**672 Omara (USA)** reared up leaving the stalls. Calling it a day over a furlong out, she is not a five-furlong performer. (2/1)

**Nattier** looked in need of the outing and showed a glimmer of ability, showing speed for three. (12/1)

**783 Gormire** showed that she was flattered by her initial effort when she was well-drawn. (16/1)

### 1034 MIDLAND BANK BRITISH OLYMPIC APPEAL H'CAP (0-70) (3-Y.O+) (Class E)
3-30 (3-30) **1m 3f 216y** £3,527.00 (£1,061.00: £513.00: £239.00) Stalls: High GOING: minus 0.35 sec per fur (F)

| Form | Horse / details | Dist | Pos | SP | RR | SF |
|---|---|---|---|---|---|---|
| | **Campaspe (39)** (JGFitzGerald) **4-8-1**(3)ow2 DaneO'Neill(3) (trckd ldrs: effrt 3f out: styd on wl to ld ins fnl f) | — | 1 | 14/1 | 48 | 23 |
| 738[8] | **Forzair (59)** (JJO'Neill) **4-9-10** JFEgan(11) (chsd ldrs: led over 2f out: hrd rdn & hdd ins fnl f) | 1½ | 2 | 6/1 | 66 | 43 |
| 788[4] | **Strategic Ploy (59)** (MrsJRRamsden) **3-8-5** MDeering(8) (hld up & bhd: hdwy over 3f out: styd on wl u.p ins fnl f: nt rch ldrs) | 1 | 3 | 13/8 [1] | 65 | 23 |
| 558[2] | **Gold Desire (33)** (MBrittain) **6-7-9**(3) DWright(10) (hld up & bhd: hrd rdn & styd on fnl 2f: nt rch ldrs) | 3½ | 4 | 4/1 [2] | 34 | 11 |
| 586[9] | **Glenvally (38)** (BWMurray) **5-7-12v**(5)ow1 FLynch(2) (hdwy on outside 6f out: chal 3f out: wknd 2f out) | 3½ | 5 | 12/1 | 34 | 10 |
| 784[5] | **Northern Clan (50)** (MWEasterby) **3-7-3**(7) RMullen(9) (dwlt s: sn prom: rdn & outpcd 3f out: n.d after) | 1¾ | 6 | 10/1 | 44 | 2 |
| 504[2] | **Never Time (IRE) (42)** (MrsVAAconley) **4-8-7** NCarlisle(6) (hdwy on outside 5f out: rdn & edgd rt over 2f out: sn wknd) | 6 | 7 | 15/2 | 28 | 5 |
| 787[13] | **Western Horizon (USA) (40)** (CEBrittain) **4-8-0**(5) MBaird(1) (sn chsng ldrs: chal over 3f out: wkng whn n.m.r over 2f out) | 2½ | 8 | 5/1 [3] | 23 | — |
| *520[3]* | **Rival Queen (IRE) (55)** (MDHammond) **4-9-6** WRyan(12) (led after 2f: edgd lft & hdd over 2f out: sn wknd) | 5 | 9 | 10/1 | 31 | 8 |
| | **Dispol Dancer (31)** (MrsVAAconley) **5-7-10** NKennedy(7) (led 2f: chsd ldrs tl lost pl 4f out: sn bhd) | 3 | 10 | 25/1 | 3 | — |
| | | | | (SP 137.2%) | | **10 Rn** |

**2m 38.3** (5.90) CSF £101.62 CT £202.01 TOTE £15.50: £3.70 £2.50 £1.10 (£109.70) Trio £157.40 OWNER Mr J. G. FitzGerald (MALTON) BRED J. G. Fitzgerald

LONG HANDICAP Northern Clan 7-2 Dispol Dancer 7-4

WEIGHT FOR AGE 3yo-19lb

STEWARDS' ENQUIRY Egan susp. 19-21/5 (excessive use of whip). Mullen susp. 19-21/5 (excessive and incorrect use of whip).

**Campaspe**, who had just four outings at three, stayed on under a most competent ride to get on top in the final 100 yards. (14/1)

**612 Forzair** bounced back in this low-class handicap, but had to admit defeat in the closing stages. (6/1)

**788 Strategic Ploy**, stepping up in distance, took a keen hold in a slowly-run race. Staying on when it was all over, she needs a much stiffer test. (13/8)
**558 Gold Desire** was set an impossible task, happy to sit last for a mile. Responding to strong pressure, he stayed on in the final quarter-mile to no avail. (4/1)

## 1035 EVERINGHAM MEDIAN AUCTION MAIDEN STKS (3-Y.O) (Class E)

4-00 (4-01) **1m 1f 207y** £3,127.25 (£938.00: £451.50: £208.25) Stalls: High GOING minus 0.35 sec per fur (F)

| | | | | SP | RR | SF |
|---|---|---|---|---|---|---|
| $584^{10}$ | **Serendipity (FR) (84)** (JLDunlop) **3-9-0** WCarson(4) (lw: mde all: shkn up over 3f out: styd on wl appr fnl f: rdn out) | — | **1** | $7/4^{2}$ | 81 | 36 |
| $544^{2}$ | **North Song** (JHMGosden) **3-9-0** LDettori(7) (lw: b: b.hind: trckd ldrs: effrt 3f out: edgd lft & nt qckn 1f out: eased ins fnl f) | 4 | **2** | $4/6^{1}$ | 75 | 30 |
| $691^{3}$ | **Blurred (IRE)** (MHTompkins) **3-9-0** NDay(2) (trckd ldrs: chal 3f out: hung rt & wl outpcd over 1f out) | 4 | **3** | $7/1^{3}$ | 68 | 23 |
| | **Hot Dogging** (MrsPSly) **3-8-9** ACulhane(5) (trckd ldrs tl wknd over 2f out) | 13 | **4** | 50/1 | 42 | — |
| $703^{8}$ | **Penygarn Guv'nor** (JAGlover) **3-9-0** GCarter(1) (trckd ldrs: edgd rt & wknd over 2f out) | 5 | **5** | 20/1 | 39 | — |
| $821^{16}$ | **Miletrian Fit-Out** (CEBrittain) **3-9-0** WHollick(6) (s.i.s: sn bhd & drvn along: t.o 3f out) | dist | **6** | 33/1 | — | — |

(SP 118.5%) **6 Rn**

**2m 6.6** (4.10) CSF £3.43 TOTE £3.30: £3.30 £1.00 (£1.40) OWNER Mr John Darby (ARUNDEL)
**OFFICIAL EXPLANATION Serendipity (FR): got worked up on his previous outing.**
**584 Serendipity (FR)**, who apparently became upset beforehand at Newcastle, was calm and well behaved this time. Allowed to set his own pace, Carson quickened up the pace and had his race won just inside the final furlong. (7/4)
**544 North Song** showed on this occasion a very poor action going to post. Happy to track the winner, when he did make his effort, he edged left under pressure and Dettori accepted it with 100 yards to go. (4/6)
**691 Blurred (IRE)** still looks and runs as though he needs plenty more time. (7/1: 5/1-8/1)
**Hot Dogging** took a strong hold in the early stages. (50/1)
**Penygarn Guv'nor** was keen to get on with it and needs to learn to settle. (20/1)
**Miletrian Fit-Out** is a desperate mover and, on the evidence of this, possesses next to no ability. (33/1)

## 1036 E.B.F. RIDINGS MEDIAN AUCTION MAIDEN STKS (2-Y.O) (Class E)

4-30 (4-35) **5f** £3,782.00 (£1,136.00: £548.00: £254.00) Stalls: Centre GOING minus 0.35 sec per fur (F)

| | | | | SP | RR | SF |
|---|---|---|---|---|---|---|
| | **Alpine Time (IRE)** (DRLoder) **2-8-9** LDettori(4) (tall: sn trckng ldrs: shkn up ½-wy: led over 1f out: readily) | — | **1** | $1/2^{1}$ | 76+ | 29 |
| | **Aybeegirl** (MrsJCecil) **2-8-9** PaulEddery(2) (cmpt: led tl over 1f out: no ch w wnr) | 2½ | **2** | $7/1^{3}$ | 68+ | 21 |
| $930^{8}$ | **Gipsy Princess** (MWEasterby) **2-8-9** JFEgan(1) (sn chsng ldrs: rdn ½-wy: kpt on wl ins fnl f) | 1¼ | **3** | 33/1 | 64 | 17 |
| $568^{2}$ | **Spondulicks (IRE)** (RHannon) **2-8-11**(3) DaneO'Neill(5) (chsd ldrs: rdn & outpcd ½-wy: one pce) | 2½ | **4** | $7/2^{2}$ | 61 | 14 |
| $643^{5}$ | **Emilyjill** (JGMO'Shea) **2-8-4**(5) FLynch(7) (unf: bkwd: in tch: outpcd fr ½-wy) | 3 | **5** | 33/1 | 46 | — |
| | **Brawling Springs** (MWEasterby) **2-8-9**(5) GParkin(3) (unf: s.i.s: sn in tch: lost pl ½-wy) | 2½ | **6** | 33/1 | 43 | — |
| | **Going For Broke** (PCHaslam) **2-9-0** GCarter(8) (s.i.s: sme hdwy ½-wy: nvr nr ldrs) | 3½ | **7** | 25/1 | 32 | — |
| | **Colonel's Pride** (RMWhitaker) **2-9-0** ACulhane(6) (w'like: str: bkwd: s.s: hdwy on outside ½-wy: rn green & sn wknd) | 6 | **8** | 33/1 | 13 | — |

(SP 117.0%) **8 Rn**

**63.7 secs** (2.20) CSF £4.75 TOTE £1.40: £1.10 £1.30 £3.10 (£3.60) OWNER Cheveley Park Stud (NEWMARKET) BRED Godolphin Management Co Ltd
**Alpine Time (IRE)** showed signs of inexperience going to post. After being given time to get her eye in, she won readily in the end, but the time was slower than the claimer. (1/2: tchd 4/5)
**Aybeegirl** certainly knew her job. In the end, the winner proved much too good, but she is sure to find a race. (7/1: op 7/2)
**930 Gipsy Princess**, awkward to load, soon confirmed the promise she showed at Thirsk, but finishing behind these two will not do her nursery mark any good in the long run. (33/1)
**568 Spondulicks (IRE)**, the most experienced in the field, was hard ridden and getting nowhere at halfway. (7/2)

## 1037 HUMBERSIDE APPRENTICE H'CAP (0-70) (4-Y.O+) (Class F)

5-00 (5-02) **1m 100y** £3,113.00 (£868.00: £419.00) Stalls: High GOING minus 0.35 sec per fur (F)

| | | | | SP | RR | SF |
|---|---|---|---|---|---|---|
| | **Euro Sceptic (IRE) (44)** (TDEasterby) **4-8-1b**(3) FLynch(6) (sn in tch: styd on wl over 1f out: led wl ins fnl f) | — | **1** | $8/1^{2}$ | 53 | 31 |
| $662^{9}$ | **Commander Glen (IRE) (52)** (MrsJRRamsden) **4-8-7**(5) TFinn(4) (hld up: hdwy on outside over 2f out: styd on wl fnl f) | 2½ | **2** | 12/1 | 56 | 34 |
| $843^{7}$ | **Comedy River (42)** (NEBerry) **9-7-11**(5) AEddery(15) (a in tch: styd on wl appr fnl f) | hd | **3** | 12/1 | 46 | 24 |
| $787^{9}$ | **Westcourt Princess (51)** (MWEasterby) **4-8-6b**(5) GParkin(11) (swtchd rt s: led & sn clr: wknd & hdd wl ins fnl f) | s.h | **4** | $4/1^{1}$ | 55 | 33 |
| $827^{11}$ | **Habeta (USA) (44)** (JWWatts) **10-8-1**(3)ow5 CTeague(9) (bhd: gd hdwy over 1f out: swtchd rt & styd on wl towards fin) | nk | **5** | 12/1 | 47 | 20 |
| *$604^{12}$* | **Grey Kingdom (36)** (MBrittain) **5-7-10** DWright(3) (bhd tl styd on fnl 2f: nt rch ldrs) | nk | **6** | 33/1 | 39 | 17 |
| $851^{9}$ | **Cee-Jay-Ay (54)** (JBerry) **9-8-9**(5) JoanneWebster(10) (s.s: bhd tl styd on fnl 2f) | ½ | **7** | 14/1 | 56 | 34 |
| $713^{11}$ | **Thatched (IRE) (51)** (REBarr) **6-8-8**(3) PFessey(2) (chsd ldrs tl wknd over 1f out) | 1¼ | **8** | $8/1^{2}$ | 51 | 29 |
| $718^{12}$ | **Sea-Ayr (IRE) (44)** (MrsSMAustin) **6-8-4** DarrenMoffatt(13) (b: chsd ldr: edgd lft & wknd 2f out) | 1¼ | **9** | $9/1^{3}$ | 41 | 19 |
| $871^{10}$ | **Silver Sleeve (IRE) (55)** (MDHammond) **4-8-10b**(5) GFaulkner(14) (in tch: hrd rdn over 2f out: wknd over 1f out) | ¾ | **10** | 25/1 | 51 | 29 |
| $615^{10}$ | **Talented Ting (IRE) (61)** (PCHaslam) **7-9-2**(5) CarolDavison(1) (prom early: sn bhd: sme hdwy over 1f out: n.d) | ½ | **11** | 16/1 | 56 | 34 |
| | **Mary Macblain (36)** (JLHarris) **7-7-5**(5) RMullen(7) (chsd ldrs: rdn over 4f out: wknd 2f out) | hd | **12** | 20/1 | 31 | 9 |
| $879^{23}$ | **Murphy's Gold (IRE) (51)** (RAFahey) **5-8-6**(5) RFfrench(5) (hdwy on outside over 4f out: sn chsng ldrs: lost pl over 2f out) | 3½ | **13** | $4/1^{1}$ | 39 | 17 |
| $853^{14}$ | **Suvalu (USA) (68)** (MGMeagher) **4-9-9**(5) RStudholme(16) (lw: s.i.s: bhd: sme hdwy 2f out: sn rdn & wknd) | 1¼ | **14** | 14/1 | 54 | 32 |
| $752^{20}$ | **Arecibo (FR) (36)** (JParkes) **4-7-5**(5) PDoe(12) (chsd ldrs tl lost pl 3f out) | 2½ | **15** | 25/1 | 17 | — |
| *$299^{8}$* | **Newgate Hush (36)** (BWMurray) **4-7-5**(5) IonaWands(8) (sn bhd: t.o) | 18 | **16** | 50/1 | — | — |
| $786^{6}$ | **Legal Brief (45)** (JSWainwright) **4-8-5v**[1] DaneO'Neill(17) (sn bhd & rdn along: t.o: lame) | dist | **17** | 14/1 | — | — |

(SP 138.5%) **17 Rn**

**1m 47.1** (3.10) CSF £102.72 CT £1,125.63 TOTE £11.30: £2.60 £5.80 £3.80 £1.70 (£95.10) Trio £376.40; £318.13 to Beverley 11/5/96.
OWNER Mr C. H. Stevens (MALTON) BRED Martyn J. McEnery

LONG HANDICAP Grey Kingdom 7-6 Arecibo (FR) 7-9 Newgate Hush 6-13 Mary Macblain 7-6
**OFFICIAL EXPLANATION Legal Brief: finished lame.**
**Euro Sceptic (IRE)** has a good record round here and stuck on to show ahead and forge clear near the line under his competent boy. (8/1)
**Commander Glen (IRE)**, dropped out in the early stages, made ground on the wide outside turning in. Sticking on strongly inside the last, he is certainly on a mark from which he can win. (12/1)
**Comedy River**, whose only success was over a mile and a quarter in the Channel Islands two years ago, stuck on strongly in the closing stages and will be suited by a step up in distance. (12/1)
**787 Westcourt Princess** raced in a tongue-strap. Smartly away and switched across to race on the rail, she soon showed in a clear lead but, treading water inside the last 200 yards, she was run out of it in the closing stages. (4/1)
**Habeta (USA)**, now getting on, stayed on strongly late in the day after having to be switched. (12/1)
**Grey Kingdom**, only lightly-raced, put in some solid work in the final quarter-mile. (33/1)
**713 Murphy's Gold (IRE)** saw a lot of daylight on the outside under his inexperienced pilot and called it a day with over two left to run. To give his best, he has to be covered up. (4/1)

T/Plpt: £17.70 (574.86 Tckts). T/Qdpt: £9.20 (71.8 Tckts). WG

# 0800-**CARLISLE (R-H) (Good to firm)**
## Friday May 10th
WEATHER: cold WIND: fresh half bhd

## 1038 E.B.F. CALDEW MAIDEN STKS (2-Y.O) (Class D)
2-10 (2-11) **5f** £3,793.70 (£1,148.60: £560.80: £266.90) Stalls: Low GOING minus 0.38 sec per fur (F)

| | | | | SP | RR | SF |
|---|---|---|---|---|---|---|
| 800[2] | **Recondite (IRE)** (MRChannon) **2-9-0** KDarley(6) (trckd ldrs: nt clr run over 1f out: swtchd & qcknd to ld cl home: cleverly) | — | 1 | 8/11[1] | 65+ | 16 |
| | **Impulsif (USA)** (DJSffrenchDavis) **2-9-0** JWeaver(2) (leggy: trckd ldrs: qcknd to ld ins fnl f: hdd & no ex towards fin) | nk | 2 | 4/1[2] | 64 | 15 |
| | **Red Romance** (DenysSmith) **2-9-0** KFallon(3) (cl up: chal ins fnl f: nt qckn) | 2 | 3 | 66/1 | 58 | 9 |
| 869[6] | **Pandiculation** (EWeymes) **2-9-0** JQuinn(1) (bhd: hdwy over 1f out: n.m.r: styd on) | ½ | 4 | 33/1 | 56 | 7 |
| | **Barnburgh Boy** (JBerry) **2-9-0** JCarroll(4) (w'like: scope: disp ld tl wknd ins fnl f) | 1¾ | 5 | 8/1 | 50 | 1 |
| | **Flotilla** (SirMarkPrescott) **2-9-0** GDuffield(5) (str: scope: bit bkwd: disp ld tl hdd & btn ins fnl f) | s.h | 6 | 11/2[3] | 50 | 1 |

(SP 108.8%) **6 Rn**

**63.3 secs** (3.10) CSF £3.83 TOTE £1.40: £1.10 £2.70 (£4.10) OWNER Mr P. D. Savill (UPPER LAMBOURN) BRED P. D. Savill
**800 Recondite (IRE)** looked a useful performer here, winning in great style after getting into all sorts of trouble. (8/11)
**Impulsif (USA)** knew his job but found the winner far too good late on. Easier opportunities will be found. (4/1)
**Red Romance**, a bit of a handful in the paddock, ran well and will no doubt pick up a race. (66/1)
**869 Pandiculation** is gradually getting the hang of things and there is certainly better to come, especially over further. (33/1)
**Barnburgh Boy** ran well until blowing up in the final furlong. (8/1: 5/1-9/1)
**Flotilla**, a well-made newcomer, needed this and showed enough to suggest that in due course better will be seen. (11/2)

## 1039 IRTHING LIMITED STKS (0-60) (3-Y.O+) (Class F)
2-40 (2-45) **5f** £2,647.00 (£742.00: £361.00) Stalls: Low GOING minus 0.38 sec per fur (F)

| | | | | SP | RR | SF |
|---|---|---|---|---|---|---|
| 997* | **Just Bob (60)** (SEKettlewell) **7-9-9** 3x JFortune(7) (lw: hld up: hdwy ½-wy: led ins fnl f: comf) | — | 1 | 9/4[1] | 72 | 55 |
| 981* | **Rockcracker (IRE) (55)** (GGMargarson) **4-9-6b** 3x PBloomfield(12) (lw: s.i.s: sn chsng ldrs: chal 1f out: nt pce of wnr) | 1¼ | 2 | 5/1[3] | 65 | 48 |
| 881[3] | **Finisterre (IRE) (40)** (JJO'Neill) **3-8-8** KFallon(1) (swtchd & effrt 2f out: styd on: nrst fin) | ½ | 3 | 40/1 | 60 | 34 |
| *897** | **Limerick Princess (IRE) (58)** (JBerry) **3-8-8** 3x JCarroll(2) (trckd ldrs: chal over 1f out: rdn & nt qckn) | ½ | 4 | 4/1[2] | 59 | 33 |
| 911[3] | **Rinus Manor (IRE) (36)** (EJAlston) **5-9-3** SDWilliams(11) (lw: chsd ldrs tl wknd appr fnl f) | 1½ | 5 | 66/1 | 54 | 37 |
| 867[2] | **Pride of Whalley (IRE) (57)** (RAFahey) **3-8-5** MBirch(13) (lw: mde most tl hdd & wknd ins fnl f) | ¾ | 6 | 7/1 | 49 | 23 |
| 812[8] | **Followmegirls (50)** (MrsALMKing) **7-9-0b** JQuinn(6) (s.s: hdwy ½-wy: sn rdn & no imp) | 1¾ | 7 | 20/1 | 43 | 26 |
| 931[8] | **Tenor (58)** (DNicholls) **5-9-6** MTebbutt(8) (prom tl lost pl ½-wy: hdwy over 1f out: no imp) | s.h | 8 | 7/1 | 49 | 32 |
| 659[5] | **Six for Luck (54)** (DANolan) **4-9-0**(3) NVarley(9) (w ldrs 3f: grad wknd) | s.h | 9 | 14/1 | 46 | 29 |
| | **Metal Boys (59)** (MissLCSiddall) **9-9-3** DHarrison(5) (prom over 3f) | 2½ | 10 | 20/1 | 38 | 21 |
| *606[11]* | **April's Joy (50)** (JNorton) **3-8-5** DaleGibson(10) (outpcd fr ½-wy) | 1¼ | 11 | 20/1 | 31 | 5 |
| 750[13] | **Static Love (30)** (HAkbary) **3-8-5** DeanMcKeown(3) (outpcd & bhd fr ½-wy) | 3 | 12 | 66/1 | 21 | — |

(SP 118.8%) **12 Rn**

**61.4 secs** (1.20) CSF £13.39 TOTE £2.90: £1.70 £2.80 £5.30 (£13.50) Trio £284.10 OWNER Mr J. Fotherby (MIDDLEHAM) BRED Mrs D. Whittingham
WEIGHT FOR AGE 3yo-9lb
**997* Just Bob** is running out of his skin at present and this was his best performance to date. (9/4)
**981* Rockcracker (IRE)**, dropped back in distance, put up a sound effort but was no match for the winner in the last furlong. (5/1)
**881 Finisterre (IRE)** keeps running well over this minimum trip. Another furlong might be the answer. (40/1)
**897* Limerick Princess (IRE)** travelled quite well, but failed to pick up when asked, and is probably better with easier ground. (4/1)
**911 Rinus Manor (IRE)** seems to be gradually improving. (66/1)
**867 Pride of Whalley (IRE)** has plenty of early speed but just found this company too hot. (7/1)
**735 Tenor** met with trouble in running and this is best ignored. (7/1)

## 1040 BORDER ESK H'CAP (0-70) (3-Y.O+) (Class E)
3-10 (3-12) **5f 207y** £3,077.55 (£932.40: £455.70: £217.35) Stalls: Low GOING minus 0.38 sec per fur (F)

| | | | | SP | RR | SF |
|---|---|---|---|---|---|---|
| 718[4] | **Selhurstpark Flyer (IRE) (70)** (JBerry) **5-9-9**(5) PRoberts(11) (lw: b: mde all: edgd lft fnl f: r.o wl) | — | 1 | 9/2[2] | 81 | 61 |
| 806[7] | **Barato (63)** (MrsJRRamsden) **5-9-7v** KFallon(1) (b.nr hind: s.i.s: swtchd rt after s: hdwy whn n.m.r 2f out: r.o fnl f) | 3 | 2 | 3/1[1] | 66 | 46 |
| 806[3] | **Sonderise (48)** (NTinkler) **7-8-6**ow4 JFortune(7) (hdwy ½-wy: sn chsng ldrs: kpt on same pce fnl f) | ¾ | 3 | 7/1[3] | 49 | 25 |
| 882[7] | **Mu-Arrik (44)** (GROldroyd) **8-7-9v**(7) MartinDwyer(13) (chsd ldrs: effrt 2f out: kpt on one pce fnl f) | hd | 4 | 8/1 | 45 | 25 |
| 956[3] | **Mister Westsound (65)** (MissLAPerratt) **4-9-9b** GDuffield(9) (hld up: effrt 2f out: hrd rdn & one pce fnl f) | hd | 5 | 9/2[2] | 65 | 45 |
| 868[18] | **Tutu Sixtysix (38)** (DonEnricoIncisa) **5-7-10** KimTinkler(6) (bhd: swtchd & effrt 2f out: nrst fin) | 1¾ | 6 | 33/1 | 34 | 14 |

| | | | | | | |
|---|---|---|---|---|---|---|
| 882[13] | **Birchwood Sun (60)** (MDods) **6-9-4b** JWeaver(10) (s.s: hdwy 2f out: nvr able to chal) | ¾ | **7** | 10/1 | 54 | 34 |
| *331*[6] | **Hi Rock (57)** (JNorton) **4-9-1** DaleGibson(12) (chsd ldrs tl wknd appr fnl f) | 2 | **8** | 20/1 | 45 | 25 |
| 806[10] | **Densben (49)** (DenysSmith) **12-8-7** JQuinn(8) (nvr trbld ldrs) | 2½ | **9** | 20/1 | 31 | 11 |
| 882[6] | **Blow Dry (IRE) (54)** (MartynWane) **6-8-12** KDarley(5) (racd wd: outpcd fr ½-wy) | 2 | **10** | 14/1 | 30 | 10 |
| 931[14] | **Dominelle (49)** (TDEasterby) **4-8-7** MBirch(2) (chsd ldrs tl rdn & wknd appr fnl f) | 2½ | **11** | 11/1 | 18 | — |
| | **Gondo (46)** (EJAlston) **9-8-4v**ow1 SDWilliams(4) (chsd ldrs tl wknd 1½f out) | 1 | **12** | 25/1 | 13 | — |
| | **Miss Aragon (53)** (MissLCSiddall) **8-8-11** DHarrison(3) (sn prom: wknd wl over 1f out) | 1¼ | **13** | 14/1 | 16 | — |
| | | | | (SP 132.0%) | **13 Rn** | |

**1m 13.9** (1.40) CSF £19.41 CT £95.31 TOTE £4.50: £1.50 £2.50 £3.00 (£12.00) Trio £58.80 OWNER Mr Chris Deuters (COCKERHAM) BRED Gay O'Callaghan
LONG HANDICAP Tutu Sixtysix 7-8

**718 Selhurstpark Flyer (IRE)**, dropped back a furlong, did it well despite hanging left in the closing stages. (9/2)
**806 Barato**, drawn wide, managed to cross over to the far rail and met with trouble but, despite finishing well, could never peg the winner back. (3/1)
**806 Sonderise** is in quite good heart at present, but is not quite doing enough at the business end. (7/1)
**806 Mu-Arrik** last won two seasons ago and, although he ran well here, he could never find a real turn of foot to take the opportunity. (8/1)
**956 Mister Westsound**, held up, then saw too much daylight too soon and was never giving it full co-operation. (9/2)
**Tutu Sixtysix** tried to come from way behind and the task was always impossible. She looks in good heart. (33/1)
**Birchwood Sun** always gives ground away at the start but his performance was certainly an improvement this time. (10/1)

## 1041 DERWENT CLAIMING STKS (I) (3-Y.O+) (Class F)
3-40 (3-43) **6f 206y** £2,283.00 (£638.00: £309.00) Stalls: Low GOING minus 0.38 sec per fur (F)

| | | | | SP | RR | SF |
|---|---|---|---|---|---|---|
| 971[5] | **First Gold (54)** (JWharton) **7-9-5b** KFallon(10) (bhd: hdwy on ins 2f out: rdn to ld wl ins fnl f) | — | **1** | 4/1[2] | 67 | 36 |
| 1020[9] | **Diet (58)** (MissLAPerratt) **10-9-2v** GDuffield(8) (led 1f: chsd ldr: led over 1f out tl wl ins fnl f: no ex) | 1¼ | **2** | 11/2[3] | 61 | 30 |
| 805[7] | **Brambles Way (33)** (WLBarker) **7-8-6v**(7) MartinDwyer(6) (chsd ldrs: rdn 2f out: kpt on: nt pce to chal) | nk | **3** | 66/1 | 57 | 26 |
| 801* | **Proud Image (65)** (APJarvis) **4-9-5v** JTate(2) (lw: led after 1f: sn clr: rdn over 2f out: wknd & hdd appr fnl f) | 1¾ | **4** | 9/4[1] | 59 | 28 |
| 971[11] | **Thwaab (48)** (FWatson) **4-9-5** JWeaver(1) (c wd st: hdwy 2f out: nvr rchd ldrs) | 1¼ | **5** | 20/1 | 57 | 26 |
| | **Simand (55)** (GMMoore) **4-9-4** JFortune(7) (sn bhd: styd on fnl 2f: nrst fin) | ½ | **6** | 11/2[3] | 54 | 23 |
| *834*[3] | **Holloway Melody (43)** (BAMcMahon) **3-7-12**(5)ow1 LNewton(5) (chsd ldrs tl wknd over 2f out) | 3½ | **7** | 8/1 | 43 | — |
| 983[6] | **Polli Pui (47)** (WMBrisbourne) **4-8-5**(5) DGriffiths(4) (in tch: effrt over 2f out: btn over 1f out) | ¾ | **8** | 33/1 | 37 | 6 |
| 742[5] | **Regal Fanfare (IRE) (62)** (MrsLStubbs) **4-9-0b** DaleGibson(9) (in tch tl outpcd fnl 2½f) | 2 | **9** | 9/1 | 36 | 5 |
| 885[6] | **Pearls of Thought (IRE) (41)** (JSHaldane) **3-7-7**(3) NVarley(3) (chsd ldrs to ½-wy: sn wknd) | 15 | **10** | 100/1 | — | — |
| | | | | (SP 112.8%) | **10 Rn** | |

**1m 28.8** (3.10) CSF £23.72 TOTE £4.30: £1.40 £2.00 £9.50 (£12.30) Trio £208.00; £266.63 to Beverley 11/5/96. OWNER Mr K. D. Standen (MELTON MOWBRAY) BRED Messinger Stud Ltd
WEIGHT FOR AGE 3yo-12lb

**971 First Gold** is a law unto himself and, getting a terrific run up the rail, flew to settle it late on. (4/1)
**661* Diet**, stuck in the mud the previous day, ran his heart out here, but had no answer to the winner's late burst. (11/2: 4/1-6/1)
**Brambles Way** has never won a race and this was his best effort for a while. (66/1)
**801* Proud Image** tried his forcing tactics again, but this fast ground was not entirely to his liking and he was picked off approaching the final furlong. (9/4)
**805 Thwaab** again showed he has ability, but was never doing enough to get into it. (20/1)
**Simand** should be all the better for the run. (11/2)

## 1042 EAMONT H'CAP (0-70) (3-Y.O) (Class E)
4-10 (4-15) **7f 214y** £3,241.35 (£982.80: £480.90: £229.95) Stalls: Low GOING minus 0.38 sec per fur (F)

| | | | | SP | RR | SF |
|---|---|---|---|---|---|---|
| 616[7] | **Mister Woodstick (IRE) (48)** (MAJarvis) **3-8-4** KDarley(17) (led 1f: cl up: led 3f out: all out) | — | **1** | 8/1 | 55 | 19 |
| 775[6] | **Sandblaster (48)** (MrsJRRamsden) **3-8-4** DHarrison(6) (bhd: hdwy & swtchd 2f out: str run fnl f: jst failed) | s.h | **2** | 14/1 | 55 | 19 |
| 662[10] | **Arabian Heights (49)** (MrsJRRamsden) **3-8-5** KFallon(15) (lw: hld up: hdwy over 2f out: sn chsng ldrs: one pce fnl f) | 2 | **3** | 12/1 | 52 | 16 |
| 754[6] | **Yeoman Oliver (64)** (BAMcMahon) **3-9-1**(5) LNewton(14) (hdwy 3f out: chsng ldrs appr fnl f: kpt on one pce) | hd | **4** | 15/2[3] | 67 | 31 |
| 769[10] | **Jimjareer (IRE) (50)** (CaptJWilson) **3-8-6** SDWilliams(9) (a chsng ldrs: outpcd 3f out: kpt on fnl f) | nk | **5** | 12/1 | 52 | 16 |
| *348*[4] | **Contract Bridge (IRE) (40)** (CWThornton) **3-7-7**(3) NVarley(10) (lw: s.i.s: nvr nrr) | 1¼ | **6** | 14/1 | 40 | 4 |
| 734[2] | **Soldier Mak (61)** (AHide) **3-9-3** MTebbutt(8) (hdwy ½-wy: one pce appr fnl f) | hd | **7** | 7/2[1] | 60 | 24 |
| 824[8] | **The Butterwick Kid (47)** (RAFahey) **3-8-3** DaleGibson(16) (chsd ldrs: effrt 3f out: wknd over 1f out) | 7 | **8** | 8/1 | 32 | — |
| *280*[4] | **Guy's Gamble (54)** (JWharton) **3-8-10** JFanning(13) (a chsng ldrs: effrt 3f out: btn wl over 1f out) | nk | **9** | 10/1 | 39 | 3 |
| *516*[6] | **Tagatay (40)** (MJCamacho) **3-7-10** LCharnock(11) (nvr trbld ldrs) | nk | **10** | 33/1 | 24 | — |
| 595[2] | **Cerise (IRE) (51)** (CWCElsey) **3-8-7b** JFortune(1) (lw: led after 1f to 3f out: wknd) | s.h | **11** | 7/1[2] | 35 | — |
| 873[5] | **Yezza (IRE) (65)** (APJarvis) **3-9-7** JTate(12) (n.d) | 1¼ | **12** | 10/1 | 47 | 11 |
| 867[6] | **Magical Midnight (40)** (NTinkler) **3-7-10** KimTinkler(2) (sn bhd: n.d) | 10 | **13** | 33/1 | 1 | — |
| 774[7] | **Miletrian City (58)** (JBerry) **3-9-0** JCarroll(4) (nvr trbld ldrs) | 10 | **14** | 33/1 | — | — |
| 827[20] | **Globe Runner (65)** (JJO'Neill) **3-9-7b**[1] JWeaver(5) (sn cl up: rdn 3f out: sn wknd) | hd | **15** | 33/1 | 6 | — |
| 740[7] | **Sis Garden (55)** (TDEasterby) **3-8-11** MBirch(3) (chsd ldrs: rdn 3f out: sn wknd) | 1¼ | **16** | 33/1 | — | — |
| 734[6] | **Supermister (55)** (TDEasterby) **3-8-11** JQuinn(7) (chsd ldrs tl wknd over 2f out) | 8 | **17** | 33/1 | — | — |
| | | | | (SP 133.3%) | **17 Rn** | |

**1m 42.5** (3.90) CSF £107.21 CT £1,260.95 TOTE £10.20: £2.60 £4.60 £2.10 £2.40 (£155.10) Trio £296.30 OWNER Mr John Sims (NEWMARKET) BRED John O'Connor
LONG HANDICAP Magical Midnight 7-5

**Mister Woodstick (IRE)**, happier on this faster ground, was given a great ride to pinch the race. (8/1)
**775 Sandblaster**, given a lot to do, found trouble in running and basically should have won this. (14/1)
**662 Arabian Heights** is at last beginning to show what he can do, but was short of a turn of foot to take it. (12/1: op 8/1)
**595 Yeoman Oliver** is fully exposed and was never doing enough in the closing stages here. (15/2)
**Jimjareer (IRE)** left the impression that further should suit. (12/1: op 8/1)
**Contract Bridge (IRE)**, last away, ran well without offering a threat. She looks in good form. (14/1)
**734 Soldier Mak** could never find the speed to get into it, despite staying on under pressure. (7/2)
**873 Yezza (IRE)** (10/1: op 6/1)

## 1043 DERWENT CLAIMING STKS (II) (3-Y.O+) (Class F)

4-40 (4-46) **6f 206y** £2,283.00 (£638.00: £309.00) Stalls: Low GOING minus 0.38 sec per fur (F)

| | | | | SP | RR | SF |
|---|---|---|---|---|---|---|
| $839^{8}$ | **Miss Charlie (43)** (TWall) **6-8-12** RLappin(5) (hld up & bhd: effrt over 2f out: led ins fnl f: styd on) | — | 1 | 14/1 | 55 | 17 |
| $834^{9}$ | **Tallulah Belle (45)** (NPLittmoden) **3-7-12** JQuinn(4) (in tch: ev ch whn hmpd 1f out: nt qckn) | 1 | 2 | 20/1 | 51 | 1 |
| | **Craigmore Magic (USA) (50)** (MissMKMilligan) **3-8-1** JFanning(8) (outpcd & bhd: hdwy over 1f out: styd on wl towards fin) | hd | 3 | 25/1 | 54 | 4 |
| | **Valiant Man** (JWharton) **5-9-1b** KFallon(7) (chsd ldrs: ev ch whn wandered u.p 1f out: sn btn) | 1¾ | 4 | 11/1$^{3}$ | 51 | 13 |
| $896^{2}$ | **Palacegate Touch (75)** (JBerry) **6-9-11b** JCarroll(1) (cl up: led 4f out: put hd in air & hung bdly lft fnl 2f: hdd ins fnl f) | 1 | 5 | 1/3$^{1}$ | 59 | 21 |
| $336^{5}$ | **Serious Fact (40)** (MrsLStubbs) **4-9-5** JFortune(3) (prom: rdn 3f out: sn btn) | 9 | 6 | 12/1 | 32 | — |
| $615^{12}$ | **Lancashire Life (IRE) (44)** (EJAlston) **5-9-5** SDWilliams(9) (led 3f: wknd 2f out) | 7 | 7 | 9/1$^{2}$ | 16 | — |
| | **Star Dancer** (JNorton) **3-8-2** DaleGibson(6) (dwlt: a bhd: t.o) | dist | 8 | 14/1 | — | — |
| | | | | (SP 123.0%) | **8 Rn** | |

**1m 30.0** (4.30) CSF £202.93 TOTE £16.60: £2.60 £4.80 £4.30 (£58.20) Trio Not won; £238.00 to Beverley 11/5/96. OWNER Mr A. H. Bennett (CHURCH STRETTON) BRED Mrs B. Bacon

WEIGHT FOR AGE 3yo-12lb

**Miss Charlie** lost her maiden tag here by staying on in most determined style. (14/1)

**Tallulah Belle** has been showing little on the All-Weather, but did run reasonably here, despite being bumped in the closing stages. (20/1)

**Craigmore Magic (USA)** really got going in the final two furlongs, suggesting that another 100 yards would have seen him winning comfortably. (25/1)

**Valiant Man** had his chances but, when an effort was required, he just hung badly and refused to run on. (11/1: 8/1-12/1)

**896 Palacegate Touch** was not happy on this fast ground and, sticking his head high in the air, finished up on the stands' rail and was easily picked off. (1/3: tchd 1/2)

## 1044 EDEN H'CAP (0-70) (3-Y.O+) (Class E)

5-10 (5-15) **1m 6f 32y** £2,968.35 (£898.80: £438.90: £208.95) Stalls: High GOING minus 0.38 sec per fur (F)

| | | | | SP | RR | SF |
|---|---|---|---|---|---|---|
| | **Persian Smoke (36)** (AHide) **5-7-8**(7) MartinDwyer(9) (lw: hld up: smooth hdwy 4f out: led over 2f out: shkn up & r.o wl) | — | 1 | 10/1 | 48 | 23 |
| $886^{6}$ | **Lostris (IRE) (33)** (MDods) **5-7-12** DaleGibson(13) (hld up & bhd: hdwy 3f out: styd on: no ch w wnr) | 5 | 2 | 20/1 | 39 | 14 |
| | **Urban Dancing (USA) (46)** (BEllison) **7-8-11** KFallon(7) (in tch: hdwy to chse ldrs 3f out: nt qckn appr fnl f) | 1¾ | 3 | 5/1$^{3}$ | 50 | 25 |
| $890^{3}$ | **High Desire (IRE) (54)** (JRArnold) **3-7-12** JQuinn(8) (in tch: effrt 3f out: sn chsng ldrs: one pce appr fnl f) | hd | 4 | 7/2$^{2}$ | 58 | 12 |
| | **Zamhareer (USA) (43)** (WStorey) **5-8-8** JFanning(11) (hld up: effrt 4f out: styd on towards fin: nvr nrr) | nk | 5 | 3/1$^{1}$ | 47 | 22 |
| 1022* | **Lord Advocate (32)** (DANolan) **8-7-8b**(3) NVarley(6) (a chsng ldrs: rdn over 3f out: outpcd fnl 2f) | 1¼ | 6 | 11/2 | 35 | 10 |
| $767^{12}$ | **Punch (45)** (NTinkler) **4-8-9b** JCarroll(5) (prom: led 4f out tl over 2f out: sn wknd: eased) | 22 | 7 | 10/1 | 23 | — |
| $852^{7}$ | **Top Prize (40)** (MBrittain) **8-8-5v** GDuffield(12) (cl up tl rdn & wknd 6f out) | 1 | 8 | 20/1 | 17 | — |
| $738^{10}$ | **Royrace (45)** (WMBrisbourne) **4-8-9** JFortune(3) (cl up early: sn bhd: effrt 4f out: n.d) | ¾ | 9 | 25/1 | 21 | — |
| $537^{9}$ | **Jabaroot (IRE) (63)** (DANolan) **5-9-7**(7) DMcGaffin(14) (dwlt: a bhd) | dist | 10 | 50/1 | — | — |
| | **Magic Times (53)** (MJohnston) **5-9-4** JWeaver(2) (led after 3f tl hdd & wknd 4f out) | 5 | 11 | 16/1 | — | — |
| | **Boundary Express (56)** (EJAlston) **4-9-6** SDWilliams(1) (led 3f: cl up tl rdn & wknd 4f out) | 2 | 12 | 7/1 | — | — |
| | | | | (SP 131.2%) | **12 Rn** | |

**3m 7.1** (6.10) CSF £178.07 CT £1,043.81 TOTE £11.10: £3.90 £3.30 £1.80 (£104.90) Trio £266.30; £195.06 to Beverley 11/5/96. OWNER Mrs Andrew Normand (NEWMARKET) BRED Brook Stud Ltd

WEIGHT FOR AGE 3yo-21lb, 4yo-1lb

**Persian Smoke** travelled particularly well here, and scored in useful fashion, suggesting that he should be able to follow up. (10/1)

**612 Lostris (IRE)** is happy on this fast ground and improved a fair bit, but found the winner far too good in the last furlong and a half. (20/1)

**Urban Dancing (USA)** has been running well on much softer surfaces than this over hurdles. This was not a bad effort here in the circumstances. (5/1)

**890 High Desire (IRE)** looked to be going well here for much of the trip but, when an effort was required in the straight, she proved short of toe. Easier ground could be the answer. (7/2)

**Zamhareer (USA)** has improved no end over hurdles but lacked the pace to get into this. (3/1: tchd 10/1)

**1022* Lord Advocate** probably found his exertions of the previous night had taken the edge off him. (11/2)

**Punch** went well until an effort was required early in the straight, from which point he cried enough. (10/1)

T/Plpt: £5,472.50 (1.7 Tckts). T/Qdpt: £637.90 (0.09 Tckts); £784.46 to Lingfield 11/5/96. AA

# 0551-LINGFIELD (L-H) (Turf Good to firm, Firm back st, AWT Standard)
## Friday May 10th

WEATHER: overcast WIND: almost nil

## 1045 MCCALL GROUP MAIDEN STKS (I) (3-Y.O+) (Class D)

1-50 (1-52) **7f** £3,427.50 (£1,020.00: £485.00: £217.50) Stalls: High GOING minus 0.30 sec per fur (GF)

| | | | | SP | RR | SF |
|---|---|---|---|---|---|---|
| | **Russian Music** (MissGayKelleway) **3-8-12** RCochrane(4) (a.p: led over 1f out: rdn out) | — | 1 | 11/10$^{1}$ | 76 | 46 |
| $842^{3}$ | **Almuhimm (USA) (75)** (EALDunlop) **4-9-10** PatEddery(10) (lw: plld hrd: hld up: chsd wnr over 1f out: ev ch ins fnl f: r.o) | hd | 2 | 4/1$^{3}$ | 76 | 58 |
| $746^{2}$ | **Major Dundee (IRE) (84)** (RHannon) **3-8-12** JReid(8) (lw: w ldr: led 2f out tl over 1f out: unable qckn) | 3½ | 3 | 11/4$^{2}$ | 68 | 38 |
| $755^{5}$ | **A Chef Too Far** (RRowe) **3-8-12** TQuinn(6) (a.p: rdn over 2f out: one pce) | ½ | 4 | 8/1 | 67 | 37 |
| $677^{11}$ | **He's My Love (IRE)** (JEBanks) **3-8-12** BDoyle(1) (lw: rdn over 1f out: hdwy fnl f: nvr nrr) | 3 | 5 | 33/1 | 60 | 30 |
| $732^{11}$ | **Scimitar** (PJMakin) **3-8-12** SSanders(7) (lw: nvr nr to chal) | s.h | 6 | 50/1 | 60 | 30 |
| $583^{9}$ | **Voodoo Rocket** (JHMGosden) **3-8-7** GHind(5) (s.s: nvr plcd to chal) | ½ | 7 | 14/1 | 54 | 24 |
| $894^{10}$ | **Samuel Scott** (MBell) **3-8-12** MFenton(9) (bit bkwd: s.s: a bhd) | 2 | 8 | 50/1 | 54 | 24 |
| | **Inaminit** (HJCollingridge) **3-8-12** FNorton(3) (led 5f) | ½ | 9 | 50/1 | 53 | 23 |

| | | | SP | RR | SF |
|---|---|---|---|---|---|
| 842[11] | **Croagh Patrick** (JCFox) **4-9-10** NAdams(2) (bhd fnl 2f) | 4 **10** | 50/1 | 44 | 26 |

(SP 122.8%) **10 Rn**

**1m 23.56** (1.96) CSF £6.33 TOTE £2.60: £1.30 £1.50 £1.20 (£5.20) Trio £3.10 OWNER The Seventh Heaven Partnership (WHITCOMBE) BRED Mrs N. F. M. Sampson
WEIGHT FOR AGE 3yo-12lb
OFFICIAL EXPLANATION **Voodoo Rocket: was hanging, changed her legs and made a noise near the finish.**
**Samuel Scott: could not act on the ground.**
**Russian Music** was heavily backed to make a winning return for his new stable and did not let his supporters down. Never far away, he struck the front below the distance and, ridden along, just held off the runner-up. (11/10)
**842 Almuhimm (USA)** looked in good shape beforehand but refused to settle in the race and took a very keen hold. Moving into second place below the distance, he threw down his challenge, but just failed to get on top. He should soon win. (4/1)
**746 Major Dundee (IRE)** looked very well beforehand. Disputing the lead until showing narrowly in front over a quarter of a mile out, he was headed below the distance and then failed to find another gear. (11/4: op 7/4)
**755 A Chef Too Far** was in the firing-line from the outset, but failed to find the necessary pace in the last two furlongs. (8/1: 12/1-7/1)
**He's My Love (IRE)** was at the back of the field until staying on in the final furlong, only to find it all over bar the shouting. (33/1)
**Voodoo Rocket** (14/1: op 6/1)

## 1046 RACING CHANNEL STEVE WOOD MEMORIAL MAIDEN STKS (2-Y.O) (Class D)
2-20 (2-21) **5f** £3,351.25 (£1,000.00: £477.50: £216.25) Stalls: High GOING minus 0.30 sec per fur (GF)

| | | | | SP | RR | SF |
|---|---|---|---|---|---|---|
| 950[2] | **Caviar Royale (IRE)** (RHannon) **2-9-0** PatEddery(3) (lw: mde virtually all: clr 1f out: eased ins fnl f) | — | **1** | 4/9[1] | 81+ | 30 |
| | **Eaton Park (IRE)** (RAkehurst) **2-9-0** SSanders(5) (leggy: outpcd: hdwy 1f out: r.o one pce) | 5 | **2** | 20/1 | 65 | 14 |
| 1003[7] | **Bold African** (PDEvans) **2-9-0** RCochrane(4) (spd over 2f) | 1¼ | **3** | 10/1 | 61 | 10 |
| | **Statuette** (BPalling) **2-8-9** TSprake(2) (b: neat: chsd wnr: ev ch wl over 1f out: sn wknd) | 3 | **4** | 9/1[3] | 46 | — |
| | **Tinkerbell** (LordHuntingdon) **2-8-9** JReid(1) (neat: a bhd) | 1 | **5** | 4/1[2] | 43 | — |

(SP 113.1%) **5 Rn**

**59.4 secs** (2.40) CSF £8.54 TOTE £1.30: £1.10 £3.20 (£5.90) OWNER Mr George Teo (MARLBOROUGH) BRED Jerry O'Brien
**950 Caviar Royale (IRE)** was by far the paddock pick and had few problems here. Making virtually all the running, he forged clear a furlong from home and, with the race well and truly in the bag, was eased in the last 100 yards. (4/9)
**Eaton Park (IRE)**, slightly on the leg but with a little bit of strength, was taken off his feet until staying on in the final furlong to snatch second. (20/1)
**829 Bold African** tried to live with the winner but had already burnt his boats at halfway. (10/1: op 6/1)
**Statuette** is sure to benefit from the outing and chased the winner. Having had every chance in the final quarter-mile, she then tired as lack of a run took its toll. (9/1: 12/1-8/1)
**Tinkerbell**, a nippy sort on looks, was far from that in the race and was always badly outpaced. (4/1: 5/2-9/2)

## 1047 BOLLINGER CHAMPAGNE CHALLENGE SERIES GENTLEMENS' H'CAP (0-70) (3-Y.O+) (Class F)
2-50 (2-52) **1m 2f** £2,928.40 (£812.40: £389.20) Stalls: Low GOING minus 0.35 sec per fur (FST)

| | | | | SP | RR | SF |
|---|---|---|---|---|---|---|
| 817* | **Zidac (70)** (PJMakin) **4-12-0** MrJDurkan(5) (a.p: chsd ldr 6f out: led over 2f out: drvn out) | — | **1** | 3/1[1] | 80 | 62 |
| *854*[2] | **Montone (IRE) (47)** (JRJenkins) **6-10-1**(4) DrMMannish(3) (a.p: chsd wnr over 1f out: r.o) | 1¾ | **2** | 8/1 | 54 | 36 |
| 593[11] | **Meltemison (68)** (CEBrittain) **3-10-7**(4) MrVLukaniuk(2) (chsd ldr 4f: rdn over 2f out: unable qckn) | 1 | **3** | 20/1 | 74 | 41 |
| 817[9] | **Scottish Bambi (63)** (PRWebber) **8-11-7** MrPScott(11) (lw: hdwy 7f out: rdn 2f out: r.o one pce) | 2 | **4** | 7/2[2] | 65 | 47 |
| 866[3] | **Bronze Maquette (IRE) (35)** (THind) **6-9-3**(4) MrRThornton(12) (lw: hdwy 7f out: rdn 2f out: one pce) | 1½ | **5** | 13/2[3] | 35 | 17 |
| *854** | **Kingchip Boy (68)** (MJRyan) **7-11-8v**(4) 5x MrSLavallin(13) (led over 7f: wknd over 1f out) | nk | **6** | 13/2[3] | 68 | 50 |
| 817[16] | **It'sthebusiness (53)** (SDow) **4-10-7v**[1](4) MrSFetherstonhaugh(14) (nvr nr to chal) | 7 | **7** | 14/1 | 41 | 23 |
| 661[9] | **Good so Fa (IRE) (35)** (CNAllen) **4-9-3h**(4) MrPClose(6) (nvr nrr) | 1 | **8** | 33/1 | 22 | 4 |
| 866[8] | **Dots Dee (41)** (JMBradley) **7-9-9**(4)ow6 MrNHOliver(10) (lw: b.nr fore: hdwy 8f out: wknd over 2f out) | ½ | **9** | 33/1 | 27 | 3 |
| 664[8] | **Shaynes Domain (40)** (RMFlower) **5-9-12** MrTMcCarthy(7) (bhd fnl 6f) | ½ | **10** | 20/1 | 25 | 7 |
| 670[7] | **Digpast (IRE) (57)** (RJO'Sullivan) **6-10-11b**(4) MrDavyJones(8) (lw: virtually ref to r: a t.o) | ½ | **11** | 16/1 | 41 | 23 |
| *364*[7] | **Colour Counsellor (50)** (RMFlower) **3-9-3**(4) MrKGoble(9) (a bhd: t.o) | 10 | **12** | 33/1 | 18 | — |
| 760[5] | **Yellow Dragon (IRE) (57)** (BAPearce) **3-9-10**(4)ow3 MrAEvans(4) (6th whn rn out over 7f out) | | **R** | 25/1 | — | — |

(SP 119.7%) **13 Rn**

**2m 9.36** (4.66) CSF £25.66 CT £366.09 TOTE £4.10: £1.50 £2.00 £5.90 (£10.60) Trio £190.10 OWNER Mr Brian Brackpool (MARLBOROUGH) BRED A. J. Struthers
LONG HANDICAP Bronze Maquette (IRE) 9-2 Dots Dee 9-1 Good so Fa (IRE) 9-6 Colour Counsellor 9-2
WEIGHT FOR AGE 3yo-15lb
STEWARDS' ENQUIRY Scott susp. 19-23/5/96 (irresponsible riding).
**817* Zidac** moved into second place at the top of the hill. Sent to the front over quarter of a mile from home, he came under pressure and continually swished his tail. However, his pilot kept him going and the combination held on well. (3/1)
**854 Montone (IRE)** struggled into second place below the distance, but his rider proved very ineffective and they failed to reel in the winner. (8/1)
**Meltemison**, in a handy position throughout, failed to find the necessary turn of foot in the last two furlongs. (20/1)
**670* Scottish Bambi** moved up to track the leaders after three furlongs. He struggled on in the final quarter-mile, but failed to get to the principals. His rider was later suspended for careless riding. (7/2)
**866 Bronze Maquette (IRE)** moved up seven furlongs from home, but could only go up and down in the same spot. (13/2)
**854* Kingchip Boy** took the field along. Collared over a quarter of a mile out, he grimly tried to hold on, but had shot his bolt below the distance. (13/2: 4/1-7/1)
**636 It'sthebusiness** (14/1: 10/1-16/1)

## 1048 BOOKER CASH & CARRY CHEFS LARDER H'CAP (0-80) (4-Y.O+) (Class D)
3-20 (3-20) **1m (Equitrack)** £3,817.50 (£1,140.00: £545.00: £247.50) Stalls: High GOING minus 0.35 sec per fur (FST)

| | | | | SP | RR | SF |
|---|---|---|---|---|---|---|
| 933[6] | **Sooty Tern (48)** (JMBradley) **9-7-10** GBardwell(6) (b.off fore: mde virtually all: hrd rdn over 1f out: r.o wl) | — | **1** | 3/1[1] | 54 | 36 |
| 765[18] | **Duke Valentino (79)** (RHollinshead) **4-9-13** MWigham(2) (hld up: rdn 2f out: unable qckn fnl f) | 1¼ | **2** | 15/2 | 83 | 65 |
| 756[4] | **Waikiki Beach (USA) (69)** (GLMoore) **5-9-3** SWhitworth(9) (b: b.hind: a.p: ev ch 2f out: one pce) | 1 | **3** | 9/2[3] | 71 | 53 |
| 851[6] | **Four of Spades (71)** (PDEvans) **5-9-0b**(5) AmandaSanders(8) (lw: hdwy over 4f out: rdn over 1f out: r.o one pce) | 1¼ | **4** | 11/1 | 70 | 52 |

| | | | | SP | RR | SF |
|---|---|---|---|---|---|---|
| 876[24] | **Ertlon (80)** (CEBrittain) **6-10-0** BDoyle(5) (lw: a.p: ev ch 2f out: wknd over 1f out) | 2½ | **5** | 5/1 | 74 | 56 |
| *261** | **Mr Teigh (69)** (BSmart) **4-9-3** RCochrane(7) (hdwy over 3f out: wknd wl over 1f out) | 5 | **6** | 4/1[2] | 53 | 35 |
| *778*[7] | **Sarum (50)** (CPWildman) **10-7-12** NAdams(3) (b.nr fore: bhd fnl 4f) | 1 | **7** | 20/1 | 32 | 14 |
| 887[14] | **Hawaii Storm (FR) (67)** (DJSffrenchDavis) **8-8-10**(5) CAdamson(4) (a bhd) | 3 | **8** | 14/1 | 43 | 25 |
| | **Yeath (IRE) (57)** (RAkehurst) **4-8-5** TQuinn(1) (lw: w wnr over 3f: t.o fnl 3f) | 27 | **9** | 9/1 | — | — |

(SP 121.4%) **9 Rn**

**1m 39.02** (1.62) CSF £25.05 CT £94.76 TOTE £5.40: £1.20 £2.70 £2.00 (£26.50) Trio £36.10 OWNER Mr J. M. Bradley (CHEPSTOW) BRED Sheikh Mohammed bin Rashid al Maktoum

LONG HANDICAP Sooty Tern 7-9

**933 Sooty Tern** made virtually all the running and, responding to pressure in the last furlong and a half, kept on well to gain his first All-Weather victory in over four years. (3/1)

**Duke Valentino** chased the leaders. Asked for his effort entering the straight, he failed to find the necessary turn of foot. (15/2: 5/1-8/1)

**756 Waikiki Beach (USA)** looked really well beforehand and raced up with the pace. Holding every chance entering the straight, he then failed to find another gear. (9/2)

**Four of Spades** moved up just before halfway. Coming under pressure below the distance, he struggled on without finding the necessary turn of foot. (11/1)

**744 Ertlon**, always close up, had every chance entering the straight before tiring approaching the final furlong. (5/1)

**Hawaii Storm (FR)** (14/1: 8/1-16/1)

**Yeath (IRE)** (9/1: 5/1-10/1)

## 1049 MAXIMS H'CAP (0-70) (3-Y.O+) (Class E)

3-50 (3-50) **5f** £3,315.90 (£991.20: £474.60: £216.30) Stalls: High GOING minus 0.30 sec per fur (GF)

| | | | | SP | RR | SF |
|---|---|---|---|---|---|---|
| 846[10] | **Judgement Call (48)** (PHowling) **9-8-6** FNorton(10) (rdn over 2f out: hdwy over 1f out: led ins fnl f: r.o wl) | — | **1** | 16/1 | 55 | 30 |
| 862[17] | **Mazzarello (IRE) (45)** (RCurtis) **6-8-3v**ow4 BDoyle(12) (lw: rdn over 2f out: hdwy over 1f out: r.o) | 1¼ | **2** | 14/1 | 48 | 19 |
| 601[11] | **Lloc (56)** (CADwyer) **4-8-11**(3) JStack(11) (a.p: hrd rdn 2f out: ev ch ins fnl f: unable qckn) | ¾ | **3** | 7/1[3] | 57 | 32 |
| 862[3] | **Friendly Brave (USA) (68)** (MissGayKelleway) **6-9-12** WJO'Connor(3) (b: lw: hld up: hrd rdn over 1f out: one pce ins fnl f) | nk | **4** | 13/2[2] | 68 | 43 |
| 862[14] | **Allwight Then (IRE) (68)** (REPeacock) **5-9-7**(5) MHenry(4) (lw: led over 3f out tl ins fnl f: one pce) | 1 | **5** | 14/1 | 64 | 39 |
| 812[17] | **Halbert (63)** (PBurgoyne) **7-9-4v**(3) DRMcCabe(5) (outpcd: hdwy over 1f out: r.o) | ¾ | **6** | 9/1 | 57 | 32 |
| 743[4] | **Dancing Jack (53)** (JJBridger) **3-8-2** DeclanO'Shea(14) (lw: stumbled over 4f out: nvr nrr) | nk | **7** | 8/1 | 46 | 12 |
| 749[11] | **Squire Corrie (66)** (GHarwood) **4-9-3v**1(7) GayeHarwood(8) (a.p: rdn over 2f out: wknd fnl f) | hd | **8** | 25/1 | 59 | 34 |
| | **The Noble Oak (IRE) (41)** (MJBolton) **8-7-8**(5) CAdamson(16) (nvr nrr) | 1¼ | **9** | 33/1 | 30 | 5 |
| 758[4] | **Man of Wit (IRE) (70)** (APJarvis) **3-9-5** TQuinn(15) (nvr nrr) | 1½ | **10** | 7/1[3] | 54 | 20 |
| 862[11] | **Miami Banker (54)** (WRMuir) **10-8-12b** GBardwell(7) (prom over 3f) | hd | **11** | 20/1 | 38 | 13 |
| 846[11] | **Allyana (IRE) (68)** (RHannon) **4-9-12b**1 JReid(9) (prom over 3f) | s.h | **12** | 8/1 | 52 | 27 |
| | **Windrush Boy (64)** (JRBosley) **6-9-1**(7) AimeeCook(2) (a.p: hrd rdn over 1f out: wknd fnl f) | 1 | **13** | 25/1 | 44 | 19 |
| 868[11] | **Diebiedale (51)** (RBoss) **4-8-9** PatEddery(6) (led over 1f: wknd wl over 1f out) | ¾ | **14** | 7/2[1] | 29 | 4 |
| *362** | **Half Tone (47)** (RMFlower) **4-8-5b** DBiggs(1) (a bhd) | ½ | **15** | 8/1 | 23 | — |
| | **Heights of Love (50)** (MSSaunders) **3-7-13** NAdams(13) (hld up: rdn 2f out: sn wknd) | nk | **16** | 50/1 | 25 | — |

(SP 140.5%) **16 Rn**

**58.94 secs** (1.94) CSF £225.24 CT £1,603.28 TOTE £35.30: £7.00 £3.60 £4.20 £3.60 (£139.10) Trio £482.40 OWNER Mr K. Weston (NEWMARKET) BRED T. P. Kelly

WEIGHT FOR AGE 3yo-9lb

OFFICIAL EXPLANATION **Half Tone: was scratchy going to post and did not stride out on the ground.**

**Judgement Call** began to pick up ground below the distance and sustained his effort to hit the front inside the final furlong. (16/1)

**664 Mazzarello (IRE)**, ridden along in midfield at halfway, picked up ground below the distance but, despite running on, was unable to master the winner. (14/1: 10/1-16/1)

**601 Lloc**, always close up, had every chance inside the final furlong before tapped for toe. (7/1)

**862 Friendly Brave (USA)** chased the leaders, but failed to find another gear inside the final furlong. (13/2)

**742 Allwight Then (IRE)** was soon at the head of affairs. Collared inside the final furlong, he then failed to find another gear. (14/1)

**Halbert**, unable to lay up with the early pace, was doing all his best work in the final furlong and a half. (9/1)

## 1050 MCCALL GROUP MAIDEN STKS (II) (3-Y.O+) (Class D)

4-20 (4-25) **7f** £3,395.00 (£1,010.00: £480.00: £215.00) Stalls: High GOING minus 0.30 sec per fur (GF)

| | | | | SP | RR | SF |
|---|---|---|---|---|---|---|
| | **Iceni (IRE)** (HCandy) **3-8-7** AMcGlone(2) (a.p: led over 2f out: pushed out) | — | **1** | 100/30[2] | 70 | 24 |
| | **Ruwy** (CJBenstead) **3-8-7** JReid(6) (bit bkwd: hld up: nt clr run over 3f out & wl over 1f out: r.o ins fnl f) | 1¼ | **2** | 9/4[1] | 67 | 21 |
| | **One In The Eye** (JRPoulton) **3-8-9**(3) PMcCabe(9) (lw: reminder over 4f out: swtchd lft & hdwy over 1f out: hrd rdn & edgd rt ins fnl f: r.o) | nk | **3** | 66/1 | 72 | 26 |
| | **Jamaican Flight (USA)** (JWHills) **3-8-7**(5) MHenry(7) (lw: led over 4f: unable qckn) | ½ | **4** | 9/4[1] | 70 | 24 |
| | **Stone Island** (CACyzer) **3-8-12** TQuinn(3) (w'like: rdn thrght: hdwy over 2f out: btn whn n.m.r ins fnl f) | ¾ | **5** | 8/1[3] | 69 | 23 |
| 669[8] | **Crimson Rosella** (WJHaggas) **3-8-7** RMcGhin(1) (hld up: rdn over 1f out: btn whn bdly hmpd ins fnl f) | 1½ | **6** | 16/1 | 60 | 14 |
| 845[12] | **Lizium** (JCFox) **4-9-5** RCochrane(4) (a bhd) | 8 | **7** | 66/1 | 42 | 8 |
| 730[10] | **Brentability (IRE)** (GLewis) **3-8-12** SWhitworth(5) (prom over 4f) | hd | **8** | 14/1 | 47 | 1 |
| 840[12] | **The Grey Weaver** (RMFlower) **3-8-12** DBiggs(8) (bit bkwd: prom 3f) | 7 | **9** | 50/1 | 31 | — |

(SP 113.2%) **9 Rn**

**1m 25.05** (3.45) CSF £10.55 TOTE £3.80: £1.30 £1.10 £4.10 (£2.70) Trio £21.90 OWNER Mrs C. M. Poland (WANTAGE) BRED C. Farrell

WEIGHT FOR AGE 3yo-12lb

**Iceni (IRE)**, sold out of Alec Stewart's stable for 12,500 guineas, gained a narrow advantage over quarter of a mile form home and needed only to be nudged along to have the situation in hand. (100/30: 2/1-7/2)

**Ruwy** had no luck in running on this reappearance. With nowhere to go at halfway and again finding her way blocked along the inside rail early in the final quarter-mile, she ran on inside the final furlong but all too late. She will come on for this and should soon gain compensation. (9/4: op 6/4)

**One In The Eye** is not very big but was certainly fit for this debut. Switched to the outside, he picked up ground below the distance and, given a reminder, drifted right inside the final furlong, causing interference. Despite this, he ran on and just failed to take second. (66/1)

**Jamaican Flight (USA)**, in good shape for this reappearance, took the field along. Collared over a quarter of a mile from home, he failed to summon up another turn of foot. (9/4)

**Stone Island**, ridden along throughout, moved up over two furlongs from home, but was held when tightened up for room by the third inside the final furlong. (8/1: 6/1-10/1)
**Crimson Rosella** chased the leaders and was battling it out for the minor honours when badly hampered inside the final furlong. (16/1)
**Brentability (IRE)** (14/1: 8/1-16/1)

## 1051 INFONET LIMITED STKS (0-80) (3-Y.O+) (Class D)
4-50 (4-57) **7f 140y** £3,882.50 (£1,160.00: £555.00: £252.50) Stalls: High GOING minus 0.30 sec per fur (GF)

| | | | | SP | RR | SF |
|---|---|---|---|---|---|---|
| | **Alhawa (USA) (80)** (CJBenstead) **3-8-8** TQuinn(3) (lw: chsd ldr: hrd rdn over 1f out: led wl ins fnl f: r.o wl) | — | **1** | 6/1[2] | 89 | 55 |
| 876* | **Yeast (80)** (WJHaggas) **4-9-11** RCochrane(4) (lw: a.p: led wl over 1f out: hrd rdn: hdd wl ins fnl f: r.o wl) | s.h | **2** | 4/9[1] | 93 | 72 |
| 491[6] | **Queen of All Birds (IRE) (75)** (RBoss) **5-9-6** PatEddery(5) (hld up: rdn over 2f out: unable qckn) | 3 | **3** | 8/1[3] | 82 | 61 |
| 809[8] | **Confronter (79)** (SDow) **7-9-7** BThomson(6) (lw: hld up: rdn over 2f out: one pce) | 1½ | **4** | 14/1 | 80 | 59 |
| 809[9] | **Sotoboy (IRE) (79)** (PWHarris) **4-9-2**(5) MHenry(2) (bhd fnl 2f) | 5 | **5** | 9/1 | 69 | 48 |
| 933[12] | **Castel Rosselo (72)** (RHarris) **6-9-7b** AMackay(1) (led 6f) | 3 | **6** | 33/1 | 63 | 42 |
| | | | | (SP 114.2%) | **6 Rn** | |

**1m 29.81** (1.01) CSF £9.19 TOTE £5.60: £2.10 £1.30 (£2.60) OWNER Mr Hamdan Al Maktoum (EPSOM) BRED Shadwell Farm Inc
WEIGHT FOR AGE 3yo-13lb
**Alhawa (USA)**, in second place virtually throughout, had a ding-dong battle with the leader in the final quarter-mile before succeeding. (6/1)
**876* Yeast** just failed to complete the hat-trick. Gaining a slender advantage early in the final quarter-mile, he had a tremendous tussle with the winner and only just lost out. (4/9)
**Queen of All Birds (IRE)** chased the leaders but failed to match the front two in the last furlong. (8/1: 6/1-9/1)
**324a Confronter** could only go up and down in the same place in the final quarter-mile. (14/1: 8/1-16/1)
**Sotoboy (IRE)** (9/1: 6/1-10/1)

T/Jkpt: £24,872.30 (0.09 Tckts); £31,878.65 to Lingfield 11/5/96. T/Plpt: £13.60 (1,087.77 Tckts). T/Qdpt: £12.80 (58.54 Tckts). AK

# 0791a-SAINT-CLOUD (France) (L-H) (Good)
## Wednesday May 1st

## 1052a PRIX DU MUGUET (Gp 2) (4-Y.O+)
3-20 (3-27) **1m** £39,526.00 (£16,469.00: £7,905.00: £3,953.00)

| | | | SP | RR | SF |
|---|---|---|---|---|---|
| **Vetheuil (USA)** (AFabre,France) **4-8-11** OPeslier (hld up: smooth hdwy 2f out: led ins fnl f: r.o wl) | — | **1** | | 124 | — |
| **Nec Plus Ultra (FR)** (AdeRoyerDupre,France) **5-8-11** TGillet (trckd ldrs: rdn to ld wl over 1f out: hdd ins fnl f: r.o) | ½ | **2** | | 123 | — |
| **Silvering (FR)** (MmeCHead,France) **4-8-11** FHead (led tl hdd wl over 1f out: styd on one pce) | 6 | **3** | | 111 | — |
| **Chato (USA)** (HSteinmetz,Germany) **4-8-11** ABest (mid div: rdn 2f out: r.o fnl f) | s.nk | **4** | | 111 | — |
| **Marie de Ken (FR)** (AdeRoyerDupre,France) **4-8-8** GMosse (chsd ldr tl no ex fnl 2f) | s.nk | **5** | | 107 | — |
| **Suivez La (USA)** (JCunnington,France) **4-8-8** FSanchez (a bhd) | 4 | **6** | | 99 | — |
| | | | | | **6 Rn** |

**1m 40.4** (1.90) P-M 7.20F: 2.50F 1.40F (21.90F) OWNER Mr D. Wildenstein (CHANTILLY) BRED Allez France Stables Ltd
**Vetheuil (USA)** would have been an automatic selection for anyone who saw him in the paddock as he looked outstanding. Produced at exactly the right moment, he won going away, and now has the Prix d'Ispahan as his next target, but is also entered in the Arlington Million.
**Nec Plus Ultra (FR)** is a game little horse who always tries his best. He took the lead inside the last quarter-mile, but could not withstand the winner's challenge. His next target is the Badener Meile.
**Silvering (FR)** was facing a difficult task in his first Group race. He tried to make all of the running but, despite running on, could not cope with the first two. He is still inexperienced, and looks capable of winning at this level.
**Chato (USA)** is a genuine performer, and may have been closer but for having little room on the rail in the straight.

# 0908a-SAN SIRO (Milan, Italy) (R-H) (Heavy)
## Wednesday May 1st

## 1053a PREMIO CERTOSA (Listed) (3-Y.O+)
4-00 (4-04) **5f** £24,360.00 (£10,718.00: £5,846.00)

| | | | SP | RR | SF |
|---|---|---|---|---|---|
| **Imprevedibile (IRE)** (PCeriotti,Italy) **6-9-7** AParravani | — | **1** | | 115 | — |
| **Leap for Joy** (JHMGosden) **4-9-0** SDettori | nse | **2** | | 108 | — |
| **Reinaldo (FR)** (GBotti,Italy) **4-9-0** EBotti | 2 | **3** | | 102 | — |
| | | | | | **8 Rn** |

**59.5 secs** (4.30) Tote 43L: 16L 17L 20L (79L) OWNER Scuderia Gianni Daniele BRED Ardenode Stud Ltd
**Imprevedibile (IRE)** won this race for the second successive year after taking the lead well inside the final furlong.
**Leap for Joy**, always prominent, took the advantage over two furlongs out. Collared well inside the last 200 yards, she rallied again close home.

# MULHEIM (Mulheim-Ruhr, Germany) (Good)
## Wednesday May 1st

## 1054a MULHEIM FRUHJARS-STEHERA-PREIS (Listed) (4-Y.O+)
2-45 (2-47) **2m** £9,009.00 (£3,604.00: £1,802.00)

| | | | | SP | RR | SF |
|---|---|---|---|---|---|---|
| | **Camp David (GER)** (AWohler,Germany) **6-9-2** ABoschert | — | **1** | | 116 | — |
| | **Flamingo Paradise** (HBlume,Germany) **5-8-3** MLarsen | ½ | **2** | | 103 | — |
| | **Moltaire (GER)** (BSchutz,Germany) **4-9-6b[1]** AStarke | 2 | **3** | | 121 | — |
| 563[4] | **Kristal's Paradise (IRE)** (JLDunlop) **4-8-9** MRimmer (btn over 31l) | | **10** | | — | — |
| | | | | | | **10 Rn** |

**3m 18.9** Tote 38DM: 17DM 23DM 18DM (SF 160DM) OWNER Mr D. Gabel BRED Frau & I. Brunotte

**Camp David (GER)** won this event for the second year in succession, narrowly outbattling the runner-up.
**563 Kristal's Paradise (IRE)** was prominent until weakening five furlongs from home.

# CHURCHILL DOWNS (Louisville, USA) (L-H) (Fast)
## Saturday May 4th

### 1055a KENTUCKY DERBY (Gp 1) (3-Y.O)
10-32 (10-34) **1m 2f** **(Dirt)** £570,839.00 (£109,677.00: £54,839.00)

| | Horse | Dist | Pos | SP | RR | SF |
|---|---|---|---|---|---|---|
| | **Grindstone (USA)** (DWLukas,USA) **3-9-0** JBailey | — | 1 | | 126 | — |
| | **Cavonnier (USA)** (BBaffert,USA) **3-9-0** CMcCarron | nse | 2 | | 126 | — |
| | **Prince of Thieves (USA)** (DWLukas,USA) **3-9-0** PDay | 3½ | 3 | | 120 | — |
| | | | | | | **19 Rn** |

**2m 1.06** P-M £13.80: PL £6.00 £6.20: SHOW £4.00 £4.40 £4.60 (£61.80) OWNER Overbrook Farm et al BRED Overbrook Farm
**Grindstone (USA)** came from well behind to snatch this right on the line. The Louisiana Derby winner followed his stablemate Prince of Thieves through, and then produced a terrific burst in the last half-furlong to get up. He has now been retired.
**Cavonnier (USA)** took over from the weakening favourite over a furlong out, and looked sure to win, but was collared in the very last stride.

# 0905a-LONGCHAMP (Paris, France) (R-H) (Good)
## Sunday May 5th

### 1056a PRIX DE SAINT-GEORGES (Gp 3) (3-Y.O+)
1-25 (1-22) **5f** £28,986.00 (£10,540.00: £5,270.00: £2,635.00)

| | Horse | Dist | Pos | SP | RR | SF |
|---|---|---|---|---|---|---|
| 790a* | **Anabaa (USA)** (MmeCHead,France) **4-9-0** FHead | — | 1 | | 116+ | 16 |
| | **Bouche Bee (USA)** (JEHammond,France) **4-8-11** GMosse | 6 | 2 | | 94 | — |
| | **Vilayet** (MmeCHead,France) **3-8-5** OPeslier | 2 | 3 | | 90 | — |
| | **Millyant** (RGuest) **6-9-5** CAsmussen | s.nk | 4 | | 95 | — |
| | | | | | | **4 Rn** |

**59.6 secs** (5.10) P-M 1.40F: 1.10F 1.10F (16.40F)
OWNER Mme A. Head (CHANTILLY) BRED Gainsborough Farm Inc
**790a* Anabaa (USA)** could prove a major force in European sprints, with no obvious contenders for the Championship having yet emerged, as his back problems seem to be over and he is improving all the time. Taking this by the scruff of the neck a furlong and a half out, he just coasted home, and now goes for the Prix du Gros Chene, followed by the King's Stand Stakes.
**Bouche Bee (USA)** was cleverly supplemented for this race, and her owners were rewarded with more than three times the entry fee, and black type for their filly to boot. She came through late to claim second place, and is capable of winning a listed event.
**Vilayet** would have preferred a longer trip.
**Millyant** was on her toes in the paddock, and almost unshipped her jockey leaving the stalls. She then raced into the lead running far too keenly, and was a spent force in the last quarter-mile. This run is best forgotten.

### 1057a PRIX HOCQUART (Gp 2) (3-Y.O C & F)
3-20 (3-27) **1m 4f** £54,084.00 (£21,410.00: £10,145.00: £3,953.00)

| | Horse | Dist | Pos | SP | RR | SF |
|---|---|---|---|---|---|---|
| 621a² | **Arbatax (IRE)** (PBary,France) **3-9-2** CAsmussen (hld up in rr: rdn over 2f: r.o to ld cl home) | — | 1 | | 105 | 68 |
| | **Dark Nile (USA)** (MmeCHead,France) **3-9-2** FHead (led: rdn clr 2f out: wknd ins fnl f: hdd cl home) | 1½ | 2 | | 103 | 66 |
| | **Stage Pass** (NClement,France) **3-9-2** OPeslier (mid div: hdwy & ev ch over 1f out: one pce) | 1 | 3 | | 102 | 65 |
| | **Halcon** (MmeMBollack-Badel,France) **3-9-2** ABadel (hld up: sme hdwy st: nt rch ldrs) | 4 | 4 | | 96 | 59 |
| | **Katun (FR)** (JForesi,France) **3-9-2** DBoeuf (cl up: rdn 2f out: one pce) | ¾ | 5 | | 95 | 58 |
| | **New York New York (FR)** (JEHammond,France) **3-9-2** WMongil (hld up: rdn & nt qckn fnl 2f) | ½ | 6 | | 95 | 58 |
| 621a⁴ | **Supreme Commander (FR)** (AFabre,France) **3-9-2** TJarnet (prom tl rdn & wknd 2f out) | 4 | 7 | | 89 | 52 |
| 797a⁴ | **Oliviero (FR)** (AMauchamp,France) **3-9-2b** GGuignard (chsd ldr tl wknd over 2f out) | 2 | 8 | | 87 | 50 |
| | **Trivellino (FR)** (PDemercastel,France) **3-9-2** TThulliez (a bhd) | 1½ | 9 | | 85 | 48 |
| | | | | | | **9 Rn** |

**2m 32.0** (6.00) P-M 5.70F: 1.40F 1.20F 1.50F (6.20F) OWNER Mme F. Boutin (CHANTILLY) BRED Citadel Stud
**621a Arbatax (IRE)** is a decent colt on the upgrade. His win looked spectacular, but it may have been due to the leaders fading as much as any acceleration on his part. He now heads for the Prix du Jockey-Club.
**Dark Nile (USA)** tried to make all the running, but had nothing left when challenged. He was not a certain stayer, so front-running tactics may not have suited, and he may come back in distance for the Prix Jean Prat.
**Stage Pass** ran a good race for one so inexperienced, and looks capable of winning a Group race.
**Halcon** was outstanding in the paddock, but never really took a hand in the finish. He may be better over a shorter trip.
DS

# 0903a-CAPANNELLE (Rome, Italy) (R-H) (Soft)
## Sunday May 5th

### 1058a PREMIO FELICE SCHEIBLER (3-Y.O)
4-00 (4-35) **1m 3f** £101,500.00 (£44,660.00: £24,360.00)

| | Horse | Dist | Pos | SP | RR | SF |
|---|---|---|---|---|---|---|
| | **Coral Reef (ITY)** (GColleo,Italy) **3-9-2** MLatorre | — | 1 | | 88 | — |
| | **Ranuncolo (ITY)** (PMozzoni,Italy) **3-9-2** BJovine | 2½ | 2 | | 84 | — |
| | **Perseo (ITY)** (LCamici,Italy) **3-9-2** JacquelineFreda | 2½ | 3 | | 81 | — |
| 677⁵ | **Robamaset (IRE)** (LMCumani) **3-9-2** FJovine (btn 6 3/4l) | | 5 | | 79 | — |
| | | | | | | **12 Rn** |

**2m 19.0** Tote 24L: 14L 31L 46L (173L) OWNER Scuderia Andy Capp BRED A. Rampa
**Coral Reef (ITY)** made all in this valuable event and, after this easy victory, goes next for the Derby Italiano.
**677 Robamaset (IRE)**, held up in the rear early, made headway two furlongs out, but could only stay on at one pace.

# DIELSDORF (Zurich, Switzerland) (L-H) (Soft)
## Sunday May 5th

### 1059a GROSSER PREIS DER ZURITEL (3-Y.O)
3-45 (1-34) **1m** £8,523.00

| | | | | SP | RR | SF |
|---|---|---|---|---|---|---|
| 611[2] | **Double Diamond (IRE)** (MJohnston) **3-9-2** JWeaver | — | 1 | | 94 | — |
| | **Shturm (RUS)** (MWeiss,Switzerland) **3-9-2** JHills | ½ | 2 | | 93 | — |
| | **Fablinix (FR)** (RStadelmann,Switzerland) **3-9-2** DRegnard | 4¾ | 3 | | 84 | — |
| | | | | | | **14 Rn** |

**1m 46.4** Tote 2.30SF: 1.50SF 2.00SF 2.00SF (25.20SF) OWNER The Second Middleham Partnership (MIDDLEHAM) BRED Dene Investments N V

**611 Double Diamond (IRE)**, always prominent, took the lead turning for home and held on well inside the final furlong to give his enterprising connections a Classic winner in the Swiss equivalent of the 2000 Guineas.

# DUSSELDORF (Germany) (R-H) (Soft)
## Sunday May 5th

### 1060a ARAG-PREIS (Gp 2) (3-Y.O F)
3-45 (3-51) **1m** £54,054.00 (£21,622.00: £10,811.00: £5,405.00)

| | | | | SP | RR | SF |
|---|---|---|---|---|---|---|
| | **La Blue (GER)** (BSchutz,Germany) **3-9-2** THellier (hld up: hdwy to ld 1f out: sn clr: easily) | — | 1 | | 103 | — |
| | **Dapprima (GER)** (BSchutz,Germany) **3-9-2** AStarke (trckd ldrs: chal 2f out: nt qckn fnl f) | 3 | 2 | | 97 | — |
| | **Salonrolle (IRE)** (MHofer,Germany) **3-9-2** ATylicki (hld up in rr: hdwy 3f out: hmpd 2f out: r.o) | ¾ | 3 | | 96 | — |
| | **Massada** (HRemmert,Germany) **3-9-2** KWoodburn (mid div: one pce fnl 2f) | 3 | 4 | | 90 | — |
| | **Kirsberry (GER)** (Germany) **3-9-2** TMundry (hmpd early: styd on st) | 3½ | 5 | | 83 | — |
| | **Masai Mara (GER)** (Germany) **3-9-2** WNewnes (rr early: hdwy 2f out: nt rch ldrs) | s.h | 6 | | 82 | — |
| | **Personal Love (USA)** (Germany) **3-9-2** ABest (led tl hdd & wknd 2f out) | ¾ | 7 | | 81 | — |
| | **Song of Peace (GER)** (Germany) **3-9-2** ILindner (prom early) | 1½ | 8 | | 78 | — |
| 905a[4] | **Motzki (FR)** (France) **3-9-2** MBoutin (nvr rchd ldrs) | 1¾ | 9 | | 74 | — |
| 572[12] | **Tamnia** (JLDunlop) **3-9-2** MRimmer (a abt same pl: btn over 15l) | | 10 | | — | — |
| | **Fag End (IRE)** (MHTompkins) **3-9-2** NDay (prom tl wknd 2f out: btn over 16l) | | 11 | | — | — |
| | | | | | | **16 Rn** |

**1m 43.11** Tote 81DM: 25DM 25DM 72DM (423DM) OWNER Gestut Wittekindshof BRED Gestut Wittekindshof

**La Blue (GER)** came from well behind and, despite hampering the third, proved an easy winner. She now goes for the Preis der Diana.

**Dapprima (GER)** ran on into second, but was no match for her stable-companion. She is, however, likely to join her at Mulheim on 27th May.

**Salonrolle (IRE)** was hampered by the winner, but managed to stay on for third. She will renew rivalry in the German Oaks.

**Tamnia** raced near the back of a tight leading group, and was never going well enough to put in a challenge.

**Fag End (IRE)** was up with the pace until dropping back in the last quarter-mile. She gave the impression that the soft ground did not suit her.

# 0860-BATH (L-H) (Good to firm)
## Saturday May 11th
WEATHER: overcast WIND: almost nil

### 1061 CHAPEL FARM MAIDEN STKS (3-Y.O F) (Class D)
2-10 (2-11) **1m 5y** £3,598.50 (£1,083.00: £524.00: £244.50) Stalls: Low GOING minus 0.45 sec per fur (F)

| | | | | SP | RR | SF |
|---|---|---|---|---|---|---|
| | **Roses In The Snow (IRE) (98)** (JWHills) **3-8-11** BThomson(4) (a.p: led over 2f out: comf) | — | 1 | 6/4[1] | 76+ | 42 |
| 842[6] | **Silver Showers (USA)** (MRStoute) **3-8-11** RCochrane(1) (b.hind: a.p: chsd wnr over 1f out: no imp) | 2½ | 2 | 6/4[1] | 71 | 37 |
| 755[4] | **Lady Bankes (IRE) (70)** (WGMTurner) **3-8-11** RPerham(5) (led over 5f: one pce fnl f) | 4 | 3 | 12/1[3] | 63 | 29 |
| | **Indian Nectar** (GBBalding) **3-8-8**(3) SDrowne(7) (rdn & hdwy 3f out: wknd over 1f out) | 4 | 4 | 33/1 | 55 | 21 |
| 921[10] | **Kowtow** (MDIUsher) **3-8-11** RStreet(9) (plld hrd: prom tl wknd over 1f out) | s.h | 5 | 66/1 | 55 | 21 |
| | **Perfect Gift** (PFICole) **3-8-4**(7) DavidO'Neill(8) (b.nr hind: bkwd: stdd s: a bhd) | ¾ | 6 | 25/1 | 54 | 20 |
| 922* | **Miss Pravda** (PTWalwyn) **3-8-11** JCarroll(3) (chsd ldr tl wknd over 2f out) | nk | 7 | 6/1[2] | 53 | 19 |
| | **On The Home Run** (JRJenkins) **3-8-11** NDay(6) (a bhd) | s.h | 8 | 66/1 | 53 | 19 |
| 943[6] | **Volare** (BJMeehan) **3-8-11** MTebbutt(2) (bhd fnl 2f) | 2 | 9 | 25/1 | 49 | 15 |
| 746[9] | **Shoemaker Levy** (RJO'Sullivan) **3-8-11** SSanders(10) (a bhd) | 9 | 10 | 66/1 | 31 | — |
| | | | | (SP 117.1%) | | **10 Rn** |

**1m 40.1** (1.60) CSF £4.00 TOTE £2.60: £1.10 £1.10 £1.70 (£2.30) Trio £6.00 OWNER Mr G. Howard-Spink (LAMBOURN) BRED Tullamaine Castle Stud and Partners

**Roses In The Snow (IRE)**, who spent the winter in Pisa, came into her own over this mile and is bred to stay further. (6/4)

**842 Silver Showers (USA)** had to be content to play second fiddle in the final furlong and a half. (6/4)

**755 Lady Bankes (IRE)** tried to make all over this longer trip. (12/1: op 6/1)

**Indian Nectar** should come on a bit for the outing. (33/1)

**921 Kowtow** was bought out of Roger Charlton's yard for 1,600 guineas, having not run as a two-year-old. She did not help her cause by running too freely. (66/1)

**922* Miss Pravda** (6/1: tchd 10/1)

### 1062 TATTERSALLS MAIDEN AUCTION STKS (2-Y.O) (Class E)
2-40 (2-42) **5f 11y** £3,031.50 (£912.00: £441.00: £205.50) Stalls: High GOING minus 0.45 sec per fur (F)

| | | | | SP | RR | SF |
|---|---|---|---|---|---|---|
| 815[5] | **Petite Danseuse** (SDow) **2-8-4**ow1 BThomson(1) (lw: w ldr: led over 1f out: rdn out) | — | 1 | 9/1 | 72 | 19 |
| 823[2] | **Enchantica** (JBerry) **2-8-2** JCarroll(6) (led over 3f: ev ch ins fnl f: r.o) | nk | 2 | 6/5[1] | 69 | 17 |
| | **What Happened Was** (MartynMeade) **2-7-7**(5) PFessey(8) (w'like: bit bkwd: s.s: rn wd bnd over 3f out: hdwy over 2f out: r.o fnl f) | 2 | 3 | 6/1[3] | 59 | 7 |
| 807[5] | **Preskidul (IRE)** (DWPArbuthnot) **2-8-4**ow2 RPerham(7) (lw: b.hind: hdwy over 2f out: r.o fnl f) | nk | 4 | 6/1[3] | 64 | 10 |

| | | | | SP | RR | SF |
|---|---|---|---|---|---|---|
| | **Cariad Cymru** (RAkehurst) **2-8-3** SSanders(9) (leggy: lt-f: a.p: r.o one pce fnl f) | ¾ | **5** | 11/2[2] | 60 | 8 |
| 815[3] | **Windborn** (KMcAuliffe) **2-8-3** JFEgan(3) (lw: dwlt: hdwy over 2f out: rdn & wknd over 1f out) | 1¼ | **6** | 7/1 | 56 | 4 |
| 465[5] | **Summer Risotto** (DJSffrenchDavis) **2-7-7**(5) CAdamson(2) (chsd ldrs 3f) | 1¼ | **7** | 33/1 | 48 | — |
| | **Rosenkavalier (IRE)** (LGCottrell) **2-8-9** RCochrane(4) (str: wl bhd fnl 2f) | 7 | **8** | 16/1 | 36 | — |
| | **Lady Sadie (IRE)** (JSMoore) **2-7-12** NAdams(5) (neat: outpcd: t.o fnl 3f) | 11 | **9** | 33/1 | — | — |

(SP 123.7%) **9 Rn**

**62.5 secs** (2.00) CSF £20.92 TOTE £9.30: £2.10 £1.40 £1.10 (£10.30) Trio £23.10 OWNER Mrs A. M. Upsdell (EPSOM) BRED I. D. Livingstone

**815 Petite Danseuse** had improved for her debut and held on well in the closing stages. (9/1: op 6/1)
**823 Enchantica** showed no tendency to go right this time and it seemed to be just a question of the winner having the edge. (6/5)
**What Happened Was** played up in the stalls and it came as no surprise to see her slowly away. Running wide in the straight, she did well to finish so close. (6/1: 8/1-9/2)
**807 Preskidul (IRE)** (6/1: op 3/1)
**Cariad Cymru** may do better over a longer trip. (11/2: 8/1-14/1)
**815 Windborn** was not knocked about when her chance had gone. (7/1: op 4/1)

## 1063 MRS HELEN HARRIS 50TH BIRTHDAY H'CAP (0-70) (4-Y.O+) (Class E)

3-10 (3-12) **2m 1f 34y** £3,109.50 (£936.00: £453.00: £211.50) Stalls: Low GOING minus 0.45 sec per fur (F)

| | | | | SP | RR | SF |
|---|---|---|---|---|---|---|
| 449[11] | **Coleridge (47)** (JJSheehan) **8-8-9b** RCochrane(6) (hld up: hdwy 9f out: led over 2f out: rdn out) | — | **1** | 16/1 | 62 | 37 |
| 944[2] | **Lalindi (IRE) (66)** (DRCElsworth) **5-10-0b** AProcter(8) (lw: a.p: chsd wnr fnl f: no imp) | 6 | **2** | 8/1[2] | 75 | 50 |
| 759[2] | **Courbaril (60)** (SDow) **4-9-5** BThomson(3) (lw: hld up: hdwy 10f out: led over 3f out tl over 2f out: one pce) | 2 | **3** | 9/1[3] | 68 | 40 |
| 759* | **The Lad (45)** (LMontagueHall) **7-8-0**(7) MartinDwyer(5) (hld up: hdwy over 3f out: hung lft & one pce fnl 2f) | 1¼ | **4** | 15/8[1] | 51 | 26 |
| 944[3] | **Durham (50)** (RSimpson) **5-8-9b**(3) SDrowne(4) (a.p: hung bdly lft 3f out: no hdwy) | 1¼ | **5** | 11/1 | 55 | 30 |
| *108*[7] | **Fabulous Mtoto (43)** (MSSaunders) **6-8-5** JFEgan(9) (lw: plld hrd: led tl over 3f out: wknd over 2f out) | 2½ | **6** | 16/1 | 46 | 21 |
| *236*[7] | **Romalito (36)** (MBlanshard) **6-7-7**(5) CAdamson(12) (nvr nrr) | 2½ | **7** | 33/1 | 37 | 12 |
| | **Raqib (43)** (PCRitchens) **5-8-5** JCarroll(14) (hdwy 10f out: rdn 8f out: wknd 7f out) | 1½ | **8** | 9/1[3] | 42 | 17 |
| *837*[6] | **Stevie's Wonder (IRE) (60)** (BJLlewellyn) **6-9-8** VSlattery(13) (a bhd) | 7 | **9** | 25/1 | 53 | 28 |
| 872[9] | **Shahrani (47)** (BJMeehan) **4-8-6**ow2 MTebbutt(11) (prom tl wknd 4f out) | 2½ | **10** | 33/1 | 37 | 7 |
| 811[9] | **Call My Guest (IRE) (57)** (REPeacock) **6-9-0**(5) MHenry(10) (bhd fnl 7f) | 3½ | **11** | 33/1 | 44 | 19 |
| 852[8] | **Brandon Prince (IRE) (61)** (IABalding) **8-9-2b**(7) CScudder(7) (lw: a bhd) | 6 | **12** | 9/1[3] | 42 | 17 |
| 759[3] | **Ikhtiraa (USA) (37)** (RJO'Sullivan) **6-7-13b** SSanders(2) (chsd ldr 9f out: sn rdn: wknd 4f out) | s.h | **13** | 12/1 | 18 | — |
| 811[12] | **Gentleman Sid (49)** (PGMurphy) **6-8-11** NAdams(1) (bhd fnl 7f) | nk | **14** | 25/1 | 30 | 5 |

(SP 120.2%) **14 Rn**

**3m 45.7** (4.70) CSF £126.58 CT £1,118.31 TOTE £10.30: £2.70 £2.20 £4.50 (£39.50) Trio £39.90 OWNER Mr P. J. Sheehan (FINDON) BRED W. and R. Barnett Ltd

WEIGHT FOR AGE 4yo-3lb

**Coleridge**, second on four successive occasions on the sand in the winter, has been sweetened up by a couple of runs over hurdles. (16/1)
**944 Lalindi (IRE)** found it impossible to concede so much weight to the winner. (8/1)
**759 Courbaril** is running consistently well at the moment, but a lack of finishing speed was again the problem. (9/1)
**759* The Lad** came off his true line in the final quarter-mile and was never going to get to grips. (15/8)
**944 Durham** may have been thinking about his recent hard race at Salisbury. (11/1)
**Fabulous Mtoto** proved impossible to settle and had little hope of lasting home. (16/1)
**647 Brandon Prince (IRE)** (9/1: 12/1-8/1)

## 1064 ROMAN CITY H'CAP (0-90) (3-Y.O+) (Class C)

3-40 (3-43) **5f 11y** £5,475.00 (£1,650.00: £800.00: £375.00) Stalls: High GOING minus 0.45 sec per fur (F)

| | | | | SP | RR | SF |
|---|---|---|---|---|---|---|
| 814[2] | **To the Roof (IRE) (79)** (PWHarris) **4-9-9** GHind(1) (a.p: swtchd rt over 2f out: r.o to ld last strides) | — | **1** | 100/30[1] | 93 | 76 |
| 812[14] | **Tart and a Half (75)** (BJMeehan) **4-9-5** MTebbutt(5) (w ldr: led 3f out: hdd last strides) | nk | **2** | 25/1 | 88 | 71 |
| | **Ann's Pearl (IRE) (73)** (JWHills) **5-9-3** BThomson(8) (a.p: edgd lft over 1f out: one pce) | 3 | **3** | 10/1 | 77 | 60 |
| 862[2] | **Jucea (63)** (JLSpearing) **7-8-7** SSanders(12) (lw: hdwy over 1f out: r.o ins fnl f) | nk | **4** | 9/2[2] | 66 | 49 |
| 928[2] | **Sir Joey (USA) (82)** (PGMurphy) **7-9-9**(3) SDrowne(10) (nvr nr to chal) | 2½ | **5** | 6/1[3] | 77 | 60 |
| 862* | **Ansellman (75)** (JBerry) **6-9-5b** JCarroll(7) (prom over 3f) | 1¼ | **6** | 8/1 | 66 | 49 |
| 862[6] | **La Belle Dominique (54)** (SGKnight) **4-7-12** FNorton(9) (stumbled s: no hdwy fnl 2f) | hd | **7** | 20/1 | 44 | 27 |
| 928[23] | **Mister Jolson (76)** (RJHodges) **7-9-6** RCochrane(11) (lw: nvr trbld ldrs) | 1¼ | **8** | 6/1[3] | 62 | 45 |
| | **Law Commission (79)** (DRCElsworth) **6-9-9** AProcter(4) (s.i.s: a bhd) | hd | **9** | 33/1 | 65 | 48 |
| 814[14] | **Louisville Belle (IRE) (52)** (MDIUsher) **7-7-10** NAdams(2) (bhd fnl 2f) | 1 | **10** | 33/1 | 35 | 18 |
| 989[4] | **Polly Golightly (82)** (MBlanshard) **3-8-12b**(5) CAdamson(6) (led 2f) | 3 | **11** | 14/1 | 55 | 29 |
| 812[11] | **Tinker Osmaston (70)** (MSSaunders) **5-9-0** JFEgan(3) (outpcd) | 6 | **12** | 20/1 | 24 | 7 |

(SP 116.0%) **12 Rn**

**60.1 secs** (0.20 under best) (-0.40) CSF £69.40 CT £690.26 TOTE £4.90: £1.40 £3.90 £3.80 (£55.60) Trio £170.20 OWNER Mrs P. W. Harris (BERKHAMSTED) BRED Pendley Farm

LONG HANDICAP Louisville Belle (IRE) 7-9

WEIGHT FOR AGE 3yo-9lb

**814 To the Roof (IRE)**, 12lb higher than when winning at Musselburgh, is in good form and it looked like matters were always under control. (100/30)
**Tart and a Half** has not yet had the blinkers re-fitted this season, but ran an honest race here. (25/1)
**Ann's Pearl (IRE)** won this race last year and seems to run some of her best races here. (10/1: 7/1-11/1)
**862 Jucea** only got going late in the day. (9/2)
**928 Sir Joey (USA)**, upped 5lb, ran better than his finishing position suggests. (6/1)
**862* Ansellman** could well have found the ground too lively. (8/1)
**989 Polly Golightly** (14/1: 10/1-16/1)

## 1065 SOMERSET CONDITIONS STKS (4-Y.O+) (Class C)

4-10 (4-10) **1m 3f 144y** £5,343.50 (£1,721.00: £835.50) Stalls: Low GOING minus 0.45 sec per fur (F)

| | | | | SP | RR | SF |
|---|---|---|---|---|---|---|
| | **Royal Scimitar (USA) (92)** (PFICole) **4-8-10** RCochrane(1) (mde all: clr over 1f out: easily) | — | **1** | 8/11[1] | 90+ | 37 |
| 751[4] | **Charter** (MajorDNChappell) **5-8-10** BThomson(3) (chsd wnr: rdn 3f out: edgd rt wl over 1f out: no imp) | 8 | **2** | 2/1[2] | 79 | 26 |
| 818[6] | **High Shot** (GLewis) **6-9-0** GHind(2) (hld up & plld hrd: rdn 2f out: no rspnse) | 6 | **3** | 5/1[3] | 75 | 22 |

919[5] **Commoner (USA) (112)** (RHannon) **4-9-2** JCarroll(4) (Withdrawn not under Starter's orders: colic) .................. **W** — —
(SP 107.9%) **3 Rn**

**2m 29.9** (3.20) CSF £2.36 TOTE £1.60: (£1.90) OWNER H R H Prince Fahd Salman (WHATCOMBE) BRED Newgate Stud Farm Inc
**Royal Scimitar (USA)** proved far too good for his two rivals. (8/11)
**751 Charter** was in trouble early in the home straight. (2/1: op 7/2)
**818 High Shot** was stepping up in distance. (5/1)

## 1066 RADSTOCK H'CAP (0-95) (3-Y.O+) (Class C)

4-40 (4-42) **1m 2f 46y** £5,280.00 (£1,590.00: £770.00: £360.00) Stalls: Low GOING minus 0.45 sec per fur (F)

| | | | | SP | RR | SF |
|---|---|---|---|---|---|---|
| 410[6] | **Bardon Hill Boy (IRE) (78)** (BHanbury) **4-8-9**(7) MartinDwyer(2) (lw: a.p: hrd rdn over 1f out: led ins fnl f: r.o) | — | **1** | 10/1 | 90 | 66 |
| 968[4] | **Zermatt (IRE) (63)** (MDIUsher) **6-8-1** NAdams(3) (lw: led over 3f: led over 2f out tl ins fnl f) | 1¼ | **2** | 10/1 | 73 | 49 |
| 581[11] | **Easy Listening (USA) (84)** (RCharlton) **4-9-8** SSanders(7) (hld up: hrd rdn 3f out: styd on fnl f) | 4 | **3** | 2/1 [1] | 88 | 64 |
| 646[3] | **Quality (IRE) (80)** (WAO'Gorman) **3-8-3b** EmmaO'Gorman(8) (chsd ldr: led 7f out tl over 2f out: sn wknd) | 4 | **4** | 9/1 | 78 | 39 |
| 580[16] | **Glide Path (USA) (90)** (JWHills) **7-10-0** BThomson(5) (lw: prom tl wknd over 2f out) | 2½ | **5** | 9/1 | 84 | 60 |
| 650[6] | **Silently (78)** (IABalding) **4-9-2** RCochrane(4) (nvr trbld ldrs) | 2½ | **6** | 3/1 [2] | 68 | 44 |
| 920[11] | **Statajack (IRE) (83)** (DRCElsworth) **8-9-7b** AProcter(1) (lw: a bhd) | 3 | **7** | 16/1 | 68 | 44 |
| 871[13] | **Fairy Knight (73)** (RHannon) **4-8-11b** JCarroll(9) (a bhd) | 3 | **8** | 11/1 | 53 | 29 |
| | **Sweet Pavlova (USA) (66)** (PFICole) **4-7-11**(7) DavidO'Neill(6) (sddle slipped s: gd hdwy 7f out: rn wd bnd over 5f out: sn lost pl: t.o) | dist | **9** | 8/1 [3] | — | — |

(SP 121.8%) **9 Rn**

**2m 7.2** (-0.30) CSF £96.34 CT £259.81 TOTE £12.00: £2.60 £1.70 £1.60 (£30.00) Trio £29.80 OWNER Ms Mary Breslin (NEWMARKET) BRED John McNamee in Ireland
WEIGHT FOR AGE 3yo-15lb
OFFICIAL EXPLANATION **Swwet Pavlove (USA): his saddle slipped coming out of the stalls.**
**Bardon Hill Boy (IRE)** was 4lb lower than when winning on the Fibresand a year ago. (10/1: op 6/1)
**968 Zermatt (IRE)** has yet to win beyond a mile. (10/1)
**Easy Listening (USA)** broke the course record here last year. Struggling early in the home straight, he plugged on in the style of a stayer. (2/1)
**646 Quality (IRE)** should have been suited by this return to ten. (9/1: op 6/1)
**Glide Path (USA)** needs to return to a mile and a half. (9/1: 5/1-10/1)
**Sweet Pavlova (USA)** (8/1: op 12/1)

T/Plpt: £24.70 (478.2 Tckts). T/Qdpt: £12.60 (38.97 Tckts). KH

# 1032-BEVERLEY (R-H) (Good to firm)

## Saturday May 11th

WEATHER: fine WIND: mod half against

## 1067 KIPLINGCOTE (S) STKS (3-Y.O) (Class F)

2-25 (2-29) **1m 1f 207y** £2,875.00 (£800.00: £385.00) Stalls: High GOING minus 0.21 sec per fur (GF)

| | | | | SP | RR | SF |
|---|---|---|---|---|---|---|
| 849[5] | **Poly My Son (IRE) (50)** (MRChannon) **3-9-0** KDarley(12) (mde all: styd on u.p fnl 2f: unchal) | — | **1** | 7/2 [1] | 51 | 7 |
| | **Irish Oasis (IRE) (50)** (BSRothwell) **3-9-0** MFenton(13) (bit bkwd: a chsng ldrs: styd on fnl f: nt rch wnr) | 1¼ | **2** | 20/1 | 49 | 5 |
| | **How Could-I (IRE) (40)** (TDEasterby) **3-8-9** MBirch(2) (bit bkwd: b.nr fore: sn chsng ldrs: one pce fnl 2f) | ½ | **3** | 10/1 | 43 | — |
| | **Lebedinski (IRE)** (MrsPSly) **3-8-9** ACulhane(14) (w'like: bit bkwd: b.nr fore: s.i.s: bhd: gd hdwy 2f out: styd on: nt rch ldrs) | 2½ | **4** | 25/1 | 39 | — |
| 899[6] | **Crystal Fast (USA) (50)** (PAKelleway) **3-9-0** KFallon(8) (lw: a.p: sn rdn along: one pce fnl 2f) | 1½ | **5** | 5/1 [2] | 42 | — |
| 525[12] | **Cinnamon Stick (IRE) (36)** (PSFelgate) **3-9-0** GDuffield(1) (bhd tl styd on u.p fnl 2f) | ½ | **6** | 15/2 [3] | 41 | — |
| 861[12] | **In Cahoots** (AGNewcombe) **3-9-0** JQuinn(9) (hld up: rdn 5f out: styd on fnl 2f) | ¾ | **7** | 8/1 | 40 | — |
| 784[8] | **Chipalata** (TWDonnelly) **3-9-0** CRutter(4) (gd hdwy over 3f out: sn prom: wknd over 1f out: eased) | 6 | **8** | 33/1 | 30 | — |
| 522[14] | **Still Here (IRE) (48)** (MJHeaton-Ellis) **3-8-9**(5) AmandaSanders(11) (lw: w ldrs: effrt over 2f out: wknd over 1f out) | ½ | **9** | 9/1 | 29 | — |
| 885[4] | **My Kind (53)** (NTinkler) **3-8-9b** KimTinkler(3) (prom: rdn along 4f out: wknd over 2f out) | nk | **10** | 8/1 | 24 | — |
| 637[5] | **Alpheton Prince (40)** (JLHarris) **3-8-11**(3) PMcCabe(10) (lw: bhd: sme hdwy over 3f out: sn wknd) | 1½ | **11** | 14/1 | 26 | — |
| 867[13] | **Turbo North (52)** (MDods) **3-9-0v[1]** DeanMcKeown(7) (hld up: sme hdwy on outside over 3f out: sn wknd) | 12 | **12** | 16/1 | 7 | — |
| 803[14] | **Panama Jive (IRE) (46)** (MJohnston) **3-8-9** JWeaver(6) (chsd ldrs: sn rdn along: lost pl over 4f out) | 2½ | **13** | 9/1 | — | — |
| 703[15] | **Kudos Blue (35)** (JDBethell) **3-8-9** TWilliams(5) (hld up & plld hrd: gd hdwy on outside to chse ldrs 7f out: lost pl over 2f out) | 18 | **14** | 16/1 | — | — |

(SP 131.9%) **14 Rn**

**2m 11.8** (9.30) CSF £70.11 TOTE £3.90: £2.00 £7.10 £3.00 (£37.40) Trio £165.40; £191.12 to Windsor 13/5/96. OWNER Sheet & Roll Convertors Ltd (UPPER LAMBOURN) BRED Newlands House Stud
Bt in 8,000 gns
**849 Poly My Son (IRE)**, given a positive ride over this two furlong shorter trip, had to be kept right up to his work but he never looked like being overhauled, even in this poor race by selling standards. (7/2)
**Irish Oasis (IRE)** looked in need of the outing but stuck on strongly inside the last. (20/1)
**How Could-I (IRE)** looked as if the outing would do him good. Flat out two furlongs from home, he could make no impression on the winner. (10/1: 8/1-12/1)
**Lebedinski (IRE)** looked on the burly side. After losing ground at the start, she made up a good deal in the final quarter-mile. Presumably she is capable of better. (25/1)
**899 Crystal Fast (USA)** is not an easy ride and needs plenty of driving. (5/1)
**658 Panama Jive (IRE)** (9/1: op 6/1)

## 1068 HYPAC H'CAP (0-70) (3-Y.O) (Class E)

2-55 (3-01) **7f 100y** £4,056.75 (£1,224.00: £594.50: £279.75) Stalls: High GOING minus 0.21 sec per fur (GF)

| | | | | SP | RR | SF |
|---|---|---|---|---|---|---|
| 851[4] | **Smarter Charter (58)** (MrsJRRamsden) **3-8-9** KFallon(6) (lw: sn outpcd & rdn along: hdwy & swtchd lft over 2f out: styd on strly to ld ins fnl f: readily) | — | **1** | 7/1 [3] | 67 | 44 |

| Form | Horse | Dist | Pos | SP | RR | SF |
|---|---|---|---|---|---|---|
| $614^{11}$ | **Ivor's Deed (51)** (CFWall) **3-8-2**$^{ow2}$ GDuffield(3) (sn chsng ldrs: edgd rt & led over 1f out: hdd & nt qckn ins fnl f) | 2½ | **2** | 13/2[2] | 43 | 30 |
| $734^{4}$ | **Mellors (IRE) (60)** (JARToller) **3-8-11** JWeaver(9) (led tl over 1f out: one pce) | 2 | **3** | 8/1 | 59 | 36 |
| $824^{15}$ | **Camionneur (IRE) (56)** (TDEasterby) **3-8-7** WJO'Connor(11) (a chsng ldrs: one pce fnl 2f) | 1¼ | **4** | 16/1 | 53 | 30 |
| | **The Barnsley Belle (IRE) (48)** (JLEyre) **3-7-13** JQuinn(15) (a chsng ldrs: one pce fnl 2f) | s.h | **5** | 20/1 | 45 | 22 |
| $976^{2}$ | **Silverdale Knight (60)** (KWHogg) **3-8-11** DeanMcKeown(4) (chsd ldrs: sn rdn along: wknd over 1f out) | 3 | **6** | 4/1[1] | 50 | 27 |
| $638^{13}$ | **Mullagh Hill Lad (IRE) (57)** (BAMcMahon) **3-8-8** GCarter(14) (lw: bhd tl styd on fnl 2f) | 1¾ | **7** | 14/1 | 43 | 20 |
| $873^{10}$ | **Katie Komaite (60)** (CaptJWilson) **3-8-11** CRutter(13) (nvr nr ldrs) | 1¾ | **8** | 16/1 | 43 | 20 |
| $827^{18}$ | **Kernof (IRE) (62)** (MDHammond) **3-8-13** JFortune(12) (lw: bhd: sme hdwy 2f out: n.d) | 1 | **9** | 20/1 | 43 | 20 |
| $775^{11}$ | **Veshca Lady (IRE) (55)** (EWeymes) **3-8-6** JFanning(7) (in tch: effrt over 2f out: sn wknd) | s.h | **10** | 16/1 | 35 | 12 |
| $686^{12}$ | **Eccentric Dancer (46)** (MPBielby) **3-7-11**$^{ow1}$ DaleGibson(2) (sn bhd) | 1 | **11** | 25/1 | 24 | — |
| $882^{15}$ | **Briganoone (45)** (SRBowring) **3-7-10** NCarlisle(10) (rr div: hmpd over 2f out: n.d) | 2 | **12** | 12/1 | 19 | — |
| *$897^{3}$* | **Miss Offset (48)** (MJohnston) **3-7-13b** TWilliams(8) (chsd ldrs tl wknd over 1f out) | s.h | **13** | 13/2[2] | 22 | — |
| $824^{13}$ | **Too Hasty (70)** (TDEasterby) **3-9-7** MBirch(16) (in tch tl wknd qckly 2f out) | 1¼ | **14** | 10/1 | 41 | 18 |
| *$605^{2}$* | **Down The Yard (45)** (MCChapman) **3-7-10** NKennedy(1) (a in rr) | s.h | **15** | 16/1 | 16 | — |
| $824^{16}$ | **Khabar (69)** (RBastiman) **3-9-1**$^{(5)}$ HBastiman(5) (s.s: a bhd) | 6 | **16** | 16/1 | 27 | 4 |

(SP 136.5%) **16 Rn**

**1m 35.0** (3.00) CSF £54.09 CT £361.21 TOTE £7.70: £2.40 £1.10 £2.10 £6.80 (£96.10) Trio £384.50; £335.84 to Windsor 13/5/96. OWNER Mrs Alison Iles (THIRSK) BRED Carlton Consultants Ltd

LONG HANDICAP Briganoone 7-9 Down The Yard 7-9

**851 Smarter Charter** was hobdayed after showing little in two starts at two. Soon struggling to go the pace, when he did pick up the bit, he flew and was able to take things easy near the line. He should keep a step ahead of the Handicapper for a while as he is still learning. (7/1: op 4/1)

**Ivor's Deed** moved up travelling strongly to show ahead over a furlong out. Galloping right as he took the lead, in the end he proved no match, but this was his best effort yet. (13/2)

**734 Mellors (IRE)** set a strong pace but could only stay on at one speed. This was a step up on his Thirsk effort. (8/1)

**Camionneur (IRE)** has yet to be re-equipped with the blinkers that helped him show improvement at two. (16/1)

**The Barnsley Belle (IRE)** proved willing but could only stick on at the one pace. (20/1)

**976 Silverdale Knight**, unable to dominate, dropped out over a furlong out. (4/1)

## 1069 ROTHMANS ROYALS NORTH SOUTH CHALLENGE SERIES H'CAP (0-85) (3-Y.O+) (Class D)

3-25 (3-30) **1m 100y** £4,510.00 (£1,360.00: £660.00: £310.00) Stalls: High GOING minus 0.21 sec per fur (GF)

| Form | Horse | Dist | Pos | SP | RR | SF |
|---|---|---|---|---|---|---|
| $827^{13}$ | **Coureur (61)** (MDHammond) **7-8-6** JQuinn(14) (chsd ldrs: styd on wl u.p to ld ins fnl f) | — | **1** | 12/1 | 71 | 30 |
| $851^{2}$ | **Bollin Frank (59)** (TDEasterby) **4-8-4** MBirch(1) (lw: racd wd: chsd ldrs: edgd rt & led over 1f out: hdd & nt qckn towards fin) | 1 | **2** | 7/1[2] | 67 | 26 |
| $933^{18}$ | **Tertium (IRE) (77)** (MartynWane) **4-9-8** JFortune(15) (sn chsng ldrs: hdwy & ev ch over 1f out: kpt on same pce) | 2 | **3** | 10/1 | 81 | 40 |
| $739^{3}$ | **Gymcrak Flyer (62)** (GHolmes) **5-8-7** KFallon(2) (b.hind: sn bhd & pushed along: gd hdwy on outside over 2f out: kpt on same pce appr fnl f) | 1¼ | **4** | 11/2[1] | 64 | 23 |
| $933^{8}$ | **Karinska (62)** (MCChapman) **6-8-4**$^{(3)}$ DRMcCabe(11) (bmpd s: bhd: hdwy whn hmpd over 2f out: kpt on ins fnl f: nrst fin) | ½ | **5** | 16/1 | 63 | 22 |
| $935^{7}$ | **Nashaat (USA) (63)** (MCChapman) **8-8-5**$^{(3)}$ PMcCabe(8) (swtg: bhd: hdwy & nt clr run over 1f out: styd on towards fin) | nk | **6** | 16/1 | 63 | 22 |
| $933^{11}$ | **Rambo Waltzer (70)** (DNicholls) **4-8-8**$^{(7)}$ JBramhill(3) (kpt on fnl 2f: nvr nr ldrs) | ½ | **7** | 10/1 | 70 | 29 |
| $827^{14}$ | **Roseate Lodge (51)** (SEKettlewell) **10-7-10** NKennedy(4) (bhd tl styd on fnl 2f) | ½ | **8** | 25/1 | 50 | 9 |
| $802^{2}$ | **Percy Braithwaite (IRE) (83)** (MJohnston) **4-10-0** JWeaver(9) (lw: swvd rt s: in tch: rdn over 4f out: n.d after) | 2 | **9** | 11/2[1] | 78 | 37 |
| $629^{10}$ | **Elpidos (69)** (MDHammond) **4-9-0** JFanning(6) (bhd & rdn along: n.d) | 4 | **10** | 12/1 | 56 | 15 |
| $765^{17}$ | **Touch a Million (USA) (71)** (EALDunlop) **4-9-2v** KDarley(17) (mde most tl hdd & wknd over 1f out) | hd | **11** | 15/2[3] | 58 | 17 |
| $935^{5}$ | **Pride of Pendle (75)** (DNicholls) **7-9-6** NConnorton(12) (hld up: effrt & n.m.r over 2f out: n.d) | 3 | **12** | 7/1[2] | 56 | 15 |
| $713^{9}$ | **Legal Issue (IRE) (60)** (WWHaigh) **4-8-5** GDuffield(7) (w ldrs tl wknd over 1f out) | 3½ | **13** | 14/1 | 35 | — |
| $763^{6}$ | **Always Happy (79)** (JRFanshawe) **3-8-11** DHarrison(16) (trckd ldrs: effrt over 2f out: wkng whn n.m.r over 1f out) | 2½ | **14** | 8/1 | 49 | — |
| $883^{14}$ | **Balata Bay (53)** (JJBirkett) **5-7-12**$^{ow2}$ TWilliams(13) (a wl bhd) | 16 | **15** | 100/1 | — | — |
| | **Mountgate (76)** (MPBielby) **4-9-7** WJO'Connor(5) (hung lft thrght: chsd ldrs tl wknd over 2f out: eased) | 10 | **16** | 16/1 | — | — |

(SP 141.4%) **16 Rn**

**1m 48.5** (4.50) CSF £99.35 CT £868.50 TOTE £15.20: £3.70 £2.20 £2.30 £1.80 (£146.30) Trio £652.10 OWNER Mr Frank Hanson (MIDDLEHAM) BRED Gainsborough Stud Management Ltd

LONG HANDICAP Balata Bay 6-9 Roseate Lodge 7-9

WEIGHT FOR AGE 3yo-13lb

**OFFICIAL EXPLANATION Mountgate: hung left throughout the race.**

**Coureur**, ridden by a lady when showing little on his previous two outings, this time was back on a track he really likes and, well handled, did just enough. (12/1)

**851 Bollin Frank** was not helped by his high draw. Forced to race wide to the first bend, he had to give best in the closing stages, but is running really well at present. (7/1)

**802 Tertium (IRE)**, badly drawn at Thirsk, ran much better and had every chance over a furlong out. (10/1)

**739 Gymcrak Flyer** struggled to go the pace. After making up a deal of ground to get onto the heels of the leaders over a furlong out, she could then find no more, but she should be spot on next time. (11/2)

**Karinska**, bumped at the start, did not have the run of the race and, in the circumstances, did well to finish so close. (16/1)

**718 Nashaat (USA)** was another to meet trouble in running. (16/1)

**802 Percy Braithwaite (IRE)** never looked a serious threat after diving right at the start. (11/2)

## 1070 DON & RAYMOND GIBBON MEMORIAL H'CAP (0-70) (4-Y.O+) (Class E)

3-55 (3-59) **2m 35y** £3,834.00 (£1,152.00: £556.00: £258.00) Stalls: High GOING minus 0.21 sec per fur (GF)

| Form | Horse | Dist | Pos | SP | RR | SF |
|---|---|---|---|---|---|---|
| *$214^{3}$* | **Royal Expression (59)** (MrsMReveley) **4-9-8** KDarley(4) (lw: hld up: hdwy on outside 6f out: led over 2f out: hld on wl towards fin) | — | **1** | 9/1 | 73 | 32 |
| $852^{*}$ | **Izza (41)** (WStorey) **5-8-7** JQuinn(13) (lw: trckd ldrs: chal over 1f out: nt qckn towards fin) | ½ | **2** | 11/4[1] | 55 | 17 |
| $872^{7}$ | **Hullbank (55)** (WWHaigh) **6-9-7b**[1] GDuffield(8) (bhd: hdwy 6f out: styd on same pce fnl 2f) | 5 | **3** | 12/1 | 64 | 26 |

625* **Sudden Spin (46)** (JNorton) **6-8-12** KFallon(7) (lw: in tch: pushed along & outpcd over 5f out: styd on fnl 3f).nk **4** 7/2 2 54 16
852 2 **Chakalak (50)** (SDow) **8-8-11**(5) ADaly(10) (b: prom: n.m.r over 2f out: one pce)...2½ **5** 15/2 56 18
625 12 **Hotspur Street (60)** (MWEasterby) **4-9-4**(5) GParkin(5) (trckd ldrs: effrt 2f out: one pce)...nk **6** 12/1 66 25
852 3 **Great Oration (IRE) (40)** (FWatson) **7-8-6** JWeaver(9) (hld up: effrt over 4f out: hdwy on ins over 2f out: sn wknd)...5 **7** 7/1 3 41 3
*898 7* **Comtec's Legend (30)** (JFBottomley) **6-7-10** NKennedy(3) (in tch: edgd lft & outpcd over 2f out: no imp after)...hd **8** 12/1 30 —
**Vain Prince (53)** (NTinkler) **9-9-5b** LCharnock(14) (bit bkwd: chsd ldrs: drvn along 4f out: lost pl over 2f out)..4 **9** 14/1 50 12
**Greystyle (31)** (MBrittain) **6-7-8**(3)ow1 DWright(2) (bit bkwd: w ldr: led over 3f out tl over 2f out: sn wknd)...¾ **10** 50/1 27 —
**French Ivy (USA) (62)** (FMurphy) **9-10-0** JFanning(12) (bit bkwd: hld up & a bhd)...5 **11** 10/1 53 15
**Victoria Day (40)** (JAHarris) **4-8-3** DHarrison(11) (sn pushed along: a in rr)...1 **12** 33/1 30 —
609 13 **Can She Can Can (37)** (CSmith) **4-8-0** NCarlisle(6) (led tl over 3f out: sn wknd)...nk **13** 20/1 27 —
*558 4* ***Tancred Mischief (30)*** (WLBarker) **5-7-7**(3) NVarley(1) (Withdrawn not under Starter's orders: distressed at s)... **W** 20/1 — —
(SP 136.4%) **13 Rn**

**3m 42.8** (12.30) CSF £35.34 CT £295.34 TOTE £8.90: £2.20 £1.50 £2.40 (£17.40) Trio £131.30 OWNER Mr Les De La Haye (SALTBURN) BRED K. Panos
LONG HANDICAP Greystyle 7-3 Tancred Mischief 7-7
WEIGHT FOR AGE 4yo-3lb

**Royal Expression**, who has been in good form over hurdles, had stamina doubts going into the race but his rider had no worries about him getting the trip. After being hotly challenged, he held on well towards the finish. (9/1)
**852* Izza**, raised 9lb, raced on the inside and never really settled. She moved almost upsides a furlong out, but had to give best near the line. (11/4: 2/1-3/1)
**625 Hullbank**, in blinkers, stayed on at the one pace in the last two furlongs. (12/1)
**625* Sudden Spin** was heavily backed. Outpaced soon after halfway, he stuck on under pressure but was never going to get near the first two. (7/2: op 6/1)
**852 Chakalak** ran his usual race, being tapped for toe some way from home, but keeping on all the way to the line. (15/2)
**474 Hotspur Street** travelled strongly but, when he came under pressure two furlongs out, he could do no more than plod on at the one pace. (12/1)

## 1071 YORKSHIRE-TYNE TEES TELEVISION LIMITED STKS (0-80) (3-Y.O) (Class D)

4-25 (4-25) **1m 3f 216y** £3,743.00 (£1,124.00: £542.00: £251.00) Stalls: High GOING minus 0.21 sec per fur (GF)

SP RR SF

593* **General Macarthur (80)** (JLDunlop) **3-9-0** GDuffield(3) (lw: b.off fore: hld up: effrt & swtchd lft 3f out: led over 1f out: pushed out)...— **1** 10/11 1 84 5
938 5 **Classic Flyer (IRE) (87)** (SCWilliams) **3-8-9** AMackay(4) (trckd ldr: led over 5f out to 4f out: nt qckn fnl f).....1¾ **2** 5/1 3 77 —
570 3 **Madame Steinlen (80)** (BWHills) **3-8-9** KFallon(1) (led tl over 5f out: led 4f out tl over 1f out: kpt on same pce)...1¼ **3** 2/1 2 75 —
702 3 **Burnt Offering (65)** (CEBrittain) **3-9-0** KDarley(2) (lw: hld up: hdwy on outside 6f out: effrt over 3f out: outpcd over 1f out)...¾ **4** 14/1 79 —
(SP 109.0%) **4 Rn**

**2m 44.4** (12.00) CSF £5.16 TOTE £1.90: (£2.50) OWNER Mr Ian Cameron (ARUNDEL) BRED Lady Richard Wellesley and Grange Nominees

**593* General Macarthur** is a progressive sort well worth keeping on the right side in handicap company, and he always looked to have the situation in hand. (10/11: 8/11-Evens)
**938 Classic Flyer (IRE)** looked on the lean side and proved no match. (5/1)
**570 Madame Steinlen** did not appeal at all in the paddock. Allowed to make the running, she was easily picked off. (2/1)
**702 Burnt Offering** was hard at work some way from home. (14/1)

## 1072 WILLIAM HILL H'CAP (0-80) (3-Y.O+) (Class D)

4-55 (4-56) **1m 1f 207y** £4,410.75 (£1,326.00: £640.50: £297.75) Stalls: High GOING minus 0.21 sec per fur (GF)

SP RR SF

920 7 **Domitia (USA) (63)** (MBell) **4-9-0** MFenton(1) (b: hdwy over 4f out: led over 1f out: all out)...— **1** 7/1 3 77 31
787* **Darling Clover (57)** (DMorley) **4-8-8** GCarter(4) (lw: chsd ldr: led over 2f out: sn rdn: hdd over 1f out: nt qckn ins fnl f)...¾ **2** 11/10 1 70 24
890 11 **Hanbitooh (USA) (68)** (EALDunlop) **3-8-4** TWilliams(3) (hdwy u.p 4f out: styd on fnl 2f: nvr able to chal).........4 **3** 9/1 74 13
988 12 **Nordic Breeze (IRE) (73)** (ABailey) **4-9-10b** KDarley(7) (chsd ldrs: drvn along over 2f out: hung rt: kpt on one pce)...¾ **4** 11/2 2 78 32
995 9 **Rushen Raider (58)** (KWHogg) **4-8-4**(5) ADaly(6) (led tl over 2f out: wknd over 1f out)...1 **5** 16/1 62 16
771 10 **Maftun (USA) (63)** (GMMoore) **4-9-0** DaleGibson(2) (sn pushed along & outpcd: sme hdwy over 1f out: n.d).nk **6** 16/1 66 20
816 6 **Dr Edgar (67)** (MDods) **4-9-4** JFortune(8) (lw: trckd ldrs: rdn & outpcd over 3f out: grad wknd)...3 **7** 8/1 65 19
**Eric's Bett (70)** (FMurphy) **3-8-6** JFanning(5) (bit bkwd: a in rr)...10 **8** 10/1 52 —
613 9 **Roussi (USA) (64)** (DNicholls) **4-9-1** MBirch(9) (sme hdwy 4f out: sn wl outpcd & bhd)...7 **9** 10/1 35 —
(SP 126.6%) **9 Rn**

**2m 8.7** (6.20) CSF £16.06 CT £72.32 TOTE £8.20: £1.80 £1.20 £2.50 (£4.50) Trio £11.10 OWNER Mr Desmond Fitzgerald (NEWMARKET) BRED Wakefield Farm
WEIGHT FOR AGE 3yo-15lb

**920 Domitia (USA)** came from off the pace to get home with nothing at all to spare. (7/1)
**787* Darling Clover** lacks substance. After hitting the front, she made very hard work of it and was held near the line. It is doubtful if she has any improvement in her. (11/10: 11/8-10/11)
**668 Hanbitooh (USA)** made his rider work hard. Tending to wander, he stuck on at the one pace and lacked anything in the way of speed. A mile and a half will suit. (9/1: op 6/1)
**Nordic Breeze (IRE)**, making a quick reappearance, again wore blinkers but gave his rider problems by hanging right. (11/2)
**Rushen Raider** met trouble on his last outing four days ago, and made sure he was clear this time by making the running, but his stride shortened coming to the final furlong. (16/1)
**816 Dr Edgar** (8/1: 6/1-10/1)
**Eric's Bett**, having his first outing since changing stables, looked burly and had a run round at the back. He is capable of making his mark in this sort of company in due course. (10/1)

T/Plpt: £106.10 (129.21 Tckts). T/Qdpt: £8.80 (82.81 Tckts). WG

# 1045-LINGFIELD (L-H) (Good to firm, Firm back st)

## Saturday May 11th

WEATHER: overcast WIND: almost nil

### 1073 UNITED HOUSE H'CAP (0-80) (3-Y.O+) (Class D)

2-15 (2-16) **6f** £4,045.00 (£1,210.00: £580.00: £265.00) Stalls: High GOING minus 0.51 sec per fur (F)

| | | | | SP | RR | SF |
|---|---|---|---|---|---|---|
| $868^{6}$ | **Prima Silk (63)** (MJRyan) **5-9-2** TIves(14) (gd hdwy over 1f out: led ins fnl f: r.o wl) | — | 1 | $7/1^{3}$ | 71 | 36 |
| $846^{4}$ | **How's Yer Father (75)** (RJHodges) **10-10-0** BDoyle(9) (lost pl over 4f out: rallied over 1f out: led ins fnl f: sn hdd: r.o wl) | s.h | 2 | 12/1 | 83 | 48 |
| $893^{3}$ | **Denbrae (IRE) (69)** (DJGMurraySmith) **4-9-8** JReid(12) (rdn over 2f out: gd hdwy fnl f: r.o wl) | 1½ | 3 | $11/2^{2}$ | 73 | 38 |
| 814* | **So Intrepid (IRE) (73)** (JMBradley) **6-9-12** LDettori(7) (lw: a.p: rdn over 2f out: led 1f out tl ins fnl f: unable qckn) | 1½ | 4 | $5/1^{1}$ | 73 | 38 |
| $692^{9}$ | **Banzhaf (USA) (75)** (GLMoore) **3-9-4** SWhitworth(6) (lw: led to 1f out: sn wknd) | nk | 5 | 20/1 | 74 | 29 |
| $850^{5}$ | **Samsolom (65)** (PHowling) **8-9-4** PatEddery(2) (lw: b.hind: racd far side: a.p: rdn over 1f out: wknd fnl f) | 1 | 6 | 9/1 | 61 | 26 |
| | **Balance of Power (65)** (RAkehurst) **4-8-11**(7) TAshley(8) (hld up: rdn over 1f out: sn wknd) | 1½ | 7 | 12/1 | 57 | 22 |
| 631* | **Agwa (68)** (RJO'Sullivan) **7-9-7** WWoods(11) (spd over 4f) | ¾ | 8 | $11/2^{2}$ | 58 | 23 |
| $554^{9}$ | **Sharp 'n Smart (70)** (BSmart) **4-9-9** TQuinn(5) (a.p: ev ch over 1f out: wknd fnl f) | 1 | 9 | 16/1 | 58 | 23 |
| *$380^{4}$* | **Sharp Imp (51)** (RMFlower) **6-8-4b** DBiggs(4) (a.p: rdn over 2f out: wknd fnl f) | ½ | 10 | 14/1 | 37 | 2 |
| $1016^{10}$ | **Ashtina (70)** (BAPearce) **11-9-9** MHills(1) (racd far side: spd over 4f) | 1 | 11 | 33/1 | 54 | 19 |
| $846^{7}$ | **Moujeeb (USA) (62)** (PatMitchell) **6-9-1v** AClark(13) (lw: a bhd) | 2½ | 12 | 14/1 | 39 | 4 |
| $893^{12}$ | **Sizzling (61)** (RHannon) **4-8-11b**[1](3) DaneO'Neill(10) (lw: prom over 3f) | 1½ | 13 | 8/1 | 34 | — |
| | **Grey Legend (60)** (RMFlower) **3-8-3** DeclanO'Shea(3) (swtg: racd far side: a bhd) | 7 | 14 | 33/1 | 14 | — |
| | | | | (SP 126.3%) | **14 Rn** | |

**1m 10.4** (1.40) CSF £83.75 CT £461.30 TOTE £7.50: £2.00 £3.00 £2.40 (£40.10) Trio £66.90 OWNER Three Ply Racing (NEWMARKET) BRED R. M. Scott

WEIGHT FOR AGE 3yo-10lb

**868 Prima Silk** only got going below the distance, but she came storming through to sweep into the lead in the last 100 yards, and just held on. (7/1)

**846 How's Yer Father** began to pick up ground below the distance but, having poked a nostril in front inside the final furlong, he was passed only a few strides later by the winner. To his credit, he stuck on well and only just failed. (12/1: 8/1-14/1)

**893 Denbrae (IRE)**, out with the washing for much of the trip, only got going in the final furlong, but came storming through to take third. (11/2)

**814* So Intrepid (IRE)** managed to get to the front a furlong out, but was soon passed by the runner-up and failed to quicken. (5/1)

**Banzhaf (USA)** attempted to make all. Collared a furlong out, he had nothing left in reserve. (20/1)

**850 Samsolom**, one of three who elected to race on the far side, was close up until tiring in the final furlong. (9/1)

### 1074 OCS LADIES' H'CAP (0-80) (3-Y.O+) (Class E)

2-45 (2-48) **7f** £3,261.30 (£974.40: £466.20: £212.10) Stalls: High GOING minus 0.51 sec per fur (F)

| | | | | SP | RR | SF |
|---|---|---|---|---|---|---|
| 742* | **Apollo Red (54)** (AMoore) **7-10-1** MrsJMoore(15) (mde virtually all: r.o wl) | — | 1 | $7/1^{2}$ | 63 | 49 |
| *$530^{5}$* | **Bubble Wings (FR) (56)** (SPCWoods) **4-10-3** MissLHide(5) (hdwy over 1f out: r.o wl ins fnl f) | 1½ | 2 | $8/1^{3}$ | 62 | 48 |
| $583^{13}$ | **Superior Force (60)** (MissBSanders) **3-9-9** MissDianaJones(3) (lw: hld up: rdn over 2f out: r.o ins fnl f) | ½ | 3 | 16/1 | 64 | 38 |
| $814^{7}$ | **Stolen Melody (64)** (SDow) **4-10-11** MissYHaynes(7) (hdwy over 2f out: r.o ins fnl f) | nk | 4 | 16/1 | 68 | 54 |
| | **Moon Strike (FR) (74)** (SCWilliams) **6-11-7** MissIFoustok(9) (hld up: chsd wnr 3f out: ev ch 1f out: wknd ins fnl f) | 1 | 5 | $8/1^{3}$ | 76 | 62 |
| *$854^{7}$* | **Love Legend (50)** (DWPArbuthnot) **11-9-11** MrsDArbuthnot(4) (hld up: rdn over 2f out: one pce) | ½ | 6 | 20/1 | 50 | 36 |
| | **Dancing Heart (69)** (BJMeehan) **4-11-2** MissJAllison(12) (chsd wnr 4f: wknd over 1f out) | ½ | 7 | 14/1 | 68 | 54 |
| $713^{4}$ | **Edgar Kirby (53)** (PWHarris) **5-10-0** MissAElsey(6) (hld up: rdn over 1f out: sn wknd) | 2½ | 8 | $8/1^{3}$ | 47 | 33 |
| $1010^{4}$ | **Mr Cube (IRE) (59)** (JMBradley) **6-10-2v**(4) MissLKerr(2) (hdwy over 1f out: wknd fnl f) | 1¼ | 9 | 14/1 | 50 | 36 |
| | **Norsong (53)** (RAkehurst) **4-10-0** MrsAPerrett(10) (prom over 4f) | s.h | 10 | $7/1^{2}$ | 44 | 30 |
| $752^{5}$ | **Breezed Well (45)** (BRCambidge) **10-9-6**ow6 MrsHNoonan(1) (a bhd) | 1 | 11 | 25/1 | 33 | 13 |
| $887^{6}$ | **Persian Affair (IRE) (57)** (TJNaughton) **5-10-4** MrsSBosley(13) (lw: bhd fnl 2f) | ½ | 12 | $9/2^{1}$ | 44 | 30 |
| | **Bold Habit (61)** (JPearce) **11-10-8** MrsLPearce(16) (a bhd) | 1¼ | 13 | $7/1^{2}$ | 45 | 31 |
| $819^{15}$ | **Craven Cottage (65)** (CJames) **3-9-10**(4) MissCCorbett(8) (bhd fnl 4f) | 8 | 14 | 33/1 | 31 | 5 |
| $755^{9}$ | **Mam'selle Bergerac (IRE) (65)** (PhilipMitchell) **3-9-10**(4) MissHMitchell(11) (a bhd) | 10 | 15 | 33/1 | 8 | — |
| *$185^{5}$* | **Thorny Bishop (40)** (BAPearce) **5-8-11b**(4) MrsSColville(14) (lw: prom 4f) | 5 | 16 | 33/1 | — | — |
| | | | | (SP 131.5%) | **16 Rn** | |

**1m 23.15** (1.55) CSF £61.80 CT £840.97 TOTE £7.70: £1.90 £2.10 £4.80 £3.70 (£31.30) Trio £529.00 OWNER Mr A. Moore (BRIGHTON) BRED Crest Stud Ltd

LONG HANDICAP Breezed Well 8-13

WEIGHT FOR AGE 3yo-12lb

**742* Apollo Red** dictated matters from the front. He may have been passed for a few strides below the distance by the runner-up, but kept on really strongly and was not going to be denied. (7/1)

**530 Bubble Wings (FR)**, making her debut on turf, at last found her feet below the distance but, despite storming through to take second prize, she found the line always beating her. (8/1)

**Superior Force** chased the leaders. He ran on inside the final furlong, but never looked like posing a serious threat. (16/1)

**814 Stolen Melody** began to take closer order over two furlongs from home. She ran on inside the final furlong and only just failed to take third prize. (16/1)

**Moon Strike (FR)**, who has changed stables since last year, moved into second place three furlongs from home, and looked a serious danger to the winner. He may well have got his head in front for a few strides below the distance, but tired inside the last 150 yards as lack of a recent run took its toll. (8/1: op 5/1)

**Love Legend** chased the leaders but failed to quicken in the last two furlongs. (20/1)

**Norsong** (7/1: op 4/1)

### 1075 TJH GROUP CHARTWELL STKS (Listed) (3-Y.O+ F & M) (Class A)

3-15 (3-16) **7f** £10,754.00 (£3,986.00: £1,918.00: £790.00: £320.00: £132.00) Stalls: High GOING minus 0.51 sec per fur (F)

| | | | | SP | RR | SF |
|---|---|---|---|---|---|---|
| | **Isla Del Rey (USA)** (SbinSuroor) **4-9-3** LDettori(6) (lw: mde all: qcknd over 1f out: rdn out) | — | 1 | $15/8^{1}$ | 104+ | 60 |

| | | | | SP | RR | SF |
|---|---|---|---|---|---|---|
| 889[4] | **Carranita (IRE) (107)** (BPalling) **6-9-8** TSprake(2) (hld up: chsd wnr over 1f out: hrd rdn: r.o wl) | ½ | **2** | 7/2[3] | 108 | 64 |
| 679[7] | **Christmas Kiss (80)** (RHannon) **4-9-3b[1]** MHills(1) (chsd wnr over 5f: unable qckn) | 2½ | **3** | 25/1 | 97 | 53 |
| 889[5] | **Branston Abby (IRE) (113)** (MJohnston) **7-9-8** JReid(3) (lw: hld up: rdn over 1f out: one pce) | 1½ | **4** | 5/2[2] | 99 | 55 |
| 874[6] | **More Than You Know (IRE)** (RHannon) **3-8-5** TQuinn(5) (lw: a bhd) | 1¼ | **5** | 11/1 | 91 | 35 |
| | **Paris Babe (93)** (DMorris) **4-9-3** PatEddery(4) (prom 5f) | 2 | **6** | 10/1 | 86 | 42 |

(SP 106.8%) **6 Rn**

**1m 21.34** (-0.26) CSF £7.92 TOTE £2.30: £1.50 £1.70 (£3.50) OWNER Godolphin (NEWMARKET) BRED Darley Stud Management Inc
WEIGHT FOR AGE 3yo-12lb

**Isla Del Rey (USA)**, winner of a maiden for John Oxx last year, has spent the winter in Dubai, where she won two of her four races. Looking in really good shape for this English debut, she was taken down some ten minutes early to the start. Making all the running, she quickened up the tempo just before the distance and, ridden along, kept the runner-up at bay. She looks useful and a step up to Group Three company is deserved. (15/8)
**889 Carranita (IRE)** ran a fine race in defeat. Throwing down her challenge from below the distance, she proved a real thorn in the side of the winner, but found that rival just a little bit too strong. (7/2)
**Christmas Kiss**, fitted with blinkers for the first time, gave chase to the winner but, collared for that position below the distance, failed to find another gear. (25/1)
**889 Branston Abby (IRE)**, covered up at the back of the field, was asked for her effort below the distance but disappointingly could only find one pace. (5/2)
**Paris Babe** (10/1: 7/1-12/1)

## 1076 TRIPLEPRINT DERBY TRIAL STKS (Gp 3) (3-Y.O) (Class A)

3-45 (3-46) **1m 3f 106y** £30,820.00 (£11,380.00: £5,440.00: £2,200.00: £850.00: £310.00) Stalls: High GOING minus 0.51 sec per fur (F)

| | | | | SP | RR | SF |
|---|---|---|---|---|---|---|
| 725[3] | **Mystic Knight (96)** (RCharlton) **3-8-7** LDettori(2) (mde all: rdn out) | — | **1** | 4/1[2] | 102 | 40 |
| 891* | **Heron Island (IRE) (105)** (PWChapple-Hyam) **3-8-7** JReid(3) (b.hind: hld up: rdn 2f out: r.o one pce) | 1¼ | **2** | 9/4[1] | 100 | 38 |
| 671[6] | **Zaforum (95)** (LMontagueHall) **3-8-7** DaneO'Neill(5) (chsd wnr: rdn over 2f out: one pce) | 1¼ | **3** | 33/1 | 99 | 37 |
| 677* | **Dovaly** (HRACecil) **3-8-7** PatEddery(1) (lw: a.p: rdn over 5f out: one pce fnl 3f) | ½ | **4** | 9/4[1] | 98 | 36 |
| | **Dismissed (USA) (106)** (PFICole) **3-8-7** TQuinn(6) (lw: nvr nr to chal) | hd | **5** | 5/1[3] | 98 | 36 |
| 903a[5] | **Acharne (103)** (CEBrittain) **3-8-7** BDoyle(4) (hld up: rdn over 2f out: 5th & btn whn nt clr run on ins ins fnl f) | 1 | **6** | 11/1 | 96 | 34 |

(SP 109.5%) **6 Rn**

**2m 25.79** (1.59) CSF £12.50 TOTE £4.60: £1.90 £1.40 (£5.60) OWNER Lady Oppenheimer (BECKHAMPTON) BRED Hascombe and Valiant Studs

IN-FOCUS: **None of these horses can be considered up to Classic standard after this race, and it was no surprise that the winner will head for the Italian Derby.**
**725 Mystic Knight** set little more than a moderate pace. Quickening things up in the straight, it turned into a three-furlong scrap and, rousted along from below the distance, he managed to keep his rivals at bay. (4/1)
**891* Heron Island (IRE)**, held up in fourth place, was asked for his effort a quarter of a mile from home. He stayed on for second but never seriously threatened the winner, and Derby hopes evaporated with this performance. (9/4)
**671 Zaforum** chased the winner from the start. Grimly trying to get on terms in the straight, he held on to second place until inside the final furlong. (33/1)
**677* Dovaly** looked absolutely superb in the paddock. Racing in third place, Eddery was already niggling him along at the top of the hill and the signs did not look good. In the straight, he could only keep on at one pace but, in a stronger-run race, he should soon regain the winning thread. (9/4)
**Dismissed (USA)**, held up at the back of the field, tried to get into the action in the straight but could never do so, and was clearly held when tightened up for room inside the final furlong. (5/1)
**903a Acharne**, held up at the back of the field, could never get in a blow. (11/1)

## 1077 CHAMPAGNE RUINART OAKS TRIAL STKS (Listed) (3-Y.O F) (Class A)

4-15 (4-15) **1m 3f 106y** £13,273.00 (£4,613.00: £2,231.50: £932.50) Stalls: High GOING minus 0.51 sec per fur (F)

| | | | | SP | RR | SF |
|---|---|---|---|---|---|---|
| | **Lady Carla** (HRACecil) **3-8-8** PatEddery(2) (lw: mde all: qcknd over 4f out: shkn up over 2f out: r.o wl) | — | **1** | 4/11[1] | 98+ | 46 |
| 813[4] | **Flame Valley (USA) (86)** (MRStoute) **3-8-8** LDettori(3) (lw: chsd wnr: rdn over 2f out: unable qckn) | 3½ | **2** | 15/2[3] | 93 | 41 |
| 723a[4] | **Moody's Cat (IRE)** (BWHills) **3-8-8** MHills(1) (lw: lost pl over 4f out: one pce fnl 3f) | 1¾ | **3** | 5/1[2] | 91 | 39 |
| | **Meribel (IRE)** (PWChapple-Hyam) **3-8-8** JReid(4) (a in rr) | 4 | **4** | 9/1 | 85 | 33 |

(SP 111.8%) **4 Rn**

**2m 25.03** (0.83) CSF £3.58 TOTE £1.40 (£3.30) OWNER Mr Wafic Said (NEWMARKET) BRED Meon Valley Stud
**Lady Carla** was all the rage in the market on this occasion and did not let her supporters down. Making it all, she quickened up the tempo running down the hill and had only the runner-up to worry about in the straight. Shaken up, she proved too strong for that rival in the final quarter-mile. This was a good performance and, whilst it did not set the world alight, she is sure to come on a lot for it. Not surprisingly, her odds were halved for the Oaks, and connections can look forward to a good run at Epsom. (4/11)
**813 Flame Valley (USA)** chased the winner and was the only horse who could stay with her when she quickened running down the hill. In the final quarter-mile, she had to accept defeat, but she should soon find a race. (15/2)
**723a Moody's Cat (IRE)**, outpaced over half a mile from home, could only struggle on in her own time in the straight. (5/1: 7/2-11/2)
**Meribel (IRE)**, a lengthy filly who looked as though she would come on for the run, was always in last place and was in trouble over half a mile from home. (9/1: 5/1-10/1)

## 1078 HSBC JAMES CAPEL H'CAP (0-100) (3-Y.O+) (Class C)

4-45 (4-45) **7f** £5,972.00 (£1,796.00: £868.00: £404.00) Stalls: High GOING minus 0.51 sec per fur (F)

| | | | | SP | RR | SF |
|---|---|---|---|---|---|---|
| 879[17] | **Neuwest (USA) (73)** (NJHWalker) **4-8-5**(3) JStack(4) (chsd ldr: led over 2f out: rdn out) | — | **1** | 14/1 | 82 | 55 |
| 876[20] | **Mister Fire Eyes (IRE) (72)** (CEBrittain) **4-8-7b** BDoyle(1) (a.p: rdn over 3f out: unable qckn fnl f) | 1½ | **2** | 8/1 | 78 | 51 |
| 876[16] | **Wild Rice (90)** (GWragg) **4-9-11** MHills(10) (lw: b: a.p: rdn over 2f out: one pce) | ¾ | **3** | 4/1[2] | 94 | 67 |
| 672[4] | **Mutamanni (USA) (82)** (HThomsonJones) **3-8-5** RHills(11) (hdwy over 2f out: rdn over 1f out: one pce) | 1½ | **4** | 7/2[1] | 82 | 43 |
| 956[4] | **Double Matt (IRE) (77)** (RHannon) **4-8-9**(3) DaneO'Neill(6) (hld up: rdn over 2f out: one pce) | 4 | **5** | 4/1[2] | 68 | 41 |
| 714* | **Golden Pound (USA) (83)** (MissGayKelleway) **4-9-4b** LDettori(3) (led over 4f) | ½ | **6** | 9/2[3] | 73 | 46 |
| 679[10] | **Prima Cominna (80)** (SPCWoods) **4-9-1** WWoods(7) (a bhd) | 1¼ | **7** | 8/1 | 67 | 40 |
| 809[18] | **Easy Choice (USA) (75)** (PhilipMitchell) **4-8-10** AClark(8) (lw: a bhd) | 2½ | **8** | 20/1 | 57 | 30 |
| 889[8] | **Shikari's Son (93)** (JCullinan) **9-10-0** TQuinn(9) (bhd fnl 2f) | hd | **9** | 20/1 | 74 | 47 |

| | | | | SP | RR | SF |
|---|---|---|---|---|---|---|
| | **Zamalek (USA) (87)** (GLMoore) **4-9-8** SWhitworth(5) (bhd fnl 3f) | 3½ | **10** | 33/1 | 60 | 33 |
| | | | | (SP 121.8%) | **10 Rn** | |

**1m 21.08** (-0.52) CSF £113.29 CT £506.29 TOTE £21.30: £3.30 £2.10 £1.90 (£27.30) Trio £51.50 OWNER Mr Paul Green (WANTAGE) BRED Robert Bloomer and Sharon L. Bloomer
WEIGHT FOR AGE 3yo-12lb
**633 Neuwest (USA)** chased the leader. Sent on over a quarter of a mile from home, he was scrubbed along to keep his rivals at bay. (14/1)
**450 Mister Fire Eyes (IRE)**, a leading light from the off, grimly tried to get on terms but was tapped for toe in the last 200 yards. (8/1)
**Wild Rice**, always well placed, failed to find the necessary turn of foot in the final quarter-mile. (4/1)
**672 Mutamanni (USA)**, held up off the pace, moved into contention over a quarter of a mile from home, but failed to find the necessary turn of foot from below the distance. A step up to a mile may be in his favour. (7/2)
**956 Double Matt (IRE)** chased the leaders but was made to look very pedestrian in the last two furlongs. (4/1)
**714* Golden Pound (USA)** took the field along but, collared over a quarter of a mile from home, was soon in trouble. (9/2)

## 1079 A A APPOINTMENTS MAIDEN STKS (3-Y.O+) (Class D)
5-15 (5-19) **1m 2f** £3,980.00 (£1,190.00: £570.00: £260.00) Stalls: High GOING minus 0.51 sec per fur (F)

| | | | | SP | RR | SF |
|---|---|---|---|---|---|---|
| | **Wot No Fax** (SDow) **3-8-11** WRyan(6) (str: scope: hld up: rdn over 2f out: led 1f out: edgd lft: r.o wl) | — | **1** | 50/1 | 78 | 28 |
| 860$^{7}$ | **Sadler's Realm** (MRStoute) **3-8-11** JReid(2) (a.p: led over 1f out: sn hdd: unable qckn) | ¾ | **2** | 11/1 | 77 | 27 |
| 820$^{3}$ | **Spartan Heartbeat (70)** (CEBrittain) **3-8-11** BDoyle(10) (swtg: s.s: hdwy 9f out: led 6f out to 4f out: led over 3f out tl over 1f out: one pce) | s.h | **3** | 4/1$^{3}$ | 77 | 27 |
| 821$^{6}$ | **Lead Him On (USA)** (PWHarris) **3-8-11** RHills(1) (hld up: rdn over 2f out: one pce) | 2½ | **4** | 5/1 | 73 | 23 |
| | **Western Playboy** (RHannon) **4-9-9**(3) DaneO'Neill(8) (nvr nr to chal) | 5 | **5** | 20/1 | 65 | 30 |
| | **Ingrina** (HRACecil) **3-8-6** PatEddery(7) (unf: scope: dwlt: hdwy 9f out: rdn over 2f out: eased whn btn over 1f out) | 3 | **6** | 11/4$^{1}$ | 55+ | 5 |
| | **Bold Classic (IRE)** (JLDunlop) **3-8-11** SWhitworth(12) (w'like: nvr nrr) | 1½ | **7** | 25/1 | 58 | 8 |
| 820$^{11}$ | **Seventh Edition** (DBurchell) **3-8-4**(7) TAshley(4) (prom over 4f) | ½ | **8** | 20/1 | 57 | 7 |
| 821$^{4}$ | **King Rufus** (JRArnold) **3-8-11** LDettori(11) (lw: led 4f: led 4f out tl over 3f out: wknd 2f out) | s.h | **9** | 7/2$^{2}$ | 57 | 7 |
| 860$^{11}$ | **Ela Agapi Mou (USA)** (GLewis) **3-8-8**(3) AWhelan(5) (a bhd) | 1¼ | **10** | 50/1 | 55 | 5 |
| 687$^{9}$ | **Liberatrice (FR)** (EALDunlop) **3-8-6** TQuinn(9) (a bhd) | 8 | **11** | 50/1 | 37 | — |
| | **Mannagar (IRE)** (JRPoulton) **4-9-12** TIves(3) (b: dwlt: a bhd: t.o) | 30 | **12** | 66/1 | — | — |
| | | | | (SP 114.6%) | **12 Rn** | |

**2m 8.06** (3.36) CSF £447.85 TOTE £31.30: £5.20 £2.80 £1.60 (£116.70) Trio £532.20 OWNER Kerniquip's Racing Partnership (EPSOM) BRED D. S. Rigby
WEIGHT FOR AGE 3yo-15lb
OFFICIAL EXPLANATION **King Rufus: was unable to act on the ground.**
**Wot No Fax**, a well-built gelding, caused a real shock here. Chasing the leaders, he came through to lead a furlong out and, despite drifting left, kept on well. (50/1)
**Sadler's Realm**, a leading light from the off, poked a nostril in front below the distance but no sooner had he got there than he was passed by the winner. (11/1: 7/1-12/1)
**820 Spartan Heartbeat** poked a whisker in front at the top of the hill. Collared below the distance, he failed to find another gear. (4/1)
**821 Lead Him On (USA)** chased the leaders, but could only struggle on at the one pace in the last two furlongs. (5/1)
**Western Playboy** stayed on past beaten horses in the straight. (20/1)
**Ingrina**, a plain filly who needs time, was soon in a handy position. Shaken up early in the straight, she failed to find the necessary turn of foot and the situation was accepted from below the distance. (11/4: 6/4-7/2)

T/Jkpt: £43,405.10 (1 Tckts). T/Plpt: £208.40 (115.31 Tckts). T/Qdpt: £30.00 (83.21 Tckts). AK

# 0895-**WOLVERHAMPTON (L-H) (Standard)**
## Saturday May 11th
WEATHER: overcast WIND: almost nil

## 1080 E.B.F. CARDIFF MEDIAN AUCTION MAIDEN STKS (2-Y.O) (Class F)
7-00 (7-04) **5f (Fibresand)** £2,846.00 (£848.00: £404.00: £182.00) Stalls: Low

| | | | | SP | RR | SF |
|---|---|---|---|---|---|---|
| *895$^{9}$* | **Just Loui** (WGMTurner) **2-9-0** TSprake(5) (bit bkwd: mde all: hrd drvn over 1f out: edgd rt fnl f: r.o wl) | — | **1** | 12/1 | 68 | 18 |
| | **Castle Ashby Jack** (PHowling) **2-9-0** FNorton(6) (w'like: bkwd: b.hind: trckd ldrs: shkn up to chal ent fnl f: unable qckn) | 1¾ | **2** | 9/4$^{1}$ | 62 | 12 |
| 848$^{9}$ | **Calchou** (CWFairhurst) **2-8-9** DeanMcKeown(7) (prom: rdn over 1f out: nt pce to chal) | ¾ | **3** | 6/1 | 55 | 5 |
| 880$^{3}$ | **Our Kevin** (KMcAuliffe) **2-9-0v$^{1}$** JFEgan(3) (prom: hrd drvn wl over 1f out: one pce) | ½ | **4** | 5/1$^{3}$ | 58 | 8 |
| | **Skelton Sovereign (IRE)** (RHollinshead) **2-8-9**(5) FLynch(8) (lt-f: dwlt: a bhd & outpcd) | 2 | **5** | 6/1 | 52 | 2 |
| 880$^{4}$ | **I'm Still Here** (JBerry) **2-8-9**(5) PRoberts(1) (prom on ins: rdn wl over 1f out: sn btn) | ¾ | **6** | 3/1$^{2}$ | 50 | — |
| *895$^{5}$* | **Colins Choice** (JLSpearing) **2-8-6**(3) SDrowne(2) (outpcd: a wl bhd) | 1½ | **7** | 8/1 | 40 | — |
| | **Master Foley** (NPLittmoden) **2-9-0** TGMcLaughlin(4) (leggy: unf: bit bkwd: swvd rt s: sn pushed along: a outpcd) | 9 | **8** | 33/1 | 16 | — |
| | | | | (SP 122.8%) | **8 Rn** | |

**64.0 secs** (5.30) CSF £40.10 TOTE £14.70: £5.10 £1.20 £2.90 (£24.20) OWNER Mr A. Poole (SHERBORNE) BRED M. A. Poole
**Just Loui** knew much more this time and, smartly into his stride, always just had the edge. (12/1)
**Castle Ashby Jack**, a late foal who looked the most backward, failed to land the gamble but must have shown something at home. (9/4: op 7/2)
**Calchou**, not yet quite right in her coat, lasted longer than she did on her debut but she will come good in time. (6/1)
**880 Our Kevin** did not benefit from the visor. (5/1)
**Skelton Sovereign (IRE)** missed the break and was always being taken off his legs. (6/1: op 4/1)
**880 I'm Still Here** had the inside berth and pressed the leaders until getting left behind from the turn into the straight. (3/1: op 2/1)

## 1081 EDINBURGH CLAIMING STKS (3-Y.O+) (Class F)
7-30 (7-33) **1m 1f 79y (Fibresand)** £2,381.00 (£656.00: £311.00) Stalls: Low

| | | | | SP | RR | SF |
|---|---|---|---|---|---|---|
| 641$^{15}$ | **Sweet Supposin (IRE) (77)** (CADwyer) **5-9-10v**(3) JStack(6) (hld up: hdwy on bit to chal 1f out: rdn to ld last stride) | — | **1** | 5/4$^{1}$ | 71 | 48 |

| | | | | SP | RR | SF |
|---|---|---|---|---|---|---|
| *654*7 | **David James' Girl (51)** (ABailey) **4-8-9**(7) IonaWands(5) (hld up: hdwy 5f out: led over 2f out: hrd drvn: ct post) | s.h | **2** | 13/2 | 60 | 37 |
| 884 10 | **Sandmoor Denim (64)** (SRBowring) **9-9-2**(5) CTeague(9) (hdwy ½-wy: ev ch 1f out: unable to qckn nr fin) | ½ | **3** | 9/2 3 | 64 | 41 |
| 821 15 | **Golden Filigree** (DTThom) **4-9-8** GHind(8) (dwlt: sme hdwy fnl 2f: nvr nrr) | 8 | **4** | 20/1 | 51 | 28 |
| *776** | **Spencer's Revenge (73)** (NTinkler) **7-9-13b** GBardwell(11) (hmpd after 2½f: sn hrd drvn: nvr nr ldrs) | 1½ | **5** | 3/1 2 | 54 | 31 |
| | **Evening Brigadier** (NMBabbage) **5-9-3** JQuinn(4) (chsd ldrs: led 4f out tl over 2f out: sn rdn & wknd) | 8 | **6** | 33/1 | 30 | 7 |
| 671 10 | **Glowing Reeds** (CNAllen) **3-8-0** TWilliams(1) (led after 2f to 4f out: sn rdn & wknd) | 4 | **7** | 20/1 | 20 | — |
| 748 12 | **Inca Bird (35)** (BAMcMahon) **3-8-4** GCarter(3) (prom 5f: wknd qckly: t.o) | 11 | **8** | 20/1 | 6 | — |
| | **Franklinsboy** (CDBroad) **4-9-1** NAdams(2) (in tch tl ½-wy: sn lost pl: t.o) | 30 | **9** | 33/1 | — | — |
| | **Rural Lad (54)** (RCSpicer) **7-9-1** DeanMcKeown(7) (led 2f: broke down & fell over 6f out: dead) | | **F** | 25/1 | — | — |
| | ***Orange Extreme*** (WClay) **5-8-7**(3) DWright(10) (Withdrawn not under Starter's orders: ref to ent stalls) | | **W** | 25/1 | — | — |
| | | | | (SP 128.8%) | **10 Rn** | |

**2m 4.2** (8.20) CSF £10.69 TOTE £2.20: £1.30 £1.80 £1.40 (£13.20) Trio £16.30 OWNER Binding Matters Ltd (NEWMARKET) BRED Ballylinch Stud Ltd
WEIGHT FOR AGE 3yo-14lb
Sweet Supposin (IRE) clmd PMiddleton £8,000
**498* Sweet Supposin (IRE)** travelled strongly throughout the race but found the filly in no mood to give best, and it was strength from the saddle that enabled him to shade it on the line. (5/4)
**521 David James' Girl** kicked for home turning in and battled on bravely, but this longer trip just caught her out. (13/2)
**778 Sandmoor Denim** was fighting for the lead until finding an extra effort beyond him nearing the line. (9/2: op 7/1)
**776* Spencer's Revenge**, badly impeded by the faller with less than a circuit to race, could never recover the lost ground. (3/1: op 2/1)

## 1082 BIRMINGHAM H'CAP (0-85) (4-Y.O+) (Class D)
8-00 (8-03) **1m 6f 166y (Fibresand)** £3,661.80 (£1,091.40: £520.20: £234.60) Stalls: High

| | | | | SP | RR | SF |
|---|---|---|---|---|---|---|
| 753 9 | **Well Arranged (IRE) (61)** (RAkehurst) **5-8-9** SSanders(3) (a.p: led over 2f out: drew clr fnl f) | — | **1** | 9/2 3 | 70 | 43 |
| 825 5 | **Hillzah (USA) (72)** (RBastiman) **8-9-1**(5) HBastiman(2) (lw: a.p: slt ld wl over 2f out: sn hdd: rallied 1f out: no ex towards fin) | 2½ | **2** | 100/30 1 | 78 | 51 |
| 647 5 | **Backview (76)** (BJLlewellyn) **4-9-8** TWilliams(1) (led after 4f tl wl over 2f out: kpt on u.p appr fnl f) | 1½ | **3** | 4/1 2 | 81 | 52 |
| 872 11 | **Iota (61)** (JLHarris) **7-8-9** JFEgan(6) (dwlt: effrt 4f out: nvr nr ldrs) | 4 | **4** | 6/1 | 61 | 34 |
| | **Unsuspicious (IRE) (48)** (CDBroad) **6-7-10** NAdams(7) (bkwd: led 4f: rdn & wknd 6f out: t.o) | 14 | **5** | 33/1 | 33 | 6 |
| 961 5 | **Shakiyr (FR) (70)** (RHollinshead) **5-8-13**(5) FLynch(5) (drvn along ½-wy: no imp: t.o) | ½ | **6** | 4/1 2 | 55 | 28 |
| 963 5 | **Greenspan (IRE) (78)** (WRMuir) **4-9-10** Jean-PierreLopez(4) (lw: s.i.s: hld up & bhd: rdn & outpcd 5f out: sn t.o) | 6 | **7** | 6/1 | 56 | 27 |
| | | | | (SP 112.8%) | **7 Rn** | |

**3m 18.3** (10.90) CSF £18.61 TOTE £5.80: £2.70 £2.50 (£16.80) OWNER Mrs Anne-Marie Hamilton (EPSOM) BRED T. G. Mooney in Ireland
LONG HANDICAP Unsuspicious (IRE) 7-7
WEIGHT FOR AGE 4yo-2lb
**Well Arranged (IRE)** stayed this trip well and, shaking off his nearest pursuer inside the final furlong, won going away. (9/2: op 11/4)
**825 Hillzah (USA)** needs less use made of him over these extended trips and that proved the deciding factor here. (100/30)
**647 Backview** ran a but too free and helped force the pace, but had nothing in the tank when the final battle got under way. (4/1)
**656* Iota** could not muster the pace to get anywhere near the principals after being sluggish leaving the stalls. (6/1)
**767 Shakiyr (FR)** may benefit from a break. (4/1)
**963 Greenspan (IRE)** got outpaced when he was about to make a move. (6/1: op 4/1)

## 1083 PLYVINE CATERING H'CAP (0-70) (3-Y.O+) (Class E)
8-30 (8-31) **6f (Fibresand)** £2,933.70 (£873.60: £415.80: £186.90) Stalls: Low

| | | | | SP | RR | SF |
|---|---|---|---|---|---|---|
| 644 10 | **Vax New Way (68)** (JLSpearing) **3-8-13b**(3) SDrowne(3) (a.p: led over 1f out: clr fnl f) | — | **1** | 6/1 3 | 75 | 36 |
| 981 4 | **Jon's Choice (39)** (BPreece) **8-7-8**(3)ow1 DWright(5) (trckd ldng pair: kpt on u.p ins fnl f: no ch w wnr) | 1¾ | **2** | 11/2 2 | 41 | 11 |
| *896*3 | **Wardara (60)** (CADwyer) **4-9-1b**(3) JStack(2) (lw: led tl over 1f out: wknd ins fnl f) | 1 | **3** | 2/1 1 | 60 | 31 |
| 893 11 | **Delrob (50)** (DHaydnJones) **5-8-8** AMackay(8) (sn hrd drvn & outpcd: kpt on appr fnl f: nvr nrr) | 1¾ | **4** | 12/1 | 45 | 16 |
| 981 7 | **Sound the Trumpet (IRE) (54)** (RCSpicer) **4-8-12** DeanMcKeown(4) (spd over 3f: sn lost tch) | 1½ | **5** | 10/1 | 45 | 16 |
| 814 10 | **Leigh Crofter (70)** (PDCundell) **7-10-0b** GHind(7) (sn outpcd & pushed along: a bhd) | 2 | **6** | 6/1 3 | 56 | 27 |
| 617 12 | **Sue Me (IRE) (60)** (WRMuir) **4-9-4b**1 Jean-PierreLopez(1) (drvn along thrght: nvr gng pce of ldrs: t.o) | 6 | **7** | 6/1 3 | 30 | 1 |
| 868 9 | **Tael of Silver (44)** (KRBurke) **4-8-2** TWilliams(6) (lw: a bhd & outpcd: t.o) | 5 | **8** | 11/2 2 | — | — |
| | | | | (SP 123.7%) | **8 Rn** | |

**1m 16.6** (5.20) CSF £38.42 CT £83.51 TOTE £6.70: £2.40 £2.20 £1.30 (£15.90) OWNER Vax Ltd (ALCESTER) BRED Aquamin Limited
LONG HANDICAP Jon's Choice 7-9
WEIGHT FOR AGE 3yo-10lb
**Vax New Way**, a previous winner over course and distance here in the autumn, was always going that bit better than the favourite and, forging through in the final furlong, won with any amount in hand. (6/1)
**981 Jon's Choice**, doing all his best work inside the distance, is crying out for a return to seven. (11/2)
**896 Wardara** gave of her best from the front, but the winner was always waiting to pounce, and had her measure approaching the final furlong. (2/1)
**Delrob**, flat to the boards from the break, did keep on in the closing stages but far too late to cause concern. (12/1)
**Sue Me (IRE)** (6/1: op 10/1)

## 1084 WOLVERHAMPTON SERIES (S) STKS (Qualifier) (2-Y.O) (Class F)
9-00 (9-00) **6f (Fibresand)** £2,381.00 (£656.00: £311.00) Stalls: Low

| | | | | SP | RR | SF |
|---|---|---|---|---|---|---|
| *895*3 | **C-Harry (IRE)** (RHollinshead) **2-8-7v**(5) FLynch(3) (lw: sn prom: led wl over 1f out: hld on wl fnl f) | — | **1** | 2/1 1 | 51 | 15 |
| 741 5 | **Don't Forget Shoka (IRE)** (JSMoore) **2-8-7** JFEgan(5) (lw: led after 1f tl wl over 1f out: rallied u.p fnl f) | ¾ | **2** | 4/1 | 44 | 8 |
| *838*6 | **Tazio Nuvolari** (WGMTurner) **2-8-7** TSprake(1) (prom: rdn 2f out: r.o one pce) | 2½ | **3** | 7/2 3 | 37 | 1 |
| 770 7 | **Run For Us (IRE)** (CADwyer) **2-8-4b**1(3) JStack(2) (lw: dwlt: hdwy over 2f out: nt rch ldrs) | 8 | **4** | 9/1 | 16 | — |
| *838*4 | **Abstone Again (IRE)** (PDEvans) **2-8-12** JFortune(4) (led 1f: rdn & outpcd 2f out) | 4 | **5** | 11/4 2 | 10 | — |
| | | | | (SP 112.2%) | **5 Rn** | |

**1m 17.9** (6.50) CSF £9.60 TOTE £2.00: £1.50 £2.00 (£6.40) OWNER Mr D. Coppenhall (UPPER LONGDON) BRED Dan O'Loughlin
No bid

**895 C-Harry (IRE)** found this extra furlong tailor-made, and had the measure of the runner-up throughout the final furlong. (2/1: op 11/10)
**569 Don't Forget Shoka (IRE)** did not go down for the want of trying and she will find her way over six furlongs when the nurseries get under way. (4/1: op 5/2)
**Tazio Nuvolari** too will come into her own when faced with a tougher test of stamina. (7/2: 5/1-3/1)
**838 Abstone Again (IRE)** (11/4: 3/1-9/2)

## 1085 LONDON H'CAP (0-70) (3-Y.O+) (Class E)
9-30 (9-30) **1m 100y (Fibresand)** £3,097.50 (£924.00: £441.00: £199.50) Stalls: Low

| | | | | SP | RR | SF |
|---|---|---|---|---|---|---|
| | **Northern Fan (IRE) (70)** (ACStewart) **4-10-0** SWhitworth(8) (lw: hld up: hdwy 4f out: led 2f out: brought wd st: comf) | — | 1 | 100/30 2 | 82 | 59 |
| *406*5 | **Sporting Risk (42)** (PWHarris) **4-8-0** JQuinn(11) (a.p: led over 3f out to 2f out: kpt on: no ch w wnr) | 3½ | 2 | 14/1 | 47 | 24 |
| *839** | **Young Benson (61)** (BAMcMahon) **4-9-5** GCarter(9) (lw: a.p: led 5f out tl over 3f out: sn rdn: kpt on) | ½ | 3 | 15/8 1 | 65 | 42 |
| 7474 | **Scathebury (65)** (SPCWoods) **3-8-10** WWoods(6) (hld up: hdwy 4f out: rdn 2f out: grad faded) | 8 | 4 | 5/1 | 54 | 18 |
| | **Penmar (56)** (TJEtherington) **4-9-0** LCharnock(5) (bit bkwd: trckd ldrs: hrd drvn & wknd over 3f out) | ½ | 5 | 14/1 | 44 | 21 |
| *839*4 | **Irchester Lass (47)** (SRBowring) **4-7-12b**(7) MartinDwyer(1) (prom tl rdn & outpcd wl over 2f out) | 3 | 6 | 11/1 | 30 | 7 |
| *654*5 | **Ring the Chief (45)** (MDIUsher) **4-8-3** NAdams(10) (a in rr) | ¾ | 7 | 14/1 | 26 | 3 |
| *839*3 | **Quinzii Martin (53)** (DHaydnJones) **8-8-11** AMackay(2) (prom: pushed along 6f out: grad wknd: t.o) | 12 | 8 | 9/2 3 | 12 | — |
| *200*7 | **Exclusive Assembly (53)** (APJames) **4-8-11** FNorton(4) (bit bkwd: dropped rr 5f out: t.o) | 4 | 9 | 14/1 | 4 | — |
| | **Lucy's Gold (39)** (MJRyan) **5-7-8**(3)ow1 DWright(7) (led over 3f: wknd qckly: t.o) | 4 | 10 | 25/1 | — | — |

(SP 131.6%) **10 Rn**

**1m 51.4** (6.40) CSF £48.92 CT £108.48 TOTE £6.80: £2.20 £4.40 £1.70 (£35.00) Trio £135.20 OWNER S Corman Ltd (NEWMARKET) BRED Mrs Max Morris
LONG HANDICAP Lucy's Gold 6-12
WEIGHT FOR AGE 3yo-13lb
**Northern Fan (IRE)**, opening his account on this seasonal debut, did not look fully wound up, but he let his class do the talking and won in a common canter. (100/30: 3/1-5/1)
**Sporting Risk** ran his best race yet and, though he was outpointed by the winner in the latter stages, he gave notice that his turn is near. (14/1)
**839* Young Benson** shared the lead and stuck on well inside the distance, but ran a bit flat, and maybe the edge has gone. (15/8)
**747 Scathebury** began a promising run on the outside on the home turn, but would not go through with his effort when the task looked hopeless on straightening up. (5/1)
**Penmar** just needed this after six months on the sidelines and was in trouble before reaching the straight. (14/1: op 8/1)

T/Plpt: £35.60 (370.4 Tckts). T/Qdpt: £5.90 (147.68 Tckts). IM

# REDCAR (L-H) (Good to firm)
## Monday May 13th
WEATHER: sunny WIND: almost nil

## 1086 AYTON MEDIAN AUCTION MAIDEN STKS (2-Y.O) (Class F)
2-15 (2-16) **5f** £2,798.00 (£778.00: £374.00) Stalls: Centre GOING minus 0.31 sec per fur (GF)

| | | | | SP | RR | SF |
|---|---|---|---|---|---|---|
| | **Hula Prince (IRE)** (MJohnston) **2-9-0** MHills(7) (w'like: str: w ldr: led ½-wy: shkn up over 1f out: r.o) | — | 1 | 4/1 1 | 70+ | 32 |
| | **The Lambton Worm** (DenysSmith) **2-9-0** KFallon(6) (wl grwn: bit bkwd: a.p: shkn up ½-wy: hdwy over 1f out: r.o) | 1½ | 2 | 6/1 3 | 65 | 27 |
| | **Dive Master (IRE)** (CMurray) **2-9-0** BDoyle(10) (str: cmpt: bhd & pushed along tl hdwy over 1f out: r.o wl towards fin) | 1½ | 3 | 9/1 | 60 | 22 |
| | **Lucky Oakwood (USA)** (MBell) **2-8-9** MFenton(5) (w'like: scope: a chsng ldrs: ev ch & rdn over 1f out: no ex) | hd | 4 | 4/1 1 | 55 | 17 |
| 9506 | **Fine Times** (CWFairhurst) **2-9-0** DeanMcKeown(9) (a.p: pushed along thrght: nvr able to chal) | hd | 5 | 25/1 | 60 | 22 |
| 8697 | **Docklands Carriage (IRE)** (NTinkler) **2-9-0** KimTinkler(14) (lw: outpcd tl styd on wl fnl f) | hd | 6 | 20/1 | 59 | 21 |
| 9303 | **Mill End Boy** (MWEasterby) **2-8-9**(5) GParkin(11) (lw: outpcd ½-wy: hdwy & swtchd over 1f out: n.d) | 2½ | 7 | 4/1 1 | 51 | 13 |
| | **Nifty Norman** (JBerry) **2-9-0** JCarroll(13) (leggy: scope: chsd ldrs tl wknd appr fnl f) | 1 | 8 | 9/2 2 | 48 | 10 |
| 9905 | **Super Sheriff** (MWEasterby) **2-9-0** JFanning(12) (slt ld to ½-wy: sn rdn & btn) | 3 | 9 | 50/1 | 39 | 1 |
| | **Pension Fund** (MWEasterby) **2-9-0** DaleGibson(1) (rangy: bit bkwd: sn outpcd) | 2 | 10 | 33/1 | 32 | — |
| | **Cala-Holme (IRE)** (TDEasterby) **2-8-9** MBirch(3) (leggy: scope: outpcd fr ½-wy) | 1¼ | 11 | 25/1 | 23 | — |
| 93010 | **Thewrightone (IRE)** (GROldroyd) **2-8-9** FNorton(2) (sn bhd) | nk | 12 | 50/1 | 22 | — |
| | **Father Eddie** (JJO'Neill) **2-9-0** SDWilliams(8) (cmpt: scope: b.nr fore: dwlt: a bhd) | 3½ | 13 | 33/1 | 16 | — |
| | **Riva La Belle** (JWharton) **2-8-9** KDarley(4) (leggy: s.s: a outpcd & bhd) | 1¾ | 14 | 10/1 | 6 | — |

(SP 133.8%) **14 Rn**

**59.8 secs** (2.30) CSF £29.77 TOTE £5.70: £2.00 £2.60 £2.90 (£46.10) Trio £183.60; £129.34 to York 14/5/96 OWNER Maktoum Al Maktoum (MIDDLEHAM) BRED Gainsborough Stud Management Ltd
**Hula Prince (IRE)**, an attractive colt, did the business well and, judging by his appearance, can only improve. (4/1: 2/1-9/2)
**The Lambton Worm** is a decent type and got better as the race progressed. Improvement now looks likely, especially over further. (6/1)
**Dive Master (IRE)** took an age to realise what was required but, when he did, he certainly finished with a flourish, and looks one to keep an eye on. (9/1)
**Lucky Oakwood (USA)** looked pretty fit for her debut here but was off the bit to take the winner on, and that finally found her out with a furlong left. She will be all the better for this. (4/1)
**950 Fine Times** was always struggling to go the pace but did keep on to show he is improving. (25/1)
**869 Docklands Carriage (IRE)**, taken off his legs for much of the trip, suddenly found his stride when it was all over. (20/1)
**930 Mill End Boy** found this a much more competitive event and, after finding some trouble, failed to get into it, despite keeping on. (4/1)
**Nifty Norman** looked likely to benefit from this and showed some useful speed. (9/2)

## 1087 KILTON CLAIMING STKS (3-Y.O+) (Class F)
2-45 (2-46) **6f** £2,756.00 (£766.00: £368.00) Stalls: Centre GOING minus 0.31 sec per fur (GF)

| | | | | SP | RR | SF |
|---|---|---|---|---|---|---|
| 8822 | **Panther (IRE) (57)** (JHetherton) **6-9-2** KFallon(10) (lw: bhd: hdwy ½-wy: led over 1f out: r.o) | — | 1 | 6/1 3 | 69 | 51 |

839$^{2}$ **Komlucky (39)** (ABMulholland) **4-8-7b** TWilliams(4) (chsd ldrs: chal over 1f out: nt qckn towards fin)..............¾ **2** 25/1 58 40
992$^{3}$ **No Monkey Nuts (80)** (JBerry) **3-8-12** JCarroll(8) (lw: led tl hdd over 1f out: rdn & fnd nil)..................................3 **3** 11/8$^{1}$ 65 37
951$^{2}$ **Sea-Deer (74)** (DWChapman) **7-9-8** DeanMcKeown(13) (lw: hdwy 2f out: styd on: nvr rchd ldrs)...................1¼ **4** 6/1$^{3}$ 62 44
*606$^{13}$* **Thorntoun Jewel (IRE) (40)** (JBalding) **3-7-13b** JFanning(12) (sn in tch: kpt on fnl f)........................................1½ **5** 50/1 45 17
**Monkey Face (33)** (WWHaigh) **5-8-9** RHills(9) (bit bkwd: chsd ldrs tl wknd fnl 2f).............................................3 **6** 100/1 37 19
*317$^{6}$* **Sense of Priority (58)** (DNicholls) **7-9-2** AlexGreaves(11) (bit bkwd: in tch tl outpcd fnl 2f) ...........................nk **7** 8/1 43 25
882$^{14}$ **Rankaidade (26)** (DonEnricoIncisa) **5-8-7** KimTinkler(6) (lw: hdwy ½-wy: no imp) ..........................................1¼ **8** 50/1 31 13
971$^{12}$ **Steel Sovereign (38)** (MDods) **5-8-7**(7) IonaWands(5) (outpcd fr ½-wy)............................................................1¼ **9** 50/1 34 16
**Naughty Pistol (USA)** (PDEvans) **4-9-7** TIves(7) (prom 4f).................................................................................½ **10** 11/2$^{2}$ 40 22
769$^{13}$ **Napoleon's Return (46)** (AHarrison) **3-8-3** BDoyle(2) (outpcd fr ½-wy)..............................................................3½ **11** 50/1 23 —
971$^{9}$ **Prime Property (IRE) (38)** (MWEasterby) **4-8-11b** DaleGibson(14) (s.s: a bhd)..................................................½ **12** 25/1 19 1
**Gone to Heaven** (TJEtherington) **4-9-4** KDarley(1) (bkwd: racd far side: gd spd 4f)..................................................6 **13** 7/1 10 —
**Redbrook Lady (45)** (JMJefferson) **3-8-3** AMackay(3) (bit bkwd: bolted gng to s: racd far side: a bhd).........dist **14** 50/1 — —
(SP 128.2%) **14 Rn**

**1m 11.8** (1.60) CSF £132.56 TOTE £9.00: £2.10 £2.90 £1.10 (£58.70) Trio £33.20 OWNER Mr K. C. West (MALTON) BRED My Treasure Ltd
WEIGHT FOR AGE 3yo-10lb
Panther (IRE) clmd JHetherton £5,000
**882 Panther (IRE)** will act on any ground and came from off the pace to win in great style. (6/1: op 12/1)
**839 Komlucky** is in really good form at present on all surfaces, and should pick up a race in due course. (25/1)
**992 No Monkey Nuts**, happy when on the bridle, was disappointing when off it. (11/8: op 4/5)
**951 Sea-Deer** again ran quite well but only ran on when it was too late. (6/1)
**Thorntoun Jewel (IRE)** showed her first signs of form here, staying on at the end. (50/1)
**Monkey Face** needed this and ran well. She has the ability to do better if she can be persuaded. (100/1)
**Sense of Priority** had not been out for almost three months and needed this. (8/1)

## 1088 KISS AND CUDDLE LADIES' H'CAP (0-70) (3-Y.O+) (Class E)

3-15 (3-16) **1m** £3,127.25 (£938.00: £451.50: £208.25) Stalls: Centre GOING minus 0.31 sec per fur (GF)

SP RR SF

713$^{12}$ **Spanish Steps (IRE) (50)** (MWEasterby) **4-8-4b**(7) JoHunnam(6) (prom: led wl over 2f out: kpt on)...............— **1** 8/1 62 46
662$^{2}$ **Pc's Cruiser (IRE) (47)** (JLEyre) **4-8-1b**(7) AimeeCook(4) (lw: bhd: jnd ldrs ½-wy: hung lft u.p: nt qckn fnl f)..........................................................................................................................1¾ **2** 11/2$^{2}$ 56 40
*1048$^{4}$* **Four of Spades (57)** (PDEvans) **5-8-13v**(5) AmandaSanders(3) (in tch: effrt 3f out: styd on: nvr able to chal) ....................................................................................................................1½ **3** 13/2$^{3}$ 63 47
1018$^{9}$ **Parliament Piece (66)** (DNicholls) **10-9-13b** AlexGreaves(2) (lw: effrt ½-wy: sn in tch: kpt on fnl f).................nk **4** 5/2$^{1}$ 71 55
995$^{5}$ **Carlton Express (IRE) (44)** (JLEyre) **6-7-12**(7)ow2 ClaireWest(7) (lw: in tch: one pce fnl 3f)...........................2½ **5** 8/1 44 26
*854$^{5}$* **Thaleros (57)** (GMMoore) **6-8-11**(7) AngelaGallimore(1) (lw: a chsng ldrs: rdn & one pce fnl 3f)......................1¾ **6** 8/1 53 37
*249$^{6}$* **Bentico (67)** (MrsNMacauley) **7-9-9v**(5) SophieMitchell(9) (cl up early: outpcd fr ½-wy)..........................................½ **7** 8/1 62 46
787$^{15}$ **Dance of Joy (45)** (JMCarr) **4-7-13**(7) CarolDavison(8) (nvr rchd ldrs)..................................................................1 **8** 16/1 38 22
884$^{6}$ **Roar on Tour (36)** (MrsMReveley) **7-7-4v**(7) JennyBenson(11) (led over 5f: sn wknd) ..........................................nk **9** 16/1 29 13
688$^{6}$ **Self Expression (47)** (JAHarris) **8-8-1**(7) JoanneWebster(12) (a bhd)...................................................................s.h **10** 10/1 40 24
806$^{11}$ **Langtonian (35)** (JLEyre) **7-7-3b**(7) IonaWands(10) (bhd: jnd ldr after 2½f: wknd over 3f out).........................3½ **11** 20/1 21 5
*782$^{7}$* **Ruby Plus (42)** (GROldroyd) **5-7-10**(7)ow7 SallySandes(13) (bhd fr ½-wy).........................................................8 **12** 50/1 12 —
**Bardia (35)** (DonEnricoIncisa) **6-7-10** KimTinkler(5) (dwlt: a bhd) ............................................................................3½ **13** 33/1 — —
(SP 132.3%) **13 Rn**

**1m 37.9** (2.20) CSF £53.22 CT £292.02 TOTE £13.50: £3.50 £2.10 £1.60 (£64.30) Trio £125.80 OWNER R O M Racing (SHERIFF HUTTON) BRED Lady McAlpine
LONG HANDICAP Langtonian 7-3 Ruby Plus 7-5 Bardia 7-7
**Spanish Steps (IRE)** had the blinkers on for the first time this season and, given a good ride, won his first race in style. (8/1)
**662 Pc's Cruiser (IRE)** had his chances from halfway but, when put under pressure, he was always inclined to go to his left, and was never doing enough. (11/2)
**1048 Four of Spades** has never won over as far as this but, judging by the way he was keeping on, it should not be a problem. (13/2)
**Parliament Piece**, given plenty to do, took time to get going and never offered a threat. Despite his years, there are still races to be picked up. (5/2)
**995 Carlton Express (IRE)** was always finding this trip a bit sharp and could never offer a serious threat. (8/1)
**854 Thaleros** needs further than this but did run quite well. (8/1)

## 1089 MACKINLAY MEMORIAL H'CAP (0-70) (3-Y.O) (Class E)

3-45 (3-48) **1m 2f** £3,491.25 (£1,050.00: £507.50: £236.25) Stalls: Low GOING minus 0.31 sec per fur (GF)

SP RR SF

658* **Hawksley Hill (IRE) (55)** (MrsJRRamsden) **3-8-9** KFallon(11) (lw: hld up: effrt 3f out: led ins fnl f: hung lft: styd on)..............................................................................................................................— **1** 3/1$^{1}$ 63 25
914$^{9}$ **Ordained (45)** (EJAlston) **3-7-13** JFanning(7) (hdwy on ins over 4f out: led 3f out tl ins fnl f: kpt on wl)............½ **2** 33/1 52 14
669$^{7}$ **Alpine Panther (IRE) (65)** (WJarvis) **3-9-5** KDarley(9) (lw: prom: effrt over 3f out: sn hrd drvn: one pce appr fnl f) ....................................................................................................................2½ **3** 100/30$^{2}$ 68 30
849$^{15}$ **Blenheim Terrace (52)** (CBBBooth) **3-8-6** ACulhane(5) (bhd: hdwy over 3f out: sn chsng ldrs: nt qckn ins fnl f)..........................................................................................................................¾ **4** 66/1 54 16
976* **Lucky Bea (59)** (MWEasterby) **3-8-8**(5) 5x GParkin(15) (lw: s.i.s: bhd tl styd on wl fnl 3f)..............................1½ **5** 14/1 59 21
819$^{4}$ **Forest Fantasy (51)** (JWharton) **3-8-5** FNorton(17) (hdwy 4f out: nt clr run over 2f out: wandered u.p & nvr able to chal).................................................................................................................½ **6** 9/2$^{3}$ 50 12
586$^{7}$ **Dispol Conqueror (IRE) (42)** (GROldroyd) **3-7-3**(7) RFfrench(1) (cl up: led over 4f out tl hdd 3f out: grad wknd fnl 2f)..................................................................................................................s.h **7** 50/1 41 3
803$^{8}$ **Six Clerks (IRE) (63)** (JGFitzGerald) **3-9-3** MWigham(6) (in tch tl hmpd & lost pl over 2f out: sme late hdwy)..............................................................................................................................s.h **8** 25/1 62 24
614$^{8}$ **Etterby Park (USA) (45)** (MrsJRRamsden) **3-7-13** NKennedy(12) (hld up & bhd: hdwy whn hmpd 2f out: nvr plcd to chal).......................................................................................................................½ **9** 20/1 43 5
763$^{4}$ **Crystal Warrior (60)** (DNicholls) **3-9-0** AlexGreaves(2) (prom: hdwy on ins to chal 4f out: wknd 2f out).........2½ **10** 12/1 54 16
761* **Safecracker (67)** (JWHills) **3-9-7** RHills(8) (lw: cl up: chal 3f out: wknd 2f out).............................................1 **11** 9/1 59 21
*782$^{12}$* **Northern Falcon (45)** (MWEasterby) **3-7-13** DaleGibson(10) (a bhd).......................................................................4 **12** 66/1 31 —
*516$^{5}$* **Shermood (55)** (MBell) **3-8-9** MFenton(14) (in tch tl wknd 3½f out)......................................................................3 **13** 14/1 36 —

775[18] **Ginger Hodgers (50)** (RMWhitaker) **3-8-4** AMackay(4) (n.d) ....nk **14** 66/1 31 —
614[3] **Phantom Haze (61)** (MissSEHall) **3-9-1** NConnorton(13) (plld hrd: a bhd) ....¾ **15** 16/1 40 2
870[10] **The Jolly Barmaid (IRE) (52)** (PCalver) **3-8-6** JCarroll(16) (prom tl wknd fnl 4f) ....2 **16** 16/1 28 —
**Recall To Mind (65)** (TDEasterby) **3-9-5** MBirch(3) (bit bkwd: led tl hdd & wknd over 4f out) ....1¾ **17** 16/1 38 —
(SP 132.9%) **17 Rn**

**2m 9.0** (5.40) CSF £93.63 CT £339.47 TOTE £5.00: £1.30 £9.40 £1.10 £8.10 (£230.30) Trio £324.50 OWNER Mr Hamish Alexander (THIRSK) BRED The Wickfield Stud Ltd

LONG HANDICAP Dispol Conqueror (IRE) 7-3

**658* Hawksley Hill (IRE)** keeps doing the business, despite not looking too happy. Judging from his action, he would seem to have some sort of a problem. (3/1)

**614 Ordained** has recently run two poor races on soft ground but, back of this surface, was in really good form. He should pick up a race in due course. (33/1)

**448 Alpine Panther (IRE)**, who qualified for handicaps over shorter trips, looked none too happy on the bend here but did keep responding to pressure, albeit in vain. He still has something to learn and will be suited by further. (100/30: 9/4-7/2)

**Blenheim Terrace** put in a much-improved performance and would seem to be getting the hang of things. (66/1)

**976* Lucky Bea**, stepping up in distance again, only got going when it was all over. (14/1)

**819 Forest Fantasy** met with all sorts of trouble in the last three furlongs and should do better in due course. (9/2)

**444 Six Clerks (IRE)** is short of a real turn of foot and being hampered with two furlongs to go spoilt any chance he had. (25/1)

**614 Etterby Park (USA)**, a stable-companion of the winner, certainly caught the eye and, but for being hampered, would have been a deal closer. Time will see a lot better from him. (20/1)

## 1090 DANBY MAIDEN STKS (3-Y.O) (Class D)

4-15 (4-23) **1m 2f** £3,873.00 (£1,164.00: £562.00: £261.00) Stalls: Low GOING minus 0.31 sec per fur (GF)

SP RR SF

820[7] **Classic Find (USA)** (SCWilliams) **3-9-0** AMackay(2) (s.i.s: swtchd & effrt 3f out: led ins fnl f: smoothly) ....— **1** 10/1 73+ 40
821[2] **Get Away With It (IRE)** (MRStoute) **3-9-0** KFallon(6) (in tch: outpcd 4f out: hdwy to ld over 1f out: hdd ins fnl f: kpt on) ....¾ **2** 2/1[1] 72 39
**Lord of The Manor** (MJohnston) **3-9-0** MHills(3) (rangy: scope: in tch: effrt 2f out: kpt on: nt pce to chal) ....3½ **3** 12/1 66 33
**Ambassadori (USA)** (CEBrittain) **3-9-0** BDoyle(7) (str: cmpt: bit bkwd: trckd ldrs: effrt 3f out: edgd lft: r.o one pce) ....¾ **4** 6/1[3] 65 32
**Viridis (USA)** (HRACecil) **3-8-9** WRyan(8) (lw: led: rdn 3f out: hdd over 1f out: one pce) ....nk **5** 7/2[2] 60 27
677[8] **Mohannad (IRE)** (JWHills) **3-9-0** RHills(1) (lw: cl up: chal over 3f out: sn rdn: btn appr fnl f) ....1 **6** 2/1[1] 63 30
826[12] **Clash of Swords** (PCalver) **3-9-0** MBirch(5) (lw: nvr nr to chal) ....9 **7** 50/1 49 16
804[5] **Respecting** (DenysSmith) **3-9-0** JCarroll(4) (bolted gng to s: lost tch fnl 3½f) ....18 **8** 250/1 20 —
(SP 122.3%) **8 Rn**

**2m 7.7** (4.10) CSF £31.09 TOTE £14.00: £2.80 £1.00 £3.70 (£34.90) OWNER Classic Bloodstock Plc (NEWMARKET) BRED Maric Bloodstock Inc

**Classic Find (USA)** needed every yard of this trip in a strongly-run race and looks a very useful prospect, especially over further. (10/1: 6/1-11/1)

**821 Get Away With It (IRE)** was the first off the bit, but he did respond well, only to get well outpointed by the winner. He is learning. (2/1)

**Lord of The Manor**, a decent type, should have learnt plenty here and did run pretty well. (12/1: op 8/1)

**Ambassadori (USA)**, a well-made individual, needed the run and the experience. Better looks likely. (6/1)

**Viridis (USA)** made this a real test, but her limitations had been exposed with a furlong left. (7/2)

**Mohannad (IRE)** tried to take the pacemaker on which proved his undoing. He should do better later on. (2/1: 6/4-9/4)

## 1091 TEES H'CAP (0-80) (4-Y.O+) (Class D)

4-45 (4-45) **2m 4y** £3,483.00 (£1,044.00: £502.00: £231.00) Stalls: Low GOING minus 0.31 sec per fur (GF)

SP RR SF

852[5] **Arian Spirit (IRE) (45)** (JLEyre) **5-8-1** RLappin(1) (lw: hld up: hdwy appr st: led jst ins fnl f: r.o) ....— **1** 5/1[3] 56 12
961[4] **Satin Lover (72)** (MrsMReveley) **8-10-0** KDarley(2) (trckd ldrs: led 3f out tl jst ins fnl f: no ex) ....1¼ **2** 4/1[2] 82 38
825[6] **Mondragon (69)** (MrsMReveley) **6-9-11** ACulhane(5) (lw: bhd: effrt 3f out: styd on towards fin) ....1¼ **3** 9/1 78 34
*236[5]* **Jalcanto (56)** (MrsMReveley) **6-8-5**(7) SCopp(4) (bhd: styd on u.p fnl 2f: nrst fin) ....hd **4** 8/1 64 20
767* **Upper Mount Clair (67)** (CEBrittain) **6-9-9** BDoyle(3) (led tl hdd 3f out: one pce) ....¾ **5** 2/1[1] 75 31
*87[4]* **Suivez (54)** (MrsNMacauley) **6-8-10** DaleGibson(6) (b: plld hrd: trckd ldr: effrt 4f out: sn btn) ....21 **6** 4/1[2] 41 —
(SP 111.1%) **6 Rn**

**3m 35.4** (10.40) CSF £22.78 TOTE £5.20: £2.20 £4.50 (£13.30) OWNER Mr Martin West (HAMBLETON) BRED M. Ervine in Ireland

**852 Arian Spirit (IRE)**, in a race full of ifs and buts, had the turn of speed that mattered. (5/1)

**961 Satin Lover** looked to be going well early in the straight but, when pressure was on, he never found as much as looked likely. (4/1)

**825 Mondragon** only got going when the race was over, but does seem to be improving. (9/1)

**Jalcanto** took some persuading to get into stride and failed to offer a threat, despite staying on. (8/1)

**767* Upper Mount Clair** needs either a stronger-run race or further and was well tapped for toe in the closing stages. (2/1)

**Suivez**, taking a big step up in distance, pulled too hard and failed to stay. (4/1: op 5/2)

## 1092 HUNTCLIFFE H'CAP (0-80) (3-Y.O+ F & M) (Class D)

5-15 (5-15) **7f** £3,769.00 (£1,132.00: £546.00: £253.00) Stalls: Centre GOING minus 0.31 sec per fur (GF)

SP RR SF

888[3] **Zelda Zonk (66)** (BJMeehan) **4-9-7** BDoyle(3) (lw: cl up: led 3f out & qcknd: styd on wl) ....— **1** 7/2[1] 75 61
613[11] **Fairywings (63)** (MrsJRRamsden) **3-8-6** KFallon(4) (swtg: hdwy over 3f out: styd on wl fnl f: nrst fin) ....½ **2** 8/1 71 45
802[7] **Best of All (IRE) (71)** (JBerry) **4-9-12** TIves(8) (a.p: effrt 3f out: kpt on: nvr able to chal) ....3 **3** 12/1 72 58
827[17] **Prudent Pet (57)** (CWFairhurst) **4-8-12b** DeanMcKeown(6) (hdwy over 2f out: n.m.r: edgd lft appr fnl f: styd on) ....1½ **4** 14/1 55 41
978[7] **Charming Bride (61)** (SCWilliams) **3-8-4**ow1 KDarley(2) (a.p: rdn & no imp fnl 2f) ....3 **5** 7/1[3] 52 25
868[2] **Maid O'Cannie (57)** (MWEasterby) **5-8-7b**(5) GParkin(10) (lw: hld up & bhd: hdwy on bit ½-wy: rdn over 2f out: sn btn) ....nk **6** 4/1[2] 47 33
689[4] **Lovely Prospect (72)** (RGuest) **3-9-1** JCarroll(7) (swtg: chsd ldrs tl wknd fnl 2f) ....2½ **7** 4/1[2] 56 30
586[13] **Hats of to Hilda (41)** (MrsMReveley) **4-7-10** FNorton(5) (bhd: hdwy over 2f out: n.d) ....3 **8** 10/1 19 5
**Respect A Secret (41)** (SEKettlewell) **4-7-10** NKennedy(1) (bit bkwd: led 4f: sn wknd) ....5 **9** 16/1 7 —
**Rupiana (IRE) (56)** (CMurray) **4-8-11** ACulhane(9) (bit bkwd: prom: rdn ½-wy: sn wknd) ....3½ **10** 33/1 14 —

Village Opera (54) (GMMoore) 3-7-11ow1 DaleGibson(11) (swtg: outpcd fr ½-wy)....5 11 50/1 1 —
(SP 120.1%) 11 Rn

1m 24.4 (1.40) CSF £30.02 CT £286.65 TOTE £4.00: £1.40 £1.80 £4.40 (£31.60) Trio £45.40 OWNER Mrs Christine Painting (UPPER LAMBOURN) BRED Mrs Christine Painting
LONG HANDICAP Respect A Secret 7-4 Village Opera 7-7
WEIGHT FOR AGE 3yo-12lb

**888 Zelda Zonk,** made plenty of use of, had her rivals in trouble some way out and was never going to stop. (7/2)
**Fairywings** behaved herself better this time and finished to some purpose, suggesting that further should suit. (8/1)
**Best of All (IRE),** happier on this faster surface, ran a deal better. (12/1)
**Prudent Pet** was inclined to wander about when the pressure was on, but was staying on at the finish. (14/1)
**686 Charming Bride** showed up, but failed to pull out any extra when the pressure was on in the last couple of furlongs. (7/1)
**868 Maid O'Cannie** travelled on the bridle but, once off it entering the last two furlongs, found little. This trip is certainly beyond her best. (4/1)

T/Jkpt: Not won; £3,322.79 to York 14/5/96. T/Plpt: £234.30 (63.89 Tckts). T/Qdpt: £42.70 (25.76 Tckts) AA

## 1026-SOUTHWELL (L-H) (Standard)
## Monday May 13th
WEATHER: warm WIND: slt half bhd

### 1093 SWEDEN MAIDEN AUCTION STKS (2-Y.O) (Class F)
2-30 (2-30) **5f (Fibresand)** £2,857.00 (£792.00: £379.00) Stalls: High GOING: 0.00 sec per fur (STD)

| | Horse | | Pos | SP | RR | SF |
|---|---|---|---|---|---|---|
| | **Just Visiting** (CaptJWilson) **2-7-9**(5) MHenry(3) (leggy: w ldrs: led wl over 1f out: edgd rt & rdn out) | — | 1 | 25/1 | 60 | 22 |
| 757[6] | **Whizz Kid** (JJBridger) **2-7-9**(3) DarrenMoffatt(7) (w ldrs: kpt on same pce appr fnl f) | 2½ | 2 | 25/1 | 50 | 12 |
| 910[2] | **Bollero (IRE)** (JBerry) **2-8-2** GCarter(8) (lw: led tl wl over 1f out: kpt on same pce) | hd | 3 | 5/6 1 | 54 | 16 |
| 865[6] | **Molly Music** (GGMargarson) **2-8-1** DBiggs(11) (w ldr: hung lft ½-wy: grad wknd) | 7 | 4 | 6/1 2 | 30 | — |
| | **Fit For The Job (IRE)** (WGMTurner) **2-8-5** AClark(5) (lengthy: unf: bit bkwd: s.i.s: sn in tch: wknd 2f out) | 1¼ | 5 | 7/1 3 | 30 | — |
| | **Nampara Bay** (GCBravery) **2-7-13**(3)ow1 DRMcCabe(10) (unf: s.i.s: nvr nr ldrs) | 4 | 6 | 7/1 3 | 15 | — |
| | **Wedding Music** (PCHaslam) **2-7-7**(5) PFessey(6) (chsd ldrs tl wknd over 1f out) | ½ | 7 | 20/1 | 9 | — |
| | **Captain Picard** (DCO'Brien) **2-8-5** GBardwell(9) (leggy: unf: dwlt: a bhd) | 5 | 8 | 10/1 | — | — |
| | **Imperial Garden (IRE)** (PCHaslam) **2-8-8** JFortune(2) (w'like: lengthy: bit bkwd: b.hind: in tch to ½-wy: sn rdn & lost pl) | 1¼ | 9 | 11/1 | — | — |
| | **Rons Revenge** (MJRyan) **2-7-13**(5) MBaird(1) (neat: s.s: a wl bhd) | 4 | 10 | 10/1 | — | — |

(SP 132.8%) 10 Rn

**60.6 secs** (3.60) CSF £445.20 TOTE £40.10: £13.90 £7.80 £1.00 (£242.70) Trio £203.60 OWNER Mrs Rosemary Moszkowicz (PRESTON) BRED Henry and Mrs Rosemary Moszkowicz

**Just Visiting,** one of the two rank outsiders in the betting, won a modest contest entirely on merit. (25/1)
**Whizz Kid,** well beaten in selling company first time, like the winner was unconsidered in the betting, This race was probably worse than a seller or claimer. (25/1)
**910 Bollero (IRE)** looked very fit and made the running but had no excuse. She was simply not good enough. (5/6)
**643 Molly Music,** who had shown only poor form on her four previous outings, hung left and faded from halfway. (6/1: op 10/1)
**Fit For The Job (IRE)** will need more time yet. (7/1)
**Captain Picard** (10/1: op 16/1)

### 1094 SPAIN CLAIMING STKS (3-Y.O+) (Class F)
3-00 (3-01) **7f (Fibresand)** £2,381.00 (£656.00: £311.00) Stalls: Low GOING: 0.00 sec per fur (STD)

| | Horse | | Pos | SP | RR | SF |
|---|---|---|---|---|---|---|
| *1029*[3] | **Awesome Venture (69)** (MCChapman) **6-9-8**(3) DRMcCabe(6) (trckd ldrs: effrt 2f out: styd on to ld ins fnl f: hld on towards fin) | — | 1 | 7/1 | 79 | 61 |
| 1024[10] | **Desert Invader (IRE) (75)** (DWChapman) **5-9-7** JFortune(5) (chsd ldrs: hrd rdn & led over 1f out: hdd ins fnl f: kpt on wl) | ½ | 2 | 13/2 | 74 | 56 |
| 662[5] | **Dancing Sioux (75)** (RGuest) **4-9-8**(5) FLynch(10) (chsd ldrs: chal over 1f out: sn rdn & nt qckn) | 1¾ | 3 | 15/8 1 | 76 | 58 |
| 1043[5] | **Palacegate Touch (80)** (JBerry) **6-9-11b** GCarter(9) (b.off fore: swtchd lft s: led tl over 1f out: grad wknd) | 1¾ | 4 | 5/1 2 | 70 | 52 |
| *1029*[2] | **Elton Ledger (IRE) (63)** (MrsNMacauley) **7-9-7v** JTate(4) (lw: b: s.i.s: hld up: effrt over 2f out: kpt on: nvr nr to chal) | 1 | 5 | 11/2 3 | 64 | 46 |
| *896*[4] | **Mustn't Grumble (IRE) (67)** (MissSJWilton) **6-9-5** MTebbutt(3) (trckd ldrs tl wknd appr fnl f) | 1 | 6 | 17/2 | 59 | 41 |
| *782*[6] | **Undawaterscubadiva (28)** (MPBielby) **4-9-0**(5) LNewton(7) (drvn along & outpcd after 2f: n.d) | 4 | 7 | 66/1 | 50 | 32 |
| | **Mamnoon (USA) (56)** (WClay) **5-8-13** NCarlisle(1) (sn bhd: t.o ½-wy: kpt on appr fnl f) | 1¾ | 8 | 25/1 | 40 | 22 |
| *1030*[2] | **Sea Devil (67)** (MJCamacho) **10-9-1** LCharnock(2) (chsd ldrs: rdn ½-wy: wknd over 1f out: eased) | 1¾ | 9 | 8/1 | 38 | 20 |
| *1030*[7] | **Justinianus (IRE) (45)** (JJBridger) **4-8-10**(5) MBaird(8) (s.i.s: racd wd: a outpcd & sn rdn along) | 11 | 10 | 50/1 | 13 | — |

(SP 121.6%) 10 Rn

**1m 30.9** (4.10) CSF £49.81 TOTE £10.30: £2.30 £2.20 £1.20 (£47.90) Trio £34.30 OWNER Market Rasen Racing Club (MARKET RASEN) BRED The Lavington Stud

**1029 Awesome Venture,** having his nineteenth run of the year, was ridden to perfection and did just enough. (7/1)
**882 Desert Invader (IRE),** back on his favourite surface, made the winner fight all the way to the line. (13/2)
**662 Dancing Sioux,** who looked very woolly, was heavily backed. Tending to edge left under pressure, he was never doing enough in the final furlong. (15/8)
**1043 Palacegate Touch,** making a quick reappearance, was soon racing on the rail, despite being drawn nine of ten. Putting his head in the air turning in, he never looked anything like happy in his work. (5/1)
**1029 Elton Ledger (IRE)** had plenty to do at these weights. (11/2)

### 1095 ITALY H'CAP (0-65) (4-Y.O+) (Class F)
3-30 (3-33) **2m (Fibresand)** £2,381.00 (£656.00: £311.00) Stalls: Low GOING: 0.00 sec per fur (STD)

| | Horse | | Pos | SP | RR | SF |
|---|---|---|---|---|---|---|
| 1044[8] | **Top Prize (29)** (MBrittain) **8-7-10v** GBardwell(6) (lw: sn pushed along: hdwy & in tch ½-wy: hrd rdn 6f out: styd on fnl 2f: led nr fin) | — | 1 | 8/1 | 41 | — |

| | | | | | |
|---|---|---|---|---|---|
| 767[7] | **Tiaphena (40)** (JMackie) **5-8-7** GCarter(2) (w ldr: led ½-wy tl over 2f out: styd on to ld ins fnl f: jst ct)..............½ | **2** | 7/1 | 52 | — |
| 753[11] | **Bella Sedona (53)** (LadyHerries) **4-9-3** AClark(5) (smooth hdwy 7f out: rdn to ld over 2f out: hdd ins fnl f: kpt on same pce)..............½ | **3** | 7/2 [1] | 64 | — |
| *1031[8]* | **Record Lover (IRE) (39)** (MCChapman) **6-8-3**(3) DRMcCabe(9) (chsd ldrs tl wknd over 1f out: eased)...........10 | **4** | 16/1 | 40 | — |
| *656[2]* | **Swordking (IRE) (38)** (JLHarris) **7-8-5v** JQuinn(10) (hld up: hdwy to chse ldrs 6f out: rdn 3f out: one pce).....hd | **5** | 9/2 [2] | 39 | — |
| *855[4]* | **Cross Talk (IRE) (57)** (RHollinshead) **4-9-2**(5) DGriffiths(4) (w ldrs: effrt over 3f out: wknd over 1f out: eased)..............19 | **6** | 8/1 | 39 | — |
| *855[3]* | **Brave Spy (57)** (CACyzer) **5-9-10** GDuffield(11) (chsd ldrs: pushed along 10f out: wknd over 2f out: eased)....2 | **7** | 8/1 | 37 | — |
| *898[6]* | **Captain Marmalade (46)** (DTThom) **7-8-13** JTate(3) (b: bhd: smooth hdwy 6f out: lost pl over 3f out: eased: fin lame)..............7 | **8** | 7/1 | 19 | — |
| 1034[10] | **Dispol Dancer (33)** (MrsVAAconley) **5-8-0**ow4 MDeering(1) (led to ½-wy: lost pl 5f out: t.o 4f out)..................s.h | **9** | 33/1 | 6 | — |
| 844[13] | **Jovie King (IRE) (50)** (PhilipMitchell) **4-9-0** CRutter(8) (chsd ldrs: rdn 9f out: wknd 6f out: t.o 4f out).............12 | **10** | 20/1 | 11 | — |
| 625[13] | **Selmeston (IRE) (45)** (PSFelgate) **4-8-6**(3) DWright(7) (sn bhd: pushed along 10f out: t.o 4f out)....................¾ | **11** | 5/1 [3] | 5 | — |
| | **Lady Risk Me (29)** (DTThom) **7-7-10** NCarlisle(12) (b: bhd & pushed along 10f out: t.o 7f out).....................dist | **12** | 33/1 | — | — |
| | | | (SP 131.9%) | | **12 Rn** |

**3m 48.4** (22.40) CSF £64.55 CT £219.90 TOTE £10.70: £3.00 £2.00 £1.40 (£51.50) Trio £333.50; £93.95 to York 14/5/96 OWNER Mr Mel Brittain (WARTHILL) BRED The Overbury Stud
LONG HANDICAP Dispol Dancer 7-1 Top Prize 7-9 Lady Risk Me 7-6
WEIGHT FOR AGE 4yo-3lb

**474 Top Prize** really made his rider earn his fee. Staying on under severe pressure, he led near the finish. He would have been much better suited by a faster pace. (8/1: op 5/1)

**767 Tiaphena** went on at halfway and soon stepped up the gallop. Proving most determined, she almost landed the gamble, despite having run poorly on her two previous outings this time. (7/1: op 16/1)

**546 Bella Sedona,** who is only small, was put into the stalls last. After moving up on the bridle at halfway and looking all over the winner, once in front, she made hard work of it and was run out of it in the last 100 yards. She certainly stayed the trip in this moderately-run event and the surface was no problem. (7/2)

## 1096 FRANCE H'CAP (0-70) (3-Y.O+ F & M) (Class E)

4-00 (4-03) **1m (Fibresand)** £3,179.40 (£949.20: £453.60: £205.80) Stalls: High GOING: 0.00 sec per fur (STD)

| | | | SP | RR | SF |
|---|---|---|---|---|---|
| 754[5] | **Distinct Beauty (IRE) (67)** (WAO'Gorman) **3-9-4v[1]** EmmaO'Gorman(5) (trckd ldrs: shkn up to ld over 2f out: sn clr)..............— | **1** | 9/1 [3] | 77 | 43 |
| 937[14] | **Hadadabble (45)** (PatMitchell) **3-7-10** NCarlisle(4) (a chsng ldrs: kpt on u.p fnl 2f: no imp) ..............4 | **2** | 25/1 | 47 | 13 |
| *857[2]* | **Grey Galava (60)** (BWHills) **3-8-11** JFEgan(2) (led 2f: rdn & outpcd over 2f out: kpt on fnl f)..............1½ | **3** | 7/2 [1] | 59 | 25 |
| *782[8]* | **Prudent Princess (60)** (AHide) **4-9-3**(7) MartinDwyer(3) (plld hrd: led after 2f tl over 2f out: wknd towards fin)..............hd | **4** | 16/1 | 59 | 38 |
| *836[2]* | **Noble Canonire (55)** (SRBowring) **4-9-0**(5) CTeague(7) (a chsng ldrs: one pce fnl 2f)..............¾ | **5** | 5/1 [2] | 52 | 31 |
| *463** | **Lady Dignity (IRE) (68)** (PJMakin) **3-9-5** SSanders(8) (hld up & bhd: hdwy 2f out: kpt on: nvr nr to chal) ......s.h | **6** | 5/1 [2] | 65 | 31 |
| 527[8] | **Jalmaid (55)** (BAMcMahon) **4-9-5** GCarter(6) (in tch: rdn & outpcd ½-wy: sme hdwy over 1f out: nvr rchd ldrs)..............5 | **7** | 9/1 [3] | 42 | 21 |
| | **Patrio (IRE) (60)** (SCWilliams) **3-8-6**(5) MHenry(11) (unruly gng to s: sn chsng ldrs: rdn over 2f out: sn wknd)11 | **8** | 10/1 | 25 | — |
| | **Toffee (64)** (JRFanshawe) **3-9-1** DHarrison(9) (swtg: bhd & rdn over 3f out: no rspnse)..............7 | **9** | 5/1 [2] | 15 | — |
| 884[7] | **Ballard Lady (IRE) (39)** (JSWainwright) **4-8-3** JQuinn(1) (prom early: rdn & outpcd ½-wy: lost pl 2f out) ..........5 | **10** | 14/1 | — | — |
| 870[6] | **Skelton Countess (IRE) (59)** (RHollinshead) **3-8-5**(5) FLynch(10) (sn bhd: t.o 4f out)..............dist | **11** | 12/1 | — | — |
| | | | (SP 125.4%) | | **11 Rn** |

**1m 45.9** (5.90) CSF £179.49 CT £867.90 TOTE £9.00: £3.60 £9.90 £1.10 (£139.60) Trio £261.20; £184.01 to York 14/5/96 OWNER Mr N. S. Yong (NEWMARKET) BRED Green Ireland Properties Ltd
LONG HANDICAP Hadadabble 7-4
WEIGHT FOR AGE 3yo-13lb

**OFFICIAL EXPLANATION Skelton Countess (IRE): had coughed, possibly due to kick-back and finished sore.**

**754 Distinct Beauty (IRE),** with a visor on this time, scored with the minimum of fuss. (9/1)

**Hadadabble,** who had an impossible task on the turf last time, had two handlers in the paddock. Responding to pressure, she stuck on to finish second best, but had no chance with the winner. (25/1)

**857 Grey Galava** broke first. In trouble and under pressure once in line for home, she stuck on in the final furlong, despite looking anything but happy in her work. (7/2)

**Prudent Princess** raced keenly. After soon showing ahead, her stride shortened noticeably towards the finish. Seven furlongs might be her trip. (16/1)

**836 Noble Canonire** stuck on under strong pressure in the final two furlongs but a mile is much too sharp for her. (5/1)

**463* Lady Dignity (IRE),** from a 4lb higher mark, looked very fit and, involved in some scrimmaging at the start, was dropped in. Picking up ground in the final two furlongs, she could never take a hand. (5/1)

**Toffee,** who wore a crossed-noseband, sweated up badly at the gate. Temperament seems to be getting the better of her and she found nothing at all under pressure at halfway. (5/1)

## 1097 DENMARK (S) STKS (2-Y.O F) (Class G)

4-30 (4-31) **5f (Fibresand)** £2,070.00 (£570.00: £270.00) Stalls: High GOING: 0.00 sec per fur (STD)

| | | | SP | RR | SF |
|---|---|---|---|---|---|
| *1026[2]* | **Come Too Mamma's** (JBerry) **2-8-9** GCarter(7) (trckd ldrs: shkn up to ld jst ins fnl f: rdn out)..............— | **1** | 100/30 [2] | 56 | 3 |
| *858[2]* | **Run Lucy Run** (RGuest) **2-8-4**(5) FLynch(3) (mde most tl jst ins fnl f: kpt on wl)..............¾ | **2** | 4/1 [3] | 54 | 1 |
| *895[2]* | **Who Told Vicky (IRE)** (JSMoore) **2-8-9** JFEgan(9) (w ldrs: nt qckn ins fnl f)..............¾ | **3** | 2/1 [1] | 51 | — |
| 990[6] | **Rahona (IRE)** (BSRothwell) **2-8-9b[1]** DHarrison(5) (a chsng ldrs: kpt on one pce fnl 2f) ..............1½ | **4** | 12/1 | 46 | — |
| 770[3] | **Face It** (WGMTurner) **2-8-9** AClark(6) (chsd ldrs tl wknd over 1f out)..............2½ | **5** | 5/1 | 38 | — |
| 823[9] | **Ramsey Pride** (CWFairhurst) **2-8-9** JTate(4) (s.i.s: nvr nr ldrs)..............5 | **6** | 14/1 | 22 | — |
| | **Midnight Times** (DCO'Brien) **2-8-9** GBardwell(1) (swvd lft s: sn chsng ldrs: edgd lft & wknd qckly over 1f out)..............¾ | **7** | 12/1 | 20 | — |
| 733[8] | **Chilled Wine** (NBycroft) **2-8-9** LCharnock(2) (chsd ldrs to ½-wy: sn wknd) ..............6 | **8** | 16/1 | 1 | — |
| *858[7]* | **Chloezymp (IRE)** (JBalding) **2-8-2b[1]**(7) JEdmunds(8) (outpcd & bhd fr ½-wy)..............9 | **9** | 33/1 | — | — |
| | | | (SP 124.0%) | | **9 Rn** |

**62.3 secs** (5.30) CSF £17.53 TOTE £3.10: £1.80 £1.90 £1.10 (£5.50) Trio £3.70 OWNER Mr J. K. Brown (COCKERHAM) BRED D. Walker
Bt in 3,200 gns

**1026 Come Too Mamma's** had much less use made of her this time. Moving up strongly to show ahead just inside the last, she had only to be kept up to her work. (100/30)
**858 Run Lucy Run** turned the tables on the third on the Folkestone form. After making the running, she proved all heart but the winner always had her measure. (4/1)
**895 Who Told Vicky (IRE)** raced under the stands' side. After having every chance inside the last, she could find no extra. (2/1)
**446 Rahona (IRE)**, in blinkers, ran better. (12/1)
**770 Face It**, having her first outing on the All-Weather, showed plenty of speed but tired over a furlong out. (5/1)

## 1098 GERMANY APPRENTICE H'CAP (0-65) (3-Y.O+) (Class G)

5-00 (5-01) **1m 3f (Fibresand)** £2,070.00 (£570.00: £270.00) Stalls: Low GOING: 0.00 sec per fur (STD)

| | | | | SP | RR | SF |
|---|---|---|---|---|---|---|
| *$898^{2}$* | **Canton Venture (64)** (SPCWoods) **4-9-7**(7) JMoon(1) (lw: mde all: styd on wl fnl 2f: rdn out) | — | **1** | $4/1^{1}$ | 76 | 37 |
| | **Silver Hunter (USA) (50)** (GCBravery) **5-9-0** LNewton(4) (lw: trckd ldrs: wnt 2nd 3f out: sn hrd rdn: kpt on: no imp) | 2½ | **2** | 8/1 | 58 | 19 |
| $884^{2}$ | **Personimus (39)** (CaptJWilson) **6-8-3** PFessey(6) (lw: sn pushed along: hdwy to chse ldrs ½-wy: rdn & outpcd over 3f out: kpt on fnl 2f) | 1¼ | **3** | $6/1^{3}$ | 46 | 7 |
| $995^{7}$ | **Watch Me Go (IRE) (46)** (BobJones) **7-8-5**(5) GFaulkner(5) (b: sn pushed along: in tch: outpcd 4f out: kpt on one pce) | 6 | **4** | 12/1 | 44 | 5 |
| *$898^{8}$* | **Carol Again (50)** (NBycroft) **4-9-0** FLynch(8) (lw: sn trckng ldrs gng wl: ev ch & rdn over 2f out: wknd over 1f out) | 2½ | **5** | $4/1^{1}$ | 44 | 5 |
| *$360^{2}$* | **Pedaltothemetal (IRE) (45)** (PhilipMitchell) **4-8-6**(3) CAdamson(3) (lw: sn outpcd & bhd: styd on fnl 2f: nvr nr ldrs) | nk | **6** | 8/1 | 39 | — |
| $979^{12}$ | **Mazilla (52)** (AStreeter) **4-9-2v** RHavlin(10) (lw: trckd ldrs: effrt 3f out: sn rdn: wknd over 1f out) | nk | **7** | 8/1 | 45 | 6 |
| *$855^{5}$* | **Milltown Classic (IRE) (32)** (JParkes) **4-7-5**(5) PDoe(9) (chsd ldrs tl lost pl over 2f out) | 2½ | **8** | 14/1 | 22 | — |
| $883^{8}$ | **Mr Moriarty (IRE) (41)** (SRBowring) **5-8-5** CTeague(7) (w wnr: rdn ½-wy: lost pl over 3f out: sn bhd) | 4 | **9** | $5/1^{2}$ | 25 | — |
| *$1031^{7}$* | **Mega Tid (50)** (BAPearce) **4-8-9**(5) JWilkinson(2) (chsd ldrs: rdn ½-wy: sn lost pl) | 2½ | **10** | 16/1 | 30 | — |
| $866^{10}$ | **Thorniwama (41)** (JJBridger) **5-8-5b** MBaird(11) (dwlt: a bhd) | ½ | **11** | 10/1 | 21 | — |
| | | | | (SP 133.6%) | **11 Rn** | |

**2m 30.5** (10.50) CSF £38.06 CT £186.82 TOTE £7.20: £3.50 £2.50 £2.00 (£42.20) Trio £194.70 OWNER Dr Frank Chao (NEWMARKET) BRED High Point B/stock Ltd & Chao Racing & B/stock Ltd
LONG HANDICAP Milltown Classic (IRE) 7-6
STEWARDS' ENQUIRY Newton susp. 22-24/5/96 (excessive use of whip).
**898 Canton Venture** showed the benefit of his initial outing. Making all the running, he was kept going by the boy who was recording his first ever success. (4/1: op 5/2)
**Silver Hunter (USA)**, fresh and well, has broken blood-vessels in the past. Responding to severe pressure, he was always second best and never going to get in a blow. (8/1)
**884 Personimus**, still a maiden on his twenty-eighth outing, struggled to go the pace. Sticking on under pressure in the final two furlongs, he was never going to get in a blow. (6/1)
**609 Watch Me Go (IRE)** struggled to go the pace throughout and was never nearer. (12/1)
**898 Carol Again**, 17lb higher than when breaking her duck here three outings ago, travelled strongly and looked a real danger turning in, but she was soon under pressure and faded over a furlong out. (4/1: 3/1-9/2)

T/Plpt: £29.10 (371.76 Tckts). T/Qdpt: £17.30 (55.78 Tckts). WG

# WINDSOR (Fig. 8) (Good to firm)

## Monday May 13th

WEATHER: fine WIND: almost nil

## 1099 BRITISH RED CROSS CLAIMING STKS (3 & 4-Y.O) (Class F)

6-05 (6-06) **1m 67y** £2,899.00 (£814.00: £397.00) Stalls: High GOING minus 0.29 sec per fur (GF)

| | | | | SP | RR | SF |
|---|---|---|---|---|---|---|
| $850^{12}$ | **Delight of Dawn (70)** (KTIvory) **4-8-9**(7) CScally(10) (hdwy over 2f out: led over 1f out: rdn out) | — | **1** | $7/1^{3}$ | 63 | 37 |
| | **Move With Edes (61)** (WGMTurner) **4-9-4** TSprake(19) (lw: rdn & hdwy over 1f out: r.o wl ins fnl f) | nk | **2** | 14/1 | 64 | 38 |
| | **Adilov (62)** (RTPhillips) **4-9-0** RPerham(18) (a.p: n.m.r on ins over 6f out: rdn over 2f out: unable qckn) | 2 | **3** | 14/1 | 57 | 31 |
| $968^{15}$ | **Desert Harvest (74)** (GMMcCourt) **4-8-8**(7) RStudholme(20) (lw: led 7f: one pce) | 3½ | **4** | 12/1 | 51 | 25 |
| $879^{31}$ | **Rockville Pike (IRE) (65)** (SDow) **4-9-0v** TQuinn(4) (a.p: rdn over 2f out: one pce fnl f) | ½ | **5** | 9/1 | 49 | 23 |
| $893^{14}$ | **Andsome Boy (41)** (CRBarwell) **3-8-0**(3) NVarley(21) (a.p: rdn over 3f out: one pce) | 1½ | **6** | 33/1 | 48 | 9 |
| *$409^{6}$* | **Considerable Charm (41)** (AMoore) **4-8-9** CandyMorris(16) (a.p: rdn over 2f out: wknd over 1f out) | 2½ | **7** | 33/1 | 36 | 10 |
| $1000^{4}$ | **Sunley Secure (66)** (MRChannon) **3-8-6** PaulEddery(2) (hld up: rdn over 2f out: one pce) | s.h | **8** | $6/1^{1}$ | 46 | 7 |
| *$531^{2}$* | **Rowlandsons Charm (IRE) (57)** (AMoore) **3-7-12v** NAdams(5) (hld up: rdn over 3f out: wknd over 1f out) | ½ | **9** | $13/2^{2}$ | 37 | — |
| $670^{11}$ | **Mystic Legend (IRE) (30)** (TJNaughton) **4-9-5** SWhitworth(14) (nvr nrr) | ¾ | **10** | 50/1 | 44 | 18 |
| $752^{22}$ | **Kama Simba (56)** (JWhite) **4-9-5** JFortune(12) (hld up: rdn over 2f out: sn wknd) | 2½ | **11** | 12/1 | 39 | 13 |
| $870^{9}$ | **Gold Lining (IRE)** (CDBroad) **3-8-3** AMcGlone(3) (a mid div) | 1¾ | **12** | 20/1 | 33 | — |
| *$141^{7}$* | **Burnt Sienna (IRE) (47)** (JSMoore) **4-8-5**(7) JKeenan(11) (nvr nrr) | 1¼ | **13** | 14/1 | 26 | — |
| $980^{8}$ | **Lahik (IRE) (45)** (KTIvory) **3-8-4** DBiggs(8) (w ldr 5f) | 3 | **14** | 50/1 | 25 | — |
| | **Welcome Brief** (WJMusson) **3-8-4**ow6 GHind(17) (neat: bkwd: s.s: nvr nrr) | 2 | **15** | 16/1 | 21 | — |
| $949^{8}$ | **Out Line** (MMadgwick) **4-8-7**(7) AEddery(7) (bhd fnl 3f) | 1¼ | **16** | 33/1 | 16 | — |
| *$776^{7}$* | **Athinar** (CPWildman) **4-8-9** RCochrane(13) (bhd fnl 4f) | 2 | **17** | 16/1 | 7 | — |
| $860^{15}$ | **Indian Wolf** (PGMurphy) **3-8-2**(3) SDrowne(6) (a bhd) | 1½ | **18** | 50/1 | 13 | — |
| $756^{9}$ | **Eurobox Boy (70)** (APJarvis) **3-8-3**(3) DaneO'Neill(9) (b.nr hind: bhd fnl 3f) | 2 | **19** | $7/1^{3}$ | 10 | — |
| | **Bromfylde Fayemaid (IRE)** (JRJenkins) **4-8-12** NDay(15) (s.s: a bhd) | 7 | **20** | 16/1 | — | — |
| $932^{12}$ | **Michelle's Ella (IRE)** (CDBroad) **4-8-11**(5) ADaly(1) (bhd fnl 5f) | 7 | **21** | 50/1 | — | — |
| | | | | (SP 137.1%) | **21 Rn** | |

**1m 46.2** (4.00) CSF £99.80 TOTE £9.70: £3.30 £3.90 £8.80 (£119.70) Trio £152.40 OWNER Mr K. T. Ivory (RADLETT) BRED John Hayter
WEIGHT FOR AGE 3yo-13lb
Delight of Dawn clmd JDewhurst £10,000; Adilov clmd TJMitchell £3,000; Desert Harvest clmd ASpargo £4,000; Welcome Brief clmd EAlston £5,000
**Delight of Dawn** moved up to hit the front below the distance and, ridden along, just managed to hold on. (7/1)

**Move With Edes** only just failed to make a winning return to action. Finding his feet below the distance, he ran on really strongly inside the final furlong but found the line coming too soon. (14/1)
**Adilov**, who has changed stables since last year, was always close up but failed to find that vital turn of foot. (14/1)
**Desert Harvest**, collared below the distance, could only keep on in his own time. (12/1)
**549* Rockville Pike (IRE)**, almost on level terms below the distance, was then tapped for toe. (9/1: op 6/1)
**Andsome Boy** was being pushed along over three furlongs from home but could only go up and down in the same place. (33/1)
**531 Rowlandsons Charm (IRE)** (13/2: 9/2-7/1)
**655 Eurobox Boy** (7/1: 9/2-8/1)

## 1100 VODAFONE H'CAP (0-70) (3-Y.O) (Class E)

6-35 (6-36) **1m 3f 135y** £3,241.25 (£980.00: £477.50: £226.25) Stalls: High GOING minus 0.29 sec per fur (GF)

| | | | | SP | RR | SF |
|---|---|---|---|---|---|---|
| 731[6] | **Atlantic Mist (56)** (BRMillman) **3-8-6**(3) SDrowne(3) (hdwy over 3f out: led over 1f out: r.o wl) | — | 1 | 14/1 | 65 | 28 |
| *1031[4]* | **State Approval (58)** (APJarvis) **3-8-11** JFortune(18) (hrd rdn over 2f out: hdwy over 1f out: r.o wl ins fnl f) | nk | 2 | 20/1 | 67 | 30 |
| 754[3] | **Classic Ballet (FR) (67)** (SCWilliams) **3-9-6** AMackay(4) (hdwy over 3f out: hrd rdn over 2f out: r.o one pce) | 4 | 3 | 9/1[3] | 70 | 33 |
| 593[12] | **Compass Pointer (60)** (JMPEustace) **3-8-13** MTebbutt(5) (rdn & hdwy 2f out: one pce fnl f) | s.h | 4 | 33/1 | 63 | 26 |
| 819[8] | **Tarry (62)** (SESherwood) **3-9-1** JReid(10) (hdwy & hmpd over 3f out: nvr nrr) | 1¼ | 5 | 8/1[2] | 63 | 26 |
| 761[4] | **Domettes (IRE) (60)** (RHannon) **3-8-10**(3) DaneO'Neill(15) (no hdwy fnl 3f) | s.h | 6 | 9/1[3] | 61 | 24 |
| | **Spinning Mouse (56)** (DMorley) **3-8-9** RCochrane(2) (gd hdwy fnl f: nvr plcd to chal) | 3 | 7 | 16/1 | 53 | 16 |
| *555[2]* | **Blueberry Fields (60)** (CFWall) **3-8-13** WWoods(9) (nvr nrr) | nk | 8 | 9/1[3] | 57 | 20 |
| *515[2]* | **Bailiwick (49)** (NAGraham) **3-8-2b**ow4 PaulEddery(17) (prom 9f) | d.h | 8 | 10/1 | 46 | 5 |
| 731[9] | **Oliver Rock (63)** (MajorDNChappell) **3-9-2** BThomson(6) (hdwy 6f out: hrd rdn over 2f out: wknd over 1f out) | nk | 10 | 14/1 | 59 | 22 |
| 640[9] | **Flame of Hope (62)** (JLDunlop) **3-9-1** TQuinn(7) (a mid div) | hd | 11 | 11/1 | 58 | 21 |
| 526[9] | **He's Got Wings (IRE) (52)** (MBell) **3-8-5v**[1] SWhitworth(11) (b.nr hind: lw: chsd ldr: led 4f out tl over 1f out: sn wknd) | ½ | 12 | 16/1 | 47 | 10 |
| 717[5] | **Charming Admiral (IRE) (64)** (CFWall) **3-9-3** GDuffield(12) (hmpd over 2f out: nvr nrr) | ½ | 13 | 8/1[2] | 59 | 22 |
| 578[13] | **Dashing Invader (USA) (53)** (PWHarris) **3-8-6** GHind(13) (led over 7f) | ½ | 14 | 25/1 | 47 | 10 |
| 821[11] | **The Boozing Brief (USA) (68)** (MAJarvis) **3-9-4**(3) AWhelan(14) (prom 9f) | 1¼ | 15 | 8/1[2] | 60 | 23 |
| 820[8] | **Le Teteu (FR) (59)** (BobJones) **3-8-12** NDay(1) (bhd fnl 6f) | 1¼ | 16 | 25/1 | 50 | 13 |
| 863[5] | **Dhulikhel (61)** (DMarks) **3-9-0** PatEddery(16) (bhd fnl 3f) | 1½ | 17 | 7/1[1] | 50 | 13 |
| 819[5] | **Ben Bowden (65)** (MBlanshard) **3-9-4** NAdams(20) (hld up: rdn over 3f out: wknd over 2f out) | 1¾ | 18 | 16/1 | 51 | 14 |
| *859[8]* | **Natatarl (IRE) (50)** (BPalling) **3-8-3** TSprake(19) (lw: prom 9f) | nk | 19 | 33/1 | 36 | — |
| *826[14]* | ***Scandator (IRE) (59)*** (PWHarris) **3-8-12b**[1] AMcGlone(8) (Withdrawn not under Starter's orders: lame) | | W | 33/1 | — | — |
| | | | | (SP 145.5%) | **19 Rn** | |

**2m 30.1** (6.10) CSF £266.37 CT £2,466.09 TOTE £19.70: £3.30 £5.80 £2.20 £13.00 (£235.40) Trio £752.60 OWNER The Wardour Partnership (CULLOMPTON) BRED R. Burton

**731 Atlantic Mist**, fitted with a crossed-noseband, took closer order early in the straight. Sent on below the distance, he just managed to hold on. (14/1)
**1031 State Approval**, making a quick reappearance, really found his feet below the distance. Running on strongly inside the final furlong, he found the line coming just too soon. (20/1)
**754 Classic Ballet (FR)** moved up over three furlongs from home. Staying on under pressure, she was unable to get to the front two. (9/1)
**Compass Pointer**, scrubbed along to pick up ground on the outside of the field two furlongs from home, was making no further impression in the last 200 yards. (33/1)
**Tarry**, hampered as she made a forward move over three furlongs from home, nevertheless stayed on, but failed to get there in time. (8/1: tchd 12/1)
**761 Domettes (IRE)** was making little impression in the last three furlongs. (9/1)
**Spinning Mouse** caught the eye in no uncertain terms. Given very tender handling, she was stoked up in the final furlong and came storming through in good style to be nearest at the line. No doubt the kindness will be repaid in due course. (16/1)
**Flame of Hope** (11/1: 6/1-12/1)
**863 Dhulikhel** (7/1: 5/1-8/1)

## 1101 PERPETUAL H'CAP (0-80) (3-Y.O) (Class D)

7-05 (7-10) **5f 217y** £4,026.00 (£1,218.00: £594.00: £282.00) Stalls: High GOING minus 0.29 sec per fur (GF)

| | | | | SP | RR | SF |
|---|---|---|---|---|---|---|
| 1006[4] | **Wildwood Flower (78)** (RHannon) **3-9-7** PatEddery(10) (a.p: led over 3f out: hrd rdn over 1f out: r.o wl) | — | 1 | 5/2[1] | 93+ | 50 |
| 850[14] | **Miss Waterline (70)** (PDEvans) **3-8-13** JFortune(6) (s.s: rdn over 3f out: hdwy over 1f out: r.o wl ins fnl f) | ½ | 2 | 40/1 | 84 | 41 |
| | **Nellie North (72)** (GMMcCourt) **3-9-1** JReid(13) (lw: hld up: rdn over 2f out: unable qckn) | 2½ | 3 | 40/1 | 79 | 36 |
| 893[2] | **Meranti (59)** (SDow) **3-7-11**(5) ADaly(7) (lw: outpcd: hdwy over 1f out: r.o wl ins fnl f) | 2½ | 4 | 13/2[3] | 59 | 16 |
| 755[7] | **Rififi (62)** (RIngram) **3-8-2**(3) PMcCabe(16) (s.s: rdn & hdwy over 3f out: one pce fnl 2f) | s.h | 5 | 25/1 | 62 | 19 |
| 824[3] | **Thai Morning (65)** (PWHarris) **3-8-8b**[1] GHind(11) (hld up: rdn over 2f out: one pce) | 1½ | 6 | 12/1 | 61 | 18 |
| 732[12] | **Charlton Imp (USA) (65)** (RJHodges) **3-8-5**(3) SDrowne(9) (outpcd: nvr nr to chal) | 3 | 7 | 25/1 | 53 | 10 |
| 887[5] | **Amber Fort (69)** (PFICole) **3-8-12b** TQuinn(18) (led over 2f: rdn over 2f out: wknd fnl f) | ½ | 8 | 5/1[2] | 56 | 13 |
| | **Power Game (64)** (JBerry) **3-8-7** WCarson(14) (a mid div) | ½ | 9 | 12/1 | 50 | 7 |
| | **Prime Partner (56)** (WRMuir) **3-7-8**(5) MHenry(1) (a mid div) | 2½ | 10 | 25/1 | 35 | — |
| | **Kossolian (60)** (BPalling) **3-8-3** TSprake(15) (spd over 3f) | nk | 11 | 11/1 | 38 | — |
| | **Faith Alone (65)** (CFWall) **3-8-8** GDuffield(4) (b: bhd fnl 2f) | 3 | 12 | 20/1 | 35 | — |
| 467[13] | **Sharp Stock (73)** (BJMeehan) **3-9-2** RHughes(12) (spd over 4f) | s.h | 13 | 40/1 | 43 | — |
| 783[5] | **Magic Mail (72)** (JMPEustace) **3-9-1** RCochrane(2) (lw: a bhd) | 1¾ | 14 | 20/1 | 37 | — |
| 992[4] | **Blue Suede Hoofs (72)** (BJMeehan) **3-9-1** MTebbutt(5) (bhd fnl 2f) | ½ | 15 | 33/1 | 36 | — |
| 832[6] | **Mindrace (70)** (KTIvory) **3-8-13** DBiggs(17) (prom tl hmpd over 3f out: sn wknd) | 1 | 16 | 33/1 | 31 | — |
| | **Beauchamp Kate (72)** (HCandy) **3-9-1** CRutter(8) (b.hind: bit bkwd: a bhd) | 7 | 17 | 14/1 | 14 | — |
| 672[8] | **Literary Society (USA) (66)** (JARToller) **3-8-9** SSanders(3) (a bhd: lame) | 3 | 18 | 33/1 | — | — |
| | | | | (SP 126.2%) | **18 Rn** | |

**1m 12.6** (2.10) CSF £88.92 CT £3,131.22 TOTE £3.40: £1.40 £4.60 £4.10 £2.00 (£143.40) Trio £640.60; £469.23 to York 15/5/96 OWNER Mr G. Howard-Spink (MARLBOROUGH) BRED Sir Stephen Hastings and G. Howard-Spink
OFFICIAL EXPLANATION **Literary Society (USA): was lame behind.**

**1006 Wildwood Flower** went on over three furlongs from home. Given a few reminders below the distance, she was not going to be denied. (5/2)
**Miss Waterline**, who lost ground at the start, came storming through from below the distance but failed to get there in time. (40/1)
**Nellie North**, on this seasonal bow, could only go up and down in the same place when ridden. (40/1)
**893 Meranti**, unable to live with the early pace, stayed on nicely in the last furlong and a half to be nearest at the line. (13/2)
**Rififi**, pushed along to take closer order just before halfway, failed to find the necessary turn of foot in the last two furlongs. (25/1)
**824 Thai Morning**, fitted with blinkers for the first time, chased the leaders but was making no impression in the last two furlongs. (12/1: op 6/1)
**Power Game** (12/1: op 8/1)
**Kossolian** (11/1: 8/1-12/1)
**Beauchamp Kate** (14/1: 8/1-16/1)

## 1102 CADOGAN GROUP LIMITED STKS (0-75) (4-Y.O+) (Class D)

7-35 (7-39) **1m 2f 7y** £3,714.00 (£1,122.00: £546.00: £258.00) Stalls: High GOING minus 0.29 sec per fur (GF)

| | | | | SP | RR | SF |
|---|---|---|---|---|---|---|
| $871^{6}$ | **Shining Example (72)** (PJMakin) **4-9-0** PatEddery(13) (swtg: hld up: hrd rdn & led over 1f out: edgd rt ins fnl f: r.o wl) | — | **1** | 9/4[1] | 83 | 62 |
| *$243^{6}$* | **Access Adventurer (IRE) (73)** (RBoss) **5-9-0** WRyan(6) (chsd ldr: led over 3f out tl over 1f out: 2nd & btn whn hmpd ins fnl f) | 1½ | **2** | 6/1 | 81 | 60 |
| $739^{11}$ | **Ma Petite Anglaise (75)** (WJarvis) **4-8-6**(5) MHenry(10) (hdwy 5f out: ev ch 2f out: hrd rdn over 1f out: one pce) | ½ | **3** | 10/1 | 77 | 56 |
| $879^{14}$ | **Country Lover (72)** (LordHuntingdon) **5-9-0v** DHarrison(5) (rdn over 2f out: hdwy over 1f out: r.o) | ½ | **4** | 11/2[3] | 79 | 58 |
| $844^{14}$ | **Gloriana (72)** (LadyHerries) **4-8-11** JReid(4) (lw: hld up: rdn over 2f out: one pce) | 2 | **5** | 12/1 | 73 | 52 |
| $670^{10}$ | **Premier League (IRE) (48)** (JELong) **6-8-7**(7) TField(8) (a.p: rdn over 2f out: wknd over 1f out) | 1¼ | **6** | 50/1 | 74 | 53 |
| $650^{14}$ | **Tappeto (73)** (HCandy) **4-9-0b1** CRutter(9) (led over 6f) | 1 | **7** | 7/1 | 72 | 51 |
| *$184^{3}$* | **Wonderful Day (66)** (HAkbary) **5-8-11** GHind(3) (hdwy over 3f out: hrd rdn over 2f out: sn wknd) | 5 | **8** | 16/1 | 61 | 40 |
| $843^{5}$ | **Master Beveled (72)** (PDEvans) **6-9-0** JFortune(11) (lw: hdwy over 3f out: wknd over 2f out) | 4 | **9** | 5/1[2] | 58 | 37 |
| | **Couchant (IRE) (62)** (JWhite) **5-8-11**(3) SDrowne(14) (bit bkwd: a bhd) | 2 | **10** | 33/1 | 55 | 34 |
| | **Printers Quill (54)** (MajorDNChappell) **4-9-0** BThomson(1) (prom over 3f) | 10 | **11** | 20/1 | 39 | 18 |
| $879^{30}$ | **Komodo (USA) (60)** (KOCunningham-Brown) **4-9-0** SWhitworth(12) (a bhd) | s.h | **12** | 33/1 | 39 | 18 |
| $817^{14}$ | **Tribal Peace (IRE) (65)** (BGubby) **4-8-13**(3) JStack(2) (bhd fnl 4f) | 6 | **13** | 33/1 | 31 | 10 |
| | | | | (SP 127.8%) | **13 Rn** | |

**2m 6.5** (1.60) CSF £16.82 TOTE £3.40: £1.50 £3.10 £3.10 (£12.30) Trio £56.50 OWNER Mr D. M. Ahier (MARLBOROUGH) BRED Stetchworth Park Stud Ltd

**871 Shining Example** drifted right inside the final furlong, hampering the second, but this did not affect the result, and he was definitely the best horse on the day. (9/4)
**Access Adventurer (IRE)**, off the track for three months, was interfered with by the winner inside the final furlong but was held in second at the time. (6/1)
**Ma Petite Anglaise** moved up entering the straight. With every chance a quarter of a mile from home, she then failed to find another gear. (10/1)
**325a Country Lover** put in some good work in the last furlong and a half but failed to get there in time. (11/2)
**Gloriana** chased the leaders but failed to find another gear in the last two furlongs. (12/1: 7/1-14/1)
**Tappeto** (7/1: 10/1-6/1)
**843 Master Beveled** (5/1: 4/1-6/1)

## 1103 SUNLEY CONDITIONS STKS (2-Y.O) (Class C)

8-05 (8-05) **5f 10y** £4,601.00 (£1,676.00: £818.00: £350.00: £155.00) Stalls: High GOING minus 0.29 sec per fur (GF)

| | | | | SP | RR | SF |
|---|---|---|---|---|---|---|
| | **Natalia Bay (IRE)** (PFICole) **2-8-4**ow1 TQuinn(5) (neat: hld up: w ldr over 2f out: led over 1f out: rdn out) | — | **1** | 14/1 | 80 | 32 |
| 930* | **Braveheart (IRE)** (MRChannon) **2-8-11** RHughes(1) (a.p: led over 2f out tl over 1f out: unable qckn) | 1¾ | **2** | 9/2[3] | 82 | 35 |
| 990* | **Grovefair Flyer (IRE)** (BJMeehan) **2-8-8**(3) DaneO'Neill(4) (hld up: rdn over 2f out: one pce) | 5 | **3** | 25/1 | 66 | 19 |
| 557* | **Sweet Emmaline** (WGMTurner) **2-8-6** TSprake(3) (lw: led over 2f: sn wknd) | 1¾ | **4** | 11/8[1] | 55 | 8 |
| 807* | **Sabotini** (BWHills) **2-8-10** PatEddery(2) (chsd ldr 2f) | 5 | **5** | 6/4[2] | 43 | — |
| | | | | (SP 110.8%) | **5 Rn** | |

**61.1 secs** (1.90) CSF £63.02 TOTE £12.50: £2.40 £1.60 (£16.80) OWNER Philip Blacker Studio Partnership (WHATCOMBE) BRED C. J. Foy
**Natalia Bay (IRE)** disputed the lead from halfway. Sent on below the distance, she was ridden along to assert. (14/1: 7/1-16/1)
**930* Braveheart (IRE)**, collared below the distance, found the winner had too many guns for him. (9/2)
**990* Grovefair Flyer (IRE)** chased the leaders but never looked like quickening up from halfway. (25/1)
**557* Sweet Emmaline**, the paddock pick, lost her race by running far too freely on the way to the post. (11/8)
**807* Sabotini** ran no race at all. In second place for the first two furlongs, she was then in trouble. (6/4)

## 1104 BOWRING GROUP MEDIAN AUCTION MAIDEN STKS (3-Y.O) (Class E)

8-35 (8-42) **1m 2f 7y** £3,095.00 (£935.00: £455.00: £215.00) Stalls: High GOING minus 0.29 sec per fur (GF)

| | | | | SP | RR | SF |
|---|---|---|---|---|---|---|
| | **Persian Punch (IRE)** (DRCElsworth) **3-9-0** AProcter(11) (wl grwn: lw: hdwy 2f out: led ins fnl f: r.o wl) | — | **1** | 20/1 | 85+ | 42 |
| $845^{6}$ | **King of Sparta** (LMCumani) **3-9-0** PatEddery(3) (led: rdn 3f out: hdd ins fnl f: unable qckn) | 2½ | **2** | 4/5[1] | 81 | 38 |
| $892^{7}$ | **Effectual** (JARToller) **3-9-0** SSanders(12) (a.p: ev ch 1f out: one pce) | 1¾ | **3** | 50/1 | 78 | 35 |
| $978^{9}$ | **Half An Inch (IRE) (73)** (BJMeehan) **3-9-0** RHughes(18) (chsd ldr: edgd rt 2f out: ev ch 1f out: sn wknd) | 2½ | **4** | 14/1 | 74 | 31 |
| | **Linda's Joy (IRE)** (RGuest) **3-8-9b1** PBloomfield(4) (w'like: bit bkwd: s.s: hdwy 2f out: r.o one pce) | 2½ | **5** | 50/1 | 65 | 22 |
| $860^{13}$ | **Absolutelystunning (45)** (MrsBarbaraWaring) **3-8-9** JFEgan(15) (b: b.off hind: no hdwy fnl 3f) | 2 | **6** | 100/1 | 62 | 19 |
| | **Tom Swift (IRE)** (RCSpicer) **3-9-0** TSprake(5) (prom over 7f) | nk | **7** | 100/1 | 67 | 24 |
| | **Prestige Lass** (BSmart) **3-8-9** RCochrane(1) (leggy: nvr nr to chal) | hd | **8** | 25/1 | 61 | 18 |
| $550^{4}$ | **Premier Censure** (JRFanshawe) **3-8-9** DHarrison(10) (b.hind: prom over 7f) | 4 | **9** | 9/1 | 55 | 12 |
| $847^{8}$ | **Hoofprints (IRE)** (GHarwood) **3-9-0** AClark(2) (4th whn hmpd & lost pl over 8f out: nt rcvr) | ¾ | **10** | 40/1 | 59 | 16 |
| $894^{6}$ | **Morning Sir** (CRBarwell) **3-9-0** GHind(14) (prom over 7f) | ¾ | **11** | 50/1 | 58 | 15 |
| | **Bellaphento** (JRinger) **3-8-9** GDuffield(13) (b: 8th whn hmpd on ins 6f out: wknd over 3f out) | 2 | **12** | 66/1 | 50 | 7 |
| | **Tathmin** (JRBosley) **3-9-0** CRutter(16) (w'like: bit bkwd: bhd fnl 4f) | 1½ | **13** | 50/1 | 52 | 9 |
| | **Parsa (USA)** (JLDunlop) **3-8-9** WCarson(9) (s.s: a bhd) | 5 | **14** | 6/1[3] | 39 | — |
| | **Russian Rose (IRE)** (AHide) **3-8-9** MTebbutt(6) (leggy: 7th whn hmpd 9f out: bhd fnl 7f) | 2½ | **15** | 50/1 | 35 | — |
| *$167^{9}$* | **Foothill (IRE)** (RTPhillips) **3-9-0** WJO'Connor(8) (bhd fnl 8f) | hd | **16** | 100/1 | 40 | — |
| $932^{11}$ | **Secondment** (LMCumani) **3-9-0** CHodgson(17) (s.s: a bhd: t.o) | 30 | **17** | 40/1 | — | — |

684[9] **Robusta (IRE)** (ACStewart) **3-8-9** SWhitworth(7) (lw: 3rd whn broke leg and fell over 8f outz) .......................... **F** 100/30[2] — —
*Ell Ell Eff* (AHide) **3-8-9** WRyan(19) (Withdrawn not under Starter's orders: uns rdr & bolted at s) .................... **W** 40/1 — —
(SP 139.8%) **18 Rn**

**2m 9.0** (4.10) CSF £37.75 TOTE £44.50: £7.30 £1.30 £11.40 (£30.40) Trio £351.40; £202.97 to York 15/5/96 OWNER Mr J. C. Smith (WHITCOMBE) BRED Adstock Manor Stud

**Persian Punch (IRE)**, a well-built newcomer, looked in good shape for this outing and sprang a surprise. Getting into top gear in the last two furlongs, he came storming through to grab the initiative inside the final furlong and soon had it sewn up. (20/1)
**845 King of Sparta**, rfidden along three furlongs from home as he tried to stretch his field, was eventually overhauled inside the last 200 yards. His turn is not far away. (4/5)
**Effectual**, never far away, had every chance a furlong from home before tapped for toe. (50/1)
**Half An Inch (IRE)**, who gave chase to the winner, was certainly close enough if good enough a furlong from home before tiring. (14/1)
**Linda's Joy (IRE)**, fitted with blinkers for this racecourse debut, looked in need of the run. Staying on in the last two furlongs, she never looked like getting there in time. (50/1)
**550 Premier Censure** (9/1: 5/1-10/1)
**Parsa (USA)** (6/1: op 14/1)

T/Plpt: £470.10 (36.5 Tckts). T/Qdpt: £32.00 (47.93 Tckts). AK

# YORK (L-H) (Good to firm, Good patches)
## Tuesday May 14th

Race 1: hand-timed
WEATHER: sunny & warm WIND: almost nil

## 1105 E.B.F. TRANSPENNINE EXPRESS MAIDEN STKS (2-Y.O F) (Class D)
2-00 (2-01) **5f** £5,796.00 (£1,728.00: £824.00: £372.00) Stalls: High GOING minus 0.24 sec per fur (GF)

| | | | | SP | RR | SF |
|---|---|---|---|---|---|---|
| | **Dance Parade (USA)** (PFICole) **2-8-11** MJKinane(4) (gd sort: cl up: led jst ins fnl f: r.o) | — | 1 | 2/1[2] | 81+ | 25 |
| | **Royal Orchid (IRE)** (RHannon) **2-8-11** JReid(6) (w'like: led: edgd lft fr ½-wy: hdd ins fnl f: no ex) | 2½ | 2 | 5/2[3] | 73 | 17 |
| | **Sketch Pad** (RCharlton) **2-8-11** KFallon(3) (w'like: scope: lw: trckd ldrs: effrt & hmpd appr fnl f: swtchd & nt rcvr) | ¾ | 3 | 7/4[1] | 71+ | 15 |
| 950[5] | **Top of The Wind (IRE)** (JJO'Neill) **2-8-11** WCarson(5) (chsd ldrs: rdn 2f out: no imp) | 2½ | 4 | 10/1 | 63 | 7 |
| 984[6] | **Amy** (CSmith) **2-8-11** NCarlisle(2) (spd to ½-wy: sn bhd) | 13 | 5 | 50/1 | 21 | — |

(SP 109.3%) **5 Rn**

**60.6 secs** (2.90) CSF £6.93 TOTE £3.00: £1.70 £1.80 (£3.20) OWNER H R H Prince Fahd Salman (WHATCOMBE) BRED Newgate Stud Farm Inc

**Dance Parade (USA)**, a good-bodied filly, looked likely to benefit from this, but still won well. The future looks very rosy. (2/1)
**Royal Orchid (IRE)** put up a decent show, but was inclined to hang off the rail from halfway, and should be all the better for the experience. (5/2)
**Sketch Pad** looked fit but did not impress on the way to post. She was messed about and would certainly have finished second with a clear run, and is one to keep in mind, especially over further. (7/4)
**950 Top of The Wind (IRE)** showed more enthusiasm this time and a repeat of this would certainly bring her success in a run-of-the-mill event. (10/1)
**Amy** moved moderately and, once the pace hotted up at halfway, she was left way behind. (50/1)

## 1106 SHEPHERD TROPHY RATED STKS H'CAP (0-100) (3-Y.O) (Class B)
2-35 (2-36) **1m 2f 85y** £12,884.80 (£4,763.20: £2,281.60: £928.00: £364.00: £138.40) Stalls: Low GOING minus 0.24 sec per fur (GF)

| | | | | SP | RR | SF |
|---|---|---|---|---|---|---|
| 575* | **Dombey (88)** (RCharlton) **3-9-2** TSprake(5) (lw: trckd ldrs: effrt over 2f out: r.o to ld nr fin) | — | 1 | 9/4[1] | 92+ | 68 |
| 766* | **Humourless (90)** (LMCumani) **3-9-4** MJKinane(7) (lw: trckd ldr: rdn to ld 2f out: r.o: hdd nr fin) | hd | 2 | 9/4[1] | 94+ | 70 |
| 970[6] | **Warning Reef (84)** (MRChannon) **3-8-12** RHughes(3) (led 1f: chsd ldrs: rdn 3f out: kpt on wl) | 1¼ | 3 | 12/1 | 86 | 62 |
| 1002[2] | **Pleasant Surprise (89)** (MJohnston) **3-9-3** KDarley(2) (plld hrd: in tch: hdwy on ins 3f out: kpt on fnl f) | 2 | 4 | 9/2[2] | 88 | 64 |
| 1059a* | **Double Diamond (IRE) (93)** (MJohnston) **3-9-7** JReid(6) (led after 1f tl hdd 2f out: one pce) | 2 | 5 | 15/2[3] | 89 | 65 |
| 947[7] | **Villeggiatura (86)** (BWHills) **3-9-0** RHills(4) (hld up: rdn 3f out: btn appr fnl f) | ½ | 6 | 14/1 | 81 | 57 |
| | **Mancini (88)** (MBell) **3-9-2** MFenton(1) (hmpd s: bhd: effrt 3f out: sn btn) | 2 | 7 | 16/1 | 80 | 56 |

(SP 111.7%) **7 Rn**

**2m 11.29** (1.59) CSF £7.35 TOTE £3.10: £1.80 £1.50 (£2.60) OWNER Lady Rothschild (BECKHAMPTON) BRED Exors of the late Mrs D. M. de Rothschild

STEWARDS' ENQUIRY Kinane susp. 23-24/5/96 (excessive use of whip)

**575* Dombey**, stepping up in distance, needed every yard of this and will get better again as he tries further yet. (9/4)
**766* Humourless**, a good-actioned colt, tried hard but was just touched off. This might well turn out to be a decent performance. (9/4)
**833 Warning Reef** enjoyed this longer trip. Judging by the way he kept battling on, he should stay further yet, and he will certainly not be a maiden for much longer. (12/1)
**1002 Pleasant Surprise** needed more use made of him than was the case here. Although keeping on well in the home straight, he could never offer a threat, but will do better in due course. (9/2)
**1059a* Double Diamond (IRE)** made most of the running, but basically did not go fast enough, and was done for toe in the last two furlongs. (15/2: 5/1-8/1)
**Villeggiatura**, a sturdy individual, is taking time to come to hand and better will be seen as he gets fitter. (14/1)
**Mancini** got messed about at the start and never took any interest thereafter. (16/1)

## 1107 PAUL CADDICK AND MACGAY SPRINT TROPHY RATED STKS H'CAP (0-105) (3-Y.O+) (Class B)
3-05 (3-07) **6f** £11,274.20 (£4,167.80: £1,996.40: £812.00: £318.50: £121.10) Stalls: High GOING minus 0.24 sec per fur (GF)

| | | | | SP | RR | SF |
|---|---|---|---|---|---|---|
| 928* | **Jayannpee (96)** (IABalding) **5-8-8**(7) MartinDwyer(2) (lw: trckd ldrs gng wl: led 1½f out: sn clr) | — | 1 | 11/2[3] | 110 | 70 |
| 940* | **Madly Sharp (97)** (JWWatts) **5-9-2** MJKinane(8) (lw: hld up & bhd: nt clr run & swtchd twice 2f out: r.o wl: too much to do) | 1½ | 2 | 11/2[3] | 107 | 67 |
| 711[2] | **Top Banana (91)** (HCandy) **5-8-10** CRutter(3) (a cl up: effrt 2f out: nt qckn) | 3 | 3 | 5/2[1] | 93 | 53 |
| | **Stylish Ways (IRE) (97)** (MissSEHall) **4-9-2** NConnorton(4) (plld hrd: effrt ½-wy: styd on: nvr able to chal) | 1¼ | 4 | 20/1 | 96 | 56 |

| | | | | SP | RR | SF |
|---|---|---|---|---|---|---|
| 940[11] | **Hello Mister (102)** (TEPowell) **5-9-4**(3) PMcCabe(1) (chsd ldrs: ev ch & edgd lft 2f out: nt qckn) | 2½ | **5** | 25/1 | 94 | 54 |
| | **Master Planner (92)** (CACyzer) **7-8-11** KFallon(5) (lw: led tl hdd 1½f out: sn btn) | nk | **6** | 7/1 | 83 | 43 |
| 679[6] | **Astrac (IRE) (95)** (RAkehurst) **5-8-7**(7) TAshley(6) (hld up: hdwy 2f out: nvr able to chal) | nk | **7** | 13/2 | 85 | 45 |
| 940[7] | **Double Blue (101)** (MJohnston) **7-9-6** JReid(9) (chsd ldrs: rdn ½-wy: sn btn) | 2½ | **8** | 9/1 | 85 | 45 |
| 889[2] | **Everglades (IRE) (96)** (RCharlton) **8-9-1** SSanders(7) (trckd ldrs gng wl tl rdn & btn wl over 1f out) | 1¼ | **9** | 5/1[2] | 76 | 36 |

(SP 120.4%) **9 Rn**

**1m 11.65** (0.65) CSF £34.55 CT £87.72 TOTE £6.80: £1.90 £2.20 £1.40 (£21.70) Trio £11.00 OWNER Mr J. Paniccia (KINGSCLERE) BRED C. H. Bothway

**928* Jayannpee** is in the form of his life just now and, once allowed to go on approaching the final furlong, there were never any doubts. (11/2)
**940* Madly Sharp**, trying to come from behind, met with all sorts of trouble and had an impossible task once free. He might well have shaken the winner up with a clear passage. (11/2)
**711 Top Banana**, badly handicapped with the winner on their Stewards' Cup running last year, ran a sound race in the circumstances. (5/2)
**Stylish Ways (IRE)** took a strong hold going down and some of the way back. Asked for an effort, he was never doing enough. (20/1)
**Hello Mister** moves, as some sprinters do, very moderately and gave problems at the start, but still showed he has ability. (25/1)
**Master Planner**, looking pretty fit, had a good blow out and should now be cherry-ripe. (7/1)
**679 Astrac (IRE)**, better on easier ground, was never doing quite enough, but did give the impression that he is coming to hand. (13/2)

## 1108 TATTERSALLS MUSIDORA STKS (Gp 3) (3-Y.O F) (Class A)

3-40 (3-40) **1m 2f 85y** £25,304.00 (£9,104.00: £4,352.00: £1,760.00: £680.00) Stalls: Low GOING minus 0.24 sec per fur (GF)

| | | | | SP | RR | SF |
|---|---|---|---|---|---|---|
| 938[3] | **Magnificient Style (USA)** (HRACecil) **3-8-8** MJKinane(3) (lw: mde all: shkn up over 2f out: r.o wl) | — | **1** | 5/2[2] | 110 | 60 |
| 708[3] | **Sil Sila (IRE) (102)** (BSmart) **3-8-8** RCochrane(2) (a.p: effrt 3f out: kpt on wl towards fin) | 1¾ | **2** | 12/1 | 107 | 57 |
| 936[4] | **Obsessive (USA) (100)** (MRStoute) **3-8-8** TQuinn(4) (trckd ldrs: effrt over 2f out: sn ev ch: nt qckn appr fnl f) | 1 | **3** | 9/1[3] | 106 | 56 |
| 938[4] | **Ruznama (USA) (109)** (BWHills) **3-8-8** WCarson(5) (hld up & bhd: hdwy over 3f out: sn rdn: btn 2f out) | 3 | **4** | 7/4[1] | 101 | 51 |
| 572* | **Sea Spray (IRE)** (PWChapple-Hyam) **3-8-8** JReid(1) (trckd wnr tl rdn & btn over 2f out) | 2 | **5** | 5/2[2] | 98 | 48 |

(SP 111.2%) **5 Rn**

**2m 11.45** (1.75) CSF £22.64 TOTE £3.10: £1.50 £2.80 (£12.10) OWNER Buckram Oak Holdings (NEWMARKET) BRED Buckram Oak Farm

**938 Magnificient Style (USA)**, who looked superb, was given the aggressive ride she needs. Responding gamely when challenged, she was well on top at the end. She will get further yet and easier ground would certainly not go amiss. A supplementary entry for the Oaks would cost £15,000 and is probably dependent on the likelihood of soft ground. (5/2)
**708 Sil Sila (IRE)** appreciated this longer trip and, given some cut in the ground, should do even better. (12/1)
**936 Obsessive (USA)** put up a decent performance, but tried to take the winner on in the straight and that proved too much. She is certainly improving. (9/1)
**938 Ruznama (USA)**, given a patient ride, was disappointing once off the bit. (7/4)
**572* Sea Spray (IRE)**, a sparely-made filly, was always in the right place here. Once the pressure was on, her limitations were there for all to see. (5/2)

## 1109 YORKSHIRE LIFE MAGAZINE H'CAP (0-90) (4-Y.O+) (Class C)

4-10 (4-10) **1m 3f 195y** £7,570.00 (£2,260.00: £1,080.00: £490.00) Stalls: Low GOING minus 0.24 sec per fur (GF)

| | | | | SP | RR | SF |
|---|---|---|---|---|---|---|
| 853* | **Remaadi Sun (72)** (MDIUsher) **4-8-10** RStreet(1) (hld up & bhd: hdwy on bit 3f out: led ins fnl f: comf) | — | **1** | 10/1 | 83 | 60 |
| 925[4] | **Polydamas (83)** (MRStoute) **4-9-7** JReid(2) (lw: led 1f: trckd ldrs: rdn to ld wl over 1f out: hdd ins fnl f: kpt on) | 1 | **2** | 4/1[1] | 93 | 70 |
| 766[6] | **Tykeyvor (IRE) (77)** (LadyHerries) **6-9-1** KDarley(3) (b.hind: bhd: effrt & swtchd 3f out: styd on u.p) | 2 | **3** | 7/1 | 84 | 61 |
| 886[2] | **Lord Hastie (USA) (67)** (CWThornton) **8-8-5** TQuinn(10) (a.p: effrt 3f out: kpt on one pce) | nk | **4** | 12/1 | 74 | 51 |
| 941[5] | **Progression (81)** (CMurray) **5-9-5b** DeanMcKeown(6) (bhd: shkn up 4f out: styd on: nvr trbld ldrs) | 2½ | **5** | 7/1 | 84 | 61 |
| 872[16] | **Advance East (62)** (MrsJRRamsden) **4-8-0** NKennedy(4) (swtg: hld up & bhd: styd on fnl 3f: nvr rchd ldrs) | hd | **6** | 13/2[3] | 65 | 42 |
| 968[6] | **Domappel (73)** (MrsJCecil) **4-8-11** BThomson(9) (lw: in tch: rdn 3f out: no imp) | nk | **7** | 7/1 | 76 | 53 |
| 871[3] | **Prize Pupil (IRE) (73)** (CFWall) **4-8-11** GDuffield(8) (trckd ldrs: effrt 3f out: hung lft over 1f out: sn wknd) | 1 | **8** | 6/1[2] | 74 | 51 |
| | **Invest Wisely (87)** (JMPEustace) **4-9-11** RCochrane(5) (in tch tl outpcd fnl 3f) | 3 | **9** | 14/1 | 84 | 61 |
| | **Elpida (USA) (60)** (JPearce) **4-7-12** FNorton(7) (led after 1f tl wl over 1f out: wknd) | 8 | **10** | 25/1 | 47 | 24 |
| | **Casual Water (IRE) (75)** (AGNewcombe) **5-8-8**(5) MHenry(11) (unruly leaving paddock: chsd ldrs tl wknd fnl 4f) | 25 | **11** | 6/1[2] | 28 | 5 |

(SP 126.7%) **11 Rn**

**2m 30.02** (2.22) CSF £50.31 CT £285.95 TOTE £14.80: £3.30 £1.80 £2.60 (£39.70) Trio £94.40 OWNER Mr Trevor Barker (SWINDON) BRED Whitsbury Manor Stud

OFFICIAL EXPLANATION **Casual Water (IRE): had been difficult to settle in the early stages and had tired four furlongs from home.**
**853* Remaadi Sun**, confidently ridden, came from behind to win with a good deal in hand. More success looks likely. (10/1)
**925 Polydamas** put up a game display but the winner was far too good for him in the closing stages. (4/1)
**766 Tykeyvor (IRE)** does not do anything quickly but he does stick to his task and was making up ground all the way up the straight. (7/1)
**886 Lord Hastie (USA)** ran well but was just short of a turn of foot to take the opportunity, and would have been better suited by some easier ground. (12/1)
**941 Progression**, off the bit a long way out, kept on but never held out any hopes of making it. (7/1)
**675 Advance East** has yet to win a race, but these shorter distances would seem to be what he wants. (13/2)
**968 Domappel**, who is happier on easier ground, came off the bit a long way out this time and took little interest. (7/1)
**Casual Water (IRE)**, who proved very awkward leaving the paddock, refused point-blank to pass the Stands and ran no sort of race. (6/1)

## 1110 YORK RACEDAY RADIO CONDITIONS STKS (3-Y.O) (Class C)

4-40 (4-40) **1m 5f 194y** £6,207.00 (£2,232.00: £1,066.00: £430.00: £165.00) Stalls: Low GOING minus 0.24 sec per fur (GF)

| | | | | SP | RR | SF |
|---|---|---|---|---|---|---|
| 588* | **Athenry (97)** (JPearce) **3-8-11** NDay(5) (lw: cl up: led wl over 3f out to 2f out: rallied to ld ins fnl f: styd on wl) | — | **1** | 3/1[3] | 96 | 57 |
| 447* | **Summer Spell (USA)** (RCharlton) **3-9-0** SSanders(3) (trckd ldrs: stdy hdwy 4f out: led 2f out tl ins fnl f: no ex) | ¾ | **2** | 5/2[2] | 98 | 59 |
| 923[2] | **Lallans (IRE)** (MJohnston) **3-9-0** JReid(2) (lw: trckd ldrs: swtchd over 2f out: sn hrd drvn: r.o wl towards fin) | s.h | **3** | 4/5[1] | 98 | 59 |
| 954[4] | **Rivercare (IRE) (58)** (MJPolglase) **3-8-11** NCarlisle(1) (led tl hdd wl over 3f out: sn btn) | 18 | **4** | 50/1 | 74? | 35 |

1068[15] **Down The Yard (44)** (MCChapman) **3-8-3**(3) PMcCabe(4) (in tch tl wknd 4f out) ....11 **5** 100/1 57? 18
(SP 112.1%) **5 Rn**

**2m 59.65** (3.45) CSF £10.36 TOTE £4.30: £1.60 £1.70 (£4.30) OWNER Mr A. J. Thompson (NEWMARKET) BRED Jeff Pearce
STEWARDS' ENQUIRY Day susp. 23-25/5/96 (excessive use of whip).
IN-FOCUS: **Nigel Day rode his first winner in Britain for three years following a spell in Singapore.**
**588* Athenry**, a real stayer in the making, has courage aplenty and that won him the day here. (3/1)
**447* Summer Spell (USA)**, whose action suggests that easier ground would suit, ran well until just outbattled in the closing stages.(5/2: 6/4-11/4)
**923 Lallans (IRE)** should basically have won this, but got messed about at a vital stage. More use should have been made of him. (4/5: Evens-8/11)
**954 Rivercare (IRE)** ran as well as could be expected, getting well outpaced in the last half-mile. (50/1)

T/Jkpt: Not won; £15,658.54 to York 15/5/96. T/Plpt: £47.30 (702.31 Tckts). T/Qdpt: £27.60 (76.38 Tckts). AA

## 1105-YORK (L-H) (Good to firm)
## Wednesday May 15th

WEATHER: overcast WIND: mod against

### 1111 EQUITY FINANCIAL COLLECTIONS MIDDLETON CONDITIONS STKS (3-Y.O F) (Class C)

2-00 (2-04) **1m 2f 85y** £6,570.00 (£2,430.00: £1,165.00: £475.00: £187.50: £72.50) Stalls: Low GOING minus 0.37 sec per fur (F)

| | Horse / details | Dist | Pos | SP | RR | SF |
|---|---|---|---|---|---|---|
| | **Bathilde (IRE)** (MRStoute) **3-8-9** MJKinane(3) (bit bkwd: hld up: pushed along 7f out: rdn 3f out: hdwy over 2f out: styd on to ld wl ins fnl f) | — | 1 | 6/1[3] | 104 | 61 |
| 826* | **Kinlochewe** (HRACecil) **3-8-12** WRyan(4) (chsd ldr: led wl over 2f out tl wl ins fnl f) | 1½ | 2 | 13/8[1] | 105 | 62 |
| | **Rouge Rancon (USA)** (PFICole) **3-8-12** TQuinn(6) (led: sn wl clr: hdd wl over 2f out: grad wknd) | 7 | 3 | 7/2[2] | 94 | 51 |
| 674[8] | **Wild Rumour (IRE)** (PWChapple-Hyam) **3-9-2** JReid(7) (dwlt: hld up & bhd: shkn up 3f out: no imp) | 7 | 4 | 13/2 | 87 | 44 |
| | **Zelzelah (USA) (85)** (PAKelleway) **3-9-2** OPeslier(5) (lw: unruly s: trckd ldrs: effrt 3f out: wknd over 2f out) | s.h | 5 | 8/1 | 87 | 44 |
| 874[4] | **Miss Riviera (86)** (GWragg) **3-8-12** PaulEddery(2) (hld up & bhd: effrt over 3f out: sn rdn: no imp) | ¾ | 6 | 9/1 | 82 | 39 |
| | ***Circled (USA)*** (BWHills) **3-8-12** RHills(1) (Withdrawn not under Starter's orders: ref to go in stalls) | | W | 14/1 | — | — |

(SP 115.7%) **6 Rn**

**2m 10.01** (0.31) CSF £14.64 TOTE £6.50: £2.50 £1.60 (£7.50) OWNER Sultan Al Kabeer (NEWMARKET) BRED Prince Sultan Al Kabeer
**Bathilde (IRE)** did not look to be fully wound up and did not impress to post, but she relished this strong gallop. With stamina her strong suit, she stayed on to take the measure of the favourite in the final 100 yards. She holds an Oaks engagement but the Ribblesdale could be her target. (6/1)
**826* Kinlochewe**, the smooth winner of her maiden, performed with credit on this big step up in class and looked all over the winner until tapped for toe in the dash to the line. She looked ill-at-ease on the way to post and will benefit from getting her toe in. (13/8)
**Rouge Rancon (USA)**, a likeable filly who has done well since last year, soon opened up a commanding lead. Tying up and headed halfway up the straight, she had obviously done too much too soon and was a spent force once collared. (7/2)
**674 Wild Rumour (IRE)**, restrained in the rear at this first attempt at the trip, failed to respond when shaken up early in the straight and was unable to get herself into the race. She still has to come in her coat. (13/2)
**Zelzelah (USA)**, looking well forward in condition for this seasonal debut, waited on the leaders but could not respond when popped the question and was in trouble from some way out. (8/1: 6/1-9/1)
**874 Miss Riviera**, knocked out of her stride in a barging match with the winner soon after straightening up, failed to pick up when shown the whip and was most disappointing. (9/1)

### 1112 HAMBLETON RATED STKS H'CAP (0-110) (Listed) (4-Y.O+) (Class A)

2-35 (2-37) **7f 202y** £13,372.00 (£4,948.00: £2,374.00: £970.00: £385.00: £151.00) Stalls: High GOING minus 0.37 sec per fur (F)

| | Horse / details | Dist | Pos | SP | RR | SF |
|---|---|---|---|---|---|---|
| 810[5] | **First Island (IRE) (107)** (GWragg) **4-9-7** RCochrane(8) (lw: hld up: swtchd rt 2f out: qcknd to ld ent fnl f: edgd lft: sn clr) | — | 1 | 11/2[3] | 121 | 79 |
| 878[3] | **Green Green Desert (FR) (98)** (LadyHerries) **5-8-12** DHarrison(7) (hld up & bhd: hdwy wl over 1f out: fin wl) | 2½ | 2 | 16/1 | 107 | 65 |
| 967[2] | **Clan Ben (IRE) (96)** (HRACecil) **4-8-10** MJKinane(9) (lw: trckd ldrs: rdn & n.m.r over 1f out: nt qckn fnl f) | 1¼ | 3 | 7/2[1] | 102 | 60 |
| 878* | **Tarawa (IRE) (106)** (NACallaghan) **4-9-6** RHughes(1) (lw: chsd ldr: ev ch over 1f out: unable qckn) | 2 | 4 | 5/1[2] | 108 | 66 |
| 679[2] | **Monaassib (104)** (EALDunlop) **5-9-4** RHills(12) (prom: rdn & ev ch whn hung lft over 1f out: sltly hmpd: one pce) | s.h | 5 | 13/2 | 106 | 64 |
| 960[3] | **Band on the Run (93)** (BAMcMahon) **9-8-7** SSanders(4) (trckd ldrs: hrd drvn over 1f out: nt pce to chal) | 2 | 6 | 16/1 | 91 | 49 |
| | **Nagnagnag (IRE) (102)** (SDow) **4-9-2** WRyan(6) (hld up: effrt & styd on fnl 2f: nvr nrr) | ½ | 7 | 33/1 | 99 | 57 |
| | **Green Perfume (USA) (97)** (PFICole) **4-8-11** TQuinn(11) (lw: led: sn clr: hrd rdn & hdd over 1f out: wknd qckly) | 2 | 8 | 20/1 | 90 | 48 |
| 876[7] | **Kayvee (96)** (GHarwood) **7-8-10** AClark(13) (hld up towards rr: nvr plcd to chal) | ½ | 9 | 10/1 | 88 | 46 |
| 810[7] | **Lap of Luxury (107)** (WJarvis) **7-9-7** BThomson(5) (trckd ldrs tl wknd over 1f out: eased whn btn) | 1 | 10 | 25/1 | 97 | 55 |
| | **Silca Blanka (IRE) (106)** (MRChannon) **4-9-6** KDarley(3) (lw: chsd ldrs: wkng whn hmpd over 2f out) | hd | 11 | 20/1 | 96 | 54 |
| 876[14] | **Jawaal (97)** (LadyHerries) **6-8-11** JReid(2) (reard s: a wl bhd: t.o) | 6 | 12 | 8/1 | 75 | 33 |
| 878[2] | **Behaviour (98)** (MrsJCecil) **4-8-12** PaulEddery(10) (hld up in rr: t.o) | s.h | 13 | 7/1 | 76 | 34 |

(SP 128.4%) **13 Rn**

**1m 36.4** (-0.40) CSF £85.74 CT £331.79 TOTE £6.40: £2.10 £3.90 £1.80 (£67.60) Trio £62.30 OWNER Mollers Racing (NEWMARKET) BRED Citadel Stud
**810 First Island (IRE)** found this step down to handicap company no problem at all and, though he did dive left after striking the front, soon drew clear for a very easy success. (11/2)
**878 Green Green Desert (FR)**, making good progress from way off the pace inside the distance, finished with a flourish and it will be surprising if he can not improve on this in the coming weeks. (16/1)
**967 Clan Ben (IRE)** had a fair pull in the weights with the winner compared to the last time they clashed, but the outcome was identical. It is doubtful if the slight interference suffered when the field bunched 200 yards out made any difference to the result. (7/2)
**878* Tarawa (IRE)**, who was trying for a hat-trick, was in the firing-line and holding every chance until done for toe in the battle to the finish. (5/1)
**679 Monaassib**, attempting a mile for the first time, was fighting for the lead when he hung left approaching the final furlong, but he appeared to be fighting a lost cause when the winner passed him just inside the distance. (13/2)

**960 Band on the Run** continues to run well and will be worth waiting for when he gets the easier ground that he requires. (16/1)
**Nagnagnag (IRE)**, sure to strip fitter for the run, stayed on in pleasing style in the latter stages and will find his way when the ground gets easier. (33/1)
**Green Perfume (USA)**, allowed to stride along in a clear lead, took a lot of pegging back and, if he had been as race-fit as the winner, he would probably not have been caught. (20/1)

## 1113 HOMEOWNERS SPRINT H'CAP (0-105) (3-Y.O+) (Class B)

3-05 (3-07) **5f** £16,310.00 (£4,880.00: £2,340.00: £1,070.00) Stalls: High GOING minus 0.20 sec per fur (GF)

| | | | | SP | RR | SF |
|---|---|---|---|---|---|---|
| | **Fairy Wind (IRE) (92)** (NACallaghan) **4-9-4** MJKinane(6) (b.hind: a.p: led 2f out: sn clr: hld on cl home) | — | **1** | 14/1 | 101 | 55 |
| $940^{5}$ | **Brave Edge (95)** (RHannon) **5-9-7** RHughes(4) (lw: trckd ldrs: rdn wl over 1f out: r.o wl ins fnl f) | ½ | **2** | $7/1^{2}$ | 102 | 56 |
| $812^{15}$ | **Twice as Sharp (84)** (PWHarris) **4-8-10** GHind(3) (w ldrs far side: kpt on wl ins fnl f) | nk | **3** | 14/1 | 90 | 44 |
| $928^{13}$ | **Sweet Magic (84)** (PHowling) **5-8-10** FNorton(7) (s.i.s: sn chsng ldrs: shkn up & unable qckn fnl f) | nk | **4** | 20/1 | 90 | 44 |
| $1016^{4}$ | **Lady Sheriff (83)** (RHollinshead) **5-8-4**(5) DGriffiths(5) (lw: sn outpcd & pushed along: gd hdwy fnl f: fin wl) | hd | **5** | 14/1 | 88 | 42 |
| $1016^{3}$ | **Ziggy's Dancer (USA) (83)** (EJAlston) **5-8-9** SDWilliams(2) (lw: chsd ldr far side: outpcd over 1f out: kpt on towards fin) | 1¾ | **6** | 11/1 | 83 | 37 |
| $928^{19}$ | **Saddlehome (USA) (75)** (TDBarron) **7-8-1** WCarson(12) (swtg: hld up: r.o appr fnl f: nvr nrr) | nk | **7** | 10/1 | 74 | 28 |
| $864^{5}$ | **Laurel Delight (85)** (JBerry) **6-8-6**(5) PRoberts(8) (b.nr fore: led 3f: sn hrd drvn & wknd) | ¾ | **8** | 25/1 | 81 | 35 |
| $735^{2}$ | **Royal Dome (IRE) (75)** (MartynWane) **4-8-1** JCarroll(14) (lw: prom: rdn over 1f out: grad wknd) | nk | **9** | $8/1^{3}$ | 70 | 24 |
| $931^{6}$ | **Insider Trader (73)** (MrsJRRamsden) **5-7-13v** SSanders(15) (trckd ldrs stands' side tl wknd over 1f out) | nk | **10** | 10/1 | 67 | 21 |
| $1016^{2}$ | **Lago Di Varano (80)** (RMWhitaker) **4-8-6v** DaleGibson(1) (sn pushed along & a outpcd) | nk | **11** | 9/1 | 73 | 27 |
| $1016^{7}$ | **Mr Oscar (100)** (MJohnston) **4-9-12** JWeaver(9) (trckd ldrs: effrt ½-wy: wknd over 1f out) | ½ | **12** | $7/1^{2}$ | 92 | 46 |
| 989* | **Pride of Brixton (84)** (GLewis) **3-8-1** 6x PaulEddery(13) (dwlt: a bhd & outpcd) | ¾ | **13** | $9/2^{1}$ | 73 | 18 |
| $716^{5}$ | **Stolen Kiss (IRE) (77)** (MWEasterby) **4-8-3v** KDarley(10) (lw: hld up: a in rr) | 3½ | **14** | 14/1 | 55 | 9 |
| | **Portelet (77)** (RGuest) **4-8-3** LCharnock(16) (racd alone stands' side: bhd fr ½-wy: t.o) | 9 | **15** | 20/1 | 26 | — |
| | | | | (SP 130.8%) | **15 Rn** | |

**59.41 secs** (1.71) CSF £107.73 CT £1,316.75 TOTE £10.90: £3.20 £3.20 £7.50 (£32.30) Trio £653.00 OWNER Mr N. A. Callaghan (NEWMARKET) BRED Ron Con Ltd
WEIGHT FOR AGE 3yo-9lb
IN-FOCUS: **Those drawn low dominated the finish.**
**Fairy Wind (IRE)**, who is thought to be in foal to Arazi, is a half-sister to Mistertopogigo. She won this race with more in hand than the verdict suggests and a trip to Royal Ascot for the King's Stand Stakes has been pencilled in. (14/1)
**940 Brave Edge** ran well and lost no caste in defeat, but he could be flattered to run the winner so close. (7/1)
**Twice as Sharp**, very keen to post, could have found the ground livelier than he cares for, but he was a leading light all the way and deserves to gain reward. (14/1)
**Sweet Magic** did not look at all happy cantering to the start but did extremely well after missing a beat at the start, and would seem to be thriving. (20/1)
**1016 Lady Sheriff** could not hold her pitch in the early stages, but was into her stride inside the distance and there is another race in the pipe-line. (14/1)
**1016 Ziggy's Dancer (USA)**, making a quick return to action, showed good pace in the centre of the track, but was hard at work and held approaching the final furlong. (11/1)
**Saddlehome (USA)** showed a return to form with by far his best effort this term and should be kept in mind. (10/1)
**989* Pride of Brixton**, flat-footed as the stalls opened, could not recover the lost ground and was taken off his legs all the way. (9/2)

## 1114 HOMEOWNERS DANTE STKS (Gp 2) (3-Y.O) (Class A)

3-40 (3-43) **1m 2f 85y** £66,526.00 (£24,962.05: £12,043.53: £5,303.42) Stalls: Low GOING minus 0.37 sec per fur (F)

| | | | | SP | RR | SF |
|---|---|---|---|---|---|---|
| $830^{2}$ | **Glory of Dancer** (PAKelleway) **3-8-11** OPeslier(2) (lw: b: hld up: swtchd rt & hdwy over 2f out: led ins fnl f: r.o wl) | — | **1** | $3/1^{2}$ | 118+ | 45 |
| 923* | **Dushyantor (USA)** (HRACecil) **3-8-11** WRyan(5) (lw: hld up & bhd: gd hdwy over 2f out: rdn to chal ins fnl f: r.o) | ½ | **2** | $5/1^{3}$ | 117++ | 44 |
| $694^{3}$ | **Jack Jennings (105)** (BAMcMahon) **3-8-11** SSanders(3) (led tl hdd ins fnl f) | 1 | **3** | 25/1 | 116 | 43 |
| 730* | **Nash House (IRE)** (PWChapple-Hyam) **3-8-11** JReid(6) (lw: hld up: hdwy 3f out: rdn over 1f out: one pce) | 1 | **4** | $5/2^{1}$ | 114 | 41 |
| $830^{4}$ | **Double Leaf** (MRStoute) **3-8-11** WCarson(4) (prom: drvn along & outpcd whn hmpd & snatched up 2f out: styd on fnl f) | hd | **5** | 16/1 | 114 | 41 |
| $926^{11}$ | **Storm Trooper (USA) (116)** (HRACecil) **3-8-11** MJKinane(1) (chsd ldrs: rdn & one pce fnl 2f) | ¾ | **6** | $5/2^{1}$ | 113 | 40 |
| $918^{2}$ | **Bahamian Knight (CAN) (106)** (DRLoder) **3-8-11** TQuinn(7) (chsd ldr tl outpcd over 2f out) | 3 | **7** | 20/1 | 108? | 35 |
| | | | | (SP 113.3%) | **7 Rn** | |

**2m 12.4** (2.70) CSF £16.97 TOTE £4.30: £2.20 £2.90 (£11.90) OWNER Gen Horse Advertizing SRL (NEWMARKET) BRED Cotswold Stud
OFFICIAL EXPLANATION **Nash House (IRE): was found to be in a distressed state after the race.**
IN-FOCUS: **A slow early pace turned this into a three-furlong sprint and produced a time over 2 seconds slower than the fillies in the opener.**
**830 Glory of Dancer** had done it all before when winning a Group One event in Italy and won with any degree of confidence. Immediately installed favourite for the Derby, he is even better when there is a bit of give in the ground. (3/1)
**923* Dushyantor (USA)** had to forfeit his unbeaten record, but was up against a class performer here and, making a race of it, showed what an improving colt he really is. (5/1)
**694 Jack Jennings** gained his revenge over Storm Trooper with a bold display of front-running and, in turning in his best display yet, gave notice that he is not far behind the best of his age. (25/1)
**730* Nash House (IRE)** covers a lot of ground and was by far the most impressive to post. Making his move three furlongs out, he soon had every chance but, made to work below the distance, lacked the speed to put his stamp on proceedings. He apparently finished distressed after what was a big test for one so short of experience and, in time, this could be considered not a bad effort. (5/2: 6/4-11/4)
**830 Double Leaf** pushed the pace but got caught out when the tempo increased early in the straight, and was already going in reverse when impeded by the winner and snatched up over two furlongs out. Driven along, he was staying on again towards the finish and should not be written off yet. (16/1)
**694* Storm Trooper (USA)**, content to be given a lead, was being made to struggle over two furlongs out and could not summon up the pace to match strides with the leaders. At this level it would seem he must have easier ground. (5/2)
**918 Bahamian Knight (CAN)** sat in behind the pacemaker waiting to pounce, but was chopped for speed when the race began in earnest entering the last quarter-mile, and was one of the first beaten. (20/1)

## 1115 YORKSHIRE-TYNE TEES TELEVISION CONDITIONS STKS (2-Y.O) (Class B)

4-10 (4-12) **6f** £6,947.00 (£2,573.00: £1,236.50: £507.50: £203.75: £82.25) Stalls: High GOING minus 0.20 sec per fur (GF)

| | | | | SP | RR | SF |
|---|---|---|---|---|---|---|
| 608* | **Proud Native (IRE)** (APJarvis) **2-8-13** MJKinane(4) (lw: mde all: shkn up over 1f out: hld on gamely) | — | **1** | 5/1 | 84 | 43 |
| 441* | **Indian Spark** (WGMTurner) **2-9-1** TSprake(1) (lw: a.p: ev ch fnl f: kpt on u.p cl home) | nk | **2** | 9/2 3 | 85 | 44 |
| 585* | **Marathon Maid** (RAFahey) **2-8-8** ACulhane(5) (trckd ldrs: hrd drvn & outpcd appr fnl f) | 1½ | **3** | 14/1 | 74 | 33 |
| 800* | **Exit To Rio (CAN)** (MrsJRRamsden) **2-8-13** KFallon(6) (s.i.s: effrt ½-wy: drifted lft 2f out: nvr able to chal) | 2 | **4** | 11/4 2 | 74 | 33 |
| | **Impetuous Air** (EWeymes) **2-8-3** KDarley(3) (w'like: cmpt: bit bkwd: s.s: hung lft: racd alone centre: nvr nr ldrs) | 3 | **5** | 16/1 | 56 | 15 |
| 984 2 | **Foot Battalion (IRE)** (RHollinshead) **2-8-11** WRyan(8) (trckd ldrs: effrt & rdn 2f out: sn outpcd) | 1¼ | **6** | 13/2 | 61 | 20 |
| 877* | **Smokey Pete** (RHannon) **2-9-3** JReid(2) (lw: w ldrs to ½-wy: wknd qckly 2f out) | 5 | **7** | 9/4 1 | 53 | 12 |

(SP 118.2%) **7 Rn**

**1m 13.66** (2.66) CSF £26.58 TOTE £6.10: £2.70 £2.80 (£11.10) OWNER Mr L. Fust (ASTON UPTHORPE) BRED Mrs B. A. Headon

IN-FOCUS: **One of the first six furlong juvenile races this year and an informative heat, featuring runners from the Brocklesby, Garter and Lily Agnes Stakes.**

**608* Proud Native (IRE)** again looked ill-at-ease on the way down but showed no ill-effects on the way back, making all up the stands' rail to ward off a persistent rival. The Norfolk Stakes is his objective. (5/1)

**441* Indian Spark**, winner of the Brocklesby on his debut, did not stride out with any freedom and could never quite force his head in front. He did keep the pressure on right to the end though, and may be allowed to take his chance at Royal Ascot. (9/2)

**585* Marathon Maid** is bred to need further and was always at full stretch to keep tabs on the leading pair. (14/1)

**800* Exit To Rio (CAN)** finished up in the centre of the track and could not muster the speed to deliver a challenge. (11/4)

**877* Smokey Pete** shared the lead for three furlongs, but then lost his pitch rather quickly and, in the end, finished well beaten. This was not his true running. (9/4)

## 1116 WILKINSON MEMORIAL H'CAP (0-90) (4-Y.O+) (Class C)

4-40 (4-40) **1m 5f 194y** £7,375.00 (£2,200.00: £1,050.00: £475.00) Stalls: Low GOING minus 0.37 sec per fur (F)

| | | | | SP | RR | SF |
|---|---|---|---|---|---|---|
| 941 6 | **Celeric (90)** (DMorley) **4-10-0** WCarson(4) (hld up & bhd: effrt on ins & hmpd over 2f out: qcknd to ld ent fnl f: readily) | — | **1** | 3/1 1 | 100+ | 85 |
| 712 6 | **Golden Arrow (IRE) (73)** (IABalding) **5-8-12** KDarley(3) (hld up in tch: drvn along 3f out: kpt on appr fnl f: no ch w wnr) | 1 | **2** | 12/1 | 82 | 68 |
| 886 8 | **Turgenev (IRE) (58)** (RBastiman) **7-7-11bow1** DaleGibson(5) (s.i.s: bhd tl hdwy over 3f out: styd on wl u.p fnl f) | hd | **3** | 25/1 | 67 | 52 |
| 816 3 | **Midyan Blue (IRE) (78)** (JMPEustace) **6-9-3** RCochrane(8) (hld up: rdn to ld over 2f out: hdd ent fnl f: no ex) | hd | **4** | 4/1 3 | 87 | 73 |
| 886* | **Sarawat (69)** (DNicholls) **8-8-8** GDuffield(9) (lw: trckd ldrs: ev ch 3f out: sn wknd) | 11 | **5** | 7/2 2 | 65 | 51 |
| 972 4 | **Hasta la Vista (57)** (MWEasterby) **6-7-3b(7)** RMullen(7) (lw: w ldr: led 4f out tl over 2f out: wknd over 1f out) | 4 | **6** | 12/1 | 48 | 34 |
| 753 5 | **Bowcliffe Court (IRE) (59)** (BWHills) **4-7-11** JQuinn(2) (hld up: hdwy 4f out: sn ev ch: wknd over 2f out: t.o) | 11 | **7** | 9/2 | 38 | 23 |
| | **Floating Line (70)** (EJAlston) **8-8-9** SDWilliams(1) (prom tl wknd over 3f out: t.o) | 12 | **8** | 12/1 | 35 | 21 |
| | **Highflying (85)** (GMMoore) **10-9-10** JTate(6) (bit bkwd: mde most 10f: wknd over 3f out: t.o) | 4 | **9** | 14/1 | 45 | 31 |

(SP 119.0%) **9 Rn**

**2m 55.77** (-0.43) CSF £35.24 CT £702.59 TOTE £3.50: £1.80 £2.40 £6.00 (£20.10) Trio £207.80 OWNER Mr Christopher Spence (NEWMARKET) BRED Chieveley Manor Enterprises

LONG HANDICAP Turgenev (IRE) 7-8 Hasta la Vista 7-7

WEIGHT FOR AGE 4yo-1lb

OFFICIAL EXPLANATION **Sarawat: was sore after the race.**

**941 Celeric** found all the trouble that was going when creeping up on the inside rail, yet he was still able to win as he pleased, so it does not say much for the opposition. (3/1: 5/2-100/3)

**573 Golden Arrow (IRE)** is not the easiest of rides over hurdles and did not appear to be giving his jockey any help whatsoever. With fitness coming into play though, he stayed on to gain a worthy runner-up prize. (12/1)

**886 Turgenev (IRE)** was the unlucky one of the race but, in turning in his best display for quite some time, showed that his turn is near at hand. (25/1)

**816 Midyan Blue (IRE)**, winner of this event twelve months ago, was ridden to show in front halfway up the straight, but had to admit the winner much too good for him in the race to the line. He does appear to need easier ground. (4/1)

**886* Sarawat** should have been thereabouts but he decided enough was enough over two furlongs out and wanted no part of it. (7/2)

**972 Hasta la Vista** likes to dictate but he had a running battle with Highflying until the turn into the straight, and it left him with nothing in reserve when the race began in earnest. (12/1)

T/Jkpt: Not won; £31,930.16 to York 16/5/96. T/Plpt: £459.30 (99 Tckts). T/Qdpt: £113.30 (22.22 Tckts). IM

# 0943-SALISBURY (R-H) (Good to firm, Firm patches)

## Thursday May 16th

WEATHER: overcast WIND: fresh half bhd

## 1117 NETHERHAMPTON MAIDEN STKS (I) (3-Y.O+ F & M) (Class D)

1-40 (1-41) **1m 1f 209y** £3,460.00 (£1,030.00: £490.00: £220.00) Stalls: High GOING minus 0.55 sec per fur (F)

| | | | | SP | RR | SF |
|---|---|---|---|---|---|---|
| 813 10 | **Stately Dancer (68)** (GWragg) **3-8-7** WWoods(11) (chsd ldr: led over 1f out: drvn out) | — | **1** | 9/2 3 | 78 | 18 |
| 640 4 | **Tart (FR)** (JRFanshawe) **3-8-4(3)** NVarley(8) (a.p: hrd rdn & ev ch 2f out: r.o one pce) | ¾ | **2** | 7/2 1 | 77 | 17 |
| 678 8 | **La Pellegrina (IRE)** (PWChapple-Hyam) **3-8-4(5)ow2** RHavlin(1) (led tl over 1f out: r.o one pce) | s.h | **3** | 11/2 | 79 | 17 |
| | **Kidston Lass (IRE)** (JARToller) **3-8-7** GDuffield(7) (lt-f: plld hrd: stdd & lost pl after 2f: rdn & hdwy 2f out: swtchd lft & r.o fnl f) | nk | **4** | 25/1 | 76 | 16 |
| 820 9 | **Arietta's Way (IRE)** (RCharlton) **3-8-7** TSprake(10) (b.nr hind: hld up & plld hrd: hdwy 3f out: nvr nr to chal) | 2½ | **5** | 8/1 | 72 | 12 |

Shining Dancer (55) (SDow) 4-9-7 WRyan(5) (plld hrd: prom tl wknd over 2f out) ....7 6 50/1 61 15
$860^{4}$ Shalateeno (MRChannon) 3-8-7 AGorman(3) (lw: hld up & plld hrd: hdwy 4f out: hrd rdn 3f out: wknd 2f out) ....nk 7 13/2 61 1
Peetsie (IRE) (LordHuntingdon) 4-9-7 TIves(6) (unf: a bhd) ....½ 8 14/1 60 14
$813^{11}$ Reiterate (GBBalding) 3-8-4$^{(3)}$ SDrowne(9) (bhd fnl 3f) ....6 9 20/1 50 —
$847^{9}$ Dance Model (JJSheehan) 3-8-2$^{(5)}$ PPMurphy(12) (rdn over 5f out: a bhd) ....½ 10 50/1 49 —
$921^{6}$ Love Bateta (IRE) (RHannon) 3-8-7 RPerham(4) (prom tl wknd over 4f out) ....2 11 4/1$^{2}$ 46 —
*$412^{9}$* Opening Range (35) (NEBerry) 5-9-0$^{(7)}$ AEddery(2) (prom over 6f) .... 12 66/1 — —
(SP 120.9%) 12 Rn

**2m 9.21** (3.91) CSF £19.93 TOTE £5.40: £1.90 £1.80 £1.80 (£7.40) Trio £30.00 OWNER Mr A. E. Oppenheimer (NEWMARKET) BRED Hascombe and Valiant Studs
WEIGHT FOR AGE 3yo-14lb

**576 Stately Dancer**, disappointing last time, stayed on well enough under pressure in this easier company. (9/2)
**640 Tart (FR)**, a half-sister to Gold Blade, showed the right sort of attitude under strong driving. (7/2: op 9/4)
**678 La Pellegrina (IRE)**, a half-sister to 1000 Guineas winner Las Meninas, kept plugging away after trying to make all over this longer trip. (11/2: 7/2-6/1)
**Kidston Lass (IRE)** ran on promisingly in the closing stages and hopefully this will have taught her to settle. (25/1)
**Arietta's Way (IRE)** is a sister to Rubhahunish and a half-sister to Italian Derby winner Court of Honour. Taking a strong hold, she shaped as if she would do better over further. (8/1)

## 1118 WARMINSTER MAIDEN STKS (2-Y.O) (Class D)
2-10 (2-12) **5f** £3,333.50 (£998.00: £479.00: £219.50) Stalls: High GOING minus 0.55 sec per fur (F)

SP RR SF
Tipsy Creek (USA) (BHanbury) 2-9-0 WRyan(4) (str: scope: hld up: led over 1f out: qcknd clr: easily) ....— 1 7/4$^{1}$ 81+ 36
Maserati Monk (BJMeehan) 2-9-0 MTebbutt(1) (w'like: a.p: chsd wnr fnl f: no imp) ....3½ 2 6/1$^{3}$ 70 25
Summer Queen (SPCWoods) 2-8-9 WWoods(6) (unf: hld up: swtchd lft over 1f out: r.o) ....¾ 3 10/1 62 17
$596^{5}$ Will To Win (PGMurphy) 2-8-6$^{(3)}$ SDrowne(7) (b.hind: a.p: led 2f out: sn hdd: one pce) ....1¼ 4 20/1 58 13
$841^{4}$ Bold Catch (USA) (RCharlton) 2-9-0 TSprake(8) (led 3f: wknd over 1f out) ....2½ 5 5/2$^{2}$ 55 10
Don Sebastian (RHannon) 2-9-0 RPerham(9) (unf: dwlt: outpcd: nvr nrr) ....½ 6 9/1 54 9
$977^{5}$ Bramble Bear (MBlanshard) 2-8-9 AClark(10) (prom over 2f) ....½ 7 14/1 47 2
$841^{8}$ Heart Full of Soul (PFICole) 2-9-0 CRutter(3) (hdwy 2f out: wknd over 1f out) ....s.h 8 10/1 52 7
Salty Jack (IRE) (SDow) 2-8-9$^{(5)}$ ADaly(11) (str: prom 3f) ....nk 9 16/1 51 6
Midatlantic (PTWalwyn) 2-9-0 GHind(5) (neat: s.s: a t.o) ....10 10 20/1 19 —
(SP 129.5%) 10 Rn

**60.97 secs** (0.97) CSF £14.01 TOTE £3.00: £1.10 £1.70 £4.20 (£9.60) Trio £64.70 OWNER Mr Abdullah Ali (NEWMARKET) BRED Airlie Stud

**Tipsy Creek (USA)**, a half-brother to Wathik and My Sovereign, was his stable's first two-year-old runner of the season. Making an impressive debut, a decision about Royal Ascot will be made following a tilt at a listed race at the Curragh on Irish 1000 Guineas day. (7/4)
**Maserati Monk**, a half-brother to mile and a half winner Mr Abbot, should improve over an extra furlong. (6/1: op 4/1)
**Summer Queen**, a half-sister to several winners, was going about her work nicely in the closing stages and should soon step up on this. (10/1: 6/1-12/1)
**Will To Win** could not raise her game after showing ahead briefly entering the last quarter-mile. (20/1)
**841 Bold Catch (USA)** was again a bit disappointing. (5/2)
**Don Sebastian**, a half-brother to All She Surveys, may not be one of his stable's leading lights but did start to get the hang of things late on. (9/1: 5/1-10/1)
**Bramble Bear** (14/1: 10/1-20/1)
**Heart Full of Soul** (10/1: 5/1-12/1)

## 1119 DRUIDS H'CAP (0-70) (3-Y.O) (Class E)
2-45 (2-48) **1m** £3,652.00 (£1,096.00: £528.00: £244.00) Stalls: High GOING minus 0.55 sec per fur (F)

SP RR SF
$819^{10}$ Sound Check (55) (BJMeehan) 3-8-11 MTebbutt(16) (hrd rdn 3f out: hdwy 2f out: led nr fin: all out) ....— 1 16/1 61 35
Dancing Image (65) (IABalding) 3-9-7 WRyan(18) (lw: hld up on ins: swtchd lft over 1f out: str run ins fnl f)..s.h 2 7/1$^{2}$ 71 45
$978^{5}$ Wilfull Lad (IRE) (60) (MartynMeade) 3-9-2 VSlattery(7) (chsd ldr: led over 2f out: hdd nr fin) ....hd 3 14/1 66 40
$763^{8}$ Bright Eclipse (USA) (54) (JWHills) 3-8-5$^{(5)}$ MHenry(6) (prom: rdn 3f out: r.o ins fnl f) ....½ 4 14/1 59 33
$888^{4}$ Mystic Dawn (60) (SDow) 3-8-11$^{(5)}$ ADaly(9) (plld hrd: a.p: ev ch over 1f out: one pce) ....nk 5 7/2$^{1}$ 64 38
$892^{9}$ Premier Generation (IRE) (64) (DWPArbuthnot) 3-9-6 SWhitworth(10) (hdwy 2f out: one pce fnl f) ....nk 6 12/1 68 42
$873^{14}$ Pride of Kashmir (56) (PWHarris) 3-8-12b$^{1}$ GHind(14) (nvr nr to chal) ....5 7 20/1 50 24
$687^{8}$ Needle Match (64) (CFWall) 3-9-6 GDuffield(11) (lw: led over 5f: wknd over 1f out) ....2½ 8 15/2$^{3}$ 53 27
$863^{9}$ Laughing Buccaneer (53) (AGFoster) 3-8-2b$^{(7)}$ RWaterfield(1) (nvr trbld ldrs) ....2 9 20/1 38 12
$761^{8}$ Spiral Flyer (IRE) (53) (MDIUsher) 3-8-9 RPrice(8) (n.d) ....2½ 10 33/1 33 7
$868^{16}$ Dil Dil (61) (RHannon) 3-9-3 RPerham(15) (rdn over 5f out: a mid div) ....1½ 11 14/1 38 12
$819^{12}$ Expeditious Way (GR) (65) (RCharlton) 3-9-7 TSprake(2) (prom tl rdn & wknd over 2f out) ....½ 12 20/1 41 15
Zdenka (63) (MBlanshard) 3-9-5 NAdams(5) (a bhd) ....nk 13 20/1 38 12
$678^{9}$ Baloustar (USA) (60) (SPCWoods) 3-9-2 WWoods(17) (bhd fnl 2f) ....3 14 10/1 29 3
*$782^{9}$* Smile Forever (USA) (64) (JARToller) 3-9-6 TIves(4) (plld hrd: prom 5f) ....1¾ 15 20/1 29 3
$873^{13}$ Night of Glass (53) (DMorris) 3-8-9 JHBrown(12) (prom tl rdn & wknd 3f out) ....3½ 16 25/1 11 —
$1025^{2}$ Dungeon Princess (IRE) (60) (MRChannon) 3-8-11$^{(5)}$ PPMurphy(3) (a bhd: t.o) ....10 17 14/1 — —
$467^{7}$ Realms of Glory (IRE) (56) (PhilipMitchell) 3-8-12 AClark(13) (rdn 4f out: a bhd: t.o) ....1¼ 18 20/1 — —
(SP 131.2%) 18 Rn

**1m 42.07** (1.67) CSF £120.58 CT £1,553.88 TOTE £36.10: £4.60 £2.40 £4.10 £3.70 (£83.90) Trio Not won; £463.50 to Newbury 17/5/96 OWNER Theobalds Stud (UPPER LAMBOURN) BRED Theobalds Stud

**Sound Check** proved a tough customer under a hard ride and Tebbutt's perseverance eventually paid off. (16/1)
**Dancing Image**, who has been gelded, had to work his way off the fence and only just failed to land the spoils. (7/1)
**978 Wilfull Lad (IRE)** lost no caste in defeat. (14/1)
**555 Bright Eclipse (USA)**, on his handicap debut, looks capable of finding a suitable opportunity especially if reverting to a longer trip. (14/1)
**888 Mystic Dawn**, backed down to favouritism, did not help her chances by refusing to settle. (7/2)
**892 Premier Generation (IRE)** could not quite sustain a promising run on the wide outside. (12/1: op 8/1)
**Dil Dil** (14/1: 10/1-16/1)
**Baloustar (USA)** (10/1: 6/1-11/1)

## 1120 DURNFORD CONDITIONS STKS (3-Y.O) (Class C)

3-15 (3-15) **1m 4f** £5,410.50 (£1,743.00: £846.50) Stalls: High GOING minus 0.55 sec per fur (F)

| | | | | SP | RR | SF |
|---|---|---|---|---|---|---|
| 948* | **Chief Contender (IRE)** (PWChapple-Hyam) **3-8-10**(5) RHavlin(1) (mde all: rdn over 3f out: r.o wl) | — | 1 | 5/6 1 | 105 | 34 |
| 847* | **Yom Jameel (IRE)** (MRStoute) **3-9-1** KBradshaw(3) (hld up: rdn to chse wnr over 2f out: no imp) | 3½ | 2 | 7/4 2 | 100 | 29 |
| 860* | **Lear Jet (USA) (87)** (PFICole) **3-9-1** CRutter(5) (plld hrd: chsd wnr: rdn 3f out: wknd 2f out) | 7 | 3 | 9/2 3 | 91 | 20 |
| | | | | (SP 109.1%) | **3 Rn** | |

**2m 35.98** (3.38) CSF £2.50 TOTE £1.50: (£1.60) OWNER Mrs John Magnier (MARLBOROUGH) BRED Jayeff 'B' Stables and Calogo Bloodstock A G

**948* Chief Contender (IRE)** goes well for his young rider and proved his course record-breaking effort earlier in the month was no fluke. (5/6)
**847* Yom Jameel (IRE)**, a half-brother to the useful Topanoora, should have been suited by this extra quarter-mile. (7/4)
**860* Lear Jet (USA)** took such a strong hold that he gave himself little chance of staying this longer trip. (9/2: 9/4-5/1)

## 1121 TRYON H'CAP (0-80) (3-Y.O+) (Class D)

3-45 (3-47) **6f 212y** £4,337.50 (£1,300.00: £625.00: £287.50) Stalls: High GOING minus 0.55 sec per fur (F)

| | | | | SP | RR | SF |
|---|---|---|---|---|---|---|
| $1001^{11}$ | **Morocco (IRE) (56)** (MRChannon) **7-8-3**(7) AEddery(14) (hld up: hdwy on ins to ld 2f out: edgd lft: r.o) | — | 1 | 20/1 | 58 | 24 |
| $887^{2}$ | **Jaazim (50)** (MMadgwick) **6-8-1**(3) NVarley(9) (a.p: rdn over 2f out: r.o wl ins fnl f) | ½ | 2 | 5/1 1 | 51 | 17 |
| $935^{13}$ | **Sand Star (70)** (DHaydnJones) **4-9-10** AMackay(13) (lw: a.p: rdn over 2f out: r.o one pce) | 1½ | 3 | 14/1 | 67 | 33 |
| $775^{13}$ | **Time Clash (64)** (BPalling) **3-8-7** TSprake(10) (led 4f: rallied over 1f out: one pce fnl f) | 1 | 4 | 14/1 | 59 | 14 |
| $747^{3}$ | **Victory Team (IRE) (66)** (GBBalding) **4-9-6** AClark(2) (hdwy over 2f out: r.o one pce fnl f) | 1 | 5 | 6/1 2 | 59 | 25 |
| | **Thatchmaster (IRE) (46)** (CAHorgan) **5-8-0** DeclanO'Shea(4) (w ldrs tl wknd 2f out) | ½ | 6 | 16/1 | 38 | 4 |
| | **Philistar (74)** (JMPEustace) **3-9-0**(3) PMcCabe(8) (nvr nr to chal) | s.h | 7 | 14/1 | 66 | 21 |
| *$1029^{6}$* | **Scissor Ridge (45)** (JJBridger) **4-7-8**(5) MBaird(1) (nvr nr ldrs) | 2½ | 8 | 14/1 | 31 | — |
| $846^{6}$ | **Ahjay (51)** (TJNaughton) **6-8-2**(3) SDrowne(3) (nvr trbld ldrs) | s.h | 9 | 5/1 1 | 37 | 3 |
| | **Twice Purple (IRE) (59)** (BJMeehan) **4-8-13** MTebbutt(6) (w ldrs: led 3f out: hdd & wknd 2f out) | nk | 10 | 20/1 | 44 | 10 |
| | **Catch The Lights (77)** (RHannon) **3-9-6** RPerham(5) (lw: a bhd) | 2½ | 11 | 9/1 3 | 56 | 11 |
| $749^{17}$ | **Amnesty Bay (53)** (MDIUsher) **4-8-7** NAdams(11) (bhd fnl 3f) | 5 | 12 | 20/1 | 21 | — |
| $893^{18}$ | **Great Hall (51)** (PDCundell) **7-8-5** WRyan(12) (b.hind: s.s: a wl bhd) | s.h | 13 | 12/1 | 19 | — |
| | **Indian Rhapsody (51)** (ABailey) **4-8-5** GBardwell(7) (rdn over 3f out: sn wl bhd) | 4 | 14 | 10/1 | 10 | — |
| | | | | (SP 121.2%) | **14 Rn** | |

**1m 28.25** (2.25) CSF £109.50 CT £1,323.58 TOTE £14.80: £3.50 £1.10 £8.70 (£24.70) Trio £160.40 OWNER Mr Martin Myers (UPPER LAMBOURN) BRED Nikita Investments

WEIGHT FOR AGE 3yo-11lb

**Morocco (IRE)** found a clear run on the inside from halfway and, after striking the front at the two-furlong marker, was never in danger, despite edging to the left in the closing stages. (20/1)
**887 Jaazim** went with the leaders. After looking beaten approaching the final furlong, he came with a renewed effort in the last 100 yards. (5/1)
**Sand Star**, always chasing the leaders, ran on at one pace when pressure was applied, but lacked a final turn of foot. (14/1)
**Time Clash** appeared beaten after making the running for half a mile, but rallied strongly and may need a longer trip. (14/1)
**747 Victory Team (IRE)** came with a promising-looking run approaching the two-furlong marker but, though staying on, lacked a final turn of foot. (6/1: op 3/1)
**Thatchmaster (IRE)** disputed the lead until past halfway, but had shot his bolt with two furlongs with race. (16/1)
**Philistar** (14/1: 10/1-16/1)
**664 Scissor Ridge** (14/1: 10/1-16/1)
**Ahjay** ran most disappointingly and never looked likely to repeat last year's win. (5/1)
**Catch The Lights** (9/1: 9/2-10/1)

## 1122 REDENHAM CLAIMING STKS (3-Y.O) (Class F)

4-20 (4-21) **6f 212y** £2,784.00 (£774.00: £372.00) Stalls: High GOING minus 0.55 sec per fur (F)

| | | | | SP | RR | SF |
|---|---|---|---|---|---|---|
| $730^{9}$ | **Flying Pennant (IRE) (60)** (RHannon) **3-9-3** RPerham(7) (a.p: r.o one pce fnl 2f: nt trble wnr: fin 2nd, 5l: awrdd r) | — | 1 | 6/1 3 | 69 | 33 |
| | **Mystical Maid** (HThomsonJones) **3-8-12** WRyan(4) (small: lt-f: hdwy over 2f out: r.o one pce fnl f: fin 3rd, 4l: plcd 2nd) | | 2 | 7/1 | 54 | 18 |
| $983^{19}$ | **Little Kenny (50)** (MJFetherston-Godley) **3-8-2b¹** GDuffield(13) (hdwy fnl 2f: nvr nrr: fin 4th, nk: plcd 3rd) | | 3 | 14/1 | 44 | 8 |
| *$857^{5}$* | **Coastguards Hero (52)** (MDIUsher) **3-9-0** NAdams(6) (sn chsng wnr: wknd over 1f out: fin 5th, hd: plcd 4th) | | 4 | 11/1 | 55 | 19 |
| $595^{16}$ | **One Shot (IRE) (58)** (WRMuir) **3-8-7** WWoods(5) (a mid div: fin 6th, 3½l: plcd 5th) | | 5 | 12/1 | 40 | 4 |
| $743^{2}$ | **Ciserano (IRE) (55)** (MRChannon) **3-8-7**(5) PPMurphy(12) (chsd ldrs: rdn over 2f out: no rspnse) | 1 | 7 | 3/1 1 | 43 | 7 |
| | **Dyanko** (MSSaunders) **3-9-0**(3) SDrowne(9) (a bhd) | 4 | 8 | 20/1 | 39 | 3 |
| $861^{13}$ | **Duet** (JSKing) **3-8-4** GBardwell(2) (bit bkwd: prom 4f) | 5 | 9 | 50/1 | 14 | — |
| | **Silhouette (IRE) (40)** (DRCElsworth) **3-8-2** FNorton(1) (bhd fnl 3f) | 2 | 10 | 14/1 | 8 | — |
| *$281^{8}$* | **Petite Annie (50)** (TGMills) **3-8-8** MarkLynch(10) (plld hrd: prom 4f) | 3½ | 11 | 14/1 | 6 | — |
| $665^{4}$ | **Lincon Twenty One (40)** (MJHaynes) **3-7-9b¹**(5) MBaird(11) (a bhd: t.o) | 11 | 12 | 14/1 | — | — |
| $892^{16}$ | **Motrib (USA)** (MMadgwick) **3-8-8**(3) NVarley(3) (bit bkwd: a bhd: t.o) | 7 | 13 | 33/1 | — | — |
| $1009^{4}$ | **Daily Risk (65)** (SDow) **3-8-2**(5) ADaly(8) (wnt rt s: mde all: pushed clr over 3f out: r.o wl: fin 1st: disq: plcd last) | | D | 5/1 2 | 70 | 34 |
| | | | | (SP 120.8%) | **13 Rn** | |

**1m 27.14** (1.14) CSF £44.72 TOTE £8.60: £3.30 £1.90 £2.80 (£21.30) Trio £104.40 OWNER Mr C. M. Hamer (MARLBOROUGH) BRED Frank Barry

STEWARDS' ENQUIRY Daly susp. 25 & 27-30/5/96 (irresponsible riding)

**Flying Pennant (IRE)**, second or third throughout, could make no impression on the winner in the closing stages and was very luckily awarded the race. (6/1: op 4/1)
**Mystical Maid** came with a run on the outside and, though not quite able to sustain it, gave the impression that she is capable of winning a race. (7/1: op 12/1)
**Little Kenny**, blinkered for the first time, was badly outpaced but stayed on well in the closing stages. (14/1)
**Coastguards Hero** disputed second place for much of the way, but weakened approaching the final furlong. He never threatened the winner. (11/1: 8/1-12/1)

**One Shot (IRE)**, struggling to go the pace for most of the way, could never improve beyond mid-division. (12/1)
**Silhouette (IRE)** (14/1: 10/1-16/1)
**Lincon Twenty One** (14/1: 10/1-16/1)
**1009 Daily Risk**, who went to the right at the start and crossed over to the rail, made the running and was driven clear approaching the three-furlong marker. It seemed very harsh that he should lose the race in the Stewards' Room. (5/1: 9/4-11/2)

## 1123 NETHERHAMPTON MAIDEN STKS (II) (3-Y.O+ F & M) (Class D)
4-50 (4-53) **1m 1f 209y** £3,460.00 (£1,030.00: £490.00: £220.00) Stalls: High GOING minus 0.55 sec per fur (F)

| | | | | SP | RR | SF |
|---|---|---|---|---|---|---|
| | **Sardonic** (HRACecil) **3-8-7** WRyan(1) (w'like: led after 1f: clr over 2f out: easily) | — | **1** | 6/5 1 | 87+ | 33 |
| 921 3 | **Seirenes** (PTWalwyn) **3-8-7** GHind(6) (hld up: hdwy over 2f out: r.o: nvr nr wnr) | 8 | **2** | 4/1 2 | 74 | 20 |
| 845 7 | **Naseem Alsahar** (MajorWRHern) **3-8-7** TSprake(10) (led 1f: chsd wnr: ev ch 3f out: wknd fnl f) | hd | **3** | 5/1 3 | 74 | 20 |
| 845 9 | **Alicia (IRE)** (JLDunlop) **3-8-7** SWhitworth(4) (lw: hdwy 3f out: rdn 2f out: one pce) | 5 | **4** | 9/1 | 66 | 12 |
| | **Turia** (MajorDNChappell) **3-8-7** AClark(11) (hdwy fnl 2f: nvr nrr) | s.h | **5** | 16/1 | 66 | 12 |
| 820 5 | **Finlana** (MRStoute) **3-8-7** KBradshaw(5) (hld up: hdwy over 2f out: nvr nr to chal) | 1¾ | **6** | 7/1 | 63 | 9 |
| | **Vendetta** (IABalding) **3-8-7** AMcGlone(7) (bkwd: hdwy 3f out: wknd over 1f out) | s.h | **7** | 12/1 | 63 | 9 |
| 957 8 | **Most Wanted (IRE)** (PFICole) **3-8-7** CRutter(9) (bit bkwd: prom tl wknd over 2f out) | 8 | **8** | 12/1 | 50 | — |
| | **Fortunes Course (IRE)** (JSKing) **7-9-7** GBardwell(3) (a wl bhd) | 5 | **9** | 33/1 | 42 | 2 |
| 964 8 | **Amber Ring** (MRChannon) **3-8-2**(5) PPMurphy(8) (prom tl wknd over 3f out) | 12 | **10** | 33/1 | 23 | — |
| 1050 7 | **Lizium** (JCFox) **4-9-7** RPerham(2) (a wl bhd: rn v.wd st: t.o) | 20 | **11** | 50/1 | — | — |

(SP 133.7%) **11 Rn**

**2m 7.19** (1.89) CSF £7.70 TOTE £1.90: £1.50 £1.20 £2.00 (£5.40) Trio £5.40 OWNER Lord Howard de Walden (NEWMARKET) BRED Lord Howard de Walden
WEIGHT FOR AGE 3yo-14lb
**Sardonic**, an attractive filly, was inclined to pull for her head in the early stages and her rider let her stride on after a furlong. She proved much too good for these and readily drew clear when pushed along over two furlongs from home. She could be very good. (6/5: Evens-7/4)
**921 Seirenes** made a forward move over two furlongs from home but, though staying on to snatch second place, was never in the same parish as the winner. (4/1)
**Naseem Alsahar** made the early running. Second for most of the way, she was the only possible danger three furlongs out but burst herself trying to match strides with the easy winner. (5/1)
**Alicia (IRE)** came with a run at the three-furlong marker but could not sustain it when pressure was applied a furlong later. (9/1)
**Turia**, in the ruck for most of the way, looked like finishing there until making good late headway. (16/1)
**820 Finlana** ran a little better than her final position of sixth would suggest. After making a forward move, she could not respond to pressure below the distance and the position was accepted. (7/1)
**Most Wanted (IRE)** (12/1: op 8/1)

## 1124 LEVY BOARD H'CAP (0-80) (3-Y.O+) (Class D)
5-20 (5-21) **1m 4f** £3,850.00 (£1,150.00: £550.00: £250.00) Stalls: High GOING minus 0.55 sec per fur (F)

| | | | | SP | RR | SF |
|---|---|---|---|---|---|---|
| 826 4 | **Old Irish (75)** (LMCumani) **3-9-0** WRyan(7) (hdwy 4f out: swvd bdly rt & lft 3 times fnl 2f: qcknd to ld cl home) | — | **1** | 2/1 1 | 92 | 44 |
| 811 5 | **Hattaafeh (IRE) (56)** (MissBSanders) **5-8-12** GHind(3) (led: clr over 3f out: hdd nr fin) | ¾ | **2** | 8/1 3 | 72 | 41 |
| 866 2 | **Soviet Bride (IRE) (66)** (SDow) **4-9-3**(5) ADaly(8) (lw: chsd ldr tl over 3f out: r.o one pce) | 6 | **3** | 9/4 2 | 74 | 43 |
| 811 11 | **Reaganesque (USA) (51)** (PGMurphy) **4-8-7** FNorton(1) (hdwy 4f out: one pce fnl 2f) | 9 | **4** | 12/1 | 47 | 16 |
| | **Blanchland (47)** (PCRitchens) **7-8-3** NAdams(9) (nvr nr to chal) | 1¾ | **5** | 25/1 | 41 | 10 |
| 879 18 | **Pistol (IRE) (60)** (CAHorgan) **6-9-2** WWoods(6) (b.hind: hld up in rr: hdwy 3f out: wknd over 1f out) | ¾ | **6** | 14/1 | 53 | 22 |
| 1011 4 | **Prerogative (61)** (RSimpson) **6-9-0**(3) SDrowne(5) (dropped rr over 3f out: no ch after) | 7 | **7** | 14/1 | 44 | 13 |
| 745 2 | **Grandes Oreilles (IRE) (52)** (NJHWalker) **4-8-8** CRutter(2) (prom tl wknd over 3f out) | 1½ | **8** | 14/1 | 33 | 2 |
| 844 6 | **Dormy Three (68)** (RJHodges) **6-9-10** AMcGlone(4) (a bhd: t.o) | 14 | **9** | 10/1 | 31 | — |

(SP 115.8%) **9 Rn**

**2m 34.2** (1.60) CSF £17.26 CT £35.05 TOTE £2.30: £1.30 £2.40 £1.30 (£22.00) Trio £7.50 OWNER Sheikh Mohammed (NEWMARKET) BRED Sheikh Mohammed bin Rashid al Maktoum
WEIGHT FOR AGE 3yo-17lb
**826 Old Irish** put up a remarkable performance. He improved smoothly to take second place at the three-furlong marker and was quickly upsides the leader. When asked for his effort, he veered from one side of the course to the other and, when his rider put down the whip, he quickened readily to win cheekily. He is far better than his present handicap mark would suggest. (2/1)
**811 Hattaafeh (IRE)** tried to make all the running. She slipped clear over three furlongs from home but, though keeping on well, found the winner too good near the finish. (8/1)
**866 Soviet Bride (IRE)**, in second place until over three furlongs out, was fighting a losing battle thereafter but was never going to surrender third place. (9/4)
**Reaganesque (USA)** made a forward move four furlongs out but the effort was not sustained in the final quarter-mile. (12/1)
**Blanchland** stayed on to be a distant fifth but was never on terms. (25/1)
**Pistol (IRE)**, last for a long way, improved on to the heels of the leading group three furlongs out, but faded approaching the final furlong. (14/1)
**1011 Prerogative** (14/1: op 8/1)

T/Plpt: £1,070.10 (7.6 Tckts). T/Qdpt: £248.80 (2.75 Tckts). KH

# 1111-YORK (L-H) (Good to firm)
## Thursday May 16th
WEATHER: overcast WIND: mod half against

## 1125 MICHAEL SEELY MEMORIAL GLASGOW CONDITIONS STKS (3-Y.O C & G) (Class B)
2-00 (2-01) **1m 2f 85y** £8,390.20 (£3,101.80: £1,485.90: £604.50: £237.25: £90.35) Stalls: Low GOING minus 0.24 sec per fur (GF)

| | | | | SP | RR | SF |
|---|---|---|---|---|---|---|
| 970* | **Dr Massini (IRE)** (MRStoute) **3-8-12** MJKinane(4) (hld up: effrt over 3f out: rdn to ld over 1f out: r.o strly) | — | **1** | 6/4 1 | 113+ | 80 |

821* **King Alex** (RCharlton) **3-8-12** PatEddery(2) (lw: led: pushed along over 3f out: hdd over 1f out: eased whn btn towards fin)....3½ **2** 9/4[2] 108 75
**Astor Place (IRE)** (PWChapple-Hyam) **3-8-12** JReid(6) (bit bkwd: hld up: effrt & outpcd 3f out: styd on ins fnl f)....4 **3** 7/2[3] 101 68
736[5] **Van Gurp (94)** (BAMcMahon) **3-8-9** SSanders(1) (bit bkwd: trckd ldrs: effrt over 3f out: one pce)....2 **4** 16/1 95 62
677[7] **Radiant Star** (GWragg) **3-8-9** PaulEddery(5) (bit bkwd: chsd ldr: chal 3f out: wknd over 1f out)....4 **5** 20/1 89 56
903a[8] **Mironov** (MRChannon) **3-8-12** RHughes(3) (trckd ldrs: effrt over 3f out: edgd lft & wknd over 2f out: eased)...9 **6** 14/1 78 45
(SP 110.3%) **6 Rn**

**2m 9.39** (-0.31) CSF £5.03 TOTE £2.30: £1.30 £1.70 (£2.50) OWNER Mr M. Tabor (NEWMARKET) BRED Mount Coote Partnership
IN-FOCUS: **A race that numbers Commander in Chief and Tamure amongst its recent winers, this event is becoming an alternative to the Dante for lightly-raced Derby hopefuls.**
**970* Dr Massini (IRE)** entered the Derby picture with an authoritative success. He won really well in the end and will be even better suited by the mile and a half and less firm ground. However he fares at Epsom, he looks a fine long-term prospect. (6/4)
**821* King Alex**, with the role of pacemaker thrust upon him, showed definite signs of inexperience. In the end, he proved no match but was eased a length when clearly held near the line. He will be well suited by a step up to a mile and a half and he too looks an excellent long-term prospect. (9/4)
**Astor Place (IRE)**, who finished fifth, beaten three lengths in the Grand Criterium on his final outing at two, is said to have undergone a wind operation in the winter. Keen to get on with it, he was left behind halfway up the straight but was staying on in the closing stages. He looked in need of the outing but will have to learn to relax if he is to fulfil his potential. (7/2: 5/2-4/1)
**736 Van Gurp** is being set some stiff tasks. Sticking on at the one pace, he will be suited by a step up to one and a half miles. (16/1)
**677 Radiant Star** dropped away after having every chance halfway up the straight. He might be better suited by some give underfoot. (20/1)
**903a Mironov**, disqualified after passing the post fifth in the Italian 2000 Guineas, showed plenty of knee-action going to post. Racing keenly, he was never on an even keel and his rider eventually gave up. He will have to learn to settle if he is to stay as far as his pedigree might suggest. (14/1: 8/1-16/1)

## 1126 LAMBSON-KNIGHT AIR H'CAP (0-95) (3-Y.O) (Class C)

2-35 (2-37) **7f 202y** £7,960.00 (£2,380.00: £1,140.00: £520.00) Stalls: Low GOING minus 0.24 sec per fur (GF)

SP RR SF

**Missile (78)** (WJHaggas) **3-8-7** RCochrane(12) (hld up: nt clr run & swtchd over 2f out: gd hdwy over 1f out: qcknd to ld ins fnl f: hld on wl)....— **1** 6/1[1] 95 54
**Winter Romance (85)** (EALDunlop) **3-9-0** PaulEddery(8) (bit bkwd: gd hdwy over 2f out: ev ch ins fnl f: r.o)..hd **2** 6/1[1] 102 61
937* **Spirito Libro (USA) (71)** (CNAllen) **3-7-7**(7) MartinDwyer(10) (bhd: effrt on outside 3f out: styd on wl fnl f)....1¾ **3** 10/1[3] 84 43
917[4] **Charlie Chang (IRE) (72)** (RHannon) **3-8-1** SSanders(6) (chsd ldr: led over 1f out tl ins fnl f: styd on same pce)....2 **4** 6/1[1] 81 40
978* **Mawingo (IRE) (69)** (GWragg) **3-7-12** 5x JQuinn(1) (sn bhd & pushed along: hdwy on ins over 3f out: styd on fnl f: nt rch ldrs)....½ **5** 15/2[2] 77 36
**Russian Rascal (IRE) (67)** (TDEasterby) **3-7-10** LCharnock(2) (a chsng ldrs: kpt on one pce fnl 2f)....s.h **6** 33/1 75 34
917[6] **Sky Dome (IRE) (80)** (MHTompkins) **3-8-9** NDay(13) (lw: bhd: effrt on outside 3f out: kpt on: nvr nr ldrs)....1 **7** 10/1[3] 86 45
709* **Therhea (IRE) (87)** (BRMillman) **3-9-2** TQuinn(4) (lw: hld up: trckd ldrs: hrd rdn 2f out: sn wknd)....5 **8** 15/2[2] 83 42
785[3] **Mybotye (78)** (GROldroyd) **3-8-7** JWeaver(5) (lw: led tl over 2f out: btn whn eased towards fin)....1 **9** 15/2[2] 72 31
833[5] **Bullfinch (92)** (PTWalwyn) **3-9-7** PatEddery(11) (hld up & bhd: sme hdwy whn n.m.r over 2f out: styd on towards fin)....½ **10** 20/1 85 44
870[7] **Indian Relative (72)** (RGuest) **3-8-1** WCarson(3) (swtg: trckd ldr: led over 2f out tl over 1f out: eased whn n.m.r ins fnl f)....½ **11** 14/1 64 23
917[9] **Truancy (90)** (MBell) **3-9-5** MFenton(7) (in tch: effrt over 3f out: wknd over 2f out)....9 **12** 25/1 64 23
768* **Promptly (IRE) (85)** (MRStoute) **3-9-0** JReid(9) (chsd ldrs: wkng whn hmpd over 2f out)....1¼ **13** 6/1[1] 56 15
(SP 128.8%) **13 Rn**

**1m 38.49** (1.69) CSF £42.20 CT £338.81 TOTE £9.50: £2.40 £2.80 £3.30 (£22.40) Trio £306.40 OWNER Mr J. W. Bogie (NEWMARKET) BRED The Duke of Marlborough
LONG HANDICAP Russian Rascal (IRE) 7-8
**Missile**, turned out in tremendous shape, overcame all sorts of difficulties. A follow up is a definite possibility. (6/1)
**Winter Romance**, who looked as if the outing might do him good, is a particularly good mover. Carrying his head high, in the end, he was only just held at bay. (6/1)
**937* Spirito Libro (USA)**, from a 4lb higher mark, proved her Newmarket effort was no fluke, staying on in most determined fashion in the final furlong. (10/1)
**917 Charlie Chang (IRE)** stepped up on his initial effort and might be even better suited by a slight step up in distance. (6/1)
**978* Mawingo (IRE)**, under a 5lb penalty and raised considerably in class, showed plenty of knee-action going to post. Struggling to go the pace, he was staying on when it was all over. (15/2)
**Russian Rascal (IRE)**, pulled up after breaking a blood-vessel on his final outing at two, was on his toes beforehand but ran with plenty of credit. (33/1)
**768* Promptly (IRE)** was on the retreat when the winner appeared to strike into her, and she was allowed to come home in her own time. Hopefully, she will be none the worse. (6/1)

## 1127 WILLIAM HILL H'CAP (0-105) (3-Y.O) (Class B)

3-05 (3-07) **6f 214y** £19,087.50 (£5,700.00: £2,725.00: £1,237.50) Stalls: Low GOING minus 0.24 sec per fur (GF)

SP RR SF

917[8] **Polish Spring (IRE) (85)** (BWHills) **3-8-6** BThomson(5) (hld up: effrt & n.m.r over 2f out: squeezed thro ins fnl f: fin strly to ld post)....— **1** 14/1 90 35
937[5] **Royal Mark (IRE) (88)** (JWWatts) **3-8-9** PatEddery(3) (lw: a chsng ldrs: led over 1f out tl nr fin)....hd **2** 5/1[1] 93 38
833[8] **Caricature (IRE) (84)** (GLewis) **3-8-5** PaulEddery(13) (hld up: effrt & hung lft over 2f out: styd on wl fnl f)....s.h **3** 8/1 89 34
732[6] **Double Bluff (IRE) (85)** (IABalding) **3-8-6** KDarley(14) (sn pushed along: hdwy on outside ½-wy: styd on wl ins fnl f)....hd **4** 7/1 89 34
960[D] **Letluce (95)** (JRArnold) **3-9-2** MJKinane(11) (hld up: effrt on outside over 2f out: kpt on: nt rch ldrs)....1 **5** 11/2[2] 97 42
705[4] **Iamus (88)** (PTWalwyn) **3-8-9** RCochrane(4) (dwlt: hdwy on ins whn bdly hmpd over 2f out: swtchd: styd on appr fnl f)....1 **6** 16/1 88 33
987[4] **Sualtach (IRE) (84)** (RHollinshead) **3-8-5** DHarrison(6) (chsd ldrs: ev ch & edgd rt 1f out: wknd towards fin)....1¾ **7** 10/1 80 25

$935^{10}$ **Jo Mell (83)** (TDEasterby) **3-8-4** MBirch(10) (led tl over 1f out: grad wknd) ....... ½ **8** 14/1 78 23
$937^{6}$ **Tarneem (USA) (88)** (MRStoute) **3-8-9** JReid(12) (in tch: pushed along ½-wy: wknd 2f out) ....... 1 **9** $13/2^{3}$ 80 25
$945^{3}$ **King of Peru (100)** (APJarvis) **3-9-7** JTate(8) (lw: prom: styd on one pce whn hmpd ins fnl f) ....... ½ **10** 20/1 91 36
$917^{7}$ **Paint It Black (85)** (RHannon) **3-8-6** TQuinn(7) (bit bkwd: chsd ldrs: sn pushed along: wkng whn hmpd over 1f out) ....... 1 **11** 10/1 74 19
$937^{15}$ **Green Bopper (USA) (84)** (MBell) **3-8-5** MFenton(9) (lw: outpcd after 2f: n.d after) ....... hd **12** 14/1 73 18
$1006^{9}$ **Whittle Rock (80)** (EJAlston) **3-8-1** JQuinn(1) (lw: chsd ldrs: wkng whn hmpd over 1f out) ....... ½ **13** 16/1 68 13
$565^{6}$ **Prince Aslia (95)** (MJohnston) **3-9-2** JWeaver(2) (w ldr tl wknd over 2f out: eased) ....... 9 **14** 20/1 62 7
(SP 128.5%) **14 Rn**

**1m 25.91** (2.91) CSF £81.79 CT £576.98 TOTE £40.10: £8.60 £2.00 £3.30 (£55.80) Trio £644.30 OWNER Marston Stud (LAMBOURN) BRED Lady Richard Wellesley and Grange Nominees

**917 Polish Spring (IRE)**, who seemed to lose her way in her three subsequent outings after winning on her debut at Newmarket in September, overcame all sorts of difficulties. Squeezing through the eye of the needle, she stuck her head in front right on the line. She is certainly willing. (14/1)

**937 Royal Mark (IRE)** made the best of his way home but, however hard he battled, he could not quite hang on. A mile might suit him better. (5/1)

**Caricature (IRE)**, dropped back in distance, gave his rider problems but, even so, in the end was only just denied. With the blinkers back on, he might be an easier ride. (8/1: 6/1-9/1)

**732 Double Bluff (IRE)**, struggling to go the pace, was putting in all his best work at the line and will be definitely suited by a step up to a mile. (7/1)

**960 Letluce** showed that the fast ground here was not a problem. (11/2)

**705 Iamus**, a frustrating individual, did not have the run of the race. After giving away ground at the start, he was knocked right back on the inner over two furlongs out. Staying on strongly late in the day, on the face of it, he would have been involved in the finish with better luck in running, but he is not one to trust. (16/1)

**935 Jo Mell**, dropped 2lb after a quiet run round at Thirsk, was allowed to get on with it this time, but faded noticeably in the closing stages. There is room for improvement yet. (14/1)

**945 King of Peru**, with plenty to do at the weights, was only sticking on at the same pace when hampered and forced to snatch up inside the last. (20/1)

## 1128 EAST COAST YORKSHIRE CUP STKS (Gp 2) (4-Y.O+) (Class A)

3-40 (3-41) **1m 5f 194y** £52,481.62 (£18,853.50: £8,989.25: £3,608.75: £1,366.88) Stalls: Low GOING minus 0.24 sec per fur (GF)

SP RR SF

**Classic Cliche (IRE)** (SbinSuroor) **4-9-0** MJKinane(5) (trckd ldrs: effrt over 4f out: led over 2f out: styd on strly fnl f) ....... — **1** $2/1^{2}$ 126 100
**Strategic Choice (USA) (120)** (PFICole) **5-9-0** TQuinn(4) (trckd ldrs: hdwy to chal over 2f out: nt qckn fnl f) ....... 1½ **2** $13/8^{1}$ 124 98
**Court of Honour (IRE) (117)** (PWChapple-Hyam) **4-9-0** JReid(3) (trckd ldr: rdn & outpcd over 3f out: kpt on fnl f) ....... 2 **3** 10/1 122 96
$875^{2}$ **Grey Shot (104)** (IABalding) **4-8-9** KDarley(1) (led tl over 2f out: one pce) ....... 3½ **4** $100/30^{3}$ 113 87
**Asterita (106)** (RHannon) **4-8-6** PatEddery(2) (lw: sn outpcd & pushed along: n.d) ....... 9 **5** 16/1 100 74
(SP 109.5%) **5 Rn**

**2m 52.77** (0.15 under best) (-3.43) CSF £5.40 TOTE £2.20: £1.30 £1.40 (£2.40) OWNER Godolphin (NEWMARKET) BRED Lord Victor Matthews in Ireland

**Classic Cliche (IRE)**, last year's St Leger winner, won this decisively in the end in record time. He looks an outstanding Gold Cup prospect but no doubt he will be campaigned over shorter trips on the continent. (2/1)

**Strategic Choice (USA)**, controversially rated Europe's top stayer last year ahead of Double Trigger, travelled strongly and looked to have the upper hand when moving upsides halfway up the straight but, inside the last, he had to give best. Third behind Lammtarra in the King George at Ascot last year, a drop back to a mile and a half should be no problem. (13/8)

**Court of Honour (IRE)**, who was carrying condition, proved he is as good as ever. (10/1: op 6/1)

**875 Grey Shot** set a strong pace but, over this trip, the first three, all Group One winners, had too much speed for him where it mattered. (100/30)

**Asterita** was never happy on this ground and was soon struggling to go the pace. (16/1)

## 1129 DUKE OF YORK STKS (Gp 3) (3-Y.O+) (Class A)

4-10 (4-10) **6f** £24,640.00 (£9,229.50: £4,439.75: £1,940.75) Stalls: High GOING minus 0.24 sec per fur (GF)

SP RR SF

$940^{2}$ **Venture Capitalist (110)** (DNicholls) **7-9-0** RCochrane(9) (lw: s.i.s: gd hdwy 2f out: swtchd & styd on strly to ld nr fin) ....... — **1** 11/1 112 68
$1075^{4}$ **Branston Abby (IRE) (109)** (MJohnston) **7-8-11** JWeaver(4) (sn bhd & pushed along: hdwy on outside ½-wy: kpt on wl fnl f) ....... hd **2** 16/1 109 65
**Royale Figurine (IRE) (102)** (MJFetherston-Godley) **5-8-11** BThomson(7) (bit bkwd: b: chsd ldrs: led over 1f out tl hdd nr fin) ....... hd **3** 20/1 109 65
$927^{2}$ **Lucky Lionel (USA) (115)** (RHannon) **3-8-11** PatEddery(2) (sn outpcd & pushed along: hdwy 2f out: styd on towards fin) ....... ½ **4** $7/1^{3}$ 116 63
$727^{5}$ **Woodborough (USA) (116)** (PWChapple-Hyam) **3-8-9** JReid(12) (sn bhd & pushed along: hdwy & nt clr run 2f out: hung rt & swtchd ins fnl f: kpt on wl) ....... ¾ **5** 12/1 112 59
673* **Passion For Life (112)** (GLewis) **3-8-5** PaulEddery(10) (trckd ldr: led over 3f out tl over 1f out: wknd towards fin) ....... 1 **6** $11/4^{2}$ 106 53
$818^{2}$ **Easy Dollar (105)** (BGubby) **4-9-0b** RHughes(1) (lw: a chsng ldrs: kpt on same pce appr fnl f) ....... 1 **7** 20/1 103 59
374a* **Diffident (FR)** (SbinSuroor) **4-9-4** MJKinane(3) (sn trckng ldrs: effrt over 1f out: sn wknd) ....... nk **8** $5/2^{1}$ 106 62
$940^{8}$ **Welsh Mist (98)** (RBoss) **5-8-11** KDarley(11) (nvr trbld ldrs) ....... 3½ **9** 50/1 90 46
$927^{3}$ **Westcourt Magic (109)** (MWEasterby) **3-8-5** TQuinn(8) (lw: led over 2f: wknd over 1f out) ....... nk **10** 10/1 92 39
674* **Thrilling Day (113)** (NAGraham) **3-8-6** DHarrison(5) (in tch: rdn along ½-wy: lost pl 2f out: eased) ....... 7 **11** 11/1 74 21
**Mubhij (IRE) (111)** (BWHills) **3-8-9** WCarson(6) (h.d.w: bkwd: dwlt: sn trckng ldrs: wknd 2f out: eased) ....... 2½ **12** 10/1 71 18
(SP 127.6%) **12 Rn**

**1m 11.72** (0.72) CSF £161.07 TOTE £11.70: £1.80 £3.90 £4.30 (£40.50) Trio £376.40 OWNER Mr W. G. Swiers (THIRSK) BRED Brook Bloodstock Plc

WEIGHT FOR AGE 3yo-9lb

**IN-FOCUS: The Classic generation were put in their place here, with the finish fought out by two fully exposed seven-year-olds.**

**940 Venture Capitalist** proved himself better than ever, picking up in a tight finish near the line (11/1)
**1075 Branston Abby (IRE)**, in this race for the third year running, bounced right back to her very best. Battling strongly all the way to the line, in the end, she was only just denied. (16/1)
**Royale Figurine (IRE)**, much improved in the second half of last season, ran a tremendous race, especially considering she looked as if this outing would bring her on. (20/1)
**927 Lucky Lionel (USA)** faced a stiff task for a three-year-old at the weights under a 6lb penalty for his victory last year. Soon struggling to go the pace, he was putting in his best work at the finish and might be worth a try over seven. (7/1)
**727 Woodborough (USA)** appreciated the six furlongs and fast ground. First impressions were that he was possibly unlucky not to be more closely involved in the finish but, in truth, he was always giving his rider problems by hanging right, and the blame was on his own doorstep. (12/1)
**673* Passion For Life** and Westcourt Magic seemed to set a very strong pace. Fading towards the finish, he might be worth a try with more patient tactics over seven. (11/4: 2/1-3/1)
**818 Easy Dollar** ran right up to his best, and seven furlongs on firm ground will probably bring out the best in him. (20/1)
**374a* Diffident (FR)** is not very big. Turned out in the pink, his stride shortened over a furlong out. He looked a potentially top-class sprinter when taking last year's Free Handicap but, in truth, has not really progressed. (5/2)
**927 Westcourt Magic**, as usual taken to post early, burst out of the stalls but had run himself into the ground with over a furlong left to run. (10/1: 8/1-12/1)

## 1130 E.B.F. RACING CHANNEL MAIDEN STKS (2-Y.O) (Class D)
4-40 (4-41) **6f** £5,744.00 (£1,712.00: £816.00: £368.00) Stalls: High GOING minus 0.24 sec per fur (GF)

| | | | | SP | RR | SF |
|---|---|---|---|---|---|---|
| | **Belgravia** (PFICole) **2-9-0** TQuinn(2) (leggy: lt-f: unruly in stalls: outpcd & rdn along after 2f: ran v.green & sn bhd: gd hdwy over 1f out: led ins fnl f) | — | **1** | 5/1 3 | 93+ | 38 |
| 706 3 | **Referendum (IRE)** (GLewis) **2-9-0** PaulEddery(1) (w ldr: hung lft: led 1f out tl ins fnl f) | ¾ | **2** | 11/4 2 | 91 | 36 |
| 924 4 | **Hawait (IRE)** (BWHills) **2-9-0** RHills(3) (trckd ldrs: led over 2f out: wandered bdly & swvd rt over 1f out: sn hdd & btn) | 3½ | **3** | 5/4 1 | 82 | 27 |
| | **Andreyev (IRE)** (RHannon) **2-9-0** RHughes(5) (w'like: leggy: bit bkwd: dwlt: hung bdly lft ½-wy: ev ch over 1f out: sn wknd) | 3 | **4** | 7/1 | 74+ | 19 |
| 815 2 | **Lucayan Beach** (BGubby) **2-9-0** JWeaver(4) (led tl over 2f out: lost pl over 1f out) | 5 | **5** | 10/1 | 60 | 5 |
| | | | | (SP 109.4%) | **5 Rn** | |

**1m 13.86** (2.86) CSF £17.31 TOTE £4.70: £1.90 £1.60 (£6.50) OWNER H R H Prince Fahd Salman (WHATCOMBE) BRED Newgate Stud Co
IN-FOCUS: **The leaders may have gone too fast in the early stages.**
**Belgravia** went to post keenly. Playing up badly in the stalls, he was soon struggling badly and flat out. Despite showing signs of inexperience, he picked up ground in good style over a furlong out to lead near the line, despite hanging left when he did hit the front. Though by Rainbow Quest, seven furlongs might be as far as he wants to go this year. (5/1)
**706 Referendum (IRE)** hung left throughout, but was only collared near the line. (11/4)
**924 Hawait (IRE)**, with a previous outing under his belt, seemed to run very green, wandering and diving right after hitting the front. After this there must be a question mark over his temperament. (5/4)
**Andreyev (IRE)** was on one rein throughout. Considering he ended up racing towards the far side, it was surprising that he was still almost upsides over a furlong out. If his steering can be sorted out, he definitely has the ability. (7/1: 5/1-8/1)
**815 Lucayan Beach**, the only one of the five to keep straight, still managed to finish stone last. (10/1)

## 1131 LEVY BOARD SEVENTH RACE RATED STKS H'CAP (0-105) (4-Y.O+) (Class B)
5-10 (5-11) **1m 2f 85y** £8,067.50 (£2,982.50: £1,428.75: £581.25: £228.13: £86.87) Stalls: Low GOING minus 0.24 sec per fur (GF)

| | | | | SP | RR | SF |
|---|---|---|---|---|---|---|
| | **Key to My Heart (IRE) (102)** (MissSEHall) **6-9-5** JWeaver(1) (bit bkwd: b: mde all: clr 1f out: styd on strly) | — | **1** | 12/1 | 117 | 77 |
| 831 10 | **Medaille Militaire (102)** (JLDunlop) **4-9-5** PatEddery(2) (stdd s: hld up: effrt & swtchd rt over 2f out: styd on ins fnl f: no ch w wnr) | 3½ | **2** | 4/1 3 | 112 | 72 |
| | **Sanoosea (USA) (104)** (MRStoute) **4-9-7** JReid(4) (bit bkwd: trckd wnr: chal over 2f out: sn rdn & hung lft: no imp) | 1 | **3** | 2/1 1 | 112 | 72 |
| 960 5 | **Moments of Fortune (USA) (98)** (BHanbury) **4-8-12**(3) JStack(7) (swtg: effrt over 4f out: sn rdn & wl outpcd) | 8 | **4** | 6/1 | 94 | 54 |
| 988 2 | **Ten Past Six (90)** (MartynWane) **4-8-7** JCarroll(5) (lw: chsd ldrs: rdn along over 3f out: lost pl over 2f out) | ½ | **5** | 7/2 2 | 85 | 45 |
| 925* | **Ball Gown (93)** (DTThom) **6-8-7**(3) DRMcCabe(6) (hld up: effrt over 2f out: eased whn no ch over 1f out) | s.h | **6** | 9/2 | 88 | 48 |
| | | | | (SP 115.7%) | **6 Rn** | |

**2m 10.63** (0.93) CSF £54.71 TOTE £12.90: £2.40 £2.10 (£18.10) OWNER Mrs Maureen Pickering (MIDDLEHAM) BRED Miss Fiona Meehan
LONG HANDICAP Ten Past Six 8-6
**Key to My Heart (IRE)**, the 1994 Yorkshire Cup winner, has been beset with training problems since and had apparently overcome a serious leg injury. Despite running over what looked an inadequate trip, he was a springer in the market to take advantage of what looked a lenient handicap mark. Waiting in front, he stepped up the gallop halfway up the straight and scored in decisive fashion in the end. Provided all stays well with him, further success will surely follow. (12/1: op 25/1)
**831 Medaille Militaire**, given a much more patient ride, stayed on nicely inside the last and is on the way back. (4/1)
**Sanoosea (USA)** proved rather disappointing, hanging left in behind the winner when asked to make a race of it. (2/1)
**960 Moments of Fortune (USA)**, who sweated up beforehand, did not have the blinkers on and was not in a co-operative mood. (6/1)
**988 Ten Past Six** ran flat, being under pressure early in the straight and dropping right out. (7/2)
**925* Ball Gown**, raised 9lb for her Newmarket success, was given a negative ride and her rider seemed very happy to call it a day. (9/2)

T/Jkpt: Not won; £67,050.80 to Newbury 17/5/96. T/Plpt: £886.90 (43.84 Tckts). T/Qdpt: £113.10 (19.15 Tckts). WG

# LES LANDES (Jersey) (L-H) (Good)
## Monday May 6th

## 1132a GEOFFREY EDWARDS MEMORIAL H'CAP (3-Y.O+)
4-50 (4-53) **1m 2f** £784.00

| | | | SP | RR | SF |
|---|---|---|---|---|---|
| **Mans Passion** (MissAVibert,Jersey) **4-8-10** SLanigan | — | **1** | | 42 | — |
| **Sunley Sparkle** (BWalford,Jersey) **8-9-2** ATucker | 15 | **2** | | 24 | — |

| | Horse | Btn | Pos | SP | RR | SF |
|---|---|---|---|---|---|---|
| | **Misinterrex** (MissAVibert,Jersey) **5-8-11** SFothergill | 3 | 3 | | 14 | — |
| | **Admiralty Way** (RBrotherton) **10-10-2** BPowell (btn 21l) | | 5 | | 27 | — |
| | | | | | | **6 Rn** |

**2m 16.0** Tote £20.40: £23.60 £2.80 (£15.60) OWNER Mr Bill Allan BRED W. Allan and Miss Y. Stead

# 1056a-LONGCHAMP (Paris, France) (R-H) (Good)
## Thursday May 9th

### 1133a PRIX DE GUICHE (Gp 3) (3-Y.O C)
3-30 (3-33) **1m 1f 55y** £28,986.00 (£10,540.00: £5,270.00)

| | Horse | Btn | Pos | SP | RR | SF |
|---|---|---|---|---|---|---|
| | **Martiniquais (IRE)** (AFabre,France) **3-9-2** OPeslier | — | 1 | | 104 | — |
| | **Kalmoss (FR)** (BRenard,France) **3-9-2** DSicaud | s.nk | 2 | | 104 | — |
| | **Rupert (FR)** (JdeRoualle,France) **3-9-2** GMosse | 2 | 3 | | 100 | — |
| | | | | | | **6 Rn** |

**1m 56.3** (4.30) P-M 1.40F: 1.20F 2.00F (SF 7.80F) OWNER Mr D. Wildenstein (CHANTILLY) BRED Allez France Stables
**Martiniquais (IRE)**, who was long odds-on, arrived late on the scene and had to be kept right up to his work to hold on. He may well go for the Prix Jean Prat, but could benefit from a longer trip.
**Kalmoss (FR)** may well have won if his jockey had been more used to the course. Although trained in the Provinces, he is certainly a decent colt.
**Rupert (FR)** made some late progress, but is not up to Group class.

# FUCHU (Tokyo, Japan) (L-H) (Firm)
## Saturday May 11th

### 1134a KEIO HAI SPRING CUP (Gp 2) (4-Y.O+)
7-40 (7-40) **7f** £382,079.00

| | Horse | Btn | Pos | SP | RR | SF |
|---|---|---|---|---|---|---|
| 374a[2] | **Heart Lake** (SbinSuroor,UAE) **5-9-4** YTake | — | 1 | 111/10[3] | 123 | — |
| | **Taiki Blizzard (USA)** (KFujisawa,Japan) **5-9-2** YOkabe | ½ | 2 | 2/1[1] | 120 | — |
| | **Trot Thunder (JPN)** (KAikawa,Japan) **7-9-4** NYokoyama | hd | 3 | 23/10[2] | 122 | — |
| | **Shaanxi (USA)** (ELellouche,France) **4-8-9** MEbina (btn 4½l) | | 7 | | 105 | — |
| | | | | | (SP 71.9%) | **15 Rn** |

**1m 21.1** OWNER Godolphin BRED Sheikh Mohammed bin Rashid al Maktoum
**374a Heart Lake** gained a second success in Japan with a workmanlike performance. Racing in mid-division until making a forward move soon after turning for home, he battled it out with the favourite Taiki Blizzard from then on, and just got home. He will stay in Japan for the Yasuda Kinen, a race he won last year. (111/10)
**Shaanxi (USA)** put up a good show against some of the top horses in Japan. She was always prominent and had every chance a quarter of a mile from home, but could only run on at one pace.

# 1058a-CAPANNELLE (Rome, Italy) (R-H) (Heavy)
## Sunday May 12th

### 1135a PREMIO PRESIDENTE DELLA REPUBLICA (Gp 1) (4-Y.O+ C & F)
3-15 (3-37) **1m 2f** £53,235.00 (£26,122.00: £15,006.00)

| | Horse | Btn | Pos | SP | RR | SF |
|---|---|---|---|---|---|---|
| | **Hollywood Dream (GER)** (UOstmann,Germany) **5-8-13** JReid (hld up: hdwy over 1f out: r.o to ld cl home) | — | 1 | | 119 | — |
| *536a[7]* | **Needle Gun (IRE)** (CEBrittain) **6-9-2** BDoyle (led tl over 1f out: rallied to ld ins fnl f: hdd cl home) | hd | 2 | | 122 | — |
| | **Montjoy (USA)** (PFICole) **4-9-2** TQuinn (a.p: led over 1f out tl ins fnl f: no ex) | ½ | 3 | | 121 | — |
| | **Concepcion (GER)** (HJentzsch,Germany) **6-9-2** PSchiergen (a cl up: chal over 1f out: r.o one pce) | 1½ | 4 | | 119 | — |
| | **Manzoni (GER)** (AWohler,Germany) **4-9-2b[1]** ABoschert (hld up in rr: hdwy to chal over 1f out: one pce) | ½ | 5 | | 118 | — |
| *535a[2]* | **Cezanne** (SbinSuroor) **7-9-2** MJKinane (trckd ldrs: chal 2f out: no ex fnl f) | 1½ | 6 | | 115 | — |
| 906a[10] | **Slicious** (VCaruso,Italy) **4-9-2** MEsposito (unruly s: a abt same pl) | 3 | 7 | | 111 | — |
| 909a* | **Tarhelm (IRE)** (GColleo,Italy) **4-9-2** MLatorre (a bhd: rdn & btn st) | 4½ | 8 | | 103 | — |
| | **Big River (ITY)** (VCaruso,Italy) **4-9-2** LFicuciello (chsd ldr tl wknd 3f out: t.o) | dist | 9 | | — | — |
| | | | | | | **9 Rn** |

**2m 6.4** Tote 39L: 22L 23L 22L (190L) OWNER Gestut Haus Ittlingen BRED Gestut Hof Ittlingen
**Hollywood Dream (GER)**, in rear until moving up from the two-furlong marker, still appeared to have a lot to do, but her jockey conjured up a tremendous run from her, and forced her head in front on the line. She acts really well on soft or heavy ground.
**536a Needle Gun (IRE)** put up a superb display in the conditions. Trying to make it all, he fought back bravely when headed by Montjoy to regain the advantage and looked sure to win, but could not withstand the winner's late rush.
**Montjoy (USA)** ran really well on this reappearance. He took the advantage over a furlong out, but lack of an outing in the testing conditions took its toll inside the last 200 yards.
**535a Cezanne** may have found the conditions too testing. He had every chance a furlong out, but could not quicken.

### 1136a PREMIO MELTON MEMORIAL TUDINI (Gp 3) (3-Y.O+)
4-05 (4-41) **6f** £30,438.00 (£14,018.00: £7,830.00: £3,915.00)

| | Horse | Btn | Pos | SP | RR | SF |
|---|---|---|---|---|---|---|
| | **Beat of Drums** (GBotti,Italy) **5-9-5** MJKinane | — | 1 | | 118 | — |
| | **Macanal (USA)** (HJentzsch,Germany) **4-9-5** PSchiergen | 3 | 2 | | 110 | — |
| | **Gentle Fan (USA)** (BAgriformi,Italy) **7-9-5** CZarroli | 1 | 3 | | 107 | — |
| 1053a* | **Imprevedibile (IRE)** (PCeriotti,Italy) **6-9-5** AParravani | hd | 4 | | 107 | — |
| | | | | | | **10 Rn** |

**1m 10.7** Tote 40L: 17L 14L 48L (47L) OWNER Dr Carlo Vittadini (ITALY) BRED Dr C. Vittadini
**Beat of Drums** continued his progress with a comfortable victory, but was forced to squeeze through between the placed horses to get a run, and then had to survive a stewards' enquiry. He is going to prove a tough opponent for any overseas raiders whilst in this form.

# 1053a-SAN SIRO (Milan, Italy) (R-H) (Heavy)
## Sunday May 12th

### 1137a PREMIO RESEGONE (3-Y.O)
**1m** £10,150.00

| | Horse | | | SP | RR | SF |
|---|---|---|---|---|---|---|
| | **Sovereign Magic (USA)** (ATavazzani,Italy) **3-8-11** LManiezzi | — | 1 | | 74 | — |
| | **Sondalo (IRE)** (LCamici,Italy) **3-8-11** MCangiano | 2¼ | 2 | | 70 | — |
| 903a[12] | **Sharp Reproach** (Ld'Auria,Italy) **3-8-11** MDemuro | hd | 3 | | 69 | — |
| | **How Long** (LMCumani) **3-8-11** LPanici | s.nk | 4 | | 69 | — |
| | | | | | | **5 Rn** |

**1m 45.5** (15.50) Tote 47L: 23L 24L (105L) OWNER Scuderia Artares BRED Hester H. Witcher
**How Long** was making his debut for Luca Cumani, and produced a creditable effort against some useful sorts. He moved up to challenge over a furlong out before unable to sustain the effort, and is one to keep an eye on.

# COLOGNE (Germany) (R-H) (Good)
## Sunday May 12th

### 1138a GERLING PREIS (Gp 2) (4-Y.O+)
3-40 (3-45) **1m 4f** £32,658.00 (£13,063.00: £6,532.00: £4,054.00)

| | Horse | | | SP | RR | SF |
|---|---|---|---|---|---|---|
| | **Laroche (GER)** (HJentzsch,Germany) **5-9-4** LHammer-Hansen (mde all: r.o wl) | — | 1 | | 125 | — |
| | **Protektor (GER)** (ALowe,Germany) **7-9-0** MRimmer (hld up: chal 2f out: r.o) | 1¼ | 2 | | 119 | — |
| | **Aratikos (GER)** (HBlume,Germany) **5-9-0** ASuborics (chsd ldr: chal over 1f out: no ex fnl f) | 3 | 3 | | 115 | — |
| 789a* | **Oxalagu (GER)** (BSchutz,Germany) **4-9-2** AStarke (mid div: chal 2f out: one pce fnl f) | nse | 4 | | 117 | — |
| | **First Hello (GER)** (Germany) **4-9-4** TMundry (prom tl rdn & one pce fnl 2f) | 3 | 5 | | 115 | — |
| 789a[2] | **Sir King (GER)** (RSuerland,Germany) **4-9-0** AHelfenbein (hld up in rr: r.o st: nt rch ldrs) | 3 | 6 | | 107 | — |
| | **Suave Tern (USA)** (JEHammond,France) **5-9-0** WMongil (hld up in rr: rdn & no imp st) | 1½ | 7 | | 105 | — |
| | **Coneybury (IRE)** (Germany) **6-9-0** NGrant (a bhd) | 2½ | 8 | | 102 | — |
| | **Caballo (GER)** (Germany) **5-9-2** ATylicki (trckd ldrs tl wknd over 2f out) | 16 | 9 | | 83 | — |
| | | | | | | **9 Rn** |

**2m 29.88** (2.88) Tote 80DM: 29DM 28DM 26DM (SF 1035DM) OWNER Gestut Ittlingen BRED Gestut Hof Ittlingen in Germany
**Laroche (GER)** carried on from where his half-brother Lando left off, with his all-the-way victory completing a memorable weekend for his owners, who had a Group One success in Rome with Hollywood Dream. With the ground drying out just in time for him, he took full advantage, and will always taken some passing when the going is on the fast side.

# 1133a-LONGCHAMP (Paris, France) (R-H) (Good)
## Sunday May 12th

### 1139a PRIX LUPIN (Gp 1) (3-Y.O C & F)
3-05 (3-08) **1m 2f 110y** £62,292.00 (£24,769.00: £12,016.00: £5,270.00)

| | Horse | | | SP | RR | SF |
|---|---|---|---|---|---|---|
| 621a* | **Helissio (FR)** (ELellouche,France) **3-9-2** DBoeuf (a.p: led 2f out: rdn & styd on wl fnl f) | — | 1 | 2/5[1] | 114 | 81 |
| | **Loup Solitaire (USA)** (AFabre,France) **3-9-2** OPeslier (hld up: rdn & hdwy over 1f out: r.o wl fnl f) | ¾ | 2 | 47/10[3] | 113 | 80 |
| | **Fort Nottingham (USA)** (JEHammond,France) **3-9-2** CAsmussen (trckd ldr: rdn 2f out: r.o) | 2½ | 3 | 42/10[2] | 109 | 76 |
| | **Le Triton (USA)** (MmeCHead,France) **3-9-2** FHead (led tl hdd 2f out: no ex u.p) | nk | 4 | 13/2 | 109 | 76 |
| | **Cachet Noir (USA)** (PBary,France) **3-9-2** FGrenet (a in rr) | 4 | 5 | 215/10 | 103 | 70 |
| | | | | | (SP 126.0%) | **5 Rn** |

**2m 10.3** (2.30) P-M 1.40F: 1.10F 1.20F (SF 5.50F) OWNER E. Sarasola BRED Ecurie Skymarc Farm
**621a* Helissio (FR)**, a fine-looking colt, won his first Group One in workmanlike style. Always up with the pace, he took the advantage halfway up the straight and, although finding little in the way of a turn of foot, was never going to be beaten. He goes for the Prix du Jockey-Club with a favourite's chance, although he is not guaranteed to stay the trip on breeding. (2/5)
**Loup Solitaire (USA)** produced a much better effort this time, although he did not get into the race until it was almost over. He will renew rivalry with the winner in the French Derby and, although he has the breeding of a miler, this performance suggests the trip may suit him. (47/10)
**Fort Nottingham (USA)** ran creditably, having made the big step up from maiden company. He was short of pace at the end, but looks up to winning a Group race. (42/10)
**Le Triton (USA)** once again tried to make all and, although he kept on after being headed, was no match for the principals. He still holds an Epsom Derby entry. (13/2)

### 1140a DUBAI POULE D'ESSAI DES POULICHES (Gp 1) (3-Y.O F)
3-35 (3-34) **1m** £131,752.00 (£52,701.00: £26,350.00: £13,175.00)

| | Horse | | | SP | RR | SF |
|---|---|---|---|---|---|---|
| 921* | **Ta Rib (USA)** (EALDunlop) **3-9-0** WCarson (a.p: 2nd st: led over 1f out: r.o wl u.p) | — | 1 | 141/10 | 108 | 58 |
| 796a* | **Shake the Yoke** (ELellouche,France) **3-9-0** DBoeuf (mid div early: n.m.r 2f out: swtchd & r.o wl fnl f) | ¾ | 2 | 3/5[1] | 107 | 57 |
| 794a[2] | **Sagar Pride (IRE)** (JGBurns,Ireland) **3-9-0** OPeslier (mid div: r.o u.p fnl f) | ½ | 3 | 21/1 | 106 | 56 |
| | **A Votre Sante (USA)** (MmeCHead,France) **3-9-0** FHead (led early: styd prom: hmpd over 2f out: no ex fnl f) | 1 | 4 | 61/10[2] | 104 | 54 |
| | **True Flare (USA)** (MmeCHead,France) **3-9-0** PatEddery (s.i.s: bhd tl r.o fnl f) | s.nk | 5 | 86/10 | 103+ | 53 |
| | **Shawanni** (SbinSuroor) **3-9-0** LDettori (led 6f out tl hdd over 1f out: wknd) | ¾ | 6 | 96/10 | 102 | 52 |
| 796a[2] | **Raisonnable** (DSepulchre,France) **3-9-0** CAsmussen (s.s: nvr rchd ldrs) | hd | 7 | 16/1 | 101 | 51 |
| | **Housa Dancer (FR)** (AFabre,France) **3-9-0** TJarnet (trckd ldrs: rdn 2f out: one pce) | nk | 8 | 13/2[3] | 101 | 51 |
| | **Parade Sauvage (FR)** (CO'Brien,Ireland) **3-9-0** CRoche (a bhd) | nk | 9 | 95/1 | 100 | 50 |
| | | | | | (SP 127.9%) | **9 Rn** |

**1m 38.7** (3.70) P-M 15.10L: 2.30L 1.10L 2.80L (10.90L) OWNER Mr Hamdan Al Maktoum (NEWMARKET) BRED Shadwell Estate Co., Ltd. and Shadwell Farm, Inc.
**921* Ta Rib (USA)** handled the big step up from maiden company successfully. Kept close to the pace to avoid any trouble, she took the advantage a furlong and a half from home and kept on really well. She may well go to Ireland in search of a Guineas double. (141/10)

**796a* Shake the Yoke,** who met a good deal of trouble at a vital stage, looked an unlucky loser, and a line through Raisonnable suggests she should have been an easy winner. She will get a chance for compensation in the Coronation Stakes at Ascot, where the likely fast ground should suit her. (3/5)
**794a Sagar Pride (IRE)** ran really well without ever looking likely to win. She may be awarded the Italian Guineas on a technicality, and is likely to return there for her next race. She deserves to win a Group race on this showing. (21/1)
**A Votre Sante (USA)** took a little while to settle, but produced disappointingly little in the straight. She will now go for the Prix de Diane, which her granddam won in 1980. (61/10)
**Shawanni** took control after two furlongs, and held on until halfway up the straight. She kept on to be beaten just over three lengths and, on this showing, should soon be in the winner's enclosure. (96/10)
**Parade Sauvage (FR)**, never able to get into the race, was out of her depth. (95/1)

## 1141a DUBAI POULE D'ESSAI DES POULAINS (Gp 1) (3-Y.O C)
4-05 (4-15) **1m** £131,752.00 (£52,701.00: £26,350.00: £13,175.00)

| | | | | SP | RR | SF |
|---|---|---|---|---|---|---|
| 798a* | **Ashkalani (IRE)** (AdeRoyerDupre,France) **3-9-2** GMosse (mid div: n.m.r over 2f out: rdn to ld ins fnl f: r.o wl) | — | 1 | 4/5$^{1}$ | 118+ | 71 |
| 798a$^{3}$ | **Spinning World (USA)** (JEPease,France) **3-9-2** CAsmussen (hld up & bhd: hdwy on ins & n.m.r 2f out: hmpd & swtchd 1f out: fin v.wl) | ¾ | 2 | 61/10$^{3}$ | 117+ | 70 |
| 727$^{3}$ | **Tagula (IRE)** (IABalding) **3-9-2** KDarley (trckd ldrs: rdn 2f out: led 1f out: hdd & no ex ins fnl f) | ½ | 3 | 414/10 | 116 | 69 |
| 681* | **Cayman Kai (IRE)** (RHannon) **3-9-2** PatEddery (mid div: styd on fnl f: nt rch ldrs) | ¾ | 4 | 5/1$^{2}$ | 114 | 67 |
| 727$^{2}$ | **Kahir Almaydan (IRE)** (JLDunlop) **3-9-2** WCarson (a.p: led 2f out to 1f out: wknd fnl f) | nk | 5 | 26/1 | 113 | 66 |
| | **Barricade (USA)** (AFabre,France) **3-9-2** TJarnet (plld hrd early: prom tl rdn & wknd 2f out) | 1½ | 6 | 11/1 | 110 | 63 |
| 798a$^{2}$ | **Eternity Range (USA)** (PBary,France) **3-9-2** FHead (bhd early: nvr nr to chal) | 1½ | 7 | 10/1 | 107 | 60 |
| | **Don Micheletto** (SbinSuroor) **3-9-2** LDettori (mid div: no ex fnl 2f) | 1½ | 8 | 12/1 | 104 | 57 |
| 926$^{6}$ | **Danehill Dancer (IRE)** (NACallaghan) **3-9-2** RHughes (a bhd) | 1½ | 9 | 14/1 | 101 | 54 |
| 681$^{4}$ | **Gothenberg (IRE)** (MJohnston) **3-9-2** JWeaver (led tl hdd 2f out: wknd) | 4 | 10 | 35/1 | 93 | 46 |
| | | | | (SP 126.9%) | **10 Rn** | |

**1m 37.6** (2.60) P-M 1.80F: 1.10F 1.70F 3.50F (4.80F) OWNER Aga Khan (CHANTILLY) BRED Aga Khan's Studs S.C.
**798a* Ashkalani (IRE)** duly won his Classic, but had to work hard to do so. He had to struggle for room early in the straight but, once he got to the front, he never looked like being beaten. He is likely to stick to a mile for the time being, with the St. James' Palace Stakes at Ascot his next target. (4/5)
**798a Spinning World (USA)** appeared an unlucky loser, with his jockey riding his usual waiting race and asking him to do an awful lot from the entrance to the straight. Asmussen tried to go through the middle of the pack when he realised he had left his run too late, and then ran into a wall of horses. Forced to pull to the outside to get a run, the race was over by that time. Post-race comments from the jockey that the colt 'may have won' were pessimistic in the extreme as, with a clear run, it would surely have been him breaking the course record. He is not certain to get the Derby trip, but is a supplementary entry for Epsom, and is in the Irish 2000 Guineas in the meantime. He looks very useful. (61/10)
**727 Tagula (IRE)**, always up with the pace, briefly showed in front a furlong out and kept on bravely after being headed to take third. Entered in the Derby, although his breeding suggests the trip may be beyond him, he seems to do particularly well in France, and may come back for the Prix Jean Prat. (414/10)
**681* Cayman Kai (IRE)** ran on well in the closing stages without ever looking likely to be involved in the finish. This effort confirmed that he is up to Group class, and he looks sure to win a race at this level before long. (5/1)
**727 Kahir Almaydan (IRE)** ran freely as usual, and kept on really well when headed. His style of racing suggests that a return to a shorter trip may be to his advantage. (26/1)
**Don Micheletto** was unable to make much impression in this company. (12/1)
**926 Danehill Dancer (IRE)** never got into the race, and this may have come too soon for him after Newmarket. It is possible that he may revert to sprinting after this. (14/1)
**1253a* Gothenberg (IRE)** set a decent early pace, but was beaten soon after entering the straight. (35/1)
DS

# 0725-NEWBURY (L-H) (Good to firm)
## Friday May 17th
WEATHER: overcast WIND: mod half bhd

## 1142 CROOKHAM MAIDEN STKS (3-Y.O) (Class D)
2-05 (2-06) **1m (straight)** £4,523.00 (£1,364.00: £662.00: £311.00) Stalls: Centre GOING: 0.16 sec per fur (G)

| | | | | SP | RR | SF |
|---|---|---|---|---|---|---|
| 962$^{2}$ | **Keltoi** (LMCumani) **3-9-0** MJKinane(17) (lw: hld up: rdn over 3f out: swtchd lft over 1f out: led nr fin) | — | 1 | 5/1$^{3}$ | 86 | 56 |
| 808$^{2}$ | **Gold Spats (USA)** (MRStoute) **3-9-0** RCochrane(16) (a.p: led over 1f out: hrd rdn fnl f: hdd nr fin) | hd | 2 | 5/2$^{1}$ | 86 | 56 |
| 860$^{5}$ | **Hismagicmoment (USA)** (PWChapple-Hyam) **3-9-0** JReid(15) (led over 6f: one pce fnl f) | 1 | 3 | 6/1 | 84 | 54 |
| | **Veridian** (PWHarris) **3-9-0** FNorton(13) (unf: hld up: rdn over 2f out: r.o ins fnl f) | 1¼ | 4 | 33/1 | 81 | 51 |
| | **Strazo (IRE)** (JHMGosden) **3-9-0** BThomson(5) (str: scope: a.p: ev ch over 1f out: one pce: bttr for r) | ¾ | 5 | 20/1 | 80 | 50 |
| 892$^{12}$ | **Don Bosio (USA)** (MRStoute) **3-9-0** KBradshaw(2) (s.s: shkn up 2f out: hdwy over 1f out: r.o) | ¾ | 6 | 33/1 | 78 | 48 |
| 544$^{10}$ | **John-T** (JLDunlop) **3-9-0** SWhitworth(12) (shkn up over 2f out: nvr plcd to chal) | s.h | 7 | 33/1 | 78 | 48 |
| | **Slip Jig (IRE)** (RHannon) **3-9-0** RHughes(7) (unf: scope: lw: shkn up over 2f out: hdwy over 1f out: r.o: bttr for rce) | 3 | 8 | 33/1 | 72 | 42 |
| | **Zurs (IRE)** (JARToller) **3-9-0** SSanders(14) (leggy: bit bkwd: a.p: ev ch 2f out: wknd over 1f out) | 2½ | 9 | 33/1 | 67 | 37 |
| 894$^{2}$ | **Dilazar (USA)** (JRFanshawe) **3-9-0** DHarrison(8) (hld up: rdn 3f out: wknd over 1f out) | 1¾ | 10 | 7/2$^{2}$ | 64 | 34 |
| | **Puce** (LMCumani) **3-8-2**(7) RFfrench(11) (neat: bit bkwd: s.s: nvr nr) | 2½ | 11 | 33/1 | 54 | 24 |
| | **Bello Carattere** (LordHuntingdon) **3-9-0** TQuinn(9) (str: scope: lw: a mid div) | 1 | 12 | 25/1 | 57 | 27 |
| | **Witherkay** (RHannon) **3-8-11**(3) DaneO'Neill(1) (leggy: unf: prom 4f) | s.h | 13 | 33/1 | 57 | 27 |
| | **Glen Parker (IRE)** (HRACecil) **3-9-0** PatEddery(3) (lw: prom over 5f) | s.h | 14 | 10/1 | 57 | 27 |
| | **Present Generation** (RGuest) **3-9-0** NDay(4) (leggy: nvr plcd to chal) | 1 | 15 | 33/1 | 55 | 25 |
| 892$^{8}$ | **Beauchamp Knight** (HCandy) **3-9-0** CRutter(18) (bhd fnl 2f) | 6 | 16 | 25/1 | 43 | 13 |
| 821$^{10}$ | **Bronhallow** (MrsBarbaraWaring) **3-9-0** WJO'Connor(10) (bhd fnl 3f) | nk | 17 | 100/1 | 42 | 12 |
| | **Hawanafa** (RHannon) **3-8-9** RPerham(6) (prom 5f) | 1¾ | 18 | 33/1 | 33 | 3 |
| 970$^{5}$ | **Lituus (USA)** (JHMGosden) **3-9-0** WCarson(19) (bhd fnl 3f) | 2 | 19 | 12/1 | 34 | 4 |

894[16] **Utmost Zeal (USA)** (PWHarris) **3-9-0** GHind(20) (a bhd) ....½ **20** 33/1 33 3
(SP 141.4%) **20 Rn**

**1m 42.3** (5.30) CSF £18.89 TOTE £5.30: £1.90 £1.60 £3.10 (£9.80) Trio £36.80 OWNER Sheikh Mohammed (NEWMARKET) BRED Sheikh Mohammed bin Rashid al Maktoum

**IN-FOCUS: Newbury maidens can often prove very hot races indeed, and this event was packed with promising performances.**
**962 Keltoi** looked in tremendous shape in the paddock. He came with a nice run inside the last 200 yards to snatch it near the line. (5/1: 7/2-11/2)
**808 Gold Spats (USA)**, who showed a lot of promise on his Sandown debut, should make no mistake next time. (5/2: 7/4-11/4)
**860 Hismagicmoment (USA)** appreciated the return to a mile, and a trip to the winner's enclosure is not far away. (6/1)
**Veridian**, a weak-looking gelding, found the line always beating him. This was a pleasing debut. (33/1)
**Strazo (IRE)**, a plain, good-bodied individual, showed a lot of promise. His jockey was certainly not hard on him and he should not take long to open his account. (20/1)
**Don Bosio (USA)** was not given a hard time. Catching the eye as he weaved through the pack in the last furlong and a half, he is going the right way. (33/1)
**John-T** caught the eye in no uncertain terms. Given considerate handling, his jockey shook him up in the final quarter-mile and the combination came through to finish a highly-encouraging seventh. With three runs under his belt, he is now qualified for handicaps and is very much one to note. (33/1)
**Slip Jig (IRE)**, a scopey sort, caught the eye on this racecourse debut. With his jockey doing a lot of knitting in the final quarter-mile, the colt ran on nicely to finish a very encouraging eighth. Sure to have learnt a lot from this, he can show marked improvement next time. (33/1)
**Zurs (IRE)**, a tall colt, showed a lot of promise, despite not looking fully wound up. He is sure to come on a lot for this. (33/1)
**Glen Parker (IRE)** (10/1: 5/1-12/1)
**Present Generation**, a tall colt, was given a nice educational run and is sure to improve on it before long. (33/1)
**970 Lituus (USA)** (12/1: op 7/1)

## 1143 HIGHCLERE STUD CONDITIONS STKS (2-Y.O F) (Class C)

2-40 (2-42) **5f 34y** £5,251.00 (£1,831.00: £890.50: £377.50) Stalls: Centre GOING: 0.16 sec per fur (G)

| | | | | SP | RR | SF |
|---|---|---|---|---|---|---|
| | **More Silver (USA)** (PFICole) **2-8-5** TQuinn(2) (scope: hld up: shkn up to ld over 1f out: qcknd: easily)....— | 1 | | 8/11 [1] | 87+ | 43 |
| 841* | **Arethusa** (RHannon) **2-8-8**(3) DaneO'Neill(4) (lw: led over 3f out tl over 1f out: unable qckn) ....5 | 2 | | 4/1 [3] | 78 | 34 |
| 1062[3] | **What Happened Was** (MartynMeade) **2-8-3**(5) RHavlin(3) (a.p: rdn over 2f out: wknd over 1f out)....5 | 3 | | 50/1 | 59 | 15 |
| 977* | **Nightbird (IRE)** (BWHills) **2-8-11** PatEddery(1) (led over 1f: rdn over 2f out: wknd over 1f out) ....3 | 4 | | 5/2 [2] | 53 | 9 |
| | | | | (SP 108.4%) | | **4 Rn** |

**63.8 secs** (3.60) CSF £3.73 TOTE £1.80: (£2.10) OWNER Mr Brereton Jones (WHATCOMBE) BRED Brereton C. Jones
**More Silver (USA)**, a half-sister to several winners in the States, is very well regarded at home and justified stable confidence in no uncertain manner. Taking a keen hold, Quinn settled her nicely and the filly quickened away when asked to win very impressively. She looks a very exciting prospect and looks a Royal Ascot banker in the Queen Mary Stakes. (8/11: 4/5-Evens)
**841* Arethusa** has a lot of substance about her for a juvenile filly. The 6lb she was conceding to the winner did not help, but she would not have beaten her off levels. (4/1: op 2/1)
**1062 What Happened Was** called it a day below the distance. (50/1)
**977* Nightbird (IRE)** cried enough over a furlong out. (5/2)

## 1144 VODAFONE GROUP TRIAL STKS (Listed) (3-Y.O F) (Class A)

3-10 (3-10) **1m 2f 6y** £12,575.00 (£3,800.00: £1,850.00: £875.00) Stalls: Low GOING: 0.16 sec per fur (G)

| | | | SP | RR | SF |
|---|---|---|---|---|---|
| 674[7] | **Mezzogiorno (112)** (GWragg) **3-8-9** RCochrane(6) (lw: hld up: led over 2f out: rdn & r.o wl) ....— | 1 | 5/2 [2] | 107 | 40 |
| 813* | **Quota** (HRACecil) **3-8-9** PatEddery(3) (lw: hld up: led 3f out tl over 2f out: unable qckn) ....3 | 2 | 5/6 [1] | 102 | 35 |
| 939[9] | **Miss Universal (IRE) (100)** (CEBrittain) **3-8-9b[1]** MJKinane(1) (lw: led 7f: hrd rdn: one pce)....1¾ | 3 | 7/1 [3] | 99 | 32 |
| 901a* | **Nimble (IRE)** (JWHills) **3-8-9** BThomson(2) (w'like: scope: lw: chsd ldr over 6f: wknd over 2f out)....3½ | 4 | 7/1 [3] | 94 | 27 |
| 454[4] | **Wight** (RHannon) **3-8-9** TQuinn(4) (a.p: rdn over 3f out: wknd over 2f out)....¾ | 5 | 25/1 | 93 | 26 |
| | | | (SP 112.0%) | | **5 Rn** |

**2m 12.0** (8.20) CSF £4.95 TOTE £3.50: £1.50 £1.20 (£1.80) OWNER Mrs R. Philipps (NEWMARKET) BRED Exors of the late Sir Robin McAlpine
**674 Mezzogiorno**, not right when flopping in the Nell Gwyn, was a totally different proposition here and won very impressively. Not surprisingly, her odds were slashed for the Oaks, and she must go into the Epsom Classic with very strong claims. (5/2)
**813* Quota** failed to live up to the hype. Unimpressive in a gallop at home three days earlier, her Oaks dreams were surely left in tatters after this thrashing, although she is still capable of lifting a decent prize this season. (5/6: 4/5-Evens)
**708 Miss Universal (IRE)**, fitted with blinkers for the first time, could only keep on at one speed when headed. (7/1)
**901a* Nimble (IRE)**, a good-bodied filly, looked in good shape for this English debut - she won recently in Italy. (7/1)
**454 Wight** had given her all over two furlongs out. (25/1)

## 1145 FURLONG CLUB H'CAP (0-80) (3-Y.O+) (Class D)

3-40 (3-43) **1m 2f 6y** £4,211.00 (£1,268.00: £614.00: £287.00) Stalls: Low GOING: 0.16 sec per fur (G)

| | | | SP | RR | SF |
|---|---|---|---|---|---|
| | **Niknaks Nephew (62)** (BJMeehan) **4-8-11** RHughes(18) (led over 1f: rdn & swtchd rt over 2f out: led over 1f out: r.o wl)....— | 1 | 50/1 | 82 | 56 |
| 955* | **Ground Game (70)** (DRLoder) **3-8-5** 5x PatEddery(16) (a.p: led over 2f out tl over 1f out: unable qckn)....2 | 2 | 2/1 [1] | 87 | 47 |
| | **Bakheta (47)** (MissGayKelleway) **4-7-10** NAdams(20) (lw: led over 8f out: sn hdd: led over 4f out tl over 2f out: one pce) ....7 | 3 | 33/1 | 53 | 27 |
| 879[7] | **Noble Sprinter (IRE) (79)** (RHannon) **4-10-0b** JReid(2) (rdn over 2f out: hdwy over 1f out: r.o) ....2 | 4 | 12/1 | 81 | 55 |
| 760* | **Ashby Hill (IRE) (47)** (RRowe) **5-7-3**(7) PDoe(5) (rdn & hdwy over 2f out: one pce)....½ | 5 | 16/1 | 49 | 23 |
| 941[12] | **Painted Hall (USA) (69)** (JARToller) **4-9-4** SSanders(7) (rdn over 3f out: nvr nr to chal)....5 | 6 | 20/1 | 63 | 37 |
| 528* | **Shu Gaa (IRE) (75)** (WJHaggas) **3-8-10** RCochrane(21) (lw: s.s: stdy hdwy fnl 2f: nvr plcd to chal) ....3½ | 7 | 10/1 [3] | 63 | 23 |
| 693[3] | **Select Few (80)** (LMCumani) **3-9-1** MJKinane(1) (b.off fore: a mid div) ....3 | 8 | 3/1 [2] | 63 | 23 |
| | **Shift Again (IRE) (66)** (SESherwood) **4-9-1** MTebbutt(9) (rdn over 3f out: nvr nrr)....hd | 9 | 33/1 | 49 | 23 |
| | **Winged Prince (65)** (AGFoster) **3-8-0** TSprake(17) (nvr nrr) ....1 | 10 | 50/1 | 47 | 7 |
| 682[7] | **Meghdoot (71)** (HJCollingridge) **4-9-6** FNorton(13) (hdwy over 3f out: wknd over 1f out) ....1¼ | 11 | 25/1 | 51 | 25 |
| 843[6] | **Sharp Consul (IRE) (69)** (HCandy) **4-9-4** CRutter(3) (nvr nrr) ....½ | 12 | 20/1 | 48 | 22 |
| | **Game Ploy (POL) (65)** (DHaydnJones) **4-8-11**(3) SDrowne(12) (hld up: rdn over 3f out: wknd over 2f out) ....1¼ | 13 | 50/1 | 42 | 16 |
| 843[3] | **I Recall (IRE) (56)** (PHayward) **5-8-5v** WJO'Connor(14) (hld up: rdn over 3f out: sn wknd) ....¾ | 14 | 20/1 | 32 | 6 |
| 876[21] | **Whatever's Right (IRE) (69)** (MDIUsher) **7-9-4** BThomson(10) (a bhd) ....1¼ | 15 | 33/1 | 43 | 17 |

| | Horse | Btn | Pos | SP | RR | SF |
|---|---|---|---|---|---|---|
| 853[8] | **Tissisat (USA) (68)** (JohnBerry) **7-9-3b**[1] RPerham(11) (b: lw: bhd fnl 3f) | 9 | **16** | 33/1 | 27 | 1 |
| | **Ottavio Farnese (67)** (AHide) **4-8-13**(3) AWhelan(15) (bhd fnl 3f) | ½ | **17** | 25/1 | 25 | — |
| | **Emily-Mou (IRE) (70)** (MJRyan) **4-9-5** TQuinn(8) (b: led 8f out tl over 4f out: wknd over 2f out) | 3 | **18** | 14/1 | 24 | — |
| 871[5] | **Yaverland (IRE) (60)** (CADwyer) **4-8-9** DHarrison(19) (b.hind: bhd fnl 3f) | 14 | **19** | 16/1 | — | — |
| 887[10] | **Serious Option (IRE) (61)** (PFICole) **5-8-3**(7) JBosley(6) (a bhd) | 4 | **20** | 50/1 | — | — |
| | | | | (SP 135.1%) | **20 Rn** | |

**2m 10.21** (6.41) CSF £148.52 CT £3332.49 TOTE £53.90: £6.40 £1.30 £8.70 £3.30 (£119.40) Trio £1704.50; £1728.55 to Thirsk 18/5/96
OWNER Mr James Blackshaw (UPPER LAMBOURN) BRED Halevale Ltd
LONG HANDICAP Ashby Hill (IRE) 7-9 Bakheta 7-8
WEIGHT FOR AGE 3yo-14lb
**OFFICIAL EXPLANATION Shu Gaa (IRE): was left at the start and never able to get into the race.**
**Nlknaks Nephew**, who has changed stables and been gelded since last year, at last lost his maiden tag. (50/1)
**955* Ground Game**, set to rise 10lb in future handicaps, should have been able to take this. (2/1)
**Bakheta** had given his all once headed. (33/1)
**766 Noble Sprinter (IRE)** weaved through the pack in the final quarter-mile for fourth. (12/1)
**760* Ashby Hill (IRE)** could make no impression in the final quarter-mile. (16/1)
**528* Shu Gaa (IRE)**, who drifted in the market, was given very tender handling on this handicap debut, but was noted staying on late to finish a very encouraging seventh. He looks one to note with interest. (10/1: op 5/1)

## 1146 WOODHAY CONDITIONS STKS (3-Y.O) (Class B)

4-10 (4-11) **6f 8y** £7,570.20 (£2,821.80: £1,370.90: £579.50: £249.75: £117.85) Stalls: Centre GOING: 0.16 sec per fur (G)

| | Horse | Btn | Pos | SP | RR | SF |
|---|---|---|---|---|---|---|
| 889[6] | **Rambling Bear (104)** (MBlanshard) **3-9-7** RCochrane(1) (hdwy 3f out: led 2f out: rdn out) | — | **1** | 13/2[3] | 114 | 56 |
| 737[2] | **Atraf (103)** (DMorley) **3-9-5** WCarson(3) (a.p: rdn over 2f out: chsd wnr over 1f out: unable qckn) | 3½ | **2** | 3/1[1] | 103 | 45 |
| 673[11] | **Warning Time (104)** (BJMeehan) **3-9-5** RHughes(2) (s.s: hdwy 2f out: rdn over 1f out: one pce) | nk | **3** | 7/1 | 102 | 44 |
| | **King of The East (IRE) (104)** (MRStoute) **3-9-2** MJKinane(5) (lw: hld up: swtchd rt over 2f out: one pce) | 2½ | **4** | 8/1 | 92 | 34 |
| 674[10] | **Marl (90)** (RAkehurst) **3-8-11** SSanders(7) (hld up: rdn over 2f out: wknd wl over 1f out) | 3 | **5** | 12/1 | 79 | 21 |
| | **Ortolan (100)** (RHannon) **3-9-2** RPerham(6) (bhd fnl 2f) | 3 | **6** | 8/1 | 76 | 18 |
| | **Fly Tip (IRE)** (BJMeehan) **3-8-9** PatEddery(8) (lw: sme hdwy wl over 1f out: sn wknd) | 1¼ | **7** | 9/1 | 66 | 8 |
| | **Chalamont (IRE) (90)** (PWChapple-Hyam) **3-9-0** JReid(10) (lw: led 4f) | 3½ | **8** | 8/1 | 62 | 4 |
| | **Amazing Bay (105)** (IABalding) **3-9-4** DHarrison(4) (lw: a.p: ev ch 2f out: wknd over 1f out) | s.h | **9** | 6/1[2] | 66 | 8 |
| | | | | (SP 116.1%) | **9 Rn** | |

**1m 16.24** (4.44) CSF £25.10 TOTE £6.60: £2.90 £1.90 £1.50 (£7.60) Trio £18.40 OWNER Mrs Michael Hill (UPPER LAMBOURN) BRED E. A. Badger
**889 Rambling Bear** moved through to lead two furlongs out and soon asserted. A listed race at Haydock is next. (13/2)
**737 Atraf** never looked like beating the winner. (3/1)
**Warning Time** could only go up and down on the spot when asked to go about his business. (7/1)
**King of The East (IRE)** never looked like winning. (8/1: 6/1-9/1)
**548 Marl** had been seen off early in the final quarter-mile. (12/1: tchd 8/1)

## 1147 MIDGHAM H'CAP (0-90) (3-Y.O+) (Class C)

4-40 (4-40) **1m 4f 5y** £5,731.50 (£1,722.00: £831.00: £385.50) Stalls: Low GOING: 0.16 sec per fur (G)

| | Horse | Btn | Pos | SP | RR | SF |
|---|---|---|---|---|---|---|
| | **Dance So Suite (78)** (PFICole) **4-9-5** TQuinn(1) (lw: hld up: led 1f out: r.o wl) | — | **1** | 16/1 | 93 | 63 |
| 866* | **Paradise Waters (59)** (RFJohnsonHoughton) **4-8-0** SSanders(9) (a.p: led 3f out to 1f out: unable qckn) | 2½ | **2** | 12/1 | 71 | 41 |
| | **Southern Power (IRE) (79)** (RAkehurst) **5-9-6** PatEddery(6) (b.nr hind: w ldr: led over 6f out to 3f out: wknd over 1f out) | 6 | **3** | 5/1[2] | 83 | 53 |
| 920[2] | **Spillo (87)** (LMCumani) **3-8-11** JReid(5) (no hdwy fnl 3f) | ¾ | **4** | 5/1[2] | 90 | 43 |
| 816* | **Riparius (USA) (81)** (HCandy) **5-9-8** CRutter(7) (lw: wl bhd 8f: hdwy fnl 2f: nvr nrr) | hd | **5** | 9/1 | 84 | 54 |
| 1019* | **Orinoco River (USA) (77)** (PWChapple-Hyam) **3-8-1v** 5x DHarrison(10) (lw: a.p: hrd rdn over 3f out: wknd over 2f out) | 8 | **6** | 7/1 | 69 | 22 |
| 925[9] | **My Learned Friend (83)** (AHide) **5-9-7**(3) DaneO'Neill(2) (led over 5f: wknd over 3f out) | 5 | **7** | 12/1 | 68 | 38 |
| 968[3] | **General Mouktar (57)** (BJMeehan) **6-7-12b**ow1 WCarson(3) (lw: a bhd) | ¾ | **8** | 4/1[1] | 41 | 10 |
| | **Stompin (64)** (MissHCKnight) **5-8-5** MJKinane(11) (lw: a bhd) | 1¾ | **9** | 6/1[3] | 46 | 16 |
| | **Spread The Word (60)** (LGCottrell) **4-8-1** FNorton(8) (lw: bhd fnl 6f) | 25 | **10** | 40/1 | 9 | — |
| 968[5] | **Dont Shoot Fairies (74)** (CEBrittain) **4-9-1** RHughes(4) (prom over 7f) | s.h | **11** | 14/1 | 23 | — |
| | | | | (SP 120.5%) | **11 Rn** | |

**2m 37.9** (7.90) CSF £173.82 CT £1013.33 TOTE £22.60: £3.90 £3.80 £2.30 (£204.10) Trio £1055.90; £59.49 to Thirsk 18/5/96 OWNER Mr J. S. Gutkin (WHATCOMBE) BRED Genesis Green Stud and Walter Swinburn Ltd
WEIGHT FOR AGE 3yo-17lb
**Dance So Suite**, without a run in six months and 7lb higher than when last winning, put up a good display. The Handicapper will not take kindly to this. (16/1)
**866* Paradise Waters**, collared a furlong out, soon had to give best. (12/1: 8/1-14/1)
**Southern Power (IRE)**, formerly with Richard Hannon, David Loder and most recently Mary Reveley, is often placed, but is not easy to win with - his only success came back in November 1993. (5/1)
**920 Spillo** could make no impression in the final three furlongs. (5/1: op 3/1)
**816* Riparius (USA)** lost all chance in the first furlong when getting himself completely detached, but stayed on in the straight. (9/1)

T/Jkpt: Not won; £116,534.43 to Newbury 18/5/96. T/Plpt: £110.80 (209.19 Tckts). T/Qdpt: £31.20 (44.81 Tckts). AK

# 0936-NEWMARKET (R-H) (Good)

## Friday May 17th

WEATHER: overcast WIND: slt against

## 1148 E.B.F. DITCH MAIDEN STKS (2-Y.O F) (Class D)

2-15 (2-15) **6f (Rowley)** £4,152.00 (£1,236.00: £588.00: £264.00) Stalls: Centre GOING minus 0.14 sec per fur (G)

| | Horse | Btn | Pos | SP | RR | SF |
|---|---|---|---|---|---|---|
| 977[2] | **Open Credit** (HRACecil) **2-8-11** WRyan(3) (keen hold: sn settled: trckd ldrs: led 2f out: sn clr: easily) | — | **1** | 4/6[1] | 81+ | 19 |

**Rich In Love (IRE)** (CACyzer) **2-8-11** JWeaver(2) (leggy: w ldr: rdn & ev ch over 2f out: kpt on one pce ins fnl f)........5 **2** 11/2[3] 68 6
**Solfegietto** (MBell) **2-8-11** MFenton(4) (b.off hind: cmpt: led: rdn over 2f out: sn hdd: one pce)........nk **3** 7/2[2] 67 5
**Stride** (DMorley) **2-8-11** GCarter(1) (leggy: unf: trckd ldrs: rdn & ev ch over 2f out: one pce)........s.h **4** 11/2[3] 67 5
(SP 113.0%) **4 Rn**

**1m 16.49** (4.69) CSF £4.55 TOTE £1.60: (£2.80) OWNER Buckram Oak Holdings (NEWMARKET) BRED Buckram Thoroughbred Enterprises Inc
**977 Open Credit** outclassed her rivals in the paddock and in the race. (4/6)
**Rich In Love (IRE)** plugged on in the final furlong to finish second, but was flattered to finish within five lengths of the winner. (11/2: 7/2-6/1)
**Solfegietto** cut out the running but was soon put in her place. (7/2: op 2/1)

## 1149 NGK SPARK PLUGS RATED STKS H'CAP (0-100) (4-Y.O+) (Class B)

2-50 (2-50) **7f (Rowley)** £7,893.50 (£2,916.50: £1,395.75: £566.25: £220.63: £82.37) Stalls: Centre GOING minus 0.14 sec (G)

| | | | | SP | RR | SF |
|---|---|---|---|---|---|---|
| 928[6] | **Saseedo (USA) (86)** (WAO'Gorman) **6-8-5** EmmaO'Gorman(3) (hld up: hdwy over 1f out: led ins fnl f: r.o wl)........— | **1** | | 11/2 | 97 | 47 |
| 728[18] | **Czarna (IRE) (81)** (CEBrittain) **5-7-9**(5) MHenry(6) (lw: trckd ldrs: led over 1f out: hdd ins fnl f: r.o)........1 | **2** | | 7/1 | 90 | 40 |
| | **Courageous Dancer (IRE) (87)** (BHanbury) **4-8-3**(3) JStack(4) (lw: trckd ldrs: rdn over 1f out: one pce)........5 | **3** | | 5/1[3] | 84 | 34 |
| 940[6] | **Cyrano's Lad (IRE) (91)** (CADwyer) **7-8-10** CDwyer(5) (keen hold: led: hdd over 1f out: sn wknd)........2 | **4** | | 9/4[1] | 84 | 34 |
| 1078[7] | **Prima Cominna (81)** (SPCWoods) **4-8-0** JTate(2) (w ldr tl rdn & wknd over 2f out)........2½ | **5** | | 33/1 | 68 | 18 |
| 876[4] | **Emerging Market (95)** (JLDunlop) **4-9-0** GCarter(1) (hld up in tch: rdn over 2f out: sn wknd)........17 | **6** | | 11/4[2] | 43 | — |

(SP 104.9%) **6 Rn**

**1m 27.08** (2.58) CSF £34.44 TOTE £5.90: £2.20 £1.90 (£13.50) OWNER Mr S. Fustok (NEWMARKET) BRED Audley Farm Incorporated
LONG HANDICAP Czarna (IRE) 7-13 Prima Cominna 7-13
OFFICIAL EXPLANATION **Emerging Market: lost his action through the last furlong and a half.**
**928 Saseedo (USA)** was given a confident and competent ride, being brought with a well-timed challenge to settle the issue inside the final furlong. (11/2)
**Czarna (IRE)** looked and ran well. He appeared likely to score when leading below the distance, but could not match the winner for a turn of foot. (7/1)
**Courageous Dancer (IRE)** ran well on this seasonal debut and can soon step up on it. (5/1)
**940 Cyrano's Lad (IRE)** dropped away disappointingly once headed. (9/4)
**876 Emerging Market** ran appallingly, weakening quickly in the final two furlongs. Something was probably amiss. (11/4: 9/4-7/2)

## 1150 EQUITY FINANCIAL COLLECTIONS H'CAP (0-80) (3-Y.O+) (Class D)

3-20 (3-26) **1m 6f (Rowley)** £4,620.00 (£1,380.00: £660.00: £300.00) Stalls: Low GOING minus 0.14 sec per fur (G)

| | | | SP | RR | SF |
|---|---|---|---|---|---|
| 872[2] | **Opaque (66)** (LMCumani) **4-9-6** JWeaver(8) (a.p: chsd ldr 6f out: led over 1f out: hrd rdn ins fnl f: all out)........— | **1** | 2/1[1] | 77 | 45 |
| 886[5] | **Fabillion (68)** (CASmith) **4-9-8** RHills(6) (hld up: gd hdwy 2f out: str run ins fnl f: jst failed)........s.h | **2** | 6/1[3] | 79 | 47 |
| 886[10] | **Rock Group (52)** (JPearce) **4-8-6** GBardwell(4) (led: hdd over 1f out: one pce)........1¼ | **3** | 14/1 | 62 | 30 |
| 972[5] | **Amiarge (47)** (MBrittain) **6-7-12**(3) DWright(9) (mid div: hdwy over 2f out: ev ch over 1f out: one pce)........½ | **4** | 14/1 | 56 | 24 |
| 1044* | **Persian Smoke (42)** (AHide) **5-7-5**(5) 4x MartinDwyer(1) (hld up: hdwy 4f out: wknd over 1f out)........10 | **5** | 3/1[2] | 40 | 8 |
| 816[5] | **Brave Patriarch (IRE) (71)** (JLDunlop) **5-9-11** GCarter(3) (mid div: rdn 3f out: wknd 2f out)........2 | **6** | 14/1 | 66 | 34 |
| *898*[3] | **Charlie Bigtime (47)** (RHarris) **6-8-1** AMackay(7) (b.hind: rr: hdwy 3f out: wknd 2f out)........nk | **7** | 12/1 | 42 | 10 |
| 972[6] | **Mr Christie (44)** (MissLCSiddall) **4-7-12** NCarlisle(5) (in tch: rdn 6f out: sn wknd)........nk | **8** | 14/1 | 39 | 7 |
| 844[4] | **Crested Knight (IRE) (59)** (CAHorgan) **4-8-13** PaulEddery(10) (hld up in rr: rdn 3f out: no hdwy)........hd | **9** | 12/1 | 53 | 21 |
| 993[9] | **Green Land (BEL) (68)** (SCWilliams) **4-9-8** BDoyle(2) (b.nr fore: chsd ldr 8f: rdn 5f out: wknd over 3f out)........11 | **10** | 14/1 | 50 | 18 |

(SP 121.3%) **10 Rn**

**3m 4.3** (8.30) CSF £14.52 CT £126.25 TOTE £2.80: £1.50 £2.50 £5.30 (£6.00) Trio £93.10 OWNER Mrs Luca Cumani (NEWMARKET) BRED Snailwell Stud Co Ltd
LONG HANDICAP Persian Smoke 7-4
**872 Opaque** races like a dour stayer and the further he goes the better he is. (2/1)
**886 Fabillion** staged a strong run in the final furlong and will be suited by two miles on this show. (6/1)
**666 Rock Group** made a brave bid to lead from pillar to post, and kept on gallantly once headed. (14/1)
**972 Amiarge** moved up to have every chance below the distance, but could not find the necessary turn of foot. (14/1)
**1044* Persian Smoke** was a bit disappointing and probably needs it firmer. (3/1)
**898 Charlie Bigtime** (12/1: 8/1-14/1)
**Mr Christie** (14/1: 20/1-33/1)
**844 Crested Knight (IRE)** (12/1: op 8/1)

## 1151 KING CHARLES II STKS (Listed) (3-Y.O) (Class A)

3-50 (3-53) **7f (Rowley)** £10,774.60 (£3,981.40: £1,905.70: £773.50: £301.75: £113.05) Stalls: Centre GOING minus 0.14 sec per fur (G)

| | | | SP | RR | SF |
|---|---|---|---|---|---|
| 736[3] | **Ali-Royal (IRE) (104)** (HRACecil) **3-8-12** WRyan(3) (lw: hld up: gd hdwy to ld over 2f out: sn clr: easily)........— | **1** | 5/1[3] | 113+ | 44 |
| | **Rabican (IRE) (100)** (MHTompkins) **3-9-2** PRobinson(2) (hld up in tch: n.m.r 2f out: rdn over 1f out: one pce).8 | **2** | 25/1 | 99 | 30 |
| 926[8] | **World Premier (112)** (CEBrittain) **3-9-2** BDoyle(4) (lw: trckd ldrs: rdn over 2f out: one pce)........s.h | **3** | 7/2[2] | 99 | 30 |
| | **Polar Eclipse** (MJohnston) **3-8-12** JWeaver(5) (lw: led 1f: styd prom: rdn over 2f out: one pce)........2 | **4** | 8/1 | 90 | 21 |
| 842* | **West Humble** (LadyHerries) **3-8-7** DeclanO'Shea(1) (hld up: hdwy 3f out: rdn over 2f out: sn btn)........3 | **5** | 5/1[3] | 78 | 9 |
| 936* | **Projection (USA) (104)** (BWHills) **3-8-12** PaulEddery(8) (lw: trckd ldrs: rdn & ev ch over 2f out: sn wknd).....3½ | **6** | 15/8[1] | 75 | 6 |
| 874[2] | **Tawaaded (IRE) (90)** (PTWalwyn) **3-8-7** RHills(7) (led 6f out: hdd over 2f out: sn wknd)........4 | **7** | 7/1 | 61 | — |

(SP 117.8%) **7 Rn**

**1m 27.92** (3.42) CSF £81.55 TOTE £7.10: £2.90 £5.00 (£58.50) OWNER Greenbay Stables Ltd (NEWMARKET) BRED C. H. WACKER III
IN-FOCUS: **This looked a decent renewal of a race which could be renamed the Jersey Stakes Trial.**
**736 Ali-Royal (IRE)** proved a revelation, leaving his previous form behind. On this showing, Group successes must surely follow. (5/1)
**Rabican (IRE)** ran well on this seasonal debut, but had caught a tartar. (25/1)
**681 World Premier**, beaten some eleven lengths in the Guineas, appeared to run his race here. His proximity in the Classic must say something for the advantage of having been drawn low. (7/2)
**Polar Eclipse** ran well until outpaced in the final two furlongs. (8/1)
**842* West Humble** found this jump in class beyond her. (5/1)
**936* Projection (USA)** could have done without the overnight rain. (15/8)

## 1152 EQUITY FINANCIAL COLLECTIONS CLAIMING STKS (3-Y.O) (Class E)

4-20 (4-20) **1m (Rowley)** £3,720.00 (£1,110.00: £530.00: £240.00) Stalls: Centre GOING minus 0.14 sec per fur (G)

| Form | Horse | Btn | Pos | SP | RR | SF |
|---|---|---|---|---|---|---|
| 917[5] | **Rebel County (IRE) (68)** (DJSCosgrove) **3-8-5**(3) JStack(10) (lw: racd far side: hld up: gd hdwy to ld over 1f out: r.o wl) | — | **1** | 15/8[1] | 63 | 38 |
| *1027** | **Eagle Canyon (IRE) (64)** (BHanbury) **3-9-2**(5) MartinDwyer(1) (trckd ldrs stands' side: led 2f out: hdd over 1f out: one pce) | 4 | **2** | 8/1[3] | 68 | 43 |
| *1027[13]* | **Ivory's Grab Hire (50)** (KTIvory) **3-8-2b**[ow1] BDoyle(6) (racd far side: a.p: rdn over 1f out: one pce) | s.h | **3** | 33/1 | 49 | 23 |
| 978[10] | **Bold Enough (65)** (BWHills) **3-8-4** PaulEddery(11) (hld up far side: hdwy 3f out: rdn over 2f out: one pce) | 3½ | **4** | 12/1 | 44 | 19 |
| 646[13] | **Lionel Edwards (IRE) (70)** (PFICole) **3-9-7** JWeaver(3) (racd stands' side: led 3f out: hdd 2f out: grad wknd) | 3 | **5** | 12/1 | 55 | 30 |
| *355[5]* | **Snow Falcon (67)** (MBell) **3-9-1** MFenton(8) (b: racd far side: prom 5f) | 2 | **6** | 11/1 | 45 | 20 |
| 914* | **Danico (57)** (SCWilliams) **3-8-2**(5) ADaly(2) (racd stands' side: led: hdd 3f out: sn wknd) | 8 | **7** | 12/1 | 21 | — |
| 955[7] | **Capture The Moment (64)** (RJRWilliams) **3-8-4b[1]** DBiggs(9) (b.nr hind: racd far side: in tch 5f) | 2 | **8** | 11/1 | 2 | — |
| | **Rogue Trader (IRE)** (DrJDScargill) **3-8-1** GBardwell(5) (w'like: bkwd: racd far side: a bhd) | 1½ | **9** | 20/1 | 8 | — |
| 1099[14] | **Lahik (IRE) (45)** (KTIvory) **3-8-2b[1]**[ow1] GDuffield(7) (racd far side: prom to ½-wy) | 9 | **10** | 33/1 | — | — |
| | **Cebwob (85)** (PFICole) **3-9-2** RHills(4) (b.hind: racd far side: in tch 5f) | 1½ | **11** | 3/1[2] | 2 | — |

(SP 121.3%) **11 Rn**

**1m 41.46** (4.16) CSF £17.17 TOTE £3.00: £1.50 £2.10 £4.70 (£15.40) Trio £309.70 OWNER Edermine Bloodstock (NEWMARKET) BRED C. Foy

**917 Rebel County (IRE)** was well suited by the longer trip and drop in class. (15/8)

**1027* Eagle Canyon (IRE)** ran well but could not match the winner's turn of foot. (8/1)

**761 Ivory's Grab Hire** raced more prominently than of late and did all the better for it. (33/1)

**Bold Enough** proved very one-paced in the final two furlongs. (12/1: op 8/1)

**Cebwob** (3/1: op 7/4)

## 1153 ASHLEY MAIDEN STKS (3-Y.O) (Class D)

4-55 (4-55) **1m 4f (Rowley)** £4,503.00 (£1,344.00: £642.00: £291.00) Stalls: Low GOING minus 0.14 sec per fur (G)

| Form | Horse | Btn | Pos | SP | RR | SF |
|---|---|---|---|---|---|---|
| 985[4] | **Arnhem** (CEBrittain) **3-9-0** BDoyle(6) (lw: chsd ldrs: led 3f out: pushed out ins fnl f) | — | **1** | 5/6[1] | 83 | 34 |
| 985[8] | **Ancient Quest** (NACallaghan) **3-9-0** PaulEddery(1) (lw: hld up: hdwy 3f out: chsd wnr 2f out: hrd rdn ins fnl f: r.o) | 1¼ | **2** | 9/1 | 81 | 32 |
| 826[3] | **Chocolate Ice** (CACyzer) **3-9-0** GDuffield(2) (chsd ldr: ev ch 3f out: sn rdn: wknd over 1f out) | 7 | **3** | 11/2[3] | 72 | 23 |
| 820[13] | **Pompier** (JLDunlop) **3-9-0** GCarter(5) (hld up: pushed along ½-wy: wknd 3f out) | 9 | **4** | 14/1 | 60 | 11 |
| | **Private Audience (USA)** (HRACecil) **3-9-0** WRyan(3) (bit bkwd: led to 3f out: sn wknd) | 19 | **5** | 100/30[2] | 35 | — |

(SP 109.7%) **5 Rn**

**2m 38.55** (8.05) CSF £7.61 TOTE £1.50: £1.10 £2.20 (£11.30) OWNER Mr W. J. Gredley (NEWMARKET) BRED Stetchworth Park Stud Ltd

**985 Arnhem** gained a deserved success, needing only to be pushed out in the closing stages. (5/6)

**Ancient Quest** ran a pleasing race and left his debut effort well behind. Staying on in promising fashion late on, he looks as though stamina is his strong suit. (9/1: 6/1-10/1)

**826 Chocolate Ice** was left behind in the final two furlongs. (11/2)

**Private Audience (USA)** looks one of his stable's lesser lights. (100/30: 2/1-7/2)

## 1154 TUDDENHAM LIMITED STKS (0-70) (4-Y.O+) (Class E)

5-25 (5-25) **7f (Rowley)** £4,503.00 (£1,344.00: £642.00: £291.00) Stalls: Centre GOING minus 0.14 sec per fur (G)

| Form | Horse | Btn | Pos | SP | RR | SF |
|---|---|---|---|---|---|---|
| 756[2] | **The Stager (IRE) (70)** (JRJenkins) **4-8-6**(5) ADaly(1) (keen hold: a.p: led 3f out: hdd 2f out: rallied to ld again ins fnl f: r.o) | — | **1** | 4/1[2] | 81 | 43 |
| | **Easy Jet (POL) (70)** (LordHuntingdon) **4-8-11** JWeaver(8) (bkwd: rr: rdn 3f out: hdwy over 1f out: styd on ins fnl f) | 1¼ | **2** | 13/2[3] | 78 | 40 |
| | **Sharpical (70)** (SirMarkPrescott) **4-8-11** GDuffield(4) (chsd ldrs: led 2f out: hdd ins fnl f: one pce) | hd | **3** | 7/2[1] | 78 | 40 |
| 879[16] | **Wild Palm (63)** (WAO'Gorman) **4-8-11b** EmmaO'Gorman(9) (lw: chsd ldrs: rdn 2f out: one pce) | nk | **4** | 11/1 | 77 | 39 |
| | **Dontforget Insight (IRE) (66)** (CPEBrooks) **5-8-11** PaulEddery(6) (b.hind: hld up: sme hdwy over 2f out: rdn & edgd lft over 1f out: wknd ins fnl f) | 5 | **5** | 14/1 | 66 | 28 |
| 920[4] | **Manabar (63)** (MJPolglase) **4-8-11** NCarlisle(2) (dwlt: a bhd) | 3 | **6** | 16/1 | 59 | 21 |
| | **Midnight Spell (66)** (JWHills) **4-8-3**(5) MHenry(3) (in tch: rdn 3f out: wknd over 1f out) | nk | **7** | 7/1 | 55 | 17 |
| | **Blockade (USA) (70)** (MBell) **7-8-11** MFenton(5) (led: hdd 3f out: sn wknd) | 8 | **8** | 7/2[1] | 40 | 2 |

(SP 111.2%) **8 Rn**

**1m 27.95** (3.45) CSF £26.61 TOTE £4.60: £1.40 £2.20 £1.50 (£13.80) Trio £27.10 OWNER Mr T. Long (ROYSTON) BRED Barronstown Bloodstock and Swettenham Stud

**756 The Stager (IRE)** put up a brave display, rallying determinedly to regain the lead inside the final furlong, having looked cooked below the distance. (4/1)

**Easy Jet (POL)** carried condition but ran well. He kept on nicely in the final furlong and a return to a mile will suit. (13/2)

**Sharpical** looked sure to score on this seasonal debut when taking it up at the two-furlong pole, but he just lost out inside the final 200 yards as lack of hard-fitness told. (7/2)

**650 Wild Palm** had every chance until tapped for speed in the closing stages. A return to further will suit. (11/1: 8/1-12/1)

**Blockade (USA)** ran poorly. (7/2: 3/1-9/2)

T/Plpt: £648.50 (17.55 Tckts). T/Qdpt: £57.50 (19.44 Tckts). SM

# 0930-THIRSK (L-H) (Good to firm)

## Friday May 17th

WEATHER: overcast WIND: fresh half against

## 1155 EASINGWOLD RATING RELATED MAIDEN STKS (0-70) (3-Y.O) (Class E)

2-00 (2-01) **1m** £3,187.50 (£960.00: £465.00: £217.50) Stalls: Low GOING minus 0.01 sec per fur (G)

| Form | Horse | Btn | Pos | SP | RR | SF |
|---|---|---|---|---|---|---|
| 786[5] | **Caribbean Dancer (70)** (MRStoute) **3-8-11** DeanMcKeown(3) (pushed along after s: sn in tch: outpcd appr st: hdwy 2f out: r.o to ld cl home) | — | **1** | 3/1[1] | 67 | 33 |

| | | | | SP | RR | SF |
|---|---|---|---|---|---|---|
| 873[19] | **Time of Night (USA) (70)** (RGuest) **3-8-11** LCharnock(5) (led: clr over 3f out tl disp ld 1f out: ct nr fin) | hd | **2** | 12/1 | 67 | 33 |
| 873[6] | **Alreeh (IRE) (70)** (JHMGosden) **3-8-11** JCarroll(6) (chsd ldrs: outpcd 3f out: hdwy 2f out: nt qckn towards fin) | 1 | **3** | 7/2[2] | 65 | 31 |
| 714[4] | **Shady Girl (IRE) (68)** (BWHills) **3-8-6**[(5)] JDSmith(2) (trckd ldrs: hdwy to disp ld 1f out: wknd nr fin) | ½ | **4** | 6/1 | 64 | 30 |
| 873[9] | **Sea Danzig (66)** (PHowling) **3-9-0** KDarley(9) (chsd ldrs tl grad wknd fnl 2½f) | ¾ | **5** | 8/1 | 65 | 31 |
| 870[8] | **Another Quarter (IRE) (60)** (SPCWoods) **3-8-11** WWoods(7) (rdn most of wy: nvr trbld ldrs) | 4 | **6** | 13/2 | 54 | 20 |
| | **Bollin Dorothy (70)** (TDEasterby) **3-8-11** MBirch(8) (plld hrd: prom to st) | 6 | **7** | 11/2[3] | 42 | 8 |
| 934[7] | **Bollin Jacob (67)** (TDEasterby) **3-9-0** TWilliams(4) (nvr nr ldrs) | ¾ | **8** | 16/1 | 44 | 10 |
| 976[7] | **Islay Brown (IRE) (62)** (CWCElsey) **3-8-6b**[1(5)] PFessey(1) (lw: drvn along appr st: sn lost tch) | ½ | **9** | 25/1 | 40 | 6 |
| | | | | (SP 118.8%) | **9 Rn** | |

**1m 42.5** (6.00) CSF £35.17 TOTE £3.90: £1.70 £1.60 £1.30 (£40.60) Trio £35.50 OWNER Mr W. H. Scott (NEWMARKET) BRED W. Scott and P. Scott

**786 Caribbean Dancer** needed every yard of this trip and looks sure to do better over further. (3/1: 2/1-100/30)
**Time of Night (USA)**, who showed a fine action, stepped up considerably on her two previous efforts this season. She should find a race before long. (12/1)
**873 Alreeh (IRE)**, who lost her footing coming off the home turn, looks likely to appreciate a more galloping track and longer distances. (7/2: op 9/4)
**714 Shady Girl (IRE)** looked fitter than last time and ran well, but failed to see out the trip. (6/1)
**525 Sea Danzig** had her chances, but was always finding things too tough in the final quarter-mile. Slightly easier ground might be more to his liking. (8/1: 6/1-9/1)
**Another Quarter (IRE)** was never on the bridle and seems to need a fair bit further. (13/2: op 20/1)
**Bollin Dorothy** spoiled her chances by pulling hard. (11/2)

## 1156 MOWBRAY (S) STKS (I) (3-Y.O+) (Class G)

2-30 (2-32) **7f** £1,970.00 (£545.00: £260.00) Stalls: Low GOING minus 0.01 sec per fur (G)

| | | | | SP | RR | SF |
|---|---|---|---|---|---|---|
| | **Lunch Party** (DNicholls) **4-9-7** AlexGreaves(8) (swtg: qckndto ld after 2f: shkn up & r.o wl nr fin) | — | **1** | 11/8[1] | 63+ | 40 |
| *1029*[8] | **Mels Baby (IRE) (53)** (JLEyre) **3-8-7**[(3)] NVarley(1) (chsd ldrs tl lost pl appr st: hdwy 2f out: ev ch wl ins fnl f: nt qckn) | ½ | **2** | 5/1 | 62 | 28 |
| | **Bold Angel (62)** (KAMorgan) **9-9-7** JFortune(9) (b: hld up: hdwy 3f out: styd on u.p: nvr able to chal) | 3½ | **3** | 3/1[2] | 54 | 31 |
| | **Lawnswood Captain (IRE) (48)** (RHollinshead) **3-8-5**[(5)] DGriffiths(2) (bhd tl styd on fnl 3f: nvr rchd ldrs) | 1¼ | **4** | 10/1 | 51 | 17 |
| 631[10] | **Southern Dominion (56)** (CNAllen) **4-9-7** CHodgson(7) (b.hind: bhd & rn wd appr st: styd on fnl 2f) | s.h | **5** | 11/1 | 51 | 28 |
| 586[8] | **Move Smartly (IRE) (47)** (FHLee) **6-9-7** KDarley(3) (lw: prom: hdwy to chal over 2f out: wknd over 1f out) | ¾ | **6** | 9/2[3] | 49 | 26 |
| *782*[14] | **Prim Lass (46)** (MissJBower) **5-9-2** AMcGlone(6) (effrt over 3f out: rdn & no imp) | 3 | **7** | 33/1 | 37 | 14 |
| *517*[7] | **Lithe Spirit (IRE) (55)** (JAHarris) **4-9-2** TGMcLaughlin(4) (led 2f: cl up: chal 3f out: wknd wl over 1f out) | hd | **8** | 12/1 | 37 | 14 |
| 1043[7] | **Lancashire Life (IRE) (44)** (EJAlston) **5-9-7** SDWilliams(5) (lw: chsd ldrs tl wknd fnl 2f) | 5 | **9** | 33/1 | 31 | 8 |
| | | | | (SP 133.0%) | **9 Rn** | |

**1m 29.6** (5.40) CSF £10.32 TOTE £2.60: £1.60 £1.70 £1.40 (£8.50) Trio £10.70 OWNER Mr S. Aitken (THIRSK) BRED Aston Park Stud
WEIGHT FOR AGE 3yo-11lb
No bid
**Lunch Party**, a winner in the Czech Republic, was too good for this company and won a shade cosily. (11/8)
**748 Mels Baby (IRE)** did not handle the turn too well but ran on well at the end to give the winner a bit of a fright. There is certainly a seller in him. (5/1)
**Bold Angel** ran a reasonable first race for his new stable, staying on determinedly up the straight. (3/1)
**Lawnswood Captain (IRE)** never got going until the race was over and would seem to need a bit further. (10/1: 7/1-12/1)
**Southern Dominion** did not handle the bend at all but did finish well to show he is in good heart. (11/1: 8/1-12/1)
**586 Move Smartly (IRE)** again had chances but failed to see it out. (9/2)

## 1157 DICK PEACOCK SPRINT H'CAP (0-70) (3-Y.O+) (Class E)

3-00 (3-01) **6f** £4,471.00 (£1,348.00: £654.00: £307.00) Stalls: High GOING minus 0.14 sec per fur (G)

| | | | | SP | RR | SF |
|---|---|---|---|---|---|---|
| 991[8] | **Benzoe (IRE) (69)** (MrsJRRamsden) **6-10-0** JFortune(4) (lw: s.i.s: swtchd rt after s: hdwy stands' side 2f out: led wl ins fnl f) | — | **1** | 10/1 | 78 | 34 |
| 868* | **Almasi (IRE) (59)** (CFWall) **4-9-4** WWoods(3) (bhd: hdwy over 1f out: r.o wl towards fin) | 1 | **2** | 7/1[3] | 65 | 21 |
| 850[10] | **Plum First (65)** (LRLloyd-James) **6-9-10** JFanning(15) (lw: cl up: nt qckn wl ins fnl f) | ¾ | **3** | 8/1 | 69 | 25 |
| 956* | **Daawe (USA) (63)** (MrsVAAconley) **5-9-8v** [7x] MDeering(9) (lw: led tl hdd & no ex wl ins fnl f) | nk | **4** | 11/2[2] | 67 | 23 |
| 971[3] | **Sallyoreally (IRE) (37)** (WStorey) **5-7-5**[(5)] PFessey(2) (lw: a chsng ldrs: one pce fnl 2f) | 2½ | **5** | 33/1 | 34 | — |
| *199*[11] | **Aquado (50)** (SRBowring) **7-8-4b**[(5)] CTeague(14) (styd on fnl 2f: nvr trbld ldrs) | 4 | **6** | 25/1 | 36 | — |
| *1028*[7] | **Freckles Kelly (44)** (TDEasterby) **4-8-3** TWilliams(7) (dwlt: styd on fnl 2f: n.d) | hd | **7** | 14/1 | 30 | — |
| *900*[5] | **Sir Tasker (54)** (JLHarris) **8-8-13** KDarley(5) (dwlt: hdwy & in tch ½-wy: n.m.r 2f out: no imp) | nk | **8** | 20/1 | 39 | — |
| 629[11] | **So Amazing (63)** (JLEyre) **4-9-8** JQuinn(6) (trckd ldrs: effrt 2f out: eased whn btn ins fnl f) | ¾ | **9** | 12/1 | 46 | 2 |
| 935[8] | **It's Academic (67)** (MrsJRRamsden) **4-9-12** KFallon(16) (swtg: racd stands' side: effrt ½-wy: no imp) | nk | **10** | 5/1[1] | 49 | 5 |
| 735[10] | **Shadow Jury (63)** (DWChapman) **6-9-8b** LCharnock(11) (trckd ldrs: effrt 2f out: nt qckn) | nk | **11** | 12/1 | 45 | 1 |
| 1040[13] | **Miss Aragon (53)** (MissLCSiddall) **8-8-12** AMcGlone(13) (dwlt: n.d) | 2 | **12** | 20/1 | 29 | — |
| 1040[6] | **Tutu Sixtysix (37)** (DonEnricoIncisa) **5-7-10** KimTinkler(12) (s.i.s: n.d) | 1½ | **13** | 20/1 | 9 | — |
| 931[19] | **Silk Cottage (61)** (RMWhitaker) **4-9-6** ACulhane(1) (s.i.s: n.d) | ¾ | **14** | 33/1 | 31 | — |
| 931[12] | **Ned's Bonanza (67)** (MDods) **7-9-12** JCarroll(10) (outpcd fr ½-wy) | 1¼ | **15** | 7/1[3] | 34 | — |
| 824[12] | **Ramsey Hope (67)** (CWFairhurst) **3-9-3** NKennedy(8) (chsd ldrs over 4f: wknd) | ¾ | **16** | 25/1 | 32 | — |
| | | | | (SP 127.2%) | **16 Rn** | |

**1m 14.3** (4.60) CSF £75.38 CT £572.12 TOTE £11.50: £3.10 £2.50 £2.60 £1.60 (£77.30) Trio £269.70 OWNER Mr Tony Fawcett (THIRSK) BRED Mrs P. Grubb
LONG HANDICAP Sallyoreally (IRE) 6-7 Tutu Sixtysix 7-9
WEIGHT FOR AGE 3yo-9lb
**IN-FOCUS: Only two of the runners took advantage of the best ground up the stands' side, and the winner was amazingly given enough room to drive a bus through.**
**991 Benzoe (IRE)** did the impossible, winning from stall four. Crossing over behind the field to get the stands' rail, he won a shade cleverly. (10/1)
**868* Almasi (IRE)** took a long time to find her stride, but she finished with a flourish and another furlong on a sharp track as this would not go amiss. (7/1)

**659 Plum First** failed to take advantage of his good draw and was done for foot late on. (8/1)
**956* Daawe (USA)** again showed bags of speed but his rider unbelievably raced down the centre of the track. That probably made all the difference. (11/2)
**971 Sallyoreally (IRE)** put up a pretty good show from a poor draw and looks likely to do better before long. (33/1)
**Aquado** was well enough drawn but never had the pace to take advantage. (25/1)
**Freckles Kelly** could never fully recover from a poor start but was making ground at the finish. (14/1)

## 1158 HELMSLEY H'CAP (0-90) (4-Y.O+) (Class C)
3-30 (3-31) **2m** £5,312.00 (£1,586.00: £758.00: £344.00) Stalls: Low GOING minus 0.01 sec per fur (G)

| | | | | SP | RR | SF |
|---|---|---|---|---|---|---|
| $872^{6}$ | **Uncle Doug (49)** (MrsMReveley) **5-7-13** JFanning(2) (lw: hld up: qcknd to ld over 1f out: carried rt: all out) | — | **1** | 5/2$^{2}$ | 62 | 25 |
| $825^{2}$ | **Great Easeby (IRE) (56)** (WStorey) **6-8-6** JQuinn(1) (lw: led: qcknd appr st: edgd rt fnl 3f: hdd over 1f out: rallied) | s.h | **2** | 6/4$^{1}$ | 69 | 32 |
| $1005^{12}$ | **Sea Victor (76)** (JLHarris) **4-9-10v** JFEgan(4) (lw: chsd wnr after 6f: swtchd lft over 2f out: one pce) | 5 | **3** | 5/1$^{3}$ | 84 | 45 |
| $1070^{9}$ | **Vain Prince (53)** (NTinkler) **9-8-3** LCharnock(5) (hld up: effrt 3f out: no imp) | 14 | **4** | 10/1 | 47 | 10 |
| $811^{13}$ | **Lear Dancer (USA) (66)** (PhilipMitchell) **5-9-2v** AClark(3) (hld up: effrt ent st: sn btn) | 10 | **5** | 11/2 | 50 | 13 |

(SP 109.7%) **5 Rn**

**3m 34.9** (11.90) CSF £6.39 TOTE £3.70: £1.40 £1.10 (£2.70) OWNER Mr D. D. Saul (SALTBURN) BRED Charlton Down Stud
WEIGHT FOR AGE 4yo-2lb
**872 Uncle Doug,** winning only his second race on the Flat, looked likely to score convincingly when going on, but it was a desperate thing in the end. (5/2)
**825 Great Easeby (IRE),** after setting his own pace, tried very hard, but was inclined to edge right and could never quite find enough. Marathon trips are surely what he needs. (6/4)
**Sea Victor,** off a much higher mark than he has previously won from, ran as well as could be expected. (5/1)
**Vain Prince** failed to make any impression, but looks to be gradually coming to himself. (10/1)
**Lear Dancer (USA)** ran moderately. (11/2)

## 1159 STATION ROAD CLAIMING STKS (4-Y.O+) (Class F)
4-00 (4-01) **1m 4f** £2,868.00 (£798.00: £384.00) Stalls: Low GOING minus 0.01 sec per fur (G)

| | | | | SP | RR | SF |
|---|---|---|---|---|---|---|
| $787^{4}$ | **Anchorena (57)** (JAHarris) **4-8-9** KFallon(14) (hld up: stdy hdwy 5f out: led over 1f out: hld on wl towards fin) | — | **1** | 9/4$^{1}$ | 64 | 33 |
| $913^{4}$ | **Loveyoumillions (IRE) (82)** (MJohnston) **4-9-6** KDarley(12) (chsd ldr: led ½-wy: rdn 2f out: hdd over 1f out: nt qckn ins fnl f) | 1 | **2** | 9/4$^{1}$ | 74 | 43 |
| | **Elite Bliss (IRE)** (MJCamacho) **4-8-11** LCharnock(6) (a chsng ldrs: chal over 2f out: one pce) | 10 | **3** | 33/1 | 51 | 20 |
| $609^{10}$ | **Goodbye Millie (45)** (JLEyre) **6-8-5** RLappin(5) (sn bhd & pushed along: styd on u.p fnl 3f: nt rch ldrs) | 1¾ | **4** | 14/1$^{3}$ | 43 | 12 |
| $787^{11}$ | **Rose Chime (IRE) (35)** (JLHarris) **4-7-12**(5) PFessey(4) (chsd ldrs: one pce fnl 2f) | 1¼ | **5** | 40/1 | 39 | 8 |
| | **Checkpoint Charlie (34)** (JMPEustace) **11-8-8** NKennedy(15) (hld up: hdwy & in tch 7f out: no imp fnl 3f) | hd | **6** | 50/1 | 44 | 13 |
| 972* | **Latvian (62)** (RAllan) **9-9-6** JFortune(8) (sn trckng ldrs: rdn over 2f out: hung lft & wandered: sn wknd) | 1¼ | **7** | 11/4$^{2}$ | 55 | 24 |
| $508^{14}$ | **Gallardini (IRE) (49)** (BSRothwell) **7-9-2** JQuinn(11) (bhd: hdwy ½-wy: styd on fnl 2f: nvr nr ldrs) | ½ | **8** | 33/1 | 50 | 19 |
| $988^{13}$ | **Sheraz (IRE) (68)** (NTinkler) **4-9-10** MBirch(1) (led to ½-wy: lost pl over 1f out) | ½ | **9** | 14/1$^{3}$ | 57 | 26 |
| | **Gentle Gambler** (LRLloyd-James) **5-8-7** JFanning(7) (sn bhd & rdn: t.o 4f out: sme hdwy fnl 2f) | 2½ | **10** | 100/1 | 37 | 6 |
| *$346^{7}$* | **Bowland Park** (EJAlston) **5-8-9** SDWilliams(10) (hld up & bhd: hdwy on outside ½-wy: lost pl 3f out) | 2½ | **11** | 100/1 | 36 | 5 |
| $993^{13}$ | **Island Cascade (34)** (DonEnricoIncisa) **4-8-3** KimTinkler(3) (sn bhd & pushed along) | nk | **12** | 25/1 | 29 | — |
| | **Sly Lady** (CWCElsey) **4-8-11** JFEgan(13) (s.i.s: a wl bhd: t.o) | 21 | **13** | 50/1 | 9 | — |
| | **Little Red** (RCraggs) **5-8-8** JCarroll(2) (chsd ldrs tl rdn & wknd over 3f out: t.o) | ¾ | **14** | 100/1 | 5 | — |
| $752^{R}$ | **Silver Samurai (48)** (MrsVAAconley) **7-9-0** MDeering(9) (ref to r: t.n.p) | | **R** | 33/1 | — | — |

(SP 123.5%) **15 Rn**

**2m 39.0** (9.00) CSF £7.51 TOTE £3.40: £1.30 £1.40 £4.80 (£5.50) Trio £41.10 OWNER Mrs J. F. Wichelow (EDINGLEY) BRED Normanby Stud Ltd
Loveyoumillions (IRE) clmd MrsKBliss £10,000; Anchorena clmd GDDeverill £7,000
STEWARDS' ENQUIRY Tinkler susp. 27-28/5/96 (improper use of whip).
**IN-FOCUS: Apart from the first two, these looked a really moderate bunch.**
**787 Anchorena,** stepped up in distance and with the visor left off, did just enough. (9/4: 3/1-2/1)
**913 Loveyoumillions (IRE),** who looked to have a good chance at the weights, was simply not good enough. Connections will not be sorry at having seen him be claimed. (9/4: 6/4-5/2)
**Elite Bliss (IRE),** who had run in two bumpers, showed plenty of knee-action going to post. (33/1)
**Goodbye Millie,** a very poor mover, ran her best race so far this time. (14/1)
**972* Latvian** had one of his non-going days. (11/4)

## 1160 GORDON FOSTER MAIDEN STKS (3-Y.O+) (Class D)
4-30 (4-31) **1m** £3,925.00 (£1,180.00: £570.00: £265.00) Stalls: Low GOING minus 0.01 sec per fur (G)

| | | | | SP | RR | SF |
|---|---|---|---|---|---|---|
| | **Chief Burundi (USA)** (LMCumani) **4-9-10** KDarley(5) (lw: mde all: shkn up over 1f out: r.o strly) | — | **1** | 7/4$^{2}$ | 81 | 55 |
| $870^{2}$ | **Dawna** (HRACecil) **3-8-7** AMcGlone(2) (lw: trckd ldrs: chal 2f out: sn rdn & nt qckn) | 2½ | **2** | 4/5$^{1}$ | 71 | 33 |
| | **Lachesis** (RHollinshead) **3-8-2**(5) DGriffiths(1) (hld up & plld hrd: sn trckng ldrs: effrt over 2f out: hung lft: kpt on fnl f: nvr nr to chal) | 6 | **3** | 20/1 | 59 | 21 |
| | **Tabl (IRE)** (HThomsonJones) **3-8-7** KFallon(3) (neat: lw: a chsng ldrs: one pce fnl 2f) | ½ | **4** | 6/1$^{3}$ | 58 | 20 |
| | **Knotty Hill** (RCraggs) **4-9-10** JCarroll(6) (bhd: sme hdwy on outside over 2f out: nvr nr ldrs) | 1¼ | **5** | 150/1 | 61 | 35 |
| | **Highfield Pet** (CWFairhurst) **3-8-12** DeanMcKeown(4) (bit bkwd: hld up: sme hdwy over 2f out: n.d) | 1¾ | **6** | 33/1 | 57 | 19 |
| $703^{10}$ | **Riccarton** (PCalver) **3-8-12** MBirch(7) (chsd ldrs tl hung lft over 1f out) | ¾ | **7** | 50/1 | 56 | 18 |
| $994^{10}$ | **Bright Pet** (MrsSJSmith) **3-8-7** NConnorton(8) (sn outpcd & pushed along: n.d) | 11 | **8** | 66/1 | 29 | — |

(SP 118.0%) **8 Rn**

**1m 41.5** (5.00) CSF £3.51 TOTE £3.00: £1.10 £1.20 £2.20 (£1.60) OWNER Mr P. A. Leonard (NEWMARKET) BRED Ross Valley Farm
WEIGHT FOR AGE 3yo-12lb
**Chief Burundi (USA),** runner-up on his two outings as a juvenile, was turned out in good trim. Setting his own pace, he scored decisively in the end, and will be an interesting proposition in handicaps over further. (7/4)
**870 Dawna** travelled strongly but, off the bridle, could do no more than stick on at the same pace. She probably wants further. (4/5)

**Lachesis** raced keenly and, despite hanging under pressure, kept on in the final furlong. (20/1)
**Tabl (IRE)**, who lacks size, looked fit and it is hard to see where the improvement will come from. (6/1)
**Knotty Hill**, making his racecourse debut, defied his odds, running with some credit. (150/1)
**Highfield Pet**, unplaced in two outings as a juvenile, looked burly and took a keen grip. He will need to learn to settle. (33/1)

## 1161 KILBURN H'CAP (0-80) (3-Y.O+) (Class D)

5-00 (5-07) **5f** £3,964.00 (£1,192.00: £576.00: £268.00) Stalls: High GOING minus 0.14 sec per fur (G)

| | | | | SP | RR | SF |
|---|---|---|---|---|---|---|
| | **Tuscan Dawn (74)** (JBerry) **6-9-7**(5) PRoberts(7) (mde all: jst hld on) | — | 1 | 14/1 | 80 | 63 |
| 1039* | **Just Bob (69)** (SEKettlewell) **7-9-7** 7x JFortune(8) (lw: dwlt: sn wl bhd: gd hdwy over 1f out: fin fast) | hd | 2 | 9/4 1 | 75 | 58 |
| 931 11 | **Here Comes a Star (76)** (JMCarr) **8-10-0** ACulhane(6) (sn outpcd & rdn: hdwy over 1f out: styd on wl nr fin) | ¾ | 3 | 15/2 | 79 | 62 |
| *1028 3* | **Ninety-Five (61)** (JGFitzGerald) **4-8-13** TIves(10) (a chsng ldrs: ev ch & rdn over 1f out: nt qckn) | ½ | 4 | 5/1 3 | 63 | 46 |
| 956 5 | **Just Dissident (IRE) (58)** (RMWhitaker) **4-8-10v1** DeanMcKeown(11) (sn rdn along: chsd ldrs: kpt on one pce fnl 2f) | ½ | 5 | 9/2 2 | 58 | 41 |
| *900 2* | **Perfect Brave (60)** (JBalding) **5-8-5**(7) JEdmunds(9) (lw: chsd ldrs: rdn over 2f out: wknd appr fnl f) | 1 | 6 | 5/1 3 | 57 | 40 |
| 931 16 | **Able Sheriff (48)** (MWEasterby) **4-8-0b** DaleGibson(4) (chsd ldrs tl rdn & wknd 2f out) | 2½ | 7 | 14/1 | 37 | 20 |
| 951 4 | **Super Rocky (70)** (RBastiman) **7-9-3**(5) HBastiman(2) (racd far side: bhd fr ½-wy: eased ins fnl f) | 3½ | 8 | 14/1 | 48 | 31 |
| 931 3 | **Kalar (49)** (DWChapman) **7-8-1b** LCharnock(3) (lw: racd far side: bhd fr ½-wy: eased 1f out) | 2½ | 9 | 7/1 | 19 | 2 |
| *1049 13* | ***Windrush Boy (64)*** (JRBosley) **6-8-9**(7) AimeeCook(5) (Withdrawn not under Starters' orders: burst out of stalls) | | W | 14/1 | — | — |
| | | | | (SP 133.2%) | **9 Rn** | |

**60.0 secs** (2.00) CSF £47.58 CT £251.28 TOTE £18.40: £3.20 £1.80 £2.00 (£23.10) Trio £81.00 OWNER Mrs Chris Deuters (COCKERHAM) BRED F. Hines

OFFICIAL EXPLANATION **Just Bob: enquiring into the running of the horse as he had finished second, beaten a head, having apparently laid well out of his ground, the Stewards were told that the horse had to be held up to come with a late run. He tends to be slow out of the stalls and if he had been asked for his effort any earlier, he would not have responded. The rider added that he had ridden the gelding in the same manner as in his two previous winning runs.**

**Tuscan Dawn**, who scored twice as a three-year-old, has taken some time to slip back down to a winning mark. Behaving himself in the stalls this time, the post came in the nick of time. (14/1)
**1039* Just Bob**, bidding to extend his winning sequence to four, missed the break as is his wont. Soon a long way behind, he made up all of eight lengths in the final furlong and just failed to get there. His rider seemed to show no sense of urgency, and there is no doubt he should have won. (9/4)
**716 Here Comes a Star** struggled to go the pace, but was staying on in good style at the line. Over five, he appreciates a stiffer track. (15/2)
**1028 Ninety-Five** is still a maiden and looks in the grip of the Handicapper. (5/1)
**956 Just Dissident (IRE)**, a poor mover, was tried in a visor and it certainly did not sharpen him up. (9/2)

## 1162 MOWBRAY (S) STKS (II) (3-Y.O+) (Class G)

5-30 (5-32) **7f** £1,952.50 (£540.00: £257.50) Stalls: Low GOING minus 0.01 sec per fur (G)

| | | | | SP | RR | SF |
|---|---|---|---|---|---|---|
| 971 2 | **Broctune Gold (60)** (MrsMReveley) **5-9-7** ACulhane(9) (trckd ldrs: led wl over 1f out: drew clr fnl f) | — | 1 | 10/11 1 | 61 | 34 |
| 971* | **My Godson (37)** (JLEyre) **6-9-12b** RLappin(2) (hdwy to chse ldrs 3f out: kpt on appr fnl f: no ch w wnr) | 5 | 2 | 7/2 2 | 55 | 28 |
| 1043 4 | **Valiant Man** (JWharton) **5-9-7v1** KFallon(6) (chsd ldrs: effrt & swtchd rt over 2f out: kpt on towards fin) | 2½ | 3 | 9/1 | 44 | 17 |
| 1087 6 | **Monkey Face (33)** (WWHaigh) **5-9-2** LCharnock(1) (chsd ldrs: led over 3f out tl wl over 1f out: edgd rt & wknd ins fnl f) | hd | 4 | 14/1 | 39 | 12 |
| *606 4* | **Monkey Zanty (IRE) (51)** (JLHarris) **3-8-0**(5) PFessey(8) (lw: led tl ½-wy: wknd 2f out) | 1½ | 5 | 8/1 3 | 35 | — |
| 1043 2 | **Tallulah Belle (45)** (NPLittmoden) **3-8-5** JQuinn(5) (lw: s.i.s: hmpd over 4f out: kpt on fnl 2f: nvr nr ldrs) | 2 | 6 | 10/1 | 31 | — |
| 805 4 | **Ohnonotagain (33)** (BWMurray) **4-9-2** TWilliams(7) (hmpd over 4f out: sme hdwy 2f out: n.d) | 4 | 7 | 50/1 | 22 | — |
| *1029 10* | **Peacefull Reply (USA) (38)** (FHLee) **6-9-7** TIves(3) (lw: hld up: hmpd over 4f out: n.d after) | 3½ | 8 | 12/1 | 19 | — |
| | **Scott's Risk** (LJBarratt) **6-9-0**(7) AngelaGallimore(4) (in tch whn hung rt over 4f out: lost pl over 3f out: t.o) | 23 | 9 | 100/1 | — | — |
| | | | | (SP 122.1%) | **9 Rn** | |

**1m 30.1** (5.90) CSF £4.96 TOTE £1.90: £1.10 £1.80 £2.60 (£2.80) Trio £7.60 OWNER Mrs M. B. Thwaites (SALTBURN) BRED A. J. Poulton (Epping) Ltd
WEIGHT FOR AGE 3yo-11lb
No bid

**971 Broctune Gold** looked nailed-on after his sound effort from a poor draw at Newcastle last time and made no mistake. All his victories to date have been recorded in the month of May. (10/11: 4/5-Evens)
**971* My Godson**, 1lb worse off with the winner on Newcastle running, did not have the draw to help this time. (7/2)
**1043 Valiant Man** has not won for over three years. (9/1)
**1087 Monkey Face** would have been 4lb better off with My Godson in a handicap, and probably ran up to her very best. (14/1)
**1043 Tallulah Belle** did best of the three hampered when Scott's Risk all but knocked them over turning out of the back straight.(10/1)

T/Plpt: £6.50 (1,523.46 Tckts). T/Qdpt: £3.50 (188.87 Tckts). AA/WG

# 1020-HAMILTON (R-H) (Good to firm, Firm patches)

## Saturday May 18th

WEATHER: overcast WIND: almost nil

## 1163 PATRICK & KATHLEEN MCCLOSKEY APPRENTICE H'CAP (0-70) (3-Y.O+) (Class F)

6-20 (6-21) **5f 4y** £2,497.50 (£710.00: £352.50) Stalls: Low GOING minus 0.24 sec per fur (GF)

| | | | | SP | RR | SF |
|---|---|---|---|---|---|---|
| 1020 5 | **Cheeky Chappy (39)** (DWChapman) **5-7-8b**(3) KSked(6) (mde all: sn clr: hung lft fr over 1f out: kpt on) | — | 1 | 10/1 | 53 | 35 |
| | **Red Five (45)** (JBerry) **5-7-11**(6) JoanneWebster(7) (bit bkwd: chsd ldrs: drvn along over 2f out: kpt on & edgd lft fnl f) | 1 | 2 | 33/1 | 56 | 38 |

| | | | | SP | RR | SF |
|---|---|---|---|---|---|---|
| 931[20] | **Natural Key (58)** (DHaydnJones) **3-8-2**(6) AnthonyBond(14) (chsd ldrs: rdn ½-wy: edgd lft u.p: nt qckn appr fnl f) | 3 | **3** | 8/1 | 59 | 33 |
| 1041[2] | **Diet (58)** (MissLAPerratt) **10-9-2v** DSweeney(12) (in tch: outpcd & drvn ½-wy: swtchd rt & hdwy over 1f out: kpt on) | s.h | **4** | 10/1 | 59 | 41 |
| 1020* | **Henry the Hawk (52)** (MDods) **5-8-7v**(3) RFfrench(11) (lw: mid div: rdn over 2f out: kpt on fnl f: nt rch ldrs) | 1½ | **5** | 9/2[1] | 48 | 30 |
| 559[5] | **Kenesha (IRE) (43)** (DANolan) **6-7-12**(3) JFowle(5) (b: chsd ldrs tl rdn & wknd over 1f out: b.b.v) | 2½ | **6** | 12/1 | 31 | 13 |
| 997[9] | **Another Nightmare (IRE) (38)** (TDyer) **4-7-7**(3) RMullen(2) (chsd ldrs tl rdn & wknd over 1f out) | ¾ | **7** | 25/1 | 24 | 6 |
| 931[17] | **Ultra Beet (66)** (PCHaslam) **4-9-4b**(6) CarolDavison(13) (sn bhd: drvn along after 2f: n.d) | s.h | **8** | 11/1 | 52 | 34 |
| 1020[4] | **Suedoro (49)** (RMMcKellar) **6-7-13**(8)ow4 DMcGaffin(9) (s.i.s: effrt over 2f out: n.d) | hd | **9** | 6/1[3] | 35 | 13 |
| 1039[3] | **Finisterre (IRE) (59)** (JJO'Neill) **3-8-6**(3) FMBerry(8) (lw: in tch: effrt wl over 2f out: btn over 1f out) | nk | **10** | 8/1 | 44 | 18 |
| 1020[8] | **Leading Princess (IRE) (45)** (MissLAPerratt) **5-8-0b**(3) JBramhill(3) (chsd ldrs: rdn & lost pl over 2f out: hung lft fnl f) | s.h | **11** | 25/1 | 29 | 11 |
| 1020[2] | **Best Kept Secret (55)** (PDEvans) **5-8-7b**(6)ow2 HayleyWilliams(10) (s.i.s: rdn along in rr ½-wy: n.d) | 1¼ | **12** | 11/2[2] | 35 | 15 |
| 997[2] | **Seconds Away (38)** (JSGoldie) **5-7-5b**(5) JMcAuley(1) (racd alone stands' side: spd 3f) | s.h | **13** | 12/1 | 18 | — |
| 1001[6] | **Millemay (42)** (PMonteith) **6-7-11**(3)ow3 RStudholme(4) (dwlt: rdn & sme hdwy ½-wy: btn wl over 1f out) | 2½ | **14** | 25/1 | 14 | — |
| | | | | (SP 126.5%) | | **14 Rn** |

**59.8 secs** (1.50) CSF £254.88 CT £2598.00 TOTE £12.70: £2.80 £6.00 £2.50 (£781.10) Trio Not won; £347.90 to 20/5/96 OWNER Mrs Jeanne Chapman (YORK) BRED Ian W. Glenton

LONG HANDICAP Seconds Away 7-7 Another Nightmare (IRE) 7-9

WEIGHT FOR AGE 3yo-8lb

**1020 Cheeky Chappy** blazed a trail down the centre and never looked like being caught, despite drifting left. (10/1)

**Red Five**, just in need of the outing, shaped well, staying on in the final furlong. (33/1)

**Natural Key** came back to some sort of form, despite showing a tendency to hang left. She had not had the best of the draw in recent runs. (8/1)

**1041 Diet**, taken off his feet at halfway, stuck on late. Eight times a course winner, he will no doubt add to that this term. (10/1)

**1020* Henry the Hawk** never looked like continuing the sequence. (9/2)

**559 Kenesha (IRE)** did not shape too badly, but is now on a losing run of twenty-nine. (12/1)

**1020 Best Kept Secret** (11/2: 4/1-6/1)

**997 Seconds Away** (12/1: 8/1-14/1)

## 1164 ISLE OF ARRAN CLAIMING STKS (2-Y.O) (Class F)

6-50 (6-50) **6f 5y** £2,521.00 (£706.00: £343.00) Stalls: Low GOING minus 0.24 sec per fur (GF)

| | | | | SP | RR | SF |
|---|---|---|---|---|---|---|
| 930[7] | **Smokey From Caplaw** (JJO'Neill) **2-8-10** KFallon(1) (dwlt: trckd ldrs: hdwy & hung rt over 2f out: led over 1f out: kpt on u.p) | — | **1** | 5/1[3] | 66 | — |
| 1021[2] | **Ekaterini Paritsi** (WGMTurner) **2-8-0**(5) CAdamson(4) (lw: cl up: led over 2f out tl over 1f out: kpt on wl u.p towards fin) | ½ | **2** | Evens[1] | 60 | — |
| 990[3] | **Contravene (IRE)** (JBerry) **2-8-7** JCarroll(3) (hung rt thrght: led tl hdd over 2f out: sn rdn: btn over 1f out) | 8 | **3** | 6/4[2] | 40 | — |
| 910[5] | **Flood's Flyer (IRE)** (NTinkler) **2-8-3** LCharnock(2) (chsd ldrs: drvn along over 2f out: btn wl over 1f out: eased) | 11 | **4** | 33/1 | 7 | — |
| | | | | (SP 109.6%) | | **4 Rn** |

**1m 15.8** (5.80) CSF £10.12 TOTE £6.20: (£3.10) OWNER Mr G. P. Bernacchi (PENRITH) BRED Gino P. Bernacchi

**Smokey From Caplaw** showed a tendency to hang right but saw it out in reasonable style. (5/1: op 3/1)

**1021 Ekaterini Paritsi**, stepping up in trip, clearly needs every yard of six furlongs. (Evens)

**990 Contravene (IRE)** did not look at all comfortable and hung right throughout. (6/4)

**624 Flood's Flyer (IRE)** was always flat out. (33/1)

## 1165 ARIZONA H'CAP (0-70) (4-Y.O+) (Class E)

7-20 (7-20) **1m 5f 9y** £3,252.00 (£984.00: £480.00: £228.00) Stalls: High GOING minus 0.52 sec per fur (F)

| | | | | SP | RR | SF |
|---|---|---|---|---|---|---|
| | **Victor Laszlo (36)** (RAllan) **4-7-13** JFanning(4) (racd keenly: hld up in tch: effrt 3f out: led wl over 1f out: drvn clr) | — | **1** | 7/2[3] | 47 | 18 |
| 1070[10] | **Greystyle (35)** (MBrittain) **6-7-9v**(3)ow2 DWright(6) (led 2f: chsd ldr: led 4f out: hdd 2f out: kpt on one pce fnl f) | 3½ | **2** | 10/1 | 42 | 11 |
| 1044[6] | **Lord Advocate (42)** (DANolan) **8-8-5b** VHalliday(1) (lw: chsd ldrs: rdn over 3f out: one pce fr wl over 1f out) | 2 | **3** | 9/4[1] | 46 | 17 |
| | **Bruz (33)** (PMonteith) **5-7-10** LCharnock(7) (racd keenly: hld up in tch: hdwy & nt clr run 3f out: swtchd & led 2f out: sn hdd & btn) | nk | **4** | 16/1 | 37 | 8 |
| 999[10] | **Guards Brigade (34)** (JHetherton) **5-7-11** NKennedy(2) (hld up: hdwy on outside 4f out: rdn & wknd fr over 2f out) | 15 | **5** | 3/1[2] | 20 | — |
| 1044[11] | **Magic Times (48)** (MJohnston) **5-8-11** JWeaver(5) (led after 2f tl rdn & hdd 4f out: btn over 2f out) | 1½ | **6** | 10/1 | 32 | 3 |
| 884[11] | **Segala (IRE) (65)** (JJO'Neill) **5-10-0** KFallon(3) (hld up in rr: effrt over 3f out: sn outpcd: eased fnl f) | 9 | **7** | 12/1 | 38 | 9 |
| | | | | (SP 109.7%) | | **7 Rn** |

**2m 50.0** (4.30) CSF £31.23 TOTE £5.50: £3.50 £3.50 (£42.60) OWNER Mr Ian Dalgleish (CORNHILL-ON-TWEED) BRED Lawers Stud

LONG HANDICAP Greystyle 7-0 Bruz 7-8

**Victor Laszlo** came through to settle it well over a furlong out and won most decisively in the end. This was only his fifth ever outing and he is open to further improvement. (7/2)

**Greystyle**, 10lb out of the handicap, carried 2lb overweight to boot, but ran an honest race and could find a run-of-the-mill event in due course. (10/1)

**1044 Lord Advocate** was under pressure and going nowhere from three furlongs out. (9/4)

**Bruz** carried his head high and was well outpointed from well over a furlong out. (16/1)

**Guards Brigade** made a short-lived effort half a mile out. (3/1)

**Segala (IRE)** (12/1: 8/1-14/1)

## 1166 TATTERSALLS MAIDEN AUCTION STKS (2-Y.O) (Class E)

7-50 (7-52) **5f 4y** £2,995.65 (£907.20: £443.10: £211.05) Stalls: Low GOING minus 0.24 sec per fur (GF)

| | | | | SP | RR | SF |
|---|---|---|---|---|---|---|
| 848[4] | **Ride Sally Ride (IRE)** (JBerry) **2-8-11** JCarroll(11) (lw: w ldrs: led over 2f out: r.o strly fnl f: readily) | — | **1** | 7/2[1] | 79+ | 22 |

| | | | | SP | RR | SF |
|---|---|---|---|---|---|---|
| 1003[8] | **Nomore Mr Niceguy** (EJAlston) **2-8-5** SDWilliams(8) (lw: s.s: sn rcvrd: trckd ldrs gng wl: effrt over 1f out: no imp whn hung lft ins fnl f) | 3½ | **2** | 11/2 | 62 | 5 |
| 930[5] | **Grate Times** (EWeymes) **2-8-6** RLappin(6) (chsd ldrs: n.m.r ½-wy: effrt 2f out: kpt on one pce fnl f) | 1¾ | **3** | 8/1 | 57 | — |
| 880[2] | **Tribal Mischief** (DMoffatt) **2-7-10**(3) DarrenMoffatt(7) (slt ld tl rdn over 2f out: wknd over 1f out) | nk | **4** | 4/1[2] | 49 | — |
| | **Ginny Wossername** (WGMTurner) **2-7-7**(5) CAdamson(2) (neat: mid div: effrt 2f out: kpt on fnl f) | 1¾ | **5** | 20/1 | 43 | — |
| | **Real Fire (IRE)** (MGMeagher) **2-8-4** JFEgan(5) (neat: scope: bit bkwd: dwlt: sn pushed along: effrt & hdwy on outside wl over 1f out: no ex ins fnl f) | 2½ | **6** | 16/1 | 41 | — |
| *895[6]* | **Jingoist (IRE)** (MJohnston) **2-8-0** TWilliams(4) (w ldrs: rdn ½-wy: btn wl over 1f out) | ¾ | **7** | 6/1 | 34 | — |
| 958[3] | **Rockaroundtheclock** (PDEvans) **2-8-10** JFortune(9) (lw: w ldrs tl rdn & outpcd fr wl over 1f out) | ½ | **8** | 9/2[3] | 43 | — |
| | **Ballydinero (IRE)** (CaptJWilson) **2-8-3** DeanMcKeown(10) (w'like: bit bkwd: dwlt: in tch & rdn ½-wy: rn green & sn wknd) | 2½ | **9** | 20/1 | 28 | — |
| | **The Orraman (IRE)** (JJO'Neill) **2-8-8** KFallon(1) (unf: s.s: a bhd) | 15 | **10** | 20/1 | — | — |
| | | | | (SP 121.4%) | **10 Rn** | |

**61.4 secs** (3.10) CSF £22.67 TOTE £4.30: £1.70 £2.30 £1.60 (£9.80) Trio £28.50 OWNER Mrs John Magnier (COCKERHAM) BRED Patrick Headon

**848 Ride Sally Ride (IRE)**, clearly all the better for his debut, was always going like a winner and scored in tremendous style. He can go on from this. (7/2)

**Nomore Mr Niceguy** again missed the kick, but tracked the leaders on the bridle until outpointed by the winner. He should not be written off yet and is certainly worth another chance. (11/2: 4/1-6/1)

**930 Grate Times** chased the leaders, but found himself in a bit of a pocket at halfway, before staying on at one pace late in the day. (8/1)

**880 Tribal Mischief** showed plenty of dash. (4/1)

**Ginny Wossername**, a newcomer, showed a little promise, staying on in the closing stages. (20/1)

**Real Fire (IRE)** showed some promise for the future. (16/1)

**958 Rockaroundtheclock** (9/2: op 3/1)

## 1167 ISLE OF BUTE (S) H'CAP (0-60) (3-Y.O+) (Class G)

8-20 (8-20) **1m 3f 16y** £2,514.00 (£704.00: £342.00) Stalls: High GOING minus 0.52 sec per fur (F)

| | | | | SP | RR | SF |
|---|---|---|---|---|---|---|
| 872[15] | **Firefighter (47)** (BPJBaugh) **7-9-4**(7) IonaWands(10) (b: mid div: pushed along 6f out: hdwy over 4f out: led wl over 2f out: hld on wl towards fin) | — | **1** | 20/1 | 59 | 44 |
| 995[14] | **I'm a Nut Man (32)** (CASmith) **5-8-10** DeanMcKeown(11) (hld up in rr: smooth hdwy fr over 3f out: rdn to chal ins fnl f: nt qckn cl home) | nk | **2** | 10/1 | 44 | 29 |
| 541[4] | **Steadfast Elite (IRE) (39)** (JJO'Neill) **5-9-3** JFortune(13) (in tch: rdn along 3f out: one pce fr over 1f out) | 3½ | **3** | 8/1[3] | 46 | 31 |
| 998[2] | **Rattle (50)** (JJO'Neill) **3-8-13b** KFallon(6) (mid div: pushed along over 6f out: hdwy 4f out: one pce fnl 2f) | 1¼ | **4** | 8/1[3] | 55 | 25 |
| *1027[3]* | **Princess Pamgaddy (44)** (CNAllen) **3-8-7** CHodgson(7) (bhd: hdwy u.p over 2f out: nt rch ldrs) | 1 | **5** | 8/1[3] | 47 | 17 |
| 883[7] | **Hawwam (45)** (EJAlston) **10-9-9** SDWilliams(4) (bhd: effrt 3f out: hdwy over 2f out: nt pce of ldrs) | 1½ | **6** | 12/1 | 46 | 31 |
| *854[10]* | **No Submission (USA) (38)** (DWChapman) **10-9-2** ACulhane(9) (bhd tl styd on fnl 2f: n.d) | 2½ | **7** | 12/1 | 36 | 21 |
| | **Mcgillycuddy Reeks (IRE) (46)** (NTinkler) **5-9-10** LCharnock(14) (bit bkwd: in tch: effrt over 4f out: btn over 2f out) | 2½ | **8** | 6/1[1] | 40 | 25 |
| *899** | **Pearl Anniversary (IRE) (54)** (MJohnston) **3-9-3** JWeaver(5) (bhd: pushed along 6f out: hdwy over 2f out: n.d) | ½ | **9** | 7/1[2] | 47 | 17 |
| 1001[9] | **Snake Plissken (IRE) (46)** (DHaydnJones) **5-9-5**(5) PPMurphy(3) (lw: chsd ldrs: rdn 3f out: btn over 2f out) | 5 | **10** | 7/1[2] | 32 | 17 |
| 620[10] | **Vintage Taittinger (IRE) (35)** (TDyer) **4-8-6**(7) RMullen(17) (chsd ldrs: rdn & ev ch 4f out: btn over 2f out) | s.h | **11** | 20/1 | 21 | 6 |
| 999[5] | **Walworth Lady (50)** (MDods) **5-10-0** JCarroll(8) (b: trckd ldrs: effrt 4f out: wknd over 2f out) | nk | **12** | 6/1[1] | 35 | 20 |
| | **Kalko (22)** (JSGoldie) **7-8-0** TWilliams(12) (bhd: effrt over 4f out: no imp) | nk | **13** | 50/1 | 7 | — |
| 998[4] | **Trumped (IRE) (34)** (PMonteith) **4-8-9**(3) DarrenMoffatt(16) (sn prom: led 7f out tl over 5f out: wknd u.p 3f out) | 1¼ | **14** | 11/1 | 17 | 2 |
| 609[6] | **Portite Sophie (33)** (MBrittain) **5-8-8**(3) DWright(15) (led: hdd 7f out: sn led again: hdd wl over 2f out: sn btn) | ¾ | **15** | 10/1 | 15 | — |
| | **Riva's Book (USA) (50)** (MGMeagher) **5-9-7**(7) RStudholme(1) (in tch tl rdn & btn over 3f out: t.o) | 20 | **16** | 33/1 | 3 | — |
| 620[15] | **Recluse (43)** (MissLAPerratt) **5-9-7b** JFanning(2) (mid div & drvn along 6f out: lost tch 4f out: t.o) | ¾ | **17** | 66/1 | — | — |
| | | | | (SP 144.7%) | **17 Rn** | |

**2m 22.7** (3.30) CSF £217.64 CT £1636.69 TOTE £63.50: £17.50 £4.90 £2.90 £2.90 (£170.50) Trio Not won; £339.98 to 20/5/96 OWNER Mr John Meredith (LITTLE HAYWOOD) BRED Sir Stephen Hastings

WEIGHT FOR AGE 3yo-15lb

No bid

**Firefighter**, well handled, held on well near the finish. (20/1)

**752 I'm a Nut Man** moved smoothly through the field from three furlongs out. He looked likely to prevail until failing to pull out any extra close home. (10/1: 8/1-12/1)

**541 Steadfast Elite (IRE)** could find only one pace when it mattered. (8/1)

**998 Rattle** could find only one insufficient speed when it mattered. (8/1)

**1027 Princess Pamgaddy** stayed on under pressure late on without looking likely to reach the leaders. (8/1)

**Hawwam** could never land a blow. (12/1)

## 1168 ARIZONA MAIDEN STKS (3-Y.O+) (Class D)

8-50 (8-50) **1m 4f 17y** £3,566.25 (£1,080.00: £527.50: £251.25) Stalls: High GOING minus 0.52 sec per fur (F)

| | | | | SP | RR | SF |
|---|---|---|---|---|---|---|
| | **Mattawan** (MJohnston) **3-8-7** JWeaver(3) (w'like: scope: lw: chsd ldr: pushed along 6f out: smooth hdwy to jn ldr over 3f out: sn led: rn green: shkn up & r.o fnl f) | — | **1** | 8/11[1] | 81+ | 28 |
| 974[2] | **Candle Smile (USA) (90)** (MRStoute) **4-9-10** DeanMcKeown(1) (lw: led: jnd over 3f out: sn hdd: kpt on u.p fr over 1f out) | 1¼ | **2** | 11/8[2] | 79 | 43 |
| | **Kuwam (IRE)** (BHanbury) **3-8-2**(5) LNewton(4) (bhd: hdwy to chse clr ldrs over 3f out: sn outpcd) | 22 | **3** | 9/1[3] | 50 | — |
| | **Calcando** (EWeymes) **4-9-5** JFortune(6) (prom tl rdn & wknd wl over 3f out) | 3 | **4** | 100/1 | 41 | 5 |
| 934[8] | **Raise A Ripple** (MrsDThomson) **3-8-7** RLappin(5) (in tch tl rdn & outpcd fnl 4f: t.o) | 15 | **5** | 25/1 | 26 | — |
| 1023[6] | **Lord Cornelious** (DANolan) **3-8-7** VHalliday(2) (hld up in rr: lost tch fr over 4f out: t.o) | 22 | **6** | 150/1 | — | — |
| | | | | (SP 115.5%) | **6 Rn** | |

**2m 35.5** (3.50) CSF £2.15 TOTE £1.80: £3.50 £1.00 (£1.20) OWNER Sheikh Mohammed (MIDDLEHAM) BRED Sheikh Mohammed Bin Rashid Al Maktoum

WEIGHT FOR AGE 3yo-17lb

**Mattawan**, an attractive son of Nashwan and entered in the Derby, won without having a hard race, but ran very green and showed a noticeably rounded action. Racing and better ground will improve him. (8/11)
**974 Candle Smile (USA)** took them along at a decent clip but was readily outpointed when the winner went on. However, he battled back when that rival ran green and did not go down without a fight. (11/8)
**Kuwam (IRE)** went in pursuit of the first two half a mile out, but was soon seen off. (9/1)

T/Plpt: £6,904.80 (1.49 Tckts). T/Qdpt: £78.20 (10.91 Tckts). O'R

# 1073-LINGFIELD (L-H) (Good to firm)
## Saturday May 18th
Race 6: hand-timed
WEATHER: overcast WIND: mod half against

## 1169 E.B.F. CIDER MAIDEN STKS (2-Y.O) (Class D)
6-00 (6-02) **5f** £3,527.35 (£1,052.80: £502.90: £227.95) Stalls: High GOING minus 0.07 sec per fur (G)

| | Horse | Dist | Pos | SP | RR | SF |
|---|---|---|---|---|---|---|
| | **Smart Boy (IRE)** (PFICole) **2-9-0** CRutter(5) (neat: hdwy 2f out: led ins fnl f: rdn out) | — | 1 | 6/1 2 | 60 t | 26 |
| | **Tough Leader** (BHanbury) **2-8-11**(3) JStack(7) (str: a.p: led over 1f out tl ins fnl f: unable qckn) | 1½ | 2 | 5/4 1 | 55 t | 21 |
| 930R | **Tear White (IRE)** (TGMills) **2-9-0b1** MarkLynch(6) (plld hrd: led over 3f: one pce) | 1 | 3 | 13/2 3 | 52 t | 18 |
| | **Sharp Return** (MJRyan) **2-9-0** DBiggs(2) (neat: a.p: ev ch ins fnl f: sn wknd) | 1½ | 4 | 15/2 | 47 t | 13 |
| | **My Beloved (IRE)** (RHannon) **2-8-9** RPerham(1) (unf: outpcd: hdwy fnl f: nvr nrr) | hd | 5 | 13/2 3 | 42 t | 8 |
| | **Talisman (IRE)** (SDow) **2-8-9**(5) ADaly(4) (cmpt: dwlt: outpcd: nvr nr to chal) | ½ | 6 | 10/1 | 45 t | 11 |
| | **Super Scravels** (DrJDScargill) **2-8-9** MFenton(3) (neat: bhd fnl 3f) | 2½ | 7 | 25/1 | 32 t | — |
| | | | | (SP 110.1%) | **7 Rn** | |

**60.77 secs** (3.77) CSF £13.14 TOTE £4.30: £1.60 £1.80 (£4.10) OWNER H R H Sultan Ahmad Shah (WHATCOMBE) BRED Peter Savill
**Smart Boy (IRE)**, slightly on the leg, drifted badly in the market but still managed to carry the day. Edging closer a quarter of a mile out, he came with a useful run to lead inside the final furlong and quickly asserted. (6/1: op 5/2)
**Tough Leader**, quite a strongly-made newcomer, raced in the front rank from the outset, but was unable to withstand the winner's challenge inside the final furlong. (5/4)
**Tear White (IRE)** looks a nightmare ride - he ran out and unseated his rider on his debut - and full marks must go to his jockey who valiantly tried to restrain him as he tore off in front and would have veered right across the course if he had had his way. Collared over a furlong out, he nevertheless kept on well to the line. He has ability but should not be touched with a barge-pole. (13/2)
**Sharp Return** is not very big and was extremely coltish leaving the paddock. Racing in the front rank from the start, he still had every chance inside the final furlong before weakening. (15/2)
**My Beloved (IRE)**. a sparely-made individual, was unable to go the pace, but did make a little late headway. (13/2: op 7/2)
**Talisman (IRE)**, a sturdy individual, failed to go the pace. (10/1)

## 1170 GIN & TONIC (S) H'CAP (0-60) (3-Y.O+) (Class G)
6-30 (6-31) **5f** £2,637.00 (£732.00: £351.00) Stalls: High GOING minus 0.07 sec per fur (G)

| | Horse | Dist | Pos | SP | RR | SF |
|---|---|---|---|---|---|---|
| 981 5 | **Halliard (53)** (TMJones) **5-9-10** RPerham(3) (b: a.p: led over 2f out: r.o wl) | — | 1 | 10/1 3 | 69 | 51 |
| 667 6 | **Lift Boy (USA) (45)** (AMoore) **7-9-2** CandyMorris(11) (a.p: hrd rdn over 2f out: ev ch ins fnl f: unable qckn) | 1¾ | 2 | 5/2 1 | 55 | 37 |
| 887 13 | **Almapa (45)** (RJHodges) **4-8-13**(3) SDrowne(9) (rdn over 2f out: hdwy over 1f out: r.o ins fnl f) | ½ | 3 | 14/1 | 54 | 36 |
| 862 18 | **Secret Miss (51)** (APJones) **4-9-8** RCochrane(12) (lw: s.s: outpcd: hdwy on ins over 1f out: r.o ins fnl f) | nk | 4 | 7/1 2 | 59 | 41 |
| 861 10 | **Jessica's Song (52)** (WGMTurner) **3-9-1** TSprake(13) (lw: a.p: hrd rdn & ev ch over 1f out: one pce) | ½ | 5 | 7/1 2 | 58 | 32 |
| 991 12 | **Rocky Two (43)** (PHowling) **5-9-0v** FNorton(7) (a.p: rdn over 2f out: one pce) | 2½ | 6 | 33/1 | 41 | 23 |
| 981 19 | **Assignment (40)** (JELong) **10-8-8**(3) PMcCabe(10) (outpcd: nvr nrr) | 1½ | 7 | 25/1 | 33 | 15 |
| 750 8 | **The Fed (42)** (JAPickering) **6-8-13** SWhitworth(8) (nvr nr to chal) | 1½ | 8 | 16/1 | 31 | 13 |
| | **Little Gent (IRE) (40)** (JELong) **5-8-4**(7) TField(14) (bit bkwd: prom over 2f) | ¾ | 9 | 50/1 | 26 | 8 |
| 949 9 | **Deardaw (39)** (MDIUsher) **4-8-10** NAdams(16) (prom over 2f) | 1½ | 10 | 20/1 | 20 | 2 |
| 1049 9 | **The Noble Oak (IRE) (39)** (MJBolton) **8-8-10** GCarter(15) (prom over 2f) | 1¼ | 11 | 7/1 2 | 16 | — |
| 644 13 | **Bouton d'Or (45)** (PHowling) **3-8-8** DBiggs(6) (hld up: rdn over 2f out: wknd fnl f) | 1½ | 12 | 20/1 | 18 | — |
| 1074 16 | **Thorny Bishop (35)** (BAPearce) **5-8-6b** GBardwell(1) (racd alone far side: outpcd) | ½ | 13 | 50/1 | 6 | — |
| 893 20 | **Admirals Realm (42)** (AGNewcombe) **7-8-13** RHughes(4) (outpcd) | 3 | 14 | 12/1 | 3 | — |
| 867 4 | **Music Mistress (IRE) (50)** (JSMoore) **3-8-13** WJO'Connor(5) (s.i.s: a bhd) | ½ | 15 | 7/1 2 | 10 | — |
| *386* 8 | **Tommy Tempest (36)** (REPeacock) **7-8-2v**(5) ADaly(2) (led over 2f) | 4 | 16 | 25/1 | — | — |
| | | | | (SP 132.0%) | **16 Rn** | |

**59.87 secs** (2.87) CSF £35.64 CT £358.18 TOTE £12.10: £2.80 £1.30 £4.90 £2.00 (£19.10) Trio £207.10; £43.77 to 20/5/96 OWNER The Rest Hill Partnership (GUILDFORD) BRED Mrs J. Brookes
WEIGHT FOR AGE 3yo-8lb
No bid
**981 Halliard** hit the front at halfway and found another gear inside the final furlong. (10/1)
**Lift Boy (USA)** still had every chance inside the final furlong before the winner found another gear. (5/2)
**470 Almapa** found this trip too sharp. Only getting going below the distance, he found the line always coming too soon. (14/1: 10/1-16/1)
**667 Secret Miss** was doing all her best work in the last furlong and a half. (7/1)
**Jessica's Song** had every chance below the distance before tapped for toe. (7/1: 5/1-8/1)
**Rocky Two** was made to look very pedestrian in the last two furlongs. One win from fifty-four starts says it all. (33/1)
**867 Music Mistress (IRE)** (7/1: 5/1-15/2)

## 1171 KIR ROYAL MAIDEN STKS (3-Y.O+) (Class D)
7-00 (7-03) **6f** £4,225.35 (£1,264.80: £606.90: £277.95) Stalls: High GOING minus 0.07 sec per fur (G)

| | Horse | Dist | Pos | SP | RR | SF |
|---|---|---|---|---|---|---|
| | **Mijas** (LMontagueHall) **3-8-7** RPerham(10) (unf: a.p: led 2f out: r.o wl) | — | 1 | 33/1 | 80 | 34 |
| 987 9 | **Alpine Hideaway (IRE) (77)** (BHanbury) **3-8-9**(3) JStack(15) (hld up: rdn over 3f out: chsd wnr fnl f: unable qckn) | 2 | 2 | 7/1 | 80 | 34 |
| | **Delphine** (MBell) **3-8-7** MFenton(9) (unf: outpcd: hdwy over 1f out: r.o wl ins fnl f) | 1¼ | 3 | 14/1 | 71 | 25 |
| 758 3 | **Blessed Spirit (69)** (CFWall) **3-8-7** RCochrane(4) (a.p: ev ch over 1f out: wknd fnl f) | 2½ | 4 | 8/1 | 65 | 19 |
| | **Onefortheditch (USA)** (JHMGosden) **3-8-7** AGarth(13) (hld up: edgd lft 2f out: one pce) | hd | 5 | 7/2 2 | 64 | 18 |

730[14] **Stoney End (USA)** (MRChannon) **3-8-12** RHughes(8) (a.p: rdn & hung lft over 2f out: wknd over 1f out) ......1¼ **6** 25/1 66 20
**Bellacardia** (GLewis) **3-8-4**(3) AWhelan(14) (hdwy over 1f out: nvr plcd to chal) ......s.h **7** 33/1 61 15
921[8] **Ember** (LMCumani) **3-8-7** SSanders(12) (lw: no hdwy fnl 3f) ......hd **8** 6/1 3 61 15
943[3] **Mellow Master** (NJHWalker) **3-8-12** CRutter(16) (lw: nvr nrr) ......2 **9** 16/1 60 14
1016[6] **Glorious Aragon (81)** (RFJohnsonHoughton) **4-9-2** TIves(2) (led over 4f out to 2f out: sn wknd) ......6 **10** 9/4 1 39 2
**Mutasarrif (IRE)** (HThomsonJones) **3-8-12** GCarter(5) (str: s.s: a bhd) ......1½ **11** 12/1 40 —
*377[8]* **Into Debt** (JRPoulton) **3-8-4**(3) PMcCabe(6) (s.s: a bhd) ......½ **12** 33/1 34 —
982[16] **Risky Baby** (THind) **4-8-13**(3) SDrowne(7) (b: lw: led over 1f: wknd over 3f out) ......2½ **13** 50/1 27 —
**Sea Idol (IRE)** (PFICole) **3-8-7** TQuinn(3) (lt-f: bhd fnl 2f) ......s.h **14** 12/1 27 —
**Nightswimming (IRE)** (SDow) **3-8-7**(5) ADaly(11) (str: scope: bit bkwd: s.s: a bhd) ......2½ **15** 33/1 26 —
(SP 136.4%) **15 Rn**

**1m 12.55** (3.55) CSF £252.73 TOTE £33.60: £6.20 £4.60 £4.00 (£566.20) Trio Not won; £313.20 to 20/5/96 OWNER The Mijas Partnership (EPSOM) BRED Roldvale Ltd
WEIGHT FOR AGE 3yo-9lb
OFFICIAL EXPLANATION **Bellacardia: the jockey reported that the filly missed the break and did not come down the hill too well, but ran on in the final two furlongs.**
**Mijas** caused a surprise on this racecourse debut. Hitting the front a quarter of a mile out, she kept up the gallop. (33/1)
**755 Alpine Hideaway (IRE)**, struggling into second place a furlong out, never looked like reeling in the winner. (7/1)
**Delphine**, unable to go the early pace, ran on nicely in the last furlong and a half only to find the line always coming too soon. (14/1: 10/1-16/1)
**758 Blessed Spirit** had every chance below the distance before tiring inside the last 200 yards. (8/1)
**Onefortheditch (USA)** chased the leaders but failed to quicken in the last two furlongs. (7/2: 9/4-4/1)
**Stoney End (USA)**, never far away, hung left over a quarter of a mile from home and had cooked his goose below the distance. (25/1)
**Bellacardia** was given a very quiet ride but caught the eye in no uncertain terms as she stayed on from below the distance to finish a promising seventh. She is now qualified for handicaps and, over further, looks one to keep an eye on. (33/1)
**Sea Idol (IRE)** (12/1: op 7/1)

## 1172 OASTWELL WINES H'CAP (0-80) (3-Y.O) (Class D)
7-30 (7-32) **7f** £4,424.25 (£1,326.00: £637.50: £293.25) Stalls: High GOING minus 0.07 sec per fur (G)

SP RR SF
709[4] **Ashjar (USA) (77)** (HThomsonJones) **3-9-7** GCarter(7) (lw: mde virtually all: rdn out) ......— **1** 13/2 88 60
861[3] **Silver Harrow (58)** (AGNewcombe) **3-8-2** SSanders(6) (a.p: rdn over 2f out: r.o one pce) ......2 **2** 14/1 64 36
1042* **Mister Woodstick (IRE) (53)** (MAJarvis) **3-7-11** GBardwell(13) (a.p: rdn over 4f out: ev ch wl over 1f out: one pce fnl f) ......2½ **3** 13/2 54 26
444[17] **Worldwide Elsie (USA) (75)** (RHarris) **3-9-5** AMackay(8) (lw: hld up: rdn over 2f out: one pce) ......¾ **4** 12/1 74 46
775[5] **White Plains (IRE) (67)** (MBell) **3-8-11** MFenton(4) (lw: hld up: rdn over 2f out: one pce) ......s.h **5** 7/2 1 66 38
978[3] **Ed's Folly (IRE) (57)** (SDow) **3-7-10**(5) ADaly(3) (lw: chsd wnr over 4f: wknd over 1f out) ......1½ **6** 6/1 3 53 25
734[5] **Nakhal (61)** (DJGMurraySmith) **3-8-2v**(3)ow2 DaneO'Neill(14) (nvr nr to chal) ......hd **7** 12/1 56 26
978[4] **Moi Canard (59)** (BAPearce) **3-7-12**(5) MHenry(10) (hld up: rdn 3f out: wknd over 1f out) ......1½ **8** 11/2 2 51 23
641[14] **Just Millie (USA) (73)** (JEBanks) **3-9-0**(3) JStack(9) (a bhd) ......s.h **9** 14/1 65 37
983[17] **Henry Otis (65)** (RAkehurst) **3-8-2**(7) DDenby(5) (lw: a bhd) ......10 **10** 16/1 34 6
888[12] **Sunset Harbour (IRE) (52)** (TJNaughton) **3-7-10** FNorton(11) (a bhd) ......¾ **11** 25/1 19 —
496[9] **Sheilana (IRE) (71)** (TGMills) **3-8-8**(7) JCornally(2) (bhd fnl 2f) ......2½ **12** 20/1 32 4
1073[14] **Grey Legend (55)** (RMFlower) **3-7-13** DeclanO'Shea(1) (lw: a bhd) ......5 **13** 25/1 5 —
(SP 125.6%) **13 Rn**

**1m 24.76** (3.16) CSF £88.12 CT £586.95 TOTE £6.40: £2.70 £3.80 £3.90 (£45.00) Trio £104.10 OWNER Mr Hamdan Al Maktoum (NEWMARKET) BRED Shadwell Estate Company Limited
**709 Ashjar (USA)** made no mistake here. Racing against the favoured stands' rail, he made all the running to give his trainer his first winner of the season. (13/2: 4/1-7/1)
**861 Silver Harrow**, always close up, struggled on to take second place, but never looked like threatening the winner. (14/1)
**1042* Mister Woodstick (IRE)** was almost on terms with the winner early in the final quarter-mile before tapped for toe. (13/2)
**Worldwide Elsie (USA)** failed to find the necessary turn of foot in the last two furlongs. (12/1: op 8/1)
**775 White Plains (IRE)** could only go up and down in the same place in the final quarter-mile. (7/2: 5/1-100/30)
**978 Ed's Folly (IRE)**, in second place until over a quarter of a mile out, had burnt his boats below the distance. (6/1)
**978 Moi Canard** (11/2: 4/1-6/1)

## 1173 S.G.B./YOUNGMAN H'CAP (0-70) (3-Y.O+) (Class E)
8-00 (8-03) **1m 2f** £3,561.60 (£1,066.80: £512.40: £235.20) Stalls: Low GOING minus 0.07 sec per fur (G)

SP RR SF
1047[7] **It'sthebusiness (51)** (SDow) **4-8-11v** TQuinn(15) (led 8f out: clr 2f out: r.o wl) ......— **1** 12/1 60 36
*553[4]* **Wet Patch (IRE) (60)** (RHannon) **4-9-6** RHughes(2) (lw: hdwy over 3f out: chsd wnr over 1f out: unable qckn) ......3½ **2** 6/1 2 63 39
*1031[5]* **Zaaleff (USA) (50)** (BHanbury) **4-8-7b**(3) JStack(8) (lw: rdn over 3f out: gd hdwy over 1f out: str run fnl f: fin wl) ......1¾ **3** 6/1 2 51 27
738[4] **Contrafire (IRE) (68)** (WJarvis) **4-10-0** SSanders(4) (lw: hld up: rdn over 2f out: one pce) ......nk **4** 6/1 2 68 44
1047[11] **Digpast (IRE) (57)** (RJO'Sullivan) **6-9-3b** DBiggs(16) (lw: s.s: hdwy over 1f out: one pce) ......nk **5** 16/1 57 33
995[10] **Mr Rough (61)** (DMorris) **5-9-7** RCochrane(13) (rdn & hdwy over 2f out: one pce) ......1½ **6** 9/2 1 58 34
817[11] **Roi de la Mer (IRE) (61)** (JAkehurst) **5-9-7** GCarter(11) (nvr plcd to chal) ......½ **7** 14/1 57 33
**Persian Conquest (IRE) (60)** (RIngram) **4-9-6b** BDoyle(12) (lw: led 2f: hrd rdn over 2f out: wknd fnl f) ......¾ **8** 10/1 55 31
1012[4] **The Little Ferret (50)** (AMoore) **6-8-10** RPerham(14) (lw: prom 8f) ......nk **9** 16/1 45 21
**East Sheen (48)** (CJBenstead) **4-8-8** CRutter(10) (bhd fnl 4f) ......6 **10** 20/1 33 9
979[10] **Abtaal (60)** (RJHodges) **6-9-6** AMcGlone(5) (lw: hld up: rdn over 3f out: wknd over 2f out) ......hd **11** 33/1 45 21
*106[4]* **Sweet Allegiance (50)** (JRPoulton) **6-8-7**(3) PMcCabe(6) (a bhd) ......¾ **12** 33/1 34 10
979[6] **Scorpius (50)** (TTClement) **6-8-10** GBardwell(7) (t: b: lw: prom over 6f) ......3½ **13** 14/1 28 4
872[20] **Rasmi (CAN) (58)** (PHowling) **5-9-4** FNorton(3) (lw: hld up: rdn over 3f out: wknd over 2f out) ......s.h **14** 25/1 36 12
635[9] **Double Rush (IRE) (50)** (TGMills) **4-8-10** MarkLynch(9) (prom over 6f) ......1¾ **15** 8/1 3 25 1
(SP 128.5%) **15 Rn**

**2m 11.43** (6.73) CSF £80.75 CT £447.94 TOTE £11.60: £3.90 £2.00 £2.70 (£49.10) Trio £61.00 OWNER Eurostrait Ltd (EPSOM) BRED Eurostrait Ltd

OFFICIAL EXPLANATION **Roi de la Mer (IRE): the jockey's instructions were to drop his mount in and cover him up for a run, but the horse did not seem suited by the course, did not come down the hill well, and was short of room late on.**
**East Sheen: lost her near-fore plate during the race and was found to be sore the following morning.**
**636 It'sthebusiness** at last came good at the fourteenth attempt. Soon at the head of affairs, he forged clear a quarter of a mile out. (12/1)
**553 Wet Patch (IRE)** never looked like reeling in the winner. (6/1: op 4/1)
**1031 Zaaleff (USA)**, in last place and with absolutely no chance entering the straight, went into turbo-drive from below the distance and came storming through to take third place. (6/1)
**738 Contrafire (IRE)** failed to find the necessary turn of foot in the last two furlongs. A mile and a half is probably better for him. (6/1: op 4/1)
**Digpast (IRE)**, as usual, lost ground at the start. He tried to get into it below the distance, but could then make no further impression. (16/1)
**636 Mr Rough** moved up over two furlongs form home, but was then only treading water. (9/2)
**649 Roi de la Mer (IRE)** was given such a quiet ride that punters would have been forgiven for thinking his jockey had fallen asleep. He caught the eye in no uncertain terms as he weaved his way through the pack in the last two furlong to finish a highly-promising seventh. The Stewards quite rightly enquired into this performance, but decided to accept the explanations given. Winner of a selling handicap at Sandown last year, he looks one to keep a very close eye on, especially if dropped in class. (14/1: 10/1-16/1)
**979 Scorpius** (14/1: 12/1-20/1)

## 1174 F. T. EVERARD & SONS MAIDEN STKS (3-Y.O+) (Class D)

8-30 (8-32) **1m 1f** £4,125.90 (£1,234.20: £591.60: £270.30) Stalls: Low GOING minus 0.07 sec per fur (G)

| | Horse | Dist | Pos | SP | RR | SF |
|---|---|---|---|---|---|---|
| 1045[3] | **Major Dundee (IRE) (84)** (RHannon) **3-8-8**(3) DaneO'Neill(5) (lw: a.p: chsd wnr fnl 2f: hrd rdn & led last stride) | — | **1** | 9/2[3] | 77 | 15 |
| 982[2] | **Kamari (USA)** (ACStewart) **3-8-11** WCarson(4) (lw: a gng wl: led: hrd hld fnl 3f: shkn up last strides: hdd line) | s.h | **2** | 4/5[1] | 77+ | 15 |
| 994[5] | **Pep Talk (USA)** (HRACecil) **3-8-11** AMcGlone(7) (chsd ldr 7f: unable qckn) | 2 | **3** | 100/30[2] | 73 | 11 |
| | **Tea Party (USA)** (KOCunningham-Brown) **3-8-6** TQuinn(11) (w'like: lw: a.p: rdn over 2f out: one pce) | 3½ | **4** | 20/1 | 62 | — |
| 892[11] | **Gain Line (USA)** (RCharlton) **3-8-11** TSprake(12) (a.p: rdn over 2f out: one pce) | 1¼ | **5** | 14/1 | 65 | 3 |
| | **Classic Affair (USA)** (RHarris) **3-8-6** AMackay(6) (hdwy over 4f out: one pce fnl 3f) | hd | **6** | 20/1 | 60 | — |
| 678[16] | **Giddy** (DMorley) **3-8-7**ow1 RCochrane(3) (nvr plcd to chal) | s.h | **7** | 20/1 | 61 | — |
| 994[12] | **Mr Speculator** (PAKelleway) **3-8-4**(7) CDomergue(10) (hld up: rdn over 2f out: wknd over 1f out) | ½ | **8** | 66/1 | 64 | 2 |
| | **African Sun (IRE)** (BHanbury) **3-8-8**(3) JStack(8) (bhd fnl 4f) | 10 | **9** | 25/1 | 46 | — |
| 745[8] | **Ela-Ment (IRE)** (BAPearce) **4-9-10** SSanders(9) (bhd fnl 3f) | 13 | **10** | 100/1 | 23 | — |
| 870[11] | **Persephone** (ICampbell) **3-8-6** MTebbutt(2) (a wl bhd) | 10 | **11** | 100/1 | — | — |
| 471[12] | **Native Song (39)** (MJHaynes) **3-8-1b**(5) MBaird(1) (lw: a wl bhd) | 2½ | **12** | 66/1 | — | — |

(SP 126.6%) **12 Rn**

**1m 58.9** (8.40) CSF £8.63 TOTE £6.10: £1.50 £1.40 £1.20 (£4.20) Trio £4.20 OWNER Mr J. A. Leek (MARLBOROUGH) BRED Brittas House Stud
WEIGHT FOR AGE 3yo-13lb
STEWARDS' ENQUIRY Carson susp. 27-31/5 & 1 & 3/6/96 (failure to obtain best possible placing).
OFFICIAL EXPLANATION **Kamari (USA): the rider admitted that he failed to see the horse challenging on his left hand side.**
**1045 Major Dundee (IRE)** will surely be one of the luckiest winners of the season and full marks must go to O'Neill for his persistence and determination. On the quarters of the winner for the final quarter-mile, that rival appeared to be toying with him, but O'Neill kept badgering away at the colt and the combination managed to catch the napping runner-up right on the line. (9/2: 5/2-5/1)
**982 Kamari (USA)** was given a diabolical ride by Carson, for which there can be no excuse, especially from such a senior jockey. Travelling well in front, Carson had a tight rein on him in the straight and began to look over his right shoulder below the distance. However, the winner was snapping at his heels on his left-hand side but, for some reason, Carson did not seem to notice. Looking over his right shoulder no less than four times in the final furlong, he was only aware of the winner in the last few strides and, by then, it was too late. The Stewards handed him a seven-day suspension which is the maximum penalty allowed for a first offence of the season of this nature, but it was too light considering Carson's seniority and the money punters must have lost on this odds-on favourite. The Jockey Club needs to sit down and have a serious rethink about penalties for this rule. Aggrieved punters should recoup losses on Kamari next time out. (4/5)
**994 Pep Talk (USA)**, in second place until the two-furlong marker, could then only struggle on at one pace. (100/30)
**Tea Party (USA)** looked in good shape for his debut. Always handy, she failed to find the necessary turn of foot in the straight. (20/1)
**Gain Line (USA)** failed to quicken in the last three furlongs. (14/1: 8/1-16/1)
**Classic Affair (USA)** was only treading water in the straight. (20/1)

T/Plpt: £186.40 (54.51 Tckts). T/Qdpt: £64.20 (11.09 Tckts). AK

# 1142-NEWBURY (L-H) (Good becoming Soft)
## Saturday May 18th

WEATHER: fine WIND: mod half bhd

## 1175 LONDON GOLD CUP RATED STKS H'CAP (0-95) (3-Y.O) (Class C)

2-00 (2-00) **1m 4f 5y** £9,539.60 (£3,556.40: £1,728.20: £731.00: £315.50: £149.30) Stalls: Low GOING: 0.33 sec per fur (G)

| | Horse | Dist | Pos | SP | RR | SF |
|---|---|---|---|---|---|---|
| 923[3] | **Samraan (USA) (90)** (JLDunlop) **3-9-5** TQuinn(9) (chsd ldrs: rdn over 4f out: swtchd rt over 1f out: r.o wl to ld last stride) | — | **1** | 4/1[2] | 101 | 59 |
| 947[4] | **Nador (88)** (DRLoder) **3-9-3** RHughes(3) (hld up & bhd: stdy hdwy 3f out: led wl over 1f out: hdd last stride) | hd | **2** | 10/1 | 99 | 57 |
| 702* | **Nabhaan (IRE) (83)** (DMorley) **3-8-12** WCarson(4) (lw: hld up: rdn 5f out: nt clr run on ins 3f out & over 1f out: swtchd rt ins fnl f: squeezed thro: fin wl) | s.h | **3** | 3/1[1] | 94+ | 52 |
| 1071[4] | **Burnt Offering (78)** (CEBrittain) **3-8-7** BDoyle(8) (a.p: wnt 2nd over 4f out: led over 2f out tl wl over 1f out: one pce fnl f) | 4 | **4** | 25/1 | 84 | 42 |
| 1002[7] | **Al's Alibi (78)** (WRMuir) **3-8-7** MJKinane(6) (led tl over 2f out: eased whn btn ins fnl f) | 6 | **5** | 4/1[2] | 76 | 34 |
| | **Warbrook (92)** (IABalding) **3-9-7** RCochrane(2) (lw: chsd ldr over 7f: sn rdn: wknd wl over 2f out) | 5 | **6** | 9/1[3] | 83 | 41 |
| 731[5] | **Nosey Native (80)** (JPearce) **3-8-9** GBardwell(1) (bhd: hrd rdn 3f out: no rspnse) | ¾ | **7** | 9/1[3] | 70 | 28 |
| | **Exalted (IRE) (89)** (SirMarkPrescott) **3-9-4** SSanders(10) (hld up: hrd rdn & wknd wl over 1f out) | 2 | **8** | 16/1 | 76 | 34 |

$969^{5}$ **Clouds Hill (FR) (78)** (RHannon) **3-8-4**(3) DaneO'Neill(7) (a bhd: t.o fnl 3f) ....................22 **9** 12/1 36 —
(SP 111.5%) **9 Rn**

**2m 40.5** (10.50) CSF £37.38 CT £119.81 TOTE £4.70: £1.80 £2.60 £1.40 (£25.30) Trio £20.00 OWNER Mr K. M. Al-Mudhaf (ARUNDEL) BRED Mrs Afaf A. Al Essa

LONG HANDICAP Burnt Offering 7-13 Clouds Hill (FR) 8-5

**923 Samraan (USA),** who is still in the Italian Derby, appreciated the drop into handicap company, but would not have scored had Nabhaan had any sort of run. (4/1: 5/2-9/2)

**947 Nador** stayed the trip well enough and, benefiting from the trouble behind, only got touched off on the line. (10/1: 7/1-11/1)

**702* Nabhaan (IRE)** encountered all sorts of trouble in running and it is hard to visualize an unluckier loser all season. This kicked off a day to forget for Carson. (3/1)

**1071 Burnt Offering** gave a good account of himself from 8lb out of the handicap. (25/1)

**731* Al's Alibi** did not like the soft ground but was 6lb higher than when successful over course and distance last month. (4/1)

**Warbrook** should have been suited by this longer trip but perhaps ground conditions were against him. (9/1)

**731 Nosey Native** (9/1: 5/1-10/1)

**969 Clouds Hill (FR)** (12/1: op 8/1)

## 1176 QUANTEL ASTON PARK STKS (Listed) (4-Y.O+) (Class A)

2-30 (2-31) **1m 5f 61y** £12,185.00 (£3,680.00: £1,790.00: £845.00) Stalls: Low GOING: 0.33 sec per fur (G)

| | | | SP | RR | SF |
|---|---|---|---|---|---|
| $1017^{2}$ | **Election Day (IRE) (111)** (MRStoute) **4-8-12** WCarson(6) (lw: a.p: led over 1f out: rdn out) .......— | **1** | 5/2 ² | 120 | 61 |
| $1017^{3}$ | **Minds Music (USA) (114)** (HRACecil) **4-9-1** PatEddery(10) (lw: chsd ldr: hrd rdn to ld wl over 1f out: sn hdd: one pce) .......4 | **2** | 9/4 ¹ | 118 | 59 |
| | **Posidonas (116)** (PFICole) **4-9-7** TQuinn(8) (lw: plld hrd early: led: rdn & hdd wl over 1f out: wknd fnl f).......9 | **3** | 8/1 | 113 | 54 |
| 828* | **Suplizi (IRE) (110)** (LMCumani) **5-8-12** RHughes(9) (hld up: rdn 3f out: wknd 2f out) .......6 | **4** | 4/1 ³ | 97 | 38 |
| | **Arctic Thunder (USA) (97)** (LadyHerries) **5-8-12** TSprake(2) (b: hld up & bhd: sme hdwy on ins over 3f out: wknd over 2f out).......5 | **5** | 16/1 | 91 | 32 |
| $929^{3}$ | **Djais (FR) (95)** (JRJenkins) **7-8-12** RCochrane(7) (a bhd: t.o fnl 3f) .......14 | **6** | 33/1 | 74 | 15 |
| | **Cuff Link (IRE) (106)** (MajorWRHern) **6-8-12** PaulEddery(11) (hld up: rdn over 4f out: wknd 3f out: t.o) .......6 | **7** | 25/1 | 67 | 8 |
| 965* | **Proposing (IRE) (96)** (JHMGosden) **4-8-12** MJKinane(4) (hld up & bhd: rdn over 3f out: sn t.o) .......28 | **8** | 7/1 | 33 | — |

(SP 115.6%) **8 Rn**

**2m 56.66** (10.16) CSF £8.35 TOTE £2.90: £1.60 £1.30 £1.50 (£3.70) Trio £11.40 OWNER Lord Weinstock & The Hon Simon Weinstock (NEWMARKET) BRED Ballymacoll Stud Farm Ltd

**1017 Election Day (IRE)** confirmed the Chester form with the second on 3lb better terms and is beginning to look the finished article, but whether he can turn the tables on Oscar Schindler should they meet in the Hardwicke at Royal Ascot remains to be seen. (5/2)

**1017 Minds Music (USA)** was 3lb worse off with the winner here than when finishing a short-head behind him in the Ormonde Stakes at Chester. (9/4)

**Posidonas** won a Group One in Milan in the mud last year, but did not help his cause by running too keen early on here. (8/1)

**828* Suplizi (IRE)** may have found the ground too soft. (4/1: 3/1-9/2)

**Arctic Thunder (USA)** found this company too hot. (16/1)

## 1177 JUDDMONTE LOCKINGE STKS (Gp 1) (4-Y.O+) (Class A)

3-00 (3-04) **1m (straight)** £74,731.00 (£27,876.05: £13,313.03: £5,714.92) Stalls: Centre GOING: 0.33 sec per fur (G)

| | | | SP | RR | SF |
|---|---|---|---|---|---|
| $810^{2}$ | **Soviet Line (IRE) (120)** (MRStoute) **6-9-0** TQuinn(1) (lw: w ldr: led & edgd lft wl over 1f out: all out).......— | **1** | 13/2 ³ | 128 | 51 |
| | **Charnwood Forest (IRE)** (SbinSuroor) **4-9-0** MJKinane(2) (lw: hld up: rdn & ev ch over 1f out: r.o ins fnl f) ..nk | **2** | 3/1 ² | 127 | 50 |
| 906a$^{4}$ | **Spectrum (IRE) (120)** (PWChapple-Hyam) **4-9-0** JReid(5) (lw: hld up: hdwy over 2f out: rdn over 1f out: r.o one pce) .......4 | **3** | 11/10 ¹ | 119 | 42 |
| $680^{2}$ | **Smart Alec (110)** (LMCumani) **4-9-0** RCochrane(7) (lw: hld up: rdn & ev ch 2f out: one pce) .......nk | **4** | 8/1 | 119 | 42 |
| 810* | **Gabr (113)** (RWArmstrong) **6-9-0** WCarson(3) (lw: led over 6f: eased whn btn ins fnl f).......8 | **5** | 10/1 | 103 | 26 |
| $810^{4}$ | **Nwaamis (USA) (110)** (JLDunlop) **4-9-0** PatEddery(4) (prom tl rdn & wknd over 2f out) .......13 | **6** | 14/1 | 77 | — |
| | **Brief Glimpse (IRE) (106)** (MajorDNChappell) **4-8-11** MHills(6) (rdn over 3f out: a bhd: t.o).......4 | **7** | 50/1 | 66 | — |

(SP 114.8%) **7 Rn**

**1m 44.22** (7.22) CSF £25.12 TOTE £6.20: £2.60 £2.20 (£9.40) OWNER Maktoum Al Maktoum (NEWMARKET) BRED Cheveley Park Stud Ltd

**810 Soviet Line (IRE),** at level weights this time, did not mind the rain-softened ground and became the first horse since Welsh Pageant to win this race two years in succession. He is probably still worth opposing when he does not have a left-hand rail to race against. (13/2: 4/1-7/1)

**Charnwood Forest (IRE)** looked in fine shape after a winter in Dubai, but would have preferred better ground and ran a fine race in defeat. He goes for the Queen Anne at Royal Ascot without any penalties and, given decent ground, will be the one they all have to beat. (3/1: 9/4-7/2)

**906a Spectrum (IRE),** back to a mile, should have been suited by the soft ground, but never really seemed likely to score. It had been a bad week for the stable and it may well be that they are not firing on all cylinders. (11/10)

**680 Smart Alec,** continuing on the comeback trail, had never encountered this sort of ground but kept plugging away to the end. (8/1)

**810* Gabr** could not go with the winner in the final quarter-mile on 6lb worse terms than when scraping home at Sandown. (10/1)

## 1178 WINCHESTER H'CAP (0-90) (3-Y.O+) (Class C)

3-30 (3-32) **6f 8y** £5,614.50 (£1,686.00: £813.00: £376.50) Stalls: Centre GOING: 0.33 sec per fur (G)

| | | | SP | RR | SF |
|---|---|---|---|---|---|
| $928^{16}$ | **Thatcherella (68)** (MajorDNChappell) **5-8-10** BThomson(14) (a.p: led over 2f out: clr over 1f out: drvn out) ..— | **1** | 10/1 | 83 | 49 |
| $692^{4}$ | **Domak Amaam (IRE) (76)** (JHMGosden) **3-8-9** MJKinane(10) (hld up: hdwy over 2f out: hrd rdn over 1f out: r.o ins fnl f) .......¾ | **2** | 13/2 ² | 89 | 46 |
| *896** | **Intiaash (IRE) (74)** (DHaydnJones) **4-8-11**(5) MartinDwyer(9) (a.p: rdn over 1f out: one pce).......4 | **3** | 16/1 | 76 | 42 |
| $928^{8}$ | **Bowden Rose (85)** (MBlanshard) **4-9-13b** RCochrane(7) (w ldrs: one pce fnl 2f) .......3½ | **4** | 20/1 | 78 | 44 |
| $1064^{10}$ | **Louisville Belle (IRE) (54)** (MDIUsher) **7-7-10** NAdams(8) (hld up: edgd rt over 1f out: nvr nr to chal).......nk | **5** | 50/1 | 46 | 12 |
| $1078^{6}$ | **Golden Pound (USA) (83)** (MissGayKelleway) **4-9-8b**(3) DaneO'Neill(13) (lw: racd alone stands' side: led 4f out tl over 2f out: wknd over 1f out).......½ | **6** | 14/1 | 74 | 40 |
| $1073^{2}$ | **How's Yer Father (79)** (RJHodges) **10-9-7** PatEddery(6) (rdn over 3f out: no hdwy fnl 2f) .......hd | **7** | 6/1 ¹ | 70 | 36 |
| $928^{20}$ | **Bayin (USA) (73)** (MDIUsher) **7-9-1** RStreet(5) (hld up: nvr nr to chal) .......nk | **8** | 14/1 | 63 | 29 |
| $648^{4}$ | **Persian Butterfly (68)** (ICampbell) **4-8-10** SSanders(11) (s.i.s: a bhd).......2½ | **9** | 12/1 | 51 | 17 |
| $1064^{2}$ | **Tart and a Half (79)** (BJMeehan) **4-9-7b** BDoyle(3) (prom over 3f).......s.h | **10** | 10/1 | 62 | 28 |
| 846* | **Latching (IRE) (85)** (RFJohnsonHoughton) **4-9-13** JReid(4) (w ldrs over 3f).......1½ | **11** | 10/1 | 64 | 30 |

| | | Dist | Pos | SP | RR | SF |
|---|---|---|---|---|---|---|
| 1064[5] | **Sir Joey (USA) (82)** (PGMurphy) **7-9-7**(3) SDrowne(1) (a bhd) | 5 | **12** | 9/1 | 48 | 14 |
| 893[10] | **Oggi (64)** (PJMakin) **5-8-6b** PaulEddery(12) (hrd rdn over 2f out: no rspnse) | ½ | **13** | 7/1[3] | 29 | — |
| 814[11] | **Sailormaite (80)** (SRBowring) **5-9-8** RPrice(2) (led 2f: wknd over 2f out) | 1 | **14** | 12/1 | 42 | 8 |
| | | | | (SP 118.7%) | **14 Rn** | |

**1m 17.0** (5.20) CSF £67.28 CT £951.41 TOTE £12.20: £3.10 £2.40 £4.80 (£37.70) Trio £331.40 OWNER Mr J. H. Widdows (WHITSBURY) BRED M. L. Page

LONG HANDICAP Louisville Belle (IRE) 7-5

WEIGHT FOR AGE 3yo-9lb

**Thatcherella** did not mind the cut in the ground and had slipped down the ratings to a mark 1lb lower than when winning at Chepstow a year ago. (10/1)

**892 Domak Amaam (IRE)**, taking on older opposition this time, is knocking at the door and a return to seven could be on the cards. (13/2)

**896* Intiaash (IRE)** again showed she is in good form in this hotter event. (16/1)

**Bowden Rose**, racing off a mark 6lb higher than her last win, ran well on ground too soft for her. (20/1)

**Louisville Belle (IRE)** has never won on ground worse than good and put up a respectable performance from 5lb out of the handicap. (50/1)

**1078 Golden Pound (USA)**, reverting to six furlongs, may have found the ground too testing. (14/1)

**1073 How's Yer Father**, not successful since October 1994, has never scored on ground worse than good to soft. (6/1)

## 1179 KINGWOOD STUD MAIDEN STKS (2-Y.O F) (Class D)

4-00 (4-03) **6f 8y** £3,574.00 (£1,072.00: £516.00: £238.00) Stalls: Centre GOING: 0.33 sec per fur (G)

| | | Dist | Pos | SP | RR | SF |
|---|---|---|---|---|---|---|
| 916[3] | **March Star (IRE)** (JARToller) **2-8-11** WCarson(6) (w ldr: led over 3f out: pushed out) | — | **1** | 11/4[1] | 68 | 41 |
| | **Maid By The Fire (USA)** (PFICole) **2-8-11** TQuinn(5) (leggy: s.i.s: hdwy & rdn over 2f out: ev ch fnl f: r.o) | nk | **2** | 3/1[2] | 67 | 40 |
| | **Simple Logic** (AGFoster) **2-8-11** TSprake(2) (tall: s.s: wl bhd tl hdwy 2f out: nrst fin) | 1¾ | **3** | 25/1 | 63 | 36 |
| | **Raindancing (IRE)** (RHannon) **2-8-11** PatEddery(4) (w'like: w ldrs: ev ch over 1f out: eased whn btn ins fnl f) | 2 | **4** | 6/1[3] | 57 | 30 |
| | **Dashing Rocksville** (MRChannon) **2-8-11** RHughes(1) (w'like: scope: outpcd: wl bhd fnl 3f) | 8 | **5** | 7/1 | 36 | 9 |
| 729[2] | **Copperbeech (IRE)** (PWChapple-Hyam) **2-8-11** JReid(3) (led over 2f: wknd qckly) | 6 | **6** | 3/1[2] | 20 | — |
| | | | | (SP 107.3%) | **6 Rn** | |

**1m 17.71** (5.91) CSF £10.28 TOTE £4.50: £1.60 £1.80 (£3.50) OWNER Mr G. M. Cobey (WHITSBURY) BRED Noel O'Callaghan

**916 March Star (IRE)** went with the leaders, despite having been difficult in the stalls. She gained a slight advantage over three furlongs out and needed only to be pushed along to win narrowly but decisively. (11/4)

**Maid By The Fire (USA)** jumped off well enough but failed to go the pace. She had to be ridden into a challenging position over two furlongs out and drew almost level with the winner, but could never force her head in front. (3/1: 7/4-100/30)

**Simple Logic** lost many lengths at the start and appeared likely to finish tailed off for a long way, but she grasped the idea from halfway and finished in fine style. She will certainly stay further. (25/1)

**Raindancing (IRE)** looked the main danger to the winner for most of the way, but lack of experience told late on, and the position was accepted. She will certainly win races. (6/1: op 4/1)

**Dashing Rocksville** failed to go the pace. (7/1: 4/1-8/1)

**729 Copperbeech (IRE)** made the early running looking to be travelling strongly, but distress signals were being shown before halfway. (3/1)

## 1180 DENNIS TOWNSEND 70TH BIRTHDAY MAIDEN STKS (I) (3-Y.O) (Class D)

4-30 (4-31) **1m 2f 6y** £3,314.00 (£992.00: £476.00: £218.00) Stalls: Low GOING: 0.33 sec per fur (G)

| | | Dist | Pos | SP | RR | SF |
|---|---|---|---|---|---|---|
| | **Harbour Dues** (LadyHerries) **3-9-0** RCochrane(2) (lw: s.s: stdy hdwy 3f out: qcknd to ld wl ins fnl f: r.o) | — | **1** | 20/1 | 80 | 20 |
| 730[6] | **Bechstein** (JLDunlop) **3-9-0** TQuinn(13) (a.p: led over 2f out tl wl ins fnl f) | nk | **2** | 15/2 | 80 | 20 |
| 845[2] | **Count Basie** (HRACecil) **3-9-0** PatEddery(6) (a.p: rdn 2f out: r.o ins fnl f) | 3 | **3** | 2/1[1] | 75 | 15 |
| | **Arctiid (USA)** (JHMGosden) **3-9-0** MJKinane(12) (w ldr: led 3f out: sn hdd: r.o one pce) | nk | **4** | 10/1 | 74 | 14 |
| 934[4] | **Battle Spark (USA)** (CACyzer) **3-9-0** WJO'Connor(5) (a.p: one pce fnl 3f) | 1¼ | **5** | 33/1 | 72 | 12 |
| | **Dalwhinnie** (JWHills) **3-8-4**(5) MHenry(7) (hld up: hdwy to chal over 1f out: btn whn n.m.r & eased ins fnl f) | 2 | **6** | 50/1 | 64 | 4 |
| 1079[9] | **King Rufus** (JRArnold) **3-9-0** DHarrison(9) (hld up & bhd: nvr nr to chal) | ¾ | **7** | 16/1 | 68 | 8 |
| | **Skillington (USA) (96)** (IABalding) **3-9-0** MHills(3) (hld up: effrt & rdn over 2f out: sn wknd) | 10 | **8** | 7/2[2] | 52 | — |
| 948[9] | **Mathon (IRE)** (MRChannon) **3-9-0** RHughes(4) (a bhd) | 5 | **9** | 50/1 | 44 | — |
| 830[7] | **Amfortas (IRE)** (CEBrittain) **3-9-0** BDoyle(8) (in tch tl wknd over 2f out) | 5 | **10** | 5/1[3] | 36 | — |
| | **Gooseberry Pie** (RCharlton) **3-8-9** TSprake(10) (unf: led tl wknd 3f out) | 1½ | **11** | 10/1 | 29 | — |
| 588[4] | **Comic's Future (USA)** (PWChapple-Hyam) **3-8-9**(5) RHavlin(11) (lw: hdwy 7f out: rdn & wknd qckly over 3f out: sn t.o) | dist | **12** | 25/1 | — | — |
| | | | | (SP 123.5%) | **12 Rn** | |

**2m 16.86** (13.06) CSF £153.67 TOTE £21.30: £4.20 £1.90 £1.30 (£61.40) Trio £35.20 OWNER Hesmonds Stud (LITTLEHAMPTON) BRED Hesmonds Stud Ltd

**Harbour Dues**, dropped out last at the start, came with a steady run from the three-furlong pole. Shaken up in earnest in the last 200 yards, he quickened readily to lead in the final 75 yards. (20/1)

**730 Bechstein**, with the leaders throughout, had a battle-royal from the three-furlong pole but, having seen off many rivals, found the winner's late run just too much. (15/2: 5/1-8/1)

**845 Count Basie**, always close up, appeared to be travelling well halfway up the straight. When rousted along, he took a while to realise what was required and it was too late when he ran on in the final 200 yards. (2/1)

**Arctiid (USA)** ran a fine race for an inexperienced colt, and was not given a hard time when it was clear his chance of winning had gone. (10/1: 7/1-12/1)

**934 Battle Spark (USA)**, always on the heels of the leaders, kept on at one pace in the closing stages. (33/1)

**Dalwhinnie** was coming with a promising run when short of room approaching the final furlong. She would probably not have finished nearer than third at best, but should be able to win a race. (50/1)

**Skillington (USA)** appeared to be travelling well enough on the heels of the leaders to the three-furlong pole but, when asked for his effort, was all at sea on the soft ground. He is worth another chance. (7/2)

**Gooseberry Pie** (10/1: 4/1-12/1)

## 1181 HEADLEY H'CAP (0-80) (3-Y.O F) (Class D)

5-00 (5-03) **7f 64y (round)** £4,029.00 (£1,212.00: £586.00: £273.00) Stalls: Low GOING: 0.33 sec per fur (G)

| | | Dist | Pos | SP | RR | SF |
|---|---|---|---|---|---|---|
| 888[8] | **Capilano Princess (72)** (DHaydnJones) **3-9-1** AMackay(1) (hmpd on ins over 4f out: hdwy 3f out: led over 1f out: r.o) | — | **1** | 20/1 | 84 | 28 |

| Form | Horse | Dist | Pos | SP | RR | SF |
|---|---|---|---|---|---|---|
| | **Commin' Up (67)** (JWHills) **3-8-10** MHills(2) (hld up in rr: stdy hdwy over 2f out: nrst fin) | 1½ | **2** | 16/1 | 76 | 20 |
| 917[2] | **Golden Pond (IRE) (71)** (RFJohnsonHoughton) **3-9-0** JReid(5) (lw: hld up: chal & ev ch over 2f out: nt qckn) | hd | **3** | 5/1[1] | 80 | 24 |
| 949[2] | **Petit Point (IRE) (70)** (RHannon) **3-8-13** PatEddery(13) (hdwy 3f out: ev ch over 1f out: wknd ins fnl f) | 7 | **4** | 15/2 | 63 | 7 |
| 686[5] | **Sondos (67)** (JWHills) **3-8-5**(5) MHenry(3) (lw: a.p: led 2f out: sn hdd: wknd fnl f) | nk | **5** | 12/1 | 60 | 4 |
| | **Al Shadeedah (USA) (78)** (LMCumani) **3-9-7** MJKinane(4) (lw: hdwy on ins over 2f out: wknd over 1f out) | 6 | **6** | 7/1[3] | 57 | 1 |
| 824* | **Antonias Melody (73)** (SRBowring) **3-8-11**(5) CTeague(6) (led tl wknd 2f out) | nk | **7** | 8/1 | 52 | — |
| 915[2] | **Green Gem (BEL) (69)** (SCWilliams) **3-8-12** BDoyle(11) (a bhd) | 3½ | **8** | 9/1 | 40 | — |
| | **Queen's Insignia (USA) (65)** (PFICole) **3-8-8** TQuinn(14) (nvr bttr than mid div) | hd | **9** | 7/1[3] | 36 | — |
| 775[3] | **Sharp 'n' Shady (59)** (CFWall) **3-8-2** WLord(12) (lw: bhd tl hdwy 3f out: wknd over 1f out) | 2½ | **10** | 6/1[2] | 24 | — |
| 840[11] | **Tiama (IRE) (62)** (SDow) **3-8-2**(3)ow2 DaneO'Neill(10) (a bhd) | 5 | **11** | 33/1 | 16 | — |
| 692[12] | **Victim of Love (65)** (RCharlton) **3-8-8** SSanders(8) (prom tl rdn & wknd qckly 3f out) | s.h | **12** | 16/1 | 19 | — |
| 888[11] | **Jubilee Place (IRE) (72)** (TThomsonJones) **3-9-1** PaulEddery(9) (b: prom tl wknd qckly 3f out: t.o) | 10 | **13** | 20/1 | 4 | — |
| 1061[9] | **Volare (56)** (BJMeehan) **3-7-13** WCarson(7) (a bhd: t.o) | nk | **14** | 16/1 | — | — |

(SP 126.6%) **14 Rn**

**1m 36.86** (8.76) CSF £280.37 CT £1156.95 TOTE £48.90: £9.60 £5.50 £1.60 (£304.10) Trio £791.40; £501.59 to Newbury 19/5/96 OWNER Mr H. G. Collis (PONTYPRIDD) BRED Mrs O. M. Collis

**Capilano Princess**, drawn on the inside, had to be snatched up on the home turn and lost several places. In the circumstances, she did well to win. (20/1)

**Commin' Up**, anchored on leaving the stalls and dropped out in last, clearly takes a strong hold and her rider skilfully settled her. Coming with a steady run in the straight, she could not quite catch the winner, but should be able to win a race. (16/1)

**917 Golden Pond (IRE)**, patiently ridden, moved up to challenge approaching the final furlong, but could find no extra near the finish. (5/1)

**949 Petit Point (IRE)** came with a steady run on the outside to look dangerous below the distance, but tired on the soft ground in the final furlong. (15/2: 5/1-8/1)

**686 Sondos** was soon beaten when headed. (12/1: 8/1-14/1)

**Al Shadeedah (USA)**, having her first run of the season, came with a promising-looking challenge on the inside halfway up the straight, but the effort petered out below the distance. She will be better for the race. (7/1: op 9/2)

**915 Green Gem (BEL)** (9/1: 12/1-8/1)

## 1182 DENNIS TOWNSEND 70TH BIRTHDAY MAIDEN STKS (II) (3-Y.O) (Class D)

5-30 (5-32) **1m 2f 6y** £3,288.00 (£984.00: £472.00: £216.00) Stalls: Low GOING: 0.33 sec per fur (G)

| Form | Horse | Dist | Pos | SP | RR | SF |
|---|---|---|---|---|---|---|
| 892[2] | **Alzeus (IRE)** (CAHorgan) **3-9-0** PaulEddery(2) (a.p: led over 2f out tl over 1f out: hrd rdn & led jst ins fnl f: sn clr) | — | **1** | 11/2[3] | 83 | 13 |
| | **Sharaf Kabeer** (SbinSuroor) **3-9-0** MJKinane(12) (gd sort: chsd ldr: led over 1f out: hdd & rn green ins fnl f) | 5 | **2** | 6/4[1] | 75 | 5 |
| | **Palamon (USA)** (RCharlton) **3-9-0** PatEddery(8) (b: rdn & hdwy 3f out: ev ch over 1f out: nt qckn) | 5 | **3** | 4/1[2] | 67 | — |
| | **Queen Bee** (JLDunlop) **3-8-9** WCarson(9) (leggy: unf: hdwy fnl 2f: nvr nrr) | 3 | **4** | 10/1 | 57 | — |
| 1079[8] | **Seventh Edition** (DBurchell) **3-9-0** AProcter(4) (nvr nr to chal) | 1¾ | **5** | 50/1 | 60 | — |
| 942[6] | **Crown Court (USA)** (LMCumani) **3-9-0** MHills(11) (prom tl wknd 2f out) | nk | **6** | 20/1 | 59 | — |
| | **Lead Story (IRE)** (EALDunlop) **3-9-0** BDoyle(7) (w'like: scope: lw: nvr plcd to chal) | hd | **7** | 25/1 | 59 | — |
| | **Shaha** (RHannon) **3-8-11**(3) DaneO'Neill(5) (bit bkwd: prom tl wknd 2f out) | nk | **8** | 25/1 | 58 | — |
| | **Regal Eagle** (IABalding) **3-9-0** DHarrison(6) (led tl wknd over 2f out) | nk | **9** | 33/1 | 58 | — |
| | **King's Academy (IRE)** (HRACecil) **3-9-0** AMcGlone(13) (leggy: prom tl rdn & wknd qckly 2f out: t.o) | 14 | **10** | 7/1 | 36 | — |
| | **Sylvella** (MAJarvis) **3-8-9** PBloomfield(10) (bkwd: rdn over 3f out: a bhd: t.o) | 8 | **11** | 50/1 | 18 | — |
| | **Crest Wing (USA)** (PWChapple-Hyam) **3-9-0** JReid(3) (rangy: prom tl wknd over 2f out: t.o) | 5 | **12** | 10/1 | 15 | — |

(SP 125.4%) **12 Rn**

**2m 17.8** (14.00) CSF £14.27 TOTE £6.40: £1.50 £1.60 £1.50 (£6.40) Trio £7.80 OWNER Mrs B. Sumner (PULBOROUGH) BRED Stilvi and Roncon Ltd

**892 Alzeus (IRE)** took it up over two furlongs out. He looked beaten when headed but, rousted up in earnest, found a tremendous spurt to go clear. (11/2)

**Sharaf Kabeer**, a magnificent individual, made an encouraging debut. Settled in second, he appeared set for victory when taking it up going to the furlong pole, but ran green when pressure was applied. He will be hard to beat next time. (6/4)

**Palamon (USA)**, two thirds of the way down the field for a long way, came with a steady run to join the leaders below the distance but, put to his best, tired in the soft ground. (4/1: 5/2-9/2)

**Queen Bee**, behind for a long way, was running on steadily in the closing stages and should win, possibly over a longer trip. (10/1)

**Seventh Edition** raced in midfield until staying on inside the final furlong. (50/1)

**942 Crown Court (USA)** was close up until gradually weakening in the last two and a half furlongs. (20/1)

**Lead Story (IRE)**, behind for a long way, made some headway at the two-furlong pole, but could not reach a challenging position. After this third run, he is one to note for a handicap. (25/1)

**King's Academy (IRE)** (7/1: 9/2-15/2)

**Crest Wing (USA)** (10/1: 4/1-12/1)

T/Jkpt: £150,868.00 (0.2 Tckts); £169,992.18 to Newbury 19/5/96. T/Plpt: £35.90 (1,383.91 Tckts). T/Qdpt: £36.90 (37.56 Tckts). Hn

# 1155-THIRSK (L-H) (Good to firm)

## Saturday May 18th

WEATHER: fine WIND: almost nil

## 1183 SKIPTON CLAIMING STKS (2-Y.O) (Class F)

2-15 (2-16) **5f** £2,687.50 (£750.00: £362.50) Stalls: High GOING minus 0.17 sec per fur (GF)

| Form | Horse | Dist | Pos | SP | RR | SF |
|---|---|---|---|---|---|---|
| *1026** | **Fonzy** (MrsLStubbs) **2-8-8** JWeaver(1) (cl up: led over 1f out: styd on wl) | — | **1** | 13/2[3] | 59 | 30 |
| 1032[3] | **Lawful Find (IRE)** (RHollinshead) **2-8-6**ow1 KFallon(9) (chsd ldrs: hdwy over 1f out: styd on: nrst fin) | 1½ | **2** | 7/1 | 52 | 22 |
| 996[9] | **Full Traceability (IRE)** (JBerry) **2-8-2** JCarroll(6) (cl up: rdn 2f out: nt qckn) | nk | **3** | 11/4[2] | 47 | 18 |
| 977[4] | **Sharp But Fair** (SirMarkPrescott) **2-8-1** GDuffield(8) (led tl appr fnl f: no ex) | 1¼ | **4** | 9/4[1] | 42 | 13 |
| | **Petrine Gray** (TDEasterby) **2-8-4** MBirch(7) (w'like: bit bkwd: dwlt: hdwy ½-wy: wknd over 1f out) | 3½ | **5** | 8/1 | 34 | 5 |
| 975[7] | **Bellaf** (MWEasterby) **2-8-9**(5) GParkin(3) (sn outpcd & a bhd) | 3 | **6** | 16/1 | 34 | 5 |

| | Horse | | SP | RR | SF |
|---|---|---|---|---|---|
| | **In Good Nick** (MWEasterby) **2-8-6** DaleGibson(5) (small: neat: s.s: n.d) ....nk | **7** | 20/1 | 26 | — |
| 685[12] | **Classic Partygoer** (MWEasterby) **2-8-11** JFEgan(4) (outpcd & lost tch after 1½f) ....2 | **8** | 12/1 | 24 | — |
| | **Samspet** (RAFahey) **2-8-9** ACulhane(2) (cmpt: s.i.s: a outpcd & bhd) ....3½ | **9** | 16/1 | 11 | — |

(SP 118.6%) **9 Rn**

**60.8 secs** (2.80) CSF £47.87 TOTE £6.20: £1.50 £1.80 £1.50 (£20.70) Trio £15.90 OWNER The West Riding Partnership (WARTHILL) BRED J. and Mrs Rose

**1026* Fonzy** is only small but has a big heart, and proved too tough for this lot. (13/2)
**1032 Lawful Find (IRE)** gives the impression that another furlong would see improvement. (7/1)
**657* Full Traceability (IRE)** had her limitations well exposed late on. (11/4: op 9/2)
**977 Sharp But Fair** is improving and should win a small race. (9/4)
**Petrine Gray** is one of the few in this race with any scope, and showed ability. She should improve for the outing. (8/1: op 5/1)

## 1184 E.B.F. CARLTON MINIOTT MAIDEN STKS (2-Y.O) (Class D)

2-45 (2-45) **5f** £3,361.25 (£1,010.00: £487.50: £226.25) Stalls: High GOING minus 0.17 sec per fur (GF)

| | Horse | | SP | RR | SF |
|---|---|---|---|---|---|
| 958[4] | **Double Action** (TDEasterby) **2-9-0** MBirch(6) (mde all: hung bdly lft fnl 2f: kpt on wl) ....— | **1** | 4/7[1] | 71 | 42 |
| 865[4] | **Fredrik The Fierce (IRE)** (JBerry) **2-9-0** KDarley(3) (lw: trckd ldrs: ev ch 1f out: nt qckn towards fin) ....½ | **2** | 11/2[2] | 69 | 40 |
| | **Rum Lad** (JJQuinn) **2-9-0** NConnorton(1) (str: s.i.s: sn prom: nt qckn fnl f) ....5 | **3** | 9/1 | 53 | 24 |
| | **Noble Dancer (IRE)** (MDHammond) **2-9-0** KFallon(4) (leggy: a.p: nt qckn fnl 2f) ....s.h | **4** | 15/2[3] | 53 | 24 |
| 1036[6] | **Brawling Springs** (MWEasterby) **2-9-0** DaleGibson(5) (chsd ldrs 3f: sn btn) ....5 | **5** | 16/1 | 37 | 8 |
| | **Veerapong (IRE)** (MWEasterby) **2-8-4**(5) GParkin(2) (lt-f: s.s: a bhd) ....5 | **6** | 16/1 | 16 | — |

(SP 112.6%) **6 Rn**

**60.4 secs** (2.40) CSF £4.26 TOTE £1.60: £1.30 £1.50 (£2.00) OWNER Mr C. H. Stevens (MALTON) BRED Whitsbury Manor Stud

**958 Double Action**, who took a strong hold, made it all, despite giving his rider all sorts of problems in the closing stages, (4/7: 10/11-8/15)
**865 Fredrik The Fierce (IRE)** is coming to himself looks-wise and ran a deal better. His turn is near. (11/2)
**Rum Lad**, a really sturdy sort, was very green in the preliminaries and early in the race, but learnt as it progressed. (9/1: op 5/1)
**Noble Dancer (IRE)**, an angular sort, showed some ability and should improve as a result. (15/2)
**Brawling Springs** looks the type who will need time to strengthen and failed to see out the trip. (16/1)

## 1185 ROTHMANS ROYALS NORTH SOUTH CHALLENGE SERIES H'CAP (0-80) (3-Y.O) (Class D)

3-15 (3-31) **1m** £8,025.00 (£2,400.00: £1,150.00: £525.00) Stalls: Low GOING minus 0.01 sec per fur (G)

| | Horse | | SP | RR | SF |
|---|---|---|---|---|---|
| 824[6] | **Royal Ceilidh (IRE) (69)** (DenysSmith) **3-8-10** JFortune(13) (in tch: led wl over 1f out: r.o) ....— | **1** | 8/1 | 77 | 44 |
| 1068* | **Smarter Charter (66)** (MrsJRRamsden) **3-8-7** KFallon(7) (outpcd & bhd: c wd & hdwy 3f out: styd on fnl f) ....2 | **2** | 5/2[1] | 70 | 37 |
| 987[5] | **Kazimiera (IRE) (72)** (CWCElsey) **3-8-8**(5) PFessey(3) (chsd ldrs: ch over 1f out: nt qckn) ....1¼ | **3** | 8/1 | 74 | 41 |
| 937[7] | **Traceability (80)** (SCWilliams) **3-9-7** KDarley(9) (bhd: hdwy ent st: chsng ldrs appr fnl f: kpt on one pce) ....s.h | **4** | 6/1[3] | 81 | 48 |
| 1068[14] | **Too Hasty (65)** (TDEasterby) **3-8-6** MBirch(5) (cl up: led appr st: hdd wl over 1f out: grad wknd) ....3 | **5** | 20/1 | 60 | 27 |
| 786[7] | **Mock Trial (IRE) (60)** (MrsJRRamsden) **3-8-1** JFEgan(6) (bhd: hdwy on outside 3f out: nvr nr to chal) ....1¾ | **6** | 20/1 | 52 | 19 |
| 810[9] | **Mr Speaker (IRE) (66)** (CFWall) **3-8-7** GDuffield(8) (lw: a.p: effrt over 2f out: btn over 1f out) ....¾ | **7** | 14/1 | 56 | 23 |
| 976[11] | **Cumbrian Maestro (60)** (TDEasterby) **3-8-1b** TWilliams(14) (cl up tl wknd fnl 2f) ....7 | **8** | 25/1 | 36 | 3 |
| 873[11] | **Gilling Dancer (IRE) (60)** (PCalver) **3-8-1** NCarlisle(10) (a rr div) ....2½ | **9** | 25/1 | 31 | — |
| *232*[2] | **Double-O-Seven (78)** (MJohnston) **3-9-5** JWeaver(11) (lw: nvr wnt pce) ....3½ | **10** | 7/1 | 42 | 9 |
| 819[2] | **Cool Fire (72)** (SPCWoods) **3-8-13** WWoods(4) (in tch: hmpd appr st: sn wknd) ....9 | **11** | 4/1[2] | 18 | — |
| | **Magic Lake (57)** (EJAlston) **3-7-12**ow2 JFanning(1) (h.d.w: led tl hdd appr st: sn lost pl) ....6 | **12** | 12/1 | — | — |
| *915*[3] | ***Tabriz (71)*** (JDBethell) **3-8-12** RHills(2) (Withdrawn not under Starter's orders: bolted & uns rider) .... | **W** | | — | — |
| *824*[9] | ***Safio (72)*** (CSmith) **3-8-13** AClark(12) (Withdrawn not under Starter's orders: spread a plate) .... | **W** | | — | — |

(SP 129.2%) **12 Rn**

**1m 41.3** (4.80) CSF £29.26 CT £162.84 TOTE £9.40: £2.40 £1.70 £2.80 (£16.90) Trio £57.70 OWNER Carlton Appointments (Aberdeen) Ltd (BISHOP AUCKLAND) BRED Thomas and Mary Shirley

LONG HANDICAP Magic Lake 7-7

OFFICIAL EXPLANATION **Cool Fire: did not act on the ground.**

**824 Royal Ceilidh (IRE)**, stepping up in trip, travelled well. Once she struck the front inside the final quarter-mile, the race was hers. (8/1)
**1068* Smarter Charter**, not really suited by this sharp track, had a lot of running to do in the straight and did well to finish so close. (5/2)
**987 Kazimiera (IRE)** is nothing special looks-wise but does have an engine, although this time was just lacking horse-power. (8/1)
**937 Traceability**, high enough in the weights, ran well. (6/1)
**Too Hasty** showed signs of a return to form. (20/1)
**786 Mock Trial (IRE)**, an exciteable sort, needed two handlers in the paddock, but does have ability and should be watched. (20/1)

## 1186 DIBB LUPTON BROOMHEAD CUP H'CAP (0-95) (4-Y.O+) (Class C)

3-45 (3-59) **6f** £16,180.00 (£4,840.00: £2,320.00: £1,060.00) Stalls: High GOING minus 0.17 sec per fur (GF)

| | Horse | | SP | RR | SF |
|---|---|---|---|---|---|
| 1064* | **To the Roof (IRE) (84)** (PWHarris) **4-9-5** GHind(4) (cl up far side: led 2f out: r.o wl) ....— | **1** | 10/1 | 96 | 54 |
| 1157* | **Benzoe (IRE) (75)** (MrsJRRamsden) **6-8-10** 6x KFallon(6) (lw: dwlt & swtchd rt after s: hdwy stands' side 2f out: r.o) ....1½ | **2** | 10/1 | 77 | 35 |
| 1040* | **Selhurstpark Flyer (IRE) (80)** (JBerry) **5-8-10**(5) PRoberts(1) (b: led far side 4f: r.o one pce) ....1½ | **3** | 16/1 | 84 | 42 |
| 1018[12] | **Fame Again (79)** (MrsJRRamsden) **4-9-0** WWoods(7) (lw: dwlt & swtchd rt after s: hdwy stands' side 2f out: nt qckn ins fnl f) ....s.h | **4** | 16/1 | 83 | 41 |
| 814[4] | **Double Splendour (IRE) (81)** (PSFelgate) **6-9-2** GDuffield(12) (lw: chsd ldrs centre: chal 2f out: nt qckn fnl f) ....hd | **5** | 7/2[1] | 85 | 43 |
| 928[5] | **Seigneurial (90)** (GHarwood) **4-9-11** AClark(20) (cl up stands' side: rdn over 2f out: r.o one pce) ....nk | **6** | 9/1[3] | 93 | 51 |
| 812[4] | **Master of Passion (85)** (JMPEustace) **7-9-6** MTebbutt(2) (racd far side: nvr rchd ldrs) ....s.h | **7** | 14/1 | 88 | 46 |
| 610[15] | **Brecongill Lad (75)** (MissSEHall) **4-8-10b** NConnorton(19) (cl up stands' side: rdn & nt qckn fnl 2f) ....nk | **8** | 12/1 | 77 | 35 |
| 1073[6] | **Samsolom (65)** (PHowling) **8-8-0** JQuinn(21) (b.hind: cl up stands' side tl rdn & btn wl over 1f out) ....2½ | **9** | 11/1 | 60 | 18 |
| 928[16] | **Rock Symphony (86)** (WJHaggas) **6-9-7** WRyan(3) (racd far side: prom 4f) ....2½ | **10** | 16/1 | 75 | 33 |
| 744* | **My Best Valentine (85)** (JWhite) **6-9-6** DaleGibson(15) (lw: nvr trbld ldrs) ....hd | **11** | 16/1 | 73 | 31 |
| | **Tedburrow (82)** (MrsAMNaughton) **4-9-3** ACulhane(9) (n.d) ....½ | **12** | 20/1 | 69 | 27 |

928[9] **Rich Glow (61)** (NBycroft) **5-7-10** NKennedy(17) (unruly s: n.d) ....s.h **13** 16/1 48 6
928[11] **Castlerea Lad (82)** (RHollinshead) **7-8-12**(5) DGriffiths(8) (n.d)....nk **14** 16/1 68 26
893* **Patsy Grimes (67)** (JSMoore) **6-8-2** JFEgan(10) (lw: prom centre 4f)....s.h **15** 16/1 53 11
928[3] **Perryston View (88)** (PCalver) **4-9-9v** MBirch(14) (lw: cl up centre tl rdn & wknd 2f out)....3 **16** 4/1[2] 66 24
850[2] **Bollin Harry (78)** (TDEasterby) **4-8-13** JCarroll(11) (chsd ldrs centre tl wknd fnl 2f)....1½ **17** 16/1 52 10
931[4] **The Scythian (73)** (BobJones) **4-8-8** LCharnock(5) (racd far side: spd to ½-wy)....2½ **18** 16/1 40 —
956[13] **Barrel of Hope (81)** (JLEyre) **4-9-2b** RLappin(13) (n.d)....2 **19** 20/1 43 1
940[10] **Shamanic (93)** (RHannon) **4-10-0** KDarley(16) (n.d)....1¼ **20** 16/1 52 10
935[W] **White Sorrel (63)** (AHarrison) **5-7-12**ow2 JFanning(18) (led stands' side over 3f: wknd qckly)....2½ **21** 25/1 15 —
(SP 165.3%) **21 Rn**

**1m 12.1** (2.40) CSF £125.77 CT £962.88 TOTE £13.00: £3.40 £3.00 £4.70 £5.50 (£59.90) Trio £409.80 OWNER Mrs P. W. Harris (BERKHAMSTED) BRED Pendley Farm
LONG HANDICAP Benzoe (IRE) 8-4 Rich Glow 7-6
**1064* To the Roof (IRE)** was one of five runners to stay on the far rail and, with that group always leading the field, he took command in the last two furlongs. (10/1)
**1157* Benzoe (IRE)** almost did the impossible two days running by crossing over to the stands' side after a slow start, but the effort was just too late on this occasion. He is in superb form. (10/1: 7/1-11/1)
**1040* Selhurstpark Flyer (IRE)** led the far-side group, but was well outpointed in the final couple of furlongs. (16/1)
**933 Fame Again**, from the same stable as Benzoe, tried similar tactics but was never doing enough in the closing stages. She is coming to form. (16/1)
**814 Double Splendour (IRE)** was always racing up the unfavoured centre of the track and ran well in the circumstances. (7/2: op 8/1)
**928 Seigneurial**, owned by the sponsors, had the best draw and raced with every chance, but this poor mover was never quite good enough. (9/1)
**812 Master of Passion**, racing on the far side where the pace was really on, always found things happening too quickly. (14/1)
**451 Brecongill Lad** ran quite well towards the stands' side, but the effort proved too much in the last couple of furlongs. (12/1)
**Tedburrow** never got into it, but ran well enough to suggest that he still retains his ability. (20/1)
**928 Perryston View** never showed anything like as much speed as last time and, racing towards the unfavoured centre of the track, was back-pedalling in the last couple of furlongs. (4/1)

## 1187 DISHFORTH CONDITIONS STKS (3-Y.O) (Class B)
4-15 (4-25) **1m** £7,991.00 (£2,969.00: £1,434.50: £597.50: £248.75: £109.25) Stalls: Low GOING minus 0.01 sec per fur (G)

SP RR SF
548[4] **L'Ami Louis (USA) (98)** (JHMGosden) **3-9-6v**[1] GHind(5) (hld up: hdwy appr st: led over 1f out: hung lft: r.o)....— **1** 9/1 109 59
934* **Hammerstein (103)** (MRStoute) **3-9-1** KDarley(2) (lw: cl up: led 3f out tl over 1f out: carried lft: rallied ins fnl f)....s.h **2** 6/4[1] 104 54
952[2] **Anthelia (102)** (GWragg) **3-8-12** WWoods(6) (lw: hmpd appr st: hdwy 2f out: nt qckn fnl f)....1¾ **3** 5/2[3] 97 47
736[4] **Tamhid (USA) (104)** (HThomsonJones) **3-9-6** WRyan(4) (hld up: hdwy 3f out: nt qckn appr fnl f)....s.h **4** 9/4[2] 105 55
**Persian Secret (FR) (100)** (JWWatts) **3-8-10** GDuffield(3) (led tl hdd 3f out: btn whn hmpd wl over 1f out)....4 **5** 12/1 87 37
(SP 117.0%) **5 Rn**

**1m 40.7** (4.20) CSF £23.15 TOTE £12.90: £3.00 £1.20 (£6.50) OWNER Oak Cliff Foals of 1993 Plus 2, LLC (NEWMARKET) BRED E. A. Cox Jr
**548 L'Ami Louis (USA)** had the Monty Roberts rug on at the start but gave a few problems. He managed to score narrowly after hanging left and looked a shade fortunate not to lose the race, but there was not even a stewards' enquiry. (9/1)
**934* Hammerstein** was beaten by the narrowest of margins with the winner continually hanging into him, and it seems very surprising that there was no objection or stewards' enquiry. (6/4)
**952 Anthelia** ran well in this decent event and should not be written off yet. (5/2)
**736 Tamhid (USA)** made his move once into the straight, but was always short of a turn of foot to go through with it. His turn will come. (9/4)
**Persian Secret (FR)** failed to handle the turn and was fighting a lost cause thereafter. She showed a good action going down though and looks on good terms with herself. (12/1)

## 1188 D.L.B. CORPORATE FINANCE H'CAP (0-100) (3-Y.O) (Class C)
4-45 (4-46) **5f** £5,630.50 (£1,684.00: £807.00: £368.50) Stalls: High GOING minus 0.17 sec per fur (GF)

SP RR SF
966[8] **Kunucu (IRE) (90)** (TDBarron) **3-8-12** KDarley(4) (a cl up: led appr fnl f: r.o)....— **1** 9/4[1] 96 54
832[8] **Swynford Dream (83)** (JFBottomley) **3-8-2**(3) DRMcCabe(3) (led tl hdd appr fnl f: sn btn)....1¼ **2** 11/4[2] 85 43
832[7] **Laafee (99)** (HThomsonJones) **3-9-7** WRyan(6) (trckd ldrs: hdwy & swtchd over 1f out: nt qckn ins fnl f)....¾ **3** 11/4[2] 99 57
989[6] **Miss Bigwig (75)** (JBerry) **3-7-6**(5) PFessey(5) (b: a chsng ldrs: rdn & btn over 1f out)....1¾ **4** 4/1[3] 69 27
989[8] **Pleasure Time (74)** (CSmith) **3-7-10b** NCarlisle(2) (s.i.s: sn in tch: outpcd fr ½-wy)....7 **5** 10/1 46 4
(SP 113.2%) **5 Rn**

**59.6 secs** (1.60) CSF £8.52 TOTE £3.80: £1.70 £1.70 (£5.40) OWNER Mr P. D. Savill (THIRSK) BRED Mrs Rita Fitzgerald
LONG HANDICAP Pleasure Time 7-4
**565 Kunucu (IRE)** took time to get on top but, once she did in the final furlong, she won most authoritatively. (9/4)
**Swynford Dream** showed all his customary speed, but failed to last out, and may still have just needed this. (11/4)
**Laafee** looked to be travelling well when in behind the leaders but, switched for room, failed to respond in the final furlong. His stable is yet to strike any sort of form. (11/4)
**989 Miss Bigwig** has plenty of speed, but is failing to see it out so far this year. (4/1)
**773 Pleasure Time** was well outclassed. (10/1)

## 1189 ELMIRE MAIDEN STKS (3-Y.O F) (Class D)
5-15 (5-15) **1m 4f** £3,665.00 (£1,100.00: £530.00: £245.00) Stalls: Low GOING minus 0.01 sec per fur (G)

SP RR SF
957[2] **Place de L'Opera** (HRACecil) **3-8-11** WRyan(4) (lw: hld up: hdwy 5f out: led wl over 1f out: r.o)....— **1** 8/11[1] 77 28
820[2] **Sunset Wells (USA)** (DRLoder) **3-8-8**(3) DRMcCabe(5) (hld up: hdwy 3f out: ch & hung lft 1f out: no ex)....1¼ **2** 5/1[3] 75 26
932[2] **Shirley Venture** (SPCWoods) **3-8-11** WWoods(2) (lw: a cl up: disp ld 3f out tl wl over 1f out: kpt on)....¾ **3** 7/1 74 25
821[3] **St Rita** (JLDunlop) **3-8-11** GDuffield(6) (led tl hdd wl over 1f out: kpt on)....hd **4** 4/1[2] 74 25
826[6] **Amusing Aside (IRE)** (JWWatts) **3-8-11** KDarley(3) (b.hind: trckd ldrs: outpcd appr st: no imp after)....3 **5** 9/1 70? 21
(SP 117.1%) **5 Rn**

**2m 40.0** (10.00) CSF £5.08 TOTE £1.70: £1.20 £1.90 (£2.70) OWNER Cliveden Stud (NEWMARKET) BRED Cliveden Stud Ltd
**957 Place de L'Opera** appreciated the extra distance and won well, but did give the impression that easier ground might help. (8/11)

**820 Sunset Wells (USA)**, looking lean and fit, came there looking dangerous entering the final furlong, only to hang left and fail to quicken. Experience is probably all she needs. (5/1)
**932 Shirley Venture** ran a fine race and, although tapped for foot in the last furlong and a half, did keep battling on, and should stay further. (7/1: op 9/2)
**821 St Rita**, made plenty of use of, stayed on well when headed and looks likely to appreciate stiffer tests of stamina. (4/1)
**826 Amusing Aside (IRE)** got outpaced before the home turn and could make no impression thereafter, but looks likely to improve for the experience. (9/1)

T/Plpt: £38.50 (362.18 Tckts). T/Qdpt: £26.20 (29.37 Tckts). AA

# 1175-NEWBURY (L-H) (Soft)
## Sunday May 19th
WEATHER: overcast WIND: str half against

## 1190 MAIL ON SUNDAY MILE H'CAP (Qualifier) (0-85) (3-Y.O+) (Class D)
2-00 (2-02) **1m (straight)** £7,360.00 (£2,230.00: £1,090.00: £520.00) Stalls: Centre GOING: 0.80 sec per fur (S)

| | | | | SP | RR | SF |
|---|---|---|---|---|---|---|
| $967^{6}$ | **Amrak Ajeeb (IRE) (85)** (BHanbury) **4-10-0** JReid(22) (lw: hld up: hdwy 3f out: led ins fnl f: r.o wl) | — | **1** | 9/1 $^{3}$ | 101 | 78 |
| $879^{20}$ | **Admirals Flame (IRE) (73)** (CFWall) **5-9-2** GDuffield(19) (b: hld up & plld hrd: hdwy 3f out: led over 2f out tl ins fnl f) | 3½ | **2** | 25/1 | 82 | 59 |
| $879^{20}$ | **Saifan (72)** (DMorris) **7-9-1b** CHodgson(9) (lw: hld up: ev ch over 1f out: hrd rdn: one pce) | 1¼ | **3** | 40/1 | 79 | 56 |
| $879^{11}$ | **Mo-Addab (IRE) (80)** (ACStewart) **6-9-9** DHarrison(15) (lw: hld up: hdwy over 2f out: r.o one pce fnl f) | 1 | **4** | 16/1 | 85 | 62 |
| 879* | **Tregaron (USA) (80)** (RAkehurst) **5-9-9** TQuinn(18) (hld up: rdn & one pce fnl 2f) | ¾ | **5** | 3/1 $^{1}$ | 83 | 60 |
| $669^{5}$ | **Diminutive (USA) (85)** (JWHills) **3-8-11**(5) MHenry(20) (lw: hld up: hdwy over 2f out: nvr nr to chal) | 8 | **6** | 25/1 | 72 | 37 |
| 888* | **Lilli Claire (83)** (AGFoster) **3-9-0** BDoyle(14) (hdwy 3f out: wknd 1f out) | ½ | **7** | 9/1 $^{3}$ | 69 | 34 |
| $887^{9}$ | **Talathath (FR) (62)** (CADwyer) **4-8-2v**(3) JStack(4) (swtchd lft to r alone far side over 4f out: wknd over 1f out) | 3½ | **8** | 20/1 | 41 | 18 |
| $967^{12}$ | **Zajko (USA) (79)** (LadyHerries) **6-9-8** RCochrane(21) (lw: nvr trbld ldrs) | 2 | **9** | 12/1 | 54 | 31 |
| $809^{17}$ | **Ron's Secret (82)** (JWPayne) **4-9-11** BThomson(17) (prom over 4f) | s.h | **10** | 20/1 | 57 | 34 |
| $765^{15}$ | **Duello (62)** (MBlanshard) **5-8-5** JQuinn(10) (plld hrd: sme hdwy 3f out: wknd 2f out) | 2½ | **11** | 10/1 | 32 | 9 |
| $967^{9}$ | **Embankment (IRE) (80)** (RHannon) **6-9-6**(3) DaneO'Neill(12) (a bhd) | nk | **12** | 10/1 | 49 | 26 |
| $786^{8}$ | **Boston Rock (IRE) (60)** (PWHarris) **4-8-3** GHind(3) (lw: led 5f) | 1¼ | **13** | 8/1 $^{2}$ | 27 | 4 |
| | **Moscow Mist (IRE) (75)** (LadyHerries) **5-9-4** TSprake(8) (prom tl wknd over 2f out) | 4 | **14** | 16/1 | 34 | 11 |
| | **Broughtons Turmoil (65)** (WJMusson) **7-8-8** RPrice(6) (lw: plld hrd: w ldr: led 3f out: sn hdd & wknd) | 1 | **15** | 20/1 | 22 | — |
| $887^{3}$ | **Desert Calm (IRE) (55)** (MrsPNDutfield) **7-7-12b** GBardwell(7) (sn rdn: bhd fnl 3f) | 9 | **16** | 14/1 | — | — |
| $713^{13}$ | **Noble Neptune (55)** (WJMusson) **4-7-12** AMackay(5) (s.s: a bhd: t.o) | 14 | **17** | 40/1 | — | — |
| $1018^{16}$ | **Hand Craft (IRE) (81)** (WJHaggas) **4-9-10** SSanders(1) (plld hrd: prom over 4f: t.o) | 26 | **18** | 20/1 | — | — |
| | | | | (SP 132.0%) | **18 Rn** | |

**1m 46.67** (9.67) CSF £199.63 CT £7,813.53 TOTE £10.90: £2.90 £8.90 £10.90 £2.90 (£232.80) Trio £672.80 OWNER Mr A. Merza (NEWMARKET) BRED Ovidstown Investments Ltd
WEIGHT FOR AGE 3yo-12lb
**967 Amrak Ajeeb (IRE)** has won over ten furlongs and found his stamina coming into play in the testing ground. (9/1)
**Admirals Flame (IRE)** has won on soft ground and stepped up on his debut, despite being rated 7lb higher than when he last won. (25/1)
**Saifan** has been dropped 9lb this season and showed he is not inconvenienced by plenty of give underfoot. (40/1)
**Mo-Addab (IRE)** had ground conditions in his favour, but may need to come down a few pounds in the handicap. (16/1)
**879* Tregaron (USA)** could not defy an 11lb hike in the weights in this rain-softened ground. (3/1)
**669 Diminutive (USA)** seemed to have his fair share of weight for this first run in handicap company. (25/1)
**888* Lilli Claire**, raised 9lb, did not get home in the testing conditions. (9/1)
**613 Boston Rock (IRE)** (8/1: op 5/1)

## 1191 CATS MAIDEN STKS (2-Y.O C & G) (Class D)
2-30 (2-32) **6f 8y** £5,485.00 (£1,660.00: £810.00: £385.00) Stalls: Centre GOING: 0.80 sec per fur (S)

| | | | | SP | RR | SF |
|---|---|---|---|---|---|---|
| | **Premier Bay** (PWHarris) **2-8-11** GHind(13) (w'like: s.s: hdwy over 2f out: led over 1f out: rdn out) | — | **1** | 8/1 $^{3}$ | 87+ | 38 |
| | **Myrmidon** (JLDunlop) **2-8-11** PatEddery(11) (a.p: led over 3f out tl over 1f out: r.o) | 1 | **2** | 8/1 $^{3}$ | 84+ | 35 |
| | **Double-J (IRE)** (KMcAuliffe) **2-8-8**(3) JStack(9) (leggy: bit bkwd: s.s: hld up & bhd: hdwy over 2f out: one pce fnl f) | 5 | **3** | 33/1 | 71 | 22 |
| $946^{3}$ | **Powder River** (RHannon) **2-8-8**(3) DaneO'Neill(8) (lw: hld up: one pce fnl 2f) | 1½ | **4** | 7/2 $^{2}$ | 67 | 18 |
| $924^{6}$ | **Puzzlement** (CEBrittain) **2-8-11** BDoyle(14) (prom: rdn over 2f out: wknd over 1f out) | 7 | **5** | 11/1 | 49 | — |
| | **Prairie Minstrel (USA)** (RDickin) **2-8-11** GDuffield(10) (w'like: lw: rdn & lost pl 4f out: hdwy over 2f out: wknd over 1f out) | 3 | **6** | 33/1 | 41 | — |
| | **Bold Oriental (IRE)** (NACallaghan) **2-8-11** RCochrane(7) (leggy: unf: sme hdwy over 2f out: wknd over 1f out) | 6 | **7** | 14/1 | 25 | — |
| | **Bold Spring (IRE)** (RHannon) **2-8-11** RPerham(5) (leggy: bhd fnl 3f) | ¾ | **8** | 16/1 | 23 | — |
| $865^{5}$ | **Sun O'Tirol (IRE)** (MRChannon) **2-8-11** RHughes(6) (led over 2f: wknd over 1f out) | 3½ | **9** | 14/1 | 13 | — |
| $841^{9}$ | **Speedfit** (GGMargarson) **2-8-11** PBloomfield(4) (a bhd) | 2½ | **10** | 25/1 | 7 | — |
| | **Sturgeon (IRE)** (PFICole) **2-8-11** TQuinn(1) (str: s.i.s: sn prom: wknd over 2f out) | ½ | **11** | 2/1 $^{1}$ | 6 | — |
| | **Merciless Cop** (BJMeehan) **2-8-11** MTebbutt(2) (cmpt: bit bkwd: s.s: outpcd) | 1¾ | **12** | 20/1 | 1 | — |
| | | | | (SP 119.8%) | **12 Rn** | |

**1m 20.77** (8.97) CSF £65.37 TOTE £7.60: £1.50 £2.20 £9.50 (£51.10) Trio £262.10 OWNER Prime Cartel (BERKHAMSTED) BRED Pendley Farm
**Premier Bay**, a half-brother to Taufan Boy, recovered from an indifferent start and needed plenty of stamina because of the ground. (8/1: op 16/1)
**Myrmidon** stuck to his task when headed, and should soon go one better. (8/1: op 5/1)
**Double-J (IRE)** should be all the better for the experience and improvement should be expected. (33/1)
**946 Powder River** deserves another chance on better ground. (7/2: 5/2-4/1)
**Puzzlement** (11/1: op 7/1)
**Bold Oriental (IRE)** (14/1: 10/1-16/1)
**Sturgeon (IRE)** did not seem to handle the soft ground and should do better in due course. (2/1: 6/4-9/4)

## 1192 STARLIGHT EXPRESS LIMITED STKS (0-80) (3-Y.O+) (Class D)

3-00 (3-00) **7f 64y (round)** £4,742.50 (£1,435.00: £700.00: £332.50) Stalls: Low GOING: 0.61 sec per fur (GS)

| | Horse | Btn | Pos | SP | RR | SF |
|---|---|---|---|---|---|---|
| 692[11] | **Xenophon of Cunaxa (IRE) (75)** (MJFetherston-Godley) **3-8-8** DHarrison(2) (mde all: rdn over 2f out: edgd rt & bmpd ins fnl f: r.o: originally fin 1st: disq: plcd 2nd: later reinstated after appeal) | — | 1 | 14/1 | 86 | 16 |
| 577[3] | **Zygo (USA) (80)** (WJarvis) **4-9-5** TQuinn(7) (lw: a.p: chsd ldr over 3f out: rdn over 2f out: ev ch whn carried rt & bmpd ins fnl f: r.o: originally fin 2nd, hd: awrdd r: later plcd 2nd) | hd | 2 | 7/2[2] | 86 | 27 |
| 876[18] | **Be Warned (73)** (NACallaghan) **5-9-5b** PatEddery(1) (hld up: hdwy over 2f out: rdn over 1f out: one pce) | 6 | 3 | 11/4[1] | 73 | 14 |
| 1064[9] | **Law Commission (79)** (DRCElsworth) **6-9-5** RCochrane(4) (hld up: rdn over 1f out: one pce) | 7 | 4 | 6/1 | 57 | — |
| 1092* | **Zelda Zonk (66)** (BJMeehan) **4-9-5** RHughes(3) (lw: hld up: rdn over 2f out: wknd over 1f out) | 2½ | 5 | 4/1[3] | 52 | — |
| 1078[2] | **Mister Fire Eyes (IRE) (74)** (CEBrittain) **4-9-8b** BDoyle(5) (lw: chsd ldr over 3f: wknd over 1f out) | ¾ | 6 | 9/2 | 53 | — |
| | | | | (SP 108.0%) | **6 Rn** | |

**1m 39.35** (11.25) CSF £36.29 TOTE £3.70: £2.10 £3.90 (£31.40) OWNER Abigail Ltd (EAST ILSLEY) BRED Newtownbarry House Stud and Miss S. Von Schilcher

WEIGHT FOR AGE 3yo-11lb

**Xenophon of Cunaxa (IRE)** certainly did it the hard way in the testing ground and, regardless of the merits of the Stewards' decision, did not deserve to lose the race. (14/1: op 8/1)

**577 Zygo (USA)** had a ding-dong battle with Xenophon of Cunaxa in the last 200 yards and got the race in the Stewards' Room. (7/2: op 2/1)

**Be Warned**, well backed in the Offices, could not go with the two principals in the last furlong and a half. (11/4)

**1092* Zelda Zonk**, attempting a quick follow-up, had to contend with totally different conditions underfoot. (4/1: 3/1-9/2)

## 1193 BY JEEVES RATED STKS H'CAP (0-105) (3-Y.O+) (Class B)

3-30 (3-32) **1m 1f** £9,529.80 (£3,568.20: £1,746.60: £753.00: £339.00: £173.40) Stalls: Low GOING: 0.61 sec per fur (GS)

| | Horse | Btn | Pos | SP | RR | SF |
|---|---|---|---|---|---|---|
| | **Night City (96)** (LadyHerries) **5-9-5** DeclanO'Shea(15) (hdwy over 3f out: led & hung rt over 2f out: r.o wl) | — | 1 | 8/1 | 108 | 48 |
| 925[3] | **Major Change (86)** (RHannon) **4-8-6**(3) DaneO'Neill(14) (a.p: rdn & ev ch over 1f out: one pce) | 3 | 2 | 14/1 | 93 | 33 |
| 809[6] | **Donna Viola (88)** (CFWall) **4-8-11** JReid(5) (hld up: hdwy over 3f out: ev ch 2f out: one pce) | ½ | 3 | 13/2[3] | 94 | 34 |
| 967[4] | **Star Manager (USA) (86)** (PFICole) **6-8-9** TQuinn(12) (bhd: hdwy & swtchd stands' side over 3f out: one pce fnl f) | ¾ | 4 | 11/2[2] | 90 | 30 |
| 728[15] | **Hoh Express (97)** (IABalding) **4-9-6** PaulEddery(10) (lw: bhd tl hdwy & swtchd stands' side 3f out: one pce fnl 2f) | ½ | 5 | 12/1 | 101 | 41 |
| 808[5] | **Censor (88)** (HRACecil) **3-7-12** AMcGlone(9) (lw: a.p: led over 3f out tl over 2f out: wknd over 1f out) | 1¾ | 6 | 5/1[1] | 88 | 15 |
| 646[9] | **Vola Via (USA) (86)** (IABalding) **3-7-5**(5) MartinDwyer(3) (hld up & bhd: hdwy over 2f out: nvr nr to chal) | nk | 7 | 33/1 | 86 | 13 |
| 580[8] | **Sheer Danzig (IRE) (88)** (RWArmstrong) **4-8-11** WWoods(13) (lw: hld up & bhd: hdwy 3f out: wknd 2f out) | 3½ | 8 | 14/1 | 82 | 22 |
| | **La Volta (100)** (JGFitzGerald) **3-8-10** RCochrane(4) (plld hrd: prom tl wknd over 3f out) | 13 | 9 | 20/1 | 71 | — |
| | **Kadamann (IRE) (95)** (RAkehurst) **4-9-4** SSanders(8) (bhd fnl 3f) | 9 | 10 | 10/1 | 50 | — |
| | **Daryabad (IRE) (100)** (TJNaughton) **4-9-9** BThomson(11) (bit bkwd: a bhd: t.o) | 20 | 11 | 20/1 | 19 | — |
| 878[5] | **Grand du Lac (USA) (94)** (DRLoder) **4-9-3** PatEddery(7) (lw: a.p: led over 5f out tl over 3f out: wknd over 2f out) | 5 | 12 | 11/2[2] | 4 | — |
| 810[8] | **Autumn Affair (96)** (CEBrittain) **4-9-5b**[1] BDoyle(2) (led over 3f: wknd over 3f out: t.o) | 13 | 13 | 16/1 | — | — |
| | | | | (SP 120.3%) | **13 Rn** | |

**2m 1.78** (11.48) CSF £102.87 CT £733.89 TOTE £9.40: £2.30 £3.10 £2.80 (£64.50) Trio £167.70 OWNER Dexam International Ltd (LITTLE-HAMPTON)

LONG HANDICAP Major Change 8-7

WEIGHT FOR AGE 3yo-13lb

**Night City** loves the mud and was in control once reaching the stands' rail. (8/1)

**925 Major Change** again ran well and his turn is near. (14/1)

**809 Donna Viola** ran well off a mark 5lb higher than when she scored at Sandown last September. (13/2)

**967 Star Manager (USA)** did not mind the soft ground but could never get to grips with the principals. (11/2)

**Hoh Express** stepped up on his two previous efforts this season. (12/1)

**808 Censor** was having his first run on ground worse than good. (5/1)

## 1194 SUNSET BOULEVARD H'CAP (0-90) (4-Y.O+) (Class C)

4-00 (4-00) **2m** £7,490.00 (£2,270.00: £1,110.00: £530.00) Stalls: Low GOING: 0.61 sec per fur (GS)

| | Horse | Btn | Pos | SP | RR | SF |
|---|---|---|---|---|---|---|
| 811[2] | **Rocky Forum (60)** (GLMoore) **4-8-0**ow1 SSanders(18) (b: a gng wl: led on bit over 2f out: clr over 1f out: rdn out) | — | 1 | 8/1[2] | 78 | 54 |
| 647[10] | **En Vacances (IRE) (71)** (AGFoster) **4-8-11** TSprake(16) (lw: hld up: outpcd 2f out: styd on fnl f) | 4 | 2 | 10/1 | 85 | 62 |
| 1005[13] | **Thaljanah (IRE) (80)** (DLWilliams) **4-9-6** DHarrison(13) (lw: hdwy 8f out: ev ch over 2f out: one pce) | hd | 3 | 20/1 | 94 | 71 |
| 825* | **Orchestra Stall (80)** (JLDunlop) **4-9-6** PatEddery(19) (b: lw: a.p: led over 6f out tl over 2f out: one pce) | 3½ | 4 | 9/4[1] | 90 | 67 |
| 811[7] | **Toy Princess (USA) (74)** (CEBrittain) **4-9-0** BDoyle(14) (lw: a.p: ev ch over 2f out: wknd over 1f out) | ½ | 5 | 25/1 | 84 | 61 |
| | **Nanton Point (USA) (79)** (LadyHerries) **4-9-5** JQuinn(7) (hld up: hdwy 3f out: one pce fnl 2f) | 3½ | 6 | 10/1 | 85 | 62 |
| 852[4] | **Kamikaze (64)** (JWhite) **6-8-6** GDuffield(5) (hld up: hdwy on ins & hmpd over 8f out: wknd 3f out) | 10 | 7 | 11/1 | 60 | 39 |
| 944[5] | **Granby Bell (56)** (PHayward) **5-7-7**(5)ow2 MHenry(2) (lw: prom tl wknd over 3f out) | 2½ | 8 | 50/1 | 50 | 27 |
| 944[4] | **Kilcoran Bay (67)** (IABalding) **4-8-7b** PaulEddery(17) (nvr trbld ldrs) | 9 | 9 | 25/1 | 52 | 29 |
| | **Greycoat Boy (66)** (BJMeehan) **4-8-6b**ow2 MTebbutt(6) (hdwy over 10f out: led over 8f out tl over 6f out: wknd over 3f out) | 9 | 10 | 14/1 | 42 | 17 |
| | **Muse (86)** (DRCElsworth) **9-10-0** AProcter(8) (a bhd) | 2½ | 11 | 20/1 | 59 | 38 |
| 961[3] | **Stalled (IRE) (54)** (PTWalwyn) **6-7-5**(5) MartinDwyer(12) (lw: a bhd) | 1¼ | 12 | 14/1 | 26 | 5 |
| | **Allmosa (54)** (TJNaughton) **7-7-10** NAdams(3) (a bhd) | ¾ | 13 | 50/1 | 25 | 4 |
| *75*[4] | **Nijmegen (65)** (JGFitzGerald) **8-8-7b** RCochrane(10) (b: lw: a bhd) | ¾ | 14 | 8/1[2] | 36 | 15 |
| 1005[16] | **Kadastrof (FR) (82)** (RDickin) **6-9-7**(3) DaneO'Neill(1) (led over 7f: wknd over 3f out) | s.h | 15 | 10/1 | 53 | 32 |
| 1005[9] | **Seasonal Splendour (IRE) (83)** (MCPipe) **6-9-11** GCarter(15) (a bhd: t.o) | 14 | 16 | 9/1[3] | 40 | 19 |
| | | | | (SP 133.1%) | **16 Rn** | |

**3m 41.09** (16.09) CSF £85.35 CT £1,452.34 TOTE £9.90: £1.50 £2.10 £9.60 £1.60 (£75.50) Trio £606.40 OWNER The Forum Ltd (EPSOM) BRED Forum Bloodstock Ltd

LONG HANDICAP Granby Bell 7-4 Stalled (IRE) 7-8 Allmosa 7-4

WEIGHT FOR AGE 4yo-2lb

**811 Rocky Forum** relished the give underfoot and was the likely winner from some way out. (8/1)
**En Vacances (IRE)** stays well and likes soft ground. (10/1)
**675 Thaljanah (IRE)** has gradually been slipping down the ratings. (20/1)
**825* Orchestra Stall** could not defy a 5lb rise in the weights. (9/4)
**666* Toy Princess (USA)**, 5lb higher than when winning at Folkestone, would have preferred better ground. (25/1)
**Nanton Point (USA)**, runner-up in last season's Cesarewitch, made a highly respectable reappearance on ground too soft for him. (10/1)

## 1195 PHANTOM MAIDEN STKS (3-Y.O) (Class D)

4-30 (4-30) **7f 64y (round)** £5,407.00 (£1,636.00: £798.00: £379.00) Stalls: Low GOING: 0.61 sec per fur (GS)

| Form | Horse | Dist | Pos | SP | RR | SF |
|---|---|---|---|---|---|---|
| $1045^{4}$ | **A Chef Too Far** (RRowe) **3-9-0** TQuinn(6) (mde all: clr over 1f out: edgd rt ins fnl f: easily) | — | 1 | $11/2^{2}$ | 76+ | 38 |
| | **Polar Prospect** (BHanbury) **3-8-11**$^{(3)}$ JStack(8) (b.hind: w'like: scope: bit bkwd: hld up: rdn & chsd wnr over 1f out: no imp) | 6 | 2 | $6/1^{3}$ | 63 | 25 |
| | **Bandit Girl** (IABalding) **3-8-9** RCochrane(10) (plld hrd: a.p: one pce fnl 2f) | 2 | 3 | $6/1^{3}$ | 53 | 15 |
| $669^{10}$ | **Shouldbegrey** (WRMuir) **3-9-0** DHarrison(4) (hld up: rdn over 3f out: sn bhd: t.o) | 16 | 4 | 25/1 | 23 | — |
| | **Cerdan (USA)** (MRStoute) **3-9-0** JReid(3) (lw: prom tl rdn & wknd over 2f out: t.o) | 8 | 5 | $4/7^{1}$ | 6 | — |

(SP 111.4%) **5 Rn**

**1m 37.84** (9.74) CSF £30.92 TOTE £5.80: £1.70 £2.60 (£18.90) Trio £8.30 OWNER Hon Mervyn Greenway (PULBOROUGH) BRED Barrettstown Stud Farms Ltd
OFFICIAL EXPLANATION **Cerdan (USA): could not handle the soft ground.**
**1045 A Chef Too Far** came into his own in the testing ground. (11/2: 3/1-6/1)
**Polar Prospect** was playing second fiddle approaching the final furlong. (6/1: 4/1-7/1)
**Bandit Girl**, a half-sister to Blue Siren amongst others, did not help her chances by refusing to settle. (6/1: op 4/1)
**Cerdan (USA)** presumably failed to handle the testing ground. (4/7)

T/Jkpt: Not won; £228,219.65 to Bath 20/5/96. T/Plpt: £10,632.20 (3.3 Tckts). T/Qdpt: £313.10 (8.7 Tckts). KH

# 0822-RIPON (R-H) (Good)
## Sunday May 19th

WEATHER: overcast WIND: str half bhd

## 1196 SUNDAY IS FUNDAY AT THE RACES (S) STKS (3-Y.O+) (Class F)

2-15 (2-17) **1m** £2,983.00 (£904.00: £442.00: £211.00) Stalls: High GOING: 0.08 sec per fur (G)

| Form | Horse | Dist | Pos | SP | RR | SF |
|---|---|---|---|---|---|---|
| $983^{W}$ | **Cicerone (49)** (JLHarris) **6-9-4v**$^{1(5)}$ PFessey(19) (led: clr ent st: hld on wl) | — | 1 | 9/1 | 72 | 51 |
| $1040^{8}$ | **Hi Rock (57)** (JNorton) **4-8-13** JFanning(18) (a chsng ldrs: chal 1f out: r.o: jst failed) | s.h | 2 | 14/1 | 62 | 41 |
| $549^{4}$ | **Scottish Park (39)** (JLHarris) **7-8-10**$^{(3)}$ PMcCabe(14) (lw: a.p: outpcd 2f out: styd on wl fnl f) | 1 | 3 | 14/1 | 60 | 39 |
| $851^{10}$ | **Harry's Treat (52)** (JLEyre) **4-8-13** RLappin(10) (hdwy over 3f out: styd on: nvr able to chal) | 5 | 4 | 8/1 | 50 | 29 |
| $822^{3}$ | **Master Ofthe House (57)** (MDHammond) **10-9-4** KFallon(8) (hdwy 3f out: styd on: nrst fin) | ½ | 5 | $11/2^{3}$ | 54 | 33 |
| $817^{5}$ | **Arcatura (62)** (CJames) **4-9-4b**$^{1}$ WJO'Connor(12) (chsd ldrs: outpcd over 2f out: no imp) | ½ | 6 | $7/2^{1}$ | 53 | 32 |
| | **Forget Paris (IRE)** (BSRothwell) **3-8-2**$^{ow1}$ MFenton(7) (unf: bit bkwd: s.i.s: styd on fnl 3f: nrst fin) | 2 | 7 | 16/1 | 45 | 11 |
| $1040^{10}$ | **Blow Dry (IRE) (54)** (MartynWane) **6-9-4** JCarroll(1) (in tch: no imp fnl 3f) | 1 | 8 | 14/1 | 47 | 26 |
| | **Whatashowman (IRE)** (SEKettlewell) **4-9-4** OUrbina(17) (bit bkwd: chsd ldrs tl wknd fnl 2½f) | 1¾ | 9 | 25/1 | 43 | 22 |
| $1041^{6}$ | **Simand (55)** (GMMoore) **4-8-13** JFortune(6) (bhd: hdwy 4f out: sn rdn & no imp) | 2½ | 10 | 8/1 | 33 | 12 |
| *$777^{4}$* | **Adaloaldo (USA) (46)** (JParkes) **4-9-4**$^{(5)}$ RHavlin(15) (s.i.s: nvr rchd ldrs) | ¾ | 11 | 20/1 | 42 | 21 |
| *$1081^{3}$* | **Sandmoor Denim (65)** (SRBowring) **9-8-13**$^{(5)}$ CTeague(2) (lw: bhd: hdwy on outside 4f out: sn btn) | 1¼ | 12 | $5/1^{2}$ | 34 | 13 |
| $1001^{13}$ | **Shareoftheaction (40)** (MrsAMNaughton) **5-8-11**$^{(7)}$ JDennis(11) (prom 5f) | 2½ | 13 | 33/1 | 29 | 8 |
| 1024* | **Pash (37)** (CWFairhurst) **4-9-4v** NKennedy(13) (lost tch fr ½-wy) | ¾ | 14 | 14/1 | 28 | 7 |
| $983^{11}$ | **Asterix (46)** (JMBradley) **8-9-4v** WRyan(16) (b: a bhd) | 6 | 15 | 12/1 | 16 | — |
| $820^{15}$ | **Formentiere** (JMBradley) **3-8-1** TWilliams(9) (s.i.s: a bhd) | ¾ | 16 | 33/1 | 9 | — |
| $784^{7}$ | **Dispol Agenda** (GROldroyd) **3-8-1** DaleGibson(20) (prom tl wknd over 3f out) | hd | 17 | 33/1 | 9 | — |
| | **Daring Ryde (48)** (JPSmith) **5-9-4** SDWilliams(3) (bit bkwd: a bhd) | 18 | 18 | 33/1 | — | — |
| $1037^{17}$ | **Legal Brief (45)** (JSWainwright) **4-9-4b** TIves(5) (lost tch fr ½-wy) | 10 | 19 | 20/1 | — | — |
| $775^{16}$ | **Percy Park (USA) (43)** (MWEasterby) **3-8-1b**$^{1(5)}$ GParkin(4) (cl up to st: sn bhd) | nk | 20 | 14/1 | — | — |

(SP 158.5%) **20 Rn**

**1m 43.8** (6.10) CSF £144.13 TOTE £10.40: £3.70 £8.30 £6.90 (£385.50) Trio £308.90; £391.64 to Bath 20/5/96 OWNER Dr C. W. Ashpole (MELTON MOWBRAY) BRED Aldershawe Stud Farm
WEIGHT FOR AGE 3yo-12lb
No bid
**545* Cicerone**, who refused to enter the stalls last time, was put in late here and had the visor fitted for the first time, and they certainly worked. (9/1)
**Hi Rock** had never tried further than seven furlongs previously, but got this mile well and another stride would probably have seen her succeed. (14/1)
**549 Scottish Park** has changed stables over the winter and seems to be coming to form. Over further or on easier ground, she should find a race or two. (14/1)
**734 Harry's Treat** has yet to win a race, but she was staying on well in the last half-mile, suggesting that an opening can be found. (8/1)
**822 Master Ofthe House** has to be caught in the right mood and was never doing enough on this occasion. (11/2)
**817 Arcatura** had the blinkers on for the first time and they never had the required response. (7/2)
**Forget Paris (IRE)**, needing this, put in a reasonable first effort and was noted making late progress. (16/1)
**Whatashowman (IRE)** showed up well until blowing up in the final couple of furlongs. (25/1)

## 1197 DELOITTE & TOUCHE MAIDEN STKS (2-Y.O) (Class D)

2-45 (2-49) **6f** £3,712.50 (£1,125.00: £550.00: £262.50) Stalls: Low GOING minus 0.20 sec per fur (GF)

| Form | Horse | Dist | Pos | SP | RR | SF |
|---|---|---|---|---|---|---|
| $848^{3}$ | **For Your Eyes Only** (TDEasterby) **2-9-0** MBirch(5) (b: lw: mde all: shkn up over 1f out: r.o wl) | — | 1 | $2/1^{2}$ | 78 | 29 |
| | **Falls O'Moness (IRE)** (KRBurke) **2-8-6**$^{(3)}$ DRMcCabe(4) (cmpt: in tch: hdwy over 1f out: r.o) | 2 | 2 | 25/1 | 68 | 19 |
| $1003^{4}$ | **Rainbow Rain (USA)** (MJohnston) **2-9-0** WRyan(9) (lw: w wnr: rdn over 1f out: wknd ins fnl f) | ¾ | 3 | $8/11^{1}$ | 70 | 22 |
| | **Rivonia (USA)** (MrsJRRamsden) **2-8-9** KFallon(1) (cmpt: bit bkwd: hdwy fnl 2f: nvr nr to chal) | 9 | 4 | 14/1 | 42+ | — |

| Form | Horse | Dist | Pos | SP | RR | SF |
|---|---|---|---|---|---|---|
| 1014[5] | **Dizzy Dancer** (ABailey) **2-8-9** JCarroll(3) (a chsng ldrs: rdn ½-wy: no imp) | ½ | **5** | 10/1[3] | 40 | — |
| | **Jack Flush (IRE)** (BSRothwell) **2-9-0** MFenton(10) (leggy: unf: s.i.s: sn in tch: nt qckn fnl 2f) | hd | **6** | 33/1 | 45 | — |
| | **Hurgill Dancer** (JWWatts) **2-9-0** NConnorton(7) (neat: bhd: hdwy over 1f out: nvr nr ldrs) | 3½ | **7** | 16/1 | 36 | — |
| | **Warrlin** (CWFairhurst) **2-9-0** JTate(2) (leggy: unf: scope: bhd tl sme late hdwy) | hd | **8** | 25/1 | 36 | — |
| | **Ninth Symphony** (PCHaslam) **2-9-0** JFortune(11) (w'like: str: bit bkwd: nvr wnt pce) | 3 | **9** | 14/1 | 28 | — |
| | **Flo's Choice (IRE)** (JAHarris) **2-8-9** JO'Reilly(8) (small: unf: chsd ldrs tl wknd 2f out) | 4 | **10** | 33/1 | 12 | — |
| | **Rich Ground** (JDBethell) **2-9-0** WJO'Connor(12) (unf: bkwd: sn outpcd & wl bhd) | 1¾ | **11** | 25/1 | 12 | — |
| 608[7] | **Foolish Flutter (IRE)** (GROldroyd) **2-8-9** FNorton(6) (s.i.s: a bhd) | 4 | **12** | 33/1 | — | — |

(SP 139.9%) **12 Rn**

**1m 14.2** (3.70) CSF £53.87 TOTE £3.50: £1.40 £3.40 £1.30 (£143.90) Trio £28.50 OWNER Mr Reg Griffin (MALTON) BRED Compton Down Stud

**848 For Your Eyes Only** knew the job this time and, given a most positive ride, ran on really well. (2/1)
**Falls O'Moness (IRE)** took time to get into the swing of things but certainly picked up well in the closing stages, and should be a different prospect next time. (25/1)
**1003 Rainbow Rain (USA)** had come on for his Chester run but, after taking the winner on, the effort proved beyond him approaching the final furlong. (8/11: 4/5-Evens)
**Rivonia (USA)** needed this and never looked likely to offer a threat, despite keeping on at the end. Time should see plenty of improvement. (14/1: op 7/1)
**Dizzy Dancer** chased the leaders, but was always a few lengths off them and never looked likely to improve. (10/1: op 13/2)
**Jack Flush (IRE)**, after a poor start, ran reasonably and should improve a little as a result. (33/1)
**Hurgill Dancer** is not very big but did show some ability, staying on at the end, and should be all the sharper for the run. (16/1)
**Warrlin** was learning as the race progressed. (25/1)

## 1198 MIDDLEHAM TRAINERS ASSOCIATION H'CAP (0-85) (3-Y.O+) (Class D)

3-15 (3-17) **1m 2f** £4,377.00 (£1,326.00: £648.00: £309.00) Stalls: High GOING: 0.08 sec per fur (G)

| Form | Horse | Dist | Pos | SP | RR | SF |
|---|---|---|---|---|---|---|
| 988[15] | **Komreyev Dancer (71)** (ABailey) **4-9-3** JCarroll(6) (chsd ldrs: effrt over 2f out: led over 1f out: all out) | — | **1** | 12/1 | 81 | 48 |
| 913[3] | **Sarmatian (USA) (65)** (MDHammond) **5-8-11** KFallon(12) (a.p: effrt & nt clr run over 1f out: swtchd lft: ev ch ins fnl f: r.o) | nk | **2** | 10/1 | 75 | 42 |
| 628[3] | **Hazard a Guess (IRE) (81)** (DNicholls) **6-9-13** AlexGreaves(8) (lw: bhd: hdwy 3f out: nt clr run ins fnl f: kpt on) | 1¼ | **3** | 7/1[3] | 89 | 56 |
| 1022[3] | **Field of Vision (IRE) (70)** (MrsASwinbank) **6-9-2** JFortune(14) (lw: chsd ldr: disp ld 4f out tl appr fnl f: kpt on) | nk | **4** | 10/1 | 77 | 44 |
| | **Current Speech (IRE) (70)** (TDEasterby) **5-8-11b**(5) RHavlin(11) (a chsng ldrs: rdn 3f out: r.o one pce) | ¾ | **5** | 14/1 | 76 | 43 |
| | **Deano's Beeno (76)** (MJohnston) **4-9-8** TWilliams(15) (lw: mde most tl hdd & wknd appr fnl f) | s.h | **6** | 12/1 | 82 | 49 |
| 982[8] | **Le Khoumf (FR) (72)** (JMBradley) **5-9-4** LCharnock(4) (hdwy 4f out: chsng ldrs 2f out: eased whn btn fnl f) | 7 | **7** | 8/1 | 67 | 34 |
| 993[15] | **Haido'hart (55)** (BSRothwell) **4-8-1** JFanning(13) (bhd: hdwy over 3f out: nvr rchd ldrs) | 4 | **8** | 33/1 | 43 | 10 |
| 967[11] | **Il Trastevere (FR) (80)** (MissGayKelleway) **4-9-12** OUrbina(10) (lw: mid div: effrt 3f out: wknd fnl 2f) | ½ | **9** | 10/1 | 67 | 34 |
| 871[11] | **Mister Rm (76)** (RGuest) **4-9-8** MFenton(9) (bit bkwd: in tch tl wknd fnl 3f) | ½ | **10** | 12/1 | 63 | 30 |
| 879[5] | **Fakih (USA) (75)** (ACStewart) **4-9-7** WCarson(2) (prom: rdn 3f out: sn btn & eased) | 1¾ | **11** | 2/1[1] | 59 | 26 |
| 504[8] | **Antarticturn (USA) (51)** (GROldroyd) **6-7-4**(7)ow1 RFfrench(1) (s.s: a bhd) | ¾ | **12** | 33/1 | 34 | — |
| 933[15] | **Celestial Choir (82)** (JLEyre) **6-10-0** RLappin(7) (bhd & rdn 4f out: n.d) | 10 | **13** | 9/1 | 49 | 16 |
| 920[5] | **Sovereign Page (USA) (76)** (BHanbury) **7-9-8** WRyan(3) (b: lost tch fnl 4f) | 12 | **14** | 5/1[2] | 23 | — |
| | **Augustan (57)** (SGollings) **5-8-0**(3)ow3 DRMcCabe(5) (a bhd) | ½ | **15** | 20/1 | 4 | — |

(SP 151.3%) **15 Rn**

**2m 10.8** (7.30) CSF £141.32 CT £870.39 TOTE £19.40: £3.30 £2.50 £2.30 (£135.70) Trio £156.60 OWNER Mr Denis Gallagher (TARPORLEY) BRED G. and Mrs Whittaker
LONG HANDICAP Antartictern (USA) 6-13

**628* Komreyev Dancer**, who ran inexplicably badly at Chester last time, came back to form here in a messy race and deservedly held on. (12/1)
**913 Sarmatian (USA)** would probably have won this had he got a gap entering the last two furlongs. He still had a chance after that, but the winner had taken first run. (10/1)
**628 Hazard a Guess (IRE)** produced a great run from three furlongs out, only to run into trouble entering the final furlong, and he is definitely one to keep on the right side. (7/1)
**1022 Field of Vision (IRE)**, dropped back in distance this time, ran another sound race, but was always inclined to edge left when the pressure was on and was just tapped for toe. (10/1)
**Current Speech (IRE)** had the blinkers that worked an odd time over hurdles on, but was never doing anything like enough. (14/1)
**Deano's Beeno**, having his first run for eight months, had a good blow, going off in front, and should be all the better for this. (12/1)
**821 Le Khoumf (FR)** would have finished a fair bit closer but for being eased when beaten in the closing stages. (8/1)
**879 Fakih (USA)** raced in a handy position but, when the pressure was on three furlongs out, soon threw in the towel. (2/1)

## 1199 RIPON SUNDAY SPRINT CHALLENGE H'CAP (0-90) (3-Y.O+) (Class C)

3-45 (3-46) **5f** £6,872.50 (£2,080.00: £1,015.00: £482.50) Stalls: Low GOING minus 0.20 sec per fur (GF)

| Form | Horse | Dist | Pos | SP | RR | SF |
|---|---|---|---|---|---|---|
| 850[13] | **Portend (78)** (SRBowring) **4-9-5b1**(5) CTeague(3) (lw: cl up: carried lft ½-wy: led 2f out: hld on wl) | — | **1** | 10/1 | 89 | 72 |
| 928[4] | **Stuffed (65)** (MWEasterby) **4-8-6**(5) GParkin(2) (prom: hmpd ½-wy: swtchd & hdwy over 1f out: chal ins fnl f: no ex towards fin) | ¾ | **2** | 3/1[1] | 74 | 57 |
| 1073[4] | **So Intrepid (IRE) (73)** (JMBradley) **6-9-5** WRyan(6) (lw: s.i.s: hdwy ½-wy: kpt on) | 3 | **3** | 13/2 | 72 | 55 |
| 1113[10] | **Insider Trader (73)** (MrsJRRamsden) **5-9-5** KFallon(4) (w ldrs: carried lft ½-wy: kpt on) | 1¼ | **4** | 7/1 | 68 | 51 |
| 931* | **Awasha (IRE) (65)** (MissGayKelleway) **4-8-11** OUrbina(7) (b: lw: w ldrs: carried lft ½-wy: r.o one pce) | nk | **5** | 5/1[3] | 59 | 42 |
| 931[13] | **Palo Blanco (73)** (TDBarron) **5-9-5** JFortune(8) (prom: shkn up 2f out: kpt on fnl f) | 1¾ | **6** | 9/2[2] | 61 | 44 |
| *335*[6] | **Celandine (85)** (JLEyre) **3-9-6**(3) DWright(1) (sn wl bhd: sme late hdwy) | 4 | **7** | 25/1 | 61 | 36 |
| 1113[9] | **Royal Dome (IRE) (75)** (MartynWane) **4-9-7** JCarroll(9) (lw: led: edgd lft ½-wy: hdd 2f out: sn wknd) | ¾ | **8** | 6/1 | 48 | 31 |
| 973[17] | **Imp Express (IRE) (59)** (GMMoore) **3-7-11**ow1 DaleGibson(5) (outpcd fr ½-wy) | 4 | **9** | 33/1 | 19 | — |
| 475[5] | **Broadstairs Beauty (IRE) (72)** (PHowling) **6-9-4b** SDWilliams(10) (lw: spd to ½-wy: sn btn) | 5 | **10** | 7/1 | 16 | — |

(SP 128.3%) **10 Rn**

**59.5 secs** (1.10) CSF £41.77 CT £204.73 TOTE £16.40: £2.90 £1.70 £2.70 (£26.80) Trio £62.20 OWNER Mr D. H. Bowring (EDWINSTOWE) BRED Hollow Hole Stud
LONG HANDICAP Imp Express (IRE) 7-7
WEIGHT FOR AGE 3yo-8lb
STEWARDS' ENQUIRY Obj. to Portend by Parkin overruled.

**716 Portend** came back to form in good style, holding on bravely when challenged. (10/1)
**928 Stuffed**, who got murdered at halfway, recovered well to challenge inside the final furlong, but was well held late on. (3/1)
**1073 So Intrepid (IRE)** is in terrific form at present, but just found this trip on this sharp track too quick. (13/2)
**931 Insider Trader** keeps running well without success. A pair of blinkers might help, as they have in the past. (7/1)
**931* Awasha (IRE)** raced with every chance, but was caught up in some scrimmaging at halfway and was fighting a lost cause thereafter. (5/1)
**Palo Blanco** was never really giving it her best until too late, and gives the impression that there is more to come if the key can be found. (9/2)
**Celandine**, a long way behind early on, was picking up at the end and should do better over further. (25/1)
**475 Broadstairs Beauty (IRE)** has changed stables and ran miserably. (7/1)

## 1200 RACING NORTH H'CAP (0-80) (3-Y.O) (Class D)

4-15 (4-16) **1m 4f 60y** £4,240.50 (£1,284.00: £627.00: £298.50) Stalls: Low GOING: 0.08 sec per fur (G)

| | | | | SP | RR | SF |
|---|---|---|---|---|---|---|
| 954[5] | **Exactly (IRE) (67)** (JLEyre) **3-8-11** TWilliams(2) (mde all: clr ½-wy: kpt on wl) | — | **1** | 5/1[3] | 76 | 29 |
| 932[6] | **Mental Pressure (76)** (MrsMReveley) **3-9-6** ACulhane(1) (hld up: hdwy 3f out: hung rt: kpt on: nvr able to chal) | 2½ | **2** | 6/1 | 82 | 35 |
| 1000[5] | **Manoy (55)** (JHetherton) **3-7-13** NKennedy(6) (chsd wnr: n.m.r 2f out: one pce) | 3 | **3** | 14/1 | 57 | 10 |
| 702[4] | **Samim (USA) (77)** (JLDunlop) **3-9-7b** WCarson(7) (lw: chsd ldrs: effrt over 3f out: hrd rdn over 2f out: btn whn hmpd over 1f out) | 4 | **4** | 11/4[1] | 74 | 27 |
| 717[4] | **Anchor Venture (64)** (SPCWoods) **3-8-8** WRyan(4) (lw: stdd s: hld up & bhd: nt clr run over 2f out: nvr plcd to chal) | nk | **5** | 7/2[2] | 60 | 13 |
| 803[10] | **Jackson Park (65)** (TDEasterby) **3-8-9** MBirch(8) (chsd ldrs: rdn over 3f out: no imp) | 1 | **6** | 5/1[3] | 60 | 13 |
| 1089[5] | **Lucky Bea (56)** (MWEasterby) **3-8-0** DaleGibson(3) (hld up: effrt 4f out: no imp) | 4 | **7** | 13/2 | 46 | — |
| 921[12] | **Atienza (USA) (65)** (SCWilliams) **3-8-9** JTate(5) (prom tl wknd fnl 4f) | 5 | **8** | 13/2 | 48 | 1 |

(SP 129.8%) **8 Rn**

**2m 45.2** (11.20) CSF £36.13 CT £379.85 TOTE £6.90: £2.00 £2.20 £4.20 (£26.30) OWNER Mr Frank Thornton (HAMBLETON) BRED Asigh Farm Ltd
**954 Exactly (IRE)**, suited by this drop back in distance, was given a fine ride. Holding a useful lead entering the straight, she never looked likely to stop. (5/1)
**932 Mental Pressure** would probably have won this had he fully co-operated with his jockey, but he was intent on hanging right all the way up the straight. (6/1)
**1000 Manoy**, a real handful in the preliminaries, ran a sound race but was short of any turn of foot. (14/1)
**702 Samim (USA)** has ability but does not seem to want to use it. (11/4)
**717 Anchor Venture**, given an educational ride, stayed on well and will do better, especially over further. (7/2)
**702 Jackson Park** never looked happy from the home turn and failed to offer a threat. (5/1)
**Atienza (USA)** (13/2: 4/1-7/1)

## 1201 STIRRING SMILES BY TOYOTA MAIDEN STKS (3-Y.O) (Class D)

4-45 (4-47) **1m 1f** £4,032.50 (£1,220.00: £595.00: £282.50) Stalls: High GOING: 0.08 sec per fur (G)

| | | | | SP | RR | SF |
|---|---|---|---|---|---|---|
| | **Cabaret (IRE)** (PWChapple-Hyam) **3-8-4**(5) RHavlin(4) (w'like: lw: a.p: led 1½f out: styd on) | — | **1** | 7/4[2] | 87 | 35 |
| 957[6] | **Nanda** (DRLoder) **3-8-6**(3) DRMcCabe(5) (led: qcknd 4f out: hdd 1½f out: no ex) | 3 | **2** | 7/2[3] | 82 | 30 |
| 970[7] | **Mawared (IRE)** (JLDunlop) **3-9-0** WCarson(6) (chsd ldrs: outpcd appr st & lost pl: hdwy u.p 3f out: no imp) | 14 | **3** | 6/4[1] | 62 | 10 |
| 994[8] | **Indiphar** (FHLee) **3-8-9** MFenton(3) (effrt over 4f out: nvr trbld ldrs) | 1¾ | **4** | 50/1 | 54 | 2 |
| 974[3] | **Beacontree** (MJohnston) **3-9-0** TWilliams(1) (plld hrd early: chsd ldrs: outpcd over 4f out: sn btn) | 21 | **5** | 8/1 | 21 | — |
| 705[12] | **Celia's Rainbow** (MPBielby) **3-8-9** JFortune(2) (outpcd & bhd fnl 4f) | 7 | **6** | 50/1 | 4 | — |

(SP 113.6%) **6 Rn**

**1m 57.4** (7.20) CSF £8.05 TOTE £2.90: £1.50 £2.10 (£6.20) OWNER Mr Ivan Allan (MARLBOROUGH) BRED Ivan W. Allan and K. C. Choo
**Cabaret (IRE)** looked fit but took time to get going but was well on top at the finish. (7/4: op Evens)
**957 Nanda** went out to make all but had no answer when tackled approaching the final furlong. She might be better over shorter distances still. (7/2: 5/2-4/1)
**Mawared (IRE)** was well-backed but never looked happy at any stage. He would seem to have a problem. (6/4)
**Indiphar** needs more time yet. (50/1)
**974 Beacontree** has an attitude problem. (8/1: op 5/1)

T/Plpt: £480.20 (29.51 Tckts). T/Qdpt: £42.30 (28.62 Tckts). AA

## 1202a-1234a (Irish Racing) - See Computer Raceform

# 1214a-CURRAGH (Newbridge, Ireland) (R-H) (Soft)

## Saturday April 13th

## 1235a GLADNESS STKS (Gp 3) (3-Y.O+)

3-55 (4-00) **7f**

| | | | SP | RR | SF |
|---|---|---|---|---|---|
| **Idris (IRE)** (JSBolger,Ireland) **6-9-7** KJManning (trckd ldrs: chal over 1f out: r.o wl u.p to ld wl ins fnl f) | — | **1** | 13/2[3] | 113 | 75 |
| **Burden Of Proof (IRE)** (CO'Brien,Ireland) **4-9-7** CRoche (trckd ldrs: led over 1f out: hdd & no ex wl ins fnl f) | ½ | **2** | 13/8[1] | 112 | 74 |
| **Rainbow Blues (IRE)** (APO'Brien,Ireland) **3-8-7** JAHeffernan (led tl over 1f out: no ex ins fnl f) | 5½ | **3** | 20/1 | 99 | 47 |
| **Aylesbury (IRE)** (JOxx,Ireland) **3-8-10** JPMurtagh (chsd ldrs: no imp fr over 1f out) | hd | **4** | 6/1[2] | 102 | 50 |
| **America's Cup (IRE)** (CO'Brien,Ireland) **4-9-4** NGMcCullagh (a cl up: ev ch 2f out: btn over 1f out) | 3½ | **5** | 16/1 | 88 | 50 |
| **No Animosity (IRE)** (APO'Brien,Ireland) **3-8-7** SCraine (hld up & bhd: hdwy fnl 2f: nvr nrr) | ½ | **6** | 10/1 | 90 | 38 |
| **Sir Silver Sox (USA)** (TStack,Ireland) **4-9-7** PJSmullen (hld up & bhd: hdwy wl over 2f out: no imp) | 1 | **7** | 20/1 | 88 | 50 |
| **Nautical Pet (IRE)** (DKWeld,Ireland) **4-9-10** MJKinane (hld up & bhd: sme hdwy over 2f out: no imp) | 3 | **8** | 6/1[2] | 84 | 46 |
| **I'm Supposin (IRE)** (KPrendergast,Ireland) **4-9-7** WJSupple (chsd ldrs tl rdn & wknd over 2f out) | ½ | **9** | 7/1 | 80 | 42 |
| **Cossack Count** (MKauntze,Ireland) **3-8-4** WJO'Connor (disp ld tl wknd qckly over 2f out) | 8 | **10** | 14/1 | 58 | 6 |

(SP 123.7%) **10 Rn**

**1m 28.7** (5.70) OWNER Mr Michael Keogh (COOLCULLEN)

**1236a-1245a** (Irish Racing) - See Computer Raceform

# 1210a-**LEOPARDSTOWN (Dublin, Ireland)** (L-H) (Soft)
## Saturday April 20th

### 1246a LEOPARDSTOWN 1000 GUINEAS TRIAL STKS (Listed) (3-Y.O F)
3-30 (3-32) **7f** £9,675.00 (£2,775.00: £1,275.00: £375.00)

| | Horse | Dist | Pos | SP | RR | SF |
|---|---|---|---|---|---|---|
| | **Sheraka (IRE)** (JOxx,Ireland) **3-8-10** JPMurtagh (rn 3rd: chsd ldrs st: sn chal: rdn to ld early ins fnl f: rdn & kpt on wl) | — | 1 | 11/8[1] | 100 | 52 |
| | **Tirol Hope (IRE)** (MKauntze,Ireland) **3-8-10b[1]** WJO'Connor (led tl ins fnl f: kpt on) | nk | 2 | 9/1 | 99 | 51 |
| | **Dance Clear (IRE)** (APO'Brien,Ireland) **3-8-10** CRoche (hld up: 5th ½-wy: 4th & chsd ldrs whn edgd lft bef st: rdn to chal 1½f out: nt trble ldrs: kpt on same pce) | 5 | 3 | 9/4[2] | 88 | 40 |
| | **Pegwood (IRE)** (DKWeld,Ireland) **3-8-10** MJKinane (chsd ldr: chal 2f out: 3rd u.p 1½f out: sn no ex) | ¾ | 4 | 5/1[3] | 86 | 38 |
| | **Highly Motivated** (APO'Brien,Ireland) **3-8-10** JAHeffernan (6th ½-wy: rdn & no imp 2f out) | 13 | 5 | 14/1 | 57 | 9 |
| | **Sliabh Bawn (USA)** (JSBolger,Ireland) **3-8-10** KJManning (in tch: 4th ½-wy: 5th & chsd ldrs whn bdly hmpd bef st: nt rcvr) | 2½ | 6 | 14/1 | 51 | 3 |
| | **In The Evening (IRE)** (NMeade,Ireland) **3-8-10** WJSupple (towards rr: bdly hmpd bef st: n.d) | 3 | 7 | 33/1 | 44 | — |

(SP 115.8%) **7 Rn**

**1m 33.3** (8.30) OWNER H H Aga Khan (CURRABEG) BRED H.H. Aga Khan's Stud S.C.

**Sheraka (IRE)** is not much to look at, but was fit enough. Leading inside the final 200 yards, she was always doing just enough. (11/8: op 4/5)

### 1247a LEOPARDSTOWN 2000 GUINEAS TRIAL STKS (Listed) (3-Y.O C)
4-00 (4-04) **1m** £9,675.00 (£2,775.00: £1,275.00: £375.00)

| | Horse | Dist | Pos | SP | RR | SF |
|---|---|---|---|---|---|---|
| | **Deed of Love (USA)** (JSBolger,Ireland) **3-8-10** KJManning (hld up: 3rd & trckd ldrs 3f out: smooth hdwy on ins to disp ld wl over 1f out: led 1f out: rdn & kpt on wl) | — | 1 | 2/1[1] | 107 | 54 |
| | **Pro Trader (USA)** (DKWeld,Ireland) **3-8-10b[1]** MJKinane (towards rr: rdn st: wnt 3rd & nt trble ldrs over 1f out: styd on u.p ins last: wnt 2nd nr fin) | 1 | 2 | 5/1[2] | 105 | 52 |
| | **Tasdid** (KPrendergast,Ireland) **3-8-10** WJSupple (sn led: rdn 3f out: jnd wl over 1f out: hdd u.p 1f out: kpt on) | hd | 3 | 10/1 | 105 | 52 |
| | **Deynawari (IRE)** (JOxx,Ireland) **3-8-13** JPMurtagh (led early: chsd ldr: chal st: 3rd, rdn & btn 1½f out) | 8 | 4 | 2/1[1] | 92 | 39 |
| 1235a[6] | **No Animosity (IRE)** (APO'Brien,Ireland) **3-8-13** CRoche (rn 3rd: 4th & rdn st: one pce & no imp 1½f out) | 1 | 5 | 6/1[3] | 90 | 37 |

(SP 106.7%) **5 Rn**

**1m 46.3** (9.30) OWNER Maktoum Al Maktoum (COOLCULLEN)

**Deed of Love (USA)**, clear on ratings, got a smooth run up the inner coming off the last bend and held on well enough. (2/1)

**Pro Trader (USA)** ran above himself and has now been put up 7lb. He stayed on under pressure to snatch second near the line. (5/1)

**Deynawari (IRE)** faded right out. (2/1)

### 1249a BALLYSAX STKS (Listed) (3-Y.O)
5-00 (5-02) **1m 2f** £9,675.00 (£2,775.00: £1,275.00: £375.00)

| | Horse | Dist | Pos | SP | RR | SF |
|---|---|---|---|---|---|---|
| | **Key Change (IRE)** (JOxx,Ireland) **3-8-11** DHogan (led briefly early: chsd ldr: led 3f out: rdn clr 1½f out: r.o) | — | 1 | 12/1 | 105 | 67 |
| | **Harghar (USA)** (JOxx,Ireland) **3-9-0** JPMurtagh (wnt 3rd after 3f: chsd ldrs 3f out: mod 2nd 1f out: kpt on: no ch w wnr) | 6 | 2 | 2/1[1] | 98 | 60 |
| | **Peace Offering (IRE)** (APO'Brien,Ireland) **3-8-11** CRoche (hld up towards rr: rdn & hdwy 3f out: 4th over 1f out: no imp fnl f) | hd | 3 | 4/1[3] | 95 | 57 |
| | **Ceirseach (IRE)** (JSBolger,Ireland) **3-8-11** KJManning (sn led: hdd 3f out: rdn & nt qckn wl over 1f out: kpt on same pce) | ¾ | 4 | 4/1[3] | 94 | 56 |
| | **Ahkaam (USA)** (DKWeld,Ireland) **3-9-5** MJKinane (hld up in tch: 4th ½-wy: towards rr & rdn 2f out: no imp) | 5½ | 5 | 100/30[2] | 93 | 55 |
| | **Rescue Time (IRE)** (KPrendergast,Ireland) **3-9-0** WJSupple (hld up towards rr: hdwy over 3f out: 4th & rdn 2f out: sn btn) | 7 | 6 | 16/1 | 77 | 39 |

(SP 110.0%) **6 Rn**

**2m 14.2** (10.20) OWNER Lady Clague (CURRABEG) BRED Collinstown Stud Farm Ltd

**Key Change (IRE)** was not ignored in the market but, in beating her better-fancied stablemate, stepped up considerably on her juvenile form. She will stay further. (12/1)

# 1232a-**CURRAGH (Newbridge, Ireland)** (R-H) (Yielding)
## Saturday April 27th

### 1252a MOORESBRIDGE STKS (Listed) (4-Y.O+)
2-50 (2-51) **1m 2f** £9,675.00 (£2,775.00: £1,275.00: £375.00)

| | Horse | Dist | Pos | SP | RR | SF |
|---|---|---|---|---|---|---|
| | **Definite Article** (DKWeld,Ireland) **4-9-4** MJKinane (rn 3rd: hdwy 4f out: effrt on outside 2f out: led over 1f out: sn rdn & wnt rt: kpt on) | — | 1 | 4/9[1] | 117 | 31 |
| | **Al Mohaajir (USA)** (JSBolger,Ireland) **5-9-4** KJManning (hld up: 4th st: 3rd & rdn over 1f out: sn chsng wnr: r.o) | ¾ | 2 | 3/1[2] | 116 | 30 |
| 1235a[9] | **I'm Supposin (IRE)** (KPrendergast,Ireland) **4-8-12** WJSupple (hld up in rr: hdwy 2f out: sn rdn: swtchd lft over 1f out: n.m.r ins fnl f: r.o) | 1 | 3 | 6/1[3] | 108 | 22 |
| | **Ger's Royale (IRE)** (PJFlynn,Ireland) **5-8-12** JPMurtagh (chsd ldr after 1½f: rdn & led 2f out: hdd over 1f out: sn btn & eased) | 6 | 4 | 14/1 | 99 | 13 |
| | **Viaticum (IRE)** (NMeade,Ireland) **4-9-1b[1]** JMorgan (hld up: 5th st: sn rdn: no imp fr 2f out) | 3½ | 5 | 14/1 | 96 | 10 |
| | **Free To Speak (IRE)** (DKWeld,Ireland) **4-8-12** PShanahan (led to 2f out: sn wknd) | 1 | 6 | 25/1 | 91 | 5 |

(SP 125.7%) **6 Rn**

**2m 13.3** (9.30) OWNER Moyglare Stud Farm (CURRAGH) BRED Dr D. Davis

**Definite Article**, runner-up in the 1995 Irish Derby, looked big and well. He found little in the way of acceleration when asked and did not win as authoritatively as he should have, and one would want to see considerable improvement when he returns to tackle the Tattersalls Rogers Gold Cup in late May. (4/9)
**I'm Supposin (IRE)** was better suited by this trip. He did not enjoy the clearest of passages though and could improve on this. (6/1)

## 1253a LEXUS TETRARCH STKS (Gp 3) (3-Y.O C & F)
3-20 (3-22) **7f** £16,250.00 (£4,750.00: £2,250.00: £750.00)

| | | | SP | RR | SF |
|---|---|---|---|---|---|
| 1141a[10] | **Gothenberg (IRE)** (MJohnston) **3-8-9** JWeaver (mde all: drew clr fr 3f out: r.o wl) .......— | **1** | 5/2[2] | 111? | 58 |
| 1235a[3] | **Rainbow Blues (IRE)** (APO'Brien,Ireland) **3-8-9** CRoche (hld up: hdwy over 2f out: rdn & wnt 3rd over 1f out: chsd wnr ent fnl f: kpt on: no imp) .......6 | **2** | 9/2[3] | 97 | 44 |
| | **Force of Will (USA)** (DKWeld,Ireland) **3-8-6** MJKinane (hld up: wnt 3rd over 2f out: 4th & no hdwy over 1f out: kpt on ins fnl f) .......3 | **3** | 7/4[1] | 87 | 34 |
| | **Nashcash (IRE)** (CCollins,Ireland) **3-8-9** PShanahan (chsd ldr: 2nd over 3f out: rdn 2f out: wknd 1f out) ......1½ | **4** | 5/1 | 87 | 34 |
| | **Mitch (USA)** (DKWeld,Ireland) **3-8-6** WJSupple (hld up in rr: 5th & n.d last 2f) .......7 | **5** | 14/1 | 68 | 15 |
| | **Party Poll (USA)** (DKWeld,Ireland) **3-8-6** DJO'Donohoe (chsd ldr: pushed along after 2f: 2nd ½-wy: wknd qckly over 2f out: sn bhd: eased) .......15 | **6** | 16/1 | 34 | — |
| | | | (SP 112.3%) | | **6 Rn** |

**1m 26.2** (3.20) OWNER Brian Yeardley Continental Ltd (MIDDLEHAM) BRED Brownstown Stud Farm
**1141a Gothenberg (IRE)** certainly underlined the likely dominance of British colts over the Irish this season. Out of the stalls like a flash, he had them all in trouble at halfway and was only being ridden to keep straight. He certainly seemed to enjoy the ground. (5/2)
**Rainbow Blues (IRE)** came through for second early inside the final furlong. (9/2)
**Force of Will (USA)** was a real market drifter, and his burly appearance told its own tale. His trainer admitted that there was still plenty to work on. (7/4: op Evens)

## 1255a ATHASI STKS (Listed) (3 & 4-Y.O F)
4-20 (4-29) **7f** £9,675.00 (£2,775.00: £1,275.00: £375.00)

| | | | SP | RR | SF |
|---|---|---|---|---|---|
| | **Proud Titania (IRE)** (APO'Brien,Ireland) **3-8-8** JAHeffernan (cl up: 3rd ½-wy: rdn to ld & drifted rt over 1f out: r.o) .......— | **1** | 10/1 | 110 | 42 |
| | **Zafzala (IRE)** (JOxx,Ireland) **3-8-8** MJKinane (6th ½-wy: 4th whn swtchd lft over 1f out: chsng wnr over 1f out: r.o wl u.p ins fnl f) .......hd | **2** | 2/1[1] | 110 | 42 |
| | **Asmara (USA)** (JOxx,Ireland) **3-8-8** DHogan (prom: 2nd ½-wy: rdn & ev ch over 1f out: outpcd 1f out: r.o) .....2 | **3** | 7/1 | 105 | 37 |
| | **Marqueta (USA)** (CO'Brien,Ireland) **4-9-7** JPMurtagh (towards rr ½-wy: hdwy fr 2f out: kpt on: nt trble ldrs) .5½ | **4** | 14/1 | 93 | 38 |
| | **Priory Belle (IRE)** (JSBolger,Ireland) **3-9-1** KJManning (cl up: 4th ½-wy: rdn over 2f out: sn btn) .......nk | **5** | 9/2[2] | 99 | 31 |
| | **Rithab** (KPrendergast,Ireland) **3-8-8** WJSupple (bhd: sme hdwy over 2f out: 6th & no imp over 1f out) .......½ | **6** | 10/1 | 91 | 23 |
| 1246a[2] | **Tirol Hope (IRE)** (MKauntze,Ireland) **3-8-8b** WJO'Connor (led: c stands' side after 2f: rdn over 2f out: hdd 1½f out: wknd) .......1½ | **7** | 7/1 | 87 | 19 |
| | **Sarah's Guest (IRE)** (NMeade,Ireland) **3-8-8** PShanahan (cl up: lost pl & 5th ½-wy: n.d last 2f) .......1½ | **8** | 20/1 | 84 | 16 |
| | **Magarah (IRE)** (APO'Brien,Ireland) **3-8-9**ow1 CRoche (hld up: eased & t.o fr 2f out: p.u ins fnl f: dead) ....... | **P** | 5/1[3] | — | — |
| | | | (SP 122.8%) | | **9 Rn** |

**1m 27.5** (4.50) OWNER Mrs John Magnier (PILTOWN)
**Proud Titania (IRE)** ran to a mark around 12lb better than her current handicap rating. She led over a furlong out and stayed on well. (10/1)
**Zafzala (IRE)** was catching the winner close home and needs further. (2/1)

## 1256a-1295a (Irish Racing) - See Computer Raceform

# 1244a-LEOPARDSTOWN (Dublin, Ireland) (L-H) (Good)
## Saturday May 11th

## 1296a AMETHYST STKS (Listed) (3-Y.O+)
5-00 (5-01) **1m** £9,675.00 (£2,775.00: £1,275.00: £375.00)

| | | | SP | RR | SF |
|---|---|---|---|---|---|
| 1235a* | **Idris (IRE)** (JSBolger,Ireland) **6-10-1** KJManning (hld up: 6th & on bridle 3f out: 5th st: effrt over 1f out: led early fnl f: kpt on wl) .......— | **1** | 7/2[2] | 113 | 51 |
| 728[3] | **Cadeaux Tryst** (EALDunlop) **4-9-10** PaulEddery (3rd st: ev ch over 1f out: rdn & no ex wl ins fnl f) .......1½ | **2** | 3/1[1] | 105 | 43 |
| | **Troysend** (APO'Brien,Ireland) **3-8-11** CRoche (hld up: hdwy on outside bef st: r.o. fr 2f out: nrst fin) .......½ | **3** | 8/1 | 104 | 29 |
| 728[12] | **Anastina** (NAGraham) **4-9-7** SCraine (cl up tl lost pl & 6th st: n.d fr 2f out: btn approx 9l) ....... | **7** | 10/1 | 87 | 25 |
| | | | | | **9 Rn** |

**1m 39.9** (2.90) OWNER Michael Keogh (COOLCULLEN)

## 1297a-1300a (Irish Racing) - See Computer Raceform

# 1061-BATH (L-H) (Good, Good to firm patches)
## Monday May 20th
WEATHER: overcast WIND: mod across

## 1301 TIMEFORM DAY AT BATH MEDIAN AUCTION MAIDEN STKS (3-Y.O) (Class F)
2-15 (2-20) **1m 5y** £2,635.00 (£735.00: £355.00) Stalls: Low GOING minus 0.39 sec per fur (F)

| | | | SP | RR | SF |
|---|---|---|---|---|---|
| | **Divina Luna** (JWHills) **3-8-9** MHills(2) (bit bkwd: a.p: led 3f out: sn hdd: led 2f out: drvn out) .......— | **1** | 12/1 | 72 | 29 |
| *856*[2] | **Young Mazaad (IRE) (68)** (DCO'Brien) **3-9-0v**[1] GBardwell(1) (plld hrd: a.p: led over 2f out: sn hdd: r.o one pce) .......1¾ | **2** | 10/1 | 74 | 31 |
| 768[3] | **Budby** (ACStewart) **3-8-9** BThomson(3) (hld up: hdwy over 1f out: nvr nrr) .......1¾ | **3** | 9/4[1] | 65 | 22 |
| 730[7] | **Banneret (USA)** (LordHuntingdon) **3-9-0** AReid(8) (lw: hld up: rdn & outpcd over 3f out: styd on fnl f) .......2½ | **4** | 5/1[3] | 65 | 22 |
| *502*[6] | **Two Socks (50)** (MMcCormack) **3-9-0** AClark(9) (rdn & hdwy 4f out: r.o one pce fnl f) .......½ | **5** | 50/1 | 64 | 21 |
| 892[14] | **Dramatic Act** (CRBarwell) **3-8-9** NAdams(4) (s.s: nrst fin) .......2½ | **6** | 12/1 | 54 | 11 |

| | | | | SP | RR | SF |
|---|---|---|---|---|---|---|
| | **Animation** (KMcAuliffe) **3-8-9** SSanders(11) (nvr nr ldrs) | 2 | **7** | 50/1 | 50 | 7 |
| $976^{8}$ | **Brandonville (70)** (NTinkler) **3-9-0** PatEddery(7) (prom tl wknd 3f out) | nk | **8** | 13/2 | 55 | 12 |
| $949^{4}$ | **Blossom Dearie** (RGFrost) **3-8-9** RStreet(5) (hld up: wknd over 3f out) | 2½ | **9** | 25/1 | 45 | 2 |
| $1010^{12}$ | **Lancashire Legend (67)** (SDow) **3-9-0** TQuinn(10) (led 5f: wknd qckly) | 2½ | **10** | 20/1 | 45 | 2 |
| $978^{12}$ | **Rapid Liner (41)** (HOliver) **3-9-0** VSlattery(6) (prom 2f: sn bhd: t.o) | dist | **11** | 66/1 | — | — |
| *$577^{7}$* | ***Atlantic Storm*** (JHMGosden) **3-9-0** GHind(12) (Withdrawn not under Starter's orders: unruly in stalls) | | **W** | 5/2 [2] | — | — |

(SP 127.8%) **11 Rn**

**1m 41.7** (3.20) CSF £72.86 TOTE £15.00: £3.20 £2.00 £1.20 (£28.20) Trio £37.30 OWNER Mr D. J. Deer (LAMBOURN) BRED Azienda Agricola Colle Cardella

**Divina Luna** may not have beaten a lot but it did look beforehand as if she would come on for the run. (12/1: 8/1-14/1)
**856 Young Mazaad (IRE)** was very keen in the first-time visor and could have been entitled to have cried enough in the last quarter-mile. (10/1: op 5/1)
**768 Budby**, stepping up to a mile, settled much better but only got going when the race was virtually over. Out of a mare who won over a mile and a half, she could need even further. (9/4)
**Banneret (USA)** got caught flat-footed entering the home straight. (5/1: 7/2-6/1)
**Two Socks** did not appear suited to reverting to a mile. (50/1)
**Dramatic Act** seems worth a try over a longer trip. (12/1: op 5/1)
**714 Brandonville** (13/2: 9/2-7/1)

## 1302 TIMEFORM BLACK BOOK & RATINGS H'CAP (0-70) (3-Y.O+) (Class E)

2-45 (2-49) **1m 5y** £3,109.50 (£936.00: £453.00: £211.50) Stalls: Low GOING minus 0.39 sec per fur (F)

| | | | | SP | RR | SF |
|---|---|---|---|---|---|---|
| $983^{3}$ | **Leguard Express (IRE) (31)** (OO'Neill) **8-7-4b**(7) JBramhill(7) (mde all: rdn over 3f out: r.o wl) | — | **1** | 8/1 | 42 | 24 |
| $983^{4}$ | **Zahran (IRE) (40)** (JMBradley) **5-8-6** TQuinn(13) (rdn over 3f out: hdwy over 1f out: nt rch wnr) | 1¼ | **2** | 13/2 [2] | 49 | 31 |
| $688^{9}$ | **Noeprob (USA) (41)** (RJHodges) **6-8-2**(5) AmandaSanders(9) (hld up: hdwy over 2f out: r.o one pce fnl f) | nk | **3** | 16/1 | 49 | 31 |
| $983^{2}$ | **Runic Symbol (34)** (MBlanshard) **5-8-0** JQuinn(8) (hdwy over 1f out: r.o wl ins fnl f) | 1¼ | **4** | 7/1 [3] | 39 | 21 |
| $1037^{7}$ | **Cee-Jay-Ay (50)** (JBerry) **9-8-11**(5) PRoberts(14) (s.s: sn rcvrd: hdwy 3f out: one pce fnl 2f) | s.h | **5** | 15/2 | 55 | 37 |
| *$319^{6}$* | **Gentle Irony (55)** (MJRyan) **4-9-7** BDoyle(12) (chsd wnr: ev ch 2f out: one pce) | hd | **6** | 25/1 | 60 | 42 |
| $873^{8}$ | **Windswept (IRE) (65)** (DJSffrenchDavis) **3-9-0**(5) CAdamson(2) (prom: hrd rdn over 2f out: wknd over 1f out) | 1¼ | **7** | 20/1 | 68 | 38 |
| $1011^{7}$ | **Zeliba (32)** (CEBrittain) **4-7-7**(5)ow2 MHenry(18) (lw: nvr nr to chal) | ½ | **8** | 33/1 | 34 | 14 |
| $995^{16}$ | **Swift Maiden (60)** (JNeville) **3-8-9**(5) PPMurphy(16) (prom tl wknd over 2f out) | ½ | **9** | 20/1 | 61 | 31 |
| $879^{15}$ | **Ever so Lyrical (62)** (PWHarris) **6-10-0** GHind(3) (nvr nrr) | ¾ | **10** | 12/1 | 61 | 43 |
| $983^{12}$ | **Helios (57)** (NJHWalker) **8-9-9** JReid(6) (lw: n.d) | ¾ | **11** | 14/1 | 55 | 37 |
| $991^{5}$ | **Soaking (50)** (PBurgoyne) **6-8-13**(3) DRMcCabe(15) (lw: bhd fnl 2f) | 5 | **12** | 5/1 [1] | 38 | 20 |
| $981^{12}$ | **Cedar Dancer (41)** (RJHodges) **4-8-7** TSprake(1) (a bhd) | ½ | **13** | 33/1 | 28 | 10 |
| *$1048^{8}$* | **Hawaii Storm (FR) (48)** (DJSffrenchDavis) **8-9-0** RHughes(17) (s.i.s: a bhd) | ¾ | **14** | 33/1 | 33 | 15 |
| $887^{17}$ | **Roka (50)** (RHannon) **4-8-13**(3) DaneO'Neill(11) (lw: prom 5f) | 6 | **15** | 20/1 | 23 | 5 |
| 1010* | **Perilous Plight (61)** (WRMuir) **5-9-13** Jean-PierreLopez(5) (prom: rdn over 3f out: wknd over 2f out) | 7 | **16** | 7/1 [3] | 20 | 2 |
| $1010^{7}$ | **Napoleon Star (IRE) (60)** (MSSaunders) **5-9-12** RPrice(10) (a bhd) | ½ | **17** | 20/1 | 18 | — |
| | **Sobeloved (44)** (NEBerry) **4-8-10** AMackay(4) (s.s: a bhd: t.o) | 16 | **18** | 25/1 | — | — |

(SP 133.7%) **18 Rn**

**1m 41.1** (2.60) CSF £59.30 CT £767.90 TOTE £10.30: £2.20 £1.90 £2.90 £2.10 (£34.50) Trio £263.40 OWNER Mr John Gilbert (CHELTENHAM) BRED Knocklong House Stud

WEIGHT FOR AGE 3yo-12lb

**983 Leguard Express (IRE)** likes to dominate from the front and kept on gamely to the finish. (8/1)
**983 Zahran (IRE)** has won over nine furlongs at Hamilton, and a mile is looking the bare minimum for him nowadays. (13/2)
**549 Noeprob (USA)** could not produce that vital extra surge. (16/1)
**983 Runic Symbol** again got going too late in the day. (7/1)
**Cee-Jay-Ay** did not take long to recover from a slow start on this occasion. (15/2: 8/1-12/1)
**Gentle Irony** has slipped down to an 11lb lower mark on the turf than on the sand. (25/1)
**991 Soaking**, dropped 12lb this season, could only manage the briefest of efforts at halfway. (5/1: 6/1-4/1)
**1010* Perilous Plight** (7/1: op 4/1)

## 1303 TIMEFORM RACE CARD CONDITIONS STKS (2-Y.O) (Class C)

3-15 (3-16) **5f 11y** £4,670.10 (£1,628.10: £791.55: £335.25) Stalls: High GOING: 0.00 sec per fur (G)

| | | | | SP | RR | SF |
|---|---|---|---|---|---|---|
| 1032* | **For Old Times Sake** (JBerry) **2-8-11** GCarter(2) (s.i.s: hdwy over 2f out: rdn to ld over 1f out: comf) | — | **1** | 6/4 [1] | 78+ | 14 |
| 865* | **Pelham (IRE)** (RHannon) **2-9-0** PatEddery(1) (led: rdn & hdd over 1f out: unable qckn) | 2½ | **2** | 2/1 [2] | 73 | 9 |
| $1103^{2}$ | **Braveheart (IRE)** (MRChannon) **2-8-11** RHughes(3) (w ldr: hrd rdn 2f out: one pce) | 2 | **3** | 9/4 [3] | 64 | — |
| | **Sir Alidaf** (OO'Neill) **2-8-8** VSlattery(4) (str: scope: rdn 3f out: sn bhd: t.o) | 22 | **4** | 50/1 | — | — |

(SP 106.1%) **4 Rn**

**63.5 secs** (3.00) CSF £4.45 TOTE £2.30: (£2.80) OWNER Mrs Bridget Blum (COCKERHAM) BRED Shutford Stud

**1032* For Old Times Sake** may not be in the major leagues but is progressive and is still improving. (6/4)
**865* Pelham (IRE)** could not hold the winner in the last furlong and a half. (2/1: op 5/4)
**1103 Braveheart (IRE)**, a half-brother to Triumph Hurdle winner Kissair, could well now be finding the minimum trip too sharp. (9/4)

## 1304 TIMEFORM PHONE SERVICE LIMITED STKS (0-75) (3-Y.O) (Class D)

3-45 (3-46) **5f 11y** £3,530.25 (£1,062.00: £513.50: £239.25) Stalls: High GOING minus 0.39 sec per fur (F)

| | | | | SP | RR | SF |
|---|---|---|---|---|---|---|
| $1006^{7}$ | **Total Aloof (70)** (WJHaggas) **3-8-11** MHills(2) (lw: chsd ldr: led over 2f out: rdn over 1f out: r.o wl) | — | **1** | 11/4 [1] | 78 | 30 |
| $949^{7}$ | **Sharp Pearl (75)** (JWhite) **3-8-11b**[1] RHughes(6) (s.i.s: hdwy 2f out: hung lft over 1f out & wl ins fnl f: r.o) | 2½ | **2** | 10/1 | 70 | 22 |
| $867^{3}$ | **The Frisky Farmer (65)** (WGMTurner) **3-9-0** AClark(8) (lw: a.p: rdn over 1f out: btn whn hmpd wl ins fnl f) | ¾ | **3** | 14/1 | 71 | 23 |
| $1101^{3}$ | **Nellie North (72)** (GMMcCourt) **3-8-8** JReid(7) (a.p: rdn over 1f out: one pce) | s.h | **4** | 100/30 [2] | 65 | 17 |
| $989^{10}$ | **Dande Flyer (74)** (DWPArbuthnot) **3-8-11** TQuinn(5) (b: hld up: rdn over 2f out: one pce) | nk | **5** | 4/1 [3] | 67 | 19 |
| $1101^{15}$ | **Blue Suede Hoofs (70)** (BJMeehan) **3-8-11b**[1] BDoyle(4) (lw: s.i.s: swtchd rt ins fnl f: nrst fin) | s.h | **6** | 14/1 | 66 | 18 |
| | **White Settler (70)** (RJHodges) **3-8-11** AMcGlone(1) (led over 2f: wkng whn n.m.r over 1f out) | 10 | **7** | 9/2 | 35 | — |

| | | | | SP | RR | SF |
|---|---|---|---|---|---|---|
| 1049[16] | **Heights of Love (45)** (MSSaunders) **3-8-8** RPrice(3) (prom tl rdn & wknd over 2f out: t.o) | 15 | **8** | 66/1 | — | — |
| | | | | (SP 111.8%) | | **8 Rn** |

**62.5 secs** (2.00) CSF £26.13 TOTE £3.90: £1.50 £2.60 £2.20 (£24.70) OWNER Total (Bloodstock) Ltd (NEWMARKET) BRED Gainsborough Stud Management Ltd

**626* Total Aloof** did not handle the tight turns at Chester last time. (11/4)

**Sharp Pearl**, gelded since leaving Roger Charlton's yard, was inclined to duck away from the whip in the first-time blinkers. (10/1: 8/1-14/1)

**867 The Frisky Farmer** would have been receiving weight from all but one of his rivals had this been a handicap. (14/1: 10/1-16/1)

**1101 Nellie North** was dropping back to the minimum trip. (100/30: op 7/4)

**Dande Flyer** did not find the anticipated response when let down. (4/1: op 5/2)

**992 Blue Suede Hoofs**, tried in blinkers, could never get into it after rather fly-jumping leaving the stalls, and may need a longer trip. (14/1)

## 1305 TIMEFORM SILVER TANKARD MAIDEN STKS (3-Y.O+) (Class D)

4-15 (4-17) **1m 2f 46y** £3,621.25 (£1,090.00: £527.50: £246.25) Stalls: Low GOING: 0.00 sec per fur (G)

| | | | | SP | RR | SF |
|---|---|---|---|---|---|---|
| 860[2] | **Private Song (USA) (86)** (RCharlton) **3-8-12** PatEddery(5) (lw: mde all: hrd rdn 2f out: r.o wl) | — | **1** | 4/5[1] | 89 | 48 |
| 918[5] | **Qasida (IRE)** (CEBrittain) **3-8-12** BDoyle(2) (sn chsng wnr: rdn & ev ch 2f out: unable to qckn ins fnl f) | ½ | **2** | 5/2[2] | 88 | 47 |
| 860[14] | **Random Kindness** (PWHarris) **3-8-12** GHind(7) (a.p: rdn over 4f out: no hdwy fnl 3f) | 7 | **3** | 66/1 | 77 | 36 |
| | **Ragsak Jameel (USA)** (MajorWRHern) **3-8-12** TSprake(6) (bkwd: prom tl rdn & wknd over 4f out) | 7 | **4** | 8/1[3] | 66 | 25 |
| 847[6] | **Code Red** (JWHills) **3-8-12** MHills(12) (hld up & bhd: rdn & sme hdwy over 3f out: n.d) | 4 | **5** | 16/1 | 60 | 19 |
| 1079[5] | **Western Playboy** (RHannon) **4-9-9**(3) DaneO'Neill(8) (nvr nr ldrs) | ½ | **6** | 16/1 | 59 | 32 |
| 821[12] | **Ghusn** (TThomsonJones) **3-8-12** JReid(4) (mid div: rdn over 3f out: sn bhd) | 2½ | **7** | 20/1 | 55 | 14 |
| | **Crandon Boulevard** (LordHuntingdon) **3-8-12** DHarrison(9) (lengthy: a bhd) | 2 | **8** | 20/1 | 52 | 11 |
| | **Dry Sea** (RGFrost) **5-9-12** RStreet(11) (bkwd: hdwy 8f out: wknd 4f out) | 3 | **9** | 100/1 | 48 | 21 |
| | **Kairine (IRE)** (MRChannon) **3-8-7** TQuinn(1) (unf: lengthy: s.s: a bhd) | 1¼ | **10** | 20/1 | 41 | — |
| | **Kings Nightclub** (JWhite) **3-8-7** AMackay(3) (bkwd: a bhd) | 7 | **11** | 100/1 | 30 | — |
| 943[12] | **Saucy Soul** (SEarle) **3-8-12** RPerham(10) (hld up: bhd fnl 4f: t.o) | 13 | **12** | 100/1 | 14 | — |
| | | | | (SP 125.8%) | | **12 Rn** |

**2m 9.7** (2.20) CSF £3.53 TOTE £1.90: £1.10 £1.30 £5.10 (£2.00) Trio £48.10 OWNER Mr K. Abdulla (BECKHAMPTON) BRED Juddmonte Farms

WEIGHT FOR AGE 3yo-14lb

OFFICIAL EXPLANATION **Western Playboy: the jockey reported that his instructions had been to settle the horse as he is a strong ride, and make his effort turning for home. The gelding proved difficult to settle and when asked a question, found nothing.**

**860 Private Song (USA)** had to work pretty hard to fend off the persistent runner-up. (4/5)

**918 Qasida (IRE)** flashed his tail a couple of times in the closing stages and may have been thinking twice about going through with it. (5/2)

**Random Kindness** could make no impression on the leading pair and it was a case of finishing best of the rest. (66/1)

**Ragsak Jameel (USA)**, a half-brother to Party Cited, should at least strip fitter for the outing. (8/1)

## 1306 TIMEFORM PERSPECTIVE & RATINGS H'CAP (0-80) (3-Y.O+ F & M) (Class D)

4-45 (4-46) **1m 5f 22y** £3,598.50 (£1,083.00: £524.00: £244.50) Stalls: High GOING minus 0.39 sec per fur (F)

| | | | | SP | RR | SF |
|---|---|---|---|---|---|---|
| 1147[2] | **Paradise Waters (59)** (RFJohnsonHoughton) **4-8-13** JReid(4) (mde all: r.o wl fnl 2f) | — | **1** | 11/4[1] | 71 | 41 |
| 1063[2] | **Lalindi (IRE) (66)** (DRCElsworth) **5-9-6b** AProcter(6) (chsd wnr: rdn over 3f out: ev ch 2f out: sn edgd rt: one pce) | 2½ | **2** | 5/1[3] | 75 | 45 |
| 995* | **Rasayel (USA) (56)** (PDEvans) **6-8-10** TQuinn(3) (lw: hld up: rdn over 2f out: swtchd lft over 1f out: one pce) | ½ | **3** | 4/1[2] | 64 | 34 |
| 1011[2] | **Uncharted Waters (52)** (CACyzer) **5-8-6** GDuffield(7) (lw: lost pl 6f out: hdwy over 2f out: nt trble ldrs) | 3½ | **4** | 7/1 | 56 | 26 |
| 1005[4] | **Unchanged (74)** (CEBrittain) **4-10-0b[1]** BDoyle(5) (prom tl wknd over 2f out) | 1½ | **5** | 4/1[2] | 76 | 46 |
| *1031[12]* | **Triple Tie (USA) (42)** (MBlanshard) **5-7-10** JQuinn(1) (swtg: rdn 3f out: a bhd) | 9 | **6** | 33/1 | 33 | 3 |
| 993[8] | **Tirolette (IRE) (57)** (RJRWilliams) **4-8-11b** MHills(2) (hld up: bhd fnl 5f: t.o) | dist | **7** | 13/2 | — | — |
| | | | | (SP 112.1%) | | **7 Rn** |

**2m 49.9** (4.20) CSF £15.47 TOTE £3.40: £1.90 £2.00 (£6.60) OWNER Mr R. Crutchley (DIDCOT) BRED R. E. Crutchley

LONG HANDICAP Triple Tie (USA) 7-5

OFFICIAL EXPLANATION **Tirolette (IRE): the trainer reported the filly to be heavily in season the following day.**

**1147 Paradise Waters**, making a quick reappearance, had probably not been suited by the heavily watered ground at Newbury. (11/4)

**1063 Lalindi (IRE)**, inclined to carry her head high, could not overhaul the winner. (5/1)

**995* Rasayel (USA)**, up 6lb, was running off a mark 11lb higher than when winning this race last year. (4/1)

**1011 Uncharted Waters** was 7lb higher than when winning at Brighton last month. (7/1: 5/1-8/1)

**1005 Unchanged**, blinkered for the first time, needs a stiffer test of stamina. (4/1: 3/1-9/2)

## 1307 TIMEFORM RACEVIEW H'CAP (0-70) (3-Y.O+) (Class E)

5-15 (5-17) **5f 161y** £3,109.50 (£936.00: £453.00: £211.50) Stalls: High GOING minus 0.39 sec per fur (F)

| | | | | SP | RR | SF |
|---|---|---|---|---|---|---|
| 1064[4] | **Jucea (63)** (JLSpearing) **7-9-8** JReid(4) (lw: hdwy over 2f out: led wl over 1f out: drvn out) | — | **1** | 11/4[1] | 75 | 55 |
| 1041[8] | **Polli Pui (40)** (WMBrisbourne) **4-7-8**(5) MartinDwyer(8) (s.s: hdwy fnl 2f: r.o) | 3 | **2** | 50/1 | 44 | 24 |
| 862[9] | **Baileys Sunset (IRE) (61)** (JMBradley) **4-9-1**(5) MHenry(9) (hdwy over 2f out: ev ch over 1f out: one pce) | hd | **3** | 9/1 | 64 | 44 |
| *1030[3]* | **Our Shadee (USA) (49)** (KTIvory) **6-8-1v**(7) CScally(14) (hdwy over 2f out: rdn over 1f out: one pce) | 3 | **4** | 20/1 | 44 | 24 |
| 814[9] | **Mousehole (62)** (RGuest) **4-9-7** GDuffield(1) (chsd ldrs: rdn 4f out: no hdwy fnl 2f) | ¾ | **5** | 11/2[3] | 55 | 35 |
| 1073* | **Prima Silk (68)** (MJRyan) **5-9-13** TIves(5) (bhd tl hdwy over 1f out: nvr nrr) | ½ | **6** | 5/1[2] | 60 | 40 |
| | **Kildee Lad (69)** (APJones) **6-10-0** GCarter(7) (hdwy over 2f out: wknd over 1f out) | ¾ | **7** | 20/1 | 58 | 38 |
| 1039[2] | **Rockcracker (IRE) (63)** (GGMargarson) **4-9-8b** PBloomfield(3) (nvr trbld ldrs) | 1¼ | **8** | 7/1 | 49 | 29 |
| 806[12] | **Petraco (IRE) (62)** (NASmith) **8-9-7** SDWilliams(2) (bhd: rdn 3f out: n.d) | 1 | **9** | 10/1 | 45 | 25 |
| | **Ashkernazy (IRE) (43)** (NEBerry) **5-8-2** NAdams(10) (bit bkwd: led over 2f) | 1½ | **10** | 20/1 | 22 | 2 |
| 997[7] | **Lord Sky (51)** (ABailey) **5-8-3**(7) AngelaGallimore(13) (a.p: led over 2f out tl wknd wl over 1f out) | 3½ | **11** | 20/1 | 20 | — |
| 1170[16] | **Tommy Tempest (37)** (REPeacock) **7-7-10v** GBardwell(11) (prom: hrd rdn 3f out: sn wknd) | nk | **12** | 66/1 | 5 | — |
| 1101[11] | **Kossolian (60)** (BPalling) **3-8-10b[1]** TSprake(6) (w ldr over 2f) | 3½ | **13** | 16/1 | 19 | — |
| *178[8]* | **Willrack Farrier (60)** (BJMeehan) **4-9-5** BDoyle(12) (bit bkwd: a bhd) | 6 | **14** | 33/1 | 2 | — |
| | | | | (SP 121.6%) | | **14 Rn** |

**1m 10.8** (1.30) CSF £106.76 CT £1,034.11 TOTE £3.80: £1.80 £11.30 £3.30 (£175.20) Trio £512.20 OWNER Mr A. A. Campbell (ALCESTER) BRED G. W. Mills and Sons

LONG HANDICAP Tommy Tempest 7-9

WEIGHT FOR AGE 3yo-9lb

**1064 Jucea** gained due reward for some good efforts on this course and had a low draw this time. (11/4)
**983 Polli Pui**, who has been dropping down the ratings, put in some good late work after a poor start. (50/1)
**750* Baileys Sunset (IRE)** fared much better than when running under a penalty here last month. (9/1)
**1030 Our Shadee (USA)** has been dropped 9lb since his run at Sandown. (20/1)
**Mousehole**, a springer in the market, has slipped back down to the sort of mark off which he won. (11/2: op 10/1)
**1073* Prima Silk** had to contend with a slightly shorter trip and a 5lb hike in the weights. (5/1)

T/Jkpt: £27,652.60 (10.64 Tckts). T/Plpt: £36.90 (824.25 Tckts). T/Qdpt: £12.00 (84.13 Tckts) KH

# 0657-MUSSELBURGH (R-H) (Good)
## Monday May 20th
WEATHER: sunny WIND: almost nil

## 1308 MAY MAIDEN STKS (2-Y.O) (Class F)
6-30 (6-30) **5f** £2,517.00 (£707.00: £345.00) Stalls: High GOING: 0.00 sec per fur (G)

| | | | | SP | RR | SF |
|---|---|---|---|---|---|---|
| 975$^{2}$ | **Bayford Thrust** (JBerry) **2-8-8** JCarroll(2) (b: cl up: led 2f out: r.o) | — | **1** | Evens$^{1}$ | 69 | 40 |
| 1038$^{3}$ | **Red Romance** (DenysSmith) **2-8-5**$^{ow2}$ KFallon(1) (lw: outpcd after 2f: styd on wl appr fnl f: nrst fin) | 2½ | **2** | 11/2$^{3}$ | 58 | 27 |
| | **Casual Cottage (IRE)** (CMurray) **2-8-5** KDarley(3) (neat: led 3f: sn btn) | 3½ | **3** | 14/1 | 47 | 18 |
| 990$^{W}$ | **Treasure Touch (IRE)** (AHarrison) **2-8-7** DeanMcKeown(4) (w'like: scope: lw: chsd ldrs: swtchd & effrt ½-wy: rn green & sn btn) | 2 | **4** | 2/1$^{2}$ | 42 | 13 |
| | **Sheraton Girl** (MJohnston) **2-8-3** TWilliams(5) (leggy: scope: bit bkwd: s.i.s: a outpcd & bhd) | hd | **5** | 20/1 | 38 | 9 |
| | | | | (SP 110.1%) | | **5 Rn** |

**60.9 secs** (3.20) CSF £6.36 TOTE £1.90: £1.10 £2.30 (£2.80) OWNER Mrs Jean Turner (COCKERHAM) BRED Mrs J. M. Berry
**975 Bayford Thrust** looked ultra-fit and, with his stable really coming to form, always had this in hand from halfway. (Evens)
**1038 Red Romance** found this track too sharp but was keeping on well at the end, suggesting that another furlong would also help. (11/2: 7/2-6/1)
**Casual Cottage (IRE)** is a sharp sort and went tearing off in front but, headed by halfway, her head then went up and she was soon left struggling. (14/1: op 6/1)
**Treasure Touch (IRE)** gave absolutely no problems at the stalls this time but, in the race, ran very green when the pressure was on at halfway and was soon beaten. (2/1)
**Sheraton Girl** needed this and, always struggling with the pace, would seem to need plenty of time. (20/1)

## 1309 EAST LOTHIAN H'CAP (0-65) (3-Y.O+) (Class F)
7-00 (7-00) **1m 3f 32y** £2,707.40 (£761.40: £372.20) Stalls: High GOING: 0.04 sec per fur (G)

| | | | | SP | RR | SF |
|---|---|---|---|---|---|---|
| 1165$^{3}$ | **Lord Advocate (42)** (DANolan) **8-8-5b** VHalliday(3) (cl up: rdn to ld 3f out: styd on wl) | — | **1** | 14/1 | 53 | 28 |
| 1034$^{4}$ | **Gold Desire (33)** (MBrittain) **6-7-10** DaleGibson(4) (mid div: hdwy over 2f out: styd on wl towards fin) | 1¼ | **2** | 11/2$^{2}$ | 42 | 17 |
| 1167$^{14}$ | **Trumped (IRE) (39)** (PMonteith) **4-8-2**$^{ow5}$ NConnorton(9) (chsd ldrs: sltly hmpd over 3f out: hdwy 2f out: nt qckn ins fnl f) | s.h | **3** | 33/1 | 48 | 18 |
| 999* | **Manful (67)** (CWCElsey) **4-10-2b** NKennedy(12) (bhd: gd hdwy 3f out: swtchd over 1f out: styd on) | nk | **4** | 7/1$^{3}$ | 76 | 51 |
| 971$^{6}$ | **Here Comes Herbie (34)** (WStorey) **4-7-11**$^{ow1}$ TWilliams(5) (hld up: hdwy on ins whn hmpd wl over 1f out: swtchd & nt rcvr) | 1½ | **5** | 14/1 | 41+ | 15 |
| 1024$^{3}$ | **Rapid Mover (35)** (DANolan) **9-7-5b**$^{(7)}$ IonaWands(10) (led tl hdd 3f out: wknd over 1f out) | 2 | **6** | 14/1 | 39 | 14 |
| 661$^{6}$ | **Funny Rose (33)** (PMonteith) **6-7-10** LCharnock(14) (chsd ldrs: effrt over 3f out: wknd 2f out) | 6 | **7** | 14/1 | 28 | 3 |
| 883$^{P}$ | **Public Way (IRE) (48)** (NChamberlain) **6-8-11** DeanMcKeown(13) (effrt ent st: nvr trbld ldrs) | ½ | **8** | 50/1 | 42 | 17 |
| *348** | **Dirab (65)** (TDBarron) **3-8-13** JFanning(15) (hld up & bhd: nvr nr to chal) | hd | **9** | 12/1 | 59 | 19 |
| 752$^{9}$ | **Northern Motto (55)** (MrsJRRamsden) **3-8-3** RLappin(6) (hld up: stdy hdwy appr st: rdn & nt qckn fnl 2f) | 1¼ | **10** | 15/8$^{1}$ | 47 | 7 |
| *1031*$^{14}$ | **Anistop (46)** (JLEyre) **4-8-6**$^{(3)}$ DWright(7) (outpcd ent st: n.d) | 8 | **11** | 10/1 | 27 | 2 |
| 995$^{6}$ | **Paronomasia (33)** (JLHarris) **4-7-5b**$^{(5)}$ PFessey(2) (lw: chsd ldrs tl wknd fnl 3f) | 5 | **12** | 16/1 | 7 | — |
| 1044$^{10}$ | **Jabaroot (IRE) (59)** (DANolan) **5-9-8** KDarley(11) (a bhd) | 6 | **13** | 40/1 | 24 | — |
| | **Ihtimaam (FR) (55)** (MrsASwinbank) **4-9-4** JFortune(8) (b: b.hind: chsd ldrs tl wknd fnl 3f) | nk | **14** | 7/1$^{3}$ | 20 | — |
| | **Blain (35)** (BSRothwell) **5-7-9**$^{(3)ow2}$ DarrenMoffatt(1) (racd wd: chsd ldrs tl wknd 5f out) | 3½ | **15** | 100/1 | — | — |
| | | | | (SP 132.8%) | | **15 Rn** |

**2m 28.8** (9.10) CSF £90.29 CT £2,356.22 TOTE £11.00: £3.10 £2.40 £13.10 (£35.00) Trio Not won; £386.19 to 22/5/96. OWNER Mrs J. McFadyen-Murray (WISHAW) BRED London Thoroughbred Services Ltd
LONG HANDICAP Here Comes Herbie 7-7 Paronomasia 7-9 Funny Rose 7-7 Blain 7-4
WEIGHT FOR AGE 3yo-15lb
**OFFICIAL EXPLANATION Funny Rose: gurgled in the race.**
**1165 Lord Advocate**, happy with the strong pace set by his stable-companion, took it up once into the straight and just kept galloping. (14/1)
**1034 Gold Desire** keeps running well but is just short of a real turn of foot to make it. (11/2)
**998 Trumped (IRE)** ran her best race to date and seems to be coming to hand. (33/1)
**999* Manful** would have been happier on a more galloping track and was never any nearer than at the finish. (7/1)
**Here Comes Herbie** looked very unlucky here, running into trouble in the last two furlongs. He had no chance of recovering fully, but is in really good heart at present. (14/1)
**1024 Rapid Mover** set the race up for his stable-companion, but was then tapped for speed in the last three furlongs. (14/1)
**661 Funny Rose** (14/1: 10/1-16/1)
**Dirab**, having his first run since his hard race at Southwell in February, showed he is in good heart and was this time certainly not knocked about. (12/1: op 6/1)

## 1310 LEVENHALL MEDIAN AUCTION MAIDEN STKS (3-Y.O) (Class F)
7-30 (7-31) **1m 3f 32y** £2,517.00 (£707.00: £345.00) Stalls: High GOING: 0.04 sec per fur (G)

| | | | | SP | RR | SF |
|---|---|---|---|---|---|---|
| 1090$^{3}$ | **Lord of The Manor** (MJohnston) **3-9-0** JWeaver(3) (mde all: pushed along & styd on wl fnl 3½f) | — | **1** | 4/9$^{1}$ | 67 | 25 |
| | **She's Simply Great (IRE) (50)** (JJO'Neill) **3-8-9** JFortune(1) (unruly s: bhd tl styd on fnl 3f: no ch w wnr) | 8 | **2** | 25/1 | 51 | 9 |
| 1104$^{5}$ | **Linda's Joy (IRE)** (RGuest) **3-8-9b** LCharnock(4) (lw: trckd ldrs: effrt appr st: sn rdn & no rspnse) | 3½ | **3** | 5/2$^{2}$ | 46 | 4 |
| 826$^{13}$ | **Dicentra (47)** (EWeymes) **3-8-9** KDarley(2) (cl up tl outpcd appr st: sn btn) | 1¾ | **4** | 14/1$^{3}$ | 43 | 1 |
| | | | | (SP 108.3%) | | **4 Rn** |

**2m 30.5** (10.80) CSF £7.54 TOTE £1.30 (£4.90) OWNER Mrs J. D. Trotter (MIDDLEHAM) BRED Mrs John Trotter

**1090 Lord of The Manor** left nothing to chance and went off in front. Really stepping up the pace early in the straight, he soon had it sewn up. Galloping tracks look likely to suit him much better. (4/9)
**She's Simply Great (IRE)** got upset in the stalls and, after bringing up the rear, only stayed on when the winner was weighed in. (25/1)
**1104 Linda's Joy (IRE)** swished her tail repeatedly and looked none too keen throughout. (5/2)
**Dicentra** has yet to show anything worthwhile. (14/1: 16/1-25/1)

## 1311 FISHERROW (S) STKS (3-Y.O+) (Class G)

8-00 (8-03) **1m 16y** £2,211.00 (£621.00: £303.00) Stalls: High GOING: 0.00 sec per fur (G)

| | | | | SP | RR | SF |
|---|---|---|---|---|---|---|
| $629^{17}$ | **Elite Racing (53)** (NTinkler) **4-9-2** LCharnock(2) (lw: cl up: led over 3f out to 2f out: hung lft: led ins fnl f: all out) | — | **1** | 5/1 3 | 42 | 18 |
| $1088^{11}$ | **Langtonian (28)** (JLEyre) **7-9-0v**(7) IonaWands(3) (a.p: led 2f out: hung lft, hdd & no ex ins fnl f) | ½ | **2** | 20/1 | 46 | 22 |
| $688^{5}$ | **Absolute Ruler (IRE) (40)** (JLHarris) **5-9-7b** KDarley(5) (lw: a.p: rdn over 3f out: styd on: nvr able to chal) | 1¼ | **3** | 9/4 1 | 44 | 20 |
| $1020^{7}$ | **Sunday Mail Too (IRE) (32)** (MissLAPerratt) **4-9-2** JFanning(4) (lw: cl up: ev ch 3f out: one pce fnl 2f) | 2½ | **4** | 20/1 | 34 | 10 |
| $998^{6}$ | **Philgem** (JHetherton) **3-8-4** NKennedy(8) (in tch: hdwy u.p 2f out: no imp) | s.h | **5** | 8/1 | 34 | — |
| $884^{14}$ | **Amnesia (IRE) (30)** (MrsSCBradburne) **5-9-2v** JWeaver(1) (nvr trbld ldrs) | 4 | **6** | 33/1 | 26 | 2 |
| $1088^{8}$ | **Dance of Joy (45)** (JMCarr) **4-9-2** ACulhane(7) (bhd tl styd on fnl 3f) | ¾ | **7** | 3/1 2 | 24 | — |
| $884^{8}$ | **Strathtore Dream (IRE) (26)** (MissLAPerratt) **5-9-2** JCarroll(9) (nvr wnt pce) | 7 | **8** | 33/1 | 10 | — |
| | **Mr Titch** (DenysSmith) **3-8-9** KFallon(10) (leggy: a outpcd & bhd) | 3 | **9** | 12/1 | 9 | — |
| | **Barik (IRE) (50)** (MrsASwinbank) **6-9-7** JFortune(11) (lw: led tl hdd & wknd over 3f out) | 2½ | **10** | 14/1 | 4 | — |
| *$1030^{13}$* | **Rebounder** (KMcAuliffe) **3-8-9b**[1] WJO'Connor(6) (chsd ldrs tl wknd qckly over 3f out) | dist | **11** | 16/1 | — | — |

(SP 119.2%) **11 Rn**

**1m 47.1** (8.50) CSF £85.70 TOTE £5.20: £1.80 £4.30 £1.60 (£28.20) Trio £88.30 OWNER Elite Racing Club (MALTON) BRED R. J. McAlpine
WEIGHT FOR AGE 3yo-12lb
Bt in 4,000 gns

**Elite Racing**, despite hanging left, won this very moderate event in which all the principals looked very iffy enthusiasm wise. (5/1)
**586 Langtonian** looked likely to win this when taking it up two furlongs out but then threw it away by hanging left even worse than the winner. (20/1)
**688 Absolute Ruler (IRE)** looked a picture and had his chances but was never doing enough when it mattered. (9/4)
**882 Sunday Mail Too (IRE)** was always up with the pace but found the struggle too much in the last quarter-mile. (20/1)
**Philgem** keeps running a shade better but there is still plenty of improvement needed. (8/1: op 12/1)
**739 Dance of Joy** always found this trip on this track too sharp. (3/1)
**Mr Titch** (12/1: op 8/1)
**Barik (IRE)** (14/1: op 6/1)

## 1312 MUSSELBURGH HONEST TOUN H'CAP (0-65) (3-Y.O) (Class F)

8-30 (8-31) **1m 16y** £2,612.20 (£734.20: £358.60) Stalls: High GOING: 0.04 sec per fur (G)

| | | | | SP | RR | SF |
|---|---|---|---|---|---|---|
| $873^{3}$ | **Mazcobar (63)** (PJMakin) **3-9-7** KDarley(1) (cl up: led over 2f out: shkn up & r.o) | — | **1** | 6/4 1 | 72 | 28 |
| | **Termon (56)** (MissLAPerratt) **3-9-0** JFanning(6) (a chsng ldrs: ev ch 2f out: nt qckn ins fnl f) | 1½ | **2** | 14/1 | 62 | 18 |
| $1087^{11}$ | **Napoleon's Return (46)** (AHarrison) **3-8-4** DeanMcKeown(9) (in tch: hdwy over 2f out: styd on: nt pce to chal) | 3 | **3** | 33/1 | 46 | 2 |
| $774^{8}$ | **Falcon's Flame (USA) (56)** (MrsJRRamsden) **3-9-0** KFallon(5) (hld up & bhd: styd on fnl 3f: nrst fin) | 2 | **4** | 11/2 3 | 52 | 8 |
| *$376^{3}$* | **Apartments Abroad (50)** (KMcAuliffe) **3-8-8v** WJO'Connor(7) (b.off hind: mid div: styd on fnl 3f: no imp) | hd | **5** | 7/1 | 46 | 2 |
| $1068^{5}$ | **The Barnsley Belle (IRE) (48)** (JLEyre) **3-8-6** RLappin(3) (prom tl lost pl appr st: hdwy u.p 3f out: no imp) | 2½ | **6** | 9/2 2 | 39 | — |
| $775^{10}$ | **Ned's Contessa (IRE) (48)** (MDods) **3-8-6** JCarroll(10) (bhd: effrt over 3f out: n.d) | 1½ | **7** | 11/1 | 36 | — |
| $595^{13}$ | **Knave (63)** (PMonteith) **3-9-7** LCharnock(2) (chsd ldrs tl wknd fnl 3f) | 4 | **8** | 16/1 | 43 | — |
| $881^{7}$ | **Swifty Nifty (IRE) (51)** (WWHaigh) **3-8-9** DaleGibson(4) (lw: plld hrd: a bhd) | 1¼ | **9** | 33/1 | 29 | — |
| $1068^{13}$ | **Miss Offset (46)** (MJohnston) **3-8-4b** TWilliams(8) (led tl hdd & wknd over 2f out) | ½ | **10** | 12/1 | 23 | — |
| | **Orange And Blue (45)** (MissJFCraze) **3-8-3c**ow2 NConnorton(11) (prom to st: wknd qckly) | 18 | **11** | 33/1 | — | — |

(SP 123.5%) **11 Rn**

**1m 46.6** (8.00) CSF £22.92 CT £468.70 TOTE £1.90: £1.60 £5.90 £2.80 (£22.80) Trio £194.10; £30.07 to 22/5/96 OWNER Mr A. W. Schiff (MARLBOROUGH) BRED A. W. Schiff

**873 Mazcobar** travelled well in the race and, once sent about his business two furlongs out, was always finding enough. (6/4)
**Termon** ran well and should be able to pick up a race in due course. (14/1)
**Napoleon's Return** ran his best race for some time and seems to be coming back to form. (33/1)
**458 Falcon's Flame (USA)**, set an impossible task, did well to finish so close, and is one to keep in mind, especially when there is a market pointer. (11/2: 4/1-6/1)
**Apartments Abroad** has yet to win on grass, and could never find the pace to get in a blow. (7/1)
**1068 The Barnsley Belle (IRE)** got shuffled back when a bit short of room approaching the straight, and lacked the pace to recover. (9/2)
**Ned's Contessa (IRE)** (11/1: 8/1-12/1)
**897 Miss Offset** (12/1: 8/1-14/1)

## 1313 MUSSELBURGH LINKS H'CAP (0-70) (3-Y.O+) (Class E)

9-00 (9-01) **7f 15y** £2,944.00 (£892.00: £436.00: £208.00) Stalls: High GOING: 0.04 sec per fur (G)

| | | | | SP | RR | SF |
|---|---|---|---|---|---|---|
| | **Murray's Mazda (IRE) (41)** (JLEyre) **7-7-11**(3) DWright(4) (in tch: hdwy 3f out: led ins fnl f: styd on u.p) | — | **1** | 25/1 | 52 | 24 |
| $1018^{2}$ | **Persian Fayre (64)** (JBerry) **4-9-9** JCarroll(9) (lw: trckd ldrs: led on bit 2f out: sn rdn: hdd & nt qckn ins fnl f) | 1½ | **2** | 5/2 1 | 72 | 44 |
| $1001^{3}$ | **Miss Pigalle (41)** (MissLAPerratt) **5-8-0b** DaleGibson(5) (a.p: chsng ldrs over 1f out: no ex) | 1¾ | **3** | 10/1 | 45 | 17 |
| $1024^{4}$ | **Hutchies Lady (38)** (RMMcKellar) **4-7-11** TWilliams(1) (hdwy 3f out: swtchd over 1f out: styd on: nrst fin) | s.h | **4** | 14/1 | 42 | 14 |
| $1163^{13}$ | **Seconds Away (37)** (JSGoldie) **5-7-10** NKennedy(3) (in tch: rdn over 2f out: kpt on one pce) | 3½ | **5** | 25/1 | 33 | 5 |
| $1037^{8}$ | **Thatched (IRE) (49)** (REBarr) **6-8-3**(5) PFessey(6) (bhd tl styd on fnl 3f) | 2½ | **6** | 12/1 | 39 | 11 |
| | **Ninia (USA) (69)** (MJohnston) **4-10-0** JWeaver(2) (chsd ldrs: outpcd 3f out: no imp after) | nk | **7** | 12/1 | 58 | 30 |
| $1001^{8}$ | **Tinklers Folly (52)** (DenysSmith) **4-8-11** LCharnock(10) (lw: chsd ldrs: led over 3f out to 2f out: sn btn) | ¾ | **8** | 13/2 3 | 40 | 12 |
| $1163^{4}$ | **Diet (58)** (MissLAPerratt) **10-9-3v** NConnorton(7) (lost pl appr st: n.d after) | 2½ | **9** | 10/1 | 40 | 12 |
| $935^{11}$ | **Allinson's Mate (IRE) (60)** (TDBarron) **8-9-5** JFortune(12) (lw: a outpcd & bhd) | nk | **10** | 8/1 | 41 | 13 |
| $687^{12}$ | **Nordisk Legend (39)** (MrsDThomson) **4-7-9**(3)ow2 DarrenMoffatt(8) (n.d) | ½ | **11** | 50/1 | 19 | — |

| | | | SP | RR | SF |
|---|---|---|---|---|---|
| 1010[6] | **Don Pepe (60)** (RBoss) **5-9-5** KDarley(11) (led tl hdd over 3f out: sn wknd)....4 | **12** | 6/1[2] | 31 | 3 |
| 1037[2] | **Commander Glen (IRE) (52)** (MrsJRRamsden) **4-8-11** KFallon(13) (dwlt: a wl bhd)....nk | **13** | 6/1[2] | 22 | — |

(SP 131.5%) **13 Rn**

**1m 31.0** (5.50) CSF £89.74 CT £664.04 TOTE £27.10: £2.90 £2.20 £2.90 (£28.50) Trio £127.60 OWNER Mr Murray Grubb (HAMBLETON) BRED Patrick Kennedy

LONG HANDICAP Nordisk Legend 7-8 Seconds Away 7-8

**Murray's Mazda (IRE)** last won a race almost three years ago but, despite an awkward head carriage, there was no fluke about this. (25/1)

**1018 Persian Fayre** sailed on the bridle for much of the trip but, when it came down to an effort, he was found wanting in the last furlong and a half. The strong early pace may have been his undoing. (5/2: op 4/1)

**1001 Miss Pigalle** keeps threatening to win a race, but is just short of that vital turn of foot. (10/1)

**1024 Hutchies Lady** ran well, but found this track a bit too sharp, and could never get in a blow, despite running on. (14/1)

**997 Seconds Away**, whose stable is going reasonably well at present, ran a decent race. (25/1)

**Thatched (IRE)** made fair late progress, suggesting that he is returning to form. (12/1)

**1037 Commander Glen (IRE)**, easy to back, surprisingly missed the break and remained at the rear. It would seem that a positive market move is the best pointer to his chances. (6/1: 7/2-7/1)

T/Plpt: £29.60 (324.1 Tckts). T/Qdpt: £7.40 (103.82 Tckts) AA

## 1099-WINDSOR (Fig. 8) (Good)
## Monday May 20th

WEATHER: sunny WIND: almost nil

### 1314 PORTLAND OUTDOOR ADVERTISING CLAIMING STKS (3-Y.O+) (Class F)

6-15 (6-16) **1m 67y** £2,801.00 (£786.00: £383.00) Stalls: High GOING: 0.00 sec per fur (G)

| | | | SP | RR | SF |
|---|---|---|---|---|---|
| 645[8] | **Cape Pigeon (USA) (63)** (LGCottrell) **11-9-0v** MFenton(13) (a.p: led ins fnl f: drvn out)....— | **1** | 13/2 | 71 | 49 |
| | **Tauten (IRE) (34)** (PBurgoyne) **6-8-10**(3) DRMcCabe(14) (gd hdwy fnl 2f: fin wl)....1½ | **2** | 100/1 | 67 | 45 |
| 1010[5] | **Orange Place (IRE) (70)** (TJNaughton) **5-9-6** PaulEddery(2) (lw: led: hrd rdn fnl 3f: hdd ins fnl f)....nk | **3** | 8/1 | 74 | 52 |
| 633[5] | **Bagshot (73)** (RHannon) **5-9-6** PatEddery(16) (rdn & hdwy 3f out: ev ch whn n.m.r 1f out: nt qckn)....1¼ | **4** | 9/2[2] | 71 | 49 |
| 1099[5] | **Rockville Pike (IRE) (65)** (SDow) **4-8-13v** BThomson(19) (lw: hdwy 3f out: rdn & one pce fnl 2f)....3½ | **5** | 12/1 | 57 | 35 |
| 960[12] | **Cim Bom Bom (IRE) (90)** (MBell) **4-9-4**(7) GFaulkner(11) (a.p: hrd rdn & ev ch over 2f out: wknd over 1f out)....2½ | **6** | 4/1[1] | 65 | 43 |
| 470[9] | **Gee Gee Tee (52)** (JAkehurst) **3-8-6** DHarrison(8) (lw: no hdwy fnl 3f)....1¾ | **7** | 33/1 | 54 | 20 |
| 747[5] | **Mr Nevermind (IRE) (64)** (GLMoore) **6-9-0**(7) ALakeman(3) (nvr nrr)....nk | **8** | 12/1 | 57 | 35 |
| 1102[12] | **Komodo (USA) (60)** (KOCunningham-Brown) **4-8-8**(7) CMunday(17) (lw: prom tl wknd over 2f out)....s.h | **9** | 25/1 | 51 | 29 |
| *1030*[4] | **Juba** (DrJDScargill) **4-8-10** RCochrane(4) (b: nrst fin)....nk | **10** | 10/1 | 45 | 23 |
| | **Kerrier (IRE)** (RHarris) **4-9-7** AMackay(15) (b: a mid div)....2 | **11** | 16/1 | 52 | 30 |
| | **Early Peace (IRE) (74)** (RHannon) **4-9-1**(3) DaneO'Neill(12) (bit bkwd: nvr nr ldrs)....2½ | **12** | 10/1 | 44 | 22 |
| | **Nordic Flash** (TJNaughton) **9-8-8**(7) TAshley(5) (b: bit bkwd: a bhd)....2 | **13** | 33/1 | 37 | 15 |
| 979[18] | **Labudd (USA) (46)** (RIngram) **6-9-2** DBiggs(1) (b: lw: rapid hdwy 6f out: wknd over 3f out)....1¼ | **14** | 100/1 | 36 | 14 |
| | **Tocco Jewel (15)** (MJRyan) **6-8-3**(7) AMcCarthy(20) (bhd fnl 3f)....nk | **15** | 100/1 | 29 | 7 |
| *836*[5] | **Northern Celadon (IRE) (72)** (MJHeaton-Ellis) **5-9-3** AClark(9) (prom tl wknd over 3f out)....2½ | **16** | 6/1[3] | 32 | 10 |
| | **Dolly Dolittle (15)** (HJCollingridge) **5-8-8** NCarlisle(7) (a bhd: t.o)....14 | **17** | 100/1 | — | — |
| 893[8] | **Newlands Corner (48)** (JAkehurst) **3-7-13** FNorton(10) (lw: bhd fnl 4f: t.o)....8 | **18** | 20/1 | — | — |
| | **Ath Cheannaithe (FR) (59)** (JNeville) **4-9-11b** RHughes(6) (lw: bhd fnl 3f: t.o)....nk | **19** | 33/1 | — | — |
| | **Miss Electra (26)** (MBlanshard) **4-8-3**(5) CAdamson(18) (lw: a bhd: t.o)....hd | **20** | 100/1 | — | — |

(SP 138.7%) **20 Rn**

**1m 47.1** (4.90) CSF £449.12 TOTE £7.40: £3.00 £49.90 £3.50 (£1234.20; £347.69 to 22/5/96) Trio £313.60; £362.22 to 22/5/96 OWNER Mr E. J. S. Gadsden (CULLOMPTON) BRED Ashwood Thoroughbreds, Inc.

WEIGHT FOR AGE 3yo-12lb

OFFICIAL EXPLANATION **Ath Cheannaithe (FR): the jockey reported that the gelding had choked three furlongs out and, as a result, did not persevere.**

**Cape Pigeon (USA)**, whose two wins last year were both in Windsor sellers, held on well. (13/2: 9/2-7/1)

**Tauten (IRE)** nearly caused a major shock on this seasonal debut. Scrubbed along and going nowhere over three furlongs from home, she came storming through to take second place. (100/1)

**1010 Orange Place (IRE)**, overhauled inside the final furlong, failed to find another gear. (8/1)

**633 Bagshot**, pushed along to take closer order three furlongs from home, did not get much room between horses entering the final furlong as he tried to mount a challenge. Not looking over-enthusiastic about the job in hand, he failed to find the necessary turn of foot. (9/2: op 3/1)

**1099 Rockville Pike (IRE)** was only treading water in the final quarter-mile. (12/1: op 7/1)

**Cim Bom Bom (IRE)** was taking a big drop in class but still ran poorly. (4/1)

**747 Mr Nevermind (IRE)** (12/1: op 8/1)

**836 Northern Celadon (IRE)** (6/1: 9/2-7/1)

### 1315 E.B.F. OASIS HOLIDAY VILLAGE MAIDEN STKS (2-Y.O) (Class D)

6-45 (6-46) **5f 10y** £3,420.00 (£1,035.00: £505.00: £240.00) Stalls: High GOING: 0.00 sec per fur (G)

| | | | SP | RR | SF |
|---|---|---|---|---|---|
| | **Saunders Wren** (MRChannon) **2-8-9** RHughes(7) (unf: hdwy 2f out: led over 1f out: drvn out)....— | **1** | 10/1 | 74 | 36 |
| | **Golden Fact (USA)** (RHannon) **2-9-0** PatEddery(4) (str: a.p: rdn & ev ch fnl 2f: r.o)....½ | **2** | 4/5[1] | 77 | 39 |
| *1080*[2] | **Castle Ashby Jack** (PHowling) **2-9-0** FNorton(2) (b.hind: bit bkwd: chsd ldr: led wl over 1f out: sn swvd rt & hdd: one pce)....5 | **3** | 6/1[3] | 62 | 24 |
| 807[7] | **Loch Dibidale** (JEBanks) **2-8-9** NDay(1) (hld up: rdn over 2f out: one pce)....1 | **4** | 12/1 | 53 | 15 |
| | **John Emms (IRE)** (MBell) **2-9-0** MFenton(6) (str: scope: bit bkwd: hld up: rdn over 2f out: sn wknd)....1¼ | **5** | 5/1[2] | 54 | 16 |
| 869[8] | **M T Vessel** (JRJenkins) **2-8-9**(5) ADaly(3) (led over 3f)....3 | **6** | 16/1 | 45 | 7 |

(SP 109.2%) **6 Rn**

**61.8 secs** (2.60) CSF £17.77 TOTE £7.00: £2.10 £1.30 (£4.10) OWNER Charles Saunders Ltd (UPPER LAMBOURN) BRED C. Scott

**Saunders Wren**, a lengthy, weak-looking newcomer who cost a mere 2,100 guineas as a yearling, was unable to go the early pace. In a tremendous battle with the runner-up, she just prevailed. (10/1: op 5/2)

**Golden Fact (USA)**, a sturdy individual, had a hard race on this debut. Vying for the lead in the final two furlongs, he just lost out. (4/5: 5/4-8/11)
**1080 Castle Ashby Jack**, still not looking fully fit, swerved right approaching the final furlong as he was shown the persuader and, after losing the advantage, could only plod on at one pace. (6/1: 7/2-8/1)
**Loch Dibidale** was only treading water in the last two furlongs. (12/1: 8/1-16/1)
**John Emms (IRE)** (5/1: op 5/2)

## 1316 EVENING STANDARD H'CAP (0-95) (3-Y.O) (Class C)

7-15 (7-16) **5f 10y** £5,270.50 (£1,594.00: £777.00: £368.50) Stalls: High GOING minus 0.16 sec per fur (GF)

| | | | | SP | RR | SF |
|---|---|---|---|---|---|---|
| | **Midnight Escape (82)** (CFWall) **3-8-8** NCarlisle(7) (mde all: r.o wl) | — | **1** | 16/1 | 93 | 60 |
| 1101* | **Wildwood Flower (85)** (RHannon) **3-8-11** 7x PatEddery(3) (a.p: chsd wnr fnl 3f: hrd rdn: no imp) | 2½ | **2** | $9/4^{1}$ | 88 | 55 |
| $966^{5}$ | **Willow Dale (IRE) (82)** (DRCElsworth) **3-8-8** TQuinn(5) (lw: hdwy over 1f out: r.o ins fnl f) | hd | **3** | $7/1^{3}$ | 85 | 52 |
| $565^{4}$ | **Music Gold (IRE) (95)** (WAO'Gorman) **3-9-7b$^{1}$** EmmaO'Gorman(1) (hld up: hdwy & rdn 2f out: btn whn swvd lft wl ins fnl f) | 2 | **4** | $5/1^{2}$ | 91 | 58 |
| 861* | **Songsheet (77)** (MartynMeade) **3-8-3** FNorton(4) (prom over 2f) | 2½ | **5** | 9/1 | 66 | 33 |
| | **Rushcutter Bay (84)** (TTClement) **3-8-10** PRobinson(6) (lw: a bhd) | ½ | **6** | 14/1 | 71 | 38 |
| 1006* | **Princely Sound (70)** (MBell) **3-7-10** JQuinn(2) (w wnr 2f: hrd rdn & wknd 2f out) | 7 | **7** | $9/4^{1}$ | 35 | 2 |
| | | | | (SP 113.3%) | **7 Rn** | |

**60.3 secs** (1.10) CSF £49.53 TOTE £19.00: £5.50 £1.60 (£45.70) OWNER Mr Mervyn Ayers (NEWMARKET) BRED M. L. Ayers
OFFICIAL EXPLANATION **Princely Sound: the jockey reported that the colt lost his action crossing the junction and he therefore did not persevere to the line.**
**Midnight Escape** made a winning return to action. Making every post a winning one, he proved too strong for his rivals in the final quarter-mile. (16/1)
**1101* Wildwood Flower**, in second place by halfway, never looked like pegging back the winner. The drop in distance was against her as both her wins have come over six. (9/4: op 6/4)
**966 Willow Dale (IRE)** began to pick up ground below the distance and, running on, only just failed to snatch second prize. (7/1)
**565 Music Gold (IRE)**, fitted with blinkers for the first time, moved up at halfway, but could make little impression in the final furlong and a half. (5/1)
**861* Songsheet** (9/1: 6/1-10/1)

## 1317 OK! WEEKLY STAR H'CAP (0-80) (3-Y.O) (Class D)

7-45 (7-48) **1m 3f 135y** £3,636.00 (£1,098.00: £534.00: £252.00) Stalls: High GOING minus 0.01 sec per fur (G)

| | | | | SP | RR | SF |
|---|---|---|---|---|---|---|
| *$856^{4}$* | **Isitoff (66)** (SCWilliams) **3-8-8**(3) PMcCabe(10) (hdwy 6f out: led 3f out: r.o wl) | — | **1** | 12/1 | 76 | 34 |
| $863^{7}$ | **Willie Rushton (56)** (GLMoore) **3-8-1** FNorton(7) (b.hind: lw: hdwy 5f out: ev ch fnl 2f: nt qckn) | 1½ | **2** | 12/1 | 64 | 22 |
| $595^{7}$ | **Ret Frem (IRE) (60)** (MAJarvis) **3-8-5** PRobinson(9) (hdwy 3f out: hrd rdn & one pce fnl 2f) | 5 | **3** | $5/1^{2}$ | 61 | 19 |
| $947^{2}$ | **Clemente (76)** (RHannon) **3-9-7** PatEddery(1) (chsd ldrs: rdn & outpcd 5f out: hdwy 2f out: nt clr run over 1f out: r.o) | ½ | **4** | $5/2^{1}$ | 76 | 34 |
| $668^{6}$ | **Alwarqa (63)** (RWArmstrong) **3-8-8** WCarson(2) (led 9f out to 3f out: one pce) | s.h | **5** | $6/1^{3}$ | 63 | 21 |
| $1104^{4}$ | **Half An Inch (IRE) (70)** (BJMeehan) **3-9-1** BDoyle(11) (prom tl wknd over 2f out) | 2 | **6** | 12/1 | 68 | 26 |
| 863* | **Meg's Memory (IRE) (59)** (JohnBerry) **3-7-13**(5) MHenry(6) (bhd fnl 4f) | 1¼ | **7** | $6/1^{3}$ | 55 | 13 |
| $471^{11}$ | **Nikita's Star (IRE) (67)** (DJGMurraySmith) **3-8-9**(3) DaneO'Neill(3) (nvr nr to chal) | 3½ | **8** | 10/1 | 58 | 16 |
| *$516^{3}$* | **Cherry Garden (IRE) (57)** (TJNaughton) **3-8-2** DHarrison(5) (swtg: bhd fnl 6f: t.o) | 18 | **9** | 14/1 | 23 | — |
| $788^{9}$ | **D'naan (IRE) (75)** (WJHaggas) **3-9-6** RHughes(4) (lw: led over 2f: wknd over 3f out: t.o) | 12 | **10** | 14/1 | 25 | — |
| *1067** | ***Poly My Son (IRE) (51)*** (MRChannon) **3-7-10** AMackay(8) (Withdrawn not under Starter's orders: unruly in stalls) | | **W** | 15/2 | — | — |
| | | | | (SP 131.1%) | **10 Rn** | |

**2m 32.8** (8.80) CSF £117.70 CT £565.17 TOTE £14.80: £2.90 £3.20 £1.90 (£147.80) Trio £305.10; £343.86 to 22/5/96 OWNER Mr James Brown (NEWMARKET) BRED Mrs Celia Miller
LONG HANDICAP Poly My Son (IRE) 7-9
**856 Isitoff** made a winning start for his new stable. Taking closer order on the long loop to the home straight, he got the better of the runner-up in the last 150 yards. (12/1: op 8/1)
**863 Willie Rushton**, still in with every chance entering the last 200 yards, was then put in her place. (12/1: op 7/1)
**595 Ret Frem (IRE)** failed to make any further impression in the final quarter-mile. (5/1)
**947 Clemente** became the meat in the sandwich approaching the final furlong and Eddery had to switch, costing his mount ground he could ill afford. He stayed on again the closing stages, and only just lost out for third. (5/2)
**668 Alwarqa**, who caught the eye last time, adopted totally different tactics on this occasion, but was collared three furlongs from home, and could then only complete in her own time. (6/1)
**D'naan (IRE)** (14/1: op 8/1)

## 1318 MARIE CLAIRE CONDITIONS STKS (2-Y.O F) (Class C)

8-15 (8-16) **5f 10y** £4,622.40 (£1,614.40: £787.20: £336.00) Stalls: High GOING minus 0.16 sec per fur (GF)

| | | | | SP | RR | SF |
|---|---|---|---|---|---|---|
| 1062* | **Petite Danseuse** (SDow) **2-8-8** BThomson(4) (hld up: led wl over 1f out: hung lft: sn clr) | — | **1** | $9/1^{3}$ | 75 | 19 |
| 1008* | **Wait For Rosie** (MRChannon) **2-8-11** RHughes(2) (hld up in rr: rdn over 2f out: r.o ins fnl f) | 3½ | **2** | $9/1^{3}$ | 67 | 11 |
| $1103^{4}$ | **Sweet Emmaline** (WGMTurner) **2-8-8** TSprake(1) (led: hrd rdn over 2f out: hdd wl over 1f out: sn wknd) | ½ | **3** | $11/2^{2}$ | 62 | 6 |
| 729* | **Cherry Blossom (IRE)** (RHannon) **2-8-11** PatEddery(3) (lw: w ldr: hrd rdn & ev ch 2f out: sn wknd: eased ins fnl f) | 5 | **4** | $4/11^{1}$ | 50 | — |
| | | | | (SP 108.7%) | **4 Rn** | |

**62.8 secs** (3.60) CSF £50.75 TOTE £6.70 (£12.90) OWNER Mrs A. M. Upsdell (EPSOM) BRED I. D. Livingstone
OFFICIAL EXPLANATION **Cherry Blossom (IRE): hung right throughout the race.**
**1062* Petite Danseuse**, held up behind the front two, hit the front early in the final quarter-mile and, despite drifting left, was soon in command. (9/1: op 5/1)
**1008* Wait For Rosie** was in last place until staying on in the latter stages to take second inside the final furlong. (9/1: op 5/1)
**1103 Sweet Emmaline** was taken down very early to avoid a recurrence of last week. (11/2: 4/1-8/1)
**729* Cherry Blossom (IRE)** was a major disappointment. Racing with the leader, she had every chance a quarter of a mile out before tamely dropping away. (4/11)

## 1319 ROYAL WINDSOR MAIDEN STKS (3-Y.O+) (Class D)

8-45 (8-46) **1m 67y** £3,967.50 (£1,200.00: £585.00: £277.50) Stalls: High GOING: 0.00 sec per fur (G)

| Form | Horse | Dist | Pos | SP | RR | SF |
|---|---|---|---|---|---|---|
| $892^{4}$ | **Crazy Chief (75)** (PFICole) **3-8-12** TQuinn(1) (mde all: rdn out) | — | **1** | 7/1 | 86 | 56 |
| | **Bend Wavy (IRE)** (LMCumani) **4-9-10** RCochrane(4) (hld up: rdn over 3f out: r.o ins fnl f) | nk | **2** | $4/1^{2}$ | 85 | 67 |
| $892^{3}$ | **Male-Ana-Mou (IRE)** (DRCElsworth) **3-8-12** PatEddery(8) (a.p: rdn over 3f out: r.o ins fnl f) | ½ | **3** | $3/1^{1}$ | 85 | 55 |
| $970^{8}$ | **Hareb (USA)** (JWHills) **3-8-12** MHills(9) (lw: chsd wnr over 6f: sn wknd) | 7 | **4** | $6/1^{3}$ | 71 | 41 |
| $833^{7}$ | **Classy Chief (85)** (RBoss) **3-8-12** RHughes(15) (hld up: rdn over 3f out: wknd wl over 1f out) | 1¾ | **5** | 8/1 | 68 | 38 |
| | **Golden Thunderbolt (FR)** (JHMGosden) **3-8-12** GHind(13) (w'like: lw: hmpd over 2f out: stdy hdwy fnl 2f: bttr for r) | nk | **6** | 9/1 | 67 | 37 |
| $892^{6}$ | **Far Dawn (USA)** (GHarwood) **3-8-12** AClark(2) (hld up: rdn over 3f out: wknd over 2f out) | 2½ | **7** | 10/1 | 62 | 32 |
| | **Naaman (IRE)** (MAJarvis) **3-8-7** PRobinson(3) (neat: nvr nrr) | 7 | **8** | 25/1 | 44 | 14 |
| | **Sandpiper** (KOCunningham-Brown) **3-8-0**(7) CMunday(19) (prom 5f) | ¾ | **9** | 50/1 | 42 | 12 |
| $842^{12}$ | **Barrack Yard** (ACStewart) **3-8-7**(5) MHumphries(10) (nvr nrr) | s.h | **10** | 33/1 | 47 | 17 |
| $840^{6}$ | **Le Bam Bam** (HAkbary) **4-9-10** DBiggs(6) (a mid div) | 1¾ | **11** | 25/1 | 44 | 26 |
| $840^{7}$ | **Formidable Partner** (RWArmstrong) **3-8-12** RPrice(7) (bit bkwd: bhd fnl 2f) | hd | **12** | 16/1 | 44 | 14 |
| $922^{2}$ | **Beau Bruno** (MBell) **3-8-12** MFenton(11) (bhd fnl 2f) | nk | **13** | 25/1 | 43 | 13 |
| | **Little Murray** (MrsJCecil) **3-8-12** TIves(17) (str: scope: bit bkwd: bhd fnl 4f) | hd | **14** | 16/1 | 43 | 13 |
| $932^{8}$ | **Induna Mkubwa** (CFWall) **3-8-12** GDuffield(12) (a bhd) | ¾ | **15** | 50/1 | 41 | 11 |
| $1045^{10}$ | **Croagh Patrick** (JCFox) **4-9-7**(3) DaneO'Neill(18) (s.s: a bhd) | 3½ | **16** | 100/1 | 35 | 17 |
| $845^{13}$ | **Emperors Wood** (PHayward) **5-9-10** TSprake(16) (a bhd) | 2½ | **17** | 66/1 | 30 | 12 |
| $982^{12}$ | **Slievenamon** (JEBanks) **3-8-12** JQuinn(14) (bhd fnl 2f) | 1¼ | **18** | 100/1 | 27 | — |

(SP 135.6%) **18 Rn**

**1m 46.2** (4.00) CSF £35.92 TOTE £7.40: £2.60 £2.90 £1.50 (£18.40) Trio £12.80 OWNER Mr David Simpson (WHATCOMBE) BRED D. J. Simpson

WEIGHT FOR AGE 3yo-12lb

**892 Crazy Chief** made every post a winning one and, ridden along, just held on. (7/1)

**Bend Wavy (IRE)** chased the leaders, but was being rowed along over three furlongs from home. He ran on in good style inside the final furlong, but found the line always beating him. (4/1)

**892 Male-Ana-Mou (IRE)**, never far away, was being pushed along over three furlongs from home. He too ran on inside the final furlong and just failed to get there. (3/1: 5/2-4/1)

**684 Hareb (USA)**, taking a drop in class, raced in second place. Collared for that position over a furlong out, he had nothing more to give. (6/1: op 3/1)

**Classy Chief** chased the leaders, but was a spent force early in the final quarter-mile. (8/1: 6/1-9/1)

**Golden Thunderbolt (FR)** was given a nice educational ride. After being hampered well over two furlongs from home, he was doing some nice work thereafter and is sure to come on for this. (9/1: op 6/1)

**892 Far Dawn (USA)** (10/1: op 6/1)

T/Plpt: £2,590.20 (5.42 Tckts). T/Qdpt: £296.90 (3.68 Tckts) AK

# 1067-BEVERLEY (R-H) (Good to firm)

## Tuesday May 21st

WEATHER: fine WIND: mod half against

## 1320 TIGER INN (S) STKS (2-Y.O) (Class F)

2-25 (2-26) **5f** £2,651.00 (£736.00: £353.00) Stalls: Centre GOING minus 0.40 sec per fur (F)

| Form | Horse | Dist | Pos | SP | RR | SF |
|---|---|---|---|---|---|---|
| $770^{4}$ | **Skyers Flyer (IRE)** (RonaldThompson) **2-8-6** NConnorton(8) (trckd ldrs: plld hrd: led 2f out: edgd lft: r.o u.p) | — | **1** | 7/1 | 47 | 6 |
| *1084** | **C-Harry (IRE)** (RHollinshead) **2-9-2v** KDarley(5) (trckd ldrs: effrt on ins & ev ch over 1f out: sn rdn & kpt on same pce) | 1¾ | **2** | $7/2^{2}$ | 51 | 10 |
| $770^{9}$ | **Lunar Music** (MartynMeade) **2-8-6** VSlattery(3) (chsd ldrs: outpcd 2f out: styd on ins fnl f) | nk | **3** | 12/1 | 40 | — |
| *$1093^{5}$* | **Fit For The Job (IRE)** (WGMTurner) **2-8-11** TSprake(7) (led to 2f out: wknd over 1f out) | 6 | **4** | $6/4^{1}$ | 26 | — |
| | **No Rush** (JBerry) **2-8-11** JCarroll(2) (leggy: lw: sn trckng ldrs: effrt ½-wy: sn wknd) | 5 | **5** | $9/2^{3}$ | 10 | — |
| | **Sparky** (MWEasterby) **2-8-6**(5) GParkin(1) (w'like: bkwd: s.s: rn green & hung rt: a wl outpcd) | 1¼ | **6** | 25/1 | 6 | — |
| $1086^{9}$ | **Super Sheriff** (MWEasterby) **2-8-11** DaleGibson(6) (chsd ldrs: rdn ½-wy: sn lost pl) | ½ | **7** | 13/2 | 5 | — |
| *$1097^{8}$* | **Chilled Wine** (NBycroft) **2-8-6** LCharnock(4) (sn outpcd) | 2½ | **8** | 12/1 | — | — |

(SP 125.5%) **8 Rn**

**64.8 secs** (3.30) CSF £32.66 TOTE £7.20: £2.00 £1.30 £1.80 (£10.50) OWNER Mrs J. Carney (DONCASTER) BRED Denis Brennan

No bid

**770 Skyers Flyer (IRE)**, a poor mover, raced keenly. Edging off the rail, in the end, she showed far more determination than the runner-up. (7/1)

**1084* C-Harry (IRE)**, dropping back to five, was left with plenty of room to challenge on the inside but, when asked for a serious effort, he did not pull out much. (7/2)

**Lunar Music**, racing towards the centre, ran green and tended to run about. Sticking on strongly at the finish, she still has something to learn. (12/1)

**1093 Fit For The Job (IRE)**, a poor mover, broke first but dropped out over a furlong out. (6/4)

**No Rush** looked the part in the paddock, but drifted badly in the betting and showed very little. (9/2)

## 1321 GREEN DRAGON CONDITIONS STKS (3-Y.O+) (Class C)

2-55 (2-56) **5f** £4,851.00 (£1,809.00: £879.50: £372.50: £161.25: £76.75) Stalls: Centre GOING minus 0.40 sec per fur (F)

| Form | Horse | Dist | Pos | SP | RR | SF |
|---|---|---|---|---|---|---|
| $927^{4}$ | **Struggler (110)** (DRLoder) **4-9-0** KDarley(6) (lw: trckd ldrs: nt clr run over 1f out: swtchd & led ins fnl f: pushed clr) | — | **1** | $4/11^{1}$ | 111 | 27 |
| $927^{9}$ | **Lucky Parkes (99)** (JBerry) **6-8-4**(5) PRoberts(7) (lw: led tl ins fnl f: kpt on wl: no ch w wnr) | 3½ | **2** | $13/2^{2}$ | 95 | 11 |
| $927^{10}$ | **Takadou (IRE) (91)** (MissLCSiddall) **5-9-6** JWeaver(1) (hld up: effrt & reminder ½-wy: hung rt & styd on fnl f) | 2 | **3** | 20/1 | 99 | 15 |

| | | | | SP | RR | SF |
|---|---|---|---|---|---|---|
| 966[4] | **Babsy Babe (90)** (JJQuinn) **3-8-3** DaleGibson(4) (chsd ldrs: rdn & outpcd ½-wy: kpt on same pce) | 1¼ | **4** | 9/1[3] | 86 | — |
| | **Tarf (USA) (90)** (PTWalwyn) **3-8-7** JCarroll(3) (lw: swvd lft s: chsd ldrs: hung rt & wknd over 1f out) | 2½ | **5** | 16/1 | 82 | — |
| 1161[3] | **Here Comes a Star (76)** (JMCarr) **8-9-0** ACulhane(5) (chsd ldrs: rdn & outpcd ½-wy: n.d after) | 1¼ | **6** | 25/1 | 77 | — |
| | **Croft Pool (100)** (JAGlover) **5-10-0** SDWilliams(2) (bit bkwd: sltly hmpd & stumbled s: a bhd) | 2½ | **7** | 20/1 | 83 | — |
| | | | | (SP 115.9%) | **7 Rn** | |

**63.9 secs** (2.40) CSF £3.69 TOTE £1.30: £1.10 £2.80 (£3.20) OWNER Sir Andrew Lloyd Webber (NEWMARKET)
WEIGHT FOR AGE 3yo-8lb

**927 Struggler**, a poor mover at the best of times, has the reputation of being a lazy individual, but he won this well in the end as he was fully entitled to. (4/11)

**507 Lucky Parkes**, who looked particularly well was, as usual, put into the stalls last. Showing all her old speed, she was meeting the winner on 6lb worse terms than on Official Ratings. Back on song, she will soon be adding to her record of fifteen victories. (13/2)

**Takadou (IRE)**, who looked fresh and on good terms with himself, stuck on, despite a marked tendency to hang right. (20/1)

**966 Babsy Babe**, awkward to load, was tapped for foot at halfway and might appreciate being put back over six. (9/1: 6/1-10/1)

**Tarf (USA)**, on her toes beforehand and keen to post, hung right and dropped out over a furlong out. Her temperament might be a problem. (16/1)

## 1322 DAVID SWANNELL MEMORIAL RATED STKS H'CAP (0-90) (3-Y.O+) (Class C)

3-25 (3-25) **1m 100y** £6,178.48 (£2,306.32: £1,123.16: £477.80: £208.90: £101.34) Stalls: High GOING minus 0.40 sec per fur (F)

| | | | | SP | RR | SF |
|---|---|---|---|---|---|---|
| 1069[3] | **Tertium (IRE) (77)** (MartynWane) **4-8-9** JCarroll(6) (lw: hld up: smooth hdwy over 2f out: led over 1f out: rdn clr) | — | **1** | 13/2[3] | 89 | 47 |
| 913* | **Clifton Fox (80)** (JAGlover) **4-8-12** SDWilliams(4) (lw: sn outpcd & pushed along: hdwy 2f out: styd on fnl f) | 2 | **2** | 5/1[1] | 88 | 46 |
| 876[9] | **Gymcrak Premiere (90)** (GHolmes) **8-9-8** KFallon(2) (b.hind: sn bhd & pushed along: hdwy 2f out: styd on towards fin) | 2½ | **3** | 15/2 | 94 | 52 |
| 802[5] | **Night Wink (USA) (78)** (DNicholls) **4-8-10** AlexGreaves(1) (a chsng ldrs: hung rt over 1f out: kpt on one pce) | ¾ | **4** | 7/1 | 80 | 38 |
| 739[2] | **Queens Consul (IRE) (79)** (BSRothwell) **6-8-11** MFenton(5) (w ldrs: one pce fnl 2f) | 1½ | **5** | 5/1[1] | 78 | 36 |
| 913[6] | **Nigel's Lad (IRE) (81)** (PCHaslam) **4-8-13** JFortune(10) (hld up: pushed along & outpcd 5f out: n.d after) | 2½ | **6** | 16/1 | 76 | 34 |
| 920[10] | **Bernard Seven (IRE) (78)** (CEBrittain) **4-8-10b** KDarley(7) (mde most tl over 1f out: wkng whn n.m.r ins fnl f) | ¾ | **7** | 12/1 | 71 | 29 |
| 933[2] | **Sandmoor Chambray (76)** (TDEasterby) **5-8-8** MBirch(9) (chsd ldrs: shkn up over 2f out: wkng whn n.m.r on ins over 1f out) | 1¼ | **8** | 11/2[2] | 67 | 25 |
| 876[23] | **Al Reet (IRE) (80)** (MDHammond) **5-8-12** JQuinn(8) (chsd ldrs: effrt over 2f out: sn wknd) | 2 | **9** | 20/1 | 67 | 25 |
| 953[6] | **Pearl Venture (80)** (SPCWoods) **4-8-12v[1]** WWoods(3) (sn pushed along: chsd ldrs tl lost pl over 2f out) | nk | **10** | 16/1 | 66 | 24 |
| *211*[10] | **Leif the Lucky (USA) (78)** (MissSEHall) **7-8-10** JWeaver(11) (trckd ldrs: effrt on ins 3f out: grad wknd) | 1½ | **11** | 15/2 | 62 | 20 |
| | | | | (SP 122.3%) | **11 Rn** | |

**1m 45.4** (1.40) CSF £37.95 CT £233.81 TOTE £8.70: £2.50 £1.30 £2.10 (£19.60) Trio £74.30 OWNER Mr W. N. Smith (RICHMOND) BRED Mrs C. A. Waters
LONG HANDICAP Sandmoor Chambray 8-5

**1069 Tertium (IRE)** wore a tongue-strap for the first time. After travelling strongly, he was ridden clear inside the last and a drop back in distance will be no problem. He apparently choked here last time but the ones who must feel really choked are those who backed him first time out at Carlisle. (13/2)

**913* Clifton Fox**, keen to post, struggled to keep up, but stuck to his guns to finish clear second best in the end. He might be happier on easier ground. (5/1)

**Gymcrak Premiere**, soon struggling in the rear, stuck on in the final two furlongs. He will do better when the visor is back on. (15/2)

**802 Night Wink (USA)**, with a tongue-strap on again, was always struggling from the number-one draw. (7/1)

**739 Queens Consul (IRE)** could never dominate. (5/1)

## 1323 WINDMILL INN MAIDEN STKS (3-Y.O) (Class D)

3-55 (3-57) **7f 100y** £3,561.00 (£1,068.00: £514.00: £237.00) Stalls: High GOING minus 0.40 sec per fur (F)

| | | | | SP | RR | SF |
|---|---|---|---|---|---|---|
| 942[3] | **Marigliano (USA)** (MRStoute) **3-9-0** KDarley(6) (trckd ldrs: shkn up & led over 2f out: rdn out) | — | **1** | 8/15[1] | 75+ | 49 |
| 921[9] | **Hannalou (FR)** (SPCWoods) **3-8-9** WWoods(3) (sn in tch: hdwy 2f out: styd on fnl f: nt rch wnr) | 1½ | **2** | 16/1 | 67 | 41 |
| 962[8] | **Dispol Diamond** (GROldroyd) **3-8-9** KFallon(4) (sn pushed along & in tch: styd on u.p fnl 3f: nvr nr to chal) | hd | **3** | 25/1 | 67 | 41 |
| 982[4] | **Melt The Clouds (CAN) (82)** (PWHarris) **3-9-0** GHind(7) (trckd ldrs: effrt over 2f out: kpt on same pce) | 1¾ | **4** | 9/2[2] | 68 | 42 |
| 987[10] | **Naissant (80)** (CEBrittain) **3-8-9** JWeaver(1) (lcd tl over 2f out: wknd over 1f out) | 3½ | **5** | 8/1[3] | 55 | 29 |
| 1045[5] | **He's My Love (IRE)** (JEBanks) **3-9-0** JQuinn(5) (unruly s: hld up & bhd: stdy hdwy 2f out: nvr nr to chal) | 3 | **6** | 8/1[3] | 54 | 28 |
| | **Skylight** (MissMKMilligan) **3-9-0** JFanning(9) (unf: bkwd: s.i.s: bhd tl sme late hdwy) | 1½ | **7** | 50/1 | 51 | 25 |
| 934[11] | **Winn Caley** (CWFairhurst) **3-8-9** DeanMcKeown(8) (sn outpcd & bhd) | 6 | **8** | 66/1 | 33 | 7 |
| | **New Regime (IRE)** (PTDalton) **3-8-9** LCharnock(2) (bkwd: s.s: a bhd) | 13 | **9** | 50/1 | 5 | — |
| | | | | (SP 120.8%) | **9 Rn** | |

**1m 33.5** (1.50) CSF £10.92 TOTE £1.50: £1.10 £2.20 £4.40 (£10.40) Trio £314.30 OWNER Sultan Al Kabeer (NEWMARKET) BRED Prince Sultan Bin Mohammed Bin Saud Al Kabeer

**942 Marigliano (USA)** is still unfurnished. Kept right up to his work, he showed a fair bit of knee-action and should do better with more time and easier ground. (8/15)

**Hannalou (FR)** stepped up considerably on her first effort. (16/1)

**Dispol Diamond**, on her toes beforehand, stuck on in determined fashion but this will have done her handicap mark no good at all. (25/1)

**982 Melt The Clouds (CAN)**, fit as a flea and keen, did not find much under pressure. (9/2)

**Naissant** made the running and was given as easy a time as possible when all chance had gone. She has not come to herself yet. (8/1)

**1045 He's My Love (IRE)**, a handful at the start, was given an educational outing, his third, which qualifies him for a handicap mark. (8/1: 5/1-9/1)

## 1324 ANGEL H'CAP (0-80) (3-Y.O F) (Class D)

4-25 (4-26) **1m 1f 207y** £3,665.00 (£1,100.00: £530.00: £245.00) Stalls: High GOING minus 0.40 sec per fur (F)

| | | | | SP | RR | SF |
|---|---|---|---|---|---|---|
| 1092[2] | **Fairywings (64)** (MrsJRRamsden) **3-8-5**ow1 KFallon(5) (stdd s: hld up & bhd: gd hdwy & nt clr run 2f out: swtchd & styd on strly to ld post) | — | **1** | 11/4[1] | 71 | 30 |
| 803[13] | **Daira (55)** (JDBethell) **3-7-5**(5) PFessey(10) (chsd ldrs: swtchd lft over 1f out: led ins fnl f: hung rt & jst ct) | s.h | **2** | 25/1 | 62 | 22 |

| | | | | | |
|---|---|---|---|---|---|
| 785[7] **Baileys First (IRE) (73)** (MJohnston) **3-9-0** JWeaver(8) (led tl hdd ins fnl f) | ¾ | **3** | 16/1 | 79 | 39 |
| 915[4] **Sweetness Herself (72)** (MJRyan) **3-8-8**(5) MBaird(7) (chsd ldrs: outpcd over 2f out: styd on fnl f) | 3½ | **4** | 5/1 3 | 72 | 32 |
| 939[10] **Portuguese Lil (80)** (DNicholls) **3-9-7** JCarroll(9) (hld up: sme hdwy over 3f out: nvr nr ldrs) | 2½ | **5** | 10/1 | 76 | 36 |
| 1100[5] **Tarry (62)** (SESherwood) **3-8-3** TSprake(2) (bhd: hdwy on outside over 4f out: one pce whn sltly hmpd over 1f out) | 1 | **6** | 10/1 | 56 | 16 |
| 937[2] **She's My Love (77)** (JEBanks) **3-9-4** JQuinn(4) (lw: sn trckng ldrs: plld hrd: effrt over 2f out: wkng whn sltly hmpd over 1f out) | 9 | **7** | 100/30 2 | 57 | 17 |
| 740[3] **Scenicris (IRE) (62)** (RHollinshead) **3-8-3** NCarlisle(11) (hld up: effrt over 3f out: n.m.r & sn wknd) | 1¾ | **8** | 20/1 | 39 | — |
| 888[2] **Honorable Estate (IRE) (72)** (RHannon) **3-8-13** JFortune(1) (chsd ldrs tl wknd wl over 1f out) | 1 | **9** | 11/2 | 48 | 8 |
| **Primrose Path (75)** (CEBrittain) **3-9-2** KDarley(6) (plld hrd: trckd ldrs: hung lft & hmpd over 3f out: sn eased) | dist | **10** | 20/1 | — | — |

(SP 119.2%) **10 Rn**

**2m 5.9** (3.40) CSF £57.76 CT £867.86 TOTE £5.60: £2.10 £2.90 £3.00 (£107.30) Trio £411.90 OWNER L C and A E Sigsworth (THIRSK) BRED L. C. and A. E. Sigsworth and The Kris Syndicate

**1092 Fairywings**, stepping up from seven, was put into the stalls late. Dropped out at the start, she overcame difficulties in running to get up on the line. There is further improvement in her. (11/4)

**Daira** was switched violently round the leader over a furlong out, bumping the winner. Hanging right near the line, she was just caught. If the photo had gone her way, she would definitely have been stood down. (25/1)

**714 Baileys First (IRE)** appreciated the step up in distance and her rider did his best to pinch it. (16/1)

**915 Sweetness Herself**, back up in distance, was on edge beforehand and looked to give her rider a problem or two. (5/1)

**Portuguese Lil**, hoisted 20lb in the weights after finishing down the track in the 1000 Guineas, came from off the pace to be staying on at the finish. Touted as a Derby runner, connections will need to come down to earth. (10/1)

**1100 Tarry** is only small. (10/1)

**937 She's My Love**, stepping up two furlongs in distance, pulled very hard due to the sedate pace and had nothing left when hampered over a furlong out. (100/30)

## 1325 ROSE & CROWN H'CAP (0-70) (3-Y.O) (Class E)

5-00 (5-02) **1m 3f 216y** £3,036.25 (£910.00: £437.50: £201.25) Stalls: Centre GOING minus 0.40 sec per fur (F)

| | | | SP | RR | SF |
|---|---|---|---|---|---|
| 1034[3] **Strategic Ploy (59)** (MrsJRRamsden) **3-9-1** KFallon(2) (hld up: hdwy & swtchd outside over 2f out: hung rt & led ins fnl f: styd on wl) | — | **1** | 5/2 1 | 68 | 33 |
| 803* **Go-Go-Power-Ranger (58)** (BEllison) **3-9-0** NKennedy(3) (trckd ldrs: hdwy on ins to ld over 1f out: hdd & nt qckn ins fnl f) | 1¼ | **2** | 5/1 3 | 65 | 30 |
| 849[2] **Champagne Warrior (IRE) (45)** (MJCamacho) **3-8-1** LCharnock(6) (lw: trckd ldrs: kpt on same pce whn n.m.r ins fnl f) | 1½ | **3** | 5/1 3 | 50 | 15 |
| 954[6] **Jump The Lights (60)** (SPCWoods) **3-9-2** WWoods(7) (in tch: effrt over 2f out: hung rt over 1f out: styd on towards fin) | 1½ | **4** | 7/1 | 63 | 28 |
| 980[5] **Mister Aspecto (IRE) (65)** (MJohnston) **3-9-7** JWeaver(4) (led tl over 5f out: led 3f out tl over 1f out: sn wknd) | 3 | **5** | 12/1 | 64 | 29 |
| 980[2] **Uoni (56)** (CEBrittain) **3-8-12** KDarley(1) (chsd ldrs: led over 5f out tl rn wd & hdd 3f out: wkng whn n.m.r ins fnl f) | 1½ | **6** | 9/2 2 | 53 | 18 |
| 955P **Tashjir (USA) (58)** (DMorley) **3-9-0** MFenton(5) (bhd: outpcd 5f out: sme hdwy 3f out: n.d) | 2½ | **7** | 20/1 | 52 | 17 |
| 826[10] **Noir Esprit (56)** (JMCarr) **3-8-12** ACulhane(9) (unruly s: chsd ldrs: rdn & outpcd 3f out: sn wknd) | ½ | **8** | 14/1 | 49 | 14 |
| 914[6] **Salsian (54)** (SCWilliams) **3-8-10** GHind(8) (b.nr hind: bhd: outpcd 5f out: n.d) | nk | **9** | 12/1 | 47 | 12 |

(SP 119.4%) **9 Rn**

**2m 37.8** (5.40) CSF £15.22 CT £54.17 TOTE £3.30: £1.70 £2.00 £1.60 (£7.20) Trio £17.50 OWNER Mrs H. M. Carr (THIRSK) BRED Miss M. Sheriffe and Exors of the late A. J. Tree

**1034 Strategic Ploy**, suited by the better pace, came from last to first, despite taxing her rider's skills by tending to hang right. She should improve further, especially when stepped up in distance. (5/2)

**803* Go-Go-Power-Ranger**, from a 3lb higher mark, took a keen grip. Sticking to the rail, he showed ahead over a furlong out but, in the end, the winner proved much too strong. (5/1: op 3/1)

**849 Champagne Warrior (IRE)** raced keenly, but was only sticking on at the same pace when the winner went slightly across her inside the last. (5/1)

**954 Jump The Lights**, down two furlongs in distance, wanted to do nothing but hang badly right, but was persuaded to stay on towards the line. (7/1)

**788 Mister Aspecto (IRE)** helped force the pace, but had nothing more to give over a furlong out. (12/1)

**980 Uoni**, pushed wide on the home turn, was weakening when forced to check slightly inside the last. (9/2)

T/Plpt: £20.10 (799.05 Tckts). T/Qdpt: £7.20 (203.05 Tckts). WG

# GOODWOOD (R-H) (Good)

## Tuesday May 21st

WEATHER: fine WIND: str half against

## 1326 TREHEARNE & NORMAN MAIDEN STKS (3-Y.O) (Class D)

2-10 (2-12) **1m** £4,793.75 (£1,430.00: £682.50: £308.75) Stalls: High GOING: 0.08 sec per fur (G)

| | | | SP | RR | SF |
|---|---|---|---|---|---|
| 894[4] **Forza Figlio** (MissGayKelleway) **3-9-0** JReid(11) (b.hind: a.p: n.m.r 2f out: swtchd lft over 1f out: str run to ld wl ins fnl f: r.o wl) | — | **1** | 3/1 1 | 82 | 51 |
| 894[7] **No-Aman** (MajorWRHern) **3-9-0** RHughes(4) (hdwy over 2f out: led over 1f out tl wl ins fnl f: unable qckn) | ¾ | **2** | 20/1 | 81 | 50 |
| 732[10] **Fasil (IRE)** (CJBenstead) **3-9-0** MWigham(6) (lw: hdwy over 1f out: r.o wl ins fnl f) | 1½ | **3** | 50/1 | 78 | 47 |
| 962[10] **Sabrak (IRE)** (MAJarvis) **3-9-0** PRobinson(5) (lw: hld up: ev ch over 1f out: one pce) | s.h | **4** | 16/1 | 77 | 46 |
| **Mua-Tab** (PTWalwyn) **3-8-9** WCarson(7) (a.p: ev ch over 1f out: wknd fnl f) | 2½ | **5** | 9/2 2 | 67 | 36 |
| 1007[8] **Ashanti Dancer (IRE) (72)** (MJHaynes) **3-8-9** RCochrane(10) (led over 5f out tl over 1f out: sn wknd) | 3 | **6** | 5/1 3 | 61 | 30 |
| 860[10] **Northern Ballet (IRE)** (RHannon) **3-8-9** PatEddery(2) (hld up: rdn over 2f out: n.m.r on ins wl over 1f out: eased whn btn over 1f out) | ½ | **7** | 16/1 | 60 | 29 |
| **Danish Rhapsody (IRE)** (LadyHerries) **3-9-0** MHills(1) (unf: scope: bkwd: s.s: a bhd) | 2½ | **8** | 9/1 | 60 | 29 |
| 813[13] **Nawaji (USA)** (WRMuir) **3-8-9** MJKinane(8) (a bhd) | ¾ | **9** | 20/1 | 54 | 23 |

| | | | Pos | SP | RR | SF |
|---|---|---|---|---|---|---|
| 1050$^{5}$ | **Stone Island** (CACyzer) **3-9-0** TQuinn(9) (led over 2f: wknd over 2f out) | 8 | **10** | 15/2 | 43 | 12 |
| 962$^{3}$ | **Roushan** (JGMO'Shea) **3-9-0** JTate(3) (s.s: hung violently lft over 5f out: c stands' side st: nt rcvr: t.o) | dist | **11** | 7/1 | — | — |

(SP 117.4%) **11 Rn**

**1m 42.38** (5.18) CSF £53.00 TOTE £3.50: £1.60 £7.00 £10.50 (£46.10) Trio £161.70 OWNER Grid Thoroughbred Racing Partnership (WHITCOMBE) BRED R. E. A. Bott (Wigmore Street) Ltd

**894 Forza Figlio** again did not have the clearest of passages but, on this occasion, managed to carry the day. Switched left, he came with a useful run to swoop into the lead in the closing stages. (3/1: 2/1-100/30)

**703 No-Aman** was unable to withstand the winner's late surge. (20/1)

**Fasil (IRE)** showed great improvement on his Newbury debut and was doing a lot of good work in the final furlong and a half. (50/1)

**Sabrak (IRE)** left his debut run well behind. Chasing the leaders, he was one of four almost in line below the distance before tapped for toe. (16/1)

**Mua-Tab** had every chance over a furlong out before lack of a recent run took its toll. (9/2)

**Ashanti Dancer (IRE),** collared below the distance, soon had bellows to mend. (5/1)

**Danish Rhapsody (IRE)** (9/1: op 6/1)

**1050 Stone Island** (15/2: 5/1-8/1)

## 1327 CHICHESTER FESTIVAL THEATRE H'CAP (0-100) (3-Y.O) (Class C)

2-40 (2-42) **7f** £10,867.50 (£3,240.00: £1,545.00: £697.50) Stalls: High GOING: 0.08 sec per fur (G)

| | | | Pos | SP | RR | SF |
|---|---|---|---|---|---|---|
| 1127$^{10}$ | **King of Peru (100)** (APJarvis) **3-9-7** PatEddery(10) (nt clr run over 3f out to 2f out: hdwy over 1f out: led ins fnl f: r.o wl) | — | **1** | 14/1 | 103 | 59 |
| 1045* | **Russian Music (95)** (MissGayKelleway) **3-9-2** RCochrane(7) (lw: nt clr run over 3f out to 2f out: hdwy over 1f out: r.o wl ins fnl) | 1 | **2** | 11/2$^{2}$ | 96+ | 52 |
| 785$^{4}$ | **State of Caution (82)** (JLDunlop) **3-8-3** DHarrison(8) (hld up: rdn 3f out: led 1f out tl ins fnl f: unable qckn) | ¾ | **3** | 13/2$^{3}$ | 81 | 37 |
| 978$^{2}$ | **Sylva Paradise (IRE) (80)** (CEBrittain) **3-8-1** BDoyle(5) (w ldr: ev ch over 1f out: one pce) | 1¾ | **4** | 7/1 | 75 | 31 |
| 785$^{5}$ | **Marjaana (IRE) (75)** (PTWalwyn) **3-7-5**(5) MartinDwyer(1) (rdn over 3f out: hdwy over 1f out: r.o wl ins fnl f) | ½ | **5** | 7/1 | 69 | 25 |
| 737$^{7}$ | **Mazeed (IRE) (95)** (HThomsonJones) **3-9-2** GCarter(11) (lw: hld up: rdn over 2f out: wknd fnl f) | 3 | **6** | 33/1 | 82 | 38 |
| 833$^{6}$ | **Kilvine (88)** (LMCumani) **3-8-9** MJKinane(6) (rdn over 3f out: nvr nr to chal) | 1 | **7** | 5/1$^{1}$ | 73 | 29 |
| 1073$^{5}$ | **Banzhaf (USA) (75)** (GLMoore) **3-7-10** FNorton(4) (lw: bhd whn stumbled bdly over 2f out: nt clr run wl over 1f out: nt rcvr) | hd | **8** | 14/1 | 60 | 16 |
| 736$^{6}$ | **Wisam (96)** (RHannon) **3-9-0b1**(3) DaneO'Neill(9) (b.off fore: a.p: rdn over 2f out: wknd 1f out) | nk | **9** | 10/1 | 80 | 36 |
| *897$^{2}$* | **Splicing (80)** (WJHaggas) **3-8-1** SSanders(3) (lw: prom over 5f) | ½ | **10** | 8/1 | 63 | 19 |
| | **La Modiste (90)** (SDow) **3-8-11** TQuinn(12) (led to 1f out: eased whn btn ins fnl f) | nk | **11** | 33/1 | 72 | 28 |
| 842$^{5}$ | **Albaha (USA) (80)** (RWArmstrong) **3-8-1** WCarson(2) (a bhd) | 3½ | **12** | 14/1 | 54 | 10 |

(SP 116.5%) **12 Rn**

**1m 29.26** (4.46) CSF £81.28 CT £503.61 TOTE £10.30: £2.90 £1.80 £2.80 (£18.40) Trio £109.10 OWNER Mr L. Fust (ASTON UPTHORPE) BRED C. R. Black

LONG HANDICAP Banzhaf (USA) 7-7

**1127 King of Peru,** a stone higher than when winning his last race back in September, was boxed in at the back of the field in the straight, but came with a good rattle to strike the front inside the final furlong. (14/1)

**1045* Russian Music,** like the winner, was boxed in at the back in the straight until finding an opening below the distance. He too ran on strongly, and losses are only lent. (11/2: 4/1-6/1)

**785 State of Caution** struck the front a furlong out, but was soon passed by the winner and tapped for toe. (13/2)

**978 Sylva Paradise (IRE),** with every chance below the distance, then failed to summon up another gear. (7/1)

**785 Marjaana (IRE),** out with the washing for much of the trip, ran on strongly in the last furlong and a half to be nearest at the line. (7/1)

**737 Mazeed (IRE)** tired in the last 200 yards. (33/1)

**736 Wisam,** in blinkers for the first time, played an active role until calling it a day a furlong from home. (10/1)

**897 Splicing** (8/1: op 5/1)

**842 Albaha (USA)** (14/1: 10/1-16/1)

## 1328 E.B.F. TEGLEAZE MAIDEN STKS (2-Y.O) (Class D)

3-10 (3-11) **5f** £6,213.50 (£1,853.00: £884.00: £399.50) Stalls: Low GOING: 0.08 sec per fur (G)

| | | | Pos | SP | RR | SF |
|---|---|---|---|---|---|---|
| | **Deadly Dudley (IRE)** (RHannon) **2-9-0** MJKinane(1) (neat: hld up: led 1f out: qcknd: r.o wl) | — | **1** | 7/1$^{3}$ | 94+ | 35 |
| 706$^{2}$ | **Granny's Pet** (PFICole) **2-9-0** TQuinn(3) (lw: a.p: led over 1f out: sn hdd: unable qckn) | 5 | **2** | 8/13$^{1}$ | 78 | 19 |
| | **Cauda Equina** (MRChannon) **2-9-0** RHughes(4) (str: scope: bkwd: led over 3f: wknd fnl f) | 4 | **3** | 5/2$^{2}$ | 65 | 6 |
| | **Mystery** (SDow) **2-8-9** BThomson(2) (str: s.s: hdwy over 3f out: ev ch 2f out: wknd over 1f out) | 3 | **4** | 33/1 | 51 | — |

(SP 105.9%) **4 Rn**

**60.68 secs** (3.98) CSF £11.33 TOTE £4.20 (£2.50) OWNER Lucayan Stud (MARLBOROUGH) BRED John Kent

**Deadly Dudley (IRE),** less impressive than his rivals but at least fit, certainly knew his job. Held up behind the front two, he moved into the lead a furlong out and showed a fine turn of foot to storm well clear. (7/1: op 4/1)

**706 Granny's Pet** stood out in the paddock and this race appeared to be a formality. Unfortunately it did not prove to be so and the winner firmly put him in his place. (8/13)

**Cauda Equina,** a very well-developed two-year-old who is a half-brother to Flying Squaw, was carrying a lot of surplus flesh. When fully fit, he should not be difficult to win with. (5/2)

**Mystery,** a sturdy filly, soon recovered from a tardy start. With every chance a quarter of a mile out, she had given her all below the distance. (33/1)

## 1329 WESTMINSTER TAXI INSURANCE PREDOMINATE STKS (Listed) (3-Y.O C & G) (Class A)

3-40 (3-40) **1m 2f** £22,515.00 (£6,720.00: £3,210.00: £1,455.00) Stalls: High GOING: 0.08 sec per fur (G)

| | | | Pos | SP | RR | SF |
|---|---|---|---|---|---|---|
| 1141a$^{8}$ | **Don Micheletto** (SbinSuroor) **3-8-8** MJKinane(4) (lw: stdy hdwy over 3f out: led over 1f out: hrd rdn: r.o wl) | — | **1** | 5/1$^{2}$ | 112 | 56 |
| 1015* | **Prize Giving (108)** (GWragg) **3-8-11** MHills(1) (lw: a.p: led over 2f out tl over 1f out: ev ch ins fnl f: r.o) | ½ | **2** | 4/1$^{1}$ | 114 | 58 |
| 986$^{2}$ | **St Mawes (FR) (107)** (JLDunlop) **3-8-8** PRobinson(3) (lw: a.p: rdn over 2f out: r.o one pce) | 2½ | **3** | 5/1$^{2}$ | 107 | 51 |

| | | | | SP | RR | SF |
|---|---|---|---|---|---|---|
| 985* | **Legal Right (USA)** (PWChapple-Hyam) **3-8-8** JReid(2) (chsd ldr: ev ch over 2f out: one pce) | 1¾ | **4** | 8/1 | 104 | 48 |
| 695[5] | **Rio Duvida (119)** (DRLoder) **3-8-8** RHughes(7) (lw: hld up: rdn 2f out: one pce) | 1¾ | **5** | 10/1 | 102 | 46 |
| 892* | **Side Note** (HRACecil) **3-8-8** PatEddery(6) (led over 7f: eased whn btn over 1f out) | 1¼ | **6** | 6/1[3] | 100 | 44 |
| 926[7] | **Masehaab (IRE) (106)** (JLDunlop) **3-8-8** WCarson(5) (6th whn squeezed out 5f out: bhd fnl 4f) | 2½ | **7** | 10/1 | 96 | 40 |
| 797a[5] | **General Academy (IRE)** (PAKelleway) **3-8-8** RCochrane(9) (w'like: scope: s.i.s: slipped bnd 5f out: a bhd) | 5 | **8** | 11/1 | 88 | 32 |
| | **Swift Fandango (USA)** (PFICole) **3-8-8** TQuinn(8) (bit bkwd: prom over 7f) | 2½ | **9** | 14/1 | 84 | 28 |

(SP 111.9%) **9 Rn**

**2m 10.81** (5.31) CSF £23.03 TOTE £6.20: £2.00 £1.50 £1.70 (£8.00) Trio £16.30 OWNER Godolphin (NEWMARKET) BRED Hascombe and Valiant Studs

**1141a Don Micheletto** had a real set-to with the runner-up but just managed to prevail. A mile and a quarter is definitely his ideal trip. (5/1: 4/1-6/1)

**1015* Prize Giving** ran a fine race in defeat. Gaining control over a quarter of a mile out, he was headed below the distance but, refusing to give way, only just lost out. (4/1: op 5/2)

**986 St Mawes (FR)** found this trip too sharp, especially in this slowly-run race. Staying is going to be his game. (5/1)

**985* Legal Right (USA)** could only keep on in his own time. A mile and a half would probably be in his favour. (8/1)

**695 Rio Duvida**, a sick horse after flopping in the Craven, chased the leaders but, when bustled along a quarter of a mile from home, failed to find the necessary turn of foot. (10/1)

**892* Side Note** took the field along at little more than a crawl. At last quickening things up in the straight, he was collared over a quarter of a mile from home, and allowed to coast in from below the distance when all chance had gone. (6/1)

**797a General Academy (IRE)** (11/1: 8/1-12/1)

## 1330 ANNE FRANCES STEVENS MEMORIAL H'CAP (0-100) (4-Y.O+) (Class C)

4-10 (4-12) **1m** £9,006.00 (£2,688.00: £1,284.00: £582.00) Stalls: High GOING: 0.08 sec per fur (G)

| | | | | SP | RR | SF |
|---|---|---|---|---|---|---|
| 988* | **Hugwity (79)** (BHanbury) **4-8-7** WRyan(5) (hld up: rdn over 2f out: str run fnl f: led last strides) | — | **1** | 7/2[1] | 89 | 75 |
| 1112[8] | **Green Perfume (USA) (97)** (PFICole) **4-9-11** TQuinn(6) (lw: led: rdn over 1f out: hdd last strides) | s.h | **2** | 10/1 | 107 | 93 |
| 935[2] | **Star Talent (USA) (82)** (MissGayKelleway) **5-8-10** RCochrane(4) (b.hind: lw: s.s: hdwy over 1f out: rdn: r.o) | 2½ | **3** | 6/1[3] | 87 | 73 |
| 879[13] | **Pay Homage (79)** (IABalding) **8-8-2**(5) MartinDwyer(8) (a.p: hrd rdn over 1f out: one pce) | ¾ | **4** | 10/1 | 82 | 68 |
| 728[16] | **Stone Ridge (IRE) (94)** (RHannon) **4-9-5**(3) DaneO'Neill(3) (a.p: rdn wl over 1f out: one pce) | ½ | **5** | 10/1 | 96 | 82 |
| 967[7] | **Wakeel (USA) (84)** (SDow) **4-8-12** BThomson(11) (lw: hld up: rdn over 2f out: one pce) | ½ | **6** | 8/1 | 85 | 71 |
| 802[6] | **Sue's Return (81)** (APJarvis) **4-8-9** JTate(1) (nvr nr to chal) | hd | **7** | 12/1 | 82 | 68 |
| 1018[11] | **Pinkerton's Pal (87)** (CEBrittain) **5-9-1** BDoyle(10) (lw: a bhd) | 1½ | **8** | 20/1 | 85 | 71 |
| 1078[10] | **Zamalek (USA) (83)** (GLMoore) **4-8-11** SSanders(9) (hld up: rdn 3f out: wknd wl over 1f out) | 3 | **9** | 33/1 | 75 | 61 |
| 967[13] | **Night Dance (91)** (GLewis) **4-9-2**(3) AWhelan(7) (sme hdwy over 2f out: wknd wl over 1f out) | 2½ | **10** | 11/1 | 78 | 64 |
| 879[2] | **Samba Sharply (80)** (AHide) **5-8-3**(5) RHavlin(2) (prom over 4f) | 7 | **11** | 11/2[2] | 53 | 39 |

(SP 114.0%) **11 Rn**

**1m 39.49** (2.29) CSF £33.98 CT £184.00 TOTE £4.20: £1.70 £1.80 £1.80 (£14.40) Trio £16.70 OWNER Mr Abdullah Ali (NEWMARKET) BRED Gainsborough Stud Management Ltd

**988* Hugwity** was almost caught out by the drop in trip. Ridden along over a quarter of a mile from home, he came with a good run in the final furlong to snatch the spoils in the last few strides and complete the hat-trick. A mile and a quarter is his best trip. (7/2)

**1112 Green Perfume (USA)** looked as if he was going to prevail, but he had not bargained on the late run of the winner and was caught out in the last few strides. (10/1)

**935 Star Talent (USA)**, held up and travelling well, was asked for his effort from below the distance. Running on nicely for third prize, he was unable to get to the front two. (6/1)

**Pay Homage**, winner of this race last year, was never far away, but failed to quicken up in the last two furlongs. (10/1)

**455* Stone Ridge (IRE)** seems to be in the Handicapper's grip at the moment. (10/1)

**325a Wakeel (USA)** was made to look rather pedestrian in the final quarter-mile. (8/1)

**455 Night Dance** (11/1: 6/1-12/1)

## 1331 EQUITY FINANCIAL COLLECTIONS CLAIMING STKS (2-Y.O) (Class D)

4-45 (4-46) **6f** £3,492.50 (£1,040.00: £495.00: £222.50) Stalls: Low GOING: 0.08 sec per fur (G)

| | | | | SP | RR | SF |
|---|---|---|---|---|---|---|
| 757* | **Without Friends (IRE)** (RHannon) **2-8-8**(3) DaneO'Neill(7) (chsd ldr: shkn up over 1f out: led ins fnl f: qcknd: comf) | — | **1** | 3/1[2] | 63 | 18 |
| 916[13] | **Miss Barcelona (IRE)** (MJPolglase) **2-8-3** WHollick(8) (lw: led tl ins fnl f: unable qckn) | 4 | **2** | 40/1 | 44 | — |
| 877[6] | **Battle Ground (IRE)** (NACallaghan) **2-9-5** PatEddery(6) (lw: hld up: rdn over 2f out: one pce) | 1 | **3** | 100/30[3] | 58 | 13 |
| 1008[3] | **Misty Cay (IRE)** (SDow) **2-7-13**(5) ADaly(3) (hld up: rdn over 2f out: wknd over 1f out) | 3 | **4** | 11/2 | 35 | — |
| 910[4] | **Alimerjam** (JWhite) **2-8-8** KRutter(5) (nvr nr to chal) | nk | **5** | 40/1 | 38 | — |
| 877[4] | **Folly Foot Fred** (BRMillman) **2-8-12**(3) SDrowne(1) (prom over 4f) | nk | **6** | 8/1 | 44 | — |
| 1062[4] | **Preskidul (IRE)** (DWPArbuthnot) **2-8-6** TQuinn(2) (b.hind: hld up: hrd rdn over 2f out: wknd fnl f) | 1½ | **7** | 11/4[1] | 31 | — |

(SP 106.1%) **7 Rn**

**1m 15.98** (5.98) CSF £62.30 TOTE £2.70: £1.80 £7.10 (£54.10) OWNER Mr R. Hannon (MARLBOROUGH) BRED Churchtown House Stud
Without Friends (IRE) clmd MrsLStubbs £10,000

**757* Without Friends (IRE)** had nothing to recommend him on looks, as he is quite small, but he certainly did the job in good style. Racing in second place, he was woken up below the distance and, leading early inside the final furlong, quickened right away for a decisive victory. (3/1)

**Miss Barcelona (IRE)**, collared early inside the final furlong, was firmly put in her place. (40/1)

**Battle Ground (IRE)** found the big drop in class not helping him. Chasing the leaders, he was woken up approaching the final quarter-mile, but failed to find the necessary turn of foot. (100/30)

**1008 Misty Cay (IRE)** chased the leaders until calling it a day below the distance. (11/2)

## 1332 COCKED HAT CONDITIONS STKS (3-Y.O+) (Class C)

5-20 (5-21) **6f** £4,931.20 (£1,820.80: £870.40: £352.00: £136.00: £49.60) Stalls: Low GOING: 0.08 sec per fur (G)

| | | | | SP | RR | SF |
|---|---|---|---|---|---|---|
| 889[3] | **Loch Patrick (104)** (MMadgwick) **6-9-6** JReid(7) (lw: hdwy 2f out: led over 1f out: all out) | — | **1** | 11/4[1] | 106 | 57 |
| 889[7] | **Montendre (104)** (MMcCormack) **9-9-2** MJKinane(5) (nt clr run over 1f out: hdwy fnl f: fin wl) | nk | **2** | 5/1[2] | 101 | 52 |
| 864[7] | **Hard to Figure (109)** (RJHodges) **10-10-0** RCochrane(6) (a.p: ev ch ins fnl f: r.o) | hd | **3** | 8/1 | 113 | 64 |
| | **Kuantan (USA) (107)** (PFICole) **3-8-13** TQuinn(1) (a.p: ev ch 1f out: unable qckn) | 1 | **4** | 5/1[2] | 104 | 46 |
| 864[2] | **Wavian (97)** (RHannon) **4-8-13**(3) DaneO'Neill(3) (led over 4f: wknd fnl f) | 1¼ | **5** | 6/1[3] | 95 | 46 |
| 1107[5] | **Hello Mister (102)** (TEPowell) **5-9-5**(3) PMcCabe(2) (nvr nr to chal) | hd | **6** | 10/1 | 101 | 52 |

| | | | SP | RR | SF |
|---|---|---|---|---|---|
| 864[4] | **That Man Again (100)** (GLewis) **4-8-13b**(3) AWhelan(4) (lw: w ldr: ev ch over 1f out: sn wknd) ....6 | **7** | 7/1 | 79 | 30 |

(SP 107.0%) **7 Rn**

**1m 13.71** (3.71) CSF £14.66 TOTE £3.30: £2.10 £2.50 (£12.20) OWNER Miss E. M. L. Coller (DENMEAD) BRED Miss E. Coller
WEIGHT FOR AGE 3yo-9lb

**889 Loch Patrick** moved through to gain a narrow advantage below the distance and, driven along, found the line only just saving him. (11/4)
**457 Montendre** had nowhere to go below the distance, but at last the gap appeared in the final furlong and he flew, only to find the line coming a few strides too soon. He would surely have prevailed with a little further to go and can be considered unlucky. (5/1)
**579* Hard to Figure**, with no easy task under topweight, was always close up. Throwing down his challenge from below the distance, he still had every chance inside the final furlong, and only just lost out. (8/1)
**Kuantan (USA)**, a very temperamental individual last year, has since been gelded and was fitted with a net-muzzle for this seasonal reappearance. Better behaved here, he was always handy and had every chance a furlong from home before tapped for toe. (5/1)
**864 Wavian** held a slender lead from the start but, collared below the distance, had nothing more to give inside the last 200 yards.(6/1: op 4/1)
**864 That Man Again** had every chance until stopping as if shot in the final furlong. He does not stay six and, back over five, should soon be adding to his tally of wins. (7/1: op 4/1)

T/Jkpt: £7,100.00 (1 Tckt). T/Plpt: £133.60 (238.04 Tckts). T/Qdpt: £46.90 (45.25 Tckts) AK

## 1326-GOODWOOD (R-H) (St Good to soft becoming Soft, Rnd Good becoming Good to soft)
## Wednesday May 22nd

vis: under 1f races 6-7 - sea fret (restricted comments)
WEATHER: raining WIND: str half against

### 1333 METSA-SERLA PAPERBOARD LTD MAIDEN STKS (3-Y.O F) (Class D)
2-10 (2-12) **7f** £5,258.50 (£1,573.00: £754.00: £344.50) Stalls: High GOING: 0.51 sec per fur (GS)

| | | | SP | RR | SF |
|---|---|---|---|---|---|
| 663[2] | **Poetry (IRE) (73)** (MHTompkins) **3-8-11** PRobinson(9) (mde all: hrd rdn fnl f: r.o wl) ....— | **1** | 12/1 | 77 | 49 |
| 982[9] | **Pomona** (PJMakin) **3-8-11** SSanders(8) (rdn & hdwy 2f out: r.o wl ins fnl f) ....¾ | **2** | 50/1 | 75 | 47 |
| | **Press On Nicky** (WRMuir) **3-8-11** RCochrane(11) (w'like: dwlt: rdn & hdwy on ins over 2f out: r.o one pce)....2 | **3** | 20/1 | 71 | 43 |
| 840[4] | **Smooth Asset (IRE)** (PWChapple-Hyam) **3-8-11** JReid(7) (a.p: rdn over 3f out: one pce) ....2½ | **4** | 5/1[2] | 65 | 37 |
| | **Highland Rhapsody (IRE)** (IABalding) **3-8-11** MHills(16) (w'like: scope: bit bkwd: chsd wnr: ev ch over 2f out: wknd over 1f out) ....1½ | **5** | 14/1 | 62 | 34 |
| | **Classic Look (IRE)** (MajorDNChappell) **3-8-11** BThomson(10) (nvr nr to chal) ....1¼ | **6** | 20/1 | 59 | 31 |
| | **All Stand** (MajorDNChappell) **3-8-11** AClark(12) (unf: hdwy on ins over 3f out: rdn over 2f out: wknd over 1f out) ....hd | **7** | 50/1 | 59 | 31 |
| 870[3] | **Lubaba (USA)** (HThomsonJones) **3-8-11** WCarson(13) (hld up: rdn over 3f out: wknd over 2f out) ....7 | **8** | 7/1[3] | 43 | 15 |
| 966[3] | **Emy Coasting (USA)** (PFICole) **3-8-11** TQuinn(15) (prom over 5f) ....1¾ | **9** | 8/1 | 39 | 11 |
| 921[2] | **Fatefully (USA)** (SbinSuroor) **3-8-11** MJKinane(2) (rdn over 3f out: a mid div) ....1¼ | **10** | 6/4[1] | 36 | 8 |
| | **Love And Kisses** (CACyzer) **3-8-11** WRyan(6) (str: scope: bit bkwd: a bhd) ....¾ | **11** | 33/1 | 34 | 6 |
| 1061[8] | **On The Home Run** (JRJenkins) **3-8-11** NDay(4) (a bhd) ....1¼ | **12** | 50/1 | 31 | 3 |
| | **Kawanin** (PTWalwyn) **3-8-11** PatEddery(5) (w'like: a bhd) ....2½ | **13** | 14/1 | 25 | — |
| 813[14] | **Mimosa (67)** (SDow) **3-8-11** RHughes(14) (prom over 3f) ....2½ | **14** | 50/1 | 20 | — |
| | **Risking** (GLewis) **3-8-8**(3) AWhelan(3) (b: a bhd) ....2½ | **15** | 50/1 | 14 | — |
| 949[10] | **Bella's Legacy** (RJHodges) **3-8-11** BDoyle(1) (bhd fnl 5f) ....15 | **16** | 50/1 | — | — |

(SP 125.5%) **16 Rn**

**1m 32.33** (7.53) CSF £430.80 TOTE £12.00: £2.70 £15.00 £5.00 (£394.40) Trio Not won; £814.40 to Goodwood 23/5/96. OWNER Mr Michael Keogh (NEWMARKET) BRED St Simon Foundation

**663 Poetry (IRE)**, well supported in the market, did not let her followers down. Making every post a winning one in poor conditions, she had her field at it early in the straight and, keeping up the gallop, held on well. (12/1)
**Pomona** ran on in good style inside the final furlong, but never looked like overhauling the winner in time. (50/1)
**Press On Nicky**, a half-sister to jumper Easy Buck, stayed on for third prize, if never looking likely to get there. (20/1)
**840 Smooth Asset (IRE)** could only plod on at the one pace in the last three furlongs. (5/1: 4/1-6/1)
**Highland Rhapsody (IRE)**, a scopey newcomer, found lack of race fitness taking its toll on the rain-softened ground below the distance. She should come on for this. (14/1: op 8/1)
**Classic Look (IRE)**, making her seasonal bow, stayed on past beaten horses in the final two furlongs. (20/1)
**921 Fatefully (USA)** ran no race at all on this rain-softened ground and was always stuck in the pack. (6/4: op 4/5)

### 1334 MARRIOTT GOODWOOD PARK HOTEL H'CAP (0-95) (3-Y.O+) (Class C)
2-40 (2-42) **6f** £9,240.00 (£2,760.00: £1,320.00: £600.00) Stalls: Low GOING: 0.38 sec per fur (GS)

| | | | SP | RR | SF |
|---|---|---|---|---|---|
| 928[6] | **Montserrat (70)** (LGCottrell) **4-8-7v** MFenton(12) (a.p: rdn over 2f out: led wl ins fnl f: r.o wl) ....— | **1** | 5/1[1] | 81 | 64 |
| | **Purple Fling (70)** (LGCottrell) **5-8-7** JQuinn(7) (a.p: led over 1f out tl wl ins fnl f: r.o) ....½ | **2** | 25/1 | 80 | 63 |
| 846[3] | **La Petite Fusee (71)** (RJO'Sullivan) **5-8-8** RHughes(3) (hld up: rdn over 2f out: r.o ins fnl f) ....¾ | **3** | 5/1[1] | 79 | 62 |
| 1073[3] | **Denbrae (IRE) (69)** (DJGMurraySmith) **4-8-6** JReid(13) (dwlt: hdwy over 1f out: r.o wl ins fnl f) ....¾ | **4** | 9/1 | 75 | 58 |
| 812[12] | **Lennox Lewis (86)** (APJarvis) **4-9-9** JTate(14) (lw: hdwy 2f out: rdn over 1f out: unable qckn) ....s.h | **5** | 10/1 | 92 | 75 |
| 876[19] | **Charlie Sillett (82)** (BWHills) **4-9-5** MHills(2) (hdwy over 1f out: r.o wl ins fnl f) ....hd | **6** | 11/2[2] | 87 | 70 |
| 1186[14] | **Castlerea Lad (82)** (RHollinshead) **7-9-5** MJKinane(8) (nvr nr to chal) ....¾ | **7** | 8/1[3] | 85 | 68 |
| 1113[3] | **Twice as Sharp (84)** (PWHarris) **4-9-7** GHind(11) (lw: led over 4f: eased whn btn ins fnl f) ....nk | **8** | 5/1[1] | 87 | 70 |
| 928[10] | **Lord Olivier (IRE) (83)** (WJarvis) **6-9-6** MTebbutt(9) (hld up: rdn over 2f out: wknd over 1f out) ....½ | **9** | 14/1 | 84 | 67 |
| 1178[7] | **How's Yer Father (79)** (RJHodges) **10-9-2** RCochrane(5) (bhd fnl 5f) ....2½ | **10** | 10/1 | 74 | 57 |
| 632[6] | **Invocation (59)** (AMoore) **9-7-10** NAdams(4) (b.nr hind: lw: dwlt: hdwy 5f out: wknd 2f out) ....3½ | **11** | 50/1 | 44 | 27 |
| | **Al Nufooth (IRE) (91)** (MajorWRHern) **4-10-0** WCarson(6) (prom over 3f) ....7 | **12** | 20/1 | 58 | 41 |
| 1078[9] | **Shikari's Son (90)** (JCullinan) **9-9-13** TQuinn(1) (bhd fnl 5f) ....4 | **13** | 33/1 | 46 | 29 |

(SP 124.9%) **13 Rn**

**1m 14.2** (4.20) CSF £108.74 CT £632.12 TOTE £6.00: £2.00 £6.00 £1.60 (£88.60) Trio £72.80 OWNER Mrs Anne Yearley (CULLOMPTON) BRED Whitsbury Manor Stud
LONG HANDICAP Invocation 7-2

**928 Montserrat** loves the mud and found the rain coming just in time. Never far away, she threw down her challenge from below the distance and eventually managed to get on top in the closing stages, (5/1)
**Purple Fling**, formally with Sir Mark Prescott, made a very pleasing reappearance for his new stable. Striking the front below the distance, he was given no peace at all by the winner in the final furlong, but was only worried out of it in the closing stages. (25/1)
**846 La Petite Fusee** ran on inside the final furlong, but was unable to get to the front two in time. (5/1)
**1073 Denbrae (IRE)**, despite running on strongly, always found the line going to beat him. (9/1)
**Lennox Lewis** has done all his winning on a fast surface. (10/1)
**Charlie Sillett** found this trip just too sharp on this track. Only finding his feet from below the distance, he ran on strongly but never looked like getting there in time. Seven is his requirement nowadays. (11/2)

## 1335 TRIPLEPRINT LUPE STKS (Listed) (3-Y.O F) (Class A)
3-10 (3-14) **1m 2f** £17,740.00 (£5,320.00: £2,560.00: £1,180.00) Stalls: High GOING: 0.51 sec per fur (GS)

| | Horse | | | SP | RR | SF |
|---|---|---|---|---|---|---|
| 964* | **Whitewater Affair** (MRStoute) **3-8-8** RCochrane(1) (hdwy over 3f out: led 1f out: r.o wl) | — | 1 | 4/1 1 | 102 | 54 |
| 1004³ | **Shemozzle (IRE)** (JHMGosden) **3-8-8** PatEddery(7) (chsd ldr 2f: chsd ldr over 3f out: led 2f out to 1f out: unable qckn) | 1¾ | 2 | 9/2 2 | 99 | 51 |
| 939¹¹ | **Papering (IRE) (100)** (LMCumani) **3-8-8** MJKinane(10) (hdwy over 3f out: squeezed thro over 1f out: one pce) | nk | 3 | 9/2 2 | 99 | 51 |
| 938⁶ | **Scarlet Plume (106)** (JLDunlop) **3-9-0** WCarson(6) (led 8f: hrd rdn: wknd 1f out) | 5 | 4 | 5/1 3 | 97 | 49 |
| 908a* | **Alzabella (IRE)** (JWHills) **3-8-8** MHills(4) (leggy: bhd fnl 5f) | 11 | 5 | 7/1 | 73 | 25 |
| 708⁶ | **Silk Masque (USA)** (PWChapple-Hyam) **3-8-8** JReid(9) (a bhd) | hd | 6 | 8/1 | 73 | 25 |
| 1060a¹¹ | **Fag End (IRE) (96)** (MHTompkins) **3-8-8** PRobinson(5) (a bhd) | 3 | 7 | 16/1 | 68 | 20 |
| 938² | **Faraway Waters (100)** (DWPArbuthnot) **3-8-8** TQuinn(2) (b: chsd ldr 8f out tl over 3f out: sn wknd) | 14 | 8 | 8/1 | 46 | — |
| 938⁷ | **Promissory** (CEBrittain) **3-8-8** BDoyle(8) (lw: hld up: rdn 4f out: sn wknd) | 9 | 9 | 25/1 | 31 | — |

(SP 117.5%) **9 Rn**

**2m 15.51** (10.01) CSF £21.40 TOTE £5.00: £1.80 £1.70 £2.20 (£11.00) Trio £10.90 OWNER Mr J. M. Greetham (NEWMARKET) BRED J. M. Greetham
**964* Whitewater Affair** put up an impressive display in searching conditions. Taking closer order as the Bugler called entering the straight, she struck the front a furlong out and soon pulled away. She is turning into a very useful filly and can progress further. (4/1)
**1004 Shemozzle (IRE)** moved into second early in the straight. Striking the front a quarter of a mile out, she was unable to cope with the winner in the final furlong. (9/2)
**939 Papering (IRE)** moved up early in the straight. Squeezing through between horses approaching the final furlong, she failed to quicken. (9/2)
**938 Scarlet Plume**, whose two wins last year both came with cut in the ground, improved on her seasonal bow but found her 6lb penalty taking its toll. (5/1)
**908a* Alzabella (IRE)**, quite a tall, neatly-made filly who won in yielding ground in Italy last time out, dropped towards the back of the field at the top of the hill. (7/1)
**708 Silk Masque (USA)** is finding life difficult this season and never threatened to get into it. (8/1: 5/1-9/1)
**938 Faraway Waters** flopped in these testing conditions and, stopping to nothing, was eased. (8/1)

## 1336 KINCSEM RATED STKS H'CAP (0-105) (4-Y.O+) (Class B)
3-40 (3-42) **1m 6f** £9,454.80 (£3,493.20: £1,671.60: £678.00: £264.00: £98.40) Stalls: High GOING: 0.51 sec per fur (GS)

| | Horse | | | SP | RR | SF |
|---|---|---|---|---|---|---|
| 828² | **Prussian Blue (USA) (97)** (HRACecil) **4-9-2** WRyan(4) (chsd ldr: led over 2f out: drvn out) | — | 1 | 4/1 3 | 108 | 42 |
| 941³ | **Backgammon (87)** (JABOld) **5-8-6**ow1 JReid(1) (led over 11f: hrd rdn fnl f: r.o) | ¾ | 2 | 6/1 | 97 | 30 |
| 961* | **Purple Splash (92)** (PJMakin) **6-8-11v** TQuinn(7) (hdwy over 2f out: ev ch over 1f out: unable qckn) | hd | 3 | 11/4 1 | 102 | 36 |
| 751³ | **Source of Light (102)** (RCharlton) **7-9-7** PatEddery(2) (s.s: hdwy & nt clr run over 2f out: nt clr run over 1f out: one pce) | 3 | 4 | 3/1 2 | 109 | 43 |
| 925⁸ | **Better Offer (IRE) (97)** (GHarwood) **4-9-2** AClark(3) (lw: hdwy over 2f out: wknd over 1f out) | 9 | 5 | 9/2 | 93 | 27 |
| 647¹¹ | **English Invader (90)** (RAkehurst) **5-8-9b¹** SSanders(5) (b.nr hind: prom over 11f) | 7 | 6 | 12/1 | 78 | 12 |

(SP 111.8%) **6 Rn**

**3m 16.58** (17.58) CSF £24.40 TOTE £6.00: £2.60 £2.40 (£16.60) OWNER Mr L. Marinopoulos (NEWMARKET) BRED E. A. Cox Jnr
**828 Prussian Blue (USA)** raced in second place. Hitting the front over a quarter of a mile out, he failed to pull away from his rivals and his rider had to keep him up to his work to hold on. (4/1: 3/1-9/2)
**941 Backgammon** showed real determination and stuck to his guns in fine style. (6/1: op 4/1)
**961* Purple Splash**, raised another 7lb for his latest success, found that counting against him. (11/4)
**751 Source of Light** tried to make a move early in the straight, but found himself with nowhere to go until below the distance. When a gap did appear, he failed to find the necessary turn of foot. (3/1)
**Better Offer (IRE)**, taking a step up in distance, moved up over a quarter of a mile from home but had given his all below the distance. (9/2)

## 1337 SOUTHERNPRINT H'CAP (0-80) (3-Y.O+) (Class D)
4-10 (4-11) **1m** £7,895.00 (£2,360.00: £1,130.00: £515.00) Stalls: High GOING: 0.51 sec per fur (GS)

| | Horse | | | SP | RR | SF |
|---|---|---|---|---|---|---|
| 983¹³ | **Young Butt (62)** (JFfitch-Heyes) **3-7-8**(5)ow3 MHenry(2) (hdwy 3f out: led over 2f out: all out) | — | 1 | 33/1 | 75 | 43 |
| 1069* | **Coureur (66)** (MDHammond) **7-9-1** JQuinn(6) (hld up: rdn over 2f out: ev ch fnl f: r.o wl) | hd | 2 | 11/2 3 | 79 | 62 |
| | **Thames Side (60)** (MMadgwick) **5-8-2**(7) AEddery(8) (hdwy on ins over 1f out: unable qckn ins fnl f) | 2½ | 3 | 16/1 | 68 | 51 |
| 713³ | **Chairmans Choice (56)** (APJarvis) **6-8-5** JTate(7) (a.p: ev ch 2f out: wknd fnl f) | 5 | 4 | 9/2 2 | 54 | 37 |
| 1126⁴ | **Charlie Chang (IRE) (72)** (RHannon) **3-8-6**(3) DaneO'Neill(10) (a.p: rdn over 2f out: one pce) | hd | 5 | 3/1 1 | 70 | 41 |
| 1121⁶ | **Thatchmaster (IRE) (47)** (CAHorgan) **5-7-10** DeclanO'Shea(4) (lw: led over 5f) | 1½ | 6 | 9/1 | 42 | 25 |
| 935⁶ | **Rakis (IRE) (76)** (MrsLStubbs) **6-9-11** RCochrane(11) (lw: nvr nr to chal) | 2½ | 7 | 8/1 | 66 | 49 |
| *298*⁵ | **Northern Grey (49)** (DrJDScargill) **4-7-12** GBardwell(5) (a bhd) | 10 | 8 | 25/1 | 19 | 2 |
| 833¹³ | **No Cliches (78)** (GLewis) **3-9-1** PaulEddery(12) (lw: a bhd) | 9 | 9 | 12/1 | 30 | 1 |
| | **Greatest (63)** (RAkehurst) **5-8-12** TQuinn(3) (chsd ldr 5f) | 8 | 10 | 10/1 | — | — |
| | **Night in a Million (57)** (SWoodman) **5-8-6** MFenton(13) (a bhd) | 5 | 11 | 16/1 | — | — |
| 1124⁶ | **Pistol (IRE) (60)** (CAHorgan) **6-8-9** WJO'Connor(9) (b.hind: bhd fnl 3f) | 3 | 12 | 16/1 | — | — |

(SP 120.9%) **12 Rn**

**1m 45.31** (8.11) CSF £192.30 CT £2,827.65 TOTE £56.60: £10.70 £1.70 £5.70 (£181.50) Trio £819.50; £727.24 to Goodwood 23/5/96.
OWNER Mr G. R. Butterfield (LEWES) BRED Llety Stud
LONG HANDICAP Young Butt 7-9 Thatchmaster (IRE) 7-9
WEIGHT FOR AGE 3yo-12lb

**Young Butt** caused a real upset here. Moving through the gloom to lead over a quarter of a mile from home, he had a tremendous ding-dong battle with the runner-up and had little to spare at the line, as he held on by the skin of his teeth. (33/1)
**1069* Coureur** threw down his challenge in the final furlong but, despite giving his all, just failed to get there. (11/2)
**Thames Side**, making his seasonal bow, picked up ground along the inside rail below the distance, but having got into third place, was making no further impression in the last 100 yards. (16/1)
**713 Chairmans Choice**, with every chance a quarter of a mile from home, had run out of gas in the final furlong. (9/2)
**1126 Charlie Chang (IRE)**, never far away, was made to look very pedestrian in the last two furlongs. (3/1)
**1121 Thatchmaster (IRE)** took the field along but, collared over a quarter of a mile from home, had little left in reserve. (9/1)
**Greatest** (10/1: 8/1-12/1)

## 1338 EQUITY FINANCIAL COLLECTIONS CLAIMING STKS (3-Y.O+) (Class D)

4-45 (4-46) **1m 2f** £4,199.25 (£1,254.00: £599.50: £272.25) Stalls: High GOING: 0.51 sec per fur (GS)

| | | | | SP | RR | SF |
|---|---|---|---|---|---|---|
| 1102$^{4}$ | **Country Lover (72)** (LordHuntingdon) **5-9-4v**(7) AimeeCook(7) (lw: w ldr 5f out: in ld ins fnl f: r.o wl) | — | **1** | 7/2$^{3}$ | 79 | 41 |
| 873$^{16}$ | **Asking For Kings (IRE) (55)** (SDow) **3-7-10**(5) ADaly(1) (lw: 5th 5f out: 2nd ins fnl f: unable qckn) | 4 | **2** | 5/1 | 63 | 11 |
| 817$^{7}$ | **Battleship Bruce (68)** (NACallaghan) **4-9-8b$^{1}$** PatEddery(9) (lw: in ld 5f out: 3rd & btn ins fnl f) | 3½ | **3** | 5/2$^{1}$ | 64 | 26 |
| 1066$^{7}$ | **Statajack (IRE) (79)** (DRCElsworth) **8-9-11b** RHughes(3) (7th 5f out) | 5 | **4** | 3/1$^{2}$ | 59 | 21 |
| 1079$^{10}$ | **Ela Agapi Mou (USA)** (GLewis) **3-8-8** PaulEddery(6) (4th 5f out) | 7 | **5** | 20/1 | 45 | — |
| 760$^{11}$ | **Northern Spruce (IRE) (25)** (AGFoster) **4-8-12**(5) MHenry(8) (lw: 3rd 5f out) | 9 | **6** | 20/1 | 25 | — |
| 968$^{13}$ | **Yet Again (45)** (BHanbury) **4-9-1b$^{1}$**(3) JStack(5) (lw: 6th 5f out) | 2½ | **7** | 14/1 | 22 | — |
| 1079$^{12}$ | **Mannagar (IRE)** (JRPoulton) **4-9-5**(3) PMcCabe(2) (8th 5f out) | 17 | **8** | 33/1 | — | — |

(SP 111.6%) **8 Rn**

**2m 19.21** (13.71) CSF £19.34 TOTE £4.80: £1.60 £1.80 £1.20 (£9.50) Trio £12.00 OWNER Sir Gordon Brunton (WEST ILSLEY) BRED Sir Gordon Brunton

WEIGHT FOR AGE 3yo-14lb

**1102 Country Lover** appreciated the drop in class. Disputing the lead at halfway, he then disappeared in the gloom, but reappeared in front inside the final furlong with a commanding lead. (7/2)
**322a Asking For Kings (IRE)**, in midfield at halfway, came out of the pack in second place inside the final furlong, with no hope of pegging back the winner. (5/1)
**817 Battleship Bruce**, fitted with blinkers for the first time, was in front at halfway as the runners disappeared into the fog. (5/2)
**682 Statajack (IRE)**, taking a drop in class and 7lb clear of his rivals on adjusted ratings, emerged from the gloom in fourth place inside the final furlong. (3/1)

## 1339 E.B.F. BOXGROVE MAIDEN STKS (2-Y.O) (Class D)

5-20 (5-21) **6f** £4,386.00 (£1,308.00: £624.00: £282.00) Stalls: Low GOING: 0.38 sec per fur (GS)

| | | | | SP | RR | SF |
|---|---|---|---|---|---|---|
| | **Falkenham** (PFICole) **2-9-0** TQuinn(1) (unf: w ldr 4f out: in ld ins fnl f: rdn out) | — | **1** | 4/1$^{2}$ | 76+ | 33 |
| 916$^{5}$ | **Latin Master (IRE)** (RHannon) **2-9-0** RHughes(10) (5th 4f out: 2nd & ev ch ins fnl f: unable qckn) | 1 | **2** | 9/2$^{3}$ | 73 | 30 |
| | **Strathmore Clear** (GLewis) **2-9-0** PatEddery(9) (str: bit bkwd: 9th & rdn 4f out: 3rd ins fnl f: one pce) | 3 | **3** | 20/1 | 65 | 22 |
| | **Ikatania** (JLDunlop) **2-9-0** WCarson(7) (b: neat: 6th & rdn 4f out: 4th ins fnl f: one pce) | ½ | **4** | 13/2 | 64 | 21 |
| | **Mister Pink** (RFJohnsonHoughton) **2-9-0** JReid(5) (unf: 3rd & rdn 4f out) | 1 | **5** | 16/1 | 61 | 18 |
| | **Goodwood Lass (IRE)** (JLDunlop) **2-8-9** GCarter(3) (neat: 4th & rdn 4f out) | 1¼ | **6** | 12/1 | 53 | 10 |
| 829$^{6}$ | **Spaniards Inn** (BJMeehan) **2-9-0** PRobinson(2) (in ld 4f out) | 1¾ | **7** | 10/1 | 53 | 10 |
| | **Generous Gift** (EALDunlop) **2-9-0** PaulEddery(8) (w'like: 8th & rdn 4f out) | 7 | **8** | 6/4$^{1}$ | 35 | — |
| | **Chakra** (SDow) **2-9-0** JQuinn(6) (str: bkwd: 7th 4f out) | 7 | **9** | 20/1 | 16 | — |

(SP 123.7%) **9 Rn**

**1m 16.86** (6.86) CSF £22.63 TOTE £6.50: £2.80 £1.60 £2.60 (£15.00) Trio £20.00 OWNER Mr T. M. Hely-Hutchinson (WHATCOMBE) BRED Kirtlington Stud Ltd

**Falkenham**, quite a lightly-made individual, was disputing the lead in the early stages before the runners disappeared into the mist. Reappearing in front inside the final furlong, he was strongly pressed by the runner-up but, ridden along, just managed to prevail. (4/1: 2/1-9/2)
**916 Latin Master (IRE)**, well supported in the market, emerged from the fog battling for the advantage with the winner. In the last 50 yards, he was tapped for toe. (9/2)
**Strathmore Clear** was in last place in the early stages but reappeared from the sea-fret in third place inside the final furlong, if then making no impression on the front two. (20/1)
**Ikatania** emerged from the fog in fourth place but was only struggling on at one pace. (13/2)
**Mister Pink** was very coltish in the paddock and was in third place in the early stages, but was held in fifth inside the final furlong. (16/1)

T/Jkpt: Not won; £6,981.51 to Goodwood 23/5/96. T/Plpt: £1,412.00 (23.54 Tckts). T/Qdpt: £21.60 (157.07 Tckts). AK

# 0971-NEWCASTLE (L-H) (Good, Good to firm patches)

## Wednesday May 22nd

Race 6: hand-timed

WEATHER: overcast WIND: fresh across

## 1340 BURRADON H'CAP (0-85) (3-Y.O) (Class D)

6-30 (6-30) **6f** £3,647.50 (£1,105.00: £540.00: £257.50) Stalls: High GOING minus 0.23 sec per fur (GF)

| | | | | SP | RR | SF |
|---|---|---|---|---|---|---|
| 934$^{2}$ | **Enchanted Guest (IRE) (70)** (PWHarris) **3-8-8** GDuffield(2) (mde all far side: all out) | — | **1** | 3/1$^{1}$ | 76 | 36 |
| 571$^{5}$ | **Mallia (76)** (TDBarron) **3-9-0** JFortune(5) (prom stands' side: rdn ½-wy: styd on wl towards fin) | nk | **2** | 6/1$^{3}$ | 81 | 41 |
| 1006$^{6}$ | **Hoh Majestic (IRE) (66)** (MartynWane) **3-8-4v** DeanMcKeown(3) (lw: swtchd far side after 1f: cl up: hrd rdn fnl 2f: nt qckn towards fin) | hd | **3** | 7/1 | 71 | 31 |
| 610$^{8}$ | **Blessingindisguise (83)** (MWEasterby) **3-9-7** MBirch(7) (outpcd & bhd stands' side: hdwy 2f out: styd on wl towards fin) | ¾ | **4** | 8/1 | 86 | 46 |
| *1028*$^{13}$ | **Hickleton Miss (58)** (MrsVAAconley) **3-7-10** NCarlisle(9) (in tch: hdwy to ld stands' side 2f out: wknd ins fnl f) | nk | **5** | 50/1 | 60 | 20 |
| 997$^{4}$ | **Precious Girl (69)** (DMoffatt) **3-8-4v$^{1}$**(3) DarrenMoffatt(6) (cl up stands' side: effrt & edgd lft over 2f out: no ex fnl f) | 1¼ | **6** | 6/1$^{3}$ | 68 | 28 |

| | | Pos | SP | RR | SF |
|---|---|---|---|---|---|
| 824[5] | **Mister Joel (60)** (MWEasterby) **3-7-12** DaleGibson(1) (racd far side: rdn ½-wy: no imp) ....hd | 7 | 10/1 | 59 | 19 |
| | **Albert The Bear (75)** (JBerry) **3-8-13** KDarley(10) (outpcd stands' side tl styd on appr fnl f: n.d) ....1 | 8 | 14/1 | 71 | 31 |
| 973* | **Desert Lynx (IRE) (72)** (TRWatson) **3-8-10** KFallon(4) (racd stands' side: drvn along thrght: no ch fr ½-wy) .3½ | 9 | 11/2[2] | 59 | 19 |
| *857** | **Mask Flower (USA) (70)** (MJohnston) **3-8-8** JWeaver(11) (led stands' side 4f: sn wknd) ....6 | 10 | 7/1 | 41 | 1 |
| 824[10] | **Amanita (75)** (JWWatts) **3-8-13** JCarroll(8) (cl up stands' side 4f: wknd qckly) ....16 | 11 | 12/1 | 3 | — |

(SP 130.5%) **11 Rn**

**1m 14.15** (2.65) CSF £22.70 CT £115.11 TOTE £4.10: £1.80 £3.20 £3.50 (£15.90) Trio £29.90 OWNER The Fillies Fanciers (BERKHAMSTED) BRED Pendley Farm
LONG HANDICAP Hickleton Miss 6-12

**934 Enchanted Guest (IRE)** found this drop back in trip just right, and the line came just in time. (3/1)
**571 Mallia**, racing on the opposite side of the course to the winner, took time to find his stride, but really flew at the finish, suggesting that a bit further might help. (6/1)
**1006 Hoh Majestic (IRE)**, whose jockey was undecided early on as to which side to race, eventually decided to chase the winner up the far side and had every chance, but was never quite doing enough. (7/1)
**Blessingindisguise** was off the bit and behind until staying on well in the closing stages. He looks to be coming to hand. (8/1)
**Hickleton Miss** ran her best race for some time, but just failed to see the trip out on this occasion. (50/1)
**997 Precious Girl**, in a visor for the first time, showed more speed, but was inclined to hang when ridden and cried enough entering the final furlong. (6/1)
**824 Mister Joel** again without the blinkers, failed to make any impression. (10/1)

## 1341 DINNINGTON H'CAP (0-80) (3-Y.O+) (Class D)

7-00 (7-03) **1m (round)** £3,810.00 (£1,155.00: £565.00: £270.00) Stalls: Low GOING minus 0.23 sec per fur (GF)

| | | Pos | SP | RR | SF |
|---|---|---|---|---|---|
| 1019[6] | **Maple Bay (IRE) (65)** (ABailey) **7-8-12**(5) PRoberts(2) (a.p: led ins fnl f: r.o u.p) ....— | 1 | 7/1[3] | 75 | 46 |
| 1024[2] | **Intendant (55)** (JGFitzGerald) **4-8-7** KFallon(12) (a.p: effrt 3f out: kpt on wl towards fin) ....½ | 2 | 9/2[1] | 64 | 35 |
| 851* | **Shaffishayes (62)** (MrsMReveley) **4-9-0** DeanMcKeown(6) (lw: lost pl appr st: hdwy u.p 2f out: swtchd & r.o towards fin) ....s.h | 3 | 5/1[2] | 71 | 42 |
| 827[7] | **Anonym (IRE) (65)** (DNicholls) **4-8-10**(7) JBramhill(15) (cl up: led over 2f out tl ins fnl f: one pce) ....1¼ | 4 | 25/1 | 71 | 42 |
| 991[10] | **Jungle Patrol (IRE) (55)** (MBrittain) **4-8-7** KDarley(8) (bhd: hdwy over 2f out: nrst fin) ....½ | 5 | 25/1 | 60 | 31 |
| 1069[12] | **Pride of Pendle (73)** (DNicholls) **7-9-11** AlexGreaves(3) (bhd: hdwy & swtchd over 1f out: nvr able to chal)...nk | 6 | 10/1 | 78 | 49 |
| 991[4] | **Special-K (62)** (EWeymes) **4-9-0** JFortune(11) (bhd & rdn over 3f out: styd on: n.d) ....½ | 7 | 7/1[3] | 66 | 37 |
| 1024[6] | **Nobby Barnes (46)** (DonEnricoIncisa) **7-7-12** KimTinkler(4) (s.i.s: hmpd after 1½f: styd on wl fnl f) ....nk | 8 | 25/1 | 49 | 20 |
| 765[5] | **Western General (73)** (MissMKMilligan) **5-9-11** NConnorton(9) (bhd tl styd on fnl 3f: n.m.r 1f out) ....½ | 9 | 10/1 | 75 | 46 |
| 1072[8] | **Eric's Bett (67)** (FMurphy) **3-8-7** JWeaver(13) (s.i.s: hdwy on outside appr st: sn rdn & no imp) ....nk | 10 | 9/1 | 69 | 28 |
| 1037* | **Euro Sceptic (IRE) (49)** (TDEasterby) **4-8-1b** TWilliams(5) (chsd ldr tl wknd fnl 3f) ....1¾ | 11 | 7/1[3] | 47 | 18 |
| 1088* | **Spanish Steps (IRE) (56)** (MWEasterby) **4-8-3b**(5) 6x GParkin(14) (w ldr tl wknd 2f out) ....nk | 12 | 10/1 | 54 | 25 |
| 933[14] | **Spanish Verdict (62)** (DenysSmith) **9-8-11**(3) CTeague(1) (led tl hdd over 2f out: sn wknd) ....2 | 13 | 20/1 | 56 | 27 |
| 805[6] | **Kashana (IRE) (50)** (WStorey) **4-8-2** JFanning(7) (lw: effrt over 2f out: n.d) ....hd | 14 | 25/1 | 43 | 14 |
| *211[7]* | **Forgotten Empress (55)** (AHarrison) **4-8-7** GDuffield(10) (cl up 3f: sn bhd) ....12 | 15 | 33/1 | 24 | — |

(SP 132.7%) **15 Rn**

**1m 42.6** (3.60) CSF £39.52 CT £170.18 TOTE £8.40: £2.80 £1.60 £2.20 (£38.40) Trio £42.20 OWNER Mr Roy Matthews (TARPORLEY) BRED Berkshire Equestrian Services Ltd
WEIGHT FOR AGE 3yo-12lb

**1019 Maple Bay (IRE)**, dropped back to his optimum trip, travelled well and saw it out determinedly. (7/1)
**1024 Intendant** again kept responding to pressure but just lacked that turn of foot to make it, and really does look likely to suit a little further. (9/2)
**851* Shaffishayes** lost a bit of ground on the home turn and then had to weave his way through. Despite some strong driving, he was never doing enough to get there. (5/1)
**Anonym (IRE)** has improved a good deal on his last couple of runs and is coming to hand. (25/1)
**Jungle Patrol (IRE)** was staying on well here, suggesting that longer trips would help. (25/1)
**935 Pride of Pendle** met with trouble in running and looks to be coming to herself. She is one to keep in mind. (10/1)
**991 Special-K** kept responding to pressure, but was never doing things quickly enough. (7/1)
**1024 Nobby Barnes** as usual gave ground away at the start and was then hampered. In the end he flew when it was too late. (25/1)
**765 Western General**, given plenty to do, made headway up the straight and ran into trouble entering the final furlong, but was certainly not knocked about. (10/1)

## 1342 GO EVENING RACING WITH THE DAILY TELEGRAPH (S) STKS (3-Y.O+) (Class G)

7-30 (7-31) **5f** £2,316.00 (£651.00: £318.00) Stalls: High GOING minus 0.23 sec per fur (GF)

| | | Pos | SP | RR | SF |
|---|---|---|---|---|---|
| 1087[4] | **Sea-Deer (69)** (DWChapman) **7-9-5** JFortune(10) (racd stands' side: a.p: styd on u.p fnl f to ld cl home) ....— | 1 | 9/4[1] | 66 | 49 |
| 911[7] | **Swan At Whalley (56)** (MartynWane) **4-9-0**(5) PRoberts(1) (racd far side: led: rdn 2f out: hdd & no ex nr fin) ...1 | 2 | 10/1 | 63 | 46 |
| | **Flashy's Son (69)** (FMurphy) **8-9-5** JFanning(9) (led stands' side: rdn 2f out: nt qckn wl ins fnl f) ....½ | 3 | 9/2[2] | 61 | 44 |
| 997[5] | **Call to the Bar (IRE) (48)** (MDods) **7-9-2**(3) CTeague(3) (racd far side: effrt ½-wy: styd on fnl f: nrst fin) ....hd | 4 | 14/1 | 61 | 44 |
| 1087[7] | **Sense of Priority (58)** (DNicholls) **7-9-10** AlexGreaves(2) (racd far side: a chsng ldrs: nt qckn appr fnl f) ....½ | 5 | 8/1[3] | 64 | 47 |
| *1030[9]* | **Tropical Beach (55)** (JBerry) **3-8-11b**[1] JCarroll(4) (racd far side: hrd drvn ½-wy: styd on: nvr rchd ldrs) ....1 | 6 | 12/1 | 56 | 31 |
| 1039[10] | **Metal Boys (56)** (MissLCSiddall) **9-9-5** JWeaver(7) (racd far side: nvr trbld ldrs) ....3 | 7 | 8/1[3] | 47 | 30 |
| 1087[13] | **Gone to Heaven** (TJEtherington) **4-9-5** KDarley(5) (chsd ldr far side: rdn 2f out: wknd fnl f) ....1¾ | 8 | 9/2[2] | 41 | 24 |
| | **Pallium (IRE) (58)** (MrsAMNaughton) **8-9-5** NConnorton(6) (racd far side: a bhd) ....¾ | 9 | 14/1 | 39 | 22 |
| *22[9]* | **Sigama (USA) (55)** (JMCarr) **10-9-0**(5) GParkin(13) (racd stands' side: cl up to ½-wy: grad wknd) ....1 | 10 | 14/1 | 35 | 18 |
| 881[4] | **Aye Ready (30)** (MissLAPerratt) **3-8-11b** LCharnock(8) (racd stands' side: a bhd) ....6 | 11 | 33/1 | 16 | — |
| | **Waverley Star (30)** (JSWainwright) **11-9-5b** DeanMcKeown(11) (racd stands' side: spd 3f) ....½ | 12 | 33/1 | 15 | — |
| *606[14]* | **Sharvic (IRE)** (MissMKMilligan) **3-8-11** DaleGibson(12) (dwlt: a bhd stands' side) ....5 | 13 | 33/1 | — | — |

(SP 135.0%) **13 Rn**

**60.4 secs** (2.00) CSF £27.36 TOTE £3.20: £1.10 £2.90 £2.10 (£40.20) Trio £98.40 OWNER Miss N. F. Thesiger (YORK) BRED Stetchworth Park Stud Ltd
WEIGHT FOR AGE 3yo-8lb
No bid

**1087 Sea-Deer** won his first race here for two years and was given a fine ride. (9/4)
**750 Swan At Whalley** did his best to make all up the far side, but the winner's late burst just proved too much. (10/1)

**Flashy's Son** ran well on his first outing of the season, and will no doubt pick up a similar race as the season progresses. (9/2)
**997 Call to the Bar (IRE)** showed here that he is improving but, despite staying on, never looked likely to get there. (14/1)
**1087 Sense of Priority** is much better on the All-Weather but ran quite well before failing to quicken in the final furlong. (8/1)
**Tropical Beach**, in blinkers for the first time, was off the bit throughout and only ran on when it was too late. (12/1)
**Gone to Heaven** (9/2: 6/1-4/1)

## 1343 REED PRINT & DESIGN H'CAP (0-80) (3-Y.O+) (Class D)

8-00 (8-01) **2m 19y** £3,501.25 (£1,060.00: £517.50: £246.25) Stalls: High GOING minus 0.23 sec per fur (GF)

| | | | | SP | RR | SF |
|---|---|---|---|---|---|---|
| 1044$^{5}$ | **Zamhareer (USA) (42)** (WStorey) **5-7-4**$^{(7)}$ IonaWands(2) (mde all: qcknd 4f out: r.o wl) | — | **1** | 11/2$^{2}$ | 57 | 17 |
| 1070* | **Royal Expression (65)** (MrsMReveley) **4-9-4** KDarley(3) (lw: in tch: styd on u.p fnl 3f: nt pce to chal) | 3 | **2** | 11/2$^{2}$ | 77 | 35 |
| 1158$^{2}$ | **Great Easeby (IRE) (56)** (WStorey) **6-8-11** JFanning(6) (lw: chsd ldrs: effrt 3f out: r.o one pce) | hd | **3** | 11/8$^{1}$ | 68 | 28 |
| 1091$^{3}$ | **Mondragon (69)** (MrsMReveley) **6-9-10** ACulhane(9) (lw: bhd: hdwy ent st: no imp) | 7 | **4** | 11/1 | 74 | 34 |
| 852$^{6}$ | **Sujud (IRE) (54)** (MrsJRRamsden) **4-8-7** KFallon(5) (prom: effrt ent st: one pce) | 5 | **5** | 6/1$^{3}$ | 54 | 12 |
| 1070$^{11}$ | **French Ivy (USA) (60)** (FMurphy) **9-9-1** TWilliams(10) (b: hld up & bhd: shkn up 3f out: n.d) | 3½ | **6** | 11/1 | 57 | 17 |
| *837** | **Jaraab (46)** (MissSJWilton) **5-8-1v** LCharnock(7) (chsd ldrs: drvn along 7f out: wknd 3f out) | 4 | **7** | 8/1 | 39 | — |
| 1034$^{8}$ | **Western Horizon (USA) (43)** (CEBrittain) **4-7-10** NCarlisle(1) (cl up tl wknd fnl 3f) | 6 | **8** | 25/1 | 30 | — |
| 1044$^{3}$ | **Urban Dancing (USA) (45)** (BEllison) **7-8-0** NKennedy(4) (lw: effrt 4f out: sn btn) | 2½ | **9** | 10/1 | 29 | — |
| | **Rodeo Star (USA) (65)** (NTinkler) **10-9-6** JFortune(8) (cl up tl wknd fnl 3f) | 3½ | **10** | 33/1 | 46 | 6 |
| | | | | (SP 130.8%) | **10 Rn** | |

**3m 35.35** (9.85) CSF £37.48 CT £61.61 TOTE £6.40: £1.90 £1.60 £1.60 (£21.40) Trio £14.10 OWNER Mr D. C. Batey (CONSETT) BRED Mrs Jackie Ward Ramos
LONG HANDICAP Western Horizon (USA) 7-3
WEIGHT FOR AGE 4yo-2lb
**1044 Zamhareer (USA)**, given a completely different ride to last time, got it right in some style and always had too much speed for the opposition in the home straight. (11/2)
**1070* Royal Expression** is in terrific form at present but he was short of a real turn of speed to get near the winner. (11/2)
**1158 Great Easeby (IRE)** looked and raced well, but his stable-companion always had too much speed for him in this muddling event. All he needs is another half-mile and a strong gallop. (11/8)
**1091 Mondragon**, waited with, needed a stronger pace than was set here and could never get into it. (11/1)
**852 Sujud (IRE)** does not look quite right as yet and was unsuited by the sprint up the straight. (6/1: op 4/1)
**French Ivy (USA)**, set an impossible task in this moderately-run event, did well to finish so close. (11/1)

## 1344 RAMSIDE HALL HOTEL AND COUNTRY CLUB MAIDEN STKS (2-Y.O) (Class D)

8-30 (8-31) **5f** £3,078.75 (£930.00: £452.50: £213.75) Stalls: High GOING minus 0.23 sec per fur (GF)

| | | | | SP | RR | SF |
|---|---|---|---|---|---|---|
| 930$^{2}$ | **Bolero Boy** (MWEasterby) **2-9-0** DaleGibson(2) (mde all: r.o strly fnl f: eased towards fin) | — | **1** | 5/1 | 58+ | 24 |
| | **Night Flight** (JJO'Neill) **2-9-0** KFallon(1) (cmpt: scope: wnt lft s: sn rcvrd & cl up: effrt 2f out: nt qckn) | 3½ | **2** | 9/2$^{3}$ | 47 | 13 |
| | **Bold Risk** (JBerry) **2-9-0** JCarroll(4) (leggy: unf: chsd ldrs: outpcd 2f out: kpt on fnl f) | ½ | **3** | 7/2$^{2}$ | 45 | 11 |
| | **Demolition Man** (JWWatts) **2-9-0** KDarley(5) (w'like: unf: lw: dwlt: jnd ldrs after 1f: rdn 2f out: nt qckn) | ½ | **4** | 11/4$^{1}$ | 44 | 10 |
| 1086$^{10}$ | **Pension Fund** (MWEasterby) **2-8-9**$^{(5)}$ GParkin(6) (bhd tl stdy hdwy fnl 2f) | 1¼ | **5** | 33/1 | 40 | 6 |
| | **Return of Amin** (JDBethell) **2-9-0** JFortune(7) (cmpt: scope: dwlt: hdwy u.p ½-wy: no imp) | nk | **6** | 7/2$^{2}$ | 39 | 5 |
| | **Our Home Land (USA)** (MJohnston) **2-9-0** JWeaver(3) (w'like: str: bit bkwd: spd to ½-wy: wknd qckly) | 2½ | **7** | 9/1 | 31 | — |
| | | | | (SP 118.9%) | **7 Rn** | |

**61.64 secs** (3.24) CSF £26.74 TOTE £6.20: £2.00 £3.90 (£26.60) OWNER Sheriff Racing (SHERIFF HUTTON) BRED R. S. A. Urquhart
OFFICIAL EXPLANATION **Pension Fund: returned home with sore shins.**
**930 Bolero Boy** is obviously improving and won this in useful style against some well-fancied newcomers. (5/1)
**Night Flight**, a sturdy sort, ran well and looks likely to be all the better for it. (9/2)
**Bold Risk**, a well-touted sort, was always a bit short of room and was not over-punished when beaten. He will benefit a good deal from the run. (7/2: op 2/1)
**Demolition Man** took the eye in the paddock and ran well after a slow start, but he had had his limitations exposed approaching the final furlong. (11/4)
**Pension Fund** never got into this, but was staying on well under tender handling and, over further, better should be seen. (33/1)
**Return of Amin**, after a poor start. failed to get into it, but looks likely to benefit for the experience. (7/2)
**Our Home Land (USA)** needed this quite badly and blew up soon after halfway. (9/1: 4/1-10/1)

## 1345 DUDLEY LIMITED STKS (0-65) (3-Y.O+) (Class F)

9-00 (9-01) **1m 1f 9y** £2,745.00 (£770.00: £375.00) Stalls: Low GOING minus 0.23 sec per fur (GF)

| | | | | SP | RR | SF |
|---|---|---|---|---|---|---|
| *859$^{2}$* | **Call Me (65)** (CWThornton) **3-8-7** DeanMcKeown(4) (lw: trckd ldrs: led wl over 1f out: r.o) | — | **1** | 5/1$^{3}$ | 72 | 33 |
| 1152$^{2}$ | **Eagle Canyon (IRE) (64)** (BHanbury) **3-8-10** JWeaver(7) (lw: cl up: led 2f out: sn hdd: kpt on wl) | ¾ | **2** | 6/4$^{1}$ | 74 | 35 |
| 1089$^{3}$ | **Alpine Panther (IRE) (65)** (WJarvis) **3-8-8** KDarley(1) (lw: bhd: hdwy on outside appr st: rdn 3f out: one pce fnl 2f) | 2½ | **3** | 15/8$^{2}$ | 67 | 28 |
| 999$^{9}$ | **Stormless (34)** (PMonteith) **5-9-7** LCharnock(2) (bhd: effrt over 3f out: nvr rchd ldrs) | 1 | **4** | 50/1 | 66? | 40 |
| 1154$^{6}$ | **Manabar (63)** (MJPolglase) **4-9-7** NCarlisle(6) (lw: lost pl appr st: styd on u.p fnl 3f: no imp) | 2½ | **5** | 9/1 | 61 | 35 |
| 885$^{5}$ | **She's A Winner (IRE) (56)** (PMonteith) **3-8-7** SDWilliams(3) (chsd ldrs tl wknd over 2f out) | 6 | **6** | 14/1 | 49 | 10 |
| 1072$^{7}$ | **Dr Edgar (64)** (MDods) **4-9-7** KFallon(5) (lw: led tl hdd & wknd 2f out) | 1¼ | **7** | 8/1 | 48 | 22 |
| | | | | (SP 121.2%) | **7 Rn** | |

**1m 56.8** (4.50) CSF £13.47 TOTE £7.70: £1.90 £1.50 (£5.10) OWNER Mr Guy Reed (MIDDLEHAM) BRED J. M. Greetham
WEIGHT FOR AGE 3yo-13lb
**859 Call Me** appreciated this step up in trip and, always travelling nicely, won in good style. (5/1)
**1152 Eagle Canyon (IRE)** ran another sound race and kept fighting back when all looked lost. (6/4)
**1089 Alpine Panther (IRE)**, surprisingly dropped back in trip, was last away. Forced to race round the outside to improve, he was never doing enough when ridden. (15/8)
**Stormless** has more ability than he cares to show sometimes and this trip looked a bit on the short side. (50/1)
**920 Manabar** looks really well but he is a funny customer and was never doing enough to offer a threat. (9/1)
**885 She's A Winner (IRE)** soon dropped out when the pressure was on early in the straight. (14/1)

T/Plpt: £33.10 (461.58 Tckts). T/Qdpt: £5.40 (184.6 Tckts). AA

# 1117-SALISBURY (R-H) (Soft)
## Wednesday May 22nd

Races 3 & 5: Flag starts
WEATHER: raining WIND: fresh across

### 1346 WHITEPARISH MAIDEN STKS (2-Y.O F) (Class D)

6-15 (6-27) **6f** £3,489.50 (£1,046.00: £503.00: £231.50) Stalls: High GOING: 0.17 sec per fur (G)

| | | | | SP | RR | SF |
|---|---|---|---|---|---|---|
| | **Witching Hour (IRE)** (MrsJCecil) **2-8-11** TIves(10) (w'like: w ldrs: rdn over 2f out: led over 1f out: r.o wl) | — | **1** | 13/2[3] | 84+ | 37 |
| | **Conspiracy** (JLDunlop) **2-8-11** TSprake(4) (w'like: plld hrd: w ldrs: led 3f out tl over 1f out: one pce) | 4 | **2** | 11/4[1] | 73 | 26 |
| | **Green Jewel** (RHannon) **2-8-11** MHills(9) (w'like: scope: rdn & hdwy 2f out: styd on fnl f) | 1 | **3** | 8/1 | 71 | 24 |
| | **Permission** (RHannon) **2-8-8**(3) DaneO'Neill(1) (w'like: a.p: rdn & outpcd over 2f out: styd on appr fnl f) | ¾ | **4** | 7/1 | 69 | 22 |
| 1062[6] | **Windborn** (KMcAuliffe) **2-8-11** JFEgan(2) (led 3f: wknd fnl f) | 2 | **5** | 14/1 | 63 | 16 |
| 916[6] | **Supercal** (DRCElsworth) **2-8-11** RCochrane(14) (s.s: hdwy over 3f out: eased whn btn ins fnl f) | 2 | **6** | 13/2[3] | 58 | 11 |
| | **Lucky Dip** (MajorDNChappell) **2-8-11** BThomson(3) (lengthy: unf: dwlt: nvr nrr) | 2 | **7** | 12/1 | 53 | 6 |
| | **Bluebell Miss** (MJRyan) **2-8-11** DBiggs(7) (w'like: bit bkwd: mid div: rdn 4f out: bhd fnl 2f) | 2 | **8** | 33/1 | 47 | — |
| | **Princess Ferdinand (IRE)** (MMcCormack) **2-8-11** RPerham(5) (neat: dwlt: sn rcvrd: bhd fnl 2f) | 2½ | **9** | 16/1 | 41 | — |
| | **Watercolour (IRE)** (PFICole) **2-8-11** CRutter(13) (prom over 3f) | 2 | **10** | 9/2[2] | 35 | — |
| | **My Precious** (MMcCormack) **2-8-11** AClark(8) (cmpt: s.s: sn rdn: a bhd) | 1½ | **11** | 33/1 | 31 | — |
| | **Advance Repro** (JAkehurst) **2-8-11** AMcGlone(11) (lengthy: unf: a bhd) | nk | **12** | 33/1 | 31 | — |
| | **Grovefair Maiden (IRE)** (BJMeehan) **2-8-11** BDoyle(15) (lt-f: bit bkwd: s.s: a bhd) | 2 | **13** | 20/1 | 25 | — |
| | **Russian Sable** (MRChannon) **2-8-11** WWoods(12) (neat: s.s: a bhd) | ¾ | **14** | 16/1 | 23 | — |
| | ***Nasscina*** (MRChannon) **2-8-11** DHarrison(6) (Withdrawn not under Starter's orders: unruly at s) | | **W** | 20/1 | — | — |

(SP 139.6%) **14 Rn**

**1m 18.3** (5.30) CSF £26.18 TOTE £8.90: £3.30 £2.50 £2.50 (£17.60) Trio £145.50; £63.56 to Brighton 24/5/96 OWNER Greenbay Stables Ltd (NEWMARKET) BRED C. H. Wacker III

**Witching Hour (IRE)** stayed on strongly in this soft ground and seems likely to eventually get much further. (13/2: 7/2-7/1)
**Conspiracy**, a well-bred filly, took a strong hold and seems sure to be better for the experience. (11/4)
**Green Jewel** will come into her own when tackling a longer trip and is looking a bargain at 4,000 guineas. (8/1)
**Permission** is another who shaped as though she already needs further. (7/1: op 3/1)
**1062 Windborn**, stepping up in class, did not see out the extra furlong in the rain-softened ground. (14/1: 12/1-20/1)
**916 Supercal** again lost ground at the start and was not knocked about when her chance had gone. Better ground might help. (13/2)
**Lucky Dip** showed promise for the future in the closing stages. (12/1: op 8/1)
**Watercolour (IRE)** (9/2: op 5/2)

### 1347 SHERBORNE CLAIMING H'CAP (0-60) (3-Y.O+) (Class F)

6-45 (6-53) **1m 4f** £3,036.00 (£846.00: £408.00) Stalls: High GOING: 0.17 sec per fur (G)

| | | | | SP | RR | SF |
|---|---|---|---|---|---|---|
| | **Glow Forum (36)** (LMontagueHall) **5-8-2**(3)ow2 DaneO'Neill(3) (led over 7f: led over 3f out: r.o wl) | — | **1** | 9/2[1] | 49 | 31 |
| 822[4] | **Kristal Breeze (38)** (WRMuir) **4-8-7**ow1 RCochrane(12) (reminders 6f out: hdwy 4f out: chsd wnr 2f out: one pce fnl f) | 5 | **2** | 10/1 | 44 | 27 |
| 546[13] | **World Express (IRE) (53)** (BRMillman) **6-9-5b**(3) SDrowne(11) (wl bhd: rdn 6f out: hdwy fnl 3f: nrst fin) | 4 | **3** | 12/1 | 54 | 38 |
| 890[6] | **Sterling Fellow (51)** (RHannon) **3-8-3** JFEgan(16) (prom: rdn 5f out: one pce fnl 3f) | 3 | **4** | 14/1 | 48 | 15 |
| | **Sinclair Lad (IRE) (39)** (RJHodges) **8-8-8b** TSprake(1) (plld hrd: no hdwy fnl 3f) | 2 | **5** | 14/1 | 33 | 17 |
| 1012[9] | **Ginka (29)** (JWMullins) **5-7-12**ow1 AMackay(2) (wl bhd tl r.o fnl 3f: nrst fin) | 3½ | **6** | 33/1 | 19 | 2 |
| 979[13] | **Fastini Gold (42)** (MDIUsher) **4-8-11** NAdams(20) (prom tl wknd 2f out) | hd | **7** | 33/1 | 32 | 16 |
| | **Duty Sergeant (IRE) (37)** (PhilipMitchell) **7-8-6** GBardwell(13) (hld up & plld hrd: hdwy over 4f out: hrd rdn & wknd 3f out) | 2½ | **8** | 20/1 | 23 | 7 |
| 999[7] | **Achilles Heel (39)** (CNAllen) **5-8-8** CHodgson(17) (plld hrd: a.p: led over 4f out tl over 3f out: wknd wl over 1f out) | 2½ | **9** | 10/1 | 22 | 6 |
| 1011[10] | **Racing Hawk (USA) (55)** (MSSaunders) **4-9-10** RPrice(5) (prom: hrd rdn over 4f out: wknd over 2f out) | ¾ | **10** | 33/1 | 37 | 21 |
| 546[18] | **Greenwich Again (57)** (TGMills) **4-9-12** MarkLynch(9) (plld hrd early: prom over 8f) | ¾ | **11** | 12/1 | 38 | 22 |
| 642[7] | **Brick Court (IRE) (42)** (RFJohnsonHoughton) **4-8-4**(7) BarrySmith(18) (a bhd) | 1½ | **12** | 33/1 | 21 | 5 |
| 944[8] | **Sails Legend (33)** (MrsMELong) **5-7-9**(7) TField(14) (a bhd) | 3 | **13** | 33/1 | 8 | — |
| 884[5] | **Chilly Lad (52)** (MJRyan) **5-9-7b** DBiggs(8) (hld up mid div: wknd over 4f out) | 1½ | **14** | 5/1[2] | 25 | 9 |
| | **King Ubad (USA) (35)** (KOCunningham-Brown) **7-8-4b**[1] BDoyle(4) (prom over 6f) | 1¼ | **15** | 20/1 | 6 | — |
| 1009[8] | **Remember Star (47)** (AGNewcombe) **3-7-13** AMcGlone(7) (plld hrd: bhd fnl 6f) | 1¼ | **16** | 16/1 | 17 | — |
| 1011[8] | **Bag of Tricks (IRE) (53)** (SDow) **6-9-3**(5) ADaly(10) (s.s: sn rcvrd: wknd 5f out) | ¾ | **17** | 10/1 | 22 | 6 |
| *898*[11] | **Bresil (USA) (30)** (KRBurke) **7-7-8**(5)ow1 MHenry(15) (a bhd) | 8 | **18** | 11/1 | — | — |
| 752[4] | **Cheveley Dancer (USA) (32)** (TJNaughton) **8-8-1** SSanders(19) (a bhd) | 4 | **19** | 8/1[3] | — | — |

(SP 140.4%) **19 Rn**

**2m 43.57** (10.97) CSF £50.27 CT £483.05 TOTE £4.90: £1.50 £2.50 £1.90 £4.20 (£56.00) Trio £419.70 OWNER The Forum Ltd (EPSOM) BRED Forum Bloodstock Ltd
WEIGHT FOR AGE 3yo-17lb
**OFFICIAL EXPLANATION Chilly Lad: was distressed after the race.**

**Glow Forum**, backed right down to favouritism, took to the soft ground like a duck to water and forged clear in the last 200 yards. (9/2: op 12/1)
**822 Kristal Breeze** does not mind give underfoot and, stepping up in distance, tried to make a race of it until finding the winner much too strong from the distance. (10/1)
**World Express (IRE)**, with ground conditions in his favour this time, is coming down the weights, but only consented to get going when it was far too late. (12/1)
**Sterling Fellow**, dropped 3lb, fared better on this ground. (14/1: op 8/1)
**Sinclair Lad (IRE)**, down to a winning mark, ran creditably on this return after proving difficult to settle. (14/1)
**Ginka** came from a long way back to reach her finishing position and seems worth a try over further. (33/1)

### 1348 BOLLINGER CHAMPAGNE CHALLENGE SERIES GENTLEMENS' H'CAP (0-70) (3-Y.O+) (Class F)

7-15 (7-20) **6f 212y** £3,054.00 (£912.00: £436.00: £198.00) GOING: 0.17 sec per fur (G)

| | | | | SP | RR | SF |
|---|---|---|---|---|---|---|
| 893[6] | **Pointer (39)** (MrsPNDutfield) **4-10-0**(4) MrLJefford(2) (a.p: led over 2f out: r.o wl) | — | **1** | 10/1 | 48 | 21 |

| Last run | Horse / details | Dist | Pos | SP | RR | SF |
|---|---|---|---|---|---|---|
| 1170[3] | **Almapa (45)** (RJHodges) **4-10-10** JCulloty(10) (rdn & hdwy over 2f out: swtchd rt ins fnl f: r.o) | ¾ | **2** | 9/2 [1] | 52 | 25 |
| 1047[10] | **Shaynes Domain (40)** (RMFlower) **5-10-5b** MrTMcCarthy(6) (hld up: hdwy on stands' side over 2f out: nt clr run & swtchd rt over 1f out: r.o ins fnl f) | ½ | **3** | 14/1 | 46 | 19 |
| 1122* | **Flying Pennant (IRE) (65)** (RHannon) **3-11-5** 5x MrMRimell(5) (a.p: ev ch over 1f out: unable qckn ins fn lf) | 1¼ | **4** | 9/1 [3] | 68 | 30 |
| 1121* | **Morocco (IRE) (61)** (MRChannon) **7-11-12** 5x MrCVigors(15) (hld up: hdwy over 2f out: ev ch over 1f out: wknd ins fnl f) | 3 | **5** | 8/1 [2] | 57 | 30 |
| 670[9] | **Kevasingo (56)** (BWHills) **4-11-3**(4) MrCBHills(3) (hdwy over 2f out: wknd fnl f) | s.h | **6** | 14/1 | 52 | 25 |
| 1047[6] | **Kingchip Boy (63)** (MJRyan) **7-11-10v**(4) MrSLavallin(8) (nvr nr to chal) | 5 | **7** | 12/1 | 48 | 21 |
| | **Mazirah (52)** (PJMakin) **5-11-3** MrJDurkan(9) (nvr trbld ldrs) | s.h | **8** | 16/1 | 37 | 10 |
| 1099[2] | **Move With Edes (61)** (WGMTurner) **4-11-8**(4) MrNMoran(1) (prom 5f) | 2½ | **9** | 10/1 | 40 | 13 |
| 981[9] | **Jigsaw Boy (57)** (PGMurphy) **7-11-4**(4) MrMatthewWells(12) (a bhd) | 1¾ | **10** | 10/1 | 32 | 5 |
| *1083[6]* | **Leigh Crofter (60)** (PDCundell) **7-11-11b** MrABalding(13) (chsd ldrs: wknd over 1f out) | 3 | **11** | 16/1 | 28 | 1 |
| 893[19] | **Winter Scout (USA) (58)** (CPEBrooks) **8-11-9** MrEJames(17) (prom over 4f) | 1¼ | **12** | 33/1 | 23 | — |
| *839[11]* | **Titanium Honda (IRE) (28)** (DCO'Brien) **5-9-3b**(4) MrVLukaniuk(4) (b: led tl wknd over 2f out) | 5 | **13** | 33/1 | — | — |
| 1122[D] | **Daily Risk (65)** (SDow) **3-11-1**(4) MrSFetherstonhaugh(16) (s.s: a bhd: t.o) | 12 | **14** | 9/2 [1] | — | — |
| *653[6]* | **Fighter Squadron (38)** (REPeacock) **7-9-13b**(4) MrAEvans(11) (s.s: hdwy over 4f out: wknd over 2f out: t.o) | 2½ | **15** | 33/1 | — | — |
| *1048[7]* | **Sarum (40)** (JELong) **10-10-1**(4) MrTWaters(14) (b: prom over 4f: t.o) | 5 | **16** | 33/1 | — | — |
| | | | | (SP 129.3%) | **16 Rn** | |

**1m 35.4** (9.40) CSF £53.27 CT £611.42 TOTE £13.00: £3.10 £1.40 £2.10 £3.00 (£47.70) Trio £172.10 OWNER In For The Crack (SEATON) BRED Darley Stud Management Co Ltd
LONG HANDICAP Titanium Honda (IRE) 9-6
WEIGHT FOR AGE 3yo-11lb

**893 Pointer** relished this return to seven and the ground put an even greater emphasis on getting the trip. (10/1)
**1170 Almapa**, back to the right sort of trip, could not peg back the winner. He does seem at his best on faster ground. (9/2: 6/1-4/1)
**Shaynes Domain** finished runner-up in this race last year, and had to be switched from under the stands' rail to get a run. (14/1)
**1122* Flying Pennant (IRE)** ran well, but could not defy a 5lb penalty for his lucky win over course and distance last week. (9/1: 6/1-10/1)
**1121* Morocco (IRE)**, another penalised for a course and distance win last week, again showed he is in good form but did not get home on ground too soft for him. (8/1: op 4/1)
**Kevasingo** likes a mile on fast ground and has dropped back down to a winning mark. (14/1)

## 1349 ST. EDMUND OF ABINGDON LIMITED STKS (0-80) (3-Y.O) (Class D)

7-45 (7-46) **1m 1f 209y** £3,606.50 (£1,082.00: £521.00: £240.50) Stalls: High GOING: 0.17 sec per fur (G)

| Last run | Horse / details | Dist | Pos | SP | RR | SF |
|---|---|---|---|---|---|---|
| 1002[11] | **Deadline Time (IRE) (79)** (MrsMReveley) **3-8-11** MHills(2) (hld up: n.m.r over 2f out: squeezed thro to ld over 1f out: rdn out) | — | **1** | 7/4 [2] | 88 | 31 |
| 842[4] | **Sandy Floss (IRE) (77)** (HRACecil) **3-8-11** PatEddery(1) (a.p: led over 3f out tl over 1f out: unable qckn) | 3 | **2** | 13/8 [1] | 83 | 26 |
| 969[8] | **Royal Diversion (IRE) (80)** (JLDunlop) **3-8-8** TQuinn(3) (hld up: rdn 3f out: ev ch over 1f out: one pce) | 2 | **3** | 9/2 [3] | 77 | 20 |
| | **Majdak Jereeb (IRE) (80)** (MajorWRHern) **3-8-11** TSprake(4) (led 2f: led over 5f out tl over 3f out: rdn whn hmpd over 2f out: sn wknd) | 1¾ | **4** | 16/1 | 77 | 20 |
| 709[5] | **Decision Maker (IRE) (80)** (RHannon) **3-8-8**(3) DaneO'Neill(5) (led 10f out tl over 5f out: rdn & edgd lft over 2f out: sn wknd) | nk | **5** | 8/1 | 77 | 20 |
| | | | | (SP 109.6%) | **5 Rn** | |

**2m 15.1** (9.80) CSF £4.79 TOTE £2.60: £1.50 £1.20 (£1.60) OWNER Mr P. D. Savill (SALTBURN) BRED Johnny Kelly

**483 Deadline Time (IRE)**, disappointing in a visor at Chester, enjoyed the give underfoot and was his trainer's first runner at the course. (7/4)
**842 Sandy Floss (IRE)**, stepping up in distance, could not cope with the winner once his rival found a gap. (13/8)
**550 Royal Diversion (IRE)** could not produce the required turn of foot. (9/2: op 3/1)
**Majdak Jereeb (IRE)**, trying a longer trip, was just starting to feel the pinch when squeezed up against the stands' rail. (16/1)
**526 Decision Maker (IRE)**, not for the first time, went left under pressure. (8/1: 5/1-9/1)

## 1350 LANDFORD MAIDEN STKS (3-Y.O) (Class D)

8-15 (8-15) **6f 212y** £4,370.00 (£1,310.00: £630.00: £290.00) GOING: 0.17 sec per fur (G)

| Last run | Horse / details | Dist | Pos | SP | RR | SF |
|---|---|---|---|---|---|---|
| 1142[8] | **Slip Jig (IRE)** (RHannon) **3-9-0** RHughes(8) (w ldrs: led wl over 1f out tl ins fnl f: led nr fin: all out) | — | **1** | 6/4 [1] | 77 | 40 |
| | **Double March** (PRWebber) **3-9-0** TQuinn(1) (wl grwn: scope: a.p: hrd rdn over 1f out: led ins fnl f: hdd nr fin) | hd | **2** | 33/1 | 77 | 40 |
| 696[3] | **Prime Light** (GWragg) **3-9-0** MHills(12) (led over 5f: one pce fnl f) | 4 | **3** | 2/1 [2] | 68 | 31 |
| | **Welsh Emblem (IRE)** (GWragg) **3-9-0** WWoods(11) (gd srt: chsd ldrs: rdn & outpcd over 2f out: styd on fnl f: btr for r) | ¾ | **4** | 16/1 | 66 | 29 |
| | **Attarikh (IRE)** (JHMGosden) **3-9-0** WCarson(14) (plld hrd: w ldrs tl wknd wl over 1f out) | 3 | **5** | 9/2 [3] | 59 | 22 |
| 1045[6] | **Scimitar** (PJMakin) **3-9-0** SSanders(13) (prom over 5f) | 4 | **6** | 20/1 | 50 | 13 |
| 1045[7] | **Voodoo Rocket** (JHMGosden) **3-8-9** GHind(6) (b.hind: no hdwy fnl 3f) | nk | **7** | 12/1 | 44 | 7 |
| 710[17] | **Alajyal (IRE)** (PTWalwyn) **3-8-9** RCochrane(10) (hld up & plld hrd: rdn 3f out: sn wknd) | 4 | **8** | 16/1 | 35 | — |
| | **Mr Hacker** (GThorner) **3-8-7**(7) AEddery(5) (str: scope: s.s: a bhd) | 3 | **9** | 50/1 | 33 | — |
| | **Blue Jumbo (IRE)** (WJMusson) **3-8-9** OUrbina(2) (str: scope: bhd fnl 3f) | 1½ | **10** | 33/1 | 25 | — |
| | **Burning Flame** (RMFlower) **3-8-6**(3) SDrowne(4) (w'like: bkwd: a bhd) | nk | **11** | 50/1 | 24 | — |
| | **Camphar** (RMFlower) **3-8-4**(5) JDSmith(7) (w'like: a bhd) | 1½ | **12** | 50/1 | 20 | — |
| 1050[9] | **The Grey Weaver** (RMFlower) **3-9-0** DBiggs(3) (sn rdn: a bhd: t.o) | 19 | **13** | 50/1 | — | — |
| | | | | (SP 129.5%) | **13 Rn** | |

**1m 32.16** (6.16) CSF £47.86 TOTE £3.50: £1.80 £3.30 £1.30 (£64.60) Trio £29.70 OWNER Mr John Horgan (MARLBOROUGH) BRED Scuderia Milano

**1142 Slip Jig (IRE)** is a half-brother to Strutting. Although inclined to carry his head over the stands' rail, he got the better of a good battle through the final furlong. (6/4)
**Double March** very nearly pulled off a big upset and it would be a surprise if this turns out to be merely a flash in the pan. (33/1)
**696 Prime Light** certainly had easier ground this time, but could not match the first two from the distance. (2/1)
**Welsh Emblem (IRE)**, a 50,000 guineas yearling, was apparently the stable's second string, but stuck on well in the closing stages, and should come into his own over a mile. (16/1)
**Attarikh (IRE)** did well to last so long given how freely he ran, and should not be written off yet. (9/2)
**Voodoo Rocket** (12/1: op 8/1)

## 1351 ROMSEY H'CAP (0-70) (3-Y.O+) (Class E)

8-45 (8-46) **5f** £3,210.00 (£960.00: £460.00: £210.00) Stalls: High GOING: 0.17 sec per fur (G)

| | | | SP | RR | SF |
|---|---|---|---|---|---|
| 981[16] | **High Domain (IRE) (58)** (JLSpearing) **5-8-13**(3) SDrowne(7) (a.p: led over 2f out: r.o wl).....— | 1 | 20/1 | 70 | 50 |
| 1049[4] | **Friendly Brave (USA) (68)** (MissGayKelleway) **6-9-12** WJO'Connor(10) (b: hld up: hdwy 2f out: edgd rt wl over 1f out: btn whn edgd lft wl ins fnl f).....2½ | 2 | 5/1 [2] | 72 | 52 |
| 582[21] | **Astral Invader (IRE) (53)** (MSSaunders) **4-8-11** RPrice(4) (led over 2f: sn rdn: edgd rt & nt clr run over 1f out: one pce).....2 | 3 | 20/1 | 51 | 31 |
| 928[15] | **Gone Savage (59)** (WJMusson) **8-9-3** RCochrane(1) (w ldr: ev ch 2f out: one pce).....½ | 4 | 2/1 [1] | 55 | 35 |
| 943[5] | **Cassimere (58)** (MajorDNChappell) **4-9-2** BThomson(9) (plld hrd: sn prom: hmpd wl over 1f out: nt rcvr).....2½ | 5 | 10/1 | 46 | 26 |
| 592[15] | **Diamond Bangle (38)** (WRMuir) **4-7-5**(5) MartinDwyer(8) (w ldrs: ev ch 2f out: wknd 1f out).....2½ | 6 | 50/1 | 18 | — |
| *338*[5] | **Robo Magic (USA) (62)** (LMontagueHall) **4-9-6** SSanders(2) (nvr trbld ldrs).....s.h | 7 | 5/1 [2] | 42 | 22 |
| 742[4] | **Giggleswick Girl (55)** (MRChannon) **5-8-6**(7) JDennis(3) (lw: n.d).....1¾ | 8 | 11/2 [3] | 29 | 9 |
| 1170[14] | **Admirals Realm (42)** (AGNewcombe) **7-8-0** AMackay(6) (hld up: a bhd).....3 | 9 | 14/1 | 7 | — |
| 1049[6] | **Halbert (61)** (PBurgoyne) **7-9-2v**(3) DRMcCabe(5) (a bhd).....½ | 10 | 10/1 | 24 | 4 |
| | | | (SP 118.4%) | **10 Rn** | |

**63.86 secs** (3.86) CSF £109.50 CT £1,912.16 TOTE £18.50: £4.80 £1.50 £4.90 (£22.20) Trio £103.10 OWNER Mr Stephen Borsberry (ALCESTER) BRED Shannon Holdings Ltd

LONG HANDICAP Diamond Bangle 6-6

**High Domain (IRE)** had registered the second of his two victories as a two-year-old over course and distance on yielding ground, but had not seen the winner's enclosure since. (20/1)

**1049 Friendly Brave (USA)**, inclined to run about a bit, was always finding the winner too much of a handful. (5/1: 3/1-11/2)

**Astral Invader (IRE)** rather caused his own trouble coming to the furlong pole. (20/1)

**812 Gone Savage** has dropped back to a mark 3lb lower than when successful at Kempton over a year ago. (2/1)

**Cassimere** would have finished closer with a trouble-free run, but would not have beaten the winner. (10/1: 6/1-12/1)

**Diamond Bangle**, including her rider's allowance, was still carrying 13lb more than her long-handicap mark. (50/1)

**Admirals Realm** (14/1: 33/1-50/1)

**1049 Halbert** (10/1: op 6/1)

T/Plpt: £174.50 (79.58 Tckts). T/Qdpt: £18.00 (56.66 Tckts). KH

# 1333-GOODWOOD (R-H) (Good to soft, Soft st)
## Thursday May 23rd

vis: poor race 4-6. Race 7 abandoned

WEATHER: overcast & fog WIND: mod half against

## 1352 ROYAL SUSSEX REGIMENT CONDITIONS STKS (2-Y.O F) (Class C)

2-10 (2-10) **6f** £4,833.75 (£1,740.00: £832.50: £337.50: £131.25) Stalls: Low GOING: 0.33 sec per fur (G)

| | | | SP | RR | SF |
|---|---|---|---|---|---|
| | **Naked Poser (IRE)** (RHannon) **2-8-2**(3)ow1 DaneO'Neill(3) (str: scope: lw: s.s: hdwy & nt clr run over 1f out: squeezed thro on ins fnl f: str run to ld last strides).....— | 1 | 4/1 [3] | 72+ | 26 |
| 1103* | **Natalia Bay (IRE)** (PFICole) **2-8-12** TQuinn(4) (stumbled s: chsd ldr: led over 2f out: rdn fnl f: hdd last strides).....hd | 2 | 13/8 [1] | 79 | 34 |
| 1318[2] | **Wait For Rosie** (MRChannon) **2-8-10** RHughes(1) (led over 3f: ev ch over 1f out: unable qckn).....1 | 3 | 5/1 | 74 | 29 |
| 815* | **Hil Rhapsody** (BPalling) **2-8-8** TSprake(6) (a.p: rdn over 2f out: one pce).....1 | 4 | 11/4 [2] | 69 | 24 |
| *1093*[2] | **Whizz Kid** (JJBridger) **2-8-5**(3) DarrenMoffatt(2) (hld up: rdn over 2f out: wknd fnl f).....5 | 5 | 14/1 | 56 | 11 |
| | | | (SP 108.1%) | **5 Rn** | |

**1m 16.47** (6.47) CSF £10.23 TOTE £4.90: £1.60 £1.30 (£3.40) OWNER Mr Peter Winfield (MARLBOROUGH) BRED R. A. Keogh

**Naked Poser (IRE)**, well muscled for an early-season two-year-old filly, stood out in the paddock with the runner-up and would have been most unlucky had she not collected. Slowly away, she was at the back of the field but trying to get closer when meeting with a wall of horses below the distance. Luckily for her, a gap did appear along the rail and she squeezed through in the final furlong before producing a useful run to snatch the spoils in the last couple of strides. (4/1: 3/1-9/2)

**1103* Natalia Bay (IRE)** found the concession of 10lb to the winner just too much. She should soon gain compensation. (13/8: Evens-7/4)

**1318 Wait For Rosie**, having her fifth race of the season, the last coming on Monday evening, held a narrow advantage until nearly quarter of a mile from home. Still battling for the lead below the distance, she was soon tapped for toe. (5/1: 7/2-6/1)

**815* Hil Rhapsody** raced in third place but, shunted along over two furlongs from home, failed to find another gear from below the distance. (11/4)

**1093 Whizz Kid**, out of her depth here, nevertheless hung on until tiring in the final furlong. (14/1: 8/1-20/1)

## 1353 PULLMAN FOODS H'CAP (0-100) (4-Y.O+) (Class C)

2-40 (2-40) **1m 4f** £7,505.00 (£2,240.00: £1,070.00: £485.00) Stalls: Low GOING: 0.46 sec per fur (GS)

| | | | SP | RR | SF |
|---|---|---|---|---|---|
| 941[2] | **Taipan (IRE) (98)** (JLDunlop) **4-10-0** LDettori(8) (hld up: chsd ldr over 3f out: led over 1f out: eased wl ins fnl f).....— | 1 | 7/2 [1] | 111 | 86 |
| 1066* | **Bardon Hill Boy (IRE) (84)** (BHanbury) **4-8-11**(3) JStack(5) (rdn & hdwy over 2f out: r.o one pce).....3 | 2 | 10/1 | 93 | 68 |
| 1065* | **Royal Scimitar (USA) (92)** (PFICole) **4-9-8** TQuinn(6) (lw: led: qcknd over 3f out: hdd over 1f out: one pce) .hd | 3 | 11/2 | 101 | 76 |
| 1005[10] | **Opera Buff (IRE) (71)** (MissGayKelleway) **5-8-1** BDoyle(1) (rdn & hdwy over 2f out: one pce).....¾ | 4 | 5/1 [3] | 79 | 54 |
| 993[4] | **Fighting Times (69)** (CASmith) **4-7-13** JQuinn(4) (b.hind: hld up: rdn over 3f out: one pce).....2½ | 5 | 7/1 | 74 | 49 |
| 968[7] | **Summerhill Special (IRE) (67)** (MrsPNDutfield) **5-7-11** GBardwell(9) (bit bkwd: prom over 8f).....1½ | 6 | 33/1 | 70 | 45 |
| 650* | **Bit on the Side (IRE) (83)** (NEBerry) **7-8-6**(7) AEddery(7) (rdn & hdwy over 3f out: wknd over 1f out).....½ | 7 | 9/2 [2] | 85 | 60 |
| 941[11] | **Lombardic (USA) (94)** (MrsJCecil) **5-9-10** JReid(10) (chsd ldrs over 8f).....22 | 8 | 14/1 | 67 | 42 |
| 1109[5] | **Progression (81)** (CMurray) **5-8-6b**(5) MBaird(3) (s.s: hdwy over 6f out: 6th whn squeezed out & lost pl over 5f out: rallied over 3f out: nt clr run over 2f out: sn wknd).....3½ | 9 | 12/1 | 49 | 24 |
| | | | (SP 111.3%) | **9 Rn** | |

**2m 42.71** (9.51) CSF £32.93 CT £165.42 TOTE £4.10: £1.70 £4.10 £1.80 (£27.50) Trio £61.10 OWNER Lord Swaythling (ARUNDEL) BRED C. H. Wacker III

**941 Taipan (IRE)** struck the front below the distance and soon shot clear. With a considerable advantage, his jockey wisely eased him down in the closing stages. (7/2)
**1066* Bardon Hill Boy (IRE)** stayed on for second but is greatly flattered to finish so close, as the winner was eased right down. (10/1: 7/1-11/1)
**1065* Royal Scimitar (USA)** stole a march on his rivals as the Bugler called entering the straight. Eventually reeled in below the distance, he kept on for third place. (11/2)
**682 Opera Buff (IRE)** was back over a more suitable trip here. Pushed along to pick up ground over two furlongs from home, he could then make no further impression. (5/1)
**993 Fighting Times** chased the leaders, but failed to find another gear in the straight. (7/1)
**650* Bit on the Side (IRE)** (9/2: op 3/1)

## 1354 KIDSONS IMPEY TROPHY H'CAP (0-90) (4-Y.O+) (Class E)
3-10 (3-11) **7f** £8,850.00 (£2,640.00: £1,260.00: £570.00) Stalls: High GOING: 0.46 sec per fur (GS)

| | | | | SP | RR | SF |
|---|---|---|---|---|---|---|
| 1314[3] | **Orange Place (IRE) (70)** (TJNaughton) **5-8-11** TQuinn(8) (lw: mde all: clr over 1f out: r.o wl) | — | **1** | 12/1 | 80 | 63 |
| 1018[15] | **Dawalib (USA) (62)** (DHaydnJones) **6-8-3** WCarson(13) (a.p: rdn 2f out: unable qckn) | 2½ | **2** | 14/1 | 66 | 49 |
| 1018[14] | **Stoppes Brow (70)** (GLMoore) **4-8-11v** SWhitworth(5) (hld up: rdn over 2f out: one pce) | 1¼ | **3** | 20/1 | 71 | 54 |
| 876[5] | **Sharp Rebuff (75)** (PJMakin) **5-9-2** LDettori(7) (rdn over 2f out: hdwy over 1f out: one pce) | ¾ | **4** | 5/1[2] | 75 | 58 |
| 1186[11] | **My Best Valentine (85)** (JWhite) **6-9-9**(3) AWhelan(3) (nt clr run on ins over 2f out: swtchd lft: hdwy fnl f: r.o wl) | s.h | **5** | 25/1 | 85 | 68 |
| 935[12] | **Knobbleeneeze (69)** (MRChannon) **6-8-10v** RHughes(12) (lw: a.p: rdn over 2f out: wknd over 1f out) | ¾ | **6** | 11/2[3] | 67 | 50 |
| 650[10] | **Captain's Day (75)** (TGMills) **4-9-2** MarkLynch(11) (lw: hld up: rdn over 2f out: sn wknd) | nk | **7** | 33/1 | 72 | 55 |
| 1149[3] | **Courageous Dancer (IRE) (87)** (BHanbury) **4-9-11**(3) JStack(6) (prom over 5f) | 1¾ | **8** | 7/2[1] | 80 | 63 |
| 1330[3] | **Star Talent (USA) (82)** (MissGayKelleway) **5-9-9** RCochrane(4) (b: b.hind: sme hdwy over 1f out: eased whn btn fnl f) | 8 | **9** | 5/1[2] | 57 | 40 |
| 850[8] | **Sea Thunder (77)** (IABalding) **4-9-4** MHills(10) (hld up: rdn over 2f out: sn wknd) | 2 | **10** | 10/1 | 47 | 30 |
| 1078[5] | **Double Matt (IRE) (75)** (RHannon) **4-8-13**(3) DaneO'Neill(1) (a bhd) | 6 | **11** | 14/1 | 32 | 15 |

(SP 112.6%) **11 Rn**

**1m 30.78** (5.98) CSF £140.74 CT £3,047.77 TOTE £13.90: £2.40 £3.40 £4.90 (£87.80) Trio £252.20 OWNER Mr G. E. Archer (EPSOM) BRED Rathvinden Stud in Ireland
OFFICIAL EXPLANATION **Star Talent (USA): was unsuited by the soft ground.**
**1314 Orange Place (IRE)**, third in a claimer at Windsor on Monday night, appreciated the cut in the ground. Adopting his usual front-running role, he had a few lengths to spare from below the distance and was not going to be caught. (12/1)
**Dawalib (USA)** tried to peg back the winner in the last two furlongs, but failed to do so. (14/1)
**887 Stoppes Brow** chased the leaders but, having got into third place in the final furlong, was making no further impression. (20/1)
**876 Sharp Rebuff** began to take closer order below the distance, but was then making no further progress. (5/1)
**744* My Best Valentine**, with nowhere to go on the inside rail over a quarter of a mile from home, had to be brought to the outside and still had it all to do below the distance. He buckled down to some really good work in the final furlong but, by then, it was all too late. (25/1)
**Knobbleeneeze** goes in these conditions, but has been out of form this season and, after showing prominently, faded below the distance. (11/2)
**1330 Star Talent (USA)**, who finished third here on Tuesday, was totally unsuited by the soft ground. (5/1)
**Sea Thunder** (10/1: 8/1-12/1)

## 1355 FESTIVAL STKS (Listed) (4-Y.O+) (Class A)
3-40 (3-41) **1m 2f** £15,270.00 (£4,560.00: £2,180.00: £990.00) Stalls: High GOING: 0.46 sec per fur (GS)

| | | | | SP | RR | SF |
|---|---|---|---|---|---|---|
| 909a[5] | **Captain Horatius (IRE) (110)** (JLDunlop) **7-9-1** TQuinn(4) (lw: hdwy over 3f out: led 1f out: rdn out) | — | **1** | 4/1[3] | 118 | 72 |
| 878[4] | **Wijara (IRE) (103)** (RHannon) **4-8-12** RHughes(9) (lw: led over 7f: led 2f out to 1f out: unable qckn) | 2½ | **2** | 4/1[3] | 111 | 65 |
| 831[5] | **Lear White (USA) (105)** (PAKelleway) **5-9-4** LDettori(5) (chsd ldr 3f: rdn over 3f out: one pce) | 1¾ | **3** | 100/30[2] | 114 | 68 |
| | **Fahal (USA) (117)** (DMorley) **4-9-4** WCarson(2) (chsd ldr 7f out: led over 2f out: sn hdd: wknd 1f out) | 2 | **4** | 11/4[1] | 111 | 65 |
| 831[8] | **Prince Arthur (IRE) (113)** (PWChapple-Hyam) **4-9-7** JReid(8) (lw: bhd fnl 6f) | 8 | **5** | 6/1 | 101 | 55 |
| | **Otto E Mezzo** (MJPolglase) **4-8-12** DHarrison(3) (hld up: rdn over 3f out: wknd over 2f out) | ½ | **6** | 25/1 | 91 | 45 |

(SP 107.9%) **6 Rn**

**2m 13.44** (7.94) CSF £17.89 TOTE £4.30: £2.20 £1.90 (£9.10) Trio £7.80 OWNER Mr D. R. Hunnisett (ARUNDEL) BRED B. W. Hills and Mrs V. Shaw
**909a Captain Horatius (IRE)** has been a grand servant to his connections and bounced back to form in fine style, despite the appalling conditions. (4/1)
**878 Wijara (IRE)**, who goes well with some cut, took the field along but was marginally headed as the runners disappeared into the fog over quarter of a mile from home. Soon back in front, he was collared a furlong out and failed to quicken. (4/1)
**831 Lear White (USA)**, who relished the mud, was always handy. Pushed along early in the straight, he failed to find the necessary turn of foot, but did hang on well for third. (100/30)
**Fahal (USA)** failed to cope with these very testing conditions. He appeared to be cruising early in the straight, and gaining a narrow advantage over a quarter of a mile from home, but was soon headed and stopped to nothing at the distance. Back on a fast surface there is certainly a Group Three race waiting for him. (11/4)
**831 Prince Arthur (IRE)** again flopped and had dropped to the back of the field by the top of the hill. His stable is not in form at present. (6/1)

## 1356 RACING CHANNEL CLAIMING STKS (3-Y.O) (Class D)
4-10 (4-11) **6f** £4,163.50 (£1,243.00: £594.00: £269.50) Stalls: Low GOING: 0.33 sec per fur (G)

| | | | | SP | RR | SF |
|---|---|---|---|---|---|---|
| 1146[6] | **Ortolan (100)** (RHannon) **3-8-13**(3) DaneO'Neill(4) (lw: 9th 4f out: hdwy over 1f out: hrd rdn fnl f: led last stride) | — | **1** | 15/8[1] | 82 | 38 |
| 1152[5] | **Lionel Edwards (IRE) (70)** (PFICole) **3-8-8** TQuinn(5) (4th 4f out: in ld ins fnl f: hrd rdn: hdd last stride) | s.h | **2** | 13/2[3] | 74 | 30 |
| 1009[3] | **Red Time (55)** (MSSaunders) **3-8-6** RPrice(6) (in ld 4f out: 3rd ins fnl f: one pce) | 1¼ | **3** | 20/1 | 69 | 25 |
| 1033[9] | **Gormire** (JHetherton) **3-8-6** RCochrane(3) (8th 4f out: 6th ins fnl f: r.o) | 1½ | **4** | 12/1 | 65 | 21 |
| *264*[3] | **Cindy Kate (IRE)** (WRMuir) **3-8-1** CRutter(10) (6th 4f out: 5th ins fnl f: one pce) | hd | **5** | 16/1 | 59 | 15 |
| 1122[7] | **Ciserano (IRE) (55)** (MRChannon) **3-7-13** NCarlisle(9) (w ldr 4f out: 2nd & ev ch ins fnl f: sn wknd) | 1½ | **6** | 8/1 | 53 | 9 |
| *859*[W] | **Elegantissima (50)** (SDow) **3-7-13** JQuinn(7) (7th 4f out) | 6 | **7** | 33/1 | 37 | — |
| 943[10] | **Dancing Man (40)** (MrsMELong) **3-8-4** NAdams(8) (5th 4f out) | nk | **8** | 66/1 | 42 | — |
| 934[5] | **Depiction (70)** (RGuest) **3-8-8** LDettori(2) (3rd 4f out) | s.h | **9** | 11/4[2] | 45 | 1 |

867[7] **Victory Commander (46)** (TJNaughton) **3-7-11**(5) MHenry(11) (swtg: a bhd)....½ **10** 33/1 38 —
(SP 111.6%) **10 Rn**

**1m 16.32** (6.32) CSF £13.09 TOTE £2.40: £2.10 £1.90 £3.80 (£6.80) Trio £40.60 OWNER Mr J. A. Lazzari (MARLBOROUGH) BRED Filletts Farm Stud

**Ortolan**, taking a big drop in class, was at the back of the field when the runners first came into view. When they came out of the fog entering the final furlong, he was picking up ground and, responding to pressure, came through to snatch the spoils right on the line. (15/8: op Evens)
**Lionel Edwards (IRE)**, who emerged from the heavy sea-fret in front inside the final furlong, looked likely to hold on until caught by the winner right on the line. (13/2)
**1009 Red Time**, in front in the early stages, reappeared from the dense fog in third place inside the final furlong and was only plodding on at one pace. (20/1)
**1033 Gormire** was running on when the runners reappeared from the fog inside the final furlong. (12/1: 10/1-16/1)
**Cindy Kate (IRE)**, making her Turf debut after a break of three and a half months, was only plodding on at one pace inside the final furlong. (16/1)
**743 Ciserano (IRE)** appeared to be disputing the lead from what could be seen, and still had every chance when they reappeared inside the final furlong before tiring. (8/1)
**934 Depiction** (11/4: op 5/1)

## 1357 A & J BULL MAIDEN STKS (3-Y.O) (Class D)
4-45 (4-47) **1m 1f** £5,047.25 (£1,508.00: £721.50: £328.25) Stalls: High GOING: 0.46 sec per fur (GS)

| | Horse / details | Dist | Pos | SP | RR | SF |
|---|---|---|---|---|---|---|
| 1035[2] | **North Song** (JHMGosden) **3-9-0** LDettori(4) (mde all: comf) | — | **1** | 13/8 [1] | 87 | 37 |
| | **Ta Awun (USA)** (ACStewart) **3-8-9** WCarson(2) (w'like: scope: in 2nd ins fnl f: unable qckn) | 2½ | **2** | 9/2 [3] | 78 | 28 |
| | **Dramatic Moment** (IABalding) **3-8-9** RCochrane(6) (lw) | 8 | **3** | 12/1 | 63 | 13 |
| 985[5] | **Chabrol (CAN)** (HRACecil) **3-9-0** AMcGlone(8) | 8 | **4** | 9/2 [3] | 54 | 4 |
| 964[4] | **Premier Night** (SDow) **3-8-9** TQuinn(1) | 13 | **5** | 5/2 [2] | 26 | — |
| | **Sherna (IRE)** (IABalding) **3-8-4**(5) MartinDwyer(3) (unf) | 2½ | **6** | 20/1 | 22 | — |
| | **Duncombe Hall** (CACyzer) **3-9-0** WJO'Connor(9) | 2½ | **7** | 25/1 | 22 | — |

(SP 119.3%) **7 Rn**

**2m 2.31** (10.91) CSF £9.60 TOTE £2.40: £1.50 £2.10 (£6.40) Trio £23.40 OWNER Mr John Gosden (NEWMARKET) BRED C. R. Mason
**1035 North Song** appears to be suited by some cut. His jockey reported that he made all and, when the runners eventually appeared from the dense fog in the last 50 yards, he had things comfortably sewn up. (13/8: 5/4-2/1)
**Ta Awun (USA)**, quite a lengthy filly with a lot of substance and scope, took the eye in the paddock gloom. When the runners did appear in the last 50 yards, she was a clear second best. She obviously has ability and, if her conformation is anything is anything to go by, she will win a race. (9/2)
**985 Chabrol (CAN)** (9/2: op 3/1)

## 1358 LEVIN DOWN APPRENTICE H'CAP (0-70) (3-Y.O+) (Class E)
**Abandoned** - Poor visibility

T/Jkpt: £10,574.80 (0.3 Tckts); £10,425.86 to Haydock 24/5/96. T/Plpt: £181.60 (142.48 Tckts). T/Qdpt: £54.20 (29.65 Tckts).
AK

# 1340-NEWCASTLE (L-H) (Good, Good to firm patches)
## Thursday May 23rd
Races 1-3 & 5: hand-timed
WEATHER: overcast WIND: fresh across

## 1359 TYNEMOUTH MAIDEN STKS (3-Y.O) (Class D)
2-25 (2-29) **1m 2f 32y** £3,728.75 (£1,130.00: £552.50: £263.75) Stalls: Low GOING minus 0.29 sec per fur (GF)

| | Horse / details | Dist | Pos | SP | RR | SF |
|---|---|---|---|---|---|---|
| 986[4] | **Sasuru (102)** (GWragg) **3-9-0** PaulEddery(7) (lw: b: a.p: led ins fnl f: r.o wl) | — | **1** | 15/8 [1] | 100 | 58 |
| | **Questonia** (HRACecil) **3-8-9** WRyan(9) (leggy: unf: prom: hdwy appr st: led over 2f out tl ins fnl f: r.o wl) | ½ | **2** | 5/2 [2] | 94 | 52 |
| | **Altamura (USA)** (JHMGosden) **3-8-9** AGarth(2) (a.p: effrt over 2f out: r.o one pce) | 5 | **3** | 7/1 | 86 | 44 |
| | **Heart** (MRStoute) **3-8-9** KFallon(8) (unf: mid div: effrt ent st: styd on: nvr able to chal) | 6 | **4** | 12/1 | 77 | 35 |
| | **Tiger Lake** (SbinSuroor) **3-9-0** KDarley(12) (w'like: dwlt: hdwy on outside ent st: styd on: nrst fin) | 3½ | **5** | 5/1 [3] | 76 | 34 |
| 1090[4] | **Ambassadori (USA)** (CEBrittain) **3-9-0** JWeaver(6) (led tl hdd over 2f out: grad wknd) | 2½ | **6** | 20/1 | 72 | 30 |
| 870[5] | **Whispered Melody** (PWHarris) **3-8-9** GHind(5) (effrt 3f out: nvr trbld ldrs) | 1¼ | **7** | 20/1 | 65 | 23 |
| 717[2] | **Nayib** (DMorley) **3-9-0** BThomson(11) (bhd: effrt over 2f out: nvr trbld ldrs) | 3½ | **8** | 16/1 | 65 | 23 |
| 1090[7] | **Clash of Swords** (PCalver) **3-9-0** MBirch(4) (bhd tl sme late hdwy) | nk | **9** | 100/1 | 64 | 22 |
| 962[9] | **Bashtheboards (61)** (JJQuinn) **3-9-0** SDWilliams(13) (chsd ldrs tl wknd over 3f out) | 3 | **10** | 100/1 | 60 | 18 |
| 974[5] | **Fiasco** (MJCamacho) **3-8-9** LCharnock(3) (bit bkwd: n.d) | 1½ | **11** | 20/1 | 52 | 10 |
| 804[7] | **Troika (IRE)** (JBerry) **3-8-4**(5) PRoberts(10) (chsd ldrs tl wknd fnl 2½f) | ½ | **12** | 50/1 | 52 | 10 |
| | **Mukeed** (JHMGosden) **3-9-0** JCarroll(14) (gd sort: bit bkwd: dwlt: a bhd) | 2½ | **13** | 12/1 | 53 | 11 |
| 885[8] | **Phar Closer (46)** (WTKemp) **3-8-6**(3) SDrowne(1) (w ldr tl wknd appr st) | hd | **14** | 100/1 | 48 | 6 |

(SP 133.0%) **14 Rn**

**2m 8.8** (2.10) CSF £7.63 TOTE £3.40: £1.40 £1.50 £2.10 (£5.10) Trio £18.00 OWNER Lady Oppenheimer (NEWMARKET) BRED Hascombe and Valiant Studs
**IN-FOCUS: This looked a useful event.**
**986 Sasuru**, suited by this drop back in distance, won with style. This should have boosted his confidence and he will get a little further in time. (15/8)
**Questonia** is only lightly-made, but still has something about her. Her determined style of racing certainly impresses and she should not be long in finding a suitable event. (5/2: 6/4-11/4)
**Altamura (USA)** is nothing to look at but does have plenty of ability. Short of toe in the last couple of furlongs, she should appreciate further yet. (7/1: 5/1-8/1)
**Heart** was staying on steadily up the straight without offering a threat, and looks likely to be all the better for the experience. (12/1: 8/1-14/1)
**Tiger Lake** is a useful type with a good action, but he was very green in the early stages and, despite keeping on well, failed to get into it. There would seem to be a lot of improvement in him. (5/1: op 3/1)

**1090 Ambassadori (USA)** was left struggling from two furlongs out and may need shorter trips. (20/1)
**870 Whispered Melody** looks the type to improve with time and, although never in the race, did give the impression that there is something to come as she strengthens. (20/1)
**717 Nayib**, dropped back in trip here, could never get into it, despite staying on. He will do better in due course. (16/1)
**Clash of Swords** should improve in time. (100/1)
**Mukeed** (12/1: 8/1-14/1)

## 1360 ANNITSFORD CLAIMING STKS (2-Y.O) (Class F)

2-55 (3-01) **6f** £2,577.00 (£722.00: £351.00) Stalls: High GOING minus 0.11 sec per fur (G)

| | | | | SP | RR | SF |
|---|---|---|---|---|---|---|
| *895*[4] | **Hello Dolly (IRE)** (KRBurke) **2-8-9** PaulEddery(7) (mde all: qcknd 2f out: r.o wl) | — | **1** | 3/1[2] | 56 | 15 |
| 1036[7] | **Going For Broke** (PCHaslam) **2-9-0** JFortune(5) (cl up: rdn 2f out: kpt on: nt pce of wnr) | 3 | **2** | 10/1 | 53 | 12 |
| 557[9] | **Silver Raj** (WTKemp) **2-8-2b**[1](3)ow1 SDrowne(8) (chsd ldrs: outpcd 2f out: kpt on towards fin) | 2 | **3** | 50/1 | 39 | — |
| *1026*[4] | **Alisadara** (NBycroft) **2-8-3** GHind(6) (prom: outpcd 2f out: kpt on ins fnl f) | ½ | **4** | 50/1 | 35 | — |
| 1183* | **Fonzy** (MrsLStubbs) **2-8-10** JWeaver(3) (trckd ldrs: rdn over 2f out: sn btn) | 1 | **5** | Evens[1] | 40 | — |
| 975[9] | **Clonavon Girl (IRE)** (MJCamacho) **2-7-13** LCharnock(2) (prom: rdn 2f out: sn outpcd) | nk | **6** | 10/1 | 28 | — |
| 770[8] | **Kuda** (JNorton) **2-7-11** DaleGibson(1) (lw: sn pushed along: lost tch after 2f: t.o) | 28 | **7** | 16/1 | — | — |
| | **Hurgill Minstrel** (JWWatts) **2-8-6v**[1] GDuffield(4) (str: reluctant to r: sn t.o) | 20 | **8** | 8/1[3] | — | — |

(SP 114.1%) **8 Rn**

**1m 16.5** (5.00) CSF £28.91 TOTE £4.40: £1.10 £2.40 £8.30 (£17.90) OWNER Mr Nigel Shields (WANTAGE) BRED Rathasker Stud
**895 Hello Dolly (IRE)** set a moderate pace and, once she quickened two furlongs out, always had the upper hand. (3/1)
**Going For Broke**, dropped in class, put in a much better performance and would probably be suited by a stronger pace. (10/1: 7/1-12/1)
**481 Silver Raj** had the blinkers on for the first time and put in a much-improved effort. (50/1)
**Alisadara**, most unruly in the paddock, ran a reasonable race, but was never able to make her presence felt. (50/1)
**1183* Fonzy**, dropped in behind the leaders presumably to get the trip, never took any interest. He needs to be right up with the pace. (Evens)
**823 Clonavon Girl (IRE)**, dropped in class, proved disappointing when the pace quickened up in the last couple of furlongs. (10/1: op 6/1)
**Hurgill Minstrel** (8/1: op 5/1)

## 1361 SCOTTISH EQUITABLE/JOCKEYS ASSOCIATION H'CAP (0-95) (3-Y.O) (Class C)

3-25 (3-27) **1m 4f 93y** £5,889.50 (£1,781.00: £868.00: £411.50) Stalls: Low GOING minus 0.29 sec per fur (GF)

| | | | | SP | RR | SF |
|---|---|---|---|---|---|---|
| 788[3] | **Pine Needle (78)** (DMorley) **3-9-3** BThomson(2) (lw: hld up: effrt over 3f out: styd on wl fnl f to ld cl home) | — | **1** | 9/2[2] | 84 | 55 |
| 788* | **Faateq (82)** (JLDunlop) **3-9-7** KDarley(7) (cl up: led 4f out: clr over 1f out: wknd & ct nr fin) | nk | **2** | 9/2[2] | 88 | 59 |
| 1079[3] | **Spartan Heartbeat (73)** (CEBrittain) **3-8-12b**[1] WRyan(3) (bhd: rdn 3f out: styd on strly fnl f: nrst fin) | nk | **3** | 6/1[3] | 78 | 49 |
| 974[4] | **Ledgendry Line (68)** (MrsMReveley) **3-8-7** ACulhane(6) (s.i.s: bhd tl hdwy over 1f out: styd on) | 1¾ | **4** | 6/1[3] | 71 | 42 |
| 766[3] | **Ladykirk (76)** (JWWatts) **3-9-1** GDuffield(4) (cl up: shkn up 3f out: r.o one pce) | 1½ | **5** | 9/1 | 77 | 48 |
| 826[5] | **Karisma (IRE) (75)** (DenysSmith) **3-9-0** JFortune(1) (lw: chsd ldrs: outpcd over 2f out: kpt on towards fin) | s.h | **6** | 14/1 | 76 | 47 |
| 1079[2] | **Sadler's Realm (73)** (MRStoute) **3-8-12** PaulEddery(8) (lw: hld up: hdwy & prom 6f out: rdn 3f out: wknd fnl 2f) | 5 | **7** | 2/1[1] | 68 | 39 |
| 920[8] | **Tissue of Lies (USA) (76)** (MJohnston) **3-9-1** JWeaver(5) (led tl hdd 4f out: ev ch tl wknd over 2f out) | 5 | **8** | 16/1 | 64 | 35 |

(SP 120.8%) **8 Rn**

**2m 41.1** (3.60) CSF £24.71 CT £114.38 TOTE £4.50: £1.40 £1.40 £2.10 (£6.50) OWNER Lord Halifax (NEWMARKET) BRED Lord Halifax
**788 Pine Needle**, stepped up in trip, needed every yard of this and proved to be a really tough sort. (9/2)
**788* Faateq** had this sewn up approaching the final furlong, but he then decided he had done enough and, idling badly, was caught near the line. (9/2)
**1079 Spartan Heartbeat**, in blinkers this time, was very coltish in the preliminaries and in the race. He took little interest until flying in the closing stages and there is plenty more ability there. (6/1)
**974 Ledgendry Line**, having his first run in a handicap, was out the back until finishing in eyecatching fashion. Better looks likely. (6/1)
**766 Ladykirk**, trying a longer trip, proved a shade disappointing under pressure in the last three furlongs. (9/1)
**826 Karisma (IRE)** is still learning to settle and, once he does, better should be seen. (14/1)
**1079 Sadler's Realm** looked in good trim and had his chances approaching the last two furlongs, but then failed to get home. It would seem he just did not stay. (2/1)

## 1362 CRAMLINGTON CONDITIONS STKS (2-Y.O) (Class D)

3-55 (3-55) **5f** £3,062.50 (£925.00: £450.00: £212.50) Stalls: High GOING minus 0.11 sec per fur (G)

| | | | | SP | RR | SF |
|---|---|---|---|---|---|---|
| 1086* | **Hula Prince (IRE)** (MJohnston) **2-9-1** JWeaver(6) (lw: dwlt: nt clr run 1½f out: qcknd fnl f to ld nr fin) | — | **1** | 5/6[1] | 76+ | 36 |
| *895** | **Young Bigwig (IRE)** (JBerry) **2-9-1** JCarroll(4) (chsd ldrs: led over 1f out: r.o: jst ct) | s.h | **2** | 4/1[3] | 76 | 36 |
| 880* | **Seaside (IRE)** (JohnBerry) **2-8-10** KFallon(3) (lw: a.p: rdn to chal 1f out: kpt on) | 1 | **3** | 8/1 | 68 | 28 |
| 1303[3] | **Braveheart (IRE)** (MRChannon) **2-9-1** KDarley(2) (lw: led tl hdd over 1f out: sn btn) | 1¼ | **4** | 7/2[2] | 69 | 29 |
| 975* | **Legend of Aragon** (JAGlover) **2-8-10** GDuffield(5) (lw: w ldr tl ½-wy: outpcd whn hmpd over 1f out: sn wl btn) | 9 | **5** | 7/1 | 35 | — |
| 880[5] | **Apiculate (IRE)** (WTKemp) **2-8-8**(3) SDrowne(1) (sn outpcd & wl bhd) | 9 | **6** | 100/1 | 7 | — |

(SP 121.4%) **6 Rn**

**61.53 secs** (3.13) CSF £5.19 TOTE £1.60: £1.20 £4.00 (£4.80) OWNER Maktoum Al Maktoum (MIDDLEHAM) BRED Gainsborough Stud Management Ltd
**1086* Hula Prince (IRE)** basically did everything wrong but still won and looks a useful sort. (5/6: 4/5-Evens)
**895* Young Bigwig (IRE)** put in a determined effort and a win on turf can not be far away. (4/1)
**880* Seaside (IRE)** ran a sound race on this much faster surface but, despite trying hard, was always being held in the closing stages. She does look to be improving. (8/1: 6/1-9/1)
**1303 Braveheart (IRE)**, an edgy sort, just jumps and runs. Once headed, there is little more in the tank. (7/2)
**975* Legend of Aragon** ran fast but was all at sea and going nowhere when being hampered well over a furlong out. (7/1)

## 1363 BOOKER CASH & CARRY H'CAP (0-70) (3-Y.O) (Class E)

4-25 (4-29) **1m** £3,152.00 (£956.00: £468.00: £224.00) Stalls: Low GOING minus 0.29 sec per fur (GF)

| | | | | SP | RR | SF |
|---|---|---|---|---|---|---|
| 976[3] | **Winston (60)** (JDBethell) **3-8-9**(3) SDrowne(14) (hld up: hdwy 3f out: styd on to ld wl ins fnl f) | — | **1** | 7/2[1] | 68 | 37 |
| 1126[6] | **Russian Rascal (IRE) (65)** (TDEasterby) **3-9-3** MBirch(17) (lw: trckd ldrs: hdwy to ld ins fnl f: sn hdd & nt qckn) | ¾ | **2** | 5/1[2] | 72 | 41 |

| | | | | SP | RR | SF |
|---|---|---|---|---|---|---|
| 1042[2] | **Sandblaster (54)** (MrsJRRamsden) **3-8-6** KFallon(12) (mid div: hdwy over 2f out: ev ch 1f out: nt qckn) | 1½ | **3** | 11/2[3] | 58 | 27 |
| 955[4] | **Dubai College (IRE) (69)** (CEBrittain) **3-9-7** JWeaver(13) (cl up: led 3f out tl ins fnl f: no ex) | 2½ | **4** | 14/1 | 68 | 37 |
| 483[6] | **Oxgang (IRE) (50)** (JGFitzGerald) **3-8-2** GHind(9) (bhd tl styd on wl fnl 3f: nrst fin) | 1½ | **5** | 20/1 | 46 | 15 |
| 614[4] | **One Life To Live (IRE) (50)** (AHarrison) **3-8-2** TWilliams(15) (chsd ldrs: shkn up over 2f out: one pce) | 1 | **6** | 14/1 | 44 | 13 |
| 1043[3] | **Craigmore Magic (USA) (50)** (MissMKMilligan) **3-8-2** JFanning(3) (led tl hdd 3f out: grad wknd) | hd | **7** | 20/1 | 43 | 12 |
| *859*[6] | **Lawn Order (49)** (MrsJRRamsden) **3-8-1** JFEgan(11) (s.i.s: bhd tl sme hdwy fnl 2f) | 1½ | **8** | 11/1 | 39 | 8 |
| 562[8] | **Generous Present (53)** (JWPayne) **3-8-5**ow1 BThomson(8) (chsd ldrs tl grad wknd fnl 2f) | hd | **9** | 20/1 | 43 | 11 |
| 1034[6] | **Northern Clan (44)** (MWEasterby) **3-7-7b**1(3) DWright(7) (s.i.s: hdwy & swtchd 2f out: n.d) | nk | **10** | 20/1 | 34 | 3 |
| 614[14] | **Energy Man (68)** (MDods) **3-9-6** JCarroll(5) (prom tl outpcd fnl 2½f) | 1½ | **11** | 50/1 | 55 | 24 |
| 973[7] | **Oriole (49)** (NTinkler) **3-8-1** KimTinkler(18) (bhd: rdn 3f out: n.d) | s.h | **12** | 16/1 | 35 | 4 |
| 1068[9] | **Kernof (IRE) (55)** (MDHammond) **3-8-7** JFortune(10) (sme hdwy 2f out: nvr rchd ldrs) | 1¼ | **13** | 16/1 | 39 | 8 |
| *859*[9] | **Any Colour (55)** (MJCamacho) **3-8-7** LCharnock(6) (nvr bttr than mid div) | 5 | **14** | 20/1 | 29 | — |
| 1042[11] | **Cerise (IRE) (51)** (CWCElsey) **3-7-12b**(5) PFessey(1) (effrt on ins whn nt clr run & swtchd over 2f out: n.d) | 1½ | **15** | 14/1 | 22 | — |
| *857*[6] | **Ballykissangel (44)** (NBycroft) **3-7-7**(3) NVarley(16) (in tch: effrt appr st: sn btn) | 6 | **16** | 33/1 | 3 | — |
| 1001[10] | **Eben Naas (USA) (59)** (SCWilliams) **3-8-11** KDarley(2) (b.hind: prom tl wknd fnl 3f) | ½ | **17** | 6/1 | 17 | — |
| 1089[14] | **Ginger Hodgers (50)** (RMWhitaker) **3-8-2v**1 DaleGibson(4) (chsd ldrs tl wknd over 2f out) | ¾ | **18** | 50/1 | 6 | — |

(SP 139.3%) **18 Rn**

**1m 42.6** (3.60) CSF £22.93 CT £95.93 TOTE £4.80: £1.50 £1.60 £1.60 £2.70 (£12.60) Trio £17.50 OWNER Mr John Galvanoni (MIDDLEHAM) BRED Benson Stud

LONG HANDICAP Ballykissangel 7-2 Northern Clan 7-8

**976 Winston** got a run when required this time, and produced a useful turn of foot to settle it. (7/2)

**1126 Russian Rascal (IRE)** is an edgy, free-running individual and put up a decent performance, but had nothing more to give late on. (5/1)

**1042 Sandblaster** ran another fine race, but failed to quicken in the final furlong and was then not over-punished. She will do better in due course. (11/2)

**955 Dubai College (IRE)**, better suited by this shorter trip, ran well until running out of steam inside the last furlong. (14/1)

**Oxgang (IRE)** found this trip a bit on the sharp side, and was putting in all his best work when it was too late. (20/1)

**614 One Life To Live (IRE)**, dropped back in distance, was always short of a turn of foot to make his presence felt. (14/1)

**1043 Craigmore Magic (USA)** came from behind in a poor event over a shorter trip last time, and burned himself out here setting the pace. (20/1)

**686 Lawn Order**, a drifter in the market, ran as expected. (11/1: op 7/1)

## 1364 SEATON BURN H'CAP (0-75) (3-Y.O+) (Class D)

5-00 (5-01) **5f** £3,647.50 (£1,105.00: £540.00: £257.50) Stalls: High GOING minus 0.11 sec per fur (G)

| | | | | SP | RR | SF |
|---|---|---|---|---|---|---|
| 956[6] | **Captain Carat (62)** (MrsJRRamsden) **5-9-5** KFallon(5) (lw: b.nr fore: racd far side: hdwy 2f out: led ins fnl f: r.o wl) | — | **1** | 11/2[2] | 71 | 47 |
| 1342[7] | **Metal Boys (56)** (MissLCSiddall) **9-8-13** JWeaver(15) (lw: chsd ldrs: led stands' side 2f out: r.o) | 2 | **2** | 20/1 | 59 | 35 |
| 704[11] | **Featherstone Lane (48)** (MissLCSiddall) **5-8-5v** GHind(4) (racd far side: a.p: ev ch over 1f out: kpt on) | s.h | **3** | 14/1 | 50 | 26 |
| 956[9] | **Colway Rake (69)** (JWWatts) **5-9-12b** NConnorton(8) (lw: trckd ldrs far side: effrt 2f out: styd on nr fin) | s.h | **4** | 10/1[3] | 71 | 47 |
| 1040[3] | **Sonderise (49)** (NTinkler) **7-8-6**ow1 JFortune(12) (lw: racd stands' side: in tch: effrt 2f out: kpt on one pce) | 1 | **5** | 10/1[3] | 48 | 23 |
| 1157[5] | **Sallyoreally (IRE) (40)** (WStorey) **5-7-11** NKennedy(13) (racd stands' side: in tch: kpt on fnl f) | nk | **6** | 12/1 | 38 | 14 |
| 1040[11] | **Dominelle (47)** (TDEasterby) **4-8-4** MBirch(2) (racd far side: led tl hdd & no ex ins fnl f) | hd | **7** | 14/1 | 45 | 21 |
| 806[5] | **Foist (45)** (MWEasterby) **4-8-2** DaleGibson(7) (swtchd stands' side: bhd tl styd on wl fnl f) | 1 | **8** | 11/2[2] | 40 | 16 |
| 1157[3] | **Plum First (65)** (LRLloyd-James) **6-9-8** JFanning(11) (b: b.hind: racd stands' side: chsd ldrs: effrt 2f out: one pce) | nk | **9** | 5/1[1] | 59 | 35 |
| 882[11] | **Dictation (USA) (71)** (JJO'Neill) **4-10-0** JFEgan(14) (racd stands' side: bhd & rdn ½-wy: sme late hdwy) | 1½ | **10** | 16/1 | 60 | 36 |
| 769[11] | **Invigilate (49)** (MartynWane) **7-8-6** DeanMcKeown(6) (racd far side: spd 3f) | 1¼ | **11** | 16/1 | 34 | 10 |
| 1157[15] | **Ned's Bonanza (67)** (MDods) **7-9-10** JCarroll(1) (chsd ldrs far side tl wknd & eased fnl f) | nk | **12** | 12/1 | 51 | 27 |
| 997[3] | **Penny's Wishing (46)** (NBycroft) **4-8-3**ow1 GDuffield(9) (b.nr hind: cl up stands' side: effrt over 2f out: wknd) | 3½ | **13** | 11/1 | 19 | — |
| 1087[8] | **Rankaidade (39)** (DonEnricoIncisa) **5-7-10** KimTinkler(3) (racd far side: a bhd) | ¾ | **14** | 50/1 | 9 | — |
| 959[7] | **Astral's Chance (55)** (KRBurke) **3-8-4** PaulEddery(10) (led stands' side 3f: wknd) | 6 | **15** | 20/1 | 6 | — |

(SP 125.9%) **15 Rn**

**61.08 secs** (2.68) CSF £101.33 CT £1,391.56 TOTE £4.90: £1.90 £6.00 £4.20 (£61.90) Trio £202.40 OWNER Mr Colin Webster (THIRSK) BRED Lt-Col J. H. Scott

LONG HANDICAP Rankaidade 6-11

WEIGHT FOR AGE 3yo-8lb

**956 Captain Carat** made no mistakes here, responding to pressure to lead and go clear in the final furlong. (11/2)

**Metal Boys**, who looked and ran well, won the race up the stands' side, but had no chance with the winner on the far side. (20/1)

**559 Featherstone Lane** had his chances up the far side, but was never finding enough under pressure. (14/1)

**Colway Rake** looked a picture and appeared to be travelling well for much of the trip but, when ridden, he failed to respond immediately and never got in a blow. He is likely to pick up a race in this mood. (10/1)

**1040 Sonderise** looked to be going quite well behind the leaders on the stands' side but, when an effort was required, he was never producing the goods. (10/1)

**1157 Sallyoreally (IRE)** was always finding this trip a bit on the sharp side, but did keep on well at the end. (12/1: op 8/1)

**Dominelle** has bags of speed, but failed to find to see it out on this occasion. (14/1)

**806 Foist** lost ground at the start, but was making up ground in eyecatching style at the finish. (11/2: 3/1-6/1)

T/Plpt: £90.90 (145.85 Tckts). T/Qdpt: £9.00 (144.9 Tckts). AA/WG

## 1365a-1387a (Irish Racing) - See Computer Raceform

## 1052a-SAINT-CLOUD (France) (L-H) (Good)
## Tuesday May 14th

## 1388a PRIX CLEOPATRE (Gp 3) (3-Y.O F)

2-15 (2-21) **1m 2f 110y** £28,986.00 (£10,540.00: £5,270.00)

| | | | | SP | RR | SF |
|---|---|---|---|---|---|---|
| | **Khalisa (IRE)** (AdeRoyerDupre,France) **3-8-9** GMosse | — | **1** | | 99 | — |
| 791a[3] | **Amiarma (IRE)** (EChevalierduFau,France) **3-8-9** TGillet | ¾ | **2** | | 98 | — |

| | | | | SP | RR | SF |
|---|---|---|---|---|---|---|
| 791a[2] | **Camille (FR)** (PDemercastel,France) **3-8-9** WMongil | nk | 3 | | 97 | — |

**9 Rn**

**2m 16.5** (6.50) P-M 4.60F: 2.00F 1.90F 2.10F (20.80F) OWNER Aga Khan (CHANTILLY) BRED H. H. Aga Khan's Studs S.C.
**Khalisa (IRE)** threw her jockey and galloped free before the race, but it did not affect her performance. She is still inexperienced, but is going the right way, and it would be no surprise to see her take her chance in the Prix de Diane.
**791a Amiarma (IRE)** has been the bridesmaid on several occasions this season. She deserves a Group race victory, and will probably take her chance in the Prix de Royaumont.
**791a Camille (FR)** was always prominent, and hit the front a furlong and a half from home. She galloped on resolutely, but could not quicken in the final 100 yards.

# DEAUVILLE (France) (R-H) (Good)
## Thursday May 16th

### 1389a PRIX LA FORCE (Gp 3) (3-Y.O)
2-50 (2-53) **1m 2f** £28,986.00 (£10,540.00: £5,270.00: £2,635.00)

| | | | | SP | RR | SF |
|---|---|---|---|---|---|---|
| 797a[3] | **Radevore** (AFabre,France) **3-9-2** TJarnet | — | 1 | | 110 | 70 |
| 323a* | **Top Glory (FR)** (FDoumen,France) **3-9-2** GMosse | ¾ | 2 | | 109 | 69 |
| 727[4] | **Henry The Fifth** (CEBrittain) **3-9-2** BDoyle | 4 | 3 | | 102 | 62 |
| | **Blueshaan (IRE)** (MmeCHead,France) **3-9-2** ODoleuze | hd | 4 | | 102 | 62 |
| 574[6] | **Line Dancer** (WJarvis) **3-9-2** OPeslier | 3 | 5 | | 97 | 57 |

**5 Rn**

**2m 7.7** (2.70) P-M 1.60F: 1.20F 1.60F (SF 4.90F) OWNER Mr K. Abdullah (CHANTILLY) BRED Juddmonte Farms
**797a Radevore** won this in good style, and had a little in hand in the closing stages. He is on the upgrade, and connections have a choice between the Prix Jean Prat and the Prix du Jockey-Club for his next engagement.
**Top Glory (FR)** came with a dangerous challenge, but was held in the final 50 yards. He is useful, but probably only listed class.
**727 Henry The Fifth** was always prominent, and showed ahead early in the straight. He could only stay on at one pace, and may need a longer trip, although he was probably out of his depth.
**574 Line Dancer** was among the leaders until early in the straight before dropping away, and appeared not to stay.

### 1390a PRIX JEAN DE CHAUDENAY - GRAND PRIX DE PRINTEMPS (Gp 2) (4-Y.O+)
3-45 (3-46) **1m 4f 110y** £39,526.00 (£15,810.00: £7,905.00: £3,953.00)

| | | | | SP | RR | SF |
|---|---|---|---|---|---|---|
| 919[3] | **Sacrament** (MRStoute) **5-8-11** OPeslier (a.p: led over 2f out: styd on wl u.p) | — | 1 | | 118 | 71 |
| 831[4] | **Punishment** (CEBrittain) **5-8-11** BDoyle (hld up: hdwy to chal over 1f out: no ex ins fnl f) | ½ | 2 | | 117 | 70 |
| 907a* | **Percutant** (DSmaga,France) **5-8-11** CAsmussen (trckd ldr: ev ch 2f out: one pce fnl f) | 2 | 3 | | 115 | 68 |
| | **Essesstee (FR)** (DSmaga,France) **5-8-11** CRamonet (led tl over 2f out: wknd) | 20 | 4 | | 89 | 42 |

**4 Rn**

**2m 41.1** (2.60) P-M 2.60F: 2.40F 3.80F (SF 10.60F) OWNER Cheveley Park Stud (NEWMARKET) BRED Cheveley Park Stud Ltd
**919 Sacrament** held on well, and this could be the prelude to a good season now he has recovered from a chipped bone in his knee. He has a choice between the Hardwicke Stakes and the Grand Prix d'Evry as his next race.
**831 Punishment** stepped up from listed class, and ran the race of his life. He would have preferred better ground, and should be able to win a Group Three on this showing.
**907a* Percutant** was disappointing, and was beaten halfway up the straight. He had been in good form prior to this, and the soft ground may not have suited him. He could possibly meet the winner again at Evry.
**Essesstee (FR)** acted as pacemaker for his stablemate.

# PIMLICO (Baltimore, USA) (L-H) (Fast)
## Saturday May 18th

### 1391a PREAKNESS STAKES (Gp 1) (3-Y.O)
10-31 (10-33) **1m 1f 110y (Dirt)** £272,826.00 (£90,942.00: £50,018.00)

| | | | | SP | RR | SF |
|---|---|---|---|---|---|---|
| | **Louis Quatorze (USA)** (NZito,USA) **3-9-0** PDay | — | 1 | 17/2 | 126 | — |
| | **Skip Away (USA)** (HHine,USA) **3-9-0** SSellers | 3¼ | 2 | 33/10 | 121 | — |
| | **Editor's Note (USA)** (DWLukas,USA) **3-9-0** GStevens | 3 | 3 | 13/2 | 116 | — |

**12 Rn**

**1m 53.4** P-M $19.00: PL $7.80 $5.60 SHOW $5.20 $4.60 $5.00 ($613.40) OWNER Condren & Cornacchia & Hofmann BRED Georgia Hofmann
**Louis Quatorze (USA)** put his disappointing Kentucky Derby performance behind him by making all the running to give his jockey a third consecutive win in the race. He was always travelling well, and drew away for an easy victory in the second fastest time ever for the event. (17/2)
**Skip Away (USA)** chased the winner from the start, but could make no impression in the straight. (33/10)

# 1137a-SAN SIRO (Milan, Italy) (R-H) (Good to soft)
## Sunday May 19th

### 1392a PREMIO ARCO DELL PACE (3-Y.O+)
3-30 (3-36) **1m 4f** £8,120.00

| | | | | SP | RR | SF |
|---|---|---|---|---|---|---|
| 828[3] | **Suranom (IRE)** (LMCumani) **4-8-11** FJovine | — | 1 | | 108 | — |
| | **Northern Chief (FR)** (LBatzella,Italy) **5-8-11** SDettori | 3½ | 2 | | 103 | — |
| | **Baujes (IRE)** (JHeloury,Italy) **6-8-11** GBietolini | s.nk | 3 | | 103 | — |
| | **Scribano** (GBotti,Italy) **6-8-13** EBotti | d.h | 3 | | 105 | — |

**6 Rn**

**2m 30.6** (10.60) Tote 32L: 19L 24L (117L) OWNER Scuderia Rencati (NEWMARKET) BRED Yeomanstown Lodge Stud
**828 Suranom (IRE)** appreciated this easier ground. Making all, he went clear approaching the two-furlong pole for an easy victory. He looks capable of stepping up to listed company on this showing.

## 1393a OAKS D'ITALIA (Gp 1) (3-Y.O F)
4-00 (4-10) **1m 3f** £90,344.00 (£46,354.00: £27,222.00: £13,611.00)

| | | | | SP | RR | SF |
|---|---|---|---|---|---|---|
| 794a5 | **Germignana (ITY)** (LCamici,Italy) **3-8-11** MCangiano (a cl up: rdn to ld ins fnl f: r.o wl) | — | 1 | | 106 | — |
| | **Blu Metemi (ITY)** (SCardaioli,Italy) **3-8-11b1** DZarroli (led tl appr fnl f: r.o wl u.p) | 1 | 2 | | 105 | — |
| 794a10 | **Bog Wild (USA)** (EBorromeo,Italy) **3-8-11** LSorrentino (prom after 3f: led appr fnl f tl ins fnl f: no ex) | ½ | 3 | | 104 | — |
| | **Karlaska** (PBary,France) **3-8-11** DBoeuf (chsd ldrs: r.o fnl 2f) | hd | 4 | | 104 | — |
| 723a2 | **Grey Way (USA)** (GBotti,Italy) **3-8-11** FJovine (hld up: r.o wl fnl 2f: nrst fin) | hd | 5 | | 104 | — |
| 723a* | **Robereva (IRE)** (APecoraro,Italy) **3-8-11** SDettori (mid div: no ex fnl 2f) | 1½ | 6 | | 101 | — |
| 8912 | **Story Line** (BWHills) **3-8-11** MHills (hld up in rr: hdwy appr str: no imp fnl 2f) | ¾ | 7 | | 100 | — |
| 719a* | **Bellflower (FR)** (LBrogi,Italy) **3-8-11** VMezzatesta (cl up fr ½-wy tl wknd st) | 2½ | 8 | | 97 | — |
| 908a2 | **Sopran Benda (ITY)** (JHeloury,Italy) **3-8-11** GBietolini (prom tl wknd 5f out) | ¾ | 9 | | 96 | — |
| | **Black Wood (USA)** (GBotti,Italy) **3-8-11** EBotti (a bhd: t.o) | 15 | 10 | | 74 | — |
| | | | | | | **10 Rn** |

**2m 18.9** (10.90) Tote 90L: 25L 29L 72L (325L) OWNER Allevamento Gialloblu BRED Allevamento Gialloblu

**Germignana (ITY)** was produced with a well-timed challenge to take the lead, and then resisted the renewed effort of the runner-up.

**Blu Metemi (ITY)** put up a game display. She made most of the running, and then came again when headed to press the winner all the way to the line.

**Bog Wild (USA)** looked the likely winner when hitting the front, but appeared not to stay.

**891 Story Line** went off an odds-on favourite but, although she was close enough turning for home, she found nothing extra in the last quarter-mile. Connections were unable to explain this disappointing display.

# 1138a-COLOGNE (Germany) (R-H) (Soft)
## Sunday May 19th

## 1394a CHARLES HEIDSIECK-FLIEGER-PREIS (Listed) (3-Y.O+)
2-30 (2-37) **5f** £10,811.00 (£4,414.00: £2,207.00)

| | | | | SP | RR | SF |
|---|---|---|---|---|---|---|
| | **Auenadler (GER)** (UOstmann,Germany) **4-9-8** GBocskai | — | 1 | | 114 | — |
| | **Adjmal (IRE)** (PLautner,Germany) **7-9-1** WNewnes | ¾ | 2 | | 105 | — |
| | **Sharp Prod (USA)** (HJentzsch,Germany) **6-9-8** PSchiergen | ½ | 3 | | 110 | — |
| 9595 | **Cross The Border** (RHannon) **3-8-8** KDarley | | 10 | | — | — |
| | | | | | | **12 Rn** |

**59.77 secs** (5.27) Tote 40DM: 16DM 40DM 14DM (SF 539DM) OWNER Gestut Auenquelle BRED Gestut Auenquelle

**Auenadler (GER)** took advantage of a favourable draw to score an all-the-way victory.

**832 Cross The Border** did his best to keep pace with the winner until halfway but, unsuited by the sticky ground, dropped away tamely.

## 1395a MEHL-MULHENS-RENNEN (Gp 2) (3-Y.O C & F)
3-40 (3-48) **1m** £85,586.00 (£34,685.00: £17,117.00: £9,009.00)

| | | | | SP | RR | SF |
|---|---|---|---|---|---|---|
| 795a2 | **Lavirco (GER)** (PRau,Germany) **3-9-2** TMundry (a.p: led 2f out: sn clr: rdn & hld on ins fnl f) | — | 1 | | 106 | — |
| | **Accento** (RSuerland,Germany) **3-9-2** AHelfenbein (led tl hdd 2f out: outpcd: r.o wl fnl f) | 1¼ | 2 | | 104 | — |
| | **Barlovento (GER)** (UOstmann,Germany) **3-9-2** GBocskai (hdwy 2f out: nt rch ldrs) | 6 | 3 | | 92 | — |
| | **Peppito (GER)** (PLautner,Germany) **3-9-2** WNewnes (hld up in rr: hdwy 2f out: nrst fin) | 3 | 4 | | 86 | — |
| 9365 | **Brandon Magic** (IABalding) **3-9-2** KDarley (prom tl rdn & wknd 2f out) | nk | 5 | | 85 | — |
| | **Happy Boy** (Germany) **3-9-2** PSchiergen (prom tl wknd over 1f out) | nk | 6 | | 84 | — |
| | **Savage (IRE)** (Germany) **3-8-11** GHuber (hdwy ½-wy: nvr rchd ldrs) | hd | 7 | | 79 | — |
| | **Jashin (IRE)** (Germany) **3-9-2** MRimmer (a abt same pl) | ½ | 8 | | 83 | — |
| | **Sambakonig (GER)** (Germany) **3-9-2** DMcCann | nk | 9 | | 83 | — |
| | | | | | | **14 Rn** |

**1m 39.85** (9.85) Tote 18DM: 12DM 24DM 21DM (SF 135DM) OWNER Gestut Fahrhof BRED Gestut Fahrhof Stiftung

**Lavirco (GER)** justified odds-on favouritism, but was made to battle. He had taken a clear advantage a quarter of a mile from home, but began to tire inside the last 200 yards.

**Accento** led and, although left behind when the winner quickened, fought back resolutely all the way to the line.

**936 Brandon Magic** raced prominently until the pace quickened in the straight.

# 1139a-LONGCHAMP (Paris, France) (R-H) (Very Soft)
## Sunday May 19th

## 1396a PRIX SAINT-ALARY (Gp 1) (3-Y.O F)
3-40 (3-47) **1m 2f** £65,119.00 (£25,856.00: £12,451.00: £5,270.00)

| | | | | SP | RR | SF |
|---|---|---|---|---|---|---|
| 905a* | **Luna Wells (IRE)** (AFabre,France) **3-9-0** TJarnet (hld up: hdwy to ld over 1f out: qcknd clr) | — | 1 | Evens 1 | 115+ | 31 |
| 796a3 | **Miss Tahiti (IRE)** (AFabre,France) **3-9-0** OPeslier (hld up: r.o fr over 1f out: nt rch wnr) | 1½ | 2 | 22/10 2 | 113 | 29 |
| 905a2 | **Ecoute (USA)** (MmeCHead,France) **3-9-0** ODoleuze (prom: rdn 2f out: one pce) | 5 | 3 | 78/10 | 105 | 21 |
| 794a* | **Beauty To Petriolo (IRE)** (LCamici,Italy) **3-9-0** MPasquale (rr early: led 6f out tl over 1f out: no ex) | 3 | 4 | 84/10 | 100 | 16 |
| | **L'Annee Folle (FR)** (FDoumen,France) **3-9-0** GMosse (prom tl wknd u.p 2f out) | 20 | 5 | 38/10 3 | 68 | — |
| | **Papalma (USA)** (MmeCHead,France) **3-9-0** NGuesdon (led 4f: t.o) | dist | 6 | 37/1 | — | — |
| | | | | | (SP 126.7%) | **6 Rn** |

**2m 13.6** (13.60) P-M 2.00F: 1.10F 1.20F (SF 4.90) OWNER Mr J-L Lagardere (CHANTILLY) BRED S.N.C. Lagardere Elevage et al

**905a* Luna Wells (IRE)** has done really well during the winter, and only had to be pushed out to ensure victory. A Sadler's Wells half-sister to Linamix, she has a choice between the Oaks and the Prix de Diane and, although she may well go to Epsom, no final decision has been made yet. (Evens)

**796a Miss Tahiti (IRE)** looked much better on this occasion, and showed a return to form. She ran on well once she saw daylight, but had no chance with the winner. She is expected to go for the Prix de Diane next. (22/10)

**905a Ecoute (USA)** was hampered when her pacemaker lost her place early in the race. She was no match for the first two, but had been closer to the winner in the Prix de la Grotte. (78/10)
**Beauty To Petriolo (IRE)**, the Italian Guineas winner, would have been better suited by a faster surface. Left in front after half a mile, she tired in the soft ground halfway up the straight. (84/10)

## 1397a PRIX VICOMTESSE VIGIER (Gp 2) (4-Y.O+)
4-10 (4-19) **1m 7f 110y** £39,526.00 (£15,810.00: £7,905.00: £3,953.00)

| | | | | SP | RR | SF |
|---|---|---|---|---|---|---|
| 902a* | **Double Eclipse (IRE)** (MJohnston) **4-8-12** JWeaver (mde all: qcknd over 5f out: r.o wl) | — | **1** | | 123 | 78 |
| | **Nononito (FR)** (JLesbordes,France) **5-8-12** OPeslier (racd 3rd: hdwy over 1f out: fin wl) | ¾ | **2** | | 121 | 77 |
| 875³ | **Always Aloof (USA)** (MRStoute) **5-8-12** CAsmussen (chsd wnr: no ex fnl 2f) | 5 | **3** | | 116 | 72 |
| 751² | **Assessor (IRE)** (RHannon) **7-8-12** GMosse (hld up in rr: rdn st: nt rch ldrs) | 4 | **4** | | 112 | 68 |
| | **Always Earnest (USA)** (MmeMBollack-Badel,France) **8-9-4** ABadel (rr early: nvr able to chal) | 2½ | **5** | | 115 | 71 |
| | **Pibarnon (FR)** (CMaillard,France) **6-8-11** SGuillot (n.d) | 3 | **6** | | 105 | 61 |
| 902a⁴ | **Affidavit (USA)** (AFabre,France) **4-9-1** TJarnet (4th tl rdn 2f out: wknd) | 4 | **7** | | 106 | 61 |
| | | | | | | **7 Rn** |

**3m 28.2** (12.20) P-M 2.40F: 1.60F 3.30F (SF 33.10F) OWNER The Middleham Partnership (MIDDLEHAM) BRED Dene Investments N V in Ireland
**902a* Double Eclipse (IRE)** made all the running, and had enough in hand to comfortably hold off the runner-up. A time breakdown indicates that he killed off his rivals with a burst of acceleration worthy of a sprinter between the two and one furlong markers. He will go straight to the Gold Cup for what looks likely to be an epic contest with his brother.
**Nononito (FR)** finished really well after being outpaced early in the straight. He showed a return to form here, and seemed to appreciate the soft ground. He may take on the winner again at Ascot.
**875 Always Aloof (USA)** kept tabs on the winner, but could not match his acceleration. He is not quite up to this class.
**751 Assessor (IRE)** does not appear quite as good as he was. He was held up for a run, but could never get in a blow.

# 1008-BRIGHTON (L-H) - Friday May 24th
**1398-1403 Abandoned-** Poor visibility

# 0957-HAYDOCK (L-H) (Good to soft)
## Friday May 24th
Race 1: hand-timed
WEATHER: fine & sunny WIND: mod half against

## 1404 PARKSIDE MAIDEN AUCTION STKS (2-Y.O) (Class D)
2-00 (2-02) **5f** £3,241.25 (£980.00: £477.50: £226.25) Stalls: High GOING: 0.37 sec per fur (GS)

| | | | | SP | RR | SF |
|---|---|---|---|---|---|---|
| 1008² | **Joint Venture (IRE)** (BJMeehan) **2-8-6b¹** PatEddery(6) (racd centre: broke smartly: mde all: comf) | — | **1** | 4/1² | 75+ | 28 |
| | **Future Prospect (IRE)** (MJohnston) **2-8-9** JWeaver(12) (w'like: leggy: s.i.s: hdwy ½-wy: shkn up to chse wnr over 1f out: r.o) | 1¾ | **2** | 7/1 | 72+ | 25 |
| 958⁶ | **Magic Blue (IRE)** (RHollinshead) **2-8-9** LDettori(7) (prom: rdn & edgd rt appr fnl f: one pce) | 4 | **3** | 16/1 | 60 | 13 |
| 996⁴ | **Osomental** (DHaydnJones) **2-8-6** AMackay(11) (bit bkwd: s.i.s: sn pushed along: r.o appr fnl f: nvr nrr) | nk | **4** | 11/8¹ | 56 | 9 |
| | **Out of Sight (IRE)** (BAMcMahon) **2-8-9** GCarter(3) (w'like: scope: bkwd: s.s: sme hdwy fnl 2f: nrst fin) | 2 | **5** | 11/1 | 52 | 5 |
| 481³ | **Perfect Bliss** (PDEvans) **2-7-12** TWilliams(10) (prom: rdn & outpcd ½-wy: sn btn) | hd | **6** | 25/1 | 41 | — |
| 975³ | **High Spirits (IRE)** (TDEasterby) **2-8-3** LCharnock(9) (dwlt: sn bhd & pushed along: n.d) | ¾ | **7** | 10/1 | 44 | — |
| 1036² | **Aybeegirl** (MrsJCecil) **2-8-2ow1** PaulEddery(1) (trckd ldrs: sn rdn & outpcd) | nk | **8** | 5/1³ | 42 | — |
| 715⁵ | **Nightingale Song** (MartynMeade) **2-7-12** FNorton(5) (outpcd: a bhd) | s.h | **9** | 25/1 | 37 | — |
| | **Heggies (IRE)** (CREgerton) **2-8-3** CRutter(2) (b.hind: small: bkwd: s.s: a bhd & outpcd) | 1¼ | **10** | 25/1 | 38 | — |
| | **Ballymote** (JBerry) **2-8-3** JCarroll(4) (leggy: lt-f: bit bkwd: unruly stalls: chsd ldrs 3f) | 2½ | **12** | 14/1 | 30 | — |
| | | | | (SP 132.8%) | | **11 Rn** |

**64.8 secs** (5.60) CSF £34.02 TOTE £4.10: £1.30 £2.50 £3.20 (£15.10) Trio £51.50 OWNER Mrs B. Bell (UPPER LAMBOURN) BRED Gay O'Callaghan
**1008 Joint Venture (IRE)**, who was not winning out of turn, responded to the first-time blinkers, and was never in any serious danger. (4/1)
**Future Prospect (IRE)**, sluggish leaving the stalls, did well in the circumstances to run the experienced winner so close. He should have little trouble in going one better. (7/1)
**Magic Blue (IRE)**, a very poor mover in his slower paces, was being bustled along at halfway and, drifting right in the latter stages, could not muster the speed to prove troublesome. (16/1)
**996 Osomental** again missed a beat at the start, and was flat to the boards all the way. He did run on inside the distance but, inclined to hang and run green, was never within striking range of the winner. (11/8)
**Out of Sight (IRE)**, a half-brother to two winners who is bred to need further, performed with credit after losing ground at the start. He will not be hard to place. (11/1: 8/1-12/1)
**481 Perfect Bliss** was being taken off her legs at halfway and soon fighting a losing battle, but she did keep on again towards the finish, and all is not lost yet. (25/1)

## 1405 SPINAL INJURIES ASSOCIATION APPRENTICE H'CAP (0-70) (3-Y.O) (Class E)
2-30 (2-32) **6f** £3,111.25 (£940.00: £457.50: £216.25) Stalls: High GOING: 0.37 sec per fur (GS)

| | | | | SP | RR | SF |
|---|---|---|---|---|---|---|
| 1039⁴ | **Limerick Princess (IRE) (58)** (JBerry) **3-8-7(5)** JoanneWebster(14) (a.p: led over 2f out: r.o wl) | — | **1** | 7/1² | 74 | 18 |
| 881* | **Maiteamia (63)** (SRBowring) **3-9-3b** GMilligan(8) (a w ldrs: ev ch fnl f: unable qckn) | 1¾ | **2** | 11/4¹ | 74 | 18 |
| 867¹⁰ | **Maysimp (IRE) (47)** (BPJBaugh) **3-7-10(5)ow5** PClarke(16) (trckd ldrs: kpt on one pce fnl 2f) | 5 | **3** | 33/1 | 45 | — |
| 973⁶ | **Doug's Folly (49)** (MWEasterby) **3-8-3b** GParkin(15) (hld up: hdwy & n.m.r 2f out: swtchd lft & r.o wl fnl f) | 1 | **4** | 10/1 | 44 | — |
| 1312¹⁰ | **Miss Offset (46)** (MJohnston) **3-7-9b(5)** KSked(6) (led tl over 2f out: sn rdn: wknd appr fnl f) | 1¾ | **5** | 9/1 | 37 | — |
| *606*⁷ | **Sharp Monty (57)** (RHollinshead) **3-8-11** MHumphries(2) (trckd ldrs: rdn wl over 1f out: nt pce to chal) | ¾ | **6** | 16/1 | 46 | — |
| 644¹¹ | **Boffy (IRE) (59)** (BPJBaugh) **3-8-13** PRoberts(12) (hld up: effrt over 2f out: nt rch ldrs) | 1¼ | **7** | 20/1 | 44 | — |
| 973¹⁰ | **Rhythmic Ball (44)** (TRWatson) **3-7-12** CAdamson(11) (prom tl rdn & wknd wl over 1f out) | 2½ | **8** | 33/1 | 23 | — |
| 973² | **Madam Zando (46)** (JBalding) **3-8-0** MartinDwyer(4) (prom tl rdn & wknd 2f out) | nk | **9** | 8/1³ | 24 | — |
| 973³ | **Pathaze (52)** (NBycroft) **3-8-3(3)** JoHunnam(7) (a outpcd) | 1¾ | **10** | 8/1³ | 25 | — |

| | | | | SP | RR | SF |
|---|---|---|---|---|---|---|
| 1007[10] | **Marjorie Rose (IRE) (65)** (ABailey) **3-9-5** IonaWands(9) (prom over 3f) | 1¼ | **11** | 7/1[2] | 35 | — |
| 1006[11] | **Montrestar (67)** (PDEvans) **3-9-4**(3) AngelaGallimore(3) (prom: rdn over 2f out: grad wknd) | ½ | **12** | 9/1 | 36 | — |
| *857*[4] | **Lapu-Lapu (54)** (MJCamacho) **3-8-8** SCopp(5) (outpcd fr ½-wy) | 2½ | **13** | 8/1[3] | 16 | — |
| | **Babyshooz (42)** (MBrittain) **3-7-5**(5) JBramhill(10) (s.s: a t.o) | dist | **14** | 25/1 | — | — |
| | | | | (SP 134.5%) | **14 Rn** | |

**1m 19.61** (7.91) CSF £28.03 CT £603.81 TOTE £6.80: £2.60 £1.80 £16.50 (£5.60) Trio £160.90 OWNER Mr Thomas Doherty (COCKERHAM) BRED Thomas Doherty

LONG HANDICAP Maysimp (IRE) 7-8 Babyshooz 7-8

**1039 Limerick Princess (IRE)** won this with the minimum amount of fuss. No doubt assisted by her high draw, she seems to be much happier when she can get her toe in. (7/1)

**881* Maiteamia**, fighting for supremacy all the way, kept battling away, but found the winner too much of a handful. (11/4)

**Maysimp (IRE)** ran much better on this step up in class, and would seem to be improving now that she is getting some sunshine on her back. (33/1)

**973 Doug's Folly**, drawn by the stands' rail, had trouble getting a run two furlongs out, but she ran on strongly after being switched and would appear to be on the upgrade. (10/1)

**492 Sharp Monty**, in the chasing group, was unable to respond when asked for his effort below the distance, but this performance should be good enough to enable him to win a seller. (16/1)

## 1406 GREENALLS PROPERTY H'CAP (0-90) (4-Y.O+) (Class C)

3-00 (3-00) **1m 30y** £5,541.75 (£1,674.00: £814.50: £384.75) Stalls: Low GOING: 0.37 sec per fur (GS)

| | | | | SP | RR | SF |
|---|---|---|---|---|---|---|
| 1069[2] | **Bollin Frank (62)** (TDEasterby) **4-8-0** LCharnock(3) (led after 2f: rdn & kpt on wl fnl f) | — | **1** | 4/1[1] | 70 | 26 |
| 1112[6] | **Band on the Run (90)** (BAMcMahon) **9-10-0** LDettori(6) (hld up: hdwy over 2f out: sn hrd drvn & hung lft: r.o wl nr fin) | 1 | **2** | 4/1[1] | 96 | 52 |
| 649* | **Reverand Thickness (72)** (ABailey) **5-8-10** KDarley(4) (led 2f: outpcd 3f out: rallied & swtchd ins 1f out: r.o) | 1¼ | **3** | 10/1 | 76 | 32 |
| 933[4] | **High Premium (69)** (RAFahey) **8-8-7b**[1] ACulhane(5) (hld up: hdwy 3f out: hrd rdn appr fnl f: nt qckn) | ½ | **4** | 7/1 | 72 | 28 |
| 988[10] | **Tatika (69)** (GWragg) **6-8-0**(7) GMilligan(11) (lw: reard s: bhd: hdwy over 2f out: nvr nr to chal) | hd | **5** | 11/2[2] | 71 | 27 |
| 933[10] | **Up in Flames (IRE) (73)** (MDHammond) **5-8-11** WCarson(2) (hld up: hdwy & nt clr run over 2f out: btn whn hmpd ins fnl f) | 2½ | **6** | 9/1 | 71 | 27 |
| 988[8] | **Barbaroja (84)** (JGFitzGerald) **5-9-8** PatEddery(9) (lw: prom tl wknd & eased 2f out) | 8 | **7** | 8/1 | 66 | 22 |
| 728[10] | **Shinerolla (81)** (CParker) **4-9-5** JCarroll(1) (lw: prom: rdn 2f out: eased whn btn appr fn lf) | 1¼ | **8** | 13/2[3] | 60 | 16 |
| 649[3] | **Q Factor (65)** (DHaydnJones) **4-8-3** AMackay(7) (a bhd & outpcd) | 2½ | **9** | 14/1 | 39 | — |
| *1048*[2] | **Duke Valentino (62)** (RHollinshead) **4-7-9**(5) PFessey(10) (trckd ldrs to ½-wy: sn lost tch: t.o) | dist | **10** | 20/1 | — | — |
| | | | | (SP 122.8%) | **10 Rn** | |

**1m 49.53** (8.93) CSF £20.43 CT £141.21 TOTE £4.60: £1.50 £1.70 £3.40 (£6.10) Trio £29.30 OWNER Sir Neil Westbrook (MALTON) BRED Sir Neil and Lady Westbrook

**1069 Bollin Frank**, a previous winner over course and distance, took advantage of his lenient handicap mark and made every post a winning one. (4/1)

**1112 Band on the Run** did not pick up as expected when asked for his effort entering the final quarter-mile, and was inclined to hang under pressure, but he did stay on particularly well inside the last 100 yards, and still has the ability to win races. (4/1)

**649* Reverand Thickness**, stepping up in class, looked to be in trouble when losing his pitch early in the straight, but he renewed his challenge inside the final furlong and went down fighting. (10/1)

**933 High Premium**, blinkered for the first time, was battling hard in an attempt to wear down the winner approaching the final furlong, but he was unable to increase his pace and was always being held. This was a decent performance in this company, and he has not stopped winning yet. (7/1)

**Tatika** reared up as the stalls opened and lost quite a lot of ground. Pulled into the centre of the track to mount a challenge, he could never quicken up and was unable to get himself into the action. (11/2)

**Up in Flames (IRE)**, making progress up the inside rail, was never getting much room in which to manoeuvre and, though he did reach a challenging position, he was held when forced to take avoiding action 150 yards out. (9/1)

## 1407 COAL PRODUCTS GROUP RATED STKS H'CAP (0-90) (3-Y.O) (Class C)

3-30 (3-30) **1m 6f** £4,653.80 (£1,734.20: £842.10: £355.50: £152.75: £71.65) Stalls: Centre GOING: 0.37 sec per fur (GS)

| | | | | SP | RR | SF |
|---|---|---|---|---|---|---|
| 1002[4] | **Bellator (71)** (GBBalding) **3-8-7** SSanders(1) (hld up: rdn 3f out: hdwy over 2f out: styd on to ld ins fnl f) | — | **1** | 6/1 | 77 | 42 |
| 932[3] | **Arctic Fancy (USA) (80)** (PWHarris) **3-9-2** GHind(2) (hld up: hdwy to ld over 1f out: drifted rt, hdd & no ex ins fnl f) | 1½ | **2** | 10/1 | 84 | 49 |
| 668* | **Sharaf (IRE) (83)** (JLDunlop) **3-9-5** WCarson(5) (lw: sn chsng ldr: rdn to chal 3f out: styd on ins fnl f) | ¾ | **3** | 9/4[1] | 86 | 51 |
| 1002[5] | **Benatom (USA) (85)** (HRACecil) **3-9-7** PatEddery(7) (led tl hdd over 1f out: rdn & no ex fnl f) | hd | **4** | 11/2[3] | 88 | 53 |
| 1002[8] | **Overruled (IRE) (84)** (DRLoder) **3-9-6** LDettori(3) (lw: hld up in tch: effrt over 2f out: sn ev ch: wknd fnl f) | 2½ | **5** | 13/2 | 85 | 50 |
| *370** | **Disc of Gold (USA) (85)** (MJohnston) **3-9-7** JWeaver(6) (hld up & bhd: rdn ent st: t.o fnl 2f) | 6 | **6** | 10/1 | 79 | 44 |
| 731[2] | **Infamous (USA) (84)** (PFICole) **3-9-6** RCochrane(4) (lw: dwlt: sn chsng ldrs: brought stands' side ent st: rdn & btn wl over 1f out) | hd | **7** | 3/1[2] | 78+ | 43 |
| | | | | (SP 117.0%) | **7 Rn** | |

**3m 12.17** (13.97) CSF £54.53 TOTE £7.50: £3.80 £3.20 (£73.10) OWNER Mr P. Richardson (ANDOVER) BRED Theakston Stud

**1002 Bellator**, tackling a more suitable trip, took advantage of his pull in the weights, and stayed on strongly to open his account. He will be a useful recruit to hurdling next season. (6/1)

**932 Arctic Fancy (USA)** looked to have the edge when nosing ahead below the distance, but he showed signs of greenness and, veering off a true line, could not withstand the powerful late thrust of the winner. He is not short on stamina and should continue to improve. (10/1)

**668* Sharaf (IRE)** proved a big disappointment for, after challenging for the lead three furlongs out, he was soon outpaced and looked done for. He was staying on as well as anything towards the finish, and is possibly better than his form suggests. (9/4)

**1002 Benatom (USA)** found this step up in distance just too much, and he had reached the end of his tether entering the final furlong. (11/2)

**1002 Overruled (IRE)**, given every chance to get the trip, failed to see it out, and was beaten approaching the last furlong. (13/2)

**731 Infamous (USA)**, pressing the leaders, decided to come over to the stands' side from the turn into the straight, but the plan back-fired, and he was never able to recover the lost ground. (3/1)

## 1408 W Y INSURANCE BROKERS (S) STKS (2-Y.O) (Class G)

4-00 (4-00) **5f** £2,220.00 (£620.00: £300.00) Stalls: High GOING: 0.37 sec per fur (GS)

| | | | | SP | RR | SF |
|---|---|---|---|---|---|---|
| 1320[2] | **C-Harry (IRE)** (RHollinshead) **2-9-2v** LDettori(2) (a.p: led ins fnl f: rdn out) | — | **1** | 9/4[2] | 51 | 17 |

| | | | | SP | RR | SF |
|---|---|---|---|---|---|---|
| | **Suave Star** (PDEvans) **2-8-6** JFortune(1) (leggy: lt-f: s.s: hdwy ½-wy: rdn 2f out: r.o wl cl home)....nk | 2 | | 11/4 3 | 40 | 6 |
| | **The Four Isles** (DHaydnJones) **2-8-11** AMackay(3) (w'like: leggy: bkwd: s.s: hld up & bhd: nt clr run 2f out: r.o wl ins fnl f)....4 | 3 | | 8/1 | 32 | — |
| 1097* | **Come Too Mamma's** (JBerry) **2-8-11** JCarroll(4) (lw: a.p: led 2f out tl rdn & hdd ins fnl f: sn btn)....1¼ | 4 | | 15/8 1 | 28 | — |
| | **Vivora** (MartynMeade) **2-8-7**ow1 VSlattery(5) (lt-f: bkwd: chsd ldrs: rdn 2f out: sn btn)....2½ | 5 | | 6/1 | 16 | — |
| | **Shotley Princess** (NBycroft) **2-8-6** LCharnock(6) (cmpt: bkwd: led 3f: sn rdn & wknd)....1¾ | 6 | | 11/1 | 10 | — |

(SP 125.9%) **6 Rn**

**66.05 secs** (6.85) CSF £9.73 TOTE £2.70: £2.20 £1.70 (£6.20) OWNER Mr D. Coppenhall (UPPER LONGDON) BRED Dan O'Loughlin
Bt in 4,000 gns

OFFICIAL EXPLANATION **The Four Isles: the jockey stated that the gelding missed the break, made up ground but had nowhere to go until the final furlong. The trained added that he had asked his rider to keep to a straight course due to the fact that the horse has suffered from sore shins.**

**1320 C-Harry (IRE)** does need further than this minimum trip but, with the ground riding testing, was able to take charge 200 yards out. Though he had to be kept up to his work, he was always going to hold on. (9/4)

**Suave Star**, a sparely-made debutante, ran a fine race after losing ground at the start, and she may eventually prove better than a selling plater. (11/4: 4/1-5/2)

**The Four Isles**, a half-brother to Media Express, did not look fully wound up for this racecourse debut, and a slow start did nothing to help his cause. Trapped on the stands' rail full of running two furlongs out, he ran on promisingly once he saw daylight, but the damage had been done. Whilst he is sure to benefit from the experience, the time of the race was slow, and he must not be overrated as yet. (8/1: op 5/1)

**1097* Come Too Mamma's** has won on the All-Weather, but she found this ground far too testing and was legless inside the final furlong. (15/8)

## 1409 LITTLETON MAIDEN STKS (3-Y.O F) (Class D)

4-30 (4-31) **1m 3f 200y** £3,558.00 (£1,074.00: £522.00: £246.00) Stalls: High GOING: 0.37 sec per fur (GS)

| | | | SP | RR | SF |
|---|---|---|---|---|---|
| 813 3 | **Ninotchka (USA)** (JLDunlop) **3-8-11** WCarson(5) (lw: chsd ldr: led over 5f out: clr appr fnl f)....— | 1 | 5/2 1 | 96 | 60 |
| 847 3 | **Generosa (84)** (HCandy) **3-8-11** RCochrane(7) (swtg: a.p: ev ch 3f out: rdn & outpcd appr fnl f)....8 | 2 | 4/1 3 | 85 | 49 |
| 1004 6 | **Berenice** (GWragg) **3-8-11** MHills(2) (lw: hld up: effrt & rdn over 2f out: wknd wl over 1f out)....3½ | 3 | 6/1 | 81 | 45 |
| | **Heronwater (IRE)** (MJohnston) **3-8-11** JWeaver(3) (w'like: scope: hld up in rr: hdwy over 3f out: nt rch ldrs)1¾ | 4 | 4/1 3 | 78 | 42 |
| 1077 4 | **Meribel (IRE)** (PWChapple-Hyam) **3-8-11** PaulEddery(1) (hld up: drvn along over 4f out: no imp: t.o)....12 | 5 | 15/2 | 62 | 26 |
| | **Marino Casino (USA)** (HRACecil) **3-8-11** PatEddery(4) (lengthy: scope: hld up & bhd: reminders & lost tch ent st: t.o)....9 | 6 | 7/2 2 | 50 | 14 |
| 932 10 | **Gildoran Sound** (TDEasterby) **3-8-11** TWilliams(6) (plld hrd: led over 6f: wknd over 3f out: t.o)....12 | 7 | 100/1 | 34 | — |

(SP 117.8%) **7 Rn**

**2m 39.01** (9.61) CSF £12.78 TOTE £3.50: £1.50 £2.30 (£5.90) OWNER Miss K. Rausing (ARUNDEL) BRED Swettenham Stud, RonCon 1 and Binfield House

**813 Ninotchka (USA)** came into her own over this longer trip and, the further she went, the easier she was going to win. She can gallop and is just about to find her way. (5/2)

**847 Generosa** joined the winner three furlongs out, but could match strides when the race began in earnest. (4/1)

**578 Berenice**, out of her class at Chester, was in with a live chance entering the last quarter-mile but, once the winner set sail for home, she was left standing. (6/1: 4/1-13/2)

**Heronwater (IRE)** looked well tuned up for this racecourse debut, and latched onto the heels of the leaders two furlongs out, but that was as far as she could get, and she may well benefit from a sounder surface. (4/1)

**1077 Meribel (IRE)** (15/2: 5/1-8/1)

**Marino Casino (USA)**, a plain-looking filly who has been slow to come to herself, is probably not ready for action judged on this very poor run, and it looks like it is back to the drawing board. (7/2: 5/2-4/1)

## 1410 BICKERSHAW CONDITIONS STKS (3-Y.O+) (Class C)

5-00 (5-00) **7f 30y** £5,095.80 (£1,855.80: £905.40: £387.00: £171.00) Stalls: Low GOING: 0.37 sec per fur (GS)

| | | | SP | RR | SF |
|---|---|---|---|---|---|
| 774* | **Master Boots** (DRLoder) **3-8-7** PatEddery(3) (lw: chsd ldrs: qcknd to ld appr fnl f: drvn clr)....— | 1 | 4/1 2 | 109 | 40 |
| 818 5 | **Fire Dome (IRE) (108)** (RHannon) **4-9-8** MHills(1) (lw: hld up: hdwy over 2f out: led over 1f out: sn hdd & one pce)....3½ | 2 | 8/1 | 105 | 47 |
| | **Takkatamm (USA)** (SbinSuroor) **4-9-4** LDettori(4) (a.p: chal over 2f out: sn rdn: outpcd appr fnl f)....7 | 3 | 4/9 1 | 86 | 28 |
| 794a 9 | **Inner Circle (USA)** (PWChapple-Hyam) **3-8-2** PaulEddery(2) (led tl hdd over 1f out: no ex)....hd | 4 | 7/1 3 | 80 | 11 |
| | **Kissel** (AHarrison) **4-8-10**(3) JStack(5) (w'like: bkwd: hld up & bhd: plld out & effrt 3f out: wknd 2f out: t.o)....11 | 5 | 25/1 | 56 | — |

(SP 116.7%) **5 Rn**

**1m 34.68** (7.18) CSF £28.31 TOTE £3.70: £1.40 £2.70 (£14.10) OWNER Mr Chris Brasher (NEWMARKET) BRED Hesmonds Stud Ltd
WEIGHT FOR AGE 3yo-11lb

**774* Master Boots**, a very progressive colt, won this readily and has booked himself a trip to Royal Ascot for a tilt at the Group Three Jersey Stakes. (4/1)

**818 Fire Dome (IRE)**, produced to win his race over a furlong out, was challenged almost immediately by the winner and the weight concession swayed the issue against him. There was no disgrace in this defeat, and he is in fine fettle. (8/1: op 4/1)

**Takkatamm (USA)** came here from the sunshine of Dubai, and looked something of a good thing, but he had quite a tussle to get past the filly, and the principals had taken his measure before reaching the final furlong. (4/9)

**794a Inner Circle (USA)** does her running from the front, and competed in a Group Two event in Italy last month, but she appeared to find this ground much too testing, and was a spent force approaching the final furlong. (7/1: 4/1-8/1)

T/Jkpt: £11,682.30 (0.9 Tckts); £1,645.40 to Haydock 25/5/96. T/Plpt: £208.10 (96.14 Tckts). T/Qdpt: £39.90 (32.8 Tckts). IM

# 0867-NOTTINGHAM (L-H) (Good to firm, Good patches)

## Friday May 24th

WEATHER: unsettled WIND: slt across

## 1411 ARNOLD (S) H'CAP (0-60) (3-Y.O+) (Class G)

2-20 (2-20) **1m 1f 213y** £2,070.00 (£570.00: £270.00) Stalls: Low GOING minus 0.20 sec per fur (GF)

| | | SP | RR | SF |
|---|---|---|---|---|
| **Marchman (45)** (JSKing) **11-9-3** TQuinn(4) (bit bkwd: hld up: hdwy on ins over 3f out: led 1f out: jst hld on)..— | 1 | 14/1 | 59 | 31 |

| | | | | SP | RR | SF |
|---|---|---|---|---|---|---|
| 883$^{9}$ | **Bobanlyn (IRE) (44)** (JSWainwright) **4-9-2** TIves(8) (swtg: hld up: hdwy & nt clr run 2f out: r.o wl ins fnl f) | hd | **2** | 6/1$^{1}$ | 58 | 30 |
| | **Diamond Crown (IRE) (44)** (MartynWane) **5-9-2** KFallon(5) (bkwd: hld up & bhd: gd hdwy 2f out: swtchd rt ins fnl f: r.o) | 2 | **3** | 14/1 | 55 | 27 |
| 1037$^{3}$ | **Comedy River (42)** (NEBerry) **9-8-7**$^{(7)}$ AEddery(9) (hdwy on ins over 2f out: nt clr run & swtchd rt ins fnl f: r.o) | hd | **4** | 7/1$^{2}$ | 53 | 25 |
| 983$^{10}$ | **Mezzoramio (41)** (KAMorgan) **4-8-6v**$^{(7)ow1}$ CScudder(12) (led tl hdd 1f out: one pce) | ¾ | **5** | 16/1 | 50 | 21 |
| 1196$^{3}$ | **Scottish Park (39)** (JLHarris) **7-8-8b**$^{(3)}$ PMcCabe(7) (hdwy & nt clr run over 2f out: nt rch ldrs) | s.h | **6** | 7/1$^{2}$ | 48 | 20 |
| | **Irrepressible (IRE) (35)** (RJHodges) **5-8-2**$^{(5)}$ AmandaSanders(1) (prom: rdn 3f out: wknd 2f out) | 5 | **7** | 50/1 | 36 | 8 |
| 983$^{5}$ | **My Handsome Prince (42)** (PJBevan) **4-9-0v** NCarlisle(6) (lw: hdwy 4f out: wknd 2f out) | hd | **8** | 11/1 | 43 | 15 |
| *1098$^{7}$* | **Mazilla (42)** (AStreeter) **4-8-9v**$^{(5)}$ RHavlin(10) (lw: a.p: ev ch over 2f out: wknd over 1f out) | ¾ | **9** | 7/1$^{2}$ | 42 | 14 |
| 843$^{11}$ | **Tony's Mist (46)** (JMBradley) **6-8-13**$^{(5)}$ MHenry(13) (prom tl wknd over 2f out) | 5 | **10** | 14/1 | 38 | 10 |
| *499** | **Awesome Power (46)** (JWHills) **10-9-4** AClark(17) (swtg: nvr trbld ldrs) | 4 | **11** | 10/1$^{3}$ | 31 | 3 |
| 991$^{15}$ | **Begger's Opera (35)** (PatMitchell) **4-8-7** GBardwell(23) (lw: nvr nr to chal) | hd | **12** | 33/1 | 20 | — |
| *855$^{8}$* | **Battery Boy (36)** (CWCElsey) **4-8-8b** DHarrison(3) (chsd ldr: rdn & ev ch 3f out: wknd over 2f out) | 1¾ | **13** | 25/1 | 18 | — |
| 1156$^{7}$ | **Prim Lass (46)** (MissJBower) **5-9-4** GDuffield(20) (prom 5f) | 1¾ | **14** | 33/1 | 26 | — |
| | **Spice and Sugar (39)** (BRCambidge) **6-8-11** DaleGibson(21) (bit bkwd: a bhd) | s.h | **15** | 33/1 | 19 | — |
| 670$^{6}$ | **Speedy Snaps Pride (39)** (PDCundell) **4-8-11** JQuinn(15) (a bhd) | s.h | **16** | 25/1 | 18 | — |
| 822$^{8}$ | **Hunza Story (36)** (NPLittmoden) **4-8-8** TGMcLaughlin(16) (b.hind: a bhd) | ½ | **17** | 20/1 | 15 | — |
| *512$^{7}$* | **Queens Stroller (IRE) (50)** (TWall) **5-9-8** RLappin(22) (a bhd) | 1¼ | **18** | 20/1 | 27 | — |
| 1167$^{7}$ | **No Submission (USA) (38)** (DWChapman) **10-8-10** SDWilliams(14) (lw: a bhd) | s.h | **19** | 12/1 | 15 | — |
| 690$^{13}$ | **Spitfire Bridge (IRE) (49)** (MMcCormack) **4-9-7** RHughes(18) (b: bhd most of way) | ¾ | **20** | 12/1 | 24 | — |
| *1094$^{8}$* | **Mamnoon (USA) (56)** (WClay) **5-10-0v** TSprake(11) (prom: rdn 5f out: wknd over 3f out) | 2 | **21** | 25/1 | 28 | — |
| 1012$^{3}$ | **Hang a Right (52)** (CADwyer) **9-9-10** CDwyer(2) (prom tl wknd over 3f out: t.o) | 12 | **22** | 14/1 | 5 | — |
| | | | | (SP 149.0%) | **22 Rn** | |

**2m 9.3** (6.80) CSF £102.75 CT £1167.42 TOTE £18.50: £3.90 £1.90 £5.60 £4.30 (£78.80) Trio £201.20 OWNER Mrs P. M. King (SWINDON) BRED Lord Edwin McAlpine
No bid
**Marchman** likes fast ground, but his suspect legs have trouble taking the strain of jumping hurdles on it now. (14/1)
**Bobanlyn (IRE)**, backed down to favourite, did not get the best of passages and could not quite peg back the winner in time. (6/1)
**Diamond Crown (IRE)** will come on for the run and made a highly promising reappearance over a trip on the short side for him. (14/1)
**1037 Comedy River** appreciated reverting to this longer distance. (7/1)
**778 Mezzoramio** is probably better forcing the pace over a mile. (16/1)
**1196 Scottish Park**, stepping up in distance, was a bit short of daylight when trying to improve and could never get to grips with the principals. (7/1)
**Mazilla** (7/1: op 14/1)

## 1412 RADCLIFFE LIMITED STKS (0-65) (3-Y.O+) (Class F)
2-50 (2-52) **6f 15y** £2,381.00 (£656.00: £311.00) Stalls: High GOING: 0.19 sec per fur (G)

| | | | | SP | RR | SF |
|---|---|---|---|---|---|---|
| 868$^{4}$ | **Faraway Lass (65)** (LordHuntingdon) **3-8-6** DHarrison(13) (hld up: hdwy 2f out: led over 1f out: edgd lft: r.o wl) | — | **1** | 9/4$^{1}$ | 68 | 42 |
| 893$^{4}$ | **Sing Up (51)** (MMcCormack) **4-9-4** RHughes(14) (a.p: led over 2f out tl over 1f out: r.o one pce) | 1½ | **2** | 10/1 | 67 | 50 |
| 1040$^{2}$ | **Barato (64)** (MrsJRRamsden) **5-9-4v** KFallon(17) (hld up: hdwy over 2f out: edgd lft & r.o ins fnl f) | nk | **3** | 13/2$^{2}$ | 66 | 49 |
| 743* | **Kings Harmony (IRE) (63)** (PJMakin) **3-8-12** TQuinn(11) (a.p: ev ch over 1f out: unable qkcn) | 1¼ | **4** | 9/1$^{3}$ | 66 | 40 |
| | **Impulsive Air (IRE) (58)** (EWeymes) **4-9-4v** TIves(3) (a.p: rdn over 1f out: one pce) | hd | **5** | 16/1 | 63 | 46 |
| *1028$^{9}$* | **Merrie le Bow (43)** (PatMitchell) **4-8-10**$^{(5)}$ AmandaSanders(15) (nvr nr to chal) | 2 | **6** | 33/1 | 54 | 37 |
| 1186$^{9}$ | **Samsolom (65)** (PHowling) **8-9-4** BThomson(10) (prom over 4f) | nk | **7** | 10/1 | 57 | 40 |
| 868$^{15}$ | **Tymeera (59)** (BPalling) **3-8-9** TSprake(18) (led over 3f: wknd over 1f out) | hd | **8** | 16/1 | 56 | 30 |
| *1028$^{5}$* | **Princess Efisio (50)** (BAMcMahon) **3-8-6** GDuffield(7) (prom over 4f) | 2 | **9** | 33/1 | 48 | 22 |
| 1307$^{9}$ | **Petraco (IRE) (62)** (NASmith) **8-9-4** SDWilliams(2) (chsd ldrs far side 4f) | nk | **10** | 20/1 | 50 | 33 |
| 1154$^{4}$ | **Wild Palm (63)** (WAO'Gorman) **4-9-4b** EmmaO'Gorman(4) (dwlt: a bhd) | hd | **11** | 10/1 | 50 | 33 |
| | **Hickory Blue (65)** (KAMorgan) **6-8-11b**$^{(7)}$ CScudder(16) (w ldrs over 3f) | nk | **12** | 20/1 | 49 | 32 |
| 956$^{2}$ | **Cretan Gift (65)** (NPLittmoden) **5-9-7b** TGMcLaughlin(6) (led far side: hung rt over 2f out: wknd over 1f out) | 3 | **13** | 9/1$^{3}$ | 44 | 27 |
| 1073$^{12}$ | **Moujeeb (USA) (60)** (PatMitchell) **6-9-4v** JQuinn(5) (a bhd) | s.h | **14** | 14/1 | 41 | 24 |
| | **Deerly (60)** (DMorris) **3-8-1**$^{(5)}$ MHenry(9) (bhd fnl 3f) | 5 | **15** | 10/1 | 25 | — |
| 951$^{6}$ | **Hannah's Usher (63)** (CMurray) **4-9-0**$^{(7)}$ GFaulkner(8) (a bhd) | ¾ | **16** | 20/1 | 29 | 12 |
| 758$^{5}$ | **Daring Venture (58)** (TJNaughton) **3-7-13**$^{(7)}$ TAshley(12) (t.o) | 14 | **17** | 25/1 | — | — |
| *1101$^{5}$* | ***Rififi (62)*** (RIngram) **3-8-6**$^{(3)}$ PMcCabe(1) (Withdrawn not under Starter's orders: rdr uns & inj.) | | **W** | 10/1 | | |
| | | | | (SP 152.0%) | **17 Rn** | |

**1m 15.1** (4.60) CSF £27.58 TOTE £3.70: £1.20 £2.90 £2.40 (£27.60) Trio £51.70 OWNER Mr J. Rose (WEST ILSLEY) BRED John Rose
WEIGHT FOR AGE 3yo-9lb
**868 Faraway Lass** made the most of being extremely well in at the weights. (9/4)
**893 Sing Up** confirmed he is back to form, and would have been receiving 17lb from the winner had this been a handicap. (10/1)
**1040 Barato** would have been getting 4lb from the winner had this been a handicap. (13/2)
**743* Kings Harmony (IRE)** found this more competitive, and there would have been a stone turn around with the winner had this been a handicap. (9/1: 6/1-10/1)
**Impulsive Air (IRE)** made a most respectable reappearance, and the winner would have been conceding him 10lb in a handicap. (16/1)
**868 Merrie le Bow** would have been receiving no less than 22lb from the winner on handicap ratings. (33/1)

## 1413 E.B.F. MAIDEN STKS (2-Y.O F) (Class D)
3-20 (3-20) **6f 15y** £3,362.60 (£1,002.80: £478.40: £216.20) Stalls: High GOING: 0.19 sec per fur (G)

| | | | | SP | RR | SF |
|---|---|---|---|---|---|---|
| | **Fernanda** (JLDunlop) **2-8-11** TSprake(5) (w'like: hld up: swtchd lft & hdwy over 1f out: qcknd to ld ins fnl f: pushed out) | — | **1** | 5/2$^{2}$ | 75 | 31 |
| | **Hakkaniyah** (DMorley) **2-8-11** RHills(1) (w'like: hld up: hdwy over 2f out: led & edgd rt over 1f out: hdd ins fnl f) | 1¼ | **2** | 7/2$^{3}$ | 72 | 28 |
| | **Seva (IRE)** (DRLoder) **2-8-11** RHughes(3) (gd sort: scope: hld up: rdn over 2f out: ev ch whn bmpd over 1f out: one pce) | 5 | **3** | 4/5$^{1}$ | 59 | 15 |

| | | | | SP | RR | SF |
|---|---|---|---|---|---|---|
| 1014[3] | **Danehill Princess (IRE)** (RHollinshead) **2-8-11** KFallon(4) (chsd ldr: led over 2f out: hdd & carried rt over 1f out: sn wknd) | hd | **4** | 9/2 | 58 | 14 |
| | **April Jackson** (PTDalton) **2-8-11** SDWilliams(2) (w'like: bkwd: s.s: a bhd) | 4 | **5** | 50/1 | 48 | 4 |
| 1036[5] | **Emilyjill** (JGMO'Shea) **2-8-11** JQuinn(6) (led over 3f: wkng whn bdly hmpd over 1f out) | 3 | **6** | 25/1 | 40 | — |

(SP 130.3%) **6 Rn**

**1m 16.2** (5.70) CSF £12.97 TOTE £5.80: £4.20 £2.60 (£12.40) OWNER Sultan Al Kabeer (ARUNDEL) BRED Mrs John Trotter
**Fernanda**, a half-sister to Chipaya, looked well tuned up and had been backed in the morning with one of the few firms betting on the race. (5/2: 2/1-3/1)
**Hakkaniyah** caused a chain reaction by jinking right after striking the front, and was unable to cope with the winner. (7/2)
**Seva (IRE)**, quite a long-backed filly, is out of a half-sister to Ya Malak, and it was a shade disappointing she came off the bit so soon after halfway. (4/5: op 2/5)
**1014 Danehill Princess (IRE)** was already feeling the pinch when meeting trouble below the distance. (9/2)
**643 Emilyjill** would not have been beaten so far had she not been murdered against the stands' rail. (25/1)

## 1414 OPTION CLAIM LEGAL EXPENSE PROTECTION H'CAP (0-70) (3-Y.O+) (Class E)
3-50 (3-51) **1m 1f 213y** £3,889.20 (£1,167.60: £562.80: £260.40) Stalls: Low GOING minus 0.20 sec per fur (GF)

| | | | | SP | RR | SF |
|---|---|---|---|---|---|---|
| 1104[6] | **Absolutelystunning (51)** (MrsBarbaraWaring) **3-7-7**(3) NVarley(7) (b: a.p: led wl over 1f out: rdn out) | — | **1** | 33/1 | 64 | 20 |
| 995[3] | **Master M-E-N (IRE) (50)** (NMBabbage) **4-8-9** AClark(6) (lw: hld up: hdwy on ins over 3f out: rdn & nt clr run over 2f out: swtchd rt over 1f out: r.o wl) | ½ | **2** | 13/2[3] | 62 | 32 |
| 1302[2] | **Zahran (IRE) (40)** (JMBradley) **5-7-13** NCarlisle(2) (lw: a.p: rdn over 3f out: hrd rdn & r.o one pce fnl f) | 3 | **3** | 6/1[2] | 47 | 17 |
| 844[3] | **George Bull (63)** (MajorWRHern) **4-9-8** TSprake(4) (plld hrd: prom tl rdn & wknd over 1f out) | 4 | **4** | 9/4[1] | 64 | 34 |
| 1047[4] | **Scottish Bambi (62)** (PRWebber) **8-9-7** RPerham(10) (lw: plld hrd: prom tl wknd over 1f out) | 3½ | **5** | 6/1[2] | 57 | 27 |
| 920[9] | **Conic Hill (IRE) (55)** (JPearce) **5-9-0** GBardwell(15) (dwlt: plld hrd: hdwy on ins over 2f out: nt rch ldrs) | 1½ | **6** | 25/1 | 48 | 18 |
| 1309[12] | **Paronomasia (37)** (JLHarris) **4-7-3b**(7) RMullen(14) (prom tl wknd over 2f out) | hd | **7** | 33/1 | 30 | — |
| 760[7] | **Fresh Look (IRE) (39)** (RCSpicer) **4-7-12** NKennedy(13) (s.s: bhd tl plld out & late hdwy: nrst fin) | 2½ | **8** | 25/1 | 28 | — |
| | **Voila Premiere (IRE) (67)** (MHTompkins) **4-9-12** PRobinson(3) (bit bkwd: led over 8f) | s.h | **9** | 12/1 | 56 | 26 |
| 963[6] | **Desert Spring (69)** (PWHarris) **4-9-9**(5) MHenry(5) (bhd fnl 2f) | ½ | **10** | 12/1 | 57 | 27 |
| 1047[5] | **Bronze Maquette (IRE) (37)** (THind) **6-7-5**(5) MBaird(1) (bhd :most of way) | 3½ | **11** | 12/1 | 19 | — |
| 1037[6] | **Grey Kingdom (38)** (MBrittain) **5-7-11**ow1 DaleGibson(11) (bhd fnl 4f) | 3½ | **12** | 25/1 | 15 | — |
| 469[10] | **Our Tom (55)** (JWharton) **4-9-0** KFallon(9) (a bhd) | 1 | **13** | 12/1 | 30 | — |
| 994[9] | **Squared Away (56)** (JWPayne) **4-9-1** BThomson(8) (a bhd) | 2 | **14** | 14/1 | 28 | — |
| 851[14] | **Bellateena (52)** (HJCollingridge) **4-8-11** JQuinn(12) (prom tl wknd qckly 3f out: t.o) | 26 | **15** | 9/1 | — | — |

(SP 137.5%) **15 Rn**

**2m 8.1** (5.60) CSF £240.70 CT £1,385.67 TOTE £36.10: £6.40 £2.80 £2.40 (£169.00) Trio £475.60; £133.98 to Kempton 25/5/96 OWNER Racehorse Owners Bath Ltd (CHIPPENHAM) BRED Mrs A. Plummer
LONG HANDICAP Bronze Maquette (IRE) 7-9 Grey Kingdom 7-7 Paronomasia 7-5 Absolutelystunning 7-4
WEIGHT FOR AGE 3yo-14lb
**Absolutelystunning**, carrying 3lb more than her long-handicap mark, knocked a joint last year and showed her first signs of ability last time. (33/1)
**995 Master M-E-N (IRE)** took time to find a clear run and was probably unlucky not to add to his stable's 75% strike-rate at the course. (13/2)
**1302 Zahran (IRE)**, trying a longer trip, is as tough as old boots and kept plugging away to the end. (6/1)
**844 George Bull**, dropping back in distance, was backed as if defeat was out of the question, but could not get his stable off the mark for the season. (9/4: 3/1-9/2)
**1047 Scottish Bambi** did not help his chances by refusing to settle. (6/1)
**Conic Hill (IRE)** has dropped to a mark 18lb lower than when he last won. (25/1)
**Voila Premiere (IRE)** (12/1: op 8/1)
**Squared Away** (14/1: op 8/1)

## 1415 GEDLING H'CAP (0-80) (3-Y.O) (Class D)
4-20 (4-20) **1m 6f 15y** £3,622.50 (£1,080.00: £515.00: £232.50) Stalls: Low GOING minus 0.20 sec per fur (GF)

| | | | | SP | RR | SF |
|---|---|---|---|---|---|---|
| 993[3] | **Ela-Yie-Mou (IRE) (73)** (LMCumani) **3-9-1** RHughes(4) (hld up: stdy hdwy 4f out: led ins fnl f: r.o) | — | **1** | 9/4[1] | 82 | 49 |
| 890[2] | **Macmorris (USA) (70)** (PFICole) **3-8-12** TQuinn(3) (chsd ldr: led 3f out: hrd rdn & hdd ins fnl f: r.o) | hd | **2** | 11/4[2] | 79 | 46 |
| 1023* | **Shooting Light (IRE) (79)** (MAJarvis) **3-9-7** PBloomfield(1) (hld up & bhd: rdn 5f out: hdwy 3f out: one pce fnl 2f) | 5 | **3** | 13/2 | 82 | 49 |
| 954* | **Influence Pedler (54)** (CEBrittain) **3-7-5**(5) MBaird(7) (swtg: led 11f: wknd 2f out) | 8 | **4** | 13/2 | 48 | 15 |
| 826[8] | **Doctor Green (FR) (68)** (LordHuntingdon) **3-8-10v**[1] DHarrison(2) (prom tl wknd over 2f out) | nk | **5** | 9/1 | 62 | 29 |
| 594[2] | **Dancing Cavalier (69)** (RHollinshead) **3-8-6**(5) DGriffiths(6) (swtg: a bhd) | 8 | **6** | 5/1[3] | 54 | 21 |
| 803[15] | **Muhtadi (IRE) (73)** (JLDunlop) **3-9-1** RHills(8) (lw: prom tl rdn & wknd 3f out) | 6 | **7** | 13/2 | 51 | 18 |
| 932[9] | **Harbet House (FR) (60)** (CACyzer) **3-8-2**ow2 GDuffield(5) (plld hrd: prom tl wknd 4f out) | 9 | **8** | 20/1 | 28 | — |

(SP 128.9%) **8 Rn**

**3m 4.6** (6.10) CSF £9.91 CT £35.09 TOTE £3.30: £2.30 £1.10 £2.60 (£7.70) OWNER Mr Andreas Michael (NEWMARKET) BRED Stonethorn Stud Farms Ltd
LONG HANDICAP Influence Pedler 7-8
**993 Ela-Yie-Mou (IRE)**, cruising in behind the leader, had his tongue out and carried his head to one side when asked to assert, but just managed to do enough. (9/4: 6/4-5/2)
**890 Macmorris (USA)** stays well and gave the reluctant winner's supporters a fright. (11/4)
**1023* Shooting Light (IRE)**, again stepping up in distance, stays all day, but does not seem over-blessed with speed. (13/2)
**954* Influence Pedler** found this more competitive than Doncaster. (13/2)

## 1416 COLWICK MAIDEN APPRENTICE H'CAP (0-70) (3-Y.O+) (Class G)
4-50 (4-51) **1m 54y** £2,090.00 (£590.00: £290.00) Stalls: Low GOING minus 0.20 sec per fur (GF)

| | | | | SP | RR | SF |
|---|---|---|---|---|---|---|
| 787[12] | **Broughton's Pride (IRE) (47)** (JLEyre) **5-8-13**(3) DSweeney(10) (lw: a.p: led wl over 1f out: r.o wl) | — | **1** | 6/1[1] | 58 | 23 |
| | **Spa Lane (47)** (PJMakin) **3-8-4** TAshley(20) (lw: hdwy over 1f out: r.o wl ins fnl f) | nk | **2** | 20/1 | 57 | 10 |
| 979[19] | **Bad News (42)** (JMBradley) **4-8-6**(5) CLowther(15) (lw: hld up: hdwy over 2f out: chsd wnr fnl f: r.o) | s.h | **3** | 10/1 | 52 | 17 |
| | **Oscar Rose (55)** (LordHuntingdon) **3-8-9**(3) JWilkinson(2) (lw: s.s: gd hdwy over 1f out: r.o wl ins fnl f) | nk | **4** | 20/1 | 65 | 18 |

| | | | | SP | RR | SF |
|---|---|---|---|---|---|---|
| *17*$^{7}$ | **Straight Thinking (USA) (59)** (PFICole) **3-8-6**(10) DavidO'Neill(19) (lw: hld up: hdwy on ins 2f out: r.o ins fnl f) | 1½ | **5** | 12/1 | 66 | 19 |
| | **El Don (44)** (MJRyan) **4-8-3b**$^{1}$(10) AMcCarthy(7) (a.p: rdn & hung lft over 1f out: one pce) | 3½ | **6** | 13/2$^{2}$ | 44 | 9 |
| | **Harvest Reaper (53)** (JLHarris) **4-9-3**(5) TField(17) (bkwd: led over 5f: wknd over 1f out) | nk | **7** | 14/1 | 53 | 18 |
| 892$^{15}$ | **Society Magic (USA) (63)** (IABalding) **3-9-0**(6) CScudder(16) (hld up: stdy hdwy 3f out: wknd over 1f out) | ½ | **8** | 10/1 | 62 | 15 |
| 887$^{7}$ | **Tarian (USA) (54)** (GBBalding) **4-8-13**(10) RGordon(13) (no hdwy fnl 2f) | ¾ | **9** | 7/1$^{3}$ | 51 | 16 |
| 887$^{18}$ | **Jona Holley (54)** (IABalding) **3-8-6**(5) RMullen(3) (n.d) | 1¾ | **10** | 20/1 | 48 | 1 |
| 1117$^{12}$ | **Opening Range (35)** (NEBerry) **5-8-4b**$^{1}$ AEddery(14) (a bhd) | 4 | **11** | 25/1 | 21 | — |
| *834*$^{5}$ | **Backhander (IRE) (55)** (MartynWane) **4-9-10** JEdmunds(6) (a.p: led over 2f out tl wl over 1f out: sn wknd) | ¾ | **12** | 10/1 | 39 | 4 |
| 1312$^{7}$ | **Ned's Contessa (IRE) (48)** (MDods) **3-8-5b**$^{1}$ JDennis(1) (s.s: a bhd) | ¾ | **13** | 16/1 | 31 | — |
| *781*$^{5}$ | **Classic Daisy (41)** (RCSpicer) **3-7-5**(7)ow1 JBosley(8) (a bhd) | 3 | **14** | 25/1 | 18 | — |
| | **Miss Toffee Nose (IRE) (30)** (DJSCosgrove) **4-7-6**(7) JMcAuley(12) (bit bkwd: sn wl bhd) | 1½ | **15** | 33/1 | 4 | — |
| 638$^{9}$ | **Rustic Song (IRE) (45)** (JWharton) **3-7-11**(5) RFfrench(9) (swtg: prom 5f) | hd | **16** | 8/1 | 19 | — |
| *1096*$^{2}$ | **Hadadabble (46)** (PatMitchell) **3-7-12**(5)ow3 JMoon(11) (prom 5f) | 2½ | **17** | 13/2$^{2}$ | 15 | — |
| 942$^{7}$ | **Prince Zizim (63)** (CADwyer) **3-8-10**(10) FTynan(18) (a bhd) | 6 | **18** | 12/1 | 21 | — |
| | | | | (SP 144.7%) | **18 Rn** | |

**1m 47.5** (6.20) CSF £125.01 CT £1,173.33 TOTE £6.10: £2.10 £9.40 £2.10 £4.80 (£116.40) Trio £340.50; £306.95 to Kempton 25/5/96
OWNER Mrs Janet Morris (HAMBLETON) BRED A. J. Poulton (Epping) Ltd
WEIGHT FOR AGE 3yo-12lb
**508 Broughton's Pride (IRE)** was nicely backed on her first run for Les Eyre. (6/1: op 4/1)
**Spa Lane**, who has changed stables, did all his best work in the last furlong and a half, and is bred to stay further. (20/1)
**645 Bad News** disappointed when tried over a longer trip last time. (10/1)
**Oscar Rose**, visored on her final outing last season, put in some excellent work in the closing stages after a poor start. (20/1)
**Straight Thinking (USA)** showed promise on his first run since the turn of the year. (12/1: op 8/1)
**El Don**, fit from jumping, went left under pressure in this first run in blinkers. (13/2)

T/Plpt: £172.80 (80.2 Tckts). T/Qdpt: £24.70 (46 Tckts). KH

# 0848-PONTEFRACT (L-H) (Good)
## Friday May 24th
WEATHER: fine WIND: almost nil

### 1417 FRIENDS OF THE NORTHERN RACING COLLEGE CLAIMING STKS (4-Y.O+) (Class F)
6-45 (6-46) **1m 4y** £3,125.50 (£868.00: £416.50) Stalls: Low GOING minus 0.22 sec per fur (GF)

| | | | | SP | RR | SF |
|---|---|---|---|---|---|---|
| | **Options Open** (MrsJRRamsden) **4-9-5** KFallon(3) (hld up: hdwy on bit to ld over 1f out: qckdn clr: eased towards fin) | — | **1** | 5/4$^{1}$ | 81 | 42 |
| 1041$^{3}$ | **Brambles Way (45)** (WLBarker) **7-8-0v**(5) MartinDwyer(5) (trckd ldrs: led over 2f out tl over 1f out: no ch w wnr) | 4 | **2** | 33/1 | 59 | 20 |
| 871$^{8}$ | **Break the Rules (71)** (MrsMReveley) **4-9-1** KDarley(9) (lw: hld up: hdwy over 2f out: kpt on same pce) | 1¾ | **3** | 6/4$^{2}$ | 66 | 27 |
| | **Stone Cross (IRE)** (RFFisher) **4-8-11** NConnorton(7) (b.off hind: hld up: styd on fnl 2f: nvr nr ldrs) | 5 | **4** | 14/1 | 52 | 13 |
| 1087$^{10}$ | **Naughty Pistol (USA)** (PDEvans) **4-8-8** RLappin(2) (chsd ldrs: outpcd over 2f out: n.d after) | 6 | **5** | 20/1 | 37 | — |
| 787$^{8}$ | **Mill Dancer (IRE) (41)** (EJAlston) **4-8-6** SDWilliams(6) (w ldr: led 3f out: sn hdd: wknd wl over 1f out) | 2 | **6** | 25/1 | 31 | — |
| | **Raased (87)** (FWatson) **4-8-13** JFortune(1) (chsd ldrs: rdn over 2f out: hung lft & wknd over 1f out) | s.h | **7** | 13/2$^{3}$ | 38 | — |
| 884$^{12}$ | **Battle Colours (IRE) (38)** (DonEnricoIncisa) **7-8-5** KimTinkler(4) (mde most to 3f out: wknd wl over 1f out) | 3½ | **8** | 50/1 | 23 | — |
| | **Royal Comedian (38)** (BWMurray) **7-8-6** TWilliams(8) (prom early: outpcd & rdn ½-wy: sn bhd) | 12 | **9** | 50/1 | — | — |
| | | | | (SP 119.9%) | **9 Rn** | |

**1m 45.9** (4.40) CSF £35.30 TOTE £2.10: £1.10 £2.90 £1.50 (£18.40) Trio £6.30 OWNER Mr Jonathan Ramsden (THIRSK) BRED D. H. Jones
**OFFICIAL EXPLANATION Raased: had choked and lost his action.**
**Options Open**, a record-breaking two-year-old and fifth in the Jersey Stakes from just two outings last year, carried plenty of condition. Travelling supremely well throughout, he won very easily indeed as he was entitled to, and he certainly gets a mile at least in this sort of company. (5/4: 4/5-11/8)
**1041 Brambles Way**, still a maiden, would have been meeting the winner on no less than 43lb better terms in a handicap and seemed to run the race of his life to finish second best. (33/1)
**537 Break the Rules**, who would have been meeting the winner on two stone better terms in a handicap, was amazingly well backed to beat him, but it was obvious some way from home that he was no match. (6/4)
**Stone Cross (IRE)**, who was having his first outing for thirteen months, was settled at the rear, and was staying on at the finish. (14/1)
**Raased**, who changed hands cheaply, hung badly left under pressure and his rider reported that he had choked and lost his action. He is obviously one to have grave reservations about. (13/2)

### 1418 TOTE H'CAP (0-70) (3-Y.O+) (Class E)
7-10 (7-12) **1m 2f 6y** £3,315.90 (£991.20: £474.60: £216.30) Stalls: Low GOING minus 0.22 sec per fur (GF)

| | | | | SP | RR | SF |
|---|---|---|---|---|---|---|
| 995$^{2}$ | **Maradata (IRE) (51)** (RHollinshead) **4-9-0** LDettori(12) (hld up: gd hdwy & swtchd outside 2f out: qcknd to ld ins fnl f: pushed out) | — | **1** | 5/1$^{2}$ | 63 | 43 |
| 1089* | **Hawksley Hill (IRE) (60)** (MrsJRRamsden) **3-8-9** 5x KFallon(8) (hld up: pushed along 5f out: gd hdwy over 2f out: rdn to ld over 1f out: hung lft & hdd ins fnl f: nt pce of wnr) | 1¾ | **2** | 9/4$^{1}$ | 69 | 35 |
| | **Essayeffsee (56)** (MrsMReveley) **7-9-5** KDarley(9) (hld up: hdwy over 3f out: effrt whn hmpd over 1f out: kpt on same pce) | 1¾ | **3** | 12/1 | 62 | 42 |
| 1309$^{2}$ | **Gold Desire (33)** (MBrittain) **6-7-10** GBardwell(1) (in tch: rdn 3f out: swtchd to outside over 1f out: styd on) | 3½ | **4** | 9/1 | 34 | 14 |
| 1024$^{9}$ | **Calder King (63)** (JLEyre) **5-9-12v** RLappin(4) (sn rdn along: a.p: led wl over 1f out: sn hdd: one pce) | 3 | **5** | 12/1 | 59 | 39 |
| 1072$^{3}$ | **Hanbitooh (USA) (67)** (EALDunlop) **3-9-2b**$^{1}$ WCarson(3) (lw: trckd ldrs: effrt over 2f out: wknd over 1f out) | 2 | **6** | 8/1 | 60 | 26 |
| 995$^{13}$ | **Alzotic (IRE) (50)** (JNorton) **3-7-13** JFanning(6) (bhd: sme hdwy over 2f out: nvr nr ldrs) | 2 | **7** | 20/1 | 40 | 6 |
| 1072$^{2}$ | **Darling Clover (61)** (DMorley) **4-9-10** PatEddery(14) (w ldr: led over 3f out tl wl over 1f out: sn wknd) | 1¾ | **8** | 11/2$^{3}$ | 48 | 28 |
| 1019$^{5}$ | **Ambidextrous (IRE) (50)** (EJAlston) **4-8-13v** SDWilliams(7) (s.i.s: a in rr) | 3 | **9** | 20/1 | 32 | 12 |
| 1034$^{5}$ | **Glenvally (35)** (BWMurray) **5-7-12v** TWilliams(11) (chsd ldrs: ev ch tl wknd wl over 1f out) | ¾ | **10** | 25/1 | 16 | — |

1098[3] **Personimus (36)** (CaptJWilson) **6-7-8**(5) PFessey(13) (in tch: rdn 4f out: lost pl 2f out) 3½ **11** 12/1 11 —
879[12] **Super High (60)** (PHowling) **4-9-9** RCochrane(2) (swtg: plld hrd: mde most tl over 3f out: sn lost pl) 3 **12** 12/1 31 11
1088[13] **Bardia (33)** (DonEnricoIncisa) **6-7-10** KimTinkler(10) (bhd: sme hdwy 4f out: sn wknd) 1½ **13** 50/1 1 —
1037[14] **Suvalu (USA) (65)** (MGMeagher) **4-10-0** JFortune(5) (chsd ldrs: rdn 4f out: wknd over 2f out) 2 **14** 33/1 30 10
(SP 133.0%) **14 Rn**

**2m 13.1** (4.80) CSF £17.48 CT £129.72 TOTE £5.40: £2.10 £1.50 £3.70 (£11.10) Trio £75.40 OWNER Mr R. Hollinshead (UPPER LONGDON) BRED His Highness the Aga Khans Studs S. C.
LONG HANDICAP Bardia 7-9
WEIGHT FOR AGE 3yo-14lb

**995 Maradata (IRE)**, who certainly does not lack ability, was given a fine ride, and won this without knowing she had been in a contest. (5/1)
**1089* Hawksley Hill (IRE)**, under a 5lb penalty, is certainly not a straightforward ride. Pushed along early on and then taking quite a tug, he hung violently left under pressure in the straight and, in the end, proved no match. (9/4)
**Essayeffsee**, who looked just in need of the outing on this reappearance, was only sticking on at the one pace when hampered by Hawksley Hill. (12/1)
**1309 Gold Desire** is running well at present. (9/1)
**912* Calder King** was flat out from start to finish. (12/1)
**1072 Hanbitooh (USA)** wore blinkers for the first time, but they had no apparent effect. (8/1)

## 1419 NORTHERN RACING COLLEGE CONDITIONS STKS (2-Y.O) (Class C)
7-35 (7-37) **6f** £4,994.40 (£1,869.60: £914.80: £394.00: £177.00: £90.20) Stalls: Low GOING minus 0.22 sec per fur (GF)

SP RR SF

1115[3] **Marathon Maid** (RAFahey) **2-8-10** ACulhane(4) (mde all: hld on towards fin) — **1** 15/2 84 41
1036* **Alpine Time (IRE)** (DRLoder) **2-8-8** LDettori(6) (a chsng wnr: hrd rdn fnl f: jst failed) s.h **2** 100/30 [2] 82 39
1038* **Recondite (IRE)** (MRChannon) **2-9-1** KDarley(7) (lw: sn trckng ldrs: effrt over 2f out: sn rdn & wandered: kpt on same pce) 2 **3** 7/2 [3] 84 41
552* **Iechyd-Da (IRE)** (MBell) **2-9-1** PatEddery(1) (chsd ldrs: rdn over 2f out: styd on same pce) 2 **4** 9/2 78 35
1115[4] **Exit To Rio (CAN)** (MrsJRRamsden) **2-9-1v[1]** KFallon(3) (s.i.s: sn pushed along: hrd rdn over 1f out: nvr nr ldrs) 2½ **5** 13/2 72 29
848* **Rude Awakening** (GLewis) **2-9-1** PaulEddery(5) (lw: hld up: effrt on outside 2f out: hung lft & no imp) 3 **6** 5/2 [1] 64 21
1115[6] **Foot Battalion (IRE)** (RHollinshead) **2-8-13** TIves(2) (trckd ldrs: effrt & outpcd whn n.m.r 2f out: sn bhd) 7 **7** 16/1 43 —
(SP 123.0%) **7 Rn**

**1m 16.9** (2.60) CSF £33.09 TOTE £10.90: £3.40 £2.40 (£13.50) OWNER Marathon Thoroughbred Racing (MALTON) BRED Shadwell Estate Company Limited

**1115 Marathon Maid** is nothing to look at, but she is very tough. Making the most of her stamina, she responded to her rider's every call to hang on bravely in a very tight finish. On breeding, she will be suited by seven furlongs. (15/2)
**1036* Alpine Time (IRE)** looked fitter than at Beverley. In second place throughout, she responded to her rider's every urging but, in the end, was just held at bay. (100/30)
**1038* Recondite (IRE)**, on his toes beforehand and troublesome to load, wandered badly under pressure and could never get in a serious blow at the first two. He probably needs gelding. (7/2)
**552* Iechyd-Da (IRE)**, who looked very fit, handled the ground all right, but had his limitations exposed. (9/2)
**1115 Exit To Rio (CAN)**, who ran flat at York, wore a visor. After missing the break, he was never going the pace and seems to have lost his way at present. (13/2)
**848* Rude Awakening** was ridden with plenty of confidence but, when asked for his effort, all he did was hang left. (5/2)

## 1420 WILLIAM HILL H'CAP (0-80) (3-Y.O) (Class D)
8-05 (8-06) **1m 4y** £4,556.75 (£1,364.00: £654.50: £299.75) Stalls: Low GOING minus 0.22 sec per fur (GF)

SP RR SF

873* **Samara (IRE) (79)** (JLDunlop) **3-9-7** PatEddery(1) (trckd ldrs: shkn up to ld over 1f out: sn qcknd clr) — **1** 7/4 [1] 102+ 61
1185[2] **Smarter Charter (66)** (MrsJRRamsden) **3-8-8** KFallon(8) (lw: trckd ldrs: effrt over 2f out: kpt on appr fnl f: no ch w wnr) 5 **2** 5/2 [2] 79 38
1119[2] **Dancing Image (65)** (IABalding) **3-8-7** KDarley(2) (swtg: led tl over 1f out: one pce) ¾ **3** 7/2 [3] 77 36
994[3] **Victory Bound (USA) (75)** (MJohnston) **3-9-3** JWeaver(9) (hld up: rdn & hung bdly lft over 1f out: nvr nr ldrs) 7 **4** 9/1 73 32
1121[7] **Philistar (74)** (JMPEustace) **3-9-2** RCochrane(4) (s.i.s: bhd tl sme hdwy 2f out: n.d) 1½ **5** 16/1 69 28
860[8] **Absolute Utopia (USA) (70)** (EALDunlop) **3-8-12** WCarson(7) (chsd ldrs tl wknd wl over 1f out) 1 **6** 10/1 63 22
**Kingfisher Brave (72)** (MGMeagher) **3-9-0** JFortune(5) (chsd ldrs: rdn 4f out: lost pl 2f out) 1½ **7** 20/1 62 21
994[7] **Gool Lee Shay (USA) (62)** (RMWhitaker) **3-8-4** DaleGibson(3) (chsd ldrs: rdn along 4f out: hung lft & lost pl over 1f out) 2½ **8** 40/1 47 6
978[13] **Fervent Fan (IRE) (70)** (MBell) **3-8-12** PaulEddery(6) (hld up: effrt 3f out: n.d) 1 **9** 33/1 53 12
(SP 122.3%) **9 Rn**

**1m 44.2** (2.70) CSF £6.85 CT £13.01 TOTE £2.20: £1.30 £1.20 £1.20 (£3.10) Trio £2.40 OWNER Aylesfield Farms Stud (ARUNDEL) BRED Mount Coote Stud

**873* Samara (IRE)**, from a 9lb higher mark, is nothing to look at and shows plenty of knee-action, but she certainly has an engine. After travelling best throughout, she quickened clear to score in tremendous style. The Handicapper will not forget this. (7/4)
**1185 Smarter Charter**, much better suited by this track, ran well, but the winner was in a different league. (5/2)
**1119 Dancing Image**, who sweated up beforehand, was taken to post quietly. Racing keenly, he had no answer when the winner swept by. (7/2)
**994 Victory Bound (USA)** wore a tongue-strap, and again hung badly under pressure. He presumably has a problem. (9/1)
**Philistar** had plenty to do at the weights. (16/1)
**703 Absolute Utopia (USA)**, having his first outing in handicap company, wore a tongue-strap, and found little under pressure. (10/1)

## 1421 MICK MCCOY MEMORIAL H'CAP (0-70) (3-Y.O+) (Class E)
8-35 (8-36) **1m 4f 8y** £3,425.10 (£1,024.80: £491.40: £224.70) Stalls: Low GOING minus 0.22 sec per fur (GF)

SP RR SF

1325* **Strategic Ploy (64)** (MrsJRRamsden) **3-8-5** 5x KFallon(11) (hld up: gd hdwy 3f out: swtchd outside over 1f out: led 1f out: rdn out) — **1** 5/2 [1] 75 40
**Welsh Mill (IRE) (64)** (MrsMReveley) **7-9-8** KDarley(16) (hld up: effrt over 3f out: styd on appr fnl f: nvr able to chal) 1½ **2** 10/1 73 55

| | | | | SP | RR | SF |
|---|---|---|---|---|---|---|
| 1088[5] | **Carlton Express (IRE) (41)** (JLEyre) **6-7-13** GBardwell(14) (a in tch: sn pushed along: hdwy to ld over 1f out: sn hdd & nt qckn) | 1½ | **3** | 12/1 | 48 | 30 |
| | **Junior Ben (IRE) (55)** (PHowling) **4-8-13** RCochrane(7) (hld up & bhd: effrt over 3f out: one pce fnl 2f) | 7 | **4** | 20/1 | 53 | 35 |
| | **Reimei (67)** (RAkehurst) **7-9-11** SSanders(2) (w ldrs: one pce appr fnl f) | ¾ | **5** | 6/1[3] | 64 | 46 |
| 1109[4] | **Lord Hastie (USA) (67)** (CWThornton) **8-9-8**(3) OPears(1) (led tl over 1f out: wknd fnl f) | 1½ | **6** | 100/30[2] | 62 | 44 |
| | **Redstella (USA) (67)** (RMWhitaker) **7-9-4**(7) PFredericks(9) (chsd ldrs: one pce fnl 2f) | 2 | **7** | 33/1 | 59 | 41 |
| 816[8] | **Slapy Dam (61)** (JMackie) **4-9-0**(5) PFessey(5) (bhd tl sme late hdwy) | ¾ | **8** | 20/1 | 52 | 34 |
| 1070[6] | **Hotspur Street (59)** (MWEasterby) **4-8-12**(5) GParkin(3) (in tch: effrt over 2f out: no imp) | ½ | **9** | 16/1 | 49 | 31 |
| | **Sharp Sensation (38)** (WLBarker) **6-7-3**(7) JBramhill(15) (in tch: drvn along 4f out: lost pl over 2f out) | ½ | **10** | 25/1 | 28 | 10 |
| 771[4] | **Admirals Secret (USA) (63)** (CFWall) **7-9-7** WLord(13) (in tch: effrt over 2f out: sn wknd) | 7 | **11** | 8/1 | 43 | 25 |
| 993[6] | **Tulu (69)** (MrsJRRamsden) **5-9-13** MDeering(12) (b: in tch tl wknd qckly over 2f out) | 7 | **12** | 11/1 | 40 | 22 |
| *268[8]* | **Hong Kong Designer (48)** (MissJFCraze) **4-8-6** NConnorton(10) (trckd ldrs tl lost pl over 2f out) | 21 | **13** | 40/1 | — | — |
| | **Soba Up (69)** (TJEtherington) **6-9-13** ACulhane(4) (bit bkwd: prom: hmpd & lost pl 7f out: bhd fnl 4f) | 7 | **14** | 20/1 | 3 | — |
| 734[7] | **Four Lane Flyer (41)** (EJAlston) **4-7-13** JFanning(8) (swtg: plld hrd: t.o 4f out) | 13 | **15** | 40/1 | — | — |

(SP 134.0%) **15 Rn**

**2m 39.3** (5.00) CSF £29.48 CT £254.16 TOTE £3.30: £1.90 £3.40 £2.40 (£28.60) Trio £159.40 OWNER Mrs H. M. Carr (THIRSK) BRED Miss M. Sheriffe and Exors of the late A. J. Tree
LONG HANDICAP Sharp Sensation 7-7
WEIGHT FOR AGE 3yo-17lb
**1325* Strategic Ploy**, given a confident ride, worked her way to the outside once in line for home and, showing a nice turn of foot, scored in decisive fashion. Trainer and jockey could probably walk on water here. (5/2)
**Welsh Mill (IRE)**, who has been in good heart over hurdles, has been fired. Coming from off the pace, he stuck on to finish clear second best, but was never going to seriously trouble the winner. He should certainly find a race or two on the Flat. (10/1)
**1088 Carlton Express (IRE)**, stepping up in distance, finished clear of the remainder. (12/1)
**Junior Ben (IRE)** is still a maiden. (20/1)
**Reimei** was made to look very one-paced. (6/1)
**1109 Lord Hastie (USA)** seemed to set a very strong pace, and was out on his legs coming to the final furlong. (100/30: op 6/1)

## 1422 RACING AND THOROUGHBRED BREEDING TRAINING BOARD MAIDEN STKS (3-Y.O) (Class D)
9-05 (9-06) **6f** £3,728.75 (£1,130.00: £552.50: £263.75) Stalls: Low GOING minus 0.22 sec per fur (GF)

| | | | | SP | RR | SF |
|---|---|---|---|---|---|---|
| 934[3] | **Mutadarra (IRE) (88)** (RWArmstrong) **3-9-0** WCarson(13) (chsd ldrs: lft in ld over 1f out: hung lft: jst hld on) | — | **1** | 8/11[1] | 86 | 37 |
| | **Old Roma (IRE)** (JohnBerry) **3-8-9** KFallon(6) (leggy: unf: s.i.s: sn wl bhd: hdwy 2f out: styd on strly ins fnl f: fin fast) | hd | **2** | 25/1 | 81 | 32 |
| 962[5] | **Look Who's Calling (IRE) (70)** (BAMcMahon) **3-9-0** SSanders(12) (lw: w ldrs: led over 2f out tl hung violently rt over 1f out: hrd rdn & styd on towards fin) | ¾ | **3** | 4/1[2] | 84 | 35 |
| 783[9] | **Wee Hope (USA) (87)** (MRStoute) **3-9-0** DeanMcKeown(8) (lw: trckd ldrs: effrt 2f out: styd on same pce) | 3 | **4** | 6/1[3] | 76 | 27 |
| 1171[6] | **Stoney End (USA)** (MRChannon) **3-9-0** KDarley(7) (led tl over 2f out: wknd over 1f out) | s.h | **5** | 12/1 | 76 | 27 |
| | **Petarina** (MissJFCraze) **3-8-9** RCochrane(5) (leggy: unf: chsd ldrs: wknd appr fnl f: eased towards fin) | 5 | **6** | 33/1 | 57 | 8 |
| 921[11] | **Desert Skimmer (USA)** (MBell) **3-8-9** PaulEddery(4) (in tch: outpcd over 2f out: n.d after) | 4 | **7** | 16/1 | 47 | — |
| 964[9] | **In The Highlands** (DJSCosgrove) **3-8-2**(7) MNutter(3) (b: sn outpcd: nvr nr ldrs) | 2 | **8** | 16/1 | 41 | — |
| 1033[10] | **Goldrill** (MissSEHall) **3-9-0** NConnorton(11) (sn outpcd: bhd fr ½-wy) | nk | **9** | 40/1 | 46 | — |
| 1033[8] | **Ameliajill** (JGMO'Shea) **3-8-9** JFanning(10) (in tch: rdn ½-way: sn outpcd) | 1½ | **10** | 33/1 | 37 | — |
| 934[13] | **Rocky Stream** (RMWhitaker) **3-8-9** ACulhane(1) (a outpcd & bhd) | nk | **11** | 50/1 | 36 | — |
| | **Present 'n Correct** (CBBBooth) **3-9-0** MBirch(2) (sn bhd & pushed along) | s.h | **12** | 50/1 | 41 | — |
| | **Clancassie** (EJAlston) **3-8-9** SDWilliams(9) (tall: s.i.s: rn green & wl bhd fr ½-wy) | 18 | **13** | 33/1 | — | — |

(SP 130.7%) **13 Rn**

**1m 17.5** (3.20) CSF £22.91 TOTE £1.80: £1.60 £2.90 £1.60 (£12.60) Trio £45.50 OWNER Mr Hamdan Al Maktoum (NEWMARKET) BRED Mrs T. V. Ryan
**934 Mutadarra (IRE)** looked very hard trained. Hanging left under pressure, in the end the post came just in time. (8/11)
**Old Roma (IRE)**, who is nothing much to look at, is bred for stamina on her sire's side, and changed hands cheaply. After missing the break, she was soon a remote last but, picking up ground in tremendous style in the straight, finished with a flourish. She would have made it in two more strides, and connections will be hoping this was not a fluke. (25/1)
**962 Look Who's Calling (IRE)**, who looked in tremendous shape, took it up going in to the turn but then hung violently right and swerved right across to end up under the stands'-side rail. Sticking on under strong pressure, in the end he was just held. He ran wide at Catterick two outings ago and clearly has a steering problem but, if he can be sorted out, he will certainly win handicaps from a mark of only 70. (4/1: op 7/1)
**783 Wee Hope (USA)**, rated 87 on his two-year-old form, looked well and travelled strongly but, at the business end, could pull out little. It is hard to know what distance will suit him best. (6/1: op 5/2)
**1171 Stoney End (USA)**, a keen-going type, faded in the final furlong. (12/1: op 8/1)

T/Plpt: £9.30 (2,035.75 Tckts). T/Qdpt: £5.60 (196.36 Tckts). WG

# 0990-DONCASTER (L-H) (Good, Rnd crse Good to firm patches)
## Saturday May 25th
WEATHER: showers WIND: fresh against

## 1423 RACING SCHOOLS FURNITURE FACTORS APPRENTICE H'CAP (0-70) (4-Y.O+) (Class F)
2-20 (2-23) **7f** £2,697.50 (£760.00: £372.50) Stalls: High GOING: 0.12 sec per fur (G)

| | | | | SP | RR | SF |
|---|---|---|---|---|---|---|
| *778[2]* | **Johnnie the Joker (46)** (JPLeigh) **5-8-5b** PFessey(15) (b: disp ld to ½-wy: sn outpcd: styd on appr fnl f: led wl ins fnl f) | — | **1** | 9/1[3] | 54 | 36 |
| 718[2] | **Ochos Rios (IRE) (58)** (BSRothwell) **5-9-3** SCopp(10) (hdwy u.p over 2f out: led ins fnl f: hrd drvn, hdd & nt qckn towards fin) | s.h | **2** | 7/1[2] | 66 | 48 |
| 991[3] | **Kid Ory (63)** (PCalver) **5-9-8** DGriffiths(1) (chsd ldrs: led wl over 1f out tl ins fnl f: no ex) | ¾ | **3** | 9/2[1] | 69 | 51 |
| 1157[10] | **It's Academic (65)** (MrsJRRamsden) **4-9-6**(4) AEddery(6) (lw: hdwy ½-wy: chsng ldrs appr fnl f: kpt on) | 2 | **4** | 10/1 | 67 | 49 |
| 508[9] | **Phase One (IRE) (52)** (JLEyre) **6-8-11** SDrowne(13) (in tch: rdn over 2f out: styd on towards fin) | nk | **5** | 16/1 | 53 | 35 |

| | | | | SP | RR | SF |
|---|---|---|---|---|---|---|
| $1186^{21}$ | **White Sorrel (59)** (AHarrison) **5-9-4** GMilligan(12) (prom: effrt over 2f out: kpt on one pce) | nk | **6** | 20/1 | 59 | 41 |
| $981^{13}$ | **Cats Bottom (58)** (AGNewcombe) **4-9-3** RPainter(7) (squeezed out s: bhd tl styd on fnl 2f) | 1¼ | **7** | 14/1 | 55 | 37 |
| $1069^{4}$ | **Gymcrak Flyer (62)** (GHolmes) **5-9-7** RHavlin(2) (bhd: hdwy 3f out: sn prom: one pce appr fnl f) | 1 | **8** | 9/2 $^{1}$ | 57 | 39 |
| $1088^{4}$ | **Parliament Piece (65)** (DNicholls) **10-9-6**$^{(4)}$ CarolDavison(5) (lw: sn bhd: sme late hdwy) | 1¾ | **9** | 10/1 | 56 | 38 |
| $1157^{6}$ | **Aquado (48)** (SRBowring) **7-8-7b** CTeague(16) (lw: disp ld to ½-wy: grad wknd) | ¾ | **10** | 12/1 | 37 | 19 |
| $1020^{3}$ | **Craigie Boy (54)** (NBycroft) **6-8-13b** IonaWands(3) (s.i.s: hdwy ½-wy: n.d) | nk | **11** | 14/1 | 43 | 25 |
| $1040^{4}$ | **Mu-Arrik (44)** (GROldroyd) **8-7-13v**$^{(4)}$ RFfrench(11) (disp ld to ½-wy: wknd 2f out) | 3½ | **12** | 12/1 | 25 | 7 |
| *$1085^{6}$* | **Irchester Lass (40)** (SRBowring) **4-7-9b**$^{(4)}$ PDoe(14) (in tch tl outpcd fnl 3f) | 1¼ | **13** | 16/1 | 18 | — |
| $991^{17}$ | **Arc Lamp (41)** (JAGlover) **10-7-6**$^{(8)}$ TThomas(4) (prom: effrt 3f out: wknd fnl 2f) | ¾ | **14** | 20/1 | 17 | — |
| $846^{12}$ | **Rise Up Singing (55)** (WJMusson) **8-8-10b**$^{(4)}$ JWilkinson(9) (bmpd s: n.d) | s.h | **15** | 16/1 | 31 | 13 |
| $718^{14}$ | **Souperficial (53)** (JAGlover) **5-8-8v**$^{(4)}$ DSweeney(8) (disp ld tl led ½-wy: hdd & wknd wl over 1f out) | 1 | **16** | 14/1 | 27 | 9 |
| | | | | (SP 139.6%) | **16 Rn** | |

**1m 28.95** (5.35) CSF £74.61 CT £319.01 TOTE £7.50: £1.50 £2.40 £2.20 £2.40 (£33.90) Trio £47.80 OWNER Miss M. Carrington-Smith (GAINSBOROUGH) BRED Miss M. Carrington-Smith

**778 Johnnie the Joker** last won on turf three years ago and it is also two years since he won on the All-Weather, but he had been running well of late and thoroughly deserved this game success. (9/1)
**718 Ochos Rios (IRE)** was given plenty of help from the saddle here and responded well, but just failed to last out. (7/1)
**991 Kid Ory**, from a yard that has not struck form as yet, ran well but just failed to get home on this occasion, and is quite well handicapped at present. (9/2)
**802 It's Academic** looked quite dangerous approaching the final furlong, but then failed to quicken enough. (10/1)
**Phase One (IRE)** was keeping on at the end here, but is not one to trust entirely. (16/1)
**718 White Sorrel** ran reasonably but is better on the All-Weather. (20/1)
**Cats Bottom** was a long way behind until running on when it was all too late to show her first signs of form for a while. (14/1)
**1157 Aquado** (12/1: op 8/1)

## 1424 E.B.F. ZETLAND MAIDEN STKS (2-Y.O) (Class D)

2-50 (2-51) **6f** £3,655.00 (£1,090.00: £520.00: £235.00) Stalls: High GOING: 0.12 sec per fur (G)

| | | | | SP | RR | SF |
|---|---|---|---|---|---|---|
| | **Hello (IRE)** (JLDunlop) **2-9-0** WRyan(7) (leggy: scope: lw: dwlt: swtchd & hdwy over 2f out: led ins fnl f: r.o) | — | **1** | 100/30 $^{1}$ | 75+ | 37 |
| $841^{3}$ | **Mantles Prince** (GLewis) **2-9-0** TIves(2) (unruly s: cl up: rdn 2f out: kpt on wl) | 2½ | **2** | 100/30 $^{1}$ | 68 | 30 |
| | **Baritone** (JWWatts) **2-9-0** NConnorton(5) (cmpt: lw: prom: outpcd over 2f out: hdwy over 1f out: styd on wl towards fin) | nk | **3** | 9/2 $^{3}$ | 68+ | 30 |
| $1169^{2}$ | **Tough Leader** (BHanbury) **2-8-11**$^{(3)}$ JStack(8) (cl up: led over 2f out tl ins fnl f: no ex) | nk | **4** | 7/2 $^{2}$ | 67 | 29 |
| | **Blonde Rock** (MRChannon) **2-8-4**$^{(5)}$ PPMurphy(1) (leggy: led tl over 2f out: grad wknd) | 4 | **5** | 10/1 | 51 | 13 |
| $1197^{9}$ | **Ninth Symphony** (PCHaslam) **2-9-0** LCharnock(6) (spd 3½f: sn btn) | 2 | **6** | 25/1 | 51 | 13 |
| | **Mac's Delight** (EALDunlop) **2-9-0** DHarrison(3) (cmpt: chsd ldrs tl rdn & btn 2f out) | 5 | **7** | 8/1 | 37 | — |
| $924^{7}$ | **Protaras Bay** (TTClement) **2-9-0** JQuinn(9) (outpcd & bhd fr ½-wy) | ½ | **8** | 50/1 | 36 | — |
| | **Wild City (USA)** (BHanbury) **2-8-9**$^{(5)}$ MHenry(4) (str: dwlt: hdwy u.p ½-wy: sn wknd) | 7 | **9** | 8/1 | 17 | — |
| | | | | (SP 123.7%) | **9 Rn** | |

**1m 16.07** (5.07) CSF £15.32 TOTE £4.10: £1.70 £2.00 £2.10 (£9.70) Trio £37.20 OWNER Mr Philip Wroughton (ARUNDEL) BRED H Volz

**Hello (IRE)** looked fit for his debut here and, coming from off the pace, won in most determined style. (100/30)
**841 Mantles Prince** was awkward at the stalls, but then ran a decent race. By the way he kept responding to pressure, his turn will come. (100/30)
**Baritone** reared up in the stalls before the start and then ran green halfway through the race but, after having to switch for a clear run, he finished in a manner that left the impression that better now looks likely. (9/2)
**1169 Tough Leader** tried to make his experience tell from halfway but was always inclined to hang when the pressure was seriously on, which spoilt his chances. (7/2)
**Blonde Rock** showed plenty of speed and this experience should stand her in good stead. (10/1)
**Ninth Symphony** showed something this time and is obviously learning. (25/1)

## 1425 MERLIN LAND ROVER H'CAP (0-100) (3-Y.O+) (Class C)

3-20 (3-20) **7f** £7,440.00 (£2,220.00: £1,060.00: £480.00) Stalls: High GOING: 0.12 sec per fur (G)

| | | | | SP | RR | SF |
|---|---|---|---|---|---|---|
| | **Hi Nod (96)** (MJCamacho) **6-10-0** LCharnock(1) (stdd s: hdwy over 2f out: r.o wl fnl f to ld cl home) | — | **1** | 11/1 | 105 | 66 |
| $1018^{6}$ | **Pengamon (80)** (HJCollingridge) **4-8-12** JQuinn(5) (a chsng ldrs: effrt 2f out: ev ch ins fnl f: r.o) | ½ | **2** | 10/1 | 88 | 49 |
| $1186^{4}$ | **Fame Again (78)** (MrsJRRamsden) **4-8-10** KFallon(9) (lw: hld up: hdwy over 2f out: rdn to ld ins fnl f: no ex & hdd towards fin) | s.h | **3** | 4/1 $^{2}$ | 86 | 47 |
| $876^{8}$ | **Delta Soleil (USA) (90)** (PWHarris) **4-9-8** WRyan(2) (trckd ldrs: led 2f out tl ins fnl f: sn btn) | 1¾ | **4** | 5/1 $^{3}$ | 94 | 55 |
| $991^{2}$ | **Sycamore Lodge (IRE) (68)** (MrsJRRamsden) **5-7-9**$^{(5)}$ MHenry(3) (s.i.s: hdwy 2f out: styng on whn nt clr run wl ins fnl f) | 1 | **5** | 5/1 $^{3}$ | 70 | 31 |
| $589^{17}$ | **Tawafij (USA) (80)** (TDyer) **7-8-9**$^{(3)}$ SDrowne(6) (hld up & bhd: hdwy 2f out: styd on towards fin) | ½ | **6** | 14/1 | 80 | 41 |
| $1322^{4}$ | **Night Wink (USA) (78)** (DNicholls) **4-8-10** AlexGreaves(7) (led 2½f: cl up: led 2½f out: hdd 2f out: sn outpcd) | 2½ | **7** | 9/1 | 73 | 34 |
| $935^{9}$ | **Somerton Boy (IRE) (71)** (PCalver) **6-8-3** NCarlisle(4) (in tch: effrt over 2f out: wknd over 1f out) | 1¼ | **8** | 12/1 | 63 | 24 |
| $956^{10}$ | **Keston Pond (IRE) (72)** (MrsVAAconley) **6-8-4** MDeering(8) (bit bkwd: chsd ldrs tl wknd fnl 2f) | 3½ | **9** | 25/1 | 56 | 17 |
| 610* | **Super Benz (80)** (JLEyre) **10-8-12** RLappin(10) (b: plld hrd: led after 2½f tl over 2f out: sn btn) | 5 | **10** | 5/2 $^{1}$ | 52 | 13 |
| | | | | (SP 127.5%) | **10 Rn** | |

**1m 28.25** (4.65) CSF £111.00 CT £491.37 TOTE £10.10: £2.80 £2.60 £1.80 (£55.30) Trio £109.50 OWNER Mr Brian Nordan (MALTON) BRED B. Nordan

OFFICIAL EXPLANATION **Super Benz: was found to be lame on returning home.**

**Hi Nod** won this muddling race off his highest ever mark and showed plenty of courage to do so. (11/1)
**1018 Pengamon** is in good form and keeps running well. He deserves a change of luck. (10/1)
**1186 Fame Again** has had so many bad luck stories in the past, but this time there were no real excuses apart from the fact she just was not good enough. (4/1)
**455 Delta Soleil (USA)** was always doing too much here and needed a much stronger pace. (5/1)
**991 Sycamore Lodge (IRE)** runs when he feels like it and, as yet this season, has never done quite enough. (5/1)
**Tawafij (USA)**, from an out-of-form yard, found the pace too slow but still ran well, and is worth keeping in mind. (14/1)
**1322 Night Wink (USA)** is just beginning to show signs of coming to form. (9/1)
**610* Super Benz**, off the track for over six weeks, came back far too fresh and ran himself into the ground a long way from home. (5/2: op 9/2)

## 1426 ROSEHILL H'CAP (0-85) (3-Y.O+) (Class D)
3-50 (3-52) **1m 4f** £4,503.00 (£1,344.00: £642.00: £291.00) Stalls: Low GOING: 0.12 sec per fur (G)

| | | | | SP | RR | SF |
|---|---|---|---|---|---|---|
| 941* | **Beauchamp Jade (84)** (HCandy) **4-9-13** CRutter(3) (lw: hld up: effrt 3f out: styd on u.p to ld wl ins fnl f) | — | 1 | 7/4 1 | 92 | 68 |
| 682 9 | **Jermyn Street (USA) (72)** (MrsJCecil) **5-8-10**(5) MHenry(6) (cl up: led over 1f out tl hdd & no ex wl ins fnl f) | 1¼ | 2 | 9/1 | 78 | 54 |
| 1145 11 | **Meghdoot (69)** (HJCollingridge) **4-8-12** JQuinn(1) (led: rdn 3f out: hdd over 1f out: sn btn) | 2 | 3 | 7/1 | 73 | 49 |
| 691 11 | **Raffles Rooster (61)** (AGNewcombe) **4-8-1**(3)ow1 SDrowne(2) (chsd ldr: ev ch 3f out: wknd appr fnl f) | 4 | 4 | 7/2 3 | 59 | 34 |
| 1109* | **Remaadi Sun (79)** (MDIUsher) **4-9-8** RStreet(5) (b.hind: hld up & bhd: effrt & swtchd 3f out: no imp) | 5 | 5 | 2/1 2 | 71 | 47 |
| 825 9 | **Blackpatch Hill (78)** (NTinkler) **7-9-7** KimTinkler(4) (hld up: effrt appr st: rdn & btn over 3f out) | 6 | 6 | 25/1 | 62 | 38 |
| | | | | (SP 118.3%) | | **6 Rn** |

**2m 37.84** (7.84) CSF £16.21 TOTE £2.00: £1.30 £2.70 (£8.50) OWNER Mr E. Penser (WANTAGE) BRED E. Penser

**941* Beauchamp Jade** needs to come from behind and, the way the race was run here, she had a lot to do, but she proved to be a real battler and got up late on. (7/4)

**Jermyn Street (USA)** was always in a good position and did his best to pinch it approaching the final furlong, but the winner proved just too strong. (9/1: 6/1-10/1)

**Meghdoot** set a steady pace and had really stepped on the gas in the straight but, once collared approaching the final furlong, she had to admit defeat. She is coming to hand. (7/1)

**Raffles Rooster**, stepped up in trip, ran his best race so far until crying enough approaching the final furlong. (7/2: 5/1-3/1)

**1109* Remaadi Sun** was completely unsuited by the small field and the steady pace and never took an interest. This is best ignored. (2/1)

**Blackpatch Hill** showed little once off the bit turning for home. (25/1)

## 1427 NAPOLEONS CASINO CONDITIONS STKS (3-Y.O) (Class B)
4-20 (4-21) **1m 2f 60y** £8,067.50 (£2,982.50: £1,428.75: £581.25: £228.13: £86.87) Stalls: Low GOING: 0.12 sec per fur (G)

| | | | | SP | RR | SF |
|---|---|---|---|---|---|---|
| 684* | **Farasan (IRE)** (HRACecil) **3-9-0** JTate(4) (a.p: led over 3f out: r.o strly) | — | 1 | 4/1 3 | 109+ | 67 |
| 830 8 | **South Salem (USA) (112)** (DRLoder) **3-9-2** DHarrison(3) (lw: outpcd 4f out: hdwy 2f out: edgd lft: styd on towards fin: no ch w wnr) | 8 | 2 | 10/1 | 99 | 57 |
| 942 2 | **Kammtarra (USA)** (SbinSuroor) **3-8-11** DeanMcKeown(8) (lw: plld hrd: in tch: effrt 4f out: hrd rdn 3f out: one pce) | s.h | 3 | 9/4 1 | 94 | 52 |
| 932* | **Smart Play (USA)** (MrsJCecil) **3-9-0** TIves(1) (lw: chsd ldrs: rdn 4f out: r.o one pce) | ¾ | 4 | 14/1 | 95 | 53 |
| | **Germano** (GWragg) **3-9-0** JQuinn(7) (prom: outpcd over 3f out: no imp after) | nk | 5 | 13/2 | 95 | 53 |
| 960 4 | **Yarob (IRE) (100)** (HThomsonJones) **3-9-0** KFallon(6) (bhd: hdwy 3f out: nt clr run over 1f out: nvr able to chal) | 1½ | 6 | 10/1 | 93 | 51 |
| 974* | **Generosus (FR)** (HRACecil) **3-9-0** WRyan(2) (lw: led tl hdd over 3f out: wknd 2f out) | 6 | 7 | 3/1 2 | 83 | 41 |
| 894* | **Manaloj (USA)** (PTWalwyn) **3-9-0** LCharnock(5) (chsd ldr tl wknd fnl 3f) | 14 | 8 | 12/1 | 61 | 19 |
| | | | | (SP 121.6%) | | **8 Rn** |

**2m 12.15** (5.15) CSF £40.10 TOTE £5.50: £1.80 £2.00 £1.20 (£23.10) OWNER Prince A A Faisal (NEWMARKET) BRED Yeomanstown Lodge Stud

**684* Farasan (IRE)** was again apparently the stable's second string but again he won, and this time in real style. He will surely make his trainer sit up and take notice as he is beginning to look extremely useful. (4/1)

**South Salem (USA)** is taking time to come to himself this year and was always inclined to hang left here but, judging by the way he stayed on, he is now getting it together. He never had a hope with the easy winner though. (10/1)

**942 Kammtarra (USA)** proved a handful in the paddock and on the way to post. In the race he spoiled any chance he had by pulling hard and refusing to settle early on. He obviously has the ability but, as yet, his temperament is getting the better of him. (9/4)

**932* Smart Play (USA)**, dropping back in distance, had his limitations exposed and this trip is surely short of his best. (14/1)

**Germano** has not been out for seven months and obviously needed this. He was left wanting for speed once the tempo increased in the last half-mile. (13/2)

**960 Yarob (IRE)**, despite the step up in trip, found the early pace too strong and again ran into trouble when staying on. (10/1)

**974* Generosus (FR)** was a big disappointment here, dropping out in the straight after setting a strong gallop. (3/1)

## 1428 HAREWOOD RATED STKS H'CAP (0-95) (4-Y.O+) (Class C)
4-50 (4-50) **2m 110y** £5,051.84 (£1,866.56: £893.28: £362.40: £141.20: £52.72) Stalls: Low GOING: 0.12 sec per fur (G)

| | | | | SP | RR | SF |
|---|---|---|---|---|---|---|
| | **Snow Princess (IRE) (81)** (LordHuntingdon) **4-8-10** DHarrison(7) (lw: pushed along ½-wy: hdwy 4f out: led appr fnl f: styd on wl) | — | 1 | 9/4 2 | 97 | 54 |
| | **Latahaab (USA) (86)** (RAkehurst) **5-9-3** TIves(3) (trckd ldrs: chal 4f out: led wl over 2f out tl appr fnl f: kpt on) | 4 | 2 | 7/1 | 98 | 57 |
| 1005 8 | **Noufari (FR) (78)** (RHollinshead) **5-8-9** KFallon(1) (hld up: effrt 3f out: styd on fnl f: nvr able to chal) | 2 | 3 | 10/1 | 88 | 47 |
| 1005 3 | **Corradini (92)** (HRACecil) **4-9-7** WRyan(6) (in tch: hdwy ½-wy: led over 4f out: sn rdn: hdd wl over 2f out: one pce) | 1½ | 4 | 2/1 1 | 101 | 58 |
| 1116 9 | **Highflying (85)** (GMMoore) **10-9-2** JTate(5) (lw: hld up: effrt 4f out: sn outpcd) | 8 | 5 | 20/1 | 86 | 45 |
| 1005 7 | **Blaze Away (USA) (78)** (IABalding) **5-8-4**(5) DGriffiths(2) (cl up tl outpcd 6f out: no imp after) | 1 | 6 | 6/1 3 | 78 | 37 |
| | **High Pyrenees (75)** (RAllan) **4-8-4** JQuinn(4) (b: trckd ldrs tl wknd fnl 3f) | 2 | 7 | 14/1 | 73 | 30 |
| 1109 9 | **Invest Wisely (87)** (JMPEustace) **4-9-2** MTebbutt(8) (led tl hdd over 4f out: sn wknd) | 5 | 8 | 6/1 3 | 80 | 37 |
| | | | | (SP 125.7%) | | **8 Rn** |

**3m 39.38** (10.38) CSF £18.96 CT £128.82 TOTE £4.20: £1.40 £2.20 £2.40 (£17.30) OWNER Lord Weinstock & The Hon Simon Weinstock (WEST ILSLEY) BRED Ballymacoll Stud Co

WEIGHT FOR AGE 4yo-2lb

**Snow Princess (IRE)**, taking a big step up in trip, got it particularly well. She looks one to follow again this year, and should pick up a top-class staying handicap before long. (9/4)

**Latahaab (USA)** ran a sound first race of the season but found the winner far too strong in the closing stages. He looks in good heart again this season. (7/1)

**837 Noufari (FR)** has only ever won on sand but is still a useful performer on turf and runs consistently in marathon events, especially when they are run at a strong pace. (10/1)

**1005 Corradini** stepped the pace up once into the home straight but, when the pressure was on, he found little and was going nowhere in the last three furlongs. (2/1)

**Highflying** looks well in himself and ran a deal better this time, but he was still beaten a long way from home. (20/1)

**1005 Blaze Away (USA)** never had enough use made of him here and, after getting outpaced approaching the straight, had no further chance. (6/1)
**High Pyrenees**, having his first run for almost a year, looked in need of it and ran reasonably until blowing up in the last half-mile. (14/1)
**Invest Wisely** looked very lean beforehand and disappointed, dropping out once passed early in the straight. (6/1)

## 1429 RIFLE BUTTS MEDIAN AUCTION MAIDEN STKS (3-Y.O) (Class E)
5-20 (5-20) **5f** £3,028.00 (£904.00: £432.00: £196.00) Stalls: High GOING: 0.12 sec per fur (G)

| | | | Pos | SP | RR | SF |
|---|---|---|---|---|---|---|
| 1028[11] | **Chalice (66)** (JBalding) **3-8-2**(7) JEdmunds(2) (bhd: hdwy 2f out: styd on to ld wl ins fnl f) | — | 1 | 10/1 | 70 | 41 |
| | **Longwick Lad** (WRMuir) **3-9-0** Jean-PierreLopez(1) (wnt lft s: sn trckng ldrs: led over 1f out tl wl ins fnl f: kpt on) | ¾ | 2 | 10/1 | 73 | 44 |
| 1033[4] | **Matam** (MWEasterby) **3-8-4**(5) GParkin(9) (lw: s.i.s: hdwy & swtchd 2f out: hrd rdn fnl f: nvr able to chal) | 1½ | 3 | 7/2[2] | 63 | 34 |
| | **Superfrills (45)** (MissLCSiddall) **3-8-9** DeanMcKeown(8) (led tl hdd & wknd over 1f out) | 2 | 4 | 20/1 | 56 | 27 |
| 783[8] | **Madrina** (JBerry) **3-8-9** LCharnock(6) (cl up tl rdn & btn appr fnl f) | nk | 5 | 6/1 | 55 | 26 |
| | **Gymcrak Gem (IRE)** (GHolmes) **3-8-9** KFallon(4) (b.hind: plld hrd: prom tl outpcd appr fnl f) | 2 | 6 | 4/1[3] | 49 | 20 |
| 1033[6] | **Nattier** (SirMarkPrescott) **3-8-9** CNutter(3) (spd over 3f) | nk | 7 | 7/2[2] | 48 | 19 |
| | **Sotonian (HOL)** (MrsLStubbs) **3-9-0** MMcAndrew(5) (b.hind: shkn up ½-wy: nvr trbld ldrs) | 1½ | 8 | 20/1 | 48 | 19 |
| 949[6] | **Arch Enemy (IRE)** (MRChannon) **3-9-0** JQuinn(7) (chsd ldrs to ½-wy: sn wknd) | 2½ | 9 | 3/1[1] | 40 | 11 |

(SP 131.4%) **9 Rn**

**62.08 secs** (3.68) CSF £102.75 TOTE £12.80: £1.90 £2.40 £2.10 (£90.90) Trio £76.30 OWNER Mrs J. T. Balding (DONCASTER) BRED Pinfold Stud and Farms Ltd
**779 Chalice**, well ridden, came from off the pace to score convincingly. (10/1)
**Longwick Lad**, having his first outing, ran green early on but then went really well and should be all the better for it. (10/1)
**1033 Matam** gave away valuable ground at the start but then had to switch round the whole field to get a run, and failed to maintain the effort in the final furlong. She certainly has the ability to win a race or two. (7/2)
**Superfrills**, having her first race of the season, made it until running out of petrol in the last furlong. (20/1)
**Madrina** ran her best race to date and would seem to be gradually improving. (6/1)
**Gymcrak Gem (IRE)**, very fresh for this first effort of the season, had run herself out with over a furlong to go. (4/1)

T/Plpt: £118.80 (193.21 Tckts). T/Qdpt: £35.20 (35.53 Tckts). AA

# 1404-HAYDOCK (L-H) (Good to soft)
## Saturday May 25th
WEATHER: cloudy WIND: fresh against

## 1430 BE FRIENDLY H'CAP (0-90) (3-Y.O+) (Class C)
2-00 (2-00) **5f** £5,400.50 (£1,634.00: £797.00: £378.50) Stalls: High GOING: 0.37 sec per fur (GS)

| | | | Pos | SP | RR | SF |
|---|---|---|---|---|---|---|
| 1178[14] | **Sailormaite (78)** (SRBowring) **5-9-4b** DeanMcKeown(9) (chsd ldrs: led wl ins fnl f: pushed clr) | — | 1 | 12/1 | 87 | 60 |
| 931[2] | **Sing With the Band (60)** (BAMcMahon) **5-8-0**ow2 GCarter(10) (lw: trckd ldrs: kpt on u.p ins fnl f) | 2½ | 2 | 13/2[3] | 61 | 32 |
| 1161* | **Tuscan Dawn (78)** (JBerry) **6-8-13**(5) PRoberts(11) (lw: set str pce tl hdd & no ex wl ins fnl f) | hd | 3 | 4/1[1] | 79 | 52 |
| 1186[12] | **Tedburrow (82)** (MrsAMNaughton) **4-9-8** PaulEddery(3) (hdwy 2f out: rdn & r.o wl fnl f) | s.h | 4 | 16/1 | 83 | 56 |
| 735[16] | **Surprise Mission (75)** (RMWhitaker) **4-9-1** ACulhane(8) (b: bit bkwd: swtchd rt sn after s: trckd ldrs: n.m.r ent fnl f: one pce) | 1¼ | 5 | 13/2[3] | 72 | 45 |
| 1171[10] | **Glorious Aragon (79)** (RFJohnsonHoughton) **4-9-5** RHills(4) (sn drvn along: nvr on terms) | ¾ | 6 | 9/1 | 73 | 46 |
| 610[24] | **Musical Season (88)** (TDBarron) **4-10-0** JFortune(6) (lw: swtchd rt & hdwy over 1f out: sn rdn: nt pce to chal) | ½ | 7 | 16/1 | 81 | 54 |
| 951[7] | **La Suquet (71)** (NTinkler) **4-8-11** MBirch(5) (prom over 3f) | 2½ | 8 | 16/1 | 56 | 29 |
| 711[10] | **Lord High Admiral (CAN) (84)** (MJHeaton-Ellis) **8-9-10v** RPerham(7) (lw: chsd ldr over 3f: wknd qckly) | 1½ | 9 | 9/2[2] | 64 | 37 |
| 1016[9] | **Hinton Rock (IRE) (80)** (ABailey) **4-9-3**(3) DWright(1) (bit bkwd: outpcd: a bhd) | ¾ | 10 | 16/1 | 57 | 30 |
| 1113[6] | **Ziggy's Dancer (USA) (84)** (EJAlston) **5-9-10** SDWilliams(2) (lw: bhd: sn drvn along: no imp) | ¾ | 11 | 8/1 | 59 | 32 |

(SP 117.2%) **11 Rn**

**63.53 secs** (4.33) CSF £80.52 CT £280.36 TOTE £11.70: £2.20 £1.80 £1.90 (£19.40) Trio £32.90 OWNER Mr S. R. Bowring (EDWINSTOWE) BRED S. R. Bowring
OFFICIAL EXPLANATION **Sailormaite: broke well and so was unable to be covered up, which is the way he has to be ridden and also, he was wearing blinkers for the first time he was a three year old.**
**711 Sailormaite**, fitted with blinkers for the first time in a couple of years and suited by the very fast early pace, took charge 150 yards out and won going away. (12/1)
**931 Sing With the Band** ran another good race, but she was unable to quicken with the winner in the closing stages, despite running on to secure the runner-up prize. (13/2)
**1161* Tuscan Dawn** needed to set a very strong gallop to prevent the other confirmed front-runner gaining control but, in this more testing ground and with a headwind to cope with, was at the end of his tether when worn down halfway through the final furlong. (4/1)
**1186 Tedburrow** could have found this softer ground just too much for him, but he ran a race full of promise, and his turn can not be far away. (16/1)
**Surprise Mission**, still needing this, did not have a lot of room in which to manoeuvre below the distance, and could do little more than keep on at the same pace. (13/2)
**1016 Glorious Aragon** struggled with the pace and was never nearer than at the finish. (9/1)
**451 Lord High Admiral (CAN)**, attempting to win this event for the third time running, could not adopt his usual trail-blazing tactics, and called enough below the distance. (9/2: op 3/1)

## 1431 SANDY LANE RATED STKS H'CAP (0-110) (Listed) (3-Y.O) (Class A)
2-30 (2-30) **6f** £12,609.20 (£4,599.20: £2,249.60: £968.00: £434.00) Stalls: High GOING: 0.37 sec per fur (GS)

| | | | Pos | SP | RR | SF |
|---|---|---|---|---|---|---|
| 945* | **Farhana (100)** (WJarvis) **3-9-1** RHills(1) (b: hld up: hdwy to ld over 1f out: edgd rt: sn clr) | — | 1 | Evens[1] | 106+ | 67 |
| 722a[5] | **April The Eighth (100)** (BWHills) **3-9-1** PRobinson(5) (led tl over 1f out: kpt on u.p fnl f: no ch w wnr) | 4 | 2 | 11/2[3] | 95 | 56 |
| 832* | **Dashing Blue (100)** (IABalding) **3-9-1** PaulEddery(3) (plld hrd: hld up & bhd: hdwy over 1f out: rdn & veered rt: no imp) | 1¼ | 3 | 5/2[2] | 92 | 53 |

| | | | Pos | SP | RR | SF |
|---|---|---|---|---|---|---|
| 939[12] | **Maid For The Hills (106)** (DRLoder) **3-9-7** DRMcCabe(2) (lw: prom: rdn & outpcd whn hmpd & swtchd lft appr fnl f: fin 5th, 1¼l: plcd 4th) | | 4 | 13/2 | 88 | 49 |
| | **Dovebrace (104)** (ABailey) **3-9-5** JFortune(4) (h.d.w: trckd ldrs: rdn & one pce appr fnl f: fin 4th, 2½l: disq: plcd 5th) | | 5 | 16/1 | 89 | 50 |

(SP 113.2%) **5 Rn**

**1m 16.22** (4.52) CSF £6.62 TOTE £1.90: £1.20 £2.20 (£4.10) OWNER Mr A. Foustok (NEWMARKET) BRED Ahmed M. Foustok
STEWARDS' ENQUIRY Fortune susp. 3-8/6/96 (irresponsible riding).
**945* Farhana** is on a roll, and seems to be well ahead of the Handicapper this season. (Evens)
**722a April The Eighth**, brought back to sprinting, stuck on willingly after being headed and, if he can steer clear of the useful winner, should soon be paying his way. (11/2)
**832* Dashing Blue**, taking a keen hold under restraint, let the winner take first run and was always fighting a lost cause. (5/2)
**939 Maid For The Hills**, struggling to hang on when becoming the meat in the sandwich over a furlong out, switched to the outside, but she had lost her momentum and was unable to recover. (13/2)
**Dovebrace**, looking well prepared for this seasonal debut, sat in behind the leaders but wandered off a true line when asked to quicken, and it is possible that he found the ground more testing than he prefers. (16/1)

## 1432 TOTE CREDIT SILVER BOWL H'CAP (0-110) (3-Y.O) (Class B)

3-00 (3-01) **1m 30y** £21,300.00 (£6,450.00: £3,150.00: £1,500.00) Stalls: Low GOING: 0.37 sec per fur (GS)

| | | | Pos | SP | RR | SF |
|---|---|---|---|---|---|---|
| 1126[2] | **Winter Romance (90)** (EALDunlop) **3-9-0** PaulEddery(8) (hld up: hdwy over 2f out: led appr fnl f: sn clr) | — | 1 | 9/4[1] | 105 | 79 |
| 1127[8] | **Jo Mell (80)** (TDEasterby) **3-8-4** MBirch(5) (plld hrd: a.p: ev ch 2f out: hrd rdn over 1f out: one pce) | 5 | 2 | 14/1 | 85 | 59 |
| 694[11] | **Believe Me (97)** (RHannon) **3-9-7** RPerham(1) (lw: a.p: rdn & outpcd 2f out: kpt on u.p fnl f) | ¾ | 3 | 20/1 | 101 | 75 |
| 785[6] | **Kala Sunrise (90)** (CSmith) **3-8-11**(3) DRMcCabe(3) (lw: bhd & outpcd tl r.o wl appr fnl f) | 1½ | 4 | 50/1 | 91 | 65 |
| 937[3] | **Polar Prince (IRE) (90)** (MAJarvis) **3-9-0** PRobinson(4) (prom: led over 2f out tl appr fnl f: sn rdn & outpcd) | nk | 5 | 5/1[2] | 90 | 64 |
| 969[2] | **Kriscliffe (82)** (MissGayKelleway) **3-8-6** NAdams(2) (lw: led tl over 2f out: sn rdn & wknd) | 6 | 6 | 15/2 | 70 | 44 |
| 1127[4] | **Double Bluff (IRE) (87)** (IABalding) **3-8-6**(5) MartinDwyer(9) (trckd ldrs tl rdn & wknd over 1f out) | ¾ | 7 | 11/2[3] | 74 | 48 |
| 937[4] | **Al Shafa (88)** (JLDunlop) **3-8-12** TSprake(10) (hld up: hdwy over 3f out: rdn & wknd fnl f) | 2½ | 8 | 6/1 | 70 | 44 |
| 1125[4] | **Van Gurp (94)** (BAMcMahon) **3-9-4** GCarter(6) (stumbled s: sn chsng ldrs: rdn & wknd over 2f out) | 4 | 9 | 7/1 | 68 | 42 |
| | **Some Horse (IRE) (93)** (MGMeagher) **3-9-3** JFortune(7) (hld up & a bhd) | ½ | 10 | 14/1 | 66 | 40 |

(SP 121.4%) **10 Rn**

**1m 46.59** (5.99) CSF £31.75 CT £489.48 TOTE £3.00: £1.50 £2.80 £3.80 (£22.30) Trio £121.50 OWNER Maktoum Al Maktoum (NEWMARKET) BRED Gainsborough Stud Management Ltd.
**OFFICIAL EXPLANATION Van Gurp: was hanging badly throughout the race and his pilot thought there was something wrong with him.**
**1126 Winter Romance** has had the misfortune to come up against some very useful animals, but it was hard to believe that he was able to break his duck in such a competitive handicap. In the end, he won with any amount in hand, and this success could be the first of many. (9/4)
**1127 Jo Mell** pushed the pace from the start, and kept on strongly under pressure, but had to admit the winner was in a class of his own. He can soon make amends. (14/1)
**Believe Me**, who ran with his tongue tied down, gave the impression that he well benefit from a longer trip by the way he was staying on after losing his pitch two furlongs out. After all, he did succeed at this trip on the much stiffer Rowley Mile Course at Newmarket in his first season. (20/1)
**785 Kala Sunrise** brought up the rear, some way off the pace, until staying on when it was all to late. He will return to form when he steps back into his own class (50/1)
**937 Polar Prince (IRE)** kicked for home over two furlongs out but, once the winner appeared on the scene, he must have wondered what had hit him. (5/1)
**969 Kriscliffe** did a good job of pacemaking, but was out of his depth when the race began in earnest. (15/2)

## 1433 E.B.F. ST HELENS MAIDEN STKS (2-Y.O F) (Class D)

3-30 (3-31) **5f** £3,434.50 (£1,036.00: £503.00: £236.50) Stalls: High GOING: 0.37 sec per fur (GS)

| | | | Pos | SP | RR | SF |
|---|---|---|---|---|---|---|
| 930[9] | **Molly Drummond** (CWCElsey) **2-8-11** MBirch(6) (led to ½-wy: rallied u.p to ld cl home) | — | 1 | 14/1 | 62 | — |
| 1014[6] | **Manhattan Diamond** (ABailey) **2-8-11** JFortune(2) (lw: a.p: ev ch fnl f: unable qckn) | hd | 2 | 9/1[3] | 62 | — |
| 1014[4] | **Ruby Tuesday** (BAMcMahon) **2-8-11** GCarter(1) (lw: led over 2f out tl ct nr fin) | hd | 3 | 4/1[2] | 61 | — |
| | **Terry's Rose** (RHollinshead) **2-8-11** JCarroll(3) (lt-f: bit bkwd: chsd ldrs over 3f: wknd appr fnl f) | 4 | 4 | 12/1 | 49 | — |
| | **E Sharp (USA)** (DRLoder) **2-8-8**(3) DRMcCabe(5) (scope: sn pushed along & outpcd: rdn & hung lft 2f out: no imp) | 1¾ | 5 | 8/15[1] | 43 | — |
| | **Whittle Times** (EJAlston) **2-8-11** SDWilliams(4) (cmpt: bkwd: s.s: hung lft: swchd rt ½-wy: a outpcd: t.o) | 11 | 6 | 14/1 | 8 | — |

(SP 116.2%) **6 Rn**

**66.84 secs** (7.64) CSF £106.11 TOTE £12.00: £3.30 £3.30 (£149.80) OWNER R V Hughes and Partners (MALTON) BRED Frank Steele
STEWARDS' ENQUIRY Birch susp. 3-6/6/96 (excessive & incorrect use of whip).
**585 Molly Drummond** proved a right madam to load into the stalls, but she put her mind to the task in hand once in action, and came out best in a thrilling battle to the line. (14/1)
**Manhattan Diamond** got away on terms this time, and remained in the firing-line with very chance until touched off in a three-way photo. She will win races. (9/1)
**1014 Ruby Tuesday** poked her nose in front at halfway, and proved a tough nut to wear down. She had learnt from her previous outing, and an early success will come as just reward. (4/1: op 6/1)
**Terry's Rose** is not bred for sprinting, but she gave a good account of herself and the experience will prove beneficial. (12/1)
**E Sharp (USA)**, a late foal who still looks to need time, was never going the pace of the leaders. (8/15)
**Whittle Times** (14/1: op 8/1)

## 1434 ECCLES MAIDEN STKS (3-Y.O) (Class D)

4-00 (4-02) **1m 2f 120y** £3,792.00 (£1,146.00: £558.00: £264.00) Stalls: Low GOING: 0.37 sec per fur (GS)

| | | | Pos | SP | RR | SF |
|---|---|---|---|---|---|---|
| 957[4] | **Mount Row** (LMCumani) **3-8-6**(3) DRMcCabe(10) (chsd ldr: hrd rdn 2f out: styd on to ld cl home) | — | 1 | 2/1[1] | 87 | 54 |
| 813[6] | **Lothlorien (USA)** (PWChapple-Hyam) **3-8-9** BThomson(7) (led: clr 4f out: wknd & hdd nr fin) | ½ | 2 | 11/2[3] | 86 | 53 |
| 813[8] | **Annecy (USA)** (HRACecil) **3-8-9** GCarter(2) (dwlt: sn chsng ldrs: effrt 2f out: kpt on same pce) | 2½ | 3 | 5/1[2] | 82 | 49 |
| | **Jaseur (USA)** (JHMGosden) **3-9-0** JCarroll(8) (w'like: scope: dwlt: sn chsng ldrs: effrt over 2f out: nt pce to chal) | ½ | 4 | 6/1 | 87 | 54 |
| 892[10] | **Alsahib (USA)** (HThomsonJones) **3-9-0** RHills(1) (trckd ldrs tl wknd wl over 1f out) | 7 | 5 | 7/1 | 76 | 43 |

| | | | | SP | RR | SF |
|---|---|---|---|---|---|---|
| 985[7] | **Crabbie's Pride** (ABailey) **3-9-0** JFanning(13) (hld up: hdwy 3f out: nt rch ldrs) | 2 | **6** | 16/1 | 73 | 40 |
| 1182[9] | **Regal Eagle** (IABalding) **3-9-0** PaulEddery(14) (bkwd: nvr plcd to chal) | hd | **7** | 14/1 | 73 | 40 |
| 994[11] | **Newbridge Boy** (MGMeagher) **3-8-7**(7) RStudholme(11) (bit bkwd: trckd ldrs over 7f) | 4 | **8** | 66/1 | 67 | 34 |
| | **So Keen** (ABailey) **3-9-0** SDWilliams(12) (w'like: bkwd: mid div: effrt & rdn over 2f out: no imp) | 2½ | **9** | 33/1 | 63 | 30 |
| 1099[12] | **Gold Lining (IRE)** (CDBroad) **3-8-9** AMackay(15) (a bhd) | 1½ | **10** | 50/1 | 56 | 23 |
| | **Aren't We Lucky (IRE)** (JJO'Neill) **3-9-0** JFortune(6) (lt-f: a bhd) | 4 | **11** | 25/1 | 55 | 22 |
| 792a[6] | **Maid To Last** (JWHills) **3-8-9** PRobinson(4) (s.s: hdwy ½-wy: wknd wl over 2f out) | ¾ | **12** | 20/1 | 49 | 16 |
| | **Alfahad** (MissGayKelleway) **3-9-0** OUrbina(5) (b.hind: lengthy: scope: bit bkwd: a in rr: t.o) | 9 | **13** | 12/1 | 40 | 7 |
| | **Kulshi Momken** (RTPhillips) **3-9-0** TSprake(9) (small: bkwd: mid div tl wknd over 3f out: t.o) | 8 | **14** | 20/1 | 28 | — |
| | **Cherry Muna** (CWFairhurst) **3-8-9** DaleGibson(3) (lt-f: bit bkwd: s.s: a bhd: t.o) | 8 | **15** | 50/1 | 11 | — |

(SP 134.1%) **15 Rn**

**2m 20.59** (9.09) CSF £14.71 TOTE £3.90: £1.80 £1.90 £1.90 (£11.30) Trio £13.30 OWNER Lord Hartington (NEWMARKET) BRED Side Hill Stud

**957 Mount Row**, in pursuit of the leader from the break, was hard at work entering the final quarter-mile but kept pulling out extra and swooped to conquer nearing the line. She will know she has been in a race. (2/1)

**813 Lothlorien (USA)** did her utmost to gallop these rivals into the ground and, for most of the trip, looked sure to do just that, but her stride shortened inside the final furlong, and she was headed in the shadow of the post. She will soon be winning. (11/2: 4/1-6/1)

**813 Annecy (USA)** soon recovered from a sluggish start and stayed on promisingly in the latter stages without ever promising to get on terms.(5/1)

**Jaseur (USA)**, a workmanlike son of a very useful mare, was flat-footed as the stalls opened. Moving onto the heels of the leaders down the back straight, he could not summon up the speed to deliver a challenge, but he was not knocked about and looks a colt who will continue to progress. (6/1: op 4/1)

**Alsahib (USA)** ran as if he failed to see this longer trip out, but he is such a huge individual that it is possible that he is still not quite 100%. (7/1: 5/1-8/1)

**566 Crabbie's Pride** was unable to get himself in to contention, but he performed with credit and is still in the process of learning. (16/1)

**Regal Eagle** (14/1: op 8/1)

**Alfahad** (12/1: op 8/1)

## 1435 SHEVINGTON MAIDEN STKS (3-Y.O+) (Class D)

4-30 (4-32) **7f 30y** £3,753.00 (£1,134.00: £552.00: £261.00) Stalls: Low GOING: 0.37 sec per fur (GS)

| | | | | SP | RR | SF |
|---|---|---|---|---|---|---|
| 1007[6] | **Sandhill (IRE)** (JHMGosden) **3-8-8** JCarroll(1) (mde virtually all: clr over 1f out: eased nr fin) | — | **1** | 11/2 | 79+ | 37 |
| | **High Cut** (IABalding) **3-8-8** PaulEddery(12) (trckd ldrs: effrt wl over 1f out: rn green & kpt on towards fin) | 3 | **2** | 4/1[2] | 72 | 30 |
| 640[7] | **Chinensis (IRE)** (LMCumani) **3-8-13** OUrbina(9) (hld up: hdwy over 2f out: nt rch ldrs) | 7 | **3** | 5/1[3] | 62 | 20 |
| 934[12] | **Surf City** (WWHaigh) **3-8-13** JFortune(13) (hld up: hdwy over 2f out: nvr nrr) | nk | **4** | 50/1 | 61 | 19 |
| | **Detachment (USA) (95)** (PWChapple-Hyam) **3-8-13** BThomson(11) (bit bkwd: prom: jnd wnr ½-wy: rdn & wknd over 1f out) | 1¾ | **5** | 11/8[1] | 57 | 15 |
| | **Rocky's Meteor** (RAFahey) **3-8-13** ACulhane(8) (bit bkwd: sme hdwy fnl 2f: nvr nrr) | 1¼ | **6** | 20/1 | 54 | 12 |
| 1159[9] | **Sheraz (IRE) (63)** (NTinkler) **4-9-10** MBirch(7) (prom tl rdn & wknd over 2f out) | 1 | **7** | 33/1 | 52 | 21 |
| | **Northgate Chief** (MBrittain) **4-9-10** GCarter(3) (bkwd: a in rr) | 2½ | **8** | 100/1 | 46 | 15 |
| 992[5] | **Angus McCoatup (IRE) (58)** (BAMcMahon) **3-8-8**(5) LNewton(2) (trckd ldrs 5f: sn lost tch) | nk | **9** | 16/1 | 46 | 4 |
| 1099[15] | **Welcome Brief** (EJAlston) **3-8-8** JFanning(5) (bit bkwd: a bhd: t.o) | 6 | **10** | 100/1 | 27 | — |
| | **Paper Maze (48)** (EHOwenjun) **3-8-5**(3) DarrenMoffatt(4) (bkwd: a bhd: t.o) | 2½ | **11** | 100/1 | 22 | — |
| | **Nexsis Star** (MrsSJSmith) **3-8-8**(5) PRoberts(10) (w'like: bkwd: a bhd: t.o) | 3½ | **12** | 40/1 | 19 | — |
| | **Celtic Lady** (MrsNMacauley) **5-9-2b**[1](3) CTeague(6) (s.s: a t.o) | dist | **13** | 40/1 | — | — |

(SP 117.6%) **13 Rn**

**1m 35.02** (7.52) CSF £25.66 TOTE £6.40: £2.30 £1.60 £2.10 (£10.90) Trio £7.70 OWNER Mr K. Abdulla (NEWMARKET) BRED Juddmonte Farms

WEIGHT FOR AGE 3yo-11lb

**1007 Sandhill (IRE)** made sure this was going to be a true test of stamina and, with the prize in safe-keeping approaching the final furlong, was eased right down towards the finish. (11/2)

**High Cut** looked in tip-top condition for this first run in over a year, and gave a brief glimpse of what she is capable of. She showed signs of greenness when the pressure was on, and can only improve on this. (4/1)

**640 Chinensis (IRE)**, who is being brought along steadily, was stepping down in distance. Staying on without threatening danger, he will soon leave this form behind. (5/1)

**774 Surf City** turned in his best display yet and is grasping what it is all about. (50/1)

**Detachment (USA)** just needed this, but ran a race full of promise, holding every chance until blowing up below the distance. (11/8)

**Rocky's Meteor**, doing all his best work late on, will be much sharper the next time he appears. (20/1)

## 1436 LADBROKE H'CAP (0-80) (4-Y.O+) (Class D)

5-05 (5-05) **1m 6f** £3,694.50 (£1,116.00: £543.00: £256.50) Stalls: Centre GOING: 0.37 sec per fur (GS)

| | | | | SP | RR | SF |
|---|---|---|---|---|---|---|
| 1091[2] | **Satin Lover (72)** (MrsMReveley) **8-9-0**(7) SCopp(4) (a.p: led 4f out: rdn & kpt on wl fnl f) | — | **1** | 15/8[1] | 83 | 46 |
| 753[3] | **Embryonic (IRE) (75)** (RFFisher) **4-9-10** JFortune(1) (hld up: hdwy ent st: jnd wnr 3f out: rdn over 1f out: no ex nr fin) | ½ | **2** | 11/4[3] | 85 | 48 |
| 972[3] | **Secret Service (IRE) (73)** (CWThornton) **4-9-8** PaulEddery(3) (lw: trckd ldrs: hrd rdn over 2f out: styd on strly cl home) | hd | **3** | 5/2[2] | 83 | 46 |
| 993[14] | **Pickens (USA) (65)** (NTinkler) **4-9-0** MBirch(2) (led 10f: rdn & wknd over 2f out) | 9 | **4** | 16/1 | 65 | 28 |
| | **Blazon of Troy (52)** (TThomsonJones) **7-8-1** AMackay(5) (hld up & bhd: hdwy 5f out: rdn 3f out: sn btn) | hd | **5** | 7/1 | 52 | 15 |
| 872[18] | **Kings Cay (IRE) (51)** (THCaldwell) **5-7-11**(3) DarrenMoffatt(6) (hld up: wnt 2nd 5f out: rdn & wknd 3f out: t.o) | 17 | **6** | 16/1 | 32 | — |

(SP 114.3%) **6 Rn**

**3m 13.84** (15.64) CSF £7.35 TOTE £2.30: £1.70 £2.20 (£3.50) OWNER Mr D. S. Hall (SALTBURN) BRED Stud-On-The-Chart

**1091 Satin Lover** threw down the gauntlet once in line for home and, though he was soon being strongly pressed, kept his head in front and ran out a worthy winner. The boy rode him well. (15/8)

**753 Embryonic (IRE)** has only won on much faster ground and, though he did not fail for the want of trying, he had met a rival who was not going to give best. (11/4)

**972 Secret Service (IRE)** was under pressure halfway up the straight, but he stuck to his task, and his spirited late challenge only just failed to get him there. This was his first attempt at the trip and he saw it out well. (5/2)

T/Jkpt: Not won; £8,514.58 to Sandown 27/5/96. T/Plpt: £346.20 (68.33 Tckts). T/Qdpt: £115.10 (6.56 Tckts). IM

# 0964-KEMPTON (R-H) (Good to soft)
## Saturday May 25th
WEATHER: fine WIND: almost nil

### 1437 NEW ENGLAND CONDITIONS STKS (2-Y.O) (Class C)
2-05 (2-05) **6f** £4,675.40 (£1,748.60: £854.30: £366.50: £163.25: £81.95) Stalls: High GOING: 0.00 sec per fur (G)

| Form | Horse / details | Dist | Pos | SP | RR | SF |
|---|---|---|---|---|---|---|
| 699* | **Statesman** (MRChannon) **2-9-0** RHughes(6) (hld up: swtchd lft over 1f out: led 1f out: comf) | — | 1 | 11/2 [3] | 88+ | 48 |
| 924* | **Abou Zouz (USA)** (DRLoder) **2-9-0** JReid(3) (lw: hld up: shkn up over 2f out: led over 1f out: sn hdd: unable qckn) | 2½ | 2 | 8/13 [1] | 81 | 41 |
| 958* | **Bali Paradise (USA)** (PFICole) **2-9-0** TQuinn(7) (lw: a.p: ev ch over 1f out: one pce) | ¾ | 3 | 4/1 [2] | 79 | 39 |
| 698[4] | **Blue Movie** (MBell) **2-9-0** WJO'Connor(2) (lw: lost pl over 3f out: r.o one pce fnl f) | 3½ | 4 | 20/1 | 70 | 30 |
| | **Palaemon** (GBBalding) **2-8-10** AClark(1) (w'like: bit bkwd: swtg: s.s: outpcd: nvr nrr) | nk | 5 | 66/1 | 65 | 25 |
| | **Palisander (IRE)** (SDow) **2-8-10** SSanders(5) (unf: scope: dwlt: bhd fnl 3f) | nk | 6 | 14/1 | 64 | 24 |
| 946[4] | **Castle House** (JAkehurst) **2-8-10** RCochrane(4) (led over 4f: wknd fnl f) | ½ | 7 | 33/1 | 63 | 23 |

(SP 113.2%) **7 Rn**

**1m 14.85** (3.55) CSF £9.09 TOTE £6.40: £2.10 £1.30 (£2.40) OWNER Mr Stephen Crown (UPPER LAMBOURN) BRED S. Crown

**699* Statesman** looks a useful tool. Traveling sweetly, he was brought to the outside below the distance and, sweeping into the lead at the furlong pole, quickly pulled away for a comfortable success. He can go on from here and complete the hat-trick. (11/2: 4/1-6/1)

**924* Abou Zouz (USA)** really took the eye in the paddock but failed to deliver the goods. He is well worth another chance as the only possible explanations for this below-par performance were the softish ground, or the fact that his stable is not quite firing as yet. (8/13)

**958* Bali Paradise (USA)** had every chance below the distance before tapped for toe. (4/1: 3/1-5/1)

**698 Blue Movie** got outpaced just before halfway, but did stay on in the final furlong, if never looking likely to get back into it. (20/1)

**Palaemon** looked as though the outing would do him good and was very coltish in the paddock. Losing ground at the start and totally outpaced, he made up a little late ground without ever posing a threat. (66/1)

**Palisander (IRE)**, a scopey individual, was getting left behind at halfway. (14/1: 6/1-16/1)

### 1438 CALIFORNIAN MAIDEN STKS (3-Y.O) (Class D)
2-35 (2-36) **1m (Jubilee)** £3,753.00 (£1,134.00: £552.00: £261.00) Stalls: High GOING: 0.26 sec per fur (G)

| Form | Horse / details | Dist | Pos | SP | RR | SF |
|---|---|---|---|---|---|---|
| 964[2] | **My Lewicia (IRE)** (PWHarris) **3-8-9** GHind(5) (hld up: led over 2f out: comf) | — | 1 | Evens [1] | 86 | 55 |
| 1142[15] | **Present Generation** (RGuest) **3-8-11**(3) DaneO'Neill(9) (hdwy over 2f out: chsd wnr wl over 1f out: unable qckn) | 5 | 2 | 16/1 | 81 | 50 |
| 894[13] | **Phonetic** (GBBalding) **3-9-0** AClark(10) (hdwy on ins over 2f out: swtchd lft wl over 1f out: r.o ins fnl f) | 2½ | 3 | 100/1 | 76 | 45 |
| | **Possessive Artiste** (MRStoute) **3-8-9** JReid(3) (rdn over 2f out: hdwy fnl f: r.o) | 1¼ | 4 | 11/2 [2] | 69 | 38 |
| 921[7] | **Passage Creeping (IRE)** (LMCumani) **3-8-9** RHughes(1) (a.p: rdn over 2f out: wknd fnl f) | 1¾ | 5 | 12/1 | 65 | 34 |
| 842[7] | **Soaked** (JRFanshawe) **3-8-11**(3) NVarley(4) (nvr nr to chal) | 2½ | 6 | 14/1 | 65 | 34 |
| 577[6] | **Warren Knight** (CAHorgan) **3-9-0** WJO'Connor(11) (lw: w ldr: led 4f out tl over 2f out: wknd fnl f) | 1 | 7 | 20/1 | 63 | 32 |
| 1319[13] | **Beau Bruno** (MBell) **3-9-0** SSanders(7) (prom over 6f) | 2½ | 8 | 100/1 | 58 | 27 |
| 1195[2] | **Polar Prospect** (BHanbury) **3-9-0** RCochrane(2) (b.hind: bhd fnl 2f) | 1½ | 9 | 7/1 [3] | 55 | 24 |
| | **Shark (IRE)** (HThomsonJones) **3-9-0** GDuffield(6) (w'like: scope: bit bkwd: led 4f: wknd 3f out) | 4 | 10 | 12/1 | 47 | 16 |
| | **Bent Raiwand (USA)** (BHanbury) **3-8-9** PBloomfield(8) (scope: bit bkwd: s.s: a bhd) | 3½ | 11 | 25/1 | 35 | 4 |

(SP 116.4%) **11 Rn**

**1m 42.96** (5.76) CSF £16.77 TOTE £1.90: £1.20 £4.10 £10.70 (£18.10) Trio £211.50 OWNER Mr G. Knight (BERKHAMSTED) BRED Pendley Farm

**964 My Lewicia (IRE)** confirmed the promise shown over this course and distance recently. Moving to the front over a quarter of a mile from home, she asserted in good style from below the distance for a comfortable success. (Evens)

**1142 Present Generation**, all the better for his informative introduction, moved through to take second place early inside the final quarter-mile. The only danger to the winner, he failed to peg back that rival, but a race should soon be found for him. (16/1)

**Phonetic** left his debut run behind. Picking up ground along the inside rail early in the straight, he had to be switched left well over a furlong out to get a clear run, but he kept on nicely in the final furlong, if never looking likely to pose a serious threat. (100/1)

**Possessive Artiste**, who did not take the eye on this reappearance, was being pushed along early in the straight, but only made headway in the final furlong. (11/2: 7/2-6/1)

**921 Passage Creeping (IRE)** played an active role until tiring in the final furlong. (12/1: op 8/1)

**Soaked** (14/1: 10/1-16/1)

### 1439 CRAWLEY WARREN H'CAP (0-90) (4-Y.O+) (Class C)
3-05 (3-06) **2m** £8,602.50 (£2,595.00: £1,260.00: £592.50) Stalls: High GOING: 0.26 sec per fur (G)

| Form | Horse / details | Dist | Pos | SP | RR | SF |
|---|---|---|---|---|---|---|
| 1194* | **Rocky Forum (67)** (GLMoore) **4-8-6** SSanders(9) (b: hdwy over 3f out: led over 2f out: rdn out) | — | 1 | 11/4 [1] | 83 | 63 |
| 944[6] | **Sea Freedom (60)** (GBBalding) **5-7-12v**(3) NVarley(4) (hdwy over 3f out: chsd wnr over 1f out: r.o) | 1¼ | 2 | 14/1 | 75 | 57 |
| 1005[5] | **Fujiyama Crest (IRE) (89)** (MRStoute) **4-10-0** JReid(1) (b.nr hind: led tl over 2f out: unable qckn) | 4 | 3 | 7/2 [2] | 100 | 80 |
| 1194[10] | **Greycoat Boy (63)** (BJMeehan) **4-8-2b** JFEgan(2) (a.p: rdn over 3f out: one pce fnl 2f) | 1 | 4 | 11/1 | 73 | 53 |
| 811[4] | **Barford Sovereign (67)** (JRFanshawe) **4-8-6** TQuinn(6) (lw: chsd ldr 7f: rdn over 3f out: wknd 1f out) | 1¼ | 5 | 9/1 | 76 | 56 |
| | **Ivor's Flutter (74)** (DRCElsworth) **7-9-1** AProcter(5) (nvr nr to chal) | 11 | 6 | 33/1 | 72 | 54 |
| 1063[3] | **Courbaril (59)** (SDow) **4-7-12** FNorton(11) (lw: chsd ldr 9f out tl over 2f out: sn wknd) | 4 | 7 | 12/1 | 53 | 33 |
| 712[8] | **Shadirwan (IRE) (81)** (RAkehurst) **5-9-1**(7) TAshley(10) (prom 12f) | 4 | 8 | 10/1 | 71 | 53 |
| 811[8] | **Paradise Navy (68)** (CREgerton) **7-8-9** RHughes(7) (lw: s.s: hdwy over 2f out: sn wknd) | 2 | 9 | 12/1 | 56 | 38 |
| 573[8] | **Salaman (FR) (81)** (JLDunlop) **4-9-6** RCochrane(3) (lw: dwlt: a bhd) | 13 | 10 | 8/1 [3] | 56 | 36 |
| 1194[13] | **Allmosa (55)** (TJNaughton) **7-7-5**(5) MBaird(8) (swtg: a bhd) | 1½ | 11 | 50/1 | 28 | 10 |

(SP 114.4%) **11 Rn**

**3m 34.4** (9.80) CSF £35.83 CT £125.11 TOTE £3.50: £1.30 £2.90 £1.90 (£17.70) Trio £24.90 OWNER The Forum Ltd (EPSOM) BRED Forum Bloodstock Ltd

LONG HANDICAP Allmosa 7-3

WEIGHT FOR AGE 4yo-2lb

**1194* Rocky Forum** hacked up in the mud at Newbury and was not going to allow a 7lb rise in the weights to stop her here, especially with a bit of cut in the ground. Cruising to the front over a quarter of a mile from home, she was ridden along to maintain her superiority. (11/4)

**647 Sea Freedom**, moving into second place below the distance, kept on well but failed to peg back the winner. He remains a winner after nineteen attempts. (14/1)
**1005 Fujiyama Crest (IRE)** adopted his usual front-running role. Collared over a quarter of a mile from home, he could only keep on in his own time. (7/2)
**Greycoat Boy**, never far away, was left for dead in the last two furlongs. (11/1: 8/1-12/1)
**811 Barford Sovereign**, in second place for the first half of the race, remained in contention until tiring at the distance. (9/1)
**Ivor's Flutter**, off the track for nearly eleven months, was at the back of the field until passing beaten horses. (33/1)
**449* Shadirwan (IRE)** (10/1: 7/1-12/1)

## 1440 NEW SOUTH WALES H'CAP (0-90) (3-Y.O+) (Class C)
3-35 (3-36) **1m 2f (Jubilee)** £5,504.50 (£1,666.00: £813.00: £386.50) Stalls: High GOING: 0.26 sec per fur (G)

| | | | | SP | RR | SF |
|---|---|---|---|---|---|---|
| 1066$^{2}$ | **Zermatt (IRE) (67)** (MDIUsher) **6-8-5** SSanders(10) (lw: mde all: clr over 2f out: rdn out) | — | **1** | 8/1$^{3}$ | 80 | 45 |
| 1072* | **Domitia (USA) (69)** (MBell) **4-8-7** WJO'Connor(13) (b: lw: a.p: chsd wnr fnl 2f: r.o) | 1¾ | **2** | 11/1 | 79 | 44 |
| 871* | **Kings Assembly (81)** (PWHarris) **4-9-5** GHind(14) (chsd ldr 8f: unable qckn) | 4 | **3** | 6/1$^{2}$ | 85 | 50 |
| | **Fieldridge (76)** (MPMuggeridge) **7-8-11**(3) DaneO'Neill(12) (plld hrd: hld up: rdn over 2f out: one pce) | 1¼ | **4** | 40/1 | 78 | 43 |
| 988$^{5}$ | **Golden Touch (USA) (65)** (NACallaghan) **4-8-3** JFEgan(15) (lw: plld hrd: nt clr run on ins wl over 1f out: nvr nr to chal) | ¾ | **5** | 8/1$^{3}$ | 66 | 31 |
| 580$^{6}$ | **Menas Gold (85)** (SDow) **4-9-9** JReid(11) (rdn over 2f out: nvr nrr) | ½ | **6** | 10/1 | 85 | 50 |
| 1051* | **Alhawa (USA) (85)** (CJBenstead) **3-8-9** MWigham(2) (lw: prom 6f) | s.h | **7** | 6/1$^{2}$ | 85 | 36 |
| | **Mystic Hill (87)** (GHarwood) **5-9-11** AClark(7) (nvr nrr) | 1¼ | **8** | 20/1 | 85 | 50 |
| 988$^{14}$ | **Romios (IRE) (85)** (PFICole) **4-9-9** TQuinn(1) (lw: hdwy over 7f out: wknd over 2f out) | s.h | **9** | 14/1 | 83 | 48 |
| 988$^{7}$ | **Conspicuous (IRE) (78)** (LGCottrell) **6-9-2** AMcGlone(3) (lw: bhd fnl 2f) | 1¾ | **10** | 8/1$^{3}$ | 73 | 38 |
| 802* | **Mokuti (74)** (GWragg) **4-8-12b$^{1}$** RCochrane(4) (bhd fnl 5f) | nk | **11** | 4/1$^{1}$ | 68 | 33 |
| 440$^{6}$ | **Seventeens Lucky (70)** (BobJones) **4-8-8** GDuffield(9) (lw: hdwy 4f out: wknd over 2f out) | 2 | **12** | 25/1 | 61 | 26 |
| 920$^{6}$ | **Errant (59)** (DJSCosgrove) **4-7-11** DeclanO'Shea(8) (b: plld hrd: bhd 3f) | 3½ | **13** | 25/1 | 45 | 10 |
| 1078$^{8}$ | **Easy Choice (USA) (65)** (PhilipMitchell) **4-8-3** GBardwell(6) (lw: bhd fnl 4f) | 21 | **14** | 20/1 | 17 | — |

(SP 125.7%) **14 Rn**

**2m 11.52** (8.02) CSF £88.05 CT £528.66 TOTE £10.20: £3.60 £4.00 £2.10 (£72.80) Trio £207.80 OWNER Clairtex Gwent (SWINDON) BRED Ivan W. Allan and K. C. Choo
WEIGHT FOR AGE 3yo-14lb
**OFFICIAL EXPLANATION Mokuti: his trainer reported that the colt had suffered interference in the first furlong of the race, and was unable to get back into the contest thereafter.**
**1066 Zermatt (IRE)** was given a fine ride. Making all the running, the combination quickened clear early in the straight and were not going to be denied. (8/1)
**1072* Domitia (USA)** moved into second place a quarter of a mile out but, despite keeping on, failed to peg back the winner. (11/1: 8/1-12/1)
**871* Kings Assembly** raced in second place until the two-furlong marker, from which point he could only go up and own in the same place. (6/1)
**Fieldridge** took a very keen hold in the early stages as he chased the leaders. Pushed along early in the straight, he failed to find the necessary turn of foot. (40/1)
**988 Golden Touch (USA)** took a keen hold in midfield but could never get in a serious blow. (8/1)
**580 Menas Gold** was at the back of the field until making a little late headway. (10/1: 7/1-12/1)

## 1441 CRAWLEY WARREN HERON STKS (Listed) (3-Y.O) (Class A)
4-05 (4-06) **1m (Jubilee)** £14,605.00 (£4,390.00: £2,120.00: £985.00) Stalls: High GOING: 0.26 sec per fur (G)

| | | | | SP | RR | SF |
|---|---|---|---|---|---|---|
| 808* | **Regal Archive (IRE)** (PWChapple-Hyam) **3-8-12** JReid(6) (b.hind: a.p: squeezed thro on ins over 1f out: led ins fnl f: drvn out) | — | **1** | 5/1$^{3}$ | 111+ | 69 |
| 833* | **Sorbie Tower (IRE) (104)** (MissGayKelleway) **3-8-12** RCochrane(8) (b.hind: lw: nt clr run on ins & snatched up 7f out: hdwy 2f out: ev ch ins fnl f: r.o) | nk | **2** | 5/2$^{1}$ | 110+ | 68 |
| 952* | **Wixim (USA) (108)** (RCharlton) **3-8-12** TQuinn(1) (lw: a.p: led over 1f out: edgd rt: hdd ins fnl f: r.o) | s.h | **3** | 100/30$^{2}$ | 110 | 68 |
| 703* | **Unreal City (IRE)** (HRACecil) **3-8-12** AMcGlone(2) (w ldr over 6f: sn wknd) | 4 | **4** | 11/1 | 102 | 60 |
| | **Quakers Field (106)** (GLMoore) **3-8-12** SWhitworth(9) (led over 6f) | s.h | **5** | 25/1 | 102 | 60 |
| 936$^{2}$ | **Hidden Oasis (98)** (SbinSuroor) **3-8-12** AClark(4) (lw: hld up: rdn over 2f out: sn wknd) | 10 | **6** | 13/2 | 82 | 40 |
| 830$^{9}$ | **Brighstone (104)** (HRACecil) **3-8-12** WJO'Connor(5) (plld hrd: some hdwy over 2f out: sn wknd) | 4 | **7** | 20/1 | 74 | 32 |
| 674$^{6}$ | **Darling Flame (USA) (106)** (JHMGosden) **3-8-7** GHind(7) (s.s: a bhd) | 3 | **8** | 12/1 | 63 | 21 |
| 939$^{13}$ | **Keepers Dawn (IRE) (104)** (RFJohnsonHoughton) **3-8-8**ow1 RHughes(3) (a bhd) | ¾ | **9** | 9/1 | 63 | 20 |

(SP 116.3%) **9 Rn**

**1m 41.89** (4.69) CSF £17.21 TOTE £5.70: £2.30 £1.10 £1.50 (£8.80) Trio £6.10 OWNER Mrs B. V. Sangster (MARLBOROUGH) BRED Studcrown Ltd
**808* Regal Archive (IRE)** showed a tremendous attitude to win this. Always close up, he had to squeeze through along the inside rail below the distance with very little room in which to manoeuvre. However, battling his heart out, he got on top inside the final furlong and just managed to hold off his very persistent rivals. This was a really good performance and he can win a bigger prize than this before long. (5/1: 7/2-11/2)
**833* Sorbie Tower (IRE)**, unbeaten in three races this season, was taking a step up in class and, although just failing to gain the day, lost nothing in defeat. He is certainly up to this class and can win a listed race before long. (5/2)
**952* Wixim (USA)** ran a very gutsy race and lost nothing in defeat. Never far away, he showed in front below the distance but edged slightly right in the process which did no favours to the winner. Headed inside the final furlong, he showed a tremendous attitude. He should find a listed race in due course. (100/30)
**703* Unreal City (IRE)**, in second pace until early in the final quarter-mile, soon had to give best. (11/1)
**Quakers Field**, making his seasonal bow, took the field along but, collared over a furlong out, was soon put in his place. (25/1)
**936 Hidden Oasis** looked an absolute picture in the paddock, but was beaten in the straight. (13/2)

## 1442 UNDERWRITING H'CAP (0-90) (3-Y.O+) (Class C)
4-35 (4-35) **6f** £5,374.50 (£1,626.00: £793.00: £376.50) Stalls: High GOING: 0.00 sec per fur (G)

| | | | | SP | RR | SF |
|---|---|---|---|---|---|---|
| 1018$^{5}$ | **Scharnhorst (73)** (SDow) **4-9-3** RHughes(3) (lw: mde all: hrd rdn over 1f out: r.o wl) | — | **1** | 5/1 | 85 | 54 |
| 1186$^{5}$ | **Double Splendour (IRE) (80)** (PSFelgate) **6-9-10** GHind(4) (a.p: chsd wnr over 2f out: hrd rdn over 1f out: unable qckn) | 2½ | **2** | 11/4$^{2}$ | 85 | 54 |
| 1348$^{11}$ | **Leigh Crofter (60)** (PDCundell) **7-8-4b** GDuffield(7) (lost pl 3f out: rallied fnl f: r.o) | 1¼ | **3** | 12/1 | 62 | 31 |

1121[10] **Twice Purple (IRE) (59)** (BJMeehan) **4-8-3** JFEgan(5) (a.p: rdn over 2f out: one pce)....nk **4** 25/1 60 29
1045[2] **Almuhimm (USA) (79)** (EALDunlop) **4-9-9** TQuinn(6) (lw: hdwy 3f out: wknd over 2f out)....9 **5** 9/4[1] 56 25
846[2] **Efra (68)** (RHannon) **7-8-9**(3) DaneO'Neill(2) (hdwy 3f out: wknd over 2f out)....3 **6** 4/1[3] 37 6
1073[7] **Balance of Power (65)** (RAkehurst) **4-8-9** SSanders(1) (prom over 3f)....7 **7** 11/1 16 —
(SP 114.0%) **7 Rn**

**1m 14.66** (3.36) CSF £18.29 TOTE £7.10: £2.70 £2.30 (£12.30) OWNER Mackenzie Print (EPSOM) BRED M. F. Kentish
**1018 Scharnhorst** looked extremely well beforehand. Making all the running, he responded to pressure below the distance and was not going to be denied. (5/1)
**1186 Double Splendour (IRE)** moved into second place soon after halfway but, despite his rider's urgings, failed to peg back the winner. (11/4: 2/1-3/1)
**418 Leigh Crofter**, making a quick reappearance, got outpaced at halfway but stayed on in the final furlong to regain third prize. (12/1: op 20/1)
**Twice Purple (IRE)** failed to find the necessary turn of foot in the last two furlongs and remains a maiden. (25/1)
**1045 Almuhimm (USA)** was taking a drop in distance which looked likely to help this hard-puller but he was very disappointing. Restrained at the back of the field, he moved up at halfway, only to soon capitulate. His fortunes may well change if allowed to bowl along in front. (9/4)
**846 Efra** made an effort at halfway but it came to little. (4/1: 3/1-9/2)
**Balance of Power** (11/1: 7/1-12/1)

T/Plpt: £36.20 (628.25 Tckts). T/Qdpt: £17.00 (77.41 Tckts). AK

## 1169-LINGFIELD (L-H) (Turf Good, Good to soft patches, AWT Standard)
## Saturday May 25th
WEATHER: cloudy WIND: almost nil

### 1443 HALL MAIDEN APPRENTICE STKS (3-Y.O) (Class F)
6-10 (6-11) **1m 2f** £2,473.00 (£703.00: £349.00) Stalls: High GOING: 0.04 sec per fur (G)

SP RR SF
894[14] **Claire's Dancer (IRE)** (AndrewTurnell) **3-8-11** CScudder(2) (chsd ldr: led 6f out: hdd 2f out: sn led again: rdn over 1f out: r.o)....— **1** 25/1[3] 76 12
982[3] **Ood Dancer (USA) (84)** (LMCumani) **3-8-8**(3) RFfrench(4) (in tch: chsd wnr over 3f out: led briefly 2f out: rdn over 1f out: unable qckn)....3½ **2** 1/10[1] 70 6
*501*[11] **Moving Up (IRE) (56)** (GLMoore) **3-8-6**(3)ow3 ALakeman(1) (b.hind: hld up: lost tch 6f out: swtchd lft 3f out: rdn 2f out: kpt on one pce ins fnl f)....3 **3** 16/1[2] 64 —
*1027*[7] **Supreme Illusion (AUS) (37)** (JohnBerry) **3-8-4b**(8)ow6 AmyQuirk(3) (led: hdd 6f out: wknd qckly over 3f out: t.o)....dist **4** 25/1[3] — —
(SP 104.5%) **4 Rn**

**2m 15.64** (10.94) CSF £28.06 TOTE £7.40 (£2.50) OWNER Mrs Claire Hollowood (WANTAGE) BRED Mrs H. M. Orpen
**Claire's Dancer (IRE)** caused a shock here but it was no fluke. He looked beaten when headed by the favourite two furlongs out, but battled back well and saw off his rival. (25/1)
**982 Ood Dancer (USA)** looked sure to land the long odds laid on him when leading two furlongs out, but the distress signals were soon out, and he found disappointingly little. (1/10)
**Moving Up (IRE)** made moderate late progress. (16/1)
**859 Supreme Illusion (AUS)** lost touch up the straight. (25/1)

### 1444 PATIO (S) H'CAP (0-60) (3-Y.O+) (Class G)
6-40 (6-40) **2m (Equitrack)** £2,343.00 (£648.00: £309.00) Stalls: High GOING minus 0.42 sec per fur (FST)

SP RR SF
1070[5] **Chakalak (49)** (SDow) **8-9-10** RHughes(5) (lw: chsd ldr: led over 3f out: rdn clr over 1f out: r.o)....— **1** 4/1[2] 63 45
*275*[3] **Milngavie (IRE) (40)** (BSmart) **6-9-1** RCochrane(2) (led: hdd over 3f out: hrd rdn fnl 2f: unable qckn)....2½ **2** 7/2[1] 52 34
666[4] **Juliasdarkinvader (40)** (AMoore) **6-8-12**(3) DaneO'Neill(1) (chsd ldrs: rdn 3f out: wknd over 1f out)....6 **3** 9/2[3] 46 28
1167[9] **Pearl Anniversary (IRE) (54)** (MJohnston) **3-8-7** GDuffield(10) (lw: chsd ldrs: rdn 3f out: wknd over 1f out)..3½ **4** 11/2 56 16
*279*[10] **Sorisky (39)** (BGubby) **4-8-12** GBardwell(7) (rr: hrd rdn & sme hdwy 5f out: no imp fnl 3f)....5 **5** 16/1 36 16
1347[12] **Brick Court (IRE) (41)** (RFJohnsonHoughton) **4-9-0** SSanders(8) (mid div: hrd rdn 5f out: sn wknd)....7 **6** 25/1 31 11
1012[8] **Hever Golf Diamond (53)** (TJNaughton) **3-8-6** DBiggs(3) (bhd fnl 5f)....5 **7** 8/1 38 —
*1082*[5] **Unsuspicious (IRE) (44)** (CDBroad) **6-9-5** DeclanO'Shea(4) (a bhd)....1¾ **8** 16/1 27 9
1174[10] **Ela-Ment (IRE) (40)** (BAPearce) **4-8-10**(3) NVarley(9) (sn rdn along: a bhd)....½ **9** 33/1 23 3
849[13] **Suparoy (48)** (TGMills) **3-8-1** FNorton(6) (bhd fnl 5f)....13 **10** 10/1 18 —
(SP 114.5%) **10 Rn**

**3m 28.01** (6.01) CSF £17.12 CT £58.68 TOTE £4.70: £1.80 £1.40 £1.30 (£7.60) Trio £6.30 OWNER Mr P. F. Chakko (EPSOM) BRED Seend Stud
WEIGHT FOR AGE 3yo-22lb, 4yo-2lb
No bid
**1070 Chakalak** made good use of his proven stamina here, setting sail for home coming down the hill, and never looking likely to be caught. (4/1)
**275 Milngavie (IRE)** kept on gamely for an honourable second, having tried to make all. (7/2)
**666 Juliasdarkinvader** was always to the fore, but had no more to give up the straight. (9/2)
**899* Pearl Anniversary (IRE)** had every chance starting down the hill, but weakened from the home turn. (11/2)
**899 Hever Golf Diamond** (8/1: op 4/1)

### 1445 E.B.F. LINGFIELD MAIDEN STKS (2-Y.O) (Class D)
7-10 (7-11) **6f** £3,649.55 (£1,090.40: £521.70: £237.35) Stalls: High GOING minus 0.26 sec per fur (GF)

SP RR SF
1118[2] **Maserati Monk** (BJMeehan) **2-9-0** JReid(5) (lw: led: edgd lft ½-wy: hdd wl over 1f out: hrd rdn ent fnl f: led last stride)....— **1** 13/8[2] 80 29
**Indian Rocket** (JLDunlop) **2-9-0** RHughes(1) (cmpt: a.p: led wl over 1f out: rdn & edgd rt ent fnl f: hdd last stride)....s.h **2** 5/4[1] 80+ 29
**Aficionado (IRE)** (RFJohnsonHoughton) **2-9-0** GDuffield(3) (neat: bit bkwd: chsd ldrs: pushed along 4f out: rdn over 1f out: styd on ins fnl f)....1¼ **3** 16/1 77 26
1046[2] **Eaton Park (IRE)** (RAkehurst) **2-9-0** SSanders(6) (prom to ½-wy)....13 **4** 9/1[3] 42 —

| | | | SP | RR | SF |
|---|---|---|---|---|---|
| **Secret Pass (USA)** (EALDunlop) **2-9-0** RCochrane(4) (w'like: bit bkwd: s.s: a outpcd) ....s.h | **5** | | 10/1 | 42 | — |
| **Riscatto (USA)** (WRMuir) **2-8-11**(3) DaneO'Neill(7) (leggy: scope: bit bkwd: sn outpcd) ....2½ | **6** | | 33/1 | 35 | — |
| **Lancashire Knight** (SDow) **2-9-0** FNorton(2) (w'like: bit bkwd: a bhd) ....8 | **7** | | 33/1 | 14 | — |

(SP 113.4%) **7 Rn**

**1m 12.26** (3.26) CSF £3.92 TOTE £2.90: £1.90 £1.30 (£1.60) OWNER The Three Bears Racing (UPPER LAMBOURN) BRED Britton House Stud

**1118 Maserati Monk** confirmed the promise of his Salisbury debut with a game display here. He looked cooked when headed below the distance, but rallied well to get back up in the shadow of the post. He was well suited by this six furlongs. (13/8)

**Indian Rocket**, a compact colt, came here with a bit of a reputation and he looked like justifying it when taking the lead over a furlong out but, though doing nothing wrong, was worn down in the final strides. (5/4)

**Aficionado (IRE)** ran a very promising race. Very green in the paddock, he showed his inexperience in the race too, having to be nudged along early to keep in touch. The penny dropped inside the final furlong and he was staying on well at the finish. He should learn a lot from this. (16/1)

**1046 Eaton Park (IRE)** (9/1: 6/1-10/1)

**Secret Pass (USA)** (10/1: op 5/1)

## 1446 BANNISTER H'CAP (0-70) (3-Y.O+) (Class E)

7-40 (7-40) **5f** £3,070.20 (£915.60: £436.80: £197.40) Stalls: High GOING minus 0.26 sec per fur (GF)

| | | | SP | RR | SF |
|---|---|---|---|---|---|
| 1170* | **Halliard (59)** (TMJones) **5-9-3** RPerham(5) (b: a.p: rdn over 1f out: led ins fnl f: r.o wl) ....— | **1** | 4/1 2 | 67 | 47 |
| 1307 7 | **Kildee Lad (69)** (APJones) **6-9-13** JReid(6) (lw: chsd ldrs: rdn over 1f out: r.o) ....½ | **2** | 9/1 | 75 | 55 |
| 582 22 | **Tauber (41)** (PatMitchell) **12-7-8**(5)ow2 MHenry(4) (a.p: led over 1f out: hdd ins fnl f: unable qckn) ....nk | **3** | 33/1 | 46 | 24 |
| 1199 5 | **Awasha (IRE) (65)** (MissGayKelleway) **4-9-9** RCochrane(10) (b: b.hind: hld up: nt clr run on ins over 2f out: hdwy over 1f out: r.o ins fnl f) ....1¾ | **4** | 11/4 1 | 65 | 45 |
| 1049* | **Judgement Call (52)** (PHowling) **9-8-10** FNorton(3) (b: lw: chsd ldrs: rdn over 2f out: one pce) ....1¾ | **5** | 11/2 3 | 46 | 26 |
| | **Pride of Hayling (IRE) (51)** (PRHedger) **5-8-6**(3) NVarley(2) (mid div: rdn 3f out: swtchd rt over 1f out: one pce) ....½ | **6** | 20/1 | 44 | 24 |
| 1064 7 | **La Belle Dominique (53)** (SGKnight) **4-8-11** SSanders(1) (led: hdd over 1f out: sn wknd) ....1¾ | **7** | 12/1 | 40 | 20 |
| 861 7 | **Rowlandsons Stud (IRE) (57)** (AMoore) **3-8-4**(3) DaneO'Neill(11) (a outpcd) ....1½ | **8** | 12/1 | 39 | 11 |
| 1073 11 | **Ashtina (70)** (BAPearce) **11-9-11**(3) PMcCabe(7) (lw: in tch tl ½-wy) ....4 | **9** | 16/1 | 39 | 19 |
| 943 9 | **King of Munster (AUS) (65)** (MrsJCecil) **4-9-9** GDuffield(8) (sn outpcd) ....nk | **10** | 6/1 | 34 | 14 |
| 862 19 | **Midnight Cookie (53)** (BAPearce) **3-8-3** GBardwell(9) (bhd fnl 3f) ....8 | **11** | 33/1 | — | — |

(SP 118.2%) **11 Rn**

**58.77 secs** (1.77) CSF £36.79 CT £941.96 TOTE £4.70: £1.30 £2.00 £7.20 (£34.20) Trio £270.20 OWNER The Rest Hill Partnership (GUILDFORD) BRED Mrs J. Brookes

WEIGHT FOR AGE 3yo-8lb

**1170* Halliard** followed up last week's course and distance win in game fashion, and is in good heart at present. (4/1)

**Kildee Lad** ran well, staying on nicely in the final furlong, and is running into form. (9/1)

**Tauber**, a winner on this course eleven times, the last being four years ago, ran his best race for ages here, and could yet sneak another course win at the age of twelve. (33/1)

**1199 Awasha (IRE)** was unlucky. Trapped behind tiring horses at halfway, she finally got clear below the distance but, although staying on very well, she had too much ground to make up. (11/4)

**1049* Judgement Call** hunted up the leaders until outpaced in the final two furlongs. (11/2: 7/2-6/1)

**743 Rowlandsons Stud (IRE)** (12/1: op 8/1)

## 1447 SUN PUNTERS CLUB H'CAP (0-80) (3-Y.O) (Class D)

8-10 (8-10) **1m 2f** £3,960.15 (£1,183.20: £566.10: £257.55) Stalls: High GOING: 0.04 sec per fur (G)

| | | | SP | RR | SF |
|---|---|---|---|---|---|
| 860 6 | **Double Up (60)** (LadyHerries) **3-8-8** DeclanO'Shea(1) (led: hdd 3f out: led again over 1f out: r.o wl) ....— | **1** | 15/2 | 68 | 25 |
| 980 4 | **Silver Wing (USA) (73)** (MBell) **3-9-7** RCochrane(4) (b.hind: chsd ldrs: led 2f out: hdd over 1f out: one pce) ...3 | **2** | 4/1 3 | 76 | 33 |
| 1337* | **Young Butt (63)** (JFfitch-Heyes) **3-8-6**(5) 5x MHenry(5) (lw: hld up: outpcd & lost tch over 4f out: hdwy over 1f out: styd on ins fnl f) ....1¼ | **3** | 100/30 2 | 64 | 21 |
| 756 6 | **Castan (IRE) (65)** (JLDunlop) **3-8-13** GDuffield(3) (chsd ldrs: ev ch 2f out: wknd ins fnl f) ....2½ | **4** | 13/2 | 62 | 19 |
| 1119* | **Sound Check (57)** (BJMeehan) **3-8-5** SSanders(6) (lw: chsd ldr: led 3f out: hdd 2f out: wknd over 1f out)....5 | **5** | 11/4 1 | 46 | 3 |
| *836** | **Law Dancer (IRE) (73)** (TGMills) **3-9-7** MarkLynch(2) (lw: hld up in tch: rdn 3f out: wknd 2f out) ....3½ | **6** | 5/1 | 57 | 14 |

(SP 111.5%) **6 Rn**

**2m 13.54** (8.84) CSF £33.68 TOTE £8.90: £3.40 £1.50 (£17.80) OWNER Mrs L. Stevens (LITTLEHAMPTON) BRED Aston Park Stud

**Double Up** rallied gamely to lead again below the distance, and soon came clear. The way she ran here suggests she will stay further. (15/2)

**980 Silver Wing (USA)** came through looking likely to win at the two-furlong pole, but was soon put in her place by the winner. (4/1)

**1337* Young Butt** got badly outpaced coming down the hill, and it was only late on that he started to close. (100/30)

**Castan (IRE)** looked one-paced in the closing stages. (13/2: 9/2-7/1)

**1119* Sound Check** dropped away disappointingly in the final two furlongs. (11/4)

## 1448 KING POST LIMITED STKS (0-70) (3-Y.O+) (Class E)

8-40 (8-40) **1m 2f (Equitrack)** £3,124.80 (£932.40: £445.20: £201.60) Stalls: High GOING minus 0.42 sec per fur (FST)

| | | | SP | RR | SF |
|---|---|---|---|---|---|
| 1154 3 | **Sharpical (70)** (SirMarkPrescott) **4-9-7** GDuffield(5) (lw: hld up: hdwy over 3f out: led 1f out: rdn out)....— | **1** | 2/1 2 | 80 | 38 |
| 1088 3 | **Four of Spades (70)** (PDEvans) **5-9-4v**(5) AmandaSanders(2) (keen hold: chsd ldr: led 4f out: hdd 1f out: unable qckn) ....3 | **2** | 13/2 3 | 77 | 35 |
| *1096** | **Distinct Beauty (IRE) (78)** (WAO'Gorman) **3-8-8v** EmmaO'Gorman(7) (a.p: ev ch 2f out: sn rdn: one pce) .....3 | **3** | 11/8 1 | 71 | 15 |
| *499 6* | **Our Eddie (60)** (BGubby) **7-9-7v** RPerham(1) (chsd ldrs tl rdn & outpcd fnl 4f) ....6 | **4** | 10/1 | 61 | 19 |
| 1047 R | **Yellow Dragon (IRE) (45)** (BAPearce) **3-8-2**(5) MHenry(8) (sn outpcd: bhd tl mod late hdwy) ....4 | **5** | 40/1 | 54 | — |
| 982 15 | **Flow Back (65)** (GPEnright) **4-9-7** RCochrane(3) (sn outpcd: a bhd) ....6 | **6** | 20/1 | 45 | 3 |
| *349 5* | **Real Madrid (45)** (GPEnright) **5-9-6v**(3) NVarley(4) (chsd ldrs tl rdn & wknd 5f out) ....1½ | **7** | 16/1 | 44 | 2 |
| | **Direct Dial (USA) (67)** (JARToller) **4-9-7** SSanders(6) (led: hdd 4f out: sn wknd) ....5 | **8** | 12/1 | 34 | — |

(SP 118.6%) **8 Rn**

**2m 8.4** (4.10) CSF £15.09 TOTE £3.50: £1.50 £1.80 £1.10 (£12.60) OWNER Mr A. S. Reid (NEWMARKET) BRED E. R. W. Stanley and New England Stud Farm Ltd

WEIGHT FOR AGE 3yo-14lb

**OFFICIAL EXPLANATION Flow Back: was outpaced early on, resented the kick back and wants further according to both jockey and trainer.**

**1154 Sharpical** always travelled like the winner and, though ridden out in the final furlong, won with a bit in hand. (2/1)
**1088 Four of Spades** runs very well on this course and put up another good display here. (13/2: 4/1-7/1)
**1096* Distinct Beauty (IRE)** had every chance but did not look very keen in the closing stages. (11/8)
**Direct Dial (USA)** (12/1: 8/1-14/1)

T/Plpt: £1,093.70 (7.69 Tckts). T/Qdpt: £26.40 (36.37 Tckts). SM

# 0977-**WARWICK (L-H) (Good)**
## Saturday May 25th
WEATHER: overcast WIND: almost nil

## 1449 LEAM AMATEUR H'CAP (0-70) (3-Y.O+) (Class G)
6-25 (6-25) **1m** £2,931.00 (£816.00: £393.00) Stalls: Low GOING minus 0.36 sec per fur (F)

| | Horse / details | Dist | Pos | SP | RR | SF |
|---|---|---|---|---|---|---|
| 1047[2] | **Montone (IRE) (48)** (JRJenkins) **6-10-0v**(5) DrMMannish(21) (chsd ldrs: led 1f out: rdn out) | — | **1** | 9/2 1 | 61 | 48 |
| 1018[3] | **Wentbridge Lad (IRE) (63)** (PDEvans) **6-11-1v**(5) MrWMcLaughlin(17) (hld up: plld out 2f out: r.o wl appr fnl f: nt rch wnr) | 1¼ | **2** | 13/2 2 | 74 | 61 |
| 1348[7] | **Kingchip Boy (63)** (MJRyan) **7-11-1v**(5) MrSLavallin(13) (chsd ldrs: led 4f out to 1f out: no ex) | 1 | **3** | 8/1 3 | 72 | 59 |
| 787[6] | **Lady Sabina (41)** (WJMusson) **6-9-12** MrTMcCarthy(11) (hdwy over 1f out: r.o) | 2 | **4** | 12/1 | 46 | 33 |
| 973[13] | **Lila Pedigo (IRE) (53)** (MissJFCraze) **3-9-7**(5) MrWWenyon(20) (r.o fnl 2f: nvr rchd ldrs) | ¾ | **5** | 50/1 | 56 | 31 |
| *184*[4] | **Benjamins Law (52)** (JAPickering) **5-10-4**(5) MissEGeorge(10) (prom: rdn 2f out: one pce) | 1¾ | **6** | 11/1 | 52 | 39 |
| 1069[8] | **Roseate Lodge (47)** (SEKettlewell) **10-10-4** MrsDKettlewell(16) (lw: in tch: rdn & r.o appr fnl f) | nk | **7** | 16/1 | 46 | 33 |
| 670[14] | **Legal Drama (USA) (54)** (JohnBerry) **4-10-6**(5)ow9 MrVCoogan(15) (s.s: r.o wl fnl 2f) | ¾ | **8** | 50/1 | 51 | 29 |
| 1196[15] | **Asterix (40)** (JMBradley) **8-9-11v** MrsLPearce(19) (plld hrd: chsd ldrs: wknd fnl f) | hd | **9** | 10/1 | 37 | 24 |
| | **Pusey Street Boy (46)** (JRBosley) **9-10-3** MrsSBosley(22) (lw: led 4f: ev ch over 1f out: sn wknd) | nk | **10** | 14/1 | 43 | 30 |
| *389*[8] | **Prince Rooney (IRE) (40)** (PButler) **8-9-6**(5) MrJGoldstein(8) (nvr nrr) | s.h | **11** | 33/1 | 37 | 24 |
| | **Little Luke (IRE) (40)** (PButler) **5-9-6**(5) MrIMongan(1) (bit bkwd: chsd ldrs 5f) | s.h | **12** | 50/1 | 36 | 23 |
| 1074[6] | **Love Legend (46)** (DWPArbuthnot) **11-10-3** MrsDArbuthnot(4) (b: in tch over 5f) | nk | **13** | 16/1 | 42 | 29 |
| 440[22] | **Don't Drop Bombs (USA) (37)** (DTThom) **7-9-8v** MissJFeilden(23) (w ldrs tl wknd wl over 1f out) | hd | **14** | 9/1 | 33 | 20 |
| 1074[11] | **Breezed Well (39)** (BRCambidge) **10-9-5**(5)ow1 MrsHNoonan(14) (prom tl wknd 2f out) | s.h | **15** | 33/1 | 35 | 21 |
| 1411[10] | **Tony's Mist (46)** (JMBradley) **6-9-12**(5) MissLKerr(7) (lw: chsd ldrs 5f) | ¾ | **16** | 50/1 | 40 | 27 |
| *1096*[4] | **Prudent Princess (60)** (AHide) **4-11-3** MissLHide(9) (prom 6f) | hd | **17** | 20/1 | 54 | 41 |
| 981[15] | **Spectacle Jim (46)** (MJHaynes) **7-10-3b** MissYHaynes(6) (hdwy 4f out: nvr rchd ldrs) | 1½ | **18** | 50/1 | 37 | 24 |
| *854*[9] | **Dream Carrier (IRE) (45)** (REPeacock) **8-9-11b**(5) MrsCPeacock(18) (in tch tl rdn & wknd 3f out) | s.h | **19** | 20/1 | 36 | 23 |
| 879[28] | **Cuban Reef (47)** (WJMusson) **4-9-13**(5) MrMBurrows(3) (in tch 5f) | 2½ | **20** | 20/1 | 33 | 20 |
| *208*[8] | **Air Command (BAR) (43)** (CTNash) **6-9-9**(5) MrPPhillips(2) (bhd fnl 3f) | 2½ | **21** | 33/1 | 24 | 11 |
| | **Ripsnorter (IRE) (48)** (KBishop) **7-10-0**(5) MissAPurdy(12) (dwlt: a bhd) | 5 | **22** | 50/1 | 19 | 6 |
| 1010[10] | **Risky Romeo (64)** (GCBravery) **4-11-2**(5) MrKSantana(5) (v.slowly away: a t.o) | 25 | **23** | 10/1 | — | — |

(SP 140.1%) **23 Rn**

**1m 40.1** (3.70) CSF £34.32 CT £222.72 TOTE £8.00: £2.00 £1.80 £2.50 £2.50 (£23.90) Trio £40.70 OWNER Mr B. Shirazi (ROYSTON) BRED Sean Gorman
WEIGHT FOR AGE 3yo-12lb
**1047 Montone (IRE)** has been threatening to win for a while and took control entering the final furlong. (9/2)
**1018 Wentbridge Lad (IRE)** proved hard to pull out wide of the pack early in the straight but, once on an even keel, finished with a real flourish. (13/2)
**1047 Kingchip Boy**, meeting the winner for the fourth time in six weeks, finds the score now stands at two apiece. (8/1)
**787 Lady Sabina** was doing some excellent work late in the day and needs further. (12/1: op 8/1)
**Lila Pedigo (IRE)**, racing beyond six furlongs for the first time, did not seem to be getting anywhere until finishing strongly. (50/1)
**Benjamins Law** is yet to score on turf, but shaped well having been off since January, and there is a race in him. (11/1)

## 1450 WEATHERBYS INSURANCE SERVICES H'CAP (0-80) (3-Y.O+) (Class D)
6-50 (6-51) **1m 2f 169y** £4,077.50 (£1,220.00: £585.00: £267.50) Stalls: Low GOING minus 0.36 sec per fur (F)

| | Horse / details | Dist | Pos | SP | RR | SF |
|---|---|---|---|---|---|---|
| 979[8] | **Myfontaine (61)** (KTIvory) **9-8-13** JCarroll(1) (lw: hld up: hdwy 3f out: led 2f out: sn clr: easily) | — | **1** | 11/2 2 | 73+ | 40 |
| 844[9] | **Typhoon Eight (IRE) (70)** (BWHills) **4-9-3b**1(5) JDSmith(6) (hld up: hdwy over 1f out: r.o wl nr fin) | 6 | **2** | 14/1 | 73 | 40 |
| 1124[9] | **Dormy Three (64)** (RJHodges) **6-9-2** ACulhane(7) (lw: hmpd after 1f: hdwy over 3f out: no imp appr fnl f) | hd | **3** | 20/1 | 67 | 34 |
| 979[3] | **Hand of Straw (IRE) (58)** (PGMurphy) **4-8-10v** NAdams(10) (in tch: hdwy 4f out: no imp fnl 2f) | 2½ | **4** | 8/1 | 57 | 24 |
| 1198[15] | **Augustan (52)** (SGollings) **5-8-4v** VHalliday(11) (dwlt: hdwy 5f out: led 3f out: sn hdd: wknd appr fnl f) | hd | **5** | 16/1 | 51 | 18 |
| 853[2] | **Another Time (71)** (SPCWoods) **4-9-4**(5) MartinDwyer(8) (chsd ldrs: ev ch 2f out: sn rdn & btn) | 1¼ | **6** | 11/4 1 | 68 | 35 |
| 1102[7] | **Tappeto (70)** (HCandy) **4-9-8** CRutter(2) (nvr trbld ldrs) | 4 | **7** | 10/1 | 61 | 28 |
| 1145[18] | **Emily-Mou (IRE) (70)** (MJRyan) **4-9-3**(5) MBaird(5) (bit bkwd: chsd ldrs: led over 2f out: sn hdd & one pce) | 3½ | **8** | 14/1 | 56 | 23 |
| 1198[6] | **Deano's Beeno (76)** (MJohnston) **4-10-0** TWilliams(9) (lw: prom tl wknd 4f out) | 4 | **9** | 6/1 3 | 56 | 23 |
| *353*[8] | **Ilandra (IRE) (47)** (RAkehurst) **4-7-13** JFEgan(12) (chsd ldrs: rdn 4f out: wknd over 2f out) | 6 | **10** | 12/1 | 18 | — |
| 995[8] | **Sarasota Storm (50)** (MBell) **4-8-2v**1ow1 PRobinson(4) (led over 7f) | 2 | **11** | 8/1 | 18 | — |
| 871[7] | **Out on a Promise (IRE) (75)** (NJHWalker) **4-9-13** WJO'Connor(13) (prom: rdn over 3f out: sn wknd) | ½ | **12** | 8/1 | 43 | 10 |
| | **Sun Circus (54)** (JLSpearing) **4-8-3**(3)ow4 SDrowne(3) (wl bhd fnl 3f) | 23 | **13** | 33/1 | — | — |

(SP 133.4%) **13 Rn**

**2m 17.3** (3.80) CSF £79.87 CT £1,364.78 TOTE £4.80: £2.00 £7.90 £5.00 (£167.90) Trio £140.70; £158.58 to Sandown 27/5/96. OWNER Mr K. T. Ivory (RADLETT) BRED Farmleigh Partners
**979 Myfontaine**, gaining his eighth course success, fairly trotted up and is in great heart. He has never won after June. (11/2)
**Typhoon Eight (IRE)**, dropping back in trip, stayed on under strong pressure past beaten horses to make the frame for the first time in ten attempts. (14/1)
**844 Dormy Three** made rapid strides on the home turn but the effort began to slacken once in line for home. (20/1)
**979 Hand of Straw (IRE)** had pulled up over hurdles since his last run on the Flat and could not match the pace of the winner from the home turn. (8/1)
**Augustan**, who has found a race in the last two summers, ran much better than of late. (16/1)
**853 Another Time**, raised for his last run, tried hard early in the straight but the winner quickly broke him. (11/4)
**Sarasota Storm** (8/1: op 12/1)

# 1451 RADWAY CLAIMING STKS (3-Y.O) (Class F)

7-20 (7-23) **1m 2f 169y** £2,690.40 (£744.40: £355.20) Stalls: Low GOING minus 0.36 sec per fur (F)

| | Horse | Dist | Pos | SP | RR | SF |
|---|---|---|---|---|---|---|
| 849[7] | **Cry Baby (49)** (NTinkler) **3-8-6b[1]** JCarroll(4) (lw: hld up: hdwy over 3f out: r.o to ld nr fin) | — | 1 | 11/2 | 49 | 3 |
| 849[9] | **Radmore Brandy (35)** (NPLittmoden) **3-8-1** NCarlisle(2) (trckd ldrs: rdn over 1f out: r.o ins fnl f: jst failed) | nk | 2 | 12/1 | 44 | — |
| 1009[6] | **Wingnut (IRE) (44)** (MJHaynes) **3-7-13b** JQuinn(8) (plld hrd: prom: led over 2f out: sn rdn: ct nr fin) | hd | 3 | 11/1 | 41 | — |
| 1099[8] | **Sunley Secure (65)** (MRChannon) **3-8-9** PaulEddery(6) (chsd ldrs: rdn 3f out: one pce) | 1¾ | 4 | 15/8[1] | 49 | 3 |
| *655[6]* | **Forliando (43)** (MSSaunders) **3-8-9** NAdams(7) (hld up: rdn 4f out: nvr rchd ldrs) | 10 | 5 | 25/1 | 34 | — |
| 863[13] | **Kinnescash (IRE) (63)** (MSSaunders) **3-8-11** RPrice(3) (led tl hdd & wknd over 2f out) | 8 | 6 | 9/2[3] | 24 | — |
| 1067[4] | **Lebedinski (IRE)** (MrsPSly) **3-8-6** ACulhane(9) (plld hrd: w ldr: rdn 4f out: hmpd over 2f out: sn btn) | 4 | 7 | 7/2[2] | 13 | — |
| 957[9] | **Alana's Ballad (IRE)** (BPJBaugh) **3-8-3**ow1 PRobinson(5) (hld up & plld hrd: nvr nr to chal) | hd | 8 | 25/1 | 10 | — |
| 849[14] | **Friendly Dreams (IRE)** (PTDalton) **3-8-2** JFEgan(1) (bit bkwd: trckd ldrs 5f: sn wknd & eased: p.u 2f out) | | P | 40/1 | — | — |
| | | | | (SP 116.7%) | **9 Rn** | |

**2m 21.6** (8.10) CSF £60.50 TOTE £5.80: £1.40 £2.10 £1.80 (£31.60) Trio £60.60 OWNER Mrs Marie Tinkler (MALTON) BRED Mrs M. Tinkler

OFFICIAL EXPLANATION **Lebedinski (IRE): was found to have pulled a muscle in her hind quarters.**

**849 Cry Baby,** blinkered for the first time, raced with his head high in the home straight and took an awful lot of persuading to go through with his effort. (11/2)

**522 Radmore Brandy** looked short of pace as the tempo quickened, but kept plugging away on the inside rail and would have won in another couple of strides. (12/1: 9/1-14/1)

**Wingnut (IRE),** stepping up half a mile in trip, pulled hard early on but nearly made the move pay as it was only in the dying strides that she was worn down. (11/1)

**1000 Sunley Secure,** stepping up in trip, failed to pick up when the chips were down. (15/8)

**Forliando** never threatened to close on the leaders as the pressure was applied. (25/1)

**Kinnescash (IRE)** moved to post far too freely and refused to settle in the race, and had nothing left for the home straight. (9/2: 2/1-5/1)

**1067 Lebedinski (IRE)** (7/2: op 8/1)

# 1452 WATCH SECURITY MAIDEN STKS (3-Y.O+) (Class D)

7-50 (7-51) **7f** £3,947.50 (£1,180.00: £565.00: £257.50) Stalls: Low GOING minus 0.36 sec per fur (F)

| | Horse | Dist | Pos | SP | RR | SF |
|---|---|---|---|---|---|---|
| 982[10] | **Pusey Street Girl** (JRBosley) **3-8-1**(7) AimeeCook(4) (plld hrd: a.p: rdn to ld nr fin) | — | 1 | 50/1 | 74 | 34 |
| 583[2] | **Civil Liberty (90)** (GLewis) **3-8-13** PaulEddery(3) (chsd ldrs: pushed along 4f out: r.o wl fnl f: jst failed) | s.h | 2 | Evens[1] | 79 | 39 |
| | **Duel At Dawn** (JHMGosden) **3-8-13** WRyan(9) (w'like: scope: b: b.hind: led: rdn over 1f out: ct nr fin) | ¾ | 3 | 7/2[3] | 77 | 37 |
| 1127[6] | **Iamus (88)** (PTWalwyn) **3-8-13** JCarroll(2) (trckd ldrs: rdn 2f out: r.o nr fin) | ½ | 4 | 5/2[2] | 76 | 36 |
| | **Panata (IRE)** (LMCumani) **3-8-8** OUrbina(1) (w'like: trckd ldrs: shkn up & r.o fnl f) | ¾ | 5 | 10/1 | 69 | 29 |
| | **Irish Kinsman** (PTWalwyn) **3-8-13** TQuinn(10) (lw: chsd ldr: hmpd over 1f out: sn btn & eased) | 8 | 6 | 40/1 | 56 | 16 |
| | **Serape** (HCandy) **3-8-8** CRutter(8) (leggy: nvr trbld ldrs) | 1½ | 7 | 14/1 | 48 | 8 |
| 1171[9] | **Mellow Master** (NJHWalker) **3-8-13** WJO'Connor(11) (dwlt: nvr nr to chal) | 2 | 8 | 25/1 | 48 | 8 |
| | **Severn Mill** (JMBradley) **5-9-7**(3) SDrowne(6) (outpcd: kpt on fnl 2f) | ½ | 9 | 66/1 | 47 | 18 |
| | **Nullahs Pet** (AStreeter) **4-9-0**(5) RHavlin(12) (neat: lengthy: trckd ldrs over 4f) | 8 | 10 | 66/1 | 24 | — |
| | **Fleeting Footsteps** (MJPolglase) **4-9-10** WHollick(5) (leggy: unf: bit bkwd: in tch over 4f) | 3½ | 11 | 66/1 | 21 | — |
| | | | | (SP 129.3%) | **11 Rn** | |

**1m 27.0** (2.40) CSF £105.29 TOTE £44.80: £4.80 £1.10 £1.80 (£46.40) Trio £93.10 OWNER Marks (Banbury) (WANTAGE) BRED M. A. Wilkins

WEIGHT FOR AGE 3yo-11lb

**Pusey Street Girl** is not a great mover but is coming to hand and, after pulling hard, fought gamely to the front. (50/1)

**583 Civil Liberty,** a class apart from these on looks, always found things happening too fast for him but nearly snatched the prize at the death. This was a disappointment, but surely he needs further. (Evens)

**Duel At Dawn** is impeccably bred but rather ordinary to look at. Nevertheless, he went close to making all and should find a small race. (7/2: 3/1-5/1)

**1127 Iamus** does not seem to enjoy his racing and would probably do better in blinkers. (5/2)

**Panata (IRE)** looked green and hung fire when initially sent about her work, only to run on near the finish. (10/1: op 4/1)

**Irish Kinsman** did show a little promise and would have finished close up but for having his ground taken. (40/1)

**Serape** (14/1: op 5/1)

# 1453 SANDRETTO MEDIAN AUCTION MAIDEN STKS (2-Y.O) (Class E)

8-20 (8-20) **5f** £3,015.60 (£898.80: £428.40: £193.20) Stalls: Low GOING minus 0.36 sec per fur (F)

| | Horse | Dist | Pos | SP | RR | SF |
|---|---|---|---|---|---|---|
| | **Deep Finesse** (MAJarvis) **2-9-0** PRobinson(1) (str: scope: lw: chsd ldrs: led ins fnl f: sn rdn clr) | — | 1 | 4/1[2] | 88+ | 33 |
| | **Ruby Princess (IRE)** (PFICole) **2-8-9** TQuinn(3) (lt-f: unf: led over 4f: sn btn) | 4 | 2 | 3/1[1] | 70 | 15 |
| 1191[12] | **Merciless Cop** (BJMeehan) **2-9-0** JQuinn(8) (in tch: c wd over 2f out: r.o fnl f) | 2 | 3 | 33/1 | 69 | 14 |
| | **Turtle Moon** (MHTompkins) **2-9-0** PaulEddery(2) (unf: scope: bit bkwd: dwlt: sn in tch: hung lft over 2f out: no ex fnl f) | 1¼ | 4 | 8/1 | 65 | 10 |
| 1191[3] | **Double-J (IRE)** (KMcAuliffe) **2-9-0** JFEgan(6) (s.i.s: c wd over 2f out: nvr trbld ldrs) | ¾ | 5 | 3/1[1] | 62 | 7 |
| 1086[3] | **Dive Master (IRE)** (CMurray) **2-9-0** MTebbutt(4) (bhd tl rdn & r.o fnl 2f) | ¾ | 6 | 5/1 | 60 | 5 |
| | **Champagne Toast** (RHannon) **2-9-0** JCarroll(5) (leggy: scope: in tch: hmpd over 2f out: sn btn) | 5 | 7 | 9/2[3] | 44 | — |
| *1080[8]* | **Master Foley** (NPLittmoden) **2-9-0** TGMcLaughlin(7) (chsd ldr: hung rt over 2f out: sn wknd) | 3 | 8 | 50/1 | 34 | — |
| | | | | (SP 120.9%) | **8 Rn** | |

**60.0 secs** (2.00) CSF £16.59 TOTE £5.80: £2.10 £1.10 £3.70 (£9.00) OWNER Mr John Sims (NEWMARKET) BRED D. A. and Mrs Hicks

**Deep Finesse** is not over-big but has sprinter written all over him. A scratchy mover in his slower paces, he picked up well once he warmed up in the last couple of furlongs of the race and could prove to be quite useful, although his half-sister Champagne Girl became disappointing after making a winning debut in 1993. (4/1)

**Ruby Princess (IRE),** not much to look at, took a good hold going down and, shooting out of the stalls, had all bar the winner in trouble after a couple of furlongs. Headed in the last 200 yards, she tied up quickly. (3/1)

**Merciless Cop** reversed last Sunday's form with Double-J but did not take the corner well, and would be better back at six furlongs. (33/1)

**Turtle Moon** looked green and in need of the experience, but showed enough in recovering quickly from a poor start to suggest that there is hope for him. (8/1)

**1191 Double-J (IRE),** reappearing just six days after his debut and dropping a furlong in trip, got quite wound up and was taken to post last. Again missing the break, he had an unhappy run which may leave its mark. (3/1)

**1086 Dive Master (IRE)** again shaped like a horse that needs considerably further. (5/1)

## 1454 BANBURY H'CAP (0-70) (3-Y.O+) (Class E)

8-50 (8-50) **1m 6f 194y** £3,315.90 (£991.20: £474.60: £216.30) Stalls: Low GOING minus 0.36 sec per fur (F)

| Form | Horse / Details | Dist | Pos | SP | RR | SF |
|---|---|---|---|---|---|---|
| 1147[9] | **Stompin (62)** (MissHCKnight) **5-9-4**(7) GFaulkner(8) (lw: prom: led 6f out: clr over 1f out: comf) | — | **1** | 3/1[3] | 75+ | 34 |
| *260** | **Sheriff (55)** (JWHills) **5-9-4** PaulEddery(6) (chsd ldrs: ev ch over 2f out: sn rdn & one pce) | 4 | **2** | 2/1[1] | 64 | 23 |
| *1095[3]* | **Bella Sedona (53)** (LadyHerries) **4-9-1** AClark(3) (hld up: hdwy 4f out: styd on fnl f) | ½ | **3** | 9/4[2] | 61 | 19 |
| 1063[6] | **Fabulous Mtoto (41)** (MSSaunders) **6-8-4** NCarlisle(9) (lw: s.i.s: plld hrd: sn chsng ldrs: rdn 2f out: sn btn) | hd | **4** | 8/1 | 49 | 8 |
| 1044[9] | **Royrace (41)** (WMBrisbourne) **4-7-12**(5) MartinDwyer(2) (lw: hld up: rdn & hdwy 5f out: nvr rchd ldrs) | 4 | **5** | 25/1 | 45 | 3 |
| *422[10]* | **Kymin (IRE) (65)** (DJGMurraySmith) **4-9-8**(5) RPainter(4) (hld up: rdn & hdwy 5f out: btn over 2f out) | hd | **6** | 20/1 | 69 | 27 |
| 504[10] | **Hatta River (USA) (46)** (PTDalton) **6-8-9** JFEgan(10) (lw: in tch: hdwy 5f out: wknd over 1f out) | 2½ | **7** | 25/1 | 47 | 6 |
| *836[10]* | **Northern Chief (33)** (JCullinan) **6-7-10** JQuinn(11) (led 9f: wknd qckly over 3f out) | dist | **8** | 50/1 | — | — |
| 1102[10] | **Couchant (IRE) (62)** (JWhite) **5-9-11** DaleGibson(7) (in tch: rdn 7f out: sn bhd) | 3½ | **9** | 20/1 | — | — |
| | **Hang Ten (65)** (SGollings) **7-10-0b[1]** VHalliday(5) (lw: prom 8f: sn wl bhd) | dist | **10** | 50/1 | — | — |
| | ***Naseer (USA) (37)*** (KBishop) **7-8-0** NAdams(1) (Withdrawn not under Starter's orders: lame at s) | | **W** | 50/1 | — | — |

(SP 123.3%) **10 Rn**

**3m 18.8** (8.80) CSF £9.47 CT £14.35 TOTE £4.00: £2.20 £1.50 £1.10 (£5.40) Trio £4.60 OWNER The Voice Group Ltd (WANTAGE) BRED Highclere Stud Ltd

LONG HANDICAP Northern Chief 7-9

WEIGHT FOR AGE 4yo-1lb

**Stompin**, on his toes, put his Newbury flop behind him over this longer trip. He has improved considerably over hurdles since his previous Flat career and may take a bit of stopping now. (3/1)

**Sheriff**, off since the Cheltenham Festival, was right in the firing-line on the home turn before being brushed aside by the winner. (2/1)

**1095 Bella Sedona** travelled well at the back but, having got close on the home turn, did not find as much as anticipated. (9/4)

**1063 Fabulous Mtoto** missed the break but it was probably deliberate as he again failed to settle. He is his own worst enemy. (8/1)

**546 Royrace**, despite taking a good hold, seemed to stay this longer trip, although rather in his own time. (25/1)

**Kymin (IRE)**, back on turf for the first time since her days in the Cumani yard, was hard ridden to close on the leaders and the effort was petering out on the home turn. (20/1)

T/Plpt: £173.90 (69.29 Tckts). T/Qdpt: £44.90 (17.45 Tckts). Dk

# 1080-WOLVERHAMPTON (L-H) (Standard)

## Saturday May 25th

WEATHER: cloudy WIND: slt half bhd

## 1455 EDGBASTON H'CAP (0-65) (3-Y.O+ F & M) (Class F)

7-00 (7-02) **5f (Fibresand)** £2,243.00 (£618.00: £293.00) Stalls: Low GOING minus 0.08 sec per fur (STD)

| Form | Horse / Details | Dist | Pos | SP | RR | SF |
|---|---|---|---|---|---|---|
| 1157[7] | **Freckles Kelly (46)** (TDEasterby) **4-9-1** MBirch(5) (lw: mde all: drvn out) | — | **1** | 9/2[1] | 53 | 36 |
| 868[10] | **Belinda Blue (46)** (RAFahey) **4-9-1** DHarrison(4) (s.i.s: sn rcvrd: r.o fnl f) | 1¼ | **2** | 6/1[3] | 49 | 32 |
| *897[5]* | **Napier Star (51)** (MrsNMacauley) **3-8-9**(3) CTeague(11) (a.p: r.o one pce fnl f) | ½ | **3** | 14/1 | 52 | 27 |
| *1028[4]* | **Little Saboteur (55)** (PJMakin) **7-9-10b** AClark(3) (trckd ldrs: ev ch over 1f out: unable qckn) | nk | **4** | 5/1[2] | 55 | 38 |
| *1083[4]* | **Delrob (47)** (DHaydnJones) **5-9-2** AMackay(7) (lw: sn rdn: outpcd over 3f out: hdwy over 1f out: r.o) | nk | **5** | 12/1 | 47 | 30 |
| *1028[8]* | **Wasblest (56)** (JBerry) **4-9-6**(5) PRoberts(13) (hld up: nvr nr to chal) | 2 | **6** | 8/1 | 49 | 32 |
| 1307[10] | **Ashkernazy (IRE) (50)** (NEBerry) **5-8-12**(7) AEddery(1) (prom: ev ch over 1f out: wknd ins fnl f) | s.h | **7** | 8/1 | 43 | 26 |
| *1083[3]* | **Wardara (59)** (CADwyer) **4-9-11v**(3) AWhelan(8) (nvr trbld ldrs) | 2 | **8** | 7/1 | 46 | 29 |
| *1028[15]* | **Fyors Gift (IRE) (60)** (BHanbury) **3-9-4**(3) JStack(2) (w wnr: ev ch over 1f out: wknd fnl f) | ¾ | **9** | 5/1[2] | 44 | 19 |
| *835[9]* | **Subfusk (60)** (WGMTurner) **3-9-7** TSprake(6) (prom over 3f) | 2½ | **10** | 12/1 | 36 | 11 |
| *780[7]* | **Dhes-C (54)** (RHollinshead) **3-8-10**(5) DGriffiths(12) (outpcd) | ½ | **11** | 14/1 | 29 | 4 |
| *900[9]* | **Highland Fawn (49)** (BAMcMahon) **3-8-10** GCarter(9) (a bhd) | 2½ | **12** | 16/1 | 16 | — |
| 587[16] | **Margaretrose Anna (46)** (PDEvans) **4-9-1b[1]** JFortune(10) (a bhd) | hd | **13** | 20/1 | 12 | — |

(SP 139.9%) **13 Rn**

**62.0 secs** (3.30) CSF £35.08 CT £359.48 TOTE £7.10: £2.20 £3.40 £4.00 (£26.50) Trio £124.10; £139.88 to Sandown 27/5/96. OWNER Mr T. H. Bennett (MALTON) BRED Bjorn Neilson

WEIGHT FOR AGE 3yo-8lb

**1157 Freckles Kelly**, back to the minimum trip, repelled all challengers in the short home straight. (9/2)

**762 Belinda Blue** was again sluggish at the start on this first run on the sand. (6/1)

**897 Napier Star** may have found the minimum trip short of her best. (14/1)

**1028 Little Saboteur** could not take advantage of being dropped a further 2lb. (5/1)

**1083 Delrob**, dropping back in distance, was 11lb lower than when previously scoring on the All-Weather. (12/1)

## 1456 TRENT BRIDGE CLAIMING STKS (3-Y.O) (Class F)

7-30 (7-30) **1m 100y (Fibresand)** £2,070.00 (£570.00: £270.00) Stalls: Low GOING minus 0.08 sec per fur (STD)

| Form | Horse / Details | Dist | Pos | SP | RR | SF |
|---|---|---|---|---|---|---|
| 540[5] | **Dragonjoy (65)** (JWPayne) **3-8-8b** AMcGlone(7) (hld up: stdy hdwy over 5f out: led wl over 1f out: qcknd clr: easily) | — | **1** | 9/4[1] | 70 | 29 |
| 1152[7] | **Danico (52)** (SCWilliams) **3-8-12** KFallon(11) (a.p: led over 2f out tl wl over 1f out: no ch w wnr) | 7 | **2** | 4/1[3] | 61 | 20 |
| 1068[11] | **Eccentric Dancer (38)** (MPBielby) **3-8-3** JFanning(9) (s.i.s: hdwy 6f out: led over 4f out tl over 2f out: one pce) | nk | **3** | 20/1 | 51 | 10 |
| 1035[5] | **Penygarn Guv'nor** (JAGlover) **3-9-4** SDWilliams(4) (lw: chsd ldr tl wknd over 2f out) | 11 | **4** | 3/1[2] | 45 | 4 |
| 1174[9] | **African Sun (IRE) (50)** (BHanbury) **3-8-5**(3) JStack(8) (prom over 4f) | 1¾ | **5** | 10/1 | 32 | — |
| 1067[7] | **In Cahoots** (AGNewcombe) **3-9-0** DHarrison(2) (hdwy 5f out: wknd over 3f out) | 1¼ | **6** | 8/1 | 36 | — |
| | **Crown And Cushion** (KSBridgwater) **3-8-10** VSlattery(1) (leggy: unf: a bhd) | 4 | **7** | 33/1 | 24 | — |
| *839[12]* | **Classic Victory (47)** (RHarris) **3-9-4hb** AMackay(5) (led: rdn & hdd over 4f out: wknd over 3f out) | 3½ | **8** | 14/1 | 26 | — |
| | **Wee Tinkerbell** (RTJuckes) **3-7-10v[1]**(3) DWright(6) (s.i.s: a bhd) | 5 | **9** | 10/1 | — | — |
| 764[8] | **Primo Lad (54)** (WGMTurner) **3-8-10** AClark(10) (a bhd: t.o) | 22 | **10** | 14/1 | — | — |

1030[14] **Bobaluna** (RFMarvin) **3-8-0**(7)ow1 TAshley(3) (sn bhd: t.o)......14 **11** 25/1 — —
(SP 129.9%) **11 Rn**

**1m 51.0** (6.00) CSF £12.71 TOTE £2.70: £1.60 £1.50 £7.40 (£4.70) Trio £66.50; £84.42 to Sandown 27/5/96. OWNER Mr T. H. Barma (NEWMARKET) BRED T. H. Barma

**540 Dragonjoy**, freshened up by a break, would have been conceding lumps of weight had this been a handicap. (9/4)
**914* Danico** got left for dead by the winner. (4/1)
**Eccentric Dancer** appreciated this drop in class for her first outing on the All-Weather. (20/1)
**1035 Penygarn Guv'nor**, lowered in class for this first try on the sand, was gambled on in the Ring. (3/1: op 5/1)
**African Sun (IRE)** (10/1: op 4/1)
**In Cahoots** (8/1: 5/1-9/1)
**540 Classic Victory** (14/1: 10/1-16/1)

## 1457 S. J. DIXON & SON MAIDEN H'CAP (0-70) (3-Y.O+) (Class E)

8-00 (8-00) **1m 1f 79y (Fibresand)** £3,236.00 (£968.00: £464.00: £212.00) Stalls: Low GOING minus 0.08 sec per fur (STD)

| | | | | SP | RR | SF |
|---|---|---|---|---|---|---|
| 1085[5] | **Penmar (56)** (TJEtherington) **4-9-6** LCharnock(5) (lw: stdy hdwy over 5f out: rdn to ld ins fnl f: r.o wl) | — | **1** | 12/1 | 66 | 46 |
| 782[3] | **Hornpipe (55)** (JWharton) **4-9-5** KFallon(2) (lw: led 1f: led over 3f out tl ins fnl f) | ½ | **2** | 7/1 | 64 | 44 |
| 979[17] | **African-Pard (IRE) (64)** (DHaydnJones) **4-10-0** AMackay(7) (lw: a.p: hrd rdn & r.o: one pce fnl 2f) | 5 | **3** | 16/1 | 65 | 45 |
| 983[8] | **Voices in the Sky (33)** (AGNewcombe) **5-7-4**(7) IonaWands(13) (hdwy 6f out: one pce fnl 2f) | 3 | **4** | 12/1 | 29 | 9 |
| 1094[7] | **Undawaterscubadiva (40)** (MPBielby) **4-7-13**(5) LNewton(9) (rdn & hdwy over 1f out: nt rch ldrs) | s.h | **5** | 20/1 | 35 | 15 |
| 1025[4] | **Flash In The Pan (IRE) (55)** (MBell) **3-8-6** GCarter(4) (lw: dropped rr 6f out: n.d after) | 3 | **6** | 9/1 | 45 | 12 |
| 863[11] | **Rostaq (56)** (DJGMurraySmith) **3-8-7b[1]** JFortune(12) (lw: nvr nr to chal) | 7 | **7** | 20/1 | 34 | 1 |
| | **Samara Song (60)** (WGMTurner) **3-8-11** TSprake(10) (prom tl wknd over 2f out) | nk | **8** | 25/1 | 38 | 5 |
| 987[11] | **School Boy (68)** (TJNaughton) **3-9-5** DHarrison(6) (b: lw: bhd tl rdn & hdwy over 3f out: eased whn btn fnl f) | ¾ | **9** | 3/1 [1] | 45 | 12 |
| 784[2] | **Phantom Dancer (IRE) (52)** (JBerry) **3-7-12**(5) PFessey(8) (led after 1f: hdd over 3f out: wknd 2f out) | nk | **10** | 6/1 [3] | 28 | — |
| 609[7] | **Remontant (IRE) (35)** (RHollinshead) **4-7-13**ow1 JFanning(11) (prom 4f) | 2½ | **11** | 16/1 | 7 | — |
| 1173[3] | **Zaaleff (USA) (50)** (BHanbury) **4-8-11b**(3) JStack(3) (lw: sn wl bhd) | ½ | **12** | 7/2 [2] | 21 | 1 |
| 1085[2] | **Sporting Risk (43)** (PWHarris) **4-8-7** GHind(1) (led 1f: wknd over 2f out) | 6 | **13** | 6/1 [3] | 4 | — |

(SP 138.8%) **13 Rn**

**2m 1.9** (5.90) CSF £99.23 CT £1,288.30 TOTE £22.90: £5.00 £2.80 £7.10 (£88.70) Trio £112.90; £15.91 to Sandown 27/5/96. OWNER Mr G. Liversidge (MALTON) BRED Worksop Manor Stud Farm
WEIGHT FOR AGE 3yo-13lb

**1085 Penmar**, still without the blinkers he wore towards the end of last year, scored a shade more decisively than the margin suggests. (12/1)
**782 Hornpipe**, stepping up in distance, ran well but could not hold the winner in the closing stages. (7/1)
**African-Pard (IRE)** could not concede the weight on this first outing on the artificial surface. (16/1)
**Voices in the Sky**, a late withdrawal at Nottingham the previous day, may need to drop into selling company. (12/1)
**782 Undawaterscubadiva** was trying a longer trip. (20/1)
**819 School Boy** was rather disappointing. (3/1)
**1173 Zaaleff (USA)** ran no race at all. (7/2)

## 1458 FOLEY STEELSTOCK H'CAP (0-70) (4-Y.O+) (Class E)

8-30 (8-30) **1m 4f (Fibresand)** £2,950.00 (£880.00: £420.00: £190.00) Stalls: Low GOING minus 0.08 sec per fur (STD)

| | | | | SP | RR | SF |
|---|---|---|---|---|---|---|
| 837[5] | **Premier Dance (68)** (DHaydnJones) **9-9-5**(7) AnthonyBond(8) (hld up: stdy hdwy over 5f out: led over 1f out: r.o wl) | — | **1** | 8/1 | 80 | 51 |
| 690[3] | **Locorotondo (IRE) (60)** (MBell) **5-9-4** KFallon(5) (hld up: hdwy over 3f out: led over 2f out: c wd ent st: hdd over 1f out: one pce) | 2 | **2** | 5/1 [2] | 69 | 40 |
| 898[12] | **Red Phantom (IRE) (66)** (SMellor) **4-9-10** MWigham(9) (hld up: hdwy 4f out: one pce fnl 2f) | 2½ | **3** | 12/1 | 72 | 43 |
| 993[7] | **In the Money (IRE) (61)** (RHollinshead) **7-9-0**(5) DGriffiths(4) (hld up: nt clr run over 3f out: no hdwy fnl 2f) | hd | **4** | 5/1 [2] | 67 | 38 |
| 1031* | **Cuban Nights (USA) (66)** (BJLlewellyn) **4-9-10** TWilliams(6) (lw: hld up: led over 3f out tl over 2f out: eased whn btn ins fnl f) | 7 | **5** | 11/2 [3] | 63 | 34 |
| 1082* | **Well Arranged (IRE) (65)** (RAkehurst) **5-9-2**(7) TAshley(2) (hld up: rdn over 4f out: no hdwy fnl 2f) | 1½ | **6** | 9/4 [1] | 60 | 31 |
| 1063[9] | **Stevie's Wonder (IRE) (67)** (BJLlewellyn) **6-9-11** VSlattery(7) (chsd ldr: led 9f out tl over 3f out: wknd 2f out) | 1¼ | **7** | 10/1 | 60 | 31 |
| | **Broom Isle (62)** (DBurchell) **8-9-6** LCharnock(3) (led 3f: eased whn btn over 1f out) | 4 | **8** | 20/1 | 50 | 21 |
| 1150[7] | **Charlie Bigtime (52)** (RHarris) **6-8-10** AMackay(1) (prom: rdn over 3f out: wknd 2f out) | 1½ | **9** | 6/1 | 38 | 9 |

(SP 126.4%) **9 Rn**

**2m 40.4** (7.90) CSF £48.23 CT £453.63 TOTE £14.20: £3.10 £1.40 £2.90 (£65.10) Trio £107.90; £60.81 to Sandown 27/5/96 OWNER J S Fox and Sons (PONTYPRIDD) BRED Brick Kiln Stud Farm

**Premier Dance** registered his sixth course win, the last being for his young rider back in February. (8/1)
**690 Locorotondo (IRE)** fared better on the sand this time, but Fallon's tactics of making for the stands' rail did not pay off. (5/1)
**Red Phantom (IRE)** only won a couple of claimers last year and does not look particularly well handicapped. (12/1)
**898* In the Money (IRE)** disappointed on the turf last time and was 5lb higher than his latest win. (5/1)
**1031* Cuban Nights (USA)** could not defy a 5lb rise in the weights. (11/2)
**1082* Well Arranged (IRE)** seemed to find this trip on the sharp side. (9/4)

## 1459 LORDS (S) STKS (2-Y.O F) (Class G)

9-00 (9-01) **6f (Fibresand)** £2,208.00 (£608.00: £288.00) Stalls: Low GOING minus 0.08 sec per fur (STD)

| | | | | SP | RR | SF |
|---|---|---|---|---|---|---|
| 1097[2] | **Run Lucy Run** (RGuest) **2-8-9** LCharnock(5) (plld hrd: led over 2f: hrd rdn over 1f out: rallied to ld last stride) | — | **1** | 6/4 [1] | 54 | 6 |
| 1164[2] | **Ekaterini Paritsi** (WGMTurner) **2-8-9b[1]** TSprake(1) (chsd ldr: led over 2f out: clr over 1f out: hrd rdn fnl f: hdd last stride) | s.h | **2** | 9/4 [2] | 54 | 6 |
| 1097[4] | **Rahona (IRE)** (BSRothwell) **2-8-9b** DHarrison(2) (a.p: rdn 2f out: r.o one pce) | 1¾ | **3** | 16/1 | 49 | 1 |
| 1164[3] | **Contravene (IRE)** (JBerry) **2-8-9**(5) PRoberts(4) (plld hrd: a.p: rn wd bnd 2f out: wknd ins fnl f) | 2½ | **4** | 3/1 [3] | 48 | — |

| | | | | SP | RR | SF |
|---|---|---|---|---|---|---|
| | **Classic Lady** (RHollinshead) **2-8-4**(5) DGriffiths(3) (lt-f: rdn over 2f out: sn wl bhd) | 12 | **5** | 8/1 | 11 | — |
| | | | | (SP 112.8%) | | **5 Rn** |

**1m 17.3** (5.90) CSF £5.22 TOTE £3.00: £1.30 £1.90 (£2.70) OWNER Matthews Breeding and Racing (NEWMARKET) BRED Lord Matthews
No bid
**1097 Run Lucy Run** fought back bravely over this extra furlong after looking well held. (6/4: op 9/4)
**1164 Ekaterini Paritsi**, tried in blinkers, seemed to be in control coming to the final furlong, but got touched off on the line. (9/4: 6/4-5/2)
**1097 Rahona (IRE)** could not reverse the Southwell form with the winner over this extra furlong. (16/1)
**1164 Contravene (IRE)** was again inclined to hang right, this time on the bend. (3/1)

## 1460 OLD TRAFFORD H'CAP (0-65) (3-Y.O+) (Class F)
9-30 (9-31) **7f (Fibresand)** £2,070.00 (£570.00: £270.00) Stalls: High GOING minus 0.08 sec per fur (STD)

| | | | | SP | RR | SF |
|---|---|---|---|---|---|---|
| 1348[10] | **Jigsaw Boy (61)** (PGMurphy) **7-9-7**(3) SDrowne(9) (hld up: hdwy over 3f out: led ins fnl f: pushed out) | — | **1** | 9/2[2] | 71 | 36 |
| *1085[8]* | **Quinzii Martin (51)** (DHaydnJones) **8-9-0v** AMackay(7) (hld up: hdwy over 2f out: led over 1f out tl ins fnl f) | 1¼ | **2** | 5/1[3] | 58 | 23 |
| 1087* | **Panther (IRE) (47)** (JHetherton) **6-8-10** KFallon(1) (lw: hld up: stdy hdwy on ins 4f out: led wl over 1f out: sn hdd: one pce) | 1¾ | **3** | 9/2[2] | 50 | 15 |
| *1083[2]* | **Jon's Choice (42)** (BPreece) **8-8-2**(3) DWright(3) (lw: led over 5f: wknd 1f out) | 8 | **4** | 5/1[3] | 27 | — |
| | **Dome Patrol (46)** (DBurchell) **5-8-9** LCharnock(8) (prom tl wknd over 1f out) | 2½ | **5** | 20/1 | 25 | — |
| *900[7]* | **Disco Boy (53)** (PDEvans) **6-9-2** JFortune(10) (prom tl wknd wl over 1f out) | ¾ | **6** | 12/1 | 30 | — |
| *1081[6]* | **Evening Brigadier (45)** (NMBabbage) **5-8-8** GHind(5) (lw: nvr nr to chal) | nk | **7** | 14/1 | 22 | — |
| 1121[14] | **Indian Rhapsody (50)** (ABailey) **4-8-6b1**(7) AngelaGallimore(2) (a bhd) | 4 | **8** | 14/1 | 18 | — |
| 645[11] | **Private Fixture (IRE) (55)** (DMarks) **5-9-4** DHarrison(4) (sn bhd) | 3 | **9** | 16/1 | 16 | — |
| *652[10]* | **All Apologies (IRE) (56)** (RHollinshead) **4-9-0**(5) DGriffiths(6) (chsd ldr tl wknd over 3f out) | 1¾ | **10** | 16/1 | 13 | — |
| 973[4] | **Silver Welcome (60)** (TDEasterby) **3-8-12** MBirch(12) (lw: nvr gng wl: sn bhd) | 2½ | **11** | 7/2[1] | 11 | — |
| | **Lotties Bid (43)** (JAGlover) **4-8-3b1**(3) AWhelan(11) (s.i.s: sn rcvrd: wknd 3f out) | 1¼ | **12** | 20/1 | — | — |
| | | | | (SP 134.2%) | | **12 Rn** |

**1m 30.2** (5.50) CSF £29.30 CT £104.75 TOTE £7.50: £3.00 £1.70 £2.40 (£14.10) Trio £12.80 OWNER The Jigsaw Puzzlers (BRISTOL) BRED Mrs J. A. Rawding
WEIGHT FOR AGE 3yo-11lb
**OFFICIAL EXPLANATION Silver Welcome: was unsuited by the all-weather surface.**
**981 Jigsaw Boy** returned to the All-Weather on a mark 2lb higher than when scoring the first of his two wins here back in November. (9/2)
**839 Quinzii Martin**, who has not won for fifteen months, simply met one too good. (5/1)
**1087* Panther (IRE)** ran his best race on the sand, but has yet to win beyond six furlongs. (9/2: op 3/1)
**1083 Jon's Choice**, stepping up in distance, was running off a mark 23lb lower than when last successful over two years ago. (5/1)
**653 Disco Boy** (12/1: op 8/1)
**Indian Rhapsody** (14/1: op 8/1)
**973 Silver Welcome** was reported by his rider to have been unsuited to the All-Weather surface. (7/2)

T/Plpt: £276.00 (35.36 Tckts). T/Qdpt: £75.20 (8.98 Tckts). KH

# CHEPSTOW (L-H) (Good to soft, Soft patches)
## Monday May 27th
WEATHER: overcast WIND: mod half bhd

## 1461 ST ARVANS MAIDEN STKS (3-Y.O+) (Class D)
2-00 (2-01) **1m 4f 23y** £3,666.75 (£1,104.00: £534.50: £249.75) Stalls: Low GOING: 0.15 sec per fur (G)

| | | | | SP | RR | SF |
|---|---|---|---|---|---|---|
| | **Royal Court (IRE)** (PWChapple-Hyam) **3-8-4**(5) RHavlin(2) (str: cmpt: scope: s.i.s: hld up: hdwy over 4f out: led over 3f out: sn rdn clr: easily) | — | **1** | 3/1[3] | 106+ | 28 |
| 845[3] | **Jiyush (89)** (HThomsonJones) **3-8-9** RHills(3) (swtg: hld up: rdn over 3f out: one pce) | 20 | **2** | 6/4[1] | 80 | 2 |
| 985[3] | **Bowled Over (86)** (CACyzer) **3-8-9** BThomson(5) (lw: plld hrd: chsd ldr: led 8f out to 3f out: one pce) | ½ | **3** | 9/4[2] | 79 | 1 |
| 1079[7] | **Bold Classic (IRE)** (JLDunlop) **3-8-9** AMcGlone(6) (prom tl wknd over 2f out) | 8 | **4** | 14/1 | 68 | — |
| | **Artic Bay** (MrsPNDutfield) **4-9-12** AProcter(4) (s.s: hld up: bhd fnl 3f) | 1¼ | **5** | 25/1 | 67 | 6 |
| 1117[8] | **Peetsie (IRE)** (LordHuntingdon) **4-9-0**(7) AimeeCook(7) (lw: plld hrd: led 4f: wknd over 4f out: t.o) | 30 | **6** | 16/1 | 22 | — |
| | | | | (SP 112.2%) | | **6 Rn** |

**2m 44.2** (11.80) CSF £7.70 TOTE £3.80: £1.70 £1.40 (£2.90) OWNER Mr R. E. Sangster (MARLBOROUGH) BRED Swettenham Stud And Ron Con Ltd.
WEIGHT FOR AGE 3yo-17lb
**Royal Court (IRE)**, a half-brother to Dr Devious and good Irish sprinter Archway, is apparently slow and lazy at home and took a walk in the market. Turning the race into a procession, he could be anything. (3/1: op 6/4)
**845 Jiyush**, stepping up in distance, got very warm in the preliminaries and is almost certainly better than this bare form suggests. (6/4)
**985 Bowled Over** should have been suited by the longer trip but found the winner in a different league. (9/4)
**Bold Classic (IRE)** (14/1: 10/1-16/1)

## 1462 ST ATHAN H'CAP (0-80) (3-Y.O+ F) (Class D)
2-30 (2-32) **1m 4f 23y** £3,575.75 (£1,076.00: £520.50: £242.75) Stalls: Low GOING: 0.15 sec per fur (G)

| | | | | SP | RR | SF |
|---|---|---|---|---|---|---|
| *312[8]* | **Roufontaine (62)** (WRMuir) **5-8-12**(5) RHavlin(8) (lw: a.p: led over 3f out: r.o wl) | — | **1** | 12/1 | 71 | 31 |
| 1306[4] | **Uncharted Waters (53)** (CACyzer) **5-8-8**ow1 RPrice(7) (lw: hld up: hdwy 4f out: chsd wnr fnl 2f: r.o ins fnl f) | 1 | **2** | 8/1[3] | 61 | 20 |
| 1102[3] | **Ma Petite Anglaise (73)** (WJarvis) **4-10-0** RHills(13) (lw: hld up & bhd: hdwy over 3f out: r.o one pce fnl f) | 1¾ | **3** | 7/1[2] | 78 | 38 |
| | **White Sea (IRE) (75)** (PFICole) **3-8-6**(7) DavidO'Neill(5) (s.i.s: hld up: hdwy over 2f out: styd on fnl f) | nk | **4** | 6/1[1] | 80 | 23 |
| | **Daily Sport Girl (52)** (BJLlewellyn) **7-8-0**(7)ow11 AnthonyBond(1) (a.p: no hdwy fnl 2f) | ¾ | **5** | 7/1[2] | 56 | 5 |
| 1117[7] | **Shalateeno (69)** (MRChannon) **3-8-2**(5) PPMurphy(12) (plld hrd: a.p: led over 4f out: sn hdd: wknd 2f out) | 3 | **6** | 8/1[3] | 69 | 12 |
| 1150[10] | **Green Land (BEL) (64)** (SCWilliams) **4-9-0**(5) DGriffiths(6) (b.nr fore: no hdwy fnl 3f) | ½ | **7** | 10/1 | 63 | 23 |
| *319[4]* | **Elly Fleetfoot (IRE) (63)** (MJRyan) **4-8-13**(5) MBaird(9) (hld up: hdwy over 5f out: led 4f out: sn hdd: wknd over 2f out) | 4 | **8** | 20/1 | 57 | 17 |

1123[9] **Fortunes Course (IRE) (49)** (JSKing) **7-8-4** AMcGlone(11) (lw: led over 7f) ....1½ **9** 14/1 41 1
528[9] **Fro (58)** (TJNaughton) **3-7-10** NAdams(3) (bhd fnl 5f) ....3 **10** 20/1 46 —
817[12] **Frankly Fran (49)** (DWPArbuthnot) **4-8-1**(3) DarrenMoffatt(4) (b: a bhd) ....nk **11** 33/1 37 —
1145[5] **Ashby Hill (IRE) (48)** (RRowe) **5-7-10**(7)ow2 RSmith(10) (hld up: hdwy on outside over 5f out: wknd over 2f out) ....hd **12** 6/1 1 36 —
1145[9] **Shift Again (IRE) (64)** (SESherwood) **4-9-5** BThomson(2) (prom 8f) ....6 **13** 12/1 44 4
(SP 119.4%) **13 Rn**

**2m 45.0** (12.60) CSF £95.82 CT £669.22 TOTE £9.80: £2.80 £2.30 £2.80 (£28.70) Trio £49.00 OWNER Mr D. J. Deer (LAMBOURN) BRED D. J. and Mrs Deer
LONG HANDICAP Daily Sport Girl 7-6 Fro 7-4
WEIGHT FOR AGE 3yo-17lb
**Roufontaine**, fit from hurdling, was 5lb lower than when finishing fourth in first-time blinkers at Salisbury last August. (12/1)
**1306 Uncharted Waters**, 7lb higher than when scoring at Brighton last month, may have preferred faster ground and should not be inconvenienced by a stiffer test of stamina. (8/1)
**1102 Ma Petite Anglaise** seemed to stay the extra quarter-mile and stuck to her guns under a big weight. (7/1)
**White Sea (IRE)**, ridden to get the trip, only got going fairly late on and more positive tactics can be employed in the future. (6/1)
**Daily Sport Girl** could never quite make her presence felt. (7/1)
**860 Shalateeno** again did her chances no good by refusing to settle. (8/1)
**1145 Ashby Hill (IRE)**, 5lb higher than when winning at Folkestone, may be at her best on faster ground. (6/1)

## 1463 DARLOWS (S) STKS (2-Y.O) (Class G)
3-00 (3-02) **6f 16y** £2,276.00 (£636.00: £308.00) Stalls: High GOING: 0.15 sec per fur (G)

SP RR SF
*1084*[2] **Don't Forget Shoka (IRE)** (JSMoore) **2-8-1**(5) PPMurphy(1) (lw: led 3f: led over 1f out: edgd lft ins fnl f: r.o) ....— **1** 7/4 1 46 9
596[7] **Heavenly Miss (IRE)** (BPalling) **2-8-6** RHills(5) (chsd ldrs: rdn over 2f out: ev ch wl ins fnl f: r.o) ....hd **2** 2/1 2 46 9
1032[5] **Nattie** (AGNewcombe) **2-8-11** AMcGlone(4) (hmpd s: hdwy over 2f out: unable qckn fnl f) ....½ **3** 7/1 49 12
**Impala** (WGMTurner) **2-8-6**(5) RHavlin(2) (neat: wnt rt s: prom: rdn & outpcd over 2f out: r.o wl ins fnl f) ....nk **4** 9/2 3 49 12
*1093*[10] **Rons Revenge** (MJRyan) **2-8-6**(5) MBaird(3) (w wnr: led 3f out tl over 1f out: one pce) ....½ **5** 12/1 47 10
(SP 108.1%) **5 Rn**

**1m 15.9** (6.70) CSF £5.29 TOTE £2.30: £1.30 £1.60 (£2.30) OWNER Mrs Victoria Goodman (HUNGERFORD) BRED Godolphin Management Co Ltd
No bid
**1084 Don't Forget Shoka (IRE)** managed to hold on, despite coming off a true line in the closing stages. (7/4: op Evens)
**Heavenly Miss (IRE)** appreciated the drop into selling company. (2/1)
**1032 Nattie** benefited from the extra furlong. (7/1: op 9/2)
**Impala**, out of a modest staying chaser, fought back well towards the finish. (9/2: 4/1-6/1)
**Rons Revenge** got away on level terms this time. (12/1: op 6/1)

## 1464 ST JOHN LIMITED STKS (0-75) (3-Y.O+) (Class D)
3-30 (3-31) **1m 14y** £3,735.00 (£1,125.00: £545.00: £255.00) Stalls: High GOING: 0.15 sec per fur (G)

SP RR SF
**Hilaala (USA) (75)** (PTWalwyn) **3-8-5** RHills(7) (hld up: rdn & wnt 2nd 2f out: led ins fnl f: r.o wl) ....— **1** 4/1 3 89 53
1319* **Crazy Chief (75)** (PFICole) **3-8-3**(7) DavidO'Neill(4) (lw: w ldr: led over 3f out tl ins fnl f) ....2 **2** 3/1 1 90 54
*1048*[6] **Mr Teigh (67)** (BSmart) **4-9-3**(5) DGriffiths(8) (led over 4f: wkng whn hung lft over 1f out) ....12 **3** 20/1 66 42
1192* **Xenophon of Cunaxa (IRE) (80)** (MJFetherston-Godley) **3-8-8** BThomson(2) (s.s: hld up: rdn over 3f out: wknd over 2f out: bdly hmpd over 1f out) ....1½ **4** 3/1 1 61 25
876[13] **Quintus Decimus (74)** (RAkehurst) **4-9-6** RPrice(3) (b.nr fore: hld up: wknd over 2f out) ....1½ **5** 7/2 2 58 34
1314[16] **Northern Celadon (IRE) (72)** (MJHeaton-Ellis) **5-9-3**(5) PPMurphy(5) (trckd ldrs: wknd over 2f out) ....2½ **6** 14/1 55 31
1099[6] **Andsome Boy (50)** (CRBarwell) **3-8-8** NAdams(1) (b.hind: prom 5f) ....6 **7** 50/1 41 5
1190[14] **Moscow Mist (IRE) (75)** (LadyHerries) **5-9-6** AMcGlone(6) (bit bkwd: s.s: a bhd) ....1¾ **8** 8/1 38 14
(SP 116.7%) **8 Rn**

**1m 37.1** (4.60) CSF £15.97 TOTE £4.60: £1.50 £1.60 £4.00 (£6.80) OWNER Mr Hamdan Al Maktoum (LAMBOURN) BRED Shadwell Estate Company
WEIGHT FOR AGE 3yo-12lb
STEWARDS' ENQUIRY Griffiths susp. 5-7/6/96 (careless riding).
**Hilaala (USA)** found no problem getting the mile. (4/1)
**1319* Crazy Chief**, again keen to force the pace, found the winner too strong in the last 150 yards. (3/1)
**Mr Teigh** did Xenophon of Cunaxa no favours coming to the furlong pole and his rider picked up a three-day ban. (20/1)
**1192* Xenophon of Cunaxa (IRE)** was unable to dictate matters from the front this time. (3/1)
**836 Northern Celadon (IRE)** (14/1: 10/1-16/1)

## 1465 ST BRIAVELS MAIDEN STKS (3-Y.O+) (Class D)
4-00 (4-04) **1m 14y** £3,712.25 (£1,118.00: £541.50: £253.25) Stalls: High GOING: 0.15 sec per fur (G)

SP RR SF
1142[5] **Strazo (IRE)** (JHMGosden) **3-8-12** BThomson(1) (lw: mde all: clr over 1f out: easily) ....— **1** 1/2 1 88+ 41
1104[3] **Effectual** (JARToller) **3-8-12** RHills(6) (a.p: pushed along over 4f out: chsd wnr over 2f out: no imp) ....5 **2** 13/2 3 78 31
1180[5] **Battle Spark (USA) (76)** (CACyzer) **3-8-12** RPrice(5) (chsd wnr: rdn over 3f out: cl 3rd whn stumbled 2f out: sn btn & eased) ....7 **3** 7/1 64 17
**Melomania (USA)** (TJNaughton) **4-9-10** NAdams(3) (w'like: chsd ldrs over 4f) ....4 **4** 5/1 2 56 21
1099[18] **Indian Wolf** (PGMurphy) **3-8-12** AMcGlone(4) (lw: bhd fnl 4f) ....10 **5** 66/1 36 —
**Baxworthy Lord** (CLPopham) **5-9-5**(5) PPMurphy(2) (s.s: a wl bhd) ....1¾ **6** 100/1 33 —
**Allez Pablo** (RRowe) **6-9-3**(7) RSmith(7) (bhd fnl 3f) ....3 **7** 100/1 27 —
(SP 112.6%) **7 Rn**

**1m 38.8** (6.30) CSF £4.35 TOTE £1.50: £1.30 £2.20 (£2.70) OWNER Mr K. Abdulla (NEWMARKET) BRED Juddmonte Farms
WEIGHT FOR AGE 3yo-12lb
**1142 Strazo (IRE)**, out of a daughter of a winner of both the Irish 1000 Guineas and Irish Oaks, can go on to better things. (1/2)
**1104 Effectual**, a half-brother to a mile and a half winner Risky Rose, was supported in the Ring for this drop back in distance. Probably catching a tartar, he may be an interesting prospect in handicaps back over a longer trip. (13/2: 9/2-7/1)

**1180 Battle Spark (USA)**, back to a mile, would have finished closer to the runner-up had he not completely lost his action at the quarter-mile marker. (7/1: 7/2-8/1)
**Melomania (USA)**, recently bought out of John Dunlop's yard for 28,000 guineas, is a half-brother to a minor winner in the States. (5/1: 4/1-6/1)

## 1466 ST BRIDES H'CAP (0-80) (3-Y.O+ F & M) (Class D)
4-30 (4-32) **6f 16y** £3,848.75 (£1,160.00: £562.50: £263.75) Stalls: High GOING: 0.15 sec per fur (G)

| | | | | SP | RR | SF |
|---|---|---|---|---|---|---|
| 1186[15] | **Patsy Grimes (67)** (JSMoore) **6-8-11**(7) AimeeCook(6) (hld up: nt clr run & swtchd stands' side over 2f out: hdwy over 1f out: led ins fnl f: r.o wl) | — | **1** | 15/2 | 79 | 61 |
| 1064[12] | **Tinker Osmaston (68)** (MSSaunders) **5-9-5** RPrice(8) (a.p: led over 2f out tl ins fnl f) | 3 | **2** | 9/1 | 72 | 54 |
| | **Rambold (51)** (NEBerry) **5-7-13**(3) DarrenMoffatt(9) (led over 3f: r.o one pce fnl f) | ½ | **3** | 16/1 | 54 | 36 |
| 1178[3] | **Intiaash (IRE) (73)** (DHaydnJones) **4-9-3**(7) AnthonyBond(10) (a.p: rdn 2f out: one pce) | 3 | **4** | 11/2[3] | 68 | 50 |
| 467[5] | **Mrs McBadger (66)** (BSmart) **3-8-3**(5)ow2 RHavlin(7) (no hdwy fnl 2f) | 1¾ | **5** | 11/1 | 56 | 27 |
| 931[5] | **Sally Slade (73)** (CACyzer) **4-9-10** RHills(2) (hld up: rdn over 2f out: wknd over 1f out) | 2½ | **6** | 5/1[2] | 57 | 39 |
| 1178[5] | **Louisville Belle (IRE) (49)** (MDIUsher) **7-8-0** NAdams(3) (prom: ev ch over 2f out: wknd over 1f out) | nk | **7** | 8/1 | 32 | 14 |
| 626[4] | **Loose Talk (66)** (WJarvis) **3-8-8** AMcGlone(4) (hld up: bhd fnl 2f) | 4 | **8** | 4/1[1] | 38 | 11 |
| 1101[7] | **Charlton Imp (USA) (62)** (RJHodges) **3-8-4**ow1 BThomson(11) (rdn over 3f out: sn bhd) | 6 | **9** | 14/1 | 19 | — |
| 1013[6] | **May Queen Megan (54)** (MrsALMKing) **3-7-5**(5) MBaird(1) (s.i.s: outpcd) | ¾ | **10** | 16/1 | 9 | — |
| | **Itsinthepost (65)** (VSoane) **3-8-2**(5) PPMurphy(5) (bit bkwd: prom 3f) | 2½ | **11** | 10/1 | 13 | — |
| | | | | (SP 120.8%) | **11 Rn** | |

**1m 12.9** (3.70) CSF £68.12 CT £968.18 TOTE £10.60: £3.30 £2.30 £4.40 (£34.00) Trio £153.10 OWNER Mr J. K. Grimes (HUNGERFORD) BRED J. C. Fox
LONG HANDICAP May Queen Megan 7-9
WEIGHT FOR AGE 3yo-9lb
**893* Patsy Grimes**, 3lb higher than when winning at Salisbury, was well ridden and found little difficulty overcoming traffic problems. (15/2)
**Tinker Osmaston**, nibbled at in the Ring, ran much better but could not cope with the winner. (9/1)
**Rambold** looked well tuned up for this reappearance. (16/1)
**1178 Intiaash (IRE)** goes well for her young rider but could not raise her game when the chips were down. (11/2)
**931 Sally Slade** has yet to win beyond the minimum trip. (5/1)

T/Plpt: £60.40 (106.16 Tckts). T/Qdpt: £10.90 (25.56 Tckts). KH

# 0814-LEICESTER (R-H) (Good to soft)
## Monday May 27th
WEATHER: overcast WIND: mod half against

## 1467 LIONESS MAIDEN STKS (2-Y.O F) (Class D)
2-20 (2-25) **5f 218y** £3,482.20 (£1,039.60: £496.80: £225.40) Stalls: Low GOING: 0.23 sec per fur (G)

| | | | | SP | RR | SF |
|---|---|---|---|---|---|---|
| 1346[8] | **Bluebell Miss** (MJRyan) **2-8-11** DBiggs(1) (a.p: rdn to ld appr fnl f: r.o wl) | — | **1** | 25/1 | 71 | — |
| 1179[2] | **Maid By The Fire (USA)** (PFICole) **2-8-11** CRutter(2) (unruly s: led tl hdd appr fnl f: kpt on u.p) | 1½ | **2** | 11/8[1] | 67 | — |
| | **Caribbean Star** (MRStoute) **2-8-11** KBradshaw(3) (lt-f: s.s: hdwy ½-wy: rdn & unable qckn fnl f) | ½ | **3** | 4/1[2] | 66 | — |
| 1169[5] | **My Beloved (IRE)** (RHannon) **2-8-11** RPerham(6) (prom tl outpcd wl over 1f out: rallied u.p fnl f) | nk | **4** | 8/1 | 65 | — |
| | **Lily Jaques** (PFICole) **2-8-11** AClark(7) (leggy: lt-f: trckd ldrs: effrt wl over 1f out: nvr able to chal) | nk | **5** | 10/1 | 64 | — |
| | **Salabatni** (EALDunlop) **2-8-11** WRyan(5) (lt-f: unf: s.s: hdwy 2f out: one pce appr fnl f) | 1½ | **6** | 7/1 | 60 | — |
| | **Maria di Castiglia** (RHannon) **2-8-11** GCarter(4) (small: unf: s.i.s: a bhd & outpcd: t.o) | 9 | **7** | 6/1[3] | 36 | — |
| | | | | (SP 112.9%) | **7 Rn** | |

**1m 18.9** (8.90) CSF £57.68 TOTE £36.30: £4.70 £1.30 (£24.50) OWNER Mr P. E. Axon (NEWMARKET) BRED Denis Bell
**IN-FOCUS: These were a group of very sparely-made fillies who do not look mature enough to handle testing ground. The form should be treated with caution.**
**Bluebell Miss**, making a quick return to action, got the better of the battle to nose ahead entering the final furlong and, kept up to her work, was not hard pressed to hold on. (25/1)
**1179 Maid By The Fire (USA)** caused problems before being loaded into the stalls and looks to have a mind of her own. Settling down in the lead, she did respond to pressure after being headed, but had to admit the winner just too good. (11/8)
**Caribbean Star**, a very lightly-made filly who will almost certainly require a sound surface to produce her best, turned in a pleasing performance after losing ground at the start. She should be able to win a race. (4/1)
**1169 My Beloved (IRE)** looked to be in trouble when losing her pitch soon after entering the final quarter-mile, but she rallied once into the last furlong and was still making up ground at the finish. (8/1: 5/1-9/1)
**Lily Jaques** could not summon up the speed to mount a challenge, but she did keep on and will be all the wiser for the experience. (10/1: op 5/1)
**Salabatni** failed to recover from a slow start but she was not knocked about, and can only improve on this. (7/1: 5/1-8/1)
**Maria di Castiglia** (6/1: op 3/1)

## 1468 ANSTEY (S) H'CAP (0-60) (3-Y.O+) (Class G)
2-55 (2-57) **1m 1f 218y** £2,910.00 (£810.00: £390.00) Stalls: Low GOING minus 0.03 sec per fur (G)

| | | | | SP | RR | SF |
|---|---|---|---|---|---|---|
| 1347[2] | **Kristal Breeze (37)** (WRMuir) **4-8-9** Jean-PierreLopez(5) (hld up in tch: shkn up to ld over 2f out: hld on wl cl home) | — | **1** | 100/30[1] | 51 | 24 |
| 1167[2] | **I'm a Nut Man (36)** (CASmith) **5-8-8** CRutter(12) (hld up: effrt on ins & n.m.r 3f out: hdwy wl over 1f out: rdn & hung rt fnl f: r.o) | ½ | **2** | 7/1[2] | 49 | 22 |
| 1167[6] | **Hawwam (43)** (EJAlston) **10-9-1** SDWilliams(11) (lw: in tch: effrt & rdn 2f out: r.o one pce) | 4 | **3** | 14/1 | 50 | 23 |
| 1411[16] | **Speedy Snaps Pride (39)** (PDCundell) **4-8-4b**(7) GFaulkner(14) (led tl hdd over 2f out: no ex fnl f) | 3½ | **4** | 20/1 | 40 | 13 |
| 1411[9] | **Mazilla (42)** (AStreeter) **4-8-7**(7) DSweeney(4) (lw: dwlt: bhd tl hdwy fnl 2f: nrst fin) | 1½ | **5** | 10/1[3] | 41 | 14 |
| *553*[13] | **She Said No (52)** (LordHuntingdon) **4-9-7**(3) AWhelan(8) (hld up mid div: styd on appr fnl f: nvr nrr) | s.h | **6** | 14/1 | 51 | 24 |
| 1196[14] | **Pash (41)** (CWFairhurst) **4-8-6v**(7) PDoe(15) (hld up: hdwy 2f out: styd on) | ½ | **7** | 16/1 | 39 | 12 |
| | **Wordsmith (IRE) (41)** (JLHarris) **6-8-13** AMackay(1) (bit bkwd: s.s: bhd tl styd on fnl 2f) | 1½ | **8** | 14/1 | 37 | 10 |

$866^{13}$ **Brown Eyed Girl (42)** (BJMeehan) **4-9-0b[1]** MTebbutt(2) (in tch: effrt over 2f out: rdn & wknd over 1f out) 1½ **9** 14/1 35 8
$1338^{7}$ **Yet Again (45)** (BHanbury) **4-9-3b** WRyan(9) (lw: hld up: hdwy over 3f out: wknd wl over 1f out) 3 **10** 20/1 33 6
$1411^{19}$ **No Submission (USA) (36)** (DWChapman) **10-8-8v** NDay(7) (chsd ldrs: rdn 4f out: grad fdd) ¾ **11** 20/1 23 —
$887^{19}$ **Nabjelsedr (40)** (AGNewcombe) **6-8-12** DBiggs(17) (s.s: a in rr) ¾ **12** 25/1 26 —
$1121^{12}$ **Amnesty Bay (46)** (MDIUsher) **4-9-4** MWigham(13) (nvr trbld ldrs) ¾ **13** 20/1 31 4
$1311^{3}$ **Absolute Ruler (IRE) (40)** (JLHarris) **5-8-9b(3)** SDrowne(18) (prom tl wknd 3f out) 2 **14** 7/1 2 22 —
*$776^{8}$* **Shuttlecock (40)** (MrsNMacauley) **5-8-12** JTate(19) (prom 7f) 4 **15** 16/1 15 —
$979^{11}$ **Kirov Protege (IRE) (38)** (HJCollingridge) **4-8-10v** RPerham(6) (hld up: effrt & hmpd 2f out: nt rcvr) 2 **16** 16/1 10 —
$1196^{18}$ **Daring Ryde (48)** (JPSmith) **5-9-6** GCarter(3) (bit bkwd: trckd ldrs tl rdn & wknd over 2f out) 3½ **17** 20/1 14 —
*$1095^{10}$* **Jovie King (IRE) (47)** (PhilipMitchell) **4-9-5b[1]** AClark(10) (prom tl wknd over 3f out: t.o) 8 **18** 25/1 1 —
$645^{13}$ **Finjan (44)** (AGFoster) **9-8-9v(7)** DLynch(16) (t.o) 30 **19** 33/1 — —
(SP 135.9%) **19 Rn**

**2m 12.1** (8.40) CSF £27.91 CT £289.60 TOTE £4.00: £1.30 £2.00 £3.10 £4.80 (£10.10) Trio £44.50 OWNER Mr S. Lamb (LAMBOURN) BRED R. and Mrs Heathcote
No bid

**1347 Kristal Breeze** has taken time to find an opening, but it arrived here and she did not need to work too hard to win a shade cosily. (100/30: 5/1-3/1)
**1167 I'm a Nut Man** was unlucky here for he was trapped on the inside rail when he should have been delivering his challenge. When he did eventually get free, he caused his own problems by hanging right and squandering a winning chance. (7/1)
**1167 Hawwam** is finding it increasingly difficult to get back to winning ways, and it would seem his stamina gives out at trips beyond a mile. (14/1)
**Speedy Snaps Pride** ran his best race for quite some time with these new forceful tactics being employed. They are certainly worth trying again. (20/1)
**Mazilla** needs to get her toe in, but she missed the kick this time and it was only in the closing stages that she began to stay on. (10/1)
**She Said No**, a very poor mover who raced with her tongue tied down, is still very much in the hands of the Handicapper and she was never able to get herself in with a shout. (14/1)

## 1469 ROTHMANS ROYALS NORTH SOUTH CHALLENGE SERIES H'CAP (0-85) (3-Y.O+) (Class D)
3-25 (3-28) **1m 8y** £5,848.00 (£1,744.00: £832.00: £376.00) Stalls: Low GOING: 0.23 sec per fur (G)

SP RR SF
786* **Freequent (85)** (LMCumani) **3-9-5** WRyan(1) (hld up & bhd: gd hdwy to ld over 1f out: sn clr) — **1** 11/8 1 87++ 30
$809^{10}$ **Blaze of Song (82)** (RHannon) **4-10-0** RPerham(3) (b: bit bkwd: hld up: rdn over 2f out: kpt on ins fnl f: no ch w wnr) 5 **2** 4/1 2 74 29
$994^{2}$ **Classic Leader (79)** (RHarris) **3-8-13** AMackay(2) (hld up: hdwy over 3f out: slt ld over 2f out tl over 1f out: r.o one pce) nk **3** 4/1 2 70 13
$1326^{11}$ **Roushan (76)** (JGMO'Shea) **3-8-10** JTate(5) (prom over 2f out: kpt on one pce fnl f) nk **4** 25/1 67 10
$937^{9}$ **Uncle George (70)** (MHTompkins) **3-8-4** NDay(4) (bit bkwd: prom tl outpcd ½-wy: sn rdn & btn: t.o) 11 **5** 10/1 39 —
$887^{15}$ **Duffertoes (65)** (MJRyan) **4-8-11** DBiggs(6) (led tl hdd & wknd over 2f out. t.o) 4 **6** 9/1 3 26 —
(SP 105.0%) **6 Rn**

**1m 43.8** (8.80) CSF £6.37 TOTE £1.60: £1.10 £2.50 (£3.50) OWNER Fittocks Stud (NEWMARKET) BRED Fittocks Stud
WEIGHT FOR AGE 3yo-12lb

**786* Freequent** did not have a lot to beat in this first handicap and, in achieving it with the minimum of effort, is certainly capable of tackling stiffer opposition. (11/8: op Evens)
**Blaze of Song** still has a bit left to work on and was out with the washing until gaining the runner-up spot near the finish. (4/1)
**994 Classic Leader** did poke his head in front over two furlongs out, but did not appear to be putting much effort into his work and was brushed aside with ease. He is short of experience but a pair of blinkers could make his mind up for him. (4/1)
**962 Roushan** pressed the leaders but was in trouble entering the final quarter-mile and could only stay on at the one pace. (25/1)

## 1470 MARKET BOSWORTH MEDIAN AUCTION MAIDEN STKS (3-Y.O) (Class F)
3-55 (3-55) **1m 8y** £3,003.00 (£833.00: £399.00) Stalls: Low GOING: 0.23 sec per fur (G)

SP RR SF
$703^{2}$ **Henry Island (IRE) (86)** (GWragg) **3-9-0** AClark(8) (hld up: hdwy 3f out: led wl over 1f out: sn clr: canter) — **1** 5/4 1 79++ 34
**Amadour (IRE)** (PhilipMitchell) **3-9-0** GCarter(1) (bit bkwd: bhd: rdn over 2f out: styd on ins fnl f) 11 **2** 33/1 57 12
$943^{11}$ **No Hiding Place (50)** (BHanbury) **3-9-0** JTate(3) (led: sn clr: edgd lft & hdd wl over 1f out: sn btn) s.h **3** 16/1 57 12
*$856^{5}$* **Spencer Stallone** (LordHuntingdon) **3-8-11(3)** AWhelan(2) (prom tl rdn & outpcd fnl 2f) 2½ **4** 8/1 52 7
$942^{8}$ **Lucky Begonia (IRE)** (CNAllen) **3-8-9** CHodgson(5) (b: bkwd: nvr trbld ldrs) 1 **5** 33/1 45 —
$1035^{3}$ **Blurred (IRE)** (MHTompkins) **3-9-0** NDay(4) (prom tl wknd u.p 2f out) ¾ **6** 11/2 3 49 4
**The Great Flood** (NTinkler) **3-9-0** MTebbutt(6) (w'like: bkwd: a in rr) 4 **7** 33/1 41 —
$976^{4}$ **Dispol Gem (72)** (GROldroyd) **3-8-9** WRyan(7) (trckd ldrs: hrd drvn over 3f out: sn wknd) 3½ **8** 2/1 2 29 —
(SP 119.0%) **8 Rn**

**1m 43.0** (8.00) CSF £33.12 TOTE £1.80: £1.20 £8.50 £3.20 (£66.70) OWNER Mr H. H. Morriss (NEWMARKET) BRED Mr and Mrs H. H. Morriss

**703 Henry Island (IRE)**, produced from off the pace, outclassed the opposition and would not realise he had been in a race. (5/4: 8/11-11/8)
**Amadour (IRE)** needed this first run in eight months, but stayed on to take the runner-up spot well inside the final furlong. (33/1)
**779 No Hiding Place** showed his first glimpse of form over this longer trip, but he gave away what chance he had by hanging badly left in the last couple of furlongs. (16/1)
**1035 Blurred (IRE)** (11/2: op 7/2)
**976 Dispol Gem** finished much closer to the winner when they clashed last month, but she faded out of contention rather quickly when shown the whip over two furlongs out, and failed to produce her true running. (2/1: op 7/2)

## 1471 LOUGHBOROUGH CLAIMING STKS (2-Y.O) (Class F)
4-25 (4-25) **5f 218y** £2,733.50 (£756.00: £360.50) Stalls: Low GOING: 0.23 sec per fur (G)

SP RR SF
$1183^{2}$ **Lawful Find (IRE)** (RHollinshead) **2-8-5** WRyan(5) (hld up gng wl: hdwy 2f out: led ent fnl f: drvn clr) — **1** 4/1 2 64 15
$984^{5}$ **Aztec Traveller** (JBerry) **2-9-3** GCarter(1) (lw: led tl rdn, hdd & no ex ent fnl f) 2½ **2** 11/4 1 69 20
$916^{9}$ **Gresatre** (CADwyer) **2-8-6(3)** SDrowne(7) (hld up: hdwy over 1f out: kpt on wl ins fnl f) 1¾ **3** 9/1 57 8
$996^{7}$ **Enchanting Eve** (CNAllen) **2-7-13(7)** IonaWands(6) (prom tl rdn & outpcd over 1f out) 4 **4** 9/1 43 —
$1036^{4}$ **Spondulicks (IRE)** (RHannon) **2-9-3** SWhitworth(3) (prom 4f: wknd qckly) 6 **5** 9/2 3 38 —
*1080** **Just Loui** (WGMTurner) **2-8-11** RPerham(4) (spd over 4f: sn rdn & fdd) 3 **6** 7/1 24 —
**Life's A Roar (IRE)** (CADwyer) **2-8-2(3)** AWhelan(2) (unf: scope: bkwd: s.s: swtchd rt: a outpcd) 6 **7** 9/1 2 —

| | | | | SP | RR | SF |
|---|---|---|---|---|---|---|
| | **Top Titfer** (AGFoster) **2-8-2** JTate(8) (small: bkwd: s.s: rdn along ½-wy: no imp) | ½ | 8 | 25/1 | — | — |

(SP 111.2%) **8 Rn**

**1m 16.7** (6.70) CSF £14.26 TOTE £3.40: £1.30 £1.10 £2.20 (£3.20) OWNER Mr J. Doxey (UPPER LONGDON) BRED Joseph O'Callaghan

**1183 Lawful Find (IRE)**, well suited by this step up to six furlongs, quickened up to take over approaching the final furlong and only needed pushing out to storm clear. (4/1)

**984 Aztec Traveller** again tried to lead from start to finish but the winner was always waiting to pounce and, once he was let loose, the writing was on the wall. (11/4)

**490 Gresatre**, doing all his best work inside the distance, showed that he does need at least this trip and there could be a race in him. (9/1: op 6/1)

**715 Enchanting Eve** has plenty of speed but the six furlongs caught her out and she obviously does not want more than the minimum trip at this stage of her career. (9/1)

**Life's A Roar (IRE)** (9/1: 5/1-10/1)

## 1472 TIGERS APPRENTICE H'CAP (0-65) (4-Y.O+) (Class F)

4-55 (4-56) **1m 3f 183y** £2,718.60 (£764.60: £373.80) Stalls: Low GOING minus 0.03 sec per fur (G)

| | | | | SP | RR | SF |
|---|---|---|---|---|---|---|
| $1347^{8}$ | **Duty Sergeant (IRE) (37)** (PhilipMitchell) **7-8-8** CAdamson(9) (hld up: hdwy 4f out: rdn to ld wl ins fnl f: r.o) | — | 1 | 9/1 | 47 | 29 |
| *$265^{4}$* | **Wottashambles (37)** (LMontagueHall) **5-8-5**(3) AEddery(7) (led tl over 2f out: rallied to ld appr fnl f: hdd towards fin) | 1¾ | 2 | $13/2^{3}$ | 45 | 27 |
| *$400^{5}$* | **Howqua River (43)** (PWChapple-Hyam) **4-8-7**(7) RCody-Boutcher(5) (hld up: hdwy over 3f out: r.o wl ins fnl f) | ½ | 3 | 16/1 | 50 | 32 |
| $1165^{2}$ | **Greystyle (35)** (MBrittain) **6-8-3v**(3) GFaulkner(11) (lw: prom: outpcd 3f out: rallied over 1f out: fin wl) | 1½ | 4 | 9/1 | 40 | 22 |
| | **Rock The Barney (IRE) (51)** (PBurgoyne) **7-9-5**(3) DSweeney(10) (s.i.s: hdwy ½-wy: ev ch over 1f out: no ex fnl f) | 1¼ | 5 | 8/1 | 54 | 36 |
| $993^{5}$ | **Cliburnel News (IRE) (57)** (AStreeter) **6-9-11**(3) DDenby(1) (lw: hld up in tch: hdwy to ld over 2f out: hdd & wknd appr fnl f) | 3½ | 6 | $13/2^{3}$ | 56 | 38 |
| 1167* | **Firefighter (52)** (BPJBaugh) **7-9-9** IonaWands(3) (b: trckd ldrs: effrt & ev ch 3f out: wknd fnl 2f) | 9 | 7 | $4/1^{1}$ | 38 | 20 |
| $1416^{6}$ | **El Don (44)** (MJRyan) **4-8-8**(7) AMcCarthy(8) (bit bkwd: mid div: effrt 3f out: sn rdn: no imp) | 1¼ | 8 | 9/1 | 29 | 11 |
| *$1031^{2}$* | **Jean de Florette (USA) (31)** (RCSpicer) **5-7-13**(3) JDennis(4) (nvr plcd to chal) | nk | 9 | $6/1^{2}$ | 15 | — |
| $1159^{5}$ | **Rose Chime (IRE) (32)** (JLHarris) **4-7-12**(5) CLowther(12) (trckd ldrs tl wknd wl over 2f out) | 2 | 10 | 20/1 | 14 | — |
| $759^{7}$ | **Imlak (IRE) (56)** (JLHarris) **4-9-10**(3) JWilkinson(6) (prom: rdn over 3f out: sn wknd: t.o) | 8 | 11 | 16/1 | 27 | 9 |
| $886^{12}$ | **Kismetim (33)** (DWChapman) **6-8-1**(3) JoHunnam(13) (in tch tl wknd 3f out: t.o) | 2½ | 12 | 16/1 | — | — |
| $995^{12}$ | **Doreen's Delight (35)** (HJCollingridge) **10-8-1**(5) PDoe(2) (b: bkwd: a bhd: t.o whn p.u & dismntd ins fnl f) | | P | 16/1 | — | — |

(SP 130.4%) **13 Rn**

**2m 38.2** (9.20) CSF £67.00 CT £875.21 TOTE £17.20: £5.00 £2.30 £6.80 (£66.80) Trio £250.10 OWNER Mr W. R. Mann (EPSOM) BRED Hibernia Farm

**Duty Sergeant (IRE)** still looked to be carrying condition for this second outing in six days, but he got the better of a stiff tussle with the runner-up to lead 75 yards out and record his first success since September '92. (9/1)

**Wottashambles** reserves his best for the All-Weather, but he put in a brave display here and certainly did not fail for the want of trying. (13/2)

**Howqua River** has not yet got off the mark, but he ran one of his better races on this first run over twelve furlongs, and it would seem this is his trip. (16/1)

**1165 Greystyle** gave the impression that he would be more suited to more patient tactics, judging by the way he was staying on after getting outpaced early in the straight. (9/1)

**Rock The Barney (IRE)**, twice a winner here over ten furlongs, performed with credit on this first run in almost seven months and, with this run under his best, he should be able to add to his score. (8/1: 6/1-9/1)

**993 Cliburnel News (IRE)** swooped to lead over two furlongs out, looking full of running, but topweight took its toll and she stopped quickly after being collared approaching the last furlong. (13/2: 4/1-7/1)

**1167* Firefighter** joined issue three furlongs out, but did not find a lot when asked to quicken and was throwing out distress signals a furlong later. (4/1)

## 1473 GROBY H'CAP (0-85) (3-Y.O+) (Class D)

5-25 (5-25) **5f 218y** £3,947.50 (£1,180.00: £565.00: £257.50) Stalls: Low GOING: 0.23 sec per fur (G)

| | | | | SP | RR | SF |
|---|---|---|---|---|---|---|
| 949* | **Pleading (80)** (HCandy) **3-9-6** CRutter(4) (lw: hdwy over 2f out: led 100y out: r.o strly) | — | 1 | $4/1^{1}$ | 97+ | 71 |
| $1327^{12}$ | **Albaha (USA) (80)** (RWArmstrong) **3-9-6b**1 WRyan(1) (led: sn clr: rdn & hdd wl ins fnl f) | 1 | 2 | 14/1 | 94 | 68 |
| $1199^{3}$ | **So Intrepid (IRE) (72)** (JMBradley) **6-9-4**(3) SDrowne(3) (hdwy ½-wy: rdn 2f out: nt pce to chal) | 5 | 3 | $4/1^{1}$ | 73 | 56 |
| $1178^{8}$ | **Bayin (USA) (72)** (MDIUsher) **7-9-7** RStreet(6) (wl bhd tl gd hdwy appr fnl f: fin wl) | 3 | 4 | $8/1^{3}$ | 65 | 48 |
| $1121^{13}$ | **Great Hall (47)** (PDCundell) **7-7-3b**(7) IonaWands(2) (b.hind: bhd: hdwy u.p wl over 1f out: nvr nrr) | s.h | 5 | 12/1 | 40 | 23 |
| | **Winsome Wooster (62)** (PGMurphy) **5-8-11** RPerham(5) (bkwd: trckd ldrs: shkn up 2f out: no imp) | 2½ | 6 | 10/1 | 48 | 31 |
| $812^{10}$ | **Multan (57)** (GLMoore) **4-8-6** SWhitworth(9) (s.s: a in rr) | 7 | 7 | $9/2^{2}$ | 25 | 8 |
| $1064^{6}$ | **Ansellman (75)** (JBerry) **6-9-10** GCarter(8) (prom tl rdn & wknd over 2f out) | nk | 8 | 10/1 | 42 | 25 |
| $1157^{8}$ | **Sir Tasker (54)** (JLHarris) **8-8-3** AClark(11) (lw: gd spd over 3f: sn lost tch: t.o) | 6 | 9 | 20/1 | 5 | — |
| $1051^{6}$ | **Castel Rosselo (68)** (RHarris) **6-9-3b** AMackay(7) (prom 4f: wknd qckly: t.o) | 1¾ | 10 | 16/1 | 14 | — |
| *$1029^{4}$* | **Maybank (IRE) (56)** (BAMcMahon) **4-8-0**(5)ow2 LNewton(10) (prom tl outpcd over 2f out: t.o) | 1¼ | 11 | $8/1^{3}$ | — | — |

(SP 123.6%) **11 Rn**

**1m 13.7** (3.70) CSF £54.84 CT £196.61 TOTE £4.30: £2.10 £3.10 £2.50 (£19.20) Trio £100.60 OWNER Mr Simon Broke (WANTAGE) BRED Cheveley Park Stud Ltd

WEIGHT FOR AGE 3yo-9lb

**949* Pleading**, a very progressive colt, won this readily and will now be stepped up to the William Hill Trophy at York next month. (4/1)

**842 Albaha (USA)**, brought back to sprinting and fitted with blinkers, set a testing gallop and held a clear lead until tying up and being collared halfway through the final furlong. These tactics should enable him to find an opening. (14/1)

**1199 So Intrepid (IRE)**, always struggling to remain in touch, was hard at work two furlongs out and never looked likely to take a hand in proceedings. (4/1)

**Bayin (USA)** came from another county to reach his finishing position and still retains some ability. (8/1)

**664 Great Hall** was only finding top gear when the race was as good as over, and was never a factor. (12/1)

**Winsome Wooster** does run well when fresh but she can be made fitter, and she should be able to step up on this. (10/1)

**Multan**, the subject of quite a gamble, lost ground at the start and, in such a fast-run race, was never able to recover. (9/2: 8/1-4/1)

T/Plpt: £15.90 (385.6 Tckts). T/Qdpt: £8.80 (35.74 Tckts). IM

# 1086-REDCAR (L-H) (Good to firm)
## Monday May 27th
WEATHER: sunny periods WIND: almost nil

## 1474 BANK HOLIDAY (S) STKS (3-Y.O+) (Class G)
2-10 (2-11) **7f** £2,600.00 (£725.00: £350.00) Stalls: High GOING minus 0.11 sec per fur (G)

| | | | | SP | RR | SF |
|---|---|---|---|---|---|---|
| | **Sakharov (56)** (MJohnston) **7-9-7** MHills(4) (mde all: hld on wl) | — | **1** | 11/4 1 | 68 | 42 |
| 1156[6] | **Move Smartly (IRE) (47)** (FHLee) **6-9-4**(3) DRMcCabe(7) (trckd ldrs: chal over 1f out: nt qckn towards fin) | ½ | **2** | 12/1 | 67 | 41 |
| 851[13] | **Mbulwa (57)** (RAFahey) **10-9-7** LCharnock(9) (hdwy & prom ½-wy: hrd rdn fnl 2f: kpt on) | ½ | **3** | 8/1 | 66 | 40 |
| 971[10] | **Blue Grit (51)** (MDods) **10-9-7b** DaleGibson(6) (hdwy ½-wy: chsng ldrs appr fnl f: nt qckn) | ½ | **4** | 16/1 | 65 | 39 |
| 1041* | **First Gold (54)** (JWharton) **7-9-10b** KFallon(10) (lw: dwlt: hdwy 2f out: nrst fin) | 1¾ | **5** | 11/2 3 | 64 | 38 |
| 1163[8] | **Ultra Beet (63)** (PCHaslam) **4-9-7b** JFortune(1) (chsd ldrs: effrt 2f out: r.o one pce) | 2 | **6** | 14/1 | 56 | 30 |
| 1162* | **Broctune Gold (55)** (MrsMReveley) **5-9-10** ACulhane(8) (a cl up: chal ½-wy: wknd appr fnl f) | ½ | **7** | 7/2 2 | 58 | 32 |
| | **Superbird** (TDEasterby) **3-8-5** MBirch(5) (neat: unf: bhd tl sme late hdwy) | 2½ | **8** | 25/1 | 44 | 7 |
| 1087[5] | **Thorntoun Jewel (IRE) (40)** (JBalding) **3-8-5b** MFenton(15) (bhd: sme hdwy 2f out: n.d) | 1 | **9** | 20/1 | 42 | 5 |
| 1067[14] | **Kudos Blue (28)** (JDBethell) **3-8-5** TSprake(2) (lw: chsd ldrs tl wknd fnl 2f) | hd | **10** | 100/1 | 42 | 5 |
| 1309[14] | **Ihtimaam (FR) (55)** (MrsASwinbank) **4-9-7b**[1] BDoyle(13) (s.i.s: n.d) | s.h | **11** | 20/1 | 47 | 21 |
| 998[3] | **Flyaway Blues (50)** (MrsMReveley) **4-9-7b** JFanning(17) (effrt & hung lft over 2f out: nt r.o) | 1½ | **12** | 8/1 | 43 | 17 |
| 971[8] | **Care And Comfort (47)** (NTinkler) **4-9-2** GBardwell(3) (a outpcd & bhd) | 1¼ | **13** | 25/1 | 35 | 9 |
| 1162[2] | **My Godson (47)** (JLEyre) **6-9-10b** RLappin(12) (bhd fr ½-wy) | 7 | **14** | 11/1 | 27 | 1 |
| 550[17] | **Domusky** (ABMulholland) **3-8-5** MMcAndrew(11) (in tch 3f: sn t.o) | 23 | **15** | 100/1 | — | — |
| 868[20] | **Crowning Tino (20)** (MrsNMacauley) **4-9-2v** NConnorton(14) (wandered bdly after 2f: sn t.o) | 19 | **16** | 200/1 | — | — |

(SP 134.8%) **16 Rn**

**1m 27.4** (4.40) CSF £37.52 TOTE £3.20: £1.50 £4.40 £2.70 (£22.90) Trio £78.70 OWNER Mr J. R. Good (MIDDLEHAM) BRED J. R. and Mrs P. Good
WEIGHT FOR AGE 3yo-11lb
No bid

**Sakharov** did well under pressure to win his first race for almost two years. (11/4: op 5/1)
**1156 Move Smartly (IRE)** keeps running well and should find a race, but is not one to be relied upon. (12/1)
**Mbulwa**, despite his years, showed here he still has the ability, and will again pay his way. (8/1: 6/1-9/1)
**850 Blue Grit** ran one of his better races this time but, once he got in behind the leaders entering the final furlong, he then decided he had done enough. (16/1)
**1041* First Gold**, who is in good form at present, makes his own mind up about things and, although keeping on well in the last two furlongs, the effort was always too late. (11/2)
**Ultra Beet** had done nearly all his winning on sand, but he did run his best race for a while here, only to find this trip just beyond him. (14/1)
**1162* Broctune Gold** tried to take the winner on, but the struggle proved too much approaching the last furlong. (7/2)
**Superbird** showed some ability, staying on well when it was all over. (25/1)
**Ihtimaam (FR)** has ability, but the blinkers being on for the first time did not work the oracle. (20/1)

## 1475 RACING CHANNEL MEDIAN AUCTION MAIDEN STKS (3-Y.O) (Class D)
2-40 (2-40) **6f** £3,717.00 (£1,116.00: £538.00: £249.00) Stalls: High GOING minus 0.11 sec per fur (G)

| | | | | SP | RR | SF |
|---|---|---|---|---|---|---|
| *304*[4] | **Shanghai Girl** (DRLoder) **3-8-6**(3) DRMcCabe(5) (lw: hld up: qcknd to ld over 2f out: r.o u.p) | — | **1** | 9/1 | 83 | 38 |
| 1007[4] | **Bollin Joanne (81)** (TDEasterby) **3-8-9** MBirch(2) (b: cl up: effrt & ev ch 2f out: nt qckn u.p) | 1¾ | **2** | 2/1 2 | 78 | 33 |
| | **Willie Miles** (JWWatts) **3-9-0** NConnorton(3) (w'like: s.i.s: shkn up ½-wy: stdy hdwy appr fnl f: nrst fin) | 1¾ | **3** | 25/1 | 79 | 34 |
| 1178[2] | **Domak Amaam (IRE) (80)** (JHMGosden) **3-9-0** AGarth(4) (b.hind: lw: cl up: outpcd over 2f out: kpt on u.p fnl f) | s.h | **4** | 11/8 1 | 79 | 34 |
| | **Merrily** (MissSEHall) **3-8-9** KFallon(1) (hld up: effrt over 2f out: nvr able to chal) | 1¾ | **5** | 25/1 | 69 | 24 |
| 1171[3] | **Delphine** (MBell) **3-8-9** MFenton(7) (mde most tl hdd over 2f out: grad wknd) | 1 | **6** | 5/1 3 | 66 | 21 |
| 453[13] | **Craignairn (70)** (JBerry) **3-9-0** JFortune(6) (disp ld to ½-wy: sn wknd) | 9 | **7** | 10/1 | 47 | 2 |

(SP 118.9%) **7 Rn**

**1m 13.4** (3.20) CSF £27.53 TOTE £11.50: £3.60 £1.40 (£16.90) OWNER Mr Wafic Said (NEWMARKET) BRED Addison Racing Ltd Inc
**Shanghai Girl** did not act on the All-Weather last time but, despite an awkward head carriage, there was nothing wrong with this performance. She should find further success. (9/1: op 6/1)
**1007 Bollin Joanne** keeps running her heart out and her consistency will pay dividends before long. (2/1)
**Willie Miles**, quite an attractive newcomer, did not move that well. After getting left behind, he was tenderly handled in the closing stages and finished in a style that suggests there is better to come. (25/1)
**1178 Domak Amaam (IRE)**, wearing a tongue-strap and bandages, got tapped for speed when the tempo increased at halfway and had no further chance, despite keeping on. Either softer ground or further could be the answer. (11/8)
**Merrily** showed a good action and travelled quite well in the first half of the race. He should do better in time. (25/1)
**1171 Delphine**, a sharp-actioned sort who came from behind last time, made it here and was done with some way out. (5/1)

## 1476 ZETLAND GOLD CUP H'CAP (0-105) (3-Y.O+) (Class B)
3-10 (3-11) **1m 2f** £14,655.00 (£4,440.00: £2,170.00: £1,035.00) Stalls: Low GOING minus 0.37 sec per fur (F)

| | | | | SP | RR | SF |
|---|---|---|---|---|---|---|
| 953* | **Migwar (90)** (LMCumani) **3-8-5**ow1 KFallon(8) (hld up: stdy hdwy 2f out: led ins fnl f: r.o wl) | — | **1** | 3/1 1 | 101 | 45 |
| 953[2] | **Billy Bushwacker (89)** (MrsMReveley) **5-9-4** ACulhane(3) (lw: hld up: hdwy on ins 3f out: led over 1f out tl ins fnl f: r.o) | 1½ | **2** | 11/1 | 98 | 57 |
| 953[4] | **Wafir (IRE) (81)** (PCalver) **4-8-10** MBirch(1) (lw: trckd ldrs: led over 2f out tl over 1f out: kpt on wl) | 1¾ | **3** | 12/1 | 87 | 46 |
| 1322* | **Tertium (IRE) (83)** (MartynWane) **4-8-12** 6x JFortune(4) (hld up & bhd: nt clr run in several positions fnl 3f: nrst fin) | ½ | **4** | 14/1 | 88 | 47 |
| 933[5] | **Lookingforarainbow (IRE) (75)** (BobJones) **8-8-4** DaleGibson(2) (a in tch: outpcd 3f out: kpt on appr st) | 1¾ | **5** | 14/1 | 77 | 36 |
| 1198[5] | **Current Speech (IRE) (70)** (TDEasterby) **5-7-13b** JFanning(6) (a chsng ldrs: one pce fnl 3f) | ½ | **6** | 25/1 | 71 | 30 |
| 879[3] | **Angus-G (71)** (MrsMReveley) **4-8-0** LCharnock(16) (bhd: effrt 4f out: kpt on: nt pce to chal) | nk | **7** | 11/2 3 | 72 | 31 |
| 941D | **Hagwah (USA) (99)** (BHanbury) **4-9-11**(3) JStack(10) (a.p: ev ch over 2f out: btn appr fnl f) | 2½ | **8** | 14/1 | 96 | 55 |
| 1330[8] | **Pinkerton's Pal (87)** (CEBrittain) **5-9-2** BDoyle(12) (led tl hdd over 2f out: one pce) | 2 | **9** | 50/1 | 81 | 40 |

| | | | | SP | RR | SF |
|---|---|---|---|---|---|---|
| 1106* | **Dombey (92)** (RCharlton) **3-8-7** TSprake(14) (hld up: hdwy on outside ent st: rdn & wknd fnl 2f) | ½ | **10** | 5/1[2] | 85 | 30 |
| 1185[4] | **Traceability (81)** (SCWilliams) **3-7-10** GBardwell(9) (bhd & hmpd ent st: n.d) | 3½ | **11** | 20/1 | 68 | 13 |
| 808[4] | **Royal Canaska (92)** (DRLoder) **3-8-4**(3) DRMcCabe(15) (nvr trbld ldrs) | hd | **12** | 12/1 | 79 | 24 |
| | **Quango (92)** (JGFitzGerald) **4-9-2**(5) PRoberts(13) (in tch tl rdn & wknd 4f out) | 6 | **13** | 20/1 | 70 | 29 |
| 967[8] | **Blue Zulu (IRE) (90)** (JRFanshawe) **4-9-2**(3) NVarley(11) (in tch tl wknd fnl 3f) | 1 | **14** | 14/1 | 66 | 25 |
| 988[6] | **Grand Selection (IRE) (80)** (MBell) **4-8-9** MFenton(7) (cl up tl wknd over 3f out) | 14 | **15** | 12/1 | 34 | — |
| 766[7] | **Sadler's Walk (80)** (GWragg) **5-8-9b[1]** MHills(5) (pushed along after s: a bhd: hmpd appr st) | hd | **16** | 14/1 | 33 | — |
| | | | | (SP 137.1%) | **16 Rn** | |

**2m 5.4** (1.80) CSF £38.40 CT £350.80 TOTE £5.00: £2.10 £2.10 £3.50 £4.50 (£20.50) Trio £121.00 OWNER Umm Qarn Racing (NEWMARKET) BRED Meon Valley Stud
LONG HANDICAP Traceability 7-9
WEIGHT FOR AGE 3yo-14lb
**OFFICIAL EXPLANATION Grand Selection (IRE): lost his action during the race.**
**953* Migwar**, given a fine ride, got the gap when required and produced a nice turn of foot to settle it. This sturdy little colt is really progressing. (3/1: op 5/1)
**953 Billy Bushwacker** found everything just right for him this time until the winner proved too strong in the closing stages. However, he looks superb and does deserve to pick up a decent race. (11/1)
**953 Wafir (IRE)** ran a cracker but was just short of a turn of foot to take it, and is now well worth keeping on the right side. (12/1)
**1322* Tertium (IRE)**, stepping up in trip, had all sorts of trouble in getting a run and appeared very unlucky. He might well have given the winner a fright. (14/1)
**933 Lookingforarainbow (IRE)** keeps running well over these shorter distances and is an amazing performer, but he does seem better over further. (14/1: op 25/1)
**1198 Current Speech (IRE)** has so much ability but has his own ideas and, although running well here, was never doing enough. (25/1)
**879 Angus-G**, a big, long-striding individual, was always struggling from an outside draw and, trying to come from behind, had little chance. A more galloping track would certainly suit, and he will show he is much better than this in due course. (11/2)
**Hagwah (USA)** travelled particularly well until getting outpaced in the last couple of furlongs. Longer trips should see better. (14/1)
**1106* Dombey**, a drifter in the market, made his ground going very wide into the straight and than cried enough two furlongs out. This was certainly not his true running. (5/1)
**808 Royal Canaska** looked to be going quite well early in the straight, but then hit a brick wall entering the last two furlongs, and would seem to have stamina problems. (12/1)

## 1477 VAUX SAMSON H'CAP (0-75) (3-Y.O) (Class D)
3-40 (3-42) **1m 3f** £7,262.50 (£2,200.00: £1,075.00: £512.50) Stalls: Low GOING minus 0.37 sec per fur (F)

| | | | | SP | RR | SF |
|---|---|---|---|---|---|---|
| 693[7] | **Hamlet (IRE) (72)** (MBell) **3-9-4** MFenton(10) (hld up & bhd: smooth hdwy to ld over 1f out: r.o wl) | — | **1** | 10/1 | 84 | 53 |
| 1317* | **Isitoff (71)** (SCWilliams) **3-9-0**(3) 5x PMcCabe(7) (lw: a.p: led 3f out tl over 1f out: sn outpcd) | 6 | **2** | 4/1[2] | 74 | 43 |
| 1089[6] | **Forest Fantasy (50)** (JWharton) **3-7-7**(3) NVarley(3) (cl up: chal 3f out: one pce appr fnl f) | ½ | **3** | 4/1[2] | 53 | 22 |
| 1145[7] | **Shu Gaa (IRE) (75)** (WJHaggas) **3-9-7** MHills(9) (in tch: outpcd ent st: styd on towards fin) | 2 | **4** | 7/2[1] | 75 | 44 |
| 1185[8] | **Cumbrian Maestro (56)** (TDEasterby) **3-8-2** JFanning(6) (hld up & bhd: styd on fnl 3f: n.d) | hd | **5** | 20/1 | 56 | 25 |
| 1067[2] | **Irish Oasis (IRE) (50)** (BSRothwell) **3-7-10** LCharnock(2) (lw: led tl hdd 3f out: grad wknd) | hd | **6** | 12/1 | 49 | 18 |
| 976[9] | **Gulf of Siam (59)** (MissSEHall) **3-8-5**ow1 NConnorton(8) (trckd ldrs: chal 3f out: wknd over 1f out) | 2½ | **7** | 14/1 | 55 | 23 |
| 1047[3] | **Meltemison (68)** (CEBrittain) **3-9-0** BDoyle(5) (swtg: cl up tl outpcd 4f out: no ch after) | 1 | **8** | 7/1[3] | 62 | 31 |
| 1312[4] | **Falcon's Flame (USA) (56)** (MrsJRRamsden) **3-7-13**(3) DRMcCabe(4) (hld up & bhd: n.d) | ½ | **9** | 7/2[1] | 50 | 19 |
| 509[8] | **Whitley Grange Boy (63)** (JLEyre) **3-8-9** RLappin(1) (lost tch fnl 4f) | 19 | **10** | 16/1 | 29 | — |
| | | | | (SP 131.0%) | **10 Rn** | |

**2m 20.6** (2.60) CSF £52.33 CT £181.04 TOTE £7.90: £3.30 £1.90 £1.80 (£22.80) Trio £62.60 OWNER Mr M. B. Hawtin (NEWMARKET) BRED Peter McCalmont
LONG HANDICAP Forest Fantasy 7-9 Irish Oasis (IRE) 7-8
**OFFICIAL EXPLANATION Falcon's Flame (USA): failed to settle in the early stages and found nothing in the straight.**
**Hamlet (IRE)**, who broke a blood-vessel last time, got everything right on this occasion and put up an amazing performance. (10/1)
**1317* Isitoff** is a real tough performer and tried particularly hard here, but had no answer to the winner's turn of foot. (4/1)
**1089 Forest Fantasy** keeps running well but is just short of a change of gear. (4/1)
**1145 Shu Gaa (IRE)**, after a promising run last time, disappointingly got outpaced turning for home here and had no further chance, despite keeping on at the end. He can be forgiven this lapse. (7/2)
**Cumbrian Maestro** showed little when in blinkers last time, but ran better over this longer trip and, ridden differently, was staying on at the end. (20/1)
**1067 Irish Oasis (IRE)**, taking on better company this time, was ridden aggressively and was done with two furlongs out. (12/1)
**Gulf of Siam** travelled well until his stamina gave out in the last couple of furlongs. (14/1)
**1312 Falcon's Flame (USA)**, although joint-favourite, was easy to back and, despite stepping up to what appeared an ideal trip, he was still not suited as the early pace was too slow. This run should be completely ignored and a positive market-move is probably the best guide. (7/2)

## 1478 ROSE GARDEN H'CAP (0-70) (3-Y.O+) (Class E)
4-10 (4-15) **1m 6f 19y** £3,208.50 (£963.00: £464.00: £214.50) Stalls: Low GOING minus 0.37 sec per fur (F)

| | | | | SP | RR | SF |
|---|---|---|---|---|---|---|
| 1091* | **Arian Spirit (IRE) (47)** (JLEyre) **5-8-13** RLappin(5) (hld up: effrt over 3f out: hung lft u.p: styd on to ld cl home) | — | **1** | 11/4[1] | 59 | 38 |
| 1421[10] | **Sharp Sensation (35)** (WLBarker) **6-7-8**(7) JBramhill(9) (in tch: led 3f out & qcknd: hdd & no ex towards fin) | nk | **2** | 9/1 | 47 | 26 |
| 961[6] | **Tremendisto (47)** (CaptJWilson) **6-8-13** KFallon(7) (cl up: led over 6f out tl hdd 3f out: one pce) | 2½ | **3** | 7/1 | 56 | 35 |
| 1158[4] | **Vain Prince (51)** (NTinkler) **9-9-3b** LCharnock(8) (lw: trckd ldrs: chal over 3f out: r.o one pce) | nk | **4** | 5/1[3] | 60 | 39 |
| | **Monaco Gold (IRE) (35)** (MrsMReveley) **4-8-1** JFanning(1) (a.p: one pce fnl 4f) | 2½ | **5** | 10/1 | 41 | 20 |
| 1044[2] | **Lostris (IRE) (33)** (MDods) **5-7-13** DaleGibson(2) (in tch: outpcd 4f out: no imp after) | nk | **6** | 9/2[2] | 38 | 17 |
| *267[4]* | **Red Spectacle (IRE) (58)** (PCHaslam) **4-9-10** JFortune(3) (led tl hdd over 6f out: sn lost pl) | 2½ | **7** | 14/1 | 61 | 40 |
| *1095** | **Top Prize (37)** (MBrittain) **8-8-3v** GBardwell(6) (wnt prom 7f out: effrt 4f out: wknd 3f out) | 1¾ | **8** | 8/1 | 38 | 17 |
| 972[8] | **Lindisfarne Lady (40)** (MrsMReveley) **4-8-6** ACulhane(10) (lw: bhd: effrt over 4f out: n.d) | 7 | **9** | 16/1 | 33 | 12 |
| | **Jundi (IRE) (57)** (JDBethell) **5-9-9** MFenton(4) (outpcd ent st: a bhd) | 6 | **10** | 20/1 | 43 | 22 |
| | | | | (SP 121.5%) | **10 Rn** | |

**3m 4.8** (5.50) CSF £26.80 CT £148.71 TOTE £3.20: £1.40 £3.90 £2.00 (£24.50) Trio £146.10 OWNER Mr Martin West (HAMBLETON) BRED M. Ervine in Ireland

**1091* Arian Spirit (IRE)**, despite the shorter trip, found a turn of foot to get there. This was a poor race. (11/4)
**Sharp Sensation** ran his best race for some time but, after looking likely to win, just failed to last home. (9/1)
**Tremendisto** brings a new dimension to one-paced, and is yet to win a race after twenty-four attempts. (7/1)
**1158 Vain Prince** is gradually improving and will find his form in due course. (5/1)
**Monaco Gold (IRE)** has changed stables and did run a shade better here, but there is still a long way to go. (10/1)
**1044 Lostris (IRE)**, a big, awkward individual, probably needs more use making of him as he certainly does not do anything quickly. (9/2)

## 1479 YARM MAIDEN AUCTION STKS (2-Y.O) (Class E)

4-40 (4-43) **5f** £3,195.50 (£959.00: £462.00: £213.50) Stalls: High GOING minus 0.11 sec per fur (G)

| | | | | SP | RR | SF |
|---|---|---|---|---|---|---|
| | **Meliksah (IRE)** (MBell) **2-8-7** MFenton(6) (str: scope: lw: sn wl bhd: rapid hdwy to ld wl over 1f out: sn clr) | — | **1** | 3/1$^{2}$ | 87+ | 30 |
| 1046$^{3}$ | **Bold African** (PDEvans) **2-8-5**$^{ow2}$ KFallon(2) (lw: led tl hdd wl over 1f out: sn rdn & btn) | 4 | **2** | 4/1$^{3}$ | 72 | 13 |
| 950$^{3}$ | **Bailieborough Boy (IRE)** (TDBarron) **2-8-7** JFortune(7) (dwlt: hdwy u.p ½-wy: hung lft & no imp) | 3 | **3** | 7/4$^{1}$ | 65 | 8 |
| | **Jack Says** (TDEasterby) **2-8-4**$^{ow1}$ MBirch(3) (cmpt: effrt ½-wy: styd on: nt trble ldrs) | nk | **4** | 20/1 | 61 | 3 |
| 946$^{5}$ | **Red Garter (IRE)** (KMcAuliffe) **2-7-13**$^{(3)}$ DRMcCabe(4) (trckd ldr 3f: sn rdn & btn) | ¾ | **5** | 9/2 | 56 | — |
| | **Star of The Road** (JMCarr) **2-8-5**$^{ow2}$ ACulhane(1) (lengthy: bit bkwd: wnt lft s: n.d) | 1 | **6** | 20/1 | 56 | — |
| | **Read Your Contract (IRE)** (JBerry) **2-8-2**$^{(5)}$ PRoberts(5) (lengthy: outpcd & bhd fr ½-wy) | 5 | **7** | 8/1 | 42 | — |
| | | | | (SP 120.2%) | **7 Rn** | |

**60.5 secs** (3.00) CSF £15.45 TOTE £4.90: £2.10 £2.80 (£14.30) OWNER Mr Yucel Birol (NEWMARKET) BRED Ron Con Ltd
**Meliksah (IRE)** is a really nice sort, but his action left something to be desired. After a furlong and a half, he was stone last and looked in trouble, but he suddenly clicked into overdrive, flew past the whole field and scored in great style. (3/1)
**1046 Bold African** has bags of toe but, once the winner appeared on the scene, there was nothing he could do about it. (4/1)
**950 Bailieborough Boy (IRE)** disappointed here. Never going that well and always inclined to hang left when the pressure was on, he failed to make any real impression. (7/4)
**Jack Says**, off the bit by halfway, never looked likely to get in a blow. (20/1)
**946 Red Garter (IRE)** sat on the leader's heels but suddenly ran out of petrol entering the last couple of furlongs. (9/2)
**Star of The Road** needed this and, after ducking left leaving the stalls, never looked likely to get anywhere near. (20/1)
**Read Your Contract (IRE)** (8/1: op 5/1)

T/Plpt: £294.40 (33.32 Tckts). T/Qdpt: £20.70 (27.46 Tckts). AA

# 0829-SANDOWN (R-H) (Rnd Good to soft, Good bk st, 5f Good, Good to soft patches)
## Monday May 27th

WEATHER: overcast WIND: mod half against

## 1480 E.B.F. MAIDEN STKS (2-Y.O F) (Class D)

2-00 (2-02) **5f 6y** £3,818.00 (£1,154.00: £562.00: £266.00) Stalls: High GOING: 0.02 sec per fur (G)

| | | | | SP | RR | SF |
|---|---|---|---|---|---|---|
| | **Moonshine Girl (USA)** (MRStoute) **2-8-11** JReid(5) (unf: lw: s.s: hld up: rdn over 1f out: chsd ldr fnl f: led last stride) | — | **1** | 9/4$^{2}$ | 85+ | 49 |
| | **Dancing Drop** (RHannon) **2-8-11** RHughes(4) (str: scope: bit bkwd: led 1f: led over 2f out: hrd rdn fnl f: hdd last stride) | s.h | **2** | 11/2$^{3}$ | 85+ | 49 |
| | **Queen's Pageant** (JLSpearing) **2-8-11** JWeaver(3) (leggy: led 4f out tl over 2f out: rdn over 1f out: one pce) | 1¾ | **3** | 20/1 | 79 | 43 |
| 977$^{3}$ | **Third Party** (SDow) **2-8-11** SSanders(2) (prom over 2f) | 11 | **4** | 14/1 | 44 | 8 |
| | **Miss Clonteen (IRE)** (MMadgwick) **2-8-11** JQuinn(1) (str: bkwd: a wl bhd) | 10 | **5** | 66/1 | 12 | — |
| 1105$^{3}$ | **Sketch Pad** (RCharlton) **2-8-11** PatEddery(6) (lw: 5th whn p.u over 2f out: lame) | | **P** | 5/6$^{1}$ | — | — |
| | | | | (SP 113.6%) | **6 Rn** | |

**62.65 secs** (2.85) CSF £13.79 TOTE £3.40: £1.60 £2.70 (£9.40) OWNER Mr Saeed Maktoum Al Maktoum (NEWMARKET) BRED Gainsborough Farm Inc
OFFICIAL EXPLANATION **Sketch Pad: was pulled up when she had injured a hind leg.**
**Moonshine Girl (USA)** needs time to develop but looked in good shape and got on top in the very last strides. The last two winners of the Queen Mary Stakes at Royal Ascot have made their debut in this race and that is where Moonshine Girl will now head. (9/4: 6/4-5/2)
**Dancing Drop**, a strongly-built filly, looked as though the run would do her good but only just lost out. Regaining the advantage at halfway, she looked to be on top in the final furlong but, despite doing nothing wrong, was caught right on the line. A half-sister to Wisam and Moon King, she should soon get in the winning groove. (11/2: op 3/1)
**Queen's Pageant** was tapped for toe from below the distance. (20/1)
**977 Third Party** showed speed to halfway before floundering. (14/1: 10/1-20/1)
**1105 Sketch Pad** was pulled up at halfway and connections fear she may have suffered a stress-fracture of her off-hind leg. (5/6)

## 1481 BONUSPHOTO H'CAP (0-100) (3-Y.O+ F & M) (Class C)

2-35 (2-35) **7f 16y** £8,635.00 (£2,605.00: £1,265.00: £595.00) Stalls: High GOING: 0.02 sec per fur (G)

| | | | | SP | RR | SF |
|---|---|---|---|---|---|---|
| 969$^{4}$ | **Aerleon Jane (85)** (JHMGosden) **3-8-10** PatEddery(2) (lw: chsd ldr: led over 1f out: rdn: r.o wl) | — | **1** | 6/1$^{3}$ | 95 | 47 |
| 966$^{9}$ | **Alpine Twist (USA) (87)** (PWChapple-Hyam) **3-8-12** JReid(3) (led over 5f: unable qckn) | 1 | **2** | 9/1 | 95 | 47 |
| 987* | **Prends Ca (IRE) (94)** (RHannon) **3-9-5** RHughes(5) (lw: plld hrd: hld up: rdn over 1f out: one pce) | 2 | **3** | 7/2$^{1}$ | 97 | 49 |
| | **Forest Cat (IRE) (92)** (MrsJCecil) **4-10-0** TIves(1) (plld hrd: hld up: rdn over 2f out: one pce) | 1½ | **4** | 7/2$^{1}$ | 92 | 55 |
| 945$^{6}$ | **Prima Volta (81)** (RHannon) **3-8-3**$^{(3)}$ DaneO'Neill(4) (lw: rdn over 2f out: nvr nr to chal) | nk | **5** | 14/1 | 80 | 32 |
| 676$^{9}$ | **Consordino (86)** (LMCumani) **3-8-11** MJKinane(6) (hld up: rdn over 2f out: one pce) | hd | **6** | 7/2$^{1}$ | 85 | 37 |
| 1121$^{3}$ | **Sand Star (70)** (DHaydnJones) **4-8-6** PRobinson(7) (a.p: rdn over 2f out: wknd over 1f out) | 6 | **7** | 11/2$^{2}$ | 55 | 18 |
| | | | | (SP 113.0%) | **7 Rn** | |

**1m 32.93** (4.33) CSF £49.27 TOTE £6.30: £2.60 £3.70 (£27.80) OWNER Mr Paul Locke (NEWMARKET) BRED P. Locke
WEIGHT FOR AGE 3yo-11lb
**969 Aerleon Jane**, sent to the front approaching the final furlong, was ridden along to assert. Connections believe a mile is her ideal trip. (6/1)
**966 Alpine Twist (USA)** took the field along and brought them over towards the stands' side in the straight. Collared over a furlong out, she found the winner a little bit too good. (9/1: 6/1-10/1)
**987* Prends Ca (IRE)** took a keen hold in the early stages as she was anchored towards the back of the field. Woken up below the distance, she failed to find the necessary turn of foot. (7/2: 9/4-4/1)

**Forest Cat (IRE)** was unable to follow up last year's success in this race on her seasonal bow. (7/2)
**945 Prima Volta** could never get in a blow. (14/1)
**676 Consordino** chased the leaders, but never looked like quickening up in the last two furlongs. (7/2)

## 1482 BONUSPRINT HENRY II STKS (Gp 3) (4-Y.O+) (Class A)

3-05 (3-05) **2m 78y** £25,120.00 (£9,506.00: £4,653.00: £2,121.00) Stalls: High GOING: 0.02 sec per fur (G)

| | | | | SP | RR | SF |
|---|---|---|---|---|---|---|
| 875* | **Double Trigger (IRE) (119)** (MJohnston) **5-9-5** JWeaver(4) (lw: mde virtually all: rdn over 3f out: clr whn edgd rt over 1f out: r.o wl) | — | **1** | 5/6[1] | 128 | 61 |
| 1397a[4] | **Assessor (IRE) (105)** (RHannon) **7-9-1** RHughes(2) (chsd wnr over 8f out tl over 2f out: chsd wnr ins fnl f: no imp) | 7 | **2** | 6/1[3] | 117 | 50 |
| 1128[3] | **Court of Honour (IRE) (117)** (PWChapple-Hyam) **4-9-3** JReid(6) (chsd wnr 8f: rdn over 3f out: chsd wnr over 2f out tl ins fnl f: one pce) | ½ | **3** | 15/8[2] | 121 | 52 |
| | **Admiral's Well (IRE) (108)** (RAkehurst) **6-8-12** SSanders(3) (bit bkwd: a bhd) | 16 | **4** | 25/1 | 98 | 31 |
| 965[2] | **Bahamian Sunshine (USA) (102)** (DRLoder) **5-8-12** MJKinane(7) (a bhd) | 12 | **5** | 25/1 | 86 | 19 |
| | | | | (SP 111.3%) | | **5 Rn** |

**3m 41.15** (9.15) CSF £5.91 TOTE £1.70: £1.30 £1.70 (£2.90) OWNER Mr R. W. Huggins (MIDDLEHAM) BRED Dene Investments N V
WEIGHT FOR AGE 4yo-2lb

**875* Double Trigger (IRE)** raised the roof with this exhilarating display. Soon at the head of affairs, he was woken up in the straight and gradually forged clear in the final quarter-mile to win this race for the second year running. Surely the only danger to him winning the Ascot Gold Cup for a second successive year is Double Eclipse. (5/6)
**1397a Assessor (IRE)** moved into second place at halfway. Alongsides the winner three furlongs from home, he was soon collared for the runner-up berth but struggled into second place again inside the final furlong, if never looking likely to get back on terms with the winner. (6/1)
**1128 Court of Honour (IRE)** was collared for the runner-up berth inside the final furlong. (15/8)
**Admiral's Well (IRE)**, off the course since pulling up over hurdles back in December, looked in need of this race and, always at the back of the field, was losing touch entering the straight. (25/1)
**965 Bahamian Sunshine (USA)** had very bad spotty skin and was at the back of the field until losing touch turning into the straight. (25/1)

## 1483 TRIPLEPRINT TEMPLE STKS (Gp 2) (3-Y.O+) (Class A)

3-40 (3-41) **5f 6y** £37,595.00 (£14,026.00: £6,700.50: £2,878.50) Stalls: High GOING: 0.02 sec per fur (G)

| | | | | SP | RR | SF |
|---|---|---|---|---|---|---|
| | **Mind Games (117)** (JBerry) **4-9-7** JCarroll(9) (w ldr: led over 2f out: rdn over 1f out: r.o wl) | — | **1** | 7/2[1] | 127 | 87 |
| 1321* | **Struggler (110)** (DRLoder) **4-9-3** RHughes(6) (lw: hld up: rdn over 2f out: chsd wnr fnl f: r.o) | ¾ | **2** | 11/2 | 121 | 81 |
| 1129[5] | **Woodborough (USA) (116)** (PWChapple-Hyam) **3-8-9** JReid(4) (lw: outpcd: gd hdwy fnl f: r.o wl) | 1 | **3** | 6/1 | 117 | 69 |
| 1053a[2] | **Leap for Joy (103)** (JHMGosden) **4-9-0** GHind(5) (lw: rdn & hdwy 2f out: r.o one pce) | 1 | **4** | 11/1 | 111 | 71 |
| 940[3] | **Espartero (IRE) (101)** (SirMarkPrescott) **4-9-3** GDuffield(8) (lw: a.p: rdn over 3f out: one pce) | 2½ | **5** | 10/1 | 106 | 66 |
| 1113* | **Fairy Wind (IRE) (92)** (NACallaghan) **4-9-0** PatEddery(10) (led over 2f: wknd fnl f) | 1¼ | **6** | 5/1[3] | 99 | 59 |
| 927[8] | **Double Quick (IRE) (102)** (MJohnston) **4-9-0** JWeaver(7) (lw: prom over 3f out) | 2 | **7** | 14/1 | 93 | 53 |
| 579[3] | **The Puzzler (IRE) (105)** (BWHills) **5-9-3** PRobinson(1) (b: bhd fnl 2f) | 2 | **8** | 25/1 | 90 | 50 |
| 927* | **Cool Jazz (114)** (CEBrittain) **5-9-3** MJKinane(3) (lw: hung lft 2f out: a bhd) | 5 | **9** | 9/2[2] | 74 | 34 |
| | | | | (SP 114.7%) | | **9 Rn** |

**60.99 secs** (1.19) CSF £21.38 TOTE £3.30: £1.80 £1.90 £1.90 (£11.80) Trio £35.40 OWNER Mr Rob Hughes (COCKERHAM) BRED Mrs V. E. Hughes
WEIGHT FOR AGE 3yo-8lb

OFFICIAL EXPLANATION **Cool Jazz: the jockey reported that the horse, who is a difficult ride, had hung severely left throughout the race so that he was unable to ride him out effectively.**

**Mind Games**, whose trainer reported the colt to be in fine form and as fit as a 'butcher's dog', put up a sparkling display and lengthened his stride well from below the distance. A lot more mature and stronger than last year, he looks set to take a real hand in the top sprints this year. (7/2)
**1321* Struggler** chased the leaders but was being niggled along from halfway. Taking second place entering the final furlong, he gradually closed the gap on the winner, but was never going to overhaul that rival in time. (11/2)
**1129 Woodborough (USA)**, who went down early, found five furlongs too sharp even on this stiff track. Totally unable to go the pace, he was doing some really good work in the final furlong, but by then it was too late. Six furlongs is his trip and he will now head for the Cork And Orrery at Royal Ascot. (6/1: op 4/1)
**1053a Leap for Joy** stayed on up the hill, if never looking likely to pose a serious threat. (11/1: 7/1-12/1)
**940 Espartero (IRE)** was made to look very pedestrian from halfway. (10/1: 8/1-12/1)
**927* Cool Jazz** proved totally unsteerable in the second half of the race and was always trailing at the back of the field. (9/2)

## 1484 DOUBLEPRINT WHITSUN CUP RATED STKS H'CAP (0-105) (3-Y.O+) (Class B)

4-10 (4-12) **1m 14y** £15,781.50 (£5,908.50: £2,891.75: £1,246.25: £560.63: £286.37) Stalls: High GOING: 0.02 sec per fur (G)

| | | | | SP | RR | SF |
|---|---|---|---|---|---|---|
| 878[7] | **Blomberg (IRE) (93)** (JRFanshawe) **4-9-1** JCarroll(8) (hld up: rdn over 2f out: led wl ins fnl f: r.o wl) | — | **1** | 20/1 | 107 | 69 |
| 960[11] | **Royal Philosopher (97)** (JWHills) **4-9-0**(5) MHenry(14) (led: styd centre st: clr over 2f out: hdd wl ins fnl f: unable qckn) | 1¼ | **2** | 15/2 | 109 | 71 |
| 1160* | **Chief Burundi (USA) (100)** (LMCumani) **4-9-8** PatEddery(3) (a.p: rdn over 2f out: r.o ins fnl f) | nk | **3** | 13/2[3] | 111 | 73 |
| 960* | **Cool Edge (IRE) (96)** (MHTompkins) **5-9-4** PRobinson(5) (lw: a.p: rdn over 2f out: one pce) | 3½ | **4** | 3/1[1] | 100 | 62 |
| 728[9] | **Wilcuma (90)** (PJMakin) **5-8-12** JWeaver(12) (swtchd rt 2f out: hdwy over 1f out: r.o) | s.h | **5** | 7/1 | 94 | 56 |
| 1193[5] | **Hoh Express (97)** (IABalding) **4-9-0**(5) MartinDwyer(2) (lw: hrd rdn 3f out: nvr nr to chal) | 2 | **6** | 12/1 | 97 | 59 |
| 1187[2] | **Hammerstein (103)** (MRStoute) **3-8-13** MJKinane(13) (a.p: rdn over 2f out: wknd over 1f out) | nk | **7** | 9/2[2] | 102 | 52 |
| 680[8] | **Beauchamp Jazz (99)** (JLDunlop) **4-9-7** JReid(11) (lw: a mid div) | s.h | **8** | 16/1 | 98 | 60 |
| 1193[12] | **Grand du Lac (USA) (90)** (DRLoder) **4-8-12** RHughes(1) (lw: a.p: rdn over 2f out: wknd wl over 1f out) | 3½ | **9** | 20/1 | 82 | 44 |
| 1126[10] | **Bullfinch (90)** (PTWalwyn) **3-8-0** SSanders(4) (bhd fnl 2f) | 1¾ | **10** | 16/1 | 79 | 29 |
| 1112[12] | **Jawaal (97)** (LadyHerries) **6-9-5** DeclanO'Shea(7) (lw: rdn & sme hdwy 2f out: eased whn btn fnl f) | 3 | **11** | 16/1 | 80 | 42 |
| 967* | **Desert Green (FR) (98)** (RHannon) **7-9-3**(3) DaneO'Neill(6) (lw: rdn & sme hdwy 2f out: wknd over 1f out) | 1¾ | **12** | 14/1 | 77 | 39 |
| 1193[11] | **Daryabad (IRE) (96)** (TJNaughton) **4-9-4** GDuffield(9) (a bhd) | 2½ | **13** | 33/1 | 70 | 32 |
| 1112[7] | **Nagnagnag (IRE) (98)** (SDow) **4-9-6** JQuinn(10) (a bhd) | 1¾ | **14** | 12/1 | 69 | 31 |
| | | | | (SP 132.9%) | | **14 Rn** |

**1m 44.36** (3.16) CSF £163.07 CT £1,042.53 TOTE £29.30: £6.40 £2.90 £2.50 (£130.10) Trio £318.40 OWNER Comet Group Plc (NEWMARKET) BRED Mrs Chris Harrington
WEIGHT FOR AGE 3yo-12lb

**679 Blomberg (IRE)** chased the leaders. Pushed along over a quarter of a mile from home, he eventually got on top in the closing stages. The Royal Hunt Cup at Royal Ascot is next on the agenda. (20/1)
**960 Royal Philosopher** attempted to make all the running and was the only runner to stay in the centre of the track in the straight. Clear of his rivals, he was not pegged back until the closing stages. (15/2)
**1160* Chief Burundi (USA)** gave a good account of himself, despite being done no favours by the Handicapper on this handicap debut. Always close up, he stuck on well inside the final furlong, if just failing to get there. (13/2)
**960* Cool Edge (IRE)**, never far away, could only keep on at one pace in the last two furlongs. He may now be in the Handicapper's grip. (3/1: op 9/2)
**Wilcuma**, racing at the back of field, put in some good work in the last furlong and a half but found it all over bar the shouting. (7/1)
**1193 Hoh Express**, shown the whip early in the straight, could never get in a serious blow. (12/1)
**967* Desert Green (FR)** never looked like posing a threat. He needs a fast surface. (14/1: 10/1-16/1)

## 1485 FAMILY DAY OUT H'CAP (0-80) (3-Y.O) (Class D)

4-45 (4-46) **7f 16y** £3,915.50 (£1,184.00: £577.00: £273.50) Stalls: High GOING: 0.02 sec per fur (G)

| | | | | SP | RR | SF |
|---|---|---|---|---|---|---|
| 976$^{5}$ | **Farmost (61)** (SirMarkPrescott) **3-8-2** GDuffield(9) (lw: chsd ldr over 5f out: rdn over 3f out: led over 1f out: r.o wl) | — | **1** | 5/2$^{1}$ | 75 | 37 |
| 646$^{12}$ | **Brighton Road (IRE) (76)** (GBBalding) **3-9-3** SSanders(10) (hld up: rdn over 3f out: r.o ins fnl f) | 3½ | **2** | 12/1 | 82 | 44 |
| 987$^{7}$ | **Menoo Hal Batal (USA) (77)** (MRStoute) **3-9-4** MJKinane(6) (hdwy 2f out: rdn over 1f out: r.o) | ½ | **3** | 4/1$^{2}$ | 82 | 44 |
| 894$^{12}$ | **Apache Len (USA) (75)** (RHannon) **3-8-13**$^{(3)}$ DaneO'Neill(4) (rdn over 3f out: hdwy over 1f out: r.o one pce) | ½ | **4** | 12/1 | 79 | 41 |
| 1074$^{3}$ | **Superior Force (61)** (MissBSanders) **3-8-2**$^{ow1}$ GHind(2) (lw: nvr nr to chal) | 1¼ | **5** | 7/1 | 62 | 23 |
| | **Playmaker (80)** (MAJarvis) **3-9-7** PatEddery(11) (b.off hind: rdn over 2f out: hdwy over 1f out: wknd fnl f) | 1¾ | **6** | 8/1 | 77 | 39 |
| | **Stop Play (IRE) (72)** (MHTompkins) **3-8-13** PRobinson(3) (led: clr 4f out: styd far side st: hdd over 1f out: wknd fnl f) | nk | **7** | 10/1 | 68 | 30 |
| 1119$^{3}$ | **Wilfull Lad (IRE) (61)** (MartynMeade) **3-8-2** JCarroll(1) (chsd ldr over 1f: rdn over 3f out: wknd over 1f out) | 1¼ | **8** | 11/2$^{3}$ | 55 | 17 |
| 1119$^{13}$ | **Zdenka (63)** (MBlanshard) **3-8-4** JQuinn(8) (hld up: rdn over 3f out: wknd over 1f out) | ¾ | **9** | 20/1 | 55 | 17 |
| 978$^{14}$ | **Western Venture (IRE) (70)** (JWPayne) **3-8-11** RHughes(7) (b: a bhd) | 16 | **10** | 33/1 | 26 | — |
| | **Janies Girl (IRE) (58)** (KRBurke) **3-7-13** WSupple(5) (lw: a bhd) | 10 | **11** | 33/1 | — | — |
| | | | | (SP 122.7%) | **11 Rn** | |

**1m 33.14** (4.54) CSF £31.37 CT £109.85 TOTE £3.80: £1.70 £2.30 £2.10 (£22.40) Trio £49.40 OWNER Mr W. E. Sturt (NEWMARKET) BRED Hesmonds Stud Ltd
**976 Farmost** looked extremely well in the paddock. In second place by the end of the back straight, he gave chase to the leader racing on the opposite side of the track and, getting on top approaching the final furlong, kept on well. He will now try for a quick double at Brighton on Thursday. (5/2)
**Brighton Road (IRE)** left his first run for his new stable well behind. Chasing the leaders, he kept on well inside the final furlong for second prize. (12/1)
**987 Menoo Hal Batal (USA)**, held up at the back of the field, still appeared to be travelling well early in the straight. Picking up ground a quarter of a mile out, he was certainly given quite a lot to do but ran on inside the final furlong, if never looking likely to get there in time. (4/1)
**Apache Len (USA)** stayed on well in the last furlong and a half to be nearest at the line. He should be stepped back up in trip. (12/1: 8/1-14/1)
**1074 Superior Force** never looked like getting in a serious blow. (7/1)
**Playmaker**, who has changed stables since last year, began to pick up ground up the stands' side below the distance but had little left to offer in the last 200 yards as this longer trip found him out. A drop back to six furlongs would be in his favour. (8/1)

## 1486 SURREY RACING H'CAP (0-80) (4-Y.O+) (Class D)

5-20 (5-20) **1m 2f 7y** £4,188.50 (£1,268.00: £619.00: £294.50) Stalls: High GOING: 0.02 sec per fur (G)

| | | | | SP | RR | SF |
|---|---|---|---|---|---|---|
| 1145$^{3}$ | **Bakheta (47)** (MissGayKelleway) **4-7-7**$^{(5)ow2}$ MHenry(13) (lw: chsd ldr: led 6f out: rdn out) | — | **1** | 9/2$^{2}$ | 57 | 46 |
| 1066$^{6}$ | **Silently (76)** (IABalding) **4-9-8**$^{(5)}$ MartinDwyer(4) (lw: rdn over 3f out: hdwy over 2f out: hung lft ins fnl f: r.o wl) | nk | **2** | 16/1 | 86 | 77 |
| 979$^{4}$ | **Koathary (USA) (55)** (LGCottrell) **5-8-6** JQuinn(8) (lw: a.p: rdn over 3f out: unable qckn fnl f) | 2½ | **3** | 16/1 | 61 | 52 |
| 1109$^{8}$ | **Prize Pupil (IRE) (73)** (CFWall) **4-9-10** GDuffield(10) (a.p: rdn over 3f out: wknd over 1f out) | 6 | **4** | 6/1$^{3}$ | 69 | 60 |
| 1145$^{4}$ | **Noble Sprinter (IRE) (77)** (RHannon) **4-10-0b** JReid(14) (lw: lost pl 7f out: no hdwy fnl 2f) | 2½ | **5** | 15/2 | 69 | 60 |
| 995$^{11}$ | **Miswaki Dancer (USA) (58)** (LadyHerries) **6-8-9** DeclanO'Shea(9) (b: nvr nr to chal) | s.h | **6** | 16/1 | 50 | 41 |
| 1051$^{5}$ | **Sotoboy (IRE) (76)** (PWHarris) **4-9-13** GHind(3) (styd far side st: hrd rdn & edgd lft 2f out: nvr nrr) | 2 | **7** | 16/1 | 65 | 56 |
| 1440$^{2}$ | **Domitia (USA) (69)** (MBell) **4-9-6** PatEddery(5) (b: stdy hdwy 7f out: wknd over 2f out) | 12 | **8** | 11/4$^{1}$ | 39 | 30 |
| 1145$^{6}$ | **Painted Hall (USA) (67)** (JARToller) **4-9-4** JWeaver(11) (led 4f: wknd over 2f out) | hd | **9** | 16/1 | 36 | 27 |
| | **Newport Knight (65)** (RAkehurst) **5-9-2** TIves(1) (a bhd) | 1 | **10** | 16/1 | 33 | 24 |
| 844$^{7}$ | **Sayitagain (55)** (JRJenkins) **4-8-3**$^{(3)ow2}$ DaneO'Neill(7) (lw: bhd fnl 3f) | 5 | **11** | 33/1 | 15 | 4 |
| *308*$^{2}$ | **New Albion (USA) (67)** (NJHenderson) **5-9-4** RHughes(6) (bhd fnl 6f) | 17 | **12** | 14/1 | — | — |
| 844$^{12}$ | **Proton (74)** (RAkehurst) **6-9-11** SSanders(2) (lw: bhd fnl 3f) | 2½ | **13** | 14/1 | 3 | — |
| | | | | (SP 122.5%) | **13 Rn** | |

**2m 11.49** (4.79) CSF £68.05 CT £984.73 TOTE £4.90: £2.00 £4.80 £4.70 (£86.30) Trio £232.30 OWNER Mr Frank O'Rourke (WHITCOMBE) BRED Haresfoot Stud
STEWARDS' ENQUIRY Hind susp. 5-6/6/96 (excessive use of whip).
**1145 Bakheta** put up a gutsy performance. Racing in second place, she went on three-quarters of a mile out and, ridden along in the straight, managed to keep her persistent rivals at bay. (9/2)
**650 Silently** moved into the action over a quarter of a mile out and, racing between the winner and third, tried to get in a challenge. Hanging left inside the final furlong, doing the third no favours, he nevertheless ran on well, if just failing to get there. (16/1)
**979 Koathary (USA)**, always close up, was almost on terms below the distance. Although the runner-up did cross him inside the final furlong, he was held in third place at the time. He remains a maiden. (16/1)
**871 Prize Pupil (IRE)**, always close up, was unable to prevent the first three from pulling away from below the distance. (6/1)
**1145 Noble Sprinter (IRE)** was making little impression on the principals in the last two furlongs. (15/2)

T/Jkpt: £13,344.80 (0.8 Tckts); £3,759.11 to Redcar 28/5/96. T/Plpt: £237.70 (185.81 Tckts). T/Qdpt: £19.70 (118.53 Tckts). AK

# 1093-SOUTHWELL (L-H) (Standard)
## Monday May 27th
WEATHER: overcast

## 1487 WOODLAND H'CAP (0-65) (3-Y.O+ F & M) (Class F)
2-15 (2-15) **1m 3f (Fibresand)** £2,070.00 (£570.00: £270.00) Stalls: Low GOING minus 0.07 sec per fur (STD)

| | | | | SP | RR | SF |
|---|---|---|---|---|---|---|
| 1022[2] | **Philmist (48)** (CWCElsey) **4-9-3b** NKennedy(2) (in tch tl lost pl 6f out: hdwy on outside over 2f out: led over 1f out: r.o wl) | — | 1 | 8/1 | 56 | 20 |
| 1159* | **Anchorena (45)** (MrsASwinbank) **4-9-0** OUrbina(12) (hld up: hdwy 5f out: rdn over 2f out: led wl over 1f out: sn hdd & one pce) | 2 | 2 | 7/1 [3] | 50 | 14 |
| *1096[7]* | **Jalmaid (55)** (BAMcMahon) **4-9-5**(5) LNewton(8) (in tch: rdn along to chse ldrs appr st: styd on one pce fr over 1f out) | hd | 3 | 20/1 | 60 | 24 |
| *1096[5]* | **Noble Canonire (55)** (SRBowring) **4-9-7**(3) CTeague(9) (bhd: hdwy & wnt prom 6f out: rdn to ld 2f out: sn hdd & one pce) | 3½ | 4 | 9/1 | 55 | 19 |
| *1098[8]* | **Milltown Classic (IRE) (28)** (JParkes) **4-7-11** NCarlisle(5) (sn bhd & drvn along: styd on fnl 3f: nt rch ldrs) | 6 | 5 | 33/1 | 19 | — |
| 1306[3] | **Rasayel (USA) (41)** (PDEvans) **6-8-10** TWilliams(11) (trckd ldrs: led over 6f out: rdn & hdd 2f out: sn wknd) | ¾ | 6 | 9/2 [2] | 31 | — |
| *1098[5]* | **Carol Again (48)** (NBycroft) **4-8-10**(7) TAshley(7) (hld up: stdy hdwy over 6f out: in tch appr st: sn rdn & btn) | nk | 7 | 10/1 | 38 | 2 |
| 1167[5] | **Princess Pamgaddy (44)** (CNAllen) **3-7-7**(5) PFessey(10) (chsd ldrs: jnd ldrs over 6f out: rdn & wknd 3f out) | 2 | 8 | 14/1 | 31 | — |
| *777[6]* | **Instantaneous (51)** (TDEasterby) **4-9-6** JFEgan(3) (dwlt: rr div: rdn along 6f out: btn over 3f out) | 8 | 9 | 7/1 [3] | 26 | — |
| *856** | **Perpetual Light (62)** (JJQuinn) **3-9-2** KDarley(6) (lw: trckd ldrs: disp ld over 6f out: rdn & wknd appr st) | 1¾ | 10 | 9/4 [1] | 35 | — |
| *424[7]* | **Palacegate Jo (IRE) (40)** (DWChapman) **5-8-9** DeanMcKeown(4) (prom tl rdn & wknd 4f out: sn bhd) | 5 | 11 | 20/1 | 5 | — |
| 763[11] | **Lucitino (45)** (SCWilliams) **3-7-10**(3) DWright(1) (b: led: sn rdn along: hdd over 6f out: sn lost pl) | 3 | 12 | 25/1 | 6 | — |

(SP 127.1%) **12 Rn**

**2m 30.8** (10.80) CSF £62.27 CT £1,016.82 TOTE £9.30: £1.70 £2.80 £6.50 (£24.10) Trio £81.50; £103.36 to Leicester 28/5/96. OWNER Mr C. D. Barber-Lomax (MALTON) BRED Mrs M. Morley
WEIGHT FOR AGE 3yo-15lb

**1022 Philmist**, racing off an 8lb higher mark than on turf, won decisively in the end. Her only other success was also gained here on the sand. (8/1)
**1159* Anchorena** had no sooner battled her way to the front than the winner pounced, and she had no answer. (7/1)
**Jalmaid** ran her best race for some time and is clearly suited to the sand. (20/1)
**1096 Noble Canonire** led briefly early in the straight but, once collared, had nothing more to give. (9/1)
**604 Milltown Classic (IRE)**, flat to the boards most of the way, made some late progress. (33/1)
**1306 Rasayel (USA)** was soon on the retreat when collared in the home straight. (9/2)
**856* Perpetual Light**, bang in the firing-line towards the end of the back straight, was soon found wanting. (9/4: 6/4-5/2)

## 1488 COPPICE CLAIMING STKS (4-Y.O+) (Class F)
2-45 (2-45) **2m (Fibresand)** £2,070.00 (£570.00: £270.00) Stalls: Low GOING minus 0.07 sec per fur (STD)

| | | | | SP | RR | SF |
|---|---|---|---|---|---|---|
| 1343[7] | **Jaraab (89)** (MissSJWilton) **5-9-10v** SWhitworth(2) (hld up: hdwy ½-wy: wnt 2nd & rdn along 5f out: led over 2f out: hld on wl cl home) | — | 1 | 4/5 [1] | 73 | — |
| | **Castle Secret (47)** (DBurchell) **10-8-12** FNorton(7) (mid div: hdwy 6f out: drvn along & outpcd appr st: styd on u.p fnl 2f: nrst fin) | ¾ | 2 | 7/1 | 60 | — |
| 886[3] | **Cutthroat Kid (IRE) (61)** (MrsMReveley) **6-9-8v** KDarley(9) (lw: a.p: jnd ldr 7f out: led 5f out: hdd over 2f out: no ex) | 4 | 3 | 100/30 [2] | 66 | — |
| *603[3]* | **Eulogy (FR) (66)** (KRBurke) **9-8-5**(7) TAshley(3) (trckd ldrs: rdn along over 3f out: sn wknd) | 17 | 4 | 5/1 [3] | 39 | — |
| *125[3]* | **Zesti (46)** (TTClement) **4-8-8** OUrbina(8) (hld up: stdy hdwy over 6f out: sn trckng ldrs: rdn & btn over 2f out) | 13 | 5 | 25/1 | 24 | — |
| *1031[6]* | **Efaad (IRE) (47)** (JNorton) **5-9-0** JFEgan(5) (in tch: rdn along & outpcd over 6f out: sn lost tch) | 3 | 6 | 33/1 | 25 | — |
| *1095[7]* | **Brave Spy (55)** (CACyzer) **5-9-6** TWilliams(6) (trckd ldr: led 8f out tl hdd 5f out: btn & eased 3f out) | 3 | 7 | 16/1 | 28 | — |
| | **Walk In The Wild** (ABailey) **4-8-5** PBloomfield(4) (led to ½-wy: sn drvn along & wknd: t.o fnl 4f) | dist | 8 | 25/1 | — | — |
| *1095[11]* | **Selmeston (IRE) (43)** (PSFelgate) **4-8-7**(3) DWright(1) (rr div: rdn along 7f out: lost tch 5f out: t.o) | 12 | 9 | 14/1 | — | — |

(SP 131.0%) **9 Rn**

**3m 48.7** (22.70) CSF £8.59 TOTE £1.80: £1.30 £1.20 £1.80 (£6.80) Trio £17.70 OWNER Gilberts Animal Feed Products (STOKE-ON-TRENT) BRED Shadwell Estate Company Limited
WEIGHT FOR AGE 4yo-2lb

**837* Jaraab**, much happier back on sand, gained his tenth All-Weather success. (4/5: 4/6-Evens)
**Castle Secret**, flat to the boards and going nowhere half a mile out, stayed on stoutly under pressure throughout the final two furlongs and would have won with a little further to go. (7/1)
**886 Cutthroat Kid (IRE)** went smoothly to the front but, strongly tackled in the straight, was clearly outpointed in the final quarter-mile. (100/30)
**603 Eulogy (FR)** beat a hasty retreat from the home turn. (5/1)

## 1489 E.B.F. ASTON MAIDEN STKS (2-Y.O) (Class D)
3-15 (3-15) **6f (Fibresand)** £3,497.50 (£1,045.00: £500.00: £227.50) Stalls: Low GOING minus 0.07 sec per fur (STD)

| | | | | SP | RR | SF |
|---|---|---|---|---|---|---|
| 950[4] | **Belle Vue** (SirMarkPrescott) **2-8-9** KDarley(5) (lw: mde all: rdn clr over 1f out: readily) | — | 1 | 2/1 [1] | 60+ | 15 |
| 975[5] | **Nostalgic Air (USA)** (EWeymes) **2-8-9** OUrbina(6) (in tch: rdn & outpcd appr st: c wd: styd on wl fr over 1f out: no ch w wnr) | 5 | 2 | 9/1 | 47 | 2 |
| | **Mystic Quest (IRE)** (KMcAuliffe) **2-9-0** JFEgan(7) (w'like: scope: cl up: rdn ½-wy: ev ch 2f out: no ex fr over 1f out) | 3 | 3 | 16/1 | 44 | — |
| | **Superquest** (WAO'Gorman) **2-9-0** EmmaO'Gorman(10) (scope: dwlt: hdwy to chse ldrs on outside ½-wy: sn ev ch: grad wknd fr over 1f out) | ½ | 4 | 5/1 | 42 | — |
| *895[8]* | **Court House** (BAMcMahon) **2-8-9**(5) LNewton(8) (leggy: chsd ldrs: effrt & ev ch over 2f out: wknd over 1f out) | 1 | 5 | 20/1 | 40 | — |
| | **Paddy Lad (IRE)** (RGuest) **2-9-0** PBloomfield(1) (leggy: s.i.s: sn drvn along & a outpcd) | 5 | 6 | 12/1 | 26 | — |

950[7] **Petula Boy** (MMcCormack) **2-8-11b[1]**(3) DWright(9) (drvn along thrght: nvr able to rch ldrs)....2 **7** 10/1 21 —
**Biba (IRE)** (RBoss) **2-8-9** FNorton(3) (w'like: scope: sn pushed along & nvr wnt pce of ldrs fr ½-wy)....1 **8** 9/2[3] 13 —
1331[3] **Battle Ground (IRE)** (NACallaghan) **2-9-0** SWhitworth(4) (chsd ldrs tl rdn & wknd fr 2f out: eased fnl f)....3 **9** 4/1[2] 10 —
800[9] **Zorba** (CWThornton) **2-9-0** DeanMcKeown(2) (s.s: a outpcd & bhd)....3 **10** 14/1 2 —
(SP 132.3%) **10 Rn**

**1m 18.9** (5.40) CSF £22.26 TOTE £2.90: £1.30 £2.00 £3.90 (£7.60) Trio £72.20; £92.66 to Leicester 28/5/96 OWNER Mrs C. R. Philipson (NEWMARKET) BRED Red House Stud

**950 Belle Vue**, all the better for her debut outing and much more at home over this extra furlong, won in fine style. Better things look likely for this daughter of Petong. (2/1)

**975 Nostalgic Air (USA)** finished to some effect down the middle of the course without ever looking likely to trouble the winner. (9/1)

**Mystic Quest (IRE)** shaped well on this debut, having every chance until outpointed from over a furlong out. The experience will not have been wasted on him. (16/1)

**Superquest** showed promise on this debut and had every chance until gradually weakening from over a furlong out. He will be better for the race. (5/1)

**Court House**, bang in with every chance over two furlongs out, could then do no more. (20/1)

## 1490 COVERT H'CAP (0-70) (3-Y.O) (Class E)

3-45 (3-48) **1m (Fibresand)** £3,261.40 (£905.40: £434.20) Stalls: Low GOING minus 0.07 sec per fur (STD)

SP RR SF

1042[4] **Yeoman Oliver (66)** (BAMcMahon) **3-9-1**(5) LNewton(16) (a.p: rdn over 2f out: styd on strly to ld last strides)....— **1** 12/1 72 41
*780[2]* **Awafeh (42)** (SMellor) **3-7-5**(5) PFessey(12) (led: rdn 2f out: hdd cl home)....hd **2** 10/1 48 17
890[8] **Princely Affair (47)** (MBell) **3-7-8**(7) RMullen(2) (rdn along appr st: hdwy on ins fnl 2f: styd on: nt rch ldrs)....8 **3** 14/1 45 6
860[12] **Quiet Arch (IRE) (62)** (CACyzer) **3-9-2** OUrbina(10) (chsd ldrs: c wd st: one pce fnl 2f)....nk **4** 25/1 60 20
*1027[6]* **Efipetite (45)** (NBycroft) **3-7-13** NKennedy(11) (s.i.s: bhd tl hdwy 3f out: one pce fnl 2f)....½ **5** 14/1 42 2
*1027[2]* **People Direct (62)** (KMcAuliffe) **3-9-2** JFEgan(9) (chsd ldrs: c wd st: drvn along & no imp fnl 2f)....hd **6** 4/1[1] 59 19
*1029** **Principal Boy (IRE) (53)** (TJEtherington) **3-8-7** KDarley(6) (chsd ldrs: rdn along & outpcd wl over 2f out: n.d after)....1¼ **7** 6/1[2] 49 8
*1030** **Klipspinger (60)** (BSRothwell) **3-8-7**(7) TAshley(7) (prom: rdn over 3f out: wknd fnl 2f)....s.h **8** 7/1[3] 56 14
738[7] **Nose No Bounds (IRE) (67)** (MJohnston) **3-9-7** TWilliams(8) (cl up: sn pushed along: lost pl & wknd fnl 2f) .1½ **9** 10/1 61 18
1042[5] **Jimjareer (IRE) (51)** (CaptJWilson) **3-8-2**(3)ow1 CTeague(4) (drvn along in mid div ½-wy: n.d)....2½ **10** 7/1[3] 43 —
914[7] **Silent Guest (IRE) (60)** (SirMarkPrescott) **3-9-0** CNutter(15) (nvr rchd ldrs)....hd **11** 14/1 52 6
1100[17] **Dhulikhel (45)** (DMarks) **3-7-13** NCarlisle(14) (in tch: rdn along 3f out: btn 2f out)....¾ **12** 10/1 36 —
*899[5]* **Sweet Amoret (55)** (PHowling) **3-8-9** FNorton(13) (chsd ldrs: rdn & lost pl over 2f out: eased fnl f)....1 **13** 12/1 45 —
658[3] **Rajah (49)** (CWThornton) **3-8-3** DeanMcKeown(5) (a outpcd & bhd)....2½ **14** 7/1[3] 36 —
**Lagan (62)** (PSFelgate) **3-8-13**(3) DWright(3) (s.i.s: a bhd: t.o & eased fnl 2f)....25 **15** 33/1 24 —
(SP 141.2%) **15 Rn**

**1m 45.7** (5.70) CSF £132.83 CT £1640.40 TOTE £16.80: £4.80 £3.70 £7.20 (£96.70) Trio Not won; £212.52 to Leicester 28/5/96 OWNER Mr Michael Stokes (TAMWORTH) BRED M. G. T. Stokes

LONG HANDICAP Awafeh 7-9

**1042 Yeoman Oliver** overcame a poor draw and clinched the verdict in the dying strides. (12/1)

**780 Awafeh** tried to make the most of his feather-weight and almost succeeded, only being pipped near the line. (10/1)

**Princely Affair** did well to finish so close, having raced on the slowest ground near the inside rail in the home straight. (14/1)

**Quiet Arch (IRE)**, never too far away, came under pressure once in line for home and could find only one pace. (25/1)

**781 Efipetite** did not help her cause by missing the break, but could pull out no extra having made ground around the home turn. (14/1)

**1027 People Direct** chased the leading group but could make no impression in the final quarter-mile. (4/1: op 6/1)

## 1491 SPINNEY (S) STKS (2-Y.O) (Class G)

4-15 (4-16) **5f (Fibresand)** £2,070.00 (£570.00: £270.00) Stalls: High GOING minus 0.07 sec per fur (STD)

SP RR SF

*1097[3]* **Who Told Vicky (IRE)** (JSMoore) **2-8-6** JFEgan(2) (a.p: led over 1f out: r.o wl u.p)....— **1** 2/1[1] 55 10
**Make Ready** (JNeville) **2-8-6** FNorton(1) (neat: stumbled s: sn chsng ldrs: rdn & ev ch ent fnl f: nt qckn)....1¼ **2** 16/1 51 6
1320[4] **Fit For The Job (IRE)** (WGMTurner) **2-8-11** KRutter(4) (a.p: rdn 2f out: one pce appr fnl f)....¾ **3** 9/2[3] 54 9
1183[4] **Sharp But Fair** (SirMarkPrescott) **2-8-6** CNutter(3) (trckd ldrs: rdn 2f out: one pce fr over 1f out)....1¼ **4** 3/1[2] 45 —
1183[3] **Full Traceability (IRE)** (JBerry) **2-8-11** KDarley(5) (led tl hdd over 1f out: no ex)....¾ **5** 2/1[1] 47 2
1166[7] **Jingoist (IRE)** (MJohnston) **2-8-6** TWilliams(6) (chsd ldrs tl rdn & wknd wl over 1f out)....8 **6** 10/1 17 —
(SP 124.8%) **6 Rn**

**61.3 secs** (4.30) CSF £27.35 TOTE £3.50: £2.50 £1.10 (£26.30) OWNER Mrs Victoria Goodman (HUNGERFORD) BRED A. M. F. Persse
No bid

**1097 Who Told Vicky (IRE)** finally found opportunity knocking and won with very little to spare. (2/1)

**Make Ready** did not help her cause by stumbling at the start, and looks capable of winning a similar event. (16/1)

**1320 Fit For The Job (IRE)**, in with every chance, was found wanting entering the final furlong. (9/2)

**1183 Sharp But Fair** received the worst of the kick-back in tracking the leaders, but was unable to pull out any extra approaching the final furlong. (3/1)

**1183 Full Traceability (IRE)** attempted to lead from pillar-to-post but was outpointed from over a furlong out. (2/1)

## 1492 FOREST H'CAP (0-70) (3-Y.O+) (Class E)

4-45 (4-48) **5f (Fibresand)** £3,235.50 (£898.00: £430.50) Stalls: High GOING minus 0.07 sec per fur (STD)

SP RR SF

1157[4] **Daawe (USA) (65)** (MrsVAAconley) **5-9-10v** MDeering(10) (led tl hdd appr fnl f: hrd rdn & rallied to ld again on line)....— **1** 7/1 78 56
1161[6] **Perfect Brave (66)** (JBalding) **5-9-4**(7) JEdmunds(3) (cl up: rdn to ld appr fnl f: hdd on line)....hd **2** 13/2[3] 79 57
*900[3]* **Rennyholme (57)** (JHetherton) **5-9-2b** NKennedy(17) (lw: hdwy stands' side 2f out: kpt on: nt rch ldrs)....4 **3** 10/1 57 35
*1094[5]* **Elton Ledger (IRE) (63)** (MrsNMacauley) **7-9-8v** EmmaO'Gorman(6) (b: mid div: hdwy over 2f out: kpt on fnl f)....¾ **4** 10/1 61 39
*1028[2]* **My Cherrywell (59)** (LRLloyd-James) **6-9-4b** TWilliams(8) (lw: b.hind: chsd ldrs: rdn along over 2f out: sn outpcd: kpt on fnl f)....nk **5** 6/1[2] 56 34
1161[8] **Super Rocky (66)** (RBastiman) **7-9-6**(5) HBastiman(12) (in tch: effrt over 2f out: nt pce to chal)....nk **6** 10/1 62 40

| | | | | |
|---|---|---|---|---|
| 1163* **Cheeky Chappy (60)** (DWChapman) **5-9-0b**(5) PFessey(11) (cl up: rdn 2f out: no ex fr over 1f out)..................½ **7** | 7/1 | 54 | 32 |
| *155*11 **Most Uppitty (52)** (JBerry) **4-8-4**(7) JoanneWebster(9) (sn drvn along & outpcd in centre: styd on fnl f).........1¼ **8** | 20/1 | 42 | 20 |
| *900*6 **Daaniera (IRE) (38)** (PHowling) **6-7-11v** FNorton(4) (in tch far side: no imp fr wl over 1f out)............................1 **9** | 16/1 | 25 | 3 |
| 997 10 **Frontman (IRE) (67)** (TDBarron) **3-9-4** KDarley(2) (sn pushed along far side: nvr rchd ldrs) ............................hd **10** | 10/1 | 53 | 23 |
| **Scored Again (60)** (MJHeaton-Ellis) **6-9-0**(5) AmandaSanders(15) (sn pushed along stands' side: n.d).........1¼ **11** | 20/1 | 42 | 20 |
| 1307 11 **Lord Sky (69)** (ABailey) **5-9-7**(7) AngelaGallimore(14) (nvr bttr than mid div)...........................nk **12** | 12/1 | 51 | 29 |
| *368*9 **Double Glow (37)** (NBycroft) **4-7-7**(3) DWright(1) (dwlt: racd far side: nvr wnt pce)..............................1¼ **13** | 33/1 | 19 | — |
| *835*6 **Mister (44)** (KMcAuliffe) **4-8-3b**1 JFEgan(16) (chsd ldrs stands' side over 3f) ..................................d.h **13** | 20/1 | 26 | — |
| 592 12 **Square Deal (FR) (65)** (SRBowring) **5-9-7b**1(3) CTeague(5) (s.i.s: a bhd) ...........................................1 **15** | 7/2 1 | 43 | 17 |
| 773 11 **Kustom Kit (IRE) (66)** (BAMcMahon) **3-8-10**(7) TAshley(13) (a outpcd stands' side) .........................................3 **16** | 25/1 | 35 | 1 |
| 868 19 **Kiwud (45)** (TWDonnelly) **3-7-10** NCarlisle(7) (in tch centre 3f) ...................................................¾ **17** | 33/1 | 11 | — |

(SP 148.8%) **17 Rn**

**59.6 secs** (2.60) CSF £58.53 CT £463.71 TOTE £11.50: £2.20 £2.10 £3.40 £3.70 (£57.40) Trio £117.50 OWNER Mrs Andrea Mallinson (WESTOW) BRED Gainsborough Farm W.C.
LONG HANDICAP Double Glow 6-7 Kiwud 7-6
WEIGHT FOR AGE 3yo-8lb

**1157 Daawe (USA)**, who is in good form at present, came back to five furlongs. He got back up in the dying strides under a very strong ride. (7/1)
**900 Perfect Brave** looked to have the measure of the winner when going on approaching the final furlong, but was denied on the stick. (13/2)
**900 Rennyholme** picked up ground two furlongs out, but could never reach the first two. (10/1)
**1094 Elton Ledger (IRE)** ran respectably but is probably better over further. (10/1)
**1028 My Cherrywell** raced in the firing-line but became outpaced well over a furlong out before staying on again towards the finish. (6/1)
**951 Super Rocky** was unable to peg back the leaders from over a furlong out. (10/1)
**Most Uppitty**, soon pushed along and outpaced, stayed on and was never nearer than at the line. (20/1)
**Square Deal (FR)**, a springer in the market and blinkered for the first time, missed the break and was never in the firing-line. (7/2: op 8/1)

T/Plpt: £760.80 (6.05 Tckts). T/Qdpt: £182.10 (0.5 Tckts); £123.10 to Redcar 28/5/96. O'R

# 1467-LEICESTER (R-H) (Good to soft)
## Tuesday May 28th

vis: poor race 5
WEATHER: showers WIND: mod half bhd

## 1493 SHARNFORD CONDITIONS STKS (3-Y.O) (Class C)
2-30 (2-31) **5f 218y** £4,889.96 (£1,807.64: £865.82: £352.10: £138.05: £52.43) Stalls: Low GOING minus 0.42 sec per fur (F)

| | SP | RR | SF |
|---|---|---|---|
| 1146 4 **King of The East (IRE) (104)** (MRStoute) **3-9-3** LDettori(1) (hld up: hdwy over 2f out: led appr fnl f: comf)....— **1** | 13/8 1 | 99+ | 34 |
| **Red Nymph (90)** (WJarvis) **3-8-12** BThomson(4) (prom: led wl over 1f out tl hdd & outpcd appr fnl f)............2½ **2** | 6/1 3 | 87 | 22 |
| **Agnella (IRE) (96)** (GLMoore) **3-8-10** TQuinn(6) (bkwd: s.i.s: pushed along thrght: kpt on ins fnl f)...............3½ **3** | 6/1 3 | 76 | 11 |
| 1146 7 **Fly Tip (IRE) (84)** (BJMeehan) **3-8-10** BDoyle(3) (dwlt: bhd & drvn: nvr nr to chal) ..........................................¾ **4** | 13/2 | 74 | 9 |
| 1188 5 **Pleasure Time (66)** (CSmith) **3-8-4**(7) AngelaGallimore(2) (slt ld over 3f: sn rdn & wknd over 1f out).............s.h **5** | 50/1 | 75 | 10 |
| 832 4 **Norwegian Blue (IRE) (91)** (APJarvis) **3-9-1** PatEddery(5) (lw: prom: led over 2f out tl wl over 1f out: wknd appr fnl f) ..............................................2½ **6** | 9/4 2 | 72 | 7 |

(SP 112.7%) **6 Rn**

**1m 12.2** (2.20) CSF £10.87 TOTE £2.10: £1.60 £2.00 (£5.00) OWNER Dr K. Shimizu (NEWMARKET) BRED Barronstown Stud And Ron Con Ltd

**1146 King of The East (IRE)**, always going easily behind the leaders, quickened up well when given the office and won readily. (13/8)
**Red Nymph**, still not quite in her coat, ran a pleasing race on this first outing in eight months and, given similar ground conditions, can soon go one better. (6/1)
**Agnella (IRE)**, placed in a listed race in Baden-Baden in the autumn, was far from fully wound up for this return to action, but she was finding her stride inside the distance and looks to need further. (6/1)
**Fly Tip (IRE)**, well behind the winner early in the month, had little chance of turning the tables on identical terms and the form was franked without much difficulty. (13/2)
**832 Norwegian Blue (IRE)** helped force the pace for over half a mile, but weakened rather quickly once headed and the position was accepted. (9/4)

## 1494 HATHERN (S) STKS (2-Y.O) (Class G)
3-00 (3-00) **5f 218y** £2,238.00 (£618.00: £294.00) Stalls: Low GOING minus 0.42 sec per fur (F)

| | SP | RR | SF |
|---|---|---|---|
| 869 5 **But Why** (CMurray) **2-8-11** MTebbutt(1) (hld up in tch: shkn up & hdwy to ld over 1f out: pushed clr)............— **1** | 3/1 1 | 59 | 19 |
| 1166 5 **Ginny Wossername** (WGMTurner) **2-8-6** TSprake(2) (bit bkwd: prom: lost pl & rdn 2f out: kpt on ins fnl f)...2½ **2** | 3/1 1 | 47 | 7 |
| *895*7 **Caviar And Candy** (DJSCosgrove) **2-8-1**(5) LNewton(3) (led over 3f: rdn & no ex appr fnl f) ...........................2 **3** | 4/1 3 | 42 | 2 |
| *1080*4 **Our Kevin** (KMcAuliffe) **2-8-11** JFEgan(4) (prom tl rdn & one pce appr fnl f) ..........................................½ **4** | 5/1 | 46 | 6 |
| **Grovefair Dancer (IRE)** (BJMeehan) **2-8-6** BDoyle(6) (leggy: scope: w ldrs: slt ld over 2f out: hdd over 1f out: eased when btn)...............................................3 **5** | 7/2 2 | 33 | — |
| 1086 14 **Riva La Belle** (JWharton) **2-8-6** PRobinson(5) (a bhd: lost tch fnl 2f)................................................1¾ **6** | 14/1 | 28 | — |

(SP 115.6%) **6 Rn**

**1m 12.9** (2.90) CSF £12.13 TOTE £3.70: £2.00 £1.80 (£9.00) OWNER Four Score Racing (NEWMARKET) BRED D. G. Mason
SoldTStafford 6,500 gns

**869 But Why**, tackling another furlong but stepping down in class, proved far too good for these rivals and has now been sold to race in France. (3/1)
**1166 Ginny Wossername**, with a bit still left to work on, got outpaced when the tempo increased two furlongs out, but she picked up again inside the distance and will win in time. (3/1)
**733 Caviar And Candy** has got plenty of speed but she possibly does too much too soon, and keeps nothing in reserve for the final battle. (4/1)
**1080 Our Kevin** wore a visor on his previous outing but raced with no headgear this time, and pressed the leaders until tapped for speed inside the distance. (5/1)
**Grovefair Dancer (IRE)** looked well tuned up but did not impress to post. In the firing-line from the start, she faded rather tamely approaching the final furlong and may well have found the ground too testing. (7/2: op 9/4)

## 1495 ABBEY PARK CONDITIONS STKS (3-Y.O) (Class C)

3-30 (3-30) **7f 9y** £5,018.39 (£1,807.64: £865.82: £352.10: £138.05) Stalls: Low GOING minus 0.42 sec per fur (F)

| | | | | SP | RR | SF |
|---|---|---|---|---|---|---|
| 870* | **Abeyr** (MAJarvis) **3-8-9** PRobinson(4) (lw: a.p: led wl over 1f out: hrd rdn & r.o strly) | — | 1 | 3/1[3] | 91 | 43 |
| 952[3] | **Lucayan Prince (USA) (97)** (DRLoder) **3-9-0b** LDettori(3) (lw: hld up: hdwy & swtchd rt over 1f out: ev ch ins fnl f: r.o) | nk | 2 | 9/4[1] | 95 | 47 |
| 1332[4] | **Kuantan (USA) (107)** (PFICole) **3-9-4** TQuinn(2) (plld hrd: a.p: effrt & ev ch appr fnl f: unable qckn) | 1¼ | 3 | 7/2 | 97 | 49 |
| 1185[W] | **Safio (72)** (CSmith) **3-9-2** AClark(5) (bit bkwd: bhd & outpcd: rdn 2f out: no imp) | 4 | 4 | 50/1 | 85 | 37 |
| 732* | **Golden Ace (IRE)** (RHannon) **3-9-0** PatEddery(1) (led tl wl over 1f out: eased whn btn fnl f) | nk | 5 | 5/2[2] | 83 | 35 |
| | | | | (SP 108.5%) | **5 Rn** | |

**1m 24.2** (1.20) CSF £9.40 TOTE £4.00: £1.30 £2.30 (£4.70) OWNER Sheikh Ahmed Al Maktoum (NEWMARKET) BRED W. H. F. Carson

**870* Abeyr** confirmed the promise shown on her debut and, not at all inconvenienced by this shorter trip, looks a very progressive filly. (3/1)

**952 Lucayan Prince (USA)**, switched to deliver his challenge approaching the final furlong, finished fast but the winner was up to the challenge and was always keeping him at bay. (9/4)

**1332 Kuantan (USA)** could have found this race coming plenty soon enough, but he was breathing down the necks of the leaders all the way and will be the one to beat from now on. (7/2)

**732* Golden Ace (IRE)** was certainly not helped by this step down to seven furlongs and, though he did attempt to make it more of a test by setting the pace, he was swamped for speed when the principals quickened, and the situation was accepted. (5/2)

## 1496 FOREST H'CAP (0-70) (3-Y.O+) (Class E)

4-00 (4-02) **1m 1f 218y** £3,643.50 (£1,092.00: £525.00: £241.50) Stalls: Low GOING minus 0.09 sec per fur (G)

| | | | | SP | RR | SF |
|---|---|---|---|---|---|---|
| 1145[12] | **Sharp Consul (IRE) (67)** (HCandy) **4-9-13** CRutter(7) (hld up & bhd: smooth hdwy to ld wl over 1f out: r.o wl) | — | 1 | 15/2[2] | 80 | 40 |
| 879[6] | **Saltando (IRE) (47)** (PatMitchell) **5-8-7** KFallon(1) (hld up: hdwy 3f out: rdn & r.o wl fnl f) | 1¾ | 2 | 9/1[3] | 57 | 17 |
| 1302[4] | **Runic Symbol (36)** (MBlanshard) **5-7-10** JQuinn(4) (hld up: hdwy 2f out: r.o wl fnl f) | ½ | 3 | 12/1 | 45 | 5 |
| | **Western Sal (68)** (JLHarris) **4-10-0** TQuinn(2) (bkwd: hld up in tch: effrt 2f out: kpt on fnl f) | 1¼ | 4 | 12/1 | 75 | 35 |
| 955[2] | **Classic Colours (USA) (68)** (RHarris) **3-9-0** AMackay(15) (trckd ldrs: rdn to ld 2f out: sn hdd & outpcd) | 5 | 5 | 9/1[3] | 67 | 13 |
| 1347[14] | **Chilly Lad (52)** (MJRyan) **5-8-12b** DBiggs(8) (hdwy ent st: rdn to chal 2f out: one pce appr fnl f) | s.h | 6 | 12/1 | 51 | 11 |
| 866[6] | **Great Tern (43)** (NMBabbage) **4-8-3**ow1 PaulEddery(9) (hld up: hdwy over 4f out: wknd wl over 1f out) | ½ | 7 | 10/1 | 42 | 1 |
| 853[10] | **Fern's Governor (42)** (WJMusson) **4-8-2** TSprake(13) (trckd ldr tl rdn & wknd fnl 2f) | 1¼ | 8 | 14/1 | 39 | — |
| 817[3] | **Hawkish (USA) (52)** (DMorley) **7-8-12** MFenton(6) (prom: ev ch over 2f out: sn rdn & btn) | hd | 9 | 5/2[1] | 48 | 8 |
| 1142[17] | **Bronhallow (57)** (MrsBarbaraWaring) **3-8-3** JFEgan(12) (b.hind: nvr trbld ldrs) | ¾ | 10 | 16/1 | 52 | — |
| | **Teen Jay (65)** (BJLlewellyn) **6-9-11** TWilliams(14) (bit bkwd: dwlt: nvr nr to chal) | nk | 11 | 12/1 | 60 | 20 |
| 1104[11] | **Morning Sir (65)** (CRBarwell) **3-8-11** GHind(10) (led tl hdd & wknd 2f out) | ¾ | 12 | 16/1 | 59 | 5 |
| *219*[11] | **Owdbetts (IRE) (56)** (GLMoore) **4-9-2** SWhitworth(11) (lw: plld hrd: chsd ldrs: ev ch over 2f out: sn wknd) | 2 | 13 | 20/1 | 46 | 6 |
| 979[5] | **Kintwyn (46)** (WRMuir) **6-8-6** DHarrison(3) (w ldrs tl wknd u.p 2f out: t.o) | 11 | 14 | 9/1[3] | 19 | — |
| *855*[9] | **Sungrove's Best (36)** (PEccles) **9-7-10** NAdams(5) (a in rr: t.o) | 1¼ | 15 | 66/1 | 7 | — |
| 853[15] | **Studio Thirty (39)** (DMorris) **4-7-8**(5)ow3 MHenry(16) (in tch: effrt 4f out: wknd 3f out: t.o) | s.h | 16 | 12/1 | 10 | — |
| | | | | (SP 142.6%) | **16 Rn** | |

**2m 11.6** (7.90) CSF £78.70 CT £777.96 TOTE £9.10: £2.60 £2.00 £2.90 £2.20 (£59.40) Trio £245.70 OWNER Mrs David Blackburn (WANTAGE) BRED B. Barnwell

LONG HANDICAP Runic Symbol 7-8 Sungrove's Best 7-1

WEIGHT FOR AGE 3yo-14lb

OFFICIAL EXPLANATION **Fern's Governor: his rider reported that he had to take a pull to avoid clipping the heels of the horse in front, rounding the bend into the straight.**

**843 Sharp Consul (IRE)** had the going in his favour and, ridden with any amount of confidence, did not need to give of his all to win with quite a bit in hand. (15/2)

**879 Saltando (IRE)** had no chance at all with the very easy winner, but he ran on strongly in the closing stages and should now be ready to strike. (9/1)

**1302 Runic Symbol** should have found this trip made to measure, but he does not appear to put his best foot forward until too late. That is probably the reason why he is still a maiden. (12/1)

**Western Sal**, successful over course and distance in the autumn, did not look fully prepared on this seasonal debut, but she ran extremely well and another win is just around the corner. (12/1)

**955 Classic Colours (USA)** continues to perform with credit, but he loses out at the business end of his races and may fare better ridden with more patient tactics. (9/1)

**884 Chilly Lad** has not won a race for almost two years but he showed here that he still retains the ability when he can get it all together. (12/1)

**817 Hawkish (USA)** runs his best races when he is produced from off the pace, but he had far too much use made of him here and was a spent force below the distance. (5/2)

## 1497 WOODHOUSE EAVES CLAIMING STKS (3-Y.O) (Class F)

4-30 (4-32) **1m 8y** £3,101.00 (£861.00: £413.00) Stalls: Low GOING minus 0.42 sec per fur (F)

| | | | | SP | RR | SF |
|---|---|---|---|---|---|---|
| 1152* | **Rebel County (IRE) (68)** (DJSCosgrove) **3-8-13**(3) JStack(5) (lw: trckd ldrs: led over 2f out: r.o wl) | — | 1 | 10/11[1] | 66 | 18 |
| 1099[19] | **Eurobox Boy (60)** (APJarvis) **3-8-12v[1]** JTate(4) (led after 2f tl over 2f out: rallied gamely fnl f) | 2 | 2 | 25/1 | 58 | 10 |
| *655*[4] | **Trianna** (LordHuntingdon) **3-7-12**(3) AWhelan(7) (hld up: hdwy over 2f out: styd on u.p fnl f) | 1 | 3 | 16/1 | 45 | — |
| 1009[7] | **May King Mayhem (47)** (MrsALMKing) **3-8-8** AGarth(11) (hld up: styd on u.p appr fnl f: nvr nrr) | nk | 4 | 33/1 | 51 | 3 |
| 1122[10] | **Silhouette (IRE) (40)** (DRCElsworth) **3-8-1** FNorton(9) (hld up: hdwy 2f out: rdn ent fnl f: one pce) | ½ | 5 | 20/1 | 43 | — |
| 1123[8] | **Most Wanted (IRE)** (PFICole) **3-8-11** TQuinn(10) (lw: in tch: effrt 3f out: sn rdn: wknd appr fnl f) | 7 | 6 | 11/2[2] | 40 | — |
| *1027*[9] | **Royal Rapport (46)** (BAMcMahon) **3-8-7**(5) LNewton(1) (trckd ldrs tl rdn & wknd over 2f out: t.o) | 12 | 7 | 14/1 | 17 | — |
| 1312[5] | **Apartments Abroad (50)** (KMcAuliffe) **3-8-5v** JFEgan(12) (in tch: rdn 3f out: sn btn & eased: t.o) | 7 | 8 | 11/1[3] | — | — |
| *1027*[4] | **Tudor Falcon** (WJHaggas) **3-9-2** KFallon(3) (lw: nvr nr ldrs: r.o fnl 3f) | 9 | 9 | 11/2[2] | — | — |
| *1456*[8] | **Classic Victory (65)** (RHarris) **3-9-2hb** AMackay(2) (led 2f: rdn & wknd wl over 2f out: t.o) | 17 | 10 | 14/1 | — | — |
| *1027*[11] | **Below The Red Line** (MrsNMacauley) **3-8-10v** JQuinn(8) (a bhd: t.o) | 20 | 11 | 33/1 | — | — |
| 1451[P] | **Friendly Dreams (IRE)** (PTDalton) **3-8-3** NAdams(6) (s.s: sn outpcd: t.o) | dist | 12 | 50/1 | — | — |
| | | | | (SP 127.2%) | **12 Rn** | |

**1m 39.5** (4.50) CSF £25.79 TOTE £1.70: £1.10 £3.90 £2.70 (£16.20) Trio £171.00 OWNER Edermine Bloodstock (NEWMARKET) BRED C. Foy

Rebel County (IRE) clmd SHolder £12,500

**1152* Rebel County (IRE)** coped adequately with this soft ground and won this very much as she pleased. (10/11)
**655 Eurobox Boy** showed a return to form with the help of the visor and a repeat could see him getting off the mark. (25/1)
**655 Trianna** looked sure to take a hand in proceedings when mounting her bid below the distance, but the progress was slow and she was unable to land a blow. (16/1)
**May King Mayhem** stayed on particularly well inside the last quarter-mile, and a further step up could be what he needs. (33/1)
**Silhouette (IRE)**, a very poor mover even on this softer ground, did not shape badly over this longer trip and there is probably a race in her. (20/1)
**Most Wanted (IRE)** (11/2: 5/2-6/1)
**1312 Apartments Abroad** (11/1: 8/1-12/1)

## 1498 CORONATION H'CAP (0-70) (3-Y.O) (Class E)

5-00 (5-03) **1m 3f 183y** £3,534.30 (£1,058.40: £508.20: £233.10) Stalls: Low GOING minus 0.09 sec per fur (G)

| | | | | SP | RR | SF |
|---|---|---|---|---|---|---|
| 1421* | **Strategic Ploy (63)** (MrsJRRamsden) **3-9-2** $^{4x}$ KFallon(6) (dwlt: smooth hdwy over 4f out: led over 2f out: drifted rt fnl f: hld on) | — | 1 | 9/4 $^{1}$ | 70 | 34 |
| $1100^{4}$ | **Compass Pointer (59)** (JMPEustace) **3-8-12** MTebbutt(12) (hld up: hdwy 4f out: sn rdn: str chal ins fnl f) | ½ | 2 | 12/1 | 65 | 29 |
| $754^{4}$ | **Ski For Gold (68)** (JLDunlop) **3-9-7** TSprake(15) (lw: hld up: hdwy 4f out: led 3f out tl over 2f out: no ex fnl f) | 2 | 3 | 17/2 $^{3}$ | 72 | 36 |
| $1100^{3}$ | **Classic Ballet (FR) (66)** (RHarris) **3-9-5** AMackay(8) (lw: settled mid div: hdwy over 4f out: ev ch 2f out: one pce) | 2½ | 4 | 10/1 | 66 | 30 |
| $1100^{7}$ | **Spinning Mouse (54)** (DMorley) **3-8-7** PaulEddery(13) (hld up: hdwy on ins 4f out: rdn 2f out: kpt on sme pce) | 1 | 5 | 9/2 $^{2}$ | 53 | 17 |
| $1045^{8}$ | **Samuel Scott (66)** (MBell) **3-9-5** MFenton(16) (lw: hld up in rr: hdwy 2f out: nt rch ldrs) | ½ | 6 | 11/1 | 64 | 28 |
| | **Contrarie (43)** (MJRyan) **3-7-5**(5) MBaird(3) (chsd ldrs: rdn over 2f out: one pce) | 1½ | 7 | 33/1 | 39 | 3 |
| $1002^{13}$ | **Backwoods (62)** (WMBrisbourne) **3-9-1** AGarth(9) (prom tl wknd ent st) | 14 | 8 | 33/1 | 39 | 3 |
| | **Umberston (IRE) (56)** (LMCumani) **3-8-9** OUrbina(17) (bit bkwd: nvr nr to chal) | ½ | 9 | 12/1 | 33 | — |
| $1100^{8}$ | **Bailiwick (46)** (NAGraham) **3-7-13b** TWilliams(5) (plld hrd: prom: rdn & faded 3f out: t.o) | 8 | 10 | 20/1 | 12 | — |
| $1044^{4}$ | **High Desire (IRE) (54)** (JRArnold) **3-8-7** JQuinn(11) (trckd ldrs 9f: sn rdn & wknd: t.o) | ½ | 11 | 20/1 | 19 | — |
| $803^{9}$ | **Quiet Moments (IRE) (43)** (PGMurphy) **3-7-10** NAdams(10) (led over 7f: wknd 3f out: t.o) | 2½ | 12 | 33/1 | 5 | — |
| $1100^{14}$ | **Dashing Invader (USA) (50)** (PWHarris) **3-8-3** GHind(14) (a in rr: t.o) | ½ | 13 | 20/1 | 11 | — |
| $1168^{3}$ | **Kuwam (IRE) (50)** (BHanbury) **3-8-0**(3)ow1 JStack(1) (trckd ldrs tl rdn & wknd over 3f out: t.o) | ¾ | 14 | 14/1 | 10 | — |
| $890^{5}$ | **Galway Blade (59)** (APJarvis) **3-8-12** JTate(7) (lw: prom tl wknd over 3f out: t.o) | 1½ | 15 | 14/1 | 17 | — |
| $1023^{4}$ | **Sedbergh (USA) (67)** (MrsMReveley) **3-9-6** WJO'Connor(4) (prom: led over 4f out to 3f out: sn rdn & wknd: t.o) | 6 | 16 | 16/1 | 17 | — |
| $1145^{10}$ | **Winged Prince (60)** (AGFoster) **3-8-13** JFEgan(2) (mid div tl wknd over 3f out: t.o) | 3 | 17 | 33/1 | 6 | — |
| *$899^{9}$* | **Chillington (43)** (WMBrisbourne) **3-7-5**(5) MartinDwyer(18) (a bhd: t.o fnl 4f) | 23 | 18 | 50/1 | — | — |

(SP 139.5%) **18 Rn**

**2m 37.8** (8.80) CSF £32.32 CT £206.00 TOTE £2.80: £2.00 £1.90 £2.40 £2.20 (£48.80) Trio £119.40 OWNER Mrs H. M. Carr (THIRSK) BRED Miss M. Sheriffe and Exors of the late A. J. Tree

LONG HANDICAP Contrarie 7-2 Chillington 7-2

**1421* Strategic Ploy** is making hay while the sun shines and, in recording her third success in eight days, showed she is very much ahead of the game. (9/4)
**1100 Compass Pointer** continues to progress and, in turning in his best performance yet, gave notice that his turn is near at hand. (12/1)
**754 Ski For Gold** ran much better on this more suitable ground but she had it all to do in attempting to concede weight all round. She is not far off her peak. (17/2)
**1100 Classic Ballet (FR)** joined issue two furlongs out but she had been made to work to get there, and was a spent force in the battle to the finish. (10/1)
**1100 Spinning Mouse** crept through on the inside early in the straight, and had her chance two furlongs out but, with no company to egg her on, she was tapped for speed in the race to the line. She is worth bearing in mind. (9/2)
**Samuel Scott** is bred to stay but was tackling this trip for the first time. Making good ground in the latter stages, he will not be long in opening his account. (11/1)

T/Plpt: £124.10 (92.76 Tckts). T/Qdpt: £21.40 (47.99 Tckts). IM

# 1474-REDCAR (L-H) (Good to firm)
## Tuesday May 28th

WEATHER: showers WIND: str bhd

## 1499 E.B.F. MEDIAN AUCTION MAIDEN STKS (2-Y.O F) (Class E)

2-15 (2-17) **6f** £3,254.00 (£977.00: £471.00: £218.00) Stalls: High GOING minus 0.84 sec per fur (HD)

| | | | | SP | RR | SF |
|---|---|---|---|---|---|---|
| | **Reunion (IRE)** (JWHills) **2-8-11** RHills(6) (w'like: leggy: lw: hung lft thrght: hld up: hdwy to ld wl over 1f out: r.o) | — | 1 | Evens $^{1}$ | 69+ | 1 |
| $1197^{2}$ | **Falls O'Moness (IRE)** (KRBurke) **2-8-11** DRMcCabe(5) (lw: cl up: chal over 2f out: r.o towards fin) | nk | 2 | 11/8 $^{2}$ | 68 | — |
| | **Taome (IRE)** (PDEvans) **2-8-11** JFortune(2) (small: led over 4f: kpt on wl u.p) | 1 | 3 | 20/1 | 66 | — |
| | **Under Pressure** (TDEasterby) **2-8-11** MBirch(4) (leggy: unf: a chsng ldrs: rdn over 1f out: kpt on) | 2 | 4 | 10/1 $^{3}$ | 60 | — |
| | **Northern Princess** (RHollinshead) **2-8-11** GCarter(1) (w'like: outpcd ½-wy: sn bhd) | 12 | 5 | 16/1 | 28 | — |
| | **Oddfellows Girl** (NBycroft) **2-8-11** GDuffield(3) (unf: s.s: sn pushed along: wl bhd fr ½-wy) | 6 | 6 | 50/1 | 12 | — |

(SP 113.8%) **6 Rn**

**1m 12.0** (1.80) CSF £2.75 TOTE £1.70: £1.10 £1.80 (£1.50) OWNER Highclere Thoroughbred Racing Ltd (LAMBOURN) BRED Dr Michael Smurfit

**Reunion (IRE)**, a useful-looking type, gave problems by hanging left all the way, but can improve once she learns to run straight. (Evens)
**1197 Falls O'Moness (IRE)** had every chance throughout, but took time to get into it and would have preferred a stronger pace or a stiffer test. (11/8)
**Taome (IRE)** is only small but certainly has an engine, and fought back well when headed. (20/1)
**Under Pressure** looks the type to improve with time, but she did run well here and battled on at the end. (10/1)
**Northern Princess** never looked happy and was left struggling by halfway. (16/1)
**Oddfellows Girl**, very green, missed the break and was always struggling. (50/1)

## 1500 REDCAR MAIDEN AMATEUR H'CAP (0-80) (3-Y.O+) (Class F)

2-45 (2-46) **6f** £2,931.00 (£816.00: £393.00) Stalls: High GOING minus 0.84 sec per fur (HD)

| | Horse | Details | Dist | Pos | SP | RR | SF |
|---|---|---|---|---|---|---|---|
| 1092[9] | **Respect A Secret (35)** | (SEKettlewell) **4-10-10** MrsDKettlewell(7) (chsd ldrs: led ins fnl f: r.o) | — | **1** | 16/1 | 42 | 34 |
| 1020[6] | **Bowcliffe Grange (IRE) (23)** | (DWChapman) **4-9-12** MissRClark(1) (led after 2f tl ins fnl f: no ex) | 1¼ | **2** | 14/1 | 27 | 19 |
| 1364[6] | **Sallyoreally (IRE) (37)** | (WStorey) **5-10-12** JCulloty(5) (styd on fnl 3f: nrst fin) | 3½ | **3** | 9/2[1] | 31 | 23 |
| 1363[10] | **Northern Clan (42)** | (MWEasterby) **3-10-8b** MrsAFarrell(10) (cl up tl outpcd fnl 2f) | ¾ | **4** | 25/1 | 34 | 17 |
| 1196[20] | **Percy Park (USA) (45)** | (MWEasterby) **3-10-11b**ow2 MrNWilson(17) (a chsng ldrs: rdn 3f out: nvr able to chal) | ¾ | **5** | 25/1 | 35 | 16 |
| 1001[17] | **Blue Lugana (33)** | (NBycroft) **4-10-8b** MissPRobson(16) (chsd ldrs tl rdn & btn over 1f out) | ½ | **6** | 20/1 | 22 | 14 |
| 1068[4] | **Camionneur (IRE) (52)** | (TDEasterby) **3-10-13b**(5) MissADeniel(15) (in tch: effrt ½-wy: no imp) | 2½ | **7** | 5/1[2] | 34 | 17 |
| *782[5]* | **Boost (40)** | (MrsNMacauley) **4-11-1b**[1] MrCBonner(6) (lw: a about same pl) | 1¼ | **8** | 20/1 | 19 | 11 |
| 1039[6] | **Pride of Whalley (IRE) (54)** | (RAFahey) **3-11-6** MrRHale(3) (racd far side: led 2f: outpcd fnl 2f) | 1¾ | **9** | 10/1 | 28 | 11 |
| 973[11] | **Polish Saga (54)** | (MDods) **3-11-6** MrSSwiers(11) (s.i.s: nvr rchd ldrs) | s.h | **10** | 16/1 | 28 | 11 |
| 1013[4] | **Chief's Lady (41)** | (JMBradley) **4-10-9**(7) MissLKerr(2) (nvr trbld ldrs) | ¾ | **11** | 20/1 | 13 | 5 |
| 1307[2] | **Polli Pui (40)** | (WMBrisbourne) **4-10-10**(5) MrWMcLaughlin(8) (dwlt: n.d) | ½ | **12** | 7/1 | 11 | 3 |
| 1088[12] | **Ruby Plus (30)** | (GROldroyd) **5-10-0v**[1](5) MrVLukaniuk(12) (a outpcd & bhd) | 2 | **13** | 50/1 | — | — |
| *129[8]* | **Florrie'm (48)** | (JLHarris) **3-10-7**(7) MrCWatson(13) (a outpcd & bhd) | 1 | **14** | 100/1 | 11 | — |
| 1416[7] | **Harvest Reaper (53)** | (JLHarris) **4-11-7**(7) MrGWoodward(18) (in tch to ½-wy) | 1 | **15** | 25/1 | 13 | 5 |
| 786[12] | **Peace House (IRE) (40)** | (JLSpearing) **3-10-1b**[1](5) MissTSpearing(9) (lw: sn bhd) | 1¼ | **16** | 100/1 | — | — |
| | **Nutcracker Suite (IRE) (53)** | (JLEyre) **4-12-0** MissDianaJones(14) (sn bhd) | 4 | **17** | 16/1 | — | — |
| 1001[5] | **Taurean Fire (43)** | (MrsMReveley) **3-10-9** MrMHNaughton(4) (t.o fnl 3f) | 18 | **18** | 6/1[3] | — | — |
| | | | | | (SP 124.8%) | **18 Rn** | |

**1m 11.3** (1.10) CSF £202.63 CT £1,086.36 TOTE £33.00: £5.00 £4.70 £1.60 £5.30 (£380.70) Trio £369.00; £311.83 to Ripon 29/5/96. OWNER Mrs P. Simpson (MIDDLEHAM) BRED James Simpson

WEIGHT FOR AGE 3yo-9lb

OFFICIAL EXPLANATION **Taureen Fire: had bolted going to the start and was later, on examination, reported to be in a distressed state.**

**Respect A Secret**, who had shown little last season, has now got it together and won this well. Although this was a moderate event, she looks to be going the right way. (16/1)

**1020 Bowcliffe Grange (IRE)** ran his best race to date and has so much early pace that he can pick up a race. (14/1)

**1364 Sallyoreally (IRE)** keeps running well, but was always struggling to go the pace here and may need a bit further. (9/2)

**784 Northern Clan** has tried all sorts of trips without success and this was not a bad effort. (25/1)

**Percy Park (USA)** showed ability when first running as a two-year-old but has done little since. This was his best effort this year. (25/1)

## 1501 JAMESON IRISH WHISKEY SPRINT H'CAP (0-90) (3-Y.O+) (Class C)

3-15 (3-16) **5f** £5,842.00 (£1,756.00: £848.00: £394.00) Stalls: High GOING minus 0.84 sec per fur (HD)

| | Horse | Details | Dist | Pos | SP | RR | SF |
|---|---|---|---|---|---|---|---|
| 1307* | **Jucea (70)** | (JLSpearing) **7-8-10** 7x JWeaver(3) (in tch: hdwy 2f out: led ins fnl f: r.o) | — | **1** | 11/2[2] | 78 | 32 |
| 1199* | **Portend (84)** | (SRBowring) **4-9-7b**(3) CTeague(4) (lw: in tch: styd on u.p fnl 2f: nrst fin) | ½ | **2** | 6/1[3] | 90 | 44 |
| 1199[4] | **Insider Trader (72)** | (MrsJRRamsden) **5-8-5**(7) ClaireWest(2) (chsd ldr: rdn ½-wy: kpt on) | ½ | **3** | 14/1 | 77 | 31 |
| 1157[11] | **Shadow Jury (61)** | (DWChapman) **6-8-1b** LCharnock(1) (lw: led tl hdd & no ex ins fnl f) | ½ | **4** | 16/1 | 64 | 18 |
| 1113[14] | **Stolen Kiss (IRE) (77)** | (MWEasterby) **4-8-12b**(5) GParkin(7) (outpcd ½-wy: hdwy over 1f out: styd on wl) | 1 | **5** | 14/1 | 77 | 31 |
| 1113[5] | **Lady Sheriff (84)** | (RHollinshead) **5-9-5**(5) FLynch(6) (lw: outpcd tl styd on fnl 2f) | ½ | **6** | 5/1[1] | 82 | 36 |
| 928[24] | **For the Present (81)** | (TDBarron) **6-9-7** JFortune(9) (drvn along & bhd tl styd on towards fin) | ½ | **7** | 20/1 | 78 | 32 |
| 1092[6] | **Maid O'Cannie (57)** | (MWEasterby) **5-7-11b** DaleGibson(5) (bhd & rdn ½-wy: sme late hdwy) | hd | **8** | 12/1 | 54 | 8 |
| 1186[8] | **Brecongill Lad (74)** | (MissSEHall) **4-9-0b** NConnorton(12) (lw: cl up stands' side tl rdn & btn wl over 1f out) | ¾ | **9** | 5/1[1] | 68 | 22 |
| 1188[2] | **Swynford Dream (84)** | (JFBottomley) **3-9-2** DRMcCabe(8) (a bhd) | 4 | **10** | 7/1 | 65 | 11 |
| 1064[3] | **Ann's Pearl (IRE) (73)** | (JWHills) **5-8-13** RHills(10) (nvr wnt pce) | 10 | **11** | 5/1[1] | 22 | — |
| | | | | | (SP 123.8%) | **11 Rn** | |

**56.9 secs** (-0.60) CSF £37.76 CT £322.92 TOTE £7.20: £2.00 £3.40 £3.50 (£21.80) Trio £63.60 OWNER Mr A. A. Campbell (ALCESTER) BRED G. W. Mills and Sons

WEIGHT FOR AGE 3yo-8lb

**1307* Jucea** is a typical sprinter in form. Patiently ridden as usual, she settled it in determined style in the final half-furlong. (11/2)

**1199* Portend** ran another fine race with the blinkers on and kept staying on in the closing stages, but the line was always going to come too soon. (6/1)

**1199 Insider Trader** again ran well, but just failed to pick up enough in the closing stages. (14/1)

**Shadow Jury** won this last year and tried hard, but just ran out of steam in the last furlong. He is on his way back to form. (16/1)

**716 Stolen Kiss (IRE)** ran well and should find another race or two, but does seem at her best when there is some cut in the ground. (14/1)

**1113 Lady Sheriff**, after finding the early pace too strong, stayed on at the end. (5/1)

**For the Present** began to pick up ground at the finish. (20/1)

**1092 Maid O'Cannie** was always finding things happening too quickly. (12/1: 10/1-16/1)

**1186 Brecongill Lad** raced on his own and then was never doing enough. If caught in the mood, he is a lot better than this. (5/1)

## 1502 DORMANSTOWN H'CAP (0-70) (3-Y.O+) (Class E)

3-45 (3-45) **1m 1f** £3,309.25 (£994.00: £479.50: £222.25) Stalls: Low GOING minus 0.36 sec per fur (F)

| | Horse | Details | Dist | Pos | SP | RR | SF |
|---|---|---|---|---|---|---|---|
| 991[14] | **Alabang (48)** | (MJCamacho) **5-8-6** LCharnock(1) (dwlt: hdwy on ins ent st: led 1f out: qcknd: comf) | — | **1** | 8/1 | 58 | 29 |
| 802[11] | **Bold Amusement (70)** | (WSCunningham) **6-10-0** ACulhane(12) (in tch: hdwy to ld wl over 1f out: hdd 1f out: kpt on) | 2½ | **2** | 25/1 | 76 | 47 |
| 1037[5] | **Habeta (USA) (44)** | (JWWatts) **10-8-2**ow1 GDuffield(7) (hld up: hdwy 3f out: sn chsng ldrs & rdn: nt qckn fnl f) | 1¼ | **3** | 7/1 | 47 | 17 |
| 1341[3] | **Shaffishayes (62)** | (MrsMReveley) **4-9-6** DeanMcKeown(10) (trckd ldrs: outpcd whn hmpd 2f out: no imp after) | 2 | **4** | 7/2[2] | 62 | 33 |
| 1414[3] | **Zahran (IRE) (40)** | (JMBradley) **5-7-9**(3) NVarley(4) (effrt over 3f out: styd on: no imp) | 1 | **5** | 11/2[3] | 38 | 9 |
| | **Champagne N Dreams (51)** | (DNicholls) **4-8-9** AlexGreaves(3) (hld up: hdwy over 2f out: nvr nr to chal) | 2 | **6** | 14/1 | 45 | 16 |
| 1092[4] | **Prudent Pet (54)** | (CWFairhurst) **4-8-5b**(7) PDoe(5) (cl up: led over 2f out tl wl over 1f out: wandered bdly & sn wknd) | ½ | **7** | 8/1 | 48 | 19 |
| 1418* | **Maradata (IRE) (56)** | (RHollinshead) **4-8-9**(5) 5x FLynch(8) (lw: hld up & bhd: hdwy on outside 3f out: rdn & no rspnse 2f out) | 1 | **8** | 5/2[1] | 48 | 19 |

| | | | | | |
|---|---|---|---|---|---|
| 1037[12] **Mary Macblain (38)** (JLHarris) **7-7-5**(5) PFessey(11) (chsd ldrs tl wknd fnl 3f)........½ | **9** | 33/1 | 29 | — |
| 1414[12] **Grey Kingdom (39)** (MBrittain) **5-7-8**(3)ow1 DWright(6) (bhd: effrt on ins 3f out: n.d)........nk | **10** | 33/1 | 29 | — |
| 1341[11] **Euro Sceptic (IRE) (49)** (TDEasterby) **4-8-2b**(5) RHavlin(2) (in tch tl outpcd fnl 2½f)........1¼ | **11** | 12/1 | 37 | 8 |
| 1001[4] **Malzoom (38)** (SEKettlewell) **4-7-10** NKennedy(9) (lw: unruly s: led tl hdd & wknd over 2f out)........11 | **12** | 33/1 | 7 | — |

(SP 127.9%) **12 Rn**

**1m 53.3** (3.50) CSF £167.49 CT £1,368.89 TOTE £12.30: £3.00 £9.60 £1.60 (£135.80) Trio £363.20; £373.46 to Ripon 29/5/96. OWNER Mr H. Roberts (MALTON) BRED Mrs S. Camacho

LONG HANDICAP Mary Macblain 7-4 Grey Kingdom 7-6 Malzoom 6-11

**OFFICIAL EXPLANATION Alabang: the trainer reported that the use of different riding tactics to those used on his previous outing, had brought about the improvement in the horse's performance.**

**Malzoom: may have been feeling the effects of being replated shortly before the race.**

**Alabang**, ridden from behind this time, did the business in style to show he has ability. (8/1)

**Bold Amusement** showed he still has the ability, but the winner was too strong for him in the closing stages. (25/1)

**1037 Habeta (USA)** ran his best race of the season, but was still not doing enough in the latter stages to make any real impression. (7/1)

**1341 Shaffishayes**, who had his chances, got messed about in the last two furlongs but was already giving his rider problems. (7/2)

**1414 Zahran (IRE)** looked short of pace but he did respond to pressure in the last quarter-mile, albeit in vain. (11/2)

**Champagne N Dreams** had a nice pipe-opener here. (14/1)

## 1503 SKELTON MAIDEN H'CAP (0-60) (3-Y.O) (Class F)

4-15 (4-16) **1m 6f 19y** £2,868.00 (£798.00: £384.00) Stalls: Low GOING minus 0.36 sec per fur (F)

| | | SP | RR | SF |
|---|---|---|---|---|
| 803[3] **Forgie (IRE) (53)** (PCalver) **3-9-6** MBirch(7) (led 2f: cl up: led wl over 1f out: styd on)........— | **1** | 4/1[2] | 62 | 24 |
| 1359[14] **Phar Closer (46)** (WTKemp) **3-8-10**(3) SDrowne(9) (a.p: effrt 3f out: hung lft ins fnl f: kpt on wl towards fin)....¾ | **2** | 20/1 | 54 | 16 |
| 849[4] **What Jim Wants (IRE) (40)** (JJO'Neill) **3-8-7** JFanning(12) (a chsng ldrs: effrt & ch 3f out: one pce)........3½ | **3** | 11/1 | 44 | 6 |
| 1200[3] **Manoy (54)** (JHetherton) **3-9-7** NKennedy(1) (bhd: hung bdly lft fnl 4f: styd on strly towards fin)........hd | **4** | 12/1 | 58 | 20 |
| 890[4] **Ship's Dancer (53)** (JLDunlop) **3-9-6** GCarter(10) (a chsng ldrs: one pce fnl 3f)........¾ | **5** | 15/8[1] | 56 | 18 |
| 890[9] **Brighter Byfaah (IRE) (44)** (NAGraham) **3-8-11b**[1] JWeaver(4) (led after 2f tl wl over 1f out: sn btn)........1¾ | **6** | 14/1 | 45 | 7 |
| 1100[12] **He's Got Wings (IRE) (50)** (MBell) **3-9-3v** DRMcCabe(6) (effrt over 4f out: nvr trbld ldrs)........1 | **7** | 9/1 | 50 | 12 |
| 640[13] **Washington Reef (USA) (54)** (JHMGosden) **3-9-7v**[1] RHills(13) (lw: mid div: rdn over 4f out: no rspnse)........2½ | **8** | 6/1[3] | 51 | 13 |
| *280*[5] **Diasafina (31)** (SCWilliams) **3-7-9b**(3) NVarley(8) (in tch: sn pushed along: wknd fnl 4f)........2 | **9** | 12/1 | 26 | — |
| 1067[3] **How Could-I (IRE) (40)** (TDEasterby) **3-8-7** LCharnock(5) (b.nr fore: a bhd)........3 | **10** | 7/1 | 32 | — |
| *859*[10] **Belacqua (USA) (32)** (DWChapman) **3-7-8b**(5) PFessey(11) (prom to st)........9 | **11** | 33/1 | 13 | — |
| 1092[11] **Village Opera (45)** (GMMoore) **3-8-12** DaleGibson(3) (a bhd)........11 | **12** | 50/1 | 14 | — |

(SP 131.6%) **12 Rn**

**3m 8.8** (9.50) CSF £77.73 CT £786.07 TOTE £4.70: £1.10 £21.70 £2.50 (£108.90) Trio £156.00 OWNER Mrs Janis MacPherson (RIPON) BRED Stilvi Compania Financiera And Roncon Ltd.

**803 Forgie (IRE)** appreciated this step up in trip and saw it out in game style. (4/1)

**588 Phar Closer** is improving but spoilt his chances by hanging left in the closing stages. (20/1)

**849 What Jim Wants (IRE)** needed the extra distance. He had his chances but was never quite doing enough. (11/1)

**1200 Manoy** has the ability and appreciated this extra trip, but his rider had a real job trying to stop him hanging left up the straight, and he only ran on when it was too late. (12/1)

## 1504 KIRKLEATHAM RATING RELATED MAIDEN STKS (0-70) (3-Y.O+) (Class E)

4-45 (4-47) **1m 2f** £2,990.75 (£896.00: £430.50: £197.75) Stalls: Low GOING minus 0.36 sec per fur (F)

| | | SP | RR | SF |
|---|---|---|---|---|
| 1155[3] **Alreeh (IRE) (70)** (JHMGosden) **3-8-7** RHills(1) (wnt prom 6f out: led over 2f out: hung lft: r.o)........— | **1** | 2/1[1] | 75 | 38 |
| 994[6] **Lady of Leisure (USA) (65)** (MrsJCecil) **4-9-7** TIves(5) (lw: a.p: effrt over 2f out: chsd wnr fnl f: kpt on)........1¼ | **2** | 4/1[3] | 73 | 50 |
| 754[7] **Salty Girl (IRE) (68)** (BWHills) **3-8-7** GCarter(3) (lw: chsd ldrs: ev ch over 2f out: nt qckn)........1½ | **3** | 10/1 | 71 | 34 |
| 947[6] **Fursan (USA) (69)** (NAGraham) **3-8-10** JWeaver(2) (lw: led tl hdd over 2f out: sn outpcd)........5 | **4** | 3/1[2] | 66 | 29 |
| 1198[7] **Le Khoumf (FR) (70)** (JMBradley) **5-9-7**(3) SDrowne(6) (chsd ldrs: stumbled ent st: one pce fnl 3f)........2½ | **5** | 9/2 | 62 | 39 |
| **Roy Boy (68)** (MrsMReveley) **4-9-10** JFortune(9) (lw: effrt over 4f out: nvr rchd ldrs)........1¾ | **6** | 20/1 | 59 | 36 |
| **Valise (48)** (MrsMReveley) **3-8-7** JFanning(4) (s.i.s: a bhd)........5 | **7** | 50/1 | 48 | 11 |
| 1072[6] **Maftun (USA) (60)** (GMMoore) **4-9-10** DaleGibson(10) (prom tl outpcd ent st: sn bhd)........2 | **8** | 25/1 | 48 | 25 |
| 1160[6] **Highfield Pet (58)** (CWFairhurst) **3-8-10** DeanMcKeown(8) (prom to st)........nk | **9** | 20/1 | 47 | 10 |
| 1420[8] **Gool Lee Shay (USA) (62)** (RMWhitaker) **3-8-10** ACulhane(7) (a bhd)........1¼ | **10** | 33/1 | 45 | 8 |

(SP 123.9%) **10 Rn**

**2m 6.6** (3.00) CSF £10.89 TOTE £2.20: £1.50 £1.60 £2.10 (£5.50) Trio £19.20 OWNER Mr Hamdan Al Maktoum (NEWMARKET) BRED Oldtown Stud

WEIGHT FOR AGE 3yo-14lb

**1155 Alreeh (IRE)** needed this extra trip but looked a bit of a character when hanging left in front. (2/1)

**994 Lady of Leisure (USA)**, back over a more suitable trip, kept trying hard but could never peg back the winner. (4/1)

**Salty Girl (IRE)** has not got the best of actions and may be suited by some give. (10/1)

**947 Fursan (USA)** set the pace up for the winner, but was well outpointed in the last two furlongs. (3/1)

**1198 Le Khoumf (FR)** had his chances but lacked a change of gear. (9/2)

**Roy Boy** made a little late headway. (20/1)

## 1505 BILLINGHAM LIMITED STKS (0-75) (3-Y.O+) (Class D)

5-15 (5-16) **7f** £3,561.00 (£1,068.00: £514.00: £237.00) Stalls: High GOING minus 0.84 sec per fur (HD)

| | | SP | RR | SF |
|---|---|---|---|---|
| 1333* **Poetry (IRE) (73)** (MHTompkins) **3-8-7** PRobinson(1) (mde all: qcknd over 2f out: r.o wl)........— | **1** | 11/8[1] | 85 | 24 |
| **Equerry (75)** (MJohnston) **5-9-4** JWeaver(5) (prom: effrt ½-wy: styd on wl: nt pce of wnr)........3 | **2** | 7/1 | 78 | 28 |
| 1154* **The Stager (IRE) (74)** (JRJenkins) **4-9-2**(5) RHavlin(7) (lw: a chsng ldrs: rdn 3f out: r.o one pce)........nk | **3** | 100/30[2] | 81 | 31 |
| 739[4] **Cashmere Lady (73)** (JLEyre) **4-9-7** RLappin(2) (in tch: effrt over 2f out: nt qckn appr fnl f)........1½ | **4** | 6/1 | 77 | 27 |
| 935[15] **Quilling (75)** (MDods) **4-9-4** DeanMcKeown(6) (chsd ldrs: effrt 3f out: no imp)........nk | **5** | 11/1 | 73 | 23 |
| 1101[2] **Miss Waterline (74)** (PDEvans) **3-8-5**ow1 JFortune(4) (in tch tl outpcd fnl 2½f)........6 | **6** | 5/1[3] | 58 | — |
| 931[15] **Call Me I'm Blue (IRE) (74)** (NTinkler) **6-9-4** MBirch(3) (outpcd ½-wy: virtually p.u fnl 2f)........30 | **7** | 25/1 | — | — |

(SP 120.8%) **7 Rn**

**1m 22.8** (-0.20) CSF £11.70 TOTE £2.10: £1.70 £3.10 (£5.40) OWNER Mr Michael Keogh (NEWMARKET) BRED St Simon Foundation

WEIGHT FOR AGE 3yo-11lb

OFFICIAL EXPLANATION **Call Me I'm Blue (IRE): was reported to have lost his action during the race but was sound afterwards.**
**1333* Poetry (IRE)** has improved tremendously and won this in real style. (11/8)
**Equerry** tried to peg the winner back from halfway, but the struggle was always beyond him over this shorter trip. (7/1)
**1154* The Stager (IRE)** kept trying hard, but was always fighting a lost cause. (100/30)
**Cashmere Lady**, after over five weeks off, failed to get into this, despite keeping on well. She will be better for this. (6/1)
**Quilling** won here twice last season when making all, but that was never on here. (11/1)

T/Jkpt: Not won; £7,300.25 to Folkestone 29/5/96. T/Plpt: £1,270.50 (12.49 Tckts). T/Qdpt: £432.40 (4.58 Tckts). AA

# 1480-SANDOWN (R-H) (Rnd Good to soft, Good bk st, 5f Good, Good to soft patches)
## Tuesday May 28th
WEATHER: overcast WIND: almost nil

## 1506 CHUNKY CLAIMING STKS (3-Y.O+) (Class E)
6-20 (6-20) **1m 14y** £3,582.50 (£1,085.00: £530.00: £252.50) Stalls: Low GOING minus 0.11 sec per fur (G)

| | | | | SP | RR | SF |
|---|---|---|---|---|---|---|
| 1314[12] | **Early Peace (IRE) (74)** (RHannon) **4-9-4**(3) DaneO'Neill(4) (s.s: rdn over 2f out: hdwy over 1f out: led wl ins fnl f: r.o wl) | — | **1** | 16/1 | 78 | 47 |
| 1159[2] | **Loveyoumillions (IRE) (80)** (NTinkler) **4-9-8** KDarley(8) (plld hrd: a.p: rdn over 2f out: led ins fnl f: sn hdd: unable qckn) | 1½ | **2** | 3/1[1] | 76 | 45 |
| 853[13] | **Denomination (USA) (57)** (IABalding) **4-9-4** LDettori(3) (a.p: ev ch over 1f out: one pce ins fnl f) | ½ | **3** | 14/1 | 71 | 40 |
| | **Monument (73)** (JSKing) **4-9-4** BDoyle(6) (rdn over 2f out: hdwy over 1f out: r.o wl ins fnl f) | s.h | **4** | 10/1 | 71 | 40 |
| 1314[6] | **Cim Bom Bom (IRE) (90)** (MBell) **4-9-1**(7) GFaulkner(2) (b: hdwy to ld 2f out: hdd ins fnl f: one pce) | hd | **5** | 9/1[3] | 75 | 44 |
| 1314[4] | **Bagshot (73)** (RHannon) **5-9-7** MJKinane(7) (chsd ldr: led over 2f out: sn hdd: wknd over 1f out) | 7 | **6** | 7/2[2] | 60 | 29 |
| 1099[3] | **Adilov (62)** (KOCunningham-Brown) **4-9-0** RPerham(1) (bhd fnl 2f) | 2½ | **7** | 14/1 | 48 | 17 |
| 988[11] | **Te Amo (IRE) (74)** (RAkehurst) **4-9-6** SSanders(5) (lw: bhd fnl 3f) | 2½ | **8** | 3/1[1] | 49 | 18 |
| 863[12] | **Duralock Fencer (50)** (PGMurphy) **3-8-5** MHills(10) (led over 5f) | ½ | **9** | 50/1 | 45 | 2 |
| | **Speedy Snaps Image (35)** (JELong) **5-8-9**(7) TField(9) (b: prom over 4f) | 7 | **10** | 66/1 | 30 | — |
| | | | | (SP 114.0%) | **10 Rn** | |

**1m 46.17** (4.97) CSF £58.87 TOTE £26.60: £5.60 £1.20 £2.50 (£37.80) Trio £184.30 OWNER Mr R. Hannon (MARLBOROUGH) BRED Barronstown Stud
WEIGHT FOR AGE 3yo-12lb
Early Peace (IRE) clmd GPhillips £11,000
OFFICIAL EXPLANATION **Te Amo (IRE): suffered slight interference due to general bunching and was unable to mount a challenge.**
**Early Peace (IRE)** lost ground at the start and was still out with the washing entering the straight. However, he came with a good run from below the distance to swoop into the lead in the closing stages. (16/1)
**1159 Loveyoumillions (IRE)** took a keen hold and was always close up. Throwing down his challenge the final quarter-mile, he eventually got on top inside the final furlong, only to be passed by the winner soon after. (3/1)
**598 Denomination (USA)** was vying for the advantage below the distance before tapped for toe. (14/1: 10/1-16/1)
**Monument**, fit from hurdling, ran on really strongly inside the final furlong. (10/1)
**1314 Cim Bom Bom (IRE)** ran his best race so far this season. (9/1)
**1314 Bagshot** looked far from enthusiastic in front and, soon headed, then chucked in the towel. (7/2)

## 1507 BETA H'CAP (0-80) (3-Y.O) (Class D)
6-50 (6-52) **1m 3f 91y** £3,915.50 (£1,184.00: £577.00: £273.50) Stalls: Low GOING minus 0.11 sec per fur (G)

| | | | | SP | RR | SF |
|---|---|---|---|---|---|---|
| 1100* | **Atlantic Mist (59)** (BRMillman) **3-8-0** GBardwell(1) (hdwy over 4f out: chsd ldr over 2f out: led ins fnl f: drvn out) | — | **1** | 7/1[3] | 69 | 43 |
| 1110[4] | **Rivercare (IRE) (58)** (MJPolglase) **3-7-13** NCarlisle(11) (led: clr 10f out: hdd ins fnl f: r.o) | ½ | **2** | 12/1 | 67 | 41 |
| 1042[7] | **Soldier Mak (61)** (AHide) **3-7-11**(5) MHenry(5) (plld hrd: hdwy over 2f out: hrd rdn over 1f out: r.o ins fnl f) | 1¼ | **3** | 14/1 | 69 | 43 |
| | **The Swan (68)** (JLDunlop) **3-8-9** SWhitworth(10) (b: s.s: hdwy over 2f out: hrd rdn over 1f out: r.o ins fnl f) | ½ | **4** | 11/1 | 75 | 49 |
| 693[10] | **Galapino (71)** (CEBrittain) **3-8-12** BDoyle(8) (swtg: chsd ldr 9f: wknd ins fnl f) | 2½ | **5** | 20/1 | 74 | 48 |
| 1349* | **Deadline Time (IRE) (82)** (MrsMReveley) **3-9-9** 5x KDarley(9) (lw: hdwy over 2f out: wknd fnl f) | 5 | **6** | 5/2[1] | 78 | 52 |
| 1100[2] | **State Approval (61)** (APJarvis) **3-8-2**ow1 DHarrison(4) (hdwy over 4f out: wknd 2f out) | 1¾ | **7** | 6/1[2] | 55 | 28 |
| 1317[4] | **Clemente (76)** (RHannon) **3-9-0b[1]**(3) DaneO'Neill(7) (bhd fnl 2f) | 8 | **8** | 7/1[3] | 59 | 33 |
| 948[7] | **Veronica Franco (65)** (JLDunlop) **3-8-6** SSanders(3) (hdwy over 4f out: wknd over 2f out) | nk | **9** | 16/1 | 47 | 21 |
| | **Gumair (USA) (74)** (RHannon) **3-9-1** PatEddery(2) (lw: bhd fnl 3f) | 4 | **10** | 7/1[3] | 51 | 25 |
| | | | | (SP 113.7%) | **10 Rn** | |

**2m 28.17** (4.77) CSF £75.09 CT £1,033.99 TOTE £8.90: £2.30 £2.20 £2.90 (£46.60) Trio £220.60 OWNER The Wardour Partnership (CULLOMPTON) BRED R. Burton
**1100* Atlantic Mist**, after reeling in the long-time leader inside the final furlong, held on well in a driving finish. (7/1: 5/1-15/2)
**1110 Rivercare (IRE)** was very well supported in the market but appeared to have set a suicidal pace as he careered off in front. He looked certain to come back to his field in the straight, but was not overhauled until inside the final furlong. Even then, he stuck to his guns in commendable fashion. (12/1)
**1042 Soldier Mak** did not seem to have a problem with this much longer trip, even though he took a very keen hold for the first half of the race. Moving up early in the straight, he ran on inside the final furlong to finish an encouraging third. (14/1: 10/1-16/1)
**The Swan**, certainly fit enough for this seasonal debut, ran on up the hill to finish fourth. (11/1: 8/1-12/1)
**693 Galapino** eventually called it a day inside the last 200 yards. (20/1)
**1349* Deadline Time (IRE)** could never get to the principals and the position was accepted in the last 200 yards. (5/2)
**1100 State Approval** (6/1: op 4/1)

## 1508 PRIME MAIDEN STKS (3-Y.O+) (Class D)
7-20 (7-26) **1m 2f 7y** £3,972.50 (£1,205.00: £590.00: £282.50) Stalls: Low GOING minus 0.11 sec per fur (G)

| | | | | SP | RR | SF |
|---|---|---|---|---|---|---|
| 985[2] | **Shantou (USA)** (JHMGosden) **3-8-11** LDettori(16) (lw: hld up: led over 1f out: pushed out) | — | **1** | 4/5[1] | 103 | 58 |

**Rocky Oasis (USA)** (MRStoute) **3-8-11** TQuinn(12) (lw: a.p: led over 2f out tl over 1f out: r.o) ¾ **2** 9/2[2] 102 57
**Ginger Fox (USA)** (HRACecil) **3-8-11** PatEddery(9) (w'like: scope: lw: led 9f out to over 2f out: unable qckn) .6 **3** 9/1[3] 92 47
**Akhla (USA)** (HRACecil) **3-8-6** AMcGlone(3) (leggy: scope: lw: hdwy over 4f out: ev ch over 1f out: wknd fnl f) 1¼ **4** 25/1 85 40
**Oops Pettie** (MrsJCecil) **3-8-6** AClark(5) (leggy: scope: bit bkwd: rdn 3f out: hdwy over 1f out: nvr nrr) 4 **5** 33/1 79 34
1326[3] **Fasil (IRE)** (CJBenstead) **3-8-11** MWigham(7) (hdwy over 1f out: nvr nrr) 1½ **6** 14/1 82 37
1065[2] **Charter** (MajorDNChappell) **5-9-11** BThomson(13) (a.p: shkn up over 2f out: eased whn btn over 1f out) 4 **7** 50/1 75 44
1117[3] **La Pellegrina (IRE)** (PWChapple-Hyam) **3-8-7**[ow1] JReid(2) (prom over 7f) s.h **8** 12/1 71 25
678[12] **Hippy** (CEBrittain) **3-8-6** BDoyle(14) (swtg: a mid div) 1¼ **9** 25/1 68 23
**Gold Lance (USA)** (MRStoute) **3-8-11** KDarley(8) (str: scope: bit bkwd: sme hdwy 2f out: wknd over 1f out) hd **10** 25/1 73 28
**Imperial Prospect (USA)** (JJSheehan) **4-9-6** MJKinane(15) (b: lw: s.s: a bhd) ¾ **11** 66/1 67 36
1104[15] **Russian Rose (IRE)** (AHide) **3-8-1**[(5)] MHenry(4) (prom over 7f) nk **12** 50/1 66 21
**Give And Take** (LordHuntingdon) **3-8-11** RPerham(6) (leggy: scope: lw: prom 6f) hd **13** 33/1 71 26
821[8] **Formidable Flame** (WJMusson) **3-8-11** RPrice(17) (lw: s.s: hdwy on ins over 4f out: wknd over 2f out) 1½ **14** 66/1 69 24
1090[5] **Viridis (USA)** (HRACecil) **3-8-6** WRyan(11) (led 1f: wknd 3f out) 7 **15** 25/1 53 8
**Conwy** (NAGraham) **3-8-6** DHarrison(1) (s.s: a wl bhd) 4 **16** 66/1 46 1
***Ectomorph (IRE)*** (JPearce) **3-8-6** GBardwell(10) (Withdrawn not under Starter's orders: veterinary advice) **W** 66/1 — —
(SP 129.3%) **16 Rn**

**2m 10.24** (3.54) CSF £5.37 TOTE £1.90: £1.40 £1.70 £2.40 (£3.10) Trio £10.60 OWNER Sheikh Mohammed (NEWMARKET) BRED Darley Stud Management Inc
WEIGHT FOR AGE 3yo-14lb

**985 Shantou (USA)** has been held up since his last run with a bruised foot and looked very well beforehand, but was not as big as some of his rivals. (4/5)
**Rocky Oasis (USA)**, a well-matured individual, was weak in the market but made a highly promising return and stuck on well to the end. He looks nailed-on for a similar event. (9/2: 5/2-5/1)
**Ginger Fox (USA)** looked very well in the paddock and showed a lot of promise. Although in fourth approaching the final furlong having made it, he regained third prize going up the hill, and should have no problems finding a race. (9/1: 5/1-10/1)
**Akhla (USA)** looked in good shape beforehand. This was a hot maiden race and she should soon be winning. (25/1)
**Oops Pettie** stayed on well in the last furlong and a half but never threatened to get to the principals. She should come on a lot for this. (33/1)
**1326 Fasil (IRE)** was doing all his best work in the final furlong and a half and is now qualified for handicaps. (14/1: 12/1-20/1)
**1117 La Pellegrina (IRE)** (12/1: op 8/1)

## 1509 SPILLERS BRIGADIER GERARD STKS (Gp 3) (4-Y.O+) (Class A)
7-50 (7-58) **1m 2f 7y** £19,650.00 (£7,440.00: £3,645.00: £1,665.00) Stalls: Low GOING minus 0.11 sec per fur (G)

SP RR SF

831[2] **Pilsudski (IRE) (105)** (MRStoute) **4-8-10** PatEddery(7) (a.p: led over 2f out: drvn out) — **1** 11/2[3] 122 86
581* **Lucky Di (USA) (113)** (LMCumani) **4-8-10** MHills(2) (b.nr fore: rdn & hdwy over 2f out: ev ch fnl 2f: r.o) ½ **2** 13/8[1] 121 85
**Song of Tara (IRE)** (PWChapple-Hyam) **4-8-10** JReid(1) (hdwy 5f out: nt clr run on ins over 2f out: r.o ins fnl f) 1½ **3** 10/1 119 83
*536a*[5] **Tamayaz (CAN)** (SbinSuroor) **4-8-10** LDettori(10) (a.p: ev ch over 2f out: unable qckn) 3½ **4** 5/2[2] 113 77
1017[4] **Poppy Carew (IRE) (105)** (PWHarris) **4-8-7** GHind(3) (lw: hdwy over 2f out: wknd over 1f out) 6 **5** 33/1 101 65
1065[W] **Commoner (USA) (110)** (RHannon) **4-8-10** RHughes(4) (lw: led over 7f) 3½ **6** 33/1 98 62
726[2] **Wayne County (IRE) (110)** (RAkehurst) **6-8-10** TQuinn(8) (hld up: rdn over 2f out: sn wknd) ½ **7** 16/1 97 61
828[4] **Star Selection (105)** (JMackie) **5-8-10** AClark(9) (s.s: a bhd) ¾ **8** 50/1 96 60
**Phantom Gold (112)** (LordHuntingdon) **4-8-12** OPeslier(11) (bhd fnl 2f) nk **9** 25/1 98 62
**Maidment** (LadyHerries) **5-8-7** PaulEddery(5) (bhd fnl 4f: t.o) 25 **10** 66/1 53 17
831[6] **Prince of Andros (USA) (113)** (DRLoder) **6-9-1** MJKinane(6) (hld up: rdn over 3f out: eased whn btn over 2f out: t.o) dist **11** 16/1 — —
(SP 116.1%) **11 Rn**

**2m 6.76** (0.06) CSF £13.94 TOTE £5.80: £1.40 £1.40 £2.20 (£5.90) Trio £9.70 OWNER Lord Weinstock/Exors of late S Weinstock (NEWMARKET) BRED Ballymacoll Stud Co

**831 Pilsudski (IRE)** continues his rise and put up a gutsy performance to land his first Group success. In front over a quarter of a mile from home, he had a ding-dong battle with the runner-up and just managed to prevail. A trip to Royal Ascot is richly deserved. (11/2)
**581* Lucky Di (USA)** ran a fine race in defeat. Moving through to have every chance in the final quarter-mile, he went at it hammer and tongs with the winner and only just lost out. He is certainly capable of winning a Group race this season, and a mile and a half would be no problem. (13/8)
**Song of Tara (IRE)** was in his box for five months after injuring himself, but showed bags of promise on this return. Moving up turning for home, he was done no favours by the winner over a quarter of a mile from home, but this made little difference to his chances. Running on inside the final furlong, he finished a highly-encouraging third and is sure to come on in leaps and bounds. A Group race is surely waiting for him this season. (10/1)
**536a Tamayaz (CAN)**, who finished fifth in the Dubai World Cup, was rather disappointing. (5/2)
**1017 Poppy Carew (IRE)** made her effort up the centre of the course over two furlongs from home, but had burnt her boats below the distance. (33/1)
**919 Commoner (USA)**, once collared over two furlongs from home, was soon beaten. (33/1)

## 1510 WINALOT NATIONAL STKS (Listed) (2-Y.O) (Class A)
8-20 (8-27) **5f 6y** £10,260.00 (£3,105.00: £1,515.00: £720.00) Stalls: High GOING minus 0.11 sec per fur (G)

SP RR SF

1328* **Deadly Dudley (IRE)** (RHannon) **2-9-1** MJKinane(7) (b: b.hind: hdwy on ins to ld over 2f out: shkn up over 1f out: qcknd fnl f: r.o wl) — **1** 7/4[1] 106 56
829* **Roman Imp (IRE)** (APJarvis) **2-9-1** PatEddery(6) (lw: led over 2f: ev ch over 1f out: unable qckn) 4 **2** 100/30[3] 93 43
706* **Daylight In Dubai (USA)** (PWChapple-Hyam) **2-9-1** KDarley(5) (lw: chsd ldr over 2f: hung lft: one pce) 5 **3** 5/2[2] 77 27
1179* **March Star (IRE)** (JARToller) **2-8-10** JReid(4) (lw: a.p: carried lft over 2f out tl swtchd rt over 1f out: one pce) 1½ **4** 9/1 68 18
**Halowing (USA)** (PAKelleway) **2-8-7** WJO'Connor(1) (w'like: scope: lw: s.s: a bhd) 4 **5** 20/1 52 2
1166* **Ride Sally Ride (IRE)** (JBerry) **2-8-12** JCarroll(2) (lw: bhd fnl 2f) ¾ **6** 14/1 55 5
(SP 109.4%) **6 Rn**

**61.83 secs** (2.03) CSF £7.42 TOTE £2.40: £1.50 £2.10 (£3.20) OWNER Lucayan Stud (MARLBOROUGH) BRED John Kent
STEWARDS' ENQUIRY Obj. to Daylight in Dubai (USA) by Reid overruled.

**1328* Deadly Dudley (IRE)** put up a very impressive display. Moving up along the far rail to strike the front over a quarter of a mile from home, he quickened right away from the runner-up in the final furlong. He now heads for Royal Ascot and six furlongs would hold no terrors. (7/4)
**829* Roman Imp (IRE)** lost nothing in defeat. In front to halfway, he was still holding on to Deadly Dudley until brushed aside in the final furlong. He would have finished closer had he not let that one up the rail, and there are more races to be won. (100/30)
**706* Daylight In Dubai (USA)**, uneasy in the market, was rather disappointing. In second place to halfway, he was soon in trouble and gave his rider steering problems as he hung to his left. (5/2: 6/4-11/4)
**1179* March Star (IRE)**, carried left by the third from halfway, was switched right from below the distance to avoid that rival. It made little difference to her chances though. (9/1)
**Halowing (USA)** lost all chance at the start. (20/1)
**1166* Ride Sally Ride (IRE)** stayed with the leaders to halfway before tiring. (14/1: 10/1-16/1)

## 1511 SUPRIUM H'CAP (0-80) (3-Y.O+) (Class D)

8-50 (8-52) **1m 6f** £3,837.50 (£1,160.00: £565.00: £267.50) Stalls: Low GOING minus 0.11 sec per fur (G)

| | | | | SP | RR | SF |
|---|---|---|---|---|---|---|
| 1347$^{3}$ | **World Express (IRE) (53)** (BRMillman) **6-8-1** BDoyle(6) (lw: hdwy over 2f out: led ins fnl f: r.o wl) | — | **1** | 12/1 | 65 | 39 |
| 1439* | **Rocky Forum (71)** (GLMoore) **4-9-5** 4x SSanders(8) (hdwy over 4f out: led 2f out tl ins fnl f: r.o) | hd | **2** | 13/8 1 | 83 | 57 |
| 1150$^{3}$ | **Rock Group (53)** (JPearce) **4-8-1** GBardwell(2) (led 12f: hrd rdn & ev ch ins fnl f: unable qckn) | 1 | **3** | 12/1 | 64 | 38 |
| 1116$^{2}$ | **Golden Arrow (IRE) (73)** (IABalding) **5-9-7b1** LDettori(1) (lw: hdwy 10f out: chsd ldr 9f out tl over 2f out: swtchd rt ins fnl f: one pce) | 2 | **4** | 5/1 3 | 82 | 56 |
| | **Requested (48)** (PBurgoyne) **9-7-10** JQuinn(4) (hdwy over 2f out: hrd rdn over 1f out: one pce) | 2 | **5** | 14/1 | 54 | 28 |
| 1116$^{4}$ | **Midyan Blue (IRE) (78)** (JMPEustace) **6-9-12** PatEddery(5) (a.p: rdn over 4f out: wknd over 2f out) | 5 | **6** | 100/30 2 | 79 | 53 |
| 968$^{10}$ | **Bolivar (IRE) (60)** (RAkehurst) **4-8-8** TQuinn(3) (lw: rdn & hdwy over 2f out: sn wknd) | 8 | **7** | 13/2 | 51 | 25 |
| 1347$^{15}$ | **King Ubad (USA) (48)** (KOCunningham-Brown) **7-7-10b** NCarlisle(7) (chsd ldr 5f: wknd over 5f out) | 13 | **8** | 66/1 | 25 | — |
| | | | | (SP 114.7%) | **8 Rn** | |

**3m 5.65** (6.75) CSF £30.81 CT £226.13 TOTE £16.50: £1.70 £1.40 £3.10 (£12.00) OWNER World Express Ltd (CULLOMPTON) BRED D. Twomey
LONG HANDICAP King Ubad (USA) 6-11
**1347 World Express (IRE)** came through to strike the front inside the final furlong. (12/1)
**1439* Rocky Forum** looked set for a quick hat-trick as she moved to the front a quarter of a mile out, but she failed to shake off her rivals and was collared inside the final furlong. To her credit, she stuck to her guns really well all the way to the line. She would prefer further. (13/8: 5/4-15/8)
**1150 Rock Group**, showing a really good attitude, refused to go down without a fight and was still in with every chance early inside the final furlong before tapped for toe. (12/1: op 8/1)
**1116 Golden Arrow (IRE)** had shot his bolt from below the distance. (5/1)
**Requested**, making his seasonal debut, failed to find another gear below the distance. (14/1)
**1116 Midyan Blue (IRE)** called it a day over two furlongs from home. (100/30)
**Bolivar (IRE)** (13/2: 9/2-7/1)

T/Plpt: £113.90 (232.85 Tckts). T/Qdpt: £3.00 (793.77 Tckts). AK

# 0755-FOLKESTONE (R-H) (Good)
## Wednesday May 29th

WEATHER: fine but cloudy WIND: slt half bhd

## 1512 BREDE H'CAP (0-70) (3-Y.O+) (Class E)

2-15 (2-20) **5f** £3,343.20 (£999.60: £478.80: £218.40) Stalls: Low GOING minus 0.47 sec per fur (F)

| | | | | SP | RR | SF |
|---|---|---|---|---|---|---|
| 911$^{5}$ | **Canovas Heart (65)** (BobJones) **7-9-9** NDay(14) (mde all: hrd rdn over 1f out: r.o wl) | — | **1** | 8/1 3 | 74 | 47 |
| 1307$^{5}$ | **Mousehole (62)** (RGuest) **4-9-6b1** PaulEddery(5) (led stands' side: hrd rdn over 1f out: r.o wl ins fnl f) | 1¼ | **2** | 9/1 | 67 | 40 |
| 1049$^{15}$ | **Half Tone (47)** (RMFlower) **4-8-5b** WWoods(11) (lw: outpcd: hdwy over 1f out: r.o wl ins fnl f) | ¾ | **3** | 20/1 | 50 | 23 |
| 1170$^{2}$ | **Lift Boy (USA) (47)** (AMoore) **7-8-5** CandyMorris(9) (swtg: hrd rdn & hdwy over 2f out: r.o one pce) | ½ | **4** | 10/1 | 48 | 21 |
| 1351$^{2}$ | **Friendly Brave (USA) (68)** (MissGayKelleway) **6-9-9**(3) DaneO'Neill(6) (b: lw: hdwy 2f out: hung lft over 1f out: one pce) | ¾ | **5** | 4/1 1 | 67 | 40 |
| 846$^{9}$ | **Dwingeloo (IRE) (66)** (MajorDNChappell) **3-9-2** BThomson(4) (racd stands' side: prom over 3f out) | 1 | **6** | 9/2 2 | 61 | 26 |
| 1412$^{14}$ | **Moujeeb (USA) (60)** (PatMitchell) **6-9-4v** JQuinn(2) (s.s: racd stands' side: outpcd: nvr nrr) | nk | **7** | 25/1 | 54 | 27 |
| 951$^{3}$ | **Barranak (IRE) (62)** (GMMcCourt) **4-9-6** JReid(7) (s.s: racd stands' side: no hdwy fnl 2f) | 1¼ | **8** | 10/1 | 52 | 25 |
| 1049$^{8}$ | **Squire Corrie (65)** (GHarwood) **4-9-2v**(7) GayeHarwood(3) (racd stands' side: no hdwy fnl 2f) | 1 | **9** | 25/1 | 52 | 25 |
| 1049$^{11}$ | **Miami Banker (52)** (WRMuir) **10-8-10b** GBardwell(12) (prom over 3f) | 1¼ | **10** | 25/1 | 35 | 8 |
| 893$^{16}$ | **Jolis Present (53)** (MJRyan) **3-8-3b** DBiggs(13) (prom over 2f) | 3½ | **11** | 20/1 | 25 | — |
| 1049$^{3}$ | **Lloc (56)** (CADwyer) **4-8-11**(3) JStack(8) (bhd fnl 2f) | hd | **12** | 11/1 | 28 | 1 |
| 1049$^{2}$ | **Mazzarello (IRE) (46)** (RCurtis) **6-7-13v**(5) MBaird(10) (prom over 3f) | 3½ | **13** | 10/1 | 7 | — |
| 861$^{8}$ | **My Mother's Local (USA) (46)** (KOCunningham-Brown) **3-7-10b** NAdams(15) (a bhd) | ½ | **14** | 66/1 | 5 | — |
| *664$^{15}$* | ***Distant Dynasty (40)*** (BAPearce) **6-7-7b1**(5)ow2 MHenry(1) (Withdrawn not under Starter's orders: lame) | | **W** | 33/1 | — | — |
| | | | | (SP 120.4%) | **14 Rn** | |

**58.7 secs** (0.10 under best) (1.10) CSF £69.96 CT £1,302.55 TOTE £8.20: £2.30 £3.20 £7.20 (£55.50) Trio £491.20; £629.62 to Brighton 30/5/96. OWNER Mr M J Osborne and Mrs J Woods (NEWMARKET) BRED M. J. Hall
LONG HANDICAP My Mother's Local (USA) 6-13 Distant Dynasty 7-8
WEIGHT FOR AGE 3yo-8lb
**911 Canovas Heart** made all the running and, responding to pressure below the distance, kept on well to beat the course record. (8/1)
**1307 Mousehole** made all the running on the stands' side, but did not have overall control. He ran on really strongly inside the final furlong, but was unable to peg back the winner racing on the opposite side of the track. (9/1)
**Half Tone**, as usual unable to go the pace, ran on really strongly but found the line always coming too soon. (20/1)
**1170 Lift Boy (USA)**, under pressure to take closer order at halfway, stayed on without ever looking likely to get there in time. He is more at home in claimers and sellers. (10/1)
**1351 Friendly Brave (USA)** picked up ground a quarter of a mile from home, but he drifted left below the distance and ended up with the stands'-side group. However, it made little difference to his chances as he was only plodding on at one pace. (4/1)
**Dwingeloo (IRE)**, one of five who raced on the stands' side, was close up until tiring approaching the final furlong. (9/2: op 5/2)
**1049 Lloc** (11/1: 8/1-12/1)

## 1513 HOTEL BURSTIN MAIDEN AUCTION STKS (2-Y.O) (Class E)

2-45 (2-47) **6f** £3,234.00 (£966.00: £462.00: £210.00) Stalls: Low GOING minus 0.47 sec per fur (F)

| | | | | SP | RR | SF |
|---|---|---|---|---|---|---|
| 1346[6] | **Supercal** (DRCElsworth) **2-8-1** BDoyle(9) (racd far side: hdwy 2f out: led over 1f out: r.o wl) | — | 1 | 11/1 | 64 | 19 |
| 848[5] | **Topatori (IRE)** (MHTompkins) **2-8-1**ow1 PRobinson(2) (lw: a.p: led over 2f out tl over 1f out: unable qckn) | 2 | 2 | 4/1[2] | 59 | 13 |
| 1339[5] | **Mister Pink** (RFJohnsonHoughton) **2-8-8** JReid(12) (racd far side: a.p: rdn over 2f out: one pce) | nk | 3 | 7/1[3] | 65 | 20 |
| | **Matoaka** (RJRWilliams) **2-8-1** DBiggs(1) (neat: hdwy over 1f out: nvr nrr: fin lame) | 3 | 4 | 12/1 | 50 | 5 |
| 1143[3] | **What Happened Was** (MartynMeade) **2-7-7**(5) MHenry(7) (a.p: ev ch over 1f out: sn wknd) | 2½ | 5 | 7/1[3] | 40 | — |
| | **Senorita Matilda (USA)** (RHannon) **2-8-0**(3) DaneO'Neill(4) (w'like: bit bkwd: a.p: ev ch over 1f out: sn wknd) | 5 | 6 | Evens[1] | 32 | — |
| *1093*[6] | **Nampara Bay** (GCBravery) **2-8-0**ow1 DRMcCabe(8) (prom over 4f) | 2½ | 7 | 25/1 | 22 | — |
| 1331[2] | **Miss Barcelona (IRE)** (MJPolglase) **2-8-0** JQuinn(13) (racd far side: a.p: ev ch over 2f out: wknd over 1f out) | ½ | 8 | 20/1 | 21 | — |
| | **Herbshan Dancer** (BRMillman) **2-8-3** MFenton(5) (neat: outpcd) | 2 | 9 | 33/1 | 19 | — |
| 1021[4] | **Janglynyve** (SPCWoods) **2-8-2** DHarrison(10) (racd far side: bhd fnl 2f) | ¾ | 10 | 16/1 | 16 | — |
| *1093*[8] | **Captain Picard** (DCO'Brien) **2-8-3** GBardwell(6) (outpcd) | 12 | 11 | 50/1 | — | — |
| | **Dasul** (GLewis) **2-8-1** NAdams(14) (leggy: unf: racd far side: led over 3f) | 1¾ | 12 | 12/1 | — | — |
| | **No Class** (RHarris) **2-7-13** AMackay(11) (unf: bit bkwd: s.s: racd far side: a bhd) | 1 | 13 | 33/1 | — | — |
| | **Whynotriskme** (RHarris) **2-8-0**ow2 DBatteate(3) (w'like: s.s: a wl bhd) | 6 | 14 | 50/1 | — | — |

(SP 143.0%) **14 Rn**

**1m 12.1** (1.90) CSF £60.61 TOTE £11.20: £2.10 £2.90 £2.90 (£25.20) Trio £28.60 OWNER The Caledonian Racing Society (WHITCOMBE) BRED Stetchworth Park Stud Ltd

**1346 Supercal**, one of six to race on the far side, came through to take overall control below the distance and proved too strong for her rivals. (11/1: 7/1-12/1)

**848 Topatori (IRE)** looked really well beforehand. Always close up on the stands' side, she went on over a quarter of a mile from home but was unable to live with the winner when collared below the distance. She should soon find a small race. (4/1: 5/2-9/2)

**1339 Mister Pink**, always close up on the far side, failed to find the necessary turn of foot in the last two furlongs. (7/1: 5/1-8/1)

**Matoaka**, a half-sister to three winners, was doing all her best work in the last furlong and a half. Unfortunately, she was found to be lame after the race. (12/1: 16/1-25/1)

**1143 What Happened Was** had every chance below the distance before tiring. (7/1: op 4/1)

**Senorita Matilda (USA)**, who looked as though the run would do her good, was always close up on the stands' side. With every chance a furlong and a half from home, she soon tired as lack of race-fitness took its toll. She should come on for this. (Evens)

**Dasul** (12/1: op 8/1)

## 1514 LYMPNE LIMITED STKS (0-50) (3-Y.O+) (Class F)

3-15 (3-16) **1m 4f** £2,381.00 (£656.00: £311.00) Stalls: High GOING minus 0.47 sec per fur (F)

| | | | | SP | RR | SF |
|---|---|---|---|---|---|---|
| *1098** | **Canton Venture (50)** (SPCWoods) **4-9-9** WWoods(14) (led over 9f: rdn over 1f out: led nr fin) | — | 1 | 9/2[2] | 61 | 27 |
| 1317W | **Poly My Son (IRE) (50)** (MRChannon) **3-8-9**ow1 RHughes(16) (a.p: led over 2f out: rdn over 1f out: hdd nr fin) | nk | 2 | 8/1 | 64 | 12 |
| 866[9] | **Pip's Dream (49)** (MJRyan) **5-9-5**(5) MBaird(17) (hdwy over 2f out: one pce fnl f) | ¾ | 3 | 10/1 | 61 | 27 |
| | **Birthday Boy (IRE) (46)** (JRJenkins) **4-9-9v** TQuinn(5) (hdwy over 1f out: r.o) | 2 | 4 | 12/1 | 57 | 23 |
| *1098*[2] | **Silver Hunter (USA) (50)** (GCBravery) **5-9-9** MHills(13) (lw: a.p: rdn over 2f out: one pce) | 1½ | 5 | 8/1 | 55 | 21 |
| 820[12] | **Breydon (48)** (MHTompkins) **3-8-6** PRobinson(6) (nvr nr to chal) | 1 | 6 | 9/1 | 54 | 3 |
| *1458*[9] | **Charlie Bigtime (46)** (RHarris) **6-9-9** AMackay(18) (b.hind: hdwy over 1f out: r.o) | ½ | 7 | 14/1 | 53 | 19 |
| 703[13] | **Miss Prism (50)** (JLDunlop) **3-8-3** SWhitworth(10) (hdwy 8f out: wknd over 1f out) | 2 | 8 | 11/1 | 47 | — |
| 760[2] | **Fast Forward Fred (50)** (LMontagueHall) **5-9-6**(3) DaneO'Neill(11) (a mid div) | nk | 9 | 9/4[1] | 50 | 16 |
| 760[10] | **Lord Ellangowan (IRE) (41)** (RIngram) **3-8-3b**(3) PMcCabe(15) (lw: hdwy over 3f out: wknd wl over 1f out) | 1¼ | 10 | 25/1 | 48 | — |
| 670[5] | **Todd (USA) (50)** (PhilipMitchell) **5-9-11** AClark(12) (hld up: rdn 3f out: sn wknd) | 1¾ | 11 | 20/1 | 48 | 14 |
| 666[9] | **Soojama (IRE) (43)** (RMFlower) **6-9-9** GHind(8) (s.s: a bhd) | 2 | 12 | 14/1 | 43 | 9 |
| 1152[10] | **Lahik (IRE) (40)** (KTIvory) **3-8-6** SSanders(9) (bhd fnl 5f) | 1¾ | 13 | 25/1 | 41 | — |
| 1019[4] | **Ajdar (50)** (MissGayKelleway) **5-9-11** WJO'Connor(3) (bhd fnl 2f) | ½ | 14 | 7/1[3] | 42 | 8 |
| 1012[6] | **Boston Tea Party (42)** (AMoore) **3-8-3** CandyMorris(2) (a bhd) | 14 | 15 | 33/1 | 19 | — |
| 546[11] | **Shy Paddy (IRE) (39)** (KOCunningham-Brown) **4-9-2**(7) CMunday(1) (lw: bhd fnl 4f) | 2½ | 16 | 33/1 | 18 | — |
| 637[12] | **Take Note (IRE) (46)** (NAGraham) **3-8-6** DHarrison(4) (bhd fnl 6f: t.o) | dist | 17 | 25/1 | — | — |

(SP 154.3%) **17 Rn**

**2m 37.7** (6.50) CSF £47.79 TOTE £6.60: £2.60 £5.30 £5.20 (£21.30) Trio £90.30 OWNER Dr Frank Chao (NEWMARKET) BRED High Point B/stock Ltd & Chao Racing & B/stock Ltd

WEIGHT FOR AGE 3yo-17lb

**1098* Canton Venture** battled his heart out to get back in front near the line and gain his first victory on turf. (9/2)

**1067* Poly My Son (IRE)** moved into a narrow lead over a quarter of a mile from home. However, he could never shake off the persistent winner and was worried out of it near the finish. (8/1: 6/1-9/1)

**760 Pip's Dream** took closer order early in the straight and was on the heels of the leader entering the final furlong before tapped for toe. (10/1)

**Birthday Boy (IRE)**, who finished fourth over hurdles recently, ran on in the last furlong and a half to take fourth place. (12/1)

**1098 Silver Hunter (USA)** could only go up and down in the same place in the straight. (8/1: 6/1-9/1)

**898 Charlie Bigtime** (14/1: 10/1-16/1)

**Miss Prism** (11/1: 7/1-12/1)

**760 Fast Forward Fred** (9/4: op 4/1)

## 1515 GLOVER INSURANCE SERVICES 50TH ANNIVERSARY CHALLENGE CUP H'CAP (0-70) (3-Y.O+) (Class E)

3-45 (3-45) **1m 1f 149y** £3,315.90 (£991.20: £474.60: £216.30) Stalls: High GOING minus 0.47 sec per fur (F)

| | | | | SP | RR | SF |
|---|---|---|---|---|---|---|
| 577[9] | **Florentino (IRE) (62)** (BWHills) **3-8-8** MHills(12) (hdwy over 1f out: nt clr run 1f out: swtchd lft: str run to ld nr fin) | — | 1 | 7/1[3] | 69 | 18 |
| 1172[5] | **White Plains (IRE) (67)** (MBell) **3-8-13** MFenton(7) (hdwy over 1f out: r.o wl ins fnl f) | nk | 2 | 6/1[2] | 74 | 23 |
| 1173* | **It'sthebusiness (60)** (SDow) **4-9-6** TQuinn(14) (hld up: rdn over 1f out: ev ch wl ins fnl f: r.o) | nk | 3 | 6/1[2] | 66 | 29 |
| 1074[10] | **Norsong (53)** (RAkehurst) **4-8-13** SSanders(15) (led 2f: led 2f out: rdn over 1f out: hdd nr fin) | nk | 4 | 12/1 | 59 | 22 |

| | | | | | SP | RR | SF |
|---|---|---|---|---|---|---|---|
| *462[7]* | **South Eastern Fred (48)** | (HJCollingridge) **5-8-8** JQuinn(10) (hld up: rdn over 2f out: one pce fnl f) | 1¼ | **5** | 14/1 | 51 | 14 |
| 1102[5] | **Gloriana (68)** | (LadyHerries) **4-10-0** JReid(2) (led over 7f out to 2f out: one pce fnl f) | nk | **6** | 6/1[2] | 71 | 34 |
| 1173[2] | **Wet Patch (IRE) (62)** | (RHannon) **4-9-8** RHughes(6) (hdwy over 1f out: nvr nrr) | 3½ | **7** | 4/1[1] | 59 | 22 |
| 827[16] | **Guesstimation (USA) (65)** | (JPearce) **7-9-11** GBardwell(5) (nvr nrr) | s.h | **8** | 10/1 | 62 | 25 |
| 1011[9] | **Total Rach (IRE) (47)** | (RIngram) **4-8-7b** WWoods(13) (prom 8f) | 1¾ | **9** | 33/1 | 41 | 4 |
| 1174[6] | **Classic Affair (USA) (62)** | (RHarris) **3-8-8** AMackay(11) (lw: a bhd) | 4 | **10** | 20/1 | 50 | — |
| 1173[15] | **Double Rush (IRE) (46)** | (TGMills) **4-8-6** MarkLynch(9) (a bhd) | 7 | **11** | 33/1 | 22 | — |
| | **Dutosky (62)** | (RJO'Sullivan) **6-9-8** AClark(4) (lw: prom 7f) | 2½ | **12** | 12/1 | 34 | — |
| 1190[17] | **Noble Neptune (52)** | (WJMusson) **4-8-12** RPrice(1) (bhd fnl 3f) | 5 | **13** | 20/1 | 16 | — |
| 1302[10] | **Ever so Lyrical (62)** | (PWHarris) **6-9-8** GHind(8) (prom 6f) | 2½ | **14** | 20/1 | 22 | — |
| | **Our Little Lady (54)** | (JCPoulton) **4-9-0** FNorton(3) (bhd fnl 5f) | 23 | **15** | 33/1 | — | — |

(SP 129.6%) **15 Rn**

**2m 2.0** (4.30) CSF £48.47 CT £250.97 TOTE £13.40: £2.90 £2.80 £3.50 (£91.50) Trio £300.20 OWNER Lady Harrison (LAMBOURN) BRED Fluorocarbon Bloodstock

WEIGHT FOR AGE 3yo-14lb

**445 Florentino (IRE)** appreciated this longer trip. Beginning his effort from below the distance, he had to be switched left after failing to get a clear run a furlong out. Nevertheless, he came with a useful run to snatch the spoils near the line. (7/1)

**1172 White Plains (IRE)** had no problem with this longer trip. Picking up ground below the distance, he ran on really strongly inside the final furlong and only just failed to get there. (6/1)

**1173* It'sthebusiness** threw down his challenge from below the distance and might have got his head in front for a couple of strides in the closing stages before passed by the winner. (6/1)

**Norsong**, the early leader, regained the advantage a quarter of a mile out. Gamely trying to fend off his challengers, he was worried out of it near the line. (12/1: op 8/1)

**South Eastern Fred**, rated 31lb lower than his last run on the All-Weather, chased the leaders. Grimly trying to mount a challenge in the home straight, he was tapped for toe in the last 200 yards. (14/1: 10/1-16/1)

**1102 Gloriana** went on just before the entrance to the back straight. Collared a quarter of a mile from home, she tried to hold on but was tapped for toe in the last 200 yards. (6/1)

**1173 Wet Patch (IRE)** (4/1: op 7/1)

**Guesstimation (USA)** (10/1: op 6/1)

## 1516 SELLINDGE CLAIMING STKS (I) (3-Y.O+) (Class F)

4-15 (4-16) **6f 189y** £2,031.00 (£556.00: £261.00) Stalls: High GOING minus 0.47 sec per fur (F)

| | | | | | SP | RR | SF |
|---|---|---|---|---|---|---|---|
| 981[10] | **Martinosky (46)** | (GCBravery) **10-9-6** NDay(5) (s.s: hrd rdn & hdwy over 1f out: led nr fin) | — | **1** | 16/1 | 60 | 35 |
| *1085[4]* | **Scathebury (60)** | (SPCWoods) **3-8-13** WWoods(2) (hdwy over 2f out: ev ch ins fnl f: r.o wl) | s.h | **2** | 9/4[2] | 64 | 28 |
| *1094[10]* | **Justinianus (IRE) (45)** | (JJBridger) **4-8-11**(3) DarrenMoffatt(8) (lw: led 5f out: hrd rdn over 1f out: hdd nr fin) | hd | **3** | 25/1 | 54 | 29 |
| 981[3] | **Milos (61)** | (TJNaughton) **5-9-10** PaulEddery(6) (hld up: rdn over 2f out: one pce fnl f) | 2½ | **4** | 5/6[1] | 58 | 33 |
| 1314[9] | **Komodo (USA) (55)** | (KOCunningham-Brown) **4-8-9b**(7) CMunday(4) (lw: a.p: rdn over 2f out: wknd over 1f out) | 5 | **5** | 16/1 | 38 | 13 |
| | **Logie (53)** | (DRGandolfo) **4-9-0v** MFenton(7) (hld up: rdn over 2f out: sn wknd) | 1¼ | **6** | 16/1 | 33 | 8 |
| | **The Atheling (IRE)** | (MHTompkins) **6-9-2** AMackay(1) (a bhd) | 2 | **7** | 20/1 | 31 | 6 |
| 1122[11] | **Petite Annie (50)** | (TGMills) **3-8-0** MarkLynch(9) (b.off hind: lw: led 2f: rdn over 2f out: wknd over 1f out) | 4 | **8** | 12/1[3] | 16 | — |
| 1351[6] | **Diamond Bangle (20)** | (WRMuir) **4-8-7** TQuinn(3) (bhd fnl 5f) | 24 | **9** | 33/1 | — | — |

(SP 122.2%) **9 Rn**

**1m 24.0** (2.40) CSF £52.42 TOTE £17.30: £4.20 £1.10 £8.20 (£21.50) Trio £135.00 OWNER Mr D. B. Clark (NEWMARKET) BRED David B. Clark

WEIGHT FOR AGE 3yo-11lb

Scathebury clmd MrNRShields £8,000

**Martinosky**, who lost several lengths at the start, picked up ground under pressure below the distance and eventually managed to get on top near the line to gain his first win in over three years. (16/1)

**1085 Scathebury** began a forward move turning for home. With every chance inside the final furlong, he only just missed out. (9/4: 6/4-5/2)

**Justinianus (IRE)** was eventually collared near the line. (25/1)

**981 Milos** chased the leaders. Trying to mount a challenge in the straight, he was tapped for toe in the final furlong. (5/6: Evens-11/10)

**Komodo (USA)** played an active role until coming to the end of his tether below the distance. (16/1)

**Petite Annie** (12/1: op 8/1)

## 1517 SELLINDGE CLAIMING STKS (II) (3-Y.O+) (Class F)

4-45 (4-47) **6f 189y** £2,031.00 (£556.00: £261.00) Stalls: High GOING minus 0.47 sec per fur (F)

| | | | | | SP | RR | SF |
|---|---|---|---|---|---|---|---|
| 1074[5] | **Moon Strike (FR) (74)** | (SCWilliams) **6-9-10** MHills(6) (b.nr fore: a gng wl: hld up: led on bit 1f out: hrd hld) | — | **1** | 10/11[1] | 77+ | 47 |
| | **Sapphire Son (IRE) (48)** | (DMorris) **4-9-0** PBloomfield(8) (lw: led 6f out to 5f out: rdn over 2f out: ev ch ins fnl f: unable qckn) | ¾ | **2** | 20/1 | 65 | 35 |
| 1314[5] | **Rockville Pike (IRE) (55)** | (SDow) **4-9-0v** WWoods(7) (led 1f: led 5f out to 1f out: one pce) | 1¾ | **3** | 9/2[3] | 61 | 31 |
| 1154[5] | **Dontforget Insight (IRE) (65)** | (CPEBrooks) **5-9-4b** PaulEddery(5) (b.hind: dwlt: plld hrd: hdwy over 1f out: one pce) | 3½ | **4** | 11/4[2] | 57 | 27 |
| 983[15] | **Forgotten Dancer (IRE) (45)** | (RIngram) **5-9-2** DRMcCabe(3) (lw: dwlt: nvr nr to chal) | 1¾ | **5** | 40/1 | 51 | 21 |
| *834[8]* | **Woolverstone Hall (IRE)** | (DJGMurraySmith) **4-8-9b** NAdams(4) (prom over 4f) | 6 | **6** | 25/1 | 30 | — |
| | **Little Wobbly** | (PCClarke) **6-8-2**(5) PPMurphy(2) (dlwt: a bhd) | 5 | **7** | 50/1 | 16 | — |
| 631[8] | **Branston Kristy (35)** | (CSmith) **4-8-2b**(5) MBaird(1) (lw: prom over 4f) | nk | **8** | 50/1 | 16 | — |

(SP 112.2%) **8 Rn**

**1m 23.3** (1.70) CSF £16.95 TOTE £1.70: £1.00 £6.10 £1.20 (£13.20) OWNER Mr A. Foustok (NEWMARKET) BRED Haras de Manneville in France

**1074 Moon Strike (FR)** had little more than an exercise gallop in this low-grade race. Always travelling supremely well, he cruised into the lead on the bridle a furlong out and, with his jockey having a very tight rein on him, won pulling the proverbial bus. (10/11: 4/6-Evens)

**Sapphire Son (IRE)**, having his first run of the season, was always handy. He may have got his head in front for a few strides inside the final furlong, but is greatly flattered to finish so close as the winner did not even break sweat. (20/1)

**1314 Rockville Pike (IRE)** was soon at the head of affairs. Collared a furlong out, he was firmly put in his place. (9/2)

**Dontforget Insight (IRE)**, who took a keen hold in the early stages, moved up below the distance but could then make no further impression. (11/4)

## 1518 SMEETHE MEDIAN AUCTION MAIDEN STKS (3-Y.O) (Class F)
5-15 (5-15) **6f 189y** £2,381.00 (£656.00: £311.00) Stalls: High GOING minus 0.47 sec per fur (F)

| | Horse | | | SP | RR | SF |
|---|---|---|---|---|---|---|
| 1301[2] | **Young Mazaad (IRE) (68)** (DCO'Brien) **3-9-0b[1]** GBardwell(6) (hdwy to chse ldr 2f out: hrd rdn & led ins fnl f: r.o wl) | — | 1 | 2/1[1] | 63 | 34 |
| *58*[3] | **Cointosser (IRE)** (SPCWoods) **3-8-9** WWoods(7) (hld up: rdn over 1f out: r.o ins fnl f) | 1¼ | 2 | 2/1[1] | 55 | 26 |
| 1045[9] | **Inaminit (62)** (HJCollingridge) **3-9-0** JQuinn(8) (lw: a.p: led 3f out tl ins fnl f: unable qckn) | 1¾ | 3 | 7/1 | 56 | 27 |
| 1326[10] | **Stone Island** (CACyzer) **3-9-0** GHind(5) (lw: nvr nr to chal) | 3½ | 4 | 9/2[2] | 48 | 19 |
| 851[11] | **Cowboy Dreams (IRE) (50)** (MHTompkins) **3-9-0** NDay(2) (led over 5f out to 3f out: wknd over 1f out) | d.h | 4 | 25/1 | 48 | 27 |
| 758[8] | **Governor's Bid** (MrsLCJewell) **3-9-0** NAdams(4) (bit bkwd: led over 1f: wknd over 2f out) | 16 | 6 | 100/1 | 11 | — |
| *503*[5] | **Baranov (IRE)** (DJGMurraySmith) **3-9-0** AClark(1) (5th whn sddle slipped over 3f out: t.o whn p.u 2f out) | | P | 6/1[3] | — | — |
| *1171*[12] | ***Into Debt*** (JRPoulton) **3-8-6**(3) PMcCabe(3) (Withdrawn not under Starter's orders: uns & inj rdr in paddock) | | W | 50/1 | — | — |
| | | | | (SP 118.4%) | **7 Rn** | |

**1m 23.6** (2.00) CSF £6.45 TOTE £2.70: £1.50 £1.90 (£2.90) OWNER Letts Green Farm Ltd (TONBRIDGE) BRED Lorcan Higgins

**1301 Young Mazaad (IRE)** at last came good. Moving through to take second early in the straight, his jockey had to get down to some serious work to get him in front inside the final furlong. (2/1: 5/4-9/4)
**Cointosser (IRE)** chased the leaders. She ran on inside the final furlong but failed to peg back the winner. (2/1: op 3/1)
**Inaminit**, collared inside the final furlong, failed to find another gear. (7/1)
**1050 Stone Island** was out with the washing until making some late headway. He may improve for a step up in distance. (9/2)
**Cowboy Dreams (IRE)** had shot his bolt below the distance. (25/1)
**Baranov (IRE)** (6/1: 4/1-13/2)

T/Jkpt: Not won; £12,052.66 to Brighton 30/5/96. T/Plpt: £134.20 (136.85 Tckts). T/Qdpt: £15.00 (97.01 Tckts). AK

# 1190-NEWBURY (L-H) (Soft)
## Wednesday May 29th
WEATHER: unsettled WIND: slt half bhd

## 1519 E.B.F. BOXFORD MAIDEN STKS (2-Y.O) (Class D)
6-30 (6-31) **5f 34y** £3,473.50 (£1,048.00: £509.00: £239.50) Stalls: Centre GOING: 0.50 sec per fur (GS)

| | Horse | | | SP | RR | SF |
|---|---|---|---|---|---|---|
| 1003[2] | **Raven Master (USA)** (PWChapple-Hyam) **2-9-0** JReid(6) (w ldr: led 3f out tl wl over 1f out: rallied to ld last strides) | — | 1 | 11/4[2] | 90 | 23 |
| | **Darb Alola (USA)** (MRStoute) **2-9-0** LDettori(2) (gd sort: hld up: nt clr run & swtchd rt over 1f out: rdn to ld ins fnl f: hdd last strides) | hd | 2 | 5/2[1] | 90+ | 23 |
| | **Cathedral (IRE)** (BJMeehan) **2-9-0** BDoyle(4) (lengthy: bit bkwd: hld up: led wl over 1f out: hdd ins fnl f: r.o wl) | s.h | 3 | 5/1 | 90+ | 23 |
| 1315[2] | **Golden Fact (USA)** (RHannon) **2-9-0** PatEddery(5) (lw: w ldrs tl wknd fnl f) | 4 | 4 | 7/2[3] | 77 | 10 |
| | **Buzzby** (AGFoster) **2-9-0** SSanders(7) (b: small: bkwd: wnt rt s: hdwy over 2f out: ev ch wl over 1f out: sn wknd) | 2 | 5 | 33/1 | 71 | 4 |
| | **Mystic Ridge** (DRCElsworth) **2-9-0** AProcter(1) (str: scope: s.s: outpcd: nvr nrr) | 1 | 6 | 10/1 | 68 | 1 |
| | **Accountancy Leader (IRE)** (BPalling) **2-8-9** TSprake(3) (unf: led 2f: wknd wl over 1f out) | 1¼ | 7 | 33/1 | 59 | — |
| | | | | (SP 109.1%) | **7 Rn** | |

**67.35 secs** (7.15) CSF £9.24 TOTE £3.10: £1.60 £2.50 (£3.30) OWNER Mr R. E. Sangster (MARLBOROUGH) BRED Swettenham Stud & Ron Con No. 1

**1003 Raven Master (USA)**, out of a close relative of Intrepidity, found the ground putting the emphasis on stamina and fought back to pull the race out of the fire virtually on the line. (11/4: op 7/4)
**Darb Alola (USA)** was friendless in the market and will soon go one better on decent ground. (5/2: Evens-11/4)
**Cathedral (IRE)** will come on for the run and looks a ready-made future winner. (5/1: tchd 8/1)
**1315 Golden Fact (USA)** probably needs better ground and should not be written off yet. (7/2: 9/4-4/1)
**Buzzby** did well to get into the picture after losing ground at the start and will strip fitter for the race. (33/1)
**Mystic Ridge**, a powerful colt, is out of a ten furlong winner and should improve when tackling further. (10/1)

## 1520 NEWBURY 400TH CHARTER ANNIVERSARY CONDITIONS STKS (4-Y.O+) (Class C)
7-00 (7-01) **1m 2f 6y** £4,933.80 (£1,834.20: £887.10: £370.50: £155.25: £69.15) Stalls: High GOING: 0.50 sec per fur (GS)

| | Horse | | | SP | RR | SF |
|---|---|---|---|---|---|---|
| 726[7] | **Murajja (USA) (104)** (PTWalwyn) **4-8-10** PatEddery(5) (led over 6f: led over 2f out: hrd rdn over 1f out: all out) | — | 1 | 6/1 | 121 | 80 |
| | **King's Theatre (IRE)** (SbinSuroor) **5-8-10** LDettori(3) (lw: a.p: chal on bit over 1f out: rdn & unable qckn ins fnl f) | hd | 2 | 7/4[1] | 121 | 80 |
| 581[7] | **Fire on Ice (IRE) (103)** (MRStoute) **4-8-13** JReid(1) (lw: hld up & plld hrd: stdy hdwy 3f out: rdn & wknd over 1f out) | 15 | 3 | 14/1 | 100 | 59 |
| 1355[2] | **Wijara (IRE) (103)** (RHannon) **4-9-1** RHughes(7) (hld up: rdn over 2f out: sn wknd) | 1½ | 4 | 4/1[2] | 100 | 59 |
| | **Dee-Lady (83)** (WGMTurner) **4-8-5** TSprake(8) (b: prom: led over 3f out tl over 2f out: sn wknd) | 3 | 5 | 40/1 | 85 | 44 |
| 878[6] | **Ki Chi Saga (USA)** (JLDunlop) **4-8-10** WJO'Connor(2) (hld up: wknd 3f out) | 3½ | 6 | 16/1 | 84 | 43 |
| 1193* | **Night City (102)** (LadyHerries) **5-9-8** DeclanO'Shea(6) (hld up & plld hrd: wknd over 2f out) | ½ | 7 | 5/1[3] | 95 | 54 |
| 929[5] | **Tremplin (USA)** (NACallaghan) **4-8-10** SWhitworth(4) (b: plld hrd in rr: rdn over 3f out: sn bhd) | 4 | 8 | 16/1 | 77 | 36 |
| | | | | (SP 108.2%) | **8 Rn** | |

**2m 10.62** (6.82) CSF £15.34 TOTE £6.90: £1.80 £1.20 £2.20 (£5.80) OWNER Mr Hamdan Al Maktoum (LAMBOURN) BRED Shadwell Farm Inc & Shadwell Estate Co Ltd in USA

**Murajja (USA)**, fitter for his run here in the John Porter, had registered both juvenile wins on soft ground. (6/1)
**King's Theatre (IRE)**, runner-up in both the English and Irish Derbies and winner of the King George, did not adapt to training and racing conditions in the States last year and consequently lost all form. Racing with his tongue tied down, he looked sure to score coming to the final furlong and may have been suffering breathing problems when put under pressure. (7/4)
**Fire on Ice (IRE)**, unproven on this sort of ground, took a keen hold and got left for dead by the main protagonists in the last furlong and a half. (14/1: 8/1-16/1)
**1355 Wijara (IRE)** may be better forcing the pace over a slightly shorter trip. (4/1: 3/1-9/2)

**Dee-Lady** was far from disgraced on her reappearance in this company. (40/1)
**Ki Chi Saga (USA)**, trying further, won twice last year in Scandinavia. (16/1)
**1193* Night City** had a tough task at the weights and compounded matters by refusing to settle. (5/1)

## 1521 CITY INDEX SPREAD BETTING H'CAP (0-80) (3-Y.O+) (Class D)
7-30 (7-31) **6f 8y** £4,185.00 (£1,260.00: £610.00: £285.00) Stalls: Centre GOING: 0.50 sec per fur (GS)

| | Horse / details | Dist | Pos | SP | RR | SF |
|---|---|---|---|---|---|---|
| $1354^{3}$ | **Stoppes Brow (70)** (GLMoore) **4-9-4v** SWhitworth(1) (lw: hld up: hdwy over 2f out: swtchd stands' side over 1f out: hrd rdn to ld ins fnl f: r.o wl) | — | **1** | $5/1^{2}$ | 77 | 59 |
| $814^{16}$ | **Bajan Rose (74)** (MBlanshard) **4-9-8** RHughes(8) (racd alone stands' side: led over 2f out: clr over 1f out: rdn & hdd ins fnl f) | 1¾ | **2** | $6/1^{3}$ | 76 | 58 |
| $1178^{6}$ | **Golden Pound (USA) (80)** (MissGayKelleway) **4-10-0** WJO'Connor(6) (swtg: a.p: rdn 2f out: one pce) | 6 | **3** | 13/2 | 67 | 49 |
| $1442^{3}$ | **Leigh Crofter (60)** (PDCundell) **7-8-8b** DHarrison(4) (a.p: rdn over 2f out: one pce) | nk | **4** | $3/1^{1}$ | 46 | 28 |
| | **Kiss Me Again (IRE) (80)** (RHannon) **3-9-2**$^{(3)}$ DaneO'Neill(5) (no hdwy fnl 2f) | 6 | **5** | 8/1 | 50 | 23 |
| $862^{12}$ | **Malibu Man (60)** (EAWheeler) **4-8-8** TSprake(3) (led over 3f: wknd over 1f out) | 7 | **6** | 15/2 | 11 | — |
| $1121^{9}$ | **Ahjay (48)** (TJNaughton) **6-7-10** DeclanO'Shea(7) (a bhd: t.o) | 10 | **7** | 13/2 | — | — |
| | **Manderella (68)** (JAkehurst) **3-8-7** LDettori(2) (bit bkwd: sn bhd: t.o) | 1½ | **8** | 12/1 | — | — |

(SP 113.2%) **8 Rn**

**1m 17.85** (6.05) CSF £31.56 CT £179.11 TOTE £6.50: £1.90 £2.00 £2.60 (£28.20) OWNER Mr C. J. Pennick (EPSOM) BRED Dodford Stud
LONG HANDICAP Ahjay 7-8
WEIGHT FOR AGE 3yo-9lb
STEWARDS' ENQUIRY Whitworth susp. 9-10/6/96 (excessive use of whip).
IN-FOCUS: **All of ten days after the last meeting, many jockeys seemed to have already forgotten the advantage of coming down the stands' rail on soft ground, the exception being Richard Hughes.**
**1354 Stoppes Brow** found the combination of six furlongs and soft ground just the ticket and was always going to catch the runner-up once he was switched to the stands' side. His rider picked up a two-day whip ban though. (5/1)
**Bajan Rose**, 3lb higher when winning at Chepstow last October, made the best of her way home in splendid isolation under the stands' rail. (6/1)
**1178 Golden Pound (USA)** again had soft ground to contend with and probably needs to be dropped a few pounds. (13/2)
**1442 Leigh Crofter**, who runs often, is now 15lb lower than when he last won on turf here two years ago. (3/1: op 9/2)
**Kiss Me Again (IRE)**, having her first run on soft ground, was 8lb higher than when winning a nursery at Windsor last season. (8/1)
**466 Malibu Man** needs faster ground to stay this trip. (15/2)

## 1522 COOPERS & LYBRAND H'CAP (0-85) (4-Y.O+) (Class D)
8-00 (8-01) **7f 64y (round)** £5,410.00 (£1,630.00: £790.00: £370.00) Stalls: High GOING: 0.50 sec per fur (GS)

| | Horse / details | Dist | Pos | SP | RR | SF |
|---|---|---|---|---|---|---|
| $1190^{11}$ | **Duello (60)** (MBlanshard) **5-8-6** JQuinn(13) (lw: a.p: c stands' side 5f out: led over 1f out: all out) | — | **1** | 8/1 | 68 | 50 |
| $1354^{6}$ | **Knobbleeneeze (69)** (MRChannon) **6-9-1v** RHughes(10) (led tl c stands' side 5f out: led over 3f out tl over 1f out: r.o) | ¾ | **2** | $11/2^{2}$ | 75 | 57 |
| $1354^{2}$ | **Dawalib (USA) (62)** (DHaydnJones) **6-8-8** JReid(5) (lw: hld up: stdy hdwy 3f out: ev ch over 2f out: one pce) | 1½ | **3** | $4/1^{1}$ | 65 | 47 |
| $1347^{7}$ | **Fastini Gold (50)** (MDIUsher) **4-7-10** NAdams(7) (bhd tl hdwy 2f out: r.o one pce fnl f) | hd | **4** | 33/1 | 53 | 35 |
| $1145^{14}$ | **I Recall (IRE) (55)** (PHayward) **5-7-10v**$^{(5)}$ MHenry(3) (s.i.s: hdwy 2f out: r.o one pce fnl f) | hd | **5** | 14/1 | 58 | 40 |
| *$1083^{7}$* | **Sue Me (IRE) (62)** (WRMuir) **4-8-8** WJO'Connor(11) (a.p: ev ch 2f out: wknd fnl f) | s.h | **6** | 12/1 | 65 | 47 |
| | **Express Routing (58)** (JAkehurst) **4-8-4** PaulEddery(14) (b: w ldrs: c stands' side 5f out: wknd over 2f out) | 6 | **7** | 20/1 | 47 | 29 |
| $983^{18}$ | **Flag Fen (USA) (62)** (MartynMeade) **5-8-3**$^{(5)}$ RHavlin(6) (c stands' side 5f out: bhd fnl 2f) | ¾ | **8** | 20/1 | 50 | 32 |
| $649^{8}$ | **Zatopek (61)** (JCullinan) **4-8-7** PatEddery(4) (lw: hdwy 2f out: eased whn btn ins fnl f) | 4 | **9** | 14/1 | 40 | 22 |
| $879^{19}$ | **Lynton Lad (73)** (CPEBrooks) **4-9-5b** BThomson(9) (lw: prom tl wknd over 2f out) | 9 | **10** | 15/2 | 32 | 14 |
| $1073^{9}$ | **Sharp 'n Smart (66)** (BSmart) **4-8-12** SSanders(8) (swtg: plld hrd: led 5f out tl over 3f out: wknd over 2f out) | 1¾ | **11** | 10/1 | 21 | 3 |
| $968^{12}$ | **Kelly Mac (51)** (DCO'Brien) **6-7-11** GBardwell(1) (lw: a bhd) | 4 | **12** | 20/1 | — | — |
| $1198^{10}$ | **Mister Rm (72)** (RGuest) **4-9-4b**$^{1}$ MFenton(2) (s.i.s: a bhd) | 4 | **13** | $13/2^{3}$ | 10 | — |

(SP 118.9%) **13 Rn**

**1m 35.28** (7.18) CSF £47.86 CT £192.80 TOTE £9.60: £2.60 £2.10 £1.90 (£16.00) Trio £12.10 OWNER H C Promotions Ltd (UPPER LAMBOURN) BRED P. D. and Mrs Player
LONG HANDICAP Fastini Gold 7-2
OFFICIAL EXPLANATION **Duello: accounting for the gelding's apparent improvement, his rider said that his mount lost interest when the field split on his previous run, and suggested a round track for this his next run.**
**496 Duello** again had ground conditions to his liking and settled much better this time. (8/1)
**1354 Knobbleeneeze** has been slipping down the ratings and bounced back to form. (11/2)
**1354 Dawalib (USA)** again ran well off a mark 4lb lower than when he last won. (4/1)
**Fastini Gold**, 8lb out of the handicap, has been racing over further and found this trip inadequate. (33/1)
**843 I Recall (IRE)** is another who did not seem suited by a drop back in distance. (14/1)
**Sue Me (IRE)**, tried in blinkers on the Fibresand last time, did not see out this longer trip. (12/1)

## 1523 BASINGSTOKE CLAIMING STKS (3-Y.O) (Class E)
8-30 (8-30) **1m 2f 6y** £3,168.00 (£954.00: £462.00: £216.00) Stalls: High GOING: 0.50 sec per fur (GS)

| | Horse / details | Dist | Pos | SP | RR | SF |
|---|---|---|---|---|---|---|
| $1302^{9}$ | **Swift Maiden (60)** (JNeville) **3-8-8** JReid(3) (a gng wl: led over 2f out: clr over 1f out: easily) | — | **1** | $9/1^{3}$ | 79+ | 35 |
| $678^{15}$ | **Cd Super Targeting (IRE) (58)** (MRChannon) **3-8-9**$^{ow1}$ RHughes(6) (a.p: chsd wnr fnl 2f: no imp) | 11 | **2** | 12/1 | 62 | 17 |
| $1002^{12}$ | **Diego (73)** (CEBrittain) **3-9-1** BDoyle(2) (sn bhd: hrd rdn 3f out: hdwy over 1f out: n.d) | 2 | **3** | 10/1 | 65 | 21 |
| $1338^{2}$ | **Asking For Kings (IRE) (55)** (SDow) **3-8-9** LDettori(8) (prom tl wknd over 2f out) | 1 | **4** | $100/30^{1}$ | 58 | 14 |
| $1324^{9}$ | **Honorable Estate (IRE) (72)** (RHannon) **3-8-7**$^{(3)}$ DaneO'Neill(5) (hld up: hdwy over 2f out: wknd over 1f out) | 8 | **5** | $100/30^{1}$ | 46 | 2 |
| $1317^{6}$ | **Half An Inch (IRE) (70)** (BJMeehan) **3-9-4b** PatEddery(4) (lw: led: rdn & hdd over 3f out: sn wknd) | 5 | **6** | $11/2^{2}$ | 46 | 2 |
| $976^{6}$ | **Forest Boy (73)** (KMcAuliffe) **3-9-7v** JFEgan(7) (prom: led over 3f out tl wknd rapidly over 2f out: t.o) | dist | **7** | $100/30^{1}$ | — | — |
| | **Storm Wind (IRE)** (KRBurke) **3-8-13** SWhitworth(1) (bkwd: dwlt: rdn over 6f out: t.o fnl 4f) | 17 | **8** | 33/1 | — | — |

(SP 114.3%) **8 Rn**

**2m 15.89** (12.09) CSF £92.06 TOTE £14.70: £2.80 £2.00 £2.00 (£65.20) OWNER Mr David Lewis (NEWPORT, GWENT)
Swift Maiden clmd RSimpson £10,000
STEWARDS' ENQUIRY Doyle susp. 7-10/6/96 (excessive use of whip).

**873 Swift Maiden** loved the give underfoot and turned the race into a procession. (9/1: op 6/1)
**Cd Super Targeting (IRE)**, upped in distance and dropped in class, proved no match in the final quarter-mile, but took second as easily as the winner took first. (12/1)
**175* Diego** stayed on under strong pressure, and his rider picked up a four-day whip ban. (10/1)
**1338 Asking For Kings (IRE)** again had ground conditions in his favour. (100/30)
**888 Honorable Estate (IRE)** may not have handled the soft ground. (100/30)
**976 Forest Boy** has won on this ground, and he stopped so quickly that one could not put it down to the longer trip. (100/30)

## 1524 KENNETH ROBERTSON H'CAP (0-80) (3-Y.O+) (Class D)
9-00 (9-01) **1m 5f 61y** £3,821.00 (£1,148.00: £554.00: £257.00) Stalls: High GOING: 0.50 sec per fur (GS)

| | | | | SP | RR | SF |
|---|---|---|---|---|---|---|
| 1194[8] | **Granby Bell (48)** (PHayward) **5-7-8**(5) MHenry(3) (a.p: led over 4f out: all out) | — | **1** | 9/1 | 61 | 41 |
| 1124* | **Old Irish (80)** (LMCumani) **3-8-12** LDettori(9) (hld up: rdn 5f out: hdwy over 2f out: ev ch whn wandered over 1f out & wl ins fnl f: r.o) | ½ | **2** | 13/8[1] | 92 | 53 |
| 1353[4] | **Opera Buff (IRE) (71)** (MissGayKelleway) **5-9-5**(3) DaneO'Neill(7) (hld up: hdwy over 6f out: ev ch over 1f out: rdn & edgd lft: one pce) | 2 | **3** | 13/2[3] | 81 | 61 |
| 1147[11] | **Dont Shoot Fairies (71)** (CEBrittain) **4-9-8** BDoyle(6) (led 7f: wknd over 2f out) | 7 | **4** | 20/1 | 73 | 53 |
| 872* | **Cuango (IRE) (58)** (RHollinshead) **5-8-4**(5) FLynch(5) (lw: s.i.s: nvr nr ldrs) | 8 | **5** | 10/1 | 50 | 30 |
| 1019[3] | **Fahs (USA) (66)** (RAkehurst) **4-9-3** RHughes(10) (lw: s.i.s: a bhd: t.o) | 23 | **6** | 6/1[2] | 30 | 10 |
| 979[15] | **Monty (53)** (MajorDNChappell) **4-8-4** SSanders(8) (hld up mid div: bhd fnl 3f: t.o) | 2½ | **7** | 50/1 | 14 | — |
| 712[5] | **Johns Act (USA) (68)** (DHaydnJones) **6-9-5** JReid(2) (a bhd: t.o) | ½ | **8** | 11/1 | 29 | 9 |
| 1436[3] | **Secret Service (IRE) (73)** (CWThornton) **4-9-10** PaulEddery(1) (lw: bhd fnl 3f: t.o) | ¾ | **9** | 6/1[2] | 33 | 13 |
| 753[15] | **Western Dynasty (52)** (EAWheeler) **10-8-3** TSprake(4) (a.p: led over 6f out tl over 4f out: wknd 3f out: t.o) | 1½ | **10** | 50/1 | 10 | — |
| | | | | (SP 116.1%) | **10 Rn** | |

**3m 0.18** (13.68) CSF £22.88 CT £94.56 TOTE £11.30: £2.00 £1.50 £2.00 (£17.10) Trio £24.50 OWNER Mr H. A. Watton (NETHERAVON) BRED L. V. Wadge
WEIGHT FOR AGE 3yo-19lb
STEWARDS' ENQUIRY Henry susp. 9-10/6/96 (excessive use of whip).
**753 Granby Bell**, back to the right sort of trip and with the stands' rail to help him, held on grimly. His rider got a two-day whip ban. (9/1)
**1124* Old Irish**, challenging in the centre, again resented the whip and could not overcome a 5lb rise in the weights. (13/8)
**1353 Opera Buff (IRE)** was inclined to come off a true line and could not match the two principals in the closing stages. (13/2: 9/2-7/1)
**968 Dont Shoot Fairies** did not see out the extended trip on such testing ground. (20/1)
**872* Cuango (IRE)** never seemed likely to defy a 10lb rise in the weights. (10/1)
**Johns Act (USA)** (11/1: 8/1-12/1)

T/Plpt: £177.70 (128.04 Tckts). T/Qdpt: £108.50 (12.84 Tckts). KH

# 1196-RIPON (R-H) (Good)
## Wednesday May 29th
WEATHER: overcast WIND: almost nil

## 1525 LISHMAN, SIDWELL, CAMPBELL AND PRICE MAIDEN STKS (2-Y.O) (Class D)
6-45 (6-46) **5f** £3,548.00 (£1,073.00: £523.00: £248.00) Stalls: Low GOING minus 0.17 sec per fur (GF)

| | | | | SP | RR | SF |
|---|---|---|---|---|---|---|
| 924[3] | **Grand Lad (IRE)** (RWArmstrong) **2-9-0** RHills(11) (mde all: qcknd ½-wy: r.o wl) | — | **1** | 4/5[1] | 86+ | 56 |
| | **Vax Star** (JLSpearing) **2-8-6**(3) SDrowne(2) (str: scope: chsd ldrs: hdwy 2f out: r.o) | 3 | **2** | 9/1[3] | 71 | 41 |
| | **Divide And Rule** (RHollinshead) **2-8-9**(5) DGriffiths(5) (neat: scope: ½-wy: no imp) | 8 | **3** | 33/1 | 51 | 21 |
| | **Tickntima** (MDHammond) **2-9-0** KFallon(7) (unf: scope: hdwy ½-wy: styd on: nrst fin) | 2½ | **4** | 33/1 | 43 | 13 |
| 1197[10] | **Flo's Choice (IRE)** (JAHarris) **2-8-9** JO'Reilly(6) (chsd ldrs: rdn ½-wy: no imp after) | 1½ | **5** | 33/1 | 33 | 3 |
| 1184[3] | **Rum Lad** (JJQuinn) **2-9-0** NConnorton(4) (lw: s.i.s: hdwy ½-wy: nvr nr to chal) | s.h | **6** | 20/1 | 38 | 8 |
| 1328[3] | **Cauda Equina** (MRChannon) **2-9-0** KDarley(3) (w wnr: rdn ½-wy: wknd wl over 1f out) | 1¼ | **7** | 2/1[2] | 34 | 4 |
| | **Sandbaggedagain** (MWEasterby) **2-9-0** DaleGibson(10) (leggy: unf: s.s: nvr nr to chal) | 1¼ | **8** | 100/1 | 30 | — |
| 1184[6] | **Veerapong (IRE)** (MWEasterby) **2-8-4**(5) GParkin(9) (nvr trbld ldrs) | 1 | **9** | 100/1 | 22 | — |
| | **Hong Kong Express (IRE)** (JBerry) **2-8-9** JCarroll(12) (w'like: bit bkwd: sn outpcd & bhd) | 1½ | **10** | 25/1 | 17 | — |
| | **Siouxrouge** (PCHaslam) **2-9-0** JWeaver(1) (leggy: scope: s.s: a bhd) | s.h | **11** | 14/1 | 22 | — |
| | **Honourable Felix** (EJAlston) **2-9-0** SDWilliams(8) (w'like: dwlt: a bhd) | 10 | **12** | 66/1 | — | — |
| | | | | (SP 126.5%) | **12 Rn** | |

**60.0 secs** (1.60) CSF £9.79 TOTE £2.00: £1.20 £2.50 £12.20 (£16.50) Trio £183.40; £232.50 to 31/5/96 OWNER Mr Hugh Hart (NEWMARKET) BRED Mrs A. Whitehead
**924 Grand Lad (IRE)** made no mistake this time and had burnt his only serious rival off soon after halfway, but was then always holding the runner-up. (4/5: Evens-5/4)
**Vax Star**, a useful sort, put in a most promising first effort but, despite running on, the winner always had her measure. She should be a different proposition next time. (9/1)
**Divide And Rule**, who looks the type to do better in time, ran quite well but failed to offer a serious threat. (33/1)
**Tickntima** showed something, staying on well in the last two furlongs to suggest that, with experience, improvement is likely. (33/1)
**Flo's Choice (IRE)** got a bit warm beforehand but was one of the few in the race to show any early pace. (33/1)
**1184 Rum Lad** threw any chances away by starting slowly. His action suggests that a bit more cut in the ground would not go amiss. (20/1)
**1328 Cauda Equina**, a heavy-topped colt, probably found this race coming too quickly after Goodwood and was done with entering the final two furlongs. He is a really nice sort and, if looks mean anything, he will do better in time. (2/1: op 5/4)
**Sandbaggedagain** never got into this, but showed enough to suggest that, with more experience, he will do a deal better. (100/1)

## 1526 RIPON THORPE PREBEND TRUST APPEAL CLAIMING STKS (3-Y.O) (Class F)
7-15 (7-16) **1m** £2,738.00 (£768.00: £374.00) Stalls: High GOING: 0.06 sec per fur (G)

| | | | | SP | RR | SF |
|---|---|---|---|---|---|---|
| *464[7]* | **Society Girl (62)** (CWThornton) **3-8-10** DeanMcKeown(7) (lw: chsd ldrs: led over 2f out tl ins fnl f: rallied to ld nr fin) | — | **1** | 11/1[3] | 66 | 26 |
| 1200[7] | **Lucky Bea (56)** (MWEasterby) **3-9-1** DaleGibson(15) (lw: in tch: swtchd & qcknd to ld ins fnl f: jst ct) | hd | **2** | 12/1 | 71 | 31 |
| 1152[4] | **Bold Enough (58)** (BWHills) **3-8-10** RHills(16) (lw: prom: squeezed thro to chal ins fnl f: no ex) | ¾ | **3** | 3/1[2] | 64 | 24 |

| | | | | SP | RR | SF |
|---|---|---|---|---|---|---|
| *$651^{6}$* | **Richard House Lad (46)** (RHollinshead) **3-8-5** WRyan(10) (lw: a.p: chal over 2f out: nt qckn ins fnl f) | 1½ | **4** | 25/1 | 56 | 16 |
| $1185^{W}$ | **Tabriz (71)** (JDBethell) **3-8-11**(3) SDrowne(2) (lw: cl up: led 4f out tl over 2f out: edgd rt: wknd fnl f) | 2½ | **5** | $13/8^{1}$ | 60 | 20 |
| $1122^{5}$ | **One Shot (IRE) (53)** (WRMuir) **3-8-7b1** Jean-PierreLopez(14) (a chsng ldrs: effrt & ch 2f out: btn appr fnl f) | 5 | **6** | 12/1 | 43 | 3 |
| $1067^{10}$ | **My Kind (45)** (NTinkler) **3-7-12b** KimTinkler(19) (plld hrd to st: sn rdn: bhd tl styd on fnl 2f) | 1¼ | **7** | 20/1 | 32 | — |
| | **Totally Yours (IRE)** (MRChannon) **3-8-10** KDarley(9) (w'like: lw: hdwy ½-wy: nvr nr to chal) | nk | **8** | 14/1 | 43 | 3 |
| | **Pulga Circo (45)** (BAMcMahon) **3-8-6** GCarter(17) (led tl hdd 4f out: wknd over 2f out) | ½ | **9** | 33/1 | 38 | — |
| $1196^{7}$ | **Forget Paris (IRE)** (BSRothwell) **3-9-0** JFanning(11) (bhd: hdwy over 3f out: nvr trbld ldrs) | 1½ | **10** | 14/1 | 43 | 3 |
| | **Shepherds Dean (IRE)** (PCHaslam) **3-7-7**(5) PFessey(3) (n.d) | 4 | **11** | 100/1 | 19 | — |
| $562^{14}$ | **Mill End Lady (49)** (MWEasterby) **3-8-5**(5) GParkin(13) (nvr trbld ldrs) | 3½ | **12** | 33/1 | 24 | — |
| | **Beacon Hill Lady** (BEllison) **3-8-10** NKennedy(1) (unf: s.s: n.d) | s.h | **13** | 33/1 | 24 | — |
| $1359^{11}$ | **Fiasco** (MJCamacho) **3-8-4** LCharnock(5) (n.d) | ½ | **14** | 12/1 | 17 | — |
| $1323^{9}$ | **New Regime (IRE)** (PTDalton) **3-8-2** GDuffield(6) (n.d) | 2 | **15** | 100/1 | 11 | — |
| $1067^{12}$ | **Turbo North (40)** (MDods) **3-7-10v**(7) IonaWands(12) (cl up: wandered u.p fnl 4f & wknd) | ¾ | **16** | 50/1 | 11 | — |
| | **Fisiostar** (MDods) **3-8-13** JCarroll(18) (b.hind: bit bkwd: chsd ldrs tl wknd fnl 4f) | ¾ | **17** | 50/1 | 19 | — |
| | **Baroness Gold (40)** (TDEasterby) **3-7-12b1** TWilliams(4) (bhd fr ½-wy: t.o) | dist | **18** | 33/1 | — | — |
| | ***The Oddfellow*** (NBycroft) **3-9-1** JFortune(8) (Withdrawn not under Starter's orders: ref to ent stalls) | | **W** | 66/1 | — | — |
| | | | | (SP 135.6%) | **18 Rn** | |

**1m 44.9** (7.20) CSF £133.89 TOTE £8.50: £2.50 £3.10 £1.50 (£31.10) Trio £17.90 OWNER Mr Guy Reed (MIDDLEHAM) BRED G. Reed

**Society Girl** has hardly set the world alight on the All-Weather, but she appreciated this return to grass, and showed fine courage to win. She should stay further. (11/1: 7/1-12/1)

**1089 Lucky Bea**, taken to post early as usual, looked to have it won when produced to lead entering the final furlong, but was just outbattled. (12/1)

**1152 Bold Enough** had her chances here, but just lacked a change of gear to take it. A bit further might help. (3/1: op 9/2)

**Richard House Lad**, who has failed to trouble the Judge previously, did show enough here to suggest that he is improving. (25/1)

**915 Tabriz** is a headstrong individual who had a lot of running to do from a poor draw, and finally cried enough in the last two furlongs. (13/8)

**1122 One Shot (IRE)**, tried in blinkers this time, called it a day with over a furlong left. (12/1)

**885 My Kind** looks a very hard ride. (20/1)

**974 Fiasco** (12/1: op 7/1)

## 1527 DELOITTE & TOUCHE H'CAP (0-70) (3-Y.O) (Class E)

7-45 (7-46) **6f** £3,225.00 (£975.00: £475.00: £225.00) Stalls: Low GOING minus 0.17 sec per fur (GF)

| | | | | SP | RR | SF |
|---|---|---|---|---|---|---|
| $1163^{10}$ | **Finisterre (IRE) (57)** (JJO'Neill) **3-8-8** KFallon(21) (lw: racd far side: in tch: hdwy to ld ins fnl f: drvn out) | — | **1** | 25/1 | 64 | 19 |
| $1101^{9}$ | **Power Game (64)** (JBerry) **3-9-1b1** JCarroll(20) (lw: chsd ldrs far side: chal over 1f out: kpt on wl) | ½ | **2** | 20/1 | 70 | 25 |
| 748* | **The Wad (62)** (DNicholls) **3-8-13** JFortune(2) (lw: led stands' side: hung bdly rt fnl 2f: kpt on) | 1¼ | **3** | $8/1^{3}$ | 64 | 19 |
| $1068^{7}$ | **Mullagh Hill Lad (IRE) (50)** (BAMcMahon) **3-8-1** GCarter(4) (chsd ldrs stands' side: carried rt fnl f: kpt on) | 2½ | **4** | $6/1^{2}$ | 46 | 1 |
| $1068^{2}$ | **Ivor's Deed (51)** (CFWall) **3-8-2** GDuffield(16) (lw: cl up far side: led wl over 1f out tl ins fnl f: no ex) | 1¾ | **5** | $11/2^{1}$ | 42 | — |
| $937^{12}$ | **Willisa (68)** (JDBethell) **3-9-5** JWeaver(9) (prom stands' side: rdn ½-wy: nt qckn) | 1 | **6** | 12/1 | 56 | 11 |
| $973^{5}$ | **Bowlers Boy (64)** (JJQuinn) **3-9-1** KDarley(15) (racd far side: chsd ldrs: led over 2f out tl wl over 1f out: grad wknd) | s.h | **7** | $8/1^{3}$ | 52 | 7 |
| $775^{14}$ | **Hobbs Choice (52)** (GMMoore) **3-8-3** DaleGibson(3) (racd stands side: nvr rchd ldrs) | hd | **8** | 16/1 | 40 | — |
| $644^{8}$ | **Mystique Smile (49)** (SCWilliams) **3-8-0**ow1 JTate(8) (racd stands' side: no imp fr ½-wy) | 1½ | **9** | 12/1 | 33 | — |
| $1363^{12}$ | **Oriole (49)** (NTinkler) **3-8-0b1** KimTinkler(5) (racd stands' side: n.d) | ¾ | **10** | 16/1 | 31 | — |
| *$857^{7}$* | **Bee Health Boy (59)** (MWEasterby) **3-8-5b**(5) GParkin(11) (chsd ldrs stands' side tl wknd fnl 2f) | hd | **11** | 25/1 | 41 | — |
| $762^{15}$ | **Harriet's Beau (45)** (MWEasterby) **3-7-10** LCharnock(1) (chsd ldrs stands' side 4f) | ¾ | **12** | 16/1 | 25 | — |
| | **Jenny's Charmer (50)** (SEKettlewell) **3-8-1** NKennedy(19) (w ldrs far side: hung lft & wknd 2½f) | 2½ | **13** | 25/1 | 23 | — |
| $1155^{7}$ | **Bollin Dorothy (70)** (TDEasterby) **3-9-7** MBirch(17) (racd far side: nvr nr to chal) | ½ | **14** | 20/1 | 42 | — |
| *$1492^{10}$* | **Frontman (IRE) (67)** (TDBarron) **3-8-11**(7) SBuckley(10) (racd stands' side: n.d) | nk | **15** | 25/1 | 38 | — |
| $867^{8}$ | **Mystic Times (55)** (MissJFCraze) **3-8-6** NConnorton(18) (led far side over 3f: wknd) | nk | **16** | 20/1 | 25 | — |
| $1340^{3}$ | **Hoh Majestic (IRE) (66)** (MartynWane) **3-9-3** DeanMcKeown(14) (lw: racd far side: bhd fr ½-wy) | s.h | **17** | 10/1 | 36 | — |
| $1312^{3}$ | **Napoleon's Return (47)** (AHarrison) **3-7-12**ow1 TWilliams(6) (racd stands' side: bhd fr ½-wy) | s.h | **18** | 16/1 | 17 | — |
| $1101^{10}$ | **Prime Partner (52)** (WRMuir) **3-8-3** RHills(13) (racd far side: n.d) | 5 | **19** | 10/1 | 9 | — |
| $1340^{5}$ | **Hickleton Miss (46)** (MrsVAAconley) **3-7-11** NCarlisle(12) (outpcd stands' side fr ½-wy) | 1¾ | **20** | 12/1 | — | — |
| $973^{12}$ | **Theatre Magic (60)** (SRBowring) **3-8-8b**(3) CTeague(7) (lw: cl up stands' side 4f: wknd qckly) | ¾ | **21** | 10/1 | 10 | — |
| | | | | (SP 155.4%) | **21 Rn** | |

**1m 14.7** (4.20) CSF £468.66 CT £4,040.52 TOTE £33.80: £6.10 £4.20 £2.10 £2.70 (£324.70) Trio £1,781.00 OWNER Les Femmes Fatales (PENRITH) BRED Mrs C. L. Weld

LONG HANDICAP Harriet's Beau 7-8

**1039 Finisterre (IRE)** needed this extra furlong and got some strong assistance from the saddle. (25/1)

**Power Game** had the blinkers on for the first time and they certainly made a difference, but the winner was just too determined for him. (20/1)

**748* The Wad** had the best of things up the stands' side, but did not help matters by hanging right in the last two furlongs. (8/1)

**Mullagh Hill Lad (IRE)** had his chances on the stands' side, but was not helped by The Wad carrying him across the track in the closing stages. (6/1: op 10/1)

**1068 Ivor's Deed**, always in the thick of things on the far side, was given plenty of encouragement from the saddle but was not good enough. (11/2)

**740* Willisa** had her chances, but always found this trip a bit too sharp. (12/1: 10/1-20/1)

**973 Bowlers Boy** has not, as yet, found luck going his way. (8/1)

**1155 Bollin Dorothy** never got into this, but was certainly not knocked about, and is one to keep an eye on. (20/1)

**1340 Hickleton Miss** (12/1: op 8/1)

## 1528 AMEC CIVIL ENGINEERING H'CAP (0-85) (3-Y.O+) (Class D)

8-15 (8-15) **1m** £3,870.00 (£1,170.00: £570.00: £270.00) Stalls: High GOING: 0.06 sec per fur (G)

| | | | | SP | RR | SF |
|---|---|---|---|---|---|---|
| $1313^{7}$ | **Ninia (USA) (69)** (MJohnston) **4-8-13** JWeaver(4) (lw: mde all: rdn & r.o wl fnl 2f) | — | **1** | 11/1 | 83 | 58 |
| $1322^{8}$ | **Sandmoor Chambray (73)** (TDEasterby) **5-9-3** MBirch(6) (chsd ldrs: hrd rdn & ch 2f out: kpt on one pce) | 4 | **2** | $7/2^{2}$ | 79 | 54 |

| | | | | SP | RR | SF |
|---|---|---|---|---|---|---|
| 967[10] | **Scaraben (69)** (SEKettlewell) **8-8-13** JFortune(2) (bhd: hdwy 3f out: chsng ldrs appr fnl f: kpt on) | 2 | **3** | 9/2[3] | 71 | 46 |
| 1157[9] | **So Amazing (63)** (JLEyre) **4-8-7** KFallon(7) (chsd ldrs: effrt 3f out: one pce) | 6 | **4** | 11/1 | 53 | 28 |
| 1069[16] | **Mountgate (76)** (MPBielby) **4-9-6** DeanMcKeown(5) (s.s: sme hdwy fnl 3f: n.d) | 6 | **5** | 25/1 | 54 | 29 |
| 994* | **Singapore Sting (USA) (77)** (HRACecil) **3-8-9** WRyan(1) (lw: hld up: effrt ½-wy: rdn & btn 2f out) | s.h | **6** | 2/1[1] | 55 | 18 |
| 682[12] | **Benfleet (82)** (RWArmstrong) **5-9-12** RHills(8) (a bhd) | 5 | **7** | 7/1 | 50 | 25 |
| *1048** | **Sooty Tern (69)** (JMBradley) **9-8-10**(3) SDrowne(3) (b.off fore: cl up tl wknd fnl 3f) | 13 | **8** | 11/2 | 11 | — |

(SP 122.1%) **8 Rn**

**1m 42.0** (4.30) CSF £49.17 CT £189.37 TOTE £10.40: £1.80 £1.70 £1.70 (£31.00) OWNER Mrs D. R. Schreiber (MIDDLEHAM) BRED Newgate Stud Farm Inc

WEIGHT FOR AGE 3yo-12lb

**Ninia (USA)**, back to her best here, got her own way out in front and won in great style. (11/1: op 7/1)

**933 Sandmoor Chambray**, a shade unlucky last time, was given every chance under some strong assistance, but found the winner too tough. (7/2)

**933 Scaraben** showed plenty of signs of coming back to form here. (9/2)

**So Amazing** has only ever won on the sand and never looked likely to rectify that here. (11/1)

**Mountgate** again gave problems by hanging, and failed to get anywhere near. (2[illegible]

**994* Singapore Sting (USA)** had plenty on here for a three-year-old and was d [illegible] tering the last couple of furlongs. (2/1)

## 1529 ST MARYGATE H'CAP (0-75) (4-Y.O+) (Class D)

8-45 (8-45) **2m** £3,690.70 (£1,117.60: £545.80: £259.90) Stalls: Low GOING: 0.06 sec per fur (G)

| | | | | SP | RR | SF |
|---|---|---|---|---|---|---|
| 1343* | **Zamhareer (USA) (47)** (WStorey) **5-7-9**(7) 5x IonaWands(6) (lw: w ldr: led over 5f out: r.o strly) | — | **1** | 11/4[2] | 62 | 37 |
| 1436[2] | **Embryonic (IRE) (75)** (RFFisher) **4-10-0** JFortune(10) (lw: in tch: effrt 4f out: styd on wl: no ch w wnr) | 6 | **2** | 9/1 | 84 | 57 |
| 1091[4] | **Jalcanto (56)** (MrsMReveley) **6-8-4**(7) SCopp(7) (hld up & bhd: hdwy 4f out: edgd rt: styd on: nvr nrr) | 1¼ | **3** | 12/1 | 64 | 39 |
| 1005[11] | **Anglesey Sea View (66)** (ABailey) **7-9-4**(3) DWright(2) (hdwy 10f out: rdn over 3f out: styd on: no imp) | 2 | **4** | 14/1 | 72 | 47 |
| 1194[14] | **Nijmegen (63)** (JGFitzGerald) **8-9-4b** KFallon(5) (b: chsd ldrs: effrt 4f out: wknd fnl 2f) | 1¾ | **5** | 8/1 | 67 | 42 |
| 1150* | **Opaque (69)** (LMCumani) **4-9-8** JWeaver(4) (lw: in tch: hdwy to chse ldrs 3f out: sn rdn & btn) | 5 | **6** | 13/8[1] | 68 | 41 |
| 1158[3] | **Sea Victor (74)** (JLHarris) **4-9-13v** WRyan(1) (chsd ldrs tl wknd over 3f out) | 1¾ | **7** | 12/1 | 71 | 44 |
| 1159[8] | **Gallardini (IRE) (44)** (BSRothwell) **7-7-13** LCharnock(8) (effrt ent st: outpcd fnl 4f) | ¾ | **8** | 33/1 | 41 | 16 |
| 1158* | **Uncle Doug (53)** (MrsMReveley) **5-8-8** KDarley(3) (swtg: lw: wnt lft s: hld up & bhd: hdwy 4f out: wknd fnl 2f) | ¾ | **9** | 11/2[3] | 49 | 24 |
| 1019[9] | **Kadari (41)** (WClay) **7-7-10v** NCarlisle(9) (led tl hdd over 5f out: sn wknd) | 8 | **10** | 50/1 | 29 | 4 |

(SP 128.2%) **10 Rn**

**3m 36.2** (11.20) CSF £28.43 CT £250.58 TOTE £4.90: £1.80 £2.10 £2.50 (£25.50) Trio £43.00 OWNER Mr D. C. Batey (CONSETT) BRED Mrs Jackie Ward Ramos

LONG HANDICAP Kadari 7-9

WEIGHT FOR AGE 4yo-2lb

**1343* Zamhareer (USA)** is getting better with every run and really enjoyed the strong pace here. (11/4)

**1436 Embryonic (IRE)** is a game sort who stays well, but the winner was always too good for him at these weights. (9/1)

**1091 Jalcanto** struggled on under pressure, but did not help matters by hanging right, and failed to get in a serious blow. (12/1)

**Anglesey Sea View** is at last beginning to drop down the handicap, but still found the effort here beyond her. (14/1)

**Nijmegen** ran a good deal better than last time but, after being up with the strong pace here, was found out entering the last couple of furlongs. (8/1: op 14/1)

**1150* Opaque** had his limitations exposed in this strongly-run event. (13/8)

**1158* Uncle Doug** was very warm beforehand and obviously not in the right mood, as he showed little. (11/2)

## 1530 ST AGNESGATE MAIDEN STKS (3-Y.O+) (Class D)

9-15 (9-17) **1m 2f** £4,028.70 (£1,221.60: £597.80: £285.90) Stalls: High GOING: 0.06 sec per fur (G)

| | | | | SP | RR | SF |
|---|---|---|---|---|---|---|
| 1180[4] | **Arctiid (USA)** (JHMGosden) **3-8-10** RHills(7) (mde all: qcknd over 3f out: easily) | — | **1** | 4/5[1] | 76+ | 19 |
| | **Irish Sea (USA)** (MRStoute) **3-8-10** DeanMcKeown(13) (unf: mid div: hdwy over 3f out: r.o: no ch w wnr) | 2½ | **2** | 14/1 | 72 | 15 |
| | **Dragon's Back (IRE)** (MrsJCecil) **3-8-10** TIves(15) (sn chsng ldrs: effrt over 3f out: r.o one pce) | 2½ | **3** | 9/1 | 68 | 11 |
| 1104[17] | **Secondment** (LMCumani) **3-8-10b**[1] OUrbina(9) (a chsng ldrs: rdn over 3f out: one pce fnl 2f) | 1¾ | **4** | 66/1 | 65 | 8 |
| 974[6] | **Baraqueta** (JLEyre) **4-9-7**(3) OPears(11) (hdwy 3f out: styd on: nrst fin) | 3 | **5** | 200/1 | 60 | 17 |
| 1182[7] | **Lead Story (IRE)** (EALDunlop) **3-8-10** KFallon(4) (mid div: outpcd over 3f out: kpt on wl appr fnl f) | s.h | **6** | 12/1 | 60 | 3 |
| | **Arktikos (IRE)** (JHMGosden) **3-8-10** JCarroll(17) (w'like: str: bit bkwd: dwlt: hdwy appr st: rdn over 3f out: kpt on one pce) | 1½ | **7** | 25/1 | 58 | 1 |
| | **Berlin Blue** (JWWatts) **3-8-10** GDuffield(16) (w'like: str: bit bkwd: hdwy appr st: sn prom: lost pl 4f out: kpt on fnl 2f) | 1½ | **8** | 33/1 | 56 | — |
| 1079[6] | **Ingrina** (HRACecil) **3-8-5** WRyan(3) (s.i.s: hdwy appr st: no imp) | 1¾ | **9** | 7/1[2] | 48 | — |
| | **Attalos** (HRACecil) **3-8-10** AMcGlone(12) (tall: lengthy: unf: b.hind: chsd ldrs tl wknd fnl 3f) | nk | **10** | 8/1[3] | 52 | — |
| | **Filly Mignonne (IRE)** (BWHills) **3-8-5** GCarter(14) (unf: s.i.s: nvr nr to chal) | ½ | **11** | 10/1 | 46 | — |
| | **Fatehalkhair (IRE) (45)** (BEllison) **4-9-10** NKennedy(2) (plld hrd: jnd ldrs appr st: wknd over 2f out) | 2½ | **12** | 66/1 | 47 | 4 |
| | **Karaylar (IRE)** (WStorey) **4-9-10** JFanning(8) (a rr div) | 2½ | **13** | 50/1 | 43 | — |
| | **South Pagoda (IRE)** (DNicholls) **3-8-10** AlexGreaves(5) (bit bkwd: s.i.s: n.d) | 7 | **14** | 33/1 | 32 | — |
| 1035[4] | **Hot Dogging** (MrsPSly) **3-8-5** ACulhane(1) (lost tch fr ½-wy) | 16 | **15** | 200/1 | 2 | — |
| | **Kayf** (LMCumani) **3-8-5** KDarley(6) (unf: s.i.s: gd hdwy 4f out: wnt lame & virtually p.u fnl 3f) | 5 | **16** | 7/1[2] | — | — |
| | **Ballysokerry (IRE)** (JParkes) **5-9-10** LCharnock(10) (bit bkwd: unruly s: cl up to ½-wy: wknd qckly) | 2½ | **17** | 300/1 | — | — |

(SP 141.1%) **17 Rn**

**2m 13.5** (10.00) CSF £16.48 TOTE £2.30: £1.20 £2.50 £2.40 (£16.90) Trio £38.80 OWNER Sheikh Mohammed (NEWMARKET) BRED Clovelly Farms

WEIGHT FOR AGE 3yo-14lb

**1180 Arctiid (USA)** looked very useful indeed here and is obviously getting the hang of things. He looks one to follow. (4/5: op 5/4)

**Irish Sea (USA)** ran a decent first race and kept responding to pressure, but the winner was in a different league. (14/1: op 8/1)

**Dragon's Back (IRE)** took a strongish hold and ran pretty well. He looks likely to be all the better for it. (9/1: 12/1-7/1)

**Secondment** had blinkers on for the first time and they made a difference, but there is still some way to go. (66/1)

**Baraqueta**, who showed nothing on his debut, put in a much-improved performance this time, making ground all the way up the straight. (200/1)

**1182 Lead Story (IRE)** was very green when the pace increased early in the straight and never looked likely to offer a threat. Experience should improve him. (12/1: op 8/1)

**Arktikos (IRE)** needed this, fitness and experience wise, and time should see better. (25/1)
**Berlin Blue** got messed about, losing ground early in the straight, and was then wisely not overpunished. (33/1)
**1079 Ingrina** (7/1: 6/1-9/1)
**Kayf** (7/1: op 4/1)

T/Plpt: £545.50 (30.93 Tckts). T/Qdpt: £76.50 (15.79 Tckts). AA

# 1398-BRIGHTON (L-H) (Good, Good to firm patches)

## Thursday May 30th

WEATHER: warm WIND: slt half bhd

## 1531 E.B.F. FRESHFIELD MEDIAN AUCTION MAIDEN STKS (2-Y.O) (Class E)

2-10 (2-10) **5f 213y** £3,042.90 (£907.20: £432.60: £195.30) Stalls: Low GOING minus 0.48 sec per fur (F)

| | | | | SP | RR | SF |
|---|---|---|---|---|---|---|
| 865[2] | **Dalmeny Dancer** (BJMeehan) **2-9-0** BDoyle(2) (mde all: clr over 1f out: comf) | — | **1** | 3/1[3] | 74+ | 15 |
| | **Kenwood Melody** (MBell) **2-9-0** MFenton(3) (leggy: lw: chsd wnr: rdn over 2f out: unable qckn) | 4 | **2** | 9/4[1] | 63 | 4 |
| | **Chain Reaction (IRE)** (MAJarvis) **2-8-9** PBloomfield(4) (w'like: scope: bit bkwd: a.p: rdn over 2f out: one pce) | 1¾ | **3** | 12/1 | 54 | — |
| | **Castles Burning (USA)** (CACyzer) **2-9-0** GDuffield(6) (str: scope: bkwd: outpcd: hdwy over 1f out: nvr nrr) | 2 | **4** | 8/1 | 53 | — |
| | **Fly Down To Rio (IRE)** (DWPArbuthnot) **2-8-6**(3) DarrenMoffatt(8) (b.hind: neat: bit bkwd: prom over 3f) | 6 | **5** | 25/1 | 32 | — |
| 1453[6] | **Dive Master (IRE)** (CMurray) **2-9-0** MTebbutt(1) (outpcd) | 1¾ | **6** | 25/1 | 32 | — |
| 590[6] | **Emmas Breeze** (CADwyer) **2-8-9** DHarrison(5) (s.s: a bhd) | 2½ | **7** | 50/1 | 21 | — |
| | **Big Ben** (RHannon) **2-9-0** RHughes(7) (neat: lw: hld up: rdn over 2f out: wknd over 1f out) | ¾ | **8** | 5/2[2] | 24 | — |
| | | | | (SP 112.8%) | **8 Rn** | |

**1m 10.0** (2.80) CSF £9.72 TOTE £3.40: £1.20 £2.00 £1.50 (£4.60) OWNER Thurloe Thoroughbreds (UPPER LAMBOURN) BRED Highclere Stud and Side Hill Stud

**865 Dalmeny Dancer** made his experience tell. In front from the start, he was ridden clear below the distance to win with plenty to spare. (3/1: 6/4-7/2)
**Kenwood Melody**, a tall colt who cost 30,000 guineas, is a half-brother to Baddi Bird who won five races in France at two and three years. A small race can be found for him. (9/4: 6/4-5/2)
**Chain Reaction (IRE)**, a good-bodied filly who would have been the pick on physical looks, unfortunately did not look fully fit. (12/1: 8/1-16/1)
**Castles Burning (USA)**, a very well-built two-year-old who could easily have been mistaken for a chaser, looked far from fit and is not the type of horse suited to this trappy switchback track. Totally taken off his feet, he stayed on in the last furlong and a half. (8/1: 12/1-5/1)
**Fly Down To Rio (IRE)**, a narrow filly carrying some condition, showed up well until tiring over two furlongs from home. (25/1)
**Big Ben** (5/2: 2/1-3/1)

## 1532 SHOREHAM LIMITED STKS (0-65) (3-Y.O+) (Class F)

2-40 (2-40) **6f 209y** £2,381.00 (£656.00: £311.00) Stalls: Low GOING minus 0.48 sec per fur (F)

| | | | | SP | RR | SF |
|---|---|---|---|---|---|---|
| 1485* | **Farmost (61)** (SirMarkPrescott) **3-8-13** 2x GDuffield(6) (lw: chsd ldr: led over 2f out: clr over 1f out: r.o wl) | — | **1** | 4/6[1] | 82 | 47 |
| 1314[8] | **Mr Nevermind (IRE) (64)** (GLMoore) **6-9-10** SWhitworth(5) (lw: rdn over 2f out: hdwy over 1f out: r.o one pce) | 5 | **2** | 25/1 | 71 | 47 |
| 1010[9] | **Crystal Heights (FR) (64)** (RJO'Sullivan) **8-9-8** SSanders(10) (hld up: rdn over 2f out: one pce) | ¾ | **3** | 20/1 | 67 | 43 |
| 1302[16] | **Perilous Plight (61)** (WRMuir) **5-9-10** Jean-PierreLopez(7) (lw: rdn over 2f out: hdwy fnl f: r.o wl) | 1½ | **4** | 14/1 | 65 | 41 |
| 1010[11] | **Office Hours (64)** (CACyzer) **4-9-6** GHind(8) (a.p: rdn over 2f out: one pce) | ½ | **5** | 16/1 | 60 | 36 |
| 1348[9] | **Move With Edes (65)** (WGMTurner) **4-9-6** TSprake(9) (prom over 4f) | 1 | **6** | 12/1[3] | 58 | 34 |
| 1074* | **Apollo Red (56)** (AMoore) **7-9-10** CandyMorris(2) (swtg: led over 4f: wknd fnl f) | ¾ | **7** | 9/2[2] | 60 | 36 |
| 1033[7] | **Pigeon Hole (60)** (RHannon) **3-8-3**(3) DaneO'Neill(1) (prom over 4f) | 2½ | **8** | 14/1 | 47 | 12 |
| | **Need You Badly (62)** (SPCWoods) **3-8-6** WWoods(4) (shkn up over 2f out: nvr plcd to chal) | 6 | **9** | 33/1 | 34 | — |
| 1348[5] | **Morocco (IRE) (60)** (MRChannon) **7-9-8** RHughes(3) (bhd fnl 3f) | 26 | **10** | 12/1[3] | — | — |
| | | | | (SP 124.3%) | **10 Rn** | |

**1m 20.7** (0.70) CSF £19.44 TOTE £1.60: £1.20 £5.20 £2.50 (£13.30) Trio £35.00 OWNER Mr W. E. Sturt (NEWMARKET) BRED Hesmonds Stud Ltd

WEIGHT FOR AGE 3yo-11lb

OFFICIAL EXPLANATION **Morocco (IRE): was never travelling throughout the race.**

**1485* Farmost** again looked extremely well and had no problems following up Monday's win at Sandown. He is obviously something of a lazy individual as Duffield was having to nudge him along for the vast majority of the race. Showing in second place until kicked into the lead over two furlongs from home, he forged clear below the distance to win with plenty in hand. (4/6: 10/11-Evens)
**747 Mr Nevermind (IRE)** began to find his feet in the last two furlongs and stayed on for second prize, if having no chance with the winner. (25/1)
**633 Crystal Heights (FR)**, a lot closer than normal, chased the leaders but failed to find a vital turn of foot in the last two furlongs. (20/1)
**1010* Perilous Plight** was still out with the washing below the distance, but he found his feet in fine style in the final furlong and came flying through for fourth prize. (14/1: 8/1-16/1)
**756 Office Hours** could only go up and down in the same place in the last two furlongs. (16/1)
**1099 Move With Edes** (12/1: 8/1-14/1)
**Need You Badly** was certainly looked after by her jockey on this seasonal bow. Held up at the back of the field, her jockey did wiggle about a bit over two furlongs from home, before allowing the filly to complete in his own time. She is sure to come on in leaps and bounds for this and certainly looks one to note in a small race, especially if tried over a bit further. (33/1)
**1348 Morocco (IRE)** (12/1: op 6/1)

## 1533 FLANAGAN AND ALLEN H'CAP (0-60) (3-Y.O+) (Class F)

3-10 (3-12) **7f 214y** £3,142.60 (£873.60: £419.80) Stalls: Low GOING minus 0.48 sec per fur (F)

| | | | | SP | RR | SF |
|---|---|---|---|---|---|---|
| 1074[2] | **Bubble Wings (FR) (57)** (SPCWoods) **4-9-11** VSmith(10) (hdwy 2f out: led ins fnl f: rdn out) | — | **1** | 7/2[1] | 69 | 41 |
| 1010[2] | **Rocky Waters (USA) (53)** (PBurgoyne) **7-9-7** CHodgson(1) (b.hind: led over 6f out tl ins fnl f: r.o) | 1 | **2** | 5/1[2] | 63 | 35 |
| 1074[8] | **Edgar Kirby (53)** (PWHarris) **5-9-7** NDay(2) (hdwy over 2f out: hrd rdn over 1f out: unable qckn) | 1½ | **3** | 12/1 | 60 | 32 |
| 1010[3] | **College Night (IRE) (51)** (CADwyer) **4-9-5** CDwyer(13) (a.p: rdn over 2f out: one pce) | ¾ | **4** | 5/1[2] | 57 | 29 |
| 1121[2] | **Jaazim (53)** (MMadgwick) **6-9-7** AProcter(6) (nt clr run & hmpd over 2f out: hdwy over 1f out: hmpd 1f out: r.o) | ¾ | **5** | 7/1[3] | 57 | 29 |

| | | | | SP | RR | SF |
|---|---|---|---|---|---|---|
| $1314^{14}$ | **Labudd (USA) (46)** (RIngram) **6-9-0** NAdams(4) (b: s.s: hdwy over 1f out: n.m.r on ins fnl f: nt rcvr) | hd | **6** | 25/1 | 50 | 22 |
| $1302^{6}$ | **Gentle Irony (55)** (MJRyan) **4-9-9** DBiggs(7) (hld up: n.m.r over 2f out: nt clr rn & swtchd rt over 1f out: one pce) | ¾ | **7** | 14/1 | 57 | 29 |
| $1302^{17}$ | **Napoleon Star (IRE) (60)** (MSSaunders) **5-10-0** RPrice(15) (lw: nvr nr to chal) | ½ | **8** | 33/1 | 61 | 33 |
| $888^{7}$ | **Miss Laughter (51)** (JWHills) **4-9-5** OUrbina(12) (swtg: led over 1f: hrd rdn over 1f out: wknd fnl f) | nk | **9** | 14/1 | 52 | 24 |
| $1074^{12}$ | **Persian Affair (IRE) (57)** (TJNaughton) **5-9-11** MWigham(5) (nvr nrr) | 2½ | **10** | 7/1 3 | 53 | 25 |
| $1092^{10}$ | **Rupiana (IRE) (55)** (CMurray) **4-9-9** CNutter(8) (prom over 4f) | s.h | **11** | 50/1 | 51 | 23 |
| *$499^{11}$* | **Tandridge (IRE) (45)** (JRJenkins) **4-8-13** Jean-PierreLopez(14) (a bhd) | ½ | **12** | 50/1 | 40 | 12 |
| | **Current Leader (58)** (RHannon) **3-9-0** RPerham(3) (prom 5f: wkng whn hmpd over 2f out & wl over 1f out) | 1¼ | **13** | 10/1 | 50 | 10 |
| $1173^{14}$ | **Rasmi (CAN) (53)** (PHowling) **5-9-7** FNorton(9) (lw: a bhd) | 2½ | **14** | 50/1 | 40 | 12 |
| | **Indian Serenade (49)** (THind) **5-9-3** JFEgan(11) (bhd fnl 2f) | 14 | **15** | 20/1 | 8 | — |
| | | | | (SP 128.1%) | **15 Rn** | |

**1m 34.6** (2.40) CSF £21.44 CT £183.66 TOTE £4.30: £1.70 £3.40 £3.10 (£14.10) Trio £152.90 OWNER Dr Frank Chao (NEWMARKET) BRED H. S. Verrerie, Gue Foulon and Florent Couturier
WEIGHT FOR AGE 3yo-12lb

**1074 Bubble Wings (FR)** began her run a quarter of a mile from home. Coming through to lead inside the final furlong, she was ridden along to assert. (7/2)
**1010 Rocky Waters (USA)** was soon at the head of affairs. Eventually overhauled inside the final furlong, he stuck on well to the line. (5/1)
**713 Edgar Kirby** picked up ground over a quarter of a mile from home, but failed to find another gear in the last 200 yards. (12/1: op 7/1)
**1010 College Night (IRE)** failed to quicken in the last two furlong. She is still looking for that elusive first victory. (5/1)
**1121 Jaazim** had more traffic problems than the M25. Having met with interference over a quarter of a mile from home, he was picking up ground when again done no favours entering the final furlong. In the circumstances, he did extremely well to finish fifth. (7/1)
**Labudd (USA)** picked up ground along the inside below the distance but, with little room in which to manoeuvre in the final furlong, his jockey had little option but to sit and suffer. (25/1)
**1302 Gentle Irony** (14/1: 10/1-16/1)
**Miss Laughter** (14/1: 10/1-16/1)
**Current Leader** (10/1: 7/1-11/1)

## 1534 SEAFORD (S) H'CAP (0-60) (3-Y.O+) (Class G)

3-40 (3-44) **1m 3f 196y** £2,070.00 (£570.00: £270.00) Stalls: High GOING minus 0.48 sec per fur (F)

| | | | | SP | RR | SF |
|---|---|---|---|---|---|---|
| $1047^{12}$ | **Colour Counsellor (42)** (RMFlower) **3-7-5**(5) CAdamson(2) (a.p: chsd ldr 5f out: led 1f out: r.o wl) | — | **1** | 20/1 | 53 | 20 |
| *$1098^{4}$* | **Watch Me Go (IRE) (40)** (BobJones) **7-8-11** MWigham(13) (b: lw: reminder 6f out: hdwy over 1f out: r.o wl ins fnl f) | 3 | **2** | 9/2 2 | 47 | 31 |
| $1347^{17}$ | **Bag of Tricks (IRE) (53)** (SDow) **6-9-10** RHughes(9) (s.s: hdwy over 2f out: hrd rdn over 1f out: r.o one pce) | s.h | **3** | 11/2 | 60 | 44 |
| $1173^{9}$ | **The Little Ferret (47)** (AMoore) **6-9-4** RPerham(5) (hld up: hrd rdn over 2f out: one pce fnl f) | 1½ | **4** | 11/1 | 52 | 36 |
| | **Hillswick (30)** (JSKing) **5-8-1** BDoyle(1) (lw: a.p: hrd rdn over 2f out: one pce fnl f) | 1½ | **5** | 33/1 | 33 | 17 |
| *$485^{4}$* | **Harlequin Walk (IRE) (34)** (RJO'Sullivan) **5-8-2b**(3)ow1 DaneO'Neill(8) (lw: led: clr 6f out: wknd & hdd 1f out) | 3 | **6** | 11/4 1 | 33 | 16 |
| $890^{10}$ | **Eskimo Kiss (IRE) (42)** (MJFetherston-Godley) **3-7-10b1** FNorton(10) (hdwy over 4f out: rdn over 3f out: one pce) | hd | **7** | 33/1 | 41 | 8 |
| $1347^{5}$ | **Sinclair Lad (IRE) (39)** (RJHodges) **8-8-10b** TSprake(14) (lw: a mid div) | 11 | **8** | 5/1 3 | 23 | 7 |
| *$54^{8}$* | **Kenyatta (USA) (25)** (AMoore) **7-7-10** NAdams(4) (b: hld up: rdn 5f out: sn wknd) | 2 | **9** | 20/1 | 6 | — |
| $1159^{6}$ | **Checkpoint Charlie (34)** (JMPEustace) **11-8-5** DRMcCabe(3) (s.s: nvr nrr) | 3 | **10** | 14/1 | 11 | — |
| $1124^{8}$ | **Grandes Oreilles (IRE) (49)** (NJHWalker) **4-9-3b1**(3) JStack(7) (lw: chsd ldr 7f) | 4 | **11** | 25/1 | 21 | 5 |
| | **Tommyknocker (IRE) (30)** (JRJenkins) **4-7-10v1**(5) MHenry(6) (a bhd) | 4 | **12** | 33/1 | — | — |
| *$23^{13}$* | **Tudor Flight (39)** (AGNewcombe) **5-8-5**(5) DGriffiths(16) (bhd fnl 6f) | 10 | **13** | 12/1 | — | — |
| *$899^{8}$* | **Driftholme (43)** (GLMoore) **3-7-6**(5)ow1 MBaird(15) (prom 6f) | 13 | **14** | 33/1 | — | — |
| $983^{7}$ | **Well Suited (34)** (THind) **6-8-5** SSanders(11) (b: a bhd) | 5 | **15** | 20/1 | — | — |
| | | | | (SP 129.5%) | **15 Rn** | |

**2m 30.9** (3.30) CSF £105.60 CT £530.17 TOTE £31.70: £7.00 £2.10 £2.50 (£49.90) Trio £147.20 OWNER Mrs G. M. Temmerman (JEVINGTON) BRED M. A. Kirby
LONG HANDICAP Eskimo Kiss (IRE) 7-0 Driftholme 6-10 Colour Counsellor 7-8
WEIGHT FOR AGE 3yo-17lb
No bid

**OFFICIAL EXPLANATION Colour Counsellor: accounting for the gelding's apparent improvement, his trainer explained that it has taken him time to recover from a hard campaign as a two-year-old, but also benefitted from being run over a mile and a half for the first time. On his last run he had suffered from interference early on and thereafter lost interest, but on this occasion he had a clear run.**
**Colour Counsellor** left previous form well behind. Moving into second place five furlongs from home, he still had it all to do to catch the clear leader but, with that rival tying up badly below the distance, he swept into the lead a furlong out and quickly asserted. (20/1)
**1098 Watch Me Go (IRE)**, given a reminder at halfway, was still miles off the leaders two furlongs from home. Picking up ground below the distance, he found his feet inside the final furlong and came through to snatch second place on the line. (9/2)
**745* Bag of Tricks (IRE)**, a quirky customer at the best of times, stayed on in the straight and only just failed to take second place. (11/2: op 7/2)
**1012 The Little Ferret** chased the leaders. Hard ridden over a quarter of a mile from home as he grimly tried to get on terms, he was tapped for toe in the last 200 yards. (11/1: 8/11-12/1)
**Hillswick**, fit from hurdling, was never far away. Coming under strong pressure over two furlongs from home, he was almost on terms entering the final furlong before tapped for toe. (33/1)
**485 Harlequin Walk (IRE)** dictated matters from the front and appeared to have an unassailable lead at halfway. She was still miles clear going to the last two furlongs but she tied up badly below the distance and, collared a furlong out, folded up in a heap. (11/4)

## 1535 REGENCY MEDIAN AUCTION MAIDEN STKS (3-Y.O) (Class F)

4-10 (4-11) **7f 214y** £2,381.00 (£656.00: £311.00) Stalls: Low GOING minus 0.48 sec per fur (F)

| | | | | SP | RR | SF |
|---|---|---|---|---|---|---|
| | **Corniche Quest (IRE) (52)** (MRChannon) **3-8-9** RHughes(6) (led 6f out: hrd rdn over 1f out: r.o wl) | — | **1** | 20/1 | 61 | 30 |
| $1119^{4}$ | **Bright Eclipse (USA) (54)** (JWHills) **3-8-9**(5) MHenry(4) (led 2f: ev ch over 2f out: hrd rdn & hung lft over 1f out: r.o ins fnl f) | ½ | **2** | 11/4 2 | 65 | 34 |
| *$856^{3}$* | **Allstars Express** (TJNaughton) **3-9-0** DHarrison(1) (hld up: rdn over 2f out: unable qckn) | 1¾ | **3** | 9/2 3 | 62 | 31 |

| | | | SP | RR | SF |
|---|---|---|---|---|---|
| 1142[13] | **Witherkay** (RHannon) **3-8-11**(3) DaneO'Neill(7) (hdwy 4f out: hung rt 3f out: wkng whn hung lft over 1f out)....5 | **4** | 8/1 | 52 | 21 |
| | **Halebid** (SPCWoods) **3-9-0** WWoods(9) (bit bkwd: nvr nr to chal)....4 | **5** | 5/2[1] | 43 | 12 |
| | **Happy Venturer (IRE)** (CMurray) **3-9-0** MTebbutt(2) (w'like: bit bkwd: nvr nrr)....nk | **6** | 20/1 | 43 | 12 |
| 1356[3] | **Red Time (55)** (MSSaunders) **3-9-0** RPrice(5) (prom over 5f)....13 | **7** | 8/1 | 17 | — |
| 1171[14] | **Sea Idol (IRE)** (PFICole) **3-8-9** JFEgan(3) (hdwy over 3f out: hrd rdn over 2f out: sn wknd)....6 | **8** | 8/1 | — | — |
| 583[16] | **Challenger (IRE)** (TJNaughton) **3-9-0** SWhitworth(8) (lw: bhd fnl 3f)....2½ | **9** | 33/1 | — | — |

(SP 119.2%) **9 Rn**

**1m 34.2** (2.00) CSF £72.64 TOTE £10.60: £1.60 £1.90 £2.20 (£19.10) Trio £26.30 OWNER Mr M. Bishop (UPPER LAMBOURN) BRED K. Molloy

**Corniche Quest (IRE)**, who failed to score as a two-year-old, made no mistake on this seasonal bow. Soon at the head of affairs, she came under pressure over a furlong out but kept on just too well for the runner-up. (20/1)

**1119 Bright Eclipse (USA)** looked ill-at-ease on this switchback course. In front early, he had every chance over a quarter of a mile from home but he did not appear to be enjoying things and hung in behind the winner below the distance. His jockey had difficulty straightening him, but the colt did run on inside the final furlong. (11/4)

**856 Allstars Express** chased the leaders, but never looked like finding the necessary turn of foot in the last two furlongs. (9/2)

**Witherkay** moved up at halfway but he hung into the centre of the track early in the straight and was already a spent force when then drifting back left below the distance. (8/1: 4/1-9/1)

**1356 Red Time** (8/1: op 9/2)

**Sea Idol (IRE)** (8/1: 7/1-14/1)

## 1536 CLAYTON H'CAP (0-70) (3-Y.O+) (Class E)

4-40 (4-40) **5f 213y** £3,042.90 (£907.20: £432.60: £195.30) Stalls: Low GOING minus 0.48 sec per fur (F)

| | | | SP | RR | SF |
|---|---|---|---|---|---|
| 981[8] | **Always Grace (56)** (MissGayKelleway) **4-8-12**(3) DaneO'Neill(3) (s.s: hdwy over 1f out: str run to ld wl ins fnl f: r.o wl)....— | **1** | 14/1 | 62 | 27 |
| 1013* | **Lorins Gold (39)** (AndrewTurnell) **6-7-7**(5)ow2 MHenry(9) (a.p: led over 2f out tl wl over 1f out: hrd rdn: ev ch wl ins fnl f: unable qckn)....1¼ | **2** | 5/1[3] | 42 | 5 |
| *461*[6] | **Random (51)** (CJames) **5-8-10** JFEgan(10) (hld up: rdn over 2f out: ev ch wl ins fnl f: one pce)....nk | **3** | 16/1 | 53 | 18 |
| 1412[W] | **Rififi (62)** (RIngram) **3-8-12** SWhitworth(4) (lw: hld up: rdn over 2f out: led wl over 1f out tl wl ins fnl f: one pce)....¾ | **4** | 11/2 | 62 | 18 |
| 1351[3] | **Astral Invader (IRE) (53)** (MSSaunders) **4-8-12** RPrice(2) (lw: a.p: rdn over 3f out: r.o ins fnl f)....nk | **5** | 12/1 | 52 | 17 |
| 1074[7] | **Dancing Heart (69)** (BJMeehan) **4-10-0b** BDoyle(6) (rdn over 2f out: hdwy over 1f out: r.o ins fnl f)....½ | **6** | 10/1 | 67 | 32 |
| 1073[10] | **Sharp Imp (51)** (RMFlower) **6-8-10b** DBiggs(7) (stumbled bdly 5f out: a bhd)....3½ | **7** | 12/1 | 39 | 4 |
| 1049[7] | **Dancing Jack (52)** (JJBridger) **3-7-13**(3) DarrenMoffatt(5) (lw: hld up: hrd rdn over 2f out: wknd over 1f out)....1¼ | **8** | 10/1 | 37 | — |
| 1073[8] | **Agwa (68)** (RJO'Sullivan) **7-9-13** SSanders(1) (led over 3f: wknd over 1f out)....1½ | **9** | 3/1[1] | 49 | 14 |
| 1009* | **No Sympathy (52)** (GLMoore) **3-8-2** MFenton(8) (lw: bhd fnl 2f)....2½ | **10** | 4/1[2] | 26 | — |

(SP 123.2%) **10 Rn**

**1m 9.2** (2.00) CSF £80.46 CT £1,081.31 TOTE £15.10: £3.30 £2.00 £9.40 (£59.40) Trio £120.20 OWNER Easy Going Partnership (WHITCOMBE) BRED Zetland Stud

LONG HANDICAP Lorins Gold 7-8

WEIGHT FOR AGE 3yo-9lb

**592 Always Grace** was certainly put to sleep at the back of the field and his jockey was still not do anything on her a quarter of a mile from home. She appeared to have absolutely no chance, but she certainly found another gear from below the distance and came storming through to snatch the spoils in the last 50 yards. (14/1: 8/1-16/1)

**1013* Lorins Gold** showed in front soon after halfway. Collared early in the final quarter-mile, he refused to give way and was back on level terms with the leader when the winner swept past in the last 50 yards. (5/1)

**Random** chased the leaders and had just poked a whisker in front in the closing stages when the winner swept by. (16/1)

**1101 Rififi** gained control early in the final quarter-mile, but he failed to pull away from his rivals and, once collared in the last 50 yards, was swamped for toe. (11/2)

**1351 Astral Invader (IRE)** was in serious trouble before halfway but, to his credit, he got his second wind inside the final furlong and kept on well. (12/1: op 7/1)

**Dancing Heart** found this trip too short for him. He was doing all his best work in the last furlong and a half but, by then, it was too late. Seven furlongs is his ideal distance. (10/1: 5/1-12/1)

**Sharp Imp** (12/1: 8/1-14/1)

T/Jkpt: Not won; £18,199.11 to Catterick 31/5/96. T/Plpt: £162.50 (94.03 Tckts). T/Qdpt: £40.50 (21.59 Tckts). AK

# 1038-CARLISLE (R-H) (Good, Good to firm patches)

## Thursday May 30th

WEATHER: fine WIND: slt half against

## 1537 TUCK SHOP MAIDEN AUCTION STKS (2-Y.O) (Class E)

2-20 (2-23) **5f 207y** £2,982.00 (£903.00: £441.00: £210.00) Stalls: Centre GOING minus 0.03 sec per fur (G)

| | | | SP | RR | SF |
|---|---|---|---|---|---|
| 1179[5] | **Dashing Rocksville** (MRChannon) **2-7-12** AMackay(9) (sn outpcd & rdn along: gd hdwy over 1f out: styd on wl to ld post)....— | **1** | 8/1[3] | 60 | 7 |
| | **Swiss Coast (IRE)** (MrsJRRamsden) **2-8-6** KFallon(3) (w'like: gd hdwy on outside over 2f out: rn green: led ins fnl f: jst ct)....hd | **2** | 10/1 | 68+ | 15 |
| 1038[4] | **Pandiculation** (EWeymes) **2-8-3** JQuinn(10) (trckd ldrs: styd on wl fnl f)....1 | **3** | 8/1[3] | 62 | 9 |
| | **Two On The Bridge** (DenysSmith) **2-8-3** LCharnock(13) (leggy: unf: s.i.s: sn in tch: carried rt ins fnl f: r.o same pce)....hd | **4** | 20/1 | 62 | 9 |
| 1086[6] | **Docklands Carriage (IRE)** (NTinkler) **2-8-6** KimTinkler(6) (mid div: hrd rdn & styd on fnl 2f: nvr rchd ldrs)....3 | **5** | 16/1 | 57 | 4 |
| 1086[5] | **Fine Times** (CWFairhurst) **2-8-6** DeanMcKeown(8) (chsd ldrs: ev ch 2f out: hung rt & wknd jst ins fnl f)....½ | **6** | 17/2 | 55 | 2 |
| 975[4] | **Plan For Profit (IRE)** (MJohnston) **2-8-6** JWeaver(14) (led tl over 1f out: wknd ins fnl f)....hd | **7** | 3/1[1] | 55 | 2 |
| 916[7] | **Ocker (IRE)** (MHTompkins) **2-8-6** PRobinson(2) (chsd ldrs: led over 1f out: hung rt & hdd ins fnl f: sn hmpd & eased)....1¾ | **8** | 7/2[2] | 50 | — |

| | | | | SP | RR | SF |
|---|---|---|---|---|---|---|
| | **Chasetown Flyer (USA)** (RHollinshead) **2-8-4**ow1 LDettori(11) (cmpt: bkwd: chsd ldrs 4f: sn wknd) | 2 | **9** | 10/1 | 43 | — |
| *1026*3 | **Komasta** (CaptJWilson) **2-8-3** RHills(15) (swtg: s.i.s: sn chsng ldrs: wknd over 1f out) | ¾ | **10** | 20/1 | 40 | — |
| 9306 | **Eager To Please** (JBerry) **2-8-10** KDarley(4) (in tch: rdn over 2f out: sn wknd) | 1 | **11** | 12/1 | 44 | — |
| | **Zagros (IRE)** (TDEasterby) **2-8-4**ow1 MBirch(12) (rangy: bit bkwd: s.s: a wl outpcd) | hd | **12** | 16/1 | 38 | — |
| | **Imperial Or Metric (IRE)** (JBerry) **2-8-6** JCarroll(7) (w'like: bit bkwd: scope: s.i.s: a outpcd) | 1 | **13** | 12/1 | 37 | — |
| 11669 | **Ballydinero (IRE)** (CaptJWilson) **2-7-12**(5) PFessey(5) (nvr wnt pce) | 1 | **14** | 33/1 | 32 | — |
| | **Dissington Times** (JNorton) **2-8-3** DaleGibson(1) (cmpt: unf: s.i.s: sn wl bhd) | 17 | **15** | 25/1 | — | — |
| | | | | (SP 141.6%) | **15 Rn** | |

**1m 17.9** (5.40) CSF £90.98 TOTE £7.00: £2.00 £6.20 £2.10 (£106.40) Trio £212.20; £209.29 to Catterick 31/5/96 OWNER The Crews Missile Syndicate (UPPER LAMBOURN) BRED B. D. Cantle

**1179 Dashing Rocksville** struggled badly to go the pace. Staying on in determined fashion, she is stoutly bred on her dam's side and will be much better suited by seven or even a mile. (8/1)

**Swiss Coast (IRE)** was very green beforehand and unseated his rider leaving the paddock. Rather marooned on the wide outside, he showed definite signs of inexperience but, even so, after showing ahead inside the last, was only just collared. He should have a deal of improvement in him. (10/1: op 6/1)

**1038 Pandiculation**, who was still carrying plenty of condition, was staying on relentlessly at the end and is crying out for seven. (8/1)

**Two On The Bridge**, on the leg and narrow, showed a poor action going down, but ran a highly creditable first race. (20/1)

**1086 Fine Times** gave his rider all sorts of problems and might be suited by a drop back to five. (17/2: 6/1-9/1)

**975 Plan For Profit (IRE)** looks to have outgrown his strength and might be seen to better advantage over seven later in the year. (3/1)

**916 Ocker (IRE)**, a good mover, was beaten when forced to snatch up inside the last. (7/2)

## 1538 MALT HOUSE VINTNERS H'CAP (0-70) (3-Y.O+) (Class E)

2-50 (2-54) **6f 206y** £3,077.55 (£932.40: £455.70: £217.35) Stalls: High GOING minus 0.03 sec per fur (G)

| | | | | SP | RR | SF |
|---|---|---|---|---|---|---|
| 131313 | **Commander Glen (IRE) (52)** (MrsJRRamsden) **4-8-12b** KFallon(3) (s.i.s: bhd: hdwy on outside over 2f out: hrd rdn & hung lft: led fnl 75y) | — | **1** | 10/1 | 65 | 44 |
| 134112 | **Spanish Steps (IRE) (54)** (MWEasterby) **4-8-9b**(5) GParkin(13) (trckd ldrs: hrd rdn to ld ins fnl f: sn hdd & nt qckn) | ½ | **2** | 14/1 | 66 | 45 |
| 10245 | **Three Arch Bridge (57)** (MJohnston) **4-9-3b** JWeaver(9) (led tl ins fnl f: one pce) | 2½ | **3** | 10/1 | 63 | 42 |
| 14172 | **Brambles Way (45)** (WLBarker) **7-8-0v**(5) MartinDwyer(11) (prom: hrd rdn over 2f out: one pce) | ½ | **4** | 12/1 | 50 | 29 |
| 13025 | **Cee-Jay-Ay (50)** (JBerry) **9-8-10** JCarroll(8) (dwlt s: bhd tl styd on fnl 2f) | ½ | **5** | 11/1 | 54 | 33 |
| 99113 | **Superpride (64)** (MrsMReveley) **4-9-10** KDarley(5) (trckd ldrs: effrt 2f out: sn wknd) | 2 | **6** | 12/1 | 63 | 42 |
| 134113 | **Spanish Verdict (62)** (DenysSmith) **9-9-8** JFortune(1) (lw: mid div: effrt over 2f out: nvr nr ldrs) | 2 | **7** | 20/1 | 57 | 36 |
| 13133 | **Miss Pigalle (41)** (MissLAPerratt) **5-8-1b** DaleGibson(6) (chsd ldrs tl wknd over 1f out) | ½ | **8** | 14/1 | 34 | 13 |
| 100112 | **Northern Spark (47)** (MissLAPerratt) **8-8-7** JFanning(12) (chsd ldrs: outpcd fnl 2f) | 2 | **9** | 16/1 | 36 | 15 |
| 14238 | **Gymcrak Flyer (62)** (GHolmes) **5-9-8** NConnorton(4) (b.hind: hld up: hmpd over 4f out: effrt & swtchd ins over 2f out: n.d) | nk | **10** | 9/1 3 | 50 | 29 |
| 991* | **Cheerful Groom (IRE) (41)** (SRBowring) **5-8-1** NKennedy(14) (hmpd & lost pl over 4f out: effrt & swtchd rt over 2f out: n.d) | 1½ | **11** | 4/1 1 | 26 | 5 |
| 10407 | **Birchwood Sun (58)** (MDods) **6-9-4b** LDettori(2) (bhd: sme hdwy over 2f out: sn wknd) | 10 | **12** | 8/1 2 | 20 | — |
| 11615 | **Just Dissident (IRE) (56)** (RMWhitaker) **4-9-2** ACulhane(10) (trckd ldrs: effrt over 2f out: sn wknd) | 1¼ | **13** | 16/1 | 15 | — |
| 10415 | **Thwaab (48)** (FWatson) **4-8-8** JQuinn(7) (chsd ldrs tl wknd over 2f out) | 1¼ | **14** | 20/1 | 4 | — |
| 10882 | **Pc's Cruiser (IRE) (47)** (JLEyre) **4-8-7b** RLappin(15) (hmpd & lost pl over 4f out: sn bhd) | 21 | **15** | 8/1 2 | — | — |
| | | | | (SP 128.7%) | **15 Rn** | |

**1m 30.0** (4.30) CSF £134.97 CT £1,350.82 TOTE £16.70: £4.30 £5.90 £2.80 (£172.30) Trio £438.30; £389.00 to Catterick 31/5/96. OWNER Mr P. A. Leonard (THIRSK) BRED Des Vere Hunt Farming Co

STEWARDS' ENQUIRY Parkin susp. 8-10/6/96 (excessive use of whip).

**1313 Commander Glen (IRE)**, who had finished last at Musselburgh on his previous outing, had the blinkers back on here. Coming from last to first, he tended to hang but was persuaded to stay on and his rider was afforded the luxury of being able to ease up in the final few strides. His trainer describes him as 'a bit of a thief'. (10/1: 6/1-11/1)

**1088* Spanish Steps (IRE)**, from a 4lb higher mark, responded to his rider's every urgings to show ahead inside the last furlong, but was definitely second best near the line. He is better suited by a mile. (14/1)

**1024 Three Arch Bridge** set out to make her stamina tell. Back to her best. she is better over slightly longer distances. (10/1)

**1417 Brambles Way** confirmed that he is flattered by the bare form of his Pontefract second. (12/1)

**1302 Cee-Jay-Ay**, who has not won for over two years, ran his usual race, forfeiting ground at the start and staying on when it was all over. (11/1)

**806 Superpride** was warm and stewed up beforehand. (12/1)

**991* Cheerful Groom (IRE)** effectively lost his chance when knocked right back after the first quarter-mile. Meeting trouble in the straight, his cause was a hopeless one. This is safely overlooked. (4/1)

## 1539 BOOKER CASH & CARRY H'CAP (0-70) (3-Y.O) (Class E)

3-20 (3-23) **7f 214y** £3,050.25 (£924.00: £451.50: £215.25) Stalls: High GOING minus 0.03 sec per fur (G)

| | | | | SP | RR | SF |
|---|---|---|---|---|---|---|
| 10426 | **Contract Bridge (IRE) (42)** (CWThornton) **3-7-7**(3) NVarley(7) (sn outpcd & rdn along: gd hdwy on ins over 2f out: led over 1f out: drvn out) | — | **1** | 8/1 | 50 | 18 |
| 13633 | **Sandblaster (54)** (MrsJRRamsden) **3-8-8** KFallon(4) (hld up: sn trckng ldrs: effrt & n.m.r over 1f out: styd on: nt rch wnr) | 2 | **2** | 13/8 1 | 58 | 26 |
| 11558 | **Bollin Jacob (62)** (TDEasterby) **3-9-2** MBirch(5) (trckd ldrs: effrt over 2f out: styd on fnl f) | ½ | **3** | 10/1 | 65 | 33 |
| 11818 | **Green Gem (BEL) (67)** (SCWilliams) **3-9-7** KDarley(2) (trckd ldrs: effrt 2f out: kpt on same pce) | 1¾ | **4** | 7/1 3 | 67 | 35 |
| 10898 | **Six Clerks (IRE) (61)** (JGFitzGerald) **3-9-1b**1 LDettori(9) (trckd ldrs: led 2f out: sn hdd: one pce) | ¾ | **5** | 11/2 2 | 59 | 27 |
| 6168 | **Boundary Bird (IRE) (55)** (MJohnston) **3-8-9b**1 JFanning(11) (led to 2f out: sn wknd) | 4 | **6** | 12/1 | 45 | 13 |
| 8853 | **Old Hush Wing (IRE) (57)** (PCHaslam) **3-8-11** JFortune(8) (s.i.s: sn drvn along & bhd: nvr nr ldrs) | 1½ | **7** | 14/1 | 44 | 12 |
| 7759 | **Nkapen Rocks (SPA) (67)** (CaptJWilson) **3-9-7** JCarroll(1) (plld hrd: trckd ldrs: wkng whn n.m.r over 1f out) | hd | **8** | 14/1 | 54 | 22 |
| | **Oare Budgie (45)** (DonEnricoIncisa) **3-7-13** KimTinkler(10) (bit bkwd: sn bhd) | 11 | **9** | 25/1 | 10 | — |
| 106816 | **Khabar (65)** (RBastiman) **3-9-0**(5) HBastiman(3) (sn outpcd: eased over 1f out) | 1¾ | **10** | 20/1 | 26 | — |
| | **Bold Future (IRE) (42)** (JWWatts) **3-7-10** LCharnock(6) (sn prom & pushed along: lost pl 3f out) | 1 | **11** | 20/1 | 1 | — |
| | | | | (SP 120.6%) | **11 Rn** | |

**1m 44.6** (6.00) CSF £20.92 CT £127.02 TOTE £9.00: £1.40 £1.40 £2.90 (£8.00) Trio £26.00 OWNER Racegoers Club Spigot Lodge Owners Group (MIDDLEHAM) BRED E. O'Leary

LONG HANDICAP Contract Bridge (IRE) 7-8 Bold Future (IRE) 7-8

**1042 Contract Bridge (IRE)**, who likes to come from behind, stuck to the inner and, as a result, found a clear run. (8/1)
**1363 Sandblaster**, tightened up at a crucial stage, is overdue a change of luck. (13/8)
**934 Bollin Jacob** has certainly been done no favours by the Handicapper. Sticking on inside the last furlong, he is still learning. (10/1)
**915 Green Gem (BEL)**, who looked very fit, looked to have a pound or two too much at present. (7/1)
**1089 Six Clerks (IRE)**, fitted with blinkers for the first time, lacked anything in the way of speed over this trip. (11/2)

## 1540 GOLD MARK MAIDEN STKS (3-Y.O+ F & M) (Class D)

3-50 (3-50) **7f 214y** £3,485.00 (£1,055.00: £515.00: £245.00) Stalls: High GOING minus 0.03 sec per fur (G)

| Form | Horse | Dist | Pos | SP | RR | SF |
|---|---|---|---|---|---|---|
| | **Magic Carousel** (MJohnston) **3-8-9** JFanning(4) (cmpt: unf: effrt over 2f out: rdn to ld over 1f out: hung rt & styd on wl towards fin) | — | 1 | 5/1$^{3}$ | 76 | 32 |
| 1007$^{3}$ | **Hulm (IRE) (82)** (HThomsonJones) **3-8-9** RHills(2) (trckd ldr: rdn to ld 2f out: nt qckn ins fnl f) | 1¼ | 2 | 8/11$^{1}$ | 74 | 30 |
| 870$^{4}$ | **Dimakya (USA) (85)** (DRLoder) **3-8-9** LDettori(1) (led: rdn & hdd 2f out: eased whn btn towards fin) | 3 | 3 | 7/4$^{2}$ | 68 | 24 |
| 1323$^{8}$ | **Winn Caley** (CWFairhurst) **3-8-9** DeanMcKeown(3) (plld hrd: trckd ldrs: rdn 3f out: sn lost pl) | 9 | 4 | 66/1 | 49? | 5 |

(SP 112.4%) **4 Rn**

**1m 44.4** (5.80) CSF £9.18 TOTE £5.20 (£4.50) OWNER Mrs S. W. O'Brien (MIDDLEHAM) BRED C. and Mrs Blackwell and P. V. Mccalmont

**Magic Carousel**, a narrow type, overcame greenness to get on top near the line. She should show improvement as she gains more experience. (5/1)
**1007 Hulm (IRE)**, who looked very fit, could never muster the pace to seriously trouble the winner. (8/11)
**870 Dimakya (USA)**, basically a disappointing sort, set her own pace but she pulled out little under pressure and Dettori gave up near the line. (7/4)
**Winn Caley**, on her toes beforehand, could never be persuaded to settle. (66/1)

## 1541 CHEF'S LARDER LIMITED STKS (0-55) (3-Y.O+) (Class F)

4-20 (4-23) **5f** £2,745.00 (£770.00: £375.00) Stalls: Centre GOING minus 0.03 sec per fur (G)

| Form | Horse | Dist | Pos | SP | RR | SF |
|---|---|---|---|---|---|---|
| 1423$^{10}$ | **Aquado (48)** (SRBowring) **7-9-3b** JQuinn(14) (w ldrs: led over 2f out: rdn clr fnl f) | — | 1 | 10/1 | 60 | 42 |
| 1342$^{4}$ | **Call to the Bar (IRE) (48)** (MDods) **7-9-0**(3) CTeague(6) (chsd ldrs: rdn & hung lft 1f out: kpt on) | 3½ | 2 | 9/2$^{2}$ | 49 | 31 |
| 1342$^{6}$ | **Tropical Beach (55)** (JBerry) **3-8-9b** JCarroll(12) (sn in tch: rdn ½-wy: hung lft & kpt on fnl f) | ½ | 3 | 8/1 | 47 | 21 |
| 1364$^{3}$ | **Featherstone Lane (48)** (MissLCSiddall) **5-9-6v** LDettori(2) (lw: hld up: hdwy over 1f out: styd on u.p: nvr nr to chal) | nk | 4 | 7/2$^{1}$ | 49 | 31 |
| 659$^{8}$ | **Serious Hurry (48)** (RMMcKellar) **8-8-10**(7) DMcGaffin(4) (led tl over 2f out: grad wknd) | 1¼ | 5 | 20/1 | 42 | 24 |
| 762$^{8}$ | **Rotherfield Park (IRE) (34)** (CSmith) **4-8-7**(7) AngelaGallimore(3) (in tch: rdn ½-wy: no imp) | ½ | 6 | 20/1 | 38 | 20 |
| 769$^{6}$ | **Lochon (53)** (JLEyre) **5-9-6** RLappin(13) (in tch: rdn ½-wy: eased whn btn 1f out) | 4 | 7 | 5/1$^{3}$ | 31 | 13 |
| 1157$^{13}$ | **Tutu Sixtysix (33)** (DonEnricoIncisa) **5-9-0v** KimTinkler(1) (lw: hld up & bhd: rdn 2f out: n.d) | ¾ | 8 | 20/1 | 22 | 4 |
| 1199$^{9}$ | **Imp Express (IRE) (50)** (GMMoore) **3-8-9** ACulhane(11) (chsd ldrs tl wknd over 1f out) | ¾ | 9 | 10/1 | 23 | — |
| 1364$^{7}$ | **Dominelle (47)** (TDEasterby) **4-9-0** MBirch(5) (lw: w ldrs: rdn 2f out: sn wknd & eased) | nk | 10 | 9/2$^{2}$ | 19 | 1 |
| 1313$^{11}$ | **Nordisk Legend (35)** (MrsDThomson) **4-9-3**(3)ow3 OPears(8) (sn bhd & rdn along) | ½ | 11 | 25/1 | 24 | 3 |
| 661$^{14}$ | **Cacharro (47)** (MissZAGreen) **5-9-3** AMackay(7) (bhd fr ½-wy) | hd | 12 | 20/1 | 20 | 2 |
| *250*$^{5}$ | **Brisas (43)** (CWFairhurst) **9-9-3** DeanMcKeown(10) (sn outpcd & rdn along) | ¾ | 13 | 16/1 | 18 | — |
| *347*$^{11}$ | **First Option (50)** (RBastiman) **6-8-12**(5) HBastiman(9) (t: s.s: a bhd) | 1 | 14 | 25/1 | 15 | — |

(SP 137.2%) **14 Rn**

**63.6 secs** (3.40) CSF £58.05 TOTE £10.90: £2.20 £2.10 £3.30 (£32.90) Trio £67.30 OWNER Mr K. Nicholls (EDWINSTOWE) BRED Lord Howard de Walden

WEIGHT FOR AGE 3yo-8lb

**1157 Aquado**, dropped back in distance, won this decisively in the end. (10/1)
**1342 Call to the Bar (IRE)** ran satisfactorily on ground softer than he truly cares for. (9/2)
**1342 Tropical Beach**, with the blinkers fitted again, was staying on at the line, despite a tendency to hang. (8/1)
**1364 Featherstone Lane** was ridden from some way off the pace and, though staying on, was never a threat. (7/2: 11/4-9/2)
**Serious Hurry**, who finished distressed last time, carried plenty of condition. (20/1)

## 1542 FAMILY CHOICE H'CAP (0-70) (4-Y.O+) (Class E)

4-50 (4-51) **1m 6f 32y** £2,927.40 (£886.20: £432.60: £205.80) Stalls: Low GOING minus 0.03 sec per fur (G)

| Form | Horse | Dist | Pos | SP | RR | SF |
|---|---|---|---|---|---|---|
| 1343$^{2}$ | **Royal Expression (65)** (MrsMReveley) **4-9-9** ACulhane(1) (lw: hld up: smooth hdwy ½-wy: led on bit 2f out: styd on wl fnl f) | — | 1 | 9/4$^{1}$ | 78 | 41 |
| 1070$^{3}$ | **Hullbank (55)** (WWHaigh) **6-8-13** JTate(9) (hld up: gd hdwy 5f out: chal 2f out: nt qckn fnl f) | 3 | 2 | 9/2$^{3}$ | 65 | 28 |
| 1034* | **Campaspe (42)** (JGFitzGerald) **4-8-0** JFanning(2) (trckd ldrs: rdn to ld 3f out: one pce fnl 2f) | 3 | 3 | 7/2$^{2}$ | 48 | 11 |
| *1095*$^{6}$ | **Cross Talk (IRE) (69)** (RHollinshead) **4-9-13** LDettori(8) (lw: hld up: effrt over 3f out: styd on u.p fnl f: nvr rchd ldrs) | 3 | 4 | 9/2$^{3}$ | 72 | 35 |
| 1070$^{W}$ | **Tancred Mischief (38)** (WLBarker) **5-7-5**(5) MartinDwyer(7) (chsd ldrs: rdn over 4f out: wl outpcd fnl 2f) | 1 | 5 | 20/1 | 40 | 3 |
| 1070$^{13}$ | **Can She Can Can (38)** (CSmith) **4-7-3**(7) IonaWands(4) (led to 3f out: wknd over 1f out) | 3 | 6 | 14/1 | 36 | — |
| | **Twin Falls (IRE) (70)** (GMMoore) **5-9-11**(3) OPears(5) (hld up: hdwy ½-wy: wknd over 2f out) | 12 | 7 | 10/1 | 55 | 18 |
| 886$^{9}$ | **Don't Cry (38)** (DonEnricoIncisa) **8-7-10** KimTinkler(6) (chsd ldrs: pushed along 7f out: lost pl over 2f out: sn bhd) | 17 | 8 | 50/1 | 4 | — |

(SP 111.8%) **8 Rn**

**3m 12.5** (11.50) CSF £11.84 CT £29.70 TOTE £2.70: £1.10 £2.30 £1.50 (£5.60) Trio £6.20 OWNER Mr Les De La Haye (SALTBURN) BRED K. Panos

LONG HANDICAP Tancred Mischief 6-13 Can She Can Can 7-7 Don't Cry 6-4

**1343 Royal Expression**, with hindsight, was tackling a tough nut in Zamhareer at Newcastle. Travelling best throughout, he had only to be kept up to his work. (9/4)
**1070 Hullbank** threw down a determined challenge two furlongs from home but it was very obvious soon after that he was booked for second spot. (9/2)
**1034* Campaspe**, from a 3lb higher mark, was warm beforehand. Under pressure, she proved painfully one-paced. (7/2)
**855 Cross Talk (IRE)**, whose two latest outings were on the All-Weather, proved awkward to load. Under pressure a long way from home, he never looked like giving Dettori his first winner here. (9/2)
**558 Tancred Mischief**, withdrawn last time after breaking a blood vessel on the way to the start, ran creditably from 11lb out of the weights (20/1)

T/Plpt: £333.10 (34.59 Tckts). T/Qdpt: £15.60 (49.01 Tckts). WG

# 1308-MUSSELBURGH (R-H) (Good to soft, Rnd crse Soft patches)
## Thursday May 30th
WEATHER: overcast WIND: almost nil

### 1543 DON'T BLINK (S) STKS (2-Y.O) (Class G)
6-45 (6-47) **5f** £2,211.00 (£621.00: £303.00) Stalls: High GOING minus 0.15 sec per fur (GF)

| | | | | SP | RR | SF |
|---|---|---|---|---|---|---|
| | **Brutal Fantasy (IRE)** (NTinkler) **2-8-11** KDarley(5) (str: cmpt: bit bkwd: chsd wnr: led on bit 2f out: easily) | — | 1 | 11/10[1] | 65+ | — |
| 1320[5] | **No Rush** (JBerry) **2-8-11** JCarroll(6) (outpcd tl styd on fnl 2f: no ch w wnr) | 1½ | 2 | 7/1[3] | 60? | — |
| 1360[5] | **Fonzy** (MrsLStubbs) **2-9-2b[1]** JFortune(2) (led 3f: sn rdn & btn) | 3 | 3 | 2/1[2] | 56 | — |
| | **Chanson d'Amour (IRE)** (MissLAPerratt) **2-8-6** NConnorton(4) (cmpt: scope: bit bkwd: sn outpcd) | 2½ | 4 | 12/1 | 38 | — |
| 1362[6] | **Apiculate (IRE)** (WTKemp) **2-8-11b[1]** KFallon(3) (dwlt: a bhd) | 1¼ | 5 | 14/1 | 39 | — |
| | **Chloe's Mark** (RMMcKellar) **2-8-6** TWilliams(1) (lt-f: bit bkwd: sn outpcd & wl bhd) | 9 | 6 | 20/1 | 5 | — |

(SP 112.6%) **6 Rn**

**62.8 secs** (5.10) CSF £8.66 TOTE £1.90: £1.30 £2.70 (£5.80) OWNER Mr P. D. Savill (MALTON) BRED Michael G. O'Brien
Bt in 6,200gns

**Brutal Fantasy (IRE)**, a useful sort for this type of race, did not look fully wound up, but proved to be different class and scored easily. (11/10)
**1320 No Rush** is a very lean individual but, after getting outpaced early on, he stayed on to prove that a similar event can be found. (7/1: op 3/1)
**1360 Fonzy**, in blinkers for the first time, really blasted out of the stalls, but he had run himself into the ground soon after halfway. (2/1: 6/4-9/4)
**Chanson d'Amour (IRE)**, a well-made filly, needed this and never went the pace. (12/1: op 6/1)
**Apiculate (IRE)**, with blinkers on for the first time, put in her best effort to date, but still never had a hope. (14/1: 8/1-16/1)

### 1544 SHERATON GRAND CLAIMING STKS (4-Y.O+) (Class F)
7-15 (7-15) **1m 4f 31y** £2,624.10 (£737.60: £360.30) Stalls: High GOING: 0.17 sec per fur (G)

| | | | | SP | RR | SF |
|---|---|---|---|---|---|---|
| 886[7] | **Bayrak (USA) (73)** (MJRyan) **6-9-7** JCarroll(5) (lw: mde all: qcknd clr 3f out: unchal) | — | 1 | 6/5[1] | 65+ | 41 |
| *401*[3] | **Pharly Dancer (56)** (WWHaigh) **7-8-13** DaleGibson(4) (swtg: a.p: chsd wnr fnl 2f: no imp) | 3½ | 2 | 6/1 | 52 | 28 |
| 1159[7] | **Latvian (66)** (RAllan) **9-9-7** JFortune(6) (in tch: effrt 4f out: no imp) | 2½ | 3 | 7/2[2] | 57 | 33 |
| 1159[4] | **Goodbye Millie (40)** (JLEyre) **6-8-5**(3) DWright(2) (in tch: effrt over 4f out: rdn & no hdwy) | ½ | 4 | 11/2[3] | 43 | 19 |
| 1418[9] | **Ambidextrous (IRE) (50)** (EJAlston) **4-8-11v** KFallon(8) (hld up: effrt appr st: n.d) | 1½ | 5 | 9/1 | 45 | 21 |
| 558[12] | **School of Science (28)** (RMMcKellar) **6-8-5b** TWilliams(7) (chsd wnr tl wknd fnl 3f) | 3½ | 6 | 100/1 | 34 | 10 |
| 1309[13] | **Jabaroot (IRE) (59)** (DANolan) **5-8-6**(3) NVarley(1) (bhd: sme hdwy 5f out: sn btn) | 14 | 7 | 33/1 | 19 | — |
| 1167[13] | **Kalko (19)** (JSGoldie) **7-8-2b**(5) PFessey(3) (a bhd) | 7 | 8 | 100/1 | 8 | — |

(SP 112.3%) **8 Rn**

**2m 44.9** (11.90) CSF £8.37 TOTE £1.90: £1.20 £1.40 £1.90 (£8.80) OWNER Mr A. S. Reid (NEWMARKET) BRED Swettenham Stud

**816 Bayrak (USA)** had it all his own way here and, once he quickened early in the straight, there were no dangers. (6/5)
**Pharly Dancer** got very warm beforehand, but still ran well, albeit without looking likely to trouble the winner. (6/1)
**1159 Latvian** has never won on ground as soft as this, so ran fairly well. (7/2)
**1159 Goodbye Millie** won this last year but never looked like repeating that. (11/2: 4/1-6/1)
**547 Ambidextrous (IRE)**, from a yard that is out of form, showed little. (9/1)

### 1545 SHERATON GRAND CUP H'CAP (0-75) (3-Y.O+) (Class E)
7-45 (7-45) **5f** £4,086.25 (£1,240.00: £607.50: £291.25) Stalls: High GOING minus 0.15 sec per fur (GF)

| | | | | SP | RR | SF |
|---|---|---|---|---|---|---|
| 911[6] | **Garnock Valley (65)** (JBerry) **6-9-6** JCarroll(3) (in tch: hdwy 2f out: styd on to ld wl ins fnl f) | — | 1 | 9/4[1] | 76 | 42 |
| 1342[2] | **Swan At Whalley (56)** (MartynWane) **4-8-6**(5) PRoberts(2) (led: hung bdly rt fnl 2f: hdd wl ins fnl f) | 1¼ | 2 | 7/2[3] | 63 | 29 |
| *900*[8] | **The Institute Boy (46)** (MissJFCraze) **6-8-1** AMackay(8) (hdwy 2f out: nrst fin) | 3 | 3 | 3/1[2] | 43 | 9 |
| 1163[7] | **Another Nightmare (IRE) (41)** (TDyer) **4-7-7**(3) DWright(4) (prom: rdn & no imp fr ½-wy) | 1¼ | 4 | 20/1 | 34 | — |
| 1161[9] | **Kalar (49)** (DWChapman) **7-8-4b** LCharnock(7) (lw: chsd ldr: hmpd & swtchd over 1f out: sn btn) | ¾ | 5 | 7/1 | 40 | 6 |
| 1039[9] | **Six for Luck (54)** (DANolan) **4-8-6**(3) NVarley(6) (nvr wnt pce) | 6 | 6 | 9/1 | 26 | — |
| 1313[5] | **Seconds Away (41)** (JSGoldie) **5-7-10b** JQuinn(5) (sn outpcd & bhd) | nk | 7 | 14/1 | 12 | — |
| | **Another Episode (IRE) (70)** (MissLAPerratt) **7-9-11** KDarley(1) (chsd ldrs tl rdn & wknd fr ½-wy) | 3½ | 8 | 25/1 | 30 | — |

(SP 115.8%) **8 Rn**

**60.5 secs** (2.80) CSF £10.28 CT £21.26 TOTE £3.20: £1.50 £1.10 £2.60 (£5.00) OWNER Mr Robert Aird (COCKERHAM) BRED Sunley Stud
LONG HANDICAP Another Nightmare (IRE) 7-2 Seconds Away 7-4

**911 Garnock Valley** likes this track, and responded to pressure to settle it late on. (9/4)
**1342 Swan At Whalley** has speed aplenty, but threw it away by hanging badly right in the final two furlongs. (7/2)
**769 The Institute Boy** has yet to win on grass, but he was staying on here and, over a bit further or on a stiffer track, might well break his duck. (3/1)
**Another Nightmare (IRE)** looked very one-paced once the pressure was on from halfway. (20/1)
**931 Kalar**, who is better on faster ground, is beginning to come to himself looks-wise and was not helped here by the leader hanging into him. (7/1)

### 1546 CASTLE H'CAP (0-60) (3-Y.O+) (Class F)
8-15 (8-15) **1m 16y** £2,766.90 (£778.40: £380.70) Stalls: High GOING: 0.17 sec per fur (G)

| | | | | SP | RR | SF |
|---|---|---|---|---|---|---|
| 999[11] | **Bowcliffe (44)** (MrsAMNaughton) **5-9-1** JCarroll(2) (sn cl up: led 3f out: kpt on wl fnl f) | — | 1 | 20/1 | 56 | 41 |
| 1313[4] | **Hutchies Lady (38)** (RMMcKellar) **4-8-9** TWilliams(4) (b.hind: hdwy over 3f out: ev ch over 1f out: no ex u.p) | 1¾ | 2 | 3/1[1] | 47 | 32 |
| 883[5] | **Waterlord (IRE) (40)** (DNicholls) **6-8-4**(7) JBramhill(5) (chsd ldrs: ev ch over 2f out: r.o one pce) | 1½ | 3 | 5/1[3] | 46 | 31 |
| 1311[4] | **Sunday Mail Too (IRE) (32)** (MissLAPerratt) **4-8-3** JQuinn(8) (a chsng ldrs: rdn & no imp fnl 3f) | 5 | 4 | 16/1 | 28 | 13 |
| 1417[6] | **Mill Dancer (IRE) (41)** (EJAlston) **4-8-12** SDWilliams(3) (led tl hdd 3f out: grad wknd) | 1 | 5 | 12/1 | 35 | 20 |
| 505[12] | **Lady Silk (50)** (MissJFCraze) **5-9-7** NConnorton(11) (nvr nr to chal) | hd | 6 | 20/1 | 44 | 29 |
| 1001[14] | **Bedazzle (39)** (MBrittain) **5-8-10** KDarley(12) (b.off fore: nvr trbld ldrs) | 5 | 7 | 7/1 | 23 | 8 |
| 1313[8] | **Tinklers Folly (52)** (DenysSmith) **4-9-9** JFortune(6) (in tch: rdn 4f out: sn wknd) | 1 | 8 | 9/1 | 34 | 19 |
| 822[9]. | **Great Bear (55)** (DWChapman) **4-9-7**(5) PFessey(9) (chsd ldrs to ½-wy: sn wknd) | 5 | 9 | 50/1 | 27 | 12 |
| 883[4] | **Raindeer Quest (47)** (JLEyre) **4-9-1**(3) DWright(10) (s.i.s: a bhd) | 1¼ | 10 | 9/2[2] | 16 | 1 |
| *839*[10] | **La Dama (USA) (38)** (ABMulholland) **4-8-9** MMcAndrew(7) (plld hrd: a bhd) | 1¾ | 11 | 20/1 | 4 | — |

| | | | | SP | RR | SF |
|---|---|---|---|---|---|---|
| $1309^{6}$ | **Rapid Mover (35)** (DANolan) **9-8-3b**(3) NVarley(1) (wl outpcd fr ½-wy) | 1¼ | **12** | 12/1 | — | — |

(SP 119.9%) **12 Rn**

**1m 45.7** (7.10) CSF £75.53 CT £330.62 TOTE £23.00: £4.50 £1.30 £2.70 (£91.20) Trio £263.10; £155.64 to 1/6/96 OWNER Mr Philip Davies (RICHMOND) BRED Lady Matthews

**Bowcliffe**, wearing a tongue-strap for the first time, looked and travelled well. When the pressure was on, he was always doing enough. (20/1)
**1313 Hutchies Lady** looked likely to win when improving going nicely in the straight but, asked for an effort approaching the final furlong, she failed to respond sufficiently. (3/1)
**883 Waterlord (IRE)** had his chances in the straight, but lacked the pace to do anything about it. (5/1)
**1311 Sunday Mail Too (IRE)** was always in pursuit of the leaders, but the effort required was always beyond her. (16/1)
**Mill Dancer (IRE)**, racing wide, set a good pace but, once passed three furlongs out, she put up little fight. (12/1)
**Lady Silk** was making some ground in the straight to suggest that there is a bit better to come. (20/1)
**662* Tinklers Folly** (9/1: op 9/2)
**883 Raindeer Quest** got warm beforehand and showed nothing in the race. (9/2)
**1309 Rapid Mover** (12/1: op 8/1)

## 1547 GULLANE RATING RELATED MAIDEN STKS (0-60) (3-Y.O+) (Class F)

8-45 (8-45) **5f** £2,493.20 (£700.20: £341.60) Stalls: High GOING minus 0.15 sec per fur (GF)

| | | | | SP | RR | SF |
|---|---|---|---|---|---|---|
| $1161^{4}$ | **Ninety-Five (60)** (JGFitzGerald) **4-9-2** KFallon(4) (cl up: led appr fnl f: kpt on u.p) | — | **1** | 4/7 1 | 55 | 45 |
| $881^{6}$ | **Ready Teddy (IRE) (38)** (MissLAPerratt) **3-8-8** KDarley(1) (lw: led tl hdd appr fnl f: kpt on) | 1 | **2** | 50/1 | 52 | 34 |
| $1157^{14}$ | **Silk Cottage (60)** (RMWhitaker) **4-9-5** ACulhane(7) (lw: cl up: rdn 2f out: r.o one pce) | 2½ | **3** | 7/2 2 | 47 | 37 |
| $1039^{5}$ | **Rinus Manor (IRE) (51)** (EJAlston) **5-9-5** SDWilliams(2) (lw: sn outpcd & bhd: styd on appr fnl f: nrst fin) | ½ | **4** | 7/1 3 | 45 | 35 |
| $704^{10}$ | **China Hand (IRE) (38)** (MartynWane) **4-9-5** JCarroll(3) (lw: cl up tl rdn & btn appr fnl f) | hd | **5** | 20/1 | 45 | 35 |
| $1342^{11}$ | **Aye Ready (30)** (MissLAPerratt) **3-8-11b** LCharnock(5) (outpcd & bhd after 2f) | 9 | **6** | 50/1 | 16 | — |
| $1168^{6}$ | **Lord Cornelious (29)** (DANolan) **3-8-8**(3) NVarley(6) (sn outpcd & bhd) | 15 | **7** | 50/1 | — | — |

(SP 109.0%) **7 Rn**

**60.1 secs** (2.40) CSF £20.26 TOTE £1.70: £1.60 £3.40 (£12.50) OWNER Mr N. H. T. Wrigley (MALTON) BRED M. H. Wrigley
WEIGHT FOR AGE 3yo-8lb

**1161 Ninety-Five** at last got it right, but needed driving out to make sure of it. (4/7)
**Ready Teddy (IRE)** got the favoured stands' side and, when headed with a furlong to go, she kept fighting back to put up by far her best performance yet. (50/1)
**Silk Cottage** ran his best race of the season but this was a modest event. (7/2: op 9/4)
**1039 Rinus Manor (IRE)**, completely outpaced early on, then stayed on well in the closing stages to suggest that, over further, there is a race to be found. (7/1: 8/1-5/1)
**China Hand (IRE)** did show reasonable early pace. (20/1)

## 1548 SHERATON GRAND H'CAP (0-70) (3-Y.O+) (Class E)

9-15 (9-15) **1m 3f 32y** £2,957.00 (£896.00: £438.00: £209.00) Stalls: High GOING: 0.17 sec per fur (G)

| | | | | SP | RR | SF |
|---|---|---|---|---|---|---|
| $1167^{3}$ | **Steadfast Elite (IRE) (39)** (JJO'Neill) **5-9-1** JFortune(7) (lw: in tch: hdwy 4f out: slt ld over 2f out: all out) | — | **1** | 9/2 2 | 53 | 33 |
| $1309^{5}$ | **Here Comes Herbie (30)** (WStorey) **4-7-13**(7) IonaWands(9) (a.p: effrt appr st: chal over 2f out: r.o) | s.h | **2** | 7/4 1 | 44 | 24 |
| $999^{2}$ | **Keep Battling (43)** (JSGoldie) **6-9-5** JQuinn(8) (hld up: stdy hdwy over 3f out: chal over 1f out: no ex u.p) | 5 | **3** | 9/2 2 | 50 | 30 |
| $1418^{4}$ | **Gold Desire (33)** (MBrittain) **6-8-9** KDarley(3) (hld up: effrt 4f out: styd on: no imp) | 5 | **4** | 5/1 3 | 33 | 13 |
| *$246^{2}$* | **Greek Gold (IRE) (45)** (WLBarker) **7-9-0**(7) JBramhill(5) (prom: led over 4f out tl over 2f out: sn btn) | 7 | **5** | 20/1 | 35 | 15 |
| $1167^{8}$ | **Mcgillycuddy Reeks (IRE) (44)** (NTinkler) **5-9-6** LCharnock(1) (hld up: effrt appr st: n.d) | 6 | **6** | 12/1 | 25 | 5 |
| $1503^{2}$ | **Phar Closer (46)** (WTKemp) **3-8-7b**1 KFallon(6) (lw: chsd ldrs tl wknd over 4f out) | 4 | **7** | 15/2 | 21 | — |
| $1472^{12}$ | **Kismetim (33)** (DWChapman) **6-8-4b**(5) PFessey(4) (lw: led: clr 7f out: hdd over 4f out: sn wknd) | 3½ | **8** | 50/1 | 3 | — |
| $1312^{8}$ | **Knave (63)** (PMonteith) **3-9-10** SDWilliams(2) (prom tl wknd fnl 4f) | 5 | **9** | 20/1 | 26 | — |

(SP 120.3%) **9 Rn**

**2m 30.9** (11.20) CSF £12.86 CT £35.13 TOTE £7.00: £1.40 £2.30 £2.00 (£16.60) Trio £16.10 OWNER Mr J. Clayton (PENRITH) BRED Cecil Harris Bloodstock Ltd
WEIGHT FOR AGE 3yo-15lb

**1167 Steadfast Elite (IRE)** was given a superb ride and, once in front approaching the final quarter-mile, she would not be denied. (9/2)
**1309 Here Comes Herbie** travelled well, but then came off the bit early in the straight. He he still had his chances throughout the last two furlongs and, despite trying hard, just failed. (7/4)
**999 Keep Battling** as usual looked likely to win this but, when it came down to a struggle, he failed to produce the goods again. He has to be ridden just right. (9/2)
**1418 Gold Desire** was off the bit too far from home and failed to get in a blow. (5/1: 4/1-6/1)
**Greek Gold (IRE)** has been off the track for almost three and a half months and, in the circumstances, ran reasonably well. (20/1)
**Mcgillycuddy Reeks (IRE)** (12/1: op 6/1)
**1503 Phar Closer** is better than this. (15/2: 5/1-8/1)

T/Plpt: £15.00 (881.73 Tckts). T/Qdpt: £4.10 (249.27 Tckts). AA

## 1549a-1564a (Irish Racing) - See Computer Raceform

# 1251a-CURRAGH (Newbridge, Ireland) (R-H) (Good to soft)
## Saturday May 25th

## 1565a ORAL B. MARBLE HILL (Listed) (2-Y.O)

2-50 (2-50) **5f** £9,675.00 (£2,775.00: £1,275.00: £375.00)

| | | | | SP | RR | SF |
|---|---|---|---|---|---|---|
| | **Raphane (USA)** (CCollins,Ireland) **2-8-9** KDarley (mde all: rdn & r.o ins fnl f) | — | **1** | Evens 1 | 93 | 49 |
| 946* | **Kingsinger (IRE)** (MRChannon) **2-9-2** PatEddery (a cl up: 3rd & rdn 2f out: no imp 1f out: r.o) | 1½ | **2** | 5/1 3 | 95 | 51 |
| | **Classic Park** (APO'Brien,Ireland) **2-8-11** CRoche (cl 2nd: effrt u.p over 1f out: no ex ins fnl f) | 1 | **3** | 5/2 2 | 87 | 43 |
| | **Mosconi (IRE)** (JSBolger,Ireland) **2-8-9** KJManning (hld up: hdwy 2f out: effrt u.p ent fnl f: no imp) | 1 | **4** | 9/1 | 82 | 38 |
| | **Scottish Mist (IRE)** (GMLyons,Ireland) **2-8-11** JPMurtagh (chsd ldrs: 4th & rdn 2f out: btn whn drifted ins fnl f) | 1½ | **5** | 12/1 | 79 | 35 |

| | | | | SP | RR | SF |
|---|---|---|---|---|---|---|
| | **Silvestrini (IRE)** (JSBolger,Ireland) **2-8-9** SCraine (n.d) | 4½ | **6** | 10/1 | 63 | 19 |
| | **Daffodil Dale (IRE)** (KPrendergast,Ireland) **2-8-11** WJSupple (n.d) | 5 | **7** | 10/1 | 49 | 5 |
| | | | | (SP 131.1%) | | **7 Rn** |

**59.6 secs** (1.60) OWNER Peter Savill (THE CURRAGH)
**Raphane (USA)** was heavily backed and made the anticipated improvement. In front all the way, he won very much as he pleased. The Norfolk Stakes is his aim. (Evens: op 2/1)
**946* Kingsinger (IRE)**, always close up on the outer, was in third place and making little impression a furlong and a half out. He ran on well but was no match for the winner under his penalty. (5/1)
**Classic Park** ran second until finding nothing under pressure from a furlong out. (5/2)
**Mosconi (IRE)** delivered his challenge under pressure just inside the last furlong but was soon beaten. (9/1: op 5/1)

## 1566a WEATHERBYS IRELAND GREENLANDS (Gp 3) (3-Y.O+)
3-20 (3-21) **6f** £16,250.00 (£4,750.00: £2,250.00: £750.00)

| | | | | SP | RR | SF |
|---|---|---|---|---|---|---|
| | **Lidanna** (DHanley,Ireland) **3-8-7**[ow1] MJKinane (hld up: hdwy on outside 2f out: led ins fnl f: rdn & drifted lft: r.o wl) | — | **1** | 5/1[3] | 109 | 45 |
| | **Catch The Blues (IRE)** (APO'Brien,Ireland) **4-9-1** WJSupple (disp ld tl led after 2f: rdn & edgd lft wl over 2f out: hdd u.p ins fnl f: no ex) | 3 | **2** | 16/1 | 100 | 46 |
| 1253a[4] | **Nashcash (IRE)** (CCollins,Ireland) **3-8-10**[ow1] PShanahan (cl up: effrt u.p 1½f out: kpt on ins fnl f) | nk | **3** | 12/1 | 103 | 39 |
| | **Petite Fantasy** (APO'Brien,Ireland) **4-9-1** LDettori (hld up: hdwy fr rr 2f out: swtchd rt & squeezed thro over 1f out: rdn & r.o ins fnl f) | s.h | **4** | 7/1 | 99 | 45 |
| 1296a* | **Idris (IRE)** (JSBolger,Ireland) **6-9-8** KJManning (chsd ldrs: 4th whn rdn & edgd rt over 1f out: nt qckn ins fnl f) | 3 | **5** | 7/1 | 98 | 44 |
| 1235a[7] | **Sir Silver Sox (USA)** (TStack,Ireland) **4-9-4** JPMurtagh (chsd ldrs: no imp 2f out: kpt on ins fnl f) | 2½ | **6** | 16/1 | 87 | 33 |
| 1129[2] | **Branston Abby (IRE)** (MJohnston) **7-9-1** JWeaver (disp ld 2f: rdn ½-wy: lost pl 2f out: btn whn hmpd over 1f out) | hd | **7** | 7/2[2] | 84 | 30 |
| 864[3] | **Warning Star** (BWHills) **4-9-1** MHills (chsd ldrs: dropped bhd bef ½-wy: rdn & hmpd 2f out: no imp) | s.h | **8** | 14/1 | 84 | 30 |
| 1235a[2] | **Burden Of Proof (IRE)** (CO'Brien,Ireland) **4-9-4** CRoche (s.s: bhd: hdwy & nt clr run wl over 1f out: 5th whn sltly hmpd & no imp 1f out: eased) | ½ | **9** | 7/4[1] | 86 | 32 |
| | | | | (SP 126.4%) | | **9 Rn** |

**1m 12.6** (2.10) OWNER McLoughlin Family Syndicate (STRAFFAN)
**Lidanna** had plenty in front of her before halfway but made good headway to join the leaders under two furlongs out. She led inside the last and, despite drifting left, had matters very much her own way. The King's Stand Stakes is her Royal Ascot target. (5/1)
**Catch The Blues (IRE)** showed improved form, going on after two furlongs and, despite edging left, was not headed until inside the final furlong. (16/1)
**1253a Nashcash (IRE)**, always close up, was under pressure a furlong and a half out and just kept on at the one pace. (12/1: op 8/1)
**Petite Fantasy**, making headway from behind, had to be switched to squeeze through between horses over a furlong out and might be considered a little unlucky. (7/1: op 9/2)
**Idris (IRE)** found the penalty and this inadequate trip against him. (7/1)
**1129 Branston Abby (IRE)** showed her usual speed to halfway but soon lost her place and was beaten when hampered over a furlong out. (7/2)
**864 Warning Star**, prominent early, had dropped right away before halfway and was going nowhere when hampered two furlongs out. (14/1)
**Burden Of Proof (IRE)**, slowly into his stride, encountered traffic problems two furlongs out and again a furlong out. He was finally eased down. (7/4)

## 1567a AIRLIE COOLMORE IRISH 1,000 GUINEAS (Gp 1) (3-Y.O F)
3-55 (3-58) **1m** £84,250.00 (£28,750.00: £13,750.00: £4,750.00)

| | | | | SP | RR | SF |
|---|---|---|---|---|---|---|
| 939[2] | **Matiya (IRE)** (BHanbury) **3-9-0** WCarson (prom: led ½-wy: rdn over 2f out: kpt on wl) | — | **1** | 5/1[3] | 117 | 32 |
| | **Dance Design (IRE)** (DKWeld,Ireland) **3-9-0** MJKinane (sn cl up: effrt fr over 2f out: 2nd u.p 1½f out: kpt on: no imp) | 3 | **2** | 5/1[3] | 111 | 26 |
| 939[4] | **My Branch** (BWHills) **3-9-0** MHills (hld up: hdwy over 3f out: rdn & wnt 3rd 1½f out: no ex ins fnl f) | ½ | **3** | 6/1 | 110 | 25 |
| 874* | **Distant Oasis (USA)** (HRACecil) **3-9-0** PatEddery (hld up: hdwy over 2f out: 4th & rdn 1½f out: no imp fnl f) | 1½ | **4** | 5/2[1] | 107 | 22 |
| 1255a[5] | **Priory Belle (IRE)** (JSBolger,Ireland) **3-9-0** KJManning (bhd: r.o u.p fnl 1½f: nrst fin) | 1½ | **5** | 25/1 | 104 | 19 |
| 1255a[2] | **Zafzala (IRE)** (JOxx,Ireland) **3-9-0** JPMurtagh (cl up: wnt 2nd 3½f out: rdn over 2f out: sn lost pl: one pce fr wl over 1f out) | ½ | **6** | 12/1 | 103 | 18 |
| 1246a* | **Sheraka (IRE)** (JOxx,Ireland) **3-9-1**[ow1] GMosse (hld up: hdwy over 3f out: rdn wl over 2f out: sn btn) | 1 | **7** | 14/1 | 102 | 16 |
| 1255a[3] | **Asmara (USA)** (JOxx,Ireland) **3-9-0** CRoche (chsd ldrs: rdn ½-wy: lost pl over 3f out: eased over 1f out) | 1 | **8** | 25/1 | 99 | 14 |
| | **Tossup (USA)** (JGBurns,Ireland) **3-9-0** PShanahan (stumbled after 1½f: n.d) | 15 | **9** | 20/1 | 69 | — |
| 964[6] | **Abir** (HThomsonJones) **3-9-0** WJSupple (sn led: hdd ½-wy: wknd qckly 3½f out: sn bhd: eased) | 5½ | **10** | 150/1 | 58 | — |
| | **Princess Tycoon (IRE)** (APO'Brien,Ireland) **3-9-0** SCraine (s.s: a bhd) | 3 | **11** | 200/1 | 52 | — |
| 939[3] | **Bint Shadayid (USA)** (SbinSuroor) **3-9-0** LDettori (prom over 3f: wknd qckly ½-wy: sn bhd: eased: t.o) | 20 | **12** | 4/1[2] | 12 | — |
| | | | | (SP 124.2%) | | **12 Rn** |

**1m 39.8** (4.80) OWNER Hamdan Al Maktoum (NEWMARKET) BRED Barronstown Stud
**939 Matiya (IRE)** took over after three and a half furlongs out and kept on really well. She might have been tying up a little towards the end and there are obvious stamina doubts. (5/1)
**Dance Design (IRE)** ran well on this reappearance. Going second under pressure a furlong and a half out, she kept on well without making any inroads on the winner's advantage. (5/1)
**939 My Branch** went third a furlong and a half out, but she found this stiff mile testing her to the limit. Her aim is the Jersey Stakes. (6/1)
**874* Distant Oasis (USA)** made headway on the outer to get into a challenging position two furlongs out. Fourth and making little impression from a furlong and a half out, she could improve a bit on this. (5/2)
**1255a Priory Belle (IRE)** ran on from a furlong and a half out to be a tail-swishing nearest at the finish. (25/1)
**1255a Zafzala (IRE)**, in second place after halfway, was beaten a furlong and a half out. (12/1)
**1246a* Sheraka (IRE)** is shaping like a stayer, but could make no impression over the last two furlongs. (14/1)
**964 Abir** ran in front until headed by the winner, and was soon behind. (150/1)
**939 Bint Shadayid (USA)** raced prominently for three furlongs until weakening quickly from halfway. Eased down and completely tailed off, she was afterwards found to be 'clinically abnormal'. (4/1)
NR

## 1568a-1572a (Irish Racing) - See Computer Raceform

# 1564a-CURRAGH (Newbridge, Ireland) (R-H) (Good to soft)
## Sunday May 26th

### 1573a CONRAD INTERNATIONAL DUBLIN SILVER STKS (Listed) (3-Y.O)
3-35 (3-36) **1m 2f** £9,675.00 (£2,775.00: £1,275.00: £375.00)

| | Horse / details | Dist | Pos | SP | RR | SF |
|---|---|---|---|---|---|---|
| | **Identify (IRE)** (JSBolger,Ireland) **3-8-9**ow1 KJManning (rn 2nd: jnd ldr appr ½-wy: led st: rdn clr 2f out: r.o wl: eased bef fin) | — | **1** | 2/1[1] | 105+ | 54 |
| 1249a[2] | **Harghar (USA)** (JOxx,Ireland) **3-8-11** JPMurtagh (hld up: wnt mod 3rd & rdn appr st: 2nd under 2f out: styd on: nt trble wnr) | 5½ | **2** | 9/2[3] | 98 | 48 |
| | **Sun Ballet (IRE)** (JOxx,Ireland) **3-8-8** LDettori (bhd: hdwy st: wnt fair 3rd over 1f out: styd on) | 4 | **3** | 9/1 | 89 | 39 |
| | **Blending Element (IRE)** (TStack,Ireland) **3-8-8** MJKinane (bhd: last ½-wy: 6th st: styd on: nvr nrr) | 4 | **4** | 12/1 | 82 | 32 |
| 1151[4] | **Polar Eclipse** (MJohnston) **3-8-11** JWeaver (led: jnd appr ½-wy: 2nd st: wknd qckly over 2f out) | 3½ | **5** | 9/2[3] | 80 | 30 |
| | **Lone Eagle (IRE)** (APO'Brien,Ireland) **3-8-11** CRoche (fair 4th & drvn along ½-wy: n.d last 2f: eased whn btn) | 1 | **6** | 7/2[2] | 78 | 28 |
| | **Safflower (IRE)** (JTGorman,Ireland) **3-8-3** RTFitzpatrick (bhd: last st: t.o) | 25 | **7** | 14/1 | 30 | — |
| | | | | (SP 116.3%) | | **7 Rn** |

**2m 8.9** (4.90) OWNER Michael Smurfit (COOLCULLEN)

**Identify (IRE)**, successful in a handicap last time, made this look ridiculously easy, leading into the straight and going clear from two furlongs out. She moves up 11lb to a new mark of 110 and joins the Dermot Weld stable. (2/1: op 3/1)

**1249a Harghar (USA)**, with a victory over the winner to his credit earlier in the season, was a one-paced second over the last two furlongs here. (9/2: op 5/2)

**Sun Ballet (IRE)** made headway in the straight to go a never-threatening third over a furlong out. (9/1: op 6/1)

**Blending Element (IRE)** (12/1: op 8/1)

**1151 Polar Eclipse** led and disputed the lead until the straight where he weakened quickly over two furlongs out. (9/2)

### 1574a FIRST NATIONAL BUILDING SOCIETY IRISH 2,000 GUINEAS (Gp 1) (3-Y.O C & F)
4-10 (4-12) **1m (New)** £112,700.00 (£38,700.00: £18,700.00: £6,700.00)

| | Horse / details | Dist | Pos | SP | RR | SF |
|---|---|---|---|---|---|---|
| 1141a[2] | **Spinning World (USA)** (JEPease,France) **3-9-0** CAsmussen (hld up: hdwy over 2f out: 2nd & rdn over 1f out: led ent fnl f: qcknd clr) | — | **1** | 7/4[1] | 127 | 68 |
| 1253a[2] | **Rainbow Blues (IRE)** (APO'Brien,Ireland) **3-9-0** CRoche (prom: pushed along ½-wy: led wl over 1f out: hdd & outpcd ins fnl f) | 2 | **2** | 50/1 | 123 | 64 |
| 926[5] | **Beauchamp King** (JLDunlop) **3-9-0** MJKinane (hld up: hdwy & swtchd lft over 2f out: r.o u.p fnl f) | 1½ | **3** | 9/2[3] | 120 | 61 |
| 926[3] | **Bijou d'Inde** (MJohnston) **3-9-0** JWeaver (prom: disp ld over 3f out: rdn & led 2½f out: hdd wl over 1f out: no ex) | 3 | **4** | 3/1[2] | 114 | 55 |
| 1141a[3] | **Tagula (IRE)** (IABalding) **3-9-0** KDarley (hld up: trckng ldrs ½-wy: rdn over 2f out: unable qckn wl over 1f out) | 1 | **5** | 11/1 | 112 | 53 |
| 942* | **Phantom Quest** (HRACecil) **3-9-0** PatEddery (hld up: chsng ldrs ½-wy: sn pushed along: no imp fr 2f out) | 2½ | **6** | 10/1 | 107 | 48 |
| | **Russian Revival (USA)** (SbinSuroor) **3-9-0** LDettori (sn led: jnd over 3f out: hdd 2½f out: sn wknd) | 9 | **7** | 12/1 | 89 | 30 |
| 962* | **Musick House (IRE)** (PWChapple-Hyam) **3-9-0** BThompson (7th & rdn ½-wy: sn n.d) | 2½ | **8** | 16/1 | 84 | 25 |
| 1247a* | **Deed of Love (USA)** (JSBolger,Ireland) **3-9-0** KJManning (a bhd) | ½ | **9** | 14/1 | 83 | 24 |
| | **Flame of Athens (IRE)** (MJGrassick,Ireland) **3-9-0** JPMurtagh (a bhd) | 7 | **10** | 20/1 | 69 | 10 |
| | | | | (SP 123.9%) | | **10 Rn** |

**1m 38.8** (3.80) OWNER Niarchos Family (CHANTILLY)

**1141a Spinning World (USA)** was not going to encounter any traffic problems this time and Asmussen made ground up the middle with two furlongs to race. Cruising in second place with a furlong to run, the response was not immediate but he quickened clear early inside the last for an emphatic win. (7/4)

**1253a Rainbow Blues (IRE)** looked like bringing off the surprise of the season for a few strides at the furlong marker. Eventually he was completely outpaced, but it was a performance which necessitated raising him 13lb to 113. (50/1)

**926 Beauchamp King**, waited with and then switched to the outer over two furlongs out, ran on under pressure but was never nearer than at the line. It is difficult to see him ever beating the winner. (9/2)

**926 Bijou d'Inde** disputed it over three furlongs out but, headed over a furlong out, found nothing. There may be possible stamina limitations. (3/1)

**1141a Tagula (IRE)**, tracking the leaders at halfway, found this ground holding and was unable to quicken in it. (11/1)

**942* Phantom Quest**, close up to halfway, was soon ridden along and could make no impression two furlongs out. (10/1)

**Russian Revival (USA)** led to over three furlongs out and soon weakened. (12/1: op 8/1)

**962* Musick House (IRE)** looked very ordinary, being ridden along at halfway and never getting into contention. (16/1)

### 1575a TATTERSALLS GOLD CUP (Gp 2) (4-Y.O+)
4-45 (4-46) **1m 2f** £32,500.00 (£9,500.00: £4,500.00: £1,500.00)

| | Horse / details | Dist | Pos | SP | RR | SF |
|---|---|---|---|---|---|---|
| 1252a* | **Definite Article** (DKWeld,Ireland) **4-8-12** MJKinane (rn 3rd: hdwy & carried wd st: led under 2f out: edgd rt: kpt on wl u.p) | — | **1** | 15/8[1] | 124 | 62 |
| | **Timarida (IRE)** (JOxx,Ireland) **4-8-12** JPMurtagh (hld up: hdwy 4f out: 4th st: effrt on outside to go 2nd over 1f out: r.o) | 1 | **2** | 2/1[2] | 122 | 60 |
| *435a*[4] | **Annus Mirabilis (FR)** (SbinSuroor) **4-8-12** LDettori (broke best: sn hdd: rn 2nd: c wd st: sn rdn: no imp fr wl over 1f out) | 3 | **3** | 5/1[3] | 118 | 56 |
| 1131[3] | **Sanoosea (USA)** (MRStoute) **4-8-12** CAsmussen (in tch tl lost pl bef st: rdn & r.o wl fnl f) | nk | **4** | 10/1 | 117 | 55 |
| | **River North (IRE)** (LadyHerries) **6-8-12** KDarley (5th st: rdn & no imp last 2f) | 4 | **5** | 10/1 | 111 | 49 |
| 1252a[5] | **Viaticum (IRE)** (NMeade,Ireland) **4-8-9b** JMorgan (sn led & wnt clr: wknd bef st: hdd 2f out: sn btn) | 4 | **6** | 33/1 | 101 | 39 |
| 1252a[2] | **Al Mohaajir (USA)** (JSBolger,Ireland) **5-8-12** KJManning (a bhd) | 2 | **7** | 10/1 | 101 | 39 |
| | **Kayaara (IRE)** (NFurlong,Ireland) **4-8-12** WJSupple (ref to r: t.n.p) | | **R** | 25/1 | — | — |
| | | | | (SP 118.8%) | | **8 Rn** |

**2m 8.9** (4.90) OWNER Moyglare Stud Farm (CURRAGH) BRED Dr D. Davis

**1252a* Definite Article**, in third place until coming steadily wide into the straight, led under two furlongs out and, despite edging towards the rail, he kept on strongly under pressure. He will come on further for this. (15/8)
**Timarida (IRE)** ran well on this reappearance, making headway to go fourth in the straight and delivering a sustained challenge to go second over a furlong out. With the sex allowance, she could well turn the tables on the winner in the future. (2/1: op 5/4)
**435a Annus Mirabilis (FR)**, settled in second place, came wide into the straight but was making no impression on the first two from a furlong out. (5/1)
**1131 Sanoosea (USA)** lost interest before the straight but ran on again inside the last. (10/1)
**River North (IRE)** could make no headway over the last two furlongs. (10/1)
**1252a Al Mohaajir (USA)**, second here earlier in the season to the winner, was a trailer throughout this time. (10/1: op 6/1)

## 1396a-LONGCHAMP (Paris, France) (R-H) (Soft)
### Thursday May 23rd

### 1577a PRIX DE LA PORTE DE MADRID (Listed) (4-Y.O+)
3-20 (3-26) **1m 4f** £18,445.00 (£6,324.00: £3,953.00)

| | Horse | Dist | Pos | SP | RR | SF |
|---|---|---|---|---|---|---|
| | **Poliglote** (MmeCHead,France) **4-8-12** FHead | — | **1** | | 117 | — |
| 907a² | **Rainbow Dancer (FR)** (PBary,France) **5-8-12** DBoeuf | 1½ | **2** | | 115 | — |
| | **Maid Of Honor (FR)** (JdeRoualle,France) **4-8-13** WMongil | ¾ | **3** | | 115 | — |
| | | | | | | **7 Rn** |

**2m 43.5** (17.50) P-M 2.30F: 1.40F 1.40F (2.50F) OWNER Wertheimer Brothers (CHANTILLY) BRED Wertheimer et Freres
**Poliglote**, second to Celtic Swing in last season's Prix Du Jockey Club, made a successful return to the track in this Listed event. He should be able to return to a higher level with confidence restored.

## 1392a-SAN SIRO (Milan, Italy) (R-H) (Good to firm)
### Friday May 24th

### 1578a PREMIO ROCCHETTA TANARO (3-Y.O)
2-30 (2-35) **7f 110y** £6,090.00

| | Horse | Dist | Pos | SP | RR | SF |
|---|---|---|---|---|---|---|
| | **Second Barrage** (LMCumani) **3-9-2** MCangiano | — | **1** | | 104+ | — |
| | **Diogene Laerzio (ITY)** (PBilleri,Italy) **3-9-2** GForte | 10 | **2** | | 83 | — |
| | **Trood** (GVerricelli,Italy) **3-9-2** LSorrentino | 2½ | **3** | | 77 | — |
| | | | | | | **12 Rn** |

**No Time Taken** TOTE 29L: 19L 82L 35L (760L) OWNER Allevamento Giailoblu (NEWMARKET) BRED Milton Park Stud Partnership
**Second Barrage** gave the impression that he will be one to follow in the future. Setting a good pace, he had all his rivals struggling with three furlongs still to go. He soon put daylight between himself and his nearest rival for a comfortable win. He is sure to go on to better things.

## 1135a-CAPANNELLE (Rome, Italy) (R-H) (Good to firm)
### Saturday May 25th

### 1579a PREMIO ELLINGTON-MEMORIAL CARLO D'ALESSIO (Gp 2) (4-Y.O+)
2-00 (2-00) **1m 4f** £42,813.00 (£19,524.00: £10,850.00: £5,425.00)

| | Horse | Dist | Pos | SP | RR | SF |
|---|---|---|---|---|---|---|
| 906a² | **Luso** (CEBrittain) **4-8-9** BDoyle (mde all: comf) | — | **1** | | 120+ | — |
| | **Tiana (ITY)** (OPacifici,Italy) **4-8-9** CFiocchi (4th tl hdwy 1f out: kpt on one pce) | 2½ | **2** | | 115 | — |
| | **Pay Me Back (IRE)** (GVerricelli,Italy) **6-8-9** LSorrentino (chsd ldrs: rdn & outpcd appr fnl f: kpt on wl nr fin) | s.h | **3** | | 115 | — |
| | **Sugarland Express (IRE)** (AVerdesi,Italy) **5-8-9** GBietolini (trckd ldr tl wknd appr fnl f) | 3½ | **4** | | 108 | — |
| | **Torrismondo (USA)** (Italy) **5-8-9** GVerricelli (a bhd) | 7 | **5** | | 94 | — |
| | | | | | | **5 Rn** |

**2m 29.8** TOTE 11L: 11L 16L (58L) OWNER Mr Saeed Manana (NEWMARKET) BRED Saeed Manana
**906a Luso** disposed of his four modest rivals with the minimum of fuss. Forced to make his own running, he quickened up when challenged two and a half furlongs out, and from then on, always had matters under control. He may come back to Italy for the Gran Premio di Milano but has the Coronation Cup as an alternative.

## 1579a-CAPANNELLE (Rome, Italy) (R-H) (Good to firm)
### Sunday May 26th

### 1580a DERBY ITALIANO (Gp 1) (3-Y.O C & F)
4-00 (4-20) **1m 4f** £209,536.00 (£106,808.00: £62,544.00: £31,272.00)

| | Horse | Dist | Pos | SP | RR | SF |
|---|---|---|---|---|---|---|
| 1114⁷ | **Bahamian Knight (CAN)** (DRLoder) **3-9-2** RHughes (7th st: hdwy over 2f out: led over 1f out: r.o) | — | **1** | | 109 | — |
| 1002* | **Backdrop (IRE)** (PWChapple-Hyam) **3-9-2** JCarroll (mid div: hdwy over 2f out: r.o wl fnl f) | 1¾ | **2** | | 107 | — |
| 1058a* | **Coral Reef (ITY)** (GColleo,Italy) **3-9-2** MLatorre (led tl over 1f out: kpt on one pce) | ¾ | **3** | | 106 | — |
| 1058a² | **Ranuncolo (ITY)** (PMazzoni,Italy) **3-9-2** BJovine (hld up: last st: gd hdwy fnl 2f: nrst fin) | 2½ | **4** | | 102 | — |
| 903a* | **Dancer Mitral** (LBrogi,Italy) **3-9-2** CFiocchi (in rr tl st: hdwy fnl 3f: nrst fin) | ½ | **5** | | 102 | — |
| | **Kafhar** (LBrogi,Italy) **3-9-2** VMezzatesta (gd hdwy over 3f out: ev ch 2f out: one pce) | ½ | **6** | | 101 | — |
| 1076⁵ | **Dismissed (USA)** (PFICole) **3-9-2** TQuinn (4th st: ev ch 2f out: sn wknd) | ¾ | **7** | | 100 | — |
| 725² | **Flyfisher (IRE)** (GLewis) **3-9-2** PaulEddery (trckd ldr: 2nd st: wknd over 2f out) | 1½ | **8** | | 98 | — |
| 793a* | **Pierrot Solaire (FR)** (AColella,Italy) **3-9-2b¹** ACorniani (prom: 8th st: no hdwy fnl 3f) | 1½ | **9** | | 96 | — |
| 1015⁴ | **Babinda** (CEBrittain) **3-9-2** BDoyle (in tch to 3f out) | 1¼ | **10** | | 94 | — |
| 1076² | **Heron Island (IRE)** (PWChapple-Hyam) **3-9-2** JReid (6th st: wknd 2f out) | 1½ | **11** | | 92 | — |
| | **Golden Agos** (GFratini,Italy) **3-9-2** MEsposito (a in rr) | 10 | **12** | | 79 | — |
| | **Anticolano (IRE)** (LBietolini,Italy) **3-9-2** GBietolini (a in rr) | 1½ | **13** | | 77 | — |
| | **Touch Judge (USA)** (DKWeld,Ireland) **3-9-2b¹** PShanahan (swtng: 5th st: wknd wl over 2f out) | 1¼ | **14** | | 75 | — |

| | | | SP | RR | SF |
|---|---|---|---|---|---|
| | **His Excellence (USA)** (APO'Brien,Ireland) **3-9-2** SCraine (3rd st: sn wknd) ........½ | **15** | | 75 | — |
| | | | | | **15 Rn** |

**2m 26.6** TOTE 165L: 51L 102L 40L (2313L) OWNER Lucayan Stud Ltd (NEWMARKET) BRED Donald F. Prowse & Don A. McIntosh

**1114 Bahamian Knight (CAN)** was ill-suited by the slow pace in the Dante but, with Coral Reef setting a cracking pace from the off, he was right back to his best. Seventh into the straight, he enjoyed a trouble-free passage before hitting the front approaching the furlong pole, and was ridden right out. The Irish Derby is now on the agenda.

**1002* Backdrop (IRE)** had plenty in front of him turning into the straight, but followed the winner through. Drifting into the centre of the track as Carroll used his whip vigorously in his right hand, he stayed on really strongly to grab second place well inside the final furlong. This was a remarkable effort for a horse who was beaten on merit in a 0-95 Chester handicap on his previous start.

**1076 Dismissed (USA)** was never far away and moved up to hold every chance at the quarter-mile pole, before fading rapidly.

**725 Flyfisher (IRE)** tracked the leaders into the straight, but was not really travelling even at that stage and soon back-pedalling.

**1015 Babinda** tried for a run up the inside but never had a great deal of room. He never threatened to take a hand in the finish, but may prove better than his finishing position suggests.

**1076 Heron Island (IRE)** fared much worse than his lesser-fancied stable-companion. Hard ridden to close on the leaders on the outside fully three furlongs out, he would not let himself down on this fast ground.

**Touch Judge (USA)** was surprisingly sent off as favourite. Sweating up badly in the preliminaries, he weakened quickly over three furlongs out and something was clearly amiss.

## 1389a-DEAUVILLE (France) (R-H) (Soft)
## Sunday May 26th

### 1581a PRIX DU GROS-CHENE (Gp 2) (3-Y.O+)
2-55 (2-51) **5f** £39,526.00 (£15,810.00: £7,905.00: £3,953.00)

| | | | SP | RR | SF |
|---|---|---|---|---|---|
| 1056a* | **Anabaa (USA)** (MmeCHead,France) **4-9-3** FHead (racd 2nd early: gd hdwy to ld over 1f out: impressive) ...— | **1** | | 121+ | 66 |
| | **Easy Option (IRE)** (SbinSuroor) **4-8-10** SGuillot (racd 5th: mde prog ½-wy: wnt rt u.p over 1f out: r.o fnl f: no ch w wnr) ........2 | **2** | | 108 | 53 |
| | **General Alan (FR)** (PTual,France) **3-8-6** TJarnet (led: rdn 2f out: hdd over 1f out: styd on wl) ........1½ | **3** | | 107 | 44 |
| 721a³ | **Titus Livius (FR)** (JEPease,France) **3-8-13** OPeslier (racd in 4th: rdn fr ½-wy: outpcd: sme late prog)........½ | **4** | | 112 | 49 |
| | **Don't Worry Me (IRE)** (GHenrot,France) **4-8-10** AJunk (racd in 3rd: rdn & unable to qckn fr over 2 out)........nk | **5** | | 100 | 45 |
| | **Phone Fee (USA)** (CLaffon-Parias,France) **3-8-6** FSanchez (in rr early on: nvr any ch) ........½ | **6** | | 103 | 40 |
| 960² | **General Monash (USA)** (PWChapple-Hyam) **4-9-0** DHarrison (in rr: outpcd fr ½-wy)........3 | **7** | | 93 | 38 |
| | | | | | **7 Rn** |

**60.0 secs** (3.50) P-M 1.30F: 1.10F 2.00F (5.20F) OWNER Mme A. Head (CHANTILLY) BRED Gainsborough Farm Inc

**1056a* Anabaa (USA)** is the best sprinter to be seen out so far in Europe this season, and dominated his first Group Two race from start to finish. Considering the state of the ground, the time of one minute dead was most respectable, and he was only coasting in the final furlong with his jockey allowed the luxury of looking over both shoulders. He is becoming more of a sprinter with each race and has now judged his start from the stalls to perfection. His jockey reported that better ground would have enabled Anabaa to be even more impressive, and he now goes for the King's Stand Stakes. It will take a decent horse to end his current run of four straight wins.

**Easy Option (IRE)** was a picture in the paddock, and she put up a decent effort, but never looked like getting on terms with the winner. Held up early, she swerved under the whip when making her challenge, but ran on well in the final furlong which suggests she might be a force over a slightly longer distance. She needs soft ground, which will govern her future programme, and she looks sure to win a decent race this year.

**General Alan (FR)** ran his heart out and put up one of the best performances of his career. He went stride for stride with Anabaa for four furlongs, but could not hold him for the fifth. He looks capable of winning a listed or even Group Three race.

**721a Titus Livius (FR)** has thickened out, but not grown since his two-year-old days. Always in mid-division but not able to go the pace in the final furlong and a half, this minimum distance seems a little sharp for him and he could be more of a force over six furlongs or possibly a little further. Despite being a three-year-old, he was only receiving two kilos from the winner as a result of his juvenile successes.

**960 General Monash (USA)** appeared outpaced throughout and was last for virtually the whole race. This five-furlongs definitely looked too sharp for him.

### 1582a PRIX DU PALAIS-ROYAL (Gp 3) (3-Y.O+)
4-00 (3-48) **7f** £28,986.00 (£10,540.00: £5,270.00: £2,635.00)

| | | | SP | RR | SF |
|---|---|---|---|---|---|
| 810³ | **Mistle Cat (USA)** (SPCWoods) **6-9-4** WWoods ........— | **1** | | 115 | 86 |
| 810⁶ | **Myself** (PWChapple-Hyam) **4-9-1** DHarrison ........2 | **2** | | 107 | 78 |
| 818* | **Young Ern** (SDow) **6-9-4** WRyan ........½ | **3** | | 109 | 80 |
| | | | | | **6 Rn** |

**1m 27.56** (3.56) P-M 5.80F: 3.40F 4.90F (34.00F) OWNER Mr P. Chu (NEWMARKET) BRED Henry H. Fitzgibbon & Overbrook Farm

**810 Mistle Cat (USA)** was produced spot on by his trainer and, after taking the lead immediately after the start, had it won by the furlong marker after galloping his five opponents into the ground. This was a thoroughly deserved first Group win for both the horse and the trainer, who thinks Mistle Cat is now at his best. The six-year-old will now be campaigned in top-class company, and heads for the Queen Anne Stakes at Royal Ascot. He is a most genuine performer who appears to be getting better with age.

**810 Myself** was putting in her best work at the end having been held up early on. She swerved when making her challenge a furlong and a half out, and could never reach the leader. It was a welcome return to form by this filly, who could come back to France for the Prix de la Porte Maillot at Longchamp next month.

**818* Young Ern** was rather disappointing and, try as he did, was never able to get on terms with Mistle Cat. He came under strong pressure a furlong and a half out and stayed on at one pace. He appeared to lack his usual zip and his trainer was slightly bemused by the effort, but he will return to Deauville for a second tilt at the Prix Maurice de Gheest.

## 0996-AYR (L-H) (Soft becoming Good)
## Friday May 31st
WEATHER: fine WIND: str

### 1583 GREIG MIDDLETON PEP MEDIAN AUCTION MAIDEN STKS (2-Y.O) (Class E)
2-00 (2-02) **6f** £3,208.75 (£970.00: £472.50: £223.75) Stalls: High GOING: 0.27 sec per fur (G)

| | | | SP | RR | SF |
|---|---|---|---|---|---|
| | **Samsung Spirit** (EWeymes) **2-8-9** JQuinn(6) (bhd: swtchd & hdwy ½-wy: led wl over 1f out: styd on wl) .....— | **1** | 10/1 | 62+ | 5 |

1191[7] **Bold Oriental (IRE)** (NACallaghan) **2-9-0** PatEddery(10) (a cl up: led 2f out: sn hdd: kpt on one pce) ..........1¾ **2** 11/4[2] 62 5
996[8] **Biff-Em (IRE)** (MissLAPerratt) **2-9-0** NCarlisle(2) (in tch: hdwy over 2f out: styd on wl: nrst fin) ..........3 **3** 25/1 54 —
1360[4] **Alisadara** (NBycroft) **2-8-9** NConnorton(3) (in tch: styd on fnl 2f: nrst fin) ..........1¼ **4** 20/1 46 —
1038[5] **Barnburgh Boy** (TDBarron) **2-9-0** JFortune(4) (led 4f: grad wknd) ..........hd **5** 2/1[1] 51 —
1086[13] **Father Eddie** (JJO'Neill) **2-9-0** DeanMcKeown(9) (outpcd ½-wy: kpt on appr fnl f: n.d) ..........1½ **6** 25/1 47 —
685[11] **Our Future (IRE)** (MJohnston) **2-9-0** TWilliams(8) (cl up over 3f: wknd) ..........¾ **7** 14/1 45 —
**Plutarch Angel** (WTKemp) **2-8-11**(3) DarrenMoffatt(7) (dwlt: sn wl bhd) ..........7 **8** 66/1 26 —
1166[10] **The Orraman (IRE)** (JJO'Neill) **2-9-0** AlexGreaves(5) (outpcd & bhd fr ½-wy) ..........1½ **9** 25/1 22 —
608[8] **Prince of Parkes** (JBerry) **2-9-0** JCarroll(1) (rdn after 2f: sn wknd) ..........2½ **10** 6/1[3] 15 —

(SP 107.8%) **10 Rn**

**1m 17.73** (7.93) CSF £33.04 TOTE £11.30: £1.60 £1.40 £2.40 (£33.50) Trio £70.00 OWNER Mr T. A. Scothern (MIDDLEHAM) BRED Red House Stud

**Samsung Spirit** is a useful-looking type and certainly stays well as she was running into an extremely strong wind here. (10/1)
**Bold Oriental (IRE)** ran a fine race from what appeared a moderate draw and was certainly not given a hard time when beaten. He is on the upgrade. (11/4: 5/4-3/1)
**996 Biff-Em (IRE)** showed much improved form this time and looks to be going the right way. (25/1)
**1360 Alisadara** was given a stiff test in the circumstances, and she appreciated this by staying well at the end. (20/1)
**1038 Barnburgh Boy** attempted to make all but facing this very strong wind found him out in the last couple of furlongs. He should be forgiven this. (2/1: op 7/2)
**Father Eddie** appreciated the extra furlong in these testing conditions, but only got going when it was too late. (25/1)
**618 Our Future (IRE)** (14/1: 7/1-16/1)
**608 Prince of Parkes** (6/1: op 7/2)

## 1584 GILT-EDGED RATING RELATED MAIDEN STKS (0-60) (3-Y.O) (Class F)

2-30 (2-34) **1m 2f** £2,722.50 (£760.00: £367.50) Stalls: Low GOING: 0.27 sec per fur (G)

SP RR SF

**Temptress (60)** (PTWalwyn) **3-8-11** DeanMcKeown(4) (mde all: qcknd 3f out: kpt on u.p towards fin) ..........— **1** 7/1[3] 56 —
1185[6] **Mock Trial (IRE) (58)** (MrsJRRamsden) **3-9-0** KFallon(3) (stdd s: hld up & bhd: hdwy 2f out: styd on: nt rch wnr) ..........1¼ **2** 2/7[1] 57 —
1167[4] **Rattle (49)** (JJO'Neill) **3-9-0** JFortune(1) (trckd wnr: ev ch over 2f out: rdn & one pce) ..........s.h **3** 11/2[2] 57 —
1042[14] **Miletrian City (56)** (JBerry) **3-9-0** JCarroll(5) (trckd ldrs tl outpcd fnl 3f) ..........20 **4** 33/1 25 —

(SP 108.6%) **4 Rn**

**2m 20.21** (15.61) CSF £9.53 TOTE £7.00: (£2.20) OWNER Mr A. D. G. Oldrey (LAMBOURN) BRED A. D. G. Oldrey

**Temptress** showed very little last year but stole this slowly-run event. (7/1: op 9/2)
**1185 Mock Trial (IRE)**, trying a distance more likely to suit, was given a poor ride in this slowly-run event and this is best forgotten. (2/7)
**1167 Rattle** was not made enough use of in this slowly-run race and was short of speed in the home straight. (11/2: 7/2-6/1)
**Miletrian City**, stepping up in trip, did not run any sort of race once the pace increased early in the straight. (33/1)

## 1585 GREIG MIDDLETON STOCKBROKERS CUP H'CAP (0-80) (3-Y.O+) (Class D)

3-00 (3-02) **1m 2f** £4,260.00 (£1,290.00: £630.00: £300.00) Stalls: Low GOING: 0.27 sec per fur (G)

SP RR SF

1198[2] **Sarmatian (USA) (69)** (MDHammond) **5-9-10** KFallon(6) (hld up & bhd: hdwy to ld appr fnl f: r.o) ..........— **1** 100/30[1] 83 43
1345[4] **Stormless (41)** (PMonteith) **5-7-10** NCarlisle(5) (a.p: smooth hdwy to ld 1½f out: sn hdd & nt qckn) ..........2 **2** 7/1 52 12
999[3] **Drummer Hicks (43)** (EWeymes) **7-7-12** JQuinn(1) (chsd ldrs tl outpcd appr st: styd on again fnl 2f) ..........2½ **3** 4/1[3] 50 10
*399*[6] **Swandale Flyer (42)** (NBycroft) **4-7-11**ow1 TWilliams(2) (led tl hdd 1½f out: wknd) ..........3 **4** 40/1 44 3
863[3] **Arcady (66)** (PTWalwyn) **3-8-7** DeanMcKeown(4) (hdwy 5f out: ch 3f out: wknd fnl 2f) ..........7 **5** 7/2[2] 57 3
**Home Counties (IRE) (68)** (DMoffatt) **7-9-6**(3) DarrenMoffatt(7) (hld up: hdwy & prom appr st: wknd over 2f out) ..........3 **6** 7/1 54 14
1092[3] **Best of All (IRE) (69)** (JBerry) **4-9-10** JCarroll(3) (chsd ldrs tl wknd over 2f out) ..........1 **7** 5/1 53 13

(SP 109.4%) **7 Rn**

**2m 15.38** (10.78) CSF £23.02 TOTE £4.00: £1.50 £3.90 (£12.50) OWNER Mr S. T. Brankin (MIDDLEHAM) BRED David Allan
LONG HANDICAP Stormless 7-3
WEIGHT FOR AGE 3yo-14lb

**1198 Sarmatian (USA)**, sitting off the pace, produced a turn of foot to settle it inside the final furlong and won most emphatically. He seems to save his best performances for racing in Scotland. (100/30)
**1345 Stormless** really travelled well but, just when he hit the front over a furlong out, the winner swept past him and he found little. He is on good terms with himself. (7/1)
**999 Drummer Hicks** is a frustrating character these days and, after losing his pitch turning for home, he ran on when it was all too late. (4/1)
**Swandale Flyer** ran his best race to date. (40/1)
**863 Arcady** is nothing much to look at and, once she had to face this strong wind in the straight, she soon cried enough. (7/2)
**1092 Best of All (IRE)**, stepped up in trip, found that and the testing conditions too much in the last two furlongs. (5/1: 4/1-6/1)

## 1586 GREIG MIDDLETON PRIVATE CLIENT H'CAP (0-70) (3-Y.O+) (Class E)

3-30 (3-34) **1m** £3,160.00 (£955.00: £465.00: £220.00) Stalls: Low GOING: 0.27 sec per fur (G)

SP RR SF

1001* **Highspeed (IRE) (52)** (SEKettlewell) **4-8-12** JFortune(5) (a.p: rdn to ld ins fnl f: styd on wl) ..........— **1** 5/2[2] 63 47
1313[2] **Persian Fayre (64)** (JBerry) **4-9-10** JCarroll(2) (led: rdn over 1f out: hdd & no ex ins fnl f) ..........1¾ **2** 3/1[3] 72 56
1001[7] **Teejay'n'aitch (IRE) (43)** (JSGoldie) **4-8-3** JQuinn(6) (hld up: effrt 3f out: sn outpcd: styd on towards fin) ..........6 **3** 14/1 39 23
769[8] **River Garnock (50)** (DNicholls) **4-8-3**(7) JBramhill(1) (chsd ldr tl wknd fnl 2f) ..........s.h **4** 16/1 45 29
1363* **Winston (66)** (JDBethell) **3-9-0** 6x KFallon(4) (outpcd & lost tch appr st: sme hdwy 2f out: no imp) ..........5 **5** 6/4[1] 51 23
1311[8] **Strathtore Dream (IRE) (36)** (MissLAPerratt) **5-7-10** NCarlisle(8) (prom tl wknd fnl 3f) ..........14 **6** 100/1 — —

(SP 107.1%) **6 Rn**

**1m 44.32** (6.92) CSF £9.37 CT £61.25 TOTE £3.10: £2.20 £1.70 (£4.30) OWNER Mr David Wright (MIDDLEHAM) BRED R.McQuillan
LONG HANDICAP Strathtore Dream (IRE) 7-0
WEIGHT FOR AGE 3yo-12lb
**OFFICIAL EXPLANATION Winston: sustained a cut to his front leg and finished lame.**

**1001* Highspeed (IRE)** got this extra furlong well and kept on most determinedly in the closing stages. (5/2)
**1313 Persian Fayre** keeps running well and deserves a change of luck. (3/1)
**Teejay'n'aitch (IRE)** gives the impression that he has more ability, and only decided to run when it was too late on this occasion. (14/1)
**River Garnock** stepped up from sprint distances here. He ran well but testing conditions just found him out in the last couple of furlongs. (16/1)
**1363* Winston** was never going at all and was later found to be lame. (6/4)

## 1587 GREIG MIDDLETON PORTFOLIO CHARITY MAIDEN STKS (3-Y.O+) (Class D)

4-00 (4-00) **1m 5f 13y** £3,779.00 (£1,142.00: £556.00: £263.00) Stalls: Low GOING: 0.27 sec per fur (G)

| Form | Horse | Dist | Pos | SP | RR | SF |
|---|---|---|---|---|---|---|
| $1168^{2}$ | **Candle Smile (USA) (86)** (MRStoute) **4-9-12** DeanMcKeown(4) (mde all: styd on gamely fnl 2f) | — | 1 | $2/1^{2}$ | 82 | 34 |
| $1153^{2}$ | **Ancient Quest** (NACallaghan) **3-8-7** PatEddery(5) (trckd wnr: chal 3f out: sn pushed along: no ex ins fnl f) | 1½ | 2 | $4/7^{1}$ | 80 | 13 |
| | **Tillyboy** (MrsMReveley) **6-9-12** JFortune(3) (dwlt: hdwy 6f out: styd on: nvr plcd to chal) | 3½ | 3 | 20/1 | 76 | 28 |
| | **Double Dash (IRE)** (MJohnston) **3-8-7** TWilliams(1) (hld up: effrt over 3f out: no imp) | 5 | 4 | $10/1^{3}$ | 70 | 3 |
| | **Little Redwing** (MDHammond) **4-9-7** KFallon(2) (prom tl wknd 3½f) | dist | 5 | 66/1 | — | — |

(SP 112.3%) **5 Rn**

**3m 0.84** (16.04) CSF £3.51 TOTE £2.90: £1.90 £1.00 (£1.10) OWNER Maktoum Al Maktoum (NEWMARKET) BRED Maple Leaf Farm
WEIGHT FOR AGE 3yo-19lb

**1168 Candle Smile (USA)** was certainly suited by this longer trip, and proved very game in the testing conditions. (2/1)
**1153 Ancient Quest** wouldn't win any prizes in a beauty contest and after stalking the winner, found the effort beyond him in the final furlong. (4/7)
**Tillyboy** has won a bumper and showed plenty here under a sympathetic ride and looks one to keep an eye on. (20/1)
**Double Dash (IRE)** looked fit but was not put into the race and looked one paced in the home straight. (10/1)

## 1588 ST VINCENT HIGH INCOME H'CAP (0-80) (3-Y.O+) (Class D)

4-30 (4-33) **6f** £3,896.00 (£1,178.00: £574.00: £272.00) Stalls: High GOING: 0.27 sec per fur (G)

| Form | Horse | Dist | Pos | SP | RR | SF |
|---|---|---|---|---|---|---|
| $1199^{6}$ | **Palo Blanco (71)** (TDBarron) **5-9-8** JFortune(3) (bhd: nt clr run ½-wy: hdwy 2f out: chal ins fnl f: led nr fin) | — | 1 | 6/1 | 79 | 53 |
| $956^{8}$ | **Amron (62)** (JBerry) **9-8-13** NCarlisle(7) (bhd: hdwy to ld appr fnl f: nt qckn cl home) | hd | 2 | 12/1 | 70 | 44 |
| $1040^{5}$ | **Mister Westsound (65)** (MissLAPerratt) **4-9-2b** TWilliams(8) (hld up: hdwy to chal ins fnl f: no ex towards fin) | s.h | 3 | 9/1 | 73 | 47 |
| $850^{3}$ | **Stand Tall (54)** (CWThornton) **4-8-5** DeanMcKeown(9) (mde most tl hdd appr fnl f: kpt on one pce) | 2½ | 4 | 6/1 | 55 | 29 |
| 1364* | **Captain Carat (68)** (MrsJRRamsden) **5-9-5** 6x KFallon(5) (hld up & bhd: hdwy 2f out: nvr rchd ldrs) | 2 | 5 | $5/1^{3}$ | 64 | 38 |
| | **Grand Chapeau (IRE) (60)** (DNicholls) **4-8-11** AlexGreaves(1) (disp ld 4f: grad wknd) | ½ | 6 | 20/1 | 54 | 28 |
| $1186^{13}$ | **Rich Glow (57)** (NBycroft) **5-8-8** JQuinn(2) (plld hrd: prom tl outpcd fnl 2f) | 1½ | 7 | 10/1 | 47 | 21 |
| 1545* | **Garnock Valley (65)** (JBerry) **6-9-2** 6x JCarroll(10) (chsd ldrs over 4f: wknd) | 4 | 8 | 10/1 | 51 | 19 |
| $1364^{4}$ | **Colway Rake (69)** (JWWatts) **5-9-6b** NConnorton(4) (trckd ldrs tl rdn & wknd fnl 2f) | 2½ | 9 | $4/1^{2}$ | 42 | 16 |
| $1192^{3}$ | **Be Warned (73)** (NACallaghan) **5-9-10b** PatEddery(6) (bhd & rdn ½-wy: n.d) | nk | 10 | $3/1^{1}$ | 45 | 19 |

(SP 130.9%) **10 Rn**

**1m 15.1** (5.30) CSF £73.92 CT £626.40 TOTE £8.40: £1.70 £4.10 £2.30 (£104.60) Trio £123.00 OWNER Mr J. G. Brown (THIRSK) BRED P. and D. H. Cockcroft

**1199 Palo Blanco**, after being short of room at halfway, found everything going his way and, given some fine assistance, got up when it mattered. (6/1)
**814 Amron** ran his best race for a long time, only just failing to last out. (12/1)
**1040 Mister Westsound** is beginning to come to himself and ran a fine race, but just failed to quicken late on. (9/1: 6/1-10/1)
**850 Stand Tall**, still looking on good terms with himself, did a lot of the donkey work and showed that a win on grass is likely in due course. (6/1: op 4/1)
**1364* Captain Carat**, with a 6lb penalty, made up a fair amount of ground, but failed to get into it with a chance, which is hardly surprising. (5/1: 4/1-6/1)
**Grand Chapeau (IRE)** ran a cracker for his new stable and will no doubt improve in due course. (20/1)
**475 Rich Glow** pulled too hard early on, but still ran quite well. (10/1)
**1545* Garnock Valley** (10/1: op 6/1)
**1364 Colway Rake** is unpredictable and decided it was not his day soon after the halfway point. (4/1)
**1192 Be Warned** was not in the right mood. (3/1: 4/1-6/1)

T/Plpt: £1,276.60 (8.19 Tckts). T/Qdpt: £39.10 (24.58 Tckts). AA

# 1301-BATH (L-H) (Good)

## Friday May 31st

WEATHER: overcast

## 1589 GRITTLETON RATING RELATED MAIDEN STKS (0-65) (3-Y.O F) (Class F)

6-35 (6-36) **1m 2f 46y** £2,565.00 (£715.00: £345.00) Stalls: Low GOING minus 0.44 sec per fur (F)

| Form | Horse | Dist | Pos | SP | RR | SF |
|---|---|---|---|---|---|---|
| $1523^{2}$ | **Cd Super Targeting (IRE) (58)** (MRChannon) **3-8-11** RHughes(3) (mde all: clr over 2f out: comf) | — | 1 | $7/1^{3}$ | 67+ | 34 |
| | **Lavender Della (IRE) (55)** (MJFetherston-Godley) **3-8-11** WJO'Connor(5) (bit bkwd: hld up: hdwy 4f out: rdn & chsd wnr over 2f out: no imp) | 2½ | 2 | 33/1 | 63 | 30 |
| $1155^{6}$ | **Another Quarter (IRE) (60)** (SPCWoods) **3-8-11** WWoods(1) (bhd: rdn over 4f out: r.o one pce fnl 2f) | 6 | 3 | $7/1^{3}$ | 54 | 21 |
| $761^{5}$ | **Basood (USA) (62)** (EALDunlop) **3-8-11v1** PaulEddery(4) (b.off hind: prom tl rdn & wknd wl over 2f out) | 10 | 4 | $4/1^{2}$ | 38 | 5 |
| $955^{3}$ | **Fijon (IRE) (65)** (BWHills) **3-8-11** MHills(2) (prom tl wknd 3f out) | 4 | 5 | $4/5^{1}$ | 32 | — |

(SP 103.5%) **5 Rn**

**2m 10.8** (3.30) CSF £82.96 TOTE £3.60: £2.20 £4.20 (£43.40) OWNER Circular Distributors Ltd (UPPER LAMBOURN) BRED J. M. Cusack

**1523 Cd Super Targeting (IRE)**, making a quick reappearance, was probably more at home on this better ground. (7/1: 5/1-8/1)
**Lavender Della (IRE)** is bred to stay this sort of trip and should at least come on for the outing. (33/1)
**1155 Another Quarter (IRE)**, stepping up from a mile, never posed a threat. (7/1: op 3/1)
**761 Basood (USA)** showed no signs of improvement in the first-time visor. (4/1)
**955 Fijon (IRE)** was most disappointing and the trainers representative could offer no explanation. (4/5)

## 1590 E.B.F. SWAINSWICK MAIDEN STKS (2-Y.O F) (Class D)

7-05 (7-06) **5f 161y** £3,949.50 (£1,191.00: £578.00: £271.50) Stalls: High GOING minus 0.10 sec per fur (G)

| | | | | SP | RR | SF |
|---|---|---|---|---|---|---|
| | **Red Embers** (RHannon) **2-8-11** MHills(3) (unf: hmpd 2f out: swtchd rt & gd hdwy over 1f out: str run to ld wl ins fnl f: r.o wl) | — | 1 | 10/1$^{3}$ | 79 | 22 |
| | **Chilling** (PGMurphy) **2-8-11** NAdams(4) (unf: bkwd: hld up & plld hrd: hdwy 2f out: ev ch ins fnl f: unable qckn) | 1¾ | 2 | 20/1 | 74 | 17 |
| | **Jilly Woo** (DRCElsworth) **2-8-11** BDoyle(8) (unf: s.s: hdwy 2f out: led ins fnl f: sn hdd: unable qkcn) | s.h | 3 | 11/1 | 74+ | 17 |
| | **Gopi** (RHannon) **2-8-8**(3) DaneO'Neill(7) (small: lt-f: led tl ins fnl f) | 1¼ | 4 | 10/1$^{3}$ | 71 | 14 |
| 1118$^{3}$ | **Summer Queen** (SPCWoods) **2-8-11** WWoods(5) (prom: rdn over 2f out: wknd over 1f out) | 3 | 5 | 5/4$^{1}$ | 62 | 5 |
| | **Incandescent** (APJones) **2-8-11** JReid(1) (lt-f: s.s: nvr nr to chal) | s.h | 6 | 25/1 | 62 | 5 |
| | **Victoria's Dream (IRE)** (MRChannon) **2-8-11** RHughes(9) (w'like: bit bkwd: prom tl wknd over 1f out) | s.h | 7 | 10/1$^{3}$ | 62 | 5 |
| | **Calamander (IRE)** (PFICole) **2-8-11** TQuinn(10) (lt-f: prom: rdn over 2f out: sn wknd) | 1¼ | 8 | 4/1$^{2}$ | 58 | 1 |
| 1480$^{5}$ | **Miss Clonteen (IRE)** (MMadgwick) **2-8-6**(5) MartinDwyer(6) (a bhd) | 9 | 9 | 50/1 | 33 | — |
| 1346$^{5}$ | **Windborn** (KMcAuliffe) **2-8-11** JFEgan(2) (prom: rdn over 3f out: sn wknd: t.o) | 8 | 10 | 14/1 | 11 | — |
| | | | | (SP 117.3%) | **10 Rn** | |

**1m 14.1** (4.60) CSF £156.79 TOTE £9.80: £2.10 £4.50 £2.40 (£293.70) Trio £164.00; £166.31 to 3/6/96 OWNER Cheveley Park Stud (MARLBOROUGH) BRED Cheveley Park Stud and Broughton Homes Ltd

**Red Embers** overcame trouble in running to win going away, and seems sure to improve. (10/1: op 5/1)
**Chilling** needs to learn to settle and will strip fitter next time. (20/1)
**Jilly Woo** did well to recover from a tardy start and should be better for the experience. (11/1: op 6/1)
**Gopi** is not very big, but showed plenty of speed to make the running, and may be better over a sharp five at the moment. (10/1: 6/1-11/1)
**1118 Summer Queen** found disappointingly little when let down. (5/4: op 5/2)
**Incandescent** missed the break and could never land a blow. (25/1)
**Victoria's Dream (IRE)** (10/1: op 9/2)
**Calamander (IRE)** (4/1: 5/2-5/1)
**1346 Windborn** (14/1: 8/1-16/1)

## 1591 FRIDAY EVENING H'CAP (0-75) (3-Y.O) (Class D)

7-35 (7-35) **2m 1f 34y** £3,507.50 (£1,055.00: £510.00: £237.50) Stalls: Low GOING minus 0.44 sec per fur (F)

| | | | | SP | RR | SF |
|---|---|---|---|---|---|---|
| 954$^{2}$ | **Flocheck (USA) (73)** (JLDunlop) **3-9-7** PatEddery(6) (a.p: led 7f out: clr 3f out: easily) | — | 1 | 11/10$^{1}$ | 89+ | 27 |
| 1317$^{5}$ | **Alwarqa (63)** (RWArmstrong) **3-8-11** RHills(9) (hld up: hdwy 8f out: rdn 4f out: wnt 2nd over 1f out: no ch w wnr) | 12 | 2 | 5/1$^{2}$ | 68 | 6 |
| *245*$^{6}$ | **Illegally Yours (48)** (LMontagueHall) **3-7-5**(5) MartinDwyer(4) (rdn 6f out: hdwy 4f out: one pce fnl 2f) | 1 | 3 | 20/1 | 52 | — |
| 1462$^{6}$ | **Shalateeno (69)** (MRChannon) **3-8-12**(5) PPMurphy(7) (led over 10f: wknd over 2f out) | 6 | 4 | 12/1 | 67 | 5 |
| 1347$^{4}$ | **Sterling Fellow (51)** (RHannon) **3-7-13** SSanders(1) (prom rdn over 5f out: sn wknd) | 3 | 5 | 6/1$^{3}$ | 47 | — |
| 1023$^{3}$ | **Ewar Bold (73)** (CEBrittain) **3-9-7** BDoyle(3) (lw: hld up: hdwy 6f out: wknd over 3f out) | s.h | 6 | 8/1 | 68 | 6 |
| 1418$^{6}$ | **Hanbitooh (USA) (67)** (EALDunlop) **3-9-1b** PaulEddery(5) (lw: hld up: hdwy 8f out: rdn over 4f out: sn wknd) | 12 | 7 | 10/1 | 51 | — |
| 1180$^{9}$ | **Mathon (IRE) (52)** (MRChannon) **3-8-0** AMackay(8) (bhd fnl 4f: t.o) | 22 | 8 | 33/1 | 16 | — |
| 637$^{13}$ | **Louisiana Purchase (48)** (MrsBarbaraWaring) **3-7-10** NAdams(2) (stdd s: plld hrd in rr: t.o fnl 4f) | dist | 9 | 50/1 | — | — |
| *899*$^{3}$ | **Shamand (USA) (50)** (BJMeehan) **3-7-12b**$^{1}$ow2 JFEgan(10) (chsd ldr 8f: wknd qckly: t.o fnl 4f) | dist | 10 | 14/1 | — | — |
| | | | | (SP 122.8%) | **10 Rn** | |

**3m 50.8** (9.80) CSF £7.60 CT £70.22 TOTE £1.90: £1.10 £2.10 £3.60 (£5.80) Trio £137.60 OWNER Stonethorn Stud Farms Ltd (ARUNDEL) BRED G. W. Jennings

LONG HANDICAP Illegally Yours 7-2 Louisiana Purchase 6-11 Shamand (USA) 7-8

**954 Flocheck (USA)** obviously relishes a real test of stamina and can go on to better things. (11/10)
**1317 Alwarqa**, trying a longer trip, had to work hard to finish best of the rest. (5/1)
**Illegally Yours**, off course since February, has taken a big step up in distance without the headgear she had worn in her last two runs. (20/1)
**1462 Shalateeno**, again stepping up in distance, at least settled better making the running. (12/1: op 7/1)
**1347 Sterling Fellow** did not find a real test of stamina doing the trick. (6/1)
**1023 Ewar Bold** showed no sign of improvement over this extended trip. (8/1: op 4/1)
**1418 Hanbitooh (USA)** (10/1: op 5/1)

## 1592 HAYMAKING CLAIMING STKS (3-Y.O) (Class F)

8-05 (8-05) **5f 11y** £2,687.50 (£750.00: £362.50) Stalls: High GOING minus 0.10 sec per fur (G)

| | | | | SP | RR | SF |
|---|---|---|---|---|---|---|
| 1356$^{6}$ | **Ciserano (IRE) (55)** (MRChannon) **3-8-5**(7) AEddery(8) (hld up: hdwy 2f out: led ins fnl f: r.o wl) | — | 1 | 11/2$^{3}$ | 72 | 42 |
| 973$^{8}$ | **Miletrian Refurb (IRE) (62)** (MRChannon) **3-8-11** RHughes(5) (lw: w ldr: led over 3f out tl ins fnl f) | 1¾ | 2 | 5/2$^{2}$ | 66 | 36 |
| 731$^{12}$ | **Wire Act (USA) (57)** (MartynMeade) **3-8-4b**$^{1}$(5) RHavlin(9) (lw: prom: rdn over 2f out: ev ch over 1f out: edgd lft ins fnl f: one pce) | ½ | 3 | 20/1 | 62 | 32 |
| 1170$^{5}$ | **Jessica's Song (51)** (WGMTurner) **3-8-4** TSprake(10) (led over 3f: ev ch over 1f out: one pce) | s.h | 4 | 11/2$^{3}$ | 57 | 27 |
| 824$^{14}$ | **Standown (68)** (JBerry) **3-9-7** TQuinn(6) (chsd ldrs: btn whn hmpd ins fnl f) | ¾ | 5 | 9/4$^{1}$ | 71 | 41 |
| *292*$^{7}$ | **Double Impression (IRE)** (JLHarris) **3-8-6** SSanders(7) (a.p: ev ch whn n.m.r over 1f out: nt clr m ins fnl f: nt rcvr) | s.h | 6 | 25/1 | 56 | 26 |
| 1122$^{9}$ | **Duet** (JSKing) **3-8-4** AMackay(3) (a bhd) | 5 | 7 | 33/1 | 38 | 8 |
| 1364$^{15}$ | **Astral's Chance (55)** (KRBurke) **3-8-10b**$^{1}$(3) DaneO'Neill(1) (a bhd) | 1¾ | 8 | 20/1 | 42 | 12 |
| 783$^{6}$ | **Farida Seconda (62)** (JLSpearing) **3-8-3**(3) SDrowne(2) (lw: prom over 2f) | 1 | 9 | 10/1 | 32 | 2 |
| 1122$^{4}$ | **Coastguards Hero (52)** (MDIUsher) **3-9-3** NAdams(4) (w ldrs over 2f) | 3½ | 10 | 12/1 | 32 | 2 |
| | | | | (SP 123.2%) | **10 Rn** | |

**63.3 secs** (2.80) CSF £19.85 TOTE £8.60: £2.30 £1.20 £4.60 (£9.80) Trio £86.60 OWNER Mr K. A. Dack (UPPER LAMBOURN) BRED Joseph O'Brien

**1356 Ciserano (IRE)**, well suited by dropping back to the minimum trip, finally lived up to being a half-sister to Polykratis. (11/2)
**973 Miletrian Refurb (IRE)** could not hold his stable-companion in the closing stages. (5/2: op 6/4)
**Wire Act (USA)**, taking a big drop in distance, did remarkably well in the first-time blinkers, despite being inclined to go left-handed. (20/1)
**1170 Jessica's Song** really needs faster ground than she encountered here. (11/2)
**652* Standown** appeared to be just held when meeting trouble in the last 200 yards. (9/4)

**Double Impression (IRE)**, an Irish import, showed nothing in one run at Lingfield in February, but got no sort of run here, and possesses some ability. (25/1)
**Farida Seconda** (10/1: 8/1-12/1)

## 1593 HAMSWELL MAIDEN STKS (3-Y.O+) (Class D)
8-35 (8-39) **1m 5y** £3,871.50 (£1,167.00: £566.00: £265.50) Stalls: Low GOING minus 0.44 sec per fur (F)

| | | | | SP | RR | SF |
|---|---|---|---|---|---|---|
| 942[4] | **The Dilettanti (USA) (85)** (JARToller) **3-8-9** SSanders(8) (mde all: rdn 2f out: r.o wl) | — | **1** | 4/1[3] | 86 | 31 |
| 1142[6] | **Don Bosio (USA)** (MRStoute) **3-8-9** JReid(2) (hld up: chsd wnr over 2f out: rdn & ev ch over 1f out: unable qckn) | 1¼ | **2** | 9/4[2] | 84 | 29 |
| | **Victorian Style** (RCharlton) **3-8-6**ow2 PatEddery(6) (lengthy: unf: hld up: hdwy over 2f out: swtchd lft & styd on ins fnl f) | 1½ | **3** | 13/8[1] | 78 | 21 |
| 970[4] | **Philosopher (IRE) (84)** (RHannon) **3-8-6**(3) DaneO'Neill(3) (a.p: r.o one pce fnl 2f) | nk | **4** | 13/2 | 80 | 25 |
| | **Shadow Casting** (BWHills) **3-8-4** MHills(4) (lengthy: scope: s.s: nvr trbld ldrs) | 5 | **5** | 33/1 | 65 | 10 |
| | **Baasm** (MajorWRHern) **3-8-9** RHills(1) (w'like: scope: chsd ldr tl wknd over 2f out) | 2½ | **6** | 33/1 | 65 | 10 |
| | **Sharp Progress** (APJones) **3-8-9** BDoyle(5) (unf: s.s: a bhd) | 4 | **7** | 50/1 | 57 | 2 |
| 1182[12] | **Crest Wing (USA)** (PWChapple-Hyam) **3-8-4**(5) RHavlin(7) (prom 4f: t.o) | 24 | **8** | 33/1 | 9 | — |
| | | | | (SP 113.0%) | | **8 Rn** |

**1m 41.1** (2.60) CSF £12.70 TOTE £5.20: £1.10 £1.50 £1.40 (£4.70) OWNER Duke of Devonshire (WHITSBURY) BRED Carmine Carcieri
**942 The Dilettanti (USA)** found this company a different kettle of fish. (4/1: 3/1-9/2)
**1142 Don Bosio (USA)** could not cope with the winner in the final quarter-mile and may need a longer trip. (9/4: 6/4-5/2)
**Victorian Style**, a half-sister to stayer Sea Victor, is certainly no oil painting and did a fair amount of tail swishing. She shaped as though she will require further. (13/8)
**970 Philosopher (IRE)** again lacked a finishing kick and may be worth a try over slightly further. (13/2: 4/1-7/1)
**Shadow Casting**, a half-sister to Solar Flight, should do better in due course. (33/1)
**Baasm** has already been gelded. (33/1)

## 1594 END OF THE DAY H'CAP (0-70) (3-Y.O) (Class E)
9-05 (9-09) **1m 5y** £3,402.00 (£1,026.00: £498.00: £234.00) Stalls: Low GOING minus 0.44 sec per fur (F)

| | | | | SP | RR | SF |
|---|---|---|---|---|---|---|
| 978[6] | **Sistar Act (58)** (MRChannon) **3-8-9** RHughes(16) (hld up: hdwy over 2f out: led ins fnl f: r.o wl) | — | **1** | 13/2[2] | 68 | 22 |
| 1348[4] | **Flying Pennant (IRE) (64)** (RHannon) **3-8-12**(3) DaneO'Neill(5) (hld up: hdwy over 2f out: ev ch over 1f out: unable qckn) | 2½ | **2** | 7/1[3] | 69 | 23 |
| 851[7] | **Classic Defence (IRE) (68)** (JWHills) **3-9-0**(5) MHenry(1) (lw: a.p: rdn & r.o one pce fnl 2f) | nk | **3** | 12/1 | 72 | 26 |
| 1119[7] | **Pride of Kashmir (54)** (PWHarris) **3-8-5** GHind(12) (lw: led tl ins fnl f) | ¾ | **4** | 14/1 | 57 | 11 |
| 1122[3] | **Little Kenny (45)** (MJFetherston-Godley) **3-7-10** FNorton(4) (lw: hld up: hdwy on ins over 2f out: rdn over 1f out: one pce) | 1¼ | **5** | 10/1 | 45 | — |
| *1096[6]* | **Lady Dignity (IRE) (68)** (PJMakin) **3-9-5** SSanders(14) (bhd tl hrd rdn & hdwy over 2f out: nt rch ldrs) | s.h | **6** | 10/1 | 68 | 22 |
| | **Unspoken Prayer (50)** (JRArnold) **3-8-1** JFEgan(15) (w ldrs tl wknd over 1f out) | 1¾ | **7** | 33/1 | 47 | 1 |
| 1122[8] | **Dyanko (46)** (MSSaunders) **3-7-11** AMackay(11) (hld up & bhd: stdd hdwy over 1f out: nvr nrr) | s.h | **8** | 20/1 | 43 | — |
| 1195[4] | **Shouldbegrey (47)** (WRMuir) **3-7-7**(5) MartinDwyer(3) (prom tl rdn & wknd 3f out) | 1 | **9** | 33/1 | 42 | — |
| 1119[10] | **Spiral Flyer (IRE) (53)** (MDIUsher) **3-8-4** TSprake(6) (lw: a bhd) | 4 | **10** | 33/1 | 40 | — |
| 1464[7] | **Andsome Boy (50)** (CRBarwell) **3-8-1** NAdams(8) (lw: prom: rdn over 3f out: wknd over 2f out) | 4 | **11** | 33/1 | 29 | — |
| 1101[17] | **Beauchamp Kate (68)** (HCandy) **3-9-5** CRutter(13) (lw: sn bhd) | 3½ | **12** | 8/1 | 40 | — |
| 758[6] | **Never Think Twice (61)** (KTIvory) **3-8-5v**(7) CScally(10) (b: bhd fnl 4f) | 1¼ | **13** | 20/1 | 30 | — |
| | **Parsis (USA) (70)** (LadyHerries) **3-9-7** DeclanO'Shea(9) (lw: a bhd) | 3 | **14** | 15/2 | 33 | — |
| 819[6] | **Goodwood Rocket (69)** (JLDunlop) **3-9-6** PatEddery(2) (prom tl n.m.r on ins over 2f out: eased whn btn over 1f out) | 3½ | **15** | 100/30[1] | 25 | — |
| *1100[18]* | ***Ben Bowden (61)*** (MBlanshard) **3-8-12** TQuinn(7) (Withdrawn not under Starter's orders: Unruly start) | | **W** | 13/2[2] | — | — |
| | | | | (SP 138.9%) | | **15 Rn** |

**1m 42.1** (3.60) CSF £44.60 CT £375.80 TOTE £5.00: £1.40 £2.70 £4.20 (£16.40) Trio £115.70 OWNER Mr Tim Corby (UPPER LAMBOURN) BRED D. S. Rigby
**978 Sistar Act**, dropped 2lb, had better ground and was back to a mile this time. (13/2: op 4/1)
**1348 Flying Pennant (IRE)**, back to a mile, continues to run consistently. (7/1)
**851 Classic Defence (IRE)** seems to have his fair share of weight for winning a little race at Musselburgh. (12/1)
**562 Pride of Kashmir** had been tried in blinkers last time having played up at the start on his previous outing. (14/1)
**1122 Little Kenny** was another who wore first-time headgear last time. (10/1)
**1096 Lady Dignity (IRE)** could not get to grips with the principals on this return to the turf. (10/1)
**Dyanko** is one to keep an eye on and may need even further. (20/1)
**Beauchamp Kate** (8/1: op 12/1)
**819 Goodwood Rocket** did not get the best of runs on the inside early in the home straight and was allowed to coast in. (100/30)

T/Plpt: £465.50 (28.33 Tckts). T/Qdpt: £4.20 (341.6 Tckts). KH

# 0769-CATTERICK (L-H) (Good, Good to firm patches)
## Friday May 31st
WEATHER: showery

## 1595 STAPLETON MAIDEN AUCTION STKS (2-Y.O) (Class F)
2-20 (2-23) **5f** £2,763.00 (£768.00: £369.00) Stalls: Low GOING minus 0.32 sec per fur (GF)

| | | | | SP | RR | SF |
|---|---|---|---|---|---|---|
| 1021[3] | **Robec Girl (IRE)** (JBerry) **2-7-13** GCarter(5) (mde all: edgd rt ½-wy: rdn clr 1f out) | — | **1** | 5/4[1] | 80 | — |
| | **Hoh Surprise (IRE)** (MBell) **2-7-6**(7) RMullen(6) (w'like: leggy: sn chsng ldrs: rdn 2f out: no imp) | 4 | **2** | 11/2 | 67 | — |
| 557[8] | **Midyans Song** (JJO'Neill) **2-8-1** JFanning(8) (sn chsng ldrs: styd on same pce appr fnl f: bmpd ins fnl f) | 2½ | **3** | 16/1 | 61 | — |
| 1036[3] | **Gipsy Princess** (MWEasterby) **2-7-13** DaleGibson(7) (chsd ldrs: rdn ½-wy: wandered & kpt on same pce) | ¾ | **4** | 9/2[2] | 57 | — |
| | **Little Blue (IRE)** (TDEasterby) **2-7-13** LCharnock(4) (neat: prom to ½-wy: sn wknd) | 1½ | **5** | 16/1 | 52 | — |
| 1308[3] | **Casual Cottage (IRE)** (CMurray) **2-8-4** KDarley(3) (w ldrs: effrt ½-wy: wknd over 1f out) | 3 | **6** | 5/1[3] | 47 | — |
| *1084[4]* | **Run For Us (IRE)** (CADwyer) **2-7-10b**(3) NVarley(1) (chsd ldrs: sn rdn along: lost pl ½-wy) | ¾ | **7** | 25/1 | 40 | — |

| | | | Pos | SP | RR | SF |
|---|---|---|---|---|---|---|
| | **Miskin Heights (IRE)** (KRBurke) **2-7-13** DRMcCabe(2) (unf: scope: s.s: a wl outpcd) | 6 | **8** | 8/1 | 21 | — |
| | **Madam Poppy** (CADwyer) **2-7-13** NKennedy(9) (cmpt: s.i.s: sn wl bhd) | nk | **9** | 10/1 | 20 | — |

(SP 130.5%) **9 Rn**

**61.2 secs** (3.70) CSF £10.02 TOTE £2.00: £1.60 £2.30 £4.20 (£7.60) Trio £63.90 OWNER Highgrove Developments Ltd (COCKERHAM) BRED Michael Fleming

**1021 Robec Girl (IRE)**, beaten by the draw in bad ground first time, took this modest contest in decisive fashion. (5/4)
**Hoh Surprise (IRE)** showed definite signs of inexperience going to post, but stuck on under pressure to finish a clear second best. (11/2)
**Midyans Song** was only staying on at the same pace when bumped inside the last. She already needs six furlongs. (16/1)
**1036 Gipsy Princess** wandered under strong pressure and, quite stoutly bred, needs six or even seven furlongs. (9/2)
**Little Blue (IRE)** is well named. (16/1)
**1308 Casual Cottage (IRE)** was too keen for her own good both on the way to the post and coming back. (5/1)

## 1596 CROFT (S) STKS (4-Y.O+) (Class G)

2-50 (2-51) **1m 2f 39y** £2,406.00 (£666.00: £318.00) Stalls: High GOING: 0.00 sec per fur (G)

| | | | Pos | SP | RR | SF |
|---|---|---|---|---|---|---|
| | **North Ardar (58)** (MrsMReveley) **6-8-5**(7) SCopp(8) (chsd ldrs: effrt & n.m.r over 2f out: led over 1f out: r.o u.p) | — | **1** | 2/1[1] | 66 | — |
| 1196[10] | **Simand (50)** (GMMoore) **4-8-7** KDarley(1) (hld up: hdwy & swtchd outside over 2f out: styd on fnl f) | 1½ | **2** | 13/2 | 59 | — |
| 1159[3] | **Elite Bliss (IRE)** (MJCamacho) **4-8-7** LCharnock(2) (a chsng ldrs: kpt on same pce fnl 2f) | 2½ | **3** | 11/4[2] | 55 | — |
| 999[8] | **Miss Zanzibar (51)** (RAFahey) **4-8-7** ACulhane(13) (hld up: hdwy on outside over 3f out: hung lft 2f out: sn wknd) | 3 | **4** | 5/1[3] | 50 | — |
| | **Mithraic (IRE) (55)** (WSCunningham) **4-8-12** JTate(11) (mid div: styd on fnl 2f: nvr nr ldrs) | ¾ | **5** | 16/1 | 54 | — |
| 884[13] | **Heathyards Magic (IRE) (60)** (MDods) **4-8-9**(3) CTeague(4) (lw: bdly hpmd & lost pl over 7f out: styd on fnl 2f: nvr nr ldrs) | 1¾ | **6** | 10/1 | 51 | — |
| 1159[11] | **Bowland Park** (EJAlston) **5-8-7** SDWilliams(9) (mde most tl over 1f out: sn wknd) | 2½ | **7** | 25/1 | 42 | — |
| 1196[9] | **Whatashowman (IRE)** (SEKettlewell) **4-8-12** OUrbina(7) (chsd ldrs: hmpd after 1f: hung lft & wknd over 1f out) | 1¼ | **8** | 20/1 | 45 | — |
| 822[5] | **Troubadour Song (55)** (WWHaigh) **4-8-12** DaleGibson(10) (bhd & rdn 4f out: no rspnse) | 8 | **9** | 7/1 | 33 | — |
| 1474[11] | **Ihtimaam (FR) (55)** (MrsASwinbank) **4-8-12v[1]** DRMcCabe(3) (b.hind: hld up: effrt over 3f out: sn wknd) | 2½ | **10** | 14/1 | 29 | — |
| 1159[14] | **Little Red** (RCraggs) **5-8-7**(5) PFessey(5) (s.i.s: a in rr) | 4 | **11** | 33/1 | 22 | — |
| 1421[15] | **Four Lane Flyer (41)** (EJAlston) **4-8-7v[1]** JFanning(12) (chsd ldrs tl lost pl 3f out) | ¾ | **12** | 20/1 | 16 | — |

(SP 140.5%) **12 Rn**

**2m 13.9** CSF £18.29 TOTE £3.50: £2.20 £3.10 £1.10 (£16.70) Trio £25.00 OWNER Laurel (Leisure) Ltd (SALTBURN) BRED Mrs H.Seddington No bid

**North Ardar**, who looked very fit, was dropped in both class and distance. (2/1)
**1041 Simand**, who had to switch to get a run, seemed to stay the trip. (13/2)
**1159 Elite Bliss (IRE)**, who has a pronounced knee-action, lacks pace, and either needs more use making of her, or a step up in distance. (11/4)
**836 Miss Zanzibar** gave her rider problems, persisting in hanging left. (5/1: op 3/1)
**805 Heathyards Magic (IRE)** lost his chance when badly hampered on the turn into the back straight. There is only a furlong run between the stalls and the paddock bend and it is inviting trouble. (10/1)

## 1597 WENSLEY SPRINT H'CAP (0-80) (3-Y.O) (Class D)

3-20 (3-22) **5f** £3,687.50 (£1,100.00: £525.00: £237.50) Stalls: Low GOING minus 0.32 sec per fur (GF)

| | | | Pos | SP | RR | SF |
|---|---|---|---|---|---|---|
| 1405[2] | **Maiteamia (63)** (SRBowring) **3-8-7b**(3) CTeague(1) (lw: w ldrs: rdn ½-wy: styd on wl to ld nr fin) | — | **1** | 9/4[1] | 67 | 29 |
| 881[2] | **Goretski (IRE) (70)** (NTinkler) **3-9-3** KDarley(7) (lw: trckd ldrs: led ½-wy: hdd post) | s.h | **2** | 5/2[2] | 74 | 36 |
| 1304[5] | **Dande Flyer (74)** (DWPArbuthnot) **3-9-7** RPerham(8) (lw: b: chsd ldrs: effrt & hung lft over 1f out: nt qckn ins fnl f) | 1 | **3** | 7/1 | 75 | 37 |
| 1493[5] | **Pleasure Time (66)** (CSmith) **3-8-6**(7) AngelaGallimore(3) (led to ½-wy: ev ch tl wknd ins fnl f) | 1¼ | **4** | 10/1 | 63 | 25 |
| 1188[4] | **Miss Bigwig (72)** (JBerry) **3-9-0**(5) PFessey(6) (chsd ldrs: outpcd ½-wy: styd on fnl f) | s.h | **5** | 8/1 | 69 | 31 |
| | **Purple Memories (66)** (MJohnston) **3-8-13** JFanning(5) (prom: rdn ½-wy: sn outpcd) | 3 | **6** | 6/1[3] | 53 | 15 |
| 881[5] | **Gwespyr (60)** (JBerry) **3-8-7v** GCarter(4) (s.s: nvr nr ldrs) | hd | **7** | 7/1 | 47 | 9 |
| | **Happy Tycoon (IRE) (70)** (CMurray) **3-9-3b[1]** MTebbutt(2) (chsd ldrs: rdn ½-wy: sn lost pl) | 8 | **8** | 12/1 | 31 | — |

(SP 126.5%) **8 Rn**

**59.7 secs** (2.20) CSF £9.09 CT £33.42 TOTE £3.10: £1.10 £1.20 £2.10 (£3.50) OWNER Mrs Zoe Grant (EDWINSTOWE) BRED Mrs Z. Grant and S. R. Bowring

**1405 Maiteamia**, due to rise 7lb in the weights after Haydock, did just enough to get up on the line. (9/4)
**881 Goretski (IRE)**, who as usual travelled strongly, was only just touched off. (5/2)
**1304 Dande Flyer** ran easily his best race so far this time. (7/1)
**1188 Pleasure Time** tended to duck and dive under pressure, and might do better with the blinkers back on. (10/1)
**1188 Miss Bigwig** ran her best race so far this time, but is still not running up to the level of her best juvenile form. (8/1)
**Purple Memories** was badly tapped for foot at halfway and probably needs a stiffer test. (6/1)

## 1598 PEN HILL CLAIMING STKS (3-Y.O+) (Class F)

3-50 (3-54) **5f** £2,763.00 (£768.00: £369.00) Stalls: Low GOING minus 0.32 sec per fur (GF)

| | | | Pos | SP | RR | SF |
|---|---|---|---|---|---|---|
| 1342* | **Sea-Deer (67)** (DWChapman) **7-8-13** ACulhane(16) (lw: hld up: hdwy 2f out: r.o u.p to ld ins fnl f) | — | **1** | 7/2[2] | 55 | 33 |
| 951* | **Bolshoi (IRE) (69)** (JBerry) **4-9-4b**(5) PRoberts(12) (w ldrs: led over 1f out tl ins fnl f) | 1½ | **2** | 6/1[3] | 60 | 38 |
| 1430[8] | **La Suquet (71)** (NTinkler) **4-9-4** MBirch(10) (w ldrs: nt qckn appr fnl f) | 2½ | **3** | 8/1 | 47 | 25 |
| 1342[3] | **Flashy's Son (69)** (FMurphy) **8-8-13** JFanning(5) (lw: b: sn rdn along: hdwy ½-wy: ev ch over 1f out: nt qckn) | ½ | **4** | 5/2[1] | 41 | 19 |
| *835*[10] | **Ivy Lilian (IRE) (32)** (WMBrisbourne) **4-7-11**(7) RMullen(3) (a chsng ldrs: rdn ½-wy: kpt on same pce) | ½ | **5** | 33/1 | 30 | 8 |
| 769[9] | **Thick as Thieves (50)** (RonaldThompson) **4-8-10**(3) CTeague(13) (sn outpcd & bhd: sme hdwy over 1f out: nvr nr ldrs) | 1 | **6** | 20/1 | 36 | 14 |
| 861[16] | **Snitch (39)** (CSmith) **3-8-2v**[ow1] MFenton(15) (sme hdwy over 1f out: nvr nr ldrs) | hd | **7** | 25/1 | 33 | 2 |
| 1412[16] | **Hannah's Usher (63)** (CMurray) **4-9-5** MTebbutt(7) (chsd ldrs to ½-wy: grad wknd) | 1¼ | **8** | 12/1 | 38 | 16 |
| 1412[12] | **Hickory Blue (65)** (KAMorgan) **6-9-0b** DRMcCabe(11) (in tch: rdn ½-wy: eased 1f out) | nk | **9** | 8/1 | 32 | 10 |
| *1028*[12] | **Born A Lady (56)** (SRBowring) **3-8-0** NKennedy(9) (in tch 3f: sn rdn & wknd) | 2½ | **10** | 16/1 | 18 | — |
| 1040[12] | **Gondo (43)** (EJAlston) **9-8-11v** SDWilliams(2) (chsd ldrs 3f: eased) | 1½ | **11** | 16/1 | 16 | — |

1364[14] **Rankaidade (26)** (DonEnricoIncisa) **5-8-4b[1]** KimTinkler(4) (sn bhd & pushed along)....½ **12** 33/1 7 —
1435[8] **Northgate Chief** (MBrittain) **4-9-2**(5) GParkin(1) (sn wl outpcd & bhd)....nk **13** 33/1 23 1
648[15] **Roxane (IRE) (30)** (ABailey) **3-7-9**(3) DWright(8) (sn bhd & outpcd)....¾ **14** 33/1 6 —
1307[3] **Baileys Sunset (IRE) (61)** (JMBradley) **4-9-1** LCharnock(14) (b: in tch to ½-wy: eased 1f out: collapsed & died after line)....4 **15** 15/2 2 —
1342[8] **Gone to Heaven** (TJEtherington) **4-8-13b[1]** KDarley(6) (led tl over 1f out: wknd qckly)....3 **16** 12/1 — —
(SP 146.6%) **16 Rn**

**59.6 secs** (2.10) CSF £28.29 TOTE £6.00: £2.00 £3.80 £2.50 (£16.10) Trio £88.60 OWNER Miss N. F. Thesiger (YORK) BRED Stetchworth Park Stud Ltd
WEIGHT FOR AGE 3yo-8lb
Sea-Deer clmd GMiddlemiss £5,000
**1342* Sea-Deer**, drawn sixteen of sixteen, came from off the pace to score readily in the end. (7/2)
**951* Bolshoi (IRE)**, drawn towards the outside, made the best of his way home, but the winner proved much too strong near the line. (6/1)
**951 La Suquet** ran better after being below form on her previous three outings. (8/1)
**1342 Flashy's Son** struggled to make ground at halfway. Only able to keep on at the same pace, this sharp five was against him. He usually runs well at Redcar where he has recorded three of his seven victories. (5/2: op 9/2)
**762 Ivy Lilian (IRE)** seemed to run easily her best ever race on turf. (33/1)

## 1599 GRINTON H'CAP (0-70) (3-Y.O) (Class E)
4-20 (4-21) **5f 212y** £3,314.00 (£992.00: £476.00: £218.00) Stalls: High GOING minus 0.32 sec per fur (GF)

SP RR SF

1405* **Limerick Princess (IRE) (58)** (JBerry) **3-8-9** GCarter(2) (dwlt s: hld up: hdwy & swtchd outside 2f out: led jst ins fnl f: eased towards fin)....— **1** 11/10[1] 66+ 36
1157[16] **Ramsey Hope (62)** (CWFairhurst) **3-8-13b[1]** NKennedy(3) (sn rdn along: led tl jst ins fnl f: kpt on: no ch w wnr)....1¾ **2** 33/1 65 35
1356[2] **Lionel Edwards (IRE) (65)** (PFICole) **3-8-13**(3) CTeague(4) (sn outpcd & bhd: styd on fnl 2f: nvr nr to chal) ..hd **3** 11/2[3] 68 38
1527[3] **The Wad (62)** (DNicholls) **3-8-13** KDarley(6) (trckd ldrs: effrt over 2f out: styd on same pce)....1¾ **4** 5/1[2] 60 30
1316[7] **Princely Sound (70)** (MBell) **3-9-7** MFenton(5) (lw: chsd ldr: rdn over 2f out: one pce)....½ **5** 11/2[3] 67 37
1527[17] **Hoh Majestic (IRE) (66)** (MartynWane) **3-8-12v**(5) PRoberts(1) (chsd ldrs tl wknd over 1f out)....hd **6** 7/1 63 33
1121[4] **Time Clash (61)** (BPalling) **3-8-12** SDWilliams(7) (s.i.s: a outpcd & bhd)....6 **7** 10/1 42 12
**Katy-Q (IRE) (55)** (PCalver) **3-8-6b** MBirch(8) (chsd ldrs: rdn & hung lft 2f out: fnd nil)....5 **8** 14/1 22 —
(SP 126.3%) **8 Rn**

**1m 13.1** (2.20) CSF £32.00 CT £157.62 TOTE £1.80: £1.10 £6.70 £1.20 (£62.70) OWNER Mr Thomas Doherty (COCKERHAM) BRED Thomas Doherty
**1405* Limerick Princess (IRE)**, due to rise 9lb in the weights after getting the better of Maiteamia at Haydock a week earlier, missed the break slightly. Confidently ridden, she scored with plenty in hand but will obviously find things much tougher in the future. (11/10: op 7/4)
**Ramsey Hope**, a tough and consistent two-year-old, showed a return to form, fitted with blinkers for the first time. (33/1)
**1356 Lionel Edwards (IRE)** struggled to keep up and needs either a stiffer six or, even better, seven. (11/2)
**1527 The Wad** had his tongue tied down. (5/1)
**1006* Princely Sound**, 6lb higher in the weights than when winning at Chester, was struggling some way from home. (11/2)
**1340 Hoh Majestic (IRE)** had the visor back on. (7/1)

## 1600 MUKER RATING RELATED MAIDEN STKS (0-60) (3-Y.O+) (Class F)
4-50 (4-51) **1m 3f 214y** £2,658.00 (£738.00: £354.00) Stalls: Low GOING minus 0.32 sec per fur (GF)

SP RR SF

1324[2] **Daira (55)** (JDBethell) **3-7-12**(5) PFessey(10) (trckd ldrs: effrt over 2f out: led ins fnl f: rdn out)....— **1** 2/1[1] 56 23
1061[6] **Perfect Gift (60)** (PFICole) **3-8-0**(3) AWhelan(3) (b.nr hind: hdwy 5f out: sn chsng ldrs: styd on ins fnl f: nt rch wnr)....nk **2** 9/2[3] 56 23
803[4] **Go With The Wind (60)** (MBell) **3-8-6v[1]** MFenton(9) (led tl ins fnl f)....1½ **3** 9/4[2] 57 24
763[5] **Batoutoftheblue (60)** (WWHaigh) **3-8-6** JTate(6) (lw: sn outpcd & pushed along: hdwy over 3f out: styd on: nt rch ldrs)....1½ **4** 13/2 55 22
1200[8] **Atienza (USA) (60)** (SCWilliams) **3-8-4**ow1 KDarley(11) (plld hrd: trckd ldrs: pushed along 5f out: wknd 2f out)....7 **5** 9/1 43 9
658[5] **The Fullbangladesh (49)** (JLEyre) **3-8-0**(3) DWright(4) (in tch: rdn over 4f out: one pce)....2 **6** 20/1 40 7
1034[7] **Never Time (IRE) (38)** (MrsVAAconley) **4-9-9** MDeering(7) (s.i.s: bhd: sme hdwy over 2f out: nvr nr ldrs) .....1¼ **7** 25/1 41 25
1042[16] **Sis Garden (48)** (TDEasterby) **3-8-5**ow2 MBirch(1) (chsd ldrs tl lost pl over 2f out)....¾ **8** 16/1 39 4
**Chik's Secret (42)** (BPalling) **3-8-4**ow1 GCarter(8) (hld up & plld hrd: a bhd: t.o 3f out)....12 **9** 16/1 22 —
*24[7]* **Saltis (IRE) (50)** (DWPArbuthnot) **4-9-9** RPerham(2) (b.hind: a bhd: t.o 2f out)....s.h **10** 16/1 24 8
619[9] **Carmenoura (IRE) (30)** (EJAlston) **4-9-6** SDWilliams(5) (bhd & reminders 6f out: t.o 3f out)....27 **11** 50/1 — —
(SP 133.8%) **11 Rn**

**2m 37.4** (6.00) CSF £13.00 TOTE £4.20: £2.40 £2.20 £1.10 (£7.10) Trio £6.10 OWNER Mr L. B. Holliday (MIDDLEHAM) BRED Cleaboy Farms Co
WEIGHT FOR AGE 3yo-17lb
**1324 Daira** did just enough after looking in two minds as to whether to go through with her effort inside the last. (2/1)
**Perfect Gift**, a smallish, narrow daughter of Generous, appreciated the step up in distance and, putting in all her best work at the end, just failed to get up. (9/2: op 3/1)
**803 Go With The Wind**, in a visor, made the running, but thrashed his tail under pressure and was edged out of it inside the last. (9/4)

T/Jkpt: £223.20 (96.91 Tckts). T/Plpt: £6.90 (2,247.57 Tckts). T/Qdpt: £3.40 (262.99 Tckts). WG

# 1455-WOLVERHAMPTON (L-H) (Standard)
## Friday May 31st
WEATHER: fine WIND: str

## 1601 CLOWN AMATEUR H'CAP (0-85) (3-Y.O+) (Class E)
2-10 (2-11) **1m 100y (Fibresand)** £3,124.80 (£932.40: £445.20: £201.60) Stalls: High GOING minus 0.15 sec per fur (FST)

SP RR SF

*1085** **Northern Fan (IRE) (80)** (ACStewart) **4-11-1**(4) MrVLukaniuk(6) (a.p: led 4f out: sn clr: rdn & hld on gamely)— **1** 9/4[1] 89 49

| | | | | | |
|---|---|---|---|---|---|
| 1505[4] | **Cashmere Lady (82)** (JLEyre) **4-11-7** MissDianaJones(7) (hdwy over 3f out: chsd wnr fnl 2f: kpt on wl nr fin) ....½ | **2** | 11/2[3] | 90 | 50 |
| 1001[2] | **My Gallery (IRE) (72)** (ABailey) **5-10-7**(4) MissBridgetGatehouse(5) (lw: outpcd: effrt 3f out: kpt on appr fnl f: nvr nrr) ....6 | **3** | 4/1[2] | 69 | 29 |
| 1149[5] | **Prima Cominna (70)** (SPCWoods) **4-10-5**(4) MissLHide(9) (outpcd: hdwy over 4f out: nt rch ldrs) ....2½ | **4** | 12/1 | 62 | 22 |
| *341*[9] | **Flashfeet (55)** (KBishop) **6-9-4**(4)ow5 MissAPurdy(10) (bit bkwd: s.s: hdwy over 2f out: nrst fin) ....2½ | **5** | 16/1 | 42 | — |
| 1172[4] | **Worldwide Elsie (USA) (80)** (RHarris) **3-10-0**(7) MrRBarrett(8) (trckd ldrs over 5f: sn lost tch) ....1½ | **6** | 6/1 | 64 | 12 |
| 469[2] | **Bellas Gate Boy (63)** (JPearce) **4-10-2** MrsLPearce(11) (outpcd: a bhd) ....4 | **7** | 7/1 | 40 | — |
| 1449[3] | **Kingchip Boy (66)** (MJRyan) **7-10-1v**(4) MrSLavallin(3) (mde most over 4f: wknd ent st) ....1 | **8** | 7/1 | 41 | 1 |
| *1094*[2] | **Desert Invader (IRE) (73)** (DWChapman) **5-10-8**(4) MissRClark(1) (lw: w ldr to ½-wy: wknd qckly over 2f out: t.o) ....11 | **9** | 12/1 | 27 | — |
| 1172[8] | **Moi Canard (82)** (BAPearce) **3-10-2**(7)ow9 MrRBlyth(4) (lw: outpcd: a bhd: t.o) ....6 | **10** | 20/1 | 25 | — |
| | | | (SP 131.5%) | | **10 Rn** |

**1m 52.2** (7.20) CSF £16.61 CT £47.77 TOTE £3.00: £1.40 £2.40 £2.80 (£9.30) Trio £28.00 OWNER S Corman Ltd (NEWMARKET) BRED Mrs Max Morris

WEIGHT FOR AGE 3yo-12lb

**1085* Northern Fan (IRE)** had more use made of him on this occasion and kicked on over half a mile out. Needing to find extra inside the distance, he did so willingly and is still very much on the upgrade. (9/4: 3/1-2/1)

**1505 Cashmere Lady** threw down a determined challenge inside the final furlong, but the winner was not stopping and she was never quite going to make it. (11/2)

**1001 My Gallery (IRE)**, trying a longer trip, stayed on relentlessly in the latter stages but could not get within striking range of the leading pair. (4/1)

**Prima Cominna** could never get herself into the race over this longer trip and her first attempt on this surface came to nothing. (12/1)

**469 Bellas Gate Boy** (7/1: op 9/2)

## 1602 GROUPER CLAIMING STKS (3-Y.O+) (Class F)

2-40 (2-40) **1m 1f 79y (Fibresand)** £2,381.00 (£656.00: £311.00) Stalls: Low GOING minus 0.15 sec per fur (FST)

| | | | SP | RR | SF |
|---|---|---|---|---|---|
| 1196[12] | **Sandmoor Denim (64)** (SRBowring) **9-9-3** LDettori(7) (a.p: rdn to chal ins fnl f: kpt on to ld cl home) ....— | **1** | 4/1[3] | 69 | 39 |
| 1198[4] | **Field of Vision (IRE) (71)** (MrsASwinbank) **6-9-6**(5) FLynch(5) (hld up: hdwy over 4f out: led wl ins fnl f: hdd nr fin) ....s.h | **2** | 9/4[2] | 77 | 47 |
| 650[15] | **Chevalier (USA) (75)** (ICampbell) **4-9-3v**1(7) GFaulkner(8) (led: clr over 2f out: hrd rdn & hdd wl ins fnl f) ....1 | **3** | 12/1 | 74 | 44 |
| *1081*[2] | **David James' Girl (54)** (ABailey) **4-8-5**(7) IonaWands(4) (trckd ldrs: rdn 2f out: sn btn) ....6 | **4** | 4/1[3] | 52 | 22 |
| 1449[2] | **Wentbridge Lad (IRE) (73)** (PDEvans) **6-9-10** GHind(1) (hdwy over 4f out: rdn over 2f out: no imp) ....5 | **5** | 13/8[1] | 55 | 25 |
| 801[4] | **Genesis Four (44)** (MrsLStubbs) **6-9-2b** JFEgan(3) (lw: nvr nr to chal) ....10 | **6** | 20/1 | 30 | — |
| 1314[11] | **Kerrier (IRE)** (RHarris) **4-9-8** AMackay(6) (b: bit bkwd: trckd ldrs: sn pushed along: wknd 3f out: t.o) ....14 | **7** | 16/1 | 12 | — |
| *1456*[7] | **Crown And Cushion** (KSBridgwater) **3-8-7**ow2 VSlattery(2) (lost pl ½-wy: sn t.o) ....6 | **8** | 50/1 | — | — |
| | **Needwood Fantasy** (BCMorgan) **3-7-11** GBardwell(9) (lw: chsd ldrs 5f: sn wknd: t.o) ....hd | **9** | 50/1 | — | — |
| | | | (SP 131.1%) | | **9 Rn** |

**2m 1.9** (5.90) CSF £14.81 TOTE £4.50: £2.40 £1.10 £3.50 (£10.70) Trio £57.20 OWNER Mr E. H. Lunness (EDWINSTOWE) BRED Rathasker Stud

WEIGHT FOR AGE 3yo-13lb

**1081 Sandmoor Denim**, winning his first race in over fourteen months, owed a lot to the skill of the man on top. (4/1)

**1198 Field of Vision (IRE)** looked likely to make it three wins over course and distance when poking his nose in front 150 yards out but, hard as he tried, the winner proved just too strong. (9/4)

**Chevalier (USA)**, visored for the first time, ran by far his best race yet and a repeat could see him opening his account. (12/1)

**1081 David James' Girl** pushed the pace but was hard at work on the home turn. (4/1)

**1449 Wentbridge Lad (IRE)** took closer order nearing the end of the back straight, but he was soon being nudged along and, failing to respond, ran no race at all. (13/8)

## 1603 REGIONAL RAILWAYS MAIDEN STKS (2-Y.O) (Class D)

3-10 (3-11) **6f (Fibresand)** £3,263.50 (£973.00: £464.00: £209.50) Stalls: Low GOING minus 0.15 sec per fur (FST)

| | | | SP | RR | SF |
|---|---|---|---|---|---|
| 1003[5] | **Burlington House (USA)** (PFICole) **2-9-0** TQuinn(5) (mde all: clr ent st: drvn out) ....— | **1** | Evens[1] | 66 | 11 |
| 1038[6] | **Flotilla** (SirMarkPrescott) **2-9-0** GDuffield(2) (trckd ldrs: effrt & rdn wl over 1f out: kpt on) ....4 | **2** | 4/1[2] | 55 | — |
| | **Saratoga Red (USA)** (WAO'Gorman) **2-9-0** EmmaO'Gorman(4) (w'like: bit bkwd: s.s: hdwy ½-wy: effrt 2f out: nt pce to chal) ....½ | **3** | 10/1 | 54 | — |
| 800[3] | **Blazing Castle** (WGMTurner) **2-9-0** TSprake(8) (chsd ldrs: rdn along fr ½-wy: kpt on one pce) ....nk | **4** | 10/1 | 53 | — |
| | **Red Test (USA)** (WAO'Gorman) **2-9-0** TIves(1) (lt-f: unf: s.s: gd hdwy on ins to chse wnr over 2f out: wknd appr fnl f) ....6 | **5** | 11/2[3] | 37 | — |
| 1408[2] | **Suave Star** (PDEvans) **2-8-9** GHind(7) (rdn along ½-wy: nvr plcd to chal) ....1¼ | **6** | 12/1 | 29 | — |
| | **Presentiment** (JBerry) **2-9-0** WRyan(6) (lt-f: unf: bkwd: outpcd: a bhd) ....½ | **7** | 9/1 | 33 | — |
| *1080*[5] | **Skelton Sovereign (IRE)** (RHollinshead) **2-9-0** LDettori(3) (bit bkwd: outpcd: a bhd) ....1¾ | **8** | 7/1 | 28 | — |
| | | | (SP 133.8%) | | **8 Rn** |

**1m 16.9** (5.50) CSF £6.87 TOTE £1.80: £1.10 £2.70 £3.60 (£7.30) OWNER Richard Green (Fine Paintings) (WHATCOMBE) BRED John A. Bell III & B. B. Williams

**1003 Burlington House (USA)**, who is only a pony, put his best foot forward at this first run on the All-Weather and galloped the opposition into the ground. (Evens)

**1038 Flotilla** still looked just short of peak-fitness but did well to win the race for second prize and he should not remain a maiden for long. (4/1)

**Saratoga Red (USA)** needed the run and lost ground leaving the stalls, so all in all, this must be considered a promising performance. (10/1: 8/1-12/1)

**800 Blazing Castle** found the task of trying to keep tabs on the winner hard work, and he was never in a position to pose a threat. (10/1: op 6/1)

**Red Test (USA)**, subject of market support, obtained a clear passage on the inside after losing ground at the start and chased the winner into the straight, but the effort of getting there had sucked his reserves. (11/2)

**1408 Suave Star** found this opposition much too good for her and was flat to the boards all the way. (12/1)

**1080 Skelton Sovereign (IRE)** (7/1: op 4/1)

## 1604 VSR LINEMANN H'CAP (0-70) (3-Y.O+) (Class E)

3-40 (3-40) **7f (Fibresand)** £3,406.50 (£1,017.00: £486.00: £220.50) Stalls: High GOING minus 0.15 sec per fur (FST)

| | | | | SP | RR | SF |
|---|---|---|---|---|---|---|
| 1127$^{7}$ | **Sualtach (IRE) (70)** (RHollinshead) **3-9-3** LDettori(1) (a.p: led over 2f out: shkn up ent fnl f: r.o wl) | — | **1** | 4/7$^{1}$ | 87 | 23 |
| *1448*$^{2}$ | **Four of Spades (70)** (PDEvans) **5-9-9v**$^{(5)}$ AmandaSanders(5) (lw: a.p: pushed along 3f out: jnd wnr appr fnl f: rdr dropped whip: unable qckn) | 4 | **2** | 11/2$^{3}$ | 78 | 25 |
| *1029*$^{9}$ | **Sea Spouse (57)** (MBlanshard) **5-9-1** NAdams(3) (led tl hdd over 2f out: rdn & outpcd wl over 1f out) | 4 | **3** | 14/1 | 56 | 3 |
| *1460*$^{2}$ | **Quinzii Martin (51)** (DHaydnJones) **8-8-9v** AMackay(2) (bhd: effrt ent st: sn rdn: no imp) | 4 | **4** | 7/2$^{2}$ | 41 | — |
| | **River Tern (68)** (JBerry) **3-9-1** GHind(4) (unf: lw: s.i.s: a in rr: lost tch over 2f out) | 6 | **5** | 16/1 | 44 | — |
| | | | | (SP 113.8%) | | **5 Rn** |

**1m 30.4** (5.70) CSF £4.31 TOTE £1.40: £1.10 £1.70 (£2.60) OWNER Mr Noel Sweeney (UPPER LONGDON) BRED Brownstown Stud
WEIGHT FOR AGE 3yo-11lb

**987 Sualtach (IRE)** won quite comfortably in the end, but he looked a very fortunate winner, gaining his initial success on the All-Weather.(4/7)
**1448 Four of Spades** cruised upsides the winner going much the better approaching the final furlong but, just when he needed a crack to go past, his rider dropped her whip and he failed to pick up without the encouragement to do so. He would have almost certainly won this. (11/2)
**470* Sea Spouse** set out to make all, but the winner took his measure on the home turn and he was soon fighting a lost cause. (14/1: op 7/1)

## 1605 LION (S) STKS (3, 4 & 5-Y.O) (Class F)

4-10 (4-10) **1m 4f (Fibresand)** £2,381.00 (£656.00: £311.00) Stalls: Low GOING minus 0.15 sec per fur (FST)

| | | | | SP | RR | SF |
|---|---|---|---|---|---|---|
| *1444*$^{4}$ | **Pearl Anniversary (IRE) (54)** (MJohnston) **3-8-11** PRobinson(6) (prom: reminders over 4f out: led over 3f out: hrd rdn: all out) | — | **1** | 15/8$^{1}$ | 69 | 3 |
| 1347$^{11}$ | **Greenwich Again (65)** (TGMills) **4-10-0** MarkLynch(3) (hld up: hdwy 6f out: ev ch fnl 2f: rdn & r.o wl cl home) | nk | **2** | 3/1$^{2}$ | 69 | 20 |
| | **Slippery Fin** (WGMTurner) **4-9-5** TSprake(9) (bkwd: hld up: hdwy 6f out: jnd wnr 2f out: hrd rdn fnl f: r.o) | ½ | **3** | 14/1 | 59 | 10 |
| *57*$^{8}$ | **Dannistar (53)** (PDEvans) **4-9-5** GHind(5) (hld up: hdwy ½-wy: ev ch 2f out: rdn & wknd over 1f out) | 13 | **4** | 9/2$^{3}$ | 42 | — |
| 688$^{16}$ | **Timely Example (USA) (46)** (BRCambidge) **5-9-3b**$^{(7)}$ IonaWands(7) (trckd ldrs tl outpcd over 3f out: t.o) | 10 | **5** | 20/1 | 33 | — |
| 1165$^{6}$ | **Magic Times (55)** (MJohnston) **5-9-10** LDettori(8) (led 5f: led 5f out tl over 3f out: sn rdn & wknd: t.o) | 9 | **6** | 11/2 | 21 | — |
| | **Minnie The Minx** (WGMTurner) **5-9-0**$^{(5)}$ CAdamson(2) (lw: chsd ldrs: led 7f out to 5f out: sn outpcd: t.o) | 13 | **7** | 20/1 | — | — |
| *162*$^{8}$ | **Laser Light Lady** (NPLittmoden) **4-9-5** TGMcLaughlin(1) (bit bkwd: dwlt: sn drvn along: t.o fr ½-wy) | 11 | **8** | 33/1 | — | — |
| *899*$^{7}$ | **Pandora's Gift** (KRBurke) **3-8-2** JFEgan(4) (a bhd: t.o fnl 4f) | 3½ | **9** | 33/1 | — | — |
| | | | | (SP 115.4%) | | **9 Rn** |

**2m 45.3** (12.80) CSF £7.67 TOTE £2.80: £1.10 £2.40 £2.70 (£5.50) Trio £35.00 OWNER Mr & Mrs A Mordain (MIDDLEHAM) BRED Ovidstown Investments Ltd
WEIGHT FOR AGE 3yo-17lb
Bt in 4,000 gns
STEWARDS' ENQUIRY Lynch susp. 9-10/6/96 (excessive use of whip)

**1444 Pearl Anniversary (IRE)** had to be bustled along to strike the front leaving the back straight and he had a battle on his hands all the way to the finish, but he responded gamely and deservedly held on. (15/8)
**486 Greenwich Again** had less use made of him and looked the likely winner when joining issue entering the last quarter-mile, but it was not until the final strides that he really started to peg the winner back. (3/1)
**Slippery Fin**, a lightly-made ex-French filly, looked far from fully wound up for her debut in this country but she ran a fine race in defeat, and she could prove better than a selling plater with this run under her belt. (14/1)
**Dannistar**, one of five fighting for the lead two furlongs out, was the first to crack and her stamina gave out approaching the final furlong. (9/2)

## 1606 ANGEL H'CAP (0-65) (3-Y.O+) (Class F)

4-40 (4-42) **6f (Fibresand)** £2,381.00 (£656.00: £311.00) Stalls: Low GOING minus 0.15 sec per fur (FST)

| | | | | SP | RR | SF |
|---|---|---|---|---|---|---|
| 601$^{18}$ | **Newington Butts (IRE) (47)** (KMcAuliffe) **6-8-10e** SSanders(5) (mde virtually all: rdn & hld on gamely nr fin) | — | **1** | 10/1 | 53 | 16 |
| *1490*$^{8}$ | **Klipspinger (60)** (BSRothwell) **3-8-11**$^{(3)}$ JStack(3) (a.p: disp ld fnl 2f: hrd rdn & no ex cl home) | hd | **2** | 4/1$^{2}$ | 66 | 20 |
| *1455*$^{8}$ | **Wardara (59)** (CADwyer) **4-9-3v**$^{(5)}$ FLynch(6) (sn bhd & rdn along: hdwy wl over 1f out: nrst fin) | 2½ | **3** | 5/1 | 58 | 21 |
| *1460*$^{4}$ | **Jon's Choice (42)** (BPreece) **8-7-12v**$^{(7)}$ IonaWands(9) (prom tl rdn & outpcd 2f out) | 5 | **4** | 7/2$^{1}$ | 28 | — |
| *1492*$^{15}$ | **Square Deal (FR) (65)** (SRBowring) **5-10-0** LDettori(7) (effrt on ins over 2f out: sn hrd: nt rch ldrs) | nk | **5** | 6/1 | 50 | 13 |
| 1500$^{2}$ | **Bowcliffe Grange (IRE) (33)** (DWChapman) **4-7-10** GBardwell(10) (lw: prom tl wknd u.p 2f out) | 1 | **6** | 7/1 | 15 | — |
| 1351* | **High Domain (IRE) (65)** (JLSpearing) **5-9-11**$^{(3)}$ 7x SDrowne(2) (lw: trckd ldrs tl outpcd over 2f out) | ¾ | **7** | 9/2$^{3}$ | 45 | 8 |
| *1460*$^{6}$ | **Disco Boy (53)** (PDEvans) **6-8-11**$^{(5)}$ AmandaSanders(8) (prom tl outpcd over 2f out) | nk | **8** | 14/1 | 33 | — |
| *1455*$^{5}$ | **Delrob (47)** (DHaydnJones) **5-8-10** AMackay(4) (outpcd: a bhd) | hd | **9** | 8/1 | 26 | — |
| 1043$^{6}$ | **Serious Fact (41)** (MrsLStubbs) **4-8-4** MMcAndrew(1) (outpcd: t.o fr ½-wy) | 13 | **10** | 14/1 | — | — |
| | | | | (SP 137.4%) | | **10 Rn** |

**1m 16.2** (4.80) CSF £54.77 CT £220.81 TOTE £15.60: £5.10 £2.60 £2.90 (£61.00) Trio £72.50 OWNER Mr D. D. Davies (LAMBOURN) BRED A. F. O. Callaghan
LONG HANDICAP Bowcliffe Grange (IRE) 7-0
WEIGHT FOR AGE 3yo-9lb

**Newington Butts (IRE)**, at her best when able to force the pace, did just that and, answering her rider's every call, held on grimly to the finish. (10/1)
**1030* Klipspinger** had plenty of use made of her and only just failed to wear down a most persistent rival. This was her best effort yet. (4/1: 3/1-9/2)
**1083 Wardara**, off the bridle from the start, stayed on to gain the minor prize inside the final furlong. (5/1)
**1460 Jon's Choice** held a pitch just behind the leaders until feeling the strain and dropping away entering the straight. (7/2)
**1492 Square Deal (FR)** made progress on the inside from halfway, but could not get himself close enough. (6/1)
**1500 Bowcliffe Grange (IRE)** took a keen tug to post and broke well to press the leaders, but he was a spent force on the home turn and faded tamely. (7/1)
**1351* High Domain (IRE)** did not think much of having dirt kicked in his face and gradually dropped himself out on the home turn. This was his first run on the All-Weather. (9/2: op 3/1)
**1455 Delrob** (8/1: op 5/1)

T/Plpt: £36.80 (234.82 Tckts). T/Qdpt: £7.10 (86.5 Tckts). IM

# 1595-CATTERICK (L-H) (Good, Good to firm home st)

## Saturday June 1st

WEATHER: cloudy

### 1607 RACING CHANNEL (S) STKS (2-Y.O) (Class G)

2-15 (2-16) **5f 212y** £2,364.00 (£654.00: £312.00) Stalls: High GOING minus 0.34 sec per fur (GF)

| | Horse / details | Btn | Pos | SP | RR | SF |
|---|---|---|---|---|---|---|
| $1494^{4}$ | **Our Kevin** (KMcAuliffe) **2-8-11b¹** JTate(7) (s.i.s: outpcd & bhd tl hdwy 2f out: led ins fnl f: r.o) | — | 1 | $3/1^{2}$ | 54 | 4 |
| $1183^{6}$ | **Bellaf** (MWEasterby) **2-8-11** DaleGibson(4) (sn bhd: hdwy 2f out: ch ins fnl f: kpt on) | 1¾ | 2 | $7/1^{3}$ | 49 | — |
| 1320* | **Skyers Flyer (IRE)** (RonaldThompson) **2-8-12** NConnorton(1) (plld hrd: sn cl up: led appr fnl f: sn hdd & no ex) | ½ | 3 | $11/10^{1}$ | 49 | — |
| *$1084^{5}$* | **Abstone Again (IRE)** (PDEvans) **2-8-11v** JFortune(2) (lw: led tl hdd appr fnl f: sn btn) | 1¾ | 4 | 12/1 | 43 | — |
| | **Moor Hall Princess** (KRBurke) **2-8-6** TWilliams(5) (small: dwlt: sn chsng ldrs: swtchd over 2f out: wknd appr fnl f) | s.h | 5 | 11/1 | 38 | — |
| $1360^{3}$ | **Silver Raj** (WTKemp) **2-8-11b** KFallon(6) (chsd ldrs tl outpcd fnl 2f) | 2 | 6 | 14/1 | 38 | — |
| $1433^{6}$ | **Whittle Times** (EJAlston) **2-8-3**(3) SDrowne(9) (outpcd fr ½-wy) | 4 | 7 | 14/1 | 22 | — |
| | **Where's Wally (IRE)** (JBerry) **2-8-6**(5) PRoberts(3) (leggy: lt-f: cl up 4f: wknd) | hd | 8 | $7/1^{3}$ | 27 | — |

(SP 127.0%) **8 Rn**

**1m 15.5** (4.60) CSF £24.78 TOTE £3.10: £1.10 £2.80 £1.70 (£17.40) Trio £6.90 OWNER Mr T. Mohan (LAMBOURN) BRED J. Vaughan
Bt in 6,600gns

**1494 Our Kevin**, in blinkers this time, never looked happy but decided to run in the home straight to settle it inside the last furlong. (3/1: 4/1-5/2)
**Bellaf**, dropped in class, ran his best race to date and could well pick up a similar event. (7/1)
**1320* Skyers Flyer (IRE)** pulled too hard for her own good early on and that probably made all the difference. (11/10: op 7/4)
**838 Abstone Again (IRE)** showed plenty of speed, but failed to see out the trip. (12/1: op 7/1)
**Moor Hall Princess** is only small, but she does use herself well and should be all the better for this. (11/1: 8/1-12/1)
**1360 Silver Raj**, having his second run in blinkers, did continue the improvement. (14/1)
**Where's Wally (IRE)** (7/1: op 4/1)

### 1608 MAURITIU'SMILE GRAND DRAW MAIDEN AUCTION STKS (3-Y.O) (Class E)

2-45 (2-46) **7f** £3,158.00 (£944.00: £452.00: £206.00) Stalls: Low GOING minus 0.34 sec per fur (GF)

| | Horse / details | Btn | Pos | SP | RR | SF |
|---|---|---|---|---|---|---|
| $714^{3}$ | **Alamein (USA) (74)** (WJHaggas) **3-9-0b¹** KFallon(2) (trckd ldrs: led wl over 1f out: comf) | — | 1 | $9/4^{1}$ | 79 | 52 |
| $1171^{4}$ | **Blessed Spirit (69)** (CFWall) **3-8-9** ACulhane(1) (lw: cl up: led over 3f out tl wl over 1f out: one pce) | 2½ | 2 | 5/1 | 68 | 41 |
| $1126^{11}$ | **Indian Relative (70)** (RGuest) **3-8-9** LCharnock(3) (lw: chsd ldrs: rdn 2f out: nt qckn) | 1¼ | 3 | $3/1^{3}$ | 65 | 38 |
| $1033^{2}$ | **Sihafi (USA) (77)** (EALDunlop) **3-9-0** JFortune(11) (led after 2f tl over 3f out: one pce) | ½ | 4 | $11/4^{2}$ | 69 | 42 |
| $1429^{7}$ | **Nattier** (SirMarkPrescott) **3-8-9** CNutter(9) (chsd ldrs tl lost pl appr st: sme late hdwy) | 11 | 5 | 20/1 | 39 | 12 |
| $971^{14}$ | **Chilly Looks (45)** (WLBarker) **3-8-9** TWilliams(14) (swtg: effrt ½-wy: rdn & no imp) | 2 | 6 | 50/1 | 35 | 8 |
| $1435^{10}$ | **Welcome Brief** (EJAlston) **3-8-6**(3) SDrowne(8) (nvr bttr than mid div) | 1¼ | 7 | 100/1 | 32 | 5 |
| $1312^{9}$ | **Swifty Nifty (IRE) (45)** (WWHaigh) **3-8-9** JTate(13) (led 2f: cl up tl wknd 2f out) | 4 | 8 | 100/1 | 23 | — |
| $1530^{14}$ | **South Pagoda (IRE)** (DNicholls) **3-9-0** AlexGreaves(4) (nvr trbld ldrs) | ½ | 9 | 20/1 | 26 | — |
| | **Mercury (IRE)** (JAGlover) **3-9-0** MBirch(5) (str: bkwd: a outpcd & bhd) | hd | 10 | 20/1 | 26 | — |
| | **Moonraking** (TJEtherington) **3-9-0** DaleGibson(12) (unf: bit bkwd: s.i.s: a bhd) | 2 | 11 | 50/1 | 22 | — |
| $626^{7}$ | **Eleanor May** (TDBarron) **3-8-9** JFanning(6) (sn wl bhd) | 1¾ | 12 | 25/1 | 13 | — |
| | **Distinctly Swingin (IRE)** (MissLAPerratt) **3-8-4**(5) PFessey(7) (bhd fr ½-wy) | hd | 13 | 33/1 | 12 | — |
| $1323^{7}$ | **Skylight** (MissMKMilligan) **3-9-0** NConnorton(10) (sn wl bhd) | ¾ | 14 | 50/1 | 16 | — |

(SP 128.0%) **14 Rn**

**1m 25.1** (1.50) CSF £14.41 TOTE £3.20: £1.30 £2.20 £1.70 (£16.90) Trio £11.20 OWNER Mr Henryk De Kwiatkowski (NEWMARKET) BRED Kennelot Stables Limited

**714 Alamein (USA)** had blinkers on for the first time and they certainly worked as he won nicely. (9/4: 7/4-11/4)
**1171 Blessed Spirit** looked well and really got into it but she lacks the change of gear at the business end. (5/1)
**Indian Relative** was edgy beforehand and although putting in her best effort of the season, she was never doing enough when it mattered. (3/1)
**1033 Sihafi (USA)**, taken to post last, behaved well but once the pressure was applied, the response was again disappointing. (11/4)
**1033 Nattier**, having her third run here, was not knocked about and will no doubt do better in handicaps in due course. (20/1)

### 1609 ROTHMANS ROYALS NORTH SOUTH CHALLENGE SERIES H'CAP (0-85) (3-Y.O+) (Class D)

3-15 (3-17) **7f** £4,659.00 (£1,392.00: £666.00: £303.00) Stalls: Low GOING minus 0.34 sec per fur (GF)

| | Horse / details | Btn | Pos | SP | RR | SF |
|---|---|---|---|---|---|---|
| $1322^{5}$ | **Queens Consul (IRE) (78)** (BSRothwell) **6-9-9** MBirch(3) (lw: chsd ldrs: led over 1f out: r.o) | — | 1 | $8/1^{3}$ | 87 | 59 |
| $718^{10}$ | **Zain Dancer (55)** (DNicholls) **4-8-0** NKennedy(14) (a chsng ldrs: styd on fnl 2f: nt pce to chal) | 2½ | 2 | 16/1 | 58 | 30 |
| $589^{13}$ | **Blue Bomber (72)** (TDBarron) **5-9-3** JFortune(4) (led tl hdd over 1f out: one pce) | hd | 3 | 10/1 | 75 | 47 |
| $1313^{10}$ | **Allinson's Mate (IRE) (55)** (TDBarron) **8-8-0** JFanning(9) (rr div tl styd on wl fnl 2f) | hd | 4 | 12/1 | 58 | 30 |
| $935^{4}$ | **Bargash (64)** (PDEvans) **4-8-2b**(7) IonaWands(7) (chsd ldrs: effrt over 2f out: one pce appr fnl f) | ¾ | 5 | 10/1 | 65 | 37 |
| $850^{9}$ | **Halmanerror (68)** (MrsJRRamsden) **6-8-13** KFallon(6) (in tch: swtchd over 1f out: nvr nr to chal) | nk | 6 | $7/2^{1}$ | 68 | 40 |
| $956^{7}$ | **Shashi (IRE) (70)** (WWHaigh) **4-9-1** JTate(1) (a in tch: no hdwy fnl 2f) | ¾ | 7 | 33/1 | 69 | 41 |
| $1341^{6}$ | **Pride of Pendle (72)** (DNicholls) **7-9-3** AlexGreaves(13) (hld up: nvr nr to chal) | ¾ | 8 | $6/1^{2}$ | 69 | 41 |
| $1423^{4}$ | **It's Academic (64)** (MrsJRRamsden) **4-8-9** MDeering(2) (bhd tl sme late hdwy) | ½ | 9 | 16/1 | 60 | 32 |
| $928^{14}$ | **Tiler (IRE) (79)** (MJohnston) **4-9-10** TWilliams(8) (sn cl up: rdn & wknd over 1f out) | 1¼ | 10 | $8/1^{3}$ | 72 | 44 |
| *$1094^{3}$* | **Dancing Sioux (67)** (DNicholls) **4-8-12** MWigham(11) (hld up & bhd: nvr plcd to chal) | 1½ | 11 | 12/1 | 57 | 29 |
| $1074^{9}$ | **Mr Cube (IRE) (55)** (JMBradley) **6-8-0v** LCharnock(10) (chsd ldrs tl wknd fnl 2½f) | ½ | 12 | 11/1 | 43 | 15 |
| $1425^{6}$ | **Tawafij (USA) (78)** (TDyer) **7-9-6**(3) SDrowne(12) (s.i.s: a rr div) | nk | 13 | $6/1^{2}$ | 66 | 38 |

(SP 129.6%) **13 Rn**

**1m 25.2** (1.60) CSF £122.34 CT £1,243.21 TOTE £11.50: £2.20 £11.40 £3.70 (£209.80) Trio £429.50; £544.56 to Leicester 3/6/96. OWNER Miss Heather Davison (MALTON) BRED Mrs Ann Galvin

**OFFICIAL EXPLANATION Dancing Sioux: his rider reported that he moved down scratchily, and after leaving the stalls seemed to be feeling something and hung to the right on the bend. He needs more give in the ground and on examination was found to be suffering from muscle sensitivity.**

**1322 Queens Consul (IRE)** got the run of the race and gained a totally deserved success, but some of her opponents did not appear over-fancied. (8/1)

**718 Zain Dancer** is certainly improving and looks to be off a useful mark at present. (16/1)
**Blue Bomber** ran pretty well to show he is on his way back to form. (10/1)
**479 Allinson's Mate (IRE)**, who showed absolutely nothing last time, decided to run here but it was always too late. (12/1)
**935 Bargash** had her chances but lacked a turn of foot to overtake them. (10/1)
**850 Halmanerror** raced in touch but did not show any real sparkle this time, but is beginning to slip down the handicap. (7/2)
**1341 Pride of Pendle** never got into this but still ran well enough to suggest that she is worth keeping in mind. (6/1)
**1094 Dancing Sioux** left the impression that she can certainly do better. (12/1)
**1425 Tawafij (USA)** failed get into this at any stage and it seems that he more suited to galloping tracks these days. (6/1)

## 1610 YORKSHIRE-TYNE TEES TEVEVISION LIMITED STKS (0-60) (3-Y.O+) (Class F)

3-45 (3-46) **7f** £2,805.00 (£780.00: £375.00) Stalls: Low GOING minus 0.34 sec per fur (GF)

| | | | | SP | RR | SF |
|---|---|---|---|---|---|---|
| $991^{7}$ | **Darcey Bussell (55)** (BWHills) **4-9-2** KFallon(2) (sn pushed along: hdwy over 2f out: led ins fnl f: hung lft: r.o) | — | **1** | 4/1 $^{3}$ | 65 | 45 |
| $1156^{2}$ | **Mels Baby (IRE) (53)** (JLEyre) **3-8-6**(3) DWright(4) (in tch: hdwy over 1f out: ch ins fnl f: kpt on) | 1 | **2** | 11/1 | 66 | 36 |
| $1069^{13}$ | **Legal Issue (IRE) (56)** (WWHaigh) **4-9-5** JTate(1) (lw: trckd ldrs: led wl over 1f to ins fnl f: no ex) | nk | **3** | 10/1 | 65 | 45 |
| $1068^{8}$ | **Katie Komaite (58)** (CaptJWilson) **3-8-1**(5) PFessey(6) (led tl hdd wl over 1f out: kpt one pce) | 3½ | **4** | 16/1 | 54 | 24 |
| $1163^{12}$ | **Best Kept Secret (53)** (PDEvans) **5-9-5** JFortune(9) (chsd ldrs: rdn over 2f out: one pce) | 1½ | **5** | 14/1 | 54 | 34 |
| | **Catwalk Girl (50)** (MissJFCraze) **3-8-6** NConnorton(5) (chsd ldrs: rdn appr s: one pce) | 1½ | **6** | 16/1 | 47 | 17 |
| *$1460^{11}$* | **Silver Welcome (60)** (TDEasterby) **3-8-9** MBirch(8) (cl up tl wknd appr fnl f) | hd | **7** | 4/1 $^{3}$ | 50 | 20 |
| $1423^{2}$ | **Ochos Rios (IRE) (62)** (BSRothwell) **5-9-5** LCharnock(3) (rr div & drvn along over 2f out: n.d) | hd | **8** | 5/2 $^{1}$ | 50 | 30 |
| $1412^{5}$ | **Impulsive Air (IRE) (58)** (EWeymes) **4-9-5v** ACulhane(7) (s.i.s: nvr wnt pce) | 3 | **9** | 3/1 $^{2}$ | 43 | 23 |
| | **Intrepid Fort (19)** (BWMurray) **7-8-12b**(7) IonaWands(10) (s.i.s: a outpcd & bhd) | 2½ | **10** | 200/1 | 37 | 17 |

(SP 129.9%) **10 Rn**

**1m 25.8** (2.20) CSF £47.34 TOTE £5.90: £2.20 £2.10 £2.90 (£26.50) Trio £109.50 OWNER Mr W. J. Gredley (LAMBOURN) BRED Stetchworth Park Stud Ltd
WEIGHT FOR AGE 3yo-10lb
**Darcey Bussell** won this authoritatively after looking none too happy early on. (4/1)
**1156 Mels Baby (IRE)** got a bit warm beforehand but again ran well, putting in all her best work at the end. (11/1)
**505 Legal Issue (IRE)** looked particularly well and ran his best race for a while, and would seem to be coming to hand. (10/1)
**Katie Komaite** showed something for the first time this season but was well outpaced approaching the final furlong. (16/1)
**1020 Best Kept Secret** was not in a co-operative mood this time. (14/1: 10/1-16/1)
**Catwalk Girl**, a real handful in the preliminaries, had used up her energy when it mattered. (16/1)
**1460 Silver Welcome** looked none too keen when asked for an effort early in the straight. (4/1)
**1423 Ochos Rios (IRE)** had a hard race last time and never took any interest here. (5/2)

## 1611 WILLIAM EDWIN NEESHAM MEMORIAL H'CAP (0-70) (4-Y.O+) (Class E)

4-20 (4-20) **1m 7f 177y** £3,106.00 (£928.00: £444.00: £202.00) Stalls: Low GOING minus 0.34 sec per fur (GF)

| | | | | SP | RR | SF |
|---|---|---|---|---|---|---|
| *$1095^{2}$* | **Tiaphena (40)** (JMackie) **5-7-12** JFanning(6) (led early: cl up: led 6f out: hld on wl fnl f) | — | **1** | 5/1 $^{3}$ | 51 | 30 |
| $1116^{7}$ | **Bowcliffe Court (IRE) (58)** (BWHills) **4-9-1** KFallon(5) (trckd ldrs: chal over 2f out: no ex u.p ins fnl f) | ½ | **2** | 2/1 $^{1}$ | 69 | 47 |
| $642^{10}$ | **Bobby's Dream (39)** (MHTompkins) **4-7-10** LCharnock(1) (in tch: hdwy 4f out: wl outpcd fnl 2f) | 14 | **3** | 10/1 | 35 | 13 |
| $1343^{4}$ | **Mondragon (68)** (MrsMReveley) **6-9-5**(7) SCopp(8) (lw: dwlt: effrt 8ft out: rdn & no imp) | 10 | **4** | 5/2 $^{2}$ | 54 | 33 |
| $1116^{6}$ | **Hasta la Vista (53)** (MWEasterby) **6-8-11b** DaleGibson(7) (lw: sn led tl hdd 6f out: sn rdn: wknd fnl 3f) | 1 | **5** | 5/1 $^{3}$ | 38 | 17 |
| $1542^{8}$ | **Don't Cry (39)** (DonEnricoIncisa) **8-7-11**ow1 KimTinkler(3) (a bhd: t.o) | 25 | **6** | 100/1 | — | — |
| $713^{16}$ | **Gymcrak Hero (IRE) (43)** (GHolmes) **4-8-0** TWilliams(2) (chsd ldrs tl wknd 6f out: t.o) | dist | **7** | 33/1 | — | — |
| | **Silverdale Count (42)** (KWHogg) **4-7-10**(3) DWright(4) (prom: outpcd 8f out: sn bhd: p.u 4f out) | | **P** | 10/1 | — | — |

(SP 117.4%) **8 Rn**

**3m 26.9** (5.40) CSF £15.23 CT £88.70 TOTE £5.90: £2.00 £1.20 £1.80 (£11.90) OWNER The Five Nations Partnership (CHURCH BROUGHTON) BRED C. J. and Mrs J. E. Small
LONG HANDICAP Don't Cry 6-4 Bobby's Dream 7-8
WEIGHT FOR AGE 4yo-1lb
**1095 Tiaphena** gained her first win here and, judging by the manner in which she did it, she should find further success. (5/1)
**753 Bowcliffe Court (IRE)**, given a fine ride, had his chances two furlongs out, but just failed to go through with the effort. (2/1)
**Bobby's Dream** looked fit and had her chances, but proved far too slow when the pressure was on in the last half-mile. (10/1)
**1343 Mondragon** was never happy on this track and never took the slightest interest. (5/2)
**1116 Hasta la Vista** has never won over this far on turf and was left struggling approaching the home turn. (5/1)

## 1612 ALDBROUGH RATING RELATED MAIDEN STKS (0-60) (3-Y.O+) (Class F)

4-50 (4-51) **5f 212y** £2,595.00 (£720.00: £345.00) Stalls: High GOING minus 0.34 sec per fur (GF)

| | | | | SP | RR | SF |
|---|---|---|---|---|---|---|
| $1068^{3}$ | **Mellors (IRE) (56)** (JARToller) **3-8-11** JFortune(3) (lw: cl up: led over 2f out: r.o) | — | **1** | 11/8 $^{1}$ | 58 | 29 |
| $1405^{9}$ | **Madam Zando (44)** (JBalding) **3-8-1**(7) JEdmunds(9) (bhd: hdwy on outside 2f out: hung lft 1f out: nt qckn) | 1¾ | **2** | 12/1 | 50 | 21 |
| | **Answers-To-Thomas (58)** (JMJefferson) **3-8-11** KFallon(1) (hld up: hdwy on ins 2f out: hrd rdn & nt qckn ins fnl f) | 1½ | **3** | 8/1 | 49 | 20 |
| $861^{4}$ | **Members Welcome (IRE) (56)** (JMBradley) **3-8-8**(3) SDrowne(8) (outpcd ½-wy: hdwy over 1f out: n.m.r ins fnl f) | 1¼ | **4** | 7/2 $^{2}$ | 46 | 17 |
| | **Time To Fly (60)** (BWMurray) **3-8-11** TWilliams(2) (lw: led tl hdd 2f out: grad wknd) | 2 | **5** | 5/1 $^{3}$ | 41 | 12 |
| *$1096^{8}$* | **Patrio (IRE) (58)** (SCWilliams) **3-8-8** JTate(4) (n.m.r after 2f: sme hdwy over 1f out: n.d) | s.h | **6** | 7/1 | 37 | 8 |
| $885^{9}$ | **Mon Pere (50)** (KMcAuliffe) **3-8-11b**$^{1}$ JFanning(7) (a outpcd & bhd) | 9 | **7** | 20/1 | 16 | — |
| | **Good To Talk (43)** (TDEasterby) **3-8-11** MBirch(6) (chsd ldrs over 3f: sn wknd) | 2 | **8** | 33/1 | 11 | — |
| $882^{16}$ | **So Natural (IRE) (48)** (EJAlston) **4-8-11b**$^{1}$(5) PPMurphy(5) (cl up tl wknd fnl 2f) | 2½ | **9** | 20/1 | 1 | — |

(SP 124.8%) **9 Rn**

**1m 13.6** (2.70) CSF £18.85 TOTE £2.20: £1.20 £2.50 £2.70 (£15.10) Trio £24.90 OWNER The B B A Fortune In Mind Partnership (WHITSBURY) BRED Jimmy Coogan
WEIGHT FOR AGE 3yo-8lb
**1068 Mellors (IRE)** was the pick on looks and did the business in determined style. (11/8)
**973 Madam Zando** looks to have plenty of ability but all she wanted to do here was hang left in the closing stages. (12/1)
**Answers-To-Thomas** raced too freely early on and, once he settles, there should be a race for him. (8/1: op 5/1)

**861 Members Welcome (IRE)**, taken off his legs at halfway, only stayed on when it was too late and then never had much room. (7/2)
**Time To Fly** looked pretty fit for this seasonal debut but, judging by the way he ran, he needed it. (5/1)
**Patrio (IRE)**, short of room early on, got shuffled back in the field and lacked the pace to recover. (7/1)

T/Plpt: £251.70 (42.12 Tckts). T/Qdpt: £104.10 (5.17 Tckts). AA

# 1437-KEMPTON (R-H) (Good to firm)
## Saturday June 1st
WEATHER: fine WIND: almost nil

## 1613 AMBITION APPRENTICE H'CAP (0-75) (3-Y.O+) (Class E)
6-25 (6-28) **1m (Jubilee)** £3,078.75 (£930.00: £452.50: £213.75) Stalls: High GOING minus 0.28 sec per fur (GF)

| Prev | Horse / details | Dist | Pos | SP | RR | SF |
|---|---|---|---|---|---|---|
| 1440[12] | **Seventeens Lucky (68)** (BobJones) **4-9-13** LNewton(10) (a.p: led over 2f out: clr over 1f out: r.o wl) | — | 1 | 7/1[3] | 78 | 54 |
| 1302* | **Leguard Express (IRE) (37)** (OO'Neill) **8-7-5b**(5) JBramhill(12) (led over 5f: unable qckn) | 3½ | 2 | 9/2[1] | 40 | 16 |
| 1449[20] | **Cuban Reef (45)** (WJMusson) **4-7-13**(5) JWilkinson(9) (dwlt: rn wd bnd over 3f out: hdwy over 2f out: one pce fnl f) | nk | 3 | 10/1 | 47 | 23 |
| 1423[7] | **Cats Bottom (56)** (AGNewcombe) **4-9-1** RPainter(7) (dwlt: rdn over 2f out: hung bdly lft over 1f out: hdwy fnl f: r.o) | 1¾ | 4 | 5/1[2] | 55 | 31 |
| *1457*[3] | **African-Pard (IRE) (64)** (DHaydnJones) **4-9-4**(5) AnthonyBond(2) (lw: hld up: rdn over 2f out: one pce) | 1½ | 5 | 14/1 | 60 | 36 |
| 765[11] | **Gadge (61)** (DMorris) **5-9-6** MHenry(6) (hld up: rdn over 2f out: wknd fnl f) | ½ | 6 | 9/1 | 56 | 32 |
| 1468[18] | **Jovie King (IRE) (47)** (PhilipMitchell) **4-8-3b**(3) CAdamson(13) (lw: hld up: rdn over 2f out: wknd over 1f out) | 1¼ | 7 | 40/1 | 39 | 15 |
| *776*[3] | **Lilac Rain (42)** (JRArnold) **4-8-1** MBaird(1) (nvr nr to chal) | 6 | 8 | 11/1 | 22 | — |
| *384*[3] | **Mislemani (IRE) (59)** (AGNewcombe) **6-9-4** DGriffiths(8) (prom over 5f) | 1¾ | 9 | 14/1 | 36 | 12 |
| 1333[14] | **Mimosa (60)** (SDow) **3-8-8v**[1] ADaly(5) (lw: hld up: rdn over 3f out: sn wknd) | 1¾ | 10 | 20/1 | 33 | — |
| | **Sharp Shuffle (IRE) (65)** (RHannon) **3-8-6**(7) KSalt(3) (bit bkwd: bhd fnl 4f) | ¾ | 11 | 8/1 | 37 | 2 |
| *308*[5] | **Oozlem (IRE) (41)** (JRPoulton) **7-7-9b**(5)ow1 TField(11) (b: s.s: a bhd) | 3 | 12 | 7/1[3] | 7 | — |
| 1172[10] | **Henry Otis (58)** (RAkehurst) **3-8-1**(5) DDenby(4) (lw: a bhd) | 1 | 13 | 20/1 | 22 | — |

(SP 123.7%) **13 Rn**

**1m 40.38** (3.18) CSF £37.41 CT £239.57 TOTE £7.50: £2.40 £1.20 £3.30 (£9.70) Trio £56.30 OWNER Mr D. M. Cameron (NEWMARKET) BRED D. E. Weeden
LONG HANDICAP Leguard Express (IRE) 7-9
WEIGHT FOR AGE 3yo-11lb

**Seventeens Lucky** struck the front over a quarter of a mile from home and soon forged clear for a decisive victory. (7/1)
**1302* Leguard Express (IRE)** attempted to make all the running, but was firmly put in his place when collared over two furlongs from home. To his credit though, he did hold on for second prize. (9/2: op 3/1)
**Cuban Reef** ran her best race so far this season. Racing at the back of the field, her jockey unwisely took her to the outside and made his effort on the filly on the outer as they were turning into the straight. The result was that the combination lost all ground they had originally made up. Nevertheless, she picked up again early in the straight and looked likely to take second place. However, she failed to find another gear in the final furlong and had to settle for third prize. (10/1)
**1423 Cats Bottom** gave her rider serious steering problems. Scrubbed along early in the straight, she hung violently left below the distance and ended up on the stands' rail. However, despite this huge handicap, she ran on in the final furlong for fourth prize. (5/1)
**1457 African-Pard (IRE)** chased the leaders but failed to find another gear in the straight. (14/1)
**Gadge** chased the leaders. Pushed along early in the straight as he tried to mount a challenge, he had nothing left to offer in the final furlong. This was not a bad effort considering he needs to get his toe in to be seen to best effect. (9/1: op 6/1)
**776 Lilac Rain** (11/1: 8/1-12/1)
**Sharp Shuffle (IRE)** (8/1: 5/1-9/1)

## 1614 KEMPTON EXHIBITION CENTRE MAIDEN STKS (3-Y.O F) (Class D)
6-55 (6-59) **1m 1f (round)** £3,850.50 (£1,164.00: £567.00: £268.50) Stalls: High GOING minus 0.28 sec per fur (GF)

| Prev | Horse / details | Dist | Pos | SP | RR | SF |
|---|---|---|---|---|---|---|
| | **Balalaika** (LMCumani) **3-8-11** PatEddery(2) (wl grwn: hld up: led 2f out: pushed out) | — | 1 | 9/4[1] | 73+ | 33 |
| 1007[5] | **Iberian Dancer (CAN) (76)** (JWHills) **3-8-11** RHughes(16) (hdwy over 2f out: ev ch ins fnl f: r.o) | nk | 2 | 7/2[2] | 73 | 33 |
| | **Wandering Star (USA)** (JRFanshawe) **3-8-11** NDay(11) (bit bkwd: a.p: nt clr run over 2f out: ev ch ins fnl f: unable qckn) | ½ | 3 | 16/1 | 72 | 32 |
| 1174[4] | **Tea Party (USA)** (KOCunningham-Brown) **3-8-11** TQuinn(15) (b: lw: hdwy & nt clr run on ins over 2f out: nt clr run on ins over 1f out: one pce) | 6 | 4 | 16/1 | 61 | 21 |
| | **Coh Sho No** (IABalding) **3-8-6**(5) MartinDwyer(14) (leggy: rdn over 2f out: hdwy over 1f out: r.o) | ¾ | 5 | 25/1 | 60 | 20 |
| | **Namouna (IRE)** (PWChapple-Hyam) **3-8-11** JReid(1) (neat: a.p: led over 2f out: sn hdd: wknd 1f out) | s.h | 6 | 5/1[3] | 60 | 20 |
| 1180[11] | **Gooseberry Pie** (RCharlton) **3-8-11** TSprake(17) (stdy hdwy over 1f out: nvr nrr) | ¾ | 7 | 20/1 | 58 | 18 |
| 705[13] | **Esquiline (USA)** (JHMGosden) **3-8-11** LDettori(9) (hld up: nt clr run over 2f out: swtchd lft: one pce) | 1¼ | 8 | 9/1 | 56 | 16 |
| | **South Wind** (MrsJCecil) **3-8-11** AClark(13) (unf: scope: a mid div) | s.h | 9 | 20/1 | 56 | 16 |
| 448[8] | **Sandicliffe (USA)** (BWHills) **3-8-11** MHills(18) (nvr nrr) | nk | 10 | 25/1 | 55 | 15 |
| 1061[4] | **Indian Nectar** (GBBalding) **3-8-11** SSanders(12) (a mid div) | hd | 11 | 25/1 | 55 | 15 |
| 1333[13] | **Kawanin** (PTWalwyn) **3-8-11** RHills(19) (lw: rdn over 4f out: hdwy & nt clr run on ins over 2f out: nt clr run on ins wl over 1f out: eased whn btn ins fnl f) | hd | 12 | 25/1 | 55+ | 15 |
| *502*[5] | **Nelly's Cousin** (NACallaghan) **3-8-8**(3) DaneO'Neill(8) (lw: bhd fnl 6f) | 1¼ | 13 | 33/1 | 53 | 13 |
| | **Giant Nipper** (IABalding) **3-8-11** WRyan(3) (small: a bhd) | 1 | 14 | 16/1 | 51 | 11 |
| 921[13] | **Mujtahida (IRE)** (RWArmstrong) **3-8-11** RPrice(7) (led 7f out to over 2f out: wkng whn nt clr run on ins over 1f out) | hd | 15 | 20/1 | 51 | 11 |
| | **Amelanchier** (GBBalding) **3-8-8**(3) NVarley(10) (prom over 7f) | hd | 16 | 66/1 | 51 | 11 |
| 1333[11] | **Love And Kisses** (CACyzer) **3-8-11** AMcGlone(5) (lw: led 2f: wkng whn n.m.r over 2f out) | 1¼ | 17 | 33/1 | 48 | 8 |
| 1117[10] | **Dance Model** (JJSheehan) **3-8-11** JQuinn(4) (swtg: hdwy 7f out: wknd over 4f out) | 15 | 18 | 66/1 | 22 | — |

(SP 135.8%) **18 Rn**

**1m 54.98** (4.38) CSF £11.27 TOTE £3.00: £1.60 £2.00 £3.60 (£7.80) Trio £79.40 OWNER Helena Springfield Ltd (NEWMARKET) BRED Meon Valley Stud

**Balalaika**, an imposing filly who cost 510,000 guineas, is by Sadler's Wells, out of 1985 1,000 Guineas third Bella Colora which makes her a sister to the very useful Stagecraft. Chasing the leaders, she moved to the front a quarter of a mile out and needed only to be nudged along to keep her rivals at bay. She will have learnt a great deal from this, and certain to be a lot fitter for the run can now go on to bigger and better things. (9/4: 5/4-11/4)
**1007 Iberian Dancer (CAN)** appreciated the step up in distance. Her turn is not far away. (7/2)
**Wandering Star (USA)** ran a fine race on this reappearance, especially considering she did not look fully wound up. Never far away, she failed to get a clear run in a tightly-packed field in the straight and her jockey had to just ease her out. Weaving her way through to have every chance inside the final furlong, she was just then tapped for toe. She should soon find a race. (16/1)
**1174 Tea Party (USA)** looked in good shape beforehand but met with real traffic problems. Stuck along the inside rail in the straight as she tried to make headway, she was tapped for toe from below the distance. (16/1)
**Coh Sho No**, a plain, rather leggy filly who is a half-sister to the useful Sought Out, winner of the Prix du Cadran in 1992, put in some really good work in the last furlong and a half to be nearest at the line. Sure to be a lot wiser for this, she will come into her own over further. (25/1)
**Namouna (IRE)**, a nippy sort, poked a nostril in front over a quarter of a mile from home but she was soon passed by the winner and came to the end of her tether a furlong from home. (5/1: op 2/1)
**Gooseberry Pie** was given considerate handling. However, she picked up ground below the distance and stayed on on the outside of the field to be nearest at the line. She looks one to bear in mind. (20/1)
**Esquiline (USA)** chased the leaders but found herself buried with nowhere to go early in the straight. Switched left, she could then only keep on at one pace under considerate handling. She is going the right way. (9/1: 8/1-12/1)

## 1615 CLUBHOUSE H'CAP (0-90) (3-Y.O) (Class C)

7-25 (7-27) **7f (round)** £5,602.00 (£1,696.00: £828.00: £394.00) Stalls: High GOING minus 0.28 sec per fur (GF)

| | | | | SP | RR | SF |
|---|---|---|---|---|---|---|
| | **Almushtarak (IRE) (85)** (MissGayKelleway) **3-9-7** JReid(5) (b.hind: hdwy 2f out: led over 1f out: rdn out) | — | **1** | 6/1$^{2}$ | 96 | 66 |
| $1181^{3}$ | **Golden Pond (IRE) (71)** (RFJohnsonHoughton) **3-8-7** AMcGlone(11) (led over 5f: unable qckn) | 2½ | **2** | 7/1$^{3}$ | 76 | 46 |
| $1327^{4}$ | **Sylva Paradise (IRE) (80)** (CEBrittain) **3-9-2** BDoyle(10) (w ldr: ev ch over 1f out: one pce) | ½ | **3** | 9/1 | 84 | 54 |
| $593^{7}$ | **Navigate (USA) (78)** (RHannon) **3-9-0** PatEddery(4) (lw: hld up: rdn over 1f out: one pce) | nk | **4** | 8/1 | 82 | 52 |
| $1172^{2}$ | **Silver Harrow (63)** (AGNewcombe) **3-7-10**(3) NVarley(6) (rdn over 3f out: hdwy & n.m.r over 1f out: one pce) | 2 | **5** | 10/1 | 62 | 32 |
| $1326^{6}$ | **Ashanti Dancer (IRE) (69)** (MJHaynes) **3-8-5**ow1 BThomson(8) (hdwy & nt clr run on ins over 2f out: wknd over 1f out) | 3 | **6** | 20/1 | 61 | 30 |
| | **Ballpoint (69)** (RHannon) **3-8-2**(3)ow2 DaneO'Neill(9) (lost pl over 4f out: sme hdwy over 1f out: sn wknd) | ¾ | **7** | 20/1 | 59 | 27 |
| $1013^{3}$ | **Time For Tea (IRE) (69)** (CACyzer) **3-8-5** TQuinn(1) (nvr nr to chal) | 3 | **8** | 7/1$^{3}$ | 53 | 23 |
| | **Star And Garter (78)** (GWragg) **3-9-0** MHills(7) (lw: prom 5f) | 2½ | **9** | 8/1 | 56 | 26 |
| $1101^{4}$ | **Meranti (60)** (SDow) **3-7-10** JQuinn(12) (prom over 5f) | nk | **10** | 9/1 | 37 | 7 |
| $1181^{2}$ | **Commin' Up (67)** (JWHills) **3-8-3** RHills(2) (a bhd) | 1 | **11** | 5/1$^{1}$ | 42 | 12 |
| $692^{5}$ | **Blue Flyer (IRE) (73)** (RIngram) **3-8-9** WWoods(3) (a bhd) | ¾ | **12** | 8/1 | 46 | 16 |

(SP 127.9%) **12 Rn**

**1m 25.78** (1.28) CSF £47.65 CT £356.11 TOTE £8.60: £3.10 £2.20 £3.90 (£27.60) Trio £288.10 OWNER Mr A. Al-Radi (WHITCOMBE) BRED Stonethorn Stud Farms Ltd
LONG HANDICAP Meranti 7-9
OFFICIAL EXPLANATION **Commin' Up: was outpaced and unable to handle the turn.**
**Almushtarak (IRE)** made a winning return to action. Coming through to lead over a furlong out, he was then ridden clear. (6/1)
**1181 Golden Pond (IRE)** attempted to make all the running but, collared below the distance, was firmly put in her place. (7/1)
**1327 Sylva Paradise (IRE)** disputed the lead from the start. Still in with every chance below the distance, he was then tapped for toe. (9/1)
**593 Navigate (USA)** chased the leaders, but failed to find the necessary turn of foot in the last two furlongs. A return to a slightly longer trip might help. (8/1)
**1172 Silver Harrow**, scrubbed along and going nowhere in last place turning for home, weaved his way through the pack below the distance but was making no further impression in the final furlong. (10/1)
**1326 Ashanti Dancer (IRE)**, who had problems as she tried to make up ground along the inside early in the straight, had nothing more to give approaching the final furlong. (20/1)
**Star And Garter** (8/1: op 5/1)
**1101 Meranti** failed to see out this longer trip. He played an active role until tiring approaching the final furlong, and a return to six furlongs is required. (9/1)

## 1616 RING & BRYMER ACHILLES STKS (Listed) (3-Y.O+) (Class A)

7-55 (7-56) **5f** £10,500.80 (£3,927.20: £1,918.60: £823.00: £366.50: £183.90) Stalls: Low GOING minus 0.28 sec per fur (GF)

| | | | | SP | RR | SF |
|---|---|---|---|---|---|---|
| $1113^{2}$ | **Brave Edge (97)** (RHannon) **5-9-2** PatEddery(1) (hdwy over 1f out: led ins fnl f: rdn out) | — | **1** | 7/1 | 113 | 56 |
| $1483^{7}$ | **Double Quick (IRE) (102)** (MJohnston) **4-9-1** JWeaver(5) (outpcd: hdwy fnl f: r.o wl) | 1¾ | **2** | 11/1 | 106 | 49 |
| $927^{7}$ | **Blue Iris (109)** (MAJarvis) **3-8-4** PRobinson(4) (a.p: led over 1f out tl ins fnl f: unable qckn) | ½ | **3** | 5/2$^{1}$ | 101 | 37 |
| $1321^{2}$ | **Lucky Parkes (99)** (JBerry) **6-8-11** JCarroll(3) (led over 3f: one pce) | ½ | **4** | 15/2 | 99 | 42 |
| $927^{5}$ | **Ya Malak (110)** (JWPayne) **5-9-6** BThomson(2) (w ldr over 3f) | 1¼ | **5** | 4/1$^{3}$ | 104 | 47 |
| $1483^{6}$ | **Fairy Wind (IRE) (97)** (NACallaghan) **4-8-11** LDettori(6) (b.hind: hld up: ev ch over 1f out: wknd fnl f) | 3 | **6** | 3/1$^{2}$ | 86 | 29 |

(SP 106.2%) **6 Rn**

**59.33 secs** (1.13) CSF £58.48 TOTE £7.20: £2.60 £3.10 (£31.90) OWNER Horris Vale Racing Partnership (MARLBOROUGH) BRED Mrs G. A. Whent
WEIGHT FOR AGE 3yo-7lb
**1113 Brave Edge** swept into the lead inside the final furlong and was ridden along to assert. (7/1)
**Double Quick (IRE)** usually races up with the pace but, on this occasion, was completely outpaced after only a furlong and a half. However, she came with a wet sail in the final furlong to storm through for second prize. (11/1: 8/1-12/1)
**927 Blue Iris** failed to find another gear once collared inside the final furlong. (5/2)
**1321 Lucky Parkes**, headed below the distance, could then only keep on in her own time. (15/2: 12/1-7/1)
**927 Ya Malak** raced with the leader until calling it a day below the distance. (4/1: op 5/2)
**1113* Fairy Wind (IRE)** had every chance below the distance before coming to the end of her tether. (3/1)

## 1617 WATERLOO MAIDEN STKS (3-Y.O) (Class D)

8-25 (8-30) **7f (Jubilee)** £3,889.50 (£1,176.00: £573.00: £271.50) Stalls: High GOING minus 0.28 sec per fur (GF)

| | | | | SP | RR | SF |
|---|---|---|---|---|---|---|
| $1142^{2}$ | **Gold Spats (USA)** (MRStoute) **3-9-0** RCochrane(16) (a.p: led over 1f out: r.o wl) | — | **1** | 4/6$^{1}$ | 80 | 39 |

| | | | Pos | SP | RR | SF |
|---|---|---|---|---|---|---|
| | **Elmi Elmak (IRE)** (LMCumani) **3-9-0** OUrbina(12) (w'like: scope: bit bkwd: hld up: rdn 2f out: n.m.r over 1f out: r.o wl ins fnl f) | 2 | **2** | 25/1 | 75 | 34 |
| 1438[8] | **Beau Bruno** (MBell) **3-9-0** RHills(9) (hdwy over 1f out: r.o ins fnl f) | 1 | **3** | 66/1 | 73 | 32 |
| 678[5] | **Nunsharpa** (JRFanshawe) **3-8-9** DHarrison(7) (rdn over 2f out: hdwy over 1f out: r.o ins fnl f) | hd | **4** | 10/1 | 68 | 27 |
| 1350[3] | **Prime Light** (GWragg) **3-9-0** MHills(13) (a.p: led 2f out tl over 1f out: wknd fnl f) | ¾ | **5** | 9/1[3] | 71 | 30 |
| | **Misrule (USA)** (JHMGosden) **3-8-9** GHind(10) (leggy: unf: scope: s.s: shkn up over 2f out: n.m.r over 1f out: hdwy fnl f: r.o: bttr for r) | nk | **6** | 16/1 | 66 | 25 |
| | **Sovereigns Court** (MajorDNChappell) **3-9-0** BThomson(2) (w'like: scope: hld up: rdn over 2f out: wknd fnl f) | 2 | **7** | 12/1 | 66 | 25 |
| 1195[3] | **Bandit Girl** (IABalding) **3-8-9** TQuinn(6) (plld hrd: prom over 5f) | 1¼ | **8** | 16/1 | 58 | 17 |
| | **Redskin Lady** (DRCElsworth) **3-8-6(3)** DaneO'Neill(15) (w'like: scope: hld up: rdn over 2f out: sn wknd) | 2 | **9** | 16/1 | 54 | 13 |
| 710[13] | **Shine** (IABalding) **3-8-9** WRyan(14) (lw: led 5f: wknd 1f out) | s.h | **10** | 33/1 | 53 | 12 |
| | **Chirico (USA)** (JHMGosden) **3-9-0** LDettori(1) (str: scope: bkwd: s.s: hdwy on ins over 2f out: eased whn btn over 1f out: bttr for r) | s.h | **11** | 6/1[2] | 58 | 17 |
| 1350[11] | **Burning Flame** (RMFlower) **3-8-9** DBiggs(8) (bit bkwd: a bhd) | 2½ | **12** | 66/1 | 48 | 7 |
| 648[14] | **Play The Tune** (KRBurke) **3-9-0** SWhitworth(3) (bit bkwd: bhd fnl 2f) | 1¼ | **13** | 66/1 | 50 | 9 |
| 1007[9] | **Covered Girl (IRE)** (BWHills) **3-8-4(5)** JDSmith(5) (a wl bhd) | ½ | **14** | 25/1 | 44 | 3 |
| | **First Law** (MissGayKelleway) **3-8-9** WJO'Connor(4) (b.hind: scope: bit bkwd: a bhd: hung bdly lft over 3f out: t.o whn virtually p.u fnl 2f) | dist | **15** | 25/1 | — | — |

(SP 137.7%) **15 Rn**

**1m 27.58** (3.08) CSF £23.43 TOTE £1.70: £1.20 £5.60 £15.40 (£21.10) Trio £175.80 OWNER Cheveley Park Stud (NEWMARKET) BRED Christiana Stables

OFFICIAL EXPLANATION **First Law: the bit went through the filly's mouth.**

**1142 Gold Spats (USA)** gained a richly-deserved success after two highly promising runs. Sent to the front below the distance, he soon asserted for a decisive victory. (4/6)

**Elmi Elmak (IRE)**, a plain colt with plenty of scope, looked as though the run would do him good but still showed a lot of promise. Chasing the leaders, he did not have a great deal of room in which to manoeuvre below the distance, but ran on strongly inside the final furlong to snatch second prize. He should soon be winning. (25/1)

**922 Beau Bruno** ran his best race to date. Finding his feet from below the distance, he ran on inside the final furlong for third prize. (66/1)

**678 Nunsharpa**, pushed along over a quarter of a mile from home, was putting in some good work in the last furlong and a half and just failed to take third prize. She is certainly going the right way. (10/1: tchd 16/1)

**1350 Prime Light** poked a nostril in front a quarter of a mile from home, but he was headed below the distance and soon in trouble. (9/1: 5/1-10/1)

**Misrule (USA)**, a tall, weak-looking filly who needs time, proved very green on this debut and was given tender handling. Shaken up early in the straight, she showed her inexperience by fly-jumping below the distance, but she ran on nicely inside the final furlong to finish a very encouraging sixth. Sure to be a lot wiser for this, she can find a race before long. (16/1)

**Chirico (USA)**, a deep-girthed individual, looked far from fit and was given sympathetic handling. Picking up ground along the inside rail early in the straight, Dettori eased him right down approaching the final furlong and allowed him to coast home in his own time. He is sure to come on in leaps and bounds as a result and should soon leave this race way behind. (6/1: 4/1-7/1)

## 1618 BLACKBIRD H'CAP (0-80) (3-Y.O+) (Class D)

8-55 (8-57) **1m 4f** £3,850.50 (£1,164.00: £567.00: £268.50) Stalls: High GOING minus 0.28 sec per fur (GF)

| | | | Pos | SP | RR | SF |
|---|---|---|---|---|---|---|
| 1019[2] | **Leading Spirit (IRE) (73)** (CFWall) **4-9-12** PatEddery(9) (lw: chsd ldr 8f out: led over 3f out: clr over 2f out: eased ins fnl f) | — | **1** | 4/1[1] | 89+ | 71 |
| 1124[2] | **Hattaafeh (IRE) (58)** (MissBSanders) **5-8-11** SSanders(11) (a.p: chsd wnr over 2f out: no imp) | 4 | **2** | 11/2[2] | 69 | 51 |
| 1147[8] | **General Mouktar (55)** (BJMeehan) **6-8-8** BDoyle(13) (rdn over 2f out: hdwy over 1f out: r.o ins fnl f) | 1½ | **3** | 8/1[3] | 64 | 46 |
| 1150[9] | **Crested Knight (IRE) (56)** (CAHorgan) **4-8-9** PaulEddery(6) (hdwy 6f out: hrd rdn over 2f out: one pce) | 3 | **4** | 9/1 | 61 | 43 |
| 1102* | **Shining Example (75)** (PJMakin) **4-9-9(5)** RHavlin(3) (hdwy over 2f out: nt clr run wl over 1f out: one pce) | s.h | **5** | 8/1[3] | 80 | 62 |
| | **Farringdon Hill (73)** (MajorWRHern) **5-9-12** RHills(4) (hld up: rdn over 3f out: wknd 2f out) | 4 | **6** | 14/1 | 72 | 54 |
| *1098*[6] | **Pedaltothemetal (IRE) (43)** (PhilipMitchell) **4-7-5(5)** CAdamson(8) (nvr nrr) | s.h | **7** | 25/1 | 42 | 24 |
| 1124[3] | **Soviet Bride (IRE) (66)** (SDow) **4-9-0(5)** ADaly(2) (led over 8f: wknd over 2f out) | nk | **8** | 10/1 | 65 | 47 |
| 670[8] | **Rising Dough (IRE) (68)** (GLMoore) **4-9-7** SWhitworth(5) (hdwy over 3f out: wknd over 2f out) | 1¼ | **9** | 14/1 | 65 | 47 |
| 1450[2] | **Typhoon Eight (IRE) (70)** (BWHills) **4-9-4b(5)** JDSmith(10) (bhd fnl 3f) | 1½ | **10** | 11/1 | 65 | 47 |
| | **White Claret (59)** (RAkehurst) **4-8-12** TQuinn(1) (b: a bhd) | ½ | **11** | 10/1 | 54 | 36 |
| 1353[5] | **Fighting Times (68)** (CASmith) **4-9-7** CRutter(14) (b.hind: bhd fnl 5f) | s.h | **12** | 11/1 | 62 | 44 |
| 1102[11] | **Printers Quill (54)** (MajorDNChappell) **4-8-7** JReid(12) (prom 4f) | ¾ | **13** | 16/1 | 47 | 29 |
| 1173[8] | **Persian Conquest (IRE) (60)** (RIngram) **4-8-13b** JWeaver(7) (chsd ldr 4f: wknd over 3f out) | 24 | **14** | 12/1 | 21 | 3 |

(SP 133.2%) **14 Rn**

**2m 33.12** (2.42) CSF £27.62 CT £165.99 TOTE £4.70: £2.20 £2.40 £2.50 (£9.70) Trio £59.10 OWNER Induna Racing Partners Two (NEWMARKET) BRED Sir Peter Nugent and Ascot Stables

**1019 Leading Spirit (IRE)** went on turning into the straight and soon shot clear. He was eased considerably inside the final furlong and is certainly worth double the official winning distance. (4/1)

**1124 Hattaafeh (IRE)** struggled into second place early in the straight but is greatly flattered to finish so close. (11/2)

**968 General Mouktar**, who disappointed last time out, stayed on in the last furlong and a half to take third prize. (8/1)

**844 Crested Knight (IRE)** moved up halfway down the back straight, but was only treading water once in line for home. He remains a maiden. (9/1: 8/1-12/1)

**1102* Shining Example**, taking a step up in distance, made an effort early in the straight, but was making no further impression from below the distance. (8/1: 6/1-9/1)

**Farringdon Hill**, off the course for over a year, chased the leaders but had burnt his boots two furlongs from home. (14/1)

**Rising Dough (IRE)** (14/1: 12/1-20/1)

**1450 Typhoon Eight (IRE)** (11/1: 8/1-12/1)

**White Claret** (10/1: 7/1-11/1)

**1353 Fighting Times** (11/1: 8/1-12/1)

T/Plpt: £153.90 (115 Tckts). T/Qdpt: £38.50 (27.78 Tckts). AK

# 1443-LINGFIELD (L-H) (Good to firm)
## Saturday June 1st
WEATHER: fine but cloudy WIND: fresh half bhd

### 1619 BET WITH THE TOTE H'CAP (0-100) (3-Y.O) (Class C)
2-00 (2-00) **1m 2f** £5,848.00 (£1,744.00: £832.00: £376.00) Stalls: Centre GOING minus 0.42 sec per fur (F)

| | | | | SP | RR | SF |
|---|---|---|---|---|---|---|
| 917[10] | **Expensive Taste (84)** (MRStoute) **3-9-4** RCochrane(4) (hld up: hdwy over 2f out: led ins fnl f: pushed out) | — | 1 | 9/1 | 91 | 45 |
| 1120[3] | **Lear Jet (USA) (87)** (PFICole) **3-9-7** TQuinn(7) (lw: led: rdn over 1f out: hdd ins fnl f: r.o) | 1 | 2 | 4/1[2] | 92 | 46 |
| 1326* | **Forza Figlio (87)** (MissGayKelleway) **3-9-7** JReid(6) (b.hind: lw: hld up in tch: lost pl 4f out: sme hdwy whn n.m.r on ins 2f out: swtchd rt over 1f out: r.o one pce ins fnl f) | 2½ | 3 | 2/1[1] | 88 | 42 |
| 1447[2] | **Silver Wing (USA) (75)** (MBell) **3-8-2**(7) GFaulkner(1) (b.hind: chsd ldrs: rdn over 2f out: one pce) | s.h | 4 | 9/1 | 76 | 30 |
| 1106[6] | **Villeggiatura (81)** (BWHills) **3-9-1** BThomson(3) (chsd ldrs: lost pl ½-wy: sme hdwy & n.m.r on ins 2f out: kpt on one pce ins fnl f) | 1½ | 5 | 4/1[2] | 80 | 34 |
| 1174* | **Major Dundee (IRE) (80)** (RHannon) **3-9-0** RHughes(2) (lw: hld up: hdwy 4f out: wknd over 1f out) | 1¼ | 6 | 13/2[3] | 77 | 31 |
| 1175[8] | **Exalted (IRE) (87)** (SirMarkPrescott) **3-9-7** GDuffield(5) (chsd ldr: rdn over 2f out: sn wknd) | 1½ | 7 | 16/1 | 82 | 36 |

(SP 112.5%) **7 Rn**

**2m 7.63** (2.93) CSF £41.03 TOTE £8.50: £2.90 £2.60 (£16.50) OWNER Mr Mohamed Suhail (NEWMARKET) BRED Gainsborough Stud Management Ltd

**Expensive Taste**, from a yard in top form, ran out a cosy winner here. Always travelling best, she was brought with a well-timed challenge to win with a bit in hand. This step up in distance suited. (9/1: 6/1-10/1)
**1120 Lear Jet (USA)** ran well under a positive ride and is obviously well suited to making the running. (4/1)
**1326* Forza Figlio** fell down the hill and was trying to recover when short of room at the two-furlong pole. He rallied in the closing stages but it is stretching it a bit to say he was unlucky. (2/1)
**1447 Silver Wing (USA)** looked one-paced in the closing stages. (9/1: op 6/1)
**1106 Villeggiatura** fell down the hill and could never recover (4/1)
**1174* Major Dundee (IRE)** appeared not to stay. (13/2)

### 1620 TOTE BOOKMAKERS CONDITIONS STKS (4-Y.O+) (Class C)
2-30 (2-30) **1m 3f 106y** £6,844.00 (£2,364.00: £1,132.00: £460.00) Stalls: Centre GOING minus 0.42 sec per fur (F)

| | | | | SP | RR | SF |
|---|---|---|---|---|---|---|
| | **Taufan's Melody (106)** (LadyHerries) **5-9-10** RCochrane(3) (hld up: hdwy to chse ldr 3f out: led 2f out: r.o wl) | — | 1 | 11/2[3] | 116 | 59 |
| 919[4] | **Midnight Legend (114)** (LMCumani) **5-9-5** JReid(1) (lw: led: hdd 2f out: hrd rdn ins fnl f: r.o) | s.h | 2 | 5/6[1] | 111 | 54 |
| 929* | **Florid (USA) (106)** (HRACecil) **5-9-1** WRyan(2) (lw: keen hold: chsd ldrs to 3f out: hrd rdn 2f out: one pce) | 2 | 3 | 5/2[2] | 104 | 47 |
| 878[8] | **Ionio (USA) (105)** (CEBrittain) **5-8-10** BDoyle(4) (b: chsd ldrs: lost tch 4f out: hrd rdn 3f out: no hdwy) | 6 | 4 | 7/1 | 91 | 34 |

(SP 111.0%) **4 Rn**

**2m 26.32** (2.12) CSF £10.44 TOTE £4.60: (£3.10) OWNER All At Sea (LITTLEHAMPTON) BRED Midhurst Farm Inc

**Taufan's Melody** put up a good performance here to give weight all round. (11/2: 4/1-6/1)
**919 Midnight Legend** tried to make all but never really stretched his rivals. He looked cooked when the winner went on two furlongs out, but to his credit, rallied gamely to make it tight. (5/6)
**929* Florid (USA)** pulled too hard for his own good. (5/2)
**456 Ionio (USA)** is running poorly at present. (7/1: 6/1-9/1)

### 1621 TOTE CREDIT LEISURE STKS (Listed) (3-Y.O+) (Class A)
3-00 (3-02) **6f** £12,661.20 (£4,690.80: £2,255.40: £927.00: £373.50: £152.10) Stalls: Centre GOING minus 0.42 sec per fur (F)

| | | | | SP | RR | SF |
|---|---|---|---|---|---|---|
| 1146* | **Rambling Bear (113)** (MBlanshard) **3-8-10** RCochrane(3) (chsd ldrs: led 1f out: r.o wl) | — | 1 | 11/2[2] | 120 | 64 |
| 889* | **Iktamal (USA) (110)** (EALDunlop) **4-9-0** PaulEddery(7) (lw: hld up: hdwy 2f out: rdn ins fnl f: r.o) | 1 | 2 | 11/10[1] | 113 | 65 |
| 810[11] | **Inzar (USA) (112)** (PFICole) **4-9-7** TQuinn(2) (led: hdd 1f out: unable qckn) | ½ | 3 | 7/1 | 119 | 71 |
| | **Averti (IRE) (95)** (WRMuir) **5-9-0** WJO'Connor(6) (bit bkwd: chsd ldrs: rdn 2f out: one pce) | 2 | 4 | 33/1 | 107 | 59 |
| 1332* | **Loch Patrick (104)** (MMadgwick) **6-9-0** JReid(11) (hld up: rdn ½-wy: styd on ins fnl f) | 1¾ | 5 | 13/2[3] | 102 | 54 |
| 582[15] | **Chewit (78)** (AMoore) **4-9-0** CandyMorris(4) (w ldrs 4f: wknd over 1f out) | 6 | 6 | 66/1 | 86 | 38 |
| 940[4] | **Domulla (103)** (RAkehurst) **6-9-0** SSanders(10) (hld up: rdn ½-wy: no hdwy) | s.h | 7 | 12/1 | 86 | 38 |
| 1332[3] | **Hard to Figure (109)** (RJHodges) **10-9-4** TSprake(8) (bhd fnl 4f) | nk | 8 | 10/1 | 89 | 41 |
| 1332[6] | **Hello Mister (99)** (TEPowell) **5-9-0** PMcCabe(9) (sn outpcd) | 1 | 9 | 14/1 | 82 | 34 |
| 876[22] | **Bold Effort (FR) (95)** (KOCunningham-Brown) **4-9-0** TIves(5) (chsd ldrs: rdn 2f out: sn wknd) | 2 | 10 | 33/1 | 77 | 29 |

(SP 119.7%) **10 Rn**

**1m 8.59** (-0.41) CSF £11.78 TOTE £6.50: £1.70 £1.40 £1.60 (£5.20) Trio £12.20 OWNER Mrs Michael Hill (UPPER LAMBOURN) BRED E. A. Badger

WEIGHT FOR AGE 3yo-8lb

**1146* Rambling Bear** continues his rise here with an emphatic win. He won well and is worth his chance in a Group race. (11/2)
**889* Iktamal (USA)** was given a confident, and possibly a shade over-confident, ride here. He did not pick up immediately when asked and was never going to get to the winner. (11/10)
**Inzar (USA)** made a brave attempt to make all but found the weight concession too much in the closing stages. He is just as effective at seven. (7/1)
**Averti (IRE)** looked as though the run would do him good and ran very well in the circumstances. (33/1)
**1332* Loch Patrick** was struggling with the pace some way from home. (13/2)
**Chewit**, a smart winner on the sand, ran really well here, racing well to the fore until below the distance. (66/1)
**1332 Hard to Figure** (10/1: 5/1-11/1)

### 1622 SMUGGLERS MAIDEN AUCTION STKS (2-Y.O) (Class D)
3-30 (3-31) **5f** £3,497.50 (£1,045.00: £500.00: £227.50) Stalls: Centre GOING minus 0.42 sec per fur (F)

| | | | | SP | RR | SF |
|---|---|---|---|---|---|---|
| 916[2] | **Magical Times** (RBoss) **2-8-4** WRyan(11) (chsd ldrs: led over 1f out: rdn ins fnl f: r.o) | — | 1 | 11/8[1] | 72 | 39 |
| 815[8] | **Class Distinction (IRE)** (RHannon) **2-8-3** SSanders(9) (a.p: ev ch ins fnl f: unable qckn) | 1¼ | 2 | 12/1 | 67 | 34 |
| | **Olympic Spirit** (JBerry) **2-8-1** GCarter(6) (neat: dwlt: sn rcvrd: hdwy ½-wy: rdn over 1f out: edgd lft ins fnl f: unable qckn) | nk | 3 | 8/1 | 64 | 31 |

**Lamarita** (JMPEustace) **2-7-13** DRMcCabe(8) (w'like: bit bkwd: rr: rdn ½-wy: hdwy over 1f out: styd on strly ins fnl f)........1 **4** 7/1[3] 59+ 26
877[5] **Mangus (IRE)** (KOCunningham-Brown) **2-7-11**(7) CMunday(4) (led: hdd over 1f out: wknd ins fnl f)........3½ **5** 16/1 53 20
585[4] **Trading Aces** (MBell) **2-8-5** TQuinn(13) (b.hind: lw: chsd ldrs: hrd rdn 2f out: wknd over 1f out)........2½ **6** 7/2[2] 46 13
**Le Shuttle** (MHTompkins) **2-7-8**(5) MHenry(2) (neat: outpcd & wl bhd: hdwy fnl f: nvr nrr)........½ **7** 10/1 38 5
1346[12] **Advance Repro** (JAkehurst) **2-7-12** NCarlisle(5) (mid div tl wknd 2f out)........¾ **8** 33/1 35 2
569[6] **Bapsford** (GLMoore) **2-8-7** SWhitworth(10) (mid div tl wknd 2f out)........nk **9** 20/1 43 10
**Be True** (AMoore) **2-8-3** CandyMorris(3) (unf: bit bkwd: a bhd)........2½ **10** 33/1 31 —
*1097*[7] **Midnight Times** (DCO'Brien) **2-7-12** GBardwell(12) (spd to ½-wy)........5 **11** 66/1 10 —
*1404*[10] ***Heggies (IRE)*** (CREgerton) **2-8-4** BThomson(7) (Withdrawn not under Starter's orders)........ **W** — —
(SP 122.7%) **11 Rn**

**57.7 secs** (0.70) CSF £18.60 TOTE £2.20: £1.20 £3.70 £2.50 (£15.20) Trio £50.80 OWNER Ms Lynn Bell (NEWMARKET) BRED White Lodge Farm Stud

**916 Magical Times** gained due reward for two previous good displays and his future probably lies in nurseries. (11/8)
**Class Distinction (IRE)** showed marked improvement from his debut and can pick up a race soon. (12/1: 6/1-14/1)
**Olympic Spirit** was green at the stalls and in the race, but showed enough to suggest she will find a race. (8/1: 5/1-9/1)
**Lamarita** ran an eyecatching race staying on very strongly, having been well adrift early. (7/1: op 12/1)
**Mangus (IRE)** showed good speed, but was put in his place in the closing stages. (16/1)
**585 Trading Aces** was struggling with the pace some way from home. (7/2)
**Le Shuttle** (10/1: 6/1-11/1)

## 1623 FERRENDONS CONDITIONS STKS (4-Y.O+) (Class C)

4-00 (4-01) **7f 140y** £5,066.28 (£1,874.52: £899.26: £367.30: £145.65: £56.99) Stalls: Centre GOING minus 0.42 sec per fur (F)

SP RR SF

1330[2] **Green Perfume (USA) (100)** (PFICole) **4-8-10** TQuinn(7) (lw: mde all: qcknd clr 1f out: comf)........— **1** 2/1[1] 111+ 48
840* **Azizzi** (CREgerton) **4-9-0** WRyan(4) (lw: prom: chsd wnr over 2f out: hrd rdn over 1f out: one pce)........5 **2** 7/1 105 42
1112[10] **Lap of Luxury (105)** (WJarvis) **7-8-13** BThomson(5) (chsd wnr 5f: rdn 2f out: one pce)........3 **3** 4/1[3] 97 34
1107[8] **Double Blue (99)** (MJohnston) **7-8-11**(7) NPollard(2) (racd far side to ½-wy: rdn & lost pl 3f out: kpt on one pce ins fnl f)........nk **4** 20/1 102 39
728[4] **Welton Arsenal (95)** (MRChannon) **4-9-2** RHughes(8) (lw: hld up gng wl: rdn over 1f out: sn wknd: eased ins fnl f)........1¾ **5** 4/1[3] 96 33
1112[5] **Monaassib (103)** (EALDunlop) **5-9-4** JReid(1) (racd far side to ½-wy: rdn over 2f out: sn wknd)........1¼ **6** 100/30[2] 95 32
1440[14] **Easy Choice (USA) (65)** (PhilipMitchell) **4-9-4b**[1] RCochrane(3) (lw: outpcd & wl bhd: sme hdwy ins fnl f: nvr nrr)........s.h **7** 20/1 50 t 32
(SP 118.4%) **7 Rn**

**1m 29.68** (0.88) CSF £15.77 TOTE £2.50: £1.60 £3.50 (£8.70) OWNER Lord Sondes (WHATCOMBE) BRED Brereton C. Jones

**1330 Green Perfume (USA)**, who had run a great race under a big weight last time, won this very easily and is right back to his best. (2/1)
**840* Azizzi** stepped up on his maiden win with a bold display here, but was no match for the winner. (7/1)
**Lap of Luxury** runs his best races in late summer and is gradually coming to hand. (4/1)
**940 Double Blue** is out of form at present. (20/1)
**728 Welton Arsenal** travelled very well but, not for the first time, did not find a lot. (4/1)
**1112 Monaassib** ran poorly, dropping away tamely in the last two furlongs. (100/30)

## 1624 MEDWAY H'CAP (0-70) (3-Y.O+) (Class E)

4-30 (4-32) **6f** £3,315.90 (£991.20: £474.60: £216.30) Stalls: Centre GOING minus 0.42 sec per fur (F)

SP RR SF

1412[6] **Merrie le Bow (45)** (PatMitchell) **4-8-1**(5) AmandaSanders(14) (a.p: led ½-wy: rdn ins fnl f: all out)........— **1** 10/1 56 39
1307[6] **Prima Silk (67)** (MJRyan) **5-10-0** TIves(12) (hld up in rr: hdwy over 1f out: str run ins fnl f: jst failed)........s.h **2** 9/1[3] 78 61
1307[4] **Our Shadee (USA) (48)** (KTIvory) **6-8-2v**(7) CScally(11) (hld up: rdn over 2f out: hdwy over 1f out: r.o ins fnl f)........1¾ **3** 10/1 54 37
1442[4] **Twice Purple (IRE) (57)** (BJMeehan) **4-9-4b**[1] BDoyle(3) (a.p: ev ch over 1f out: rdn ins fnl f: one pce)........1¼ **4** 9/1[3] 60 43
1412[2] **Sing Up (64)** (MMcCormack) **4-9-11** JReid(7) (chsd ldrs: rdn over 1f out: one pce)........½ **5** 11/2[1] 66 49
1446[3] **Tauber (41)** (PatMitchell) **12-7-11**(5) MHenry(15) (mid div: hdwy 3f out: ev ch 2f out: faultered & eased ins fnl f)........2 **6** 11/2[1] 37 20
1351[7] **Robo Magic (USA) (60)** (LMontagueHall) **4-9-7** RPerham(6) (prom: ev ch 2f out: rdn & wknd over 1f out)........¾ **7** 12/1 54 37
*607*[6] **Adamton (45)** (MrsJCecil) **4-8-6** DRMcCabe(8) (led to ½-wy: ev ch 2f out: sn wknd)........2 **8** 10/1 34 17
1307[8] **Rockcracker (IRE) (63)** (GGMargarson) **4-9-10v**[1] PBloomfield(10) (mid div tl wknd 2f out)........1¾ **9** 12/1 47 30
893[9] **Anita's Contessa (IRE) (58)** (BPalling) **4-9-5** TSprake(4) (mid div: rdn over 2f out: sn wknd)........nk **10** 20/1 41 24
1172[6] **Ed's Folly (IRE) (57)** (SDow) **3-8-10** RHughes(9) (prom to ½-wy)........1 **11** 7/1[2] 38 13
*780*[8] **Monsieur Culsyth (48)** (JBerry) **3-8-1** GCarter(5) (a bhd)........2½ **12** 14/1 22 —
981[2] **Dashing Dancer (IRE) (59)** (RAkehurst) **5-9-6** SSanders(1) (lw: chsd ldrs tl wknd over 2f out)........¾ **13** 7/1[2] 31 14
1302[15] **Roka (44)** (RHannon) **4-8-5b**[1] BThomson(2) (bhd fr ½-wy)........9 **14** 16/1 — —
***Ichor (49)*** (JSMoore) **3-7-13**(3) NVarley(13) (Withdrawn not under Starter's orders: ref to ent stalls)........ **W** 25/1 — —
(SP 139.6%) **14 Rn**

**1m 10.02** (1.02) CSF £99.41 CT £604.42 TOTE £13.30: £4.50 £3.40 £3.90 (£70.20) Trio £116.90 OWNER Mrs Anna Sanders (NEWMARKET) BRED Mrs J. R. Hine and Miss J. Bunting
WEIGHT FOR AGE 3yo-8lb
OFFICIAL EXPLANATION **Adamton: the jockey could not ride the gelding as he was hanging badly on the ground.**

**1412 Merrie le Bow** took it up at halfway and held on by the skin of her teeth. (10/1)
**1307 Prima Silk** finished strongly and would have won in another stride. (9/1)
**1307 Our Shadee (USA)** is running well at present and ran another sound race here. (10/1)
**1442 Twice Purple (IRE)**, blinkered for the first time, was up with the pace throughout but could not quicken up when needed. (9/1)
**1412 Sing Up** ran well until being tapped for foot in the closing stages. (11/2)
**1446 Tauber** looked as though something was amiss in the final furlong. (11/2)
**607 Adamton** (10/1: 6/1-12/1)
**1172 Ed's Folly (IRE)** showed up to halfway before dropping away tamely. (7/1)
**Monsieur Culsyth** (14/1: 10/1-16/1)

T/Plpt: £348.60 (50.73 Tckts). T/Qdpt: £13.10 (82.46 Tckts). SM

# 1148-NEWMARKET (R-H) (Good to firm)
## Saturday June 1st
WEATHER: overcast WIND: fresh half bhd

### 1625 COUNTRYSIDE MOVEMENT H'CAP (0-80) (4-Y.O+) (Class D)
2-10 (2-13) **1m (Rowley)** £4,125.90 (£1,234.20: £591.60: £270.30) Stalls: Centre GOING minus 0.40 sec per fur (F)

| | | | | SP | RR | SF |
|---|---|---|---|---|---|---|
| $1190^{3}$ | **Saifan (72)** (DMorris) **7-9-6b** CHodgson(9) (hdwy over 2f out: led over 1f out: sn clr: rdn out) | — | **1** | $13/2^{1}$ | 83 | 58 |
| $1450^{8}$ | **Emily-Mou (IRE) (68)** (MJRyan) **4-9-2** JWeaver(14) (b: a.p: rdn 2f out: unable qckn appr fnl f) | 1½ | **2** | 16/1 | 76 | 51 |
| $1190^{8}$ | **Talathath (FR) (60)** (CADwyer) **4-8-8** RHills(3) (hdwy over 3f out: r.o fnl f) | 1 | **3** | 25/1 | 66 | 41 |
| $598^{11}$ | **Dance King (62)** (RHarris) **4-8-5**(5) ADaly(4) (hdwy fnl 2f: fin wl) | nk | **4** | 33/1 | 67 | 42 |
| $1051^{3}$ | **Queen of All Birds (IRE) (75)** (RBoss) **5-9-9** PatEddery(10) (chsd ldrs tl rdn & btn appr fnl f) | 1½ | **5** | $13/2^{1}$ | 77 | 52 |
| $879^{27}$ | **Deevee (71)** (CJBenstead) **7-9-5** PRobinson(13) (lw: hdwy 2f out: r.o) | 1¼ | **6** | $7/1^{2}$ | 71 | 46 |
| $1440^{5}$ | **Golden Touch (USA) (65)** (NACallaghan) **4-8-8**(5) FLynch(6) (hld up: hdwy over 1f out: nvr rchd ldrs) | hd | **7** | $7/1^{2}$ | 65 | 40 |
| $1173^{13}$ | **Scorpius (48)** (TTClement) **6-7-10b** JQuinn(7) (b: led: clr over 2f out: rdn & hdd over 1f out: sn wknd) | ¾ | **8** | 40/1 | 46 | 21 |
| | **Concer Un (78)** (SCWilliams) **4-9-12** MHills(2) (b.nr fore: trckd ldrs: effrt 3f out: wknd appr fnl f) | 1¼ | **9** | 16/1 | 74 | 49 |
| $1190^{4}$ | **Mo-Addab (IRE) (79)** (ACStewart) **6-9-13** DHarrison(15) (lw: hdwy 3f out: wknd & eased appr fnl f) | 2 | **10** | $8/1^{3}$ | 71 | 46 |
| $636^{13}$ | **Mediate (IRE) (55)** (AHide) **4-8-0**(3)ow3 JStack(8) (bhd: effrt 4f out: no imp) | 1¾ | **11** | 50/1 | 43 | 15 |
| | **Shayim (USA) (77)** (RHannon) **4-9-8**(3) DaneO'Neill(5) (lw: prom: rdn over 2f out: sn wknd) | s.h | **12** | 14/1 | 65 | 40 |
| $1192^{5}$ | **Zelda Zonk (70)** (BJMeehan) **4-9-4** MTebbutt(11) (dwlt: in tch: rdn over 2f out: sn btn) | ½ | **13** | $8/1^{3}$ | 57 | 32 |
| $1190^{10}$ | **Ron's Secret (80)** (JWPayne) **4-10-0** LDettori(1) (a bhd) | 4 | **14** | 16/1 | 59 | 34 |
| $1414^{9}$ | **Voila Premiere (IRE) (67)** (MHTompkins) **4-9-1** NDay(12) (prom 2f: sn lost pl) | 2 | **15** | 16/1 | 42 | 17 |
| $1072^{4}$ | **Nordic Breeze (IRE) (71)** (ABailey) **4-9-5b** JCarroll(16) (dwlt: rdn 4f out: sn bhd) | ¾ | **16** | 14/1 | 45 | 20 |

(SP 121.9%) **16 Rn**

**1m 38.56** (1.26) CSF £95.43 CT £2,323.11 TOTE £6.90: £1.80 £3.30 £5.00 £8.90 (£90.90) Trio £806.30 OWNER Mrs L. Brook (NEWMARKET) BRED M. M. Nashar

LONG HANDICAP Scorpius 7-9

**1190 Saifan** won off this mark last year and, after running well off it at Newbury, burst clear after the trailblazer tied up in the Dip. He has done his winning close to his Newmarket base, namely here, Yarmouth and Leicester. (13/2)

**Emily-Mou (IRE)**, dropping back in trip, ran a cracker, although short of speed at a vital time, and should win before long. (16/1)

**495 Talathath (FR)**, whose Newbury failure owed more to racing on the far side than the soft ground, bounced back here and may still have a little improvement in him given his lack of racing. (25/1)

**Dance King**, who won over hurdles last month, found a fine turn of foot in the Dip to finish best of all. (33/1)

**1051 Queen of All Birds (IRE)** ran a sound race but is beginning to look as if she is better on Equitrack than turf. (13/2)

**Deevee**, who often runs well here, finished with his usual flourish, although it was a case of too little, too late. He carries weight well and would be a major contender for any 0-70 handicap. (7/1)

### 1626 E.B.F. SUNLEY BUILDS MAIDEN STKS (2-Y.O) (Class D)
2-40 (2-42) **6f (Rowley)** £4,620.00 (£1,380.00: £660.00: £300.00) Stalls: Centre GOING minus 0.40 sec per fur (F)

| | | | | SP | RR | SF |
|---|---|---|---|---|---|---|
| | **Shock Value (IRE)** (MRStoute) **2-9-0** LDettori(7) (cmpt: scope: w ldr: led over 1f out: comf) | — | **1** | $5/4^{1}$ | 80+ | 45 |
| | **Barrier King (USA)** (PFICole) **2-9-0** PatEddery(9) (neat: scope: led over 4f: eased whn btn nr fin) | 3 | **2** | $9/2^{2}$ | 72 | 37 |
| | **Silver Widget (USA)** (RCharlton) **2-9-0** MHills(2) (gd sort: dwlt: hdwy 2f out: r.o fnl f) | 2½ | **3** | $5/1^{3}$ | 65+ | 30 |
| $1339^{7}$ | **Spaniards Inn** (BJMeehan) **2-9-0** PRobinson(6) (lw: plld hrd: w ldrs: no ex appr fnl f) | 1 | **4** | 7/1 | 63 | 28 |
| | **Briska (IRE)** (RHannon) **2-8-6**(3) DaneO'Neill(4) (w'like: lw: trckd ldrs: outpcd over 2f out: kpt on fnl f) | 5 | **5** | 14/1 | 44 | 9 |
| | **Carlton (IRE)** (GLewis) **2-9-0** DHarrison(8) (B: cmpt: scope: chsd ldrs over 3f) | 2 | **6** | 20/1 | 44 | 9 |
| | **Ile Distinct (IRE)** (MrsASwinbank) **2-9-0** JWeaver(5) (w'like: leggy: dwlt: hdwy 3f out: nvr able to chal) | hd | **7** | 50/1 | 44 | 9 |
| | **Barnwood Crackers** (NACallaghan) **2-9-0** AMackay(10) (small: cmpt: s.i.s: sn in tch: rdn 2f out: no imp) | 6 | **8** | 25/1 | 28 | — |
| | **No Comment** (MBell) **2-9-0** AClark(1) (cmpt: in tch: rdn 3f out: sn btn) | 2 | **9** | 33/1 | 22 | — |
| | **Doubly-H (IRE)** (MBell) **2-9-0** MFenton(3) (cmpt: scope: a bhd) | dist | **10** | 20/1 | — | — |

(SP 116.7%) **10 Rn**

**1m 13.17** (1.37) CSF £7.23 TOTE £2.30: £1.40 £1.70 £1.40 (£4.00) Trio £2.50 OWNER Mr Seisuke Hata (NEWMARKET) BRED Dr J. J. Ryan

**Shock Value (IRE)**, a slightly long-backed good walker, moved to post as well as any. Let down in the Dip, he came clear with some ease and goes to the Coventry not merely to make up the numbers. (5/4: op 9/4)

**Barrier King (USA)**, rather green and keen going to post, shaped really well and was not knocked about once headed. He looks sure to get further once he learns to settle. (9/2: op 5/2)

**Silver Widget (USA)**, sure to get further in time, did some good late work and this good mover looks the type to progress. (5/1: 9/4-11/2)

**Spaniards Inn** needs to learn to settle as he virtually ran away going to post. However, he is gradually showing improvement. (7/1: 5/1-12/1)

**Briska (IRE)** looked ready but only made any impact in the final furlong. (14/1: op 8/1)

**Carlton (IRE)** was struggling to go with the leaders from some way out, but there was something left to work on and a little improvement can be expected. (20/1)

### 1627 FORTUNE CENTRE MAIDEN STKS (3-Y.O) (Class D)
3-10 (3-11) **1m (Rowley)** £4,737.00 (£1,416.00: £678.00: £309.00) Stalls: Centre GOING minus 0.40 sec per fur (F)

| | | | | SP | RR | SF |
|---|---|---|---|---|---|---|
| $970^{2}$ | **Wall Street (USA)** (SbinSuroor) **3-9-0** LDettori(6) (lw: trckd ldrs: led 2f out: sn qcknd clr: easily) | — | **1** | $2/7^{1}$ | 78++ | 61 |
| | **Russian Request (IRE)** (MRStoute) **3-8-9** RHills(4) (w'like: leggy: hld up: hdwy over 1f out: r.o: no ch w wnr) | 7 | **2** | $8/1^{2}$ | 59 | 42 |
| $1465^{3}$ | **Battle Spark (USA) (76)** (CACyzer) **3-9-0** JWeaver(7) (led 4f: chsd wnr 2f out: sn outpcd) | 1¾ | **3** | $11/1^{3}$ | 61 | 44 |
| $710^{12}$ | **Larissa (IRE)** (GWragg) **3-8-9** MHills(2) (chsd ldrs: rdn 3f out: no imp) | 1¾ | **4** | $11/1^{3}$ | 52 | 35 |
| | **Polar Champ** (SPCWoods) **3-9-0** WWoods(3) (prom 4f: sn lost pl: styd on again fnl f) | 1½ | **5** | 50/1 | 54 | 37 |
| $684^{17}$ | **Shavinsky** (PHowling) **3-9-0** FNorton(5) (bhd: effrt 4f out: no imp) | 1½ | **6** | 50/1 | 51 | 34 |
| $1319^{14}$ | **Little Murray** (MrsJCecil) **3-9-0** AClark(1) (lw: b.off hind: plld hrd: w ldr: led 4f out to 2f out: sn wknd) | 1¼ | **7** | 33/1 | 49 | 32 |

(SP 112.4%) **7 Rn**

**1m 37.65** (0.35) CSF £3.40 TOTE £1.30: £1.10 £2.00 (£2.20) OWNER Maktoum Al Maktoum / Godolphin (NEWMARKET) BRED Darley Stud Management Inc

**970 Wall Street (USA)**, whose initial defeat by Dr Massini has taken on a different complexion, needed two handlers in the paddock. He disposed of these in most impressive fashion and the three-year-old weight-for-age allowance should help him when he steps into Group company. (2/7)

**Russian Request (IRE)** did some good work once the winner had flown and will appreciate a longer trip. (8/1)

**1465 Battle Spark (USA)**, up with the pace throughout, was made to look pedestrian once the chips were down. (11/1: 7/1-12/1)
**Larissa (IRE)**, a tail flasher, at least broke on terms this time, but lacks speed over this trip. (11/1: 7/1-12/1)
**Polar Champ** dropped back at halfway, only to stay on past a couple of beaten rivals. (50/1)
**Shavinsky**, not too well away, was never a factor. (50/1)

## 1628 CORAL SPRINT H'CAP (0-105) (3-Y.O) (Class B)

3-40 (3-42) **6f (Rowley)** £22,125.00 (£6,600.00: £3,150.00: £1,425.00) Stalls: Centre GOING minus 0.40 sec per fur (F)

| | | | | SP | RR | SF |
|---|---|---|---|---|---|---|
| $1146^{2}$ | **Atraf (104)** (DMorley) **3-9-7** RHills(4) (w ldrs: led ins fnl f: drvn out) | — | **1** | 8/1 | 110 | 73 |
| $1181^{7}$ | **Antonias Melody (79)** (SRBowring) **3-7-5**(5) MartinDwyer(14) (a.p: ev ch 2f out: r.o wl ins fnl f) | ¾ | **2** | 25/1 | 83 | 46 |
| $992^{*}$ | **Hoh Returns (IRE) (87)** (MBell) **3-8-4** MFenton(10) (lw: prom: led 3f out to ins fnl f: unable qckn) | s.h | **3** | 6/1 $^{3}$ | 91 | 54 |
| $945^{5}$ | **White Emir (81)** (BJMeehan) **3-7-12** JFEgan(9) (prom: ev ch 2f out: no ex ins fnl f) | ¾ | **4** | 9/1 | 83 | 46 |
| $1321^{4}$ | **Babsy Babe (90)** (JJQuinn) **3-8-2**(5) FLynch(12) (s.i.s: hdwy over 1f out: r.o) | ½ | **5** | 15/2 | 91 | 54 |
| $1006^{5}$ | **Angaar (IRE) (80)** (ACStewart) **3-7-11** CRutter(11) (hdwy over 1f out: nt rch ldrs) | s.h | **6** | 4/1 $^{1}$ | 80 | 43 |
| $1316^{6}$ | **Rushcutter Bay (80)** (TTClement) **3-7-11** JQuinn(3) (lw: hdwy 3f out: sn rdn: hdwy over 1f out: nvr rchd ldrs) | ½ | **7** | 50/1 | 79 | 42 |
| $758^{*}$ | **Spotted Eagle (87)** (RHannon) **3-8-1**(3)ow1 DaneO'Neill(13) (spd 4f) | 3½ | **8** | 8/1 | 77 | 39 |
| $945^{4}$ | **Depreciate (89)** (CJames) **3-8-6**ow1 PatEddery(7) (lw: chsd ldrs over 3f) | nk | **9** | 5/1 $^{2}$ | 78 | 40 |
| $1006^{8}$ | **Air Wing (79)** (MHTompkins) **3-7-10** AMackay(8) (b: led 3f) | nk | **10** | 10/1 | 67 | 30 |
| $966^{7}$ | **Forentia (92)** (JRFanshawe) **3-8-9** DHarrison(1) (bhd: rdn 2f out: no imp) | 2½ | **11** | 33/1 | 74 | 37 |
| $960^{8}$ | **Tropical Dance (USA) (98)** (MrsJCecil) **3-9-1** LDettori(5) (chsd ldrs 4f) | 1¼ | **12** | 14/1 | 76 | 39 |
| | **Double Oscar (IRE) (90)** (MJohnston) **3-8-7** JWeaver(6) (w ldrs tl wknd 2f out) | 2 | **13** | 33/1 | 63 | 26 |
| | | | | (SP 122.4%) | **13 Rn** | |

**1m 11.69** (-0.11) CSF £163.95 CT £1,221.82 TOTE £8.40: £2.60 £6.40 £2.40 (£92.40) Trio £693.70 OWNER Mr Hamdan Al Maktoum (NEWMARKET) BRED R. T. and Mrs Watson
LONG HANDICAP Antonias Melody 7-4 Air Wing 7-8
**1146 Atraf** won this handicap with a real display of determination and looks up to listed class at least. (8/1)
**824* Antonias Melody** was not helped by racing wide apart from the winner and won the battle towards that side. (25/1)
**992* Hoh Returns (IRE)** travelled well until put to work in the Dip, and then just lacked enough to maintain the advantage. (6/1)
**945 White Emir** ran right up to his best and looks to get the sixth furlong. (9/1)
**1321 Babsy Babe** forfeited her chance at the start, but for which she would surely have gone close. (15/2)
**1006 Angaar (IRE)** again lacked speed when asked to make his move and may need another furlong still. (4/1)
**945 Depreciate** lost his pitch in the last quarter-mile and pulled up sore. (5/1)

## 1629 WILLIAMS DE BROE CHARLOTTE STKS (Listed) (3-Y.O+ F & M) (Class A)

4-15 (4-15) **6f (Rowley)** £11,366.20 (£4,205.80: £2,017.90: £824.50: £327.25: £128.35) Stalls: Centre GOING minus 0.40 sec per fur (F)

| | | | | SP | RR | SF |
|---|---|---|---|---|---|---|
| $1566a^{7}$ | **Branston Abby (IRE) (108)** (MJohnston) **7-9-6** JWeaver(7) (bhd: hdwy over 1f out: str run to ld nr fin) | — | **1** | 7/2 $^{2}$ | 101 | 83 |
| $939^{8}$ | **My Melody Parkes (108)** (JBerry) **3-8-8** JCarroll(6) (w ldrs: led 2f out: rdn fnl f: ct nr fin) | hd | **2** | 5/2 $^{1}$ | 97 | 71 |
| $987^{2}$ | **React (92)** (WJarvis) **3-8-8** PatEddery(1) (lw: chsd ldrs: rdn 2f out: r.o wl ins fnl f) | ½ | **3** | 11/2 | 95 | 69 |
| $940^{9}$ | **Cheyenne Spirit (105)** (BHanbury) **4-9-6** JStack(2) (b: w ldrs: ev ch over 1f out: edgd lft: no ex ins fnl f) | ½ | **4** | 4/1 $^{3}$ | 98 | 80 |
| $1431^{4}$ | **Maid For The Hills (106)** (DRLoder) **3-8-12v**[1] LDettori(4) (lw: led 4f: wknd ins fnl f) | 2½ | **5** | 9/1 | 91 | 65 |
| $1177^{7}$ | **Brief Glimpse (IRE) (106)** (MajorDNChappell) **4-9-6** MHills(5) (dwlt: nvr trbld ldrs) | 3½ | **6** | 7/1 | 82 | 64 |
| $1041^{9}$ | **Regal Fanfare (IRE) (62)** (MrsLStubbs) **4-9-2b** PRobinson(8) (spd 3f) | 7 | **7** | 100/1 | 59 t | 41 |
| | **Femme Savante (100)** (RHannon) **4-9-2** RHills(3) (lw: bhd fnl 3f) | 4 | **8** | 25/1 | 49 t | 31 |
| | | | | (SP 113.5%) | **8 Rn** | |

**1m 10.92** (-0.88) CSF £12.04 TOTE £4.00: £1.70 £1.60 £1.30 (£5.50) OWNER Mr David Abell (MIDDLEHAM) BRED John David Abell
WEIGHT FOR AGE 3yo-8lb
**1566a Branston Abby (IRE)** put the Irish disappointment behind her and gave her fans a real thrill, swooping late to conquer and gaining her seventh listed event, her twentieth in all. The fast early pace, which had her off the bit early on, suited her ideally. (7/2)
**939 My Melody Parkes** probably ran her best ever race over this trip when second in the Lowther and looked all set when going on, only to be collared on the line. (5/2)
**987 React**, dropping in trip, was doing all her best work at the end and looks sure to win races when going back in trip. (11/2)
**Cheyenne Spirit** is not the greatest of movers in her slower paces and ruined a bright chance by hanging in the Dip. (4/1: 3/1-9/2)
**1431 Maid For The Hills** did not look happy on the way down and seems in the process of losing her way. (9/1)
**Brief Glimpse (IRE)**, back sprinting for the first time since her two-year-old days, never fully recovered from a tardy start, despite briefly flattering soon after halfway. (7/1)

## 1630 NGK SPARK PLUGS H'CAP (0-100) (3-Y.O+) (Class C)

4-45 (4-46) **5f (Rowley)** £5,848.00 (£1,744.00: £832.00: £376.00) Stalls: Centre GOING minus 0.40 sec per fur (F)

| | | | | SP | RR | SF |
|---|---|---|---|---|---|---|
| $1107^{3}$ | **Top Banana (91)** (HCandy) **5-9-5** CRutter(4) (lw: hdwy over 1f out: qcknd to ld wl ins fnl f: rdn out) | — | **1** | 3/1 $^{1}$ | 101 | 70 |
| $1178^{4}$ | **Bowden Rose (83)** (MBlanshard) **4-8-11b** JQuinn(9) (chsd ldrs: led ins fnl f: sn hdd & unable qckn) | ½ | **2** | 7/1 $^{3}$ | 91 | 60 |
| $1321^{7}$ | **Croft Pool (100)** (JAGlover) **5-10-0** SDWilliams(10) (a.p: led 1f out: sn hdd & no ex) | ½ | **3** | 25/1 | 107 | 76 |
| $1178^{10}$ | **Tart and a Half (79)** (BJMeehan) **4-8-7b** LDettori(12) (chsd ldrs: ev ch over 1f out: no ex ins fnl f) | hd | **4** | 6/1 $^{2}$ | 86 | 55 |
| $1113^{4}$ | **Sweet Magic (84)** (PHowling) **5-8-12** FNorton(2) (chsd ldrs: rdn & no ex appr fnl f) | ¾ | **5** | 6/1 $^{2}$ | 88 | 57 |
| $1149^{4}$ | **Cyrano's Lad (IRE) (89)** (CADwyer) **7-9-3** CDwyer(1) (led 4f: one pce) | s.h | **6** | 12/1 | 93 | 62 |
| $1113^{13}$ | **Pride of Brixton (88)** (GLewis) **3-8-9** PatEddery(3) (dwlt: nvr nrr) | nk | **7** | 8/1 | 91 | 53 |
| $1321^{3}$ | **Takadou (IRE) (95)** (MissLCSiddall) **5-9-9** JWeaver(6) (lw: nvr trbld ldrs) | ¾ | **8** | 12/1 | 96 | 65 |
| $1113^{8}$ | **Laurel Delight (83)** (JBerry) **6-8-11** JCarroll(7) (b.nr fore: chsd ldrs over 3f) | 2 | **9** | 20/1 | 77 | 46 |
| $1446^{9}$ | **Ashtina (68)** (BAPearce) **11-7-5**(5) MartinDwyer(8) (lw: outpcd) | 5 | **10** | 50/1 | 46 | 15 |
| $1186^{7}$ | **Master of Passion (83)** (JMPEustace) **7-8-11** MTebbutt(5) (b: prom: stumbled after 2f: no ch after) | 2½ | **11** | 9/1 | 53++ | 22 |
| $1430^{*}$ | **Sailormaite (85)** (SRBowring) **5-8-13b** DeanMcKeown(11) (ref to r: t.n.p) | | **R** | 7/1 $^{3}$ | — | — |
| | | | | (SP 125.6%) | **12 Rn** | |

**58.62 secs** (-0.08) CSF £24.45 CT £428.80 TOTE £3.40: £1.60 £2.30 £7.50 (£25.50) Trio £205.90 OWNER Major M. G. Wyatt (WANTAGE) BRED Dunchurch Lodge Stud Co
LONG HANDICAP Ashtina 7-8
WEIGHT FOR AGE 3yo-7lb
**IN-FOCUS: The stalls were placed in the centre for both sprints on the card, but were dominated by horses racing closer to either rail.**

**1107 Top Banana** found a fine turn of speed to pass the field in the last couple of furlongs and goes to Royal Ascot with every chance, although it must be remembered that he finished second in last year's Stewards' Cup off just 79. (3/1)
**1178 Bowden Rose**, who ran a cracker from a bad draw last time, went to post really well. Racing wide apart from the winner, she is having no luck and must surely win soon. (7/1)
**Croft Pool**, off a 12lb higher mark than he has ever won, ran a terrific race and would have prospects in listed company over this trip. (25/1)
**1064 Tart and a Half** is in good form at present but does not exactly make a habit of winning. (6/1)
**1113 Sweet Magic**, lightly-raced for a five-year-old, ran well and should soon find an opportunity. (6/1)
**1149 Cyrano's Lad (IRE)** ran well but found this trip too short. (12/1)
**1186 Master of Passion** last all chance when clipping the heels of a rival and pulling off a front shoe. (9/1)

## 1631 MILTON PARK STUD MAIDEN STKS (3-Y.O) (Class D)
5-20 (5-21) **1m 6f (Rowley)** £4,308.00 (£1,284.00: £612.00: £276.00) Stalls: High GOING minus 0.40 sec per fur (F)

| | | | | SP | RR | SF |
|---|---|---|---|---|---|---|
| 671³ | **Valedictory** (HRACecil) **3-9-0** PatEddery(7) (lw: b: trckd ldr: led over 3f out: rdn clr fnl f) | — | 1 | 4/9 ¹ | 85 | 48 |
| 804⁴ | **Classic Colleen (IRE)** (RHarris) **3-8-9** AMackay(4) (hld up: hdwy 3f out: edgd rt & kpt on appr fnl f) | 3 | 2 | 25/1 | 77 | 40 |
| | **Belmarita (IRE)** (MHTompkins) **3-8-9** PRobinson(3) (chsd ldrs: rdn 3f out: styd on fnl f) | nk | 3 | 25/1 | 76 | 39 |
| 948⁴ | **Desert Dunes** (NAGraham) **3-9-0** LDettori(5) (led over 10f: wknd & eased ins fnl f) | 3½ | 4 | 11/2 ² | 77 | 40 |
| 1153³ | **Chocolate Ice (75)** (CACyzer) **3-9-0** JWeaver(1) (lw: trckd ldrs: ev ch 3f out: wknd 2f out) | 5 | 5 | 13/2 ³ | 72 | 35 |
| 932⁴ | **Velmez** (RGuest) **3-8-9**(5) FLynch(2) (hld up: rdn 6f out: nvr trbld ldrs) | 3½ | 6 | 16/1 | 68 | 31 |
| | | | | (SP 111.5%) | **6 Rn** | |

**2m 59.28** (3.28) CSF £10.56 TOTE £1.40: £1.20 £1.90 (£6.00) OWNER Lord Howard de Walden (NEWMARKET) BRED Lord Howard de Walden
**671 Valedictory** did not impress on the way to post and took some time to win his race, only drawing away on meeting the rising ground. On this evidence, cut in the ground, a flat track and a long trip are his requirements. (4/9)
**804 Classic Colleen (IRE)** certainly has some ability, but her head carriage and the fact that she tended to drift in behind the winner when asked to challenge gave some cause for concern. (25/1)
**Belmarita (IRE)**, doubling the distance of her two previous outings, did appear to stay. (25/1)
**948 Desert Dunes** tried to force the pace but was shaken off by the winner in the Dip, and Dettori's acceptance of this may have cost him third place. (11/2)
**1153 Chocolate Ice** is becoming disappointing as he is stepped up in trip and found nothing after travelling well to the three-furlong pole. (13/2)

T/Jkpt: £3,966.40 (1.79 Tckts). T/Plpt: £59.50 (573.65 Tckts). T/Qdpt: £8.50 (220.53 Tckts). Dk

# 1163-HAMILTON (R-H) (Good)
## Monday June 3rd
WEATHER: overcast WIND: fresh half bhd

## 1632 E.B.F. MANDORA MEDIAN AUCTION MAIDEN STKS (2-Y.O) (Class E)
2-30 (2-33) **5f 4y** £3,060.30 (£926.40: £452.20: £215.10) Stalls: Low GOING minus 0.31 sec per fur (GF)

| | | | | SP | RR | SF |
|---|---|---|---|---|---|---|
| 1583³ | **Biff-Em (IRE)** (MissLAPerratt) **2-9-0** JWeaver(3) (mde most: kpt on wl fnl f) | — | 1 | 6/1 | 61 | 23 |
| *1093*³ | **Bollero (IRE)** (JBerry) **2-8-9** JCarroll(5) (lw: trckd ldrs: n.m.r 2f out: hdwy over 1f out: nt pce of wnr) | 1¼ | 2 | 5/2 ¹ | 52 | 14 |
| 975¹⁰ | **Antares** (NTinkler) **2-9-0** LCharnock(6) (cl up: rdn over 1f out: nt qckn ins fnl f) | 3 | 3 | 9/2 ³ | 47 | 9 |
| 476³ | **Wagga Moon (IRE)** (JJO'Neill) **2-9-0** KFallon(4) (s.i.s: hdwy ½-wy: rdn & no imp) | 2 | 4 | 10/1 | 41 | 3 |
| | **Bonnie Lassie** (CWThornton) **2-8-9** DeanMcKeown(2) (leggy: lt-f: dwlt: hdwy & prom ½-wy: sn wknd) | nk | 5 | 9/2 ³ | 35 | — |
| 1169³ | **Tear White (IRE)** (TGMills) **2-9-0b** MarkLynch(1) (sn cl up: rdn ½-wy: nt r.o) | 7 | 6 | 3/1 ² | 18 | — |
| | | | | (SP 113.3%) | **6 Rn** | |

**61.2 secs** (2.90) CSF £20.40 TOTE £4.80: £4.90 £1.50 (£4.00) OWNER Miss L. A. Perratt (AYR) BRED J. C. Lett
**1583 Biff-Em (IRE)** won in really good style and is certainly going the right way. (6/1)
**1093 Bollero (IRE)** raced a bit too freely and then found the winner too strong in the closing stages. (5/2)
**Antares** has plenty of speed but, when the pressure was on, was never up to it. Time should see improvement. (9/2)
**476 Wagga Moon (IRE)** is now a sturdy individual, but this was his first run for over two months, and he ran as though it was needed.(10/1: op 4/1)
**Bonnie Lassie** does not live up to her name and, after a slow start, had no chance, though she did show something. (9/2: 4/1-6/1)
**1169 Tear White (IRE)** ran straighter this time. (3/1)

## 1633 NADINE PRENTICE H'CAP (0-70) (3-Y.O+) (Class E)
3-00 (3-00) **1m 1f 36y** £3,376.80 (£1,022.40: £499.20: £237.60) Stalls: High GOING minus 0.31 sec per fur (GF)

| | | | | SP | RR | SF |
|---|---|---|---|---|---|---|
| 1538³ | **Three Arch Bridge (57)** (MJohnston) **4-9-1b** JWeaver(6) (lw: mde most: kpt on wl u.p fnl 2f) | — | 1 | 7/2 ² | 71 | 53 |
| 1502* | **Alabang (53)** (MJCamacho) **5-8-11** 5x LCharnock(2) (lw: trckd ldrs: chal over 2f out: sn rdn: no ex ins fnl f) | 2½ | 2 | 5/2 ¹ | 63 | 45 |
| 1418¹¹ | **Personimus (38)** (CaptJWilson) **6-7-5**(5) PFessey(8) (a chsng ldrs: one pce fnl 3f) | 2 | 3 | 14/1 | 44 | 26 |
| 1546² | **Hutchies Lady (38)** (RMMcKellar) **4-7-10** TWilliams(7) (b.hind: trckd ldrs: swtchd & effrt over 2f out: rdn & nt qckn) | 1¼ | 4 | 5/1 ³ | 42 | 24 |
| 1502² | **Bold Amusement (70)** (WSCunningham) **6-10-0** ACulhane(4) (bhd: effrt ½-wy: nvr trbld ldrs) | 4 | 5 | 8/1 | 67 | 49 |
| 1411⁴ | **Comedy River (42)** (NEBerry) **9-7-11**(3) DarrenMoffatt(10) (s.i.s: rdn ½-wy: n.d) | 2½ | 6 | 8/1 | 35 | 17 |
| 1341⁸ | **Nobby Barnes (44)** (DonEnricoIncisa) **7-8-2** KimTinkler(5) (dwlt: hdwy ½-wy: sn btn) | 2 | 7 | 14/1 | 33 | 15 |
| 1468⁷ | **Pash (41)** (CWFairhurst) **4-7-13v** NKennedy(9) (led early: outpcd appr st: sn bhd) | 3½ | 8 | 12/1 | 24 | 6 |
| 1546¹² | **Rapid Mover (38)** (DANolan) **9-7-3b**(7) IonaWands(1) (chsd ldrs tl wknd fnl 4f) | 3½ | 9 | 25/1 | 15 | — |
| | | | | (SP 114.6%) | **9 Rn** | |

**1m 56.7** (2.40) CSF £12.02 CT £96.42 TOTE £4.10: £1.60 £1.20 £2.60 (£8.00) Trio £50.40 OWNER Mr R. N. Pennell (MIDDLEHAM) BRED R. Taylor
LONG HANDICAP Personimus 7-8 Rapid Mover 7-7
**1538 Three Arch Bridge** was soon dictating things as she likes to and, getting the best ground against the far rails in the straight, she would not be denied. (7/2)
**1502* Alabang** did little wrong other than find one too good and, now he has found the secret, further success should come his way. (5/2)
**1098 Personimus**, although without a win in thirty attempts, has been placed a dozen times, but does seem to bring a new meaning to the phrase 'one-paced'. (14/1)
**1546 Hutchies Lady** travelled quite well but, once a real effort was required in the final two furlongs, this little filly again failed to produce the goods. (5/1)

**1502 Bold Amusement** was trying the impossible coming from off the pace on a track that suits front-runners, and it was never on. (8/1: 6/1-9/1)
**1411 Comedy River**, slowly out, never got going until too late. (8/1: tchd 12/1)

## 1634 ADAIR HOUSTON HIGH JINKS LIMITED STKS (0-55) (3-Y.O+) (Class F)

3-30 (3-30) **6f 5y** £2,535.00 (£710.00: £345.00) Stalls: Low GOING minus 0.31 sec per fur (GF)

| | | | | SP | RR | SF |
|---|---|---|---|---|---|---|
| 1466$^{3}$ | **Rambold (51)** (NEBerry) **5-8-12**$^{(3)}$ DarrenMoffatt(6) (w ldr: led ½-wy: r.o) | — | **1** | 3/1$^{2}$ | 54 | 26 |
| 1423$^{11}$ | **Craigie Boy (54)** (NBycroft) **6-9-7b** TWilliams(5) (lw: trckd ldrs: effrt 2f out: nt qckn ins fnl f) | 3½ | **2** | 3/1$^{2}$ | 51 | 23 |
| 973$^{9}$ | **Penny Parkes (46)** (JBerry) **3-8-7** JCarroll(4) (lw: chsd ldrs: effrt ½-wy: btn appr fnl f) | 2½ | **3** | 6/1$^{3}$ | 38 | 2 |
| | **Croeso Cynnes (55)** (BPalling) **3-8-7** TSprake(2) (lw: hld up: effrt 2f out: wandered u.p & nt qckn) | 1 | **4** | 9/4$^{1}$ | 35 | — |
| 1040$^{9}$ | **Densben (48)** (DenysSmith) **12-9-4** KFallon(1) (lw: in tch: effrt ½-wy: n.d) | 5 | **5** | 10/1 | 25 | — |
| 1163$^{14}$ | **Millemay (37)** (PMonteith) **6-9-1** LCharnock(3) (led to ½-wy: sn rdn & btn) | 3½ | **6** | 33/1 | 13 | — |

(SP 107.1%) **6 Rn**

**1m 13.3** (3.30) CSF £11.14 TOTE £4.80: £1.30 £1.40 (£6.60) OWNER Mr Ron Collins (UPPER LAMBOURN) BRED Sydney Mason
WEIGHT FOR AGE 3yo-8lb

**1466 Rambold** turned down the option of going to the far side but still had too much pace for this bunch. (3/1)
**1020 Craigie Boy** looked set to go to the far side but was trapped towards the stands' side by the winner, and was then well held in the final furlong. (3/1)
**Penny Parkes** showed up behind the leaders but once off the bit there was never any real spark. (6/1)
**Croeso Cynnes** travelled on the bridle but, once an effort was required soon after halfway, she looked none too happy. (9/4)
**Densben** is beginning to come to himself looks-wise. (10/1)

## 1635 AGAS H'CAP (0-70) (3-Y.O+) (Class E)

4-00 (4-01) **6f 5y** £3,392.40 (£1,027.20: £501.60: £238.80) Stalls: Low GOING minus 0.31 sec per fur (GF)

| | | | | SP | RR | SF |
|---|---|---|---|---|---|---|
| 1546$^{4}$ | **Sunday Mail Too (IRE) (37)** (MissLAPerratt) **4-7-10** NKennedy(12) (lw: racd far side: hdwy ½-wy: led ins fnl f: styd on wl) | — | **1** | 16/1 | 46 | 29 |
| 1588$^{4}$ | **Stand Tall (54)** (CWThornton) **4-8-13** DeanMcKeown(2) (racd centre: led over 1f out tl ins fnl f: kpt on) | 1¼ | **2** | 5/1$^{2}$ | 60 | 43 |
| *1460*$^{3}$ | **Panther (IRE) (62)** (JHetherton) **6-9-7** KFallon(11) (disp ld far side tl hdd & no ex ins fnl f) | 1½ | **3** | 4/1$^{1}$ | 64 | 47 |
| 1588$^{3}$ | **Mister Westsound (65)** (MissLAPerratt) **4-9-10b** JCarroll(6) (lw: dwlt: racd centre tl swtchd rt ½-wy: swtchd lft over 1f out: nrst fin) | hd | **4** | 4/1$^{1}$ | 66 | 49 |
| *781*$^{6}$ | **Amoeba (IRE) (48)** (JBerry) **3-7-8**$^{(5)}$ PFessey(5) (cl up centre: kpt on fnl f) | ½ | **5** | 20/1 | 48 | 23 |
| 1163$^{5}$ | **Henry the Hawk (52)** (MDods) **5-8-8**$^{(3)}$ CTeague(10) (b: disp ld far side tl wknd over 1f out) | hd | **6** | 11/2$^{3}$ | 52 | 35 |
| 1163$^{9}$ | **Suedoro (45)** (RMMcKellar) **6-8-1**$^{(3)}$ DarrenMoffatt(8) (sn dispng ld far side: wknd fnl 2f) | 5 | **7** | 8/1 | 32 | 15 |
| 1042$^{15}$ | **Globe Runner (60)** (JJO'Neill) **3-8-11** JFanning(9) (racd far side: nvr trbld ldrs) | 3½ | **8** | 50/1 | 37 | 12 |
| 1313$^{9}$ | **Diet (58)** (MissLAPerratt) **10-9-3v** NConnorton(4) (led centre 4f: wknd) | ¾ | **9** | 12/1 | 33 | 16 |
| 1364$^{13}$ | **Penny's Wishing (44)** (NBycroft) **4-8-3** TWilliams(3) (racd centre: outpcd fr ½-wy) | 3½ | **10** | 12/1 | 10 | — |
| 1545$^{7}$ | **Seconds Away (37)** (JSGoldie) **5-7-3b**$^{(7)}$ IonaWands(1) (hld up centre: lost tch fr ½-wy) | 1½ | **11** | 16/1 | — | — |
| 1538$^{12}$ | **Birchwood Sun (58)** (MDods) **6-9-3b** JWeaver(7) (sn outpcd & bhd: p.u lame ins fnl f) | | **P** | 14/1 | — | — |

(SP 123.7%) **12 Rn**

**1m 11.8** (1.80) CSF £91.04 CT £365.65 TOTE £18.20: £3.00 £2.70 £2.10 (£81.90) Trio £75.00 OWNER Scottish Daily Record & Sunday Mail Ltd (AYR) BRED Miss Ruth Lonergan in Ireland
LONG HANDICAP Sunday Mail Too (IRE) 7-4 Seconds Away 7-5
WEIGHT FOR AGE 3yo-8lb

**1546 Sunday Mail Too (IRE)**, dropped back to sprinting, had the best draw and, sticking to the far rails, won well. (16/1)
**1588 Stand Tall** ran a super race from a poor draw and would have won had he been on the right side. (5/1)
**1460 Panther (IRE)** had the right draw but was always struggling to make it and was comfortably picked off in the final furlong. (4/1)
**1588 Mister Westsound** travelled on most parts of the track and, although finishing well, the effort was always too late. He is never one to ignore. (4/1)
**781 Amoeba (IRE)** ran well for a three-year-old and from a moderate draw. (20/1)
**1163 Henry the Hawk** has gone up the handicap and is better over the minimum trip. (11/2)

## 1636 RAMILLES RATING RELATED MAIDEN STKS (0-60) (3-Y.O) (Class F)

4-30 (4-30) **1m 3f 16y** £2,521.00 (£706.00: £343.00) Stalls: High GOING minus 0.31 sec per fur (GF)

| | | | | SP | RR | SF |
|---|---|---|---|---|---|---|
| 1503$^{4}$ | **Manoy (54)** (JHetherton) **3-9-0b**$^{1}$ KFallon(3) (trckd ldr: rdn to ld 2f out: drvn clr) | — | **1** | Evens$^{1}$ | 60 | 20 |
| 1155$^{9}$ | **Islay Brown (IRE) (54)** (CWCElsey) **3-8-11b** NConnorton(1) (lw: led tl hdd 2f out: sn outpcd) | 6 | **2** | 6/1 | 48 | 8 |
| 1548$^{7}$ | **Phar Closer (46)** (WTKemp) **3-8-11** TWilliams(4) (prom tl outpcd over 3f out: sn btn) | 11 | **3** | 7/2$^{3}$ | 32 | — |
| 1310$^{2}$ | **She's Simply Great (IRE) (56)** (JJO'Neill) **3-8-11** JFanning(2) (prom tl rdn & btn over 3f out) | 3½ | **4** | 11/4$^{2}$ | 27 | — |

(SP 113.2%) **4 Rn**

**2m 27.0** (7.60) CSF £6.49 TOTE £1.80 (£5.80) OWNER Mr C. D. Barber-Lomax (MALTON) BRED John Rose

**1503 Manoy** had blinkers on for the first time, but had to work hard to get the advantage. Once in front, staying was the name of the game and he certainly does that. (Evens)
**Islay Brown (IRE)**, stepped up in distance, tried to make all but looked none too keen under pressure and was well beaten when headed two furlongs out. (6/1)
**1548 Phar Closer**, without the blinkers this time, was always finding this trip too short. (7/2)
**1310 She's Simply Great (IRE)** showed next to nothing. (11/4)

## 1637 BLENHEIM H'CAP (0-70) (4-Y.O+) (Class E)

5-00 (5-00) **1m 5f 9y** £3,252.00 (£984.00: £480.00: £228.00) Stalls: High GOING minus 0.31 sec per fur (GF)

| | | | | SP | RR | SF |
|---|---|---|---|---|---|---|
| 1421$^{2}$ | **Welsh Mill (IRE) (67)** (MrsMReveley) **7-10-0** ACulhane(1) (lw: trckd ldrs: smooth hdwy 3f out: rdn to ld wl ins fnl f) | — | **1** | 7/4$^{1}$ | 76 | 39 |
| *1487** | **Philmist (42)** (CWCElsey) **4-8-3b** 4x NKennedy(4) (led tl hdd over 5f out: led over 2f out tl wl ins fnl f: kpt on) | nk | **2** | 6/1$^{3}$ | 51 | 14 |
| 912$^{4}$ | **Me Cherokee (44)** (CWThornton) **4-8-5** DeanMcKeown(2) (cl up: led over 5f out tl over 2f out: sn btn) | 6 | **3** | 7/1 | 45 | 8 |
| 1034$^{2}$ | **Forzair (60)** (JJO'Neill) **4-9-7** KFallon(3) (lw: bhd: sme hdwy u.p fnl 3f: n.d) | 5 | **4** | 6/1$^{3}$ | 55 | 18 |
| 1421$^{6}$ | **Lord Hastie (USA) (67)** (CWThornton) **8-9-11**$^{(3)}$ OPears(6) (lw: hld up: effrt 3f out: sn rdn & no imp) | 4 | **5** | 5/2$^{2}$ | 57 | 20 |

1165[4] **Bruz (35)** (PMonteith) **5-7-3**(7) IonaWands(5) (dwlt: effrt 4f out: n.d) ....13 **6** 16/1 9 —
(SP 111.9%) **6 Rn**

**2m 53.7** (8.00) CSF £11.50 TOTE £2.70: £1.50 £4.70 (£9.40) OWNER Mr D. S. Hall (SALTBURN) BRED Ballymacoll Stud Farm Ltd
LONG HANDICAP Bruz 7-6
**1421 Welsh Mill (IRE)** gained his first win on the Flat for three years here, and had a real battle to do so. (7/4: 5/4-2/1)
**1487* Philmist** has never won on Turf but she did try really hard here and should pick up a race in due course. (6/1)
**912 Me Cherokee** tried to pinch this by kicking on early in the straight, but could never get away and was left struggling once passed approaching the last two furlongs. (7/1: 5/1-8/1)
**1034 Forzair**, an All-Weather specialist, was never doing enough to get into this. (6/1: op 7/2)

T/Plpt: £21.00 (537.69 Tckts). T/Qdpt: £11.30 (62.87 Tckts). AA

# 1493-LEICESTER (R-H) (Good to firm)
## Monday June 3rd
WEATHER: overcast & showers WIND: fresh half bhd

## 1638 SWANNINGTON CLAIMING STKS (3-Y.O+) (Class F)
2-15 (2-22) **1m 8y** £3,095.00 (£860.00: £413.00) Stalls: High GOING minus 0.54 sec per fur (F)

| | Horse | Dist | Pos | SP | RR | SF |
|---|---|---|---|---|---|---|
| 1411[6] | **Scottish Park (39)** (JLHarris) **7-8-7b** SSanders(2) (hld up: stdy hdwy over 3f out: led over 1f out: rdn out) | — | **1** | 7/1 | 54 | 32 |
| | **Return To Brighton** (JMBradley) **4-8-4**(3) SDrowne(6) (bit bkwd: a.p: ev ch appr fnl f: r.o) | ½ | **2** | 25/1 | 53 | 31 |
| 1154[8] | **Blockade (USA) (70)** (MBell) **7-9-4** MFenton(8) (t: lw: led tl over 1f out: r.o one pce) | 1¾ | **3** | 4/1 [2] | 61 | 39 |
| 1449[16] | **Tony's Mist (43)** (JMBradley) **6-8-12** AMackay(5) (disp ld: rdn & one pce fnl 2f) | 1½ | **4** | 25/1 | 52 | 30 |
| 1043* | **Miss Charlie (49)** (TWall) **6-8-11** RLappin(7) (plld hrd: trckd ldrs: no hdwy appr fnl f) | 1½ | **5** | 12/1 | 48 | 26 |
| 1468[17] | **Daring Ryde (48)** (JPSmith) **5-9-4** GCarter(1) (lw: prom: effrt over 2f out: sn rdn: nt qckn) | ½ | **6** | 25/1 | 54 | 32 |
| 1474[5] | **First Gold (54)** (JWharton) **7-9-4b** JReid(10) (s.i.s: effrt & hung lft over 2f out: no imp) | hd | **7** | 6/1 | 53 | 31 |
| 1069[6] | **Nashaat (USA) (62)** (MCChapman) **8-9-6** DRMcCabe(15) (hld up: effrt 3f out: one pce fnl 2f) | ½ | **8** | 3/1 [1] | 54 | 32 |
| *1457*[13] | **Sporting Risk (42)** (PWHarris) **4-9-6** GHind(14) (lw: trckd ldrs 5f: sn hrd rdn & btn) | 4 | **9** | 25/1 | 46 | 24 |
| 645[7] | **Reed My Lips (IRE) (32)** (BPJBaugh) **5-8-7**(5) MHumphries(9) (b: s.s: a bhd) | 3 | **10** | 66/1 | 32 | 10 |
| 1526[4] | **Richard House Lad (46)** (RHollinshead) **3-8-3** WRyan(12) (lw: a in rr) | 2½ | **11** | 5/1 [3] | 29 | — |
| 1434[15] | **Cherry Muna** (CWFairhurst) **3-8-4** JTate(13) (a bhd: t.o) | 7 | **12** | 33/1 | 17 | — |
| *1460*[7] | **Evening Brigadier (45)** (NMBabbage) **5-9-5**(7)ow6 MartinSmith(3) (lw: in tch: hdwy over 3f out: wknd fnl 2f: t.o) | s.h | **13** | 16/1 | 27 | — |
| | **Pats Folly (17)** (FJYardley) **5-8-7** NAdams(4) (bkwd: trckd ldrs over 5f: sn wknd: t.o) | 1 | **14** | 66/1 | 6 | — |
| 1122[13] | **Motrib (USA)** (MMadgwick) **3-8-2v**[1](3) NVarley(11) (plld hrd: w ldrs 4f: sn wknd: t.o) | 23 | **15** | 50/1 | — | — |

(SP 125.3%) **15 Rn**

**1m 36.3** (1.30) CSF £150.50 TOTE £8.10: £2.80 £17.30 £1.70 (£318.60) Trio £321.30; £316.84 to Pontefract 4/6/96 OWNER Cleartherm Ltd (MELTON MOWBRAY) BRED J. B. H. Stevens
WEIGHT FOR AGE 3yo-11lb
Scottish Park clmd CWylie £4,000
**1411 Scottish Park** moved poorly to post but came back in fine style, and this return to a mile suited her admirably. (7/1)
**Return To Brighton**, seeing a racecourse for the first time in over twelve months, did not look fully tuned up but she ran exceptionally well on this initial outing for her new stable and looks a ready-made winner. (25/1)
**1154 Blockade (USA)** cut out the running, but could never establish a clear advantage and was well outpaced inside the distance. (4/1: 9/4-9/2)
**Tony's Mist** took the leader on but failed to win that battle and was made to look very onepaced when the principals came on the scene. (25/1)
**1043* Miss Charlie**, trying a longer trip this time, did not really get into top gear until the race was as good as over. (12/1: op 8/1)
**Daring Ryde**, winner of this event twelve months ago, performed much better than he has of late but he was hard at work approaching the final furlong and failed to make much impact. (25/1)
**1474 First Gold** (6/1: 4/1-8/1)
**1069 Nashaat (USA)** runs his best races when produced from off the pace but his effort was very short-lived and he was never a serious contender. (3/1: op 7/4)
**1526 Richard House Lad** (5/1: 4/1-7/1)

## 1639 SILVER PHEASANT CONDITIONS STKS (3-Y.O F) (Class C)
2-45 (2-45) **7f 9y** £4,978.12 (£1,841.08: £882.54: £359.70: £141.85: £54.71) Stalls: High GOING minus 0.54 sec per fur (F)

| | Horse | Dist | Pos | SP | RR | SF |
|---|---|---|---|---|---|---|
| | **Bewitching (USA) (95)** (JARToller) **3-9-0** SSanders(2) (lw: hld up: hdwy on bit to ld 2f out: edgd rt fnl f: r.o wl) | — | **1** | 14/1 | 105 | 38 |
| 1144[3] | **Miss Universal (IRE) (99)** (CEBrittain) **3-8-10b** BDoyle(4) (mde most to 2f out: rallied ent fnl f: no ex nr fin) | 1½ | **2** | 11/4 [2] | 98 | 31 |
| 1151[5] | **West Humble (88)** (LadyHerries) **3-9-0** PatEddery(1) (stdd s: swtchd rt: hdwy 3f out: ev ch 2f out: one pce fnl f) | 2½ | **3** | 3/1 [3] | 96 | 29 |
| 708[7] | **Najiya (106)** (JLDunlop) **3-9-6** RHills(3) (hld up: ev ch 2f out: sn rdn: one pce) | nk | **4** | 9/4 [1] | 101 | 34 |
| 1075[5] | **More Than You Know (IRE) (94)** (RHannon) **3-8-11**(3) DaneO'Neill(6) (lw: trckd ldrs: rdn & outpcd over 2f out) | 3½ | **5** | 9/1 | 87 | 20 |
| 1410[4] | **Inner Circle (USA) (92)** (PWChapple-Hyam) **3-9-0** JReid(5) (w ldr over 4f: sn wknd) | 4 | **6** | 6/1 | 78 | 11 |

(SP 113.4%) **6 Rn**

**1m 24.2** (1.20) CSF £49.21 TOTE £9.30: £1.40 £1.60 (£22.10) OWNER Mr P. C. J. Dalby (WHITSBURY) BRED B. Ned Jones and Dr James R. Cook
**Bewitching (USA)**, highly tried in her first season, was produced fit and well for her return to action and won this readily. She does seem to be a very progressive filly. (14/1)
**1144 Miss Universal (IRE)**, taking a step down in distance, made the majority of the running and stuck to her task willingly but the winner proved much too good. (11/4)
**1151 West Humble**, who wore a tongue-strap, was restrained leaving the stalls and switched to race on the far rail. With a chance as good as any entering the final quarter-mile, she was unable to increase her pace and was soon struggling to hold on. (3/1: op 7/4)
**Najiya** cut no ice in a Group race on her seasonal debut and, though she did fare a bit better here, was being ridden and in trouble before reaching the final furlong. (9/4)

**874 More Than You Know (IRE)** failed to hold her pitch when the pace increased two furlongs out and, as she has proved that she gets a mile, obviously needs a stiffer test of stamina. (9/1: op 6/1)
**1410 Inner Circle (USA)** has not progressed from her first outing this term and it could be that she is not up to this class. (6/1: op 7/2)

## 1640 JOHN FERNELEY H'CAP (0-70) (4-Y.O+) (Class E)
3-15 (3-18) **1m 3f 183y** £3,343.20 (£999.60: £478.80: £218.40) Stalls: High GOING minus 0.38 sec per fur (F)

| | | | | SP | RR | SF |
|---|---|---|---|---|---|---|
| *1458$^{4}$* | **In the Money (IRE) (55)** (RHollinshead) **7-8-13**$^{(5)}$ FLynch(7) (lw: hld up: stdy hdwy 4f out: str chal fnl f: led post) | — | **1** | 14/1 | 70 | 47 |
| 1462$^{5}$ | **Daily Sport Girl (37)** (BJLlewellyn) **7-7-9**$^{(5)}$ MBaird(9) (led tl over 1f out: led ins fnl f: ct last stride) | s.h | **2** | 8/1$^{3}$ | 52 | 29 |
| 1514$^{3}$ | **Pip's Dream (49)** (MJRyan) **5-8-12** DBiggs(10) (a.p: led over 1f out tl ins fnl f) | 1½ | **3** | 8/1$^{3}$ | 62 | 39 |
| 968$^{2}$ | **Nordansk (48)** (MMadgwick) **7-8-8**$^{(3)}$ NVarley(15) (b: dwlt: plld hrd: hdwy 2f out: kpt on u.p fnl f) | 1¼ | **4** | 7/1$^{2}$ | 59 | 36 |
| 1462$^{2}$ | **Uncharted Waters (52)** (CACyzer) **5-9-1** JReid(8) (prom tl rdn & one pce fnl 2f) | 3½ | **5** | 6/1$^{1}$ | 59 | 36 |
| 1472$^{6}$ | **Cliburnel News (IRE) (57)** (AStreeter) **6-9-1**$^{(5)}$ RHavlin(14) (hld up: effrt over 2f out: no imp appr fnl f) | 1½ | **6** | 10/1 | 62 | 39 |
| 1421$^{11}$ | **Admirals Secret (USA) (63)** (CFWall) **7-9-5**$^{(7)}$ PClarke(12) (lw: prom tl wknd fnl 2f) | 1½ | **7** | 11/1 | 65 | 42 |
| 1306$^{6}$ | **Triple Tie (USA) (37)** (MBlanshard) **5-8-0** JQuinn(13) (swtg: trckd ldrs: rdn 2f out: grad wknd) | 1¼ | **8** | 33/1 | 38 | 15 |
| 1421$^{8}$ | **Slapy Dam (58)** (JMackie) **4-9-7** SSanders(6) (nvr plcd to chal) | 6 | **9** | 10/1 | 51 | 28 |
| | **Solatium (IRE) (57)** (MCPipe) **4-9-6b** TQuinn(1) (prom to ½-wy: sn rdn & wknd) | 2½ | **10** | 16/1 | 46 | 23 |
| | **Lawful Love (IRE) (35)** (TWDonnelly) **6-7-12** CRutter(11) (trckd ldrs tl wknd 3f out) | 1½ | **11** | 50/1 | 22 | — |
| *365$^{11}$* | **Sacred Mirror (IRE) (53)** (CEBrittain) **5-9-2** BDoyle(2) (b: bkwd: prom 7f) | 3 | **12** | 20/1 | 36 | 13 |
| *1458$^{7}$* | **Stevie's Wonder (IRE) (59)** (BJLlewellyn) **6-9-8** VSlattery(4) (hld up: mid div: wknd over 3f out: t.o) | 7 | **13** | 20/1 | 33 | 10 |
| 546$^{17}$ | **Pennine Wind (IRE) (62)** (SDow) **4-9-6**$^{(5)}$ ADaly(16) (plld hrd: a bhd: t.o) | hd | **14** | 33/1 | 36 | 13 |
| 1496$^{2}$ | **Saltando (IRE) (47)** (PatMitchell) **5-8-10** LDettori(5) (lw: bhd: hrd rdn 3f out: no imp: t.o) | nk | **15** | 6/1$^{1}$ | 20 | — |
| 1305$^{6}$ | **Western Playboy (65)** (RHannon) **4-9-11**$^{(3)}$ DaneO'Neill(3) (a in rr: t.o) | 3 | **16** | 6/1$^{1}$ | 34 | 11 |

(SP 134.0%) **16 Rn**

**2m 32.7** (3.70) CSF £121.92 CT £906.50 TOTE £23.10: £5.40 £2.70 £2.20 £1.20 (£39.50) OWNER Mr J. E. Bigg (UPPER LONGDON) BRED Cheveley Park Stud Ltd

**1458 In the Money (IRE)**, in no hurry to take on the leaders, had to battle hard when he did mount his challenge and it was only on the nod that he did eventually emerge the winner. (14/1)
**1462 Daily Sport Girl** looked to have slipped her field when holding a three-length lead entering the last quarter-mile and, though she fought gamely right to the finish, to the amazement of many only came out second best in the photo. (8/1: op 5/1)
**1514 Pip's Dream** worked hard to take the measure of the runner-up below the distance but she was unable to shake her off and had to admit the tempo too hot for her in the last one hundred yards. (8/1)
**968 Nordansk**, settled in the rear after being sluggish at the start, always had too much to do and he is still striving to make his mark at this game. (7/1)
**1462 Uncharted Waters**, never far off the pace, could not respond when shaken up well over a furlong out and was brushed aside with ease. (6/1: op 4/1)
**1472 Cliburnel News (IRE)** tried to get herself into the action two furlongs out but the pace was being stepped up all the time and she was unable to land a blow. (10/1: op 6/1)
**512 Slapy Dam** (10/1: 6/1-12/1)
**1496 Saltando (IRE)** has yet to prove that he stays this trip but he ran such a poor race here that he told no-one anything. (6/1: op 4/1)
**1079 Western Playboy**, a maiden carrying top weight in a handicap on this step up in distance, never figured at all and there were plenty of punters who got their fingers burnt. (6/1: 4/1-7/1)

## 1641 OLD DALBY H'CAP (0-70) (3-Y.O) (Class E)
3-45 (3-49) **1m 1f 218y** £3,698.10 (£1,108.80: £533.40: £245.70) Stalls: High GOING minus 0.38 sec per fur (F)

| | | | | SP | RR | SF |
|---|---|---|---|---|---|---|
| 1104$^{14}$ | **Parsa (USA) (54)** (JLDunlop) **3-8-6** PatEddery(2) (hld up & bhd: gd hdwy over 2f out: rdn to ld ins fnl f: r.o wl) | — | **1** | 5/1$^{3}$ | 64 | 32 |
| 1182$^{8}$ | **Shaha (64)** (RHannon) **3-8-13**$^{(3)}$ DaneO'Neill(19) (a.p: led wl over 1f out tl hdd & no ex ins fnl f) | 1¼ | **2** | 10/1 | 72 | 40 |
| 1301$^{3}$ | **Budby (61)** (ACStewart) **3-8-13** RHills(6) (hld up mid div: gd hdwy 2f out: ev ch 1f out: unable qckn) | ½ | **3** | 3/1$^{1}$ | 68 | 36 |
| | **Tart (65)** (RFJohnsonHoughton) **3-9-3** JReid(12) (a.p: sltly hmpd 3f out: styd on ins fnl f) | hd | **4** | 12/1 | 72 | 40 |
| 1089$^{2}$ | **Ordained (50)** (EJAlston) **3-8-2** SSanders(18) (hld up: hdwy over 2f out: nt rch ldrs) | 3½ | **5** | 20/1 | 51 | 19 |
| 1068$^{6}$ | **Silverdale Knight (58)** (KWHogg) **3-8-5**$^{(5)}$ ADaly(8) (lw: led: clr ½-wy: hdd wl over 1f out: one pce) | ½ | **6** | 14/1 | 59 | 27 |
| 1042$^{3}$ | **Arabian Heights (50)** (MrsJRRamsden) **3-8-2** JFEgan(14) (plld hrd: hld up: no hdwy fnl 2f) | 6 | **7** | 8/1 | 41 | 9 |
| 1319$^{15}$ | **Induna Mkubwa (58)** (CFWall) **3-8-10** WLord(4) (hld up: nvr nrr) | 1¾ | **8** | 33/1 | 46 | 14 |
| 1182$^{5}$ | **Seventh Edition (64)** (DBurchell) **3-9-2** AProcter(7) (b.nr fore: nvr trbld ldrs) | 4 | **9** | 14/1 | 46 | 14 |
| 1100$^{8}$ | **Blueberry Fields (57)** (CFWall) **3-8-9** WWoods(17) (trckd ldrs over 7f) | 2 | **10** | 25/1 | 36 | 4 |
| 1050$^{8}$ | **Brentability (IRE) (58)** (GLewis) **3-8-10** SWhitworth(9) (swtg: bhd: swtchd lft & hdwy 3f out: hmpd over 2f out: sn btn) | 1¼ | **11** | 9/2$^{2}$ | 35 | 3 |
| 1104$^{7}$ | **Tom Swift (IRE) (63)** (RCSpicer) **3-9-1** TQuinn(10) (trckd ldrs tl wknd 3f out) | 1½ | **12** | 33/1 | 37 | 5 |
| 1301$^{6}$ | **Dramatic Act (69)** (CRBarwell) **3-9-7** NAdams(3) (mid div: rn wd ent st: sn bhd) | 3½ | **13** | 16/1 | 38 | 6 |
| 1447* | **Double Up (66)** (LadyHerries) **3-9-4** DeclanO'Shea(15) (s.i.s: plld hrd: effrt ent st: wknd over 2f out) | 2 | **14** | 15/2 | 31 | — |
| *1448$^{5}$* | **Yellow Dragon (IRE) (54)** (BAPearce) **3-8-6** GBardwell(16) (a bhd) | 1¾ | **15** | 33/1 | 17 | — |
| 932$^{7}$ | **Sharp Command (65)** (RWArmstrong) **3-9-3** RPrice(11) (prom over 7f: eased whn btn) | 2½ | **16** | 20/1 | 24 | — |
| 894$^{15}$ | **Jelali (IRE) (68)** (DJGMurraySmith) **3-9-6** LDettori(13) (prom: rdn 4f out: wknd over 1f out: eased whn btn) | ¾ | **17** | 14/1 | 25 | — |
| | **Needwood Epic (65)** (BCMorgan) **3-9-3** CHodgson(1) (bkwd: hld up in tch: wknd over 2f out) | ¾ | **18** | 33/1 | 21 | — |

(SP 150.5%) **18 Rn**

**2m 7.1** (3.40) CSF £60.77 CT £173.30 TOTE £10.50: £2.80 £4.60 £1.50 £4.00 (£57.60) Trio £70.20 OWNER Mrs Brenda Gudgeon (ARUNDEL) BRED Alec Head and Wertheimer and Frere

**Parsa (USA)** has shown very little sign of ability in any of her three previous outings but, in this first handicap, she delivered a sustained challenge to take command inside the distance. (5/1: op 3/1)
**Shaha** ran his best race yet and he could be very much on the way up. (10/1: op 6/1)
**1301 Budby**, continuing her step up in distance, had her chance entering the final furlong but could not quite produce sufficient speed to poke her nose in front. Her turn is overdue. (3/1)
**Tart**, bred to need middle distances, ran a fine race on this seasonal debut and she should not be long in troubling the judge again. (12/1)
**1089 Ordained** was unable to pose a serious threat but she did keep staying on and will come into her own when tackling twelve furlongs plus. (20/1)

**1068 Silverdale Knight** set a telling gallop and was the one to catch from some way out but stamina appeared to desert him and he was a spent force when collared just inside the quarter-mile pole. (14/1)
**1042 Arabian Heights** (8/1: op 5/1)
**Brentability (IRE)**, subject of substantial support in his first handicap, must have got word of what was expected of him for he was lathered by the time he reached the start. Attempting to make progress from off the pace, he was already doomed when squeezed for room two furlongs out. (9/2: 16/1-4/1)
**1447* Double Up** (15/2: 5/1-8/1)

## 1642 HICKLING (S) H'CAP (0-60) (3-Y.O+) (Class G)

4-15 (4-22) **5f 218y** £2,889.00 (£804.00: £387.00) Stalls: High GOING minus 0.54 sec per fur (F)

| | | | | SP | RR | SF |
|---|---|---|---|---|---|---|
| 1405[6] | **Sharp Monty (54)** (RHollinshead) **3-9-2** LDettori(5) (hld up: gd hdwy wl over 1f out: led ins fnl f: r.o) | — | **1** | 8/1[3] | 64 | 41 |
| *1083*[5] | **Sound the Trumpet (IRE) (53)** (RCSpicer) **4-9-4**(5) RHavlin(14) (a.p: led over 2f out tl ins fnl f) | 1¾ | **2** | 12/1 | 58 | 43 |
| | **Bee Dee Best (IRE) (37)** (JPSmith) **5-8-7** GCarter(12) (chsd ldrs: rdn over 2f out: r.o ins fnl f) | 1 | **3** | 14/1 | 40 | 25 |
| 1500[11] | **Chief's Lady (41)** (JMBradley) **4-8-8**(3) SDrowne(7) (a.p: rdn wl over 1f out: kpt on) | ¾ | **4** | 25/1 | 42 | 27 |
| 1541[6] | **Rotherfield Park (IRE) (34)** (CSmith) **4-8-4** WWoods(15) (lw: a.p: ev ch 2f out: one pce fnl f) | nk | **5** | 12/1 | 34 | 19 |
| 981[17] | **Blushing Grenadier (IRE) (50)** (MJFetherston-Godley) **4-9-6b** WJO'Connor(2) (hld up: hdwy over 1f out: nvr nrr) | 2 | **6** | 8/1[3] | 45 | 30 |
| 1474[9] | **Thorntoun Jewel (IRE) (40)** (JBalding) **3-8-2b** CRutter(20) (hdwy 2f out: nrst fin) | hd | **7** | 20/1 | 34 | 11 |
| 1162[3] | **Valiant Man (42)** (JWharton) **5-8-12v** JReid(9) (trckd ldrs: no hdwy fnl 2f) | ¾ | **8** | 14/1 | 34 | 19 |
| 1087[2] | **Komlucky (44)** (ABMulholland) **4-9-0b** WRyan(6) (mid div: sn pushed along: n.d) | nk | **9** | 7/2[1] | 35 | 20 |
| *1030*[10] | **Niteowl Raider (IRE) (51)** (JAHarris) **3-8-13** JO'Reilly(13) (led over 3f: wknd wl over 1f out) | 1 | **10** | 14/1 | 40 | 17 |
| *780*[6] | **Arlington Lady (40)** (NACallaghan) **3-8-2** GBardwell(3) (b.hind: nvr nr ldrs) | ¾ | **11** | 10/1 | 27 | 4 |
| *1028*[6] | **Nadwaty (IRE) (45)** (MCChapman) **4-9-1** DRMcCabe(8) (nvr nr ldrs) | 1 | **12** | 20/1 | 29 | 14 |
| 1314[18] | **Newlands Corner (40)** (JAkehurst) **3-8-2** FNorton(19) (prom over 3f) | 3 | **13** | 25/1 | 16 | — |
| 1423[12] | **Mu-Arrik (43)** (GROldroyd) **8-8-13v** PatEddery(22) (lw: a in rr) | ¾ | **14** | 8/1[3] | 17 | 2 |
| 1500[12] | **Polli Pui (41)** (WMBrisbourne) **4-8-6**(5) MartinDwyer(1) (s.s: a bhd) | nk | **15** | 14/1 | 14 | — |
| 1517[8] | **Branston Kristy (35)** (CSmith) **4-8-0b**(5) MBaird(17) (prom over 3f) | 1¼ | **16** | 33/1 | 5 | — |
| 1473[5] | **Great Hall (47)** (PDCundell) **7-9-3b** DHarrison(11) (b.hind: s.s: a bhd) | 1¾ | **17** | 7/1[2] | 12 | — |
| 1342[12] | **Waverley Star (30)** (JSWainwright) **11-8-0v** JFEgan(10) (bhd fr ½-wy) | 4 | **18** | 25/1 | — | — |
| 981[18] | **Bold Time Monkey (37)** (MTate) **5-8-7** GHind(16) (outpcd) | ¾ | **19** | 33/1 | — | — |
| 1473[9] | **Sir Tasker (54)** (JLHarris) **8-9-10** SSanders(18) (in tch to ½-wy: sn lost pl) | s.h | **20** | 16/1 | 6 | — |
| 1170[10] | **Deardaw (39)** (MDIUsher) **4-8-9** NAdams(21) (prom far side over 3f: wknd qckly) | ¾ | **21** | 25/1 | — | — |
| | | | | (SP 155.9%) | **21 Rn** | |

**1m 10.9** (0.90) CSF £112.64 CT £1,305.26 TOTE £11.40: £3.00 £3.20 £4.80 £12.70 (£66.30) Trio £2,662.50; £450.01 to Pontefract 4/6/96
OWNER Mr R. Leah (UPPER LONGDON) BRED R. Leah
WEIGHT FOR AGE 3yo-8lb
No bid
**1405 Sharp Monty** seemed to appreciate this faster ground and swooped to lead two hundred yards out for a very comfortable first success. (8/1)
**981 Sound the Trumpet (IRE)** kicked for home over two furlongs out and soon had the measure of his nearest pursuers but the determined late challenge of the winner proved much too strong. (12/1: op 6/1)
**Bee Dee Best (IRE)**, brought back to sprinting, was into his stride inside the last furlong and there could be a small race to be found. (14/1)
**1013 Chief's Lady**, pressing the leaders from the break, kept on gamely inside the last furlong and all is not lost yet. (25/1)
**Rotherfield Park (IRE)** is taking time to regain her true form but she showed up prominently here and she will get it right one of these days. (12/1: op 7/1)
**Blushing Grenadier (IRE)** ran much better here without being able to get himself contention and he has the ability to win more races if he puts his mind to it. (8/1: op 12/1)
**1087 Komlucky** ran no race at all and she seems to have a mind of her own. (7/2)
**1473 Great Hall** (7/1: 5/1-8/1)

## 1643 E.B.F. WOLVEY MAIDEN STKS (2-Y.O F) (Class D)

4-45 (4-47) **5f 2y** £3,655.00 (£1,090.00: £520.00: £235.00) Stalls: High GOING minus 0.54 sec per fur (F)

| | | | SP | RR | SF |
|---|---|---|---|---|---|
| **Cowrie** (RFJohnsonHoughton) **2-8-11** JReid(2) (unf: scope: unruly s: hld up: qcknd to ld ins fnl f: sn clr) | — | **1** | 11/8[1] | 67+ | 7 |
| **Kustom Kit Xpres** (MMcCormack) **2-8-11** LDettori(1) (unf: led to ½-wy: rdn & ev ch 1f out: sn outpcd) | 2½ | **2** | 4/1[3] | 59 t | — |
| **Venetian Scene** (PFICole) **2-8-11** TQuinn(3) (small: unf: s.i.s: sn prom: rdn & ev ch over 1f out: one pce) | 2 | **3** | 13/8[2] | 53 t | — |
| **Oneknight With You** (MJFetherston-Godley) **2-8-11** WJO'Connor(4) (leggy: w'like: prom: led ½-wy tl hdd & outpcd ins fnl f) | ¾ | **4** | 7/1 | 50 t | — |
| **Madame Chinnery** (JMPEustace) **2-8-11** MHills(5) (lengthy: unf: s.s: a bhd & outpcd) | s.h | **5** | 7/1 | 50 t | — |
| | | | (SP 125.2%) | **5 Rn** | |

**61.1 secs** (2.60) CSF £7.93 TOTE £2.90: £1.60 £2.50 (£7.60) OWNER Lady Rothschild (DIDCOT) BRED Lord Rothschild
**Cowrie** came here with quite a reputation and proceeded to turn in a very impressive display. She was very troublesome at the start and it is to be hoped temperament does not get the better of her. (11/8)
**Kustom Kit Xpres**, an unfurnished half-sister to a couple of winners, helped share the pace and was still fighting for supremacy when the winner struck and left her stranded. (4/1: 5/2-9/2)
**Venetian Scene** did not break quite as fast as some but she soon recovered to put herself in with every chance until tapped for toe in the dash to the line. (13/8: 11/10-7/4)
**Oneknight With You**, who may well benefit from a slightly longer trip, had no answer when the winner was let loose but she should be all the wiser for the experience. (7/1: 5/1-8/1)
**Madame Chinnery** lost her chance with a very tardy start and was never able to make her presence felt. (7/1: op 7/2)

## 1644 LEVY BOARD MAIDEN STKS (3-Y.O) (Class D)

5-15 (5-18) **1m 3f 183y** £4,192.20 (£1,254.60: £601.80: £275.40) Stalls: High GOING minus 0.38 sec per fur (F)

| | | | | SP | RR | SF |
|---|---|---|---|---|---|---|
| 813[7] | **Forest Heights** (MrsJCecil) **3-8-9** LDettori(4) (mde all: rdn over 1f out: kpt on gamely) | — | **1** | 20/1 | 92 | 45 |
| 1359[2] | **Questonia** (HRACecil) **3-8-9** PatEddery(5) (a.p: rdn over 2f out: ev ch over 1f out: unable qckn) | ¾ | **2** | 4/5[1] | 91 | 44 |
| | **Fancy Heights** (LadyHerries) **3-8-9** DeclanO'Shea(1) (lw: dwlt: hdwy over 3f out: rdn & r.o wl fnl f) | ¾ | **3** | 20/1 | 90 | 43 |

| | | | | SP | RR | SF |
|---|---|---|---|---|---|---|
| | **Flying Legend (USA)** (HRACecil) **3-9-0** WRyan(2) (leggy: hld up: hdwy 4f out: ev ch 2f out: sn rdn: one pce) | hd | **4** | 12/1 | 95 | 48 |
| 1117[5] | **Arietta's Way (IRE)** (RCharlton) **3-8-2**(7) RBrisland(6) (b.nr hind: s.s: hdwy 4f out: swtchd rt over 2f out: styd on) | 1¼ | **5** | 33/1 | 88 | 41 |
| *502*[3] | **State Circus** (LordHuntingdon) **3-8-9** DHarrison(8) (trckd ldrs over 9f) | 11 | **6** | 33/1 | 73 | 26 |
| | **Trilby** (PFICole) **3-8-9** TQuinn(13) (bit bkwd: sn prom: wknd over 2f out) | 3 | **7** | 11/1[3] | 69 | 22 |
| 1180[2] | **Bechstein** (JLDunlop) **3-9-0** MHills(12) (hld up: rdn over 4f out: wknd over 2f out) | 1 | **8** | 9/4[2] | 73 | 26 |
| | **State Theatre (IRE)** (PWChapple-Hyam) **3-9-0** JReid(3) (prom: rdn 6f out: wknd over 2f out) | 9 | **9** | 12/1 | 61 | 14 |
| 1357[7] | **Duncombe Hall** (CACyzer) **3-9-0** DRMcCabe(11) (a bhd) | 4 | **10** | 66/1 | 55 | 8 |
| 1035[6] | **Miletrian Fit-Out** (CEBrittain) **3-9-0b**[1] BDoyle(9) (s.s: a bhd: t.o) | dist | **11** | 66/1 | — | — |
| | **Action Replay** (RHollinshead) **3-8-9**(5) DGriffiths(10) (leggy: unf: a bhd: t.o fr ½-wy) | nk | **12** | 66/1 | — | — |
| | **Precious Island** (PTDalton) **3-8-9** SDWilliams(7) (unf: bkwd: prom to ½-wy: sn wknd: t.o) | nk | **13** | 66/1 | — | — |

(SP 131.4%) **13 Rn**

**2m 31.7** (2.70) CSF £38.28 TOTE £22.70: £6.60 £1.10 £4.60 (£15.00) Trio £36.10 OWNER Mr George Ward (NEWMARKET) BRED Coral's Farm and Stud

**Forest Heights**, a rare 20/1 winner for substitute Frankie Dettori, is a long-striding filly who is well suited by being allowed to dictate from the front and she only needed to be kept up to her work to outstay the efforts of the favourite. (20/1)

**1359 Questonia**, a most impressive mover, threw down a determined challenge inside the final quarter-mile, but could not muster the pace to get to terms. (4/5)

**Fancy Heights** stayed on in fine style inside the distance and an early success could be very much on the cards. (20/1)

**Flying Legend (USA)**, a leggy, weak-looking colt who could still need time, did pose a serious threat two furlongs out but he showed signs of greenness and failed to go through with his effort. He can only improve on this. (12/1)

**1117 Arietta's Way (IRE)** did not impress to post on this first try at this extended trip but she was finding her stride in the latter stages and is going the right way. (33/1)

**Trilby**, a half-sister to Chester Cup winner Merit, sat on the tail of the leaders until fading over two furlongs out as lack of peak fitness caught her out. She will not remain a maiden for long. (11/1: op 6/1)

**State Theatre (IRE)** (12/1: op 6/1)

T/Jkpt: Not won; £2,802.61 to Pontefract 4/6/96. T/Plpt: £1,048.90 (16.85 Tckts). T/Qdpt: £46.20 (27.5 Tckts). IM

## 1183-THIRSK (L-H) (Firm, Good to firm patches)
## Monday June 3rd

WEATHER: overcast WIND: fresh half bhd

### 1645 PICKERING (S) STKS (2-Y.O F) (Class G)

6-45 (6-46) **6f** £2,355.00 (£655.00: £315.00) Stalls: High GOING minus 0.50 sec per fur (F)

| | | | | SP | RR | SF |
|---|---|---|---|---|---|---|
| 823[6] | **Clara Bliss (IRE)** (BJMeehan) **2-8-9** MTebbutt(4) (mde virtually all: wandered u.p ins fnl f: hld on wl) | — | **1** | 13/2 | 59 | 10 |
| *838*[9] | **Cantsaynowt** (RAFahey) **2-8-9** JQuinn(5) (trckd ldrs: effrt & ev ch over 1f out: nt qckn ins fnl f) | 1¼ | **2** | 14/1 | 56 | 7 |
| *1491*[5] | **Full Traceability (IRE)** (JBerry) **2-9-0v**[1] JCarroll(9) (a chsng ldrs: rdn 2f out: kpt on same pce) | 3 | **3** | 11/2[3] | 53 | 4 |
| 1424[5] | **Blonde Rock** (MRChannon) **2-8-4**(5) PPMurphy(8) (trckd ldrs: effrt 2f out: sn rdn & outpcd: kpt on ins fnl f) | nk | **4** | 13/8[1] | 47 | — |
| *1459*[3] | **Rahona (IRE)** (BSRothwell) **2-8-3b**(7)ow1 SCopp(10) (sn outpcd & bhd: hrd rdn ½-wy: styd on) | 1¾ | **5** | 16/1 | 43 | — |
| 1315[4] | **Loch Dibidale** (JEBanks) **2-8-6**(3) JStack(6) (lw: in tch: hdwy over 2f out: nvr rchd ldrs) | s.h | **6** | 5/1[2] | 42 | — |
| *1459*[2] | **Ekaterini Paritsi** (WGMTurner) **2-8-4**(5) ADaly(3) (chsd ldrs: rdn ½-wy: sn wknd) | 4 | **7** | 5/1[2] | 31 | — |
| 848[7] | **Loxley's Girl (IRE)** (MWEasterby) **2-8-4b**[1](5) GParkin(2) (prom: rdn & outpcd ½-wy: wnt rt: sn lost pl) | ½ | **8** | 14/1 | 30 | — |
| 1086[12] | **Thewrightone (IRE)** (GROldroyd) **2-8-9** RLappin(7) (a outpcd & bhd) | 4 | **9** | 33/1 | 19 | — |
| 823[5] | **Morritt Magic** (CWThornton) **2-8-9** LCharnock(1) (sn wl outpcd & bhd) | 6 | **10** | 16/1 | 3 | — |

(SP 128.2%) **10 Rn**

**1m 12.6** (2.90) CSF £87.68 TOTE £9.20: £2.00 £3.30 £2.00 (£124.20) Trio £147.10; £93.24 to 5/6/96 OWNER Mr Gary Catchpole (UPPER LAMBOURN) BRED Martyn J. McEnery

Bt in 8,000gns. Cantsaynowt clmd WGraham £6,000

**823 Clara Bliss (IRE)**, dropped in trip, wandered under pressure and seemed not to appreciate this undulating track, but held on well to the finish. (13/2: op 10/1)

**838 Cantsaynowt** travelled strongly on the heels of the leaders but, after having every chance, had to give best in the last 100 yards. (14/1)

**1491 Full Traceability (IRE)** went to post keenly in a visor for the first time. (11/2)

**1424 Blonde Rock**, who had shown ability in much better company first time, was disappointing. Tracking the leaders, she was suddenly outpaced two furlongs from home and her chance had gone. (13/8)

**1459 Rahona (IRE)**, soon behind, stayed on late in the day. She will not forget this in a hurry. (16/1)

**1459 Ekaterini Paritsi** (5/1: op 3/1)

### 1646 LEEMING BAR H'CAP (0-75) (3-Y.O+) (Class D)

7-15 (7-24) **5f** £3,717.00 (£1,116.00: £538.00: £249.00) Stalls: High GOING minus 0.50 sec per fur (F)

| | | | | SP | RR | SF |
|---|---|---|---|---|---|---|
| 1161[7] | **Able Sheriff (45)** (MWEasterby) **4-8-1b** DaleGibson(3) (chsd ldrs: rdn over 1f out: r.o wl to ld ins fnl f) | — | **1** | 10/1 | 55 | 37 |
| 1501[3] | **Insider Trader (72)** (MrsJRRamsden) **5-9-7**(7) ClaireWest(1) (w ldrs on outside: led over 1f out tl ins fnl f) | 1½ | **2** | 6/1[3] | 77 | 59 |
| 1501[4] | **Shadow Jury (61)** (DWChapman) **6-9-3b** LCharnock(6) (s.i.s: sn chsng ldrs: ev ch over 1f out: edgd lft & nt qckn ins fnl f) | 1 | **3** | 100/30[2] | 63 | 45 |
| 443[17] | **Chemcast (66)** (DNicholls) **3-9-1** AlexGreaves(5) (led tl over 1f out: styd on same pce) | s.h | **4** | 7/1 | 68 | 43 |
| 1364[11] | **Invigilate (47)** (MartynWane) **7-8-3** JQuinn(7) (sn outpcd & bhd: styd on appr fnl f) | 2½ | **5** | 16/1 | 41 | 23 |
| 1364[12] | **Ned's Bonanza (64)** (MDods) **7-9-6** JCarroll(4) (lw: in tch: rdn over 2f out: no imp) | s.h | **6** | 7/1 | 58 | 40 |
| | **Clincher Club (74)** (MJohnston) **3-9-9** JWeaver(8) (hld up: a bhd) | 3 | **7** | 8/1 | 58 | 33 |
| 1304* | **Total Aloof (75)** (WJHaggas) **3-9-10** KDarley(2) (chsd ldrs: rdn & outpcd over 2f out: sn lost pl) | hd | **8** | 5/2[1] | 59 | 34 |
| | ***Just Lady (70)*** (WGMTurner) **3-9-0**(5) ADaly(9) (Withdrawn not under Starter's orders: burst out of front of stalls) | | **W** | 12/1 | — | — |

(SP 124.7%) **8 Rn**

**58.3 secs** (0.30) CSF £63.23 CT £225.26 TOTE £13.80: £2.50 £2.20 £1.80 (£27.50) Trio £83.90 OWNER Early Morning Breakfast Syndicate (SHERIFF HUTTON) BRED Theakston Stud

WEIGHT FOR AGE 3yo-7lb

**704 Able Sheriff** disappointed on his last two outings but appreciated this firm ground and bounced right back to his best, scoring in decisive fashion in the end. (10/1)
**1501 Insider Trader**, worst drawn, one of eight, raced up the centre and his cause was not helped by a slipping noseband, but he would not have beaten the winner anyway. (6/1: 4/1-6/1)
**1501 Shadow Jury** missed the break slightly. Moving up to race on the stands' side which is normally favoured, he edged left under pressure and was not good enough on the day. (100/30)
**Chemcast**, absent for 74 days, showed a very poor action going down but showed plenty of speed to lead them for over three furlongs. (7/1: 5/1-8/1)
**Invigilate** looked particularly well in the paddock. With his stable struggling to find form, he was by no means disgraced and, significantly, all his seven career wins have been recorded in June and July. (16/1)
**Ned's Bonanza** (7/1: 13/2-10/1)
**1304* Total Aloof**, a tail swisher, showed a poor action going down. Struggling at halfway, her rider soon gave up. Connections were at a loss for a reason. (5/2)

## 1647 BUSINESS FURNITURE CENTRE (HOLDINGS) H'CAP (0-80) (3-Y.O+) (Class D)

7-45 (7-46) **1m 4f** £3,812.75 (£1,142.00: £548.50: £251.75) GOING minus 0.34 sec per fur (GF)

| | | | | SP | RR | SF |
|---|---|---|---|---|---|---|
| 1109[7] | **Domappel (70)** (MrsJCecil) **4-9-11** JWeaver(10) (led 3f: led over 2f out: sn drvn clr: unchal) | — | **1** | 7/2[1] | 81 | 56 |
| 979[2] | **Beaumont (IRE) (59)** (JEBanks) **6-9-0** JQuinn(8) (lw: sn pushed along: hdwy 3f out: styd on fnl f) | 2½ | **2** | 11/2 | 67 | 42 |
| 1200[2] | **Mental Pressure (78)** (MrsMReveley) **3-9-4** KDarley(7) (hld up: effrt over 3f out: styd on appr fnl f) | nk | **3** | 9/2[3] | 85 | 45 |
| 1418[5] | **Calder King (62)** (JLEyre) **5-9-3v** RLappin(2) (a.p: sn pushed along: one pce fnl 3f) | s.h | **4** | 8/1 | 69 | 44 |
| 1200[5] | **Anchor Venture (62)** (SPCWoods) **3-8-2** WWoods(5) (lw: trckd ldrs: rdn over 2f out: one pce) | 1½ | **5** | 4/1[2] | 67 | 27 |
| 1436[6] | **Kings Cay (IRE) (46)** (THCaldwell) **5-8-1** DaleGibson(4) (a in rr: hmpd over 7f out) | 3 | **6** | 25/1 | 47 | 22 |
| 1309[9] | **Dirab (65)** (TDBarron) **3-8-5** JFanning(3) (lw: hld up: hmpd over 7f out: nvr nr ldrs) | 1 | **7** | 8/1 | 65 | 25 |
| 1109[6] | **Advance East (60)** (MrsJRRamsden) **4-8-8**(7) TFinn(6) (led after 3f: sddle slipped: hdd over 2f out: eased) | 6 | **8** | 6/1 | 52 | 27 |
| 1421[14] | **Soba Up (69)** (TJEtherington) **6-9-10** ACulhane(9) (bit bkwd: chsd ldrs: rdn along over 3f out: lost pl over 2f out: eased) | 7 | **9** | 14/1 | 52 | 27 |

(SP 122.8%) **9 Rn**

**2m 33.8** (3.80) CSF £23.05 CT £83.16 TOTE £4.40: £2.10 £1.80 £1.90 (£4.80) Trio £8.90 OWNER Mr M. C. Banks (NEWMARKET) BRED Bolton Grange
WEIGHT FOR AGE 3yo-15lb
OFFICIAL EXPLANATION **Anchor Venture: had been struck into.**
**Advance East: his jockey reported that his saddle slipped turning into the home straight, which prevented him from riding it out.**
**1109 Domappel** was given an enterprising ride. Kicking clear early in the straight, he was never in any danger. (7/2)
**979 Beaumont (IRE)** stuck on under pressure and seems to stay this trip all right. (11/2)
**1200 Mental Pressure** tended to run in snatches. Kept to the wide outside, he was staying on when it was all over and would be worth a try at a mile and six. (9/2)
**1418 Calder King**, soon pushed along to go the pace, seemed to stay the trip all right. (8/1)
**1200 Anchor Venture** looked particularly well. Struck into turning into the back straight, a mile from home, he can be forgiven. It would be interesting to see him ridden from the front over further. (4/1)
**1309 Dirab**, dropped out, seemed to run into the back of horses a mile from home and his rider never got serious with him. He looks capable of a good deal better. (8/1)
**1109 Advance East**, racing keenly, went on turning into the back straight, but his saddle slipped some way from home and the boy did well to stay with him. (6/1)

## 1648 BEDALE LIMITED STKS (0-75) (3-Y.O) (Class D)

8-15 (8-16) **7f** £3,613.00 (£1,084.00: £522.00: £241.00) GOING minus 0.34 sec per fur (GF)

| | | | | SP | RR | SF |
|---|---|---|---|---|---|---|
| 1608* | **Alamein (USA) (74)** (WJHaggas) **3-9-0b** [3x] KFallon(1) (trckd ldrs: outpcd over 2f out: hdwy over 1f out: led wl ins fnl f) | — | **1** | 9/4[1] | 84 | 40 |
| 1301* | **Divina Luna (70)** (JWHills) **3-8-6**(5) MHenry(3) (lw: w ldr: led over 3f out tl nr fin) | ½ | **2** | 6/1[3] | 80 | 36 |
| 1185* | **Royal Ceilidh (IRE) (75)** (DenysSmith) **3-8-11** KDarley(5) (trckd ldrs: styd on sme pce whn sltly hmpd jst ins fnl f) | 2½ | **3** | 7/2[2] | 74 | 30 |
| 1327[5] | **Marjaana (IRE) (75)** (PTWalwyn) **3-8-8** RHills(2) (led tl over 3f out: wknd jst ins fnl f) | 1¼ | **4** | 9/4[1] | 68 | 24 |
| 1172[9] | **Just Millie (USA) (70)** (JEBanks) **3-8-5**(3) JStack(6) (hld up: effrt & outpcd over 2f out: nvr nr ldrs) | ½ | **5** | 10/1 | 67 | 23 |
| 1495[4] | **Safio (72)** (CSmith) **3-8-11** WWoods(4) (hld up: effrt 3f out: n.d) | 4 | **6** | 7/1 | 61 | 17 |

(SP 119.6%) **6 Rn**

**1m 26.7** (2.50) CSF £15.48 TOTE £2.90: £2.40 £2.50 (£11.00) OWNER Mr Henryk De Kwiatkowski (NEWMARKET) BRED Kennelot Stables Limited
**1608* Alamein (USA)** recorded his second victory in three days. The blinkers have worked to good effect. (9/4)
**1301* Divina Luna**, who looked particularly well, went on at halfway and soon stepped up the pace but the winning combination proved too strong near the line. (6/1: op 4/1)
**1185* Royal Ceilidh (IRE)** took a keen grip on the heels of the leaders. She was only staying on at the same pace when the winner brushed her slightly aside, just inside the last. She needs the mile. (7/2: op 9/4)
**1327 Marjaana (IRE)**, an unfurnished filly, set a moderate pace, but her stride shortened just inside the last. It is hard to see where any improvement is going to come from. (9/4: op 4/1)
**Safio** was too keen for his own good. (7/1: op 4/1)

## 1649 SPROXTON MAIDEN STKS (3-Y.O+) (Class D)

8-45 (8-46) **1m** £3,795.00 (£1,140.00: £550.00: £255.00) Stalls: High GOING minus 0.34 sec per fur (GF)

| | | | | SP | RR | SF |
|---|---|---|---|---|---|---|
| 1190[6] | **Diminutive (USA) (82)** (JWHills) **3-8-7**(5) MHenry(6) (lw: trckd ldrs: effrt & outpcd 3f out: styd on to ld wl ins fnl f) | — | **1** | 13/8[1] | 72 | 36 |
| 1160[5] | **Knotty Hill** (RCraggs) **4-9-9** JCarroll(2) (plld hrd: trckd ldr: rdn to ld over 1f out: hdd wl ins fnl f) | 1¼ | **2** | 16/1 | 70 | 45 |
| 1155[2] | **Time of Night (USA) (71)** (RGuest) **3-8-7** LCharnock(3) (led: clr over 3f out: hdd over 1f out: one pce) | 1¼ | **3** | 100/30[3] | 62 | 26 |
| 1350[5] | **Attarikh (IRE)** (JHMGosden) **3-8-12** RHills(7) (trckd ldrs: outpcd over 3f out: styd on same pce appr fnl f) | ¾ | **4** | 7/4[2] | 66 | 30 |
| | **Magic Heights** (JEBanks) **3-8-12** JQuinn(5) (bit bkwd: s.i.s: sme hdwy 2f out: nvr nr ldrs) | 9 | **5** | 9/1 | 48 | 12 |
| 1530[13] | **Karaylar (IRE)** (WStorey) **4-9-9** JFanning(8) (in tch: sn pushed along: outpcd fr ½-wy) | 1½ | **6** | 50/1 | 45 | 20 |
| 1350[8] | **Alajyal (IRE)** (PTWalwyn) **3-8-7** KDarley(1) (dwlt s: a bhd) | 3 | **7** | 14/1 | 34 | — |

| | | | | SP | RR | SF |
|---|---|---|---|---|---|---|
| | **Lady Seren (IRE)** (SEKettlewell) **4-9-4** NRodgers(4) (bkwd: s.i.s: a in rr) | nk | **8** | 50/1 | 33 | 8 |

(SP 124.0%) **8 Rn**

**1m 39.6** (3.10) CSF £26.11 TOTE £2.30: £1.10 £2.00 £1.20 (£14.30) OWNER Gainsbury Partnership (LAMBOURN) BRED Mr & Mrs James W. Phillips

WEIGHT FOR AGE 3yo-11lb

**1190 Diminutive (USA)**, tapped for foot early in the straight, stayed on to get on top inside the last. Rated 82, he probably ran some way below that here. (13/8)

**1160 Knotty Hill**, who showed ability first time, was a springer in the market. Taking a keen grip after hitting the front, he only gave best near the line. He could be worth a try over seven and letting him get on with it. (16/1)

**1155 Time of Night (USA)** did her best to pinch the race, quickening clear off the bend, but in the end, she was simply not good enough. (100/30)

**1350 Attarikh (IRE)** raced with his tongue tied down, his head came up under pressure, and he looks like he has problems. (7/4)

**Magic Heights** looked backward and was never in the contest. She ought to do better in time. (9/1: op 6/1)

**Karaylar (IRE)** was having his third run to qualify for handicaps. (50/1)

## 1650 SALTERSGATE H'CAP (0-70) (3-Y.O+) (Class E)

9-15 (9-15) **1m** £3,367.75 (£1,012.00: £488.50: £226.75) Stalls: Low GOING minus 0.34 sec per fur (GF)

| | | | | SP | RR | SF |
|---|---|---|---|---|---|---|
| $1538^{7}$ | **Spanish Verdict (59)** (DenysSmith) **9-9-4** JWeaver(7) (chsd ldrs: hrd rdn over 2f out: edgd rt: led jst ins fnl f: jst hld on) | — | **1** | 8/1 | 67 | 39 |
| $1341^{2}$ | **Intendant (57)** (JGFitzGerald) **4-9-2** KFallon(6) (lw: hld up: hdwy over 2f out: hrd rdn over 1f out: r.o) | s.h | **2** | $5/2^{1}$ | 65 | 37 |
| $1345^{7}$ | **Dr Edgar (60)** (MDods) **4-9-5** JCarroll(3) (led after 2f tl jst ins fnl f: nt qckn) | 1¼ | **3** | 16/1 | 65 | 37 |
| $1500^{3}$ | **Sallyoreally (IRE) (37)** (WStorey) **5-7-3**(7) IonaWands(1) (hld up: hdwy ½-wy: nt clr run over 1f out: kpt on same pce) | ½ | **4** | 11/2 | 41 | 13 |
| $1341^{4}$ | **Anonym (IRE) (65)** (DNicholls) **4-9-10** AlexGreaves(2) (lw: trckd ldrs: effrt 2f out: kpt on same pce) | nk | **5** | $4/1^{2}$ | 69 | 41 |
| *$122^{11}$* | **Whackford Squeers (56)** (DNicholls) **4-8-8**(7) JBramhill(10) (chsd ldrs: outpcd over 2f out: grad wknd) | 7 | **6** | 25/1 | 46 | 18 |
| $1185^{5}$ | **Too Hasty (63)** (TDEasterby) **3-8-11** KDarley(4) (trckd ldrs: effrt over 2f out: wkng whn n.m.r over 1f out) | s.h | **7** | 6/1 | 53 | 14 |
| $801^{8}$ | **Kummel King (56)** (EJAlston) **8-9-1** SDWilliams(5) (led 2f: chsd ldrs tl lost pl 3f out: sn bhd) | 16 | **8** | 16/1 | 14 | — |
| $1087^{12}$ | **Prime Property (IRE) (38)** (MWEasterby) **4-7-11b** DaleGibson(8) (s.i.s: sn rdn along & wl bhd) | 7 | **9** | 33/1 | — | — |
| 1416* | **Broughton's Pride (IRE) (50)** (JLEyre) **5-8-9** RLappin(9) (chsd ldrs: pushed along & lost pl ½-wy: p.u over 2f out: b.b.v) | | **P** | $5/1^{3}$ | — | — |

(SP 124.6%) **10 Rn**

**1m 39.9** (3.40) CSF £28.82 CT £302.06 TOTE £11.20: £3.00 £1.60 £2.20 (£8.70) Trio £67.80 OWNER Cox & Allen (Kendal) Ltd (BISHOP AUCKLAND) BRED Hyde Stud

WEIGHT FOR AGE 3yo-11lb

STEWARDS' ENQUIRY Fallon susp. 12-13/6/96 (excessive use of whip).

**Spanish Verdict**, who had slipped down the weights, had the firm ground he loves. Given a most determined ride, he held on by the skin of his teeth. (8/1)

**1341 Intendant** had everything thrown at him in the final furlong. To his credit, he knuckled down to it but could not quite force his head in front. It was no surprise when his rider was suspended. (5/2: op 4/1)

**816 Dr Edgar** showed a very poor action going down but ran well, making the best of his way home and only giving best inside the last. (16/1)

**1500 Sallyoreally (IRE)**, on the face of it, looked a shade unlucky, having no room in which to work. Her best trip these days is anyone's guess. (11/2)

**1341 Anonym (IRE)** looked well, and with the ground to suit he ran creditably, but this is probably as good as he is now. (4/1)

**1185 Too Hasty** (6/1: op 4/1)

**1416* Broughton's Pride (IRE)** suddenly came under pressure and looked distressed at halfway. Soon pulled up, she was brought back in the horse ambulance but had broken a blood-vessel. (5/1)

T/Plpt: £102.10 (159 Tckts). T/Qdpt: £4.20 (363.5 Tckts). WG

# 1314-WINDSOR (Fig. 8) (Good to firm)

## Monday June 3rd

WEATHER: sunny WIND: almost nil

## 1651 BARCLAYS BANK (S) STKS (3-Y.O+) (Class G)

6-30 (6-30) **1m 67y** £2,542.00 (£712.00: £346.00) GOING minus 0.28 sec per fur (GF)

| | | | | SP | RR | SF |
|---|---|---|---|---|---|---|
| $1302^{3}$ | **Noeprob (USA) (43)** (RJHodges) **6-8-13**(3) SDrowne(4) (a.p: qcknd to ld wl over 1f out: r.o) | — | **1** | $11/2^{3}$ | 66 | 48 |
| $1497^{2}$ | **Eurobox Boy (60)** (APJarvis) **3-8-10v** JTate(11) (b.nr hind: led tl wl over 1f out: nt qckn) | 5 | **2** | $5/1^{2}$ | 61 | 32 |
| $1156^{3}$ | **Bold Angel (60)** (KAMorgan) **9-9-7** GDuffield(3) (b: a.p: hrd rdn & one pce fnl 2f) | 2½ | **3** | $5/1^{2}$ | 57 | 39 |
| $1347^{10}$ | **Racing Hawk (USA) (52)** (MSSaunders) **4-9-7** RPrice(14) (hdwy over 2f out: hrd rdn over 1f out: styd on) | 2 | **4** | 33/1 | 53 | 35 |
| 1314* | **Cape Pigeon (USA) (63)** (LGCottrell) **11-9-12v** MFenton(9) (lw: a.p: ev ch 2f out: nt qckn) | nk | **5** | $100/30^{1}$ | 57 | 39 |
| *$1457^{8}$* | **Samara Song (60)** (WGMTurner) **3-8-10** RPerham(10) (w ldr: rdn over 2f out: wknd over 1f out) | 1¼ | **6** | 16/1 | 50 | 21 |
| $1526^{8}$ | **Totally Yours (IRE)** (MRChannon) **3-8-5** AGorman(13) (nvr nr to chal) | ¾ | **7** | 14/1 | 43 | 14 |
| $1174^{12}$ | **Native Song (39)** (MJHaynes) **3-8-5** PaulEddery(17) (nvr nrr) | hd | **8** | 33/1 | 43 | 14 |
| | **Mustahil (IRE) (49)** (RJHodges) **7-9-7** FNorton(15) (a mid div) | hd | **9** | 33/1 | 48 | 30 |
| $1099^{13}$ | **Burnt Sienna (IRE) (47)** (JSMoore) **4-8-13**(3) NVarley(2) (lw: hdwy over 4f out: wknd over 2f out) | ¾ | **10** | 12/1 | 41 | 23 |
| | **Doodies Pool (IRE) (49)** (PBurgoyne) **6-9-4v**(3) PMcCabe(6) (a bhd) | 8 | **11** | 33/1 | 31 | 13 |
| $1301^{10}$ | **Lancashire Legend (60)** (SDow) **3-8-10v$^{1}$** SSanders(8) (prom tl wknd 3f out) | 15 | **12** | 11/1 | 2 | — |
| $1496^{15}$ | **Sungrove's Best (27)** (PEccles) **9-9-7** SWhitworth(1) (lw: a bhd: t.o) | 2½ | **13** | 66/1 | — | — |
| $1338^{8}$ | **Mannagar (IRE)** (JRPoulton) **4-9-7b$^{1}$** AMorris(5) (a bhd: t.o) | 1¼ | **14** | 33/1 | — | — |
| $1009^{10}$ | **Simply Seven** (PButler) **3-8-7**(3) DaneO'Neill(7) (bhd fnl 4f: t.o) | 6 | **15** | 33/1 | — | — |
| | **Winning Wonder** (MissJacquelineDoyle) **4-8-13**(3) AWhelan(16) (prom 4f: t.o) | 1 | **16** | 33/1 | — | — |

(SP 122.5%) **16 Rn**

**1m 45.2** (3.00) CSF £31.05 TOTE £5.90: £1.80 £1.50 £1.70 (£9.80) Trio £18.40 OWNER Mrs P. A. Bradshaw (SOMERTON) BRED Charles Cyzer

WEIGHT FOR AGE 3yo-11lb

Bt in 4,600 gns

**1302 Noeprob (USA)**, tracking the leaders, then found a good turn of foot to settle the issue in a few strides below the distance. (11/2)
**1497 Eurobox Boy** made a gallant effort to lead all the way and, though easily outpaced by the winner approaching the final furlong, kept on well for second. (5/1: 3/1-11/2)
**1156 Bold Angel**, never out of the leading group, stayed on at one pace under strong pressure in the final two furlongs. (5/1)
**Racing Hawk (USA)** was in midfield until improving under pressure from the junction, but although staying on, was never in the race with a chance. (33/1)
**1314* Cape Pigeon (USA)** laid close up as usual, but failed to quicken when asked for his effort at the two furlong marker. (100/30)
**Samara Song** disputed the lead but, under pressure two furlongs from home, was beaten approaching the final furlong. (16/1)
**Totally Yours (IRE)** (14/1: op 7/1)
**Lancashire Legend** (11/1: 7/1-12/1)

## 1652 SUNLEY LIMITED STKS (0-80) (3-Y.O+) (Class D)

7-00 (7-03) **5f 217y** £3,597.00 (£1,086.00: £528.00: £249.00) GOING minus 0.28 sec per fur (GF)

| | | | | SP | RR | SF |
|---|---|---|---|---|---|---|
| | **My Cadeaux (78)** (RGuest) **4-9-1** DHarrison(2) (a.p: led wl over 1f out: drvn out) | — | **1** | 10/1 | 85 | 54 |
| $1064^{8}$ | **Mister Jolson (75)** (RJHodges) **7-9-4**(3) SDrowne(1) (lw: b.nr fore: hdwy 2f out: ev ch fnl f: nt qckn) | 2½ | **2** | 12/1 | 84 | 53 |
| $1521^{5}$ | **Kiss Me Again (IRE) (80)** (RHannon) **3-8-4**(3) DaneO'Neill(3) (prom tl outpcd & n.m.r over 1f out: swtchd lft: r.o ins fnl f) | ¾ | **3** | $5/1^{2}$ | 76 | 37 |
| | **Youdontsay (80)** (TJNaughton) **4-9-1** RHughes(4) (led tl wknd wl over 1f out) | 2 | **4** | 8/1 | 71 | 40 |
| $1064^{11}$ | **Polly Golightly (79)** (MBlanshard) **3-8-7b** SSanders(7) (a.p: no hdwy fnl 2f) | 2 | **5** | $11/2^{3}$ | 66 | 27 |
| 1171* | **Mijas (80)** (LMontagueHall) **3-8-10** RPerham(6) (w ldr: ev ch 2f out: sn wknd) | 4 | **6** | 7/1 | 58 | 19 |
| $648^{3}$ | **Smithereens (79)** (PTWalwyn) **3-8-7** PatEddery(9) (lw: chsd ldrs: n.m.r over 1f out: eased whn btn) | ½ | **7** | 8/1 | 54 | 15 |
| $928^{22}$ | **French Grit (IRE) (78)** (MDods) **4-9-4** SWhitworth(8) (s.s: a bhd) | 2 | **8** | 8/1 | 51 | 20 |
| $1334^{7}$ | **Castlerea Lad (80)** (RHollinshead) **7-9-4** LDettori(5) (a bhd) | ½ | **9** | $7/2^{1}$ | 50 | 19 |
| | | | | (SP 116.9%) | | **9 Rn** |

**1m 12.0** (1.50) CSF £106.21 TOTE £15.40: £4.70 £3.50 £1.50 (£87.70) Trio £78.40 OWNER Mr C. J. Mills (NEWMARKET) BRED Jim and Mrs Strange
WEIGHT FOR AGE 3yo-8lb
OFFICIAL EXPLANATION **Mister Jolson: spread a plate during the race.**
**My Cadeaux** found a useful turn of foot when asked to win her race below the distance, and battled on well when strongly challenged in the final furlong. (10/1: 7/1-11/1)
**928 Mister Jolson** looked much like winning when coming with a steady run from two furlongs out, but after taking second place, and reaching the winner's quarters entering the final furlong, was easily held over the last 100 yards. (12/1: op 7/1)
**1521 Kiss Me Again (IRE)**, was chasing the leaders until squeezed for room approaching the final furlong. After looking well-beaten, she ran on again strongly for third. (5/1)
**Youdontsay** faded after leading until the final furlong. (8/1)
**989 Polly Golightly**, though never far behind the leaders, was soon being driven along and could find no extra in the last quarter-mile. (11/2: 12/1-5/1)
**1171* Mijas** disputed the lead for four furlongs and then weakened. (7/1)
**648 Smithereens** appeared to be travelling well enough on the heels of the leaders, but when denied a clear run approaching the final furlong, the position was quickly accepted. She can do much better. (8/1)
**716 French Grit (IRE)** (8/1: op 9/2)

## 1653 VANGUARD LEASE COMPANY CONDITIONS STKS (2-Y.O) (Class D)

7-30 (7-31) **5f 10y** £3,160.00 (£955.00: £465.00: £220.00) GOING minus 0.28 sec per fur (GF)

| | | | | SP | RR | SF |
|---|---|---|---|---|---|---|
| $1130^{4}$ | **Andreyev (IRE)** (RHannon) **2-8-11** RHughes(3) (b.off hind: lw: a.p: led over 1f out: all out) | — | **1** | $3/1^{2}$ | 88 | 54 |
| 916* | **Dame Laura (IRE)** (PFICole) **2-8-12** TQuinn(1) (w ldr: led wl over 1f out: sn hdd: hrd rdn: r.o) | nk | **2** | $13/8^{1}$ | 88 | 54 |
| 1453* | **Deep Finesse** (MAJarvis) **2-9-3** PRobinson(6) (lw: led over 3f: ev ch 1f out: nt qckn) | 1½ | **3** | $4/1^{3}$ | 88 | 54 |
| | **Rudi's Pet (IRE)** (RHannon) **2-8-11** PatEddery(5) (w'like: bit bkwd: hdwy 2f out: rdn 1f out: wknd ins fnl f) | 3 | **4** | 13/2 | 73 | 39 |
| $1404^{4}$ | **Osomental** (DHaydnJones) **2-8-11b**[1] AMackay(4) (lw: hdwy over 2f out: hrd rdn & wknd over 1f out) | s.h | **5** | 8/1 | 73 | 39 |
| $1318^{3}$ | **Sweet Emmaline** (WGMTurner) **2-8-10** TSprake(2) (spd 3f) | 6 | **6** | 20/1 | 53 | 19 |
| $1315^{3}$ | **Castle Ashby Jack** (PHowling) **2-8-11** FNorton(7) (b.hind: bhd fnl 2f) | 1¼ | **7** | 20/1 | 50 | 16 |
| | | | | (SP 117.1%) | | **7 Rn** |

**60.2 secs** (1.00) CSF £8.35 TOTE £5.30: £2.20 £1.50 (£4.90) OWNER Mr J. Palmer-Brown (MARLBOROUGH) BRED T. F. Moorhead
STEWARDS' ENQUIRY Hughes susp. 12-14/6/96 (excessive use of whip).
**1130 Andreyev (IRE)**, close up from the start, had to be hard driven to gain a narrow lead at the distance and the pressure was maintained all the way to the line. (3/1)
**916* Dame Laura (IRE)**, always in the first two, led momentarily below the distance and fought back well when headed. (13/8)
**1453* Deep Finesse** made the running for over three furlongs. He had another crack inside the last furlong but was being held near the finish. (4/1: 9/4-9/2)
**Rudi's Pet (IRE)** loomed up in the centre of the course and looked like taking a hand at the distance, but could not sustain the effort inside the last furlong. (13/2: 2/1-7/1)
**1404 Osomental**, blinkered for the first time, made a forward move at halfway but the effort petered out below the distance. (8/1: 5/1-10/1)

## 1654 SCHWEPPES H'CAP (0-70) (3-Y.O) (Class E)

8-00 (8-01) **1m 67y** £3,338.75 (£1,010.00: £492.50: £233.75) GOING minus 0.28 sec per fur (GF)

| | | | | SP | RR | SF |
|---|---|---|---|---|---|---|
| $1317^{3}$ | **Ret Frem (IRE) (58)** (MAJarvis) **3-8-12** LDettori(4) (chsd ldr: led wl over 1f out: r.o wl) | — | **1** | $8/1^{3}$ | 68 | 34 |
| $1319^{12}$ | **Formidable Partner (65)** (RWArmstrong) **3-9-5** JReid(10) (a.p: wnt 2nd over 1f out: no imp) | 2 | **2** | $8/1^{3}$ | 71 | 37 |
| $1447^{5}$ | **Sound Check (57)** (BJMeehan) **3-8-11b**[1] BDoyle(19) (a.p: rdn 2f out: r.o one pce) | 1¾ | **3** | 10/1 | 60 | 26 |
| $1594^{9}$ | **Shouldbegrey (47)** (WRMuir) **3-8-1** DRMcCabe(5) (hdwy fnl 3f: nrst fin) | 1 | **4** | 33/1 | 48 | 14 |
| $1466^{9}$ | **Charlton Imp (USA) (61)** (RJHodges) **3-8-12**(3) SDrowne(15) (a.p: r.o one pce fnl 2f) | nk | **5** | 33/1 | 61 | 27 |
| $1119^{5}$ | **Mystic Dawn (60)** (SDow) **3-9-0** PaulEddery(6) (led tl wknd wl over 1f out) | 1½ | **6** | $15/2^{2}$ | 57 | 23 |
| $1485^{5}$ | **Superior Force (60)** (MissBSanders) **3-9-0** SSanders(2) (lw: chsd ldrs: eased whn btn over 1f out: sddle slipped) | ½ | **7** | 12/1 | 56 | 22 |
| $1174^{7}$ | **Giddy (63)** (DMorley) **3-9-3** RCochrane(17) (a mid div: hrd rdn over 1f out: one pce) | s.h | **8** | 11/1 | 59 | 25 |
| 1594* | **Sistar Act (64)** (MRChannon) **3-9-4** 6x RHughes(13) (hdwy 4f out: wknd fnl f) | nk | **9** | $6/1^{1}$ | 60 | 26 |

1152[3] **Ivory's Grab Hire (53)** (KTIvory) **3-8-2b**(5) MartinDwyer(20) (prom over 4f) ........1 **10** 25/1 47 13
**Mono Lady (IRE) (55)** (DHaydnJones) **3-8-9** AMackay(11) (nvr nr to chal) ........1¾ **11** 33/1 45 11
701[6] **Catherine's Choice (67)** (JDBethell) **3-9-7** DHarrison(12) (b.hind: nvr nr ldrs) ........s.h **12** 12/1 57 23
1416[18] **Prince Zizim (58)** (CADwyer) **3-8-9**(3) NVarley(21) (lw: prom over 4f) ........½ **13** 33/1 47 13
1451[6] **Kinnescash (IRE) (60)** (MSSaunders) **3-9-0** RPrice(9) (b: nvr on terms) ........1½ **14** 33/1 47 13
**Mac Oates (65)** (DWPArbuthnot) **3-9-5** SWhitworth(16) (a bhd) ........hd **15** 33/1 51 17
**Seven Crowns (USA) (65)** (RHannon) **3-9-5** PatEddery(7) (a bhd) ........1¼ **16** 12/1 49 15
1172[12] **Sheilana (IRE) (65)** (TGMills) **3-8-12**(7) JCornally(14) (a bhd) ........hd **17** 33/1 49 15
1185[7] **Mr Speaker (IRE) (64)** (CFWall) **3-9-4** GDuffield(1) (lw: a bhd) ........6 **18** 33/1 36 2
978[8] **Welcome Royale (IRE) (64)** (MHTompkins) **3-9-4** PRobinson(3) (lw: a bhd) ........2½ **19** 14/1 31 —
761[2] **Efficacious (IRE) (48)** (CJBenstead) **3-8-2** AMcGlone(18) (lw: b.off hind: snatched up after 2f: a bhd) ........s.h **20** 12/1 15 —
1416[5] **Straight Thinking (USA) (59)** (PFICole) **3-8-13** TQuinn(8) (lw: chsd ldrs: wkng whn hmpd over 2f out: eased whn btn) ........6 **21** 6/1[1] 15 —
(SP 144.8%) **21 Rn**

**1m 46.3** (4.10) CSF £70.52 CT £613.89 TOTE £11.20: £1.90 £2.20 £2.50 £10.60 (£58.90) Trio £372.60 OWNER Mrs Anita Green (NEWMARKET) BRED Miss Audrey F. Thompson

**Straight Thinking (USA): his rider reported that the colt was hanging left-handed from three furlongs out.**

**1317 Ret Frem (IRE)** appeared well-suited by this drop in distance and was able to comfortably sit in second. Sent about his business from the two furlong marker, he quickly settled the issue. (8/1: tchd 12/1)

**Formidable Partner** ran easily his best race to date. Always close up, he took second place when the winner went on approaching the final furlong but could make no impression. (8/1)

**1447 Sound Check**, blinkered for the first time, was always chasing up the leaders and stayed on at one pace when hard driven form the two furlong marker. (10/1: 7/1-11/1)

**Shouldbegrey** was switched to the wide outside of the junction, and ran past several beaten horses in the final three furlongs to reach fourth place. (33/1)

**550 Charlton Imp (USA)**, always tucked in behind the leaders, kept on at one pace in the final quarter-mile. (33/1)

**1119 Mystic Dawn** set a strong pace but his chance had quickly gone when headed below the distance. (15/2: 6/1-10/1)

**1485 Superior Force**, always chasing the leading group, would have finished closer had the rider not been stricken with a slipping saddle in the closing stages. (12/1: 8/1-14/1)

**Seven Crowns (USA)** (12/1: op 7/1)

**761 Efficacious (IRE)** (12/1: 7/1-14/1)

## 1655 R. MEARS & CO. H'CAP (0-60) (3-Y.O+) (Class F)

8-30 (8-32) **1m 3f 135y** £2,997.00 (£842.00: £411.00) GOING minus 0.28 sec per fur (GF)

SP RR SF

1454[4] **Fabulous Mtoto (41)** (MSSaunders) **6-8-9** RPrice(8) (b: hdwy 4f out: led over 1f out: r.o wl) ........— **1** 16/1 56 32
1011[5] **Scenic Dancer (43)** (AHide) **8-8-8**(3) AWhelan(14) (rapid hdwy fnl 2f: fin fast) ........1¼ **2** 15/2[2] 56 32
1102[6] **Premier League (IRE) (59)** (JELong) **6-9-6**(7) TField(6) (led after 4f: sn clr: hdd over 1f out: edgd bdly lft: nt qckn) ........1½ **3** 12/1 70 46
1421[4] **Junior Ben (IRE) (53)** (PHowling) **4-9-7** RCochrane(11) (hdwy on ins over 2f out: nrst fin) ........3 **4** 8/1[3] 60 36
**Hamilton Silk (49)** (MCPipe) **4-9-3** PatEddery(15) (led 2f: styd prom: ev ch over 1f out: wknd fnl f) ........1¼ **5** 12/1 54 30
1472[5] **Rock The Barney (IRE) (51)** (PBurgoyne) **7-9-5** DRMcCabe(4) (nvr nrr) ........3½ **6** 4/1[1] 52 28
1440[13] **Errant (56)** (DJSCosgrove) **4-9-10** MRimmer(10) (b: hdwy over 2f out: nvr nrr) ........3 **7** 14/1 52 28
1498[15] **Galway Blade (59)** (APJarvis) **3-8-12** JTate(18) (nvr nrr) ........¾ **8** 16/1 54 15
1507[2] **Rivercare (IRE) (58)** (MJPolglase) **3-8-11** LDettori(9) (lw: prom tl wknd over 2f out) ........1¼ **9** 4/1[1] 52 13
**Star Fighter (46)** (MJHaynes) **4-9-0b** JReid(16) (lw: nvr nr to chal) ........hd **10** 20/1 40 16
1449[12] **Little Luke (IRE) (38)** (PButler) **5-8-3**(3) DaneO'Neill(1) (nvr bttr than mid div) ........1¾ **11** 33/1 29 5
1109[10] **Elpida (USA) (56)** (JPearce) **4-9-10** GBardwell(20) (a mid div) ........½ **12** 20/1 46 22
1173[10] **East Sheen (46)** (CJBenstead) **4-9-0** PRobinson(2) (bhd fnl 5f) ........5 **13** 25/1 30 6
546[9] **Full Quiver (41)** (MrsBarbaraWaring) **11-8-6v**(3) SDrowne(3) (b: b.hind: prom tl wknd over 2f out) ........2 **14** 20/1 22 —
1100[11] **Flame of Hope (60)** (JLDunlop) **3-8-13** TQuinn(12) (prom tl rdn & wknd over 2f out) ........s.h **15** 10/1 41 2
546[19] **Braydon Forest (57)** (CJDrewe) **4-9-11** SSanders(17) (a bhd) ........hd **16** 16/1 38 14
745[4] **Park Ridge (45)** (TGMills) **4-8-6**(7) DToole(19) (a bhd) ........hd **17** 25/1 25 1
1099[10] **Mystic Legend (IRE) (37)** (TJNaughton) **4-8-5** SWhitworth(13) (wl bhd fnl 5f: t.o) ........23 **18** 33/1 — —
**Prince of Spades (59)** (FJordan) **4-9-13** RHughes(5) (lw: wl bhd fnl 6f: t.o) ........1¼ **19** 25/1 6 —
**Prince de Berry (51)** (BJMeehan) **5-9-5** BDoyle(7) (bit bkwd: led after 2f tl after 4f: wknd 4f out: t.o) ........4 **20** 33/1 — —
(SP 146.3%) **20 Rn**

**2m 29.6** (5.60) CSF £139.29 CT £1,419.16 TOTE £19.90: £3.40 £2.00 £4.50 £1.90 (£42.00) Trio £525.10; £554.73 to 5/6/96 OWNER Mr N. R. Pike (WELLS)

WEIGHT FOR AGE 3yo-15lb

STEWARDS' ENQUIRY Price susp. 12-13/6/96 (excessive use of whip).

**1454 Fabulous Mtoto** came with a long run from the four furlong marker. He struck the front approaching the final furlong and, hard driven, stayed on well. (16/1)

**1011 Scenic Dancer** is a law unto himself and has to be allowed to run his own race. He did not elect to co-operate until the final quarter-mile but finished extremely strongly. (15/2)

**Premier League (IRE)** went to the front after two furlongs and was clear before the home turn. He and his rider began to tire approaching the final furlong and, when headed, veered left across the track. (12/1: 12/1-8/1)

**1421 Junior Ben (IRE)** came with a good run on the inside of the junction, but though staying on, lacked the pace to trouble the leading trio. (8/1)

**Hamilton Silk**, after making the early run, remained on the heels of the leaders. He still had every chance approaching the final furlong, but then began to weaken. (12/1: op 6/1)

**1472 Rock The Barney (IRE)** stayed on in the last two furlongs, without troubling the leaders. (4/1: op 6/1)

**920 Errant** (14/1: 10/1-16/1)

**1507 Rivercare (IRE)** hunted up the leading group until gradually weakening in the last two and a half furlongs. (4/1)

## 1656 STORACALL MEDIAN AUCTION MAIDEN STKS (3-Y.O) (Class E)

9-00 (9-02) **1m 2f 7y** £3,176.25 (£960.00: £467.50: £221.25) GOING minus 0.28 sec per fur (GF)

SP RR SF

1180[3] **Count Basie** (HRACecil) **3-9-0** PatEddery(1) (a.p: led over 2f out: rdn out) ........— **1** 11/8[1] 88 49

| | | | | | | |
|---|---|---|---|---|---|---|
| | **Kitty Kitty Cancan** (LadyHerries) **3-8-9** PaulEddery(2) (mid div tl stdy hdwy over 2f out: r.o: nt rch wnr)......1¼ | **2** | 9/1 | 81 | 42 |
| 269[4] | **Shenango (IRE)** (GWragg) **3-9-0** MHills(13) (lw: a.p: swtchd rt 3f out: ev ch over 1f out: nt qckn) ....................3 | **3** | 12/1 | 81 | 42 |
| 1465[2] | **Effectual** (JARToller) **3-9-0** SSanders(5) (a.p: ev ch 2f out: one pce) ....................3 | **4** | 12/1 | 76 | 37 |
| 1004[5] | **Smilin N Wishin (USA) (85)** (PWChapple-Hyam) **3-8-9** JReid(14) (lw: led tl over 2f out: one pce)..........1¾ | **5** | 5/1[2] | 69 | 30 |
| 445[8] | **Village King (IRE) (78)** (RHannon) **3-8-11**(3) DaneO'Neill(8) (prom tl lost pl after 5f: sme hdwy over 1f out: nt rch ldrs) ....................7 | **6** | 20/1 | 63 | 24 |
| | **Full Throttle** (MHTompkins) **3-9-0** NDay(6) (w'like: bit bkwd: nvr nr to chal) ....................¾ | **7** | 50/1 | 61 | 22 |
| 1104[8] | **Prestige Lass** (BSmart) **3-8-9** RCochrane(9) (lost pl 6f out: no ch after) ....................1½ | **8** | 14/1 | 54 | 15 |
| | **El Presidente** (GPEnright) **3-9-0** TQuinn(10) (str: scope: bit bkwd: prom tl outpcd over 3f out) ....................2½ | **9** | 50/1 | 55 | 16 |
| 982[14] | **Parrot's Hill (IRE)** (MHTompkins) **3-9-0** PRobinson(12) (s.s: nrst fin) ....................½ | **10** | 50/1 | 54 | 15 |
| 1123[2] | **Seirenes (80)** (PTWalwyn) **3-8-9** LDettori(11) (prom tl wknd over 2f out: eased whn btn) ....................1½ | **11** | 11/2[3] | 47 | 8 |
| 1305[10] | **Kairine (IRE)** (MRChannon) **3-8-9** JFEgan(4) (a bhd) ....................s.h | **12** | 50/1 | 47 | 8 |
| | **Cortes** (BGubby) **3-8-9** RPerham(15) (w'like: bkwd: wl bhd fnl 4f) ....................½ | **13** | 50/1 | 46 | 7 |
| | **Aqua Star (IRE)** (JLDunlop) **3-9-0** SWhitworth(3) (w'like: s.s: a bhd)....................3½ | **14** | 9/1 | 45 | 6 |
| | **Canadian Jive** (DWPArbuthnot) **3-8-9** BDoyle(7) (b: b.hind: unf: a bhd: t.o)....................27 | **15** | 50/1 | — | — |

(SP 132.7%) **15 Rn**

**2m 8.2** (3.30) CSF £15.39 TOTE £2.30: £1.60 £4.10 £3.00 (£19.80) Trio £110.30 OWNER Lucayan Stud (NEWMARKET) BRED Equideal Ltd

**1180 Count Basie** was always close up. He was already under pressure when taking the lead approaching the two furlong marker, and kept staying on without appearing to quicken. (11/8)

**Kitty Kitty Cancan** raced in midfield until improving under pressure over two furlongs from home. Gradually drifting out to the centre of the course, she ran on to take second place but could not reach the winner. (9/1: 5/1-10/1)

**Shenango (IRE)** was always close up. Switched to the inside three furlongs from home, he came with every chance at the distance but failed to quicken inside the last furlong. (12/1)

**1465 Effectual**, always on the heels of the leaders, looked the main danger when the winner went on over two furlongs from home, but could find no extra from the distance. (12/1: 10/1-16/1)

**1004 Smilin N Wishin (USA)** made the running until over two furlongs from home, but probably found the fast ground against her and was easily held for finishing speed. (5/1: 3/1-11/2)

**Village King (IRE)** lost his place at about halfway and seemed to have no chance, but did make some headway in the closing stages. (20/1)

**Prestige Lass** was pulling so hard that her rider had to give away ground to settle her approaching the straight. She ran rather better than her placing would suggest. (14/1: 20/1-33/1)

**1123 Seirenes** (11/2: 7/2-6/1)

**Aqua Star (IRE)** (9/1: 8/1-16/1)

T/Plpt: £239.10 (77.58 Tckts). T/Qdpt: £46.30 (32.69 Tckts). AK/Hn

## 1531-BRIGHTON (L-H) (Firm)
## Tuesday June 4th

WEATHER: fine WIND: almost nil

## 1657 MOULSECOOMB MEDIAN AUCTION MAIDEN STKS (3-Y.O) (Class E)

2-30 (2-30) **5f 213y** £3,070.20 (£915.60: £436.80: £197.40) Stalls: Low GOING minus 0.36 sec per fur (F)

| | | | SP | RR | SF |
|---|---|---|---|---|---|
| 1422[5] | **Stoney End (USA) (70)** (MRChannon) **3-9-0** RHughes(1) (a.p: led 3f out to 1f out: unable qckn: fin 2nd, 4l: awrdd r) ....................— | **1** | 7/1[3] | 75 | 26 |
| 1304[6] | **Blue Suede Hoofs (66)** (BJMeehan) **3-9-0b** MTebbutt(4) (a.p: rdn over 2f out: edgd lft over 1f out: wknd fnl f: fin 3rd, 3½l: plcd 2nd).................... | **2** | 12/1 | 66 | 17 |
| 1518[4] | **Stone Island** (CACyzer) **3-9-0** TQuinn(5) (lw: outpcd: nvr nr to chal: fin 4th, 1 1/4l: plcd 3rd) .................... | **3** | 9/1 | 63 | 14 |
| 758[7] | **Extra Hour (IRE) (65)** (WRMuir) **3-9-0** WJO'Connor(7) (outpcd: fin 5th, 1 1/4l: plcd 4th) .................... | **4** | 12/1 | 59 | 10 |
| 783[4] | **Solo Symphony (IRE) (65)** (PWChapple-Hyam) **3-8-4**(5) RHavlin(2) (lw: a.p: rdn over 2f out: 4th & btn whn hmpd over 1f out: fin 6th, s.h: plcd 5th).................... | **5** | 9/2[2] | 53 | 4 |
| | **Embroidered** (RMFlower) **3-8-9** DBiggs(6) (bhd fnl 2f) ....................12 | **7** | 50/1 | 21 | — |
| 672[5] | **Statoyork (82)** (BWHills) **3-9-0** AClark(3) (dwlt: stdd hdwy over 2f out: swtchd lft wl over 1f out: squeezed thro to ld 1f out: comf: plcd 1st: disq) .................... | **D** | 10/11[1] | 86 | 37 |

(SP 110.4%) **7 Rn**

**1m 9.2** (2.00) CSF £67.87 TOTE £10.50: £3.70 £3.00 (£25.50) OWNER Mr Martin Myers (UPPER LAMBOURN) BRED Bud Boschert's Stables Inc.

STEWARDS' ENQUIRY Clark susp.13-15 &17/6/96 (irresponsible riding).

**1422 Stoney End (USA)** went on at halfway but was firmly put in his place by Statoyork when passed a furlong from home. He was undoubtedly second best and can thank Clark's error of judgement for this victory. (7/1: 4/1-8/1)

**1304 Blue Suede Hoofs**, in the front ranks throughout, was battling hard for the advantage until tiring in the final furlong. (12/1: op 4/1)

**1518 Stone Island** failed to go the pace but did make a little late headway. This trip is too sharp for him. (9/1)

**Extra Hour (IRE)** (12/1: op 6/1)

**783 Solo Symphony (IRE)**, always close up, was being pushed along but was feeling the pinch in fourth when hampered by Statoyork approaching the final furlong. (9/2)

**672 Statoyork**, taken down early, looked really well and was certainly a cut above these in the race. Content to bide his time at the back of the field, he steadily crept into the action over a quarter of a mile from home and was switched to the rails well over a furlong out. He then found he had nowhere to go and his jockey had to squeeze him through a marginal gap approaching the final furlong, causing interference. Soon in front, he strolled away to win with plenty in hand. Although the best horse on the day, the Stewards were left with no choice but to disqualify him for his rider's error of judgment. (10/11: 4/6-Evens)

## 1658 PEACEHAVEN APPRENTICE H'CAP (0-60) (3-Y.O+) (Class F)

3-00 (3-01) **6f 209y** £2,405.00 (£680.00: £335.00) Stalls: Low GOING minus 0.36 sec per fur (F)

| | | | SP | RR | SF |
|---|---|---|---|---|---|
| 1337[4] | **Chairmans Choice (56)** (APJarvis) **6-9-2**(8) KHopkins(3) (led 6f out: edgd rt fnl f: r.o wl)....................— | **1** | 9/2[1] | 72 | 55 |
| 487[6] | **Fort Knox (IRE) (53)** (RMFlower) **5-9-7b** RSmith(1) (s.s: hdwy 2f out: chsd wnr over 1f out: ev ch whn hung lft ins fnl f: r.o)....................¾ | **2** | 13/2[3] | 67 | 50 |
| 1449[9] | **Asterix (39)** (JMBradley) **8-8-7v** CLowther(7) (s.s: rdn over 2f out: hdwy over 1f out: r.o)....................4 | **3** | 10/1 | 44 | 27 |
| 1042[8] | **The Butterwick Kid (47)** (RAFahey) **3-8-5b**[1] RFfrench(4) (a.p: hrd rdn & edgd lft over 1f out: wknd fnl f)......3½ | **4** | 13/2[3] | 44 | 17 |

| | | | | SP | RR | SF |
|---|---|---|---|---|---|---|
| 1536[10] | **No Sympathy (52)** (GLMoore) **3-8-5**(5) JCornally(8) (hdwy over 2f out: rdn over 1f out: one pce) | ¾ | **5** | 7/1 | 47 | 20 |
| 1411[22] | **Hang a Right (48)** (CADwyer) **9-8-8**(8) NicolaCole(9) (stdy hdwy over 1f out: nt clr run on ins ins fnl f: nt rcvr) | 1½ | **6** | 12/1 | 40 | 23 |
| 1348* | **Pointer (43)** (MrsPNDutfield) **4-8-11** ALakeman(5) (no hdwy fnl 2f) | 1½ | **7** | 5/1[2] | 31 | 14 |
| 1517[5] | **Forgotten Dancer (IRE) (45)** (RIngram) **5-8-13** RMullen(2) (lw: hdwy over 4f out: wknd over 1f out) | ¾ | **8** | 12/1 | 32 | 15 |
| 1356[10] | **Victory Commander (46)** (TJNaughton) **3-7-10**(8) RachaelMoody(10) (bhd fnl 2f) | 4 | **9** | 50/1 | 23 | — |
| 1170[9] | **Little Gent (IRE) (36)** (JELong) **5-8-4** TField(13) (bhd fnl 2f) | 2½ | **10** | 40/1 | 8 | — |
| 981[6] | **Courting Newmarket (42)** (NMBabbage) **8-8-5**(5) RCody-Boutcher(6) (lw: prom 4f) | ½ | **11** | 8/1 | 13 | — |
| 1416[11] | **Opening Range (37)** (NEBerry) **5-8-5b**[ow7] CScudder(11) (prom over 4f) | ½ | **12** | 50/1 | 6 | — |
| | **Oscilights Gift (30)** (PBurgoyne) **4-7-7**(5) JBosley(12) (b.off hind: led 1f: wknd 5f out: t.o) | 25 | **13** | 40/1 | — | — |

(SP 118.4%) **13 Rn**

**1m 21.7** (1.70) CSF £31.31 CT £262.39 TOTE £3.80: £1.30 £2.00 £2.80 (£11.80) Trio £31.10 OWNER Mrs D. B. Brazier (ASTON UPTHORPE) BRED D. V. Wakefield

WEIGHT FOR AGE 3yo-10lb

**1337 Chairmans Choice** was much happier on this faster surface. Soon at the head of affairs, he drifted to his right in the final furlong but proved just too strong for the runner-up. (9/2: 4/1-6/1)

**464* Fort Knox (IRE)** began to get going a quarter of a mile from home and threw down his challenge in the final furlong. He hung left though over to the far rails, doing his cause no good, and was unable to get the better of the winner. (13/2)

**Asterix** lost ground at the start but stayed on well in the final furlong and a half to take third. (10/1)

**824 The Butterwick Kid**, always close up, came under pressure and drifted left below the distance. He was soon done with. (13/2: op 4/1)

**1009* No Sympathy** began a forward move over two furlongs from home but was making no further impression from below the distance. (7/1)

**1012 Hang a Right** was given no assistance whatsoever form the saddle. The gelding nevertheless picked up ground steadily below the distance, but had nowhere to go along the inside rail inside the final furlong. (12/1)

**981 Courting Newmarket** (8/1: op 5/1)

## 1659 BRIGHTON MILE CHALLENGE TROPHY H'CAP (0-80) (3-Y.O+) (Class D)

3-30 (3-31) **7f 214y** £4,092.00 (£1,221.00: £583.00: £264.00) Stalls: Low GOING minus 0.36 sec per fur (F)

| | | | | SP | RR | SF |
|---|---|---|---|---|---|---|
| 1302[11] | **Helios (51)** (NJHWalker) **8-8-2** JQuinn(4) (a.p: led 3f out: rdn out) | — | **1** | 10/1 | 63 | 41 |
| 1435[3] | **Chinensis (IRE) (72)** (LMCumani) **3-8-12** OUrbina(1) (hld up: rdn & bmpd over 2f out: r.o ins fnl f) | 5 | **2** | 9/4[1] | 74 | 41 |
| 1497* | **Rebel County (IRE) (73)** (MCPipe) **3-8-13**[5x] TQuinn(3) (hld up: rdn & bdly hmpd over 2f out: r.o ins fnl f) | s.h | **3** | 5/2[2] | 75 | 42 |
| 1532[4] | **Perilous Plight (61)** (WRMuir) **5-8-12** Jean-PierreLopez(7) (lw: hdwy 3f out: chsd wnr fnl 2f: unable qckn) | s.h | **4** | 6/1[3] | 63 | 41 |
| 1528[8] | **Sooty Tern (69)** (JMBradley) **9-9-3**(3) SDrowne(2) (b.off fore: a.p: led over 4f out to 3f out: one pce fnl 2f) | 2½ | **5** | 10/1 | 66 | 44 |
| 1354[7] | **Captain's Day (73)** (TGMills) **4-9-10** MarkLynch(5) (lw: hld up: rdn over 2f out: sn wknd) | 8 | **6** | 10/1 | 54 | 32 |
| 1533[4] | **College Night (IRE) (51)** (CADwyer) **4-7-9**(7) IonaWands(6) (lw: led over 3f: wknd over 2f out) | 3 | **7** | 6/1[3] | 26 | 4 |

(SP 115.2%) **7 Rn**

**1m 33.5** (1.30) CSF £31.79 TOTE £16.50: £5.50 £1.90 (£29.60) OWNER Box 40 Racing (WANTAGE) BRED Sunley Stud

WEIGHT FOR AGE 3yo-11lb

**Helios** was sent into the lead three furlongs from home and, ridden along, asserted his authority from below the distance. (10/1)

**1435 Chinensis (IRE)** chased the leaders but was engaged in a bumping match with Rebel County over two furlongs from home. Tapped for toe, he was really struggling until getting his second wind inside the final furlong and snatching second place right on the line. (9/4: op 6/4)

**1497* Rebel County (IRE)**, claimed out of David Cosgrove's stable for £12,500 last week, was badly hampered at the back of the field over a quarter of a mile from home. Despite this, she ran on nicely inside the final furlong and only just failed in a blanket finish for second place. (5/2)

**1532 Perilous Plight** came through to take second place a quarter of a mile out, although unable to contain the winner, he held on to the runner-up berth until caught right on the line. (6/1)

**1048* Sooty Tern** went on just before halfway but, collared three furlongs from home, was only treading water in the final quarter-mile. (10/1: op 6/1)

## 1660 LEVY BOARD H'CAP (0-70) (3-Y.O+) (Class E)

4-00 (4-03) **1m 3f 196y** £3,315.90 (£991.20: £474.60: £216.30) Stalls: High GOING minus 0.36 sec per fur (F)

| | | | | SP | RR | SF |
|---|---|---|---|---|---|---|
| 871[12] | **Renown (64)** (LordHuntingdon) **4-9-11** DHarrison(4) (hld up: chsd ldr over 5f out: led 2f out: hrd rdn over 1f out: r.o wl) | — | **1** | 13/2 | 75 | 52 |
| 1618[3] | **General Mouktar (55)** (BJMeehan) **6-9-2** RHughes(5) (lw: hdwy over 4f out: chsd wnr over 1f out: ev ch ins fnl f: r.o) | nk | **2** | 5/2[1] | 66 | 43 |
| 1011* | **Prince Danzig (IRE) (66)** (DJGMurraySmith) **5-9-10**(3) DaneO'Neill(3) (lw: a.p: rdn 4f out: unable qckn fnl 2f) | 2½ | **3** | 7/2[2] | 73 | 50 |
| 635[6] | **Guest Alliance (IRE) (48)** (AMoore) **4-8-9** CandyMorris(2) (led over 1f: lost pl over 4f out: r.o one pce fnl 2f) | ¾ | **4** | 10/1 | 54 | 31 |
| 1347[9] | **Achilles Heel (37)** (CNAllen) **5-7-12b**[1] JQuinn(1) (led over 10f out to 2f out: wknd over 1f out) | 2½ | **5** | 5/1 | 40 | 17 |
| 1515[3] | **It'sthebusiness (60)** (SDow) **4-9-7v** TQuinn(6) (lw: hdwy over 3f out: wknd over 1f out) | 3½ | **6** | 9/2[3] | 58 | 35 |

(SP 108.1%) **6 Rn**

**2m 31.6** (4.00) CSF £21.03 TOTE £7.20: £3.50 £1.10 (£18.70) OWNER The Queen (WEST ILSLEY) BRED The Queen

**462* Renown** bounced back to form to gain his first victory on Turf. Moving into second place soon after halfway, he struck the front a quarter of a mile out and, responding to pressure, kept on well. (13/2: 4/1-7/1)

**1618 General Mouktar**, making a quick reappearance, moved up at the top of the hill. Taking second place approaching the final furlong, he had every chance but just failed to master the winner. (5/2)

**1011* Prince Danzig (IRE)**, never far away, failed to find the necessary turn of foot in the last two furlongs. (7/2)

**498 Guest Alliance (IRE)**, in front for a furlong or so early on, got outpaced at the top of the hill but did stay on from below the distance. (10/1: 6/1-12/1)

**Achilles Heel**, fitted with blinkers for the first time, was soon at the head of affairs but, collared a quarter of a mile out, soon had bellows to mend. (5/1)

**1515 It'sthebusiness** found this trip beyond him. Easing his way into the action over three furlongs from home, he ran out of stamina below the distance. (9/2: op 9/4)

## 1661 HOVE CLAIMING STKS (3-Y.O+) (Class F)

4-30 (4-31) **1m 1f 209y** £2,381.00 (£656.00: £311.00) Stalls: High GOING minus 0.36 sec per fur (F)

| | | | | SP | RR | SF |
|---|---|---|---|---|---|---|
| 1012* | **Roman Reel (USA) (65)** (GLMoore) **5-9-8** SWhitworth(7) (lw: hld up: led 2f out: clr over 1f out: comf) | — | **1** | 5/2[1] | 76 | 47 |

*262** **Multi Franchise (54)** (BGubby) **3-8-5** JQuinn(2) (hld up: rdn over 2f out: r.o one pce) ....7 **2** 8/1 61 19
1451[4] **Sunley Secure (60)** (MRChannon) **3-8-11** RHughes(5) (led 3f: led over 2f out: sn hdd: hrd rdn over 1f out: wknd fnl f) ....4 **3** 10/1 60 18
1301[5] **Two Socks (55)** (MMcCormack) **3-8-7** AClark(1) (lw: lost pl 8f out: rallied fnl f: r.o) ....½ **4** 11/1 56 14
1012[2] **Araboybill (58)** (RSimpson) **5-9-1b**(3) SDrowne(9) (led 6f out tl over 2f out: wknd over 1f out) ....1½ **5** 7/2[3] 51 22
853[5] **Curtelace (57)** (MrsMReveley) **6-9-12** DHarrison(8) (rdn & hdwy 3f out: wknd 2f out) ....7 **6** 3/1[2] 48 19
1099[7] **Considerable Charm (41)** (AMoore) **4-8-11** CandyMorris(6) (led 7f out to 6f out: wknd 4f out: t.o) ....dist **7** 33/1 — —
1451[3] **Wingnut (IRE) (40)** (MJHaynes) **3-7-9b**(5) MBaird(4) (lw: prom over 5f: t.o) ....6 **8** 16/1 — —
**Garlandhayes** (NMBabbage) **4-8-11** WRyan(3) (s.s: a t.o) ....dist **9** 25/1 — —
(SP 117.0%) **9 Rn**

**2m 1.6** (3.30) CSF £21.39 TOTE £2.60: £1.60 £3.60 £3.00 (£13.10) Trio £32.90 OWNER Mr K. Higson (EPSOM) BRED Dorothy Price, Jackie W. Ramos & Ken Hickson
WEIGHT FOR AGE 3yo-13lb

**1012* Roman Reel (USA)** put up a polished display. Sent on a quarter of a mile out, he soon forged clear for a comfortable success. (5/2)
**Multi Franchise**, off the track for nearly four months, chased the leaders. He struggled into second place inside the final furlong but had no hope of reeling in the winner. (8/1: 6/1-11/1)
**1451 Sunley Secure** disputed the lead from the outset. Collared a quarter of a mile from home, he was soon in trouble. (10/1)
**1301 Two Socks** lost his pitch after only a couple of furlongs. He did stay on in the last furlong but by then it was all over. (11/1: 7/1-12/1)
**1012 Araboybill** failed to take revenge on the winner on 4lb better terms for a short head beating. Disputing the lead for much of the race, he finally gave best below the distance. (7/2)
**853 Curtelace** failed to make the long journey down from the North pay off. Pushed along to take closer order three furlongs out, he had come to the end of his tether a quarter of a mile from home. (3/1)

## 1662 BEVENDEAN MAIDEN STKS (3-Y.O+) (Class D)
5-00 (5-00) **6f 209y** £3,720.00 (£1,110.00: £530.00: £240.00) Stalls: Low GOING minus 0.36 sec per fur (F)

SP RR SF
**El Opera (IRE)** (PFICole) **3-8-6** TQuinn(2) (a gng wl: hld up: led ins fnl f: comf) ....— **1** 11/4[2] 73+ 44
1142[3] **Hismagicmoment (USA) (85)** (PWChapple-Hyam) **3-8-6**(5) RHavlin(5) (lw: led tl hdd ins fnl f: unable qckn) .1½ **2** 10/11[1] 75 46
1009[2] **Velvet Jones (52)** (GFHCharles-Jones) **3-8-11** SWhitworth(4) (rdn over 2f out: hdwy over 1f out: one pce ins fnl f) ....1½ **3** 66/1 71 42
964[5] **Divine Quest** (HRACecil) **3-8-6** WRyan(3) (lw: hld up: rdn over 2f out: one pce) ....1¼ **4** 11/2 63 34
1319[5] **Classy Chief (78)** (RBoss) **3-8-11** RHughes(1) (w ldr over 5f: eased whn btn fnl f) ....8 **5** 4/1[3] 50 21
(SP 115.9%) **5 Rn**

**1m 21.2** (1.20) CSF £5.86 TOTE £3.70: £1.90 £1.10 (£3.30) OWNER Mr Faisal Salman (WHATCOMBE) BRED Islanmore Stud
**El Opera (IRE)**, looking big and well for this reappearance, was always travelling nicely. Held up, she was eased onto the quarters of the leader below the distance and shaken up to lead inside the final furlong. She won with plenty in hand and can go on from here. (11/4)
**1142 Hismagicmoment (USA)** attempted to make all the running. With the winner travelling supremely well below the distance, it was only a matter of time before he was passed. He should soon be winning. (10/11: 4/6-Evens)
**1009 Velvet Jones** picked up ground from the back of the field below the distance but, having got into third place, could then make no further impression. (66/1)
**964 Divine Quest** chased the leaders but was made to look pedestrian in the last two furlongs. (11/2: 3/1-6/1)
**1319 Classy Chief**, with the leader until well over a furlong from home, was eased down when all chance had gone. (4/1)

## 1663 KEMP TOWN H'CAP (0-70) (3-Y.O) (Class E)
5-30 (5-30) **5f 59y** £3,070.20 (£915.60: £436.80: £197.40) Stalls: Low GOING minus 0.36 sec per fur (F)

SP RR SF
1304[2] **Sharp Pearl (70)** (JWhite) **3-9-7b** RHughes(4) (lw: stdy hdwy 2f out: led ins fnl f: rdn out) ....— **1** 5/2[2] 81 38
1597[2] **Goretski (IRE) (70)** (NTinkler) **3-9-7** TQuinn(2) (led: rdn 2f out: hdd ins fnl f: unable qckn) ....2 **2** 11/10[1] 75 32
1527[9] **Mystique Smile (48)** (SCWilliams) **3-7-8**(5) MHenry(5) (b.hind: hld up: ev ch 2f out: hrd rdn over 1f out: one pce) ....1¼ **3** 4/1[3] 49 6
1181[14] **Volare (55)** (BJMeehan) **3-8-6** MTebbutt(1) (lost pl over 3f out: rallied 2f out: wknd over 1f out) ....5 **4** 33/1 41 —
1446[11] **Midnight Cookie (45)** (BAPearce) **3-7-5**(5) MartinDwyer(7) (nvr nr to chal) ....1¼ **5** 33/1 27 —
*142*[7] **Double Or Bust (45)** (AGNewcombe) **3-7-7**(3) NVarley(6) (swtg: prom 3f) ....1¼ **6** 66/1 23 —
861[11] **Beeny (55)** (APJarvis) **3-8-6v**[1] JTate(3) (spd 3f) ....6 **7** 12/1 15 —
(SP 111.3%) **7 Rn**

**62.1 secs** (2.10) CSF £5.35 TOTE £4.40: £1.10 £1.50 (£2.00) OWNER Mr Dennis Yardy (ASTON ROWANT) BRED D. MacRae
LONG HANDICAP Double Or Bust 7-7
**1304 Sharp Pearl**, held up travelling well, cruised into the action a quarter of a mile out and, shaken up between horses below the distance, came through to lead inside the final furlong. (5/2: 7/2-9/4)
**1597 Goretski (IRE)**, making the long journey down from Malton, attempted to make all the running. Collared inside the final furlong, he found the winner too strong. (11/10: 4/5-5/4)
**Mystique Smile**, with every chance a quarter of a mile from home, failed to find another gear from below the distance. (4/1)
**943 Volare**, outpaced over three furlong from home, tried to get back into it a quarter of a mile out, but was soon a spent force. (33/1)
**461 Beeny** (12/1: 8/1-16/1)

T/Plpt: £206.40 (68.76 Tckts). T/Qdpt: £11.20 (96.34 Tckts). AK

# 1417-PONTEFRACT (L-H) (Good to firm)
## Tuesday June 4th
WEATHER: sunny WIND: mod half bhd

## 1664 E.B.F. THORNE MAIDEN STKS (2-Y.O F) (Class D)
2-45 (2-52) **6f** £4,162.50 (£1,260.00: £615.00: £292.50) Stalls: Low GOING minus 0.38 sec per fur (F)

SP RR SF
**Lycility (IRE)** (CEBrittain) **2-8-11** BDoyle(9) (w'like: cmpt: bit bkwd: cl up: led ins fnl f: r.o) ....— **1** 16/1 68 19
**Native Rhythm (IRE)** (PWChapple-Hyam) **2-8-11** WCarson(2) (leggy: b.nr hind: led tl hdd ins fnl f: kpt on) ....2 **2** 4/5[1] 63 14
**Vagabond Chanteuse** (TJEtherington) **2-8-11** LCharnock(1) (rangy: bit bkwd: prom: outpcd over 2f out: kpt on ins fnl f) ....1½ **3** 50/1 59 10

| | | | | SP | RR | SF |
|---|---|---|---|---|---|---|
| 1413[4] | **Danehill Princess (IRE)** (RHollinshead) **2-8-11** LDettori(6) (chsd ldrs tl outpcd over 2f out: kpt on wl towards fin) | nk | **4** | 10/1 | 58 | 9 |
| | **Mystic Circle (IRE)** (JWWatts) **2-8-11** BThomson(7) (w'like: hld up: hdwy over 1f out: nvr nr to chal) | ½ | **5** | 16/1 | 57+ | 8 |
| | **Dundel (IRE)** (BWHills) **2-8-11** PatEddery(4) (str: scope: bit bkwd: stdd s: shkn up & hdwy ½-wy: chal over 1f out: wknd ins fnl f) | hd | **6** | 7/1[2] | 56 | 7 |
| | **Princess of Hearts** (WJHaggas) **2-8-11** MHills(10) (w'like: scope: dwlt: n.d) | 4 | **7** | 7/1[2] | 46 | — |
| | **Auction Hall** (MBell) **2-8-11** MFenton(3) (w'like: bit bkwd: s.s: a bhd) | 1½ | **8** | 9/1[3] | 42 | — |
| | **Dance Melody** (GROldroyd) **2-8-11** KFallon(8) (unf: bit bkwd: dwlt: a bhd) | 1¼ | **9** | 50/1 | 38 | — |
| 1413[5] | **April Jackson** (PTDalton) **2-8-11** SDWilliams(5) (bit bkwd: spd 4f: sn wknd) | 5 | **10** | 66/1 | 25 | — |

(SP 116.8%) **10 Rn**

**1m 17.8** (3.50) CSF £28.29 TOTE £35.30: £4.90 £1.20 £9.80 (£14.30) Trio £301.30; £101.87 to Yarmouth 5/6/96 OWNER Mr Saeed Manana (NEWMARKET) BRED Lodge Park Stud

**Lycility (IRE)** looked likely to be better for this but won well, and should find further success. (16/1)

**Native Rhythm (IRE)** tried her heart out to make all. When headed, she struggled on well, and should be all the better for the experience. (4/5: 11/18-6/4)

**Vagabond Chanteuse** was a bit of a handful beforehand but she ran well, and by the way she stayed on she will appreciate further yet. (50/1)

**1413 Danehill Princess (IRE)** got tapped for toe at a vital stage, and despite keeping on at the end, it was always too late. Her turn will come. (10/1: 7/1-12/1)

**Mystic Circle (IRE)**, a useful sort, moved well and had a quiet introduction. Better now looks likely. (16/1)

**Dundel (IRE)** needed this and, after blowing up, was given an easy time late on. (7/1: op 4/1)

**Princess of Hearts** (7/1: op 4/1)

**Auction Hall** (9/1: op 6/1)

## 1665 PONTEFRACT SERIES (ROUND 2) APPRENTICE (S) H'CAP (0-60) (3-Y.O+) (Class G)

3-15 (3-20) **1m 4y** £2,763.00 (£768.00: £369.00) Stalls: Low GOING minus 0.38 sec per fur (F)

| | | | | SP | RR | SF |
|---|---|---|---|---|---|---|
| 999[12] | **Percy Parrot (37)** (RMWhitaker) **4-8-2**(7)ow7 PFredericks(16) (mde all: clr over 1f out: styd on wl) | — | **1** | 33/1 | 53 | 24 |
| 1468[14] | **Absolute Ruler (IRE) (40)** (JLHarris) **5-8-12b** AEddery(8) (hdwy on ins 3f out: swtchd 2f out: r.o wl towards fin) | 5 | **2** | 12/1 | 46 | 24 |
| 995[15] | **Tame Deer (52)** (MCChapman) **4-9-5**(5) MSemple(17) (chsd wnr: one pce fnl 2f) | 1¾ | **3** | 16/1 | 55 | 33 |
| *1096*[10] | **Ballard Lady (IRE) (39)** (JSWainwright) **4-8-6**(5) PDoe(15) (lw: chsd ldrs: hmpd after 1f out: wknd 2f out) | 3½ | **4** | 16/1 | 35 | 13 |
| 1468[5] | **Mazilla (40)** (AStreeter) **4-8-12v** DSweeney(13) (lw: hmpd after 1f: sn chsng ldrs: one pce fnl 2f) | nk | **5** | 12/1 | 35 | 13 |
| 1502[6] | **Champagne N Dreams (51)** (DNicholls) **4-9-4**(5) JBramhill(2) (lw: trckd ldrs: effrt 3f out: hung rt & grad wknd) | 1½ | **6** | 9/4[1] | 43 | 21 |
| 1418[10] | **Glenvally (32)** (BWMurray) **5-7-13v**(5) JoanneWebster(11) (nvr rchd ldrs) | 2½ | **7** | 16/1 | 19 | — |
| 1156[4] | **Lawnswood Captain (IRE) (48)** (RHollinshead) **3-8-2**(7) SCrawford(9) (bhd: c wd st: sme late hdwy) | nk | **8** | 11/1 | 34 | 1 |
| 1047[8] | **Good so Fa (IRE) (32)** (CNAllen) **4-8-4h** JWilkinson(5) (nvr nr ldrs) | ½ | **9** | 20/1 | 17 | — |
| 1502[9] | **Mary Macblain (32)** (JLHarris) **7-8-1**(3) KSked(12) (n.d) | nk | **10** | 14/1 | 17 | — |
| 1311[2] | **Langtonian (33)** (JLEyre) **7-8-5b** AngelaGallimore(18) (b.nr hind: s.i.s: hdwy on outside ½-wy: wknd 2f out) | nk | **11** | 10/1[3] | 17 | — |
| 1311* | **Elite Racing (38)** (NTinkler) **4-8-10b** AimeeCook(14) (lw: hmpd after 1f: prom tl wknd fnl 2½f) | 1¾ | **12** | 10/1[3] | 19 | — |
| 1411[17] | **Hunza Story (32)** (NPLittmoden) **4-8-4v**[1] JoHunnam(6) (b.hind: s.i.s: n.d) | nk | **13** | 20/1 | 12 | — |
| 1500[13] | **Ruby Plus (30)** (GROldroyd) **5-7-11v**(5) JFowle(7) (n.d) | 1 | **14** | 33/1 | 8 | — |
| 1538[4] | **Brambles Way (48)** (WLBarker) **7-9-6v** JEdmunds(1) (hmpd after 1f: in tch 5f) | 1 | **15** | 8/1[2] | 24 | 2 |
| 522[11] | **Kai's Lady (IRE) (35)** (SWCampion) **3-7-5**(5) CCogan(4) (s.i.s: n.d) | 1 | **16** | 50/1 | 9 | — |
| 1196[11] | **Adaloaldo (USA) (46)** (JParkes) **4-8-13v**(5) SBuckley(19) (a bhd) | 3½ | **17** | 25/1 | 13 | — |
| 1092[8] | **Hats of to Hilda (36)** (MrsMReveley) **4-8-8** JDennis(3) (n.d) | 1 | **18** | 16/1 | 1 | — |
| 1421[13] | **Hong Kong Designer (44)** (MissJFCraze) **4-8-11**(5) PClarke(20) (swtg: prom 4f: sn bhd) | 3 | **19** | 50/1 | 3 | — |
| | **My Millie (58)** (RBoss) **3-9-5** GFaulkner(10) (bit bkwd: hmpd after 1f: in tch 4f: sn bhd) | 5 | **20** | 14/1 | 7 | — |

(SP 143.8%) **20 Rn**

**1m 45.6** (4.10) CSF £391.13 CT £6,045.22 TOTE £179.60: £26.00 £2.60 £6.60 £6.80 (£828.90) Trio £2,653.80; £2,616.46 to Yarmouth 5/6/96 OWNER Mrs Juliet Thompson (LEEDS) BRED J. Young

LONG HANDICAP Kai's Lady (IRE) 7-0

WEIGHT FOR AGE 3yo-11lb

No bid

OFFICIAL EXPLANATION **Ballard Lady: had been struck into on her off-fore leg.**

**Percy Parrot** went out in front leaving all the trouble behind and there were no challengers in the last couple of furlongs. (33/1)

**1311 Absolute Ruler (IRE)** took a long time to get going but he certainly finished well and, if he can be persuaded, he undoubtedly has the ability. (12/1: op 8/1)

**425 Tame Deer** was the only one to keep tabs on the winner but his stamina gave out approaching the final furlong. (16/1)

**586 Ballard Lady (IRE)** was involved in some bumping early on. He then ran on well, but was going nowhere in the last couple of furlongs. (16/1)

**1468 Mazilla** is a funny customer and was never doing enough. (12/1)

**1502 Champagne N Dreams** sat in behind the leaders going well but, once off the bit, her response was disappointing. (9/4)

**1156 Lawnswood Captain (IRE)** was again finishing quite well, suggesting that even stiffer tests are needed. (11/1)

## 1666 KALAMAZOO G.M.S. SECURITY TICKET H'CAP (0-90) (3-Y.O) (Class C)

3-45 (3-47) **1m 2f 6y** £6,160.00 (£1,840.00: £880.00: £400.00) Stalls: Low GOING minus 0.38 sec per fur (F)

| | | | | SP | RR | SF |
|---|---|---|---|---|---|---|
| 808[7] | **Gold Disc (USA) (85)** (BWHills) **3-9-6** PatEddery(3) (lw: hld up & bhd: shkn up over 2f out: qcknd to ld ins fnl f) | — | **1** | 12/1 | 92 | 47 |
| 1324* | **Fairywings (69)** (MrsJRRamsden) **3-8-4**ow1 KFallon(5) (hld up: shkn up over 3f out: gd hdwy 2f out: kpt on: nt pce of wnr) | 2 | **2** | 2/1[1] | 73 | 27 |
| 1496[5] | **Classic Colours (USA) (68)** (RHarris) **3-8-3** AMackay(1) (trckd ldrs: effrt over 2f out: ev ch over 1f out: kpt on one pce) | 1½ | **3** | 33/1 | 69 | 24 |
| 1035* | **Serendipity (FR) (86)** (JLDunlop) **3-9-7** WCarson(4) (lw: chsd ldrs: chal over 3f out: rdn & nt qckn fnl f) | 2½ | **4** | 11/4[2] | 83 | 38 |
| 1155* | **Caribbean Dancer (74)** (MRStoute) **3-8-9** LDettori(2) (led tl hdd & wknd ins fnl f) | ½ | **5** | 3/1[3] | 71 | 26 |
| 1324[3] | **Baileys First (IRE) (74)** (MJohnston) **3-8-9** JWeaver(6) (chsd ldrs tl outpcd 3f out: sn btn) | 1 | **6** | 12/1 | 69 | 24 |
| 1363[2] | **Russian Rascal (IRE) (69)** (TDEasterby) **3-8-4** LCharnock(8) (dwlt: hld up & a bhd) | 1½ | **7** | 12/1 | 62 | 17 |

| | Horse | Details | Dist | Pos | SP | RR | SF |
|---|---|---|---|---|---|---|---|
| 1323$^{5}$ | **Naissant (75)** | (CEBrittain) **3-8-10** BDoyle(7) (chsd ldrs tl wknd 4f out: virtually p.u) | dist | **8** | 33/1 | — | — |

(SP 114.0%) **8 Rn**

**2m 11.7** (3.40) CSF £34.65 CT £710.25 TOTE £12.40: £2.10 £1.40 £4.20 (£29.80) OWNER Mr K. Abdulla (LAMBOURN) BRED Juddmonte Farms

**Gold Disc (USA)** apparently likes to be ridden from behind, and produced a terrific burst to settle inside the final furlong. (12/1)
**1324* Fairywings**, excitable as she can be, nevertheless ran a sound race, but just found one too good. (2/1)
**1496 Classic Colours (USA)** has plenty of ability but he is his own worst enemy. Racing too freely, he must learn to settle. (33/1)
**1035* Serendipity (FR)** has plenty of ability but seem to like to have his own way, and that was never on here. (11/4)
**1155* Caribbean Dancer**, stepping up in trip, made it this time but had run herself out when caught entering the final furlong. (3/1)
**1324 Baileys First (IRE)** seems at her best when allowed to dictate and had her limitations exposed here in the final furlong. (12/1)

## 1667 FERRYBRIDGE FLYERS' MAIDEN STKS (3-Y.O+) (Class D)

4-15 (4-17) **6f** £3,631.25 (£1,100.00: £537.50: £256.25) Stalls: Low GOING minus 0.38 sec per fur (F)

| | Horse | Details | Dist | Pos | SP | RR | SF |
|---|---|---|---|---|---|---|---|
| 783$^{3}$ | **Dark Deed (USA) (80)** | (BWHills) **3-8-9** PatEddery(1) (chsd ldrs: rdn over 2f out: chal over 1f out: r.o to ld wl ins fnl f) | — | **1** | 7/1 | 84 | 40 |
| 1452$^{3}$ | **Duel At Dawn** | (JHMGosden) **3-9-0** LDettori(5) (b: b.hind: lw: led: qcknd over 1f out: hdd & no ex wl ins fnl f) | 1¼ | **2** | 5/4$^{1}$ | 86 | 42 |
| 1475$^{5}$ | **Merrily** | (MissSEHall) **3-8-9** KFallon(2) (hld up: stdy hdwy 2f out: nvr plcd to chal) | 5 | **3** | 20/1 | 67 | 23 |
| 1438$^{11}$ | **Bent Raiwand (USA)** | (BHanbury) **3-8-6**$^{(3)}$ JStack(8) (b.hind: hld up & bhd: stdy hdwy 2f out: nvr nr to chal) | ¾ | **4** | 33/1 | 65 | 21 |
| 1435$^{5}$ | **Detachment (USA) (90)** | (PWChapple-Hyam) **3-9-0** BThomson(11) (cl up tl outpcd fnl 2f) | s.h | **5** | 7/2$^{2}$ | 70 | 26 |
| 1350$^{4}$ | **Welsh Emblem (IRE)** | (GWragg) **3-9-0** MHills(13) (lw: in tch: no hdwy fnl 2f) | 4 | **6** | 6/1$^{3}$ | 60 | 16 |
| 840$^{10}$ | **Spandrel** | (HCandy) **4-9-3** CRutter(4) (s.i.s: bhd tl sme late hdwy) | 1 | **7** | 16/1 | 52 | 16 |
| | **Hamilton Gold** | (MGMeagher) **3-8-2**$^{(7)}$ RStudholme(9) (cl up 4f: wknd) | 2 | **8** | 250/1 | 47 | 3 |
| | **Taragona** | (RHollinshead) **3-8-5**$^{(5)ow1}$ DGriffiths(7) (unf: bit bkwd: nvr trbld ldrs) | hd | **9** | 33/1 | 47 | 2 |
| 1429$^{9}$ | **Arch Enemy (IRE)** | (MRChannon) **3-9-0** KDarley(14) (prom to ½-wy) | 1½ | **10** | 33/1 | 47 | 3 |
| | **Gretna Green (USA)** | (LadyHerries) **3-8-9** DeclanO'Shea(6) (angular: bit bkwd: s.i.s: a rr div) | 3½ | **11** | 12/1 | 33 | — |
| 1350$^{10}$ | **Blue Jumbo (IRE)** | (WJMusson) **3-8-9** RPrice(12) (outpcd fr ½-wy) | 1¼ | **12** | 50/1 | 30 | — |
| | **Datum (USA)** | (MBell) **3-9-0** MFenton(3) (str: cmpt: bkwd: dwlt: a bhd) | hd | **13** | 14/1 | 34 | — |
| 1452$^{10}$ | **Nullahs Pet** | (AStreeter) **4-9-3** SDWilliams(10) (bhd fr ½-wy) | 11 | **14** | 100/1 | — | — |

(SP 130.6%) **14 Rn**

**1m 16.0** (1.70) CSF £16.56 TOTE £7.40: £1.90 £1.40 £3.30 (£6.00) Trio £26.60 OWNER Mr K. Abdulla (LAMBOURN) BRED Juddmonte Farms
WEIGHT FOR AGE 3yo-8lb

**783 Dark Deed (USA)** needed some determined assistance from the saddle to get going from halfway, and in the end she did it well. (7/1)
**1452 Duel At Dawn**, a sturdy colt, attempted to make all, but was just tapped for toe late on and was certainly not over-punished. (5/4: 6/4-Evens)
**1475 Merrily**, who got a bit warm beforehand, again impressed with a good action on the way down and was not given a hard time in the race. He should be better for this. (20/1)
**Bent Raiwand (USA)** showed plenty of promise this time and is one to keep an eye on now he is getting the hang of things. (33/1)
**1435 Detachment (USA)**, wearing a tongue strap, had his chances but looked very one-paced when the pressure was on in the last couple of furlongs. (7/2)
**1350 Welsh Emblem (IRE)**, dropped back in trip and on faster ground, found things happening far too quickly. (6/1)
**Spandrel** showed plenty here and is one to watch. (16/1)

## 1668 ROPERGATE MAIDEN STKS (I) (3-Y.O) (Class D)

4-45 (4-50) **1m 2f 6y** £3,192.50 (£965.00: £470.00: £222.50) Stalls: Low GOING minus 0.38 sec per fur (F)

| | Horse | Details | Dist | Pos | SP | RR | SF |
|---|---|---|---|---|---|---|---|
| 985$^{6}$ | **Ambassador (USA) (85)** | (BWHills) **3-9-0** PatEddery(9) (lw: trckd ldrs: led 5f out: rdn & r.o wl fnl f) | — | **1** | 5/2$^{1}$ | 86 | 46 |
| 671$^{8}$ | **Lakeline Legend (IRE)** | (MAJarvis) **3-9-0** EmmaO'Gorman(4) (s.i.s: hdwy ½-wy: chal over 2f out: nt qckn ins fnl f) | 1¼ | **2** | 4/1$^{2}$ | 84 | 44 |
| | **Fitzwilliam (USA)** | (IABalding) **3-9-0** LDettori(8) (rangy: cl up: led 7f out: sn hdd: ev ch tl outpcd fnl 2½f) | 3½ | **3** | 13/2 | 78 | 38 |
| | **Upper Gallery (IRE)** | (PWChapple-Hyam) **3-9-0** BThomson(3) (w'like: chsd ldrs: rdn over 3f out: one pce) | 6 | **4** | 5/1$^{3}$ | 69 | 29 |
| | **Flamanda** | (CEBrittain) **3-8-9** BDoyle(5) (lt-f: unf: led tl hdd 7f out: wknd fnl 3f) | 1 | **5** | 14/1 | 62 | 22 |
| 687$^{10}$ | **Elashath (USA)** | (JHMGosden) **3-9-0** WCarson(7) (in tch: outpcd over 3f out: n.d after) | 14 | **6** | 25/1 | 45 | 5 |
| 1305$^{7}$ | **Ghusn** | (TThomsonJones) **3-9-0** RHills(10) (in tch: rdn over 3f out: sn btn) | 3 | **7** | 25/1 | 40 | — |
| 962$^{7}$ | **Northern Judge (75)** | (BHanbury) **3-8-11**$^{(3)}$ JStack(11) (hld up & bhd: effrt over 3f out: n.d) | 1 | **8** | 14/1 | 39 | — |
| | **Sing And Dance** | (EWeymes) **3-8-9** KFallon(2) (bit bkwd: bhd: hmpd 4f out: n.d) | 13 | **9** | 66/1 | 13 | — |
| 820$^{10}$ | **Charnwood Jack (USA)** | (RHarris) **3-9-0** AMackay(1) (in tch: rdn 4f out: sn btn) | 3 | **10** | 15/2 | 13 | — |
| | **Mr Gold (IRE)** | (RonaldThompson) **3-9-0** TWilliams(12) (leggy: unf: dwlt: plld hrd & hdwy to ld 6½f out: hung rt & hdd 5f out: sn bhd: t.o: bit slipped) | dist | **11** | 100/1 | — | — |

(SP 113.8%) **11 Rn**

**2m 11.2** (2.90) CSF £11.88 TOTE £3.30: £1.50 £1.70 £2.10 (£7.50) Trio £11.30 OWNER Maktoum Al Maktoum (LAMBOURN) BRED John R. Gaines

**OFFICIAL EXPLANATION Mr Gold (IRE): on leaving the stalls the bit slipped through his mouth.**
**985 Ambassador (USA)** left nothing to chance here and, made plenty of use of, stayed on really well and was nicely on top at the end. (5/2)
**Lakeline Legend (IRE)** is certainly improving but, after trying hard, was well held. (4/1)
**Fitzwilliam (USA)** ran well until lack of experience told in the home straight. (13/2)
**Upper Gallery (IRE)** had a nice introduction here and looks one likely to improve a fair bit. (5/1)
**Flamanda** put in a reasonable first effort but was tapped for speed in the last three furlongs. (14/1)
**Elashath (USA)** is gradually learning and was not given a hard time here. (25/1)

## 1669 IRONBRIDGE H'CAP (0-80) (3-Y.O) (Class D)

5-15 (5-20) **1m 4f 8y** £4,012.50 (£1,200.00: £575.00: £262.50) Stalls: Low GOING minus 0.38 sec per fur (F)

| | Horse | Details | Dist | Pos | SP | RR | SF |
|---|---|---|---|---|---|---|---|
| 1147$^{6}$ | **Orinoco River (USA) (79)** | (PWChapple-Hyam) **3-9-7v** KDarley(6) (a.p: led 2½f out: r.o) | — | **1** | 10/1 | 92 | 64 |
| 738$^{3}$ | **Ceilidh Star (IRE) (67)** | (BWHills) **3-8-9** PatEddery(5) (in tch: hdwy 3f out: styd on fnl f: nvr able to chal) | 3 | **2** | 9/2$^{2}$ | 76 | 48 |
| 1145$^{2}$ | **Ground Game (78)** | (DRLoder) **3-9-6** LDettori(4) (b.hind: trckd ldrs: effrt over 3f out: one pce fnl 2f) | 3 | **3** | 11/8$^{1}$ | 83 | 55 |

| | | | | SP | RR | SF |
|---|---|---|---|---|---|---|
| 1100[15] | **The Boozing Brief (USA) (65)** (MAJarvis) **3-8-7** PRobinson(9) (swtg: rr div: pushed along & hdwy over 3f out: styd on wl towards fin) | hd | **4** | 16/1 | 70 | 42 |
| 1175[7] | **Nosey Native (76)** (JPearce) **3-9-4** GBardwell(11) (sn in tch: effrt & ev ch 3f out: wknd appr fnl f) | 3½ | **5** | 11/1 | 76 | 48 |
| 1200* | **Exactly (IRE) (73)** (JLEyre) **3-9-1** TWilliams(8) (cl up: led 5f out tl over 2f out: sn wknd) | 1½ | **6** | 10/1 | 71 | 43 |
| 1309[10] | **Northern Motto (55)** (MrsJRRamsden) **3-7-11** LCharnock(3) (plld hrd: hld up & bhd: nvr trbld ldrs) | 2½ | **7** | 14/1 | 50 | 22 |
| 1477[9] | **Falcon's Flame (USA) (54)** (MrsJRRamsden) **3-7-10** NKennedy(2) (plld hrd: hld up & bhd: nvr nr to chal) | 2½ | **8** | 20/1 | 46 | 18 |
| | **Skram (65)** (RDickin) **3-8-7** DaleGibson(7) (sn outpcd & wl bhd) | 21 | **9** | 50/1 | 29 | 1 |
| 1089[17] | **Recall To Mind (62)** (TDEasterby) **3-8-4** KFallon(10) (in tch tl outpcd fnl 4f) | 4 | **10** | 50/1 | 20 | — |
| 1310* | **Lord of The Manor (76)** (MJohnston) **3-9-4** JWeaver(1) (led tl hdd 5f out: wknd qckly) | 12 | **11** | 7/1[3] | 18 | — |

(SP 120.5%) **11 Rn**

**2m 36.0** (1.70) CSF £52.32 CT £92.94 TOTE £10.10: £2.50 £2.00 £1.20 (£20.80) Trio £20.70 OWNER Mr R. E. Sangster (MARLBOROUGH) BRED Poole Investments

**1019* Orinoco River (USA)** is a funny customer but has plenty of ability and, under a fine ride, did the business this time. (10/1)
**738 Ceilidh Star (IRE)** was putting in all her best in the closing stages suggesting that further should improve her. (9/2)
**1145 Ground Game** has a superb action but, when it comes down to it, is basically one-paced. (11/8: 2/1-5/4)
**The Boozing Brief (USA)** took a long time to get going and when he did it was always too late. (16/1)
**731 Nosey Native** had his chances but was found wanting in the last couple of furlongs. (11/1)
**1200* Exactly (IRE)** was always struggling to gain the initiative this time and, once passed over two furlongs out, soon gave up altogether. (10/1)
**752 Northern Motto** showed something without getting into it. (14/1)

## 1670 ROPERGATE MAIDEN STKS (II) (3-Y.O) (Class D)

5-45 (5-50) **1m 2f 6y** £3,176.25 (£960.00: £467.50: £221.25) Stalls: Low GOING minus 0.38 sec per fur (F)

| | | | | SP | RR | SF |
|---|---|---|---|---|---|---|
| 1180[8] | **Skillington (USA) (90)** (IABalding) **3-9-0** MHills(4) (mde all: qcknd 3f out: styd on wl) | — | **1** | 7/2[3] | 96 | 56 |
| 1002[9] | **Three Hills (84)** (BWHills) **3-9-0** PatEddery(6) (lw: trckd ldrs: effrt over 3f out: rdn & nt pce of wnr fnl 2f) | 5 | **2** | 13/8[1] | 88 | 48 |
| 1305[3] | **Random Kindness** (PWHarris) **3-9-0** GHind(10) (prom: outpcd over 3f out: styd on fnl 2f) | 7 | **3** | 16/1 | 77 | 37 |
| 1189[5] | **Amusing Aside (IRE)** (JWWatts) **3-8-9** JCarroll(3) (b: b.hind: in tch: effrt 4f out: kpt on fnl 2f) | 2 | **4** | 20/1 | 69 | 29 |
| 1160[4] | **Tabl (IRE)** (HThomsonJones) **3-8-9** RHills(5) (chsd ldrs tl wknd fnl 3f) | 6 | **5** | 25/1 | 59 | 19 |
| | **Secret Gift** (BHanbury) **3-8-9** PBloomfield(8) (tall: unf: sn bhd: sme hdwy over 2f out: nvr nr ldrs) | 6 | **6** | 16/1 | 50 | 10 |
| | **Mallooh** (JHMGosden) **3-9-0** LDettori(7) (w'like: leggy: b.hind: s.i.s: hdwy & prom ½-wy: outpcd fnl 2½f) | 2½ | **7** | 3/1[2] | 51 | 11 |
| 1508[10] | **Gold Lance (USA)** (MRStoute) **3-9-0** KFallon(11) (bhd: pushed along 4f out: n.d) | 3 | **8** | 16/1 | 46 | 6 |
| | **Namoodaj** (ACStewart) **3-8-9**(5) MHumphries(9) (w'like: bkwd: s.i.s: a bhd) | nk | **9** | 25/1 | 45 | 5 |
| 1435[12] | **Nexsis Star** (MrsSJSmith) **3-8-9**(5) PRoberts(2) (prom tl wknd 4f out) | 2½ | **10** | 200/1 | 41 | 1 |
| | ***Sufuf*** (DMorley) **3-8-9** WCarson(1) (Withdrawn not under Starter's orders: veterinary advice) | | **W** | 16/1 | — | — |

(SP 121.8%) **10 Rn**

**2m 9.9** (1.60) CSF £9.12 TOTE £4.30: £1.40 £1.40 £4.50 (£3.60) Trio £15.70 OWNER Mr George Strawbridge (KINGSCLERE) BRED George Strawbridge Jr

**1180 Skillington (USA)** won in tremendous style, in a much faster time than the other two races at this trip. (7/2)
**1002 Three Hills** had his chances but, when the winner quickened, had no answer. (13/8)
**1305 Random Kindness** is gradually improving and would seem likely to appreciate further. (16/1)
**1189 Amusing Aside (IRE)**, having her third run here, was staying on and looks likely to do better in handicaps. (20/1)
**1160 Tabl (IRE)**, stepping up in trip, failed to get home. (25/1)
**Secret Gift** showed something and looks likely to improve with experience. (16/1)
**Gold Lance (USA)** had an educational run out the back. (16/1)

T/Jkpt: Not won; £7,721.60 to Warwick 5/6/96. T/Plpt: £189.90 (109.42 Tckts). T/Qdpt: £6.20 (234.97 Tckts). AA

# 1320-BEVERLEY (R-H) (Good to firm)
## Wednesday June 5th

WEATHER: fine

## 1671 COTTINGHAM MAIDEN LIMITED STKS (0-70) (3-Y.O) (Class E)

6-30 (6-30) **1m 100y** £2,945.25 (£882.00: £423.50: £194.25) Stalls: Low GOING minus 0.64 sec per fur (F)

| | | | | SP | RR | SF |
|---|---|---|---|---|---|---|
| 1000[2] | **Alambar (IRE) (70)** (PTWalwyn) **3-9-0** WCarson(5) (mde most: kpt on well fnl 2f) | — | **1** | 6/4[1] | 76 | 26 |
| 1061[3] | **Lady Bankes (IRE) (68)** (WGMTurner) **3-8-11** RPerham(4) (a chsng ldrs: hdwy over 2f out: no ex fnl f) | 3 | **2** | 7/1 | 67 | 17 |
| 1361[8] | **Tissue of Lies (USA) (70)** (MJohnston) **3-9-0** JWeaver(1) (chsd ldrs: outpcd over 2f out: kpt on fnl f) | ½ | **3** | 5/1[3] | 69 | 19 |
| 1101[8] | **Amber Fort (67)** (PFICole) **3-9-0** TQuinn(3) (cl up: effrt over 2f out: nt r.o) | 1½ | **4** | 7/2[2] | 67 | 17 |
| *241*[3] | **Anak-Ku (69)** (MissGayKelleway) **3-9-0** KFallon(7) (sn outpcd & bhd: sme late hdwy) | 3 | **5** | 5/1[3] | 61 | 11 |
| 1429[3] | **Matam (67)** (MWEasterby) **3-8-6**(5) GParkin(2) (hld up: hdwy over 2f out: no imp) | 3½ | **6** | 12/1 | 51 | 1 |
| *1490*[15] | **Lagan (65)** (PSFelgate) **3-8-11**(3) DWright(6) (nvr wnt pce) | 23 | **7** | 25/1 | 11 | — |

(SP 119.6%) **7 Rn**

**1m 46.2** (2.20) CSF £12.43 TOTE £2.50: £1.50 £3.20 (£6.20) OWNER Mr Hamdan Al Maktoum (LAMBOURN) BRED Mrs J. Martin-Smith

**1000 Alambar (IRE)**, a free-runner, settled better out in front and responded to pressure in the last two furlongs to score decisively. (6/4)
**1061 Lady Bankes (IRE)** was happy to sit in behind the leaders this time but, after looking dangerous approaching the final furlong, the stiff finish found her out. (7/1)
**Tissue of Lies (USA)** seems to have connections in a quandary about what trip he needs, and this would certainly seem to be too short. (5/1)
**887 Amber Fort** looked really well and had his chances, but failed to respond when pressure was applied. (7/2)
**241 Anak-Ku**, having his first run on grass, failed to go the early pace but was picking up ground at the end to suggest that further might help. (5/1)
**1429 Matam** probably just found this trip too far. (12/1)

## 1672 DERBY WEEK H'CAP (0-80) (4-Y.O+) (Class D)

7-00 (7-01) **1m 100y** £3,691.00 (£1,108.00: £534.00: £247.00) Stalls: Low GOING minus 0.64 sec per fur (F)

| | | | | SP | RR | SF |
|---|---|---|---|---|---|---|
| 1505[2] | **Equerry (75)** (MJohnston) **5-9-12** JWeaver(5) (led 1f: cl up: led 2f out: r.o u.p) | — | **1** | 15/8[1] | 85 | 45 |
| 1625[16] | **Nordic Breeze (IRE) (71)** (ABailey) **4-9-8** KDarley(3) (trckd ldrs: effrt over 2f out: r.o: nt pce to chal) | 1¼ | **2** | 6/1 | 79 | 39 |
| 1337[2] | **Coureur (70)** (MDHammond) **7-9-7** JQuinn(2) (hld up: effrt 3f out: ch over 1f out: nt qckn) | 1 | **3** | 2/1[2] | 76 | 36 |
| 1502[11] | **Euro Sceptic (IRE) (49)** (TDEasterby) **4-8-0b** WCarson(1) (led after 1f out to 2f out: one pce) | ½ | **4** | 7/2[3] | 54 | 14 |

1088[6] **Thaleros (54)** (GMMoore) **6-8-5** DeanMcKeown(4) (hld up: outpcd over 3f out: rdn & no imp after).................4 **5** 9/1 51 11
(SP 114.6%) **5 Rn**

**1m 45.3** (1.30) CSF £12.03 TOTE £3.00: £1.60 £3.00 (£11.80) OWNER Mr J. R. Good (MIDDLEHAM) BRED J. R. and Mrs P. Good
**1505 Equerry**, happier over this trip, was not going to be denied once he struck the front early in the straight. (15/8: op 3/1)
**1072 Nordic Breeze (IRE)** has his chances, but was short of a real turn of foot to take it on this occasion. (6/1)
**1337 Coureur**, off a mark 9lb above which he has previously won, just found this too much. (2/1)
**1037* Euro Sceptic (IRE)** is a track specialist but, after making it, was well tapped for toe in the final furlong and a half. (7/2)
**1088 Thaleros**, with no real pace early on, found this trip far too sharp when the tempo increased dramatically in the home straight. (9/1)

## 1673 HILARY NEEDLER TROPHY CONDITIONS STKS (2-Y.O F) (Class B)

7-30 (7-30) **5f** £9,820.00 (£3,420.00: £1,660.00: £700.00) GOING minus 0.64 sec per fur (F)

| | | | | SP | RR | SF |
|---|---|---|---|---|---|---|
| 1105* | **Dance Parade (USA)** (PFICole) **2-8-12** TQuinn(4) (mde all: pushed along & r.o wl fnl 2f) | — | **1** | 2/5[1] | 74+ | 18 |
| 1115[5] | **Impetuous Air** (EWeymes) **2-8-8** KDarley(1) (chsd ldrs: rdn 2f out: kpt on: nvr able to chal) | 2½ | **2** | 9/2[2] | 62 | 6 |
| 1607[3] | **Skyers Flyer (IRE)** (RonaldThompson) **2-8-8** NConnorton(2) (hld up: hdwy ½-wy: rdn & no ex appr fnl f) | ¾ | **3** | 33/1 | 60? | 4 |
| 1318* | **Petite Danseuse** (SDow) **2-9-0** BThomson(3) (w wnr tl rdn & btn over 1f out) | 2½ | **4** | 5/1[3] | 58 | 2 |
| | | | | (SP 109.2%) | **4 Rn** | |

**63.2 secs** (1.70) CSF £2.59 TOTE £1.30 (£1.90) OWNER H R H Prince Fahd Salman (WHATCOMBE) BRED Newgate Stud Farm Inc
**1105* Dance Parade (USA)**, who looks likely to appreciate further, got better as the race went on, but did need to be vigorously pushed along to put in beyond doubt. (2/5)
**Impetuous Air** looked the part, but took time to get going, and should improve over further. (9/2)
**1607 Skyers Flyer (IRE)** ran by far her best race to date and, if she ever learns to settle, she could prove this was no fluke. (33/1)
**1318* Petite Danseuse** got pretty warm beforehand and, after taking the winner on, was a spent force approaching the last furlong. (5/1)

## 1674 COMPUTER SPORTS SERVICES H'CAP (0-70) (3-Y.O+) (Class E)

8-00 (8-00) **7f 100y** £3,860.00 (£1,160.00: £560.00: £260.00) Stalls: Low GOING minus 0.64 sec per fur (F)

| | | | | SP | RR | SF |
|---|---|---|---|---|---|---|
| 1633* | **Three Arch Bridge (63)** (MJohnston) **4-9-13b** 6x JWeaver(5) (bhd: hdwy over 2f out: r.o to ld cl home) | — | **1** | 7/1 | 74 | 58 |
| 1502[10] | **Grey Kingdom (34)** (MBrittain) **5-7-12** DaleGibson(10) (disp ld tl ld over 1f out: nt qckn towards fin) | ½ | **2** | 33/1 | 44 | 28 |
| *1094** | **Awesome Venture (50)** (MCChapman) **6-9-0** KFallon(1) (hdwy 3f out: styd on wl fnl f: nrst fin) | ¾ | **3** | 7/1 | 58 | 42 |
| 1037[13] | **Murphy's Gold (IRE) (48)** (RAFahey) **5-8-12** ACulhane(14) (mid div: hdwy 2f out: swtchd & ch appr fnl f: kpt on) | ½ | **4** | 6/1[2] | 55 | 39 |
| 1313* | **Murray's Mazda (IRE) (46)** (JLEyre) **7-8-7**(3) DWright(8) (disp ld tl hdd over 1f out: one pce) | ½ | **5** | 8/1 | 52 | 36 |
| *1601[3]* | **My Gallery (IRE) (55)** (ABailey) **5-8-12**(7) AngelaGallimore(4) (bhd: hmpd over 2f out & wl over 1f out: swtchd twice & r.o wl) | 1 | **6** | 13/2[3] | 59 | 43 |
| 1546[3] | **Waterlord (IRE) (40)** (DNicholls) **6-7-11**(7) JBramhill(13) (a chsng ldrs: hmpd after 1f: wknd 2f out) | ¾ | **7** | 12/1 | 42 | 26 |
| 1423* | **Johnnie the Joker (51)** (JPLeigh) **5-8-10b**(5) PFessey(15) (a in tch: hung rt u.p over 2f out: one pce) | ¾ | **8** | 15/2 | 52 | 36 |
| 1198[8] | **Haido'hart (52)** (BSRothwell) **4-9-2** JFanning(3) (bhd tl sme late hdwy) | nk | **9** | 20/1 | 52 | 36 |
| 469[15] | **Canary Falcon (56)** (HJCollingridge) **5-9-6v** VSmith(11) (prom: hmpd after 1f: wknd fnl 2½f) | s.h | **10** | 20/1 | 56 | 40 |
| 1341[7] | **Special-K (60)** (EWeymes) **4-9-10** KDarley(9) (bhd: effrt 3f out: no imp) | 1½ | **11** | 5/1[1] | 57 | 41 |
| 1423[13] | **Irchester Lass (39)** (SRBowring) **4-8-3** NCarlisle(2) (prom 5f) | 2 | **12** | 20/1 | 32 | 16 |
| 1500[7] | **Camionneur (IRE) (52)** (TDEasterby) **3-8-6** WCarson(6) (cl up over 4f: wknd) | 2 | **13** | 8/1 | 40 | 14 |
| *1028[10]* | **Dancing Rainbow (52)** (MJCamacho) **3-8-6** LCharnock(7) (chsd ldrs tl wknd fnl 2f) | 2 | **14** | 16/1 | 36 | 10 |
| 1363[11] | **Energy Man (65)** (MDods) **3-9-5** DeanMcKeown(12) (a bhd) | 5 | **15** | 33/1 | 38 | 12 |
| | | | | (SP 137.0%) | **15 Rn** | |

**1m 32.0** (0.00) CSF £200.35 CT £1,604.48 TOTE £7.60: £2.50 £5.60 £2.60 (£153.40) Trio £708.80; £29.95 to 7/6/96 OWNER Mr R. N. Pennell (MIDDLEHAM) BRED R. Taylor
WEIGHT FOR AGE 3yo-10lb
**1633* Three Arch Bridge**, because of her poor draw, had to come from behind and proved to be very determined to get there. (7/1)
**1037 Grey Kingdom** put in a solid effort here and seems to be getting it together. (33/1)
**1094* Awesome Venture** has not won on grass for three years and is well handicapped. Judging by the way he finished, he should pick up a race before long. (7/1)
**1037 Murphy's Gold (IRE)** likes this track and is quite well handicapped, but does need things to go just right. (6/1)
**1313* Murray's Mazda (IRE)** tried to make it, but could never fully gain the initiative and finally gave up approaching the final furlong. This was still not a bad effort. (8/1)
**1601 My Gallery (IRE)** found more trouble here than an England football team on tour and may well have won with any luck. (13/2)
**Haido'hart** keeps staying on at the end of his races, suggesting there is some ability. (20/1)

## 1675 WELTON MAIDEN STKS (3-Y.O+) (Class D)

8-30 (8-31) **7f 100y** £3,457.00 (£1,036.00: £498.00: £229.00) GOING minus 0.64 sec per fur (F)

| | | | | SP | RR | SF |
|---|---|---|---|---|---|---|
| 1443[2] | **Ood Dancer (USA) (82)** (LMCumani) **3-8-11** KDarley(1) (mde all: qcknd over 2f out: r.o wl) | — | **1** | 5/4[1] | 83 | 11 |
| | **Mubariz (IRE)** (EALDunlop) **4-9-7** WCarson(2) (chsd wnr: chal over 2f out: hrd rdn: hung lft & nt qckn nr fin) | 1 | **2** | 7/4[2] | 81 | 19 |
| 1323[3] | **Dispol Diamond (80)** (GROldroyd) **3-8-6** KFallon(5) (chsd ldrs: rdn 3f out: no imp) | 4 | **3** | 5/2[3] | 67 | — |
| 1470[7] | **The Great Flood** (NTinkler) **3-8-11** KimTinkler(3) (nvr wnt pce) | 11 | **4** | 33/1 | 49 | — |
| | | | | (SP 112.3%) | **4 Rn** | |

**1m 35.1** (3.10) CSF £3.81 TOTE £2.30 (£1.90) OWNER Sheikh Ahmed Al Maktoum (NEWMARKET) BRED Fares Farms Inc
WEIGHT FOR AGE 3yo-10lb
**1443 Ood Dancer (USA)** left nothing to chance this time and, given a forceful ride, proved game under pressure. (5/4)
**Mubariz (IRE)** looked fit and was certainly given some strong assistance from the saddle, but it all proved in vain as he just wanted to hang left. (7/4)
**1323 Dispol Diamond** ran another decent race, but was never quite good enough to worry the front two. (5/2)
**The Great Flood** showed little and probably still needed it. (33/1)

## 1676 DRIFTERS NIGHT H'CAP (0-60) (3-Y.O+) (Class F)

9-00 (9-08) **1m 3f 216y** £3,050.00 (£850.00: £410.00) Stalls: Low GOING minus 0.64 sec per fur (F)

| | | | | SP | RR | SF |
|---|---|---|---|---|---|---|
| 1584[2] | **Mock Trial (IRE) (58)** (MrsJRRamsden) **3-9-5** KFallon(10) (hld up: hdwy & swtchd outside over 2f out: hrd rdn to ld cl home) | — | **1** | 15/8[1] | 67 | 28 |

1411[2] **Bobanlyn (IRE) (47)** (JSWainwright) **4-9-2**(7) JBramhill(15) (a.p: rdn to ld 1½f out: nt qckn towards fin)..........nk **2** 8/1[3] 56 32
886[11] **Bold Elect (40)** (EJAlston) **8-9-2** SDWilliams(7) (bhd: hdwy on ins 3f out: nt clr run over 1f out: r.o wl towards fin)..........½ **3** 20/1 48 24
1647[6] **Kings Cay (IRE) (46)** (THCaldwell) **5-9-8** JWeaver(1) (led 2f: cl up: led wl over 2f out to 1½f out: one pce)......1 **4** 12/1 53 29
**Abalene (37)** (TWDonnelly) **7-8-13** CRutter(14) (a chsng ldrs: one pce fnl 3f)..........¾ **5** 16/1 43 19
1529[8] **Gallardini (IRE) (44)** (BSRothwell) **7-9-6b**[1] LCharnock(8) (mid div: hdwy 3f out: rdn & btn appr fnl f)..........1½ **6** 25/1 48 24
1548[4] **Gold Desire (33)** (MBrittain) **6-8-9** DaleGibson(12) (chsd ldrs: effrt 3f out: wknd over 1f out)..........½ **7** 10/1 36 12
*1456*[5] **African Sun (IRE) (45)** (BHanbury) **3-8-6** JQuinn(3) (hld up: effrt 3f out: no imp)..........2 **8** 10/1 45 6
1411[3] **Diamond Crown (IRE) (44)** (MartynWane) **5-9-6** BThomson(5) (bhd: effrt 3f out: n.d)..........4 **9** 7/1[2] 39 15
1544[4] **Goodbye Millie (40)** (JLEyre) **6-9-2** RLappin(9) (a rr div)..........1½ **10** 16/1 33 9
1044[7] **Punch (42)** (NTinkler) **4-9-4b** KDarley(11) (hld up: hdwy & prom 3f out: sn rdn & fnd nil)..........3½ **11** 25/1 30 6
**Longcroft (34)** (KWHogg) **4-8-7**(3) DWright(2) (uns rdr & bolted bef s: a bhd)..........4 **12** 20/1 17 —
*1487*[9] **Instantaneous (48)** (TDEasterby) **4-9-10** WCarson(13) (cl up tl wknd 2f out)..........5 **13** 10/1 24 —
1600[7] **Never Time (IRE) (38)** (MrsVAAconley) **4-9-0** MDeering(4) (led after 2f tl hdd & wknd qckly over 2f out).......1¼ **14** 20/1 13 —
(SP 127.1%) **14 Rn**

**2m 36.3** (3.90) CSF £17.86 CT £222.58 TOTE £2.80: £2.00 £3.00 £6.50 (£17.70) Trio £314.30 OWNER Mr P. A. Leonard (THIRSK) BRED Sheikh Mohammed Bin Rashid Al Maktoum
WEIGHT FOR AGE 3yo-15lb

**1584 Mock Trial (IRE)**, very excitable beforehand, was given a ride and a half and showed fine courage to get up. (15/8: 5/2-13/8)
**1411 Bobanlyn (IRE)** is in good form just now but, despite a valiant effort, just failed to last home. (8/1)
**625 Bold Elect**, from a yard that can do nothing right this season, was very unlucky and may well have won had a gap appeared sooner. (20/1)
**Kings Cay (IRE)** ran well but was just done for foot late on. (12/1: op 8/1)
**Abalene** ran a fine race after a lengthy lay-off and should be all the better for it. (16/1)
**440 Gallardini (IRE)** had blinkers on for the first time and ran a bit better, but was still not doing enough in the final furlong and a half. (25/1)
**African Sun (IRE)** (10/1: op 6/1)
**777 Instantaneous** (10/1: 8/1-16/1)

T/Plpt: £61.00 (182.93 Tckts). T/Qdpt: £25.40 (30.11 Tckts). AA

## 1512-FOLKESTONE (R-H) (Good to firm)
## Wednesday June 5th

WEATHER: warm WIND: nil

### 1677 CO STEEL AMATEUR LIMITED STKS (0-70) (3-Y.O+) (Class F)

6-15 (6-16) **6f 189y** £2,714.20 (£751.20: £358.60) Stalls: Low GOING minus 0.46 sec per fur (F)

SP RR SF

1532* **Farmost (61)** (SirMarkPrescott) **3-10-10** MrPScott(3) (lw: led 5f out: rdn out)..........— **1** 10/11[1] 84 56
1518* **Young Mazaad (IRE) (68)** (DCO'Brien) **3-10-1b**(5) MrVLukaniuk(5) (swtg: a.p: chsd wnr fnl 2f: ev ch 1f out: unable qckn)..........1½ **2** 6/1[3] 77 49
1521* **Stoppes Brow (70)** (GLMoore) **4-10-11v**(5) MrKGoble(6) (hdwy over 3f out: rdn over 1f out: one pce)..........2½ **3** 5/2[2] 71 53
*854*[12] **Super Park (62)** (JPearce) **4-11-0** MrsLPearce(1) (a.p: rdn over 1f out: sn wknd)..........3 **4** 14/1 62 44
1449[18] **Spectacle Jim (44)** (MJHaynes) **7-11-0b** MissYHaynes(8) (prom over 3f)..........3½ **5** 33/1 54 36
1536[6] **Dancing Heart (69)** (BJMeehan) **4-11-0b** MissJAllison(7) (nvr nr to chal)..........hd **6** 10/1 53 35
1348[16] **Sarum (40)** (JELong) **10-10-11**(5) MrTWaters(9) (b: mid div whn hmpd on ins 4f out: bhd fnl 3f)..........1½ **7** 50/1 52 34
1012[13] **Red Sky Delight (IRE) (35)** (PButler) **3-9-10**(5) MrIMongan(10) (led 2f out: wknd 3f out)..........9 **8** 66/1 26 —
**Wagon Load (40)** (JWhite) **11-10-9**(5) MissSBrown(2) (a bhd)..........½ **9** 50/1 28 10
1449[11] **Prince Rooney (IRE) (38)** (PButler) **8-10-9**(5) MrJGoldstein(4) (a bhd)..........3½ **10** 66/1 19 1
(SP 120.8%) **10 Rn**

**1m 23.7** (2.10) CSF £7.31 TOTE £2.00: £1.10 £1.20 £1.20 (£4.10) OWNER Mr W. E. Sturt (NEWMARKET) BRED Hesmonds Stud Ltd
WEIGHT FOR AGE 3yo-10lb
STEWARDS' ENQUIRY Lukaniuk susp.14-15 &17/6/96 (careless riding).

**1532* Farmost** continues in sparkling form, despite his hectic schedule, and was completing a quick hat-trick. He proved far more resolute than the runner-up in the final furlong. (10/11: tchd Evens)
**1518* Young Mazaad (IRE)**, still in with every chance entering the final furlong, was unable to get past the winner. (6/1)
**1521* Stoppes Brow**, whose new rating is 77 which made him theoretically well in as this was a 0-70 race, was tapped for toe from below the distance. (5/2)
**Super Park** played an active role until left for dead by the front three from below the distance. (14/1: 8/1-16/1)
**582 Spectacle Jim** was close up to halfway. One win from 52 starts says it all. (33/1)
**1536 Dancing Heart** could never get in a blow. (10/1: op 5/1)

### 1678 E.B.F. SEEBOARD MAIDEN STKS (2-Y.O F) (Class D)

6-45 (6-46) **6f** £3,409.75 (£1,018.00: £486.50: £220.75) Stalls: Low GOING minus 0.46 sec per fur (F)

SP RR SF

**Passiflora** (JLDunlop) **2-8-11** GDuffield(3) (w'like: rdn over 3f out: hdwy over 1f out: led ins fnl f: r.o wl).......— **1** 11/8[1] 78+ 7
1328[4] **Mystery** (SDow) **2-8-11** SSanders(4) (chsd ldr: led 2f out tl ins fnl f: unable qckn)..........¾ **2** 5/1[3] 76 5
1413[3] **Seva (IRE)** (DRLoder) **2-8-11** DRMcCabe(1) (lw: led 4f: hrd rdn: one pce)..........2½ **3** 3/1[2] 69 —
1148[4] **Stride** (DMorley) **2-8-8**(3) JStack(6) (hld up: rdn over 2f out: one pce)..........¾ **4** 13/2 67 —
**Aegean Sound** (RHannon) **2-8-8**(3) DaneO'Neill(7) (hld up: rdn 2f out: wknd over 1f out)..........3½ **5** 6/1 58 —
**Rise 'n Shine** (CACyzer) **2-8-11** AClark(2) (str: bit bkwd: prom 3f)..........8 **6** 14/1 37 —
**First Page** (WJarvis) **2-8-11** MTebbutt(5) (str: scope: bit bkwd: s.s: hdwy over 2f out: sn wknd)..........1½ **7** 12/1 33 —
(SP 125.8%) **7 Rn**

**1m 13.8** (3.60) CSF £9.62 TOTE £2.20: £1.30 £2.00 (£10.00) OWNER Mrs Karen Grieve (Susan Racing) (ARUNDEL) BRED The Lavington Stud

**Passiflora**, whose dam is a half-sister to In the Groove, was being pushed along and going nowhere at the back of the field at halfway. At last finding her feet below the distance, she came through to lead inside the final furlong and proved far too strong for the runner-up. (11/8)
**1328 Mystery** was unable to contain the winner inside the final furlong. (5/1: 4/1-6/1)
**1413 Seva (IRE)**, collared two furlongs out, was soon tapped for toe. (3/1: op 6/4)
**Stride** failed to quicken in the last two furlongs. (13/2)

**Aegean Sound**, a small, sparely-made filly with no scope, chased the leaders until tiring below the distance. (6/1: 4/1-7/1)
**Rise 'n Shine**, a well-built filly, did not look fully wound up and had given her all from halfway. (14/1: 8/1-16/1)
**First Page** (12/1: 8/1-14/1)

## 1679 CHARNLEY FAMILY H'CAP (0-65) (3-Y.O+) (Class F)
7-15 (7-15) **2m 93y** £2,785.60 (£771.60: £368.80) Stalls: Low GOING minus 0.46 sec per fur (F)

| | | | | SP | RR | SF |
|---|---|---|---|---|---|---|
| *365*[3] | **Mr Copyforce (36)** (MissBSanders) **6-8-2**(3) AWhelan(5) (hld up: chsd ldr 6f out: led 3f out: sn clr: easily) | — | 1 | 8/1 | 51 | 31 |
| 1415[4] | **Influence Pedler (52)** (CEBrittain) **3-8-0** DRMcCabe(7) (swtg: hld up: rdn over 3f out: chsd wnr wl over 1f out: no imp) | 7 | 2 | 7/2[2] | 60 | 19 |
| *1444** | **Chakalak (49)** (SDow) **8-8-13**(5) ADaly(1) (lw: lost pl over 11f out: r.o one pce: bhd fnl 3f) | ¾ | 3 | 4/1[3] | 56 | 36 |
| 1511[3] | **Rock Group (53)** (JPearce) **4-9-7** GBardwell(6) (led: rdn 6f out: hdd 3f out: sn wknd) | 17 | 4 | 100/30[1] | 44 | 23 |
| *206*[8] | **Chez Catalan (47)** (RAkehurst) **5-9-2b** SSanders(4) (chsd ldr 12f out to 6f out: sn wknd) | 11 | 5 | 8/1 | 27 | 7 |
| 1618[7] | **Pedaltothemetal (IRE) (43)** (PhilipMitchell) **4-8-6**(5) CAdamson(3) (7th whn b.d bend over 9f out) | | B | 14/1 | — | — |
| 1063* | **Coleridge (55)** (JJSheehan) **8-9-7b**(3) DaneO'Neill(2) (5th whn s.u bend over 9f out) | | S | 7/2[2] | — | — |
| | | | | (SP 116.4%) | **7 Rn** | |

**3m 35.9** (4.90) CSF £34.51 TOTE £6.70: £3.40 £2.40 (£19.30) OWNER Copyforce Ltd (EPSOM) BRED Highclere Stud Ltd
WEIGHT FOR AGE 3yo-21lb, 4yo-1lb
**Mr Copyforce**, whose last victory was on the All-Weather two years ago off a mark of 57, has been below-par since and as a result was racing off just 36 here.He cruised into the lead three furlongs from home and soon pulled clear to win very easily. (8/1)
**1415 Influence Pedler**, taking a step up in distance, had no chance of reeling in the winner. (7/2)
**1444* Chakalak** had lost his pitch with fully a circuit to race, but did plod on in the last three furlongs for third prize. (4/1)
**1511 Rock Group** failed to see out this longer trip and a return to a mile and three-quarters is required. (100/30)
**Chez Catalan** (8/1: op 5/1)

## 1680 DOUGAL BROS H'CAP (0-85) (3-Y.O+) (Class D)
7-45 (7-45) **6f** £3,590.00 (£1,070.00: £510.00: £230.00) Stalls: Low GOING minus 0.46 sec per fur (F)

| | | | | SP | RR | SF |
|---|---|---|---|---|---|---|
| 1192[4] | **Law Commission (79)** (DRCElsworth) **6-9-11**(3) DaneO'Neill(5) (stdy hdwy over 2f out: led 1f out: r.o wl) | — | 1 | 10/1 | 87 | 49 |
| 1334[4] | **Denbrae (IRE) (69)** (DJGMurraySmith) **4-8-13**(5) RPainter(3) (swtg: dwlt: outpcd: hrd rdn & hdwy over 1f out: r.o) | 1¼ | 2 | 9/2[3] | 74 | 36 |
| 1078* | **Neuwest (USA) (78)** (NJHWalker) **4-9-10**(3) JStack(1) (lw: w ldr: led over 3f out to 2f out: led over 1f out: sn hdd: unable qckn) | nk | 3 | 4/1[2] | 82 | 44 |
| 1624[2] | **Prima Silk (67)** (MJRyan) **5-9-2** TIves(4) (lost pl over 3f out: swtchd rt over 2f out: one pce fnl f) | 1 | 4 | 2/1[1] | 68 | 30 |
| 846[13] | **Bashful Brave (74)** (JWPayne) **5-9-9** AClark(7) (lw: a.p: led 2f out tl over 1f out: wknd fnl f) | 3½ | 5 | 9/2[3] | 66 | 28 |
| 1522[11] | **Sharp 'n Smart (66)** (BSmart) **4-9-1** MTebbutt(6) (swtg: prom over 3f) | 5 | 6 | 20/1 | 45 | 7 |
| 1464[5] | **Quintus Decimus (74)** (RAkehurst) **4-9-9b**[1] SSanders(2) (b.off fore: led over 2f) | 13 | 7 | 10/1 | 18 | — |
| | | | | (SP 112.6%) | **7 Rn** | |

**1m 11.8** (1.60) CSF £49.32 TOTE £10.00: £4.20 £3.10 (£28.60) OWNER Mr Raymond Tooth (WHITCOMBE) BRED Airlie Stud
**Law Commission** eased his way into the action in the second half of the race and, striking the front a furlong from home, kept on nicely. (10/1)
**1334 Denbrae (IRE)** at last got going below the distance and, responding to pressure, came through for second prize. (9/2)
**1078* Neuwest (USA)** as usual looked very well in the paddock. (4/1)
**1624 Prima Silk** was tapped for toe in the final furlong. (2/1)
**632* Bashful Brave** went on a quarter of a mile out, but this was too soon for him. Collared below the distance, he needs to be held up much longer than this. (9/2)
**Quintus Decimus** (10/1: 6/1-11/1)

## 1681 GRAYLINE INTERNATIONAL REMOVAL & STORAGE (S) STKS (3-Y.O+) (Class G)
8-15 (8-15) **5f** £2,301.00 (£636.00: £303.00) Stalls: Low GOING minus 0.46 sec per fur (F)

| | | | | SP | RR | SF |
|---|---|---|---|---|---|---|
| 1512[4] | **Lift Boy (USA) (47)** (AMoore) **7-9-10** CandyMorris(2) (lw: led over 2f: led ins fnl f: r.o wl) | — | 1 | 11/4[3] | 56 | 20 |
| | **Myasha (USA)** (AlexVanderhaeghen,Belgium) **7-9-3b** MServranckx(3) (w ldr: led over 2f out tl ins fnl f: r.o) | ¾ | 2 | 5/2[2] | 47 | 11 |
| 664[13] | **Superlao (BEL) (38)** (JJBridger) **4-8-9**(3) DarrenMoffatt(1) (b.nr hind: lost pl over 3f out: rallied fnl f: r.o) | 2½ | 3 | 12/1 | 34 | — |
| *1455*[4] | **Little Saboteur (60)** (PJMakin) **7-8-12b** AClark(6) (b.nr hind: hld up: ev ch wl over 1f out: wknd fnl f) | 3 | 4 | 7/4[1] | 24 | — |
| 1013[8] | **Old Gold N Tan (33)** (JRPoulton) **3-8-7b**[1](3) PMcCabe(4) (a bhd) | 5 | 5 | 33/1 | 13 | — |
| 1099[20] | **Bromfylde Fayemaid (IRE)** (JRJenkins) **4-8-9b**[1](3) DaneO'Neill(7) (hld up: rdn over 2f out: sn wknd) | 2 | 6 | 33/1 | 2 | — |
| 1171[15] | **Nightswimming (IRE)** (SDow) **3-8-5**(5) ADaly(5) (lw: dwlt: hld up: rdn over 2f out: sn wknd) | nk | 7 | 12/1 | 6 | — |
| | | | | (SP 112.9%) | **7 Rn** | |

**60.4 secs** (2.80) CSF £9.62 TOTE £3.30: £2.30 £1.20 (£6.50) OWNER Mr A. Moore (BRIGHTON) BRED Paul & Arnold Bryant in USA
WEIGHT FOR AGE 3yo-7lb
No bid
**1512 Lift Boy (USA)** is at his best in this grade or in claiming company. (11/4)
**Myasha (USA)**, who proved very troublesome on the way out onto the course, was unable to get back at the winner. (5/2: op 6/4)
**Superlao (BEL)** was soon outpaced but did stay on in the final furlong for third prize. (12/1: 10/1-16/1)
**1455 Little Saboteur** was unable to take advantage of the drop in class. She is on the downgrade. (7/4)

## 1682 SUPAGLAZING H'CAP (0-70) (3-Y.O+ F & M) (Class E)
8-45 (8-45) **1m 1f 149y** £3,234.00 (£966.00: £462.00: £210.00) Stalls: Low GOING minus 0.46 sec per fur (F)

| | | | | SP | RR | SF |
|---|---|---|---|---|---|---|
| 1462[12] | **Ashby Hill (IRE) (46)** (RRowe) **5-8-11** AClark(7) (lw: hld up: led over 1f out: pushed out) | — | 1 | 4/1[2] | 50 | — |
| 1357[3] | **Dramatic Moment (60)** (IABalding) **3-8-12** PaulEddery(8) (lw: led 2f: led 4f out tl over 1f out: unable qckn) | 3 | 2 | 9/4[1] | 59 | — |
| 1302[8] | **Zeliba (31)** (CEBrittain) **4-7-10** GBardwell(4) (lost pl over 3f out: one pce fnl 2f) | 3½ | 3 | 7/1[3] | 24 | — |
| 1061[7] | **Miss Pravda (58)** (PTWalwyn) **3-8-10** SSanders(6) (lw: rdn over 2f out: hdwy 1f out: one pce) | hd | 4 | 8/1 | 51 | — |
| 1181[11] | **Tiama (IRE) (55)** (SDow) **3-8-2**(5) ADaly(2) (s.s: rdn & hdwy on ins 2f out: one pce) | nk | 5 | 20/1 | 48 | — |
| 979[14] | **Miss Iron Heart (USA) (38)** (DJSCosgrove) **4-8-0**(3) AWhelan(5) (hld up: rdn over 2f out: wknd fnl f) | 3½ | 6 | 10/1 | 25 | — |
| | **Evidence In Chief (60)** (DRCElsworth) **3-8-9**(3) DaneO'Neill(1) (bhd fnl 5f) | 1¼ | 7 | 4/1[2] | 45 | — |

| | | | SP | RR | SF |
|---|---|---|---|---|---|
| 1462[8] | **Elly Fleetfoot (IRE) (63)** (MJRyan) **4-10-0** TIves(3) (lw: hdwy 8f out: led over 7f out to 4f out: wkng whn n.m.r over 2f out) ....4 | 8 | 9/1 | 41 | — |

(SP 118.2%) **8 Rn**

**2m 5.7** (8.00) CSF £13.36 CT £56.07 TOTE £4.30: £1.50 £1.20 £2.30 (£6.10) OWNER Miss Meriel Tufnell (PULBOROUGH) BRED Patrick Aspell
LONG HANDICAP Zeliba 7-9
WEIGHT FOR AGE 3yo-13lb
**1462 Ashby Hill (IRE)** put up a very polished display. Always travelling sweetly, she was bustled into the lead below the distance and soon pulled clear for a decisive victory. (4/1)
**Dramatic Moment** was unable to stop the winner storming clear. (9/4)
**Zeliba** could only keep on in her own time in the last two furlongs and remains a maiden. (7/1: op 4/1)
**922* Miss Pravda**, ridden along and going nowhere turning into the straight, made some headway a furlong out but could then make no further impression. (8/1: op 4/1)
**Tiama (IRE)** made an effort along the inside rail early in the straight, but was then only treading water. (20/1)
**739 Miss Iron Heart (USA)** had nothing more to offer in the final furlong. (10/1: 7/1-12/1)
**Evidence In Chief** (4/1: 3/1-5/1)
**Elly Fleetfoot (IRE)** (9/1: 6/1-10/1)

T/Plpt: £152.10 (68.9 Tckts). T/Qdpt: £62.80 (11.07 Tckts). AK

# 1449-WARWICK (L-H) (Firm)
## Wednesday June 5th
WEATHER: sunny & warm WIND: mod half bhd

## 1683 KENILWORTH MAIDEN AUCTION STKS (2-Y.O) (Class D)
2-30 (2-32) **6f** £3,263.50 (£973.00: £464.00: £209.50) Stalls: Low GOING minus 0.57 sec per fur (F)

| | | | SP | RR | SF |
|---|---|---|---|---|---|
| | **Lamorna** (MRChannon) **2-7-12** AGorman(2) (w'like: scope: bit bkwd: trckd ldrs: led over 1f out: sn clr: comf) ....— | 1 | 10/1 | 64+ | 21 |
| 1513[3] | **Mister Pink** (RFJohnsonHoughton) **2-8-6v**[1ow1] JReid(1) (a.p: led wl over 1f out: hdd appr fnl f: one pce) ....1¼ | 2 | 4/1[2] | 69 | 25 |
| *1489*[4] | **Superquest** (WAO'Gorman) **2-8-5** EmmaO'Gorman(7) (sn drvn along: hdwy ent st: one pce fnl 2f) ....5 | 3 | 8/1 | 54 | 11 |
| 1118[6] | **Don Sebastian** (RHannon) **2-8-5** SSanders(8) (s.i.s: sn bhd & outpcd: effrt u.p over 1f out: nvr nrr) ....s.h | 4 | 5/1[3] | 54 | 11 |
| 1404[8] | **Aybeegirl** (MrsJCecil) **2-7-9**(5) MHenry(4) (mde most tl hdd wl over 1f out: sn outpcd) ....1¼ | 5 | 2/1[1] | 46 | 3 |
| 1346[9] | **Princess Ferdinand (IRE)** (MMcCormack) **2-8-0** GCarter(3) (gd spd 4f: wknd qckly) ....2 | 6 | 14/1 | 41 | — |
| 1531[5] | **Fly Down To Rio (IRE)** (DWPArbuthnot) **2-8-2** JCarroll(5) (outpcd: a bhd) ....3½ | 7 | 20/1 | 33 | — |
| 1346[10] | **Watercolour (IRE)** (PFICole) **2-8-5** TQuinn(6) (in tch tl outpcd over 2f out) ....½ | 8 | 9/1 | 35 | — |

(SP 111.6%) **8 Rn**

**1m 13.1** (1.10) CSF £45.19 TOTE £10.10: £1.90 £1.10 £2.90 (£19.70) OWNER Mr W. H. Ponsonby (UPPER LAMBOURN) BRED E. M. Thornton
**Lamorna** made a good start to her racing career with a smoothly-gained success and, as she can only improve on this, her future looks bright. (10/1: op 4/1)
**1513 Mister Pink** was once again very coltish in the paddock. Visored for the first time, he looked all over the winner until the filly proved much too good for him at the weights. (4/1: 3/1-9/2)
**1489 Superquest** may well need further to find his true form and could be well worth waiting for. (8/1)
**1118 Don Sebastian**, sluggish leaving the stalls, did not really get going until far too late and was never a threat to the principals. (5/1: op 3/1)
**1036 Aybeegirl**, having her first try at this slightly longer trip, forced the pace until getting left behind from below the distance. (2/1: op 3/1)
**Princess Ferdinand (IRE)**, smartly into her stride to press the leader, was feeling the strain soon after straightening up and faded tamely. (14/1)

## 1684 QUEEN BESS APPRENTICE CLAIMING STKS (3-Y.O+) (Class F)
3-00 (3-01) **6f** £2,928.40 (£812.40: £389.20) Stalls: Low GOING minus 0.57 sec per fur (F)

| | | | SP | RR | SF |
|---|---|---|---|---|---|
| 1635[3] | **Panther (IRE) (62)** (JHetherton) **6-9-3** MartinDwyer(8) (mde all: clr ½-wy: pushed out) ....— | 1 | 7/2[2] | 63 | 45 |
| 1334[10] | **How's Yer Father (77)** (RJHodges) **10-9-3** AmandaSanders(7) (lw: trckd ldrs: effrt & rdn 2f out: r.o wl ins fnl f) ....1¼ | 2 | Evens[1] | 60 | 42 |
| 1333[15] | **Risking** (GLewis) **3-8-3**(3) DSweeney(4) (bit bkwd: chsd wnr: rdn over 1f out: one pce) ....1¾ | 3 | 20/1 | 52 | 26 |
| 1624[3] | **Our Shadee (USA) (48)** (KTIvory) **6-9-7v** CScally(5) (sn bhd & pushed along: kpt on ins fnl f: nvr nrr) ....1½ | 4 | 10/1 | 55 | 37 |
| 1592[9] | **Farida Seconda (62)** (JLSpearing) **3-7-12**(5)ow1 SRighton(6) (hdwy 2f out: rdn & kpt on ins fnl f) ....nk | 5 | 40/1 | 44 | 17 |
| 1417[5] | **Naughty Pistol (USA)** (PDEvans) **4-9-1**(5) HayleyWilliams(1) (chsd ldrs 4f: sn rdn & outpcd) ....1¾ | 6 | 25/1 | 49 | 31 |
| 951[5] | **John O'Dreams (50)** (MrsALMKing) **11-8-13** SophieMitchell(2) (b: s.s: a bhd & outpcd) ....3 | 7 | 10/1 | 34 | 16 |
| 1013[9] | **Victoria Sioux (47)** (JAPickering) **3-7-9**(3) AngelaGallimore(3) (outpcd: a bhd: t.o) ....8 | 8 | 40/1 | 5 | — |
| 1516[4] | **Milos (61)** (TJNaughton) **5-9-4**(3) TAshley(9) (outpcd: drvn along & sme hdwy whn s.u & fell ent st) .... | F | 9/1[3] | — | — |

(SP 113.9%) **9 Rn**

**1m 12.6** (0.60) CSF £6.98 TOTE £3.80: £1.10 £1.20 £4.50 (£2.60) Trio £46.20 OWNER Mr K. C. West (MALTON) BRED My Treasure Ltd
WEIGHT FOR AGE 3yo-8lb
Panther (IRE) clmd PDEvans £6,000
**1635 Panther (IRE)** handled this fast ground particularly well and was always going much too fast for his pursuers. He was claimed after the race and will now operate from the Welsh borders. (7/2)
**1178 How's Yer Father** struggles a bit on ground as lively as this and did not find top gear until well inside the final furlong. (Evens)
**Risking**, very short on experience and still not fully wound up, shaped promisingly, being in pursuit of the winner until calling enough approaching the final furlong. (20/1)
**1624 Our Shadee (USA)**, taken off his legs in the early stages, did begin to stay on inside the distance but the principals were beyond recall. (10/1: op 6/1)
**Farida Seconda**, who has not got much mileage on the clock, was out with the washing until running on in the closing stages. (40/1)
**1516 Milos** (9/1: 6/1-10/1)

## 1685 BOLLINGER CHAMPAGNE CHALLENGE SERIES GENTLEMENS' H'CAP (0-70) (3-Y.O+) (Class E)
3-30 (3-45) **1m** £3,288.60 (£982.80: £470.40: £214.20) Stalls: Low GOING minus 0.57 sec per fur (F)

| | | | SP | RR | SF |
|---|---|---|---|---|---|
| 1449* | **Montone (IRE) (53)** (JRJenkins) **6-10-7v**(4) DrMMannish(5) (hld up: hdwy ½-wy: led appr fnl f: r.o wl) ....— | 1 | 11/2[2] | 65 | 41 |

| | | | | SP | RR | SF |
|---|---|---|---|---|---|---|
| | **Raven's Roost (IRE) (52)** (AJChamberlain) **5-10-6**(4)ow2 MrACharles-Jones(11) (trckd ldrs: kpt on u.p ins fnl f) | 2 | **2** | 66/1 | 60 | 34 |
| 1348[6] | **Kevasingo (56)** (BWHills) **4-10-10**(4) MrCBHills(1) (trckd ldrs: rdn & effrt appr fnl f: r.o) | s.h | **3** | 8/1 | 64 | 40 |
| 1449[6] | **Benjamins Law (50)** (JAPickering) **5-10-4**(4) MrOMcPhail(10) (a.p: rdn & ev ch wl over 1f out: no ex fnl f) | 1 | **4** | 9/1 | 56 | 32 |
| *1601[8]* | **Kingchip Boy (63)** (MJRyan) **7-11-3v**(4) MrSLavallin(2) (dwlt: hdwy over 1f out: fin wl) | 1 | **5** | 9/1 | 67 | 43 |
| 1190[16] | **Desert Calm (IRE) (55)** (MrsPNDutfield) **7-10-9b**(4) MrLJefford(4) (hld up: hdwy 2f out: nrst fin) | ½ | **6** | 10/1 | 58 | 34 |
| | **Fluidity (USA) (50)** (JGMO'Shea) **8-10-4**(4) MrNBradley(3) (bkwd: nvr nr to chal) | 1¼ | **7** | 66/1 | 50 | 26 |
| 1613[2] | **Leguard Express (IRE) (36)** (OO'Neill) **8-9-4b**(4) MrCWatson(7) (b: s.i.s: sn led: hdd & wknd appr fnl f) | 1¼ | **8** | 7/1[3] | 34 | 10 |
| 1348[2] | **Almapa (48)** (RJHodges) **4-10-6** JCulloty(14) (hld up: effrt 2f out: no imp) | nk | **9** | 9/2[1] | 45 | 21 |
| 1496[11] | **Teen Jay (65)** (BJLlewellyn) **6-11-9** MrJLLlewellyn(6) (s.s: a in rr) | 1 | **10** | 12/1 | 60 | 36 |
| 1613[10] | **Mimosa (60)** (SDow) **3-10-3v**(4) MrSFetherstonhaugh(9) (swtg: in tch tl wknd qckly 2f out) | ½ | **11** | 20/1 | 54 | 19 |
| | **Indrapura (IRE) (62)** (PFICole) **4-11-6b** MrJDurkan(16) (prom: c wd ent st: sn lost tch) | 1½ | **12** | 7/1[3] | 53 | 29 |
| | **Bite the Bullet (39)** (AJChamberlain) **5-9-7**(4)ow4 MrKWheate(13) (b: bkwd: a bhd: t.o) | 5 | **13** | 50/1 | 20 | — |
| | **Royal Thimble (IRE) (69)** (NoelChance) **5-11-13** MrRFCoonan(8) (bkwd: trckd ldrs tl wknd over 3f out: t.o) | hd | **14** | 16/1 | 50 | 26 |
| 1610[5] | **Best Kept Secret (53)** (PDEvans) **5-10-7b**(4) MrAEvans(12) (prom tl rdn & wknd ent st: t.o) | 2½ | **15** | 14/1 | 29 | 5 |
| | **Swedish Invader (70)** (JWhite) **5-11-10**(4) MrJCrowley(15) (t: bit bkwd: a bhd: t.o) | 3½ | **16** | 20/1 | 39 | 15 |
| | | | | (SP 133.5%) | **16 Rn** | |

**1m 39.7** (3.30) CSF £261.84 CT £2,804.42 TOTE £5.40: £1.50 £19.80 £2.20 £2.00 (£445.60) Trio £775.10; £764.27 to Goodwood 6/6/96
OWNER Mr B. Shirazi (ROYSTON) BRED Sean Gorman
LONG HANDICAP Bite the Bullet 8-11
WEIGHT FOR AGE 3yo-11lb
STEWARDS' ENQUIRY Lavallin susp. 14-15 & 17-19/6/96 (failure to secure best possible placing).
OFFICIAL EXPLANATION **Teen Jay: the jockey reported that his instructions were to be in the first four, not to hit his mount and to finish as close as he could but, after missing the break, he was unable to carry them out.**

**1449* Montone (IRE)**, winner of a similar event over course and distance eleven days ago, followed up with an almost identical ride, and could be on a roll. (11/2)
**Raven's Roost (IRE)**, fit from hurdling but with no form at all to his name, ran as if he is just about to find his way. (66/1)
**1348 Kevasingo** performed much better on this return to a mile and had every chance until having to admit the winner too good for him. (8/1)
**1449 Benjamins Law**, in the firing-line from the start, was hard at work entering the final furlong and found an extra effort beyond him. (9/1: op 6/1)
**1449 Kingchip Boy** ran extremely well after losing ground at the start and, with a level break, would have gone close. (9/1)
**887 Desert Calm (IRE)**, staying on when the race was all but decided, showed that he has got ability when he wants to put it to use. (10/1: op 6/1)
**1613 Leguard Express (IRE)** (7/1: op 4/1)
**1348 Almapa** could not go the pace on this firm ground and was always nearer last than first. (9/2)
**Teen Jay** (12/1: op 7/1)
**Indrapura (IRE)** (7/1: op 4/1)

## 1686 MIDSUMMER H'CAP (0-80) (3-Y.O+) (Class D)

4-00 (4-09) **1m 2f 169y** £4,077.50 (£1,220.00: £585.00: £267.50) Stalls: Low GOING minus 0.57 sec per fur (F)

| | | | | SP | RR | SF |
|---|---|---|---|---|---|---|
| 1198[14] | **Sovereign Page (USA) (73)** (BHanbury) **7-9-10** JReid(2) (trckd ldrs: shkn up to ld ent fnl f: rdn out) | — | **1** | 11/2[3] | 83 | 20 |
| 1486[2] | **Silently (76)** (IABalding) **4-9-8**(5) MartinDwyer(1) (hld up: hdwy on ins & hmpd over 1f out: swtchd rt: fin wl) | 1 | **2** | 7/2[2] | 85 | 22 |
| 979* | **Harvey White (IRE) (59)** (JPearce) **4-8-10** AMcGlone(6) (hld up: hdwy u.p over 1f out: fin wl) | ½ | **3** | 6/1 | 67 | 4 |
| 1450[3] | **Dormy Three (64)** (RJHodges) **6-9-1** PaulEddery(3) (led: rdn & drifted lft over 1f out: sn hdd: kpt on one pce) | s.h | **4** | 17/2 | 72 | 9 |
| 1450* | **Myfontaine (69)** (KTIvory) **9-9-6** JCarroll(8) (hld up & bhd: gd hdwy wl over 1f out: no ex fnl f) | 1½ | **5** | 2/1[1] | 75 | 12 |
| 1416[9] | **Tarian (USA) (51)** (GBBalding) **4-7-13**(3) NVarley(5) (prom tl rdn & wknd wl over 1f out) | 1½ | **6** | 12/1 | 54 | — |
| 1450[4] | **Hand of Straw (IRE) (58)** (PGMurphy) **4-8-9v** NAdams(9) (hld up: hdwy 3f out: rdn & outpcd fnl 2f) | 6 | **7** | 12/1 | 52 | — |
| *1469[4]* | ***Roushan (76)*** (JGMO'Shea) **3-8-13v**[1] JTate(4) (Withdrawn not under Starter's orders: bolted bef s) | | **W** | 16/1 | — | — |
| | | | | (SP 117.0%) | **7 Rn** | |

**2m 19.2** (5.70) CSF £22.98 CT £103.74 TOTE £6.20: £2.50 £2.00 (£7.60) Trio £12.90 OWNER Mrs Ben Hanbury (NEWMARKET) BRED T. Holland Martin
WEIGHT FOR AGE 3yo-14lb
OFFICIAL EXPLANATION **Sovereign Page (USA): regarding the apparent improvent in form of the winner compared to his previous run at Ripon, the trainer's representative reported that the gelding had missed the break and had lost interest.**

**920 Sovereign Page (USA)**, at his best at this time of year, was given a positive ride by Reid and, given no chance to duck the issue, was kept up to his work to the finish. (11/2: op 7/2)
**1486 Silently** was a most unlucky loser, losing far more ground when forced to check than he was beaten by. (7/2)
**979* Harvey White (IRE)** needed to be stoked up to go about his work inside the last quarter-mile and, though he finished strongly, he had mistimed his run. (6/1: 4/1-13/2)
**1450 Dormy Three** attempted more forceful tactics this time and held the call until edging left and forfeiting his advantage approaching the final furlong. (17/2: 6/1-9/1)
**1450* Myfontaine**, set alight early in the home straight, briefly looked capable of wearing the leaders down but the pace never dropped and he was unable to land a blow. (2/1)
**Tarian (USA)**, still to get off the mark, pushed the pace until finding demands too great from below the distance. (12/1: op 8/1)
**1450 Hand of Straw (IRE)** (12/1: op 8/1)

## 1687 WORTHINGTON DRAUGHT BITTER LIMITED STKS (0-80) (3-Y.O) (Class D)

4-30 (4-32) **1m 2f 169y** £3,622.50 (£1,080.00: £515.00: £232.50) Stalls: Low GOING minus 0.57 sec per fur (F)

| | | | | SP | RR | SF |
|---|---|---|---|---|---|---|
| 1476[11] | **Traceability (80)** (SCWilliams) **3-8-11** GCarter(2) (hld up & bhd: gd hdwy to ld 2f out: drvn out) | — | **1** | 9/4[2] | 83 | 40 |
| | **Present Arms (USA) (73)** (PFICole) **3-8-11** PaulEddery(1) (hld up: effrt & sltly hmpd 3f out: chsd wnr appr fnl f: no imp) | 1¾ | **2** | 4/1[3] | 80 | 37 |
| 1349[4] | **Majdak Jereeb (IRE) (77)** (MajorWRHern) **3-8-11** TSprake(3) (lw: led after 2f: sn hdd: ev ch wl after 1f out: one pce) | 2 | **3** | 8/1 | 77 | 34 |
| 847[4] | **Raed (79)** (PTWalwyn) **3-8-11** WCarson(6) (led 7f out to 2f out: sn rdn & outpcd) | 7 | **4** | 2/1[1] | 67 | 24 |
| 1443* | **Claire's Dancer (IRE) (74)** (AndrewTurnell) **3-8-11** JReid(5) (lw: led 2f: prom tl outpcd fnl 2f) | ½ | **5** | 8/1 | 66 | 23 |
| 1069[14] | **Always Happy (77)** (JRFanshawe) **3-8-5**(3) NVarley(4) (trckd ldrs tl rdn & wknd 2f out) | 4 | **6** | 7/1 | 57 | 14 |
| | | | | (SP 118.8%) | **6 Rn** | |

**2m 14.7** (1.20) CSF £11.66 TOTE £3.10: £1.70 £2.40 (£13.30) OWNER Mr J. W. Lovitt (NEWMARKET) BRED J. S. A. and Mrs Shorthouse

**1185 Traceability**, stepping down in class and ridden with plenty of confidence, stormed through from the rear to take it up passing the quarter-mile marker and, running on strongly, ran out a comfortable winner. (9/4)
**Present Arms (USA)**, a very well-bred colt making his seasonal debut, did not enjoy the smoothest of passages on the home turn but he stayed on strongly towards the finish and that initial first success can not be far away. (4/1)
**1349 Majdak Jereeb (IRE)** is bred to need at least this trip and, though he has still to score, gave notice that he is getting his act together. (8/1)
**847 Raed** faded very quickly after doing his share of the pacemaking to the straight, and is not yet getting it together. (2/1)

## 1688 PRINCE RUPERT MAIDEN H'CAP (0-75) (3-Y.O+ F & M) (Class D)

5-00 (5-02) **5f** £2,415.00 (£2,415.00: £530.00: £240.00) Stalls: Low GOING minus 0.75 sec per fur (HD)

| | | | | SP | RR | SF |
|---|---|---|---|---|---|---|
| | **Step On Degas (63)** (MJFetherston-Godley) **3-9-6**(5) FLynch(2) (led tl over 1f out: rdn to ld ins fnl f: all out) | — | **1** | 3/1[1] | 70 | 46 |
| *1455[9]* | **Fyors Gift (IRE) (63)** (BHanbury) **3-9-11** MRimmer(8) (a.p: led over 1f out tl ins fnl f: hrd rdn & r.o wl) | — | **1** | 17/2 | 70 | 46 |
| 648[5] | **Lillibella (62)** (IABalding) **3-9-5**(5) MartinDwyer(3) (trckd ldrs: rdn wl over 1f out: r.o wl nr fin) | 1 | **3** | 4/1[2] | 66 | 42 |
| 1412[9] | **Princess Efisio (50)** (BAMcMahon) **3-8-12b[1]** GCarter(5) (bhd: effrt u.p wl over 1f out: nvr nrr) | 1¾ | **4** | 11/2[3] | 48 | 24 |
| 1429[5] | **Madrina (63)** (JBerry) **3-9-11** JCarroll(6) (bhd: rdn 2f out: nt pce to chal) | 2 | **5** | 7/1 | 55 | 31 |
| 943[7] | **Incatinka (62)** (JLSpearing) **3-9-10** JReid(4) (prom tl rdn & outpcd appr fnl f) | 1½ | **6** | 6/1 | 49 | 25 |
| 1170[12] | **Bouton d'Or (40)** (PHowling) **3-8-2** PaulEddery(1) (prom tl rdn & outpcd fnl 2f) | 3½ | **7** | 12/1 | 16 | — |
| 1446[7] | **La Belle Dominique (50)** (SGKnight) **4-9-5** VSlattery(7) (prom to ½-wy: sn lost pl: t.o) | 20 | **8** | 7/1 | — | — |
| | | | | (SP 117.9%) | **8 Rn** | |

**57.9 secs** (-0.10) CSF £16.65 FG & SOD £13.25 SOD & FG CT FG, SOD & L £55.36 SOD, FG & L £47.90 TOTE £6.20 FG £1.60 SOD: £2.60 FG £1.30 SOD £1.60 (£41.80) OWNER The Degas Partnership (EAST ILSLEY)/Maktoum Al Maktoum (NEWMARKET) BRED A. J. Poulton (Epping) Ltd
WEIGHT FOR AGE 3yo-7lb

**Step On Degas**, produced in tip-top condition for this first outing since changing stables, looked to have held on in a nail-biting finish but the photo only gave her half of the spoils which still gave connections a tremendous thrill. (3/1)
**1028 Fyors Gift (IRE)** appreciated this return to racing on turf and showed her gratitude with a very courageous performance that enabled her to open her account. (17/2: 5/1-9/1)
**648 Lillibella**, who proved a bit of a handful when mounted, did not put her best foot forward until well inside the final furlong and another try at six furlongs could be what she really requires. (4/1: op 5/2)
**1028 Princess Efisio** struggled with the pace and did not make any impact until late in the day. She seemed ill-at-ease cantering to post. (11/2)
**1429 Madrina** needs more cut in the ground than she had here and was never going the pace of the leaders. (7/1)
**Incatinka**, having her first try at the minimum trip, sat in behind the leaders until getting left behind approaching the final furlong. (6/1)

## 1689 KINGSBURY LIMITED STKS (0-60) (3-Y.O+) (Class F)

5-30 (5-32) **7f** £3,190.20 (£887.20: £426.60) Stalls: Low GOING minus 0.57 sec per fur (F)

| | | | | SP | RR | SF |
|---|---|---|---|---|---|---|
| | **Paddy's Rice (56)** (MMcCormack) **5-9-3** JReid(6) (chsd ldrs: led over 1f out: hld on wl cl home) | — | **1** | 8/1 | 66 | 48 |
| 868[5] | **Morning Surprise (58)** (APJarvis) **3-7-11**(7) CCarver(8) (lw: hld up: hdwy 2f out: str run fnl f: jst failed) | hd | **2** | 8/1 | 63 | 35 |
| 1536* | **Always Grace (56)** (MissGayKelleway) **4-8-12**(5) MHenry(11) (hld up: hdwy over 1f out: r.o wl fnl f) | 3 | **3** | 5/2[1] | 59 | 41 |
| | **Jareer Do (IRE) (60)** (BPalling) **4-9-0** TSprake(13) (led tl over 1f out: kpt on u.p fnl f) | nk | **4** | 16/1 | 55 | 37 |
| *403[6]* | **Fairelaine (56)** (KCBailey) **4-8-9**(5) PPMurphy(10) (bit bkwd: hld up in tch: effrt u.p 2f out: kpt on) | hd | **5** | 14/1 | 55 | 37 |
| 1142[18] | **Hawanafa (60)** (RHannon) **3-8-4** JTate(14) (chsd ldr: brought wd over 1f out: sn btn) | 1 | **6** | 11/2[2] | 53 | 25 |
| 1348[12] | **Winter Scout (USA) (58)** (CPEBrooks) **8-8-10**(7) SCopp(4) (lw: sme hdwy fnl 2f: nvr nrr) | nk | **7** | 33/1 | 55 | 37 |
| 1007[11] | **Nicola's Princess (56)** (BAMcMahon) **3-8-4** GCarter(9) (nvr nr ldrs) | hd | **8** | 8/1 | 52 | 24 |
| 1324[8] | **Scenicris (IRE) (60)** (RHollinshead) **3-7-13**(5) FLynch(3) (a in rr) | 2 | **9** | 14/1 | 47 | 19 |
| 1416[8] | **Society Magic (USA) (60)** (IABalding) **3-8-7** PaulEddery(5) (swtg: mid div tl wknd wl over 1f out) | 2 | **10** | 7/1[3] | 46 | 18 |
| 955[6] | **Bullpen Belle (60)** (PTWalwyn) **3-8-4** JCarroll(7) (a in rr) | 1¼ | **11** | 12/1 | 40 | 12 |
| 1518[P] | **Baranov (IRE) (60)** (DJGMurraySmith) **3-8-7** NAdams(1) (prom tl wknd qckly 2f out) | ½ | **12** | 14/1 | 42 | 14 |
| 1074[14] | **Craven Cottage (60)** (CJames) **3-8-7** AMcGlone(2) (in tch 4f: wknd qckly t.o) | 9 | **13** | 33/1 | 21 | — |
| | | | | (SP 129.2%) | **13 Rn** | |

**1m 25.1** (0.50) CSF £70.11 TOTE £8.50: £2.40 £2.00 £1.50 (£47.40) Trio £48.50 OWNER Mrs R. G. Wellman (WANTAGE) BRED Mrs H. Lawson
WEIGHT FOR AGE 3yo-10lb

**Paddy's Rice**, looking well tuned up and wearing boots, quickened up to gain command over a furlong out and, though he had to find extra nearing the line, he was always in control. (8/1)
**868 Morning Surprise** produced a sustained last-furlong challenge that only just failed to gain the day. She should not be long in going one better. (8/1)
**1536* Always Grace** took too long to find top gear and the race was over when she did eventually get going. (5/2)
**Jareer Do (IRE)** has not shown much in previous races but, adopting new tactics on this seasonal debut, she ran by far her best race yet. She does look to be coming to herself. (16/1)
**Fairelaine** has been tried at several different trip and has still not got it right. Having her first outing since changing stables, she did stay on in the latter stages but needed plenty of encouragement to do so. (14/1)
**Hawanafa** sat on the tail of the leader until brought to race on the stands' side below the distance and, from then on, she was fighting a lost cause. (11/2)
**Bullpen Belle** (12/1: op 8/1)

T/Jkpt: Not won; £12,590.78 to Goodwood 6/6/96. T/Plpt: £76.60 (210.59 Tckts). T/Qdpt: £14.80 (83.45 Tckts). IM

# YARMOUTH (L-H) (Firm)

## Wednesday June 5th

WEATHER: fine WIND: mod half against

## 1690 SUFFOLK MAIDEN STKS (3-Y.O) (Class D)

2-15 (2-21) **1m 3y** £4,125.90 (£1,234.20: £591.60: £270.30) Stalls: High GOING minus 0.20 sec per fur (GF)

| | | | | SP | RR | SF |
|---|---|---|---|---|---|---|
| 1160[2] | **Dawna** (HRACecil) **3-8-9** PatEddery(7) (a gng wl: nt clr run over 1f out: swtchd lft: qcknd to ld ins fnl f: comf) | — | **1** | 13/8[1] | 74+ | 25 |

| | | | | SP | RR | SF |
|---|---|---|---|---|---|---|
| | **Sea of Stone (USA)** (LMCumani) **3-8-2**$^{(7)}$ RFfrench(5) (unf: hld up: hdwy over 1f out: r.o ins fnl f) | 2 | **2** | 33/1 | 70 | 21 |
| 826$^{7}$ | **Royal Action** (JEBanks) **3-9-0** JQuinn(3) (a.p: led over 1f out tl ins fnl f) | nk | **3** | 25/1 | 74 | 25 |
| 1319$^{6}$ | **Golden Thunderbolt (FR)** (JHMGosden) **3-9-0** LDettori(11) (w ldr: led over 2f out tl over 1f out: one pce) | ½ | **4** | 9/2$^{2}$ | 73 | 24 |
| | **Alrayyih (USA)** (JHMGosden) **3-9-0** RHills(10) (wl grwn: s.s: plld hrd in rr: hdwy 2f out: nt clr run 1f out: swtchd lft: r.o wl: bttr for r) | 1½ | **5** | 12/1 | 70 | 21 |
| 1470$^{5}$ | **Lucky Begonia (IRE)** (CNAllen) **3-8-9** CHodgson(8) (rdn & hdwy over 1f out: nvr nr to chal) | ½ | **6** | 40/1 | 64 | 15 |
| 1319$^{8}$ | **Naaman (IRE)** (MAJarvis) **3-8-9** PRobinson(13) (no hdwy fnl 2f) | 2 | **7** | 20/1 | 60 | 11 |
| 1004$^{8}$ | **Lunda (IRE)** (CEBrittain) **3-8-9** BDoyle(9) (led over 5f: wknd over 1f out) | ½ | **8** | 20/1 | 59 | 10 |
| | **Go Britannia** (DRLoder) **3-9-0** DRMcCabe(12) (cmpt: hld up & bhd: nvr plcd to chal) | ½ | **9** | 10/1 | 63 | 14 |
| | **Bourbonist (FR)** (LMCumani) **3-9-0** OUrbina(6) (wl grwn: hld up mid div: bhd fnl 2f) | ½ | **10** | 20/1 | 62 | 13 |
| | **Great Chief** (HRACecil) **3-9-0** WRyan(4) (str: hld up & plld hrd: bhd fnl 2f) | 4 | **11** | 10/1 | 54 | 5 |
| 730$^{4}$ | **Raise A Prince (FR)** (RWArmstrong) **3-9-0** WWoods(1) (prom over 5f) | 2 | **12** | 5/1$^{3}$ | 50 | 1 |
| | **Silky Smooth (IRE)** (MrsNMacauley) **3-8-6**$^{(3)}$ CTeague(2) (wl grwn: dwlt: a bhd: t.o) | dist | **13** | 40/1 | — | — |
| | | | | (SP 124.8%) | **13 Rn** | |

**1m 40.3** (5.00) CSF £50.44 TOTE £2.00: £1.10 £4.80 £5.90 (£35.90) Trio £256.10; £165.96 to Goodwood 6/6/96 OWNER Mr K. Abdulla (NEWMARKET) BRED Juddmonte Farms

**1160 Dawna**, a half-sister to a useful French middle-distance performer, showed a nice turn of foot to settle this and is bred to stay further. (13/8)

**Sea of Stone (USA)**, out of a mare who won twice over a mile and a half, ran a race full of promise over what should have been an inadequate trip. (33/1)

**826 Royal Action** should have stayed last time, but ran better on this return to a mile. (25/1)

**1319 Golden Thunderbolt (FR)**, out of a French listed winner over a mile and a half, should do better when trying a longer trip. (9/2: 4/1-6/1)

**Alrayyih (USA)** will have learnt a lot from this and is one to note. (12/1: op 8/1)

**Lucky Begonia (IRE)**, a sister to a mile juvenile winner, shaped as though she needs a stiffer test of stamina and should at least get a reasonable handicap mark. (40/1)

**Go Britannia**, a 185,000 guineas yearling, was given an educational outing, and will come into his own over longer trips. (10/1: op 5/1)

**Great Chief** (10/1: op 5/1)

## 1691 FLEGGS (S) H'CAP (0-60) (3-Y.O+) (Class G)

2-45 (2-49) **1m 3y** £2,805.00 (£780.00: £375.00) Stalls: High GOING minus 0.20 sec per fur (GF)

| | | | | SP | RR | SF |
|---|---|---|---|---|---|---|
| 1411$^{7}$ | **Irrepressible (IRE) (33)** (RJHodges) **5-8-1**$^{(5)}$ ADaly(12) (mde all: qcknd clr 2f out: easily) | — | **1** | 20/1 | 48+ | 35 |
| 1337$^{8}$ | **Northern Grey (46)** (DrJDScargill) **4-9-5** MFenton(10) (s.s: gd hdwy & n.m.r over 1f out: nt trble wnr) | 4 | **2** | 16/1 | 53 | 40 |
| 1468$^{10}$ | **Yet Again (40)** (BHanbury) **4-8-13** WRyan(18) (s.s: gd hdwy & nt clr run over 1f out: r.o) | 2½ | **3** | 9/1$^{3}$ | 42 | 29 |
| 1515$^{9}$ | **Total Rach (IRE) (47)** (RIngram) **4-9-6b** WWoods(9) (lw: hld up & bhd: hdwy over 2f out: nt rch ldrs) | 1½ | **4** | 6/1$^{2}$ | 46 | 33 |
| 1517$^{2}$ | **Sapphire Son (IRE) (48)** (DMorris) **4-9-7** PBloomfield(16) (lw: a.p: one pce fnl 2f) | 1¾ | **5** | 4/1$^{1}$ | 44 | 31 |
| 998$^{7}$ | **Sylvan Princess (44)** (CNAllen) **3-8-6b$^{1}$** LDettori(4) (lw: hdwy & nt clr run over 1f out: r.o) | hd | **6** | 10/1 | 39 | 15 |
| | **Overpower (51)** (MHTompkins) **12-9-10** PRobinson(8) (hdwy 2f out: nvr nr to chal) | hd | **7** | 10/1 | 46 | 33 |
| 920$^{12}$ | **Buddy's Friend (IRE) (48)** (RJRWilliams) **8-9-0**$^{(7)}$ AimeeCook(5) (b.nr fore: lw: hld up: swtchd lft over 3f out: no hdwy fnl 2f) | 2½ | **8** | 14/1 | 38 | 25 |
| 595$^{8}$ | **Farfeste (50)** (DMorris) **3-8-12** DHarrison(14) (prom over 6f) | 1¼ | **9** | 11/1 | 38 | 14 |
| 1642$^{11}$ | **Arlington Lady (40)** (NACallaghan) **3-8-2** JFEgan(6) (lw: prom over 6f) | hd | **10** | 11/1 | 27 | 3 |
| 1468$^{15}$ | **Shuttlecock (40)** (MrsNMacauley) **5-8-10**$^{(3)}$ CTeague(17) (lw: hld up & bhd: nt clr run over 3f out: nvr nrr) | hd | **11** | 33/1 | 27 | 14 |
| | **Glorious Island (46)** (MrsNMacauley) **6-9-5** CRutter(15) (b: n.d) | 3 | **12** | 16/1 | 27 | 14 |
| 1022$^{9}$ | **Pinkerton Polka (47)** (CEBrittain) **4-9-6** BDoyle(7) (lw: nvr trbld ldrs) | d.h | **12** | 12/1 | 34 | 21 |
| 1416$^{3}$ | **Bad News (44)** (JMBradley) **4-9-0**$^{(3)}$ SDrowne(1) (b: prom over 5f) | 5 | **14** | 10/1 | 15 | 2 |
| 1411$^{12}$ | **Begger's Opera (32)** (PatMitchell) **4-8-5** FNorton(2) (lw: prom 5f) | nk | **15** | 33/1 | 3 | — |
| | **Binlaboon (IRE) (35)** (KGWingrove) **5-8-8b** KRutter(3) (b: bhd fnl 2f) | hd | **16** | 33/1 | 6 | — |
| *274*$^{10}$ | **Red Adair (IRE) (50)** (BobJones) **4-9-9** NDay(13) (lw: a bhd) | hd | **17** | 9/1$^{3}$ | 20 | 7 |
| 1067$^{5}$ | **Crystal Fast (USA) (44)** (PAKelleway) **3-8-6** WJO'Connor(11) (prom over 5f) | 1½ | **18** | 11/1 | 11 | — |
| | | | | (SP 146.3%) | **18 Rn** | |

**1m 39.0** (3.70) CSF £315.89 CT £2,916.64 TOTE £28.20: £4.90 £5.70 £3.60 £2.40 (£303.10) Trio £1,317.60 OWNER Mr R. Callow (SOMERTON) BRED Ron Con Ltd

WEIGHT FOR AGE 3yo-11lb

No bid

**Irrepressible (IRE)**, who has undergone a wind operation, showed signs of a return to form last time and made the long journey from Somerset pay off in no uncertain fashion over this shorter trip. (20/1)

**Northern Grey**, sold out of Jack Berry's yard for 2,100 guineas, appreciated the drop into selling company on this second run for his new stable. (16/1)

**Yet Again** ran better without the blinkers and appreciated the fast ground, but a mile is on the sharp side for him. (9/1: op 6/1)

**Total Rach (IRE)**, 1lb lower than when winning a similar event over course and distance last October, was never going to get there in time on this drop back to a mile. (6/1)

**1517 Sapphire Son (IRE)** may have found this trip just beyond his best. (4/1)

**560 Sylvan Princess**, dropped into selling company, was tried in blinkers but probably found this shorter trip inadequate. (10/1)

**Buddy's Friend (IRE)** (14/1: 10/1-16/1)

**Farfeste** (11/1: 8/1-12/1)

**488 Arlington Lady** (11/1: 6/1-12/1)

**1067 Crystal Fast (USA)** (11/1: 8/1-12/1)

## 1692 ROYAL ANGLIAN REGIMENT MEDIAN AUCTION MAIDEN STKS (3-Y.O F) (Class E)

3-15 (3-16) **7f 3y** £2,961.00 (£882.00: £420.00: £189.00) Stalls: High GOING minus 0.20 sec per fur (GF)

| | | | | SP | RR | SF |
|---|---|---|---|---|---|---|
| 1452$^{5}$ | **Panata (IRE)** (LMCumani) **3-8-11** OUrbina(1) (chsd ldr: led wl over 1f out: pushed out) | — | **1** | 6/5$^{1}$ | 81 | 49 |
| 1475$^{6}$ | **Delphine** (MBell) **3-8-11** MFenton(3) (lw: hld up: hdwy 2f out: chsd wnr fnl f: no imp) | 5 | **2** | 3/1$^{2}$ | 70 | 38 |
| 686$^{15}$ | **Ewar Sunrise (72)** (CEBrittain) **3-8-11** BDoyle(4) (led over 5f: one pce) | 1¼ | **3** | 6/1$^{3}$ | 67 | 35 |
| 1171$^{8}$ | **Ember** (LMCumani) **3-8-4**$^{(7)}$ RFfrench(6) (hld up: wknd over 1f out) | 3½ | **4** | 10/1 | 59 | 27 |
| 1405$^{8}$ | **Rhythmic Ball (42)** (TRWatson) **3-8-6**$^{(5)}$ CAdamson(5) (b: prom: rdn over 2f out: wknd wl over 1f out) | 2 | **5** | 50/1 | 54 | 22 |
| | **Jeanne Cutrona** (NACallaghan) **3-8-11** WRyan(2) (w'like: lw: hld up: bhd fnl 2f: t.o) | 22 | **6** | 14/1 | 4 | — |
| | | | | (SP 102.5%) | **6 Rn** | |

**1m 26.7** (2.50) CSF £4.42 TOTE £2.00: £1.30 £1.50 (£1.70) OWNER Mrs Angie Silver (NEWMARKET) BRED Dr J. J. Ryan

**1452 Panata (IRE)** made short work of these rivals and should continue to progress. (6/5)
**1475 Delphine** had to be content to play second fiddle. (3/1: op 5/1)
**550 Ewar Sunrise** is bred to stay at least a mile, so it was surprising to see her drop back to six last time. (6/1: op 4/1)
**921 Ember** should require at least a mile on breeding. (10/1: 8/1-12/1)

## 1693 LODDON H'CAP (0-80) (3-Y.O) (Class D)

3-45 (3-47) **6f 3y** £3,993.30 (£1,193.40: £571.20: £260.10) Stalls: High GOING minus 0.20 sec per fur (GF)

| | | | | SP | RR | SF |
|---|---|---|---|---|---|---|
| 937$^{11}$ | **Jerry Cutrona (IRE) (66)** (NACallaghan) **3-8-9** JFEgan(6) (lw: hld up: swtchd stands' side & hdwy 2f out: led 1f out: comf) | — | **1** | 9/1 | 75+ | 38 |
| 773$^{5}$ | **Green Barries (78)** (MJohnston) **3-9-7** MHills(8) (hld up: hdwy & nt clr run over 1f out: swtchd lft: r.o: nt trble wnr) | 2½ | **2** | 4/1$^{2}$ | 80 | 43 |
| 1485$^{7}$ | **Stop Play (IRE) (72)** (MHTompkins) **3-9-1** PRobinson(13) (a.p: ev ch over 1f out: unable qckn) | ¾ | **3** | 6/1$^{3}$ | 72 | 35 |
| 1152$^{6}$ | **Snow Falcon (65)** (MBell) **3-8-8b$^{1}$** MFenton(5) (lw: hdwy & hmpd wl over 1f out: swtchd lft: r.o ins fnl f) | 1¾ | **4** | 25/1 | 61 | 24 |
| 571$^{13}$ | **Welsh Mountain (72)** (MJHeaton-Ellis) **3-8-12v$^{1}$**(3) SDrowne(11) (a.p: led over 1f out: sn hdd: one pce) | s.h | **5** | 25/1 | 68 | 31 |
| 676$^{13}$ | **Missile Toe (IRE) (70)** (JEBanks) **3-8-13** LDettori(7) (lw: no hdwy fnl 2f) | 1¼ | **6** | 9/1 | 62 | 25 |
| 1473$^{2}$ | **Albaha (USA) (75)** (RWArmstrong) **3-9-4b** RHills(12) (led over 4f) | 1 | **7** | 9/4$^{1}$ | 65 | 28 |
| 1142$^{20}$ | **Utmost Zeal (USA) (65)** (PWHarris) **3-8-8** FNorton(9) (lw: bhd: sn rdn along: nvr nr to chal) | ½ | **8** | 25/1 | 53 | 16 |
| 1536$^{4}$ | **Rififi (62)** (RIngram) **3-8-5** SWhitworth(2) (bhd fnl 2f) | hd | **9** | 9/1 | 50 | 13 |
| 1101$^{16}$ | **Mindrace (66)** (KTIvory) **3-8-9** BDoyle(10) (chsd ldr over 3f) | 6 | **10** | 14/1 | 38 | 1 |
| 692$^{14}$ | **Badger Bay (IRE) (64)** (CADwyer) **3-8-7** WRyan(1) (a bhd) | ¾ | **11** | 25/1 | 34 | — |
| | **Times of Times (IRE) (78)** (MJRyan) **3-9-7** CRutter(3) (bit bkwd: prom 3f) | 3½ | **12** | 14/1 | 39 | 2 |

(SP 123.8%) **12 Rn**

**1m 13.6** (2.70) CSF £43.15 CT £215.26 TOTE £13.40: £4.20 £1.70 £1.80 (£42.40) Trio £49.10 OWNER Mr Michael Hill (NEWMARKET) BRED Dr Paschal Carmody
**756 Jerry Cutrona (IRE)**, dropped 3lb, ran out a convincing winner over this shorter trip. (9/1: 9/2-10/1)
**773 Green Barries** does not mind fast ground and bounced back to form, but it is doubtful whether he would have beaten the winner even with a trouble-free run. (4/1)
**Stop Play (IRE)** did race on her own last time, but looked more at home over this shorter trip and should now be approaching her peak. (6/1)
**Snow Falcon**, blinkered for the first time, had already been tried in a visor on the All-Weather and appeared to find this sprint trip inadequate. (25/1)
**Welsh Mountain**, tried in a visor, seems better suited to the minimum trip. (25/1)
**Missile Toe (IRE)**, without the headgear this time, was making no impression when the Stewards found he was accidentally interfered with by the runner-up approaching the final furlong. (9/1)
**1473 Albaha (USA)** was apparently due to go up 10lb following his good run in first-time blinkers last week, so the Handicapper may have to have a rethink. (9/4)
**Utmost Zeal (USA)**, last in two runs over a mile this season, showed signs of improvement over an inadequate trip. (25/1)
**1536 Rififi** (9/1: 6/1-10/1)
**Times of Times (IRE)** (14/1: 8/1-16/1)

## 1694 E.B.F. BRECKLAND MAIDEN STKS (2-Y.O) (Class D)

4-15 (4-16) **6f 3y** £3,362.60 (£1,002.80: £478.40: £216.20) Stalls: High GOING minus 0.20 sec per fur (GF)

| | | | | SP | RR | SF |
|---|---|---|---|---|---|---|
| | **Quest Express** (MBell) **2-9-0** MFenton(4) (w'like: scope: hld up: stdy hdwy over 2f out: led ins fnl f: pushed out) | — | **1** | 11/2$^{2}$ | 76+ | 23 |
| | **Air Express (IRE)** (CEBrittain) **2-9-0** BDoyle(5) (gd sort: s.i.s: hld up: hdwy 2f out: led over 1f out: hdd ins fnl f) | ½ | **2** | 13/2$^{3}$ | 75 | 22 |
| 697$^{6}$ | **Maraud** (RWArmstrong) **2-9-0** MHills(1) (led over 4f: one pce) | 5 | **3** | 20/1 | 61 | 8 |
| | **Regal Patrol** (MRStoute) **2-9-0** LDettori(6) (w'like: scope: sn chsng ldr: ev ch whn rn green & hit rails wl over 1f out: nt rcvr) | 2 | **4** | 1/2$^{1}$ | 56+ | 3 |
| | **Admonish** (MAJarvis) **2-8-9** PRobinson(3) (w'like: b.nr hind: dwlt: bhd fnl 2f) | ¾ | **5** | 25/1 | 49 | — |
| | **A Breeze** (DMorris) **2-9-0** DHarrison(2) (unf: hld up: rdn over 2f out: wknd wl over 1f out) | 1¼ | **6** | 14/1 | 51 | — |
| 1169$^{4}$ | **Sharp Return** (MJRyan) **2-9-0** DBiggs(7) (prom over 3f) | 8 | **7** | 12/1 | 29 | — |

(SP 118.4%) **7 Rn**

**1m 15.1** (4.20) CSF £37.71 TOTE £8.40: £2.00 £2.50 (£19.80) OWNER Mr R. P. B. Michaelson (NEWMARKET) BRED Hamish Alexander
**Quest Express** ran out a decisive winner. Well regarded by his trainer, he could go for the July Stakes and an extra furlong should not be a problem. (11/2: 4/1-6/1)
**Air Express (IRE)**, a good-looking half-brother to three winners including Aljazzaf, found the winner too much of a handful in the closing stages, but should not always find one so smart. (13/2)
**Maraud** is a half-brother to hurdler Forgetful. (20/1)
**Regal Patrol**, a first foal out of a mare from a good family, completely lost his action inside the quarter-mile marker. Reported to have been working well at home, he should be given a chance to atone. (1/2)

## 1695 RIVER YARE LIMITED STKS (0-65) (4-Y.O+) (Class F)

4-45 (4-46) **1m 6f 17y** £2,660.00 (£735.00: £350.00) Stalls: Low GOING minus 0.39 sec per fur (F)

| | | | | SP | RR | SF |
|---|---|---|---|---|---|---|
| | **Frozen Sea (USA) (65)** (GPEnright) **5-8-10** BDoyle(3) (hld up: led over 2f out: clr 1f out: pushed out) | — | **1** | 3/1$^{2}$ | 72 | 29 |
| 968$^{14}$ | **Lucky Coin (64)** (PHowling) **4-8-7** FNorton(6) (hld up: hrd rdn & outpcd over 3f out: chsd wnr fnl f: no imp) | 4 | **2** | 6/1$^{3}$ | 65 | 22 |
| 759$^{5}$ | **Mizyan (IRE) (60)** (JEBanks) **8-8-10** LDettori(5) (lw: led after 1f: hdd over 2f out: one pce) | 1¼ | **3** | 15/8$^{1}$ | 66 | 23 |
| 1462$^{7}$ | **Green Land (BEL) (64)** (SCWilliams) **4-8-7** MHills(2) (lw: b.nr fore: led 1f: one pce fnl 2f) | nk | **4** | 3/1$^{2}$ | 63 | 20 |
| | **Red Light (65)** (JRJenkins) **4-8-10v** MFenton(4) (hld up & bhd: hung lft & wknd over 2f out) | 16 | **5** | 10/1 | 48 | 5 |
| | **Noble Society (30)** (KGWingrove) **8-8-10** KRutter(1) (b: hld up: rdn over 4f out: sn bhd: t.o) | 15 | **6** | 33/1 | 31 | — |

(SP 111.1%) **6 Rn**

**3m 5.7** (6.30) CSF £18.57 TOTE £4.70: £1.90 £2.70 (£9.20) OWNER The Oaks Partners (LEWES) BRED Darley Stud Management Co Ltd
**Frozen Sea (USA)**, who won over hurdles at Fontwell in April, scored readily on this fast ground and his trainer is thinking in terms of the Bessborough at Royal Ascot, and the Ebor if he can get into the respective handicaps. (3/1)
**Lucky Coin**, bought out of Clive Brittain's stable for 12,500 guineas at Ascot October Sales, likes fast ground and fared better than on her first run for her new connections. (6/1)

**Mizyan (IRE)** was twice a winner from three attempts for Dettori last year, but the Italian could not work the oracle this time. (15/8)
**Green Land (BEL)** seemed better suited to this faster surface. (3/1)

## 1696 HEYDON HALL APPRENTICE H'CAP (0-70) (3-Y.O+) (Class G)
5-15 (5-17) **1m 2f 21y** £2,154.50 (£612.00: £303.50) Stalls: Low GOING minus 0.39 sec per fur (F)

| | | | | SP | RR | SF |
|---|---|---|---|---|---|---|
| *1490[3]* | **Princely Affair (49)** (MBell) **3-7-2**(8) RMullen(7) (hld up: hdwy over 2f out: led 1f out: r.o) | — | **1** | 13/2[3] | 55 | 24 |
| 1173[4] | **Contrafire (IRE) (68)** (WJarvis) **4-9-4**(10) TThomas(6) (lw: a.p: led over 1f out: sn hdd: r.o one pce) | 1¼ | **2** | 4/1[2] | 72 | 54 |
| 1496[16] | **Studio Thirty (37)** (DMorris) **4-7-11**ow1 AEddery(2) (hdwy over 2f out: ev ch over 1f out: r.o one pce) | s.h | **3** | 12/1 | 41 | 22 |
| 1449[4] | **Lady Sabina (40)** (WJMusson) **6-7-11**(3) JWilkinson(8) (lw: rdn over 3f out: hdwy 2f out: one pce fnl f) | 1½ | **4** | 3/1[1] | 42 | 24 |
| 1450[5] | **Augustan (50)** (SGollings) **5-8-10v** JEdmunds(9) (s.i.s: sn prom: hrd rdn 3f out: no hdwy fnl 2f) | 1 | **5** | 8/1 | 50 | 32 |
| 1343[8] | **Western Horizon (USA) (36)** (CEBrittain) **4-7-5**(5) PDoe(1) (lw: a.p: led over 2f out tl over 1f out: wknd ins fnl f) | s.h | **6** | 12/1 | 36 | 18 |
| 1414[6] | **Conic Hill (IRE) (52)** (JPearce) **5-8-4**(8) SGaillard(10) (hld up: hdwy over 2f out: wknd over 1f out) | ½ | **7** | 8/1 | 51 | 33 |
| 1472[8] | **El Don (42)** (MJRyan) **4-7-6b**(10) AMcCarthy(5) (prom tl wknd over 2f out) | 4 | **8** | 16/1 | 35 | 17 |
| 1174[8] | **Mr Speculator (65)** (PAKelleway) **3-8-2**(10)ow5 CDomergue(4) (wl bhd fnl 4f) | 8 | **9** | 16/1 | 45 | 9 |
| 1174[11] | **Persephone (49)** (ICampbell) **3-7-7b**[1](3) KSked(3) (led: clr over 4f out: hdd over 2f out: sn wknd) | 2 | **10** | 11/1 | 26 | — |

(SP 116.0%) **10 Rn**

**2m 7.6** (3.20) CSF £30.59 CT £279.53 TOTE £8.10: £2.90 £1.80 £2.80 (£17.20) Trio £103.40 OWNER Mr S. C. Sampson (NEWMARKET) BRED P. T. Tellwright
LONG HANDICAP Princely Affair 7-8 Persephone 7-1
WEIGHT FOR AGE 3yo-13lb
**1490 Princely Affair** goes well for his young rider and appreciated the return to a longer trip. (13/2: 5/1-8/1)
**1173 Contrafire (IRE)** probably now finds this distance the bare minimum. (4/1: 3/1-9/2)
**Studio Thirty** has been slipping down the ratings and bounced back to form on this fast ground. (12/1)
**1449 Lady Sabina**, 2lb higher than when winning a similar event last season, was back to the right sort of trip but could never quite get to grips with the principles. (3/1)
**1450 Augustan** was 10lb lower than when winning a similar event over a mile and a half at York last August and this trip looked on the short side for him. (8/1: op 4/1)
**Western Horizon (USA)** (12/1: 9/1-14/1)

T/Plpt: £335.90 (35.85 Tckts). T/Qdpt: £25.70 (32.83 Tckts). KH

# 1671-BEVERLEY (R-H) (Good to firm, Firm patches)
## Thursday June 6th
WEATHER: fine & sunny WIND: mod half bhd

## 1697 HURN CLAIMING STKS (4-Y.O+) (Class F)
2-20 (2-21) **1m 3f 216y** £2,798.00 (£778.00: £374.00) Stalls: High GOING minus 0.49 sec per fur (F)

| | | | | SP | RR | SF |
|---|---|---|---|---|---|---|
| | **Cante Chico (64)** (OBrennan) **4-7-13**(7) JoHunnam(3) (lw: trckd ldrs: led over 1f out: styd on u.p) | — | **1** | 10/1 | 51 | 28 |
| | **Viardot (IRE) (69)** (MrsMReveley) **7-9-1** KDarley(2) (hld up: effrt over 3f out: styd on u.p ins fnl f: nt rch wnr) | 1¼ | **2** | 4/6[1] | 58 | 35 |
| 872[19] | **Bold Top (35)** (BSRothwell) **4-8-3b**(3) JStack(4) (trckd ldr: led over 3f out tl over 1f out: one pce) | s.h | **3** | 12/1 | 49 | 26 |
| 822[2] | **Castletown Count (52)** (KWHogg) **4-8-4** NKennedy(6) (trckd ldrs: outpcd 2f out: styd on same pce ins fnl f) | ½ | **4** | 3/1[2] | 47 | 24 |
| 1159[12] | **Island Cascade (30)** (DonEnricoIncisa) **4-7-11** KimTinkler(7) (hld up & plld hrd: effrt 3f out: nvr nr ldrs) | 8 | **5** | 33/1 | 29 | 6 |
| *1457[11]* | **Remontant (IRE) (34)** (RHollinshead) **4-7-12**(5)ow2 FLynch(1) (trckd ldrs: rdn over 3f out: sn wknd) | 6 | **6** | 9/1[3] | 25 | 2 |
| | **Venture Fourth (21)** (MissMKMilligan) **7-8-2** JTate(5) (led tl over 3f out: sn wknd) | 11 | **7** | 33/1 | 11 | — |

(SP 117.7%) **7 Rn**

**2m 36.1** (3.70) CSF £17.51 TOTE £8.90: £3.10 £2.00 (£7.40) OWNER Miss V. Haigh (WORKSOP) BRED Sheikh Mohammed bin Rashid al Maktoum
Castletown Count clmd RArmitage £4,000
**Cante Chico**, who had shown next to nothing in three outings in selling hurdles during the winter, looked particularly well and was capably handled. (10/1: op 6/1)
**Viardot (IRE)**, a winner over hurdles this winter, was in one of his unco-operative moods. When his rider got serious with him, he was never putting his best foot forward, although he did stay on inside the last. (4/6)
**504 Bold Top**, who would have been 29lb better off with the winner in a handicap, seemed to run the race of his life. (12/1)
**822 Castletown Count** never settled at any stage but showed his Ripon effort was no fluke. (3/1: op 2/1)
**609 Remontant (IRE)** (9/1: op 6/1)

## 1698 TOUCH ABOVE H'CAP (0-70) (3-Y.O+) (Class E)
2-50 (2-50) **1m 1f 207y** £3,127.25 (£938.00: £451.50: £208.25) Stalls: High GOING minus 0.49 sec per fur (F)

| | | | | SP | RR | SF |
|---|---|---|---|---|---|---|
| 1418[3] | **Essayeffsee (56)** (MrsMReveley) **7-9-2** KDarley(7) (hld up: effrt over 3f out: styd on u.p to ld jst ins fnl f) | — | **1** | 11/10[1] | 67 | 36 |
| 1641[6] | **Silverdale Knight (58)** (KWHogg) **3-8-5** DeanMcKeown(1) (led tl over 2f out: rallied & ev ch 1f out: kpt on same pce) | ½ | **2** | 7/2[2] | 68 | 24 |
| | **Efizia (60)** (GMMoore) **6-9-6** JTate(6) (bit bkwd: trckd ldrs: led over 2f out tl jst ins fnl f) | 2 | **3** | 15/2[3] | 67 | 36 |
| 979[7] | **Reefa's Mill (IRE) (64)** (JNeville) **4-9-7v**(3) SDrowne(3) (chsd ldrs: rdn over 3f out: edgd lft & sn wknd) | 6 | **4** | 9/1 | 61 | 30 |
| 1341[5] | **Jungle Patrol (IRE) (54)** (MBrittain) **4-9-0** GCarter(2) (trckd ldrs: effrt over 3f out: sn wknd) | 3 | **5** | 7/2[2] | 47 | 16 |
| *1241[2]* | **Elite Justice (61)** (SGollings) **4-9-7** VHalliday(4) (pushed along 5f out: sn bhd) | 1¼ | **6** | 10/1 | 52 | 21 |

(SP 122.9%) **6 Rn**

**2m 5.5** (3.00) CSF £6.01 TOTE £1.70: £1.40 £1.80 (£3.20) OWNER Mrs S. D. Murray (SALTBURN) BRED Mrs L. F. Rathbone
WEIGHT FOR AGE 3yo-13lb
**1418 Essayeffsee** did just enough. The Handicapper has his form summed up to a pound. (11/10)
**1641 Silverdale Knight** did not force the pace. Proving determined under pressure, the winner always had his measure in the closing stages. (7/2)
**Efizia**, who has not won for two and a half years, ran well considering she looked very big. (15/2: 5/1-8/1)
**Reefa's Mill (IRE)** looked very lean and has slipped down the weights. The visor had little effect though. (9/1)

**1341 Jungle Patrol (IRE)**, stepped up in distance, wore a tongue-strap. (7/2)
**Elite Justice** (10/1: op 6/1)

## 1699 BRIAN YEARDLEY CONTINENTAL TWO YEAR OLD TROPHY CONDITIONS STKS (2-Y.O C & G) (Class B)

3-20 (3-21) **5f** £7,468.40 (£2,795.60: £1,367.80: £589.00: £264.50: £134.70) Stalls: High GOING minus 0.78 sec per fur (HD)

| | | | | SP | RR | SF |
|---|---|---|---|---|---|---|
| 1197* | **For Your Eyes Only** (TDEasterby) **2-8-13** KDarley(4) (lw: b: chsd ldr: led 1f out: r.o strly) | — | 1 | 11/4$^{1}$ | 91+ | 57 |
| 996$^{2}$ | **Superior Premium** (RAFahey) **2-8-9** ACulhane(6) (lw: led to 1f out: kpt on wl) | 2½ | 2 | 4/1$^{2}$ | 79 | 45 |
| 1184* | **Double Action** (TDEasterby) **2-8-13** KFallon(3) (lw: drvn along & outpcd over 3f out: styd on wl appr fnl f) | 1 | 3 | 10/1 | 80 | 46 |
| 1344* | **Bolero Boy** (MWEasterby) **2-8-13** DaleGibson(5) (chsd ldrs: rdn ½-wy: styd on wl fnl f) | hd | 4 | 7/1$^{3}$ | 80 | 46 |
| 1303* | **For Old Times Sake** (JBerry) **2-9-1** GCarter(2) (lw: sn outpcd & pushed along: hdwy on outside ½-wy: nvr nr to chal) | 3½ | 5 | 11/4$^{1}$ | 70 | 36 |
| 950* | **Ice Age** (RJRWilliams) **2-8-13** MHills(1) (sn trckng ldrs: rdn & hung rt 2f out: sn wknd & eased) | 17 | 6 | 11/4$^{1}$ | 14 | — |

(SP 121.6%) **6 Rn**

**61.6 secs** (0.10) CSF £14.32 TOTE £4.00: £2.50 £1.40 (£9.50) OWNER Mr Reg Griffin (MALTON) BRED Compton Down Stud
OFFICIAL EXPLANATION **Ice Age: was found to be lame on his near-fore on returning home.**
**1197* For Your Eyes Only**, who has thrived physically since Ripon, scored in most decisive fashion in the end from five previous winners, and is fully entitled to take his chance in the Norfolk Stakes at Royal Ascot. He would have to be seriously considered. (11/4)
**996 Superior Premium** showed a poor action going down. Racing keenly, he showed bags of toe but, in the end, the winner proved much superior. He would not want the ground any firmer. (4/1: 6/1-7/2)
**1184* Double Action**, who has a scratchy action, struggled to go the pace. Staying on inside the last, he will be suited by six and easier ground. (10/1: op 5/1)
**1344* Bolero Boy** was sticking on strongly at the finish and will be suited by six. (7/1: 5/1-8/1)
**1303* For Old Times Sake** was dwarfed by the winner in the paddock and the race. (11/4)
**950* Ice Age** did not take the eye in the paddock and only wanted to hang right. (11/4: op 7/4)

## 1700 111TH YEAR OF THE WATT MEMORIAL H'CAP (0-90) (3-Y.O+) (Class C)

3-50 (3-50) **1m 3f 216y** £5,540.00 (£1,670.00: £810.00: £380.00) Stalls: High GOING minus 0.49 sec per fur (F)

| | | | | SP | RR | SF |
|---|---|---|---|---|---|---|
| 1109$^{3}$ | **Tykeyvor (IRE) (77)** (LadyHerries) **6-9-3** KDarley(3) (lw: b.hind: trckd ldr: rdn to ld over 2f out: styd on wl fnl f) | — | 1 | 7/4$^{1}$ | 89 | 50 |
| 1353$^{2}$ | **Bardon Hill Boy (IRE) (84)** (BHanbury) **4-9-7**(3) JStack(5) (trckd ldrs: effrt over 2f out: nt qckn fnl f) | 1½ | 2 | 4/1$^{3}$ | 94 | 55 |
| 1450$^{9}$ | **Deano's Beeno (76)** (MJohnston) **4-9-2** JWeaver(2) (lw: led tl over 2f out: one pce) | 5 | 3 | 11/2 | 79 | 40 |
| 963$^{4}$ | **Tessajoe (72)** (MJCamacho) **4-8-12** LCharnock(4) (trckd ldrs: effrt over 2f out: no imp) | 8 | 4 | 5/2$^{2}$ | 65 | 26 |
| | **Faugeron (56)** (NTinkler) **7-7-10** KimTinkler(1) (dwlt s: sn chsng ldrs: rdn & hung rt over 2f out: sn wknd) | 2½ | 5 | 20/1 | 45 | 6 |
| | **Harbour Island (88)** (MRStoute) **4-10-0v**$^{1}$ KFallon(6) (a last: pushed along over 3f out: sn bhd) | 11 | 6 | 11/2 | 63 | 24 |

(SP 120.5%) **6 Rn**

**2m 34.3** (1.90) CSF £9.49 TOTE £3.00: £1.60 £2.10 (£5.10) OWNER Seymour Bloodstock (UK) Ltd (LITTLEHAMPTON) BRED H. Key
**1109 Tykeyvor (IRE)**, on really good terms with himself, was given a first-class attacking ride and always had it under control. He will now go for the Bessborough at Royal Ascot. (7/4)
**1353 Bardon Hill Boy (IRE)** had plenty to do at the weights with the winner on Sandown running last year. (4/1)
**1198 Deano's Beeno** looked particularly well and made the running, but proved one-paced. (11/2)
**963 Tessajoe** took a keen grip but fell in a heap with two furlongs to go. (5/2)

## 1701 ETTON MAIDEN STKS (3-Y.O+) (Class D)

4-20 (4-23) **1m 100y** £3,561.00 (£1,068.00: £514.00: £237.00) Stalls: High GOING minus 0.49 sec per fur (F)

| | | | | SP | RR | SF |
|---|---|---|---|---|---|---|
| | **Fahim** (ACStewart) **3-8-10** RHills(5) (trckd ldrs: shkn up to ld over 1f out: pushed clr fnl f: easily) | — | 1 | 2/5$^{1}$ | 85+ | 56 |
| | **Shehab (IRE)** (WJHaggas) **3-8-10** RMcGhin(6) (w'like: trckd ldrs: outpcd & swtchd outside over 1f out: styd on towards fin) | 3 | 2 | 12/1 | 79 | 50 |
| 1182$^{6}$ | **Crown Court (USA)** (LMCumani) **3-8-10** KDarley(3) (b: trckd ldrs: rdn over 2f out: one pce) | nk | 3 | 6/1$^{3}$ | 79 | 50 |
| | **Desert Frolic (IRE)** (MJohnston) **3-8-5** PRobinson(2) (a chsng ldrs: rdn & outcpd over 2f out: styd on one pce) | 3 | 4 | 11/2$^{2}$ | 68 | 39 |
| 1154$^{7}$ | **Midnight Spell (65)** (JWHills) **4-9-2** MHills(4) (led tl over 1f out: sn wknd) | 6 | 5 | 12/1 | 57 | 39 |
| | **Arabian Design** (GMMoore) **4-9-7** JTate(1) (bit bkwd: unruly s: swvd lft s: a last: rdn over 5f out: bhd fnl 2f) | 7 | 6 | 25/1 | 49 | 31 |

(SP 120.3%) **6 Rn**

**1m 43.8** (-0.20) CSF £6.80 TOTE £1.60: £1.10 £3.40 (£7.10) OWNER Mr Hamdan Al Maktoum (NEWMARKET) BRED Shadwell Estate Company Limited
WEIGHT FOR AGE 3yo-11lb
**Fahim** showed plenty of promise on one outing at two and is a fluent mover. Confidently ridden, he won this with plenty to spare. The Handicapper looks unlikely to take any chances with him. (2/5: op 8/11)
**Shehab (IRE)**, who has a reputation of being difficult in the stalls, took plenty of loading. Showing signs of inexperience, he was staying on at the end and should improve. (12/1: op 5/1)
**1182 Crown Court (USA)**, a good-topped colt, showed a poor action on the ground. His future lies in handicaps on better going. (6/1: op 3/1)
**Desert Frolic (IRE)** was not disgraced on her reappearance as she probably needs further and handicap company. (11/2)
**Midnight Spell** misbehaved coming out of the paddock. (12/1: op 7/1)
**Arabian Design** showed a poor action and behaved badly at the stalls. (25/1)

## 1702 FIGHAM MAIDEN APPRENTICE H'CAP (0-75) (3-Y.O+) (Class G)

4-50 (4-51) **5f** £2,133.50 (£606.00: £300.50) Stalls: High GOING minus 0.78 sec per fur (HD)

| | | | | SP | RR | SF |
|---|---|---|---|---|---|---|
| *1606*$^{6}$ | **Bowcliffe Grange (IRE) (23)** (DWChapman) **4-8-1** JoanneWebster(7) (lw: mde all: clr ½-wy: unchal) | — | 1 | 5/2$^{2}$ | 31 | 12 |
| 1592$^{3}$ | **Wire Act (USA) (57)** (MartynMeade) **3-9-9**(5) ClaireAngell(8) (sn outpcd & bhd: styd on fnl 2f: nt rch wnr) | 2 | 2 | 6/1 | 59 | 33 |
| 1642$^{16}$ | **Branston Kristy (35)** (CSmith) **4-8-13b** CCogan(6) (chsd ldrs: hrd rdn & wnt rt jst ins fnl f: kpt on) | 1½ | 3 | 20/1 | 32 | 13 |
| *1455*$^{2}$ | **Belinda Blue (46)** (RAFahey) **4-9-10** RFfrench(9) (v.unruly leaving paddock: chsd ldrs: styng on sme pce whn bmpd jst ins fnl f) | ¾ | 4 | 11/8$^{1}$ | 40 | 21 |
| 1422$^{11}$ | **Rocky Stream (45)** (RMWhitaker) **3-8-11**(5) PFredericks(2) (sn drvn along: hdwy ½-wy: hrd rdn & hung lft: no imp) | 1¼ | 5 | 9/1 | 35 | 9 |

1500[6] **Blue Lugana (33)** (NBycroft) **4-8-11b** CScudder(3) (hdwy ½-wy: hrd rdn & hmpd 1f out: n.d) ....½ **6** 10/1 22 3
1547[5] **China Hand (IRE) (38)** (MartynWane) **4-9-2** KSked(4) (chsd wnr: hung rt 2f out: sn wknd)....3½ **7** 11/2[3] 16 —
**Sharp Holly (IRE) (49)** (JABennett) **4-9-13** RMullen(5) (s.i.s: a bhd) ....1 **8** 12/1 23 4
*607*[13] **Young Ben (IRE) (42)** (JSWainwright) **4-9-1**(5) TSiddall(1) (b: b.hind: sn bhd) ....3½ **9** 20/1 5 —
(SP 136.7%) **9 Rn**

**62.2 secs** (0.70) CSF £20.42 CT £247.31 TOTE £4.20: £1.40 £2.00 £4.20 (£10.80) Trio £68.20 OWNER Mr David Chapman (YORK) BRED Rosemount House Stud
WEIGHT FOR AGE 3yo-7lb
OFFICIAL EXPLANATION **Belinda Blue: was found to be in season on returning home.**
**1606 Bowcliffe Grange (IRE)**, rated only 23, made the most of a first-class opportunity. Soon showing his rivals a clean pair of heels, he was never in any danger of being caught. (5/2)
**1592 Wire Act (USA)**, who has run at up to twelve furlongs, had the blinkers left off. Making up a fair amount of ground in the final furlong, he was never going to reach the winner. (6/1)
**Branston Kristy**, still a maiden after twenty-four outings, dived right with her inexperienced rider being very free with the whip. (20/1)
**1455 Belinda Blue** rolled over and unseated her rider coming out of the paddock. Starting on terms for once, she was not doing much when bumped by the third inside the last. (11/8)
**Rocky Stream**, drawn two, tended to hang left and made her effort up the middle. (9/1)
**Blue Lugana** was staying on when knocked out of his stride. (10/1)

T/Plpt: £47.30 (179.69 Tckts). T/Qdpt: £19.90 (23.39 Tckts). WG

## 1014-CHESTER (L-H) (Good to firm)
## Thursday June 6th
WEATHER: cloudy

## 1703 PEEPING TOM H'CAP (0-90) (3-Y.O+) (Class C)
6-45 (6-45) **7f 2y** £6,645.00 (£2,010.00: £980.00: £465.00) Stalls: Low GOING minus 0.33 sec per fur (GF)

SP RR SF
1522[2] **Knobbleeneeze (67)** (MRChannon) **6-8-5v** LDettori(3) (hld up in tch: qcknd to ld 1f out: sn clr) ....— **1** 4/1[1] 79 57
933* **New Century (USA) (87)** (DNicholls) **4-9-11** AlexGreaves(11) (swtg: dwlt: hld up mid div: hdwy & nt clr run ent st: kpt on fnl f: no ch w wnr) ....3½ **2** 11/1 91 69
1522* **Duello (66)** (MBlanshard) **5-8-4** 6x JQuinn(1) (bhd & pushed along: brought wd ent st: fin wl)....½ **3** 12/1 69 47
1018* **Highborn (IRE) (88)** (PSFelgate) **7-9-12** KDarley(7) (lw: s.i.s: sn chsng ldrs: effrt 2f out: nt pce to chal) ....½ **4** 7/1[2] 90 68
971[4] **Sagebrush Roller (70)** (JWWatts) **8-8-8** NConnorton(4) (hld up & bhd: hdwy over 1f out & n.m.r: swtchd rt: r.o) ....½ **5** 12/1 71 49
1613[4] **Cats Bottom (58)** (AGNewcombe) **4-7-7**(3) NVarley(9) (sn drvn along: nvr nr to chal)....3 **6** 14/1 52 30
935* **I'm Your Lady (72)** (BAMcMahon) **5-8-10** GCarter(6) (lw: a.p: led wl over 1f out: sn hdd: rdn & outpcd fnl f)..hd **7** 10/1 66 44
1609[10] **Tiler (IRE) (79)** (MJohnston) **4-9-3** JWeaver(5) (led tl hdd wl over 1f out: eased whn btn fnl f)....¾ **8** 9/1[3] 71 49
987[6] **Le Sport (76)** (ABailey) **3-8-1**(3) DWright(2) (lw: outpcd: a bhd: t.o) ....7 **9** 16/1 52 20
1078[3] **Wild Rice (90)** (GWragg) **4-10-0** MHills(8) (b: prom tl wknd wl over 1f out: t.o)....nk **10** 4/1[1] 65 43
1586[2] **Persian Fayre (66)** (JBerry) **4-8-4** JCarroll(12) (lw: trckd ldrs 5f: sn outpcd: t.o)....6 **11** 12/1 27 5
1354* **Orange Place (IRE) (75)** (TJNaughton) **5-8-13** TQuinn(10) (b.hind: prom: sn drvn along: wknd 2f out: t.o) ...dist **12** 10/1 — —
(SP 124.6%) **12 Rn**

**1m 25.68** (0.48) CSF £45.72 CT £466.12 TOTE £3.40: £1.90 £5.70 £4.60 (£45.10) Trio £147.30 OWNER Mr Anthony Andrews (UPPER LAMBOURN) BRED A. and Mrs Andrews
LONG HANDICAP Cats Bottom 7-8
WEIGHT FOR AGE 3yo-10lb
**1522 Knobbleeneeze** gained his revenge over Duello on 8lb better terms and, in winning his first race since the autumn, did so impressively. He will win again. (4/1)
**933* New Century (USA)**, very much on his toes and sweating beforehand, recovered from a sluggish start and ran on strongly in the latter stages after being squeezed for room when about to deliver his challenge. (11/1)
**1522* Duello** had the best of the draw but was unable to take advantage of it. Switched to the outside entering the straight, he finished strongly and should not be long in getting back to winning ways. (12/1)
**1018* Highborn (IRE)** recovered from a tardy start and was soon chasing the leaders but, when a final effort was called for, he just lacked the extra pace to deliver his challenge. (7/1)
**971 Sagebrush Roller** always runs well here, but he found the ground more lively than he really needs and, after a none too clear passage, did extremely well in the circumstances to finish so close. (12/1)
**1078 Wild Rice** had plenty on his plate, attempting to concede weight in this competitive event, and his run had come to an end soon after straightening up. (4/1)

## 1704 RABBIT CATCHER H'CAP (0-80) (3-Y.O+) (Class D)
7-15 (7-16) **1m 2f 75y** £4,201.50 (£1,272.00: £621.00: £295.50) Stalls: High GOING minus 0.33 sec per fur (GF)

SP RR SF
1502[8] **Maradata (IRE) (57)** (RHollinshead) **4-8-9** LDettori(1) (hld up & prom: led over 1f out: r.o wl) ....— **1** 11/4[1] 66 16
*1602*[5] **Wentbridge Lad (IRE) (65)** (PDEvans) **6-9-3b** KFallon(3) (hld up: hdwy on ins whn hmpd wl over 1f out: fin wl: unlucky) ....1½ **2** 5/1[3] 72 22
1496[4] **Western Sal (68)** (JLHarris) **4-9-6** TQuinn(5) (lw: hld up: effrt & pushed along 3f out: kpt on u.p ins fnl f) ....1¼ **3** 3/1[2] 73 23
1173[6] **Mr Rough (60)** (DMorris) **5-8-12** DHarrison(2) (plld hrd: chsd ldr: lft in ld wl over 1f out: sn hdd: rdn & no ex fnl f) ....nk **4** 11/2 64 14
1538[5] **Cee-Jay-Ay (50)** (JBerry) **9-8-2** JCarroll(6) (s.s: hdwy 3f out: rdn & unable qckn appr fnl f)....nk **5** 8/1 54 4
1406[3] **Reverand Thickness (72)** (ABailey) **5-9-10** KDarley(4) (led: drvn along whn broke leg & uns rdr wl over 1f out: destroyed) .... **U** 5/1[3] — —
(SP 111.5%) **6 Rn**

**2m 15.34** (6.64) CSF £15.18 TOTE £2.80: £1.80 £2.90 (£6.80) OWNER Mr R. Hollinshead (UPPER LONGDON) BRED His Highness the Aga Khans Studs S. C.
**1418* Maradata (IRE)**, waiting on the leaders, was fortunate to find a way through when the leader departed the scene early in the straight. Quickening up readily when sent about his work, he was soon well on top. (11/4)

**1602 Wentbridge Lad (IRE)**, mounting his challenge on the inside rail, was the main sufferer when the leader broke down and, though he did run on strongly inside the final furlong, the damage had already been done. This was a very good effort and he deserves to find consolation. (5/1)
**1496 Western Sal** was always struggling with the pace and it says much that she was able to get so close at the finish. (3/1)
**1173 Mr Rough**, still to win beyond a mile, raced freely and was in the thick of the action until outpaced in the dash to the line. (11/2: 4/1-6/1)
**1538 Cee-Jay-Ay** could never quite recover from a slow start, but was within striking range from the turn into the straight, if unable to summon up the speed to mount a challenge. (8/1)
**1406 Reverand Thickness** gave concern cantering to post and only took part after the Vet had given permission. Leading the way, he was at full stretch but still held the call when he broke his off-fore soon after entering the straight. (5/1)

## 1705 TARRAGON MAIDEN STKS (2-Y.O) (Class D)

7-45 (7-45) **5f 16y** £4,045.50 (£1,224.00: £597.00: £283.50) Stalls: Low GOING minus 0.33 sec per fur (GF)

| | | | | SP | RR | SF |
|---|---|---|---|---|---|---|
| | **Omaha City (IRE)** (BGubby) **2-9-0** LDettori(3) (b: w'like: dwlt: hdwy ½-wy: n.m.r wl over 1f out: str run to ld nr fin) | — | **1** | 5/1$^{3}$ | 73 | 29 |
| $1479^{2}$ | **Bold African** (PDEvans) **2-9-0b$^{1}$** KFallon(5) (led tl hdd wl ins fnl f) | nk | **2** | 6/1 | 72 | 28 |
| $1003^{3}$ | **Mujova (IRE)** (RHollinshead) **2-9-0** JWeaver(2) (prom: rdn & ev ch ins fnl f: unable qckn nr fin) | nk | **3** | 10/11$^{1}$ | 71 | 27 |
| $1404^{12}$ | **Ballymote** (JBerry) **2-9-0** JCarroll(1) (lw: stirrup broke leaving stalls: chsd ldr: ev ch over 1f out: wknd fnl f) | 7 | **4** | 15/2 | 49 | 5 |
| $1433^{2}$ | **Manhattan Diamond** (ABailey) **2-8-9** KDarley(4) (s.i.s: a bhd & outpcd) | 4 | **5** | 4/1$^{2}$ | 31 | — |
| | | | | (SP 115.1%) | | **5 Rn** |

**62.52 secs** (2.52) CSF £29.04 TOTE £5.10: £2.20 £2.00 (£19.30) OWNER Brian Gubby Ltd (BAGSHOT) BRED Brownstown Stud Farm
OFFICIAL EXPLANATION **Ballymote: his stirrup broke on leaving the stalls.**
**Omaha City (IRE)**, a quick-actioned May foal, had a nightmare run when poised to challenge over a furlong out but he stuck to his work and found a better turn of finishing speed to forge ahead nearing the line. (5/1: op 3/1)
**1479 Bold African** raced very freely in his first-time blinkers and held the call until worn down inside the final 50 yards. (6/1)
**1003 Mujova (IRE)** looked likely to justify his market support when putting in a determined challenge 200 yards out, but a turn of finishing speed was missing when it was most needed. (10/11)
**Ballymote**, whose rider showed his true skills as a horseman after the pin came out of a stirrup on leaving the stalls, still had every chance approaching the final furlong before the position had to be accepted. His finishing position can safely be ignored. (15/2)

## 1706 BIRD LIME CONDITIONS STKS (4-Y.O+) (Class C)

8-15 (8-15) **1m 4f 66y** £5,602.50 (£2,040.00: £995.00: £425.00: £187.50) Stalls: Low GOING minus 0.33 sec per fur (GF)

| | | | | SP | RR | SF |
|---|---|---|---|---|---|---|
| | **Kalabo (USA)** (SbinSuroor) **4-8-11** LDettori(2) (swtg: hld up: hdwy to jn ldr 2f out: led over 1f out: drvn clr) | — | **1** | 6/4$^{1}$ | 112 | 70 |
| 1131* | **Key to My Heart (IRE) (110)** (MissSEHall) **6-9-5** JWeaver(5) (b: led 9f out tl rdn & hdd over 1f out: one pce) | 2½ | **2** | 2/1$^{2}$ | 117 | 75 |
| $919^{8}$ | **Juyush (USA) (108)** (BWHills) **4-9-11** RHills(4) (b.hind: led over 3f: prom tl outpcd over 2f out: sn btn) | 3½ | **3** | 7/1$^{3}$ | 118 | 76 |
| *263** | **Rainbow Top** (WJHaggas) **4-9-5** MHills(1) (s.s: hdwy over 7f out: wknd 2f out) | 6 | **4** | 8/1 | 104 | 62 |
| 1392a* | **Suranom (IRE)** (LMCumani) **4-9-5** KDarley(3) (lw: hld up: dropped rr 7f out: drvn along 3f out: no imp) | 5 | **5** | 8/1 | 98 | 56 |
| | | | | (SP 108.1%) | | **5 Rn** |

**2m 36.51** (-0.09) CSF £4.59 TOTE £2.20: £1.40 £1.30 (£2.00) OWNER Godolphin (NEWMARKET) BRED Darley Stud Management Inc
**Kalabo (USA)**, a classy-looking colt who carried plenty of condition, overcame his absence from the racecourse since January and turned in a most impressive display to win going away in the style of a very progressive individual. (6/4: op Evens)
**1131* Key to My Heart (IRE)** hardly knows how to run a bad race and he was the only one able to make the winner extend himself. (2/1)
**919 Juyush (USA)** was trying the impossible in attempting to concede so much weight to the very useful winner and he was left for dead before reaching the home turn. (7/1)
**Rainbow Top**, twice successful on the All-Weather and returning after a lengthy break, did not shape badly after losing ground at the start, but he was out of his class when the contest really got under way. (8/1)
**1392a* Suranom (IRE)** could not handle the fast-ground conditions and, after dropping to the rear going out on the final circuit, was soon hard at work and making no impression. (8/1)

## 1707 FLASH IN THE PAN CLAIMING STKS (3-Y.O) (Class E)

8-45 (8-46) **6f 18y** £3,512.50 (£1,060.00: £515.00: £242.50) Stalls: Low GOING minus 0.33 sec per fur (GF)

| | | | | SP | RR | SF |
|---|---|---|---|---|---|---|
| $1592^{5}$ | **Standown (68)** (JBerry) **3-8-12** KDarley(5) (hdwy over 2f out: led ent fnl f: jst hld on) | — | **1** | 10/1 | 76 | 50 |
| $1599^{4}$ | **The Wad (62)** (DNicholls) **3-8-6** KFallon(6) (trckd ldrs: barged thro to ld over 1f out: sn hdd: rallied strly nr fin) | s.h | **2** | 13/2 | 70 | 44 |
| $867^{11}$ | **U-No-Harry (IRE) (57)** (RHollinshead) **3-7-13**(5) FLynch(3) (trckd ldrs: sn pushed along: nt clr run over 1f out: swtchd rt: kpt on fnl f) | 3 | **3** | 16/1 | 60 | 34 |
| $1628^{13}$ | **Double Oscar (IRE) (90)** (MJohnston) **3-9-8** JWeaver(10) (dwlt: wl bhd & outpcd tl r.o strly appr fnl f) | 3½ | **4** | 5/1$^{3}$ | 69 | 43 |
| $1304^{3}$ | **The Frisky Farmer (69)** (WGMTurner) **3-8-4** TSprake(4) (disp ld tl rdn & one pce appr fnl f) | ¾ | **5** | 9/2$^{2}$ | 49 | 23 |
| $1087^{3}$ | **No Monkey Nuts (74)** (JBerry) **3-8-10** JCarroll(9) (led after 2f tl hdd & n.m.r over 1f out: eased whn btn) | 1½ | **6** | 4/1$^{1}$ | 51 | 25 |
| 1592* | **Ciserano (IRE) (55)** (MRChannon) **3-8-11** DHarrison(7) (dwlt: a outpcd) | 1¼ | **7** | 6/1 | 49 | 23 |
| $1435^{9}$ | **Angus McCoatup (IRE) (58)** (BAMcMahon) **3-8-7b$^{1}$**(5) LNewton(1) (sn drvn along: a outpcd) | ¾ | **8** | 20/1 | 48 | 22 |
| $1405^{7}$ | **Boffy (IRE) (55)** (BPJBaugh) **3-8-3**(7) IonaWands(11) (outpcd: t.o) | 6 | **9** | 16/1 | 30 | 4 |
| $773^{9}$ | **Little Noggins (IRE) (75)** (CADwyer) **3-9-0**(3) NVarley(2) (led 2f: hrd drvn & ev ch 2f out: wknd ent st: t.o) | 6 | **10** | 8/1 | 21 | — |
| | **Palacegate Chief** (NPLittmoden) **3-8-5** TGMcLaughlin(8) (chsd ldrs 3f: sn lost tch: t.o) | 1¼ | **11** | 33/1 | 6 | — |
| | | | | (SP 122.1%) | | **11 Rn** |

**1m 14.65** (1.35) CSF £70.25 TOTE £16.10: £4.40 £2.00 £3.70 (£73.40) Trio £482.00 OWNER Mrs Chris Deuters (COCKERHAM) BRED Alan Gibson
**1592 Standown**, winning for the first time at the trip, found the post arriving not a stride too soon after nosing ahead entering the final furlong. (10/1)
**1599 The Wad**, full of running when denied a clear run below the distance, did eventually barge his way through and his determined late rally looked to have succeeded right on the line but, to the dismay of many, the print went against him. (13/2)
**748 U-No-Harry (IRE)**, never far away, was short of room approaching the final furlong but it is doubtful if he had the speed to take advantage even with a clear run. (16/1)
**Double Oscar (IRE)**, making a quick reappearance, was taken off his legs for most of the way but, pulled wide into the straight, finished strongly and would seem to be on the way back. (5/1: 4/1-6/1)

**1304 The Frisky Farmer** shared the lead until tapped for toe in the sprint to the finish. (9/2)
**1087 No Monkey Nuts** was the meat in the sandwich after being headed approaching the final furlong and, forced to check, had little hope of recovery. (4/1)

## 1708 DOGE OF VENICE H'CAP (0-85) (3-Y.O+) (Class D)

9-15 (9-16) **5f 16y** £4,279.50 (£1,296.00: £633.00: £301.50) Stalls: Low GOING minus 0.33 sec per fur (GF)

| | | | | SP | RR | SF |
|---|---|---|---|---|---|---|
| $1521^{2}$ | **Bajan Rose (74)** (MBlanshard) **4-9-4** JQuinn(12) (hdwy on outside 2f out: qcknd to ld ins fnl f: edgd lft: r.o wl) | — | **1** | $7/1^{2}$ | 82 | 52 |
| $1501^{6}$ | **Lady Sheriff (84)** (RHollinshead) **5-9-9**(5) FLynch(4) (chsd ldrs: effrt over 1f out: kpt on ins fnl f) | 1¾ | **2** | $7/1^{2}$ | 87 | 57 |
| $1016^{11}$ | **Palacegate Jack (IRE) (80)** (JBerry) **5-9-5**(5) PRoberts(2) (led tl hdd ins fnl f: no ex towards fin) | s.h | **3** | 16/1 | 82 | 52 |
| $1430^{10}$ | **Hinton Rock (IRE) (78)** (ABailey) **4-9-8b** JCarroll(3) (hdwy 2f out: swtchd ins ent st: ev ch 1f out: unable qckn) | ¾ | **4** | $10/1^{3}$ | 78 | 48 |
| 704* | **Chadwell Hall (65)** (SRBowring) **5-8-6b**(3) CTeague(10) (lw: hdwy ½-wy: rdn whn sltly impeded 1f out: sn btn) | ¾ | **5** | $7/1^{2}$ | 63 | 33 |
| $711^{W}$ | **Macfarlane (70)** (MJFetherston-Godley) **8-9-0** DHarrison(11) (b: dwlt: hdwy on ins over 1f out: nrst fin) | nk | **6** | 11/1 | 67 | 37 |
| $1006^{2}$ | **Myttons Mistake (74)** (ABailey) **3-8-11** KDarley(1) (hdwy ½-wy: ev ch over 1f out: wknd fnl f) | ½ | **7** | $9/4^{1}$ | 69 | 32 |
| $1598^{11}$ | **Gondo (52)** (EJAlston) **9-7-3v**(7) IonaWands(6) (bhd & outpcd tl kpt on ins fnl f) | 2 | **8** | 25/1 | 41 | 11 |
| $1018^{8}$ | **Little Ibnr (62)** (PDEvans) **5-8-6**ow2 KFallon(9) (lw: sn drvn along: a outpcd) | 1½ | **9** | 14/1 | 46 | 14 |
| $1430^{2}$ | **Sing With the Band (60)** (BAMcMahon) **5-7-13**(5) LNewton(7) (gd spd over 3f) | 1¼ | **10** | $7/1^{2}$ | 40 | 10 |
| $1049^{5}$ | **Allwight Then (IRE) (67)** (REPeacock) **5-8-8**(3) SDrowne(5) (swtg: spd 3f: sn rdn & wknd) | 1¾ | **11** | $10/1^{3}$ | 42 | 12 |
| $1307^{12}$ | **Tommy Tempest (52)** (REPeacock) **7-7-7v**(3) NVarley(8) (mid div 3f: sn rdn & outpcd) | 1½ | **12** | 66/1 | 22 | — |
| | | | | (SP 125.2%) | **12 Rn** | |

**61.3 secs** (1.30) CSF £53.99 CT £717.95 TOTE £6.50: £2.60 £3.10 £4.20 (£41.50) Trio £282.90 OWNER Mr C. McKenna (UPPER LAMBOURN) BRED E. A. Badger
LONG HANDICAP Gondo 7-1 Tommy Tempest 6-2
WEIGHT FOR AGE 3yo-7lb

**1521 Bajan Rose**, thought to be better when she can get her toe in, achieved the almost impossible by producing a telling burst of speed from off the pace to lead 100 yards out and win going away, despite edging left. (7/1)
**1501 Lady Sheriff**, who had to work hard to hold her pitch, gave her all in a good race to the line and certainly lost no caste in defeat. (7/1)
**Palacegate Jack (IRE)** gave notice that he is back to something like his best with a bold display of front-running that only came to an end late in the final furlong. (16/1)
**Hinton Rock (IRE)** delivered his challenge on the inside rail once in line for home and posed a serious threat passing the furlong pole, but just could not go through with his effort. This was a very promising performance. (10/1)
**704* Chadwell Hall** had to work hard to reach the leaders and he was struggling to hold his pitch when slightly impeded by the winner just inside the last furlong. (7/1)
**Macfarlane** always performs well here and did extremely well to finish so close after losing ground at the start. He does require a more yielding surface to produce his best but this effort would suggest his turn is near. (11/1: 8/1-12/1)
**1006 Myttons Mistake** joined issue approaching the final furlong but could not find the necessary turn of speed to put his stamp on proceedings. (9/4)
**1049 Allwight Then (IRE)** (10/1: 8/1-12/1)

T/Plpt: £906.90 (20.49 Tckts). T/Qdpt: £135.00 (8.72 Tckts). IM

# 1352-GOODWOOD (R-H) (St Good, Rnd Good to firm)

## Thursday June 6th

WEATHER: very hot WIND: almost nil

## 1709 ALBERT MEDIAN AUCTION MAIDEN STKS (3-Y.O) (Class D)

2-00 (2-02) **7f** £3,915.00 (£1,170.00: £560.00: £255.00) Stalls: High GOING minus 0.24 sec per fur (GF)

| | | | | SP | RR | SF |
|---|---|---|---|---|---|---|
| $1599^{3}$ | **Lionel Edwards (IRE) (70)** (PFICole) **3-9-0** TQuinn(6) (a.p: led over 2f out: wandered fnl f: drvn out) | — | **1** | $5/1^{2}$ | 81 | 34 |
| | **Lucky Revenge (65)** (MartynMeade) **3-8-4**(5) RHavlin(8) (swtg: hld up: rdn over 2f out: chsd wnr over 1f out: unable qckn) | 1¼ | **2** | 20/1 | 73 | 26 |
| | **Diamond Beach (78)** (BWHills) **3-9-0** BThomson(11) (bit bkwd: hld up: rdn over 2f out: one pce) | 2 | **3** | $5/1^{2}$ | 74 | 27 |
| $1327^{3}$ | **State of Caution (85)** (JLDunlop) **3-9-0** PatEddery(1) (nvr gng wl: chsd ldrs: rdn over 5f out: one pce fnl 2f) | 3 | **4** | $5/6^{1}$ | 67 | 20 |
| $1333^{7}$ | **All Stand** (MajorDNChappell) **3-8-9** AClark(7) (lw: a.p: rdn over 2f out: wknd over 1f out) | 1¼ | **5** | 20/1 | 59 | 12 |
| $1007^{12}$ | **Bombay Sapphire** (RHannon) **3-8-6**(3) DaneO'Neill(9) (nvr nr to chal) | 1¼ | **6** | 50/1 | 56 | 9 |
| | **Muhandam (IRE) (70)** (BHanbury) **3-9-0** WRyan(3) (b.hind: swtg: led over 4f: wknd over 1f out) | s.h | **7** | $10/1^{3}$ | 61 | 14 |
| | **Memphis Beau (IRE)** (JARToller) **3-9-0** DHarrison(12) (w'like: s.s: a bhd) | 1½ | **8** | 20/1 | 58 | 11 |
| | **Cross of Valour** (JARToller) **3-9-0** SSanders(10) (leggy: scope: s.s: a bhd) | 1¾ | **9** | 20/1 | 54 | 7 |
| $669^{12}$ | **Governance (IRE)** (KMcAuliffe) **3-8-4**(5) MHenry(4) (lw: a bhd) | 5 | **10** | 50/1 | 37 | — |
| $1617^{13}$ | **Play The Tune** (KRBurke) **3-9-0** SWhitworth(2) (s.s: a bhd) | 1 | **11** | 50/1 | 40 | — |
| | | | | (SP 121.9%) | **11 Rn** | |

**1m 28.57** (3.77) CSF £87.45 TOTE £6.10: £1.90 £3.00 £2.00 (£31.30) Trio £44.00 OWNER Richard Green (Fine Paintings) (WHATCOMBE) BRED Fluorocarbon Bloodstock

**1599 Lionel Edwards (IRE)** struck the front over a quarter of a mile out, but was given no peace by the runner-up in the final furlong. Wandering about all over the place under pressure, he nevertheless held on well. (5/1: 7/2-11/2)
**Lucky Revenge**, having her first run of the season, chased the leaders. Moving into second place approaching the final furlong, she made sure the winner did not have things all his own way but was unable to get on terms. (20/1)
**Diamond Beach**, carrying condition for this reappearance, chased the leaders. Despite his rider's efforts, he failed to find the necessary turn of foot. (5/1)
**1327 State of Caution** found the ground too lively and, as a result, was never travelling. Chasing the leaders, he was soon being niggled along and failed to find the necessary turn of foot in the last two furlongs. (5/6)
**All Stand** had shot her bolt below the distance. (20/1)
**Muhandam (IRE)** (10/1: op 6/1)

## 1710 MORTAR MILL H'CAP (0-85) (3-Y.O+) (Class D)

2-30 (2-31) **2m** £4,464.00 (£1,332.00: £636.00: £288.00) Stalls: High GOING minus 0.24 sec per fur (GF)

| Form | Horse | Dist | Pos | SP | RR | SF |
|---|---|---|---|---|---|---|
| 811[3] | **Speed to Lead (IRE) (79)** (HRACecil) **4-9-10** PatEddery(2) (swtg: mde all: pushed out) | — | 1 | 5/2[1] | 93 | 71 |
| 1194[2] | **En Vacances (IRE) (73)** (AGFoster) **4-9-4** SSanders(1) (swtg: chsd wnr: hrd rdn 3f out: unable qckn) | 1½ | 2 | 7/1 | 86 | 64 |
| 1439[6] | **Ivor's Flutter (72)** (DRCElsworth) **7-9-4** AProcter(8) (rdn over 3f out: hdwy over 1f out: r.o) | 3½ | 3 | 12/1 | 81 | 60 |
| 1511[7] | **Bolivar (IRE) (60)** (RAkehurst) **4-8-5b[1]** TQuinn(4) (a.p: rdn 3f out: one pce) | s.h | 4 | 12/1 | 69 | 47 |
| 1454[2] | **Sheriff (56)** (JWHills) **5-8-2** DHarrison(7) (lw: lost pl over 5f out: sme hdwy over 2f out: sn wknd) | 14 | 5 | 7/2[2] | 51 | 30 |
| 1524* | **Granby Bell (53)** (PHayward) **5-7-8**(5) 5x MHenry(5) (swtg: hdwy over 6f out: wknd 4f out) | 1¾ | 6 | 8/1 | 46 | 25 |
| | **Supreme Star (USA) (68)** (PRHedger) **5-8-11**(3) DaneO'Neill(3) (swtg: bhd fnl 6f) | 13 | 7 | 12/1 | 48 | 27 |
| 1194[3] | **Thaljanah (IRE) (82)** (DLWilliams) **4-9-13** WCarson(6) (bhd fnl 6f) | 9 | 8 | 6/1[3] | 53 | 31 |
| | | | | (SP 111.8%) | **8 Rn** | |

**3m 27.51** (3.51) CSF £18.23 CT £154.91 TOTE £2.70: £1.60 £1.90 £2.50 (£10.40) OWNER Buckram Oak Holdings (NEWMARKET) BRED Buckram Thoroughbred Enterprises

WEIGHT FOR AGE 4yo-1lb

**811 Speed to Lead (IRE)** at last came good, having been placed on all her previous starts. Making all the running, she quickened things up entering the straight, and needed only to be nudged along to have things nicely in hand. (5/2)

**1194 En Vacances (IRE)**, whose two wins to date have both been with some cut in the ground, did not have conditions in her favour here, but still ran well. Giving chase to the winner, she came under pressure early in the straight but failed to get on terms with that rival. (7/1: 5/1-8/1)

**1439 Ivor's Flutter** is not an easy individual to deal with, but stayed on from below the distance to snatch third right on the line. (12/1)

**Bolivar (IRE)** found the application of blinkers helping him to leave his two previous runs this season well behind. (12/1: 8/1-14/1)

**1454 Sheriff** was rather disappointing. Having lost his pitch at the top of the hill, he tried to pick up ground over a quarter of a mile out, but the effort proved short-lived. (7/2)

**1524* Granby Bell** (8/1: op 5/1)

## 1711 BELMOREDEAN MAIDEN STKS (3-Y.O) (Class D)

3-00 (3-04) **1m 2f** £4,240.00 (£1,270.00: £445.00: £445.00) Stalls: High GOING minus 0.24 sec per fur (GF)

| Form | Horse | Dist | Pos | SP | RR | SF |
|---|---|---|---|---|---|---|
| 1319[3] | **Male-Ana-Mou (IRE)** (DRCElsworth) **3-9-0** TQuinn(13) (swtg: lost pl over 3f out: rallied over 2f out: hrd rdn: led ins fnl f: r.o wl) | — | 1 | 13/2 | 85 | 36 |
| 1182[3] | **Palamon (USA)** (RCharlton) **3-9-0** PatEddery(3) (b: hld up: rdn over 2f out: led 1f out tl ins fnl f: unable qckn) | 1¾ | 2 | 5/1[2] | 82 | 33 |
| 1182[10] | **King's Academy (IRE)** (HRACecil) **3-9-0** WRyan(5) (swtg: a.p: led over 3f out to 1f out: ev ch ins fnl f: one pce) | 1¼ | 3 | 20/1 | 80 | 31 |
| | **Serenus (USA)** (LordHuntingdon) **3-9-0** BDoyle(8) (w'like: bit bkwd: lost pl 7f out: rallied over 1f out: r.o wl) | d.h | 3 | 40/1 | 82 | 33 |
| 860[3] | **Illuminate** (JARToller) **3-9-0** SSanders(1) (dwlt: hld up: rdn over 2f out: one pce) | 2 | 5 | 11/2[3] | 77 | 28 |
| 1530[2] | **Irish Sea (USA)** (MRStoute) **3-9-0** JReid(12) (rdn over 2f out: hdwy & nt clr run wl over 1f out: one pce) | 3 | 6 | 6/1 | 72 | 23 |
| 892[13] | **Firbur** (NAGraham) **3-9-0** RHughes(6) (swtg: s.s: nt clr run 3f out & 2f out: hdwy fnl f: nvr nrr) | s.h | 7 | 66/1 | 72 | 23 |
| 957[3] | **Classic Parisian (IRE)** (RHarris) **3-8-9** AMackay(14) (s.s: nt clr run over 3f out: nvr nr to chal) | ¾ | 8 | 7/1 | 66 | 17 |
| 1182[4] | **Queen Bee** (JLDunlop) **3-8-9** WCarson(2) (b: swtg: lost pl over 5f out: rallied over 3f out: wknd over 1f out) | 1¼ | 9 | 100/30[1] | 64 | 15 |
| 684[11] | **Lepikha (USA)** (BWHills) **3-8-4**(5) JDSmith(4) (hld up: rdn over 2f out: sn wknd) | nk | 10 | 16/1 | 63 | 14 |
| 821[9] | **Future's Trader** (RHannon) **3-8-11**(3) DaneO'Neill(9) (led 5f: wknd 3f out) | 3 | 11 | 33/1 | 64 | 15 |
| 1359[13] | **Mukeed** (JHMGosden) **3-9-0** AMcGlone(11) (bit bkwd: bhd fnl 3f) | 2½ | 12 | 33/1 | 60 | 11 |
| 1333[6] | **Classic Look (IRE)** (MajorDNChappell) **3-8-9** BThomson(7) (mid div whn hmpd over 2f out: sn wknd) | 3 | 13 | 33/1 | 50 | 1 |
| 1061[10] | **Shoemaker Levy** (RJO'Sullivan) **3-8-9** AClark(10) (a bhd) | 9 | 14 | 66/1 | 35 | — |
| | **Sylvan Heights** (RTPhillips) **3-9-0** MFenton(15) (w'like: s.s: hdwy 9f out: led 5f out tl over 3f out: sn wknd) | 7 | 15 | 66/1 | 29 | — |
| | | | | (SP 121.6%) | **15 Rn** | |

**2m 10.97** (5.47) CSF £36.54 TOTE £5.80: £1.60 £2.40 £3.70 KA £4.50 S (£18.60) Trio £90.30 w KA, £207.20 w S OWNER Oh So Bright Syndicate (WHITCOMBE) BRED John Corcoran

**1319 Male-Ana-Mou (IRE)** appreciated the step up in trip. Rather tapped for toe early in the straight, he soon managed to get back into it and, responding to pressure, swooped into the lead inside the final furlong. (13/2)

**1182 Palamon (USA)** chased the leaders. Poking a nostril in front a furlong out, he did not remain there for long as the winner came between him and the third. (5/1)

**King's Academy (IRE)**, a half-brother to King's Theatre, was much happier on this faster ground and left his initial run well behind. He should soon find a race. (20/1)

**Serenus (USA)** did not look fully wound up for this initial run but broke well enough before losing his pitch after about three furlongs out. Getting his second wind from below the distance, he finished with a real wet sail to dead-heat for third place. (40/1)

**860 Illuminate** could only go up and down in the same place in the final two furlongs. (11/2)

**1530 Irish Sea (USA)** tried to weave his way through the field, but failed get a clear run early in the final quarter-mile and could then only plod on in his own time. (6/1: op 7/2)

## 1712 EQUITY FINANCIAL COLLECTIONS H'CAP (0-95) (3-Y.O) (Class C)

3-30 (3-32) **1m 4f** £5,791.25 (£1,730.00: £827.50: £376.25) Stalls: Low GOING minus 0.24 sec per fur (GF)

| Form | Horse | Dist | Pos | SP | RR | SF |
|---|---|---|---|---|---|---|
| 1180* | **Harbour Dues (83)** (LadyHerries) **3-9-1** PaulEddery(3) (rdn over 2f out: str run fnl f: led nr fin) | — | 1 | 6/1 | 94+ | 59 |
| 717[3] | **Clerkenwell (USA) (84)** (MRStoute) **3-9-2** JReid(4) (lw: led: hrd rdn fnl f: hdd nr fin) | nk | 2 | 5/1[3] | 95 | 60 |
| 1090* | **Classic Find (USA) (85)** (RHarris) **3-9-3** AMackay(6) (b: b.hind: rdn over 2f out: hdwy over 1f out: one pce) | 2½ | 3 | 16/1 | 92 | 57 |
| 1477* | **Hamlet (IRE) (77)** (MBell) **3-8-9** 5x MFenton(2) (hdwy 4f out: rdn over 2f out: one pce) | 1¾ | 4 | 7/2[2] | 82 | 47 |
| 1071* | **General Macarthur (89)** (JLDunlop) **3-9-7** PatEddery(5) (hld up: hung rt fnl 2f: nt rcvr) | 1¼ | 5 | 5/1[3] | 92 | 57 |
| 1175[3] | **Nabhaan (IRE) (88)** (DMorley) **3-9-6** WCarson(1) (chsd ldr: rdn over 2f out: eased whn btn ins fnl f) | 1¼ | 6 | 2/1[1] | 90 | 55 |
| 1407[7] | **Infamous (USA) (84)** (PFICole) **3-9-2** TQuinn(7) (a.p: rdn over 2f out: wknd over 1f out) | 4 | 7 | 16/1 | 80 | 45 |
| | | | | (SP 114.9%) | **7 Rn** | |

**2m 36.5** (3.30) CSF £33.12 TOTE £8.20: £2.80 £3.10 (£17.50) OWNER Hesmonds Stud (LITTLEHAMPTON) BRED Hesmonds Stud Ltd

**1180* Harbour Dues** showed a very impressive turn of foot, for he was still last of all a furlong and a half from home. Eating up the ground in the last 200 yards, he quickened up in really impressive style to snatch the spoils near the line. He is certainly better than handicap company and connections should now be looking to win with him in a listed race. (6/1: 4/1-13/2)

**717 Clerkenwell (USA)** once again had to settle for being the bridesmaid. Attempting to make all the running, it looked as if he was at last going to break his duck, only to be worried out of it near the line. He richly deserves a change of luck. (5/1)
**1090* Classic Find (USA)** began to pick up ground below the distance, but was making no further impression in the final furlong. (16/1)
**1477* Hamlet (IRE)** moved up half a mile from home but, ridden over two furlongs out, the writing was soon on the wall. (7/2)
**1071* General Macarthur** chased the leaders, but gave his rider serious problems in the final quarter-mile and, hanging badly, proved virtually unsteerable. (5/1)
**1175 Nabhaan (IRE)**, who has been raised 5lb for his unlucky defeat at Newbury recently, raced in second place. Still battling for that position entering the final furlong, he was eased down when all chance had evaporated. (2/1)

## 1713 BUSTER HASLAM AND PADDY MORRISSEY CLAIMING STKS (2-Y.O) (Class E)

4-00 (4-00) **6f** £3,557.50 (£1,060.00: £505.00: £227.50) Stalls: Low GOING minus 0.24 sec per fur (GF)

| | | | | SP | RR | SF |
|---|---|---|---|---|---|---|
| 1346[14] | **Russian Sable** (MRChannon) **2-8-6** WCarson(6) (outpcd: hdwy over 2f out: led over 1f out: r.o wl) | — | 1 | 12/1 | 72 | 16 |
| 551[5] | **Impulsion (IRE)** (RHannon) **2-9-2** PatEddery(7) (led over 4f: unable qckn: fin 3rd, 3½l: plcd 2nd) | | 2 | 8/1 | — | 15 |
| 1494[3] | **Caviar And Candy** (DJSCosgrove) **2-7-12**(5) MHenry(4) (a.p: rdn over 2f out: wknd 1f out: fin 4th, 2½l: plcd 3rd) | | 3 | 12/1 | — | — |
| 1360* | **Hello Dolly (IRE)** (KRBurke) **2-8-8** PaulEddery(2) (a.p: rdn & bmpd 2f out: nt clr run over 1f out: nt rcvr: fin 5th, 3/4l: plcd 4th) | | 4 | 5/1 | — | — |
| 1437[7] | **Castle House** (JAkehurst) **2-9-0**(5) JDSmith(1) (swtg: a.p: wkng whn bmpd 2f out & n.m.r on ins over 1f out: fin 6th, 12l: plcd 5th) | | 5 | 9/2[3] | — | — |
| 1103[3] | **Grovefair Flyer (IRE)** (BJMeehan) **2-9-5** BDoyle(5) (a.p: rdn over 2f out: wknd over 1f out) | 2½ | 7 | 3/1[2] | — | — |
| 1331* | **Without Friends (IRE)** (MrsLStubbs) **2-8-13**(3) DaneO'Neill(3) (a.p: barged thro 2f out: hrd rdn over 1f out: r.o: fin 2nd, 3/4l: disq: plcd last) | | D | 9/4[1] | 71 | 24 |
| | | | | (SP 117.1%) | **7 Rn** | |

**1m 13.82** (3.82) CSF £90.21 TOTE £11.00: £3.30 £3.60 (£19.10) OWNER Mr T. S. M. Cunningham (UPPER LAMBOURN) BRED The Duke of Marlborough
STEWARDS' ENQUIRY O'Neill susp. 15, 17-22 & 24-26/6/96 (reckless riding).
**Russian Sable** left her debut run well behind. Completely outpaced in the early stages, she picked up ground over a quarter of a mile out and, hitting the front below the distance, soon asserted. (12/1)
**551 Impulsion (IRE)** attempted to make all the running. Collared approaching the final furlong, he was firmly put in his place by the winner. (8/1)
**1494 Caviar And Candy** had nothing more to offer in the final furlong. (12/1)
**1360* Hello Dolly (IRE)**, always close up, was given a nasty bump a quarter of mile out and was then chopped off by the same rival below the distance. Not surprisingly she could never recover. (5/1: 7/2-11/2)
**946 Castle House** was sending out distress signals when bumped as a result of Without Friends trying to barge through a quarter of a mile out. (9/2)
**1331* Without Friends (IRE)**, claimed out of Richard Hannon's stable for £10,000 after winning here last month, did not have a very happy time. Never far away, he found his passage blocked and his rider decided to barge through a non-existent gap, causing all kinds of trouble. However, the colt ran on in good style inside the final furlong, but was unable to peg back the winner. The Stewards quite rightly decided to suspend O'Neill for careless riding. (9/4)

## 1714 DARNLEY LIMITED STKS (0-80) (3-Y.O) (Class D)

4-30 (4-31) **1m 1f** £7,570.00 (£2,260.00: £1,080.00: £490.00) Stalls: High GOING minus 0.24 sec per fur (GF)

| | | | | SP | RR | SF |
|---|---|---|---|---|---|---|
| 1464* | **Hilaala (USA) (75)** (PTWalwyn) **3-8-11** WCarson(1) (lw: chsd ldr: led over 2f out: sn hdd: hrd rdn: led 1f out: r.o wl) | — | 1 | 6/4[1] | 87 | 25 |
| 969[6] | **Docklands Limo (77)** (BJMcMath) **3-9-2** MTebbutt(3) (lw: hld up: led 2f out to 1f out: hrd rdn: r.o) | nk | 2 | 6/1 | 92 | 30 |
| 1654[16] | **Seven Crowns (USA) (65)** (RHannon) **3-8-9**(3) DaneO'Neill(6) (lw: hld up: rdn over 3f out: unable qckn) | 7 | 3 | 40/1 | 75 | 13 |
| 1438[4] | **Possessive Artiste (77)** (MRStoute) **3-8-9** JReid(2) (swtg: hdwy 3f out: rdn over 2f out: one pce) | nk | 4 | 5/1[3] | 72 | 10 |
| 1589* | **Cd Super Targeting (IRE) (58)** (MRChannon) **3-8-11** RHughes(5) (led over 6f) | 9 | 5 | 11/1 | 58 | — |
| 1142[7] | **John-T (80)** (JLDunlop) **3-8-12** PatEddery(4) (a bhd) | 2½ | 6 | 3/1[2] | 54 | — |
| | | | | (SP 106.7%) | **6 Rn** | |

**1m 57.1** (5.70) CSF £9.44 TOTE £2.00: £1.20 £2.60 (£7.40) OWNER Mr Hamdan Al Maktoum (LAMBOURN) BRED Shadwell Estate Company
**1464* Hilaala (USA)** raced in second place until gaining a slender advantage over a quarter of a mile from home. Narrowly passed by the runner-up soon after, she battled her way back to the front again a furlong out and proved just too strong for that rival. (6/4)
**969 Docklands Limo**, engaged in a tremendous ding-dong battle with the winner in the last two furlongs, showed marginally in front until the furlong pole before that rival just had the measure of him. (6/1: op 10/1)
**Seven Crowns (USA)**, making a quick reappearance, chased the leaders but just failed to find the necessary turn of foot in the last three furlongs. (40/1)
**1438 Possessive Artiste** took closer order in the straight but failed to raise her game in the last two furlongs. (5/1: 3/1-11/2)
**1589* Cd Super Targeting (IRE)** attempted to make all the running but, collared over a quarter of a mile from home, had soon cooked her goose. (11/1)
**1142 John-T** was always trailing and lost touch entering the straight. The ground may well have been too lively for him and he is worth another chance on an easier surface. (3/1: op 7/4)

## 1715 ROOKWOOD APPRENTICE H'CAP (0-70) (3-Y.O+) (Class E)

5-00 (5-03) **6f** £4,077.50 (£1,220.00: £585.00: £267.50) Stalls: Low GOING minus 0.24 sec per fur (GF)

| | | | | SP | RR | SF |
|---|---|---|---|---|---|---|
| 1313[12] | **Don Pepe (56)** (RBoss) **5-8-12**(3) GFaulkner(13) (hdwy over 2f out: led ins fnl f: r.o wl) | — | 1 | 8/1[3] | 67 | 50 |
| 1121[8] | **Scissor Ridge (42)** (JJBridger) **4-7-8**(7) RBrisland(12) (swtg: a.p: led over 2f out tl ins fnl f: unable qckn) | ¾ | 2 | 20/1 | 51 | 34 |
| | **Jobie (62)** (BWHills) **6-9-7** JDSmith(7) (hrd rdn & hdwy over 2f out: one pce fnl f) | 1½ | 3 | 6/1[1] | 67 | 50 |
| 1334[11] | **Invocation (51)** (AMoore) **9-8-5**(5) TField(6) (b.nr hind: a.p: rdn over 2f out: one pce) | 1¼ | 4 | 16/1 | 53 | 36 |
| 1624* | **Merrie le Bow (52)** (PatMitchell) **4-8-8**(3) 7x AmandaSanders(3) (outpcd: hdwy over 1f out: r.o) | 1¼ | 5 | 6/1[1] | 50 | 33 |
| 862[10] | **Efficacy (42)** (APJarvis) **5-7-8**(7) CCarver(5) (b: swtg: a.p: rdn over 2f out: one pce) | s.h | 6 | 20/1 | 40 | 23 |
| 1536[7] | **Sharp Imp (51)** (RMFlower) **6-8-10b** RHavlin(2) (outpcd: nvr nrr) | 1 | 7 | 7/1[2] | 47 | 30 |
| 1304[4] | **Nellie North (70)** (GMMcCourt) **3-9-2**(5) RStudholme(4) (lw: prom 3f) | 1½ | 8 | 9/1 | 62 | 37 |
| 1536[9] | **Agwa (68)** (RJO'Sullivan) **7-9-13** MHenry(10) (led over 3f: wknd 1f out) | s.h | 9 | 7/1[2] | 59 | 42 |
| | **Don't Tell Vicki (50)** (JSMoore) **3-7-8**(7) JKeenan(9) (bhd fnl 3f) | 2½ | 10 | 33/1 | 35 | 10 |

1348$^{3}$ **Shaynes Domain (42)** (RMFlower) **5-8-1b** MBaird(14) (b.nr hind: s.s: a bhd) ....1¾ **11** 12/1 22 5
**Dark Menace (56)** (EAWheeler) **4-9-1** ADaly(8) (reard s: a bhd)....1 **12** 20/1 33 16
1170$^{11}$ **The Noble Oak (IRE) (37)** (MJBolton) **8-7-5**$^{(5)}$ PDoe(1) (a bhd)....4 **13** 33/1 4 —
*1536$^{5}$* ***Astral Invader (IRE) (51)*** (MSSaunders) **4-8-5b**$^{1(5)}$ AEddery(11) (Withdrawn not under Starter's orders: inj in stalls) .... **W** 8/1$^{3}$ — —
(SP 119.5%) **13 Rn**

**1m 12.0** (2.00) CSF £112.80 CT £687.36 TOTE £8.10: £2.90 £6.90 £2.00 (£89.80) Trio £445.30 OWNER Mrs Elaine Aird (NEWMARKET) BRED Patrick Eddery Ltd
WEIGHT FOR AGE 3yo-8lb
**1010 Don Pepe** bounced back to form to register his first win over six, his previous five victories having all come over seven. (8/1)
**664 Scissor Ridge**, despite giving his all, found the winner too strong in the last 150 yards. (20/1)
**Jobie**, having his first run of the season, was under pressure to take closer order over a quarter of a mile from home. Having moved into third place entering the final furlong, he could then make no further impression. (6/1)
**632 Invocation**, always close up, was, as on many other occasions, made to look very one-paced in the last two furlongs. (16/1)
**1624* Merrie le Bow**, unable to go the pace, was doing all her best work in the last furlong and a half. (6/1)
**769 Efficacy**, always close up, could only plod on in her own time in the last two furlongs. (20/1)

T/Jkpt: £18,325.60 (0.4 Tckts): £15,486.47 to Epsom 7/6/96. T/Plpt: £2,801.00 (6.26 Tckts). T/Qdpt: £356.60 (3.2 Tckts). AK

## 1487-SOUTHWELL (L-H) (Standard)
## Thursday June 6th
WEATHER: fine

## 1716 LION H'CAP (0-65) (3-Y.O+) (Class F)
2-10 (2-12) **5f** **(Fibresand)** £2,381.00 (£656.00: £311.00) GOING minus 0.13 sec per fur (FST)

SP RR SF
*1455** **Freckles Kelly (51)** (TDEasterby) **4-9-0** JQuinn(7) (lw: w ldr: led ins fnl f: r.o wl)....— **1** 9/2$^{2}$ 59 23
*1492$^{4}$* **Elton Ledger (IRE) (63)** (MrsNMacauley) **7-9-12v** EmmaO'Gorman(3) (b: chsd ldrs: ev ch ins fnl f: r.o)....nk **2** 9/1 70 34
*1606$^{9}$* **Delrob (46)** (DHaydnJones) **5-8-2v**$^{1(7)}$ AnthonyBond(10) (lw: sn pushed along: gd hdwy fnl f: fin wl)....1¼ **3** 10/1 49 13
**Kung Frode (65)** (BAMcMahon) **4-10-0** GDuffield(8) (chsd ldrs stands' side: r.o fnl f)....½ **4** 14/1 66 30
1351$^{10}$ **Halbert (44)** (PBurgoyne) **7-8-7v** DRMcCabe(1) (prom far side: r.o one pce fnl 2f)....hd **5** 12/1 45 9
*1455$^{3}$* **Napier Star (51)** (MrsNMacauley) **3-8-4**$^{(3)}$ CTeague(6) (led tl wknd ins fnl f)....1½ **6** 6/1$^{3}$ 47 4
1598$^{5}$ **Ivy Lilian (IRE) (35)** (WMBrisbourne) **4-7-5**$^{(7)}$ RMullen(2) (prom far side: no hdwy fnl 2f)....nk **7** 20/1 30 —
644$^{9}$ **General Equation (62)** (JBalding) **3-8-11**$^{(7)}$ JEdmunds(5) (prom over 3f)....3½ **8** 8/1 46 3
*1492$^{5}$* **My Cherrywell (59)** (LRLloyd-James) **6-9-1b**$^{(7)}$ CWebb(9) (b.off hind: hld up: a bhd)....s.h **9** 8/1 43 7
1446* **Halliard (55)** (TMJones) **5-9-4** RPerham(11) (swtg: s.i.s: reminders after 1f: outpcd)....1¾ **10** 4/1$^{1}$ 33 —
*1492$^{3}$* **Rennyholme (57)** (JHetherton) **5-9-6b** NAdams(4) (bhd fnl 2f)....nk **11** 15/2 34 —
(SP 124.7%) **11 Rn**

**60.7 secs** (3.70) CSF £43.41 CT £369.97 TOTE £4.20: £1.90 £1.30 £5.00 (£25.20) Trio £80.90 OWNER Mr T. H. Bennett (MALTON) BRED Bjorn Neilson
WEIGHT FOR AGE 3yo-7lb
**1455* Freckles Kelly**, taken to post steadily, likes this surface and held on well to defy a 5lb rise in the weights for a win last time. (9/2)
**1492 Elton Ledger (IRE)** has still to win over the minimum trip, but went close on this occasion. (9/1)
**1455 Delrob** ran better in the first-time visor, but only found top gear late in the day. (10/1: 7/1-11/1)
**Kung Frode**, lightly-raced, looked well tuned up for this reappearance and it came as no surprise to see him give a good account of himself. (14/1)
**1049 Halbert** was rated 7lb lower on the sand than his last run at Salisbury. (12/1)
**1455 Napier Star** was reverting to the minimum trip. (6/1)
**1446* Halliard** (4/1: 11/4-9/2)

## 1717 PUMA CLAIMING STKS (4-Y.O+) (Class F)
2-40 (2-44) **2m** **(Fibresand)** £2,381.00 (£656.00: £311.00) GOING minus 0.13 sec per fur (FST)

SP RR SF
1529$^{7}$ **Sea Victor (76)** (JLHarris) **4-9-5** TIves(9) (a gng wl: led wl over 1f out: r.o wl)....— **1** 10/11$^{1}$ 60 —
*73$^{6}$* **Gunmaker (30)** (BJLlewellyn) **7-8-10** TWilliams(7) (b: a.p: led 8f out tl wl over 1f out: unable qckn fnl f)....2½ **2** 14/1 48 —
666$^{10}$ **Ready to Draw (IRE) (45)** (RJO'Sullivan) **7-8-10** DBiggs(6) (hdwy 6f out: wknd over 1f out)....7 **3** 12/1 41 —
*1095$^{4}$* **Record Lover (IRE) (37)** (MCChapman) **6-8-5**$^{(5)}$ PFessey(5) (led 6f: wknd 6f out: t.o)....dist **4** 14/1 — —
*275$^{5}$* **Desert President (26)** (PMooney) **5-8-8** JQuinn(13) (bhd fnl 6f: t.o)....14 **5** 20/1 — —
**Club Elite (28)** (MFBarraclough) **4-7-11**$^{(3)}$ NVarley(8) (bhd fnl 6f: t.o)....¾ **6** 33/1 — —
*1488$^{6}$* **Efaad (IRE) (47)** (JNorton) **5-8-10v**$^{1}$ JFEgan(12) (lw: bhd fnl 6f: t.o)....3 **7** 33/1 — —
*284$^{6}$* **Kindred Greeting (33)** (JAHarris) **4-8-7** JO'Reilly(2) (bhd fnl 6f: t.o)....3½ **8** 25/1 — —
**Celtic Lilley** (PMooney) **6-8-3** JFanning(1) (a bhd: t.o fnl 8f)....hd **9** 33/1 — —
994$^{13}$ **Comedie Arrete (FR)** (MCChapman) **4-8-1**$^{(3)}$ PMcCabe(11) (swtg: a bhd: t.o fnl 5f)....29 **10** 25/1 — —
*1605$^{3}$* **Slippery Fin** (WGMTurner) **4-8-4** TSprake(4) (swtg: prom: led after 6f to 8f out: wknd 6f out: t.o)....5 **11** 11/1$^{3}$ — —
**Kirkadian** (NBycroft) **6-9-1** GDuffield(10) (a bhd: t.o fnl 8f)....dist **12** 33/1 — —
*837$^{4}$* **Old Provence (72)** (RHarris) **6-9-2** DBatteate(3) (b: hdwy after 6f: 3rd & ev ch whn p.u lame 3f out: broke leg: dead) .... **P** 7/2$^{2}$ — —
(SP 128.2%) **13 Rn**

**3m 47.6** (21.60) CSF £15.55 TOTE £1.80: £1.50 £2.70 £2.60 (£27.10) Trio £29.70 OWNER Mr David Abell (MELTON MOWBRAY) BRED Juddmonte Farms
WEIGHT FOR AGE 4yo-1lb
**1158 Sea Victor** would have been conceding much more weight to these in a handicap, with the exception of Old Provence, and his task was made easier when misfortune struck that rival. (10/11: Evens-11/10)
**Gunmaker** found his form over hurdles last month and would have been receiving two and a half stone off the winner had this been a handicap. (14/1)
**489 Ready to Draw (IRE)** would have been a stone and a half better off with the winner had this been a handicap. (12/1: op 6/1)
**Record Lover (IRE)** (14/1: op 9/1)
**837 Old Provence** was bang in contention when breaking his off-fore just before the home turn. (7/2: 2/1-4/1)

## 1718 CHEETAH H'CAP (0-65) (3-Y.O+) (Class F)

3-10 (3-12) **7f (Fibresand)** £2,381.00 (£656.00: £311.00) GOING minus 0.13 sec per fur (FST)

| | | | | SP | RR | SF |
|---|---|---|---|---|---|---|
| *1604[3]* | **Sea Spouse (57)** (MBlanshard) **5-9-1**(5) CAdamson(7) (mde all: qcknd clr over 2f out: rdn 1f out: r.o wl) | — | **1** | 11/1 | 70 | 37 |
| 1677* | **Farmost (69)** (SirMarkPrescott) **3-9-8** 6x GDuffield(4) (lw: hmpd after 1f: sn rdn: hdwy over 3f out: chsd wnr over 2f out: r.o one pce) | 2½ | **2** | 6/4 1 | 76 | 33 |
| | **Moneghetti (45)** (RHollinshead) **5-8-8** NCarlisle(9) (bhd tl gd hdwy over 1f out: nvr nrr) | 3 | **3** | 12/1 | 45 | 12 |
| *1490[7]* | **Principal Boy (IRE) (53)** (TJEtherington) **3-8-6** CRutter(13) (hdwy 3f out: one pce fnl 2f) | 1¼ | **4** | 7/1 | 51 | 8 |
| *1604[4]* | **Quinzii Martin (56)** (DHaydnJones) **8-8-12v**(7) AnthonyBond(10) (hdwy 2f out: rdn & edgd lft over 1f out: n.d) | 8 | **5** | 12/1 | 35 | 2 |
| 1473[11] | **Maybank (IRE) (61)** (BAMcMahon) **4-9-10** JFEgan(1) (lw: hld up: n.m.r over 4f out: hdwy 3f out: wknd 2f out) | ½ | **6** | 8/1 | 39 | 6 |
| *1029[7]* | **Fred's Delight (IRE) (33)** (MrsVAAconley) **5-7-10** JQuinn(2) (lw: nvr trbld ldrs) | 5 | **7** | 33/1 | — | — |
| 1348[13] | **Titanium Honda (IRE) (33)** (DCO'Brien) **5-7-10b** GBardwell(5) (b: chsd ldrs over 4f) | hd | **8** | 33/1 | — | — |
| 1586[4] | **River Garnock (50)** (DNicholls) **4-8-6**(7) JBramhill(6) (lw: chsd wnr over 4f: sn wknd) | hd | **9** | 10/1 | 16 | — |
| 1446[10] | **King of Munster (AUS) (59)** (MrsJCecil) **4-9-8** TIves(12) (prom 5f) | ¾ | **10** | 6/1 2 | 24 | — |
| *186[14]* | **Verro (USA) (33)** (KBishop) **9-7-10e** NAdams(11) (lw: a bhd) | nk | **11** | 33/1 | — | — |
| 1548[8] | **Kismetim (45)** (DWChapman) **6-8-8b** SDWilliams(3) (prom over 3f) | 1¾ | **12** | 20/1 | 5 | — |
| 1196[2] | **Hi Rock (45)** (JNorton) **4-8-8** JFanning(8) (prom over 4f: eased whn btn over 1f out) | 12 | **13** | 13/2 3 | — | — |

(SP 137.6%) **13 Rn**

**1m 31.7** (4.90) CSF £30.44 CT £210.30 TOTE £13.60: £3.20 £1.10 £5.30 (£9.80) Trio £124.40; £157.80 to Goodwood 7/6/96 OWNER Seven Seas Racing (UPPER LAMBOURN) BRED Cheveley Park Stud Ltd
LONG HANDICAP Verro (USA) 6-6 Fred's Delight (IRE) 7-3
WEIGHT FOR AGE 3yo-10lb

**1604 Sea Spouse** likes to force the pace and had his field in trouble when throwing down the gauntlet once in line for home. (11/1: 8/1-12/1)
**1677* Farmost** was attempting his fourth win in eleven days and his second within twenty-four hours. Done no favours early on, he returned with a cut to his leg and the plan of running again the next day was abandoned. (6/4: op 4/5)
**Moneghetti**, fit from hurdling, was 7lb higher than when winning here over a mile last July and may need to return to that trip. (12/1)
**1029* Principal Boy (IRE)** is more effective over seven furlongs. (7/1: op 13/1)
**1460 Quinzii Martin** had been raised 5lb since his last two runs, but was due to drop 2lb in the future. (12/1: op 8/1)
**1029 Maybank (IRE)** disappointed on the turf last time when dropped back to six. (8/1)
**King of Munster (AUS)** (6/1: 3/1-7/1)

## 1719 TIGER MAIDEN H'CAP (0-70) (3-Y.O+) (Class E)

3-40 (3-41) **1m (Fibresand)** £3,370.50 (£1,008.00: £483.00: £220.50) GOING minus 0.13 sec per fur (FST)

| | | | | SP | RR | SF |
|---|---|---|---|---|---|---|
| 1435[7] | **Sheraz (IRE) (58)** (NTinkler) **4-9-11** CRutter(16) (lw: hdwy over 3f out: led 1f out: rdn out) | — | **1** | 11/1 | 65 | 38 |
| 928[18] | **La Tansani (IRE) (66)** (RHannon) **3-9-8** JFEgan(4) (lw: a.p: led 2f out to 1f out: unable qckn) | 2½ | **2** | 9/1 | 68 | 30 |
| 1468[4] | **Speedy Snaps Pride (33)** (PDCundell) **4-8-0b** JQuinn(14) (a.p: ev ch over 2f out: r.o one pce fnl f) | 1 | **3** | 14/1 | 33 | 6 |
| 1416[17] | **Hadadabble (46)** (PatMitchell) **3-8-2** NCarlisle(13) (a.p: ev ch 2f out: one pce) | 1¾ | **4** | 12/1 | 43 | 5 |
| 1497[7] | **Royal Rapport (46)** (BAMcMahon) **3-8-2b** GDuffield(7) (led 6f: wknd over 1f out) | 6 | **5** | 14/1 | 31 | — |
| *499[5]* | **Nivasha (37)** (PMooney) **4-8-4** JFanning(10) (no hdwy fnl 2f) | 1 | **6** | 16/1 | 20 | — |
| 969[10] | **Disallowed (IRE) (65)** (MBell) **3-9-7** RPerham(8) (nvr nr to chal) | 5 | **7** | 4/1 1 | 38 | — |
| | **Careful (IRE) (64)** (BWHills) **3-9-6** TSprake(15) (bkwd: no hdwy fnl 3f) | 1½ | **8** | 11/2 3 | 34 | — |
| 1613[7] | **Jovie King (IRE) (45)** (PhilipMitchell) **4-8-7v**1(5) CAdamson(6) (n.d) | nk | **9** | 25/1 | 14 | — |
| 1449[17] | **Prudent Princess (60)** (AHide) **4-9-8**(5) MartinDwyer(2) (s.i.s: a bhd) | 1½ | **10** | 14/1 | 26 | — |
| 1522[4] | **Fastini Gold (47)** (MDIUsher) **4-9-0** NAdams(1) (chsd ldrs over 5f) | ½ | **11** | 8/1 | 12 | — |
| | **Tip it In (38)** (ASmith) **7-8-2**(3)ow3 CTeague(9) (b: bkwd: a bhd) | ½ | **12** | 25/1 | 2 | — |
| *1457[2]* | **Hornpipe (58)** (JWharton) **4-9-11** WJO'Connor(3) (prom 4f) | 5 | **13** | 9/2 2 | 12 | — |
| 1314[2] | **Tauten (IRE) (59)** (PBurgoyne) **6-9-12** DRMcCabe(11) (a bhd) | 6 | **14** | 10/1 | 1 | — |
| 1314[10] | **Juba (50)** (DrJDScargill) **4-9-3** TIves(12) (prom over 5f) | ¾ | **15** | 11/1 | — | — |
| 1359[10] | **Bashtheboards (61)** (JJQuinn) **3-9-3** SDWilliams(5) (dwlt: a bhd: t.o) | dist | **16** | 25/1 | — | — |

(SP 145.5%) **16 Rn**

**1m 46.0** (6.00) CSF £115.12 CT £1,368.65 TOTE £18.50: £3.10 £3.00 £2.90 £2.30 (£161.60) Trio £175.50; £224.96 to Goodwood 7/6/96. OWNER Speedlith Group (MALTON) BRED Ardenode Stud Ltd
WEIGHT FOR AGE 3yo-11lb

**738 Sheraz (IRE)** scored at the first time of asking on the Sand and seemed well suited to the mile. (11/1)
**La Tansani (IRE)**, another trying his luck on the Sand, appreciated the return to a mile in easier company. (9/1)
**1468 Speedy Snaps Pride** kept on again in the closing stages and may have found this trip on the short side. (14/1)
**1096 Hadadabble** seems better on the All-Weather than the turf. (12/1)
**637 Royal Rapport**, trying different tactics, did not last home. (14/1)
**499 Nivasha** was 2lb lower than when second in a seller back in February. (16/1)
**588 Disallowed (IRE)**, 9lb lower than on the turf, could never land a blow on this return to a mile. (4/1)

## 1720 LEOPARD (S) STKS (2-Y.O) (Class G)

4-10 (4-10) **6f (Fibresand)** £2,070.00 (£570.00: £270.00) GOING minus 0.13 sec per fur (FST)

| | | | | SP | RR | SF |
|---|---|---|---|---|---|---|
| 1471[4] | **Enchanting Eve** (CNAllen) **2-8-7**(5) LNewton(3) (led over 4f out: clr 1f out: r.o wl) | — | **1** | 7/2 3 | 66 | 11 |
| 1463[4] | **Impala** (WGMTurner) **2-8-11** TSprake(4) (led over 1f: rdn & hung rt fnl 2f: nt rcvr) | 8 | **2** | 6/4 1 | 44 | — |
| 1463[5] | **Rons Revenge** (MJRyan) **2-8-11** JFEgan(5) (lw: chsd ldrs 4f) | 10 | **3** | 13/2 | 17 | — |
| 1543[2] | **No Rush** (JBerry) **2-8-11** SDWilliams(7) (lw: b.off hind: w ldrs: wknd 2f out) | 1¼ | **4** | 3/1 2 | 14 | — |
| 590[8] | **Dozen Roses** (TMJones) **2-8-6** RPerham(2) (prom 4f) | 1¼ | **5** | 16/1 | 5 | — |
| | **Hazy Dayz** (DCO'Brien) **2-8-6** GBardwell(6) (s.s: a wl bhd: t.o) | 11 | **6** | 9/1 | — | — |

(SP 116.4%) **6 Rn**

**1m 19.1** (5.60) CSF £9.30 TOTE £5.20: £1.60 £1.50 (£4.60) OWNER Mr Alexander MacGillivray (NEWMARKET) BRED P. Young
No bid

**1471 Enchanting Eve**, dropped into selling company, appreciated this surface and was in control when the runner-up started to go walkabout.(7/2)
**1463 Impala** seemed to be getting the worst of the argument when starting to drift to the stands' rail. (6/4)
**1543 No Rush** (3/1: 7/4-7/2)
**Hazy Dayz** (9/1: 5/1-10/1)

## 1721 BET WITH THE TOTE H'CAP (0-60) (3-Y.O) (Class F)

4-40 (4-42) **1m (Fibresand)** £2,381.00 (£656.00: £311.00) GOING minus 0.13 sec per fur (FST)

| | | | SP | RR | SF |
|---|---|---|---|---|---|
| 1487$^{8}$ | **Princess Pamgaddy (44)** (CNAllen) **3-8-5**$^{(5)}$ MartinDwyer(15) (hld up: hdwy 3f out: squeezed thro to ld over 1f out: r.o wl)..........— | 1 | 8/1$^{3}$ | 52 | 23 |
| 1030$^{8}$ | **Seeking Destiny (IRE) (48)** (MCChapman) **3-8-9**$^{(5)}$ PFessey(14) (a.p: led 3f out to 2f out: r.o one pce)..........3 | 2 | 11/1 | 50 | 21 |
| 1110$^{5}$ | **Down The Yard (43)** (MCChapman) **3-8-6**$^{(3)}$ PMcCabe(8) (dwlt: hdwy 4f out: btn whn sddle slipped fnl f).....1½ | 3 | 11/1 | 42 | 13 |
| 1490$^{10}$ | **Jimjareer (IRE) (50)** (CaptJWilson) **3-9-2** SDWilliams(12) (lw: hdwy over 3f out: c wd ent st: r.o one pce fnl f)..........hd | 4 | 11/1 | 49 | 20 |
| 1119$^{18}$ | **Realms of Glory (IRE) (52)** (PhilipMitchell) **3-9-4v$^{1}$** JQuinn(16) (a.p: rdn & one pce fnl 2f)..........s.h | 5 | 20/1 | 51 | 22 |
| 1443$^{4}$ | **Supreme Illusion (AUS) (37)** (JohnBerry) **3-8-3b** GDuffield(13) (prom: ev ch 2f out: wknd over 1f out)..........5 | 6 | 25/1 | 26 | — |
| 1490$^{2}$ | **Awafeh (41)** (SMellor) **3-8-7** NAdams(9) (lw: swtg: led 5f: led 2f out: sn hdd & wknd)..........nk | 7 | 13/8$^{1}$ | 29 | — |
| 1490$^{5}$ | **Efipetite (45)** (NBycroft) **3-8-11** NKennedy(7) (s.i.s: hdwy over 3f out: wknd 2f out)..........3½ | 8 | 13/2$^{2}$ | 26 | — |
| 237$^{5}$ | **Cocoon (IRE) (36)** (CWThornton) **3-8-2** NCarlisle(2) (hmpd on ins 6f out: sn rdn along: n.d)..........1¾ | 9 | 14/1 | 14 | — |
| 387$^{10}$ | **Classic Delight (USA) (55)** (RHarris) **3-9-7** DBatteate(3) (a bhd)..........9 | 10 | 25/1 | 15 | — |
| 1503$^{10}$ | **How Could-I (IRE) (40)** (TDEasterby) **3-8-6** WJO'Connor(10) (lw: bhd fnl 3f)..........6 | 11 | 9/1 | — | — |
| 1526$^{9}$ | **Pulga Circo (45)** (BAMcMahon) **3-8-11** JFEgan(5) (bhd fnl 3f)..........2 | 12 | 25/1 | — | — |
| 522$^{7}$ | **Digwana (IRE) (40)** (TMJones) **3-8-6** RPerham(6) (prom: hrd rdn over 4f out: wknd over 3f out)..........3 | 13 | 25/1 | — | — |
| 1363$^{7}$ | **Craigmore Magic (USA) (55)** (MissMKMilligan) **3-9-7** JFanning(11) (lw: a bhd)..........1 | 14 | 16/1 | — | — |
| 1487$^{12}$ | **Lucitino (45)** (SCWilliams) **3-8-11b$^{1}$** OUrbina(1) (b: dwlt: a bhd)..........5 | 15 | 25/1 | — | — |
| 1512$^{11}$ | **Jolis Present (53)** (MJRyan) **3-9-5b** GBardwell(4) (prom early: p.u lame over 5f out: dead).......... | P | 14/1 | — | — |

(SP 140.7%) **16 Rn**

**1m 46.2** (6.20) CSF £93.46 CT £943.67 TOTE £10.80: £1.70 £4.30 £2.80 £2.30 (£94.90) Trio £93.50 OWNER Theobalds Stud (NEWMARKET) BRED K. Panos

**1167 Princess Pamgaddy**, set to drop 2lb in future handicaps, relished reverting to a mile. (8/1)
**780 Seeking Destiny (IRE)**, tried in blinkers last time, appeared to stay the mile well enough. (11/1: 7/1-12/1)
**605 Down The Yard**, back to a more suitable trip, managed to hold on for third, despite a slipping saddle. (11/1)
**1042 Jimjareer (IRE)** may still be worth a try over further. (11/1)
**Realms of Glory (IRE)** was sharpened up by the first-time visor. (20/1)

T/Plpt: £723.60 (10.13 Tckts). T/Qdpt: £132.00 (3.3 Tckts). KH

## 1722a-1748a (Irish Racing) - See Computer Raceform

# 1577a-LONGCHAMP (Paris, France) (R-H) (Very Soft)
## Monday May 27th

## 1749a PRIX D'ISPAHAN (Gp 1) (4-Y.O+)

2-50 (2-47) **1m 1f** £65,876.00 (£26,350.00: £13,175.00: £6,588.00)

| | | | SP | RR | SF |
|---|---|---|---|---|---|
| 536a$^{11}$ | **Halling (USA)** (SbinSuroor) **5-9-2** LDettori (mde all: qcknd st: rdn over 1f out: r.o wl fnl f)..........— | 1 | | 128 | — |
| 622a$^{6}$ | **Gunboat Diplomacy (FR)** (ELellouche,France) **5-9-2** DBoeuf (plld wd 2f out: chal 1f out: no ex fnl f)..........1½ | 2 | | 125 | — |
| 1052a* | **Vetheuil (USA)** (AFabre,France) **4-9-2** OPeslier (trckd ldrs: rdn st: kpt on one pce: no imp)..........1½ | 3 | | 123 | — |
| 1135a$^{3}$ | **Montjoy (USA)** (PFICole) **4-9-2** TQuinn (bhd tl st: nvr able to chal)..........1½ | 4 | | 120 | — |

**4 Rn**

**2m 2.9** (14.90) P-M 2.10F: 1.40F 1.40F (5.60F) OWNER Godolphin (NEWMARKET) BRED Cyril Humphries

**536a Halling (USA)** looked a picture in the paddock. He was asked to make all the running and did so in style, but was given a slight fright when Gunboat Diplomacy made his challenge halfway up the straight. He found another gear though and, after a few reminders, went on to win in excellent style. Nearly ten months of being trained on the dirt has evidently had no negative effect, and he relished this return to grass. He looks likely to have another highly successful season in top-class company over distances up to twelve furlongs, and his target is again the Eclipse Stakes, which he won last year, but he may be seen out at Royal Ascot in the Prince Of Wales's Stakes in the meantime.
**438a* Gunboat Diplomacy (FR)** looked extremely dangerous as he made his challenge a furlong and a half out, but he was held comfortably in the closing stages by the winner. Even though the ground was riding very soft, it was not truly testing enough for this mudlark. He has been difficult to get fit because of the firm state of the training tracks at Chantilly, but this was a good effort, and he will probably next be seen out in the Grand Prix d'Evry, providing there is plenty of cut in the ground.
**1052a* Vetheuil (USA)** tracked the leader until early in the straight and was then outpaced before running on again near the finish. He was running in a Group One for the first time and he does not really look this class, although he did not seem at his best on this soft ground. He looks the perfect sort to race in America, and holds an engagement in the Arlington Million.
**1135a Montjoy (USA)** was disappointing. Racing in last place, he made a half-hearted effort up the rail soon after entering the straight and, when switched to the outside, just stayed on at the same pace. He now goes for the Prince Of Wales's Stakes at Royal Ascot.

# 1054a-MULHEIM (Mulheim-Ruhr, Germany) (Heavy)
## Monday May 27th

## 1750a PREIS DER DIANA (Gp 2) (3-Y.O F)

4-15 **1m 3f** £98,198.00 (£39,340.00: £19,820.00: £10,909.00)

| | | | SP | RR | SF |
|---|---|---|---|---|---|
| | **Night Petticoat (GER)** (BSchutz,Germany) **3-9-2** AStarke (racd in 3rd: led 1f out: r.o wl)..........— | 1 | | 104 | — |
| 791a* | **Tulipa (USA)** (AFabre,France) **3-9-2** SGuillot (trckd ldr: led 2f out to 1f out: one pce)..........2½ | 2 | | 100 | — |
| | **Anno Luce** (UOstmann,Germany) **3-9-2** GBocskai (led to 2f out: wknd)..........5 | 3 | | 93 | — |
| 1060a* | **La Blue (GER)** (BSchutz,Germany) **3-9-2** THellier (late hdwy: nt rch ldrs)..........2 | 4 | | 90 | — |
| 1060a$^{5}$ | **Kirsberry (GER)** (Germany) **3-9-2** TMundry (nvr bttr than mid div)..........¾ | 5 | | 89 | — |
| 1060a$^{2}$ | **Dapprima (GER)** (Germany) **3-9-2** WWoods (hld up in rr: late hdwy)..........1½ | 6 | | 87 | — |
| | **Aiyana (GER)** (Germany) **3-9-2** PSchiergen (last st: styd on fnl 2f)..........1½ | 7 | | 84 | — |
| | **Morning Queen (GER)** (Germany) **3-9-2** JPMurtagh (n.d)..........1¾ | 8 | | 82 | — |
| 1060a$^{4}$ | **Massada** (Germany) **3-9-2** KWoodburn (mid div: wknd over 2f out)..........2½ | 9 | | 78 | — |

| | | | | SP | RR | SF |
|---|---|---|---|---|---|---|
| 1060a[6] | **Masai Mara (GER)** (Germany) **3-9-2** WNewnes (n.d) | | 10 | | — | — |
| | **Dakota (GER)** (Germany) **3-9-2** ABest (4th st: sn wknd) | | 11 | | — | — |
| | **Ice Cream (GER)** (Germany) **3-9-2** MRimmer (5th st: sn btn) | | 12 | | — | — |
| | **Pradilla (GER)** (Germany) **3-9-2** DMcCann (a in rr) | | 13 | | — | — |
| | **Purple Sun (GER)** (Germany) **3-9-2** StephenDavies (a in rr) | | 14 | | — | — |
| | **Dark Lady (GER)** (Germany) **3-9-2** NGrant (t.o ½-wy: p.u) | | P | | — | — |

**15 Rn**

**2m 31.8** TOTE 30DM: 13DM 18DM 32DM (125DM) OWNER Gestut Wittekindshof BRED Gestut Wittekindshof
**Night Petticoat (GER)**, a German-bred daughter of Petoski, showed her appreciation for the heavy ground and proved too strong for this field. Racing in third place, she took the lead a furlong out and eventually came home a comfortable winner.
**791a* Tulipa (USA)** tracked the leader for most of the way and made an effort two furlongs from home. She was swallowed up by the impressive winner with a furlong left to travel, and could then only run on at one pace.

# MUNICH (Germany) (L-H) (Very Soft)
## Monday May 27th

### 1751a GROSSER PREIS VON DEUTSCHLAND (Gp 3) (3-Y.O)
3-25 (3-30) **1m 3f** £66,216.00 (£26,126.00: £13,514.00: £6,757.00)

| | | | | SP | RR | SF |
|---|---|---|---|---|---|---|
| 904a[2] | **Mongol Warrior (USA)** (LordHuntingdon) **3-9-2** DHarrison (racd in 3rd: rdn to ld 2f out: drvn out) | — | 1 | | 94 | — |
| | **Agnelli** (HJentzsch,Germany) **3-9-2** LHammer-Hansen (led: qcknd 4f out: hdd 2f out: styd on one pce) | 2 | 2 | | 91 | — |
| | **Flamingo Garden (GER)** (HBlume,Germany) **3-9-2** MLarsen (prom tl outpcd fnl 3f) | 18 | 3 | | 65 | — |
| 904a[3] | **Sir Warren (IRE)** (HBlume,Germany) **3-9-2** ASuborics (a mid div) | 1 | 4 | | 64 | — |
| | **Daubigny (GER)** (Germany) **3-9-2** JHillis (n.d) | 3 | 5 | | 59 | — |
| | **Lorcan (GER)** (Germany) **3-9-2** PaulEddery (n.d) | 8 | 6 | | 48 | — |
| | **Apia (USA)** (Germany) **3-9-2** SEccles (racd in 2nd: wknd fr 4f out) | 7 | 7 | | 37 | — |
| | **Magic Mahal (GER)** (Germany) **3-9-2** PPiatkowski (n.d) | ¾ | 8 | | 36 | — |
| | **Bad Bertrich Again (IRE)** (Germany) **3-9-2** AHelfenbein (a bhd) | 1½ | 9 | | 34 | — |

**9 Rn**

**2m 30.8** TOTE 59DM: 15DM 13DM 20DM (199DM) OWNER H De Kwiatkowski (WEST ILSLEY) BRED Kennelot Stables Limited
**904a Mongol Warrior (USA)** relished the testing ground. Always close up, he went clear with the pace-setting Agnelli with over three furlongs to run and took the measure of that rival passing the quarter-mile pole. He is entered in the King Edward VII Stakes at Royal Ascot.

# BADEN-BADEN (Germany) (L-H) (Good)
## Saturday June 1st

### 1752a OLEANDER RENNEN (Gp 3) (4-Y.O+)
3-43 (3-43) **2m** £33,784.00 (£13,514.00: £6,757.00: £3,604.00)

| | | | | SP | RR | SF |
|---|---|---|---|---|---|---|
| 1054a* | **Camp David (GER)** (AWohler,Germany) **6-8-12** PSchiergen | — | 1 | | 117 | — |
| 1138a[5] | **First Hello (GER)** (PRau,Germany) **4-9-2** TMundry | 2 | 2 | | 120 | — |
| | **Little Smart (GER)** (PLautner,Germany) **4-8-7** WNewnes | 1¾ | 3 | | 109 | — |
| 875[5] | **Old Rouvel (USA)** (DJGMurraySmith) **5-8-7b[1]** KWoodburn | 2 | 4 | | 106 | — |
| 1128[4] | **Grey Shot** (IABalding) **4-9-0** THellier | 1½ | 5 | | 113 | — |
| 1005[2] | **Daraydan (IRE)** (LadyHerries) **4-8-7** KDarley (btn 21½l) | | 8 | | — | — |

**12 Rn**

**3m 22.31** TOTE 58DM: 20DM 31DM 97DM (481DM) OWNER D. Gabel BRED Frau & I. Brunotte
**1054a* Camp David (GER)** was in touch throughout. Making steady progress three furlongs from home, he was ridden to lead at the distance and, despite hanging right, ran on strongly in the final furlong.
**875 Old Rouvel (USA)** put in a performance which really pleased his connections. Racing in mid-division, he gradually made headway from five furlongs out, and with two furlongs to go he looked to have every chance, but he was just unable to quicken enough.
**1128 Grey Shot** disappointed connections with his run here. As normal, he was very prominent and took up the running at halfway but, having turned into the straight, he soon came under pressure and could find nothing when asked. Plans for him running at Royal Ascot have now been put on hold and he may be given a break.
**1005 Daraydan (IRE)** may have run his race prior to going into the stalls. He played up in the paddock and became very coltish. However, he raced in touch with the leaders before, like Grey Shot, found nothing from two furlongs out. He is capable of much better.

### 1753a SCHERPING RENNEN (Listed) (3-Y.O)
4-55 (4-56) **6f** £18,018.00 (£7,207.00: £4,505.00: £2,703.00)

| | | | | SP | RR | SF |
|---|---|---|---|---|---|---|
| | **Waky Nao** (HBlume,Germany) **3-8-11** ASuborics | — | 1 | | 93 | — |
| | **My King (GER)** (HRemmert,Germany) **3-8-9** KWoodburn | 1¾ | 2 | | 86 | — |
| | **Woodfighter (IRE)** (CSprengel,Germany) **3-8-9** SHeller | 1 | 3 | | 84 | — |
| | **Greek Icon** (MRChannon) **3-8-11** KDarley (btn 19¼l) | 4 | 9 | | 75 | — |

**11 Rn**

**1m 16.44** TOTE 29DM: 16DM 29DM 42DM (276DM) OWNER H. von Finck BRED H. von Finck
**Greek Icon** was having her first run for her trainer having formerly been trained with John Dunlop, but disappointed connections with a fairly lack-lustre display. Prominent to halfway, she weakened quite quickly soon after and just kept on at the same pace.

# 1749a-LONGCHAMP (Paris, France) (R-H) (Good)
## Saturday June 1st

### 1754a PRIX DE LA JONCHERE (Gp 3) (3-Y.O C & G)
2-45 (2-45) **1m** £28,986.00 (£10,540.00: £5,270.00: £2,635.00)

| | | | | SP | RR | SF |
|---|---|---|---|---|---|---|
| | **Android (USA)** (AFabre,France) **3-8-12** OPeslier | — | 1 | | 108 | 29 |

| | | | | | | |
|---|---|---|---|---|---|---|
| | **Manninamix** (AFabre,France) **3-9-1** TJarnet | 1 | **2** | | 109 | 30 |
| 903a[2] | **Dankeston (USA)** (MBell) **3-8-12** CAsmussen | 1½ | **3** | | 103 | 24 |
| | | | | | | **6 Rn** |

**1m 43.4** (8.40) P-M 4.40F: 1.70F 1.20F OWNER D. Wildenstein (CHANTILLY)
**Android (USA)** looked a colt who is going the right way when winning this Group event on only his third racecourse performance and did it in good style. He always plays up at the start but he does nothing wrong when the gates open, and moved smoothly into the lead a furlong and a half out. He had the race wrapped up shortly after and was never put under the slightest pressure. Sure to improve, he might stay a little further and may be allowed to take his chance in the Grand Prix de Paris.
**Manninamix** put up a superb performance considering he was making his seasonal debut and giving 3lb to the winner. He was set the task of making all and did so at a leisurely pace, but was outpaced early in the straight before running on again in the final furlong. Not given a hard time, he should definitely be followed in the future and could go for the Grand Prix de Paris.
**903a Dankeston (USA)** was totally unsuited by the way the race went. There was not enough pace and he could not accelerate when speed was injected in the straight, but he did run on in the final stages if only at the same pace. He needs a tough mile and shows his best when hidden until the last moment.
DS

# 1752a-BADEN-BADEN (Germany) (L-H) (Soft)
## Sunday June 2nd

### 1755a BADENER MEILE (Gp 3) (3-Y.O+)
3-25 (3-30) **1m** £33,784.00 (£13,514.00: £6,757.00: £3,604.00)

| | | | | SP | RR | SF |
|---|---|---|---|---|---|---|
| | **Sinyar** (BSchutz,Germany) **4-9-2** THellier | — | **1** | | 114 | — |
| | **Kalatos (GER)** (AWohler,Germany) **4-9-2** GBocskai | ½ | **2** | | 113 | — |
| | **Devil River Peek (USA)** (BSchutz,Germany) **4-9-2** AStarke | ¾ | **3** | | 112 | — |
| 1112[11] | **Silca Blanka (IRE)** (MRChannon) **4-9-2** KDarley (btn 8 3/4l) | | **6** | | — | — |
| | | | | | | **13 Rn** |

**1m 44.82** TOTE 103DM: 25DM 20DM 21DM (2713DM) OWNER Mr J. Abdullah
**Silca Blanka (IRE)** had the conditions against him after considerable overnight rain. He raced prominently and moved into third position with two furlongs left, but could not quicken on the rain-softened ground. He is suited more by firmer conditions.

# CHANTILLY (France) (R-H) (Firm)
## Sunday June 2nd

### 1756a PRIX JEAN PRAT (Gp 1) (3-Y.O C & F)
2-30 (2-34) **1m 1f** £52,701.00 (£21,080.00: £10,540.00: £5,270.00)

| | | | | SP | RR | SF |
|---|---|---|---|---|---|---|
| 1139a[4] | **Le Triton (USA)** (MmeCHead,France) **3-9-2** FHead (mde all: r.o wl) | — | **1** | /1 | 111 | 82 |
| 1133a* | **Martiniquais (IRE)** (AFabre,France) **3-9-2** OPeslier (racd in 5th: rdn over 2f out: stdy prog fr over 1f out: wnt 2nd cl home) | 2 | **2** | | 107 | 78 |
| | **Blackwater (USA)** (MZilber,France) **3-9-2** GGuignard (hld up in rr: rdn 2f out: hdwy to go 2nd 1f out: no imp) | ½ | **3** | | 107 | 78 |
| 1133a[2] | **Kalmoss (FR)** (BRenard,France) **3-9-2** DSicaud (racd in 2nd: rdn over 2f out: one pce) | 2 | **4** | | 103 | 74 |
| 1441* | **Regal Archive (IRE)** (PWChapple-Hyam) **3-9-2** JReid (racd in 4th: 3rd st: rdn 2f out: unable qckn) | ½ | **5** | | 102 | 73 |
| 1133a[3] | **Rupert (FR)** (JdeRoualle,France) **3-9-2** GMosse (racd in 3rd:4th st: rdn over 2f out: one pce) | nk | **6** | | 102 | 73 |
| | | | | (SP 100.0%) | | **6 Rn** |

**1m 48.6** (-1.40) P-M 2.50F: 1.70F 1.80F (11.10F) OWNER Maktoum Al Maktoum (CHANTILLY) BRED West Star Bloodstock
**1139a Le Triton (USA)** made every yard of the running to win his first Group One race impressively, beating the course record in the process. He accelerated early in the straight and had the race wrapped up a furlong from home. He had problems early in the season with colic, but is now back to his very best and, although not the easiest of characters, he is out of the top drawer. He now goes for the Grand Prix de Paris, and another main target is the Jacques le Marois at Deauville. (/1)
**1133a* Martiniquais (IRE)** never looked like catching the winner, but he did stay on well to take second place inside the final furlong. Ten furlongs should be within his grasp, and he is an honest colt, but probably not quite of Group One level.
**Blackwater (USA)** started slowly and nearly put the brakes on when he saw a path seven furlongs out. He remained in last place until the straight when bought wide to challenge, but was one-paced. His trainer thinks he is much better than he showed on this occasion, and certainly the incident with the path did not help. He is still inexperienced and will be allowed to take his chance in the Grand Prix de Paris.
**1133a Kalmoss (FR)** was second early on, but proved very one-paced in the straight. He is not up to this standard and could probably do with more cut in the ground
**1441* Regal Archive (IRE)** raced on the rail behind Le Triton, but was a beaten force soon after entering the straight. This race was just eight days after his previous start, and it was probably asking too much in Group One company. He may also have preferred some cut in the ground.

### 1757a LES EMIRATS ARABES UNIS PRIX DU JOCKEY-CLUB (Gp 1) (3-Y.O C & F)
3-50 (3-51) **1m 4f** £329,381.00 (£131,752.00: £68,876.00: £32,928.00)

| | | | | SP | RR | SF |
|---|---|---|---|---|---|---|
| 797a* | **Ragmar (FR)** (PBary,France) **3-9-2** GMosse (hld up in rr: hdwy wl over 2f out: led appr fnl f r.o wl) | — | **1** | | 116 | 66 |
| 903a[9] | **Polaris Flight (USA)** (PWChapple-Hyam) **3-9-2** MJKinane (in rr to st: hdwy on outside 2f out: swtchd rt 1f out: hrd rdn & jst failed) | s.h | **2** | | 116 | 66 |
| | **Le Destin (FR)** (PDemercastel,France) **3-9-2** TGillet (dwlt: last st: gd hdwy on outside fnl 2f: fin strly) | nk | **3** | | 116 | 66 |
| 1329* | **Don Micheletto** (SbinSuroor) **3-9-2** LDettori (mid div: hdwy over 2f out: r.o) | 2 | **4** | | 113 | 63 |
| 1057a[8] | **Oliviero (FR)** (AMauchamp,France) **3-9-2b** TThulliez (last str: nt clr run over 2f out: r.o fnl f: nrst fin) | ¾ | **5** | | 112 | 62 |
| 1139a* | **Helissio (FR)** (ELellouche,France) **3-9-2** DBoeuf (plld hrd: 3rd ½-wy: nt clr run over 1f out: no ex) | d.h | **5** | | 112 | 62 |
| | **Grape Tree Road** (AFabre,France) **3-9-2** TJarnet (a.p: 2nd st: led 2f out tl appr fnl f: one pce) | nk | **7** | | 112 | 62 |
| 1125[3] | **Astor Place (IRE)** (PWChapple-Hyam) **3-9-2** PatEddery (mid-div: prog u.p fnl 2f: nvr nrr) | ¾ | **8** | | 111 | 61 |
| 986* | **High Baroque (IRE)** (PWChapple-Hyam) **3-9-2** JReid (prom: 8th st: 4th over 1f out: one pce) | nk | **9** | | 110 | 60 |
| 1057a* | **Arbatax (IRE)** (PBary,France) **3-9-2** CAsmussen (hld up in rr: hdwy & 6th st: ev ch over 1f out: one pce) | 1½ | **10** | | 108 | 58 |
| | **L'Africain Bleu (FR)** (MmeCHead,France) **3-9-2** GGuignard (prom: led ent st to 2f out: sn wknd) | 2 | **11** | | 105 | 55 |

| | | | SP | RR | SF |
|---|---|---|---|---|---|
| | **Water Poet (IRE)** (AFabre,France) **3-9-2** SGuillot (prom: 5th st: wknd appr fnl f: eased)..........3 | **12** | | 101 | 51 |
| 1389a* | **Radevore** (AFabre,France) **3-9-2** OPeslier (7th st: wkng whn bdly hmpd over 2f out)..........2 | **13** | | 99 | 49 |
| 1057a[2] | **Dark Nile (USA)** (MmeCHead,France) **3-9-2** FHead (bhd fnl 3f)..........10 | **14** | | 85 | 35 |
| 797a[6] | **Hoist To Heaven (USA)** (MmeCHead,France) **3-9-2** NGuesdon (led to wl over 2f out)..........15 | **15** | | 65 | 15 |

**15 Rn**

**2m 27.2** (0.40) P-M 10.30F: 4.70F 10.20F 8.50F (280.30F) OWNER Mr J-L Bouchard (CHANTILLY) BRED Dr G. & Mme J. Sandor

**797a* Ragmar (FR)**, a really tough individual, held on by a nostril to win this Classic in the gamest of styles. In the rear early, he moved up round the turn before making an effort at the two-furlong marker and, after accelerating to lead 200 yards out, just held on. One could not say he was a brilliant winner, but he is a fine-looking colt who always gives his best and, although the first nine were covered by four lengths, the time was excellent. He is a lightly raced, very laid back individual, who shows nothing in the morning gallops and he is not fashionably bred, but possesses both stamina and acceleration. This seems to be his perfect trip and he will now go on to run in the Grand Prix de Saint-Cloud, although his breeder is pushing for a supplement into the Irish Derby. The main target though is the Prix de l'Arc de Triomphe, and he is the sort of horse who will always catch out a more classy opponent on a bad day.

**903a Polaris Flight (USA)**, who tracked Ragmar, came with a devastating late burst but, unlike when the pair met in the Criterium de Saint-Cloud, he got the worse of the photo. His jockey thought that the winner caused slight interference a furlong out, but the Stewards would have none of it and left the result unaltered. He was not a well horse in the Italian 2,000 Guineas, but showed much improved form over this distance and is now being aimed at the Irish Derby.

**Le Destin (FR)**, who was slowly away, trailed the field until the straight, a tactic employed on purpose as he is inclined to pull. Once given his head, he finished fastest of all but just too late. He is a very consistent colt, and is being aimed at the Arc de Triomphe, although the Grand Prix de Saint-Cloud is an option.

**1329* Don Micheletto** produced a good run in the straight having been in mid-division early on, but did not have the pace to go with the first three, although he did prove that twelve furlongs was no problem. He may take his chance in the Grand Prix de Paris or go on to the Irish Derby.

**1125 Astor Place (IRE)** was well up for the first four furlongs but then lost his place at the six-furlong marker. He made some progress in the straight, but never looked like taking a hand in the finish.

**986* High Baroque (IRE)** was in mid-division early on, and came with a promising challenge in the straight, but it petered out in the final furlong. He was almost certainly feeling the firm ground and will do much better on a softer surface.

## 1758a PRIX DE SANDRINGHAM (Gp 3) (3-Y.O F)
5-15 (5-15) **1m** £28,986.00 (£10,540.00: £5,270.00: £2,635.00)

| | | | SP | RR | SF |
|---|---|---|---|---|---|
| | **Sensation** (MmeCHead,France) **3-8-11** LDettori ..........— | **1** | | 114 | 51 |
| | **Patch Of Blue** (AFabre,France) **3-8-11** OPeslier ..........2½ | **2** | | 109 | 46 |
| 1140a[5] | **True Flare (USA)** (MmeCHead,France) **3-8-11** FHead ..........1 | **3** | | 107 | 44 |
| 1140a[3] | **Sagar Pride (IRE)** (JGBurns,Ireland) **3-8-11** WCarson (btn over 5½l) .......... | **5** | | — | — |

**9 Rn**

**1m 37.7** (1.20) P-M 3.10F: 1.30F 1.70F 1.40F (16.10F) OWNER Sheikh Mohammed (CHANTILLY) BRED Sheikh Mohammed

**Sensation** lived up to her name with a pillar-to-post victory in her first Group event and won in style and by no means fully extended. This filly has really blossomed over the past two months, and it is a shame she was not entered into the Coronation Stakes at Royal Ascot. She may go for the Falmouth Stakes at Newmarket followed by the Jacques le Marois or the Prix d'Astarte at Deauville.

**Patch Of Blue** ran with much credit considering it was only her second racecourse appearance. She began to understand things in the straight and ran on really well without threatening the winner, and looks to have a bright future. She is certainly of Group quality and may next be seen out in the Prix Chloe at Evry.

**True Flare (USA)** was waited with on the rail before running on really well in the straight. She has shown her best form when allowed to make all the running and a return to her favourite tactics might be beneficial. She could go for the Prix de la Porte Maillot.

**1140a Sagar Pride (IRE)** ran well until halfway up the straight. She might have been a little tired after travelling for the third occasion this season, and she certainly did not run up to her true form. Her jockey thought she may need a longer distance now.
DS

# 1578a-SAN SIRO (Milan, Italy) (R-H) (Good to firm)
**Sunday June 2nd**

## 1759a PREMIO EMILIO TURATI (Gp 2) (3-Y.O+ C & F)
4-40 (5-18) **1m** £38,915.00 (£17,859.00: £9,957.00: £4,979.00)

| | | SP | RR | SF |
|---|---|---|---|---|
| **Morigi** (ITellini,Italy) **5-9-4** MTellini (a cl up: 3rd st: r.o wl u.p to ld at fin)..........— | **1** | | 117 | — |
| **Ravier (ITY)** (EBorromeo,Italy) **5-9-4** FJovine (led over 6f out: hrd rdn appr fnl f: ct on line)..........s.h | **2** | | 117 | — |
| **Tres Heureux (GER)** (FrauEMader,Germany) **6-9-4** LMader (led over 2f: 2nd st: hrd rdn & ev ch over 1f out: one pce)..........4¾ | **3** | | 107 | — |
| **Lake Storm (IRE)** (GBotti,Italy) **5-9-2** EBotti (4th st: wknd wl over 1f out)..........1½ | **4** | | 102 | — |
| **Tatas** (Italy) **3-8-7** MCandiano (hld up: 5th st: chal over 2f out: sn one pce)..........4¼ | **5** | | 96 | — |
| **Welsh Liberty (IRE)** (Italy) **7-9-4** MEsposito (a in rr: wl bhd fnl 3f)..........2½ | **6** | | 91 | — |

**6 Rn**

**1m 38.8** (8.80) TOTE 52L: 14L 12L (21L) OWNER Razza Giallorosso

**Morigi**, a son of Rousillon, was always in a challenging position and got up in the last stride to nose out the favourite.

**Ravier (ITY)** took over from the German raider Tres Heureux after two and a half furlongs, and was still racing in front entering the final furlong. He hung on bravely but was just pipped on the line.

**Tres Heureux (GER)**, the early leader, was demoted to second place by the favourite after two and a half furlongs. Always handy, he had every chance over a furlong out, but could only run on at the one pace.

# 1607-CATTERICK (L-H) (Good to firm, Good patches)
**Friday June 7th**
WEATHER: unsettled

## 1760 E.B.F. MAIDEN STKS (2-Y.O F) (Class D)
2-10 (2-11) **5f** £3,149.75 (£938.00: £446.50: £200.75) Stalls: Low GOING minus 0.39 sec per fur (F)

| | | | SP | RR | SF |
|---|---|---|---|---|---|
| 1525[2] | **Vax Star** (JLSpearing) **2-8-8**(3) SDrowne(3) (trckd ldr: led 2f out: shkn up & qcknd clr 1f out: readily)..........— | **1** | 11/10[1] | 78 | 6 |

| | | | | | |
|---|---|---|---|---|---|
| 715[2] **Double Park (FR)** (MJohnston) **2-8-11** JWeaver(4) (lw: chsd ldrs: outpcd ½-wy: styd on wl ins fnl f)............1¼ | **2** | 15/8[2] | 74 | 2 |
| 1062[2] **Enchantica** (JBerry) **2-8-11** JCarroll(2) (lw: b.hind: led 3f: hung rt & kpt on same pce)..................................1½ | **3** | 3/1[3] | 69 | — |
| 630[6] **Singforyoursupper** (GGMargarson) **2-8-11** PBloomfield(1) (s.i.s: outpcd tl styd on appr fnl f)......................2½ | **4** | 20/1 | 61 | — |
| *1080*[3] **Calchou** (CWFairhurst) **2-8-11** DeanMcKeown(5) (unruly: trckd ldrs: plld hrd: wknd over 1f out)......................2 | **5** | 14/1 | 55 | — |
| | | (SP 118.8%) | | **5 Rn** |

**60.8 secs** (3.30) CSF £3.86 TOTE £1.90: £1.40 £1.10 (£2.10) OWNER Vax Ltd (ALCESTER) BRED A. Brazier
**1525 Vax Star** was entitled to take this after her good effort first time at Ripon, and she did it nicely. (11/10)
**715 Double Park (FR)**, who showed plenty of knee-action going down, stayed on in determined fashion late in the day. She will be much better suited by six. (15/8)
**1062 Enchantica** has plenty of pace, but she again showed a marked tendency to hang. (3/1)
**630 Singforyoursupper**, edgy beforehand, was never in the contest and probably needs at least six. (20/1)
**1080 Calchou**, a tail-swisher, proved too keen, both on the way down, and in the race itself. (14/1)

## 1761 JERVAULX H'CAP (0-65) (3-Y.O) (Class F)

2-40 (2-48) **5f** £2,889.00 (£804.00: £387.00) Stalls: Low GOING minus 0.39 sec per fur (F)

| | | SP | RR | SF |
|---|---|---|---|---|
| 1340[7] **Mister Joel (58)** (MWEasterby) **3-8-9b**(5) GParkin(1) (lw: mde all: clr ½-wy: hrd rdn over 1f out: all out).........— | **1** | 11/2[2] | 64 | 18 |
| *1492*[17] **Kiwud (41)** (TWDonnelly) **3-7-6b**[1](5) PFessey(4) (a chsng wnr: bmpd over 1f out: nt qckn wl ins fnl f).............½ | **2** | 25/1 | 45 | — |
| 1541[9] **Imp Express (IRE) (50)** (GMMoore) **3-8-6b**[1] JWeaver(5) (prom: rdn & hung lft over 1f out: kpt on)...............1¼ | **3** | 8/1 | 50 | 4 |
| 1597[7] **Gwespyr (60)** (JBerry) **3-9-2** JCarroll(15) (s.i.s: hdwy u.p ½-wy: hung lft: styd on same pce fnl f)....................½ | **4** | 14/1 | 59 | 13 |
| 1612[2] **Madam Zando (44)** (JBalding) **3-8-0** TWilliams(12) (prom early: sn outpcd: hdwy & n.m.r over 1f out: styd on: nvr nr ldrs)..........1 | **5** | 7/1 | 40 | — |
| 1598[7] **Snitch (40)** (CSmith) **3-7-10v** AMackay(11) (a chsng ldrs: sn rdn along: no imp fnl 2f)..................................hd | **6** | 20/1 | 35 | — |
| 1152[8] **Capture The Moment (55)** (RJRWilliams) **3-8-11** DaleGibson(6) (b.nr hind: bhd: hdwy over 1f out: nvr nr ldrs)..........2½ | **7** | 9/1 | 42 | — |
| 1356[4] **Gormire (62)** (JHetherton) **3-9-4** NKennedy(2) (b.hind: in tch: sn rdn along & outpcd).......................................1 | **8** | 12/1 | 46 | — |
| 1527[13] **Jenny's Charmer (50)** (SEKettlewell) **3-8-6** NRodgers(10) (s.i.s: bhd: sme hdwy over 1f out: n.d)................hd | **9** | 16/1 | 34 | — |
| 1527[16] **Mystic Times (55)** (MissJFCraze) **3-8-11** NConnorton(13) (sn outpcd & bhd)..................................................7 | **10** | 16/1 | 16 | — |
| 1429[4] **Superfrills (55)** (MissLCSiddall) **3-8-11** DeanMcKeown(3) (s.s: a bhd)...........................................................1¼ | **11** | 12/1 | 12 | — |
| *430*[8] **Ping-Pong Ball (40)** (TRWatson) **3-7-5**(5) CAdamson(14) (sn bhd).................................................................2 | **12** | 50/1 | — | — |
| *989*[5] ***Don't Tell Anyone (52)*** (PDEvans) **3-8-1**(7) IonaWands(8) (Withdrawn not under Starter's orders: v.unruly in stalls)........ | **W** | 11/1 | — | — |
| *1592*[2] ***Miletrian Refurb (IRE) (62)*** (MRChannon) **3-8-13**(5) PPMurphy(9) (Withdrawn not under Starter's orders: kicked & played up bdly in stalls)........ | **W** | 13/2[3] | — | — |
| *665** ***Lady Caroline Lamb (IRE) (65)*** (RBastiman) **3-9-2**(5) HBastiman(7) (Withdrawn not under Starter's orders: kicked & played up bdly in stalls)........ | **W** | 3/1[1] | — | — |
| | | (SP 140.0%) | | **12 Rn** |

**60.2 secs** (2.70) CSF £58.02 CT £243.57 TOTE £4.20: £2.40 £8.00 £1.30 (£69.20) Trio £87.80 OWNER Mr Philip Jarvis (SHERIFF HUTTON) BRED Roldvale Ltd
LONG HANDICAP Snitch 7-9 Ping-Pong Ball 7-5
**1340 Mister Joel**, with the blinkers back on, did just enough. (11/2)
**Kiwud**, with blinkers fitted for the first time, showed her first worthwhile form. (25/1)
**Imp Express (IRE)**, fitted with blinkers for the first time, ran easily his best race so far this year. (8/1)
**881 Gwespyr** ran his best race for some time, despite a marked tendency to hang left. (14/1)
**1612 Madam Zando**, on edge beforehand, was putting in her best work at the finish after meeting interference. (7/1)
**Capture The Moment**, who ran over ten furlongs on her previous outing, stayed on late in the day and six might suit her better. (9/1: op 6/1)
**1356 Gormire** (12/1: op 8/1)

## 1762 SCORTON CLAIMING STKS (3-Y.O) (Class F)

3-10 (3-20) **1m 5f 175y** £2,637.00 (£732.00: £351.00) Stalls: Low GOING minus 0.39 sec per fur (F)

| | | SP | RR | SF |
|---|---|---|---|---|
| 1498[16] **Sedbergh (USA) (67)** (MrsMReveley) **3-9-3** WJO'Connor(4) (trckd ldrs gng wl: led on bit over 1f out: rdn out)..........— | **1** | 5/4[1] | 68 | 25 |
| 1591[8] **Mathon (IRE) (52)** (MRChannon) **3-8-6v**[1](5) PPMurphy(3) (a chsng ldrs: kpt on same pce fnl 2f: no ch w wnr).4 | **2** | 15/2 | 57 | 14 |
| *1457*[10] **Phantom Dancer (IRE) (52)** (JBerry) **3-8-9** JCarroll(6) (led tl over 1f out: sn wknd)..........................................8 | **3** | 5/1[2] | 46 | 3 |
| 537[10] **Brogans Brush** (JSHaldane) **3-8-1** JFanning(2) (bhd & rdn 8f out: sme hdwy over 3f out: nvr nr ldrs).............3 | **4** | 50/1 | 35 | — |
| 1504[7] **Valise (48)** (MrsMReveley) **3-8-4** ACulhane(1) (plld hrd: trckd ldrs tl lost pl over 6f out)..................................hd | **5** | 6/1 | 38 | — |
| 1311[9] **Mr Titch** (DenysSmith) **3-8-3** LCharnock(7) (swtg: sn chsng ldrs: outpcd over 5f out: n.d after).......................nk | **6** | 25/1 | 36 | — |
| 1474[8] **Superbird** (TDEasterby) **3-8-0** TWilliams(8) (hld up: hdwy 7f out: dmv along over 5f out: wknd 4f out)...........¾ | **7** | 8/1 | 32 | — |
| 1477[6] **Irish Oasis (IRE) (48)** (BSRothwell) **3-8-13** MBirch(5) (plld hrd: trckd ldrs tl wknd qckly over 5f out: sn t.o)...dist | **8** | 11/2[3] | — | — |
| | | (SP 119.5%) | | **8 Rn** |

**3m 3.5** (8.00) CSF £11.30 TOTE £2.30: £1.00 £2.10 £2.90 (£10.80) OWNER Mr P. D. Savill (SALTBURN) BRED Mulholland Brothers
**1023 Sedbergh (USA)**, stepped up in distance, was heavily backed to take this dire contest. After looking likely to win very easily at one stage, in the end he had to be kept right up to his work. (5/4: op 9/4)
**Mathon (IRE)**, in a visor after finishing tailed off last time, kept on to finish clear second best. (15/2: 9/2-8/1)
**784 Phantom Dancer (IRE)** made the running until his stamina gave out. (5/1)
**Brogans Brush**, who wore a crossed-noseband, was under pressure before halfway. (50/1)
**Valise** (6/1: op 7/2)
**1474 Superbird** (8/1: op 4/1)
**1477 Irish Oasis (IRE)** (11/2: 4/1-6/1)

## 1763 LESLIE PETCH H'CAP (0-70) (3-Y.O+) (Class E)

3-40 (3-42) **1m 3f 214y** £2,976.00 (£888.00: £424.00: £192.00) Stalls: Low GOING minus 0.39 sec per fur (F)

| | | SP | RR | SF |
|---|---|---|---|---|
| 1548[2] **Here Comes Herbie (37)** (WStorey) **4-7-5**(5) PFessey(6) (hld up: hdwy 6f out: led 3f out tl over 1f out: styd on wl to ld ins fnl f)..........— | **1** | 7/4[1] | 48 | 8 |
| 1647[4] **Calder King (62)** (JLEyre) **5-9-7b** KFallon(2) (trckd ldrs: rdn to ld over 1f out: hdd ins fnl f)..............................1 | **2** | 2/1[2] | 72 | 32 |
| 1544[2] **Pharly Dancer (56)** (WWHaigh) **7-9-1** DaleGibson(3) (plld hrd: trckd ldrs: pushed along 6f out: one pce fnl 3f)..........1½ | **3** | 5/1[3] | 64 | 24 |

1309[8] **Public Way (IRE) (45)** (NChamberlain) **6-8-4** DeanMcKeown(7) (trckd ldrs: effrt over 2f out: kpt on same pce) ....2½ **4** 33/1 49 9
1542[4] **Cross Talk (IRE) (69)** (RHollinshead) **4-9-9**(5) FLynch(1) (hld up: stumbled over 7f out: pushed along 5f out: nvr nr ldrs) ....½ **5** 5/1[3] 73 33
1504[6] **Roy Boy (68)** (MrsMReveley) **4-9-13** ACulhane(4) (led to 3f out: sn lost pl & bhd) ....26 **6** 8/1 37 —
1325[7] **Tashjir (USA) (55)** (DMorley) **3-7-13** LCharnock(5) (chsd ldrs: chal 4f out: wknd over 2f out: sn bhd) ....s.h **7** 12/1 24 —
(SP 124.8%) **7 Rn**

**2m 37.9** (6.50) CSF £6.26 TOTE £2.90: £1.20 £2.30 (£5.10) OWNER Mr H. S. Hutchinson (CONSETT) BRED H. Hutchinson
LONG HANDICAP Here Comes Herbie 7-5
WEIGHT FOR AGE 3yo-15lb
**1548 Here Comes Herbie**, 5lb out of the weights, fought back strongly to regain the initiative. His trainer feels he is better waited with longer. (7/4)
**1647 Calder King**, who showed a very poor action going down, was outbattled in the end. (2/1)
**1544 Pharly Dancer**, who refused to settle, is better suited by the All-Weather. (5/1)
**Public Way (IRE)**, on ground plenty firm enough for him, was far from disgraced. (33/1)
**1542 Cross Talk (IRE)** stumbled on the turn into the back straight, and this is best overlooked. (5/1)
**Tashjir (USA)** (12/1: op 8/1)

## 1764 ELLERY HILL RATING RELATED MAIDEN APPRENTICE STKS (0-60) (3-Y.O+) (Class F)
4-15 (4-15) **7f** £2,469.50 (£702.00: £348.50) Stalls: Low GOING minus 0.39 sec per fur (F)

SP RR SF
1527[5] **Ivor's Deed (51)** (CFWall) **3-8-10** PClarke(4) (lw: trckd ldrs: hdwy to ld ins fnl f: r.o wl) ....— **1** 11/8[1] 65 1
1416[12] **Backhander (IRE) (51)** (MartynWane) **4-9-6** KSked(5) (sn chsng ldr: rdn over 2f out: styd on one pce fnl f)..1½ **2** 7/2[2] 62 8
660[2] **Carmosa (USA) (57)** (DNicholls) **3-8-7** JBramhill(1) (set moderate pce: rdn & qcknd over 2f out: hdd ins fnl f: one pce) ....nk **3** 11/8[1] 58 —
1500[17] **Nutcracker Suite (IRE) (53)** (JLEyre) **4-9-3** ClaireWest(2) (chsd ldrs: pushed along over 3f out: sn wl outpcd) ....12 **4** 16/1 31 —
*782*[16] **Haute Cuisine (60)** (JBerry) **3-8-10** CLowther(3) (reard up bdly in stalls: s.v.s: hdwy to chse ldrs ½-wy: sn wknd) ....15 **5** 8/1[3] — —
(SP 123.4%) **5 Rn**

**1m 28.9** (5.30) CSF £7.16 TOTE £1.90: £1.10 £2.90 (£5.60) OWNER Mr Mervyn Ayers (NEWMARKET) BRED David Sinden, Mervyn Ayers and Richard Brunger
WEIGHT FOR AGE 3yo-10lb
**1527 Ivor's Deed** looked in a different league to his rivals and showed a good fluent action going down. Confidently ridden in what was in effect a two and a half furlong sprint, he won well in the end. (11/8)
**834 Backhander (IRE)** stuck on under pressure to get the better of the pacesetter in the final strides, but the winner swept by them both on the outside. (7/2)
**660 Carmosa (USA)**, who showed a very poor action going to post, set just a modest pace. Quickening off the bend, she was worn down in the last 150 yards. (11/8)

## 1765 SCOTCH CORNER H'CAP (0-70) (3-Y.O+) (Class E)
4-45 (4-45) **5f 212y** £3,028.00 (£904.00: £432.00: £196.00) Stalls: High GOING minus 0.39 sec per fur (F)

SP RR SF
1364[5] **Sonderise (47)** (NTinkler) **7-8-10** JWeaver(2) (lw: hld up: hdwy ½-wy: rdn to ld over 1f out: wandered: rdn out) ....— **1** 5/1[3] 56 42
1541* **Aquado (55)** (SRBowring) **7-9-1b**(3) 7x CTeague(4) (chsd ldrs: rdn & outpcd over 2f out: styd on fnl f) ....2 **2** 3/1[1] 59 45
1364[9] **Plum First (65)** (LRLloyd-James) **6-9-7b**(7) CWebb(6) (b: b.hind: bhd: hdwy u.p 2f out: n.m.r over 1f out: kpt on same pce) ....2½ **3** 6/1 62 48
1635[6] **Henry the Hawk (52)** (MDods) **5-8-12**(3) PMcCabe(7) (b: swtg: chsd ldrs: outpcd 2f out: n.d after) ....5 **4** 17/2 36 22
*1492*[12] **Lord Sky (48)** (ABailey) **5-8-11** SDWilliams(8) (mde most tl over 2f out: wknd over 1f out) ....2 **5** 11/1 26 12
*1083** **Vax New Way (64)** (JLSpearing) **3-9-2b**(3) SDrowne(1) (w ldr: led over 2f tl over 1f out: sn wknd) ....¾ **6** 9/2[2] 40 18
1545[3] **The Institute Boy (46)** (MissJFCraze) **6-8-9** AMackay(3) (lw: hld up: hdwy ½-wy: wknd 2f out) ....1½ **7** 6/1 18 4
1500[18] **Taurean Fire (43)** (MrsMReveley) **3-7-12** LCharnock(10) (hld up: nvr nr ldrs) ....1½ **8** 11/1 11 —
1087[9] **Steel Sovereign (38)** (MDods) **5-7-10b**(5) PFessey(5) (sn bhd & rdn along) ....¾ **9** 20/1 4 —
1541[7] **Lochon (53)** (JLEyre) **5-9-2** TWilliams(9) (sn drvn along: chsd ldrs tl lost pl 2f out: fin lame) ....2 **10** 10/1 14 —
(SP 129.5%) **10 Rn**

**1m 12.3** (1.40) CSF £21.67 CT £90.30 TOTE £7.50: £1.70 £1.40 £3.60 (£17.70) Trio £47.60 OWNER Mrs D. Wright (MALTON) BRED Doublet Ltd
WEIGHT FOR AGE 3yo-8lb
**1364 Sonderise** gained his first success for three years. Having nothing to do with the frantic early dash, he wandered under pressure, but his rider had all the answers. (5/1)
**1541* Aquado**, raised 12lb after his Carlisle success, had difficulties handling the bend. Staying on at the finish, it turned out he had spread a plate during the race. (3/1)
**1157 Plum First** is an inconsistent individual. (6/1)
**1635 Henry the Hawk** was badly tapped for foot on this ground. (17/2)
**997 Lord Sky** went very keenly to post and did too much in the race. (11/1)

T/Plpt: £12.70 (599.34 Tckts). T/Qdpt: £9.50 (39.42 Tckts). WG

# EPSOM (L-H) (Good, Good to firm patches back st)
## Friday June 7th
WEATHER: hot WIND: slt across

## 1766 VODATA CONDITIONS STKS (2-Y.O C & G) (Class B)
2-15 (2-15) **5f** £9,162.37 (£3,340.50: £1,632.75: £701.25: £313.13) Stalls: High GOING minus 0.14 sec per fur (G)

SP RR SF
1328[2] **Granny's Pet** (PFICole) **2-8-9** TQuinn(4) (hld up: hung lft thrght: hdwy over 2f out: led over 1f out: r.o wl) ....— **1** 5/2[1] 84 48
916[4] **Hangover Square (IRE)** (RHannon) **2-8-9** MJKinane(1) (lw: chsd ldr 3f: r.o one pce) ....3½ **2** 4/1[3] 73 37

| | | | | | | |
|---|---|---|---|---|---|---|
| 1404* | **Joint Venture (IRE)** (BJMeehan) **2-8-12b** PatEddery(6) (led over 3f: one pce) | 1¼ | **3** | 4/1[3] | 72 | 36 |
| 1419[6] | **Rude Awakening** (GLewis) **2-8-12b[1]** LDettori(5) (prom: hung lft over 1f out: wknd ins fnl f) | 2½ | **4** | 3/1[2] | 64 | 28 |
| 1169[6] | **Talisman (IRE)** (SDow) **2-8-9** WRyan(2) (outpcd) | 13 | **5** | 25/1 | 19 | — |
| 946[2] | **Herecomestheknight** (MartynMeade) **2-8-12** JReid(3) (sn bhd: p.u lame over 1f out: broke leg: dead) | | **P** | 9/1 | — | — |

(SP 107.4%) **6 Rn**

**56.28 secs** (1.78) CSF £11.43 TOTE £2.50: £1.40 £2.20 (£6.70) OWNER Mrs D. M. Arbib (WHATCOMBE) BRED Fluorocarbon Bloodstock

**1328 Granny's Pet** caught a tartar last time, and had previously found the ground too soft at Newbury. Hanging down the camber from the word go, the bit eventually slipped through his mouth, but he still scored well enough. The Windsor Castle at Royal Ascot is now on the agenda. (5/2)

**916 Hangover Square (IRE)** now seems ready to tackle an extra furlong. (4/1)

**1404* Joint Venture (IRE)** again tried to make all, but this company was a bit hotter than at Haydock. (4/1)

**1419 Rude Awakening**, tried in blinkers, again hung left which was fairly predictable on this course. (3/1)

## 1767 VODAPAGE RATED STKS H'CAP (0-105) (4-Y.O+) (Class B)

2-50 (2-50) **1m 4f 10y** £21,221.20 (£7,940.80: £3,882.90: £1,669.50: £747.25: £378.35) Stalls: Low GOING minus 0.14 sec per fur (G)

| | | | | SP | RR | SF |
|---|---|---|---|---|---|---|
| 1336[2] | **Backgammon (90)** (JABOld) **5-8-0** JQuinn(4) (chsd ldr over 8f: outpcd over 2f out: rallied 1f out: hrd rdn to ld nr fin) | — | **1** | 6/1 | 101 | 66 |
| 941[8] | **Son of Sharp Shot (IRE) (98)** (JLDunlop) **6-8-8** WCarson(6) (lw: hld up & bhd: hdwy on ins & plld out over 2f out: r.o wl ins fnl f) | hd | **2** | 11/2[3] | 109 | 74 |
| 925[12] | **Korambi (92)** (CEBrittain) **4-8-2**ow2 MFenton(1) (led tl nr fin) | 1 | **3** | 20/1 | 102 | 65 |
| 919[7] | **Naked Welcome (104)** (MJFetherston-Godley) **4-9-0** JReid(7) (hld up: rdn 3f out: styd on fnl f) | nk | **4** | 5/1[2] | 113 | 78 |
| 1440[8] | **Mystic Hill (90)** (GHarwood) **5-7-9**(5) MHenry(5) (lw: no hdwy fnl 2f) | 4 | **5** | 8/1 | 94 | 59 |
| 1176[5] | **Arctic Thunder (USA) (97)** (LadyHerries) **5-8-7** JPMurtagh(2) (b: lw: nvr nr to chal) | 1¼ | **6** | 7/1 | 99 | 64 |
| 1336[4] | **Source of Light (102)** (RCharlton) **7-8-12** PatEddery(9) (prom: wnt 2nd over 2f out: eased whn btn ins fnl f) | ½ | **7** | 4/1[1] | 104 | 69 |
| 925[6] | **At Liberty (IRE) (90)** (RHannon) **4-7-11**(3) AWhelan(3) (a bhd) | nk | **8** | 14/1 | 91 | 56 |
| 1193[10] | **Kadamann (IRE) (93)** (RAkehurst) **4-8-3** SSanders(8) (lw: prom tl wknd over 2f out) | 11 | **9** | 10/1 | 80 | 45 |

(SP 110.5%) **9 Rn**

**2m 36.27** (1.27) CSF £34.40 CT £530.13 TOTE £5.20: £1.40 £2.10 £7.70 (£17.00) Trio £200.30 OWNER Mr W. E. Sturt (WROUGHTON) BRED Stilvi Compania Financiera S A

LONG HANDICAP Mystic Hill 7-11 At Liberty (IRE) 7-8 Backgammon 7-13

**1336 Backgammon** appreciated the faster ground, but his rider reported that he did not come down the hill, and he certainly looked tapped for toe early in the home straight. (6/1)

**Son of Sharp Shot (IRE)**, 8lb higher than winning last season's Bessborough at Royal Ascot, subsequently finished fourth off this mark in the Ebor. (11/2: 4/1-6/1)

**Korambi** only got worn down at the death, and his turn would appear to be near. (20/1)

**919 Naked Welcome** was back in handicap company, but his four wins have come on more galloping courses than this. (5/1)

**Mystic Hill**, bought for 28,000 guineas out of Roger Charlton's yard last autumn, appears to be coming to hand. (8/1)

**1176 Arctic Thunder (USA)** hinted at a return to form, but may need to come down the handicap a few pounds. (7/1)

**1336 Source of Light** looks handicapped up to the hilt at the moment. (4/1: 3/1-5/1)

**925 At Liberty (IRE)** (14/1: 10/1-16/1)

## 1768 VODAFONE DIOMED STKS (Gp 3) (3-Y.O+) (Class A)

3-20 (3-21) **1m 114y** £28,850.00 (£10,905.00: £5,327.50: £2,417.50) Stalls: Low GOING minus 0.14 sec per fur (G)

| | | | | SP | RR | SF |
|---|---|---|---|---|---|---|
| 1484* | **Blomberg (IRE) (93)** (JRFanshawe) **4-9-4** DHarrison(4) (rdn 3f out: hdwy to ld 2f out: sn clr: drvn out) | — | **1** | 6/1[3] | 112 | 75 |
| 1112[13] | **Behaviour (95)** (MrsJCecil) **4-9-4** JReid(8) (lw: dwlt: hld up & bhd: hdwy 2f out: chsd wnr over 1f out: r.o one pce) | 1¼ | **2** | 14/1 | 110 | 73 |
| | **Mr Martini (IRE) (113)** (CEBrittain) **6-9-7** CAsmussen(5) (a.p: r.o one pce fnl f) | 2½ | **3** | 6/1[3] | 108 | 71 |
| 1755a[6] | **Silca Blanka (IRE) (106)** (MRChannon) **4-9-4** KDarley(7) (lw: hld up: hdwy on ins 3f out: sn rdn: nt clr run over 1f out & ins fnl f: nt rcvr) | 1¾ | **4** | 7/1 | 102 | 65 |
| 1329[5] | **Rio Duvida (112)** (DRLoder) **3-8-6** PatEddery(3) (chsd ldr: rdn over 2f out: wknd over 1f out) | ½ | **5** | 100/30[1] | 101 | 52 |
| 1410[3] | **Takkatamm (USA) (111)** (SbinSuroor) **4-9-4** LDettori(2) (lw: led over 6f) | 2½ | **6** | 4/1[2] | 96 | 59 |
| 1580a[7] | **Dismissed (USA) (105)** (PFICole) **3-8-6** TQuinn(1) (prom tl wknd over 2f out) | 1¾ | **7** | 7/1 | 93 | 44 |
| 1395a[5] | **Brandon Magic (105)** (IABalding) **3-8-6** MHills(6) (s.i.s: bhd fnl 2f) | 9 | **8** | 14/1 | 76 | 27 |

(SP 110.0%) **8 Rn**

**1m 43.59** (1.59) CSF £67.86 TOTE £7.90: £1.80 £2.70 £2.40 (£44.60) OWNER Comet Group Plc (NEWMARKET) BRED Mrs Chris Harrington

WEIGHT FOR AGE 3yo-12lb

**1484* Blomberg (IRE)** is certainly in fine form and will still go for the Royal Hunt Cup under a penalty. (6/1)

**878 Behaviour** is becoming something of an in-and-out performer. (14/1)

**Mr Martini (IRE)** could not repeat last year's win in this event without a previous run behind him. (6/1)

**1755a Silca Blanka (IRE)** had finished sixth in a similar event on soft ground at Baden-Baden five days ago. (7/1)

**1329 Rio Duvida** found no joy on this return to a mile. (100/30)

**1410 Takkatamm (USA)** found his front-running bid coming to an end at the quarter-mile pole. (4/1: op 5/2)

## 1769 VODAFONE OAKS STKS (Gp 1) (3-Y.O F) (Class A)

4-05 (4-06) **1m 4f 10y** £201,000.00 (£75,200.00: £36,100.00: £15,700.00) Stalls: Low GOING minus 0.14 sec per fur (G)

| | | | | SP | RR | SF |
|---|---|---|---|---|---|---|
| 1077* | **Lady Carla** (HRACecil) **3-9-0** PatEddery(9) (lw: a.p: wnt 2nd 7f out: shkn up to ld wl over 2f out: sn qckndclr: r.o wl) | — | **1** | 100/30[2] | 120+ | 84 |
| 938* | **Pricket (USA)** (SbinSuroor) **3-9-0** LDettori(4) (lw: a.p: rdn & chsd wnr over 2f out: no imp) | 9 | **2** | 7/4[1] | 108 | 72 |
| 1144* | **Mezzogiorno (112)** (GWragg) **3-9-0** CAsmussen(8) (hdwy over 2f out: styd on fnl f) | ½ | **3** | 14/1 | 107 | 71 |
| 957* | **Camporese (IRE)** (PWChapple-Hyam) **3-9-0** JReid(2) (hld up & bhd: hdwy over 2f out: styd on fnl f) | ½ | **4** | 9/1[3] | 107 | 71 |
| 1077[3] | **Moody's Cat (IRE) (90)** (BWHills) **3-9-0** MHills(10) (led tl hdd wl over 2f out: sn wknd) | 7 | **5** | 100/1 | 97 | 61 |
| 1335* | **Whitewater Affair (105)** (MRStoute) **3-9-0** TQuinn(3) (lw: rdn over 3f out: no hdwy) | nk | **6** | 9/1[3] | 97 | 61 |
| 1335[8] | **Faraway Waters (100)** (DWPArbuthnot) **3-9-0** KDarley(1) (b.hind: prom tl wknd over 2f out) | ½ | **7** | 100/1 | 96 | 60 |
| 939[5] | **Honest Guest (IRE) (110)** (MHTompkins) **3-9-0** PRobinson(7) (lw: hld up: stdy hdwy 5f out: wknd over 2f out) | 5 | **8** | 14/1 | 90 | 54 |
| 1573a* | **Identify (IRE)** (DKWeld,Ireland) **3-9-0** MJKinane(5) (lengthy: lw: hld up mid div: wknd over 2f out) | 2½ | **9** | 16/1 | 86 | 50 |

| | | | | SP | RR | SF |
|---|---|---|---|---|---|---|
| 1189[3] | **Shirley Venture** (SPCWoods) **3-9-0** WWoods(11) (prom 6f: t.o fnl 5f) | 22 | **10** | 200/1 | 57 | 21 |
| 939[7] | **Bint Salsabil (USA) (115)** (JLDunlop) **3-9-0** WCarson(6) (prom 6f: t.o fnl 3f) | dist | **11** | 10/1 | — | — |
| | | | | (SP 110.2%) | **11 Rn** | |

**2m 35.55** (0.55) CSF £8.45 TOTE £4.50: £1.70 £1.40 £3.20 (£4.00) Trio £30.90 OWNER Mr Wafic Said (NEWMARKET) BRED Meon Valley Stud

OFFICIAL EXPLANATION **Bint Salsabil (USA): her trainer reported that following an ECG, the filly was found to have a slight heart strain.**

**1077* Lady Carla**, with no stamina doubts, threw down the gauntlet early in the home straight. Showing a classy turn of foot to spreadeagle the field in a matter of strides, she won by the widest margin since Sun Princess in 1983, and would seem well up to taking on the colts should connections wish to do so. (100/30)
**938* Pricket (USA)** may be a very useful filly but, once the winner was given the green light, it soon became apparent she was not going to emulate her sister Diminuendo who won this race in 1988. (7/4)
**1144* Mezzogiorno** lacked nothing on the stamina front, but was only playing for the places. (14/1)
**957* Camporese (IRE)**, a touch warm on a hot day, had faster ground and inexperience to contend with, but stayed on from off the pace to contest the minor honours. (9/1: 12/1-8/1)
**1077 Moody's Cat (IRE)** had no answer to the winner going to the quarter-mile pole. (100/1)
**939 Honest Guest (IRE)** did not appear to get the trip. (14/1: 10/1-16/1)
**1573a* Identify (IRE)**, a really long-backed filly, did look an ideal sort to handle this course, and needs softer ground. (16/1)
**939 Bint Salsabil (USA)**, rather warm on a hot day, ran as if something was amiss. It later transpired she was suffering from heart problems.(10/1)

## 1770 VODAC VICTRESS STKS (Listed) (3-Y.O+ F & M) (Class A)

4-40 (4-41) **1m 114y** £17,425.00 (£5,275.00: £2,575.00: £1,225.00) Stalls: Low GOING minus 0.14 sec per fur (G)

| | | | | SP | RR | SF |
|---|---|---|---|---|---|---|
| 1193[3] | **Donna Viola (88)** (CFWall) **4-9-6** WWoods(2) (hdwy on ins over 2f out: r.o wl to ld last strides) | — | **1** | 9/1[3] | 107 | 87 |
| 1476[8] | **Hagwah (USA) (99)** (BHanbury) **4-9-9** WRyan(3) (led: clr 3f out: wknd ins fnl f: ct last strides) | nk | **2** | 10/1 | 109 | 89 |
| 1484[14] | **Nagnagnag (IRE) (98)** (SDow) **4-9-6** BThomson(4) (hld up & bhd: hdwy over 2f out: r.o fnl f) | 1 | **3** | 14/1 | 105 | 85 |
| | **Tereshkova (USA)** (SbinSuroor) **4-9-9** LDettori(1) (hld up: hdwy 3f out: chsd wnr over 2f out: one pce fnl f) | 1¾ | **4** | 5/2[1] | 104 | 84 |
| | **Louis' Queen (IRE) (101)** (JLDunlop) **4-9-6** JReid(11) (hld up & bhd: hdwy 2f out: nvr nr to chal) | 3½ | **5** | 9/1[3] | 95 | 75 |
| 581[10] | **Musetta (IRE) (110)** (CEBrittain) **4-9-9** CAsmussen(5) (prom: hmpd over 2f out: nt rcvr) | ¾ | **6** | 12/1 | 96 | 76 |
| 1190[7] | **Lilli Claire (83)** (AGFoster) **3-8-8** SSanders(9) (nvr trbld ldrs) | 1¼ | **7** | 20/1 | 91 | 59 |
| 1335[7] | **Fag End (IRE) (96)** (MHTompkins) **3-8-8** PRobinson(8) (lw: prom tl wknd 3f out) | 15 | **8** | 12/1 | 63 | 31 |
| 960[9] | **Alessia (90)** (WRMuir) **4-9-6b[1]** MJKinane(6) (lw: prom tl wknd over 2f out) | 3½ | **9** | 25/1 | 56 | 36 |
| 1075[3] | **Christmas Kiss (93)** (RHannon) **4-9-6b** MHills(7) (a bhd: t.o fnl 2f) | dist | **10** | 20/1 | — | — |
| 1007* | **Aunty Jane** (BWHills) **3-8-8** PatEddery(10) (prom tl wknd 3f out: p.u lame over 1f out) | | **P** | 100/30[2] | — | — |
| | | | | (SP 116.2%) | **11 Rn** | |

**1m 42.62** (0.62) CSF £84.87 TOTE £13.50: £2.50 £4.80 £3.20 (£141.80) Trio £795.30 OWNER Mr Kieran Scott (NEWMARKET) BRED Lady Juliet de Chair

WEIGHT FOR AGE 3yo-12lb

OFFICIAL EXPLANATION **Aunty Jane: her jockey reported that the filly lost her action.**

**1193 Donna Viola** bridged the gap into listed company, and seems well suited to a stiff or extended mile. (9/1)
**1476 Hagwah (USA)** was given an enterprising ride over this shorter trip, and seemed to have the race won until she began to die in the latter stages. (10/1)
**1112 Nagnagnag (IRE)** likes this course and bounced back to form. (14/1: 10/1-16/1)
**Tereshkova (USA)**, a smart performer for Andre Fabre, has since won three of her four starts in Dubai. She might need more cut in the ground to be really at her best. (5/2: op 6/4)
**Louis' Queen (IRE)** did not manage to win last season, but ran some useful races and should soon step up on this performance. (9/1)
**Musetta (IRE)**, fourth in last year's Oaks, had not run over this trip since making her reappearance last year, and it was rather surprising she did not have more use made of her. Stopped in her tracks with over a quarter mile to go, this run is best forgotten. (12/1)

## 1771 VODACOM H'CAP (0-100) (3-Y.O) (Class C)

5-15 (5-17) **1m 2f 18y** £17,831.25 (£5,400.00: £2,637.50: £1,256.25) Stalls: Low GOING minus 0.14 sec per fur (G)

| | | | | SP | RR | SF |
|---|---|---|---|---|---|---|
| 1126[3] | **Spirito Libro (USA) (73)** (CNAllen) **3-7-6**(5) MBaird(12) (hld up: led over 1f out: r.o wl) | — | **1** | 8/1[3] | 84 | 53 |
| 969* | **Trojan Risk (75)** (GLewis) **3-7-10**(3) AWhelan(5) (dwlt: hdwy over 1f out: r.o wl ins fnl f) | 1¼ | **2** | 15/2[2] | 84 | 53 |
| 1193[7] | **Vola Via (USA) (84)** (IABalding) **3-8-3**(5) MartinDwyer(11) (lw: a.p: r.o one pce fnl f) | ½ | **3** | 12/1 | 92 | 61 |
| 1432[3] | **Believe Me (97)** (RHannon) **3-9-4**(3) DaneO'Neill(7) (lw: prom: outpcd over 2f out: r.o ins fnl f) | ¾ | **4** | 10/1 | 104 | 73 |
| 1175[4] | **Burnt Offering (75)** (CEBrittain) **3-7-8**(5) MHenry(1) (hld up & bhd: hdwy 2f out: r.o ins fnl f) | 1 | **5** | 20/1 | 80 | 49 |
| 1345* | **Call Me (72)** (CWThornton) **3-7-7**(3) NVarley(10) (chsd ldrs: rdn & outpcd over 2f out: styd on ins fnl f) | hd | **6** | 16/1 | 77 | 46 |
| 1142[19] | **Lituus (USA) (80)** (JHMGosden) **3-8-4v[1]** LDettori(8) (plld hrd: led tl hdd over 1f out: wknd fnl f) | ½ | **7** | 9/1 | 85 | 54 |
| 1469* | **Freequent (89)** (LMCumani) **3-8-13** 4x WRyan(3) (hld up & bhd: c wd ent st: late hdwy: nrst fin) | ½ | **8** | 7/4[1] | 93 | 62 |
| 1106[3] | **Warning Reef (84)** (MRChannon) **3-8-8** MJKinane(4) (nvr nrr) | 2½ | **9** | 15/2[2] | 84 | 53 |
| 1050[4] | **Jamaican Flight (USA) (73)** (JWHills) **3-7-11** WCarson(6) (a bhd) | 9 | **10** | 16/1 | 58 | 27 |
| 1327[11] | **La Modiste (88)** (SDow) **3-8-12** TQuinn(2) (plld hrd: prom tl wknd over 2f out) | 2 | **11** | 25/1 | 70 | 39 |
| 1106[7] | **Mancini (84)** (MBell) **3-8-8** MFenton(9) (lw: chsd ldr tl wandered & wknd 3f out) | ¾ | **12** | 20/1 | 65 | 34 |
| | | | | (SP 122.9%) | **12 Rn** | |

**2m 6.56** (2.16) CSF £63.66 CT £667.72 TOTE £10.00: £2.60 £2.60 £4.80 (£40.00) Trio £208.50 OWNER Camelot Racing (NEWMARKET) BRED T. J. Rooney

LONG HANDICAP Call Me 7-8

**1126 Spirito Libro (USA)**, raised a further 2lb, certainly saw out the extra quarter-mile well enough. (8/1)
**969* Trojan Risk**, upped 3lb, had quite a bit to do in the last furlong and a half, and could not peg back the winner. (15/2)
**Vola Via (USA)** has been dropped 4lb this season and looked much more at home on this faster ground. (12/1: op 20/1)
**1432 Believe Me** again got caught flat-footed at a vital stage, but the longer trip meant he was coming back at the finish. (10/1)
**1175 Burnt Offering** did not appear suited to this drop back in distance. (20/1)
**1345* Call Me** has found her niche over this sort of trip, and gave a decent account of herself, despite possibly not handling the camber in the home straight. (16/1)
**970 Lituus (USA)**, a $220,000 brother to Young Senor, was tried in a visor over this longer trip. (9/1)
**1469* Freequent**, due to go up 8lb as of the following day, came around the houses at Tattenham Corner and ran on nicely at the death without being knocked about. (7/4: 11/10-15/8)

T/Jkpt: £23,668.70 (0.1 Tckts); £30,002.59 to Epsom 8/6/96. T/Plpt: £1,319.50 (29.07 Tckts). T/Qdpt: £223.80 (9.91 Tckts). KH

# 1709-GOODWOOD (R-H) (St crse Good, Rnd crse Good to firm)
## Friday June 7th
WEATHER: fine

## 1772 WEALD & DOWNLAND MUSEUM CLAIMING STKS (4-Y.O+) (Class E)
6-30 (6-30) **1m 4f** £3,720.00 (£1,110.00: £530.00: £240.00) Stalls: Low GOING minus 0.20 sec per fur (GF)

| Form | Horse | Dist | Pos | SP | RR | SF |
|---|---|---|---|---|---|---|
| $1338^{4}$ | **Statajack (IRE) (72)** (DRCElsworth) **8-9-7b** TQuinn(2) (lw: stdy hdwy over 2f out: edgd rt & led over 1f out: edgd rt ins fnl f: r.o wl) | — | **1** | 5/2$^{1}$ | 71 | 52 |
| | **Shabanaz (60)** (WRMuir) **11-8-9** WJO'Connor(3) (hld up: rdn 3f out: r.o ins fnl f) | 1¾ | **2** | 5/1$^{3}$ | 57 | 38 |
| *$145^{2}$* | **Ultimate Warrior (70)** (CACyzer) **6-9-1** MFenton(7) (a.p: led over 6f out tl over 1f out: unable qckn) | 1 | **3** | 4/1$^{2}$ | 61 | 42 |
| | **Peter Monamy (58)** (MCPipe) **4-8-12** LDettori(4) (led over 5f: hrd rdn over 3f out: 4th & btn whn squeezed out over 1f out) | 2 | **4** | 5/2$^{1}$ | 56 | 37 |
| *$1444^{3}$* | **Juliasdarkinvader (39)** (AMoore) **6-8-8** AClark(1) (b: swtg: lost pl 5f out: no hdwy fnl 3f) | s.h | **5** | 33/1 | 52 | 33 |
| | **Johns Joy (40)** (JJBridger) **11-8-6** JQuinn(5) (b: bit bkwd: a bhd) | 23 | **6** | 33/1 | 19 | — |
| *$1448^{6}$* | **Flow Back (60)** (GPEnright) **4-9-1** NAdams(8) (a bhd) | 3½ | **7** | 8/1 | 23 | 4 |

(SP 110.8%) **7 Rn**

**2m 38.91** (5.71) CSF £13.97 TOTE £2.80: £2.10 £3.00 (£8.10) OWNER Mrs M. E. Slade (WHITCOMBE) BRED Princess Oettingen-Spielberg

**1338 Statajack (IRE)** was given a lovely ride by Quinn who did no more than coax this old rogue to victory. (5/2)
**Shabanaz**, last seen out over hurdles in December, may be eleven years old, but he looked fit enough for this return and still retains ability. This is his class as his last seven wins have come in sellers or claimers, and a similar event can be found for this old stager in the near future. (5/1)
**Ultimate Warrior** was without a run in over four months. (4/1: 3/1-9/2)
**Peter Monamy**, winner of two selling hurdles last month, was feeling the pinch in fourth place when becoming the meat in the sandwich below the distance. (5/2)
**1444 Juliasdarkinvader** lost his pitch at the top of the hill and was making no further impression in the straight. (33/1)

## 1773 WILEY EUROPE H'CAP (0-80) (3-Y.O) (Class D)
7-00 (7-03) **1m 2f** £6,230.00 (£1,865.00: £895.00: £410.00) Stalls: High GOING minus 0.20 sec per fur (GF)

| Form | Horse | Dist | Pos | SP | RR | SF |
|---|---|---|---|---|---|---|
| $873^{12}$ | **Get Tough (57)** (SDow) **3-7-13** JFEgan(5) (hdwy, nt clr run & swtchd rt over 2f out: squeezed thro on ins ins fnl f: led wl ins fnl f: r.o wl) | — | **1** | 25/1 | 66 | 33 |
| $1326^{2}$ | **No-Aman (79)** (MajorWRHern) **3-9-7** WCarson(17) (hdwy over 2f out: led ins fnl f: sn hdd: r.o) | ½ | **2** | 5/1$^{1}$ | 87 | 54 |
| $1515^{2}$ | **White Plains (IRE) (67)** (MBell) **3-8-9** MFenton(12) (swtg: hdwy over 2f out: ev ch 1f out: r.o) | 1 | **3** | 8/1$^{3}$ | 74 | 41 |
| $1345^{2}$ | **Eagle Canyon (IRE) (72)** (BHanbury) **3-8-11**(3) JStack(1) (a.p: led over 3f out to 1f out: unable qckn) | ¾ | **4** | 12/1 | 77 | 44 |
| $755^{6}$ | **Mighty Phantom (USA) (70)** (JWHills) **3-8-12** MHills(3) (led 8f out tl over 3f out: hrd rdn over 2f out: led 1f out tl ins fnl f: one pce) | 1¾ | **5** | 16/1 | 73 | 40 |
| $1180^{7}$ | **King Rufus (72)** (JRArnold) **3-9-0** DRMcCabe(7) (lw: rdn over 3f out: hdwy over 1f out: r.o) | 2½ | **6** | 14/1 | 71 | 38 |
| $1312^{*}$ | **Mazcobar (70)** (PJMakin) **3-8-12** LDettori(10) (led 2f: rdn over 3f out: eased whn btn fnl f) | 1¼ | **7** | 6/1$^{2}$ | 67 | 34 |
| $1641^{2}$ | **Shaha (64)** (RHannon) **3-8-3**(3) DaneO'Neill(15) (lost pl over 5f out: rdn over 3f out: one pce) | 1¾ | **8** | 5/1$^{1}$ | 58 | 25 |
| $1185^{11}$ | **Cool Fire (72)** (SPCWoods) **3-9-0** WWoods(16) (swtg: prom 8f) | 6 | **9** | 25/1 | 56 | 23 |
| $1420^{5}$ | **Philistar (71)** (JMPEustace) **3-8-13** MTebbutt(6) (swtg: prom over 6f) | 1 | **10** | 20/1 | 54 | 21 |
| | **Matthias Mystique (54)** (MissBSanders) **3-7-10** JQuinn(13) (a bhd) | nk | **11** | 33/1 | 36 | 3 |
| $1304^{7}$ | **White Settler (68)** (RJHodges) **3-8-10** AMcGlone(4) (a bhd) | d.h | **11** | 33/1 | 50 | 17 |
| $1349^{3}$ | **Royal Diversion (IRE) (74)** (JLDunlop) **3-9-2** TQuinn(8) (swtg: bhd fnl 2f) | 3½ | **13** | 10/1 | 51 | 18 |
| $1324^{4}$ | **Sweetness Herself (70)** (MJRyan) **3-8-12** GCarter(14) (bhd fnl 5f) | 3 | **14** | 14/1 | 42 | 9 |
| $894^{9}$ | **Lazali (USA) (74)** (EALDunlop) **3-9-2** JReid(2) (bhd fnl 2f) | 5 | **15** | 20/1 | 38 | 5 |
| $894^{8}$ | **Sam Rockett (63)** (CAHorgan) **3-8-5** AClark(9) (s.s: a bhd) | 4 | **16** | 25/1 | 20 | — |
| $948^{5}$ | **Royal Expose (USA) (60)** (RHannon) **3-8-2** SSanders(11) (lw: p.u 9f out: sddle slipped) | | **P** | 12/1 | — | — |

(SP 129.4%) **17 Rn**

**2m 9.82** (4.32) CSF £141.49 CT £1,032.20 TOTE £42.40: £6.50 £1.70 £1.70 £2.10 (£143.50) Trio £457.80 OWNER Gravy Boys Racing (EPSOM) BRED Highfield Stud Ltd and The Glen Andred Stud
LONG HANDICAP Matthias Mystique 7-6

**616 Get Tough**, who had anything but a clear run, eventually managed to pick up ground and squeeze through a narrow gap inside the final furlong. Soon in front, he kept on well. (25/1)
**1326 No-Aman** appreciated the step up in distance. (5/1)
**1515 White Plains (IRE)** may even have got his head in front for a few strides around the furlong pole before the front two passed him. (8/1)
**1345 Eagle Canyon (IRE)**, collared a furlong out, then failed to raise his work-rate. (12/1)
**Mighty Phantom (USA)** came into her own over this much longer trip. (16/1)
**821 King Rufus** was doing all his best work in the last furlong and a half. (14/1)
**1641 Shaha** could only plod on at the one pace in the straight. (5/1)

## 1774 E.B.F. RUINART CHAMPAGNE MAIDEN STKS (2-Y.O) (Class D)
7-30 (7-31) **6f** £4,542.00 (£1,356.00: £648.00: £294.00) Stalls: Low GOING minus 0.20 sec per fur (GF)

| Form | Horse | Dist | Pos | SP | RR | SF |
|---|---|---|---|---|---|---|
| | **Tuscany** (PFICole) **2-9-0** TQuinn(2) (str: scope: lw: mde virtually all: hung rt fnl 2f: drvn out) | — | **1** | 5/4$^{1}$ | 82+ | 53 |
| | **Close Relative (IRE)** (RCharlton) **2-9-0** TSprake(1) (str: bkwd: rdn over 2f out: hdwy over 1f out: r.o wl ins fnl f) | ¾ | **2** | 16/1 | 80+ | 51 |
| $1445^{3}$ | **Aficionado (IRE)** (RFJohnsonHoughton) **2-9-0** JReid(5) (a.p: ev ch fnl 2f: unable qckn wl ins fnl f) | nk | **3** | 5/1 | 79 | 50 |
| | **Maladerie (IRE)** (MRChannon) **2-9-0** JFEgan(3) (str: bkwd: a.p: ev ch fnl 2f: one pce wl ins fnl f) | hd | **4** | 14/1 | 79 | 50 |
| $1424^{2}$ | **Mantles Prince** (GLewis) **2-9-0** SWhitworth(9) (hld up: rdn over 2f out: wknd 1f out) | 4 | **5** | 14/1 | 68 | 39 |
| $1191^{2}$ | **Myrmidon** (JLDunlop) **2-9-0** WCarson(4) (hld up: rdn over 2f out: wknd over 1f out) | 1 | **6** | 4/1$^{2}$ | 66 | 37 |
| $1531^{4}$ | **Castles Burning (USA)** (CACyzer) **2-9-0** MFenton(6) (bit bkwd: prom 4f) | 3½ | **7** | 25/1 | 56 | 27 |
| | **Blue Ridge** (RHannon) **2-9-0** LDettori(8) (w'like: prom over 4f) | ¾ | **8** | 9/2$^{3}$ | 54 | 25 |
| | **Littlestone Rocket** (WRMuir) **2-9-0** WJO'Connor(7) (unf: bhd fnl 2f: t.o) | dist | **9** | 25/1 | — | — |

(SP 126.2%) **9 Rn**

**1m 11.96** (1.96) CSF £22.13 TOTE £3.00: £1.30 £4.00 £1.50 (£50.80) Trio £127.80 OWNER Highclere Thoroughbred Racing Ltd (WHATCOMBE) BRED Whitsbury Manor Stud

**Tuscany**, a very well matured two-year-old, had been showing up well at home, and transferred that to the racecourse although he gave his rider real steering problems. Making virtually all, he shied away from the Stands in the final quarter-mile but, to his credit, he responded to pressure and held on well. He is sure to have learnt a lot from this, and has now earned a tilt at the Coventry Stakes at Royal Ascot. (5/4)
**Close Relative (IRE)**, a strongly-made colt, looked far from fit, but ran a race full of promise. Only finding his feet from below the distance, he ran on really strongly inside the final furlong, and may have even overhauled the winner with a little further to go. Sure to come on a lot for this, it should not take him long to get in the winner's enclosure. (16/1)
**1445 Aficionado (IRE)** lost nothing in defeat. Battling hard for the lead in the final quarter-mile, he gave his all, and was only worried out of it in the closing stages. His turn is not far away. (5/1)
**Maladerie (IRE)**, a strongly-made gelding, looked very burly but still showed a lot of promise. He should soon find a suitable opportunity. (14/1)
**1424 Mantles Prince** was hung out to dry a furlong from home. (14/1)
**1191 Myrmidon** had shot his bolt below the distance. (4/1: 3/1-9/2)
**Blue Ridge** (9/2: 3/1-5/1)

## 1775 THREE KEYS H'CAP (0-90) (3-Y.O+) (Class C)

8-00 (8-04) **1m** £5,888.75 (£1,760.00: £842.50: £383.75) Stalls: High GOING minus 0.20 sec per fur (GF)

| | | | | SP | RR | SF |
|---|---|---|---|---|---|---|
| | **Belfry Green (IRE) (89)** (CAHorgan) **6-10-0** AClark(10) (s.s: stdy hdwy over 1f out: led ins fnl f: rdn out) | — | **1** | 16/1 | 100 | 79 |
| | **Serious (84)** (LadyHerries) **6-9-9** JReid(15) (nt clr run over 2f out: hdwy over 1f out: ev ch ins fnl f: unable qckn) | ¾ | **2** | 8/1$^{3}$ | 94 | 73 |
| $1337^{7}$ | **Rakis (IRE) (74)** (MrsLStubbs) **6-8-13** JFEgan(11) (nt clr run over 2f out: hdwy wl over 1f out: 3rd & btn whn n.m.r wl ins fnl f) | ¾ | **3** | 20/1 | 82 | 61 |
| *$306^{2}$* | **King of Tunes (FR) (72)** (JJSheehan) **4-8-11** JQuinn(13) (swtg: hdwy & nt clr run on ins over 2f out: swtchd lft: nt clr run 1f out: swtchd rt: r.o) | hd | **4** | 7/1$^{2}$ | 80 | 59 |
| $1354^{4}$ | **Sharp Rebuff (75)** (PJMakin) **5-9-0** LDettori(3) (a.p: led 2f out tl ins fnl f: one pce) | 1½ | **5** | 4/1$^{1}$ | 80 | 59 |
| $1190^{15}$ | **Broughtons Turmoil (65)** (WJMusson) **7-8-4** RPrice(6) (hld up: hmpd 2f out: one pce) | 3½ | **6** | 14/1 | 63 | 42 |
| $1625^{12}$ | **Shayim (USA) (77)** (RHannon) **4-8-13**(3) DaneO'Neill(2) (lw: a.p: led 5f out to 2f out: wknd fnl f) | 1¼ | **7** | 12/1 | 72 | 51 |
| $1520^{5}$ | **Dee-Lady (83)** (WGMTurner) **4-9-8** TSprake(4) (b: prom 6f) | 9 | **8** | 20/1 | 60 | 39 |
| $1613^{6}$ | **Gadge (61)** (DMorris) **5-8-0** WCarson(12) (nt clr run on ins over 2f out: nvr nrr) | 6 | **9** | 12/1 | 26 | 5 |
| $888^{5}$ | **Little Black Dress (USA) (71)** (RCharlton) **3-7-8**(5) MHenry(7) (bhd fnl 2f) | 2 | **10** | 10/1 | 32 | — |
| $1625^{2}$ | **Emily-Mou (IRE) (68)** (MJRyan) **4-8-7** GCarter(5) (b: led 3f: wknd over 2f out) | 3 | **11** | 4/1$^{1}$ | 23 | 2 |
| | **Fionn de Cool (IRE) (74)** (RAkehurst) **5-8-13** SSanders(1) (prom over 5f) | s.h | **12** | 16/1 | 29 | 8 |
| $1522^{8}$ | **Flag Fen (USA) (62)** (MartynMeade) **5-8-1** FNorton(8) (bhd fnl 3f) | 1¾ | **13** | 33/1 | 14 | — |
| $1198^{9}$ | **Il Trastevere (FR) (76)** (MissGayKelleway) **4-9-1** RHughes(14) (swtg: prom over 4f) | 2½ | **14** | 16/1 | 23 | 2 |
| | **Ethbaat (USA) (82)** (WRMuir) **5-9-7** WJO'Connor(9) (bhd fnl 5f: t.o fnl 3f) | dist | **15** | 33/1 | — | — |
| | | | | (SP 127.8%) | **15 Rn** | |

**1m 38.75** (1.55) CSF £133.28 CT £2,374.54 TOTE £19.60: £4.60 £2.60 £2.90 (£50.60) Trio £193.40 OWNER Mr John Kelsey-Fry (PULBOROUGH) BRED G. J. King
WEIGHT FOR AGE 3yo-11lb
OFFICIAL EXPLANATION **Ethbaat (USA): the gelding ran too freely to post which may have affected his running.**
**Belfry Green (IRE),** whose rider adopted very patient tactics, steadily inched closer from below the distance and came with a useful run to lead inside the final furlong. (16/1)
**Serious**, who won over hurdles at Uttoxeter in December, found the winner too strong. (8/1)
**744 Rakis (IRE)** was being tapped for toe in third place when slightly squeezed for room in the closing stages. (20/1)
**King of Tunes (FR)** had no luck in running and continually met with traffic problems. Despite this, he ran on inside the final furlong to finish a highly creditable fourth. A return to a mile and a quarter would be a help. (7/1)
**1354 Sharp Rebuff** gave his all but was swamped for toe inside the final furlong. (4/1)
**Broughtons Turmoil** was hampered a quarter of a mile from home. This did him no good at all, but he could only plod on at one pace from that point. (14/1)
**Shayim (USA)** was a spent force in the last 200 yards. (12/1: 8/1-14/1)

## 1776 HALL AND COMPANY BUILDING MATERIALS SUPPLIER CLAIMING STKS (3-Y.O) (Class E)

8-30 (8-34) **7f** £3,850.00 (£1,150.00: £550.00: £250.00) Stalls: High GOING minus 0.20 sec per fur (GF)

| | | | | SP | RR | SF |
|---|---|---|---|---|---|---|
| $1523^{5}$ | **Honorable Estate (IRE) (72)** (RHannon) **3-8-2**(3) DaneO'Neill(2) (lw: nt clr run over 2f out: hdwy over 1f out: str run to ld nr fin) | — | **1** | 4/1$^{2}$ | 63 | 30 |
| $1592^{10}$ | **Coastguards Hero (52)** (MDIUsher) **3-8-4** SSanders(9) (stdy hdwy 2f out: led ins fnl f: hrd rdn: hdd nr fin) | nk | **2** | 20/1 | 61 | 28 |
| $1654^{10}$ | **Ivory's Grab Hire (53)** (KTIvory) **3-7-13b**(5) MartinDwyer(13) (hld up: nt clr run 3f out: rdn over 2f out: led over 1f out tl ins fnl f: one pce) | 1¾ | **3** | 20/1 | 57 | 24 |
| *$272^{5}$* | **Hever Golf Express (75)** (TJNaughton) **3-8-11** RHughes(3) (rdn 3f out: hdwy over 1f out: r.o one pce) | 3 | **4** | 5/1$^{3}$ | 58 | 25 |
| $1526^{6}$ | **One Shot (IRE) (53)** (WRMuir) **3-8-3b** WWoods(11) (lw: hld up: rdn over 2f out: nt clr run over 1f out: one pce) | 2½ | **5** | 20/1 | 44 | 11 |
| $1497^{5}$ | **Silhouette (IRE) (40)** (DRCElsworth) **3-7-12** FNorton(10) (hld up: rdn over 2f out: one pce) | 1¾ | **6** | 16/1 | 35 | 2 |
| | **Moylough Rebel (45)** (JELong) **3-7-13**(7) TField(12) (bit bkwd: nt clr run on ins 2f out: nvr nr to chal) | nk | **7** | 40/1 | 42 | 9 |
| $1122^{2}$ | **Mystical Maid** (HThomsonJones) **3-8-1** GCarter(8) (lw: chsd ldr: led over 2f out tl hrd rdn, hung bdly lft & hdd over 1f out: nt rcvr) | s.h | **8** | 6/1 | 37 | 4 |
| $1155^{4}$ | **Shady Girl (IRE) (68)** (BWHills) **3-8-3** WCarson(5) (a.p: rdn over 2f out: 3rd & btn whn hung rt & eased over 1f out) | 3 | **9** | 2/1$^{1}$ | 32 | — |
| $1651^{7}$ | **Totally Yours (IRE)** (MRChannon) **3-8-3** CandyMorris(4) (s.s: a wl bhd) | 6 | **10** | 16/1 | 18 | — |
| | **Rock Daisy** (MMadgwick) **3-7-12** NAdams(6) (b.off fore: s.s: a bhd) | 6 | **11** | 40/1 | — | — |
| $1122^{12}$ | **Lincon Twenty One (40)** (MJHaynes) **3-7-7b**(5) MBaird(7) (lw: led over 4f: wkng whn n.m.r on ins 2f out) | s.h | **12** | 40/1 | — | — |
| | | | | (SP 117.7%) | **12 Rn** | |

**1m 28.45** (3.65) CSF £69.81 TOTE £4.90: £2.10 £6.20 £3.00 (£63.80) Trio £250.90 OWNER Mr R. A. Bernard (MARLBOROUGH) BRED James W. Ryan
**1523 Honorable Estate (IRE)**, who flopped in the mud last time, came with a rattle from below the distance to sweep into the lead near the line. (4/1: 3/1-9/2)
**1122 Coastguards Hero** was worried out of it near the line. (20/1)
**1152 Ivory's Grab Hire**, making a quick reappearance, was collared inside the final furlong and could only keep on at one pace. (20/1)
**Hever Golf Express**, without a run in nearly four months, stayed on in the last furlong and a half without posing a serious threat. (5/1)
**1526 One Shot (IRE)**, done no favours by the hanging Shady Girl below the distance, could then only struggle on at one pace. (20/1)

**1497 Silhouette (IRE)** could only go up and down in the same place in the last two furlongs. (16/1)
**1155 Shady Girl (IRE)** was held in third place when hanging right below the distance. Her jockey quite rightly accepted the situation and allowed her to coast in from that point. (2/1)

## 1777 GEORGE STUBBS H'CAP (0-75) (3-Y.O+) (Class D)

9-00 (9-04) **5f** £4,056.25 (£1,210.00: £577.50: £261.25) Stalls: High GOING minus 0.20 sec per fur (GF)

| | Horse / details | | Pos | SP | RR | SF |
|---|---|---|---|---|---|---|
| 1466$^{6}$ | **Sally Slade (73)** (CACyzer) **4-10-0** LDettori(2) (nt clr run & swtchd rt over 2f out: swtchd rt 2f out: hdwy over 1f out: led ins fnl f: rdn out) | — | **1** | 9/1 | 81 | 62 |
| 1334$^{3}$ | **La Petite Fusee (72)** (RJO'Sullivan) **5-9-10**(3) DaneO'Neill(6) (led over 3f: hrd rdn: r.o) | 1¼ | **2** | 100/30$^{1}$ | 76 | 57 |
| 1446$^{6}$ | **Pride of Hayling (IRE) (49)** (PRHedger) **5-8-1**(3) NVarley(5) (lw: hdwy over 1f out: r.o wl ins fnl f) | s.h | **3** | 14/1 | 53 | 34 |
| 1512$^{3}$ | **Half Tone (47)** (RMFlower) **4-8-2b** DBiggs(11) (outpcd: hdwy over 1f out: r.o ins fnl f) | hd | **4** | 5/1$^{2}$ | 51 | 32 |
| 1512$^{5}$ | **Friendly Brave (USA) (68)** (MissGayKelleway) **6-9-9** WJO'Connor(7) (b.hind: lw: hld up: hrd rdn over 1f out: r.o ins fnl f) | ½ | **5** | 9/1 | 70 | 51 |
| | **Walk the Beat (63)** (MartynMeade) **6-9-4** RPerham(13) (hld up: led over 1f out tl ins fnl f: unable qckn) | 1½ | **6** | 20/1 | 60 | 41 |
| 1446$^{2}$ | **Kildee Lad (70)** (APJones) **6-9-11** JReid(9) (lw: hld up: rdn 2f out: wknd fnl f) | 2½ | **7** | 5/1$^{2}$ | 59 | 40 |
| 1466$^{2}$ | **Tinker Osmaston (68)** (MSSaunders) **5-9-9** JFEgan(4) (hld up: rdn over 2f out: wknd wl over 1f out) | ½ | **8** | 8/1$^{3}$ | 56 | 37 |
| 1446$^{5}$ | **Judgement Call (52)** (PHowling) **9-8-7** FNorton(3) (b: bhd fnl 3f) | ½ | **9** | 12/1 | 38 | 19 |
| 893$^{17}$ | **Bryan Robson (USA) (54)** (GBBalding) **5-8-9** SSanders(8) (prom over 3f) | 1½ | **10** | 16/1 | 35 | 16 |
| 1630$^{10}$ | **Ashtina (66)** (BAPearce) **11-9-2**(5) MartinDwyer(1) (bhd fnl 3f) | 1 | **11** | 20/1 | 44 | 25 |
| 1512$^{13}$ | **Mazzarello (IRE) (46)** (RCurtis) **6-7-10v**(5) MBaird(10) (spd over 3f) | 1½ | **12** | 9/1 | 19 | — |

(SP 127.3%) **12 Rn**

**58.51 secs** (1.81) CSF £39.58 CT £395.86 TOTE £7.50: £2.70 £1.60 £4.20 (£13.10) Trio £303.70 OWNER Mr R. M. Cyzer (HORSHAM) BRED C. A. Cyzer

**1466 Sally Slade** started off on the rail but had to be switched to the outside a quarter of a mile from home. Soon picking up ground, she came through to lead inside the final furlong and kept on well. (9/1)
**1334 La Petite Fusee** stuck to her task well to the bitter end. (100/30)
**Pride of Hayling (IRE)** ran on strongly but was never going to get there in time. (14/1)
**1512 Half Tone** was not surprisingly outpaced as usual. Finding his feet from below the distance, he ran on but found the line always coming too soon. (5/1)
**1512 Friendly Brave (USA)** ran on inside the final furlong. (9/1)
**Walk the Beat**, having his first run of the season, showed narrowly in front below the distance before tapped for toe. (20/1)

T/Plpt: £651.40 (22.95 Tckts). T/Qdpt: £260.10 (3.31 Tckts). AK

# 1430-**HAYDOCK (L-H) (Good)**
## Friday June 7th

WEATHER: showery WIND: slt half against

## 1778 RED ROSE AMATEUR H'CAP (0-70) (3-Y.O+) (Class G)

6-45 (6-48) **1m 2f 120y** £2,416.00 (£676.00: £328.00) Stalls: Low GOING minus 0.11 sec per fur (G)

| | Horse / details | | Pos | SP | RR | SF |
|---|---|---|---|---|---|---|
| 1585$^{3}$ | **Drummer Hicks (43)** (EWeymes) **7-10-8**(4) MrJWeymes(14) (lw: hld up & bhd: gd hdwy to ld 2f out: sn clr) | — | **1** | 8/1$^{3}$ | 60 | 42 |
| 752* | **Gold Blade (48)** (JPearce) **7-11-3** MrsLPearce(16) (hld up: hdwy over 3f out: kpt on appr fnl f: no ch w wnr) | 5 | **2** | 9/4$^{1}$ | 57 | 39 |
| *1487$^{6}$* | **Rasayel (USA) (56)** (PDEvans) **6-11-4**(7) MrAEvans(2) (dwlt: sn rcvrd to chse ldrs: styd on u.p fnl 2f) | 1 | **3** | 9/1 | 64 | 46 |
| 1423$^{5}$ | **Phase One (IRE) (51)** (JLEyre) **6-11-6** MissDianaJones(1) (a.p: led over 4f out to 2f out: sn rdn: one pce) | ¾ | **4** | 9/1 | 58 | 40 |
| | **Salska (47)** (AStreeter) **5-10-9**(7)ow2 MrPClinton(13) (bit bkwd: in tch: effrt over 2f out: nt rch ldrs) | 1 | **5** | 16/1 | 52 | 32 |
| *57$^{13}$* | **Nord Lys (IRE) (25)** (BJLlewellyn) **5-9-4**(4) MissEJJones(6) (mid div: effrt over 2f out: no imp) | 6 | **6** | 25/1 | 21 | 3 |
| | **Ice Magic (24)** (FJYardley) **9-9-0v**(7) MissSYardley(7) (b.nr hind: nvr trbld ldrs) | 7 | **7** | 33/1 | 10 | — |
| *854$^{3}$* | **Royal Acclaim (32)** (JMBradley) **11-9-8v**(7) MissLKerr(15) (wl bhd tl styd on appr fnl f) | ½ | **8** | 20/1 | 17 | — |
| *1458$^{5}$* | **Cuban Nights (USA) (59)** (BJLlewellyn) **4-12-0** MrJLLlewellyn(4) (bhd: rdn over 3f out: no imp) | ½ | **9** | 10/1 | 43 | 25 |
| 1449$^{21}$ | **Air Command (BAR) (41)** (CTNash) **6-10-6**(4) MrPPhillips(9) (led 2f: wknd 3f out) | 5 | **10** | 33/1 | 17 | — |
| *420$^{7}$* | **Florismart (56)** (BPJBaugh) **4-11-4**(7) MrCWatson(10) (sn pushed along: a bhd) | ¾ | **11** | 33/1 | 31 | 13 |
| 1325$^{2}$ | **Go-Go-Power-Ranger (62)** (BEllison) **3-10-10**(7) MissDeborahHall(8) (trckd ldrs 7f: sn wknd) | 1¼ | **12** | 5/1$^{2}$ | 35 | 3 |
| 1047$^{9}$ | **Dots Dee (29)** (JMBradley) **7-9-8**(4) MissBridgetGatehouse(3) (b.nr fore: chsd ldrs over 7f: sn wknd) | hd | **13** | 20/1 | 2 | — |
| | **Highfield Fizz (52)** (CWFairhurst) **4-11-7** MrsSBosley(11) (bit bkwd: a in rr) | hd | **14** | 16/1 | 25 | 7 |
| 1411$^{13}$ | **Battery Boy (33)** (CWCElsey) **4-10-2b** MissAElsey(5) (swtg: led after 2f tl rn wd & wknd over 4f out) | 2 | **15** | 20/1 | 3 | — |
| 1625$^{8}$ | **Scorpius (47)** (TTClement) **6-10-12**(4) MrVLukaniuk(12) (b: t: trckd ldrs over 6f: sn lost tch: t.o) | 7 | **16** | 16/1 | 6 | — |

(SP 132.2%) **16 Rn**

**2m 21.03** (9.53) CSF £26.74 CT £162.20 TOTE £7.70: £1.20 £1.10 £2.10 £2.20 (£9.50) Trio £15.00 OWNER Mrs N. Napier (MIDDLEHAM) BRED Mrs N. Napier
LONG HANDICAP Ice Magic 8-11
WEIGHT FOR AGE 3yo-14lb

**1585 Drummer Hicks**, taken to post steadily and given a very patient ride, came up the centre of the track to lead passing the quarter-mile marker and the race was soon his. (8/1)
**752* Gold Blade** began to close early in the straight, but did not make much impression until staying on inside the distance. (9/4)
**1487 Rasayel (USA)** soon pulled his way into contention after missing a beat at the start, but he was under strong pressure over two furlongs out and could only plug on at the one pace. (9/1)
**1423 Phase One (IRE)** helped share the pace, but had little left when headed two furlongs out. (9/1: op 6/1)
**Salska**, a winner here over a longer trip in the autumn, ran promisingly after over seven months on the sidelines. (16/1)

## 1779 E.B.F. WEAVER MAIDEN STKS (2-Y.O) (Class D)

7-15 (7-15) **6f** £3,629.50 (£1,096.00: £533.00: £251.50) Stalls: Low GOING minus 0.11 sec per fur (G)

| | Horse / details | | Pos | SP | RR | SF |
|---|---|---|---|---|---|---|
| 1537$^{3}$ | **Pandiculation** (EWeymes) **2-9-0** KFallon(1) (a.p: led over 1f out: hld on u.p) | — | **1** | 9/1 | 62 | 14 |
| 1424$^{6}$ | **Ninth Symphony** (PCHaslam) **2-9-0** LCharnock(6) (led 2f: swtchd rt & rallied u.p ins fnl f) | nk | **2** | 25/1 | 61 | 13 |
| | **General's Star** (MRStoute) **2-9-0** DeanMcKeown(7) (neat: hld up: effrt & nt clr run over 1f out: rdn & r.o ins fnl f) | 1¼ | **3** | 9/2$^{2}$ | 58+ | 10 |

**Groom's Gordon (FR)** (JLDunlop) **2-9-0** PatEddery(4) (lt-f: unf: bit bkwd: dwlt: sn chsng ldrs: pushed along ½-wy: rdn wl over 1f out: sn btn) ....3 **4** 8/11$^1$ 50+ 2
1166$^8$ **Rockaroundtheclock** (PDEvans) **2-9-0** KDarley(5) (nvr trbld ldrs) ....3 **5** 14/1 42 —
**Toronto** (JBerry) **2-9-0** JCarroll(3) (w'like: leggy: lw: sn pushed along: a outpcd) ....4 **6** 7/1$^3$ 31 —
**Midyan Queen** (RHollinshead) **2-8-4**(5) FLynch(2) (leggy: lt-f: unf: led after 2f tl over 1f out: eased whn btn) ..¾ **7** 25/1 24 —
**Bankers Order** (TDEasterby) **2-9-0** MBirch(8) (lt-f: chsd ldrs tl ½-wy: sn wknd t.o) ....12 **8** 14/1 — —
(SP 119.6%) **8 Rn**

**1m 17.2** (5.50) CSF £152.01 TOTE £7.40: £1.70 £4.60 £1.60 (£96.10) OWNER Mrs R. L. Heaton (MIDDLEHAM) BRED Mrs Celia Miller
STEWARDS' ENQUIRY Charnock susp. 17-19/6/96 (excessive use of whip).
**1537 Pandiculation**, the most experienced member of the field, kicked on entering the final furlong and only needed to be kept up to his work to hold on. (9/1)
**1424 Ninth Symphony**, switched to the stands' rail to renew his challenge inside the final furlong, kept on well but was never quite going to make it. (25/1)
**General's Star**, very coltish in the paddock, was denied a clear run when about to mount a challenge below the distance and, when he did get free, ran on well. He will win races. (9/2: op 3/1)
**Groom's Gordon (FR)**, supported as if defeat was out of the question, had neither come to himself or in his coat and, running green, does look to need time. (8/11)
**958 Rockaroundtheclock**, settled in behind the leaders, got outpaced when the contest really got under way and was never a factor. (14/1)
**Midyan Queen**, a very sparely-made late foal, showed up well until being eased when beaten in the final furlong. (25/1)

## 1780 PLP VAUXHALL MOTORS H'CAP (0-70) (3-Y.O) (Class E)

7-45 (7-49) **1m 30y** £3,241.25 (£980.00: £477.50: £226.25) Stalls: High GOING minus 0.11 sec per fur (G)

SP RR SF
1100$^{16}$ **Le Teteu (FR) (55)** (BobJones) **3-8-6** NConnorton(6) (hld up: hdwy over 2f out: led ins fnl f: qcknd clr) ....— **1** 11/1 67 18
*1490** **Yeoman Oliver (70)** (BAMcMahon) **3-9-2**(5) 6x LNewton(2) (led after 2f tl over 3f out: led over 1f out: edgd lft u.p: sn hdd & one pce) ....4 **2** 10/1 74 25
1527$^2$ **Power Game (64)** (JBerry) **3-9-1v$^1$** JCarroll(9) (stdd s: hdwy 4f out: ev ch whn hmpd over 1f out: nt rcvr) ....¾ **3** 5/1$^1$ 67 18
1447$^4$ **Castan (IRE) (63)** (JLDunlop) **3-9-0** PatEddery(5) (led 2f: led over 3f out tl over 1f out: one pce) ....2 **4** 5/1$^1$ 62 13
1160$^7$ **Riccarton (55)** (PCalver) **3-8-6** NCarlisle(3) (plld hrd: trckd ldrs: rdn wl over 1f out: one pce) ....1¼ **5** 16/1 51 2
1539$^3$ **Bollin Jacob (62)** (TDEasterby) **3-8-13** MBirch(14) (hld up & bhd: hdwy on ins & nt clr run appr fnl f: nt rcvr) ....hd **6** 7/1$^3$ 58 9
1452$^8$ **Mellow Master (65)** (NJHWalker) **3-9-2** CRutter(12) (hld up: hdwy & ev ch 3f out: sn rdn & wknd) ....2½ **7** 16/1 56 7
1079$^4$ **Lead Him On (USA) (70)** (PWHarris) **3-9-7** GHind(13) (lw: hld up: effrt 3f out: sn rdn & no imp) ....nk **8** 11/2$^2$ 61 12
1447$^6$ **Law Dancer (IRE) (70)** (TGMills) **3-9-0**(7) DToole(10) (lw: trckd ldrs: rdn over 2f out: eased whn btn appr fnl f) ....5 **9** 9/1 51 2
1435$^6$ **Rocky's Meteor (64)** (RAFahey) **3-9-1** ACulhane(11) (hld up in rr: plld wd & effrt 3f out: no imp) ....nk **10** 12/1 44 —
*531$^6$* **Flood's Fancy (60)** (LJBarratt) **3-8-11** LCharnock(4) (chsd ldrs 5f: sn wknd: t.o) ....5 **11** 25/1 30 —
1405$^4$ **Doug's Folly (46)** (MWEasterby) **3-7-11** DaleGibson(8) (trckd ldrs over 5f: sn wknd: t.o) ....½ **12** 12/1 15 —
382$^5$ ***Ebony Boy* (55)** (JWharton) **3-8-6v$^1$** KFallon(1) (Withdrawn not under Starter's orders: veterinary advice) .... **W** 20/1 — —
(SP 124.4%) **12 Rn**

**1m 47.06** (6.46) CSF £105.71 CT £579.29 TOTE £12.00: £2.30 £2.90 £2.00 (£159.40) Trio £344.30; £179.48 to Epsom 9/6/96 OWNER Mrs Judit Woods (NEWMARKET) BRED Pillar Stud
**Le Teteu (FR)** readily landed a gamble on this step down to a mile and left one wandering what he has been up to in the past. (11/1: 16/1-10/1)
**1490* Yeoman Oliver**, still to win on turf, was in and out of the lead until he veered left when ridden entering the final furlong. Soon headed, he could only keep on at the one pace. (10/1)
**1527 Power Game** ran much better than his final placing might suggest on this first attempt at this longer trip, and is one to keep in mind. (5/1)
**1447 Castan (IRE)** helped force the pace, but was hard at work approaching the final furlong and is plenty high enough in the handicap for a maiden. (5/1)
**Riccarton** raced freely in behind the leaders, and had every chance until unable to step up his pace inside the distance. (16/1)
**1539 Bollin Jacob**, given plenty to do, had no luck when trying to force his way through up the inside rail approaching the final furlong, and the position had to be accepted. There is a race in him. (7/1)

## 1781 MOSCHINOS CHEAP AND CHIC H'CAP (0-80) (3-Y.O+) (Class D)

8-15 (8-15) **6f** £3,753.00 (£1,134.00: £552.00: £261.00) Stalls: Low GOING minus 0.11 sec per fur (G)

SP RR SF
*1606$^7$* **High Domain (IRE) (64)** (JLSpearing) **5-8-12** JWeaver(10) (mde all: qcknd clr fnl f) ....— **1** 10/1 75 55
**Bold Street (IRE) (64)** (ABailey) **6-8-9b**(3) DWright(9) (b: bit bkwd: a.p: rdn 2f out: kpt on ins fnl f) ....3½ **2** 14/1 66 46
1321$^6$ **Here Comes a Star (76)** (JMCarr) **8-9-10** ACulhane(8) (lw: hld up: hdwy & n.m.r over 1f out: rdn & r.o wl fnl f) ....s.h **3** 7/1 78 58
1635$^2$ **Stand Tall (54)** (CWThornton) **4-8-2** GDuffield(3) (lw: chsd ldrs: rdn over 1f out: unable qckn) ....hd **4** 9/2$^1$ 55 35
1473$^3$ **So Intrepid (IRE) (72)** (JMBradley) **6-9-3**(3) SDrowne(5) (hld up: rdn along ½-wy: kpt on wl ins fnl f) ....½ **5** 6/1$^3$ 72 52
1412$^3$ **Barato (64)** (MrsJRRamsden) **5-8-12v** KFallon(1) (b.nr hind: stumbled s: hld up & bhd: swtchd & hdwy appr fnl f: r.o) ....¾ **6** 5/1$^2$ 62 42
1588$^2$ **Amron (62)** (JBerry) **9-8-10** NCarlisle(7) (hld up in tch: effrt & bdly hmpd over 1f out: nt rcvr) ....2 **7** 9/2$^1$ 55 35
**Lough Erne (65)** (CFWall) **4-8-13** PatEddery(2) (bit bkwd: hld up & bhd: effrt over 2f out: sn rdn: wknd appr fnl f) ....hd **8** 6/1$^3$ 57 37
1609$^5$ **Bargash (64)** (PDEvans) **4-8-12b** KDarley(4) (gd spd over 4f) ....hd **9** 14/1 56 36
1186$^{18}$ **The Scythian (72)** (BobJones) **4-9-6** DaleGibson(6) (lw: prom over 4f) ....1 **10** 10/1 61 41
(SP 125.6%) **10 Rn**

**1m 13.95** (2.25) CSF £128.50 CT £692.49 TOTE £15.80: £4.20 £3.30 £2.30 (£102.10) Trio £212.80 OWNER Mr Stephen Borsberry (ALCESTER) BRED Shannon Holdings Ltd
**1606 High Domain (IRE)** appreciated this return to the turf and, taking advantage of his stands'-side draw, was always going far too well for his pursuers. (10/1)
**Bold Street (IRE)** has not won a race in almost two years, but he performed with credit on this first outing in six months and, if there is any improvement to come, should be able to find an opening. (14/1)
**1161 Here Comes a Star**, having another try at this slightly longer trip, had to contend with traffic problems when about to launch his bid, and his finishing position was as close as he was able to get. There is another prize beckoning. (7/1)
**1635 Stand Tall**, in the action in the centre of the track, was unable to respond when shaken up, but he did keep battling away and deserves to win another race. (9/2)

**1473 So Intrepid (IRE)** was always struggling with the pace and, though he was within striking range, he did not pick up until the race was as good as over. (6/1)
**1412 Barato**, down on his knees as he left the stalls, was pulled towards the centre of the track to make his effort below the distance, but could not quicken sufficiently to land a blow. (5/1)
**1588 Amron**, stopped in his tracks when poised to challenge below the distance, had no chance of recovery and the position had to be accepted. (9/2)
**931 The Scythian** (10/1: 8/1-12/1)

## 1782 WINWICK MAIDEN STKS (3-Y.O+) (Class D)

8-45 (8-46) **1m 6f** £3,538.50 (£1,068.00: £519.00: £244.50) Stalls: Centre GOING minus 0.11 sec per fur (G)

| | Horse / details | Dist | Pos | SP | RR | SF |
|---|---|---|---|---|---|---|
| 1407[2] | **Arctic Fancy (USA) (81)** (PWHarris) **3-8-7** GHind(5) (hld up in tch: hdwy over 2f out: led & drifted rt over 1f out: styd on) | — | **1** | 4/1[2] | 79 | 26 |
| 1439[2] | **Sea Freedom (62)** (GBBalding) **5-9-12v** PatEddery(9) (sn bhd & drvn along: styd on fnl 2f: nvr nrr) | 3½ | **2** | 8/1 | 75 | 41 |
| 1409[4] | **Heronwater (IRE)** (MJohnston) **3-8-2** MRoberts(6) (trckd ldrs: led over 2f out tl over 1f out: sn rdn & outpcd) | .5 | **3** | 2/1[1] | 64 | 11 |
| 1415[2] | **Macmorris (USA) (75)** (PFICole) **3-8-7** CRutter(4) (chsd ldrs: effrt 3f out: wknd appr fnl f) | 4 | **4** | 9/2[3] | 65 | 12 |
| | **Salamander King** (LadyHerries) **4-9-12** KDarley(7) (bit bkwd: in tch: reminders 7f out: wknd wl over 1f out) | 2½ | **5** | 20/1 | 62 | 28 |
| 1189[4] | **St Rita** (JLDunlop) **3-8-2** GDuffield(1) (led tl rdn & hdd over 2f out: sn btn) | hd | **6** | 9/2[3] | 57 | 4 |
| | **Stage Fright** (FMurphy) **5-9-12** JFanning(8) (bkwd: dwlt: a bhd) | 2½ | **7** | 50/1 | 59 | 25 |
| 1359[8] | **Nayib** (DMorley) **3-8-7** RHills(3) (chsd ldr 9f: sn lost tch: t.o) | 13 | **8** | 12/1 | 44 | — |
| 1305[4] | **Ragsak Jameel (USA)** (MajorWRHern) **3-8-7** MBirch(10) (lw: a bhd & outpcd: t.o) | 4 | **9** | 14/1 | 40 | — |
| | **Apache Raider** (FMurphy) **4-9-12** JWeaver(2) (bkwd: s.s: a bhd & outpcd: t.o) | 9 | **10** | 20/1 | 29 | — |

(SP 126.7%) **10 Rn**

**3m 8.39** (10.19) CSF £36.00 TOTE £5.10: £1.80 £2.00 £1.50 (£13.50) Trio £19.20 OWNER The Cool Customers (BERKHAMSTED) BRED Woodrow D. Marriott
WEIGHT FOR AGE 3yo-19lb

**1407 Arctic Fancy (USA)**, in a race that did not take a deal of winning, again ran about after striking the front, but this time he was soon well on top, and at last was able to open his account. (4/1: 5/2-9/2)
**1439 Sea Freedom**, off the bridle all the way, had the right man on top to get him to extend himself in the latter stages, but the winner by then was beyond recall. (8/1)
**1409 Heronwater (IRE)** waited on the leaders over this longer trip, and nosed ahead halfway up the straight, but the winner brushed her aside with ease and she quite simply had no answer. (2/1: op 3/1)
**1415 Macmorris (USA)** continues to run well but, on this occasion, he was a spent force approaching the final furlong and was eased when beaten. (9/2)
**Salamander King** did keep tabs on the leaders and closed up two furlongs out, but he was at the end of his tether approaching the final furlong. (20/1)
**1189 St Rita** continued her step up in distance and again forced the pace, but she was legless when collared over two furlongs out. (9/2)

## 1783 MATTHEW PEACOCK H'CAP (0-80) (3-Y.O) (Class D)

9-15 (9-16) **1m 6f** £3,655.50 (£1,104.00: £537.00: £253.50) Stalls: Centre GOING minus 0.11 sec per fur (G)

| | Horse / details | Dist | Pos | SP | RR | SF |
|---|---|---|---|---|---|---|
| | **Double Agent (65)** (MJohnston) **3-8-7** JWeaver(4) (h.d.w: a.p: led over 2f out: styd on strly) | — | **1** | 8/1 | 77 | 32 |
| 1591* | **Flocheck (USA) (77)** (JLDunlop) **3-9-5** 4x PatEddery(6) (lw: set str pce: sn clr: hdd over 3f out: sn lost pl: rallied u.p fnl f) | 3 | **2** | 11/8[1] | 86 | 41 |
| 1415* | **Ela-Yie-Mou (IRE) (79)** (LMCumani) **3-9-7** KDarley(9) (s.s: hdwy 10f out: led over 3f out tl over 2f out: one pce) | 2 | **3** | 13/2[3] | 85 | 40 |
| 1361[4] | **Ledgendry Line (68)** (MrsMReveley) **3-8-10** ACulhane(8) (wl bhd tl hdwy 4f out: rdn & wknd appr fnl f) | 3 | **4** | 7/1 | 71 | 26 |
| 1477[2] | **Isitoff (74)** (SCWilliams) **3-8-13**(3) PMcCabe(5) (trckd ldrs tl wknd over 2f out) | 11 | **5** | 10/1 | 64 | 19 |
| 1407* | **Bellator (74)** (GBBalding) **3-8-13**(3) SDrowne(7) (in tch tl ½-wy: renewed effrt 3f out: no imp) | 4 | **6** | 5/1[2] | 60 | 15 |
| 1503* | **Forgie (IRE) (57)** (PCalver) **3-7-13** 4x NCarlisle(3) (lw: trckd ldrs: drvn along ent st: eased whn btn) | 2 | **7** | 12/1 | 40 | — |
| 1498[6] | **Samuel Scott (66)** (MBell) **3-8-8** KFallon(1) (hld up: a bhd) | 1¾ | **8** | 10/1 | 47 | 2 |
| 1477[5] | **Cumbrian Maestro (56)** (TDEasterby) **3-7-12** LCharnock(2) (s.s: rdn 4f out: t.o) | 16 | **9** | 20/1 | 19 | — |

(SP 126.4%) **9 Rn**

**3m 7.31** (9.11) CSF £20.52 CT £77.00 TOTE £9.20: £2.00 £1.40 £2.40 (£9.20) Trio £20.10 OWNER Mr R. W. Huggins (MIDDLEHAM) BRED Mrs R. D. Peacock

**Double Agent**, who was gelded during the winter, came into his own over this extended trip with a comfortable success, and he will improve further with this outing under his belt. (8/1)
**1591* Flocheck (USA)** took off at a rate of knots and held a clear advantage until worn down soon after turning in. Getting his second wind, he was coming back for more towards the finish, but the winner had got away. (11/8)
**1415* Ela-Yie-Mou (IRE)** kicked on over three furlongs out and promised to come away, but the winner proved the stronger once they were engaged in battle, and the concession of 14lb took its toll. (13/2: 4/1-7/1)
**1361 Ledgendry Line**, dropped out at the start, took closer order entering the straight, but his run had come to an end well over a furlong out. (7/1)
**1477 Isitoff** was fighting for the lead early in the straight, but he faded quickly over a quarter of a mile out as lack of stamina took its toll. (10/1)
**1407* Bellator** tried hard to get himself into the race three furlongs out but, on this more lively ground, lacked the speed to do so. (5/1)

T/Plpt: £352.50 (43.74 Tckts). T/Qdpt: £75.30 (14.17 Tckts). IM

# 1423-DONCASTER (L-H) (Good)

## Saturday June 8th

WEATHER: fine and sunny WIND: almost nil

## 1784 VODAFONE DERBY DAY H'CAP (0-70) (4-Y.O+) (Class E)

2-00 (2-00) **2m 110y** £4,110.00 (£1,230.00: £590.00: £270.00) Stalls: Low GOING minus 0.04 sec per fur (G)

| | Horse / details | Dist | Pos | SP | RR | SF |
|---|---|---|---|---|---|---|
| 872[8] | **Greek Night Out (IRE) (45)** (JLEyre) **5-7-12**(5) MHenry(2) (lw: trckd ldrs: qcknd to ld 6f out: hld on wl fnl f) | — | **1** | 6/1 | 54 | 31 |
| 1542* | **Royal Expression (71)** (MrsMReveley) **4-10-0** ACulhane(4) (lw: trckd ldrs: hdwy on bit 4f out: effrt over 1f out: rdn & one pce) | 1 | **2** | 11/8[1] | 79 | 55 |

| Form | Horse and details | Dist | Pos | SP | RR | SF |
|---|---|---|---|---|---|---|
| $1070^{7}$ | **Great Oration (IRE) (41)** (FWatson) **7-7-13**$^{ow2}$ JFanning(1) (trckd ldrs: effrt 2f out: n.m.r: no ex ins fnl f) | ½ | **3** | 10/1 | 49 | 24 |
| $1439^{4}$ | **Greycoat Boy (62)** (BJMeehan) **4-9-5** JFEgan(3) (lw: chsd ldrs: ev ch 3f out: n.m.r 2f out: wknd appr fnl f) | 6 | **4** | $3/1^{2}$ | 64 | 40 |
| $1150^{4}$ | **Amiarge (47)** (MBrittain) **6-8-2**(3) DWright(8) (hld up & bhd: hdwy 4f out: prom 2f out: sn rdn & btn) | 2 | **5** | $5/1^{3}$ | 47 | 24 |
| $1676^{12}$ | **Longcroft (39)** (KWHogg) **4-7-10** NKennedy(7) (bhd: effrt 5f out: sn rdn: nvr able to chal) | 1¾ | **6** | 25/1 | 37 | 13 |
| $1478^{10}$ | **Jundi (IRE) (53)** (JDBethell) **5-8-11v** KFallon(6) (rr div: pushed along ent st: no imp) | 1¾ | **7** | 14/1 | 49 | 26 |
| $1168^{4}$ | **Calcando (40)** (EWeymes) **4-7-6**(5) PFessey(9) (cl up: led 7f out to 6f out: wknd 4f out: t.o) | dist | **8** | 20/1 | — | — |
| | **Icanspell (38)** (WStorey) **5-7-10b** GBardwell(5) (led tl hdd 7f out: sn t.o) | dist | **9** | 33/1 | — | — |

(SP 125.4%) **9 Rn**

**3m 40.15** (11.15) CSF £15.41 CT £81.10 TOTE £5.90: £1.50 £1.30 £1.90 (£6.70) Trio £9.10 OWNER Sunpak Potatoes (HAMBLETON) BRED Airlie Stud

LONG HANDICAP Longcroft 7-5 Icanspell 7-7

WEIGHT FOR AGE 4yo-1lb

**767 Greek Night Out (IRE)**, after almost six weeks off, was brought back here looking a picture and proved too tough for the runner-up. (6/1)

**1542* Royal Expression** appeared for most of the trip to be going best of all but, when it came down to a struggle in the last furlong and a half, he failed to produce the goods. (11/8)

**852 Great Oration (IRE)** travelled pretty well and tried for a run up the inner but, once a real effort was required, failed to do any more. (10/1)

**1439 Greycoat Boy** had his chances, but was a bit short of room two furlongs out and then well short of pace. (3/1)

**1150 Amiarge**, given plenty to do, almost got into it two furlongs out, but the effort of getting there sapped all reserves. (5/1)

**Longcroft**, at her first attempt at this trip, ran reasonably without getting into it and looks likely to do better before long. (25/1)

## 1785 STONES BITTER H'CAP (0-100) (3-Y.O) (Class C)

2-50 (2-52) **1m (round)** £7,505.00 (£2,240.00: £1,070.00: £485.00) Stalls: High GOING minus 0.04 sec per fur (G)

| Form | Horse and details | Dist | Pos | SP | RR | SF |
|---|---|---|---|---|---|---|
| $833^{4}$ | **Mushahid (USA) (99)** (JLDunlop) **3-9-7** GCarter(1) (lw: bdly hmpd & lost pl after 2f: hdwy 2f out: r.o: fin 2nd, 1 3/4l: awrdd r) | — | **1** | $100/30^{2}$ | 103 | 46 |
| 1181* | **Capilano Princess (75)** (DHaydnJones) **3-7-11** TWilliams(6) (hld up: hdwy over 3f out: led wl over 1f out: r.o: fin 1st: disq: plcd 2nd) | | **2** | 9/1 | 82 | 25 |
| 1323* | **Marigliano (USA) (90)** (MRStoute) **3-8-12** KFallon(4) (lw: b.hind: hmpd after 2f: prom: effrt 2f out: nt qckn ins fnl f) | ½ | **3** | $5/2^{1}$ | 93 | 36 |
| $1432^{2}$ | **Jo Mell (82)** (TDEasterby) **3-8-4** JFanning(5) (led tl hdd wl over 1f out: r.o one pce) | ½ | **4** | 9/2 | 84 | 27 |
| $1528^{6}$ | **Singapore Sting (USA) (75)** (HRACecil) **3-7-11** NCarlisle(2) (w ldrs tl rdn & btn appr fnl f) | 14 | **5** | 13/2 | 49 | — |
| 1000* | **Bold Patriot (IRE) (76)** (JWHills) **3-7-7**(5)$^{ow2}$ MHenry(7) (lw: w ldrs to ½-wy: sn rdn & btn) | ¾ | **6** | 7/1 | 48 | — |
| 845* | **Murheb (90)** (RWArmstrong) **3-8-12** RPrice(3) (hmpd after 2f: hdwy over 2f out: sn wknd & eased) | nk | **7** | $4/1^{3}$ | 61 | 4 |

(SP 125.7%) **7 Rn**

**1m 41.72** (5.22) CSF £31.57 TOTE £4.60: £2.60 £4.00 (£16.20) OWNER Mr Hamdan Al Maktoum (ARUNDEL) BRED Courtney and Congleton

STEWARDS' ENQUIRY Williams susp. 17-19/6/96 (careless riding).

**833 Mushahid (USA)** got absolutely murdered early on and did well to finish second and, as the winner was blamed for the interference, he had to get the race. (100/30)

**1181* Capilano Princess**, being on the outside, was adjudged to have crowded the three runners on her inside approaching the home straight, causing a lot of trouble. After winning convincingly, she was put back to second in the Stewards' Room. (9/1)

**1323* Marigliano (USA)** got badly squeezed early on and was short of room again two furlongs out, but he had his chance after that, only to prove too slow. (5/2)

**1432 Jo Mell** has proved disappointing so far this season and is taking time to come to himself. (9/2)

**1528 Singapore Sting (USA)**, very warm beforehand, raced with every chance until stopping approaching the final furlong. (13/2)

**1000* Bold Patriot (IRE)**, very edgy in the preliminaries, raced with the leaders but his nervous energy had sapped all reserves soon after halfway. (7/1)

**845* Murheb** got badly hampered early on and, never happy thereafter, was eased a good deal in the last couple of furlongs. (4/1)

## 1786 INOVAR H'CAP (0-80) (4-Y.O+ F & M) (Class D)

3-20 (3-22) **6f** £5,117.00 (£1,526.00: £728.00: £329.00) Stalls: High GOING minus 0.04 sec per fur (G)

| Form | Horse and details | Dist | Pos | SP | RR | SF |
|---|---|---|---|---|---|---|
| $1157^{2}$ | **Almasi (IRE) (62)** (CFWall) **4-8-12** WWoods(4) (lw: hld up: hdwy 2f out: chal ins fnl f: r.o to ld post) | — | **1** | $4/1^{2}$ | 70 | 52 |
| 1588* | **Palo Blanco (74)** (TDBarron) **5-9-10** JFanning(5) (trckd ldrs: led 1½f out: r.o u.p: jst ct) | s.h | **2** | $9/2^{3}$ | 82 | 64 |
| $956^{11}$ | **Premium Gift (60)** (CBBBooth) **4-8-10** ACulhane(3) (lw: hld up: hdwy ½-wy: ev ch 2f out: sn rdn & nt qckn) | 3½ | **3** | 14/1 | 59 | 41 |
| $1609^{7}$ | **Shashi (IRE) (68)** (WWHaigh) **4-9-4** RLappin(6) (chsd ldrs: outpcd 2f out: kpt on fnl f) | 1¼ | **4** | 10/1 | 63 | 45 |
| $1157^{12}$ | **Miss Aragon (50)** (MissLCSiddall) **8-8-0** NCarlisle(1) (lw: hld up: effrt ½-wy: n.m.r & nvr able to chal) | ½ | **5** | 16/1 | 44 | 26 |
| $1609^{9}$ | **It's Academic (63)** (MrsJRRamsden) **4-8-13** KFallon(2) (lw: prom: outpcd ½-wy: hdwy 2f out: nt qckn fnl f) | hd | **6** | $11/4^{1}$ | 57 | 39 |
| $1680^{4}$ | **Prima Silk (71)** (MJRyan) **5-9-7** DBiggs(9) (chsd ldrs: led 2f out: sn hdd & nt qckn) | 2½ | **7** | $9/2^{3}$ | 58 | 40 |
| *$1492^{8}$* | **Most Uppitty (46)** (JBerry) **4-7-5**(5) PFessey(7) (lw: disp ld 4f: wknd) | ½ | **8** | 20/1 | 32 | 14 |
| *$170^{7}$* | **Encore M'Lady (IRE) (60)** (FHLee) **5-8-10** GCarter(8) (disp ld 4f: btn whn hmpd 1f out) | 6 | **9** | 7/1 | 30 | 12 |

(SP 121.9%) **9 Rn**

**1m 13.88** (2.88) CSF £22.28 CT £215.34 TOTE £4.20: £1.80 £1.50 £5.60 (£6.70) Trio £47.80 OWNER The Equema Partnership (NEWMARKET) BRED Newtownbarry House Stud

**1157 Almasi (IRE)** puts in all her best work late on and, once she got a run here, flew to lead on the line. (4/1)

**1588* Palo Blanco** seems to relish tight finishes and, after looking the likely winner, was just touched off this time. (9/2)

**868 Premium Gift** is certainly coming to hand, but she just failed to see out the final furlong. (14/1)

**956 Shashi (IRE)** keeps running well but is short of a turn of foot to do anything serious about it. (10/1)

**Miss Aragon** is gradually coming to hand, but her effort was always too late on this occasion. (16/1)

**1423 It's Academic** ran reasonably but that final dash was never forthcoming. She has not as yet hit form this season but looks now to be coming to hand. (11/4: op 5/1)

**Encore M'Lady (IRE)**, after a lengthy lay-off, showed all her old speed and was eased when beaten. (7/1)

## 1787 ST JOHN AMBULANCE MAIDEN STKS (3-Y.O+) (Class D)

3-55 (3-56) **5f** £3,687.50 (£1,100.00: £525.00: £237.50) Stalls: High GOING minus 0.04 sec per fur (G)

| Form | Horse and details | Dist | Pos | SP | RR | SF |
|---|---|---|---|---|---|---|
| $1422^{4}$ | **Wee Hope (USA) (78)** (MRStoute) **3-9-0v**$^{1}$ KFallon(10) (lw: hld up: hdwy over 1f out: r.o wl to ld wl ins fnl f) | — | **1** | $9/4^{2}$ | 78 | 37 |
| $1333^{9}$ | **Emy Coasting (USA) (85)** (PFICole) **3-8-4**(5) MHenry(5) (a.p: rdn to ld ins fnl f: sn hdd & nt qckn) | 1½ | **2** | $6/4^{1}$ | 68 | 27 |
| | **Time To Tango** (GMMoore) **3-8-9** JFEgan(1) (cl up: led wl over 1f out tl ins fnl f: no ex) | 1 | **3** | $4/1^{3}$ | 65 | 24 |

| | | | SP | RR | SF |
|---|---|---|---|---|---|
| | **Fancy Clancy (40)** (MissLCSiddall) **3-8-6**(3) PMcCabe(2) (lw: hld up: hdwy ½-wy: ev ch over 1f out: wknd) .....4 | **4** | 25/1 | 52 | 11 |
| 1422[6] | **Petarina** (MissJFCraze) **3-8-9** NConnorton(8) (chsd ldrs tl btn appr fnl f) ........3 | **5** | 9/1 | 43 | 2 |
| | **Forzara** (JBerry) **3-8-9** GCarter(9) (in tch over 3f) ........2½ | **6** | 14/1 | 35 | — |
| | **Chelwood** (LRLloyd-James) **4-9-2** TWilliams(6) (b: bhd: effrt & swtchd ½-wy: n.d) ........2 | **7** | 20/1 | 28 | — |
| | **Fig Tree Bay** (TTClement) **3-9-0** JFanning(3) (b: b.hind: dwlt: n.d) ........1½ | **8** | 16/1 | 28 | — |
| 1162[9] | **Scott's Risk** (LJBarratt) **6-9-7** SDWilliams(7) (lw: b: led over 3f: eased whn btn) ........3 | **9** | 50/1 | 19 | — |
| | | | (SP 123.9%) | **9 Rn** | |

**61.78 secs** (3.38) CSF £6.34 TOTE £2.50: £1.30 £1.30 £1.20 (£2.60) Trio £2.70 OWNER Maktoum Al Maktoum (NEWMARKET) BRED James G. Bell

WEIGHT FOR AGE 3yo-7lb

**1422 Wee Hope (USA)** had the visor on for the first time and, given a fine ride, did the business well. (9/4)
**966 Emy Coasting (USA)** is nothing special to look at, but she did try quite hard here, only to find the winner too strong late doors. (6/4)
**Time To Tango** ran a decent first race of the season and should be all the better for it. (4/1)
**Fancy Clancy** looked in great shape and ran reasonably until running out of steam approaching the final furlong. (25/1)
**Petarina** again showed speed but, even over this shorter trip, failed to last home. (9/1)
**Forzara** had a nice pipe-opener and should improve for it. (14/1)

## 1788 WHITBY CLAIMING STKS (3-Y.O+) (Class E)
4-35 (4-35) **1m 4f** £2,950.00 (£880.00: £420.00: £190.00) Stalls: Low GOING minus 0.04 sec per fur (G)

| | | | SP | RR | SF |
|---|---|---|---|---|---|
| 1523[3] | **Diego (73)** (CEBrittain) **3-8-8** KFallon(1) (lw: trckd ldrs: led wl over 2f out: styd on strly) ........— | **1** | 3/1[2] | 71 | 41 |
| *1602[6]* | **Genesis Four (40)** (MrsLStubbs) **6-9-3** JFEgan(4) (lw: hld up: effrt 4f out: styd on: no ch w wnr) ........4 | **2** | 20/1 | 60 | 45 |
| 1544* | **Bayrak (USA) (73)** (MJRyan) **6-9-9** GCarter(2) (lw: led tl hdd wl over 2f out: sn btn) ........2 | **3** | 8/15[1] | 63 | 48 |
| 1019[7] | **Ela Man Howa (54)** (NTinkler) **5-9-4**(5) MHenry(3) (cl up tl wknd 4f out) ........dist | **4** | 6/1[3] | — | — |
| | | | (SP 109.3%) | **4 Rn** | |

**2m 37.17** (7.17) CSF £25.92 TOTE £3.50 (£27.80) OWNER Mr C. E. Brittain (NEWMARKET) BRED T. R. Lock

WEIGHT FOR AGE 3yo-15lb

**1523 Diego** looked the pick and did the business well. The further they went, the stronger he got. (3/1)
**801 Genesis Four** has only won one race in forty-five starts and that was on sand, but he did appreciate this longer trip and stayed on well towards the finish. (20/1)
**1544* Bayrak (USA)** was never allowed to get away from his field this time and, once passed over two furlongs out, he soon gave in. (8/15)
**Ela Man Howa** has shown next to nothing since changing stables and was again disappointing here. (6/1)

## 1789 KNOWSLEY H'CAP (0-75) (3-Y.O+) (Class D)
5-10 (5-11) **7f** £4,485.25 (£1,342.00: £643.50: £294.25) Stalls: High GOING minus 0.04 sec per fur (G)

| | | | SP | RR | SF |
|---|---|---|---|---|---|
| 1610[3] | **Legal Issue (IRE) (56)** (WWHaigh) **4-8-9** RLappin(3) (lw: trckd ldrs: led 2f out: hld on wl) ........— | **1** | 10/1 | 65 | 33 |
| 1638[8] | **Nashaat (USA) (62)** (MCChapman) **8-8-12**(3) PMcCabe(6) (trckd ldrs gng wl: chal over 1f out: kpt on) ........½ | **2** | 14/1 | 70 | 38 |
| 1425[5] | **Sycamore Lodge (IRE) (68)** (MrsJRRamsden) **5-9-7** KFallon(9) (lw: dwlt: hdwy over 2f out: chsng ldrs appr fnl f: nt qckn) ........1¼ | **3** | 100/30[1] | 73 | 41 |
| 1609[4] | **Allinson's Mate (IRE) (55)** (TDBarron) **8-8-8** JFanning(10) (lw: bhd: hdwy 2f out: sn prom: nt qckn fnl f) ......1¼ | **4** | 9/2[2] | 57 | 25 |
| 1538[15] | **Pc's Cruiser (IRE) (47)** (JLEyre) **4-8-0b** TWilliams(1) (b.off fore: disp ld tl hdd 2f out: wandered u.p: sn btn) 3½ | **5** | 10/1 | 41 | 9 |
| 1505[5] | **Quilling (73)** (MDods) **4-9-12** WWoods(2) (disp ld 4f: grad wknd fnl 2f) ........3½ | **6** | 11/1 | 59 | 27 |
| 1423[3] | **Kid Ory (64)** (PCalver) **5-9-3** ACulhane(11) (lw: effrt over 2f out: nvr trbld ldrs) ........1¾ | **7** | 6/1 | 46 | 14 |
| 1522[3] | **Dawalib (USA) (64)** (DHaydnJones) **6-9-3** JFEgan(5) (prom: rdn over 2f out: wknd over 1f out) ........nk | **8** | 5/1[3] | 46 | 14 |
| 1517* | **Moon Strike (FR) (74)** (SCWilliams) **6-9-8**(5) MHenry(8) (lw: reard s: hdwy ½-wy: hung lft over 1f out: sn btn) ........nk | **9** | 9/2[2] | 55 | 23 |
| *1606[4]* | **Jon's Choice (44)** (BPreece) **8-7-8**(3)ow1 DWright(7) (disp ld 5f: sn wknd) ........2½ | **10** | 25/1 | 19 | — |
| 1598[13] | **Northgate Chief (50)** (MBrittain) **4-8-3** GBardwell(4) (lost tch fr ½-wy) ........14 | **11** | 33/1 | — | — |
| | | | (SP 130.4%) | **11 Rn** | |

**1m 28.4** (4.80) CSF £134.44 CT £537.69 TOTE £12.30: £2.90 £4.90 £1.70 (£174.80) Trio £138.70 OWNER Mr B. Valentine (MALTON) BRED Naver Enterprises Ltd

LONG HANDICAP Jon's Choice 7-9

**1610 Legal Issue (IRE)** travelled well and, once in front, proved determined under pressure. (10/1)
**1638 Nashaat (USA)** spent most of the race swinging off the bit but, when it came down to a struggle, he was never doing enough. He looks in good heart at present. (14/1)
**1425 Sycamore Lodge (IRE)** ran his usual race, but was yet again never doing enough when it mattered. (100/30)
**1609 Allinson's Mate (IRE)** is coming back to form and may need the blinkers on again to produce the goods, as he is certainly very well handicapped. (9/2)
**1088 Pc's Cruiser (IRE)** had his chances, but was inclined to wander about when the pressure was applied. (10/1)
**1505 Quilling**, a funny customer, is running pretty well at present. (11/1: 8/1-12/1)
**1517* Moon Strike (FR)** got things wrong throughout here and can be forgiven this. (9/2)

T/Plpt: £226.50 (43.99 Tckts). T/Qdpt: £26.80 (15.47 Tckts). AA

# 1766-EPSOM (L-H) (Good, Good to firm back st)
## Saturday June 8th
WEATHER: fine WIND: almost nil

## 1790 VODAPAGE H'CAP (0-100) (3-Y.O+) (Class C)
1-45 (1-50) **6f** £18,400.00 (£5,575.00: £2,725.00: £1,300.00) Stalls: High GOING minus 0.21 sec per fur (GF)

| | | | SP | RR | SF |
|---|---|---|---|---|---|
| 1186[3] | **Selhurstpark Flyer (IRE) (79)** (JBerry) **5-8-8**(5) PRoberts(9) (b: swtg: w ldr: led over 2f out: rdn out) ........— | **1** | 12/1 | 92 | 72 |
| 1354[5] | **My Best Valentine (85)** (JWhite) **6-9-2**(3) AWhelan(3) (lw: a.p: chsd wnr wl over 1f out: ev ch ins fnl f: unable qckn) ........2 | **2** | 16/1 | 93 | 73 |
| 1628[12] | **Tropical Dance (USA) (92)** (MrsJCecil) **3-9-4** JReid(4) (lw: hdwy over 1f out: r.o one pce) ........2½ | **3** | 25/1 | 93 | 65 |
| 1186[20] | **Shamanic (90)** (RHannon) **4-9-7**(3) DaneO'Neill(2) (swtg: hdwy on ins 3f out: edgd rt over 1f out: one pce).....¾ | **4** | 25/1 | 89 | 69 |
| 876[10] | **Jo Maximus (75)** (SDow) **4-8-4**(5) ADaly(5) (a.p: rdn 3f out: one pce) ........2 | **5** | 20/1 | 69 | 49 |

| | | | | SP | RR | SF |
|---|---|---|---|---|---|---|
| 1334[8] | **Twice as Sharp (85)** (PWHarris) **4-9-5** GHind(14) (lw: no hdwy fnl 2f) | hd | **6** | 12/1 | 78 | 58 |
| 1521[3] | **Golden Pound (USA) (78)** (MissGayKelleway) **4-8-12** OPeslier(16) (swtg: nvr nr to chal) | ½ | **7** | 14/1 | 70 | 50 |
| 1016[5] | **The Happy Fox (IRE) (84)** (BAMcMahon) **4-9-4b** JPMurtagh(11) (plld hrd: nvr nrr) | 2½ | **8** | 14/1 | 69 | 49 |
| 1334[13] | **Shikari's Son (90)** (JCullinan) **9-9-10** TQuinn(12) (lw: nvr nrr) | hd | **9** | 33/1 | 75 | 55 |
| 1630[2] | **Bowden Rose (84)** (MBlanshard) **4-9-4b** JQuinn(8) (lw: nvr nrr) | 1½ | **10** | 11/2[1] | 65 | 45 |
| 1354[10] | **Sea Thunder (75)** (IABalding) **4-8-9v[1]** LDettori(13) (nvr nrr) | d.h | **10** | 20/1 | 56 | 36 |
| | **Silent Expression (85)** (BJMeehan) **6-9-5** MJKinane(10) (bit bkwd: prom 4f) | ½ | **12** | 20/1 | 65 | 45 |
| 1178* | **Thatcherella (75)** (MajorDNChappell) **5-8-9** BThomson(17) (swtg: a bhd) | ¾ | **13** | 8/1[3] | 53 | 33 |
| 1113[11] | **Lago Di Varano (85)** (RMWhitaker) **4-9-5v** DaleGibson(15) (plld hrd: bhd fnl 2f) | s.h | **14** | 25/1 | 63 | 43 |
| 1334[5] | **Lennox Lewis (86)** (APJarvis) **4-9-6** PatEddery(7) (lw: mid div over 4f) | s.h | **15** | 6/1[2] | 64 | 44 |
| 928[12] | **Go Hever Golf (90)** (TJNaughton) **4-9-10** CAsmussen(1) (b.hind: swtg: led over 3f) | ¾ | **16** | 11/1 | 66 | 46 |
| 1630[5] | **Sweet Magic (84)** (PHowling) **5-9-4** PaulEddery(6) (prom 3f) | 8 | **17** | 14/1 | 38 | 18 |
| | | | | (SP 119.1%) | **17 Rn** | |

**1m 8.48** (0.48) CSF £165.98 CT £4,231.50 TOTE £12.20: £2.20 £3.40 £5.30 £8.30 (£154.70) Trio £2,465.80; £937.71 to Epsom 9/6/96
OWNER Mr Chris Deuters (COCKERHAM) BRED Gay O'Callaghan
WEIGHT FOR AGE 3yo-8lb

**1186 Selhurstpark Flyer (IRE)** disputed the lead until showing in front over a quarter of a mile from home. Ridden along, he just managed to get the better of the runner-up in the closing stages. (12/1)

**1354 My Best Valentine** ran well over a trip which looked as if it would be too sharp, especially on this track. Moving into second place early in the final quarter-mile, he threw down a determined challenge and made the winner fight hard until tapped for toe in the closing stages. All five of his victories have come over seven furlongs. (16/1)

**Tropical Dance (USA)** ran her best race so far this season. Only finding her feet from below the distance, she stayed on well for third. (25/1)

**Shamanic** moved up along the inside rail early in the straight, but he drifted right on the camber below the distance and failed to find another gear. (25/1)

**744 Jo Maximus** was unable to dominate on this occasion. Never far away, he was ridden along early in the straight but could only go up and down in the same place. Seven furlongs is his trip nowadays. (20/1)

**1113 Twice as Sharp** chased the leaders but was making no impression in the last two furlongs. (12/1)

## 1791 VODAFONE DERBY STKS (Gp 1) (3-Y.O C & F) (Class A)

2-25 (2-33) **1m 4f 10y** £523,100.00 (£197,130.00: 95,815.00: £42,955.00) Stalls: Low GOING minus 0.21 sec per fur (GF)

| | | | | SP | RR | SF |
|---|---|---|---|---|---|---|
| | **Shaamit (IRE)** (WJHaggas) **3-9-0** MHills(9) (lw: gd hdwy over 2f out: led wl over 1f out: drvn out) | — | **1** | 12/1 | 127+ | 82 |
| 1114[2] | **Dushyantor (USA) (112)** (HRACecil) **3-9-0** PatEddery(4) (lw: plld hrd: hmpd & lost pl 9f out: hmpd 5f out: swtchd rt & gd hdwy over 2f out: str run fnl f: fin wl) | 1¼ | **2** | 9/2[1] | 125+ | 80 |
| 1508* | **Shantou (USA)** (JHMGosden) **3-9-0** LDettori(6) (lw: swtchd rt 3f out: rdn & hdwy over 2f out: r.o wl ins fnl f) | 1¼ | **3** | 25/1 | 124 | 79 |
| 1114* | **Glory of Dancer** (PAKelleway) **3-9-0** OPeslier(8) (lw: a.p: led over 2f out tl wl over 1f out: unable qckn) | 1 | **4** | 6/1[3] | 122 | 77 |
| 926[4] | **Alhaarth (IRE) (118)** (MajorWRHern) **3-9-0** WCarson(14) (swtg: hld up: bmpd 9f out: rdn over 2f out: r.o one pce) | hd | **5** | 15/2 | 122 | 77 |
| 1076* | **Mystic Knight (108)** (RCharlton) **3-9-0** KDarley(19) (swtg: a.p: hrd rdn over 2f out: one pce) | 1¼ | **6** | 14/1 | 121 | 76 |
| 1114[3] | **Jack Jennings (110)** (BAMcMahon) **3-9-0** JReid(7) (led over 9f) | 1 | **7** | 25/1 | 119 | 74 |
| 1076[6] | **Acharne (103)** (CEBrittain) **3-9-0** WJO'Connor(11) (swtg: hdwy on ins over 3f out: rdn over 2f out: one pce) | 1¼ | **8** | 200/1 | 118 | 73 |
| 1120* | **Chief Contender (IRE) (104)** (PWChapple-Hyam) **3-9-0** DHarrison(21) (lw: a.p: rdn over 3f out: wknd over 2f out) | 1¾ | **9** | 15/1 | 115 | 70 |
| 1114[5] | **Double Leaf (109)** (MRStoute) **3-9-0** JPMurtagh(5) (swtg: nvr nrr) | ½ | **10** | 16/1 | 115 | 70 |
| 986[6] | **Classic Eagle (89)** (RHarris) **3-9-0** AMackay(3) (nvr nrr) | nk | **11** | 200/1 | 114 | 69 |
| 1247a[3] | **Tasdid** (KPrendergast,Ireland) **3-9-0** WJSupple(15) (hdwy over 4f out: wknd over 2f out) | s.h | **12** | 200/1 | 114 | 69 |
| 926[2] | **Even Top (IRE) (120)** (MHTompkins) **3-9-0** PRobinson(13) (lw: plld hrd: hld up: bmpd 9f out: hmpd 5f out: wknd 3f out) | hd | **13** | 11/2[2] | 114 | 69 |
| 1361[3] | **Spartan Heartbeat (73)** (CEBrittain) **3-9-0** MBirch(1) (swtg: nvr nrr) | 6 | **14** | 200/1 | 106 | 61 |
| 1114[6] | **Storm Trooper (USA) (114)** (HRACecil) **3-9-0** MJKinane(17) (lw: bhd fnl 3f) | 1½ | **15** | 15/2 | 104 | 59 |
| 1076[3] | **Zaforum (103)** (LMontagueHall) **3-9-0** DaneO'Neill(2) (swtg: bhd fnl 5f) | 1¾ | **16** | 150/1 | 102 | 57 |
| 1329[3] | **St Mawes (FR) (107)** (JLDunlop) **3-9-0** TQuinn(16) (bhd fnl 2f) | 1 | **17** | 20/1 | 100 | 55 |
| 830[6] | **Busy Flight (109)** (BWHills) **3-9-0** CAsmussen(20) (lw: prom 6f) | 5 | **18** | 25/1 | 94 | 49 |
| 986[3] | **Prince of My Heart (103)** (BWHills) **3-9-0** BThomson(18) (prom over 8f) | 7 | **19** | 100/1 | 84 | 39 |
| 1324[5] | **Portuguese Lil (80)** (DNicholls) **3-8-9** AlexGreaves(10) (swtg: a bhd) | 3 | **20** | 500/1 | 75 | 30 |
| | | | | (SP 118.0%) | **20 Rn** | |

**2m 35.05** (0.05) CSF £57.00 TOTE £16.60: £4.90 £2.80 £4.60 (£36.50) Trio £313.50 OWNER Mr Khalifa Dasmal (NEWMARKET) BRED Khalifa Abdulla Dasmal

**Shaamit (IRE)**, who had an abscess on his withers in the spring and then suffered with an overreach, had to miss the Dante and, as a result, came into this event without a run under his belt this season. Making giant strides over a quarter of a mile from home, he swept into the lead well over a furlong out but, with the second and third finishing really fast, found the line only just coming in time. He may now be supplemented for the Irish Derby. (12/1)

**1114 Dushyantor (USA)** was certainly the hard luck story of the race. Taking a keen hold, he was one of several to get involved in scrimmaging after only three furlongs, and as a result, was soon losing his pitch. At the top of the hill, the colt was hardly in a good position and things certainly did not look good for him - he was only fourteenth coming into the straight. Switched to the outside, he picked up ground in tremendous style over a quarter of a mile from home and, absolutely flying in the final furlong, would surely have prevailed with a little further to go. He looks destined for a big prize. (9/2)

**1508* Shantou (USA)**, who only the week before had won a hot maiden at Sandown, ran out of his skin especially considering he was another who did not have the run of the race. Only thirteenth entering the straight and with it all to do, having been involved in general bunching running down Tattenham Hill, he picked up ground over a quarter of a mile from home and, together with the runner-up, finished really strongly. A Group race is his for the taking this year. (25/1)

**1114* Glory of Dancer** ran a tremendous race but probably found the trip a bit beyond him. In a handy position throughout, he gained a narrow lead over a quarter of a mile from home but, passed by the winner well over a furlong out, failed to find another gear. He will now return to a mile and a quarter with the Grand Prix de Paris a possibility. (6/1)

**926 Alhaarth (IRE)**, whose stamina was in doubt before the race, had no problems with this trip. Involved in a bit of scrimmaging after only three furlongs, he chased the leaders and, ridden along in the straight, was actually staying on well in the closing stages. Although unbeaten Champion two-year-old last season, he has been caught up by his contemporaries but, having said that, this was no mean feat and he is still a very good horse. (15/2)

**1076* Mystic Knight** did not run at all badly. Never far away, he came under pressure over quarter of a mile from home, but lacked that vital turn of foot. (14/1)
**1114 Jack Jennings** ran really well and took them along until collared over two furlongs from home. (25/1)
**1076 Acharne** did not run at all badly for a 200/1 shot. Moving up along the inside around Tattenham Corner, he failed to find another gear in the straight. (200/1)
**1120* Chief Contender (IRE)**, taking a decided step up in class, was never far away but had given his all over two furlongs from home. (15/1: op 25/1)
**926 Even Top (IRE)**, involved in scrimmaging after only three furlongs, chased the leaders but was hung out to dry in the straight. It later transpired that he had been struck into and returned with a gash on a back leg. He is well worth another chance. (11/2)
**1114 Storm Trooper (USA)** was very disappointing and was towards of the back of the field early in the straight. (15/2)

## 1792 PAKNET 'TOTE DIRECT' APPRENTICE H'CAP (0-90) (4-Y.O+) (Class C)

3-10 (3-16) **1m 4f 10y** £10,796.25 (£3,270.00: £1,597.50: £761.25) Stalls: Low GOING minus 0.21 sec per fur (GF)

| Form | Horse | Dist | Pos | SP | RR | SF |
|---|---|---|---|---|---|---|
| 1147* | **Dance So Suite (86)** (PFICole) **4-9-6**(7) DavidO'Neill(7) (b: a.p: led over 1f out: r.o wl) | — | **1** | 6/1$^{2}$ | 96 | 78 |
| 1660$^{5}$ | **Achilles Heel (55)** (CNAllen) **5-7-10** MartinDwyer(2) (hdwy over 1f out: r.o wl ins fnl f) | 1½ | **2** | 66/1 | 63 | 45 |
| 1618$^{2}$ | **Hattaafeh (IRE) (60)** (MissBSanders) **5-8-1** MBaird(12) (lw: a.p: led over 2f out tl over 1f out: unable qckn) | nk | **3** | 8/1 | 68 | 50 |
| 968* | **Artic Courier (80)** (DJSCosgrove) **5-9-7** AWhelan(1) (lw: hdwy 2f out: edgd rt 1f out: r.o one pce) | 1 | **4** | 13/2$^{3}$ | 86 | 68 |
| 1109$^{11}$ | **Casual Water (IRE) (75)** (AGNewcombe) **5-9-2** SDrowne(11) (lw: rdn & hdwy over 2f out: one pce) | 1½ | **5** | 7/1 | 79 | 61 |
| 1528$^{7}$ | **Benfleet (80)** (RWArmstrong) **5-9-7** DGriffiths(6) (hdwy over 1f out: nvr nrr) | 1¼ | **6** | 15/2 | 83 | 65 |
| 1462$^{3}$ | **Ma Petite Anglaise (71)** (WJarvis) **4-8-12** RHavlin(8) (lw: a.p: rdn over 2f out: wkng whn hmpd wl over 1f out) | s.h | **7** | 10/1 | 74 | 56 |
| 1338* | **Country Lover (70)** (LordHuntingdon) **5-8-8v**(3) AimeeCook(10) (lw: no hdwy fnl 2f) | ½ | **8** | 7/1 | 72 | 54 |
| 844* | **Roisin Clover (72)** (SDow) **5-8-10**(3) ADaly(14) (swtg: hdwy 8f out: rdn over 2f out: btn whn bdly hmpd 1f out) | ¾ | **9** | 11/2$^{1}$ | 73 | 55 |
| 1194$^{5}$ | **Toy Princess (USA) (74)** (CEBrittain) **4-8-12**(3) JGotobed(13) (hdwy 6f out: wknd over 2f out) | ¾ | **10** | 16/1 | 74 | 56 |
| | **Global Dancer (73)** (SDow) **5-8-7**(7) DSalt(9) (swtg: led over 9f) | 3 | **11** | 12/1 | 69 | 51 |
| 580$^{15}$ | **Cedez le Passage (FR) (87)** (KOCunningham-Brown) **5-9-11**(3) CMunday(4) (lw: bhd fnl 3f) | 8 | **12** | 33/1 | 72 | 54 |
| 1330$^{9}$ | **Zamalek (USA) (80)** (GLMoore) **4-9-7** PPMurphy(5) (swtg: bhd fnl 6f) | 21 | **13** | 33/1 | 37 | 19 |
| | | | | (SP 120.9%) | **13 Rn** | |

**2m 37.54** (2.54) CSF £242.86 CT £2,901.17 TOTE £6.10: £2.70 £6.60 £2.00 (£146.50) Trio £905.30 OWNER Mr J. S. Gutkin (WHATCOMBE) BRED Genesis Green Stud and Walter Swinburn Ltd
LONG HANDICAP Achilles Heel 6-6
STEWARDS' ENQUIRY Whelan susp. 17-19/6/96 (careless riding).
**1147* Dance So Suite**, never far away, hit the front over a furlong out and kept on strongly. (6/1)
**1660 Achilles Heel** ran well from 18lb out of the handicap. Only finding his feet from below the distance, he ran on really strongly inside the final furlong, but found the line always coming too soon. (66/1)
**1618 Hattaafeh (IRE)** went for home over a quarter of a mile out but, headed below the distance, failed to find another gear. (8/1)
**968* Artic Courier** picked up ground a quarter of a mile from home but, edging slightly right a furlong out, failed to find the necessary turn of foot. He is not easy to win with, and has scored just twice, the second coming last month when he was awarded a race at Kempton. (13/2)
**1109 Casual Water (IRE)**, ridden along to take closer order over two furlongs from home, could then make no further impression. (7/1)
**Benfleet** stayed on in the last furlong and a half, but found it all over bar the shouting. (15/2)

## 1793 RACING CHANNEL H'CAP (4-Y.O+) (Class B)

3-50 (3-52) **1m 2f 18y** £31,795.00 (£11,905.00: £5,827.50: £2,512.50: £1,131.25: £578.75) Stalls: Low GOING minus 0.21 sec per fur (GF)

| Form | Horse | Dist | Pos | SP | RR | SF |
|---|---|---|---|---|---|---|
| 831$^{11}$ | **Ela-Aristokrati (IRE) (109)** (LMCumani) **4-9-10** PRobinson(8) (lw: gd hdwy over 1f out: str run fnl f: led nr fin) | — | **1** | 16/1 | 118 | 89 |
| 1476$^{4}$ | **Tertium (IRE) (84)** (MartynWane) **4-7-10**(3) AWhelan(4) (hld up: led over 1f out: hrd rdn: hdd nr fin) | ½ | **2** | 7/1$^{2}$ | 92 | 63 |
| 1484$^{6}$ | **Hoh Express (94)** (IABalding) **4-8-9** LDettori(12) (hdwy over 1f out: r.o ins fnl f) | 1¼ | **3** | 8/1$^{3}$ | 100 | 71 |
| 1440$^{10}$ | **Conspicuous (IRE) (81)** (LGCottrell) **6-7-10** JQuinn(2) (hdwy over 1f out: one pce) | 1¼ | **4** | 20/1 | 85 | 56 |
| | **Ellie Ardensky (94)** (JRFanshawe) **4-8-6**(3) NVarley(6) (a.p: one pce fnl 2f) | 2 | **5** | 14/1 | 95 | 66 |
| 988$^{3}$ | **Hardy Dancer (91)** (GLMoore) **4-8-6** SWhitworth(11) (lw: a.p: led over 2f out tl over 1f out: wknd fnl f: sddle slipped) | hd | **6** | 7/1$^{2}$ | 92 | 63 |
| 1198$^{3}$ | **Hazard a Guess (IRE) (82)** (DNicholls) **6-7-4**(7) JBramhill(10) (dwlt: nvr nr to chal) | 1 | **7** | 7/1$^{2}$ | 81 | 52 |
| 1440$^{4}$ | **Fieldridge (81)** (MPMuggeridge) **7-7-5**(5) MartinDwyer(9) (a mid div) | ¾ | **8** | 25/1 | 79 | 50 |
| 831$^{9}$ | **Maralinga (IRE) (100)** (LadyHerries) **4-9-1** PaulEddery(16) (prom over 8f) | 1¼ | **9** | 16/1 | 96 | 67 |
| 1330$^{6}$ | **Wakeel (USA) (86)** (SDow) **4-7-10**(5)ow4 ADaly(13) (lw: a mid div) | 1¼ | **10** | 16/1 | 80 | 47 |
| 1476$^{9}$ | **Pinkerton's Pal (84)** (CEBrittain) **5-7-8**(5) MBaird(5) (led over 7f) | 3 | **11** | 40/1 | 73 | 44 |
| 1484$^{13}$ | **Daryabad (IRE) (90)** (TJNaughton) **4-8-5** TQuinn(7) (hdwy over 2f out: wknd over 1f out) | 1½ | **12** | 40/1 | 77 | 48 |
| 1440* | **Zermatt (IRE) (81)** (MDIUsher) **6-7-10** NAdams(14) (swtg: chsd ldr over 7f) | 1½ | **13** | 25/1 | 66 | 37 |
| | **Danegold (IRE) (83)** (MRChannon) **4-7-12v** AMackay(15) (bit bkwd: swtg: a bhd) | 2½ | **14** | 40/1 | 64 | 35 |
| 1330$^{5}$ | **Stone Ridge (IRE) (93)** (RHannon) **4-8-5**(3) DaneO'Neill(3) (lw: a bhd: t.o) | 25 | **15** | 14/1 | 34 | 5 |
| 1330* | **Hugwity (84)** (BHanbury) **4-7-13** WCarson(1) (b: b.hind: prom 6f: t.o) | 6 | **16** | 11/4$^{1}$ | 16 | — |
| | | | | (SP 126.0%) | **16 Rn** | |

**2m 4.62** (0.22) CSF £117.60 CT £894.91 TOTE £18.80: £3.50 £2.40 £1.70 £4.70 (£85.00) Trio £323.40 OWNER Mr Andreas Michael (NEWMARKET) BRED M. Ervine
LONG HANDICAP Fieldridge 7-5 Conspicuous (IRE) 7-5 Zermatt (IRE) 7-3
**Ela-Aristokrati (IRE)**, racing at the back of the field, found his feet in no uncertain terms from below the distance. Coming with a storming run, he swept into the lead near the line. (16/1)
**1476 Tertium (IRE)** chased the leaders. Sent on below the distance, it looked as if he was going to prevail until caught by the fast-finishing winner near the line. (7/1)
**1484 Hoh Express** found his feet from below the distance but, despite running on, was never going to get there in time. (8/1)
**Conspicuous (IRE)** took closer order below the distance, but could make no further impression in the final furlong. (20/1)
**Ellie Ardensky**, making her seasonal bow, was never far away, but failed to increase her work-rate in the last two furlongs. (14/1)
**988 Hardy Dancer** went on over two furlongs from home but, headed below the distance, soon ran out of gas. (7/1)

## 1794 VODAFONE CORONATION CUP STKS (Gp 1) (4-Y.O+) (Class A)

4-25 (4-27) **1m 4f 10y** £106,560.00 (£39,691.75: £18,908.38: £8,064.87) Stalls: Low GOING minus 0.21 sec per fur (GF)

| | | | | SP | RR | SF |
|---|---|---|---|---|---|---|
| 906a[3] | **Swain (IRE)** (AFabre,France) **4-9-0** LDettori(2) (gd sort: mde all: rdn out) | — | 1 | 11/10[1] | 124+ | 48 |
| 831* | **Singspiel (IRE) (120)** (MRStoute) **4-9-0** MJKinane(1) (chsd wnr: ev ch fnl 2f: r.o) | nk | 2 | 9/4[2] | 124 | 48 |
| 907a[0] | **De Quest** (AFabre,France) **4-9-0** PatEddery(3) (hld up: rdn over 2f out: unable qckn) | 5 | 3 | 7/2[3] | 117 | 41 |
| 1390a[2] | **Punishment** (CEBrittain) **5-9-0** TQuinn(4) (hld up: rdn over 2f out: one pce) | s.h | 4 | 14/1 | 117 | 41 |

(SP 107.3%) **4 Rn**

**2m 40.27** (5.27) CSF £3.67 TOTE £1.90 (£1.70) OWNER Sheikh Mohammed (CHANTILLY) BRED Sheikh Mohammed
STEWARDS' ENQUIRY Quinn susp. 17-19/6/96 (failure to obtain best possible placing).
OFFICIAL EXPLANATION **Regal Patrol: his jockey reported that the colt was running green approaching the two furlong marker, and collided with the rail which caused him to lose his action.**

**906a Swain (IRE)** ran a tremendous race. Making all the running, he was engaged in a ding-dong battle with the runner-up in the final quarter-mile but, sticking to his task in admirable style, held on well. His rider added later that he would be even better on soft, and he will head for the King George at Royal Ascot for which he will be a leading contender. (11/10)

**831* Singspiel (IRE)** lost nothing in defeat. Chasing the winner, he threw down his challenge in the final quarter-mile and appeared to be going better than that rival. However, he had met a real tartar and, despite giving his all, he failed to get past. He will now go for the Eclipse and must have a good chance. (9/4: op 6/4)

**907a De Quest**, held up in fourth place, got completely outpaced over a quarter of a mile from home as the race developed in earnest but, struggling on, snatched third prize right on the line. (7/2)

**1390a Punishment**, racing in third place, failed to quicken once the race began in earnest over two furlongs out and lost third place right on the line. (14/1)

## 1795 VODATA WOODCOTE STKS (Listed) (2-Y.O) (Class A)

5-00 (5-00) **6f** £13,680.00 (£4,140.00: £2,020.00: £960.00) Stalls: Low GOING minus 0.21 sec per fur (GF)

| | | | | SP | RR | SF |
|---|---|---|---|---|---|---|
| 1115* | **Proud Native (IRE)** (APJarvis) **2-9-4** MJKinane(3) (chsd ldr: led over 1f out: drvn out) | — | 1 | 5/2[1] | 97 | 51 |
| 1191* | **Premier Bay** (PWHarris) **2-9-0** GHind(2) (s.s: hdwy over 3f out: rdn over 2f out: r.o wl ins fnl) | hd | 2 | 4/1[2] | 93 | 47 |
| 1046* | **Caviar Royale (IRE)** (RHannon) **2-9-0** PatEddery(5) (lw: led over 4f: unable qckn fnl f) | 3 | 3 | 5/2[1] | 85 | 39 |
| 1303[2] | **Pelham (IRE)** (RHannon) **2-9-0** JReid(1) (hld up: rdn over 2f out: wknd over 1f out) | 5 | 4 | 10/1 | 71 | 25 |
| *1603** | **Burlington House (USA)** (PFICole) **2-9-0** TQuinn(6) (lw: hld up: rn v.wd bnd over 3f out: wknd 2f out) | 2 | 5 | 12/1 | 66 | 20 |
| 1531* | **Dalmeny Dancer** (BJMeehan) **2-8-11** LDettori(4) (hld up: rn wd bnd over 3f out: wknd 2f out) | 6 | 6 | 11/2[3] | 47 | 1 |

(SP 109.3%) **6 Rn**

**1m 10.19** (2.19) CSF £11.66 TOTE £2.80: £1.70 £3.00 (£6.20) OWNER Mr L. Fust (ASTON UPTHORPE) BRED Mrs B. A. Headon

**1115* Proud Native (IRE)** maintained his unbeaten record but had to fight for it. He went on below the distance but, with the runner-up finishing really well, had to be driven right out to prevail. He has certainly earned a trip to Royal Ascot. (5/2)

**1191* Premier Bay** took closer order early in the straight and, running on really strongly inside the final furlong, only just failed to get there. (4/1)

**1046* Caviar Royale (IRE)** attempted to make all the running. Collared below the distance, he failed to find another gear. (5/2)

**1303 Pelham (IRE)** chased the leaders, but was left for dead from below the distance. (10/1: 7/1-11/1)

**1603* Burlington House (USA)** totally failed to negotiate Tattenham Corner and came extremely wide into the straight. He was hung out to dry two furlongs from home. (12/1: 8/1-14/1)

**1531* Dalmeny Dancer** was another who failed to handle the Corner and was swept aside two furlongs from home. (11/2)

## 1796 VODACOM CONDITIONS STKS (3-Y.O) (Class B)

5-30 (5-32) **7f** £12,196.00 (£4,564.00: £2,232.00: £960.00: £430.00: £218.00) Stalls: Low GOING minus 0.21 sec per fur (GF)

| | | | | SP | RR | SF |
|---|---|---|---|---|---|---|
| 918[3] | **Ramooz (USA) (104)** (BHanbury) **3-9-4** WRyan(1) (lw: hdwy over 1f out: hrd rdn: led wl ins fnl f: r.o wl) | — | 1 | 5/2[1] | 104 | 33 |
| 1146[3] | **Warning Time (104)** (BJMeehan) **3-9-5** MJKinane(4) (hld up: led over 1f out tl wl ins fnl f: unable qckn) | 1¼ | 2 | 13/2 | 102 | 31 |
| 1615* | **Almushtarak (IRE) (85)** (MissGayKelleway) **3-9-0** JReid(3) (b.hind: lw: hdwy over 1f out: r.o wl ins fnl f) | nk | 3 | 7/2[2] | 97 | 26 |
| 1481[3] | **Prends Ca (IRE) (94)** (RHannon) **3-8-9** LDettori(5) (led over 5f: one pce) | 2½ | 4 | 9/2[3] | 86 | 15 |
| 936[3] | **Lucky Archer (90)** (CEBrittain) **3-8-11** CAsmussen(2) (lw: prom over 5f) | 1 | 5 | 14/1 | 86 | 15 |
| *1601[6]* | **Worldwide Elsie (USA) (75)** (RHarris) **3-8-6** AMackay(7) (lw: chsd ldr over 5f) | s.h | 6 | 50/1 | 80 | 9 |
| 1327* | **King of Peru (105)** (APJarvis) **3-9-0** PatEddery(6) (sme hdwy over 2f out: sn wknd) | 1½ | 7 | 5/2[1] | 85 | 14 |

(SP 119.5%) **7 Rn**

**1m 24.43** (4.13) CSF £18.41 TOTE £3.50: £2.10 £4.10 (£16.80) OWNER Mr Hilal Salem (NEWMARKET) BRED Gainsborough Stud Management Ltd

**918 Ramooz (USA)**, who failed to stay a mile and a quarter last time, almost found this trip too sharp. Finding his feet from below the distance, he eventually responded gamely to pressure and managed to get on top in the closing stages. The Jersey Stakes at Ascot is next on the agenda, but a mile is probably his ideal trip. (5/2)

**1146 Warning Time** chased the leaders. Sent on below the distance, he gamely tried to hold on, but was just worried out of it in the closing stages. (13/2)

**1615* Almushtarak (IRE)**, taking a step up in class, only got going below the distance. Running on strongly inside the final furlong, he just failed to get there. His trainer insists that this is a very good horse and promises to have him right for the Jersey Stakes. (7/2)

**1481 Prends Ca (IRE)** attempted to make all the running. Collared below the distance, she could only go up and own in the same place. (9/2)

**936 Lucky Archer** was close up until calling it a day early in the final quarter-mile. (14/1: 10/1-16/1)

T/Jkpt: Not won; £49,009.23 to Epsom 9/6/96. T/Plpt: £1,813.40 (31.17 Tckts). T/Qdpt: £60.10 (40.54 Tckts). AK

# 1778-HAYDOCK (L-H) (Good to soft)

## Saturday June 8th

WEATHER: fine & sunny WIND: slt half against

## 1797 HALSALL MAIDEN STKS (3-Y.O) (Class D)

2-10 (2-10) **1m 30y** £3,714.00 (£1,122.00: £546.00: £258.00) Stalls: Low GOING: 0.30 sec per fur (G)

| | | | | SP | RR | SF |
|---|---|---|---|---|---|---|
| 1593[3] | **Victorian Style** (RCharlton) **3-8-9** TSprake(1) (a.p: led wl over 1f out: drvn clr fnl f) | — | 1 | 3/1[2] | 78 | 28 |

| | | | SP | RR | SF |
|---|---|---|---|---|---|
| 1137a[4] | **How Long** (LMCumani) **3-9-0** OUrbina(8) (hld up: hdwy 4f out: chal 2f out: kpt on fnl f: no ch w wnr) ..............6 | **2** | 5/1[3] | 71 | 21 |
| 1594[14] | **Parsis (USA) (70)** (LadyHerries) **3-9-0h** TIves(9) (lw: plld hrd: led tl over 2f out: rdn & one pce appr fnl f) .......¾ | **3** | 14/1 | 70 | 20 |
| 1617[11] | **Chirico (USA)** (JHMGosden) **3-9-0** JCarroll(3) (bit bkwd: a.p: led over 2f out: sn hdd: wknd ins fnl f).............nk | **4** | 7/1 | 69 | 19 |
| | **Unitus (IRE)** (MRStoute) **3-9-0** DeanMcKeown(4) (w'like: scope: bkwd: trckd ldrs: rdn wl over 1f out: one pce) ..........1¼ | **5** | 11/4[1] | 67 | 17 |
| 1530[8] | **Berlin Blue** (JWWatts) **3-9-0** GDuffield(2) (bit bkwd: hld up: a in rr).........6 | **6** | 25/1 | 55 | 5 |
| | **El Bardador (IRE)** (WJarvis) **3-9-0** AMcGlone(7) (w'like: scope: s.s: a bhd)..........hd | **7** | 20/1 | 55 | 5 |
| 1434[9] | **So Keen** (ABailey) **3-9-0** LCharnock(11) (bit bkwd: a bhd)..........1½ | **8** | 33/1 | 52 | 2 |
| 1422[2] | **Old Roma (IRE)** (JohnBerry) **3-8-9** MFenton(5) (a in rr)..........s.h | **9** | 6/1 | 47 | — |
| 1627[6] | **Shavinsky** (PHowling) **3-9-0** FNorton(6) (plld hrd: prom tl wknd qckly over 2f out)..........2½ | **10** | 33/1 | 47 | — |
| 1434[12] | **Maid To Last** (JWHills) **3-8-9** AClark(10) (dwlt: effrt 4f out: sn rdn & wknd: t.o)..........12 | **11** | 33/1 | 18 | — |
| | | | (SP 119.2%) | | **11 Rn** |

**1m 49.63** (9.03) CSF £17.72 TOTE £3.40: £1.20 £2.30 £2.00 (£6.20) Trio £33.50 OWNER Mr K. Abdulla (BECKHAMPTON) BRED Juddmonte Farms

OFFICIAL EXPLANATION **Old Roma (IRE): failed to handle the going.**

**1593 Victorian Style** appreciated the rain-softened ground better than most and, taking over just inside the quarter-mile pole, gradually extended her advantage to win very much as she pleased. (3/1)

**1137a How Long** was successful in a ten-furlong race in France at Cagnes-Sur-Mer in January, so how was it he was able to compete in a maiden event some four months later. An impressive-looking colt, he posed a serious threat two furlongs out, but then seemed to get outpaced until staying on inside the final furlong. (5/1: op 3/1)

**Parsis (USA)**, fitted with a hood, raced freely and made the running for over five furlongs. Ridden along, he did stay on and would seem to be better than he has shown so far. (14/1)

**1617 Chirico (USA)**, still with a bit left to work on, was one of the principals until his stride shortened inside the last furlong. He should soon leave this form behind. (7/1)

**Unitus (IRE)**, a son of Oaks winner Unite, did not look fully wound up for this racecourse debut, but showed up in the chasing group until calling enough approaching the final furlong. (11/4)

## 1798 DOUGLAS RATED STKS H'CAP (0-95) (3-Y.O) (Class C)

2-55 (2-56) **1m 2f 120y** £6,303.76 (£2,353.84: £1,146.92: £488.60: £214.30: £104.58) Stalls: High GOING: 0.30 sec per fur (G)

| | | | SP | RR | SF |
|---|---|---|---|---|---|
| 1106[4] | **Pleasant Surprise (91)** (MJohnston) **3-9-3b[1]** JWeaver(7) (led 1f: brought stands' side st: led wl over 2f out: hrd rdn: jst hld on)..........— | **1** | 9/2[2] | 102 | 57 |
| 1619[7] | **Exalted (IRE) (82)** (SirMarkPrescott) **3-8-8** GDuffield(6) (a.p: rdn over 2f out: kpt on doggedly fnl f)..........hd | **2** | 20/1 | 93 | 48 |
| 1349[2] | **Sandy Floss (IRE) (77)** (HRACecil) **3-8-3** AMcGlone(9) (a.p: effrt u.p wl over 1f out: wknd fnl f)..........7 | **3** | 4/1[1] | 77 | 32 |
| 1126[12] | **Truancy (87)** (MBell) **3-8-13** MFenton(10) (lw: bhd: hdwy over 2f out: sn hrd rdn: nt rch ldrs)..........2 | **4** | 20/1 | 84 | 39 |
| | **A-Aasem (74)** (HThomsonJones) **3-8-0** RHills(1) (bit bkwd: led 7f out tl wl over 2f out: sn rdn: grad wknd)......½ | **5** | 11/1 | 70 | 25 |
| *555** | **Prince Kinsky (80)** (LordHuntingdon) **3-8-6** TSprake(2) (lw: hld up in rr: effrt over 2f out: nvr nrr)..........2½ | **6** | 11/2[3] | 73 | 28 |
| 1002[10] | **Misky Bay (78)** (JHMGosden) **3-8-4** JCarroll(5) (dwlt: a in rr)..........8 | **7** | 10/1 | 59 | 14 |
| 1432[4] | **Kala Sunrise (90)** (CSmith) **3-9-2** AClark(11) (a in rr: t.o)..........10 | **8** | 16/1 | 55 | 10 |
| 1619[2] | **Lear Jet (USA) (90)** (PFICole) **3-8-11(5)** FLynch(4) (led after 1f to 7f out: wknd qckly & eased 3f out: t.o).........6 | **9** | 9/2[2] | 46 | 1 |
| 611[4] | **Salmis (80)** (JRFanshawe) **3-8-3(3)** JStack(12) (hld up in tch: wknd wl over 2f out: t.o)..........s.h | **10** | 11/1 | 36 | — |
| 1619[5] | **Villeggiatura (79)** (BWHills) **3-8-5b[1]** SSanders(3) (trckd ldrs over 6f: sn wknd & eased: t.o)..........18 | **11** | 8/1 | 8 | — |
| | | | (SP 124.0%) | | **11 Rn** |

**2m 20.47** (8.97) CSF £80.69 CT £359.18 TOTE £4.50: £1.80 £3.10 £1.80 (£25.80) Trio £48.40 OWNER Mr Abdullah Ali (MIDDLEHAM) BRED Highclere Stud Ltd

OFFICIAL EXPLANATION **Lear Jet (USA): lost his action due to the ground.**

**1106 Pleasant Surprise**, wearing blinkers for the first time and running with his tongue tied down, raced alone on the stands' side from the turn in to the straight, but some of the others realised that was the place to be and gradually worked their way over. In control from some way out, he had to dig deep close home to hold on. (9/2)

**Exalted (IRE)**, returning to something like his best, put in a sustained late challenge that was to fail by a stride. This easy ground seemed to suit and he deserves to gain reward. (20/1)

**1349 Sandy Floss (IRE)** sat on the tails of the leaders and put in his bid below the distance but, failing to make much of an impact, tied up rather quickly inside the final furlong. (4/1)

**Truancy**, held up in the rear at this first attempt at the trip, did close up two furlongs out, but he always had far too much to do, and was unable to make his presence felt. He is bred to stay at least this trip. (20/1)

**A-Aasem** just needed this airing, but made his full share of the pacemaking until feeling the strain entering the last quarter-mile. (11/1: op 7/1)

**555* Prince Kinsky** had more on his plate than when winning on the All-Weather two months ago, and was never able to get within striking range. (11/2)

**611 Salmis** (11/1: 8/1-12/1)

**1619 Villeggiatura** (8/1: op 5/1)

## 1799 ROTHMANS ROYALS NORTH SOUTH CHALLENGE SERIES H'CAP (0-100) (3-Y.O+) (Class C)

3-30 (3-30) **1m 30y** £7,103.00 (£2,144.00: £1,042.00: £491.00) Stalls: Low GOING: 0.30 sec per fur (G)

| | | | SP | RR | SF |
|---|---|---|---|---|---|
| 1406* | **Bollin Frank (66)** (TDEasterby) **4-8-1** LCharnock(3) (lw: a.p: led 3f out: hrd rdn fnl f: r.o wl)..........— | **1** | 11/4[1] | 74 | 33 |
| 455[10] | **Moving Arrow (93)** (MissSEHall) **5-10-0** JWeaver(9) (lw: led to 3f out: rallied u.p appr fnl f: unable qckn) ......nk | **2** | 13/2[3] | 100 | 59 |
| 1609* | **Queens Consul (IRE) (84)** (BSRothwell) **6-9-5** MFenton(8) (a.p: pushed along 4f out: kpt on u.p fnl f)..........1¼ | **3** | 6/1[2] | 89 | 48 |
| 1078[4] | **Mutamanni (USA) (82)** (HThomsonJones) **3-8-6** RHills(4) (lw: hld up: hdwy & nt clr run over 2f out: swtchd lft & kpt on u.p)..........2½ | **4** | 13/2[3] | 82 | 30 |
| 1354[8] | **Courageous Dancer (IRE) (85)** (BHanbury) **4-9-3(3)** JStack(7) (hld up in rr: swtchd lft & hdwy over 2f out: sn rdn: nvr able to chal)..........3½ | **5** | 13/2[3] | 78 | 37 |
| 1672[2] | **Nordic Breeze (IRE) (69)** (ABailey) **4-8-4** SSanders(1) (lw: prom tl rdn & wknd over 1f out)..........6 | **6** | 8/1 | 50 | 9 |
| | **Lay The Blame (85)** (WJarvis) **3-8-9** MTebbutt(5) (h.d.w: bit bkwd: trckd ldrs tl wknd over 2f out)..........¾ | **7** | 13/2[3] | 65 | 13 |
| 1522[6] | **Sue Me (IRE) (64)** (WRMuir) **4-7-13ow3** DRMcCabe(2) (bhd: effrt 3f out: sn rdn: no imp: t.o)..........7 | **8** | 12/1 | 30 | — |
| 1322[9] | **Al Reet (IRE) (77)** (MDHammond) **5-8-12** JCarroll(6) (lw: hld up in rr: rdn 3f out: no imp: t.o)..........hd | **9** | 14/1 | 43 | 2 |
| | | | (SP 119.8%) | | **9 Rn** |

**1m 48.33** (7.73) CSF £20.39 CT £93.14 TOTE £3.40: £1.20 £3.10 £2.60 (£12.80) Trio £51.50 OWNER Sir Neil Westbrook (MALTON) BRED Sir Neil and Lady Westbrook

WEIGHT FOR AGE 3yo-11lb

**1406* Bollin Frank** made it win number three over course and distance with a hard-fought success, and he certainly does not lack anything in courage. (11/4)
**455 Moving Arrow** turned in a bold display under topweight, and was only forced to concede defeat nearing the line. He looks in tremendous fettle, and will soon make amends. (13/2)
**1609* Queens Consul (IRE)** ran possibly her best race yet, and really stuck to her task inside the distance. She would appear to be at the top of her form. (6/1)
**1078 Mutamanni (USA)**, given every chance to stay this slightly longer tip, had trouble obtaining a clear run when about to mount his challenge two furlongs out and, though he did stay on after being switched, he could not muster the speed to throw down his bid. (13/2)
**1149 Courageous Dancer (IRE)**, in no hurry to take the leaders on, had to weave her way through to deliver her challenge but, once there, could not increase her pace enough to land a blow. (13/2)
**1672 Nordic Breeze (IRE)**, stepping up in class, showed up prominently until finding demands too hot for him when the race began in earnest. (8/1)
**Lay The Blame**, sure to strip fitter for the run, pushed the pace until blowing up approaching the last quarter-mile. (13/2)

## 1800 JOHN OF GAUNT STKS (Listed) (3-Y.O+) (Class A)

4-05 (4-06) **7f 30y** £12,965.00 (£3,920.00: £1,910.00: £905.00) Stalls: Low GOING: 0.30 sec per fur (G)

| | | | | SP | RR | SF |
|---|---|---|---|---|---|---|
| 1621[3] | **Inzar (USA) (112)** (PFICole) **4-9-5** RHills(8) (lw: mde all: shkn up 2f out: jst hld on) | — | **1** | 7/2[2] | 118 | 55 |
| 1629* | **Branston Abby (IRE) (108)** (MJohnston) **7-8-12** JWeaver(1) (hld up & bhd: swtchd & hdwy appr fnl f: fin wl) | hd | **2** | 100/30[1] | 111 | 48 |
| 1075[2] | **Carranita (IRE) (105)** (BPalling) **6-8-12** TSprake(7) (lw: a.p: rdn ent fnl f: r.o wl) | nk | **3** | 7/1[3] | 110 | 47 |
| 1406[2] | **Band on the Run (92)** (BAMcMahon) **9-8-12** SSanders(5) (lw: prom: rdn wl over 1f out: sltly hmpd ent fnl f: r.o one pce) | 1½ | **4** | 14/1 | 107 | 44 |
| 1483[5] | **Espartero (IRE) (102)** (SirMarkPrescott) **4-8-12** GDuffield(10) (plld hrd: hld up: hdwy over 2f out: nt clr run appr fnl f: nt rcvr) | nk | **5** | 15/2 | 106 | 43 |
| 1481[4] | **Forest Cat (IRE) (91)** (MrsJCecil) **4-8-7** JCarroll(4) (hld up: effrt over 2f out: nt pce to chal) | 1 | **6** | 14/1 | 99 | 36 |
| 1410* | **Master Boots (110)** (DRLoder) **3-8-2** DRMcCabe(2) (s.i.s: hld up in rr: effrt & nt clr run 2f out: no imp) | 1¾ | **7** | 7/2[2] | 100 | 27 |
| 1129* | **Venture Capitalist (112)** (DNicholls) **7-9-5** TIves(6) (lw: dwlt: hld up in rr: reminders 3f out: no imp) | 7 | **8** | 9/1 | 91 | 28 |
| 1431[5] | **Dovebrace (102)** (ABailey) **3-8-2** MFenton(9) (chsd wnr tl wknd over 2f out: t.o) | 5 | **9** | 20/1 | 73 | — |

(SP 119.9%) **9 Rn**

**1m 33.79** (6.29) CSF £15.48 TOTE £4.10: £1.50 £1.90 £2.40 (£7.50) Trio £15.90 OWNER H R H Prince Fahd Salman (WHATCOMBE) BRED Newgate Stud Farm Inc in USA
WEIGHT FOR AGE 3yo-10lb
**1621 Inzar (USA)** returned to form on this more suitable ground with a brave front-running performance that was diminishing with every stride nearing the finish. (7/2)
**1629* Branston Abby (IRE)** had to barge her way through a narrow gap entering the final furlong, and her determined late challenge was only a stride down at the line. All in all, she was possibly a shade unlucky not to win. (100/30)
**1075 Carranita (IRE)**, narrowly beaten in this race last year, once again had to taste defeat, but she gave of her all as usual, and there is more success to be had. (7/1)
**1406 Band on the Run** was the main sufferer when the runner-up made room for herself passing the furlong marker, but he was flat to the boards at the time, and it is doubtful if it cost him the race. (14/1)
**1483 Espartero (IRE)** took a fearsome tug over this slightly longer trip, but did not get the run of the race when making his move approaching the final furlong, and the contest was as good as over when he did find top gear. He was the unlucky one and deserves compensation. (15/2)
**1481 Forest Cat (IRE)** performed with credit in this higher grade event, and was only found wanting for a turn of finishing speed inside the distance. She should not be long in returning to form. (14/1)
**1410* Master Boots** tried for an almost impossible run on the stands'-side rail two furlongs out, but got stopped for his cheek more than once and, with little hope of recovery, just had to sit and suffer. Whether he would have been good enough had a gap presented itself, only time will tell. (7/2: op 9/4)

## 1801 E.B.F. LEYLAND MAIDEN STKS (2-Y.O) (Class D)

4-45 (4-46) **5f** £3,415.00 (£1,030.00: £500.00: £235.00) Stalls: High GOING: 0.30 sec per fur (G)

| | | | | SP | RR | SF |
|---|---|---|---|---|---|---|
| 1404[2] | **Future Prospect (IRE)** (MJohnston) **2-9-0** JWeaver(6) (dwlt: hdwy 2f out: qcknd to ld ent fnl f: r.o strly) | — | **1** | 4/5[1] | 81+ | 40 |
| 1003[6] | **Swino** (PDEvans) **2-9-0** MFenton(4) (led: rdn & hdd 1f out: one pce) | 3 | **2** | 8/1 | 71 | 30 |
| 1404[3] | **Magic Blue (IRE)** (RHollinshead) **2-8-9**(5) FLynch(5) (hld up: swtchd lft over 1f out: kpt on u.p towards fin) | hd | **3** | 12/1 | 71 | 30 |
| 1424[4] | **Tough Leader** (BHanbury) **2-8-11**(3) JStack(1) (lw: chsd ldng pair: rdn over 1f out: one pce) | ¾ | **4** | 5/1[3] | 69 | 28 |
| 1344[3] | **Bold Risk** (JBerry) **2-9-0** JCarroll(2) (lw: w ldr: ev ch over 1f out: wknd fnl f) | 2½ | **5** | 4/1[2] | 61 | 20 |
| | **Cumbrian Quest** (TDEasterby) **2-9-0** LCharnock(3) (w'like: scope: bkwd: s.s: a bhd & outpcd: t.o) | 15 | **6** | 14/1 | 13 | — |

(SP 117.7%) **6 Rn**

**64.16 secs** (4.96) CSF £7.89 TOTE £1.80: £1.70 £2.80 (£5.00) OWNER Mr C. C. Buckley (MIDDLEHAM) BRED Mrs C. L. Weld
**1404 Future Prospect (IRE)** again lost ground leaving the stalls, but made good headway soon after halfway and, shaken up to lead into the final furlong, had little trouble forging clear. He will probably be better suited to a step up to six furlongs. (4/5)
**848 Swino**, taking the runner-up prize for the fourth time in six races, adopted more forceful tactics this time, but the outcome was just the same and he must wonder if his turn will ever come. (8/1)
**1404 Magic Blue (IRE)**, four lengths behind the winner last month, had a 5lb pull in the weights, but the improvement was only marginal, and he gives the impression that he needs a longer trip. (12/1: op 8/1)
**1424 Tough Leader** was not helped by this step back to the minimum trip, and he was hard at work and held approaching the final furlong. (5/1)
**1344 Bold Risk** had a running battle for the lead which he eventually lost, and his stride shortened dramatically inside the last furlong. It is possible the ground was more testing than he needs. (4/1)

## 1802 PENNY LANE H'CAP (0-90) (4-Y.O+) (Class C)

5-20 (5-20) **1m 6f** £5,452.50 (£1,650.00: £805.00: £382.50) Stalls: Centre GOING: 0.30 sec per fur (G)

| | | | | SP | RR | SF |
|---|---|---|---|---|---|---|
| 1116[3] | **Turgenev (IRE) (58)** (RBastiman) **7-7-13b** DaleGibson(6) (hld up & bhd: rdn & hdwy 3f out: led ent fnl f: styd on str) | — | **1** | 6/1 | 72 | 54 |
| | **Istabraq (IRE) (83)** (JHMGosden) **4-9-10** RHills(1) (b: b.hind: bit bkwd: led to 1f out: rdn & no ex towards fin) | 1 | **2** | 9/2[2] | 96 | 78 |
| 1147[5] | **Riparius (USA) (81)** (HCandy) **5-9-8** CRutter(8) (hld up & bhd: hdwy over 3f out: styd on u.p) | 5 | **3** | 15/2 | 88 | 70 |
| 1529[4] | **Anglesey Sea View (64)** (ABailey) **7-8-5** MFenton(3) (hld up mid div: outpcd 3f out: styd on again ins fnl f) | ¾ | **4** | 14/1 | 70 | 52 |

1524$^{5}$ **Cuango (IRE) (62)** (RHollinshead) **5-7-12**$^{(5)ow4}$ FLynch(11) (bhd: effrt & n.m.r over 2f out: swtchd & styd on fnl f) ....1¼ **5** 12/1 67 45
1436* **Satin Lover (75)** (MrsMReveley) **8-8-9**$^{(7)}$ SCopp(2) (lw: trckd ldrs: rdn over 2f out: wknd appr fnl f) ....s.h **6** 100/30$^{1}$ 80 62
1150$^{2}$ **Fabillion (70)** (CASmith) **4-8-11** DeanMcKeown(9) (plld hrd: prom tl wknd 3f out) ....½ **7** 8/1 74 56
1529$^{2}$ **Embryonic (IRE) (76)** (RFFisher) **4-9-3** JCarroll(12) (hld up: effrt & rdn 3f out: sn no imp) ....1¾ **8** 5/1$^{3}$ 78 60
**Tudor Island (80)** (CEBrittain) **7-9-7** JWeaver(5) (b.hind: bkwd: chsd ldr 6f: prom tl wknd wl over 2f out) ....2½ **9** 9/1 79 61
1428$^{5}$ **Highflying (83)** (GMMoore) **10-9-10** JTate(7) (bit bkwd: trckd ldrs over 10f: grad wknd) ....1¾ **10** 12/1 80 62
(SP 127.1%) **10 Rn**

**3m 7.7** (9.50) CSF £33.98 CT £196.66 TOTE £9.20: £2.30 £2.50 £2.00 (£38.60) Trio £53.90 OWNER Mrs Bridget Tranmer (WETHERBY)

**1116 Turgenev (IRE)** showed his promising York performance was no fluke and, enjoying a much smoother passage this time, won with a fair bit in hand. (6/1: op 4/1)

**Istabraq (IRE)**, usually better with a run under his belt, tried hard to lead from pillar-to-post, but the race-fit, well-handicapped winner took his measure inside the final furlong. This was a very promising effort and he looks as good as ever. (9/2)

**1147 Riparius (USA)** stayed on under pressure in the latter stages, but could not get close enough to cause concern. (15/2)

**1529 Anglesey Sea View** found this trip inadequate, and was only getting into her stride when the race was as good as over. (14/1)

**1524 Cuango (IRE)** had trouble getting through when poised to challenge from three furlongs out, but did not find a lot when a gap did appear, and he only does as much as he wants to. (12/1)

**1436* Satin Lover**, waiting on the leaders, was being bustled along over two furlongs out and, though he did hold his pitch, he had reached the end of his tether below the distance. (100/30: op 5/1)

**Tudor Island**, much more effective on a sounder surface, usually runs best when fresh, but he was in trouble early in the straight and was allowed to complete in his own time. (9/1)

T/Plpt: £47.00 (322.58 Tckts). T/Qdpt: £16.90 (36.71 Tckts). IM

## 1625-NEWMARKET (R-H) (Good to firm)
## Saturday June 8th

WEATHER: fine WIND: almost nil

## 1803 NEWMARKET LADIES DERBY LADIES' H'CAP (0-60) (4-Y.O+) (Class F)

6-40 (6-43) **1m 4f (July)** £5,127.00 (£1,536.00: £738.00: £339.00) Stalls: Low GOING minus 0.52 sec per fur (F)

SP RR SF

1514$^{12}$ **Soojama (IRE) (42)** (RMFlower) **6-10-4b** MrsAFarrell(13) (hdwy 2f out: led ins fnl f: sn pushed clr) ....— **1** 16/1 57 47
**Make a Stand (59)** (MCPipe) **5-11-2**$^{(5)}$ MissERamsden(9) (hdwy over 2f out: ev ch 1f out: unable qckn) ....4 **2** 9/2$^{1}$ 69 59
**Sloe Brandy (34)** (JWharton) **6-9-5**$^{(5)}$ MissHCarrington(12) (swtg: prom: led 6f out tl wknd & hdd ins fnl f) ....5 **3** 33/1 37 27
1347$^{19}$ **Cheveley Dancer (USA) (30)** (TJNaughton) **8-9-6** MissPRobson(21) (swtg: bhd: hdwy fnl 2f: nrst fin) ....¾ **4** 33/1 32 22
1696$^{5}$ **Augustan (50)** (SGollings) **5-10-7**$^{(5)}$ MrsJMGollings(18) (lw: prom: one pce fnl 3f) ....1¾ **5** 11/1 50 40
1514$^{7}$ **Charlie Bigtime (46)** (RHarris) **6-10-3**$^{(5)}$ MissKWright(6) (b.nr hind: bhd: hdwy 3f out: nrst fin) ....1¼ **6** 16/1 44 34
*1487*$^{2}$ **Anchorena (57)** (MrsASwinbank) **4-11-5** MissJFeilden(23) (prom: rdn 6f out: one pce fnl 3f) ....4 **7** 8/1$^{3}$ 50 40
1640$^{15}$ **Saltando (IRE) (48)** (PatMitchell) **5-10-10** MrsAPerrett(4) (lw: dwlt: hdwy 5f out: wknd over 1f out) ....1 **8** 20/1 39 29
1347* **Glow Forum (46)** (LMontagueHall) **5-10-8** MrsLPearce(5) (led 6f) ....½ **9** 9/2$^{1}$ 37 27
1514$^{14}$ **Ajdar (49)** (MissGayKelleway) **5-10-6**$^{(5)}$ MissSKelleway(20) (hld up: hdwy 6f out: wknd over 1f out) ....1¾ **10** 20/1 37 27
1548$^{6}$ **Mcgillycuddy Reeks (IRE) (40)** (NTinkler) **5-10-2** MrsDKettlewell(2) (swtg: s.s: nvr nr to chal) ....nk **11** 33/1 28 18
1194$^{12}$ **Stalled (IRE) (52)** (PTWalwyn) **6-10-9**$^{(5)}$ MarchionessBlandford(11) (lw: hld up: hdwy 3f out: nvr trbld ldrs) ....3½ **12** 14/1 35 25
1691$^{15}$ **Begger's Opera (32)** (PatMitchell) **4-9-3**$^{(5)}$ MissCCarcary(14) (prom 6f) ....1¾ **13** 50/1 13 3
1655$^{2}$ **Scenic Dancer (43)** (AHide) **8-10-5** MissLHide(16) (swtg: v.slowly away: wl bhd tl r.o fnl 4f) ....½ **14** 5/1$^{2}$ 23 13
**Superhoo (36)** (RCraggs) **5-9-7**$^{(5)}$ MissJNCraggs(3) (in tch 7f) ....1 **15** 25/1 15 5
1347$^{18}$ **Bresil (USA) (41)** (KRBurke) **7-9-12**$^{(5)ow14}$ MrsHSweeting(19) (lw: s.i.s: a bhd) ....2½ **16** 33/1 17 —
1685$^{4}$ **Benjamins Law (50)** (JAPickering) **5-10-7**$^{(5)}$ MissEGeorge(8) (prom 7f) ....1 **17** 16/1 24 14
1414$^{14}$ **Squared Away (50)** (JWPayne) **4-10-7**$^{(5)}$ MissCLake(7) (lw: bhd fnl 5f) ....¾ **18** 33/1 23 13
*1098*$^{10}$ **Mega Tid (37)** (BAPearce) **4-9-8**$^{(5)}$ MrsSColville(15) (s.i.s: a bhd) ....nk **19** 33/1 10 —
*85*$^{15}$ **Keep Quiet (34)** (WJMusson) **4-9-5b**$^{(5)}$ MissEJJones(22) (lw: prom 5f: sn bhd) ....dist **20** 33/1 — —
1486$^{11}$ **Sayitagain (50)** (JRJenkins) **4-10-7**$^{(5)}$ MrsSEddery(1) (sn bhd) ....15 **21** 25/1 — —
**Lofty Deed (USA) (25)** (WJMusson) **6-9-1b** MrsDArbuthnot(10) (swtg: prom 6f) ....5 **22** 33/1 — —
(SP 139.5%) **22 Rn**

**2m 33.96** (3.96) CSF £87.53 CT £2,260.85 TOTE £20.60: £3.20 £2.40 £6.80 £10.70 (£148.50) Trio Not won; £528.30 to 7-00 Windsor 10/6/96 OWNER Mr M. G. Rogers (JEVINGTON) BRED E. and Mrs Hanley

**OFFICIAL EXPLANATION Scenic Dancer: was reluctant to leave the stalls and was tailed off in the early stages.**

**Soojama (IRE)**, over a trip short of his best, wore blinkers for the first time since 1993 and these had a considerable effect. (16/1)

**Make a Stand**, who ran up a hat-trick over hurdles last month, swept through towards the centre of the track to dispute the lead, but then could not quicken again to hold the winner. (9/2)

**Sloe Brandy**, starting from her fourth different stable in four starts, looked fit but got warm. Quickening clear at halfway, her stamina gave out approaching the final furlong. She is certainly worth bearing in mind. (33/1)

**752 Cheveley Dancer (USA)**, as has so often been the case, was doing his best work when the race was over. (33/1)

**1696 Augustan** is struggling to recapture his best form of last year, on which he would now be very well handicapped. (11/1: 7/1-12/1)

**898 Charlie Bigtime**, a poor mover, stayed on well towards the finish but too late to do much damage. (16/1)

## 1804 CECIL BOYD ROCHFORT MAIDEN STKS (3-Y.O) (Class D)

7-05 (7-11) **1m 2f (July)** £4,542.00 (£1,356.00: £648.00: £294.00) Stalls: Low GOING minus 0.52 sec per fur (F)

SP RR SF

1508$^{4}$ **Akhla (USA)** (HRACecil) **3-8-11** PatEddery(9) (hld up: hdwy 3f out: led ins fnl f: rdn out) ....— **1** 11/10$^{1}$ 86 42
**Dancing Debut** (JHMGosden) **3-8-11** LDettori(10) (b.hind: trckd ldrs: nt clr run wl over 1f out: plld out & r.o fnl f) ....1¼ **2** 10/1 84 40
1409$^{3}$ **Berenice (80)** (GWragg) **3-8-11** MHills(6) (hdwy 3f out: led over 1f out: sn hdd & no ex) ....nk **3** 8/1$^{3}$ 84 40
**Lady Lucre (IRE)** (MRStoute) **3-8-11** KBradshaw(1) (leggy: hld up: hdwy & n.m.r wl over 1f out: no imp) ....4 **4** 33/1 77 33
1359$^{4}$ **Heart** (MRStoute) **3-8-11** JReid(4) (trckd ldr: led 3f out: edgd rt & hdd over 1f out: sn btn) ....nk **5** 5/1$^{2}$ 77 33
957$^{7}$ **Dear Life (USA)** (MrsJCecil) **3-8-11** TIves(11) (led over 5f) ....1¾ **6** 20/1 74 30
**Veiled Dancer (IRE)** (JLDunlop) **3-8-11** KDarley(3) (lw: hld up: hdwy over 3f out: no imp appr fnl f) ....nk **7** 14/1 73 29
**Adelaide (IRE)** (LMCumani) **3-8-11** OUrbina(5) (scope: bit bkwd: hld up: effrt over 3f out: nvr nr to chal) ....1½ **8** 20/1 71 27

| | | | | SP | RR | SF |
|---|---|---|---|---|---|---|
| 1180[6] | **Dalwhinnie** (JWHills) **3-8-11** RHills(8) (plld hrd: prom 6f) | 1¾ | **9** | 14/1 | 68 | 24 |
| 957[5] | **Aethra (USA)** (LadyHerries) **3-8-11b[1]** PRobinson(7) (plld hrd: prom: rdn over 1f out: sn wknd) | 2 | **10** | 5/1[2] | 65 | 21 |
| 1515[10] | **Classic Affair (USA) (62)** (RHarris) **3-8-11** DBatteate(2) (prom: led over 4f out to 3f out: sn wknd) | 4 | **11** | 33/1 | 59 | 15 |
| | | | | (SP 129.9%) | **11 Rn** | |

**2m 6.48** (1.48) CSF £14.39 TOTE £2.20: £1.30 £1.90 £2.30 (£7.10) Trio £40.90 OWNER Mr L. Marinopoulos (NEWMARKET) BRED John C. and Mrs Mabee

STEWARDS' ENQUIRY Obj. to Akhla (USA) by Dettori overruled.

**1508 Akhla (USA)** went to post rather too freely and had to win what was probably an ordinary maiden. Now she is off the mark, she ought to progress. (11/10: op 2/1)

**Dancing Debut**, lightly-made, was done no favours by Heart in the Dip, but stayed on well once seeing daylight. Her pilot erroneously objected to the winner. (10/1: op 6/1)

**1409 Berenice** moved down keenly and this is probably her trip as she looked dangerous until inside the final furlong. (8/1: 6/1-10/1)

**Lady Lucre (IRE)**, only seriously put to work in the last quarter-mile, lacked the pace to take a hand but will improve on this debut effort, probably over further. (33/1)

**1359 Heart** tried to go for home early, but was looking short of pace when briefly coming off a true line and causing the runner-up problems. (5/1: 3/1-6/1)

**826 Dear Life (USA)** moved down keenly and did not have the pace to prove dangerous once her lead had gone. (20/1)

**Veiled Dancer (IRE)** (14/1: 6/1-16/1)

**1180 Dalwhinnie** (14/1: 7/1-16/1)

**957 Aethra (USA)**, tried in blinkers, flatly refused to settle either in the race or on the way to post. (5/1: 5/2-11/2)

## 1805 NGK SPARK PLUGS H'CAP (0-80) (3-Y.O) (Class D)

7-35 (7-37) **6f (July)** £4,659.00 (£1,392.00: £666.00: £303.00) Stalls: Low GOING minus 0.29 sec per fur (GF)

| | | | | SP | RR | SF |
|---|---|---|---|---|---|---|
| 1101[12] | **Faith Alone (61)** (CFWall) **3-8-4** GDuffield(3) (lw: prom: led over 1f out: rdn out) | — | **1** | 20/1 | 71 | 39 |
| 812[7] | **Galine (75)** (WAO'Gorman) **3-9-4** EmmaO'Gorman(5) (trckd ldrs: ev ch 1f out: unable qckn) | ¾ | **2** | 4/1[3] | 83 | 51 |
| 1693* | **Jerry Cutrona (IRE) (72)** (NACallaghan) **3-9-1** 6x JFEgan(6) (lw: hld up: hdwy & edgd lft over 1f out: one pce fnl f) | 1½ | **3** | 6/4[1] | 76 | 44 |
| 1340* | **Enchanted Guest (IRE) (73)** (PWHarris) **3-9-2** GHind(8) (lw: raced alone centre: prom: led 3f out tl over 1f out: wknd ins fnl f) | s.h | **4** | 3/1[2] | 77 | 45 |
| 1485[6] | **Playmaker (78)** (MAJarvis) **3-9-7** PRobinson(7) (b.off hind: hld up: effrt 2f out: nvr trbld ldrs) | 8 | **5** | 9/1 | 61 | 29 |
| 1181[13] | **Jubilee Place (IRE) (70)** (TThomsonJones) **3-8-13** PaulEddery(4) (b: w ldr tl wknd over 2f out) | 7 | **6** | 12/1 | 34 | 2 |
| 539[6] | **Beldray Park (IRE) (70)** (MrsALMKing) **3-8-13** JQuinn(1) (in tch tl rdn & btn over 2f out) | 2½ | **7** | 20/1 | 27 | — |
| 824[11] | **Shontaine (71)** (MJohnston) **3-9-0** MHills(2) (lw: led 3f) | s.h | **8** | 16/1 | 28 | — |
| | | | | (SP 118.1%) | **8 Rn** | |

**1m 13.83** (1.83) CSF £93.31 CT £178.76 TOTE £16.90: £2.90 £1.80 £1.60 (£40.60) OWNER Mrs R. M. S. Neave (NEWMARKET) BRED J. R. Mitchell

**Faith Alone**, arguably a good thing for this on All-Weather form, had shown nothing in three previous turf runs. (20/1)

**692* Galine**, back at six furlongs, did nothing wrong but found one too good. (4/1)

**1693* Jerry Cutrona (IRE)** moved down well and again settled but, asked to make his move, did not find as much as three days ago and hung towards the far rail. He is a hard horse to predict but may be suited by racing against a right-hand rail. (6/4)

**1340* Enchanted Guest (IRE)**, a poor mover, raced alone in the centre of the course and showed plenty of speed. (3/1)

**1485 Playmaker**, restrained off the pace, stayed on when let down but without really quickening. Blazing a trail was his game last year and he has yet to try those tactics this season. (9/1)

**Jubilee Place (IRE)** won her races last year from the front and, unable to establish a definite advantage, was among the first beaten. (12/1)

## 1806 WALTER EARL (S) STKS (3-Y.O) (Class E)

8-05 (8-06) **1m (July)** £3,785.00 (£1,130.00: £540.00: £245.00) Stalls: Low GOING minus 0.29 sec per fur (GF)

| | | | | SP | RR | SF |
|---|---|---|---|---|---|---|
| 1310[3] | **Linda's Joy (IRE)** (RGuest) **3-8-6b** PBloomfield(5) (swtg: hld up: hdwy 2f out: led 1f out: all out) | — | **1** | 8/1 | 65 | 5 |
| *515[7]* | **Home Cookin' (57)** (DrJDScargill) **3-8-6** LDettori(3) (swtg: chsd ldrs: ev ch over 2f out: nt qckn nr fin) | nk | **2** | 11/2[3] | 64 | 4 |
| | **Titchwell Lass** (JEBanks) **3-8-3**(3) JStack(1) (neat: unf: hdwy 5f out: styd on fnl f: nrst fin) | nk | **3** | 10/1 | 64 | 4 |
| 1526[7] | **My Kind (45)** (NTinkler) **3-8-6** JQuinn(10) (chsd ldrs: one pce fnl 2f) | 5 | **4** | 16/1 | 54 | — |
| 1535* | **Corniche Quest (IRE) (52)** (MRChannon) **3-8-11** PatEddery(4) (lw: trckd ldrs: rdn to ld over 2f out: hdd 1f out: found nil) | 2 | **5** | 9/4[1] | 55 | — |
| *131[8]* | **Balpare (56)** (NACallaghan) **3-8-6** GDuffield(9) (b.off hind: hld up & plld hrd: effrt over 2f out: no imp) | 1 | **6** | 6/1 | 48 | — |
| 1089[13] | **Shermood (52)** (KTIvory) **3-8-1**(5) MartinDwyer(7) (lw: chsd ldr over 5f: wknd over 1f out) | 2½ | **7** | 20/1 | 43 | — |
| *1456[2]* | **Danico (57)** (SCWilliams) **3-9-2** KDarley(8) (in tch over 5f) | 3 | **8** | 4/1[2] | 47 | — |
| 1497[10] | **Classic Victory (63)** (RHarris) **3-8-11hb** AMackay(2) (led over 5f: sn wknd) | 8 | **9** | 16/1 | 26 | — |
| *460[7]* | **Casino Chip (42)** (TTClement) **3-8-11** KMarks(6) (b: lw: plld hrd: prom 4f: sn bhd) | 17 | **10** | 40/1 | — | — |
| | | | | (SP 119.6%) | **10 Rn** | |

**1m 43.37** (6.17) CSF £49.00 TOTE £8.40: £1.90 £1.70 £2.70 (£35.40) Trio £208.60; £14.69 to 7-00 Windsor 10/6/96 OWNER Mr M. G. Hill (NEWMARKET) BRED E. O'Leary

Sold MPipe 6,700 gns; Home Cookin' clmd MPipe £8,000

**1310 Linda's Joy (IRE)** swished her tail furiously early in the race, but battled on well enough to put her head in front. She will continue for the all-conquering Pipe team. (8/1)

**Home Cookin'** had the advantage of the rail in a driving finish, but could not make it pay. (11/2: 4/1-6/1)

**Titchwell Lass** moved to post nicely but got stirred up in the stalls. Staying on better than any in the final furlong after looking well held, her turn should come. (10/1: 6/1-14/1)

**1526 My Kind** ran her best race of the year, but will struggle to find a much easier opportunity. (16/1)

**1535* Corniche Quest (IRE)** appeared to get this trip down the hill at Brighton but certainly did not get home here, folding tamely on meeting the rising ground. (9/4)

**Balpare**, off since January, was held up for a late effort which came to very little. (6/1: op 3/1)

## 1807 BAILEYS IRISH CREAM LIQUEUR H'CAP (0-90) (3-Y.O+) (Class C)

8-35 (8-35) **1m (July)** £8,155.00 (£2,440.00: £1,170.00: £535.00) Stalls: Low GOING minus 0.29 sec per fur (GF)

| | | | | SP | RR | SF |
|---|---|---|---|---|---|---|
| 1126[5] | **Mawingo (IRE) (69)** (GWragg) **3-8-1** JQuinn(1) (lw: hld up & plld hrd: hdwy & squeezed thro over 1f out: sn led: rdn out) | — | **1** | 3/1[2] | 80 | 29 |

| | | | SP | RR | SF |
|---|---|---|---|---|---|
| 876[2] | **Master Charter (76)** (MrsJRRamsden) **4-9-5** KFallon(7) (lw: trckd ldrs: edgd lft & led over 1f out: sn hdd & no ex) 1½ | **2** | 11/4[1] | 84 | 44 |
| | **Insatiable (IRE) (85)** (MRStoute) **3-9-3** JReid(10) (lw: hld up: hdwy 3f out: r.o fnl f) 1½ | **3** | 4/1[3] | 90+ | 39 |
| 1625* | **Saifan (78)** (DMorris) **7-9-7b** CHodgson(4) (s.i.s: rdn 4f out: styng on whn edgd lft fnl f) ½ | **4** | 7/1 | 82 | 42 |
| 1469[3] | **Classic Leader (78)** (RHarris) **3-8-10b[1]** AMackay(9) (hld up: hdwy 2f out: no ex ins fnl f) 1¾ | **5** | 25/1 | 79 | 28 |
| 1528[5] | **Mountgate (74)** (MPBielby) **4-9-3** DRMcCabe(6) (hld up & plld hrd: effrt 2f out: no imp) 1¼ | **6** | 20/1 | 72 | 32 |
| 1412[11] | **Wild Palm (69)** (WAO'Gorman) **4-8-12b** EmmaO'Gorman(2) (lw: dwlt: sn prom: wknd over 1f out) 3 | **7** | 25/1 | 61 | 21 |
| 1506[5] | **Cim Bom Bom (IRE) (70)** (MBell) **4-8-13** PatEddery(8) (led over 5f out tl over 1f out: sn wknd) nk | **8** | 12/1 | 61 | 21 |
| *132[13]* | **Toujours Riviera (84)** (JPearce) **6-9-13** GBardwell(5) (plld hrd: prom: wkng whn hmpd over 1f out) 4 | **9** | 16/1 | 67 | 27 |
| 1088[7] | **Bentico (65)** (MrsNMacauley) **7-8-8** PBloomfield(3) (led over 2f: wknd 2f out) 2½ | **10** | 25/1 | 43 | 3 |
| 1449[23] | **Risky Romeo (64)** (GCBravery) **4-8-7** MHills(11) (rel to race: a t.o) 20 | **11** | 14/1 | 2 | — |
| | | | (SP 120.7%) | **11 Rn** | |

**1m 40.39** (3.19) CSF £11.51 CT £29.36 TOTE £4.10: £1.90 £1.70 £2.00 (£5.50) Trio £9.20 OWNER Mrs Claude Lilley (NEWMARKET) BRED Miss Geraldine Browne

WEIGHT FOR AGE 3yo-11lb

**1126 Mawingo (IRE)**, in a much easier race than last time, moved down well and showed good battling qualities when the chips were down. (3/1: op 9/2)

**876 Master Charter** moved to post quite dreadfully, but this would seem to be his way as he still ran a sound race. (11/4)

**Insatiable (IRE)** took a good hold going to post but moved smoothly through the field when initially let down. His head carriage again did not entirely impress in the last furlong, although he stayed on well and he ought to stay another quarter-mile. (4/1: op 5/2)

**1625* Saifan** walked around the paddock with his ears flat back and missed the break, but still ran respectably off a 6lb higher mark than last time, beaten only by three improving types. (7/1)

**1469 Classic Leader**, tried in blinkers, came through late in the race and was not unduly punished as his measure was taken. His Leicester form took a real knock at Epsom a day earlier, and he probably needs some help from the Handicapper. (25/1)

**1528 Mountgate** needs a faster-run race than this to make his turn of foot effective. (20/1)

## 1808 FRANK BUTTERS MAIDEN STKS (2-Y.O F) (Class D)

9-05 (9-05) **6f (July)** £4,386.00 (£1,308.00: £624.00: £282.00) Stalls: Low GOING minus 0.29 sec per fur (GF)

| | | | SP | RR | SF |
|---|---|---|---|---|---|
| 1413[2] | **Hakkaniyah** (DMorley) **2-8-11** RHills(5) (lw: hld up: hdwy to ld over 1f out: drew clr fnl f: easily) — | **1** | 11/10[1] | 62+ | — |
| | **Hen Harrier** (JLDunlop) **2-8-11** KDarley(4) (unf: trckd ldr: ev ch over 1f out: one pce) 3 | **2** | 11/4[2] | 54 | — |
| | **Leitrim Lodge (IRE)** (NACallaghan) **2-8-11** LDettori(3) (leggy: hld up: hdwy over 1f out: no ex ins fnl) 1 | **3** | 3/1[3] | 51 | — |
| | **Baby Jane** (RGuest) **2-8-11** MWigham(1) (leggy: unf: bit bkwd: chsd ldrs: kpt on ins fnl f) hd | **4** | 12/1 | 51 | — |
| | **Rock Fantasy** (CMurray) **2-8-11** CHodgson(2) (leggy: scope: led over 4f: sn wknd) 1½ | **5** | 33/1 | 47 | — |
| | | | (SP 109.9%) | **5 Rn** | |

**1m 19.4** (7.40) CSF £4.34 TOTE £2.30: £2.00 £1.60 (£2.70) OWNER Mr Hamdan Al Maktoum (NEWMARKET) BRED Shadwell Estate Company Limited

**1413 Hakkaniyah** dismissed an ordinary-looking bunch in considerable style and this will have done her nothing but good. (11/10: 4/5-5/4)

**Hen Harrier** has stamina in her pedigree and ran as well as could have been hoped given that the race developed into a two-furlong sprint. (11/4: 2/1-3/1)

**Leitrim Lodge (IRE)**, a short-backed newcomer, was in last place when the race proper started and never looked like making up the leeway. (3/1)

**Baby Jane** needs very much further on pedigree and should leave this behind in time. (12/1: 10/1-16/1)

**Rock Fantasy** set a steady pace but was the first in trouble when the race finally started. (33/1)

T/Plpt: £164.90 (78.35 Tckts). T/Qdpt: £22.10 (28.48 Tckts). Dk

# 1601-WOLVERHAMPTON (L-H) (Standard)

## Saturday June 8th

WEATHER: fine

## 1809 SURCINGLE MAIDEN H'CAP (0-70) (3-Y.O+) (Class E)

7-00 (7-02) **7f (Fibresand)** £3,206.70 (£957.60: £457.80: £207.90) Stalls: High GOING minus 0.19 sec per fur (FST)

| | | | SP | RR | SF |
|---|---|---|---|---|---|
| 962[6] | **Oberon's Dart (IRE) (66)** (PJMakin) **3-9-4** AClark(5) (a.p: led over 3f out: r.o wl) — | **1** | 7/2[2] | 71 | 43 |
| *1719[2]* | **La Tansani (IRE) (66)** (RHannon) **3-9-4** SSanders(12) (lw: hld up: hdwy over 3f out: rdn over 1f out: styd on same pce) 2 | **2** | 5/2[1] | 66 | 38 |
| 1617[3] | **Beau Bruno (76)** (MBell) **3-9-7**(7) GFaulkner(2) (trckd ldrs: rdn over 1f out: unable qckn) ¾ | **3** | 15/2[3] | 75 | 47 |
| 1416[16] | **Rustic Song (IRE) (44)** (JWharton) **3-7-10** FNorton(1) (swtg: chsd ldrs: ev ch over 2f out: wknd appr fnl f) 7 | **4** | 25/1 | 27 | — |
| 1539[8] | **Nkapen Rocks (SPA) (64)** (CaptJWilson) **3-9-2** GCarter(7) (lw: hld up: hdwy over 2f out: wknd fnl f) s.h | **5** | 16/1 | 47 | 19 |
| *1085[7]* | **Ring the Chief (38)** (MDIUsher) **4-8-0** NAdams(11) (b: nvr nr to chal) 2½ | **6** | 8/1 | 15 | — |
| 1319[11] | **Le Bam Bam (65)** (HAkbary) **4-9-13** DBiggs(3) (led: hdd over 3f out: wknd over 1f out) 2 | **7** | 14/1 | 37 | 19 |
| *387[4]* | **Taniyar (FR) (42)** (RHollinshead) **4-8-4** NCarlisle(6) (prom over 3f) 1 | **8** | 14/1 | 12 | — |
| 1506[9] | **Duralock Fencer (52)** (PGMurphy) **3-8-1**(3)ow2 SDrowne(4) (nvr trbld ldrs) ¾ | **9** | 16/1 | 20 | — |
| 1500[10] | **Polish Saga (51)** (MDods) **3-8-3** LCharnock(9) (prom: rdn over 3f out: grad lost pl) 1¼ | **10** | 9/1 | 17 | — |
| 1539[6] | **Boundary Bird (IRE) (52)** (MJohnston) **3-8-4b** AMcGlone(10) (prom: rdn over 3f out: wknd 2f out) 5 | **11** | 9/1 | 6 | — |
| 1642[19] | **Bold Time Monkey (34)** (MTate) **5-7-3**(7) JFowle(8) (dwlt: a outpcd) 1¼ | **12** | 50/1 | — | — |
| | | | (SP 124.6%) | **12 Rn** | |

**1m 28.4** (3.70) CSF £12.76 CT £59.99 TOTE £4.70: £1.90 £1.30 £3.20 (£4.40) Trio £10.60 OWNER Mr Peter Wragg (MARLBOROUGH) BRED Ballysheehan Stud

LONG HANDICAP Rustic Song (IRE) 7-8 Bold Time Monkey 6-10

WEIGHT FOR AGE 3yo-10lb

**Oberon's Dart (IRE)**, who has been gelded, won with a little more in hand than the verdict suggests on this his first venture into handicap company. (7/2: op 6/1)

**1719 La Tansani (IRE)** seems to be having trouble finding a trip that suits. (5/2)

**1617 Beau Bruno** came there nearly running away but found precious little when off the bridle. (15/2)

**Le Bam Bam** (14/1: 10/1-20/1)

**638 Polish Saga** (9/1: 6/1-10/1)

## 1810 SADDLE CLAIMING STKS (3-Y.O+) (Class F)

7-30 (7-31) **7f (Fibresand)** £2,381.00 (£656.00: £311.00) Stalls: High GOING minus 0.19 sec per fur (FST)

| | | | | SP | RR | SF |
|---|---|---|---|---|---|---|
| 1406[4] | **High Premium (77)** (RAFahey) **8-9-11** ACulhane(3) (sn outpcd: hdwy over 2f out: styd on to ld wl ins fnl f) | — | 1 | 5/4[1] | 88 | 56 |
| 1412[13] | **Cretan Gift (87)** (NPLittmoden) **5-9-11v** TGMcLaughlin(2) (trckd ldrs: outpcd 3f out: rallied & ev ch ins fnl f: kpt on) | ½ | 2 | 9/4[2] | 87 | 55 |
| *1094[4]* | **Palacegate Touch (75)** (JBerry) **6-9-9v** GCarter(7) (prom: led over 5f out: clr 3f out: wknd & hdd ins fnl f) | 5 | 3 | 3/1[3] | 73 | 41 |
| 1677[6] | **Dancing Heart (72)** (BJMeehan) **4-9-11b** MTebbutt(6) (lw: chsd ldrs tl rdn & wknd over 2f out) | 16 | 4 | 7/1 | 39 | 7 |
| | **Trouble's Brewing** (PRWebber) **5-8-8** RPerham(5) (s.i.s: sn prom: wknd over 3f out) | 3 | 5 | 66/1 | 15 | — |
| *1460[10]* | **All Apologies (IRE) (51)** (RHollinshead) **4-8-6**(5) FLynch(1) (led: hdd over 5f out: wknd over 2f out) | nk | 6 | 20/1 | 17 | — |
| 1435[13] | **Celtic Lady** (MrsNMacauley) **5-8-5**(3) CTeague(4) (b: s.i.s: a outpcd) | dist | 7 | 66/1 | — | — |
| | | | | (SP 120.5%) | **7 Rn** | |

**1m 27.8** (3.10) CSF £4.80 TOTE £2.40: £1.40 £1.80 (£3.00) OWNER Mr J. C. Parsons (MALTON) BRED M.E Wates

**1406 High Premium** finds this trip plenty short enough. (5/4)

**956 Cretan Gift**, who has done all his winning over shorter trips, seemed to last this out. (9/4)

**1094 Palacegate Touch** looked to have stolen this, but folded tamely in the latter stages. (3/1)

## 1811 CYRIL TERRY 60TH BIRTHAY H'CAP (0-75) (3-Y.O+) (Class D)

8-00 (8-02) **1m 1f 79y (Fibresand)** £3,915.00 (£1,170.00: £560.00: £255.00) Stalls: Low GOING minus 0.19 sec per fur (FST)

| | | | | SP | RR | SF |
|---|---|---|---|---|---|---|
| 1464[3] | **Mr Teigh (67)** (BSmart) **4-9-6** MTebbutt(6) (chsd ldr: rdn over 1f out: styd on to ld nr fin) | — | 1 | 20/1 | 76 | 58 |
| 1674* | **Three Arch Bridge (62)** (MJohnston) **4-9-1b** 5x JWeaver(4) (lw: led: rdn over 1f out: hdd nr fin) | 1 | 2 | 3/1[1] | 69 | 51 |
| 1418[12] | **Super High (75)** (PHowling) **4-10-0b[1]** FNorton(9) (hld up in tch: outpcd over 2f out: r.o ins fnl f) | 2½ | 3 | 16/1 | 78 | 60 |
| *1602[2]* | **Field of Vision (IRE) (71)** (MrsASwinbank) **6-9-5**(5) FLynch(1) (hld up: r.o appr fnl f: nvr nrr) | 2½ | 4 | 5/1[3] | 70 | 52 |
| *1457** | **Penmar (60)** (TJEtherington) **4-8-13** LCharnock(3) (lw: trckd ldrs: rdn over 3f out: r.o one pce fnl 2f) | 2 | 5 | 9/1 | 55 | 37 |
| *1602[4]* | **David James' Girl (54)** (ABailey) **4-8-4**(3) DWright(10) (mid div: rdn 5f out: nvr able to chal) | 1 | 6 | 12/1 | 48 | 30 |
| 1704[2] | **Wentbridge Lad (IRE) (68)** (PDEvans) **6-9-7v** SSanders(8) (lw: hmpd s: hld up: hdwy 4f out: wknd 2f out) | 2½ | 7 | 7/2[2] | 57 | 39 |
| | **Ayunli (66)** (SCWilliams) **5-9-5** GCarter(2) (chsd ldrs 6f) | 5 | 8 | 12/1 | 47 | 29 |
| *1456** | **Dragonjoy (65)** (JWPayne) **3-8-6b** AMcGlone(11) (lw: hld up: hdwy 6f out: wknd over 3f out) | 1¼ | 9 | 8/1 | 44 | 14 |
| 508[10] | **Able Choice (IRE) (73)** (RWArmstrong) **6-9-12** RPrice(7) (sn pushed along & bhd: a in rr) | 15 | 10 | 12/1 | 26 | 8 |
| *1602[3]* | **Chevalier (USA) (70)** (ICampbell) **4-9-9v** AClark(5) (prom 6f) | dist | 11 | 8/1 | — | — |
| | | | | (SP 129.8%) | **11 Rn** | |

**1m 59.5** (3.50) CSF £82.19 CT £960.07 TOTE £29.20: £7.80 £1.40 £4.60 (£39.00) Trio £223.60; £220.45 to 7-00 Windsor 10/6/96 OWNER Mrs Hannah McAuliffe (LAMBOURN) BRED K. G. Bridges

WEIGHT FOR AGE 3yo-12lb

**1464 Mr Teigh** can progress now that connections have found that he does stay. (20/1)

**1674* Three Arch Bridge**, who races in a pricker, made a valiant attempt to land the three-timer within a week but, racing on the slower ground on the inside, was just run out of it. (3/1)

**Super High**, equipped with first-time blinkers, put in some sterling late work. (16/1)

**1602 Field of Vision (IRE)** was given plenty to do. (5/1)

**1602 David James' Girl** (12/1: op 8/1)

**1704 Wentbridge Lad (IRE)** again proved a disappointment here. Previously a six times course winner, it may be that he has had enough of Wolverhampton for the time being. (7/2)

## 1812 EXPRESS AND STAR H'CAP (0-70) (3-Y.O+) (Class E)

8-30 (8-32) **6f (Fibresand)** £3,015.60 (£898.80: £428.40: £193.20) Stalls: Low GOING minus 0.19 sec per fur (FST)

| | | | | SP | RR | SF |
|---|---|---|---|---|---|---|
| *1606[3]* | **Wardara (58)** (CADwyer) **4-8-11v**(5) FLynch(3) (dwlt: hdwy over 2f out: r.o to ld nr fin) | — | 1 | 7/1[3] | 66 | 46 |
| *1606[2]* | **Klipspinger (64)** (BSRothwell) **3-9-0v[1]** MFenton(11) (a.p: led over 1f out: hdd nr fin) | hd | 2 | 5/1[1] | 72 | 44 |
| *1604[2]* | **Four of Spades (70)** (PDEvans) **5-9-9v**(5) AmandaSanders(9) (mid div: r.o appr fnl f: nt pce to chal) | 5 | 3 | 5/1[1] | 64 | 44 |
| 1412[8] | **Tymeera (58)** (BPalling) **3-8-8** TSprake(8) (a.p: rdn over 1f out: no imp) | ¾ | 4 | 20/1 | 50 | 22 |
| *1460** | **Jigsaw Boy (67)** (PGMurphy) **7-9-8**(3) SDrowne(7) (nvr nrr) | 2½ | 5 | 11/2[2] | 53 | 33 |
| 1635[8] | **Globe Runner (60)** (JJO'Neill) **3-8-10** JWeaver(12) (nvr trbld ldrs) | nk | 6 | 20/1 | 45 | 17 |
| *1492[11]* | **Scored Again (60)** (MJHeaton-Ellis) **6-9-4** AClark(10) (lw: b: led over 2f: wknd wl over 1f out) | s.h | 7 | 14/1 | 45 | 25 |
| 1624[4] | **Twice Purple (IRE) (56)** (BJMeehan) **4-9-0b** MTebbutt(5) (chsd ldrs: rdn over 1f out: r.o one pce) | s.h | 8 | 8/1 | 41 | 21 |
| *1606** | **Newington Butts (IRE) (52)** (KMcAuliffe) **6-8-10e** SSanders(1) (chsd ldrs: rdn 2f out: sn btn) | 4 | 9 | 8/1 | 26 | 6 |
| 1765[5] | **Lord Sky (67)** (ABailey) **5-9-4**(7) AngelaGallimore(6) (led over 3f out: hdd over 1f out: wknd ins fnl) | ½ | 10 | 12/1 | 40 | 20 |
| 1423[16] | **Souperficial (65)** (JAGlover) **5-9-9v** SDWilliams(2) (bhd: hdwy ½-wy: wknd over 1f out) | 3½ | 11 | 8/1 | 28 | 8 |
| 1642[9] | **Komlucky (39)** (ABMulholland) **4-7-11b** NAdams(4) (sn rdn along: outpcd fr ½-wy) | ½ | 12 | 9/1 | 1 | — |
| | | | | (SP 128.4%) | **12 Rn** | |

**1m 14.1** (2.70) CSF £42.52 CT £182.02 TOTE £9.90: £3.30 £2.40 £1.70 (£26.10) Trio £33.00 OWNER Binding Matters Ltd (NEWMARKET) BRED G. B. Turnbull Ltd

WEIGHT FOR AGE 3yo-8lb

**1606 Wardara** came from last to first and may well be suited by another furlong. (7/1)

**1606 Klipspinger**, with the first-time visor, did nothing wrong but was only just worried out of it. (5/1)

**1604 Four of Spades**, stepping down in trip, found these too sharp. (5/1)

**1460* Jigsaw Boy** (11/2: 4/1-6/1)

**Globe Runner**, who was well detached at halfway, did stay on once in line for home, and will be interesting when tackling trips in excess of a mile. (20/1)

## 1813 MARTINGALE (S) STKS (2-Y.O F) (Class G)

9-00 (9-02) **6f (Fibresand)** £2,208.00 (£608.00: £288.00) Stalls: Low GOING minus 0.19 sec per fur (FST)

| | | | | SP | RR | SF |
|---|---|---|---|---|---|---|
| *1720** | **Enchanting Eve** (CNAllen) **2-8-9**(5) LNewton(4) (mde all: qcknd clr over 1f out: impressive) | — | 1 | 5/2[2] | 70 | 27 |
| 1032[4] | **Shandana** (PCHaslam) **2-8-9** JWeaver(3) (chsd wnr: rdn 2f out: sn outpcd) | 4 | 2 | 6/1 | 54 | 11 |
| 1404[6] | **Perfect Bliss** (PDEvans) **2-8-6**(3) SDrowne(1) (w wnr: rdn 2f out: r.o one pce) | ¾ | 3 | 5/1 | 52 | 9 |
| 1408[4] | **Come Too Mamma's** (JBerry) **2-9-0** GCarter(2) (hld up: hdwy over 2f out: sn rdn & outpcd) | ½ | 4 | 7/2[3] | 56 | 13 |
| 1494[2] | **Ginny Wossername** (WGMTurner) **2-8-9** TSprake(6) (chsd ldrs: rdn 2f out: sn outpcd) | 7 | 5 | 15/8[1] | 32 | — |

1459[5] **Classic Lady** (RHollinshead) **2-8-7**(5)ow3 DGriffiths(5) (trckd ldrs: outpcd fr ½-wy) ....17 **6** 33/1 — —
(SP 119.5%) **6 Rn**

**1m 15.4** (4.00) CSF £16.97 TOTE £2.70: £1.70 £2.10 (£11.40) OWNER Mr Alexander MacGillivray (NEWMARKET) BRED P. Young
Bt in 7,600 gns

**1720* Enchanting Eve** followed up her Southwell victory in emphatic style. (5/2: 7/4-11/4)
**1032 Shandana**, dropped into a seller, caught a real tartar in the winner and no doubt her astute trainer will place her to advantage. (6/1)
**1404 Perfect Bliss** was easily shaken off once in line for home. (5/1)
**1408 Come Too Mamma's**, stepping up in trip, raced keenly and looked a big danger a quarter of a mile out, but found nothing off the bridle. (7/2)

## 1814 GIRTH H'CAP (0-60) (3-Y.O) (Class F)

9-30 (9-31) **1m 6f 166y (Fibresand)** £2,381.00 (£656.00: £311.00) Stalls: High GOING minus 0.19 sec per fur (FST)

| | | | | SP | RR | SF |
|---|---|---|---|---|---|---|
| 912[3] | **Old School House (45)** (TJNaughton) **3-8-10** TSprake(3) (trckd ldrs: led over 3f out: sn clr) | — | **1** | 7/2[2] | 62 | 20 |
| *1605** | **Pearl Anniversary (IRE) (56)** (MJohnston) **3-9-7** JWeaver(10) (lw: hld up: hdwy 6f out: nvr able to chal) | 7 | **2** | 11/4[1] | 65 | 23 |
| 1415[8] | **Harbet House (FR) (55)** (CACyzer) **3-9-1**(5) FLynch(1) (hld up: hdwy to ld 4f out: sn hdd & outpcd) | 7 | **3** | 10/1 | 57 | 15 |
| *1081[7]* | **Glowing Reeds (45)** (CNAllen) **3-8-5**(5) LNewton(4) (led: hdd 5f out: sn wknd) | 5 | **4** | 16/1 | 41 | — |
| 1503[9] | **Diasafina (31)** (SCWilliams) **3-7-10b** LCharnock(7) (prom: led over 5f out: hdd 4f out: wknd over 2f out) | 4 | **5** | 11/1 | 23 | — |
| *1457[6]* | **Flash In The Pan (IRE) (52)** (MBell) **3-9-3** MFenton(2) (b: trckd ldrs: drvn along over 4f out: sn lost pl) | 3 | **6** | 9/1 | 41 | — |
| 1591[10] | **Shamand (USA) (51)** (BJMeehan) **3-9-2** MTebbutt(5) (mid div: drvn along ½-wy: sn lost tch) | nk | **7** | 8/1 | 40 | — |
| *899[11]* | **Balmoral Princess (31)** (JHPeacock) **3-7-10** NAdams(9) (prom: rdn & lost pl ½-wy: sn wl bhd) | 10 | **8** | 50/1 | 9 | — |
| 1584[3] | **Rattle (50)** (JJO'Neill) **3-9-1** SSanders(8) (mid div: lost pl ½-wy: sn bhd) | hd | **9** | 4/1[3] | 28 | — |
| 1325[9] | **Salsian (51)** (SCWilliams) **3-9-2** GCarter(6) (lw: chsd ldrs over 10f) | 12 | **10** | 14/1 | 16 | — |

(SP 121.9%) **10 Rn**

**3m 18.6** (11.20) CSF £13.63 CT £82.73 TOTE £4.70: £1.80 £1.10 £5.10 (£6.40) Trio £31.20 OWNER Just For The Crack Partnership (EPSOM) BRED Miss G. Abbey
LONG HANDICAP Balmoral Princess 7-5

**912 Old School House** ran out a very easy winner and was value for at least double the winning margin. Staying is clearly his forte. (7/2)
**1605* Pearl Anniversary (IRE)**, who has had to work hard to win a couple of sellers, was attempting the impossible task of giving weight to the winner. (11/4)
**Harbet House (FR)**, showing his first sign of form, was made to look leaden-footed in the final half-mile. (10/1: op 20/1)
**1584 Rattle** (4/1: op 6/1)

T/Plpt: £28.90 (267.68 Tckts). T/Qdpt: £16.90 (23.52 Tckts). CR

# 1790-EPSOM (L-H) (Good to firm, Firm patches)

## Sunday June 9th

WEATHER: warm & sunny WIND: mod half against

## 1815 ASTEC MEDIAN AUCTION CONDITIONS STKS (2-Y.O) (Class C)

2-00 (2-00) **6f** £6,801.00 (£2,381.00: £1,165.50: £502.50) Stalls: High GOING minus 0.36 sec per fur (F)

| | | | | SP | RR | SF |
|---|---|---|---|---|---|---|
| 1513* | **Supercal** (DRCElsworth) **2-8-6** KFallon(4) (s.s: hdwy to ld over 1f out: rdn out) | — | **1** | 2/1[1] | 64 | 17 |
| 1622* | **Magical Times** (RBoss) **2-9-1** LDettori(3) (chsd ldr: led over 2f out tl over 1f out: ev ch ins fnl f: r.o) | ½ | **2** | 2/1[1] | 72 | 25 |
| 643* | **Bettynouche** (RHannon) **2-8-10** RHughes(1) (lw: led over 3f: wknd over 1f out) | 5 | **3** | 11/4[2] | 53 | 6 |
| | **Last Chance** (GLewis) **2-8-8** PaulEddery(2) (str: hld up: 3rd & rdn whn bmpd on ins 2f out: wknd over 1f out) | 2 | **4** | 15/2[3] | 46 | — |

(SP 105.1%) **4 Rn**

**1m 10.91** (2.91) CSF £5.71 TOTE £2.90 (£2.70) OWNER The Caledonian Racing Society (WHITCOMBE) BRED Stetchworth Park Stud Ltd

**1513* Supercal**, who lost ground at the start, came with a good run on the outside of the field to strike the front approaching the final furlong and, ridden along, just managed to get the better of a real tussle with the runner-up. (2/1)
**1622* Magical Times** chased the leader until going on soon after halfway. Marginally collared below the distance, he refused to give way without a struggle and was only beaten in the last 50 yards. (2/1)
**643* Bettynouche** attempted to make all the running. Collared over two furlongs from home, she was brushed aside below the distance. (11/4)
**Last Chance**, a sturdy individual, had his tongue tied down for this debut and was very coltish in the paddock. Held up in third place, he was bumped against the rail a quarter of a mile out but this made little difference to his chances. (15/2: 3/1-8/1)

## 1816 TALKLAND LADIES' H'CAP (0-80) (4-Y.O+) (Class D)

2-35 (2-36) **1m 2f 18y** £7,197.50 (£2,180.00: £1,065.00: £507.50) Stalls: Low GOING minus 0.36 sec per fur (F)

| | | | | SP | RR | SF |
|---|---|---|---|---|---|---|
| 1618[9] | **Rising Dough (IRE) (65)** (GLMoore) **4-10-6**(5) MrsJMoore(4) (hdwy over 6f out: led over 1f out: r.o wl) | — | **1** | 12/1 | 75 | 63 |
| *108[3]* | **Hever Golf Lady (56)** (TJNaughton) **4-9-11**(5) MrsJNaughton(9) (b: a.p: rdn over 2f out: r.o ins fnl f) | 4 | **2** | 16/1 | 60 | 48 |
| 1102[2] | **Access Adventurer (IRE) (73)** (RBoss) **5-11-5** MissYHaynes(8) (led over 1f: led 2f out tl over 1f out: wknd fnl f) | 2 | **3** | 9/2[2] | 74 | 62 |
| 953[3] | **Carlito Brigante (75)** (MrsJRRamsden) **4-11-2**(5) MissERamsden(3) (lw: hdwy over 1f out: r.o) | ¾ | **4** | 4/1[1] | 74 | 62 |
| | **Amlah (USA) (65)** (PJHobbs) **4-10-11** MrsSHobbs(2) (nvr nr to chal) | hd | **5** | 10/1 | 64 | 52 |
| 1449[14] | **Don't Drop Bombs (USA) (40)** (DTThom) **7-9-0v** MissJFeilden(1) (lw: led over 8f out to 2f out: wknd 1f out) | 3½ | **6** | 9/1 | 34 | 22 |
| 1515[4] | **Norsong (53)** (RAkehurst) **4-9-13** MissJAllison(7) (b.nr fore: bhd fnl 3f) | 3½ | **7** | 6/1 | 41 | 29 |
| *216[8]* | **Yubralee (USA) (70)** (MCPipe) **4-11-2** MrsLPearce(6) (lw: bhd fnl 3f) | 2 | **8** | 10/1 | 55 | 43 |
| 1486[8] | **Domitia (USA) (72)** (MBell) **4-11-4** MrsAPerrett(5) (lw: a bhd) | 4 | **9** | 5/1[3] | 51 | 39 |

(SP 110.9%) **9 Rn**

**2m 8.0** (3.60) CSF £148.09 CT £873.46 TOTE £11.20: £2.60 £2.30 £2.00 (£60.00) Trio £111.80 OWNER Mr Bryan Pennick (EPSOM) BRED David John Brown
LONG HANDICAP Don't Drop Bombs (USA) 8-9

**Rising Dough (IRE)**, in third place by halfway, had a considerable amount of ground to make up on the front two in the straight. He gradually reeled them in though and, striking the front approaching the final furlong, soon pulled away. (12/1)
**Hever Golf Lady**, given a five-month break, was never far away but the front two then quickened entering the straight. Soon ridden along, she ran on inside the final furlong for second but was unable to get to the winner. (16/1)

**1102 Access Adventurer (IRE)**, the early leader, then raced in second place and, together with Don't Drop Bombs, pulled away from the rest of the field. Sent to the front a quarter of a mile from home, he was headed below the distance and soon capitulated. (9/2)
**953 Carlito Brigante**, racing at the back of the field, did all his best work in the last furlong and a half, but found it all over bar the shouting. (4/1)
**Amlah (USA)**, second over hurdles recently, raced at the back of the field and never threatened to get in a serious blow. (10/1)
**Don't Drop Bombs (USA)** was soon at the head of affairs and, together with Access Adventurer, pulled well clear of the remainder entering the straight. Collared a quarter of a mile out, he grimly tried to hold on, but had burnt his boats a furlong out. (9/1)
**1515 Norsong** (6/1: 4/1-13/2)
**1440 Domitia (USA)** was always at the back of the field and proved very disappointing. (5/1)

## 1817 MARTIN DAWES CONDITIONS STKS (3-Y.O+) (Class B)

3-10 (3-12) **1m 2f 18y** £12,486.00 (£4,674.00: £2,287.00: £985.00: £442.50: £225.50) Stalls: Low GOING minus 0.36 sec per fur (F)

| | | | | SP | RR | SF |
|---|---|---|---|---|---|---|
| | **Bal Harbour (106)** (HRACecil) **5-9-7** PatEddery(1) (lw: mde all: rdn out) | — | **1** | 5/2[1] | 111 | 77 |
| 1427[6] | **Yarob (IRE) (98)** (HThomsonJones) **3-8-4** RHills(5) (lw: hdwy on ins over 3f out: chsd wnr over 1f out: unable qckn) | 2 | **2** | 12/1 | 104 | 57 |
| 1079* | **Wot No Fax** (SDow) **3-8-4** SSanders(2) (lw: a.p: chsd wnr 4f out tl over 1f out: one pce) | 2 | **3** | 20/1 | 101 | 54 |
| 1120[2] | **Yom Jameel (IRE) (97)** (MRStoute) **3-8-4** PaulEddery(4) (lw: chsd wnr 6f: wknd over 1f out) | 2½ | **4** | 9/2[2] | 97 | 50 |
| 1015[6] | **Tawkil (USA) (102)** (BWHills) **3-8-4** MHills(7) (bhd fnl 3f) | 17 | **5** | 6/1 | 70 | 23 |
| 1509[7] | **Wayne County (IRE) (110)** (RAkehurst) **6-9-5** JWeaver(3) (lw: bhd fnl 3f) | 2 | **6** | 5/1[3] | 69 | 35 |
| | **Tarte Aux Pommes (USA)** (CEBrittain) **4-8-9** MRoberts(6) (hld up: rdn 4f out: sn wknd) | 4 | **7** | 6/1 | 52 | 18 |
| | | | | (SP 104.4%) | **7 Rn** | |

**2m 4.24** (-0.16) CSF £24.82 TOTE £2.90: £2.10 £4.90 (£22.60) OWNER Mr K. Abdulla (NEWMARKET) BRED Juddmonte Farms
WEIGHT FOR AGE 3yo-13lb

**Bal Harbour** made a very pleasing return to action. Adopting his usual front-running role, he was set alight in the straight and proved too strong for his rivals in the final quarter-mile. He is well up to landing a listed event to add to the one he secured as a juvenile. (5/2)
**1427 Yarob (IRE)** handled Tattenham Corner very well and moved up entering the straight. Sent into second approaching the final furlong, he was unable to reel in the winner. (12/1)
**1079* Wot No Fax** was taking a huge step up in class and, in the circumstances, ran really well. Moving into second rounding the Corner, he was collared for that position below the distance and could only plod on in his own time. (20/1)
**1120 Yom Jameel (IRE)**, in second place until Tattenham Corner, grimly tried to hold on but was left standing from below the distance. (9/2: op 3/1)
**1015 Tawkil (USA)** was getting left behind in the straight. (6/1)
**726 Wayne County (IRE)** ran a lifeless race and lost touch in the straight. This is the second bad race he has run in a row. (5/1: 3/1-11/2)

## 1818 VODAC 'DASH' RATED STKS H'CAP (0-105) (Listed) (3-Y.O+) (Class A)

3-40 (3-41) **5f** £25,180.80 (£9,427.20: £4,613.60: £1,988.00: £894.00: £456.40) Stalls: High GOING minus 0.36 sec per fur (F)

| | | | | SP | RR | SF |
|---|---|---|---|---|---|---|
| 1186* | **To the Roof (IRE) (91)** (PWHarris) **4-8-3** GHind(14) (lw: a.p: hrd rdn over 1f out: led last stride) | — | **1** | 6/1[1] | 98 | 60 |
| 1616[4] | **Lucky Parkes (96)** (JBerry) **6-8-8** JCarroll(6) (lw: a.p: led over 2f out: hrd rdn over 1f out: hdd last stride) | s.h | **2** | 11/1[3] | 103 | 65 |
| 1016[8] | **Crowded Avenue (96)** (PJMakin) **4-8-8** SSanders(5) (hdwy 2f out: rdn over 1f out: unable qckn) | 3 | **3** | 6/1[1] | 93 | 55 |
| 1146[5] | **Marl (91)** (RAkehurst) **3-7-10** JQuinn(10) (lost pl over 2f out: rallied fnl f: r.o) | hd | **4** | 16/1 | 88 | 43 |
| 1616[2] | **Double Quick (IRE) (102)** (MJohnston) **4-9-0** JWeaver(13) (a.p: 3rd & rdn whn n.m.r over 1f out: one pce) | 1 | **5** | 6/1[1] | 96 | 58 |
| 1616* | **Brave Edge (107)** (RHannon) **5-9-5** PatEddery(1) (hld up: rdn over 2f out: one pce) | s.h | **6** | 15/2[2] | 101 | 63 |
| 1332[7] | **That Man Again (98)** (GLewis) **4-8-10b** AWhelan(11) (lw: nvr nr to chal) | nk | **7** | 6/1[1] | 91 | 53 |
| 1321[5] | **Tarf (USA) (91)** (PTWalwyn) **3-7-10** LCharnock(9) (lw: a.p: rdn 2f out: one pce) | nk | **8** | 20/1 | 83 | 38 |
| 1107* | **Jayannpee (104)** (IABalding) **5-9-2** LDettori(8) (lw: hld up: rdn over 2f out: wknd over 1f out) | 1¼ | **9** | 6/1[1] | 92 | 54 |
| 1113[12] | **Mr Oscar (98)** (MJohnston) **4-8-10** MRoberts(12) (lw: s.s: stumbled over 3f out: bdly hmpd on ins over 2f out: a bhd) | ¾ | **10** | 15/2[2] | 83 | 45 |
| 1332[5] | **Wavian (97)** (RHannon) **4-8-9** RHughes(3) (a bhd) | s.h | **11** | 20/1 | 82 | 44 |
| 1501[10] | **Swynford Dream (91)** (JFBottomley) **3-7-10** AMackay(2) (led over 2f: wknd over 1f out) | 2½ | **12** | 50/1 | 68 | 23 |
| | | | | (SP 120.7%) | **12 Rn** | |

**54.21 secs** (-0.29) CSF £64.68 CT £387.28 TOTE £7.50: £1.90 £4.50 £2.40 (£59.90) Trio £247.90 OWNER Mrs P. W. Harris (BERKHAMSTED) BRED Pendley Farm
LONG HANDICAP To the Roof (IRE) 8-2 Tarf (USA) 7-8 Marl 7-9 Swynford Dream 7-3
WEIGHT FOR AGE 3yo-7lb

**1186* To the Roof (IRE)**, never far away, had a ding-dong battle for the lead from below the distance and managed to get up right on the line. (6/1)
**1616 Lucky Parkes**, the ultimate conditions race specialist, bounced back to form and failed by only a whisker to land her first handicap. Sent on at halfway, she had a tremendous battle with the winner from below the distance and only lost out right on the line. (11/1)
**Crowded Avenue** began to pick up ground a quarter of a mile out. Rousted along below the distance, he failed to reel in the front two. (6/1)
**1146 Marl**, who got rather outpaced at halfway, stayed on again in the final furlong and only just failed for third prize. (16/1)
**1616 Double Quick (IRE)**, winner of this race last year, was always handy but failed to quicken in the last two furlongs. (6/1)
**1616* Brave Edge** chased the leaders but, bustled along from halfway, could only go up and own in the same place. (15/2)
**1107* Jayannpee** chased the leaders until calling it a day below the distance. Six furlongs is probably his trip nowadays. (6/1)

## 1819 MAIL ON SUNDAY MILE H'CAP (Qualifier) (0-90) (3-Y.O+) (Class C)

4-10 (4-14) **1m 114y** £14,330.00 (£4,340.00: £2,120.00: £1,010.00) Stalls: Low GOING minus 0.36 sec per fur (F)

| | | | | SP | RR | SF |
|---|---|---|---|---|---|---|
| 1474[3] | **Mbulwa (55)** (RAFahey) **10-7-12** GCarter(2) (a.p: led 2f out: r.o wl) | — | **1** | 25/1 | 65 | 48 |
| 1354[9] | **Star Talent (USA) (82)** (MissGayKelleway) **5-9-11** KFallon(11) (b.hind: lw: stdy hdwy on ins 3f out: chsd wnr over 1f out: unable qckn) | 1¼ | **2** | 10/1[3] | 90 | 73 |
| 1528[2] | **Sandmoor Chambray (73)** (TDEasterby) **5-9-2** MBirch(16) (lw: rdn over 2f out: hdwy over 1f out: r.o wl ins fnl f) | 1 | **3** | 14/1 | 79 | 62 |
| 987[8] | **Proud Monk (77)** (GLMoore) **3-8-8** JWeaver(4) (gd hdwy over 1f out: str run fnl f: fin wl) | hd | **4** | 14/1 | 83 | 54 |
| 1406[6] | **Up in Flames (IRE) (71)** (MDHammond) **5-9-0** JQuinn(9) (rdn & hdwy over 2f out: unable qckn) | hd | **5** | 10/1[3] | 76 | 59 |
| 1330[4] | **Pay Homage (78)** (IABalding) **8-9-7** LDettori(12) (lw: rdn over 2f out: hdwy over 1f out: r.o ins fnl f) | 1¼ | **6** | 8/1[2] | 81 | 64 |
| 1018[10] | **Apollono (77)** (JRFanshawe) **4-9-6** JCarroll(5) (a.p: rdn over 2f out: wknd fnl f) | 1¾ | **7** | 10/1[3] | 77 | 60 |

| | | | | SP | RR | SF |
|---|---|---|---|---|---|---|
| 1609$^{8}$ | **Pride of Pendle (71)** (DNicholls) **7-9-0** AlexGreaves(13) (nvr nr to chal) | nk | **8** | 5/1$^{1}$ | 70 | 53 |
| 1593$^{4}$ | **Philosopher (IRE) (84)** (RHannon) **3-8-12**$^{(3)}$ DaneO'Neill(8) (prom over 4f) | nk | **9** | 16/1 | 83 | 54 |
| 1337$^{10}$ | **Greatest (60)** (RAkehurst) **5-8-3** SSanders(3) (chsd ldr: led over 3f out to 2f out: wknd over 1f out) | 1¼ | **10** | 11/1 | 56 | 39 |
| 1613* | **Seventeens Lucky (75)** (BobJones) **4-8-13**$^{(5)}$ LNewton(14) (lw: prom 7f) | nk | **11** | 8/1$^{2}$ | 71 | 54 |
| 1625$^{6}$ | **Deevee (69)** (CJBenstead) **7-8-12** PRobinson(17) (lw: a bhd) | 3½ | **12** | 14/1 | 58 | 41 |
| 1353$^{6}$ | **Summerhill Special (IRE) (64)** (MrsPNDutfield) **5-8-7** GBardwell(18) (bhd fnl 3f) | 2½ | **13** | 33/1 | 49 | 32 |
| 1051$^{4}$ | **Confronter (78)** (SDow) **7-9-7** MRoberts(15) (lw: bhd fnl 3f) | 1 | **14** | 14/1 | 61 | 44 |
| 1330$^{7}$ | **Sue's Return (79)** (APJarvis) **4-9-8** PatEddery(10) (a bhd) | ½ | **15** | 8/1$^{2}$ | 61 | 44 |
| 1613$^{9}$ | **Mislemani (IRE) (57)** (AGNewcombe) **6-8-0** DRMcCabe(1) (led 5f) | 1¼ | **16** | 25/1 | 36 | 19 |

(SP 128.8%) **16 Rn**

**1m 42.5** (0.50) CSF £243.27 CT £3,471.02 TOTE £63.40: £10.50 £3.10 £5.70 £4.40 (£386.90) Trio £1,102.70 OWNER Northumbria Leisure Ltd (MALTON) BRED Hascombe and Valiant Studs

WEIGHT FOR AGE 3yo-12lb

**1474 Mbulwa** made the long journey down from the North pay off. Always in a handy position, he went on a quarter of a mile out and kept up the gallop too well for his rivals. (25/1)

**1354 Star Talent (USA)**, who failed to handle the mud at Goodwood last time out, was far happier on this fast ground. Steadily creeping into the action early in the straight, he moved into second place below the distance but failed to reel in the winner. (10/1)

**1528 Sandmoor Chambray** ran on really strongly in the last furlong and a half, but found the line always beating him. (14/1)

**646 Proud Monk** raced at the back of the field and was still there a quarter of a mile from home. He went into overdrive though below the distance, and sprouted wings in the final furlong, only to find the line coming too soon. (14/1)

**1406 Up in Flames (IRE)**, pushed along to take closer order over two furlongs from home, then failed to find that vital turn of foot. (10/1)

**1330 Pay Homage** stayed on in the last furlong and a half without posing a serious threat. (8/1)

## 1820 VODACALL TOKYO TROPHY H'CAP (0-95) (3-Y.O) (Class C)

4-40 (4-43) **7f** £18,400.00 (£5,575.00: £2,725.00: £1,300.00) Stalls: Low GOING minus 0.36 sec per fur (F)

| | | | | SP | RR | SF |
|---|---|---|---|---|---|---|
| 1432$^{5}$ | **Polar Prince (IRE) (90)** (MAJarvis) **3-8-11**$^{(5)}$ FLynch(14) (hdwy over 2f out: led over 1f out: r.o wl) | — | **1** | 6/1$^{1}$ | 99 | 60 |
| 1327$^{8}$ | **Banzhaf (USA) (72)** (GLMoore) **3-7-12** JQuinn(6) (a.p: rdn over 2f out: ev ch over 1f out: unable qckn) | 2½ | **2** | 10/1 | 75 | 36 |
| 1485$^{3}$ | **Menoo Hal Batal (USA) (78)** (MRStoute) **3-8-4**$^{ow1}$ KFallon(11) (lw: rdn & hdwy over 2f out: r.o one pce) | ½ | **3** | 6/1$^{1}$ | 80 | 40 |
| 1327$^{7}$ | **Kilvine (85)** (LMCumani) **3-8-11** LDettori(3) (a.p: rdn over 2f out: one pce) | 2 | **4** | 9/1 | 83 | 44 |
| 1172* | **Ashjar (USA) (86)** (HThomsonJones) **3-8-12** RHills(5) (lw: chsd ldr: ev ch over 1f out: wknd fnl f) | 2½ | **5** | 13/2$^{2}$ | 78 | 39 |
| 1527$^{6}$ | **Willisa (70)** (JDBethell) **3-7-5**$^{(5)}$ PFessey(10) (nvr nr to chal) | 1¼ | **6** | 33/1 | 59 | 20 |
| 1121$^{11}$ | **Catch The Lights (73)** (RHannon) **3-7-13** SSanders(2) (led over 5f) | ½ | **7** | 20/1 | 61 | 22 |
| 1599* | **Limerick Princess (IRE) (71)** (JBerry) **3-7-11** GCarter(13) (nvr nrr) | s.h | **8** | 13/2$^{2}$ | 59 | 20 |
| 1127$^{3}$ | **Caricature (IRE) (87)** (GLewis) **3-8-13** PaulEddery(12) (a bhd) | 7 | **9** | 6/1$^{1}$ | 59 | 20 |
| 1452$^{4}$ | **Iamus (88)** (PTWalwyn) **3-9-0v$^{1}$** JCarroll(15) (a bhd) | 1 | **10** | 14/1 | 58 | 19 |
| 1050* | **Iceni (IRE) (78)** (HCandy) **3-8-4** AMcGlone(8) (hdwy on ins over 3f out: wknd over 2f out) | nk | **11** | 8/1$^{3}$ | 47 | 8 |
| 989$^{9}$ | **Eastern Prophets (95)** (TJNaughton) **3-9-7** PatEddery(7) (hld up: rdn over 2f out: sn wknd) | ¾ | **12** | 16/1 | 62 | 23 |

(SP 120.0%) **12 Rn**

**1m 20.98** (0.68) CSF £59.55 CT £351.68 TOTE £9.50: £2.30 £4.10 £2.90 (£67.00) Trio £263.30 OWNER Mrs Christine Stevenson (NEWMARKET) BRED Michael Morrin

LONG HANDICAP Willisa 7-6

**1432 Polar Prince (IRE)** moved up over a quarter of a mile from home. Striking the front below the distance, he soon had the race in the bag. (6/1)

**1073 Banzhaf (USA)**, in a handy position throughout, had every chance below the distance before the winner was let loose. (10/1)

**1485 Menoo Hal Batal (USA)**, scrubbed along to take closer order over two furlongs from home, stayed on without finding that vital turn of foot. (6/1)

**833 Kilvine** raced in a handy position, but as usual was made to look very pedestrian when the real race began in earnest. (9/1)

**1172* Ashjar (USA)** chased the leader. With every chance below the distance, he soon had bellows to mend. (13/2)

**1527 Willisa** made some late headway without posing a threat. (33/1)

T/Jkpt: Not won; £65,380.30 to Nottingham 10/6/96. T/Plpt: £2,196.20 (13.63 Tckts). T/Qdpt: £185.40 (15.33 Tckts). AK

# 1411-NOTTINGHAM (L-H) (Good to firm)

## Monday June 10th

WEATHER: overcast WIND: mod against

## 1821 MILES 33 20TH ANNIVERSARY APPRENTICE LIMITED STKS (0-50) (3-Y.O+) (Class F)

2-30 (2-32) **1m 1f 213y** £3,351.00 (£936.00: £453.00) Stalls: Low GOING minus 0.36 sec per fur (F)

| | | | | SP | RR | SF |
|---|---|---|---|---|---|---|
| 1416$^{2}$ | **Spa Lane (49)** (PJMakin) **3-8-3**$^{(3)ow2}$ RHavlin(5) (hld up: hdwy 3f out: led ins fnl f: r.o wl) | — | **1** | 13/2$^{3}$ | 60 | 26 |
| *1457*$^{12}$ | **Zaaleff (USA) (50)** (BHanbury) **4-9-3b** JStack(16) (lw: hld up: stdy hdwy 4f out: led wl over 1f out tl ins fnl f: fin 3rd, 2l: plcd 2nd) | | **2** | 8/1 | 54 | 35 |
| 1414$^{8}$ | **Fresh Look (IRE) (37)** (RCSpicer) **4-8-9b$^{1(5)}$** MartinDwyer(1) (a.p: effrt u.p over 1f out: unable qckn nr fin: fin 4th, s.h: plcd 3rd) | | **3** | 14/1 | 51 | 32 |
| 1633$^{2}$ | **Alabang (55)** (MJCamacho) **5-9-5** AWhelan(19) (swtg: s.s: hdwy over 2f out: no ex wl ins fnl f: fin 5th, nk: plcd 4th) | | **4** | 7/2$^{1}$ | 55 | 36 |
| 1548$^{5}$ | **Greek Gold (IRE) (43)** (WLBarker) **7-8-12**$^{(5)}$ JBramhill(11) (lw: led after 3f tl wl over 1f out: one pce fnl f: fin 6th, hd: plcd 5th) | | **5** | 14/1 | 47 | 28 |
| | **Chieftain's Crown (USA) (32)** (MissKMGeorge) **5-8-10**$^{(7)}$ CCarver(8) (hld up in tch: effrt over 2f out: nt rch ldrs) | 3 | **7** | 5/1$^{2}$ | 42 | 23 |
| 1119$^{9}$ | **Laughing Buccaneer (49)** (AGFoster) **3-8-4** DaneO'Neill(18) (mid div tl r.o fnl 2f: nvr nrr) | ½ | **8** | 14/1 | 41 | 9 |
| 1651$^{10}$ | **Burnt Sienna (IRE) (47)** (JSMoore) **4-8-9**$^{(5)}$ AimeeCook(20) (lw: hdwy over 3f out: wknd over 1f out) | nk | **9** | 25/1 | 38 | 19 |
| | **Bronze Runner (36)** (EAWheeler) **12-9-0b**$^{(3)}$ ADaly(10) (bit bkwd: trckd ldrs tl wknd 2f out) | ½ | **10** | 33/1 | 40 | 21 |
| 1451$^{2}$ | **Radmore Brandy (40)** (NPLittmoden) **3-7-10**$^{(5)}$ CAdamson(14) (hdwy 4f out: wknd 2f out) | ½ | **11** | 12/1 | 36 | 4 |
| *1487*$^{3}$ | **Jalmaid (43)** (BAMcMahon) **4-8-11**$^{(3)}$ LNewton(3) (led 1f: ev ch & rdn 3f out: hmpd & wknd over 1f out) | ¾ | **12** | 14/1 | 35 | 16 |
| 1089$^{16}$ | **The Jolly Barmaid (IRE) (47)** (PCalver) **3-8-1** NVarley(7) (nvr nr to chal) | nk | **13** | 16/1 | 35 | 3 |
| 1311$^{7}$ | **Dance of Joy (30)** (JMCarr) **4-8-9**$^{(7)}$ MDavies(15) (nvr nr ldrs) | 1¼ | **14** | 14/1 | 35 | 16 |

| | | | | | | |
|---|---|---|---|---|---|---|
| 597[9] | **Dauphin (IRE) (48)** (WJMusson) **3-7-13**(5) JWilkinson(13) (led after 1f: sn hdd: wknd over 3f out) ....1½ | **15** | 14/1 | 33 | 1 |
| 983[20] | **Ranger Sloane (29)** (GFierro) **4-8-12**(5) JDennis(2) (swtg: a bhd: t.o)....7 | **16** | 33/1 | 22 | 3 |
| 1363[5] | **Oxgang (IRE) (47)** (JGFitzGerald) **3-8-4** CTeague(17) (a in rr)....2 | **17** | 9/1 | 19 | — |
| *1460*[8] | **Indian Rhapsody (50)** (ABailey) **4-8-9**(5) AngelaGallimore(12) (a in rr: t.o fnl 3f)....16 | **18** | 14/1 | — | — |
| 993[11] | **Ring of Vision (IRE) (50)** (MrsMReveley) **4-8-12**(5) GFaulkner(6) (bit bkwd: hld up: hdwy 3f out: shkn up to chal ent fnl f: r.o: fin 2nd, 1/2l: disq: plcd last).... | **D** | 8/1 | 57 | 38 |
| 1196[4] | **Harry's Treat (50)** (JLEyre) **4-9-0** SDrowne(4) (swtg: stumbled & uns rdr after 1f).... | **U** | 14/1 | — | — |
| | | | (SP 161.1%) | | **19 Rn** |

**2m 6.9** (4.40) CSF £69.09 TOTE £8.10: £3.40 £3.60 £5.80 (£96.80) Trio £370.20; £172.10 to Salisbury 11/6/96 OWNER Mr R. J. K. Roberts (MARLBOROUGH) BRED R. J. K. Roberts

WEIGHT FOR AGE 3yo-13lb

STEWARDS' ENQUIRY Faulkner susp. 19-22/6/96 (irresponsible riding).

**1416 Spa Lane**, well suited to this longer trip, came from a long way off the pace to strike the front 100 yards out and win a shade cleverly. (13/2: op 4/1)

**1457 Zaaleff (USA)** looked to be travelling best when taking over soon after passing the quarter-mile marker but, when the race was on inside the final furlong, he lacked that bit of acceleration that was needed in the battle to the finish. (8/1: op 5/1)

**Fresh Look (IRE)**, never far away, stuck on gamely inside the final furlong and there is a race of this description there for the taking. (14/1)

**1633 Alabang** stood still as the stalls were released and lost at least fifteen lengths. Sent about his business entering the last quarter-mile, he could not quite land a blow but there was no doubting what an unlucky loser he really was. (7/2)

**1548 Greek Gold (IRE)** made most of the running until the race began in earnest just inside the last couple of furlongs, and then he struggled to hang on. (14/1)

**Chieftain's Crown (USA)**, fit from hurdling, was the only one the punters wanted to know. He moved very scratchily to post and could not muster the pace to mount a challenge. (5/1: 20/1-9/2)

**1311 Dance of Joy** (14/1: 10/1-16/1)

**Ring of Vision (IRE)** had an outing last month but still looked to be carrying excess condition. Ridden from off the pace, he put in a sustained last-furlong challenge and, after passing the post in second place, was disqualified and placed last for some infringement that was alleged to have taken place on the approach to the final furlong. He should not be long in winning again. (8/1: op 4/1)

## 1822 E.B.F. MAIDEN STKS (2-Y.O) (Class D)

3-00 (3-00) **5f 13y** £3,752.50 (£1,120.00: £535.00: £242.50) Stalls: High GOING minus 0.36 sec per fur (F)

| | | | SP | RR | SF |
|---|---|---|---|---|---|
| 1118[5] | **Bold Catch (USA)** (RCharlton) **2-9-0** KDarley(7) (a.p: led ins fnl f: drvn clr) ....— | **1** | 5/2[2] | 71 | 13 |
| 829[7] | **Cadeaux Cher** (BWHills) **2-9-0** MHills(1) (swvd lft s: sn prom: hung bdly lft fr ½-wy: r.o) ....2 | **2** | 7/2[3] | 65 | 7 |
| 1653[7] | **Castle Ashby Jack** (PHowling) **2-9-0b**[1] FNorton(8) (mde most tl hdd & rdn over 1f out: kpt on towards fin) ....1¼ | **3** | 12/1 | 61 | 3 |
| 865[3] | **Just Nick** (MMcCormack) **2-9-0** JReid(6) (lw: w ldrs: slt ld over 1f out tl hdd & no ex ins fnl f) ....½ | **4** | 6/4[1] | 59 | 1 |
| | **Step N Go (IRE)** (MrsJRRamsden) **2-8-9** WWoods(3) (w'like: leggy: bkwd: s.s: effrt 2f out: nt rch ldrs)....3 | **5** | 12/1 | 45 | — |
| | **Suite Factors** (JAGlover) **2-9-0** SDWilliams(2) (lt-f: unf: prom: rdn 2f out: wknd appr fnl f) ....½ | **6** | 16/1 | 48 | — |
| | **Geordie Lad** (JABennett) **2-9-0** TSprake(4) (lt-f: unf: dwlt: outpcd: a bhd)....2 | **7** | 10/1 | 42 | — |
| | **Cocoloba (IRE)** (PDEvans) **2-8-6**(3) SDrowne(5) (small: lt-f: outpcd: a bhd)....3½ | **8** | 12/1 | 26 | — |
| | | | (SP 128.8%) | | **8 Rn** |

**61.9 secs** (3.30) CSF £12.87 TOTE £4.10: £1.40 £1.60 £3.30 (£4.30) OWNER Mr K. Abdulla (BECKHAMPTON) BRED Juddmonte Farms

**1118 Bold Catch (USA)**, ridden with restraint on this occasion, quickened up well when set alight approaching the final furlong and, galloping on strongly, won comfortably. (5/2: 9/4-7/2)

**Cadeaux Cher** swerved left leaving the stalls and persisted in hanging left throughout the race. Finishing alone on the far side, he gave away far more ground than he was beaten by and, once he gets his steering sorted out, should have little trouble making it pay. (7/2: op 6/4)

**1315 Castle Ashby Jack**, keener than ever in the blinkers, was a leading light from the off and he battled back inside the distance to go down fighting. (12/1: 8/1-14/1)

**865 Just Nick** went with the pace and showed ahead inside the last furlong, but he was tapped for toe in the sprint to the line. (6/4)

**Step N Go (IRE)**, a May filly far from fully wound up, lost ground at the start and was unable to get herself into contention. (12/1: 8/1-14/1)

**Suite Factors**, a late foal, did not shape badly on this debut but he will always be at a big disadvantage throughout his career. (16/1)

## 1823 SUN CHEMICAL H'CAP (0-80) (3-Y.O) (Class D)

3-30 (3-30) **5f 13y** £3,817.50 (£1,140.00: £545.00: £247.50) Stalls: High GOING minus 0.36 sec per fur (F)

| | | | SP | RR | SF |
|---|---|---|---|---|---|
| 1628[7] | **Rushcutter Bay (79)** (TTClement) **3-9-3**(3) JStack(6) (lw: hmpd s: hdwy 2f out: str run to ld ins fnl f) ....— | **1** | 6/1[3] | 89 | 39 |
| 1597* | **Maiteamia (68)** (SRBowring) **3-8-6b**(3) CTeague(7) (swvd lft s: hdwy ½-wy: ev ch ins fnl f: unable qckn)....1¼ | **2** | 3/1[1] | 74 | 24 |
| 1597[4] | **Pleasure Time (66)** (CSmith) **3-8-7** AClark(1) (lw: a.p centre: rdn over 1f out: kpt on) ....1¼ | **3** | 7/1 | 68 | 18 |
| 700[6] | **Comic Fantasy (AUS) (80)** (MartynWane) **3-9-7b** JReid(9) (trckd ldrs: effrt & ev ch wl over 1f out: one pce u.p) ....1¼ | **4** | 14/1 | 78 | 28 |
| 1646[4] | **Chemcast (66)** (DNicholls) **3-8-0**(7) JBramhill(5) (lw: prom: rdn along ½-wy: led 2f out tl ins fnl f) ....nk | **5** | 4/1[2] | 63 | 13 |
| 931[18] | **Gagajulu (65)** (PDEvans) **3-8-3**(3) SDrowne(4) (drvn along & effrt 2f out: nvr able to chal) ....½ | **6** | 20/1 | 61 | 11 |
| 1652[5] | **Polly Golightly (79)** (MBlanshard) **3-9-6** KDarley(2) (trckd ldrs: effrt & rdn over 1f out: nt pce to chal)....1½ | **7** | 15/2 | 70 | 20 |
| 1412[4] | **Kings Harmony (IRE) (64)** (PJMakin) **3-8-5** LDettori(8) (trckd ldrs: sn pushed along: outpcd fnl 2f)....3½ | **8** | 3/1[1] | 44 | — |
| 773[8] | **Johayro (70)** (WGMTurner) **3-8-11v**[1] TSprake(3) (led 3f: sn rdn & wknd) ....4 | **9** | 16/1 | 37 | — |
| | | | (SP 125.9%) | | **9 Rn** |

**60.6 secs** (2.00) CSF £25.26 CT £124.79 TOTE £9.00: £2.20 £1.40 £2.10 (£22.50) Trio £26.50 OWNER Treasure Seekers Partnership (NEWMARKET) BRED Lloyd Bros

STEWARDS' ENQUIRY Clark susp. 21-22/6/96 (excessive use of whip).

**Rushcutter Bay**, a nice, easy mover, was knocked out of his stride on leaving the start. Switched towards the stands' side, he produced a good burst of speed to lead inside the final furlong and won going away. (6/1)

**1597* Maiteamia** came out of the stalls sideways and was unable to get himself into the race until two furlongs out. Engaged in a battle with Chemcast entering the final furlong, the powerful late challenge of the winner proved too much for both of them. (3/1)

**1597 Pleasure Time**, nudged along to keep tabs on the leaders, stuck to the task in hand but just lacked that bit extra to get to terms. (7/1)

**700 Comic Fantasy (AUS)**, at full stretch all the way, looked a serious threat below the distance but she had had to work hard, and her measure had been taken entering the final furlong. (14/1: op 8/1)

**1646 Chemcast** does look to need stronger handling but he did nothing wrong and had his chance until outpaced in the sprint to the post. (4/1)

**1412 Kings Harmony (IRE)** (3/1: 7/4-100/30)

## 1824 NOTTINGHAM EVENING POST CONDITIONS STKS (3-Y.O+) (Class C)

4-00 (4-01) **1m 54y** £5,300.80 (£1,967.20: £948.60: £393.00: £161.50: £68.90) Stalls: Low GOING minus 0.36 sec per fur (F)

| | | | | SP | RR | SF |
|---|---|---|---|---|---|---|
| 680[5] | **Restructure (IRE) (106)** (MrsJCecil) **4-10-0** PaulEddery(8) (swtg: trckd ldrs: rdn to ld 1f out: r.o strly) | — | **1** | 9/2[3] | 119 | 68 |
| | **Lower Egypt (USA) (105)** (MajorWRHern) **6-9-4** RHills(5) (bit bkwd: hld up in tch: styd on wl ins fnl f: no ch w wnr) | 1½ | **2** | 8/1 | 106 | 55 |
| 613* | **Polinesso** (BWHills) **3-8-10** MHills(3) (lw: mde most tl hdd ent fnl f: one pce) | 1¼ | **3** | 6/1 | 107 | 45 |
| 1417* | **Options Open (100)** (MrsJRRamsden) **4-9-4** WWoods(1) (lw: hld up: hdwy on ins & squeezed for room over 1f out: swtchd rt: r.o towards fin) | 1½ | **4** | 8/1 | 101 | 50 |
| | **Jarah (USA)** (SbinSuroor) **3-8-10** LDettori(6) (bit bkwd: w ldr: drvn along 3f out: wknd over 1f out) | nk | **5** | 3/1[1] | 103 | 41 |
| | **Leonato (FR)** (PDEvans) **4-9-4** DRMcCabe(4) (bhd: effrt over 2f out: no imp) | 3½ | **6** | 10/1 | 93 | 42 |
| 1142* | **Keltoi** (LMCumani) **3-8-10** KDarley(7) (trckd ldrs: pushed along over 2f out: sn btn) | hd | **7** | 4/1[2] | 96 | 34 |
| 1495[3] | **Kuantan (USA) (102)** (PFICole) **3-9-0** JReid(9) (stdd s: hld up: outpcd fnl 2f) | 1¼ | **8** | 15/2 | 98 | 36 |
| | | | | (SP 120.5%) | | **8 Rn** |

**1m 42.8** (1.50) CSF £37.64 TOTE £3.10: £1.30 £2.00 £1.60 (£18.80) Trio £62.60 OWNER Mr Martin Myers (NEWMARKET) BRED J. H. Stone

WEIGHT FOR AGE 3yo-11lb

**680 Restructure (IRE)**, a big, handsome colt who gave the impression that he would benefit from easier ground, turned in a very impressive display here to concede so much weight to some highly thought-of individuals. He has earned himself a trip to Royal Ascot for the Queen Anne Stakes. (9/2)

**Lower Egypt (USA)** did all his racing on the continent last year and, though he ran with his tongue tied down, did not look fully wound up. Doing all his best work late on, he was never going to catch the winner, but he filled a highly respectable runner-up spot and there is still life in him yet. (8/1)

**613* Polinesso** was taking a giant step up in class here, but was only forced to give best entering the final furlong. He is open to plenty of improvement. (6/1: 4/1-7/1)

**1417* Options Open**, forced to switch to find room to deliver his challenge, lacked the pace to prove troublesome but, in this class, was far from disgraced. (8/1: 6/1-9/1)

**Jarah (USA)**, who is not very big, looked to need this race and had had enough before reaching the last furlong. (3/1)

## 1825 HARLAND SIMON H'CAP (0-80) (3-Y.O+ F & M) (Class D)

4-30 (4-30) **1m 54y** £4,012.50 (£1,200.00: £575.00: £262.50) Stalls: Low GOING minus 0.36 sec per fur (F)

| | | | | SP | RR | SF |
|---|---|---|---|---|---|---|
| 1615[2] | **Golden Pond (IRE) (72)** (RFJohnsonHoughton) **3-8-12** JReid(4) (mde all: drvn clr fnl f) | — | **1** | 9/2[2] | 86 | 53 |
| | **High Note (75)** (RCharlton) **3-9-1** KDarley(5) (hld up in tch: disp ld fr 3f out: rdn & one pce appr fnl f) | 3½ | **2** | 5/1[3] | 82 | 49 |
| 1674[6] | **My Gallery (IRE) (55)** (ABailey) **5-7-13**(7) AngelaGallimore(2) (plld hrd: trckd ldrs: struck into heels of rival 5f out: kpt on u.p fnl 2f) | ½ | **3** | 7/1 | 61 | 39 |
| 1610* | **Darcey Bussell (56)** (BWHills) **4-8-7** MHills(7) (b.hind: hld up: hdwy 2f out: nvr nrr) | 2 | **4** | 4/1[1] | 58 | 36 |
| 1533* | **Bubble Wings (FR) (62)** (SPCWoods) **4-8-13** WWoods(3) (hld up: swtchd ins wl over 2f out: sn rdn: nt pce to chal) | 1 | **5** | 11/2 | 62 | 40 |
| 1625[5] | **Queen of All Birds (IRE) (74)** (RBoss) **5-9-4**(7) GFaulkner(9) (hld up in rr: effrt on outside 3f out: sn no imp) | 5 | **6** | 9/1 | 65 | 43 |
| | **Racing Brenda (57)** (BCMorgan) **5-8-8** GCarter(10) (bkwd: prom tl wknd 3f out) | ½ | **7** | 10/1 | 47 | 25 |
| 1420[9] | **Fervent Fan (IRE) (66)** (MBell) **3-8-6** MFenton(1) (lw: hld up: a bhd: t.o fnl 3f) | 12 | **8** | 14/1 | 33 | — |
| 689[6] | **Threesome (USA) (76)** (LMCumani) **3-9-2** LDettori(8) (prom tl wknd over 2f out: eased: t.o) | 1¾ | **9** | 9/2[2] | 39 | 6 |
| | | | | (SP 126.7%) | | **9 Rn** |

**1m 42.7** (1.40) CSF £28.02 CT £149.06 TOTE £5.30: £1.10 £3.20 £2.60 (£10.20) Trio £36.90 OWNER Mr John Horgan (DIDCOT) BRED Tullamaine Castle Stud and Partners

WEIGHT FOR AGE 3yo-11lb

**1615 Golden Pond (IRE)**, tackling the trip for the first time, was not afraid to put the emphasis on stamina and the style in which she drew clear after making all would suggest this is what she really needed. (9/2)

**High Note** would not have been helped when a rival clipped her heels on the home turn, but she produced a very promising display on this seasonal reappearance and can only go on from this. (5/1)

**1674 My Gallery (IRE)**, racing very freely, was fortunate not to be brought down when she struck into the heels of High Note entering the straight. Undeterred, she battled on willingly right to the finish and seems on extremely good terms with herself. (7/1)

**1610* Darcey Bussell** was up against better rivals that she beat at Catterick ten days ago, and was never able to hold out much hope for her supporters. (4/1)

**1533* Bubble Wings (FR)**, hard at work to improve from some way out, kept staying on but never looked capable of getting herself into the action. (11/2)

## 1826 USHER WALKER H'CAP (0-70) (3-Y.O+) (Class E)

5-00 (5-00) **1m 6f 15y** £3,288.00 (£984.00: £472.00: £216.00) Stalls: Low GOING minus 0.36 sec per fur (F)

| | | | | SP | RR | SF |
|---|---|---|---|---|---|---|
| 1783* | **Double Agent (69)** (MJohnston) **3-9-0**[4x] JWeaver(1) (led 6f: led over 2f out: clr whn edgd lft fnl f) | — | **1** | 11/10[1] | 80+ | 49 |
| 1778[5] | **Salska (45)** (AStreeter) **5-8-4**(5) LNewton(13) (prom tl lost pl over 4f out: rallied u.p appr fnl f) | 3 | **2** | 12/1 | 53 | 41 |
| 1436[5] | **Blazon of Troy (50)** (TThomsonJones) **7-8-7**(7) AimeeCook(8) (b: bit bkwd: hld up: hdwy on ins 4f out: kpt on wl fnl f) | nk | **3** | 33/1 | 57 | 45 |
| | **Mim-Lou-and (45)** (MissHCKnight) **4-8-2**(7)[ow2] GFaulkner(9) (hld up: hdwy 4f out: hrd rdn 2f out: one pce) | 1 | **4** | 7/1[2] | 51 | 37 |
| *1082[4]* | **Iota (51)** (JLHarris) **7-9-1** PaulEddery(2) (led 8f out tl over 2f out: kpt on u.p fnl f) | hd | **5** | 12/1 | 57 | 45 |
| | **Quest Again (63)** (DWPArbuthnot) **5-9-13** MHills(7) (hld up in tch: hdwy to jn wnr 2f out: wknd appr fnl f) | 1 | **6** | 12/1 | 68 | 56 |
| 1150[5] | **Persian Smoke (42)** (AHide) **5-8-1**(5) MartinDwyer(14) (nvr plcd to chal) | 5 | **7** | 8/1[3] | 41 | 29 |
| 1542[3] | **Campaspe (42)** (JGFitzGerald) **4-8-6** JFanning(6) (hld up: hdwy over 3f out: rdn 2f out: no imp) | 2 | **8** | 12/1 | 39 | 27 |
| 1655[14] | **Full Quiver (41)** (MrsBarbaraWaring) **11-8-2v**(3) SDrowne(12) (b: b.hind: a in rr: t.o) | 17 | **9** | 20/1 | 19 | 7 |
| 1472[4] | **Greystyle (35)** (MBrittain) **6-7-13v** GCarter(11) (prom: rdn ent st: sn wknd: t.o) | 3 | **10** | 12/1 | 9 | — |
| 1641[9] | **Seventh Edition (64)** (DBurchell) **3-8-9** SDWilliams(10) (b.nr fore: trckd ldrs 11f: sn rdn & wknd: t.o) | 1½ | **11** | 16/1 | 36 | 5 |
| 1514[9] | **Fast Forward Fred (50)** (LMontagueHall) **5-9-0** RHills(3) (trckd ldrs 9f: sn wknd & eased: t.o) | 20 | **12** | 9/1 | — | — |
| 1665[9] | **Good so Fa (IRE) (34)** (CNAllen) **4-7-7h**(5)[ow2] MBaird(4) (sn wl bhd: t.o) | dist | **13** | 16/1 | — | — |
| | | | | (SP 139.2%) | | **13 Rn** |

**3m 2.2** (3.70) CSF £18.33 CT £334.29 TOTE £1.70: £1.10 £2.20 £12.90 (£9.10) Trio £37.30 OWNER Mr R. W. Huggins (MIDDLEHAM) BRED Mrs R. D. Peacock

WEIGHT FOR AGE 3yo-19lb

**1783* Double Agent**, brought out very quickly after getting off the mark four days ago, was able to brush aside these older rivals just as easily as he had done with his own age group and he looks a real star in the making. (11/10: Evens-5/4)
**1778 Salska**, another making a good return to action, ran possibly her best race yet and, with stamina no problem, should be able to add to her single score. (12/1)
**Blazon of Troy**, beavering his way up the inside rail, was never going to trouble the winner, but he does try and he looks to be on the way back. (33/1)
**Mim-Lou-and**, winner of two hurdle races last month, has still to open his account at this game and he had a punishing race to finish as close as he did. (7/1)
**1082 Iota** is a regular at this venue and, though she has not won here for two or so years, she is not short of courage and, when she comes down in the weights, will find her true form. (12/1)
**Quest Again** had obviously done plenty of work and, moving upsides the winner two furlongs out, found the concession of almost a stone too much against a race-fit rival. He is worth keeping on the right side. (12/1)
**1542 Campaspe** (12/1: 8/1-20/1)

T/Jkpt: £49,107.70 (1.54 Tckts). T/Plpt: £136.10 (142.8 Tckts). T/Qdpt: £11.80 (93 Tckts). IM

# 1664-PONTEFRACT (L-H) (Good to firm)
## Monday June 10th
WEATHER: sunny periods & warm WIND: slt half bhd

## 1827 JUNE MAIDEN AUCTION STKS (2-Y.O) (Class F)
2-45 (2-48) **5f** £2,780.00 (£780.00: £380.00) Stalls: Low GOING minus 0.18 sec per fur (GF)

| | | | | SP | RR | SF |
|---|---|---|---|---|---|---|
| 1622[2] | **Class Distinction (IRE)** (RHannon) **2-8-5** RPerham(6) (mde most: rdn & r.o fnl f) | — | **1** | 6/4[1] | 67 | 16 |
| 1086[8] | **Nifty Norman** (JBerry) **2-8-5** JCarroll(10) (a.p: hdwy 2f out: sn chsng wnr: kpt on wl) | 1½ | **2** | 6/1[2] | 62 | 11 |
| | **Burkes Manor** (TDBarron) **2-8-8** JFortune(4) (cmpt: scope: a chsng ldrs: kpt on u.p fnl f) | 1¾ | **3** | 7/1[3] | 60 | 9 |
| 1537[10] | **Komasta** (CaptJWilson) **2-7-13**(5)ow1 FLynch(8) (a.p: kpt on same pce appr fnl f) | nk | **4** | 33/1 | 55 | 3 |
| 975[6] | **Bold Brief** (DenysSmith) **2-8-5** PatEddery(2) (bhd: hdwy 2f out: kpt on wl fnl f) | hd | **5** | 16/1 | 55 | 4 |
| 1499[4] | **Under Pressure** (TDEasterby) **2-8-0** TWilliams(3) (disp ld to ½-wy: wknd ins fnl f) | 1¼ | **6** | 7/1[3] | 46 | — |
| 1166[6] | **Real Fire (IRE)** (MGMeagher) **2-8-5** SSanders(11) (a.p: effrt ½-wy: nt qckn) | 2½ | **7** | 33/1 | 43 | — |
| | **Ultra Boy** (PCHaslam) **2-8-8** JWeaver(9) (leggy: bit bkwd: chsd ldrs over 3f: grad wknd) | 2½ | **8** | 8/1 | 38 | — |
| 1632[3] | **Antares** (NTinkler) **2-8-8** KimTinkler(1) (lw: nvr bttr than mid div) | nk | **9** | 25/1 | 37 | — |
| | **Lady Salome** (JGFitzGerald) **2-8-6**ow3 KFallon(7) (neat: bit bkwd: rdn ½-wy: nvr trbld ldrs) | nk | **10** | 16/1 | 34 | — |
| | **Budding Prospect** (WJHaggas) **2-8-0** AMcGlone(12) (unf: scope: chsd ldrs: effrt over 2f out: nt qckn) | hd | **11** | 8/1 | 28 | — |
| 1344[5] | **Pension Fund** (MWEasterby) **2-8-3** DaleGibson(5) (s.i.s: sme late hdwy) | 1¾ | **12** | 25/1 | 26 | — |
| | **The Deejay (IRE)** (MBrittain) **2-8-4**ow1 MBirch(15) (unf: s.i.s: n.d) | 2 | **13** | 20/1 | 20 | — |
| | **Impish (IRE)** (TJEtherington) **2-8-3** LCharnock(14) (str: cmpt: bit bkwd: nvr wnt pce) | 1¾ | **14** | 100/1 | 14 | — |
| | **Stravano** (BPJBaugh) **2-8-0**ow2 WLord(13) (neat: unf: scope: bit bkwd: outpcd fr ½-wy) | 2½ | **15** | 200/1 | 3 | — |
| | **T-N-T Express** (MGMeagher) **2-7-12**(7) RStudholme(16) (unf: scope: s.i.s: a bhd) | 1¼ | **16** | 66/1 | 4 | — |
| | | | | (SP 134.6%) | **16 Rn** | |

**64.5 secs** (3.70) CSF £12.27 TOTE £2.40: £1.30 £2.30 £3.70 (£8.80) Trio £52.50 OWNER The E M A Partnership (MARLBOROUGH)
**1622 Class Distinction (IRE)** did the job required in determined fashion and should be the type to do well in nurseries. (6/4)
**1086 Nifty Norman** has come on a good deal for his initial outing and should not be long in going one better. (6/1: op 4/1)
**Burkes Manor**, a decent type, showed a moderate action but still ran well and should be all the better for it. (7/1)
**1026 Komasta** was again warm beforehand but this time he ran much better, and ought to find a race. (33/1)
**Bold Brief** showed his first signs of form here, running on splendidly from halfway, and looks one to watch. (16/1)
**1499 Under Pressure** went far too freely to post and, in the circumstances, ran well. (7/1)
**Ultra Boy** needed this and showed useful speed until blowing up in the last furlong and a half. (8/1)
**Budding Prospect** (8/1: op 9/2)

## 1828 DEWSBURY (S) STKS (3-Y.O+) (Class G)
3-15 (3-26) **1m 2f 6y** £2,469.00 (£684.00: £327.00) Stalls: Low GOING minus 0.18 sec per fur (GF)

| | | | | SP | RR | SF |
|---|---|---|---|---|---|---|
| 1596* | **North Ardar (58)** (MrsMReveley) **6-9-3**(7) SCopp(7) (trckd ldrs: led over 2f out: sn clr: rdn out) | — | **1** | 4/5[1] | 59 | 46 |
| 1697[6] | **Remontant (IRE) (34)** (RHollinshead) **4-8-8**(5) FLynch(2) (in tch: hdwy & swtchd over 2f out: r.o wl towards fin) | nk | **2** | 33/1 | 48 | 35 |
| 1665[2] | **Absolute Ruler (IRE) (38)** (JLHarris) **5-9-4b** SSanders(5) (lw: bhd: hdwy 3f out: sn chsng ldrs: one pce appr fnl f) | 6 | **3** | 9/1[3] | 43 | 30 |
| 1596[3] | **Elite Bliss (IRE)** (MJCamacho) **4-8-13** LCharnock(10) (lw: trckd ldrs: effrt whn bdly hmpd over 2f out: nt rcvr) | 3½ | **4** | 11/2[2] | 32 | 19 |
| 1451* | **Cry Baby (49)** (NTinkler) **3-8-11b** JCarroll(9) (hld up: effrt 3f out: no imp fnl 2f) | nk | **5** | 9/1[3] | 43 | 17 |
| 1665[13] | **Hunza Story (32)** (NPLittmoden) **4-8-6**(7) JoHunnam(8) (b.hind: in tch tl outpcd fnl 2½f) | 8 | **6** | 100/1 | 19 | 6 |
| 1529[10] | **Kadari (36)** (WClay) **7-8-13v** NCarlisle(1) (cl up: chal 5f out: edgd lft over 2f out: sn btn) | 2½ | **7** | 20/1 | 15 | 2 |
| 1526[13] | **Beacon Hill Lady** (BEllison) **3-8-0** NKennedy(3) (bhd: effrt over 3f out: n.d) | 8 | **8** | 50/1 | 2 | — |
| 1546[5] | **Mill Dancer (IRE) (39)** (EJAlston) **4-8-13** KFallon(4) (unruly gng to s: led tl hdd, hmpd & wknd over 2f out) | 3½ | **9** | 9/1[3] | — | — |
| | **Risky Rose (35)** (RHollinshead) **4-8-8**(5) DGriffiths(6) (hld up: effrt whn bdly hmpd & uns rdr 2½f) | | **U** | 20/1 | — | — |
| | | | | (SP 116.4%) | **10 Rn** | |

**2m 14.5** (6.20) CSF £24.91 TOTE £1.90: £1.10 £5.40 £1.90 (£31.30) Trio £66.80 OWNER Laurel (Leisure) Ltd (SALTBURN) BRED Mrs H.Seddington
WEIGHT FOR AGE 3yo-13lb
Bt in 5,600gns
STEWARDS' ENQUIRY Charnock susp. 24-30/6 (improper riding).
**1596* North Ardar**, well handled, kicked clear when there was trouble behind and that won him the race. (4/5: tchd Evens)
**609 Remontant (IRE)** had trouble getting a run and then flew in the closing stages to give the winner quite a fright. (33/1)
**1665 Absolute Ruler (IRE)** had his chances, but decided he had done enough approaching the final furlong. (9/1)
**1596 Elite Bliss (IRE)** was sat on the heels of the leaders when she almost got brought down over two furlongs out, and then did well to finish so close. (11/2: 7/2-6/1)
**1451* Cry Baby**, after his hard race last time, was never doing enough here. (9/1)

## 1829 TAVERN WHOLESALING H'CAP (0-90) (3-Y.O+) (Class C)

3-45 (3-56) **6f** £7,765.00 (£2,320.00: £1,110.00: £505.00) Stalls: Low GOING minus 0.18 sec per fur (GF)

| Form | Horse | Dist | Pos | SP | RR | SF |
|---|---|---|---|---|---|---|
| 1186[17] | **Bollin Harry (78)** (TDEasterby) **4-9-4** MBirch(10) (mde most: hld on wl u.p fnl f) | — | 1 | 10/1 | 84 | 65 |
| 1598[2] | **Bolshoi (IRE) (72)** (JBerry) **4-8-7b**(5) PRoberts(9) (trckd ldrs: disp ld over 1f out: no ex ins fnl f) | ½ | 2 | 14/1 | 77 | 58 |
| 1652[9] | **Castlerea Lad (80)** (RHollinshead) **7-9-1**(5) FLynch(6) (prom: effrt 2f out: edgd lft over 1f out: r.o towards fin) | s.h | 3 | 8/1 | 85 | 66 |
| 1186[10] | **Rock Symphony (84)** (WJHaggas) **6-9-10** PatEddery(7) (lw: s.i.s: hdwy 2f out: styd on towards fin) | nk | 4 | 7/1 | 88 | 69 |
| 1126[9] | **Mybotye (76)** (GROldroyd) **3-8-8** AMackay(2) (hld up & bhd: hdwy over 1f out: nrst fin) | 1¾ | 5 | 7/1 | 75 | 48 |
| 1425[3] | **Fame Again (78)** (MrsJRRamsden) **4-9-4** SSanders(3) (prom tl outpcd ½-wy: styd on appr fnl f: n.d) | 1 | 6 | 4/1[1] | 74 | 55 |
| 1609[6] | **Halmanerror (67)** (MrsJRRamsden) **6-8-7** KFallon(4) (lw: bhd: effrt whn hmpd wl over 1f out: no imp) | ½ | 7 | 9/2[2] | 62 | 43 |
| 1501* | **Jucea (73)** (JLSpearing) **7-8-13** GHind(8) (trckd ldrs tl outpcd fnl 1½f) | 1¼ | 8 | 11/2[3] | 65 | 46 |
| 1609[3] | **Blue Bomber (72)** (TDBarron) **5-8-12** JFortune(5) (cl up: effrt 2½f out: wknd over 1f out) | 3 | 9 | 7/1 | 56 | 37 |
| 1199[7] | **Celandine (81)** (JLEyre) **3-8-10**(3) DWright(1) (spd 4f: wknd) | 8 | 10 | 20/1 | 43 | 16 |

(SP 122.7%) **10 Rn**

**1m 16.0** (1.70) CSF £126.01 CT £1,084.31 TOTE £19.40: £3.10 £4.40 £2.30 (£47.90) Trio £184.00 OWNER Sir Neil Westbrook (MALTON) BRED Sir Neil and Lady Westbrook

WEIGHT FOR AGE 3yo-8lb

STEWARDS' ENQUIRY Birch susp. 19-22 & 24/6/96 (excessive & improper use of whip).

**850 Bollin Harry**, in front virtually throughout, proved game under pressure and was certainly given some strong assistance. (10/1)
**1598 Bolshoi (IRE)** travelled well and may just have got his head in front approaching the final furlong, but was then outbattled. (14/1)
**737 Castlerea Lad** ran well in a race that did not suit his style of running. (8/1)
**812 Rock Symphony** took the eye in the paddock and ran his best race for a while. He would have preferred a stronger gallop. (7/1)
**785 Mybotye**, dropped out the back, was given no chance the way the race was run. (7/1)
**1425 Fame Again** needs a strong pace and all the luck going, and got neither here. (4/1)
**1609 Halmanerror**, who needed a stronger pace, also met with trouble in the home straight. (9/2)
**1501* Jucea**, high enough in the weights, has never won over this trip and ran out of steam in the final furlong. (11/2)

## 1830 BOROUGH H'CAP (0-70) (3-Y.O+) (Class E)

4-15 (4-22) **1m 4y** £3,314.00 (£992.00: £476.00: £218.00) Stalls: Low GOING minus 0.18 sec per fur (GF)

| Form | Horse | Dist | Pos | SP | RR | SF |
|---|---|---|---|---|---|---|
| 1502[3] | **Habeta (USA) (44)** (JWWatts) **10-8-10** PatEddery(11) (lw: a.p: led ins fnl f: styd on u.p) | — | 1 | 5/1[3] | 56 | 38 |
| 1538* | **Commander Glen (IRE) (57)** (MrsJRRamsden) **4-9-9b** KFallon(5) (lw: bhd: hmpd & squeezed thro over 1f out: fin strly) | hd | 2 | 9/4[1] | 69 | 51 |
| 1665* | **Percy Parrot (30)** (RMWhitaker) **4-7-10** NCarlisle(1) (led tl hdd ins fnl f: one pce) | 2 | 3 | 4/1[2] | 38 | 20 |
| 1546[10] | **Raindeer Quest (45)** (JLEyre) **4-8-11** RLappin(8) (chsd ldrs: edgd rt over 1f out: one pce) | 1¼ | 4 | 11/1 | 50 | 32 |
| 853[12] | **Java Red (IRE) (53)** (JGFitzGerald) **4-9-5** JFortune(4) (lw: in tch: effrt 3f out: rdn & no ex appr fnl f) | ½ | 5 | 16/1 | 57 | 39 |
| | **Heathyards Lady (USA) (57)** (RHollinshead) **5-9-4**(5) FLynch(6) (in tch: hdwy & hung lft over 2f out: hmpd over 1f out: kpt on) | 2½ | 6 | 20/1 | 56 | 38 |
| 1417[8] | **Battle Colours (IRE) (38)** (DonEnricoIncisa) **7-8-4** KimTinkler(2) (bhd tl sme late hdwy) | 2½ | 7 | 33/1 | 32 | 14 |
| 1665[3] | **Tame Deer (52)** (MCChapman) **4-8-11**(7) MSemple(13) (s.i.s: nvr rchd ldrs) | ¾ | 8 | 25/1 | 45 | 27 |
| 1515[14] | **Ever so Lyrical (56)** (PWHarris) **6-9-8** GHind(9) (chsd lrs tl n.m.r & lost pl wl over 1f out) | 2 | 9 | 9/1 | 45 | 27 |
| 1638[10] | **Reed My Lips (IRE) (34)** (BPJBaugh) **5-7-7**(7)ow2 JoHunnam(7) (b: drvn along over 3f out: n.d) | ½ | 10 | 50/1 | 22 | 2 |
| | **Cottage Prince (IRE) (43)** (JJQuinn) **3-7-12**ow1 TWilliams(12) (s.s: a bhd) | 6 | 11 | 50/1 | 19 | — |
| 1704[4] | **Mr Rough (60)** (DMorris) **5-9-12** CHodgson(10) (chsd ldrs: ev ch 2f out: sn wknd) | 1¼ | 12 | 15/2 | 33 | 15 |
| 1650[8] | **Kummel King (56)** (EJAlston) **8-9-8** WJO'Connor(3) (prom 5f) | 9 | 13 | 25/1 | 11 | — |

(SP 122.7%) **13 Rn**

**1m 45.8** (4.30) CSF £16.20 CT £47.69 TOTE £5.30: £2.10 £1.40 £2.00 (£8.30) Trio £13.40 OWNER Mr R. D. Bickenson (RICHMOND) BRED Spendthrift Farm, Inc

WEIGHT FOR AGE 3yo-11lb

**1502 Habeta (USA)** looked the part and this grand old performer pinched it by getting first run. (5/1)
**1538* Commander Glen (IRE)** should have won this, but he got messed about twice in the last three furlongs and, despite flying at the end, it was always too late. (9/4)
**1665* Percy Parrot** tried hard to repeat his all-the-way win of last week, but was just tapped for toe in the final furlong. (4/1)
**1546 Raindeer Quest** was back to something like her form here, but she was always short of a turn of foot in the last furlong a half. (11/1)
**Java Red (IRE)** looked and ran well, but could never quicken enough when it mattered. He is coming to hand. (16/1)
**Heathyards Lady (USA)** ran a fair first effort of the season. (20/1)

## 1831 YOUNGSTERS CONDITIONS STKS (2-Y.O) (Class D)

4-45 (4-47) **6f** £3,093.50 (£938.00: £459.00: £219.50) Stalls: Low GOING minus 0.18 sec per fur (GF)

| Form | Horse | Dist | Pos | SP | RR | SF |
|---|---|---|---|---|---|---|
| 1419[2] | **Alpine Time (IRE)** (DRLoder) **2-8-11** PatEddery(3) (mde all: qcknd 2f out: r.o) | — | 1 | 2/5[1] | 65+ | 23 |
| *1093** | **Just Visiting** (CaptJWilson) **2-8-9** JFortune(1) (lw: trckd ldrs: hdwy 2f out: sn chsng wnr: one pce fnl f) | 1¾ | 2 | 10/1 | 58 | 16 |
| *1603[3]* | **Saratoga Red (USA)** (WAO'Gorman) **2-8-10** EmmaO'Gorman(4) (lw: trckd ldrs: c wd st: r.o towards fin) | s.h | 3 | 8/1[3] | 59 | 17 |
| 1038[2] | **Impulsif (USA)** (DJSffrenchDavis) **2-8-10** WJO'Connor(2) (plld hrd: chsd wnr 4f: sn btn) | 12 | 4 | 5/1[2] | 27 | — |

(SP 108.3%) **4 Rn**

**1m 18.7** (4.40) CSF £4.29 TOTE £1.40 (£3.50) OWNER Cheveley Park Stud (NEWMARKET) BRED Godolphin Management Co Ltd

OFFICIAL EXPLANATION **Impulsif (USA): was found to be badly bruised under the tongue having got it over the bit during the race.**

**1419 Alpine Time (IRE)** won this well, but it was hardly a stunning performance. (2/5)
**1093* Just Visiting**, a winner on the All-Weather recently, ran well here but always found the winner too strong. (10/1)
**1603 Saratoga Red (USA)** has not got the best action and did not handle the home turn too well, but he did stay on at the end suggesting that there is better to come. (8/1)
**1038 Impulsif (USA)** disappointed here, but probably ran too freely early on. (5/1)

## 1832 BATLEY H'CAP (0-70) (3-Y.O+) (Class E)

5-15 (5-19) **1m 2f 6y** £3,158.00 (£944.00: £452.00: £206.00) Stalls: Low GOING minus 0.18 sec per fur (GF)

| Form | Horse | Dist | Pos | SP | RR | SF |
|---|---|---|---|---|---|---|
| 995[4] | **Seattle Alley (USA) (58)** (MrsJRRamsden) **3-8-8** KFallon(1) (cl up: led over 2f out: pushed along & r.o) | — | 1 | Evens[1] | 69 | 18 |

| | | | | | | |
|---|---|---|---|---|---|---|
| 1548* | **Steadfast Elite (IRE) (45)** (JJO'Neill) **5-8-8** JFortune(3) (chsd ldrs: styd on u.p fnl 2f: no imp)........................2½ | **2** | 11/4 2 | 52 | 14 |
| 629 8 | **Irie Mon (IRE) (53)** (MPBielby) **4-9-2** DeanMcKeown(2) (trckd ldrs: effrt 3f out: kpt on: nvr able to chal).........nk | **3** | 16/1 | 60 | 22 |
| 1069 5 | **Karinska (61)** (MCChapman) **6-9-3**(7) MSemple(6) (hld up: nt clr run 3f out tl wl ins fnl f: r.o) ........................s.h | **4** | 11/2 3 | 68 | 30 |
| 1418 13 | **Bardia (33)** (DonEnricoIncisa) **6-7-10** KimTinkler(5) (hld up: hdwy 3f out: one pce appr fnl f) ..........................1 | **5** | 33/1 | 38 | — |
| 1414 10 | **Desert Spring (65)** (PWHarris) **4-10-0** GHind(4) (lw: led tl hdd & wknd over 2f out).........................................3½ | **6** | 10/1 | 64 | 26 |

(SP 110.0%) **6 Rn**

**2m 16.3** (8.00) CSF £3.96 TOTE £1.70: £1.10 £1.30 (£1.90) OWNER Mr P. A. Leonard (THIRSK) BRED Hermitage Farm Inc.
LONG HANDICAP Bardia 7-5
WEIGHT FOR AGE 3yo-13lb

**995 Seattle Alley (USA)**, unusually ridden for this yard, was up with the pace and, pushed along in the straight, always had the situation in hand. (Evens)
**1548* Steadfast Elite (IRE)** ran a sound race and kept plugging away, but lacked the speed to get on terms. (11/4)
**Irie Mon (IRE)**, stepping up in trip, ran reasonably, but was always short of a real turn of foot. (16/1)
**1069 Karinska** found all sorts of trouble in the last three furlongs, and may well have given the winner something to think about with any luck. (11/2)
**Bardia** was always short of toe when it mattered. (33/1)
**963 Desert Spring** is yet to show anything positive this season. (10/1)

T/Plpt: £34.10 (377.84 Tckts). T/Qdpt: £15.10 (46.16 Tckts). AA

## 1683-WARWICK (L-H) (Firm)
## Monday June 10th
WEATHER: fine & cloudy WIND: slt bhd

## 1833 HAZY DAYS RATING RELATED MAIDEN APPRENTICE STKS (0-70) (3-Y.O+) (Class E)
6-15 (6-16) **1m 4f 115y** £3,002.00 (£896.00: £428.00: £194.00) Stalls: Low GOING minus 0.54 sec per fur (F)

| | | | SP | RR | SF |
|---|---|---|---|---|---|
| 863 10 | **One Pound (66)** (BWHills) **3-8-4**(3) JDSmith(1) (chsd clr ldr 9f out: led wl over 1f out: r.o wl) ......................— | **1** | 3/1 2 | 78 | 41 |
| 1591 4 | **Shalateeno (66)** (MRChannon) **3-8-1**(3) PPMurphy(4) (led: sn clr: rdn over 4f out: hdd wl over 1f out: one pce)..........................5 | **2** | 100/30 3 | 69 | 32 |
| 1305 5 | **Code Red (66)** (JWHills) **3-8-5**(3)ow1 DGriffiths(2) (lw: chsd clr ldr over 3f: sn lost pl: hdwy over 2f out: nt rch ldrs)..........................nk | **3** | 10/11 1 | 72 | 34 |
| 1641 17 | **Jelali (IRE) (68)** (DJGMurraySmith) **3-8-7** DaneO'Neill(3) (hld up: hdwy fnl 2f: n.d)..........................1¾ | **4** | 8/1 | 69 | 32 |
| | **Ewar Imperial (50)** (KOCunningham-Brown) **4-9-5**(5) CMunday(5) (bkwd: a bhd: t.o fnl 3f) ..........................29 | **5** | 50/1 | 32 | 12 |

(SP 113.5%) **5 Rn**

**2m 39.8** (1.30) CSF £12.51 TOTE £4.10: £2.40 £1.80 (£6.50) OWNER Mr Michael Goodbody (LAMBOURN) BRED GAINSBOROUGH STUD MANAGEMENT LTD
WEIGHT FOR AGE 3yo-17lb

**One Pound** appreciated the drop in class and longer trip. (3/1)
**1591 Shalateeno** is a free-running sort and it may be time to call on a more experienced pilot. (100/30)
**847 Code Red**, stepping up in distance, had a lot to do passing the three-furlong pole and could not overhaul the runner-up, let alone the winner. (10/11: 10/11-Evens)
**Jelali (IRE)** (8/1: op 5/1)

## 1834 E.B.F. ROYAL MAIDEN STKS (2-Y.O F) (Class D)
6-45 (6-49) **5f** £3,460.00 (£1,030.00: £490.00: £220.00) Stalls: Low GOING minus 0.54 sec per fur (F)

| | | | SP | RR | SF |
|---|---|---|---|---|---|
| 1622 3 | **Olympic Spirit** (JBerry) **2-8-11** JCarroll(3) (b.hind: lw: led over 2f: led 1f out: r.o wl)..........................— | **1** | 13/8 1 | 81+ | 39 |
| 1590 4 | **Gopi** (RHannon) **2-8-8**(3) DaneO'Neill(1) (a.p: led over 2f out to 1f out: one pce)..........................3 | **2** | 5/1 3 | 71 | 29 |
| 910 3 | **Life On The Street** (RHannon) **2-8-11** KDarley(2) (hld up: swtchd rt & hdwy over 1f out: rdn & one pce fnl f) ..........................¾ | **3** | 9/2 2 | 69 | 27 |
| 1643 2 | **Kustom Kit Xpres** (MMcCormack) **2-8-11** JReid(6) (w ldr: rdn over 2f out: one pce) ..........................1½ | **4** | 9/2 2 | 64 | 22 |
| | **Eye Shadow** (BJMeehan) **2-8-11** RHughes(4) (lengthy: unf: s.s: nvr trbld ldrs)..........................2½ | **5** | 7/1 | 56 | 14 |
| | **Miss St Kitts** (JRJenkins) **2-8-6**(5) MartinDwyer(5) (w'like: rdn over 3f out: bhd fnl 2f)..........................10 | **6** | 20/1 | 24 | — |

(SP 108.4%) **6 Rn**

**58.6 secs** (0.10 under 2y best) (0.60) CSF £9.09 TOTE £1.90: £1.40 £2.70 (£4.20) OWNER William Hill Organization Ltd (COCKERHAM) BRED W. H. Joyce

**1622 Olympic Spirit** is a half-sister to Naked Welcome. The form of the race she ran in at Lingfield is working out well and she can score again in this sort of company. (13/8)
**1590 Gopi** is going to find lack of substance a problem as the season progresses. (5/1: op 5/2)
**910 Life On The Street** had fast ground to contend with for the first time, but did not show significant improvement. (9/2)
**1643 Kustom Kit Xpres** did not progress from her debut last week. (9/2: 3/1-5/1)
**Eye Shadow** is a half-sister to a winner over a mile and had been supported. She is probably better than this. (7/1)

## 1835 'NURSERY WOOD' H'CAP (0-70) (3-Y.O+) (Class E)
7-15 (7-16) **2m 20y** £3,314.00 (£992.00: £476.00: £218.00) Stalls: Low GOING minus 0.54 sec per fur (F)

| | | | SP | RR | SF |
|---|---|---|---|---|---|
| 1454* | **Stompin (70)** (MissHCKnight) **5-9-7**(7) GFaulkner(6) (b: a.p: wnt 2nd 10f out: led 6f out: r.o wl)..........................— | **1** | Evens 1 | 85+ | 68 |
| *365* 8 | **Royal Circus (38)** (PRWebber) **7-7-7**(3) NVarley(9) (led 1f: hrd rdn over 3f out: rallied over 1f out: styd on fnl f) ..........................1½ | **2** | 9/1 | 52 | 35 |
| 1439 9 | **Paradise Navy (66)** (CREgerton) **7-9-10** RHughes(10) (hld up & bhd: hdwy 7f out: one pce fnl 2f)..........................2 | **3** | 8/1 3 | 78 | 61 |
| | **Sophism (USA) (38)** (MCPipe) **7-7-5**(5) MartinDwyer(8) (hld up & bhd: hdwy 6f out: one pce fnl 2f)..........................1 | **4** | 16/1 | 49 | 32 |
| 1454 6 | **Kymin (IRE) (59)** (DJGMurraySmith) **4-8-11v**(5) RPainter(1) (hld up: hdwy 8f out: rdn 5f out: wknd 2f out)......11 | **5** | 16/1 | 59 | 41 |
| | **Chris's Lad (60)** (BJMeehan) **5-9-4** JReid(2) (hld up: hdwy 7f out: rdn over 2f out: sn wknd) ..........................1 | **6** | 14/1 | 59 | 42 |
| | **Runaway Pete (USA) (68)** (MCPipe) **6-9-12** AMcGlone(4) (nvr nr ldrs)..........................1½ | **7** | 5/1 2 | 65 | 48 |
| 1063 11 | **Call My Guest (IRE) (53)** (REPeacock) **6-8-11** MHills(11) (led after 1f: hdd 6f out: wknd over 3f out)..........1¾ | **8** | 16/1 | 48 | 31 |
| 1439 11 | **Allmosa (49)** (TJNaughton) **7-8-2**(5)ow1 JDSmith(7) (s.s: a bhd) ..........................3 | **9** | 25/1 | 41 | 23 |
| 1063 14 | **Gentleman Sid (47)** (PGMurphy) **6-8-5** KDarley(3) (a bhd)..........................6 | **10** | 20/1 | 33 | 16 |

| | | | | SP | RR | SF |
|---|---|---|---|---|---|---|
| 1498[17] | **Winged Prince (61)** (AGFoster) **3-7-7**(5)ow2 MBaird(5) (hld up: hdwy 8f out: rdn & wknd 6f out: t.o) | dist | **11** | 50/1 | — | — |

(SP 122.7%) **11 Rn**

**3m 26.4** (0.40) CSF £11.21 CT £49.56 TOTE £2.10: £1.10 £3.60 £1.60 (£11.30) Trio £19.10 OWNER The Voice Group Ltd (WANTAGE) BRED Highclere Stud Ltd

LONG HANDICAP Royal Circus 7-7 Winged Prince 7-6

WEIGHT FOR AGE 3yo-21lb, 4yo-1lb

**1454* Stompin**, with his rider offsetting most of an 8lb rise in the weights, stayed the trip well enough. A tilt at the Ascot Stakes over an extra half-mile could well be on the cards. (Evens)

**Royal Circus** won a hurdles race over two and a half miles here last month and proved very game under pressure. (9/1: 6/1-10/1)

**811 Paradise Navy** has only ever scored once on the Flat and found disappointingly little in the home straight. (8/1: 6/1-10/1)

**Sophism (USA)** had refused in his last two jumps outings, and this may have sweetened him up. (16/1)

**Chris's Lad** (14/1: 10/1-16/1)

## 1836 WARWICK FESTIVAL CLAIMING STKS (3-Y.O) (Class F)

7-45 (7-58) **7f** £2,721.00 (£756.00: £363.00) Stalls: Low GOING minus 0.54 sec per fur (F)

| | | | | SP | RR | SF |
|---|---|---|---|---|---|---|
| 665[5] | **Bag And A Bit (43)** (BJMeehan) **3-7-12**(5)ow4 FLynch(1) (hld up: gd hdwy over 1f out: edgd lft & led ins fnl f: comf) | — | **1** | 25/1 | 57 | 27 |
| 1668[8] | **Northern Judge (75)** (BHanbury) **3-8-11b[1]** MRimmer(9) (a.p: led over 1f out tl ins fnl f) | 1¼ | **2** | 7/2[2] | 62 | 36 |
| 1707[4] | **Double Oscar (IRE) (84)** (MJohnston) **3-9-7** JWeaver(4) (chsd ldr: led 3f out: hrd rdn & hdd over 1f out: one pce) | hd | **3** | 11/10[1] | 72 | 46 |
| 1497[6] | **Most Wanted (IRE) (55)** (PFICole) **3-7-5**(5) MartinDwyer(11) (swtg: s.s: hdwy over 3f out: one pce fnl 2f) | 1 | **4** | 5/1[3] | 45 | 19 |
| 1651[6] | **Samara Song (60)** (WGMTurner) **3-8-4b[1]**(5) RHavlin(8) (swtg: plld hrd: led 4f: one pce fnl 2f) | hd | **5** | 20/1 | 57 | 31 |
| 1466[10] | **May Queen Megan (51)** (MrsALMKing) **3-8-12b[1]** FNorton(2) (nvr nr to chal) | 3 | **6** | 20/1 | 54 | 28 |
| 1196[16] | **Formentiere** (JMBradley) **3-8-4** LCharnock(7) (a bhd) | 4 | **7** | 50/1 | 36 | 10 |
| 1806[8] | **Danico (57)** (SCWilliams) **3-8-11** KDarley(10) (s.s: a bhd) | 2 | **8** | 15/2 | 39 | 13 |
| 1512[14] | **My Mother's Local (USA) (35)** (KOCunningham-Brown) **3-8-2b** DRMcCabe(5) (bhd fnl 3f) | nk | **9** | 40/1 | 29 | 3 |
| | ***Queen's Charter*** (MFBarraclough) **3-7-13**(3) NVarley(3) (Withdrawn not under Starter's orders: uns rdr & bolted bef s: veterinary advice) | | **W** | 50/1 | — | — |

(SP 118.0%) **9 Rn**

**1m 26.0** (1.40) CSF £103.79 TOTE £20.30: £2.20 £1.60 £1.20 (£100.20) Trio £22.00 OWNER Mr P. F. Boggis (UPPER LAMBOURN) BRED P. F. Boggis

Most Wanted(IRE) clmd TPeters £2,000

**Bag And A Bit**, stepping up from the minimum trip, has obviously come to herself and it sometimes pays to follow a filly in form. (25/1)

**Northern Judge** probably failed to stay ten furlongs last time and was sharpened up by the blinkers here. (7/2)

**1707 Double Oscar (IRE)** was disappointing on this return to seven and may need more cut. (11/10)

**Most Wanted (IRE)** at least finished closer over this shorter distance, but never really looked like winning. (5/1)

**1651 Samara Song** was much too free in the first-time blinkers but was not beaten that far in the end. (20/1)

**686 May Queen Megan**, tried in headgear, could never land a blow over this extra furlong. (20/1)

## 1837 GAVESTON H'CAP (0-80) (3-Y.O+) (Class D)

8-15 (8-19) **1m 4f 115y** £3,655.00 (£1,090.00: £520.00: £235.00) Stalls: Low GOING minus 0.54 sec per fur (F)

| | | | | SP | RR | SF |
|---|---|---|---|---|---|---|
| 1514* | **Canton Venture (51)** (SPCWoods) **4-8-5** WWoods(2) (a.p: led over 1f out: edgd lft: r.o wl) | — | **1** | 5/2[2] | 63 | 44 |
| 1647* | **Domappel (75)** (MrsJCecil) **4-10-1** 5x JWeaver(3) (w ldr: led 5f out tl over 1f out: one pce) | 2 | **2** | 7/4[1] | 84 | 65 |
| 1660[2] | **General Mouktar (55)** (BJMeehan) **6-8-9** KDarley(4) (hld up: hdwy 3f out: r.o one pce fnl f) | 1¼ | **3** | 3/1[3] | 63 | 44 |
| 1124[4] | **Reaganesque (USA) (46)** (PGMurphy) **4-8-0** FNorton(1) (nvr trbld ldrs) | 5 | **4** | 16/1 | 48 | 29 |
| 993[2] | **Outstayed Welcome (59)** (MJHaynes) **4-8-8**(5) MBaird(5) (led over 7f: sn wknd) | 4 | **5** | 9/2 | 55 | 36 |

(SP 114.0%) **5 Rn**

**2m 39.0** (0.50) CSF £7.26 TOTE £4.50: £1.70 £1.50 (£2.30) OWNER Dr Frank Chao (NEWMARKET) BRED High Point B/stock Ltd & Chao Racing & B/stock Ltd

**1514* Canton Venture**, 13lb lower than when winning on the Fibresand at Southwell last month, looked more at home on this left-handed course than when successful at Folkestone last time. (5/2)

**1647* Domappel** could not concede the weight to the well-handicapped winner. (7/4)

**1660 General Mouktar** again finished in the prizemoney, but has not won since his two-year-old days. (3/1)

**1124 Reaganesque (USA)** has come down 12lb in the weights this season. (16/1)

## 1838 GALLOWS HILL H'CAP (0-70) (3-Y.O+) (Class E)

8-45 (8-45) **1m 2f 169y** £3,236.00 (£968.00: £464.00: £212.00) Stalls: Low GOING minus 0.54 sec per fur (F)

| | | | | SP | RR | SF |
|---|---|---|---|---|---|---|
| 843[9] | **Rival Bid (USA) (64)** (MrsNMacauley) **8-9-7**(3) CTeague(5) (s.s: hdwy on ins over 2f out: pulled out over 1f out: led ins fnl f: rdn out) | — | **1** | 14/1 | 76 | 32 |
| 1515[7] | **Wet Patch (IRE) (60)** (RHannon) **4-9-6** RHughes(7) (hld up: hdwy 3f out: ev ch ins fnl f: r.o) | ¾ | **2** | 5/1[2] | 71 | 27 |
| 1515* | **Florentino (IRE) (65)** (BWHills) **3-8-11** MHills(6) (hld up: hdwy over 3f out: led over 1f out tl ins fnl f) | nk | **3** | 10/11[1] | 75 | 17 |
| 1686[7] | **Hand of Straw (IRE) (58)** (PGMurphy) **4-9-4v** KDarley(4) (hdwy 3f out: wknd over 1f out) | 6 | **4** | 11/1 | 60 | 16 |
| 1686[3] | **Harvey White (IRE) (59)** (JPearce) **4-9-5** AMcGlone(2) (chsd ldr: led over 2f out tl over 1f out: wknd fnl f) | ½ | **5** | 5/1[2] | 60 | 16 |
| 1502[5] | **Zahran (IRE) (40)** (JMBradley) **5-8-0** LCharnock(9) (no hdwy fnl 3f) | 3 | **6** | 9/1[3] | 36 | — |
| 787[17] | **Last Spin (47)** (JRJenkins) **4-8-2v[1]**(5) ADaly(1) (led over 2f: hrd rdn & wknd over 2f out) | 5 | **7** | 25/1 | 36 | — |
| 1534[15] | **Well Suited (36)** (THind) **6-7-7b**(3) NVarley(8) (b: a bhd) | 1½ | **8** | 50/1 | 23 | — |
| 1665[5] | **Mazilla (39)** (AStreeter) **4-7-13v** FNorton(3) (sddle slipped: led 8f out: sn clr: hdd over 2f out: sn wknd) | ¾ | **9** | 20/1 | 25 | — |

(SP 121.3%) **9 Rn**

**2m 17.9** (4.40) CSF £79.43 CT £119.30 TOTE £24.00: £4.90 £1.10 £1.50 (£27.50) Trio £41.10 OWNER Mr G. Wiltshire (MELTON MOWBRAY) BRED Marvin L. Warner Jnr.

LONG HANDICAP Well Suited 7-3

WEIGHT FOR AGE 3yo-14lb

**184 Rival Bid (USA)** bounced back to form, despite not being fancied by his trainer. (14/1: 10/1-16/1)

**1173 Wet Patch (IRE)**, well backed last time, likes fast ground but could not withstand the winner's late run. (5/1)

**1515* Florentino (IRE)** could not confirm the Folkestone form with the runner-up on 5lb worse terms. (10/11)

**1450 Hand of Straw (IRE)** is still 3lb higher than when winning over course and distance last summer. (11/1: op 7/1)

**1686 Harvey White (IRE)**, 6lb higher than when winning over course and distance last month, had much more use made of him on this occasion. (5/1)
**1502 Zahran (IRE)** possibly found the trip beyond his best. (9/1)

T/Plpt: £9.80 (829.89 Tckts). T/Qdpt: £2.30 (269.55 Tckts). KH

## 1651-WINDSOR (Fig. 8) (Good to firm)
## Monday June 10th

WEATHER: fine WIND: almost nil

### 1839 ARISTON ONANDONANDON CLAIMING STKS (3-Y.O+) (Class F)

6-30 (6-36) **1m 3f 135y** £2,843.00 (£798.00: £389.00) Stalls: High GOING minus 0.51 sec per fur (F)

| Form | Horse | Dist | Pos | SP | RR | SF |
|---|---|---|---|---|---|---|
| 641$^{11}$ | **Westminster (IRE) (63)** (MHTompkins) **4-9-11v** PRobinson(1) (chsd ldr: led ins fnl f: drvn out) | — | 1 | 13/2$^{3}$ | 72 | 34 |
| 1772* | **Statajack (IRE) (72)** (DRCElsworth) **8-10-0b** AProcter(13) (hld up: hdwy 3f out: ev ch fnl f: nt qckn) | 1 | 2 | 5/2$^{1}$ | 74 | 36 |
| 1788$^{3}$ | **Bayrak (USA) (73)** (MJRyan) **6-9-9** WCarson(8) (lw: led tl ins fnl f: nt qckn) | ¾ | 3 | 3/1$^{2}$ | 68 | 30 |
| 1506$^{8}$ | **Te Amo (IRE) (70)** (RAkehurst) **4-9-9** SSanders(5) (a.p: hrd rdn 2f out: one pce) | 2 | 4 | 15/2 | 65 | 27 |
| 948$^{8}$ | **Forever Noble (IRE) (64)** (MRChannon) **3-8-8** RPerham(9) (hdwy fnl 2f: nvr nrr) | 1 | 5 | 8/1 | 64 | 11 |
| 597$^{10}$ | **Sister Kit (IRE) (64)** (BPalling) **3-8-3** JQuinn(4) (nvr nr to chal) | 4 | 6 | 33/1 | 53 | — |
| 1461$^{5}$ | **Artic Bay** (MrsPNDutfield) **4-10-0** GBardwell(6) (hdwy 3f out: hrd rdn 2f out: wknd fnl f) | hd | 7 | 50/1 | 63 | 25 |
| 1534$^{3}$ | **Bag of Tricks (IRE) (53)** (SDow) **6-9-5** BThomson(3) (chsd ldrs: ev ch over 2f out: sn wknd) | 1¼ | 8 | 7/1 | 52 | 14 |
| | **Panto Queen** (CRBarwell) **5-8-13** TSprake(12) (a bhd) | 2½ | 9 | 50/1 | 43 | 5 |
| *9*$^{9}$ | **Fattash (USA) (45)** (PMooney) **4-9-9** JFEgan(2) (swtg: a bhd) | 4 | 10 | 33/1 | 47 | 9 |
| 1123$^{10}$ | **Amber Ring (49)** (MissKMGeorge) **3-8-3**$^{ow1}$ DHarrison(11) (lw: prom tl rdn & wknd over 2f out) | 1½ | 11 | 50/1 | 40 | — |
| 1009$^{9}$ | **Baker (42)** (JAkehurst) **3-8-1** CRutter(10) (b.hind: a bhd: t.o) | 16 | 12 | 50/1 | 16 | — |
| 1517$^{7}$ | **Little Wobbly** (PCClarke) **6-8-11** NAdams(7) (lw: a bhd: t.o & hrd rdn 4f out) | 20 | 13 | 50/1 | — | — |

(SP 118.0%) **13 Rn**

**2m 29.0** (5.00) CSF £21.39 TOTE £8.40: £2.30 £1.50 £1.50 (£10.80) Trio £12.70 OWNER Mr John Bull (NEWMARKET) BRED Ballymacarney Stud

WEIGHT FOR AGE 3yo-15lb

**Westminster (IRE)** settled down in second place. He struck the front just inside the final furlong and ran on for a clear-cut win. (13/2)
**1772* Statajack (IRE)** moved smoothly onto the heels of the leaders over two furlongs from home. He found a clear run on the rail to challenge entering the final furlong, but failed to find the pace to pass the winner. (5/2)
**1788 Bayrak (USA)** tried to lead all the way and, collared just inside the final furlong, kept on well. (3/1)
**Te Amo (IRE)** was always on the heels of the leaders. He came under pressure a long way out and, though staying on, never threatened to find the necessary speed. (15/2: 5/1-8/1)
**746 Forever Noble (IRE)** came with a good late run in the centre of the course, but could not quite reach the leaders. (8/1)
**Sister Kit (IRE)**, always in midfield, could never find the pace to reach a challenging position. (33/1)
**1534 Bag of Tricks (IRE)** (7/1: 5/1-15/2)

### 1840 SCHOLTES H'CAP (0-70) (3-Y.O F) (Class E)

7-00 (7-04) **5f 217y** £3,208.75 (£970.00: £472.50: £223.75) Stalls: High GOING minus 0.51 sec per fur (F)

| Form | Horse | Dist | Pos | SP | RR | SF |
|---|---|---|---|---|---|---|
| 1181$^{4}$ | **Petit Point (IRE) (70)** (RHannon) **3-9-7** PatEddery(15) (a.p: led 2f out: drvn out) | — | 1 | 9/2$^{1}$ | 76 | 50 |
| 1634$^{4}$ | **Croeso Cynnes (55)** (BPalling) **3-8-6** TSprake(12) (led 4f: ev ch 1f out: r.o) | 1½ | 2 | 10/1 | 57 | 31 |
| *230*$^{4}$ | **Mystery Matthias (50)** (MissBSanders) **3-8-1b** SSanders(4) (a.p: r.o ins fnl f) | hd | 3 | 14/1 | 52 | 26 |
| 686$^{11}$ | **Daffodil Express (IRE) (48)** (MJRyan) **3-7-13** WCarson(13) (prom tl outpcd over 2f out: gd hdwy fnl f) | 1¾ | 4 | 11/1 | 45 | 19 |
| 1594$^{7}$ | **Unspoken Prayer (47)** (JRArnold) **3-7-12**$^{ow1}$ JFEgan(9) (gd hdwy fnl f: nvr nrr) | hd | 5 | 20/1 | 44 | 17 |
| 1521$^{8}$ | **Manderella (65)** (JAkehurst) **3-9-2** MWigham(11) (b.off hind: swtg: nrst fin) | 1 | 6 | 20/1 | 59 | 33 |
| 1615$^{8}$ | **Time For Tea (IRE) (69)** (CACyzer) **3-9-6** WRyan(10) (b: nvr nrr) | nk | 7 | 9/1 | 62 | 36 |
| 1707$^{7}$ | **Ciserano (IRE) (64)** (MRChannon) **3-8-8**$^{(7)}$ AEddery(6) (hdwy over 1f out: nt rch ldrs) | ¾ | 8 | 10/1 | 55 | 29 |
| 1119$^{11}$ | **Dil Dil (57)** (WJHaggas) **3-8-8** BThomson(16) (lw: hdwy over 1f out: nt rch ldrs) | 1 | 9 | 8/1$^{3}$ | 46 | 20 |
| 686$^{14}$ | **Pharaoh's Joy (56)** (JWPayne) **3-8-7** MTebbutt(1) (hdwy over 2f out: eased whn btn fnl f) | 1 | 10 | 25/1 | 42 | 16 |
| 1356$^{5}$ | **Cindy Kate (IRE) (57)** (WRMuir) **3-8-8** CRutter(5) (nvr on terms) | 2 | 11 | 14/1 | 38 | 12 |
| 1301$^{9}$ | **Blossom Dearie (50)** (RGFrost) **3-8-1** RStreet(8) (a bhd) | hd | 12 | 10/1 | 30 | 4 |
| 1172$^{11}$ | **Sunset Harbour (IRE) (49)** (TJNaughton) **3-8-0** JQuinn(7) (gd spd over 3f) | s.h | 13 | 16/1 | 29 | 3 |
| | **Truth (61)** (SirMarkPrescott) **3-8-12** GDuffield(3) (bhd fnl 3f) | 1 | 14 | 6/1$^{2}$ | 39 | 13 |
| | **Donington Park (46)** (PTDalton) **3-7-11** NAdams(2) (lw: a wl bhd) | 1½ | 15 | 50/1 | 20 | — |
| 1663$^{4}$ | **Volare (55)** (BJMeehan) **3-8-6** PRobinson(14) (prom 3f) | 3½ | 16 | 11/1 | 19 | — |

(SP 132.1%) **16 Rn**

**1m 11.3** (0.80) CSF £49.32 CT £583.64 TOTE £4.60: £1.70 £3.00 £3.70 £1.90 (£26.30) Trio £268.80 OWNER Lady Tennant (MARLBOROUGH) BRED Mrs E. M. Burke

**1181 Petit Point (IRE)**, always going well on the stands' rail, took a narrow lead two furlongs out and, driven along, kept finding what was required. (9/2)
**1634 Croeso Cynnes** made the running for half a mile. She fought back well when headed, but found the winner carrying too many guns. (10/1: 6/1-11/1)
**Mystery Matthias**, always one of the leaders, was slightly outpaced at the two-furlong marker as the leading pair went clear, but she ran on well inside the final furlong. (14/1)
**Daffodil Express (IRE)**, well placed until past halfway, then dropped back and looked well beaten, but came again in the closing stages. (11/1)
**Unspoken Prayer** made good late headway and would have troubled the leading pair with a bit further to go. (20/1)
**Manderella** stayed on at the finish, but too late to trouble the leaders. (20/1)
**Truth** (6/1: 4/1-13/2)

### 1841 INDESIT H'CAP (0-80) (3-Y.O+) (Class D)

7-30 (7-30) **1m 2f 7y** £2,469.00 (£2,469.00: £558.00: £264.00) Stalls: High GOING minus 0.51 sec per fur (F)

| Form | Horse | Dist | Pos | SP | RR | SF |
|---|---|---|---|---|---|---|
| 1117$^{6}$ | **Shining Dancer (55)** (SDow) **4-8-3** SSanders(7) (lw: a.p: led cl home: all out) | — | 1 | 20/1 | 66 | 41 |
| 1486* | **Bakheta (51)** (MissGayKelleway) **4-7-13** NAdams(6) (led tl nr fin: r.o again) | — | 1 | 7/2$^{1}$ | 62 | 37 |

| | | | | SP | RR | SF |
|---|---|---|---|---|---|---|
| 1524[6] | **Fahs (USA) (65)** (RAkehurst) **4-8-13** RPerham(10) (lw: a.p: r.o one pce fnl 2f) | 1½ | **3** | 5/1[2] | 74 | 49 |
| 1686[5] | **Myfontaine (69)** (KTIvory) **9-9-3** MWigham(12) (b: lw: hdwy 3f out: rdn 2f out: one pce) | 4 | **4** | 10/1 | 71 | 46 |
| 1190[18] | **Hand Craft (IRE) (80)** (WJHaggas) **4-10-0** BThomson(9) (hld up in rr: hdwy & rdn 2f out: nrst fin) | nk | **5** | 10/1 | 82 | 57 |
| 1515[8] | **Guesstimation (USA) (63)** (JPearce) **7-8-11** GBardwell(13) (a mid div) | ¾ | **6** | 8/1[3] | 64 | 39 |
| 1099* | **Delight of Dawn (70)** (RMStronge) **4-9-4** JFEgan(11) (b: lw: nvr nrr) | nk | **7** | 14/1 | 70 | 45 |
| 1625[14] | **Ron's Secret (77)** (JWPayne) **4-9-11** LDettori(1) (prom tl wknd 2f out) | hd | **8** | 12/1 | 77 | 52 |
| 1515[5] | **South Eastern Fred (48)** (HJCollingridge) **5-7-10** JQuinn(4) (nvr on terms) | 4 | **9** | 10/1 | 42 | 17 |
| | **Prague Spring (67)** (LadyHerries) **4-9-1** DHarrison(3) (bit bkwd: a bhd) | nk | **10** | 10/1 | 60 | 35 |
| 1486[7] | **Sotoboy (IRE) (73)** (PWHarris) **4-9-7** GDuffield(2) (bhd fnl 5f) | 1½ | **11** | 14/1 | 64 | 39 |
| 1145[19] | **Yaverland (IRE) (60)** (CADwyer) **4-8-8** PatEddery(5) (b.hind: a bhd) | 10 | **12** | 12/1 | 35 | 10 |
| 1623[7] | **Easy Choice (USA) (60)** (PhilipMitchell) **4-8-8v¹** WRyan(8) (lw: a bhd: t.o) | 30 | **13** | 16/1 | — | — |

(SP 125.7%) **13 Rn**

**2m 5.7** (0.80) CSF £43.73 SD & B £33.25 B & SD CT £194.60 SD, B & F £166.55 B, SD & F TOTE £23.10 SD £2.00 B: £9.10 SD £2.20 B £2.60 (£55.10) Trio £86.20 OWNER The Lalemaha Partnership (EPSOM)/Mr Frank O'Rourke (WHITCOMBE) BRED Gainsborough Stud Management Ltd/Harsefoot Stud Royal

LONG HANDICAP South Eastern Fred 7-8

**Shining Dancer** was always close up. She drew level with the leader under strong pressure inside the final furlong, and in a battle royale forced a dead-heat. (20/1)

**1486* Bakheta** tried to make all the running. She was joined inside the final furlong, but kept sticking her head out, and fully deserved to share the spoils. (7/2)

**1019 Fahs (USA)** was always close up and had every chance, but just ran on at one pace under pressure in the final quarter-mile. (5/1)

**1686 Myfontaine** came with a promising challenge three furlongs out but, having reached the heels of the leading group a furlong later, could make no further progress. (10/1)

**Hand Craft (IRE)** was jumped off quietly and settled in the rear. He made steady headway three furlongs out and stayed on without enjoying the most brilliant of runs. He should be able to win off his present mark. (10/1)

**Guesstimation (USA)**, always in the group chasing the leaders, ran on at one pace in the final quarter-mile. (8/1)

## 1842 NEW WORLD MAIDEN AUCTION STKS (2-Y.O) (Class E)

8-00 (8-02) **5f 217y** £3,176.25 (£960.00: £467.50: £221.25) Stalls: High GOING minus 0.51 sec per fur (F)

| | | | | SP | RR | SF |
|---|---|---|---|---|---|---|
| 1339[2] | **Latin Master (IRE)** (RHannon) **2-8-5**ow1 PatEddery(3) (lw: a.p: led over 1f out: r.o wl) | — | **1** | 10/11[1] | 73 | 25 |
| | **Largesse** (JohnBerry) **2-8-10** MFenton(7) (w'like: bit bkwd: hdwy over 3f out: ev ch over 1f out: nt qckn) | 2½ | **2** | 9/1 | 71 | 23 |
| | **Jack The Lad (IRE)** (CMurray) **2-8-6** MTebbutt(9) (str: a.p: r.o ins fnl f) | 1½ | **3** | 7/1[2] | 63 | 16 |
| 1062[7] | **Summer Risotto** (DJSffrenchDavis) **2-7-12** NCarlisle(11) (a.p: ev ch over 1f out: nt qckn) | hd | **4** | 14/1 | 55 | 8 |
| | **Threeplay (IRE)** (JAkehurst) **2-8-6** GDuffield(12) (b.hind: neat: bit bkwd: led over 4f) | hd | **5** | 16/1 | 63 | 16 |
| | **Broadgate Flyer (IRE)** (WJarvis) **2-8-8** BThomson(6) (unf: s.s: hdwy 2f out: nt rch ldrs) | hd | **6** | 8/1[3] | 65 | 17 |
| 1408[3] | **The Four Isles** (DHaydnJones) **2-8-4** AMackay(5) (nvr nr to chal) | 3½ | **7** | 10/1 | 51 | 5 |
| | **Miss Stamper (IRE)** (RHannon) **2-8-1** SSanders(14) (unf: nvr bttr than mid div) | 1¼ | **8** | 10/1 | 45 | — |
| 706[12] | **Classic Mystery (IRE)** (BJMeehan) **2-8-7** JFEgan(10) (prom tl wknd over 1f out: eased whn btn) | 1 | **9** | 16/1 | 48 | 2 |
| | **Hever Golf Stormer (IRE)** (TJNaughton) **2-8-10** PaulEddery(1) (swtg: unf: bhd fnl 2f) | 1¼ | **10** | 16/1 | 48 | 2 |
| 1595[8] | **Miskin Heights (IRE)** (KRBurke) **2-7-12** JQuinn(8) (bhd fnl 2f) | nk | **11** | 33/1 | 35 | — |
| | **Hever Golf Dancer** (TJNaughton) **2-8-9** PRobinson(13) (w'like: bit bkwd: a wl bhd) | 5 | **12** | 10/1 | 33 | — |

(SP 140.5%) **12 Rn**

**1m 12.1** (1.60) CSF £12.70 TOTE £2.00: £1.30 £4.50 £1.40 (£9.70) Trio £52.40 OWNER Mr John Perry (MARLBOROUGH) BRED Mrs W. Hanson

**1339 Latin Master (IRE)** was always close up. Plenty appeared to be going as well at the quarter-mile marker but, when he was picked up in earnest, he soon asserted his superiority. (10/11: 4/6-Evens)

**Largesse** looked in need of the race. He moved up approaching halfway and, after having every chance at the distance, could make no impression on the winner. (9/1)

**Jack The Lad (IRE)** was never far behind the leaders but it was not until the last furlong that he really found top gear. He should be better for the outing. (7/1: op 12/1)

**465 Summer Risotto** was always close up and had every chance, but could not quicken under pressure in the closing stages. (14/1: op 6/1)

**Threeplay (IRE)** made the running until weakening approaching the final furlong. He looked just in need of the race and, as he clearly holds plenty of speed, he should be able to win a similar event. (16/1)

**Broadgate Flyer (IRE)** did well to reach his final position after a slow start. (8/1: 5/1-10/1)

**1408 The Four Isles** (10/1: 8/1-12/1)

**Hever Golf Dancer** (10/1: op 5/1)

## 1843 ARISTON BUILT-IN LIMITED STKS (0-80) (3-Y.O+) (Class D)

8-30 (8-30) **1m 67y** £3,480.00 (£1,050.00: £510.00: £240.00) Stalls: High GOING minus 0.51 sec per fur (F)

| | | | | SP | RR | SF |
|---|---|---|---|---|---|---|
| 1145[8] | **Select Few (80)** (LMCumani) **3-8-9** LDettori(5) (b.off fore: lw: hdwy 3f out: led over 1f out: r.o wl) | — | **1** | 11/4[2] | 87 | 38 |
| 1192[2] | **Zygo (USA) (80)** (WJarvis) **4-9-6** WRyan(6) (lw: hld up in rr: hdwy over 2f out: hrd rdn over 1f out: r.o ins fnl f) | 1¼ | **2** | 7/2[3] | 85 | 47 |
| 1190[12] | **Embankment (IRE) (77)** (RHannon) **6-9-6** PatEddery(1) (a.p: hrd rdn over 1f out: r.o ins fnl f) | nk | **3** | 8/1 | 84 | 46 |
| 1464[2] | **Crazy Chief (80)** (PFICole) **3-8-4**(7) DavidO'Neill(4) (2nd tl led over 2f out: hdd over 1f out: one pce) | ¾ | **4** | 5/2[1] | 85 | 36 |
| 755* | **Arterxerxes (80)** (MJHeaton-Ellis) **3-8-9** RPerham(3) (led tl over 2f out: wknd fnl f) | 3 | **5** | 9/1 | 77 | 28 |
| 450[15] | **Mihriz (IRE) (78)** (RAkehurst) **4-9-6** SSanders(2) (a bhd) | 5 | **6** | 9/1 | 67 | 29 |

(SP 108.6%) **6 Rn**

**1m 43.7** (1.50) CSF £11.55 TOTE £2.50: £1.60 £1.90 (£5.60) OWNER Sheikh Mohammed (NEWMARKET) BRED Sheikh Mohammed bin Rashid al Maktoum

WEIGHT FOR AGE 3yo-11lb

**693 Select Few**, patiently ridden, moved up steadily two furlongs from home. He soon took the lead and ran on for a decisive win. (11/4: 2/1-3/1)

**1192 Zygo (USA)**, settled in last place, came with a long run from the three-furlong marker and, though staying on, lacked the pace to trouble the winner. (7/2)

**Embankment (IRE)** was in third place for much of the way. He came under pressure approaching the final furlong and, though staying on, failed to quicken. (8/1: 5/1-9/1)

**1464 Crazy Chief** travelled strongly in second place until taking the lead over two furlongs from home. Headed approaching the final furlong, he was soon beaten. (5/2)
**755* Arterxerxes** attempted to make all the running and, after being headed over two furlongs from home, hung on until weakening in the final furlong. (9/1)
**Mihriz (IRE)** ran most disappointingly and was always behind. (9/1: 5/1-10/1)

## 1844 MERLONI LIMITED STKS (0-60) (3-Y.O+) (Class F)
9-00 (9-01) **5f 10y** £2,717.00 (£762.00: £371.00) Stalls: High GOING minus 0.51 sec per fur (F)

| | | | | SP | RR | SF |
|---|---|---|---|---|---|---|
| 1512[2] | **Mousehole (64)** (RGuest) **4-9-2b** PaulEddery(4) (hdwy over 2f out: led & edgd rt over 1f out: r.o) | — | **1** | 11/4[2] | 69 | 42 |
| 1521[6] | **Malibu Man (58)** (EAWheeler) **4-9-2** TSprake(6) (led over 3f: r.o) | 1 | **2** | 11/2[3] | 66 | 39 |
| 1351[4] | **Gone Savage (58)** (WJMusson) **8-9-2** LDettori(10) (hdwy over 1f out: r.o ins fnl f) | 2 | **3** | 11/2[3] | 60 | 33 |
| 1412[10] | **Petraco (IRE) (60)** (NASmith) **8-9-2** SDWilliams(3) (hdwy 2f out: r.o ins fnl f) | nk | **4** | 12/1 | 59 | 32 |
| | **Clan Chief (57)** (JRArnold) **3-8-9** CRutter(5) (hld up: ev ch whn bdly bmpd over 1f out: nt rcvr) | nk | **5** | 12/1 | 58 | 24 |
| 1512[10] | **Miami Banker (50)** (WRMuir) **10-9-2b** GBardwell(9) (gd spd over 3f) | 1¼ | **6** | 20/1 | 54 | 27 |
| 1547* | **Ninety-Five (60)** (JGFitzGerald) **4-9-2** KFallon(13) (hld up: hdwy & ev ch over 1f out: wknd ins fnl f) | s.h | **7** | 9/4[1] | 54 | 27 |
| *1716*[5] | **Halbert (60)** (PBurgoyne) **7-8-13v**(3) PMcCabe(14) (no hdwy fnl 2f) | 1 | **8** | 20/1 | 50 | 23 |
| 1642[21] | **Deardaw (39)** (MDIUsher) **4-8-13** SSanders(2) (outpcd & t.o tl r.o fnl f) | 1¼ | **9** | 25/1 | 43 | 16 |
| 981[11] | **Speedy Classic (USA) (59)** (MJHeaton-Ellis) **7-9-5b** BThomson(11) (nvr nr to chal: eased whn btn fnl f) | 1 | **10** | 14/1 | 46 | 19 |
| 1536[8] | **Dancing Jack (50)** (JJBridger) **3-8-9** JQuinn(12) (a bhd) | nk | **11** | 20/1 | 42 | 8 |
| 943[8] | **Little Pilgrim (42)** (TMJones) **3-8-9** RPerham(8) (prom over 2f) | 4 | **12** | 50/1 | 30 | — |
| | | | | (SP 130.3%) | **12 Rn** | |

**60.1 secs** (0.90) CSF £19.41 TOTE £3.60: £1.60 £2.60 £1.90 (£20.30) Trio £24.50 OWNER Mrs Janet Kent (NEWMARKET) BRED T. H. Rossiter
WEIGHT FOR AGE 3yo-7lb
**1512 Mousehole** made good headway at halfway. He had just taken the lead when he veered sharply to the right, bumping a rival, approaching the final furlong and, once straightened, ran on for a clear-cut win. (11/4)
**1521 Malibu Man** made the running until approaching the final furlong and, though he kept on well under pressure, the winner was always holding him. (11/2)
**1351 Gone Savage** raced in mid-pack until staying on to reach third place inside the final furlong. (11/2)
**762 Petraco (IRE)** came with a good run in the centre of the course two furlongs out but, though staying on, could not trouble the leading pair. (12/1: 8/1-14/1)
**Clan Chief** was going strongly on the heels of the leaders when badly bumped by the winner approaching the final furlong. In the circumstances, he did well to finish so close and is one to note. (12/1: op 8/1)
**Miami Banker** raced fast on the stands' rail while all the action was in the centre of the track, but could not quicken inside the final furlong. (20/1)
**1547* Ninety-Five** travelled well in midfield. She quickened when asked for her effort below the distance, but failed to sustain the run in the final furlong. (9/4: op 4/1)
**981 Speedy Classic (USA)** (14/1: op 7/1)

T/Plpt: £21.80 (692.3 Tckts). T/Qdpt: £10.20 (69.04 Tckts). Hn/AK

# 1499-REDCAR (L-H) (Good to firm, Good patches)
## Tuesday June 11th
WEATHER: drizzle WIND: str bhd

## 1845 HARTLEPOOL UNITED (S) STKS (2-Y.O) (Class G)
2-15 (2-17) **7f** £2,267.50 (£630.00: £302.50) Stalls: Centre GOING minus 0.74 sec per fur (HD)

| | | | | SP | RR | SF |
|---|---|---|---|---|---|---|
| | **Dee Pee Tee Cee (IRE)** (MWEasterby) **2-8-6**(5) GParkin(4) (leggy: scope: hld up: hdwy to ld & hung lft ins fnl f: qcknd: comf) | — | **1** | 10/1 | 59+ | — |
| 1645[4] | **Blonde Rock** (MRChannon) **2-8-6** KDarley(2) (cl up: led wl over 1f out tl jst ins fnl f: btn whn hmpd ins fnl f) | 1¼ | **2** | 4/5[1] | 51 | — |
| | **Fearless Cavalier** (RHollinshead) **2-8-6**(5) FLynch(1) (unf: cl up: chal 2f out: nt qckn ins fnl f) | hd | **3** | 6/1[3] | 56 | — |
| 1183[9] | **Samspet** (RAFahey) **2-8-11** ACulhane(6) (lw: led tl hdd wl over 1f out: nt qckn) | 1½ | **4** | 12/1 | 53 | — |
| | **Maremma** (DonEnricoIncisa) **2-8-6** KimTinkler(7) (neat: bit bkwd: s.i.s: effrt ½-wy: sn btn) | 3½ | **5** | 50/1 | 40 | — |
| 1086[11] | **Cala-Holme (IRE)** (TDEasterby) **2-8-6** MBirch(5) (prom tl outpcd fnl 2f) | 4 | **6** | 9/2[2] | 30 | — |
| *1097*[6] | **Ramsey Pride** (CWFairhurst) **2-8-6** NKennedy(3) (lw: hld up: effrt 3f out: sn btn) | 1¾ | **7** | 12/1 | 26 | — |
| | | | | (SP 114.5%) | **7 Rn** | |

**1m 26.2** (3.20) CSF £18.31 TOTE £12.60: £4.20 £1.10 (£7.10) OWNER Early Morning Breakfast Syndicate (SHERIFF HUTTON) BRED Michael and Heather Scott
No bid
**Dee Pee Tee Cee (IRE)** was easily the paddock pick and, despite running green, won with ease. (10/1)
**1645 Blonde Rock**, an edgy sort, was awkward at the start. She had her chances throughout, but her attitude left something to be desired, and being hampered made absolutely no difference. (4/5)
**Fearless Cavalier** ran a reasonable first race, but he was short of toe in the closing stages. (6/1: op 4/1)
**Samspet** dictated things but, once passed well over a furlong out, proved one-paced. (12/1)
**Maremma** needed this, and never looked likely to take a real hand in things. (50/1)
**Cala-Holme (IRE)** (9/2: op 5/2)

## 1846 EVENING GAZETTE H'CAP (0-70) (3-Y.O+) (Class E)
2-45 (2-45) **1m** £3,579.00 (£1,077.00: £521.00: £243.00) Stalls: Centre GOING minus 0.74 sec per fur (HD)

| | | | | SP | RR | SF |
|---|---|---|---|---|---|---|
| 1172[3] | **Mister Woodstick (IRE) (53)** (MAJarvis) **3-8-9** PRobinson(8) (cl up: led over 2f out: hld on wl fnl f) | — | **1** | 5/2[2] | 60 | 31 |
| 1586* | **Highspeed (IRE) (57)** (SEKettlewell) **4-9-10** JFortune(4) (lw: hld up & bhd: hdwy over 2f out: ch ins fnl f: r.o) | ½ | **2** | 7/4[1] | 63 | 45 |
| 1527[10] | **Oriole (43)** (NTinkler) **3-7-13b** KimTinkler(9) (trckd ldrs: ev ch over 2f out: r.o one pce) | 1½ | **3** | 14/1 | 46 | 17 |
| 1500[5] | **Percy Park (USA) (42)** (MWEasterby) **3-7-12** DaleGibson(2) (a in tch: kpt on one pce fnl 2f) | 1½ | **4** | 9/1 | 42 | 13 |

| | | | | SP | RR | SF |
|---|---|---|---|---|---|---|
| $1650^{4}$ | **Sallyoreally (IRE) (37)** (WStorey) **5-8-4** JFanning(6) (lw: in tch: effrt 3f out: no imp) | 3½ | **5** | 4/1 $^{3}$ | 30 | 12 |
| | **Bulsara (56)** (CWFairhurst) **4-9-9** DeanMcKeown(7) (led tl hdd over 2f out: sn btn) | 2½ | **6** | 16/1 | 44 | 26 |
| $1596^{12}$ | **Four Lane Flyer (37)** (EJAlston) **4-8-4** GDuffield(3) (dwlt: raced alone far side: bhd fr ½-wy) | 8 | **7** | 16/1 | 9 | — |
| | **Upex le Gold Too (38)** (LRLloyd-James) **4-7-12**(7) CWebb(5) (bhd fnl 3f) | 3 | **8** | 20/1 | 4 | — |
| *$84^{10}$* | **Macaroon Lady (29)** (NBycroft) **5-7-5**(5) PFessey(1) (lw: in tch 4f: sn bhd) | 6 | **9** | 66/1 | — | — |
| | | | | (SP 119.6%) | | **9 Rn** |

**1m 35.8** (0.10) CSF £7.33 CT £46.09 TOTE £3.10: £1.10 £1.60 £2.60 (£3.10) Trio £79.50 OWNER Mr John Sims (NEWMARKET) BRED John O'Connor

LONG HANDICAP Macaroon Lady 7-8

WEIGHT FOR AGE 3yo-11lb

**1172 Mister Woodstick (IRE)**, well ridden, was made plenty use of, and proved game under pressure. (5/2)

**1586* Highspeed (IRE)** was given plenty to do and, when he looked likely to get on terms inside the final furlong, the winner had a bit more in the tank. He goes on this ground, but is certainly better suited by some give. (7/4: op 11/10)

**973 Oriole** raced freely and had his chances, but failed to quicken in the last couple of furlongs. This was his best effort for some time. (14/1)

**1500 Percy Park (USA)** ran another decent race, and was staying on determinedly at the end. (9/1: op 6/1)

**1650 Sallyoreally (IRE)** does not seem to have a trip that suits, and is still a maiden after twenty-four starts. (4/1)

**Bulsara**, having his first run of the season over a trip just short of his best, ran well enough. (16/1)

## 1847 SUNDERLAND CLAIMING STKS (3-Y.O+) (Class F)

3-15 (3-16) **2m 4y** £2,714.00 (£754.00: £362.00) Stalls: Low GOING minus 0.74 sec per fur (HD)

| | | | | SP | RR | SF |
|---|---|---|---|---|---|---|
| | **Good Hand (USA) (70)** (JWWatts) **10-10-0** NConnorton(3) (lw: b: trckd ldrs: led 2f out: r.o) | — | **1** | Evens $^{1}$ | 65 | 20 |
| | **Brodessa (60)** (MrsMReveley) **10-9-11** KDarley(1) (lw: led: qcknd 4f out: hdd 2f out: no ex) | 2½ | **2** | 4/1 $^{3}$ | 60 | 15 |
| $1529^{3}$ | **Jalcanto (55)** (MrsMReveley) **6-9-7**(7) SCopp(9) (lw: bdly hmpd bnd after 3½f: styd on fnl 3f: nrst fin) | 1 | **3** | 100/30 $^{2}$ | 62 | 17 |
| $1784^{6}$ | **Longcroft (34)** (KWHogg) **4-9-1** NKennedy(2) (hld up: effrt 4f out: styd on: nvr rchd ldrs) | 1 | **4** | 25/1 | 49 | 3 |
| | **Iron Gent (USA) (66)** (SEKettlewell) **5-10-0** JFortune(7) (a.p: kpt on one pce fnl 3f) | 2½ | **5** | 8/1 | 58 | 13 |
| $1542^{5}$ | **Tancred Mischief (31)** (WLBarker) **5-8-12**(5) MartinDwyer(8) (chsd ldrs tl outpcd fnl 4f) | 3½ | **6** | 50/1 | 44 | — |
| $1474^{12}$ | **Flyaway Blues (49)** (MrsMReveley) **4-9-10v** DeanMcKeown(4) (bdly hmpd bnd after 3½f: n.d) | ½ | **7** | 25/1 | 51 | 5 |
| $1611^{6}$ | **Don't Cry (15)** (DonEnricoIncisa) **8-9-1** KimTinkler(10) (chsd ldrs tl ½-wy: sn lost pl) | 9 | **8** | 100/1 | 32? | — |
| $1638^{12}$ | **Cherry Muna** (CWFairhurst) **3-8-1v**[1] JTate(5) (wnt prom ½-wy: ev ch ent st: sn wknd t.o) | dist | **9** | 200/1 | — | — |
| | **Bitter Moon** (NChamberlain) **5-9-2** JFanning(6) (prom whn fell bnd after 3½f: dead) | | **F** | 200/1 | — | — |
| | | | | (SP 115.8%) | | **10 Rn** |

**3m 32.3** (7.30) CSF £5.36 TOTE £1.90: £1.50 £1.30 £1.10 (£4.20) Trio £3.90 OWNER Mrs M. M. Haggas (RICHMOND) BRED Tauner Dunlap, Jr. and Brereton C. Jones

WEIGHT FOR AGE 3yo-21lb, 4yo-1lb

Good Hand (USA) clmd J Hughes £10,000

**Good Hand (USA)**, dropped in class, enjoyed himself and won nicely, but this game old performer was then claimed. (Evens)

**Brodessa**, the same age as the winner, loves this type of race but, despite trying hard, had certainly met one too good. (4/1)

**1529 Jalcanto**, quite badly hampered by a faller early on, never got going until the race was over. (100/30)

**1784 Longcroft**, having her second race of the week, was warm in the preliminaries, but still ran reasonably, staying on well at the end. (25/1)

**Iron Gent (USA)** showed something here and should be all the better for it. (8/1: 6/1-9/1)

**1542 Tancred Mischief** had no chance at these weights, and ran quite well in the circumstances. (50/1)

## 1848 STANLEY JACKSON 50TH RACING ANNIVERSARY H'CAP (0-70) (3-Y.O+) (Class E)

3-45 (3-49) **6f** £3,265.50 (£984.00: £477.00: £223.50) Stalls: Centre GOING minus 0.74 sec per fur (HD)

| | | | | SP | RR | SF |
|---|---|---|---|---|---|---|
| $1646^{5}$ | **Invigilate (49)** (MartynWane) **7-8-7**ow2 KFallon(8) (lw: hdwy over 2f out: swtchd rt: r.o to ld wl ins fnl f) | — | **1** | 9/2 $^{2}$ | 54 | 40 |
| $1425^{9}$ | **Keston Pond (IRE) (70)** (MrsVAAconley) **6-10-0** MDeering(3) (cl up: led over 1f out tl wl ins fnl f: kpt on) | 1 | **2** | 20/1 | 72 | 60 |
| $1538^{6}$ | **Superpride (62)** (MrsMReveley) **4-9-6b**[1] MBirch(2) (led 4f: kpt on u.p) | 1¼ | **3** | 5/1 $^{3}$ | 61 | 49 |
| $1765^{3}$ | **Plum First (65)** (LRLloyd-James) **6-9-2**(7) CWebb(6) (b: b.hind: sn outpcd & bhd: hung lft over 2f out: styd on wl: nrst fin) | ¾ | **4** | 4/1 $^{1}$ | 62 | 50 |
| $1634^{5}$ | **Densben (48)** (DenysSmith) **12-8-6** KDarley(4) (outpcd & bhd tl styd on wl appr fnl f) | hd | **5** | 9/1 | 45 | 33 |
| $1588^{9}$ | **Colway Rake (69)** (JWWatts) **5-9-13b** NConnorton(1) (lw: a chsng ldrs: ev ch 2f out: r.o one pce) | ¾ | **6** | 5/1 $^{3}$ | 64 | 52 |
| $1650^{9}$ | **Prime Property (IRE) (38)** (MWEasterby) **4-7-5**(5) MartinDwyer(5) (sn drvn along: no imp fr ½-wy) | 1¾ | **7** | 16/1 | 28 | 16 |
| | **Formidable Liz (56)** (MDHammond) **6-9-0** JFortune(9) (bit bkwd: bhd: effrt u.p over 2f out: n.d) | ¾ | **8** | 12/1 | 44 | 32 |
| $1588^{5}$ | **Captain Carat (68)** (MrsJRRamsden) **5-9-5**(7) ClaireWest(7) (b.nr fore: s.i.s: hdwy ½-wy: led 2f out: sn hdd & wknd) | ½ | **9** | 5/1 $^{3}$ | 55 | 43 |
| $1598^{12}$ | **Rankaidade (38)** (DonEnricoIncisa) **5-7-10b** KimTinkler(10) (spd to ½-wy: sn wnd) | 5 | **10** | 50/1 | 11 | — |
| | | | | (SP 118.5%) | | **10 Rn** |

**1m 9.4** (-0.80) CSF £75.91 CT £439.44 TOTE £4.80: £1.30 £4.00 £3.10 (£43.50) Trio £67.70 OWNER David Kay Racing (RICHMOND) BRED Bechmann Stud

LONG HANDICAP Rankaidade 6-12

**1646 Invigilate**, who failed to score last season, came from off the pace here to win nicely. (9/2: op 3/1)

**956 Keston Pond (IRE)** is now coming to form, and should be kept on the right side. (20/1)

**1538 Superpride**, in blinkers for the first time, was really fired up. Taken to post early, he led on the way back until tapped for toe in the final furlong. (5/1)

**1765 Plum First** got outpaced early on and, after hanging badly left two furlongs out, finished quite well (4/1)

**1634 Densben** is gradually coming to hand, but is was all over before he ran on. (9/1)

**1588 Colway Rake** has the ability, but as yet this season has not been caught in the right mood. (5/1)

**Formidable Liz** needed this and should improve as a result. (12/1)

## 1849 MIDDLESBROUGH MEDIAN AUCTION MAIDEN STKS (2-Y.O) (Class D)

4-15 (4-21) **6f** £3,491.25 (£1,050.00: £507.50: £236.25) Stalls: Centre GOING minus 0.74 sec per fur (HD)

| | | | | SP | RR | SF |
|---|---|---|---|---|---|---|
| | **Nigrasine** (JLEyre) **2-9-0** DeanMcKeown(3) (w'like: unf: bit bkwd: cl up: led over 2f out: hld on wl) | — | **1** | 8/1 $^{3}$ | 73 | 34 |
| $1086^{2}$ | **The Lambton Worm** (DenysSmith) **2-9-0** KFallon(1) (lw: cl up: chal 2f out: nt qckn towards fin) | nk | **2** | 2/1 $^{2}$ | 72 | 33 |
| $1424^{3}$ | **Baritone** (JWWatts) **2-9-0** GDuffield(10) (lw: a.p: effrt 2f out: r.o fnl f: nrst fin) | nk | **3** | 11/10 $^{1}$ | 71 | 32 |
| | **Floating Devon** (TDEasterby) **2-9-0** MBirch(11) (cmpt: hld up: hdwy 2f out: nvr nr to chal) | 4 | **4** | 20/1 | 61 | 22 |
| $1525^{3}$ | **Divide And Rule** (RHollinshead) **2-8-9**(5) DGriffiths(5) (led tl hdd over 2f out: sn outpcd) | 3½ | **5** | 14/1 | 51 | 12 |

Fruitana (IRE) (JBerry) 2-9-0 JCarroll(4) (unf: a.p: nt qckn fnl 2f) ½ **6** 16/1 50 11
**Not A Lot** (MWEasterby) **2-9-0** DaleGibson(12) (lt-f: in tch: no hdwy fnl 2f) 1¼ **7** 50/1 47 8
**Woodetto (IRE)** (EWeymes) **2-9-0** KDarley(7) (cmpt: dwlt: hdwy ½-wy: nvr rchd ldrs) ½ **8** 25/1 45 6
**Kingdom Emperor** (MJCamacho) **2-9-0** LCharnock(2) (cmpt: bit bkwd: unruly s: sn in tch: wknd fnl 2f) 9 **9** 33/1 21 —
**Mon Performer** (MJCamacho) **2-9-0** JFortune(8) (leggy: scope: bit bkwd: s.i.s: a bhd) nk **10** 40/1 21 —
**Chateauherault (IRE)** (PCHaslam) **2-9-0** PRobinson(9) (w'like: leggy: bit bkwd: sn outpcd & bhd) hd **11** 20/1 20 —
**Smoke'n'jo (IRE)** (MWEasterby) **2-8-9**(5) GParkin(6) (cmpt: sn outpcd & bhd) 1½ **12** 50/1 16 —
(SP 127.3%) **12 Rn**

**1m 10.3** (0.10) CSF £24.86 TOTE £10.60: £2.40 £1.40 £1.20 (£16.10) Trio £3.10 OWNER Mr M. Gleason (HAMBLETON) BRED Lady Jennifer Green

**Nigrasine** is not the best of lookers, but does move well and showed fine courage to win this. There is still something to work on. (8/1)
**1086 The Lambton Worm** looked tremendously well, and was with the winner throughout, but just found him too tough. (2/1)
**1424 Baritone** took a long time to get going, and would seem to be crying out for further, where he should really make his mark. (11/10: 4/5-5/4)
**Floating Devon** had a nice quiet introduction here, and looks likely to do a deal better before long. (20/1)
**1525 Divide And Rule** knew more about it this time, but was well tapped for speed in the closing stages. (14/1)
**Fruitana (IRE)** looked fit, but this stable's runners are generally needing an outing or two this season, and he should improve for this. (16/1)

## 1850 NEWCASTLE UNITED H'CAP (0-65) (3-Y.O) (Class F)
4-45 (4-53) **1m 2f** £3,071.00 (£856.00: £413.00) Stalls: Low GOING minus 0.74 sec per fur (HD)

SP RR SF
1641[5] **Ordained (50)** (EJAlston) **3-8-7** KFallon(5) (bhd: hdwy over 2f out: r.o to ld ins fnl f) — **1** 6/1[2] 60 15
1696* **Princely Affair (47)** (MBell) **3-7-11**(7) RMullen(15) (lw: bhd: hdwy on outside 2f out: ev ch ins fnl f: kpt on) 1¼ **2** 4/1[1] 55 10
1698[2] **Silverdale Knight (58)** (KWHogg) **3-8-10**(5) ADaly(10) (led after 2f: qcknd clr 4f out: hdd & no ex ins fnl f) 1¼ **3** 7/1[3] 64 19
1089[4] **Blenheim Terrace (51)** (CBBBooth) **3-8-8** ACulhane(8) (hdwy on ins over 3f out: styd on: nrst fin) 1 **4** 10/1 55 10
1089[12] **Northern Falcon (40)** (MWEasterby) **3-7-11b**[1] DaleGibson(16) (in tch: effrt & hmpd 2f out: kpt on one pce) 2½ **5** 33/1 40 —
1363[8] **Lawn Order (45)** (MrsJRRamsden) **3-8-2** NKennedy(17) (lw: bhd tl styd on fnl 2f) 1½ **6** 10/1 43 —
1363[13] **Kernof (IRE) (50)** (MDHammond) **3-8-7** JFortune(9) (nvr trbld ldrs) 1 **7** 14/1 46 1
1539* **Contract Bridge (IRE) (48)** (CWThornton) **3-8-5** DeanMcKeown(14) (lw: prom: bmpd appr st: effrt 4f out: hmpd 2f out: one pce) s.h **8** 4/1[1] 44 —
1636[4] **She's Simply Great (IRE) (56)** (JJO'Neill) **3-8-13** GDuffield(3) (in tch: hmpd appr st: effrt & hung rt 2f out: sn btn) 2½ **9** 50/1 48 3
1363[9] **Generous Present (49)** (JWPayne) **3-8-6** PRobinson(11) (mid div: nt clr run over 3f out: hmpd 2f out: n.d) 2½ **10** 11/1 37 —
*859[7]* **Alfayza (60)** (JDBethell) **3-8-12**(5) PFessey(7) (led 2f: chsd ldr: effrt 4f out: wknd 2f out) nk **11** 33/1 48 3
1359[9] **Clash of Swords (64)** (PCalver) **3-9-7** MBirch(4) (n.d) 3 **12** 20/1 47 2
1359[12] **Troika (IRE) (52)** (JBerry) **3-8-4**(5) PRoberts(1) (a bhd) 2½ **13** 33/1 31 —
*1456[3]* **Eccentric Dancer (39)** (MPBielby) **3-7-5**(5) MartinDwyer(13) (prom tl wknd fnl 3f) 3 **14** 14/1 13 —
1363[6] **One Life To Live (IRE) (50)** (AHarrison) **3-8-7** TWilliams(6) (chsd ldrs: effrt 4f out: btn whn bdly hmpd & eased fnl 2f) 6 **15** 12/1 15 —
**Stoleamarch (48)** (MrsMReveley) **3-8-5** KDarley(2) (bit bkwd: unruly s: prom to st) 1¾ **16** 14/1 10 —
1539[9] **Oare Budgie (40)** (DonEnricoIncisa) **3-7-11** KimTinkler(12) (a bhd) 13 **17** 100/1 — —
(SP 137.5%) **17 Rn**

**2m 5.9** (2.30) CSF £31.73 CT £171.26 TOTE £8.50: £1.70 £1.10 £1.60 £3.40 (£16.70) Trio £25.30 OWNER Edges Farm Racing Stables (PRESTON) BRED Sheikh Mohammed Bin Rashid Al Maktoum
LONG HANDICAP Eccentric Dancer 7-9

**1641 Ordained** had a lot of running to do from the home turn, and did pretty well to win. (6/1)
**1696* Princely Affair** took an age to get going in the straight, but then found the winner too strong in the closing stages. He is on particularly good terms with himself. (4/1)
**1698 Silverdale Knight** almost stole this when quickening clear early in the straight, but he just ran out of petrol in the last furlong. Surely his turn in near. (7/1)
**1089 Blenheim Terrace** ran another decent race without offering a serious threat, and looks to be coming right. (10/1)
**Northern Falcon** ran better with the blinkers on here, but still looked short of toe in the last couple of furlongs. (33/1)
**1363 Lawn Order** is getting better as she tries longer trips, and made up a fair amount of ground this time. (10/1)
**1539* Contract Bridge (IRE)** was involved in a lot of scrimmaging at various stages, and can be forgiven this. (4/1)
**Generous Present** found all sorts of trouble throughout the race, and this effort is best ignored. (11/1)
**Stoleamarch** (14/1: op 9/1)

T/Plpt: £8.20 (1,541.85 Tckts). T/Qdpt: £4.90 (165.59 Tckts). AA

# 1346-SALISBURY (R-H) (Good, Good to firm patches)
## Tuesday June 11th
Race 4: Flip start
WEATHER: overcast WIND: fresh across

## 1851 EDDIE REAVEY MAIDEN AUCTION STKS (2-Y.O F) (Class F)
2-00 (2-02) **6f** £3,018.50 (£908.00: £439.00: £204.50) Stalls: High GOING minus 0.39 sec per fur (F)

SP RR SF
1346[3] **Green Jewel** (RHannon) **2-8-1**(3)ow1 DaneO'Neill(4) (a.p: led over 1f out: r.o wl) — **1** 15/8[1] 71 25
**Smugurs (IRE)** (RJRWilliams) **2-8-3** GHind(3) (w'like: scope: wnt lft s: sn chsng ldrs: r.o ins fnl f) 4 **2** 4/1[3] 59 14
1118[4] **Will To Win** (PGMurphy) **2-8-3** MRoberts(9) (led over 4f: one pce) s.h **3** 7/1 59 14
639[6] **Hever Golf Lily** (TJNaughton) **2-8-7** JWeaver(11) (hld up & bhd: hdwy over 2f out: one pce fnl f) 1¼ **4** 14/1 60 15
1590[3] **Jilly Woo** (DRCElsworth) **2-8-3** BDoyle(1) (hld up: hdwy over 2f out: rdn & hung rt over 1f out: btn whn hung rt fnl f) 3½ **5** 100/30[2] 47 2
**Dizzy Tilly** (TJNaughton) **2-8-7** PaulEddery(2) (w'like: scope: s.s: swtchd rt: hdwy 4f out: n.m.r on ins 2f out: sn wknd) 5 **6** 16/1 37 —
**Shall We Go (IRE)** (RHannon) **2-8-3** RPerham(10) (w'like: bit bkwd: dwlt: sn rdn: bhd fnl 3f) hd **7** 20/1 33 —
1346[11] **My Precious** (MMcCormack) **2-8-3** JFEgan(7) (prom over 3f) 3½ **8** 33/1 24 —
1519[7] **Accountancy Leader (IRE)** (BPalling) **2-8-0** TSprake(8) (chsd ldr: tl rdn & wknd 2f out) 2½ **9** 20/1 14 —
**Mystical Island** (CACyzer) **2-8-3** MFenton(6) (w'like: bit bkwd: s.i.s: a bhd) 2½ **10** 20/1 10 —

| | | | | SP | RR | SF |
|---|---|---|---|---|---|---|
| | **Double Gold** (BJMeehan) **2-8-7** MTebbutt(5) (leggy: lt-f: prom 3f) | 2½ | **11** | 16/1 | 8 | — |
| | | | | (SP 126.0%) | | **11 Rn** |

**1m 15.35** (2.35) CSF £10.39 TOTE £2.90: £1.40 £1.70 £1.50 (£7.70) Trio £15.70 OWNER Mr T. E. Bucknall (MARLBOROUGH) BRED Stetchworth Park Stud Ltd

**1346 Green Jewel** had learnt a lot from her debut last month, and stayed on strongly in this easier company. (15/8: 6/4-9/4)
**Smugurs (IRE)**, out of an unraced half-sister to Polykratis, showed the right sort of attitude to snatch second place on the line. (4/1: 5/2-5/1)
**1118 Will To Win** kept on when headed over this extra furlong. (7/1)
**639 Hever Golf Lily**, given time to come on from her debut, was better suited to this longer trip. (14/1: 7/1-16/1)
**1590 Jilly Woo** did herself no favours by repeatedly hanging right. (100/30: 9/4-7/2)
**Dizzy Tilly** should be better for the experience. (16/1)

## 1852 CITY BOWL H'CAP (0-80) (3-Y.O+ F & M) (Class D)
2-30 (2-31) **1m 4f** £4,077.50 (£1,220.00: £585.00: £267.50) Stalls: Low GOING minus 0.39 sec per fur (F)

| | | | | SP | RR | SF |
|---|---|---|---|---|---|---|
| 1462[4] | **White Sea (IRE) (74)** (PFICole) **3-8-12** TQuinn(2) (a.p: led over 2f out: rdn out) | — | **1** | 7/2[1] | 85 | 52 |
| 1640[5] | **Uncharted Waters (53)** (CACyzer) **5-8-6** JWeaver(8) (hld up & bhd: hdwy & swtchd lft wl over 1f out: r.o wl ins fnl f) | ½ | **2** | 10/1 | 63 | 45 |
| | **Tonys Gift (65)** (MCPipe) **4-9-4** MRoberts(1) (lw: a.p: ev ch over 2f out: styd on fnl f) | 1 | **3** | 7/1 | 74 | 56 |
| 1306[2] | **Lalindi (IRE) (67)** (DRCElsworth) **5-9-6b** AProcter(6) (led: clr 8f out: hdd over 2f out: wknd fnl f) | 3½ | **4** | 7/1 | 71 | 53 |
| | **Rocquaine Bay (43)** (MJBolton) **9-7-10** JQuinn(9) (bkwd: rdn over 4f out: hdwy over 2f out: one pce fnl f) | s.h | **5** | 12/1 | 47 | 29 |
| 642[13] | **Victoria's Secret (IRE) (55)** (MRChannon) **4-8-8** JFEgan(4) (hld up: rdn over 3f out: hdwy over 2f out: one pce fnl f) | 1 | **6** | 20/1 | 58 | 40 |
| 968[9] | **Quivira (71)** (HAkbary) **5-9-10** MRimmer(3) (mid div: rdn 6f out: no hdwy fnl 3f) | nk | **7** | 20/1 | 74 | 56 |
| 1585[5] | **Arcady (66)** (PTWalwyn) **3-8-4** GHind(11) (hld up: rdn over 5f out: bhd fnl 3f) | 1¼ | **8** | 9/1 | 67 | 34 |
| 1640[3] | **Pip's Dream (50)** (MJRyan) **5-8-3** WCarson(5) (prom: rdn over 5f out: wknd over 2f out: eased whn btn fnl f) | 3 | **9** | 11/2[3] | 47 | 29 |
| 1117* | **Stately Dancer (74)** (GWragg) **3-8-12** MHills(7) (hld up: hdwy over 3f out: rdn & wknd over 2f out) | 2 | **10** | 9/2[2] | 68 | 35 |
| 1117[9] | **Reiterate (58)** (GBBalding) **3-7-10** NAdams(10) (a bhd: t.o fnl 3f) | 13 | **11** | 12/1 | 35 | 2 |
| | | | | (SP 124.8%) | | **11 Rn** |

**2m 34.73** (2.13) CSF £37.46 CT £216.84 TOTE £4.40: £1.90 £3.50 £1.50 (£21.80) Trio £78.50 OWNER Mr T. M. Hely-Hutchinson (WHATCOMBE) BRED Rathbarry Stud
LONG HANDICAP Rocquaine Bay 7-9 Reiterate 7-7
WEIGHT FOR AGE 3yo-15lb

**1462 White Sea (IRE)**, with no stamina doubts this time, reversed the Chepstow form with the runner-up. (7/2)
**1640 Uncharted Waters** was given a fair bit to do and could not peg back the winner. (10/1)
**Tonys Gift**, five times a winner over hurdles, stands her racing well, and found the trip no problem on this return to the Flat. (7/1)
**1306 Lalindi (IRE)** forced the pace over this shorter distance, but had given her all in the last 200 yards. (7/1)
**Rocquaine Bay**, a springer with some of the Independents, had finished second and fourth in the last two runnings of this event, but had no previous outing this time. (12/1)
**491 Victoria's Secret (IRE)**, still a maiden, needed the blinkers to show her best when trained by David Elsworth last year. (20/1)

## 1853 COURAGE BEST H'CAP (0-90) (3-Y.O+) (Class C)
3-00 (3-02) **6f** £5,735.00 (£1,730.00: £840.00: £395.00) Stalls: High GOING minus 0.39 sec per fur (F)

| | | | | SP | RR | SF |
|---|---|---|---|---|---|---|
| 1178[12] | **Sir Joey (USA) (81)** (PGMurphy) **7-9-8** MRoberts(4) (hld up & bhd: swtchd lft & gd hdwy over 1f out: str run to ld nr fin) | — | **1** | 10/1 | 88 | 54 |
| 1473[4] | **Bayin (USA) (69)** (MDIUsher) **7-8-10** RStreet(2) (b: hld up & bhd: gd hdwy over 1f out: r.o ins fnl f) | ½ | **2** | 10/1 | 75 | 41 |
| 1781* | **High Domain (IRE) (71)** (JLSpearing) **5-8-12** 7x JWeaver(12) (led tl nr fin) | s.h | **3** | 5/1[1] | 77 | 43 |
| 1624[5] | **Sing Up (61)** (MMcCormack) **4-8-2** NCarlisle(3) (b: hld up: hdwy over 1f out: r.o ins fnl f) | 1½ | **4** | 14/1 | 63 | 29 |
| 1466* | **Patsy Grimes (76)** (JSMoore) **6-9-3** RHughes(6) (lw: hdwy over 1f out: squeezed thro ins fnl f: nt rch ldrs) | 1 | **5** | 10/1 | 75 | 41 |
| 1334[2] | **Purple Fling (73)** (LGCottrell) **5-9-0** JQuinn(10) (prom tl wknd fnl f) | 2 | **6** | 13/2[3] | 67 | 33 |
| | **Mr Bergerac (IRE) (83)** (BPalling) **5-9-10** TSprake(1) (lw: hdwy over 2f out: one pce fnl f) | nk | **7** | 20/1 | 76 | 42 |
| 1652[2] | **Mister Jolson (75)** (RJHodges) **7-9-2** WCarson(7) (lw: nvr nr to chal) | 1½ | **8** | 7/1 | 64 | 30 |
| | **Double Bounce (82)** (PJMakin) **6-9-9** LDettori(14) (lost pl 3f out: rallied on ins & nt clr run 1f out: eased whn btn) | ¾ | **9** | 13/2[3] | 69 | 35 |
| | **Bangles (66)** (LordHuntingdon) **6-8-7** DHarrison(5) (prom: eased whn btn ins fnl f) | 3½ | **10** | 25/1 | 43 | 9 |
| *500*[6] | **Spender (71)** (PWHarris) **7-8-12** GHind(9) (lw: s.i.s: sn chsng ldrs: eased whn btn ins fnl f) | ½ | **11** | 20/1 | 47 | 13 |
| 1316[3] | **Willow Dale (IRE) (81)** (DRCElsworth) **3-9-0** TQuinn(13) (prom: rdn over 2f out: swtchd lft & wknd 1f out) | ½ | **12** | 6/1[2] | 56 | 14 |
| 744[8] | **Dry Point (70)** (JARToller) **10-8-11** SSanders(11) (b: rdn over 3f out: bhd fnl 2f) | ½ | **13** | 25/1 | 43 | 9 |
| 1192[6] | **Mister Fire Eyes (IRE) (74)** (CEBrittain) **4-9-1b** BDoyle(8) (prom over 3f) | 1¾ | **14** | 14/1 | 43 | 9 |
| | | | | (SP 127.9%) | | **14 Rn** |

**1m 14.45** (1.45) CSF £102.41 CT £533.42 TOTE £18.60: £4.60 £2.90 £2.50 (£67.20) Trio £260.50 OWNER Mrs A. G. Sims (BRISTOL) BRED William Plescia & Natalie Plescia
WEIGHT FOR AGE 3yo-8lb

**1064 Sir Joey (USA)**, whose trainer was full of praise for Roberts, came with a storming late run and now heads for the Wokingham. (10/1)
**1473 Bayin (USA)**, dropped 3lb, came with his usual late flourish, but it was the winner who was finishing best. (10/1)
**1781* High Domain (IRE)**, penalised for his recent win at Haydock, was running off a mark 13lb higher than when successful over the minimum trip here last month, but very nearly pulled it off. (5/1)
**1624 Sing Up**, up 13lb for his good second when badly in at the weights in a non-handicap at Nottingham, was still 10lb higher here. (14/1)
**1466* Patsy Grimes** had been raised 9lb for winning at Chepstow last time. (10/1)
**1334 Purple Fling** had gone up 3lb for his good second at Goodwood, and may need even faster ground to show his best. (13/2)
**Double Bounce**, 5lb higher than when winning at York last October, ran better than his finishing position suggests. (13/2)

## 1854 BISHOPSTONE CONDITIONS STKS (3-Y.O) (Class C)
3-30 (3-33) **1m 6f** £4,977.75 (£1,809.00: £879.50: £372.50: £161.25) GOING minus 0.39 sec per fur (F)

| | | | | SP | RR | SF |
|---|---|---|---|---|---|---|
| 1104* | **Persian Punch (IRE)** (DRCElsworth) **3-9-0** TQuinn(2) (lw: chsd ldr: hrd rdn to ld wl ins fnl f: r.o) | — | **1** | 5/2[2] | 96 | 44 |
| 1524[2] | **Old Irish (82)** (LMCumani) **3-8-11** LDettori(1) (led: hrd rdn & hdd wl ins fnl f) | 1½ | **2** | 11/10[1] | 91 | 39 |
| 1415[3] | **Shooting Light (IRE) (79)** (MAJarvis) **3-9-0** PBloomfield(4) (hld up: reminder over 5f out: hrd rdn & hung rt over 2f out: sn wknd) | 12 | **3** | 7/1 | 81 | 29 |

| | | | Pos | SP | RR | SF |
|---|---|---|---|---|---|---|
| 1644$^{9}$ | **State Theatre (IRE)** (PWChapple-Hyam) **3-8-11** JReid(5) (lw: bhd fnl 5f) | 4 | **4** | 12/1 | 73 | 21 |
| 1111$^{W}$ | **Circled (USA)** (BWHills) **3-8-11** MHills(6) (hld up: hrd rdn over 3f out: sn bhd) | 5 | **5** | 11/2$^{3}$ | 67 | 15 |

(SP 111.8%) **5 Rn**

**3m 2.98** (4.28) CSF £5.59 TOTE £3.10: £1.50 £1.10 (£2.30) OWNER Mr J. C. Smith (WHITCOMBE) BRED Adstock Manor Stud

**1104* Persian Punch (IRE)**, a half-brother to Solario Stakes winner Island Magic, is out of a mare who won over this trip, and took a long time to wear down the favourite. (5/2: 7/4-11/4)

**1524 Old Irish** had the far rail to help this time, but could not hold the winner in the final 100 yards. (11/10)

**1415 Shooting Light (IRE)** could not go with the two principals after wanting to hang in to the rail. (7/1: op 9/2)

**Circled (USA)** (11/2: 3/1-6/1)

## 1855 LAVERSTOCK MAIDEN STKS (I) (3-Y.O F) (Class D)

4-00 (4-02) **1m** £3,427.50 (£1,020.00: £485.00: £217.50) Stalls: High GOING minus 0.39 sec per fur (F)

| | | | Pos | SP | RR | SF |
|---|---|---|---|---|---|---|
| 1614$^{3}$ | **Wandering Star (USA)** (JRFanshawe) **3-8-11** NDay(8) (a.p: led 2f out: r.o wl) | — | **1** | 7/2$^{2}$ | 84 | 40 |
| 1007$^{7}$ | **Tillyard (IRE)** (PWChapple-Hyam) **3-8-11** JReid(2) (lw: hld up: gd hdwy over 1f out: nt trble wnr) | 1¾ | **2** | 15/2 | 81 | 37 |
| | **Duchesse de Berri (USA)** (JHMGosden) **3-8-11** LDettori(10) (gd sort: hld up: rdn to chse wnr over 1f out: one pce) | 3½ | **3** | 7/1$^{3}$ | 74 | 30 |
| 964$^{3}$ | **Saleemah (USA)** (JLDunlop) **3-8-11** WCarson(6) (led 6f: wknd fnl f) | 3½ | **4** | 6/4$^{1}$ | 67 | 23 |
| 894$^{5}$ | **Tsarskaya (USA)** (MrsJCecil) **3-8-11** BThomson(12) (hld up: rdn 3f out: no hdwy) | 2 | **5** | 14/1 | 63 | 19 |
| | **Wolf Cleugh (IRE)** (AHide) **3-8-11** AMcGlone(3) (nvr nr to chal) | nk | **6** | 33/1 | 62 | 18 |
| | **Idle Fancy** (LordHuntingdon) **3-8-11** DHarrison(5) (prom tl wknd qckly fnl f) | nk | **7** | 25/1 | 61 | 17 |
| 1333$^{3}$ | **Press On Nicky** (WRMuir) **3-8-11** JWeaver(4) (lw: hdwy 3f out: wknd 2f) | 2½ | **8** | 7/1$^{3}$ | 56 | 12 |
| 1614$^{7}$ | **Gooseberry Pie** (RCharlton) **3-8-11** TSprake(9) (a bhd) | 3½ | **9** | 14/1 | 49 | 5 |
| | **Soufriere (IRE)** (LMCumani) **3-8-11** OUrbina(7) (gd sort: lw: a bhd) | 1½ | **10** | 14/1 | 46 | 2 |
| | **Early Warning** (CREgerton) **3-8-11** RHughes(1) (w'like: a bhd) | 12 | **11** | 25/1 | 22 | — |
| | **Daydream Island** (RJBaker) **3-8-11** NAdams(11) (prom over 4f: t.o) | dist | **12** | 100/1 | — | — |

(SP 130.6%) **12 Rn**

**1m 42.86** (2.46) CSF £31.11 TOTE £5.80: £1.60 £2.20 £2.10 (£50.90) Trio £35.00 OWNER Aylesfield Farms Stud (NEWMARKET) BRED Mr and Mrs R. Lyons

**1614 Wandering Star (USA)** fulfilled the promise shown last time, and the winner of that Kempton race, Balalaika, could well turn out to be quite useful. (7/2: 3/1-9/2)

**1007 Tillyard (IRE)**, a half-sister to Castillian Queen, is going the right way on this evidence. (15/2: 5/1-8/1)

**Duchesse de Berri (USA)**, from the same family as those good fillies Forest Flower and Leap Lively, should soon step up on this. (7/1: op 3/1)

**964 Saleemah (USA)**, a $100,000 half-sister to a couple of winners in the States, just set up the race for the winner on this occasion. (6/4)

**894 Tsarskaya (USA)** is now qualified for handicaps, and may do better when tackling further. (14/1)

**Wolf Cleugh (IRE)**, a sister to a seven-furlong juvenile winner in Ireland, is out of a mare that stayed a mile and a half, and she should do better over a longer trip. (33/1)

**Idle Fancy** ran well for a long way, and the jury is still out as to whether she lasted the trip. (25/1)

**Soufriere (IRE)** (14/1: op 5/1)

## 1856 DORSET H'CAP (0-70) (3-Y.O+) (Class E)

4-30 (4-32) **6f 212y** £3,444.00 (£1,032.00: £496.00: £228.00) Stalls: High GOING minus 0.39 sec per fur (F)

| | | | Pos | SP | RR | SF |
|---|---|---|---|---|---|---|
| 1533$^{7}$ | **Gentle Irony (53)** (MJRyan) **4-9-1** BDoyle(4) (lw: hdwy & swtchd lft over 2f out: r.o wl to ld last strides) | — | **1** | 14/1 | 62 | 38 |
| 1533$^{5}$ | **Jaazim (53)** (MMadgwick) **6-9-1** TQuinn(16) (a.p: led wl over 1f out: hdd last strides) | hd | **2** | 7/2$^{1}$ | 62 | 38 |
| 1658$^{7}$ | **Pointer (43)** (MrsPNDutfield) **4-8-5** CRutter(10) (hld up: hdwy over 2f out: ev ch over 1f out: unable qckn fnl f) | ¾ | **3** | 10/1 | 50 | 26 |
| 527$^{11}$ | **Artful Dane (IRE) (66)** (MJHeaton-Ellis) **4-10-0** AClark(5) (hdwy over 2f out: ev ch over 1f out: r.o one pce) | hd | **4** | 25/1 | 73 | 49 |
| 893$^{13}$ | **Ca'd'oro (56)** (GBBalding) **3-8-8** SSanders(6) (hld up: swtchd lft & hdwy over 2f out: one pce fnl f) | 2 | **5** | 16/1 | 58 | 24 |
| 1522$^{7}$ | **Express Routing (58)** (JAkehurst) **4-9-6** PaulEddery(2) (b: b.hind: nvr nrr) | 1¼ | **6** | 16/1 | 57 | 33 |
| 1715$^{11}$ | **Shaynes Domain (42)** (RMFlower) **5-8-4b** DBiggs(3) (bmpd s: hdwy over 3f out: wknd over 1f out) | ½ | **7** | 16/1 | 40 | 16 |
| 1689* | **Paddy's Rice (62)** (MMcCormack) **5-9-10** 6x JReid(7) (no hdwy fnl 2f) | ½ | **8** | 11/2$^{2}$ | 59 | 35 |
| 1302$^{12}$ | **Soaking (50)** (PBurgoyne) **6-8-12** DRMcCabe(13) (lw: a.p: led over 2f out tl wl over 1f out: sn wknd) | 3½ | **9** | 6/1$^{3}$ | 39 | 15 |
| 1533$^{8}$ | **Napoleon Star (IRE) (56)** (MSSaunders) **5-9-4** RPrice(11) (lw: bhd fnl 2f) | ¾ | **10** | 20/1 | 43 | 19 |
| 1506$^{7}$ | **Adilov (60)** (KOCunningham-Brown) **4-9-1**(7) CMunday(9) (a bhd) | 3½ | **11** | 20/1 | 39 | 15 |
| 1689$^{6}$ | **Hawanafa (60)** (RHannon) **3-8-9**(3) DaneO'Neill(12) (lw: bhd fnl 2f) | 1 | **12** | 14/1 | 37 | 3 |
| 1521$^{7}$ | **Ahjay (46)** (TJNaughton) **6-8-8** MRoberts(1) (lw: a bhd) | 10 | **13** | 8/1 | — | — |
| 1532$^{5}$ | **Office Hours (57)** (CACyzer) **4-9-5** JWeaver(14) (led tl eased over 2f out) | 5 | **14** | 12/1 | — | — |
| 1469$^{6}$ | **Duffertoes (58)** (MJRyan) **4-9-6b$^{1}$** RHughes(15) (w ldr 4f: eased & p.u over 1f out) | | **P** | 14/1 | — | — |

(SP 130.8%) **15 Rn**

**1m 28.61** (2.61) CSF £63.02 CT £507.80 TOTE £19.10: £5.00 £1.40 £3.60 (£54.50) Trio £230.20 OWNER Mr A. S. Reid (NEWMARKET) BRED Red House Stud

WEIGHT FOR AGE 3yo-10lb

**1302 Gentle Irony** registered her first win in a handicap having previously won four claimers, the last three with the aid of blinkers. (14/1: 10/1-16/1)

**1533 Jaazim**, very well backed, was running off a mark 3lb higher than when twice a runner-up over course and distance last month. (7/2: 5/1-3/1)

**1348* Pointer**, raised 4lb for his course and distance victory last month, may have found the ground too fast at Brighton next time. (10/1)

**Artful Dane (IRE)** is slipping down the ratings, but still had to contend with a big weight in this company. (25/1)

**Ca'd'oro** showed improved form over this extra furlong off a 4lb lower mark. (16/1)

**Express Routing** only got going when the race was virtually over, and seems worth a try over a longer trip. (16/1)

**1121 Ahjay** (8/1: op 12/1)

## 1857 LAVERSTOCK MAIDEN STKS (II) (3-Y.O F) (Class D)

5-00 (5-02) **1m** £3,395.00 (£1,010.00: £480.00: £215.00) Stalls: High GOING minus 0.39 sec per fur (F)

| | | | Pos | SP | RR | SF |
|---|---|---|---|---|---|---|
| 1007$^{2}$ | **Charlotte Corday (85)** (GWragg) **3-8-11** MHills(3) (stdd s: a gng wl: led on bit 2f out: shkn up & qcknd clr ins fnl f) | — | **1** | 5/6$^{1}$ | 83+ | 34 |
| 1357$^{5}$ | **Premier Night** (SDow) **3-8-11** MRoberts(2) (a.p: rdn & ev ch over 1f out: unable qckn) | 3½ | **2** | 9/1 | 76 | 27 |

| Form | Horse / details | Dist | Pos | SP | RR | SF |
|---|---|---|---|---|---|---|
| 1326[5] | **Mua-Tab** (PTWalwyn) **3-8-11** WCarson(9) (rdn & hdwy 2f out: r.o one pce fnl f) | 1¾ | **3** | 6/1[3] | 73 | 24 |
| | **Kentucky Fall (FR)** (LadyHerries) **3-8-11** PaulEddery(1) (str: scope: lw: hld up & bhd: hdwy 3f out: rdn & ev ch over 1f out: one pce) | ½ | **4** | 11/2[2] | 72 | 23 |
| 1644[7] | **Trilby** (PFICole) **3-8-11** TQuinn(4) (prom: rdn over 3f out: one pce fnl 2f) | 3 | **5** | 8/1 | 66 | 17 |
| 1614[16] | **Amelanchier** (GBBalding) **3-8-11** SSanders(7) (hld up & plld hrd: no hdwy fnl 2f) | nk | **6** | 66/1 | 65 | 16 |
| | **Snowpoles** (MrsJCecil) **3-8-11** JReid(5) (led 6f) | 3 | **7** | 20/1 | 59 | 10 |
| | **Soldier's Song** (RJHodges) **3-8-11** TSprake(10) (w'like: s.s: nrst fin) | 1 | **8** | 50/1 | 57 | 8 |
| 1617[9] | **Redskin Lady** (DRCElsworth) **3-8-8**(3) DaneO'Neill(11) (lw: prom over 5f) | 1¾ | **9** | 10/1 | 53 | 4 |
| 1617[12] | **Burning Flame** (RMFlower) **3-8-11** DBiggs(12) (a bhd) | 2½ | **10** | 50/1 | 48 | — |
| | **Isla Glen** (MMcCormack) **3-8-11** MFenton(6) (s.s: a bhd) | 1½ | **11** | 50/1 | 45 | — |
| | **Persian Dawn** (MajorDNChappell) **3-8-11** BThomson(8) (chsd ldr: rdn over 2f out: wknd over 2f out) | 2½ | **12** | 20/1 | 40 | — |

(SP 131.3%) **12 Rn**

**1m 43.53** (3.13) CSF £10.74 TOTE £2.00: £1.10 £2.80 £1.60 (£10.30) Trio £9.00 OWNER Mr A. E. Oppenheimer (NEWMARKET) BRED Hascombe and Valiant Studs

**1007 Charlotte Corday** relished the mile, and proved far too good for this opposition. (5/6)

**964 Premier Night**, a half-sister to Italian Oaks third Bunting, must have got bogged down in the ground at Goodwood last time. She is bred to stay further. (9/1: 6/1-10/1)

**1326 Mua-Tab** could not get to grips with the runner-up, let alone the winner. (6/1: op 4/1)

**Kentucky Fall (FR)**, a half-sister to ten-furlong winner Minatina, was bought for 10,000 guineas at Newmarket December Sales. She seems sure to win a race, but the dam side suggests she may need a longer trip. (11/2)

**1644 Trilby** was surprisingly dropped back to a mile, but will now be qualified for handicaps. (8/1)

**Amelanchier** proved a handful to settle, but still ran her best race to date. (66/1)

T/Jkpt: Not won; £4,138.68 to Kempton 12/6/96. T/Plpt: £198.60 (105.86 Tckts). T/Qdpt: £29.10 (35.93 Tckts). KH

## 1697-BEVERLEY (R-H) (Good to firm)
## Wednesday June 12th

WEATHER: sunny WIND: fresh half against

### 1858 GEORGE HUTCHINSON & DENISE GUTHERLESS JUST MARRIED CLAIMING STKS (2-Y.O) (Class F)

2-00 (2-00) **5f** £2,672.00 (£742.00: £356.00) Stalls: High GOING minus 0.04 sec per fur (G)

| Form | Horse / details | Dist | Pos | SP | RR | SF |
|---|---|---|---|---|---|---|
| 1471[2] | **Aztec Traveller** (JBerry) **2-9-1** JCarroll(2) (chsd ldr: led over 1f out: r.o u.p) | — | **1** | 11/8[1] | 69 | 13 |
| 1471* | **Lawful Find (IRE)** (RHollinshead) **2-8-6**(5) FLynch(9) (trckd ldrs: n.m.r & swtchd lft over 1f out: styd on: nvr nr to chal) | 1 | **2** | 7/4[2] | 62 | 6 |
| 1183[7] | **In Good Nick** (MWEasterby) **2-8-12** DaleGibson(7) (bit bkwd: s.i.s: hdwy ½-wy: styd on fnl f) | 1¼ | **3** | 16/1 | 59 | 3 |
| | **Five Live** (MDHammond) **2-8-7** JWeaver(6) (w'like: bit bkwd: trckd ldrs: effrt 2f out: kpt on same pce appr fnl f) | hd | **4** | 8/1[3] | 54 | — |
| | **Superboots** (WWHaigh) **2-8-4** RLappin(8) (cmpt: bit bkwd: s.s: bhd & pushed along: hdwy ½-wy: wknd appr fnl f) | 3½ | **5** | 20/1 | 39 | — |
| 1525[9] | **Veerapong (IRE)** (MWEasterby) **2-8-12** MBirch(3) (trckd ldrs: effrt & wandered over 1f out: grad wknd) | 2½ | **6** | 12/1 | 39 | — |
| 1607[4] | **Abstone Again (IRE)** (PDEvans) **2-8-6b**[1ow1] JFortune(5) (led tl over 1f out: sn wknd) | hd | **7** | 12/1 | 33 | — |
| 1184[5] | **Brawling Springs** (MWEasterby) **2-8-12**(5) GParkin(1) (chsd ldrs: effrt ½-wy: wknd over 1f out) | 5 | **8** | 16/1 | 28 | — |
| | **Madam Lucy** (WWHaigh) **2-8-8** DeanMcKeown(4) (w'like: bkwd: s.s: a last) | 5 | **9** | 20/1 | 3 | — |

(SP 126.3%) **9 Rn**

**66.7 secs** (5.20) CSF £4.60 TOTE £2.30: £1.10 £1.10 £3.80 (£1.80) Trio £20.60 OWNER Mr J. K. Brown (COCKERHAM) BRED J. R. Thompson

Aztec Traveller clmd PSmithEccles £9,000; Lawful Find (IRE) clmd LParkes £7,000

**1471 Aztec Traveller**, 8lb better off with the runner-up, continually swished his tail in the paddock. Showing a good action on the fast ground, he had the better luck in running. (11/8)

**1471* Lawful Find (IRE)** found himself trapped on the inner but, when he did see daylight, he lacked the pace to get in a serious blow. He is better suited by six. (7/4)

**In Good Nick** looked in need of this, but was putting in some solid work in the final furlong. (16/1)

**Five Live** looked burly, but would have hung on for third had her rider been more determined in the closing stages. She should improve and win a similar event of a seller. (8/1)

**Superboots**, a backward newcomer, showed a poor action going down but, after a slow start, did show some ability. (20/1)

**Veerapong (IRE)** definitely possesses some ability. (12/1: op 8/1)

### 1859 POLYGON (HUMBERSIDE) H'CAP (0-70) (3-Y.O+ F & M) (Class E)

2-30 (2-30) **5f** £3,036.25 (£910.00: £437.50: £201.25) Stalls: High GOING minus 0.04 sec per fur (G)

| Form | Horse / details | Dist | Pos | SP | RR | SF |
|---|---|---|---|---|---|---|
| 1541[10] | **Dominelle (45)** (TDEasterby) **4-9-2** MBirch(12) (trckd ldr: led over 1f out: hld on wl) | — | **1** | 4/1[1] | 52 | 34 |
| 1642[5] | **Rotherfield Park (IRE) (34)** (CSmith) **4-8-5** WWoods(11) (chsd ldrs: squeezed thro & ev ch ins fnl f: unable qckn) | nk | **2** | 7/1 | 40 | 22 |
| 1500* | **Respect A Secret (42)** (SEKettlewell) **4-8-13** JFortune(1) (lw: sn trckng ldrs: effrt 2f out: hung rt & nt qckn fnl f) | ¾ | **3** | 4/1[1] | 46 | 28 |
| 1541[8] | **Tutu Sixtysix (33)** (DonEnricoIncisa) **5-8-4b** KimTinkler(2) (s.i.s: bhd tl hrd rdn & styd on fnl 2f) | 1¾ | **4** | 20/1 | 31 | 13 |
| 1527[20] | **Hickleton Miss (52)** (MrsVAAconley) **3-9-2** NCarlisle(10) (a in tch: rdn ½-wy: no imp) | 2½ | **5** | 10/1 | 42 | 17 |
| *1455*[12] | **Highland Fawn (45)** (BAMcMahon) **3-8-9** DRMcCabe(4) (sn outpcd: sme hdwy over 1f out: nvr nr ldrs) | nk | **6** | 14/1 | 34 | 9 |
| 1848[7] | **Prime Property (IRE) (38)** (MWEasterby) **4-8-4b**(5) GParkin(6) (sn outpcd & rdn: sme hdwy 2f out: n.d) | nk | **7** | 16/1 | 26 | 8 |
| 1702[3] | **Branston Kristy (35)** (CSmith) **4-8-1b**(5) FLynch(7) (chsd ldrs over 3f: sn wknd) | 3 | **8** | 12/1 | 14 | — |
| 1634[3] | **Penny Parkes (46)** (JBerry) **3-8-10** JCarroll(8) (lw: chsd ldrs: edgd lft & wknd over 1f out) | 1½ | **9** | 5/1[2] | 20 | — |
| 1405[11] | **Marjorie Rose (IRE) (63)** (ABailey) **3-9-13** KDarley(3) (lw: s.i.s: hdwy on outside ½-wy: sn wknd) | ¾ | **10** | 13/2[3] | 34 | 9 |
| 1635[10] | **Penny's Wishing (44)** (NBycroft) **4-9-1b**[1] JWeaver(9) (unruly gng to s: led tl over 1f out: wknd) | nk | **11** | 8/1 | 14 | — |
| *1492*[13] | **Double Glow (38)** (NBycroft) **4-8-9** LCharnock(5) (s.s: a wl bhd) | 10 | **12** | 25/1 | — | — |

(SP 131.6%) **12 Rn**

**65.4 secs** (3.90) CSF £33.55 CT £117.36 TOTE £5.90: £2.20 £1.70 £2.30 (£12.30) Trio £61.00 OWNER Sandmoor Textiles Co Ltd (MALTON) BRED Gymcrak Thoroughbred Breeding Ltd

WEIGHT FOR AGE 3yo-7lb

**1364 Dominelle**, drawn twelve of twelve, won well, despite some tail-swishing. (4/1)
**1642 Rotherfield Park (IRE)**, drawn eleven of twelve, squeezed through to challenge inside the last, but she was never doing quite enough to worry the winner out of it. (7/1)
**1500* Respect A Secret**, raised 7lb, dropped back a furlong and, worst drawn, showed a marked tendency to hang. (4/1)
**1040 Tutu Sixtysix** ran easily her best race so far this year. (20/1)
**Highland Fawn**, a poor mover, ran her best race so far on turf, coming from off the pace and staying on when it was all over. (14/1)

## 1860 ELTHERINGTON H'CAP (0-70) (3-Y.O+) (Class E)

3-00 (3-00) **7f 100y** £3,873.00 (£1,164.00: £562.00: £261.00) Stalls: High GOING minus 0.31 sec per fur (GF)

| | | | | SP | RR | SF |
|---|---|---|---|---|---|---|
| $1674^{2}$ | **Grey Kingdom (34)** (MBrittain) **5-7-12** DaleGibson(5) (mde all: styd on wl fnl f) | — | **1** | 6/1 | 45 | 32 |
| $1674^{4}$ | **Murphy's Gold (IRE) (48)** (RAFahey) **5-8-12** ACulhane(3) (lw: hld up: effrt over 3f out: hrd rdn & nt qckn ins fnl f) | 1¼ | **2** | $4/1^{2}$ | 56 | 43 |
| *$1811^{2}$* | **Three Arch Bridge (63)** (MJohnston) **4-9-13b** $^{6x}$ JWeaver(1) (sn chsng ldrs: kpt on same pce appr fnl f) | 2 | **3** | $2/1^{1}$ | 67 | 54 |
| $1674^{11}$ | **Special-K (60)** (EWeymes) **4-9-10** KDarley(8) (chsd ldrs: rdn & outpcd 5f out: kpt on fnl 2f) | ¾ | **4** | 11/2 | 62 | 49 |
| $1674^{3}$ | **Awesome Venture (50)** (MCChapman) **6-9-0** DRMcCabe(4) (hld up: effrt over 2f out: kpt on: nvr nr to chal) | .hd | **5** | $9/2^{3}$ | 52 | 39 |
| $1674^{13}$ | **Camionneur (IRE) (51)** (TDEasterby) **3-8-5** MBirch(7) (stdd s: hld up & plld hrd: bhd tl kpt on fnl 2f) | s.h | **6** | 12/1 | 53 | 30 |
| | **Pleasure Trick (USA) (55)** (DonEnricoIncisa) **5-9-5** KimTinkler(2) (bit bkwd: chsd ldrs: hung rt & wknd qckly over 2f out) | 18 | **7** | 20/1 | 19 | 6 |
| $1530^{17}$ | **Ballysokerry (IRE) (32)** (JParkes) **5-7-10** LCharnock(6) (chsd ldrs tl lost pl over 3f out: virtually p.u over 2f out) | dist | **8** | 33/1 | — | — |
| | | | | (SP 116.6%) | **8 Rn** | |

**1m 34.4** (2.40) CSF £28.78 CT £59.63 TOTE £7.80: £1.90 £1.40 £1.20 (£9.70) OWNER Mr Mel Brittain (WARTHILL) BRED Northgate Lodge Stud Ltd
LONG HANDICAP Ballysokerry (IRE) 7-6
WEIGHT FOR AGE 3yo-10lb
**1674 Grey Kingdom** was allowed to set his own pace and, intelligently ridden, was always doing just enough. (6/1)
**1674 Murphy's Gold (IRE)** looked particularly well beforehand, but was always seeing too much daylight. Clawing back the winner inside the last, he will win again off this sort of mark when everything goes his way. (4/1)
**1811 Three Arch Bridge**, who gets no respite, showed a scratchy action going down. (2/1)
**1341 Special-K** hobbled to post. Badly outpaced starting the home turn, she seemed to slip more than once. To her credit, she kept on strongly in the final quarter-mile. (11/2)
**1674 Awesome Venture** was carrying plenty of condition on this, his twenty-first outing already this year. Not suited by the modest pace, he could not take up a challenging position. (9/2)

## 1861 UNIVERSITY OF LINCOLNSHIRE AND HUMBERSIDE H'CAP (0-80) (3-Y.O+) (Class D)

3-30 (3-31) **1m 1f 207y** £3,873.00 (£1,164.00: £562.00: £261.00) Stalls: High GOING minus 0.31 sec per fur (GF)

| | | | | SP | RR | SF |
|---|---|---|---|---|---|---|
| $1666^{2}$ | **Fairywings (68)** (MrsJRRamsden) **3-8-8** JFortune(7) (hld up: hdwy on ins over 4f out: shkn up to ld 2f out: wnt rt: pushed out) | — | **1** | $11/8^{1}$ | 78 | 28 |
| *$1490^{9}$* | **Nose No Bounds (IRE) (72)** (MJohnston) **3-8-12b¹** JWeaver(8) (led to 3f out: sltly hmpd over 1f out: rallied ins fnl f: no ch w wnr) | 1¼ | **2** | 11/1 | 80 | 30 |
| 1198* | **Komreyev Dancer (75)** (ABailey) **4-10-0** JCarroll(2) (lw: hld up: effrt on outside 2f out: hung rt & kpt on ins fnl f) | 1 | **3** | $9/2^{2}$ | 81 | 44 |
| $1672^{4}$ | **Euro Sceptic (IRE) (50)** (TDEasterby) **4-7-12**$^{(5)ow2}$ FLynch(5) (chsd ldrs: led 3f out to 2f out: one pce) | ¾ | **4** | 10/1 | 55 | 16 |
| $1507^{5}$ | **Galapino (69)** (CEBrittain) **3-8-9** BDoyle(6) (chsd ldrs: rdn over 3f out: outpcd fnl 2f) | 5 | **5** | $7/1^{3}$ | 66 | 16 |
| *$120^{7}$* | **Far Ahead (75)** (JLEyre) **4-10-0** KDarley(1) (chsd ldrs: rdn over 3f out: outpcd fnl 2f) | 1¾ | **6** | 12/1 | 69 | 32 |
| $1676^{4}$ | **Kings Cay (IRE) (46)** (THCaldwell) **5-7-10**$^{(3)}$ DarrenMoffatt(3) (chsd ldrs: rdn over 3f out: wknd 2f out) | 4 | **7** | 12/1 | 34 | — |
| $1526^{5}$ | **Tabriz (69)** (JDBethell) **3-8-9b¹** WJO'Connor(4) (trckd ldrs: rdn 3f out: sn lost pl) | 1 | **8** | 14/1 | 55 | 5 |
| $1102^{8}$ | **Wonderful Day (64)** (HAkbary) **5-9-3** MRimmer(9) (chsd ldrs tl wknd 3f out: eased & sn wl bhd) | dist | **9** | 14/1 | — | — |
| | | | | (SP 118.9%) | **9 Rn** | |

**2m 7.4** (4.90) CSF £16.54 CT £53.06 TOTE £2.30: £1.30 £2.60 £2.20 (£17.40) Trio £27.90 OWNER L C and A E Sigsworth (THIRSK) BRED L. C. and A. E. Sigsworth and The Kris Syndicate
WEIGHT FOR AGE 3yo-13lb
**1666 Fairywings** had a dream run towards the inner. On the bridle when taking it up, she then dived right onto the rail. Idling in front, she had to kept right up to her work. (11/8)
**702 Nose No Bounds (IRE)** wore blinkers after three poor shows. Setting his own pace, he was slightly hampered when the winner went across him. Rallying inside the last, he was never a real threat. (11/1)
**1198* Komreyev Dancer** ran as well as could be expected from a 4lb higher mark. (9/2)
**1672 Euro Sceptic (IRE)** likes it round here and seemed to get the extra distance. (10/1)

## 1862 ERNEST NORRIS MEMORIAL H'CAP (0-80) (3-Y.O+) (Class D)

4-00 (4-00) **1m 3f 216y** £3,795.00 (£1,140.00: £550.00: £255.00) Stalls: High GOING minus 0.31 sec per fur (GF)

| | | | | SP | RR | SF |
|---|---|---|---|---|---|---|
| $1421^{12}$ | **Tulu (67)** (MrsJRRamsden) **5-9-6** MDeering(3) (b: hld up: nt clr run over 2f out: qcknd ins fnl f: r.o to ld post) | — | **1** | 8/1 | 77 | 41 |
| $816^{7}$ | **Chatham Island (68)** (CEBrittain) **8-9-7** BDoyle(2) (trckd ldr: effrt over 3f out: rdn to ld 1f out: jst ct) | s.h | **2** | 13/2 | 78 | 42 |
| $1700^{3}$ | **Deano's Beeno (75)** (MJohnston) **4-10-0** JWeaver(1) (lw: trckd ldrs: effrt over 3f out: nt qckn fnl f) | 1¼ | **3** | $3/1^{2}$ | 83 | 47 |
| $863^{4}$ | **Cheerful Aspect (IRE) (80)** (EALDunlop) **3-9-4** KDarley(6) (trckd ldrs: effrt over 3f out: hrd rdn over 2f out: styng on same pce whn nt clr run over 1f out) | 2½ | **4** | $2/1^{1}$ | 85 | 34 |
| | **Mansur (IRE) (66)** (DRLoder) **4-9-5** DRMcCabe(4) (led: qcknd 4f out: hdd 1f out: grad wknd) | 1 | **5** | 6/1 | 70 | 34 |
| $1672^{5}$ | **Thaleros (54)** (GMMoore) **6-8-7** DeanMcKeown(5) (unruly in paddock: ref to r: t.n.p) | | **R** | $11/2^{3}$ | — | — |
| | | | | (SP 112.4%) | **6 Rn** | |

**2m 38.4** (6.00) CSF £49.67 TOTE £11.90: £4.20 £4.00 (£27.70) OWNER Mr Mark Houlston (THIRSK) BRED M. Houlston
WEIGHT FOR AGE 3yo-15lb
**993 Tulu** barely stays a mile and a half, and was ideally suited by the modest pace. Having to bide her time for an opening, she did enough to put her head in front on the line. (8/1)
**Chatham Island** showed a return to form and, in the end, was only just pipped. (13/2)
**1700 Deano's Beeno** surprisingly did not make the running in what was a modestly-run affair. (3/1)

**863 Cheerful Aspect (IRE)**, hard at work once in line for home, was only sticking on at the same pace when denied a run on the inner. He was in no way unlucky. (2/1)
**Mansur (IRE)**, a fluent mover, was allowed to set his own pace but found precious little at the business end. (6/1)

## 1863 NEW UNIVERSITY MAIDEN STKS (3-Y.O+) (Class D)

4-30 (4-30) **1m 3f 216y** £3,978.00 (£1,108.00: £534.00) Stalls: High GOING minus 0.31 sec per fur (GF)

| | | | | SP | RR | SF |
|---|---|---|---|---|---|---|
| | **Bequeath** (HRACecil) **4-9-10** WRyan(1) (lw: hld up: qckngd to ld 1f out: r.o strly) | — | 1 | 4/7 $^{1}$ | 85+ | 22 |
| $948^{2}$ | **Wilawander (97)** (BWHills) **3-8-4**(5) JDSmith(2) (led: qcknd 3f out: sn rdn: hdd 1f out: no ch w wnr) | 2½ | 2 | 13/8 $^{2}$ | 82 | 4 |
| $1530^{5}$ | **Baraqueta** (JLEyre) **4-9-7**(3) OPears(3) (trckd ldrs: lost pl over 2f out: eased & sn bhd) | 16 | 3 | 20/1 $^{3}$ | 60 | — |

(SP 106.5%) **3 Rn**

**2m 42.0** (9.60) CSF £1.73 TOTE £1.50 (£1.20) OWNER Mr K. Abdulla (NEWMARKET) BRED Juddmonte Farms
WEIGHT FOR AGE 3yo-15lb
**Bequeath**, a half-brother to Bal Harbour, looked in a different class in the paddock. Quickening to hit the front, he stretched out in really good style and should go higher than this. (4/7)
**948 Wilawander** raced keenly in front. Setting only a modest pace, he set sail for home off the bend, but it was soon clear the winner was in a different class. (13/8)
**1530 Baraqueta**, having his third run to qualify for a handicap mark, was sensibly allowed to drop away once in line for home. (20/1)

## 1864 OPEN LEARNING INSTITUTE MAIDEN STKS (3-Y.O+) (Class D)

5-00 (5-01) **7f 100y** £3,691.00 (£1,108.00: £534.00: £247.00) Stalls: High GOING minus 0.31 sec per fur (GF)

| | | | | SP | RR | SF |
|---|---|---|---|---|---|---|
| $1438^{9}$ | **Polar Prospect** (BHanbury) **3-8-11** WRyan(3) (b: chsd ldrs: styd on u.p fnl 2f: led wl ins fnl f) | — | 1 | 6/1 $^{3}$ | 72 | 39 |
| $1323^{2}$ | **Hannalou (FR)** (SPCWoods) **3-8-6** WWoods(9) (led: rdn clr 3f out: wknd & hdd wl ins fnl f) | nk | 2 | 2/1 $^{2}$ | 66 | 33 |
| | **Accondy (IRE)** (CEBrittain) **4-9-7** BDoyle(7) (tall: rangy: s.s: bhd & rn green: styd on wl appr fnl f: nt rch ldrs) | 1¼ | 3 | 10/1 | 69 | 46 |
| $1160^{3}$ | **Lachesis** (RHollinshead) **3-8-1**(5) FLynch(5) (trckd ldrs: kpt on same pce fnl 2f) | 1¼ | 4 | 13/2 | 61 | 28 |
| | **Tango Teaser** (ACStewart) **3-8-6** MRoberts(8) (cmpt: unf: hld up & plld v.hrd: in tch: hdwy over 2f out: sn rdn & hung rt: no imp) | 6 | 5 | 7/4 $^{1}$ | 48 | 15 |
| | **Shalta Chief** (EHOwenjun) **4-9-0**(7) FTynan(4) (bhd fr ½-wy) | 9 | 6 | 100/1 | 34 | 11 |
| | **Brownie's Promise** (MBrittain) **3-8-6**(5) GParkin(1) (unf: bit bkwd: s.i.s: a bhd) | 4 | 7 | 33/1 | 25 | — |
| | **Totally Different** (GROldroyd) **3-8-11** DRMcCabe(6) (sn bhd) | 5 | 8 | 50/1 | 15 | — |
| | **Dancing Jazztime** (JSWainwright) **5-9-2** NKennedy(2) (plld hrd: trckd ldrs: rn wd & lost pl 4f out: sn bhd) | 12 | 9 | 50/1 | — | — |

(SP 114.3%) **9 Rn**

**1m 34.9** (2.90) CSF £17.42 TOTE £7.60: £2.20 £1.10 £2.90 (£8.30) Trio £19.90 OWNER Ellway Racing Partnership (NEWMARKET) BRED C. H. Bothway
WEIGHT FOR AGE 3yo-10lb
**1195 Polar Prospect** showed a poor action going down. Sticking to his guns, he wore down the runner-up near the line. (6/1)
**1323 Hannalou (FR)** set just a fair pace. Driven clear off the bend, she began to tread water coming to the final furlong and was worn down near the line. She might have been better waiting rather than committing herself. (2/1)
**Accondy (IRE)**, an almost white son of Sadler's Wells, was very coltish in the paddock on this belated debut. Very green after starting slowly, he took an age to pick up but, putting in some solid work near the line, will beat the first two on his next outing. (10/1: op 5/1)
**Tango Teaser** looked very green going to post. Taking a fierce grip, she did nothing but hang right in the straight and her rider gave up over a furlong out. (7/4: op Evens)

T/Plpt: £78.90 (154.32 Tckts). T/Qdpt: £51.80 (12.74 Tckts). WG

# 1632-HAMILTON (R-H) (Good, Good to soft patches)
## Wednesday June 12th

WEATHER: sunny WIND: fresh half against

## 1865 HAMILTON ADVERTISER AMATEUR H'CAP (0-75) (3-Y.O+) (Class E)

7-00 (7-02) **5f 4y** £3,501.25 (£1,060.00: £517.50: £246.25) Stalls: Low GOING minus 0.39 sec per fur (F)

| | | | | SP | RR | SF |
|---|---|---|---|---|---|---|
| $1541^{3}$ | **Tropical Beach (53)** (JBerry) **3-10-9** MrsLPearce(11) (hdwy far side ½-wy: r.o to ld ins fnl f) | — | 1 | 5/1 $^{1}$ | 62 | 38 |
| $1541^{5}$ | **Serious Hurry (48)** (RMMcKellar) **8-10-4b**(7) MrsCWilliams(10) (lw: cl up far side: chal ins fnl f: nt qckn) | 2½ | 2 | 8/1 $^{3}$ | 49 | 32 |
| *$1492^{7}$* | **Cheeky Chappy (45)** (DWChapman) **5-10-8b** MissRClark(5) (led tl hdd & no ex ins fnl f) | ½ | 3 | 5/1 $^{1}$ | 44 | 27 |
| $1547^{4}$ | **Rinus Manor (IRE) (51)** (EJAlston) **5-11-0** MissPRobson(9) (outpcd & bhd far side tl styd on fnl f) | ½ | 4 | 6/1 $^{2}$ | 49 | 32 |
| $1765^{4}$ | **Henry the Hawk (52)** (MDods) **5-10-10v**(5) MissEMaude(6) (b: w ldrs tl rdn & btn appr fnl f) | 4 | 5 | 5/1 $^{1}$ | 37 | 20 |
| $559^{12}$ | **Coolowen Flash (IRE) (50)** (JLEyre) **5-10-13** MissDianaJones(8) (chsd ldrs far side: outpcd fr ½-wy) | 2½ | 6 | 8/1 $^{3}$ | 27 | 10 |
| 1635* | **Sunday Mail Too (IRE) (36)** (MissLAPerratt) **4-9-13** 5x MrsDKettlewell(4) (lw: swtchd stands' side: a outpcd & bhd) | 2 | 7 | 6/1 $^{2}$ | 7 | — |
| $1545^{8}$ | **Another Episode (IRE) (65)** (MissLAPerratt) **7-12-0** MrRHale(2) (raced stands' side: sn outpcd & bhd) | 3 | 8 | 50/1 | 26 | 9 |
| $1545^{6}$ | **Six for Luck (53)** (DANolan) **4-11-2b** MrAParker(3) (cl up tl wandered & wknd fnl 2f) | 3½ | 9 | 33/1 | 3 | — |
| $1163^{3}$ | **Natural Key (58)** (DHaydnJones) **3-10-7**(7)ow3 MrJDelahunt(1) (s.s: a bhd) | 7 | 10 | 14/1 | — | — |

(SP 112.4%) **10 Rn**

**61.2 secs** (2.90) CSF £39.25 CT £194.06 TOTE £4.60: £1.70 £2.40 £2.10 (£17.00) Trio £30.30 OWNER Mr Jim Unsworth (COCKERHAM) BRED P. Balding
WEIGHT FOR AGE 3yo-7lb
**1541 Tropical Beach**, without the blinkers this time, was well drawn and, given a fine ride, surged through to settle it emphatically. (5/1)
**1541 Serious Hurry** is coming to form fast and should be kept on the right side. (8/1)
**1163* Cheeky Chappy** showed tremendous early pace, but was always racing on the slightly slower ground off the far rail, and that eventually found him out. (5/1)
**1547 Rinus Manor (IRE)** found this trip too sharp, but was keeping on well at the end. (6/1)
**1765 Henry the Hawk** has all the early pace but, at the moment, is just failing to see it out. (5/1: op 8/1)
**Coolowen Flash (IRE)** had a good draw, but was not really firing. (8/1)
**1635* Sunday Mail Too (IRE)**, over a trip too short, switched to the stands' rail which put paid to any hopes he had. (6/1: op 4/1)
**1163 Natural Key** (14/1: op 7/1)

## 1866 AKELER (SCOTLAND) (S) STKS (3-Y.O+) (Class E)

7-30 (7-32) **1m 1f 36y** £3,186.05 (£964.40: £470.70: £223.85) Stalls: High GOING minus 0.39 sec per fur (F)

| | | | | SP | RR | SF |
|---|---|---|---|---|---|---|
| 1538[9] | **Northern Spark (44)** (MissLAPerratt) **8-9-2** JWeaver(9) (chsd ldrs: outpcd over 2f out: styd on u.p fnl f to ld nr fin) | — | 1 | 16/1 | 57 | 39 |
| | **Sir Arthur Hobbs (57)** (JLEyre) **9-9-2** RLappin(11) (trckd ldrs: led wl over 2f out tl ct cl home) | hd | 2 | 7/2[2] | 57 | 39 |
| 1417[7] | **Raased (70)** (FWatson) **4-9-2** TQuinn(12) (led tl hdd wl over 2f out: hrd rdn & one pce) | 3½ | 3 | 8/1 | 51 | 33 |
| 1548[9] | **Knave (57)** (PMonteith) **3-8-4v** AMackay(10) (in tch: chsng ldrs 4f out: one pce appr fnl f) | ¾ | 4 | 14/1 | 49 | 19 |
| 1596[6] | **Heathyards Magic (IRE) (58)** (MDods) **4-9-2** JFortune(2) (bhd: styd on fnl 3f: nvr able to chal) | 2½ | 5 | 8/1 | 45 | 27 |
| 1546[6] | **Lady Silk (48)** (MissJFCraze) **5-8-11** NConnorton(5) (bhd tl styd on fnl 2f) | ½ | 6 | 12/1 | 39 | 21 |
| 1311[6] | **Amnesia (IRE) (30)** (MrsSCBradburne) **5-8-11v** AlexGreaves(8) (hdwy 6f out: sn chsng ldrs: wknd appr fnl f) | 2½ | 7 | 50/1 | 35 | 17 |
| 1468[3] | **Hawwam (43)** (EJAlston) **10-9-2** SDWilliams(3) (chsd ldrs: outpcd over 3f out: no imp after) | 1¾ | 8 | 6/1[3] | 37 | 19 |
| 1587[5] | **Little Redwing** (MDHammond) **4-8-11** DaleGibson(7) (chsd ldrs: pushed along 5f out: wknd fnl 4f) | 5 | 9 | 20/1 | 23 | 5 |
| 1544[7] | **Jabaroot (IRE) (45)** (DANolan) **5-8-11b[1](5)** PFessey(4) (a bhd) | 1 | 10 | 50/1 | 26 | 8 |
| 1596[2] | **Simand (50)** (GMMoore) **4-8-11** KDarley(1) (mid div & c wd st: sn rdn: wknd over 2f out) | 1¾ | 11 | 5/2[1] | 18 | — |
| 1345[6] | **She's A Winner (IRE) (55)** (PMonteith) **3-8-4** JFanning(6) (effrt & c wd st: sn rdn & btn) | 21 | 12 | 10/1 | — | — |

(SP 125.3%) **12 Rn**

**1m 57.8** (3.50) CSF £70.71 TOTE £16.90: £3.90 £2.00 £2.40 (£47.40) Trio £213.80 OWNER Scottish Daily Record & Sunday Mail Ltd (AYR) BRED I. Thoday
WEIGHT FOR AGE 3yo-12lb
No bid

**661 Northern Spark**, trying his longest trip to date, needed every yard of it and should go on from here. (16/1)
**Sir Arthur Hobbs**, after ten months off the track, this track specialist ran a cracker, but the lack of a recent run probably just made the difference. (7/2)
**1417 Raased**, with a tongue-strap this time, had his chances but looked none too keen when the pressure was applied and swished his tail. (8/1)
**453 Knave** ran his best race since changing stables and seems to be getting it together. (14/1: op 8/1)
**1596 Heathyards Magic (IRE)** has the ability to do better if he can be persuaded. (8/1)
**1546 Lady Silk** was again putting in her best work when it was all over and may need a bit further. (12/1: op 8/1)

## 1867 LANGS SUPREME CONDITIONS STKS (3-Y.O+) (Class C)

8-00 (8-01) **1m 1f 36y** £5,410.74 (£2,025.66: £991.33: £427.15: £192.08: £98.04) Stalls: High GOING minus 0.39 sec per fur (F)

| | | | | SP | RR | SF |
|---|---|---|---|---|---|---|
| | **Salmon Ladder (USA) (100)** (PFICole) **4-9-4** TQuinn(3) (lw: mde all: qcknd 3f out: pushed out) | — | 1 | Evens[1] | 94+ | 67 |
| 1476[2] | **Billy Bushwacker (93)** (MrsMReveley) **5-9-4** KDarley(6) (lw: trckd ldrs: effrt 4f out: r.o: no ch w wnr) | 8 | 2 | 7/4[2] | 80 | 53 |
| 1355[6] | **Otto E Mezzo** (MJPolglase) **4-9-4** JWeaver(4) (chsd wnr tl outpcd fnl 3f) | 6 | 3 | 12/1 | 70 | 43 |
| 1131[5] | **Ten Past Six (90)** (MartynWane) **4-9-4** DeanMcKeown(2) (lw: prom tl outpcd fr ½-wy) | 2½ | 4 | 5/1[3] | 65 | 38 |
| 1410[5] | **Kissel** (AHarrison) **4-9-3** TWilliams(1) (nvr trbld ldrs) | 5 | 5 | 50/1 | 56 | 29 |
| 1633[4] | **Hutchies Lady (40)** (RMMcKellar) **4-8-6(7)** DMcGaffin(5) (sn bhd) | 2½ | 6 | 100/1 | 47 | 20 |

(SP 113.7%) **6 Rn**

**1m 54.8** (0.50) CSF £3.15 TOTE £1.80: £1.50 £1.50 (£1.60) OWNER Mr M. Arbib (WHATCOMBE) BRED Robert N. Clay and Michael J. & Mrs Ryan

**Salmon Ladder (USA)**, given a most aggressive ride, left nothing to chance and, although clear, was pushed out all the way home to win in a fast time. (Evens)
**1476 Billy Bushwacker** went after the winner approaching the last three furlongs, but once under pressure, the struggle was always beyond him. This was probably not a bad effort. (7/4)
**Otto E Mezzo** burnt himself out by chasing the winner and, once his sights are lowered, should improve. (12/1)
**1131 Ten Past Six** was disappointing, dropping out tamely from halfway. (5/1)
**Kissel** soon realised she had no chance here and was not overpunished. (50/1)

## 1868 SAINTS AND SINNERS CHALLENGE CUP H'CAP (0-85) (3-Y.O+) (Class D)

8-30 (8-30) **1m 65y** £4,621.00 (£1,399.00: £683.00: £325.00) Stalls: High GOING minus 0.39 sec per fur (F)

| | | | | SP | RR | SF |
|---|---|---|---|---|---|---|
| 1341[9] | **Western General (71)** (MissMKMilligan) **5-9-9** KDarley(6) (bhd: hdwy ½-wy: led ins fnl f: r.o) | — | 1 | 6/1 | 77 | 50 |
| 1037[11] | **Talented Ting (IRE) (60)** (PCHaslam) **7-8-12** JWeaver(5) (lw: cl up: led 2½f out tl ins fnl f: kpt on) | ¾ | 2 | 6/1 | 65 | 38 |
| 1528[3] | **Scaraben (68)** (SEKettlewell) **8-9-6** JFortune(3) (lw: s.i.s: hdwy over 2f out: ev ch ins fnl f: kpt on) | hd | 3 | 3/1[2] | 72 | 45 |
| 509[6] | **Give Me A Ring (IRE) (70)** (CWThornton) **3-8-11** DeanMcKeown(1) (lw: chsd ldrs: ev ch & rdn 2f out: r.o one pce) | nk | 4 | 7/1 | 74 | 36 |
| *1601*[2] | **Cashmere Lady (72)** (JLEyre) **4-9-10** RLappin(2) (trckd ldrs gng wl: effrt 2f out: r.o one pce) | hd | 5 | 5/1[3] | 76 | 49 |
| 1406[5] | **Tatika (69)** (GWragg) **6-9-0(7)** GMilligan(4) (lw: hld up: hdwy on outside ½-wy: effrt 2f out: nt qckn) | ½ | 6 | 11/4[1] | 72 | 45 |
| 817[19] | **King Curan (USA) (54)** (DHaydnJones) **5-8-6** AMackay(7) (hdwy ½-wy: n.m.r 2f out: hdwy over 1f out: no imp) | ½ | 7 | 14/1 | 56 | 29 |
| 1633[9] | **Rapid Mover (44)** (DANolan) **9-7-5b(5)** PFessey(8) (led tl hdd 2½f out: wknd over 1f out) | 5 | 8 | 66/1 | 36 | 9 |

(SP 117.6%) **8 Rn**

**1m 46.8** (2.70) CSF £38.97 CT £118.56 TOTE £8.80: £2.20 £1.60 £1.10 (£24.00) OWNER Mr J. D. Gordon (LEYBURN) BRED Fluorocarbon Bloodstock
LONG HANDICAP Rapid Mover 6-13
WEIGHT FOR AGE 3yo-11lb

**1341 Western General** again came from behind and, taking a narrow gap approaching the final furlong, showed fine courage to hang on. (6/1)
**537 Talented Ting (IRE)**, seven times a winner on this track, showed his first signs of form this season and, now well handicapped, should be kept on the right side of. (6/1)
**1528 Scaraben** is looking big and well, but is not quite firing as he did last season. He will no doubt come to hand before long. (3/1)
**Give Me A Ring (IRE)** ran well and, judging by the way he stayed on, should get further. (7/1)
**1601 Cashmere Lady** failed to produce the goods when the pressure was applied. (5/1)
**1406 Tatika** (11/4: op 7/4)

## 1869 WILCON HOMES MAIDEN AUCTION STKS (2-Y.O) (Class E)
9-00 (9-01) **6f 5y** £3,436.25 (£1,040.00: £507.50: £241.25) Stalls: Low GOING minus 0.39 sec per fur (F)

| | | | | SP | RR | SF |
|---|---|---|---|---|---|---|
| 1632[2] | **Bollero (IRE)** (JBerry) **2-7-9**(5) PFessey(5) (lw: led after 1½f: hld on wl fnl f) | — | 1 | 3/1[2] | 62 | 6 |
| 1653[5] | **Osomental** (DHaydnJones) **2-8-10b** AMackay(6) (lw: trckd ldrs: hdwy & ev ch over 1f out: rdn & nt qckn) | 1¾ | 2 | 3/1[2] | 67 | 11 |
| 996[3] | **Ben's Ridge** (PCHaslam) **2-8-10** JWeaver(9) (in tch: hdwy whn hmpd wl over 1f out: swtchd & nvr able to chal) | 1¼ | 3 | 11/4[1] | 64 | 8 |
| | **Back In The Ussr (IRE)** (MJohnston) **2-8-5** TWilliams(7) (unf: in tch: rdn over 2f out: kpt on one pce) | ¾ | 4 | 14/1 | 57 | 1 |
| 1513[8] | **Miss Barcelona (IRE)** (MJPolglase) **2-8-0** WHollick(8) (disp ld 1½f: chsd ldrs: hung rt 2f out: sn btn) | 6 | 5 | 25/1 | 36 | — |
| 1583[8] | **Plutarch Angel** (WTKemp) **2-8-5** RLappin(4) (a outpcd & bhd) | 4 | 6 | 150/1 | 31 | — |
| 1308[2] | **Red Romance** (DenysSmith) **2-8-5** KDarley(3) (in tch tl wknd fnl 2f) | hd | 7 | 4/1[3] | 30 | — |
| 1645[2] | **Cantsaynowt** (RMMcKellar) **2-8-0** DaleGibson(1) (disp ld 1½f: cl up tl wknd 2f out) | 7 | 8 | 20/1 | 7 | — |
| 1595[3] | **Midyans Song** (JJO'Neill) **2-8-0** JFanning(2) (a outpcd & wl bhd) | 6 | 9 | 14/1 | — | — |
| | | | | (SP 119.3%) | **9 Rn** | |

**1m 13.3** (3.30) CSF £12.35 TOTE £3.90: £1.30 £1.80 £1.80 (£6.60) Trio £8.10 OWNER Mr Ian Bolland (COCKERHAM) BRED Mrs G. Donnelly
**1632 Bollero (IRE)** enjoyed this longer trip and was nicely on top by the finish. (3/1: op 5/1)
**1653 Osomental** has plenty of ability but, when it comes down to it, he fails to do the business. (3/1)
**996 Ben's Ridge** was just starting to pick up when he was almost put over the rail entering the final two furlongs, and had no hope from then on. (11/4)
**Back In The Ussr (IRE)** looks likely to need time and possibly further. (14/1: op 8/1)

## 1870 TENNENT CALEDONIAN BREWERIES HAMILTON GOLD CUP H'CAP (0-80) (3-Y.O+) (Class D)
9-30 (9-32) **1m 5f 9y** £4,513.75 (£1,366.00: £666.50: £316.75) Stalls: Low GOING minus 0.39 sec per fur (F)

| | | | | SP | RR | SF |
|---|---|---|---|---|---|---|
| 1309* | **Lord Advocate (45)** (DANolan) **8-7-9b**(7) KSked(7) (chsd ldrs: led over 2f out: hung lft: styd on strly) | — | 1 | 11/2 | 59 | 39 |
| 999[13] | **Askern (65)** (DHaydnJones) **5-9-8** AMackay(8) (hld up: smooth hdwy over 3f out: rdn over 1f out: nt pce of wnr) | 5 | 2 | 8/1 | 73 | 53 |
| 1640[2] | **Daily Sport Girl (44)** (BJLlewellyn) **7-8-1** TWilliams(5) (lw: b: cl up: led 4f out tl over 2f out: one pce) | 1½ | 3 | 4/1[3] | 50 | 30 |
| 1637* | **Welsh Mill (IRE) (72)** (MrsMReveley) **7-10-1** 5x KDarley(3) (lw: trckd ldrs: effrt over 3f out: rdn & one pce) | 3½ | 4 | 3/1[2] | 74 | 54 |
| 1478[7] | **Red Spectacle (IRE) (57)** (PCHaslam) **4-8-9**(5) PFessey(4) (led tl hdd 4f out: grad wknd) | 1 | 5 | 14/1 | 58 | 38 |
| | **Moonlight Calypso (44)** (MGMeagher) **5-8-1** FNorton(2) (in tch tl outpcd fnl 3f) | 9 | 6 | 16/1 | 34 | 14 |
| 1345[5] | **Manabar (60)** (MJPolglase) **4-9-3** JWeaver(6) (s.i.s: n.d) | 8 | 7 | 14/1 | 40 | 20 |
| 1165* | **Victor Laszlo (41)** (RAllan) **4-7-12** JFanning(1) (chsd ldr tl wknd over 3f out) | 8 | 8 | 5/2[1] | 11 | — |
| | | | | (SP 119.3%) | **8 Rn** | |

**2m 48.6** (2.90) CSF £44.96 CT £180.22 TOTE £5.50: £1.80 £3.60 £2.10 (£35.30) OWNER Mrs J. McFadyen-Murray (WISHAW) BRED London Thoroughbred Services Ltd
**1309* Lord Advocate** is in terrific form at present and, the further they went, the better he got. (11/2)
**920 Askern** was in a co-operative mood and looked to be going well early in the straight but, once the pressure was on in the last two furlongs, he could never match the winner. (8/1: 6/1-9/1)
**1640 Daily Sport Girl** tried to pinch this by kicking on over half a mile out but, headed two furlongs later, then proved very one-paced. (4/1)
**1637* Welsh Mill (IRE)** was always seeing too much daylight too soon and cried enough with two furlongs left. (3/1)
**Red Spectacle (IRE)** is gradually improving but there is still some way to go. (14/1: 10/1-16/1)
**Moonlight Calypso** has been off the track for over a year and this found her out. (16/1)
**1345 Manabar** (14/1: op 8/1)

T/Plpt: £63.30 (238.45 Tckts). T/Qdpt: £7.70 (153.13 Tckts). AA

# 1613-KEMPTON (R-H) (St crse Good, Rnd crse Good to firm)
# Wednesday June 12th
WEATHER: sunny WIND: almost nil

## 1871 MARS MAIDEN AUCTION STKS (2-Y.O) (Class E)
6-45 (6-47) **6f** £2,957.00 (£896.00: £438.00: £209.00) Stalls: High GOING minus 0.41 sec per fur (F)

| | | | | SP | RR | SF |
|---|---|---|---|---|---|---|
| 1179[3] | **Simple Logic** (AGFoster) **2-7-13**ow1 TSprake(13) (lw: w ldr: led over 2f out: hrd rdn over 1f out: r.o wl) | — | 1 | 5/2[1] | 67 | 15 |
| 1643[5] | **Madame Chinnery** (JMPEustace) **2-8-1** JTate(10) (swtg: a.p: hrd rdn over 2f out: r.o ins fnl f) | ½ | 2 | 10/1 | 68 | 17 |
| 1626[5] | **Briska (IRE)** (RHannon) **2-8-2**(3) DaneO'Neill(2) (a.p: rdn over 2f out: unable qckn) | 1¾ | 3 | 8/1[3] | 67 | 16 |
| 1513[5] | **What Happened Was** (MartynMeade) **2-7-9**(3) MHenry(11) (led over 3f: rdn: one pce) | nk | 4 | 14/1 | 59 | 8 |
| | **Select Choice (IRE)** (APJarvis) **2-8-3** DHarrison(7) (w'like: bit bkwd: a.p: rdn over 2f out: one pce) | 3 | 5 | 5/2[1] | 56 | 5 |
| | **River of Fortune (IRE)** (MHTompkins) **2-8-2**ow1 PRobinson(4) (neat: dwlt: hdwy over 1f out: nvr nrr) | 1½ | 6 | 20/1 | 51 | — |
| | **Shaken Up** (MrsDHaine) **2-8-3** GCarter(9) (b.nr hind: str: bit bkwd: dwlt: rdn & hdwy over 1f out: one pce) | ½ | 7 | 14/1 | 51 | — |
| 916[11] | **Grovefair Lad (IRE)** (BJMeehan) **2-8-6** JReid(12) (bit bkwd: hld up: rdn over 2f out: wknd wl over 1f out) | ½ | 8 | 33/1 | 53 | 2 |
| 1590[7] | **Victoria's Dream (IRE)** (MRChannon) **2-8-0**(5) PPMurphy(8) (nvr nr to chal) | 1½ | 9 | 7/1[2] | 48 | — |
| | **William Wallace** (CMurray) **2-8-6** MTebbutt(6) (w'like: bit bkwd: hld up: rdn whn bmpd 2f out: sn wknd) | hd | 10 | 25/1 | 48 | — |
| | **Rumbustious** (RHannon) **2-8-5** RPerham(5) (leggy: a bhd) | nk | 11 | 20/1 | 47 | — |
| 1445[4] | **Eaton Park (IRE)** (RAkehurst) **2-8-6** SSanders(1) (racd alone stands' side: a bhd) | 4 | 12 | 25/1 | 37 | — |
| | **Amarella (IRE)** (MJHaynes) **2-7-12** JQuinn(3) (neat: a bhd) | 1¾ | 13 | 33/1 | 24 | — |
| | **Not Out Lad** (PButler) **2-8-3** JFEgan(14) (str: bkwd: prom over 3f: t.o) | 28 | 14 | 66/1 | — | — |
| | | | | (SP 127.8%) | **14 Rn** | |

**1m 13.88** (2.58) CSF £28.05 TOTE £3.40: £1.40 £3.20 £2.60 (£12.50) Trio £47.50 OWNER Miss Juliet Reed (LAMBOURN) BRED The Woodhaven Stud
**1179 Simple Logic** was the paddock pick and did not let supporters down, despite the difference in going between this and on her debut. Disputing the lead until sent on soon after halfway, she responded to pressure from below the distance and was not going to be denied. (5/2: op 5/4)
**1643 Madame Chinnery** was shown the persuader over a quarter of a mile from home but, to her credit, stuck on gamely to the bitter end. (10/1: 4/1-11/1)

**1626 Briska (IRE)**, in the firing line throughout, failed to raise her work-rate in the final quarter-mile. (8/1: op 4/1)
**1513 What Happened Was**, who had a whisker in front until over a quarter of a mile from home, could then only keep on at one pace. (14/1: 7/1-16/1)
**Select Choice (IRE)** did not look fully fit for this debut but was nevertheless backed down to go off joint-favourite. Never far away, he was scrubbed along over two furlongs from home, but failed to find that vital turn of foot. (5/2: op 9/2)
**River of Fortune (IRE)** was doing all her best work in the final furlong and a half. (20/1)

## 1872 ALLIED DUNBAR H'CAP (0-80) (3-Y.O+) (Class D)

7-10 (7-12) **1m (Jubilee)** £3,712.50 (£1,125.00: £550.00: £262.50) Stalls: High GOING minus 0.41 sec per fur (F)

| | | | | SP | RR | SF |
|---|---|---|---|---|---|---|
| 1420[3] | **Dancing Image (66)** (IABalding) **3-8-5** LDettori(4) (stdy hdwy 2f out: led over 1f out: easily) | — | **1** | 7/2[1] | 79+ | 31 |
| 1654* | **Ret Frem (IRE) (63)** (MAJarvis) **3-8-2** 5x PRobinson(11) (led over 6f: unable qckn) | 2½ | **2** | 5/1[3] | 71 | 23 |
| 1496* | **Sharp Consul (IRE) (74)** (HCandy) **4-9-10** CRutter(5) (carried wd & lost pl st: hdwy over 1f out: r.o) | 1 | **3** | 10/1 | 80 | 43 |
| 1190[2] | **Admirals Flame (IRE) (74)** (CFWall) **5-9-10** GDuffield(3) (b: hld up: rdn 2f out: r.o one pce) | 1½ | **4** | 4/1[2] | 77 | 40 |
| 1775[9] | **Gadge (58)** (DMorris) **5-8-8b[1]** DHarrison(1) (a.p: rdn over 2f out: one pce) | s.h | **5** | 16/1 | 61 | 24 |
| 1485[4] | **Apache Len (USA) (74)** (RHannon) **3-8-10**(3) DaneO'Neill(6) (rdn & hdwy 2f out: one pce) | 2½ | **6** | 8/1 | 72 | 24 |
| 987[13] | **Desert Cat (IRE) (75)** (HThomsonJones) **3-9-0** WCarson(9) (lw: chsd ldr 6f: wknd over 1f out) | ½ | **7** | 14/1 | 72 | 24 |
| *553[5]* | **Robellion (67)** (DWPArbuthnot) **5-9-3v** JReid(7) (hld up: rdn over 1f out: sn wknd) | 3½ | **8** | 16/1 | 57 | 20 |
| 1533[2] | **Rocky Waters (USA) (56)** (PBurgoyne) **7-8-3**(3) PMcCabe(10) (prom 6f) | 3 | **9** | 8/1 | 40 | 3 |
| 1423[15] | **Rise Up Singing (53)** (WJMusson) **8-8-3** AMcGlone(8) (a bhd) | 10 | **10** | 33/1 | 17 | — |
| 575[15] | **Naval Hunter (USA) (75)** (PWHarris) **3-9-0** GHind(2) (lw: prom tl rn wd & wknd st 3f out) | ¾ | **11** | 16/1 | 37 | — |
| | | | | (SP 117.5%) | | **11 Rn** |

**1m 39.7** (2.50) CSF £20.14 CT £148.83 TOTE £3.20: £1.20 £2.40 £3.70 (£7.10) Trio £34.40 OWNER The Queen (KINGSCLERE) BRED The Queen
WEIGHT FOR AGE 3yo-11lb

**1420 Dancing Image** hacked up. Cruising into the lead over a furlong from home, he pulled clear to win with any amount in hand and the winning distance is no reflection of his superiority. (7/2)
**1654* Ret Frem (IRE)** attempted to make all the running but, passed by the winner below the distance, was firmly put in his place. (5/1)
**1496* Sharp Consul (IRE)**, raised 7lb for his latest victory, was not helped by the drop in distance or the fact that he was carried wide entering the straight costing him ground he could ill-afford. (10/1: 7/1-11/1)
**1190 Admirals Flame (IRE)** took a keen hold early on and chased the leaders. He stayed on in the final quarter-mile, but never threatened to get into it. (4/1)
**1613 Gadge**, never far away, got outpaced when the real race developed over a quarter of a mile from home, and could then only plod on in his own time. He needs some rain. (16/1)
**1485 Apache Len (USA)** took closer order two furlongs from home, but could then make no further impression. (8/1)

## 1873 VENUS MAIDEN STKS (3-Y.O) (Class D)

7-40 (7-41) **1m 4f** £3,694.50 (£1,116.00: £543.00: £256.50) Stalls: High GOING minus 0.41 sec per fur (F)

| | | | | SP | RR | SF |
|---|---|---|---|---|---|---|
| 1182[2] | **Sharaf Kabeer** (SbinSuroor) **3-9-0** LDettori(6) (lw: chsd ldr: led 4f out: clr over 2f out: v.easily) | — | **1** | 7/4[2] | 94+ | 58 |
| | **Time Allowed** (MRStoute) **3-8-9** JReid(3) (hdwy 2f out: chsd wnr fnl f: no imp) | 6 | **2** | 20/1 | 81 | 45 |
| | **Hayaain (70)** (MajorWRHern) **3-9-0** WCarson(2) (bkwd: a.p: rdn over 3f out: one pce) | ½ | **3** | 20/1 | 85 | 49 |
| 1123[5] | **Turia** (MajorDNChappell) **3-8-9** TSprake(1) (hld up: rdn over 3f out: one pce) | 4 | **4** | 25/1 | 75 | 39 |
| 1508[3] | **Ginger Fox (USA)** (HRACecil) **3-9-0** PatEddery(7) (led 8f: wknd 2f out) | ¾ | **5** | 6/4[1] | 79 | 43 |
| | **Psicossis** (HRACecil) **3-9-0** AMcGlone(9) (str: scope: bkwd: stdy hdwy 5f out: wknd 2f out) | 4 | **6** | 25/1 | 74 | 38 |
| 1123[7] | **Vendetta** (IABalding) **3-8-9** PaulEddery(4) (nvr nr to chal) | 2 | **7** | 20/1 | 66 | 30 |
| | **Mischief Star (70)** (DRCElsworth) **3-8-6**(3) DaneO'Neill(5) (bhd fnl 5f) | s.h | **8** | 20/1 | 66 | 30 |
| 1508[5] | **Oops Pettie** (MrsJCecil) **3-8-9** AClark(10) (prom over 10f) | nk | **9** | 13/2[3] | 66 | 30 |
| 1656[7] | **Full Throttle** (MHTompkins) **3-9-0** PRobinson(11) (a bhd) | 3 | **10** | 33/1 | 67 | 31 |
| 1656[14] | **Aqua Star (IRE)** (JLDunlop) **3-9-0** SWhitworth(8) (a bhd) | 14 | **11** | 50/1 | 48 | 12 |
| | | | | (SP 121.3%) | | **11 Rn** |

**2m 31.88** (1.18) CSF £34.16 TOTE £2.80: £1.30 £2.60 £3.40 (£33.70) Trio £120.70 OWNER Sheikh Ahmed Al Maktoum (NEWMARKET) BRED Sheikh Ahmed Bin Rashid Al Maktoum

**1182 Sharaf Kabeer** looked magnificent and put up a thoroughly-impressive display. Racing in second place, he went on turning for home and, clear early in the straight, won with any amount in hand. He can certainly go on to better things. (7/4: 6/4-9/4)
**Time Allowed**, having her first run of the season, made some headway a quarter of a mile from home. She struggled into second place a furlong out, but had no hope of reeling in the very easy winner. (20/1)
**Hayaain** looked far from fit for this reappearance. Nevertheless, he was close up until tapped for toe in the straight. His stable is still looking for its first win of the season. (20/1)
**1123 Turia** chased the leaders. Ridden along turning for home, she could only plod on in her own time. (25/1)
**1508 Ginger Fox (USA)** did not look as well as at Sandown and was disappointing over this longer trip. Bowling along in front, he soon had the field well strung out but, collared turning for home, the writing was soon on the wall. (6/4)
**Psicossis**, a good-bodied and deep girthed individual, was carrying a lot of surplus flesh for this debut, but still showed some promise. Creeping closer to the leaders turning out of the back straight, he had given his all a quarter of a mile from home. He should come on a lot for this. (25/1)

## 1874 GUARDIAN PROPERTIES H'CAP (0-70) (3-Y.O+) (Class E)

8-10 (8-10) **1m 4f** £3,615.00 (£1,095.00: £535.00: £255.00) Stalls: High GOING: minus 0.41 sec per fur (F)

| | | | | SP | RR | SF |
|---|---|---|---|---|---|---|
| 1306* | **Paradise Waters (64)** (RFJohnsonHoughton) **4-9-9** JReid(10) (mde all: rdn out) | — | **1** | 100/30[1] | 74 | 57 |
| 1498[11] | **High Desire (IRE) (54)** (JRArnold) **3-7-9**(3) MHenry(16) (nt clr run over 2f out: hdwy 2f out: chsd wnr over 1f out: unable qckn) | 1¼ | **2** | 20/1 | 62 | 30 |
| 1472[2] | **Wottashambles (39)** (LMontagueHall) **5-7-12** JFEgan(1) (b: a.p: hrd rdn over 2f out: r.o one pce) | 2½ | **3** | 9/1[3] | 44 | 27 |
| 1414[11] | **Bronze Maquette (IRE) (37)** (THind) **6-7-3**(7) IonaWands(8) (lw: hdwy over 3f out: rdn over 1f out: one pce) | hd | **4** | 25/1 | 42 | 25 |
| 1462[13] | **Shift Again (IRE) (60)** (SESherwood) **4-9-5b[1]** LDettori(9) (a.p: nt clr run 2f out: swtchd lft: rdn over 1f out: r.o one pce) | s.h | **5** | 12/1 | 65 | 48 |
| 1837[3] | **General Mouktar (55)** (BJMeehan) **6-9-0** PatEddery(15) (lw: hdwy over 2f out: n.m.r on ins 2f out: r.o one pce) | s.h | **6** | 5/1[2] | 60 | 43 |
| 1450[7] | **Tappeto (68)** (HCandy) **4-9-13** CRutter(2) (hdwy over 2f out: nt clr run on ins over 1f out: one pce) | 1¾ | **7** | 14/1 | 70 | 53 |

| | Horse | Dist | Pos | SP | RR | SF |
|---|---|---|---|---|---|---|
| | **Double Echo (IRE) (54)** (JDBethell) **8-8-13** WCarson(6) (nt clr run over 2f out: hdwy & nt clr run over 1f out: nt clr run ins fnl f: one pce) | s.h | **8** | 16/1 | 56 | 39 |
| 1472* | **Duty Sergeant (IRE) (41)** (PhilipMitchell) **7-7-9**(5) CAdamson(14) (a mid div) | 2 | **9** | 10/1 | 41 | 24 |
| 1066[8] | **Fairy Knight (69)** (RHannon) **4-9-11v**[1](3) DaneO'Neill(3) (lw: a mid div) | 1¼ | **10** | 16/1 | 67 | 50 |
| 1618[12] | **Fighting Times (65)** (CASmith) **4-9-10** MWigham(12) (nvr nrr) | 1¾ | **11** | 12/1 | 61 | 44 |
| 1655[8] | **Galway Blade (58)** (APJarvis) **3-8-2** DHarrison(4) (a bhd) | 1¼ | **12** | 20/1 | 52 | 20 |
| 1655[10] | **Star Fighter (46)** (MJHaynes) **4-8-5b** GDuffield(11) (b.nr fore: lw: a bhd) | ½ | **13** | 20/1 | 39 | 22 |
| 1686[4] | **Dormy Three (64)** (RJHodges) **6-9-9** PaulEddery(13) (lw: prom over 10f) | 1½ | **14** | 9/1[3] | 57 | 40 |
| 1498[13] | **Dashing Invader (USA) (52)** (PWHarris) **3-7-10** JQuinn(5) (lw: prom over 9f) | d.h | **14** | 33/1 | 43 | 11 |
| | **Nothing Doing (IRE) (37)** (WJMusson) **7-7-10** NAdams(7) (bkwd: a bhd) | 10 | **16** | 20/1 | 15 | — |

(SP 128.5%) **16 Rn**

**2m 33.34** (2.64) CSF £65.43 CT £530.76 TOTE £3.80: £1.30 £4.90 £1.80 £4.80 (£85.90) Trio £466.30 OWNER Mr R. Crutchley (DIDCOT) BRED R. E. Crutchley

LONG HANDICAP Bronze Maquette (IRE) 7-8 Dashing Invader (USA) 7-3 Nothing Doing (IRE) 7-9

WEIGHT FOR AGE 3yo-15lb

**1306* Paradise Waters** is in tremendous form at present and, adopting her usual front-running role, was not going to be passed. (100/30)

**1044 High Desire (IRE)**, who failed to get a clear run early in the straight, soon picked up ground. Moving into second place at the distance, she was unable to reel in the winner. (20/1)

**1472 Wottashambles**, never far away, got rather outpaced early in the straight but did stay on for third prize. (9/1)

**1047 Bronze Maquette (IRE)** moved up turning for home but, ridden along below the distance, could only go up and down in the same place. Her only victory from thirty-four starts came nearly three years ago. (25/1)

**Shift Again (IRE)** was fitted with blinkers for the first time. Not getting the best run a quarter of a mile from home, she stayed on and only just failed to make the prize money. (12/1)

**1837 General Mouktar**, making a quick reappearance, moved up along the inside rail only to get slightly tightened up a quarter of a mile from home. It made little difference to his chances although he did stay on. He has become very frustrating, and without a win in nearly three years, is not one to back with any confidence. (5/1)

**Double Echo (IRE)**, off the course for nearly fourteen months, encountered problems en masse. Continually failing to get a clear run in the straight, the situation eventually had to be accepted inside the final furlong. (16/1)

## 1875 JUPITER LIMITED STKS (0-75) (3-Y.O+) (Class D)

8-40 (8-40) **1m 6f 92y** £3,538.50 (£1,068.00: £519.00: £244.50) Stalls: High GOING: minus 0.41 sec per fur (F)

| | Horse | Dist | Pos | SP | RR | SF |
|---|---|---|---|---|---|---|
| *1717** | **Sea Victor (73)** (JLHarris) **4-9-12** LDettori(1) (chsd ldr 12f out: rdn over 2f out: led ins fnl f: r.o wl) | — | **1** | 3/1[2] | 86 | 24 |
| 1322[10] | **Pearl Venture (75)** (SPCWoods) **4-9-7** WWoods(2) (stdy hdwy 2f out: ev ch fnl f: r.o) | hd | **2** | 7/1 | 81 | 19 |
| 1524[9] | **Secret Service (IRE) (74)** (CWThornton) **4-9-10** PaulEddery(6) (lw: led: rdn over 1f out: hdd ins fnl f: unable qckn) | 1¼ | **3** | 7/2[3] | 83 | 21 |
| 1631[3] | **Belmarita (IRE) (75)** (MHTompkins) **3-8-2** PRobinson(4) (lw: hld up: hrd rdn 2f out: one pce) | nk | **4** | 9/4[1] | 79 | — |
| 1508[15] | **Viridis (USA) (68)** (HRACecil) **3-8-2** AMcGlone(5) (chsd ldr 2f: wknd over 2f out) | 12 | **5** | 11/2 | 66 | — |
| | **Yacht (67)** (THind) **4-9-10** PatEddery(3) (a bhd) | 16 | **6** | 14/1 | 51 | — |

(SP 112.5%) **6 Rn**

**3m 13.07** (10.07) CSF £20.90 TOTE £3.90: £1.40 £3.00 (£27.00) OWNER Mr David Abell (MELTON MOWBRAY) BRED Juddmonte Farms

WEIGHT FOR AGE 3yo-19lb

**1717* Sea Victor**, soon racing in second place, was asked for his effort in the straight and eventually got on top inside the final furlong. He was given no peace by the runner-up though but just held on to give Dettori his sixth winner of the day. (3/1)

**953 Pearl Venture** eased her way into the action in the straight, and may even have got her head in front for a few strides inside the final furlong. Despite giving her all, she found the winner too strong. (7/1)

**1436 Secret Service (IRE)** attempted to make all. Collared inside the final furlong, he failed to find another gear. (7/2)

**1631 Belmarita (IRE)** was asked to mount her challenge in the straight, but failed to find a turn of foot in the final two furlongs. (9/4)

**1090 Viridis (USA)** (11/2: op 7/2)

**Yacht** (14/1: 10/1-16/1)

## 1876 DIANA H'CAP (0-70) (3-Y.O+ F & M) (Class E)

9-10 (9-11) **7f (Jubilee)** £3,420.00 (£1,035.00: £505.00: £240.00) Stalls: High GOING: minus 0.41 sec per fur (F)

| | Horse | Dist | Pos | SP | RR | SF |
|---|---|---|---|---|---|---|
| 1625[13] | **Zelda Zonk (68)** (BJMeehan) **4-10-0** JReid(10) (hld up: led 2f out: rdn out) | — | **1** | 5/1[1] | 77 | 51 |
| 1689[2] | **Morning Surprise (58)** (APJarvis) **3-8-1**(7) CCarver(6) (lw: hld up: chsd wnr over 1f out: unable qckn) | 3 | **2** | 5/1[1] | 60 | 24 |
| 1508[9] | **Hippy (67)** (CEBrittain) **3-9-3** WCarson(3) (swtg: a.p: ev ch wl over 1f out: one pce) | 2½ | **3** | 9/1 | 63 | 27 |
| 1074[4] | **Stolen Melody (64)** (SDow) **4-9-5**(5) ADaly(5) (a.p: rdn over 2f out: one pce) | 1¾ | **4** | 5/1[1] | 56 | 30 |
| 1412[15] | **Deerly (60)** (DMorris) **3-8-10** LDettori(13) (hld up: rdn over 2f out: one pce) | 1 | **5** | 8/1[3] | 50 | 14 |
| 1302[7] | **Windswept (IRE) (63)** (DJSffrenchDavis) **3-8-8**(5) CAdamson(2) (no hdwy fnl 3f) | 2½ | **6** | 10/1 | 47 | 11 |
| 1171[7] | **Bellacardia (69)** (GLewis) **3-9-5** PaulEddery(4) (nvr nr to chal) | ¾ | **7** | 11/2[2] | 52 | 16 |
| 559[13] | **Bella Coola (43)** (MartynMeade) **4-8-3** RPerham(9) (led 5f) | ¾ | **8** | 20/1 | 24 | — |
| *123*[15] | **Killatty Lark (IRE) (46)** (WJMusson) **3-7-10** NAdams(1) (bit bkwd: a bhd) | ¾ | **9** | 20/1 | 25 | — |
| | **Fayre Holly (IRE) (65)** (MJHeaton-Ellis) **3-9-1** WWoods(12) (a bhd) | 2½ | **10** | 20/1 | 39 | 3 |
| 1171[13] | **Risky Baby (45)** (THind) **4-8-5** AClark(11) (b: lw: a bhd) | ¾ | **11** | 33/1 | 17 | — |
| *897*[6] | **Again Together (60)** (GLMoore) **3-8-10** JQuinn(8) (prom over 5f) | hd | **12** | 10/1 | 32 | — |

(SP 121.9%) **12 Rn**

**1m 26.75** (2.25) CSF £29.21 CT £208.24 TOTE £4.40: £1.80 £2.20 £2.30 (£11.70) Trio £55.50 OWNER Mrs Christine Painting (UPPER LAMBOURN) BRED Mrs Christine Painting

LONG HANDICAP Killatty Lark (IRE) 7-4

WEIGHT FOR AGE 3yo-10lb

**1192 Zelda Zonk** chased the leaders. Sent on a quarter of a mile from home, she was ridden along to assert her authority. (5/1)

**1689 Morning Surprise** chased the leaders. Taking second place below the distance, she failed to get on terms with the winner. (5/1)

**Hippy** got her head in front for a few strides around the two-furlong marker before tapped for toe. (9/1)

**1074 Stolen Melody**, never far away, could only plod on in her own time in the last two furlongs. (5/1)

**Deerly** chased the leaders but failed to raise her game in the last two furlongs. (8/1: 6/1-9/1)

T/Jkpt: £311.60 (22.78 Tckts). T/Plpt: £40.70 (513.34 Tckts). T/Qdpt: £22.00 (43.21 Tckts). AK

# 1690-YARMOUTH (L-H) (Firm)
## Wednesday June 12th
WEATHER: sunny WIND: mod half bhd

### 1877 CHARTER H'CAP (0-70) (3-Y.O) (Class E)
2-15 (2-15) **1m 6f 17y** £3,261.30 (£974.40: £466.20: £212.10) Stalls: Centre GOING minus 0.62 sec per fur (F)

| | | | | SP | RR | SF |
|---|---|---|---|---|---|---|
| $1591^{2}$ | **Alwarqa (60)** (RWArmstrong) **3-9-5** RHills(3) (lw: hld up gng wl: led 2f out: styd on strly) | — | **1** | $3/1^{2}$ | 68 | 27 |
| $1600^{3}$ | **Go With The Wind (62)** (MBell) **3-9-7** MFenton(4) (hld up in rr: hdwy to jn wnr over 1f out: hrd rdn & swished tail: nt qckn) | ¾ | **2** | $11/2^{3}$ | 69 | 28 |
| $1503^{5}$ | **Ship's Dancer (53)** (JLDunlop) **3-8-12b$^{1}$** PatEddery(5) (hld up: dropped rr ent st: hdwy 3f out: sn rdn: nt pce to chal) | 1½ | **3** | $3/1^{2}$ | 58 | 17 |
| $1325^{6}$ | **Uoni (56)** (CEBrittain) **3-9-1** LDettori(2) (chsd ldr: led 3f out to 2f out: sn rdn & outpcd) | 5 | **4** | $11/4^{1}$ | 56 | 15 |
| 1534* | **Colour Counsellor (47)** (RMFlower) **3-8-6e** DBiggs(1) (lw: led to 3f out: sn drvn along: wknd wl over 1f out) | 8 | **5** | 6/1 | 38 | — |
| | | | | (SP 106.3%) | **5 Rn** | |

**3m 4.6** (5.20) CSF £16.05 TOTE £3.10: £1.70 £2.80 (£7.30) OWNER Mr Hamdan Al Maktoum (NEWMARKET) BRED Shadwell Estate Company Limited

**1591 Alwarqa** looked head and shoulders above the rest in the paddock, and only needed pushing out to open her account. (3/1)
**1600 Go With The Wind**, ridden with more restraint then he was at Catterick, moved upsides and looked likely to be a serious threat below the distance, but he again did a fair bit of tail-swishing under pressure and either would not or could not quicken. (11/2: 4/1-6/1)
**890 Ship's Dancer** is proving hard to win with and, though she did stay on in the latter stages, lacked the pace to carry her through. (3/1)
**1325 Uoni** looked ill-at-ease cantering to post and this firm ground is not for her. (11/4)
**1534* Colour Counsellor** cut out the running on this first attempt at the trip, but he was in trouble soon after being headed and appeared not to see it out. (6/1)

### 1878 E.B.F. RIVER BURE MEDIAN AUCTION MAIDEN STKS (2-Y.O) (Class E)
2-45 (2-47) **6f 3y** £3,124.80 (£932.40: £445.20: £201.60) Stalls: Centre GOING minus 0.62 sec per fur (F)

| | | | | SP | RR | SF |
|---|---|---|---|---|---|---|
| | **Isle of Corregidor (USA)** (MrsJCecil) **2-9-0** LDettori(4) (lw: s.i.s: hdwy ½-wy: led wl over 1f out: pushed clr) | — | **1** | $8/11^{1}$ | 74+ | 31 |
| $1510^{5}$ | **Halowing (USA)** (PAKelleway) **2-8-9** MWigham(5) (lw: outpcd & bhd: rdn 2f out: r.o wl ins fnl f: no ch w wnr) | 2½ | **2** | 10/1 | 62 | 19 |
| $1583^{2}$ | **Bold Oriental (IRE)** (NACallaghan) **2-9-0** PatEddery(1) (w ldrs: rdn over 1f out: one pce) | 2 | **3** | $7/2^{2}$ | 62 | 19 |
| $1683^{3}$ | **Superquest** (WAO'Gorman) **2-9-0** EmmaO'Gorman(3) (mde most over 4f: outpcd fnl f) | 1¾ | **4** | 20/1 | 57 | 14 |
| $1531^{2}$ | **Kenwood Melody** (MBell) **2-9-0** MFenton(2) (prom tl rdn & wknd over 1f out) | 2 | **5** | $5/1^{3}$ | 52 | 9 |
| | | | | (SP 110.6%) | **5 Rn** | |

**1m 12.0** (1.10) CSF £7.44 TOTE £1.60: £1.10 £2.80 (£6.40) OWNER Mr George Ohrstrom (NEWMARKET) BRED Whitewood Stable Inc

**Isle of Corregidor (USA)**, a fine-looking individual who is bred to need much further, let his class do the talking on this debut and his future looks very bright indeed. (8/11: 4/6-Evens)
**1510 Halowing (USA)** could not go the early pace, but she was picking up promisingly inside the distance, and she is beginning to grasp what is needed. (10/1: 6/1-11/1)
**1583 Bold Oriental (IRE)**, whose two previous runs have been on soft ground, did not seem inconvenienced by the faster surface, but the winner had taken his measure by the final furlong and he could do little or nothing about it. (7/2: 5/2-4/1)
**1683 Superquest** is gradually improving with experience, but he still has a long way to go and does seem to need easier ground. (20/1)
**1531 Kenwood Melody** showed plenty of speed to press the leaders until the quickening tempo proved too much for him. (5/1)

### 1879 HOPTON CONDITIONS STKS (3-Y.O+) (Class C)
3-15 (3-15) **6f 3y** £5,804.26 (£1,854.16: £888.58) Stalls: Centre GOING minus 0.62 sec per fur (F)

| | | | | SP | RR | SF |
|---|---|---|---|---|---|---|
| 1566a$^{8}$ | **Warning Star (97)** (BWHills) **4-8-9** MHills(3) (lw: hld up in rr: shkn up to ld over 1f out: r.o wl) | — | **1** | $5/2^{3}$ | 103 | 45 |
| $1629^{4}$ | **Cheyenne Spirit (105)** (BHanbury) **4-9-4v$^{1}$**(3) JStack(1) (plld hrd: led tl hdd appr fnl f: sn btn) | 2 | **2** | $11/8^{1}$ | 110 | 52 |
| $1129^{7}$ | **Easy Dollar (105)** (BGubby) **4-9-4b** LDettori(2) (gd sort: chsd ldr: drvn ½-wy: outpcd fr bel dist) | 1¼ | **3** | $7/4^{2}$ | 103 | 45 |
| | | | | (SP 107.0%) | **3 Rn** | |

**1m 10.6** (-0.30) CSF £5.56 TOTE £2.90 (£1.60) OWNER Mr Stephen Crown (LAMBOURN) BRED Snailwell Stud Co Ltd

**1566a Warning Star**, winning for the first time beyond the minimum trip, came from last to first between horses and was well on top at the finish. (5/2: 7/4-11/4)
**1629 Cheyenne Spirit**, keen to get on with it, in her first-time visor, looked as though she would win as she pleased but found nothing when let down. Her trainer expressed doubts about her soundness after the race. (11/8)
**1129 Easy Dollar**, off the bridle and bustled along some way out, did keep running on, but was fighting a lost cause from below the distance. (7/4)

### 1880 TOLLHOUSE (S) STKS (2-Y.O) (Class G)
3-45 (3-46) **6f 3y** £2,280.00 (£630.00: £300.00) Stalls: Centre GOING minus 0.62 sec per fur (F)

| | | | | SP | RR | SF |
|---|---|---|---|---|---|---|
| $1626^{8}$ | **Barnwood Crackers** (NACallaghan) **2-8-11** PatEddery(4) (racd alone stands' side: mde most tl drifted lft & hdd over 1f out: rallied u.p to ld last stride) | — | **1** | $4/5^{1}$ | 56 | 16 |
| $1713^{3}$ | **Caviar And Candy** (DJSCosgrove) **2-8-1**(5) LNewton(2) (led far side: overall ldr over 1f out: hrd drvn & ct post) | s.h | **2** | $7/2^{2}$ | 51 | 11 |
| $1169^{7}$ | **Super Scravels** (DrJDScargill) **2-8-6** MFenton(3) (chsd ldr far side: rdn 2f out: outpcd appr fnl f) | 7 | **3** | $4/1^{3}$ | 32 | — |
| | **Victory At Hart** (ICampbell) **2-8-4**(7) GFaulkner(1) (s.s: a bhd & outpcd) | 5 | **4** | 6/1 | 24 | — |
| | | | | (SP 112.1%) | **4 Rn** | |

**1m 12.9** (2.00) CSF £3.91 TOTE £1.50 (£2.00) OWNER Mr Yahya Nasib (NEWMARKET) BRED Hamilton Bloodstock (UK) Ltd
Bt in 4,000gns

**Barnwood Crackers**, taking a big drop in grade, gave away any amount of ground during the race, but he did respond willingly to Eddery's strong driving and regained the lead right on the line. (4/5: tchd Evens)
**1713 Caviar And Candy** looked sure to score when going at least a length up approaching the final furlong, but the sustained late dash of the winner proved just too much. (7/2)
**Super Scravels** (4/1: 3/1-9/2)

## 1881 POTTER HEIGHAM H'CAP (0-70) (3-Y.O+) (Class E)

4-15 (4-15) **6f 3y** £2,961.00 (£882.00: £304.00: £304.00) Stalls: Centre GOING minus 0.62 sec per fur (F)

| | | | | SP | RR | SF |
|---|---|---|---|---|---|---|
| 1598* | **Sea-Deer (67)** (CADwyer) **7-10-0** LDettori(6) (leggy: lt-f: unf: hld up: hdwy over 1f out: str chal to ld nr fin) | — | 1 | 11/4 $^{1}$ | 78 | 59 |
| 1844* | **Mousehole (71)** (RGuest) **4-10-4b** $^{7x}$ GDuffield(7) (lw: led & sn clr: rdn over 1f out: ct cl home) | hd | 2 | 3/1 $^{2}$ | 82 | 63 |
| $1715^{5}$ | **Merrie le Bow (50)** (PatMitchell) **4-8-6**$^{(5)}$ AmandaSanders(4) (prom: rdn over 1f out: one pce) | 2½ | 3 | 8/1 | 61 | 42 |
| $1715^{7}$ | **Sharp Imp (50)** (RMFlower) **6-8-11b** DBiggs(5) (bhd & outpcd: rdn 2f out: r.o wl ins fnl f) | d.h | 3 | 8/1 | 54 | 35 |
| $1412^{7}$ | **Samsolom (61)** (PHowling) **8-9-8** PaulEddery(3) (prom: rdn over 1f out: one pce) | 1 | 5 | 9/2 $^{3}$ | 62 | 43 |
| 1516* | **Martinosky (53)** (GCBravery) **10-9-0** NDay(8) (trckd ldrs: hrd drvn over 2f out: grad wknd) | 2½ | 6 | 9/1 | 48 | 29 |
| $1806^{6}$ | **Balpare (56)** (NACallaghan) **3-8-9** PatEddery(2) (outpcd: a bhd) | 1¾ | 7 | 10/1 | 46 | 19 |
| | **Mad About The Girl (IRE) (38)** (DJSCosgrove) **4-7-13** GBardwell(1) (s.s: a outpcd) | hd | 8 | 33/1 | 28 | 9 |

(SP 114.1%) **8 Rn**

**1m 10.9** (0.00) CSF £10.92 CT SD, M, MLB £25.75 SD, M, SI £25.75 TOTE £3.40: £1.10 £1.30 SI £1.00 MLB £0.90 (£4.00) OWNER Binding Matters Ltd (NEWMARKET) BRED Stetchworth Park Stud Ltd

WEIGHT FOR AGE 3yo-8lb

**1598* Sea-Deer**, who is on a roll, was able to step up in class and, though he left it late, had his head in front when it mattered most. (11/4)

**1844* Mousehole**, successful at Windsor two days earlier, tried hard to make it all but, over this extra furlong, could not quite last home. With a 7lb penalty to contend with, he was a shade unfortunate to lose this. (3/1)

**1715 Merrie le Bow** could not get the better of the leader. Though she never stopped trying, she had run her race entering the final furlong. (8/1)

**354 Sharp Imp**, taken off his legs for most of the way, ran on particularly well inside the last furlong and a return to seven would be the obvious solution. (8/1)

**1073 Samsolom** usually runs well here, but he is at his best from mid-summer onwards, and he looks to be heading in the right direction. (9/2)

**1516* Martinosky** (9/1: 6/1-10/1)

## 1882 JOHN HOLDRICH MAIDEN STKS (3-Y.O F) (Class D)

4-45 (4-46) **7f 3y** £4,125.90 (£1,234.20: £591.60: £270.30) Stalls: Centre GOING minus 0.62 sec per fur (F)

| | | | | SP | RR | SF |
|---|---|---|---|---|---|---|
| $1333^{10}$ | **Fatefully (USA)** (SbinSuroor) **3-8-11** LDettori(7) (lw: a.p: chal 2f out: sn led: r.o wl) | — | 1 | 5/2 $^{1}$ | 81 | 53 |
| $921^{5}$ | **Royal Jade** (BWHills) **3-8-11** MHills(2) (lw: brought stands' side: sn led: rdn & hdd over 1f out: kpt on) | 1½ | 2 | 7/2 $^{2}$ | 78 | 50 |
| $1033^{5}$ | **Omara (USA) (80)** (HRACecil) **3-8-11** PatEddery(6) (hld up in tch: effrt over 1f out: unable qckn) | 2 | 3 | 5/1 | 73 | 45 |
| $1050^{2}$ | **Ruwy** (CJBenstead) **3-8-11** RHills(3) (b.off hind: led early: prom: rdn over 2f out: sn outpcd) | 2½ | 4 | 6/1 | 67 | 39 |
| $1617^{6}$ | **Misrule (USA)** (JHMGosden) **3-8-11** GHind(1) (stdd s: swtchd rt: chsd ldrs tl rdn & wknd 2f out) | 1 | 5 | 4/1 $^{3}$ | 65 | 37 |
| | **True Joy (IRE)** (MRStoute) **3-8-11** PaulEddery(9) (s.s: pushed along ½-wy: a bhd) | 1 | 6 | 7/1 | 63 | 35 |
| | **Blossomville** (MAJarvis) **3-8-11** PBloomfield(5) (outpcd: a bhd) | 4 | 7 | 33/1 | 54 | 26 |

(SP 117.2%) **7 Rn**

**1m 23.4** (-0.80) CSF £11.57 TOTE £3.40: £2.40 £2.60 (£4.80) Trio £8.40 OWNER Godolphin (NEWMARKET) BRED Darley Stud Management Co Ltd

OFFICIAL EXPLANATION **Fatefully (USA): the firm ground and the addition of a tongue strap were attributed to the improvement in the filly's form.**

**1333 Fatefully (USA)**, running with her tongue tied down and back on more suitable ground, had the measure of her rivals over a furlong out and won readily. (5/2: 2/1-3/1)

**921 Royal Jade**, a quick-actioned filly, finished much closer to the winner than she did on her seasonal reappearance and should not be long in going one better. (7/2)

**1033 Omara (USA)** was given the opportunity to show her true colours over this longer trip but, after travelling really well, was unable to quicken with the principals, and is not yet firing. (5/1: 3/1-6/1)

**1050 Ruwy** still looks as though she would be made fitter and the way she ran would only confirm this. (6/1)

**1617 Misrule (USA)**, taken to post early and switched right to race on the stands' side, showed up in the chasing group until fading inside the last quarter-mile. (4/1: 3/1-9/2)

**True Joy (IRE)** lost ground at the start and was unable to get herself into the action. (7/1: op 7/2)

## 1883 HORNING H'CAP (0-70) (3-Y.O F) (Class E)

5-15 (5-15) **1m 2f 21y** £3,179.40 (£949.20: £453.60: £205.80) Stalls: Low GOING minus 0.62 sec per fur (F)

| | | | | SP | RR | SF |
|---|---|---|---|---|---|---|
| $1654^{9}$ | **Sistar Act (65)** (MRChannon) **3-8-9**$^{(7)}$ AEddery(1) (s.i.s: hld up & bhd: gd hdwy over 2f out: str run to ld wl ins fnl f) | — | 1 | 6/1 $^{3}$ | 75 | 32 |
| 1641* | **Parsa (USA) (59)** (JLDunlop) **3-8-10** $^{5x}$ PatEddery(4) (chsd ldr: led over 2f out: sn rdn: hdd & no ex wl ins fnl f) | 1½ | 2 | Evens $^{1}$ | 67 | 24 |
| 1504* | **Alreeh (IRE) (70)** (JHMGosden) **3-9-7** RHills(2) (leggy: lt-f: unf: led tl over 2f out: sn rdn: kpt on) | 1¼ | 3 | 11/4 $^{2}$ | 76 | 33 |
| $1654^{20}$ | **Efficacious (IRE) (49)** (CJBenstead) **3-8-0**$^{ow1}$ DBiggs(5) (b.off hind: trckd ldrs: effrt wl over 1f out: unable qckn fnl f) | s.h | 4 | 8/1 | 55 | 11 |
| $1317^{7}$ | **Meg's Memory (IRE) (59)** (JohnBerry) **3-8-7**$^{(3)}$ NVarley(3) (prom: rdn 2f out: no ex fnl f) | hd | 5 | 14/1 | 64 | 21 |
| $1333^{12}$ | **On The Home Run (55)** (JRJenkins) **3-8-6** NDay(6) (bit bkwd: hld up & bhd: lost tch 4f out: t.o) | 22 | 6 | 33/1 | 26 | — |

(SP 111.7%) **6 Rn**

**2m 6.7** (2.30) CSF £12.15 TOTE £6.30: £1.60 £1.40 (£4.50) OWNER Mr Tim Corby (UPPER LAMBOURN) BRED D. S. Rigby

**1594* Sistar Act**, patiently ridden over this longer trip, made up a lot of ground in the final quarter-mile and, striking the front 100 yards out, soon had the race sewn up. (6/1)

**1641* Parsa (USA)** did not look happy on this lively ground and, after having far more use made of her than when successful on her previous outing, had nothing left to repel the strong-finishing winner. (Evens)

**1504* Alreeh (IRE)** adopted front-running tactics in this first handicap, but was feeling the strain once collared and could only plod on at the one pace. (11/4)

**761 Efficacious (IRE)** is still having problems finding the correct trip, but she is showing promise and will get it right one of these days. (8/1)

**863* Meg's Memory (IRE)** did not look right in her coat, but ran up to her mark and will benefit from some sun on her back. (14/1: op 8/1)

T/Plpt: £158.10 (63.92 Tckts). T/Qdpt: £24.10 (30.24 Tckts). IM

# 1537-CARLISLE (R-H) (Firm)
## Thursday June 13th
WEATHER: sunny periods WIND: slt across

## 1884 BOWRING INSURANCE BROKERS MEDIAN AUCTION MAIDEN STKS (2-Y.O) (Class E)
2-15 (2-15) **5f** £2,941.05 (£890.40: £434.70: £206.85) Stalls: Low GOING minus 0.80 sec per fur (HD)

| | | | | SP | RR | SF |
|---|---|---|---|---|---|---|
| | **Bride's Reprisal** (MRChannon) **2-8-9** KDarley(3) (leggy: lw: a w ldr: rdn to ld cl home) | — | 1 | 6/4[1] | 68 | 15 |
| 1705[2] | **Bold African** (PDEvans) **2-9-0b** JFortune(7) (lw: led: rdn 2f out: r.o: jst ct) | nk | 2 | 5/1[3] | 72 | 19 |
| 1525[4] | **Tickntima** (MDHammond) **2-9-0** GDuffield(2) (cl up: outpcd 2f out: kpt on fnl f) | 1 | 3 | 9/1 | 69 | 16 |
| | **Harmony In Red** (JBerry) **2-9-0** JCarroll(5) (w'like: leggy: scope: sn prom: effrt 2f out: nt qckn fnl f) | ½ | 4 | 11/4[2] | 67 | 14 |
| | **Epic Stand** (MrsJRRamsden) **2-9-0** MDeering(4) (w'like: bit bkwd: s.i.s: hdwy 2f out: nvr nr to chal) | 3½ | 5 | 20/1 | 56 | 3 |
| *1603*[8] | **Skelton Sovereign (IRE)** (RHollinshead) **2-9-0** DeanMcKeown(1) (outpcd fr ½-wy) | 1¼ | 6 | 50/1 | 52 | — |
| | **Baileys Imp (IRE)** (MJohnston) **2-9-0** JWeaver(6) (str: cmpt: bit bkwd: chsd ldrs: effrt & hung rt ½-wy: sn btn) | ½ | 7 | 14/1 | 50 | — |
| | | | | (SP 106.7%) | **7 Rn** | |

**61.0 secs** (0.80) CSF £8.30 TOTE £2.10: £1.20 £1.80 (£2.70) OWNER Mrs Jean Keegan (UPPER LAMBOURN) BRED J. K. Keegan

**Bride's Reprisal** has not got a lot to recommend her looks wise, but she was very fit and, despite showing a tendency to look about, she led where it mattered. (6/4)

**1705 Bold African**, having his seventh run of the season, did his usual and led, but was again worried out of it. He really does deserve to win a race. (5/1)

**1525 Tickntima** ran as though another furlong should bring improvement. (9/1: 5/1-10/1)

**Harmony In Red**, a fair sort, ran well and looks likely to improve as a result. (11/4)

**Epic Stand** needed this, both fitness and experience wise, and time should bring plenty of improvement. (20/1)

**1080 Skelton Sovereign (IRE)**, after two moderate runs on sand, did show a little here. (50/1)

**Baileys Imp (IRE)** needed this, but his action left something to be desired and he never seemed happy on the fast ground. (14/1: 6/1-16/1)

## 1885 BURNETTS CLAIMING STKS (3-Y.O+) (Class F)
2-45 (2-45) **5f 207y** £2,647.00 (£742.00: £361.00) Stalls: Low GOING minus 0.80 sec per fur (HD)

| | | | | SP | RR | SF |
|---|---|---|---|---|---|---|
| 1689[7] | **Winter Scout (USA) (58)** (CPEBrooks) **8-8-6b[1](7)** SCopp(5) (hdwy 2f out: qcknd to ld wl ins fnl f) | — | 1 | 10/1 | 66 | 32 |
| 1635[5] | **Amoeba (IRE) (48)** (JBerry) **3-7-13(5)** PFessey(9) (led after 2f tl ct wl ins fnl f) | 2 | 2 | 9/1 | 60 | 18 |
| | **Masafah (USA) (82)** (MrsMReveley) **4-9-4** KDarley(7) (lw: chsd ldrs: effrt 2f out: one pce fnl f) | 3 | 3 | 5/2[1] | 58 | 24 |
| 1598[4] | **Flashy's Son (64)** (FMurphy) **8-8-13** JFanning(4) (lw: b: b.hind: cl up tl outpcd ½-wy: nt clr run & swtchd 1½f out: r.o towards fin) | s.h | 4 | 5/2[1] | 52 | 18 |
| 1538[14] | **Thwaab (45)** (FWatson) **4-8-13** JFortune(8) (bhd: hdwy u.p 2f out: nvr able to chal) | 3 | 5 | 33/1 | 44 | 10 |
| 764[4] | **Brookhead Lady (55)** (PDEvans) **5-8-4** NConnorton(2) (lw: b.nr fore: cl up tl grad wknd appr fnl f) | nk | 6 | 13/2[2] | 35 | 1 |
| 1635[9] | **Diet (58)** (MissLAPerratt) **10-8-11v** JCarroll(3) (chsd ldrs tl outpcd fnl 2f) | ¾ | 7 | 11/1 | 40 | 6 |
| 973[14] | **Jambo (55)** (JLEyre) **3-7-13b[1](3)** DWright(6) (led 2f: cl up tl wknd over 1f out) | ½ | 8 | 8/1[3] | 37 | — |
| 1541[12] | **Cacharro (45)** (MissZAGreen) **5-8-9** FNorton(1) (sn outpcd & bhd) | 11 | 9 | 50/1 | 7 | — |
| | | | | (SP 113.9%) | **9 Rn** | |

**1m 12.5** (0.00) CSF £84.03 TOTE £16.10: £2.80 £2.10 £1.70 (£40.90) Trio £175.30 OWNER Mrs S. M. Russell (LAMBOURN) BRED Virginia Kraft Payson

WEIGHT FOR AGE 3yo-8lb

**Winter Scout (USA)** had the blinkers on for the first time in a long time, and scored in really good style. (10/1)

**1635 Amoeba (IRE)** ran another sound race, but just found the winner too strong in the closing stages. (9/1)

**Masafah (USA)**, having her first run since changing stables, looked fit and had her chances, but just failed to quicken late on. (5/2: op 6/4)

**1598 Flashy's Son** got outpaced and was then short of room at a vital stage and, although finishing well, his chance had gone. He is coming to hand. (5/2)

**1041 Thwaab** only decided to stay on when it was too late. (33/1)

**764 Brookhead Lady** (13/2: 5/1-8/1)

**Jambo** (8/1: 12/1-7/1)

## 1886 BARCLAYS BANK CUMBRIA H'CAP (0-80) (3-Y.O+) (Class D)
3-15 (3-15) **7f 214y** £3,550.00 (£1,075.00: £525.00: £250.00) Stalls: Low GOING minus 0.80 sec per fur (HD)

| | | | | SP | RR | SF |
|---|---|---|---|---|---|---|
| 1860[3] | **Three Arch Bridge (62)** (MJohnston) **4-9-13b** 5x JWeaver(1) (led after 1f: kpt on wl fnl 2f) | — | 1 | 6/1 | 75 | 44 |
| 1650* | **Spanish Verdict (64)** (DenysSmith) **9-9-12(3)** 5x CTeague(2) (lw: led 1f: cl up: chal 3f out: rdn & nt qckn) | 1½ | 2 | 11/2[3] | 74 | 43 |
| 1313[6] | **Thatched (IRE) (44)** (REBarr) **6-8-4v(5)** PFessey(5) (chsd ldrs: effrt over 3f out: nt qckn fnl 2f) | 2 | 3 | 11/4[2] | 50 | 19 |
| 1526* | **Society Girl (60)** (CWThornton) **3-9-0** DeanMcKeown(6) (lw: a chsng ldrs: one pce fnl 3f) | ¾ | 4 | 8/1 | 65 | 23 |
| 1830[2] | **Commander Glen (IRE) (57)** (MrsJRRamsden) **4-9-8b** JFortune(4) (dwlt: hdwy 3f out: nvr nr to chal) | ½ | 5 | 2/1[1] | 61 | 30 |
| 1698[5] | **Jungle Patrol (IRE) (54)** (MBrittain) **4-9-0(5)** GParkin(3) (effrt ½-wy: sn rdn & btn) | 6 | 6 | 14/1 | 45 | 14 |
| | | | | (SP 107.4%) | **6 Rn** | |

**1m 38.8** (0.20) CSF £32.51 TOTE £6.20: £3.20 £2.80 (£13.30) OWNER Mr R. N. Pennell (MIDDLEHAM) BRED R. Taylor

WEIGHT FOR AGE 3yo-11lb

**1860 Three Arch Bridge** was having her sixth run in fifteen days here and looked very edgy in the preliminaries, but there was nothing wrong with her performance in the race. (6/1)

**1650* Spanish Verdict** loves this track and this ground, and will no doubt be back here later this month for another crack at the Carlisle Bell. (11/2)

**1313 Thatched (IRE)** did not impress on looks and, after holding every chance, failed to sparkle when ridden. (11/4)

**1526* Society Girl** gives the impression that she is improving. (8/1)

**1830 Commander Glen (IRE)** failed to stride out on his way to post and was not suited by this race. He should be forgiven this. (2/1)

## 1887 SAINTS H'CAP (0-70) (3-Y.O) (Class E)
3-45 (3-45) **1m 4f** £3,022.95 (£915.60: £447.30: £213.15) Stalls: High GOING minus 0.80 sec per fur (HD)

| | | | | SP | RR | SF |
|---|---|---|---|---|---|---|
| 1089[9] | **Etterby Park (USA) (44)** (MJohnston) **3-8-2** JFanning(5) (lw: cl up: led 7f out: clr over 2f out: eased ins fnl f) | — | 1 | 5/1[3] | 50+ | 30 |

803[12] **Marsayas (IRE) (50)** (MJCamacho) **3-8-8** JFortune(1) (lw: bhd: swtchd lft 2f out: r.o towards fin)....................2½ **2** 11/1 53 33
1325[5] **Mister Aspecto (IRE) (63)** (MJohnston) **3-9-7** JWeaver(3) (bhd: brought wd over 2f out: styd on wl towards fin)....................1 **3** 10/1 64 44
1201[4] **Indiphar (48)** (FHLee) **3-8-6** GDuffield(4) (hdwy 4f out: styd on one pce fnl 3f: no imp)....................hd **4** 11/1 49 29
1850[3] **Silverdale Knight (58)** (KWHogg) **3-9-2** DeanMcKeown(6) (a chsng ldrs: wnt 2nd 3f out: wknd over 1f out) .1¾ **5** 6/1 57 37
1363[18] **Ginger Hodgers (40)** (RMWhitaker) **3-7-12** FNorton(2) (rr div tl sme hdwy fnl 3f)....................5 **6** 33/1 32 12
1850[6] **Lawn Order (45)** (MrsJRRamsden) **3-8-3** JCarroll(9) (bhd: hdwy over 3f out: n.d)....................3 **7** 3/1[1] 33 13
1778[12] **Go-Go-Power-Ranger (62)** (BEllison) **3-9-6** NKennedy(7) (lw: chsd ldrs tl wknd fnl 3f)....................13 **8** 4/1[2] 33 13
1636* **Manoy (59)** (JHetherton) **3-9-3b** 5x NConnorton(8) (led 5f: cl up tl rdn & wknd wl over 2f out)....................¾ **9** 8/1 29 9
1503[11] **Belacqua (USA) (38)** (DWChapman) **3-7-5b**(5) PFessey(10) (cl up tl wknd over 3f out)....................8 **10** 66/1 — —

(SP 117.3%) **10 Rn**

**2m 30.1** (0.20 under best) (-0.90) CSF £52.63 CT £485.37 TOTE £6.90: £2.20 £3.40 £3.20 (£35.40) Trio £72.20 OWNER Crowther Homes Ltd (MIDDLEHAM) BRED Jayeff "B" Stables

LONG HANDICAP Belacqua (USA) 7-0

**1089 Etterby Park (USA)** has changed stables and, adopting different tactics, won with a great deal in hand to show just how good he really is. (5/1)

**614 Marsayas (IRE)** took the eye in the paddock and, judging from the way he finished, he will pick up a race or two, probably over further. (11/1)

**1325 Mister Aspecto (IRE)**, a stable-companion of the winner, looked to be going nowhere until suddenly staying on at the end. He has never won on grass and probably needs further. (10/1)

**1201 Indiphar**, trying a longer trip, ran better and seems to be on the upgrade. (11/1)

**1850 Silverdale Knight** ran quite well, but probably just found this trip too far. (6/1)

**Ginger Hodgers** ran a bit better, staying on at the end. (33/1)

**1850 Lawn Order**, over a trip that looked likely to suit, did not impress with her action and was not overpunished. (3/1)

## 1888 NEWS & STAR RATING RELATED MAIDEN STKS (0-60) (3-Y.O) (Class F)

4-15 (4-19) **5f 207y** £2,661.00 (£746.00: £363.00) Stalls: Low GOING minus 0.80 sec per fur (HD)

SP RR SF

1702[2] **Wire Act (USA) (56)** (MartynMeade) **3-9-0** FNorton(9) (lw: a.p: hdwy 2f out: r.o fnl f to ld nr fin)....................— **1** 3/1[1] 64 34
1608[5] **Nattier (60)** (SirMarkPrescott) **3-8-11** GDuffield(8) (lw: mde most tl ct nr fin)....................hd **2** 11/2[3] 61 31
862[13] **Fairy Prince (IRE) (50)** (MrsALMKing) **3-8-9**(5) PFessey(7) (lw: cl up: effrt over 2f out: kpt on same pce)......1½ **3** 50/1 60 30
*531[7]* **Fairy Highlands (IRE) (58)** (SCWilliams) **3-8-11** JWeaver(3) (hld up: stdy hdwy over 1f out: sn chsng ldrs: eased towards fin)....................2½ **4** 11/2[3] 50 20
1761[5] **Madam Zando (53)** (JBalding) **3-8-4**(7) JEdmunds(5) (bhd: effrt over 2f out: rdn & nvr able to chal)....................½ **5** 9/1 49 19
1610[2] **Mels Baby (IRE) (56)** (JLEyre) **3-9-0** RLappin(6) (sn outpcd & bhd: sme hdwy 2f out: nvr able to chal).........2½ **6** 4/1[2] 45 15
1612[5] **Time To Fly (58)** (BWMurray) **3-8-9**(5) GParkin(2) (lw: chsd ldrs over 4f: wknd)....................3 **7** 9/1 37 7
1610[4] **Katie Komaite (55)** (CaptJWilson) **3-8-11** JFortune(10) (chsd ldrs tl outpcd fnl 2f)....................s.h **8** 10/1 34 4
1612[3] **Answers-To-Thomas (56)** (JMJefferson) **3-9-0** DeanMcKeown(1) (in tch tl rdn & wknd wl over 1f out).........3½ **9** 8/1 27 —
1042[13] **Magical Midnight (35)** (NTinkler) **3-8-11b**[1] KimTinkler(4) (s.i.s: a outpcd & bhd)....................6 **10** 100/1 8 —
*1764[5]* ***Haute Cuisine (60)*** (JBerry) **3-9-0** JCarroll(11) (Withdrawn not under Starter's orders: Veterinary advice)......... **W** 16/1 — —

(SP 124.8%) **10 Rn**

**1m 12.4** (-0.10) CSF £19.18 TOTE £4.30: £1.40 £2.40 £21.80 (£14.70) Trio £153.10 OWNER Mr M. Freti (MALMESBURY) BRED Ken Opstein, M. W. Sims and L. W. Sims

**1702 Wire Act (USA)** looked the part and needed every yard of this trip to make it. He looked game. (3/1)

**1608 Nattier** is doing well and, given a real chance here, just failed to hang on. (11/2: op 7/2)

**Fairy Prince (IRE)** ran his best race by far and seems to be getting it together. (50/1)

**Fairy Highlands (IRE)** has not been out for over two months and was given a very sympathetic ride. He should be all the better for this. (11/2)

**1761 Madam Zando**, an edgy sort, was never doing enough to get into it. (9/1)

**1610 Mels Baby (IRE)** was always finding things happening too quickly at this trip. (4/1)

## 1889 JENNINGS BITTER APPRENTICE H'CAP (0-65) (4-Y.O+) (Class F)

4-45 (4-45) **5f** £2,703.00 (£758.00: £369.00) Stalls: Low GOING minus 0.80 sec per fur (HD)

SP RR SF

1163[11] **Leading Princess (IRE) (44)** (MissLAPerratt) **5-8-4b**(5) JBramhill(1) (in tch: hdwy 2f out: c stands' side & r.o wl to ld wl ins fnl f)....................— **1** 33/1 50 32
1545[2] **Swan At Whalley (59)** (MartynWane) **4-9-10** PRoberts(4) (a chsg ldrs: chal ins fnl f: nt qckn towards fin)........2 **2** 7/1 59 41
1702* **Bowcliffe Grange (IRE) (34)** (DWChapman) **4-7-13** 7x PFessey(12) (lw: led after 1f tl ct wl ins fnl f)....................½ **3** 5/2[1] 32 14
1865[2] **Serious Hurry (48)** (RMMcKellar) **8-8-8b**(5) KSked(11) (lw: led 1f: chsd ldrs: outpcd over 1f out: kpt on towards fin)....................hd **4** 11/2[3] 46 28
1342[9] **Pallium (IRE) (56)** (MrsAMNaughton) **8-9-7** OPears(9) (hdwy 2f out: kpt on: nt pce to chal)....................½ **5** 16/1 52 34
1541[2] **Call to the Bar (IRE) (53)** (MDods) **7-9-4** CTeague(3) (hdwy over 1f out: nvr rchd ldrs)....................s.h **6** 6/1 49 31
1541[14] **First Option (47)** (RBastiman) **6-8-12**ow2 HBastiman(8) (t: nvr nrr)....................¾ **7** 25/1 41 21
1786[8] **Most Uppitty (46)** (JBerry) **4-8-6**(5) JoanneWebster(7) (lw: outpcd tl sme hdwy 2f out: n.d)....................1½ **8** 20/1 35 17
1598[6] **Thick as Thieves (50)** (RonaldThompson) **4-9-1v**[1] ADaly(2) (in tch tl rdn & btn over 1f out)....................1 **9** 14/1 36 18
1545[4] **Another Nightmare (IRE) (33)** (RMMcKellar) **4-7-12** DWright(5) (spd 3f)....................6 **10** 16/1 — —
*317[7]* **Respectable Jones (45)** (RHollinshead) **10-8-3b**(7) SCrawford(10) (a outpcd & bhd)....................1½ **11** 20/1 7 —
1646* **Able Sheriff (52)** (MWEasterby) **4-9-0b**(3) 7x GParkin(6) (sn bhd: p.u 2f out: lame).................... **P** 4/1[2] — —

(SP 125.5%) **12 Rn**

**59.9 secs** (-0.30) CSF £237.47 CT £748.02 TOTE £37.80: £6.60 £1.60 £1.40 (£167.10) Trio £210.30 OWNER Mrs Ruth Wyllie (AYR) BRED Woodford Stud

**997 Leading Princess (IRE)** showed here just how much ability she really has but, in doing so, hung all the way across the track and finished up under the stands' rail. (33/1)

**1545 Swan At Whalley** keeps running well, but just lacked the finishing dash. (7/1)

**1702* Bowcliffe Grange (IRE)** has blistering speed and his patient trainer will no doubt find him plenty of opportunities on sharper tracks. (5/2)

**1865 Serious Hurry** ran another sound race and his turn is surely near. (11/2)

**Pallium (IRE)**, coming from off a strong pace as he likes to, just failed to get into it. (16/1)

**1541 Call to the Bar (IRE)** struggled on from halfway, but was never doing enough to make it. (6/1)

T/Plpt: £314.00 (34.86 Tckts). T/Qdpt: £117.30 (6.1 Tckts). AA

# 1461-CHEPSTOW (L-H) (Good, Good to soft patches)
## Thursday June 13th
WEATHER: fine WIND: almost nil

### 1890 ORSINO AMATEUR H'CAP (0-70) (3-Y.O+) (Class G)
6-45 (6-50) **7f 16y** £2,486.00 (£696.00: £338.00) Stalls: High GOING minus 0.24 sec per fur (GF)

| | | | | SP | RR | SF |
|---|---|---|---|---|---|---|
| 1825$^{3}$ | **My Gallery (IRE) (55)** (ABailey) **5-10-12**$^{(3)}$ MissBridgetGatehouse(14) (lw: a.p: led 2f out: r.o wl) | — | **1** | 13/2$^{2}$ | 71 | 53 |
| *1811$^{7}$* | **Wentbridge Lad (IRE) (65)** (PDEvans) **6-11-8v**$^{(3)}$ MrWMcLaughlin(11) (b.off hind: a.p: ev ch over 1f out: one pce) | 3½ | **2** | 12/1 | 73 | 55 |
| 1651* | **Noeprob (USA) (48)** (RJHodges) **6-10-8** $^{5x}$ JCulloty(15) (lw: gd hdwy stands' side over 1f out: r.o ins fnl f) | nk | **3** | 100/30$^{1}$ | 55 | 37 |
| 1536$^{2}$ | **Lorins Gold (39)** (AndrewTurnell) **6-9-13** MrJRees(17) (b.hind: lw: a.p: r.o one pce fnl f) | 2½ | **4** | 10/1 | 41 | 23 |
| | **Super Serenade (52)** (GBBalding) **7-10-7**$^{(5)}$ MrJThatcher(3) (lw: hdwy over 1f out: nvr nrr) | 1 | **5** | 33/1 | 52 | 34 |
| *1094$^{6}$* | **Mustn't Grumble (IRE) (58)** (MissSJWilton) **6-11-1v$^{1}$**$^{(3)}$ MissEJJones(2) (chsd ldr: led over 2f out: sn hdd: one pce) | nk | **6** | 25/1 | 57 | 39 |
| 1449$^{15}$ | **Breezed Well (37)** (BRCambidge) **10-9-11** MrsHNoonan(10) (no hdwy fnl 2f) | 1¼ | **7** | 66/1 | 33 | 15 |
| 1609$^{12}$ | **Mr Cube (IRE) (53)** (JMBradley) **6-10-8v**$^{(5)}$ MissLKerr(12) (nvr nr to chal) | ½ | **8** | 25/1 | 48 | 30 |
| 1348$^{15}$ | **Fighter Squadron (38)** (REPeacock) **7-9-7b**$^{(5)}$ MrsCPeacock(9) (led over 4f: sn wknd) | nk | **9** | 66/1 | 32 | 14 |
| 1658$^{3}$ | **Asterix (39)** (JMBradley) **8-9-13v** MrsLPearce(4) (dwlt: nvr nrr) | s.h | **10** | 10/1 | 33 | 15 |
| 1449$^{13}$ | **Love Legend (44)** (DWPArbuthnot) **11-10-4** MrsDArbuthnot(8) (n.d) | 3½ | **11** | 20/1 | 30 | 12 |
| 1532$^{2}$ | **Mr Nevermind (IRE) (61)** (GLMoore) **6-11-7** MrKGoble(7) (nvr nr ldrs) | hd | **12** | 10/1 | 47 | 29 |
| 1449$^{7}$ | **Roseate Lodge (45)** (SEKettlewell) **10-10-5** MrsDKettlewell(6) (edgd lft & bhd fnl 2f) | 1½ | **13** | 16/1 | 28 | 10 |
| 1348$^{8}$ | **Mazirah (52)** (PJMakin) **5-10-12** MrPScott(1) (n.d) | s.h | **14** | 16/1 | 34 | 16 |
| 1685$^{3}$ | **Kevasingo (56)** (BWHills) **4-10-11**$^{(5)}$ MrCBHills(16) (prom over 4f) | s.h | **15** | 8/1$^{3}$ | 38 | 20 |
| *1718$^{11}$* | **Verro (USA) (34)** (KBishop) **9-9-5**$^{(3)ow1}$ MissAPurdy(5) (a bhd) | s.h | **16** | 100/1 | 16 | — |
| 1522$^{13}$ | **Mister Rm (68)** (RGuest) **4-11-9**$^{(5)}$ MissZBurkett(18) (swtg: dwlt: a bhd) | 3½ | **17** | 20/1 | 42 | 24 |
| 1356$^{7}$ | **Elegantissima (47)** (SDow) **3-9-6**$^{(5)ow2}$ MrSFetherstonhaugh(13) (swvd badly rt s: a bhd) | nk | **18** | 40/1 | 21 | — |

(SP 120.8%) **18 Rn**

**1m 24.1** (4.10) CSF £73.55 CT £282.19 TOTE £8.40: £2.10 £1.80 £1.80 £2.60 (£61.70) Trio £56.10 OWNER Mr Robert Cox (TARPORLEY) BRED East Riding Sack and Paper Co
LONG HANDICAP Verro (USA) 8-3
WEIGHT FOR AGE 3yo-10lb

**1825 My Gallery (IRE)**, still rated 17lb lower than on the sand, made amends in good style for a couple of recent unlucky runs. (13/2)
**1811 Wentbridge Lad (IRE)** has won six times at Wolverhampton, but seems to be running much better on grass at the moment. (12/1)
**1651* Noeprob (USA)**, penalised for winning a seller, was due to go up a further 12lb, but seemed to find this trip on the short side. (100/30)
**1536 Lorins Gold** was again 9lb higher than when breaking his duck at Brighton. (10/1)
**Super Serenade** looked in good shape for this reappearance and would have preferred a mile. (33/1)
**896 Mustn't Grumble (IRE)** showed plenty of dash in the first-time visor. (25/1)
**1685 Kevasingo** (8/1: 6/1-9/1)

### 1891 SECOND SEVERN CROSSING CLAIMING STKS (3-Y.O) (Class F)
7-15 (7-17) **7f 16y** £2,792.50 (£780.00: £377.50) Stalls: High GOING minus 0.24 sec per fur (GF)

| | | | | SP | RR | SF |
|---|---|---|---|---|---|---|
| | **Finsbury Flyer (IRE)** (RJHodges) **3-8-12**$^{(5)}$ PPMurphy(4) (w'like: s.s: gd hdwy 3f out: hrd rdn over 1f out: r.o to ld nr fin) | — | **1** | 33/1 | 68 | 20 |
| 1836$^{3}$ | **Double Oscar (IRE) (84)** (MJohnston) **3-9-7b$^{1}$** MRoberts(9) (a.p: led over 3f out: hrd rdn fnl f: hdd nr fin: r.o) | s.h | **2** | 9/4$^{1}$ | 72 | 24 |
| 1776$^{4}$ | **Hever Golf Express (75)** (TJNaughton) **3-9-7** JReid(11) (a.p: r.o one pce fnl f) | 3½ | **3** | 100/30$^{2}$ | 64 | 16 |
| 1612$^{4}$ | **Members Welcome (IRE) (56)** (JMBradley) **3-8-9** TQuinn(5) (hdwy 3f out: ev ch 2f out: one pce) | 1½ | **4** | 6/1 | 49 | 1 |
| 1594$^{11}$ | **Andsome Boy (45)** (CRBarwell) **3-8-9** DHarrison(13) (nvr nr to chal) | nk | **5** | 14/1 | 48 | — |
| 1100$^{19}$ | **Natatarl (IRE) (45)** (BPalling) **3-8-2** TSprake(6) (nvr nr to chal) | hd | **6** | 16/1 | 41 | — |
| 1776$^{5}$ | **One Shot (IRE) (48)** (WRMuir) **3-8-11b** WWoods(12) (led 2f: wknd 2f out) | 9 | **7** | 10/1 | 29 | — |
| 1617$^{10}$ | **Shine** (IABalding) **3-7-11**$^{(5)}$ MartinDwyer(14) (lw: rdn 3f out: bhd fnl 2f) | ¾ | **8** | 7/2$^{3}$ | 19 | — |
| | **Lady Rambo** (LJBarratt) **3-8-2** NAdams(3) (lt-f: a bhd) | 5 | **9** | 50/1 | 7 | — |
| 861$^{14}$ | **Toe Tappin Music (USA) (40)** (MartynMeade) **3-8-5** RPerham(2) (chsd ldrs over 4f) | 1½ | **10** | 50/1 | 7 | — |
| 1465$^{5}$ | **Indian Wolf (42)** (PGMurphy) **3-8-9b$^{1}$** JQuinn(8) (plld hrd: bhd fnl 3f) | 3½ | **11** | 50/1 | 3 | — |
| 1518$^{W}$ | **Into Debt** (JRPoulton) **3-8-4** AMorris(10) (dwlt: sn rcvrd: led 5f out tl over 3f out: sn wknd) | 2 | **12** | 50/1 | — | — |

(SP 122.8%) **12 Rn**

**1m 24.9** (4.90) CSF £103.97 TOTE £50.80: £7.90 £1.30 £1.70 (£38.80) Trio £184.30 OWNER Mr P. Slade (SOMERTON) BRED Gordon Patterson

**Finsbury Flyer (IRE)**, out of an unraced half-sister to four winners, surprised everybody, including connections. (33/1)
**1836 Double Oscar (IRE)**, tried in blinkers for this third outing in eight days, fought back after being headed in the last 50 yards. (9/4)
**1776 Hever Golf Express** again seemed to get the seven well enough, but could not keep tabs on the two principals. (100/30)
**1612 Members Welcome (IRE)** may have found this trip beyond his best. (6/1)
**1099 Andsome Boy** did not seem suited to this drop back from a mile. (14/1)
**Natatarl (IRE)** ran over just short of a mile and a half last time. (16/1)

### 1892 E.B.F. MAIDEN STKS (2-Y.O) (Class D)
7-45 (7-47) **6f 16y** £3,579.00 (£1,077.00: £521.00: £243.00) Stalls: High GOING minus 0.24 sec per fur (GF)

| | | | | SP | RR | SF |
|---|---|---|---|---|---|---|
| 1445$^{2}$ | **Indian Rocket** (JLDunlop) **2-9-0** WCarson(1) (a.p: led over 1f out: edgd lft: r.o wl) | — | **1** | 2/1$^{2}$ | 83+ | 40 |
| 1626$^{2}$ | **Barrier King (USA)** (PFICole) **2-9-0** TQuinn(2) (led over 4f: one pce) | 4 | **2** | 7/2$^{3}$ | 73 | 30 |
| | **Imperial President** (HRACecil) **2-9-0** PatEddery(7) (w'like: lw: dwlt: hdwy 3f out: rdn & one pce fnl 2f) | 3 | **3** | 11/8$^{1}$ | 65+ | 22 |
| 1191$^{8}$ | **Bold Spring (IRE)** (RHannon) **2-9-0** RPerham(4) (lw: w ldrs: one pce fnl 2f) | 1½ | **4** | 25/1 | 61 | 18 |
| 841$^{7}$ | **Kewarra** (BRMillman) **2-9-0** MRoberts(6) (plld hrd: prom tl wknd over 1f out) | 2½ | **5** | 50/1 | 54 | 11 |
| 1046$^{5}$ | **Tinkerbell** (LordHuntingdon) **2-8-9** JReid(3) (dwlt: a bhd) | 3½ | **6** | 25/1 | 40 | — |
| *1603$^{2}$* | **Flotilla** (SirMarkPrescott) **2-9-0** WWoods(5) (sn rdn & outpcd) | 1¼ | **7** | 16/1 | 42 | — |

| | | | Pos | SP | RR | SF |
|---|---|---|---|---|---|---|
| | **Surprise Event** (WGMTurner) **2-9-0** TSprake(8) (small: lt-f: prom 3f) | nk | **8** | 50/1 | 41 | — |

(SP 115.2%) **8 Rn**

**1m 11.8** (2.60) CSF £9.16 TOTE £2.90: £1.20 £1.40 £1.10 (£3.30) OWNER Mr Khalil Alsayegh (ARUNDEL) BRED Red House Stud
**1445 Indian Rocket**, described as being very green last time, was the best-backed horse in the race and can score again. (2/1: op 3/1)
**1626 Barrier King (USA)** only succeeded in setting up the race for the winner. (7/2)
**Imperial President** looked well enough prepared, but made a tardy start. Never able to get to grips with the front two, he was not given a hard time. (11/8: 4/5-6/4)
**Bold Spring (IRE)** fared better than when encountering soft ground on his Newbury debut. (25/1)
**Kewarra** will last longer when he learns to settle. (50/1)

## 1893 EVENING (S) H'CAP (0-60) (3-Y.O+) (Class G)

8-15 (8-22) **1m 14y** £2,570.00 (£720.00: £350.00) Stalls: High GOING minus 0.24 sec per fur (GF)

| | | | Pos | SP | RR | SF |
|---|---|---|---|---|---|---|
| $1533^{9}$ | **Miss Laughter (48)** (JWHills) **4-9-4** OUrbina(1) (mde all: r.o wl) | — | **1** | 20/1 | 62 | 44 |
| | **Queen of Shannon (IRE) (44)** (AWCarroll) **8-9-0** DHarrison(10) (lw: hdwy 3f out: chsd wnr fnl f: r.o) | 1 | **2** | 50/1 | 56 | 38 |
| $1638^{4}$ | **Tony's Mist (43)** (JMBradley) **6-8-13** TQuinn(18) (chsd wnr: one pce fnl f) | 1½ | **3** | 15/2 $^{3}$ | 52 | 34 |
| $1821^{18}$ | **Indian Rhapsody (50)** (ABailey) **4-9-6** PBloomfield(17) (hdwy 2f out: r.o ins fnl f) | 1½ | **4** | 25/1 | 56 | 38 |
| $1691^{4}$ | **Total Rach (IRE) (43)** (RIngram) **4-8-13b** WWoods(20) (stdd & swtchd lft s: swtchd far side over 3f out: hdwy over 2f out: one pce fnl f) | ½ | **5** | 4/1 $^{2}$ | 48 | 30 |
| | **Beyond Our Reach (50)** (RJHodges) **8-9-1**(5) PPMurphy(11) (hdwy over 1f out: nvr nrr) | 1½ | **6** | 16/1 | 52 | 34 |
| $1642^{15}$ | **Polli Pui (41)** (WMBrisbourne) **4-8-6**(5) MartinDwyer(8) (hld up & plld hrd: hdwy 3f out: one pce fnl 2f) | ½ | **7** | 20/1 | 42 | 24 |
| $1468^{13}$ | **Amnesty Bay (43)** (MDIUsher) **4-8-13v¹** MWigham(19) (lw: nvr nr to chal) | nk | **8** | 20/1 | 44 | 26 |
| $1411^{8}$ | **My Handsome Prince (40)** (PJBevan) **4-8-10v** NCarlisle(6) (lw: hdwy 3f out: wknd 2f out) | hd | **9** | 14/1 | 40 | 22 |
| 1474* | **Sakharov (58)** (MJohnston) **7-10-0** MRoberts(15) (lw: prom over 5f) | hd | **10** | 3/1 $^{1}$ | 58 | 40 |
| $1651^{9}$ | **Mustahil (IRE) (49)** (RJHodges) **7-9-5** TSprake(5) (rdn & hdwy over 3f out: wknd over 2f out) | 2 | **11** | 40/1 | 45 | 27 |
| $1533^{15}$ | **Indian Serenade (49)** (THind) **5-9-2**(3) PMcCabe(4) (lw: prom over 5f) | 1½ | **12** | 33/1 | 42 | 24 |
| $561^{11}$ | **Warning Shot (49)** (MartynMeade) **4-9-5** RPerham(7) (n.d) | 1 | **13** | 16/1 | 40 | 22 |
| $1654^{14}$ | **Kinnescash (IRE) (60)** (MSSaunders) **3-9-5** NAdams(14) (n.d) | 2 | **14** | 40/1 | 47 | 18 |
| $1516^{5}$ | **Komodo (USA) (48)** (KOCunningham-Brown) **4-9-4b** JQuinn(13) (lw: prom over 5f) | 1½ | **15** | 40/1 | 32 | 14 |
| $1443^{3}$ | **Moving Up (IRE) (56)** (GLMoore) **3-9-1** SWhitworth(12) (b.hind: prom 5f) | 2 | **16** | 20/1 | 36 | 7 |
| $1651^{11}$ | **Doodies Pool (IRE) (49)** (PBurgoyne) **6-9-5v** PatEddery(16) (a bhd) | 8 | **17** | 16/1 | 13 | — |
| $1685^{2}$ | **Raven's Roost (IRE) (50)** (AJChamberlain) **5-9-6** JReid(3) (t.o) | dist | **18** | 9/1 | — | — |
| *$1319^{17}$* | ***Emperors Wood (40)*** (PHayward) **5-8-7**(3) DaneO'Neill(9) (Withdrawn not under Starter's orders: uns rdr & bolted bef s) | | **W** | 66/1 | — | — |

(SP 127.7%) **18 Rn**

**1m 35.9** (3.40) CSF £631.90 CT £7,393.39 TOTE £19.40: £3.50 £6.00 £1.90 £5.60 (£868.00) Trio £486.90; £617.31 to 14/6/96. OWNER Miss J. Wilkinson (LAMBOURN) BRED Miss J. Wilkinson
WEIGHT FOR AGE 3yo-11lb
Bt in 7,200gns
**Miss Laughter**, dropped 3lb, appreciated this lower grade and seems at her best when allowed to dictate matters from the front. (20/1)
**Queen of Shannon (IRE)** had been pulled up over hurdles on her only visit to a racecourse in the last eighteen months. (50/1)
**1638 Tony's Mist** has been slipping down the ratings but could not take advantage of this drop into a seller. (15/2)
**Indian Rhapsody**, three times a winner for Mick Channon last year, ran easily her best race for her new connections. (25/1)
**1691 Total Rach (IRE)**, covered up from his stands'-side draw, was given a strange ride and finished up on the far rail. (4/1: 7/1-7/2)
**Beyond Our Reach**, fit from hurdling, was very well handicapped on some of his old Flat form, but may need further now. (16/1)
**983 My Handsome Prince** (14/1: 10/1-16/1)
**1474* Sakharov**, 5lb higher than when winning his last handicap in August 1994, seems better suited to faster ground than this. (3/1)
**1685 Raven's Roost (IRE)** (9/1: 5/1-10/1)

## 1894 WELSH BREWERS H'CAP (0-80) (3-Y.O+) (Class D)

8-45 (8-50) **1m 2f 36y** £3,689.50 (£1,111.00: £538.00: £251.50) Stalls: Low GOING minus 0.24 sec per fur (GF)

| | | | Pos | SP | RR | SF |
|---|---|---|---|---|---|---|
| 1462* | **Roufontaine (64)** (WRMuir) **5-8-8**(5) RHavlin(2) (lw: hld up: rdn & hdwy over 3f out: led over 2f out: r.o wl) | — | **1** | 11/2 $^{3}$ | 79 | 40 |
| | **Alaflak (IRE) (75)** (MajorWRHern) **5-9-10** WCarson(8) (lw: hld up & bhd: stdy hdwy 3f out: chsd wnr over 1f out: rdn & r.o wl) | nk | **2** | 10/1 | 90 | 51 |
| 1507* | **Atlantic Mist (63)** (BRMillman) **3-7-13** GBardwell(1) (lw: plld hrd: prom: rdn over 3f out: one pce fnl 2f) | 5 | **3** | 100/30 $^{1}$ | 70 | 18 |
| $1145^{13}$ | **Game Ploy (POL) (63)** (DHaydnJones) **4-8-12** PatEddery(5) (hdwy 4f out: ev ch 3f out: wknd wl over 1f out) | 1¾ | **4** | 10/1 | 67 | 28 |
| $1414^{2}$ | **Master M-E-N (IRE) (56)** (NMBabbage) **4-8-5v** JQuinn(7) (no hdwy fnl 3f) | ¾ | **5** | 100/30 $^{1}$ | 59 | 20 |
| $1661^{5}$ | **Araboybill (58)** (RSimpson) **5-8-7b** SWhitworth(3) (chsd ldr: led over 3f out tl over 2f out: sn wknd) | 1¾ | **6** | 10/1 | 58 | 19 |
| $1515^{6}$ | **Gloriana (66)** (LadyHerries) **4-9-1** JReid(4) (led over 6f) | 3½ | **7** | 7/2 $^{2}$ | 61 | 22 |
| $1496^{12}$ | **Morning Sir (62)** (CRBarwell) **3-7-12** NAdams(6) (hld up: a bhd) | s.h | **8** | 25/1 | 56 | 4 |

(SP 114.9%) **8 Rn**

**2m 10.0** (4.70) CSF £51.10 CT £192.03 TOTE £5.60: £2.30 £2.20 £1.80 (£29.20) OWNER Mr D. J. Deer (LAMBOURN) BRED D. J. and Mrs Deer
WEIGHT FOR AGE 3yo-13lb
**1462* Roufontaine**, only raised 2lb for her course win last month, sees to like a bit of cut and held on well over this shorter trip. (11/2)
**Alaflak (IRE)** ran three times in Dubai last year and was rated 12lb lower than when he last ran here. Unable to quite peg back the winner, he should not be inconvenienced by a longer trip. (10/1)
**1507* Atlantic Mist**, upped 7lb for his two wins, was a bit keen early on in this first run against older horses. (100/30: 2/1-7/2)
**Game Ploy (POL)**, trained by Ferdy Murphy last season, fared better on this second outing for his new stable. (10/1)
**1414 Master M-E-N (IRE)**, raised 6lb, had no traffic problems to contend with this time, but he did not appear to benefit from having the visor refitted. (100/30)
**1661 Araboybill** found this company a bit more competitive. (10/1)

## 1895 THURSDAY NIGHT MAIDEN STKS (3-Y.O F) (Class D)

9-15 (9-16) **1m 4f 23y** £3,803.25 (£1,146.00: £555.50: £260.25) Stalls: Low GOING minus 0.24 sec per fur (GF)

| | | | Pos | SP | RR | SF |
|---|---|---|---|---|---|---|
| $1004^{4}$ | **Alessandra (95)** (BWHills) **3-8-11** PatEddery(5) (mde all: r.o wl) | — | **1** | 5/4 $^{1}$ | 88 | 38 |

| | | | | SP | RR | SF |
|---|---|---|---|---|---|---|
| 1614[12] | **Kawanin** (PTWalwyn) **3-8-11** WCarson(2) (a.p: styd on ins fnl f: nt trble wnr) | 1½ | **2** | 14/1 | 86 | 36 |
| 1434[2] | **Lothlorien (USA) (84)** (PWChapple-Hyam) **3-8-11** JReid(7) (chsd wnr: no imp fnl 2f) | nk | **3** | 15/8[2] | 86 | 36 |
| | **Grand Splendour** (LadyHerries) **3-8-11** DHarrison(8) (w'like: scope: hld up: rdn over 3f out: rn green: no hdwy fnl 2f) | 2½ | **4** | 20/1 | 82 | 32 |
| | **On The Piste** (RCharlton) **3-8-11** TSprake(3) (lengthy: hld up & bhd: nvr nr ldrs) | 5 | **5** | 5/1[3] | 76 | 26 |
| | **Lady Magnum (IRE)** (JNeville) **3-8-8**(3) DaneO'Neill(6) (w'like: wl bhd fnl 3f) | 7 | **6** | 66/1 | 67 | 17 |
| 1614[5] | **Coh Sho No** (IABalding) **3-8-6**(5) MartinDwyer(1) (hld up: rdn over 4f out: sn wl bhd) | 9 | **7** | 10/1 | 55 | 5 |
| | | | | (SP 117.9%) | **7 Rn** | |

**2m 38.2** (5.80) CSF £17.41 TOTE £2.10: £1.50 £2.60 (£10.50) OWNER Mr D. J. Deer (LAMBOURN) BRED D. J. and Mrs Deer
**1004 Alessandra** appreciated this easier company and had matters under control in the final quarter-mile. (5/4: 8/11-11/8)
**Kawanin** only secured the runner-up spot towards the finish and should stay further. (14/1)
**1434 Lothlorien (USA)** could not reverse the Sandown form with the winner over this longer trip. (15/8)
**Grand Splendour** has plenty of scope about her but looked a big baby in the race. (20/1)
**On The Piste** (5/1: 3/1-6/1)
**1614 Coh Sho No** (10/1: op 5/1)

T/Plpt: £45.10 (394.7 Tckts). T/Qdpt: £34.00 (23.87 Tckts). KH

## 1519-NEWBURY (L-H) (Good to firm)
## Thursday June 13th
WEATHER: warm WIND: almost nil

### 1896 E.B.F. KENNETT MAIDEN STKS (2-Y.O) (Class D)
2-00 (2-01) **6f 8y** £3,727.00 (£1,126.00: £548.00: £259.00) Stalls: High GOING minus 0.52 sec per fur (F)

| | | | SP | RR | SF |
|---|---|---|---|---|---|
| **Ocean Ridge (USA)** (PWChapple-Hyam) **2-8-9** JReid(8) (unf: scope: plld hrd: mde all: clr over 1f out: comf) | — | **1** | 6/4[1] | 82+ | 34 |
| **Eurolink Excaliber (USA)** (JLDunlop) **2-9-0** TQuinn(9) (leggy: scope: a.p: rdn over 3f out: chsd wnr over 1f out: no imp) | 4 | **2** | 14/1 | 76 t | 28 |
| **State Fair** (BWHills) **2-9-0** RStreet(4) (w'like: bit bkwd: s.s: swtchd lft & hdwy over 2f out: rdn over 1f out: one pce) | 1¼ | **3** | 25/1 | 73 t | 25 |
| **Papua** (IABalding) **2-9-0** LDettori(12) (leggy: scope: lw: hld up: rdn over 3f out: swtchd lft over 1f out: one pce) | s.h | **4** | 3/1[2] | 73 t | 25 |
| **Mr Bombastique (IRE)** (BWHills) **2-8-9**(5) JDSmith(6) (w'like: scope: bit bkwd: rdn & hdwy over 2f out: one pce) | ¾ | **5** | 33/1 | 71 t | 23 |
| **Marsad (IRE)** (CJBenstead) **2-9-0** RHills(13) (w'like: scope: bit bkwd: rdn 3f out: nt clr run on ins over 2f out: nvr nrr) | 3 | **6** | 25/1 | 63 t | 15 |
| **Faringdon Future** (BWHills) **2-9-0** MHills(1) (str: scope: bit bkwd: nvr nr to chal) | ½ | **7** | 10/1 | 62 t | 14 |
| **Ellens Lad (IRE)** (RHannon) **2-9-0** PatEddery(10) (leggy: scope: lw: chsd wnr over 2f: rdn over 2f out: eased whn btn ins fnl f) | s.h | **8** | 8/1[3] | 62 t | 14 |
| **Abacaxi (IRE)** (RCharlton) **2-9-0** SSanders(5) (w'like: scope: s.s: a bhd) | 1¼ | **9** | 33/1 | 58 t | 10 |
| **Share Delight (IRE)** (BWHills) **2-9-0** BThomson(7) (w'like: scope: chsd wnr over 3f out tl over 1f out: sn wknd) | 1¼ | **10** | 10/1 | 55 t | 7 |
| **Maftool** (JHMGosden) **2-9-0** WCarson(3) (str: scope: lw: s.s: hdwy over 3f out: wkng whn squeezed out wl over 1f out) | ½ | **11** | 8/1[3] | 54 t | 6 |
| **Prince of Fortune** (MMcCormack) **2-9-0** JFEgan(11) (w'like: bit bkwd: bhd fnl 2f) | 1¾ | **12** | 25/1 | 49 t | 1 |
| **Rupert's Double (IRE)** (BJMeehan) **2-9-0** BDoyle(2) (unf: s.s: a bhd) | 20 | **13** | 20/1 | — | — |
| | | | (SP 134.3%) | **13 Rn** | |

**1m 12.97** (1.17) CSF £25.52 TOTE £2.40: £1.30 £3.10 £6.80 (£16.20) Trio Not won; £373.20 to York 14/6/96 OWNER Mr R. E. Sangster (MARLBOROUGH) BRED Swettenham Stud
**Ocean Ridge (USA)**, quite a tall filly who needs time to develop, nevertheless took the colts on and gave them a real drubbing. Taking a keen hold, she made all the running and, forging clear in the final quarter-mile, won with plenty in hand. She looks useful and can go on to better things. (6/4)
**Eurolink Excaliber (USA)** did not look totally clued up on this debut and Quinn was pushing him along before halfway. Nevertheless, he struggled into second place below the distance, if having no chance of reeling in the winner. The experience will not be lost. (14/1: op 6/1)
**State Fair**, a plain colt who looked as though the run was needed, was switched towards the outside to begin his effort over a quarter of a mile from home. He did struggle on for third, but never looked like posing a real threat. (25/1)
**Papua**, a half-brother to numerous winners, failed to find the necessary turn of foot in the final quarter-mile. (3/1: 2/1-100/30)
**Mr Bombastique (IRE)** did not look fully fit and, ridden along to take closer order on the outside of the field over quarter of a mile from home, could then make no further impression. (33/1)
**Marsad (IRE)** looked big and well for his debut. Racing at the back of the field, he did not have much room over a quarter of a mile from home, but did make up some late headway to be nearest at the line. (25/1)
**Faringdon Future** (10/1: op 6/1)
**Ellens Lad (IRE)** (8/1: op 5/1)
**Maftool** (8/1: op 4/1)

### 1897 KINGSCLERE CONDITIONS STKS (2-Y.O) (Class B)
2-30 (2-30) **6f 8y** £6,011.00 (£2,249.00: £1,099.50: £472.50: £211.25: £106.75) Stalls: High GOING minus 0.52 sec per fur (F)

| | | | | SP | RR | SF |
|---|---|---|---|---|---|---|
| | **Fun Galore (USA)** (BWHills) **2-8-11** MHills(6) (str: scope: hld up: swtchd lft over 1f out: led ins fnl f: rdn out) | — | **1** | 7/1 | 82+ | 33 |
| | **Wolf Mountain** (RHannon) **2-8-11** LDettori(4) (unf: scope: lw: chsd ldr: led over 1f out tl ins fnl f: r.o) | hd | **2** | Evens[1] | 82+ | 33 |
| 1352[4] | **Hil Rhapsody** (BPalling) **2-8-9** TSprake(5) (led over 4f: unable qckn) | 4 | **3** | 10/1 | 69 | 20 |
| | **Peartree House (IRE)** (BWHills) **2-8-11** PatEddery(1) (wl grwn: bit bkwd: a.p: rdn 2f out: wknd over 1f out) | 3½ | **4** | 5/1[2] | 62 | 13 |
| | **Tisima (FR)** (IABalding) **2-8-6** WRyan(2) (leggy: scope: lw: s.i.s: hdwy over 2f out: wknd over 1f out) | 2 | **5** | 8/1 | 52 | 3 |
| | **Ihtiyati (USA)** (JLDunlop) **2-8-11** WCarson(3) (w'like: scope: bit bkwd: bhd fnl 2f) | 23 | **6** | 13/2[3] | — | — |
| | | | | (SP 112.7%) | **6 Rn** | |

**1m 13.15** (1.35) CSF £14.26 TOTE £7.50: £2.20 £1.30 (£4.20) OWNER Miss H Al Maktoum (LAMBOURN) BRED Gainsborough Farm Inc

**Fun Galore (USA)**, a well made colt, was settled in behind the leaders. Switched left below the distance, he was soon throwing down his challenge and, getting on top inside the final furlong, just managed to hold off the persistent runner-up. (7/1)
**Wolf Mountain** looked in good shape beforehand. Racing in second place, he went on below the distance and, although marginally collared inside the final furlong, battled his heart out to the bitter end. He looks a ready-made winner. (Evens)
**1352 Hil Rhapsody**, the only runner with experience on her side, dictated matters from the front. Collared below the distance, she was left standing by the front two. (10/1)
**Peartree House (IRE)** is such a big individual he could be mistaken for a three-mile chaser. Looking as though the run was needed, he showed up until tiring below the distance. (5/1)
**Tisima (FR)**, a flashy filly, was very slow to find her stride. Picking up ground on the outside of the field, she had shot her bolt below the distance. (8/1: op 5/1)
**Ihtiyati (USA)** (13/2: 5/2-7/1)

## 1898 GEORGE SMITH MEMORIAL RATED STKS H'CAP (0-100) (3-Y.O+) (Class B)

3-00 (3-01) **7f** £8,136.00 (£3,024.00: £1,462.00: £610.00: £255.00: £113.00) Stalls: High GOING minus 0.52 sec per fur (F)

| | Horse / details | Dist | Pos | SP | RR | SF |
|---|---|---|---|---|---|---|
| 1107[9] | **Everglades (IRE) (96)** (RCharlton) **8-9-5** PatEddery(5) (rdn over 2f out: hdwy over 1f out: led ins fnl f: r.o wl) | — | **1** | 9/2[2] | 101 | 62 |
| 1425* | **Hi Nod (98)** (MJCamacho) **6-9-7** LCharnock(2) (hld up: rdn over 2f out: ev ch fnl f: r.o wl) | s.h | **2** | 2/1[1] | 103 | 64 |
| 1149[2] | **Czarna (IRE) (84)** (CEBrittain) **5-8-7** BDoyle(3) (rdn over 2f out: hdwy over 1f out: unable qckn) | 2 | **3** | 13/2 | 84 | 45 |
| 933[13] | **Primo Lara (84)** (PWHarris) **4-8-7** GHind(6) (lw: led: clr over 3f out: hrd rdn over 1f out: hdd ins fnl f: sn wknd) | 1½ | **4** | 11/2[3] | 81 | 42 |
| 959[3] | **Ocean Grove (IRE) (86)** (PWChapple-Hyam) **3-7-13** JQuinn(7) (lw: chsd ldr over 3f out to 2f out: wknd over 1f out) | s.h | **5** | 7/1 | 83 | 34 |
| 1334[6] | **Charlie Sillett (84)** (BWHills) **4-8-7** MHills(4) (swtg: chsd ldr over 3f) | 26 | **6** | 9/2[2] | 21 | — |
| | ***Classic Sky (IRE) (96)*** (EALDunlop) **5-9-5** RHills(1) (Withdrawn not under Starter's orders: veterinary advice) | | **W** | 10/1 | — | — |
| | | | | (SP 120.0%) | | **6 Rn** |

**1m 24.27** (-0.23) CSF £13.21 TOTE £6.40: £2.90 £1.40 (£5.20) OWNER Mrs Stephen Lussier (BECKHAMPTON) BRED Hascombe and Valiant Studs
LONG HANDICAP Czarna (IRE) 8-4 Charlie Sillett 8-5
WEIGHT FOR AGE 3yo-10lb
**889 Everglades (IRE)**, whose last win nearly two years ago came off this mark, picked up ground from below the distance and, gaining control inside the final furlong, just managed to get the better in a ding-dong battle with the runner-up. (9/2)
**1425* Hi Nod** chased the leaders. He may well have got his head in front for a few strides early insides the final furlong but, in a tremendous battle with the winner, just lost out. (2/1: 7/4-11/4)
**1149 Czarna (IRE)** picked up ground below the distance, but then failed to find another gear in the final furlong. (13/2)
**718* Primo Lara** took the field along and established a clear advantage by halfway. Coming under pressure below the distance, he was eventually reeled in inside the final furlong and had nothing more to offer. (11/2)
**959 Ocean Grove (IRE)**, 5lb out of the handicap, moved into second place at halfway. Collared for that position a quarter of a mile out, she had soon cooked her goose. (7/1)

## 1899 BALLYMACOLL STUD STKS (Listed) (3-Y.O F) (Class A)

3-30 (3-33) **1m 2f 6y** £11,990.00 (£3,620.00: £1,760.00: £830.00) Stalls: Low GOING minus 0.52 sec per fur (F)

| | Horse / details | Dist | Pos | SP | RR | SF |
|---|---|---|---|---|---|---|
| 1123* | **Sardonic** (HRACecil) **3-8-9** WRyan(10) (lw: led 9f out: edgd rt over 3f out: rdn over 2f out: all out) | — | **1** | 5/2[1] | 106 | 51 |
| | **Min Alhawa (USA)** (MajorWRHern) **3-8-9** WCarson(7) (hld up: chsd wnr over 2f out: ev ch ins fnl f: r.o wl) | hd | **2** | 20/1 | 106 | 51 |
| 1187[3] | **Anthelia (98)** (GWragg) **3-8-9** MHills(1) (rdn over 2f out: hdwy over 1f out: r.o wl ins fnl f) | ½ | **3** | 16/1 | 105 | 50 |
| 1201* | **Cabaret (IRE)** (PWChapple-Hyam) **3-8-9** JReid(5) (lw: led 1f: rdn over 3f out: unable qckn) | 5 | **4** | 15/2 | 97 | 42 |
| 1614* | **Balalaika** (LMCumani) **3-8-9** PatEddery(6) (rdn over 3f out: hdwy over 1f out: nvr nrr) | hd | **5** | 11/4[2] | 97 | 42 |
| | **Caribbean Quest** (BHanbury) **3-8-9** BDoyle(11) (nvr nr to chal) | nk | **6** | 14/1 | 96 | 41 |
| | **Witch of Fife (USA) (104)** (BWHills) **3-8-9** BThomson(4) (bhd fnl 2f) | 4 | **7** | 25/1 | 90 | 35 |
| 794a[7] | **Parrot Jungle (IRE) (104)** (JLDunlop) **3-8-9** WJO'Connor(3) (lw: a bhd) | 1¼ | **8** | 8/1 | 88 | 33 |
| 1111[2] | **Kinlochewe** (HRACecil) **3-8-9** AMcGlone(9) (lw: prom over 7f) | 4 | **9** | 7/1 | 82 | 27 |
| 1077[2] | **Flame Valley (USA) (93)** (MRStoute) **3-8-9** RHills(8) (lw: prom 8f) | 1 | **10** | 5/1 | 80 | 25 |
| *1140a[6]* | ***Shawanni*** (SbinSuroor) **3-8-9** LDettori(2) (Withdrawn not under Starter's orders: reard up, uns & inj rdr in paddock) | | **W** | 4/1[3] | — | — |
| | | | | (SP 148.4%) | | **10 Rn** |

**2m 3.76** (-0.04) CSF £48.54 TOTE £3.30: £1.60 £4.20 £4.70 (£35.50) Trio £93.90 OWNER Lord Howard de Walden (NEWMARKET) BRED Lord Howard de Walden
**1123* Sardonic** had a real fight on her hands here. Soon at the head of affairs, she drifted out towards the centre of the track in the straight and, with the second throwing down a mighty challenge in the final furlong, she was all out to hold on. This was a very game performance however, and further success awaits her. (5/2)
**Min Alhawa (USA)** made an extremely promising return, but was still unable to change her stable's bad luck at present. Taking second place over a quarter of a mile from home, she threw down a massive challenge inside the final furlong and may well have prevailed in a few more strides. She should soon be winning. (20/1)
**1187 Anthelia** at last found her feet from below the distance. Running on strongly inside the final furlong, she found the line always coming too soon. (16/1)
**1201* Cabaret (IRE)**, taking a big step up in class, was always to the fore, but failed to quicken in the last two furlongs. (15/2)
**1614* Balalaika**, taking a step up in class following her debut win at Kempton, was being rousted along and going nowhere at the back of the field early in the straight. She at last found her feet below the distance but, despite staying on, never threatened to get there. A mile and a half might help her. (11/4: 2/1-100/30)
**Caribbean Quest** (14/1: 12/1-20/1)
**794a Parrot Jungle (IRE)** (8/1: 6/1-9/1)

## 1900 FURLONG CLUB H'CAP (0-80) (3-Y.O) (Class D)

4-00 (4-01) **1m 4f 5y** £3,974.00 (£1,202.00: £586.00: £278.00) Stalls: Low GOING minus 0.52 sec per fur (F)

| | Horse / details | Dist | Pos | SP | RR | SF |
|---|---|---|---|---|---|---|
| 1584* | **Temptress (60)** (PTWalwyn) **3-8-8** SSanders(9) (mde all: drvn out) | — | **1** | 12/1 | 68 | 35 |
| 1687[2] | **Present Arms (USA) (73)** (PFICole) **3-9-7** TQuinn(3) (lw: a.p: rdn over 4f out: ev ch fnl 2f: unable qckn wl ins fnl f) | ¾ | **2** | 11/4[2] | 80 | 47 |

| | | | | SP | RR | SF |
|---|---|---|---|---|---|---|
| 1669[2] | **Ceilidh Star (IRE) (67)** (BWHills) **3-9-1** PatEddery(6) (rdn & hdwy 3f out: r.o ins fnl f) | s.h | **3** | 5/2[1] | 74 | 41 |
| 1507[10] | **Gumair (USA) (72)** (RHannon) **3-9-3**(3) DaneO'Neill(4) (lw: a.p: rdn 4f out: r.o ins fnl f) | ½ | **4** | 14/1 | 78 | 45 |
| 1434[7] | **Regal Eagle (70)** (IABalding) **3-9-4** WRyan(2) (lw: a.p: rdn 4f out: n.m.r on ins over 1f out: r.o) | nk | **5** | 10/1 | 76 | 43 |
| | **Sally's Twins (64)** (JSMoore) **3-8-12** JFEgan(5) (nvr nr to chal) | 8 | **6** | 33/1 | 59 | 26 |
| 1317[8] | **Nikita's Star (IRE) (63)** (DJGMurraySmith) **3-8-11b** JReid(7) (bhd fnl 2f) | 2 | **7** | 12/1 | 56 | 23 |
| 1317[2] | **Willie Rushton (60)** (GLMoore) **3-8-8** SWhitworth(10) (b.hind: bhd fnl 3f) | 8 | **8** | 10/1 | 42 | 9 |
| 1415[7] | **Muhtadi (IRE) (73)** (JLDunlop) **3-9-7b**[1] WCarson(8) (hdwy 9f out: wkng whn hmpd over 2f out) | 6 | **9** | 16/1 | 47 | 14 |
| 849* | **Four Weddings (USA) (51)** (MCPipe) **3-7-13v** GBardwell(1) (lw: s.s: a bhd) | 10 | **10** | 9/1[3] | 12 | — |

(SP 114.3%) **10 Rn**

**2m 32.42** (2.42) CSF £41.90 CT £101.25 TOTE £10.50: £2.30 £1.50 £1.70 (£13.40) Trio £13.50 OWNER Mr A. D. G. Oldrey (LAMBOURN) BRED A. D. G. Oldrey

**1584* Temptress** made every post a winning one and, responding to pressure, kept her rivals at bay. (12/1: op 8/1)

**1687 Present Arms (USA)**, a leading light from the off, threw down a determined challenge in the final quarter-mile. Despite all his rider's efforts, he failed to get the better of the persistent winner. (11/4)

**1669 Ceilidh Star (IRE)**, ridden along to pick up ground three furlongs from home, was running on nicely in the closing stages and failed by only a whisker to take second prize. (5/2)

**Gumair (USA)**, never far away, was being pushed along early in the straight but, to his credit, he stuck to his task well inside the final furlong. (14/1)

**Regal Eagle** did not have a great deal of room in which to manoeuvre along the inside rail below the distance, but stuck on nicely inside the final furlong. (10/1: 7/1-12/1)

**385* Nikita's Star (IRE)** (12/1: 8/1-14/1)

## 1901 BUCKLEBURY MAIDEN STKS (3-Y.O) (Class D)

4-30 (4-36) **7f** £4,045.50 (£1,224.00: £597.00: £283.50) Stalls: High GOING minus 0.52 sec per fur (F)

| | | | | SP | RR | SF |
|---|---|---|---|---|---|---|
| | **Medieval Lady** (LadyHerries) **3-8-9** JReid(13) (hdwy over 2f out: led ins fnl f: rdn out) | — | **1** | 10/1 | 85 | 48 |
| 1333[5] | **Highland Rhapsody (IRE)** (IABalding) **3-8-9** MHills(12) (lw: led: hrd rdn & edgd lft over 1f out: edgd rt & hdd ins fnl f: unable qckn) | 1¼ | **2** | 11/4[1] | 82 | 45 |
| | **High Summer (USA)** (RCharlton) **3-8-9** PatEddery(16) (leggy: scope: lw: s.s: hdwy over 2f out: rdn over 1f out: one pce) | 1¾ | **3** | 4/1[3] | 78 | 41 |
| | **Supamova (USA)** (PFICole) **3-8-9** TQuinn(6) (a.p: rdn over 2f out: one pce) | 1½ | **4** | 7/2[2] | 75 | 38 |
| 1323[4] | **Melt The Clouds (CAN) (82)** (PWHarris) **3-9-0** GHind(14) (lw: rdn over 2f out: hdwy over 1f out: r.o) | s.h | **5** | 20/1 | 80 | 43 |
| | **Santella Katie** (MajorDNChappell) **3-8-9** WWoods(11) (leggy: rdn over 2f out: nvr nr to chal) | 1¼ | **6** | 33/1 | 72 | 35 |
| 1709[2] | **Lucky Revenge (65)** (MartynMeade) **3-8-4**(5) RHavlin(5) (prom over 5f) | hd | **7** | 33/1 | 72 | 35 |
| | **Mezzanotte (IRE)** (LMCumani) **3-9-0** OUrbina(3) (w'like: bit bkwd: hld up: rdn 2f out: wknd fnl f) | 2½ | **8** | 14/1 | 71 | 34 |
| | **Baydah** (ACStewart) **3-8-9** WCarson(19) (w'like: s.s: nvr nrr) | 2½ | **9** | 16/1 | 60 | 23 |
| | **Rivers Magic** (MajorDNChappell) **3-9-0** WJO'Connor(2) (w'like: bit bkwd: a mid div) | 1¼ | **10** | 33/1 | 62 | 25 |
| | **Red Tie Affair (USA)** (MBell) **3-9-0** MFenton(10) (b.nr fore: nvr nrr) | s.h | **11** | 50/1 | 62 | 25 |
| | **Sabaah Elfull** (ACStewart) **3-8-9** MRoberts(15) (prom over 4f) | ¾ | **12** | 12/1 | 55 | 18 |
| 1171[2] | **Alpine Hideaway (IRE) (80)** (BHanbury) **3-9-0** WRyan(17) (bhd fnl 3f) | 2½ | **13** | 20/1 | 55 | 18 |
| 1050[3] | **One In The Eye** (JRPoulton) **3-8-11**(3) PMcCabe(8) (s.s: a bhd) | ¾ | **14** | 33/1 | 53 | 16 |
| | **Flying Harold** (MRChannon) **3-9-0** CandyMorris(4) (a bhd) | 2½ | **15** | 50/1 | 47 | 10 |
| 1617[7] | **Sovereigns Court** (MajorDNChappell) **3-9-0** BThomson(7) (lw: prom over 4f) | nk | **16** | 20/1 | 47 | 10 |
| 663[3] | **Proud Look** (BWHills) **3-9-0** RHills(18) (a bhd) | 1¼ | **17** | 14/1 | 44 | 7 |

(SP 134.9%) **17 Rn**

**1m 24.69** (0.19) CSF £38.56 TOTE £13.60: £3.40 £1.90 £1.80 (£26.00) Trio £163.00 OWNER Summertree Stud (LITTLEHAMPTON) BRED Summertree Stud

OFFICIAL EXPLANATION **Flying Harold: his rider reported that the colt ran too freely early on, though he had to be settled and when asked for an effort two furlongs out, changed his legs and produced very little.**

**Medieval Lady** made a winning return to action. Picking up ground over a quarter of a mile from home, she swooped into the lead inside the final furlong and, ridden along, soon asserted. (10/1)

**1333 Highland Rhapsody (IRE)** attempted to make all. Grimly trying to hold off her rivals, she was only worried out of it inside the final furlong. She should soon be winning. (11/4: 6/1-5/2)

**High Summer (USA)** looked very well in the paddock, but drifted ominously in the betting. Taking closer order over a furlong from home, she tried to mount a challenge but was just tapped for toe. She should not be difficult to win with. (4/1: op 2/1)

**Supamova (USA)** was never far away, but failed to find the necessary turn of foot in the final quarter-mile. (7/2)

**1323 Melt The Clouds (CAN)** never looked like getting there in time. (20/1)

**Santella Katie** made some late headway without posing a threat. (33/1)

**Mezzanotte (IRE)** (14/1: op 8/1)

**Sabaah Elfull** (12/1: op 8/1)

**663 Proud Look** (14/1: op 8/1)

## 1902 LEVY BOARD APPRENTICE H'CAP (0-80) (3-Y.O+) (Class E)

5-00 (5-01) **1m** £3,501.25 (£1,060.00: £517.50: £246.25) Stalls: High GOING minus 0.52 sec per fur (F)

| | | | | SP | RR | SF |
|---|---|---|---|---|---|---|
| 1659* | **Helios (57)** (NJHWalker) **8-8-10** 6x AWhelan(5) (hdwy over 3f out: hrd rdn over 1f out: led ins fnl f: r.o wl) | — | **1** | 5/1[2] | 67 | 36 |
| 1154[2] | **Easy Jet (POL) (70)** (LordHuntingdon) **4-9-4**(5) AimeeCook(8) (a.p: led over 2f out tl ins fnl f: unable qckn) | 1¼ | **2** | 5/1[2] | 78 | 47 |
| 1594[2] | **Flying Pennant (IRE) (66)** (RHannon) **3-8-8** DaneO'Neill(7) (hdwy & hung lft over 1f out: one pce) | 2 | **3** | 9/2[1] | 70 | 28 |
| 1703* | **Knobbleeneeze (77)** (MRChannon) **6-9-11v**(5) 6x AEddery(2) (lw: a.p: led over 3f out tl over 2f out: wknd wl over 1f out) | 6 | **4** | 9/2[1] | 69 | 38 |
| | **Set the Fashion (58)** (DLWilliams) **7-8-8**(3) DGriffiths(3) (hdwy & hung lft over 2f out: sn wknd) | 1½ | **5** | 16/1 | 47 | 16 |
| 1485[8] | **Wilfull Lad (IRE) (61)** (MartynMeade) **3-8-0**(3) MHenry(1) (led over 4f: wknd over 2f out) | ½ | **6** | 11/2[3] | 49 | 7 |
| 1642[17] | **Great Hall (44)** (PDCundell) **7-7-6b**(5) IonaWands(6) (a bhd) | 5 | **7** | 25/1 | 22 | — |
| 1508[8] | **La Pellegrina (IRE) (73)** (PWChapple-Hyam) **3-8-12**(3) RHavlin(4) (prom over 4f) | 4 | **8** | 5/1[2] | 43 | 1 |

(SP 111.5%) **8 Rn**

**1m 38.54** (1.54) CSF £27.15 CT £105.88 TOTE £6.30: £1.90 £2.20 £1.70 (£27.30) OWNER Box 40 Racing (WANTAGE) BRED Sunley Stud

WEIGHT FOR AGE 3yo-11lb

**1659* Helios** moved up to the leaders soon after halfway. Responding to pressure below the distance, he struck the front inside the final furlong and kept on well. (5/1)

**1154 Easy Jet (POL)** went to the front over a quarter of a mile from home but, collared inside the final furlong, found the winner too strong. (5/1: 7/2-11/2)
**1594 Flying Pennant (IRE)** hung left as he picked up ground below the distance and could make no further impression in the final furlong. (9/2)
**1703* Knobbleeneeze** has been raised 10lb for his Chester win last week and was sent on over three furlongs from home. Headed over a quarter of a mile out, he soon had bellows to mend. (9/2)
**Set the Fashion** was just picking up ground when drifting badly to his left over a quarter of a mile from home and, not surprisingly, he was soon a spent force. (16/1)

T/Jkpt: Not won; £3,164.13 to York 14/6/96. T/Plpt: £22.70 (792.42 Tckts). T/Qdpt: £5.40 (211.82 Tckts). AK

# 1877-YARMOUTH (L-H) (Firm)
## Thursday June 13th
WEATHER: sunny WIND: fresh half bhd

### 1903 SEA PALLING APPRENTICE H'CAP (0-60) (3-Y.O+) (Class G)
6-30 (6-31) **1m 2f 21y** £2,144.00 (£609.00: £302.00) Stalls: Low GOING minus 0.72 sec per fur (HD)

| | | | | SP | RR | SF |
|---|---|---|---|---|---|---|
| 1821[7] | **Chieftain's Crown (USA) (32)** (MissKMGeorge) **5-8-1b** PDoe(4) (chsd ldr: led wl over 2f out: drifted rt appr fnl f: r.o) | — | **1** | 13/2 | 42 | 25 |
| 1614[13] | **Nelly's Cousin (56)** (NACallaghan) **3-8-4**(8) MDavies(8) (dwlt: hdwy 2f out: r.o strly wl ins fnl f) | ½ | **2** | 13/2 | 65 | 35 |
| 1838[5] | **Harvey White (IRE) (59)** (JPearce) **4-9-11**(3) SGaillard(5) (hld up & bhd: hdwy 3f out: r.o wl ins fnl f) | 1½ | **3** | 9/2[3] | 66 | 49 |
| 999[4] | **Giftbox (USA) (54)** (SirMarkPrescott) **4-9-1**(8) TPengkerego(9) (lw: trckd ldrs: effrt 2f out: kpt on ins fnl f) | hd | **4** | 4/1[2] | 61 | 44 |
| 1067[9] | **Still Here (IRE) (43)** (MJHeaton-Ellis) **3-7-10**(3) JFowle(2) (led tl hdd wl over 2f out: edgd rt over 1f out: wknd fnl f) | 1 | **5** | 12/1 | 48 | 18 |
| *1448*[7] | **Real Madrid (37)** (GPEnright) **5-8-6v** RFfrench(6) (hld up: hdwy over 3f out: wknd wl over 1f out) | 5 | **6** | 16/1 | 34 | 17 |
| 1696[3] | **Studio Thirty (32)** (DMorris) **4-8-1** RMullen(3) (hld up: hdwy 5f out: rdn over 2f out: sn btn) | 1¾ | **7** | 3/1[1] | 26 | 9 |
| *35*[11] | **Fortuitious (IRE) (40)** (JRJenkins) **3-7-10** CCogan(7) (bit bkwd: chsd ldrs tl rn wd ent st: sn bhd: t.o) | 16 | **8** | 33/1 | 9 | — |
| 1691[12] | **Pinkerton Polka (47)** (CEBrittain) **4-8-13**(3) JGotobed(1) (lw: a in rr: lost tch fnl 3f: t.o) | nk | **9** | 20/1 | 16 | — |
| | | | | (SP 111.1%) | **9 Rn** | |

**2m 4.7** (0.30) CSF £42.45 CT £183.80 TOTE £5.80: £3.40 £2.10 £1.30 (£62.30) Trio £60.70 OWNER Miss J. Rumford (WENDOVER) BRED Ronald K. Kirk
LONG HANDICAP Fortuitious (IRE) 7-5
WEIGHT FOR AGE 3yo-13lb
**1821 Chieftain's Crown (USA)**, getting off the mark on the Flat, made a beeline for the stands' rail after taking over and, in the end, only just held the runner-up's strong late challenge. (13/2)
**Nelly's Cousin**, taking on handicappers for the first time, remained on the far side and only just failed to peg back the winner. (13/2)
**1838 Harvey White (IRE)**, having his third run in less than a fortnight, was doing all his best work inside the final furlong but always had just too much to do. (9/2)
**999 Giftbox (USA)**, unproven on such fast ground, could not get in a blow against the principals but looked as though he would benefit from stronger handling. (4/1: 5/2-9/2)
**Still Here (IRE)** made the majority of the running, but was inclined to follow the winner entering the final furlong and forfeited what chance he had. (12/1: 8/1-14/1)
**Real Madrid** posed a threat entering the final quarter-mile, but did not appear to be giving his best when the whips started cracking. (16/1)
**1696 Studio Thirty** reserves his best for easier ground and could not get close enough to deliver a challenge. (3/1: op 7/4)

### 1904 REPPS (S) STKS (2-Y.O) (Class G)
7-00 (7-00) **7f 3y** £2,301.00 (£636.00: £303.00) Stalls: Centre GOING minus 0.72 sec per fur (HD)

| | | | | SP | RR | SF |
|---|---|---|---|---|---|---|
| 1032[2] | **Irish Fiction (IRE)** (MRChannon) **2-8-11** KDarley(6) (mde virtually all: hrd drvn wl over 1f out: hld on) | — | **1** | 11/8[1] | 60 | 9 |
| 1607* | **Our Kevin** (KMcAuliffe) **2-9-2b** JTate(4) (a.p: chal 2f out: hrd rdn & edgd lft ins fnl f: unable qckn) | ½ | **2** | 3/1[3] | 64 | 13 |
| *858*[3] | **Fan of Vent-Axia** (CNAllen) **2-8-11b**[1] CHodgson(1) (prom: rdn over 2f out: rallied ins fnl f) | 1 | **3** | 5/2[2] | 57 | 6 |
| 1494[6] | **Riva La Belle** (JWharton) **2-8-6** PRobinson(2) (swvd rt s: prom tl rdn & wknd 2f out) | 3½ | **4** | 12/1 | 44 | — |
| 1531[7] | **Emmas Breeze** (CADwyer) **2-8-3**(3) JStack(3) (hmpd s: plld hrd: chsd ldrs: rdn 3f out: grad fdd) | 4 | **5** | 16/1 | 35 | — |
| 1595[9] | **Madam Poppy** (CADwyer) **2-8-0v**[1](7)ow1 NicolaCole(5) (outpcd: a bhd: t.o) | 12 | **6** | 33/1 | 8 | — |
| | | | | (SP 112.2%) | **6 Rn** | |

**1m 26.6** (2.40) CSF £5.75 TOTE £2.10: £1.50 £1.50 (£2.20) OWNER Mr Michael Foy (UPPER LAMBOURN) BRED Miss Peg Farrington
Sold Camelot Racing 8,000gns
**1032 Irish Fiction (IRE)** came good at this first attempt at this extended trip, but needed to pull out all the stops to hang on. (11/8)
**1607* Our Kevin**, very much on his toes, joined issue two furlongs out and, had he not edged left under pressure in the final furlong, would almost certainly have won. (3/1: op 2/1)
**858 Fan of Vent-Axia** was going nowhere when put under pressure over two furlongs out, but stayed on strongly towards the finish and seems well suited by a test of stamina. (5/2)
**Riva La Belle**, soon chasing up the leaders, was throwing out distress signals entering the final quarter-mile and her chance soon evaporated. (12/1)

### 1905 WEATHERBYS VAT SERVICES H'CAP (0-70) (3-Y.O+) (Class E)
7-30 (7-31) **6f 3y** £3,525.00 (£1,050.00: £500.00: £225.00) Stalls: Centre GOING minus 0.72 sec per fur (HD)

| | | | | SP | RR | SF |
|---|---|---|---|---|---|---|
| 1881* | **Sea-Deer (73)** (CADwyer) **7-10-6** 6x RHills(5) (trckd ldrs: led over 1f out: rdn & r.o wl) | — | **1** | 4/1[2] | 77 | 53 |
| 1715* | **Don Pepe (56)** (RBoss) **5-8-10**(7) GFaulkner(8) (s.i.s: hdwy ½-wy: ev ch ins fnl f: unable qckn) | ½ | **2** | 2/1[1] | 65 | 41 |
| 1881[5] | **Samsolom (61)** (PHowling) **8-9-8** PaulEddery(9) (hld up: in tch: effrt & nt clr run over 1f out: r.o wl fnl f) | 1½ | **3** | 12/1 | 66 | 42 |
| | **Red Admiral (62)** (CMurray) **6-9-9** MTebbutt(6) (swtg: bkwd: led tl rdn & hdd over 1f out: one pce) | nk | **4** | 14/1 | 66 | 42 |
| 1693[6] | **Missile Toe (IRE) (70)** (JEBanks) **3-9-6**(3) JStack(7) (lw: a.p: rdn appr fnl f: no ex towards fin) | ½ | **5** | 10/1[3] | 73 | 41 |
| 1684[4] | **Our Shadee (USA) (48)** (KTIvory) **6-8-2b**(7) CScally(1) (racd centre: prom tl rdn & outpcd wl over 1f out) | ¾ | **6** | 10/1[3] | 49 | 25 |
| 1612* | **Mellors (IRE) (64)** (JARToller) **3-9-3** KDarley(2) (chsd ldrs over 4f) | 2½ | **7** | 4/1[2] | 58 | 26 |
| 1674[12] | **Irchester Lass (39)** (SRBowring) **4-8-0v** GCarter(3) (lw: outpcd: a bhd) | s.h | **8** | 20/1 | 33 | 9 |

*1027[10]* **Welcome Lu (43)** (PSFelgate) **3-7-10b[1]** AMackay(4) (outpcd in rr: t.o) ....25 **9** 40/1 — —
(SP 113.1%) **9 Rn**

**1m 10.7** (-0.20) CSF £11.63 CT £77.53 TOTE £5.10: £1.60 £1.80 £2.40 (£5.10) Trio £15.50 OWNER Binding Matters Ltd (NEWMARKET) BRED Stetchworth Park Stud Ltd
LONG HANDICAP Irchester Lass 7-8 Welcome Lu 7-1
WEIGHT FOR AGE 3yo-8lb

**1881* Sea-Deer** obviously likes the sea air and followed up his previous day's win with another game performance. He is proving a real money-spinner for his new stable. (4/1)
**1715* Don Pepe** looked sure to add to his recent success when throwing down a determined last-furlong challenge, but the winner stuck his neck out and would not be denied. (2/1)
**1881 Samsolom**, trying to gain his revenge on the winner, had no luck at all in running, otherwise he would have gone very close. (12/1)
**Red Admiral** did not look fully wound up for this seasonal debut, but he ran a fine race in defeat and, if he could be trusted, there is reward waiting. (14/1)
**1693 Missile Toe (IRE)**, a badly-handicapped colt, ran really well here and, if he is given a chance, will soon be winning again. (10/1: 8/1-12/1)
**1684 Our Shadee (USA)**, racing up the centre of the track, could not get in a serious blow against the principals but he will find his way again when he can get his toe in. (10/1: 8/1-12/1)

## 1906 AMEC CELEBRATION MAIDEN STKS (3-Y.O) (Class D)
8-00 (8-00) **1m 3y** £3,893.85 (£859.35: £859.35: £252.45) Stalls: Centre GOING minus 0.72 sec per fur (HD)

| | | | | SP | RR | SF |
|---|---|---|---|---|---|---|
| 1333[8] | **Lubaba (USA)** (HThomsonJones) **3-8-9** RHills(1) (lw: brought stands' side: mde all: hrd drvn fnl f: all out) | — | **1** | 5/2[1] | 67 | 19 |
| 1627[5] | **Polar Champ** (SPCWoods) **3-9-0** DBiggs(5) (hld up: pushed along over 3f out: swtchd lft appr fnl f: r.o wl nr fin) | hd | **2** | 16/1[3] | 72 | 24 |
| 1090[6] | **Mohannad (IRE) (75)** (JWHills) **3-9-0** KDarley(3) (hld up: hdwy to chse wnr 3f out: hrd drvn & ev ch fnl f: r.o) | d.h | **2** | 3/1[2] | 72 | 24 |
| 1627[4] | **Larissa (IRE)** (GWragg) **3-8-9** PaulEddery(4) (lw: chsd wnr 5f: wknd over 2f out) | 7 | **4** | 3/1[2] | 53 | 5 |
| | **Reticent** (JHMGosden) **3-9-0** GHind(2) (w'like: scope: b: b.hind: s.i.s: racd alone centre: in tch tl wknd over 2f out) | 7 | **5** | 5/2[1] | 44 | — |

(SP 113.0%) **5 Rn**

**1m 36.7** (1.40) CSF L, M £4.94 L, PC £13.30 TOTE £3.00: £2.00 M £0.80 PC £1.90 (L, M £1.80 L, PC £9.00) OWNER Mr Hamdan Al Maktoum (NEWMARKET) BRED Shadwell Farm Inc

**870 Lubaba (USA)**, brought back to a mile and fairly bouncing off the ground, settled down in the lead. She had a hard fight on her hands throughout the final furlong, but buckled down to the task in hand and found the post arriving just in time. (5/2)
**1627 Polar Champ**, not at all happy on the way down, was never really going in the race until putting in a sustained late challenge to be only a stride down at the line. He had no trouble in turning the tables on the fourth horse and is only now realising what the game is about. (16/1)
**1090 Mohannad (IRE)**, a tall colt stepping down in distance, took time to find top gear but was really into his stride in the last furlong and, though he still showed signs of greenness, only just failed to peg back the winner. He ran with his tongue tied down. (3/1: 4/1-5/2)
**1627 Larissa (IRE)** moved impressively to the start and sat in behind the winner, waiting to pounce. When push turned to shove though, she failed to respond and was easily brushed aside. (3/1)
**Reticent** (5/2: Evens-11/4)

## 1907 SOMERTON CLAIMING STKS (3-Y.O) (Class F)
8-30 (8-30) **2m** £2,586.50 (£714.00: £339.50) Stalls: Centre GOING minus 0.72 sec per fur (HD)

| | | | | SP | RR | SF |
|---|---|---|---|---|---|---|
| 1762* | **Sedbergh (USA) (64)** (MrsMReveley) **3-9-7** KDarley(1) (lw: hld up: hdwy to ld over 2f out: sn clr: canter) | — | **1** | 8/13[1] | 72+ | 21 |
| 1762[2] | **Mathon (IRE) (48)** (MRChannon) **3-8-11v** JFEgan(5) (dwlt: bhd: rdn 4f out: styd on fnl 2f: no ch w wnr) | 6 | **2** | 100/30[2] | 56 | 5 |
| *1814[7]* | **Shamand (USA) (46)** (BJMeehan) **3-8-5** MTebbutt(3) (chsd ldr: led over 3f out tl over 2f out: sn rdn & outpcd) | 6 | **3** | 9/1 | 44 | — |
| 1762[5] | **Valise (48)** (MrsMReveley) **3-8-2** PRobinson(2) (led: qcknd clr 5f out: hdd over 3f out: wknd fnl 2f) | 3½ | **4** | 7/1[3] | 38 | — |
| 1514[13] | **Lahik (IRE) (39)** (KTIvory) **3-8-11** RHills(4) (lw: prom tl rdn & outpcd over 3f out) | 6 | **5** | 20/1 | 41 | — |

(SP 112.2%) **5 Rn**

**3m 29.2** (2.60 under best) (5.70) CSF £3.14 TOTE £1.70: £2.00 £1.10 (£2.30) OWNER Mr P. D. Savill (SALTBURN) BRED Mulholland Brothers

**1762* Sedbergh (USA)** had nothing to beat and did not need to be let down to win with his head in his chest. (8/13)
**1762 Mathon (IRE)**, hard at work from the turn into the straight, kept staying on but had already been thrashed by the winner last week, and was never able to make much impact. (100/30: 2/1-7/2)
**899 Shamand (USA)** is big and slow and, though he did strike the front early in the straight, he was out of his depth when the winner set sail. (9/1: 9/2-10/1)

## 1908 APPLEGATE H'CAP (0-70) (3-Y.O F) (Class E)
9-00 (9-02) **1m 3y** £3,752.50 (£1,120.00: £535.00: £242.50) Stalls: Centre GOING minus 0.72 sec per fur (HD)

| | | | | SP | RR | SF |
|---|---|---|---|---|---|---|
| 1498[4] | **Classic Ballet (FR) (66)** (RHarris) **3-9-3** AMackay(7) (hld up: drvn along 3f out: hdwy over 1f out: shkn up to ld nr fin) | — | **1** | 3/1[2] | 70 | 19 |
| 1119[17] | **Dungeon Princess (IRE) (60)** (MRChannon) **3-8-11** KDarley(5) (hld up: hdwy over 2f out: led wl ins fnl f tl ct cl home) | ¾ | **2** | 13/2 | 63 | 12 |
| 1693[11] | **Badger Bay (IRE) (64)** (CADwyer) **3-8-12**(3) NVarley(2) (chsd ldrs: ev ch ins fnl f: r.o) | s.h | **3** | 20/1 | 66 | 15 |
| 1691[6] | **Sylvan Princess (47)** (CNAllen) **3-7-7b**(5)ow2 MBaird(4) (lw: hld up: hdwy 2f out: r.o wl nr fin) | ¾ | **4** | 6/1[3] | 48 | — |
| 1182[11] | **Sylvella (53)** (MAJarvis) **3-8-4** PRobinson(10) (hld up: effrt u.p wl over 1f out: fin wl) | hd | **5** | 8/1 | 54 | 3 |
| 1363[15] | **Cerise (IRE) (51)** (CWCElsey) **3-7-11b**(5) FLynch(3) (dwlt: sn trckng ldrs: led over 2f out: edgd lft & hdd wl ins fnl f) | ½ | **6** | 8/1 | 51 | — |
| 1598[10] | **Born A Lady (53)** (SRBowring) **3-8-4** GCarter(8) (hld up: effrt 2f out: nt pce to chal) | 1 | **7** | 10/1 | 51 | — |
| 1648[5] | **Just Millie (USA) (70)** (JEBanks) **3-9-4**(3) JStack(11) (hld up in rr: effrt over 2f out: no imp) | nk | **8** | 9/4[1] | 67 | 16 |
| | **Maraschino (56)** (BJMeehan) **3-8-7** MTebbutt(1) (lw: plld hrd: led after 1f tl over 2f out: sn wknd: t.o) | 16 | **9** | 14/1 | 21 | — |
| | **Eternally Grateful (45)** (CADwyer) **3-7-10** EJohnson(6) (still unf: led 1f: rdn & wknd over 3f out: t.o) | 15 | **10** | 25/1 | — | — |

(SP 130.0%) **10 Rn**

**1m 37.5** (2.20) CSF £24.17 CT £331.59 TOTE £3.70: £1.30 £2.00 £4.00 (£6.70) Trio £60.80 OWNER Classic Bloodstock Plc (NEWMARKET) BRED Inversiones Gonfi Inc
LONG HANDICAP Sylvan Princess 7-9 Eternally Grateful 7-5

**1498 Classic Ballet (FR)** has been performing well without being able to catch the Judge's eye but, on this step down to a mile, produced a telling burst of speed inside the distance to forge ahead in the dying strides. (3/1)
**1025 Dungeon Princess (IRE)** appears to have two ways of running, but she did put her best foot forward here, only to be touched off nearing the line. (13/2)
**Badger Bay (IRE)** has done the majority of her running at sprint distances, but she coped well with this step up to a mile and only just failed in a fierce set-to to the finish. (20/1)
**1691 Sylvan Princess** has shown little, but was getting down to some serious work here in the closing stages. (6/1)
**Sylvella**, in her first handicap, did not get going until far too late, and a small race looks to be in her grasp. (8/1: op 7/2)
**595 Cerise (IRE)** looked the likely winner when nosing ahead over two furlongs out, but she gave away all chance by veering over towards the far rail in the closing stages. She would have won had she kept straight. (8/1: op 5/1)
**Just Millie (USA)** went to post like a crab and did not come back any better. (9/4)

T/Plpt: £34.00 (318.32 Tckts). T/Qdpt: £9.70 (81.06 Tckts). IM

# 1551a-LEOPARDSTOWN (Dublin, Ireland) (L-H) (Good)
## Monday June 3rd

### 1910a SILVER FLASH STKS (Listed) (2-Y.O)
3-00 (3-01) **6f** £9,675.00 (£2,775.00: £1,275.00: £375.00)

| | | | | SP | RR | SF |
|---|---|---|---|---|---|---|
| | **Azra (IRE)** (JSBolger,Ireland) **2-8-11** TEDurcan (mde all: rdn & r.o wl fnl f) | — | 1 | 8/1 3 | 89 | 26 |
| 1565a3 | **Classic Park** (APO'Brien,Ireland) **2-8-11** CRoche (hld up pllng hrd: chsd ldr & rdn over 1f out: kpt on u.p: no imp) | 2½ | 2 | 11/4 2 | 82 | 19 |
| 1565a5 | **Scottish Mist (IRE)** (GMLyons,Ireland) **2-8-11b** PJSmullen (chsd ldrs: 4th over 1f out: rdn & r.o ins fnl f) | hd | 3 | 12/1 | 82 | 19 |
| | **Via Verbano (IRE)** (JSBolger,Ireland) **2-8-11** KJManning (chsd ldr: rdn & lost pl over 1f out: no imp ins fnl f) | 1½ | 4 | 2/1 1 | 78 | 15 |
| | **Alma Latina (IRE)** (PJFlynn,Ireland) **2-8-8** WJSmith (bhd: swtchd & veered lft 2f out: sn rdn: kpt on ins fnl f) | ¾ | 5 | 14/1 | 73 | 10 |
| | **Luisa Di Camerata (IRE)** (APO'Brien,Ireland) **2-8-8** JAHeffernan (cl up tl lost pl over 2f out: no imp over 1f out) | 2½ | 6 | 8/1 3 | 66 | 3 |
| | | | | (SP 96.6%) | **6 Rn** | |

**1m 14.6** (3.90) OWNER D. H. W. Dobson (COOLCULLEN)
**Azra (IRE)** made all and this improved animal has the Group Three Railway Stakes at the Curragh as his main summer objective. (8/1)
**1565a Classic Park** took a real tug early on, proving difficult to settle. Second over a furlong out, she was not going to get to the winner and was not subjected to a hard race. (11/4)
**Scottish Mist (IRE)**, fourth and making little impression a furlong and a half out, sprouted wings inside the last and almost snatched second. (12/1)
**Via Verbano (IRE)**, a better fancied stable-companion of the winner, ran second until losing her place over a furlong out. She was subsequently found to be slightly lame. (2/1)

### 1911a BALLYOGAN STKS (Gp 3) (3-Y.O+)
3-30 (3-30) **5f** £16,250.00 (£4,750.00: £2,250.00: £750.00)

| | | | | SP | RR | SF |
|---|---|---|---|---|---|---|
| 1016* | **Anzio (IRE)** (MissGayKelleway) **5-9-2b** RCochrane (bhd & outpcd: hdwy over 1f out: r.o wl to ld last stride) | — | 1 | 7/2 2 | 101 | 60 |
| | **Ailleacht (USA)** (JSBolger,Ireland) **4-8-13** KJManning (a.p: rdn to ld 1f out: kpt on wl u.p: hdd last stride) | s.h | 2 | 7/2 2 | 98 | 57 |
| | **Sunset Reigns (IRE)** (APO'Brien,Ireland) **3-8-6** JAHeffernan (led: rdn ½-wy: hdd 1f out: r.o) | hd | 3 | 8/1 | 96 | 50 |
| | **Almaty (IRE)** (CCollins,Ireland) **3-9-2** KDarley (edgd lft s: sn prom: 3rd & rdn 1f out: wknd ins fnl f) | 1 | 4 | 4/1 3 | 102 | 56 |
| 1056a4 | **Millyant** (RGuest) **6-9-6** MJKinane (cl up tl lost pl over 2f out: kpt on ins fnl f) | ¾ | 5 | 3/1 1 | 99 | 58 |
| | **Slayjay (IRE)** (JCHayden,Ireland) **3-8-3** WJSupple (chsd ldrs: 4th 2f out: rdn & no imp over 1f out) | 2 | 6 | 7/1 | 81 | 35 |
| | | | | (SP 113.1%) | **6 Rn** | |

**58.9 secs** (1.40) OWNER Tommy Staunton (WHITCOMBE) BRED Rathduff Stud
**1016* Anzio (IRE)** got himself well behind early on, but appeared to be travelling well within himself when making headway inside the two-furlong mark. He ran on really well between horses well inside the last furlong to get his head in front in the last stride. (7/2)
**Ailleacht (USA)** went with the pace and was second from halfway. Leading a furlong out, she pulled out all the stops inside the last 200 yards, but was headed virtually on the line. (7/2)
**Sunset Reigns (IRE)** set off in front and was being driven along from halfway. Headed a furlong out, he stuck to his task well. (8/1)
**Almaty (IRE)**, very easy in the market, went left when the stalls opened. He went fast, but was a beaten third a furlong out. (4/1: op 6/4)
**1056a Millyant** ran with the pace until dropping away after halfway. She was well behind over a furlong out, but stayed on again towards the end. (3/1)

### 1912a GLENCAIRN STKS (4-Y.O+)
4-00 (4-00) **1m 1f** £9,675.00 (£2,775.00: £1,275.00: £375.00)

| | | | | SP | RR | SF |
|---|---|---|---|---|---|---|
| 1566a5 | **Idris (IRE)** (JSBolger,Ireland) **6-9-2** KJManning (hld up: hdwy 4f out: sn trckng ldrs: 4th st: effrt on ins over 1f out: sn led: rdn & kpt on wl ins fnl f) | — | 1 | Evens 1 | 103 | 53 |
| 1252a6 | **Free To Speak (IRE)** (DKWeld,Ireland) **4-8-9** MJKinane (a in tch: 3rd st: 2nd & ev ch fr over 1f out: no ex u.p wl ins fnl f) | ¾ | 2 | 11/2 3 | 95 | 45 |
| 1252a3 | **I'm Supposin (IRE)** (KPrendergast,Ireland) **4-8-9** WJSupple (led & disp ld tl led st: hdd over 1f out: unable qckn) | 3½ | 3 | 9/4 2 | 88 | 38 |
| 1255a4 | **Marqueta (USA)** (CO'Brien,Ireland) **4-8-6** NGMcCullagh (chsd ldrs: rdn ½-wy: sn lost pl: last st: kpt on last 2f) | 4 | 4 | 10/1 | 78 | 28 |
| 1575a6 | **Viaticum (IRE)** (NMeade,Ireland) **4-8-11b** JMorgan (sn disp ld: rdn & hdd bef st: wknd qckly over 1f out) | 14 | 5 | 12/1 | 58 | 8 |
| | | | | (SP 112.9%) | **5 Rn** | |

**1m 54.1** (3.60) OWNER Michael Keogh (COOLCULLEN)
**1566a Idris (IRE)** again proved his liking for the track. Held up early on, he was tracking the leaders in fourth place turning in. He got the break on the inside early in the straight and, in front a furlong and a half out, was always in control. (Evens)
**Free To Speak (IRE)**, in third place going into the straight, held every chance and kept on under pressure. This was a return to something like his best form. (11/2)
**1252a I'm Supposin (IRE)** led the way and, for a few strides early in the straight, looked as though he had slipped the field, but he was headed a furlong and a half out and was quickly outpaced. (9/4)

**1255a Marqueta (USA)** (10/1: op 3/1)
NR

## 1913a-1937a (Irish Racing) - See Computer Raceform

## 1570a-CURRAGH (Newbridge, Ireland) (R-H) (Good)
### Saturday June 8th

### 1938a GALLINULE STKS (Gp 2) (3-Y.O+ C & F)
3-45 (3-45) **1m 2f** £26,000.00 (£7,600.00: £3,600.00: £1,200.00)

| Form | Horse | Btn | Pos | SP | RR | SF |
|---|---|---|---|---|---|---|
| 1135a[2] | **Needle Gun (IRE)** (CEBrittain) **6-9-7** MRoberts (sn led: rdn clr over 2f out: r.o wl) | — | 1 | 9/4[1] | 122 | 87 |
| 1509[11] | **Prince of Andros (USA)** (DRLoder) **6-9-7** RHughes (hld up: trckd ldrs st: hdwy 2f out: 4th & rdn 1f out: kpt on: no ch w wnr) | 2½ | 2 | 10/1 | 118 | 84 |
| 1580a[15] | **His Excellence (USA)** (APO'Brien,Ireland) **3-8-8b[1]** JAHeffernan (chsd wnr: effrt 3f out: nt trble wnr fr 2f out) | nk | 3 | 16/1 | 118 | 71 |
| 1575a[7] | **Al Mohaajir (USA)** (JSBolger,Ireland) **5-9-7** KJManning (hld up towards rr: hdwy over 4f out: chal over 2f out: 3rd & nt trble wnr 1f out: kpt on) | d.h | 3 | 10/1 | 118 | 83 |
| 1567a[7] | **Sheraka (IRE)** (JOxx,Ireland) **3-8-5** WJSmith (hld up towards rr: hdwy st: chsng ldrs 2f out: kpt on) | 1½ | 5 | 8/1 | 112 | 66 |
| | **Truth Or Dare** (CO'Brien,Ireland) **3-8-8** CRoche (hld up: 6th ½-wy: towards rr & rdn 3f out: 7th over 1f out: kpt on: nt trble ldrs) | s.h | 6 | 5/2[2] | 115 | 68 |
| | **Ashbal (USA)** (KPrendergast,Ireland) **3-8-8** SCraine (hld up in tch: 5th & chsd ldrs 3f out: 3rd & rdn 2f out: 5th & no ex over 1f out: kpt on same pce) | ¾ | 7 | 14/1 | 114 | 67 |
| | **Humbel (USA)** (DKWeld,Ireland) **4-9-12** PShanahan (cl up: rdn & effrt 3f out: btn & wknd 2f out) | 5½ | 8 | 6/1[3] | 110 | 77 |
| | | | | (SP 115.5%) | **8 Rn** | |

**2m 6.0** (2.00) OWNER Saeed Manana (NEWMARKET) BRED Saeed Manana
**1135a Needle Gun (IRE)** with the ground to suit him, popped off in front and made all the running. Asked to quicken at the two furlong marker, he produced the goods and won almost unchallenged. (9/4)
**831 Prince of Andros (USA)**, sixth into the straight, made steady headway to take second place inside the last. This was a major improvement on his Sandown effort and although he never got on terms with the winner, he seems to be finding his form. (10/1: op 5/1)
**His Excellence (USA)** chased the winner, was being ridden along two furlongs out and although unable to quicken, put up his best performance and had to be hiked up 11lb to 110. (16/1)
**1575a Al Mohaajir (USA)** was another who put a previous moderate run well behind him here. Making headway throughout the last half mile, he turned into the straight in fourth place and kept on under pressure. (10/1)
**1567a Sheraka (IRE)**, behind turning in, stayed on under pressure over the last two furlongs without ever posing a threat. (8/1: op 5/1)
**Truth Or Dare** towards the rear and ridden along at halfway, proved a real disappointment. He made his effort on the outer early in the straight, but it was a brief one and he was eased inside the last furlong. His jockey suggested that he is nowhere near as effective on a right-handed track as he is going the other way. His Irish Derby hopes seem slim if that is the case. (5/2)
**Ashbal (USA)**, fifth into the straight, went third under pressure two furlongs out but was soon done with. He was another to rise in the ratings, going up 10lb to 105. (14/1)
**Humbel (USA)** went second just before the straight but dropped away quickly over two furlongs out and was soon outpaced. He needs further. (6/1: op 7/2)
NR

## 1939a-1941a (Irish Racing) - See Computer Raceform

## 1388a-SAINT-CLOUD (France) (L-H) (Soft)
### Monday June 3rd

### 1942a PRIX DE ROYAUMONT (Gp 3) (3-Y.O F)
3-05 (3-15) **1m 4f** £28,986.00 (£10,540.00: £5,270.00)

| Horse | Btn | Pos | SP | RR | SF |
|---|---|---|---|---|---|
| **Spanish Falls** (MmeCHead,France) **3-9-0** FHead | — | 1 | | 100? | — |
| **Silversword (FR)** (AFabre,France) **3-9-0** TJarnet (fin 3rd, 2 3/4l: plcd 2nd) | | 2 | | 97? | — |
| **Met Mech Nich (FR)** (J-PPelat,France) **3-9-0** JBoisnard (fin 4th, 4 1/4l: plcd 3rd) | | 3 | | 92? | — |
| **Leonila (IRE)** (RCollet,France) **3-9-0** OPeslier (fin 2nd, shd: plcd 4th) | | 4 | | 100? | — |
| | | | | | **6 Rn** |

**2m 46.7** (17.40) P-M 3.10F: 3.10F 3.20F (23.90F) OWNER Sheikh Mohammed (CHANTILLY) BRED Sheikh Mohammed
**Spanish Falls**, held up, was brought with a finely-timed run by her jockey. The race looked sewn up well inside the final furlong, but the runner-up found a second wind and almost pinched the race on the line. She relaxed on this occasion, and will now be taking her chance in the Prix de Malleret at the end of the month.
**Silversword (FR)** raced in second place before taking the lead in the straight, but she did not have the pace to take part in the finish. She was awarded the runner-up position after a stewards' enquiry.
**Met Mech Nich (FR)** was hampered when making her effort and proved unable to challenge for the lead. Her jockey did not persevere and she coasted home in fourth position before being moved up to third. She is a little better than this performance suggests.
**Leonila (IRE)** led halfway up the straight, but was passed at the furlong marker by the winner. However, she did not give in and battled on to go under by a nose. In one more stride, she would have taken the race, but would have been disqualified anyway, as she interfered with Met Mech Nich a furlong and a half out. She will have a chance for revenge in the Prix de Malleret.

## TABY (Stockholm, Sweden) (L-H) (Good)
### Tuesday June 4th

### 1943a IBM PC TABY VARSPRINT (Listed) (4-Y.O+)
7-20 (7-49) **6f** £29,155.00 (£7,775.00: £5,831.00)

| Horse | Btn | Pos | SP | RR | SF |
|---|---|---|---|---|---|
| **Windmachine (SWE)** (BjoernOlsen,Norway) **5-8-12** JohnFortune | — | 1 | | 101 | — |

| | | | | SP | RR | SF |
|---|---|---|---|---|---|---|
| 927[11] | **Hever Golf Rose** (TJNaughton) **5-8-12** PaulEddery | s.h | **2** | | 101 | — |
| | **Hakiki (IRE)** (WNeuroth,Norway) **4-9-2** PCeron | 1 | **3** | | 102 | — |
| | | | | | | **15 Rn** |

**1m 9.5** TOTE 58.40KR: 17.30KR 13.10KR 33.80KR (164.50KR) OWNER Stall Fagernes BRED S. Pilroth & J. O. Engelbrektsson
**Hever Golf Rose** showed that her flop in the Palace House Stakes was just an aberration. Breaking smartly to take the lead, she was never able to shake off the attentions of Windmachine, but really stuck her neck out in the closing stages and only lost out by a nostril.

## 1944a IBM STOCKHOLMS STORA PRIS (Listed) (4-Y.O+)
7-55 (8-23) **1m 1f 165y** £34,985.00 (£9,718.00: £7,775.00)

| | | | | SP | RR | SF |
|---|---|---|---|---|---|---|
| | **Philidor** (ALund,Norway) **7-9-2** FDiaz | — | **1** | | 99 | — |
| 1190* | **Amrak Ajeeb (IRE)** (BHanbury) **4-9-2** JReid | hd | **2** | | 99 | — |
| | **Dulford Lad** (JFretheim,Norway) **5-9-2** MSantos | 1 | **3** | | 97 | — |
| | | | | | | **14 Rn** |

**1m 57.7** TOTE 50.10KR: 19.50KR 32.10KR 38.30KR (164.50KR) OWNER Stall Bonne Nuit BRED John A. Jones Morgan
**1190* Amrak Ajeeb (IRE)** almost made a successful step up to listed class. Beginning his run passing the two-furlong marker, he was bang there at the furlong pole and just lost out in a driving finish. In great heart at present, he can win again when returned to handicap company.

# 1755a-BADEN-BADEN (Germany) (L-H) (Good)
### Friday June 7th

## 1945a BENAZET-RENNEN (Gp 3) (3-Y.O+)
3-25 (3-53) **6f** £33,784.00 (£13,514.00: £6,757.00)

| | | | | SP | RR | SF |
|---|---|---|---|---|---|---|
| 1129[6] | **Passion For Life** (GLewis) **3-8-11** PaulEddery | — | **1** | | 118 | — |
| 1943a[2] | **Hever Golf Rose** (TJNaughton) **5-9-2** RHughes | ¾ | **2** | | 113 | — |
| | **Munaaji (USA)** (AWohler,Germany) **5-9-6** THellier | nk | **3** | | 116 | — |
| | | | | | | **13 Rn** |

**1m 9.02** TOTE 47DM: 21DM 19DM 31DM (197DM) OWNER Highclere Thoroughbred Racing Ltd (EPSOM) BRED G. R. Smith (Thriplow) Ltd
**1129 Passion For Life** made all to score a three-quarters of a length victory. Connections hope that the horse will stay further and are looking at a similar race over seven furlongs at Longchamp next.
**1943a Hever Golf Rose**, always prominent, made progress to be a close second with every chance inside the final furlong, but seemed to tire in the final 100 yards. This tough mare still has the King's Stand as her mid-summer target.

# BELMONT PARK (New York, USA) (L-H) (Fast)
### Saturday June 8th

## 1946a BELMONT STKS (Gp 1) (3-Y.O)
10-30 (10-33) **1m 4f (Dirt)** £284,439.00 (£94,813.00: £52,147.00)

| | | | | SP | RR | SF |
|---|---|---|---|---|---|---|
| *1391a[3]* | **Editor's Note (USA)** (DWLukas,USA) **3-9-0** RDouglas | — | **1** | | 128 | — |
| *1391a[2]* | **Skip Away (USA)** (HHine,USA) **3-9-0** JSantos | 1 | **2** | | 127 | — |
| | **My Flag (USA)** (CMcGaughey,USA) **3-8-9** MSmith | 4 | **3** | | 116 | — |
| 1427[2] | **South Salem (USA)** (DRLoder) **3-9-0** JulieKrone | | **P** | | — | — |
| | | | | | | **14 Rn** |

**2m 28.96** P-M £13.60: PL (1-2) £6.50 £8.20 SHOW (1-2-3) £4.30 £6.20 £5.50 (£107.50) OWNER Overbrook Farm et al BRED Fawn Leap Farm
**Editor's Note (USA)** broke a nine-race losing streak in this, the final leg of the US Triple Crown. He made his challenge halfway up the straight to take over at the front, but the eventual runner-up battled on gamely, only going down by a length in the end.
**1427 South Salem (USA)** battled for the lead in the early stages but showed a total dislike for the surface, dropping back to last after only a mile, and being pulled up with two furlongs to run. His jockey reported that he resented the kickback, and Loder was disappointed at the way he ran. He will now return to England and will stay on grass.

# 0790a-EVRY (France) (R-H) (Good)
### Saturday June 8th

## 1947a GRAND PRIX D'EVRY (Gp 2) (4-Y.O+)
3-35 (3-46) **1m 4f** £46,113.00 (£18,445.00: £9,223.00)

| | | | | SP | RR | SF |
|---|---|---|---|---|---|---|
| 1577a* | **Poliglote** (MmeCHead,France) **4-8-9** FHead (mde all: rdn whn chal 1f out: r.o wl u.p) | — | **1** | | 117 | — |
| | **Luna Mareza** (AFabre,France) **4-8-6** TJarnet (trckd ldr: 2nd st: gng wl 2f out: chal 1f out: just failed) | s.h | **2** | | 114 | — |
| | **Danseur Landais** (JLesbordes,France) **5-8-9** GMosse (hld up in rr: rdn 2f out: r.o fnl f) | 2 | **3** | | 114 | — |
| 1390a[3] | **Percutant** (DSmaga,France) **5-8-9** DBoeuf (racd 4th tl st: rdn 2f out: unable qckn: kpt on) | s.h | **4** | | 114 | — |
| 906a[5] | **Muncie (IRE)** (AFabre,France) **4-8-7**ow1 SGuillot (racd in 3rd tl st: plld wd over 2f out: ev ch over 1f out: one pce) | 1 | **5** | | 111 | — |
| | | | | | | **5 Rn** |

**2m 36.03** (6.53) P-M 1.80F: 1.40F 1.50F (5.50F) OWNER Wertheimer Brothers (CHANTILLY) BRED Wertheimer et Freres
**1577a* Poliglote** is a truly brave horse who always does it the hard way by making all the running. He led from pillar-to-post and gallantly held off the runner-up by a short-head. He is one of his trainer's favourite horses and she plans to run him in the Grand Prix de Saint-Cloud, where he could again stretch all his rivals now that he is back to his best form.
**Luna Mareza** ran a really decent race considering she was moving up in class. This filly has never been out of the first two and her challenge on this occasion only failed by inches. She looks the perfect sort for the Prix Maurice de Nieuil next month.
**Danseur Landais** is not quite up to this class, but he put in a decent performance after making up a lot of late ground to steal third place on the line.
**1390a Percutant** looks to have lost his appetite for racing a little. He was given every chance but did not go through with his challenge in the final furlong. He is another to go for the Prix Maurice de Nieuil.
DS

# 1945a-BADEN-BADEN (Germany) (L-H) (Soft)
## Sunday June 9th

## 1948a GROSSER PREIS DER WIRTSCHAFT (Gp 2) (4-Y.O+)
3-25 (3-33) **1m 3f** £72,072.00 (£29,279.00: £13,513.00)

| | | | | SP | RR | SF |
|---|---|---|---|---|---|---|
| | **Germany (USA)** (BSchutz,Germany) **5-9-6** AStarke (mde all: clr 3f out: r.o strly) | — | 1 | | 125 | — |
| 1138a4 | **Oxalagu (GER)** (BSchutz,Germany) **4-9-2** THellier (mid div: styd on fnl 2f: no ch w wnr) | 2½ | 2 | | 117 | — |
| 1575a5 | **River North (IRE)** (LadyHerries) **6-9-0** KDarley (racd 3rd: chsd wnr fr 2f out: wknd cl home) | 1¾ | 3 | | 113 | — |
| | **Artan (IRE)** (MRolke,Germany) **4-9-0** JTandari (chsd ldrs: lost pl ½-wy: rallied fnl f) | 1¾ | 4 | | 110 | — |
| 1135a* | **Hollywood Dream (GER)** (UOstmann,Germany) **5-9-2** JReid (mid div: 4th st: sn rdn & one pce) | 2½ | 5 | | 109 | — |
| | **Hondero (GER)** (BoerjeOlsson,Sweden) **6-9-2** DRegnard (a bhd) | 1 | 6 | | 107 | — |
| 789a3 | **Kornado** (BSchutz,Germany) **6-9-0b1** GBocskai (2nd tl wknd qckly 2f out) | 3 | 7 | | 101 | — |
| | **Upper Heights (GER)** (FrauEMader,Germany) **8-9-0** LMader (a bhd) | 10 | 8 | | 86 | — |
| | | | | | | **8 Rn** |

**2m 20.97** TOTE 17DM: 13DM 15DM 23DM (84DM) OWNER Mr J. Abdullah BRED Curative Ltd
**Germany (USA)** proved that his racing ability remains undiminished after a brief spell at stud, by making all and beating his stablemate Oxalagu.
**1575a River North (IRE)** raced in third and began to chase the winner from two furlongs out. He looked booked for second, but Darley was unable to switch him to the better ground as he was hanging left, and he weakened close home.

# 1756a-CHANTILLY (France) (R-H) (Good)
## Sunday June 9th

## 1949a PRIX DE DIANE HERMES (Gp 1) (3-Y.O F)
2-25 (2-24) **1m 2f 110y** £184,453.00 (£73,781.00: £36,891.00: £18,445.00)

| | | | | SP | RR | SF |
|---|---|---|---|---|---|---|
| 1108[2] | **Sil Sila (IRE)** (BSmart) **3-9-0** CAsmussen (hld up: hmpd 2f out: swtchd outside: hdwy to ld ins fnl f: r.o wl) | — | 1 | 296/10 | 117 | 86 |
| 1396a[2] | **Miss Tahiti (IRE)** (AFabre,France) **3-9-0** OPeslier (hld up early: chal 2f out: r.o to ld ins fnl f: sn hdd: r.o) | 1 | 2 | 53/10[3] | 116 | 85 |
| 1567a* | **Matiya (IRE)** (BHanbury) **3-9-0** WCarson (mid div: hmpd 6f out: 6th st: effrt to ld 1½f out: hdd ins fnl f: wknd) | 2½ | 3 | 11/2 | 112 | 81 |
| | **Averring (USA)** (JCunnington,France) **3-9-0** FSanchez (last & outpcd early: gd hdwy fr 2f out: swtchd lft 1f out: r.o wl cl home) | hd | 4 | 63/1 | 112 | 81 |
| 905a[3] | **Wedding Gift (FR)** (PDemercastel,France) **3-9-0** TGillet (mid div early: 8th st: hdwy 2f out: r.o one pce ins fnl f) | 1½ | 5 | 18/1 | 109 | 78 |
| 1388a* | **Khalisa (IRE)** (AdeRoyerDupre,France) **3-9-0** GMosse (mid div early: hdwy 2f out: r.o one pce) | ½ | 6 | 38/10[2] | 109 | 78 |
| 1396a* | **Luna Wells (IRE)** (AFabre,France) **3-9-0** TJarnet (bhd early: hdwy 2f out: btn 1f out) | ½ | 7 | Evens[1] | 108 | 77 |
| 1004[2] | **Solar Crystal (IRE)** (HRACecil) **3-9-0** WRyan (led tl over 1f out: sn btn & eased) | 5 | 8 | 21/1 | 100 | 69 |
| 1140a[4] | **A Votre Sante (USA)** (MmeCHead,France) **3-9-0** FHead (a.p: 4th st: effrt 2f out: wknd fnl f) | 1 | 9 | 88/10 | 99 | 68 |
| | **Whenby (USA)** (MmeCHead,France) **3-9-0** DBoeuf (prom: 2nd st: wknd 2f out) | ¾ | 10 | 88/10 | 97 | 66 |
| | **Melina Mou (IRE)** (GMikhalides,France) **3-9-0** MBoutin (prom early: 3rd st: wkng qckly whn hmpd 2f out: virtually t.o) | dist | 11 | 38/1 | — | — |
| | **Restless Mixa (IRE)** (AFabre,France) **3-9-0** SGuillot (prom early: btn 10th st: t.o) | 5 | 12 | Evens[1] | — | — |
| | | | | (SP 189.7%) | | **12 Rn** |

**2m 7.3** (-0.70) P-M 30.60F: 7.30F 2.50F 3.50F (124.70F) OWNER Alvarez Cervera (LAMBOURN) BRED L A C
IN-FOCUS: **For Betting purposes, Luna Wells (IRE) cpld w Restless Mixa (IRE); A Votre Sante (USA) cpld w Whenby (USA)**
**1108 Sil Sila (IRE)**, whose previous Musidora form gave her a chance, was given a brilliant waiting ride and she ended up beating a high-class field in this Classic. Great credit must go to her Lambourn trainer who always had confidence in this top-class filly, and she was winning her first Group event. Connections have not yet decided on plans, but the Prix Vermeille is a possible target. There was no fluke about this victory and there were few excuses for the beaten horses. (296/10)
**1396a Miss Tahiti (IRE)** was given every chance, and looked all over the winner at the furlong marker, but she did not have enough acceleration in the closing stages. She is now back to the form which won her the Prix Marcel Boussac and, while there are no plans for her, she will almost certainly be running over a shorter distance next time out, as her stamina appeared to be stretched in the closing stages. (53/10)
**1567a* Matiya (IRE)** was another who was given every chance by her jockey. After being in mid-division for much of the race, she moved up to take the lead a furlong and a half out, but her stamina then petered out, although she stuck to her guns. She will now go back to a mile, and will probably next be seen in the Sussex Stakes at Goodwood. (11/2)
**Averring (USA)** was several lengths last with six furlongs left to run. Sneaking up on the rail in the straight, she was then switched close home to make her challenge and finished really well. She could be heading for the Prix Minerve at Evry next month. (63/1)

## 1950a PRIX DU CHEMIN DE FER DU NORD (Gp 3) (4-Y.O+)
3-35 (3-38) **1m** £28,986.00 (£10,540.00: £5,270.00)

| | | | | SP | RR | SF |
|---|---|---|---|---|---|---|
| 1052a[2] | **Nec Plus Ultra (FR)** (AdeRoyerDupre,France) **5-9-1** TGillet | — | 1 | | 123 | 51 |
| 1135a[5] | **Manzoni (GER)** (AWohler,Germany) **4-8-12** CAsmussen | ½ | 2 | | 119 | 47 |
| 1749a[3] | **Vetheuil (USA)** (AFabre,France) **4-9-0** OPeslier | 1½ | 3 | | 118 | 46 |
| | | | | | | **7 Rn** |

**1m 39.3** (2.80) P-M 5.10F: 2.50F 6.30F (73.20F) OWNER Marquesa de Moratalla (CHANTILLY) BRED Mrs G Forien & Marquise de Moratalla in France
**1052a Nec Plus Ultra (FR)** came right back to his best. He is one of the most genuine and consistent horses in training and will be difficult to beat in this company for the rest of the season, providing the ground is not testing. He now heads for the Prix Messidor.
**Manzoni (GER)** was given every chance, but did not have the acceleration to go with the winner in the final stages.
**1749a Vetheuil (USA)** was most disappointing. He never looked like mounting a real challenge and was very one-paced in the final furlong.

DS

## 1759a-SAN SIRO (Milan, Italy) (R-H) (Good to firm)
## Sunday June 9th

### 1951a PREMIO LEGNANO MEMORIAL MARIO INCISA (Gp 3) (3-Y.O+ F & M)
5-30 (5-45) **1m** £26,065.00 (£11,997.00: £6,699.00)

| Form | Horse | Dist | Pos | SP | RR | SF |
|---|---|---|---|---|---|---|
| | **Bemont Track (ITY)** (RBrogi,Italy) **5-9-3** GBietolini | — | 1 | | 109 | — |
| | **Lara (GER)** (BSchutz,Germany) **4-9-3** NGrant | 1¼ | 2 | | 107 | — |
| | **Tycoon Lady (IRE)** (Ld'Auria,Italy) **5-9-3** SDettori | 1 | 3 | | 105 | — |
| | | | | | | **10 Rn** |

**1m 38.9** (8.90) TOTE 68L: 20L 14L 35L (87L) OWNER Bernardini & Martellino BRED M. Bernardini

## 1134a-FUCHU (Tokyo, Japan) (L-H) (Firm)
## Sunday June 9th

### 1952a YASUDA KINEN (Gp 1) (3-Y.O+)
7-35 **1m** £611,077.00

| Form | Horse | Dist | Pos | SP | RR | SF |
|---|---|---|---|---|---|---|
| 1134a[3] | **Trot Thunder (JPN)** (KAikawa,Japan) **7-9-2** NYokoyama | — | 1 | | 125 | — |
| 1134a[2] | **Taiki Blizzard (USA)** (KFujisawa,Japan) **5-9-2** YOkabe | s.h | 2 | | 125 | — |
| | **Hishi Akebono (USA)** (MSayama,Japan) **4-9-2** KTsunoda | nk | 3 | | 124 | — |
| 1134a* | **Heart Lake** (SbinSuroor,UAE) **5-9-2** YTake (btn 6l) | | 12 | | — | — |
| 1134a[7] | **Shaanxi (USA)** (ELellouche,France) **4-8-12** MEbina (btn 8l) | | 15 | | — | — |
| | | | | | | **17 Rn** |

**1m 33.1** TOTE 340Y: 140Y 160Y 650Y (1060Y) OWNER T. Fujimoto

**Trot Thunder (JPN)** justified favouritism to take this valuable prize by the narrowest of margins.

**1134a* Heart Lake**, winner of this race a year ago, broke badly from stall fifteen and was forced to race on the wide outside. He stayed on, but was never able to challenge.

**1134a Shaanxi (USA)** was unfortunately trapped on the inside rail and was tenth turning into the straight, but proved unable to get in a blow.

## 1772-GOODWOOD (R-H) (St crse Good, Rnd crse Good to firm)
## Friday June 14th
WEATHER: fine WIND: nil

### 1953 SOUTH COAST RADIO AMATEUR H'CAP (0-70) (3-Y.O+) (Class E)
6-35 (6-36) **1m 1f** £4,207.50 (£1,260.00: £605.00: £277.50) Stalls: High GOING minus 0.31 sec per fur (GF)

| Form | Horse | Dist | Pos | SP | RR | SF |
|---|---|---|---|---|---|---|
| 1533[10] | **Persian Affair (IRE) (55)** (TJNaughton) **5-10-8**(5) MrsJMoore(8) (swtg: hdwy over 3f out: led ins fnl f: r.o) | — | 1 | 12/1 | 68 | 33 |
| 1190[13] | **Boston Rock (IRE) (57)** (PWHarris) **4-11-1** MissAElsey(9) (lw: a.p: r.o ins fnl f) | 1¼ | 2 | 4/1[2] | 68 | 33 |
| 1658[2] | **Fort Knox (IRE) (53)** (RMFlower) **5-10-11b** MrTMcCarthy(7) (hdwy 2f out: r.o ins fnl f) | nk | 3 | 11/4[1] | 63 | 28 |
| 1337[3] | **Thames Side (60)** (MMadgwick) **5-10-13**(5) MrPMiddleton(11) (hdwy over 4f out: led over 1f out tl ins fnl f) | 1 | 4 | 11/2[3] | 69 | 34 |
| 759[8] | **All the Joys (40)** (CACyzer) **5-9-7**(5) MissAWilcox(15) (lw: hdwy fnl 2f: r.o) | 1 | 5 | 20/1 | 47 | 12 |
| | **Indian Jockey (63)** (MCPipe) **4-11-7** MrJDurkan(13) (a.p: led over 3f out tl over 1f out: wknd fnl f) | 2½ | 6 | 13/2 | 65 | 30 |
| 1685[11] | **Mimosa (55)** (SDow) **3-9-10**(5) MrSFetherstonhaugh(14) (wl bhd tl gd hdwy over 1f out: nrst fin) | 1 | 7 | 33/1 | 56 | 9 |
| 1685[6] | **Desert Calm (IRE) (55)** (MrsPNDutfield) **7-10-8b**(5) MrLJefford(10) (lw: no hdwy fnl 2f) | 2 | 8 | 12/1 | 52 | 17 |
| | **Safety (USA) (38)** (JWhite) **9-9-5**(5) MrJCrowley(1) (bit bkwd: led 1f: wknd over 2f out) | 1¼ | 9 | 33/1 | 33 | — |
| 1449[8] | **Legal Drama (USA) (50)** (JohnBerry) **4-10-3**(5)ow5 MrVCoogan(6) (hld up: a bhd) | s.h | 10 | 33/1 | 45 | 5 |
| *1601*[7] | **Bellas Gate Boy (63)** (JPearce) **4-11-7** MrsLPearce(12) (lw: plld out over 2f out: a bhd) | 1¼ | 11 | 13/2 | 55 | 20 |
| 1655[20] | **Prince de Berry (51)** (BJMeehan) **5-10-9** MissJAllison(3) (hdwy over 3f out: wknd 2f out) | 5 | 12 | 33/1 | 35 | — |
| 1677[9] | **Wagon Load (40)** (JWhite) **11-9-7**(5) MissSBrown(5) (a bhd) | 3½ | 13 | 33/1 | 17 | — |
| 1677[7] | **Sarum (40)** (JELong) **10-9-7**(5) MrTWaters(2) (led after 1f to 7f out: wkng whn hmpd on ins over 3f out) | 1¼ | 14 | 33/1 | 15 | — |
| 1772[6] | **Johns Joy (49)** (JJBridger) **11-10-2**(5)ow9 MrDBridger(16) (bhd fnl 4f) | 1 | 15 | 33/1 | 22 | — |
| 1173[5] | **Digpast (IRE) (57)** (RJO'Sullivan) **6-10-10b**(5) MrDavyJones(4) (plld hrd: sddle slipped: led 7f out tl over 3f out: sn wknd) | 7 | 16 | 16/1 | 18 | — |
| | | | | (SP 135.3%) | | **16 Rn** |

**1m 58.83** (7.43) CSF £58.94 CT £158.45 TOTE £24.90: £4.00 £2.20 £1.10 £1.50 (£129.40) Trio £242.60 OWNER Mr John Connor (EPSOM) BRED Barronstown Bloodstock Ltd. in Ireland

WEIGHT FOR AGE 3yo-12lb

**887 Persian Affair (IRE)**, 8lb lower than when winning over seven at Brighton over a year ago, appreciated this longer trip. (12/1)

**613 Boston Rock (IRE)**, dropped 3lb, had less use made of him this time than at Newbury and appreciated the better ground. (4/1)

**1658 Fort Knox (IRE)**, due to go up 7lb, has yet to win beyond a mile, and may well have been ridden with that in mind. (11/4)

**1337 Thames Side** was 9lb higher than when winning a maiden handicap at Bath last September. (11/2)

**All the Joys** gave a good account of herself over a trip that should have been inadequate. (20/1)

**Indian Jockey** was fit from hurdling. (13/2: 4/1-7/1)

**Mimosa** came from the next parish to reach this position. (33/1)

### 1954 GOODWOOD GOLF CLUB MAIDEN STKS (2-Y.O F) (Class D)
7-05 (7-07) **6f** £4,542.00 (£1,356.00: £648.00: £294.00) Stalls: Low GOING minus 0.31 sec per fur (GF)

| Form | Horse | Dist | Pos | SP | RR | SF |
|---|---|---|---|---|---|---|
| | **Moonlight Paradise (USA)** (JLDunlop) **2-8-11** TSprake(4) (rangy: scope: s.s: hdwy: swtchd rt & nt clr run 2f out: qcknd to ld wl ins fnl f: r.o) | — | 1 | 2/1[1] | 77+ | 41 |
| 1179[4] | **Raindancing (IRE)** (RHannon) **2-8-8**(3) DaneO'Neill(2) (a.p: rdn & ev ch ins fnl f: r.o) | 1 | 2 | 8/1 | 74 | 38 |
| | **Sambac (USA)** (HRACecil) **2-8-11** PatEddery(5) (w'like: lw: a.p: led over 1f out tl wl ins fnl f) | nk | 3 | 2/1[1] | 74 | 38 |
| 1467[3] | **Caribbean Star** (MRStoute) **2-8-11** JReid(6) (s.s: sn chsng ldrs: one pce fnl 2f) | 3 | 4 | 7/1[3] | 66 | 30 |
| 1467[2] | **Maid By The Fire (USA)** (PFICole) **2-8-11b**[1] TQuinn(7) (led over 4f: wknd fnl f) | 1¾ | 5 | 5/1[2] | 23 | 25 |
| | **Catria (IRE)** (JHMGosden) **2-8-11** GHind(1) (w'like: prom 4f) | 7 | 6 | 14/1 | 42 | 6 |

1590[6] **Incandescent** (APJones) **2-8-11** JFEgan(3) (bhd fnl 3f)....4 **7** 50/1 32 —
1331[5] **Alimerjam** (JWhite) **2-8-8**(3) AWhelan(9) (a bhd)....¾ **8** 66/1 30 —
1678[2] **Mystery** (SDow) **2-8-11** BThomson(8) (rdn over 3f out: sn bhd)....½ **9** 14/1 28 —
(SP 123.7%) **9 Rn**

**1m 11.93** (1.93) CSF £18.70 TOTE £3.80: £1.60 £1.90 £1.30 (£14.70) Trio £11.20 OWNER Sir Eric Parker (ARUNDEL) BRED Allen E. Paulson
**Moonlight Paradise (USA)** had to overcome her fair share of problems, but did it nicely enough in the end. The form may not be that good. (2/1)
**1179 Raindancing (IRE)** showed the right sort of application under pressure. (8/1)
**Sambac (USA)** was travelling well enough when taking it up, but was worn down in the closing stages. (2/1)
**1467 Caribbean Star** again lost ground at the start, but soon recovered to be in pursuit of the front rank. (7/1)
**1467 Maid By The Fire (USA)**, a shade isolated in the centre, failed to last home in the first-time blinkers. (5/1)
**Catria (IRE)** is out of a Cheveley Park winner. (14/1: op 8/1)

## 1955 EQUITY FINANCIAL COLLECTIONS H'CAP (0-85) (3-Y.O) (Class D)

7-35 (7-35) **1m 2f** £3,984.75 (£1,188.00: £566.50: £255.75) Stalls: High GOING minus 0.31 sec per fur (GF)

SP RR SF
1594[3] **Classic Defence (IRE) (69)** (JWHills) **3-8-7**(3) MHenry(5) (mde all: all out)....— **1** 8/1 80 32
863[6] **Daunting Destiny (BEL) (74)** (RHannon) **3-8-12**(3) DaneO'Neill(4) (lw: a.p: chsd wnr fnl 2f: hrd rdn: one pce) ¾ **2** 8/1 84 36
1773* **Get Tough (61)** (SDow) **3-8-2** 4x JFEgan(1) (lw: hld up & bhd: hdwy over 2f out: hrd rdn over 1f out: one pce)hd **3** 9/2 2 71 23
1530[3] **Dragon's Back (IRE) (70)** (MrsJCecil) **3-8-11** BThomson(8) (plld hrd: a.p: chsd wnr 3f out to 2f out: one pce)....1¼ **4** 13/2 3 78 30
1659[2] **Chinensis (IRE) (72)** (LMCumani) **3-8-13** TQuinn(6) (hld up & plld hrd: rdn & hdwy 3f out: one pce fnl 2f)....½ **5** 11/4 1 79 31
701[3] **Taufan Boy (75)** (PWHarris) **3-9-2** GHind(9) (nvr nr to chal)....2 **6** 9/2 2 79 31
1447[3] **Young Butt (67)** (JFfitch-Heyes) **3-8-5**(3) AWhelan(7) (hld up: rdn over 3f out: no hdwy)....1 **7** 14/1 69 21
969[7] **Dance On A Cloud (USA) (80)** (MRStoute) **3-9-7** JReid(2) (lw: chsd ldr: wkng whn hmpd over 2f out)....7 **8** 12/1 71 23
(SP 112.9%) **8 Rn**

**2m 10.27** (4.77) CSF £60.97 CT £293.26 TOTE £11.50: £2.90 £2.30 £1.70 (£28.10) Trio £47.90 OWNER Mr J. W. Robb (LAMBOURN) BRED James Hennessy
**1594 Classic Defence (IRE)** seems at his best when allowed to dictate matters from the front. (8/1)
**863 Daunting Destiny (BEL)**, dropped 2lb, could not peg back the winner, but ought to be capable of staying further. (8/1)
**1773* Get Tough** could not defy his penalty, but was due to go up a further pound. (9/2: op 3/1)
**1530 Dragon's Back (IRE)** may have settled better with a stronger gallop, and ran a good race in the circumstances. (13/2)
**1659 Chinensis (IRE)**, stepping up in distance, was another who proved difficult to settle due to the early pace. (11/4)

## 1956 SOUTHERN FM CLAIMING STKS (3-Y.O) (Class E)

8-05 (8-05) **1m** £3,655.00 (£1,090.00: £520.00: £235.00) Stalls: High GOING minus 0.31 sec per fur (GF)

SP RR SF
1661[3] **Sunley Secure (60)** (MRChannon) **3-8-7** PatEddery(9) (hld up: hrd rdn & hdwy over 2f out: led over 1f out: drvn out)....— **1** 9/4 1 62 24
1776[2] **Coastguards Hero (52)** (MDIUsher) **3-8-7** SSanders(8) (s.s: hld up: hdwy 2f out: chsd wnr fnl f: rdn & r.o one pce)....1 **2** 100/30 3 60 22
*856[10]* **Condor Ridge (47)** (BJMeehan) **3-8-5** BDoyle(1) (led over 6f: wknd fnl f)....4 **3** 33/1 50 12
1641[13] **Dramatic Act (69)** (CRBarwell) **3-8-6** TQuinn(6) (s.s: sn rcvrd: outpcd over 2f out: styd on ins fnl f)....¾ **4** 3/1 2 50 12
544[12] **Only (USA) (55)** (RHannon) **3-8-11**(3) DaneO'Neill(4) (plld hrd: prom: rdn over 3f out: wknd 2f out)....nk **5** 13/2 57 19
1776[7] **Moylough Rebel (45)** (JELong) **3-8-2**(7) TField(7) (b: mid div: rdn & hung rt 3f out: no hdwy)....2 **6** 25/1 48 10
**Areish (IRE)** (JFfitch-Heyes) **3-8-6**(3) MHenry(2) (leggy: a bhd)....11 **7** 20/1 26 —
914[5] **Hever Golf Eagle (52)** (TJNaughton) **3-9-0b**[1] PaulEddery(3) (chsd ldr tl wknd over 2f out)....2½ **8** 8/1 26 —
1776[11] **Rock Daisy** (MMadgwick) **3-8-0** NAdams(5) (a bhd: t.o fnl 3f)....dist **9** 40/1 — —
(SP 117.3%) **9 Rn**

**1m 41.36** (4.16) CSF £9.99 TOTE £3.00: £1.10 £1.60 £9.10 (£4.00) Trio £165.40 OWNER Mr Sunley Tice (UPPER LAMBOURN) BRED Sunley Stud
**1661 Sunley Secure**, backed down to favouritism, responded well to a forceful ride. (9/4)
**1776 Coastguards Hero** again ran well, but could not overhaul the winner. (100/30: 9/4-7/2)
**Condor Ridge** showed his first signs of ability. (33/1)
**1301 Dramatic Act**, dropped in class, again seemed to find a mile on the short side. (3/1)
**Only (USA)** ran too freely in this lower grade. (13/2)

## 1957 SUSSEX ENTERPRISE MAIDEN STKS (3-Y.O) (Class D)

8-35 (8-37) **1m 4f** £4,092.00 (£1,221.00: £583.00: £264.00) Stalls: Low GOING minus 0.31 sec per fur (GF)

SP RR SF
1359[5] **Tiger Lake** (SbinSuroor) **3-9-0** TQuinn(6) (a.p: led 3f out: edgd rt over 1f out: rdn out)....— **1** 5/4 1 79 37
847[5] **Nuzu (IRE)** (BWHills) **3-9-0** BThomson(8) (hld up & bhd: hdwy 2f out: edgd rt fnl f: r.o: nt rch wnr)....1 **2** 13/2 3 78 36
**Caballus (USA)** (LordHuntingdon) **3-9-0** JReid(5) (w'like: scope: led 9f: wknd fnl f)....3 **3** 12/1 74 32
1530[7] **Arktikos (IRE)** (JHMGosden) **3-9-0** GHind(2) (b.hind: s.s: sn rcvrd: btn whn edgd lft over 1f out)....3 **4** 8/1 70 28
1593[7] **Sharp Progress** (APJones) **3-9-0** BDoyle(7) (stdd after 1f: bhd fnl 2f)....3½ **5** 33/1 65 23
1587[2] **Ancient Quest (83)** (NACallaghan) **3-9-0** PatEddery(4) (chsd ldr 5f: rdn over 3f out: btn whn bmpd over 1f out: eased ins fnl f)....2½ **6** 9/4 2 62 20
1357[6] **Sherna (IRE)** (IABalding) **3-8-9** PaulEddery(1) (s.s: a bhd: t.o)....14 **7** 25/1 38 —
(SP 114.1%) **7 Rn**

**2m 38.93** (5.73) CSF £9.45 TOTE £2.30: £1.50 £2.90 (£6.20) OWNER Godolphin (NEWMARKET) BRED Sheikh Mohammed Bin Rashid Al Maktoum
**1359 Tiger Lake**, more at home over this longer trip, displayed quite a high head-carriage and had to be kept up to his work. (5/4)
**847 Nuzu (IRE)** is improving, and would have given the winner more to think about had he got going earlier. (13/2)
**Caballus (USA)** made a reasonable start to his career, but may need less use made of him over this distance. (12/1)
**1530 Arktikos (IRE)** was trying an extra quarter-mile. (8/1)

## 1958 AMBROSE HARCOURT'S HEART AND SOUL H'CAP (0-75) (3-Y.O+) (Class D)

9-05 (9-05) **6f** £4,056.25 (£1,210.00: £577.50: £261.25) Stalls: Low GOING minus 0.31 sec per fur (GF)

SP RR SF
1777[5] **Friendly Brave (USA) (67)** (MissGayKelleway) **6-9-7** WJO'Connor(2) (lw: hld up: rdn to ld ins fnl f: r.o)....— **1** 5/1 3 75 57

| | | | | SP | RR | SF |
|---|---|---|---|---|---|---|
| 1073$^{13}$ | **Sizzling (59)** (RHannon) **4-8-10**$^{(3)}$ DaneO'Neill(3) (hld up: rdn & n.m.r 2f out: hdwy fnl f: r.o) | ¾ | **2** | 10/1 | 65 | 47 |
| 1715$^{4}$ | **Invocation (51)** (AMoore) **9-8-2**$^{(3)}$ AWhelan(10) (b.nr hind: lw: hld up: stdy hdwy over 2f out: led over 1f out tl ins fnl f) | hd | **3** | 12/1 | 57 | 39 |
| 1680$^{2}$ | **Denbrae (IRE) (69)** (DJGMurraySmith) **4-9-9** JReid(6) (lw: hdwy over 1f out: ev ch ins fnl f: unable qckn nr fin) | 1¼ | **4** | 7/2$^{1}$ | 71 | 53 |
| 1715$^{2}$ | **Scissor Ridge (42)** (JJBridger) **4-7-7**$^{(3)}$ DarrenMoffatt(8) (a.p: ev ch over 1f out: one pce) | ½ | **5** | 7/1 | 43 | 25 |
| 1536$^{3}$ | **Random (51)** (CJames) **5-8-5** JFEgan(1) (swtg: hdwy, n.m.r & swtchd rt over 1f out: unable qckn nr fin) | nk | **6** | 9/1 | 51 | 33 |
| 1624$^{7}$ | **Robo Magic (USA) (57)** (LMontagueHall) **4-8-11** SSanders(5) (lw: nvr nr to chal) | 1¼ | **7** | 7/1 | 54 | 36 |
| 1588$^{10}$ | **Be Warned (71)** (NACallaghan) **5-9-11** PaulEddery(7) (lw: dwlt: hdwy over 1f out: nt rch ldrs) | hd | **8** | 9/1 | 68 | 50 |
| *203*$^{9}$ | **Classic Pet (IRE) (46)** (CAHorgan) **4-8-0** NAdams(4) (led: sn clr: hdd over 1f out: wknd qckly) | ½ | **9** | 20/1 | 41 | 23 |
| 1715$^{3}$ | **Jobie (62)** (BWHills) **6-9-2** BThomson(9) (swtg: prom: ev ch over 1f out: wknd qckly) | 3 | **10** | 4/1$^{2}$ | 49 | 31 |

(SP 125.4%) **10 Rn**

**1m 11.45** (1.45) CSF £52.19 CT £549.10 TOTE £6.30: £1.90 £2.60 £3.80 (£54.60) Trio £165.20 OWNER Grid Thoroughbred Racing Partnership (WHITCOMBE) BRED Foxfield

**1777 Friendly Brave (USA)** gained due reward for some consistent performances and seemed well suited to the extra furlong. (5/1)
**893 Sizzling,** tried in blinkers last time, bounced back to form. (10/1)
**1715 Invocation,** due to go down 2lb, went smoothly to the front, but failed to hold on. (12/1)
**1680 Denbrae (IRE)** delivered a good challenge, but was being held at the death. (7/2)
**1715 Scissor Ridge** again gave a good account of himself and was due to be raised 1lb in future handicaps. (7/1)
**1536 Random** may not have had the run of the race, but did not look really unlucky. (9/1)

T/Plpt: £196.20 (74.51 Tckts). T/Qdpt: £65.20 (13.66 Tckts). KH

## 1506-SANDOWN (R-H) (Good to firm, Firm patches)
## Friday June 14th

WEATHER: warm WIND: almost nil

### 1959 SUN BANK MAIDEN STKS (2-Y.O) (Class D)

2-15 (2-17) **5f 6y** £3,257.50 (£985.00: £480.00: £227.50) Stalls: Low GOING minus 0.59 sec per fur (F)

| | | | | SP | RR | SF |
|---|---|---|---|---|---|---|
| 1774$^{8}$ | **Blue Ridge** (RHannon) **2-9-0** PatEddery(4) (chsd ldr: led over 2f out: r.o wl) | — | **1** | 7/4$^{1}$ | 78 | 29 |
| 1822$^{2}$ | **Cadeaux Cher** (BWHills) **2-9-0** MHills(3) (lw: led over 2f: unable qckn fnl f) | 4 | **2** | 5/1$^{2}$ | 65 | 16 |
| | **Sinecure (USA)** (JHMGosden) **2-9-0** JReid(7) (w'like: rdn & hdwy over 1f out: r.o one pce) | 1 | **3** | 11/2$^{3}$ | 62 | 13 |
| 1014$^{2}$ | **Swift Refusal** (MJHaynes) **2-8-9** CRutter(2) (lw: swvd lft s: a.p: rdn over 2f out: one pce) | 2 | **4** | 11/1 | 51 | 2 |
| | **Tigrello** (GLewis) **2-9-0** PaulEddery(8) (str: s.s: wl bhd over 3f: gd hdwy fnl f: r.o) | 1 | **5** | 8/1 | 53+ | 4 |
| | **Smokebush** (LordHuntingdon) **2-9-0** DHarrison(1) (str: bkwd: s.s: rdn & hdwy over 2f out: wknd fnl f) | 1 | **6** | 8/1 | 49 | — |
| 1315$^{6}$ | **M T Vessel** (JRJenkins) **2-9-0** TQuinn(6) (prom over 3f) | nk | **7** | 33/1 | 48 | — |
| 1519$^{5}$ | **Buzzby** (AGFoster) **2-9-0** SSanders(9) (b: bit bkwd: outpcd) | 2 | **8** | 25/1 | 42 | — |
| | **Commander Jones (IRE)** (BJMeehan) **2-9-0** BDoyle(5) (str: scope: bit bkwd: bhd fnl 3f) | ¾ | **9** | 8/1 | 40 | — |

(SP 116.9%) **9 Rn**

**61.02 secs** (1.22) CSF £10.71 TOTE £2.50: £1.10 £1.40 £2.50 (£4.90) Trio £5.40 OWNER Mr Saleh Al Homeizi (MARLBOROUGH) BRED Al Dahlawi Stud Co Ltd

OFFICIAL EXPLANATION **Tigrello: his jockey reported that his instructions were not to be hard on the colt which did not move well early on, but began to pick up on the rising ground over a furlong out and ran on through beaten horses. The trainer added that the colt has had trouble with sore shins and needs cut in the ground to show his best.**

**Blue Ridge** raced in second place until going on at halfway. Running on strongly, he disposed of the runner-up inside the final furlong. (7/4)
**1822 Cadeaux Cher**, making a quick reappearance, held the advantage to halfway. Grimly trying to hold on to the winner, he was put in his place in the final furlong. (5/1)
**Sinecure (USA)**, a plain individual, was pushed along to pick up ground below the distance but, despite staying on for third, never looked like threatening the winner. (11/2: 5/2-6/1)
**1014 Swift Refusal**, who jinked badly soon after leaving the stalls, was never far away, but failed to quicken in the last two furlongs. (11/1: 7/1-12/1)
**Tigrello**, a sturdy, close-coupled colt, threw his race away with a very slow start. Soon tailed off with no chance, he found his stride below the distance and ran on really strongly to finish an encouraging fifth in the circumstances. Connections say that he needs an easier surface than this for his sore shins. Given those conditions, he certainly looks up to landing a race. (8/1: 3/1-10/1)
**Smokebush** looked far from fit. Pushed along to take closer order at halfway, he had shot his bolt entering the final furlong. (8/1: 6/1-9/1)
**Commander Jones (IRE)** (8/1: 9/2-10/1)

### 1960 SBJ GROUP MAIDEN STKS (2-Y.O) (Class D)

2-50 (2-51) **7f 16y** £3,533.75 (£1,070.00: £522.50: £248.75) Stalls: High GOING minus 0.59 sec per fur (F)

| | | | | SP | RR | SF |
|---|---|---|---|---|---|---|
| | **Putra (USA)** (PFICole) **2-9-0** TQuinn(4) (leggy: scope: lw: chsd ldr: led over 1f out: pushed out) | — | **1** | 9/2$^{2}$ | 96+ | 58 |
| | **Benny The Dip (USA)** (JHMGosden) **2-9-0** AGarth(5) (scope: w'like: s.s: rdn & hdwy 2f out: chsd wnr fnl f: no imp) | 3½ | **2** | 8/1 | 88 | 50 |
| 1191$^{4}$ | **Powder River** (RHannon) **2-9-0b$^{1}$** PatEddery(2) (lw: led over 5f: wknd fnl f) | 5 | **3** | 13/2 | 77 | 39 |
| 1694$^{4}$ | **Regal Patrol** (MRStoute) **2-9-0** MRoberts(7) (a.p: rdn over 2f out: wknd fnl f) | 2 | **4** | 11/8$^{1}$ | 72 | 34 |
| | **Bandore (IRE)** (DRLoder) **2-9-0** JReid(8) (scope: lw: a.p: rdn over 2f out: wknd fnl f) | 1¼ | **5** | 5/1$^{3}$ | 69 | 31 |
| | **Sheer Face** (WRMuir) **2-9-0** WWoods(6) (str: rdn & hdwy 2f out: wknd 1f out) | 1¼ | **6** | 20/1 | 67 | 29 |
| | **Head Gardener (IRE)** (JLDunlop) **2-9-0** TSprake(1) (w'like: bkwd: s.s: a bhd) | 1½ | **7** | 16/1 | 63 | 25 |
| | **Lady Godiva** (MJPolglase) **2-8-9** DHarrison(10) (unf: a bhd) | ½ | **8** | 33/1 | 57 | 19 |
| 1694$^{3}$ | **Maraud** (RWArmstrong) **2-9-0** MHills(9) (bhd fnl 4f) | ½ | **9** | 16/1 | 61 | 23 |

(SP 120.9%) **9 Rn**

**1m 27.95** (0.20 under 2y best) (-0.65) CSF £38.15 TOTE £4.80: £1.50 £2.90 £1.30 (£28.30) Trio £52.50 OWNER H R H Sultan Ahmad Shah (WHATCOMBE) BRED John Sullivan and Hargus Sexton

**Putra (USA)**, a tall good-looking colt, made a highly promising debut. Racing in second place in an extremely fast-run race, he overhauled the long-time leader approaching the final furlong, and needed only to be nudged along to secure victory and smash the juvenile record set thirteen years ago. There are more races to be won with him. (9/2: op 2/1)

**Benny The Dip (USA)** lost ground at the start and was unable to live with the blistering pace. Pushed along to pick up ground a quarter of a mile from home, he took second place entering the final furlong and, although having no chance of reeling in the winner, finished well clear of the rest. With this experience under his belt, he should not be difficult to win with. (8/1)
**1191 Powder River**, in blinkers for the first time, looked very well beforehand. Setting a blistering pace, he quickly had the field strung out. Overhauled below the distance, he not surprisingly had little left in the locker. (13/2)
**1694 Regal Patrol** again disappointed. Racing in fourth place, he was being pushed along over quarter of a mile from home, but did not look completely co-operative and had nothing more to give in the final furlong. (11/8)
**Bandore (IRE)** looked very well, but his stable has not been really firing this year. Ridden along, he tired in the last 200 yards. (5/1)

## 1961 DEVITT DA DIAMOND JUBILEE H'CAP (0-100) (3-Y.O+) (Class C)

3-20 (3-25) **1m 2f 7y** £7,165.00 (£2,170.00: £1,060.00: £505.00) Stalls: High GOING minus 0.59 sec per fur (F)

| | | | | SP | RR | SF |
|---|---|---|---|---|---|---|
| 1193[2] | **Major Change (87)** (RHannon) **4-9-7**(3) DaneO'Neill(7) (swtg: hdwy 3f out: chsd wnr over 1f out: hrd rdn: led last stride) | — | **1** | 8/1 | 97 | 69 |
| 1841[3] | **Fahs (USA) (65)** (RAkehurst) **4-8-2** SSanders(4) (led 9f out: clr 3f out: rdn over 2f out: hdd last stride) | s.h | **2** | 5/1[2] | 75 | 47 |
| 1193[8] | **Sheer Danzig (IRE) (85)** (RWArmstrong) **4-9-8** WWoods(8) (rdn & hdwy over 1f out: r.o ins fnl f) | 2½ | **3** | 10/1 | 91 | 63 |
| 1440[3] | **Kings Assembly (81)** (PWHarris) **4-9-4** GHind(9) (a.p: hrd rdn over 2f out: one pce) | 2 | **4** | 7/1[3] | 84 | 56 |
| 1807[2] | **Master Charter (76)** (MrsJRRamsden) **4-8-13** PatEddery(6) (swtg: hdwy over 1f out: nvr nrr) | 2½ | **5** | 2/1[1] | 75 | 47 |
| 1686[2] | **Silently (79)** (IABalding) **4-9-2** MHills(1) (nvr nr to chal) | 5 | **6** | 5/1[2] | 70 | 42 |
| 1019[10] | **Horesti (73)** (CEBrittain) **4-8-10** BDoyle(2) (lw: prom 6f) | 4 | **7** | 25/1 | 57 | 29 |
| | **Willie Conquer (78)** (RAkehurst) **4-9-1** BThomson(3) (led 1f: wknd 3f out) | 1 | **8** | 12/1 | 61 | 33 |
| 1440[6] | **Menas Gold (84)** (SDow) **4-9-7** MRoberts(5) (a bhd) | 1¼ | **9** | 10/1 | 65 | 37 |
| | | | | (SP 120.0%) | | **9 Rn** |

**2m 5.71** (-0.99) CSF £45.86 CT £376.30 TOTE £9.70: £2.10 £1.50 £3.40 (£26.20) Trio £45.20 OWNER Mrs C. J. Powell (MARLBOROUGH) BRED Shanbally House Stud
**1193 Major Change** began to pick up ground early in the straight, but had it all to do as the leader had shot clear. Taking second place below the distance, he gradually overhauled his rival and got on top right on the line. (8/1)
**1841 Fahs (USA)**, making a quick reappearance, was given a highly enterprisingly ride and failed by only a whisker to succeed. Soon at the head of affairs, he was asked to quicken up the tempo in the straight and soon shot clear. The race looked in the bag in the final furlong, but for the winner coming with a wet sail right on the line. He is a winner without a penalty. (5/1)
**Sheer Danzig (IRE)** at last got going below the distance but, despite running on up the hill, was never going to get there in time. (10/1)
**1440 Kings Assembly** was shown the persuader over two furlongs from home, but could only go up and down in the same place. (7/1)
**1807 Master Charter**, taking a step up in trip, was not given a hard time but stayed on from below the distance to be nearest at the line. (2/1)
**Willie Conquer** (12/1: 8/1-14/1)
**1440 Menas Gold** (10/1: 8/1-12/1)

## 1962 SUN LIFE OF CANADA H'CAP (0-90) (3-Y.O+) (Class C)

3-55 (3-57) **7f 16y** £7,067.50 (£2,140.00: £1,045.00: £497.50) Stalls: High GOING minus 0.59 sec per fur (F)

| | | | | SP | RR | SF |
|---|---|---|---|---|---|---|
| 1775[3] | **Rakis (IRE) (72)** (MrsLStubbs) **6-9-2** JFEgan(11) (lw: hdwy over 5f out: led wl over 1f out: hrd rdn: r.o wl) | — | **1** | 9/2[1] | 85 | 67 |
| 1680[3] | **Neuwest (USA) (78)** (NJHWalker) **4-9-5**(3) JStack(9) (lw: hdwy over 1f out: r.o ins fnl f) | 2½ | **2** | 9/1 | 85 | 67 |
| 1703[3] | **Duello (64)** (MBlanshard) **5-8-8** MRoberts(6) (rdn over 2f out: hdwy over 1f out: r.o ins fnl f) | 1½ | **3** | 6/1[3] | 68 | 50 |
| 1775[7] | **Shayim (USA) (75)** (RHannon) **4-9-5** PatEddery(10) (lw: led over 5f out tl wl over 1f out: unable qckn) | 1¼ | **4** | 12/1 | 76 | 58 |
| 1789[3] | **Sycamore Lodge (IRE) (68)** (MrsJRRamsden) **5-8-12** JReid(8) (lw: hdwy over 1f out: nvr nrr) | ½ | **5** | 11/2[2] | 68 | 50 |
| 1018[13] | **Elite Hope (USA) (78)** (CREgerton) **4-9-3**(5) RHavlin(5) (hdwy over 2f out: ev ch wl over 1f out: hrd rdn: wknd fnl f) | 2½ | **6** | 20/1 | 72 | 54 |
| 1018[4] | **Chickawicka (IRE) (83)** (BPalling) **5-9-13** TSprake(1) (lw: hld up: rdn over 2f out: wknd over 1f out) | nk | **7** | 9/1 | 77 | 59 |
| *1048[5]* | **Ertlon (80)** (CEBrittain) **6-9-10** BDoyle(2) (lw: prom over 5f) | 7 | **8** | 20/1 | 58 | 40 |
| 1442* | **Scharnhorst (78)** (SDow) **4-9-3**(5) ADaly(4) (lw: hld up: rdn over 2f out: sn wknd) | 1¼ | **9** | 11/2[2] | 53 | 35 |
| 1628[11] | **Forentia (87)** (JRFanshawe) **3-9-7** DHarrison(12) (swtg: hld up: rdn over 2f out: wknd over 1f out) | nk | **10** | 10/1 | 61 | 33 |
| 1703[12] | **Orange Place (IRE) (75)** (TJNaughton) **5-9-5** MHills(7) (lw: b.hind: led over 1f: wkng whn n.m.r over 2f out) | 13 | **11** | 14/1 | 20 | 2 |
| 1481[7] | **Sand Star (70)** (DHaydnJones) **4-9-0** AMackay(3) (s.s: a t.o) | dist | **12** | 14/1 | — | — |
| | | | | (SP 122.9%) | | **12 Rn** |

**1m 27.35** (-1.25) CSF £42.70 CT £228.44 TOTE £6.00: £2.60 £3.20 £2.30 (£28.00) Trio £89.20 OWNER Mr P. G. Shorrock (WARTHILL) BRED The Mount Coote Partnership
WEIGHT FOR AGE 3yo-10lb
**1775 Rakis (IRE)** made the journey down from Yorkshire pay off. Soon in a handy position, he went on early in the final quarter-mile and, responding to pressure, kept on well. (9/2)
**1680 Neuwest (USA)** again looked really well. Only finding his feet from below the distance, he ran on for second but was unable to get to the winner in time. (9/1)
**1703 Duello**, ridden along at the back of the field over a quarter of a mile from home, put in some good work in the last furlong and a half but, by then, it was all too late. This was good effort considering both his wins have come in the mud. (6/1)
**1775 Shayim (USA)** was soon at the head of affairs. Collared early in the final quarter-mile, he failed to find another gear. (12/1)
**1789 Sycamore Lodge (IRE)** stayed on in the final furlong and a half, but found it all over bar the shouting. (11/2)
**Elite Hope (USA)** moved up over quarter of a mile from home. With every chance over a furlong out, she came under hard riding, but her boy had problems with his whip and they faded in the final furlong. (20/1)
**Forentia** (10/1: 7/1-11/1)
**1354* Orange Place (IRE)** (14/1: 10/1-16/1)

## 1963 POLICYHOLDERS MAIDEN STKS (3-Y.O) (Class D)

4-30 (4-32) **1m 2f 7y** £3,728.75 (£1,130.00: £552.50: £263.75) Stalls: High GOING minus 0.59 sec per fur (F)

| | | | | SP | RR | SF |
|---|---|---|---|---|---|---|
| | **Shanaladee** (MRStoute) **3-9-0** TQuinn(8) (w'like: scope: hdwy & n.m.r over 2f out: led over 1f out: pushed out) | — | **1** | 12/1[3] | 72 | 41 |
| 1627[2] | **Russian Request (IRE)** (MRStoute) **3-8-9** JReid(9) (lw: a.p: led over 2f out: edgd rt & hdd over 1f out: unable qckn ins fnl f) | 2 | **2** | 8/13[1] | 64 | 33 |
| 1670[7] | **Mallooh** (JHMGosden) **3-9-0** GHind(5) (hdwy over 2f out: ev ch wl over 1f out: one pce) | 4 | **3** | 6/1[2] | 62 | 31 |
| 1530[10] | **Attalos** (HRACecil) **3-9-0** PatEddery(4) (lw: led over 8f out tl over 2f out: 4th & btn whn n.m.r on ins over 1f out) | 5 | **4** | 6/1[2] | 55 | 24 |

| | | | | | | |
|---|---|---|---|---|---|---|
| $730^{11}$ | **Hever Golf Classic** (TJNaughton) **3-9-0** PaulEddery(3) (bit bkwd: nvr nr to chal) ....½ | **5** | 40/1 | 54 | 23 |
| $860^{9}$ | **Windyedge (USA)** (BWHills) **3-8-7**(7) GBrace(2) (lw: prom over 7f) ....hd | **6** | 33/1 | 54 | 23 |
| | **Notaire (IRE)** (IABalding) **3-9-0** MHills(7) (w'like: bit bkwd: a bhd) ....1½ | **7** | 12/1$^{3}$ | 51 | 20 |
| $1514^{10}$ | **Lord Ellangowan (IRE) (41)** (RIngram) **3-9-0** WWoods(6) (lw: a bhd) ....6 | **8** | 50/1 | 42 | 11 |
| $849^{3}$ | **Noble Lord** (RHBuckler) **3-9-0** CRutter(1) (lw: led over 1f: wknd over 2f out) ....2½ | **9** | 33/1 | 38 | 7 |
| | | | (SP 116.1%) **9 Rn** | | |

**2m 8.05** (1.35) CSF £19.35 TOTE £12.10: £1.90 £1.10 £2.00 (£6.10) Trio £16.10 OWNER Maktoum Al Maktoum (NEWMARKET) BRED Gainsborough Stud Management Ltd

**Shanaladee** overturned his stable-companion who was the hot favourite. Easing into the action over a quarter of a mile from home, he went on approaching the final furlong and needed only to be nudged along to dispose of his rival in the last 100 yards. (12/1: op 4/1)
**1627 Russian Request (IRE)**, tackling a longer trip, gained a narrow advantage over a quarter of a mile from home. Headed below the distance, she grimly tried to live with her rival but was put in her place in the last 100 yards. The slow pace was probably not in her favour and it was later reported that she raced with no shoes on her hind feet. (8/13)
**Mallooh** moved up to have every chance well over a furlong from home before tapped for toe. (6/1: 6/1-4/1)
**Attalos**, an imposing individual who is half-brother to Backgammon, was soon at the head of affairs. Collared over a quarter of a mile from home, he was beginning to go in reverse when tightened up for room below the distance. (6/1: tchd 9/1)
**Notaire (IRE)** (12/1: 6/1-14/1)

## 1964 BASING VIEW CLAIMING STKS (3-Y.O+) (Class F)

5-00 (5-03) **5f 6y** £2,879.00 (£872.00: £426.00: £203.00) Stalls: Low GOING minus 0.59 sec per fur (F)

| | | | SP | RR | SF |
|---|---|---|---|---|---|
| $1430^{9}$ | **Lord High Admiral (CAN) (82)** (MJHeaton-Ellis) **8-9-5** MRoberts(7) (mde virtually all: pushed out) ....— | **1** | 7/2$^{2}$ | 76 | 55 |
| | **Spaniards Close (96)** (PJMakin) **8-9-10** MHills(5) (lw: hld up: hrd rdn over 1f out: r.o ins fnl f) ....1¼ | **2** | 11/8$^{1}$ | 77 | 56 |
| $1598^{3}$ | **La Suquet (67)** (NTinkler) **4-9-0** PatEddery(8) (hld up: hrd rdn over 1f out: r.o one pce) ....nk | **3** | 5/1$^{3}$ | 66 | 45 |
| $1364^{2}$ | **Metal Boys (56)** (MissLCSiddall) **9-8-11**(3) PMcCabe(2) (b.off hind: lost pl over 2f out: rallied fnl f: r.o) ....2½ | **4** | 12/1 | 58 | 37 |
| $1592^{6}$ | **Double Impression (IRE)** (JLHarris) **3-8-4** PRobinson(9) (hdwy over 2f out: wknd fnl f) ....½ | **5** | 20/1 | 54 | 26 |
| $1715^{9}$ | **Agwa (68)** (RJO'Sullivan) **7-9-0** SSanders(4) (spd over 2f) ....1½ | **6** | 10/1 | 52 | 31 |
| $1684^{3}$ | **Risking** (GLewis) **3-8-2**(3) AWhelan(3) (b: lw: w wnr: hrd rdn over 1f out: wknd fnl f) ....hd | **7** | 12/1 | 49 | 21 |
| $1351^{5}$ | **Cassimere (58)** (MajorDNChappell) **4-8-7** WWoods(1) (s.s: a bhd) ....5 | **8** | 20/1 | 29 | 8 |
| | | | (SP 115.0%) **8 Rn** | | |

**59.71 secs** (-0.09) CSF £8.48 TOTE £5.30: £1.80 £1.40 £1.10 (£4.00) Trio £5.10 OWNER Elite Racing Club (WROUGHTON) BRED Windfields Farm

WEIGHT FOR AGE 3yo-7lb

**1430 Lord High Admiral (CAN)**, bucking and kicking in the paddock, bounced back to form. Making virtually all the running, he needed only to be nudged along to have the situation in hand. (7/2)
**Spaniards Close** was an uneasy favourite on this reappearance. Held up travelling nicely, he was asked for his effort below the distance but, despite running on up the hill, was never going to catch the winner. He should soon be winning. (11/8: 4/5-6/4)
**1598 La Suquet** chased the leaders. Under pressure below the distance, she stayed on up the hill, and only just lost out for second prize. (5/1)
**1364 Metal Boys** got rather outpaced at halfway, but did stay on again in the final furlong. (12/1)

## 1965 SURREY RACING H'CAP (0-70) (4-Y.O+) (Class E)

5-35 (5-40) **1m 3f 91y** £3,436.25 (£1,040.00: £507.50: £241.25) Stalls: High GOING minus 0.59 sec per fur (F)

| | | | SP | RR | SF |
|---|---|---|---|---|---|
| $1625^{4}$ | **Dance King (62)** (RHarris) **4-9-1**(5) ADaly(1) (hld up: led 2f out: hrd rdn: r.o wl) ....— | **1** | 10/1 | 72 | 50 |
| $1655^{*}$ | **Fabulous Mtoto (46)** (MSSaunders) **6-8-4** 5x RPrice(14) (b: 7th whn stumbled on ins bnd 10f out: hdwy over 2f out: ev ch over 1f out: r.o wl) ....nk | **2** | 5/1$^{2}$ | 56 | 34 |
| $1514^{5}$ | **Silver Hunter (USA) (48)** (GCBravery) **5-8-6** MHills(7) (lw: rdn over 2f out: hdwy over 1f out: r.o wl) ....1¼ | **3** | 10/1 | 56 | 34 |
| $1524^{4}$ | **Dont Shoot Fairies (70)** (CEBrittain) **4-10-0** BDoyle(8) (w ldr: ev ch over 1f out: unable qckn) ....1 | **4** | 8/1 | 76 | 54 |
| | **Rising Spray (49)** (CAHorgan) **5-8-2**(5) AmandaSanders(9) (swtg: lost pl 6f out: rallied over 2f out: r.o) ....nk | **5** | 16/1 | 55 | 33 |
| | **Flight Master (64)** (PJMakin) **4-9-8** SSanders(10) (b: rdn & hdwy over 2f out: one pce) ....3½ | **6** | 10/1 | 65 | 43 |
| $1472^{9}$ | **Jean de Florette (USA) (38)** (RCSpicer) **5-7-10** AMackay(5) (hdwy over 1f out: nvr nrr) ....1½ | **7** | 25/1 | 37 | 15 |
| $1685^{10}$ | **Teen Jay (63)** (BJLlewellyn) **6-9-7** VSlattery(3) (lw: nvr nr to chal) ....¾ | **8** | 14/1 | 61 | 39 |
| $1486^{3}$ | **Koathary (USA) (55)** (LGCottrell) **5-8-13** MRoberts(2) (lw: a.p: led over 3f out to 2f out: wknd over 1f out) ....2½ | **9** | 4/1$^{1}$ | 49 | 27 |
| $1640^{8}$ | **Triple Tie (USA) (38)** (MBlanshard) **5-7-5**(5) CAdamson(12) (swtg: hdwy 7f out: wknd over 4f out) ....hd | **10** | 33/1 | 32 | 10 |
| $1655^{6}$ | **Rock The Barney (IRE) (51)** (PBurgoyne) **7-8-9** DRMcCabe(13) (lw: hld up: rdn 6f out: eased whn btn over 1f out) ....3 | **11** | 4/1$^{1}$ | 41 | 19 |
| $1486^{10}$ | **Newport Knight (63)** (RAkehurst) **5-9-0**(7) DDenby(15) (b.off fore: b.off hind: led 8f) ....1¼ | **12** | 12/1 | 51 | 29 |
| *$1719^{14}$* | **Tauten (IRE) (59)** (PBurgoyne) **6-9-0**(3) JStack(11) (a bhd: t.o) ....dist | **13** | 16/1 | — | — |
| | **Smocking (45)** (MissKMGeorge) **6-8-0**(3)ow7 DarrenMoffatt(6) (prom 8f: t.o) ....1¾ | **14** | 33/1 | — | — |
| | ***Lidhama (USA) (59)*** (GLewis) **4-9-3** PaulEddery(4) (Withdrawn not under Starter's orders).... | **W** | 6/1$^{3}$ | — | — |
| | | | (SP 145.2%) **14 Rn** | | |

**2m 24.29** (0.89) CSF £60.15 CT £488.96 TOTE £17.50: £4.20 £1.80 £2.90 (£24.20) Trio £128.50 OWNER Mr Terry Connors (NEWMARKET) BRED A. Aikin

LONG HANDICAP Jean de Florette (USA) 7-3 Triple Tie (USA) 7-9 Smocking 6-13

STEWARDS' ENQUIRY Price fined £60 (obj. to Dance King by Price overruled).

**1625 Dance King** chased the leaders. Sent on over quarter of a mile from home, he responded to pressure and just managed to keep the runner-up at bay. (10/1: op 5/1)
**1655* Fabulous Mtoto**, who clipped the heels of another rival turning into the back straight, moved up over quarter of a mile from home. Throwing down his challenge below the distance, he only just failed to overhaul the winner. (5/1)
**1514 Silver Hunter (USA)** at last found his feet from below the distance but, despite running on strongly, was never going to get there in time. (10/1)
**1524 Dont Shoot Fairies** disputed the lead. Still in with every chance over a furlong from home, he was then tapped for toe. (8/1)
**Rising Spray** lost his pitch turning out of the back straight. Trying to get back into it over a quarter of a mile from home, he ran on and only just missed out on the prizemoney. He remains a maiden. (16/1)
**Teen Jay** (14/1: 10/1-16/1)
**Newport Knight** (12/1: op 6/1)

T/Plpt: £28.70 (450.27 Tckts). T/Qdpt: £9.80 (84.36 Tckts). AK

# 1716-SOUTHWELL (L-H) (Standard)

## Friday June 14th

Race 6: stalls low due to inj horse
WEATHER: fine WIND: almost nil

## 1966 AMETHYST AMATEUR H'CAP (0-65) (3-Y.O+) (Class G)

2-00 (2-00) **7f (Fibresand)** £2,070.00 (£570.00: £270.00) Stalls: Low GOING minus 0.07 sec per fur (STD)

| Form | Horse | Dist | Pos | SP | RR | SF |
|---|---|---|---|---|---|---|
| 1685* | **Montone (IRE) (54)** (JRJenkins) **6-10-10v**(5) 6x DrMMannish(12) (chsd ldrs: led 2f out: clr fnl f: drvn out) | — | **1** | 5/2[1] | 67 | 52 |
| *1809[6]* | **Ring the Chief (38)** (MDIUsher) **4-9-8**(5) MrsAUsher(11) (lw: b: a.p: chsd wnr fnl 2f: no imp) | 3½ | **2** | 14/1 | 43 | 28 |
| *1811[6]* | **David James' Girl (54)** (ABailey) **4-10-10**(5) MissBridgetGatehouse(6) (lw: sn pushed along & bhd: hdwy over 2f out: one pce fnl f) | ¾ | **3** | 9/2[3] | 57 | 42 |
| 1789[5] | **Pc's Cruiser (IRE) (46)** (JLEyre) **4-10-7v** MissDianaJones(7) (dwlt: hdwy over 1f out: nvr able to chal) | 3 | **4** | 4/1[2] | 42 | 27 |
| 1312[11] | **Orange And Blue (43)** (MissJFCraze) **3-9-3c**(5) MrWWenyon(8) (w ldrs: led over 2f out: sn hdd & btn) | 4 | **5** | 25/1 | 30 | 5 |
| *1601[5]* | **Flashfeet (50)** (KBishop) **6-10-6**(5) MissAPurdy(9) (lw: s.s: nvr nrr) | 2½ | **6** | 12/1 | 32 | 17 |
| | **Spanish Stripper (USA) (43)** (MCChapman) **5-10-4** MrsSBosley(2) (swtg: led over 4f) | 1¼ | **7** | 14/1 | 22 | 7 |
| 1763[4] | **Public Way (IRE) (45)** (NChamberlain) **6-10-1**(5) MissCMetcalfe(5) (b.off hind: dwlt: nvr rchd ldrs) | nk | **8** | 16/1 | 23 | 8 |
| | **Star of Gold (60)** (CREgerton) **4-11-7** JCulloty(3) (w ldr 4f: sn wknd) | ½ | **9** | 7/1 | 37 | 22 |
| *1718[12]* | **Kismetim (45)** (DWChapman) **6-10-6v[1]** MissRClark(10) (in tch: effrt & hung rt over 2f out: sn btn) | 1½ | **10** | 25/1 | 19 | 4 |
| 1196[8] | **Blow Dry (IRE) (50)** (MartynWane) **6-10-6**(5) MrRDGreen(4) (chsd ldrs tl wknd 3f out) | ¾ | **11** | 10/1 | 22 | 7 |
| *347[9]* | **Caherass Court (IRE) (33)** (BPreece) **5-9-3**(5)ow1 MissLBoswell(1) (sn chsng ldrs: rdn & wknd 3f out) | 10 | **12** | 33/1 | — | — |

(SP 125.9%) **12 Rn**

**1m 32.7** (5.90) CSF £36.69 CT £148.19 TOTE £2.70: £1.10 £3.70 £1.90 (£12.40) Trio £48.20 OWNER Mr B. Shirazi (ROYSTON) BRED Sean Gorman
WEIGHT FOR AGE 3yo-10lb

**1685* Montone (IRE)**, in the form of his life, was kept right up to his work once in front, but never looked likely to be beaten. (5/2: 6/4-11/4)
**654 Ring the Chief**, who shows plenty of knee-action, ran his best race of the year. He seems to be kept to artificial surfaces now. (14/1)
**1602 David James' Girl**, a poor mover, ran well despite finding the trip on the sharp side. (9/2)
**1789 Pc's Cruiser (IRE)**, after four runs on turf, lost only a length or so at the start but the faster early pace on this surface soon saw him well off the lead. (4/1)
**Orange And Blue** tied up badly in the straight and has yet to prove she gets this trip. (25/1)
**Flashfeet** could win a small race if he could be cured of missing the break. (12/1)

## 1967 DIAMOND CLAIMING STKS (4-Y.O+) (Class F)

2-30 (2-33) **1m 6f (Fibresand)** £2,381.00 (£656.00: £311.00) Stalls: High GOING minus 0.07 sec per fur (STD)

| Form | Horse | Dist | Pos | SP | RR | SF |
|---|---|---|---|---|---|---|
| 1763[3] | **Pharly Dancer (66)** (WWHaigh) **7-8-4**(5) LNewton(5) (hld up: hdwy 7f out: led on bit 5f out: edgd rt over 2f out: sn rdn & r.o) | — | **1** | 7/4[1] | 71 | 13 |
| *1717[3]* | **Ready to Draw (IRE) (45)** (RJO'Sullivan) **7-8-1** DBiggs(8) (b: lw: hld up: hdwy 5f out: kpt on one pce fnl 2f) | 5 | **2** | 9/2[3] | 57 | — |
| *1458[3]* | **Red Phantom (IRE) (66)** (SMellor) **4-9-3** MWigham(10) (bhd: pushed along & hdwy 8f out: rdn 3f out: one pce) | 2½ | **3** | 100/30[2] | 70 | 12 |
| 1534[8] | **Sinclair Lad (IRE) (35)** (RJHodges) **8-7-12b**(5) PPMurphy(11) (lw: in tch: hdwy 7f out: rdn & wknd over 3f out) | 15 | **4** | 16/1 | 39 | — |
| | **Urban Lily** (RJHodges) **6-8-0b** FNorton(4) (lw: bhd: rdn 5f out: nvr trbld ldrs) | 25 | **5** | 16/1 | 8 | — |
| *1458[8]* | **Broom Isle (60)** (DBurchell) **8-8-4** DeanMcKeown(2) (prom: ev ch 5f out: sn wknd) | 9 | **6** | 9/2[3] | 1 | — |
| 1676[14] | **Never Time (IRE) (32)** (MrsVAAconley) **4-8-11** MDeering(7) (prom: led 7f out to 5f out: sn wknd) | 10 | **7** | 50/1 | — | — |
| *1488[5]* | **Zesti (43)** (TTClement) **4-8-5** MFenton(6) (b: led 7f: sn wknd) | 20 | **8** | 25/1 | — | — |
| *1717[12]* | **Kirkadian** (NBycroft) **6-8-12** AlexGreaves(9) (sn bhd) | 25 | **9** | 50/1 | — | — |
| | **Gildoran Palace** (TTBill) **5-9-7** WHollick(1) (sn t.o: virtually p.u fnl 3f) | dist | **10** | 40/1 | — | — |
| *1719[12]* | **Tip it In (35)** (ASmith) **7-9-7** MBirch(3) (b: bit bkwd: chsd ldrs: wkng whn p.u over 3f out) | | **P** | 12/1 | — | — |

(SP 125.5%) **11 Rn**

**3m 12.6** (13.60) CSF £10.64 TOTE £2.60: £1.10 £1.40 £1.90 (£6.20) Trio £7.90 OWNER Mr A. Marucci (MALTON) BRED Stud-On-The-Chart
**OFFICIAL EXPLANATION Tip It In: finished distressed.**

**1763 Pharly Dancer**, back on his favoured surface, broke a frustrating run of placings. Travelling much the best when hitting the front, he started to hang as pressure was applied early in the straight, but was given a cracking ride and, once balanced, the issue was beyond doubt. (7/4)
**1717 Ready to Draw (IRE)** looked exceptionally well and ran soundly, but would have met the winner on 13lb better terms in a handicap. (9/2: op 8/1)
**1458 Red Phantom (IRE)**, taken down steadily, never travelled particularly well. (100/30: 7/4-7/2)
**1347 Sinclair Lad (IRE)**, keen to post, had shot his bolt by the home turn. (16/1)
**Tip it In** (12/1: 33/1-50/1)

## 1968 LANGLEYS INSURANCE CLAIMS DEPARTMENT MEDIAN AUCTION MAIDEN STKS (2-Y.O) (Class F)

3-05 (3-06) **5f (Fibresand)** £2,381.00 (£656.00: £311.00) Stalls: High GOING minus 0.07 sec per fur (STD)

| Form | Horse | Dist | Pos | SP | RR | SF |
|---|---|---|---|---|---|---|
| 1760[5] | **Calchou** (CWFairhurst) **2-8-9** DeanMcKeown(3) (mde all: clr over 1f out: pushed out) | — | **1** | 9/1 | 55 | 2 |
| *1603[5]* | **Red Test (USA)** (WAO'Gorman) **2-9-0** EmmaO'Gorman(4) (dwlt: sn chsng ldrs: rdn & no imp fnl f) | 2½ | **2** | 5/2[2] | 52 | — |
| 1479[4] | **Jack Says** (TDEasterby) **2-9-0** MBirch(5) (hdwy over 1f out: nvr rchd ldrs) | 4 | **3** | 11/2[3] | 39 | — |
| 1408[6] | **Shotley Princess** (NBycroft) **2-8-9** AlexGreaves(1) (in tch: no hdwy fnl 2f) | 5 | **4** | 25/1 | 18 | — |
| 1869[5] | **Miss Barcelona (IRE)** (MJPolglase) **2-8-9** WHollick(9) (chsd ldrs 3f: sn rdn & btn) | 1¼ | **5** | 14/1 | 14 | — |
| *1491[2]* | **Make Ready** (JNeville) **2-8-9** FNorton(10) (lw: s.i.s: nvr rchd ldrs) | 10 | **6** | 9/1 | — | — |
| | **Emma's Risk** (RJRWilliams) **2-8-4**(5) LNewton(6) (leggy: unf: sn outpcd) | 1¼ | **7** | 8/1 | — | — |
| 1086[4] | **Lucky Oakwood (USA)** (MBell) **2-8-9** MFenton(2) (dwlt: sn trcking ldrs: wknd & eased 2f out) | hd | **8** | 7/4[1] | — | — |
| *858[6]* | **Nefertiti** (RFMarvin) **2-8-9** SDWilliams(7) (lw: sn pushed along: in tch over 2f: hung lft & virtually p.u appr fnl f) | 17 | **9** | 20/1 | — | — |
| | ***Rising Glory*** (SRBowring) **2-9-0** ACulhane(8) (Withdrawn not under Starter's orders: uns rdr in stalls) | | **W** | 12/1 | — | — |

(SP 134.4%) **9 Rn**

**62.0 secs** (5.00) CSF £31.79 TOTE £12.60: £3.20 £1.30 £2.30 (£7.80) Trio £37.40 OWNER Mr W. J. Dobson (MIDDLEHAM) BRED George Hinnigan

STEWARDS' ENQUIRY Williams susp. 24-25/6/96 (improper & incorrect use of whip). McKeown fined £200 (failing to keep to the draw).
**OFFICIAL EXPLANATION Lucky Oakford (USA): the jockey reported that the filly began to hang right and would not let herself down.**
**1760 Calchou**, whose inability to settle had been costing her dear, was mounted on the track and then allowed to bowl along. This clearly did the trick, although her rider was punished for not keeping straight. (9/1: 6/1-10/1)
**1603 Red Test (USA)** again missed the break but did stick on to the end, although not given an unduly hard time after swishing his tail entering the final furlong. (5/2)
**1479 Jack Says** did his best work at the end and looks to need further. (11/2: 7/2-6/1)
**Shotley Princess** got slightly warm and moved freely to post, but could never get into the race. (25/1)
**1331 Miss Barcelona (IRE)** raced towards the stands' side which seems slower at the moment, but only tied up below the distance. (14/1)
**1491 Make Ready** again hindered her chance with a moderate start. (9/1)
**Emma's Risk** (8/1: 6/1-10/1)
**1086 Lucky Oakwood (USA)** (7/4: 6/4-5/2)

## 1969 JAMES LATHAM MIDLAND/CSC CABERBOARD MEDIAN AUCTION MAIDEN STKS (I) (3-Y.O) (Class E)
3-35 (3-35) **1m (Fibresand)** £2,717.90 (£807.20: £382.60: £170.30) Stalls: Low GOING minus 0.07 sec per fur (STD)

| Form | Horse | Dist | Pos | SP | RR | SF |
|---|---|---|---|---|---|---|
| 1608$^{10}$ | **Mercury (IRE)** (JAGlover) **3-9-0** SDWilliams(9) (plld hrd: trckd ldrs: led over 2f out: clr over 1f out: easily) | — | **1** | 8/1 | 77+ | 25 |
| 1434$^{8}$ | **Newbridge Boy** (MGMeagher) **3-9-0** FNorton(8) (led 3f: outpcd 3f out: styd on appr fnl f) | 12 | **2** | 3/1$^{1}$ | 53 | 1 |
| *856*$^{6}$ | **Tonto** (CWThornton) **3-9-0** DeanMcKeown(6) (lw: plld hrd: in tch: effrt 3f out: r.o fnl f) | nk | **3** | 12/1 | 52 | — |
| 1649$^{5}$ | **Magic Heights** (JEBanks) **3-9-0** DBiggs(5) (hld up: rdn 3f out: styd on appr fnl f) | 1½ | **4** | 4/1$^{2}$ | 49 | — |
| *1719*$^{4}$ | **Hadadabble (46)** (PatMitchell) **3-8-9** NCarlisle(3) (chsd ldrs: rdn & btn 3f out) | 2½ | **5** | 4/1$^{2}$ | 39 | — |
| | **New Technique (FR)** (KMcAuliffe) **3-8-9** JFanning(4) (dwlt: led after 3f: hdd over 2f out: wknd ins fnl f) | 5 | **6** | 25/1 | 29 | — |
| | **Bites (45)** (TTBill) **3-8-9** WHollick(7) (bit bkwd: chsd ldrs over 4f) | 5 | **7** | 20/1 | 19 | — |
| | **Larry Lambrusco (62)** (RChampion) **3-9-0** AMcGlone(2) (lw: bhd fnl 4f) | 20 | **8** | 13/2 | — | — |
| | **Qualitair Beauty** (WAO'Gorman) **3-8-9** EmmaO'Gorman(1) (unf: bit bkwd: s.i.s: rdn after 3f: a bhd) | 10 | **9** | 9/2$^{3}$ | — | — |
| | | | | (SP 123.9%) | **9 Rn** | |

**1m 46.8** (6.80) CSF £32.78 TOTE £16.70: £2.50 £1.10 £2.60 (£91.50) Trio £101.20; £129.71 to York 15/6/96 OWNER Mr B. Dixon (WORKSOP) BRED M. B. J. Dolan
**Mercury (IRE)** left his debut effort behind him and took an admittedly moderate contest in great style. He looks like he can progress further. (8/1)
**Newbridge Boy** looks short of pace and needs further. (3/1)
**Tonto** showed improved form. (12/1)
**1649 Magic Heights**, taken down steadily, was settled towards the rear, but lacked the pace to make much impression at this trip. (4/1: op 2/1)
**1719 Hadadabble** seemed to lose his action and his place on the home turn. (4/1)
**New Technique (FR)**, a poor mover, was dashed up to the leaders after missing the break, but only surrendered second place in the final furlong. (25/1)
**Qualitair Beauty** (9/2: 3/1-5/1)

## 1970 PEARL (S) H'CAP (0-60) (3, 4 & 5-Y.O) (Class G)
4-05 (4-06) **1m 3f (Fibresand)** £2,070.00 (£570.00: £270.00) Stalls: Low GOING minus 0.07 sec per fur (STD)

| Form | Horse | Dist | Pos | SP | RR | SF |
|---|---|---|---|---|---|---|
| 1641$^{15}$ | **Yellow Dragon (IRE) (45)** (BAPearce) **3-7-13** NCarlisle(10) (b: lw: dwlt: hdwy over 4f out: c wd & rdn st: styd on to ld ins fnl f: eased nr fin) | — | **1** | 5/1$^{1}$ | 54 | — |
| *1487*$^{11}$ | **Palacegate Jo (IRE) (35)** (DWChapman) **5-8-3** GDuffield(7) (chsd ldrs: lost pl 6f out: rallied 4f out: r.o wl fnl f) | 3½ | **2** | 12/1 | 39 | — |
| 1600$^{8}$ | **Sis Garden (51)** (TDEasterby) **3-8-5b1ow3** MBirch(1) (led after 1f: rdn over 1f out: wknd & hdd ins fnl f) | 1½ | **3** | 8/1$^{2}$ | 53 | — |
| 1314$^{7}$ | **Gee Gee Tee (46)** (JAkehurst) **3-8-0** TWilliams(12) (b.hind: a.p: ev ch 3f out: sn rdn & btn) | 3 | **4** | 10/1$^{3}$ | 43 | — |
| *426*$^{4}$ | **Trumble (43)** (MrsNMacauley) **4-8-11** EmmaO'Gorman(9) (chsd ldrs: no imp fnl 2f) | 5 | **5** | 5/1$^{1}$ | 33 | — |
| 1496$^{6}$ | **Chilly Lad (60)** (MJRyan) **5-10-0b** DBiggs(11) (lw: hdwy over 4f out: btn 2f out) | 5 | **6** | 5/1$^{1}$ | 43 | — |
| | **Hannahs Bay (42)** (MGMeagher) **3-7-10** FNorton(13) (prom: rdn 7f out: btn 4f out) | s.h | **7** | 20/1 | 25 | — |
| 1302$^{13}$ | **Cedar Dancer (35)** (RJHodges) **4-7-12**(5) PPMurphy(6) (lw: in tch 6f) | 9 | **8** | 14/1 | 5 | — |
| 1665$^{17}$ | **Adaloaldo (USA) (53)** (JParkes) **4-9-2**(5) LNewton(4) (s.i.s: sn in tch: wknd 4f out) | 2½ | **9** | 5/1$^{1}$ | 19 | — |
| 1067$^{6}$ | **Cinnamon Stick (IRE) (43)** (PSFelgate) **3-7-8**(3)ow1 DWright(2) (led 1f: wknd 6f out) | hd | **10** | 11/1 | 9 | — |
| 801$^{9}$ | **Thrushwood (28)** (NChamberlain) **4-7-10** NKennedy(3) (a bhd) | 15 | **11** | 33/1 | — | — |
| 1665$^{14}$ | **Ruby Plus (28)** (GROldroyd) **5-7-3v**(7) JFowle(14) (a bhd) | 1½ | **12** | 25/1 | — | — |
| *1460*$^{5}$ | **Dome Patrol (44)** (DBurchell) **5-8-12** DeanMcKeown(8) (prom tl wknd 5f out) | 2 | **13** | 10/1$^{3}$ | — | — |
| *1462*$^{11}$ | ***Frankly Fran (43)*** (DWPArbuthnot) **4-8-11** SWhitworth(5) (Withdrawn not under Starter's orders: Veterinary advice) | | **W** | 14/1 | — | — |
| | | | | (SP 136.9%) | **13 Rn** | |

**2m 32.1** (12.10) CSF £63.06 CT £451.77 TOTE £7.40: £1.60 £2.80 £2.70 (£57.50) Trio £98.70; £1.39 to York 15/6/96 OWNER Mr C. M. Kwai (LIMPSFIELD) BRED J. N. McCaffrey
LONG HANDICAP Thrushwood 7-2 Ruby Plus 7-7 Cinnamon Stick (IRE) 7-4 Hannahs Bay 7-8
WEIGHT FOR AGE 3yo-14lb
Bt in 5,200gns
**760 Yellow Dragon (IRE)** landed a gamble but looked held until his stamina came into play in the final furlong. He eased down in the last few strides, but for which he would have won by a couple of strides. (5/1)
**Palacegate Jo (IRE)** made the frame for the first time in almost a year and looks on the way back. (12/1)
**Sis Garden** drew clear with Gee Gee Tee leaving the back straight and, once that rival folded, looked to have the race won. She found nothing further though and stopped dramatically in the final furlong. (8/1)
**Gee Gee Tee** was bang in contention until the pressure was applied turning for home. This was his first run beyond an extended mile. (10/1)
**426 Trumble** gave chase to the two clear leaders but this quickly took its toll. (5/1)

## 1971 EMERALD H'CAP (0-65) (3-Y.O+) (Class F)
4-35 (4-45) **5f (Fibresand)** £2,381.00 (£656.00: £311.00) Stalls: High GOING minus 0.07 sec per fur (STD)

| Form | Horse | Dist | Pos | SP | RR | SF |
|---|---|---|---|---|---|---|
| *1716*$^{2}$ | **Elton Ledger (IRE) (63)** (MrsNMacauley) **7-9-12v** EmmaO'Gorman(5) (b: lw: dwlt: hdwy over 2f out: led ins fnl f: pushed out) | — | **1** | 3/1$^{2}$ | 72 | 49 |
| 862$^{15}$ | **Raisa Point (40)** (WRMuir) **5-8-3** FNorton(3) (trckd ldrs: led 2f out: hdd & no ex ins fnl f) | 1 | **2** | 20/1 | 46 | 23 |

| Form | Horse / Details | Dist | Pos | SP | RR | SF |
|---|---|---|---|---|---|---|
| *1716$^{3}$* | **Delrob (45)** (DHaydnJones) **5-8-3v**$^{(5)}$ PPMurphy(7) (dwlt: edgd rt & bmpd s: hdwy over 1f out: nrst fin) | 2½ | **3** | 9/2 | 43 | 20 |
| *1492$^{9}$* | **Daaniera (IRE) (36)** (PHowling) **6-7-13v** TWilliams(4) (b.hind: led 3f: one pce) | nk | **4** | 12/1 | 33 | 10 |
| *1716$^{4}$* | **Kung Frode (65)** (BAMcMahon) **4-10-0** GDuffield(2) (lw: trckd ldrs: rdn over 1f out: wknd ins fnl f) | 1¼ | **5** | Evens$^{1}$ | 58 | 35 |
| 1663$^{5}$ | **Midnight Cookie (53)** (BAPearce) **3-8-9** NCarlisle(6) (w ldrs over 3f) | 4 | **6** | 8/1 | 33 | 3 |
| 1708$^{12}$ | **Tommy Tempest (35)** (REPeacock) **7-7-12v** GBardwell(1) (spd 3f) | hd | **7** | 25/1 | 15 | — |
| 1545$^{5}$ | **Kalar (63)** (DWChapman) **7-9-9b**$^{(3)}$ OPears(10) (w ldrs stands' side over 3f) | hd | **8** | 6/1 | 42 | 19 |
| *1716$^{8}$* | **General Equation (62)** (JBalding) **3-8-11**$^{(7)}$ JEdmunds(9) (wnt lft s: nvr trbld ldrs) | ¾ | **9** | 10/1 | 39 | 9 |
| 1716* | **Freckles Kelly (58)** (TDEasterby) **4-9-7** $^{7x}$ MBirch(8) (Withdrawn not under Starter's orders: cocussed in stalls) | | **W** | 7/2$^{3}$ | — | — |

(SP 166.2%) **9 Rn**

**60.1 secs** (3.10) CSF £60.89 CT £275.94 TOTE £3.80: £1.50 £4.70 £1.80 (£116.90) Trio £47.50 OWNER The Posse (MELTON MOWBRAY) BRED Thomas Doherty

WEIGHT FOR AGE 3yo-7lb

**1716 Elton Ledger (IRE)**, given a confident ride, always looked to be travelling well and put his head in front in the last 100 yards for a first win at the minimum trip. (3/1)

**Raisa Point**, taken to post early, nearly broke her duck on this All-Weather debut and ought to find a suitable race. (20/1)

**1716 Delrob** again ran well in the visor and produced a spirited finish under the slower stands' rail. (9/2)

**900 Daaniera (IRE)**, with what proved a favourable low draw, held the call on that side of the track to past halfway, and stuck on better than usual once headed. (12/1)

**1716 Kung Frode** moved to post poorly and found nothing when let down. (Evens)

**1716* Freckles Kelly** (7/2: 5/2-4/1)

## 1972 JAMES LATHAM MIDLAND/CSC CABERBOARD MEDIAN AUCTION MAIDEN STKS (II) (3-Y.O) (Class E)

5-05 (5-09) **1m (Fibresand)** £2,690.60 (£798.80: £378.40: £168.20) Stalls: Low GOING minus 0.07 sec per fur (STD)

| Form | Horse / Details | Dist | Pos | SP | RR | SF |
|---|---|---|---|---|---|---|
| 1319$^{10}$ | **Barrack Yard** (ACStewart) **3-9-0** SWhitworth(2) (trckd ldr: led 3f out: rdn over 1f out: r.o) | — | **1** | 5/2$^{1}$ | 66 | 26 |
| 1608$^{11}$ | **Moonraking** (TJEtherington) **3-9-0** MBirch(7) (swtg: rdn & hdwy over 3f out: r.o fnl f: nt rch wnr) | 3 | **2** | 16/1 | 60 | 20 |
| | **Safa Dancer** (BAMcMahon) **3-8-9** GDuffield(8) (w'like: neat: a.p: ev ch over 2f out: sn rdn: btn over 1f out) | 4 | **3** | 7/1$^{3}$ | 47 | 7 |
| | **Snowy Mantle** (JDBethell) **3-8-9** FNorton(1) (leggy: unf: s.i.s: hdwy after 3f: one pce fnl 3f) | 10 | **4** | 10/1 | 27 | — |
| | **Veni Vidi Vici (IRE)** (MJHeaton-Ellis) **3-8-7**$^{(7)}$ JFowle(4) (led 5f: sn wknd) | 7 | **5** | 3/1$^{2}$ | 18 | — |
| 1526$^{W}$ | **The Oddfellow** (NBycroft) **3-9-0** AlexGreaves(5) (unf: scope: bit bkwd: b.off hind: chsd ldrs 3f) | 3 | **6** | 20/1 | 12 | — |
| 1667$^{8}$ | **Hamilton Gold** (MGMeagher) **3-8-2**$^{(7)}$ RStudholme(6) (lw: stdd s: plld hrd: nvr nr to chal) | hd | **7** | 10/1 | 7 | — |
| 1535$^{6}$ | **Happy Venturer (IRE)** (CMurray) **3-9-0** CHodgson(3) (swtg: prom 4f: sn rdn & wknd) | 20 | **8** | 5/2$^{1}$ | — | — |

(SP 123.5%) **8 Rn**

**1m 46.7** (6.70) CSF £37.40 TOTE £3.20: £1.80 £3.30 £2.30 (£30.10) OWNER Mr Ricky George (NEWMARKET) BRED Britton House Stud

OFFICIAL EXPLANATION **Happy Venturer (IRE): became upset in the stalls which caused him to not run his true race.**

**Barrack Yard**, taking a big drop in class, moved poorly to post but was always in command once hitting the front. (5/2: op 6/4)

**Moonraking** looked an awkward ride, racing with his head at an angle, but stayed on well in the final furlong. (16/1)

**Safa Dancer** ran respectably until being left behind in the last quarter-mile. (7/1)

**Snowy Mantle** showed a little ability to recover from a tardy start. (10/1: 8/1-12/1)

**Veni Vidi Vici (IRE)** moved keenly to post and stopped quickly once headed. (3/1: op 6/4)

**The Oddfellow**, who went down quite keenly and showed some knee-action, was in trouble by halfway. (20/1)

**Happy Venturer (IRE)** got worked up after being in the stalls a long time. (5/2: op 6/1)

T/Plpt: £274.50 (22.87 Tckts). T/Qdpt: £94.60 (3.49 Tckts). Dk

# 1125-YORK (L-H) (Good)

## Friday June 14th

Race 3-6: Stalls moved to centre: false ground

WEATHER: sunny & warm WIND: slt half bhd

## 1973 MARKETING WEEK MEDIAN AUCTION MAIDEN STKS (3-Y.O) (Class E)

2-10 (2-20) **1m 3f 195y** £4,230.00 (£1,260.00: £600.00: £270.00) Stalls: Low GOING minus 0.30 sec per fur (GF)

| Form | Horse / Details | Dist | Pos | SP | RR | SF |
|---|---|---|---|---|---|---|
| 1461$^{3}$ | **Bowled Over (85)** (CACyzer) **3-9-0** KFallon(4) (hld up: hdwy 4f out: rdn to ld appr fnl f: r.o) | — | **1** | 11/8$^{2}$ | 78 | 25 |
| 1104$^{2}$ | **King of Sparta** (LMCumani) **3-9-0** KDarley(3) (led tl swvd lft, hit rails & hdd appr fnl f: sn btn) | 3½ | **2** | 10/11$^{1}$ | 73 | 20 |
| 1600$^{4}$ | **Batoutoftheblue (60)** (WWHaigh) **3-9-0** JTate(5) (lw: chsd ldr tl outpcd over 3f out) | 9 | **3** | 10/1$^{3}$ | 61 | 8 |
| 1434$^{11}$ | **Aren't We Lucky (IRE)** (JJO'Neill) **3-9-0** JFortune(1) (hld up: effrt over 4f out: n.d) | 3½ | **4** | 33/1 | 57 | 4 |
| | **Happy Taipan (IRE)** (CMurray) **3-9-0** MTebbutt(2) (reard s & s.s: wnt prom after 2f: wknd 6f out: t.o) | 30 | **5** | 25/1 | 16 | — |

(SP 110.4%) **5 Rn**

**2m 35.07** (7.27) CSF £2.90 TOTE £2.20: £1.30 £1.10 (£1.20) OWNER Mr R. M. Cyzer (HORSHAM) BRED Side Hill Stud

**1461 Bowled Over** pulled too hard on the way down and his saddle slipped, causing a long delay. In the race, he did nothing wrong though, and won really well. (11/8)

**1104 King of Sparta** is a superb-looking animal, but he still looks as though there is something to work on, and threw his chance away by hanging into the rail approaching the final furlong. (10/11)

**763 Batoutoftheblue** ran as well as could be expected in this company. (10/1)

**Aren't We Lucky (IRE)** ran reasonably without getting into this. (33/1)

**Happy Taipan (IRE)**, wearing a net-muzzle, was on his hind legs once the stalls opened and obviously has his problems. (25/1)

## 1974 NAPOLEONS CASINO H'CAP (0-100) (3-Y.O+) (Class C)

2-40 (2-45) **5f** £7,765.00 (£2,320.00: £1,110.00: £505.00) Stalls: Low GOING minus 0.30 sec per fur (GF)

| Form | Horse / Details | Dist | Pos | SP | RR | SF |
|---|---|---|---|---|---|---|
| 1512* | **Canovas Heart (70)** (BobJones) **7-8-5** NDay(7) (lw: a.p: led wl over 1f out: hld on wl) | — | **1** | 12/1 | 77 | 50 |
| 1501$^{2}$ | **Portend (85)** (SRBowring) **4-9-3b**$^{(3)}$ CTeague(11) (a chsng ldrs: hdwy u.p 2f out: ev ch ins fnl f: r.o) | hd | **2** | 10/1 | 92 | 65 |
| 1430$^{5}$ | **Surprise Mission (75)** (MrsJRRamsden) **4-8-10** KFallon(5) (trckd ldrs: effrt 2f out: kpt on u.p fnl f: nt pce to chal) | 1¾ | **3** | 6/1$^{1}$ | 76 | 49 |
| 1708* | **Bajan Rose (85)** (MBlanshard) **4-9-6** $^{7x}$ JQuinn(10) (bhd: hdwy ½-wy: kpt on wl fnl f) | hd | **4** | 14/1 | 86 | 59 |

| | | | | SP | RR | SF |
|---|---|---|---|---|---|---|
| 1199[2] | **Stuffed (70)** (MWEasterby) **4-8-5** DaleGibson(12) (lw: hld up: hdwy u.p 2f out: nt pce to chal) | nk | **5** | 15/2[2] | 70 | 43 |
| 1646[3] | **Shadow Jury (61)** (DWChapman) **6-7-10b** LCharnock(4) (led tl hdd wl over 1f out: kpt on one pce) | ½ | **6** | 20/1 | 59 | 32 |
| | **Crofters Ceilidh (88)** (BAMcMahon) **4-9-9** GCarter(9) (in tch: rdn ½-wy: no imp) | 2½ | **7** | 33/1 | 78 | 51 |
| 1708[2] | **Lady Sheriff (83)** (RHollinshead) **5-8-13**(5) FLynch(13) (lw: in tch: effrt ½-wy: nvr able to chal) | ¾ | **8** | 10/1 | 71 | 44 |
| 989[3] | **Tadeo (96)** (MJohnston) **3-9-10** KDarley(6) (chsd ldrs tl grad wknd fnl 2f) | nk | **9** | 14/1 | 83 | 49 |
| 1501[7] | **For the Present (79)** (TDBarron) **6-9-0** JFortune(2) (chsd ldrs: effrt 2f out: wknd fnl f) | ½ | **10** | 14/1 | 64 | 37 |
| 1430[3] | **Tuscan Dawn (78)** (JBerry) **6-8-8**(5) PRoberts(15) (early spd: outpcd fr ½-wy) | nk | **11** | 12/1 | 62 | 35 |
| 1113[7] | **Saddlehome (USA) (73)** (TDBarron) **7-8-8** WCarson(14) (a bhd) | 2½ | **12** | 6/1[1] | 49 | 22 |
| | **Desert Tiger (90)** (MJohnston) **3-9-4** JWeaver(16) (sn outpcd) | ½ | **13** | 9/1 | 65 | 31 |
| 1630[4] | **Tart and a Half (78)** (BJMeehan) **4-8-13b** MTebbutt(3) (spd to ½-wy) | ¾ | **14** | 8/1[3] | 50 | 23 |
| 1186[2] | **Benzoe (IRE) (77)** (MrsJRRamsden) **6-8-12** WJO'Connor(1) (lw: dwlt: hdwy ½-wy: wknd appr fnl f) | ½ | **15** | 11/1 | 48 | 21 |
| 1708[6] | **Macfarlane (70)** (MJFetherston-Godley) **8-8-5** WRyan(8) (b: wl bhd fr ½-wy: b.b.v) | 30 | **16** | 12/1 | — | — |

(SP 138.7%) **16 Rn**

**58.49 secs** (0.79) CSF £130.23 CT £752.96 TOTE £22.40: £3.70 £3.30 £2.40 £4.60 (£75.70) Trio £318.80 OWNER Mr M J Osborne and Mrs J Woods (NEWMARKET) BRED M. J. Hall

LONG HANDICAP Shadow Jury 7-9

WEIGHT FOR AGE 3yo-7lb

**1512* Canovas Heart** is a typical sprinter in form and, once in front, he refused to give in. (12/1)

**1501 Portend** keeps running his heart out, but he just met one too tough this time. (10/1)

**1430 Surprise Mission** travelled well but the front two got first run on him and he could never peg them back. His new stable will no doubt find a race for him before long. (6/1)

**1708* Bajan Rose** did not get the best of starts and, always struggling to recover, did well to finish so close. (14/1)

**1199 Stuffed**, held up off the pace, could never find the pace to get to terms, despite staying on. (15/2)

**1646 Shadow Jury** again showed tremendous early pace and is knocking at the door. (20/1)

**Desert Tiger** turned out to have a bad draw because of the false patch of ground on the stands' rail. (9/1)

## 1975 SHEPHERD SPRINT RATED STKS H'CAP (0-100) (3-Y.O+) (Class B)

3-10 (3-12) **6f** £12,792.00 (£4,728.00: £2,264.00: £920.00: £360.00: £136.00) Stalls: Centre GOING minus 0.30 sec per fur (GF)

| | | | | SP | RR | SF |
|---|---|---|---|---|---|---|
| 1630[6] | **Cyrano's Lad (IRE) (87)** (CADwyer) **7-8-9** KFallon(1) (lw: mde all: qcknd 2f out: edgd lft: kpt on wl) | — | **1** | 7/4[1] | 94 | 61 |
| 1430[4] | **Tedburrow (85)** (MrsAMNaughton) **4-8-7** JCarroll(4) (hld up: stdy hdwy & ev ch wl over 1f out: sn rdn & no ex) | 1¼ | **2** | 9/2[3] | 89 | 56 |
| 1623[4] | **Double Blue (99)** (MJohnston) **7-9-7** JWeaver(3) (lw: cl up tl outpcd over 2f out: r.o towards fin) | s.h | **3** | 8/1 | 103 | 70 |
| 1107[4] | **Stylish Ways (IRE) (95)** (MissSEHall) **4-9-3** NConnorton(5) (hld up: hdwy over 2f out: sn rdn & no imp) | 1½ | **4** | 4/1[2] | 95 | 62 |
| 1430[7] | **Musical Season (86)** (TDBarron) **4-8-8** KDarley(2) (chsd ldrs: effrt over 2f out: wknd over 1f out) | nk | **5** | 8/1 | 85 | 52 |
| 1628[5] | **Babsy Babe (89)** (JJQuinn) **3-7-12**(5) FLynch(6) (s.s: hdwy ½-wy: sn btn) | 2½ | **6** | 11/2 | 81 | 40 |

(SP 112.2%) **6 Rn**

**1m 11.48** (0.48) CSF £9.42 TOTE £2.80: £1.60 £2.30 (£5.50) OWNER Mr M. M. Foulger (NEWMARKET) BRED J. C. Condon

LONG HANDICAP Tedburrow 8-4

WEIGHT FOR AGE 3yo-8lb

**1630 Cyrano's Lad (IRE)** has always promised to win over this trip and made full use of his tremendous early speed. (7/4)

**1430 Tedburrow** got pretty warm beforehand but he often does. He ran his heart out, but just found the winner too good in the final furlong and a half. (9/2: op 3/1)

**1623 Double Blue** is on his way back and, after getting well outpaced, finished to some effect. (8/1)

**1107 Stylish Ways (IRE)**, edgy beforehand, was held up in the race and failed to quicken when asked. (4/1)

**Musical Season**, a soft ground specialist of a few years ago, failed to win last year but keeps showing signs of returning to form. (8/1: 6/1-9/1)

**1628 Babsy Babe** gave her chance away at the start again. (11/2)

## 1976 INTERNATIONAL FACTORS RATED STKS H'CAP (0-95) (4-Y.O+) (Class C)

3-40 (3-40) **1m 5f 194y** £8,183.50 (£3,026.50: £1,450.75: £591.25: £233.13: £89.87) Stalls: Low GOING minus 0.30 sec per fur (GF)

| | | | | SP | RR | SF |
|---|---|---|---|---|---|---|
| 1428[4] | **Corradini (91)** (HRACecil) **4-9-3** WRyan(6) (lw: hld up: hdwy 4f out: rdn to chal over 1f out: r.o to ld post) | — | **1** | 5/1[2] | 104 | 77 |
| 1116* | **Celeric (95)** (DMorley) **4-9-7** WCarson(1) (lw: in tch: hdwy on ins 3f out: led 2f out: sn hrd drvn: jst ct) | s.h | **2** | 4/5[1] | 108 | 81 |
| 1353[3] | **Royal Scimitar (USA) (92)** (PFICole) **4-9-4** KDarley(7) (chsd ldr: led over 4f out to 2f out: sn outpcd) | 8 | **3** | 5/1[2] | 96 | 69 |
| 1428[8] | **Invest Wisely (85)** (JMPEustace) **4-8-11** JTate(8) (in tch: effrt 4f out: sn outpcd: kpt on fnl f) | s.h | **4** | 12/1[3] | 89 | 62 |
| | **Lord Jim (IRE) (93)** (LordHuntingdon) **4-9-5** TIves(5) (bhd: effrt ent st: n.d) | 15 | **5** | 14/1 | 79 | 52 |
| 1700[6] | **Harbour Island (88)** (MRStoute) **4-9-0b** KFallon(4) (lw: chsd ldrs: rdn 4f out: sn wknd) | 8 | **6** | 14/1 | 65 | 38 |
| 1194[15] | **Kadastrof (FR) (81)** (RDickin) **6-8-2**(5) FLynch(2) (led & sn clr: hdd over 4f out: wknd qckly) | 18 | **7** | 14/1 | 37 | 10 |

(SP 116.6%) **7 Rn**

**2m 56.33** (0.13) CSF £9.49 CT £19.23 TOTE £4.80: £2.10 £1.40 (£2.80) OWNER Mr K. Abdulla (NEWMARKET) BRED Juddmonte Farms

LONG HANDICAP Kadastrof (FR) 8-6

**1428 Corradini**, dropping back in distance, was well suited by the very strong pace and just got there. (5/1)

**1116* Celeric**, racing off his highest mark to date, was struggling some way out but kept answering his rider's every call to just be touched off. (4/5)

**1353 Royal Scimitar (USA)**, stepping up in distance, was going well enough early in the straight, but failed to get home. (5/1)

**1428 Invest Wisely** ran miserably last time, but showed more here and seems to be getting it together. (12/1)

**Lord Jim (IRE)**, having his first run of the season, showed little. (14/1)

**Harbour Island** (14/1: op 8/1)

## 1977 MONKS CROSS APPRENTICE H'CAP (0-75) (4-Y.O+) (Class E)

4-10 (4-12) **1m 3f 195y** £5,162.50 (£1,540.00: £735.00: £332.50) Stalls: Low GOING minus 0.30 sec per fur (GF)

| | | | | SP | RR | SF |
|---|---|---|---|---|---|---|
| 1792[2] | **Achilles Heel (37)** (CNAllen) **5-7-13** MartinDwyer(6) (lw: hld up: hdwy ent st: led 2½f out: r.o wl) | — | **1** | 7/4[1] | 54 | 36 |
| 1676[2] | **Bobanlyn (IRE) (47)** (JSWainwright) **4-8-4**(5) JBramhill(1) (a.p: ev ch over 2f out: nt pce of wnr) | 4 | **2** | 6/1[3] | 59 | 41 |
| 1803[5] | **Augustan (50)** (SGollings) **5-8-12** AimeeCook(4) (s.s: hdwy ent st: chsng ldrs 2f out: kpt on one pce) | 6 | **3** | 9/1 | 54 | 36 |
| 1763* | **Here Comes Herbie (40)** (WStorey) **4-8-2** 5x IonaWands(8) (w ldrs: chal 4f out: outpcd fnl 2f) | nk | **4** | 5/1[2] | 43 | 25 |
| 1421[7] | **Redstella (USA) (65)** (RMWhitaker) **7-9-8**(5) PFredericks(12) (lw: bhd: hdwy appr st: sn chsng ldrs: one pce fnl 2f) | 3½ | **5** | 20/1 | 63 | 45 |

1676$^{6}$ **Gallardini (IRE) (40)** (BSRothwell) **7-7-13v$^{1}$**$^{(3)}$ CWebb(3) (in tch: hdwy to chse ldrs over 3f out: rdn & btn 2f out) ....5 **6** 20/1 32 14
**Pepitist (45)** (MDHammond) **5-8-0**$^{(7)ow3}$ JO'Leary(2) (bhd: sme hdwy fnl 3f: n.d) ....½ **7** 33/1 36 15
**Pendolino (IRE) (43)** (MBrittain) **5-8-5b** SCopp(11) (chsd ldrs: led over 4f out tl over 2f out: sn btn) ....1¾ **8** 33/1 32 14
**Special Beat (55)** (PFICole) **4-8-12**$^{(5)}$ DavidO'Neill(7) (led tl hdd over 4f out: sn wknd) ....3 **9** 14/1 40 22
1647$^{8}$ **Advance East (60)** (MrsJRRamsden) **4-9-3**$^{(5)}$ TFinn(10) (in tch: hdwy to chal ent st: wknd over 3f out) ....3½ **10** 15/2 40 22
1585$^{4}$ **Swandale Flyer (38)** (NBycroft) **4-7-11**$^{(3)}$ JoHunnam(9) (prom tl wknd 4f out) ....5 **11** 25/1 11 —
**Woodrising (59)** (CREgerton) **4-9-7** GFaulkner(5) (lost tch appr st: n.d after) ....½ **12** 10/1 32 14
**Eire Leath-Sceal (57)** (MBrittain) **9-9-5** GParkin(13) (lw: b: chsd ldrs tl wknd over 5f out) ....25 **13** 25/1 — —
(SP 127.9%) **13 Rn**

**2m 31.36** (3.56) CSF £13.47 CT £73.86 TOTE £2.40: £1.40 £1.80 £2.50 (£7.70) Trio £30.80 OWNER Camelot Racing (NEWMARKET) BRED Winning Post Racing Ltd

**1792 Achilles Heel** looked a certainty after his effort last week, and came with a smooth run from the back of the field to settle it in a few strides approaching the last quarter-mile. (7/4)
**1676 Bobanlyn (IRE)** keeps running well, but the winner was far too good for her. (6/1)
**1803 Augustan**, trying to win this for the second year running, gave away a lot of ground at the start and then ran his best race for some time. (9/1)
**1763* Here Comes Herbie** ran well but was always racing too keenly, and got tapped for toe in the last two furlongs. (5/1)
**Redstella (USA)** is going quite well and, though he was short of toe in the home straight, he did plug on. (20/1)
**1676 Gallardini (IRE)**, in a visor this time, had his chances early in the straight, but soon cried enough. (20/1)
**Pepitist** stayed on well in the closing stages and will appreciate further. (33/1)

## 1978 UNIVERSITY OF YORK CONDITIONS STKS (2-Y.O F) (Class C)
4-45 (4-47) **6f** £4,878.37 (£1,756.50: £840.75: £341.25: £133.13) Stalls: Centre GOING minus 0.30 sec per fur (GF)

SP RR SF

1413* **Fernanda** (JLDunlop) **2-9-2** WCarson(4) (lw: hld up: qcknd to ld wl over 1f out: r.o) ....— **1** 6/4$^{2}$ 87+ 54
1346* **Witching Hour (IRE)** (MrsJCecil) **2-9-2** TIves(1) (lw: cl up: led 2f out: sn hdd: r.o: nt pce of wnr) ....1¼ **2** Evens$^{1}$ 84 51
1583* **Samsung Spirit** (EWeymes) **2-8-11** JQuinn(2) (trckd ldrs tl outpcd 2f out: no imp after) ....5 **3** 7/1$^{3}$ 65 32
**Heathyards Pearl (USA)** (RHollinshead) **2-8-3**$^{(5)}$ FLynch(3) (w'like: leggy: bit bkwd: s.i.s: hdwy ½-wy: wknd over 1f out) ....½ **4** 20/1 61 28
1433* **Molly Drummond** (CWCElsey) **2-9-2** KDarley(5) (led 4f: sn outpcd) ....2½ **5** 16/1 62 29
(SP 113.1%) **5 Rn**

**1m 12.42** (1.42) CSF £3.40 TOTE £2.20: £1.50 £1.10 (£1.30) OWNER Sultan Al Kabeer (ARUNDEL) BRED Mrs John Trotter
**1413* Fernanda**, suited by this moderately-run event, had the best turn of foot to settle it. (6/4)
**1346* Witching Hour (IRE)** was not made enough use of and was tapped for toe in the closing stages. (Evens)
**1583* Samsung Spirit** had no chance the way the race was run and should have been forcing the pace. (7/1)
**Heathyards Pearl (USA)** needed this and was green, but did show some ability and should improve. (20/1)
**1433* Molly Drummond** was well outclassed once the tap was turned on in the final two furlongs. (16/1)

T/Jkpt: £7,100.00 (0.3 Tckts); £6,996.62 to York 15/6/96. T/Plpt: £9.60 (2,533.76 Tckts). T/Qdpt: £2.30 (457.18 Tckts). AA

# 1589-BATH (L-H) (Good to firm)
## Saturday June 15th
WEATHER: fine WIND: slt bhd

## 1979 JUNE (S) H'CAP (0-60) (3, 4 & 5-Y.O) (Class G)
2-00 (2-01) **1m 2f 46y** £2,388.00 (£668.00: £324.00) Stalls: Low GOING minus 0.62 sec per fur (F)

SP RR SF

1496$^{13}$ **Owdbetts (IRE) (53)** (GLMoore) **4-9-9** SWhitworth(1) (stdd s: hdwy on ins 3f out: plld out 2f out: led & wnt lft over 1f out: r.o) ....— **1** 7/1$^{3}$ 64 46
*1457*$^{4}$ **Voices in the Sky (28)** (AGNewcombe) **5-7-5**$^{(7)}$ IonaWands(6) (lw: hdwy fnl 2f: r.o) ....¾ **2** 8/1 38 20
1534$^{7}$ **Eskimo Kiss (IRE) (39)** (MJFetherston-Godley) **3-7-10b** FNorton(4) (lw: a.p: r.o ins fnl f) ....nk **3** 33/1 48 17
1661$^{2}$ **Multi Franchise (56)** (BGubby) **3-8-13** RPerham(3) (w ldr: led 5f out tl over 1f out: one pce) ....½ **4** 5/1$^{2}$ 65 34
1468$^{2}$ **I'm a Nut Man (42)** (CASmith) **5-8-12**$^{ow2}$ RHughes(10) (lw: hld up: wknd over 1f out: eased whn btn ins fnl f)..5 **5** 3/1$^{1}$ 43 23
1411$^{20}$ **Spitfire Bridge (IRE) (45)** (MMcCormack) **4-9-1** WJO'Connor(11) (lw: hld up: c wd 4f out: hdwy over 2f out: eased whn btn fnl f) ....¾ **6** 15/2 45 27
*1456*$^{6}$ **In Cahoots (42)** (AGNewcombe) **3-7-13** TSprake(2) (lw: plld hrd: prom tl wknd 2f out) ....1 **7** 12/1 40 9
1778$^{6}$ **Nord Lys (IRE) (27)** (BJLlewellyn) **5-7-8**$^{(3)ow1}$ DWright(7) (led over 5f: rdn 3f out: wknd over 1f out) ....1½ **8** 33/1 23 4
1821$^{9}$ **Burnt Sienna (IRE) (40)** (JSMoore) **4-8-5**$^{(5)}$ PPMurphy(8) (prom tl wknd 2f out) ....nk **9** 16/1 35 17
1451$^{5}$ **Forliando (39)** (MSSaunders) **3-7-7**$^{(3)}$ NVarley(13) (a bhd) ....4 **10** 33/1 28 —
1682$^{8}$ **Elly Fleetfoot (IRE) (58)** (MJRyan) **4-9-9**$^{(5)}$ MBaird(5) (bhd fnl 3f) ....1½ **11** 11/1 45 27
**La Belle Shyanne (26)** (RJBaker) **5-7-10** NAdams(9) (bkwd: a bhd) ....hd **12** 25/1 12 —
1893$^{8}$ **Amnesty Bay (43)** (MDIUsher) **4-8-13v** RPrice(12) (a bhd) ....7 **13** 12/1 18 —
(SP 119.3%) **13 Rn**

**2m 8.9** (1.40) CSF £57.04 CT £1,557.91 TOTE £7.70: £3.10 £2.90 £8.10 (£40.50) Trio £217.40; £245.02 to 17/6/96 OWNER Mr K. Higson (EPSOM) BRED Maria Goglio
LONG HANDICAP Eskimo Kiss (IRE) 7-6 Nord Lys (IRE) 7-6 La Belle Shyanne 7-9
WEIGHT FOR AGE 3yo-13lb
Bt in 4,500gns
**Owdbetts (IRE)**, dropped out at the start to get the trip, gave her supporters an anxious moment when cutting across at the elbow a furlong out. Fortunately, she was forging ahead at the time. (7/1: op 4/1)
**1457 Voices in the Sky**, in at the right end of the handicap, can take a similar event. (8/1)
**522 Eskimo Kiss (IRE)**, 4lb out of the handicap, stepped up on her previous effort this season and seems to have come to hand. (33/1)
**1661 Multi Franchise** again ran well but was not quite good enough. (5/1)
**1468 I'm a Nut Man** had gone up 8lb for finishing second in his last two runs. (3/1)
**Spitfire Bridge (IRE)**, dropped 6lb this season, won this race last year when it was a non-handicap. (15/2)
**Elly Fleetfoot (IRE)** (11/1: op 7/1)
**Amnesty Bay** (12/1: op 8/1)

## 1980 PUMP ROOM CONDITIONS STKS (2-Y.O) (Class D)

2-30 (2-31) **5f 11y** £3,172.75 (£952.00: £458.50: £211.75) Stalls: High GOING minus 0.62 sec per fur (F)

| | | | | SP | RR | SF |
|---|---|---|---|---|---|---|
| | **Compton Place** (JARToller) **2-8-11** WJO'Connor(6) (leggy: a gng wl: led wl ins fnl f: r.o) | — | 1 | 9/2[3] | 73+ | 34 |
| 1510[6] | **Ride Sally Ride (IRE)** (JBerry) **2-9-3** GCarter(3) (led: hrd rdn & hdd wl ins fnl f) | hd | 2 | 11/4[2] | 79 | 40 |
| | **Dayville (USA)** (RCharlton) **2-8-6** TSprake(5) (b: w'like: lw: s.s: hdwy 3f out: rdn over 1f out: one pce) | 5 | 3 | 7/4[1] | 52 | 13 |
| 869* | **Mirror Four Life (IRE)** (MHTompkins) **2-8-10** PRobinson(4) (chsd ldrs: rdn over 2f out: wknd fnl f) | 2½ | 4 | 9/2[3] | 48 | 9 |
| 1537* | **Dashing Rocksville** (MRChannon) **2-8-12** RHughes(2) (hld up: rdn & wknd over 2f out) | 2½ | 5 | 11/2 | 42 | 3 |
| 1331[6] | **Folly Foot Fred** (BRMillman) **2-8-12**(3) SDrowne(1) (w ldr tl rdn & wknd over 2f out) | ½ | 6 | 20/1 | 43 | 4 |
| | | | | (SP 119.5%) | | **6 Rn** |

**61.1 secs** (0.60) CSF £17.37 TOTE £6.70: £3.20 £2.50 (£31.40) OWNER Duke of Devonshire (WHITSBURY) BRED R. J. Turner

**Compton Place**, a 92,000 guinea purchase, had only to be shown the whip to poke his head in front, and won more decisively than the margin suggests. (9/2)

**1510 Ride Sally Ride (IRE)** could not hold the winner in the closing stages and looked a shade flattered by the narrow margin of defeat. (11/4)

**Dayville (USA)** was disappointing and the fact that he wore bandages might suggest he needs softer ground. (7/4)

**1537* Dashing Rocksville** was surprisingly dropped back to the minimum trip. (11/2: 4/1-6/1)

## 1981 ABBEY H'CAP (0-80) (4-Y.O+) (Class D)

3-05 (3-05) **2m 1f 34y** £3,598.50 (£1,083.00: £524.00: £244.50) Stalls: High GOING minus 0.62 sec per fur (F)

| | | | | SP | RR | SF |
|---|---|---|---|---|---|---|
| 1679* | **Mr Copyforce (42)** (MissBSanders) **6-7-11** GBardwell(3) (a.p: rdn over 4f out: led over 2f out tl ins fnl f: led nr fin: all out) | — | 1 | 2/1[1] | 52 | — |
| *1488*[2] | **Castle Secret (53)** (DBurchell) **10-8-3**(5)ow1 RHavlin(5) (lw: a.p: hrd rdn over 2f out: led ins fnl f: hdd nr fin) | hd | 2 | 5/2[2] | 63 | — |
| 1679[3] | **Chakalak (48)** (SDow) **8-7-12**(5) ADaly(6) (lw: led after 3f: qcknd 4f out: sn rdn: hdd over 2f out: one pce fnl f) | 2½ | 3 | 3/1[3] | 56 | — |
| 1679[B] | **Pedaltothemetal (IRE) (42)** (PhilipMitchell) **4-7-5**(5) CAdamson(1) (stdd s: rdn 3f out: no hdwy fnl 2f) | 1 | 4 | 14/1 | 49 | — |
| 1511* | **World Express (IRE) (56)** (BRMillman) **6-8-8**(3) SDrowne(2) (hld up: outpcd 4f out: sn bhd) | ½ | 5 | 6/1 | 62 | — |
| | **Dtoto (74)** (RJBaker) **4-10-0** NAdams(4) (plld hrd: led 3f: wknd 4f out: t.o) | 28 | 6 | 25/1 | 54 | — |
| | | | | (SP 111.7%) | | **6 Rn** |

**3m 53.8** (12.80) CSF £7.12 TOTE £2.80: £1.40 £2.00 (£5.00) OWNER Copyforce Ltd (EPSOM) BRED Highclere Stud Ltd

LONG HANDICAP Pedaltothemetal (IRE) 7-9

WEIGHT FOR AGE 4yo-1lb

**1679* Mr Copyforce**, raised 6lb for his Folkestone win, responded gamely to a fine ride in a race which developed into a sprint from the half-mile marker. (2/1)

**1488 Castle Secret** was 26lb lower in the ratings than when last winning on the Flat at Ascot six years ago. Running well over hurdles and on the Sand recently, he found the winner would not be denied. (5/2)

**1679 Chakalak** only started to up the moderate tempo with half a mile to go. (3/1)

**Pedaltothemetal (IRE)**, in a slowly-run race, did not really prove she gets the trip. (14/1: op 8/1)

**1511* World Express (IRE)**, raised 3lb, needs far more give in the ground. (6/1: op 3/1)

## 1982 CHARLCOMBE MAIDEN AUCTION STKS (2-Y.O) (Class E)

3-35 (3-35) **5f 11y** £2,973.00 (£894.00: £432.00: £201.00) Stalls: High GOING minus 0.62 sec per fur (F)

| | | | | SP | RR | SF |
|---|---|---|---|---|---|---|
| 1815[4] | **Last Chance** (GLewis) **2-8-9** SWhitworth(5) (w ldr: rdn to ld 2f out: r.o wl) | — | 1 | 2/1[1] | 72 | 26 |
| 1404[9] | **Nightingale Song** (MartynMeade) **2-8-2** FNorton(4) (led 3f: one pce) | 3½ | 2 | 11/2 | 54 | 8 |
| | **Victory Dancer** (BJMeehan) **2-8-7** MTebbutt(1) (unf: s.s: wl bhd tl hdwy over 1f out: nrst fin) | ¾ | 3 | 7/2[3] | 57 | 11 |
| 1622[9] | **Bapsford** (GLMoore) **2-8-12**v1ow2 RHughes(3) (lw: hld up: rdn over 2f out: one pce) | nk | 4 | 12/1 | 61 | 13 |
| | **Municipal Girl (IRE)** (BPalling) **2-7-13** TSprake(2) (lengthy: prom over 2f) | 6 | 5 | 11/1 | 29 | — |
| | **Tailwind** (WRMuir) **2-8-6** WJO'Connor(6) (leggy: wnt rt s: hdwy over 3f out: wknd over 2f out) | 1½ | 6 | 5/2[2] | 31 | — |
| | | | | (SP 115.5%) | | **6 Rn** |

**61.5 secs** (1.00) CSF £12.65 TOTE £2.60: £1.80 £1.90 (£5.20) OWNER E and B Productions (Theatre) Ltd (EPSOM) BRED Matthew Sharkey

**1815 Last Chance**, a half-brother to Orange Place, carried his head high through greenness, but did prove much too good for these. (2/1: 5/4-9/4)

**715 Nightingale Song** was unable to cope with the winner. (11/2)

**Victory Dancer**, who had already been gelded, put in some good late work to show promise for the future. (7/2)

**Bapsford** did not improve for the visor. (12/1)

**Municipal Girl (IRE)** (11/1: 8/1-12/1)

## 1983 BECKFORD TOWER H'CAP (0-85) (3-Y.O+) (Class D)

4-05 (4-06) **1m 5y** £3,462.00 (£1,041.00: £503.00: £234.00) Stalls: Low GOING minus 0.62 sec per fur (F)

| | | | | SP | RR | SF |
|---|---|---|---|---|---|---|
| 1625[9] | **Concer Un (78)** (SCWilliams) **4-10-0** JTate(2) (b.nr fore: a.p: rdn to ld wl ins fnl f: r.o) | — | 1 | 9/2[3] | 88 | 62 |
| 1615[4] | **Navigate (USA) (78)** (RHannon) **3-9-3** RHughes(7) (hld up: led over 2f out: edgd rt over 1f out: hdd wl ins fnl f) | nk | 2 | 2/1[1] | 87 | 50 |
| 1890* | **My Gallery (IRE) (60)** (ABailey) **5-8-7**(3) 5x DWright(4) (hld up: hdwy on ins over 1f out: r.o) | ½ | 3 | 7/2[2] | 68 | 42 |
| 1775[11] | **Emily-Mou (IRE) (69)** (MJRyan) **4-9-0**(5) MBaird(1) (led 7f out tl over 2f out: sn nt clr run & swtchd rt: sn wknd) | 8 | 4 | 11/2 | 61 | 35 |
| 1522[9] | **Zatopek (59)** (JCullinan) **4-8-9** GCarter(3) (t.o fnl 4f) | 11 | 5 | 12/1 | 30 | 4 |
| 1775[15] | **Ethbaat (USA) (77)** (WRMuir) **5-9-13** MRichards(5) (lw: bhd fnl 3f) | 2½ | 6 | 33/1 | 43 | 17 |
| 1659[5] | **Sooty Tern (67)** (JMBradley) **9-9-3** GBardwell(6) (lw: led 1f: rdn & wknd wl over 2f out) | 2 | 7 | 11/2 | 29 | 3 |
| | | | | (SP 115.1%) | | **7 Rn** |

**1m 38.4** (0.50 under best) (-0.10) CSF £13.64 TOTE £5.50: £2.50 £1.30 (£6.80) OWNER Miss L. J. Ward (NEWMARKET) BRED Lloyd Bros

WEIGHT FOR AGE 3yo-11lb

**Concer Un** progressed nicely last season and was 6lb higher than when winning at Kempton last September. (9/2: 5/2-5/1)

**1615 Navigate (USA)**, trying a mile, slipped through on the inside to strike the front, but did not help his cause by edging away from the rail at the elbow. (2/1)

**1890* My Gallery (IRE)**, making a rapid reappearance under a penalty, took advantage of the gap left by the runner-up, but could not get there in time. (7/2)

**1625 Emily-Mou (IRE)** scored four times last season, the first being over this trip, but the rest were over an extra quarter-mile. (11/2: 7/2-6/1)

**1984** GIVE WEMBLEY A MISS LIMITED STKS (0-65) (3-Y.O) (Class F)
4-40 (4-40) **1m 3f 144y** £2,845.00 (£795.00: £385.00) Stalls: Low GOING minus 0.62 sec per fur (F)

| | | | | SP | RR | SF |
|---|---|---|---|---|---|---|
| 995[17] | **Labeed (USA) (62)** (MajorWRHern) **3-8-11** SWhitworth(1) (chsd ldr: hrd rdn to ld over 2f out: edgd lft over 1f out: r.o) | — | **1** | 9/1 | 72 | 34 |
| 1415[5] | **Doctor Green (FR) (64)** (LordHuntingdon) **3-8-11v** RPerham(6) (lw: led: hrd rdn & hdd over 2f out: bmpd over 1f out: unable qckn) | 1¾ | **2** | 13/2 | 70 | 32 |
| 1507[3] | **Soldier Mak (62)** (AHide) **3-8-11** MTebbutt(3) (swtg: a.p: r.o one pce fnl 3f) | 4 | **3** | 4/1[2] | 64 | 26 |
| 740[5] | **Belzao (65)** (MRChannon) **3-8-11** RHughes(7) (lw: stdd s: hdwy 4f out: sn rdn: wknd over 2f out: eased whn btn) | 9 | **4** | 4/1[2] | 52 | 14 |
| 1589[5] | **Fijon (IRE) (65)** (BWHills) **3-8-8b[1]** GBardwell(2) (bhd fnl 4f) | 12 | **5** | 5/1[3] | 32 | — |
| 980[3] | **Minnisam (65)** (JLDunlop) **3-8-11** TSprake(8) (swtg: prom tl wknd 3f out) | nk | **6** | 5/2[1] | 35 | — |
| 1594[8] | **Dyanko (44)** (MSSaunders) **3-8-11** RPrice(4) (hld up: rn wd bnd over 4f out: sn bhd) | 2 | **7** | 16/1 | 32 | — |
| | | | | (SP 114.5%) | | **7 Rn** |

**2m 28.5** (1.80) CSF £58.38 TOTE £8.90: £3.40 £3.70 (£21.80) OWNER Mr Hamdan Al Maktoum (LAMBOURN) BRED Shadwell Farm Inc
**863 Labeed (USA)** comes from a stable who have only just got off the mark for the season. (9/1)
**Doctor Green (FR)** may have found the right trip now, but also met one too good. (13/2)
**1507 Soldier Mak** could only plug on at the same speed. (4/1)
**740 Belzao** had been hobdayed and was dropped out at the start in an attempt to cope with this big step up in distance. (4/1)
**1589 Fijon (IRE)** (5/1: 4/1-6/1)
**980 Minnisam** was most disappointing. (5/2)

**1985** TETBURY H'CAP (0-85) (3-Y.O+) (Class D)
5-10 (5-13) **5f 161y** £3,780.50 (£1,139.00: £552.00: £258.50) Stalls: High GOING minus 0.62 sec per fur (F)

| | | | | SP | RR | SF |
|---|---|---|---|---|---|---|
| 931[9] | **Beau Venture (USA) (64)** (BPalling) **8-9-2** TSprake(2) (mde all: clr 2f out: r.o wl) | — | **1** | 7/1[3] | 76 | 39 |
| 1340[8] | **Albert The Bear (75)** (JBerry) **3-9-5** GCarter(1) (a.p: rdn over 2f out: r.o fnl f: nt trble wnr) | 2½ | **2** | 9/2[1] | 80 | 35 |
| 1597[3] | **Dande Flyer (75)** (DWPArbuthnot) **3-9-5** RPerham(4) (b: lw: a.p: r.o one pce fnl 2f) | 3 | **3** | 9/2[1] | 72 | 27 |
| 1777[7] | **Kildee Lad (70)** (APJones) **6-9-8** JTate(5) (rdn over 2f out: hdwy fnl f: r.o) | ¾ | **4** | 7/1[3] | 65 | 28 |
| 1316[5] | **Songsheet (72)** (MartynMeade) **3-8-11**(5) RHavlin(10) (prom 3f) | 1 | **5** | 14/1 | 64 | 19 |
| 1466[7] | **Louisville Belle (IRE) (47)** (MDIUsher) **7-7-13** NAdams(8) (nvr nr to chal) | 1¼ | **6** | 20/1 | 35 | — |
| 1693[5] | **Welsh Mountain (70)** (MJHeaton-Ellis) **3-8-11v**(3) SDrowne(13) (chsd ldrs 3f) | s.h | **7** | 10/1 | 58 | 13 |
| *109*[10] | **Colston-C (68)** (RJBaker) **4-9-1**(5) PPMurphy(3) (s.s: hdwy over 1f out: nvr nrr) | hd | **8** | 14/1 | 56 | 19 |
| 1844[9] | **Deardaw (44)** (MDIUsher) **4-7-10** GBardwell(11) (nvr trbld ldrs) | nk | **9** | 50/1 | 31 | — |
| *308*[10] | **Master Millfield (IRE) (68)** (RJBaker) **4-9-6** FNorton(9) (bit bkwd: n.d) | 1¾ | **10** | 16/1 | 50 | 13 |
| 1693[12] | **Times of Times (IRE) (74)** (MJRyan) **3-8-13**(5) MBaird(6) (a bhd) | 1½ | **11** | 16/1 | 52 | 7 |
| 1777[8] | **Tinker Osmaston (69)** (MSSaunders) **5-9-7** RPrice(14) (chsd ldrs tl wknd over 2f out) | 5 | **12** | 10/1 | 33 | — |
| 1501[11] | **Ann's Pearl (IRE) (72)** (JWHills) **5-9-10** RHughes(15) (lw: hld up: bhd fnl 2f) | ¾ | **13** | 6/1[2] | 34 | — |
| | | | | (SP 125.7%) | | **13 Rn** |

**1m 10.2** (0.70) CSF £38.03 CT £133.78 TOTE £9.90: £4.20 £1.40 £2.40 (£29.40) Trio £44.20 OWNER Mrs A. L. Stacey (COWBRIDGE) BRED Mrs C. Oliver Iselin III
LONG HANDICAP Deardaw 7-5
WEIGHT FOR AGE 3yo-8lb
**587 Beau Venture (USA)**, who had been slipping down the ratings, showed signs of tying up in the closing stages but had run this field ragged. (7/1)
**Albert The Bear** never had much hope of catching the winner and was not knocked about in the last 100 yards. (9/2: 6/1-4/1)
**1597 Dande Flyer** seems more effective over the minimum trip. (9/2)
**1446 Kildee Lad**, without a win last season, is still 2lb higher than when he last visited the winner's enclosure. (7/1)
**861* Songsheet** found this a bit hotter than the seller she won over the bare minimum here in April. (14/1)
**1178 Louisville Belle (IRE)** needs further. (20/1)

T/Plpt: £1,487.10 (5.52 Tckts). T/Qdpt: £189.30 (2.72 Tckts). KH

## 1638-LEICESTER (R-H) (Good, Good to firm patches)
### Saturday June 15th
WEATHER: sunny & v.warm WIND: slt half against

**1986** SPORTING GREEN H'CAP (0-80) (3-Y.O) (Class D)
6-45 (6-46) **7f 9y** £3,694.95 (£1,101.60: £525.30: £237.15) Stalls: Low GOING minus 0.35 sec per fur (F)

| | | | | SP | RR | SF |
|---|---|---|---|---|---|---|
| 1709* | **Lionel Edwards (IRE) (73)** (PFICole) **3-8-12**(7) DavidO'Neill(5) (lw: a.p: led over 1f out: hld on wl cl home) | — | **1** | 4/1[1] | 81 | 31 |
| 1438[5] | **Passage Creeping (IRE) (70)** (LMCumani) **3-9-2** JWeaver(1) (in tch: hdwy over 1f out: swtchd rt appr fnl f: fin wl) | nk | **2** | 9/2[2] | 77 | 27 |
| *1457*[9] | **School Boy (68)** (TJNaughton) **3-9-0** DHarrison(7) (hld up in tch: hdwy & ev ch fr 2f out: no ex fnl f) | ½ | **3** | 13/2 | 74 | 24 |
| 1615[6] | **Ashanti Dancer (IRE) (67)** (MJHaynes) **3-8-13** JReid(4) (hdwy over 2f out: kpt on u.p ins fnl f) | 2 | **4** | 9/1 | 69 | 19 |
| 1707[8] | **Angus McCoatup (IRE) (56)** (BAMcMahon) **3-7-11b**(5) LNewton(8) (prom: led over 2f out tl over 1f out: wknd ins fnl f) | 1½ | **5** | 20/1 | 54 | 4 |
| 1693[4] | **Snow Falcon (64)** (MBell) **3-8-10b** MFenton(9) (hld up: effrt & rdn over 2f out: no imp appr fnl f) | 1¾ | **6** | 15/2 | 58 | 8 |
| | **Maristax (75)** (PJMakin) **3-9-7** WCarson(10) (still unf: hdwy ½-wy: rdn 2f out: eased whn btn) | 2½ | **7** | 7/1 | 64 | 14 |
| 1594[15] | **Goodwood Rocket (67)** (JLDunlop) **3-8-13b[1]** PatEddery(3) (led to ½-wy: sn rdn & lost pl: eased whn btn) | 3½ | **8** | 6/1[3] | 48 | — |
| 1185[12] | **Magic Lake (52)** (EJAlston) **3-7-12** JQuinn(2) (led over 3f out tl over 2f out: wknd appr fnl f) | 1 | **9** | 7/1 | 30 | — |
| 1671[7] | **Lagan (60)** (PSFelgate) **3-8-3**(3) DWright(6) (s.i.s: a in rr: t.o fnl 2f) | 7 | **10** | 50/1 | 22 | — |
| | | | | (SP 119.3%) | | **10 Rn** |

**1m 26.5** (3.50) CSF £21.62 CT £108.42 TOTE £5.20: £1.80 £1.90 £2.70 (£10.60) Trio £20.30 OWNER Richard Green (Fine Paintings) (WHATCOMBE) BRED Fluorocarbon Bloodstock
STEWARDS' ENQUIRY Weaver susp. 24-27/6/96 (careless riding).
**1709* Lionel Edwards (IRE)** has found his true form in recent weeks, but he again had to do battle to hold on close home. (4/1)

**1438 Passage Creeping (IRE)** looked a shade unlucky but it was probably her inability to pick up which left her with too much to do. Experience is all she needs. (9/2)
**1457 School Boy**, in an all-out battle in the final quarter-mile, just could not quicken sufficiently inside the distance to stake his claim. His turn is near at hand. (13/2)
**1615 Ashanti Dancer (IRE)** produces her best when brought late but, by doing so, is more likely to find trouble. With the runner-up taking her ground entering the final furlong, she lost her momentum and whatever chance remained. (9/1)
**992 Angus McCoatup (IRE)**, trying a longer trip, again shared the lead until fading inside the last furlong. (20/1)
**1693 Snow Falcon** moved to post badly and never got himself into it. (15/2)
**1594 Goodwood Rocket** ran much too freely in his first-time blinkers and was a spent force approaching the final quarter-mile. Eased when beaten, he is capable of much better. (6/1)

## 1987 TIPSTERS TABLE MEDIAN AUCTION MAIDEN STKS (2-Y.O) (Class F)
7-15 (7-16) **5f 2y** £2,880.80 (£798.80: £382.40) Stalls: Low GOING minus 0.35 sec per fur (F)

| | | | | SP | RR | SF |
|---|---|---|---|---|---|---|
| | **Easycall** (BJMeehan) **2-9-0** BDoyle(1) (unf: scope: dwlt: sn rcvrd: led 3f out: clr appr fnl f: v.easily) | — | 1 | 10/1 | 92+ | 41 |
| 1705[3] | **Mujova (IRE)** (RHollinshead) **2-9-0** KFallon(7) (trckd ldrs: effrt & ev ch 2f out: rdn & one pce appr fnl f) | 5 | 2 | 5/1[2] | 76 | 25 |
| 1531[3] | **Chain Reaction (IRE)** (MAJarvis) **2-8-9** PBloomfield(4) (trckd ldrs: effrt 2f out: sn hrd drvn: no imp) | 1¾ | 3 | 12/1 | 65 | 14 |
| 869[2] | **Bold Welcome** (JWharton) **2-9-0** JQuinn(2) (s.i.s: hdwy 2f out: sn rdn: nt rch ldrs) | 1¼ | 4 | 11/2[3] | 66 | 15 |
| 1766[2] | **Hangover Square (IRE)** (RHannon) **2-9-0** PatEddery(5) (led 2f: rdn & outpcd wl over 1f out) | 1½ | 5 | 4/6[1] | 62 | 11 |
| | **Silver Spell** (DrJDScargill) **2-8-9** MFenton(3) (lt-f: s.s: wl bhd tl sme late hdwy) | ¾ | 6 | 25/1 | 54 | 3 |
| 1105[5] | **Amy** (CSmith) **2-8-9** JFortune(6) (in rr tl p.u & dismntd wl over 1f out) | | P | 50/1 | — | — |

(SP 114.6%) **7 Rn**

**60.09 secs** (1.59) CSF £53.90 TOTE £13.90: £4.50 £2.30 (£47.00) OWNER Easycall Partnership (UPPER LAMBOURN) BRED Mrs Susan Feddern
OFFICIAL EXPLANATION **Amy: her jockey reported that when she lost her action three furlongs out, he pulled her up thinking something was wrong, but on dismounting found her to be sound.**
**Easycall** soon recovered from a sluggish start and, in front before halfway, stormed clear for a very impressive debut. He could be anything. (10/1: op 6/1)
**1705 Mujova (IRE)**, the most experienced of the field, tried hard to keep tabs on the winner but he was brushed aside with ease. (5/1)
**1531 Chain Reaction (IRE)** did not really find top gear until far too late on this step down to the minimum trip, and was never nearer than at the finish. (12/1)
**1766 Hangover Square (IRE)** held the call early on, but had no answer to the superior speed of the winner. (4/6)

## 1988 LEICESTER MERCURY STKS (Listed) (4-Y.O+) (Class A)
7-45 (7-45) **1m 3f 183y** £11,508.00 (£4,272.00: £2,061.00: £855.00: £352.50: £151.50) GOING minus 0.35 sec per fur (F)

| | | | | SP | RR | SF |
|---|---|---|---|---|---|---|
| 1620[2] | **Midnight Legend (113)** (LMCumani) **5-8-12** JWeaver(2) (lw: mde virtually all: hrd drvn fnl 2f: hld on gamely) | — | 1 | 9/4[2] | 117 | 67 |
| 1620* | **Taufan's Melody (115)** (LadyHerries) **5-8-12** RCochrane(4) (lw: trckd ldrs: jnd wnr over 2f out: rdn & unable qckn towards fin) | ¾ | 2 | 13/8[1] | 116 | 66 |
| 1620[3] | **Florid (USA) (106)** (HRACecil) **5-8-12** PatEddery(6) (lw: hmpd sn after s: hld up & bhd: hdwy 2f out: r.o u.p ins fnl f) | s.h | 3 | 5/1[3] | 116 | 66 |
| 726[6] | **Blushing Flame (USA) (103)** (MRStoute) **5-8-12** JReid(3) (bit bkwd: prom: shkn up 2f out: one pce appr fnl f) | 3½ | 4 | 7/1 | 111 | 61 |
| 1509[5] | **Poppy Carew (IRE) (105)** (PWHarris) **4-8-7** GHind(5) (hld up & bhd: effrt 3f out: wknd 2f out) | 5 | 5 | 11/1 | 99 | 49 |
| 1128[5] | **Asterita (106)** (RHannon) **4-8-7** MHills(1) (lw: trckd ldrs tl wknd over 2f out: t.o) | 17 | 6 | 20/1 | 76 | 26 |

(SP 111.1%) **6 Rn**

**2m 29.2** (0.20) CSF £6.07 TOTE £3.10: £1.90 £1.70 (£2.30) OWNER Umm Qarn Racing (NEWMARKET) BRED Limestone Stud
**1620 Midnight Legend** gained his revenge over the runner-up on 5lb worse terms with a gutsy all-the-way success in a time not far off the record. He could be back to his best. (9/4)
**1620* Taufan's Melody** moved upsides the winner early in the straight and looked to be travelling just the better but, in a spirited battle to the post, was always destined to be second best. (13/8)
**1620 Florid (USA)**, slightly impeded leaving the start, was soon trailing his rivals. Pulled out to deliver his challenge two furlongs out, he responded to a forceful ride and kept staying on, if just short of a burst of finishing speed. (5/1)
**Blushing Flame (USA)** still needed this, but remained in close contention until feeling the strain approaching the last furlong. He comes good in the autumn. (7/1)

## 1989 PROPERTY GUIDE MEDIAN AUCTION MAIDEN STKS (2-Y.O) (Class D)
8-15 (8-16) **5f 218y** £3,752.50 (£1,120.00: £535.00: £242.50) Stalls: Low GOING minus 0.35 sec per fur (F)

| | | | | SP | RR | SF |
|---|---|---|---|---|---|---|
| 1801[3] | **Magic Blue (IRE)** (RHollinshead) **2-8-9**(5) FLynch(1) (hld up: hdwy 3f out: led ins fnl f: r.o wl) | — | 1 | 9/2[2] | 71 | 17 |
| | **Assume (USA)** (JWHills) **2-9-0** MHills(7) (w'like: a.p: led 2f out tl ins fnl f: kpt on) | ¾ | 2 | 5/1[3] | 69 | 15 |
| 829[8] | **Supercharmer** (CEBrittain) **2-9-0** BDoyle(2) (led tl hdd 2f out: hrd drvn & one pce fnl f) | 1 | 3 | 8/1 | 66 | 12 |
| | **Three For A Pound** (JAGlover) **2-9-0** JReid(11) (w'like: leggy: bit bkwd: trckd ldrs tl wknd over 1f out) | 5 | 4 | 5/1[3] | 53 | — |
| 1622[W] | **Heggies (IRE)** (CREgerton) **2-9-0** CRutter(8) (bit bkwd: bhd: rdn 3f out: styd on appr fnl f: nt rch ldrs) | ¾ | 5 | 33/1 | 51 | — |
| | **Silk St John** (MJRyan) **2-9-0** JQuinn(3) (w'like: scope: bit bkwd: s.s: hdwy 2f out: kpt on wl ins fnl f) | hd | 6 | 20/1 | 51 | — |
| 1694[7] | **Sharp Return** (MJRyan) **2-9-0** NDay(6) (trckd ldrs: no imp fnl 2f) | 1½ | 7 | 14/1 | 47 | — |
| 1499[3] | **Taome (IRE)** (PDEvans) **2-8-9** JFortune(4) (in tch tl rdn & wknd over 2f out) | ½ | 8 | 4/1[1] | 40 | — |
| | **Pretty Sally (IRE)** (DJGMurraySmith) **2-8-9** JWeaver(9) (unf: bit bkwd: bhd fr ½-wy: t.o) | 6 | 9 | 11/1 | 24 | — |
| 1760[4] | **Singforyoursupper** (GGMargarson) **2-8-9** PBloomfield(5) (unruly s: a bhd: t.o) | 1½ | 10 | 10/1 | 20 | — |
| 1445[7] | **Lancashire Knight** (SDow) **2-8-9**(5) ADaly(10) (bit bkwd: sn pushed along: drifted lft ½-wy: t.o) | 12 | 11 | 20/1 | — | — |

(SP 119.2%) **11 Rn**

**1m 13.7** (3.70) CSF £25.99 TOTE £5.20: £2.20 £1.30 £3.20 (£10.80) Trio £32.10 OWNER Mr G. A. Johnson (UPPER LONGDON) BRED Lodge Park Stud
**1801 Magic Blue (IRE)** came good at the first time of asking over this longer trip with a readily-gained success and can go on from here. (9/2)
**Assume (USA)** looked set to make a winning start to his career when leading into the final furlong, but the more experienced winner took his measure on the run to the line. He should not have much trouble in going one better. (5/1)
**Supercharmer** still just needed this, but stuck on promisingly after being headed, and he could make it third time lucky. (8/1)

**Three For A Pound**, coltish in the paddock, pushed the pace and had every chance until lack of a previous outing began to tell approaching the final furlong. (5/1)
**Heggies (IRE)**, struggling with the pace and driven along at halfway, did stay on below the distance and seems to be getting the hang of the game. (33/1)
**Silk St John** did well to finish so close after missing the break and more will be heard of him. (20/1)
**1169 Sharp Return** (14/1: 10/1-16/1)
**Pretty Sally (IRE)** (11/1: 8/1-12/1)

## 1990 SPORTS MERCURY CONDITIONS STKS (3-Y.O) (Class C)
8-45 (8-45) **1m 3f 183y** £5,185.32 (£1,790.92: £857.46: £348.30) Stalls: Low GOING minus 0.35 sec per fur (F)

| | | | | SP | RR | SF |
|---|---|---|---|---|---|---|
| 1189* | **Place de L'Opera (85)** (HRACecil) **3-8-9** PatEddery(3) (hld up: hdwy to ld over 2f out: sn clr: impressive) | — | 1 | 2/1[1] | 94++ | 53 |
| 1168* | **Mattawan** (MJohnston) **3-9-0** JWeaver(4) (lw: chsd ldrs: ev ch 3f out: outpcd appr fnl f) | 7 | 2 | 85/40[2] | 90 | 49 |
| 793a[2] | **Camp Follower** (JLDunlop) **3-9-0** WCarson(2) (bit bkwd: hld up & bhd: outpcd ent st: sn rdn: styd on appr fnl f: nvr nr to chal) | 6 | 3 | 9/2 | 81 | 40 |
| 1644* | **Forest Heights** (MrsJCecil) **3-8-9** JReid(1) (lw: led tl hdd over 2f out: sn drvn along & wknd) | ¾ | 4 | 3/1[3] | 75 | 34 |
| | | | | (SP 108.5%) | | **4 Rn** |

**2m 30.9** (1.90) CSF £6.12 TOTE £2.30 (£2.50) OWNER Cliveden Stud (NEWMARKET) BRED Cliveden Stud Ltd
**1189* Place de L'Opera** is certainly progressing the right way and, handing out a thorough thrashing to these rivals, will now be aimed at the Lancashire Oaks. (2/1: 5/4-9/4)
**1168* Mattawan** shows plenty of knee-action, but held his pitch to have every chance until the useful winner said go. From then on, the battle was only for the places. (85/40)
**793a Camp Follower** had not raced on ground as lively as this and, off the bridle a long way out, was unable to get himself into contention. (9/2)
**1644* Forest Heights** had much more on her plate this time than when winning her maiden. (3/1)

## 1991 MERCURY RACE NIGHT H'CAP (0-70) (3-Y.O+ F & M) (Class E)
9-15 (9-15) **5f 218y** £3,234.00 (£966.00: £462.00: £210.00) Stalls: Low GOING minus 0.35 sec per fur (F)

| | | | | SP | RR | SF |
|---|---|---|---|---|---|---|
| *1812** | **Wardara (58)** (CADwyer) **4-8-11v**(5) FLynch(9) (swtchd lft 4f out: hdwy to ld over 1f out: r.o wl) | — | 1 | 8/1 | 69 | 51 |
| 1412* | **Faraway Lass (66)** (LordHuntingdon) **3-9-2** DHarrison(5) (lw: a.p: ev ch over 1f out: no ex ins fnl f) | 1¼ | 2 | 11/4[1] | 74 | 48 |
| 1786* | **Almasi (IRE) (68)** (CFWall) **4-9-12** GDuffield(1) (lw: swvd lft s: bhd tl hdwy over 1f out: fin wl) | ½ | 3 | 9/2[3] | 74 | 56 |
| 1786[6] | **It's Academic (62)** (MrsJRRamsden) **4-9-6** KFallon(10) (lw: hld up: hdwy over 2f out: hrd drvn & n.m.r appr fnl f: nvr able to chal) | 2 | 4 | 15/2 | 63 | 45 |
| 1473[6] | **Winsome Wooster (62)** (PGMurphy) **5-9-3**(3) SDrowne(4) (bit bkwd: trckd ldrs: rdn 2f out: r.o one pce) | nk | 5 | 14/1 | 62 | 44 |
| 1708[10] | **Sing With the Band (60)** (BAMcMahon) **5-8-13**(5) LNewton(6) (prom: led wl over 1f out: sn hdd: wknd fnl f) | 2 | 6 | 10/1 | 55 | 37 |
| 768[12] | **Power Princess (46)** (JAPickering) **3-7-10** JQuinn(2) (b: outpcd: a bhd) | 6 | 7 | 40/1 | 25 | — |
| 1634* | **Rambold (57)** (NEBerry) **5-8-12**(3) DarrenMoffatt(8) (racd alone: led tl hdd & wknd wl over 1f out) | 2½ | 8 | 8/1 | 29 | 11 |
| 1840* | **Petit Point (IRE) (76)** (RHannon) **3-9-12** 6x PatEddery(7) (prom 4f) | hd | 9 | 7/2[2] | 48 | 22 |
| 1761[7] | **Capture The Moment (55)** (RJRWilliams) **3-8-5** MFenton(3) (b.nr hind: chsd ldrs 4f: sn wknd) | 1½ | 10 | 16/1 | 23 | — |
| | | | | (SP 125.1%) | | **10 Rn** |

**1m 11.3** (1.30) CSF £30.90 CT £109.97 TOTE £10.00: £3.10 £1.80 £1.40 (£22.00) Trio £32.40 OWNER Binding Matters Ltd (NEWMARKET) BRED G. B. Turnbull Ltd
LONG HANDICAP Power Princess 7-4
WEIGHT FOR AGE 3yo-8lb
**1812* Wardara** looked ill-at-ease cantering to post, but she worked her way across the course to deliver her challenge, and had the measure of her rivals entering the final furlong. (8/1)
**1412* Faraway Lass**, always in the firing-line, looked to be going as well as anything until the winner appeared on the scene. (11/4)
**1786* Almasi (IRE)** gave away valuable ground by swerving left leaving the stalls and, though she did finish best of all, she was never going to get there. (9/2)
**1786 It's Academic** is better over further when the ground rides fast and, denied a clear run when about to launch her bid, was never nearer than at the line. (15/2)
**1473 Winsome Wooster** could not get in a blow at the principals, but showed promise. (14/1)

T/Plpt: £66.40 (162.89 Tckts). T/Qdpt: £8.60 (76.34 Tckts). IM

# 1619-LINGFIELD (L-H) (Turf Firm, AWT Standard)
## Saturday June 15th
WEATHER: fine WIND: almost nil

## 1992 RETRIEVER (S) H'CAP (0-60) (3-Y.O+) (Class G)
6-00 (6-04) **7f** £2,826.00 (£786.00: £378.00) Stalls: Centre GOING minus 0.57 sec per fur (F)

| | | | | SP | RR | SF |
|---|---|---|---|---|---|---|
| 887* | **King Parrot (IRE) (47)** (LordHuntingdon) **8-8-8**(7) AimeeCook(13) (lw: a.p: led over 1f out: r.o) | — | 1 | 7/2[1] | 59 | 41 |
| 1337[6] | **Thatchmaster (IRE) (45)** (CAHorgan) **5-8-13** PaulEddery(9) (lw: a.p: ev ch wl over 1f out: r.o one pce ins fnl f) | 1¼ | 2 | 4/1[2] | 54 | 36 |
| *896[9]* | **Dahiyah (USA) (60)** (GLMoore) **5-9-11v**(3) AWhelan(17) (led: hdd over 1f out: r.o one pce ins fnl f) | ½ | 3 | 14/1 | 68 | 50 |
| 1317[9] | **Cherry Garden (IRE) (51)** (TJNaughton) **3-8-4**(5) JDSmith(10) (lw: chsd ldrs: rdn over 2f out: one pce) | 1¼ | 4 | 14/1 | 56 | 28 |
| 1685[9] | **Almapa (48)** (RJHodges) **4-9-2** AMackay(7) (chsd ldrs: rdn over 2f out: one pce) | nk | 5 | 12/1 | 53 | 35 |
| 1691[2] | **Northern Grey (51)** (DrJDScargill) **4-9-2**(3) JStack(15) (mid div: rdn ½-wy: kpt on one pce fnl 2f) | 5 | 6 | 6/1[3] | 44 | 26 |
| 1681* | **Lift Boy (USA) (50)** (AMoore) **7-9-4** CandyMorris(1) (led far side group: no ch w stands' side group fnl 2f) | 1¼ | 7 | 15/2 | 40 | 22 |
| *1721[6]* | **Supreme Illusion (AUS) (42)** (JohnBerry) **3-7-7b**(7)ow4 JoHunnam(6) (chsd ldrs: rdn 3f out: wknd over 2f out) | ½ | 8 | 50/1 | 31 | — |
| 1516[3] | **Justinianus (IRE) (46)** (JJBridger) **4-8-11**(3) DarrenMoffatt(3) (chsd far side ldr: wknd over 1f out) | 4 | 9 | 14/1 | 26 | 8 |
| 1681[5] | **Old Gold N Tan (38)** (JRPoulton) **3-7-3b**(7) RMullen(12) (a bhd) | 4 | 10 | 50/1 | 9 | — |
| 1506[10] | **Speedy Snaps Image (35)** (JELong) **5-8-3** JFEgan(2) (b: racd far side: a wl bhd) | 3 | 11 | 50/1 | — | — |
| 1658[10] | **Little Gent (IRE) (30)** (JELong) **5-7-12** DaleGibson(11) (a bhd) | 3 | 12 | 50/1 | — | — |
| 1170[7] | **Assignment (36)** (JELong) **10-8-4** LeesaLong(8) (dwlt: a bhd) | 1½ | 13 | 33/1 | — | — |
| 1517[3] | **Rockville Pike (IRE) (52)** (JohnBerry) **4-9-6** MRimmer(4) (lw: prom to ½-wy) | 7 | 14 | 10/1 | — | — |

| | | | | SP | RR | SF |
|---|---|---|---|---|---|---|
| 1502[12] | **Malzoom (28)** (SEKettlewell) **4-7-10** NKennedy(5) (b.hind: reard & uns rdr s) | | **U** | 14/1 | — | — |

(SP 122.5%) **15 Rn**

**1m 22.32** (0.72) CSF £17.00 CT £161.73 TOTE £3.70: £1.60 £1.80 £6.30 (£10.70) Trio £48.40 OWNER Lord Huntingdon (WEST ILSLEY) BRED W. Hastings-Bass in Ireland
LONG HANDICAP Old Gold N Tan 7-5 Supreme Illusion (AUS) 7-4 Malzoom 7-7
WEIGHT FOR AGE 3yo-10lb
Bt in 4,400gns
**887* King Parrot (IRE)** always looked to going best and his able pilot did not have to get too serious. (7/2)
**1337 Thatchmaster (IRE)** looked very dangerous below the distance, but could not match the winner's turn of foot. (4/1)
**631 Dahiyah (USA)** made a brave attempt to make all and kept on well once headed. (14/1)
**516 Cherry Garden (IRE)** tracked the leaders, but came under pressure shortly after halfway, and then could only plod on at the one speed. (14/1)
**1685 Almapa** (12/1: op 8/1)
**1517 Rockville Pike (IRE)** (10/1: 6/1-12/1)
**1001 Malzoom** (14/1: op 8/1)

## 1993 UNION TRANSPORT GROUP FREIGHT FORWARDING LIMITED STKS (0-65) (3-Y.O+) (Class F)

6-30 (6-32) **1m (Equitrack)** £2,928.40 (£812.40: £389.20) Stalls: Centre GOING minus 0.63 sec per fur (FST)

| | | | | SP | RR | SF |
|---|---|---|---|---|---|---|
| *1490*[4] | **Quiet Arch (IRE) (60)** (CACyzer) **3-8-9** MRoberts(10) (chsd ldrs: led over 1f out: rdn ins fnl f: r.o wl) | — | **1** | 8/1 | 75 | 24 |
| 1659[4] | **Perilous Plight (65)** (WRMuir) **5-9-10** WJO'Connor(2) (lw: a.p: chsd wnr over 1f out: rdn ins fnl f: r.o) | 1 | **2** | 7/2[1] | 77 | 37 |
| *836*[7] | **Red Rusty (USA) (64)** (DMorris) **3-8-11** PaulEddery(3) (led: hdd over 1f out: wknd ins fnl f) | 5 | **3** | 13/2 | 65 | 14 |
| 1641[16] | **Sharp Command (60)** (RWArmstrong) **3-8-9** RHills(6) (lw: chsd ldrs: rdn over 1f out: one pce) | hd | **4** | 12/1 | 63 | 12 |
| 1000[3] | **General Haven (65)** (TJNaughton) **3-8-6**(5) JDSmith(11) (hld up in rr: hdwy over 1f out: styd on ins fnl f: nvr nrr) | 1¾ | **5** | 11/2[3] | 61 | 10 |
| *1719** | **Sheraz (IRE) (63)** (NTinkler) **4-9-8** JFEgan(7) (mid div: rdn 4f out: no hdwy) | 3 | **6** | 9/2[2] | 55 | 15 |
| *1490*[6] | **People Direct (62)** (KMcAuliffe) **3-8-11**(3) JStack(9) (prom tl wknd qckly over 1f out) | 2 | **7** | 12/1 | 54 | 3 |
| 1804[11] | **Classic Affair (USA) (58)** (RHarris) **3-8-6** AMackay(5) (a bhd) | 6 | **8** | 20/1 | 34 | — |
| 1856[11] | **Adilov (60)** (KOCunningham-Brown) **4-9-6** DBiggs(4) (a bhd) | ¾ | **9** | 25/1 | 36 | — |
| 1348[14] | **Daily Risk (65)** (DWChapman) **3-8-9** ACulhane(8) (a bhd) | 16 | **10** | 7/1 | 4 | — |
| 887[20] | **Little Millie (60)** (PHayward) **3-8-6** DaleGibson(1) (bhd fnl 4f) | 6 | **11** | 33/1 | — | — |

(SP 119.7%) **11 Rn**

**1m 39.19** (1.79) CSF £34.69 TOTE £9.60: £3.00 £1.70 £1.80 (£13.70) Trio £175.00; £73.94 to Windsor 17/6/96 OWNER Mr R. M. Cyzer (HORSHAM) BRED E. and Mrs Flannery
WEIGHT FOR AGE 3yo-11lb
**1490 Quiet Arch (IRE)** got first run on the favourite and made it tell. (8/1)
**1659 Perilous Plight** was hemmed in slightly when the winner went on but, try as he might, he could not make up the leeway. (7/2)
**Red Rusty (USA)** made the running but was soon left behind in the straight. (13/2: 10/1-6/1)
**528 Sharp Command** raced in touch, but only had the one speed to offer in the straight. (12/1: op 8/1)
**1000 General Haven** won here in March. He was never really put in the race here, but the way he kept on in the closing stages suggested he could find another race soon. (11/2)
**1490 People Direct** (12/1: op 8/1)

## 1994 UNION TRANSPORT GROUP 50TH ANNIVERSARY MAIDEN STKS (3-Y.O+) (Class D)

7-00 (7-05) **6f** £4,045.00 (£1,210.00: £580.00: £265.00) Stalls: Centre GOING minus 0.57 sec per fur (F)

| | | | | SP | RR | SF |
|---|---|---|---|---|---|---|
| 1667[2] | **Duel At Dawn** (JHMGosden) **3-8-12** WRyan(7) (lw: b: b.hind: w ldr: led 4f out: brought far side over 3f out: rdn over 1f out: r.o wl) | — | **1** | 5/6[1] | 88 | 32 |
| 672[7] | **Woodbury Lad (USA)** (WRMuir) **3-8-12** MRoberts(1) (racd far side: chsd wnr 2f out: sn rdn: unable qckn) | 2½ | **2** | 7/2[2] | 81 | 25 |
| 1693[7] | **Albaha (USA) (85)** (RWArmstrong) **3-8-12b** RHills(3) (lw: racd far side: led 2f: rdn 2f out: one pce) | 2½ | **3** | 5/1[3] | 75 | 19 |
| 1099[16] | **Out Line** (MMadgwick) **4-8-12**(3) NVarley(14) (hdwy 4f out: edgd lft over 1f out: styd on ins fnl f) | 2½ | **4** | 50/1 | 63 | 15 |
| 1422[8] | **In The Highlands** (DJSCosgrove) **3-8-7** DaleGibson(2) (b: racd far side: sn outpcd) | 7 | **5** | 50/1 | 44 | — |
| 1617[15] | **First Law** (MissGayKelleway) **3-8-7** WJO'Connor(12) (b.hind: chsd ldrs tl wknd 3f out) | 4 | **6** | 33/1 | 34 | — |
| 672[11] | **Cadeau Elegant** (NACallaghan) **3-8-7** AMackay(8) (in tch to ½-wy) | s.h | **7** | 33/1 | 34 | — |
| 949[12] | **Doth Protest (IRE)** (NoelChance) **4-8-10**(5) MartinDwyer(10) (bhd fnl 4f) | ½ | **8** | 50/1 | 32 | — |
| 1518[6] | **Governor's Bid** (MrsLCJewell) **3-8-12** JFEgan(6) (bhd fnl 4f) | 6 | **9** | 50/1 | 21 | — |
| 1667[6] | **Welsh Emblem (IRE)** (GWragg) **3-8-12** PaulEddery(4) (lw: a bhd) | ½ | **10** | 8/1 | 20 | — |
| 1690[13] | **Silky Smooth (IRE)** (MrsNMacauley) **3-8-4**(3) CTeague(11) (b: sn rdn along: a bhd) | 9 | **11** | 50/1 | — | — |
| | **Wey River Mist** (JJBridger) **3-8-7** ACulhane(5) (lt-f: bit bkwd: a bhd) | 1¼ | **12** | 50/1 | — | — |
| 1452[11] | **Fleeting Footsteps** (MJPolglase) **4-9-6** WHollick(9) (bhd fr ½-wy) | 1¼ | **13** | 50/1 | — | — |
| | **Allstars Rocket** (TJNaughton) **3-8-7**(5) JDSmith(13) (leggy: scope: bit bkwd: v.slowly away: a bhd) | 4 | **14** | 25/1 | — | — |

(SP 128.0%) **14 Rn**

**1m 10.03** (1.03) CSF £4.48 TOTE £1.90: £1.10 £1.70 £1.80 (£4.00) Trio £4.60 OWNER Sheikh Mohammed (NEWMARKET) BRED Sheikh Mohammed bin Rashid al Maktoum
WEIGHT FOR AGE 3yo-8lb
**1667 Duel At Dawn** was not hard pressed to open his account. (5/6: 4/5-Evens)
**672 Woodbury Lad (USA)** could not peg back the winner in the final two furlongs, but ran easily his best race to date. He is improving. (7/2: op 7/1)
**1693 Albaha (USA)** showed his usual early pace. (5/1: op 3/1)
**Out Line** kept on in promising fashion in the final two furlongs and can find a small race. (50/1)
**1667 Welsh Emblem (IRE)** (8/1: tchd 12/1)

## 1995 POINTER H'CAP (0-70) (3-Y.O) (Class E)

7-30 (7-32) **7f** £3,534.30 (£1,058.40: £508.20: £233.10) Stalls: Centre GOING minus 0.57 sec per fur (F)

| | | | | SP | RR | SF |
|---|---|---|---|---|---|---|
| 1776[3] | **Ivory's Grab Hire (53)** (KTIvory) **3-8-7b**(5) MartinDwyer(6) (hld up in tch: led 3f out: rdn over 1f out: r.o) | — | **1** | 7/1 | 68 | 23 |
| 1764* | **Ivor's Deed (54)** (CFWall) **3-8-6**(7) PClarke(3) (hld up: swtchd rt after 2f: hdwy 3f out: ev ch ent fnl f: unable qckn) | 2½ | **2** | 7/4[1] | 63 | 18 |
| 934[6] | **Classic Beauty (IRE) (62)** (RHarris) **3-9-7** AMackay(1) (lw: chsd ldrs: rdn 2f out: one pce) | 1¼ | **3** | 13/2[3] | 68 | 23 |

1693[10] **Mindrace (61)** (KTIvory) **3-8-13**(7) CScally(7) (led: hdd 3f out: rdn 2f out: one pce) ........2½ **4** 14/1 62 17
1119[16] **Night of Glass (48)** (DMorris) **3-8-7** JHBrown(10) (chsd ldrs: rdn & outpcd over 3f out: kpt on one pce ins fnl f) ........2½ **5** 33/1 43 —
1050[6] **Crimson Rosella (57)** (WJHaggas) **3-9-2** RHills(8) (dwlt: rdn ½-wy: nvr nrr) ........½ **6** 11/4[2] 51 6
1612[6] **Patrio (IRE) (55)** (SCWilliams) **3-8-11**(3) MHenry(9) (chsd ldrs: ev ch 3f out: wknd over 1f out) ........s.h **7** 9/1 49 4
1684[5] **Farida Seconda (52)** (JLSpearing) **3-8-8**(3) JStack(2) (stdd s: sn bhd: t.o) ........21 **8** 14/1 — —
1350[13] **The Grey Weaver (50)** (RMFlower) **3-8-9** DBiggs(4) (bhd fnl 4f: t.o) ........22 **9** 33/1 — —
1657[7] **Embroidered (37)** (RMFlower) **3-7-7**(3) NVarley(5) (bhd fnl 4f: t.o) ........3 **10** 33/1 — —
(SP 121.0%) **10 Rn**

**1m 23.63** (2.03) CSF £19.54 CT £78.44 TOTE £6.00: £1.90 £1.30 £1.70 (£4.30) Trio £8.20 OWNER Mr Dean Ivory (RADLETT) BRED Japan Bloodstock Ltd
LONG HANDICAP Embroidered 7-8
**1776 Ivory's Grab Hire** has flattered to deceive a few times, but did nothing wrong here. (7/1)
**1764* Ivor's Deed** loomed up threateningly below the distance, but the winner proved too strong. (7/4)
**934 Classic Beauty (IRE)**, always to the fore, found a quickening touch beyond him in the last two furlongs. (13/2)

## 1996 UNION TRANSPORT GROUP SHIPPING H'CAP (0-70) (3-Y.O+) (Class E)

8-00 (8-01) **1m 2f** £3,288.60 (£982.80: £470.40: £214.20) Stalls: Centre GOING minus 0.57 sec per fur (F)

SP RR SF

1535[3] **Allstars Express (55)** (TJNaughton) **3-8-0**ow2 AMcGlone(2) (chsd ldrs: led 2f out: rdn out) ........— **1** 6/1[3] 67 19
1337[12] **Pistol (IRE) (56)** (CAHorgan) **6-9-0** PaulEddery(6) (hld up: hdwy over 2f out: rdn over 1f out: unable qckn) .....2 **2** 14/1 65 32
1655[7] **Errant (54)** (DJSCosgrove) **4-8-12** MRimmer(4) (hld up: hdwy 3f out: r.o one pce ins fnl f) ........4 **3** 10/1 56 23
1660[6] **It'sthebusiness (60)** (SDow) **4-9-4v** MRoberts(9) (carried wd after 2f: led 7f out: hdd 2f out: one pce) ........1¼ **4** 4/1[2] 60 27
1625[7] **Golden Touch (USA) (64)** (NACallaghan) **4-9-8** WRyan(10) (hld up: hdwy 4f out: rdn over 2f out: one pce) ..hd **5** 7/2[1] 64 31
1807[10] **Bentico (62)** (MrsNMacauley) **7-9-3**(3) CTeague(1) (hld up: sme hdwy over 2f out: eased whn btn ins fnl f)...1½ **6** 12/1 60 27
**Striffolino (70)** (JohnBerry) **4-9-11**(3) PMcCabe(11) (hdwy 7f out: rdn over 3f out: wknd over 2f out) ........3 **7** 14/1 63 30
1685[14] **Royal Thimble (IRE) (60)** (NoelChance) **5-9-4** WJO'Connor(5) (in tch to ½-wy) ........4 **8** 16/1 47 14
1655[3] **Premier League (IRE) (60)** (JELong) **6-8-13**(5) MartinDwyer(7) (sn led: rn wd after 2f: hdd 7f out: wknd over 3f out) ........4 **9** 4/1[2] 40 7
**Heretical Miss (38)** (JFfitch-Heyes) **6-7-7**(3) MHenry(8) (bhd fnl 4f) ........6 **10** 40/1 9 —
1465[7] **Allez Pablo (38)** (RRowe) **6-7-3**(7) PDoe(3) (bhd fnl 3f) ........1¼ **11** 66/1 7 —
(SP 116.4%) **11 Rn**

**2m 7.27** (2.57) CSF £75.47 CT £753.47 TOTE £6.70: £2.00 £2.90 £3.00 (£58.40) Trio £143.00 OWNER The Allstars Club (EPSOM) BRED P. and Mrs Blacker
LONG HANDICAP Heretical Miss 7-7 Allez Pablo 7-4
WEIGHT FOR AGE 3yo-13lb
Bt in 4,400gns
**1535 Allstars Express** handled the course better than most, and ran out an emphatic winner. (6/1)
**1124 Pistol (IRE)** made good headway in the final two furlongs, but could never get to grips with the winner. (14/1: 10/1-16/1)
**920 Errant** kept on in the final two furlongs without looking likely to take a hand in the finish. (10/1)
**1660 It'sthebusiness** proved very one-paced in the final two furlongs. (4/1)
**1440 Golden Touch (USA)**, under pressure up the home straight, only had the one pace to give and appears in the Handicapper's grip at present. (7/2)
**Bentico** appeared ill-at-ease on the sharp downhill run and could never recover. (12/1: op 8/1)

## 1997 SETTER MAIDEN RATING RELATED MAIDEN STKS (0-70) (3-Y.O+) (Class E)

8-30 (8-30) **2m (Equitrack)** £3,015.60 (£898.80: £428.40: £193.20) Stalls: Centre GOING minus 0.63 sec per fur (FST)

SP RR SF

1773[5] **Mighty Phantom (USA) (68)** (JWHills) **3-7-13**(3) MHenry(6) (chsd ldr ½-wy: led over 2f out: rdn clr over 1f out: eased nr fin) ........— **1** 5/2[2] 55+ 14
1591[3] **Illegally Yours (39)** (LMontagueHall) **3-8-2** JFEgan(5) (chsd ldrs: rdn 4f out: kpt on to go 2nd nr fin) ........3½ **2** 4/1[3] 52 11
1503[8] **Washington Reef (USA) (51)** (JHMGosden) **3-8-5v** WRyan(2) (rr: rdn ½-wy: outpcd 5f out: hdwy 3f out: sn hrd rdn: kpt on one pce fnl 2f) ........s.h **3** 9/2 54 13
1647[5] **Anchor Venture (60)** (SPCWoods) **3-8-5** WWoods(4) (keen hold: led 2f: led again 9f out: sn clr: hdd over 2f out: wknd fnl f) ........¾ **4** 7/4[1] 54 13
1514[15] **Boston Tea Party (38)** (AMoore) **3-7-13**(3) AWhelan(1) (rr: hdwy ½-wy: rdn 4f out: one pce fnl 3f) ........½ **5** 40/1 50 9
1655[9] **Rivercare (IRE) (57)** (MJPolglase) **3-8-5** WHollick(3) (bhd fnl 5f) ........16 **6** 11/2 37 —
1833[5] **Ewar Imperial (50)** (KOCunningham-Brown) **4-9-11b**[1] DBiggs(7) (led after 2f: hdd 9f out: wknd qckly: t.o & virtually p.u 5f out) ........dist **7** 50/1 — —
(SP 122.9%) **7 Rn**

**3m 26.74** (4.74) CSF £13.42 TOTE £3.10: £2.00 £1.90 (£7.50) OWNER Mr Michael Wauchope (LAMBOURN) BRED Michael S. Anderson and Brick Kiln Stud
WEIGHT FOR AGE 3yo-21lb, 4yo-1lb
**1773 Mighty Phantom (USA)** won this very poor race comfortably. (5/2: 7/4-11/4)
**1591 Illegally Yours** was under pressure a long way out and plugged on late for second. (4/1: op 6/1)
**Washington Reef (USA)** ran in snatches and, although staying on late, is obviously slow. (9/2: 4/1-13/2)
**1647 Anchor Venture** ran a bit free and burnt himself out by the two-furlong pole. (7/4)

T/Plpt: £135.80 (72.12 Tckts). T/Qdpt: £19.60 (32.9 Tckts). SM

# 1959-SANDOWN (R-H) (Firm, Good to firm patches)

## Saturday June 15th

WEATHER: warm WIND: almost nil

## 1998 E.B.F. PORTMAN SQUARE MAIDEN STKS (2-Y.O F) (Class D)

1-50 (1-52) **5f 6y** £3,650.00 (£1,025.00: £500.00) Stalls: Low GOING minus 0.45 sec per fur (F)

SP RR SF

1346[2] **Conspiracy** (JLDunlop) **2-8-11** PaulEddery(2) (chsd ldr: led over 2f out: comf) ........— **1** 2/7[1] 69+ 20

| | | | | SP | RR | SF |
|---|---|---|---|---|---|---|
| 1678$^{6}$ | **Rise 'n Shine** (CACyzer) **2-8-11** MRoberts(1) (lw: led over 2f: rdn: chsd wnr over 1f out: unable qckn) | 1½ | **2** | 10/1$^{3}$ | 64 | 15 |
| | **Fanny's Choice (IRE)** (RHannon) **2-8-11** RHills(4) (scope: hld up: chsd wnr over 2f out tl over 1f out: wknd fnl f) | 1¾ | **3** | 7/2$^{2}$ | 59 | 10 |
| | | | | (SP 109.1%) | **3 Rn** | |

**62.09 secs** (2.29) CSF £2.98 TOTE £1.30 (£1.80) OWNER Lord Chelsea (ARUNDEL) BRED Somerhall Bloodstock Ltd and Lord Chelsea
**1346 Conspiracy** won with the minimum of fuss. Racing in second place, she went on at halfway and comfortably had the measure of her two opponents. (2/7)
**1678 Rise 'n Shine** looked in good shape in the paddock and stepped up on her initial run. (10/1)
**Fanny's Choice (IRE)**, a half-sister to three winners, does have scope to develop. (7/2)

## 1999 BERKELEY SQUARE CLAIMING STKS (3-Y.O) (Class F)

2-20 (2-24) **1m 2f 7y** £2,736.00 (£828.00: £404.00: £192.00) Stalls: High GOING minus 0.45 sec per fur (F)

| | | | | SP | RR | SF |
|---|---|---|---|---|---|---|
| 1701$^{2}$ | **Shehab (IRE)** (WJHaggas) **3-9-3** RHills(3) (mde all: clr over 2f out: easily) | — | **1** | 7/4$^{2}$ | 89+ | 49 |
| 1659$^{3}$ | **Rebel County (IRE) (73)** (MCPipe) **3-8-9** MRoberts(2) (lw: plld hrd: hdwy over 3f out: chsd wnr over 2f out: eased whn btn ins fnl f) | 7 | **2** | 6/4$^{1}$ | 70 | 30 |
| 1100$^{6}$ | **Domettes (IRE) (59)** (RHannon) **3-8-4** KDarley(6) (lw: hld up: rdn over 3f out: one pce) | 2 | **3** | 11/2$^{3}$ | 62 | 22 |
| 1676$^{8}$ | **African Sun (IRE) (43)** (BHanbury) **3-8-2**$^{(3)}$ JStack(4) (b.hind: rdn & hdwy over 2f out: sn wknd) | 3 | **4** | 20/1 | 58 | 18 |
| 1416$^{10}$ | **Jona Holley (51)** (IABalding) **3-7-13**$^{(5)}$ MartinDwyer(1) (stdd s: rdn over 3f out: nvr nr to chal) | nk | **5** | 20/1 | 56 | 16 |
| 1651$^{8}$ | **Native Song (39)** (MJHaynes) **3-8-0** NCarlisle(7) (chsd wnr over 7f) | 1¾ | **6** | 66/1 | 50 | 10 |
| 1104$^{W}$ | **Ell Ell Eff** (AHide) **3-7-13** DBiggs(5) (w'like: bit bkwd: prom over 6f) | 23 | **7** | 25/1 | 12 | — |
| | | | | (SP 106.6%) | **7 Rn** | |

**2m 8.73** (2.03) CSF £4.25 TOTE £2.70: £1.50 £1.40 (£1.40) OWNER Mr Ali K Al Jafleh (NEWMARKET) BRED Ali K. Al Jafleh
Shehab(IRE) clmd WJDunphy £18,000
**1701 Shehab (IRE)**, more amenable at the stalls this time, made every post a winning one. Breezing clear over a quarter of a mile from home, he won with plenty in hand. (7/4)
**1659 Rebel County (IRE)**, taking a step up in distance, took a keen hold at the back of the field. Moving up entering the straight, she struggled into second approaching the final quarter-mile but, when it was clear she was not going to reel in the winner, she was eased. (6/4)
**1100 Domettes (IRE)** was made to look woefully one-paced in the last three furlongs. (11/2: 4/1-6/1)
**African Sun (IRE)** made an effort on the outside of the field over two furlongs from home, but it came to little. (20/1)

## 2000 JOHNSTONE DOUGLAS H'CAP (0-75) (3-Y.O+) (Class D)

2-55 (2-57) **1m 14y** £3,954.50 (£1,196.00: £583.00: £276.50) Stalls: High GOING minus 0.45 sec per fur (F)

| | | | | SP | RR | SF |
|---|---|---|---|---|---|---|
| 879$^{4}$ | **Autumn Cover (55)** (PRHedger) **4-8-9** DBiggs(7) (lw: led over 4f: led 2f out: r.o wl) | — | **1** | 3/1$^{1}$ | 64 | 46 |
| 1615$^{7}$ | **Ballpoint (67)** (RHannon) **3-8-10** MRoberts(6) (a.p: led over 3f out to 2f out: unable qckn) | 2½ | **2** | 12/1 | 71 | 42 |
| *366*$^{10}$ | **Bakers Daughter (47)** (JRArnold) **4-7-10b**$^{1(5)}$ MartinDwyer(5) (lw: a.p: rdn over 2f out: one pce) | ¾ | **3** | 20/1 | 50 | 32 |
| 1682* | **Ashby Hill (IRE) (53)** (RRowe) **5-8-7** PaulEddery(4) (lw: nt clr run on ins 5f out: hmpd on ins bnd 4f out: swtchd lft & hdwy over 2f out: hrd rdn over 1f out: one pce) | 1¼ | **4** | 5/1$^{2}$ | 53 | 35 |
| 1654$^{2}$ | **Formidable Partner (69)** (RWArmstrong) **3-8-12** RHills(2) (a.p: rdn 3f out: one pce) | hd | **5** | 3/1$^{1}$ | 69 | 40 |
| 1803$^{8}$ | **Saltando (IRE) (47)** (PatMitchell) **5-7-12**$^{(3)}$ MHenry(8) (s.i.s: nvr nrr) | 6 | **6** | 9/1$^{3}$ | 35 | 17 |
| 1872$^{5}$ | **Gadge (58)** (DMorris) **5-8-12v** NDay(1) (bhd fnl 2f: fin lame) | 2 | **7** | 10/1 | 42 | 24 |
| | **Jolto (74)** (KMcAuliffe) **7-9-11**$^{(3)}$ JStack(3) (carried wd bnd 4f out: hdwy over 2f out: sn wknd) | 2½ | **8** | 16/1 | 53 | 35 |
| 1155$^{5}$ | **Sea Danzig (69)** (PHowling) **3-8-12** KDarley(9) (lw: prom tl hmpd & wknd 4f out) | 13 | **9** | 10/1 | 22 | — |
| | | | | (SP 113.2%) | **9 Rn** | |

**1m 42.38** (1.18) CSF £33.44 CT £549.34 TOTE £4.00: £1.20 £2.60 £3.10 (£27.20) Trio £194.50 OWNER Mr G. A. Alexander (CHICHESTER) BRED P. and Mrs Venner
WEIGHT FOR AGE 3yo-11lb
**879 Autumn Cover** made a winning debut for his new stable. Keeping up the gallop in good style, he was not going to be denied. (3/1)
**Ballpoint** went on early in the straight but, collared a quarter of a mile from home, found the winner too strong. (12/1)
**Bakers Daughter**, fitted with blinkers for the first time after a three and a half month rest, was never far away. Asked for her effort over two furlongs from home though, she could only go up and down in the same place. (20/1)
**1682* Ashby Hill (IRE)** met trouble in running and was not helped by the drop in distance. Failing to get a clear run turning out of the back straight, she was badly hampered along the inside rail going into the home straight. Switched left to pick up ground over two furlongs from home, she came under pressure below the distance but was only treading water then. Back over a mile and a quarter, she should soon be winning again. (5/1)
**1654 Formidable Partner**, never far away, was bustled along early in the straight but could only keep on in his own time. (3/1)

## 2001 ROTHMANS ROYALS NORTH SOUTH CHALLENGE SERIES H'CAP (0-95) (3-Y.O) (Class C)

3-30 (3-30) **1m 1f** £7,002.50 (£2,120.00: £1,035.00: £492.50) Stalls: High GOING minus 0.45 sec per fur (F)

| | | | | SP | RR | SF |
|---|---|---|---|---|---|---|
| 1432$^{8}$ | **Al Shafa (88)** (JLDunlop) **3-9-7** KDarley(2) (hld up: led wl over 1f out: r.o wl) | — | **1** | 7/2$^{3}$ | 100 | 61 |
| 1671* | **Alambar (IRE) (76)** (PTWalwyn) **3-8-9** RHills(6) (lw: hld up: nt clr run & swtchd lft over 2f out: 4th whn nt clr run & swtchd lft over 1f out: r.o ins fnl f) | 1¾ | **2** | 11/2 | 85 | 46 |
| *1719*$^{7}$ | **Disallowed (IRE) (72)** (MBell) **3-8-5** MRoberts(4) (lw: led over 6f: unable qckn) | 1¼ | **3** | 16/1 | 79 | 40 |
| 1771* | **Spirito Libro (USA) (77)** (CNAllen) **3-8-5**$^{(5)}$ MartinDwyer(5) (dwlt: rdn & hdwy over 2f out: r.o one pce) | nk | **4** | 3/1$^{2}$ | 83 | 44 |
| 1771$^{7}$ | **Lituus (USA) (78)** (JHMGosden) **3-8-11** WRyan(3) (chsd ldr: led over 2f out tl wl over 1f out: edgd rt: one pce) | s.h | **5** | 7/2$^{3}$ | 84 | 45 |
| 1434$^{6}$ | **Crabbie's Pride (70)** (ABailey) **3-8-3** PaulEddery(1) (lw: hld up: rdn over 3f out: sn wknd) | 12 | **6** | 11/4$^{1}$ | 55 | 16 |
| | | | | (SP 117.4%) | **6 Rn** | |

**1m 54.01** (0.22 under best) (0.91) CSF £21.31 TOTE £3.90: £2.20 £2.80 (£9.50) OWNER Prince A A Faisal (ARUNDEL) BRED Fonthill Stud
**937 Al Shafa** failed to handle the soft ground last time out but bounced back to form here. Tracking the leaders, he moved to the front early in the final quarter-mile, and kept on too well for his rivals to break the course record which had stood for five years. (7/2: 5/2-4/1)
**1671* Alambar (IRE)** did not have a trouble-free run. With nowhere to go over a quarter of a mile out, he had to be switched left and did not have the best of runs below the distance. He ran on inside the final furlong, but it would not be entirely true to say he was unlucky. (11/2)
**1719 Disallowed (IRE)**, collared over a quarter of a mile from home, could then only keep on at one pace. (16/1)
**1771* Spirito Libro (USA)** moved up on the outside over quarter of a mile from home and, staying on, only just failed to take third prize. (3/1: 7/4-100/30)
**1771 Lituus (USA)** could never shake off his rivals and, collared well over a furlong out, could only stay on at one pace. (7/2)
**1434 Crabbie's Pride** (11/4: op 5/1)

## 2002 SURREY RACING H'CAP (0-80) (3-Y.O+) (Class D)

4-00 (4-01) **1m 6f** £3,915.50 (£1,184.00: £577.00: £273.50) Stalls: High GOING minus 0.45 sec per fur (F)

| | | | | SP | RR | SF |
|---|---|---|---|---|---|---|
| 1618$^{6}$ | **Farringdon Hill (71)** (MajorWRHern) **5-9-5b** RHills(6) (led 13f out: hrd rdn 1f out: r.o wl) | — | **1** | 13/2 | 83 | 42 |
| | **Bold Resolution (IRE) (70)** (CACyzer) **8-9-4** MRoberts(5) (a.p: chsd wnr over 4f out: unable qckn) | 4 | **2** | 10/1 | 77 | 36 |
| 1511$^{6}$ | **Midyan Blue (IRE) (76)** (JMPEustace) **6-9-5**(5) MartinDwyer(9) (led 1f: rdn over 3f out: one pce) | 4 | **3** | 11/2 | 79 | 38 |
| 1687$^{3}$ | **Majdak Jereeb (IRE) (75)** (MajorWRHern) **3-8-4**ow1 KDarley(8) (lw: hld up: rdn over 3f out: one pce) | ½ | **4** | 5/1$^{3}$ | 77 | 16 |
| 1660$^{3}$ | **Prince Danzig (IRE) (66)** (DJGMurraySmith) **5-9-0** PaulEddery(2) (lw: hld up: rdn over 3f out: one pce) | ½ | **5** | 9/1 | 68 | 27 |
| 573* | **Wannaplantatree (66)** (NMBabbage) **5-9-0** AMcGlone(4) (a bhd: b.b.v) | 6 | **6** | 100/30$^{1}$ | 61 | 20 |
| 1524$^{3}$ | **Opera Buff (IRE) (71)** (MissGayKelleway) **5-9-2**(3) MHenry(1) (hdwy over 4f out: wknd over 2f out) | 5 | **7** | 9/2$^{2}$ | 60 | 19 |
| 1695$^{2}$ | **Lucky Coin (62)** (PHowling) **4-8-7**(3) JStack(7) (a bhd) | 6 | **8** | 7/1 | 44 | 3 |
| | | | | (SP 118.2%) | | **8 Rn** |

**3m 3.5** (4.60) CSF £61.33 CT £350.30 TOTE £9.10: £2.00 £2.60 £1.90 (£42.80) Trio £144.90 OWNER Mr J. R. Wallis (LAMBOURN) BRED Wick-Dromdiah Investments Ltd

WEIGHT FOR AGE 3yo-19lb

**1618 Farringdon Hill**, soon at the head of affairs, had only the runner-up to worry about in the straight and, with that rival not given a hard time, he kept up the gallop to break his stable's duck for the season. (13/2)

**Bold Resolution (IRE)** had not been out since finishing second in a valuable handicap at Ascot in '94, but he is clearly no back-number. Given very tender handling, he moved into second place turning into the straight, but his jockey was anything but hard on him from then on. He needs time to recover from this, but is certainly capable of winning before long, and has won off a 3lb higher mark than his present one. (10/1: 8/1-12/1)

**1511 Midyan Blue (IRE)** could only keep on at one pace. (11/2)

**1687 Majdak Jereeb (IRE)** looked very pedestrian in the last two furlongs. (5/1)

**573* Wannaplantatree** (100/30: op 5/1)

**1524 Opera Buff (IRE)** (9/2: op 3/1)

## 2003 LEICESTER SQUARE CONDITIONS STKS (3-Y.O+) (Class C)

4-35 (4-36) **5f 6y** £4,948.00 (£1,852.00: £906.00: £390.00: £175.00: £89.00) Stalls: Low GOING minus 0.45 sec per fur (F)

| | | | | SP | RR | SF |
|---|---|---|---|---|---|---|
| 1818$^{5}$ | **Double Quick (IRE) (102)** (MJohnston) **4-8-9** MRoberts(7) (lw: hdwy 2f out: led 1f out: rdn: r.o wl) | — | **1** | 5/2$^{1}$ | 98 | 63 |
| 1033* | **Speed On** (HCandy) **3-8-11** WRyan(6) (lw: hdwy over 1f out: r.o wl ins fnl f) | 1 | **2** | 5/2$^{1}$ | 104 | 62 |
| 1818$^{3}$ | **Crowded Avenue (96)** (PJMakin) **4-9-0** PaulEddery(4) (hdwy over 1f out: r.o wl ins fnl f) | nk | **3** | 6/1$^{3}$ | 99 | 64 |
| 1818$^{7}$ | **That Man Again (98)** (GLewis) **4-8-11b**(3) AWhelan(3) (a.p: led over 2f out to 1f out: unable qckn) | hd | **4** | 9/1 | 99 | 64 |
| 1616$^{5}$ | **Ya Malak (107)** (JWPayne) **5-9-0** AMcGlone(5) (lw: a.p: ev ch 1f out: one pce) | 1½ | **5** | 9/2$^{2}$ | 94 | 59 |
| 1483$^{8}$ | **The Puzzler (IRE) (103)** (BWHills) **5-9-0** RHills(1) (led over 2f: wkng whn n.m.r 1f out) | 7 | **6** | 12/1 | 72 | 37 |
| 1394a$^{10}$ | **Cross The Border (95)** (RHannon) **3-8-7** KDarley(2) (a.p: ev ch 2f out: wkng whn squeezed out 1f out) | 3½ | **7** | 16/1 | 60 | 18 |
| | | | | (SP 113.2%) | | **7 Rn** |

**59.35 secs** (-0.45) CSF £8.83 TOTE £2.80: £1.70 £2.00 (£3.60) OWNER The 2nd Middleham Partnership (MIDDLEHAM)

WEIGHT FOR AGE 3yo-7lb

STEWARDS' ENQUIRY Ryan susp. 24-25/6/96 (careless riding).

**1818 Double Quick (IRE)**, weighted to beat the third and fourth on Epsom form last Sunday, did so. (5/2)

**1033* Speed On** only began to get going from below the distance and, in the process, caused some interference. Running on strongly inside the final furlong, he came through for second prize. This was a good effort for one so inexperienced, and he should soon return to the winner's enclosure. (5/2)

**1818 Crowded Avenue** began a good run up the rail below the distance and, running on strongly, only just failed to get second prize. (6/1)

**1332 That Man Again** went on at halfway but, collared a furlong from home, failed to find another gear. (9/1)

**1616 Ya Malak**, always handy, threatened to take the lead below the distance, but just failed to do so, and was tapped for toe in the last 200 yards. (9/2: 4/1-6/1)

**579 The Puzzler (IRE)** was giving best when slightly tightened up a furlong from home. (12/1: 7/1-14/1)

## 2004 GROSVENOR SQUARE MAIDEN STKS (3-Y.O) (Class D)

5-05 (5-09) **7f 16y** £3,993.50 (£1,208.00: £589.00: £279.50) Stalls: High GOING minus 0.45 sec per fur (F)

| | | | | SP | RR | SF |
|---|---|---|---|---|---|---|
| 1797$^{2}$ | **How Long** (LMCumani) **3-9-0** OUrbina(2) (hld up: led over 1f out: comf) | — | **1** | 9/2$^{3}$ | 95+ | 63 |
| 1690$^{9}$ | **Go Britannia** (DRLoder) **3-9-0** DRMcCabe(4) (lw: rdn over 3f out: gd hdwy over 1f out: r.o wl ins fnl f) | 3 | **2** | 9/1 | 88 | 56 |
| | **Jumairah Sunset** (ACStewart) **3-8-9** MRoberts(7) (str: scope: bit bkwd: gd hdwy over 1f out: r.o wl ins fnl f: nvr plcd to chal) | 3 | **3** | 11/2 | 76 | 44 |
| | **Divine** (ACStewart) **3-8-9** RHills(1) (rdn over 3f out: hdwy over 1f out: nvr nrr) | 1¾ | **4** | 12/1 | 73 | 41 |
| 1432$^{7}$ | **Double Bluff (IRE) (87)** (IABalding) **3-9-0** KDarley(9) (lw: led 3f: ev ch over 1f out: wknd fnl f) | nk | **5** | 11/4$^{1}$ | 77 | 45 |
| 1796$^{5}$ | **Lucky Archer (90)** (CEBrittain) **3-8-11**(3) MHenry(6) (lw: w ldr: led 4f out tl over 1f out: wknd fnl f) | 2 | **6** | 7/2$^{2}$ | 72 | 40 |
| 1350$^{2}$ | **Double March** (PRWebber) **3-9-0** WRyan(8) (hld up: rdn 3f out: wknd fnl f) | ½ | **7** | 9/2$^{3}$ | 71 | 39 |
| 1350$^{9}$ | **Mr Hacker** (GThorner) **3-8-7**(7) AEddery(5) (a bhd) | 9 | **8** | 66/1 | 51 | 19 |
| | | | | (SP 119.8%) | | **8 Rn** |

**1m 28.55** (-0.05) CSF £40.81 TOTE £4.30: £1.70 £2.60 £1.40 (£23.20) Trio £51.30 OWNER Dr M. Boffa (NEWMARKET) BRED Scuderia Giocri

OFFICIAL EXPLANATION **Jumairah Sunset: the jocked reported that his instructions were to look after the filly as she had had leg problems. She was unable to go the early pace and, although changing her legs up the straight, ran on through beaten horses.**

**1797 How Long**, held up in fourth place in an extremely fast-run race, came through to lead below the distance as the front two tired badly, and comfortably strode away for victory. (9/2)

**1690 Go Britannia** was rather surprisingly taking a step down in distance. Racing at the back of the field, he was rousted along entering the straight and certainly had it all to do. With the leaders tiring, he picked up ground from below the distance and ran on really strongly for second prize. He will find a race over further. (9/1: 8/1-12/1)

**Jumairah Sunset**, a well built, good looking filly, who looked as though the run was needed, was given extremely tender handling, indeed, punters would have been forgiven for thinking that Roberts had fallen asleep. Held up at the back of a suicidally run race, she picked up below the distance extremely well, but this of course was exaggerated as the leaders tired very badly. She should come on in leaps and bounds for this and should not be difficult to win with. (11/2: 7/2-6/1)

**Divine**, ridden along at the back of the field entering the straight, stayed on for fourth prize. (12/1: op 8/1)

**1127 Double Bluff (IRE)**, together with Lucky Archer, set a suicidal pace and the two cut each other's throats. (11/4)

T/Plpt: £69.00 (156.96 Tckts). T/Qdpt: £51.10 (11.83 Tckts). AK

## 1973-YORK (L-H) (Good)
## Saturday June 15th
WEATHER: sunny & v.warm WIND: almost nil

### 2005 MICHAEL SOBELL SILVER TANKARD H'CAP (0-75) (3-Y.O+) (Class D)
1-45 (1-46) **6f** £7,522.50 (£2,280.00: £1,115.00: £532.50) Stalls: Centre GOING minus 0.43 sec per fur (F)

| | | | | SP | RR | SF |
|---|---|---|---|---|---|---|
| *1492** | **Daawe (USA) (63)** (MrsVAAconley) **5-9-4v** MDeering(5) (lw: mde all: hld on wl) | — | **1** | 10/1[2] | 72 | 52 |
| *1810[2]* | **Cretan Gift (65)** (NPLittmoden) **5-9-1b**(5) FLynch(3) (in tch: hdwy ½-wy: r.o: nrst fin) | ¾ | **2** | 14/1 | 72 | 52 |
| 1635[4] | **Mister Westsound (67)** (MissLAPerratt) **4-9-8b** JWeaver(19) (lw: s.i.s: gd hdwy 2f out: hung rt ins fnl f: r.o) | s.h | **3** | 12/1 | 74 | 54 |
| 1708[5] | **Chadwell Hall (65)** (SRBowring) **5-9-3b**(3) CTeague(15) (a cl up: kpt on u.p fnl 2f) | ¾ | **4** | 14/1 | 70 | 50 |
| 1765[2] | **Aquado (59)** (SRBowring) **7-9-0b** JQuinn(10) (a.p: kpt on fnl 2f) | 1½ | **5** | 14/1 | 60 | 40 |
| 1707* | **Standown (73)** (JBerry) **3-9-1**(5) PRoberts(18) (hdwy ½-wy: styd on: nvr nrr) | 1¾ | **6** | 14/1 | 69 | 41 |
| 1905[2] | **Don Pepe (61)** (RBoss) **5-9-2** GDuffield(20) (bhd: hdwy 2f out: nrst fin) | 1¾ | **7** | 6/1[1] | 53 | 33 |
| 1790[10] | **Sea Thunder (73)** (IABalding) **4-10-0** TQuinn(12) (hld up & bhd: hdwy 2f out: nvr rchd ldrs) | 1¼ | **8** | 25/1 | 61 | 41 |
| 1610[8] | **Ochos Rios (IRE) (61)** (BSRothwell) **5-9-2** MFenton(17) (sme hdwy 2f out: nvr able to chal) | 1 | **9** | 20/1 | 47 | 27 |
| 1538[13] | **Just Dissident (IRE) (56)** (RMWhitaker) **4-8-11** DeanMcKeown(23) (dwlt: hdwy ½-wy: rdn & no imp) | ½ | **10** | 33/1 | 40 | 20 |
| 1588[6] | **Grand Chapeau (IRE) (60)** (DNicholls) **4-9-1** AlexGreaves(4) (lw: chsd ldrs tl grad wknd fnl 2f) | 1½ | **11** | 16/1 | 40 | 20 |
| 1527* | **Finisterre (IRE) (63)** (JJO'Neill) **3-8-10** KFallon(11) (lw: nvr rchd ldrs) | ¾ | **12** | 12/1 | 41 | 13 |
| 1501[9] | **Brecongill Lad (73)** (MissSEHall) **4-9-7b**(7) PTurner(7) (prom 4f: sn wknd) | ¾ | **13** | 12/1 | 49 | 29 |
| 1588[7] | **Rich Glow (55)** (NBycroft) **5-8-10** GHind(1) (s.i.s: sme hdwy ½-wy: n.d) | s.h | **14** | 25/1 | 31 | 11 |
| 1848[4] | **Plum First (64)** (LRLloyd-James) **6-9-5b** DHarrison(2) (b.hind: prom to ½-wy: wknd) | ¾ | **15** | 16/1 | 38 | 18 |
| 1781[7] | **Amron (64)** (JBerry) **9-9-5** MHills(8) (lw: s.i.s: hmpd after 1½f: n.d) | 1 | **16** | 16/1 | 35 | 15 |
| 1646[6] | **Ned's Bonanza (62)** (MDods) **7-9-3** JCarroll(14) (n.d) | ½ | **17** | 16/1 | 32 | 12 |
| 1829[9] | **Blue Bomber (72)** (TDBarron) **5-9-13** JFortune(6) (spd 3f: sn bhd) | ¾ | **18** | 14/1 | 40 | 20 |
| 1885[7] | **Diet (57)** (MissLAPerratt) **10-8-7v**(5) PFessey(16) (chsd ldrs to ½-wy: wknd) | ½ | **19** | 33/1 | 24 | 4 |
| 1178[13] | **Oggi (62)** (PJMakin) **5-9-3b** PatEddery(9) (chsd ldrs: rdn ½-wy: sn wknd) | 3½ | **20** | 11/1[3] | 19 | — |
| 1364[10] | **Dictation (USA) (70)** (JJO'Neill) **4-9-11** JFEgan(22) (n.d) | hd | **21** | 50/1 | 27 | 7 |
| 1777[10] | **Bryan Robson (USA) (50)** (GBBalding) **5-8-5** SSanders(13) (bhd fr ½-wy) | 1½ | **22** | 33/1 | 3 | — |
| *1505[7]* | ***Call Me I'm Blue (IRE) (72)*** (NTinkler) **6-9-13** MBirch(21) (Withdrawn not under Starter's orders: veterinary advice at s) | | **W** | 50/1 | — | — |

(SP 136.8%) **22 Rn**

**1m 11.93** (0.93) CSF £137.49 CT £1,613.64 TOTE £8.90: £2.50 £3.40 £2.50 £3.80 (£39.70) Trio £120.70 OWNER Mrs Andrea Mallinson (WESTOW) BRED Gainsborough Farm W.C.
WEIGHT FOR AGE 3yo-8lb
OFFICIAL EXPLANATION **Grand Chapeau (IRE): lost both his front shoes.**
**Plum First: his saddle slipped and the jockey could not ride him out thereafter.**
**Blue Bomber: lost his action at halfway.**
**1492* Daawe (USA)** keeps improving and proved really determined. (10/1)
**1810 Cretan Gift** ran another sound race on turf and deserves a change of luck. (14/1)
**1635 Mister Westsound**, poorly drawn, came from a mile behind and, had he really put his heart into it, might well have won. (12/1)
**1708 Chadwell Hall** hardly ever runs a bad race but he was always struggling from his draw here, and had to fight to keep in it. (14/1)
**1765 Aquado** is a funny customer, but is in good heart just now. (14/1)
**1707* Standown** ran well from a poor draw. (14/1)
**1905 Don Pepe** had a lot of running to do from his draw and was never any nearer than at the finish. He is in good heart now. (6/1)
**Sea Thunder** has a poor action but he did show something, keeping on at the end. (25/1)
**1588 Grand Chapeau (IRE)**, from a yard that is out of form at the moment, still showed plenty of speed. (16/1)

### 2006 DANIEL PRENN ROYAL YORKSHIRE RATED STKS H'CAP (0-100) (3-Y.O) (Class B)
2-15 (2-15) **1m 2f 85y** £9,251.40 (£3,462.60: £1,693.80: £729.00: £327.00: £166.20) Stalls: Low GOING minus 0.43 sec per fur (F)

| | | | | SP | RR | SF |
|---|---|---|---|---|---|---|
| 1359* | **Sasuru (100)** (GWragg) **3-9-7** MHills(4) (lw: b: hld up: qcknd to ld appr fnl f: r.o: comf) | — | **1** | 13/2 | 110+ | 79 |
| 1670* | **Skillington (USA) (90)** (IABalding) **3-8-11** TQuinn(3) (led: qcknd 3f out: hdd appr fnl f: kpt on) | 2½ | **2** | 7/4[1] | 96 | 65 |
| 1147[4] | **Spillo (87)** (LMCumani) **3-8-8** JWeaver(5) (swtg: hld up: effrt & n.m.r 2f out: styd on appr fnl f) | 2½ | **3** | 6/1[3] | 89 | 58 |
| 1619* | **Expensive Taste (90)** (MRStoute) **3-8-11** DHarrison(8) (lw: trckd ldrs: effrt over 2f out: rdn & one pce) | 3 | **4** | 5/1[2] | 88 | 57 |
| 1798[2] | **Exalted (IRE) (86)** (SirMarkPrescott) **3-8-7** GDuffield(9) (prom: effrt over 3f out: outpcd fnl 2f) | 1¾ | **5** | 7/1 | 81 | 50 |
| 1798[4] | **Truancy (84)** (MBell) **3-8-5v**[1] MFenton(1) (trckd ldrs: effrt 3f out: rdn & no rspnse) | 1¼ | **6** | 20/1 | 77 | 46 |
| 1639[5] | **More Than You Know (IRE) (90)** (RHannon) **3-8-11** JCarroll(6) (swtg: bhd: effrt over 3f out: no imp) | nk | **7** | 20/1 | 83 | 52 |
| | **Ski Academy (IRE) (94)** (PWChapple-Hyam) **3-9-1** JReid(7) (hld up & bhd: rdn over 3f out: n.d) | 2 | **8** | 12/1 | 84 | 53 |
| 1593* | **The Dilettanti (USA) (90)** (JARToller) **3-8-11** SSanders(2) (trckd ldr tl wknd fnl 3f) | 6 | **9** | 8/1 | 70 | 39 |

(SP 121.5%) **9 Rn**

**2m 8.57** (-1.13) CSF £18.51 CT £66.81 TOTE £6.80: £1.80 £1.40 £2.10 (£7.60) Trio £16.80 OWNER Lady Oppenheimer (NEWMARKET) BRED Hascombe and Valiant Studs
**1359* Sasuru** has really got his act together and his easy style of travelling and a tremendous turn of foot will stand him in good stead. (13/2)
**1670* Skillington (USA)**, trying his best to gallop his rivals into the ground, had nothing to match the winner's turn of foot. (7/4)
**1147 Spillo** was given no chance in trying to come from behind, and was probably second best. (6/1)
**1619* Expensive Taste** travels like a dream but, when asked a question, proves disappointing. To give her the benefit, this could have been a hot race. (5/1)
**1798 Exalted (IRE)** is in good heart but is basically just short of a turn of foot. Softer ground would probably help. (7/1)
**1798 Truancy** was wearing a visor for the first time and looked to be travelling well until an effort was required in the last three furlongs. (20/1)
**Ski Academy (IRE)** got really upset when following a filly round in the paddock, and this effort is best ignored. (12/1: op 8/1)
**1593* The Dilettanti (USA)** (8/1: op 5/1)

### 2007 WILLIAM HILL TROPHY H'CAP (0-105) (3-Y.O) (Class B)
2-45 (2-45) **6f** £34,238.00 (£10,379.00: £5,077.00: £2,426.00) Stalls: Centre GOING minus 0.43 sec per fur (F)

| | | | | SP | RR | SF |
|---|---|---|---|---|---|---|
| 1340[2] | **Mallia (79)** (TDBarron) **3-7-10** LCharnock(17) (in tch: styd on to ld ins fnl f) | — | **1** | 14/1 | 90 | 36 |
| 1473* | **Pleading (87)** (HCandy) **3-8-4** 7x CRutter(11) (lw: hld up & bhd: gd hdwy over 2f out: r.o towards fin) | s.h | **2** | 6/1[2] | 98 | 44 |

1316$^{2}$ **Wildwood Flower (85)** (RHannon) **3-8-2** JCarroll(8) (chsd ldr: hmpd & lft in ld wl over 2f out: hdd & no ex ins fnl f)....1¼ **3** 14/1 93 39
1188$^{3}$ **Laafee (98)** (HThomsonJones) **3-9-1** WCarson(18) (hld up: hdwy over 2f out: sn rdn: one pce fnl f) ....hd **4** 16/1 105 51
1693$^{2}$ **Green Barries (79)** (MJohnston) **3-7-10** TWilliams(10) (lw: sn pushed along: hdwy 2f out: nvr able to chal) ...nk **5** 12/1 86 32
1126$^{13}$ **Promptly (IRE) (85)** (MRStoute) **3-7-11**(5) FLynch(13) (bhd: hdwy 2f out: r.o towards fin)....hd **6** 14/1 91 37
1431$^{3}$ **Dashing Blue (100)** (IABalding) **3-9-3** TQuinn(15) (lw: bhd: styd on fnl 2f: nvr rchd ldrs)....hd **7** 17/2 106 52
1796$^{2}$ **Warning Time (104)** (BJMeehan) **3-9-7** BDoyle(16) (lw: prom: effrt over 2f out: sn wknd) ....5 **8** 16/1 97 43
1493$^{6}$ **Norwegian Blue (IRE) (91)** (APJarvis) **3-8-8** JFortune(2) (nvr bttr than mid div) ....1¼ **9** 20/1 80 26
1820$^{12}$ **Eastern Prophets (95)** (TJNaughton) **3-8-12** JWeaver(1) (spd over 3f) ....4 **10** 33/1 74 20
959$^{2}$ **Major Quality (97)** (JRFanshawe) **3-9-0** DHarrison(4) (lw: chsd ldrs tl wknd appr fnl f)....1¾ **11** 8/1$^{3}$ 71 17
1629$^{3}$ **React (92)** (WJarvis) **3-8-9** PatEddery(9) (chsd ldrs: drvn along thrght: wknd over 2f out)....4 **12** 3/1$^{1}$ 55 1
**Oh Whataknight (88)** (JWHills) **3-8-5** MHills(14) (bit bkwd: n.d) ....6 **13** 33/1 35 —
1340$^{4}$ **Blessingindisguise (83)** (MWEasterby) **3-8-0** JQuinn(5) (prom: hmpd wl over 2f out: n.d after) ....1½ **14** 16/1 26 —
1628$^{3}$ **Hoh Returns (IRE) (87)** (MBell) **3-8-4** MFenton(7) (lw: prom tl bdly hmpd wl over 2f out: nt rcvr) ....10 **15** 11/1 4 —
1493$^{2}$ **Red Nymph (90)** (WJarvis) **3-8-7** BThomson(3) (prom whn bdly hmpd wl over 2f out: nt rcvr)....1½ **16** 14/1 3 —
989$^{7}$ **Secret Voucher (79)** (BAMcMahon) **3-7-5**(5) PFessey(12) (led tl fell wl over 2f out: dead).... **F** 33/1 — —
1628$^{8}$ **Spotted Eagle (86)** (RHannon) **3-8-3** SSanders(6) (mid div whn bdly hmpd & uns rdr wl over 2f out) .... **U** 25/1 — —
(SP 138.7%) **18 Rn**

**1m 11.61** (0.61) CSF £98.69 CT £1,171.58 TOTE £51.40: £8.70 £1.90 £3.70 £2.00 (£226.10) Trio £918.60 OWNER Mr H. T. Duddin (THIRSK) BRED B. J. McAllister
LONG HANDICAP Green Barries 7-9 Secret Voucher 7-1 Mallia 7-7
**1340 Mallia** is a game sort and, once in front inside the final furlong, he gave his all to hold on. (14/1)
**1473* Pleading** was ridden with bags of confidence but, as it proved, he had just been set too stiff a test. He should make up for this. (6/1)
**1316 Wildwood Flower** is not the best of movers, but she ran her usual game race and being hampered can not have helped. (14/1)
**1188 Laafee** travels well on the bit but so far this season has disappointed. (16/1)
**1693 Green Barries** ran as though he either needs further or softer ground. (12/1)
**1126 Promptly (IRE)** ran as though she would be suited by further. (14/1)
**1628 Hoh Returns (IRE)** (11/1: 8/1-12/1)

## 2008 QUEEN MOTHER'S CUP LADIES' H'CAP (0-95) (3-Y.O+) (Class C)

3-20 (3-21) **1m 3f 195y** £10,747.50 (£3,255.00: £1,590.00: £757.50) Stalls: Low GOING minus 0.43 sec per fur (F)
SP RR SF
1803$^{2}$ **Make a Stand (62)** (MCPipe) **5-9-4** MrsLPearce(5) (lw: trckd ldrs: led 2½f out: rdn & r.o wl)....— **1** 5/2$^{1}$ 76 41
1198$^{13}$ **Celestial Choir (80)** (JLEyre) **6-10-8** MissDianaJones(3) (hld up: hdwy 3f out: chsng wnr appr fnl f: kpt on)..2½ **2** 9/1 91 56
1440$^{9}$ **Romios (IRE) (82)** (PFICole) **4-10-10** MrsSBosley(2) (hdwy 4f out: chsng ldrs 2f out: kpt on: nt pce to chal) .2½ **3** 16/1 89 54
**Dreams End (80)** (PBowen) **8-10-3**(5) MrsKBowen(4) (hdwy 4f out: sn in tch: kpt on one pce appr fnl f) ....3 **4** 14/1 83 48
**Mellaby (USA) (82)** (MRStoute) **8-10-10** MrsSEddery(1) (hld up: effrt 4f out: nvr able to chal) ....3 **5** 8/1 81 46
1700$^{2}$ **Bardon Hill Boy (IRE) (86)** (BHanbury) **4-11-0** MissYHaynes(8) (lw: bhd & rdn 4f out: nvr rchd ldrs)....2½ **6** 13/2$^{3}$ 82 47
**Philgun (57)** (CWCElsey) **7-8-13v** MissAElsey(12) (cl up tl wknd 2f out)....1¼ **7** 50/1 51 16
944$^{9}$ **Witney-de-Bergerac (IRE) (63)** (JSMoore) **4-9-5** MrsSMoore(13) (prom to st: sn bhd)....¾ **8** 12/1 56 21
1476$^{5}$ **Lookingforarainbow (IRE) (74)** (BobJones) **8-9-11**(5) MissGJones(6) (lw: plld hrd: led tl hdd & wknd over 2f out)....5 **9** 11/2$^{2}$ 60 25
1428$^{7}$ **High Pyrenees (73)** (RAllan) **4-10-1** MissPRobson(10) (in tch tl rdn & wknd 4f out)....¾ **10** 25/1 58 23
1697* **Cante Chico (64)** (OBrennan) **4-9-6** MissVHaigh(7) (chsd ldrs tl rdn & wknd fnl 2½f) ....hd **11** 16/1 49 14
440$^{14}$ **Silktail (IRE) (67)** (MissGayKelleway) **4-9-9** MissSKelleway(9) (hld up & bhd: c wd st: n.d)....6 **12** 10/1 44 9
1802$^{10}$ **Highflying (81)** (GMMoore) **10-10-4**(5) MissDVRussell(14) (prom tl wknd ent st) ....4 **13** 20/1 53 18
1803$^{14}$ **Scenic Dancer (54)** (AHide) **8-8-10v** MissLHide(11) (virtually ref to r) ....dist **14** 16/1 — —
(SP 130.1%) **14 Rn**

**2m 31.73** (3.93) CSF £26.21 CT £296.80 TOTE £3.00: £1.50 £2.40 £9.30 (£11.10) Trio £307.90 OWNER Mr P. A. Deal (WELLINGTON) BRED R. M. West
LONG HANDICAP Scenic Dancer 8-2
**1803 Make a Stand** was always in a good position and, once he quickened approaching the final quarter-mile, the race was soon his. (5/2)
**765 Celestial Choir** ran well and, as she keeps her enthusiasm, she is worth keeping in mind. (9/1: 6/1-10/1)
**Romios (IRE)**, stepping up in trip, ran his best race of the season but he was treading water in the final furlong. (16/1)
**Dreams End** has not won on the Flat for a couple of years but he showed enough here to prove that he is not done with. (14/1)
**Mellaby (USA)**, having his first run for almost two years, showed a little without getting into it. (8/1: 6/1-9/1)

## 2009 LEONARD SAINER E.B.F. MAIDEN STKS (2-Y.O) (Class D)

3-50 (3-50) **6f** £4,045.50 (£1,224.00: £597.00: £283.50) Stalls: Centre GOING minus 0.43 sec per fur (F)
SP RR SF
**Sahm (USA)** (JLDunlop) **2-9-0** WCarson(4) (w'like: scope: rn green early: qcknd to ld over 2f out: pushed along & r.o wl) ....— **1** 8/13$^{1}$ 103+ 38
1774$^{4}$ **Maladerie (IRE)** (MRChannon) **2-9-0** PatEddery(1) (lw: led tl hdd over 2f out: no ch w wnr)....9 **2** 5/2$^{2}$ 79 14
841$^{10}$ **Zaretski** (CEBrittain) **2-9-0** BDoyle(2) (cl up tl outpcd fnl 2f)....3 **3** 16/1 71 6
**Zugudi** (BHanbury) **2-9-0** JReid(3) (str: scope: bit bkwd: chsd ldrs tl rdn & wknd 2f out) ....3 **4** 5/1$^{3}$ 63 —
(SP 113.0%) **4 Rn**

**1m 12.66** (1.66) CSF £2.64 TOTE £1.60 (£1.40) OWNER Mr Hamdan Al Maktoum (ARUNDEL) BRED Shadwell Farm Inc
**Sahm (USA)** was very coltish in the preliminaries and then ran very green in the race. Taught his job well though, he won in the style of a useful horse and hopefully will now go the right way. (8/13)
**1774 Maladerie (IRE)** was completely outclassed by the winner, but should find an ordinary event. (5/2)
**Zaretski** is obviously learning and there is scope for improvement. (16/1)
**Zugudi** needed this and will no doubt want a good bit further. (5/1)

## 2010 CADOGAN SILVER SALVER H'CAP (0-90) (3-Y.O+) (Class C)

4-25 (4-26) **1m 205y** £11,040.00 (£3,345.00: £1,635.00: £780.00) Stalls: Low GOING minus 0.43 sec per fur (F)
SP RR SF
1819$^{3}$ **Sandmoor Chambray (73)** (TDEasterby) **5-8-13** MBirch(11) (lw: a.p: led & qcknd 2f out: all out)....— **1** 6/1$^{1}$ 83 59
1816$^{4}$ **Carlito Brigante (74)** (MrsJRRamsden) **4-9-0** KFallon(13) (lw: pushed along & bhd: hdwy over 2f out: r.o u.p fnl f: jst failed)....hd **2** 6/1$^{1}$ 84 60

1819[11] **Seventeens Lucky (75)** (BobJones) **4-9-1** MWigham(4) (hdwy 4f out: chsng wnr over 1f out: nt qckn) ....1½ **3** 11/1 82 58
1069[9] **Percy Braithwaite (IRE) (82)** (MJohnston) **4-9-8** JWeaver(14) (chsd ldrs: outpcd over 2f out: kpt on u.p appr fnl f) ....3½ **4** 10/1[3] 83 59
1686* **Sovereign Page (USA) (76)** (BHanbury) **7-9-2** JReid(10) (lw: b: cl up: led 2½f out: sn hdd & btn) ....hd **5** 10/1[3] 77 53
1799[3] **Queens Consul (IRE) (84)** (BSRothwell) **6-9-10** MFenton(5) (chsd ldrs: rdn 3f out: one pce) ....1¼ **6** 16/1 82 58
1819[5] **Up in Flames (IRE) (71)** (MDHammond) **5-8-11** JQuinn(3) (lw: effrt on ins whn nt clr run 3f out: styd on fnl f) ....1¼ **7** 10/1[3] 67 43
1843[3] **Embankment (IRE) (77)** (RHannon) **6-9-3** PatEddery(8) (chsd ldrs: drvn along 3f out: no imp after) ....nk **8** 7/1[2] 73 49
1793[7] **Hazard a Guess (IRE) (82)** (DNicholls) **6-9-8** AlexGreaves(1) (bhd: hdwy on ins whn n.m.r 3f out: n.d) ....hd **9** 7/1[2] 78 54
1819[6] **Pay Homage (77)** (IABalding) **8-9-3** TQuinn(12) (prom tl outpcd & nt clr run over 2f out: sn lost pl) ....¾ **10** 11/1 71 47
1322[11] **Leif the Lucky (USA) (75)** (MissSEHall) **7-8-10**(5) GParkin(7) (outpcd ½-wy: bhd after) ....4 **11** 33/1 62 38
1330[11] **Samba Sharply (78)** (AHide) **5-9-4** WWoods(6) (a bhd) ....1 **12** 12/1 63 39
988[4] **Secret Aly (CAN) (82)** (CEBrittain) **6-9-8** BDoyle(2) (led tl hdd & wknd 2½f out) ....1 **13** 16/1 65 41
1661[6] **Curtelace (57)** (MrsMReveley) **6-7-11b** LCharnock(9) (bhd: effrt 3f out: rdn & no rspnse) ....½ **14** 20/1 40 16
1704* **Maradata (IRE) (62)** (RHollinshead) **4-7-11**(5) FLynch(15) (lw: hld up & bhd: effrt on outside 3f out: sn btn)...2½ **15** 10/1[3] 40 16
(SP 133.8%) **15 Rn**

**1m 49.5** (0.30) CSF £43.22 CT £381.83 TOTE £8.10: £2.20 £2.50 £4.10 (£18.60) Trio £270.20 OWNER Sandmoor Textiles Co Ltd (MALTON) BRED P. and Mrs Venner

**1819 Sandmoor Chambray** got the run of the race this time and received plenty of help from the saddle when it mattered. (6/1)
**1816 Carlito Brigante**, after looking none too happy early on, suddenly picked up approaching the final furlong, but this trip was probably a shade short of his best. (6/1)
**1613* Seventeens Lucky** ran well and might just be a pound or two high enough in the weights. (11/1)
**1069 Percy Braithwaite (IRE)** could not get to the front from his outside draw, and that probably made all the difference. (10/1)
**1686* Sovereign Page (USA)** won a messy race last time and found this a different proposition. (10/1)
**1799 Queens Consul (IRE)** has never won over quite this far and is high enough in the weights just now. (16/1)
**1819 Up in Flames (IRE)** never had any luck in running and should be kept in mind. (10/1)
**1198 Hazard a Guess (IRE)** met with trouble in running. (7/1)

## 2011 JACK HANSON & GUY REED MAIDEN STKS (3-Y.O) (Class D)
4-55 (4-55) **7f 202y** £4,123.50 (£1,248.00: £609.00: £289.50) Stalls: Low GOING minus 0.43 sec per fur (F)

SP RR SF
845[4] **Kuala Lipis (USA)** (PFICole) **3-9-0** TQuinn(1) (trckd ldrs: effrt 3f out: styd on u.p to ld ins fnl f) ....— **1** 4/1[3] 87 47
1475[2] **Bollin Joanne (80)** (TDEasterby) **3-8-9** MBirch(3) (lw: hld up: shkn up & hdwy over 2f out: ev ch ins fnl f: nt qckn) ....1¾ **2** 5/1 79 39
**Pearl d'Azur (USA)** (DRLoder) **3-9-0** PatEddery(6) (lengthy: scope: led: shkn up over 2f out: hdd & no ex ins fnl f) ....1¼ **3** 9/4[1] 81 41
1326[4] **Sabrak (IRE)** (MAJarvis) **3-9-0** PRobinson(2) (lw: hld up & bhd: effrt 3f out: styd on: nvr rchd ldrs) ....1 **4** 11/2 79 39
1142[4] **Veridian** (PWHarris) **3-9-0** GHind(4) (chsd ldrs: hdwy 3f out: wknd 2f out) ....2½ **5** 5/2[2] 74 34
1709[8] **Memphis Beau (IRE)** (JARToller) **3-9-0** TWilliams(5) (s.i.s: sn cl up: rdn & wknd over 2f out) ....12 **6** 25/1 50 10
(SP 115.2%) **6 Rn**

**1m 38.32** (1.52) CSF £22.21 TOTE £5.00: £2.20 £1.80 (£8.40) OWNER H R H Sultan Ahmad Shah (WHATCOMBE) BRED Gallaghers Stud

**845 Kuala Lipis (USA)** certainly does not do anything quickly, but he kept answering his rider's call and eventually got there. (4/1: op 5/2)
**1475 Bollin Joanne**, stepping up in distance, again did her best but failed to quicken late on. (5/1)
**Pearl d'Azur (USA)** looked to have this won until running out of fuel inside the final furlong. He either needed this or just did not stay. (9/4)
**1326 Sabrak (IRE)**, settled out the back, could never find the speed to get into it, despite staying on. (11/2)
**1142 Veridian**, put in the race this time, was found out when pressure was applied. (5/2: op 5/4)
**Memphis Beau (IRE)** has plenty to learn. (25/1)

T/Jkpt: Not won; £13,410.37 to Musselburgh 17/6/96. T/Plpt: £147.20 (270.58 Tckts). T/Qdpt: £32.20 (40.11 Tckts). AA

# 1657-BRIGHTON (L-H) (Firm)
## Monday June 17th
WEATHER: warm WIND: almost nil

## 2012 MONTPELIER (S) STKS (2-Y.O) (Class G)
2-00 (2-02) **5f 213y** £2,070.00 (£570.00: £270.00) Stalls: Low GOING minus 0.35 sec per fur (F)

SP RR SF
1331[4] **Misty Cay (IRE)** (SDow) **2-8-6** MRoberts(1) (s.i.s: n.m.r & swtchd rt 2f out: hdwy to ld 1f out: comf) ....— **1** 9/4[2] 52+ 6
1494[5] **Grovefair Dancer (IRE)** (BJMeehan) **2-8-6** BDoyle(2) (led to 1f out: r.o) ....nk **2** 2/1[1] 51 5
*1491** **Who Told Vicky (IRE)** (JSMoore) **2-8-11** SWhitworth(4) (chsd ldr over 4f: sn wknd) ....7 **3** 7/2[3] 37 —
1842[4] **Summer Risotto** (DJSffrenchDavis) **2-8-6** NCarlisle(3) (s.i.s: hdwy over 3f out: wknd 2f out) ....8 **4** 4/1 11 —
(SP 106.3%) **4 Rn**

**1m 10.9** (3.70) CSF £6.45 TOTE £2.80 (£3.20) OWNER Mrs A. M. Upsdell (EPSOM) BRED T. Ward
Bt in 6,400gns

**1331 Misty Cay (IRE)** looked ill-at-ease on this switch-back course, especially negotiating the downhill turn. Nevertheless, she picked up ground below the distance to sweep into the lead a furlong from home and, only playing with the long-time leader, had far more in hand than the official distance suggests. (9/4)
**1494 Grovefair Dancer (IRE)** attempted to make all. Collared by the winner a furlong out, that rival was only toying with her and she is greatly flattered to finish so close. (2/1)
**1491* Who Told Vicky (IRE)** raced in second place until approaching the final furlong before tiring. (7/2: 5/2-4/1)
**1842 Summer Risotto** moved up just before halfway but tamely dropped away over a quarter of a mile out. (4/1)

## 2013 A. R. DENNIS BOOKMAKERS JUNE MAIDEN H'CAP (0-70) (3-Y.O) (Class E)
2-30 (2-33) **6f 209y** £3,343.20 (£999.60: £478.80: £218.40) Stalls: Low GOING minus 0.35 sec per fur (F)

SP RR SF
1780[4] **Castan (IRE) (63)** (JLDunlop) **3-9-2** PatEddery(10) (nt clr run over 2f out: squeezed thro & hdwy over 1f out: led nr fin) ....— **1** 9/2[1] 73 43

1013[2] **Flagstaff (USA) (54)** (GLMoore) **3-8-7v** MRoberts(3) (swtchd rt & hdwy 2f out: led wl ins fnl f: sn hdd: unable qckn)....1¼ **2** 11/2[3] 61 31
1688[3] **Lillibella (63)** (IABalding) **3-8-11**(5) MartinDwyer(6) (hld up: rdn over 2f out: led ins fnl f: sn hdd: one pce)....hd **3** 5/1[2] 70 40
1662[3] **Velvet Jones (60)** (GFHCharles-Jones) **3-8-13** SWhitworth(11) (lw: hdwy, nt clr run & swtchd lft over 1f out: nt clr run ins fnl f: nt rcvr)....¾ **4** 15/2 65 35
1671[4] **Amber Fort (67)** (PFICole) **3-9-6b** CRutter(4) (chsd ldr 5f out: led over 2f out tl ins fnl f: 4th & btn whn hmpd wl ins fnl f)....½ **5** 8/1 71 41
1986[3] **School Boy (68)** (TJNaughton) **3-9-7** DHarrison(9) (lw: nt clr run over 2f out tl swtchd rt 2f out: hdwy over 1f out: r.o)....1¼ **6** 13/2 69 39
1594[4] **Pride of Kashmir (54)** (PWHarris) **3-8-7** GHind(7) (lw: hld up: hrd rdn over 2f out: sn wknd)....1 **7** 6/1 53 23
1840[5] **Unspoken Prayer (46)** (JRArnold) **3-7-13** JFEgan(2) (lw: prom over 5f)....4 **8** 10/1 36 6
1665[20] **My Millie (58)** (RBoss) **3-8-11** GDuffield(1) (led over 4f: wkng whn n.m.r on ins over 1f out)....nk **9** 25/1 47 17
1333[16] **Bella's Legacy (51)** (RJHodges) **3-8-1**(3)ow1 SDrowne(5) (prom over 4f)....5 **10** 33/1 28 —
1657[2] **Blue Suede Hoofs (64)** (BJMeehan) **3-9-3b** BDoyle(8) (prom 4f)....½ **11** 12/1 40 10
(SP 124.3%) **11 Rn**

**1m 22.1** (2.10) CSF £29.29 CT £123.54 TOTE £3.90: £1.90 £2.90 £2.40 (£7.20) Trio £30.10 OWNER Mr James Hartnett (ARUNDEL) BRED Taupo Ltd

**1780 Castan (IRE)** had anything but a clear run. Eventually squeezing through a gap and picking up ground below the distance, he came with a useful run to snatch the spoils in the closing stages. (9/2: 3/1-5/1)
**1013 Flagstaff (USA)**, switched to get a clear run, picked up ground a quarter of a mile from home and came though to poke his head in front in the last 100 yards. No sooner had he got there though than the winner went by. (11/2)
**1688 Lillibella**, taking a step up in distance, chased the leaders. Rousted along in the final quarter-mile, she got on top inside the final furlong, but remained there for only a few strides before, first the runner-up, then the winner, went by. (5/1)
**1662 Velvet Jones** had no luck in running. Picking up ground, he met a wall of horses just below the distance and was switched left to get a clear run. Again trying to pick up ground, he was shut out inside the final furlong and could never recover. (15/2)
**1671 Amber Fort** went on over a quarter of a mile from home. Collared inside the final furlong, he was held when hampered in the closing stages. (8/1: 6/1-9/1)
**1986 School Boy**, third at Leicester the previous Saturday, was another who failed to get a good run. He eventually picked up ground below the distance but, despite running on, found it all over bar the shouting. (13/2)
**1594 Pride of Kashmir** (6/1: op 7/2)

## 2014 LEWES LIMITED STKS (0-60) (3-Y.O+) (Class F)

3-00 (3-00) **1m 1f 209y** £2,381.00 (£656.00: £311.00) Stalls: High GOING minus 0.35 sec per fur (F)

SP RR SF

1655[12] **Elpida (USA) (53)** (JPearce) **4-9-5** GBardwell(4) (hrd rdn & hdwy 2f out: led wl ins fnl f: edgd lft: r.o wl)....— **1** 25/1 66 44
1868[2] **Talented Ting (IRE) (60)** (PCHaslam) **7-9-5** JFortune(7) (a.p: led over 3f out: hrd rdn over 2f out: hdd wl ins fnl f: r.o)....nk **2** 5/2[2] 66 44
*1096[3]* **Grey Galava (60)** (BWHills) **3-8-4** MHills(8) (led over 6f: hrd rdn: ev ch ins fnl f: 3rd & btn whn squeezed out nr fin)....½ **3** 100/30[3] 62 28
1838[2] **Wet Patch (IRE) (60)** (RHannon) **4-9-7** PatEddery(3) (lw: lost pl 6f out: r.o one pce fnl 2f)....1½ **4** 15/8[1] 64 42
1682[4] **Miss Pravda (56)** (PTWalwyn) **3-8-4** BDoyle(6) (lw: hdwy over 3f out: wknd over 1f out)....5 **5** 12/1 51 17
*1605[2]* **Greenwich Again (53)** (TGMills) **4-9-7** MarkLynch(9) (hld up: rdn over 3f out: wknd over 2f out)....¾ **6** 10/1 55 33
1534[4] **The Little Ferret (46)** (AMoore) **6-9-5** RPerham(5) (w ldr over 6f)....3 **7** 33/1 48 26
1856[14] **Office Hours (57)** (CACyzer) **4-9-5b**[1] MFenton(2) (lw: hdwy 5f out: rdn over 1f out: sn wknd)....1½ **8** 12/1 46 24
*1490[11]* **Silent Guest (IRE) (58)** (SirMarkPrescott) **3-8-7** GDuffield(1) (prom over 4f)....2½ **9** 14/1 42 8
(SP 124.4%) **9 Rn**

**2m 1.8** (3.50) CSF £88.23 TOTE £52.40: £9.50 £1.50 £1.30 (£69.20) Trio £183.90 OWNER Mr A. J. Thompson (NEWMARKET) BRED Bluefield Farms Corp
WEIGHT FOR AGE 3yo-12lb

**Elpida (USA)**, under pressure to pick up ground a quarter of a mile out, kept responding to his rider's severe urgings and eventually got on top in the closing stages, although he then drifted left doing the second and third no favours. (25/1)
**1868 Talented Ting (IRE)** only just failed. Gaining a narrow lead over three furlongs from home, he was given absolutely no peace by the determined third and was eventually overhauled by the winner in the closing stages. (5/2)
**1096 Grey Galava** set the pace and, although headed three furlongs out, simply refused to give way. She was still battling away for the advantage inside the final furlong, but was just getting the worst of the argument in third place when tightened up against the rail near the line. (100/30)
**1838 Wet Patch (IRE)**, who got outpaced after half a mile, stayed on in the final two furlongs without ever posing a threat. (15/8)
**1682 Miss Pravda** moved up over three furlongs from home, but had shot her bolt below the distance. (12/1: 7/1-14/1)
**Silent Guest (IRE)** (14/1: 10/1-16/1)

## 2015 OPERATIC SOCIETY CHALLENGE CUP MEDIAN AUCTION MAIDEN STKS (3 & 4-Y.O) (Class F)

3-30 (3-32) **1m 3f 196y** £2,547.60 (£703.60: £334.80) Stalls: High GOING minus 0.35 sec per fur (F)

SP RR SF

**Jazz King** (MissGayKelleway) **3-8-10** WJO'Connor(1) (wl grwn: hld up: chsd ldr 5f out: led over 1f out: easily)....— **1** 4/11[1] 72+ 35
*355[7]* **Bath Knight (59)** (DJSffrenchDavis) **3-8-10** DHarrison(3) (led: rdn over 3f out: hdd over 1f out: unable qckn)....10 **2** 5/1[2] 59 22
**Red Viper** (NMLampard) **4-9-5**(5) RHavlin(2) (chsd ldr over 7f out to 5f out: wknd over 3f out)....6 **3** 33/1 51 28
1656[12] **Kairine (IRE)** (MRChannon) **3-8-6**ow1 PatEddery(5) (chsd ldr over 4f: t.o)....23 **4** 11/2[3] 16 —
1104[12] **Bellaphento** (JRinger) **3-8-5** GDuffield(4) (lw: bhd fnl 5f: t.o)....4 **5** 16/1 9 —
(SP 114.2%) **5 Rn**

**2m 32.2** (4.60) CSF £2.94 TOTE £1.50: £1.10 £1.10 (£2.00) OWNER Whitcombe Manor Racing Stables Ltd (WHITCOMBE) BRED Casterbridge Stud and Brook Stud Ltd
WEIGHT FOR AGE 3yo-14lb

**Jazz King**, a huge boat of a horse, was totally unsuited by this switch-back track but proved far too good for these very bad horses. Shaken up a mile from home as he looked ill-at-ease, he moved into second place at the top of the hill but still looked very uncomfortable. He cruised into the lead though approaching the final furlong and strode clear to win an appalling race. Sure to be wiser for this, he will be much better suited by a galloping course. (4/11: op 4/7)

**Bath Knight** attempted to make all the running. Rousted along over three furlongs from home, he was collared below the distance and firmly put in his place. (5/1: op 5/2)
**Red Viper** moved into second place over seven furlongs from home, but was collared for that position at the top of the hill and was a spent force over three furlongs out. (33/1)

## 2016 HAILSHAM H'CAP (0-70) (3-Y.O+ F & M) (Class E)

4-00 (4-01) **7f 214y** £3,097.50 (£924.00: £441.00: £199.50) Stalls: Low GOING minus 0.35 sec per fur (F)

| | | | | SP | RR | SF |
|---|---|---|---|---|---|---|
| 1856* | **Gentle Irony (58)** (MJRyan) **4-10-1** 5x BDoyle(2) (lw: mde all: rdn out) | — | 1 | $5/1^{3}$ | 67 | 49 |
| *1721** | **Princess Pamgaddy (50)** (CNAllen) **3-8-6**(5) MartinDwyer(5) (lw: rdn & hdwy over 2f out: chsd wnr ins fnl f: r.o one pce) | 1¼ | 2 | $9/2^{2}$ | 57 | 29 |
| $1654^{6}$ | **Mystic Dawn (60)** (SDow) **3-9-7** MRoberts(6) (a.p: chsd wnr over 3f out tl ins fnl f: r.o one pce) | nk | 3 | $5/2^{1}$ | 66 | 38 |
| $1876^{12}$ | **Again Together (60)** (GLMoore) **3-9-4**(3) SDrowne(7) (rdn & hdwy over 2f out: r.o one pce) | 1 | 4 | 14/1 | 64 | 36 |
| $1526^{3}$ | **Bold Enough (55)** (BWHills) **3-9-2** PatEddery(1) (swtg: lost pl 4f out: rallied 2f out: wknd over 1f out) | 7 | 5 | $5/2^{1}$ | 45 | 17 |
| $1682^{6}$ | **Miss Iron Heart (USA) (36)** (DJSCosgrove) **4-8-2**(5) MBaird(4) (lw: hdwy over 3f out: wknd 2f out) | 1 | 6 | 7/1 | 24 | 6 |
| $1658^{13}$ | **Oscilights Gift (25)** (PBurgoyne) **4-7-10** NAdams(3) (b.off hind: swtg: chsd wnr over 4f) | 3½ | 7 | 40/1 | 6 | — |
| $1696^{10}$ | **Persephone (40)** (ICampbell) **3-8-1** GBardwell(8) (bhd fnl 3f) | 14 | 8 | 20/1 | — | — |
| | | | | (SP 118.4%) | **8 Rn** | |

**1m 35.2** (3.00) CSF £26.73 CT £64.15 TOTE £5.30: £1.10 £2.60 £1.10 (£8.60) OWNER Mr A. S. Reid (NEWMARKET) BRED Red House Stud
WEIGHT FOR AGE 3yo-10lb
**1856* Gentle Irony** made every post a winning one and, rousted along, was not going to be passed. (5/1)
**1721* Princess Pamgaddy**, rousted along to take closer order over two furlongs from home, struggled into second place early inside the final furlong, but failed to reel in the winner. (9/2)
**1654 Mystic Dawn** went into second place soon after halfway, but she was collared for the runner-up berth inside the final furlong and failed to quicken. (5/2)
**897 Again Together**, pushed along to pick up ground over a quarter of a mile out, stayed on without ever threatening to get there in time. (14/1: 10/1-16/1)
**1526 Bold Enough**, outpaced at halfway, threatened to get back into it a quarter of a mile out, but was soon struggling. (5/2)

## 2017 PALACE H'CAP (0-80) (3-Y.O+) (Class D)

4-30 (4-30) **5f 213y** £3,562.35 (£1,060.80: £504.90: £226.95) Stalls: Low GOING minus 0.35 sec per fur (F)

| | | | | SP | RR | SF |
|---|---|---|---|---|---|---|
| $1881^{3}$ | **Sharp Imp (48)** (RMFlower) **6-7-7b**(3) NVarley(2) (hld up: led 1f out: rdn out) | — | 1 | $4/1^{3}$ | 57 | 23 |
| *$278^{10}$* | **Pearl Dawn (IRE) (68)** (GLMoore) **6-9-2** SWhitworth(1) (chsd ldr: led over 2f out to 1f out: unable qckn) | 1½ | 2 | 10/1 | 73 | 39 |
| $1680^{5}$ | **Bashful Brave (73)** (JWPayne) **5-9-7** AMcGlone(6) (a.p: ev ch ins fnl f: one pce) | ¾ | 3 | 5/1 | 76 | 42 |
| $928^{21}$ | **Tafahhus (74)** (MJPolglase) **4-9-8** DHarrison(5) (hdwy 3f out: wknd over 1f out) | 3½ | 4 | 13/2 | 68 | 34 |
| $1621^{6}$ | **Chewit (80)** (AMoore) **4-10-0** CandyMorris(7) (dwlt: hdwy 3f out: wknd over 1f out) | 4 | 5 | $7/4^{1}$ | 63 | 29 |
| $1806^{7}$ | **Shermood (55)** (KTIvory) **3-7-5**(5) MartinDwyer(4) (b.hind: lw: a bhd) | 3½ | 6 | 40/1 | 29 | — |
| $992^{6}$ | **Akalim (80)** (DMorley) **3-9-7** WCarson(3) (led over 3f) | hd | 7 | $7/2^{2}$ | 53 | 12 |
| | | | | (SP 120.1%) | **7 Rn** | |

**1m 9.0** (1.80) CSF £38.40 TOTE £5.40: £2.60 £3.60 (£18.90) OWNER Mrs G. M. Temmerman (JEVINGTON) BRED James Wigan
LONG HANDICAP Shermood 7-2
WEIGHT FOR AGE 3yo-7lb
**1881 Sharp Imp** usually gets outpaced, but on this occasion he managed to race in fourth. Coming through to lead between horses a furlong out, he was ridden along to assert. (4/1)
**Pearl Dawn (IRE)**, given a four-month break, proved troublesome going down. Sent on over a quarter of a mile from home, she was collared a furlong out and failed to quicken. (10/1)
**1680 Bashful Brave** saw too much daylight. Racing in third place, he threw down his challenge in the final quarter-mile but this was really too early for him. Battling hard for the lead, he was still in with every chance early inside the final furlong before tapped for toe. (5/1)
**632 Tafahhus** moved up at halfway but had shot his bolt approaching the final furlong. (13/2)
**1621 Chewit** had bellows to mend below the distance. He has yet to win on grass. (7/4)

T/Plpt: £67.40 (136.1 Tckts). T/Qdpt: £9.30 (99.95 Tckts). AK

# 1543-MUSSELBURGH (R-H) (Firm, Good to firm patches)

## Monday June 17th

WEATHER: sunny WIND: almost nil

## 2018 E.B.F. MEDIAN AUCTION MAIDEN STKS (2-Y.O F) (Class F)

1-45 (1-45) **5f** £2,697.00 (£816.00: £398.00: £189.00) Stalls: High GOING minus 0.46 sec per fur (F)

| | | | | SP | RR | SF |
|---|---|---|---|---|---|---|
| $930^{4}$ | **Top of The Form (IRE)** (MJohnston) **2-8-11** JWeaver(4) (mde all: shkn up & r.o fnl f) | — | 1 | $5/4^{2}$ | 70+ | 32 |
| $1513^{2}$ | **Topatori (IRE)** (MHTompkins) **2-8-11** NDay(2) (lw: chsd wnr: rdn ½-wy: no imp fnl f) | 3½ | 2 | $4/5^{1}$ | 59 | 21 |
| | **My Girl** (JBerry) **2-8-6**(5) PRoberts(1) (neat: scope: bit bkwd: dwlt: n.d) | 13 | 3 | $12/1^{3}$ | 17 | — |
| $1869^{8}$ | **Cantsaynowt** (RMMcKellar) **2-8-11** DaleGibson(3) (spd 2f: sn wkd) | 12 | 4 | 50/1 | — | — |
| | | | | (SP 109.7%) | **4 Rn** | |

**59.8 secs** (2.10) CSF £2.56 TOTE £3.10 (£1.20) OWNER Mr R. W. Huggins (MIDDLEHAM) BRED Sean Beston
**930 Top of The Form (IRE)**, very fit, knew her job this time and made no mistake. She looks quite speedy. (5/4)
**1513 Topatori (IRE)** was flat to the boards by halfway and then proved no match for the winner. (4/5: tchd Evens)
**My Girl** needed this and, after a poor start, never showed a thing. (12/1: op 8/1)
**1645 Cantsaynowt** could only keep tabs on the leaders for two furlongs before stopping as though shot. (50/1)

## 2019 WIMPEY HOMES FARRIERS GAIT RATING RELATED MAIDEN STKS (0-60) (3-Y.O+) (Class F)

2-15 (2-15) **1m 16y** £2,682.00 (£752.00: £366.00) Stalls: High GOING minus 0.46 sec per fur (F)

| | | | | SP | RR | SF |
|---|---|---|---|---|---|---|
| $1908^{2}$ | **Dungeon Princess (IRE) (60)** (MRChannon) **3-8-8** KDarley(4) (lw: hld up: shkn up & qcknd 3f out: led ins fnl f: r.o) | — | 1 | $11/4^{1}$ | 66 | 31 |

1312² **Termon (60)** (MissLAPerratt) **3-8-8** JFanning(7) (lw: a chsng ldrs: effrt 3f out: ev ch 1f out: kpt on one pce) ....2 **2** 7/2 3 62 27
1888⁴ **Fairy Highlands (IRE) (58)** (SCWilliams) **3-8-8** KFallon(5) (led tl hdd ins fnl f: no ex) ....¾ **3** 3/1 2 61 26
1185⁹ **Gilling Dancer (IRE) (57)** (PCalver) **3-8-11** JQuinn(2) (rr div: effrt on outside 3f out: nvr able to chal) ....¾ **4** 12/1 62 27
*300*⁴ **Creeking (60)** (SirMarkPrescott) **3-8-8** CNutter(1) (bit bkwd: sn chsng ldr: outpcd fnl 2f) ....hd **5** 9/2 59 24
1584⁴ **Miletrian City (50)** (JBerry) **3-8-6**(5) PRoberts(3) (lw: bhd: effrt 3f out: no imp) ....½ **6** 66/1 61 26
1764³ **Carmosa (USA) (57)** (DNicholls) **3-8-8** AlexGreaves(6) (chsd ldrs tl wknd & eased fnl 2f) ....14 **7** 10/1 30 —
(SP 110.3%) **7 Rn**

**1m 41.0** (2.40) CSF £11.77 TOTE £3.10: £1.30 £2.10 (£4.60) OWNER The Irish Connection (UPPER LAMBOURN) BRED A. Steigenberger
OFFICIAL EXPLANATION **Carmosa (USA): got upset in the starting stalls and was later found to have been bleeding from her mouth.**
**1908 Dungeon Princess (IRE)** got it right at last here and, well handled, did the business in style. This should have done her confidence no end of good. (11/4)
**1312 Termon** ran a sound race and kept responding to pressure, but always found the winner too strong. (7/2)
**1888 Fairy Highlands (IRE)**, upped in trip and wearing a tongue-strap, was ridden aggressively this time and ran out of fuel inside the final furlong. (3/1)
**Gilling Dancer (IRE)** showed something here and seems to be improving. (12/1)
**Creeking** had not been out for almost four months and needed this. (9/2)
**1584 Miletrian City** ran his best race for a while. (66/1)
**1764 Carmosa (USA)** injured herself in the stalls and this is best forgotten. (10/1: op 5/1)

## 2020 WIMPEY HOMES EDINBURGH GOLD CUP H'CAP (0-70) (3-Y.O+) (Class E)

2-45 (2-46) **1m 4f 31y** £5,881.00 (£1,768.00: £854.00: £397.00) Stalls: High GOING minus 0.46 sec per fur (F)

SP RR SF
1548³ **Keep Battling (43)** (JSGoldie) **6-8-4** JQuinn(5) (hld up & bhd: hdwy on bit 3f out: qcknd to ld ins fnl f) ....— **1** 6/1 53 11
1870* **Lord Advocate (49)** (DANolan) **8-8-3b**(7) 4x IonaWands(4) (lw: cl up: led 4f out: qcknd: hdd ins fnl f: kpt on wl) ....2 **2** 4/1 2 56 14
1695⁴ **Green Land (BEL) (60)** (SCWilliams) **4-9-7** KFallon(6) (b.nr fore: lw: bhd: effrt & swtchd over 2f out: styd on wl towards fin) ....½ **3** 9/2 3 67 25
1839* **Westminster (IRE) (67)** (MHTompkins) **4-10-0v** 4x NDay(9) (a.p: ev ch 3f out: r.o one pce) ....1¼ **4** 3/1 1 72 30
1309³ **Trumped (IRE) (42)** (PMonteith) **4-8-3**ow3 NConnorton(7) (chsd ldrs: ev ch & rdn over 2f out: btn appr fnl f) ....¾ **5** 10/1 46 1
1676⁷ **Gold Desire (36)** (MBrittain) **6-7-11**ow1 DaleGibson(3) (b: mid div: effrt ent st: no imp) ....½ **6** 25/1 39 —
1544³ **Latvian (66)** (RAllan) **9-9-13** JWeaver(8) (led tl hdd 4f out: sn btn) ....nk **7** 12/1 69 27
1309⁴ **Manful (67)** (CWCElsey) **4-10-0b** NKennedy(1) (bhd: brought wd st: rdn & no imp) ....1½ **8** 9/1 68 26
1647⁹ **Soba Up (67)** (TJEtherington) **6-10-0** ACulhane(2) (trckd ldrs: outpcd appr st: sn wknd) ....6 **9** 12/1 60 18
(SP 115.8%) **9 Rn**

**2m 39.5** (6.50) CSF £28.46 CT £108.05 TOTE £7.40: £1.30 £1.50 £2.30 (£14.10) Trio £64.10 OWNER Mr J. S. Goldie (GLASGOW) BRED Mrs E. Campbell
LONG HANDICAP Gold Desire 7-6
**1548 Keep Battling** was given the ride he needs and he settled it in good style in the closing stages. (6/1)
**1870* Lord Advocate** ran his usual game race but had no answer to the winner's turn of foot in the final furlong. (4/1: 3/1-9/2)
**1695 Green Land (BEL)** took the eye in the paddock and picked up well in the closing stages, and would appear to be coming to hand. (9/2)
**1839* Westminster (IRE)** had everything in his favour but, when it came down to it in the final two furlongs, he was not good enough. (3/1)
**1309 Trumped (IRE)** had her chances here, but failed to quicken when the pressure was applied. (10/1)
**1548 Gold Desire** has yet to win over further than a mile and a quarter. (25/1)
**1544 Latvian** (12/1: op 8/1)

## 2021 WIMPEY HOMES KINGS RIDINGS H'CAP (0-70) (3-Y.O) (Class E)

3-15 (3-16) **5f** £3,074.00 (£932.00: £456.00: £218.00) Stalls: High GOING minus 0.46 sec per fur (F)

SP RR SF
1823⁵ **Chemcast (65)** (DNicholls) **3-9-2b**1 AlexGreaves(4) (a cl up: led ins fnl f: drvn out) ....— **1** 4/1 1 72 18
1657* **Stoney End (USA) (70)** (MRChannon) **3-9-7** KFallon(2) (hmpd s: hdwy ½-wy: r.o towards fin) ....nk **2** 5/1 3 76 22
1761⁴ **Gwespyr (58)** (JBerry) **3-8-9** KDarley(5) (lw: led tl hdd ins fnl f: hrd rdn & kpt on) ....s.h **3** 9/2 2 64 10
1599⁸ **Katy-Q (IRE) (55)** (PCalver) **3-8-6b** NConnorton(6) (lw: a chsng ldrs: rdn 2f out: nt qckn) ....1¾ **4** 12/1 55 1
1761³ **Imp Express (IRE) (48)** (GMMoore) **3-7-13v**1 DaleGibson(1) (hmpd s: hdwy ½-wy: no imp) ....¾ **5** 7/1 46 —
1663³ **Mystique Smile (46)** (SCWilliams) **3-7-11** JQuinn(9) (b.hind: sn outpcd: sme hdwy 2f out: nt trble ldrs) ....1½ **6** 9/2 2 39 —
1547⁷ **Lord Cornelious (45)** (DANolan) **3-7-3**(7) IonaWands(3) (wnt lft s: n.d) ....1¾ **7** 100/1 33 —
1547² **Ready Teddy (IRE) (50)** (MissLAPerratt) **3-8-1** JFanning(8) (cl up tl wknd fnl 2f) ....s.h **8** 8/1 37 —
1646W **Just Lady (70)** (WGMTurner) **3-9-7** JWeaver(7) (spd to ½-wy: eased fnl 2f) ....12 **9** 8/1 19 —
(SP 116.4%) **9 Rn**

**60.2 secs** (2.50) CSF £22.94 CT £85.17 TOTE £5.50: £1.10 £2.50 £1.50 (£17.50) Trio £12.30 OWNER Mr B. L. Cassidy (THIRSK) BRED C. R. and V. M. Withers
LONG HANDICAP Lord Cornelious 6-8
**1823 Chemcast**, from a yard that has been out of form for a month, was sporting blinkers for the first time and did just enough in the closing stages. (4/1)
**1657* Stoney End (USA)** took a hefty bump leaving the stalls which, in the end, probably made all the difference. His rider might well have been advised to cross over to the stands' side. (5/1)
**1761 Gwespyr** managed to get the required break this time, but then failed to last out. (9/2)
**Katy-Q (IRE)** looked very fit, but proved short of a turn of foot after racing prominently. (12/1)
**1761 Imp Express (IRE)**, in a visor for the first time, took a bump leaving the stalls and raced in the centre of the track instead of the stands' side, which probably made all the difference. (7/1: 5/1-8/1)
**1663 Mystique Smile** was short of pace and room early on, and could never offer a threat. (9/2)
**1547 Ready Teddy (IRE)** (8/1: op 5/1)

## 2022 WIMPEY HOMES HOLYGATE CLAIMING STKS (3-Y.O+) (Class F)

3-45 (3-45) **7f 15y** £2,724.00 (£764.00: £372.00) Stalls: High GOING minus 0.46 sec per fur (F)

SP RR SF
1474⁷ **Broctune Gold (55)** (MrsMReveley) **5-9-2** ACulhane(1) (mde all: r.o wl fnl f) ....— **1** 8/1 3 67 30
1789⁹ **Moon Strike (FR) (74)** (SCWilliams) **6-9-12** KFallon(5) (lw: trckd ldrs: effrt & swtchd over 1f out: styd on: nvr able to chal) ....3½ **2** 7/4 2 69 32

| | | | SP | RR | SF |
|---|---|---|---|---|---|
| $1891^{2}$ | **Double Oscar (IRE) (76)** (MJohnston) **3-9-3b** JWeaver(3) (sn trckng wnr: rdn & hung lft 2f out: r.o one pce) .nk | **3** | Evens $^{1}$ | 68 | 22 |
| *$1455^{6}$* | **Wasblest (57)** (JBerry) **4-8-10**$^{(5)}$ PRoberts(6) (trckd ldrs: nt qckn appr fnl f)....1¾ | **4** | 12/1 | 53 | 16 |
| $688^{17}$ | **Prince Rudolf (IRE) (38)** (WGMTurner) **4-9-0** JQuinn(2) (lw: bhd: effrt over 2f out: nvr able to chal).....nk | **5** | 66/1 | 52 | 15 |
| $1642^{7}$ | **Thorntoun Jewel (IRE) (38)** (MissZAGreen) **3-7-12** DaleGibson(4) (a bhd)....11 | **6** | 25/1 | 20 | — |
| | | | (SP 110.5%) | | **6 Rn** |

**1m 28.3** (2.80) CSF £21.26 TOTE £11.10: £3.80 £1.90 (£10.10) OWNER Mrs M. B. Thwaites (SALTBURN) BRED A. J. Poulton (Epping) Ltd
WEIGHT FOR AGE 3yo-9lb

**1474 Broctune Gold**, taken early to post, got things all his own way in the race and really enjoyed himself. (8/1: op 9/2)
**1789 Moon Strike (FR)** took a good hold and then took time to respond and, when he did, the winner had flown. (7/4)
**1891 Double Oscar (IRE)** looks to have plenty of ability, but has his own ideas about how to use it. (Evens)
**835 Wasblest**, who has done almost all her running over the minimum trip, travelled well here before failing to quicken when it mattered. (12/1: op 8/1)
**Prince Rudolf (IRE)** has not done much for a while, but did look well here and ran reasonably. (66/1)

## 2023 WIMPEY HOMES WESTHOLME H'CAP (0-70) (3-Y.O+) (Class E)

4-15 (4-16) **1m 16y** £3,517.50 (£1,065.00: £520.00: £247.50) Stalls: High GOING minus 0.46 sec per fur (F)

| | | | SP | RR | SF |
|---|---|---|---|---|---|
| $1546^{8}$ | **Tinklers Folly (50)** (DenysSmith) **4-9-4** KFallon(6) (hdwy ½-wy: hrd rdn to ld ins fnl f: hung rt: styd on wl) ....— | **1** | 10/1 | 62 | 40 |
| $1538^{8}$ | **Miss Pigalle (39)** (MissLAPerratt) **5-8-7b** JWeaver(4) (led after 1f tl ins fnl f: no ex)....2 | **2** | 10/1 | 47 | 25 |
| 1860* | **Grey Kingdom (41)** (MBrittain) **5-8-9** $^{5x}$ DaleGibson(9) (lw: led 1f: chsd ldrs: ev ch over 1f out: nt qckn) ..........2 | **3** | 9/4 $^{1}$ | 45 | 23 |
| $1846^{6}$ | **Bulsara (56)** (CWFairhurst) **4-9-10** RLappin(7) (a.p: effrt & ch 2f out: r.o one pce)....½ | **4** | 14/1 | 59 | 37 |
| *$1718^{9}$* | **River Garnock (46)** (DNicholls) **4-9-0** AlexGreaves(10) (lw: chsd ldrs: n.m.r 2f out: nt qckn)....nk | **5** | 16/1 | 49 | 27 |
| $1865^{7}$ | **Sunday Mail Too (IRE) (42)** (MissLAPerratt) **4-8-10** JQuinn(5) (chsd ldrs: effrt over 3f out: btn wl over 1f out)....5 | **6** | 16/1 | 35 | 13 |
| 1546* | **Bowcliffe (49)** (MrsAMNaughton) **5-9-3** KDarley(2) (bhd: rdn over 3f out: n.d)....1¾ | **7** | 3/1 $^{2}$ | 38 | 16 |
| $1867^{6}$ | **Hutchies Lady (40)** (RMMcKellar) **4-8-1**$^{(7)}$ KSked(8) (b.off hind: bhd & rn wd st: n.d)....nk | **8** | 9/1 $^{3}$ | 29 | 7 |
| $1530^{12}$ | **Fatehalkhair (IRE) (45)** (BEllison) **4-8-13v$^{1}$** NKennedy(3) (bhd & rn wd st: n.d)....½ | **9** | 10/1 | 33 | 11 |
| $1527^{18}$ | **Napoleon's Return (45)** (AHarrison) **3-8-3** JFanning(1) (chsd ldrs tl wknd over 2f out)....s.h | **10** | 20/1 | 32 | — |
| $1868^{8}$ | **Rapid Mover (33)** (DANolan) **9-7-8b**$^{(7)}$ IonaWands(11) (a bhd)....hd | **11** | 25/1 | 20 | — |
| | | | (SP 120.1%) | | **11 Rn** |

**1m 41.0** (2.40) CSF £96.73 CT £284.38 TOTE £13.40: £4.50 £2.90 £1.80 (£39.30) Trio £42.80 OWNER Mr R. O. Manners (BISHOP AUCKLAND) BRED Qualitair Stud Ltd
WEIGHT FOR AGE 3yo-10lb

**662* Tinklers Folly** is a difficult performer to work out, but he does like this track. Even then, some of his efforts here are indifferent to say the least. (10/1)
**1313 Miss Pigalle** again ran one of her better races, but she was well outpointed late on. (10/1)
**1860* Grey Kingdom** could never get his own way on this occasion and was finally done for toe in the last furlong. (9/4)
**1846 Bulsara** is gradually coming to hand. (14/1)
**1586 River Garnock** showed some ability here and was always a bit short of room in the last couple of furlongs. (16/1)
**1546* Bowcliffe** never seemed happy here and probably found the ground too fast. (3/1)
**1633 Hutchies Lady** (9/1: op 6/1)

## 2024 WIMPEY HOMES APPRENTICE H'CAP (0-60) (3-Y.O+) (Class G)

4-45 (4-45) **1m 3f 32y** £2,332.00 (£652.00: £316.00) Stalls: High GOING minus 0.46 sec per fur (F)

| | | | SP | RR | SF |
|---|---|---|---|---|---|
| $1544^{5}$ | **Ambidextrous (IRE) (43)** (EJAlston) **4-9-7** DWright(4) (lw: bhd & pushed along: hdwy over 3f out: styd on to ld wl ins fnl f)....— | **1** | 10/1 | 54 | 35 |
| $1861^{7}$ | **Kings Cay (IRE) (46)** (THCaldwell) **5-9-5**$^{(5)}$ SCopp(2) (chsd ldrs: led wl over 1f out: rdn & hdd wl ins fnl f)......½ | **2** | 12/1 | 56 | 37 |
| $1586^{3}$ | **Teejay'n'aitch (IRE) (40)** (JSGoldie) **4-9-1**$^{(3)}$ PRoberts(8) (bhd: rdn appr st: styd on fnl 2f: nrst fin)....6 | **3** | 7/1 $^{2}$ | 42 | 23 |
| 890* | **Serious Trust (58)** (SirMarkPrescott) **3-9-2**$^{(7)}$ TPengkerego(3) (lw: cl up: outpcd ent st: no imp after)...........1½ | **4** | Evens $^{1}$ | 58 | 26 |
| $1821^{5}$ | **Greek Gold (IRE) (43)** (WLBarker) **7-9-2**$^{(5)}$ JBramhill(7) (set str pce: clr ent st: hdd & wknd wl over 1f out) ...2½ | **5** | 9/1 $^{3}$ | 39 | 20 |
| $1309^{7}$ | **Funny Rose (30)** (PMonteith) **6-8-3**$^{(5)}$ IonaWands(6) (lw: bhd: sme hdwy 3f out: n.d)....3½ | **6** | 16/1 | 21 | 2 |
| $1762^{3}$ | **Phantom Dancer (IRE) (48)** (JBerry) **3-8-8**$^{(5)}$ CLowther(9) (chsd ldrs tl wknd fnl 3f)....3½ | **7** | 7/1 $^{2}$ | 34 | 2 |
| $1866^{7}$ | **Amnesia (IRE) (30)** (MrsSCBradburne) **5-8-3**$^{(5)}$ KSked(1) (b.nr fore: a rr div)....4 | **8** | 25/1 | 10 | — |
| $1167^{15}$ | **Portite Sophie (30)** (MBrittain) **5-8-3**$^{(5)}$ GParkin(5) (b: b.hind: a bhd)....nk | **9** | 14/1 | 10 | — |
| | | | (SP 118.2%) | | **9 Rn** |

**2m 24.3** (4.60) CSF £107.19 CT £821.18 TOTE £8.90: £2.20 £4.20 £4.30 (£47.10) Trio £63.30 OWNER Mrs Carol McPhail (PRESTON) BRED Saeed Manana
WEIGHT FOR AGE 3yo-13lb

**1544 Ambidextrous (IRE)** came from a long way behind in a strongly-run event and stayed on well, despite his rider dropping his whip some way out. (10/1: 8/1-12/1)
**1676 Kings Cay (IRE)** always held a good position but, despite responding to pressure, he had to admit he had met one too good. (12/1: op 8/1)
**1586 Teejay'n'aitch (IRE)** only decided to stay on once it was all too late. (7/1)
**890* Serious Trust** had the most inexperienced rider in the race and that probably made quite a bit of difference. (Evens)
**661 Funny Rose** was never co-operating sufficiently. (16/1)

T/Plpt: £101.50 (80.82 Tckts). T/Qdpt: £13.70 (74.17 Tckts). AA

# 1827-PONTEFRACT (L-H) (Good to firm)

## Monday June 17th

WEATHER: fine & sunny WIND: mod half bhd

## 2025 TATTERSALLS MAIDEN AUCTION STKS (2-Y.O F) (Class E)

6-45 (6-45) **6f** £3,165.00 (£960.00: £470.00: £225.00) Stalls: Low GOING minus 0.38 sec per fur (F)

| | | | SP | RR | SF |
|---|---|---|---|---|---|
| *$1489^{2}$* | **Nostalgic Air (USA)** (EWeymes) **2-8-0** JQuinn(9) (chsd ldrs: styd on wl to ld ins fnl f)....— | **1** | 6/1 $^{3}$ | 65 | 17 |
| $1664^{4}$ | **Danehill Princess (IRE)** (RHollinshead) **2-7-13**$^{(5)}$ FLynch(10) (racd wd: led tl ins fnl f)....½ | **2** | 7/2 $^{1}$ | 68 | 20 |

1851[4] **Hever Golf Lily** (TJNaughton) **2-8-1** DRMcCabe(7) (chsd ldrs: outpcd 2f out: styd on fnl f) ........1¾ **3** 4/1[2] 60 12
1827[6] **Under Pressure** (TDEasterby) **2-7-10**(3) MHenry(6) (w ldrs: rdn & hung lft over 1f out: sn wknd) ........5 **4** 6/1[3] 45 —
**Music Express (IRE)** (AHarrison) **2-8-4**ow4 DeanMcKeown(5) (cmpt: chsd ldrs: rdn & outpcd 2f out: swtchd & styd on ins fnl f) ........s.h **5** 33/1 50 —
**Debonair** (GLewis) **2-8-2** DaleGibson(4) (leggy: unf: dwlt s: effrt ½-wy: nvr nr ldrs) ........6 **6** 7/2[1] 32 —
**Bloomsy Babe** (JJQuinn) **2-8-0**ow1 MDeering(8) (cmpt: bit bkwd: s.i.s: bhd & pushed along: sme late hdwy)..1 **7** 33/1 27 —
**Poly Dancer** (MRChannon) **2-8-2** AGorman(2) (leggy: unf: sn drvn along & outpcd) ........hd **8** 8/1 29 —
**My Dear Watson** (JBerry) **2-8-0** AGarth(3) (w ldrs tl wknd over 2f out) ........2½ **9** 12/1 20 —
1583[4] **Alisadara** (NBycroft) **2-7-12** FNorton(11) (sn bhd) ........8 **10** 25/1 — —
**Common Rock (IRE)** (JNorton) **2-8-0** JFanning(1) (unf: sn outpcd & pushed along) ........5 **11** 33/1 — —
(SP 124.5%) **11 Rn**

**1m 17.1** (2.80) CSF £27.37 TOTE £6.30: £2.00 £1.30 £1.70 (£14.00) Trio £9.20 OWNER Mr T. A. Scothern (MIDDLEHAM) BRED Wakefield Farm

**1489 Nostalgic Air (USA)** stuck on strongly to get well on top in the closing stages. She looks a likely nursery type and will be suited by seven. (6/1)
**1664 Danehill Princess (IRE)**, drawn wide, showed bags of toe to lead them but, in the end, the winner proved too strong. (7/2)
**1851 Hever Golf Lily** is improving with every outing. She pounds the ground and would not want the going any firmer than this. (4/1)
**1827 Under Pressure**, a keen-going type, hung left under pressure and than faded in the straight. (6/1)
**Music Express (IRE)**, a lean sort, came again after being outpaced and forced to switch. She will be suited by seven. (33/1)
**Debonair**, who did not take the eye in the paddock, is a keen-going type. After missing the break, she was being driven along and making no impression at halfway. (7/2)
**My Dear Watson** (12/1: 8/1-14/1)

## 2026 BEECH (S) STKS (3-Y.O) (Class G)

7-15 (7-16) **1m 4y** £2,658.00 (£738.00: £354.00) Stalls: Low GOING minus 0.38 sec per fur (F)

SP RR SF

985[9] **Loch Style (50)** (RHollinshead) **3-8-9**(5) FLynch(9) (chsd ldrs: rdn to ld 2f out: styd on) ........— **1** 9/2[2] 61 20
*1721[11]* **How Could-I (IRE) (40)** (TDEasterby) **3-8-9** FNorton(10) (led 2f: led over 2f out: sn hdd: kpt on same pce)......2 **2** 11/1 52 11
1162[6] **Tallulah Belle (45)** (NPLittmoden) **3-8-9** JQuinn(14) (a in tch: styd on wl appr fnl f) ........1 **3** 9/1 50 9
1068[10] **Veshca Lady (IRE) (48)** (EWeymes) **3-8-10**(5) DGriffiths(1) (bhd: hdwy on outside 2f out: styd on fnl f: nt rch ldrs) ........1½ **4** 11/2[3] 53 12
*1721[14]* **Craigmore Magic (USA) (50)** (MissMKMilligan) **3-9-0** KDarley(5) (chsd ldrs: rdn & outpcd over 2f out: styd on fnl f) ........4 **5** 11/1 44 3
1836* **Bag And A Bit (43)** (BJMeehan) **3-9-1** MTebbutt(15) (chsd ldrs: rdn & outpcd 2f out: sn btn) ........hd **6** 7/4[1] 45 4
1864[7] **Brownie's Promise** (MBrittain) **3-9-0** MWigham(4) (bit bkwd: s.i.s: bhd & sn rdn along: sme late hdwy)........5 **7** 33/1 34 —
1474[15] **Domusky (35)** (ABMulholland) **3-8-9** DaleGibson(3) (bhd: sme hdwy appr fnl f: n.d) ........1¼ **8** 50/1 26 —
1850[14] **Eccentric Dancer (38)** (MPBielby) **3-8-9b[1]** JFanning(8) (chsd ldrs tl wknd 2f out) ........3 **9** 14/1 20 —
**Boy Blakeney** (MrsSJSmith) **3-9-0** AGorman(11) (sn bhd: rdn 5f out) ........1¼ **10** 33/1 23 —
1762[7] **Superbird** (TDEasterby) **3-8-9b[1]** KFallon(6) (sn pushed along: nvr nr ldrs) ........¾ **11** 9/1 16 —
1762[6] **Mr Titch** (DenysSmith) **3-9-0** JWeaver(7) (dwlt s: a in rr) ........6 **12** 20/1 9 —
1422[12] **Present 'n Correct** (CBBBooth) **3-9-0** ACulhane(16) (chsd ldrs tl wknd 2f out: eased) ........3½ **13** 33/1 2 —
**Miss Express (BEL)** (MrsSJSmith) **3-8-9** PBloomfield(13) (unf: bit bkwd: in tch: rdn 4f out: sn lost pl)........1¾ **14** 33/1 — —
637[4] **Madonna da Rossi (44)** (MDods) **3-8-9** DeanMcKeown(12) (plld v.hrd: led after 2f tl over 2f out: sn lost pl)...nk **15** 10/1 — —
**Alis Princess** (MPBielby) **3-8-9** DRMcCabe(2) (bit bkwd: sn bhd: t.o ½-wy) ........12 **16** 33/1 — —
(SP 143.8%) **16 Rn**

**1m 46.5** (5.00) CSF £58.34 TOTE £7.00: £2.00 £4.60 £2.70 (£151.90) Trio £241.70; £204.34 to 19/6/96 OWNER Mr J. B. Wilcox (UPPER LONGDON) BRED Longdon Stud Ltd
No bid

**781 Loch Style**, who had plenty on his plate on his first outing on turf, landed a gamble with something to spare under an excellent ride from his apprentice. (9/2: op 8/1)
**1067 How Could-I (IRE)**, who looked very fit, has been tried over a variety of trips. She kept on, but was never going to be anything other than second best. (11/1)
**1162 Tallulah Belle** only found her stride late in the day. (9/1)
**Veshca Lady (IRE)**, who won two sellers as a juvenile, was dropped in class. Set a stiff task, she made ground on the outer turning in, and was putting in some solid work at the line. (11/2)
**1363 Craigmore Magic (USA)**, badly tapped for toe turning in, will be suited by a step up in distance. (11/1)
**1836* Bag And A Bit** is possibly better suited by seven. (7/4)

## 2027 LANDBRIDGE SHIPPING H'CAP (0-75) (3-Y.O) (Class D)

7-45 (7-47) **1m 2f 6y** £5,526.50 (£1,652.00: £791.00: £360.50) Stalls: Low GOING minus 0.38 sec per fur (F)

SP RR SF

1832* **Seattle Alley (USA) (63)** (MrsJRRamsden) **3-8-10** 5x KFallon(11) (hld up: hdwy on outside over 2f out: rdn to ld wl ins fnl f: jst hld on) ........— **1** 3/1[1] 74 27
1089[15] **Phantom Haze (60)** (MissSEHall) **3-8-4**(3) MHenry(5) (s.i.s: sn chsng ldrs: rdn to ld 2f out: hdd wl ins fnl f: rallied towards fin) ........s.h **2** 12/1[3] 71 24
1861[2] **Nose No Bounds (IRE) (72)** (MJohnston) **3-9-5b** JWeaver(6) (led to 2f out: one pce) ........3 **3** 5/1[2] 78 31
1434[5] **Alsahib (USA) (74)** (HThomsonJones) **3-9-7** RHills(10) (effrt u.p 4f out: sn chsng ldrs: wknd over 1f out) ........9 **4** 5/1[2] 66 19
1883* **Sistar Act (70)** (MRChannon) **3-9-3** 5x KDarley(9) (sn bhd & rdn along: hdwy 5f out: sn chsng ldrs: wknd over 1f out) ........s.h **5** 3/1[1] 62 15
*1721[2]* **Seeking Destiny (IRE) (49)** (MCChapman) **3-7-10** JQuinn(2) (in tch: lost pl over 3f out: n.d after) ........4 **6** 25/1 34 —
1089[10] **Crystal Warrior (58)** (DNicholls) **3-8-5** JFanning(1) (chsd ldrs tl lost pl over 3f out) ........5 **7** 16/1 35 —
1317[10] **D'naan (IRE) (69)** (WJHaggas) **3-9-2b** DeanMcKeown(8) (chsd ldrs tl lost pl 2f out) ........½ **8** 14/1 46 —
1636[2] **Islay Brown (IRE) (55)** (CWCElsey) **3-7-11b**(5)ow5 FLynch(4) (chsd ldrs tl lost pl over 2f out) ........5 **9** 20/1 24 —
1420[7] **Kingfisher Brave (70)** (MGMeagher) **3-9-3** JFortune(7) (chsd ldrs: rdn 5f out: wknd over 2f out) ........1¼ **10** 20/1 37 —
1780[6] **Bollin Jacob (63)** (TDEasterby) **3-8-10** MWigham(3) (lw: a bhd) ........7 **11** 12/1[3] 18 —
(SP 124.6%) **11 Rn**

**2m 13.2** (4.90) CSF £37.63 CT £167.32 TOTE £3.70: £1.70 £2.70 £1.80 (£26.10) Trio £70.80 OWNER Mr P. A. Leonard (THIRSK) BRED Hermitage Farm Inc.
LONG HANDICAP Seeking Destiny (IRE) 7-6

**1832* Seattle Alley (USA)**, only gelded six weeks ago, defied a 5lb penalty. Ridden differently this time, he seemed to hang fire when he hit the front and was almost worried out of it. (3/1)
**614 Phantom Haze**, who pulled too hard last time, was much more settled here. Supported in the market, he was only just denied in the end. (12/1)
**1861 Nose No Bounds (IRE)**, with the blinkers on again, could not match the first two in the final furlong. (5/1)
**1434 Alsahib (USA)**, who has a rounded action, looked to have been given plenty of weight on his handicap debut. (5/1: op 8/1)
**1883* Sistar Act** rather ran in snatches and her rider never looked comfortable. (3/1)
**D'naan (IRE)** (14/1: 8/1-16/1)
**1780 Bollin Jacob** (12/1: op 7/1)

## 2028 PONTEFRACT CUP H'CAP (0-70) (4-Y.O+) (Class E)
8-15 (8-15) **2m 1f 216y** £3,785.00 (£1,130.00: £540.00: £245.00) Stalls: Centre GOING minus 0.38 sec per fur (F)

| | | | | SP | RR | SF |
|---|---|---|---|---|---|---|
| 1784[3] | **Great Oration (IRE) (41)** (FWatson) **7-9-3** JWeaver(1) (lw: hld up: smooth hdwy over 3f out: shkn up to ld over 1f out: sn clr) | — | **1** | 4/1[2] | 56 | 38 |
| 1478[6] | **Lostris (IRE) (33)** (MDods) **5-8-9** DaleGibson(2) (trckd ldrs: led over 3f out tl over 1f out: no ch w wnr) | 5 | **2** | 10/1 | 44 | 26 |
| *1717[2]* | **Gunmaker (26)** (BJLlewellyn) **7-8-2** FNorton(3) (chsd ldrs: pushed along 7f out: one pce fnl 2f) | 3 | **3** | 7/1 | 34 | 16 |
| 1070[2] | **Izza (46)** (WStorey) **5-9-8** JQuinn(4) (lw: hld up: stdy hdwy over 3f out: rdn 2f out: sn wknd) | 7 | **4** | 9/4[1] | 48 | 30 |
| 1784* | **Greek Night Out (IRE) (48)** (JLEyre) **5-9-7**(3) MHenry(8) (sn trckng ldr: led over 3f out to 2f out: wknd over 1f out) | 1¾ | **5** | 4/1[2] | 48 | 30 |
| *1717[4]* | **Record Lover (IRE) (31)** (MCChapman) **6-8-7** DRMcCabe(5) (led 3f: pushed along 5f out: lost pl over 3f out) | 5 | **6** | 20/1 | 27 | 9 |
| 1828[2] | **Remontant (IRE) (33)** (RHollinshead) **4-8-3**(5) FLynch(6) (dwlt s: hld up & bhd: rdn over 3f out: sn wknd) | 13 | **7** | 14/1 | 17 | — |
| 1611* | **Tiaphena (47)** (JMackie) **5-9-9** JFanning(7) (led after 3f tl over 3f out: wknd over 2f out) | 5 | **8** | 9/2[3] | 27 | 9 |
| | | | | (SP 122.0%) | **8 Rn** | |

**3m 59.9** (7.90) CSF £40.21 CT £254.62 TOTE £4.60: £1.20 £2.70 £1.80 (£43.20) OWNER M D Hetherington (Packaging) Ltd (SEDGEFIELD) BRED P. F. I. Cole
WEIGHT FOR AGE 4yo-1lb
**1784 Great Oration (IRE)**, who has to be put in the stalls last of all, wanted nothing to do with the suicidal gallop. Produced on the bridle, he had only to be nudged clear. (4/1)
**1478 Lostris (IRE)** certainly seemed to be suited by this extreme trip. (10/1)
**1717 Gunmaker** tried hard, but proved woefully one-paced. (7/1)
**1070 Izza** came there with the winner but, when the cards were played, she dropped away. She may not have been at her best here, but she does seem high in the weights now. (9/4)
**1784* Greek Night Out (IRE)** proved very keen. Pulling her way to the front soon after halfway, it was no surprise to see her fall in a heap once in line for home. (4/1)
**1611* Tiaphena** set off far too quick and the wheels fell off going into the final turn. (9/2)

## 2029 CEDAR LIMITED STKS (0-65) (3-Y.O+) (Class F)
8-45 (8-46) **5f** £2,598.00 (£728.00: £354.00) Stalls: Low GOING minus 0.38 sec per fur (F)

| | | | | SP | RR | SF |
|---|---|---|---|---|---|---|
| 1781[6] | **Barato (64)** (MrsJRRamsden) **5-9-3** KFallon(7) (b.nr hind: hld up: hdwy over 1f out: rdn to ld ins fnl f: hld on towards fin) | — | **1** | 6/4[1] | 70 | 32 |
| 1527[7] | **Bowlers Boy (61)** (JJQuinn) **3-8-6**(5) FLynch(9) (hld up: effrt 2f out: r.o ins fnl f) | nk | **2** | 8/1 | 69 | 25 |
| 1429[6] | **Gymcrak Gem (IRE) (63)** (GHolmes) **3-8-8b[1]** DeanMcKeown(5) (b.hind: racd wd: led tl ins fnl f) | ¾ | **3** | 17/2 | 64 | 20 |
| 1840[8] | **Ciserano (IRE) (64)** (MRChannon) **3-8-11** KDarley(8) (sn outpcd & pushed along: hdwy over 1f out: styd on) | 1¼ | **4** | 6/1[3] | 63 | 19 |
| 1823[6] | **Gagajulu (65)** (PDEvans) **3-8-8** JFortune(3) (a chsng ldrs: rdn ½-wy: styd on same pce) | 1 | **5** | 8/1 | 56 | 12 |
| 1859[5] | **Hickleton Miss (52)** (MrsVAAconley) **3-8-8** MDeering(1) (a chsng ldrs: one pce fnl 2f) | ½ | **6** | 25/1 | 55 | 11 |
| 1844[4] | **Petraco (IRE) (60)** (NASmith) **8-9-3** MRimmer(2) (lw: w ldrs: rdn ½-wy: kpt on same pce) | ½ | **7** | 6/1[3] | 56 | 18 |
| 2005[17] | **Ned's Bonanza (62)** (MDods) **7-9-3** JWeaver(4) (trckd ldrs: effrt ½-wy: styng on whn nt clr run jst ins fnl f: eased) | 3 | **8** | 11/2[2] | 47 | 9 |
| | **February (45)** (AJChamberlain) **3-8-8** JQuinn(6) (bit bkwd: sn outpcd & bhd) | 15 | **9** | 33/1 | — | — |
| | | | | (SP 123.5%) | **9 Rn** | |

**63.1 secs** (2.30) CSF £14.54 TOTE £2.60: £1.40 £2.40 £2.40 (£14.90) Trio £80.40 OWNER Mr David Young (THIRSK) BRED J. Carr and Miss L. Charlton
WEIGHT FOR AGE 3yo-6lb
**1781 Barato** ended a losing sequence of eighteen. His jockey rides this track to perfection. (6/4)
**1527 Bowlers Boy**, dropping back to five, travelled strongly just off the pace. Despite running with his head high, he stuck on strongly inside the last and had the winner at full stretch at the line. (8/1)
**1429 Gymcrak Gem (IRE)**, in blinkers for the first time, raced wide to the turn. (17/2)
**1592* Ciserano (IRE)** struggled to go the pace and needs six. (6/1)
**Gagajulu** ran her best race so far this year but, overall, her form is still some way below that of her juvenile days. (8/1)
**1340 Hickleton Miss** was far from disgraced after running poorly on her last two efforts. (25/1)
**Ned's Bonanza** found himself trapped in on the inner inside the last. (11/2)

## 2030 WALNUT H'CAP (0-70) (3-Y.O+) (Class E)
9-15 (9-16) **6f** £3,106.00 (£928.00: £444.00: £202.00) Stalls: Low GOING minus 0.38 sec per fur (F)

| | | | | SP | RR | SF |
|---|---|---|---|---|---|---|
| 1786[9] | **Encore M'Lady (IRE) (57)** (FHLee) **5-9-4** DRMcCabe(9) (lw: hld up: hdwy on outside over 2f out: led jst ins fnl f: jst hld on) | — | **1** | 10/1 | 65 | 33 |
| 1829[7] | **Halmanerror (67)** (MrsJRRamsden) **6-10-0** KFallon(2) (hld up: hdwy & nt clr run over 1f out: swtchd outside & styd on strly ins fnl f: jst failed) | nk | **2** | 3/1[1] | 74 | 42 |
| 1765* | **Sonderise (55)** (NTinkler) **7-9-2** JFortune(3) (lw: hld up: hdwy & nt clr run over 1f out: swtchd & styd on ins fnl f) | ¾ | **3** | 7/2[2] | 60 | 28 |
| 1474[4] | **Blue Grit (53)** (MDods) **10-9-0b** JWeaver(5) (trckd ldrs: chal over 1f out: sn rdn & nt qckn) | 1 | **4** | 11/2 | 56 | 24 |
| *1601[9]* | **Desert Invader (IRE) (50)** (DWChapman) **5-8-11** ACulhane(4) (lw: mde most: hung rt fr ½-wy: hdd jst ins fnl f: kpt on same pce) | ¾ | **5** | 14/1 | 51 | 19 |
| 1848[5] | **Densben (46)** (DenysSmith) **12-8-7** KDarley(1) (lw: chsd ldrs: one pce whn n.m.r ins fnl f) | 1¼ | **6** | 9/2[3] | 43 | 11 |

| | | | | SP | RR | SF |
|---|---|---|---|---|---|---|
| *$1812^{11}$* | **Souperficial (50)** (JAGlover) **5-8-6v$^{(5)}$** FLynch(7) (sn bhd: sme hdwy over 1f out: nvr nr to chal) | ½ | **7** | 11/2 | 46 | 14 |
| $1765^{9}$ | **Steel Sovereign (36)** (MDods) **5-7-11** DaleGibson(6) (sn rdn along: w ldr: wkng whn n.m.r ins fnl f) | 1 | **8** | 33/1 | 29 | — |

(SP 114.9%) **8 Rn**

**1m 17.2** (2.90) CSF £38.03 CT £117.45 TOTE £11.10: £2.80 £1.80 £1.20 (£12.00) Trio £20.30 OWNER Mr F. H. Lee (WILMSLOW) BRED Irish National Stud Co Ltd in Ireland

**1786 Encore M'Lady (IRE)** won the William Hill Trophy at York two years ago from a 19lb higher mark, and looked in great shape here beforehand. Different tactics were tried and, settled off the pace, she did just enough, though she did have luck on her side. (10/1)
**1829 Halmanerror**, held up in what was a three-furlong dash, met all the trouble going. Eventually switched outside, he needed three more strides. He undoubtedly has the ability to win over this distance in a truly-run race, but seven may prove his optimum trip. (3/1)
**1765* Sonderise**, raised a harsh 8lb after his overdue Catterick success, was another not to have the best of luck in running. (7/2)
**1474 Blue Grit** reserves his best for here and has won five times. He shaped better this time and the yard seems to be on the way back. (11/2)
**1094 Desert Invader (IRE)**, allowed to set his own pace, gave his rider problems by hanging away from the rail throughout. (14/1)

T/Plpt: £98.60 (160.4 Tckts). T/Qdpt: £16.10 (72.22 Tckts). WG

# 1839-WINDSOR (Fig. 8) (Good to firm)
## Monday June 17th
WEATHER: warm WIND: nil

## 2031 BOWRING MARSH & MCLENNAN (S) STKS (2-Y.O) (Class G)
6-30 (6-31) **5f 10y** £2,318.00 (£648.00: £314.00) Stalls: High GOING minus 0.33 sec per fur (GF)

| | | | | SP | RR | SF |
|---|---|---|---|---|---|---|
| $1352^{5}$ | **Whizz Kid** (JJBridger) **2-8-3$^{(3)}$** DarrenMoffatt(11) (mde virtually all: drvn out) | — | **1** | 15/2 | 67 | 10 |
| | **Charlton Spring (IRE)** (RJHodges) **2-8-3$^{(3)}$** SDrowne(2) (leggy: s.s: gd hdwy over 1f out: r.o: nt rch wnr) | 1½ | **2** | 8/1 | 62+ | 5 |
| *$1813^{4}$* | **Come Too Mamma's** (JBerry) **2-8-11** JCarroll(10) (lw: a.p: ev ch 2f out: nt qckn) | 3 | **3** | 13/2$^{2}$ | 58 | 1 |
| $490^{7}$ | **Tinker's Surprise (IRE)** (BJMeehan) **2-8-11** BDoyle(4) (a.p: hrd rdn fnl 2f: one pce) | nk | **4** | 7/1$^{3}$ | 57 | — |
| | **Vickys Double** (JSMoore) **2-8-6** WJO'Connor(9) (neat: bit bkwd: hdwy & rdn over 1f out: nvr nr to chal) | 2 | **5** | 33/1 | 45 | — |
| $1683^{6}$ | **Princess Ferdinand (IRE)** (MMcCormack) **2-8-6** WWoods(7) (spd 3f) | 1½ | **6** | 14/1 | 41 | — |
| | **Kilcullen Lad (IRE)** (PMooney) **2-8-11** MFenton(8) (cmpt: bit bkwd: nvr nrr) | ¾ | **7** | 33/1 | 43 | — |
| $1408^{5}$ | **Vivora** (MartynMeade) **2-8-6** RPerham(6) (spd 3f) | 2 | **8** | 33/1 | 32 | — |
| $990^{7}$ | **Classic Services** (BPalling) **2-8-11b$^{1}$** TSprake(1) (b: lw: spd over 2f) | 2½ | **9** | 33/1 | 29 | — |
| $1808^{3}$ | **Leitrim Lodge (IRE)** (NACallaghan) **2-8-6** PatEddery(3) (b.off hind: w ldrs: hung lft thrght: eased whn btn 2f out) | ½ | **10** | 10/11$^{1}$ | 22 | — |
| | **Lochinvar** (JSMoore) **2-8-11** JFEgan(5) (leggy: bit bkwd: a bhd: t.o) | 20 | **11** | 25/1 | — | — |

(SP 123.4%) **11 Rn**

**62.4 secs** (3.20) CSF £62.05 TOTE £9.30: £2.40 £2.30 £1.50 (£77.30) Trio £40.70 OWNER Mr J. J. Bridger (LIPHOOK) BRED S. V. Wadsworth
Bt in 7,100gns

OFFICIAL EXPLANATION **Leitrim Lodge (IRE): his rider explained that he rode the filly vigorously until the final one and a half furlongs when she lost her action, he then felt it prudent to hold her together.**

**1352 Whizz Kid**, fast away on the stands' rail, made virtually all the running. She was clear soon after the two-furlong pole and stayed on strongly. (15/2)
**Charlton Spring (IRE)**, the subject of a gamble, failed to start smartly and had plenty to do at halfway. She made good headway below the distance and, though staying on, could not reach the winner. She should certainly be able to win a similar event. (8/1)
**1813 Come Too Mamma's** looked the only danger to the winner two furlongs out, but was soon ridden and beaten. (13/2)
**Tinker's Surprise (IRE)**, always chasing the leaders, was hard ridden fully two furlongs from home and lacked a turn of foot. (7/1: op 9/2)
**1683 Princess Ferdinand (IRE)**, dropped in trip, ran fast but faded soon after the two-furlong marker. (14/1)
**1808 Leitrim Lodge (IRE)**, dropped to selling company, was a warm order but, after showing early speed, was hanging badly to the left, and her rider gave up the unequal struggle soon after the two-furlong marker. (10/11: 4/5-Evens)

## 2032 WINTERTHUR LIFE UK H'CAP (0-70) (3-Y.O+) (Class E)
7-00 (7-04) **1m 67y** £3,111.25 (£940.00: £457.50: £216.25) Stalls: High GOING minus 0.49 sec per fur (F)

| | | | | SP | RR | SF |
|---|---|---|---|---|---|---|
| $756^{10}$ | **Antarctic Storm (60)** (EALDunlop) **3-8-10** MRoberts(7) (a.p: led over 1f out: drvn out) | — | **1** | 16/1 | 74 | 26 |
| $1890^{8}$ | **Mr Cube (IRE) (53)** (JMBradley) **6-8-13v** AMackay(9) (s.s: gd hdwy 2f out: r.o ins fnl f) | 1 | **2** | 25/1 | 65 | 27 |
| 1691* | **Irrepressible (IRE) (49)** (RJHodges) **5-8-4$^{(5)}$** ADaly(3) (a.p: hrd rdn & r.o one pce fnl 2f) | 3 | **3** | 6/1$^{3}$ | 55 | 17 |
| *$1812^{3}$* | **Four of Spades (55)** (PDEvans) **5-8-10v$^{(5)}$** AmandaSanders(15) (led tl over 1f out: one pce) | hd | **4** | 11/1 | 61 | 23 |
| $1449^{22}$ | **Ripsnorter (IRE) (44)** (KBishop) **7-8-4** EmmaO'Gorman(8) (lw: s.s: wl bhd tl styd on fnl 2f) | 5 | **5** | 33/1 | 41 | 3 |
| 1776* | **Honorable Estate (IRE) (70)** (RHannon) **3-9-6** PatEddery(6) (lw: hdwy 3f out: rdn 2f out: wknd over 1f out) | 2 | **6** | 5/1$^{1}$ | 63 | 15 |
| $964^{7}$ | **Kalao Tua (IRE) (70)** (JRFanshawe) **3-9-6** JCarroll(10) (prom tl wknd 2f out) | 1 | **7** | 14/1 | 61 | 13 |
| $1613^{3}$ | **Cuban Reef (45)** (WJMusson) **4-8-5** OUrbina(13) (hdwy 4f out: hrd rdn & wknd 2f out) | nk | **8** | 11/2$^{2}$ | 35 | — |
| $1145^{15}$ | **Whatever's Right (IRE) (67)** (MDIUsher) **7-9-13** BThomson(4) (nvr bttr than mid div) | 2½ | **9** | 10/1 | 52 | 14 |
| $1685^{12}$ | **Indrapura (IRE) (60)** (PFICole) **4-9-6** CRutter(2) (prom tl wknd over 3f out) | 2½ | **10** | 16/1 | 41 | 3 |
| | **Ism (55)** (MajorWRHern) **4-9-1** TSprake(11) (a bhd) | 2½ | **11** | 11/1 | 31 | — |
| $1689^{5}$ | **Fairelaine (56)** (KCBailey) **4-8-11$^{(5)}$** PPMurphy(12) (a bhd) | 4 | **12** | 14/1 | 24 | — |
| $1654^{7}$ | **Superior Force (59)** (MissBSanders) **3-8-9** GBardwell(5) (lw: bdly hmpd over 6f out: no ch after) | 1¼ | **13** | 5/1$^{1}$ | 25 | — |
| $1594^{W}$ | **Ben Bowden (61)** (MBlanshard) **3-8-11** RHughes(1) (prom tl wknd over 2f out) | 2½ | **14** | 12/1 | 22 | — |
| $1625^{11}$ | **Mediate (IRE) (50)** (AHide) **4-8-7b$^{(3)}$** JStack(14) (a bhd) | 3 | **15** | 25/1 | 5 | — |

(SP 132.2%) **15 Rn**

**1m 45.2** (3.00) CSF £331.15 CT £2,500.21 TOTE £35.10: £8.30 £4.60 £2.20 (£169.40) Trio £607.30 OWNER Mr Jimmy Strauss (NEWMARKET) BRED N. and Mrs Bryce-Smith
WEIGHT FOR AGE 3yo-10lb

OFFICIAL EXPLANATION **Mediate (IRE): finished lame.**

**528 Antarctic Storm** took second place soon after halfway. He collared the leader approaching the final furlong and stayed on under pressure. (16/1)
**1010 Mr Cube (IRE)** did extremely well to reach second place after a slow start. He improved rapidly two furlongs out and, though staying on, could not quite catch the winner. (25/1)
**1691* Irrepressible (IRE)**, always in the leading group, was under pressure some way from the finish. Though staying on, he lacked a turn of foot. (6/1)

**1812 Four of Spades** tried to make all the running and fought back when headed approaching the final furlong. He is still capable of winning a similar event. (11/1: 8/1-12/1)
**Ripsnorter (IRE)** looked a picture but, after a slow start, was hopelessly placed for most of the way. In the circumstances, he did well to finish fifth and looks to be on an attractive mark at present. (33/1)
**1776* Honorable Estate (IRE)** made ground three furlongs out. Hard ridden a furlong later, her effort soon petered out. (5/1)
**1613 Cuban Reef** (11/2: 4/1-6/1)
**Ism** (11/1: 8/1-12/1)
**1689 Fairelaine** (14/1: op 8/1)
**819 Ben Bowden** (12/1: op 8/1)

## 2033 EL CAMINO RESOURCES H'CAP (0-80) (3-Y.O) (Class D)

7-30 (7-32) **1m 2f 7y** £4,411.00 (£1,333.00: £649.00: £307.00) Stalls: High GOING minus 0.49 sec per fur (F)

| | | | | SP | RR | SF |
|---|---|---|---|---|---|---|
| 947$^{5}$ | **Punkah (USA) (72)** (LordHuntingdon) **3-9-2** DHarrison(10) (swtg: a.p: led over 2f out: drvn out) | — | **1** | 7/1 | 77 | 47 |
| 1773$^{8}$ | **Shaha (66)** (RHannon) **3-8-10b$^{1}$** PatEddery(1) (led: hrd rdn fnl 4f: hdd over 2f out: r.o wl) | nk | **2** | 5/1$^{2}$ | 71 | 41 |
| 1771$^{2}$ | **Trojan Risk (77)** (GLewis) **3-9-7** PaulEddery(3) (hld up & bhd: gd hdwy 2f out: no ex ins fnl f) | 1½ | **3** | 7/4$^{1}$ | 79 | 49 |
| 1654$^{11}$ | **Mono Lady (IRE) (55)** (DHaydnJones) **3-7-13** AMackay(6) (hdwy 2f out: nvr nrr) | 1¾ | **4** | 50/1 | 54 | 24 |
| 1903$^{2}$ | **Nelly's Cousin (56)** (NACallaghan) **3-8-0** GCarter(4) (a.p: hrd rdn & one pce fnl 2f) | s.h | **5** | 6/1$^{3}$ | 55 | 25 |
| 1649$^{4}$ | **Attarikh (IRE) (74)** (JHMGosden) **3-9-4** WCarson(11) (lw: prom tl wknd over 2f out) | 10 | **6** | 13/2 | 57 | 27 |
| 1669$^{5}$ | **Nosey Native (72)** (JPearce) **3-9-2v$^{1}$** GBardwell(7) (nvr nr to chal) | 1¼ | **7** | 8/1 | 53 | 23 |
| 1654$^{5}$ | **Charlton Imp (USA) (60)** (RJHodges) **3-8-1**$^{(3)ow1}$ SDrowne(8) (in tch tl wknd over 3f out) | 3½ | **8** | 12/1 | 36 | 5 |
| 1533$^{13}$ | **Current Leader (56)** (RHannon) **3-8-0** JFEgan(5) (prom tl wknd over 3f out) | 1 | **9** | 20/1 | 30 | — |
| 1654$^{15}$ | **Mac Oates (65)** (DWPArbuthnot) **3-8-9** BDoyle(9) (a bhd) | 3½ | **10** | 25/1 | 34 | 4 |
| 1668$^{7}$ | **Ghusn (55)** (TThomsonJones) **3-7-13v$^{1}$**$^{ow3}$ DBiggs(2) (sn t.o) | dist | **11** | 33/1 | — | — |
| | | | | (SP 125.5%) | **11 Rn** | |

**2m 6.6** (1.70) CSF £41.82 CT £82.99 TOTE £9.90: £2.30 £1.50 £1.40 (£29.00) Trio £29.50 OWNER The Queen (WEST ILSLEY) BRED The Queen
LONG HANDICAP Ghusn 7-9
**947 Punkah (USA)**, although very warm before the race, was always close up and travelling well. He took up the running over two furlongs from home, but had to fight pretty hard to hold off the renewed challenge of the runner-up. (7/1)
**1773 Shaha**, blinkered for the first time, tried to make all the running. He was under fierce driving half a mile from home, and all looked lost when he was headed approaching the two-furlong marker, but he kept battling on and might have pulled it off with a little further to go. (5/1)
**1771 Trojan Risk**, held up at the back of the field, improved quickly two furlongs out but, having reached third place, he could find no extra inside the last furlong. (7/4)
**Mono Lady (IRE)** stayed on in the centre of the course to reach fourth place, but was never on terms with the leading pair. (50/1)
**1903 Nelly's Cousin**, close up throughout, kept on at one pace under hard driving in the last two furlongs. (6/1)
**1649 Attarikh (IRE)** looked a picture and seemed to be travelling well in second place until past halfway. Asked for his effort over two furlongs from home, he petered out tamely. (13/2)
**1654 Charlton Imp (USA)** (12/1: op 8/1)

## 2034 TOTE CREDIT SPRINT H'CAP (0-75) (3-Y.O+) (Class D)

8-00 (8-05) **5f 217y** £5,238.00 (£1,584.00: £772.00: £366.00) Stalls: High GOING minus 0.33 sec per fur (GF)

| | | | | SP | RR | SF |
|---|---|---|---|---|---|---|
| 1781$^{5}$ | **So Intrepid (IRE) (71)** (JMBradley) **6-9-13** PatEddery(4) (swtchd rt s: chsd ldrs: rdn to ld ins fnl f: r.o) | — | **1** | 8/1 | 78 | 61 |
| *1810*$^{4}$ | **Dancing Heart (65)** (BJMeehan) **4-9-7** BDoyle(11) (a.p: led 1f out tl ins fnl f: r.o) | ¾ | **2** | 20/1 | 70 | 53 |
| 1881$^{2}$ | **Mousehole (71)** (RGuest) **4-9-13b** $^{7x}$ PaulEddery(12) (a.p: led 2f out to 1f out: unable qckn) | 1 | **3** | 13/8$^{1}$ | 73 | 56 |
| 1995* | **Ivory's Grab Hire (60)** (KTIvory) **3-8-4**$^{(5)}$ $^{7x}$ MartinDwyer(10) (chsd ldrs: rdn 2f out: one pce) | ½ | **4** | 8/1 | 61 | 37 |
| 1178$^{9}$ | **Persian Butterfly (66)** (ICampbell) **4-9-5**$^{(3)}$ JStack(9) (hld up: hdwy 1f out: r.o one pce ins fnl f) | ½ | **5** | 20/1 | 66 | 49 |
| 1684* | **Panther (IRE) (65)** (PDEvans) **6-9-7** RHughes(13) (led 4f: wknd ins fnl f) | ½ | **6** | 7/1$^{3}$ | 63 | 46 |
| 1777$^{6}$ | **Walk the Beat (61)** (MartynMeade) **6-9-3** OUrbina(8) (chsd ldrs: rdn 2f out: one pce) | 1¼ | **7** | 12/1 | 56 | 39 |
| 1780$^{3}$ | **Power Game (68)** (JBerry) **3-9-3v** JCarroll(7) (dwlt: nvr nrr) | 2 | **8** | 8/1 | 58 | 34 |
| 1777$^{4}$ | **Half Tone (48)** (RMFlower) **4-8-4b** DBiggs(6) (chsd ldrs tl rdn & wknd 2f out) | 2 | **9** | 11/2$^{2}$ | 32 | 15 |
| 1594$^{13}$ | **Never Think Twice (57)** (KTIvory) **3-8-6** NAdams(1) (s.i.s: a bhd) | 1¾ | **10** | 40/1 | 37 | 13 |
| 1789$^{8}$ | **Dawalib (USA) (64)** (DHaydnJones) **6-9-6** WCarson(2) (sn rdn along: in tch tl wknd 2f out) | 1¼ | **11** | 12/1 | 40 | 23 |
| | **Silver Tzar (60)** (RTPhillips) **4-9-2** GCarter(5) (bhd fnl 3f: t.o) | dist | **12** | 33/1 | — | — |
| | | | | (SP 129.6%) | **12 Rn** | |

**1m 12.0** (1.50) CSF £143.85 CT £365.91 TOTE £9.20: £3.00 £3.90 £1.20 (£67.10) Trio £87.70 OWNER Mr E. A. Hayward (CHEPSTOW) BRED Crest Stud Ltd
WEIGHT FOR AGE 3yo-7lb
**1781 So Intrepid (IRE)** was switched to the stands' rail soon after the start and sat in behind until quickening to take the lead well inside the final furlong. (8/1: op 5/1)
**1677 Dancing Heart** disputed the lead throughout. He gained a narrow advantage entering the final furlong, but could not hold the winner in the last 100 yards. (20/1)
**1881 Mousehole**, though none too fast away, was soon with the leader. He had his head just in front under strong pressure at the two-furlong marker, but could find no extra when headed entering the final furlong. (13/8)
**1995* Ivory's Grab Hire**, successful two days previously, was on the heels of the leaders throughout and kept on under pressure in the closing stages. (8/1)
**648 Persian Butterfly** came with a run at the distance, but lacked an extra turn of foot inside the final furlong. (20/1)
**1684* Panther (IRE)** made the running for half a mile and hung on to the leaders until weakening inside the final furlong. (7/1)
**1777 Walk the Beat** (12/1: 8/1-14/1)
**1777 Half Tone** (11/2: 4/1-6/1)

## 2035 STEAMSHIP MUTUAL CONDITIONS STKS (2-Y.O F) (Class C)

8-30 (8-31) **5f 10y** £4,721.60 (£1,649.60: £804.80: £344.00) Stalls: High GOING minus 0.49 sec per fur (F)

| | | | | SP | RR | SF |
|---|---|---|---|---|---|---|
| | **Queen Sceptre (IRE)** (BWHills) **2-8-6** WCarson(2) (unf: bit bkwd: w ldr: led ins fnl f: rdn out) | — | **1** | 11/2 | 79 | 26 |
| 1595* | **Robec Girl (IRE)** (JBerry) **2-8-9** JCarroll(4) (led tl ins fnl f: nt qckn) | ½ | **2** | 13/8$^{1}$ | 80 | 27 |
| 1713* | **Russian Sable** (MRChannon) **2-8-11** RHughes(1) (prom over 2f) | 3½ | **3** | 5/1$^{3}$ | 71 | 18 |

| | Horse | Btn | Pos | SP | RR | SF |
|---|---|---|---|---|---|---|
| | **Song Mist (IRE)** (PFICole) **2-8-6** PatEddery(3) (leggy: s.s: gd hdwy 3f out: wknd over 1f out) | ¾ | **4** | 7/4[2] | 64 | 11 |
| | | | | (SP 106.5%) | | **4 Rn** |

**61.4 secs** (2.20) CSF £13.44 TOTE £6.50 (£5.70) OWNER Sceptre Racing (LAMBOURN) BRED Mrs E. McMahon
STEWARDS' ENQUIRY Carson susp. 26-27/6/96 (excessive use of whip).
**Queen Sceptre (IRE)** raced with the leader. Under hard driving, she gained a narrow advantage inside the final furlong, and held on well. (11/2: 7/2-6/1)
**1595* Robec Girl (IRE)** tried to make all the running, but could never shake off the winner. (13/8)
**1713* Russian Sable** dropped back last after showing prominently to halfway, but stayed on to snatch third near the finish. (5/1)
**Song Mist (IRE)** missed the break and was soon being chased along. She made good headway to join the leaders two furlongs out, but the effort took too much out of her and she weakened in the final furlong. (7/4: op Evens)

## 2036 CHAMPAGNE PERRIER JOUET BELLE EPOQUE MAIDEN STKS (3-Y.O+) (Class D)

9-00 (9-07) **1m 2f 7y** £3,928.50 (£1,188.00: £579.00: £274.50) Stalls: High GOING minus 0.49 sec per fur (F)

| | Horse | Btn | Pos | SP | RR | SF |
|---|---|---|---|---|---|---|
| | **Annaba (IRE)** (JHMGosden) **3-8-7** GHind(1) (a.p: led 3f out: hld on wl) | — | **1** | 9/2[2] | 89 | 42 |
| | **Dacha (IRE)** (HRACecil) **4-9-10** WRyan(11) (hdwy 3f out: swtchd rt over 1f out: ev ch ins fnl f: r.o) | s.h | **2** | 9/2[2] | 94 | 59 |
| | **Canon Can (USA) (74)** (HRACecil) **3-8-12** PatEddery(5) (led to 3f out: r.o one pce) | 8 | **3** | 8/1[3] | 81 | 34 |
| 1773[2] | **No-Aman (82)** (MajorWRHern) **3-8-12** WCarson(14) (a.p: hrd rdn over 2f out: one pce) | nk | **4** | 11/10[1] | 81 | 34 |
| | **Alisura** (JRFanshawe) **3-8-7** DHarrison(16) (mid div tl styd on fnl 2f) | 5 | **5** | 14/1 | 68 | 21 |
| 1349[5] | **Decision Maker (IRE) (77)** (RHannon) **3-8-12b[1]** RHughes(4) (w ldr tl wknd over 2f out) | ¾ | **6** | 10/1 | 72 | 25 |
| 845[11] | **Scottish Hero** (JRFanshawe) **3-8-9**(3) NVarley(6) (nvr nrr) | 3 | **7** | 20/1 | 67 | 20 |
| 1465[4] | **Melomania (USA)** (TJNaughton) **4-9-10** GCarter(9) (wl bhd tl hdwy fnl 2f) | 4 | **8** | 33/1 | 60 | 25 |
| 1839[9] | **Panto Queen** (CRBarwell) **5-9-5** TSprake(15) (nvr bttr than mid div) | hd | **9** | 66/1 | 55 | 20 |
| 1530[6] | **Lead Story (IRE)** (EALDunlop) **3-8-12** MRoberts(12) (prom tl wknd 3f out) | 1½ | **10** | 12/1 | 58 | 11 |
| 691[10] | **Rex Mundi** (PDEvans) **4-9-10** OUrbina(7) (nvr nr ldrs) | 6 | **11** | 66/1 | 48 | 13 |
| | **Nails Tails** (SDow) **3-8-12** BThomson(2) (a bhd) | 1¾ | **12** | 40/1 | 45 | — |
| 1452[9] | **Severn Mill** (JMBradley) **5-9-10** AMackay(10) (prom tl wknd 4f out) | 3½ | **13** | 66/1 | 40 | 5 |
| | **Star Anise** (MrsDHaine) **4-9-5** JTate(13) (dwlt: a bhd) | 3½ | **14** | 66/1 | 29 | — |
| | **Royal Intrusion** (RJHodges) **3-8-9**(3) SDrowne(8) (a bhd: t.o) | 13 | **15** | 40/1 | 14 | — |
| | | | | (SP 137.1%) | | **15 Rn** |

**2m 6.1** (1.20) CSF £26.90 TOTE £7.90: £2.20 £1.90 £2.60 (£14.70) Trio £36.20 OWNER Sheikh Mohammed (NEWMARKET) BRED Sheikh Mohammed Bin Rashid Al Maktoum
WEIGHT FOR AGE 3yo-12lb
**Annaba (IRE)** travelled well in third place. She took up the running three furlongs out and appeared set for a clear-cut victory entering the final furlong, but had to be driven out to hold the strong finish of the second. (9/2)
**Dacha (IRE)** has done extremely well physically since last year and this lightly-raced four-year-old has plenty of races in him. He made ground three furlongs out and, switched to the stands' rail, put in a sustained bid which failed by the narrowest margin. (9/2)
**Canon Can (USA)** made the running until three furlongs out, but it was quickly clear that he had no chance with the winner. (8/1: 5/1-9/1)
**1773 No-Aman**, well placed throughout, came under hard driving from over two furlongs out and, although he kept on, he was always fighting a losing battle. (11/10)
**Alisura**, ridden along in midfield for much of the way, stayed on without causing the leaders any anxiety. (14/1)
**1349 Decision Maker (IRE)**, blinkered for the first time, disputed the lead until three furlongs out but soon dropped back beaten. (10/1)

T/Jkpt: Not won; £20,198.36 to Ascot 18/6/96. T/Plpt: £1,971.20 (8.59 Tckts). T/Qdpt: £58.00 (17.89 Tckts). Hn

# 0874-ASCOT (R-H) (Good to firm)
## Tuesday June 18th

WEATHER: sunny periods WIND: almost nil

## 2037 QUEEN ANNE STKS (Gp 2) (3-Y.O+) (Class A)

2-30 (2-31) **1m (straight)** £59,890.00 (£22,418.25: £10,771.63: £4,695.12) Stalls: Centre GOING minus 0.40 sec per fur (F)

| | Horse | Btn | Pos | SP | RR | SF |
|---|---|---|---|---|---|---|
| 1177[2] | **Charnwood Forest (IRE) (119)** (SbinSuroor) **4-9-2** MJKinane(6) (lw: hld up: hdwy to ld over 1f out: edgd rt: sn clr) | — | **1** | 10/11[1] | 130 | 95 |
| 1824* | **Restructure (IRE) (106)** (MrsJCecil) **4-9-2** PaulEddery(8) (swtg: a.p: rdn over 2f out: unable qckn fnl f) | 4 | **2** | 11/1 | 122 | 87 |
| 1582a* | **Mistle Cat (USA) (117)** (SPCWoods) **6-9-2** WWoods(1) (led tl over 1f out: one pce) | hd | **3** | 20/1 | 122 | 87 |
| 1582a[3] | **Young Ern (119)** (SDow) **6-9-2** CAsmussen(4) (hld up & bhd: hdwy 2f out: kpt on ins fnl f) | 1¼ | **4** | 20/1 | 119 | 84 |
| 1177* | **Soviet Line (IRE) (120)** (MRStoute) **6-9-7** JReid(2) (b.off hind: s.i.s: sn chsng ldrs: hrd rdn 2f out: no imp) | 1½ | **5** | 13/2[3] | 121 | 86 |
| 1768[3] | **Mr Martini (IRE) (113)** (CEBrittain) **6-9-2** BDoyle(5) (hld up: effrt & rdn over 2f out: nvr nr to chal) | 4 | **6** | 40/1 | 108 | 73 |
| | **Prince of India (107)** (LordHuntingdon) **4-9-2** JWeaver(9) (lw: hld up & bhd: effrt over 2f out: no imp) | ½ | **7** | 50/1 | 107 | 72 |
| 1575a[2] | **Timarida (IRE)** (JOxx,Ireland) **4-9-2** JPMurtagh(7) (lw: prom tl wknd over 3f out: t.o: b.b.v) | 15 | **8** | 6/1[2] | 77 | 42 |
| 1177[5] | **Gabr (113)** (RWArmstrong) **6-9-5** WCarson(3) (plld hrd: prom tl wknd over 2f out. t.o) | hd | **9** | 12/1 | 80 | 45 |
| | | | | (SP 109.9%) | | **9 Rn** |

**1m 38.71** (-2.49) CSF £10.32 TOTE £2.00: £1.10 £2.20 £2.60 (£9.60) Trio £51.60 OWNER Godolphin (NEWMARKET) BRED Sheikh Mohammed bin Rashid al Maktoum
**1177 Charnwood Forest (IRE)** won this in the style expected, and it is hard to imagine an easier winner of such a prestigious race. Fitted with a tongue-strap for the first time, his jockey thought it was that that made him edge off a true line inside the final furlong. (10/11: tchd Evens)
**1824* Restructure (IRE)** ran a fine race on this step up to Group company, being in the action all the way and only losing out when the winner quickened up. (11/1: 8/1-12/1)
**1582a* Mistle Cat (USA)** tried to slip his field but, on ground possibly faster than he needs, could not respond when the winner threw down his challenge, although it must be said he did nothing wrong. He is a credit to his connections. (20/1)
**1582a Young Ern**, still to succeed at this trip, made good progress from off the pace inside the final quarter-mile, but lacked the speed to deliver a serious challenge. (20/1)
**1177* Soviet Line (IRE)**, third in this event last year, took a keen hold and pressed the leaders, but he was being made to work entering the last quarter-mile and was short of a turn of speed to carry him through. (13/2)
**1768 Mr Martini (IRE)** needs easier ground than he had here and, taken along faster than he wished, could never get himself close enough to cause concern. (40/1)

**1575a Timarida (IRE)**, a high-class filly from Ireland, gave chase to the clear leader until weakening quickly and finishing tailed off. It was later reported she had broken a blood-vessel and lost a shoe. (6/1)
**1177 Gabr** (12/1: op 8/1)

## 2038 PRINCE OF WALES'S STKS (Gp 2) (3-Y.O+) (Class A)

3-05 (3-06) **1m 2f** £63,325.00 (£23,735.00: £11,430.00: £5,010.00) Stalls: High GOING minus 0.40 sec per fur (F)

SP RR SF

1112* **First Island (IRE) (114)** (GWragg) **4-9-3** MHills(3) (hld up: hdwy over 2f out: led ent fnl f: drvn out) ............... — **1** 9/1 125 103
1749a$^{4}$ **Montjoy (USA) (119)** (PFICole) **4-9-6** RHills(13) (plld hrd: a.p: led wl over 1f out: sn hdd: no ex nr fin) ..........1¼ **2** 16/1 126 104
1509$^{4}$ **Tamayaz (CAN)** (SbinSuroor) **4-9-3** OPeslier(11) (mid div: hdwy over 2f out: r.o ins fnl f) ...........................1¼ **3** 12/1 121 99
1754a$^{3}$ **Dankeston (USA) (101)** (MBell) **3-8-5** MRoberts(12) (lw: trckd ldrs: outpcd ent st: styd on again appr fnl f)...3½ **4** 50/1 115 81
1135a$^{6}$ **Cezanne** (SbinSuroor) **7-9-3** JPMurtagh(1) (lw: hld up & bhd: hdwy over 2f out: nrst fin) ...............................nk **5** 25/1 115 93
1355$^{4}$ **Fahal (USA) (117)** (DMorley) **4-9-3** WCarson(5) (lw: hld up mid div: nvr nr to chal)........................................s.h **6** 7/1 115 93
680$^{6}$ **Desert Shot (115)** (MRStoute) **6-9-3** CAsmussen(4) (hld up in rr: hdwy over 2f out: nt rch ldrs)....................1¼ **7** 20/1 113 91
1509* **Pilsudski (IRE) (105)** (MRStoute) **4-9-3** PatEddery(9) (b.nr hind: lw: chsd ldr: disp ld fr 3f out tl wknd over 1f out) ..........................................................................................1¼ **8** 4/1$^{1}$ 111 89
1509$^{2}$ **Lucky Di (USA) (113)** (LMCumani) **4-9-3** JWeaver(10) (b.nr fore: mid div: rdn over 4f out: bhd fnl 3f) ...........2½ **9** 9/2$^{2}$ 107 85
918$^{4}$ **Clever Cliche** (HRACecil) **3-8-6**$^{ow1}$ JReid(7) (lw: chsd ldrs: rdn 3f out: wkng when hmpd 2f out) ....................½ **10** 16/1 107 72
**Cap Juluca (IRE) (112)** (RCharlton) **4-9-3** RHughes(8) (lw: led tl over 2f out: eased whn btn appr fnl f)..........nk **11** 5/1$^{3}$ 106 84
1938a* **Needle Gun (IRE) (118)** (CEBrittain) **6-9-6** MJKinane(6) (prom: hrd rdn ent st: sn wknd: t.o)............................9 **12** 14/1 94 72

(SP 114.0%) **12 Rn**

**2m 2.76** (0.55 under best) (-4.04) CSF £121.20 **TOTE** £11.20: £2.70 £4.60 £5.90 (£73.90) Trio £412.60 OWNER Mollers Racing (NEWMARKET) BRED Citadel Stud
WEIGHT FOR AGE 3yo-12lb

**1112* First Island (IRE)** goes from strength to strength and, in winning his first race at this trip, broke the course record that had stood for twenty years. (9/1)
**1749a Montjoy (USA)** looked sure to win when taking control below the distance, but the winner did not let him get away and had the legs of him in a good race to the line. (16/1)
**1509 Tamayaz (CAN)**, very much on his toes, was ridden with more restraint. Staying on particularly well inside the final furlong, this was possibly his best performance yet. (12/1: 8/1-14/1)
**1754a Dankeston (USA)** is in the form of his life this season, but he is just missing out in an effort to get black-type by his name for winning a Group race. He seemed well suited by this longer trip, staying on strongly after getting tapped for speed soon after turning in. (50/1)
**1135a Cezanne**, much better when he can get his toe in, did well to finish so close in such a hot event, and his turn will come. (25/1)
**1355 Fahal (USA)**, struggling to make any impression from the turn in to the straight, did keep staying on, but he was never able to get within striking range of the principals. (7/1)
**1509* Pilsudski (IRE)** ranged upsides the leader before reaching the home straight, and looked to be travelling best, but he was fighting a losing battle once Montjoy struck the front, and was eased when beaten inside the final furlong. (4/1)

## 2039 ST JAMES'S PALACE STKS (Gp 1) (3-Y.O C & F) (Class A)

3-45 (3-47) **1m (round)** £135,720.00 (£50,546.00: £24,073.00: £10,261.00) Stalls: High GOING minus 0.40 sec per fur (F)

SP RR SF

1574a$^{4}$ **Bijou d'Inde (120)** (MJohnston) **3-9-0** JWeaver(7) (led after 2f tl over 1f out: rallied gamely to ld last stride) ........................................................................................................ — **1** 9/1 126 78
1141a* **Ashkalani (IRE)** (AdeRoyerDupre,France) **3-9-0** MJKinane(9) (w'like: scope: lw: hld up: a.p: led over 1f out: hrd rdn: ct post)..............................................................................................hd **2** 13/8$^{1}$ 126 78
1441$^{2}$ **Sorbie Tower (IRE) (108)** (MissGayKelleway) **3-9-0** RHughes(6) (b.hind: lw: hld up: hdwy on outside over 2f out: drifted rt fnl f: styd on) ..........................................................................................1 **3** 33/1 124 76
1574a$^{3}$ **Beauchamp King (115)** (JLDunlop) **3-9-0** JReid(8) (trckd ldrs: hrd drvn wl over 1f out: nt pce to chal) ..........1¼ **4** 14/1 121 73
1141a$^{4}$ **Cayman Kai (IRE) (117)** (RHannon) **3-9-0** PatEddery(3) (lw: bhd: drvn along ent st: styd on wl appr fnl f).....1¼ **5** 12/1 119 71
1574a* **Spinning World (USA)** (JEPease,France) **3-9-0** CAsmussen(5) (leggy: scope: hld up in tch: outpcd 2f out: sn btn) ..........................................................................................................1¾ **6** 100/30$^{2}$ 115 67
1627* **Wall Street (USA)** (SbinSuroor) **3-9-0** BThomson(2) (swtg: prom tl wknd over 2f out) .......................................5 **7** 16/1 105 57
926* **Mark of Esteem (IRE) (120)** (SbinSuroor) **3-9-0** OPeslier(1) (mid div tl rdn & outpcd 2f out) ..........................1½ **8** 11/2$^{3}$ 102 54
1151$^{3}$ **World Premier (111)** (CEBrittain) **3-9-0** BDoyle(4) (led 2f: wknd fnl 2f) ..............................................................½ **9** 100/1 101 53

(SP 110.7%) **9 Rn**

**1m 39.7** (-1.10) CSF £22.09 TOTE £9.70: £2.10 £1.30 £4.70 (£12.80) Trio £111.30 OWNER Mr J. S. Morrison (MIDDLEHAM) BRED Whitsbury Manor Stud

IN-FOCUS: **What looked the race of the week on paper did not disappoint as a spectacle, but neither Spinning World not Mark of Esteem ran their race.**

**1574a Bijou d'Inde**, a winner at this trip in his first season, won this by seeing the trip out better than the favourite, and this success was just reward for the narrow defeat he suffered in the 2000 Guineas. (9/1)
**1141a* Ashkalani (IRE)** did not let himself down on the way to post, but he travelled strongly throughout the race, and looked to have control when leading into the final furlong, but the winner, with the help of the inside rail, proved too much of a terrier, and touched him off on the line. (13/8)
**1441 Sorbie Tower (IRE)** almost caused a major upset with by far his best performance yet, and the Sussex Stakes is next on the agenda for this rapidly-improving colt. (33/1)
**1574a Beauchamp King**, poised to challenge all the way, did look to be in trouble when the pace lifted into the straight, but he put his head down and gave of his all to go down fighting. (14/1)
**1141a Cayman Kai (IRE)**, the backmarker turning in, did a lot of running to reach his final placing, and success at this trip is definitely within his reach. (12/1)
**1574a* Spinning World (USA)**, ill-at-ease cantering to the start, stalked the favourite and made his move at the same time, but he failed to pick up when the tempo was increased early in the straight, and was one of the first beaten. He is better than this. (100/30: 9/4-7/2)
**926* Mark of Esteem (IRE)** (11/2: op 7/2)

## 2040 COVENTRY STKS (Gp 3) (2-Y.O) (Class A)

4-20 (4-21) **6f** £26,560.00 (£10,058.00: £4,929.00: £2,253.00) Stalls: Centre GOING minus 0.40 sec per fur (F)

SP RR SF

**Verglas (IRE)** (KPrendergast,Ireland) **2-8-12** WJSupple(3) (leggy: scope: hld up: hdwy 2f out: led over 1f out: sn clr: r.o strly)..........................................................................................................— **1** 9/1 109 59

| Form | Horse | Btn | Pos | SP | RR | SF |
|---|---|---|---|---|---|---|
| 1510[3] | **Daylight In Dubai (USA)** (PWChapple-Hyam) **2-8-12** KDarley(7) (lw: hld up: hdwy wl over 1f out: kpt on u.p: no ch w wnr) | 2½ | **2** | 25/1 | 102 | 52 |
| 1510* | **Deadly Dudley (IRE)** (RHannon) **2-8-12** MJKinane(8) (b: b.hind: hld up: hdwy 2f out: rdn & one pce fnl f) | 1¾ | **3** | 7/4[1] | 98 | 48 |
| 1362* | **Hula Prince (IRE)** (MJohnston) **2-8-12** JWeaver(9) (lw: led 2f: hrd drvn 2f out: kpt on) | hd | **4** | 20/1 | 97 | 47 |
| 1424* | **Hello (IRE)** (JLDunlop) **2-8-12** WRyan(13) (swtg: hdwy 2f out: rdn & one pce fnl f) | nk | **5** | 20/1 | 97 | 47 |
| 1626* | **Shock Value (IRE)** (MRStoute) **2-8-12** JReid(5) (mid div: drvn along ½-wy: kpt on appr fnl f) | 1¼ | **6** | 7/1[3] | 93 | 43 |
| 697* | **Fletcher** (PFICole) **2-8-12** PatEddery(4) (trckd ldrs over 4f) | 1¼ | **7** | 11/2[2] | 90 | 40 |
| | **Kumait (USA)** (SbinSuroor) **2-8-12** OPeslier(15) (w'like: scope: led after 2f tl hdd & wknd over 1f out) | nk | **8** | 14/1 | 89+ | 39 |
| 1774* | **Tuscany** (PFICole) **2-8-12** MHills(14) (lw: trckd ldrs: hrd rdn & wknd over 1f out) | 1¾ | **9** | 14/1 | 85 | 35 |
| 1445* | **Maserati Monk** (BJMeehan) **2-8-12** BDoyle(10) (plld hrd: prom tl rdn & wknd over 2f out) | 3½ | **10** | 33/1 | 75 | 25 |
| 1831[3] | **Saratoga Red (USA)** (WAO'Gorman) **2-8-12** EmmaO'Gorman(2) (lw: s.i.s: a in rr) | 1½ | **11** | 100/1 | 71 | 21 |
| 1842[3] | **Jack The Lad (IRE)** (CMurray) **2-8-12** MTebbutt(1) (lw: nvr gng pce of ldrs) | 2 | **12** | 100/1 | 66 | 16 |
| 1801* | **Future Prospect (IRE)** (MJohnston) **2-8-12** MRoberts(12) (prom: ev ch over 2f out: wknd qckly over 1f out) | 1¼ | **13** | 25/1 | 63 | 13 |
| | **Kaiser Kache (IRE)** (KMcAuliffe) **2-8-12** JFEgan(11) (w'like: bhd fr ½-wy) | 1½ | **14** | 100/1 | 59 | 9 |
| 1437* | **Statesman** (MRChannon) **2-8-12** RHughes(6) (mid div tl wknd over 2f out) | 2½ | **15** | 8/1 | 52 | 2 |
| | | | | (SP 121.8%) | **15 Rn** | |

**1m 14.34** (0.34) CSF £184.83 TOTE £16.20: £3.60 £6.00 £1.40 (£240.50) Trio £126.80 OWNER Mrs A. J. F. O'Reilly

IN-FOCUS: **Perhaps not up to the standard of last year's Renewal, but sure to have a bearing on the top juvenile events to come.**

**Verglas (IRE)** kept up the impressive Prendergast record in this race with a runaway victory, and was immediately installed favourite for next year's 2000 Guineas. He still has plenty of room for improvement physically and could be some horse as a three-year-old. (9/1)

**1510 Daylight In Dubai (USA)** gained his revenge over the favourite at this slightly longer trip, but he was unable to match strides with the very useful winner, and will do well to avoid him in the future. (25/1)

**1510* Deadly Dudley (IRE)** took a very keen hold but was restrained off the pace. Set alight approaching the final furlong, he did run on, but lacked anything like the speed he would have needed to trouble the winner. (7/4)

**1362* Hula Prince (IRE)** had to forfeit his unbeaten record, but he turned in easily his best performance yet, and will always be the one to beat from now on. (20/1)

**1424* Hello (IRE)** was finding his stride inside the distance and will be all the wiser with this experience under his belt. (20/1)

**1626* Shock Value (IRE)** moved scratchily to post, and was struggling with the pace all the way. He did stay on towards the finish, but was never going to take a hand in proceedings. (7/1)

**Kumait (USA)**, a scopey son of useful mare Colour Chart, showed plenty of promise on this debut in top-class company, and he will soon leave this form behind. (14/1: 10/1-16/1)

**1437* Statesman** (8/1: 6/1-9/1)

## 2041 BRITANNIA H'CAP (0-105) (3-Y.O C & G) (Class B)

4-55 (4-59) **1m (straight)** £27,011.25 (£8,190.00: £4,007.50: £1,916.25) Stalls: Centre GOING minus 0.40 sec per fur (F)

| Form | Horse | Btn | Pos | SP | RR | SF |
|---|---|---|---|---|---|---|
| 1357* | **North Song (84)** (JHMGosden) **3-8-1** GHind(23) (a.p far side: led over 2f out: hrd rdn & hld on nr fin) | — | **1** | 14/1 | 94 | 63 |
| 1807[3] | **Insatiable (IRE) (86)** (MRStoute) **3-8-3** KDarley(4) (in tch stands' side: effrt over 2f out: rdn & r.o wl nr fin) | hd | **2** | 13/2[1] | 96 | 65 |
| 1327[2] | **Russian Music (99)** (MissGayKelleway) **3-9-2** OPeslier(6) (lw: racd stands' side: trckd ldrs: kpt on u.p fnl f) | 1 | **3** | 11/1[3] | 107 | 76 |
| 1441[6] | **Hidden Oasis (98)** (SbinSuroor) **3-9-1** MJKinane(5) (lw: a.p stands' side: ev ch 1f out: unable qckn) | 1½ | **4** | 16/1 | 103 | 72 |
| 1106[5] | **Double Diamond (IRE) (90)** (MJohnston) **3-8-7** JWeaver(29) (trckd ldrs far side: rdn over 1f out: kpt on) | hd | **5** | 25/1 | 95 | 64 |
| 1648* | **Alamein (USA) (85)** (WJHaggas) **3-8-2b** MRoberts(14) (trckd ldrs stands' side: one pce appr fnl f) | ½ | **6** | 16/1 | 89 | 58 |
| 1440[7] | **Alhawa (USA) (84)** (CJBenstead) **3-8-1** PRobinson(20) (racd far side: hdwy 2f out: styd on) | ¾ | **7** | 16/1 | 86 | 55 |
| 1476[12] | **Royal Canaska (92)** (DRLoder) **3-8-9v[1]ow2** RHughes(12) (swtg: hld up stands' side: hdwy over 1f out: nvr nrr) | nk | **8** | 25/1 | 94 | 61 |
| 1768[8] | **Brandon Magic (100)** (IABalding) **3-9-3** WRyan(2) (hld up stands' side: sme hdwy fnl 2f: nvr nrr) | 2½ | **9** | 33/1 | 97 | 66 |
| 1484[10] | **Bullfinch (87)** (PTWalwyn) **3-8-4** DHolland(15) (hld up far side: sme hdwy fnl 2f: nvr nrr) | hd | **10** | 33/1 | 84 | 53 |
| 808[6] | **Al Abraq (IRE) (94)** (JWHills) **3-8-11** MHills(8) (hld up: hdwy & nt clr run over 2f out: nvr nr ldrs) | nk | **11** | 20/1 | 91 | 60 |
| 1785* | **Mushahid (USA) (103)** (JLDunlop) **3-9-6** WCarson(28) (racd far side: prom tl rdn & wknd over 1f out) | hd | **12** | 16/1 | 99 | 68 |
| 1432* | **Winter Romance (102)** (EALDunlop) **3-9-5** PaulEddery(13) (lw: nvr trbld ldrs) | 1¼ | **13** | 13/2[1] | 96 | 65 |
| 969[3] | **Forest Robin (86)** (RFJohnsonHoughton) **3-8-3** AMcGlone(24) (racd far side: n.d) | 1¾ | **14** | 25/1 | 76 | 45 |
| 1593[2] | **Don Bosio (USA) (89)** (MRStoute) **3-8-6**ow1 JReid(21) (lw: n.d) | hd | **15** | 25/1 | 79 | 47 |
| | **Slightly Speedy (IRE) (89)** (JTGorman,Ireland) **3-8-6** PShanahan(11) (w'like: scope: lw: led stands' side: sn wknd) | hd | **16** | 40/1 | 79 | 48 |
| 1127[2] | **Royal Mark (IRE) (91)** (JWWatts) **3-8-8** CAsmussen(27) (lw: racd far side: a in rr) | 2 | **17** | 14/1 | 77 | 46 |
| 1712[7] | **Infamous (USA) (81)** (PFICole) **3-7-12** CRutter(3) (a in rr) | s.h | **18** | 25/1 | 67 | 36 |
| 1127[11] | **Paint It Black (85)** (RHannon) **3-8-2** JFEgan(16) (lw: mid div stands' side tl wknd 3f out) | 1½ | **19** | 33/1 | 68 | 37 |
| 1452[2] | **Civil Liberty (90)** (GLewis) **3-8-7** PatEddery(22) (lw: racd far side: a bhd) | ½ | **20** | 10/1[2] | 72 | 41 |
| 1470* | **Henry Island (IRE) (90)** (GWragg) **3-8-0**(7) GMilligan(31) (swtg: prom far side tl wknd 2f out) | s.h | **21** | 25/1 | 72 | 41 |
| 1771[4] | **Believe Me (97)** (RHannon) **3-9-0** WJO'Connor(26) (led far side tl hdd & wknd over 2f out) | ½ | **22** | 25/1 | 78 | 47 |
| 1798[8] | **Kala Sunrise (88)** (CSmith) **3-8-5** AClark(30) (lw: racd stands' side: bhd fr ½-wy) | hd | **23** | 50/1 | 69 | 38 |
| 1649* | **Diminutive (USA) (82)** (JWHills) **3-7-10**(3) MHenry(7) (prom stands' side 5f) | ¾ | **24** | 33/1 | 61 | 30 |
| 1126[8] | **Therhea (IRE) (85)** (BRMillman) **3-8-2** JQuinn(17) (a bhd) | ½ | **25** | 25/1 | 63 | 32 |
| 1799[7] | **Lay The Blame (85)** (WJarvis) **3-8-2** SSanders(1) (bhd fnl 3f) | hd | **26** | 33/1 | 63 | 32 |
| | **Oberons Boy (IRE) (100)** (BJMeehan) **3-8-12**(5) FLynch(9) (lw: trckd ldrs stands' side over 5f) | nk | **27** | 50/1 | 77 | 46 |
| 1667[5] | **Detachment (USA) (84)** (PWChapple-Hyam) **3-8-1v[1]**ow1 DHarrison(25) (lw: a bhd) | 1½ | **28** | 16/1 | 59 | 27 |
| 1389a[3] | **Henry The Fifth (104)** (CEBrittain) **3-9-7** BDoyle(19) (prom far side 5f: eased whn btn) | 1½ | **29** | 50/1 | 76 | 45 |
| 1296[3] | **Troysend (102)** (APO'Brien,Ireland) **3-9-5v[1]** CRoche(10) (leggy: scope: prom stands' side tl wknd 3f out) | hd | **30** | 20/1 | 74 | 43 |
| 1427[8] | **Manaloj (USA) (88)** (PTWalwyn) **3-8-5** RHills(32) (prom 5f: sn wknd) | 7 | **31** | 50/1 | 46 | 15 |
| | | | | (SP 152.1%) | **31 Rn** | |

**1m 39.9** (-1.30) CSF £105.68 CT £1010.19 TOTE £16.10: £3.30 £2.00 £3.60 £5.20 (£62.80) Trio £344.10 OWNER Mr John Gosden (NEWMARKET) BRED C. R. Mason

OFFICIAL EXPLANATION **Forest Robin: was found to be lame next morning.**

IN-FOCUS: **Subsequent events made the performance of North Song in winning from a high draw all the more meritorious, but emphasised that three year old only handicaps are not as 'tight' as all aged ones.**

**1357* North Song** won his maiden last month and followed up in this first handicap with a hard-fought success which was richly deserved. (14/1)

**1807 Insatiable (IRE)** runs as if he does need further, but he did win the race on the stands' side and lost nothing in defeat. (13/2)

**1327 Russian Music** put up a bold display at this first attempt at a mile and, had he been drawn on the faster far side, would have taken all the beating. (11/1)
**1441 Hidden Oasis**, delivered his challenge and had every chance passing the furlong marker, but he was tapped for speed in the sprint to the post. He should not be long in making amends. (16/1)
**1106 Double Diamond (IRE)** is not so effective on this lively ground, but he turned in a very courageous performance, and when he gets conditions in his favour will soon get back to winning ways. (25/1)
**1648* Alamein (USA)**, in pursuit of the leaders under the stands' rail, battled on willingly to the end but could not summon up the pace to mount a challenge. (16/1)
**1051* Alhawa (USA)** was doing all his best work late on, and this lightly raced colt is only just beginning to realise what the game is all about. (16/1)
**1432* Winter Romance** could not handle the fast ground and was never able to get himself in to contention. (13/2)

## 2042 ASCOT STKS H'CAP (0-95) (4-Y.O+) (Class C)

5-30 (5-34) **2m 4f** £26,442.50 (£8,015.00: £3,920.00: £1,872.50) Stalls: Low GOING minus 0.40 sec per fur (F)

| | | | | SP | RR | SF |
|---|---|---|---|---|---|---|
| 1147[3] | **Southern Power (IRE) (79)** (RAkehurst) **5-9-7** OPeslier(9) (lw: hld up: hdwy over 2f out: rdn to ld 1f out: r.o strly) | — | **1** | 25/1 | 91 | 74 |
| | **Mirador (54)** (RCurtis) **5-7-10** GBardwell(24) (trckd ldrs: effrt & rdn over 2f out: fin strly) | ¾ | **2** | 100/1 | 65 | 48 |
| 1587* | **Candle Smile (USA) (86)** (MRStoute) **4-9-12** JReid(26) (a.p: rdn & sltly outpcd over 1f out: styd on u.p fnl f) | nk | **3** | 25/1 | 97 | 78 |
| 1875* | **Sea Victor (76)** (JLHarris) **4-9-2** 3x JWeaver(27) (led tl hdd over 1f out: rallied u.p fnl f) | ½ | **4** | 20/1 | 87 | 68 |
| 1511[4] | **Golden Arrow (IRE) (72)** (MCPipe) **5-9-0** MRoberts(11) (hld up: hdwy 3f out: styd on u.p ins fnl f) | ¾ | **5** | 25/1 | 82 | 65 |
| 1005* | **Merit (IRE) (83)** (PFICole) **4-9-9** JQuinn(23) (lw: prom: rdn over 2f out: sn btn) | ½ | **6** | 3/1[1] | 93 | 74 |
| 1511[2] | **Rocky Forum (73)** (GLMoore) **4-8-13** RHughes(3) (b: lw: hld up in tch: effrt 2f out: nvr able to chal) | s.h | **7** | 16/1 | 83 | 64 |
| 1439[8] | **Shadirwan (IRE) (80)** (RAkehurst) **5-9-8** SSanders(22) (trckd ldrs: shkn up 2f out: no ex) | ¾ | **8** | 20/1 | 89 | 72 |
| 1439[3] | **Fujiyama Crest (IRE) (88)** (MRStoute) **4-10-0v** PatEddery(20) (b.nr hind: prom: rdn to ld over 1f out: sn hdd: wknd fnl f) | ½ | **9** | 14/1 | 97 | 78 |
| 1640[10] | **Solatium (IRE) (56)** (MCPipe) **4-7-7v**[1(3)] MHenry(17) (nvr nrr) | nk | **10** | 66/1 | 65 | 46 |
| 1782[2] | **Sea Freedom (65)** (GBBalding) **5-8-4v**[(3)] NVarley(25) (in tch: effrt u.p 4f out: wknd over 2f out) | 5 | **11** | 33/1 | 70 | 53 |
| 1977* | **Achilles Heel (55)** (CNAllen) **5-7-6**[(5)] MartinDwyer(18) (nvr nr ldrs) | 1¼ | **12** | 16/1 | 59 | 42 |
| 1835[3] | **Paradise Navy (66)** (CREgerton) **7-8-8b** WRyan(21) (lw: nvr trbld ldrs) | 2 | **13** | 20/1 | 68 | 51 |
| 1343[3] | **Great Easeby (IRE) (59)** (WStorey) **6-8-1** DRMcCabe(19) (hld up & bhd: hdwy 4f out: rdn & wknd over 2f out) | 3½ | **14** | 8/1[2] | 58 | 41 |
| 1194[16] | **Seasonal Splendour (IRE) (80)** (MCPipe) **6-9-8** CAsmussen(13) (mid div: bmpd 6f out: n.d) | s.h | **15** | 20/1 | 79 | 62 |
| 1816[2] | **Hever Golf Lady (57)** (TJNaughton) **4-7-6**[(5)] MBaird(6) (b: lw: a in rr) | 10 | **16** | 20/1 | 48 | 29 |
| 1802[4] | **Anglesey Sea View (63)** (ABailey) **7-7-12**[(7)] IonaWands(2) (hdwy over 4f out: wknd 3f out) | 5 | **17** | 33/1 | 50 | 33 |
| 1428[3] | **Noufari (FR) (77)** (RHollinshead) **5-9-5** KDarley(7) (a bhd) | 1¾ | **18** | 25/1 | 63 | 46 |
| 1784[4] | **Greycoat Boy (61)** (BJMeehan) **4-8-1b** JFEgan(5) (prom tl wknd 4f out) | ¾ | **19** | 20/1 | 46 | 27 |
| 1679[S] | **Coleridge (55)** (JJSheehan) **8-7-11b** NCarlisle(4) (hdwy 6f out: rdn & wknd 4f out) | 4 | **20** | 33/1 | 37 | 20 |
| | **Our Kris (67)** (NJHenderson) **4-8-7** MHills(15) (chsd ldrs tl wknd 3f out) | hd | **21** | 20/1 | 49 | 30 |
| 1835[6] | **Chris's Lad (60)** (BJMeehan) **5-8-2** WCarson(12) (a bhd) | 1½ | **22** | 25/1 | 41 | 24 |
| 1306[5] | **Unchanged (73)** (CEBrittain) **4-8-13** BDoyle(8) (swtg: prom: rdn 6f out: grad wknd) | ¾ | **23** | 20/1 | 53 | 34 |
| 1710[2] | **En Vacances (IRE) (73)** (AGFoster) **4-8-13** TSprake(10) (lw: trckd ldrs tl wknd 3f out) | ½ | **24** | 16/1 | 53 | 34 |
| 1835* | **Stompin (73)** (MissHCKnight) **5-8-8**[(7)] 3x GFaulkner(14) (lw: in tch tl wknd 4f out: t.o) | dist | **25** | 9/1[3] | — | — |
| 767[10] | **Imad (USA) (60)** (JWhite) **6-8-2b**[1] CRutter(1) (a bhd: t.o fnl 4f) | 15 | **26** | 16/1 | — | — |

(SP 144.9%) **26 Rn**

**4m 20.2** (0.20) CSF £1,230.79 CT £40,665.11 TOTE £54.00: £9.00 £21.80 £6.00 £4.10 (£8,237.50) Trio Not won; £7,905.80 to Royal Ascot 19/6/96 OWNER Lucayan Stud (EPSOM) BRED Gay O'Callaghan
LONG HANDICAP Mirador 7-2 Solatium (IRE) 7-9
WEIGHT FOR AGE 4yo-2lb

**1147 Southern Power (IRE)** had obviously been crying out for an extended trip and, buried in the pack until asked for his effort two furlongs out, stayed on to lead entering the final furlong, and won a shade more easily than the margin suggests. (25/1)
**Mirador**, carrying 8lb more than her long-handicap weight, came here fit from hurdling and, finishing strongly, gave notice that there is more success to be gained in races over extreme distances. (100/1)
**1587* Candle Smile (USA)**, taking on handicappers for the first time and taking a big step up in distance, pushed the pace all the way. Slightly outpaced soon after entering the straight, he battled on gamely nearing the finish, and stamina is his strong suit. (25/1)
**1875* Sea Victor** set out to make it all and did not fail for the want of trying, only being forced to admit defeat nearing the finish. (20/1)
**1511 Golden Arrow (IRE)**, having his first outing for his new stable, came from out of the pack in the latter stages to be nearest at the finish. He is at his best when the ground is more yielding. (25/1)
**1005* Merit (IRE)** has risen considerably in the weights since gaining such an easy success in the Chester Cup and, coming off the bridle soon after entering the straight, had to admit his measure had been taken. (3/1)
**1511 Rocky Forum**, waiting on the leaders, did not find the expected response when let down soon after straightening up, but she kept galloping, and will return to form when the ground gets easier. (16/1)
**1439 Fujiyama Crest (IRE)** wore Sea Victor down below the distance and, at that stage, looked the likely winner, but he was unable to hang on for long, and the position was accepted after being collared passing the furlong pole. He always has his share of weight, but perhaps he will be given a fair chance one of these days. (14/1)

T/Jkpt: Not won; £52,275.12 to Royal Ascot 19/6/96. T/Plpt: £2,959.00 (32.67 Tckts). T/Qdpt: £137.10 (39.98 Tckts). IM

# 1645-THIRSK (L-H) (St crse Good to firm, Rnd crse Firm)
## Tuesday June 18th

WEATHER: Overcast WIND: mod half against

## 2043 NORTH SIDES (S) STKS (2-Y.O) (Class G)

2-15 (2-16) **6f** £2,372.50 (£660.00: £317.50) Stalls: High GOING minus 0.57 sec per fur (F)

| | | | | SP | RR | SF |
|---|---|---|---|---|---|---|
| 1537[5] | **Docklands Carriage (IRE)** (NTinkler) **2-8-11b**[1] KFallon(5) (mde most: clr over 1f out: eased ins fnl f) | — | **1** | 4/7[1] | 70+ | — |
| | **Retoto** (CWFairhurst) **2-8-6** DeanMcKeown(8) (unf: bit bkwd: hdwy ½-wy: kpt on wl: no ch w wnr) | 2½ | **2** | 20/1 | 58 | — |
| 975[12] | **Soviet Lady (IRE)** (JLEyre) **2-8-6** RLappin(6) (a chsng ldrs: rdn 2f out: nt qckn) | nk | **3** | 20/1 | 58 | — |

| | | | | SP | RR | SF |
|---|---|---|---|---|---|---|
| 1320[6] | **Sparky** (MWEasterby) **2-8-6**(5) GParkin(9) (s.i.s: hdwy & wnt lft 2f out: nrst fin) | 1¾ | **4** | 25/1 | 58 | — |
| | **Kitty Galore (IRE)** (MDods) **2-8-3**(3) CTeague(10) (neat: unf: chsd ldrs tl lost pl ½-wy: styd on again appr fnl f) | hd | **5** | 25/1 | 53+ | — |
| 1845[3] | **Fearless Cavalier** (RHollinshead) **2-8-6**(5) DGriffiths(1) (in tch: no hdwy fnl 2f) | 1¾ | **6** | 5/2 2 | 53 | — |
| 1845[6] | **Cala-Holme (IRE)** (TDEasterby) **2-8-6** GCarter(3) (cl up 4f: wknd) | 8 | **7** | 25/1 | 27 | — |
| 1607[8] | **Where's Wally (IRE)** (JBerry) **2-8-11** JCarroll(2) (in tch tl outpcd fnl 2f) | 1¾ | **8** | 14/1 3 | 27 | — |
| | **Joyful Joy** (BPJBaugh) **2-8-6** ACulhane(4) (leggy: lt-f: dwlt: a bhd) | 2½ | **9** | 50/1 | 15 | — |
| | **Billycan (IRE)** (BPJBaugh) **2-8-11** WLord(7) (cmpt: unf: outpcd & bhd fr ½-wy) | 5 | **10** | 50/1 | 7 | — |

(SP 123.9%) **10 Rn**

**1m 14.4** (4.70) CSF £14.50 TOTE £1.40: £1.10 £4.00 £3.30 (£32.20) Trio £77.90 OWNER Mrs Lisa Olley (MALTON) BRED Topazio Est Vaduz
Bt in 13,800 gns; Retoto clmd BMcMath £6,000

OFFICIAL EXPLANATION **Kitty Galore (IRE): was found to have sore shins the morning after the race.**

**1086 Docklands Carriage (IRE)** had a change of jockey and blinkers for the first time and, despite his moderate action, looked different class, and proved it. (4/7)
**Retoto**, slow to realise what was required early on, picked up well from halfway, but could never get a sniff of the winner. (20/1)
**Soviet Lady (IRE)** has improved a fair deal from her first effort, and might well win a similar event. (20/1)
**Sparky** again showed signs of greenness but, the further they went, the better he got. (25/1)
**Kitty Galore (IRE)** was given a nice, kind introduction, and will obviously improve as a result. (25/1)
**1845 Fearless Cavalier** was always struggling from his draw, and this is best forgotten. (5/2)

## 2044 MOOR HILL MEDIAN AUCTION MAIDEN STKS (2-Y.O) (Class F)
2-50 (2-51) **7f** £2,915.00 (£815.00: £395.00) Stalls: Low GOING minus 0.57 sec per fur (F)

| | | | | SP | RR | SF |
|---|---|---|---|---|---|---|
| 1801[4] | **Tough Leader** (BHanbury) **2-8-11**(3) JStack(10) (lw: mid div: hdwy over 2f out: led 1½f out: r.o wl) | — | **1** | 5/2 2 | 66 | 9 |
| 1827[13] | **The Deejay (IRE)** (MBrittain) **2-8-9**(5) GParkin(4) (cl up: disp ld over 1f out: rdn & one pce) | 3½ | **2** | 33/1 | 58 | 1 |
| 1166[3] | **Grate Times** (EWeymes) **2-9-0** KFallon(6) (outpcd appr st: styd on wl fnl 2f: nrst fin) | ½ | **3** | 4/1 3 | 57 | — |
| 1197[6] | **Jack Flush (IRE)** (BSRothwell) **2-9-0** MFenton(5) (a chsng ldrs: ev ch over 1f out: nt qckn) | 1¼ | **4** | 20/1 | 54 | — |
| 1842[6] | **Broadgate Flyer (IRE)** (WJarvis) **2-9-0** NDay(7) (chsd ldrs: effrt 3f out: no imp) | hd | **5** | 9/4 1 | 54 | — |
| 1537[13] | **Imperial Or Metric (IRE)** (JBerry) **2-9-0** JCarroll(3) (led tl hdd & wknd 1½f out) | 1½ | **6** | 16/1 | 50 | — |
| | **Gablesea** (BPJBaugh) **2-9-0** WLord(1) (leggy: unf: prom: effrt 3f out: wknd over 1f out) | 4 | **7** | 50/1 | 41 | — |
| | **Coral Springs (USA)** (PWChapple-Hyam) **2-8-4**(5) RHavlin(9) (lt-f: unruly in paddock: s.i.s: a bhd) | 2 | **8** | 6/1 | 32 | — |
| | **Cajun Sunset (IRE)** (TDEasterby) **2-9-0** GCarter(8) (w'like: s.i.s: n.d) | 2½ | **9** | 16/1 | 31 | — |
| 1849[11] | **Chateauherault (IRE)** (PCHaslam) **2-9-0** JFortune(2) (bit bkwd: hmpd & lost pl after 1f: rdn & bhd after) | 1¾ | **10** | 25/1 | 27 | — |
| | **Nordico Melody (IRE)** (MrsLStubbs) **2-9-0** MMcAndrew(11) (neat: s.i.s: racd wd & a bhd) | 3 | **11** | 50/1 | 20 | — |

(SP 120.9%) **11 Rn**

**1m 27.9** (3.70) CSF £67.65 TOTE £3.10: £1.50 £11.60 £1.80 (£49.10) Trio £64.80 OWNER Mr Abdullah Ali (NEWMARKET) BRED Gainsborough Stud Management Ltd

**1801 Tough Leader** need this trip. Once he got his head in front, he did it well. (5/2: 6/4-11/4)
**The Deejay (IRE)** has come on a ton for his first spin, and also relished this step up in trip. (33/1)
**1166 Grate Times**, stepping up two furlongs in trip, needed every yard of it and only got going when the race was over. (4/1)
**1197 Jack Flush (IRE)** ran pretty well and is going the right way. (20/1)
**1842 Broadgate Flyer (IRE)** held a good position but, when asked a question, the response was a shade disappointing. (9/4)
**Imperial Or Metric (IRE)** is learning. After doing the donkey-work, he ran out of steam going to the furlong pole. (16/1)
**Coral Springs (USA)** (6/1: op 7/2)

## 2045 BBC RADIO YORK H'CAP (0-80) (3-Y.O+ F & M) (Class D)
3-25 (3-25) **1m** £3,968.75 (£1,190.00: £572.50: £263.75) Stalls: Low GOING minus 0.57 sec per fur (F)

| | | | | SP | RR | SF |
|---|---|---|---|---|---|---|
| 1825[4] | **Darcey Bussell (56)** (BWHills) **4-8-8** KFallon(1) (lw: trckd ldr: rdn 3f out: led over 1f out: all out) | — | **1** | 2/1 1 | 65 | 9 |
| 1868[5] | **Cashmere Lady (72)** (JLEyre) **4-9-7**(3) OPears(2) (lw: hld up: effrt 3f out: chal ins fnl f: r.o) | s.h | **2** | 3/1 2 | 81 | 25 |
| 1665[6] | **Champagne N Dreams (49)** (DNicholls) **4-7-8**(7) JBramhill(5) (led: qcknd appr st: hdd over 1f out: no ex) | 3½ | **3** | 8/1 | 51 | — |
| 1665[4] | **Ballard Lady (IRE) (44)** (JSWainwright) **4-7-3**(7) PDoe(3) (trckd ldrs: effrt 3f out: sn outpcd) | 5 | **4** | 20/1 | 36 | — |
| 1502[7] | **Prudent Pet (52)** (CWFairhurst) **4-8-4b** JTate(4) (hld up: effrt over 3f out: no imp) | 4 | **5** | 6/1 3 | 36 | — |
| 1481[5] | **Prima Volta (78)** (RHannon) **3-9-6b1** JCarroll(6) (hld up: effrt 3f out: no imp) | 1¾ | **6** | 3/1 2 | 58 | — |

(SP 113.5%) **6 Rn**

**1m 40.2** (3.70) CSF £8.18 TOTE £2.80: £1.60 £1.50 (£4.40) OWNER Mr W. J. Gredley (LAMBOURN) BRED Stetchworth Park Stud Ltd
LONG HANDICAP Ballard Lady (IRE) 6-13
WEIGHT FOR AGE 3yo-10lb

**1825 Darcey Bussell** always held a good pitch in a muddling race and did just enough to hold on. (2/1)
**1868 Cashmere Lady** has yet to win on turf, but tried hard here, to only just fail. (3/1)
**1665 Champagne N Dreams**, normally held up, had to make it as nobody else wanted to. Passed approaching the final furlong, she soon cried enough. (8/1)
**1665 Ballard Lady (IRE)**, 11lb out of the handicap, ran well enough. (20/1)
**1092 Prudent Pet** has the ability, but seems none too keen at present. (6/1)
**1481 Prima Volta** had blinkers on for the first time and, in a race that turned into a sprint, never took the slightest interest. (3/1)

## 2046 BRAWBY PARKS H'CAP (0-80) (4-Y.O+) (Class D)
4-00 (4-00) **1m 4f** £3,910.25 (£1,172.00: £563.50: £259.25) Stalls: High GOING minus 0.57 sec per fur (F)

| | | | | SP | RR | SF |
|---|---|---|---|---|---|---|
| 1837* | **Canton Venture (56)** (SPCWoods) **4-8-12** 5x DBiggs(5) (mde all: qcknd appr st: pushed out cl home) | — | **1** | 6/4 1 | 67 | 31 |
| 1862[2] | **Chatham Island (68)** (CEBrittain) **8-9-10** KFallon(3) (lw: a.p: effrt over 3f out: styd on u.p towards fin) | ½ | **2** | 9/4 2 | 78 | 42 |
| 1676[13] | **Instantaneous (47)** (TDEasterby) **4-8-3** GCarter(1) (hld up & bhd: effrt over 3f out: styd on fnl f: no imp) | 9 | **3** | 16/1 | 45 | 9 |
| 1852[6] | **Victoria's Secret (IRE) (55)** (MRChannon) **4-8-6**(5) PPMurphy(4) (trckd ldrs: effrt ent st: one pce) | nk | **4** | 15/2 | 53 | 17 |
| 1647[2] | **Beaumont (IRE) (59)** (JEBanks) **6-8-12**(3) JStack(2) (lw: hld up: effrt appr st: n.d) | 1¼ | **5** | 7/2 3 | 55 | 19 |
| 1421[9] | **Hotspur Street (55)** (MWEasterby) **4-8-6**(5) GParkin(6) (cl up tl outpcd appr st: sn wknd) | 1 | **6** | 16/1 | 50 | 14 |

(SP 116.5%) **6 Rn**

**2m 33.1** (3.10) CSF £5.43 TOTE £2.20: £1.10 £1.80 (£3.50) OWNER Dr Frank Chao (NEWMARKET) BRED High Point B/stock Ltd & Chao Racing & B/stock Ltd

**1837* Canton Venture**, in tremendous form, really enjoyed this. Allowed to dictate matters, he stole a useful advantage early in the straight and, despite the runner-up proving determined, did enough. (6/4)
**1862 Chatham Island** is in good heart and, judged by the way he finished, should not be long in going one better. (9/4)
**777 Instantaneous** gave her rider problems last time by pulling hard, but settled here. She struggled on in the closing stages to sneak the minor berth. (16/1)
**1852 Victoria's Secret (IRE)** has yet to have the blinkers fitted this season and they could well make a difference. (15/2: 12/1-7/1)
**1647 Beaumont (IRE)** ran a bit flat and this is not his form. (7/2)
**1070 Hotspur Street** had his chances but looked very slow. (16/1)

## 2047 OKELD LADIES' H'CAP (0-70) (3-Y.O+) (Class G)

4-35 (4-36) **7f** £2,425.00 (£675.00: £325.00) Stalls: Low GOING minus 0.57 sec per fur (F)

| | | | | SP | RR | SF |
|---|---|---|---|---|---|---|
| $1674^{5}$ | **Murray's Mazda (IRE) (46)** (JLEyre) **7-10-1** MissDianaJones(14) (rr div: hdwy 2f out: qcknd to ld wl ins fnl f) | — | **1** | 8/1 | 57 | 40 |
| $1789^{2}$ | **Nashaat (USA) (66)** (MCChapman) **8-11-7** MissYHaynes(2) (swtg: trckd ldrs: led 2f out tl hdd wl ins fnl f) | 1¼ | **2** | 8/1 | 74 | 57 |
| $1789^{7}$ | **Kid Ory (64)** (PCalver) **5-11-5** MrsFNeedham(10) (a chsng ldrs: styd on u.p fnl 2f) | 2½ | **3** | 12/1 | 66 | 49 |
| $1610^{7}$ | **Silver Welcome (56)** (TDEasterby) **3-9-12**(4) MissADeniel(5) (led tl hdd 2f out: kpt on one pce) | s.h | **4** | 9/1 | 58 | 32 |
| $1860^{5}$ | **Awesome Venture (50)** (MCChapman) **6-10-5** MrsSBosley(3) (hmpd appr st: effrt over 2f out: no imp) | 1¾ | **5** | 8/1 | 48 | 31 |
| $1789^{4}$ | **Allinson's Mate (IRE) (55)** (TDBarron) **8-10-10b** MrsAFarrell(6) (lw: hld up: hmpd appr st: hdwy 2f out: nvr able chal) | 2½ | **6** | 5/1 2 | 48 | 31 |
| $1417^{9}$ | **Royal Comedian (38)** (BWMurray) **7-9-0**(7) MrsCWilliams(4) (hmpd after 2f: hdwy 2f out: no imp) | 2 | **7** | 16/1 | 26 | 9 |
| $1650^{5}$ | **Anonym (IRE) (65)** (DNicholls) **4-11-6** MrsAPerrett(9) (lw: chsd ldrs: effrt 3f out: wknd over 1f out) | ¾ | **8** | 4/1 1 | 51 | 34 |
| $1890^{9}$ | **Fighter Squadron (42)** (REPeacock) **7-9-4b**(7)ow4 MrsCPeacock(1) (in tch: rdn 3f out: n.d) | 4 | **9** | 20/1 | 19 | — |
| $1677^{4}$ | **Super Park (64)** (JPearce) **4-11-5** MrsLPearce(8) (trckd ldrs tl wknd fnl 2f) | 2½ | **10** | 10/1 | 36 | 19 |
| $1865^{5}$ | **Henry the Hawk (50)** (MDods) **5-10-1**(4) MissEMaude(11) (b: hdwy & c wd st: sn rdn & btn) | 1 | **11** | 25/1 | 19 | 2 |
| $1532^{10}$ | **Morocco (IRE) (60)** (MRChannon) **7-11-1** MissJWinter(13) (a bhd) | 2½ | **12** | 12/1 | 24 | 7 |
| $1859^{3}$ | **Respect A Secret (44)** (SEKettlewell) **4-9-13** MrsDKettlewell(12) (sn bhd: eased fnl 2f) | 10 | **13** | 13/2 3 | — | — |

(SP 132.3%) **13 Rn**

**1m 26.4** (2.20) CSF £62.76 CT £751.58 TOTE £11.50: £3.30 £4.20 £4.40 (£58.60) Trio £247.80 OWNER Mr Murray Grubb (HAMBLETON) BRED Patrick Kennedy
WEIGHT FOR AGE 3yo-9lb
**OFFICIAL EXPLANATION Super Park: had been struck into behind.**
**1674 Murray's Mazda (IRE)**, given a fine ride, came with a run in the last two furlongs to settle it, despite showing a tendency to hang left. (8/1)
**1789 Nashaat (USA)** ran another good race but just saw too much daylight too soon. (8/1)
**1423 Kid Ory** was always battling away in front as usual, but was again short of a real turn of foot. (12/1)
**1610 Silver Welcome**, taken early to post, ran quite well. (9/1)
**1860 Awesome Venture** was short of room at various stages and never got in a blow. (8/1)
**1789 Allinson's Mate (IRE)** had the blinkers on but, in a messy race, never found any room. (5/1: 9/2-11/1)
**Royal Comedian** got chopped for room early and failed to recover fully. (16/1)

## 2048 INGS MAIDEN STKS (3-Y.O) (Class D)

5-10 (5-11) **7f** £3,821.00 (£1,148.00: £554.00: £257.00) Stalls: Low GOING minus 0.57 sec per fur (F)

| | | | | SP | RR | SF |
|---|---|---|---|---|---|---|
| $840^{2}$ | **Sabot (102)** (BWHills) **3-9-0** KFallon(2) (lw: a gng wl: led 2f out: easily) | — | **1** | 1/4 1 | 71 | 26 |
| $1567a^{10}$ | **Abir** (HThomsonJones) **3-8-9** GCarter(4) (led tl hdd 2f out: hung rt & no ch w wnr) | 3½ | **2** | 6/1 2 | 58 | 13 |
| $1688^{5}$ | **Madrina (61)** (JBerry) **3-8-9** JCarroll(6) (a.p: effrt 3f out: one pce) | 1¼ | **3** | 11/1 | 55 | 10 |
| | **Belbay Star** (JLEyre) **3-8-9** RLappin(8) (unf: pushed along appr st: nvr trbld ldrs) | 3 | **4** | 50/1 | 48 | 3 |
| $1901^{11}$ | **Red Tie Affair (USA)** (MBell) **3-9-0** MFenton(5) (b.nr fore: s.i.s: stdy hdwy 2f out: n.d) | 4 | **5** | 9/1 3 | 44 | — |
| | **Messalina (IRE)** (BMactaggart) **3-8-9** NConnorton(3) (bkwd: dwlt: n.d) | 2½ | **6** | 100/1 | 33 | — |
| | **Truly Bay** (TDBarron) **3-9-0** JFortune(1) (lengthy: bit bkwd: dwlt: a bhd) | 4 | **7** | 20/1 | 29 | — |
| $1422^{13}$ | **Clancassie** (EJAlston) **3-8-9** SDWilliams(7) (chsd ldrs over 4f: wknd) | 4 | **8** | 150/1 | 15 | — |

(SP 121.0%) **8 Rn**

**1m 26.4** (2.20) CSF £3.02 TOTE £1.30: £1.00 £2.90 £2.40 (£1.60) OWNER Mr J. Hanson (LAMBOURN) BRED Mrs B. Skinner
**840 Sabot** won this very easily as he should have done, and it should have boosted his confidence no end. Much better looks likely. (1/4)
**1567a Abir** was well outclassed again, and looked a funny customer when hanging right in the straight. (6/1: op 4/1)
**1688 Madrina**, stepping up in distance, tried to get on terms in the straight, but was soon put in her place. (11/1)
**Belbay Star** never got into this, but showed enough to suggest that time should see better. (50/1)
**Red Tie Affair (USA)** had a nice educational without looking likely to trouble the leaders and improvement looks likely. (9/1)
**Messalina (IRE)**, very burly, will need plenty of time. (100/1)

## 2049 FRANKLAND H'CAP (0-70) (3-Y.O) (Class E)

5-40 (5-41) **6f** £3,419.75 (£1,028.00: £496.50: £230.75) Stalls: High GOING minus 0.57 sec per fur (F)

| | | | | SP | RR | SF |
|---|---|---|---|---|---|---|
| $1707^{3}$ | **U-No-Harry (IRE) (57)** (RHollinshead) **3-8-8** ACulhane(18) (racd stands' side: led after 2f: r.o u.p appr fnl f) | — | **1** | 7/1 3 | 58 | 33 |
| $997^{11}$ | **Middle East (70)** (TDBarron) **3-9-7** JFortune(16) (chsd ldrs stands' side: kpt on fnl f) | 2 | **2** | 7/1 3 | 66 | 41 |
| $1405^{10}$ | **Pathaze (49)** (NBycroft) **3-8-0** DaleGibson(17) (bhd: hdwy stands' side over 2f out: styd on wl) | s.h | **3** | 10/1 | 45 | 20 |
| $973^{15}$ | **Opening Chorus (53)** (DNicholls) **3-8-4** JFanning(14) (lw: hdwy stands' side ½-wy: kpt on fnl f) | nk | **4** | 12/1 | 48 | 23 |
| $1658^{4}$ | **The Butterwick Kid (48)** (RAFahey) **3-7-13b**ow1 GCarter(1) (sn outpcd & wl bhd far side: styd on wl fnl 2f) | 2½ | **5** | 9/1 | 36 | 10 |
| *$1812^{4}$* | **Tymeera (58)** (BPalling) **3-8-6**(3) SDrowne(6) (racd far side: chsd ldrs: nt qckn fnl 2f) | 1 | **6** | 16/1 | 43 | 18 |
| $1650^{7}$ | **Too Hasty (58)** (TDEasterby) **3-8-9** DMcKeown(3) (led far side 4f: wknd) | 2½ | **7** | 8/1 | 37 | 12 |
| $1692^{3}$ | **Ewar Sunrise (67)** (CEBrittain) **3-9-4** GDuffield(5) (racd far side: nvr trbld ldrs) | hd | **8** | 12/1 | 46 | 21 |
| $1707^{2}$ | **The Wad (66)** (DNicholls) **3-9-3** KFallon(10) (lw: prom stands' side tl wknd over 1f out) | 1½ | **9** | 4/1 1 | 41 | 16 |
| $1405^{3}$ | **Maysimp (IRE) (49)** (BPJBaugh) **3-7-7**(7)ow4 JoHunnam(13) (raced stands' side: n.d) | 1¾ | **10** | 14/1 | 19 | — |
| $1599^{2}$ | **Ramsey Hope (67)** (CWFairhurst) **3-9-4b** NKennedy(11) (w ldrs stands' side: wandered 2f out: sn btn) | 1¾ | **11** | 10/1 | 32 | 7 |
| $1610^{6}$ | **Catwalk Girl (48)** (MissJFCraze) **3-7-13v** AMackay(4) (prom far side 4f) | ½ | **12** | 14/1 | 12 | — |
| 1865* | **Tropical Beach (60)** (JBerry) **3-8-11** 7x JCarroll(9) (s.i.s: racd stands' side: pushed along thrght: n.d) | 1¾ | **13** | 6/1 2 | 19 | — |
| $1608^{8}$ | **Swifty Nifty (IRE) (45)** (WWHaigh) **3-7-3**(7) PDoe(7) (lw: racd alone centre: w ldrs over 4f: wknd) | 2½ | **14** | 20/1 | — | — |

| | | | | SP | RR | SF |
|---|---|---|---|---|---|---|
| 1518[3] | **Inaminit (62)** (HJCollingridge) **3-8-13** FNorton(12) (prom stands' side to ½-wy) | ¾ | **15** | 7/1[3] | 13 | — |
| 1405[14] | **Babyshooz (46)** (MBrittain) **3-7-8**(3)ow1 DWright(15) (dwlt: a bhd stands' side) | ¾ | **16** | 33/1 | — | — |
| 1470[3] | **No Hiding Place (65)** (BHanbury) **3-8-13**(3) JStack(2) (lw: w ldr far side 4f: wknd qckly) | nk | **17** | 12/1 | 13 | — |

(SP 161.1%) **17 Rn**

**1m 11.7** (2.00) CSF £67.23 CT £363.43 TOTE £7.10: £2.40 £2.50 £5.00 £3.90 (£41.30) Trio £41.80 OWNER Mr D. Coppenhall (UPPER LONGDON) BRED A. J. Poulton (Epping) Ltd
LONG HANDICAP Maysimp (IRE) 7-9 Babyshooz 7-5
**OFFICIAL EXPLANATION Inaminit: a blood test taken after the race showed the horse to be slightly anaemic.**
**1707 U-No-Harry (IRE)** had the best draw and made full use of it. (7/1)
**Middle East**, well drawn, kept battling away, but was never quite up to it. (7/1: 6/1-9/1)
**973 Pathaze** had plenty to do after a moderate start, but battled on well near the finish. (10/1)
**Opening Chorus** ran his best race of the season and seems to be improving. (12/1)
**1658 The Butterwick Kid** was left struggling on the far side and soon well behind, but he picked up tremendously well late on. Given a high draw, he must have gone close. (9/1)
**644 Tymeera** ran well on the far side, but the stands'-side group had a big advantage in the last couple of furlongs. (16/1)

T/Plpt: £18.80 (508.46 Tckts). T/Qdpt: £6.90 (102.39 Tckts). AA

## 2037-ASCOT (R-H) (Good to firm)
## Wednesday June 19th
WEATHER: warm WIND: almost nil

### 2050 JERSEY STKS (Gp 3) (3-Y.O) (Class A)
2-30 (2-31) **7f** £34,400.00 (£13,032.50: £6,391.25: £2,926.25) Stalls: Centre GOING minus 0.25 sec per fur (GF)

| | | | | SP | RR | SF |
|---|---|---|---|---|---|---|
| 1495[2] | **Lucayan Prince (USA) (97)** (DRLoder) **3-8-10b** RHughes(2) (dwlt: gd hdwy on bit over 1f out: n.m.r & squeezed thro: led wl ins fnl f: r.o wl) | — | **1** | 50/1 | 114 | 55 |
| 1796* | **Ramooz (USA) (106)** (BHanbury) **3-8-10** PatEddery(4) (nt clr run, swtchd lft & bmpd 2f out: hdwy over 1f out: led ins fnl f: sn hdd: unable qckn) | 1½ | **2** | 4/1[1] | 111 | 52 |
| 1639* | **Bewitching (USA) (102)** (JARToller) **3-8-7** SSanders(14) (hld up: rdn over 2f out: one pce) | ¾ | **3** | 25/1 | 106 | 47 |
| 1796[3] | **Almushtarak (IRE) (99)** (MissGayKelleway) **3-8-10** WJO'Connor(12) (b.hind: lw: a.p: led over 2f out tl ins fnl f: one pce) | s.h | **4** | 20/1 | 109 | 50 |
| 1151* | **Ali-Royal (IRE) (114)** (HRACecil) **3-8-13** WRyan(10) (swtg: nt clr run 3f out to 1f out: gd hdwy fnl f: fin wl) | 2 | **5** | 9/2[2] | 107 | 48 |
| 1329[8] | **General Academy (IRE)** (PAKelleway) **3-8-10** KFallon(16) (lw: rdn over 4f out: hdwy over 1f out: nvr nrr) | s.h | **6** | 66/1 | 104 | 45 |
| | **Helsingor (IRE)** (TStack,Ireland) **3-8-10** MRoberts(17) (hld up: rdn over 2f out: one pce) | 2½ | **7** | 66/1 | 98 | 39 |
| 1567a[3] | **My Branch (112)** (BWHills) **3-8-10** MHills(11) (hdwy over 2f out: wknd 1f out) | ½ | **8** | 4/1[1] | 97 | 38 |
| 1493* | **King of The East (IRE) (105)** (MRStoute) **3-8-10** KDarley(6) (hdwy over 3f out: wkng whn hmpd ins fnl f) | 1 | **9** | 20/1 | 95 | 36 |
| 1574a[8] | **Musick House (IRE) (98)** (PWChapple-Hyam) **3-8-10** JReid(8) (hld up: n.m.r 2f out: wknd over 1f out) | nk | **10** | 33/1 | 94 | 35 |
| 1574a[7] | **Russian Revival (USA)** (SbinSuroor) **3-8-10** OPeslier(7) (lw: plld hrd: hdwy over 5f out: led 4f out tl over 2f out: wknd over 1f out) | ½ | **11** | 14/1 | 93 | 34 |
| 966* | **Please Suzanne (100)** (RHannon) **3-8-7** CAsmussen(3) (bmpd 2f out: hdwy over 1f out: sn wknd) | hd | **12** | 20/1 | 90 | 31 |
| 1435* | **Sandhill (IRE) (90)** (JHMGosden) **3-8-7** WCarson(15) (led 3f: wknd wl over 1f out) | 3½ | **13** | 25/1 | 82 | 23 |
| 1187[4] | **Tamhid (USA) (104)** (HThomsonJones) **3-8-10** RHills(9) (prom 5f) | ¾ | **14** | 25/1 | 83 | 24 |
| | **Requin Bleu (IRE)** (APO'Brien,Ireland) **3-8-10v**[1] CRoche(1) (leggy: a bhd) | nk | **15** | 16/1 | 83 | 24 |
| 926[9] | **Leonine (IRE) (105)** (PFICole) **3-8-10** MJKinane(13) (prom 5f) | 1¾ | **16** | 11/1[3] | 79 | 20 |

(SP 112.8%) **16 Rn**

**1m 28.35** (1.15) CSF £208.20 TOTE £56.20: £11.80 £1.40 £4.90 (£100.40) Trio £752.40 OWNER Lucayan Stud (NEWMARKET) BRED Airdrie Partnership
**1495 Lucayan Prince (USA)** caused a major surprise. Still out with the washing a quarter of a mile out, he did not have the best of runs below the distance but, despite this, made giant strides on the bridle. Showing a tremendous turn of foot, he swept into the lead in then last 75 yards and quickly had it sewn up. (50/1)
**1796* Ramooz (USA)**, who found a clear run and picked up ground below the distance, moved to the front inside the final furlong. He did nothing wrong but, like everyone else, was not prepared for the winner's turn of foot. (4/1)
**1639* Bewitching (USA)** stayed on for third prize without finding that vital turn of foot (25/1)
**1796 Almushtarak (IRE)** was taking a step up in class and ran the race of his life. (20/1)
**1151* Ali-Royal (IRE)** was the unlucky horse of the race. Well supported in the market, he found his way blocked three furlongs from home and, every time his jockey tried to extricate him, he met with more interference. Eventually he found a clear passage entering the final furlong and the combination finished in tremendous style. With a clear run, he would surely have gone very close, and he is certainly up to winning a Group race. (9/2)
**797a General Academy (IRE)** was unable to cope with the drop in distance, and stayed on to be nearest at the line. His only win to date came over nine furlongs and a return to a longer trip is definitely required. (66/1)
**Leonine (IRE)** (11/1: 8/1-12/1)

### 2051 QUEEN MARY STKS (Gp 3) (2-Y.O F) (Class A)
3-05 (3-08) **5f** £25,960.00 (£9,828.00: £4,814.00: £2,198.00) Stalls: Centre GOING minus 0.25 sec per fur (GF)

| | | | | SP | RR | SF |
|---|---|---|---|---|---|---|
| 1673* | **Dance Parade (USA)** (PFICole) **2-8-8** MJKinane(2) (lw: s.s: rdn & hdwy over 1f out: led ins fnl f: r.o wl) | — | **1** | 8/1[3] | 94 | 34 |
| 1653[2] | **Dame Laura (IRE)** (PFICole) **2-8-8** CAsmussen(12) (rdn & hdwy over 1f out: r.o ins fnl f) | 1 | **2** | 20/1 | 91 | 31 |
| 1480* | **Moonshine Girl (USA)** (MRStoute) **2-8-8** JReid(9) (lw: a.p: led 3f out: rdn over 1f out: hdd ins fnl f: unable qckn nr fin) | nk | **3** | 6/1[2] | 90 | 30 |
| 984* | **Connemara (IRE)** (CADwyer) **2-8-8** KFallon(3) (lw: hdwy over 2f out: hrd rdn over 1f out: ev ch ins fnl f: one pce) | ½ | **4** | 6/1[2] | 88 | 28 |
| 1510[4] | **March Star (IRE)** (JARToller) **2-8-8** WCarson(11) (lw: a.p: rdn & ev ch over 1f out: wknd fnl f) | 2½ | **5** | 33/1 | 80 | 20 |
| 1910a[2] | **Classic Park** (APO'Brien,Ireland) **2-8-8** CRoche(13) (a.p: rdn & ev ch over 1f out: wknd fnl f) | nk | **6** | 20/1 | 79 | 19 |
| 1143* | **More Silver (USA)** (PFICole) **2-8-8** MHills(14) (lw: hdwy over 1f out: wknd fnl f) | ½ | **7** | 5/2[1] | 78 | 18 |
| | **Rihan (USA)** (SbinSuroor) **2-8-8** RHills(4) (leggy: lt-f: nvr nrr) | nk | **8** | 10/1 | 77 | 17 |
| 1480[2] | **Dancing Drop** (RHannon) **2-8-8** PatEddery(5) (hld up: rdn 3f out: wknd 1f out) | hd | **9** | 9/1 | 76 | 16 |

| | | | | SP | RR | SF |
|---|---|---|---|---|---|---|
| 1664* | **Lycility (IRE)** (CEBrittain) **2-8-8** OPeslier(8) (lw: rdn 3f out: sme hdwy over 1f out: wknd fnl f) | 1¾ | **10** | 33/1 | 71 | 11 |
| 1315* | **Saunders Wren** (MRChannon) **2-8-9**ow1 RHughes(7) (a bhd) | 1¾ | **11** | 40/1 | 66 | 5 |
| 715* | **Jennelle** (CADwyer) **2-8-8** JStack(10) (prom over 2f) | 1½ | **12** | 33/1 | 60 | — |
| 1479[5] | **Red Garter (IRE)** (KMcAuliffe) **2-8-8b[1]** WJO'Connor(6) (swtg: led 2f: wknd over 2f out) | 10 | **13** | 100/1 | 28 | — |
| *1643** | ***Cowrie*** (RFJohnsonHoughton) **2-8-8** TSprake(1) (Withdrawn not under Starter's orders: ref to ent stalls) | | **W** | 20/1 | — | — |
| | | | | (SP 113.9%) | | **13 Rn** |

**61.94 secs** (1.94) CSF £125.02 TOTE £7.40: £2.10 £3.30 £2.00 (£42.10) Trio £119.60 OWNER H R H Prince Fahd Salman (WHATCOMBE) BRED Newgate Stud Farm Inc

**IN-FOCUS: A very strong, early pace played into the winner's hands.**

**1673* Dance Parade (USA)** maintained her unbeaten record with a fine performance. Picking up nicely from below the distance, she swept into the lead inside the final furlong, proving just too strong for her very persistent rivals. She will have a break now before coming back for the big juvenile races in the autumn. (8/1)

**1653 Dame Laura (IRE)** is a real trier and ran a tremendous race. Ridden along to pick up ground below the distance, she ran on and just won the battle for second prize. Her trainer thinks she will do best as a two-year-old and so will be given plenty of opportunities this year. (20/1)

**1480* Moonshine Girl (USA)** lost nothing in defeat. Showing in front three furlongs from home, she grimly tried to hold off allcomers and, although headed inside the final furlong, managed to live with the winner until tapped for toe in the last 50 yards. She will be better suited by six and will now go for the Cherry Hinton Stakes at Newmarket. (6/1)

**984* Connemara (IRE)** ran a blinder. Picking up ground over a quarter of a mile from home, she was one of four battling for honours inside the final furlong before tapped for toe. Further success awaits her and her jockey thinks she will be even better with some cut. (6/1)

**1510 March Star (IRE)** had to accept defeat inside the final furlong. (33/1)

**1910a Classic Park** had every chance below the distance before tiring. (20/1)

**1143* More Silver (USA)**, an uneasy favourite, made her effort below the distance and then tamely faded in the final furlong. She had not been working well at home though, and all is not quite right with her. Hopefully she can bounce back from this. (5/2: 6/4-11/4)

**Rihan (USA)** (10/1: op 6/1)

## 2052 CORONATION STKS (Gp 1) (3-Y.O F) (Class A)

3-45 (3-46) **1m (round)** £120,726.00 (£44,890.80: £21,320.40: £9,022.80) Stalls: High GOING minus 0.25 sec per fur (GF)

| | | | | SP | RR | SF |
|---|---|---|---|---|---|---|
| 1140a[2] | **Shake the Yoke** (ELellouche,France) **3-9-0** OPeslier(4) (unf: hld up: shkn up 3f out: led ins fnl f: comf) | — | **1** | Evens[1] | 112 | 76 |
| | **Last Second (IRE)** (SirMarkPrescott) **3-9-0** GDuffield(7) (swtchd lft over 2f out: hdwy over 1f out: str run fnl f: fin wl) | nk | **2** | 12/1 | 111 | 75 |
| 1567a[2] | **Dance Design (IRE)** (DKWeld,Ireland) **3-9-0** MJKinane(1) (leggy: lw: led: rdn 2f out: hdd ins fnl f: unable qckn) | ½ | **3** | 9/2[3] | 110 | 74 |
| 1140a* | **Ta Rib (USA) (113)** (EALDunlop) **3-9-0** WCarson(2) (swtg: chsd ldr 6f out to 1f out: sn wknd) | 2½ | **4** | 100/30[2] | 105 | 69 |
| 1639[2] | **Miss Universal (IRE) (99)** (CEBrittain) **3-9-0** BDoyle(5) (lw: chsd ldr 2f: rdn over 2f out: r.o one pce fnl f) | ¾ | **5** | 50/1 | 104 | 68 |
| 1129[11] | **Thrilling Day (110)** (NAGraham) **3-9-0** DHarrison(3) (a bhd) | 4 | **6** | 16/1 | 96 | 60 |
| 1567a[5] | **Priory Belle (IRE)** (JSBolger,Ireland) **3-9-0** KJManning(6) (lengthy: scope: bhd fnl 2f) | 2 | **7** | 16/1 | 92 | 56 |
| | | | | (SP 112.7%) | | **7 Rn** |

**1m 40.45** (-0.35) CSF £12.21 TOTE £2.30: £1.60 £3.10 (£12.50) OWNER Mr S. Brunswick BRED Sussex Stud & Calogo Bloodstock

**IN-FOCUS: Maybe not a vintage Coronation, but a fine ride from Peslier, who must surely be one of the world's best young jockeys.**

**1140a Shake the Yoke** gained revenge on Ta Rib in impressive style. Racing in fourth place, she had to be woken up turning into the straight, but was going ominously well again below the distance and, cruising into the lead inside the final furlong, won with quite a bit up her sleeve, despite the winning distance of only a neck. She will have a rest before going to Longchamp for the Prix de Moulin in September, followed by a return visit here for the Queen Elizabeth II Stakes. (Evens)

**Last Second (IRE)**, unbeaten in two runs as a juvenile, made a tremendous return to action. Very well supported in the market, she was still out with the washing a quarter of a mile from home and the signs looked far from good. She showed a tremendous turn of foot in the final furlong though, and swept through to fail by only a neck. (12/1)

**1567a Dance Design (IRE)** ran a fine race in defeat. Bowling along merrily in the lead, she was asked to step up the tempo in the straight, and was not overhauled until inside the final furlong. (9/2)

**1140a* Ta Rib (USA)** had no excuses. Soon racing in second place, she appeared to be travelling well entering the straight, but was collared for the runner-up berth a furlong from home and had nothing more to offer. (100/30: 7/4-7/2)

**1639 Miss Universal (IRE)**, in second place early, got rather tapped for toe in the straight, but was staying on again at the death. (50/1)

**674* Thrilling Day** was always towards the rear of the field and did not stay. She will now revert to seven. (16/1)

## 2053 ROYAL HUNT CUP H'CAP (3-Y.O+) (Class B)

4-20 (4-24) **1m (straight)** £55,584.60 (£20,711.40: £10,055.70: £4,243.50: £1,821.75: £853.05) Stalls: Centre GOING minus 0.25 sec per fur (GF)

| | | | | SP | RR | SF |
|---|---|---|---|---|---|---|
| 1051[2] | **Yeast (87)** (WJHaggas) **4-8-6** KFallon(3) (mde virtually all: hrd rdn over 1f out: r.o wl) | — | **1** | 8/1[1] | 108 | 84 |
| 1793[2] | **Tertium (IRE) (85)** (MartynWane) **4-8-4**ow1 JFortune(2) (hld up: rdn over 2f out: unable qckn) | 2½ | **2** | 12/1[2] | 101 | 76 |
| 967[3] | **Crumpton Hill (IRE) (82)** (NAGraham) **4-8-1** MRoberts(1) (a.p: rdn over 2f out: one pce) | hd | **3** | 20/1 | 98 | 74 |
| 1770* | **Donna Viola (95)** (CFWall) **4-9-0** 7x WWoods(4) (lw: hdwy over 1f out: r.o) | 2 | **4** | 20/1 | 107 | 83 |
| 1193[4] | **Star Manager (USA) (86)** (PFICole) **6-8-5** CRutter(8) (s.s: rdn & hdwy over 1f out: nvr nrr) | nk | **5** | 33/1 | 97 | 73 |
| 1296[2] | **Cadeaux Tryst (103)** (EALDunlop) **4-9-8** RHills(6) (b: rdn over 2f out: hdwy over 1f out: r.o one pce) | 1¼ | **6** | 33/1 | 112 | 88 |
| 1484[8] | **Beauchamp Jazz (99)** (JLDunlop) **4-9-4** CAsmussen(10) (lw: hld up: rdn over 2f out: one pce) | 1 | **7** | 20/1 | 106 | 82 |
| 1775[2] | **Serious (84)** (LadyHerries) **6-8-3** PaulEddery(20) (racd far side: hdwy over 3f out: rdn over 2f out: one pce) | ½ | **8** | 16/1 | 90 | 66 |
| 1898[3] | **Czarna (IRE) (82)** (CEBrittain) **5-8-1**ow1 BDoyle(32) (racd far side: a.p: hrd rdn over 1f out: wknd fnl f) | 1¾ | **9** | 40/1 | 84 | 59 |
| 1625[10] | **Mo-Addab (IRE) (79)** (ACStewart) **6-7-12** GCarter(5) (rdn over 2f out: hdwy over 1f out: nvr nrr) | 3 | **10** | 40/1 | 75 | 51 |
| 1484[12] | **Desert Green (FR) (98)** (RHannon) **7-9-3** RPerham(27) (swtg: racd far side: hdwy over 1f out: nvr nrr) | 1½ | **11** | 33/1 | 91 | 67 |
| 1112[9] | **Kayvee (94)** (GHarwood) **7-8-13** AClark(30) (racd far side: hdwy over 1f out: one pce) | ½ | **12** | 12/1[2] | 86 | 62 |
| 1944a[2] | **Amrak Ajeeb (IRE) (92)** (BHanbury) **4-8-11** JReid(19) (nvr nrr) | ½ | **13** | 14/1[3] | 83 | 59 |
| | **Silvian Bliss (USA) (89)** (DKWeld,Ireland) **4-8-8** MJKinane(17) (a mid div) | 1¾ | **14** | 16/1 | 77 | 53 |
| 1793[15] | **Stone Ridge (IRE) (93)** (RHannon) **4-8-12** PatEddery(9) (lw: nvr nrr) | 1 | **15** | 20/1 | 79 | 55 |
| 1703[2] | **New Century (USA) (87)** (DNicholls) **4-8-6** AlexGreaves(29) (lw: swtchd lft 7f out: prom over 5f) | s.h | **16** | 16/1 | 73 | 49 |
| 1112[4] | **Tarawa (IRE) (105)** (NACallaghan) **4-9-10** RHughes(16) (a mid div) | ¾ | **17** | 16/1 | 89 | 65 |
| 1112[2] | **Green Green Desert (FR) (100)** (LadyHerries) **5-9-5** KDarley(31) (lw: racd far side: hdwy over 1f out: wknd fnl f) | nk | **18** | 16/1 | 84 | 60 |

| | | | | SP | RR | SF |
|---|---|---|---|---|---|---|
| 1962[7] | **Chickawicka (IRE) (83)** (BPalling) **5-8-2** TSprake(7) (prom over 4f) | 2 | **19** | 50/1 | 63 | 39 |
| 1131[4] | **Moments of Fortune (USA) (96)** (BHanbury) **4-9-1** WRyan(15) (hld up: rdn over 3f out: wknd over 2f out) | 2½ | **20** | 33/1 | 71 | 47 |
| 1703[10] | **Wild Rice (90)** (GWragg) **4-8-9v[1]** MHills(25) (b: lw: racd far side: hdwy over 2f out: wknd over 1f out) | 1½ | **21** | 33/1 | 62 | 38 |
| 1799[2] | **Moving Arrow (93)** (MissSEHall) **5-8-12** JWeaver(18) (prom 5f) | 1 | **22** | 16/1 | 63 | 39 |
| 967[5] | **Akil (IRE) (88)** (RWArmstrong) **4-8-7** WCarson(22) (racd far side: prom over 6f) | 5 | **23** | 16/1 | 48 | 24 |
| 1425[2] | **Pengamon (80)** (HJCollingridge) **4-7-13** NAdams(28) (racd far side: prom over 4f) | s.h | **24** | 33/1 | 39 | 15 |
| 1843[2] | **Zygo (USA) (80)** (WJarvis) **4-7-13** AMcGlone(12) (prom over 4f) | s.h | **25** | 40/1 | 39 | 15 |
| 1469[2] | **Blaze of Song (82)** (RHannon) **4-8-1** SSanders(26) (racd far side: bhd fnl 3f) | ½ | **26** | 33/1 | 40 | 16 |
| 1792[12] | **Cedez le Passage (FR) (87)** (KOCunningham-Brown) **5-8-1**(5) MBaird(14) (bhd fnl 4f) | 1¼ | **27** | 66/1 | 43 | 19 |
| 1819[2] | **Star Talent (USA) (82)** (MissGayKelleway) **5-7-12**(3) MHenry(13) (b: swtg: a bhd) | 2 | **28** | 25/1 | 34 | 10 |
| 1252a[4] | **Ger's Royale (IRE) (99)** (PJFlynn,Ireland) **5-9-4** MDuffy(11) (bhd fnl 2f) | 1 | **29** | 25/1 | 49 | 25 |
| 1322[3] | **Gymcrak Premiere (89)** (GHolmes) **8-8-8v** WNewnes(23) (racd far side: a bhd) | 3½ | **30** | 40/1 | 32 | 8 |
| 1768* | **Blomberg (IRE) (100)** (JRFanshawe) **4-9-5** 7x DHarrison(24) (lw: racd far side: bhd fnl 3f) | 2½ | **31** | 12/1[2] | 38 | 14 |
| | | | | (SP 142.6%) | **31 Rn** | |

**1m 39.39** (-1.81) CSF £98.16 CT £1,085.80 TOTE £8.00: £2.40 £3.90 £6.10 £5.30 (£46.30) Trio £344.60 OWNER Mr B. Haggas (NEWMARKET) BRED R. T. and Mrs Watson

OFFICIAL EXPLANATION **Blomberg (IRE): was found to be lame the following morning.**

IN-FOCUS: **A remarkable advantage was conferred by a low draw, especially with the pace up that rail.**

**1051 Yeast** turned in a tremendous front-running display. Making virtually all the running, he began to assert from below the distance and, responding to pressure, proved far too good for his rivals. He is certainly an improving individual and will probably go next for the Royal Hong Kong Jockey Club at Sandown in July, although his trainer is not sure whether he will get the extra two furlongs. (8/1)

**1793 Tertium (IRE)**, pushed along over two furlongs from home, was unable to live with the winner but still finished a very creditable second. (12/1)

**967 Crumpton Hill (IRE)**, never far away, was battling for the runner-up berth from below the distance, but was unable to get to the winner. He will now head for the Bunbury Cup over seven at Newmarket. (20/1)

**1770* Donna Viola** at last found her feet from below the distance but, despite running on, found the leaders were already home and dry. (20/1)

**1193 Star Manager (USA)**, who lost ground at the start, was doing all his best work in the final furlong and a half. This ground may have been a bit too lively for him. (33/1)

**728 Cadeaux Tryst**, pushed along over a quarter of a mile from home, stayed on in the final furlong but found it all over bar the shouting. (33/1)

## 2054 QUEEN'S VASE STKS (Gp 3) (3-Y.O) (Class A)

4-55 (4-56) **2m 45y** £32,150.00 (£12,170.00: £5,960.00: £2,720.00) Stalls: High GOING minus 0.25 sec per fur (GF)

| | | | | SP | RR | SF |
|---|---|---|---|---|---|---|
| | **Gordi (USA)** (DKWeld,Ireland) **3-8-11** MJKinane(4) (lengthy: hld up: n.m.r over 2f out: rdn over 1f out: led ins fnl f: r.o wl) | — | **1** | 7/1[3] | 113 | 63 |
| 1110* | **Athenry (97)** (JPearce) **3-8-11** GBardwell(11) (a.p: rdn 4f out: r.o ins fnl f) | 1 | **2** | 12/1 | 112 | 62 |
| 1854* | **Persian Punch (IRE)** (DRCElsworth) **3-8-11** RHughes(9) (lw: rdn over 2f out: hdwy over 1f out: r.o wl ins fnl f) | ½ | **3** | 12/1 | 112 | 62 |
| 1863? | **Wilawander (97)** (BWHills) **3-8-11** MHills(10) (hdwy 4f out: led over 1f out tl ins fnl f: unable qckn) | s.h | **4** | 33/1 | 112 | 62 |
| 1580a[2] | **Backdrop (IRE) (106)** (PWChapple-Hyam) **3-8-11** JReid(14) (b.off fore: rdn 5f out: hdwy over 1f out: r.o) | ¾ | **5** | 5/1[2] | 111 | 61 |
| 1631* | **Valedictory** (HRACecil) **3-8-11** CAsmussen(7) (led to 2f out: wknd over 1f out) | 2½ | **6** | 9/1 | 108 | 58 |
| 1712[2] | **Clerkenwell (USA) (88)** (MRStoute) **3-8-11** WCarson(3) (hdwy over 5f out: led 2f out tl over 1f out: wknd fnl f) | 1 | **7** | 14/1 | 107 | 57 |
| 1153* | **Arnhem (85)** (CEBrittain) **3-8-11** KDarley(5) (lw: nvr nr to chal) | 6 | **8** | 33/1 | 101 | 51 |
| 1407[4] | **Benatom (USA) (85)** (HRACecil) **3-8-11** WRyan(2) (lw: prom tl wknd over 1f out) | hd | **9** | 33/1 | 101 | 51 |
| 671* | **Sherpas (IRE)** (HRACecil) **3-8-11** PatEddery(8) (bhd fnl 3f) | 10 | **10** | 11/4[1] | 91 | 41 |
| 1110[3] | **Lallans (IRE) (99)** (MJohnston) **3-8-11** JWeaver(12) (lw: stdy hdwy 9f out: wknd 3f out) | 9 | **11** | 5/1[2] | 83 | 33 |
| 1305[2] | **Qasida (IRE) (86)** (CEBrittain) **3-8-11** BDoyle(13) (bhd fnl 4f) | 1 | **12** | 40/1 | 82 | 32 |
| 1791[16] | **Zaforum (103)** (LMontagueHall) **3-8-11** OPeslier(1) (bhd fnl 5f) | 8 | **13** | 25/1 | 74 | 24 |
| 1957* | **Tiger Lake** (SbinSuroor) **3-8-11** JCarroll(6) (prom 12f) | 1 | **14** | 14/1 | 73 | 23 |
| | | | | (SP 126.3%) | **14 Rn** | |

**3m 28.75** (1.55) CSF £83.77 TOTE £9.70: £2.50 £4.30 £3.50 (£87.20) Trio £194.60 OWNER Mr Allen Paulson (CURRAGH)

OFFICIAL EXPLANATION **Sherpas (IRE): failed to let himself down on the ground.**

**Gordi (USA)** was taking a big step up in distance but was very impressive. Asked for his effort from below the distance, he swept into the lead inside the final furlong. He will have a month break and then one more run before the St Leger at Doncaster. (7/1)

**1110* Athenry** ran an absolute blinder. Never far away, he was pushed along at least four furlongs from home, but his stamina really came into play and he ran on nicely inside the final furlong. The St Leger is his target and connections believe he will be a Cup horse next season. (12/1)

**1854* Persian Punch (IRE)** ran creditably. Only finding his feet from below the distance, he ran on really strongly inside the final furlong, but found the line always coming too soon. (12/1)

**1863 Wilawander** moved up half a mile from home and grabbed a narrow advantage below the distance. Headed inside the final furlong, he failed to summon up another gear. (33/1)

**1580a Backdrop (IRE)** stayed on nicely in the last furlong and a half but found the line always beating him. (5/1)

**671* Sherpas (IRE)** (11/4: 2/1-3/1)

**1110 Lallans (IRE)** should have appreciated the step up in trip. Easing his way into the action on the final circuit, he disappointingly dropped away three furlongs from home. (5/1)

## 2055 BESSBOROUGH H'CAP (0-105) (3-Y.O+) (Class B)

5-30 (5-32) **1m 4f** £25,191.25 (£7,630.00: £3,727.50: £1,776.25) Stalls: High GOING minus 0.25 sec per fur (GF)

| | | | | SP | RR | SF |
|---|---|---|---|---|---|---|
| 1700* | **Tykeyvor (IRE) (82)** (LadyHerries) **6-8-1**(5) FLynch(14) (b.hind: a.p: hrd rdn over 2f out: led over 1f out: r.o wl) | — | **1** | 14/1 | 93 | 66 |
| 1147[7] | **My Learned Friend (81)** (AHide) **5-8-5** AMcGlone(15) (lw: hdwy over 4f out: ev ch over 1f out: unable qckn) | 3 | **2** | 20/1 | 88 | 61 |
| 1767[8] | **At Liberty (IRE) (84)** (RHannon) **4-8-8** JFEgan(12) (lw: hrd rdn & hdwy over 1f out: r.o wl ins fnl f) | ½ | **3** | 20/1 | 90 | 63 |
| 1426* | **Beauchamp Jade (87)** (HCandy) **4-8-11** GCarter(1) (nt clr run over 2f out tl over 1f out: hdwy 1f out: str run fnl f: fin wl) | 1½ | **4** | 15/2 | 91 | 64 |
| 875[6] | **Sanmartino (IRE) (101)** (BWHills) **4-9-11** PatEddery(9) (lw: a.p: ev ch over 2f out: wknd over 1f out) | 2½ | **5** | 13/2[2] | 102 | 75 |
| 1426[5] | **Remaadi Sun (79)** (MDIUsher) **4-8-3** RStreet(16) (hdwy & nt clr run on ins over 1f out: r.o wl ins fnl f) | s.h | **6** | 20/1 | 80 | 53 |

| | | | Pos | SP | RR | SF |
|---|---|---|---|---|---|---|
| 1961* | **Major Change (94)** (RHannon) **4-9-4** 7x KDarley(11) (a.p: led 5f out tl over 1f out: sn wknd) | hd | **7** | 16/1 | 95 | 68 |
| | **Shadow Leader (80)** (CREgerton) **5-8-4** WRyan(13) (led 7f: btn whn hmpd on ins 4f out) | 3 | **8** | 25/1 | 77 | 50 |
| 1620[4] | **Ionio (USA) (100)** (CEBrittain) **5-9-10** BDoyle(10) (nvr nrr) | nk | **9** | 40/1 | 96 | 69 |
| 1767[4] | **Naked Welcome (104)** (MJFetherston-Godley) **4-10-0** JReid(6) (nvr nrr) | ½ | **10** | 12/1 | 100 | 73 |
| 1792* | **Dance So Suite (89)** (PFICole) **4-8-13** WCarson(8) (lw: a mid div) | nk | **11** | 7/1 [3] | 84 | 57 |
| 913[5] | **Efharisto (72)** (JWhite) **7-7-10b** NCarlisle(20) (lw: rdn & hdwy over 1f out: nt clr run 1f out: one pce) | nk | **12** | 50/1 | 67 | 40 |
| 1793[6] | **Hardy Dancer (91)** (GLMoore) **4-9-1** SWhitworth(17) (prom over 10f) | ½ | **13** | 14/1 | 85 | 58 |
| 1767[2] | **Son of Sharp Shot (IRE) (100)** (JLDunlop) **6-9-10** PaulEddery(19) (lw: hdwy over 2f out: wknd over 1f out) | 1¾ | **14** | 6/1 [1] | 92 | 65 |
| 1353[8] | **Lombardic (USA) (92)** (MrsJCecil) **5-9-2** TIves(4) (lw: prom over 10f) | 1¼ | **15** | 33/1 | 82 | 55 |
| 1792[6] | **Benfleet (78)** (RWArmstrong) **5-8-2** MRoberts(3) (hdwy & nt clr run wl over 1f out: no ch whn nt clr run ins fnl f) | hd | **16** | 12/1 | 68 | 41 |
| | **Cockney Lad (IRE) (87)** (NMeade,Ireland) **7-8-11** MJKinane(2) (lw: a bhd) | ½ | **17** | 12/1 | 77 | 50 |
| 941[10] | **Burning (USA) (90)** (GHarwood) **4-9-0** MHills(18) (swtg: bhd fnl 2f) | 2½ | **18** | 20/1 | 76 | 49 |
| 1476[3] | **Wafir (IRE) (82)** (PCalver) **4-8-6** JCarroll(5) (bhd fnl 2f) | 7 | **19** | 14/1 | 59 | 32 |
| 941[9] | **Bob's Ploy (85)** (MHTompkins) **4-8-9** PRobinson(7) (hdwy over 3f out: wknd over 2f out) | 10 | **20** | 25/1 | 49 | 22 |
| | | | | (SP 134.9%) | **20 Rn** | |

**2m 29.88** (-0.12) CSF £254.06 CT £5,064.48 TOTE £20.80: £4.10 £5.00 £9.30 £2.10 (£473.30) Trio £5,412.90; £4,574.36 to Royal Ascot 20/6/96. OWNER Seymour Bloodstock (UK) Ltd (LITTLEHAMPTON) BRED H. Key

**1700* Tykeyvor (IRE)**, grabbing the initiative below the distance, soon asserted. The Ulster Harp Derby at Down Royal is next on the agenda. (14/1)

**My Learned Friend** left previous form this season well behind. Moving up over half a mile from home, he had every chance below the distance before left standing by the winner. (20/1)

**925 At Liberty (IRE)** at last found his feet below the distance but, despite running on strongly, found the winner was already home and dry. (20/1)

**1426* Beauchamp Jade** had absolutely no luck in running and must have gone very close with a clear passage. With nowhere to go in the straight, she eventually found an opening a furlong out but, despite finishing really strongly, was never going to get there in time. (15/2)

**875 Sanmartino (IRE)**, always well placed, had every chance early in the straight before having to give best approaching the final furlong. (13/2: op 10/1)

**1426 Remaadi Sun** was another who had no luck in running. (20/1)

T/Jkpt: £67,488.20 (0.2 Tckts); £76,043.08 to Royal Ascot 20/6/96. T/Plpt: £2,555.30 (40.59 Tckts). T/Qdpt: £262.60 (20.5 Tckts). AK

## 1821-NOTTINGHAM (L-H) (Good to firm, Firm patches)
## Wednesday June 19th

WEATHER: fine WIND: mod bhd

## 2056 BURTON JOYCE (S) H'CAP (0-60) (3-Y.O+) (Class G)

6-30 (6-30) **1m 1f 213y** £2,070.00 (£570.00: £270.00) Stalls: Low GOING minus 0.46 sec per fur (F)

| | | | Pos | SP | RR | SF |
|---|---|---|---|---|---|---|
| 1838[9] | **Mazilla (37)** (AStreeter) **4-8-2**(5) RHavlin(2) (lw: trckd ldrs: led 2f out: rdn out) | — | **1** | 6/1 [3] | 48 | 19 |
| 1633[6] | **Comedy River (42)** (NEBerry) **9-8-12** GHind(7) (hld up: plld out 2f out: hdwy appr fnl f: nt rch wnr) | ½ | **2** | 9/1 | 52 | 23 |
| 1691[11] | **Shuttlecock (36)** (MrsNMacauley) **5-8-6**ow1 RPrice(21) (hdwy 5f out: no ex ins fnl f) | 1 | **3** | 16/1 | 45 | 15 |
| 1669[7] | **Northern Motto (52)** (MrsJRRamsden) **3-8-10** MRimmer(20) (chsd ldrs: rdn 3f out: styd on fnl f) | 1¾ | **4** | 5/1 [2] | 58 | 17 |
| 2024[5] | **Greek Gold (IRE) (43)** (WLBarker) **7-8-6**(7) JBramhill(14) (prom: hmpd after 2f: ev ch 3f out: wknd ins fnl f) | nk | **5** | 12/1 | 48 | 19 |
| 1893[17] | **Doodies Pool (IRE) (42)** (PBurgoyne) **6-8-9v**(3) PMcCabe(16) (lw: hld up: hdwy 4f out: rdn over 2f out: one pce) | 1¼ | **6** | 20/1 | 45 | 16 |
| *1970[5]* | **Trumble (44)** (MrsNMacauley) **4-8-11**(3) CTeague(18) (in tch: no hdwy fnl 2f) | ½ | **7** | 12/1 | 47 | 18 |
| 1828[3] | **Absolute Ruler (IRE) (38)** (JLHarris) **5-8-5b**(3) NVarley(6) (lw: chsd ldrs tl rdn & wknd appr fnl f) | nk | **8** | 7/1 | 40 | 11 |
| 613[16] | **Clytha Hill Lad (40)** (JMBradley) **5-8-5**(5) PPMurphy(8) (prom: led 3f out to 2f out: sn wknd) | ½ | **9** | 33/1 | 41 | 12 |
| 1821[10] | **Bronze Runner (36)** (EAWheeler) **12-8-1b**(5) ADaly(13) (hdwy 6f out: wknd over 2f out) | 6 | **10** | 9/1 | 28 | — |
| 1894[6] | **Araboybill (58)** (RSimpson) **5-10-0b** JHBrown(3) (chsd ldrs 6f) | 1½ | **11** | 14/1 | 47 | 18 |
| *246[5]* | **Lawnswood Junior (41)** (JLSpearing) **9-8-6**(5) DGriffiths(4) (trckd ldrs 8f: sn wknd) | 1¾ | **12** | 33/1 | 27 | — |
| *1457[5]* | **Undawaterscubadiva (38)** (MPBielby) **4-8-3**(5) LNewton(10) (b: lw: reard s: nvr trbld ldrs) | 1¼ | **13** | 20/1 | 22 | — |
| 1600[10] | **Saltis (IRE) (46)** (DWPArbuthnot) **4-8-13**(3) DarrenMoffatt(5) (b.hind: hld up: rdn 4f out: nvr rchd ldrs) | s.h | **14** | 20/1 | 30 | 1 |
| 1691[3] | **Yet Again (40)** (BHanbury) **4-8-7**(3) JStack(17) (a bhd) | 3 | **15** | 4/1 [1] | 20 | — |
| 1828[U] | **Risky Rose (35)** (RHollinshead) **4-8-5** JFanning(12) (lw: led 3f: ev ch 4f out: sn wknd) | 2 | **16** | 16/1 | 11 | — |
| 1533[11] | **Rupiana (IRE) (50)** (CMurray) **4-9-6** MTebbutt(1) (led 7f out to 3f out: sn wknd) | 2 | **17** | 33/1 | 23 | — |
| 1454[W] | **Naseer (USA) (37)** (KBishop) **7-8-7** CRutter(11) (b: a bhd) | 4 | **18** | 33/1 | 4 | — |
| | **Pillow Talk (IRE) (38)** (SWCampion) **5-8-8** SDWilliams(9) (in tch 6f) | 1½ | **19** | 14/1 | 2 | — |
| 1534[11] | **Grandes Oreilles (IRE) (43)** (NJHWalker) **4-8-13** DaleGibson(22) (prom 4f: sn lost pl) | 1¾ | **20** | 16/1 | 4 | — |
| *1030[6]* | **At the Savoy (IRE) (42)** (MrsLStubbs) **5-8-12** MMcAndrew(23) (s.s: a bhd) | 1½ | **21** | 12/1 | 1 | — |
| 1196[19] | **Legal Brief (42)** (JSWainwright) **4-8-12b** DRMcCabe(15) (a bhd) | 28 | **22** | 20/1 | — | — |
| 1500[8] | **Boost (38)** (MrsNMacauley) **4-8-8b** AMackay(19) (prom: rdn 5f out: wknd qckly) | 5 | **23** | 33/1 | — | — |
| | | | | (SP 171.3%) | **23 Rn** | |

**2m 6.9** (4.40) CSF £71.87 CT £830.86 TOTE £7.20: £1.40 £3.00 £5.00 £2.60 (£34.90) Trio Not won; £159.04 to 21/6/96 OWNER Mr M. Rhodes (UTTOXETER) BRED Mrs H. MacFarlane

WEIGHT FOR AGE 3yo-12lb

Bt in 4,000gns. Northern Motto clmd MBielby £6,000

**1665 Mazilla**, below form in recent races, looked in great shape and landed quite a touch with the visor removed. (6/1)

**1633 Comedy River**, taken to the centre of the course for daylight halfway up the straight, suddenly hit his stride and was closing right on the line. (9/1)

**521 Shuttlecock** has run well here in the past but took his losing run to nineteen after briefly looking dangerous. (16/1)

**1669 Northern Motto**, dropped in trip and class, found very little daylight between horses in the last couple of furlongs before staying on once extricated. (5/1)

**1821 Greek Gold (IRE)** lost half a dozen places soon after the start when appearing to clip the heels of a rival soon after the start, but soon recovered. The incident prevented him from getting to the head of affairs until early in the straight which can not have helped his chances. (12/1)

**Doodies Pool (IRE)** ran much better than of late, but is a hard horse to win with. (20/1)

## 2057 E.B.F. MAIDEN STKS (2-Y.O) (Class D)

7-00 (7-01) **6f 15y** £3,450.50 (£1,034.00: £497.00: £228.50) Stalls: High GOING minus 0.46 sec per fur (F)

| | Horse | | Pos | SP | RR | SF |
|---|---|---|---|---|---|---|
| $1774^{2}$ | **Close Relative (IRE)** (RCharlton) **2-9-0** TSprake(7) (plld hrd: trckd ldrs: rdn over 1f out: led ins fnl f: r.o) | — | **1** | $2/1^{2}$ | 78 | 27 |
| | **Juwwi** (MajorWRHern) **2-9-0** RHills(6) (neat: str: bkwd: led: edgd lft & hdd ins fnl f: unable qckn) | ½ | **2** | $5/4^{1}$ | 77+ | 26 |
| | **Canadian Fantasy** (MJohnston) **2-9-0** JFanning(2) (leggy: bit bkwd: w ldrs tl rdn & btn appr fnl f) | 4 | **3** | 12/1 | 66 | 15 |
| | **Chingachgook** (PWHarris) **2-9-0** GHind(5) (lengthy: scope: dwlt: hdwy 2f out: rdn & no imp fnl f) | s.h | **4** | $9/4^{3}$ | 66 | 15 |
| | **Mutabari (USA)** (DMorley) **2-9-0** BThomson(3) (leggy: unf: s.i.s: bhd tl r.o fnl f) | nk | **5** | 12/1 | 65 | 14 |
| $1467^{5}$ | **Lily Jaques** (PFICole) **2-8-9** CRutter(4) (chsd ldrs: rdn over 2f out: sn btn) | 12 | **6** | 14/1 | 29 | — |
| | **Nominator Lad** (BAMcMahon) **2-9-0** SSanders(1) (str: bit bkwd: chsd ldrs 4f) | 1½ | **7** | 33/1 | 30 | — |

(SP 133.5%) **7 Rn**

**1m 12.8** (2.30) CSF £5.87 TOTE £3.60: £2.00 £1.20 (£5.10) OWNER Mr Wafic Said (BECKHAMPTON) BRED Addison Racing Ltd Inc

**1774 Close Relative (IRE)** made his experience and the stands' rail count but not without a struggle. He failed to find as much as looked likely once let down and carried his head rather high as he quickened, the first two rapidly putting daylight between themselves and the rest. (2/1)

**Juwwi** tended to edge right, away from off the rail, on the way to post. He hung left, away from the rail at the business end of the race, but for which he might have won. (5/4: op 3/1)

**Canadian Fantasy** looked to need this, but showed plenty of speed until lack of an outing took its toll. There are races to be won with him. (12/1: 8/1-14/1)

**Chingachgook** showed a fine action on the way to post. Missing a beat as the stalls opened, he did enough to suggest that he is worth bearing in mind. (9/4)

**Mutabari (USA)** looked green on the way down and missed the break, but he showed something by staying on late in the day. (12/1)

**1467 Lily Jaques** raced towards the centre of the track and was one of the first beaten. (14/1)

## 2058 KPMG PASAS H'CAP (0-70) (4-Y.O+) (Class E)

7-30 (7-31) **1m 54y** £3,366.00 (£1,008.00: £484.00: £222.00) Stalls: Low GOING minus 0.46 sec per fur (F)

| | Horse | | Pos | SP | RR | SF |
|---|---|---|---|---|---|---|
| $1406^{9}$ | **Q Factor (62)** (DHaydnJones) **4-9-7**(3) SDrowne(8) (lw: w ldr: chal over 1f out: sn rdn: led nr fin) | — | **1** | 14/1 | 66 | 60 |
| | **Yoxall Lodge (60)** (HJCollingridge) **6-9-8** MRimmer(6) (led: rdn over 1f out: hdd & unable qckn nr fin) | hd | **2** | 14/1 | 64 | 58 |
| $1173^{7}$ | **Roi de la Mer (IRE) (61)** (JAkehurst) **5-9-9** SSanders(12) (plld hrd: hdwy 3f out: nt clr run & plld out ins fnl f: nrst fin) | ½ | **3** | $11/4^{2}$ | 64 | 58 |
| 1902* | **Helios (59)** (NJHWalker) **8-9-4**(3) JStack(11) (a.p: rdn & ev ch over 3f out: btn appr fnl f) | 1¾ | **4** | $5/2^{1}$ | 58 | 52 |
| | **Coven Moon (35)** (DMorris) **6-7-11v**ow1 DaleGibson(5) (bit bkwd: prom: rdn 2f out: sn btn) | 1½ | **5** | 20/1 | 32 | 25 |
| $1838^{6}$ | **Zahran (IRE) (40)** (JMBradley) **5-8-2** GHind(9) (chsd ldrs 5f: sn btn) | nk | **6** | 10/1 | 36 | 30 |
| $1473^{10}$ | **Castel Rosselo (66)** (RHarris) **6-10-0** AMackay(13) (lw: in tch: rdn 2f out: r.o ins fnl f) | s.h | **7** | 16/1 | 62 | 56 |
| $1821^{2}$ | **Zaaleff (USA) (50)** (BHanbury) **4-8-12b** RHills(1) (lw: stdd s: plld hrd: hdwy after 2f: one pce fnl 3f) | 6 | **8** | 11/2 | 34 | 28 |
| $1886^{5}$ | **Commander Glen (IRE) (57)** (MrsJRRamsden) **4-9-5b** KFallon(7) (lw: stdd s: effrt 3f out: nt trble ldrs: eased fnl f) | 1¼ | **9** | $9/2^{3}$ | 39 | 33 |
| $1414^{13}$ | **Our Tom (52)** (JWharton) **4-9-0b** BThomson(3) (lw: chsd ldrs: rdn 3f out: sn btn) | 6 | **10** | 20/1 | 22 | 16 |
| *1085*$^{10}$ | **Lucy's Gold (34)** (MJRyan) **5-7-10** FNorton(4) (hld up: a bhd) | 10 | **11** | 25/1 | — | — |
| $1860^{8}$ | **Ballysokerry (IRE) (34)** (JParkes) **5-7-5b**1(5) CAdamson(2) (prom over 4f) | 3 | **12** | 33/1 | — | — |

(SP 133.4%) **12 Rn**

**1m 42.3** (1.00) CSF £188.90 CT £661.45 TOTE £20.80: £5.90 £4.80 £1.40 (£154.40) Trio £128.10; £126.38 to 21/6/96 OWNER Mr H. G. Collis (PONTYPRIDD) BRED A. Sofroniou and H. Collis

LONG HANDICAP Coven Moon 7-9 Lucy's Gold 7-2 Ballysokerry (IRE) 7-4

**649 Q Factor** was not winning out of turn and had run the odd good race on this fast ground. Never out of the first two, she won a protracted battle in the dying strides. (14/1)

**Yoxall Lodge** won on his debut two years ago and almost repeated the feat. Looking well in his coat and pretty fit, he tried to make all and only just failed. (14/1)

**1173 Roi de la Mer (IRE)** was the unlucky horse of the race. Threading his way through in the straight, he was sat behind the two principals waiting for the gap that never came. Pulled to the outside in the last half-furlong, he had little time to respond. His turn must be close at hand. (11/4: 9/2-5/2)

**1902* Helios** failed in his hat-trick bid, but remains in good form, only giving best entering the final furlong. (5/2)

**Coven Moon** looked to need this, but ran well when pressure was applied. (20/1)

**1838 Zahran (IRE)** has a lack of gears which was soon exposed. (10/1)

**1886 Commander Glen (IRE)** (9/2: 3/1-5/1)

## 2059 TATTERSALLS MAIDEN AUCTION STKS (2-Y.O) (Class E)

8-00 (8-00) **5f 13y** £3,275.00 (£980.00: £470.00: £215.00) Stalls: High GOING minus 0.46 sec per fur (F)

| | Horse | | Pos | SP | RR | SF |
|---|---|---|---|---|---|---|
| $1834^{5}$ | **Eye Shadow** (BJMeehan) **2-7-12** CRutter(5) (a.p: rdn to ld wl ins fnl f) | — | **1** | $6/1^{3}$ | 69 | 21 |
| $1822^{6}$ | **Suite Factors** (JAGlover) **2-8-5** SDWilliams(6) (wnt rt s: led tl hdd & unable qckn wl ins fnl f) | ¾ | **2** | 8/1 | 74 | 26 |
| $1683^{5}$ | **Aybeegirl** (MrsJCecil) **2-8-3** RHills(7) (lw: w ldr over 3f) | 1¾ | **3** | $9/4^{1}$ | 66 | 18 |
| $1871^{9}$ | **Victoria's Dream (IRE)** (MRChannon) **2-7-13**(5) PPMurphy(9) (hmpd sn after s: chsd ldrs: no hdwy fnl 2f) | 1¼ | **4** | $6/1^{3}$ | 63 | 15 |
| | **Trulyfan (IRE)** (RAFahey) **2-8-1** GHind(4) (lt-f: unf: s.i.s: hdwy over 1f out: nrst fin) | nk | **5** | $6/1^{3}$ | 59 | 11 |
| $1842^{7}$ | **The Four Isles** (DHaydnJones) **2-8-4** FNorton(1) (lw: bhd tl r.o appr fnl f) | 1¼ | **6** | 7/1 | 58 | 10 |
| $1842^{10}$ | **Hever Golf Stormer (IRE)** (TJNaughton) **2-8-10** TSprake(8) (hmpd sn after s: prom 3f) | hd | **7** | 14/1 | 64 | 16 |
| | **Sharazamataz** (WJHaggas) **2-8-1** SSanders(10) (w'like: bit bkwd: outpcd) | 5 | **8** | $5/1^{2}$ | 39 | — |
| $1513^{13}$ | **No Class** (RHarris) **2-7-13** AMackay(3) (in tch: rdn over 2f out: sn btn) | 1½ | **9** | 14/1 | 32 | — |
| $1537^{9}$ | **Chasetown Flyer (USA)** (RHollinshead) **2-8-5**ow1 KFallon(2) (edgd lft thrght: nvr nr ldrs) | 1¾ | **10** | 7/1 | 38 | — |

(SP 139.7%) **10 Rn**

**59.9 secs** (1.30) CSF £57.73 TOTE £7.80: £3.00 £2.10 £1.10 (£27.30) Trio £49.80 OWNER Mrs D. E. Blackshaw (UPPER LAMBOURN) BRED Mrs Amanda Skiffington

**1834 Eye Shadow** is rather small and hardly took the eye on the way down, but she found a decisive turn of foot to gain the day. (6/1)

**1822 Suite Factors** showed plenty of early pace, despite steering none too straight a course, and should win a race. (8/1: 6/1-9/1)

**1683 Aybeegirl** all but bolted on the way to post and raced freely until dropping away in the final furlong. (9/4)

**Victoria's Dream (IRE)** did not lose much ground when hampered by the runner-up early in the race, but could not make her presence felt, despite racing on the favoured stands'-side rail. (6/1)

**Trulyfan (IRE)** made eyecatching late progress and should come on plenty for this. (6/1)
**1408 The Four Isles**, from what was probably the worst draw, showed enough to suggest that he possesses some ability. (7/1)
**Sharazamataz** (5/1: op 2/1)
**No Class** (14/1: op 25/1)

## 2060 SHADWELL STUD SERIES APPRENTICE H'CAP (0-70) (3-Y.O+) (Class F)

8-30 (8-30) **1m 6f 15y** £2,742.00 (£762.00: £366.00) Stalls: Low GOING minus 0.46 sec per fur (F)

| Form | Horse | Dist | Pos | SP | RR | SF |
|---|---|---|---|---|---|---|
| 1063[5] | **Durham (48)** (RSimpson) **5-8-7b** AimeeCook(5) (a.p: led over 3f out: edgd lft over 1f out: comf) | — | **1** | 12/1 | 62 | 35 |
| 1835[2] | **Royal Circus (37)** (PRWebber) **7-7-10** CAdamson(7) (lw: led over 10f: swtchd ins fnl f: r.o) | 1¼ | **2** | 3/1[2] | 50 | 23 |
| | **Atherton Green (IRE) (52)** (JAGlover) **6-8-8**(3) JEdmunds(10) (bit bkwd: plld hrd: in tch: r.o wl appr fnl f) | 6 | **3** | 14/1 | 58 | 31 |
| 1802[5] | **Cuango (IRE) (59)** (RHollinshead) **5-9-4** FLynch(6) (trckd ldrs: rdn over 3f out: no imp) | 1 | **4** | 9/4[1] | 64 | 37 |
| 1472[3] | **Howqua River (44)** (PWChapple-Hyam) **4-7-10**(7) RCody-Boutcher(9) (hdwy 5f out: wknd over 3f out) | hd | **5** | 6/1 | 49 | 22 |
| 1640[6] | **Cliburnel News (IRE) (56)** (AStreeter) **6-9-1** RHavlin(2) (lw: hdwy over 3f out: no imp fnl 2f) | nk | **6** | 10/1 | 60 | 33 |
| 1529[6] | **Opaque (69)** (LMCumani) **4-9-9**(5) RFfrench(1) (lw: hld up: rdn 4f out: nvr nr to chal) | 12 | **7** | 4/1[3] | 60 | 33 |
| 1414[7] | **Paronomasia (37)** (JLHarris) **4-7-5**(5) PDoe(3) (bhd fnl 6f) | 1¼ | **8** | 33/1 | 26 | — |
| | **Leap in the Dark (IRE) (55)** (MissLCSiddall) **7-8-7**(7)ow18 TSiddall(8) (lw: prom 10f) | 10 | **9** | 16/1 | 33 | — |
| 1497[12] | **Friendly Dreams (IRE) (54)** (PTDalton) **3-7-5b**[1](5) JBramhill(4) (plld hrd: hdwy after 5f: drvn & btn 3f out) | nk | **10** | 40/1 | 31 | — |
| | | | | (SP 124.8%) | | **10 Rn** |

**3m 2.2** (3.70) CSF £48.50 CT £490.39 TOTE £10.70: £2.30 £1.20 £2.90 (£16.50) Trio £74.90 OWNER The Secret Partnership (WELLINGTON) BRED Highclere Stud Ltd
LONG HANDICAP Royal Circus 7-8 Paronomasia 7-3 Leap in the Dark (IRE) 6-13 Friendly Dreams (IRE) 6-0
WEIGHT FOR AGE 3yo-17lb
STEWARDS' ENQUIRY Brahmhill susp. 28-29/6 & 1-2/7/96 (excessive use of the whip).
**1063 Durham** was given a peach of a ride and scored for only the second ever time in his life, and the first on the level. Proving a handful to stop from leaning on the runner-up once in front, he never really had to race. (12/1)
**1835 Royal Circus** looked something of a good thing for this on his recent Warwick run and beat the rest convincingly, but was unlucky to run into a rival who possesses far more ability than he cares to show on a rare going day. (3/1: tchd 7/1)
**Atherton Green (IRE)**, probably being prepared for hurdles, ran a cracker, making up good late ground, and is no forlorn hope on the level off this sort of mark. (14/1)
**1802 Cuango (IRE)**, ridden much closer to the pace than usual, found nothing once let down. (9/4)
**1529 Opaque** (4/1: op 5/2)

## 2061 OLD LENTON H'CAP (0-70) (3-Y.O) (Class E)

9-00 (9-03) **1m 54y** £3,548.00 (£1,064.00: £512.00: £236.00) Stalls: Low GOING minus 0.46 sec per fur (F)

| Form | Horse | Dist | Pos | SP | RR | SF |
|---|---|---|---|---|---|---|
| 1773[7] | **Mazcobar (69)** (PJMakin) **3-9-7** SSanders(3) (chsd ldrs: led over 1f out: sn rdn clr) | — | **1** | 5/1 | 80 | 44 |
| 1671[3] | **Tissue of Lies (USA) (68)** (MJohnston) **3-9-6** JFanning(5) (lw: a.p: led over 2f out tl over 1f out: one pce) | 3 | **2** | 3/1[1] | 73 | 37 |
| 1654[3] | **Sound Check (57)** (BJMeehan) **3-8-9b** MTebbutt(2) (led over 5f: kpt on) | 1½ | **3** | 9/2[3] | 59 | 23 |
| 1638[11] | **Richard House Lad (53)** (RHollinshead) **3-8-0**(5)ow7 FLynch(10) (lw: hld up & bhd: hdwy 3f out: wandered & no imp appr fnl f) | hd | **4** | 20/1 | 55 | 12 |
| | **Indira (55)** (HCandy) **3-8-7** CRutter(9) (bit bkwd: chsd ldrs: rdn & no hdwy fnl 3f) | ½ | **5** | 8/1 | 56 | 20 |
| 1692[5] | **Rhythmic Ball (52)** (TRWatson) **3-7-13**(5) CAdamson(1) (chsd ldrs: effrt over 2f out: btn over 1f out) | 1½ | **6** | 25/1 | 50 | 14 |
| 1702[5] | **Rocky Stream (45)** (RMWhitaker) **3-7-11**ow1 NCarlisle(11) (hld up: hdwy over 3f out: nvr able to chal) | ½ | **7** | 20/1 | 42 | 5 |
| 1500[14] | **Florrie'm (45)** (JLHarris) **3-7-11** JQuinn(13) (lw: bhd tl sme hdwy fnl 2f) | nk | **8** | 33/1 | 42 | 6 |
| 1669[8] | **Falcon's Flame (USA) (53)** (MrsJRRamsden) **3-8-5**ow2 KFallon(8) (hld up: hdwy 4f out: edgd rt 2f out: sn btn) | 2 | **9** | 4/1[2] | 46 | 8 |
| 2000[9] | **Sea Danzig (69)** (PHowling) **3-9-7** AMcGlone(4) (prom: rdn over 4f out: sn btn) | 1½ | **10** | 10/1 | 59 | 23 |
| 1780[W] | **Ebony Boy (55)** (JWharton) **3-8-7** SDWilliams(6) (lw: chsd ldrs 5f) | 3½ | **11** | 12/1 | 38 | 2 |
| *1780[7]* | ***Mellow Master (60)*** *(NJHWalker)* ***3-8-9**(3)* *JStack(7) (Withdrawn not under Starter's orders: ref to ent stalls)* | | **W** | 16/1 | — | — |
| | | | | (SP 129.9%) | | **11 Rn** |

**1m 43.7** (2.40) CSF £20.48 CT £69.04 TOTE £6.60: £2.20 £1.10 £2.60 (£10.30) Trio £10.90 OWNER Mr A. W. Schiff (MARLBOROUGH) BRED A. W. Schiff
LONG HANDICAP Rocky Stream 7-8
**1312* Mazcobar**, brought back to a mile, scored decisively and looks a decent handicapper in the making. (5/1)
**1671 Tissue of Lies (USA)** looked a picture of health and moved to post well, but lacks the turn of foot to provide the killer punch at this trip. (3/1)
**1654 Sound Check** adopted front-running tactics for the first time since winning at Warwick last July, but could only plug on at the same pace once headed. (9/2)
**1526 Richard House Lad** is inconsistent and rather hung fire when his chance came. (20/1)
**Indira** looked in need of this and never posed a threat. (8/1)
**1477 Falcon's Flame (USA)** (4/1: 3/1-9/2)

T/Plpt: £389.50 (24.15 Tckts). T/Qdpt: £66.60 (12.06 Tckts). Dk

# 1525-RIPON (R-H) (Good to firm)
# Wednesday June 19th

WEATHER: overcast WIND: almost nil

## 2062 MASHAM MEDIAN AUCTION MAIDEN STKS (3-Y.O) (Class E)

2-15 (2-16) **1m 2f** £3,069.10 (£929.80: £454.40: £216.70) Stalls: High GOING minus 0.47 sec per fur (F)

| Form | Horse | Dist | Pos | SP | RR | SF |
|---|---|---|---|---|---|---|
| 1508[12] | **Russian Rose (IRE)** (AHide) **3-8-9** MTebbutt(9) (in tch: hdwy over 3f out: rn green: styd on to ld ins fnl f) | — | **1** | 14/1 | 68 | 18 |
| 677[6] | **Rusk** (JPearce) **3-9-0** MWigham(5) (chsd ldrs: outpcd ent st: hdwy 3f out: led over 1f out: hdd & no ex ins fnl f) | 1½ | **2** | 10/11[1] | 71 | 21 |
| 1530[4] | **Secondment (67)** (LMCumani) **3-9-0b** OUrbina(6) (led: rdn over 2f out: hdd over 1f out: sn btn) | 3 | **3** | 5/1[3] | 66 | 16 |

$1614^{9}$ **South Wind** (MrsJCecil) **3-8-9** NDay(4) (lw: chsd ldrs: hmpd appr st: one pce fnl 4f)....3½ **4** 6/1 55 5
$1614^{10}$ **Sandicliffe (USA) (60)** (BWHills) **3-8-9** BThomson(1) (lw: chsd ldrs: 2nd & rdn over 4f out: wknd fnl 3f)....6 **5** 9/2 $^{2}$ 46 —
$1797^{8}$ **So Keen** (ABailey) **3-9-0** SDWilliams(7) (mid div & rdn ½-wy: n.d)....2 **6** 20/1 47 —
**Ballet de Cour** (CWCElsey) **3-9-0** ACulhane(2) (unf: s.i.s: sn wl bhd)....11 **7** 50/1 30 —
**Landfall** (JGFitzGerald) **3-9-0** JQuinn(3) (w'like: bit bkwd: dwlt: a wl bhd)....4 **8** 20/1 23 —
**Countess of Cadiz (USA)** (TKersey) **3-8-9** DRMcCabe(8) (unf: bkwd: b: dwlt: a wl bhd)....4 **9** 150/1 12 —
(SP 120.3%) **9 Rn**

**2m 8.2** (4.70) CSF £27.43 TOTE £19.90: £3.70 £1.10 £1.80 (£20.60) Trio £39.50 OWNER Ash Partnership (NEWMARKET) BRED Edward Keyes

**Russian Rose (IRE)**, down the field in a couple of better maidens, found the strong pace to her liking and, despite looking about, won convincingly. (14/1)
**677 Rusk**, after a two-month lay-off, looked fit but was off the bit a long way and, despite battling on, was picked off in the closing stages. (10/11: 4/5-Evens)
**1530 Secondment** attempted to gallop his rivals into the ground, but he was always tending to hang into the rail in the straight and was out on his feet approaching the last furlong. (5/1: 11/4-11/2)
**South Wind** tried to lay up with the strong pace and, after getting chopped for room on the home turn, was treading water thereafter. (6/1)
**Sandicliffe (USA)**, very much on his toes beforehand, raced with every chance until she suddenly ran out of fuel approaching the last quarter-mile. (9/2)
**So Keen** was not given a hard time and should improve a bit for this. (20/1)

## 2063 RICHMOND CONDITIONS STKS (2-Y.O) (Class C)

2-50 (2-50) **6f** £4,549.06 (£1,702.54: £832.77: £358.35: £160.68: £81.60) Stalls: Low GOING minus 0.47 sec per fur (F)

SP RR SF

$1148^{2}$ **Rich In Love (IRE)** (CACyzer) **2-8-6** MFenton(3) (s.i.s: hdwy ½-wy: led ins fnl f: r.o)....— **1** 10/1 73 19
$1362^{2}$ **Young Bigwig (IRE)** (JBerry) **2-8-11** DeanMcKeown(7) (led: hung lft u.p ent fnl f: sn hdd: kpt on)....1 **2** 5/1 $^{3}$ 75 21
$1699^{4}$ **Bolero Boy** (MWEasterby) **2-8-10(5)** GParkin(1) (lw: w ldr: edgd rt most of wy: rdn 2f out: nt qckn ins fnl f)....2 **3** 11/4 $^{2}$ 74 20
1831* **Alpine Time (IRE)** (DRLoder) **2-8-12** DRMcCabe(5) (sn chsng ldrs: rdn ½-wy: wknd fnl 2f)....9 **4** 4/5 $^{1}$ 47 —
1858* **Aztec Traveller** (MJRyan) **2-8-13** NDay(6) (lw: prom tl outpcd fr ½-wy)....3 **5** 16/1 40 —
1779* **Pandiculation** (EWeymes) **2-9-1** JQuinn(2) (lw: chsd ldrs: outpcd ½-wy: no imp after)....3½ **6** 12/1 33 —
(SP 121.6%) **6 Rn**

**1m 12.8** (2.30) CSF £55.27 TOTE £8.00: £2.40 £2.00 (£15.20) OWNER Mr R. M. Cyzer (HORSHAM) BRED Floors Farming

**1148 Rich In Love (IRE)**, despite a slow start, won in good style and is obviously on the upgrade. (10/1)
**1362 Young Bigwig (IRE)** has plenty of speed, but his attitude leaves something to be desired when put under pressure. Blinkers might help. (5/1)
**1699 Bolero Boy** was always feeling the fast ground, hanging off the rail, and will do better with some cut. (11/4)
**1831* Alpine Time (IRE)** was never really firing here and would seem to have passed her best. (4/5: Evens-11/10)
**1858* Aztec Traveller** found this company far too hot from halfway. (16/1)
**1779* Pandiculation** would probably be much happier on easier ground. (12/1)

## 2064 ACC CO-OP H'CAP (0-80) (3-Y.O+) (Class D)

3-25 (3-26) **5f** £3,640.00 (£1,102.00: £538.00: £256.00) Stalls: Low GOING minus 0.47 sec per fur (F)

SP RR SF

$1646^{2}$ **Insider Trader (73)** (MrsJRRamsden) **5-9-2v(7)** TFinn(3) (lw: a chsng ldrs: rdn to ld ins fnl f: styd on)....— **1** 7/2 $^{1}$ 80 44
*$1971^{8}$* **Kalar (48)** (DWChapman) **7-7-9(3)** DWright(2) (lw: cl up: led ½-wy: hdd & nt qckn ins fnl f)....1¼ **2** 10/1 51 15
$1889^{P}$ **Able Sheriff (50)** (MWEasterby) **4-8-0b** DaleGibson(10) (hld up: hdwy 2f out: ch 1f out: kpt on)....s.h **3** 10/1 53 17
$1781^{3}$ **Here Comes a Star (77)** (JMCarr) **8-9-13** ACulhane(4) (lw: pushed along & hdwy ½-wy: ev ch 1f out: nt qckn)....s.h **4** 4/1 $^{2}$ 80 44
1777* **Sally Slade (78)** (CACyzer) **4-10-0** MFenton(1) (lw: hdwy ½-wy: styd on: nrst fin)....1½ **5** 9/2 $^{3}$ 76 40
$1547^{3}$ **Silk Cottage (57)** (RMWhitaker) **4-8-2v(5)** RHavlin(8) (lw: hld up: hdwy ½-wy: nt qckn fnl f)....d.h **5** 20/1 55 19
$1974^{6}$ **Shadow Jury (60)** (DWChapman) **6-8-10b** DeanMcKeown(7) (cl up tl wknd appr fnl f)....¾ **7** 9/2 $^{3}$ 56 20
$1848^{8}$ **Formidable Liz (56)** (MDHammond) **6-8-6** JQuinn(6) (bhd tl sme late hdwy)....nk **8** 14/1 51 15
$1708^{11}$ **Allwight Then (IRE) (66)** (REPeacock) **5-8-11(5)** ADaly(5) (led to ½-wy: sn rdn: wknd wl over 1f out)....4 **9** 20/1 48 12
$1889^{7}$ **First Option (46)** (RBastiman) **6-7-10** FNorton(11) (t: chsd ldrs to ½-wy: sn wknd)....¾ **10** 20/1 25 —
*$1492^{16}$* **Kustom Kit (IRE) (65)** (BAMcMahon) **3-8-4(5)** LNewton(9) (a outpcd & bhd)....s.h **11** 33/1 44 2
(SP 120.7%) **11 Rn**

**59.7 secs** (1.30) CSF £36.14 CT £303.73 TOTE £3.40: £2.10 £4.20 £3.10 (£26.30) Trio £93.50 OWNER Mrs H. M. Carr (THIRSK) BRED Lord Victor Matthews

LONG HANDICAP First Option 7-9
WEIGHT FOR AGE 3yo-6lb

**1646 Insider Trader** had the visor back on here which he needs, and had the race set up for him with plenty of early pace. He swooped to conquer inside the final furlong. (7/2)
**1545 Kalar** looked a picture and will surely not be long in getting back on the winning trail. (10/1: 8/1-12/1)
**1646* Able Sheriff** made a miraculous recovery after pulling up lame last time, and attempted to come from off the pace, but could not quicken enough inside the final furlong. (10/1)
**1781 Here Comes a Star** had to work hard to improve from halfway and, having got there too soon, cried enough inside the final furlong. (4/1)
**1777* Sally Slade** looks like she needs some cut and failed to get into this, despite staying on. (9/2)
**1547 Silk Cottage** takes a strong hold and never quite finds enough when pressure is applied. (20/1)
**1974 Shadow Jury** showed plenty of speed and keeps running well without winning, so should not be written off yet. (9/2)
**1848 Formidable Liz** caught the eye finishing well, and is worth keeping in mind. (14/1)

## 2065 CITY OF RIPON H'CAP (0-90) (3-Y.O) (Class C)

4-00 (4-01) **1m** £7,035.00 (£2,130.00: £1,040.00: £495.00) Stalls: High GOING minus 0.47 sec per fur (F)

SP RR SF

1872* **Dancing Image (72)** (IABalding) **3-8-5(5)** 6x MartinDwyer(6) (plld hrd: trckd ldrs: led 3f out: edgd lft 2f out: all out)....— **1** 4/6 $^{1}$ 85 35
$1820^{3}$ **Menoo Hal Batal (USA) (78)** (MRStoute) **3-9-2** DeanMcKeown(5) (lw: hld up & bhd: hdwy whn swtchd lft 2f out: swtchd rt over 1f out: r.o wl towards fin)....nk **2** 7/1 90 40
$1820^{4}$ **Kilvine (83)** (LMCumani) **3-9-7** OUrbina(4) (lw: hld up: outpcd over 3f out: styd on appr fnl f)....5 **3** 5/1 $^{2}$ 85 35

| | | | | | |
|---|---|---|---|---|---|
| 1185[3] | **Kazimiera (IRE) (72)** (CWCElsey) **3-8-10** JQuinn(2) (lw: cl up tl outpcd fnl f) ½ | **4** | 14/1 | 73 | 23 |
| 1666[7] | **Russian Rascal (IRE) (67)** (TDEasterby) **3-8-5** BThomson(3) (lw: led tl hdd 3f out: wknd over 2f out) 6 | **5** | 10/1 | 56 | 6 |
| 1648[3] | **Royal Ceilidh (IRE) (75)** (DenysSmith) **3-8-10**(3) CTeague(1) (trckd ldrs: outpcd over 3f out: n.d after) 3 | **6** | 6/1 3 | 58 | 8 |
| | | | (SP 119.2%) | | **6 Rn** |

**1m 39.7** (2.00) CSF £6.37 TOTE £1.50: £1.10 £2.10 (£3.50) OWNER The Queen (KINGSCLERE) BRED The Queen
**1872* Dancing Image** would have been better suited by a stronger pace and, in front plenty long enough, only just got home. (4/6)
**1820 Menoo Hal Batal (USA)** obviously has his problems as he wears a net-muzzle, but he was unlucky here as he switched just as the leader hung left and, then having to switch again, had lost valuable ground. (7/1)
**1820 Kilvine** was putting in his best work when the race was over, and may need a bit further. (5/1)
**1185 Kazimiera (IRE)** had her chances but, when the pressure was on in the last three furlongs, had little to offer. (14/1)
**1363 Russian Rascal (IRE)**, after racing freely out in front, soon gave up when headed. (10/1)

## 2066 BEAUMONTS INSURANCE LADIES' DERBY H'CAP (0-70) (3-Y.O+) (Class E)
4-35 (4-37) **1m 4f 60y** £3,000.85 (£908.80: £443.90: £211.45) Stalls: Low GOING minus 0.47 sec per fur (F)

| | | | SP | RR | SF |
|---|---|---|---|---|---|
| 2024[2] | **Kings Cay (IRE) (46)** (THCaldwell) **5-9-7**(4) MrsPWharfe(9) (in tch: swtchd 3f out: led ins fnl f: styd on strly) — | **1** | 8/1 | 61 | 39 |
| 1676[3] | **Bold Elect (42)** (EJAlston) **8-9-7** MissPRobson(13) (hdwy ½-wy: chsng ldrs 4f out: kpt on wl fnl f) 2½ | **2** | 7/1 2 | 54 | 32 |
| 1837[5] | **Outstayed Welcome (59)** (MJHaynes) **4-10-10** MissYHaynes(12) (led tl hdd over 2f out: kpt on wl) hd | **3** | 8/1 | 71 | 49 |
| 1778[2] | **Gold Blade (49)** (JPearce) **7-10-0** MrsLPearce(3) (lw: a.p: led over 2f out tl ins fnl f: no ex) hd | **4** | 5/2 1 | 61 | 39 |
| 1637[2] | **Philmist (48)** (CWCElsey) **4-9-13b** MissAElsey(5) (a.p: ev ch over 2f out: wknd appr fnl f) 2 | **5** | 12/1 | 57 | 35 |
| 1763[2] | **Calder King (63)** (JLEyre) **5-10-10v**(4) MissDJJones(14) (lost tch appr st: styd on fnl 3f: n.d) 10 | **6** | 15/2 3 | 59 | 37 |
| 1839[3] | **Bayrak (USA) (70)** (MJRyan) **6-11-7** MissJAllison(11) (b: chsd ldrs tl wknd fnl 3f) 3½ | **7** | 14/1 | 61 | 39 |
| 1866[5] | **Heathyards Magic (IRE) (58)** (MDods) **4-10-9** MrsDKettlewell(7) (lost pl appr st: sme hdwy over 2f out: n.d) nk | **8** | 33/1 | 49 | 27 |
| 1953[5] | **All the Joys (43)** (CACyzer) **5-9-4**(4)ow3 MissAWilcox(16) (sn bhd: sme hdwy fnl 3f) 3 | **9** | 10/1 | 30 | 5 |
| 1778[7] | **Ice Magic (35)** (FJYardley) **9-8-10v**(4) MissSYardley(15) (b.nr hind: chsd ldrs tl wknd fnl 3f) 5 | **10** | 100/1 | 16 | — |
| 1196[5] | **Master Ofthe House (55)** (MDHammond) **10-10-6** MissMCarson(1) (s.i.s: n.d) 3 | **11** | 16/1 | 32 | 10 |
| | **Dancing Destiny (51)** (RBastiman) **4-9-12**(4)ow1 MissRBastiman(4) (prom to st) hd | **12** | 25/1 | 27 | 4 |
| 1803[3] | **Sloe Brandy (35)** (JWharton) **6-8-10**(4) MissHCarrington(8) (s.i.s: hdwy appr st: sn wknd) 1½ | **13** | 12/1 | 10 | — |
| 1821[D] | **Ring of Vision (IRE) (50)** (MrsMReveley) **4-10-1** MissHDudgeon(2) (s.i.s: hdwy & rn wd st: sn wknd) s.h | **14** | 7/1 2 | 24 | 2 |
| | **Never so Brave (39)** (JDBethell) **6-9-0**(4) MrsDWilkinson(10) (s.i.s: hdwy & rn wd st: sn btn) 7 | **15** | 50/1 | 4 | — |
| *1641[7]* | ***Arabian Heights (49)*** (MrsJRRamsden) **3-9-0** MissERamsden(6) (Withdrawn not under Starter's orders: veterinary advice at s) | **W** | 10/1 | — | — |
| | | | (SP 143.4%) | | **15 Rn** |

**2m 38.9** (4.90) CSF £64.64 CT £444.74 TOTE £16.00: £4.10 £2.70 £3.50 (£33.90) Trio £117.80 OWNER Mr R. S. G. Jones (WARRINGTON) BRED The Woodhaven Stud in Ireland
LONG HANDICAP Sloe Brandy 8-13 Ice Magic 7-7
WEIGHT FOR AGE 3yo-14lb
**2024 Kings Cay (IRE)** is a tough sort and really stays. That won him the day. (8/1)
**1676 Bold Elect** took some persuading to get going, but he did stay on particularly well at the end. Although it is almost three years since he won, he still retains the ability. (7/1)
**993 Outstayed Welcome** won this last year but, off a mark 13lb higher this time, was just found out, despite a valiant effort. (8/1)
**1778 Gold Blade** loves these type of races but, after trying hard, was not quite good enough this time. (5/2)
**1637 Philmist** again ran a decent race, but she found the effort beyond her in the last couple of furlongs. (12/1)
**1763 Calder King** got left way behind approaching the straight and had an impossible task thereafter. (15/2)

## 2067 LEVY BOARD H'CAP (0-80) (3-Y.O) (Class D)
5-10 (5-11) **1m 4f 60y** £3,758.30 (£1,138.40: £556.20: £265.10) Stalls: Low GOING minus 0.47 sec per fur (F)

| | | | SP | RR | SF |
|---|---|---|---|---|---|
| 1773[4] | **Eagle Canyon (IRE) (72)** (BHanbury) **3-9-5** PBloomfield(12) (hld up: hdwy 3f out: led ins fnl f: r.o) — | **1** | 12/1 | 79 | 46 |
| 1833* | **One Pound (66)** (BWHills) **3-8-13** OUrbina(5) (hld up: effrt 3f out: r.o wl fnl f: t.m.t.d) 1 | **2** | 7/2 2 | 72 | 39 |
| 1887* | **Etterby Park (USA) (49)** (MJohnston) **3-7-10** 5x JQuinn(6) (cl up: led 4f out: qcknd 3f out: hdd & no ex ins fnl f) ¾ | **3** | 11/8 1 | 54 | 21 |
| 1973[3] | **Batoutoftheblue (60)** (WWHaigh) **3-8-7** JTate(10) (lw: bhd: hdwy on outside 3f out: nrst fin) 1¾ | **4** | 11/1 | 62 | 29 |
| 1498[9] | **Umberston (IRE) (54)** (LMCumani) **3-7-8**(7) JoHunnam(2) (lw: a.p: one pce fnl 3f) 1½ | **5** | 25/1 | 55 | 22 |
| 1647[7] | **Dirab (64)** (TDBarron) **3-8-11** NConnorton(11) (hld up: nvr plcd to chal) nk | **6** | 16/1 | 64 | 31 |
| 1631[5] | **Chocolate Ice (73)** (CACyzer) **3-9-6** MFenton(7) (bhd: sme hdwy 2f out: n.d) 3 | **7** | 12/1 | 69 | 36 |
| 1477[3] | **Forest Fantasy (50)** (JWharton) **3-7-11** FNorton(9) (led 2f: cl up tl wknd fnl 3f) 2 | **8** | 16/1 | 44 | 11 |
| 1361[6] | **Karisma (IRE) (74)** (DenysSmith) **3-9-7** DeanMcKeown(4) (chsd ldrs tl outpcd fnl 3f) 2 | **9** | 12/1 | 65 | 32 |
| 693[9] | **Jean Pierre (57)** (JPearce) **3-8-4**ow2 NDay(1) (s.i.s: a bhd) 7 | **10** | 20/1 | 39 | 4 |
| 1200[6] | **Jackson Park (62)** (TDEasterby) **3-8-9** ACulhane(3) (lw: led after 2f tl hdd 4f out: wknd 3f out) 1¾ | **11** | 16/1 | 42 | 9 |
| 1600* | **Daira (62)** (JDBethell) **3-8-6**(3) SDrowne(8) (hdwy appr st: sn prom: wknd fnl 3f) nk | **12** | 8/1 3 | 41 | 8 |
| | | | (SP 133.1%) | | **12 Rn** |

**2m 36.9** (2.90) CSF £56.65 CT £92.32 TOTE £16.00: £2.90 £1.80 £1.60 (£17.90) Trio £19.60 OWNER Mr Clinton Lane Jnr (NEWMARKET) BRED Mount Coote Stud
STEWARDS' ENQUIRY Hunnam susp. 28/6/96 (excessive use of the whip).
**1773 Eagle Canyon (IRE)**, stepping up in trip, got it really well and getting first run on the runner-up won him the day. (12/1)
**1833* One Pound**, not made enough of here, finished well but had been set an impossible task. He will make amends and should stay still further. (7/2)
**1887* Etterby Park (USA)** tried to pinch this by quickening in the home straight, but he had to admit defeat when collared inside the final furlong. He will find other opportunities. (11/8)
**1973 Batoutoftheblue** just gallops and stays and had an impossible task from the home turn here, but did well to finish so close. His turn will come as he tries longer distances. (11/1)
**Umberston (IRE)** had her chances, but proved too slow when pressure was applied. (25/1)
**1647 Dirab** never got into this. (16/1)

## 2068 BEDALE LIMITED STKS (0-70) (4-Y.O+) (Class E)
5-40 (5-40) **1m 2f** £2,918.95 (£883.60: £431.30: £205.15) Stalls: High GOING minus 0.47 sec per fur (F)

| | | | SP | RR | SF |
|---|---|---|---|---|---|
| 1450[6] | **Another Time (70)** (SPCWoods) **4-8-11** DBiggs(1) (hld up: hdwy 3f out: rdn to ld ins fnl f: r.o) — | **1** | 15/8 2 | 79 | 37 |

1417[3] **Break the Rules (68)** (MrsMReveley) **4-8-11** ACulhane(4) (lw: cl up: led over 2f out tl ins fnl f: hrd rdn & kpt on) ....1 **2** 13/2 77 35
*1448** **Sharpical (70)** (SirMarkPrescott) **4-8-13** JQuinn(5) (lw: hld up: effrt over 2f out: sn chsng ldrs: nt qckn fnl f) ....1 **3** 13/8[1] 78 36
1116[8] **Floating Line (70)** (EJAlston) **8-8-11** MWigham(2) (lw: led tl hdd over 2f out: wknd appr fnl f) ....3 **4** 9/2[3] 71 29
1841[6] **Guesstimation (USA) (63)** (JPearce) **7-8-11** NDay(3) (chsd ldrs tl outpcd fnl 2½f) ....5 **5** 10/1 63 21
(SP 113.5%) **5 Rn**

**2m 6.0** (2.50) CSF £12.52 TOTE £2.20: £1.50 £1.80 (£11.80) OWNER Mr D. Sullivan (NEWMARKET) BRED W. G. Barker

**1450 Another Time**, in a slowly-run event, had the best turn of foot when it mattered. (15/8)

**1417 Break the Rules** always held a good position but, when the pressure was on, he was inclined to hang right and failed to quicken enough. (13/2)

**1448* Sharpical** looked to be going best of all for much of the trip but, when it came down to a sprint, was found wanting. (13/8)

**Floating Line** set a steady pace and was then outsprinted in the final two furlongs. He was beaten when hit in the face by another jockey's whip. (9/2: op 7/1)

**1841 Guesstimation (USA)** found this company too hot once the pace was really on in the final two and a half furlongs. (10/1)

T/Plpt: £194.80 (51.07 Tckts). T/Qdpt: £33.30 (25.73 Tckts). AA

# 2050-ASCOT (R-H) (Good to firm)
## Thursday June 20th

WEATHER: overcast WIND: almost nil

### 2069 RIBBLESDALE STKS (Gp 2) (3-Y.O F) (Class A)

2-30 (2-31) **1m 4f** £61,426.00 (£23,007.05: £11,066.03: £4,835.92) Stalls: Low GOING minus 0.25 sec per fur (GF)

SP RR SF

1750a[2] **Tulipa (USA)** (AFabre,France) **3-8-8** SGuillot(10) (leggy: hld up: hdwy to ld over 1f out: hung rt: rdn out cl home) ....— **1** 15/2 111 63
1249a* **Key Change (IRE)** (JOxx,Ireland) **3-8-8** CRoche(6) (leggy: scope: s.i.s: pushed along ½-wy: gd hdwy over 1f out: r.o wl nr fin) ....nk **2** 13/2[3] 111 63
1335[2] **Shemozzle (IRE) (102)** (JHMGosden) **3-8-8** MHills(2) (a.p: led over 2f out tl over 1f out: rallied fnl f) ....1¼ **3** 12/1 109 61
1335[5] **Alzabella (IRE)** (JWHills) **3-8-8** TQuinn(4) (lost tch after 4f: hdwy u.p over 3f out: styd on appr fnl f) ....7 **4** 66/1 100 52
1111* **Bathilde (IRE)** (MRStoute) **3-8-8** MJKinane(9) (trckd ldrs: effrt & rdn over 2f out: sn outpcd) ....2½ **5** 9/2[2] 96 48
1108* **Magnificient Style (USA) (106)** (HRACecil) **3-8-8** PatEddery(3) (b: led tl over 2f out: sn rdn & wknd) ....1½ **6** 13/8[1] 94 46
1895* **Alessandra (95)** (BWHills) **3-8-8** DHolland(8) (lw: prom: rdn over 3f out: wknd fnl 2f) ....1½ **7** 40/1 92 44
1249a[4] **Ceirseach (IRE)** (JSBolger,Ireland) **3-8-8** KJManning(7) (leggy: prom tl wknd over 3f out: sn t.o) ....10 **8** 20/1 79 31
1409* **Ninotchka (USA) (98)** (JLDunlop) **3-8-8** WCarson(1) (swtg: hld up: effrt 4f out: sn rdn: btn over 2f out) ....¾ **9** 10/1 78 30
1108[5] **Sea Spray (IRE) (100)** (PWChapple-Hyam) **3-8-8** JReid(5) (hld up: rdn 4f out: sn lost tch: t.o) ....13 **10** 20/1 61 13
(SP 111.6%) **10 Rn**

**2m 31.41** (1.41) CSF £48.92 TOTE £9.70: £2.30 £2.20 £2.20 (£26.00) Trio £66.20 OWNER Sheikh Mohammed (CHANTILLY) BRED Fares Farm Inc

STEWARDS' ENQUIRY Guillot susp. 29/6 - 1/7/96 (incorrect use of whip).

**IN-FOCUS: Fabre did not miss the target with this his only runner of the meeting.**

**1750a Tulipa (USA)**, a lightly-made challenger form France, winning her first race on such fast ground, would have won more easily had she not hung towards Shemozzle after taking command. The narrow margin of her success is no reflection of her superiority. (15/2)

**1249a* Key Change (IRE)**, who has been in top form back home in Ireland, took a long time to pick up after missing the beat at the start, and her determined late challenge only just failed. (13/2)

**1335 Shemozzle (IRE)**, in the firing line all the way, proved a tough challenger to shake off after being collared below the distance, and success at this trip is merely delayed. (12/1)

**1335 Alzabella (IRE)** lacks experience as yet and this first attempt at the trip, she was trying for the first time on ground she has not encountered before, proved too much of a burden. (66/1)

**1111* Bathilde (IRE)** is bred to need this trip but failed to respond when asked to quicken early in the straight, and was always being comfortably held. (9/2)

**1108* Magnificient Style (USA)** adopted tactics that were successful at York, but over this longer trip, she was galloping on the spot after being collared soon after straightening up, and lack of stamina seemed to be the main cause. (13/8)

### 2070 NORFOLK STKS (Gp 3) (2-Y.O) (Class A)

3-05 (3-06) **5f** £25,720.00 (£9,736.00: £4,768.00: £2,176.00) Stalls: Centre GOING minus 0.25 sec per fur (GF)

SP RR SF

1118* **Tipsy Creek (USA)** (BHanbury) **2-8-12** WRyan(11) (b.hind: lw: hld up far side: hdwy to ld over 1f out: rdn out) ....— **1** 7/2[1] 104 52
1565a* **Raphane (USA)** (CCollins,Ireland) **2-8-12** KDarley(7) (cmpt: lw: led: drifted lft fnl 2f: hdd over 1f out: rdn & r.o wl: unlucky) ....1 **2** 9/1 101 49
698* **Muchea** (MRChannon) **2-8-12** RHughes(6) (lw: led stands' side: rdn & sltly hmpd 1f out: kpt on) ....1¾ **3** 6/1[2] 95 43
1510[2] **Roman Imp (IRE)** (APJarvis) **2-8-12** MJKinane(5) (lw: trckd ldrs stands' side: rdn & r.o fnl f) ....½ **4** 8/1[3] 94 42
1525* **Grand Lad (IRE)** (RWArmstrong) **2-8-12** RHills(8) (lw: prom far side: edgd lft 2f out: sn rdn: one pce) ....s.h **5** 8/1[3] 93 41
1519[2] **Darb Alola (USA)** (MRStoute) **2-8-12** PatEddery(4) (lw: dwlt: racd stands' side: effrt & hrd rdn wl over 1f out: nt pce to chal) ....½ **6** 8/1[3] 92 40
1143[2] **Arethusa** (RHannon) **2-8-7** MRoberts(3) (lw: racd stands' side: effrt ½-wy: outpcd fnl 2f) ....1¾ **7** 16/1 81 29
1766* **Granny's Pet** (PFICole) **2-8-12** TQuinn(9) (lw: racd far side: sn outpcd) ....2 **8** 8/1[3] 80 28
1699* **For Your Eyes Only** (TDEasterby) **2-8-12** WCarson(10) (b: chsd ldrs far side: sn rdn along & outpcd) ....2½ **9** 6/1[2] 72 20
1519* **Raven Master (USA)** (PWChapple-Hyam) **2-8-12** JReid(1) (lw: stumbled s: rdn along ½-wy: sn outpcd) ....1 **10** 14/1 69 17
(SP 117.8%) **10 Rn**

**61.37 secs** (1.37) CSF £32.34 TOTE £4.80: £1.90 £3.70 £2.60 (£25.60) Trio £49.70 OWNER Mr Abdullah Ali (NEWMARKET) BRED Airlie Stud

**1118* Tipsy Creek (USA)**, a very mature colt bred for speed, gained control on the far side over a furlong out and, driven out strongly, ran out a comfortable winner. (7/2)

**1565a* Raphane (USA)**, a very speedy colt who has already won in Ireland, had the speed to make the running but with the field splitting into two groups, he drifted from one side of the track to the other. The fact that he was only just beaten stamps him as a very unlucky loser, and he will next run in the Molecomb Stakes at Goodwood. (9/1)

**698* Muchea**, slightly impeded when the runner-up edged across him approaching the final furlong, battled on willingly to the finish and he should not have much trouble picking up a race when he gets the easier ground that he needs. (6/1)
**1510 Roman Imp (IRE)**, very fractious at the start, ran extremely well to finish on the heels of the leaders, and looks sure to win his share of races. (8/1)
**1525* Grand Lad (IRE)** veered off a true line in company with the runner-up two furlongs out and, despite giving of his best, was unable to deliver his challenge on ground that could prove to be too lively for him. (8/1)
**1519 Darb Alola (USA)** did not hit the traps and though he did try hard to get into the action below the distance, failed to muster the pace to do so. (8/1: 6/1-9/1)

## 2071 GOLD CUP STKS (Gp 1) (4-Y.O+) (Class A)

3-45 (3-46) **2m 4f** £118,872.00 (£44,087.60: £20,843.80: £8,716.60) Stalls: Low GOING minus 0.25 sec per fur (GF)

| | | | | SP | RR | SF |
|---|---|---|---|---|---|---|
| 1128* | **Classic Cliche (IRE) (120)** (SbinSuroor) **4-9-0** MJKinane(7) (lw: hld up in tch: chal on bit 2f out: led wl over 1f out: drvn out) | — | **1** | 3/1[2] | 119+ | 66 |
| 1482* | **Double Trigger (IRE) (119)** (MJohnston) **5-9-2** JWeaver(2) (lw: led tl wl over 1f out: sn hrd rdn: styd on) | 1½ | **2** | 1/2[1] | 118 | 67 |
| 1397a[2] | **Nononito (FR)** (JLesbordes,France) **5-9-2** SGuillot(4) (hld up: hdwy over 2f out: rdn & no ex appr fnl f) | 3 | **3** | 16/1[3] | 115 | 64 |
| 1397a[3] | **Always Aloof (USA) (106)** (MRStoute) **5-9-2** WCarson(5) (hld up & bhd: effrt ent st: styd on u.p fnl 2f) | 1½ | **4** | 16/1[3] | 114 | 63 |
| 1428[2] | **Latahaab (USA) (87)** (RAkehurst) **5-9-2** TQuinn(3) (lw: chsd ldr: hrd drvn 2f out: one pce) | ¾ | **5** | 50/1 | 79 t | 63 |
| 1091[5] | **Upper Mount Clair (67)** (CEBrittain) **6-8-13** BDoyle(6) (hld up & bhd: pushed along 5f out: wknd ent st: t.o) | 13 | **6** | 66/1 | 66 t | 49 |
| 1482[2] | **Assessor (IRE) (105)** (RHannon) **7-9-2** RHughes(1) (b: trckd ldrs: rdn over 3f out: sn btn: t.o) | 5 | **7** | 20/1 | 65 t | 48 |

(SP 111.6%) **7 Rn**

**4m 23.2** (3.20) CSF £4.64 TOTE £3.60: £1.70 £1.30 (£1.80) OWNER Godolphin (NEWMARKET) BRED Lord Victor Matthews in Ireland
WEIGHT FOR AGE 4yo-2lb
OFFICIAL EXPLANATION **Double Trigger (IRE): returned to the unsaddling enclosure without his off-fore plate.**
IN-FOCUS: **Interestingly, Classic Cliche's victory was the first in the Gold Cup by an English Classic winner since Ocean Swell in 1945.**
**1128* Classic Cliche (IRE)** proved himself at the very top when he won last year's St Leger, but this was his initial attempt at such a trip and he showed just how versatile he really is by robbing last year's champion of his crown. (3/1: 2/1-100/30)
**1482* Double Trigger (IRE)** lost his off fore shoe during the race but did his utmost to make all, but courage was not enough to hold off such a talented rival as the winner, in an all out duel to the finish. (1/2)
**1397a Nononito (FR)** handled this fast ground surprisingly well and ran up to his mark. Connections believe he is so much better when the conditions are testing. (16/1)
**1397a Always Aloof (USA)** did not impress going to post but he stayed on doggedly in the closing stages and was far from disgraced in defeat. (16/1)
**1428 Latahaab (USA)** turned in by far his best race yet and was only shaken off below the distance. After such a bold effort, it would seem his days as a handicapper are numbered. (50/1)

## 2072 CORK AND ORRERY STKS (Gp 3) (3-Y.O+) (Class A)

4-20 (4-21) **6f** £34,400.00 (£13,032.50: £6,391.25: £2,926.25) Stalls: Centre GOING minus 0.25 sec per fur (GF)

| | | | | SP | RR | SF |
|---|---|---|---|---|---|---|
| 1628* | **Atraf (109)** (DMorley) **3-8-6** WCarson(2) (trckd ldrs stands' side: rdn to ld wl ins fnl f: r.o) | — | **1** | 12/1 | 120 | 69 |
| 1566a[2] | **Catch The Blues (IRE)** (APO'Brien,Ireland) **4-8-10v[1]** CRoche(14) (racd far side: bhd & rdn over 2f out: gd hdwy fnl f: fin wl) | 1 | **2** | 20/1 | 114 | 70 |
| 943* | **Watch Me (IRE) (92)** (RHannon) **3-8-3** MHills(1) (racd stands' side: overall ldr tl wl ins fnl f) | nk | **3** | 20/1 | 114 | 63 |
| 1483[3] | **Woodborough (USA) (116)** (PWChapple-Hyam) **3-8-10** JReid(10) (a in tch stands' side: rdn over 1f out: r.o wl) | nk | **4** | 5/1[1] | 120 | 69 |
| 1621[2] | **Iktamal (USA) (110)** (EALDunlop) **4-8-13** PaulEddery(3) (lw: racd stands' side: hdwy u.p wl over 1f out: nrst fin) | ¾ | **5** | 11/2[2] | 114 | 70 |
| 1075* | **Isla Del Rey (USA)** (SbinSuroor) **4-8-10** SGuillot(15) (led far side tl ins fnl f) | 2½ | **6** | 14/1 | 104 | 60 |
| 1800[8] | **Venture Capitalist (112)** (DNicholls) **7-9-3b** AlexGreaves(9) (swtg: hld up stands' side: effrt wl over 1f out: nt pce to chal) | ¾ | **7** | 20/1 | 109 | 65 |
| 939[6] | **Dance Sequence (USA) (110)** (MRStoute) **3-8-11** PatEddery(17) (swtg: far side: effrt & rdn over 1f out: nt rch ldrs) | ¾ | **8** | 9/1 | 108 | 57 |
| 1629[2] | **My Melody Parkes (105)** (JBerry) **3-8-3** JCarroll(12) (chsd ldr far side 4f) | ¾ | **9** | 20/1 | 98 | 47 |
| 1431[2] | **April The Eighth (100)** (BWHills) **3-8-6** DHolland(18) (chsd ldrs far side over 4f) | 1¼ | **10** | 33/1 | 98 | 47 |
| 1056a[2] | **Bouche Bee (USA) (93)** (JEHammond,France) **4-8-10** KFallon(16) (lw: racd far side: nvr gng pce of ldrs) | 1¼ | **11** | 25/1 | 91 | 47 |
| 1483[9] | **Cool Jazz (114)** (CEBrittain) **5-9-3** MJKinane(7) (lw: racd stands' side: outpcd fr ½-wy) | 1¼ | **12** | 16/1 | 95 | 51 |
| 1332[2] | **Montendre (102)** (MMcCormack) **9-8-13** WJO'Connor(11) (racd stands' side: sn pushed along: n.d) | ½ | **13** | 33/1 | 90 | 46 |
| 1621* | **Rambling Bear (113)** (MBlanshard) **3-8-6** JQuinn(5) (s.i.s: sn rcvrd to trck ldrs stands' side: wknd wl over 1f out) | hd | **14** | 6/1[3] | 90 | 39 |
| 1800[2] | **Branston Abby (IRE) (108)** (MJohnston) **7-8-10** MRoberts(13) (dwlt: a outpcd) | nk | **15** | 8/1 | 86 | 42 |
| 926[12] | **Tumbleweed Ridge (110)** (BJMeehan) **3-8-10b[1]** BDoyle(8) (lw: stands' side: outpcd fnl 2f) | 5 | **16** | 16/1 | 79 | 28 |
| 1441[9] | **Keepers Dawn (IRE) (100)** (RFJohnsonHoughton) **3-8-3** KDarley(4) (lw: outpcd) | 7 | **17** | 66/1 | 54 | 3 |

(SP 123.8%) **17 Rn**

**1m 14.07** (0.07) CSF £205.70 TOTE £13.30: £3.90 £7.40 £4.40 (£233.60) Trio £2349.30 OWNER Mr Hamdan Al Maktoum (NEWMARKET)
BRED R. T. and Mrs Watson
WEIGHT FOR AGE 3yo-7lb
OFFICIAL EXPLANATION **Rambling Bear: the jockey reported that the colt was very wound up at the start and never going in the race.**
**1628* Atraf** confirmed the promise shown at Newmarket and he is definitely on the way up. Another furlong should be well within his reach. (12/1)
**1566a Catch The Blues (IRE)**, towards the rear and off the bridle a long way out, burst through to take charge of the far side group 200 yards out and, forging clear, was unfortunate to have the winner under the stands' rails matching her for pace. (20/1)
**943* Watch Me (IRE)** set a scorching gallop on the stands' side that had burned off most of her challengers entering the final furlong, but the progressive winner had enough in hand to take her measure nearing the line. She looks to be very much on the upgrade. (20/1)
**1483 Woodborough (USA)** appreciated this return to a slightly longer trip, but he did not find top gear until too late and will be more at home when he can get his toe in. (5/1)
**1621 Iktamal (USA)** does from time to time just give himself too much to do, and though he went into overdrive inside the final furlong, found the line arriving too soon. (11/2)
**1075* Isla Del Rey (USA)** held the call on the far side and remained there until overtaken by the runner-up just inside the last furlong. This would seem to be her right trip. (14/1)

## 2073 CHESHAM STKS (Listed) (2-Y.O) (Class A)

4-55 (4-56) **7f** £24,508.75 (£7,420.00: £3,622.50: £1,723.75) Stalls: Centre GOING minus 0.25 sec per fur (GF)

| | Horse | Dist | Pos | SP | RR | SF |
|---|---|---|---|---|---|---|
| | **Shamikh** (SbinSuroor) **2-8-12** RHills(4) (str: scope: hld up: hdwy to ld over 1f out: drvn out) | — | **1** | 8/1$^{3}$ | 96+ | 38 |
| 1896$^{3}$ | **State Fair** (BWHills) **2-8-12** MHills(3) (hld up: hdwy 2f out: rdn & r.o wl fnl f) | 1 | **2** | 12/1 | 94+ | 36 |
| 1130* | **Belgravia** (PFICole) **2-9-0** TQuinn(9) (lw: a.p: ev ch 2f out: sn rdn & sltly outpcd: rallied fnl f) | ½ | **3** | 6/4$^{1}$ | 95 | 37 |
| | **Party Romance (USA)** (BHanbury) **2-8-12** WRyan(7) (str: scope: bit bkwd: s.s: hdwy 3f out: rdn & r.o ins fnl f) | ½ | **4** | 12/1 | 91+ | 33 |
| 1795$^{6}$ | **Dalmeny Dancer** (BJMeehan) **2-8-12** BDoyle(8) (led tl over 1f out: kpt on one pce) | nk | **5** | 33/1 | 91 | 33 |
| 1851* | **Green Jewel** (RHannon) **2-8-7** MRoberts(6) (prom tl rdn & wknd appr fnl f) | 3 | **6** | 9/1 | 79 | 21 |
| 1419* | **Marathon Maid** (RAFahey) **2-8-11** ACulhane(2) (prom tl wknd wl over 1f out) | hd | **7** | 12/1 | 83 | 25 |
| | **Bob The Broker (IRE)** (PJFlynn,Ireland) **2-9-0** MJKinane(5) (str: scope: plld hrd: chsd ldrs tl rdn & lost pl over 2f out) | 5 | **8** | 15/2$^{2}$ | 74 | 16 |
| 1892$^{2}$ | **Barrier King (USA)** (PFICole) **2-8-12** RHughes(1) (prom over 4f) | 3 | **9** | 20/1 | 65 | 7 |
| | **Soura (USA)** (PAKelleway) **2-8-7** KFallon(11) (unf: scope: trckd ldrs 5f: sn lost tch) | 3 | **10** | 33/1 | 54 | — |
| 1339$^{3}$ | **Strathmore Clear** (GLewis) **2-8-12** PatEddery(10) (s.i.s: drvn along 3f out: grad wknd) | nk | **11** | 12/1 | 58 | — |
| 1815* | **Supercal** (DRCElsworth) **2-8-11** WCarson(12) (a rr div) | ¾ | **12** | 12/1 | 55 | — |
| | | | | (SP 122.0%) | **12 Rn** | |

**1m 30.57** (3.37) CSF £91.93 TOTE £8.90: £2.70 £4.00 £1.60 (£61.50) Trio £41.80 OWNER Mr Hamdan Al Maktoum (NEWMARKET) BRED Shadwell Estate Company Limited

**IN-FOCUS: The first running of this event at seven furlongs, and the success of the debutant Shamikh, could herald a trend of unexposed sorts being kept for this.**

**Shamikh**, a strongly-made debutant with plenty of stamina in his breeding, powered through to take it up approaching the final furlong and soon made sure the prize was his. (8/1)

**1896 State Fair** could have found this race coming just too soon, but he stayed on strongly inside the distance and looks a ready made winner. (12/1)

**1130* Belgravia**, up with the pace in the centre of the track, got tapped for speed below the distance but he was back into his stride again inside the final 100 yards, and can improve on this. (6/4)

**Party Romance (USA)** almost belied his burly appearance with a promising, staying-on performance after losing ground at the start and he could be out of the top drawer. (12/1)

**1795 Dalmeny Dancer** blazed a trail from the start but could not withstand the strong-challenging winner, but he did not go down without a fight. (33/1)

**1851* Green Jewel**, taking a big step up in class, pressed the leaders and was in with a live chance until being shaken off inside the final furlong. (9/1)

## 2074 KING GEORGE V H'CAP (0-105) (3-Y.O) (Class B)

5-30 (5-31) **1m 4f** £26,215.00 (£7,945.00: £3,885.00: £1,855.00) Stalls: Low GOING minus 0.25 sec per fur (GF)

| | Horse | Dist | Pos | SP | RR | SF |
|---|---|---|---|---|---|---|
| 1175* | **Samraan (USA) (94)** (JLDunlop) **3-9-3** TQuinn(17) (lw: hld up in tch: hdwy to chal 1f out: kpt on u.p to ld nr fin) | — | **1** | 14/1 | 105 | 74 |
| 1305* | **Private Song (USA) (87)** (RCharlton) **3-8-10** PatEddery(19) (led: rdn 2f out: ct wl ins fnl f) | ½ | **2** | 8/1$^{2}$ | 97 | 66 |
| 1712* | **Harbour Dues (89)** (LadyHerries) **3-8-12** PaulEddery(2) (hld up & bhd: hdwy over 2f out: styd on strly towards fin) | 2 | **3** | 6/1$^{1}$ | 97 | 66 |
| 1798* | **Pleasant Surprise (96)** (MJohnston) **3-9-5** JWeaver(14) (lw: chsd ldr: rdn over 2f out: one pce appr fnl f) | 2½ | **4** | 20/1 | 100 | 69 |
| 1175$^{2}$ | **Nador (91)** (DRLoder) **3-9-0** RHughes(4) (trckd ldrs: outpcd 4f out: styd on again fnl 2f) | ½ | **5** | 16/1 | 95 | 64 |
| 1002$^{D}$ | **Montecristo (75)** (RGuest) **3-7-12** JQuinn(8) (hld up & bhd: hdwy on ins fnl 2f: nvr nrr) | hd | **6** | 12/1 | 79 | 48 |
| 1771$^{9}$ | **Warning Reef (84)** (MRChannon) **3-8-2**$^{(5)}$ PPMurphy(15) (hld up: hdwy & sltly hmpd 3f out: kpt on appr fnl f) | 1 | **7** | 33/1 | 86 | 55 |
| 1666$^{4}$ | **Serendipity (FR) (84)** (JLDunlop) **3-8-7** MJKinane(9) (prom tl rdn & wknd over 1f out) | 1 | **8** | 14/1 | 85 | 54 |
| 1711* | **Male-Ana-Mou (IRE) (87)** (DRCElsworth) **3-8-10** MRoberts(20) (hld up: hdwy over 4f out: 7th & styng on whn hmpd 3f out) | ½ | **9** | 16/1 | 87 | 56 |
| 1195* | **A Chef Too Far (75)** (RRowe) **3-7-7**$^{(5)}$ MBaird(13) (trckd ldrs: rdn over 3f out: wknd 2f out) | 3 | **10** | 25/1 | 71 | 40 |
| 1666* | **Gold Disc (USA) (90)** (BWHills) **3-8-13** DHolland(3) (a in rr: t.o) | 16 | **11** | 14/1 | 65 | 34 |
| 1711$^{5}$ | **Illuminate (79)** (JARToller) **3-8-2** SSanders(18) (lw: hld up: effrt 4f out: wknd over 2f out: t.o) | 5 | **12** | 12/1 | 47 | 16 |
| 1175$^{6}$ | **Warbrook (90)** (IABalding) **3-8-13** KDarley(10) (lw: trckd ldrs: 8th whn hmpd & lost pl 3f out: t.o) | 1½ | **13** | 33/1 | 56 | 25 |
| 1090$^{2}$ | **Get Away With It (IRE) (80)** (MRStoute) **3-8-3v**$^{1}$ WCarson(6) (lw: hld up: hdwy 5f out: rdn over 3f out: sn wknd: t.o) | 1¼ | **14** | 8/1$^{2}$ | 45 | 14 |
| 1669* | **Orinoco River (USA) (86)** (PWChapple-Hyam) **3-8-9v** JReid(1) (trckd ldrs: rdn 5f out: carried wd ent st: sn bhd: t.o) | 4 | **15** | 16/1 | 45 | 14 |
| 1782* | **Arctic Fancy (USA) (81)** (PWHarris) **3-8-4** GHind(5) (dwlt: hdwy 5f out: wkng whn hmpd 3f out: t.o) | 21 | **16** | 16/1 | 12 | — |
| 1656$^{3}$ | **Shenango (IRE) (80)** (GWragg) **3-8-3** MHills(7) (hld up: a in rr: t.o) | 3½ | **17** | 20/1 | 7 | — |
| 1656* | **Count Basie (88)** (HRACecil) **3-8-11** WRyan(12) (trckd ldrs: 6th & drvn along whn slipped & almost fell 3f out: t.o) | ¾ | **18** | 14/1 | 14 | — |
| 1476* | **Migwar (98)** (LMCumani) **3-9-7** KFallon(16) (lw: hld up: effrt whn bdly hmpd 3f out: eased: t.o) | 17 | **19** | 10/1$^{3}$ | 1 | — |
| 1687* | **Traceability (80)** (SCWilliams) **3-8-0**$^{(3)}$ MHenry(11) (mid div tl lost pl ½-wy: t.o) | dist | **20** | 33/1 | — | — |
| | | | | (SP 133.4%) | **20 Rn** | |

**2m 31.11** (1.11) CSF £118.61 CT £698.77 TOTE £17.70: £3.90 £2.50 £2.00 £3.90 (£92.80) Trio £175.00 OWNER Mr K. M. Al-Mudhaf (ARUNDEL) BRED Mrs Afaf A. Al Essa

**1175* Samraan (USA)** had to work hard to wear down the long time leader, and it was possibly due to the ground being much faster than he really requires. (14/1)

**1305* Private Song (USA)** produced a very game attempt to make all in this first handicap, and he certainly did not deserve to be touched off in the dying strides. (8/1)

**1712* Harbour Dues** came from another county to reach his final placing and he had set himself an impossible task. (6/1)

**1798* Pleasant Surprise** did not stride out to the start and was without the blinkers he wore when successful at Haydock. Keeping tabs on the leader, he just could not get past him and with the weight taking its toll, had run his race approaching the final furlong. (20/1)

**1175 Nador**, under hard driving and going backwards before the home straight, looked destined to finish in the pack but stayed on strongly again once he got his second wind. (16/1)

**1002 Montecristo** tried for a run up the inner once in the straight but found the inevitable trouble and could not make his presence felt. (12/1)

**1106 Warning Reef** did not fare badly on ground much too lively for him. (33/1)

**1711 Illuminate** (12/1: op 20/1)
**1656* Count Basie** tracked the leaders but was being bustled along when he stumbled and almost fell three furlongs out and that put paid to his chance. (14/1)

T/Jkpt: Not won; £155,565.21 to Ascot 21/6/96. T/Plpt: £504.80 (210.7 Tckts). T/Qdpt: £54.30 (122.58 Tckts) IM

# 2062-RIPON (R-H) (Good to firm, Firm patches)
## Thursday June 20th
WEATHER: overcast WIND: almost nil

## 2075 NORTHALLERTON APPRENTICE (S) H'CAP (0-60) (3-Y.O+) (Class F)
7-00 (7-02) **1m** £2,837.60 (£798.60: £390.80) Stalls: High GOING minus 0.43 sec per fur (F)

| | | | | SP | RR | SF |
|---|---|---|---|---|---|---|
| 1638$^{2}$ | **Return To Brighton (45)** (JMBradley) **4-9-1** AEddery(15) (in tch: hdwy ½-wy: led ins fnl f: r.o) | — | 1 | 5/1$^{1}$ | 53 | 31 |
| 1546$^{7}$ | **Bedazzle (37)** (MBrittain) **5-8-7** GParkin(7) (hdwy ½-wy: ev ch ins fnl f: kpt on) | ¾ | 2 | 20/1 | 44 | 22 |
| 1847$^{7}$ | **Flyaway Blues (49)** (MrsMReveley) **4-9-5v** SCopp(10) (lw: hld up: effrt over 3f out: hrd rdn & kpt on: nt pce to chal) | ½ | 3 | 16/1 | 55 | 33 |
| 1596$^{4}$ | **Miss Zanzibar (49)** (RAFahey) **4-9-0**(5) RFfrench(20) (cl up: led over 3f out tl ins fnl f: no ex) | hd | 4 | 11/1 | 54 | 32 |
| 1474$^{2}$ | **Move Smartly (IRE) (55)** (FHLee) **6-9-8**(3) JDennis(5) (bhd: hdwy 3f out: styd on: nvr able to chal) | 4 | 5 | 10/1$^{3}$ | 52 | 30 |
| 1691$^{8}$ | **Buddy's Friend (IRE) (40)** (RJRWilliams) **8-8-10** AimeeCook(14) (b.nr fore: styd on u.p fnl 3f: nrst fin) | nk | 6 | 14/1 | 37 | 15 |
| 1642$^{4}$ | **Chief's Lady (39)** (JMBradley) **4-8-4**(5) CLowther(12) (in tch: no imp fnl 3f) | ½ | 7 | 16/1 | 35 | 13 |
| 1890$^{13}$ | **Roseate Lodge (45)** (SEKettlewell) **10-9-1** MartinDwyer(6) (hdwy 3f out: nvr rchd ldrs) | 1 | 8 | 11/1 | 39 | 17 |
| 1162$^{8}$ | **Peacefull Reply (USA) (38)** (FHLee) **6-8-5**(3) JWilkinson(19) (cl up tl wknd fnl 2½f) | nk | 9 | 33/1 | 31 | 9 |
| *1812*$^{12}$ | **Komlucky (44)** (ABMulholland) **4-9-0b** CAdamson(17) (led: hung lft over 3f out: sn hdd & btn) | 2½ | 10 | 20/1 | 32 | 10 |
| 1908$^{7}$ | **Born A Lady (53)** (SRBowring) **3-8-10**(3) JEdmunds(11) (mid div & rn wd st: n.d after) | ½ | 11 | 14/1 | 40 | 8 |
| 1449$^{10}$ | **Pusey Street Boy (45)** (JRBosley) **9-8-10**(5) PDoe(8) (lw: b.hind: in tch tl outpcd fnl 3f) | nk | 12 | 12/1 | 32 | 10 |
| 1088$^{9}$ | **Roar on Tour (33)** (MrsMReveley) **7-7-12**(5) KSked(16) (chsd ldrs tl wknd over 2f out) | ¾ | 13 | 16/1 | 18 | — |
| 1830$^{3}$ | **Percy Parrot (45)** (RMWhitaker) **4-8-10**(5) PFredericks(13) (b: b.hind: cl up tl wknd over 3f out) | 1 | 14 | 7/1$^{2}$ | 28 | 6 |
| 2022$^{5}$ | **Prince Rudolf (IRE) (38)** (WGMTurner) **4-8-8** AmandaSanders(1) (bhd & rn wd st: n.d) | ¾ | 15 | 16/1 | 20 | — |
| 1610$^{10}$ | **Intrepid Fort (30)** (BWMurray) **7-7-11v**(3) JoHunnam(9) (a bhd) | nk | 16 | 33/1 | 11 | — |
| 1608$^{6}$ | **Chilly Looks (51)** (WLBarker) **3-8-8**(3) DSweeney(18) (prom tl wknd 3f out) | ½ | 17 | 20/1 | 31 | — |
| *1718*$^{13}$ | **Hi Rock (52)** (JNorton) **4-9-1**(7) AmyGosden(3) (bhd & rn wd st: n.d) | 2 | 18 | 25/1 | 28 | 6 |
| 1674$^{7}$ | **Waterlord (IRE) (40)** (DNicholls) **6-8-5**(5) JBramhill(4) (lw: bhd & rn wd ent st: n.d) | ½ | 19 | 10/1$^{3}$ | 15 | — |

(SP 132.6%) **19 Rn**

**1m 41.0** (3.30) CSF £97.18 CT £1437.43 TOTE £5.40: £1.30 £4.80 £5.30 £3.20 (£153.70) Trio Not won; £344.42 to 22/6/96 OWNER Mr D. A. Morris (CHEPSTOW) BRED D. A. Morris
WEIGHT FOR AGE 3yo-10lb
No bid
**1638 Return To Brighton** continued her improvement and responded to pressure. She scored in most determined fashion. (5/1)
**662 Bedazzle** came back to form here but despite struggling on under pressure, he could never quite match the winner. (20/1)
**998 Flyaway Blues** looked the part and was certainly given some strong assistance, but was never doing enough to get there. (16/1)
**1596 Miss Zanzibar** went for home a long way out and was inclined to edge left, and was finally tapped for toe in the final furlong. (11/1)
**1474 Move Smartly (IRE)** has not much of an action but keeps running well and, from his draw, this was not a bad effort. (10/1)
**Buddy's Friend (IRE)** has gone a long time without winning but he did finish well here, to show he does retain some ability. (14/1)

## 2076 GO EVENING RACING WITH THE DAILY TELEGRAPH MEDIAN AUCTION MAIDEN STKS (2-Y.O) (Class E)
7-30 (7-30) **5f** £3,028.15 (£917.20: £448.10: £213.55) Stalls: Low GOING minus 0.43 sec per fur (F)

| | | | | SP | RR | SF |
|---|---|---|---|---|---|---|
| 1849$^{5}$ | **Divide And Rule** (RHollinshead) **2-8-9**(5) DGriffiths(2) (lw: trckd ldrs: qcknd to ld ins fnl f) | — | 1 | 11/2$^{3}$ | 71 | 36 |
| 1705$^{4}$ | **Ballymote** (JBerry) **2-9-0** GCarter(3) (led: hmpd appr fnl f: hdd & no ex ins fnl f) | 2 | 2 | 5/2$^{2}$ | 65 | 30 |
| *1968*$^{2}$ | **Red Test (USA)** (WAO'Gorman) **2-9-0** EmmaO'Gorman(7) (lw: w ldr: hung lft most of wy: no ex ins fnl f) | 1¾ | 3 | 6/1 | 59 | 24 |
| 1525$^{6}$ | **Rum Lad** (JJQuinn) **2-9-0** NConnorton(9) (lw: in tch: outpcd ½-wy: kpt on wl towards fin) | s.h | 4 | 14/1 | 59 | 24 |
| | **Teddy's Bow (IRE)** (MWEasterby) **2-8-4**(5) GParkin(6) (leggy: sn outpcd & bhd: styd on appr fnl f) | 1 | 5 | 33/1 | 51 | 16 |
| | **Krystal Davey (IRE)** (TDBarron) **2-9-0** JFortune(5) (w'like: scope: dwlt: hdwy 2f out: nvr trbld ldrs) | s.h | 6 | 6/1 | 56 | 21 |
| 1036$^{8}$ | **Colonel's Pride** (RMWhitaker) **2-9-0** DeanMcKeown(1) (s.i.s: effrt ½-wy: no imp) | 1½ | 7 | 33/1 | 51 | 16 |
| | **Perpetual** (SirMarkPrescott) **2-8-9** GDuffield(8) (neat: bit bkwd: in tch: outpcd ½-wy: sn wknd) | 1½ | 8 | 2/1$^{1}$ | 41 | 6 |
| | **Strelitza (IRE)** (MWEasterby) **2-8-9** DaleGibson(4) (leggy: dwlt: n.d) | 1½ | 9 | 33/1 | 36 | 1 |

(SP 121.4%) **9 Rn**

**59.9 secs** (1.50) CSF £19.75 TOTE £8.50: £2.40 £1.20 £1.90 (£12.90) Trio £6.60 OWNER Mrs A. Mutch (UPPER LONGDON) BRED Mrs O. R. Mutch
**1849 Divide And Rule**, using more patient tactic this time, produced a lovely run to settle it inside the final furlong. (11/2)
**1705 Ballymote** takes quite a hold but does move particularly well, and after attempting to make all he was going nowhere when the third was hanging into him in the closing stases. (5/2: op 6/4)
**1968 Red Test (USA)** has a moderate action and just wanted to hang left in the race, but he has speed and if his problems are straightened out, there are certainly races to be won with him. (6/1)
**1525 Rum Lad** ran well and by the way he picked up at the end, better will be seen over further. (14/1)
**Teddy's Bow (IRE)** has an action that suggests easier ground will suit and, after getting completely outpaced, she did pick up well at the end. (33/1)
**Krystal Davey (IRE)** is a decent sort but has a poor action, nevertheless he showed some promise and was not knocked about. He should improve especially on easier ground. (6/1)
**Perpetual** looked in need of this and ran disappointingly, dropping away from halfway. (2/1)

## 2077 PRICE WATERHOUSE H'CAP (0-80) (3-Y.O+) (Class D)
8-00 (8-07) **1m 2f** £3,741.40 (£1,133.20: £553.60: £263.80) Stalls: High GOING minus 0.43 sec per fur (F)

| | | | | SP | RR | SF |
|---|---|---|---|---|---|---|
| 933$^{17}$ | **Rory (72)** (MrsJCecil) **5-9-5**(5) AmandaSanders(9) (trckd ldrs: led wl over 1f out: edgd lft: hld on wl) | — | 1 | 7/2$^{2}$ | 83 | 49 |
| 1698* | **Essayeffsee (57)** (MrsMReveley) **7-8-9** DHarrison(5) (lw: prom: outpcd over 2f out: r.o fnl f) | 1 | 2 | 3/1$^{1}$ | 66 | 32 |
| 1650$^{3}$ | **Dr Edgar (61)** (MDods) **4-8-13** FNorton(3) (lw: set slow pce: qcknd 3f out: hdd wl over 1f out: kpt on) | 1½ | 3 | 7/2$^{2}$ | 68 | 34 |

| | | | | SP | RR | SF |
|---|---|---|---|---|---|---|
| 1977[8] | **Pendolino (IRE) (44)** (MBrittain) **5-7-10b** LCharnock(1) (chsd ldrs: chal 3f out: wknd over 1f out) | 2 | **4** | 33/1 | 48 | 14 |
| 1504[8] | **Maftun (USA) (57)** (GMMoore) **4-8-9** JTate(8) (outpcd 4f out: styd on fnl 2f: n.d) | 2 | **5** | 25/1 | 58 | 24 |
| 1633[5] | **Bold Amusement (72)** (WSCunningham) **6-9-10** DeanMcKeown(7) (hld up: effrt over 2f out: no imp) | 1 | **6** | 13/2 | 71 | 37 |
| 649[11] | **Indonesian (IRE) (68)** (PCalver) **4-9-3**(3) NVarley(4) (pushed along 6f out: nvr trbld ldrs) | ½ | **7** | 12/1 | 66 | 32 |
| 1504[5] | **Le Khoumf (FR) (66)** (JMBradley) **5-9-1**(3) SDrowne(2) (trckd ldrs tl rdn & wknd over 2f out) | 8 | **8** | 5/1[3] | 51 | 17 |
| 1649[6] | **Karaylar (IRE) (54)** (WStorey) **4-8-6** JFanning(10) (wl bhd fnl 4f) | 9 | **9** | 25/1 | 25 | — |
| | ***Colway Rock (USA) (58)*** (DenysSmith) **6-8-10** JFortune(11) (Withdrawn not under Starter's orders: collapsed at s: dead) | | **W** | 33/1 | — | — |

(SP 120.7%) **9 Rn**

**2m 6.4** (2.90) CSF £14.08 CT £35.82 TOTE £4.60: £1.40 £1.40 £1.60 (£6.20) Trio £5.00 OWNER Mrs J. Cecil (NEWMARKET) BRED Lady Murless

LONG HANDICAP Pendolino (IRE) 7-9

**765 Rory,** given a chance by the Handicapper, won this messy event by getting first run and then battled on, despite showing a tendency to edge left. (7/2)

**1698* Essayeffsee** got outpaced when the tempo picked up but he did stay on at the end, albeit too late. He looks in really good form at present. (3/1)

**1650 Dr Edgar** moved poorly to post but ran well, setting a very moderate pace and then trying to pinch it in the straight, but was outpointed in the last couple of furlongs. (7/2)

**Pendolino (IRE)** ran much better and would seem to be coming right. (33/1)

**Maftun (USA)** looked slow when the pace increased, but to his credit he did keep on well at the end. (25/1)

**1633 Bold Amusement** needs a stronger pace and certainly did not get that here. (13/2)

## 2078 NORMAN WELLS CENTENARY MEMORIAL CHALLENGE TROPHY H'CAP (0-95) (3-Y.O) (Class C)

8-30 (8-31) **6f** £7,230.00 (£2,190.00: £1,070.00: £510.00) Stalls: Low GOING minus 0.43 sec per fur (F)

| | | | | SP | RR | SF |
|---|---|---|---|---|---|---|
| 1127[13] | **Whittle Rock (80)** (EJAlston) **3-8-11** JFanning(2) (disp ld: styd on u.p to ld wl ins fnl f) | — | **1** | 14/1 | 87 | 35 |
| 1475* | **Shanghai Girl (85)** (DRLoder) **3-9-2** PatEddery(8) (lw: disp ld: hrd drvn appr fnl f: nt qckn towards fin) | 1 | **2** | 5/2[1] | 89 | 37 |
| 1452* | **Pusey Street Girl (85)** (JRBosley) **3-8-9**(7) AimeeCook(5) (chsd ldrs: hdwy 2f out: n.m.r ins fnl f: kpt on) | ¾ | **3** | 12/1 | 87 | 35 |
| 1805[2] | **Galine (78)** (WAO'Gorman) **3-8-9** EmmaO'Gorman(4) (lw: chsd ldrs: effrt & edgd lft over 1f out: kpt on same pce) | hd | **4** | 9/2[3] | 80 | 28 |
| 1006[10] | **Krystal Max (IRE) (78)** (TDBarron) **3-8-9** JFortune(3) (hdwy 2f out: styd on wl fnl f: nvr nr to chal) | 2 | **5** | 11/1 | 75 | 23 |
| 1820[8] | **Limerick Princess (IRE) (71)** (JBerry) **3-8-2** GCarter(7) (lw: chsd ldrs: rdn ½-wy: no imp after) | ¾ | **6** | 6/1 | 66 | 14 |
| 1708[7] | **Myttons Mistake (74)** (ABailey) **3-8-2b**(3) DWright(6) (sn prom: outpcd fnl 2f) | ½ | **7** | 6/1 | 67 | 15 |
| 1628[2] | **Antonias Melody (81)** (SRBowring) **3-8-9**(3) CTeague(9) (cl up over 3f: wknd) | 5 | **8** | 4/1[2] | 61 | 9 |
| 1974[13] | **Desert Tiger (90)** (MJohnston) **3-9-7** TWilliams(1) (w ldrs: sn drvn along: wknd 2f out) | 7 | **9** | 7/1 | 51 | — |

(SP 130.5%) **9 Rn**

**1m 12.2** (1.70) CSF £52.47 CT £431.23 TOTE £15.50: £2.50 £1.60 £3.80 (£42.10) Trio £246.60; £177.18 to 22/6/96 OWNER Bay Horse Racing Syndicate (PRESTON) BRED J. Needham

**686 Whittle Rock** proved to be very persistent and gained a definite advantage late on after a rare battle with the runner-up. (14/1)

**1475* Shanghai Girl** forced the pace this time which may have been a mistake, as she had a battle on her hands throughout and it proved too much late on. (5/2)

**1452* Pusey Street Girl** was a shade unlucky when being short of room in the final furlong, but it was her lack of pace that really caused the problem and she is probably better over further. (12/1)

**1805 Galine** had her chances from halfway, but she was always inclined to hang in behind the leaders and could never get out of trouble. (9/2)

**443 Krystal Max (IRE)** had a terrific time on the All Weather this winter and looks to be carrying that on. (11/1)

**1708 Myttons Mistake** (6/1: 9/2-7/1)

**1974 Desert Tiger** (7/1: 5/1-8/1)

## 2079 MIDDLEHAM MAIDEN STKS (3-Y.O) (Class D)

9-00 (9-00) **1m** £3,582.50 (£1,085.00: £530.00: £252.50) Stalls: High GOING minus 0.43 sec per fur (F)

| | | | | SP | RR | SF |
|---|---|---|---|---|---|---|
| | **Nasrudin (USA)** (DRLoder) **3-9-0** PatEddery(8) (lw: hld up: hdwy 2f out: swtchd & qcknd to ld ins fnl f: r.o wl) | — | **1** | 2/1[2] | 82 | 15 |
| 1127[9] | **Tarneem (USA) (85)** (MRStoute) **3-8-4**(5) FLynch(5) (lw: hld up: shkn up over 2f out: chal over 1f out: r.o wl) | hd | **2** | 10/11[1] | 77 | 10 |
| 1807[5] | **Classic Leader (76)** (RHarris) **3-9-0b** AMackay(3) (trckd ldrs: led 2f out tl ins fnl f: no ex) | 2 | **3** | 10/1[3] | 78 | 11 |
| 1675[3] | **Dispol Diamond (80)** (GROldroyd) **3-8-9** DaleGibson(6) (led tl hdd 2f out: one pce) | 3 | **4** | 16/1 | 67 | — |
| 1614[8] | **Esquiline (USA)** (JHMGosden) **3-8-9** GHind(4) (cl up: effrt 3f out: outpcd & bmpd wl over 1f out: sn wknd) | 3½ | **5** | 12/1 | 60 | — |
| 1797[9] | **Old Roma (IRE)** (JohnBerry) **3-8-9** MFenton(2) (hld up: effrt 3f out: no imp) | 5 | **6** | 10/1[3] | 50 | — |
| 870[12] | **Mustard** (ABMulholland) **3-8-9** TWilliams(1) (plld hrd: a bhd) | 22 | **7** | 40/1 | 6 | — |

(SP 119.9%) **7 Rn**

**1m 42.5** (4.80) CSF £4.37 TOTE £3.00: £1.40 £1.30 (£2.10) OWNER Mr B. E. Nielsen (NEWMARKET) BRED Daniel M. Galbreath

**Nasrudin (USA)** showed a good turn of foot to win this slowly run event and should find further success. (2/1)

**937 Tarneem (USA)** looked ultra fit. In a messy race, he tried hard but, despite finishing well, the winner was always too good. (10/11: op 6/4)

**1807 Classic Leader** always held a good position but when the chips were down, he was inclined to edge right and was never doing enough. (10/1: op 6/1)

**1675 Dispol Diamond** keeps running consistently well but is just short of a real turn of foot. (16/1)

**1614 Esquiline (USA)** does not as yet look fully wound up and once the pace increased in the final two furlongs, she received a bump and was soon beaten. (12/1)

**1422 Old Roma (IRE)** gave the impression that she would be happier on easier ground. (10/1)

## 2080 LEYBURN MAIDEN STKS (3-Y.O+) (Class D)

9-30 (9-32) **1m 4f 60y** £3,582.50 (£1,085.00: £530.00: £252.50) Stalls: Low GOING minus 0.43 sec per fur (F)

| | | | | SP | RR | SF |
|---|---|---|---|---|---|---|
| 1644[4] | **Flying Legend (USA)** (HRACecil) **3-8-10** PatEddery(5) (mde all: qcknd 4f out: r.o strly) | — | **1** | 2/5[1] | 85 | 32 |
| 1670[3] | **Random Kindness (74)** (PWHarris) **3-8-10** GHind(9) (chsd wnr: rdn over 3f out: r.o one pce) | 4 | **2** | 14/1[3] | 80 | 27 |
| 1631[2] | **Classic Colleen (IRE)** (RHarris) **3-8-5** AMackay(1) (lw: s.i.s: sn prom: effrt 4f out: one pce) | ½ | **3** | 6/1[2] | 74 | 21 |
| 1711[12] | **Mukeed** (JHMGosden) **3-8-10** DaleGibson(8) (in tch tl lost pl appr st: stdy hdwy 2f out: nvr nr to chal) | 1 | **4** | 33/1 | 78 | 25 |
| 1711[10] | **Lepikha (USA)** (BWHills) **3-8-5** DeanMcKeown(3) (bhd: styd on fnl 3f: nvr rchd ldrs) | 2 | **5** | 16/1 | 70 | 17 |

| | | | | SP | RR | SF |
|---|---|---|---|---|---|---|
| 1864[3] | **Accondy (IRE)** (CEBrittain) **4-9-10** MFenton(4) (lw: chsd ldrs tl wknd over 3f out) | 19 | **6** | 6/1[2] | 51 | 12 |
| | **Lomond Lassie (USA)** (TKersey) **3-8-5** TWilliams(7) (b: s.i.s: a bhd) | 4 | **7** | 100/1 | 40 | — |
| 1701[6] | **Arabian Design** (GMMoore) **4-9-10** JTate(6) (in tch: rdn 4f out: sn wknd) | nk | **8** | 100/1 | 45 | 6 |
| | | | | (SP 117.5%) | **8 Rn** | |

**2m 38.4** (4.40) CSF £7.55 TOTE £1.60: £1.10 £2.70 £1.20 (£6.30) Trio £5.80 OWNER Mr Jim Browne (NEWMARKET) BRED Fares Farms Inc
WEIGHT FOR AGE 3yo-14lb

**1644 Flying Legend (USA)** left nothing to chance and, in the frame throughout, he really stepped up the pace in the last half mile and had shaken off all rivals in the last two furlongs. (2/5)
**1670 Random Kindness** got this trip well and kept responding to pressure but the winner was always far too good. (14/1: 6/1-16/1)
**1631 Classic Colleen (IRE)** lost ground at the start. Shed had to work to improve and was given some determined assistance in the straight, but proved too slow. (6/1)
**Mukeed** showed promise and, not given a hard time of it, will surely improve. (33/1)
**Lepikha (USA)** appreciated this extra distance and was putting in her best work at the end of the race. (16/1)
**1864 Accondy (IRE)**, taking a big step up in distance, appeared not to stay. (6/1: op 5/2)

T/Plpt: £13.90 (992.11 Tckts). T/Qdpt: £2.70 (375.04 Tckts) AA

## 1966-SOUTHWELL (L-H) (Standard)
## Thursday June 20th

WEATHER: overcast WIND: mod half bhd

### 2081 ST TROPEZ H'CAP (0-65) (3-Y.O+) (Class F)
2-15 (2-16) **1m (Fibresand)** £2,381.00 (£656.00: £311.00) Stalls: Low GOING: 0.08 sec per fur (STD)

| | | | | SP | RR | SF |
|---|---|---|---|---|---|---|
| *1487[10]* | **Perpetual Light (62)** (JJQuinn) **3-9-3** AMcGlone(11) (chsd ldrs: led over 1f out: edgd lft: rdn out) | — | **1** | 7/1[3] | 74 | 45 |
| *1966** | **Montone (IRE) (54)** (JRJenkins) **6-9-0v**(5) 6x ADaly(8) (chsd ldrs: rdn ½-wy: styd on ins fnl f) | 1½ | **2** | 9/4[1] | 63 | 44 |
| *1718[5]* | **Quinzii Martin (54)** (DHaydnJones) **8-9-5v** AMackay(13) (lw: a chsng ldrs: styd on same pce u.p fnl 2f) | hd | **3** | 16/1 | 63 | 44 |
| 1691[5] | **Sapphire Son (IRE) (48)** (DMorris) **4-8-13** PBloomfield(9) (led 1f: chsd ldrs styd on sme pace fnl 2f: n.m.r nr fin) | hd | **4** | 12/1 | 57 | 38 |
| *1718[3]* | **Moneghetti (45)** (RHollinshead) **5-8-10** NCarlisle(3) (chsd ldrs: rdn ½-wy: wknd over 1f out) | 3 | **5** | 7/2[2] | 48 | 29 |
| *1809[7]* | **Le Bam Bam (55)** (HAkbary) **4-8-13**(7) CWebb(4) (bhd: hung rt & styd on appr fnl f: nvr nr ldrs) | 1¼ | **6** | 25/1 | 55 | 36 |
| 2000[6] | **Saltando (IRE) (52)** (PatMitchell) **5-9-3** DRMcCabe(1) (a.p: sn rdn along: one pce fnl 2f) | 1 | **7** | 10/1 | 50 | 31 |
| 1613[8] | **Lilac Rain (47)** (JRArnold) **4-8-7**(5) FLynch(7) (dwlt s: nvr nrr) | 2½ | **8** | 14/1 | 40 | 21 |
| 1866[6] | **Lady Silk (50)** (MissJFCraze) **5-9-1** NConnorton(10) (led after 1f tl over 1f out: sn wknd) | nk | **9** | 16/1 | 43 | 24 |
| 1533[3] | **Edgar Kirby (53)** (PWHarris) **5-9-4** NDay(16) (prom: rdn over 2f out: sn wknd) | 1½ | **10** | 10/1 | 43 | 24 |
| 1468[11] | **No Submission (USA) (59)** (DWChapman) **10-9-10v** JFortune(15) (lw: s.i.s: racd wd: a bhd) | 1¼ | **11** | 16/1 | 46 | 27 |
| 1903[7] | **Studio Thirty (51)** (DMorris) **4-8-9b**1(7) AEddery(6) (sn bhd & rdn along) | 1¾ | **12** | 16/1 | 35 | 16 |
| 1638[7] | **First Gold (55)** (JWharton) **7-9-6** PRobinson(14) (sn bhd: effrt on outside over 2f out: n.d) | nk | **13** | 16/1 | 38 | 19 |
| 1830[7] | **Battle Colours (IRE) (47)** (DonEnricoIncisa) **7-8-12** KimTinkler(2) (sn bhd & rdn along) | 3 | **14** | 25/1 | 24 | 5 |
| 914[8] | **Petite Heritiere (54)** (MJRyan) **3-8-9** DBiggs(5) (chsd ldrs tl lost pl 3f out: sn bhd) | 2 | **15** | 16/1 | 27 | — |
| *688[13]* | ***Pine Essence (USA) (51)*** (JLEyre) **5-9-2** TWilliams(12) (Withdrawn not under Starter's orders: lame) | | **W** | | — | — |
| | | | | (SP 141.0%) | **15 Rn** | |

**1m 46.2** (6.20) CSF £25.38 CT £249.95 TOTE £13.70: £3.00 £1.50 £4.70 (£40.70) Trio £144.60 OWNER The Four Point Partnership (MALTON) BRED Lord Matthews
WEIGHT FOR AGE 3yo-10lb

**1487 Perpetual Light**, who has a pronounced knee action, recorded her second victory here in her last three starts. (7/1)
**1966* Montone (IRE)**, in good form at present, struggled to stay in contention but kept on inside the last. (9/4)
**1718 Quinzii Martin** extended his losing sequence to 26 runs. (16/1)
**1691 Sapphire Son (IRE)** was only staying on at the same pace when tightened up near the finish. (12/1: op 8/1)
**1718 Moneghetti**, well-supported in the market, was thought to be suited by the step up to a mile, but he was under pressure to hold his place at the halfway mark. (7/2: 6/1-3/1)

### 2082 MONTE CARLO CLAIMING STKS (3-Y.O+) (Class F)
2-50 (2-50) **1m 3f (Fibresand)** £2,381.00 (£656.00: £311.00) Stalls: Low GOING: 0.08 sec per fur (STD)

| | | | | SP | RR | SF |
|---|---|---|---|---|---|---|
| 1596[9] | **Troubadour Song (61)** (WWHaigh) **4-8-13**(3) PMcCabe(11) (bhd: gd hdwy over 2f out: led over 1f out: sn clr: eased towards fin) | — | **1** | 9/1 | 64+ | 16 |
| *1488[4]* | **Eulogy (FR) (64)** (KRBurke) **9-9-8** DRMcCabe(2) (trckd ldrs: led over 2f out tl over 1f out: no ch w wnr) | 4 | **2** | 9/2[2] | 64 | 16 |
| *1967[3]* | **Red Phantom (IRE) (66)** (SMellor) **4-10-0** MWigham(7) (bhd: hdwy 5f out: styd on one pce fnl 2f) | 2½ | **3** | 8/1[3] | 67 | 19 |
| 1600[9] | **Chik's Secret (42)** (BPalling) **3-8-2** TSprake(10) (a chsng ldrs: one pce fnl 2f) | 1¾ | **4** | 20/1 | 51 | — |
| *1719[13]* | **Hornpipe (58)** (JWharton) **4-9-7** PRobinson(9) (w ldrs: led 8f out tl over 2f out: wknd over 1f out) | 5 | **5** | 8/1[3] | 50 | 2 |
| 1526[10] | **Forget Paris (IRE)** (BSRothwell) **3-8-8** MFenton(14) (in tch: effrt over 3f out: wknd 2f out) | 2½ | **6** | 14/1 | 46 | — |
| *1970[6]* | **Chilly Lad (60)** (MJRyan) **5-9-4b** DBiggs(1) (hdwy to chse ldrs ½-wy: wknd 2f out) | 2 | **7** | 9/1 | 40 | — |
| *1966[10]* | **Kismetim (45)** (DWChapman) **6-9-0v** GDuffield(4) (led to 8f out: chsd ldrs tl over 2f out) | 3 | **8** | 16/1 | 32 | — |
| 1778[14] | **Highfield Fizz (48)** (CWFairhurst) **4-9-5** DeanMcKeown(6) (prom: sn drvn along: lost pl 6f out) | 6 | **9** | 14/1 | 28 | — |
| 1839[4] | **Te Amo (IRE) (70)** (RAkehurst) **4-10-0** RPerham(5) (lw: chsd ldrs: drvn along 7f out: lost pl over 3f out) | 3 | **10** | 7/2[1] | 33 | — |
| 1503[12] | **Village Opera (41)** (GMMoore) **3-8-2** JTate(12) (sn bhd & rdn along: t.o 4f out) | dist | **11** | 25/1 | — | — |
| *136[12]* | **P G Tips (IRE) (68)** (MrsNMacauley) **5-9-11**(3) CTeague(13) (b: carried wd by loose horse after 1f: sddle slipped: sn t.o: p.u lame over 4f out) | | **P** | 20/1 | — | — |
| 1821[12] | **Jalmaid (56)** (BAMcMahon) **4-8-10**(5) LNewton(3) (stumbled & uns rdr s) | | **U** | 9/2[2] | — | — |
| | | | | (SP 133.4%) | **13 Rn** | |

**2m 32.9** (12.90) CSF £51.44 TOTE £12.60: £3.70 £1.50 £3.60 (£74.00) Trio £79.80 OWNER Spring Cottage Racing Partnership (MALTON) BRED Paul Mellon
WEIGHT FOR AGE 3yo-13lb

**822 Troubadour Song**, who had reportedly broken blood vessels when running badly on his two previous outings, came from off the pace to score in tremendous style. (9/1)
**1488 Eulogy (FR)**, who presumably needed it last time after a long absence, stuck on to finish second but the winner left him for dead. (9/2)
**1967 Red Phantom (IRE)**, dropping back in distance, stuck on at the one pace under pressure. (8/1)

**Chik's Secret** had previously only shown form over five but ran easily her best race here. (20/1)
**1196 Forget Paris (IRE)** (14/1: 20/1-12/1)
**1496 Chilly Lad** (9/1: 6/1-10/1)
**1839 Te Amo (IRE)**, on his sand debut, dropped right away turning out of the back stretch and was allowed to come home in his own time. (7/2: 7/4-4/1)

## 2083 '96 TRENT FM MAIDEN AUCTION STKS (2-Y.O) (Class F)

3-25 (3-26) **5f (Fibresand)** £2,381.00 (£656.00: £311.00) Stalls: High GOING: 0.08 sec per fur (STD)

| | | | | SP | RR | SF |
|---|---|---|---|---|---|---|
| | **Jupiter (IRE)** (GCBravery) **2-8-5** NDay(4) (tall: sn trckng ldrs: shkn up to ld over 1f out: sn clr: eased fin) | — | 1 | 9/4[1] | 65+ | 22 |
| *1968*[3] | **Jack Says** (TDEasterby) **2-8-5** TWilliams(5) (a chsng ldrs: rdn ½-wy: kpt on: no ch w wnr) | 3 | 2 | 7/1[3] | 55 | 12 |
| 1827[4] | **Komasta** (CaptJWilson) **2-7-12**(5) FLynch(10) (a chsng ldrs: rdn & outpcd ½-wy: kpt on) | hd | 3 | 3/1[2] | 53 | 10 |
| 1595[5] | **Little Blue (IRE)** (TDEasterby) **2-8-0** LCharnock(1) (chsd ldrs: led ½-wy tl over 1f out: one pce) | 2½ | 4 | 10/1 | 42 | — |
| 557[6] | **Super Saint** (TDBarron) **2-8-7** JFortune(3) (unruly s: led to ½-wy: sn wl outpcd) | 5 | 5 | 10/1 | 33 | — |
| | **Tom Pladdey** (RBastiman) **2-8-3** DeanMcKeown(9) (cmpt: bit bkwd: w ldrs tl wknd ½-wy) | 2½ | 6 | 7/1[3] | 21 | — |
| 1880[3] | **Super Scravels** (DrJDScargill) **2-7-12** NAdams(8) (sn pushed along: hung lft & lost pl ½-wy) | 1¼ | 7 | 12/1 | 12 | — |
| | **Frandickbob** (JAHarris) **2-8-7** SDWilliams(2) (cmpt: unruly s: outpcd fr ½-wy) | ¾ | 8 | 12/1 | 19 | — |
| | **Pet Express** (PCHaslam) **2-8-3** GCarter(6) (w'like: bit bkwd: hung lft thrght: sn wl bhd) | 5 | 9 | 10/1 | — | — |
| 1827[14] | **Impish (IRE)** (TJEtherington) **2-8-3** GDuffield(7) (bit bkwd: unruly in stalls: reard s: virtually t.n.p) | dist | 10 | 33/1 | — | — |
| | | | | (SP 126.4%) | **10 Rn** | |

**61.3 secs** (4.30) CSF £19.15 TOTE £3.00: £1.20 £2.10 £1.70 (£14.70) Trio £9.30 OWNER Mr G. C. Bravery (NEWMARKET) BRED Mrs C. A. Moore

**Jupiter (IRE)** was coltish in the paddock but certainly knew his job. Though it was a modest event he won easing up and can go on from here. (9/4: 4/1-2/1)
**1968 Jack Says** stuck on under strong pressure and would be much better suited by six or even seven. (7/1: op 5/2)
**1827 Komasta**, struggling to keep up, kept on and will be better suited by six. (3/1: 2/1-7/2)
**1595 Little Blue (IRE)**, drawn wide, ran much better than she had done on her debut. She should win a seller or claimer. (10/1: op 6/1)
**557 Super Saint** (10/1: op 6/1)
**Tom Pladdey** (7/1: op 14/1)
**Frandickbob** (12/1: 16/1-10/1)
**Pet Express** (10/1: 7/1-12/1)

## 2084 R-BEE CHILDRENS WEAR LIMITED STKS (0-70) (3-Y.O+) (Class E)

4-00 (4-04) **6f (Fibresand)** £3,206.70 (£957.60: £457.80: £207.90) Stalls: Low GOING: 0.08 sec per fur (STD)

| | | | | SP | RR | SF |
|---|---|---|---|---|---|---|
| 1991* | **Wardara (63)** (CADwyer) **4-9-0v**(5) FLynch(10) (lw: hld up & plld hrd: hdwy ½-wy: led 2f out: edgd lft: drvn out) | — | 1 | 6/1[2] | 79 | 56 |
| 1848[2] | **Keston Pond (IRE) (70)** (MrsVAAconley) **6-9-2** MDeering(11) (bhd: hdwy on outside over 2f out: hrd rdn & hung lft: styd on towards fin) | 1¼ | 2 | 6/4[1] | 73 | 50 |
| *1812*[2] | **Klipspinger (68)** (BSRothwell) **3-8-9v** MFenton(9) (a chsng ldrs: styd on same pce fnl 2f) | hd | 3 | 7/1[3] | 72 | 42 |
| *1971** | **Elton Ledger (IRE) (66)** (MrsNMacauley) **7-9-11v** EmmaO'Gorman(7) (b: hld up: effrt 2f out: kpt on: nvr nr to chal) | 1¾ | 4 | 9/1 | 77 | 54 |
| 1674[8] | **Johnnie the Joker (70)** (JPLeigh) **5-9-2b** DeanMcKeown(6) (b: in tch: hrd rdn & outpcd over 2f out: kpt on) | 2½ | 5 | 10/1 | 61 | 38 |
| 1598[8] | **Hannah's Usher (70)** (CMurray) **4-9-5** MTebbutt(8) (hld up: bhd tl styd on fnl 2f) | 3 | 6 | 14/1 | 56 | 33 |
| *1718*[6] | **Maybank (IRE) (60)** (BAMcMahon) **4-9-5** GDuffield(5) (lw: n.m.r after 1f: sn drvn along & outpcd: nvr nr ldrs) | 1¼ | 7 | 10/1 | 53 | 30 |
| 1844[2] | **Malibu Man (70)** (EAWheeler) **4-9-2** TSprake(4) (lw: sn chsng ldrs: rdn over 2f out: wknd over 1f out) | ½ | 8 | 15/2 | 48 | 25 |
| *1716*[6] | **Napier Star (51)** (MrsNMacauley) **3-8-6**(3) CTeague(3) (led to 2f out: wknd over 1f out) | 1¼ | 9 | 25/1 | 45 | 15 |
| 1707[6] | **No Monkey Nuts (70)** (JBerry) **3-8-9** GCarter(2) (hld up: effrt over 3f out: wknd 2f out) | nk | 10 | 12/1 | 44 | 14 |
| 1642[10] | **Niteowl Raider (IRE) (67)** (JAHarris) **3-9-1** JO'Reilly(1) (prom early: bhd fr ½-wy) | 12 | 11 | 20/1 | 18 | — |
| | | | | (SP 129.7%) | **11 Rn** | |

**1m 17.4** (3.90) CSF £16.31 TOTE £4.50: £1.60 £1.30 £2.60 (£5.10) Trio £15.90 OWNER Binding Matters Ltd (NEWMARKET) BRED G. B. Turnbull Ltd

WEIGHT FOR AGE 3yo-7lb

STEWARDS' ENQUIRY Deering susp. 29/6 - 5/7/96 (excessive & incorrect use of whip).

**1991* Wardara**, who did not win at all last year, completed the hat-trick and, after racing keenly, had only to be kept up to her work. Her confidence must be sky high now. (6/1: 4/1-13/2)
**1848 Keston Pond (IRE)** dwarfed his rivals in the paddock. Marooned on the outside, he proved to be something of a handful and his rider did not spare the stick. Closing the gap all the way to the line, he was never going to get there. (6/4: op 5/2)
**1812 Klipspinger**, with the visor fitted again, again ran well. (7/1: 4/1-8/1)
**1971* Elton Ledger (IRE)**, making ground from off the pace, at these weights could never find sufficient to land a blow. (9/1)
**1844 Malibu Man** (15/2: 5/1-8/1)

## 2085 CHATEAU LAFITE APPRENTICE (S) H'CAP (0-60) (3-Y.O+) (Class G)

4-35 (4-35) **7f (Fibresand)** £2,095.00 (£595.00: £295.00) Stalls: Low GOING: 0.08 sec per fur (STD)

| | | | | SP | RR | SF |
|---|---|---|---|---|---|---|
| *1966*[3] | **David James' Girl (52)** (ABailey) **4-9-9** RStudholme(11) (hld up: gd hdwy on outside over 2f out: r.o to ld wl ins fnl f: pushed out) | — | 1 | 100/30[2] | 69 | 45 |
| | **Have a Nightcap (30)** (NPLittmoden) **7-8-1b** DavidO'Neill(9) (in tch: sn drvn along: styd on to ld 1f out: hdd & nt qckn towards fin) | 1¼ | 2 | 25/1 | 44 | 20 |
| 1642[8] | **Valiant Man (41)** (JWharton) **5-8-12v** PDoe(14) (w ldrs: led over 2f out to 1f out: one pce) | 3½ | 3 | 8/1 | 47 | 23 |
| 1830[8] | **Tame Deer (57)** (MCChapman) **4-10-0** TPField(6) (led after 1f tl over 1f out: hrd rdn & edgd rt appr fnl f: grad wknd) | 5 | 4 | 10/1 | 52 | 28 |
| *1966*[2] | **Ring the Chief (35)** (MDIUsher) **4-8-1**(5) RBrisland(7) (b: sn pushed along: hdwy ½-wy: one pce fnl 2f) | ½ | 5 | 3/1[1] | 29 | 5 |
| 1886[6] | **Jungle Patrol (IRE) (52)** (MBrittain) **4-9-9e** RMullen(13) (sn bhd & drvn along: sme hdwy 2f out: n.d) | ½ | 6 | 10/1 | 44 | 20 |
| 545[7] | **Cledeschamps (33)** (MWEllerby) **7-8-4** JFowle(10) (bhd: gd hdwy on ins over 2f out: sn rdn: wknd over 1f out) | ½ | 7 | 25/1 | 24 | — |
| 983[9] | **Ladybower (IRE) (44)** (LordHuntingdon) **4-9-1** CCogan(12) (sn outpcd & bhd: sme hdwy 2f out: sn wknd) | 4 | 8 | 4/1[3] | 26 | 2 |
| 1162[7] | **Ohnonotagain (33)** (BWMurray) **4-8-4b**[1] SBuckley(4) (sn bhd) | 4 | 9 | 25/1 | 6 | — |

| | | | | | |
|---|---|---|---|---|---|
| $1789^{10}$ **Jon's Choice (40)** (BPreece) **8-8-6**$^{(5)}$ SCrawford(1) (led 1f: chsd ldrs tl wknd over 1f out)....1¾ | **10** | 9/1 | 9 | — |
| *$1456^{10}$* **Primo Lad (54)** (WGMTurner) **3-9-2b**$^{1}$ GHannon(5) (w ldrs: hrd rdn & lost pl over 2f out)....3½ | **11** | 14/1 | 15 | — |
| *$50^{7}$* **Rainbows Rhapsody (37)** (DWChapman) **5-8-8** JoanneWebster(2) (s.i.s: a in rr)....5 | **12** | 16/1 | — | — |
| $1533^{14}$ **Rasmi (CAN) (46)** (PHowling) **5-9-3** RSmith(3) (s.i.s: a wl outpcd & bhd)....9 | **13** | 25/1 | — | — |

(SP 135.3%) **13 Rn**

**1m 32.7** (5.90) CSF £83.08 CT £585.77 TOTE £5.40: £1.70 £5.60 £1.90 (£71.00) Trio £139.70; £157.47 to Royal Ascot 21/6/96 OWNER One In Ten Racing Club (TARPORLEY) BRED Miss P. E. Decker
WEIGHT FOR AGE 3yo-9lb
No bid
**1966 David James' Girl** came from last to first. This trip is her bare minimum these days. (100/30)
**Have a Nightcap**, still a maiden on the Flat, had won over hurdles on the sand here. After getting his head in front, he was outpaced by the winner near the line. He had no answer to the winner near the line. (25/1)
**1162 Valiant Man** is only as good as he showed here nowadays. (8/1)
**1665 Tame Deer** edged right and weakened in the final furlong. He is possibly better over six. (10/1)
**1966 Ring the Chief** lacked the pace to take anything like a serious hand. (3/1)
**983 Ladybower (IRE)** (4/1: 5/2-9/2)

## 2086 BORDEAUX H'CAP (0-65) (3-Y.O) (Class F)

5-10 (5-11) **1m 4f (Fibresand)** £2,381.00 (£656.00: £311.00) Stalls: Low GOING: 0.08 sec per fur (STD)

| | | SP | RR | SF |
|---|---|---|---|---|
| *$1814^{3}$* **Harbet House (FR) (51)** (CACyzer) **3-8-5**$^{(5)}$ FLynch(7) (hld up: hdwy ½-wy: rdn to ld over 1f out: styd on wl)— | **1** | 12/1 | 62 | 15 |
| *1814** **Old School House (53)** (TJNaughton) **3-8-12** TSprake(6) (lw: trckd ldrs: led 4f out tl over 1f out: one pce)...3½ | **2** | 9/4$^{1}$ | 59 | 12 |
| $1850^{2}$ **Princely Affair (45)** (MBell) **3-8-4** MFenton(8) (sn bhd & pushed along: hdwy 3f out: kpt on: nvr nr to chal)..3½ | **3** | 3/1$^{2}$ | 47 | — |
| $1325^{3}$ **Champagne Warrior (IRE) (47)** (MJCamacho) **3-8-6** LCharnock(2) (hld up: hdwy 5f out: rdn & edgd rt over 2f out: sn wknd)....7 | **4** | 7/1$^{3}$ | 39 | — |
| $1641^{11}$ **Brentability (IRE) (54)** (GLewis) **3-8-13** SWhitworth(5) (sn pushed along: chsd ldrs: wkng whn hmpd over 2f out)....2½ | **5** | 7/1$^{3}$ | 43 | — |
| 1025* **Domino Flyer (62)** (MrsASwinbank) **3-9-7** JFortune(4) (lw: plld hrd: led to 4f out: wknd over 1f out)....nk | **6** | 8/1 | 51 | 4 |
| *1970** **Yellow Dragon (IRE) (50)** (BAPearce) **3-8-9** 5x NCarlisle(1) (b: hld up: lost tch 5f out: hung rt & t.o 3f out)...dist | **7** | 7/1$^{3}$ | — | — |
| $1498^{10}$ **Bailiwick (53)** (NAGraham) **3-8-12b** DHarrison(3) (chsd ldrs: rdn 7f out: sn lost pl: t.o 3f out)....14 | **8** | 14/1 | — | — |
| $1498^{7}$ **Contrarie (37)** (MJRyan) **3-7-3**$^{(7)}$ AMcCarthy(9) (chsd ldrs tl rdn & lost pl ½-wy: t.o 4f out)....5 | **9** | 10/1 | — | — |

(SP 127.8%) **9 Rn**

**2m 45.7** (13.20) CSF £41.34 CT £101.01 TOTE £18.80: £4.30 £1.70 £1.20 (£21.70) Trio £15.40 OWNER Mr R. M. Cyzer (HORSHAM)
LONG HANDICAP Contrarie 7-8
**1814 Harbet House (FR)**, meeting the runner-up on 12lb better terms compared with Wolverhampton, scored decisively in the end. (12/1)
**1814* Old School House** made the best of his way home but, over this shorter trip on the revised terms, the winner proved much too strong. (9/4)
**1850 Princely Affair**, 2lb lower in the weights than when runner-up at Redcar on terms, struggled to keep up and never looked like getting near the first two. (3/1: op 2/1)
**1325 Champagne Warrior (IRE)** came off a true line under pressure early in the straight, causing problems for the next horse. (7/1)
**1641 Brentability (IRE)** (7/1: op 4/1)

T/Plpt: £19.60 (454.59 Tckts). T/Qdpt: £6.30 (114.77 Tckts). WG

## 2087a-2091a (Irish Racing) - See Computer Raceform

# 0033a-LEOPARDSTOWN (Dublin, Ireland) (L-H) (Good)
## Wednesday June 12th

## 2092a HORIZONS BALLYCORUS STKS (Gp 3) (3-Y.O+)

6-30 (6-33) **7f** £21,775.00 (£6,365.00: £3,015.00: £1,005.00)

| | | SP | RR | SF |
|---|---|---|---|---|
| 1912a* **Idris (IRE)** (JSBolger,Ireland) **6-9-9** KJManning (hld up trckng ldrs: led over 1f out: rdn & r.o)....— | **1** | 7/4$^{1}$ | 114 | 22 |
| $1566a^{9}$ **Burden Of Proof (IRE)** (CO'Brien,Ireland) **4-9-5** CRoche (hld up: 4th & effrt over 1f out: ev ch appr fnl f: no ex)....hd | **2** | 9/4$^{2}$ | 110 | 18 |
| $1151^{6}$ **Projection (USA)** (BWHills) **3-8-9** BThompson (sn led: hdd over 1f out: no ex)....3 | **3** | 9/4$^{2}$ | 103 | 1 |
| **Force Of Will (USA)** (DKWeld,Ireland) **3-8-9b**$^{1}$ MJKinane (chsd ldr: effrt & ev ch 1½f out: btn 1f out)....4 | **4** | 7/1$^{3}$ | 94 | — |

(SP 110.4%) **4 Rn**

**1m 30.9** (5.90) OWNER Michael Keogh (COOLCULLEN)
**1912a* Idris (IRE)** held up as usual early on, went second over four furlongs out. Challenging between horses with over a furlong to race, he ran on best over the last half furlong. (7/4)
**1566a Burden Of Proof (IRE)**, held up, was last into the straight and delivered his challenge on the outside from over a furlong out. He stuck to it well and held every chance, but the winner was just that bit stronger. With some ease in the ground and a pair of blinkers, he could improve on this effort. The first two might clash again in the Group Two Sea World International at the Curragh. (9/4)
**1151 Projection (USA)**, well backed, popped of in front to dictate the pace. He didn't find anything extra when asked to quicken after the final bend and was outpaced over the last furlong. (9/4: op 7/2)
**Force Of Will (USA)** was second until crying enough well over a furlong out, and was eased down near the finish. (7/1)

## 2093a-2101a (Irish Racing) - See Computer Raceform

# 1273a-GOWRAN PARK (Kilkenny, Ireland) (R-H) (Good to firm)
## Saturday June 15th

## 2102a VICTOR MCCALMONT MEMORIAL STKS (Listed) (3-Y.O+ F & M)

4-00 (4-01) **1m 4f** £9,825.00 (£2,775.00: £1,275.00: £375.00)

| | | SP | RR | SF |
|---|---|---|---|---|
| 1004* **Tout A Coup (IRE)** (GACusack,Ireland) **3-8-10** MJKinane (plld hrd early: hld up: hdwy 3f out: jnd ldrs over 1f out: shkn up & r.o to ld last stides)....— | **1** | 11/10$^{1}$ | 98 | — |

2069$^{8}$ **Ceirseach (IRE)** (JSBolger,Ireland) **3-8-7** KJManning (led: jnd 3f out: hdd over 2f out: led over 1f out: kpt on u.p: hdd last stides) ... s.h **2** 7/2$^{2}$ 95 —
1573a$^{3}$ **Sun Ballet (IRE)** (JOxx,Ireland) **3-8-7** WJSupple (towards rr: hdwy to 4th ½-wy: disp ld 3f out: led over 2f out: hdd u.p over 1f out: no ex ins fnl f) ... 1½ **3** 7/1 93 —
1573a$^{4}$ **Blending Element (IRE)** (TStack,Ireland) **3-8-7b$^{1}$** PJSmullen (cl up: 3rd ½-wy: 4th & rdn 3f out: 5th & nt rch ldrs over 1f out: kpt on ins fnl f) ... 1½ **4** 16/1 91 —
**Bakiya (USA)** (JOxx,Ireland) **3-8-8**ow1 JPMurtagh (hld up in tch: 5th 4f out: 4th & effrt fr over 2f out: no ex ins fnl f) ... ½ **5** 5/1$^{3}$ 91 —
1246a$^{4}$ **Pegwood (IRE)** (DKWeld,Ireland) **3-8-7** PShanahan (hld up towards rr: hdwy 3f out: 6th, rdn & nt trble ldrs fr over 1f out) ... 2 **6** 12/1 88 —
**Serene Swing (USA)** (CO'Brien,Ireland) **3-8-7** NGMcCullagh (prom: 2nd ½-wy: 3rd & rdn 3f out: wknd over 2f out: n.d) ... 13 **7** 8/1 70 —
(SP 123.7%) **7 Rn**

**2m 38.7** OWNER Edmund Loder (NAAS) BRED E. J. Loder
**1004* Tout A Coup (IRE)**, faced with an easy task on paper, had a harder race than connections might have expected. Making headway on the outside turning in, she was cruising in third place with a furlong and a half to race but when asked the question, didn't respond immediately and it was only in the last couple of strides that she got her head in front. It was disclosed after the race that she had been held up in her work, but she still has the Irish Oaks as her target. (11/10)
**Ceirseach (IRE)** went of in front and, ridden along for the last furlong and a half, kept pulling out all the stops until headed in the last few strides. (7/2)
**1573a Sun Ballet (IRE)**, in second place with half a mile to race, had every chance until finding nothing under pressure in the last furlong. (7/1)
**Blending Element (IRE)** showed improved form but could not make any impression over the last half furlong. (16/1)
**Bakiya (USA)** was eased down inside the final furlong after finding herself unable to quicken with the leaders from half a furlong out. (5/1)

## **2103a-2107a** (Irish Racing) - See Computer Raceform

## 1942a-**SAINT-CLOUD (France)** (L-H) (Good)
### Friday June 14th

### 2108a PRIX DU LYS (Gp 3) (3-Y.O)
3-15 (3-14) **1m 6f** £28,986.00 (£10,540.00: £5,270.00)

SP RR SF
1139a$^{5}$ **Cachet Noir (USA)** (PBary,France) **3-8-11** FGrenet ... — **1** 103 —
1057a$^{3}$ **Stage Pass** (NClement,France) **3-8-11** OPeslier ... ¾ **2** 102 —
**Irish Woman (FR)** (MmeMBollack-Badel,France) **3-8-10**ow1 ABadel ... 1½ **3** 99 —
**5 Rn**

**3m 11.8** (13.80) P-M 5.80F: 1.10F 1.10F 11.20F OWNER Exors of the late J Garcia-Roady (CHANTILLY) BRED G. Player
**Cachet Noir (USA)** raced in behind the leaders during most of this event and took the lead two furlongs from home. This son of Theatrical then held on well inside the final furlong to repel the challenge of the short-priced favourite. He showed improved form on this occasion and was notably not wearing blinkers this time. He is obviously a horse with ability who maybe thinks a bit about racing. He now heads for the Group Two Hubert de Chaudenay on July 6th at Longchamp.
**1057a Stage Pass** disappointed connections by failing to land the odds on this occasion. After coming with a serious-looking challenge at the two furlong marker, he was only staying on in the closing stages. The odds on favourite lost quite a lot of ground coming wide into the straight but he seems to be a colt who does not quite go through with his challenge.
**Irish Woman (FR)** was in last place for most of this race but made some late progress to take third close home. She is of Listed class and has done well to get her black type by being placed in a Group race.

## 1394a-**COLOGNE (Germany)** (R-H) (Good)
### Sunday June 16th

### 2109a OPPENHEIM-COLONIA-UNION-RENNEN (Gp 2) (3-Y.O)
3-40 (3-51) **1m 3f** £54,054.00 (£21,622.00: £10,811.00: £5,405.00)

SP RR SF
1395a* **Lavirco (GER)** (PRau,Germany) **3-9-2** TMundry (hld up: prog to ld 2f out: impressive) ... — **1** 96+ —
795a* **Surako (GER)** (HJentzsch,Germany) **3-9-2** PSchiergen (racd in 3rd: kpt on wl fnl 2f: no ex fnl f) ... 2½ **2** 92 —
**Bon Jovi (GER)** (HJentzsch,Germany) **3-9-2** WRyan (led tl hdd 2f out: kpt on one pce) ... 2½ **3** 89 —
**Zero Problemo (IRE)** (BSchutz,Germany) **3-9-2** AStarke (racd mid div: ev ch fr 2f out: no cl home) ... ½ **4** 88 —
**My Happy Guest (IRE)** (Germany) **3-9-2b$^{1}$** MRoberts (trckd ldr tl wknd fr 2f out) ... 5 **5** 81 —
**Ocean Sea (USA)** (Germany) **3-9-2** THellier (a rr: little hdwy) ... 1½ **6** 79 —
**Abaton (GER)** (Germany) **3-9-2** KWoodburn (mid div tl st: wknd qckly fr 2f out) ... 14 **7** 58 —
**7 Rn**

**2m 15.52** (5.52) TOTE 27DM: 18DM 15DM 31DM (79DM) OWNER Gestut Fahrhof BRED Gestut Fahrhof Stiftung
**1395a* Lavirco (GER)**, the winner of the German 2,000 Guineas, went into clear favouritism for the Deutsches Derby with an impressive win in this event. Taking the lead over two furlongs out, he galloped on strongly to win this Derby trial very convincingly. The first three in this event are all sons of the 1979 Triple Crown winner Konigsstuhl and they may all meet again in the Derby.
**Surako (GER)** ran a fine race but could not cope with the winner.

## **FRAUENFELD (Zurich, Switzerland)** (R-H) (Good)
### Sunday June 16th

### 2110a BANKVEREIN SWISS DERBY (3-Y.O C & F)
3-00 (3-04) **1m 4f** £26,816.00 (£10,726.00: £8,045.00)

SP RR SF
1751a* **Mongol Warrior (USA)** (LordHuntingdon) **3-9-2** DHarrison ... — **1** 94 —
1059a$^{2}$ **Shturm (RUS)** (MWeiss,Switzerland) **3-9-2** SGuillot ... 5½ **2** 87 —

| | | | | SP | RR | SF |
|---|---|---|---|---|---|---|
| | **Northern Soul (USA)** (MWeiss,Switzerland) **3-9-2** RHughes | ½ | **3** | | 86 | — |

**12 Rn**

**2m 31.8** TOTE 1.70F: 1.20F 1.80F 1.70F (22.80) OWNER H De Kwiatkowski (WEST ILSLEY) BRED Kennelot Stables Limited
**1751a* Mongol Warrior (USA)**, despite finding the ground slightly too quick, put up a fine display. Racing in third, he quickened to take the lead two furlongs out and soon put distance between himself and his rivals to score a comfortable win. He could go on to be a real force in Pattern races later in the season on his preferred softer ground.

# 1951a-SAN SIRO (Milan, Italy) (R-H) (Good)
## Sunday June 16th

## 2111a GRAN PREMIO DI MILANO (Gp 1) (3-Y.O+)
5-00 (5-35) **1m 4f** £111,549.00 (£56,916.00: £33,343.00: £16,671.00)

| | | | | SP | RR | SF |
|---|---|---|---|---|---|---|
| 1128² | **Strategic Choice (USA)** (PFICole) **5-9-6** TQuinn (trckd ldr: led after 5f: gng wl ent st: r.o wl fnl 2f) | — | **1** | | 128 | — |
| 1579a* | **Luso** (CEBrittain) **4-9-6** MJKinane (led early: hdd after 5f: rdn to chal over 2f out: nvr able to chal ins fnl f) | 1½ | **2** | | 126 | — |
| 1520² | **King's Theatre (IRE)** (SbinSuroor) **5-9-6** JReid (racd in 3rd: rdn & btn over 2f out) | 4¾ | **3** | | 120 | — |
| 1579a³ | **Pay Me Back (IRE)** (GVerricelli,Italy) **6-9-6** LSorrentino (a in rr: kpt one pce fnl 2f) | 1½ | **4** | | 118 | — |

**4 Rn**

**2m 27.2** (7.20) TOTE 21L: 12L 14L (55L) OWNER Mr M. Arbib (WHATCOMBE) BRED M. Arbib
**1128 Strategic Choice (USA)** raced in second behind Luso before making headway to take the lead over five furlongs out. He was going well turning into the straight and ran on to an impressive victory. He will now go straight to the King George VI and Queen Elizabeth Diamond Stakes.
**1579a* Luso** set the early pace but was headed five furlongs out. Kinane rode him up to challenge the leader but was never able to get on terms.
**1520 King's Theatre (IRE)**, with John Reid in the saddle deputising for the injured Dettori, raced in third place but was ridden over and beaten two furlongs out.

# 2069-ASCOT (R-H) (Good to firm, Firm patches)
## Friday June 21st
WEATHER: Fine WIND: almost nil

## 2112 WINDSOR CASTLE STKS (2-Y.O) (Class B)
2-30 (2-30) **5f** £17,247.60 (£6,458.40: £3,161.70: £1,363.50: £614.25: £314.55) Stalls: Centre GOING minus 0.19 sec per fur (GF)

| | | | | SP | RR | SF |
|---|---|---|---|---|---|---|
| | **Dazzle** (MRStoute) **2-8-5**ow2 KFallon(11) (leggy: scope: dwlt: hdwy over 1f out: led ins fnl f: pushed out) | — | **1** | 7/2 1 | 94+ | 55 |
| 1760* | **Vax Star** (JLSpearing) **2-8-8** JWeaver(9) (led: rdn over 1f out: hdd ins fnl f: unable qckn) | 2½ | **2** | 12/1 | 89 | 52 |
| 1834* | **Olympic Spirit** (JBerry) **2-8-8** JCarroll(4) (b.hind: a.p: ev ch over 1f out: one pce) | 1¼ | **3** | 11/1 | 85 | 48 |
| 924² | **Taufan Rookie (IRE)** (RHannon) **2-8-11** RHughes(3) (dwlt: rdn over 2f out: hdwy & n.m.r over 1f out: r.o one pce) | 2 | **4** | 9/2 2 | 82 | 45 |
| 1795³ | **Caviar Royale (IRE)** (RHannon) **2-8-13** PatEddery(5) (a.p: rdn over 2f out: wknd 1f out) | ¾ | **5** | 6/1 3 | 81 | 44 |
| 1699² | **Superior Premium** (RAFahey) **2-8-11** MJKinane(7) (lw: a.p: rdn 2f out: wknd 1f out) | s.h | **6** | 8/1 | 79 | 42 |
| 1479* | **Meliksah (IRE)** (MBell) **2-8-11** MFenton(2) (lw: rdn over 2f out: n.m.r over 1f out: nvr nr to chal) | 1¼ | **7** | 7/1 | 75 | 38 |
| 1774³ | **Aficionado (IRE)** (RFJohnsonHoughton) **2-8-11** JReid(1) (lw: s.i.s: hdwy over 3f out: wknd over 2f out) | 1¾ | **8** | 16/1 | 69 | 32 |
| 1683* | **Lamorna** (MRChannon) **2-8-8** TQuinn(6) (lw: bhd fnl 2f) | ¾ | **9** | 20/1 | 64 | 27 |
| 1884* | **Bride's Reprisal** (MRChannon) **2-8-6** KDarley(8) (prom over 3f) | ½ | **10** | 20/1 | 60 | 23 |

(SP 109.7%) **10 Rn**

**61.09 secs** (1.09) CSF £37.69 TOTE £4.50: £2.00 £3.10 £3.10 (£38.50) Trio £160.60 OWNER Cheveley Park Stud (NEWMARKET) BRED Cheveley Park Stud Ltd
**Dazzle**, a sturdy filly who had to be led round by two handlers in the paddock, was certainly thrown in at the deep end on this debut, although this race was won by a newcomer in 1991 and 1995. Picking up really nicely inside the distance, she swooped into the lead inside the final furlong and needed only to be nudged along for a very impressive display. Further success awaits her. (7/2)
**1760* Vax Star** was taking a big step up in class, but ran really well. Dictating from the front, she was rousted along from the distance, but was not overhauled until inside the final furlong. She should soon return to the winning trail. (12/1)
**1834* Olympic Spirit**, who went down very freely, played an active role from the start and had every chance below the distance before tapped for toe. (11/1)
**924 Taufan Rookie (IRE)**, held up towards the back of the field, did not have a great deal of room in which to manoeuvre as he began to pick up ground below the distance. He did stay on to take fourth place, but it would be unfair to say he was unlucky. (9/2: op 5/2)
**1795 Caviar Royale (IRE)** had given his all entering the final furlong. (6/1)
**1699 Superior Premium** played an active role until calling it a day below the distance. (8/1)

## 2113 HARDWICKE STKS (Gp 2) (4-Y.O+) (Class A)
3-05 (3-06) **1m 4f** £70,970.00 (£26,588.50: £12,794.25: £5,597.25) Stalls: High GOING minus 0.19 sec per fur (GF)

| | | | | SP | RR | SF |
|---|---|---|---|---|---|---|
| 1017* | **Oscar Schindler (IRE)** (KPrendergast,Ireland) **4-8-9** MJKinane(8) (hdwy over 2f out: led 1f out: hrd rdn: r.o wl) | — | **1** | 7/4 1 | 122 | 94 |
| 1575a³ | **Annus Mirabilis (FR) (119)** (SbinSuroor) **4-8-9** JCarroll(2) (lw: chsd ldr: led 3f out to 1f out: r.o) | ½ | **2** | 5/1 3 | 121 | 93 |
| 1176³ | **Posidonas (116)** (PFICole) **4-9-0** TQuinn(7) (b.off hind: lw: a.p: hrd rdn & edgd lft over 2f out: unable qckn) | 3½ | **3** | 16/1 | 122 | 94 |
| 1355³ | **Lear White (USA) (106)** (PAKelleway) **5-8-9** JWeaver(5) (lw: led 9f: rdn: one pce) | s.h | **4** | 33/1 | 117 | 89 |
| 1509⁹ | **Phantom Gold (112)** (LordHuntingdon) **4-8-9** MHills(1) (hld up: rdn & n.m.r over 2f out: one pce) | 1¼ | **5** | 10/1 | 115 | 87 |
| 1017⁵ | **Dance a Dream (116)** (MRStoute) **4-8-6** PatEddery(6) (rdn over 4f out: a bhd) | 1 | **6** | 8/1 | 111 | 83 |
| 1794⁴ | **Punishment** (CEBrittain) **5-8-9** BDoyle(3) (lw: bhd fnl 2f) | hd | **7** | 16/1 | 114 | 86 |
| 1176* | **Election Day (IRE) (115)** (MRStoute) **4-8-9** WCarson(4) (lw: nvr gng wl: rdn thrght: a bhd: t.o fnl 5f) | dist | **8** | 100/30 2 | — | — |

(SP 111.0%) **8 Rn**

**2m 27.84** (-2.16) CSF £10.06 TOTE £2.20: £1.20 £1.50 £3.30 (£3.90) OWNER Mr Oliver Lehane BRED Oliver Lehane
**OFFICIAL EXPLANATION Election Day (IRE): his rider reported that the colt was never going.**

**1017* Oscar Schindler (IRE)** put up a very useful display. Beginning his run on the outside of the field in the straight, he snatched the lead a furlong from home and, responding to pressure, kept the persistent runner-up at bay. The Irish St Leger in which he finished third last year is his main objective. (7/4)
**1575a Annus Mirabilis (FR)** lost nothing in defeat. In second place until going on turning for home, he was collared a furlong out but, to his credit, showed real battling qualities and made sure the winner did not have things all his own way. His turn is surely near at hand. (5/1)
**1176 Posidonas,** who had to shoulder a 5lb Group One penalty, raced in third place. Edging slightly left under pressure early in the straight, he could then only plod on at one pace. The ground was probably a bit too lively for him. (16/1)
**1355 Lear White (USA)** ran well on ground too fast for him. Taking a step up in distance, he dictated matters from the front but, collared turning for home, could only keep on at one pace. He should be able to find a race when the ground rides soft. (33/1)
**Phantom Gold** raced in fourth place. She got slightly tightened up early in the straight, but it made not the slightest bit of difference as she was only plodding on in her own time. (10/1)
**1017 Dance a Dream** was always at the back of the field. (8/1)
**1176* Election Day (IRE)** found this ground far too fast and ran appallingly. He was subsequently found to have injured his off-fore. (100/30: 9/4-7/2)

## 2114 WOKINGHAM H'CAP (0-110) (3-Y.O+) (Class B)
3-45 (3-50) **6f** £49,533.75 (£14,895.00: £7,197.50: £3,348.75) Stalls: Centre GOING minus 0.19 sec per fur (GF)

| | | | SP | RR | SF |
|---|---|---|---|---|---|
| 1149[6] | **Emerging Market (95)** (JLDunlop) **4-8-13** KDarley(7) (hdwy over 1f out: led ins fnl f: rdn out)........................— | **1** | 33/1 | 104 | 85 |
| 876[3] | **Prince Babar (86)** (JEBanks) **5-8-1**(3) JStack(4) (rdn & hdwy over 1f out: ev ch ins fnl f: r.o)..............................½ | **2** | 10/1[2] | 94 | 75 |
| 1853[9] | **Double Bounce (82)** (PJMakin) **6-8-0** MRoberts(10) (b: lw: rdn over 3f out: hdwy over 1f out: r.o ins fnl f)......nk | **3** | 11/1[3] | 89 | 70 |
| 1623* | **Green Perfume (USA) (105)** (PFICole) **4-9-9** 5x TQuinn(2) (lw: a.p: rdn over 2f out: led 1f out tl ins fnl f: unable qckn)....................½ | **4** | 13/2[1] | 111 | 92 |
| 1853* | **Sir Joey (USA) (86)** (PGMurphy) **7-8-1**(3) 5x SDrowne(29) (racd far side: hld up: rdn over 1f out: r.o).............s.h | **5** | 50/1 | 91 | 72 |
| 1818* | **To the Roof (IRE) (98)** (PWHarris) **4-9-2** 8x GHind(25) (racd far side: hld up: rdn over 1f out: r.o)....................hd | **6** | 14/1 | 103 | 84 |
| 1107[7] | **Astrac (IRE) (93)** (RAkehurst) **5-8-11** SSanders(28) (racd far side: a.p: hrd rdn over 1f out: one pce)............1¼ | **7** | 25/1 | 95 | 76 |
| 1623[6] | **Monaassib (103)** (EALDunlop) **5-9-7** MHills(19) (swtchd lft s: hdwy over 2f out: hrd rdn over 1f out: one pce)hd | **8** | 33/1 | 105 | 86 |
| 1630[11] | **Master of Passion (83)** (JMPEustace) **7-8-1** JTate(14) (lw: chsd ldr: led over 2f out to 1f out: sn wknd)...........1 | **9** | 33/1 | 82 | 63 |
| 1818[9] | **Jayannpee (103)** (IABalding) **5-9-7** CAsmussen(6) (b.off hind: lw: prom 4f)..........................................½ | **10** | 12/1 | 101 | 82 |
| 1149* | **Saseedo (USA) (88)** (WAO'Gorman) **6-8-6** EmmaO'Gorman(18) (swtchd rt s: racd far side: nvr nrr) .............s.h | **11** | 33/1 | 85 | 66 |
| 1178[11] | **Latching (IRE) (85)** (RFJohnsonHoughton) **4-8-3** AMcGlone(27) (racd far side: a.p: rdn over 2f out: one pce) ...........................s.h | **12** | 50/1 | 82 | 63 |
| | **Coastal Bluff (88)** (TDBarron) **4-8-6** JFortune(24) (b.hind: racd far side: a.p: rdn over 2f out: one pce) ..........nk | **13** | 12/1 | 85 | 66 |
| 1680* | **Law Commission (84)** (DRCElsworth) **6-7-13**(3) 5x MHenry(30) (racd far side: nvr nrr).................................nk | **14** | 25/1 | 80 | 61 |
| 1790* | **Selhurstpark Flyer (IRE) (87)** (JBerry) **5-8-0**(5) 8x PRoberts(12) (b: lw: led over 3f: wknd over 1f out)..............1 | **15** | 25/1 | 80 | 61 |
| 1790[12] | **Silent Expression (85)** (BJMeehan) **6-8-3** BDoyle(3) (b: a mid div)..........................................nk | **16** | 33/1 | 77 | 58 |
| 1911a* | **Anzio (IRE) (104)** (MissGayKelleway) **5-9-8b** 8x MJKinane(23) (lw: racd far side: a mid div)...........................½ | **17** | 14/1 | 95 | 76 |
| 1107[2] | **Madly Sharp (101)** (JWWatts) **5-9-5** PatEddery(15) (a mid div)..........................................nk | **18** | 14/1 | 91 | 72 |
| 1853[7] | **Mr Bergerac (IRE) (83)** (BPalling) **5-8-1** TSprake(5) (lw: rdn thrght: nvr nrr) ........................1½ | **19** | 33/1 | 69 | 50 |
| 1566a[6] | **Sir Silver Sox (USA) (101)** (TStack,Ireland) **4-9-5v** KFallon(26) (racd far side: nvr nrr) ..............................½ | **20** | 40/1 | 86 | 67 |
| 1975[4] | **Stylish Ways (IRE) (95)** (MissSEHall) **4-8-8**(5) MartinDwyer(17) (b: lw: bhd fnl 2f)..............................hd | **21** | 50/1 | 80 | 61 |
| 1790[8] | **The Happy Fox (IRE) (84)** (BAMcMahon) **4-8-2** WCarson(1) (hld up: rdn over 2f out: wknd wl over 1f out) ....hd | **22** | 33/1 | 68 | 49 |
| 1621[8] | **Hard to Figure (110)** (RJHodges) **10-10-0** JReid(9) (bhd fnl 3f)..........................................hd | **23** | 40/1 | 94 | 75 |
| 1818[6] | **Brave Edge (105)** (RHannon) **5-9-9** 8x RHughes(22) (racd far side: spd over 4f) ..............................½ | **24** | 20/1 | 88 | 69 |
| 1790[9] | **Shikari's Son (90)** (JCullinan) **9-8-5**(3) AWhelan(13) (s.s: a bhd).............................................1½ | **25** | 66/1 | 69 | 50 |
| 1652[4] | **Youdontsay (80)** (TJNaughton) **4-7-7**(5) MBaird(11) (prom 4f).............................................½ | **26** | 50/1 | 57 | 38 |
| 1800[5] | **Espartero (IRE) (102)** (SirMarkPrescott) **4-9-6** GDuffield(8) (lw: bhd fnl 2f).................................1¾ | **27** | 14/1 | 75 | 56 |
| 1630* | **Top Banana (96)** (HCandy) **5-9-0** 5x CRutter(21) (racd far side: a bhd) ...................................12 | **28** | 10/1[2] | 37 | 18 |
| 1621[10] | **Bold Effort (FR) (95)** (KOCunningham-Brown) **4-8-13** JWeaver(20) (racd far side: a bhd) ............................10 | **29** | 50/1 | 9 | — |
| *1621[4]* | ***Averti (IRE) (94)*** (WRMuir) **5-8-12** WJO'Connor(16) (Withdrawn not under starters' orders: panicked in stalls) .. | **W** | 20/1 | — | — |
| | | | (SP 139.7%) | **29 Rn** | |

**1m 13.83** (-0.17) CSF £312.16 CT £3,557.40 TOTE £56.20: £10.50 £3.00 £2.50 £1.70 (£122.60) Trio £419.40 OWNER Mr Philip Wroughton (ARUNDEL) BRED R. T. and Mrs Watson
STEWARDS' ENQUIRY Darley susp. 30/6 - 3/7/96 (careless riding).
**IN-FOCUS: The winner had been running over seven of late, and a strongly-run and stiff six proved ideal.**
**1149 Emerging Market,** put to sleep at the back of the field, had to weave his way through the pack below the distance, but he managed to do so and, striking the front inside the final furlong, was rousted along for victory. (33/1)
**876 Prince Babar,** ridden along to take closer order below the distance, threatened to take the lead inside the final furlong but was just unable to cope with the winner. (10/1)
**1853 Double Bounce,** pushed along and going nowhere at the back of the field at halfway, ran on nicely in the last furlong and a half and only just failed. (11/1)
**1623* Green Perfume (USA)** ran a fine race considering this trip was a bit too sharp for him. A leading light from the off, he struck the front a furlong from home but was soon passed by the winner. (13/2)
**1853* Sir Joey (USA),** racing on the unfavoured far side, chased the leaders. He did best of those runners, but was just unable to get to his counterparts on the opposite side of the track. (50/1)
**1818* To the Roof (IRE),** racing on the unfavoured far rail, chased the leaders and stayed on nicely in the final furlong. (14/1)
**Coastal Bluff,** the only runner without a previous run under his belt, was up with the pace on the far side but failed to find the necessary turn of foot in the last two furlongs. (12/1)
**1911a* Anzio (IRE),** who lost seventeen kilos after winning a Group Three in Ireland recently, has obviously not recovered and could not get out of the ruck on the far side. (14/1)
**1800 Espartero (IRE)** was very disappointing and was getting left behind in the last two and a half furlongs. (14/1)
**1630* Top Banana** (10/1: 12/1-8/1)

## 2115 KING'S STAND STKS (Gp 2) (3-Y.O+) (Class A)
4-20 (4-24) **5f** £65,390.00 (£24,449.50: £11,724.75: £5,085.75) Stalls: Centre GOING minus 0.19 sec per fur (GF)

| | | | SP | RR | SF |
|---|---|---|---|---|---|
| | **Pivotal (104)** (SirMarkPrescott) **3-8-10** GDuffield(7) (h.d.w: a.p: rdn over 1f out: led last strides)...................— | **1** | 13/2[3] | 128 | 88 |
| 1483* | **Mind Games (117)** (JBerry) **4-9-2** JCarroll(14) (lw: racd far side: led: clr over 1f out: hrd rdn: hdd last stride) ..½ | **2** | 3/1[1] | 126 | 92 |
| 1911a[4] | **Almaty (IRE)** (CCollins,Ireland) **3-8-10** KDarley(10) (lw: racd far side: a.p: rdn over 2f out: one pce) ............3½ | **3** | 20/1 | 115 | 75 |

| | | | | SP | RR | SF |
|---|---|---|---|---|---|---|
| 1945a2 | **Hever Golf Rose (119)** (TJNaughton) **5-9-2** PatEddery(11) (lw: racd far side: a.p: rdn over 2f out: one pce) .1¾ | **4** | | 11/1 | 110 | 76 |
| 11293 | **Royale Figurine (IRE) (107)** (MJFetherston-Godley) **5-8-13** JReid(16) (racd far side: rdn over 2f out: hdwy fnl f: nvr nrr) ....hd | **5** | | 25/1 | 106 | 72 |
| 92610 | **Royal Applause (120)** (BWHills) **3-8-13** MHills(6) (hld up: rdn over 2f out: one pce) ....nk | **6** | | 11/2 2 | 111 | 71 |
| 16215 | **Loch Patrick (105)** (MMadgwick) **6-9-2** AMcGlone(18) (lw: racd far side: nvr nr to chal) ....hd | **7** | | 50/1 | 108 | 74 |
| 1566a* | **Lidanna** (DHanley,Ireland) **3-8-7** MJKinane(15) (lt-f: racd far side: a.p: rdn over 2f out: wknd fnl f) ....nk | **8** | | 9/1 | 104 | 64 |
| 1581a4 | **Titus Livius (FR)** (JEPease,France) **3-8-10** CAsmussen(12) (unf: racd far side: nvr nrr) ....hd | **9** | | 20/1 | 107 | 67 |
| 9276 | **Eveningperformance (112)** (HCandy) **5-8-13** WNewnes(5) (lw: spd over 3f) ....½ | **10** | | 14/1 | 102 | 68 |
| 112912 | **Mubhij (IRE) (111)** (BWHills) **3-8-10** WCarson(4) (a.p: rdn over 2f out: wknd fnl f) ....nk | **11** | | 25/1 | 104 | 64 |
| 11294 | **Lucky Lionel (USA) (115)** (RHannon) **3-8-10** TQuinn(13) (lw: racd far side: a bhd) ....½ | **12** | | 14/1 | 103 | 63 |
| 181811 | **Wavian (97)** (RHannon) **4-9-2** WJO'Connor(9) (lw: bhd fnl 3f) ....nk | **13** | | 100/1 | 102 | 68 |
| 1911a2 | **Ailleacht (USA)** (JSBolger,Ireland) **4-8-13** KJManning(3) (lw: bhd fnl 3f) ....nk | **14** | | 33/1 | 98 | 64 |
| 2003* | **Double Quick (IRE) (102)** (MJohnston) **4-8-13** JWeaver(2) (lw: a bhd) ....1¼ | **15** | | 25/1 | 94 | 60 |
| 14832 | **Struggler (110)** (DRLoder) **4-9-2v1** RHughes(1) (stumbled s: a bhd) ....2½ | **16** | | 15/2 | 89 | 55 |
| 20035 | **Ya Malak (110)** (JWPayne) **5-9-2b1** BThomson(8) (spd 3f) ....11 | **17** | | 50/1 | 53 | 19 |
| | | | | (SP 126.1%) | | **17 Rn** |

**59.49 secs** (-0.51) CSF £25.20 TOTE £12.70: £3.10 £1.80 £9.50 (£21.50) Trio £519.70 OWNER Cheveley Park Stud (NEWMARKET) BRED Cheveley Park Stud Ltd
WEIGHT FOR AGE 3yo-6lb

**IN-FOCUS: An up-to-standard edition of this race, won by easily the least experienced contender.**

**Pivotal** was not only taking a huge step up in class, but was also making his seasonal debut - he had a temperature in the spring. This was certainly a tall order to ask, but he proved more than up to it. Always close up on the stands' side, he broke away from that group below the distance but did not look like he would get to the leader racing on the opposite side of the track. Nevertheless, he buckled down to work in tremendous style and got up in the last few strides to win in a very fast time. The July Cup is next on the agenda. (13/2)

**1483* Mind Games** ran an absolute blinder and had the race won everywhere but the line. Clear below the distance, the race looked certain to be his, but he was caught by the winner, racing on the opposite side of the track, in the last few strides. His main target is the Nunthorpe at York and, with his trainer vowing 'we have not seen the best of him', he is still the one they all have to beat, despite this narrow defeat. (3/1)

**1911a Almaty (IRE)**, fitted with a tongue-strap, was always close up on the far side. Pushed along over a quarter of a mile from home, he was unable to cope with the very speedy Mind Games. (20/1)

**1945a Hever Golf Rose**, always close up on the far side, failed to find the necessary turn of foot in the last two furlongs. She will now return abroad for the Holsten Trophy over six furlongs at Hamburg in early July. (11/1: 8/1-12/1)

**1129 Royale Figurine (IRE)**, racing on the far side, stayed on in the final furlong, but never looked like getting into it. (25/1)

**926 Royal Applause**, who failed to stay a mile in the Guineas, may have found this trip a bit sharp. Chasing the leaders on the stands' side, he failed to quicken in the last two furlongs. Three of his four wins last year came over six furlongs and that looks like being his trip. (11/2: 4/1-6/1)

## 2116 KING EDWARD VII STKS (Gp 2) (3-Y.O C & G) (Class A)

4-55 (4-55) **1m 4f** £70,204.00 (£26,371.95: £12,748.48: £5,640.57) Stalls: High GOING minus 0.19 sec per fur (GF)

| | | | SP | RR | SF |
|---|---|---|---|---|---|
| 118010 | **Amfortas (IRE) (86)** (CEBrittain) **3-8-8** BDoyle(6) (mde virtually all: drvn out) ....— | **1** | 66/1 | 118 | 79 |
| 10152 | **Desert Boy (IRE) (106)** (PWChapple-Hyam) **3-8-8** JReid(5) (hld up: chsd wnr fnl 2f: hrd rdn: r.o) ....½ | **2** | 13/2 3 | 117 | 78 |
| 17913 | **Shantou (USA)** (JHMGosden) **3-8-8** MJKinane(1) (lw: n.m.r over 2f out: rdn & hdwy over 1f out: r.o) ....nk | **3** | 9/4 1 | 117 | 78 |
| 14275 | **Germano (95)** (GWragg) **3-8-8** PaulEddery(7) (lw: stdy hdwy on ins 3f out: wknd over 1f out) ....7 | **4** | 16/1 | 108 | 69 |
| 13292 | **Prize Giving (112)** (GWragg) **3-8-8** MHills(2) (lw: stdy hdwy 9f out: wknd 2f out) ....1½ | **5** | 9/4 1 | 106 | 67 |
| 691* | **Don Vito** (RCharlton) **3-8-8** PatEddery(4) (lw: plld hrd: bhd fnl 3f) ....3 | **6** | 7/2 2 | 102 | 63 |
| 13294 | **Legal Right (USA) (102)** (PWChapple-Hyam) **3-8-10ow2** RHughes(3) (lw: chsd wnr 10f: sn wknd) ....1 | **7** | 11/1 | 102 | 61 |
| | | | (SP 112.8%) | | **7 Rn** |

**2m 29.85** (-0.15) CSF £377.45 TOTE £50.00: £9.50 £2.80 (£144.60) OWNER Mr B. H. Voak (NEWMARKET) BRED Sir Thomas Pilkington and Mrs E. Burke

**684 Amfortas (IRE)** caused the biggest shock of the meeting, as he left all of his previous form well behind with this pillar-to-post victory. Responding to pressure, he managed to keep his closest rivals at bay. (66/1: tchd 100/1)

**1015 Desert Boy (IRE)** moved into second place a quarter of a mile from home but, despite gradually getting to the winner, was unable to overhaul him in time. (13/2)

**1791 Shantou (USA)** again did not have the clearest of runs but, unlike in the Derby, there were no excuses here, for he had plenty of daylight in the last furlong and a half. He did pick up ground, but was not quick enough to make up the leeway in time. (9/4: Evens-5/2)

**1427 Germano** made his effort turning for home, but had bellows to mend below the distance. (16/1)

**1329 Prize Giving** ran very flat. Soon in a handy position, he tamely dropped away two furlongs from home. (9/4)

**691* Don Vito**, taking a big step up in class, was getting left behind entering the straight. (7/2: op 11/2)

## 2117 QUEEN ALEXANDRA STKS (4-Y.O+) (Class B)

5-30 (5-30) **2m 6f 34y** £19,338.00 (£7,242.00: £3,546.00: £1,530.00: £690.00: £354.00) Stalls: High GOING minus 0.19 sec per fur (GF)

| | | | SP | RR | SF |
|---|---|---|---|---|---|
| 14824 | **Admiral's Well (IRE) (108)** (RAkehurst) **6-9-3** TQuinn(1) (lw: a.p: led over 2f out: rdn out) ....— | **1** | 100/30 1 | 95 | 80 |
| 1710* | **Speed to Lead (IRE) (81)** (HRACecil) **4-8-7** PatEddery(3) (led tl over 2f out: unable qckn fnl f) ....2½ | **2** | 7/2 2 | 83 | 68 |
| 1752a4 | **Old Rouvel (USA) (102)** (DJGMurraySmith) **5-9-3v1** MJKinane(5) (a.p: rdn over 2f out: hung rt over 1f out: r.o) ....hd | **3** | 4/1 3 | 93 | 78 |
| 14825 | **Bahamian Sunshine (USA) (100)** (DRLoder) **5-9-3** RHughes(8) (lw: hld up: rdn over 2f out: r.o one pce) ....hd | **4** | 12/1 | 93 | 78 |
| | **Dance d'Ore (SWE)** (LReuterskjold,Sweden) **4-8-12** KAndersen(6) (lw: nvr nrr to chal) ....5 | **5** | 20/1 | 84 | 69 |
| 17103 | **Ivor's Flutter (69)** (DRCElsworth) **7-9-0** AProcter(9) (lw: nvr nrr) ....2 | **6** | 12/1 | 85 | 70 |
| 11766 | **Djais (FR) (95)** (JRJenkins) **7-9-0** JFortune(7) (hdwy over 3f out: wknd over 1f out) ....4 | **7** | 20/1 | 82 | 67 |
| 17063 | **Juyush (USA) (108)** (BWHills) **4-9-4** WCarson(10) (chsd ldr tl wknd over 2f out: t.o) ....23 | **8** | 6/1 | 70 | 55 |
| 17847 | **Jundi (IRE) (47)** (JDBethell) **5-9-0v** JWeaver(2) (a bhd: t.o) ....13 | **9** | 25/1 | 56 | 41 |
| | **Dajraan (IRE)** (NATwiston-Davies) **7-9-0** JReid(4) (bhd fnl 4f: t.o) ....6 | **10** | 16/1 | 52 | 37 |
| | | | (SP 114.2%) | | **10 Rn** |

**4m 52.05** (2.05) CSF £14.34 TOTE £4.40: £1.70 £1.30 £1.70 (£6.70) Trio £6.90 OWNER Mr A. D. Spence (EPSOM) BRED Barronstown Bloodstock Ltd

**OFFICIAL EXPLANATION Ivor's Flutter: his rider explained that the gelding lost his action and he felt it prudent not to persevere.**

**1482 Admiral's Well (IRE)** bounced back to form here. A leading light from the off, he went on over a quarter of a mile from home and was ridden along to win in a time only half a second outside the course record. (100/30)

**1710* Speed to Lead (IRE)** showed real courage over this severe trip. Bowling along in front, she was collared over a quarter of a mile from home but, showing a tremendous never-say-die attitude, was only seen off in the final furlong. (7/2)
**1752a Old Rouvel (USA)**, a leading light from the off, appeared to be travelling well half a mile from home. Asked for his effort in the straight, he hung right below the distance, but did struggle on to take third place. He is consistent but lacks any turn of foot. (4/1: op 5/2)
**1482 Bahamian Sunshine (USA)** saw out this marathon trip. Chasing the leaders, he stayed on in the straight and only just lost out for third prize. (12/1: 8/1-14/1)
**Dance d'Ore (SWE)** made a little late headway without posing a threat. (20/1)
**1710 Ivor's Flutter** (12/1: op 20/1)
**1706 Juyush (USA)** failed to stay this extreme trip. Racing in second place, he was collared for that position over two furlongs from home and stopped as if shot, eventually finishing tailed off. (6/1: 4/1-13/2)

T/Jkpt: £212,292.60 (0.1 Tckts); £269,103.32 to Ascot 22/6/96. T/Plpt: £477.10 (222.14 Tckts). T/Qdpt: £94.50 (52.58 Tckts) AK

## 1583-AYR (L-H) (Good to firm)
## Friday June 21st
WEATHER: Fine

## 2118 SEAFIELD MAIDEN AUCTION STKS (2-Y.O) (Class F)
2-15 (2-16) **5f** £2,584.00 (£724.00: £352.00) Stalls: High GOING: 0.02 sec per fur (G)

| | | | | SP | RR | SF |
|---|---|---|---|---|---|---|
| 1827$^{5}$ | **Bold Brief** (DenysSmith) **2-8-5** LCharnock(3) (mde all: pushed along & styd on wl) | — | **1** | 2/1$^{2}$ | 63 | 2 |
| 1827$^{2}$ | **Nifty Norman** (JBerry) **2-8-7** GCarter(1) (unruly s: w wnr tl outpcd ½-wy: styd on fnl f) | 1½ | **2** | 8/13$^{1}$ | 60 | — |
| 1543$^{4}$ | **Chanson d'Amour (IRE)** (MissLAPerratt) **2-8-5** JFanning(2) (sn chsng ldrs: rdn & btn appr fnl f) | 4 | **3** | 33/1 | 45 | — |
| | **Skippy Was A Kiwi (IRE)** (APJarvis) **2-7-7**(7) CCarver(4) (neat: outpcd ½-wy: sme late hdwy) | 1¼ | **4** | 7/1$^{3}$ | 36 | — |
| | | | | (SP 110.7%) | **4 Rn** | |

**62.19 secs** (5.19) CSF £3.61 TOTE £3.50: (£2.00) OWNER P & I Darling (BISHOP AUCKLAND) BRED J. K. S. Cresswell
**1827 Bold Brief** was a different proposition this time. Flying out of the stalls and always having the edge on the favourite, he just needed pushing out to make sure of it. (2/1)
**1827 Nifty Norman** spoilt his chances by being edgy in the preliminaries and then played up in the stalls. To give him credit, he did keep on after looking well beaten. (8/13)
**1543 Chanson d'Amour (IRE)** ran a shade better than on her debut and is continually improving. (33/1)
**Skippy Was A Kiwi (IRE)**, a sharp sort, needed the experience and was never in it from halfway. (7/1)

## 2119 BEN H'CAP (0-80) (4-Y.O+) (Class D)
2-45 (2-45) **5f** £3,517.50 (£1,065.00: £520.00: £247.50) Stalls: High GOING: 0.02 sec per fur (G)

| | | | | SP | RR | SF |
|---|---|---|---|---|---|---|
| 1588$^{8}$ | **Garnock Valley (71)** (JBerry) **6-9-9** GCarter(1) (bhd: hdwy 2f out: r.o to ld cl home) | — | **1** | 7/1$^{3}$ | 80 | 55 |
| 1889* | **Leading Princess (IRE) (44)** (MissLAPerratt) **5-7-3b**(7) JBramhill(2) (led: rdn & qcknd 2f out: ct cl home) | ½ | **2** | 4/1$^{1}$ | 51 | 26 |
| 2005$^{14}$ | **Rich Glow (55)** (NBycroft) **5-8-7** NConnorton(7) (hld up & bhd: nt clr run & swtchd wl over 1f out: kpt on: nvr able to chal) | 1¾ | **3** | 6/1$^{2}$ | 57 | 32 |
| 1199$^{8}$ | **Royal Dome (IRE) (73)** (MartynWane) **4-9-11** LCharnock(5) (lw: chsd ldrs: rdn 2f out: nt qckn fnl f) | 3 | **4** | 7/1$^{3}$ | 65 | 40 |
| 2064$^{3}$ | **Able Sheriff (50)** (MWEasterby) **4-7-13b**(3) DWright(8) (lw: bhd: hdwy ½-wy: sn chsng ldrs: rdn & btn appr fnl f) | ½ | **5** | 4/1$^{1}$ | 41 | 16 |
| 1541$^{4}$ | **Featherstone Lane (51)** (MissLCSiddall) **5-8-3v** DeanMcKeown(6) (prom tl outpcd fnl 2f) | ¾ | **6** | 8/1 | 39 | 14 |
| 1974$^{12}$ | **Saddlehome (USA) (73)** (TDBarron) **7-9-11** JFanning(3) (prom: effrt ½-wy: sn outpcd) | 2 | **7** | 4/1$^{1}$ | 55 | 30 |
| 1865$^{8}$ | **Another Episode (IRE) (65)** (MissLAPerratt) **7-9-3** NDay(4) (chsd ldrs over 3f: wknd) | 4 | **8** | 33/1 | 34 | 9 |
| | | | | (SP 113.3%) | **8 Rn** | |

**60.01 secs** (3.01) CSF £32.45 CT £162.36 TOTE £7.30: £2.20 £2.10 £1.70 (£14.60) OWNER Mr Robert Aird (COCKERHAM) BRED Sunley Stud
**1545* Garnock Valley** had to really knuckle down and work to win this, and came from virtually last at halfway to get there late on. (7/1)
**1889* Leading Princess (IRE)** is really on good terms with herself now and this time went tearing off in front but, despite trying hard, just failed to last out. (4/1)
**1588 Rich Glow**, a track specialist, was given plenty to do and then met with trouble in the last couple of furlongs and, despite staying on, could never get in a blow. (6/1: op 7/2)
**735 Royal Dome (IRE)** showed plenty of speed, but is high enough in the weights just now and was going nowhere in the last furlong and a half. (7/1)
**2064 Able Sheriff**, having his second run in three days, ran reasonably until crying enough approaching the last furlong. (4/1: 6/1-7/2)
**1541 Featherstone Lane** had his chances until finding things too competitive soon after halfway. (8/1)

## 2120 BRITISH ENSIGN MAIDEN H'CAP (0-70) (3-Y.O+) (Class E)
3-20 (3-20) **1m 5f 13y** £3,100.00 (£940.00: £460.00: £220.00) Stalls: Low GOING: 0.02 sec per fur (G)

| | | | | SP | RR | SF |
|---|---|---|---|---|---|---|
| 1478$^{5}$ | **Monaco Gold (IRE) (35)** (MrsMReveley) **4-8-7** LCharnock(2) (trckd ldrs: led wl over 2f out: r.o) | — | **1** | 14/1 | 45 | 28 |
| 1507$^{7}$ | **State Approval (60)** (APJarvis) **3-9-3** NConnorton(3) (in tch: hdwy appr st: chal over 3f out: one pce) | 3½ | **2** | 6/1$^{3}$ | 66 | 34 |
| 1100$^{13}$ | **Charming Admiral (IRE) (62)** (CFWall) **3-9-5** WLord(7) (lw: hmpd after 1f: bhd: gd hdwy 2f out: r.o) | 3 | **3** | 9/4$^{1}$ | 64 | 32 |
| 620$^{12}$ | **Fanadiyr (IRE) (52)** (WStorey) **4-9-3**(7) IonaWands(11) (hdwy to chal 7f out: led over 3f out: sn hdd & wknd) | 6 | **4** | 10/1 | 47 | 30 |
| 1833$^{3}$ | **Code Red (66)** (JWHills) **3-9-9** OUrbina(9) (lw: prom: effrt ent st: rdn & btn 3f out) | 5 | **5** | 5/1$^{2}$ | 55 | 23 |
| 2024$^{3}$ | **Teejay'n'aitch (IRE) (40)** (JSGoldie) **4-8-5**(7) JBramhill(8) (hmpd after s: nvr trbld ldrs) | 1½ | **6** | 14/1 | 27 | 10 |
| 1478$^{3}$ | **Tremendisto (47)** (CaptJWilson) **6-9-5** GCarter(1) (led after 1f to 6f out: cl up tl wknd over 3f out) | 1¾ | **7** | 11/1 | 32 | 15 |
| 803$^{6}$ | **General Glow (45)** (NBycroft) **3-7-13**(3) DarrenMoffatt(10) (chsd ldrs tl outpcd 4f out: sn btn) | 7 | **8** | 50/1 | 21 | — |
| 1784$^{8}$ | **Calcando (37)** (EWeymes) **4-8-9** JFanning(4) (led 1f: cl up: led 6f out tl over 3f out: wknd qckly) | 1¼ | **9** | 66/1 | 12 | — |
| 1887$^{4}$ | **Indiphar (48)** (FHLee) **3-8-5** RLappin(5) (a bhd) | 2½ | **10** | 5/1$^{2}$ | 19 | — |
| 1877$^{2}$ | **Go With The Wind (62)** (MBell) **3-9-5b**$^{1}$ NDay(6) (hmpd bnd after s: lost tch appr st: t.o) | dist | **11** | 7/1 | — | — |
| | | | | (SP 125.1%) | **11 Rn** | |

**2m 53.03** (8.23) CSF £93.35 CT £244.51 TOTE £23.60: £5.30 £3.00 £2.40 (£67.20) Trio £101.50 OWNER Mr D. McGonagle (SALTBURN) BRED Miss M. Tucker
WEIGHT FOR AGE 3yo-15lb
**OFFICIAL EXPLANATION Go With The Wind: finished distressed.**

**1478 Monaco Gold (IRE)** travelled well and, once he kicked on early in the straight, he soon spreadeagled this bunch. (14/1)
**1100 State Approval** had his chances and kept struggling on, but lacks any turn of foot. (6/1: op 7/2)
**717 Charming Admiral (IRE)** got messed about on the first bend and seemed to lose all interest, but he certainly picked up well late on and made up an amazing amount of ground. It would seem he really stays, and he could need further yet. (9/4)
**Fanadiyr (IRE)** had his chances from halfway until running out of fuel in the last three furlongs. (10/1: op 25/1)
**1833 Code Red** is beginning to look hard-trained and is certainly short of speed. (5/1)
**2024 Teejay'n'aitch (IRE)**, hampered at the start, never took any interest thereafter. (14/1)
**1887 Indiphar** (5/1: 4/1-6/1)
**1877 Go With The Wind** (7/1: op 4/1)

## 2121 DALMILLING CLAIMING STKS (3-Y.O+) (Class E)

3-55 (3-59) **1m** £2,931.00 (£888.00: £434.00: £207.00) Stalls: Low GOING minus 0.17 sec per fur (GF)

| | Horse / details | Dist | Pos | SP | RR | SF |
|---|---|---|---|---|---|---|
| 1866² | **Sir Arthur Hobbs (57)** (JLEyre) **9-9-1** RLappin(5) (led after 1f: hld on gamely fnl f) | — | 1 | 5/2 1 | 62 | 33 |
| 1423⁹ | **Parliament Piece (63)** (DNicholls) **10-9-13** DeanMcKeown(7) (lw: a.p: effrt 3f out: ev ch over 1f out: styd on) | nk | 2 | 11/2 | 73 | 44 |
| | **Open Affair** (APJarvis) **3-8-2** GCarter(3) (bhd: hdwy over 2f out: styd on: nt pce to chal) | 2 | 3 | 25/1 | 54 | 15 |
| 1506² | **Loveyoumillions (IRE) (70)** (NTinkler) **4-9-13** JOsborne(1) (w ldr: rdn over 2f out: grad wknd) | 3½ | 4 | 11/4 2 | 62 | 33 |
| 1893⁴ | **Indian Rhapsody (50)** (ABailey) **4-8-3**(7) IonaWands(4) (prom: effrt 3f out: one pce) | s.h | 5 | 5/1 3 | 45 | 16 |
| 1866* | **Northern Spark (44)** (MissLAPerratt) **8-9-1** JFanning(6) (lw: b: chsd ldrs tl wknd fnl 3f) | 3½ | 6 | 7/1 | 43 | 14 |
| 1866¹² | **She's A Winner (IRE) (55)** (PMonteith) **3-8-4** LCharnock(2) (led 1f: chsd ldrs tl wknd 3f out) | ½ | 7 | 66/1 | 41 | 2 |

(SP 105.1%) **7 Rn**

**1m 42.52** (5.12) CSF £14.08 TOTE £2.90: £1.20 £6.10 (£23.20) OWNER Miss Donna-Marie Lappin (HAMBLETON) BRED A. Tarry
WEIGHT FOR AGE 3yo-10lb
**1866 Sir Arthur Hobbs** showed all of his old battling qualities to win this, and thoroughly deserved it. (5/2)
**1088 Parliament Piece** took the eye in the paddock and was trying to win this for a second year running but, despite a valiant attempt, just failed to get there. (11/2: op 7/2)
**Open Affair** put in a useful first effort here, staying on well in the straight to show that similar events are well within her capabilities. (25/1)
**1506 Loveyoumillions (IRE)** again raced keenly up with the pace but, when an effort was required in the last two furlongs, he was soon found out. (11/4)
**1893 Indian Rhapsody** was always chasing the leaders, but could never find the pace to take them on. (5/1)
**1866* Northern Spark** moved poorly to post here and was never happy in the race. (7/1: 5/1-8/1)
**1345 She's A Winner (IRE)**, from a yard whose charges generally look superb, must be the odd one out, and she has gone backwards for the time being. (66/1)

## 2122 E.B.F. MAIDEN STKS (2-Y.O) (Class D)

4-30 (4-34) **7f** £3,875.00 (£1,175.00: £575.00: £275.00) Stalls: Low GOING: 0.02 sec per fur (G)

| | Horse / details | Dist | Pos | SP | RR | SF |
|---|---|---|---|---|---|---|
| 1673² | **Impetuous Air** (EWeymes) **2-8-9** OUrbina(7) (lw: trckd ldrs: stdy hdwy to ld wl over 1f out: r.o) | — | 1 | 2/1 1 | 65 | 10 |
| | **Select Star (IRE)** (APJarvis) **2-8-11**(3) DWright(3) (leggy: unf: chsd ldrs: outpcd 3f out: styd on strly fnl f) | 2½ | 2 | 25/1 | 64 | 9 |
| 1869³ | **Ben's Ridge** (PCHaslam) **2-9-0** DeanMcKeown(8) (chsd ldrs: squeezed thro to ld over 2f out: hdd wl over 1f out: one pce) | nk | 3 | 9/4 2 | 64 | 9 |
| 1197⁸ | **Warrlin** (CWFairhurst) **2-9-0** LCharnock(6) (cl up: bmpd wl over 2f out: one pce) | 2½ | 4 | 33/1 | 58 | 3 |
| | **Ivan Luis (FR)** (MBell) **2-9-0** NDay(5) (leggy: bit bkwd: s.s: hdwy & hung rt over 2f out: nvr rchd ldrs) | 2½ | 5 | 9/1 | 52 | — |
| 1166⁴ | **Tribal Mischief** (DMoffatt) **2-8-6**(3) DarrenMoffatt(1) (led tl hdd over 2f out: grad wknd) | 1¾ | 6 | 5/1 3 | 43 | — |
| 848⁶ | **Fast Spin** (TDBarron) **2-9-0** JFanning(4) (lw: rr div: hmpd over 2f out: n.d) | 3½ | 7 | 16/1 | 40 | — |
| 2025¹⁰ | **Alisadara** (NBycroft) **2-8-9** NConnorton(9) (prom 4f: sn wknd) | nk | 8 | 50/1 | 35 | — |
| | **Don't Worry Mike** (FHLee) **2-9-0** RLappin(2) (w'like: s.i.s: n.d) | 3½ | 9 | 16/1 | 32 | — |
| 1479⁷ | **Read Your Contract (IRE)** (JBerry) **2-9-0** GCarter(10) (a bhd) | 5 | 10 | 25/1 | 20 | — |

(SP 115.1%) **10 Rn**

**1m 29.95** (5.95) CSF £42.22 TOTE £2.30: £1.40 £4.70 £1.10 (£33.90) Trio £17.30 OWNER Mr T. A. Scothern (MIDDLEHAM) BRED D. J. and Mrs Deer
**1673 Impetuous Air** was a shade fractious at the start, but then put up a smooth performance, winning comfortably, and is obviously progressing. (2/1: op 11/10)
**Select Star (IRE)** was very green when the tempo increased early in the straight but, judging by the way he picked up at the finish, he will be a different proposition next time. (25/1)
**1869 Ben's Ridge**, a bit of a handful in the paddock, ran a sound race, but was tapped for speed in the last couple of furlongs. (9/4)
**1197 Warrlin** put up an improved performance, racing up with the pace but, when the race really began in the last three furlongs, he did not possess a change of gear. (33/1)
**Ivan Luis (FR)** needed this and was awkward at the start. He threw away all chances by missing the break, but he did show ability, running on in the last three furlongs. (9/1: op 11/4)
**1166 Tribal Mischief**, a moderate-actioned filly, was stepping up in distance here and failed to see it out. (5/1)

## 2123 SNODGRASS APPRENTICE H'CAP (0-70) (3-Y.O) (Class E)

5-05 (5-05) **1m** £2,970.00 (£900.00: £440.00: £210.00) Stalls: Low GOING minus 0.17 sec per fur (GF)

| | Horse / details | Dist | Pos | SP | RR | SF |
|---|---|---|---|---|---|---|
| 2023¹⁰ | **Napoleon's Return (45)** (AHarrison) **3-7-6v**(7) JennyBenson(1) (mde virtually all: styd on wl fnl f) | — | 1 | 12/1 | 56 | 26 |
| 1668⁹ | **Sing And Dance (42)** (EWeymes) **3-7-10** IonaWands(8) (outpcd & bhd: hdwy 2f out: styd on wl towards fin) | ¾ | 2 | 5/1 3 | 52 | 22 |
| 1526² | **Lucky Bea (60)** (MWEasterby) **3-9-0b** GParkin(2) (hld up: hdwy 2f out: ch & rdn appr fnl f: no ex) | hd | 3 | 5/2 1 | 69 | 39 |
| 2019² | **Termon (60)** (MissLAPerratt) **3-8-9**(5) JBramhill(7) (chsd ldrs: rdn over 2f out: btn over 1f out) | 5 | 4 | 6/1 | 59 | 29 |
| 1651² | **Eurobox Boy (59)** (APJarvis) **3-8-8v**(5) KHopkins(3) (w ldrs tl wknd fnl 2f) | 2½ | 5 | 9/2 2 | 53 | 23 |
| 1599⁶ | **Hoh Majestic (IRE) (67)** (MartynWane) **3-9-4v**(3) JEdmunds(6) (w ldrs tl wknd over 2f out) | 10 | 6 | 10/1 | 41 | 11 |
| 660⁵ | **Yuppy Girl (IRE) (55)** (CaptJWilson) **3-8-2**(7) AngelaHartley(5) (a bhd) | 9 | 7 | 16/1 | 11 | — |
| 1608¹³ | **Distinctly Swingin (IRE) (45)** (MissLAPerratt) **3-7-10**(3) AngelaGallimore(4) (cl up tl wknd over 3f out) | 19 | 8 | 25/1 | — | — |

(SP 104.2%) **8 Rn**

**1m 41.69** (4.29) CSF £59.40 CT £142.78 TOTE £29.80: £2.50 £1.60 £1.30 (£112.40) Trio £142.70 OWNER Mr Martin Graham (MIDDLEHAM) BRED T. K. Knox
LONG HANDICAP Sing And Dance 7-8
**1312 Napoleon's Return** enjoyed himself out in front and was kept going in really good style. (12/1: op 8/1)

**Sing And Dance** ran as though this trip was on the short side and, despite finishing well, here was never going to make it. Her turn will come. (5/1)
**1526 Lucky Bea**, patiently ridden, had his chances approaching the final furlong, but then failed to come up with the goods. (5/2)
**2019 Termon** got a shade warm beforehand and was never firing this time. This should be forgiven. (6/1: op 4/1)
**1651 Eurobox Boy** could never gain the initiative on this occasion and he then threw in the towel fully two furlongs out. (9/2)
**1599 Hoh Majestic (IRE)** found this trip beyond him. (10/1: op 6/1)

T/Plpt: £165.60 (41.95 Tckts). T/Qdpt: £11.10 (54.53 Tckts) AA

# 1953-GOODWOOD (R-H) (St crse Good, Rnd crse Good to firm)
## Friday June 21st
WEATHER: Fine but cloudy

## 2124 FESTIVAL OF SPEED CLASSIC MAIDEN STKS (3-Y.O+) (Class D)
6-30 (6-41) **1m 1f** £4,235.00 (£1,265.00: £605.00: £275.00) Stalls: Low GOING minus 0.24 sec per fur (GF)

| | Horse | Dist | Pos | SP | RR | SF |
|---|---|---|---|---|---|---|
| 1614[2] | **Iberian Dancer (CAN) (76)** (JWHills) **3-8-4**(3) MHenry(2) (swtg: hld up & bhd: hdwy over 3f out: rdn to ld over 1f out: r.o wl) | — | **1** | 5/4[1] | 75 | 17 |
| 1142[11] | **Puce** (LMCumani) **3-8-7** SWhitworth(6) (hld up: rdn 3f out: r.o one pce fnl f) | 1¾ | **2** | 6/1[3] | 72 | 14 |
| 1690[4] | **Golden Thunderbolt (FR)** (JHMGosden) **3-8-12** GHind(5) (hdwy over 4f out: led over 2f out tl over 1f out: one pce) | ½ | **3** | 11/4[2] | 76 | 18 |
| 1627[3] | **Battle Spark (USA) (74)** (CACyzer) **3-8-12** KFallon(9) (chsd ldr over 5f: hrd rdn over 2f out: one pce) | 2 | **4** | 13/2 | 72 | 14 |
| *204*[3] | **Fresh Fruit Daily (74)** (PAKelleway) **4-9-4** MFenton(10) (led over 6f: wknd ins fnl f) | 1¼ | **5** | 9/1 | 65 | 18 |
| 1839[7] | **Artic Bay** (MrsPNDutfield) **4-9-9** CRutter(3) (hld up & plld hrd: hdwy over 3f out: wknd 2f out: eased whn btn fnl f) | 9 | **6** | 40/1 | 54 | 7 |
| 634[6] | **Followthe Allstars** (TJNaughton) **3-8-12** TSprake(4) (bhd fnl 3f) | 2 | **7** | 50/1 | 51 | — |
| 1434[13] | **Alfahad** (MissGayKelleway) **3-8-12** RPerham(1) (pushed along 6f out: a bhd) | 5 | **8** | 12/1 | 42 | — |
| 1656[8] | **Prestige Lass** (BSmart) **3-8-7** SSanders(8) (swtg: uns rdr & bolted bef s: bhd fnl 3f) | 6 | **9** | 16/1 | 26 | — |
| | **Bagby Boy (35)** (PRHedger) **4-9-9** MRichards(7) (bit bkwd: plld hrd: prom over 5f: t.o) | 16 | **10** | 50/1 | 3 | — |
| | | | | (SP 128.7%) | **10 Rn** | |

**1m 57.65** (6.25) CSF £10.45 TOTE £2.40: £1.20 £2.50 £1.60 (£9.70) Trio £15.10 OWNER Mr G. R. Collister (LAMBOURN) BRED Josham Farms Ltd.
WEIGHT FOR AGE 3yo-11lb
**1614 Iberian Dancer (CAN)**, confidently ridden, came with a nicely-timed run, but looked green and got a shade unbalanced after striking the front. (5/4: 11/10-7/4)
**Puce** seems to be going the right way and should do even better over a mile and a quarter. (6/1)
**1690 Golden Thunderbolt (FR)** again lacked the necessary finishing speed and may need even further. (11/4: 7/4-3/1)
**1627 Battle Spark (USA)** kept plugging away over what seemed an inadequate trip. (13/2)
**Fresh Fruit Daily** could need more patient tactics to stay beyond a mile. (9/1: 6/1-10/1)

## 2125 NATIONAL GRID (S) STKS (2-Y.O) (Class E)
7-00 (7-07) **5f** £3,460.00 (£1,030.00: £490.00: £220.00) Stalls: High GOING minus 0.24 sec per fur (GF)

| | Horse | Dist | Pos | SP | RR | SF |
|---|---|---|---|---|---|---|
| 2031[4] | **Tinker's Surprise (IRE)** (BJMeehan) **2-8-11b**[1] KDarley(3) (mde virtually all: rdn out) | — | **1** | 4/1[3] | 69 | — |
| 1543[3] | **Fonzy** (MrsLStubbs) **2-9-2b** KFallon(4) (w wnr: ev ch whn edgd rt wl over 1f out: r.o wl ins fnl f) | hd | **2** | 3/1[2] | 74 | 4 |
| 568[6] | **Senate Swings** (WRMuir) **2-8-11** WJO'Connor(1) (chsd ldrs: rdn 3f out: r.o one pce fnl f) | 2½ | **3** | 4/1[3] | 61 | — |
| 1880[2] | **Caviar And Candy** (DJSCosgrove) **2-8-3**(3) MHenry(2) (w ldrs: rdn & ev ch 2f out: wknd over 1f out) | ½ | **4** | 9/4[1] | 54 | — |
| 465[9] | **Anatomic** (MRChannon) **2-8-6** TQuinn(5) (a bhd: t.o) | 24 | **5** | 5/1 | — | — |
| | | | | (SP 112.4%) | **5 Rn** | |

**61.13 secs** (4.43) CSF £15.18 TOTE £4.50: £2.30 £1.50 (£6.80) OWNER Mr Stephen Molloy (UPPER LAMBOURN) BRED C. J. Foy
**2031 Tinker's Surprise (IRE)**, tried in blinkers, had the help of the stands' rail and just managed to hold a rival who gave ground away by coming off a true line. (4/1: 3/1-9/2)
**1543 Fonzy** would probably have prevailed had he not drifted into the centre of the course. (3/1)
**568 Senate Swings** is the first foal of the sprinter Heaven-Liegh-Grey. (4/1)
**1880 Caviar And Candy** could not cope with the two principals in the final quarter mile. (9/4)

## 2126 LUFTHANSA CARGO H'CAP (0-85) (3-Y.O) (Class D)
7-30 (7-32) **1m** £4,962.75 (£1,482.00: £708.50: £321.75) Stalls: Low GOING minus 0.24 sec per fur (GF)

| | Horse | Dist | Pos | SP | RR | SF |
|---|---|---|---|---|---|---|
| 2061* | **Mazcobar (76)** (PJMakin) **3-9-0** 7x SSanders(4) (swtg: hld up: n.m.r over 2f out: edgd lft over 1f out: led 1f out: drvn out) | — | **1** | 11/4[1] | 75 | 49 |
| 1770[7] | **Lilli Claire (83)** (AGFoster) **3-9-7** TSprake(2) (hld up: hdwy over 2f out: ev ch over 1f out: r.o ins fnl f) | nk | **2** | 5/1 | 81 | 55 |
| 1675* | **Ood Dancer (USA) (82)** (LMCumani) **3-9-6** KDarley(3) (lw: w ldr: led over 3f out to 1f out: unable qckn) | 1½ | **3** | 100/30[2] | 77 | 51 |
| 1820[7] | **Catch The Lights (65)** (RHannon) **3-8-3** RPerham(1) (lw: a.p: ev ch whn sltly hmpd over 1f out: one pce) | ¾ | **4** | 4/1[3] | 59 | 33 |
| 1657[3] | **Stone Island (60)** (CACyzer) **3-7-12** FNorton(6) (hld up: rdn & lost pl 4f out: btn whn hmpd on ins & swchtd lft over 2f out) | 14 | **5** | 11/1 | 26 | — |
| 1319[4] | **Hareb (USA) (75)** (JWHills) **3-8-13** TQuinn(5) (led: hrd rdn & hdd over 3f out: hmpd on ins over 2f out: sn wknd & eased: t.o) | 19 | **6** | 100/30[2] | 3 | — |
| | | | | (SP 117.8%) | **6 Rn** | |

**1m 40.03** (2.83) CSF £16.10 TOTE £4.30: £2.10 £2.30 (£10.80) OWNER Mr A. W. Schiff (MARLBOROUGH) BRED A. W. Schiff
**2061* Mazcobar** defied a penalty and could well have been feeling the effects of his win two days ago in the closing stages. (11/4)
**1190 Lilli Claire** had been highly tried since winning at Salisbury off a 9lb lower mark. (5/1)
**1675* Ood Dancer (USA)** looked tremendously well, but has possibly been overrated a few pounds by the Handicapper. (100/30)
**Catch The Lights** has been dropped 12lb this season and may be coming to hand. (4/1)

## 2127 A T KEARNEY H'CAP (0-80) (4-Y.O+) (Class D)
8-05 (8-06) **1m 2f** £4,503.00 (£1,344.00: £642.00: £291.00) Stalls: Low GOING minus 0.24 sec per fur (GF)

| | Horse | Dist | Pos | SP | RR | SF |
|---|---|---|---|---|---|---|
| 1839[2] | **Statajack (IRE) (75)** (DRCElsworth) **8-9-9b** TQuinn(6) (lw: hld up & bhd: stdy hdwy 3f out: led ins fnl f: r.o) | — | **1** | 11/2[3] | 87 | 58 |

1775$^{4}$ **King of Tunes (FR) (72)** (JJSheehan) **4-9-6** RHughes(3) (hld up & bhd: hdwy on bit over 3f out: led over 1f out tl ins fnl f: r.o)........nk **2** 13/8$^{1}$ 84 55
1841* **Bakheta (57)** (MissGayKelleway) **4-8-5** 6x KFallon(9) (prom: led 5f out tl over 1f out: one pce)........5 **3** 4/1$^{2}$ 61 32
1486$^{5}$ **Noble Sprinter (IRE) (74)** (RHannon) **4-9-8b** RPerham(10) (lw: a.p: rdn & ev ch 2f out: wknd over 1f out)......½ **4** 9/1 77 48
1819$^{13}$ **Summerhill Special (IRE) (60)** (MrsPNDutfield) **5-8-8** CRutter(1) (stdd after s: swtchd lft over 3f out: hdwy & edgd rt over 2f out: wknd over 1f out)........2 **5** 25/1 60 31
1793$^{8}$ **Fieldridge (76)** (MPMuggeridge) **7-9-10** PaulEddery(11) (prom tl wknd wl over 1f out)........1 **6** 11/1 64 35
888$^{9}$ **Princess Danielle (60)** (WRMuir) **4-8-8** WJO'Connor(7) (hld up: hdwy 3f out: wknd 2f out)........1½ **7** 16/1 46 17
1640$^{14}$ **Pennine Wind (IRE) (58)** (SDow) **4-8-6** SSanders(4) (lw: a bhd)........2½ **8** 33/1 40 11
1953* **Persian Affair (IRE) (61)** (TJNaughton) **5-8-6**(3) 6x AWhelan(2) (hld up & bhd: stdy hdwy over 4f out: wknd 3f out)........¾ **9** 8/1 42 13
1792$^{13}$ **Zamalek (USA) (74)** (GLMoore) **4-9-8v$^{1}$** SWhitworth(5) (led 5f: rdn & wknd 4f out: t.o fnl 2f)........dist **10** 20/1 — —
1145$^{17}$ **Ottavio Farnese (65)** (AHide) **4-8-13** KDarley(8) (swtg: w ldrs over 5f: t.o fnl 2f)........8 **11** 16/1 — —
(SP 126.2%) **11 Rn**

**2m 9.16** (3.66) CSF £15.28 CT £39.29 TOTE £5.00: £1.40 £1.40 £1.40 (£7.20) Trio £4.70 OWNER Mrs M. E. Slade (WHITCOMBE) BRED Princess Oettingen-Spielberg

**1839 Statajack (IRE)**, dropping back in distance, had come down 8lb in the handicap and was given a masterly ride by Quinn who kidded him along. (11/2)
**1775 King of Tunes (FR)**, back to ten furlongs, looked in control until the winner arrived on the scene. (13/8: op 5/2)
**1841* Bakheta** could not complete the hat-trick off a mark 12lb higher than when she won at Sandown. (4/1)
**1486 Noble Sprinter (IRE)** has dropped 6lb in the Ratings this season and seems to need to come down further. (9/1: 6/1-10/1)
**Summerhill Special (IRE)** has slipped 10lb in the Ratings this season, but could never land a blow. (25/1)

## 2128 OSBORNE REFRIGERATORS LIMITED STKS (0-80) (3-Y.O+) (Class D)

8-35 (8-37) **1m 2f** £3,984.75 (£1,188.00: £566.50: £255.75) Stalls: Low GOING minus 0.24 sec per fur (GF)

SP RR SF
1508$^{6}$ **Fasil (IRE) (77)** (CJBenstead) **3-8-8** TQuinn(9) (hld up: gd hdwy over 1f out: str run to ld nr fin)........— **1** 8/1 89 36
1507$^{6}$ **Deadline Time (IRE) (80)** (MrsMReveley) **3-8-10** KDarley(3) (hld up: rdn 3f out: gd hdwy to ld ins fnl f: hdd nr fin)........nk **2** 13/2$^{3}$ 91 38
1319$^{2}$ **Bend Wavy (IRE) (80)** (LMCumani) **4-9-6** SSanders(8) (hld up & plld hrd: hdwy 3f out: led over 1f out tl ins fnl f: r.o)........hd **3** 5/2$^{2}$ 88 47
1714* **Hilaala (USA) (80)** (PTWalwyn) **3-8-9** WCarson(4) (lw: led: hrd rdn & hdd over 1f out: wknd ins fnl f)........5 **4** 2/1$^{1}$ 81 28
613$^{8}$ **Bakers' Gate (USA) (80)** (JHMGosden) **4-9-6** GHind(5) (hld up in rr: hdwy on ins over 2f out: nt trble ldrs)........1½ **5** 7/1 78 37
1476$^{15}$ **Grand Selection (IRE) (79)** (MBell) **4-9-6** MFenton(2) (a.p: rdn & ev ch 2f out: wknd fnl f)........6 **6** 11/1 68 27
953$^{5}$ **Swallows Dream (IRE) (77)** (JLDunlop) **5-9-6** PaulEddery(6) (prom: rdn over 3f out: wknd over 2f out)........8 **7** 13/2$^{3}$ 56 15
1772$^{3}$ **Ultimate Warrior (67)** (CACyzer) **6-9-6** KFallon(1) (rdn over 3f out: a bhd)........4 **8** 20/1 49 8
(SP 125.3%) **8 Rn**

**2m 10.13** (4.63) CSF £57.59 TOTE £15.00: £3.20 £2.00 £1.70 (£51.60) Trio £46.90 OWNER Mr Hamdan Al Maktoum (EPSOM) BRED Ballyvolane Stud
WEIGHT FOR AGE 3yo-12lb

**1508 Fasil (IRE)** has been brought along quietly and really relished the mile and a quarter. His trainer thinks he may have preferred slightly softer ground. (8/1)
**1507 Deadline Time (IRE)** came with a good run to lead, but could not withstand the winner's late flourish. (13/2)
**1319 Bend Wavy (IRE)** did not help his cause by taking a keen tug, but certainly stayed this longer distance well enough. (5/2)
**1714* Hilaala (USA)** may need more patient tactics to get this trip. (2/1)
**Bakers' Gate (USA)** displayed an awkward head carriage and did not appear to be relishing the task in hand. (7/1)
**988 Grand Selection (IRE)** (11/1: 8/1-12/1)

## 2129 ARGUS CLASSIFIED H'CAP (0-75) (3-Y.O+) (Class D)

9-05 (9-06) **6f** £4,056.25 (£1,210.00: £577.50: £261.25) Stalls: High GOINGminus 0.24 sec per fur (GF)

SP RR SF
1958$^{5}$ **Scissor Ridge (43)** (JJBridger) **4-8-2** SSanders(11) (led over 1f: chsd ldr: led over 1f out: r.o wl)........— **1** 10/1 58 34
**Another Batchworth (54)** (EAWheeler) **4-8-13** TSprake(12) (led over 4f out tl over 1f out: one pce)........4 **2** 20/1 58 34
2034$^{9}$ **Half Tone (48)** (RMFlower) **4-8-7b** DBiggs(10) (hdwy over 2f out: r.o one pce fnl f)........1 **3** 9/1 50 26
1958$^{4}$ **Denbrae (IRE) (69)** (DJGMurraySmith) **4-9-9**(5) RPainter(6) (swtg: wl bhd tl hdwy over 1f out: nvr nrr)........s.h **4** 8/1 71 47
1958$^{2}$ **Sizzling (59)** (RHannon) **4-9-4** RHughes(9) (lw: hld up: rdn & hdwy over 2f out: one pce fnl f)........½ **5** 4/1$^{2}$ 59 35
1958$^{6}$ **Random (51)** (CJames) **5-8-10** TQuinn(3) (hdwy over 1f out: nvr nr to chal)........1 **6** 7/1$^{3}$ 49 25
1958* **Friendly Brave (USA) (74)** (MissGayKelleway) **6-10-5** 7x WJO'Connor(7) (b.hind: lw: hld up: rdn over 1f out: wknd fnl f)........hd **7** 7/1$^{3}$ 71 47
1958$^{3}$ **Invocation (49)** (AMoore) **9-8-5**(3) AWhelan(4) (hld up: lost pl over 3f out: rdn over 1f out: no hdwy)........nk **8** 7/1$^{3}$ 46 22
2017$^{2}$ **Pearl Dawn (IRE) (68)** (GLMoore) **6-9-13** SWhitworth(1) (prom: rdn over 2f out: wknd over 1f out)........1¼ **9** 9/1 61 37
1985$^{9}$ **Deardaw (39)** (MDIUsher) **4-7-12** NAdams(5) (rdn over 2f out: a bhd)........nk **10** 50/1 31 7
1905$^{3}$ **Samsolom (61)** (PHowling) **8-9-6** PaulEddery(8) (rdn 2f out: no rspnse: eased whn btn fnl f)........8 **11** 7/2$^{1}$ 32 8
1512$^{8}$ **Barranak (IRE) (60)** (GMMcCourt) **4-9-5b$^{1}$** KDarley(2) (prom 4f: t.o)........12 **12** 14/1 — —
(SP 133.3%) **12 Rn**

**1m 12.23** (2.23) CSF £180.41 CT £1,146.72 TOTE £15.70: £4.30 £4.10 £3.70 (£143.80) Trio £593.10; £584.77 to 24/6/96 OWNER Mr Donald Smith (LIPHOOK) BRED J. K. Keegan

**1958 Scissor Ridge**, due to go up 2lb, broke smartly and quickly crossed to the stands' rail. Running on strongly from the distance, the Handicapper may need to have a rethink. (10/1)
**Another Batchworth**, quickly away, tacked over to the stands' side with the winner, but found her rival much too strong in the later stages. (20/1)
**1777 Half Tone** could not overhaul the runner-up, let alone bother the winner. (9/1)
**1958 Denbrae (IRE)** came from well off the pace up the centre of the course, but was never going to trouble the principals. (8/1)
**1958 Sizzling**, off the same mark as when runner-up over course and distance a week ago, was due to go 1lb in future handicaps. (4/1)
**1958 Random** was already set to come down 1lb in the future. (7/1)
**1905 Samsolom** never looked likely to justify the market support. (7/2: op 7/1)

T/Plpt: £211.70 (55.36 Tckts). T/Qdpt: £189.30 (4.16 Tckts) KH

# 1803-NEWMARKET (R-H) (Good to firm)

**Friday June 21st**
WEATHER: Fine WIND: slt bhd

## 2130 HISTON APPRENTICE H'CAP (0-70) (3-Y.O+) (Class E)

6-45 (6-46) **1m (July)** £3,680.00 (£1,115.00: £545.00: £260.00) Stalls: High GOING minus 0.32 sec per fur (GF)

| Form | Horse | Dist | Pos | SP | RR | SF |
|---|---|---|---|---|---|---|
| 2045* | **Darcey Bussell (61)** (BWHills) **4-9-5** 5x JDSmith(12) (hld up: hdwy over 2f out: led over 1f out: rdn clr fnl f) | — | 1 | 6/1$^{2}$ | 73 | 40 |
| 2016$^{8}$ | **Persephone (48)** (ICampbell) **3-7-5v$^{1}$**(5) RMullen(5) (trckd ldrs far side: led 2f out: hdd over 1f out: unable qckn) | 3½ | 2 | 40/1 | 53 | 12 |
| 1830$^{12}$ | **Mr Rough (59)** (DMorris) **5-9-0**(3) AEddery(8) (lw: prom far side: ev ch over 2f out: kpt on) | ½ | 3 | 14/1 | 63 | 31 |
| | **La Fille de Cirque (46)** (RJRWilliams) **4-8-1**(3) AimeeCook(4) (hdwy far side 3f out: no imp appr fnl f) | s.h | 4 | 16/1 | 50 | 19 |
| 616$^{4}$ | **Soviet King (IRE) (56)** (PhilipMitchell) **3-8-1**(3) CAdamson(15) (b: lw: hdwy over 1f out: nrst fin) | nk | 5 | 20/1 | 59 | 18 |
| 1846* | **Mister Woodstick (IRE) (58)** (MAJarvis) **3-8-6** 5x FLynch(18) (lw: prom: led stands' side over 2f out: sn hdd & no ex) | 3½ | 6 | 100/30$^{1}$ | 54 | 14 |
| 1024$^{8}$ | **Monte Cavo (38)** (MBrittain) **5-7-10** MBaird(13) (led stands' side over 5f) | ¾ | 7 | 33/1 | 33 | 4 |
| 1659$^{6}$ | **Captain's Day (70)** (TGMills) **4-9-9**(5) DToole(2) (chsd ldrs far side: rdn & wknd over 2f out) | ¾ | 8 | 16/1 | 63 | 32 |
| | **Action Jackson (60)** (BJMcMath) **4-8-13**(5) DSweeney(14) (bit bkwd: chsd ldrs 6f) | s.h | 9 | 16/1 | 53 | 22 |
| *13$^{3}$* | **Kaafih Homm (IRE) (61)** (NACallaghan) **5-8-12**(7) MDavies(17) (lw: sn prom: led stands' side 3f out: sn hdd: wknd over 1f out) | nk | 10 | 6/1$^{2}$ | 54 | 23 |
| 1659$^{7}$ | **College Night (IRE) (59)** (CADwyer) **4-8-10**(7)ow8 STynan(1) (led far side 6f) | hd | 11 | 12/1 | 51 | 21 |
| 1821$^{15}$ | **Dauphin (IRE) (48)** (WJMusson) **3-7-5**(5) RFfrench(16) (prom 5f) | ½ | 12 | 33/1 | 39 | 1 |
| 1696$^{6}$ | **Western Horizon (USA) (38)** (CEBrittain) **4-7-5**(5) PDoe(3) (chsd ldrs far side 4f) | 1 | 13 | 20/1 | 27 | — |
| 1965* | **Dance King (67)** (RHarris) **4-9-11** 5x ADaly(11) (lw: in tch: rdn 3f out: hung lft & sn btn) | 1 | 14 | 8/1$^{3}$ | 54 | 24 |
| 1658$^{6}$ | **Hang a Right (42)** (CADwyer) **9-7-7**(7)ow1 NicolaCole(9) (lw: racd far side: a bhd) | 5 | 15 | 16/1 | 19 | — |
| 1992$^{6}$ | **Northern Grey (51)** (DrJDScargill) **4-8-2**(7) SHoughton(10) (a bhd) | 16 | 16 | 16/1 | — | — |
| | **Elraas (USA) (46)** (HJCollingridge) **4-7-11**(7)ow6 SMcKenna(6) (bit bkwd: bhd fnl 3f) | 17 | 17 | 33/1 | — | — |
| *1908$^{4}$* | ***Sylvan Princess (48)*** (CNAllen) **3-7-7b**(3) MartinDwyer(7) (Withdrawn not under starter's orders) | | W | 14/1 | — | — |
| | | | | (SP 134.0%) | **17 Rn** | |

**1m 40.83** (3.63) CSF £193.33 CT £2,969.86 TOTE £5.20: £1.60 £15.80 £2.10 £2.70 (£150.30) Trio £294.40; £373.29 to 24/6/96 OWNER Mr W. J. Gredley (LAMBOURN) BRED Stetchworth Park Stud Ltd

LONG HANDICAP Western Horizon (USA) 7-6 Persephone 7-2 Monte Cavo 7-7 Sylvan Princess 7-6

WEIGHT FOR AGE 3yo-10lb

**2045* Darcey Bussell** made her move by the stands' rail, which might have been an advantage, but she won in fine style anyway, and is still improving. (6/1: op 4/1)

**Persephone** showed much-improved form from 8lb out of the handicap and was a clear winner of the far-side group. (40/1)

**1704 Mr Rough** scored his three wins at this trip on this ground, but lacked a change of gear in the last quarter-mile. Despite having lost his last thirteen races, he was still on a higher mark than he has ever won off - 58 - courtesy of three placed efforts off marks in the 60s. (14/1)

**La Fille de Cirque** looked just in need of this and a promising forward move petered out entering the final furlong. (16/1)

**616 Soviet King (IRE)** did some good late work under the stands' rail and, as he was tried over ten furlongs at two, is worth another chance at that trip. (20/1)

**1846* Mister Woodstick (IRE)**, despite his draw, made his move towards the centre of the track and was soon in trouble once headed. The penalty for a hard-fought success proved his undoing. (100/30)

## 2131 SAXON STREET H'CAP (0-90) (3-Y.O+) (Class C)

7-15 (7-15) **1m 4f (July)** £5,900.00 (£1,760.00: £840.00: £380.00) Stalls: High GOING minus 0.32 sec per fur (GF)

| Form | Horse | Dist | Pos | SP | RR | SF |
|---|---|---|---|---|---|---|
| 1704$^{3}$ | **Western Sal (67)** (JLHarris) **4-8-5** JQuinn(5) (hld up: hdwy 4f out: rdn over 1f out: led ins fnl f) | — | 1 | 7/1 | 77 | 53 |
| 2008$^{9}$ | **Lookingforarainbow (IRE) (74)** (BobJones) **8-8-12** MWigham(4) (hld up: nt clr run over 2f out: swtchd & led over 1f out: hdd & unable qckn ins fnl f) | ½ | 2 | 9/2$^{2}$ | 83 | 59 |
| 1767$^{5}$ | **Mystic Hill (87)** (GHarwood) **5-9-11** RHills(9) (hld up: nt clr run fr over 2f out: r.o fnl f: nt pce to chal) | 2 | 3 | 7/1 | 94 | 69 |
| 1874* | **Paradise Waters (69)** (RFJohnsonHoughton) **4-8-7** 5x JReid(3) (led over 10f: one pce) | 5 | 4 | 4/1$^{1}$ | 69 | 46 |
| 1361* | **Pine Needle (82)** (DMorley) **3-8-6** BThomson(1) (lw: trckd ldrs: rdn 2f out: sn btn) | 3½ | 5 | 4/1$^{1}$ | 77 | 41 |
| 1439$^{5}$ | **Barford Sovereign (66)** (JRFanshawe) **4-8-4** MRoberts(2) (swtg: trckd ldr: ev ch 3f out: wknd appr fnl f) | 5 | 6 | 7/1 | 55 | 33 |
| 844$^{8}$ | **Petoskin (67)** (JPearce) **4-8-5** GBardwell(8) (chsd ldrs over 9f) | 3½ | 7 | 20/1 | 51 | 30 |
| 925$^{10}$ | **Time for Action (IRE) (85)** (MHTompkins) **4-9-9** PRobinson(7) (plld hrd: chsd ldrs: rdn 2f out: sn wknd) | 3 | 8 | 5/1$^{3}$ | 65 | 43 |
| | **Peter Quince (90)** (MBrittain) **6-10-0** WRyan(6) (b: bit bkwd: bhd fnl 4f) | 30 | 9 | 20/1 | 30 | 13 |
| | | | | (SP 121.9%) | **9 Rn** | |

**2m 31.74** (1.74) CSF £37.90 CT £210.99 TOTE £9.20: £2.10 £1.60 £2.50 (£17.70) Trio £122.00 OWNER Mrs James McAllister (MELTON MOWBRAY) BRED Fluorocarbon Bloodstock

WEIGHT FOR AGE 3yo-14lb

**1704 Western Sal** shows plenty of knee-action, but goes on this fast ground and stayed on in determined fashion to hit the front near the line. (7/1)

**1476 Lookingforarainbow (IRE)**, who beat Bold Gait in this race two seasons ago and finished second in 1995, repeated last year's feat after bursting through on the stands' side once he found daylight, only to be run out of it close home. (9/2)

**1767 Mystic Hill**, never brought into the paddock, was mounted in the chute onto the course. All dressed up with nowhere to go in the last half-mile, he finally got daylight too late, but did not pick up particularly well in any case. (7/1: 4/1-15/2)

**1874* Paradise Waters** looked one-paced once headed, and it would be no surprise to see her tackling longer trips. (4/1: op 5/2)

**1361* Pine Needle** sat in behind the leaders travelling strongly, but she suddenly came of the bridle approaching the final quarter-mile and was quickly in trouble. (4/1)

**1439 Barford Sovereign,** dropping half a mile in trip, was struggling to go the pace in the last quarter-mile. (7/1)

**Time for Action (IRE)** (5/1: op 10/1)

## 2132 NGK SPARK PLUGS MAIDEN STKS (2-Y.O) (Class D)

7-45 (7-48) **6f (July)** £4,464.00 (£1,332.00: £636.00: £288.00) Stalls: High GOING minus 0.32 sec per fur (GF)

| Form | Horse | Dist | Pos | SP | RR | SF |
|---|---|---|---|---|---|---|
| | **Makhbar** (RWArmstrong) **2-9-0** RHills(11) (unf: scope: mde virtually all: drew clr fnl f: comf) | — | 1 | 9/4$^{2}$ | 79 | 37 |

| | | | Pos | SP | RR | SF |
|---|---|---|---|---|---|---|
| | **Pun** (DMorley) **2-8-9** BThomson(3) (leggy: unf: w wnr tl rdn & btn appr fnl f) | 5 | **2** | 14/1 | 61 | 20 |
| | **Millroy (USA)** (PAKelleway) **2-9-0** MWigham(8) (leggy: scope: sn rdn along: hdwy 2f out: nvr rchd ldrs) | 2 | **3** | 14/1 | 60 | 20 |
| 1808[5] | **Rock Fantasy** (CMurray) **2-8-9** MTebbutt(2) (lw: sn pushed along: r.o fnl 2f: nrst fin) | s.h | **4** | 20/1 | 55 | 16 |
| | **Shimazu (IRE)** (JHMGosden) **2-9-0** JCarroll(10) (leggy: unf: dwlt: rdn & hdwy over 2f out: r.o fnl f) | ¾ | **5** | 9/2[3] | 58 | 18 |
| | **Drive Assured** (CEBrittain) **2-9-0** BDoyle(5) (leggy: unruly s: chsd ldrs 4f) | 1¼ | **6** | 25/1 | 55 | 15 |
| | **Multitone** (JMPEustace) **2-9-0** JTate(7) (scope: bkwd: chsd ldrs: rdn 2f out: one pce) | nk | **7** | 33/1 | 54 | 15 |
| | **Fancy A Fortune (IRE)** (JPearce) **2-9-0** GBardwell(9) (w'like: lw: rdn 3f out: a bhd) | 2½ | **8** | 25/1 | 47 | 9 |
| | **Gibb's Beach (IRE)** (CADwyer) **2-8-9** JQuinn(1) (lt-f: unf: bhd fnl 3f) | 25 | **9** | 16/1 | — | — |
| | ***Sunbeam Dance (USA)*** (SbinSuroor) **2-9-0** JReid(4) (gd sort: leggy: Withdrawn not under Starter's orders: kicked & injured in stalls) | | **W** | 6/4[1] | — | — |

(SP 123.6%) **9 Rn**

**1m 14.52** (2.52) CSF £14.09 TOTE £2.20: £1.20 £2.90 £2.70 (£16.00) Trio £37.90 OWNER Mr Hamdan Al Maktoum (NEWMARKET) BRED Mrs N. Cunliffe-Lister

**Makhbar**, with the favourite withdrawn, had little to beat, but did the job well and there is more to come. There is plenty of speed on the dam's side of his pedigree and he may not stay much further. (9/4: 3/1-2/1)

**Pun** took a good hold on the way to the post and raced upsides the winner until running out of petrol in the Dip. (14/1: 10/1-20/1)

**Millroy (USA)**, a tail-flasher who moved rather keenly to post, needed a couple of sharp reminders to get him racing early on. Staying on well towards the finish, he did show some promise. (14/1: 8/1-20/1)

**1808 Rock Fantasy**, allowed to set the pace at a virtual walk on her debut, was taken off her feet here until staying on really well in the latter stages and finishing best of all. (20/1)

**Shimazu (IRE)**, out of Oaks runner-up Shamshir, is not much to look at and looked to be getting nowhere when let down, but did begin to close nicely late on as her stamina finally became useful. She already needs further. (9/2)

**Drive Assured** panicked and went down in the stalls, lashing out to such effect that he injured the favourite, causing his withdrawal. Until he proves himself of sound mind, he is one to be wary of. (25/1)

**Sunbeam Dance (USA)** (6/4: Evens-13/8)

## 2133 KIDSONS IMPEY CLAIMING STKS (3-Y.O) (Class E)

8-15 (8-17) **1m (July)** £3,752.50 (£1,120.00: £535.00: £242.50) Stalls: High GOING: minus 0.32 sec per fur (GF)

| | | | Pos | SP | RR | SF |
|---|---|---|---|---|---|---|
| 1687[6] | **Always Happy (70)** (JRFanshawe) **3-8-9** DHarrison(9) (lw: led stands' side over 5f: led over 1f out: rdn out) | — | **1** | 8/1 | 71 | 27 |
| 1518[2] | **Cointosser (IRE)** (SPCWoods) **3-8-5** WWoods(12) (hld up: plld out over 2f out: ev ch over 1f out: hung lft & nt qckn) | 1¼ | **2** | 100/30[1] | 65 | 22 |
| 1908[8] | **Just Millie (USA) (68)** (JEBanks) **3-8-8**(3) JStack(5) (dwlt: hdwy 4f out: led over 2f out tl over 1f out: no ex) | 2½ | **3** | 4/1[3] | 66 | 23 |
| 1654[8] | **Giddy (60)** (DMorley) **3-8-4**ow1 BThomson(10) (chsd ldrs: rdn 4f out: one pce fnl 2f) | 5 | **4** | 11/2 | 49 | 8 |
| 1991[10] | **Capture The Moment (55)** (RJRWilliams) **3-7-10**(5) FLynch(1) (b.nr hind: chsd ldrs centre tl led over 3f out: hdd over 2f out: wknd appr fnl f) | ½ | **5** | 16/1 | 45 | 4 |
| 2016[2] | **Princess Pamgaddy (50)** (CNAllen) **3-7-8**(5) MartinDwyer(7) (bhd: rdn & r.o fnl 2f: nrst fin) | ½ | **6** | 7/2[2] | 42 | 1 |
| 1883[5] | **Meg's Memory (IRE) (59)** (JohnBerry) **3-7-12**(3) NVarley(4) (chsd ldrs: wkng whn bmpd over 2f out) | 1¼ | **7** | 13/2 | 41 | 1 |
| | **Princesse Lyphard** (MJPolglase) **3-8-5** WHollick(2) (w'like: unf: bkwd: racd centre: a bhd) | 17 | **8** | 33/1 | 11 | — |
| 1039[12] | **Static Love (30)** (HAkbary) **3-7-13** AMackay(6) (led centre over 4f) | 2 | **9** | 33/1 | 1 | — |
| 1956[5] | **Only (USA) (55)** (RHannon) **3-9-4** JCarroll(3) (chsd ldrs centre tl rdn & wknd 3f out) | ¾ | **10** | 14/1 | 19 | — |
| 1654[21] | **Straight Thinking (USA) (59)** (PFICole) **3-9-4** MHills(8) (prom 3f: edgd lft & sn bhd) | 6 | **11** | 12/1 | 7 | — |

(SP 131.3%) **11 Rn**

**1m 41.14** (3.94) CSF £36.77 TOTE £8.80: £2.00 £1.40 £1.70 (£18.30) Trio £37.70 OWNER Cheveley Park Stud (NEWMARKET) BRED Cheveley Park Stud Ltd

Always Happy clmd JPearce £10,000, Giddy clmd JHetherton £7,000

STEWARDS' ENQUIRY Harrison susp. 30/6 - 4/7/96 (excessive use of whip).

**763 Always Happy**, on his toes beforehand, looked in good shape and moved to post well. Making the pace on the stands' rail, he did not quit once headed and battled his way back to the front in the Dip. (8/1)

**1518 Cointosser (IRE)**, pulled off the stand rail to make her move approaching the last quarter-mile, never stopped hanging, first bumping Meg's Memory and then making a bee-line for the High Street as she mounted her challenge. She left the impression that, had she put her best foot forward and kept straight, she would have won. (100/30)

**1908 Just Millie (USA)** ran well, but did not confirm conclusively that she gets the trip. (4/1)

**Giddy**, dropped in class and rather keen going to post, looked short of any change of pace as the pressure was applied. (11/2: 3/1-6/1)

**1761 Capture The Moment** went to post freely and ran fast in the centre of the course for just over six furlongs. (16/1)

**2016 Princess Pamgaddy** ran well as she would have met most of these on better terms in a handicap but, not for the first time in her life, she did good late work when the race was all but over. (7/2)

## 2134 KENTFORD H'CAP (0-95) (3-Y.O+) (Class C)

8-45 (8-46) **7f (July)** £7,895.00 (£2,360.00: £1,130.00: £515.00) Stalls: High GOING minus 0.32 sec per fur (GF)

| | | | Pos | SP | RR | SF |
|---|---|---|---|---|---|---|
| 1442[5] | **Almuhimm (USA) (79)** (EALDunlop) **4-9-7** RHills(13) (lw: hld up & plld hrd: hdwy 2f out: rdn & r.o wl to ld nr fin) | — | **1** | 7/1[3] | 90 | 73 |
| 1807[6] | **Mountgate (72)** (MPBielby) **4-9-0** DRMcCabe(5) (hld up: hdwy over 2f out: led over 1f out tl hdd & unable qckn nr fin) | nk | **2** | 8/1 | 82 | 65 |
| 1775[6] | **Broughtons Turmoil (63)** (WJMusson) **7-8-5** AMcGlone(10) (trckd ldrs: rdn over 1f out: r.o wl ins fnl f) | nk | **3** | 8/1 | 73 | 56 |
| 1876* | **Zelda Zonk (73)** (BJMeehan) **4-9-1** 5x JReid(11) (lw: stdd & reard s: hdwy 4f out: no ex ins fnl f) | 2½ | **4** | 6/1[2] | 77 | 60 |
| 1807[7] | **Wild Palm (66)** (WAO'Gorman) **4-8-8v**[1] EmmaO'Gorman(12) (lw: hdwy over 2f out: hung lft over 1f out: no imp) | ¾ | **5** | 25/1 | 68 | 52 |
| 1807[4] | **Saifan (78)** (DMorris) **7-9-6b** CHodgson(4) (s.i.s: rdn 4f out: styng on whn hung lft fnl 2f) | 3 | **6** | 7/1[3] | 73 | 57 |
| | **Rumba Rhythm (CAN) (73)** (RWArmstrong) **3-8-6** MRoberts(16) (led: clr 2f out: hdd over 1f out: eased whn btn) | nk | **7** | 14/1 | 68 | 43 |
| 1793[12] | **Daryabad (IRE) (86)** (TJNaughton) **4-10-0** DHarrison(1) (chsd ldrs tl wknd appr fnl f) | 3½ | **8** | 33/1 | 73 | 57 |
| 1962* | **Rakis (IRE) (79)** (MrsLStubbs) **6-9-7** 5x JFEgan(3) (lw: trckd ldrs tl wknd wl over 1f out) | hd | **9** | 5/1[1] | 65 | 50 |
| 1807[9] | **Toujours Riviera (84)** (JPearce) **6-9-12** GBardwell(2) (s.i.s: nvr trbld ldrs) | 1¼ | **10** | 16/1 | 68 | 52 |
| 876[12] | **Safey Ana (USA) (73)** (BHanbury) **5-9-1** WRyan(15) (b: b.hind: nvr trbld ldrs) | hd | **11** | 14/1 | 56 | 42 |
| 1528* | **Ninia (USA) (77)** (MJohnston) **4-9-5** JWeaver(9) (chsd ldrs: wkng whn hmpd over 2f out) | nk | **12** | 5/1[1] | 60 | 45 |
| 1890[17] | **Mister Rm (68)** (RGuest) **4-8-10** PBloomfield(7) (prom: rdn over 2f out: sn wknd) | 1¼ | **13** | 33/1 | 48 | 34 |

| | | | | SP | RR | SF |
|---|---|---|---|---|---|---|
| 1962[12] | **Sand Star (70)** (DHaydnJones) **4-8-12** PRobinson(14) (lw: prom over 5f: eased whn btn) | 15 | **14** | 20/1 | 16 | 4 |
| 1853[14] | **Mister Fire Eyes (IRE) (74)** (CEBrittain) **4-9-2b** BDoyle(6) (chsd ldrs 5f) | 3½ | **15** | 16/1 | 12 | 1 |
| 1962[4] | **Shayim (USA) (74)** (RHannon) **4-9-2** PatEddery(8) (a bhd) | 1¾ | **16** | 8/1 | 8 | — |

(SP 145.5%) **16 Rn**

**1m 25.53** (0.53) CSF £68.31 CT £463.68 TOTE £7.80: £2.00 £3.00 £2.50 £1.60 (£112.40) Trio £305.70 OWNER Maktoum Al Maktoum (NEWMARKET) BRED Gainsborough Farm Inc.

WEIGHT FOR AGE 3yo-9lb

**1442 Almuhimm (USA)** continues to look a hard ride, but was handled well and swooped late to break his duck. A strongly-run race will surely help him, and he will be interesting in big fields. (7/1)

**1807 Mountgate** raced closer to the pace than is often the case and kicked for home in the Dip, but did not quite last home. Ideally he needs holding up a little longer. (8/1: 6/1-9/1)

**1775 Broughtons Turmoil** came back to form after looking full of beans going to post, and should not be long in winning. (8/1)

**1876* Zelda Zonk** seemed to resent being settled at the start, and nearly unshipped her pilot. Close enough if good enough in the last couple of furlongs, her 5lb penalty had her measure and the intended 11lb rise in her Rating for her win in a bad race last time looks unduly harsh. (6/1)

**1154 Wild Palm**, visored for the first time although blinkered of late, was taken to post last and very quietly. He hung once let down and looks in dire need of some better ground. (25/1)

**1807 Saifan**, who missed the break, was never travelling quite well enough to mount a challenge and hung in the closing stages. (7/1: 5/1-8/1)

**Rumba Rhythm (CAN)**, having her first race for over twelve months and making her handicap debut, looked to have a winning lead at the two-furlong pole, but lost her action and was not knocked about once headed. She certainly has the ability to win a similar contest if things go right. (14/1: op 8/1)

**1962* Rakis (IRE)** (5/1: 7/2-6/1)

## 2135 GAZELEY MAIDEN STKS (3-Y.O+) (Class D)

9-15 (9-19) **1m 2f (July)** £5,010.00 (£1,500.00: £720.00: £330.00) Stalls: High GOING minus 0.32 sec per fur (GF)

| | | | | SP | RR | SF |
|---|---|---|---|---|---|---|
| 1668[2] | **Lakeline Legend (IRE) (83)** (MAJarvis) **3-9-0** EmmaO'Gorman(14) (trckd ldrs: led 1f out: pushed out) | — | **1** | 4/1[3] | 88 | 48 |
| 1711[8] | **Classic Parisian (IRE)** (RHarris) **3-8-9** AMackay(11) (a.p: led 2f out tl over 1f out: unable qckn) | 3 | **2** | 16/1 | 78 | 39 |
| 1125[5] | **Radiant Star (87)** (GWragg) **3-9-0** MHills(3) (trckd ldrs: rdn over 1f out: one pce) | 1¾ | **3** | 11/8[1] | 80 | 41 |
| | **Lear Express (USA)** (HRACecil) **3-9-0** WRyan(8) (w'like: leggy: bit bkwd: in tch: pushed along & outpcd 4f out: r.o strly appr fnl f) | nk | **4** | 12/1 | 80 | 41 |
| 1711[3] | **King's Academy (IRE)** (HRACecil) **3-9-0** PatEddery(9) (w ldr: led over 1f out: sn hdd: wknd ins fnl f) | hd | **5** | 2/1[2] | 80 | 41 |
| 1656[6] | **Village King (IRE) (72)** (RHannon) **3-9-0** JReid(12) (chsd ldrs: rdn 4f out: btn whn edgd lft fnl f) | 1¼ | **6** | 33/1 | 78 | 39 |
| 1359[6] | **Ambassadori (USA)** (CEBrittain) **3-9-0** BDoyle(2) (led 8f) | 2½ | **7** | 33/1 | 74 | 36 |
| 1804[8] | **Adelaide (IRE)** (LMCumani) **3-8-9** OUrbina(6) (hld up & bhd: shkn up & r.o wl fnl f) | 4 | **8** | 16/1 | 62 | 25 |
| 1438[6] | **Soaked** (JRFanshawe) **3-9-0** DHarrison(7) (lw: hld up: effrt 4f out: no imp) | nk | **9** | 33/1 | 67 | 30 |
| 1104[9] | **Premier Censure** (JRFanshawe) **3-8-6**(3) NVarley(5) (in tch: rdn 4f out: no imp) | 2½ | **10** | 33/1 | 58 | 21 |
| | **Double Niner (USA)** (HRACecil) **3-9-0** AMcGlone(13) (unf: scope: b.hind: hld up: shkn up 3f out: no imp) | 4 | **11** | 20/1 | 57 | 21 |
| | **Foreign Judgement (USA)** (WJMusson) **3-9-0** TIves(1) (lw: chsd ldrs 4f) | ½ | **12** | 33/1 | 56 | 20 |
| 1873[10] | **Full Throttle** (MHTompkins) **3-9-0** PRobinson(10) (lw: bhd fnl 4f) | 4 | **13** | 33/1 | 49 | 14 |
| | ***High Atlas*** (BWHills) **3-8-9** RHills(4) (Withdrawn not under Starter's orders: panicked in stalls) | | **W** | 12/1 | — | — |

(SP 145.0%) **13 Rn**

**2m 8.12** (3.12) CSF £59.71 TOTE £6.30: £1.80 £3.70 £1.40 (£75.80) Trio £44.40 OWNER Mr Jerry Sung (NEWMARKET) BRED Jerry Sung

**1668 Lakeline Legend (IRE)** broke his duck in decisive style and looks to have more improvement in him. (4/1: 6/1-10/1)

**957 Classic Parisian (IRE)**, always close to the pace, looks short of gears at the business end. (16/1)

**1125 Radiant Star**, unable to capitalise on the drop in class, did his best in the last quarter mile but didn't quicken appreciably. (11/8: 4/5-7/4)

**Lear Express (USA)**, a leggy newcomer, was taken down steadily and looked a lesser light when left behind as the tempo quickened. However, once stamina came into play, he really began to motor and finished to great effect. (12/1: 6/1-14/1)

**1711 King's Academy (IRE)** probably has the ability to win a similar race but it was a disappointment to see his stride shortening inside the final furlong. (2/1)

**1656 Village King (IRE)** showed some promise in good maidens at two and came back to something approaching that form without threatening to win. (33/1)

**Adelaide (IRE)** travelled sweetly at the back of the field but tended to wander as the tempo quickened. She finished with quite a flourish and is worth keeping an eye on. (16/1)

**High Atlas** (12/1: 6/1-14/1)

T/Plpt: £158.50 (81.16 Tckts). T/Qdpt: £11.70 (99.78 Tckts) Dk

# 1845-REDCAR (L-H) (Firm, Good to firm patches)

## Friday June 21st

WEATHER: Overcast WIND: fresh half against

## 2136 NEWTON CLAIMING STKS (3-Y.O+) (Class F)

2-25 (2-26) **1m 2f** £2,826.00 (£786.00: £378.00) Stalls: Low GOING minus 0.61 sec per fur (F)

| | | | | SP | RR | SF |
|---|---|---|---|---|---|---|
| 1828* | **North Ardar (58)** (MrsMReveley) **6-8-13**(5) SCopp(11) (hdwy on outside over 3f out: led 2f out: edgd lft: rdn out) | — | **1** | 4/6[1] | 66 | 33 |
| 1596[5] | **Mithraic (IRE) (53)** (WSCunningham) **4-9-3** DHarrison(10) (led to 2f out: kpt on wl) | 1¼ | **2** | 12/1 | 63 | 30 |
| | **Willy Star (BEL)** (MrsSJSmith) **6-9-3** PBloomfield(1) (in tch: effrt over 3f out: r.o one pce) | 4 | **3** | 25/1 | 57 | 24 |
| | **Toulston Lady (IRE)** (MJCamacho) **4-9-8** DaleGibson(6) (dwlt s: bhd & rdn along: styd on fnl 3f: nt rch ldrs) | ½ | **4** | 33/1 | 61 | 28 |
| | **Anorak (USA) (44)** (GMMoore) **6-9-3v** JFEgan(5) (trckd ldrs: rdn 4f out: one pce) | hd | **5** | 14/1 | 56 | 23 |
| 1832[5] | **Bardia (28)** (DonEnricoIncisa) **6-8-12** KimTinkler(8) (s.i.s: bhd: hdwy 3f out: sn rdn & no imp) | 1 | **6** | 50/1 | 49 | 16 |
| *303*[8] | **Museum (IRE) (64)** (DNicholls) **5-9-7** AlexGreaves(2) (hld up: effrt on ins over 3f out: sn chsng ldrs: rdn 2f out: no imp) | nk | **7** | 6/1[2] | 58 | 25 |
| 1669[10] | **Recall To Mind (56)** (TDEasterby) **3-8-1b**[1] TWilliams(12) (plld hrd: trckd ldrs tl rdn & wknd over 2f out) | 11 | **8** | 15/2[3] | 32 | — |
| 1596[8] | **Whatashowman (IRE)** (SEKettlewell) **4-8-13** NRodgers(9) (prom: rdn over 4f out: sn wknd) | 3 | **9** | 25/1 | 27 | — |
| | **Mamlouk** (JWPayne) **4-9-2** WWoods(3) (sn wl outpcd & bhd) | 2½ | **10** | 25/1 | 26 | — |
| 1596[11] | **Little Red** (RCraggs) **5-9-0** NKennedy(4) (chsd ldrs tl lost pl 3f out) | nk | **11** | 50/1 | 24 | — |

| | | | | | | |
|---|---|---|---|---|---|---|
| 1421[3] | **Carlton Express (IRE) (42)** (JLEyre) **6-9-0**(3) CTeague(7) (p.u after 2f: broke down) | P | 8/1 | — | — |
| | | | (SP 129.9%) | **12 Rn** | | |

**2m 6.0** (2.40) CSF £11.43 TOTE £1.80: £1.20 £2.40 £6.60 (£13.30) Trio £159.50 OWNER Laurel (Leisure) Ltd (SALTBURN) BRED Mrs H.Seddington
WEIGHT FOR AGE 3yo-12lb
Museum (IRE) clmd DRObank £7,000
**1828* North Ardar** made it nine wins on his fiftieth appearance. Making his effort on the outside, he drifted across and his rider was lucky he did not cause any interference with the runner-up, as he did not seem to do much about it. (4/6: op Evens)
**Mithraic (IRE)**, eight lengths behind North Ardar at Catterick, showed that he is going the right way. (12/1: op 7/1)
**Willy Star (BEL)**, who has been running on the flat in Belgium, was by no means disgraced. (25/1)
**Toulston Lady (IRE)**, a backward looking newcomer, lost ground at the start and ran green. Staying on at the finish, she is not without ability. (33/1)
**303 Museum (IRE)** (6/1: op 3/1)
**Recall To Mind** (15/2: 4/1-8/1)

## 2137 SUTER H'CAP (0-90) (3-Y.O+) (Class C)

2-55 (2-59) **6f** £5,601.50 (£1,682.00: £811.00: £375.50) Stalls: Centre GOING minus 0.61 sec per fur (F)

| | | | | | SP | RR | SF |
|---|---|---|---|---|---|---|---|
| 1974[10] | **For the Present (79)** (TDBarron) **6-9-9** ACulhane(4) (lw: trckd ldrs: led 2f out: r.o wl u.p) | — | 1 | 9/1 | 86 | 27 |
| 2007[5] | **Green Barries (79)** (MJohnston) **3-9-2** TWilliams(5) (lw: a chsng ldrs: nt qckn ins fnl f) | ¾ | 2 | 9/4 1 | 84 | 18 |
| 1974[15] | **Benzoe (IRE) (77)** (MrsJRRamsden) **6-9-7** WWoods(3) (dwlt s: hld up: effrt over 2f out: kpt on fnl f) | 1¼ | 3 | 5/1 | 79 | 20 |
| 1790[14] | **Lago Di Varano (84)** (RMWhitaker) **4-9-9v**(5) RHavlin(6) (w ldrs: rdn ½-wy: kpt on same pce) | s.h | 4 | 11/1 | 86 | 27 |
| 1829[2] | **Bolshoi (IRE) (72)** (JBerry) **4-9-2b** SDWilliams(8) (trckd ldrs: effrt 2f out: sn rdn: nvr nr to chal) | 1¼ | 5 | 7/2 2 | 70 | 11 |
| 1786[4] | **Shashi (IRE) (66)** (WWHaigh) **4-8-10** JFEgan(7) (sn chsng ldrs: effrt ½-wy: edgd rt & lost pl over 1f out) | 2 | 6 | 8/1 | 59 | — |
| 1853[3] | **High Domain (IRE) (73)** (JLSpearing) **5-9-3** AlexGreaves(2) (led to 2f out: sn wknd) | ½ | 7 | 4/1 3 | 65 | 6 |
| | **Branston Danni (75)** (MrsJRRamsden) **3-8-12** DHarrison(1) (v.unruly in stalls: s.s: a bhd: eased over 1f out) | 21 | 8 | 10/1 | 11 | — |
| | | | | (SP 128.2%) | **8 Rn** | |

**1m 12.2** (2.00) CSF £31.65 CT £111.53 TOTE £13.50: £2.80 £1.40 £1.90 (£19.50) OWNER Mrs J. Hazell (THIRSK) BRED R. Barber
WEIGHT FOR AGE 3yo-7lb
**1501 For the Present**, who really took the eye in the paddock, scored for the first time since he took the 1994 Stewards' Cup off a 2lb higher mark. (9/1: op 6/1)
**2007 Green Barries** is running right up to his best at present. (9/4)
**1186 Benzoe (IRE)**, as usual, was put into the stalls late and put in some encouraging work towards the finish. (5/1)
**1016 Lago Di Varano**, under strong pressure at halfway, is probably better suited by five. (11/1)

## 2138 INGS MAIDEN STKS (2-Y.O) (Class D)

3-30 (3-30) **5f** £3,104.50 (£931.00: £448.00: £206.50) Stalls: Centre GOING minus 0.61 sec per fur (F)

| | | | | | SP | RR | SF |
|---|---|---|---|---|---|---|---|
| 1827[3] | **Burkes Manor** (TDBarron) **2-9-0** DHarrison(1) (chsd ldrs: effrt over 2f out: r.o u.p to ld ins fnl f) | — | 1 | 7/2 2 | 81 | — |
| 1884[2] | **Bold African** (PDEvans) **2-9-0b** DHolland(7) (led: hrd rdn 1f out: hdd & no ex ins fnl f) | 1¼ | 2 | 11/10 1 | 77 | — |
| 1197[4] | **Rivonia (USA)** (MrsJRRamsden) **2-8-9** MDeering(3) (hld up: hdwy 2f out: styd on ins fnl f) | nk | 3 | 6/1 | 71+ | — |
| | **Naivasha** (JBerry) **2-8-9** SDWilliams(6) (unf: bkwd: sn chsng ldrs: rdn & hung lft ½-wy: kpt on fnl f) | hd | 4 | 10/1 | 71 | — |
| | **Eastern Firedragon (IRE)** (TDEasterby) **2-8-9** ACulhane(5) (cmpt: bit bkwd: s.s: rn v.green & sn wl bhd: hdwy over 1f out: fin wl) | 4 | 5 | 12/1 | 58+ | — |
| | **Lord Discord** (TDEasterby) **2-9-0** TWilliams(2) (w'like: bit bkwd: sn chsng ldrs: effrt over 2f out: wknd over 1f out) | ½ | 6 | 9/2 3 | 61 | — |
| | **Prince Dome (IRE)** (MartynWane) **2-9-0** RHills(4) (cmpt: unf: s.i.s: hdwy u.p ½-wy: wknd over 1f out) | 2 | 7 | 8/1 | 55 | — |
| | | | | (SP 130.2%) | **7 Rn** | |

**60.6 secs** (3.10) CSF £8.85 TOTE £5.40: £1.40 £1.30 (£2.50) OWNER M P Burke Developments Ltd (THIRSK) BRED Messinger Stud Ltd
**1827 Burkes Manor** had clearly learned from his initial outing. He showed the right sort of spirit to get up in the closing stages to win what was probably a modest prize. (7/2: op 7/4)
**1884 Bold African** has plenty of speed but was run out of it in the closing stages for the fourth time in succession. (11/10: 6/4-Evens)
**1197 Rivonia (USA)**, happy to sit off the pace, put in some pleasing work inside the last and will be better suited by six or even seven. She appeals as a mid-term prospect. (6/1: 5/1-8/1)
**Naivasha**, a backward looking filly, was very keen going to post. Despite hanging left, she ran a satisfactory first race. (10/1: op 6/1)
**Eastern Firedragon (IRE)**, who looked burly, was very green going down. After missing the break, she was tailed off after halfway but came flying through at the finish. (12/1: op 6/1)
**Lord Discord**, a backward looking type, his action leaves a lot to be desired, but he showed ability, chasing the leader for over three furlongs. (9/2)
**Prince Dome (IRE)** (8/1: 6/1-9/1)

## 2139 NRS H'CAP (0-80) (3-Y.O) (Class D)

4-05 (4-05) **7f** £3,736.50 (£1,122.00: £541.00: £250.50) Stalls: Centre GOING minus 0.61 sec per fur (F)

| | | | | | SP | RR | SF |
|---|---|---|---|---|---|---|---|
| 1829[5] | **Mybotye (76)** (GROldroyd) **3-9-7** DaleGibson(8) (lw: hung lft thrght: swtchd rt & hdwy over 2f out: led ins fnl f: hld on towards fin) | — | 1 | 11/8 1 | 83 | 10 |
| 1006[12] | **Oriel Lad (67)** (PDEvans) **3-8-12b** DHolland(5) (trckd ldrs: led 2f out: hdd & nt qckn ins fnl f) | hd | 2 | 16/1 | 74 | 1 |
| 1805[8] | **Shontaine (65)** (MJohnston) **3-8-10** TWilliams(6) (a chsng ldrs: rdn to chal over 2f out: r.o same pce) | 2 | 3 | 10/1 | 67 | — |
| 1846[3] | **Oriole (51)** (NTinkler) **3-7-10** KimTinkler(4) (hdwy ½-wy: sn hrd rdn: kpt on one pce) | hd | 4 | 20/1 | 53 | — |
| 1527[8] | **Hobbs Choice (53)** (GMMoore) **3-7-12**ow2 JFEgan(7) (a chsng ldrs: rdn ½-wy: one pce) | 2½ | 5 | 9/1 | 49 | — |
| 1435[4] | **Surf City (66)** (WWHaigh) **3-8-11** DHarrison(9) (hdwy u.p ½-wy: sn chsng ldrs: wknd over 1f out) | 2 | 6 | 6/1 2 | 58 | — |
| 1806[5] | **Corniche Quest (IRE) (52)** (MRChannon) **3-7-11** AMackay(2) (lw: mde most to 2f out: hung lft & sn wknd) | 3 | 7 | 6/1 2 | 37 | — |
| 1608[9] | **South Pagoda (IRE) (56)** (DNicholls) **3-8-1** NKennedy(3) (trckd ldrs tl lost pl ½-wy) | 2 | 8 | 7/1 3 | 36 | — |
| 1885[2] | **Amoeba (IRE) (51)** (JBerry) **3-7-7**(3) NVarley(1) (w ldr tl wknd 2f out) | ½ | 9 | 6/1 2 | 30 | — |
| | | | | (SP 127.2%) | **9 Rn** | |

**1m 26.8** (3.80) CSF £24.11 CT £168.26 TOTE £2.20: £1.10 £6.80 £3.30 (£28.00) Trio £101.70 OWNER Mr Anthony Moroney (YORK) BRED R. S. A. Urquhart
LONG HANDICAP Oriole 7-2 Amoeba (IRE) 7-5

**1829 Mybotye** on this ground gave his rider all sorts of problems, hanging badly left throughout. (11/8)
**Oriel Lad** bounced right back to his best and fought back all the way to the line. (16/1)
**Shontaine** ran easily his best race for some time. (10/1)
**1846 Oriole** did remarkably well considering he was carrying 8lb more than his true handicap mark. (20/1)
**1435 Surf City** (6/1: op 4/1)
**South Pagoda (IRE)** (7/1: op 4/1)
**1885 Amoeba (IRE)** (6/1: op 4/1)

## 2140 STAITHES MAIDEN STKS (3-Y.O+) (Class D)

4-40 (4-40) **1m 6f 19y** £3,530.25 (£1,062.00: £513.50: £239.25) Stalls: Low GOING minus 0.61 sec per fur (F)

| | | | SP | RR | SF |
|---|---|---|---|---|---|
| 1957² **Nuzu (IRE)** (BWHills) **3-8-4** DHolland(3) (chsd ldrs: rdn along over 5f out: hrd rdn & led wl ins fnl f: all out) | — | 1 | 6/4¹ | 82 | 27 |
| 1647³ **Mental Pressure (78)** (MrsMReveley) **3-8-4** DHarrison(5) (hld up & plld hrd: stdy hdwy over 3f out: rdn & ev ch fnl f: edgd rt & no ex nr fin) | s.h | 2 | 7/2³ | 82 | 27 |
| 1670⁶ **Secret Gift** (BHanbury) **3-7-6**(7) RMullen(4) (b: sn chsng ldrs: effrt over 4f out: rdn to ld 3f out: hung rt: edgd lft & hdd wl ins fnl f: n.m.r nr fin) | ½ | 3 | 8/1 | 76 | 21 |
| 2002⁴ **Majdak Jereeb (IRE) (74)** (MajorWRHern) **3-8-4** RHills(1) (led to 3f out: wknd over 1f out) | 4 | 4 | 5/1 | 77 | 22 |
| 1644⁵ **Arietta's Way (IRE) (77)** (RCharlton) **3-7-6**(7) RBrisland(7) (b.nr hind: hmpd bnd after 2f: hdwy on outside 6f out: pushed wd over 4f out: wnt lft & wknd over 3f out) | 7 | 5 | 5/2² | 64 | 9 |
| **Precedency** (KMcAuliffe) **4-9-7** JFEgan(6) (lengthy: sn chsng ldrs: rn wd over 4f out: sn lost pl & bhd: t.o) | dist | 6 | 16/1 | — | — |

(SP 124.5%) **6 Rn**

**3m 1.8** (2.50) CSF £7.91 TOTE £1.90: £1.10 £2.50 (£2.40) OWNER Sheikh Mohammed (LAMBOURN) BRED Darley Stud Management Co Ltd
WEIGHT FOR AGE 3yo-17lb
**1957 Nuzu (IRE)**, a poor walker, proved suited by the step up in distance but in a desperate three way battle he got there with not an ounce to spare. (6/4: tchd Evens)
**1647 Mental Pressure**, stepping up in distance, took a keen grip. He came through between horses looking sure to win coming to the final furlong, but in the dash to the line seemed somewhat reluctant to put his head in front. (7/2)
**1670 Secret Gift** hung out towards the centre when taking it up. Soon flat out, he got in a bumping match with the runner-up near the line and the pair were pipped by Nuzu who came on the outer. (8/1)
**2002 Majdak Jereeb (IRE)**, nothing much to look at, made the running but dropped away over a furlong out. (5/1)
**1644 Arietta's Way (IRE)** was withdrawn the previous night with a Vet's certificate. A poor walker, she proved a bit of a handful for the boy after being pushed wide on the turn and soon dropped away. (5/2)

## 2141 GRIBDALE RATING RELATED MAIDEN STKS (0-65) (3-Y.O) (Class F)

5-15 (5-16) **1m 3f** £3,172.75 (£952.00: £458.50: £211.75) Stalls: Low GOING minus 0.61 sec per fur (F)

| | | | SP | RR | SF |
|---|---|---|---|---|---|
| 1701⁴ **Desert Frolic (IRE) (60)** (MJohnston) **3-8-11** TWilliams(7) (lw: w ldr: rdn to ld over 2f out: styd on fnl f) | — | 1 | 7/2³ | 69 | 46 |
| 1782⁹ **Ragsak Jameel (USA) (65)** (MajorWRHern) **3-9-0b¹** RHills(2) (swtg: trckd ldrs: effrt 3f out: styd on same pce fnl f) | 1¼ | 2 | 10/1 | 70 | 47 |
| 873¹⁷ **Rossel (USA) (65)** (MRStoute) **3-9-0v¹** JFEgan(3) (hld up: effrt over 4f out: styd on towards fin) | 1 | 3 | 10/1 | 69 | 46 |
| 1984² **Doctor Green (FR) (64)** (LordHuntingdon) **3-9-0v** DHarrison(6) (led tl over 2f out: one pce fnl f) | hd | 4 | 3/1² | 69 | 46 |
| 1771¹⁰ **Jamaican Flight (USA) (65)** (JWHills) **3-9-0** WWoods(4) (trckd ldrs: effrt 4f out: wknd 2f out) | 2½ | 5 | 6/1 | 65 | 42 |
| 1504³ **Salty Girl (IRE) (65)** (BWHills) **3-8-11** DHolland(1) (trckd ldrs: effrt over 4f out: fnd little: lost pl over 2f out: eased) | 10 | 6 | 7/4¹ | 47 | 24 |
| 576¹³ **Suitor (60)** (WJarvis) **3-9-0** DaleGibson(5) (sn pushed along: lost pl over 5f out: n.d) | 1¼ | 7 | 11/1 | 49 | 26 |

(SP 124.4%) **7 Rn**

**2m 18.1** (0.10) CSF £35.13 TOTE £5.20: £3.10 £3.60 (£27.30) OWNER Maktoum Al Maktoum (MIDDLEHAM) BRED Gainsborough Stud Management Ltd
**1701 Desert Frolic (IRE)** appreciated the step up in distance and showed the right sort of spirit under a determined ride. (7/2: 3/1-9/2)
**1305 Ragsak Jameel (USA)** wore blinkers after running badly last time. He consented to stay on in the final furlong but was never doing enough to get in a real blow at the winner. (10/1)
**Rossel (USA)**, stepped up in distance and wearing a visor for the first time, decided to stay on late in the day. He started the year badly handicapped. (10/1)
**1984 Doctor Green (FR)** who had everything his own way at Bath, proved woefully one paced. (3/1)
**1050 Jamaican Flight (USA)**, a keen going sort, never looked to be enjoying himself. (6/1: op 4/1)
**1504 Salty Girl (IRE)**, who is not a fluent mover, found little under pressure and her rider gave up (7/4)

T/Plpt: £48.60 (156.54 Tckts). T/Qdpt: £22.70 (18.8 Tckts) WG

# 2112-ASCOT (R-H) (Good to firm, Firm patches)
## Saturday June 22nd

WEATHER: unsettled WIND: alm nil

## 2142 LONDON CLUBS FERN HILL RATED STKS H'CAP (0-105) (Listed) (3-Y.O F) (Class A)

2-00 (2-00) **1m (straight)** £12,486.00 (£4,674.00: £2,287.00: £985.00: £442.50: £225.50) Stalls: Centre GOING minus 0.39 sec per fur (F)

| | | | SP | RR | SF |
|---|---|---|---|---|---|
| 1690* **Dawna (90)** (HRACecil) **3-9-3** PatEddery(4) (nt clr run over 2f out: swtchd rt & hdwy over 1f out: led ins fnl f: pushed out) | — | 1 | 9/2² | 100 | 58 |
| 1111⁶ **Miss Riviera (86)** (GWragg) **3-8-13** MHills(9) (lw: a.p: led wl over 1f out tl ins fnl f: unable qckn) | ¾ | 2 | 20/1 | 95 | 53 |
| 1901* **Medieval Lady (80)** (LadyHerries) **3-8-7** DHarrison(7) (lw: nt clr run on ins over 2f out & wl over 1f out: hdwy 1f out: r.o wl ins fnl f) | hd | 3 | 9/2² | 88 | 46 |
| 1420* **Samara (IRE) (91)** (JLDunlop) **3-9-4** TQuinn(3) (a.p: rdn & ev ch over 1f out: sn wknd) | 7 | 4 | 7/4¹ | 85 | 43 |
| 1796⁴ **Prends Ca (IRE) (94)** (RHannon) **3-9-7** JReid(1) (a.p: rdn over 2f out: wknd over 1f out) | nk | 5 | 20/1 | 88 | 46 |
| 1061* **Roses In The Snow (IRE) (92)** (JWHills) **3-9-5** RHughes(6) (lw: hld up: rdn over 2f out: wknd over 1f out) | 2½ | 6 | 20/1 | 81 | 39 |
| 1481⁶ **Consordino (83)** (LMCumani) **3-8-10** KDarley(8) (lw: w ldr: led 3f out tl wl over 1f out: sn wknd) | 3 | 7 | 20/1 | 66 | 24 |
| 1127* **Polish Spring (IRE) (90)** (BWHills) **3-9-3** BThomson(5) (a bhd) | 2½ | 8 | 12/1³ | 68 | 26 |

1151[7] **Tawaaded (IRE) (90)** (PTWalwyn) **3-9-3** WCarson(2) (led 5f: wknd 2f out)....2½ **9** 16/1 63 21
(SP 105.3%) **9 Rn**

**1m 41.86** (0.66) CSF £68.49 CT £312.94 TOTE £3.50: £1.30 £3.80 £1.80 (£44.30) Trio £67.60 OWNER Mr K. Abdulla (NEWMARKET) BRED Juddmonte Farms
LONG HANDICAP Medieval Lady 8-5

**1690* Dawna** put up a very useful display especially considering she did not have a clear run. Her jockey wisely pulled her to the outside early in the final quarter mile and the filly picked up in good style to hit the front inside the final furlong. Further success awaits her. (9/2)

**1111 Miss Riviera** struck the front early inside the final quarter mile but was unable to cope with the winner inside the last 150 yards. (20/1)

**1901* Medieval Lady** did not have luck on her side. With nowhere to go along the inside rail over a quarter of a mile from home, she eventually managed to get through and picked up ground a furlong out. Running on really strongly, she failed to get to the winner in time. Compensation awaits. (9/2)

**1420* Samara (IRE)** who has been raised 21lb for her two victories this season, was rather disappointing. A leading light from the off, she had every chance from below the distance but then tamely dropped away. (7/4)

**1796 Prends Ca (IRE)** played an active role until finally coming to the end of her tether below the distance. (20/1)

**1061* Roses In The Snow (IRE)** chased the leaders but had bellows to mend over a furlong from home. (20/1)

## 2143 PALAN H'CAP (0-105) (3-Y.O) (Class B)
2-30 (2-30) **5f** £14,265.00 (£4,320.00: £2,110.00: £1,005.00) Stalls: Centre GOING minus 0.39 sec per fur (F)

| | | | SP | RR | SF |
|---|---|---|---|---|---|
| 1316* | **Midnight Escape (89)** (CFWall) **3-8-5** NCarlisle(5) (a.p: led over 1f out: all out)....— | **1** | 13/2[2] | 97 | 33 |
| 1615[3] | **Sylva Paradise (IRE) (80)** (CEBrittain) **3-7-10** GBardwell(9) (a.p: rdn over 2f out: ev ch ins fnl f: r.o wl) ....hd | **2** | 12/1 | 88 | 24 |
| 2007[15] | **Hoh Returns (IRE) (89)** (MBell) **3-8-5** MFenton(10) (lw: a.p: rdn over 1f out: ev ch ins fnl f: unable qckn)....1¼ | **3** | 8/1[3] | 93 | 29 |
| 1985[3] | **Dande Flyer (80)** (DWPArbuthnot) **3-7-10** JQuinn(3) (b: nt clr run over 2f out: rdn & hdwy over 1f out: r.o)....1¼ | **4** | 25/1 | 80 | 16 |
| 1628[4] | **White Emir (82)** (BJMeehan) **3-7-12**ow1 JFEgan(13) (lw: led over 3f: one pce fnl f) ....1 | **5** | 10/1 | 79 | 14 |
| 1566a[3] | **Nashcash (IRE) (103)** (CCollins,Ireland) **3-9-5** PShanahan(11) (lw: hld up: rdn over 2f out: one pce) ....1 | **6** | 5/1[1] | 96 | 32 |
| 1823* | **Rushcutter Bay (85)** (TTClement) **3-8-1** MRoberts(4) (lw: nvr nrr) ....hd | **7** | 13/2[2] | 78 | 14 |
| 1974[9] | **Tadeo (93)** (MJohnston) **3-8-9** JWeaver(6) (lw: nvr nrr) ....s.h | **8** | 12/1 | 86 | 22 |
| 1853[12] | **Willow Dale (IRE) (80)** (DRCElsworth) **3-7-10v[1]** FNorton(2) (rdn & hdwy over 1f out: one pce) ....1 | **9** | 14/1 | 70 | 6 |
| 1146[9] | **Amazing Bay (105)** (IABalding) **3-9-2**(5) MartinDwyer(14) (lw: hdwy over 2f out: wknd fnl f) ....½ | **10** | 25/1 | 93 | 29 |
| 1663* | **Sharp Pearl (80)** (JWhite) **3-7-7b**(3) MHenry(12) (lw: sme hdwy over 1f out: wknd fnl f) ....¾ | **11** | 20/1 | 66 | 2 |
| 1818[8] | **Tarf (USA) (87)** (PTWalwyn) **3-8-3** WCarson(7) (lw: spd over 3f) ....2½ | **12** | 10/1 | 65 | 1 |
| 1188* | **Kunucu (IRE) (95)** (TDBarron) **3-8-11** KDarley(8) (lw: bhd fnl 2f) ....1¾ | **13** | 9/1 | 67 | 3 |
| 2007[10] | **Eastern Prophets (89)** (TJNaughton) **3-8-5** TQuinn(1) (bhd fnl 2f) ....3 | **14** | 33/1 | 51 | — |

(SP 120.1%) **14 Rn**

**61.37 secs** (1.37) CSF £74.35 CT £583.90 TOTE £6.00: £2.20 £4.20 £2.90 (£79.90) Trio £308.60 OWNER Mr Mervyn Ayers (NEWMARKET) BRED M. L. Ayers
LONG HANDICAP Dande Flyer 7-5 Sharp Pearl 7-8
OFFICIAL EXPLANATION **Kunucu (IRE): lost her action at the furlong marker.**

**1316* Midnight Escape**, who was off his food earlier in the week and had a border line blood test, had another test the night before that showed perfect blood. In the front rank throughout, he hit the front approaching the final furlong and, in a tremendous battle, just managed to prevail. (13/2)

**1615 Sylva Paradise (IRE)** coped well with the drop in distance. Always close up, he threw down his challenge from below the distance and, proving a real thorn in the winner's side, only just failed to get up. (12/1)

**1628 Hoh Returns (IRE)**, a leading light from the off, mounted his challenge from below the distance. With every chance inside the final furlong, he got tapped for toe inside the closing stages. (8/1)

**1985 Dande Flyer** failed to get a clear run along the inside rail at halfway. He stayed on inside the last furlong and a half but found the leaders had got first run and were not for catching (25/1)

**1628 White Emir** attempted to make all the running towards the centre of the track. Collared over a furlong from home, he was then only treading water. (10/1)

**1566a Nashcash (IRE)** chased the leaders but failed to find another gear in the last two furlongs. (5/1)

## 2144 MILCARS CONDITIONS STKS (3-Y.O) (Class B)
3-00 (3-00) **1m 4f** £9,922.50 (£3,472.50: £1,698.75: £731.25) Stalls: High GOING minus 0.39 sec per fur (F)

| | | | SP | RR | SF |
|---|---|---|---|---|---|
| 1757a[8] | **Astor Place (IRE) (110)** (PWChapple-Hyam) **3-8-11** JReid(3) (lw: hdwy to chse ldr wl over 1f out: hrd rdn: led last stride) ....— | **1** | 5/6[1] | 109 | 41 |
| 1791[8] | **Acharne (109)** (CEBrittain) **3-9-0** BDoyle(5) (led: clr over 7f out: rdn over 1f out: hdd last stride)....s.h | **2** | 4/1[3] | 112 | 44 |
| 1329[7] | **Masehaab (IRE) (105)** (JLDunlop) **3-9-0** WCarson(1) (chsd ldr tl wl over 1f out: sn wknd)....5 | **3** | 6/1 | 105 | 37 |
| 1015[3] | **Weet-A-Minute (IRE) (106)** (RHollinshead) **3-9-4** KDarley(2) (lw: hld up: rdn 3f out: wknd over 1f out) ....1¾ | **4** | 7/2[2] | 107 | 39 |

(SP 111.1%) **4 Rn**

**2m 33.18** (3.18) CSF £4.32 TOTE £1.90: (£2.70) OWNER Mr R. E. Sangster (MARLBOROUGH) BRED Roncon Ltd
IN-FOCUS: **It is a shame that the traditional title of this race, the Churchill Stakes, has been dropped now the race is sponsored.**

**1757a Astor Place (IRE)**, who did not have the best of runs in the French Derby, certainly gave his connections some very anxious moments. Moving up to take second place early in the final quarter mile, he still had a few lengths to make up on the leader. Although making very heavy weather of it, he managed to get in front right on the line. (5/6: 4/6-11/8)

**1791 Acharne** was given a very enterprising ride but only just failed to succeed. Bowling along in front, he had a useful advantage in the straight and although the winner moved into second place early in the final quarter mile, he appeared to be home and dried. However, despite doing nothing wrong, he was caught right on the line. (4/1: 11/4-9/2)

**926 Masehaab (IRE)** raced in second place until well over a furlong from home before tiring. (6/1)

**1015 Weet-A-Minute (IRE)** chased the leaders but was a spent force early in the final quarter mile. (7/2: 5/1-3/1)

## 2145 LADBROKE H'CAP (0-105) (4-Y.O+) (Class B)
3-35 (3-35) **1m 2f** £21,202.50 (£6,420.00: £3,135.00: £1,492.50) Stalls: High GOING minus 0.39 sec per fur (F)

| | | | SP | RR | SF |
|---|---|---|---|---|---|
| 1867* | **Salmon Ladder (USA) (102)** (PFICole) **4-10-0** TQuinn(5) (led over 3f: led 3f out: drvn out)....— | **1** | 3/1[1] | 113 | 96 |
| 1793[5] | **Ellie Ardensky (94)** (JRFanshawe) **4-9-6** DHarrison(10) (lw: a.p: rdn over 2f out: ev ch over 1f out: unable qckn) ....1 | **2** | 15/2[3] | 103 | 86 |

1793[4] **Conspicuous (IRE) (80)** (LGCottrell) **6-8-6** JQuinn(11) (lw: hdwy on ins over 3f out: hrd rdn over 1f out: one pce) ....2½ **3** 13/2[2] 85 68
1486[4] **Prize Pupil (IRE) (71)** (CFWall) **4-7-11** NCarlisle(7) (hrd rdn & hdwy over 1f out: one pce) ....1¾ **4** 8/1 74 57
2010[4] **Percy Braithwaite (IRE) (82)** (MJohnston) **4-8-8** JWeaver(4) (lw: a.p: rdn over 2f out: one pce) ....1½ **5** 11/1 82 65
1505[3] **The Stager (IRE) (75)** (JRJenkins) **4-7-10**(5)ow1 ADaly(9) (lw: nvr nr to chal) ....8 **6** 25/1 62 44
1816[3] **Access Adventurer (IRE) (74)** (RBoss) **5-8-0**ow1 MRoberts(3) (led over 6f out to 3f out: wknd 2f out) ....1½ **7** 12/1 59 41
1131[6] **Ball Gown (92)** (DTThom) **6-9-4** DRMcCabe(2) (a bhd) ....¾ **8** 10/1 76 59
1793[3] **Hoh Express (95)** (IABalding) **4-9-7** KDarley(6) (hld up: rdn over 3f out: wknd over 2f out) ....s.h **9** 15/2[3] 79 62
1861[3] **Komreyev Dancer (75)** (ABailey) **4-8-1** GBardwell(8) (bhd fnl 2f) ....2 **10** 12/1 56 39
2008[4] **Dreams End (80)** (PBowen) **8-8-6** JReid(1) (bhd fnl 3f) ....10 **11** 16/1 45 28
(SP 115.5%) **11 Rn**

**2m 4.78** (-2.02) CSF £23.62 CT £123.90 TOTE £3.40: £1.50 £2.60 £3.00 (£11.10) Trio £44.30 OWNER Mr M. Arbib (WHATCOMBE) BRED Robert N. Clay and Michael J. & Mrs Ryan

**1867* Salmon Ladder (USA)** took the field along but was marginally collared coming out of Swinley Bottom. Regaining the advantage turning for home, he responded to pressure and kept on well. Connections are now considering the Royal Hong Kong Jockey Club Handicap at Sandown next month. (3/1: 2/1-100/30)

**1793 Ellie Ardensky** a leading player from the start, mounted her challenge in the straight and had every chance below the distance before the winner found a bit extra. (15/2)

**1793 Conspicuous (IRE)** moved up along the inside rail over three furlongs from home. Almost on terms below the distance, he was then tapped for toe. (13/2)

**1486 Prize Pupil (IRE)** under pressure to pick up ground below the distance, could then make no further impression. (8/1)

**2010 Percy Braithwaite (IRE)**, in a handy position throughout, failed to quicken in the last two furlongs. (11/1)

## 2146 TRIUMVIRATE LIMITED STKS (0-80) (3-Y.O) (Class D)

4-10 (4-10) **1m (round)** £6,359.00 (£2,381.00: £1,165.50: £502.50: £226.25: £115.75) Stalls: High GOING minus 0.39 sec per fur (F)

SP RR SF

1825* **Golden Pond (IRE) (80)** (RFJohnsonHoughton) **3-8-10** JReid(8) (mde all: drvn out) ....— **1** 6/1[2] 88 54
1709[3] **Diamond Beach (76)** (BWHills) **3-8-11** PatEddery(9) (rdn & hdwy on ins 2f out: r.o) ....1¾ **2** 15/2 86 52
1648[2] **Divina Luna (80)** (JWHills) **3-8-7**(3) MHenry(12) (a.p: rdn over 2f out: unable qckn) ....1½ **3** 10/1 82 48
1652[3] **Kiss Me Again (IRE) (78)** (RHannon) **3-8-8** TQuinn(11) (hld up: rdn over 2f out: one pce) ....2 **4** 14/1 76 42
1066[4] **Quality (IRE) (79)** (WAO'Gorman) **3-8-13b** EmmaO'Gorman(6) (nvr nr to chal) ....hd **5** 33/1 80 46
1825[2] **High Note (77)** (RCharlton) **3-8-8** KDarley(5) (hld up: hrd rdn over 2f out: one pce) ....1½ **6** 6/1[2] 72 38
1324[7] **She's My Love (77)** (JEBanks) **3-8-8** JQuinn(4) (lw: prom over 6f) ....3 **7** 13/2[3] 66 32
1785[2] **Capilano Princess (80)** (DHaydnJones) **3-8-10** AMackay(7) (hld up: rdn 3f out: sn wknd) ....14 **8** 7/1 40 6
1771[12] **Mancini (79)** (MBell) **3-8-11v[1]** MFenton(3) (bhd fnl 3f) ....2 **9** 25/1 37 3
1843* **Select Few (83)** (LMCumani) **3-8-13** JWeaver(1) (bhd fnl 3f) ....nk **10** 7/2[1] 39 5
1819[4] **Proud Monk (77)** (GLMoore) **3-8-11** SWhitworth(2) (a bhd) ....1¼ **11** 10/1 34 —
(SP 120.0%) **11 Rn**

**1m 41.61** (0.81) CSF £47.39 TOTE £5.50: £1.80 £2.50 £3.60 (£23.50) Trio £169.40 OWNER Mr John Horgan (DIDCOT) BRED Tullamaine Castle Stud and Partners

**1825* Golden Pond (IRE)** has been a model of consistency this year. Making all the running, she responded to pressure and was not going to be denied. (6/1)

**1709 Diamond Beach** began to pick up ground along the inside rail a quarter of a mile from home but despite running on to snatch second place was not going to get to the winner in time. (15/2)

**1648 Divina Luna**, a leading light from the start, was asked for her effort early in the straight but failed to find the necessary turn of foot. (10/1)

**1652 Kiss Me Again (IRE)** chased the leaders but could only go up and down in the same place in the last two furlongs. (14/1)

**1066 Quality (IRE)** stayed on in the straight without posing a threat. (33/1)

**1825 High Note** chased the leaders but, shown the persuader over two furlongs from home, was making no further impression. (6/1)

**1324 She's My Love** (13/2: 9/2-7/1)

## 2147 E.B.F. MAIDEN STKS (Unraced 2-Y.O F) (Class D)

4-40 (4-41) **6f** £5,524.00 (£1,672.00: £816.00: £388.00) Stalls: Centre GOING minus 0.39 sec per fur (F)

SP RR SF

**Khassah** (JHMGosden) **2-8-11** RHills(7) (w'like: scope: lw: dwlt: hdwy over 2f out: led over 1f out: r.o wl) ....— **1** 4/1[2] 86+ 34
**Well Warned** (BWHills) **2-8-11** PatEddery(3) (w'like: scope: a.p: ev ch over 1f out: unable qckn) ....2 **2** 6/1 81 t 29
**Kalinka (IRE)** (PFICole) **2-8-11** TQuinn(4) (w'like: a.p: rdn & n.m.r over 1f out: one pce) ....¾ **3** 8/1 79 t 27
**Carati** (RBoss) **2-8-11** MRoberts(5) (leggy: bit bkwd: hld up: rdn over 2f out: r.o one pce fnl f) ....1 **4** 25/1 76 t 24
**Hanan (USA)** (PAKelleway) **2-8-11** JWeaver(8) (w'like: scope: led over 4f: wknd fnl f) ....2 **5** 16/1 71 t 19
**Stone Flower (USA)** (PWChapple-Hyam) **2-8-11** JReid(9) (w'like: scope: lw: prom 4f) ....1¾ **6** 9/2[3] 66 t 14
**Hadawah (USA)** (JLDunlop) **2-8-11** WCarson(1) (neat: hld up: rdn over 2f out: wknd over 1f out) ....5 **7** 11/8[1] 53 t 1
**Logica (IRE)** (PAKelleway) **2-8-11** KDarley(6) (w'like: dwlt: a bhd) ....1¼ **8** 33/1 49 t —
**French Mist** (CEBrittain) **2-8-11** BDoyle(2) (str: a bhd) ....2½ **9** 12/1 43 t —
(SP 126.0%) **9 Rn**

**1m 16.11** (2.11) CSF £28.66 TOTE £6.40: £1.90 £1.60 £2.20 (£18.60) Trio £31.10 OWNER Mr Hamdan Al Maktoum (NEWMARKET) BRED Shadwell Estate Company Limited

**Khassah**, a scopey newcomer, looked in good shape beforehand. Moving up on the outside to strike the front over a furlong out, she soon stamped her authority on the race. (4/1)

**Well Warned**, a scopey filly, was always close up. Threatening to take the lead below the distance, she was unable to cope with the winner. She should soon go one better. (6/1)

**Kalinka (IRE)**, a half sister to mile and a half winner Dancing Tralthee, was always close up. With not a great deal of room in which to manoeuvre over a furlong out, she could then only keep on at one pace. (8/1: 6/1-9/1)

**Carati**, a tall filly who looked as though the run would do her good, chased the leaders. Rather outpaced over two furlongs from home, she did stay on again in the final furlong. (25/1)

**Hanan (USA)**, an attractive filly, attempted to make all the running. Collared over a furlong out, she found lack of a previous run taking its toll in the closing stages. (16/1)

**Stone Flower (USA)**, a quality filly who is a full sister to Group 2 Coventry Stakes winner Stonehatch, played an active role until forced to give best a quarter of a mile from home. (9/2)

**Hadawah (USA)** (11/8: Evens-6/4)
**French Mist** (12/1: op 20/1)

## 2148 CHURCHILL H'CAP (0-80) (3-Y.O+) (Class D)

5-10 (5-10) **2m 45y** £5,992.00 (£1,816.00: £888.00: £424.00) Stalls: High GOING minus 0.39 sec per fur (F)

| | | | | SP | RR | SF |
|---|---|---|---|---|---|---|
| 1710[4] | **Bolivar (IRE) (56)** (RAkehurst) **4-8-4b** TQuinn(6) (led over 1f: led over 2f out: rdn out) | — | **1** | 9/2[1] | 69 | 35 |
| 1511[5] | **Requested (48)** (PBurgoyne) **9-7-10** JQuinn(4) (hdwy 3f out: chsd wnr over 1f out: unable qckn) | 3½ | **2** | 16/1 | 58 | 24 |
| 1343[6] | **French Ivy (USA) (58)** (FMurphy) **9-8-6**ow1 JReid(9) (b: lw: n.m.r. 3f out: hrd rdn & hdwy over 1f out: r.o) | 1¼ | **3** | 5/1[2] | 66 | 31 |
| 2042[13] | **Paradise Navy (66)** (CREgerton) **7-9-0b** RHughes(12) (hdwy over 6f out: ev ch 2f out: eased whn btn ins fnl f) | 2½ | **4** | 12/1 | 72 | 38 |
| 2008[8] | **Witney-de-Bergerac (IRE) (61)** (JSMoore) **4-8-9** JFEgan(7) (hdwy over 1f out: nvr nrr) | s.h | **5** | 20/1 | 67 | 33 |
| 1529* | **Zamhareer (USA) (55)** (WStorey) **5-7-10**(7) IonaWands(11) (a.p: rdn over 2f out: wknd wl over 1f out) | 1 | **6** | 9/2[1] | 60 | 26 |
| 1439[10] | **Salaman (FR) (80)** (JLDunlop) **4-10-0** WCarson(1) (nvr nr to chal) | ½ | **7** | 8/1[3] | 84 | 50 |
| 1847* | **Good Hand (USA) (70)** (SEKettlewell) **10-9-4** KDarley(8) (prom over 8f) | hd | **8** | 9/1 | 74 | 40 |
| 1852[2] | **Uncharted Waters (55)** (CACyzer) **5-8-3** MRoberts(13) (a bhd) | hd | **9** | 8/1[3] | 59 | 25 |
| 1788* | **Diego (70)** (CEBrittain) **3-7-12** GBardwell(10) (hld up: rdn over 3f out: wknd over 2f out) | 2 | **10** | 10/1 | 72 | 18 |
| 1835[10] | **Gentleman Sid (48)** (PGMurphy) **6-7-10** NAdams(3) (led 15f out tl over 2f out: sn wknd) | 3½ | **11** | 33/1 | 47 | 13 |
| 1514[4] | **Birthday Boy (IRE) (53)** (JRJenkins) **4-7-10v**(5)ow5 ADaly(5) (hld up: rdn 4f out: wknd over 2f out) | 1 | **12** | 20/1 | 51 | 12 |
| | | | | (SP 120.4%) | **12 Rn** | |

**3m 31.63** (4.43) CSF £66.65 CT £346.24 TOTE £4.90: £1.80 £4.80 £1.80 (£63.50) Trio £168.50 OWNER BEL Leisure Ltd (EPSOM) BRED A. Hanahoe
LONG HANDICAP Requested 7-9 Gentleman Sid 7-5 Birthday Boy (IRE) 7-8
WEIGHT FOR AGE 3yo-20lb
**1710 Bolivar (IRE)**, a leading light from the off, hit the front early in the straight and, ridden along, proved too good for his rivals. (9/2)
**1511 Requested** began his effort turning for home. Struggling into second place approaching the final furlong, he was unable to reel in the winner. (16/1)
**1343 French Ivy (USA)**, under pressure as he picked up ground in the last two furlongs, stayed on for third prize. (5/1)
**1835 Paradise Navy**, making a quick reappearance, took closer order coming out of Swinley Bottom. With every chance a quarter of a mile from home, he was soon in trouble and his jockey took things easy on him when all chance had gone in the final furlong. (12/1)
**712 Witney-de-Bergerac (IRE)** stayed on past beaten horses in the last two furlongs. (20/1)
**1529* Zamhareer (USA)**, a leading light from the off, had shot his bolt early in the final quarter mile. (9/2: 3/1-5/1)
**Salaman (FR)** (8/1: 6/1-9/1)

T/Jkpt: £19,505.10 (19.15 Tckts). T/Plpt: £166.50 (419.48 Tckts). T/Qdpt: £36.00 (63.67 Tckts) AK

# 2118-AYR (L-H) (Good to firm)
## Saturday June 22nd

5th race was hand timed
WEATHER: fine WIND: mod against

## 2149 ARRAN H'CAP (0-85) (3-Y.O+) (Class D)

2-15 (2-19) **7f** £3,566.25 (£1,080.00: £527.50: £251.25) Stalls: Low GOING minus 0.09 sec per fur (G)

| | | | | SP | RR | SF |
|---|---|---|---|---|---|---|
| 1425[8] | **Somerton Boy (IRE) (68)** (PCalver) **6-9-8** NDay(4) (lw: in tch: hdwy u.p over 1f out: r.o wl to ld wl ins fnl f) | — | **1** | 12/1 | 78 | 51 |
| 1789[6] | **Quilling (67)** (MDods) **4-9-7** DeanMcKeown(5) (led tl disp ld 1f out: no ex towards fin) | 1 | **2** | 11/1 | 75 | 48 |
| 2047* | **Murray's Mazda (IRE) (52)** (JLEyre) **7-8-6** 6x TWilliams(6) (chsd ldrs: disp led 1f out: nt qckn towards fin) | nk | **3** | 9/2[2] | 59 | 32 |
| 1703[5] | **Sagebrush Roller (70)** (JWWatts) **8-9-10** NConnorton(9) (lw: hld up: hdwy on outside 2f out: sn prom: one pce ins fnl f) | 1¼ | **4** | 10/1 | 74 | 47 |
| 2005[3] | **Mister Westsound (70)** (MissLAPerratt) **4-9-10b** WJO'Connor(7) (hld up: hdwy over 2f out: nt qckn fnl f) | nk | **5** | 7/1 | 74 | 47 |
| 1983[3] | **My Gallery (IRE) (62)** (ABailey) **5-9-2** PaulEddery(2) (w ldr: rdn over 2f out: wknd appr fnl f) | nk | **6** | 7/2[1] | 65 | 38 |
| 2047[6] | **Allinson's Mate (IRE) (55)** (TDBarron) **8-8-9b** JFortune(3) (lw: bhd: effrt over 2f out: hrd drvn & no imp) | ½ | **7** | 5/1[3] | 57 | 30 |
| 1585[7] | **Best of All (IRE) (67)** (JBerry) **4-9-7** JCarroll(1) (chsd ldrs tl wknd 2f out) | 4 | **8** | 8/1 | 60 | 33 |
| 1876[2] | **Morning Surprise (63)** (APJarvis) **3-8-1**(7) CCarver(8) (s.i.s: a bhd) | 2½ | **9** | 10/1 | 50 | 14 |
| | | | | (SP 114.9%) | **9 Rn** | |

**1m 27.57** (3.57) CSF £116.71 CT £625.15 TOTE £15.10: £2.70 £3.00 £1.50 (£55.30) Trio £191.40 OWNER Mrs Janis MacPherson (RIPON) BRED Mrs A. Whitehead
WEIGHT FOR AGE 3yo-9lb
**Somerton Boy (IRE)** likes this track and made up a fair amount in the last two furlongs to win decisively. (12/1)
**1789 Quilling** put up a useful display and looks to be coming to hand fast. (11/1)
**2047* Murray's Mazda (IRE)** is in tremendous form this season and ran another good race here, but just failed to see it out. (9/2)
**1703 Sagebrush Roller** is a law unto himself and was never giving it his best shot here. (10/1)
**2005 Mister Westsound** ran well but is yet to win over this trip. (7/1: 5/1-8/1)
**1983 My Gallery (IRE)** has had an extremely busy season and that is beginning to show looks wise. (7/2)
**2047 Allinson's Mate (IRE)** looked the part and had the required blinkers on but did not show the required sparkle here. (5/1)

## 2150 ROMAN WARRIOR SHIELD MAIDEN STKS (3-Y.O+) (Class D)

2-45 (2-46) **7f** £3,598.75 (£1,090.00: £532.50: £253.75) Stalls: Low GOING minus 0.09 sec per fur (G)

| | | | | SP | RR | SF |
|---|---|---|---|---|---|---|
| 1657D | **Statoyork (82)** (BWHills) **3-8-12** PaulEddery(5) (lw: trckd ldr: led 1½f out: pushed along & r.o) | — | **1** | 4/7[1] | 70+ | 7 |
| 1994[2] | **Woodbury Lad (USA)** (WRMuir) **3-8-12** WJO'Connor(2) (lw: led tl hdd 1½f out: one pce) | 1¾ | **2** | 7/4[2] | 66 | 3 |
| 2048[7] | **Truly Bay** (TDBarron) **3-8-12** JFortune(4) (hld up & bhd: styd on fnl 2f: nvr nr to chal) | 6 | **3** | 33/1 | 52 | — |
| 934[14] | **Nordic Gift (DEN)** (MrsDThomson) **3-8-12** RLappin(1) (chsd ldrs tl outpcd fnl 3f) | nk | **4** | 100/1 | 52 | — |
| | **Blazing Imp (USA)** (WSCunningham) **3-8-12** DeanMcKeown(3) (w'like: s.i.s: wl outpcd fr ½-wy) | 5 | **5** | 20/1[3] | 40 | — |
| | | | | (SP 108.7%) | **5 Rn** | |

**1m 30.68** (6.68) CSF £1.83 TOTE £1.60: £1.00 £2.30 (£1.30) OWNER Mr Seymour Cohn (LAMBOURN) BRED C. W. Rogers
**1657 Statoyork**, robbed of victory last time, made no mistake here and won under hands and heels driving. (4/7)

**1994 Woodbury Lad (USA)** is an excitable sort who needed two attendants in the paddock. After racing freely he had no more to give in the final furlong. (7/4)
**Truly Bay** is improving with racing and there looks to be better to come. (33/1)
**Nordic Gift (DEN)** was well short of pace once the tempo increased early in the straight. (100/1)
**Blazing Imp (USA)** needed this and was behind from halfway. (20/1)

## 2151 HIGH SPEED PRODUCTION H'CAP (0-80) (3-Y.O) (Class D)

3-15 (3-15) **5f** £4,201.50 (£1,272.00: £621.00: £295.50) Stalls: Low GOING minus 0.09 sec per fur (G)

| | | | | SP | RR | SF |
|---|---|---|---|---|---|---|
| $1340^{6}$ | **Precious Girl (67)** (DMoffatt) **3-8-8v**$^{(3)}$ DarrenMoffatt(3) (bhd: hdwy to ld appr fnl f: sn clr & eased) | — | **1** | 7/1 | 81+ | 24 |
| $2049^{3}$ | **Pathaze (55)** (NBycroft) **3-7-13**$^{ow3}$ JFanning(8) (s.i.s: hdwy 2f out: styd on: no ch w wnr) | 5 | **2** | 12/1 | 53 | — |
| $1823^{4}$ | **Comic Fantasy (AUS) (77)** (MartynWane) **3-9-7** JFortune(6) (a chsng ldrs: rdn 2f out: kpt on one pce) | 1½ | **3** | $11/2^{3}$ | 70 | 13 |
| $1049^{10}$ | **Man of Wit (IRE) (66)** (APJarvis) **3-8-10v**$^{1}$ WJO'Connor(4) (lw: hld up: hdwy 2f out: nt qckn fnl f) | ¾ | **4** | 14/1 | 57 | — |
| 1761* | **Mister Joel (62)** (MWEasterby) **3-8-1b**$^{(5)}$ GParkin(5) (lw: cl up: rdn ½-wy: one pce) | 1 | **5** | $7/2^{1}$ | 50 | — |
| $1663^{2}$ | **Goretski (IRE) (74)** (NTinkler) **3-9-4b**$^{1}$ PaulEddery(2) (lw: cl up: disp ld 2f out tl wknd 1f out) | nk | **6** | $4/1^{2}$ | 61 | 4 |
| $2021^{3}$ | **Gwespyr (59)** (JBerry) **3-8-3**$^{ow1}$ JCarroll(1) (mde most tl hdd appr fnl f: wknd) | 1¼ | **7** | $7/2^{1}$ | 42 | — |
| $1761^{11}$ | **Superfrills (53)** (MissLCSiddall) **3-7-11**$^{ow1}$ TWilliams(7) (spd over 3f) | 16 | **8** | 33/1 | — | — |
| | | | | (SP 109.6%) | **8 Rn** | |

**60.63 secs** (3.63) CSF £70.14 CT £419.80 TOTE £7.30: £1.40 £2.40 £1.60 (£22.80) OWNER Mr P. G. Airey (CARTMEL) BRED P. G. Airey and R. R. Whitton
LONG HANDICAP Pathaze 7-7 Superfrills 7-9
OFFICIAL EXPLANATION **Superfrills: his rider reported that the horse had not liked the ground.**
**1340 Precious Girl**, having her second run in a visor, was ridden from behind this time. The improvement was amazing as she won easily. (7/1)
**2049 Pathaze** again gave ground away at the start and, despite finishing well, had no chance with the winner. (12/1: op 8/1)
**1823 Comic Fantasy (AUS)** ran a sound race and is now beginning to slip down the handicap. (11/2)
**758 Man of Wit (IRE)**, wearing a visor for the first time, travelled well but failed to pick up when asked a question. (14/1: 10/1-16/1)
**1761* Mister Joel** likes to dictate and that was never on here. (7/2)
**1663 Goretski (IRE)**, in blinkers for the first time, ran fast until crying enough with a furlong left. (4/1: 3/1-9/2)
**2021 Gwespyr** made it but proved disappointing when ridden. (7/2: 5/2-4/1)

## 2152 ALLOWAY H'CAP (0-80) (3-Y.O+) (Class D)

3-45 (3-46) **1m 2f** £3,615.00 (£1,095.00: £535.00: £255.00) Stalls: Low GOING minus 0.14 sec per fur (G)

| | | | | SP | RR | SF |
|---|---|---|---|---|---|---|
| $1585^{2}$ | **Stormless (43)** (PMonteith) **5-7-7**$^{(3)}$ DarrenMoffatt(4) (lw: hld up & bhd: hdwy to join ldrs ent st: led over 1f out: all out) | — | **1** | $9/2^{2}$ | 53 | 35 |
| 2020* | **Keep Battling (48)** (JSGoldie) **6-8-1**$^{5x}$ TWilliams(5) (hld up & bhd: hdwy on bit 3f out: swtchd outside over 1f out: ev ch ins fnl f: kpt on) | hd | **2** | $9/4^{1}$ | 58 | 40 |
| $1861^{6}$ | **Far Ahead (73)** (JLEyre) **4-9-12** RLappin(3) (chsd ldrs: hdwy & ev ch ins fnl f: nt qckn) | 1¼ | **3** | 14/1 | 81 | 63 |
| $2077^{3}$ | **Dr Edgar (61)** (MDods) **4-9-0** JCarroll(6) (led tl hdd over 1f out: wknd ins fnl f) | 2½ | **4** | $11/2^{3}$ | 65 | 47 |
| $1698^{3}$ | **Efizia (60)** (GMMoore) **6-8-13** JFortune(7) (chsd ldrs tl outpcd fnl 2f) | 3½ | **5** | 6/1 | 58 | 40 |
| $1772^{2}$ | **Shabanaz (60)** (WRMuir) **11-8-13** WJO'Connor(2) (cl up tl wknd over 2f out) | s.h | **6** | $11/2^{3}$ | 58 | 40 |
| $2123^{3}$ | **Lucky Bea (60)** (MWEasterby) **3-8-1** JFanning(1) (lw: plld hrd: trckd ldrs: outpcd over 2f out: sn btn) | 2½ | **7** | 8/1 | 54 | 24 |
| | | | | (SP 111.8%) | **7 Rn** | |

**2m 8.9** (4.30) CSF £14.21 TOTE £7.10: £3.00 £1.60 (£6.90) OWNER Mr D. St Clair (ROSEWELL) BRED D. V. St Clair
WEIGHT FOR AGE 3yo-12lb
**1585 Stormless** made his ground on the outside of the field on the home turn and, once in front approaching the final furlong, he just had too much determination for the runner-up. (9/2)
**2020* Keep Battling** always looked to be going best but, brought to the outside to challenge, he saw too much daylight too soon and just failed to quicken enough. (9/4)
**Far Ahead** ran pretty well and it would appear that he is fast coming to form. (14/1)
**2077 Dr Edgar** ran another decent race out in front but finally cried enough inside the final furlong. (11/2)
**1698 Efizia** was a shade disappointing this time but should she get it together, she is certainly well enough handicapped. (6/1)
**1772 Shabanaz** is at his best in claimers and sellers. (11/2)
**2123 Lucky Bea** (8/1: op 4/1)

## 2153 BELLEISLE MEDIAN AUCTION MAIDEN STKS (2-Y.O) (Class F)

4-15 (4-15) **6f** £2,775.00 (£840.00: £410.00: £195.00) Stalls: Low GOING minus 0.09 sec per fur (G)

| | | | | SP | RR | SF |
|---|---|---|---|---|---|---|
| $1897^{4}$ | **Peartree House (IRE)** (BWHills) **2-9-0** PaulEddery(1) (mde all: qcknd over 1f out: easily) | — | **1** | $4/11^{1}$ | 60+ | 12 |
| | **Brave Montgomerie** (MissLAPerratt) **2-9-0** WJO'Connor(3) (w'like: scope: bit bkwd: dwlt: sn in tch: kpt on wl fnl f: no ch w wnr) | 6 | **2** | $6/1^{2}$ | 44 | — |
| | **Select Lady** (APJarvis) **2-8-9** JFortune(4) (neat: scope: lw: sn cl up: effrt 2f out: sn rdn & btn) | 3 | **3** | $7/1^{3}$ | 31 | — |
| | **Sweeping Statement** (JBerry) **2-8-9** JCarroll(2) (cmpt: str: spd 4f: wknd) | 2½ | **4** | 10/1 | 24 | — |
| | | | | (SP 109.2%) | **4 Rn** | |

**1m 15.4** (5.60) CSF £2.93 TOTE £1.40 (£2.60) OWNER Newbyth Stud (LAMBOURN) BRED Cocomo American Thoroughbred Exports Inc
**1897 Peartree House (IRE)** may not have beaten much here, but the way he did it had to impress and he looks one to follow. (4/11)
**Brave Montgomerie**, a useful looking sort, needed this both fitness and experience wise and was getting the hang of the things by the end. (6/1: 4/1-7/1)
**Select Lady**, a handy sort, looked pretty straight but ran as though it was needed. (7/1: op 4/1)
**Sweeping Statement** needed this and, after showing speed, blew up in the last couple of furlongs. (10/1: op 6/1)

## 2154 DOONFOOT H'CAP (0-65) (3-Y.O+) (Class F)

4-45 (4-46) **6f** £2,918.00 (£884.00: £432.00: £206.00) Stalls: Low GOING minus 0.09 sec per fur (G)

| | | | | SP | RR | SF |
|---|---|---|---|---|---|---|
| $1885^{5}$ | **Thwaab (45)** (FWatson) **4-8-12v**$^{1}$ JFanning(9) (lw: bhd: hdwy to ld ins fnl f: r.o wl) | — | **1** | 33/1 | 56 | 38 |
| $2023^{6}$ | **Sunday Mail Too (IRE) (42)** (MissLAPerratt) **4-8-9** WJO'Connor(6) (cl up: led 1½f out tl ins fnl f: no ex) | 1¾ | **2** | 20/1 | 48 | 30 |
| $1889^{8}$ | **Most Uppitty (41)** (JBerry) **4-8-8** JCarroll(8) (bhd: hdwy 2f out: styd on wl) | 1½ | **3** | 16/1 | 43 | 25 |
| $2029^{8}$ | **Ned's Bonanza (59)** (MDods) **7-9-12** PaulEddery(5) (trckd ldrs: effrt over 1f out: rdn & nt qckn ins fnl f) | ½ | **4** | $6/1^{3}$ | 60 | 42 |
| $1364^{8}$ | **Foist (45)** (MWEasterby) **4-8-7**$^{(5)}$ GParkin(15) (bhd: hdwy 2f out: sn rdn & no imp) | 1¾ | **5** | $9/4^{1}$ | 41 | 23 |

| | | | | SP | RR | SF |
|---|---|---|---|---|---|---|
| 1635[11] | **Seconds Away (32)** (JSGoldie) **5-7-13b** TWilliams(11) (in tch: rdn over 2f out: no imp) | s.h | **6** | 20/1 | 28 | 10 |
| 2119[2] | **Leading Princess (IRE) (49)** (MissLAPerratt) **5-9-2b** NDay(4) (lw: led tl hdd 1½f out: wknd) | 1¼ | **7** | 13/2 | 42 | 24 |
| 1342[5] | **Sense of Priority (56)** (DNicholls) **7-9-9** MWigham(2) (chsd ldrs: rdn over 2f out: wknd over 1f out) | 1 | **8** | 9/1 | 46 | 28 |
| 1889[5] | **Pallium (IRE) (55)** (MrsAMNaughton) **8-9-8** NConnorton(7) (lw: hld up & bhd: hdwy 2f out: n.d) | s.h | **9** | 14/1 | 45 | 27 |
| 1848[3] | **Superpride (61)** (MrsMReveley) **4-9-9b**(5) SCopp(13) (s.i.s: effrt ½-wy: sn rdn & btn) | s.h | **10** | 8/1 | 51 | 33 |
| 1848* | **Invigilate (54)** (MartynWane) **7-9-7** JFortune(3) (lw: outpcd fr ½-wy) | s.h | **11** | 9/2 [2] | 44 | 26 |
| 1363[16] | **Ballykissangel (36)** (NBycroft) **3-7-7**(3) DarrenMoffatt(1) (in tch 4f: wknd) | 2½ | **12** | 66/1 | 19 | — |
| 2005[19] | **Diet (55)** (MissLAPerratt) **10-9-1v**(7) AngelaGallimore(10) (prom 4f) | 1¼ | **13** | 25/1 | 35 | 17 |
| 1715[6] | **Efficacy (41)** (APJarvis) **5-8-1**(7) CCarver(14) (b: chsd ldrs tl rdn & btn 2f out) | 2½ | **14** | 20/1 | 14 | — |

(SP 132.8%) **14 Rn**

**1m 13.3** (3.50) CSF £529.24 CT £9,538.73 TOTE £79.70: £16.00 £5.40 £8.00 (£443.00) Trio Not won; £456.69 to 4.45 Nottingham 24/6/96
OWNER Mr J. D. Blythe (SEDGEFIELD) BRED Shadwell Estate Company Limited
WEIGHT FOR AGE 3yo-7lb

**1885 Thwaab** had the visor on for the first time and the transformation was amazing. It will be interesting to see whether it works again. (33/1)
**1865 Sunday Mail Too (IRE)**, back to something like her best trip, ran much better but was short of toe in the final furlong. (20/1)
**2029 Ned's Bonanza** travelled well but just failed to quicken when ridden in the final furlong. He seems to be coming to hand. (6/1)
**1364 Foist** looked to be going well but then failed to stride out fully on this fast ground, when asked a serious question in the last two furlongs. (9/4)
**1313 Seconds Away** showed up behind the leaders, but was always struggling with the pace and failed to made any serious impression from halfway. (20/1)
**2119 Leading Princess (IRE)**, having her second run in consecutive days, found it all too much in the final furlong and a half. (13/2: 4/1-7/1)
**1889 Pallium (IRE)** never got into this but left the impression that he is getting it together gradually. (14/1)

T/Plpt: £2,010.10 (4.55 Tckts). T/Qdpt: £484.80 (0.58 Tckts); £275.16 to 24/6/96 AA

# 1992-**LINGFIELD** (L-H) (Turf Firm, AWT Standard)
## Saturday June 22nd

1st & 5th races were handtimed
WEATHER: overcast WIND: nil

## 2155 TAIWAN AMATEUR H'CAP (0-70) (3-Y.O+) (Class F)
6-15 (6-16) **1m 3f 106y** £3,047.40 (£846.40: £406.20) Stalls: High GOING minus 0.73 sec per fur (HD)

| | | | | SP | RR | SF |
|---|---|---|---|---|---|---|
| 1852[4] | **Lalindi (IRE) (66)** (DRCElsworth) **5-11-7b** PHenley(11) (lw: a.p: led 5f out: qcknd clr 3f out: rdn & r.o wl fnl f) | — | **1** | 11/2 | 79 | 68 |
| *2086[2]* | **Old School House (49)** (TJNaughton) **3-9-0**(5)ow3 MrsJNaughton(2) (hdwy 7f out: chsd wnr 2f out: r.o one pce fnl f) | 3½ | **2** | 9/2 [3] | 57 | 30 |
| 1953[12] | **Prince de Berry (45)** (BJMeehan) **5-10-0** MissJAllison(10) (hld up & bhd: hdwy 7f out: r.o one pce fnl 2f) | 10 | **3** | 33/1 | 39 | 28 |
| 1655[5] | **Hamilton Silk (48)** (MCPipe) **4-10-3** MrsLPearce(8) (hld up & plld hrd: hdwy 6f out: wknd over 1f out) | 1¼ | **4** | 4/1 [2] | 40 | 29 |
| 1902[5] | **Set the Fashion (55)** (DLWilliams) **7-10-5**(5) MissSHiggins(1) (prom: led 7f out to 5f out: wknd over 1f out) | ½ | **5** | 12/1 | 47 | 36 |
| 1674[10] | **Canary Falcon (52)** (HJCollingridge) **5-10-2**(5) MrPClose(12) (b: lw: no hdwy fnl 4f) | hd | **6** | 25/1 | 44 | 33 |
| 1874[4] | **Bronze Maquette (IRE) (40)** (THind) **6-9-9**ow3 MrTMcCarthy(14) (nvr nr ldrs) | 7 | **7** | 8/1 | 22 | 8 |
| 1439[7] | **Courbaril (58)** (SDow) **4-10-8**(5) MrSFetherstonhaugh(5) (lw: s.i.s: plld hrd: a bhd) | 1¼ | **8** | 15/2 | 38 | 27 |
| 1534[9] | **Kenyatta (USA) (31)** (AMoore) **7-8-9**(5) MrsJMoore(6) (prom tl wknd 3f out) | 2 | **9** | 50/1 | 8 | — |
| 1826[6] | **Quest Again (63)** (DWPArbuthnot) **5-11-4** MrsDArbuthnot(7) (prom 6f) | 3 | **10** | 100/30 [1] | 36 | 25 |
| 1778[10] | **Air Command (BAR) (42)** (CTNash) **6-9-6**(5)ow6 MrPPhillips(9) (a bhd) | 4 | **11** | 25/1 | 10 | — |
| | **Written Agreement (40)** (REPeacock) **8-9-4**(5)ow9 MrsCPeacock(4) (a bhd) | 3½ | **12** | 50/1 | 3 | — |
| 1803[19] | **Mega Tid (34)** (BAPearce) **4-8-12**(5) MrsSColville(13) (b: a bhd) | ¾ | **13** | 20/1 | — | — |
| 1953[10] | **Legal Drama (USA) (52)** (JohnBerry) **4-10-2**(5)ow7 MrVCoogan(3) (led over 4f: wknd qckly) | 5 | **14** | 33/1 | 7 | — |

(SP 129.5%) **14 Rn**

**2m 24.9** (0.70) CSF £30.86 CT £714.04 TOTE £6.80: £2.10 £1.70 £14.80 (£8.90) Trio Not won; £300.43 to 4.45 Nottingham 24/6/96 OWNER White Horse Racing Ltd (WHITCOMBE) BRED Hascombe and Valiant Studs
LONG HANDICAP Kenyatta (USA) 8-6 Written Agreement 7-12
WEIGHT FOR AGE 3yo-13lb

**1852 Lalindi (IRE)**, with no doubts about stamina, was enterprisingly ridden and she slipped her field once in line for home. (11/2)
**2086 Old School House**, making a quick reappearance, is now 6lb lower on the turf than on the sand. (9/2: op 3/1)
**Prince de Berry** ran better over this longer trip than at Goodwood last week but could only plod on for the minor place. (33/1)
**1655 Hamilton Silk**, too keen for his own good, seems better over hurdles than on the Flat. (4/1)
**1902 Set the Fashion** will need a more patient ride to last this trip. (12/1)
**Canary Falcon** is probably better at shorter distances. (25/1)
**1826 Quest Again** may have found this coming a bit soon after his reappearance. (100/30)

## 2156 SINGAPORE H'CAP (0-70) (3-Y.O+) (Class E)
6-45 (6-48) **5f** £3,152.10 (£940.80: £449.40: £203.70) Stalls: High GOING minus 0.73 sec per fur (HD)

| | | | | SP | RR | SF |
|---|---|---|---|---|---|---|
| 1889[3] | **Bowcliffe Grange (IRE) (38)** (DWChapman) **4-7-5b**1(5) CAdamson(2) (mde all: sn clr: r.o wl) | — | **1** | 5/1 [2] | 45 | 10 |
| 1844[5] | **Clan Chief (58)** (JRArnold) **3-8-10** CRutter(6) (b.hind: swtg: prom centre: r.o wl ins fnl f) | 1¾ | **2** | 7/1 [3] | 59 | 18 |
| 1681[3] | **Superlao (BEL) (41)** (JJBridger) **4-7-6**(7) RBrisland(14) (b.nr hind: hdwy over 1f out: r.o ins fnl f) | s.h | **3** | 20/1 | 42 | 7 |
| 1985* | **Beau Venture (USA) (72)** (BPalling) **8-10-2** TSprake(13) (a.p stands' side: r.o ins fnl f) | nk | **4** | 7/2 [1] | 72 | 37 |
| 1777[9] | **Judgement Call (51)** (PHowling) **9-8-9** MRoberts(5) (b: hld up: hdwy over 1f out: fin wl) | s.h | **5** | 11/1 | 51 | 16 |
| *1971[7]* | **Tommy Tempest (43)** (REPeacock) **7-7-10**(5)ow5 ADaly(11) (hld up stands' side: hdwy & n.m.r fnl f: r.o wl) | s.h | **6** | 40/1 | 43 | 3 |
| *900[4]* | **Tee-Emm (38)** (THind) **6-7-10** JQuinn(10) (b: prom stands' side: one pce fnl f) | hd | **7** | 9/1 | 38 | 3 |
| 1958[9] | **Classic Pet (IRE) (43)** (CAHorgan) **4-8-1** NAdams(7) (hdwy 2f out: one pce fnl f) | 1¼ | **8** | 12/1 | 39 | 4 |
| 1761[2] | **Kiwud (44)** (TWDonnelly) **3-7-10b** DeclanO'Shea(1) (chsd wnr tl one pce ins fnl f) | s.h | **9** | 12/1 | 40 | — |
| *1716[10]* | **Halliard (62)** (TMJones) **5-9-6** RPerham(9) (swtg: prom stands' side: rdn over 2f out: no hdwy) | hd | **10** | 7/1 [3] | 57 | 22 |
| 1512[9] | **Squire Corrie (63)** (GHarwood) **4-9-0v**(7) GayeHarwood(3) (prom centre: wknd over 1f out) | 2 | **11** | 20/1 | 52 | 17 |
| | **Tachycardia (48)** (RJO'Sullivan) **4-8-6** SSanders(8) (bit bkwd: bhd fnl 2f) | 3½ | **12** | 20/1 | 26 | — |

| Last | Horse / details | Dist | Pos | SP | RR | SF |
|---|---|---|---|---|---|---|
| 1663[6] | **Double Or Bust (44)** (AGNewcombe) **3-7-3**(7) IonaWands(4) (swtg: prom over 2f) | hd | **13** | 20/1 | 21 | — |
| 1844[6] | **Miami Banker (50)** (WRMuir) **10-8-8b** GBardwell(12) (s.i.s: a bhd) | 2 | **14** | 8/1 | 21 | — |
| | | | | (SP 130.2%) | **14 Rn** | |

**57.48 secs** (0.48) CSF £40.38 CT £633.44 TOTE £5.30: £2.10 £3.10 £8.50 (£42.50) Trio Not won; £404.44 to 4.45 Nottingham 24/6/96
OWNER Mr David Chapman (YORK) BRED Rosemount House Stud
LONG HANDICAP Tommy Tempest 7-2 Bowcliffe Grange (IRE) 7-6 Kiwud 7-9 Double Or Bust 7-5 Tee-Emm 7-9
WEIGHT FOR AGE 3yo-6lb

**1889 Bowcliffe Grange (IRE)**, including his rider's allowance, was effectively running off a mark a stone higher than when successful at Beverley. Blazing a trail up the centre in the first time blinkers, he never really appeared likely to be caught. (5/1)
**1844 Clan Chief** again showed he is in good heart but the winner was not for the catching. (7/1)
**1681 Superlao (BEL)** had run over six the time before last and might be more effective at that trip. (20/1)
**1985* Beau Venture (USA)**, raised 8lb, just about led those on the stands side but all the pace was up the centre. (7/2)
**1446 Judgement Call**, 3lb higher than when winning over course and distance in May, did all his best work in the closing stages. (11/1: 7/1-12/1)
**Tommy Tempest**, carrying 8lb more than his long-handicap mark, showed signs of a return to form. (40/1)
**1761 Kiwud** ran better than her finishing position suggests. (12/1: 8/1-14/1)

## 2157 TATTERSALLS MAIDEN AUCTION STKS (2-Y.O) (Class E)
7-15 (7-19) **5f** £3,318.75 (£990.00: £472.50: £213.75) Stalls: High GOING minus 0.73 sec per fur (HD)

| Last | Horse / details | Dist | Pos | SP | RR | SF |
|---|---|---|---|---|---|---|
| 1982[3] | **Victory Dancer** (BJMeehan) **2-8-6** BDoyle(3) (s.i.s: sn prom: led 3f out: clr over 1f out: rdn out) | — | **1** | 2/1[1] | 74 | 21 |
| | **Pat Said No (IRE)** (DJSCosgrove) **2-8-5** MRoberts(4) (neat: s.i.s: hdwy over 1f out: r.o ins fnl f) | 4 | **2** | 2/1[1] | 60 | 7 |
| 1851[3] | **Will To Win** (PGMurphy) **2-7-13** JQuinn(1) (led 2f: one pce fnl 2f) | hd | **3** | 2/1[1] | 54 | 1 |
| 1622[7] | **Le Shuttle** (MHTompkins) **2-8-1**ow1 PRobinson(2) (prom tl rdn & wknd over 1f out) | 3½ | **4** | 8/1[2] | 45 | — |
| | ***Hever Golf Charger (IRE)*** (TJNaughton) **2-8-9** DHarrison(5) (Withdrawn not under Starter's orders: ref to ent stalls) | | **W** | 12/1[3] | — | — |
| | | | | (SP 118.8%) | **4 Rn** | |

**57.33 secs** (0.33) CSF £5.89 TOTE £3.20: £2.30 (£4.30) OWNER Mr Alan Cunliffe (UPPER LAMBOURN) BRED D. J. Simpson
**1982 Victory Dancer** had obviously learnt a lot from his debut at Bath last week. (2/1)
**Pat Said No (IRE)**, a half-sister to El Conquistador, is out of a half-sister to Irish St Leger winner Mountain Lodge, so she is bred to need further. (2/1: op 3/1)
**1851 Will To Win** was reverting to the minimum trip. (2/1: 11/10-9/4)
**Le Shuttle** is out of a sister to Paris House. (8/1: 5/1-10/1)
**Hever Golf Charger (IRE)** (12/1: op 5/1)

## 2158 BEIJING MAIDEN H'CAP (0-65) (3-Y.O+) (Class F)
7-45 (7-47) **1m (Equitrack)** £3,047.40 (£846.40: £406.20) Stalls: High GOING minus 0.60 sec per fur (FST)

| Last | Horse / details | Dist | Pos | SP | RR | SF |
|---|---|---|---|---|---|---|
| 2032[13] | **Superior Force (59)** (MissBSanders) **3-9-4** SSanders(3) (a.p: led ins fnl f: drvn out) | — | **1** | 8/1 | 69 | 29 |
| 1530[15] | **Hot Dogging (42)** (MrsPSly) **3-8-1** DBiggs(1) (led tl ins fnl f) | 1¾ | **2** | 25/1 | 49 | 9 |
| *1719*[6] | **Nivasha (37)** (PMooney) **4-8-6** RPerham(10) (swtg: wl bhd tl gd hdwy fnl f: fin wl) | 1¾ | **3** | 20/1 | 40 | 10 |
| 1535[2] | **Bright Eclipse (USA) (55)** (JWHills) **3-8-11**(3) MHenry(11) (lw: hdwy over 2f out: edgd lft wl over 1f out: r.o one pce) | hd | **4** | 9/2[2] | 58 | 18 |
| *1721*[7] | **Awafeh (48)** (SMellor) **3-8-7** NAdams(9) (prom: btn whn hmpd wl over 1f out) | 3 | **5** | 12/1 | 45 | 5 |
| 949[5] | **Rawi (61)** (MissGayKelleway) **3-9-6** BDoyle(2) (no hdwy fnl 2f) | 1¾ | **6** | 11/2[3] | 54 | 14 |
| 1350[7] | **Voodoo Rocket (65)** (JHMGosden) **3-9-10** GHind(4) (b.hind: s.i.s: sn rcvrd: rdn over 3f out: wknd over 1f out) | 1 | **7** | 11/8[1] | 56 | 16 |
| 1797[10] | **Shavinsky (60)** (PHowling) **3-9-5** MRoberts(8) (swtg: led 1f: wknd over 1f out) | 1¼ | **8** | 11/1 | 49 | 9 |
| 1527[19] | **Prime Partner (48)** (WRMuir) **3-8-7** DHarrison(12) (a bhd) | 1¼ | **9** | 12/1 | 34 | — |
| 1995[5] | **Night of Glass (38)** (DMorris) **3-7-11** GBardwell(6) (lw: prom tl wknd over 2f out) | 1¾ | **10** | 12/1 | 21 | — |
| *1721*[5] | **Realms of Glory (IRE) (52)** (PhilipMitchell) **3-8-11** JQuinn(5) (lw: rdn 5f out: sn bhd) | ¾ | **11** | 12/1 | 33 | — |
| 1522[5] | **I Recall (IRE) (54)** (PHayward) **5-9-9v** TSprake(7) (lw: prom tl rdn & wknd over 3f out) | ¾ | **12** | 11/1 | 34 | 4 |
| | | | | (SP 142.8%) | **12 Rn** | |

**1m 39.71** (2.31) CSF £182.53 CT £3633.81 TOTE £16.60: £3.40 £4.80 £8.20 (£216.60) Trio Not won; £239.93 to 24/6/96 OWNER Copyforce Ltd (EPSOM) BRED Ahmed M. Foustok
WEIGHT FOR AGE 3yo-10lb
**1654 Superior Force**, unlucky in his last two starts, handled the Equitrack well enough. (8/1)
**1035 Hot Dogging** showed improved form on the sand and ran a sound race from the front. (25/1)
**1719 Nivasha** was really motoring at the death but set herself an impossible task. (20/1)
**1535 Bright Eclipse (USA)** again showed a tendency to go left-handed. (9/2)
**1490 Awafeh** was going nowhere when the fourth leant on her in the home straight. (12/1: op 8/1)
**949 Rawi** (11/2: 7/2-6/1)
**Voodoo Rocket**, trying the artificial surface, was never travelling particularly well after a sluggish start. (11/8)
**1627 Shavinsky** (11/1: 7/1-12/1)
**Prime Partner** (12/1: op 8/1)
**Night of Glass** (12/1: op 7/1)
**1721 Realms of Glory (IRE)** (12/1: 8/1-16/1)

## 2159 CHATS MARRIAGE H'CAP (0-60) (3-Y.O+) (Class F)
8-15 (8-19) **1m 1f** £3,333.00 (£928.00: £447.00) Stalls: Low GOING minus 0.73 sec per fur (HD)

| Last | Horse / details | Dist | Pos | SP | RR | SF |
|---|---|---|---|---|---|---|
| 1638[9] | **Sporting Risk (42)** (PWHarris) **4-9-0** GHind(4) (mde all: clr 2f out: r.o wl) | — | **1** | 16/1 | 52 | 11 |
| 1696[7] | **Conic Hill (IRE) (49)** (JPearce) **5-9-7** GBardwell(5) (rdn & hdwy 3f out: r.o ins fnl f) | 2½ | **2** | 11/2[2] | 55 | 14 |
| 1996* | **Allstars Express (62)** (TJNaughton) **3-9-9** DHarrison(6) (lw: plld hrd: a.p: r.o one pce fnl 2f) | hd | **3** | 2/1[1] | 67 | 15 |
| 1655[15] | **Flame of Hope (57)** (JLDunlop) **3-9-4** TSprake(1) (hld up: hdwy over 2f out: r.o one pce fnl f) | hd | **4** | 10/1 | 62 | 10 |
| 1803[17] | **Benjamins Law (48)** (JAPickering) **5-9-6** JQuinn(12) (hld up: hdwy on ins 3f out: n.m.r over 2f out: nt rch ldrs) | ¾ | **5** | 10/1 | 52 | 11 |
| 1515[11] | **Double Rush (IRE) (42)** (TGMills) **4-9-0** MarkLynch(9) (prom: rdn & no hdwy fnl 3f) | nk | **6** | 14/1 | 45 | 4 |
| 1533[6] | **Labudd (USA) (45)** (RIngram) **6-9-3** NAdams(11) (b: lw: nvr nr to chal) | 2½ | **7** | 9/1 | 44 | 3 |

**Sir Oliver (IRE) (30)** (BAPearce) **7-8-2** LeesaLong(3) (hld up & plld hrd: sme hdwy over 2f out: wknd over 1f out) ....5 **8** 25/1 20 —
1497$^{4}$ **May King Mayhem (52)** (MrsALMKing) **3-8-13** AGarth(8) (a bhd) ....10 **9** 7/1$^{3}$ 24 —
650$^{8}$ **Ketabi (USA) (52)** (RAkehurst) **5-9-10b** SSanders(7) (w wnr tl wknd over 2f out) ....¾ **10** 8/1 23 —
1302$^{18}$ **Sobeloved (40)** (NEBerry) **4-8-7**$^{(5)}$ CAdamson(2) (prom tl wknd over 2f out) ....1½ **11** 25/1 8 —
1711$^{14}$ **Shoemaker Levy (39)** (RJO'Sullivan) **3-8-0** DBiggs(14) (s.s: a bhd) ....¾ **12** 25/1 6 —
**Tout de Val (27)** (KBishop) **7-7-10**$^{(3)}$ MHenry(10) (prom: rn wd bnd after 2f: sn rcvd: rn wd bnd over 3f out: wknd over 2f out) ....nk **13** 25/1 — —
1826$^{13}$ **Good so Fa (IRE) (27)** (CNAllen) **4-7-13v** CRutter(13) (rel to race: a bhd) ....2½ **14** 25/1 — —
(SP 132.3%) **14 Rn**

**1m 53.7** (3.20) CSF £99.20 CT £234.18 TOTE £18.60: £4.60 £2.40 £1.60 (£74.50) Trio £61.00 OWNER Mrs P. W. Harris (BERKHAMSTED) BRED Roldvale Ltd
WEIGHT FOR AGE 3yo-11lb

**1085 Sporting Risk** broke his duck at his seventeenth attempt off a mark 4lb lower than when he last ran in a handicap on the turf. (16/1)
**1414 Conic Hill (IRE)** had slipped to a rating 24lb lower than when winning at Beverley nearly two years ago. (11/2)
**1996* Allstars Express** was 7lb higher than when winning here over an extra furlong a week ago. (2/1)
**Flame of Hope**, coming back in distance, had dropped 5lb since making her handicap debut two outings ago. (10/1: 6/1-11/1)
**1685 Benjamins Law** would probably have finished a bit closer with an uninterrupted run. (10/1)
**Double Rush (IRE)** has come down 8lb in the handicap this season. (14/1: 12/1-20/1)
**Ketabi (USA)** (8/1: op 5/1)

## 2160 HONG KONG LIMITED STKS (0-80) (3-Y.O) (Class D)

8-45 (8-45) **7f** £3,975.00 (£1,100.00: £525.00) Stalls: High GOING minus 0.73 sec per fur (HD)

SP RR SF

1505* **Poetry (IRE) (79)** (MHTompkins) **3-9-0** PRobinson(3) (mde virtually all: rdn 1f out: r.o wl) ....— **1** Evens$^{1}$ 88 36
1843$^{5}$ **Arterxerxes (80)** (MJHeaton-Ellis) **3-8-11** MRoberts(2) (w wnr: rdn over 1f out: unable qckn) ....2 **2** 13/8$^{2}$ 80 28
1464$^{4}$ **Xenophon of Cunaxa (IRE) (80)** (MJFetherston-Godley) **3-9-0** DHarrison(1) (hdwy 3f out: rdn over 2f out: r.o one pce) ....s.h **3** 4/1$^{3}$ 83 31
(SP 108.1%) **3 Rn**

**1m 21.58** (-0.02) CSF £2.76 TOTE £2.00: (£1.70) OWNER Mr Michael Keogh (NEWMARKET) BRED St Simon Foundation

**1505* Poetry (IRE)** completed a hat-trick of front-running victories. (Evens)
**1843 Arterxerxes** was dropping back from an extended mile last time. (13/8)
**1464 Xenophon of Cunaxa (IRE)** could not find an extra gear. (4/1: op 2/1)

T/Plpt: £836.90 (11.73 Tckts). T/Qdpt: £192.50 (2.69 Tckts) KH

# 2136-REDCAR (L-H) (Firm, Good to firm patches)

## Saturday June 22nd

WEATHER: fine WIND: slt half against

## 2161 LIVERTON (S) STKS (2-Y.O) (Class G)

1-50 (1-54) **7f** £2,495.00 (£695.00: £335.00) Stalls: Centre GOING minus 0.64 sec per fur (F)

SP RR SF

1678$^{4}$ **Stride** (DMorley) **2-8-6** KFallon(3) (trckd ldrs: led over 2f out: clr 1f out: eased towards fin) ....— **1** Evens$^{1}$ 65+ —
1849$^{8}$ **Woodetto (IRE)** (EWeymes) **2-8-11** PBloomfield(8) (hdwy over 2f out: styd on appr fnl f: no ch w wnr) ....2 **2** 6/1$^{3}$ 65 —
1360$^{6}$ **Clonavon Girl (IRE)** (MJCamacho) **2-8-6** LCharnock(10) (hdwy over 2f out: styd on same pce) ....1¾ **3** 25/1 56 —
975$^{8}$ **Emily-Jayne** (MrsMReveley) **2-8-6** GCarter(11) (in tch: styd on fnl 2f: nvr nr to chal) ....hd **4** 12/1 56 —
1871$^{8}$ **Grovefair Lad (IRE)** (BJMeehan) **2-8-8**$^{(3)}$ DWright(2) (a.p: effrt over 2f out: wandered & wknd over 1f out) ....4 **5** 4/1$^{2}$ 52 —
1645$^{5}$ **Rahona (IRE)** (BSRothwell) **2-8-4v**$^{1(7)ow5}$ GFaulkner(7) (sn chsng ldrs: ev ch over 2f out: sn wknd) ....2½ **6** 14/1 46 —
1845$^{5}$ **Maremma** (DonEnricoIncisa) **2-8-6** KimTinkler(5) (s.s: sn in tch: rdn & hung lft 3f out: n.d) ....1¾ **7** 25/1 37 —
1543$^{5}$ **Apiculate (IRE)** (WTKemp) **2-8-4**$^{(7)}$ JBramhill(5) (led tl over 2f out: edgd lft & sn wknd) ....1 **8** 25/1 40 —
1845$^{4}$ **Samspet** (RAFahey) **2-8-11** ACulhane(6) (w ldrs tl wknd over 2f out) ....2 **9** 13/2 36 —
2043$^{4}$ **Sparky** (MWEasterby) **2-8-11** DaleGibson(12) (swvd rt s: a outpcd & wl bhd) ....1¾ **10** 12/1 32 —
1858$^{9}$ **Madam Lucy** (WWHaigh) **2-8-6** JTate(14) (s.s: a wl bhd) ....3 **11** 25/1 20 —
*1813*$^{2}$ **Shandana** (PCHaslam) **2-8-1**$^{(5)}$ MBaird(1) (chsd ldrs: edgd lft & wknd over 2f out) ....hd **12** 9/1 19 —
(SP 145.1%) **12 Rn**

**1m 26.8** (3.80) CSF £9.94 TOTE £2.00: £1.40 £1.80 £10.60 (£5.20) Trio Not won; £200.20 to 4.45 Nottingham 24/6/96 OWNER Lord Hartington (NEWMARKET) BRED Side Hill Stud
Sold DWalker 9,400gns

**1678 Stride**, taking a big drop in class, showed a fair bit of knee action going down. She proved different class to her rivals and won easing up, attracting a fair amount of interest at the auction. (Evens)
**Woodetto (IRE)**, who ran in better company on his debut, still carried a fair bit of condition. Sticking on strongly, he should surely find a similar event. (6/1: 4/1-7/1)
**1360 Clonavon Girl (IRE)**, a narrow type, showed a knee action going to post. In a seller for the first time, she was staying on when it was all over. (25/1)
**Emily-Jayne** looked in need of the outing and was putting in some good late work at the line. She will be suited by a stiffer track. (12/1)
**Grovefair Lad (IRE)** wandered badly under pressure. (4/1)
**1645 Rahona (IRE)** (14/1: op 8/1)

## 2162 TEES COMPONENTS MAIDEN LADIES' H'CAP (0-70) (3-Y.O+) (Class F)

2-20 (2-21) **1m** £2,792.50 (£780.00: £377.50) Stalls: Centre GOING minus 0.64 sec per fur (F)

SP RR SF

1803$^{18}$ **Squared Away (47)** (JWPayne) **4-9-7b**$^{1(7)}$ MissCLake(11) (sn bhd: swtchd rt over 2f out: rapid hdwy appr fnl f: fin fast to ld nr fin) ....— **1** 25/1 55 18
1888$^{6}$ **Mels Baby (IRE) (56)** (JLEyre) **3-9-13** MissDianaJones(13) (a in tch: hdwy over 2f out: led wl ins fnl f: jst ct) ....½ **2** 4/1$^{3}$ 63 16
2026$^{2}$ **How Could-I (IRE) (46)** (TDEasterby) **3-8-13b**$^{1(4)ow3}$ MissADeniel(10) (led: clr ½-wy: edgd lft: hdd wl ins fnl f) ....1 **3** 9/1 51 1

| Horse | Dist | Pos | SP | RR | SF |
|---|---|---|---|---|---|
| 1674[9] **Haido'hart (48)** (BSRothwell) **4-10-1** MrsAFarrell(12) (sn outpcd: styd on wl fnl 2f: nt rch ldrs) | 2 | **4** | 9/1 | 49 | 12 |
| 1615[11] **Commin' Up (67)** (JWHills) **3-10-10** MissEJohnsonHoughton(7) (chsd ldrs: ev ch over 1f out: one pce) | ½ | **5** | 6/1 | 67 | 20 |
| 1962[5] **Sycamore Lodge (IRE) (68)** (MrsJRRamsden) **5-11-3**(4) MissERamsden(15) (hld up: sddle slipped: effrt & edgd lft 2f out: nvr nr ldrs) | 5 | **6** | 100/30[2] | 58 | 21 |
| 2019[4] **Gilling Dancer (IRE) (57)** (PCalver) **3-10-0** MrsFNeedham(4) (prom: rdn & outpcd over 2f out: kpt on) | hd | **7** | 12/1 | 47 | — |
| 1778[15] **Battery Boy (33)** (CWCElsey) **4-9-0b** MissAElsey(3) (in tch: rdn & outpcd ½-wy: n.d) | s.h | **8** | 20/1 | 23 | — |
| 1806[2] **Home Cookin' (57)** (MCPipe) **3-10-0** MrsLPearce(5) (chsd ldrs: rdn & edgd lft ½-wy: lost pl over 2f out) | hd | **9** | 3/1[1] | 47 | — |
| 2075[16] **Intrepid Fort (33)** (BWMurray) **7-8-7b**(7) MrsCWilliams(6) (bmpd s: sn outpcd & drvn along) | 1¼ | **10** | 25/1 | 20 | — |
| **Shaa Spin (60)** (JBerry) **4-10-9**(4) MissVMarshall(2) (bhd fr ½-wy) | 1 | **11** | 25/1 | 45 | 8 |
| 1596[7] **Bowland Park (36)** (EJAlston) **5-9-3** MissPRobson(14) (rdn & outpcd fr ½-wy) | 7 | **12** | 33/1 | 7 | — |
| 594[8] **Fergal (USA) (50)** (TKersey) **3-9-0**(7)ow7 MissLGeorge(1) (b: sn bhd: hrd rdn & hung rt fr ½ wy) | 6 | **13** | 50/1 | 9 | — |
| 1450[13] **Sun Circus (45)** (JLSpearing) **4-9-8**(4) MissTSpearing(8) (sn bhd & drvn along) | 2 | **14** | 14/1 | — | — |

(SP 137.9%) **14 Rn**

**1m 39.7** (4.00) CSF £129.57 CT £946.04 TOTE £103.40: £15.30 £1.60 £3.20 (£188.10) Trio £111.20 OWNER Mrs E. Lake (NEWMARKET) BRED Mrs W. A. and Miss C. J. Lake

LONG HANDICAP Intrepid Fort 8-11 How Could-I (IRE) 8-11 Fergal (USA) 8-11 Battery Boy 8-9

WEIGHT FOR AGE 3yo-10lb

STEWARDS' ENQUIRY George susp. 1-6/7/96 (incorrect use of the whip).

**Squared Away**, dropped back half a mile in trip and fitted with blinkers for the first time, made up at least ten lengths and passed half a dozen horses in the final furlong. Finishing like the proverbial train, he gave his partner her first ever Flat success. (25/1)

**1888 Mels Baby (IRE)** stepped up in distance and was driven to the front in the final 75 yards, only to have the prize whipped from under his nose on the line. (4/1)

**2026 How Could-I (IRE)**, 3lb out of the handicap and fitted with blinkers for the first time, had them all in trouble at halfway but, edging left under pressure, was run out of it in the final stages. (9/1)

**1674 Haido'hart** stayed on in good style in the closing stages and should be suited by another step up in distance. (9/1)

**1181 Commin' Up** put a disappointing effort last time well behind. (6/1)

**1962 Sycamore Lodge (IRE)**, carrying three stone of dead weight, lost his chance when his saddle slipped leaving the stalls. (100/30)

**1806 Home Cookin'**, having her first outing for Martin Pipe, was in trouble at halfway. (3/1)

## 2163 WEATHERBYS BANKING SERVICE H'CAP (0-70) (3-Y.O) (Class E)

2-50 (2-51) **1m 1f** £3,886.00 (£1,168.00: £564.00: £262.00) Stalls: Low GOING: minus 0.64 sec per fur (F)

| Horse | Dist | Pos | SP | RR | SF |
|---|---|---|---|---|---|
| 1668[6] **Elashath (USA) (53)** (JHMGosden) **3-9-2** GHind(8) (lw: chsd ldr: led 3f out: drvn out) | — | **1** | 7/2[2] | 67 | 17 |
| 1477[7] **Gulf of Siam (56)** (MissSEHall) **3-9-5** MTebbutt(5) (trckd ldrs: effrt & hung lft over 2f out: nt qckn fnl f) | 1¾ | **2** | 7/1 | 67 | 17 |
| 1850* **Ordained (54)** (EJAlston) **3-9-3** GDuffield(1) (a in tch: styd on same pce fnl 2f) | 5 | **3** | 7/2[2] | 56 | 6 |
| 1846[4] **Percy Park (USA) (42)** (MWEasterby) **3-8-5b** DaleGibson(2) (trckd ldrs: rdn over 2f out: wknd over 1f out) | 2½ | **4** | 9/1 | 40 | — |
| 1089[7] **Dispol Conqueror (IRE) (38)** (GROldroyd) **3-7-12**(3) NVarley(4) (led to 3f out: wknd over 1f out) | 2 | **5** | 20/1 | 32 | — |
| 1539[2] **Sandblaster (56)** (MrsJRRamsden) **3-9-5** KFallon(9) (hld up: nvr nr ldrs) | 3½ | **6** | 9/4[1] | 44 | — |
| 1806* **Linda's Joy (IRE) (58)** (MCPipe) **3-9-7b** PBloomfield(3) (lw: s.s: bhd: effrt over 3f out: hung lft & sn wknd) | 1 | **7** | 6/1[3] | 44 | — |
| 1986[10] **Lagan (53)** (PSFelgate) **3-8-13**(3) DWright(6) (s.i.s: drvn along 4f out: n.d) | 2½ | **8** | 25/1 | 35 | — |
| 1527[12] **Harriet's Beau (39)** (MWEasterby) **3-8-2** LCharnock(7) (hld up: effrt over 3f out: n.d) | ¾ | **9** | 20/1 | 19 | — |

(SP 125.4%) **9 Rn**

**1m 53.3** (3.50) CSF £28.33 CT £87.85 TOTE £5.00: £1.90 £1.80 £1.50 (£15.70) Trio £26.60 OWNER Mr Hamdan Al Maktoum (NEWMARKET) BRED Poole Investments and Chris Smith

**1668 Elashath (USA)**, having his first run in a handicap, scored in decisive fashion and should go on from here. (7/2)

**1477 Gulf of Siam**, a keen going type, was dropped in distance. Showing a marked tendency to hang left under pressure, he was never doing anything enough to trouble the winner. (7/1)

**1850* Ordained**, over this trip, never looked finding the pace to get in a blow. (7/2)

**1846 Percy Park (USA)**, with the blinkers back on, proved very keen. (9/1)

**1539 Sandblaster**, held up to get the trip, was by no means knocked about. (9/4)

## 2164 VAUX GOLD TANKARD H'CAP (0-90) (3-Y.O+) (Class C)

3-25 (3-28) **1m 2f** £13,940.00 (£4,220.00: £2,060.00: £980.00) Stalls: Low GOING minus 0.64 sec per fur (F)

| Horse | Dist | Pos | SP | RR | SF |
|---|---|---|---|---|---|
| 1361[2] **Faateq (85)** (JLDunlop) **3-9-2** GCarter(4) (lw: unruly s: chsd ldrs: led 2f out: edgd lft ins fnl f: jst hld on) | — | **1** | 3/1[1] | 93 | 44 |
| 2010[9] **Hazard a Guess (IRE) (81)** (DNicholls) **6-9-10** AlexGreaves(8) (lw: hld up: effrt & swtchd over 2f out: hung lft over 1f out: r.o wl) | s.h | **2** | 15/2 | 89 | 52 |
| 1476[7] **Angus-G (70)** (MrsMReveley) **4-8-13** ACulhane(7) (s.i.s: drvn along over 5f out: hdwy over 3f out: sn hrd rdn: ev ch fnl f: nt qckn nr fin) | s.h | **3** | 4/1[3] | 78 | 41 |
| 2010[2] **Carlito Brigante (79)** (MrsJRRamsden) **4-9-8** KFallon(2) (hld up: effrt over 3f out: styng on same pce whn n.m.r wl ins fnl f) | 1¾ | **4** | 7/2[2] | 84 | 47 |
| 1799* **Bollin Frank (69)** (TDEasterby) **4-8-12** LCharnock(5) (lw: chsd ldr: led 3f out: hdd 2f out: wkng whn sltly hmpd ins fnl f) | 3 | **5** | 7/1 | 69 | 32 |
| 1862[4] **Cheerful Aspect (IRE) (80)** (EALDunlop) **3-8-11** WRyan(3) (mid div: drvn along & outpcd 4f out: kpt on fnl 2f) | hd | **6** | 8/1 | 80 | 31 |
| 1585* **Sarmatian (USA) (74)** (MDHammond) **5-8-10**(7) GFaulkner(6) (lw: chsd ldrs: rdn & outpcd fnl 2f) | nk | **7** | 12/1 | 74 | 37 |
| 1819* **Mbulwa (60)** (RAFahey) **10-8-3** GDuffield(1) (led to 3f out: wknd over 1f out) | ¾ | **8** | 12/1 | 58 | 21 |
| 1322[6] **Nigel's Lad (IRE) (79)** (PCHaslam) **4-9-3**(5) MBaird(9) (lw: hdwy on outside 6f out: sn chsng ldrs: rdn & wknd over 2f out) | nk | **9** | 12/1 | 77 | 40 |

(SP 125.7%) **9 Rn**

**2m 4.1** (0.50) CSF £26.02 CT £87.64 TOTE £3.30: £1.30 £2.60 £1.50 (£25.20) Trio £43.20 OWNER Mr Hamdan Al Maktoum (ARUNDEL) BRED Shadwell Estate Company Limited

WEIGHT FOR AGE 3yo-12lb

**1361 Faateq**, who gave plenty of trouble at the stalls, was dropped back two furlongs in distance. After a tremendous five cornered battle, he got there by a whisker. (3/1)

**2010 Hazard a Guess (IRE)**, suited by the fast run race, might have got there but for hanging left and hanging fire for a few strides coming to the final furlong. (15/2)

**1476 Angus-G**, flat to the boards on the home turn, had every chance in the end but should be suited by a step up in distance. He certainly has more ability than he has shown so far. (4/1)

**2010 Carlito Brigante**, raised 5lb after York, battled on under pressure but was only on the quarters of the first three before running out of room near the line. (7/2)
**1799* Bollin Frank**, raised 3lb, was weakening when hampered inside the last. Nine may be as far as he wants to go. (7/1)
**1862 Cheerful Aspect (IRE)**, flat to the boards and left behind turning in, was staying on when it was all over and should be better over a mile and a half. (8/1)
**1585* Sarmatian (USA)** (12/1: op 8/1)

## 2165 FROSTREE WINDOWS 15TH ANNIVERSARY H'CAP (0-60) (3-Y.O+) (Class F)

3-55 (3-57) **1m 6f 19y** £4,224.00 (£1,272.00: £616.00: £288.00) Stalls: Low GOING minus 0.64 sec per fur (F)

| | | | | SP | RR | SF |
|---|---|---|---|---|---|---|
| 2066² | **Bold Elect (42)** (EJAlston) **8-8-10** KFallon(1) (lw: hld up: hdwy over 3f out: hrd rdn & styd on fnl f: led post) | — | **1** | 3/1 ¹ | 56 | 36 |
| 1529⁹ | **Uncle Doug (52)** (MrsMReveley) **5-9-6** ACulhane(6) (hld up: hdwy over 4f out: led over 1f out: jst ct) | s.h | **2** | 11/2 ³ | 66 | 46 |
| *219⁹* | **Tragic Hero (58)** (MCPipe) **4-9-12b** GCarter(14) (sn drvn along: hdwy 3f out: ev ch fnl f: r.o) | ½ | **3** | 4/1 ² | 71 | 51 |
| 1783⁷ | **Forgie (IRE) (58)** (PCalver) **3-8-6**(3) NVarley(2) (w ldr: led over 2f out tl over 1f out: styd on one pce ins fnl f) | ¾ | **4** | 12/1 | 71 | 34 |
| 1542² | **Hullbank (55)** (WWHaigh) **6-9-9** JTate(4) (b: bhd: styd on fnl 2f: nvr rchd ldrs) | 2½ | **5** | 8/1 | 65 | 45 |
| 1826⁵ | **Iota (51)** (JLHarris) **7-9-5** GDuffield(15) (mid div: hdwy over 4f out: hung lft & wknd 2f out) | 3 | **6** | 12/1 | 57 | 37 |
| 1826² | **Salska (46)** (AStreeter) **5-8-11**(3) CTeague(11) (trckd ldrs: led 6f out tl over 2f out: sn wknd) | nk | **7** | 13/2 | 52 | 32 |
| 1803⁷ | **Anchorena (57)** (MrsASwinbank) **4-9-11** WRyan(3) (hld up & bhd: sme hdwy on outside over 2f out: nvr nr ldrs) | 3½ | **8** | 12/1 | 59 | 39 |
| 1478² | **Sharp Sensation (38)** (WLBarker) **6-7-13**(7) JBramhill(5) (bhd: sme hdwy 3f out: n.d) | s.h | **9** | 9/1 | 40 | 20 |
| 1676⁹ | **Diamond Crown (IRE) (44)** (MartynWane) **5-8-12** GHind(10) (a in rr) | 2½ | **10** | 12/1 | 43 | 23 |
| 1965⁷ | **Jean de Florette (USA) (33)** (RCSpicer) **5-8-1b** NKennedy(7) (trckd ldrs: effrt over 3f out: sn wknd) | 1 | **11** | 20/1 | 31 | 11 |
| 2060⁸ | **Paronomasia (30)** (JLHarris) **4-7-12** LCharnock(16) (a bhd) | 3 | **12** | 25/1 | 25 | 5 |
| 1665¹⁹ | **Hong Kong Designer (44)** (MissJFCraze) **4-8-12** MTebbutt(13) (a bhd) | nk | **13** | 33/1 | 38 | 18 |
| 1870⁵ | **Red Spectacle (IRE) (56)** (PCHaslam) **4-9-5**(5) MBaird(8) (chsd ldrs tl rdn & lost pl over 4f out) | 3 | **14** | 16/1 | 47 | 27 |
| *1717⁸* | **Kindred Greeting (33)** (JAHarris) **4-8-1b** JO'Reilly(12) (led to 6f out: sn lost pl: t.o) | 15 | **15** | 20/1 | 7 | — |
| | **Salutation (IRE) (30)** (TKersey) **5-7-12** DaleGibson(9) (b: sn wl bhd: t.o) | 12 | **16** | 50/1 | — | — |

(SP 149.8%) **16 Rn**

**3m 0.7** (1.40) CSF £23.76 CT £71.95 TOTE £3.90: £1.40 £1.80 £3.20 £3.10 (£11.50) Trio £32.40 OWNER Mr G. Lowe (PRESTON) BRED Home Stud Ltd
WEIGHT FOR AGE 3yo-17lb
**2066 Bold Elect** never flinched under his rider's use of the whip and got there in the last stride. (3/1: 5/1-5/2)
**1529 Uncle Doug** was pipped on the line. (11/2)
**Tragic Hero**, much improved over hurdles and a big race winner at Aintree and Haydock, never looked happy on the ground. Staying on to have every chance in the final furlong, he might appreciate more give underfoot. (4/1)
**1503* Forgie (IRE)** ran well but was edged out of it by the older horses in the closing stages. (12/1)
**1542 Hullbank** seems to be in the Handicapper's grip. (8/1)
**1826 Iota** (12/1: op 8/1)

## 2166 LEVY BOARD MAIDEN STKS (3-Y.O+) (Class D)

4-30 (4-30) **1m** £4,049.50 (£1,132.00: £548.50) Stalls: Centre GOING minus 0.64 sec per fur (F)

| | | | | SP | RR | SF |
|---|---|---|---|---|---|---|
| 1174² | **Kamari (USA) (86)** (ACStewart) **3-8-11** WRyan(3) (lw: mde all: clr ½-wy: canter) | — | **1** | 1/28 ¹ | 60++ | 11 |
| 1668¹¹ | **Mr Gold (IRE)** (RonaldThompson) **3-8-11** LCharnock(1) (chsd wnr: rdn ½-wy: sn lost tch) | 25 | **2** | 33/1 ² | 10 | — |
| | **Mirus** (RonaldThompson) **3-8-11** NKennedy(2) (unf: s.s: sn pushed along & wl bhd) | 7 | **3** | 33/1 ² | — | — |

(SP 102.4%) **3 Rn**

**1m 38.8** (3.10) CSF £1.73 TOTE £1.10: (£1.40) OWNER Mr Hamdan Al Maktoum (NEWMARKET) BRED Ballydoyle Stud
**1174 Kamari (USA)** had no more than an exercise gallop. (1/28)
**Mr Gold (IRE)**, a keen going type, was left for dead at halfway. (33/1)
**Mirus**, a narrow newcomer, was last throughout. This will probably be his biggest ever pay day. (33/1)

## 2167 UGTHORPE RATING RELATED MAIDEN STKS (0-70) (3-Y.O+) (Class E)

5-00 (5-00) **6f** £2,945.25 (£882.00: £423.50: £194.25) Stalls: Centre GOING minus 0.64 sec per fur (F)

| | | | | SP | RR | SF |
|---|---|---|---|---|---|---|
| 1608³ | **Indian Relative (69)** (RGuest) **3-8-6**(5) DGriffiths(4) (trckd ldrs: led over 2f out: drvn clr jst ins fnl f) | — | **1** | 6/4 ² | 74 | 30 |
| *1604⁵* | **River Tern (68)** (JBerry) **3-9-0** GCarter(2) (b: led tl over 2f out: edgd lft u.p: no ch w wnr) | 5 | **2** | 9/2 ³ | 64 | 20 |
| 1692² | **Delphine (70)** (MBell) **3-8-4**(7) GFaulkner(5) (chsd ldr: rdn & ev ch 2f out: one pce) | 2 | **3** | 11/8 ¹ | 55 | 11 |
| 1764² | **Backhander (IRE) (51)** (MartynWane) **4-9-0**(7) JEdmunds(3) (chsd ldrs: rdn & outpcd ½-wy: n.d after) | nk | **4** | 8/1 | 58 | 21 |

(SP 111.4%) **4 Rn**

**1m 11.0** (0.80) CSF £7.48 TOTE £2.20: (£7.10) OWNER Mr Vijay Mallya (NEWMARKET) BRED Barrettstown Stud Farms Ltd
WEIGHT FOR AGE 3yo-7lb
**1608 Indian Relative**, whose Catterick third is from a race that is working out really well, proved different geared than her three rivals. (6/4)
**River Tern** carried his head high and edged left as if feeling the firm ground. (9/2)
**1692 Delphine** showed a poor action going to post. (11/8)
**1764 Backhander (IRE)** was struggling to keep up at halfway. (8/1)

T/Plpt: £51.20 (197.3 Tckts). T/Qdpt: £13.00 (34.3 Tckts) WG

# 1809-WOLVERHAMPTON (L-H) (Standard)

## Saturday June 22nd

WEATHER: fine WIND: fresh half against

## 2168 WALSALL MAIDEN H'CAP (0-65) (3-Y.O) (Class F)

7-00 (7-04) **1m 1f 79y (Fibresand)** £2,381.00 (£656.00: £311.00) Stalls: Low GOING minus 0.06 sec per fur (STD)

| | | | | SP | RR | SF |
|---|---|---|---|---|---|---|
| 1535⁵ | **Halebid (60)** (SPCWoods) **3-9-5** WWoods(2) (a.p: led over 2f out: drvn clr appr fnl f) | — | **1** | 5/1 ² | 76 | 44 |
| *1970³* | **Sis Garden (50)** (TDEasterby) **3-8-4b**(5) RHavlin(3) (lw: chsd ldr: rdn & effrt wl over 1f out: one pce) | 6 | **2** | 9/1 | 56 | 24 |
| 748⁸ | **Ragtime Cowgirl (37)** (CWThornton) **3-7-10** FNorton(10) (hld up: hdwy 3f out: styd on ins fnl f) | ¾ | **3** | 33/1 | 42 | 10 |

1654[4] **Shouldbegrey (47)** (WRMuir) **3-8-6**ow2 KFallon(5) (lw: hld up: hdwy ½-wy: sn rdn: nt rch ldrs) ........................6 **4** 3/1[1] 41 7
1503[7] **He's Got Wings (IRE) (48)** (MBell) **3-8-7b**[1] MFenton(1) (b.hind: bit bkwd: led tl hdd & wknd over 2f out) .........5 **5** 12/1 34 2
1497[3] **Trianna (46)** (LordHuntingdon) **3-8-2**(3) AWhelan(7) (chsd ldrs over 5f)..........................................................1 **6** 11/2[3] 30 —
*1814*[10] **Salsian (45)** (SCWilliams) **3-8-1b**[1](3) DWright(6) (sn wl bhd & drvn along: sme late hdwy: n.d) .....................s.h **7** 20/1 29 —
1995[3] **Classic Beauty (IRE) (62)** (RHarris) **3-9-7** AMackay(4) (trckd ldrs: rdn over 2f out: eased whn btn).................4 **8** 5/1[2] 39 7
1887[10] **Belacqua (USA) (37)** (DWChapman) **3-7-3b**(7) PDoe(8) (a bhd: t.o)..............................................................1¾ **9** 33/1 11 —
*1809*[11] **Boundary Bird (IRE) (47)** (MJohnston) **3-7-13b**(7) KSked(12) (lw: mid div tl wknd over 3f out: t.o).....................6 **10** 16/1 11 —
1821[11] **Radmore Brandy (37)** (NPLittmoden) **3-7-10v**[1] NCarlisle(9) (a bhd: t.o).................................................4 **11** 8/1 — —
1301[7] **Animation (50)** (KMcAuliffe) **3-8-9e** JTate(11) (dwlt: a bhd: t.o)..........................................................dist **12** 25/1 — —
(SP 122.9%) **12 Rn**

**2m 2.3** (6.30) CSF £47.15 CT £1,235.49 TOTE £5.00: £1.90 £2.40 £11.20 (£19.40) Trio £79.30; £91.68 to 4.45 Nottingham 24/6/96 OWNER Mr S. P. C. Woods (NEWMARKET) BRED Top Spin Co Ltd
LONG HANDICAP Ragtime Cowgirl 7-8 Radmore Brandy 7-9 Belacqua (USA) 6-9

**Halebid** stripped fitter than he did at Brighton and, set alight once in line for home, drew right away for a very comfortable success. (5/1)
**1970 Sis Garden,** brought back to a shorter trip, tried hard to get to terms below the distance, but the winner proved much the stronger and she was soon fighting a losing battle. (9/1: op 6/1)
**Ragtime Cowgirl** showed her first glimpse of form over this longer trip, and the way she was staying on at the finish would suggest she may still need a stiffer test of stamina. (33/1)
**1654 Shouldbegrey** took closer order down the back straight but could not get close enough to mount a serious challenge and proved a big disappointment. (3/1)
**He's Got Wings (IRE)** adopted forceful tactics on this step down in distance but he was flat to the boards when overtaken on the home turn and faded out of contention. (12/1)
**1497 Trianna** struggling to hold her pitch at the end of the back straight, could do little more than gallop on the spot and she is still not firing. (11/2)
**1995 Classic Beauty (IRE)** is not robust enough to carry big weights and she is going to have difficulty in finding an opening. (5/1)

## 2169 WILLENHALL CLAIMING STKS (3-Y.O+) (Class F)
7-30 (7-36) **1m 100y (Fibresand)** £2,381.00 (£656.00: £311.00) Stalls: Low GOING minus 0.06 sec per fur (STD)
SP RR SF

*1811*[9] **Dragonjoy (65)** (JWPayne) **3-8-7b** AMcGlone(10) (trckd ldrs: led wl over 1f out tl wl ins fnl f: rallied to ld last stride)..........................................................— **1** 5/1[3] 77 29
*1081** **Sweet Supposin (IRE) (77)** (MissSJWilton) **5-9-9v** SWhitworth(3) (hld up: hdwy 4f out: str chal fnl f: r.o).......hd **2** 3/1[1] 83 45
1983[6] **Ethbaat (USA) (77)** (WRMuir) **5-9-9** MRichards(11) (hdwy over 5f out: rdn to ld wl ins fnl f: hdd nr fin) ..........s.h **3** 20/1 83 45
1589[3] **Another Quarter (IRE) (57)** (SPCWoods) **3-8-6b**[1] WWoods(13) (b: hdwy over 4f out: hrd rdn 2f out: one pce)..........................................................2 **4** 7/1 72 24
1099[4] **Desert Harvest (70)** (JCullinan) **4-8-8**(7) AimeeCook(8) (led tl hdd wl over 1f out: sn outpcd).........................2½ **5** 12/1 66 28
1464[6] **Northern Celadon (IRE) (60)** (MJHeaton-Ellis) **5-9-0**(3) SDrowne(6) (lw: prom tl rdn & wknd 2f out) ................6 **6** 5/1[3] 57 19
*521*[11] **Fiaba (34)** (MrsNMacauley) **8-8-8** JTate(12) (hdwy 4f out: sn rdn: no imp) ................................................7 **7** 25/1 35 —
*1602** **Sandmoor Denim (64)** (SRBowring) **9-9-1**(3) CTeague(4) (trckd ldrs: hrd drvn ½-wy: sn lost pl: fin lame).........9 **8** 7/2[2] 28 —
*1605*[7] **Minnie The Minx** (WGMTurner) **5-8-3**(5)ow1 RHavlin(1) (outpcd: a bhd t.o) ..................................................2 **9** 50/1 14 —
1411[18] **Queens Stroller (IRE) (51)** (TWall) **5-8-5**(3) PMcCabe(2) (a bhd: t.o) .......................................................¾ **10** 20/1 12 —
**Marshall Pindari** (TTBill) **6-8-11** WHollick(5) (bkwd: prom: rdn over 3f out: sn wknd: t.o) ............................1¾ **11** 50/1 12 —
1891[9] **Lady Rambo** (LJBarratt) **3-8-2** FNorton(7) (prom 5f: sn rdn & wknd: t.o)....................................................nk **12** 40/1 13 —
1707[11] **Palacegate Chief** (NPLittmoden) **3-8-7** NCarlisle(9) (chsd ldrs to ½-wy: sn lost pl: t.o).................................¾ **13** 25/1 16 —
(SP 124.3%) **13 Rn**

**1m 51.9** (6.90) CSF £20.09 TOTE £6.00: £2.70 £1.40 £7.00 (£6.60) Trio £41.30 OWNER Mr T. H. Barma (NEWMARKET) BRED T. H. Barma
WEIGHT FOR AGE 3yo-10lb
Sweet Supposin (IRE) clmd PWilliams £8,000; Dragonjoy clmd NPLittmoden £5,000

**1456* Dragonjoy,** scoring for the fourth time this season, needed to dig deep to gain the spoils in the final stride and he is certainly not short on courage. (5/1)
**1081* Sweet Supposin (IRE)** looked set to repeat last month's success over course and distance when cruising up on the bridle to deliver his challenge inside the final furlong but the photo verdict went against him this time. (3/1)
**Ethbaat (USA)** responded to a forceful ride on this step down in class and poked his head in front fifty yards out but only emerged third best in an all out scrap to the line. (20/1)
**1589 Another Quarter (IRE),** very unruly going out on to the racecourse in her first time blinkers, was eventually led to the start. Hard at work in an effort to deliver a challenge turning in, she did stay on but lacked the speed to land a blow. (7/1)
**1099 Desert Harvest** found his front-running tactics had come to an end on straightening up and it would seem less forceful tactics might prove beneficial. (12/1)

## 2170 ROTHMANS ROYALS NORTH SOUTH CHALLENGE SERIES H'CAP (0-85) (3-Y.O+) (Class F)
8-00 (8-01) **1m 100y (Fibresand)** £4,542.00 (£1,356.00: £648.00: £294.00) Stalls: Low GOING minus 0.06 sec per fur (STD)
SP RR SF

1996[6] **Bentico (68)** (MrsNMacauley) **7-8-9**(3) CTeague(7) (lw: hld up & bhd: hdwy 4f out: sn hrd rdn: led appr fnl f: r.o wl)..........................................................— **1** 14/1 75 43
1780[9] **Law Dancer (IRE) (76)** (TGMills) **3-8-10** KFallon(4) (lw: a.p: led 2f out tl appr fnl f: one pce) .........................1¼ **2** 9/1 81 39
*1811*[3] **Super High (75)** (PHowling) **4-9-5b** FNorton(6) (lw: hdwy 3f out: rdn & r.o wl ins fnl f) ......................................nk **3** 7/1[3] 79 47
*1048*[3] **Waikiki Beach (USA) (69)** (GLMoore) **5-8-13** SWhitworth(3) (b: b.hind: trckd ldrs: drvn along 3f out: one pce appr fnl f)..........................................................3 **4** 7/1[3] 67 35
*1604** **Sualtach (IRE) (78)** (RHollinshead) **3-8-7**(5) FLynch(1) (lw: led 2f: led 5f out to 2f out: sn rdn & btn) ...............1½ **5** 4/1[2] 74 32
1703[9] **Le Sport (85)** (ABailey) **3-9-2**(3) DWright(8) (bhd: hrd rdn ½-wy: nvr nrr) .................................................2½ **6** 8/1 76 34
1856[4] **Artful Dane (IRE) (66)** (MJHeaton-Ellis) **4-8-7**(3) SDrowne(5) (prom tl rdn & wknd over 2f out)..........................¾ **7** 10/1 55 23
1024[11] **Houghton Venture (USA) (67)** (SPCWoods) **4-8-11** WWoods(2) (hdwy over 4f out: rdn & wknd ent st) ........1¾ **8** 14/1 53 21
1341* **Maple Bay (IRE) (84)** (ABailey) **7-9-9**(5) PRoberts(9) (lw: led after 2f to 5f out: rdn & wknd 3f out).....................2 **9** 3/1[1] 66 34
1796[6] **Worldwide Elsie (USA) (83)** (RHarris) **3-9-3** AMackay(10) (hdwy 5f out: rdn & wknd over 2f out)......................nk **10** 10/1 65 23
1876[7] **Bellacardia (68)** (GLewis) **3-7-13**(3)ow3 AWhelan(11) (a bhd: rdn over 3f out: t.o) ....................................5 **11** 8/1 40 —
(SP 133.7%) **11 Rn**

**1m 50.8** (5.80) CSF £134.97 CT £903.55 TOTE £11.60: £2.80 £2.40 £2.50 (£137.00) Trio £136.30; £136.33 to 4.45 Nottingham 24/6/96 OWNER Twenty Twenty Racing (MELTON MOWBRAY) BRED Britton House Stud
WEIGHT FOR AGE 3yo-10lb

**1996 Bentico**, mounting his challenge from off the pace, had to work hard to get to the front, but once he had made it, the rest was easy. (14/1)
**836* Law Dancer (IRE)**, whose previous couple of appearances here have been successful, could not quite hold on over a slightly shorter trip. (9/1)
**1811 Super High** could not find top gear until far too late and his finishing position was as close as he could get. (7/1)
**1048 Waikiki Beach (USA)**, poised to challenge but at full stretch on the home turn, had to admit the principals had the legs of him. (7/1)
**1604* Sualtach (IRE)** did his share of the pacemaking but appeared to find lack of stamina a problem when the chips were down. (4/1)
**987 Le Sport** did well to finish so close after struggling in the rear for most of the way. (8/1)
**1341* Maple Bay (IRE)** was throwing out distress signals towards the end of the back straight and this return to the sand proved a big let down. (3/1)

## 2171 PLYVINE CATERING H'CAP (0-85) (3-Y.O+) (Class D)
8-30 (8-31) **6f (Fibresand)** £3,993.30 (£1,193.40: £571.20: £260.10) Stalls: Low GOING minus 0.06 sec per fur (STD)

| | | | | SP | RR | SF |
|---|---|---|---|---|---|---|
| 2005² | **Cretan Gift (85)** (NPLittmoden) **5-9-9b**(5) FLynch(2) (s.i.s: hdwy over 2f out: r.o to ld wl ins fnl f) | — | 1 | 7/1 3 | 92 | 68 |
| 1765⁶ | **Vax New Way (73)** (JLSpearing) **3-8-6b**(3) SDrowne(7) (led over 4f out tl hdd wl ins fnl f) | 2 | 2 | 10/1 | 73 | 43 |
| 1991⁶ | **Sing With the Band (73)** (BAMcMahon) **5-9-2** GCarter(11) (lw: led over 1f: hrd drvn over 1f out: r.o wl) | hd | 3 | 14/1 | 73 | 49 |
| 2030⁵ | **Desert Invader (IRE) (70)** (DWChapman) **5-8-13** ACulhane(10) (hdwy 2f out: r.o u.p ins fnl f) | s.h | 4 | 14/1 | 70 | 46 |
| 1781⁴ | **Stand Tall (82)** (CWThornton) **4-9-11** DeanMcKeown(8) (lw: trckd ldrs: drvn & outpcd 2f out: kpt on nr fin) | ¾ | 5 | 9/1 | 80 | 56 |
| 1974² | **Portend (80)** (SRBowring) **4-9-6b**(3) CTeague(4) (lw: prom: ev ch wl over 1f out: sn wknd) | 3½ | 6 | 5/2 1 | 67 | 43 |
| 1708⁹ | **Little Ibnr (73)** (PDEvans) **5-9-2** MFenton(12) (chsd ldrs over 4f) | 1¼ | 7 | 14/1 | 56 | 32 |
| 1652⁶ | **Mijas (80)** (LMontagueHall) **3-9-2** JFEgan(13) (swtg: in tch: hrd drvn over 2f out: no imp) | 3 | 8 | 25/1 | 52 | 22 |
| *1810*³ | **Palacegate Touch (75)** (JBerry) **6-8-13b**(5) PRoberts(5) (prom: rdn 2f out: wknd appr fnl f) | d.h | 8 | 12/1 | 48 | 24 |
| 1707⁹ | **Boffy (IRE) (77)** (BPJBaugh) **3-8-13** NCarlisle(3) (mid div tl outpcd wl over 1f out) | 4 | 10 | 50/1 | 36 | 6 |
| 1327¹⁰ | **Splicing (82)** (WJHaggas) **3-9-4** KFallon(6) (sn pushed along: nvr nr ldrs) | 1½ | 11 | 7/1 3 | 36 | 6 |
| 1708⁴ | **Hinton Rock (IRE) (76)** (ABailey) **4-9-2b**(3) DWright(9) (outpcd) | 1 | 12 | 6/1 2 | 28 | 4 |
| 1707¹⁰ | **Little Noggins (IRE) (73)** (CADwyer) **3-8-9b¹** FNorton(1) (prom early: sn outpcd: t.o) | 5 | 13 | 20/1 | 8 | — |
| | | | | (SP 125.2%) | | **13 Rn** |

**1m 14.9** (3.50) CSF £71.73 CT £918.42 TOTE £6.60: £3.00 £3.20 £4.40 (£56.70) Trio £172.30; £172.32 to 4.45 Nottingham 24/6/96 OWNER R A M Racecourses Ltd (WOLVERHAMPTON) BRED Hesmonds Stud Ltd
WEIGHT FOR AGE 3yo-7lb
**2005 Cretan Gift** has been performing well and this success was richly deserved after forfeiting ground at the start. (7/1)
**1083* Vax New Way** may have had too much use made of him, but having said that he did run up to his best and could be on the way up. (10/1)
**1430 Sing With the Band** appeared to be in trouble when being slightly outpaced entering the straight, but she rallied inside the distance and another success is long overdue. (14/1)
**2030 Desert Invader (IRE)** reserves his best for the All Weather but he is possibly better over a slightly longer trip and a spirited late flourish was never going to succeed. (14/1)
**1781 Stand Tall**, so much better handicapped on the turf, could not hold his pitch on the home turn, but he did renew his effort inside the final furlong and, if the Handicapper does relent, he could get back to winning ways. (9/1)
**1974 Portend** could not retain his good form on this return to the sand and it is possible that the Handicapper has his measure. (5/2)

## 2172 DERRY BUILDING SERVICES (S) STKS (2-Y.O) (Class G)
9-00 (9-03) **6f (Fibresand)** £2,070.00 (£570.00: £270.00) Stalls: Low GOING minus 0.06 sec per fur (STD)

| | | | | SP | RR | SF |
|---|---|---|---|---|---|---|
| 1537¹¹ | **Eager To Please** (JBerry) **2-8-11** GCarter(6) (a.p: led over 2f out tl ins fnl f: rallied u.p to ld last stride) | — | 1 | 6/1 | 53 | 13 |
| 1904² | **Our Kevin** (KMcAuliffe) **2-9-2v** JTate(5) (swtg: hld up: hdwy 2f out: led ins fnl f: ct post) | s.h | 2 | 11/4 2 | 58 | 18 |
| 624³ | **Abstone Queen** (PDEvans) **2-8-6** KFallon(8) (hld up: hdwy over 2f out: kpt on ins fnl f) | 1¾ | 3 | 4/1 3 | 43 | 3 |
| 2043⁶ | **Fearless Cavalier** (RHollinshead) **2-8-6**(5) FLynch(3) (outpcd: hdwy over 2f out: rdn & one pce appr fnl f) | 3½ | 4 | 5/2 1 | 39 | — |
| | **Tycoon Tina** (WMBrisbourne) **2-7-13**(7) RMullen(7) (leggy: bit bkwd: b: b.hind: s.s: wl bhd tl hdwy 2f out: nvr nrr) | 4 | 5 | 20/1 | 23 | — |
| 1607⁵ | **Moor Hall Princess** (KRBurke) **2-8-6** SWhitworth(4) (bit bkwd: prom: hrd drvn 2f out: sn wknd) | 1¼ | 6 | 9/1 | 20 | — |
| *895*¹⁰ | **Dancing Star (IRE)** (PDEvans) **2-8-6b¹** MFenton(2) (led over 3f: sn rdn along: outpcd fnl 2f) | hd | 7 | 12/1 | 20 | — |
| | **Ditty Box** (MDIUsher) **2-8-6** AMcGlone(1) (b: lt-f: s.i.s: sn rcvrd: spd over 3f: wknd qckly: t.o) | 13 | 8 | 14/1 | — | — |
| | | | | (SP 118.6%) | | **8 Rn** |

**1m 17.2** (5.80) CSF £22.58 TOTE £6.20: £2.50 £1.50 £1.80 (£12.60) OWNER The Totally Original Partnership (COCKERHAM) BRED Mrs Sara Hood
No bid
**930 Eager To Please**, in a seller for the first time and making his debut on the Fibresand, showed his true grit to force his head back in front again after looking to have shot his bolt inside the last furlong. (6/1)
**1904 Our Kevin** looked to have timed his run to perfection when showing ahead a hundred yards out, but the determined late rally of the winner shaded him on the line. (11/4)
**624 Abstone Queen**, having her first run beyond the minimum trip, was pegging back the principals nearing the finish and there could be a similar race in store. (4/1)
**2043 Fearless Cavalier**, taken off his legs in the early stages, tried hard to reach the leaders in the straight but lacked the speed to deliver a challenge. (5/2)
**Ditty Box** (14/1: op 5/1)

## 2173 JOHN SANDERS MEMORIAL H'CAP (0-65) (3-Y.O+) (Class F)
9-30 (9-35) **1m 4f (Fibresand)** £2,381.00 (£656.00: £311.00) Stalls: Low GOINGminus 0.06 sec per fur (STD)

| | | | | SP | RR | SF |
|---|---|---|---|---|---|---|
| 1022⁸ | **Claque (60)** (DWChapman) **4-9-11b** ACulhane(12) (led after 2f: rdn & edgd rt fnl f: hld on wl) | — | 1 | 14/1 | 73 | 38 |
| 1965W | **Lidhama (USA) (59)** (GLewis) **4-9-10** SWhitworth(8) (hdwy 6f out: chal ent fnl f: hld whn n.m.r & swtchd lft nr fin) | 1½ | 2 | 7/2 1 | 70 | 35 |
| 1803⁶ | **Charlie Bigtime (51)** (RHarris) **6-9-2b** AMackay(11) (b.hind: s.i.s: hdwy u.p 8f out: styd on one pce fnl 2f) | 4 | 3 | 8/1 | 57 | 22 |
| | **Wadada (40)** (DBurchell) **5-8-2**(3) SDrowne(7) (led 2f: rdn 3f out: wknd over 2f out) | 5 | 4 | 16/1 | 39 | 4 |
| 1640* | **In the Money (IRE) (61)** (RHollinshead) **7-9-7**(5) FLynch(4) (lw: hld up: hdwy 5f out: hrd drvn & one pce appr fnl f) | ¾ | 5 | 4/1 2 | 59 | 24 |
| *1458*² | **Locorotondo (IRE) (63)** (MBell) **5-9-7**(7) RMullen(2) (hld up in rr: effrt & rdn 3f out: nvr nr to chal) | 2 | 6 | 4/1 2 | 43 | 23 |

| | | | | SP | RR | SF |
|---|---|---|---|---|---|---|
| 1031[11] | **Sommersby (IRE) (58)** (MrsNMacauley) **5-9-6v**[1(3)] CTeague(10) (lw: prom tl rdn & wknd wl over 1f out) ......1¼ | **7** | 20/1 | 37 | 17 |
| 1637[3] | **Me Cherokee (46)** (CWThornton) **4-8-11** DeanMcKeown(3) (jnd wnr over 7f out: wknd over 2f out)................¾ | **8** | 12/1 | 24 | 4 |
| 668[10] | **Topanga (62)** (JABennett) **4-9-13** AMcGlone(1) (bit bkwd: prom tl wknd over 3f out).......................................nk | **9** | 20/1 | 19 | 19 |
| 1870[3] | **Daily Sport Girl (44)** (BJLlewellyn) **7-8-4**(5) MBaird(6) (b: chsd ldrs tl lost pl 5f out) ..........................................2 | **10** | 7/1[3] | — | — |
| | **Coast Along (IRE) (36)** (PJBevan) **4-8-1** NCarlisle(9) (a in rr: t.o)..................................................................5 | **11** | 16/1 | — | — |
| | **Frontier Flight (USA) (54)** (MissLCSiddall) **6-9-2**(3)ow2 OPears(5) (sn drvn along: a bhd: t.o) ........................2½ | **12** | 20/1 | — | — |

(SP 126.2%) **12 Rn**

**2m 42.6** (10.10) CSF £62.52 CT £391.59 TOTE £29.50: £5.10 £1.50 £2.10 (£87.00) Trio £124.90; £158.34 to 4.45 Nottingham 24/6/96
OWNER Mr Michael Hill (YORK) BRED Lord Howard de Walden

**Claque** made the majority of the running and, finding more when strongly pressed in the final furlong, had the measure of the favourite in the battle to the line. (14/1: op 9/1)

**Lidhama (USA),** gambled on on this first attempt since the autumn, looked set to land the spoils when putting in a sustained challenge entering the final furlong but the race winner just would not be denied. She will be on a recovery mission in the near future. (7/2)

**1803 Charlie Bigtime,** off the bridle from the break, kept battling away, but his one pace was just not good enough when the race was on in earnest. (8/1)

**Wadada,** fit from hurdling, did not run badly and there could be a small race to be had. (16/1)

**1640* In the Money (IRE)** running away when reaching the heels of the leaders turning out of the back straight, did not find a lot when let down and was fighting a lost cause from below the distance. (4/1)

**1458 Locorotondo (IRE)** could not summon up the pace to make her presence felt and she will need to come down the handicap. (4/1)

T/Plpt: £3,256.50 (3.88 Tckts). T/Qdpt: £142.40 (5.57 Tckts) IM

# 2018-**MUSSELBURGH (R-H) (Good to firm)**
## Monday June 24th
WEATHER: sunny WIND: almost nil

## 2174 CRAIGLEITH CLAIMING STKS (2-Y.O) (Class F)
2-30 (2-31) **5f** £2,552.70 (£717.20: £350.10) Stalls: High GOING minus 0.40 sec per fur (F)

| | | | SP | RR | SF |
|---|---|---|---|---|---|
| 2125[2] | **Fonzy** (MrsLStubbs) **2-8-8b** KFallon(3) (mde most: kpt on wl fnl 2f)...............................................................— | **1** | 3/1[2] | 70 | 9 |
| 1645[3] | **Full Traceability (IRE)** (JBerry) **2-8-6** JCarroll(4) (stumbled s: hdwy whn carried bdly lft 2f out: swtchd & styd on)..........................................................3 | **2** | 7/2[3] | 58 | — |
| 1471[6] | **Just Loui** (WGMTurner) **2-8-12** JFortune(6) (lw: disp ld early: rdn ½-wy: no imp after) ...................................nk | **3** | 7/2[3] | 63 | 2 |
| 1869[4] | **Back In The Ussr (IRE)** (MJohnston) **2-8-12** TWilliams(2) (drvn along thrght: nvr trbld ldrs)...........................2 | **4** | 9/4[1] | 57 | — |
| 1607[7] | **Whittle Times** (EJAlston) **2-8-7** JFanning(5) (chsd ldrs: hung bdly lft 2f out: sn btn) .......................................7 | **5** | 33/1 | 30 | — |
| 1543[6] | **Chloe's Mark** (RMMcKellar) **2-7-11** NCarlisle(1) (sn outpcd & bhd)....................................................................4 | **6** | 100/1 | 7 | — |

(SP 104.1%) **6 Rn**

**60.6 secs** (2.90) CSF £11.96 TOTE £2.60: £1.10 £2.60 (£3.00) OWNER The West Riding Partnership (WARTHILL) BRED J. and Mrs Rose

**2125 Fonzy** got a shade warm before the start as he often does, but his performance was good enough as he won convincingly. (3/1: op 7/4)

**1645 Full Traceability (IRE)** found everything going wrong in the race but still ran well and, with a trouble-free passage, might well have shaken the winner up. (7/2)

**1080* Just Loui,** running for the first time on fast ground, showed a poor action and was struggling for speed from halfway. (7/2)

**1869 Back In The Ussr (IRE)** found this trip far too sharp. (9/4)

**Whittle Times** just wanted to hang left from halfway, throwing all chance away. (33/1)

## 2175 YVONNE MURRAY M.B.E. H'CAP (0-65) (3-Y.O+) (Class F)
3-00 (3-00) **1m 7f 16y** £2,588.40 (£727.40: £355.20) Stalls: High GOING minus 0.40 sec per fur (F)

| | | | SP | RR | SF |
|---|---|---|---|---|---|
| 1450[11] | **Sarasota Storm (46)** (MBell) **4-9-5** MFenton(6) (lw: hld up & bhd: gd hdwy 3f out: r.o wl to ld ins fnl f) ..........— | **1** | 20/1 | 56 | 14 |
| 1887[3] | **Mister Aspecto (IRE) (63)** (MJohnston) **3-9-3** TWilliams(3) (lw: cl up: led ½-wy: rdn over 3f out: r.o: jst ct) .....½ | **2** | 11/2[3] | 73 | 12 |
| 2165[9] | **Sharp Sensation (38)** (DWBarker) **6-8-4**(7) JBramhill(7) (lw: cl up: chal over 2f out: kpt on one pce fnl f).......1¼ | **3** | 7/1 | 46 | 4 |
| 1887[2] | **Marsayas (IRE) (50)** (MJCamacho) **3-8-4** JFanning(9) (lw: hld up & bhd: hdwy u.p 3f out: nvr able to chal)...2½ | **4** | 5/2[1] | 56 | — |
| 1866[9] | **Little Redwing (35)** (MDHammond) **4-8-8** KFallon(1) (lw: hld up & bhd: effrt over 3f out: styd on: nrst fin).......¾ | **5** | 20/1 | 40 | — |
| 1478[4] | **Vain Prince (51)** (NTinkler) **9-9-10b** JFortune(5) (lw: trckd ldrs: disp ld over 4f out tl outpcd fnl 2½f)...............½ | **6** | 3/1[2] | 55 | 13 |
| 2020[5] | **Trumped (IRE) (39)** (PMonteith) **4-8-12** JCarroll(2) (swtg: bhd: effrt over 3f out: rdn & no imp) .......................½ | **7** | 10/1 | 43 | 1 |
| | **Yaakum (30)** (SEKettlewell) **7-8-3b** NCarlisle(4) (in tch tl outpcd appr st: sn btn)...............................................5 | **8** | 12/1 | 28 | — |
| 1762[4] | **Brogans Brush (43)** (JSHaldane) **3-7-8**(3)ow1 DarrenMoffatt(10) (led to ½-wy: sn wknd) .....................................19 | **9** | 100/1 | 21 | — |
| 1167[17] | **Recluse (38)** (MissLAPerratt) **5-8-11b** NDay(8) (prom tl wknd 3f out)..........................................................16 | **10** | 50/1 | — | — |

(SP 110.7%) **10 Rn**

**3m 21.8** (11.30) CSF £110.59 CT £749.02 TOTE £13.00: £3.30 £3.00 £2.70 (£16.20) Trio £59.30 OWNER Mr B. J. Warren (NEWMARKET)
BRED B. J. Warren
LONG HANDICAP Brogans Brush 7-5
WEIGHT FOR AGE 3yo-19lb

**Sarasota Storm,** in a slowly-run event, had the turn of foot to come from way off the pace and settle it late on. He is now off a decent mark. (20/1)

**1887 Mister Aspecto (IRE),** trying a longer trip, lay up with the pace and, although this was a muddling event, he still ran well enough to suggest there is a race to be found on turf. (11/2)

**1478 Sharp Sensation** looked and ran well and can pick up a modest race. (7/1)

**1887 Marsayas (IRE),** who is just a stayer, was unsuited by the slow pace here and pointlessly tried to come from behind. (5/2)

**Little Redwing,** trying her longest trip to date, showed something and would seem to be improving. (20/1)

**1478 Vain Prince,** the winner of this event last year, was most disappointing. (3/1)

## 2176 HADDINGTON RATING RELATED MAIDEN STKS (0-65) (3-Y.O+) (Class F)
3-30 (3-33) **5f** £2,517.00 (£707.00: £345.00) Stalls: High GOING minus 0.40 sec per fur (F)

| | | | SP | RR | SF |
|---|---|---|---|---|---|
| 1787[3] | **Time To Tango (64)** (GMMoore) **3-8-8** JFortune(5) (mde most: edgd lft fr ½-wy: r.o)....................................— | **1** | 4/5[1] | 66 | 39 |
| 2021[8] | **Ready Teddy (IRE) (50)** (MissLAPerratt) **3-8-8** KFallon(3) (hdwy ½-wy: chsd wnr fnl f: edgd rt & r.o) ...............1 | **2** | 12/1[3] | 63 | 36 |
| 1532[9] | **Need You Badly (59)** (SPCWoods) **3-8-8** DBiggs(8) (chsd ldrs: swtchd lft ½-wy: nt qckn fnl f).......................2½ | **3** | 11/4[2] | 55 | 28 |

| Form | Horse / details | Dist | Pos | SP | RR | SF |
|---|---|---|---|---|---|---|
| 1787$^{6}$ | **Forzara (45)** (JBerry) **3-8-8** JCarroll(2) (w ldrs: edgd lft ½-wy: btn over 1f out) | 5 | **4** | 25/1 | 39 | 12 |
| 1761$^{6}$ | **Snitch (39)** (CSmith) **3-8-11v** MFenton(1) (disp ld to ½-wy: rdn & btn appr fnl f) | ½ | **5** | 20/1 | 40 | 13 |
| 1787$^{4}$ | **Fancy Clancy (46)** (MissLCSiddall) **3-8-8** TWilliams(4) (lw: prom: effrt & n.m.r 2f out: no imp) | 1½ | **6** | 14/1 | 32 | 5 |
| *2085*$^{11}$ | **Primo Lad (54)** (WGMTurner) **3-8-11b** JFanning(7) (s.i.s: a outpcd & bhd) | 3½ | **7** | 20/1 | 24 | — |
| 2049$^{14}$ | **Swifty Nifty (IRE) (45)** (WWHaigh) **3-8-8** NCarlisle(6) (outpcd & bhd fr ½-wy) | hd | **8** | 50/1 | 21 | — |
| | | | | (SP 111.9%) | | **8 Rn** |

**58.8 secs** (1.10) CSF £10.21 TOTE £1.50: £1.10 £2.10 £1.40 (£4.40) OWNER Mrs D. N. B. Pearson (MIDDLEHAM) BRED Mrs D. N. B. Pearson

**1787 Time To Tango** took a fierce hold going to post but made no mistake on the way back, despite showing a tendency to hang left. (4/5)

**1547 Ready Teddy (IRE)**, from a yard that is going well at present, put in another sound effort, but just spoiled her chances by edging right late on. (12/1: 10/1-16/1)

**1532 Need You Badly** was a bit short of toe here and, as a result, got short of room. She may need further. (11/4: 9/4-7/2)

**1787 Forzara** showed plenty of speed, but just wanted to hang left from halfway, which was her undoing. (25/1)

**Snitch** has plenty of early pace, but has yet to see the trip out. (20/1)

**1787 Fancy Clancy** was short of room two furlongs out and then lost all interest. (14/1)

## 2177 EAST LOTHIAN COUNCIL HOUSE CONTENTS INSURANCE H'CAP (0-65) (3-Y.O+) (Class F)

4-00 (4-00) **1m 3f 32y** £2,576.50 (£724.00: £353.50) Stalls: High GOING minus 0.40 sec per fur (F)

| Form | Horse / details | Dist | Pos | SP | RR | SF |
|---|---|---|---|---|---|---|
| 2024* | **Ambidextrous (IRE) (43)** (EJAlston) **4-9-4** KFallon(6) (lw: outpcd & bhd: hdwy 3f out: led 1f out: r.o) | — | **1** | 9/4$^{1}$ | 54 | 36 |
| 1850$^{7}$ | **Kernof (IRE) (47)** (MDHammond) **3-8-9** JFanning(5) (lw: a.p: rdn to ld 2f out: hdd 1f out: kpt on) | 1½ | **2** | 7/2$^{3}$ | 56 | 25 |
| 1965$^{3}$ | **Silver Hunter (USA) (49)** (GCBravery) **5-9-10** NDay(2) (outpcd 5f out: styd on u.p fnl 2f: nvr able to chal) | 5 | **3** | 11/4$^{2}$ | 51 | 33 |
| 1832$^{2}$ | **Steadfast Elite (IRE) (45)** (JJO'Neill) **5-9-6** JFortune(4) (in tch: rdn over 3f out: nt pce to chal) | hd | **4** | 5/1 | 47 | 29 |
| 1633$^{3}$ | **Personimus (38)** (CaptJWilson) **6-8-13** DBiggs(7) (lw: chsd ldrs: led 4f out to 2f out: sn outpcd) | 1 | **5** | 14/1 | 38 | 20 |
| 1676$^{11}$ | **Punch (39)** (NTinkler) **4-9-0b** JCarroll(1) (lw: hld up: hdwy to chal 3f out: rdn & no rspnse 2f out) | 2½ | **6** | 20/1 | 36 | 18 |
| 2024$^{8}$ | **Amnesia (IRE) (30)** (MrsSCBradburne) **5-8-5v** TWilliams(3) (b.nr fore: set str pce tl hdd & wknd qckly 4f out: t.o) | 27 | **7** | 66/1 | — | — |
| | | | | (SP 109.2%) | | **7 Rn** |

**2m 24.5** (4.80) CSF £9.63 TOTE £2.90: £1.20 £1.80 (£5.50) OWNER Mrs Carol McPhail (PRESTON) BRED Saeed Manana

WEIGHT FOR AGE 3yo-13lb

**2024* Ambidextrous (IRE)** got the required strong pace and again came from off the pace to settle it late on. (9/4)

**Kernof (IRE)** keeps stepping up in trip and certainly put up an improved performance but, despite responding to pressure, found the winner too good. (7/2: op 7/1)

**1965 Silver Hunter (USA)** banged his head leaving the stalls and was never happy until staying on when it was all over. (11/4)

**1832 Steadfast Elite (IRE)** was always close enough if good enough, but she could never summon the necessary turn of foot. (5/1)

**1633 Personimus** had his chances, but yet again failed to take them. (14/1)

## 2178 LINLITHGOW CLAIMING STKS (3-Y.O+) (Class F)

4-30 (4-30) **1m 16y** £2,540.80 (£713.80: £348.40) Stalls: High GOING minus 0.40 sec per fur (F)

| Form | Horse / details | Dist | Pos | SP | RR | SF |
|---|---|---|---|---|---|---|
| *1993*$^{2}$ | **Perilous Plight (68)** (WRMuir) **5-9-11** KFallon(1) (lw: a.p: rdn to ld wl over 1f out: r.o) | — | **1** | 8/13$^{1}$ | 70 | 13 |
| 2154$^{13}$ | **Diet (55)** (MissLAPerratt) **10-9-3v** JCarroll(4) (led: qcknd appr st: hdd wl over 1f out: kpt on) | 2½ | **2** | 12/1 | 57 | — |
| 1866$^{11}$ | **Simand (50)** (GMMoore) **4-9-0** JFortune(3) (in tch: effrt 3f out: chsng ldrs 2f out: nt qckn) | 1¼ | **3** | 11/2$^{3}$ | 52 | — |
| 2010$^{14}$ | **Curtelace (55)** (MrsMReveley) **6-9-11** ACulhane(2) (trckd ldr: ev ch over 2f out: sn rdn & nt r.o) | 1¼ | **4** | 4/1$^{2}$ | 60 | 3 |
| | | | | (SP 105.0%) | | **4 Rn** |

**1m 45.0** (6.40) CSF £6.10 TOTE £1.50: (£3.60) OWNER The Sun Punters Club (LAMBOURN) BRED Crest Stud Ltd

**1993 Perilous Plight**, in good heart, has won over shorter trips and had the required speed in this slowly-run event. (8/13)

**1163 Diet**, given a fine ride, tried to pinch this by setting a slow pace and quickening on the turn, but was never quite good enough. (12/1)

**1596 Simand** sat last early on and then improved to have a chance two furlongs out, but the final step proved beyond her. (11/2: op 7/2)

**1661 Curtelace** did his usual to have every chance, but then refused point-blank to struggle. (4/1)

## 2179 FIRTH OF FORTH H'CAP (0-65) (3-Y.O) (Class F)

5-00 (5-02) **7f 15y** £2,612.20 (£734.20: £358.60) Stalls: High GOING minus 0.40 sec per fur (F)

| Form | Horse / details | Dist | Pos | SP | RR | SF |
|---|---|---|---|---|---|---|
| 1416$^{13}$ | **Ned's Contessa (IRE) (44)** (MDods) **3-8-3** JCarroll(4) (hdwy ent st: led over 1f out: hung lft: r.o) | — | **1** | 10/1 | 52 | 21 |
| *1809*$^{5}$ | **Nkapen Rocks (SPA) (62)** (CaptJWilson) **3-9-7** JFortune(7) (bhd: gd hdwy ent st: led 2f out: hdd & hung lft appr fnl f: kpt on) | ½ | **2** | 16/1 | 69 | 38 |
| 1995$^{2}$ | **Ivor's Deed (54)** (CFWall) **3-8-13** NCarlisle(8) (prom: hung lft appr st: hdwy over 2f out: hmpd & swtchd over 1f out: kpt on one pce) | 4 | **3** | 6/4$^{1}$ | 52 | 21 |
| 1526$^{17}$ | **Fisiostar (38)** (MDods) **3-7-8b**$^{1(3)ow1}$ DarrenMoffatt(6) (b.hind: hmpd appr st & lost pl: hdwy 2f out: no imp) | ¾ | **4** | 100/1 | 34 | 2 |
| 1363$^{17}$ | **Eben Naas (USA) (55)** (SCWilliams) **3-9-0b**$^{1}$ NDay(5) (lw: b.hind: led 1f: cl up: led over 3f out to 2f out: sn outpcd) | 6 | **5** | 9/2$^{3}$ | 38 | 7 |
| 1840$^{9}$ | **Dil Dil (54)** (WJHaggas) **3-8-13** KFallon(2) (lw: chsd ldrs tl hmpd & lost pl appr st: hdwy 3f out: sn btn) | s.h | **6** | 7/2$^{2}$ | 36 | 5 |
| 1405$^{5}$ | **Miss Offset (42)** (MJohnston) **3-8-1b** TWilliams(3) (drvn along thrght: prom to st: sn bhd) | 6 | **7** | 8/1 | 11 | — |
| 1547$^{6}$ | **Aye Ready (37)** (MissLAPerratt) **3-7-3b**$^{(7)}$ JBramhill(1) (led after 1f: rn wd st: sn hdd & wknd) | 7 | **8** | 33/1 | — | — |
| | | | | (SP 110.4%) | | **8 Rn** |

**1m 28.4** (2.90) CSF £120.19 CT £325.62 TOTE £12.50: £1.60 £2.50 £1.40 (£22.30) OWNER Mr Ned Jones (DARLINGTON) BRED Rathasker Stud

LONG HANDICAP Fisiostar 7-9 Aye Ready 7-3

**Ned's Contessa (IRE)**, after showing nothing this season, won his first race here and, although it may have been a moderate event, it was no fluke. (10/1: 6/1-12/1)

**562 Nkapen Rocks (SPA)** got a fantastic run up the inner on the home turn and made dramatic improvement, but was outbattled in the closing stages. (16/1)

**1995 Ivor's Deed** seemed to get unbalanced on the home turn, losing a few places. Getting messed about again in the last two furlongs, he soon cried enough. This should be ignored. (6/4)

**Fisiostar** had shown next to nothing previously but, after getting messed about on the home turn, was staying on well at the end. (100/1)

**1001 Eben Naas (USA)**, in blinkers for the first time, did not give his running. (9/2)

**Dil Dil** looked very fit but, after getting hampered on the home turn, never took any interest. (7/2)

T/Plpt: £32.00 (301.7 Tckts). T/Qdpt: £4.70 (138.95 Tckts). AA

## 2056-NOTTINGHAM (L-H) (Good to firm, Firm patches)

### Monday June 24th

WEATHER: overcast & warm WIND: almost nil

### 2180 SANDIACRE (S) H'CAP (0-60) (3-Y.O) (Class G)

2-15 (2-15) **1m 54y** £2,070.00 (£570.00: £270.00) Stalls: Low GOING minus 0.58 sec per fur (F)

| | | | | SP | RR | SF |
|---|---|---|---|---|---|---|
| 2162$^{3}$ | **How Could-I (IRE) (40)** (TDEasterby) **3-8-7b** GDuffield(3) (lw: mde all: rdn & r.o wl fnl f) | — | **1** | 5/1$^{1}$ | 52 | 27 |
| 1449$^{5}$ | **Lila Pedigo (IRE) (51)** (MissJFCraze) **3-9-4** NConnorton(12) (hld up: hdwy over 2f out: r.o wl ins fnl f) | 2 | **2** | 12/1 | 59 | 34 |
| 2075$^{11}$ | **Born A Lady (51)** (SRBowring) **3-9-1b**(3) CTeague(8) (a.p: rdn & ev ch over 1f out: unable qckn) | hd | **3** | 12/1 | 59 | 34 |
| 2026$^{3}$ | **Tallulah Belle (45)** (NPLittmoden) **3-8-12** JQuinn(13) (hld up: hdwy 4f out: effrt over 1f out: unable qckn) | s.h | **4** | 9/1 | 53 | 28 |
| 2061$^{4}$ | **Richard House Lad (46)** (RHollinshead) **3-8-8**(5) FLynch(15) (lw: hld up: hdwy u.p 2f out: nvr able to chal) | 2½ | **5** | 13/2$^{3}$ | 49 | 24 |
| 1992$^{4}$ | **Cherry Garden (IRE) (49)** (TJNaughton) **3-8-11**(5) JDSmith(19) (swtg: hld up & bhd: styd on fnl 2f: nvr nrr) | 4 | **6** | 14/1 | 44 | 19 |
| 1806$^{4}$ | **My Kind (47)** (NTinkler) **3-9-0** KimTinkler(6) (bhd: hdwy 3f out: nvr nrr) | 1¼ | **7** | 16/1 | 40 | 15 |
| 1836$^{8}$ | **Danico (54)** (SCWilliams) **3-9-2**(5) ADaly(10) (mid div: hdwy & drvn along 3f out: wknd appr fnl f) | 1¼ | **8** | 10/1 | 44 | 19 |
| *1721*$^{9}$ | **Cocoon (IRE) (48)** (CWThornton) **3-9-1** DeanMcKeown(5) (dwlt: sn rcvrd: prom tl wknd wl over 1f out) | s.h | **9** | 16/1 | 38 | 13 |
| 1876$^{9}$ | **Killatty Lark (IRE) (37)** (WJMusson) **3-8-4** DRMcCabe(9) (nvr trbld ldrs) | 2½ | **10** | 8/1 | 22 | — |
| *1602*$^{9}$ | **Needwood Fantasy (42)** (BCMorgan) **3-8-9v**$^{1}$ GBardwell(2) (chsd ldrs tl rdn & wknd over 2f out) | 1¾ | **11** | 16/1 | 24 | — |
| 1991$^{7}$ | **Power Princess (40)** (JAPickering) **3-8-0**(7) AngelaGallimore(17) (b: hld up & bhd: effrt over 2f out: no imp) | ½ | **12** | 25/1 | 21 | — |
| 2026$^{4}$ | **Veshca Lady (IRE) (48)** (EWeymes) **3-9-1** KDarley(7) (hld up: effrt over 3f out: no imp) | hd | **13** | 6/1$^{2}$ | 29 | 4 |
| 1891$^{6}$ | **Natatari (IRE) (45)** (BPalling) **3-8-12** TSprake(4) (chsd ldrs tl wknd wl over 2f out) | 2½ | **14** | 16/1 | 21 | — |
| 1891$^{5}$ | **Andsome Boy (45)** (CRBarwell) **3-8-9**(3) NVarley(16) (hld up: effrt over 3f out: no imp) | hd | **15** | 14/1 | 21 | — |
| 1836$^{7}$ | **Formentiere (37)** (JMBradley) **3-8-1**(3)ow1 SDrowne(20) (s.i.s: rdn & rn wd ent st: a bhd) | 1½ | **16** | 16/1 | 10 | — |
| *1721*$^{12}$ | **Pulga Circo (40)** (BAMcMahon) **3-8-7** GCarter(11) (mid div: drvn along 4f out: wknd) | ½ | **17** | 20/1 | 12 | — |
| *1081*$^{8}$ | **Inca Bird (35)** (TWall) **3-7-11**(5) CAdamson(1) (effrt u.p 4f out: nt rch ldrs) | nk | **18** | 33/1 | 6 | — |
| *1970*$^{10}$ | **Cinnamon Stick (IRE) (36)** (PSFelgate) **3-8-0**(3) DWright(14) (mid div: rdn 4f out: wknd qckly over 4f out: t.o) | 5 | **19** | 14/1 | — | — |
| 1416$^{14}$ | **Classic Daisy (37)** (RCSpicer) **3-8-4** NKennedy(18) (bhd fnl 3f: t.o) | 6 | **20** | 20/1 | — | — |
| | | | | (SP 155.6%) | **20 Rn** | |

**1m 43.9** (2.60) CSF £73.32 CT £704.20 TOTE £5.80: £1.70 £3.20 £3.60 £2.50 (£42.40) Trio £199.30 OWNER Mr M. H. Easterby (MALTON) BRED Michael Dargan

Sold GWiltshire 5,000gns

**2162 How Could-I (IRE)**, who has been kept very busy, was always calling the tune here and only needed to be driven out to open her account. (5/1)

**1449 Lila Pedigo (IRE)** came out of the pack approaching the final furlong and finished well. The winner had the prize sewn up by then and she was never going to prove troublesome. (12/1)

**606 Born A Lady** showed signs of a return to form, but she has not troubled the Judge for thirteen months and is certainly not one to trust. (12/1: op 8/1)

**2026 Tallulah Belle** was meeting the winner on 5lb worse terms than when finishing a length behind a week ago and, on unsuitably fast ground, was unable to take her revenge. (9/1)

**2061 Richard House Lad** just will not let himself down on this firm ground and was never able to get within striking range. (13/2)

**1992 Cherry Garden (IRE)** took a long time to pick up and the race was as good as over when he did eventually get going. (14/1)

**Killatty Lark (IRE)** (8/1: 5/1-9/1)

### 2181 RADCLIFFE MAIDEN STKS (3-Y.O+) (Class D)

2-45 (2-47) **1m 54y** £4,435.00 (£1,330.00: £640.00: £295.00) Stalls: Low GOING minus 0.58 sec per fur (F)

| | | | | SP | RR | SF |
|---|---|---|---|---|---|---|
| 1820$^{10}$ | **Iamus (87)** (PTWalwyn) **3-8-11** JReid(8) (led to 2f out: rallied u.p to ld ins fnl f: r.o) | — | **1** | 9/2$^{3}$ | 68 | 31 |
| 1675$^{2}$ | **Mubariz (IRE)** (EALDunlop) **4-9-7** WCarson(6) (a.p: led 2f out: edgd lft & hdd ins fnl f) | 2 | **2** | 5/2$^{1}$ | 64 | 37 |
| | **Seeking Fortune (USA)** (JRFanshawe) **3-8-6** TQuinn(5) (still unf: chsd ldr: ev ch 2f out: rdn & no ex fnl f) | nk | **3** | 3/1$^{2}$ | 59 | 22 |
| | **Blatant Outburst** (GCBravery) **6-9-7** DRMcCabe(2) (hld up: styd on appr fnl f: fin wl) | 1 | **4** | 20/1 | 62 | 35 |
| 2036$^{13}$ | **Severn Mill** (JMBradley) **5-9-4**(3) SDrowne(10) (chsd ldrs: rdn 3f out: sn outpcd) | 3½ | **5** | 50/1 | 55 | 28 |
| | **The Polymath** (HCandy) **3-8-11** CRutter(1) (leggy: unf: bkwd: bhd tl styd on fnl 2f: nvr nrr) | 1 | **6** | 14/1 | 53 | 16 |
| 1690$^{11}$ | **Great Chief** (HRACecil) **3-8-11** PatEddery(9) (bit bkwd: hld up in tch: hdwy & ev ch 2f out: nt clr run over 1f out: nt rcvr) | ½ | **7** | 3/1$^{2}$ | 52 | 15 |
| | **Road Racer (IRE)** (MrsJRRamsden) **3-8-11** MDeering(3) (w'like: bkwd: nvr nr to chal) | ½ | **8** | 16/1 | 51 | 14 |
| 1797$^{7}$ | **El Bardador (IRE)** (WJarvis) **3-8-11** AMcGlone(12) (s.i.s: a in rr) | 3½ | **9** | 12/1 | 44 | 7 |
| | **Dragon Rose** (TPTate) **4-9-7** DeanMcKeown(13) (b.hind: bkwd: s.s: a bhd: t.o) | 9 | **10** | 33/1 | 27 | — |
| *1972*$^{3}$ | **Safa Dancer** (BAMcMahon) **3-8-6** GCarter(11) (hld up: bhd fnl 4f: t.o) | 1½ | **11** | 14/1 | 19 | — |
| 1994$^{13}$ | **Fleeting Footsteps** (MJPolglase) **4-9-7** WHollick(4) (trckd ldrs tl wknd 3f out: t.o) | 5 | **12** | 50/1 | 14 | — |
| | **Myfanwy Bethesda** (BJLlewellyn) **3-8-8**ow2 VSlattery(7) (neat: bkwd: a bhd: t.o) | 2½ | **13** | 33/1 | 6 | — |
| | | | | (SP 138.2%) | **13 Rn** | |

**1m 43.5** (2.20) CSF £17.94 TOTE £5.50: £1.20 £1.40 £1.70 (£7.70) Trio £4.20 OWNER Hesmonds Stud (LAMBOURN) BRED Hesmonds Stud Ltd

WEIGHT FOR AGE 3yo-10lb

**1452 Iamus** gained a well-deserved first success with quite a comfortable win in the end, but he had to put his best foot forward to get the better of the favourite. (9/2)

**1675 Mubariz (IRE)**, trying a mile for the first time, looked set to get off the mark when leading into the final furlong, but he edged off a true line when sent about his work, and that was just sufficient to enable the winner to regain the initiative. (5/2)

**Seeking Fortune (USA)** has not improved physically since last year, but did look well tuned up. One of four upsides passing the quarter-mile marker, she gave of her best but had to admit the colts too strong for her inside the final furlong. She may be better suited by a longer trip. (3/1: op 7/4)

**Blatant Outburst**, winner of a bumper twelve months ago but disappointing over hurdles, was fairly eating up ground at the finish. When he is put back over a more suitable trip, he will be worth bearing in mind. (20/1)

**Severn Mill**, settled behind the leaders, was unable to respond when the tempo was stepped up, but he was not disgraced and is capable of finding a small race. (50/1)

**The Polymath**, a debutant, moved badly to post and was doing all his best work late on. When he gets the soft ground that he requires, more will be heard of him. (14/1)

## 2182 LENTON ABBEY CLAIMING STKS (4-Y.O+) (Class F)

3-15 (3-16) **2m 9y** £2,385.00 (£660.00: £315.00) Stalls: Low GOING minus 0.58 sec per fur (F)

| Form | Horse | Dist | Pos | SP | RR | SF |
|---|---|---|---|---|---|---|
| 1847$^{2}$ | **Brodessa (60)** (MrsMReveley) **10-9-3** KDarley(9) (lw: hld up in tch: hdwy ½-wy: led over 3f out: sn clr: eased nr fin) | — | **1** | 9/4$^{1}$ | 63 | 26 |
| | **Akiymann (USA)** (MCPipe) **6-9-6** MRoberts(2) (lw: wl bhd tl styd on fnl 2f: no ch w wnr) | 5 | **2** | 9/1 | 61 | 24 |
| 1788$^{2}$ | **Genesis Four (48)** (MrsLStubbs) **6-8-11** JFEgan(11) (hdwy over 4f out: chsd wnr over 2f out: no imp) | s.h | **3** | 16/1 | 52 | 15 |
| | **Access Sun (37)** (JSKing) **9-8-8** BDoyle(3) (a.p: rdn 4f out: one pce fnl 3f) | 1 | **4** | 16/1 | 48 | 11 |
| | **Erlemo** (WClay) **7-8-5** TSprake(8) (hld up: hmpd 6f out: styd on fnl 2f: nvr rchd ldrs) | 1 | **5** | 25/1 | 44 | 7 |
| 1697$^{2}$ | **Viardot (IRE) (69)** (MrsMReveley) **7-8-12**(5) GLee(12) (in tch tl lost pl ½-wy: styd on again fnl 2f) | 6 | **6** | 9/2$^{3}$ | 50 | 13 |
| 2165$^{15}$ | **Kindred Greeting (33)** (JAHarris) **4-8-8b** JO'Reilly(6) (prom: led over 4f out tl over 3f out: wknd 2f out) | 1¼ | **7** | 25/1 | 40 | 3 |
| 1835$^{5}$ | **Kymin (IRE) (56)** (DJGMurraySmith) **4-8-9** PatEddery(13) (lw: prom: pushed along 9f out: wknd over 4f out) | s.h | **8** | 11/2 | 41 | 4 |
| 1542$^{6}$ | **Can She Can Can (32)** (CSmith) **4-7-10**(7) IonaWands(14) (lw: mid div tl wknd 5f out) | 3½ | **9** | 25/1 | 31 | — |
| 753$^{18}$ | **Astrolabe (75)** (JMBradley) **4-8-8v**(3) SDrowne(10) (lw: led tl over 4f out: sn rdn & wknd) | nk | **10** | 14/1 | 39 | 2 |
| 1124$^{7}$ | **Prerogative (58)** (RSimpson) **6-9-2**(7) AimeeCook(4) (b: lw: trckd ldrs tl wknd 5f out: t.o) | 10 | **11** | 25/1 | 41 | 4 |
| | **Station Express (IRE)** (BJLlewellyn) **8-7-11**(5) MBaird(7) (s.i.s: a bhd: t.o) | 17 | **12** | 25/1 | 3 | — |
| 1700$^{5}$ | **Faugeron (54)** (NTinkler) **7-9-3** TQuinn(1) (w ldr: rdn 7f out: wknd over 4f out: eased whn btn: t.o) | 2 | **13** | 4/1$^{2}$ | 16 | — |
| 1611$^{3}$ | **Bobby's Dream (35)** (MHTompkins) **4-8-9** PRobinson(5) (wl bhd ½-wy: t.o) | dist | **14** | 12/1 | — | — |
| | | | | (SP 139.7%) | **14 Rn** | |

**3m 29.0** (6.00) CSF £24.65 TOTE £3.70: £1.60 £4.10 £3.90 (£23.40) Trio £78.80 OWNER Mr R. W. S. Jevon (SALTBURN) BRED B. Fairs

**1847 Brodessa** made short work of this field and could have won by a furlong had he not been steadied right down inside the final furlong. (9/4)

**Akiymann (USA)**, a winner on the level in France two years ago and fit from hurdling, did not like this lively ground and was lobbing along in the rear until staying on past beaten rivals to gain the runner-up prize right on the line. (9/1)

**1788 Genesis Four**, attempting this extended trip for the first time, moved into second place two furlongs out, but he failed to make any impression on the winner and was just touched off by the runner-up. (16/1)

**Access Sun**, out of action for almost a year, did not fare badly in the circumstances and, with this run to put an edge on him, should not have too much trouble in winning a similar event. (16/1)

**Erlemo**, fit from jumping, was staying on well in the closing stages, but far too late to cause concern. (25/1)

## 2183 BILBOROUGH H'CAP (0-70) (3-Y.O+) (Class E)

3-45 (3-46) **1m 1f 213y** £3,288.00 (£984.00: £472.00: £216.00) Stalls: Low GOING minus 0.58 sec per fur (F)

| Form | Horse | Dist | Pos | SP | RR | SF |
|---|---|---|---|---|---|---|
| 1496$^{3}$ | **Runic Symbol (37)** (MBlanshard) **5-7-10** JQuinn(7) (hld up in tch: hdwy 2f out: edgd lft fnl f: rdn to ld cl home) | — | **1** | 10/1 | 48 | 1 |
| 2058$^{6}$ | **Zahran (IRE) (39)** (JMBradley) **5-7-12** AMackay(9) (s.s: bhd: hdwy over 2f out: led wl ins fnl f: ct post) | hd | **2** | 16/1 | 50 | 3 |
| 1977$^{3}$ | **Augustan (49)** (SGollings) **5-8-8** VHalliday(4) (hld up: hdwy on ins over 2f out: n.m.r ent fnl f: r.o wl nr fin) | s.h | **3** | 12/1 | 60 | 13 |
| 1496$^{8}$ | **Fern's Governor (40)** (WJMusson) **4-7-13** DRMcCabe(11) (a.p: rdn to ld over 1f out: hdd wl ins fnl f) | 1¼ | **4** | 12/1 | 49 | 2 |
| 1411* | **Marchman (49)** (JSKing) **11-8-8** TQuinn(8) (trckd ldrs: n.m.r 2f out: hrd rdn & kpt on fnl f) | 1¼ | **5** | 8/1$^{3}$ | 56 | 9 |
| 2077$^{4}$ | **Pendolino (IRE) (41)** (MBrittain) **5-8-0b**ow1 GCarter(3) (led over 5f: rdn over 2f out: btn whn hmpd ins fnl f) | hd | **6** | 16/1 | 48 | — |
| 1838* | **Rival Bid (USA) (69)** (MrsNMacauley) **8-9-11**(3) CTeague(10) (hld up: hdwy over 2f out: nt rchd ldrs) | ½ | **7** | 10/1 | 75 | 28 |
| 1977$^{6}$ | **Gallardini (IRE) (40)** (BSRothwell) **7-7-13v**ow1 JFEgan(1) (trckd ldrs: drvn along 3f out: one pce fnl 2f) | 2½ | **8** | 16/1 | 42 | — |
| | **Spring Campaign (IRE) (69)** (MCPipe) **3-9-2** MRoberts(5) (w'like: leggy: bkwd: trckd ldr: led over 4f out tl over 1f out: btn whn hmpd ins fnl f) | ½ | **9** | 10/1 | 70 | 11 |
| 2014* | **Elpida (USA) (59)** (JPearce) **4-9-4** 6x GBardwell(12) (prom: rdn over 4f out: grad wknd) | s.h | **10** | 7/1$^{2}$ | 60 | 13 |
| 1955$^{4}$ | **Dragon's Back (IRE) (70)** (MrsJCecil) **3-9-3** JReid(15) (w'like: scope: chsd ldrs: rdn over 2f out: sn btn) | 1½ | **11** | 2/1$^{1}$ | 69 | 10 |
| *248*$^{6}$ | **Bold Joker (38)** (GROldroyd) **5-7-11**ow1 DaleGibson(2) (a in rr: t.o) | 10 | **12** | 50/1 | 20 | — |
| 1965$^{8}$ | **Teen Jay (61)** (BJLlewellyn) **6-9-6** VSlattery(13) (s.i.s: a in rr: t.o) | 3 | **13** | 14/1 | 39 | — |
| *138*$^{5}$ | **Acquittal (IRE) (56)** (AStreeter) **4-8-10**(5) RHavlin(14) (w'like: scope: hld up: hdwy 4f out: wknd wl over 2f out: t.o) | s.h | **14** | 20/1 | 34 | — |
| 1832$^{3}$ | **Irie Mon (IRE) (53)** (MPBielby) **4-8-12** DeanMcKeown(6) (trckd ldrs tl wknd 3f out: t.o) | 3½ | **15** | 14/1 | 25 | — |
| | | | | (SP 137.3%) | **15 Rn** | |

**2m 6.8** (4.30) CSF £159.07 CT £1819.38 TOTE £10.00: £2.90 £4.50 £3.50 (£31.80) Trio £66.90 OWNER Mr D. Sloan (UPPER LAMBOURN) BRED Worksop Manor Stud Farm

LONG HANDICAP Bold Joker 6-12 Runic Symbol 7-9

WEIGHT FOR AGE 3yo-12lb

**1496 Runic Symbol** has been a long time in winning a race but, produced just at the right time, he nosed ahead in the shadow of the post. (10/1)

**2058 Zahran (IRE)** lost so much ground at the start that he looked to have forfeited any chance of winning, but he worked hard to poke his head in front 100 yards out, and did not deserve to be touched off right on the line. (16/1)

**1977 Augustan** was probably an unlucky loser, for he had anything but a clear run when delivering his challenge up the inside and yet still only went down in a three-way photo. (12/1)

**Fern's Governor**, still to get off the mark, showed the way into the final furlong before getting tapped for speed close home. (12/1)

**1411* Marchman**, winner of a seller over course and distance last month, was tightened up when in full stride entering the last quarter-mile. Forced to check, he could not regain his momentum. (8/1)

**2077 Pendolino (IRE)** set the pace until halfway, but then found all the trouble going. He will benefit from easier ground, and there is a race in him. (16/1)

**1838* Rival Bid (USA)** (10/1: 7/1-12/1)

**2014* Elpida (USA)** (7/1: op 4/1)

**Teen Jay** (14/1: 10/1-16/1)

## 2184 E.B.F. MAIDEN STKS (2-Y.O) (Class D)

4-15 (4-16) **6f 15y** £2,176.45 (£2,176.45: £475.40: £213.70) Stalls: High GOING minus 0.58 sec per fur (F)

| Form | Horse | Dist | Pos | SP | RR | SF |
|---|---|---|---|---|---|---|
| | **Boojum** (BWHills) **2-8-9** MHills(1) (bit bkwd: s.s: hdwy ½-wy: led wl ins fnl f: r.o) | — | **1** | 13/8$^{1}$ | 61+ | 8 |
| 1779$^{4}$ | **Groom's Gordon (FR)** (JLDunlop) **2-9-0** PatEddery(2) (drvn along thrght: swtchd rt over 1f out: hrd rdn to jn ldr on line) | — | **1** | 7/4$^{2}$ | 66 | 13 |

| Form | Horse | Dist | Pos | SP | RR | SF |
|---|---|---|---|---|---|---|
| 1831[4] | **Impulsif (USA)** (DJSffrenchDavis) **2-9-0** RHughes(4) (led: edgd lft over 1f out: hdd wl ins fnl f) | ¾ | **3** | 13/2 | 64 | 11 |
| 1842[9] | **Classic Mystery (IRE)** (BJMeehan) **2-9-0** BDoyle(6) (lw: chsd ldr: rdn over 2f out: sn outpcd) | 3½ | **4** | 14/1 | 55 | 2 |
| | **Philosophic** (SirMarkPrescott) **2-9-0** GDuffield(3) (s.i.s: sn drvn along: outpcd fr ½-wy) | 8 | **5** | 7/1 | 34 | — |
| | **Kweilo** (JWPayne) **2-9-0** BThomson(5) (lw: s.s: hdwy ½-wy: wknd wl over 1f out) | 6 | **6** | 4/1[3] | 18 | — |

(SP 127.0%) **6 Rn**

**1m 13.1** (2.60) CSF £2.87 GG & B £2.80 B & GG TOTE £1.90 B £1.40 GG: £2.30 B £1.60 GG (£3.10) OWNER Mrs A. D. Bourne (LAMBOURN)/Mrs H. Focke (ARUNDEL) BRED W. H. F. Carson/Haras d'Etreham

**Boojum** would have won this easily had she got away on terms, but she had to do it the hard way. (13/8)

**1779 Groom's Gordon (FR)**, bustled along from the break, needed to be switched to obtain a clear run over a furlong out. With ground to make up, he responded to firm handling and got up on the line to share the spoils. (7/4)

**1831 Impulsif (USA)** made the running, but drifted off a true line approaching the final furlong and had shot his bolt 100 yards out. (13/2: 4/1-7/1)

**Classic Mystery (IRE)** (14/1: op 8/1)

**Philosophic** (7/1: op 7/2)

## 2185 RIVER TRENT H'CAP (0-60) (3-Y.O+) (Class F)

4-45 (4-46) **6f 15y** £2,385.00 (£660.00: £315.00) Stalls: High GOING minus 0.58 sec per fur (F)

| Form | Horse | Dist | Pos | SP | RR | SF |
|---|---|---|---|---|---|---|
| 1865[3] | **Cheeky Chappy (45)** (DWChapman) **5-8-13b** GDuffield(14) (mde all stands' side: overall ldr 2f out: drvn clr) | — | **1** | 3/1[1] | 62 | 24 |
| 1991[8] | **Rambold (57)** (NEBerry) **5-9-6**(5) CAdamson(6) (chsd ldrs far side: led ½-wy to 2f out: r.o one pce) | 2 | **2** | 10/1 | 69 | 31 |
| 1881[6] | **Martinosky (53)** (GCBravery) **10-9-7b** MHills(17) (racd stands' side: hdwy over 1f out: fin wl) | 4 | **3** | 10/1 | 54 | 16 |
| 1859[2] | **Rotherfield Park (IRE) (37)** (CSmith) **4-7-12**(7) IonaWands(19) (lw: trckd ldrs stands' side: kpt on u.p fnl f) | 1¼ | **4** | 9/1 | 35 | — |
| 1890[10] | **Asterix (39)** (JMBradley) **8-8-4v**(3) SDrowne(7) (hdwy over 1f out: nrst fin) | nk | **5** | 12/1 | 36 | — |
| 2030[3] | **Sonderise (55)** (NTinkler) **7-9-9** JOsborne(8) (hdwy far side over 2f out: one pce appr fnl f) | ½ | **6** | 8/1[3] | 51 | 13 |
| 2005[5] | **Aquado (59)** (SRBowring) **7-9-13b** JQuinn(16) (lw: trckd ldrs stands' side: no hdwy fnl 2f) | 2½ | **7** | 5/1[2] | 48 | 10 |
| 1642[14] | **Mu-Arrik (42)** (GROldroyd) **8-8-10v** DaleGibson(12) (in tch stands' side: rdn & one pce appr fnl f) | ½ | **8** | 16/1 | 30 | — |
| 2005[10] | **Just Dissident (IRE) (54)** (RMWhitaker) **4-9-8** DeanMcKeown(15) (lw: spd stands' side over 4f) | s.h | **9** | 10/1 | 42 | 4 |
| 1761[10] | **Mystic Times (48)** (MissJFCraze) **3-8-9v[1]** AMackay(9) (nvr trbld ldrs) | hd | **10** | 25/1 | 36 | — |
| 1787[9] | **Scott's Risk (37)** (LJBarratt) **6-8-5** NAdams(1) (b: nvr nr to chal) | 2 | **11** | 50/1 | 19 | — |
| 1876[8] | **Bella Coola (38)** (MartynMeade) **4-8-6** RPerham(18) (prom stands' side over 4f) | nk | **12** | 14/1 | 19 | — |
| *2084*[11] | **Niteowl Raider (IRE) (49)** (JAHarris) **3-8-10** JO'Reilly(2) (led far side to ½-wy: rdn & wknd 2f out) | ½ | **13** | 25/1 | 29 | — |
| *1606*[8] | **Disco Boy (45)** (PDEvans) **6-8-13b** CHodgson(5) (lw: in tch far side over 4f) | hd | **14** | 20/1 | 25 | — |
| 1170[8] | **The Fed (42)** (JAPickering) **6-8-3**(7) AngelaGallimore(3) (racd far side: effrt over 2f out: wknd wl over 1f out) | nk | **15** | 20/1 | 21 | — |
| | **Christian Flight (IRE) (46)** (SGollings) **7-9-0** VHalliday(10) (bkwd: prom centre 4f) | ¾ | **16** | 20/1 | 23 | — |
| 1840[15] | **Donington Park (42)** (PTDalton) **3-8-3** DRMcCabe(11) (outpcd fr ½-wy) | 1 | **17** | 33/1 | 16 | — |
| 1859[11] | **Penny's Wishing (43)** (NBycroft) **4-8-11** GBardwell(13) (a outpcd) | nk | **18** | 14/1 | 17 | — |
| *517*[6] | **Infiraaj (USA) (49)** (MrsDHaine) **4-9-3b** AMcGlone(4) (bit bkwd: racd far side: bhd fnl 3f: t.o) | 7 | **19** | 20/1 | 4 | — |

(SP 148.6%) **19 Rn**

**1m 12.2** (1.70) CSF £37.95 CT £287.16 TOTE £5.60: £1.80 £4.70 £2.20 £2.40 (£114.10) Trio £529.50 OWNER Mrs Jeanne Chapman (YORK) BRED Ian W. Glenton

WEIGHT FOR AGE 3yo-7lb

**1865 Cheeky Chappy**, winning his first race beyond the minimum trip, held the call up the stands' rail and, seeing off his rivals in the centre of the track inside the distance, was well on top nearing the line. (3/1)

**1634* Rambold** moved into the lead on the far side at halfway, but the winner proved much the stronger and had his measure inside the distance. (10/1)

**1516* Martinosky** is finding it hard to win at this trip nowadays and he was only finding his stride when the contest was nearly over. (10/1)

**1859 Rotherfield Park (IRE)** did not get going until far too late and the leading pair had got away. (9/1)

**1658 Asterix**, back to sprinting, was really into his stride inside the distance but, by then, the winner was beyond recall. (12/1)

T/Jkpt: £3,550.00 (2 Tckts). T/Plpt: £47.70 (302.6 Tckts). T/Qdpt: £31.50 (32.12 Tckts). IM

# 1833-WARWICK (L-H) (Firm)

## Monday June 24th

WEATHER: fine WIND: nil

## 2186 GO RACING WITH THE DAILY TELEGRAPH H'CAP (0-70) (3-Y.O+ F & M) (Class E)

6-15 (6-17) **5f** £3,206.70 (£957.60: £457.80: £207.90) Stalls: Low GOING minus 0.63 sec per fur (F)

| Form | Horse | Dist | Pos | SP | RR | SF |
|---|---|---|---|---|---|---|
| *2171*[3] | **Sing With the Band (58)** (BAMcMahon) **5-9-5** GCarter(1) (lw: mde all: clr over 2f out: easily) | — | **1** | 9/2[3] | 70+ | 48 |
| 1859* | **Dominelle (49)** (TDEasterby) **4-8-10** WJO'Connor(6) (a.p: chsd wnr fnl 2f: no imp) | 3 | **2** | 7/2[1] | 51 | 29 |
| *1971*[2] | **Raisa Point (40)** (WRMuir) **5-8-1** FNorton(7) (hmpd & lost pl after 1f: hdwy over 1f out: one pce fnl f) | 3½ | **3** | 6/1 | 31 | 9 |
| 1840[2] | **Croeso Cynnes (57)** (BPalling) **3-8-12** TSprake(8) (lw: stumbled s: hdwy 2f out: one pce fnl f) | 3 | **4** | 4/1[2] | 39 | 11 |
| 1715[8] | **Nellie North (67)** (GMMcCourt) **3-9-8** RHughes(9) (w ldrs over 3f) | 1¼ | **5** | 9/1 | 45 | 17 |
| 1170[4] | **Secret Miss (51)** (APJones) **4-8-12** JTate(5) (lw: dwlt: outpcd) | 2 | **6** | 10/1 | 22 | — |
| 1859[6] | **Highland Fawn (43)** (BAMcMahon) **3-7-12**ow1 JFEgan(2) (outpcd) | nk | **7** | 14/1 | 13 | — |
| 2021[9] | **Just Lady (70)** (WGMTurner) **3-9-8**(3) PMcCabe(4) (swtg: w wnr 3f: sn wknd) | 3½ | **8** | 11/1 | 29 | 1 |
| 1039[7] | **Followmegirls (50)** (MrsALMKing) **7-8-11** MRoberts(3) (bit bkwd: dwlt: bhd whn broke leg & uns rdr 3f out: dead) | | **U** | 14/1 | — | — |

(SP 115.4%) **9 Rn**

**58.0 secs** (0.00) CSF £19.52 CT £86.83 TOTE £3.40: £1.20 £2.00 £2.50 (£12.10) Trio £17.90 OWNER Mr D. J. Allen (TAMWORTH) BRED D. J. Allen

WEIGHT FOR AGE 3yo-6lb

**2171 Sing With the Band**, rated 15lb lower on turf than when third on the Sand two evenings ago, was certainly calling the tune from halfway and won with plenty in hand. (9/2)

**1859* Dominelle,** 4lb higher than when bouncing back to form at Beverley, was clearly second best on this occasion. (7/2)

**1971 Raisa Point** was running off the same mark as when runner-up on the All-Weather last time. (6/1)

**1840 Croeso Cynnes**, not helped by a miss-cue at the start, may need a return to six furlongs. (4/1)
**1304 Nellie North** has already been dropped 5lb this season. (9/1)
**1170 Secret Miss** is still 6lb higher than when winning on soft ground at Lingfield last September. (10/1)
**1859 Highland Fawn** (14/1: op 8/1)
**Just Lady** (11/1: 7/1-12/1)

## 2187 RAYNSFORD MAIDEN AUCTION STKS (2-Y.O F) (Class E)

6-45 (6-47) **7f** £2,988.30 (£890.40: £424.20: £191.10) Stalls: Low GOING minus 0.63 sec per fur (F)

| Form | Horse | Dist | Pos | SP | RR | SF |
|---|---|---|---|---|---|---|
| 1871[3] | **Briska (IRE)** (RHannon) **2-8-7** MRoberts(5) (lw: mde all: rdn 2f out: r.o wl) | — | 1 | 15/8[1] | 76 | 15 |
| 1871[2] | **Madame Chinnery** (JMPEustace) **2-8-3** JTate(4) (swtg: rdn over 3f out: rn wd bnd over 2f out: hdwy fnl f: r.o) | 1¾ | 2 | 2/1[2] | 68 | 7 |
| 1871[6] | **River of Fortune (IRE)** (MHTompkins) **2-8-3** PRobinson(6) (a.p: chsd wnr over 1f out: no imp) | nk | 3 | 5/2[3] | 67 | 6 |
| 1851[6] | **Dizzy Tilly** (TJNaughton) **2-8-3** GCarter(2) (jnd wnr over 5f out: wknd fnl f) | 2½ | 4 | 9/1 | 62 | 1 |
| 1851[8] | **My Precious** (MMcCormack) **2-7-12**(5)ow1 FLynch(3) (hdwy on ins over 2f out: wknd ins fnl f) | nk | 5 | 25/1 | 61 | — |
| 2031[8] | **Vivora** (MartynMeade) **2-8-5**ow3 RPerham(1) (hld up & plld hrd: carried wd over 2f out: sn bhd) | 11 | 6 | 33/1 | 38 | — |

(SP 113.5%) **6 Rn**

**1m 26.8** (2.20) CSF £5.96 TOTE £2.90: £1.60 £1.40 (£2.40) OWNER Lord Carnarvon (MARLBOROUGH) BRED A. M. F. Persse
**1871 Briska (IRE)** stayed on well over this extra furlong. (15/8)
**1871 Madame Chinnery** looked all at sea on the home turn and should be better suited to a more galloping course. (2/1)
**1851 Dizzy Tilly** could have found this trip beyond her at this stage of her career. (9/1)

## 2188 UGLY BRIDGE H'CAP (0-80) (3-Y.O+) (Class D)

7-15 (7-16) **1m** £3,720.00 (£1,110.00: £530.00: £240.00) Stalls: Low GOING minus 0.63 sec per fur (F)

| Form | Horse | Dist | Pos | SP | RR | SF |
|---|---|---|---|---|---|---|
| 1181[6] | **Al Shadeedah (USA) (78)** (LMCumani) **3-9-2** OUrbina(8) (lw: a.p: hrd rdn to ld last stride) | — | 1 | 3/1[2] | 84 | 46 |
| 1322[7] | **Bernard Seven (IRE) (75)** (CEBrittain) **4-9-6b**(3) HKYim(5) (chsd ldr: rdn to ld 1f out: hdd last stride) | s.h | 2 | 14/1 | 81 | 53 |
| 2032[2] | **Mr Cube (IRE) (53)** (JMBradley) **6-8-1v** AMackay(6) (bhd tl hdwy over 1f out: r.o ins fnl f) | 2½ | 3 | 7/2[3] | 54 | 26 |
| *55[11]* | **Pab's Choice (57)** (MMcCormack) **5-8-0**(5) MBaird(3) (a.p: rdn 2f out: one pce) | ½ | 4 | 16/1 | 57 | 29 |
| 1902[4] | **Knobbleeneeze (80)** (MRChannon) **6-10-0v** RHughes(1) (led: clr after 2f: hdd 1f out: wknd) | s.h | 5 | 8/1 | 80 | 52 |
| 1341[10] | **Eric's Bett (65)** (FMurphy) **3-7-12**(5) FLynch(4) (hld up & plld hrd: hdwy 3f out: wknd over 1f out) | 2 | 6 | 6/1 | 61 | 23 |
| 1886* | **Three Arch Bridge (68)** (MJohnston) **4-9-2b** MRoberts(7) (bhd fnl 3f) | 6 | 7 | 9/4[1] | 52 | 24 |
| | **Mapengo (68)** (JCullinan) **5-9-2** GCarter(9) (bkwd: a bhd: t.o fnl 3f) | dist | 8 | 33/1 | — | — |

(SP 118.9%) **8 Rn**

**1m 36.6** (0.20) CSF £38.54 CT £142.27 TOTE £4.90: £1.60 £2.20 £1.20 (£47.90) Trio £53.80 OWNER Umm Qarn Racing (NEWMARKET) BRED Swettenham Stud
WEIGHT FOR AGE 3yo-10lb
**1181 Al Shadeedah (USA)**, looking particularly well, appreciated this faster ground and snatched the verdict on the nod. (3/1)
**Bernard Seven (IRE)**, dropped 10lb following a couple of disappointing runs, bounced back to form but got pipped on the post. (14/1)
**2032 Mr Cube (IRE)** likes fast ground and seems to have struck form, but was never going to get there in time. (7/2)
**Pab's Choice** was 3lb lower than when scoring at Lingfield nearly two years ago. (16/1)
**1902 Knobbleeneeze**, upped a further 3lb, was nearly a stone higher than when winning at Chester, and went off too quickly for his own good. (8/1: 5/1-10/1)
**1072 Eric's Bett** proved difficult to settle, despite the strong pace. (6/1)
**1886* Three Arch Bridge**, upped 6lb, could not dominate, and Roberts reported the filly was hanging and never moving well. (9/4)

## 2189 GAVESTON (S) STKS (3-Y.O+) (Class G)

7-45 (7-45) **1m 2f 169y** £2,070.00 (£570.00: £270.00) Stalls: Low GOING minus 0.63 sec per fur (F)

| Form | Horse | Dist | Pos | SP | RR | SF |
|---|---|---|---|---|---|---|
| 2056[15] | **Yet Again (40)** (BHanbury) **4-9-7b** MRimmer(13) (lw: carried rt s: hdwy 9f out: led wl over 1f out: rdn out) | — | 1 | 8/1 | 49 | 31 |
| 2056[16] | **Risky Rose (35)** (RHollinshead) **4-8-11**(5) DGriffiths(7) (swtg: hld up & bhd: hdwy over 1f out: r.o ins fnl f: nt trble wnr) | 2 | 2 | 20/1 | 41 | 23 |
| | **Siesta Time (USA)** (RJO'Sullivan) **6-9-2** AProcter(6) (a.p: rdn & hung lft 2f out: swtchd rt over 1f out: r.o one pce) | 1½ | 3 | 25/1 | 39 | 21 |
| | **Trade Wind (70)** (JGMO'Shea) **5-9-7b** VSlattery(4) (a.p: n.m.r on ins 1f out: r.o one pce) | 1½ | 4 | 9/1 | 42 | 24 |
| 1996[7] | **Striffolino (70)** (JohnBerry) **4-9-4**(3) PMcCabe(11) (chsd ldr: ev ch wl over 1f out: wknd fnl f) | ½ | 5 | 6/1[3] | 41 | 23 |
| 2033[7] | **Nosey Native (72)** (JPearce) **3-8-8** GBardwell(10) (lw: hld up: rdn over 3f out: no hdwy) | ½ | 6 | 9/4[1] | 40 | 9 |
| 1828[6] | **Hunza Story (25)** (NPLittmoden) **4-8-9**(7) JoHunnam(8) (nvr nr to chal) | 1½ | 7 | 25/1 | 33 | 15 |
| 1984[5] | **Fijon (IRE) (62)** (BWHills) **3-8-3** DHolland(3) (led tl wl over 1f out: btn whn hmpd & swtchd rt ins fnl f) | nk | 8 | 100/30[2] | 32 | 1 |
| 1411[15] | **Spice and Sugar (35)** (BRCambidge) **6-8-9**(7) IonaWands(1) (prom tl rdn & wknd over 2f out) | 3½ | 9 | 50/1 | 27 | 9 |
| 1698[4] | **Reefa's Mill (IRE) (60)** (JNeville) **4-9-4v**(3) SDrowne(14) (lw: carried rt s: a bhd) | nk | 10 | 8/1 | 32 | 14 |
| 2026[14] | **Miss Express (BEL)** (MrsSJSmith) **3-8-4**ow1 PBloomfield(9) (b: a bhd) | 3½ | 11 | 50/1 | 23 | — |
| *1602[8]* | **Crown And Cushion** (KSBridgwater) **3-8-8** WJO'Connor(12) (wnt rt s: prom over 4f out: t.o) | 12 | 12 | 33/1 | 9 | — |
| 2036[9] | **Panto Queen** (CRBarwell) **5-9-2** TSprake(5) (hld up: a bhd: t.o) | 5 | 13 | 16/1 | — | — |

(SP 125.6%) **13 Rn**

**2m 16.7** (3.20) CSF £141.48 TOTE £8.60: £1.60 £3.10 £5.40 (£62.00) Trio £163.60; £207.42 to 26/6/96 OWNER Mr G. G. Grayson (NEWMARKET) BRED Aston Park Stud
WEIGHT FOR AGE 3yo-13lb
No bid
**1691 Yet Again** had the blinkers refitted after his disappointing run last time. (8/1)
**Risky Rose** seems to have come to hand and really needs a stiffer test of stamina. (20/1)
**Siesta Time (USA)** disappointed over hurdles recently and had only run on soft ground on the Flat in Ireland. He did not look an easy ride. (25/1)
**Trade Wind**, sold out of David Elsworth's yard for 7,400 guineas last November, did not get the best of passages up the inner in the home straight. (9/1)
**Striffolino** has yet to win beyond nine furlongs. (6/1)
**1669 Nosey Native**, tried in a visor last time, never really appeared likely to justify favouritism. (9/4)
**1698 Reefa's Mill (IRE)** (8/1: 6/1-9/1)

## 2190 F. A. SIMMS H'CAP (0-80) (3-Y.O+) (Class D)

8-15 (8-15) **1m 6f 194y** £3,752.50 (£1,120.00: £535.00: £242.50) Stalls: Low GOING minus 0.63 sec per fur (F)

| | Horse / details | | Pos | SP | RR | SF |
|---|---|---|---|---|---|---|
| 1852[3] | **Tonys Gift (65)** (MCPipe) **4-9-4** MRoberts(2) (lw: led 1f: hld up: led wl over 1f out: cleverly) | — | 1 | 11/4[2] | 75+ | 39 |
| 1875[2] | **Pearl Venture (72)** (SPCWoods) **4-9-11** RHughes(5) (hld up: hdwy on ins 2f out: ev ch 1f out: rdn & unable qckn ins fnl f) | nk | 2 | 3/1[3] | 82 | 46 |
| 1862[3] | **Deano's Beeno (75)** (MJohnston) **4-10-0** PRobinson(4) (lw: led after 1f to 12f out: rdn & ev ch 2f out: one pce) | 2½ | 3 | 5/1 | 82 | 46 |
| 1981* | **Mr Copyforce (48)** (MissBSanders) **6-7-12**(3)ow2 AWhelan(3) (plld hrd: a.p: led over 2f out tl wl over 1f out: one pce) | ½ | 4 | 5/2[1] | 55 | 17 |
| 1695[3] | **Mizyan (IRE) (60)** (JEBanks) **8-8-13** GCarter(1) (led 12f out: rdn & hdd over 2f out: eased whn btn fnl f) | 3½ | 5 | 5/1 | 63 | 27 |
| | | | | (SP 113.6%) | **5 Rn** | |

**3m 12.5** (2.50) CSF £10.83 TOTE £3.10: £2.20 £1.70 (£6.90) OWNER The Blue Chip Group (WELLINGTON) BRED Mrs Sean Kelly and West Lodge Stud

**1852 Tonys Gift**, stepping up in distance, scored more decisively than the margin suggests. (11/4)
**1875 Pearl Venture** found the winner too strong in the closing stages. (3/1)
**1862 Deano's Beeno**, trying a longer trip, again found lack of a turn of foot the problem in a slowly-run race. (5/1)
**1981* Mr Copyforce**, raised a further 4lb, could not complete the hat-trick in what turned out to be another slowly-run affair. (5/2)
**1695 Mizyan (IRE)** has dropped again to the mark at which he was last successful. (5/1)

## 2191 BLACKBRAKE PLANTATION MAIDEN H'CAP (0-60) (3-Y.O+) (Class F)

8-45 (8-46) **1m 4f 115y** £3,285.40 (£914.40: £440.20) Stalls: Low GOING minus 0.63 sec per fur (F)

| | Horse / details | | Pos | SP | RR | SF |
|---|---|---|---|---|---|---|
| 1837[4] | **Reaganesque (USA) (42)** (PGMurphy) **4-8-11**(3) SDrowne(5) (lw: mde all: clr 2f out: r.o wl) | — | 1 | 11/2[1] | 53 | 29 |
| 1661[4] | **Two Socks (55)** (MMcCormack) **3-8-12** RHughes(11) (lw: hld up & bhd: hdwy 3f out: chsd wnr over 1f out: r.o one pce) | 1¾ | 2 | 8/1[3] | 64 | 25 |
| 1591[5] | **Sterling Fellow (49)** (RHannon) **3-8-6b[1]** JFEgan(7) (lw: hld up: stdy hdwy 5f out: r.o ins fnl f) | 1¾ | 3 | 8/1[3] | 56 | 17 |
| 1514[8] | **Miss Prism (47)** (JLDunlop) **3-8-4** SWhitworth(13) (hld up: stdy hdwy 5f out: one pce fnl 2f) | 2 | 4 | 11/2[1] | 51 | 12 |
| 1696[9] | **Mr Speculator (56)** (PAKelleway) **3-8-13** GBardwell(1) (prom: rdn over 4f out: wknd over 1f out) | 2½ | 5 | 20/1 | 57 | 18 |
| 1883[4] | **Efficacious (IRE) (48)** (CJBenstead) **3-8-5** AMcGlone(3) (b.hind: hld up: chsd wnr over 2f out tl over 1f out: eased whn btn ins fnl f) | 1½ | 6 | 11/2[1] | 47 | 8 |
| 1655[4] | **Junior Ben (IRE) (52)** (PHowling) **4-9-10** FNorton(12) (lw: hld up & bhd: hdwy on ins over 2f out: sn rdn: one pce) | 3 | 7 | 11/2[1] | 47 | 23 |
| 2028[7] | **Remontant (IRE) (42)** (RHollinshead) **4-8-9**(5) FLynch(10) (hld up & bhd: nvr trbld ldrs) | 1¾ | 8 | 8/1[3] | 35 | 11 |
| 1534[5] | **Hillswick (28)** (JSKing) **5-8-0** AMackay(9) (prom tl wknd over 2f out) | 2½ | 9 | 14/1 | 18 | — |
| 660[7] | **Shirley Sue (52)** (MJohnston) **3-8-9** MRoberts(2) (lw: hld up mid div: wknd qckly 3f out) | 1¼ | 10 | 7/1[2] | 40 | 1 |
| | **Lorcanjo (36)** (AJChamberlain) **5-8-8** PRobinson(6) (b: prom 9f: t.o) | 19 | 11 | 14/1 | — | — |
| | | | | (SP 125.5%) | **11 Rn** | |

**2m 41.6** (3.10) CSF £48.02 CT £331.06 TOTE £6.20: £1.80 £1.50 £4.10 (£24.50) Trio £151.90 OWNER Mrs John Spielman (BRISTOL) BRED Gainsborough Farm Inc

WEIGHT FOR AGE 3yo-15lb

**1837 Reaganesque (USA),** dropped a further 4lb, took full advantage and justified market support in fine style. (11/2)
**1661 Two Socks** seemed well suited to the longer trip, but the winner was not for the catching. (8/1: op 12/1)
**1591 Sterling Fellow** was tried in blinkers after failing to stay two miles plus last time. (8/1)
**Miss Prism** was making her handicap debut off a low mark in lowly company. (11/2)
**Mr Speculator** did not seem suited to this stiffer test of stamina. (20/1)
**1883 Efficacious (IRE)** is another who may be better at shorter trips. (11/2)
**1655 Junior Ben (IRE)** could not take advantage of coming down 3lb this season, despite a couple of reasonable efforts. (11/2)

T/Plpt: £597.50 (18.47 Tckts). T/Qdpt: £619.80 (1.2 Tckts). KH

# 2031-WINDSOR (Fig. 8) (Good to firm)
## Monday June 24th

WEATHER: fine & sunny WIND: nil

## 2192 ROSE (S) H'CAP (0-60) (3-Y.O+) (Class G)

6-30 (6-33) **1m 2f 7y** £2,710.00 (£760.00: £370.00) Stalls: High GOING minus 0.41 sec per fur (F)

| | Horse / details | | Pos | SP | RR | SF |
|---|---|---|---|---|---|---|
| 1979[2] | **Voices in the Sky (30)** (AGNewcombe) **5-8-0**ow1 SSanders(7) (lw: a.p: led wl over 1f out: r.o wl) | — | 1 | 13/2[2] | 42 | 30 |
| 1682[3] | **Zeliba (29)** (CEBrittain) **4-7-10**(3) MHenry(4) (hdwy 4f out: chsd wnr fnl f: no imp) | 4 | 2 | 10/1 | 35 | 24 |
| *1967*[4] | **Sinclair Lad (IRE) (35)** (RJHodges) **8-8-0b**(5) PPMurphy(3) (lw: chsd ldr: led 3f out tl wl over 1f out: nt qckn) | 2½ | 3 | 14/1 | 37 | 26 |
| 1979[3] | **Eskimo Kiss (IRE) (40)** (MJFetherston-Godley) **3-7-9**(3) NVarley(12) (a.p: rdn 2f out: nt qckn) | ¾ | 4 | 12/1 | 40 | 17 |
| 1953[15] | **Johns Joy (38)** (JJBridger) **11-8-8** GHind(15) (b: lw: mid div whn hmpd 6f out: gd hdwy fnl 2f) | 1 | 5 | 33/1 | 37 | 26 |
| 2056[10] | **Bronze Runner (36)** (EAWheeler) **12-8-1b**(5) ADaly(2) (a.p: r.o one pce fnl 2f) | 1 | 6 | 12/1 | 33 | 22 |
| 1999[5] | **Jona Holley (45)** (IABalding) **3-7-12**(5) MartinDwyer(10) (hdwy fnl 2f: nt rch ldrs) | hd | 7 | 12/1 | 42 | 19 |
| | **Excelled (IRE) (35)** (CJDrewe) **7-8-5** KDarley(19) (no hdwy fnl 3f) | s.h | 8 | 20/1 | 32 | 21 |
| *1719*[11] | **Fastini Gold (49)** (MDIUsher) **4-9-5** TQuinn(8) (lw: nvr nr to chal) | 3 | 9 | 20/1 | 41 | 30 |
| 2056[3] | **Shuttlecock (35)** (MrsNMacauley) **5-8-5** RPrice(9) (b: lw: nvr nrr) | ¾ | 10 | 8/1[3] | 26 | 15 |
| 1893[6] | **Beyond Our Reach (48)** (RJHodges) **8-9-4** PatEddery(6) (prom tl wknd over 2f out) | 1¼ | 11 | 6/1[1] | 37 | 26 |
| | **Orchard Gold (42)** (JPearce) **5-8-12** CRutter(21) (b: nvr bttr than mid div) | 2½ | 12 | 20/1 | 27 | 16 |
| | **Pink Petal (27)** (RJBaker) **4-7-11** NKennedy(22) (led tl wknd 3f out) | 3 | 13 | 40/1 | 7 | — |
| 1893[16] | **Moving Up (IRE) (56)** (GLMoore) **3-9-0** SWhitworth(13) (lw: sme late hdwy) | nk | 14 | 16/1 | 36 | 13 |
| 1903[5] | **Still Here (IRE) (42)** (MJHeaton-Ellis) **3-7-7**(7) JFowle(14) (a bhd) | ¾ | 15 | 16/1 | 21 | — |
| | **John Tufty (38)** (JPearce) **5-8-1**(7) SGaillard(17) (a bhd) | ½ | 16 | 33/1 | 16 | 5 |
| 1314[17] | **Dolly Dolittle (26)** (HJCollingridge) **5-7-3**(7) PDoe(11) (a bhd) | ½ | 17 | 40/1 | 3 | — |
| 1411[11] | **Awesome Power (43)** (JWHills) **10-8-13** AClark(16) (nvr trbld ldrs) | 2 | 18 | 14/1 | 17 | 6 |
| 1965[13] | **Tauten (IRE) (55)** (PBurgoyne) **6-9-8**(3) JStack(20) (wl bhd fnl 6f) | hd | 19 | 20/1 | 29 | 18 |

| | | | | SP | RR | SF |
|---|---|---|---|---|---|---|
| 1870$^{7}$ | **Manabar (58)** (MJPolglase) **4-10-0v$^{1}$** DHarrison(18) (s.s: nvr on terms) | ½ | **20** | 20/1 | 31 | 20 |
| *1993*$^{9}$ | **Adilov (57)** (KOCunningham-Brown) **4-9-6**(7) CMunday(5) (lw: wl bhd fnl 6f) | nk | **21** | 25/1 | 29 | 18 |
| 508$^{12}$ | **Joli's Great (43)** (MJRyan) **8-8-13b** MTebbutt(23) (wl bhd fnl 6f) | 8 | **22** | 25/1 | 3 | — |
| *2082*$^{7}$ | **Chilly Lad (50)** (MJRyan) **5-9-6v** TIves(1) (lw: wl bhd fnl 6f: t.o) | 12 | **23** | 20/1 | — | — |

(SP 143.0%) **23 Rn**

**2m 7.7** (2.80) CSF £72.26 CT £852.25 TOTE £5.30: £1.60 £2.60 £5.60 £2.60 (£30.70) Trio £205.10 OWNER Mr J. A. F. Cairns (BARNSTAPLE) BRED Kiplingcotes Stud

LONG HANDICAP Dolly Dolittle 6-13

WEIGHT FOR AGE 3yo-12lb

No bid; Zeliba clmd RPeters £6,000

**1979 Voices in the Sky**, always handily placed, went to the front below the distance and, shaken up, readily drew clear. (13/2)

**1682 Zeliba** made a forward move early in the straight. She took second place entering the final furlong, but could make no impression on the winner. (10/1)

**1967 Sinclair Lad (IRE)** raced in second place until leading three furlongs out. Quickly outpaced below the distance, he kept on under pressure. (14/1)

**1979 Eskimo Kiss (IRE)**, always chasing the leaders, stayed on at one pace in the final quarter-mile. (12/1: op 8/1)

**Johns Joy**, badly hampered approaching the straight, did extremely well to reach fifth place and, despite his age, may still be capable of winning a similar event. (33/1)

**Bronze Runner** went with the leaders from the start. He could find no extra in the last two furlongs, but usually comes to hand at this time of year and can be followed against similar company. (12/1)

**2056 Shuttlecock** (8/1: 6/1-10/1)

**1893 Beyond Our Reach** was well placed until weakening over two furlongs out. (6/1)

## 2193 RAFFLES NIGHTCLUB AND PIPER CHAMPAGNE H'CAP (0-70) (3-Y.O+) (Class E)

7-00 (7-03) **5f 217y** £3,062.50 (£925.00: £450.00: £212.50) Stalls: High GOING minus 0.18 sec per fur (GF)

| | | | | SP | RR | SF |
|---|---|---|---|---|---|---|
| 1856$^{3}$ | **Pointer (44)** (MrsPNDutfield) **4-8-4**ow1 TQuinn(2) (hdwy over 2f out: led over 1f out: drvn out) | — | **1** | 13/2$^{3}$ | 55 | 32 |
| 1890$^{4}$ | **Lorins Gold (39)** (AndrewTurnell) **6-7-10**(3) MHenry(6) (w ldrs: led wl over 1f out: sn hdd: r.o) | 2½ | **2** | 8/1 | 43 | 21 |
| 1985$^{6}$ | **Louisville Belle (IRE) (44)** (MDIUsher) **7-8-4** DHarrison(5) (hdwy 2f out: ev ch 1f out: nt qckn) | ½ | **3** | 8/1 | 47 | 25 |
| 1840$^{3}$ | **Mystery Matthias (51)** (MissBSanders) **3-8-4b** SSanders(10) (lw: led over 4f: kpt on) | ½ | **4** | 8/1 | 53 | 24 |
| 2034$^{2}$ | **Dancing Heart (65)** (BJMeehan) **4-9-4**(7) DSweeney(11) (a.p: one pce fnl 2f) | 1½ | **5** | 11/2$^{1}$ | 63 | 41 |
| 1881$^{3}$ | **Merrie le Bow (49)** (PatMitchell) **4-8-4**(5) AmandaSanders(12) (nvr nrr) | ¾ | **6** | 9/1 | 45 | 23 |
| 1667$^{7}$ | **Spandrel (60)** (HCandy) **4-9-6** CRutter(13) (hdwy 2f out: nvr nr to chal) | 1¼ | **7** | 13/2$^{3}$ | 52 | 30 |
| 1844$^{3}$ | **Gone Savage (58)** (WJMusson) **8-9-4** JReid(4) (w ldrs tl wknd wl over 1f out) | s.h | **8** | 6/1$^{2}$ | 50 | 28 |
| 2129$^{11}$ | **Samsolom (60)** (PHowling) **8-9-6** PaulEddery(8) (b.hind: a bhd) | 1½ | **9** | 10/1 | 48 | 26 |
| 1715$^{10}$ | **Don't Tell Vicki (47)** (JSMoore) **3-7-7**(7)ow2 JKeenan(7) (lw: a bhd) | nk | **10** | 25/1 | 34 | 3 |
| 1840$^{6}$ | **Manderella (62)** (JAkehurst) **3-9-1** SWhitworth(3) (b.hind: bhd fnl 3f) | 6 | **11** | 14/1 | 33 | 4 |
| 2049$^{11}$ | **Ramsey Hope (67)** (CWFairhurst) **3-9-6b** NKennedy(9) (prom 3f) | 3½ | **12** | 14/1 | 29 | — |
| *531*$^{9}$ | **Subtle One (IRE) (43)** (TTClement) **3-7-7**(3) NVarley(1) (swtg: t.o fnl 4f) | 30 | **13** | 33/1 | — | — |

(SP 128.9%) **13 Rn**

**1m 13.4** (2.90) CSF £57.41 CT £400.80 TOTE £9.50: £2.50 £3.00 £4.00 (£73.70) Trio £226.80 OWNER In For The Crack (SEATON) BRED Darley Stud Management Co Ltd

LONG HANDICAP Subtle One (IRE) 7-6

WEIGHT FOR AGE 3yo-7lb

**1856 Pointer** moved up soon after halfway. He gained a narrow lead at the distance and drew clear under pressure in the last furlong. (13/2)

**1890 Lorins Gold** went with the leaders. He put his head in front momentarily below the distance but, soon headed, could not quicken with the winner. (8/1: 6/1-9/1)

**1985 Louisville Belle (IRE)** loomed up in the centre of the course two furlongs out but, after looking dangerous entering the final furlong, could not quicken when pressure was applied. (8/1)

**1840 Mystery Matthias** held a narrow lead on the stands' rail and kept on when headed below the distance. (8/1: 5/1-8/1)

**2034 Dancing Heart**, always tracking the leaders on the stands' rail, kept on at one pace when pressure was applied. (11/2)

**1881 Merrie le Bow** ran on in the last two furlongs, but too late to trouble the leaders. (9/1)

**1667 Spandrel** came with a run on the stands' rail two furlongs out, but it was soon clear she could not reach the leaders, and the position was accepted. (13/2)

## 2194 PRINCESS MARY OBOLENSKY UNDERWOOD FOUNDATION CONDITIONS STKS (3-Y.O+) (Class C)

7-30 (7-33) **1m 2f 7y** £4,930.60 (£1,845.40: £902.70: £388.50: £174.25: £88.55) Stalls: High GOING minus 0.41 sec per fur (F)

| | | | | SP | RR | SF |
|---|---|---|---|---|---|---|
| 1770$^{6}$ | **Musetta (IRE) (102)** (CEBrittain) **4-8-13** BDoyle(6) (b.off fore: lw: led tl over 2f out: led over 1f out: r.o wl) | — | **1** | 6/1 | 89 | 36 |
| 919$^{6}$ | **Valley of Gold (FR)** (SbinSuroor) **4-9-3** JReid(3) (lw: chsd wnr: led over 2f out tl over 1f out: hrd rdn: r.o) | ½ | **2** | 100/30$^{2}$ | 92 | 39 |
| 1948a$^{3}$ | **River North (IRE) (110)** (LadyHerries) **6-9-4** KDarley(2) (a.p: outpcd over 2f out: rallied over 1f out: nt qckn) | 1½ | **3** | 7/2$^{3}$ | 91 | 38 |
| | **Kings Witness (USA) (109)** (WJHaggas) **3-8-10** BThomson(7) (a.p: rdn over 3f out: wknd fnl f) | 3 | **4** | 9/4$^{1}$ | 90 | 25 |
| 1824$^{6}$ | **Leonato (FR)** (PDEvans) **4-9-4** TIves(1) (lw: plld hrd: hdwy 4f out: wknd over 1f out) | 1¼ | **5** | 25/1 | 84 | 31 |
| 1817$^{3}$ | **Wot No Fax** (SDow) **3-8-10** SSanders(5) (lw: nvr nr to chal) | ½ | **6** | 11/2 | 87 | 22 |
| 1867$^{3}$ | **Otto E Mezzo** (MJPolglase) **4-9-4** DHarrison(4) (a bhd) | s.h | **7** | 20/1 | 83 | 30 |
| 2015$^{3}$ | **Red Viper** (NMLampard) **4-8-11**(7) RBrisland(8) (a bhd: t.o) | 11 | **8** | 66/1 | 31 t | 13 |

(SP 115.8%) **8 Rn**

**2m 8.4** (3.50) CSF £25.13 TOTE £7.80: £1.70 £1.40 £1.70 (£11.00) OWNER Mr B. H. Voak (NEWMARKET) BRED Gainsborough Stud Management Ltd

WEIGHT FOR AGE 3yo-12lb

**1770 Musetta (IRE)** set off in front. She looked beaten when headed over two furlongs from home, but ran on to regain the advantage at the distance. In a great fight to the line, she held on bravely. (6/1)

**919 Valley of Gold (FR)** raced in second place until leading over two furlongs from home. Headed at the distance, she could not hold the winner's renewed challenge. (100/30)

**1948a River North (IRE)** settled down in third place, but was chopped for speed approaching the junction. Rallying below the distance, he stayed on but could not peg back the first two. (7/2)

**Kings Witness (USA)**, making his seasonal debut, looked fit and well and travelled strongly in fourth place to the straight. He came under pressure over three furlongs from home, and weakened in the last furlong. He should be better for the outing. (9/4)

## 2195 E.B.F. MEDIAN AUCTION MAIDEN STKS (2-Y.O) (Class D)

8-00 (8-02) **5f 217y** £3,403.75 (£1,030.00: £502.50: £238.75) Stalls: High GOING minus 0.18 sec per fur (GF)

| | | | | SP | RR | SF |
|---|---|---|---|---|---|---|
| 2009[2] | **Maladerie (IRE)** (MRChannon) **2-9-0** TQuinn(3) (a.p: led over 1f out: all out) | — | **1** | 9/2[2] | 76 | 27 |
| 1622[4] | **Lamarita** (JMPEustace) **2-8-9** MTebbutt(8) (a.p: ev ch fnl f: edgd lft: r.o) | nk | **2** | 9/2[2] | 70 | 21 |
| 1896[6] | **Marsad (IRE)** (CJBenstead) **2-9-0** RHills(7) (bit bkwd: led: edgd lft & hdd over 1f out: r.o) | hd | **3** | 6/1[3] | 75 | 26 |
| | **Craigievar** (JRFanshawe) **2-9-0** DHarrison(1) (lt-f: hdwy 2f out: r.o ins fnl f) | 1½ | **4** | 12/1 | 71 | 22 |
| 1878[5] | **Kenwood Melody** (MBell) **2-9-0** MFenton(4) (lw: no hdwy fnl 2f) | 3 | **5** | 20/1 | 63 | 14 |
| 1653[4] | **Rudi's Pet (IRE)** (RHannon) **2-9-0** PatEddery(5) (lw: rdn along: w ldrs tl wknd over 1f out) | 1 | **6** | 5/2[1] | 60 | 11 |
| 1437[6] | **Palisander (IRE)** (SDow) **2-9-0** SSanders(6) (w ldrs: wkng whn nt clr run over 1f out) | 2½ | **7** | 16/1 | 54 | 5 |
| | **Secret Ballot (IRE)** (RHannon) **2-9-0** BThomson(2) (w'like: nvr nrr) | 1¼ | **8** | 16/1 | 50 | 1 |
| | **Petrel** (LordHuntingdon) **2-8-9** JReid(11) (leggy: unf: nvr bttr than mid div) | ¾ | **9** | 9/1 | 43 | — |
| | **Harmony Hall** (JRFanshawe) **2-8-11**(3) NVarley(13) (b.hind: str: bit bkwd: a bhd) | 1½ | **10** | 20/1 | 44 | — |
| | **Royal Blackbird** (JEBanks) **2-8-6**(3) JStack(9) (leggy: lt-f: prom tl wknd over 2f out) | ½ | **11** | 8/1 | 38 | — |
| | **Diamond Lil** (CEBrittain) **2-8-9** BDoyle(12) (neat: s.s: a bhd) | 5 | **12** | 16/1 | 25 | — |
| 1896[13] | **Rupert's Double (IRE)** (BJMeehan) **2-9-0** JQuinn(10) (prom tl wknd over 2f out) | nk | **13** | 40/1 | 29 | — |
| | **Sharp Poppet** (MBell) **2-8-2**(7) GFaulkner(14) (a bhd) | | **14** | 20/1 | — | — |
| | | | | (SP 142.4%) | **14 Rn** | |

**1m 14.5** (4.00) CSF £28.26 TOTE £5.20: £1.60 £1.70 £2.70 (£8.80) Trio £45.60 OWNER Mr R. M. Brehaut (UPPER LAMBOURN) BRED Yeomanstown Lodge Stud

**2009 Maladerie (IRE)** was always close up. He gained a narrow lead at the distance and held on well enough. (9/2: 3/1-5/1)

**1622 Lamarita** tracked the leaders and looked the winner when moving up to challenge entering the final furlong. She edged left under pressure and gave away more ground than she was beaten by. (9/2)

**1896 Marsad (IRE)** looked in need of the race and, in the circumstances, ran extremely well. He made the running until edging left approaching the final furlong and kept on well to the end. (6/1)

**Craigievar** came with a promising effort two furlongs out and, after hanging fire, ran on again inside the final furlong. (12/1: 8/1-16/1)

**1878 Kenwood Melody** loomed up on the outside to challenge two furlongs out, but she could make no further progress in the final furlong and a half. (20/1)

**1653 Rudi's Pet (IRE)**, racing up with the leaders, was being ridden along virtually from the start and his chance had gone before the furlong marker. (5/2)

## 2196 RAFFLES NIGHTCLUB H'CAP (0-70) (3-Y.O) (Class E)

8-30 (8-31) **1m 3f 135y** £3,143.75 (£950.00: £462.50: £218.75) Stalls: High GOING minus 0.41 sec per fur (F)

| | | | | SP | RR | SF |
|---|---|---|---|---|---|---|
| 2033[2] | **Shaha (66)** (RHannon) **3-9-3b** PatEddery(8) (mde all: rdn 4f out: styd on wl: eased nr fin) | — | **1** | 2/1[1] | 74+ | 30 |
| 1874[2] | **High Desire (IRE) (56)** (JRArnold) **3-8-4**(3) MHenry(3) (hld up in rr: gd hdwy to chse wnr 2f out: r.o wl) | ½ | **2** | 7/2[2] | 63 | 19 |
| 1887[9] | **Manoy (61)** (JHetherton) **3-8-12b** KDarley(9) (chsd wnr: rdn 4f out: one pce fnl 2f) | 7 | **3** | 12/1 | 59 | 15 |
| 1485[9] | **Zdenka (58)** (MBlanshard) **3-8-9** JQuinn(7) (hdwy 3f out: one pce fnl 2f) | 2 | **4** | 25/1 | 53 | 9 |
| 1855[5] | **Tsarskaya (USA) (63)** (MrsJCecil) **3-9-0** BThomson(6) (lw: in tch tl wknd 3f out) | ½ | **5** | 6/1 | 57 | 13 |
| 1591[6] | **Ewar Bold (70)** (CEBrittain) **3-9-7b**[1] BDoyle(5) (prom tl wknd over 3f out) | 9 | **6** | 16/1 | 52 | 8 |
| 1089[11] | **Safecracker (66)** (JWHills) **3-9-3** RHills(2) (lw: a bhd) | 7 | **7** | 8/1 | 38 | — |
| 1514[2] | **Poly My Son (IRE) (53)** (MRChannon) **3-8-4** TQuinn(1) (lw: prom 6f: wknd qckly: t.o fnl 3f) | dist | **8** | 5/1[3] | — | — |
| | | | | (SP 115.0%) | **8 Rn** | |

**2m 29.5** (5.50) CSF £9.15 CT £58.64 TOTE £2.60: £1.20 £1.30 £3.00 (£4.10) Trio £16.50 OWNER Mr Salem Suhail (MARLBOROUGH) BRED G. S. Haywood and Darley Stud Management Co Ltd

OFFICIAL EXPLANATION **Poly My Son (IRE): was found to be lame on his near-fore the following morning.**

**2033 Shaha**, well suited by the extra distance, made the running and set off to make it a real test of stamina. Kicking for home early in the straight, he had most of his rivals in trouble in a short space of time and had only the runner-up to worry about from the two-furlong marker. He was able to ease up near the line. (2/1)

**1874 High Desire (IRE)**, held up in last place, came with a good run to go four lengths second at the two-furlong marker. Gamely as she strove, she never appeared likely to catch the winner. (7/2)

**1636* Manoy** was soon racing in second, but was under pressure early in the straight when the winner kicked on. He kept on at one pace in the last two furlongs. (12/1: 7/1-14/1)

**Zdenka** made a forward move three furlongs out, but could make no further progress in the final quarter-mile. (25/1)

**1855 Tsarskaya (USA)**, in mid-division throughout, was under pressure four furlongs from home and could make no headway. (6/1: 4/1-7/1)

**1591 Ewar Bold** was in touch with the leaders until weakening three furlongs from home. (16/1)

## 2197 FINANCIAL ADVISER MAIDEN STKS (3-Y.O) (Class D)

9-00 (9-02) **1m 67y** £3,987.00 (£1,206.00: £588.00: £279.00) Stalls: High GOING minus 0.41 sec per fur (F)

| | | | | SP | RR | SF |
|---|---|---|---|---|---|---|
| 1427[3] | **Kammtarra (USA)** (SbinSuroor) **3-9-0** JReid(1) (lw: mde all: pushed out: unchal) | — | **1** | Evens[1] | 88+ | 35 |
| 1855[7] | **Idle Fancy** (LordHuntingdon) **3-8-9** TIves(6) (hdwy 3f out: chsd wnr fnl 2f: no imp) | 9 | **2** | 25/1 | 66 | 13 |
| 1142[10] | **Dilazar (USA)** (JRFanshawe) **3-9-0** DHarrison(13) (lw: a.p: rdn 3f out: r.o one pce) | 1½ | **3** | 6/1[3] | 68 | 15 |
| | **Danish Circus (IRE) (82)** (MJHeaton-Ellis) **3-9-0** AClark(10) (a.p. r.o one pce fnl 2f) | ½ | **4** | 16/1 | 67 | 14 |
| 1690[3] | **Royal Action (73)** (JEBanks) **3-8-11**(3) JStack(15) (a.p: no hdwy fnl 2f) | hd | **5** | 9/1 | 67 | 14 |
| 1901[8] | **Mezzanotte (IRE)** (LMCumani) **3-9-0** KDarley(12) (stdy hdwy over 2f out: swtchd rt over 1f out: r.o) | 1 | **6** | 8/1 | 65 | 12 |
| 1117[11] | **Love Bateta (IRE) (70)** (RHannon) **3-8-9** TQuinn(16) (prom tl grad wknd fnl 3f) | 1¼ | **7** | 20/1 | 57 | 4 |
| 1963[9] | **Noble Lord** (RHBuckler) **3-9-0** CandyMorris(14) (b.off hind: hdwy 3f out: one pce fnl 2f) | nk | **8** | 50/1 | 62 | 9 |
| | **Chesteine** (PJMakin) **3-8-9** SSanders(18) (w'like: nrst fin) | hd | **9** | 33/1 | 57 | 4 |
| | **Llyswen** (JHMGosden) **3-9-0** GHind(2) (w'like: scope: s.s: gd hdwy 3f out: eased whn btn fnl f) | 3 | **10** | 14/1 | 56 | 3 |
| 1335[9] | **Promissory (72)** (CEBrittain) **3-8-9** BDoyle(8) (lw: prom tl wknd qckly over 2f out) | 2 | **11** | 20/1 | 47 | — |
| 1994[14] | **Allstars Rocket** (TJNaughton) **3-9-0** PaulEddery(4) (bit bkwd: nvr nr to chal) | 1 | **12** | 50/1 | 50 | — |
| 1857[11] | **Isla Glen** (MMcCormack) **3-8-9** MFenton(17) (nvr trbld ldrs) | s.h | **13** | 50/1 | 45 | — |
| | **On The Wildside** (MRChannon) **3-8-4**(5) PPMurphy(19) (lw: dwlt: plld hrd & gd hdwy 5f out: wknd 2f out) | 1¼ | **14** | 50/1 | 42 | — |
| 1797[4] | **Chirico (USA)** (JHMGosden) **3-9-0** PatEddery(3) (lw: a bhd: rdn 3f out: no hdwy) | nk | **15** | 5/1[2] | 47 | — |
| | **Colebrook Willie** (JRBosley) **3-9-0** CRutter(5) (leggy: unf: outpcd) | 10 | **16** | 50/1 | 28 | — |
| 1994[12] | **Wey River Mist** (JJBridger) **3-8-4**(5) ADaly(20) (lw: chsd wnr tl wknd qckly 4f out: t.o) | 15 | **17** | 50/1 | — | — |
| 1787[8] | **Fig Tree Bay** (TTClement) **3-9-0** JQuinn(9) (a bhd: t.o) | hd | **18** | 50/1 | — | — |

| | | | | SP | RR | SF |
|---|---|---|---|---|---|---|
| | **Desert Scout** (KMcAuliffe) **3-9-0v1** MTebbutt(7) (str: scope: a bhd: t.o fnl 3f: virtually p.u) | dist | **19** | 50/1 | — | — |
| | | | | (SP 146.6%) | | **19 Rn** |

**1m 45.3** (3.10) CSF £31.42 TOTE £2.20: £1.60 £5.80 £2.30 (£63.30) Trio £92.10 OWNER Mr Saeed Maktoum Al Maktoum (NEWMARKET) BRED Gainsborough Farm Inc.

STEWARDS' ENQUIRY Darley susp. 4-6/7/96 (failure to obtain the best possible placing).

**1427 Kammtarra (USA)** tried new tactics. He was sent off in front and, although not handling the right hand turn into the straight too well, was always going too strongly for his rivals. He drew right away in the final three furlongs. (Evens)

**1855 Idle Fancy** improved from the mid-division to take second place two furlongs out but, though she ran on, she had no chance with the easy winner. (25/1)

**894 Dilazar (USA)** was always close up and had every chance. Ridden along three furlongs out, he stayed on at one pace. (6/1: 7/2-7/1)

**Danish Circus (IRE)**, always in the first four, kept on at one pace under pressure in the final quarter-mile. (16/1)

**1690 Royal Action** tracked the leaders, but could make no headway under pressure in the last three furlongs. (9/1)

**Mezzanotte (IRE)** ran far better than his final position suggests. He threaded his way through the pack from over two and a half furlongs out, and is capable of considerable improvement. (8/1: 6/1-10/1)

**Llyswen** has scope for improvement. Very slowly away, he made good headway three furlongs out, but the effort took its toll and he was eased into tenth in the last furlong. (14/1)

T/Plpt: £43.10 (354.3 Tckts). T/Qdpt: £4.00 (298.71 Tckts). Hn

# 2155-LINGFIELD (L-H) (Turf Firm, AWT Standard)

## Tuesday June 25th

WEATHER: warm WIND: almost nil

## 2198 KELLY SERVICES GOLDEN ANNIVERSARY MAIDEN STKS (3-Y.O) (Class D)

2-30 (2-30) **1m 2f** £3,785.00 (£1,130.00: £540.00: £245.00) Stalls: Low GOING minus 0.57 sec per fur (F)

| | | | | SP | RR | SF |
|---|---|---|---|---|---|---|
| 948⁶ | **Set Adrift** (HRACecil) **3-9-0** AMcGlone(5) (lw: mde virtually all: shkn up over 2f out: comf) | — | **1** | Evens 1 | 76+ | 30 |
| | **Typhoon Lad** (SDow) **3-9-0** TQuinn(7) (str: scope: lw: a.p: chsd wnr over 2f out: unable qckn) | 1¾ | **2** | 15/2 3 | 73 | 27 |
| | **St Adele (USA)** (DRLoder) **3-8-9** DRMcCabe(4) (nt grwn: rdn over 3f out: hdwy over 1f out: r.o) | 1¼ | **3** | 8/1 | 66 | 20 |
| 1906² | **Polar Champ (75)** (SPCWoods) **3-9-0** DBiggs(3) (rdn 8f out: hdwy over 1f out: r.o one pce) | 1 | **4** | 2/1 2 | 70 | 24 |
| 1857⁸ | **Soldier's Song** (RJHodges) **3-8-6**(3) SDrowne(1) (s.s: hdwy 8f out: wknd 2f out) | 5 | **5** | 33/1 | 57 | 11 |
| 819¹⁴ | **Classic Lover (IRE) (63)** (RHarris) **3-8-9** JHBrown(6) (a.p: chsd wnr 8f out tl over 2f out: sn wknd) | ½ | **6** | 16/1 | 56 | 10 |
| | | | | (SP 115.0%) | | **6 Rn** |

**2m 7.57** (2.87) CSF £8.68 TOTE £1.90: £1.20 £2.10 (£5.60) OWNER Lord Howard de Walden (NEWMARKET) BRED Lord Howard de Walden

**948 Set Adrift** looked well beforehand but showed a scratchy action going to post, and was a very uneasy favourite. Nevertheless, he made virtually all the running and, shaken up in the straight, comfortably had the measure of his rivals to win a terrible race. (Evens)

**Typhoon Lad**, an ex-Irish colt, was making his debut in this country. He struggled into second two furlongs from home, but never looked like reeling in the winner. (15/2)

**St Adele (USA)** has not grown at all since last year. Rousted along at the rear early in the straight, she stayed on in the last furlong and a half without ever threatening. (8/1)

**1906 Polar Champ** was already being niggled along after a couple of furlongs. He did stay on from below the distance but never threatened. (2/1)

## 2199 CROWHURST (S) STKS (2-Y.O) (Class F)

3-00 (3-01) **6f** £2,571.40 (£710.40: £338.20) Stalls: High GOING minus 0.57 sec per fur (F)

| | | | | SP | RR | SF |
|---|---|---|---|---|---|---|
| 2031⁷ | **Kilcullen Lad (IRE)** (PMooney) **2-8-11** TQuinn(3) (led 5f out: drvn out) | — | **1** | 100/30 3 | 48 | — |
| *2172** | **Eager To Please** (JBerry) **2-9-3** 6x GCarter(2) (lw: w wnr over 4f out: rdn & ev ch fnl 3f: r.o) | nk | **2** | Evens 1 | 53 | 1 |
| *1968⁷* | **Emma's Risk** (RJRWilliams) **2-8-1**(5) LNewton(1) (a.p: rdn over 2f out: wknd over 1f out) | 9 | **3** | 12/1 | 18 | — |
| 2031⁵ | **Vickys Double** (JSMoore) **2-8-6** WJO'Connor(4) (led 1f: wknd over 3f out) | 5 | **4** | 3/1 2 | 5 | — |
| | | | | (SP 105.8%) | | **4 Rn** |

**1m 12.69** (3.69) CSF £6.63 TOTE £3.30 (£3.20) OWNER Ms Ann Cully (LEWES) BRED S. W. D. McIlveen

No bid

**Kilcullen Lad (IRE)** was well supported in the market and did not let his backers down. Soon in a narrow lead, he was given no peace by the runner-up and, in the tussle with that rival, just prevailed to win this bad race. (100/30)

**2172* Eager To Please**, making a quick reappearance after his All-Weather victory the previous Saturday, was soon alongsides the winner. With every chance in the second half of the race, he just failed to master his rival. (Evens)

**Vickys Double** (3/1: op 6/4)

## 2200 DEC-FAX H'CAP (0-80) (3-Y.O) (Class D)

3-30 (3-30) **6f** £3,720.00 (£1,110.00: £530.00: £240.00) Stalls: High GOING minus 0.57 sec per fur (F)

| | | | | SP | RR | SF |
|---|---|---|---|---|---|---|
| 2049* | **U-No-Harry (IRE) (63)** (RHollinshead) **3-8-4**(5) 6x FLynch(7) (lw: rdn over 2f out: hdwy over 1f out: led ins fnl f: r.o wl) | — | **1** | 9/2 3 | 71 | 47 |
| 1836⁶ | **May Queen Megan (51)** (MrsALMKing) **3-7-11** NAdams(9) (a.p: led over 2f out tl ins fnl f: unable qckn) | 1¼ | **2** | 33/1 | 56 | 32 |
| 2005⁶ | **Standown (73)** (JBerry) **3-9-5** GCarter(6) (bmpd s: rdn over 3f out: hdwy over 1f out: r.o) | 1½ | **3** | 4/1 2 | 74 | 50 |
| 1615¹⁰ | **Meranti (58)** (SDow) **3-8-4** TQuinn(8) (lw: rdn 3f out: hdwy & nt clr run ins fnl f: swtchd rt: r.o one pce) | 1½ | **4** | 4/1 2 | 55 | 31 |
| 992² | **Thordis (75)** (PJMakin) **3-9-7** SSanders(5) (lw: hld up: rdn over 2f out: r.o one pce) | ½ | **5** | 6/1 | 70 | 46 |
| 1844¹¹ | **Dancing Jack (50)** (JJBridger) **3-7-3**(7) RBrisland(4) (lw: led over 3f: wknd 1f out) | 2½ | **6** | 25/1 | 39 | 15 |
| | **Village Native (FR) (68)** (KOCunningham-Brown) **3-9-0** WJO'Connor(3) (b: a bhd) | 1½ | **7** | 25/1 | 53 | 29 |
| 1905⁵ | **Missile Toe (IRE) (67)** (JEBanks) **3-8-13b** KFallon(1) (spd over 4f) | 2½ | **8** | 13/2 | 45 | 21 |
| 1805* | **Faith Alone (67)** (CFWall) **3-8-13** GDuffield(2) (dwlt: sme hdwy over 2f out: wknd wl over 1f out) | ½ | **9** | 3/1 1 | 44 | 20 |
| | | | | (SP 121.4%) | | **9 Rn** |

**1m 8.78** (-0.22) CSF £104.01 CT £596.04 TOTE £5.10: £1.10 £7.00 £2.10 (£58.70) Trio £86.60 OWNER Mr D. Coppenhall (UPPER LONGDON) BRED A. J. Poulton (Epping) Ltd

**OFFICIAL EXPLANATION Faith Alone: her trainer reported that she had not travelled well to the course, and her jockey reported that she did not let herself down on the ground.**

**2049* U-No-Harry (IRE)**, held up in midfield, began his effort from below the distance and came through to lead inside the final furlong. (9/2)

**1836 May Queen Megan** went on over a quarter of a mile from home, but was unable to cope with the winner inside the final furlong. (33/1)

**2005 Standown**, pushed along at the back of the field before halfway, was doing all his best work in the last furlong and a half. (4/1: 3/1-9/2)
**1615 Meranti**, pushed along at the back of the field at halfway, was just beginning to pick up ground when not getting the clearest of runs inside the final furlong. It made little difference to his chance, although he did plod on for fourth prize. (4/1: 6/1-7/2)
**992 Thordis** chased the leaders, but never looked like finding the necessary turn of foot in the final quarter-mile. (6/1: 4/1-13/2)
**743 Dancing Jack** took the field along. Collared over two furlongs from home, he grimly tried to hold on, but got forced to concede defeat inside the distance. (25/1)

## 2201 HENRY STREETER LIMITED STKS (0-70) (3-Y.O+) (Class E)

4-00 (4-02) **1m (Equitrack)** £3,179.40 (£949.20: £453.60: £205.80) Stalls: High GOING minus 0.60 sec per fur (FST)

| | | | | SP | RR | SF |
|---|---|---|---|---|---|---|
| *2170*$^{4}$ | **Waikiki Beach (USA) (69)** (GLMoore) **5-9-7** SWhitworth(12) (b: b.hind: lw: mde virtually all: cl wl over 1f out: comf) | — | **1** | 11/2$^{3}$ | 86+ | 43 |
| 1868$^{4}$ | **Give Me A Ring (IRE) (70)** (CWThornton) **3-8-9** DeanMcKeown(1) (a.p: chsd wnr over 5f out: rdn 3f out: unable qckn fnl 2f) | 5 | **2** | 7/2$^{1}$ | 74 | 21 |
| *1993** | **Quiet Arch (IRE) (65)** (CACyzer) **3-8-11** TQuinn(6) (a.p: rdn 3f out: one pce fnl 2f) | 3 | **3** | 7/2$^{1}$ | 70 | 17 |
| 2032$^{4}$ | **Four of Spades (70)** (PDEvans) **5-9-0v**(5) AmandaSanders(8) (lw: a.p: rdn 3f out: wknd over 2f out) | 3 | **4** | 5/1$^{2}$ | 62 | 19 |
| 1773$^{10}$ | **Philistar (67)** (JMPEustace) **3-8-9** MTebbutt(10) (no hdwy fnl 3f) | 3 | **5** | 16/1 | 56 | 3 |
| 1776$^{9}$ | **Shady Girl (IRE) (68)** (BWHills) **3-8-6** KFallon(2) (no hdwy fnl 3f) | 3 | **6** | 10/1 | 47 | — |
| *1601*$^{4}$ | **Prima Cominna (66)** (SPCWoods) **4-9-2b**$^{1}$ DBiggs(4) (a mid div) | nk | **7** | 10/1 | 46 | 3 |
| 1893$^{12}$ | **Indian Serenade (55)** (THind) **5-8-12**(7) IonaWands(5) (lw: rdn thrght: nvr nr to chal) | 1½ | **8** | 33/1 | 46 | 3 |
| 1841$^{11}$ | **Sotoboy (IRE) (69)** (PWHarris) **4-9-5** GHind(7) (bhd fnl 3f) | nk | **9** | 12/1 | 46 | 3 |
| 2130$^{8}$ | **Captain's Day (70)** (TGMills) **4-9-5** MarkLynch(9) (lw: bhd fnl 5f) | ½ | **10** | 12/1 | 45 | 2 |
| | **Hong Kong Dollar (45)** (BAPearce) **4-9-5** SSanders(3) (b: a bhd) | 18 | **11** | 50/1 | 9 | — |
| 1965$^{14}$ | **Smocking (25)** (MissKMGeorge) **6-9-2** GCarter(11) (bhd fnl 5f) | 2½ | **12** | 33/1 | 1 | — |
| | | | | (SP 123.8%) | | **12 Rn** |

**1m 38.57** (1.17) CSF £24.78 TOTE £6.70: £1.90 £1.90 £2.40 (£19.30) Trio £19.70 OWNER Pennine Partners (EPSOM) BRED Dan C. Pitts & Frank Ramos
WEIGHT FOR AGE 3yo-10lb
**2170 Waikiki Beach (USA)**, making a quick reappearance, looked well beforehand and treated these rivals with contempt. Making virtually all the running, he forged clear turning into the straight and won with plenty in hand. (11/2)
**1868 Give Me A Ring (IRE)** moved into second place over five furlongs out. Turning for home, he started to hold his head very high and threw it around, and it was debatable whether this was due to the kick-back or being under pressure. He was then left standing by the winner and looks one to avoid on this surface. (7/2)
**1993* Quiet Arch (IRE)**, a leading light from the off, was made to look very pedestrian in the last quarter-mile. (7/2)
**2032 Four of Spades** was close up until calling it a day over two furlongs from home. (5/1)

## 2202 KNIGHT FRANK CENTENARY H'CAP (0-80) (3-Y.O F) (Class D)

4-30 (4-31) **1m 3f 106y** £3,655.00 (£1,090.00: £520.00: £235.00) Stalls: High GOING minus 0.57 sec per fur (F)

| | | | | SP | RR | SF |
|---|---|---|---|---|---|---|
| 1804$^{6}$ | **Dear Life (USA) (73)** (MrsJCecil) **3-9-3** AClark(3) (swtg: hld up: led over 2f out: r.o wl) | — | **1** | 5/1$^{2}$ | 86 | 33 |
| 1852$^{8}$ | **Arcady (64)** (PTWalwyn) **3-8-8** SSanders(2) (lw: led 9f: unable qckn) | 3½ | **2** | 7/1 | 72 | 19 |
| 1852* | **White Sea (IRE) (77)** (PFICole) **3-9-7** TQuinn(4) (lw: chsd ldr: ev ch 2f out: one pce) | nk | **3** | 4/6$^{1}$ | 85 | 32 |
| 2016$^{4}$ | **Again Together (55)** (GLMoore) **3-7-13** FNorton(5) (hld up: rdn 3f out: one pce) | ½ | **4** | 11/2$^{3}$ | 62 | 9 |
| 739$^{9}$ | **Classic Romance (73)** (RHarris) **3-9-3** DBatteate(1) (t.o 6f out: r.o one pce fnl 3f) | 2½ | **5** | 10/1 | 77 | 24 |
| | | | | (SP 113.6%) | | **5 Rn** |

**2m 27.48** (3.28) CSF £31.47 TOTE £6.00: £2.80 £3.60 (£20.70) OWNER Lady Howard de Walden (NEWMARKET) BRED Lord Howard de Walden
**1804 Dear Life (USA)**, taking a step up in trip, chased the leaders. Gaining control over a quarter of a mile from home, she proved too strong for her rivals. (5/1)
**1585 Arcady** attempted to make all. Collared approaching the final quarter-mile, she failed to find another gear. (7/1)
**1852* White Sea (IRE)** raced in second place. Throwing down her challenge in the straight, she still had every chance two furlongs from home before left standing. (4/6)

## 2203 VENNER SHIPLEY APPRENTICE H'CAP (0-70) (3-Y.O+) (Class F)

5-00 (5-00) **1m 2f** £2,557.50 (£720.00: £352.50) Stalls: Low GOING minus 0.57 sec per fur (F)

| | | | | SP | RR | SF |
|---|---|---|---|---|---|---|
| 1773$^{3}$ | **White Plains (IRE) (68)** (MBell) **3-8-11**(5) RMullen(7) (a.p: chsd ldr 6f out: led 1f out: drvn out) | — | **1** | 3/1$^{1}$ | 80 | 40 |
| 1903* | **Chieftain's Crown (USA) (37)** (MissKMGeorge) **5-7-6b**(5) PDoe(1) (lw: led 9f: r.o) | 1 | **2** | 3/1$^{1}$ | 47 | 19 |
| 1654$^{17}$ | **Sheilana (IRE) (60)** (TGMills) **3-8-1**(7) JCornally(6) (a.p: rdn over 2f out: unable qckn) | 7 | **3** | 20/1 | 59 | 19 |
| 439$^{4}$ | **Almuhtaram (64)** (MissGayKelleway) **4-9-10b** MartinDwyer(8) (b: hdwy over 1f out: r.o) | ½ | **4** | 4/1$^{2}$ | 62 | 34 |
| 1874$^{14}$ | **Dormy Three (63)** (RJHodges) **6-9-9** AmandaSanders(3) (lw: hdwy 2f out: one pce) | 2½ | **5** | 10/1$^{3}$ | 57 | 29 |
| *603*$^{6}$ | **Bobby Blue (IRE) (38)** (THind) **5-7-12** IonaWands(4) (b: chsd ldr 4f: wknd over 2f out) | ½ | **6** | 40/1 | 32 | 4 |
| 1696$^{4}$ | **Lady Sabina (40)** (WJMusson) **6-7-11**(3)ow1 JWilkinson(5) (nvr nr to chal) | ½ | **7** | 4/1$^{2}$ | 33 | 4 |
| 1903$^{6}$ | **Real Madrid (36)** (GPEnright) **5-7-10v** CAdamson(9) (bhd fnl 2f) | 4 | **8** | 16/1 | 22 | — |
| *1098*$^{11}$ | **Thorniwama (36)** (JJBridger) **5-7-3b**(7) RBrisland(2) (a bhd) | 1½ | **9** | 25/1 | 20 | — |
| | | | | (SP 116.0%) | | **9 Rn** |

**2m 6.43** (1.73) CSF £11.96 CT £136.44 TOTE £4.10: £1.10 £1.50 £3.20 (£6.50) Trio £118.80 OWNER Deln Ltd (NEWMARKET) BRED Howard Kaskel
LONG HANDICAP Real Madrid 7-8 Thorniwama 7-8
WEIGHT FOR AGE 3yo-12lb
STEWARDS' ENQUIRY Mullen susp. 4-6 & 8/7/96 (excessive & incorrect use of whip).
**1773 White Plains (IRE)** moved into second at the top of the hill. Eventually coming through to lead a furlong from home, he responded to stern pressure to keep the runner-up at bay, but his rider was later suspended for misuse of the whip. (3/1)
**1903* Chieftain's Crown (USA)** attempted to make all of the running. Collared a furlong out, he kept on, if finding the winner a bit too strong. (3/1)
**Sheilana (IRE)** was never far away, but failed to quicken in the straight. (20/1)
**439 Almuhtaram**, given a three-month break, was held up at the back of the field until staying on from below the distance. (4/1)
**1686 Dormy Three** made an effort a quarter of a mile from home, but could only plod on in his own time. (10/1)

T/Plpt: £1,024.30 (12.54 Tckts). T/Qdpt: £48.80 (27.91 Tckts). AK

# 1903-YARMOUTH (L-H) (Firm)

## Tuesday June 25th

WEATHER: warm WIND: almost nil

### 2204 TOTE DUAL FORECAST H'CAP (0-70) (3-Y.O) (Class E)

2-15 (2-15) **1m 6f 17y** £3,179.40 (£949.20: £453.60: £205.80) Stalls: Low GOING minus 0.66 sec per fur (HD)

| | | | | SP | RR | SF |
|---|---|---|---|---|---|---|
| 1679[2] | **Influence Pedler (52)** (CEBrittain) **3-8-9** BDoyle(3) (hld up gng wl: hdwy to ld 4f out: rdn clr over 2f out: eased ins fnl f) | — | **1** | 11/4[1] | 65+ | 36 |
| *1814[4]* | **Glowing Reeds (45)** (CNAllen) **3-8-2v[1]** JQuinn(5) (s.i.s: bhd 10f: drvn & nt keen after: mod late hdwy to take 2nd nr fin) | 7 | **2** | 25/1 | 50 | 21 |
| 1984[3] | **Soldier Mak (62)** (AHide) **3-9-2(3)** MHenry(2) (hld up: wnt 2nd 4f out: drvn & no ch w wnr fnl 2f) | nk | **3** | 6/1 | 67 | 38 |
| 1877* | **Alwarqa (64)** (RWArmstrong) **3-9-7** WCarson(4) (chsd ldrs: pushed along ½-wy: rdn & v.onepcd fnl 3f) | 2½ | **4** | 3/1[2] | 66 | 37 |
| *1814[2]* | **Pearl Anniversary (IRE) (51)** (MJohnston) **3-8-8** DHarrison(6) (sn pushed along: prom tl hrd rdn & no rspnse 4f out) | 3 | **5** | 5/1 | 50 | 21 |
| 1877[3] | **Ship's Dancer (53)** (JLDunlop) **3-8-10b** PatEddery(1) (led 10f: sn btn: t.o 2f out: sn eased) | dist | **6** | 7/2[3] | — | — |
| | | | | (SP 108.7%) | | **6 Rn** |

**3m 0.5** (1.10) CSF £40.85 TOTE £3.10: £1.80 £5.90 (£27.60) OWNER Mr C. E. Brittain (NEWMARKET) BRED Stetchworth Park Stud Ltd

**1679 Influence Pedler** was the one runner prepared to work for the money and won unchallenged, although kept about his business from a long way out until eased close home. (11/4)

**Glowing Reeds** was carrying her head high and looking reluctant all the way up the straight, and it was only the persistence of the jockey which forced her into second place. (25/1)

**1984 Soldier Mak** was placed for the fourth time this year but is devoid of acceleration. (6/1)

**1877* Alwarqa**, gifted a race here last time, had her limitations fully exposed. (3/1)

**1877 Ship's Dancer** is going from bad to worse. (7/2)

### 2205 TOTE CREDIT MAIDEN STKS (3-Y.O) (Class D)

2-45 (2-45) **1m 6f 17y** £3,628.65 (£1,081.20: £515.10: £232.05) Stalls: Low GOING minus 0.66 sec per fur (HD)

| | | | | SP | RR | SF |
|---|---|---|---|---|---|---|
| 702[7] | **Hal Hoo Yaroom (67)** (MajorWRHern) **3-9-0** RHills(4) (sn led: rdn clr fnl f) | — | **1** | 5/2[2] | 73 | 33 |
| 1461[4] | **Bold Classic (IRE)** (JLDunlop) **3-9-0** TSprake(3) (hld up: chsd wnr fnl 3f: wknd 1f out) | 5 | **2** | 11/1 | 67 | 27 |
| *1997[4]* | **Anchor Venture (60)** (SPCWoods) **3-9-0** PatEddery(2) (hld up last: hrd rdn over 3f out: no rspnse & sn btn) | 11 | **3** | Evens[1] | 55 | 15 |
| 2036[7] | **Scottish Hero** (JRFanshawe) **3-9-0** DHarrison(1) (chsd wnr: rdn 4f out: wknd qckly 3f out) | 1¾ | **4** | 4/1[3] | 53 | 13 |
| | | | | (SP 106.9%) | | **4 Rn** |

**3m 1.8** (2.40) CSF £17.54 TOTE £2.90 (£9.60) OWNER Sheikh Ahmed Al Maktoum (LAMBOURN) BRED Sheikh Ahmed Bin Rashid Al Maktoum

**Hal Hoo Yaroom** had given hints of ability at two and won this easily, as the others put up absolutely no fight. (5/2)

**Bold Classic (IRE)** was trying a longer trip and it proved beyond him. (11/1: 7/1-12/1)

**1997 Anchor Venture** was a hopeless favourite and had given up the ghost over half a mile from the finish. (Evens)

### 2206 TOTE BOOKMAKERS H'CAP (0-80) (3-Y.O+) (Class D)

3-15 (3-15) **1m 2f 21y** £4,386.00 (£1,308.00: £624.00: £282.00) Stalls: Low GOING minus 0.66 sec per fur (HD)

| | | | | SP | RR | SF |
|---|---|---|---|---|---|---|
| 2010[5] | **Sovereign Page (USA) (76)** (BHanbury) **7-9-7(3)** JStack(6) (trckd ldr gng wl: led 3f out: clr over 1f out: readily) | — | **1** | 5/2[1] | 87 | 50 |
| 1819[7] | **Apollono (75)** (JRFanshawe) **4-9-9** NDay(5) (hld up: outpcd 3f out: rdn over 2f out: drvn & kpt on to go 2nd cl home) | 1¼ | **2** | 5/1 | 84 | 47 |
| 1440[11] | **Mokuti (73)** (GWragg) **4-9-7b** PRobinson(1) (cl up: hrd rdn to chse wnr wl over 2f out: no imp) | nk | **3** | 4/1[3] | 82 | 45 |
| 1908* | **Classic Ballet (FR) (68)** (RHarris) **3-8-4** AMackay(2) (hld up: rdn over 3f out: one pce & btn 2f out) | 2 | **4** | 7/2[2] | 73 | 24 |
| 1798[11] | **Villeggiatura (77)** (BWHills) **3-8-13b** MHills(4) (led & racd freely early: hdd 3f out: lost pl qckly: eased fnl 100y) | 12 | **5** | 7/2[2] | 63 | 14 |
| 508[8] | **Sea God (48)** (MCChapman) **5-7-10** GBardwell(3) (sddle slipped & dropped back last ½-wy: n.d after) | s.h | **6** | 25/1 | 34 | — |
| | | | | (SP 113.5%) | | **6 Rn** |

**2m 4.9** (0.50) CSF £14.19 TOTE £3.10: £2.30 £1.60 (£8.70) OWNER Mrs Ben Hanbury (NEWMARKET) BRED T. Holland Martin

LONG HANDICAP Sea God 7-6

WEIGHT FOR AGE 3yo-12lb

**2010 Sovereign Page (USA)** had gained all his seven wins at or around this trip on good or firm ground, and found things suitable, landing a gamble here. (5/2)

**633 Apollono** appeared to get this trip well enough and might manage to win before too long. (5/1)

**802* Mokuti** was a beaten favourite when blinkered for the first time a month ago, and they again did little for him here. (4/1)

### 2207 TOTE PLACEPOT (S) STKS (2-Y.O) (Class G)

3-45 (3-45) **5f 43y** £2,427.00 (£672.00: £321.00) Stalls: High GOING minus 0.66 sec per fur (HD)

| | | | | SP | RR | SF |
|---|---|---|---|---|---|---|
| 1904[5] | **Emmas Breeze** (CADwyer) **2-8-6** DHarrison(4) (mde all: drvn out fnl f) | — | **1** | 5/2[2] | 49 | — |
| *1491[6]* | **Jingoist (IRE)** (JLHarris) **2-8-6** MRoberts(2) (chsd wnr: rdn over 2f out: swished tail & fnd nil) | 5 | **2** | 7/4[1] | 34 | — |
| 1595[7] | **Run For Us (IRE)** (CADwyer) **2-8-6** TGMcLaughlin(1) (trckd ldng pair: drvn over 2f out: btn wl over 1f out) | 4 | **3** | 7/4[1] | 21 | — |
| *1968[9]* | **Nefertiti** (RFMarvin) **2-8-6** AMackay(3) (bhd: hung rt fr ½-wy: sn no ch: t.o) | 12 | **4** | 14/1[3] | — | — |
| | | | | (SP 108.0%) | | **4 Rn** |

**64.4 secs** (3.90) CSF £6.74 TOTE £3.30 (£3.10) OWNER Mrs Christine Dunnett (NEWMARKET) BRED Mrs C. A. Dunnett

No bid

**590 Emmas Breeze** did not stay seven last time, but could probably have beaten this trio at any trip. (5/2)

**895 Jingoist (IRE)** was having her first run for the new yard. (7/4)

**858 Nefertiti** (14/1: op 8/1)

### 2208 TOTE PLACE ONLY MAIDEN STKS (3-Y.O F) (Class D)

4-15 (4-15) **1m 3y** £4,092.75 (£1,224.00: £586.50: £267.75) Stalls: High GOING minus 0.66 sec per fur (HD)

| | | | | SP | RR | SF |
|---|---|---|---|---|---|---|
| 1876[3] | **Hippy (66)** (CEBrittain) **3-8-11** BDoyle(5) (cl up: led 2f out: clr ins fnl f: rdn out) | — | **1** | 20/1 | 85 | 28 |

| | | | | SP | RR | SF |
|---|---|---|---|---|---|---|
| 1804[10] | **Aethra (USA) (79)** (LadyHerries) **3-8-11** DHarrison(4) (stdd s: plld hrd: racd freely & sn chsng ldrs: drvn & no imp on wnr fnl f) | 2½ | 2 | 7/2 2 | 80 | 23 |
| 1540[2] | **Hulm (IRE) (82)** (HThomsonJones) **3-8-11** RHills(7) (plld hrd: hld up in rr early: rdn & effrt 2f out: no ex fnl f) | 1¾ | 3 | 9/2 3 | 77 | 20 |
| 1882[3] | **Omara (USA) (78)** (HRACecil) **3-8-11** PatEddery(1) (led: edgd rt 3f out: rdn & hdd 2f out: wknd) | 4 | 4 | 11/2 | 69 | 12 |
| 1123[3] | **Naseem Alsahar (78)** (MajorWRHern) **3-8-11b**[1] TSprake(8) (chsd ldr 5f: rdn & sn btn) | 1¼ | 5 | 7/1 | 66 | 9 |
| | **Square Mile Miss (IRE)** (PHowling) **3-8-11** JQuinn(9) (rn green in rr: nvr nr ldrs) | 2½ | 6 | 50/1 | 61 | 4 |
| | **Flying Flowers** (RHannon) **3-8-11** MRoberts(6) (bhd & rdn after 2f: nvr gng wl) | 5 | 7 | 14/1 | 51 | — |
| 1882[7] | **Blossomville** (MAJarvis) **3-8-11** PBloomfield(10) (struggling in rr after 3f) | ½ | 8 | 50/1 | 50 | — |
| 1667[4] | **Bent Raiwand (USA)** (BHanbury) **3-8-8**(3) JStack(2) (sn bhd: rdn & struggling after 3f: t.o) | 5 | 9 | 14/1 | 40 | — |
| 1882[2] | **Royal Jade (79)** (BWHills) **3-8-11** MHills(3) (cl up: rdn 3f out: no rspnse: virtually p.u 1f out: t.o) | hd | 10 | 9/4 1 | 40 | — |

(SP 121.1%) **10 Rn**

**1m 36.5** (1.20) CSF £86.38 TOTE £18.90: £5.40 £1.90 £1.80 (£90.90) Trio £132.50 OWNER Mr D. Sieff (NEWMARKET) BRED Wooditton Stud Ltd

OFFICIAL EXPLANATION **Royal Jade: was unable to handle the firm ground.**

**1876 Hippy**, happy on the firm ground unlike several of her rivals, could be named the winner a long way out. (20/1)
**1804 Aethra (USA)** has the ability to win if she can learn to settle. (7/2)
**1540 Hulm (IRE)** is a puller who does not save anything for the closing stages. (9/2)
**1882 Omara (USA)** failed to stay seven last time and this extra furlong put even greater stress on her lack of stamina. (11/2)
**Flying Flowers** (14/1: 10/1-16/1)
**1882 Royal Jade** was most disappointing. (9/4: 6/4-5/2)

## 2209 TOTE TRIO H'CAP (0-70) (3-Y.O+) (Class E)

4-45 (4-48) **7f 3y** £2,988.30 (£890.40: £424.20: £191.10) Stalls: High GOING minus 0.66 sec per fur (HD)

| | | | | SP | RR | SF |
|---|---|---|---|---|---|---|
| 2047[2] | **Nashaat (USA) (66)** (MCChapman) **8-9-11**(3) PMcCabe(8) (hld up in rr: stdy hdwy 2f out: str run fnl 100y: rdn to ld nr fin) | — | 1 | 3/1 2 | 77 | 46 |
| 1363[4] | **Dubai College (IRE) (67)** (CEBrittain) **3-9-6** BDoyle(5) (cl up: led over 2f out: 3l clr 1f out: drvn along & jst ct) | ½ | 2 | 7/1 | 77 | 37 |
| 1881[7] | **Balpare (50)** (NACallaghan) **3-8-3** WCarson(6) (rdn & effrt 3f out: one pce & btn over 1f out) | 6 | 3 | 8/1 | 46 | 6 |
| 2130* | **Darcey Bussell (62)** (BWHills) **4-9-5**(5) 6x JDSmith(4) (in tch: rdn & effrt over 2f out: wknd over 1f out) | hd | 4 | 2/1 1 | 58 | 27 |
| 1624[9] | **Rockcracker (IRE) (62)** (GGMargarson) **4-9-10** PBloomfield(1) (rdn ½-wy: n.d after) | 6 | 5 | 20/1 | 44 | 13 |
| 1856[13] | **Ahjay (44)** (TJNaughton) **6-8-6** MRoberts(2) (led 1f: sn rdn & struggling) | hd | 6 | 11/2 3 | 26 | — |
| *1966*[7] | **Spanish Stripper (USA) (62)** (MCChapman) **5-9-3**(7) TField(3) (prom to ½-wy: rdn & sn btn) | 1 | 7 | 20/1 | 42 | 11 |
| 1825[8] | **Fervent Fan (IRE) (60)** (MBell) **3-8-13v**[1] MFenton(9) (prom 3f: sn bhd) | 1½ | 8 | 20/1 | 36 | — |
| 1778[16] | **Scorpius (42)** (TTClement) **6-8-4b** JQuinn(7) (led after 1f tl hdd 2½f out: lost pl qckly: t.o & eased) | 6 | 9 | 12/1 | 5 | — |

(SP 119.3%) **9 Rn**

**1m 25.1** (0.90) CSF £23.30 CT £135.35 TOTE £4.40: £1.70 £1.80 £2.30 (£11.40) Trio £27.30 OWNER Mr Tony Satchell (MARKET RASEN) BRED Echo Valley Horse Farm and Swettenham Stud

WEIGHT FOR AGE 3yo-9lb

OFFICIAL EXPLANATION **Scorpius: would not let himself down on the firm ground.**

**2047 Nashaat (USA)**, a small gelding with a big weight, was given a great ride. Patiently handled in the rear, he quickened on the bridle to put his head in front close home and can hardly have known he had had a race. (3/1)
**1363 Dubai College (IRE)** tried to steal a march on his rivals with a bold move to take a three-length lead a furlong out, but he was worn down close home. (7/1)
**1806 Balpare** stretched her losing sequence to thirteen and would be more at home in the selling company she has been in of late. (8/1)
**2130* Darcey Bussell** has been running really well recently, but did not perform to her usual standards. (2/1)

## 2210 TOTE JACKPOT CONDITIONS STKS (2-Y.O) (Class C)

5-15 (5-15) **6f 3y** £4,793.76 (£1,654.56: £791.28: £320.40) GOING minus 0.66 sec per fur (HD)

| | | | | SP | RR | SF |
|---|---|---|---|---|---|---|
| 1795[4] | **Pelham (IRE)** (RHannon) **2-9-0** PatEddery(2) (shkn up early: cl up tl led over 2f out: drvn & kpt on wl fnl f: readily) | — | 1 | 2/1 2 | 78 | 9 |
| 1982* | **Last Chance** (GLewis) **2-8-11** PaulEddery(1) (2nd pl virtually thrght: ev ch 1f out: drvn & a hld after) | ¾ | 2 | 7/4 1 | 73 | 4 |
| 1169* | **Smart Boy (IRE)** (PFICole) **2-9-0** CRutter(3) (in tch tl wknd tamely over 2f out) | 7 | 3 | 11/4 3 | 57 | — |
| 1989[3] | **Supercharmer** (CEBrittain) **2-8-11b**[1] BDoyle(4) (led tl over 2f out: lost pl rapidly) | 5 | 4 | 13/2 | 41 | — |

(SP 109.7%) **4 Rn**

**1m 13.4** (2.50) CSF £5.60 TOTE £2.90 (£3.30) OWNER Mr D. A. Lucie-Smith (MARLBOROUGH) BRED Golden Vale Stud

**1795 Pelham (IRE)** looked extremely well in the paddock and won in better style than the margin suggests. (2/1)
**1982* Last Chance**, wearing a tongue-strap, tried to make a fight of it with the winner but was quite comfortably held. (7/4)
**1169* Smart Boy (IRE)** was beaten a long way out and did not impress in the paddock. (11/4: op 7/4)
**1989 Supercharmer** (13/2: 7/2-7/1)

T/Jkpt: £7,100.00 (0.19 Tckts); £4,389.87 to Carlisle 26/6/96. T/Plpt: £758.50 (16.53 Tckts). T/Qdpt: £45.90 (20.01 Tckts). Mk

# 1884-CARLISLE (R-H) (Firm)
## Wednesday June 26th

WEATHER: sunny WIND: slt across

## 2211 E.B.F. SILLOTH MAIDEN STKS (2-Y.O) (Class D)

2-15 (2-16) **5f 207y** £3,916.55 (£1,186.40: £579.70: £276.35) Stalls: High GOING minus 0.78 sec per fur (HD)

| | | | | SP | RR | SF |
|---|---|---|---|---|---|---|
| | **Red Camellia** (SirMarkPrescott) **2-8-9** GDuffield(6) (neat: unf: scope: led after 2f: hld on wl fnl f) | — | 1 | 9/4 1 | 71 | 25 |
| 2025[2] | **Danehill Princess (IRE)** (RHollinshead) **2-8-4**(5) FLynch(8) (lw: cl up: disp ld over 2f out: nt qckn ins fnl f) | 1 | 2 | 9/4 1 | 68 | 22 |
| 1626[7] | **Ile Distinct (IRE)** (MrsASwinbank) **2-9-0** JFortune(3) (s.i.s: sn chsng ldrs: wl outpcd fnl 2f) | 3½ | 3 | 12/1 | 64 | 18 |
| | **Can Can Lady** (MJohnston) **2-8-9** TWilliams(2) (w'like: leggy: cl up: rdn ½-wy: sn outpcd) | 8 | 4 | 12/1 | 37 | — |
| | **Nant Y Gamer (FR)** (JBerry) **2-9-0** JCarroll(4) (leggy: bit bkwd: s.i.s: pushed along most of wy: nvr trbld ldrs) | ½ | 5 | 10/1 | 41 | — |
| 1884[5] | **Epic Stand** (MrsJRRamsden) **2-9-0** KFallon(1) (lw: s.i.s: sn wl bhd: hdwy whn nt clr run 1½f out: nt rcvr) | ¾ | 6 | 5/1 2 | 39 | — |
| | **Barresbo** (CWFairhurst) **2-9-0** DeanMcKeown(7) (w'like: hld up: rdn ½-wy: sn btn) | 3½ | 7 | 6/1 3 | 30 | — |

**Megan Carew** (DMoffatt) **2-8-6**(3) DarrenMoffatt(5) (neat: bit bkwd: led 2f: wknd over 2f out)........................1¾ **8** 25/1 20 —
(SP 120.8%) **8 Rn**

**1m 12.9** (0.40) CSF £8.01 TOTE £2.80: £1.80 £1.10 £3.10 (£3.10) OWNER Cheveley Park Stud (NEWMARKET) BRED Cheveley Park Stud Ltd
**Red Camellia** looks weak at present, but she certainly put up a stout performance, and looks likely to improve further. (9/4)
**2025 Danehill Princess (IRE)** keeps running well and, although outbattled here, does deserve a change of luck. (9/4)
**Ile Distinct (IRE)** ran as though he is learning and this have helped bring him on. (12/1)
**Can Can Lady** gave the impression that time will bring improvement. (12/1)
**Nant Y Gamer (FR)** needed this and could never get into it. (10/1)
**1884 Epic Stand** missed the break and, in the first half of the race, seemed clueless and got further behind. When he did pick up, his rider ran him into a pocket, but for which he would have been a lot closer. (5/1)
**Barresbo** took the eye in the paddock, and should be given another chance. (6/1)

## 2212 BBC RADIO CUMBRIA (S) STKS (3-Y.O+) (Class G)
2-45 (2-47) **5f 207y** £2,388.00 (£668.00: £324.00) Stalls: High GOING minus 0.78 sec per fur (HD)

| | | | SP | RR | SF |
|---|---|---|---|---|---|
| 2154[8] | **Sense of Priority (56)** (DNicholls) **7-9-10** AlexGreaves(4) (trckd ldrs: led 1f out: r.o) .......— | **1** | 4/1[2] | 72 | 34 |
| 1893[10] | **Sakharov (58)** (MJohnston) **7-9-10** KDarley(6) (bhd: hdwy over 2f out: chsng ldrs 1f out: nt qckn).......2 | **2** | 3/1[1] | 67 | 29 |
| 1685[15] | **Best Kept Secret (52)** (PDEvans) **5-9-5v** KFallon(7) (lw: bhd: hdwy 2f out: sn chsng ldrs: kpt on one pce fnl f).......nk | **3** | 17/2 | 61 | 23 |
| 2139[9] | **Amoeba (IRE) (52)** (JBerry) **3-8-7**(5) PRoberts(8) (lw: mde most tl hdd 1f out: sn btn).......1¾ | **4** | 6/1 | 56 | 11 |
| 1885[6] | **Brookhead Lady (53)** (PDEvans) **5-9-0** JFortune(2) (b.nr fore: disp ld early: cl up tl wknd appr fnl f).......1½ | **5** | 8/1 | 47 | 9 |
| 2064[10] | **First Option (45)** (RBastiman) **6-9-0**(5) HBastiman(13) (t: s.i.s: styd on fnl 2f: nvr rchd ldrs).......3 | **6** | 14/1 | 44 | 6 |
| *2085*[6] | **Jungle Patrol (IRE) (51)** (MBrittain) **4-9-5** MBirch(9) (hld up: swtchd & effrt 2f out: sn rdn & no imp).......½ | **7** | 12/1 | 43 | 5 |
| 2030[8] | **Steel Sovereign (36)** (MDods) **5-9-5** DaleGibson(1) (prom over 3f: sn outpcd).......s.h | **8** | 33/1 | 43 | 5 |
| 2022[6] | **Thorntoun Jewel (IRE) (38)** (MissZAGreen) **3-8-7b** JFanning(3) (spd to ½-wy: grad wknd).......1¾ | **9** | 33/1 | 33 | — |
| | **Time For A Glass** (DMoffatt) **3-8-4**(3) DarrenMoffatt(10) (lw: a bhd).......9 | **10** | 25/1 | 9 | — |
| 2026[7] | **Brownie's Promise** (MBrittain) **3-8-7**(5) GParkin(5) (sn outpcd & bhd: no ch whn hmpd 2f out).......hd | **11** | 33/1 | 13 | — |
| 1889[11] | **Respectable Jones (45)** (RHollinshead) **10-8-12b**(7) SCrawford(11) (chsd ldrs 4f: wknd).......1¾ | **12** | 20/1 | 9 | — |
| 1889[6] | **Call to the Bar (IRE) (52)** (MDods) **7-9-5** JCarroll(12) (trckd ldrs tl p.u 2f out: dead)....... | **P** | 5/1[3] | — | — |

(SP 129.4%) **13 Rn**

**1m 13.2** (0.70) CSF £16.98 TOTE £8.70: £2.60 £2.20 £3.00 (£11.70) Trio £18.80 OWNER Mr S. Schofield (THIRSK) BRED Cheveley Park Stud Ltd
WEIGHT FOR AGE 3yo-7lb
No bid
**1342 Sense of Priority** came back to form here, winning decisively, and is always one to be considered when dropped into this company. (4/1)
**1893 Sakharov**, who just found this trip too sharp, had to really work to get on terms and had nothing more to give at the finish. (3/1)
**1610 Best Kept Secret** looks in good form if he can be persuaded to put his best foot forward. (17/2)
**1885 Amoeba (IRE)** attempted to make all, but was outbattled in the final furlong. (6/1)
**764 Brookhead Lady** showed plenty of speed, but was never doing enough in the closing stages. (8/1)
**First Option** is running as though he is coming back to form. (14/1)
**1698 Jungle Patrol (IRE)** travels well on the bridle but, at present, his performance off it leaves a lot to be desired. (12/1)

## 2213 RACING CHANNEL H'CAP (0-80) (3-Y.O+) (Class D)
3-15 (3-16) **6f 206y** £3,533.75 (£1,070.00: £522.50: £248.75) Stalls: High GOING minus 0.78 sec per fur (HD)

| | | | SP | RR | SF |
|---|---|---|---|---|---|
| 1610[9] | **Impulsive Air (IRE) (58)** (EWeymes) **4-9-2** JFortune(1) (lw: set slow pce: qcknd 2f out: r.o wl).......— | **1** | 11/1[3] | 63 | — |
| 2034[8] | **Power Game (68)** (JBerry) **3-9-3** JCarroll(4) (trckd wnr: effrt over 2f out: kpt on).......1 | **2** | 3/1[2] | 71 | — |
| 2030[2] | **Halmanerror (66)** (MrsJRRamsden) **6-9-10** KFallon(2) (plld hrd: effrt 2f out: nt pce to chal).......2 | **3** | 10/11[1] | 64 | — |
| 1885* | **Winter Scout (USA) (60)** (CPEBrooks) **8-8-13b**(5) SCopp(3) (hld up: hdwy 3f out: outpcd fnl 2f).......½ | **4** | 3/1[2] | 57 | — |

(SP 110.7%) **4 Rn**

**1m 29.7** (4.00) CSF £36.66 TOTE £12.30: (£11.40) OWNER Mr T. A. Scothern (MIDDLEHAM) BRED Rathasker Stud
WEIGHT FOR AGE 3yo-9lb
OFFICIAL EXPLANATION **Impulsive Air (IRE): his trainer put the horse's apparent improvement down to the fact that he had had longer between races on this occasion, and he also enjoyed being able to dominate.**
**1412 Impulsive Air (IRE)** pinched a slowly-run event by holding pole position throughout and getting first run. (11/1)
**1780 Power Game** kept tabs on the winner throughout but, when it came down to a struggle, he was found wanting. (3/1)
**2030 Halmanerror** needs a strong pace and, in this two-furlong sprint, had no chance. (10/11: 4/5-Evens)
**1885* Winter Scout (USA)** is at his best in conditions races. (3/1)

## 2214 S. P. GRAHAM BOOKMAKERS CARLISLE BELL H'CAP (0-80) (3-Y.O+) (Class D)
3-45 (3-46) **7f 214y** £4,713.00 (£1,428.00: £698.00: £333.00) Stalls: High GOING minus 0.78 sec per fur (HD)

| | | | SP | RR | SF |
|---|---|---|---|---|---|
| 1830* | **Habeta (USA) (48)** (JWWatts) **10-8-2** GDuffield(6) (lw: in tch: effrt 2f out: r.o fnl f to ld post).......— | **1** | 7/1 | 56 | 36 |
| 1886[2] | **Spanish Verdict (67)** (DenysSmith) **9-9-7** KFallon(9) (lw: trckd ldrs: effrt 3f out: styd on to ld wl ins fnl f: jst ct).......s.h | **2** | 7/2[2] | 75 | 55 |
| 2023[4] | **Bulsara (54)** (CWFairhurst) **4-8-8** DeanMcKeown(10) (a chsng ldrs: rdn to ld ins fnl f: sn hdd: kpt on).......½ | **3** | 9/1 | 61 | 41 |
| 1872[2] | **Ret Frem (IRE) (65)** (MAJarvis) **3-8-9** PRobinson(2) (lw: chsd ldrs: led wl over 1f out tl wl ins fnl f: nt qckn)..1¼ | **4** | 5/2[1] | 69 | 39 |
| 1886[3] | **Thatched (IRE) (44)** (REBarr) **6-7-12** DaleGibson(8) (hld up: effrt & n.m.r appr fnl f: kpt on).......1¼ | **5** | 9/2[3] | 46 | 26 |
| | **Course Fishing (42)** (BAMcMahon) **5-7-10** GBardwell(3) (bhd: styd on fnl 2f: nrst fin).......½ | **6** | 14/1 | 43 | 23 |
| 1704[5] | **Cee-Jay-Ay (48)** (JBerry) **9-8-2** JCarroll(5) (s.s: hdwy 3f out: nvr trbld ldrs).......1¾ | **7** | 7/1 | 45 | 25 |
| 1486[12] | **New Albion (USA) (62)** (MissZAGreen) **5-9-2** JFanning(4) (w ldr tl wknd fnl 2f).......5 | **8** | 33/1 | 49 | 29 |
| 1596[10] | **Ihtimaam (FR) (45)** (MrsASwinbank) **4-7-13** JQuinn(1) (led tl hdd & wknd wl over 1f out).......3 | **9** | 50/1 | 26 | 6 |
| | **Red Valerian (70)** (GMMoore) **5-9-10b** JFortune(7) (stumbled & uns rdr leaving stalls)....... | **U** | 12/1 | — | — |

(SP 123.2%) **10 Rn**

**1m 37.4** (0.70 under best) (-1.20) CSF £31.70 CT £211.24 TOTE £8.30: £3.00 £1.30 £1.90 (£18.70) Trio £46.20 OWNER Mr R. D. Bickenson (RICHMOND) BRED Spendthrift Farm, Inc
WEIGHT FOR AGE 3yo-10lb
STEWARDS' ENQUIRY Duffield susp. 5-9/7/96 (excessive use of whip).

**1830* Habeta (USA),** looking as well as ever, was brought with a well-timed run to snatch it on the line, but his rider was judged to have been over-keen with his whip. (7/1)
**1886 Spanish Verdict** won this race four years ago and always gives a good account of himself here. Despite a valiant effort though, he was just touched off. (7/2)
**2023 Bulsara** ran a game race, being in the thick of things throughout, but just failing to quicken when it mattered. (9/1)
**1872 Ret Frem (IRE)** ran a sound race against older horses here and is not done with yet. (5/2)
**1886 Thatched (IRE)** ran better and did not have the best of runs. (9/2)
**Course Fishing** found this too sharp. (14/1)

## 2215 C. G. TRUCK H'CAP (0-70) (3-Y.O) (Class E)

4-15 (4-17) **5f 207y** £3,036.60 (£919.80: £449.40: £214.20) Stalls: High GOING minus 0.78 sec per fur (HD)

| | | | | SP | RR | SF |
|---|---|---|---|---|---|---|
| 1888$^{3}$ | **Fairy Prince (IRE) (54)** (MrsALMKing) **3-8-7**$^{(5)}$ FLynch(4) (disp ld: led 2f out: styd on wl) | — | **1** | 9/1 | 60 | 34 |
| 2151$^{2}$ | **Pathaze (49)** (NBycroft) **3-8-7** JFanning(8) (disp ld 4f: kpt on one pce) | 1¾ | **2** | 5/1$^{3}$ | 50 | 24 |
| 1780$^{12}$ | **Doug's Folly (46)** (MWEasterby) **3-8-4b** DaleGibson(2) (a chsng ldrs: kpt on u.p fnl f & edgd rt) | nk | **3** | 12/1 | 47 | 21 |
| 2049$^{4}$ | **Opening Chorus (53)** (DNicholls) **3-8-11** KDarley(3) (hdwy ½-wy: sn chsng ldrs: nt qckn fnl f) | ¾ | **4** | 7/4$^{1}$ | 52 | 26 |
| 2029$^{4}$ | **Ciserano (IRE) (63)** (MRChannon) **3-9-2**$^{(5)}$ PPMurphy(1) (a in tch: no hdwy fnl 2f) | 1¼ | **5** | 8/1 | 58 | 32 |
| 1527$^{4}$ | **Mullagh Hill Lad (IRE) (49)** (BAMcMahon) **3-8-7** GCarter(5) (sn outpcd & bhd: styd on wl fnl 2f) | hd | **6** | 6/1 | 44 | 18 |
| 2049$^{13}$ | **Tropical Beach (59)** (JBerry) **3-9-3** JCarroll(7) (s.i.s: nvr trbld ldrs) | 1½ | **7** | 14/1 | 50 | 24 |
| 1888$^{9}$ | **Answers-To-Thomas (54)** (JMJefferson) **3-8-12** KFallon(6) (chsd ldrs 4f) | 6 | **8** | 12/1 | 29 | 3 |
| 2049$^{5}$ | **The Butterwick Kid (47)** (RAFahey) **3-8-5v$^{1}$** JQuinn(9) (chsd ldrs 4f: wknd) | nk | **9** | 4/1$^{2}$ | 21 | — |
| | | | | (SP 130.5%) | **9 Rn** | |

**1m 12.4** (-0.10) CSF £55.61 CT £521.53 TOTE £11.70: £1.60 £2.00 £6.10 (£20.70) Trio £137.90 OWNER Mr A. Stennett (STRATFORD-UPON-AVON) BRED Jim O'Hara and Christian Healy
**1888 Fairy Prince (IRE)** continues his improvement and, although this was never easy, he did it well. (9/1: op 6/1)
**2151 Pathaze** jumped off on terms for a change and, although she tried hard, was always second best in the last two furlongs. (5/1)
**1405 Doug's Folly,** after a miserable run last time over probably too long a trip, ran better here and looks to be on the way back. (12/1)
**2049 Opening Chorus** was a shade disappointing and always struggling to improve. (7/4)
**2029 Ciserano (IRE)** was always in pursuit of the leaders but could never find the speed to take them on. (8/1)
**1527 Mullagh Hill Lad (IRE)** might have found this ground too firm in the early stages. (6/1)
**2049 The Butterwick Kid** ran indifferently in the visor. (4/1)

## 2216 WETHERAL RATING RELATED MAIDEN STKS (0-60) (3-Y.O+) (Class F)

4-45 (4-46) **2m 1f 52y** £2,563.00 (£718.00: £349.00) Stalls: High GOING minus 0.78 sec per fur (HD)

| | | | | SP | RR | SF |
|---|---|---|---|---|---|---|
| | **Royal Vacation (46)** (GMMoore) **7-9-12** JFortune(4) (lw: mde all: rdn & styd on wl fnl 3f) | — | **1** | 4/1$^{3}$ | 55 | — |
| | **Uplift (50)** (SirMarkPrescott) **3-8-2** GDuffield(3) (hdwy to chse wnr ½-wy: rdn 4f out: one pce) | 2½ | **2** | 3/1$^{2}$ | 49 | — |
| *1997*$^{3}$ | **Washington Reef (USA) (51)** (JHMGosden) **3-8-5b$^{1}$** JCarroll(5) (lw: chsd ldrs: rdn 4f out: nt r.o fnl 2f) | 6 | **3** | 7/4$^{1}$ | 46 | — |
| 1907$^{2}$ | **Mathon (IRE) (50)** (MRChannon) **3-8-0v**$^{(5)}$ PPMurphy(2) (outpcd & bhd ½-wy: sme hdwy 4f out: sn btn) | 21 | **4** | 3/1$^{2}$ | 27 | — |
| 1847$^{6}$ | **Tancred Mischief (35)** (DWBarker) **5-9-9** RLappin(1) (cl up tl outpcd ½-wy: sn bhd) | 7 | **5** | 10/1 | 18 | — |
| | | | | (SP 115.5%) | **5 Rn** | |

**3m 46.3** CSF £15.57 TOTE £5.80: £2.10 £1.90 (£5.70) OWNER Mr G. P. Edwards (MIDDLEHAM) BRED Small Breeders' Group
WEIGHT FOR AGE 3yo-20lb
**Royal Vacation,** a useful staying chaser, had no trouble with this trip and galloped his rivals into the ground. (4/1)
**Uplift** is slow but honest, which was never enough here. (3/1: 2/1-7/2)
**1997 Washington Reef (USA)** had the blinkers on for the first time, which had little effect once the pressure was on. (7/4)
**1907 Mathon (IRE)** was off the bit by halfway and took little interest thereafter. (3/1)
**1847 Tancred Mischief** got warm beforehand and was soon found out in the latter part of the race. (10/1)

## 2217 S. P. GRAHAM BOOKMAKERS BURGH BARONY RACES GENTLEMENS' LIMITED STKS (0-60) (3-Y.O+) (Class F)

5-15 (5-15) **1m 4f** £2,535.00 (£710.00: £345.00) Stalls: Low GOING minus 0.78 sec per fur (HD)

| | | | | SP | RR | SF |
|---|---|---|---|---|---|---|
| 2066* | **Kings Cay (IRE) (45)** (THCaldwell) **5-11-2** JCulloty(4) (trckd ldr: smooth hdwy to ld ins fnl f: pushed along & r.o: cheekily) | — | **1** | 10/11$^{1}$ | 68 | 49 |
| 2014$^{3}$ | **Grey Galava (60)** (BWHills) **3-9-7**$^{(4)}$ MrVLukaniuk(3) (led tl hdd ins fnl f: kpt on) | ½ | **2** | 9/4$^{2}$ | 62 | 29 |
| 2165$^{8}$ | **Anchorena (57)** (MrsASwinbank) **4-10-13** PHenley(2) (lw: trckd ldrs: effrt 3f out: sn rdn & one pce) | 6 | **3** | 3/1$^{3}$ | 56 | 37 |
| | **Jalore (28)** (SCoathup) **7-11-0**$^{(4)ow4}$ MrGJones(1) (t.o after 4f) | dist | **4** | 50/1 | — | — |
| | | | | (SP 110.1%) | **4 Rn** | |

**2m 33.3** (2.30) CSF £3.25 TOTE £1.90: (£1.80) OWNER Mr R. S. G. Jones (WARRINGTON) BRED The Woodhaven Stud in Ireland
WEIGHT FOR AGE 3yo-14lb
**2066* Kings Cay (IRE),** given a splendid ride, won a shade comfortably. (10/11: op Evens)
**2014 Grey Galava** just stays and gallops, but was always second best in the closing stages. (9/4)
**1487 Anchorena** travelled well on the bridle but, once off it in the last three furlongs, the required response was never there. (3/1)
**Jalore** looked extremely slow. (50/1)

T/Jkpt: Not won; £8,394.40 to Salisbury 27/6/96. T/Plpt: £1,723.80 (7.59 Tckts). T/Qdpt: £622.60 (1.2 Tckts). AA

# 1703-CHESTER (L-H) (Good to firm)

## Wednesday June 26th

WEATHER: sunny WIND: mod against

## 2218 YELLOW LABEL CLAIMING STKS (3-Y.O+) (Class D)

6-55 (6-56) **1m 2f 75y** £4,120.00 (£1,240.00: £600.00: £280.00) Stalls: High GOING minus 0.28 sec per fur (GF)

| | | | | SP | RR | SF |
|---|---|---|---|---|---|---|
| 1999$^{2}$ | **Rebel County (IRE) (71)** (MCPipe) **3-8-6** MRoberts(4) (chsd ldr: led over 3f out: qcknd clr ent fnl f: easily) | — | **1** | 2/5$^{1}$ | 59+ | 15 |
| *371*$^{3}$ | **Second Colours (USA) (66)** (MrsMReveley) **6-9-12** KDarley(1) (bit bkwd: led 1f: chsd wnr fnl 2f: no imp) | 6 | **2** | 9/4$^{2}$ | 58 | 26 |
| | **Ttyfran (35)** (BPJBaugh) **6-8-9**$^{(7)}$ IonaWands(2) (led after 1f tl over 3f out: sn drvn along & outpcd) | 3 | **3** | 50/1 | 43 | 11 |

| | | | | SP | RR | SF |
|---|---|---|---|---|---|---|
| 1830[10] | **Reed My Lips (IRE) (30)** (BPJBaugh) **5-8-13b** ACulhane(3) (b: lw: squeezed out s: sn pushed along: a outpcd) | 12 | **4** | 25/1[3] | 22 | — |
| | | | | (SP 108.0%) | | **4 Rn** |

**2m 15.65** (6.95) CSF £1.61 TOTE £1.40: (£1.10) OWNER Elite Racing Club (WELLINGTON) BRED C. J. Foy
WEIGHT FOR AGE 3yo-12lb
Rebel County (IRE) clmd ABailey £12,000
**1999 Rebel County (IRE),** faced with a comparatively easy task with her only serious rival being in need of a run, was able to complete it in the simplest possible fashion. (2/5: op 8/13)
**Second Colours (USA)** has done the majority of his racing at a mile in recent years. Carrying surplus condition for this first outing in almost four months, he was unable to offer a threat to the winner inside the distance. (9/4: op 11/8)
**Ttyfran** last saw the racecourse in April '95 and, though he did force the pace for quite some way, was soon in trouble after being collared three furlongs out. (50/1)
**Reed My Lips (IRE),** with rivals either side of him converging as the stalls opened, was forced to check. Nudged along to keep tabs on the leaders going out into the country, he was always fighting a lost cause. (25/1)

## 2219 WIDOW MAIDEN STKS (2-Y.O) (Class D)
7-25 (7-27) **5f 16y** £3,434.50 (£1,036.00: £503.00: £236.50) Stalls: Low GOING minus 0.28 sec per fur (GF)

| | | | | SP | RR | SF |
|---|---|---|---|---|---|---|
| 1184[2] | **Fredrik The Fierce (IRE)** (JBerry) **2-9-0** KDarley(1) (lw: mde all: shkn up wl over 1f out: r.o wl) | — | **1** | 7/2[2] | 76 | 34 |
| 1954[5] | **Maid By The Fire (USA)** (PFICole) **2-8-9** JCarroll(6) (bhd: drvn along ½-wy: effrt on ins ent st: nt rch wnr) | 1¼ | **2** | 9/4[1] | 67 | 25 |
| 1959[9] | **Commander Jones (IRE)** (BJMeehan) **2-9-0** MTebbutt(2) (bit bkwd: w wnr: rn wd ent st: sn rdn: kpt on fnl f) | 1 | **3** | 11/1 | 69 | 27 |
| 1166[2] | **Nomore Mr Niceguy** (EJAlston) **2-9-0** KFallon(4) (lw: trckd ldrs: effrt & ev ch appr fnl f: no ex) | ¾ | **4** | 13/2 | 67 | 25 |
| 1987[2] | **Mujova (IRE)** (RHollinshead) **2-8-9**(5) FLynch(3) (prom tl rdn & wknd over 1f out) | 2 | **5** | 9/2[3] | 60 | 18 |
| 1884[7] | **Baileys Imp (IRE)** (MJohnston) **2-9-0** MRoberts(5) (bhd: rdn 2f out: sn outpcd) | 1¼ | **6** | 14/1 | 56 | 14 |
| 1664[7] | **Princess of Hearts** (WJHaggas) **2-8-9** MHills(7) (s.s: a bhd & outpcd) | 2½ | **7** | 8/1 | 43 | 1 |
| | | | | (SP 110.6%) | | **7 Rn** |

**62.42 secs** (2.42) CSF £11.04 TOTE £3.20: £1.90 £1.70 (£3.20) OWNER Mr Chris Deuters (COCKERHAM) BRED Mrs J. M. Berry
**1184 Fredrik The Fierce (IRE)** was gelded after his previous outing. He gained the initiative from his inside stall and proceeded to make all for a comfortable first success. (7/2)
**1954 Maid By The Fire (USA),** having her first try at the minimum trip, was taken off her legs in the early stages and, though she did her best to mount a challenge into the final furlong, she lacked the speed to pose a serious threat. (9/4)
**Commander Jones (IRE),** who comes from a winning family, knew much more this time and, had he been able to handle the bend into the straight, would certainly have made a race of it. (11/1: 8/1-12/1)
**1166 Nomore Mr Niceguy,** an improving individual who should come into his own over further, found himself chopped for speed when the sprint to the line really got underway. (13/2)
**1987 Mujova (IRE),** if anything, would appear to be going backwards, for he was poised to challenge before getting well outpaced approaching the final furlong. (9/2)
**1884 Baileys Imp (IRE)** was always struggling here. (14/1)
**Princess of Hearts** (8/1: 6/1-9/1)

## 2220 PRIX DE LA GRANDE DAME RATED STKS H'CAP (0-95) (3-Y.O+) (Class C)
7-55 (7-56) **6f 18y** £8,321.60 (£3,094.40: £1,497.20: £626.00: £263.00: £117.80) Stalls: Low GOING minus 0.28 sec per fur (GF)

| | | | | SP | RR | SF |
|---|---|---|---|---|---|---|
| 1975* | **Cyrano's Lad (IRE) (91)** (CADwyer) **7-9-7** KFallon(4) (lw: mde all: clr 1f out: r.o wl) | — | **1** | 9/2[2] | 99 | 73 |
| 2114[15] | **Selhurstpark Flyer (IRE) (88)** (JBerry) **5-8-13**(5) PRoberts(10) (lw: chsd wnr thrght: rdn over 1f out: r.o ins fnl f) | 1 | **2** | 9/1 | 93 | 67 |
| 1703[8] | **Tiler (IRE) (78)** (MJohnston) **4-8-8** MRoberts(6) (a.p: hrd drvn over 1f out: kpt on wl ins fnl f) | nk | **3** | 14/1 | 83 | 57 |
| 1703[4] | **Highborn (IRE) (88)** (PSFelgate) **7-9-4** KDarley(5) (a.p: hrd drvn 2f out: nt pce to chal) | nk | **4** | 7/1[3] | 92 | 66 |
| 1430[11] | **Ziggy's Dancer (USA) (83)** (EJAlston) **5-8-13** JFortune(7) (trckd ldrs: effrt & rdn over 1f out: no imp) | 2½ | **5** | 8/1 | 80 | 54 |
| 1974[8] | **Lady Sheriff (84)** (RHollinshead) **5-8-9**(5) FLynch(2) (bhd & outpcd tl r.o appr fnl f) | 2 | **6** | 9/1 | 76 | 50 |
| 1829[4] | **Rock Symphony (84)** (WJHaggas) **6-9-0v[1]** MHills(1) (s.i.s: sn bhd & outpcd: rdn 2f out: no rspnse) | hd | **7** | 7/2[1] | 76 | 50 |
| 1799[5] | **Courageous Dancer (IRE) (82)** (BHanbury) **4-8-9**(3) JStack(3) (outpcd: effrt & rdn 2f out: no imp) | hd | **8** | 14/1 | 73 | 47 |
| 1974[4] | **Bajan Rose (85)** (MBlanshard) **4-9-1** JQuinn(8) (in tch: pushed along ½-wy: nvr gng pce of ldrs) | hd | **9** | 7/1[3] | 76 | 50 |
| 1334[9] | **Lord Olivier (IRE) (81)** (WJarvis) **6-8-11** MTebbutt(9) (outpcd: a bhd: t.o) | 6 | **10** | 14/1 | 56 | 30 |
| | | | | (SP 116.5%) | | **10 Rn** |

**1m 13.9** (0.60) CSF £40.46 CT £489.45 TOTE £7.20: £2.80 £2.20 £3.30 (£26.40) Trio £111.90 OWNER Mr M. M. Foulger (NEWMARKET) BRED J. C. Condon
**1975* Cyrano's Lad (IRE)** got the start which is so crucial on this track and, running away in front, did not need to get serious until the weight began to take its toll inside the last 100 yards. (9/2)
**1790* Selhurstpark Flyer (IRE)** ran well all the way and stuck to the task in hand inside the distance. He should soon be able to get back to winning ways. (9/1: op 6/1)
**610 Tiler (IRE)** gave notice that his turn is near with his best performance this season. A return to seven could see him back to form. (14/1)
**1703 Highborn (IRE)** can win at this trip but he has to work hard all the way. Another furlong is more suitable. (7/1: 6/1-9/1)
**1113 Ziggy's Dancer (USA),** at full stretch to hold his pitch in the chasing group, had to admit he had met his match below the distance. (8/1)
**1708 Lady Sheriff** was always being taken along much too fast. (9/1)
**1829 Rock Symphony,** in a visor, could not go the pace and was always struggling towards the rear. He did look at all happy on these bends. (7/2)

## 2221 CLIQUOT ROSE H'CAP (0-85) (3-Y.O+) (Class D)
8-25 (8-26) **1m 4f 66y** £4,068.00 (£1,224.00: £592.00: £276.00) Stalls: Low GOING minus 0.28 sec per fur (GF)

| | | | | SP | RR | SF |
|---|---|---|---|---|---|---|
| 2020[9] | **Soba Up (67)** (TJEtherington) **6-9-10** ACulhane(3) (hld up: hdwy to chse ldr 4f out: rdn to ld ent fnl f: hld on gamely) | — | **1** | 5/1[3] | 79 | 60 |
| 2046* | **Canton Venture (60)** (SPCWoods) **4-9-3** 5x DBiggs(4) (led to 1f out: rallied u.p towards fin) | nk | **2** | 4/5[1] | 72 | 53 |
| 872[3] | **Ciracusa (IRE) (64)** (JMackie) **4-9-7** GCarter(1) (lw: s.i.s: sn chsng ldrs: rdn & outpcd 3f out) | 8 | **3** | 9/2[2] | 65 | 46 |
| *1082*[3] | **Backview (60)** (BJLlewellyn) **4-9-3** TWilliams(2) (lw: chsd ldr 8f: sn rdn & lost pl) | 3½ | **4** | 11/2 | 57 | 38 |
| | | | | (SP 105.8%) | | **4 Rn** |

**2m 40.52** (3.92) CSF £8.95 TOTE £3.70: (£2.20) OWNER Mrs M. Hills (MALTON) BRED Mrs M. J. Hills
**OFFICIAL EXPLANATION Soba Up: the course and faster pace on this occasion appeared to suit the mare.**

**Soba Up** reserves her best for this track and returned to form with a courageous first success of the season which was richly deserved. (5/1)
**2046* Canton Venture** has been on a roll but he has been going up the weights and, though he went down fighting, could have found the penalty his undoing. (4/5)
**872 Ciracusa (IRE)**, restrained after losing ground at the start, had no answer when the leading pair quickened things up three furlongs out, and he was soon outpaced. (9/2)
**1082 Backview** found this ground a problem. (11/2)

## 2222 ST. PETERSBURG H'CAP (0-80) (3-Y.O) (Class D)

8-55 (8-55) **7f 2y** £4,380.00 (£1,320.00: £640.00: £300.00) Stalls: Low GOING minus 0.28 sec per fur (GF)

| | | | | SP | RR | SF |
|---|---|---|---|---|---|---|
| 1985[2] | **Albert The Bear (77)** (JBerry) **3-9-7** KDarley(7) (lw: mde virtually all: hrd drvn fnl f: hld on wl) | — | **1** | 3/1[1] | 83 | 40 |
| 2005[12] | **Finisterre (IRE) (63)** (JJO'Neill) **3-8-7** KFallon(2) (lw: hld up: gd hdwy wl over 1f out: str chal fnl f: r.o) | ½ | **2** | 9/2[3] | 68 | 25 |
| 1689[9] | **Scenicris (IRE) (60)** (RHollinshead) **3-7-13**(5)ow3 FLynch(4) (hld up: hdwy to chse wnr ½-wy: rdn over 1f out: sn btn) | 2½ | **3** | 10/1 | 59 | 13 |
| 1823[7] | **Polly Golightly (75)** (MBlanshard) **3-9-5** JQuinn(1) (lw: s.i.s: hld up & bhd: effrt 2f out: nvr nr to chal) | 2½ | **4** | 7/1 | 68 | 25 |
| 2078[7] | **Myttons Mistake (74)** (ABailey) **3-9-1**(3) DWright(3) (prom: rdn over 1f out: wknd fnl f) | 2 | **5** | 4/1[2] | 63 | 20 |
| 1597[6] | **Purple Memories (64)** (MJohnston) **3-8-8** MRoberts(5) (bit bkwd: dropped rr 3f out: sn hrd drvn: no imp) | s.h | **6** | 3/1[1] | 53 | 10 |

(SP 109.8%) **6 Rn**

**1m 28.8** (3.60) CSF £15.05 TOTE £2.50: £1.80 £1.90 (£6.10) OWNER Mr Chris Deuters (COCKERHAM) BRED Rockhouse Farms Ltd
**1985 Albert The Bear** seemed well suited to this step up to seven and, though he was forced to put his best foot forward in the latter stages, he was conceding 14lb to the runner-up. (3/1)
**1527* Finisterre (IRE)**, inclined to run his race in snatches, did deliver a determined last-furlong challenge but the winner had enough in the tank to hold him at bay. (9/2)
**740 Scenicris (IRE)**, still struggling to get off the mark, was on the heels of the winner below the distance, but that rival kept up the gallop and she was unable to respond. (10/1)
**1652 Polly Golightly**, held up to get the trip after missing the beat at the start, did not enjoy the best of passages when asked for her effort entering the straight, and was never able to mount a challenge. (7/1)
**1708 Myttons Mistake**, a previous winner at this trip, pushed the pace and had every chance until fading under pressure approaching the final furlong. (4/1)
**1597 Purple Memories** looked far from fully wound up. Blinkers may help. (3/1)

## 2223 PONSARDIN MAIDEN STKS (3-Y.O) (Class D)

9-25 (9-28) **1m 5f 89y** £4,120.00 (£1,240.00: £600.00: £280.00) Stalls: Low GOING minus 0.28 sec per fur (GF)

| | | | | SP | RR | SF |
|---|---|---|---|---|---|---|
| | **Haleakala (IRE)** (MJohnston) **3-8-9** MRoberts(3) (w'like: leggy: s.i.s: pushed along thrght: hdwy over 3f out: led appr fnl f: qcknd clr: impressive) | — | **1** | 5/1 | 93+ | — |
| 1644[3] | **Fancy Heights** (LadyHerries) **3-8-9** KDarley(2) (lw: a.p: led over 2f out: rdn & hdd appr fnl f: one pce) | 6 | **2** | 7/4[1] | 86 | — |
| 1895[2] | **Kawanin (82)** (PTWalwyn) **3-8-9** JCarroll(5) (chsd ldr 8f: rdn & outpcd fnl 2f) | 3 | **3** | 3/1[3] | 82 | — |
| 1071[3] | **Madame Steinlen (79)** (BWHills) **3-8-9** MHills(4) (led & sn clr: pushed along 4f out: hdd over 2f out: sn wknd: t.o) | 10 | **4** | 5/2[2] | 70 | — |
| 2062[6] | **So Keen** (ABailey) **3-9-0** JFortune(1) (lw: s.s: a bhd: lost tch ½-wy: t.o) | 1¾ | **5** | 33/1 | — | — |

(SP 109.5%) **5 Rn**

**3m 26.72** (36.72) CSF £13.38 TOTE £5.40: £2.40 £1.70 (£5.70) OWNER Sheikh Mohammed (MIDDLEHAM) BRED Sheikh Mohammed Bin Rashid Al Maktoum
**Haleakala (IRE)**, a well-bred filly making her belated racecourse debut, proved very green and was being bustled along from the start. Taking closer order inside the last half-mile, she got the better of the favourite entering the final furlong, and showed a rare turn of foot to forge clear and win going away. She may not have beaten much but can only get better and looks very useful. (5/1)
**1644 Fancy Heights**, an impressive and easy mover, looked to have matters in hand early in the straight, but was swamped for speed when the winner found top gear and was made to look very ordinary. (7/4)
**1895 Kawanin** should have been in her element over this extended trip, but was hard at work entering the straight, and her measure had been taken. (3/1)
**1071 Madame Steinlen** again adopted front-running tactics, but was flat to the boards before being headed, and was down to a walk on reaching the straight. (5/2)

T/Plpt: £275.60 (41.51 Tckts). T/Qdpt: £83.70 (5.82 Tckts). IM

# 1871-KEMPTON (R-H) (Good to firm)
## Wednesday June 26th

WEATHER: warm WIND: almost nil

## 2224 E.B.F. MAIDEN STKS (2-Y.O) (Class D)

6-40 (6-40) **7f (Jubilee)** £3,550.00 (£1,075.00: £525.00: £250.00) Stalls: High GOING: minus 0.36 sec per fur (F)

| | | | | SP | RR | SF |
|---|---|---|---|---|---|---|
| | **Sheer Folly (USA)** (PFICole) **2-9-0** TQuinn(7) (leggy: scope: lw: dwlt: hdwy 6f out: rdn over 2f out: n.m.r on ins & swtchd lft over 1f out: led ins fnl f: rn green) | — | **1** | 4/1[2] | 88+ | 20 |
| 1896[2] | **Eurolink Excaliber (USA)** (JLDunlop) **2-9-0** PatEddery(4) (lw: a.p: led over 2f out tl ins fnl f: unable qckn) | 1¾ | **2** | 11/8[1] | 84 | 16 |
| 1683[2] | **Mister Pink** (RFJohnsonHoughton) **2-9-0** JReid(6) (rdn over 2f out: hdwy over 1f out: r.o) | 1¾ | **3** | 12/1 | 80 | 12 |
| 1960[7] | **Head Gardener (IRE)** (JLDunlop) **2-9-0** TSprake(3) (rdn over 2f out: hdwy over 1f out: r.o) | 3 | **4** | 20/1 | 73 | 5 |
| 1960[6] | **Sheer Face** (WRMuir) **2-9-0** WJO'Connor(1) (a.p: ev ch wl over 1f out: sn wknd) | 2½ | **5** | 20/1 | 67 | — |
| 1871[10] | **William Wallace** (CMurray) **2-9-0** AMackay(11) (a.p: rdn over 2f out: wknd over 1f out) | 2 | **6** | 40/1 | 63 | — |
| | **Elhafid (USA)** (MajorWRHern) **2-9-0** RHills(12) (lw: hld up: rdn 4f out: eased whn btn ins fnl f) | ¾ | **7** | 5/1[3] | 61 | — |
| 1191[9] | **Sun O'Tirol (IRE)** (MRChannon) **2-9-0** RPerham(9) (mid div whn n.m.r on ins over 2f out tl wl over 1f out: nvr nr to chal) | 1½ | **8** | 20/1 | 58 | — |
| 815[7] | **Yangtze (IRE)** (BRMillman) **2-9-0** JFEgan(2) (bhd whn hmpd over 1f out) | 1 | **9** | 40/1 | 55 | — |
| | **Tirage** (CEBrittain) **2-9-0** BDoyle(10) (str: scope: bit bkwd: led over 4f) | 5 | **10** | 9/1 | 44 | — |
| | **Silca's My Key (IRE)** (MRChannon) **2-9-0** DHolland(8) (w'like: prom 2f) | 4 | **11** | 14/1 | 35 | — |
| | **Mutahadeth** (NAGraham) **2-9-0** AMcGlone(5) (w'like: scope: bit bkwd: a bhd) | 1¾ | **12** | 16/1 | 31 | — |

| | Horse | Dist | Pos | SP | RR | SF |
|---|---|---|---|---|---|---|
| | **Tulsa (IRE)** (BGubby) **2-9-0** GHind(13) (cmpt: s.s: a bhd) | 5 | **13** | 25/1 | 19 | — |

(SP 132.0%) **13 Rn**

**1m 28.66** (4.16) CSF £10.47 TOTE £5.90: £1.90 £1.60 £1.10 (£4.40) Trio £10.70 OWNER Al Muallim Partnership (WHATCOMBE) BRED T. F. Van Meter & L. B. Van Meter

**Sheer Folly (USA)** cost $180,000 as a yearling. Not clued up for this, he still proved up to the task and, recovering from a tardy start, began to get going in the straight, but did not have much room along the inside rail behind the leader. Switched left, he ran very green indeed, but nevertheless came through to lead inside the final furlong. He showed a very high knee-action and may be better with a bit of cut. (4/1)

**1896 Eurolink Excaliber (USA)** was unable to withstand the winner inside the final furlong, though he did finish clear second best. He should make no mistakes next time out. (11/8)

**1683 Mister Pink**, pushed along early in the straight, stayed on in the last furlong and a half but was unable to get there in time. (12/1: 10/1-16/1)

**Head Gardener (IRE)** stepped up on his initial run last week, despite still looking in need of the run. Shaken up early in the straight, he was doing some pleasing late work in the last furlong and a half. (20/1)

**Sheer Face** tired approaching the final furlong. (20/1)

**William Wallace** played an active role until coming to the end of his tether below the distance. (40/1)

**Elhafid (USA)** (5/1: op 5/2)

**Tirage** (9/1: 6/1-10/1)

## 2225 SUMMER CONDITIONS STKS (3-Y.O F) (Class C)

7-10 (7-10) **1m (Jubilee)** £5,033.50 (£1,763.50: £864.25: £373.75) Stalls: High GOING minus 0.36 sec per fur (F)

| | Horse | Dist | Pos | SP | RR | SF |
|---|---|---|---|---|---|---|
| 1855* | **Wandering Star (USA) (86)** (JRFanshawe) **3-8-12** NDay(1) (hld up: rdn to chse ldr 2f out: led ins fnl f: r.o wl) | — | **1** | 13/8[2] | 93 | 36 |
| 1060a[10] | **Tamnia (102)** (JLDunlop) **3-9-6** TQuinn(3) (hld up: led over 2f out: rdn over 1f out: hdd ins fnl f: unable qckn) | 1½ | **2** | 4/1[3] | 98 | 41 |
| 1771[11] | **La Modiste (83)** (SDow) **3-9-0** PatEddery(4) (led over 5f: wknd wl over 1f out) | 11 | **3** | 8/1 | 70 | 13 |
| 1335[6] | **Silk Masque (USA) (96)** (PWChapple-Hyam) **3-8-12** JReid(2) (lw: w ldr over 5f) | 2 | **4** | 5/4[1] | 64 | 7 |

(SP 113.7%) **4 Rn**

**1m 40.18** (2.98) CSF £7.64 TOTE £2.20: (£3.10) OWNER Aylesfield Farms Stud (NEWMARKET) BRED Mr and Mrs R. Lyons

**1855* Wandering Star (USA)**, pushed along to take second place a quarter of a mile from home, threw down the gauntlet and eventually managed to get on top inside the final furlong to win readily. (13/8)

**1060a Tamnia** bounced back to form here. Moving into the lead approaching the final quarter-mile, she was given no peace whatsoever by the winner and eventually had to concede defeat inside the final furlong. (4/1: 9/4-9/2)

**La Modiste** looked very dry in her coat. (8/1: tchd 12/1)

**1335 Silk Masque (USA)** does not appear to have trained on and flopped. (5/4)

## 2226 VANGUARD PARTNERSHIP H'CAP (0-70) (3-Y.O+) (Class E)

7-40 (7-51) **1m 4f** £3,696.25 (£1,120.00: £547.50: £261.25) Stalls: High GOING: minus 0.36 sec per fur (F)

| | Horse | Dist | Pos | SP | RR | SF |
|---|---|---|---|---|---|---|
| 1640[4] | **Nordansk (48)** (MMadgwick) **7-8-3**(3) NVarley(2) (lw: hdwy over 3f out: led over 2f out: r.o wl) | — | **1** | 7/1[3] | 61 | 46 |
| 2008* | **Make a Stand (69)** (MCPipe) **5-9-13** PatEddery(6) (a.p: led 4f out tl over 2f out: hrd rdn: r.o wl ins fnl f) | hd | **2** | 5/2[1] | 82 | 67 |
| 1486[6] | **Miswaki Dancer (USA) (55)** (LadyHerries) **6-8-13** DeclanO'Shea(9) (b: hld up: rdn over 2f out: unable qckn) | 6 | **3** | 10/1 | 60 | 45 |
| 1965[2] | **Fabulous Mtoto (49)** (MSSaunders) **6-8-7** RPrice(1) (hdwy 6f out: rdn over 2f out: sn wknd) | 3½ | **4** | 9/2[2] | 49 | 34 |
| 2155[7] | **Bronze Maquette (IRE) (38)** (THind) **6-7-10** FNorton(5) (lw: hld up: rdn over 2f out: wknd fnl f) | 3 | **5** | 16/1 | 34 | 19 |
| 1874[8] | **Double Echo (IRE) (54)** (JDBethell) **8-8-12** JReid(12) (hdwy over 3f out: wknd over 1f out) | 2½ | **6** | 9/2[2] | 47 | 32 |
| 1965[11] | **Rock The Barney (IRE) (50)** (PBurgoyne) **7-8-8** DRMcCabe(3) (lw: hdwy over 2f out: nvr nrr) | ½ | **7** | 8/1 | 42 | 27 |
| 968[11] | **Edan Heights (70)** (SDow) **4-9-9**(5) ADaly(8) (hdwy over 2f out: sn wknd) | 7 | **8** | 20/1 | 53 | 38 |
| 1961[7] | **Horesti (70)** (CEBrittain) **4-10-0b[1]** BDoyle(14) (bhd fnl 5f) | 3 | **9** | 12/1 | 49 | 34 |
| *1444[5]* | **Sorisky (38)** (BGubby) **4-7-10** NAdams(4) (led over 9f out to 4f out: sn wknd) | hd | **10** | 33/1 | 17 | 2 |
| *69[9]* | **Broughtons Formula (48)** (WJMusson) **6-7-13**(7) JWilkinson(10) (lw: a bhd) | 11 | **11** | 12/1 | 12 | — |
| | **Warspite (57)** (RJO'Sullivan) **6-9-1** DHarrison(7) (led over 2f: wknd 5f out) | 10 | **12** | 33/1 | 8 | — |
| 1996[8] | **Royal Thimble (IRE) (57)** (NoelChance) **5-9-1** WJO'Connor(11) (prom 7f) | 9 | **13** | 33/1 | — | — |
| *1852[5]* | ***Rocquaine Bay (41)*** (MJBolton) **9-7-10**(3) MHenry(13) (Withdrawn not under Starter's orders: crowd noise startled horse, which uns rdr & bolted) | | **W** | 8/1 | — | — |

(SP 143.6%) **13 Rn**

**2m 33.1** (2.40) CSF £26.11 CT £170.54 TOTE £11.70: £2.20 £1.70 £2.70 (£22.20) Trio £117.00 OWNER Mr T. Smith (DENMEAD) BRED George and Mrs Steinberg

LONG HANDICAP Bronze Maquette (IRE) 7-9 Sorisky 7-6

OFFICIAL EXPLANATION **Royal Thimble (IRE): was found to be in season the following morning.**

**1640 Nordansk** gained compensation for his disqualification here last month. Moving up turning for home, he hit the front over a quarter of a mile out and just managed to hold off the persistent runner-up. (7/1)

**2008* Make a Stand** went for home half a mile out. Collared approaching the last two furlongs, that appeared to be that as far as he was concerned, but he rallied in splendid style inside the final furlong and only just failed to get back up. He should soon gain compensation. (5/2)

**Miswaki Dancer (USA)** chased the leaders and, although struggling on for third prize, was left for dead by the front two. (10/1)

**1965 Fabulous Mtoto**, ridden along early in the straight, soon had bellows to mend. (9/2)

**1874 Bronze Maquette (IRE)**, making a quick reappearance, chased the leaders but was being scrubbed along early in the straight, and had run out of gas entering the final furlong. (16/1)

**1874 Double Echo (IRE)** had cooked his goose below the distance. (9/2)

## 2227 GALA STKS (Listed) (3-Y.O+) (Class A)

8-10 (8-15) **1m 2f (Jubilee)** £12,990.00 (£3,640.00: £1,770.00) Stalls: Low GOING: minus 0.36 sec per fur (F)

| | Horse | Dist | Pos | SP | RR | SF |
|---|---|---|---|---|---|---|
| 1817* | **Bal Harbour (106)** (HRACecil) **5-9-4** PatEddery(1) (lw: mde all: shkn up over 1f out: comf) | — | **1** | 1/2[1] | 105 | 56 |
| 929[2] | **Jural (105)** (SbinSuroor) **4-8-13** JReid(3) (swtg: hld up: chsd wnr over 3f out: rdn over 1f out: unable qckn) | 2½ | **2** | 3/1[2] | 96 | 47 |
| 1580a[8] | **Flyfisher (IRE) (104)** (GLewis) **3-8-6** TQuinn(2) (swtg: chsd wnr over 6f: wknd over 2f out) | 2½ | **3** | 5/1[3] | 97? | 36 |

(SP 108.3%) **3 Rn**

**2m 5.5** (2.00) CSF £2.21 TOTE £1.50: (£1.40) OWNER Mr K. Abdulla (NEWMARKET) BRED Juddmonte Farms

WEIGHT FOR AGE 3yo-12lb

**1817* Bal Harbour** had little more than a nice workout here. Making all the running, he needed only to be shaken up below the distance to dispose of the runner-up. (1/2: op 4/5)
**929 Jural** moved into second place over three furlongs from home and grimly tried to get in a challenge, but she was put in her place from below the distance. (3/1: op 6/4)
**1580a Flyfisher (IRE)** raced in second place until over three furlongs from home, and the writing was then on the wall. (5/1: op 3/1)

## 2228 '1812' OVERTURE H'CAP (0-80) (3-Y.O+) (Class D)
8-40 (8-41) **6f** £3,636.00 (£1,098.00: £534.00: £252.00) Stalls: High GOING: minus 0.36 sec per fur (F)

| | | | | SP | RR | SF |
|---|---|---|---|---|---|---|
| 2034* | **So Intrepid (IRE) (77)** (JMBradley) **6-10-0** 6x PatEddery(10) (lw: s.s: hdwy over 1f out: hrd rdn: led last strides) | — | **1** | 6/1 | 84 | 63 |
| 1905* | **Sea-Deer (77)** (CADwyer) **7-10-0** RHughes(6) (lw: hld up: rdn to ld over 1f out: hdd last strides) | nk | **2** | 4/1 1 | 83 | 62 |
| 1777 2 | **La Petite Fusee (73)** (RJO'Sullivan) **5-9-10** TQuinn(3) (b.nr hind: led over 4f: one pce) | 3 | **3** | 9/2 2 | 71 | 50 |
| 1958 8 | **Be Warned (70)** (NACallaghan) **5-9-7** PaulEddery(8) (lw: s.s: hdwy over 1f out: r.o ins fnl f) | ½ | **4** | 12/1 | 67 | 46 |
| 1624 13 | **Dashing Dancer (IRE) (59)** (RAkehurst) **5-8-10** SSanders(7) (lw: hdwy over 2f out: rdn wl over 1f out: one pce) | 1¼ | **5** | 9/1 | 53 | 32 |
| 1958 7 | **Robo Magic (USA) (54)** (LMontagueHall) **4-8-5** JFEgan(1) (a.p: rdn over 2f out: one pce) | s.h | **6** | 11/1 | 47 | 26 |
| 2193 5 | **Dancing Heart (65)** (BJMeehan) **4-9-2** BDoyle(2) (lw: prom over 4f) | 1 | **7** | 9/1 | 56 | 35 |
| 1853 13 | **Dry Point (68)** (JARToller) **10-9-5** JReid(9) (rdn & hdwy over 1f out: sn wknd) | 1½ | **8** | 16/1 | 55 | 34 |
| 1799 8 | **Sue Me (IRE) (60)** (WRMuir) **4-8-11** WJO'Connor(4) (a.p: rdn over 2f out: eased whn btn fnl f) | 3 | **9** | 14/1 | 39 | 18 |
| 824 4 | **Dummer Golf Time (62)** (LordHuntingdon) **3-8-6** DHarrison(5) (prom over 4f) | hd | **10** | 5/1 3 | 41 | 13 |
| 1805 4 | **Enchanted Guest (IRE) (73)** (PWHarris) **3-9-3** GHind(11) (lw: spd over 4f) | 15 | **11** | 9/1 | 12 | — |
| | | | | (SP 127.7%) | | **11 Rn** |

**1m 12.58** (1.28) CSF £31.03 CT £115.84 TOTE £7.20: £2.20 £1.70 £1.60 (£9.60) Trio £7.10 OWNER Mr E. A. Hayward (CHEPSTOW) BRED Crest Stud Ltd
WEIGHT FOR AGE 3yo-7lb
**2034* So Intrepid (IRE)**, who lost ground at the start, began to weave his way through the pack below the distance and, though he had several lengths to make up on the leader, managed to wear him down and get to the front in the last few strides. (6/1)
**1905* Sea-Deer**, ridden along to gain the initiative approaching the final furlong, looked set to complete the five-timer in the final furlong, but he had not bargained on the late run of the winner and was caught in the last few strides. He should soon return to the winner's enclosure. (4/1)
**1777 La Petite Fusee** was collared approaching the final furlong and left for dead. (9/2)
**1588 Be Warned** weaved his way through the pack in the last furlong and a half to be nearest at the line. (12/1: op 8/1)
**981 Dashing Dancer (IRE)** failed to summon up another gear below the distance. (9/1)
**266* Robo Magic (USA)** failed to quicken in the last two furlongs. (11/1)
**2193 Dancing Heart** (9/1: 6/1-10/1)

## 2229 FIREWORKS H'CAP (0-80) (3-Y.O+) (Class D)
9-10 (9-11) **7f (round)** £3,753.00 (£1,134.00: £552.00: £261.00) Stalls: High GOING: minus 0.36 sec per fur (F)

| | | | | SP | RR | SF |
|---|---|---|---|---|---|---|
| | **Young Duke (IRE) (65)** (RJBaker) **8-8-12**(3) PMcCabe(6) (hdwy over 4f out: led over 2f out: rdn out) | — | **1** | 16/1 | 74 | 49 |
| 1775 5 | **Sharp Rebuff (74)** (PJMakin) **5-9-10** PatEddery(1) (a.p: ev ch over 2f out: unable qckn) | 1½ | **2** | 5/1 3 | 80 | 55 |
| 2134 3 | **Broughtons Turmoil (63)** (WJMusson) **7-8-13** AMcGlone(7) (b: hdwy over 1f out: r.o) | 1¼ | **3** | 4/1 2 | 66 | 41 |
| 1991 5 | **Winsome Wooster (60)** (PGMurphy) **5-8-7**(3) SDrowne(2) (lw: hld up: rdn over 2f out: one pce) | 1 | **4** | 12/1 | 60 | 35 |
| 1617 4 | **Nunsharpa (71)** (JRFanshawe) **3-8-12** DHarrison(4) (hld up: rdn over 2f out: one pce) | 1¼ | **5** | 7/2 1 | 69 | 35 |
| 2005 8 | **Sea Thunder (69)** (IABalding) **4-9-0**(5) MartinDwyer(9) (a.p: rdn over 2f out: wknd fnl f) | ½ | **6** | 8/1 | 65 | 40 |
| 1121 5 | **Victory Team (IRE) (65)** (GBBalding) **4-9-1** AClark(12) (swtg: nvr nr to chal) | 1 | **7** | 9/1 | 59 | 34 |
| 1532 3 | **Crystal Heights (FR) (61)** (RJO'Sullivan) **8-8-11** RHughes(5) (lw: s.s: hdwy over 3f out: wknd over 2f out) | 2 | **8** | 16/1 | 51 | 26 |
| 1693 8 | **Utmost Zeal (USA) (62)** (PWHarris) **3-8-3** GHind(10) (bhd fnl 5f) | nk | **9** | 25/1 | 51 | 17 |
| 2032 10 | **Indrapura (IRE) (60)** (PFICole) **4-8-10** TQuinn(3) (lw: led over 4f) | ¾ | **10** | 16/1 | 47 | 22 |
| 1442 7 | **Balance of Power (63)** (RAkehurst) **4-8-13b** SSanders(8) (s.s: a bhd) | 3 | **11** | 14/1 | 43 | 18 |
| | **Hurtleberry (IRE) (75)** (LordHuntingdon) **3-8-13**(3) MHenry(11) (bhd fnl 2f) | s.h | **12** | 10/1 | 55 | 21 |
| | | | | (SP 124.9%) | | **12 Rn** |

**1m 26.18** (1.68) CSF £91.90 CT £366.31 TOTE £19.50: £3.90 £2.10 £1.70 (£51.30) Trio £143.30 OWNER Mrs Sarah Williams (TIVERTON) BRED Mrs P. F. McQuillan
WEIGHT FOR AGE 3yo-9lb
**Young Duke (IRE)** made a tremendous return, having been off the course for a year. Having his first run for his new stable, he moved up turning for home and, sent on over a quarter of a mile out, was ridden along to secure victory. (16/1)
**1775 Sharp Rebuff** had every chance early in the straight before the winner was let loose. (5/1)
**2134 Broughtons Turmoil** stayed on in the last furlong and a half but, by then, it was all too late. (4/1)
**1991 Winsome Wooster** chased the leaders, but failed to find another gear in the last two furlongs. (12/1)
**1617 Nunsharpa** chased the leaders but, pushed along early in the straight, could only go up and down in the same place. (7/2)
**2005 Sea Thunder** played an active role. Ridden along early in the straight, she had come to the end of her tether a furlong from home. (8/1)
**Balance of Power** (14/1: 10/1-16/1)

T/Plpt: £12.40 (1,166.26 Tckts). T/Qdpt: £7.00 (103.08 Tckts). AK

# 1851-SALISBURY (R-H) (Good to firm, Firm patches)
## Wednesday June 26th
Race 6: hand timed
WEATHER: overcast & showers WIND: almost nil

## 2230 E.B.F. WEYHILL MAIDEN STKS (2-Y.O F) (Class D)
2-00 (2-00) **5f** £3,600.00 (£1,080.00: £520.00: £240.00) Stalls: High GOING minus 0.31 sec per fur (GF)

| | | | | SP | RR | SF |
|---|---|---|---|---|---|---|
| | **Arruhan (IRE)** (PTWalwyn) **2-8-11** RHills(8) (leggy: lw: s.i.s: wl bhd tl gd hdwy & swtchd rt over 1f out: str run to ld wl ins fnl f) | — | **1** | 9/2 2 | 81+ | 32 |

| | | | | SP | RR | SF |
|---|---|---|---|---|---|---|
| | **Chili Concerto** (PJMakin) **2-8-11** SSanders(3) (small: lt-f: bkwd: w ldr: led over 1f out: hdd wl ins fnl f) | ¾ | 2 | 50/1 | 79 | 30 |
| 1998[2] | **Rise 'n Shine** (CACyzer) **2-8-11** TQuinn(7) (trckd ldrs: rdn over 2f out: one pce fnl f) | 2½ | 3 | 10/1 | 71 | 22 |
| 1480[4] | **Third Party** (SDow) **2-8-6**(5) ADaly(1) (hld up: no hdwy fnl 2f) | 2 | 4 | 33/1 | 64 | 15 |
| | **Head Over Heels (IRE)** (JHMGosden) **2-8-11** PatEddery(2) (str: scope: prom over 3f) | nk | 5 | 7/1 3 | 63 | 14 |
| 1105[2] | **Royal Orchid (IRE)** (RHannon) **2-8-11** JReid(5) (lw: led over 3f: eased whn btn ins fnl) | 3 | 6 | 4/7 1 | 54 | 5 |
| | **Quibbling** (HCandy) **2-8-11** CRutter(4) (leggy: a bhd) | hd | 7 | 11/1 | 53 | 4 |
| | **Lucy of Arabia (IRE)** (JJSheehan) **2-8-8**(3) SDrowne(6) (outpcd) | 1½ | 8 | 33/1 | 49 | — |
| | | | | (SP 119.6%) | **8 Rn** | |

**62.27 secs** (2.27) CSF £117.84 TOTE £5.80: £1.60 £3.70 £1.30 (£78.50) OWNER Mr Hamdan Al Maktoum (LAMBOURN) BRED Shadwell Estate Company Limited

OFFICIAL EXPLANATION **Royal Orchid (IRE): lost her action in the final furlong, and then appeared lame behind after the race.**

**Arruhan (IRE)**, very green early on - she jumped a path after a furlong and a half - looked a totally different proposition once grasping what was required. Entered for both the Lowther and the Cheveley Park, she could be anything on this showing. (9/2: 3/1-5/1)

**Chili Concerto**, though not very big, did look in need of this and can be expected to win a race on this showing. (50/1)

**1998 Rise 'n Shine**, a half-sister to Crazy Paving, could not answer her wake-up call and may need a return to six. (10/1: 8/1-12/1)

**1480 Third Party** is a half-sister to Passion For Life. (33/1)

**Head Over Heels (IRE)** is likely to need further, but was not knocked about once her chance had gone. (7/1: 3/1-8/1)

**1105 Royal Orchid (IRE)** lost her action in the closing stages and the Vet reported that the filly appeared lame behind. (4/7)

## 2231 MARGADALE CONDITIONS STKS (3-Y.O) (Class C)

2-30 (2-31) **6f 212y** £4,822.00 (£1,798.00: £874.00: £370.00: £160.00: £76.00) Stalls: High GOING minus 0.31 sec per fur (GF)

| | | | | SP | RR | SF |
|---|---|---|---|---|---|---|
| 1465* | **Strazo (IRE)** (JHMGosden) **3-9-0** PatEddery(1) (lw: chsd ldr: led over 3f out: all out) | — | 1 | 5/4 1 | 90 | 50 |
| | **Oleana (IRE)** (PFICole) **3-8-9** TQuinn(3) (hld up: chsd wnr over 2f out: hrd rdn over 1f out: ev ch fnl f: unable qckn) | ½ | 2 | 7/2 2 | 84 | 44 |
| 1350* | **Slip Jig (IRE) (85)** (RHannon) **3-9-0** JReid(2) (hld up: rdn & one pce fnl 2f) | 5 | 3 | 6/1 | 77 | 37 |
| 1891* | **Finsbury Flyer (IRE)** (RJHodges) **3-8-7**(3) SDrowne(4) (s.i.s: nvr trbld ldrs) | 4 | 4 | 20/1 | 64 | 24 |
| 768[5] | **Mishaweer** (JRFanshawe) **3-8-5** DHarrison(5) (rdn 3f out: wl bhd fnl 2f) | 5 | 5 | 33/1 | 48 | 8 |
| 1578a* | **Second Barrage** (LMCumani) **3-9-2** OUrbina(6) (tall: scope: led over 3f: sn wknd) | 1¼ | 6 | 9/2 3 | 56 | 16 |
| | | | | (SP 106.8%) | **6 Rn** | |

**1m 27.93** (1.93) CSF £5.46 TOTE £2.20: £2.30 £1.80 (£2.20) OWNER Mr K. Abdulla (NEWMARKET) BRED Juddmonte Farms

**1465* Strazo (IRE)** made hard work of this but had to contend with a combination of faster ground and a shorter trip. (5/4)

**Oleana (IRE)**, well backed, did not look all that enthusiastic, but still forced the winner to pull out all the stops. She could well have been feeling the ground and deserves another chance. (7/2: 6/1-3/1)

**1350* Slip Jig (IRE)** could not go with the two principals from below the distance. (6/1: 7/2-13/2)

**1891* Finsbury Flyer (IRE)** found this company a different kettle of fish. (20/1)

**1578a* Second Barrage** dropped away once tackled at halfway. (9/2: 3/1-5/1)

## 2232 SOLENT PREMIER CLUB SPRINT H'CAP (0-85) (3-Y.O+) (Class D)

3-00 (3-01) **5f** £3,580.50 (£1,074.00: £517.00: £238.50) Stalls: High GOING minus 0.31 sec per fur (GF)

| | | | | SP | RR | SF |
|---|---|---|---|---|---|---|
| 1853[8] | **Mister Jolson (75)** (RJHodges) **7-9-2**(3) SDrowne(5) (a.p: rdn over 1f out: led nr fin) | — | 1 | 4/1 3 | 84 | 50 |
| 1974[14] | **Tart and a Half (78)** (BJMeehan) **4-9-1b**(7) DSweeney(1) (led: rdn over 1f out: hdd nr fin) | hd | 2 | 5/1 | 87 | 53 |
| 1790[7] | **Golden Pound (USA) (77)** (MissGayKelleway) **4-9-7** WJO'Connor(4) (swtg: a.p: hrd rdn over 1f out: r.o ins fnl f) | ½ | 3 | 9/2 | 84 | 50 |
| 1790[10] | **Bowden Rose (84)** (MBlanshard) **4-9-9b**(5) CAdamson(2) (lw: hdwy 3f out: hung bdly lft over 1f out: nt rcvr) | 1¼ | 4 | 11/4 1 | 87 | 53 |
| 2064[5] | **Sally Slade (78)** (CACyzer) **4-9-8** PatEddery(3) (lw: rdn & no hdwy fnl 2f) | 1½ | 5 | 3/1 2 | 76 | 42 |
| | | | | (SP 106.5%) | **5 Rn** | |

**61.59 secs** (1.59) CSF £19.77 TOTE £4.40: £1.70 £1.90 (£7.50) OWNER Mr Bob Froome (SOMERTON) BRED Mrs D. D. Scott

**1652 Mister Jolson** is considered well handicapped by his trainer and, although he has only once scored over six, he will have one more outing before a tilt at the Stewards' Cup. (4/1)

**1630 Tart and a Half** put up a spirited bid to make all, but could not quite hold the winner. (5/1: op 3/1)

**1521 Golden Pound (USA)** seemed to find this minimum trip on the sharp side. (9/2)

**1630 Bowden Rose**, whose rider seemed to take an age to pull his whip through, eventually finished up under the stands' rail and could well have won had she kept a straight course. (11/4)

**2064 Sally Slade** was 5lb higher than when winning at Goodwood. (3/1)

## 2233 GIBBS MEW BIBURY CUP H'CAP (0-95) (3-Y.O) (Class C)

3-30 (3-30) **1m 4f** £5,540.00 (£1,670.00: £810.00: £380.00) Stalls: Low GOING minus 0.31 sec per fur (GF)

| | | | | SP | RR | SF |
|---|---|---|---|---|---|---|
| 2135[6] | **Village King (IRE) (72)** (RHannon) **3-8-1** JFEgan(3) (hld up: rdn 4f out: hdwy over 2f out: r.o to ld nr fin) | — | 1 | 13/2 | 78 | 46 |
| 1409[2] | **Generosa (84)** (HCandy) **3-8-13** TQuinn(1) (chsd ldr: led 3f out: hdd nr fin) | ½ | 2 | 3/1 2 | 89 | 57 |
| 1973* | **Bowled Over (86)** (CACyzer) **3-9-1** JReid(2) (hld up: hrd rdn over 1f out: one pce) | 6 | 3 | 3/1 2 | 83 | 51 |
| 1783[3] | **Ela-Yie-Mou (IRE) (82)** (LMCumani) **3-8-11** PatEddery(4) (swtg: hld up & plld hrd: swtchd lft over 2f out: sn rdn: fnd nil) | 7 | 4 | 2/1 1 | 70 | 38 |
| 2006[8] | **Ski Academy (IRE) (92)** (PWChapple-Hyam) **3-9-2**(5) RHavlin(5) (lw: led: rn wd bnd over 6f out: rdn & hdd 3f out: wknd 2f out) | 2 | 5 | 5/1 3 | 77 | 45 |
| | | | | (SP 113.3%) | **5 Rn** | |

**2m 34.94** (2.34) CSF £24.20 TOTE £6.30: £2.00 £1.50 (£10.80) OWNER Mr N. Ahamad (MARLBOROUGH) BRED Gerry Canavan

**2135 Village King (IRE)** was inclined to edge a shade left in the closing stages and scored more decisively than the margin indicates. (13/2)

**1409 Generosa** gets the trip well enough, but got worn down towards the finish. (3/1)

**1973* Bowled Over** lacked the necessary acceleration in the final furlong and a half. (3/1)

**1783 Ela-Yie-Mou (IRE)**, dropping back in distance, was rather too keen for his own good but this was still very disappointing. (2/1)

## 2234 MARTIN CLAIMING STKS (3-Y.O+) (Class F)

4-00 (4-01) **1m** £2,721.00 (£756.00: £363.00) Stalls: High GOING minus 0.31 sec per fur (GF)

| | | | | SP | RR | SF |
|---|---|---|---|---|---|---|
| 1506[4] | **Monument (68)** (JSKing) **4-9-8** BDoyle(7) (a.p: led wl over 1f out: rdn out) | — | 1 | 4/1 3 | 68 | 46 |
| 1535[4] | **Witherkay** (RHannon) **3-9-0** PatEddery(4) (lw: hld up: rdn & hdwy 2f out: swtchd lft ins fnl f: r.o) | ¾ | 2 | 8/1 | 69 | 37 |

1638[3] **Blockade (USA) (67)** (MBell) **7-9-5** MFenton(6) (t: swtg: led over 6f: r.o one pce) ....1 **3** 5/2[2] 62 40
982[5] **Reinhardt (IRE) (82)** (PWChapple-Hyam) **3-8-7**(7) RCody-Boutcher(1) (lw: prom: rdn over 3f out: r.o one pce fnl 2f) ....¾ **4** 9/4[1] 65 33
1953[8] **Desert Calm (IRE) (53)** (MrsPNDutfield) **7-9-3b** CRutter(2) (nvr nrr) ....4 **5** 8/1 50 28
2133[10] **Only (USA) (52)** (RHannon) **3-9-0** WJO'Connor(8) (lw: prom: rdn over 3f out: wknd over 2f out) ....4 **6** 16/1 49 17
*2081*[8] **Lilac Rain (39)** (JRArnold) **4-8-7** TQuinn(5) (prom: rdn over 4f out: wknd over 2f out) ....2 **7** 20/1 28 6
**Ebony T-A-P-S** (JSMoore) **3-7-8**(7)ow2 JKeenan(3) (bit bkwd: bhd whn rdn & hung rt over 3f out: t.o) ....23 **8** 50/1 — —
(SP 114.2%) **8 Rn**

**1m 43.89** (3.49) CSF £31.96 TOTE £6.10: £2.50 £2.00 £1.60 (£16.20) OWNER Mrs P. M. King (SWINDON) BRED Exors of the late Mrs D. M. de Rothschild

WEIGHT FOR AGE 3yo-10lb
**1506 Monument** was not exactly head and shoulders above these, but held on well to the line. (4/1: 3/1-9/2)
**1535 Witherkay** seems to have got the hang of racing, but could not peg back the winner in time. (8/1)
**1638 Blockade (USA)**, very warm in the paddock, did not cave in when headed. (5/2)
**982 Reinhardt (IRE)**, dropped in class, would have had much more to do had this been a handicap. (9/4)
**1685 Desert Calm (IRE)** has twice scored over nine furlongs in Ireland, and seems to find a mile inadequate these days. (8/1: 6/1-9/1)

## 2235 SHREWTON RATING RELATED MAIDEN STKS (0-65) (3-Y.O) (Class F)

4-30 (4-31) **6f 212y** £2,784.00 (£774.00: £372.00) Stalls: High GOING minus 0.31 sec per fur (GF)

SP RR SF

1617[8] **Bandit Girl (62)** (IABalding) **3-8-11** JReid(8) (hld up: rdn over 2f out: r.o to ld last strides) ....— **1** 100/30[1] 66 24
1671[5] **Anak-Ku (65)** (MissGayKelleway) **3-9-0** WJO'Connor(10) (lw: w ldrs: rdn 3f out: led ins fnl f: hdd last strides) ....hd **2** 8/1 69 27
1773[11] **White Settler (64)** (RJHodges) **3-8-11**(3) SDrowne(1) (lw: hld up & bhd: swtchd lft & hdwy over 2f out: ev ch ins fnl f: unable qckn) ....¾ **3** 20/1 67 25
2013[4] **Velvet Jones (60)** (GFHCharles-Jones) **3-9-0** SWhitworth(2) (hld up & bhd: hdwy 3f out: rdn over 2f out: one pce fnl f) ....2½ **4** 100/30[1] 61 19
1119[8] **Needle Match (62)** (CFWall) **3-9-0** PatEddery(6) (led tl ins fnl f) ....1¼ **5** 5/1[3] 58 16
1901[15] **Flying Harold (63)** (MRChannon) **3-9-0** CandyMorris(5) (lw: hld up: bhd fnl 2f) ....9 **6** 20/1 38 —
1657[4] **Extra Hour (IRE) (62)** (WRMuir) **3-8-9**(5) RHavlin(7) (w ldrs tl wknd qckly 2f out) ....1¼ **7** 14/1 35 —
1984[4] **Belzao (65)** (MRChannon) **3-9-0** TQuinn(3) (lw: rdn over 3f out: sn bhd) ....4 **8** 9/2[2] 26 —
539[8] **Ya Marhaba (40)** (JWPayne) **3-9-0** BThomson(4) (hld up: rdn & wknd over 2f out) ....¾ **9** 33/1 24 —
1908[9] **Maraschino (53)** (BJMeehan) **3-8-11** BDoyle(9) (prom 4f) ....9 **10** 33/1 — —
(SP 114.2%) **10 Rn**

**1m 30.0** (4.00) CSF £27.19 TOTE £3.60: £2.00 £2.10 £3.70 (£25.30) Trio £131.30 OWNER Mr J. C. Smith (KINGSCLERE) BRED Littleton Stud
**1195 Bandit Girl** responded to pressure to land the spoils near the line. (100/30)
**1671 Anak-Ku** benefited from his first run on turf last time. (8/1: op 5/1)
**White Settler**, dropping back to seven, came with a dangerous-looking run on the outside but could not sustain his effort. (20/1)
**2013 Velvet Jones** could not produce an extra gear. (100/30: 5/1-3/1)
**528 Needle Match** did not last home over this shorter trip. (5/1: op 3/1)
**Extra Hour (IRE)** (14/1: 7/1-16/1)
**1984 Belzao** (9/2: 3/1-5/1)

T/Plpt: £555.30 (19.92 Tckts). T/Qdpt: £33.20 (35.89 Tckts). KH

# 2211-CARLISLE (R-H) (Firm)

## Thursday June 27th

WEATHER: overcast WIND: mod across

## 2236 WALTON MEDIAN AUCTION MAIDEN STKS (3 & 4-Y.O) (Class E)

2-15 (2-15) **5f 207y** £2,845.50 (£861.00: £420.00: £199.50) Stalls: High GOING minus 0.70 sec per fur (HD)

SP RR SF

1475[7] **Craignairn (66)** (JBerry) **3-9-0b[1]** JCarroll(3) (mde all: hld on wl fnl f) ....— **1** 7/2[2] 64 29
1888[2] **Nattier (57)** (SirMarkPrescott) **3-8-9** GDuffield(2) (lw: chsd wnr: rdn 2f out: kpt on u.p towards fin) ....½ **2** 4/5[1] 58 23
*531*[8] **Marino Street** (PDEvans) **3-8-9** JFortune(5) (a chsng ldrs: styd on u.p fnl 2f: nrst fin) ....hd **3** 7/1 57 22
1860[6] **Camionneur (IRE) (49)** (TDEasterby) **3-9-0** KDarley(1) (s.i.s: hdwy ½-wy: rdn & no imp fnl 2f) ....6 **4** 9/2[3] 46 11
1764[4] **Nutcracker Suite (IRE) (45)** (JLEyre) **4-9-2** RLappin(4) (outpcd ½-wy: no imp after) ....2 **5** 33/1 36 8
(SP 111.4%) **5 Rn**

**1m 13.4** (0.90) CSF £6.66 TOTE £5.30: £1.40 £1.20 (£1.70) OWNER Mr Murray Grubb (COCKERHAM) BRED Llety Stud
WEIGHT FOR AGE 3yo-7lb
**Craignairn** had blinkers on for the first time and was back to form. It will be interesting to see if they work again. (7/2)
**1888 Nattier** had her chances and was staying on at the finish, but left the distinct impression that, had she fully co-operated, she would certainly have won. (4/5)
**515 Marino Street**, having her first run on turf in this country, put up a reasonable show and was keeping on at the end. (7/1)
**1068 Camionneur (IRE)** has his own ideas and was never doing enough. (9/2)
**Nutcracker Suite (IRE)** has yet to show anything positive this season. (33/1)

## 2237 CUMREW (S) STKS (2-Y.O) (Class G)

2-45 (2-46) **5f** £2,248.00 (£628.00: £304.00) Stalls: High GOING minus 0.70 sec per fur (HD)

SP RR SF

1989[8] **Taome (IRE)** (PDEvans) **2-8-6** JFortune(3) (mde most: hld on wl fnl f) ....— **1** 9/4[2] 66 3
1543* **Brutal Fantasy (IRE)** (NTinkler) **2-9-4** KDarley(2) (trckd ldrs gng wl: effrt & wandered over 1f out: r.o towards fin) ....nk **2** 8/15[1] 77 14
*1720*[4] **No Rush** (JBerry) **2-8-11** JCarroll(1) (disp ld over 3f: hung lft & sn btn) ....7 **3** 6/1[3] 48 —
**Timely Touch** (MWEllerby) **2-8-3**(3) CTeague(4) (small: lt-f: bkwd: s.s: sn wl t.o) ....30 **4** 50/1 — —
(SP 112.2%) **4 Rn**

**62.1 secs** (1.90) CSF £3.91 TOTE £3.70 (£1.50) OWNER Mr M. W. Lawrence (WELSHPOOL) BRED Thomas Doherty
Bt in 7,700gns; Brutal Fantasy (IRE) clmd JLEyre £6,000

**1499 Taome (IRE)**, dropped in class, proved to be made of the right stuff, despite her size. Taking first run, she refused to give in. (9/4)
**1543* Brutal Fantasy (IRE)** should have won this but his rider was overconfident, and then his mount ran green and could never quite make it. (8/15)
**1543 No Rush** was well outpointed here when the pace hotted up and probably added to the favourite's downfall by hanging into him approaching the final furlong. (6/1)
**Timely Touch** looked useless but, where there's life, there's hope. (50/1)

## 2238 LADBROKES LUCKY CHOICE H'CAP (0-70) (3-Y.O) (Class E)

3-15 (3-16) **5f** £2,954.70 (£894.60: £436.80: £207.90) Stalls: High GOING minus 0.70 sec per fur (HD)

| | | | SP | RR | SF |
|---|---|---|---|---|---|
| 1840$^{10}$ | **Pharaoh's Joy (52)** (JWPayne) **3-8-6**$^{ow1}$ KFallon(3) (lw: cl up: led 2f out & edgd rt: rdn out) ........................— | **1** | 5/1$^{3}$ | 64 | 28 |
| 2193$^{12}$ | **Ramsey Hope (67)** (CWFairhurst) **3-9-7b** NKennedy(5) (prom: nt clr run & swtchd 2f out: r.o wl fnl f)............nk | **2** | 20/1 | 78 | 43 |
| 2021$^{4}$ | **Katy-Q (IRE) (55)** (PCalver) **3-8-9b** MBirch(7) (lw: chsd ldrs: kpt on one pce fnl 2f) ......................................3½ | **3** | 4/1$^{2}$ | 55 | 20 |
| 1612$^{8}$ | **Good To Talk (45)** (TDEasterby) **3-7-13**$^{ow2}$ JFanning(4) (disp ld 3f: sltly hmpd wl over 1f out: nt qckn) ............1 | **4** | 20/1 | 42 | 5 |
| 2151* | **Precious Girl (74)** (DMoffatt) **3-9-11v**$^{(3)}$ 7x DarrenMoffatt(9) (hld up: effrt 2f out: nvr rchd ldrs).........................1 | **5** | 13/8$^{1}$ | 67 | 32 |
| 2029$^{5}$ | **Gagajulu (60)** (PDEvans) **3-9-0** JFortune(8) (effrt whn hmpd 2f out: sn btn).......................................................2 | **6** | 7/1 | 47 | 12 |
| 2021$^{6}$ | **Mystique Smile (46)** (SCWilliams) **3-7-11b**$^{1(3)}$ DWright(6) (b.hind: disp ld 3f: wknd over 1f out) ....................hd | **7** | 8/1 | 33 | — |
| 1674$^{14}$ | **Dancing Rainbow (50)** (MJCamacho) **3-8-4b**$^{1}$ GDuffield(2) (racd wd: spd 3f: sn btn) .......................................2 | **8** | 16/1 | 30 | — |
| | | | (SP 113.8%) | **8 Rn** | |

**60.5 secs** (0.30) CSF £75.09 CT £396.79 TOTE £8.00: £1.90 £2.80 £1.20 (£52.10) OWNER Pyramid Racing Club (NEWMARKET) BRED Mrs L. Popely
OFFICIAL EXPLANATION **Precious Girl: her trainer reported that the race had come too quickly for her, and she had not enjoyed the firm going.**
**Pharaoh's Joy** showed a useful turn of foot to get away two furlongs out, and that was just enough to see her home. (5/1)
**1599 Ramsey Hope** might have won this but for getting messed about entering the final two furlongs, but he is a funny customer who can not be relied upon. (20/1)
**2021 Katy-Q (IRE)** is in reasonable form, but is short of a real turn of foot. (4/1)
**Good To Talk** ran better this time, but was short of toe when the winner crossed him well over a furlong out. (20/1)
**2151* Precious Girl** never got into this and may have been feeling this very firm ground. (13/8)
**2029 Gagajulu** was already struggling when being chopped for room entering the last two furlongs. (7/1)

## 2239 UCB FILMS CUMBERLAND PLATE H'CAP (0-80) (3-Y.O+) (Class D)

3-45 (3-46) **1m 4f** £6,840.00 (£2,070.00: £1,010.00: £480.00) Stalls: Low GOING minus 0.70 sec per fur (HD)

| | | | SP | RR | SF |
|---|---|---|---|---|---|
| 2141* | **Desert Frolic (IRE) (65)** (MJohnston) **3-8-5** 5x TWilliams(5) (trckd ldr: led & qcknd over 3f out: r.o wl) ...........— | **1** | 7/4$^{1}$ | 84 | 48 |
| 2217* | **Kings Cay (IRE) (50)** (THCaldwell) **5-8-4** 5x GCarter(2) (hld up: hdwy to chse wnr 2f out: r.o wl).....................¾ | **2** | 11/4$^{2}$ | 68 | 46 |
| 2060$^{2}$ | **Royal Circus (42)** (PRWebber) **7-7-7**$^{(3)}$ DWright(3) (prom tl lost pl 6f out: hdwy & ch 3f out: sn rdn & one pce) ........................................................................8 | **3** | 7/1 | 49 | 27 |
| 2068$^{4}$ | **Floating Line (70)** (EJAlston) **8-9-10** KFallon(4) (led tl hdd over 3f out: sn outpcd)...........................................8 | **4** | 8/1 | 67 | 45 |
| 2020$^{3}$ | **Green Land (BEL) (60)** (SCWilliams) **4-9-0** KDarley(6) (trckd ldrs: effrt over 3f out: no rspnse) .....................1½ | **5** | 4/1$^{3}$ | 55 | 33 |
| 2020$^{7}$ | **Latvian (66)** (RAllan) **9-9-6** JFortune(1) (hld up: effrt over 3f out: sn rdn & btn) ...............................................1½ | **6** | 14/1 | 59 | 37 |
| | | | (SP 113.3%) | **6 Rn** | |

**2m 28.8** (1.50 under best) (-2.20) CSF £6.83 TOTE £2.90: £1.70 £1.70 (£3.20) OWNER Maktoum Al Maktoum (MIDDLEHAM) BRED Gainsborough Stud Management Ltd
LONG HANDICAP Royal Circus 7-8
WEIGHT FOR AGE 3yo-14lb
**2141* Desert Frolic (IRE)** is getting better as she goes over further and this was a particularly good performance in which she broke the track record. (7/4)
**2217* Kings Cay (IRE)** is on tremendous form but, despite a gallant effort, could never overhaul the useful winner. (11/4: 2/1-3/1)
**2060 Royal Circus** is running well at the moment but the first two were too good for him in the last two furlongs. (7/1)
**2068 Floating Line** is coming to hand looks-wise, but was well outclassed here. (8/1)
**2020 Green Land (BEL)** has her own ideas about the game. (4/1)

## 2240 RED MILLS IRISH HORSEFEEDS LADIES' H'CAP (0-65) (3-Y.O+) (Class G)

4-15 (4-16) **6f 206y** £2,276.00 (£636.00: £308.00) Stalls: High GOING minus 0.70 sec per fur (HD)

| | | | SP | RR | SF |
|---|---|---|---|---|---|
| 2023* | **Tinklers Folly (55)** (DenysSmith) **4-10-9**$^{(5)}$ 5x MissMCarson(2) (bhd: hdwy 3f out: r.o to ld wl ins fnl f) ...........— | **1** | 9/2 | 66 | 45 |
| 2149$^{6}$ | **My Gallery (IRE) (62)** (ABailey) **5-11-2**$^{(5)}$ MissBridgetGatehouse(6) (chsd ldrs: led wl over 1f out tl wl ins fnl f: no ex) .............................................................................................1 | **2** | 7/2$^{2}$ | 71 | 50 |
| 2047$^{4}$ | **Silver Welcome (56)** (TDEasterby) **3-10-1**$^{(5)}$ MissADeniel(7) (set str pce tl hdd wl over 1f out: sn btn) .............3 | **3** | 4/1$^{3}$ | 58 | 28 |
| 1778$^{4}$ | **Phase One (IRE) (50)** (JLEyre) **6-10-9** MissDianaJones(5) (chsd ldr: ev ch 2f out: sn rdn & btn).......................4 | **4** | 11/4$^{1}$ | 43 | 22 |
| 2022$^{4}$ | **Wasblest (57)** (JBerry) **4-11-2** MrsLPearce(1) (bhd: hdwy over 2f out: nvr rchd ldrs) ..........................................2 | **5** | 8/1 | 45 | 24 |
| 1684$^{6}$ | **Naughty Pistol (USA) (52)** (PDEvans) **4-10-11** MrsDKettlewell(3) (rdn ½-wy: nvr trbld ldrs) ...............................1 | **6** | 16/1 | 38 | 17 |
| 1865$^{4}$ | **Rinus Manor (IRE) (51)** (EJAlston) **5-10-10** MissPRobson(4) (lw: dwlt: rdn ½-wy: a bhd)...............................1¾ | **7** | 9/1 | 33 | 12 |
| | | | (SP 114.1%) | **7 Rn** | |

**1m 27.7** (2.00) CSF £19.48 TOTE £4.10: £2.40 £1.30 (£6.20) OWNER Mr R. O. Manners (BISHOP AUCKLAND) BRED Qualitair Stud Ltd
WEIGHT FOR AGE 3yo-9lb
**2023* Tinklers Folly**, well suited by the strong pace, quickened in useful style to settle it late on. (9/2)
**2149 My Gallery (IRE)**, who again did not impress on looks, does not know how to run a bad race but she had no answer to the winner's late surge. (7/2: 3/1-9/2)
**2047 Silver Welcome** went off at a breakneck pace and was picked off in the last two furlongs. (4/1)
**1778 Phase One (IRE)** had her chances but failed to go through with the effort when ridden in the last two furlongs. (11/4)
**1865 Rinus Manor (IRE)** missed the break and never showed a thing. (9/1)

## 2241 RAYOPHANE H'CAP (0-70) (3-Y.O) (Class E)

4-45 (4-46) **7f 214y** £3,118.50 (£945.00: £462.00: £220.50) Stalls: High GOING minus 0.70 sec per fur (HD)

| | | | SP | RR | SF |
|---|---|---|---|---|---|
| 1850$^{10}$ | **Generous Present (46)** (JWPayne) **3-7-8**$^{(3)}$ DWright(1) (lw: bhd: effrt 3f out: r.o u.p to ld wl ins fnl f: hung rt).......................................................................................— | **1** | 5/1$^{2}$ | 57 | 29 |

2123* **Napoleon's Return (45)** (AHarrison) **3-7-3v**(7) JennyBenson(2) (led: qcknd over 2f out: hdd & no ex wl ins fnl f) ....1 **2** 9/2 1 54 26
*1721*4 **Jimjareer (IRE) (50)** (CaptJWilson) **3-8-1** GCarter(3) (a chsng ldrs: effrt & ch 2f out: one pce)....1¼ **3** 6/1 57 29
18864 **Society Girl (59)** (CWThornton) **3-8-10** DeanMcKeown(5) (b.nr hind: lw: sn in tch: hdwy & ev ch 2f out: sn rdn & btn) ....2 **4** 5/1 2 62 34
20275 **Sistar Act (70)** (MRChannon) **3-9-2**(5) PPMurphy(7) (lw: outpcd & lost tch 4f out: styd on fnl 2f: n.d) ....3 **5** 11/2 3 67 39
185011 **Alfayza (57)** (JDBethell) **3-8-8** KFallon(8) (chsd ldrs tl wknd fnl 2f) ....s.h **6** 8/1 53 25
18509 **She's Simply Great (IRE) (50)** (JJO'Neill) **3-8-1** GDuffield(9) (cl up tl wknd fnl 2f)....1¾ **7** 16/1 43 15
15394 **Green Gem (BEL) (65)** (SCWilliams) **3-9-2** KDarley(6) (lw: chsd ldrs tl wknd 2f out)....1¾ **8** 6/1 54 26
**No More Hassle (IRE) (46)** (MrsMReveley) **3-7-11**ow1 TWilliams(4) (sn outpcd & bhd)....14 **9** 33/1 7 —
(SP 115.4%) **9 Rn**

**1m 38.3** (-0.30) CSF £25.97 CT £113.49 TOTE £8.20: £1.70 £2.00 £2.00 (£21.70) Trio £112.70 OWNER Mr Alex Penman (NEWMARKET) BRED Snowdrop Stud Co Ltd
LONG HANDICAP No More Hassle (IRE) 7-1
**1850 Generous Present** loves to come from behind and made up a lot of ground in the straight to snatch it in the final 100 yards, despite giving his rider problems by hanging right. (5/1)
**2123* Napoleon's Return** is in particularly good heart and, after trying hard, was just touched off. (9/2)
**1721 Jimjareer (IRE)** had his chances and kept staying on, but is short of a turn of foot. There would seem to be a race in him. (6/1)
**1886 Society Girl** was never really allowed to settle here and, after getting into it two furlongs out, was then soon ridden and beaten. (5/1)
**2027 Sistar Act** has ability but likes things to go her way and never took any interest this time until staying on when it was all over. (11/2)

## 2242 CARLISLE RACE CLUB LIMITED STKS (0-60) (3-Y.O+) (Class F)
5-15 (5-17) **7f 214y** £2,717.00 (£762.00: £371.00) Stalls: High GOING minus 0.70 sec per fur (HD)

SP RR SF

153810 **Gymcrak Flyer (60)** (GHolmes) **5-9-2** KFallon(2) (b.hind: hld up: hdwy 3f out: led wl over 1f out: pushed along & r.o) ....— **1** 8/11 1 67 34
20195 **Creeking (60)** (SirMarkPrescott) **3-8-6** GDuffield(3) (led tl hdd wl over 1f out: kpt on u.p) ....½ **2** 9/4 2 66 23
44514 **Tirols Tyrant (IRE) (60)** (MrsASwinbank) **3-8-9** JFortune(1) (chsd ldr tl outpcd fnl 2½f) ....4 **3** 10/1 61 18
16385 **Miss Charlie (49)** (TWall) **6-9-4** RLappin(4) (plld hrd: effrt & swtchd 2f out: rdn & no imp) ....hd **4** 7/1 3 60 27
(SP 110.3%) **4 Rn**

**1m 39.6** (1.00) CSF £2.71 TOTE £1.90 (£1.70) OWNER The Gymcrak Thoroughbred Racing Club (PICKERING) BRED D. G. Mason
WEIGHT FOR AGE 3yo-10lb
**1069 Gymcrak Flyer** looked big and well and won nicely, suggesting that there is more to come. (8/11: Evens-11/10)
**2019 Creeking** tried all she could out in front and kept fighting back when headed, but it was always in vain. (9/4: op 6/4)
**Tirols Tyrant (IRE)** showed up well but, once the pace increased in the straight, looked well short of speed. (10/1)
**1638 Miss Charlie** pulled too hard for her own good and was never doing enough when it mattered. (7/1)

T/Plpt: £158.70 (57.75 Tckts). T/Qdpt: £28.30 (33.9 Tckts). AA

# 1896-NEWBURY (L-H) (Good to firm)
## Thursday June 27th
WEATHER: fine WIND: slt half against

## 2243 POTHUNTERS/RAINBOW TRUST MAIDEN STKS (2-Y.O C & G) (Class D)
6-30 (6-34) **6f 8y** £3,850.00 (£1,150.00: £550.00: £250.00) Stalls: High GOING minus 0.48 sec per fur (F)

SP RR SF

20572 **Juwwi** (MajorWRHern) **2-8-11** RHills(5) (hld up: shkn up to ld over 1f out: comf) ....— **1** 9/4 1 79+ 25
**Flaming West (USA)** (HRACecil) **2-8-11** PatEddery(8) (scope: lw: a.p: led over 2f out tl over 1f out: rn green)....5 **2** 9/4 1 66 12
**Rehearsal (IRE)** (CACyzer) **2-8-11** MRoberts(6) (leggy: scope: outpcd: hdwy fnl f: r.o) ....2½ **3** 25/1 59 5
111810 **Midatlantic** (PTWalwyn) **2-8-11** DHolland(3) (a.p: ev ch over 2f out: wknd over 1f out) ....1 **4** 33/1 57 3
**Soda Pop (IRE)** (CEBrittain) **2-8-11** BDoyle(7) (leggy: scope: bhd fnl 2f) ....½ **5** 25/1 55 1
**Effervescence** (RHannon) **2-8-8**(3) DaneO'Neill(2) (b.nr hind: w'like: scope: led over 3f: wknd over 1f out) ..1½ **6** 16/1 51 —
**Aim Seven** (RHannon) **2-8-11** RHughes(4) (leggy: scope: hld up: ev ch over 2f out: wknd over 1f out)....¾ **7** 5/1 3 49 —
***Soviet State (USA)*** (PWChapple-Hyam) **2-8-11** JReid(1) (Withdrawn not under Starter's orders: lame at s) ..... **W** 11/4 2 — —
(SP 121.4%) **7 Rn**

**1m 14.03** (2.23) CSF £5.03 TOTE £2.30: £1.40 £2.00 (£2.00) OWNER Mr Hamdan Al Maktoum (LAMBOURN) BRED Shadwell Estate Company Limited
**2057 Juwwi** put his experience to good use. Tucked in behind the principals, he was shaken up to come through and lead below the distance, and comfortably disposed of his rivals. (9/4)
**Flaming West (USA)** was the subject on encouraging home reports, but was as green as grass. Sent on over a quarter of a mile from home, he was headed below the distance and then fly-jumped a couple of times and changed his legs in the final furlong. Eddery allowed him to coast in when all chance had gone, but the colt should make no mistakes next time out after this experience. (9/4)
**Rehearsal (IRE)** was soon outpaced, but did stay on in the final furlong past beaten horses. (25/1)
**Midatlantic** left his debut well behind. A leading light from the off, he had every chance over a quarter of a mile from home before tiring approaching the final furlong. (33/1)
**Soda Pop (IRE)** was getting left behind in the last two furlongs. (25/1)
**Effervescence** dictated things from the front on this debut. Collared over a quarter of a mile from home, he had shot his bolt below the distance. (16/1)

## 2244 KINGSTON SMITH H'CAP (0-75) (3-Y.O+) (Class D)
7-00 (7-02) **5f 34y** £4,175.00 (£1,250.00: £600.00: £275.00) Stalls: High GOING minus 0.48 sec per fur (F)

SP RR SF

16847 **John O'Dreams (48)** (MrsALMKing) **11-8-10** MRoberts(5) (b: hmpd s: hdwy over 1f out: led ins fnl f: rdn out) ....— **1** 13/2 3 54 30
21562 **Clan Chief (58)** (JRArnold) **3-9-0** TQuinn(6) (b.hind: led: rdn over 1f out: hdd ins fnl f: r.o wl)....s.h **2** 4/1 2 64 34
110118 **Literary Society (USA) (64)** (JARToller) **3-9-6** SSanders(4) (stumbled s: hld up: rdn over 1f out: ev ch ins fnl f: unable qckn)....1 **3** 16/1 67 37

| | | | SP | RR | SF |
|---|---|---|---|---|---|
| 2119[6] | **Featherstone Lane (51)** (MissLCSiddall) **5-8-13v** GHind(10) (hdwy over 2f out: ev ch ins fnl f: one pce).......1¼ | **4** | 10/1 | 50 | 26 |
| 1688* | **Step On Degas (67)** (MJFetherston-Godley) **3-9-4**(5) FLynch(7) (a.p: ev ch wl over 1f out: one pce)................¾ | **5** | 4/1[2] | 64 | 34 |
| 2156[14] | **Miami Banker (50)** (WRMuir) **10-8-12** GBardwell(8) (swtg: prom over 3f)..........................................................4 | **6** | 14/1 | 34 | 10 |
| 1853[10] | **Bangles (64)** (LordHuntingdon) **6-9-12** DHarrison(1) (a.p: rdn over 2f out: eased whn btn ins fnl f) ................s.h | **7** | 5/2[1] | 48 | 24 |
| 1844[8] | **Halbert (58)** (PBurgoyne) **7-9-6v** DRMcCabe(9) (a bhd).................................................................................1¼ | **8** | 14/1 | 38 | 14 |
| 1101[14] | **Magic Mail (72)** (JMPEustace) **3-10-0** MTebbutt(2) (lw: prom 3f)..........................................................................s.h | **9** | 14/1 | 52 | 22 |
| | | | (SP 116.9%) | **9 Rn** | |

**61.62 secs** (1.42) CSF £31.04 CT £366.79 TOTE £7.40: £1.70 £1.30 £7.20 (£10.70) Trio £375.00; £84.52 to 29/6/96 OWNER Mr Peter Brazier (STRATFORD-UPON-AVON) BRED Stephen Stanhope

WEIGHT FOR AGE 3yo-6lb

**951 John O'Dreams**, put to sleep at the back of the field, began his effort from below the distance and, sweeping into the lead 75 yards from the line, was ridden along to keep the persistent runner-up at bay. (13/2)

**2156 Clan Chief** attempted to make all. Passed by the winner inside the final furlong, he refused to give way and, although only beaten a short-head, was always being held by the winner. Compensation awaits. (4/1: op 5/2)

**672 Literary Society (USA)** chased the leaders. Throwing down his challenge from below the distance, he was close enough if good enough before tapped for toe. (16/1)

**2119 Featherstone Lane** may well have got his head in front for a few strides around the furlong pole before tapped for toe. (10/1)

**1688* Step On Degas** was left standing from below the distance. (4/1)

**1844 Miami Banker** played an active role until coming to the end of his tether early inside the final quarter-mile. (14/1)

**Bangles** was in trouble below the distance and was allowed to coast in in her own time inside the final furlong. (5/2)

## 2245 CITY INDEX SPREAD BETTING MAIDEN STKS (2-Y.O F) (Class D)

7-30 (7-31) **6f 8y** £4,370.00 (£1,310.00: £630.00: £290.00) Stalls: High GOING minus 0.48 sec per fur (F)

| | | | SP | RR | SF |
|---|---|---|---|---|---|
| | **Fig Tree Drive (USA)** (PFICole) **2-8-11** TQuinn(8) (b.nr hind: unf: scope: bit bkwd: a.p: led 2f out: rdn out)..— | **1** | 7/2[2] | 85 | 33 |
| | **Crystal Crossing (IRE)** (PWChapple-Hyam) **2-8-11** JReid(7) (leggy: scope: unf: a.p: ev ch fnl 2f: r.o) ..........nk | **2** | 4/7[1] | 84 | 32 |
| | **Ikdam (USA)** (MajorWRHern) **2-8-11** RHills(1) (leggy: rdn & hdwy over 1f out: r.o ins fnl f) ..........................1¼ | **3** | 10/1[3] | 81 | 29 |
| | **Tumbleweed Pearl** (BJMeehan) **2-8-11** BDoyle(9) (leggy: dwlt: rdn & hdwy over 1f out: r.o)............................nk | **4** | 14/1 | 80 | 28 |
| 1834[4] | **Kustom Kit Xpres** (MMcCormack) **2-8-11** MHills(5) (lw: led 4f: wknd over 1f out) ..........................................6 | **5** | 14/1 | 64 | 12 |
| | **Bathe In Light (USA)** (LordHuntingdon) **2-8-11** DHarrison(6) (leggy: scope: lw: bhd fnl 2f)..........................1¼ | **6** | 16/1 | 61 | 9 |
| 1643[4] | **Oneknight With You** (MJFetherston-Godley) **2-8-6**(5) FLynch(2) (hld up: rdn 2f out: sn wknd)........................½ | **7** | 33/1 | 60 | 8 |
| | **Dayrella** (WRMuir) **2-8-11** RHughes(3) (leggy: lt-f: hld up: rdn 2f out: sn wknd) .............................................11 | **8** | 33/1 | 30 | — |
| | | | (SP 120.0%) | **8 Rn** | |

**1m 13.4** (1.60) CSF £6.00 TOTE £4.50: £1.30 £1.10 £1.70 (£2.70) Trio £3.40 OWNER Mr Christopher Wright (WHATCOMBE) BRED Dr and Mrs R. S. West and Mr and Mrs Mackenzie Mil

**Fig Tree Drive (USA)** looked as though this run was just needed. A leading light from the off, she gained a narrow advantage a quarter of a mile from home, but was given no peace by the odds-on favorite. Engaged in a battle with that rival, she only just prevailed, and will come on a lot for this. (7/2)

**Crystal Crossing (IRE)** does need time to strengthen and develop but was heavily backed. Throwing down her challenge in the final quarter-mile, she went at it hammer and tongs with the winner and only just lost out. (4/7)

**Ikdam (USA)** picked up ground below the distance and stayed on inside the final furlong, if unable to get to the front two in time. (10/1: 6/1-12/1)

**Tumbleweed Pearl**, a half-sister to Tumbleweed Ridge, began a forward move below the distance and stayed on determinedly, only just failing to take third prize. (14/1: 7/1-16/1)

**1834 Kustom Kit Xpres** dictated matters from the front. Collared a quarter of a mile from home, she had soon shot her bolt. (14/1: 10/1-16/1)

## 2246 TARMAC H'CAP (0-75) (3-Y.O+ F & M) (Class D)

8-00 (8-01) **1m 2f 6y** £4,662.50 (£1,400.00: £675.00: £312.50) Stalls: Low GOING minus 0.48 sec per fur (F)

| | | | SP | RR | SF |
|---|---|---|---|---|---|
| 2127[3] | **Bakheta (57)** (MissGayKelleway) **4-8-5**(5) FLynch(1) (mde all: rdn over 3f out: r.o wl).......................................— | **1** | 7/2[1] | 72 | 50 |
| 1883[3] | **Alreeh (IRE) (70)** (JHMGosden) **3-8-11** RHills(4) (lw: hdwy 3f out: chsd wnr fnl 2f: unable qckn) ...................2½ | **2** | 4/1[2] | 81 | 47 |
| 731[8] | **Ailesbury Hill (USA) (69)** (PWChapple-Hyam) **3-8-10** JReid(6) (lw: a.p: hrd rdn over 2f out: one pce) ..........2½ | **3** | 10/1 | 76 | 42 |
| 2127[5] | **Summerhill Special (IRE) (60)** (MrsPNDutfield) **5-8-13b1** CRutter(3) (hld up: hrd rdn over 2f out: one pce) ..........................................................................................1½ | **4** | 20/1 | 65 | 43 |
| 1857[5] | **Trilby (65)** (PFICole) **3-7-13**(7) DavidO'Neill(7) (lw: lost pl 9f out: hdwy over 2f out: one pce).............................2 | **5** | 13/2 | 66 | 32 |
| | **Miss Haversham (75)** (CACyzer) **4-10-0** TSprake(2) (prom over 7f) ...................................................................7 | **6** | 20/1 | 65 | 43 |
| 988[9] | **Aldaneh (72)** (RHannon) **4-9-8**(3) DaneO'Neill(5) (bhd fnl 5f)..............................................................................nk | **7** | 14/1 | 62 | 40 |
| 1682[7] | **Evidence In Chief (58)** (DRCElsworth) **3-7-13** FNorton(10) (hrd rdn & hdwy over 2f out: sn wknd)................1¼ | **8** | 20/1 | 46 | 12 |
| 687[11] | **South Sea Bubble (IRE) (70)** (LMCumani) **4-9-9** PatEddery(9) (prom 7f) ..........................................................3½ | **9** | 6/1 | 52 | 30 |
| 1841* | **Shining Dancer (61)** (SDow) **4-9-0** SSanders(8) (bhd fnl 3f: lame) ......................................................................12 | **10** | 11/2[3] | 24 | 2 |
| | | | (SP 115.3%) | **10 Rn** | |

**2m 4.44** (0.64) CSF £16.76 CT £112.44 TOTE £3.50: £1.20 £1.90 £2.30 (£5.10) Trio £25.70 OWNER Mr Frank O'Rourke (WHITCOMBE) BRED Haresfoot Stud

WEIGHT FOR AGE 3yo-12lb

**2127 Bakheta** put up a gutsy display from the front. Rousted along over three furlongs from home, she was not going to be denied. (7/2)

**1883 Alreeh (IRE)** smoothly moved up over three furlongs from home. Taking second place a quarter of a mile out, she failed to reel in the winner. (4/1)

**Ailesbury Hill (USA)** ran her best race so far this season. A leading light from the off, she was shown the persuader over two furlongs from home, but could only go and down in the same place. (10/1)

**2127 Summerhill Special (IRE)** chased the leaders but, under pressure over two furlongs from home, could only keep on in her own time. (20/1)

**1857 Trilby** quickly lost her pitch and made an effort on the outside over two furlongs from home, but was then only treading water. (13/2: op 4/1)

**Miss Haversham**, making her seasonal debut, played an active role until coming to the end of her tether over two furlongs out. (20/1)

**Aldaneh** (14/1: 10/1-16/1)

## 2247 COOPERS & LYBRAND H'CAP (0-80) (3-Y.O) (Class D)

8-30 (8-31) **1m 5f 61y** £4,370.00 (£1,310.00: £630.00: £290.00) Stalls: Low GOING minus 0.48 sec per fur (F)

| | | | SP | RR | SF |
|---|---|---|---|---|---|
| 578[6] | **Steamroller Stanly (65)** (CACyzer) **3-8-12** TQuinn(3) (a.p: rdn over 3f out: led ins fnl f: r.o wl) .......................— | **1** | 16/1 | 75 | 43 |
| 1504[4] | **Fursan (USA) (67)** (NAGraham) **3-9-0** RHills(6) (hdwy over 2f out: led wl over 1f out tl ins fnl f: unable qckn) .¾ | **2** | 12/1 | 76 | 44 |
| 1804[9] | **Dalwhinnie (67)** (JWHills) **3-9-0** MHills(5) (swtg: led: rdn over 2f out: hdd over 1f out: sn wknd) ........................8 | **3** | 12/1 | 67 | 35 |

| | | | SP | RR | SF |
|---|---|---|---|---|---|
| 1854[4] **State Theatre (IRE) (73)** (PWChapple-Hyam) **3-9-6** JReid(4) (a.p: rdn over 3f out: wknd over 1f out) | 1¾ | **4** | 10/1 | 70 | 38 |
| 1826* **Double Agent (74)** (MJohnston) **3-9-7** MRoberts(8) (a.p: rdn 8f out: wknd 2f out) | 4 | **5** | 7/4[1] | 67 | 35 |
| 1783[5] **Isitoff (71)** (SCWilliams) **3-9-1**(3) PMcCabe(7) (hld up: rdn over 3f out: wknd over 1f out) | nk | **6** | 16/1 | 63 | 31 |
| 1900[5] **Regal Eagle (71)** (IABalding) **3-9-4** WRyan(2) (lw: rdn over 3f out: sme hdwy over 2f out: sn wknd) | 4 | **7** | 9/2[2] | 58 | 26 |
| 1804[7] **Veiled Dancer (IRE) (73)** (JLDunlop) **3-9-6** PatEddery(10) (lw: bhd fnl 4f) | 3 | **8** | 6/1[3] | 57 | 25 |
| 1498[2] **Compass Pointer (63)** (JMPEustace) **3-8-10** MTebbutt(9) (a bhd) | 6 | **9** | 13/2 | 40 | 8 |

(SP 118.4%) **9 Rn**

**2m 48.91** (2.41) CSF £166.80 CT £2,174.18 TOTE £18.40: £3.10 £3.20 £3.80 (£62.20) Trio £163.80 OWNER Mr R. M. Cyzer (HORSHAM) BRED R. D. Hubbard

OFFICIAL EXPLANATION **Double Agent: his jockey reported that the gelding was never travelling and hung right-handed.**

**Steamroller Stanly**, given an eleven-week break, was always close up. Eventually throwing down his challenge from below the distance, he got on top inside the final furlong. (16/1)

**1504 Fursan (USA)** moved through to gain the initiative early inside the final quarter-mile. Soon tackled by the runner-up, he was collared inside the final furlong. (12/1)

**1180 Dalwhinnie**, collared below the distance, was left standing by the front two. (12/1)

**State Theatre (IRE)** played an active role until coming to the end of his tether below the distance. (10/1)

**1826* Double Agent**, never far away, was being pushed along fully a mile from home and had nothing more to give two furlongs out. (7/4)

**1783 Isitoff** chased the leaders but had come to the end of his tether below the distance. (16/1)

## 2248 WFT CONDITIONS STKS (3-Y.O+) (Class C)

9-00 (9-01) **1m 7y (round)** £4,735.00 (£1,765.00: £857.50: £362.50: £156.25: £73.75) Stalls: Low GOING minus 0.48 sec per fur (F)

| | | | SP | RR | SF |
|---|---|---|---|---|---|
| 1770[5] **Louis' Queen (IRE) (101)** (JLDunlop) **4-8-9** JReid(2) (chsd ldr: rdn over 2f out: led wl ins fnl f: r.o wl) | — | **1** | 5/1[3] | 99 | 51 |
| 1824[3] **Polinesso (96)** (BWHills) **3-8-8** MHills(1) (lw: led: rdn over 2f out: hdd wl ins fnl f: unable qckn) | ¾ | **2** | 7/2[1] | 107 | 49 |
| 2004* **How Long** (LMCumani) **3-8-8** OUrbina(3) (hld up: rdn over 2f out: r.o one pce) | 1 | **3** | 9/2[2] | 105 | 47 |
| 1520[7] **Night City (102)** (LadyHerries) **5-9-10** DeclanO'Shea(5) (rdn over 1f out: hdwy fnl f: nvr nrr) | ¾ | **4** | 16/1 | 109 | 61 |
| 2053[13] **Amrak Ajeeb (IRE) (94)** (BHanbury) **4-9-0** MRoberts(7) (hld up: rdn over 2f out: r.o one pce) | nk | **5** | 7/2[1] | 98 | 50 |
| 1824[8] **Kuantan (USA) (100)** (PFICole) **3-8-4** TQuinn(4) (lw: s.s: hdwy 6f out: hrd rdn over 2f out: wknd over 1f out) | 2½ | **6** | 14/1 | 93 | 35 |
| 1796[7] **King of Peru (105)** (APJarvis) **3-8-8** PatEddery(8) (a bhd) | 3½ | **7** | 9/2[2] | 91 | 33 |
| 1817[7] **Tarte Aux Pommes (USA)** (CEBrittain) **4-8-9** BDoyle(6) (bhd fnl 2f) | 7 | **8** | 12/1 | 68 | 20 |

(SP 117.7%) **8 Rn**

**1m 36.18** (0.18) CSF £22.20 TOTE £5.80: £2.00 £1.50 £1.80 (£10.20) OWNER Mr Peter Winfield (ARUNDEL) BRED Snowdrop Stud Co Ltd. in Ireland

WEIGHT FOR AGE 3yo-10lb

**1770 Louis' Queen (IRE)** chased the leader. Pushed along over two furlongs out, she found another gear inside the final furlong to sweep into the lead. (5/1)

**1824 Polinesso** set a good pace. Grimly trying to fend off his rivals, he was eventually worried out of it in the closing stages. (7/2)

**2004* How Long** chased the leaders but, despite staying on for third prize, never threatened to find that vital turn of foot. (9/2: op 3/1)

**1520 Night City** was at the back of the field until staying on in the final furlong past beaten horses. (16/1)

**1944a Amrak Ajeeb (IRE)** chased the leaders and, although staying on, never posed a serious threat. (7/2)

**1495 Kuantan (USA)** (14/1: 10/1-16/1)

**Tarte Aux Pommes (USA)** (12/1: op 6/1)

T/Plpt: £139.20 (136.51 Tckts). T/Qdpt: £48.70 (29.05 Tckts). AK

# 2230-SALISBURY (R-H) (Good to firm, Firm patches)

## Thursday June 27th

Flip start: 5th race

WEATHER: fine WIND: almost nil

## 2249 NOEL CANNON MEMORIAL TROPHY H'CAP (0-100) (3-Y.O+) (Class C)

2-00 (2-01) **1m** £5,475.00 (£1,650.00: £800.00: £375.00) Stalls: High GOING minus 0.46 sec per fur (F)

| | | | SP | RR | SF |
|---|---|---|---|---|---|
| 1190[5] **Tregaron (USA) (79)** (RAkehurst) **5-9-3** TQuinn(3) (lw: hld up: led on bit over 2f out: qcknd clr over 1f out: easily) | — | **1** | 8/11[1] | 92+ | 45 |
| 1962[3] **Duello (64)** (MBlanshard) **5-8-2** JQuinn(2) (lw: hld up: hdwy over 2f out: ev ch wl over 1f out: no imp) | 3½ | **2** | 4/1[2] | 70 | 23 |
| 2010[12] **Samba Sharply (77)** (AHide) **5-8-10b**[1](5) MartinDwyer(5) (led over 5f: wknd over 1f out) | 1¾ | **3** | 9/2[3] | 80 | 33 |
| 809[14] **Above the Cut (USA) (86)** (PWHarris) **4-9-10b**[1] GHind(1) (b.off hind: hld up: rdn over 2f out: no hdwy) | 1¾ | **4** | 14/1 | 56 t | 38 |
| **Sticks and Stones (IRE) (79)** (MrsJCecil) **4-9-3** JReid(4) (swtg: chsd ldr tl wknd over 2f out) | 8 | **5** | 11/1 | 33 t | 15 |

(SP 111.1%) **5 Rn**

**1m 42.35** (1.95) CSF £3.99 TOTE £1.60: £1.10 £1.50 (£2.50) OWNER Mr Hefin Jones (EPSOM) BRED Stonethorn Stud Farms

**1190 Tregaron (USA)**, who just missed the cut in last week's Royal Hunt Cup, looked much more at home on this faster ground and won easing up. The Golden Mile at Goodwood would seem a logical target. (8/11: 10/11-Evens)

**1962 Duello** again had to contend with fast ground and is flattered by his proximity to the winner. (4/1)

**879 Samba Sharply**, 10lb better off with Tregaron than when beaten three and a half lengths at Ascot in May, has disappointed since and was tried in blinkers here. (9/2)

**Above the Cut (USA)** was also blinkered for the first time. (14/1: 8/1-16/1)

**Sticks and Stones (IRE)** (11/1: 7/1-12/1)

## 2250 HERBERT AND GWEN BLAGRAVE MEMORIAL CONDITIONS STKS (3-Y.O+) (Class C)

2-30 (2-37) **1m 6f** £4,799.25 (£1,743.00: £846.50: £357.50: £153.75) GOING minus 0.46 sec per fur (F)

| | | | SP | RR | SF |
|---|---|---|---|---|---|
| 1976[5] **Lord Jim (IRE) (90)** (LordHuntingdon) **4-9-6v**[1] DHarrison(4) (mde all: hrd rdn over 2f out: r.o wl) | — | **1** | 7/1 | 96 | 62 |
| **Edipo Re** (PJHobbs) **4-9-6** JReid(5) (lw: w'like: hld up: rdn & hdwy fnl 2f: r.o) | 4 | **2** | 11/1 | 91 | 57 |
| 1767[6] **Arctic Thunder (USA) (94)** (LadyHerries) **5-9-6** TSprake(3) (b: swtg: hld up: hdwy over 4f out: chsd wnr over 3f out: rdn over 2f out: no imp) | 2 | **3** | 7/4[1] | 89 | 55 |

| | | | Pos | SP | RR | SF |
|---|---|---|---|---|---|---|
| 1990[3] | **Camp Follower** (JLDunlop) **3-8-7** TQuinn(2) (lw: hld up: chsd wnr over 4f out tl over 3f out: hrd rdn over 2f out: wknd over 1f out: eased ins fnl f) | 15 | **4** | 7/2[3] | 76 | 25 |
| 1899[7] | **Witch of Fife (USA) (100)** (BWHills) **3-8-8** PatEddery(1) (chsd wnr over 9f: wknd over 3f out: t.o) | 10 | **5** | 9/4[2] | 66 | 15 |
| | | | | (SP 110.2%) | **5 Rn** | |

**2m 59.77** (1.07) CSF £53.89 TOTE £7.80: £2.30 £2.50 (£44.60) OWNER Mrs S. Y. Thomas (WEST ILSLEY) BRED Woodcote Stud Ltd
WEIGHT FOR AGE 3yo-17lb
**1976 Lord Jim (IRE)** has been gelded and stepped up on his first run for his new stable, with the visor doing the trick. (7/1: 5/1-8/1)
**Edipo Re** won twice as a two-year-old on soft ground in Italy and took time to get going on this faster surface. Stamina is not a problem and he will most likely go over hurdles in future. (11/1: 6/1-12/1)
**1767 Arctic Thunder (USA)** seemed well in at the weights, so this was not very good. (7/4: Evens-15/8)
**1990 Camp Follower** is not bred to stay this sort of trip (7/2)
**Witch of Fife (USA)** (9/4: op 7/2)

## 2251 DEVERILL MAIDEN H'CAP (0-65) (3-Y.O+) (Class F)
3-00 (3-03) **1m 1f 209y** £3,099.00 (£864.00: £417.00) Stalls: High GOING minus 0.46 sec per fur (F)

| | | | Pos | SP | RR | SF |
|---|---|---|---|---|---|---|
| 1682[2] | **Dramatic Moment (60)** (IABalding) **3-8-12**(5) MartinDwyer(3) (hld up: gd hdwy over 2f out: led wl over 1f out: sn swvd bdly lft: r.o wl) | — | **1** | 15/2 | 75 | 41 |
| 1686[6] | **Tarian (USA) (49)** (GBBalding) **4-9-4** AClark(8) (lw: hld up: rdn 3f out: r.o ins fnl f: nt trble wnr) | 5 | **2** | 12/1 | 56 | 34 |
| 1651[4] | **Racing Hawk (USA) (48)** (MSSaunders) **4-9-3** RPrice(18) (a.p: led 2f out: sn hdd: one pce) | 1 | **3** | 20/1 | 53 | 31 |
| 1839[5] | **Forever Noble (IRE) (64)** (MRChannon) **3-9-7** RHughes(14) (hld up: rdn over 3f out: hdwy fnl 2f: r.o) | 2½ | **4** | 12/1 | 65 | 31 |
| 1776[10] | **Totally Yours (IRE) (39)** (MRChannon) **3-7-10** AGorman(7) (hld up: hdwy on ins over 4f out: one pce fnl 2f) | 1¾ | **5** | 16/1 | 38 | 4 |
| 1953[2] | **Boston Rock (IRE) (59)** (PWHarris) **4-10-0** GHind(17) (plld hrd: a.p: led 3f out to 2f out: wknd over 1f out) | hd | **6** | 7/2[1] | 57 | 35 |
| | **Docklands Courier (45)** (BJMcMath) **4-9-0** JReid(16) (led over 6f: wknd over 2f out) | s.h | **7** | 16/1 | 43 | 21 |
| 1714[3] | **Seven Crowns (USA) (65)** (RHannon) **3-9-5**(3) DaneO'Neill(15) (swtg: prom: rdn over 3f out: wknd 2f out) | s.h | **8** | 10/1 | 63 | 29 |
| | **Supermick (32)** (WRMuir) **5-8-1** CRutter(12) (nvr trbld ldrs) | d.h | **8** | 25/1 | 30 | 8 |
| 1873[8] | **Mischief Star (65)** (DRCElsworth) **3-9-8** TQuinn(10) (hdwy 4f out: wknd 2f out) | 3 | **10** | 12/1 | 58 | 24 |
| 1010[8] | **Hank-a-chief (50)** (BSmart) **3-8-7** MTebbutt(6) (lw: a bhd) | s.h | **11** | 25/1 | 43 | 9 |
| 1856[6] | **Express Routing (53)** (JAkehurst) **4-9-8** PaulEddery(13) (swtg: b: b.hind: chsd ldr: led over 3f out: sn hrd rdn, hdd & wknd) | s.h | **12** | 12/1 | 46 | 24 |
| 595[17] | **Pleasureland (IRE) (65)** (PJMakin) **3-9-8** SSanders(2) (bhd fnl 2f) | 2½ | **13** | 25/1 | 54 | 20 |
| 1416[4] | **Oscar Rose (57)** (LordHuntingdon) **3-9-0** DHarrison(5) (lw: hld up: a bhd) | ½ | **14** | 7/1[3] | 45 | 11 |
| 1692[4] | **Ember (61)** (LMCumani) **3-9-4** PatEddery(9) (prom tl wknd 2f out) | 1 | **15** | 6/1[2] | 48 | 14 |
| 1589[2] | **Lavender Della (IRE) (62)** (MJFetherston-Godley) **3-9-5** WJO'Connor(11) (prom 7f) | 4 | **16** | 12/1 | 42 | 8 |
| 1649[7] | **Alajyal (IRE) (52)** (PTWalwyn) **3-8-9** TSprake(1) (bhd fnl 3f: t.o) | dist | **17** | 16/1 | — | — |
| | | | | (SP 142.3%) | **17 Rn** | |

**2m 8.2** (2.90) CSF £99.18 CT £1,632.14 TOTE £5.90: £1.50 £4.40 £7.10 £3.70 (£48.60) Trio £627.50; £371.25 to Newmarket 28/6/96.
OWNER Mrs Richard Plummer (KINGSCLERE) BRED Mrs A. Plummer
LONG HANDICAP Totally Yours (IRE) 7-7
WEIGHT FOR AGE 3yo-12lb
**1682 Dramatic Moment** gave her rider an anxious moment before running on strongly to win a race where quantity rather than quality was the order of the day. (15/2)
**1686 Tarian (USA)**, over a slightly shorter trip, kept on to secure the runner-up spot in the closing stages. (12/1: op 8/1)
**1651 Racing Hawk (USA)** was bought out of Henry Cecil's yard for 6,000 guineas during the winter. Dropped 12lb this season, this was his best effort for his new connections. (20/1)
**1839 Forever Noble (IRE)**, making his handicap debut, seems to need a return to a mile and a half. (12/1)
**Totally Yours (IRE)**, 3lb wrong at the weights on her first appearance in a handicap, could not sustain her effort over this longer trip. (16/1)
**1953 Boston Rock (IRE)**, well backed, was trying an extra furlong and did not settle too well. (7/2: op 7/1)
**1589 Lavender Della (IRE)** (12/1: op 7/1)

## 2252 CHAMPAGNE AUCTION STKS (2-Y.O) (Class B)
3-30 (3-32) **6f 212y** £9,451.50 (£3,538.50: £1,731.75: £746.25: £335.63: £171.37) Stalls: High GOING minus 0.46 sec per fur (F)

| | | | Pos | SP | RR | SF |
|---|---|---|---|---|---|---|
| 1339* | **Falkenham** (PFICole) **2-8-11** TQuinn(7) (stdd s: hdwy 4f out: hrd rdn 3f out: led 2f out: edgd rt over 1f out: r.o wl) | — | **1** | 4/7[1] | 89+ | 32 |
| 1960[8] | **Lady Godiva** (MJPolglase) **2-7-13** NCarlisle(4) (a.p: ev ch 2f out: edgd rt over 1f out: no imp) | 4 | **2** | 33/1 | 68 | 11 |
| 1827* | **Class Distinction (IRE)** (RHannon) **2-8-4** RPerham(5) (led 5f: one pce) | 2½ | **3** | 7/2[2] | 67 | 10 |
| 2025[6] | **Debonair** (GLewis) **2-7-13** AWhelan(1) (dwlt: hld up & plld hrd: wknd over 2f out) | 6 | **4** | 8/1[3] | 48 | — |
| | **Noble Hero** (JJSheehan) **2-8-1** SSanders(8) (leggy: scope: bit bkwd: prom over 4f) | ¾ | **5** | 20/1 | 49 | — |
| 1191[6] | **Prairie Minstrel (USA)** (RDickin) **2-8-4** DaneO'Neill(3) (hld up: rdn over 3f out: sn bhd) | ¾ | **6** | 20/1 | 50 | — |
| | **Fistral Flame** (JSMoore) **2-7-10** JQuinn(2) (w'like: str: bhd fnl 3f) | 4 | **7** | 20/1 | 33 | — |
| | **Mujadil Express (IRE)** (JSMoore) **2-7-12**ow2 JFEgan(6) (cmpt: a bhd: t.o fnl 2f) | 20 | **8** | 33/1 | — | — |
| | | | | (SP 117.1%) | **8 Rn** | |

**1m 28.22** (2.22) CSF £18.48 TOTE £1.60: £1.10 £2.40 £1.60 (£24.70) OWNER Mr T. M. Hely-Hutchinson (WHATCOMBE) BRED Kirtlington Stud Ltd
STEWARDS' ENQUIRY Obj. to Lady Godiva by Perham overruled.
**1339* Falkenham** made pretty hard work of this, but he stays well, and his rider admitted he had not learnt much on his winning debut at Goodwood. (4/7)
**Lady Godiva** fared much better than on her Sandown debut and briefly looked like springing a surprise. (33/1)
**1827* Class Distinction (IRE)** was stepping up from the minimum trip. (7/2)
**2025 Debonair** is bred to stay, but needs to learn to switch off in her races. (8/1: 6/1-9/1)

## 2253 CARNARVON CHALLENGE CUP AMATEUR H'CAP (0-70) (3-Y.O) (Class F)
4-00 (4-01) **1m** £2,735.00 (£760.00: £365.00) Stalls: High GOING minus 0.46 sec per fur (F)

| | | | Pos | SP | RR | SF |
|---|---|---|---|---|---|---|
| 1953[7] | **Mimosa (50)** (SDow) **3-10-3**(5) MrSFetherstonhaugh(5) (lw: a.p: rdn over 2f out: r.o to ld wl ins fnl f) | — | **1** | 14/1 | 58 | 32 |
| *2158** | **Superior Force (64)** (MissBSanders) **3-11-8** 5x MrsJMoore(7) (lw: hld up & bhd: hdwy 2f out: edgd lft & nt clr run 1f out: swtchd rt ins fnl f: r.o wl) | ½ | **2** | 5/1[3] | 71 | 45 |

| | | | | SP | RR | SF |
|---|---|---|---|---|---|---|
| 1956* | **Sunley Secure (55)** (MRChannon) **3-10-13** MissJWinter(6) (w ldrs: hung lft over 1f out: r.o one pce) | 1¼ | **3** | 9/2 [2] | 60 | 34 |
| 2061[3] | **Sound Check (57)** (BJMeehan) **3-11-1b** MissJAllison(1) (lw: a.p: led 3f out: hung rt wl over 1f out: hdd wl ins fnl f) | s.h | **4** | 7/2 [1] | 61 | 35 |
| *1993*[5] | **General Haven (65)** (TJNaughton) **3-11-9** MrsJNaughton(4) (lw: hld up: rdn 3f out: hdwy 2f out: r.o one pce fnl f) | 1¼ | **5** | 7/1 | 67 | 41 |
| 2033[9] | **Current Leader (56)** (RHannon) **3-11-0** MrMRimell(2) (led 5f: sn wknd) | 11 | **6** | 7/1 | 36 | 10 |
| 1350[6] | **Scimitar (70)** (PJMakin) **3-12-0** MrPScott(8) (a bhd) | 3½ | **7** | 12/1 | 43 | 17 |
| 2016[5] | **Bold Enough (55)** (BWHills) **3-10-8**(5) MrCBHills(3) (swtg: w ldrs over 4f) | 1 | **8** | 7/1 | 26 | — |
| 1658[5] | **No Sympathy (52)** (GLMoore) **3-10-10** MrKGoble(9) (swtg: a bhd) | 1¼ | **9** | 12/1 | 20 | — |
| | | | | (SP 116.6%) | **9 Rn** | |

**1m 45.55** (5.15) CSF £76.63 CT £339.25 TOTE £12.90: £3.10 £2.50 £1.70 (£18.80) Trio £57.80 OWNER Mr G. Steinberg (EPSOM) BRED S. Tindall and Stowell Hill Ltd

STEWARDS' ENQUIRY Winter susp. 8-9/7/96 (excessive use of whip).

**1953 Mimosa**, dropped 5lb, was able to lay up with the pace this time. (14/1)

**2158* Superior Force** rather caused his own trouble at the furlong pole, and may have scored with a trouble-free run. (5/1: 7/2-11/2)

**1956* Sunley Secure** seems the type who needs stronger handling. (9/2)

**2061 Sound Check** appeared in control until drifting over to the far rail. (7/2)

**1993 General Haven** looks ready to go further. (7/1: 6/1-10/1)

## 2254 SOUTHAMPTON CLAIMING STKS (2-Y.O) (Class F)

4-30 (4-31) **6f 212y** £2,714.00 (£754.00: £362.00) Stalls: High GOING minus 0.46 sec per fur (F)

| | | | | SP | RR | SF |
|---|---|---|---|---|---|---|
| | **Avinalarf** (WGMTurner) **2-7-10**(7) DSweeney(4) (w'like: a.p: led wl over 1f out: rdn out) | — | **1** | 11/2 [2] | 51 | — |
| 1467[7] | **Maria di Castiglia** (RHannon) **2-8-9** RPerham(3) (b: lw: plld hrd: w ldr: led over 3f out tl wl over 1f out: unable qckn fnl f) | 1¾ | **2** | 11/1 | 53 | — |
| 2035[3] | **Russian Sable** (MRChannon) **2-8-9** TQuinn(1) (lw: hld up: hdwy over 3f out: hrd rdn & ev ch over 1f out: unable qckn) | hd | **3** | 10/11 [1] | 53 | — |
| 1471[5] | **Spondulicks (IRE)** (RHannon) **2-8-11**(3) DaneO'Neill(7) (s.s: rdn 2f out: hdwy over 1f out: r.o ins fnl f) | 2 | **4** | 11/2 [2] | 53 | — |
| 757[4] | **Rebuke** (RFJohnsonHoughton) **2-8-10** JReid(6) (lw: led over 3f: wknd over 1f out) | nk | **5** | 13/2 [3] | 49 | — |
| 1513[9] | **Herbshan Dancer** (BRMillman) **2-8-11**(3) SDrowne(2) (no hdwy fnl 3f) | 1 | **6** | 16/1 | 50 | — |
| 1471[8] | **Top Titfer** (AGFoster) **2-8-3** TSprake(5) (b.nr hind: lw: bhd fnl 3f) | 2 | **7** | 33/1 | 23 | — |
| | | | | (SP 113.6%) | **7 Rn** | |

**1m 30.92** (4.92) CSF £52.35 TOTE £7.60: £2.30 £3.10 (£34.00) OWNER Gongolfin (SHERBORNE) BRED Crichel Farms Ltd

**Avinalarf** was not unfancied and proved good enough, despite carrying her head high through greenness. (11/2)

**Maria di Castiglia,** taking a keen hold, stepped up on her debut but could not cope with the winner. (11/1: 6/1-12/1)

**2035 Russian Sable** does not really seem to be progressing, and this was disappointing. (10/11: 4/5-Evens)

**1036 Spondulicks (IRE)** lost around ten lengths at the start. (11/2: op 3/1)

**757 Rebuke** has been gelded since being tried in blinkers last time. (13/2: op 4/1)

## 2255 ALINGTON H'CAP (0 70) (3-Y.O+ F & M) (Class E)

5-00 (5-02) **6f** £3,522.00 (£1,056.00: £508.00: £234.00) GOING minus 0.46 sec per fur (F)

| | | | | SP | RR | SF |
|---|---|---|---|---|---|---|
| 1991[2] | **Faraway Lass (67)** (LordHuntingdon) **3-8-13**(7) AimeeCook(1) (hld up: hdwy over 3f out: led over 2f out: hung lft wl over 1f out: edgd rt 1f out: r.o wl) | — | **1** | 9/4 [1] | 83 | 41 |
| 1994[4] | **Out Line (67)** (MMadgwick) **4-9-13** JQuinn(5) (hld up: rdn 3f out: hdwy 2f out: r.o one pce fnl f) | 3 | **2** | 16/1 | 75 | 40 |
| 2139[7] | **Corniche Quest (IRE) (52)** (MRChannon) **3-7-12**(7) AEddery(6) (lost pl over 3f out: swtchd lft 2f out: hdwy over 1f out: r.o one pce) | 1¾ | **3** | 10/1 | 55 | 13 |
| 2013[3] | **Lillibella (63)** (IABalding) **3-8-11**(5) MartinDwyer(11) (w ldr: ev ch 2f out: one pce) | ½ | **4** | 4/1 [2] | 65 | 23 |
| 1876[6] | **Windswept (IRE) (58)** (DJSffrenchDavis) **3-8-11** DHarrison(3) (prom: rdn over 2f out: one pce) | 1 | **5** | 8/1 [3] | 57 | 15 |
| 1422[10] | **Ameliajill (54)** (RHannon) **3-8-4**(3) DaneO'Neill(8) (dwlt: nvr nrr) | ¾ | **6** | 12/1 | 51 | 9 |
| 1901[7] | **Lucky Revenge (65)** (MartynMeade) **3-8-13**(5) RHavlin(2) (chsd ldrs: rdn over 2f out: no hdwy) | 1¾ | **7** | 4/1 [2] | 58 | 16 |
| 2016[7] | **Oscilights Gift (36)** (PBurgoyne) **4-7-10** NAdams(4) (led over 3f: sn wknd) | 1 | **8** | 40/1 | 26 | — |
| 1776[6] | **Silhouette (IRE) (44)** (DRCElsworth) **3-7-11** FNorton(7) (prom over 3f) | ½ | **9** | 14/1 | 33 | — |
| 1840[12] | **Blossom Dearie (51)** (RGFrost) **3-8-1**(3)ow1 PMcCabe(9) (prom 3f) | 2½ | **10** | 14/1 | 33 | — |
| 1466[5] | **Mrs McBadger (62)** (BSmart) **3-9-1** MTebbutt(10) (dwlt: a bhd) | 3 | **11** | 12/1 | 36 | — |
| | | | | (SP 128.0%) | **11 Rn** | |

**1m 14.86** (1.86) CSF £37.76 CT £303.19 TOTE £2.90: £1.80 £5.60 £2.40 (£42.50) Trio £179.50 OWNER Mr J. Rose (WEST ILSLEY) BRED John Rose

LONG HANDICAP Oscilights Gift 6-13

WEIGHT FOR AGE 3yo-7lb

**1991 Faraway Lass** continues to progress and proved too sharp for these rivals, despite running about quite a bit. (9/4)

**1994 Out Line** ran a sound race under a big weight on her handicap debut. (16/1)

**1806 Corniche Quest (IRE)** did not seem suited by the return to sprinting. (10/1)

**2013 Lillibella** was trying her luck at six this time. (4/1)

**Windswept (IRE)**, dropped 5lb, was another coming back in trip. (8/1: 6/1-9/1)

**Ameliajill** possibly needs a longer trip. (12/1)

T/Jkpt: Not won; £17,842.58 to Newmarket 28/6/96. T/Plpt: £4,057.30 (3.54 Tckts). T/Qdpt: £247.50 (6.18 Tckts). KH

## 2256a-2268a (Irish Racing) - See Computer Raceform

# 1947a-EVRY (France) (R-H) (Good to firm)

## Monday June 17th

## 2269a PRIX LA FLECHE (Listed) (2-Y.O)

1-55 (1-56) **5f 110y** £18,445.00 (£6,324.00: £3,953.00)

| | | | | SP | RR | SF |
|---|---|---|---|---|---|---|
| 1653[3] | **Deep Finesse** (MAJarvis) **2-9-2** PRobinson | — | **1** | | 88+ | — |

| | Horse | Btn | Pos | SP | RR | SF |
|---|---|---|---|---|---|---|
| | **Joyeuse Entree** (AdeRoyerDupre,France) **2-8-13** GMosse | 1 | **2** | | 82 | — |
| | **Nombre Premier** (AdeRoyerDupre,France) **2-9-2** TGillet | 2½ | **3** | | 78 | — |

**8 Rn**

**63.92 secs** (-0.48) P-M 10.20F: 3.00F 1.50F 1.80F (25.60F) OWNER J. E. Sims (NEWMARKET) BRED D. A. and Mrs Hicks
**1653 Deep Finesse**, in his first Listed event, was always prominent. Wandering a furlong from home, he got back to his task and ran on well close home. He has turned into a useful colt and looks capable of further improvement.

## 2270a PRIX HAMPTON (Listed) (3-Y.O+)
2-25 (2-26) **5f** £18,445.00 (£6,324.00: £3,953.00)

| | Horse | Btn | Pos | SP | RR | SF |
|---|---|---|---|---|---|---|
| | **Kistena (FR)** (MmeCHead,France) **3-8-7** ODoleuze | — | **1** | | 104 | — |
| 1630[3] | **Croft Pool** (JAGlover) **5-9-2** SDWilliams | s.h | **2** | | 107 | — |
| 1581a[5] | **Don't Worry Me (IRE)** (GHenrot,France) **4-8-13** OPeslier | ¾ | **3** | | 101 | — |
| 1616[3] | **Blue Iris** (MAJarvis) **3-8-7** PRobinson | 3 | **4** | | 92 | — |

**12 Rn**

**56.88 secs** (-1.62) P-M 7.00F: 2.30F 3.10F 1.90F (30.80F) OWNER Wertheimer Brothers (CHANTILLY) BRED J.Wertheimer & Frere
**1630 Croft Pool**, stepping up in class following his recent third to Top Banana, was always in a prominent position. He was ridden two furlongs out, and took up the running at the furlong pole but, despite running on well inside the final furlong, was just caught close home.
**1616 Blue Iris** broke well and led during the early stages. Ridden two furlongs from home, she was headed with a furlong left, and could then only keep on at the one pace.

# 1754a-LONGCHAMP (Paris, France) (R-H) (Good)
## Thursday June 20th

## 2271a PRIX DE LA PORTE MAILLOT (Gp 3) (4-Y.O+)
4-00 (4-03) **7f** £28,986.00 (£10,540.00: £5,270.00: £2,635.00)

| | Horse | Btn | Pos | SP | RR | SF |
|---|---|---|---|---|---|---|
| | **A Magicman (FR)** (HSteguweit,Germany) **4-9-7** NGrant | — | **1** | | 123 | — |
| | **Bashaayeash (IRE)** (CLaffon-Parias,France) **4-9-2** ODoleuze | 2 | **2** | | 113 | — |
| 1141a[10] | **Gothenberg (IRE)** (MJohnston) **3-8-10** OPeslier | hd | **3** | | 116 | — |
| 1950a* | **Nec Plus Ultra (FR)** (AdeRoyerDupre,France) **5-9-7** TGillet | 1½ | **4** | | 115 | — |
| 1141a[5] | **Kahir Almaydan (IRE)** (JLDunlop) **3-8-13** CAsmussen | s.h | **5** | | 116 | — |
| 1945a* | **Passion For Life** (GLewis) **3-8-10** FHead | 5 | **6** | | 101 | — |

**6 Rn**

**1m 20.3** (1.30) P-M 22.30F: 7.10F 3.80F (132.00F) OWNER Stall Dagobert BRED H. Voegele & Maria Koenig
**A Magicman (FR)** came right back to his best. Held up in rear early on and coming sweeping through to lead well over a furlong out, the further they went, the more distance he put between himself and the runner-up. Apparently he has suffered from infections during the beginning of he season and has taken time to come to himself, but he is now on course for the Group Two Berlin Brandenburg Trophy at Hoppegarten.
**Bashaayeash (IRE)** ran his usual game race. Normally a front-runner, he had to settle for third place early as he could not keep up with the break-neck pace set by the English pair. He looked dangerous two furlongs out, but did not have the pace of the winner in the final furlong. A consistent Group Three horse, he did very well considering the rain-softened ground was against him.
**1141a Gothenberg (IRE)** ran a lot better than in the French 2000 Guineas. Usually a free-running sort, he settled well in behind the leaders, and relaxed during the early part of the race. Although unable to master the older generation, he ran best of the three-year-olds and heads next for the Seaworld International at the Curragh.
**1141a Kahir Almaydan (IRE)** ran very freely early on and was a beaten force when headed well over a furlong from home. Perhaps he needs to be able to dominate.
**1945a* Passion For Life** led the field at a very fast pace and faded when they entered the straight. This improved colt looks better suited by six furlongs.
DS

# 2111a-SAN SIRO (Milan, Italy) (R-H) (Good)
## Thursday June 20th

## 2272a PREMIO VALCAVA (2-Y.O F)
3-00 **5f** £6,902.00

| | Horse | Btn | Pos | SP | RR | SF |
|---|---|---|---|---|---|---|
| | **Star Fairy (IRE)** (MCiciarelli,Italy) **2-9-0** AParravani | — | **1** | | — | — |
| | **Tonga Island (ITY)** (Italy) **2-9-0** EBotti | nk | **2** | | — | — |
| | **Lill Niagara (IRE)** (Italy) **2-9-0** MLatorre | nk | **3** | | — | — |
| | **Iolanta (IRE)** (CCollins,Ireland) **2-9-0** GForte | 1 | **4** | | — | — |

**7 Rn**

**59.9 secs** (4.70) TOTE 74L: 26l 18L (131L) OWNER Scuderia Briantea BRED D. P. O'Brien
**Iolanta (IRE)** was prominent on the outside, but ran green and was unable to quicken inside the final furlong.

# 2108a-SAINT-CLOUD (France) (L-H) (Good)
## Saturday June 22nd

## 2273a LA COUPE (Gp 3) (4-Y.O+)
3-30 (3-32) **1m 2f** £28,986.00 (£10,540.00: £5,270.00: £2,635.00)

| | Horse | Btn | Pos | SP | RR | SF |
|---|---|---|---|---|---|---|
| | **Dance Treat (USA)** (DSepulchre,France) **4-8-8** ODoleuze | — | **1** | | 119 | — |
| | **Bulington (FR)** (H-APantall,France) **4-8-11** CAsmussen | hd | **2** | | 122 | — |
| 906a[6] | **Diamond Mix (IRE)** (AFabre,France) **4-8-11** TJarnet | 2½ | **3** | | 118 | — |
| 1938a[2] | **Prince of Andros (USA)** (DRLoder) **6-8-11** DHolland | ¾ | **4** | | 117 | — |

**9 Rn**

**2m 3.4** (-0.10) P-M 44.10F: 5.00F 1.30F 2.00F (54.30F) OWNER Mr P. Pritchard BRED John C. and Mrs Mabee

**Dance Treat (USA)** showed vastly improved form to take this. The rank outsider of the field, she was second last coming into the straight, and came through right at the death to snatch victory on the line. Plans have not yet been made as to where to go with the filly, but the Prix Maurice de Nieuil or the Grand Prix de Vichy are possibilities.
**Bulington (FR)** came to win his race at the furlong pole, but was just caught on the line. An improving sort, a Group Three should come his way, with the Grand Prix de Vichy probably his next target.
**438a Diamond Mix (IRE)** looked very well in himself before the race and ran better than he has for a long time. Although he is not the same horse that won the Prix Greffulhe as a three-year-old, he is coming back to form and is one to watch next time out, especially if the going is soft.
**1938a Prince of Andros (USA)** was very unlucky on this occasion and would have been a lot closer if the race had gone his way. Close up early on, his jockey was boxed on the rail until a furlong out and, when the horse finally had some room, the principals had got first run. Obviously well in himself, he should score in Group company soon.
DS

# DORTMUND (Germany) (R-H) (Good)
## Sunday June 23rd

### 2274a GROSSER PREIS DER DORTMUNDER WIRTSCHAFT (Gp 3) (3-Y.O+)
4-00 (4-03) **1m 1f** £32,658.00 (£13,063.00: £6,532.00)

| | | | | SP | RR | SF |
|---|---|---|---|---|---|---|
| 1755a[3] | **Devil River Peek (USA)** (BSchutz,Germany) **4-9-2** AStarke | — | **1** | | 110 | — |
| 1395a[2] | **Accento** (RSuerland,Germany) **3-8-3** AHelfenbein | 2 | **2** | | 104 | — |
| 1793[9] | **Maralinga (IRE)** (LadyHerries) **4-8-12** PaulEddery | ½ | **3** | | 102 | — |
| 1441[5] | **Quakers Field** (GLMoore) **3-8-3** SWhitworth (btn approx 6½l) | | **7** | | 95 | — |
| | | | | | | **10 Rn** |

**1m 42.9** TOTE 47DM: 15DM 13DM 30DM (117DM) OWNER Stall Hoppegarten BRED Fares Farm Inc.
**Maralinga (IRE)** led the way until the two-furlong marker when Accento took the lead. He could not get back on terms, but ran on well to finish third.
**1441 Quakers Field** raced at the back of the field during the early stages of the race and never looked like being a danger to the principals.

# FREUDENAU (Vienna, Austria) (R-H) (Good)
## Sunday June 23rd

### 2275a MAGNA AUSTRIAN DERBY (3-Y.O C & F)
4-30 (4-33) **1m 4f** £44,757.00 (£15,985.00: £9,591.00)

| | | | | SP | RR | SF |
|---|---|---|---|---|---|---|
| | **Commanche Court (IRE)** (NClement,France) **3-8-13** J-MBreux | — | **1** | | 97 | — |
| | **Dancing Fred (USA)** (DKWeld,Ireland) **3-8-13** PShanahan | ¾ | **2** | | 96 | — |
| 1769[9] | **Identify (IRE)** (DKWeld,Ireland) **3-8-10** MJKinane | ¾ | **3** | | 92 | — |
| | | | | | | **8 Rn** |

**2m 36.2** TOTE 85S: 18S 14S 13S (197S) OWNER D. Khan (CHANTILLY) BRED Cambremont Ltd Partnership

# 2271a-LONGCHAMP (Paris, France) (R-H) (Good)
## Sunday June 23rd

### 2276a GRAND PRIX DE PARIS (Gp 1) (3-Y.O C & F)
3-45 (3-43) **1m 2f** £158,103.00 (£63,241.00: £31,621.00: £15,810.00)

| | | | | SP | RR | SF |
|---|---|---|---|---|---|---|
| 1757a[7] | **Grape Tree Road** (AFabre,France) **3-9-2** TJarnet (rr early: n.m.r over 1f out: swtchd rt ins fnl f: r.o strly to ld post) | — | **1** | 10/1 | 118 | 80 |
| 1791[4] | **Glory of Dancer** (PAKelleway) **3-9-2** CAsmussen (mid div: hdwy & rdn to ld 1f out: r.o: hdd nr fin) | s.h | **2** | 24/10[1] | 118 | 80 |
| 1754a* | **Android (USA)** (AFabre,France) **3-9-2** OPeslier (rr tl hdwy 2f out: r.o wl fnl f) | 2 | **3** | 46/10 | 115 | 77 |
| 1756a* | **Le Triton (USA)** (MmeCHead,France) **3-9-2** FHead (led tl hdd 1f out: kpt on one pce fnl f: fin 5th, 2½l: plcd 4th) | | **4** | 37/10[3] | 107 | 69 |
| 1756a[3] | **Blackwater (USA)** (MZilber,France) **3-9-2** GGuignard (mid div: rdn over 2f out: chal over 1f out: hmpd ins fnl f: kpt on: fin 6th, 2 3/4l: plcd 5th) | | **5** | 245/10 | 103 | 65 |
| 1427* | **Farasan (IRE)** (HRACecil) **3-9-2** JReid (n.m.r tl over 1f out: chal between horses 1f out: r.o fnl f: fin 4th, 2¼l: disq: plcd 6th) | | **6** | 26/10[2] | 111 | 73 |
| 1757a[5] | **Oliviero (FR)** (PDemercastel,France) **3-9-2** TThulliez (rr st: n.m.r tl over 1f out: sme late hdwy) | nk | **7** | 30/1 | 102 | 64 |
| | **Milford Track (IRE)** (HVandePoele,France) **3-9-2** ODoleuze (mid div: rdn fr 2f out: unable qckn) | 1½ | **8** | 127/10 | 100 | 62 |
| 1139a[3] | **Fort Nottingham (USA)** (JEHammond,France) **3-9-2** GMosse (prom early: 3rd st: rdn 2f out: hmpd wl over 1f out: no ex) | 6 | **9** | 126/10 | 90 | 52 |
| 1756a[2] | **Martiniquais (IRE)** (AFabre,France) **3-9-2** SGuillot (plld hrd: chsd ldr to st: wknd qckly fr 2f out) | 8 | **10** | 49/10 | 77 | 39 |
| | | | | (SP 144.2%) | | **10 Rn** |

**2m 2.3** (2.30) P-M 11.00F: 2.50F 1.40F 1.80F (19.00F) OWNER Mr M. Tabor (CHANTILLY)
**IN-FOCUS: For Betting purposes, Android (USA) cpld w Martiniquais (IRE)**
**Grape Tree Road**, who was outstanding in the paddock, was in behind turning into the straight, and then blocked for some time after but, once a gap appeared, he showed a blistering turn of foot to steal this on the line. Seventh in the Prix du Jockey-Club when he did not stay, he comfortably won the Prix de Suresnes over course and distance earlier in the season from Cachet Noire, who has since picked up the Prix Du Lys. He is going from strength to strength and will be a danger in all top events around ten furlongs. His future has not been decided yet, but the International at York must be a possibility. (10/1)
**1791 Glory of Dancer** just failed to hold on after looking all over the winner when he took the lead at the furlong marker. He raced on the outside and was coasting in the straight before taking the advantage, and his jockey admitted that, with hindsight, he might have taken the lead a little too soon as the colt can idle in front. This appears to be his perfect distance, and he will probably be rested before a tilt at York's International and a possible rematch with the winner. He is thoroughly consistent and genuine and was just a shade unlucky on this occasion. (24/10)
**1754a* Android (USA)** was slowly into his stride and, not surprisingly, his jockey decided to track Glory of Dancer for much of the race. When pace was injected halfway up the straight, he could not accelerate as well as the others, but he kept on at one pace in the final furlong. He is still a little green, but is an improving colt and will next be seen in the Prix Eugene Adam. (46/10)

**1756a* Le Triton (USA)**, who looked well in the paddock, as usual attempted to make all the running and did a pretty good job until the furlong marker, where he was hampered. When things go his way, he is a top-class performer and will now be given a rest before being allowed a tilt at Deauville's Prix Jacques le Marois over a stiff mile. He may be best when fresh. (37/10)
**1427* Farasan (IRE)**, stepping up enormously in class on this occasion, had a wretched race but, even if things had gone perfectly, it is doubtful he would have been in the first two. In mid-division early on, he had nowhere to go in the straight and, when a minute gap did appear between Le Triton and Blackwater just over a furlong out, Reid went for it. Sadly it closed and there was a fair amount of argy bargy between the three at the furlong marker. The Stewards shared the opinion that it was Farasan's fault, and so disqualified him from fourth place and gave Reid a four-day suspension. He is a very decent colt in the making and the obvious target would be the Prix Eugene Adam, but his ambitious owner may run him in the King George VI and Queen Elizabeth Diamond Stakes. (26/10)

## 2277a PRIX DE MALLERET (Gp 2) (3-Y.O F)
4-20 (4-18) **1m 4f** £39,526.00 (£15,810.00: £7,905.00: £3,953.00)

| | | | | SP | RR | SF |
|---|---|---|---|---|---|---|
| | **Shamadara (IRE)** (AdeRoyerDupre,France) **3-8-9** GMosse (trckd ldr to st: led over 1f out: pushed clr: impressive) | — | 1 | | 113+ | 65 |
| 1942a⁴ | **Leonila (IRE)** (RCollet,France) **3-8-9** OPeslier (mid div: hdwy to chse wnr over 1f out: hung lft u.p 1f out: kpt on fnl f: no ch w wnr) | 3 | 2 | | 109 | 61 |
| 1942a* | **Spanish Falls** (MmeCHead,France) **3-8-9** FHead (hld up last early: sme late hdwy) | 2½ | 3 | | 106 | 58 |
| | **Arel (FR)** (ELellouche,France) **3-8-9** TThulliez (racd in 4th: kpt on wl cl home: nt rch ldrs) | 1 | 4 | | 104 | 56 |
| 1769³ | **Mezzogiorno** (GWragg) **3-8-9** CAsmussen (led: u.p 2f out: hdd over 1f out: wknd) | nk | 5 | | 104 | 56 |
| 1942a³ | **Met Mech Nich (FR)** (J-PPelat,France) **3-8-9** TJarnet (swvd lft s & uns rdr) | | U | | — | — |

**6 Rn**

**2m 30.0** (4.00) P-M 4.30F: 2.40F 2.60F (28.30F) OWNER Aga Khan (CHANTILLY) BRED His Highness the Aga Khans Studs S. C.
**Shamadara (IRE)** moved from maiden company to a Group Two race without the slightest difficulty. She was in second place until halfway up the straight and, although green when asked to challenge, dominated the final stages. She is certainly a top-class filly in the making, and her previous form shows how much she has improved. All being well, she might now turn out for the Irish Oaks and she will certainly be one of the favourites for the Prix Vermeille in September.
**1942a Leonila (IRE)** is a very consistent, genuine filly and is always thereabouts in decent company, but she is not the easiest of rides and often hangs under pressure. She tracked the winner, but did not have the necessary speed to challenge the winner. She will probably next be seen in the Prix Minerve at Evry.
**1942a* Spanish Falls** was held up for a late run which she made on the rail, but her challenge began to falter at the furlong marker. It appears that she may not stay this distance when there is a strong pace.
**Arel (FR)** battled on well in the straight, but never looked like finishing in the first three.
**1769 Mezzogiorno** led until halfway up the straight and then went into reverse rather quickly. This was almost certainly not her best form and she might have been feeling the effects of a hard race in the Oaks. She will now be given a rest and this performance is best forgotten.
DS

# 2272a-SAN SIRO (Milan, Italy) (R-H) (Very Soft)
## Sunday June 23rd

## 2278a PREMIO CION DEL DUCA (4-Y.O+)
4-30 (4-33) **1m 4f** £12,180.00

| | | | | SP | RR | SF |
|---|---|---|---|---|---|---|
| 1706⁵ | **Suranom (IRE)** (LMCumani) **4-8-11** FJovine | — | 1 | | 109 | — |
| 1392a³ | **Scribano** (Italy) **6-8-11** EBotti | 1¼ | 2 | | 107 | — |
| 1579a² | **Tiana (ITY)** (Italy) **4-9-1** CFiocchi | 2¼ | 3 | | 108 | — |

**6 Rn**

**2m 34.2** (14.20) TOTE 30L: 19L 25L (80L) OWNER Scuderia Rencati (NEWMARKET) BRED Yeomanstown Lodge Stud
**1706 Suranom (IRE)** seems to run well on this course, and made all to win for the fourth time here in two seasons. He ran on well in the last furlong to hold off the challenge of Scribano.

# 1677-FOLKESTONE (R-H) (Firm)
## Friday June 28th
WEATHER: unsettled WIND: mod half against

## 2279 SCANIA 4-SERIES (S) STKS (2-Y.O) (Class G)
2-10 (2-10) **5f** £2,238.00 (£618.00: £294.00) Stalls: Low GOING minus 0.50 sec per fur (F)

| | | | | SP | RR | SF |
|---|---|---|---|---|---|---|
| 1622⁸ | **Advance Repro** (JAkehurst) **2-8-6b¹** GDuffield(1) (chsd ldr: led over 2f out: hrd rdn over 1f out: r.o wl) | — | 1 | 9/2³ | 48 | 1 |
| *1968⁵* | **Miss Barcelona (IRE)** (MJPolglase) **2-8-6** NCarlisle(2) (chsd ldrs: rdn over 3f out: chsd wnr wl over 1f out: hrd rdn: unable qckn) | 1¼ | 2 | 15/2 | 44 | — |
| | **Summerville Wood** (PMooney) **2-8-11** SSanders(4) (w'like: s.s: wl bhd over 3f out: hdwy fnl f: nvr nrr) | 6 | 3 | 11/4² | 30 | — |
| *1720⁵* | **Dozen Roses** (TMJones) **2-8-6** RPerham(3) (lw: chsd ldrs: rdn 3f out: wknd over 1f out) | ¾ | 4 | 50/1 | 22 | — |
| 2125* | **Tinker's Surprise (IRE)** (BJMeehan) **2-9-3b** MTebbutt(6) (hld up: rdn over 2f: wknd over 1f out) | 5 | 5 | 4/5¹ | 17 | — |
| 1834⁶ | **Miss St Kitts** (JRJenkins) **2-8-6v¹** CRutter(5) (lw: led over 2f) | 7 | 6 | 33/1 | — | — |

(SP 117.1%) **6 Rn**

**60.4 secs** (2.80) CSF £32.90 TOTE £7.40: £2.80 £1.80 (£14.80) OWNER Advance Reprographic Printers (LAMBOURN) BRED Roldvale Ltd
No bid
**Advance Repro** found the application of blinkers working the oracle. Racing in second place, she went on at halfway and, responding to pressure below the distance, proved far too good for the runner-up. (9/2)
**1968 Miss Barcelona (IRE)** was soon being bustled along, but struggled into second early inside the final quarter-mile. Trying to get on terms with the winner, she failed to do so. (15/2)
**Summerville Wood**, a sturdy colt, lost all chances with an extremely slow start. Still last below the distance, he stayed on well past beaten horses in the final furlong. (11/4: 2/1-3/1)
**Dozen Roses** chased the leaders, but was hung out to dry below the distance. (50/1)
**2125* Tinker's Surprise (IRE)** disappointed following last week's selling victory. Tracking the leaders, he tamely dropped away below the distance. (4/5)

## 2280 SCANIA 4-SERIES 'KING OF THE ROAD' TROPHY H'CAP (0-70) (3-Y.O+) (Class E)

2-40 (2-40) **5f** £2,933.70 (£873.60: £415.80: £186.90) Stalls: Low GOING minus 0.50 sec per fur (F)

| Form | Horse / Details | Dist | Pos | SP | RR | SF |
|---|---|---|---|---|---|---|
| $2129^{7}$ | **Friendly Brave (USA) (70)** (MissGayKelleway) **6-10-0** RHughes(3) (b.hind: lw: hld up: chsd ldr over 2f out: rdn over 1f out: led wl ins fnl f: r.o wl) | — | **1** | $7/4^{1}$ | 76 | 49 |
| $2129^{2}$ | **Another Batchworth (54)** (EAWheeler) **4-8-12** RPerham(1) (led: rdn over 1f out: hdd wl ins fnl f: nt qckn) | ¾ | **2** | $3/1^{3}$ | 58 | 31 |
| $2129^{3}$ | **Half Tone (48)** (RMFlower) **4-8-6b** DBiggs(2) (lw: rdn over 2f out: hdwy over 1f out: r.o) | hd | **3** | 7/2 | 51 | 24 |
| $1905^{4}$ | **Red Admiral (62)** (CMurray) **6-9-6** MTebbutt(4) (chsd ldr over 2f: wknd over 1f out) | 7 | **4** | $9/4^{2}$ | 43 | 16 |

(SP 114.4%) **4 Rn**

**58.7 secs** (0.10 under best) (1.10) CSF £6.97 TOTE £2.90 (£5.20) OWNER Grid Thoroughbred Racing Partnership (WHITCOMBE) BRED Foxfield

**1958* Friendly Brave (USA)** was given a lovely ride by Hughes. Nicely covered up in third, he went second at halfway and, asked for his effort from below the distance, managed to get on top in the last 75 yards. (7/4)

**2129 Another Batchworth** attempted to make all the running. Challenged by the winner entering the final furlong, she grimly stuck her neck out, but was eventually overhauled in the final 75 yards. (3/1: op 2/1)

**2129 Half Tone** picked up ground on the outside below the distance but, despite running on, was unable to overhaul the front two in time. (7/2)

**1905 Red Admiral**, in second place to halfway, tamely dropped away below the distance. (9/4)

## 2281 SCANTRUCK FOR SCANIA MEDIAN AUCTION MAIDEN STKS (3-Y.O) (Class F)

3-10 (3-15) **6f** £2,666.60 (£737.60: £351.80) Stalls: Low GOING minus 0.50 sec per fur (F)

| Form | Horse / Details | Dist | Pos | SP | RR | SF |
|---|---|---|---|---|---|---|
| $1709^{9}$ | **Cross of Valour** (JARToller) **3-9-0** SSanders(8) (lw: hld up: chsd ldr over 2f out: rdn wl over 1f out: led wl ins fnl f: r.o wl) | — | **1** | $8/1^{3}$ | 81 | 27 |
| $1608^{4}$ | **Sihafi (USA) (77)** (EALDunlop) **3-9-0** RHills(4) (lw: led: clr 3f out: rdn over 1f out: hdd wl ins fnl f: nt qckn) | 1½ | **2** | $8/15^{1}$ | 77 | 23 |
| $1356^{9}$ | **Depiction (68)** (RGuest) **3-9-0** GDuffield(3) (rdn & no hdwy fnl 3f) | 10 | **3** | $6/1^{2}$ | 50 | — |
| | **Tonic Chord** (JRFanshawe) **3-8-6**(3) NVarley(6) (unf: rdn over 3f out: sme hdwy over 1f out: one pce) | ½ | **4** | $6/1^{2}$ | 44 | — |
| $1689^{13}$ | **Craven Cottage (55)** (CJames) **3-9-0v[1]** CRutter(7) (b. unf: bit bkwd: bhd fnl 3f) | 5 | **5** | 50/1 | 36 | — |
| *$1721^{13}$* | **Digwana (IRE) (36)** (TMJones) **3-9-0** RPerham(5) (bhd fnl 3f) | 4 | **6** | 50/1 | 25 | — |
| $1681^{7}$ | **Nightswimming (IRE)** (SDow) **3-8-9**(5) ADaly(2) (lw: s.s: hdwy over 4f out: wknd over 2f out: b.b.v) | 15 | **7** | 16/1 | — | — |
| | ***Amazon Princess*** (JFfitch-Heyes) **3-8-6**(3) MHenry(1) (Withdrawn not under Starter's orders: Veterinary advice) | | **W** | 33/1 | — | — |

(SP 117.6%) **7 Rn**

**1m 12.2** (2.00) CSF £12.66 TOTE £8.80: £1.80 £1.40 (£3.60) OWNER Mr P. C. J. Dalby (WHITSBURY) BRED Cheveley Park Stud Ltd

**Cross of Valour** moved into second soon after halfway, but had about five lengths to make up on the clear leader. Buckling down to his task well, he got on top in the closing stages to win a very bad race. (8/1)

**1608 Sihafi (USA)** was certainly the paddock pick and, strolling along in front, had established a clear advantage of about five lengths going to the two-furlong pole. It looked as though the race was his, but the winner gradually wore him down and he had no more in the final 75 yards. (8/15)

**934 Depiction** was made to look extremely moderate as he plodded on from halfway. (6/1: 4/1-7/1)

**Tonic Chord** did not look tuned up at all and never threatened to get into it. (6/1: op 4/1)

## 2282 SCANIA 1996 TRUCK OF THE YEAR TROPHY H'CAP (0-65) (3-Y.O+) (Class F)

3-40 (3-40) **1m 4f** £2,761.80 (£764.80: £365.40) Stalls: Low GOING minus 0.50 sec per fur (F)

| Form | Horse / Details | Dist | Pos | SP | RR | SF |
|---|---|---|---|---|---|---|
| $1640^{12}$ | **Sacred Mirror (IRE) (50)** (CEBrittain) **5-8-13** SSanders(2) (b: lw: hdwy 6f out: led over 2f out: r.o wl) | — | **1** | 7/1 | 65 | 40 |
| $2008^{12}$ | **Silktail (IRE) (65)** (MissGayKelleway) **4-10-0** RHughes(3) (lw: s.s: hdwy over 3f out: chsd wnr wl over 1f out: unable qckn) | 3½ | **2** | $5/1^{3}$ | 75 | 50 |
| $1903^{4}$ | **Giftbox (USA) (54)** (SirMarkPrescott) **4-9-3** GDuffield(5) (lw: chsd ldr: led over 3f out tl over 2f out: wknd over 1f out) | 8 | **3** | $5/4^{1}$ | 54 | 29 |
| $1468^{16}$ | **Kirov Protege (IRE) (35)** (HJCollingridge) **4-7-12** NCarlisle(4) (nvr nr to chal) | 6 | **4** | 14/1 | 27 | 2 |
| $1803^{16}$ | **Bresil (USA) (33)** (KRBurke) **7-7-7v[1]**(3) NVarley(8) (lw: s.s & hmpd s: nvr nrr) | 1 | **5** | 33/1 | 23 | — |
| | **Riva Rock (39)** (TPMcGovern) **6-7-11**(5)ow6 ADaly(1) (lw: hld up: rdn over 5f out: sn wknd) | nk | **6** | 16/1 | 29 | — |
| $1877^{5}$ | **Colour Counsellor (47)** (RMFlower) **3-7-5b**(5) CAdamson(9) (led: rn wd bnd over 9f out: hdd over 3f out: wknd over 2f out) | 2 | **7** | 9/1 | 34 | — |
| $1874^{3}$ | **Wottashambles (39)** (LMontagueHall) **5-8-2** JFEgan(6) (b: rn wd bnd over 9f out: bhd fnl 5f) | 8 | **8** | $7/2^{2}$ | 16 | — |
| $1996^{10}$ | **Heretical Miss (35)** (JFfitch-Heyes) **6-7-9**(3) MHenry(7) (stumbled & uns rdr s) | | **U** | 40/1 | — | — |

(SP 123.8%) **9 Rn**

**2m 33.9** (2.70) CSF £41.59 CT £67.52 TOTE £7.10: £2.10 £2.50 £1.50 (£18.80) Trio £7.70 OWNER Mr C. E. Brittain (NEWMARKET) BRED Saeed Manana

LONG HANDICAP Bresil (USA) 7-4 Riva Rock 7-7

WEIGHT FOR AGE 3yo-14lb

**206 Sacred Mirror (IRE)** moved up at halfway. Striking the front entering the short home straight, she soon asserted her authority. (7/1)

**Silktail (IRE)** gradually got into the race and moved into second early inside the final quarter-mile. Try as she might, she was unable to reel in the winner. (5/1)

**1903 Giftbox (USA)** raced in second place in a fast-run race. Sent on over three furlongs from home, he was collared early in the straight and soon in trouble. (5/4)

## 2283 ARGLES & COURT H'CAP (0-80) (3-Y.O+) (Class D)

4-10 (4-10) **6f 189y** £3,590.00 (£1,070.00: £510.00: £230.00) Stalls: Low GOING minus 0.50 sec per fur (F)

| Form | Horse / Details | Dist | Pos | SP | RR | SF |
|---|---|---|---|---|---|---|
| $1962^{2}$ | **Neuwest (USA) (78)** (NJHWalker) **4-10-0** RHughes(7) (lw: a.p: led on bit over 1f out: shkn up ins fnl f: qcknd: comf) | — | **1** | $11/4^{1}$ | 89+ | 64 |
| $1677^{2}$ | **Young Mazaad (IRE) (68)** (DCO'Brien) **3-8-9b** GBardwell(4) (hdwy 2f out: ev ch 1f out: unable qckn) | 1¼ | **2** | $7/2^{2}$ | 76 | 42 |
| $1962^{8}$ | **Ertlon (78)** (CEBrittain) **6-10-0** JFEgan(3) (lw: led over 5f: one pce) | 2 | **3** | 7/1 | 81 | 56 |
| $1843^{6}$ | **Mihriz (IRE) (75)** (RAkehurst) **4-9-11** SSanders(8) (rdn over 3f out: hdwy over 1f out: r.o) | 2 | **4** | $5/1^{3}$ | 74 | 49 |
| $1953^{3}$ | **Fort Knox (IRE) (60)** (RMFlower) **5-8-10b** DBiggs(2) (lw: nvr nr to chal) | hd | **5** | 6/1 | 59 | 34 |
| $1876^{4}$ | **Stolen Melody (64)** (SDow) **4-9-0** BThomson(6) (prom over 5f) | 3 | **6** | 11/2 | 56 | 31 |
| $1872^{8}$ | **Robellion (65)** (DWPArbuthnot) **5-9-1v** MTebbutt(5) (a bhd) | 3 | **7** | 14/1 | 50 | 25 |

| | | | SP | RR | SF |
|---|---|---|---|---|---|
| 1836[2] | **Northern Judge (60)** (BHanbury) **3-7-12b**(3) MHenry(1) (chsd ldr 5f out to 3f out: sn wknd)...16 | **8** | 13/2 | 7 | — |

(SP 127.7%) **8 Rn**

**1m 22.0** (0.40) CSF £13.89 CT £60.26 TOTE £5.10: £1.30 £1.10 £2.40 (£8.40) OWNER Mr Paul Green (WANTAGE) BRED Robert Bloomer and Sharon L. Bloomer

WEIGHT FOR AGE 3yo-9lb

**1962 Neuwest (USA)** as usual looked really well beforehand and put up a polished display. Always in the front four, he cruised into the lead on the bridle approaching the final furlong. Although the runner-up proved a serious threat, he needed only to be shaken up inside the final furlong to score in style. (11/4: 3/1-10/1)

**1677 Young Mazaad (IRE)** moved up in the straight and threw down his challenge from below the distance. With every chance entering the final furlong, he yet again found one too good for him and does not look one to place a good deal of faith in. (7/2)

**1048 Ertlon** attempted to make all. Collared below the distance, he could only keep on in his own time. (7/1)

**1843 Mihriz (IRE)** stayed on in the last furlong and a half without ever threatening. (5/1)

**1876 Stolen Melody** (11/2: 7/2-6/1)

**553 Robellion** (14/1: op 8/1)

**1836 Northern Judge** (13/2: 9/2-7/1)

## 2284 SCANIA 4-SERIES 'HORSEPOWER' TROPHY AMATEUR H'CAP (0-60) (3-Y.O+) (Class G)

4-40 (4-40) **1m 1f 149y** £2,511.00 (£696.00: £333.00) Stalls: Low GOING minus 0.50 sec per fur (F)

| | | | SP | RR | SF |
|---|---|---|---|---|---|
| *2081*[2] | **Montone (IRE) (59)** (JRJenkins) **6-11-7v** DrMMannish(10) (chsd ldr 2f: swtchd lft over 2f out: chsd ldr over 1f out: led last stride)...— | **1** | 3/1 [1] | 68 | 50 |
| 1816[6] | **Don't Drop Bombs (USA) (35)** (DTThom) **7-9-11v** MissJFeilden(9) (lw: led: rdn over 1f out: hdd last stride) s.h | **2** | 6/1 [3] | 44 | 26 |
| 1979* | **Owdbetts (IRE) (56)** (GLMoore) **4-10-13**(5) MrJGoldstein(13) (stdy hdwy 3f out: rdn over 1f out: r.o wl ins fnl f)...1½ | **3** | 13/2 | 62 | 44 |
| 1890[5] | **Super Serenade (52)** (GBBalding) **7-10-9**(5) MrJThatcher(14) (a.p: rdn over 2f out: r.o one pce)...2½ | **4** | 8/1 | 54 | 36 |
| 1816[7] | **Norsong (52)** (RAkehurst) **4-11-0** MrTMcCarthy(12) (b.nr fore: chsd ldr over 7f out tl over 1f out: sn wknd) ..2½ | **5** | 3/1 [1] | 50 | 32 |
| 1778[8] | **Royal Acclaim (29)** (JMBradley) **11-9-0v**(5) MissLKerr(8) (b: nvr nr to chal)...2 | **6** | 20/1 | 24 | 6 |
| 1890[15] | **Kevasingo (56)** (BWHills) **4-10-13**(5) MrCBHills(4) (lw: a mid div)...nk | **7** | 8/1 | 50 | 32 |
| 2127[8] | **Pennine Wind (IRE) (58)** (SDow) **4-11-1**(5) MrSFetherstonhaugh(11) (nvr nrr)...½ | **8** | 20/1 | 52 | 34 |
| 1778[13] | **Dots Dee (25)** (JMBradley) **7-9-1** MrsLPearce(3) (a mid div)...1¼ | **9** | 5/1 [2] | 17 | — |
| 2155[14] | **Legal Drama (USA) (46)** (JohnBerry) **4-10-3**(5)ow1 MrVCoogan(1) (lw: s.s: a bhd)...2½ | **10** | 33/1 | 33 | 14 |
| 1953[14] | **Sarum (40)** (JELong) **10-9-11**(5) MrTWaters(6) (b: a bhd)...12 | **11** | 25/1 | 8 | — |
| 1903[9] | **Pinkerton Polka (44)** (CEBrittain) **4-10-6** MrVLukaniuk(2) (lw: prom over 4f)...s.h | **12** | 16/1 | 11 | — |
| 1803[13] | **Begger's Opera (28)** (PatMitchell) **4-8-13v**1(5) MissCCarcary(7) (a bhd)...8 | **13** | 33/1 | — | — |
| 1677[8] | **Red Sky Delight (IRE) (36)** (PButler) **3-8-9**(5) MrIMongan(5) (a bhd)...24 | **14** | 33/1 | — | — |

(SP 144.6%) **14 Rn**

**2m 2.4** (4.70) CSF £24.93 CT £112.22 TOTE £5.20: £1.80 £2.40 £3.10 (£19.30) Trio £17.20 OWNER Mr B. Shirazi (ROYSTON) BRED Sean Gorman

LONG HANDICAP Red Sky Delight (IRE) 8-13

WEIGHT FOR AGE 3yo-12lb

**2081 Montone (IRE)**, in a handy position throughout, regained second place below the distance and, although his rider proved to be of little help, the gelding got up right on the line. (3/1)

**1816 Don't Drop Bombs (USA)** attempted to make all the running. His rider did make an effort to ride him in the straight, but the combination was collared right on the line. (6/1)

**1979* Owdbetts (IRE)** steadily crept closer running down the hill. Running on nicely inside the final furlong, she failed to get there in time. (13/2)

**1890 Super Serenade** was never far away and stayed on in the last two furlongs without ever threatening. (8/1)

**1515 Norsong**, second entering the back straight, was collared for the runner-up berth below the distance and was soon out on his feet. (3/1)

T/Plpt: £170.50 (46.12 Tckts). T/Qdpt: £4.70 (227.47 Tckts). AK

# 2124-GOODWOOD (R-H) (Good to firm)

## Friday June 28th

Abandoned after Race 2 - poor visibility

WEATHER: mist WIND: almost nil

## 2285 MIDSUMMER APPRENTICE H'CAP (0-80) (4-Y.O+) (Class E)

6-40 (6-44) **7f** £3,752.50 (£1,120.00: £535.00: £242.50) Stalls: High GOING minus 0.18 sec per fur (GF)

| | | | SP | RR | SF |
|---|---|---|---|---|---|
| *513*[4] | **Present Situation (55)** (LordHuntingdon) **5-8-2**(3) AimeeCook(9) (8th ½-wy: hdwy to ld ins fnl f: r.o)...— | **1** | 10/1 | 69 | 28 |
| 1856[2] | **Jaazim (54)** (MMadgwick) **6-8-1**(3) AEddery(7) (lw: 7th ½-wy: hdwy & ev ch ins fnl f: r.o)...1 | **2** | 7/2 [1] | 66 | 25 |
| 1658* | **Chairmans Choice (65)** (APJarvis) **6-8-10**(5) KHopkins(4) (chsd ldr: led over 1f out tl ins fnl f)...¾ | **3** | 13/2 | 75 | 34 |
| 2129* | **Scissor Ridge (47)** (JJBridger) **4-7-11** 6x MBaird(8) (swtg: led over 5f: one pce)...2 | **4** | 5/1 [3] | 52 | 11 |
| | **Audrey Grace (47)** (MissGayKelleway) **5-7-11** ADaly(6) (3rd ½-wy: wknd over 1f out)...2 | **5** | 8/1 | 48 | 7 |
| 2134[11] | **Safey Ana (USA) (73)** (BHanbury) **5-9-9** DGriffiths(5) (b: swtg: 6th ½-wy: no hdwy fnl 2f)...4 | **6** | 8/1 | 65 | 24 |
| *1719*[9] | **Jovie King (IRE) (47)** (PhilipMitchell) **4-7-8v**(3)ow1 MartinDwyer(3) (5th ½-wy: wknd 2f out)...hd | **7** | 50/1 | 39 | — |
| 1775[12] | **Fionn de Cool (IRE) (74)** (RAkehurst) **5-9-5**(5) DDenby(10) (last ½-wy: a bhd)...¾ | **8** | 14/1 | 64 | 23 |
| 1856[8] | **Paddy's Rice (63)** (MMcCormack) **5-8-13** JDSmith(1) (9th ½-wy: a bhd)...1 | **9** | 10/1 | 51 | 10 |
| 2005[7] | **Don Pepe (60)** (RBoss) **5-8-7**(3) GFaulkner(2) (lw: 4th ½-wy: wknd over 2f out)...3½ | **10** | 9/2 [2] | 40 | — |

(SP 119.4%) **10 Rn**

**1m 28.82** (4.02) CSF £43.40 CT £234.95 TOTE £7.30: £1.90 £1.20 £2.60 (£14.10) Trio £30.90 OWNER Mr Chris van Hoorn (WEST ILSLEY) BRED The Queen

LONG HANDICAP Jovie King (IRE) 7-4

**513 Present Situation**, five times a winner on the All-Weather, took advantage of being rated 16lb lower to get off the mark on turf. (10/1: 6/1-11/1)

**1856 Jaazim**, raised a further pound, is running well without being able to get his head in front where it matters most. (7/2)

**1658* Chairmans Choice** did his best to defy a 9lb hike in the weights for winning a similar event at Brighton earlier in the month. (13/2)

**2129* Scissor Ridge**, after his win here a week ago, was due to go up a further 5lb in future handicaps. (5/1: 3/1-11/2)

**Safey Ana (USA)** (8/1: op 12/1)

**2005 Don Pepe** (9/2: op 3/1)

## 2286 HANNINGTONS MACMILLAN CHAPEL APPEAL (S) H'CAP (0-60) (3-Y.O+) (Class E)

7-10 (7-15) **6f** £4,402.50 (£1,320.00: £635.00: £292.50) Stalls: High GOING minus 0.18 sec per fur (GF)

| Form | Horse | Dist | Pos | SP | RR | SF |
|---|---|---|---|---|---|---|
| 1992[3] | **Dahiyah (USA) (60)** (GLMoore) **5-9-11v**(3) SDrowne(1) (led 2f: led ins fnl f: r.o) | — | **1** | 8/1[2] | 70 | 45 |
| *1812*[8] | **Twice Purple (IRE) (56)** (BJMeehan) **4-9-10b** BDoyle(10) (led 4f out: hdd ins fnl: r.o) | nk | **2** | 14/1 | 65 | 40 |
| 1777[3] | **Pride of Hayling (IRE) (50)** (PRHedger) **5-9-4** TQuinn(6) (chsd ldrs stands' side: unable qckn ins fnl f) | 1 | **3** | 5/2[1] | 57 | 32 |
| 1642[2] | **Sound the Trumpet (IRE) (54)** (RCSpicer) **4-9-3**(5) MartinDwyer(3) (chsd ldrs stands' side: one pce fnl 2f) | 3½ | **4** | 10/1[3] | 51 | 26 |
| 2029[7] | **Petraco (IRE) (58)** (NASmith) **8-9-7**(5) DGriffiths(2) (prom stands' side: wknd fnl f) | ½ | **5** | 16/1 | 54 | 29 |
| *1970*[8] | **Cedar Dancer (35)** (RJHodges) **4-7-12**(5) PPMurphy(12) (hdwy 2f out: one pce fnl f) | s.h | **6** | 20/1 | 31 | 6 |
| 2013[10] | **Bella's Legacy (50)** (RJHodges) **3-8-6**(5) JDSmith(8) (nvr nr to chal) | nk | **7** | 50/1 | 45 | 13 |
| 1642[13] | **Newlands Corner (40)** (JAkehurst) **3-8-1** AMcGlone(14) (nvr nrr) | 1¼ | **8** | 33/1 | 32 | — |
| 2129[10] | **Deardaw (39)** (MDIUsher) **4-8-7** MRimmer(5) (m.n.s) | 1½ | **9** | 33/1 | 27 | 2 |
| *406*[9] | **Pair of Jacks (IRE) (28)** (TJNaughton) **6-7-7**(3) MHenry(11) (prom 4f) | nk | **10** | 16/1 | 15 | — |
| 1856[12] | **Hawanafa (55)** (RHannon) **3-8-13**(3) DaneO'Neill(17) (m.n.s) | 2 | **11** | 20/1 | 37 | 5 |
| 1715[W] | **Astral Invader (IRE) (51)** (MSSaunders) **4-9-5** RPrice(16) (lw: spd centre 4f) | 1 | **12** | 8/1[2] | 30 | 5 |
| 1446[8] | **Rowlandsons Stud (IRE) (56)** (PBurgoyne) **3-8-10**(7) JBosley(13) (m.n.s) | hd | **13** | 25/1 | 35 | 3 |
| 1013[5] | **Dantean (35)** (RJO'Sullivan) **4-8-3b**ow1 SSanders(21) (prom far side over 3f) | hd | **14** | 25/1 | 13 | — |
| 1992[9] | **Justinianus (IRE) (46)** (JJBridger) **4-8-11**(3) DarrenMoffatt(9) (chsd ldrs 4f) | nk | **15** | 25/1 | 24 | — |
| 2156[8] | **Classic Pet (IRE) (43)** (CAHorgan) **4-8-11** NAdams(18) (prom far side 3f) | 2 | **16** | 16/1 | 15 | — |
| 1992[13] | **Assignment (32)** (JELong) **10-8-0** LeesaLong(23) (m.n.s) | ½ | **17** | 50/1 | 3 | — |
| 1677[5] | **Spectacle Jim (50)** (MJHaynes) **7-9-4b** DRMcCabe(22) (m.n.s) | 1½ | **18** | 25/1 | 17 | — |
| 1715[12] | **Dark Menace (50)** (EAWheeler) **4-8-13**(5) ADaly(24) (led far side 3f) | 5 | **19** | 25/1 | 4 | — |
| 1592[4] | **Jessica's Song (51)** (WGMTurner) **3-8-5**(7) DSweeney(19) (m.n.s) | ¾ | **20** | 12/1 | 3 | — |
| | **Coalisland (28)** (RIngram) **6-7-7b**(3) NVarley(4) (a bhd) | 1½ | **21** | 50/1 | — | — |
| 2133[5] | **Capture The Moment (52)** (RJRWilliams) **3-8-13** RHughes(20) (prom far side 3f) | ¾ | **22** | 16/1 | — | — |
| 1663[7] | **Beeny (52)** (APJarvis) **3-8-13v** WJO'Connor(7) (prom stands' side 4f) | 4 | **23** | 25/1 | — | — |
| 1777[12] | **Mazzarello (IRE) (42)** (RCurtis) **6-8-10v** PatEddery(15) (a bhd) | 3 | **24** | 10/1[3] | — | — |

(SP 151.2%) **24 Rn**

**1m 13.56** (3.56) CSF £122.87 CT £352.16 TOTE £13.10: £3.50 £4.30 £1.50 £2.80 (£130.30) Trio £121.40 OWNER Mr Bryan Pennick (EPSOM) BRED Foxfield

LONG HANDICAP Pair of Jacks (IRE) 7-9 Coalisland 6-11
WEIGHT FOR AGE 3yo-7lb
Bt in 6,200gns

**1992 Dahiyah (USA)** was coming back to his best trip in a race where a low draw proved a big help. (8/1)
**1624 Twice Purple (IRE)** disappointed on the Fibresand last time, but again ran well in the blinkers back on turf. (14/1)
**1777 Pride of Hayling (IRE)**, back to her optimum trip, won this event last year off an 8lb lower mark. (5/2: op 4/1)
**1642 Sound the Trumpet (IRE)** was 1lb higher than when second at Leicester. (10/1: 8/1-12/1)
**1844 Petraco (IRE)**, dropped into selling company, has slipped down to a rating 1lb lower than when he won last year. (16/1)

## 2287 SOUTHERN DAILY ECHO H'CAP (0-90) (3-Y.O+) (Class C)

**Abandoned** - Fog

## 2288 WEATHERBYS H'CAP (0-80) (3-Y.O+) (Class D)

**Abandoned** - Fog

## 2289 E.B.F. CELER ET AUDAX MAIDEN STKS (2-Y.O) (Class D)

**Abandoned** - Fog

## 2290 GRATWICK MEDIAN AUCTION MAIDEN STKS (3-Y.O) (Class D)

**Abandoned** - Fog

T/Plpt: £2.50 (7,829.87 Tckts). KH

# 1359-NEWCASTLE (L-H) (Firm, Good to firm patches)

## Friday June 28th

3rd, 4th & 6th races hand-timed
WEATHER: changeable & cool WIND: mod half against

## 2291 YORKSHIRE TYNE-TEES TELEVISION CONDITIONS STKS (2-Y.O) (Class C)

6-15 (6-15) **7f** £5,978.80 (£1,661.20) Stalls: High GOING minus 0.09 sec per fur (G)

| Form | Horse | Dist | Pos | SP | RR | SF |
|---|---|---|---|---|---|---|
| 1897* | **Fun Galore (USA)** (BWHills) **2-9-5** MHills(1) (b.nr hind: plld hrd: qckd to ld over 1f out: pushed clr: v.easily) | — | **1** | 2/9[1] | 81 | 32 |
| 1978[3] | **Samsung Spirit** (EWeymes) **2-8-8** JQuinn(2) (lw: led: rdn over 2f out: hdd over 1f out: no ch w wnr) | 2 | **2** | 7/2[2] | 65 | 16 |

(SP 104.0%) **2 Rn**

**1m 29.87** (5.37) TOTE £1.10 OWNER Miss H Al Maktoum (LAMBOURN) BRED Gainsborough Farm Inc

**1897* Fun Galore (USA)**, on his toes beforehand, proved in a completely different league to his sole opponent, winning with his head in his chest. He now goes for a seven-furlong listed race at the Newmarket July Meeting. (2/9)
**1978 Samsung Spirit**, in good nick, tried hard to make a race of it, but the winner was in a different class. (7/2)

## 2292 NORTHERN ROCK GOSFORTH PARK CUP H'CAP (0-105) (3-Y.O+) (Class B)

6-50 (6-52) **5f** £14,200.00 (£4,300.00: £2,100.00: £1,000.00) Stalls: High GOING minus 0.09 sec per fur (G)

| Form | Horse | Dist | Pos | SP | RR | SF |
|---|---|---|---|---|---|---|
| 1790[6] | **Twice as Sharp (84)** (PWHarris) **4-8-10** GHind(4) (lw: chsd ldr far side: carried rt & led jst ins fnl f: r.o wl) | — | **1** | 11/2[2] | 94 | 59 |
| 2220[5] | **Ziggy's Dancer (USA) (83)** (EJAlston) **5-8-9** KFallon(12) (chsd ldr stands' side: styd on wl fnl f) | 1½ | **2** | 12/1 | 88 | 53 |

| | | | | SP | RR | SF |
|---|---|---|---|---|---|---|
| 1964* | **Lord High Admiral (CAN) (82)** (MJHeaton-Ellis) **8-8-8** MRoberts(2) (led far side: hung rt & hdd jst ins fnl f: kpt on same pce) | nk | **3** | 9/1 | 86 | 51 |
| 1975[2] | **Tedburrow (85)** (MrsAMNaughton) **4-8-11** JCarroll(11) (chsd ldrs stands' side: styd on same pce appr fnl f) | 1 | **4** | 7/1[3] | 86 | 51 |
| 2143[8] | **Tadeo (93)** (MJohnston) **3-8-8**(5) KMChin(1) (a chsng ldrs: nt qckn fnl 2f) | 1½ | **5** | 25/1 | 89 | 48 |
| 1974[11] | **Tuscan Dawn (78)** (JBerry) **6-8-4**ow1 JFortune(10) (dwlt s: sn chsng ldrs: wknd fnl f) | 1¼ | **6** | 11/1 | 70 | 34 |
| 1818[10] | **Mr Oscar (97)** (MJohnston) **4-9-9** JWeaver(9) (lw: led stands' side tl wknd 1f out) | hd | **7** | 8/1 | 89 | 54 |
| | **Saint Express (100)** (MrsMReveley) **6-9-12** KDarley(7) (swtchd lft s: drvn along & hdwy ½-wy: no imp) | 1½ | **8** | 8/1 | 87 | 52 |
| 2003[3] | **Crowded Avenue (97)** (PJMakin) **4-9-9** PaulEddery(6) (trckd ldrs: effrt over 1f out: sn wknd) | nk | **9** | 4/1[1] | 83 | 48 |
| 1630[8] | **Takadou (IRE) (94)** (MissLCSiddall) **5-9-6** MHills(5) (lw: dwlt s: outpcd & bhd: sme hdwy over 1f out: n.d) | 1¾ | **10** | 14/1 | 75 | 40 |
| 2003[4] | **That Man Again (97)** (GLewis) **4-9-6b**(3) AWhelan(3) (sn outpcd) | 1 | **11** | 7/1[3] | 74 | 39 |
| 1790[17] | **Sweet Magic (84)** (PHowling) **5-8-10** JQuinn(8) (racd stands' side: nvr wnt pce) | 2½ | **12** | 10/1 | 53 | 18 |
| | | | | (SP 128.2%) | | **12 Rn** |

**60.01 secs** (1.61) CSF £67.83 CT £560.62 TOTE £9.40: £3.00 £3.10 £2.30 (£51.50) Trio £169.00 OWNER Formula Twelve (BERKHAMSTED) BRED R. and A. Craddock
WEIGHT FOR AGE 3yo-6lb

**1790 Twice as Sharp**, surprisingly for a son of Sharpo, revels on fast ground. Despite being pushed towards the centre by the third, he scored in decisive fashion. (11/2)
**2220 Ziggy's Dancer (USA)**, having his second race in three days, stepped up on his Chester effort. (12/1)
**1964* Lord High Admiral (CAN)**, who always runs well for Roberts, showed all his old speed, but hung off a true line under pressure, causing the winner a problem or two. (9/1)
**1975 Tedburrow** seemed to run right up to his best. (7/1)
**989 Tadeo** gave his apprentice a good first ride in England. (25/1)
**1430 Tuscan Dawn,** on his toes beforehand, not for the first time gave away ground at the start. (11/1)
**1016 Mr Oscar** looked very fit and led them a merry dance on the stands' side. The feeling is we have yet to see the best of him this year. (8/1)
**Saint Express** looked as if the outing would do him good and his run confirmed this impression. (8/1)
**2003 Crowded Avenue** as usual travelled strongly but, when picked up over a furlong out, found nothing. (4/1)

## 2293 STEPHEN EASTEN DOBSON PEACOCK H'CAP (0-85) (3-Y.O+) (Class D)

7-25 (7-26) **1m (round)** £6,840.00 (£2,070.00: £1,010.00: £480.00) Stalls: Low GOING minus 0.09 sec per fur (G)

| | | | | SP | RR | SF |
|---|---|---|---|---|---|---|
| 1672* | **Equerry (79)** (MJohnston) **5-9-11** JWeaver(6) (lw: sn led: styd on u.p fnl 2f: all out) | — | **1** | 5/1[3] | 88 | 40 |
| 2010* | **Sandmoor Chambray (79)** (TDEasterby) **5-9-11** MBirch(3) (lw: led early: trckd ldrs: rdn & outpcd 2f out: styd on wl ins fnl f) | nk | **2** | 7/2[2] | 87 | 39 |
| 2005[9] | **Ochos Rios (IRE) (58)** (BSRothwell) **5-8-4** MFenton(2) (chsd ldrs: chal over 2f out: kpt on same pce fnl f) | ½ | **3** | 14/1 | 65 | 17 |
| 1868[3] | **Scaraben (68)** (SEKettlewell) **8-9-0** JFortune(1) (lw: dwlt s: hld up: hdwy over 1f out: styd on towards fin) | ½ | **4** | 11/4[1] | 74 | 26 |
| | **Final Stab (IRE) (80)** (PWHarris) **3-9-2** GHind(4) (hld up: effrt & wandered over 2f out: hung lft & no imp) | 3½ | **5** | 13/2 | 79 | 21 |
| 1420[2] | **Smarter Charter (69)** (MrsJRRamsden) **3-8-5**ow1 KFallon(5) (trckd ldrs: effrt & ev ch over 2f out: sn wknd & eased) | 5 | **6** | 11/4[1] | 58 | — |
| | | | | (SP 112.2%) | | **6 Rn** |

**1m 45.1** (6.10) CSF £21.06 TOTE £4.50: £1.70 £2.20 (£6.90) OWNER Mr J. R. Good (MIDDLEHAM) BRED J. R. and Mrs P. Good
WEIGHT FOR AGE 3yo-10lb

**1672* Equerry** was allowed to set his own pace. Setting sail for home with over two furlongs left to run, he just managed to hang on. His rider deserves full marks for this. (5/1)
**2010* Sandmoor Chambray,** 6lb higher than at York, jumped off first. Having made the running in the past, here he was pulled back in behind the winner. Tapped for foot when the race began in earnest, he stayed on strongly inside the last and would have made it in a few more strides. (7/2)
**1610 Ochos Rios (IRE)**, like the winner, was given an enterprising ride but, on a losing run of twenty-one, he could find no more inside the last. (14/1: 10/1-16/1)
**1868 Scaraben** won six times last year including this one, but lost ground at the start. Happy to sit off the pace, he was only asked for an effort over a furlong out. Running on strongly at the finish, he ought to have been concerned in the finish. He seems to be back on song. (11/4)
**Final Stab (IRE)** had just two outings last year and was caught out in this falsely-run race. Wandering under pressure and then hanging left, his rider had no option but to give up. (13/2: 7/2-6/1)
**1420 Smarter Charter** did not look at his best in the paddock and is said to have injured his back at Pontefract last time. After being upsides two furlongs out, he soon began to feel the strain and was eased up. He should do much better next time. (11/4: 13/8-3/1)

## 2294 HAMLET CIGARS H'CAP (0-95) (3-Y.O) (Class C)

7-55 (7-56) **1m 2f 32y** £6,905.00 (£2,090.00: £1,020.00: £485.00) Stalls: Low GOING minus 0.09 sec per fur (G)

| | | | | SP | RR | SF |
|---|---|---|---|---|---|---|
| 1712[4] | **Hamlet (IRE) (80)** (MBell) **3-8-11** MFenton(6) (hld up: effrt over 2f out: styd on to ld post) | — | **1** | 100/30[2] | 88 | 46 |
| 2027[3] | **Nose No Bounds (IRE) (74)** (MJohnston) **3-8-5b** MRoberts(7) (mde most: qcknd over 3f out: hrd rdn: jst ct) | s.h | **2** | 13/2 | 82 | 40 |
| 1586[5] | **Winston (65)** (JDBethell) **3-7-10** JQuinn(2) (chsd ldrs: chal over 1f out: kpt on one pce) | 3 | **3** | 6/1 | 68 | 26 |
| 2006[4] | **Expensive Taste (90)** (MRStoute) **3-9-7** JWeaver(4) (trckd ldrs: effrt over 2f out: kpt on one pce) | 3 | **4** | 7/2[3] | 89 | 47 |
| 1861* | **Fairywings (74)** (MrsJRRamsden) **3-8-5** KFallon(5) (lw: hld up: effrt 3f out: kpt on same pce: nvr nr to chal) | s.h | **5** | 9/4[1] | 72 | 30 |
| 1337[9] | **No Cliches (75)** (GLewis) **3-8-6b**[1] PaulEddery(3) (dwlt s: bhd & rdn over 3f out: hung lft & nt r.o) | 4 | **6** | 8/1 | 67 | 25 |
| 2163[3] | **Ordained (65)** (EJAlston) **3-7-7**(3) DWright(1) (plld hrd: trckd ldrs: rdn 3f out: sn lost pl & eased) | 17 | **7** | 20/1 | 30 | — |
| | | | | (SP 119.6%) | | **7 Rn** |

**2m 12.0** (5.30) CSF £23.92 TOTE £4.10: £2.30 £2.70 (£12.80) OWNER Mr M. B. Hawtin (NEWMARKET) BRED Peter McCalmont
LONG HANDICAP Ordained 6-13

**1712 Hamlet (IRE)** stuck on in most determined fashion and got up right on the line. (100/30)
**2027 Nose No Bounds (IRE)** made the running. He seemed to have some difficulty like some of the others in making the home turn and, though his rider did not spare the whip in the last two furlongs, they were pipped on the line. It was surprising that the Stewards did not have Roberts in over his use of the whip. (13/2)
**1586 Winston**, who was found to be very lame after running badly last time, was handy all the way. Almost upsides over a furlong out, he soon found the first two going away from him. It is just possible that he did not truly stay the trip. (6/1)
**2006 Expensive Taste** tended to carry her head high under pressure. (7/2)
**1861* Fairywings**, 6lb higher than at Beverley, tried to get into it two furlongs out, but it was clear that she could not take a hand this time and she was by no means knocked about. She will soon step up on this. (9/4)
**No Cliches,** in blinkers for the first time, looked anything but keen. (8/1)

## 2295 RAMAGE TRANSPORT MAIDEN STKS (2-Y.O) (Class D)
8-25 (8-25) **6f** £3,485.00 (£1,055.00: £515.00: £245.00) Stalls: High GOING minus 0.09 sec per fur (G)

| | Horse | Details | Dist | Pos | SP | RR | SF |
|---|---|---|---|---|---|---|---|
| 1197[11] | **Rich Ground** | (JDBethell) **2-9-0** PaulEddery(7) (hdwy u.p over 2f out: styd on to ld wl ins fnl f) | — | **1** | 25/1 | 75 | 31 |
| 2057[3] | **Canadian Fantasy** | (MJohnston) **2-9-0** JWeaver(2) (led far side: rdn & nt qckn ins fnl f) | ½ | **2** | 6/4[1] | 74 | 30 |
| 1849[2] | **The Lambton Worm** | (DenysSmith) **2-9-0** JFortune(4) (swtchd rt s: led stands' side: clr over 2f out: wknd & hdd wl ins fnl f) | ½ | **3** | 5/2[2] | 72 | 28 |
| | **Hurgill Times** | (JWWatts) **2-9-0** NConnorton(6) (leggy: dwlt s: stdy hdwy over 2f out: kpt on wl fnl f) | 1¾ | **4** | 12/1 | 68 | 24 |
| 1537[2] | **Swiss Coast (IRE)** | (MrsJRRamsden) **2-9-0** KFallon(8) (hdwy ½-wy: sn rdn & no imp: eased towards fin) | 6 | **5** | 4/1[3] | 52 | 8 |
| 1884[4] | **Harmony In Red** | (JBerry) **2-9-0** JCarroll(1) (chsd ldr far side: rdn 2f out: sn wknd) | 1¾ | **6** | 9/2 | 47 | 3 |
| 1849[9] | **Kingdom Emperor** | (MJCamacho) **2-9-0** JQuinn(3) (swtchd lft s: trckd ldrs: rdn over 2f out: sn wl outpcd) | 1¼ | **7** | 20/1 | 44 | — |
| 1801[6] | **Cumbrian Quest** | (TDEasterby) **2-9-0** MBirch(5) (sltly hmpd s: lost pl ½-wy: virtually p.u 2f out) | dist | **8** | 20/1 | — | — |

(SP 127.8%) **8 Rn**

**1m 15.79** (4.29) CSF £67.18 TOTE £24.70: £3.30 £1.30 £1.30 (£43.40) Trio £112.60 OWNER Mrs J. E. Vickers (MIDDLEHAM) BRED C. J. Hill

**Rich Ground** had clearly learnt a lot from his first run. Staying on in determined fashion, he got up near the line to win what looked a modest contest. (25/1)

**2057 Canadian Fantasy**, soon showing his two rivals on the far side a clean pair of heels, carried his head high under pressure inside the last and seemed to lose his action slightly. (6/4)

**1849 The Lambton Worm**, clear on the stands' side at halfway, weakened badly inside the last. (5/2)

**Hurgill Times**, an excitable type, stayed on in promising fashion in the final furlong under an educational ride. (12/1: 6/1-14/1)

**1537 Swiss Coast (IRE)** looks as though he requires time, but can do better in time. (4/1: 11/4-9/2)

## 2296 STANLEY RACING CELEBRATION H'CAP (0-75) (4-Y.O+) (Class D)
8-55 (8-56) **1m 2f 32y** £3,793.75 (£1,150.00: £562.50: £268.75) Stalls: Low GOING minus 0.09 sec per fur (G)

| | Horse | Details | Dist | Pos | SP | RR | SF |
|---|---|---|---|---|---|---|---|
| 1821[4] | **Alabang (55)** | (MJCamacho) **5-8-12** JFortune(2) (dwlt: hld up: smooth hdwy to ld over 1f out: rdn out) | — | **1** | 2/1[2] | 68 | 48 |
| 2020[8] | **Manful (67)** | (CWCElsey) **4-9-10b** NKennedy(5) (lw: led: clr 6f out: hdd over 1f out: kpt on same pce) | 1¾ | **2** | 9/2[3] | 77 | 57 |
| 2077[2] | **Essayeffsee (57)** | (MrsMReveley) **7-9-0** KDarley(1) (lw: sn trckng ldrs: effrt & outpcd 2f out: styd on ins fnl f) | 3 | **3** | 7/4[1] | 63 | 43 |
| 1861[4] | **Euro Sceptic (IRE) (48)** | (TDEasterby) **4-8-5b** MBirch(3) (hld up: stdy hdwy over 2f out: sn ev ch: rdn over 1f out: fnd little) | 1¼ | **4** | 11/2 | 52 | 32 |
| 2121[6] | **Northern Spark (50)** | (MissLAPerratt) **8-8-7** JWeaver(4) (trckd ldrs: rdn over 3f out: lost pl over 1f out: eased nr fin) | 6 | **5** | 9/1 | 44 | 24 |

(SP 113.3%) **5 Rn**

**2m 11.9** (5.20) CSF £10.46 TOTE £3.30: £1.80 £1.90 (£7.10) OWNER Mr H. Roberts (MALTON) BRED Mrs S. Camacho

**1821 Alabang**, 7lb higher in the weights than when recording his first success at Redcar three runs ago, was inclined to get warm beforehand. Patiently ridden, he took it up on the bridle but had to be kept up to his work. He gives the impression that he needs restraining for longer. (2/1)

**1309 Manful**, allowed to set his own pace, stuck on under pressure but the winner always had the legs of him. (9/2)

**2077 Essayeffsee** seemed to have trouble handling the bend and, after going in second, was last on straightening up. Picking up ground inside the last, he looks in the Handicapper's grasp. (7/4)

**1861 Euro Sceptic (IRE)** showed a scratchy action going down, and came there with the winner on the bridle to challenge but, under pressure, he found next to nothing. (11/2)

**2121 Northern Spark** almost ran away going to the start. Racing keenly, he dropped out over a furlong out and sensibly was allowed to ease up. (9/1: op 5/1)

T/Plpt: £175.10 (71.52 Tckts). T/Qdpt: £19.00 (63.76 Tckts). WG

# 2130-NEWMARKET (R-H) (Good to firm)
## Friday June 28th
WEATHER: unsettled WIND: slt across

## 2297 ST. ANDREWS BUSINESS PARK CLAIMING STKS (3-Y.O) (Class E)
2-00 (2-00) **1m 2f (July)** £3,200.00 (£950.00: £450.00: £200.00) Stalls: High GOING minus 0.36 sec per fur (F)

| | Horse | Details | Dist | Pos | SP | RR | SF |
|---|---|---|---|---|---|---|---|
| 1806[3] | **Titchwell Lass** | (JEBanks) **3-8-3**(3) JStack(3) (lw: hld up & plld hrd: hdwy over 3f out: led wl over 1f out: comf) | — | **1** | 5/4[1] | 63+ | 40 |
| *2169*[4] | **Another Quarter (IRE) (57)** | (SPCWoods) **3-8-2b** MRoberts(5) (b: a.p: led 3f out: to wl over 1f out: one pce) | 2½ | **2** | 9/4[2] | 55 | 32 |
| 1999[6] | **Native Song (37)** | (MJHaynes) **3-7-13**ow1 WCarson(2) (chsd ldr: rdn over 3f out: ev ch over 2f out: one pce) | 1¼ | **3** | 16/1 | 50 | 26 |
| 2026[10] | **Boy Blakeney** | (MrsSJSmith) **3-8-4**(3) DaneO'Neill(6) (lost pl 5f out: styd on fnl 2f) | 9 | **4** | 33/1 | 44 | 21 |
| 1999[4] | **African Sun (IRE) (43)** | (BHanbury) **3-8-0**(3) HKYim(4) (prom: rdn & outpcd 5f out: n.d after) | 1 | **5** | 6/1[3] | 38 | 15 |
| 1508[W] | **Ectomorph (IRE)** | (JPearce) **3-8-0** GBardwell(7) (leggy: plld hrd: led 7f: sn wknd) | 17 | **6** | 7/1 | 8 | — |
| 1999[7] | **Ell Ell Eff** | (AHide) **3-7-12v**1 JQuinn(1) (plld hrd: wl bhd fnl 3f) | 23 | **7** | 25/1 | — | — |

(SP 114.7%) **7 Rn**

**2m 7.68** (2.68) CSF £4.45 TOTE £2.20: £1.40 £2.10 (£2.40) OWNER Mr John Rutter (NEWMARKET) BRED Kirtlington Stud Ltd

**1806 Titchwell Lass** gave no trouble in the stalls this time and, always going best in the race, won with a fair amount in hand. (5/4)

**2169 Another Quarter (IRE)**, much calmer in the blinkers second time, still took a good hold on the way to post. Going for home some way out, she was made to look pedestrian as the winner went by. (9/4)

**Native Song** looked on good terms with herself, but failed to quicken when it mattered. (16/1)

**Boy Blakeney** stayed on to the bitter end after getting outpaced and, if there is a race in him, it will be over a longer trip. (33/1)

**1999 African Sun (IRE)**, taken quietly to post some time after the others, was in trouble a long way out and failed to reproduce his slightly improved Sandown effort. (6/1)

**Ectomorph (IRE)**, on her toes beforehand, moved down keenly and folded quickly once headed in the race. (7/1: 5/1-10/1)

## 2298 MERIVALE MOORE CONDITIONS STKS (3-Y.O+ F & M) (Class C)
2-30 (2-30) **6f (July)** £4,977.60 (£1,838.40: £879.20: £356.00: £138.00: £50.80) Stalls: Low GOING minus 0.14 sec per fur (G)

| | Horse | Details | Dist | Pos | SP | RR | SF |
|---|---|---|---|---|---|---|---|
| 960[6] | **Daring Destiny (97)** | (KRBurke) **5-8-10b** DHolland(6) (hld up: hdwy over 2f out: led over 1f out: rdn clr fnl f) | — | **1** | 7/2[2] | 100 | 71 |
| 2114[16] | **Silent Expression (85)** | (BJMeehan) **6-8-10** BDoyle(1) (chsd ldrs: kpt on appr fnl f: nt pce of wnr) | 2½ | **2** | 11/1 | 93 | 64 |

| | | | | SP | RR | SF |
|---|---|---|---|---|---|---|
| | **Prancing (102)** (DRLoder) **3-8-7** PatEddery(2) (led after 2f to 2f out: sn rdn & one pce) | 1½ | 3 | 5/2 1 | 93 | 57 |
| 1334* | **Montserrat (75)** (LGCottrell) **4-8-10v** MFenton(4) (lw: led 2f: rdn & lost pl 3f out: styd on wl fnl f) | ¾ | 4 | 10/1 | 87 | 58 |
| 1129 9 | **Welsh Mist (98)** (RBoss) **5-8-10** WRyan(7) (w ldrs: led 2f out: sn hdd & btn) | 1¼ | 5 | 7/2 2 | 84 | 55 |
| | **Wollstonecraft (IRE)** (JHMGosden) **3-8-3** GHind(3) (hld up: shkn up & no imp fnl 2f) | s.h | 6 | 13/2 3 | 84 | 48 |
| 1770 10 | **Christmas Kiss (93)** (RHannon) **4-8-7b**(3) DaneO'Neill(5) (trckd ldrs over 3f) | 9 | 7 | 10/1 | 60 | 31 |
| | | | | (SP 112.9%) | **7 Rn** | |

**1m 12.86** (0.86) CSF £34.29 TOTE £4.50: £2.70 £3.90 (£27.00) OWNER Mrs Ann Wright (WANTAGE) BRED Mrs Ann E. M. Wright
WEIGHT FOR AGE 3yo-7lb

**711 Daring Destiny**, whose form with Anzio two outings ago is really working out, can be forgiven last time's effort as she was pulled wide when the action was on the inside. Moving forward and pulling double, she did not find quite as much as she threatened, but enough to score. (7/2: 5/2-4/1)

**Silent Expression**, in good form last summer, bounced back here and is ready to score, although the Handicapper will make it harder than a year ago. (11/1: 8/1-12/1)

**Prancing** looked big and well. (5/2: 7/4-11/4)

**1334* Montserrat**, as in the Abernant earlier this year, ran very much better than her mark suggests, and she ought to find another handicap when she can get her toe in. (10/1)

**673 Welsh Mist** blazed the trail in the centre before capitulating in the Dip. This extends her losing sequence to seventeen. (7/2)

**Wollstonecraft (IRE)** looked fit and was taken to post early. She found little when asked to improve, but had not run since finishing third to Blue Duster thirteen months ago. (13/2)

## 2299 SCOTTISH EQUITABLE/JOCKEYS ASSOCIATION H'CAP (0-90) (3-Y.O+) (Class C)

3-00 (3-01) **1m 2f (July)** £5,246.72 (£1,940.48: £930.24: £379.20: £149.60: £57.76) Stalls: High GOING minus 0.14 sec per fur (G)

| | | | | SP | RR | SF |
|---|---|---|---|---|---|---|
| 1961 5 | **Master Charter (79)** (MrsJRRamsden) **4-9-6** KFallon(3) (dwlt: hld up: hdwy over 3f out: rdn to ld ins fnl f) | — | 1 | 7/2 1 | 88 | 61 |
| 2010 13 | **Secret Aly (CAN) (81)** (CEBrittain) **6-9-8** BDoyle(1) (a.p: ev ch 4f out: led over 1f out: hdd ins fnl f: r.o) | s.h | 2 | 8/1 3 | 90 | 63 |
| 2145 10 | **Komreyev Dancer (75)** (ABailey) **4-9-2** DHolland(2) (trckd ldrs: rdn 2f out: r.o wl fnl f) | ¾ | 3 | 10/1 | 83 | 56 |
| 1994 3 | **Albaha (USA) (80)** (RWArmstrong) **3-8-9** WRyan(6) (led: sn clr: hdd over 1f out: sn btn) | 1¾ | 4 | 14/1 | 85 | 46 |
| | **Silver Groom (IRE) (75)** (RAkehurst) **6-9-2** JQuinn(7) (chsd ldrs: rdn over 1f out: one pce) | s.h | 5 | 5/1 2 | 80 | 53 |
| 2041 7 | **Alhawa (USA) (84)** (CJBenstead) **3-8-13** WCarson(4) (lw: in tch: shkn up 4f out: r.o appr fnl f) | 1¼ | 6 | 7/2 1 | 87 | 48 |
| 2127* | **Statajack (IRE) (78)** (DRCElsworth) **8-9-5b** 3x TQuinn(5) (hld up: rdn 3f out: no rspnse) | 8 | 7 | 7/2 1 | 68 | 41 |
| | | | | (SP 110.2%) | **7 Rn** | |

**2m 8.88** (3.88) CSF £26.74 TOTE £4.10: £1.90 £4.00 (£35.10) OWNER Mr Jonathan Ramsden (THIRSK) BRED Carlton Consultants Ltd
WEIGHT FOR AGE 3yo-12lb

**1961 Master Charter** may well have been helped by the rain easing the ground a little. He stayed the trip well enough to win, but the runner-up was coming back for more. He was the only one to come from off the pace in this muddling race, suggesting that this performance is better than it appears. (7/2)

**988 Secret Aly (CAN)** battled for the lead from the four-furlong pole, but could not hold the initiative for long once in front. Battling back at the line, he showed his courage. (8/1)

**1861 Komreyev Dancer**, caught short of speed as the tempo quickened with two furlongs left, stuck on well in the final furlong. A stronger pace would help him. (10/1)

**1994 Albaha (USA)** must have connections baffled. Without the blinkers, he was upped half a mile in trip here after one good and two poor efforts, and did not seem to stay here, though running well. (14/1)

**Silver Groom (IRE)**, off since March, failed to pick up sufficiently in the final two furlongs. (5/1: 3/1-11/2)

**2041 Alhawa (USA)**, pushed along at halfway, got going when it was all over. This could have come too soon after his Ascot exertions. (7/2)

## 2300 TARTAN GROUP H'CAP (0-80) (3-Y.O+) (Class D)

3-30 (3-31) **1m 4f (July)** £6,970.00 (£2,110.00: £1,030.00: £490.00) Stalls: High GOING minus 0.14 sec per fur (G)

| | | | | SP | RR | SF |
|---|---|---|---|---|---|---|
| 1421 5 | **Reimei (65)** (RAkehurst) **7-9-2** TQuinn(2) (lw: trckd ldrs: rdn 2f out: led over 1f out: r.o wl) | — | 1 | 9/2 2 | 73 | 56 |
| 2131 2 | **Lookingforarainbow (IRE) (72)** (BobJones) **8-9-9** MWigham(5) (trckd ldrs: effrt over 3f out: r.o fnl f: nt trble wnr) | 1½ | 2 | 4/1 1 | 78 | 61 |
| 1852 7 | **Quivira (68)** (HAkbary) **5-9-5** MRimmer(10) (swtg: led 2f: led over 2f out: hdd over 1f out: no ex ins fnl f) | hd | 3 | 14/1 | 74 | 57 |
| 2130 10 | **Kaafih Homm (IRE) (61)** (NACallaghan) **5-8-9**(3) DaneO'Neill(1) (lw: hld up: stdy hdwy 3f out: rdn & no ex appr fnl f) | s.h | 4 | 16/1 | 67 | 50 |
| 1711 7 | **Firbur (72)** (NAGraham) **3-8-9** JReid(3) (hld up: hdwy 6f out: rdn over 2f out: no ex ins fnl f) | ½ | 5 | 10/1 | 77 | 46 |
| 2131* | **Western Sal (71)** (JLHarris) **4-9-8** 4x JQuinn(9) (hld up: effrt 3f out: nvr rch ldrs) | 2½ | 6 | 11/2 3 | 73 | 56 |
| 1792 5 | **Casual Water (IRE) (73)** (AGNewcombe) **5-9-10** MRoberts(8) (chsd ldrs 9f) | 1¾ | 7 | 7/1 | 73 | 56 |
| 2020 4 | **Westminster (IRE) (70)** (MHTompkins) **4-9-7v** PRobinson(7) (nvr nr to chal) | nk | 8 | 12/1 | 69 | 52 |
| *1811* 8 | **Ayunli (69)** (SCWilliams) **5-9-6** GHind(4) (led after 2f tl over 2f out: eased whn btn fnl f) | 9 | 9 | 20/1 | 56 | 39 |
| 1498* | **Strategic Ploy (70)** (MrsJRRamsden) **3-8-7** KFallon(6) (hld up: rdn 3f out: sn btn & eased) | 13 | 10 | 9/2 2 | 40 | 9 |
| | | | | (SP 118.3%) | **10 Rn** | |

**2m 34.91** (4.91) CSF £21.93 CT £215.01 TOTE £5.10: £2.00 £1.40 £6.30 (£15.70) Trio £117.70 OWNER Mr I. Goldsmith (EPSOM) BRED A. L. and J. Chapman
WEIGHT FOR AGE 3yo-14lb

**1421 Reimei**, in a race which his yard likes to win, looked the part and bounced right back to his best after a long spell in the doldrums. (9/2: 3/1-5/1)

**2131 Lookingforarainbow (IRE)** continues to knock at the door and must surely find a race before long. (4/1)

**Quivira** got into a muck-sweat, but ran her best race of the year, only giving way inside the final furlong. (14/1)

**Kaafih Homm (IRE)** had only run over this trip twice - a win and a defeat at Brighton. Cruising into contention going like the winner, he failed to pick up when asked the question. (16/1)

**Firbur**, with something still left to work on, ran well on this handicap debut, though being shown no mercy by the Handicapper. He should continue to improve. (10/1: 8/1-12/1)

**2131* Western Sal** found life harder under a penalty. (11/2)

## 2301 GIRDLESTONE PUMPS H'CAP (0-85) (3-Y.O) (Class D)

4-00 (4-00) **5f (July)** £5,026.00 (£1,498.00: £714.00: £322.00) Stalls: Low GOING minus 0.14 sec per fur (G)

| | | | | SP | RR | SF |
|---|---|---|---|---|---|---|
| 2078 4 | **Galine (78)** (WAO'Gorman) **3-9-0** EmmaO'Gorman(4) (swtg: hld up: rdn over 1f out: led ins fnl f: comf) | — | 1 | 13/2 3 | 90 | 67 |
| 2143 7 | **Rushcutter Bay (85)** (TTClement) **3-9-4v**(3) JStack(8) (lw: trckd ldr: led over 2f out: hdd & no ex ins fnl f) | 1¾ | 2 | 10/1 | 91 | 68 |

1646[8] **Total Aloof (75)** (WJHaggas) **3-8-11** BDoyle(5) (b.off fore: chsd ldrs: outpcd 2f out: kpt on fnl f)....................3½ **3** 9/1 70 47
2143[4] **Dande Flyer (75)** (DWPArbuthnot) **3-8-11** TQuinn(2) (b: hld up: effrt over 1f out: no imp)..............................nk **4** 7/2[2] 69 46
1823[3] **Pleasure Time (66)** (CSmith) **3-8-2v**[1ow1] MFenton(7) (led over 2f: rdn & btn appr fnl f)..................................hd **5** 12/1 60 36
1628[6] **Angaar (IRE) (79)** (ACStewart) **3-9-1** MRoberts(6) (chsd ldrs: outpcd 2f out: r.o again nr fin)...........................½ **6** 3/1[1] 71 48
1805[5] **Playmaker (74)** (MAJarvis) **3-8-10** PRobinson(9) (lw: b.off hind: chsd ldrs 3f)..............................................8 **7** 16/1 41 18
2021[2] **Stoney End (USA) (70)** (MRChannon) **3-8-6** PatEddery(3) (a bhd)..........................................................7 **8** 7/2[2] 14 —
(SP 115.4%) **8 Rn**

**59.62 secs** (1.12) CSF £60.05 CT £538.29 TOTE £9.70: £2.20 £2.90 £2.70 (£61.80) Trio £425.30; £125.81 to Newcastle 29/6/96 OWNER Mr S. Fustok (NEWMARKET) BRED Deerfield Farm
OFFICIAL EXPLANATION **Stoney End (USA): the jockey reported that the colt started slowly and was reluctant to race thereafter.**
**2078 Galine,** who does like racing at home and has run well all four times here, won with a little in hand. (13/2)
**1823* Rushcutter Bay,** who has come with a late rattle in most of his recent races, all but bolted in his only try in a visor last season, but this time was under more control and raced close to the pace. He lost nothing in defeat and continues in good form. (10/1: 8/1-12/1)
**1646 Total Aloof** was never travelling well, but did stick on to the end. (9/1)
**2143 Dande Flyer** again failed to pick up in the manner expected once let down. (7/2)
**1823 Pleasure Time** has the ability but is losing his way. He started to miss the break in blinkers, but may be worth a try in a visor. (12/1)
**1628 Angaar (IRE)** surely needs further. (3/1)

## 2302 E.B.F. EQUITY FINANCIAL COLLECTIONS MAIDEN STKS (2-Y.O) (Class D)
4-30 (4-30) **6f (July)** £4,308.00 (£1,284.00: £612.00: £276.00) Stalls: Low GOING minus 0.14 sec per fur (G)

SP RR SF
**Yashmak (USA)** (HRACecil) **2-8-9** PatEddery(2) (gd sort: scope: sn trckng ldr: led over 1f out: rdn out).......— **1** 2/5[1] 86+ 46
**Man Howa (IRE)** (LMCumani) **2-9-0** OUrbina(4) (gd sort: bhd: gd hdwy over 2f out: edgd rt & r.o wl fnl f: nt rch wnr)..........................................................................1½ **2** 20/1 87+ 47
**Grapeshot (USA)** (LMCumani) **2-9-0** JReid(6) (wl grwn: plld hrd: trckd ldrs: rdn over 1f out: one pce)..........3½ **3** 5/1[2] 78 38
2009[3] **Zaretski** (CEBrittain) **2-9-0** WCarson(3) (led over 4f: wknd ins fnl f)..............................................2½ **4** 7/1[3] 71 31
**Green Power** (JRFanshawe) **2-9-0** DHarrison(5) (str: cmpt: bkwd: trckd ldrs 4f).....................................s.h **5** 20/1 71 31
**Real Estate** (CFWall) **2-9-0** AMcGlone(1) (w'like: bkwd: sn pushed along: outpcd after 3f)...........................10 **6** 20/1 44 4
(SP 114.9%) **6 Rn**

**1m 14.58** (2.58) CSF £8.97 TOTE £1.40: £1.60 £3.00 (£8.70) OWNER Mr K. Abdulla (NEWMARKET) BRED Juddmonte Farms
**Yashmak (USA),** a half-sister to a string of top-class horses, looked rather green beforehand. She won the race in no more than tidy fashion, but badly needed the experience and looks sure to improve. (2/5: 1/2-1/3)
**Man Howa (IRE)** looked the less forward of the Cumani pair but, despite edging towards the centre of the track, he found a decent turn of foot to close on the winner in the final furlong. (20/1)
**Grapeshot (USA)** looked fit and went to post freely. Once let down at the two pole, he had no more to give but will learn from this. (5/1: 3/1-7/1)
**2009 Zaretski** tried to make his experience tell, but was easily brushed aside. His stride shortened in the last 100 yards and he may be better over five for now. (7/1)
**Green Power** was outpaced at the business end and looks to need further. (20/1)
**Real Estate** could not live with these, but will probably do better over further. (20/1)

T/Jkpt: £4,878.90 (5.36 Tckts). T/Plpt: £257.20 (72.8 Tckts). T/Qdpt: £48.00 (27.11 Tckts). Dk

# 2168-WOLVERHAMPTON (L-H) (Standard)
## Friday June 28th
visibility: poor race 6
WEATHER: overcast & showers WIND: slt across

## 2303 WOLVERHAMPTON CHAMBERS OF COMMERCE H'CAP (0-60) (3-Y.O+) (Class F)
2-20 (2-22) **1m 100y (Fibresand)** £2,381.00 (£656.00: £311.00) Stalls: Low GOING: 0.08 sec per fur (STD)

SP RR SF
2134[13] **Mister Rm (60)** (RGuest) **4-10-0** PBloomfield(13) (led over 4f: led appr fnl f: rdn out)..........................— **1** 16/1 69 49
*534*[6] **Shanghai Lil (40)** (MJFetherston-Godley) **4-8-8** WJO'Connor(10) (hld up: hdwy over 3f out: str chal fnl f: r.o) ¾ **2** 16/1 48 28
*2085*[5] **Ring the Chief (35)** (MDIUsher) **4-8-3** TSprake(6) (b: trckd ldrs: effrt & ev ch appr fnl f: kpt on u.p)..........s.h **3** 7/1 43 23
1986[5] **Angus McCoatup (IRE) (58)** (BAMcMahon) **3-8-9**(7) KYu(3) (b: trckd ldrs: led 2f out tl over 1f out: unable qckn fnl f)..........................................................................1½ **4** 13/2 63 33
1893[9] **My Handsome Prince (40)** (PJBevan) **4-8-8** DeanMcKeown(2) (hdwy 5f out: rdn over 2f out: grad wknd).......6 **5** 20/1 33 13
*2081*[3] **Quinzii Martin (54)** (DHaydnJones) **8-9-8v** AMackay(9) (hld up in tch: effrt & rdn 2f out: sn btn)..............s.h **6** 11/2[2] 47 27
2075[4] **Miss Zanzibar (45)** (RAFahey) **4-8-13** ACulhane(7) (bhd: hrd drvn ½-wy: nvr nrr)...................................3½ **7** 6/1[3] 32 12
2023[8] **Hutchies Lady (41)** (RMMcKellar) **4-8-4**(5)ow1 RHavlin(5) (b.hind: a in rr)............................................nk **8** 14/1 27 6
*2081*[5] **Moneghetti (45)** (RHollinshead) **5-8-8**(5) FLynch(1) (s.i.s: hld up: hdwy 4f out: rdn 2f out: sn wknd)...............¾ **9** 11/4[1] 30 10
*1490*[13] **Sweet Amoret (54)** (PHowling) **3-8-12** FNorton(4) (b.off hind: prom: led 4f out tl hdd & wknd 2f out)...............3 **10** 14/1 33 3
**Causley (55)** (DMHyde) **11-9-2**(7) RBrisland(11) (b: chsd ldrs 5f: sn lost tch: t.o)........................................4 **11** 33/1 26 6
**Diamond Market (54)** (BRCambidge) **4-9-8** TIves(8) (bkwd: prom over 5f: sn wknd: t.o)..............................1¾ **12** 12/1 22 2
*1969*[7] **Bites (45)** (TTBill) **3-8-3** WHollick(12) (a bhd: t.o)..........................................................................17 **13** 33/1 — —
(SP 125.6%) **13 Rn**

**1m 52.2** (7.20) CSF £226.13 CT £1,850.74 TOTE £11.00: £5.60 £3.90 £3.00 (£119.80) Trio £240.90 OWNER Mr J. W. Biswell (NEWMARKET) BRED Major and Mrs R. B. Kennard
WEIGHT FOR AGE 3yo-10lb
**Mister Rm** caught the eye as he looked so poor in his coat even in mid-summer. Gaining control for a second time over a furlong out, he responded to pressure to settle it nearing the line. (16/1)
**534 Shanghai Lil** ran well after a lengthy break and put in a determined late challenge, but the winner refused to be denied. (16/1)
**2085 Ring the Chief** continues to perform with credit and that elusive first success can not be far away. (7/1)
**1986 Angus McCoatup (IRE),** attempting the trip for the first time, ran without the blinkers. Driven along to poke his nose in front turning for home, he was unable to quicken when challenged and was getting the worst of the argument in the battle to the finish. (13/2)
**2081 Quinzii Martin** would have slaughtered these rivals at the top of his form, but he only does what he wants nowadays and, once the whips were out, he wanted no part. (11/2: op 7/2)
**2081 Moneghetti,** under strong pressure to hold his pitch on the home turn, failed to maintain his progress once straightened up and was one of the first beaten. (11/4)

## 2304 TAYLOR & CO ACCOUNTANTS CLAIMING STKS (3-Y.O+) (Class F)

2-50 (2-51) **1m 4f (Fibresand)** £2,381.00 (£656.00: £311.00) Stalls: Low GOING: 0.08 sec per fur (STD)

| Form | Horse | Dist | Pos | SP | RR | SF |
|---|---|---|---|---|---|---|
| *2082** | **Troubadour Song (61)** (WWHaigh) **4-9-6**(3) PMcCabe(5) (lw: hld up & bhd: hdwy 4f out: led over 1f out: hld on) | — | **1** | $5/2^{1}$ | 78 | 37 |
| | **Princely Gait (75)** (MJPolglase) **5-9-11** WHollick(3) (hld up & bhd: gd hdwy 5f out: r.o wl ins fnl f) | hd | **2** | 12/1 | 80 | 39 |
| *$365^{12}$* | **Heighth of Fame (55)** (AJWilson) **5-9-2**(5) FLynch(9) (a.p: led 3f out: hrd rdn & hdd over 1f out: one pce) | 4 | **3** | 13/2 | 71 | 30 |
| *$1811^{11}$* | **Chevalier (USA) (68)** (ICampbell) **4-9-6**(7) RMullen(8) (a.p: led 7f to 3f out: ev ch over 1f out: sn rdn & wknd) | 3 | **4** | 8/1 | 73 | 32 |
| *$2082^{3}$* | **Red Phantom (IRE) (66)** (SMellor) **4-9-13** DeanMcKeown(1) (hld up: hdwy 4f out: nt rch ldrs) | hd | **5** | $5/1^{3}$ | 72 | 31 |
| *$2082^{4}$* | **Chik's Secret (42)** (BPalling) **3-8-2** TSprake(4) (swtg: led 1f: prom tl rdn & wknd wl over 3f out: t.o) | 20 | **6** | 12/1 | 35 | — |
| $1640^{13}$ | **Stevie's Wonder (IRE) (65)** (BJLlewellyn) **6-9-9v** VSlattery(10) (trckd ldrs: rdn along after 3f: wknd over 3f out: t.o) | nk | **7** | 12/1 | 41 | — |
| *$1811^{5}$* | **Penmar (60)** (TJEtherington) **4-9-9** GCarter(2) (dwlt: a bhd: t.o) | 15 | **8** | $9/2^{2}$ | 21 | — |
| $1866^{8}$ | **Hawwam (65)** (EJAlston) **10-9-1** SDWilliams(7) (lw: trckd ldrs over 8f: sn wknd: t.o) | 7 | **9** | 8/1 | 4 | — |
| *$2169^{10}$* | **Queens Stroller (IRE) (51)** (TWall) **5-8-10b**[1] AMackay(6) (led after 1f to 7f out: wknd qckly ½-wy: t.o) | dist | **10** | 16/1 | — | — |

(SP 127.9%) **10 Rn**

**2m 44.1** (11.60) CSF £32.69 TOTE £4.50: £1.30 £2.60 £2.60 (£19.80) Trio £67.40 OWNER Spring Cottage Racing Partnership (MALTON) BRED Paul Mellon

WEIGHT FOR AGE 3yo-14lb

**2082* Troubadour Song** had to work much harder to succeed here than at Southwell, but he always looked likely to hold on and is at the top of his form at present. (5/2)

**Princely Gait**, making a belated return to action and stepping down in distance, was eating up ground at the distance and should not have much trouble in going one better. (12/1: op 8/1)

**Heighth of Fame**, who had run over hurdles last month, kicked for home turning out of the back straight but the pack would not let him get away. With his tongue hanging out, he was forced to give best approaching the final furlong. (13/2: 9/2-7/1)

**1602 Chevalier (USA)**, still struggling to get off the mark, was in and out of the lead for most of the way and only called enough on the approach to the final furlong. (8/1)

**2082 Red Phantom (IRE)** was meeting the winner on 8lb better terms than when finishing six and a half lengths behind him on his previous outing. The outcome was just the same here and he is proving a big disappointment. (5/1)

**Stevie's Wonder (IRE)** (12/1: op 7/1)

## 2305 C.F.C. MAIDEN H'CAP (0-80) (3-Y.O+) (Class D)

3-20 (3-20) **5f (Fibresand)** £3,557.50 (£1,060.00: £505.00: £227.50) Stalls: Low GOING: 0.08 sec per fur (STD)

| Form | Horse | Dist | Pos | SP | RR | SF |
|---|---|---|---|---|---|---|
| $1688^{4}$ | **Princess Efisio (45)** (BAMcMahon) **3-8-3** GCarter(7) (swtg: a.p: rdn to ld wl ins fnl f: r.o) | — | **1** | 7/1 | 53 | 25 |
| $2064^{5}$ | **Silk Cottage (62)** (RMWhitaker) **4-9-12v** DeanMcKeown(5) (led tl hdd wl ins fnl f) | 1¼ | **2** | $5/1^{3}$ | 66 | 44 |
| $2029^{2}$ | **Bowlers Boy (61)** (JJQuinn) **3-9-5** DaleGibson(1) (lost pl ½-wy: hdwy u.p 2f out: nt pce to chal) | 7 | **3** | $11/4^{1}$ | 43 | 15 |
| $1688^{7}$ | **Bouton d'Or (51)** (PHowling) **3-8-9** FNorton(6) (lw: prom tl rdn & outpcd wl over 1f out) | 1¾ | **4** | 8/1 | 27 | — |
| $1049^{14}$ | **Diebiedale (49)** (RBoss) **4-8-8**(5) FLynch(2) (sn pushed along: nvr gng pce of ldrs) | ½ | **5** | $4/1^{2}$ | 23 | 1 |
| $1709^{7}$ | **Muhandam (IRE) (70)** (BHanbury) **3-10-0** WJO'Connor(8) (spd 3f: rdn & edgd lft wl over 1f out: sn btn) | 3 | **6** | 8/1 | 35 | 7 |
| $1702^{8}$ | **Sharp Holly (IRE) (46)** (JABennett) **4-8-7b**[1](3) DWright(4) (outpcd: a bhd) | ¾ | **7** | 16/1 | 8 | — |
| $2176^{4}$ | **Forzara (45)** (JBerry) **3-8-3** JFanning(3) (b.hind: outpcd: a in rr: t.o fnl 2f) | 16 | **8** | 7/1 | — | — |

(SP 116.4%) **8 Rn**

**62.8 secs** (4.10) CSF £39.15 CT £110.16 TOTE £7.20: £2.10 £2.20 £2.40 (£9.20) OWNER Mr J. D. Graham (TAMWORTH) BRED J. D. Graham

WEIGHT FOR AGE 3yo-6lb

**1688 Princess Efisio**, much happier on this return to the sand, consented to put her best foot forward and opened her account with a fairly straightforward success. (7/1)

**2064 Silk Cottage** performs much better when allowed to stride along with the pace and, though he was forced to give best late on, a repeat could see him getting winning brackets by his name. (5/1)

**2029 Bowlers Boy** broke smartly but did not remain with the pace for long and, though he did renew his effort entering the straight, he could not get close enough to mount a challenge. (11/4)

**Bouton d'Or**, taken to post early, showed plenty of speed, but failed to quicken it up when the sprint to the line really got under way. (8/1)

**Diebiedale** could not match strides with the leaders and was always flat to the boards and going nowhere. (4/1)

**Muhandam (IRE)** wore a tongue-strap and was coltish in the preliminaries. Pressing the leaders for three furlongs, he then found the concession of weight all round too much. (8/1)

## 2306 THORPE VERNON H'CAP (0-85) (3-Y.O+) (Class D)

3-50 (3-51) **7f (Fibresand)** £4,012.50 (£1,200.00: £575.00: £262.50) Stalls: High GOING: 0.08 sec per fur (STD)

| Form | Horse | Dist | Pos | SP | RR | SF |
|---|---|---|---|---|---|---|
| *$2084^{5}$* | **Johnnie the Joker (70)** (JPLeigh) **5-9-5b** DeanMcKeown(8) (hld up: hdwy 3f out: str chal to ld wl ins fnl f) | — | **1** | 11/1 | 79 | 40 |
| *1809** | **Oberon's Dart (IRE) (72)** (PJMakin) **3-8-12** AClark(2) (lw: led 4f out tl hdd wl ins fnl f) | nk | **2** | $11/2^{3}$ | 80 | 32 |
| $1703^{7}$ | **I'm Your Lady (72)** (BAMcMahon) **5-9-7** GCarter(7) (lw: led after 1f to 4f out: ev ch 1f out: no ex fnl f) | 2 | **3** | 9/1 | 76 | 37 |
| $1466^{4}$ | **Intiaash (IRE) (75)** (DHaydnJones) **4-9-5**(5) PRoberts(9) (hdwy 3f out: rdn & one pce appr fnl f) | 2½ | **4** | 6/1 | 73 | 34 |
| $1830^{6}$ | **Heathyards Lady (USA) (70)** (RHollinshead) **5-9-0**(5) FLynch(1) (dwlt: sn rcvrd to trck ldrs: rdn over 1f out: one pce) | 1 | **5** | 9/1 | 66 | 27 |
| *$371^{8}$* | **What a Nightmare (IRE) (59)** (PHowling) **4-8-8b** FNorton(5) (bit bkwd: disp ld after 1f tl wknd 2f out) | 16 | **6** | 25/1 | 18 | — |
| *$2171^{2}$* | **Vax New Way (73)** (JLSpearing) **3-8-10b**(3) SDrowne(3) (s.i.s: sn chsng ldrs: lost pl wl over 2f out) | ½ | **7** | $7/2^{1}$ | 31 | — |
| *$1085^{3}$* | **Young Benson (61)** (TWall) **4-8-10b** AMackay(4) (led 1f: wknd over 2f out) | nk | **8** | 7/1 | 18 | — |
| *$1972^{5}$* | **Veni Vidi Vici (IRE) (65)** (MJHeaton-Ellis) **3-7-12**(7) JFowle(6) (trckd ldrs 4f) | ½ | **9** | 33/1 | 21 | — |
| $1432^{6}$ | **Kriscliffe (82)** (MissGayKelleway) **3-9-8** WJO'Connor(10) (b: swtg: s.s: a bhd: t.o) | 15 | **10** | $4/1^{2}$ | 4 | — |

(SP 119.5%) **10 Rn**

**1m 30.6** (5.90) CSF £66.56 CT £536.37 TOTE £13.80: £3.20 £3.60 £2.10 (£50.60) Trio £121.30 OWNER Miss M. Carrington-Smith (GAINSBOROUGH) BRED Miss M. Carrington-Smith

WEIGHT FOR AGE 3yo-9lb

OFFICIAL EXPLANATION **Kriscliffe: jumped out of the stalls slowly and resented the kick-back.**

**1423* Johnnie the Joker**, produced from off the pace, responded to a forceful ride to land the spoils nearing the finish. (11/1)

**1809* Oberon's Dart (IRE)** was not easy to pass once in front, but the winner timed his run to perfection, and had his measure in the shadow of the post. (11/2)

**935* I'm Your Lady** has not really produced her true form on this surface yet, but did nothing wrong here and her turn will come. (9/1: op 6/1)
**1466 Intiaash (IRE)** got herself into a challenging position on the home turn, but was unable to increase her pace when the chips were down, and she was fighting a lost cause approaching the final furlong. (6/1)
**1830 Heathyards Lady (USA)**, sluggish leaving the start, soon recovered to press the leaders, but she was at full stretch on straightening up and proved unable to carry her effort through. (9/1: 6/1-10/1)
**2171 Vax New Way**, restrained on his first attempt at seven, did race very freely but found nothing when the pace quickened, and was in trouble before reaching the straight. (7/2)
**1432 Kriscliffe**, bred to need much further, missed the break on this first appearance on the Fibresand and, refusing to face the kick-back, was soon some way adrift. (4/1)

## 2307 BEECH (S) STKS (2-Y.O) (Class G)
4-20 (4-21) **7f (Fibresand)** £2,070.00 (£570.00: £270.00) Stalls: High GOING: 0.08 sec per fur (STD)

| | | | | SP | RR | SF |
|---|---|---|---|---|---|---|
| 2012² | **Grovefair Dancer (IRE)** (BJMeehan) **2-8-6** AClark(8) (led over 5f out: hrd rdn & edgd rt fnl f: r.o) | — | **1** | 13/8 1 | 48 | 3 |
| 1445⁶ | **Riscatto (USA)** (WRMuir) **2-8-11** WJO'Connor(3) (led over 1f: rdn & ev ch ent fnl f: r.o) | 1 | **2** | 7/1 | 51 | 6 |
| *2172³* | **Abstone Queen** (PDEvans) **2-8-6** GCarter(4) (hld up: effrt 3f out: ev ch 1f out: unable qckn) | 1¼ | **3** | 4/1 2 | 43 | — |
| *2172⁴* | **Fearless Cavalier** (RHollinshead) **2-8-6**(5) FLynch(5) (hdwy ½-wy: rdn to chal 2f out: one pce appr fnl f) | 1¼ | **4** | 9/2 3 | 45 | — |
| 2161⁹ | **Samspet** (RAFahey) **2-8-11** ACulhane(1) (chsd ldrs over 4f: sn wknd) | 7 | **5** | 7/1 | 29 | — |
| | **Bali-Pet** (WGMTurner) **2-8-8**(3) SDrowne(6) (lengthy: unf: bkwd: s.s: a bhd & outpcd) | 4 | **6** | 20/1 | 20 | — |
| | **True Vision** (WGMTurner) **2-8-6** TSprake(2) (neat: scope: bit bkwd: dwlt: a in rr: t.o fnl 3f) | 7 | **7** | 7/1 | — | — |
| 1827¹⁵ | **Stravano** (BPJBaugh) **2-8-6** WLord(7) (trckd ldrs 4f: sn lost tch: t.o) | 2 | **8** | 33/1 | — | — |

(SP 121.5%) **8 Rn**

**1m 32.9** (0.30 under 2y best) (8.20) CSF £13.70 TOTE £2.20: £1.00 £4.20 £2.10 (£15.20) OWNER Grovefair plc (UPPER LAMBOURN) BRED Thomas Doherty
Sold JPointon 3,000gns
**2012 Grovefair Dancer (IRE)** seemed well suited to the step up to seven furlongs and, making sure it was a true test, was always going that bit better than her nearest pursuers. (13/8)
**Riscatto (USA)** ran much better than he did on his debut and did his best to make a race of it, but the winner was always going too well for him. He should be able to win a seller. (7/1: 5/1-8/1)
**2172 Abstone Queen** is finding it harder to get her head in front and, though she did run up to her mark over the slightly longer trip, was found wanting in the race to the line. (4/1)
**2172 Fearless Cavalier** tried his hardest to get at the leaders entering the straight but, with the pace being maintained, could not find the speed to do so. (9/2: op 3/1)

## 2308 OAK H'CAP (0-65) (3-Y.O+) (Class F)
4-50 (4-51) **6f (Fibresand)** £2,381.00 (£656.00: £311.00) Stalls: Low GOING: 0.08 sec per fur (STD)

| | | | | SP | RR | SF |
|---|---|---|---|---|---|---|
| *1971³* | **Delrob (45)** (DHaydnJones) **5-8-8v** AMackay(7) (bhd: rdn & hdwy over 2f out: r.o to ld wl ins fnl f) | — | **1** | 6/1 3 | 49 | 31 |
| *530²* | **Yo Kiri-B (57)** (TJNaughton) **5-9-6** AClark(6) (a.p: ev ch ins fnl f: r.o) | ¾ | **2** | 8/1 | 59 | 41 |
| 1624¹⁰ | **Anita's Contessa (IRE) (56)** (BPalling) **4-9-5** TSprake(8) (a.p: led wl over 2f out tl hdd fnl 50y) | s.h | **3** | 16/1 | 58 | 40 |
| 1020¹⁰ | **Aljaz (42)** (MissGayKelleway) **6-8-5** WJO'Connor(5) (hld up in tch: effrt over 1f out: rdn & nt qckn nr fin) | nk | **4** | 9/2 2 | 43 | 25 |
| 1702⁴ | **Belinda Blue (47)** (RAFahey) **4-8-10** ACulhane(9) (effrt u.p over 2f out: kpt on: nvr able to chal) | 2½ | **5** | 7/2 1 | 41 | 23 |
| 1876⁵ | **Deerly (57)** (DMorris) **3-8-13** TIves(12) (prom: hrd rdn appr fnl f: no ex) | nk | **6** | 10/1 | 51 | 26 |
| 1890⁶ | **Mustn't Grumble (IRE) (65)** (MissSJWilton) **6-9-9**(5) LNewton(1) (prom: jnd ldrs 2f out: rdn & wknd appr fnl f) | 2½ | **7** | 14/1 | 52 | 34 |
| 1612⁹ | **So Natural (IRE) (48)** (EJAlston) **4-8-8**(3) SDrowne(13) (prom: rdn 2f out: wknd over 1f out) | ¾ | **8** | 12/1 | 33 | 15 |
| 1905⁷ | **Mellors (IRE) (60)** (JARToller) **3-9-2** DaleGibson(3) (prom: led ½-wy: sn hdd: wknd 2f out) | 1¾ | **9** | 9/1 | 40 | 15 |
| 1689⁸ | **Nicola's Princess (56)** (BAMcMahon) **3-8-12** GCarter(2) (s.i.s: a bhd & outpcd) | ¾ | **10** | 11/1 | 34 | 9 |
| *1455¹¹* | **Dhes-C (53)** (RHollinshead) **3-8-4**(5) FLynch(4) (s.i.s: a bhd & outpcd) | 3 | **11** | 12/1 | 23 | — |
| *1812⁶* | **Globe Runner (53)** (JJO'Neill) **3-8-9** DeanMcKeown(11) (outpcd) | 2½ | **12** | 8/1 | 17 | — |
| *1028¹⁴* | **Avant Huit (50)** (MrsNMacauley) **4-8-10v**(3) CTeague(10) (led to ½-wy: sn lost pl) | 2 | **13** | 14/1 | 8 | — |

(SP 138.9%) **13 Rn**

**1m 16.3** (4.90) CSF £57.36 CT £711.56 TOTE £9.70: £3.60 £4.30 £5.00 (£46.10) Trio £276.80 OWNER Mrs E. M. HaydnJones (PONTYPRIDD) BRED J. K. S. Cresswell
WEIGHT FOR AGE 3yo-7lb
**1971 Delrob**, winning her first race beyond the minimum trip, needed to battle hard to nose ahead in the last 50 yards. (6/1: op 7/2)
**530 Yo Kiri-B** came here fresh and well after two months off and ran exceptionally well to fail narrowly. She should not be long in going one better. (8/1: 6/1-10/1)
**Anita's Contessa (IRE)** was always the one to beat and she did not go down without a fight. She would seem to be reaching her peak. (16/1)
**Aljaz**, the subject of some inspired support, delivered a sustained challenge entering the final furlong, but just failed to quicken sufficiently to get to terms. He is not over-raced and there must be a prize in store. (9/2: 8/1-3/1)
**1702 Belinda Blue** continues to knock at the door but is just failing to get her head in front. (7/2)
**1876 Deerly**, beavering away just behind the leaders, was always close enough to cause a threat but, when a final effort was called for, she was unable to deliver. (10/1: 8/1-12/1)
**1890 Mustn't Grumble (IRE)** stuck to the inside and joined issue in the straight. He looked sure to take a hand in proceedings over a furlong out but, once the pace lifted, he had no answer. He is taking time to get back to winning ways. (14/1)

T/Plpt: £236.90 (38.64 Tckts). T/Qdpt: £10.50 (75.97 Tckts). IM

# 1979-BATH (L-H) (Firm)
## Saturday June 29th
WEATHER: unsettled WIND: fresh against

## 2309 WESTON MAIDEN AUCTION STKS (2-Y.O) (Class E)
2-15 (2-16) **5f 161y** £2,992.50 (£900.00: £435.00: £202.50) Stalls: High GOING: 0.16 sec per fur (G)

| | | | | SP | RR | SF |
|---|---|---|---|---|---|---|
| 1467⁴ | **My Beloved (IRE)** (RHannon) **2-7-13**(3) AWhelan(8) (hdwy 2f out: hrd rdn over 1f out: led ins fnl f: r.o) | — | **1** | 11/2 3 | 79 | 32 |
| | **Secret Combe (IRE)** (PJMakin) **2-7-12** NCarlisle(9) (str: scope: bkwd: a.p: led over 1f out tl ins fnl f: r.o) | ½ | **2** | 11/2 3 | 74 | 27 |

$2138^{2}$ **Bold African** (PDEvans) **2-8-1v**$^{(3)ow1}$ SDrowne(6) (led tl over 1f out: one pce) ....3½ **3** 3/1 $^{1}$ 70 22
$1982^{2}$ **Nightingale Song** (MartynMeade) **2-8-2** FNorton(10) (w ldr tl wknd over 1f out) ....1¾ **4** 12/1 63 16
$2040^{14}$ **Kaiser Kache (IRE)** (KMcAuliffe) **2-8-7** JFEgan(5) (lw: no hdwy fnl 2f) ....1½ **5** 5/1 $^{2}$ 64 17
$2059^{4}$ **Victoria's Dream (IRE)** (MRChannon) **2-8-1**$^{(5)}$ PPMurphy(3) (s.i.s: hdwy on ins over 2f out: wknd over 1f out) ....4 **6** 14/1 52 5
$1851^{7}$ **Shall We Go (IRE)** (RHannon) **2-8-2** NAdams(7) (nvr trbld ldrs) ....1½ **7** 10/1 43 —
$1987^{6}$ **Silver Spell** (DrJDScargill) **2-8-6** GBardwell(4) (s.s: a bhd) ....s.h **8** 10/1 47 —
$1822^{7}$ **Geordie Lad** (JABennett) **2-8-3** CRutter(2) (prom tl wknd over 2f out) ....½ **9** 50/1 43 —
$2051^{13}$ **Red Garter (IRE)** (KMcAuliffe) **2-8-3**$^{(3)}$ MHenry(1) (lw: prom tl rdn & wknd over 2f out) ....9 **10** 11/1 21 —

(SP 115.3%) **10 Rn**

**1m 14.2** (4.70) CSF £32.93 TOTE £6.60: £2.40 £2.20 £1.30 (£32.60) Trio £62.40 OWNER Mr Peter Hammond (MARLBOROUGH) BRED Roseberry Ltd

**1467 My Beloved (IRE)** needed every yard of this extended five, and the lack of experience of the runner-up helped tip the balance in her favour. (11/2)
**Secret Combe (IRE)** was a springer in the market. She will come on for the outing and seems well up to taking a similar event. (11/2: 8/1-5/1)
**2138 Bold African** is probably more effective at the bare minimum trip. (3/1)
**1982 Nightingale Song** is another who did not seem to appreciate the extended trip. (12/1: op 8/1)
**Kaiser Kache (IRE)** had only beaten one home on his debut in the Coventry last week. (5/1)
**2059 Victoria's Dream (IRE)** is certainly not one of her stable's leading lights. (14/1)

## 2310 STAYERS (S) H'CAP (0-60) (3-Y.O+) (Class F)

2-50 (2-51) **2m 1f 34y** £2,810.00 (£785.00: £380.00) Stalls: High GOING minus 0.28 sec per fur (GF)

SP RR SF

*$2173^{4}$* **Wadada (40)** (DBurchell) **5-8-8**$^{(3)}$ SDrowne(4) (lw: hld up: hdwy 8f out: led over 2f out: all out) ....— **1** 9/2 $^{2}$ 52 32
$2042^{10}$ **Solatium (IRE) (55)** (MCPipe) **4-9-12v** GBardwell(3) (hld up & bhd: hdwy 6f out: rdn over 4f out: ev ch fnl f. r.o) ....nk **2** 5/1 $^{3}$ 67 47
$1835^{4}$ **Sophism (USA) (38)** (MCPipe) **7-8-4**$^{(5)}$ MartinDwyer(2) (hld up & bhd: hdwy 6f out: rdn over 4f out: ev ch fnl f: unable qckn) ....nk **3** 7/1 49 29
$1511^{8}$ **King Ubad (USA) (31)** (KOCunningham-Brown) **7-8-2b** JFEgan(5) (b: trckd ldrs: btn whn hrd rdn & hung rt over 1f out) ....6 **4** 33/1 37 17
$2182^{4}$ **Access Sun (37)** (JSKing) **9-8-5**$^{(3)}$ MHenry(8) (plld hrd: a.p: ev ch over 2f out: wknd over 1f out) ....½ **5** 7/2 $^{1}$ 42 22
**Coochie (25)** (RJBaker) **7-7-10b** NAdams(13) (s.s: gd hdwy on ins 8f out: led 4f out tl over 2f out: sn wknd) ...9 **6** 33/1 22 2
**Bahrain Queen (IRE) (25)** (CSmith) **8-7-10** NCarlisle(10) (b: hld up & bhd: nvr nrr) ....8 **7** 20/1 15 —
$2056^{14}$ **Saltis (IRE) (42)** (DWPArbuthnot) **4-8-13** RPrice(1) (b.hind: led over 7f: led 8f out to 4f out: wknd over 2f out) ....s.h **8** 25/1 32 12
$1839^{10}$ **Fattash (USA) (45)** (PMooney) **4-9-2** RPerham(9) (lw: hld up: bhd fnl 6f) ....1¾ **9** 25/1 33 13
$1893^{11}$ **Mustahil (IRE) (42)** (RJHodges) **7-8-8b**$^{(5)}$ PPMurphy(14) (prom 11f) ....7 **10** 25/1 23 3
*$1717^{6}$* **Club Elite (25)** (MFBarraclough) **4-7-3**$^{(7)}$ RFfrench(15) (hld up: bhd fnl 6f) ....2 **11** 25/1 4 —
**Chucklestone (36)** (JSKing) **13-8-7** AClark(7) (bkwd: prom 6f) ....nk **12** 12/1 15 —
$2182^{9}$ **Can She Can Can (32)** (CSmith) **4-8-3b**$^{1}$ FNorton(11) (plld hrd: prom tl wknd 5f out) ....8 **13** 25/1 4 —
$1953^{9}$ **Safety (USA) (38)** (JWhite) **9-8-9b** AMackay(12) (plld hrd: stdy hdwy to ld 10f out: hdd 8f out: wknd over 5f out) ....21 **14** 8/1 — —

(SP 118.2%) **14 Rn**

**3m 50.3** (9.30) CSF £25.10 CT £141.13 TOTE £5.00: £1.60 £2.40 £2.00 (£17.60) Trio £26.70 OWNER Mrs Ruth Burchell (EBBW VALE) BRED A. Snipe

LONG HANDICAP Club Elite 7-6 Coochie 7-7

Bt in 4,000gns

**2173 Wadada** had struck form over hurdles this spring, and took advantage of a mark 8lb lower than when he last ran in a handicap on turf. (9/2: op 3/1)
**Solatium (IRE)**, only beaten just over four lengths in last week's Ascot Stakes, was running off a 1lb lower mark here. (5/1)
**1835 Sophism (USA)**, off the same rating as at Warwick, just lacked that vital extra surge. (7/1: 5/1-8/1)
**King Ubad (USA)** scored the second of his two victories in the French Provinces in soft ground over thirteen furlongs back in March '93 and may have been feeling the ground. (33/1)
**2182 Access Sun** took a strong hold off a rating 1lb lower than when narrowly beaten in this race last year. (7/2)
**Chucklestone** (12/1: op 8/1)

## 2311 LITTLE SOMERFIELD STKS (3-Y.O+) (Class E)

3-20 (3-23) **5f 161y** £2,914.50 (£876.00: £423.00: £196.50) Stalls: High GOING: 0.16 sec per fur (G)

SP RR SF

2167* **Indian Relative (73)** (RGuest) **3-8-2**$^{(5)}$ DGriffiths(3) (lw: hdwy 3f out: led over 2f out: r.o wl) ....— **1** 2/1 $^{1}$ 80 54
$1786^{7}$ **Prima Silk (70)** (MJRyan) **5-9-0** TIves(4) (a.p: rdn 3f out: ev ch over 1f out: no imp) ....2 **2** 4/1 $^{2}$ 74 55
$1985^{10}$ **Master Millfield (IRE) (68)** (RJBaker) **4-8-11**$^{(3)}$ SDrowne(5) (lw: rdn & outpcd 3f out: gd hdwy fnl f: fin wl) .....hd **3** 8/1 74 55
$1985^{4}$ **Kildee Lad (69)** (APJones) **6-9-0** AClark(2) (lw: hld up & bhd: hdwy over 2f out: r.o one pce fnl f) ....s.h **4** 4/1 $^{2}$ 74 55
$2129^{9}$ **Pearl Dawn (IRE) (68)** (GLMoore) **6-8-8**$^{(3)}$ AWhelan(1) (swtg: led 1f: ev ch 2f out: sn drvn & hung rt: nt r.o)..1¼ **5** 11/2 $^{3}$ 68 49
$1985^{13}$ **Ann's Pearl (IRE) (69)** (JWHills) **5-8-8b**$^{1(3)}$ MHenry(6) (led over 4f out tl over 2f out: wknd qckly) ....10 **6** 6/1 40 21

(SP 114.1%) **6 Rn**

**1m 13.0** (3.50) CSF £10.00 TOTE £2.30: £1.50 £1.90 (£5.10) OWNER Mr Vijay Mallya (NEWMARKET) BRED Barrettstown Stud Farms Ltd

WEIGHT FOR AGE 3yo-7lb

**2167* Indian Relative** has certainly found sprinting to be her game. (2/1)
**1680 Prima Silk** is probably better over six these days. (4/1)
**Master Millfield (IRE)** showed definite signs of a return to form over a trip that is the bare minimum for him. (8/1)
**1985 Kildee Lad** never appeared likely to really get to grips with the winner. (4/1)
**2017 Pearl Dawn (IRE)** did not seem to relish the battle on this occasion. (11/2: 4/1-6/1)
**1064 Ann's Pearl (IRE)** did not find the blinkers doing the trick. (6/1)

## 2312 ROTHMANS ROYALS NORTH SOUTH CHALLENGE SERIES H'CAP (0-90) (3-Y.O+) (Class C)

3-55 (3-55) **1m 5y** £6,830.00 (£2,060.00: £1,000.00: £470.00) Stalls: Low GOING minus 0.28 sec per fur (GF)

SP RR SF

1983* **Concer Un (81)** (SCWilliams) **4-9-11**$^{(3)}$ MHenry(1) (b.nr fore: a.p: led wl over 1f out: eased nr fin) ....— **1** 3/1 $^{1}$ 89+ 71

1819[10] **Greatest (58)** (RAkehurst) **5-8-5** RPerham(4) (led over 6f: one pce)........¾ **2** 5/1 65 47
1902[2] **Easy Jet (POL) (74)** (LordHuntingdon) **4-9-0**(7) AimeeCook(2) (lw: hld up: hdwy on ins 3f out: nt clr run 2f out: r.o ins fnl f)........1½ **3** 7/2[2] 78 60
1819[14] **Confronter (76)** (SDow) **7-9-9** SWhitworth(3) (chsd ldrs: one pce fnl 2f)........2 **4** 14/1 76 58
2010[10] **Pay Homage (75)** (IABalding) **8-9-3**(5) MartinDwyer(6) (lw: prom: ev ch over 2f out: edgd rt & wknd wl over 1f out)........1½ **5** 9/2[3] 72 54
1793[14] **Danegold (IRE) (80)** (MRChannon) **4-9-8v**(5) PPMurphy(5) (hld up & bhd: hdwy 2f out: nvr nr to chal)........1½ **6** 11/1 74 56
1703[6] **Cats Bottom (57)** (AGNewcombe) **4-8-1**(3)ow2 SDrowne(8) (hld up: bhd fnl 4f)........5 **7** 8/1 41 21
2283[2] **Young Mazaad (IRE) (68)** (DCO'Brien) **3-8-5b** GBardwell(7) (lw: plld hrd: prom over 5f: t.o)........11 **8** 8/1 30 2
(SP 119.3%) **8 Rn**

**1m 40.2** (1.70) CSF £18.03 CT £50.54 TOTE £4.10: £1.70 £1.70 £1.50 (£14.70) OWNER Miss L. J. Ward (NEWMARKET) BRED Lloyd Bros
WEIGHT FOR AGE 3yo-10lb

**1983* Concer Un**, raised a further 3lb, registered his third course and distance win and did not have to work so hard as last time. (3/1)
**Greatest**, 1lb lower than when winning at Brighton a year ago, is flattered by his proximity to the winner. (5/1)
**1902 Easy Jet (POL)**, raised 4lb for his second last time, remains a maiden but could have given the winner more to think about with a better run up the inner. (7/2: 5/2-4/1)
**1051 Confronter** has slipped down the ratings but is still 1lb higher than when registering the second of his two victories last summer. He has never won on ground as fast as this. (14/1: 7/1-16/1)
**1819 Pay Homage** is down to a mark 6lb lower than when he won at Goodwood last year. (9/2: op 3/1)
**Danegold (IRE)** has been gelded and had one run over hurdles since his final outing last season. (11/1: op 7/1)

## 2313 CLAVERTON CLAIMING H'CAP (0-70) (3-Y.O+) (Class E)
4-30 (4-31) **1m 5y** £3,187.50 (£960.00: £465.00: £217.50) Stalls: Low GOING minus 0.28 sec per fur (GF)

SP RR SF

1953[6] **Indian Jockey (61)** (MCPipe) **4-9-7**(3) MHenry(5) (lw: chsd ldr: led over 4f out: drvn out)........— **1** 9/2[2] 70 58
*334*[8] **Tomal (44)** (RIngram) **4-8-7** SWhitworth(1) (lw: hdwy on ins 2f out: swtchd rt over 1f out: r.o)........¾ **2** 20/1 52 40
2000[3] **Bakers Daughter (47)** (JRArnold) **4-8-5**(5) MartinDwyer(4) (a.p: ev ch whn n.m.r on ins over 1f out: r.o ins fnl f)........1 **3** 10/1 53 41
2075* **Return To Brighton (48)** (JMBradley) **4-8-8**(3) SDrowne(11) (lw: a.p: ev ch over 1f out: one pce)........½ **4** 11/2[3] 53 41
2121[2] **Parliament Piece (63)** (DNicholls) **10-9-12b** TIves(13) (a.p: ev ch over 2f out: wknd over 1f out)........1¾ **5** 5/2[1] 64 52
2075[2] **Bedazzle (38)** (MBrittain) **5-8-1** NCarlisle(12) (lw: no hdwy fnl 2f)........1 **6** 7/1 37 25
2056[9] **Clytha Hill Lad (37)** (JMBradley) **5-8-0** CRutter(2) (nvr trbld ldrs)........2½ **7** 50/1 31 19
2234[6] **Only (USA) (50)** (RHannon) **3-7-10**(7) KSalt(8) (no hdwy fnl 3f)........1¼ **8** 16/1 42 20
1594[10] **Spiral Flyer (IRE) (48)** (MDIUsher) **3-8-1** JFEgan(6) (b: n.d)........1 **9** 50/1 38 16
2056[6] **Doodies Pool (IRE) (40)** (PBurgoyne) **6-7-12v**(5) PPMurphy(14) (prom over 5f)........2½ **10** 14/1 25 13
1979[12] **La Belle Shyanne (33)** (RJBaker) **5-7-10** NAdams(3) (a bhd)........¾ **11** 25/1 16 4
1691[14] **Bad News (44)** (JMBradley) **4-8-7** DBiggs(9) (lw: a bhd)........1½ **12** 25/1 24 12
1893* **Miss Laughter (53)** (JWHills) **4-9-2** OUrbina(7) (led over 3f: wknd 3f out)........¾ **13** 7/1 32 20
1685[16] **Swedish Invader (65)** (JWhite) **5-10-0** AMackay(10) (a bhd: t.o)........19 **14** 33/1 6 —
(SP 128.1%) **14 Rn**

**1m 41.1** (2.60) CSF £85.47 CT £585.21 TOTE £5.90: £2.10 £5.90 £2.60 (£119.50) Trio £367.90; £108.84 to Doncaster 30/6/96 OWNER Mr Darren Mercer (WELLINGTON) BRED John Hayter
LONG HANDICAP La Belle Shyanne 7-2
WEIGHT FOR AGE 3yo-10lb

**1953 Indian Jockey**, whose two previous wins have been over ten furlongs, was certainly not inconvenienced by the drop back to a mile. (9/2)
**Tomal** disappointed in the winter on the Sand, but looked in good fettle for this comeback. (20/1)
**2000 Bakers Daughter**, without the headgear this time, got rather cramped for room on the inside at a vital stage. (10/1: 7/1-12/1)
**2075* Return To Brighton** was 3lb higher than when winning a seller last week. (11/2)
**2121 Parliament Piece** was a little disappointing following his narrow defeat last week. (5/2)
**2075 Bedazzle** had finished closer to the fourth at Ripon last week and may have found the ground too fast. (7/1)
**1893* Miss Laughter** (7/1: 5/1-8/1)

## 2314 ST JOHN AMBULANCE MAIDEN STKS (3-Y.O+) (Class D)
5-00 (5-01) **1m 3f 144y** £3,780.50 (£1,139.00: £552.00: £258.50) Stalls: Low GOING minus 0.28 sec per fur (GF)

SP RR SF

1873[3] **Hayaain (78)** (MajorWRHern) **3-8-10** SWhitworth(6) (mde all: rdn over 2f out: r.o wl)........— **1** Evens[1] 87 47
2074[7] **Warning Reef (83)** (MRChannon) **3-8-5**(5) PPMurphy(2) (hld up: rdn 3f out: chsd wnr fnl 2f: no imp)........3 **2** 9/4[2] 83 43
1711[6] **Irish Sea (USA)** (MRStoute) **3-8-5**(5) MartinDwyer(4) (chsd wnr: hrd rdn over 2f out: wknd wl over 1f out)........8 **3** 3/1[3] 72 32
1963[7] **Notaire (IRE)** (IABalding) **3-8-5**(5) DGriffiths(5) (prom tl wknd 4f out)........4 **4** 12/1 66 26
1305[11] **Kings Nightclub** (JWhite) **3-8-2**(3) SDrowne(3) (wl bhd fnl 4f)........10 **5** 66/1 48 8
**Song For Jess (IRE)** (FJordan) **3-8-5** AMackay(1) (w'like: bkwd: wl bhd fnl 4f)........1¼ **6** 25/1 46 6
(SP 118.8%) **6 Rn**

**2m 30.3** (3.60) CSF £3.94 TOTE £2.30: £1.50 £1.70 (£2.50) OWNER Mr Hamdan Al Maktoum (LAMBOURN) BRED Shadwell Estate Company Limited

**1873 Hayaain** has developed into a strongly-made sort and held on well to the end. (Evens)
**2074 Warning Reef** was playing second fiddle in the final quarter-mile. (9/4)
**1711 Irish Sea (USA)** did not benefit from this step up from a mile and a quarter. (3/1)

T/Plpt: £43.80 (261.18 Tckts). T/Qdpt: £13.70 (47.2 Tckts). KH

# 1784-DONCASTER (L-H) (Good, Good to firm patches)
## Saturday June 29th
WEATHER: overcast & dry WIND: mod across

## 2315 E.B.F. LONSDALE MAIDEN STKS (2-Y.O F) (Class D)
6-45 (6-47) **7f** £3,463.50 (£1,038.00: £499.00: £229.50) Stalls: High GOING: minus 0.10 sec per fur (G)

SP RR SF

**Ryafan (USA)** (JHMGosden) **2-8-11** PatEddery(7) (w'like: leggy: scope: mde all: qcknd over 1f out: easily).— **1** 5/4[1] 91++ 4

| | | | | SP | RR | SF |
|---|---|---|---|---|---|---|
| | **Ajayib (USA)** (JLDunlop) **2-8-11** WCarson(2) (gd sort: lengthy: scope: trckd ldrs: effrt over 2f out: r.o: no ch w wnr) | 1¼ | **2** | 6/4[2] | 88+ | 1 |
| | **Elrayahin** (MajorWRHern) **2-8-11** RHills(3) (lt-f: trckd ldrs: hdwy 2f out: styd on) | 1¾ | **3** | 5/1[3] | 84+ | — |
| | **Amid The Stars** (RBoss) **2-8-11** GDuffield(4) (leggy: unf: s.s: styd on fnl 2f: nvr trbld ldrs) | 3½ | **4** | 16/1 | 76 | — |
| 1664[8] | **Auction Hall** (MBell) **2-8-11** MFenton(1) (hld up: hdwy over 2f out: sn rdn & btn) | ¾ | **5** | 16/1 | 74 | — |
| 2043[3] | **Soviet Lady (IRE)** (JLEyre) **2-8-11** RLappin(5) (b.off hind: plld hrd: cl up 5f: sn lost pl) | 7 | **6** | 20/1 | 58 | — |
| 1525[5] | **Flo's Choice (IRE)** (JAHarris) **2-8-11** JO'Reilly(6) (cl up 5f: wknd) | 1¾ | **7** | 25/1 | 54 | — |
| | | | | (SP 121.5%) | **7 Rn** | |

**1m 30.72** (7.12) CSF £3.79 TOTE £2.40: £1.80 £1.80 (£1.50) OWNER Mr K. Abdulla (NEWMARKET) BRED Juddmonte Farms

**Ryafan (USA)**, despite this being a slowly-run event, looked more than a bit special, and is one to keeping following wherever she goes. (5/4)

**Ajayib (USA)** is a most attractive filly who was not suited by the slow pace here, and plenty of improvement can now be expected. (6/4)

**Elrayahin**, lightly-made, still has an engine and was keeping on to the end to suggest she can improve. (5/1)

**Amid The Stars**, after a slow start, took a long time to realise what was required, but was getting the hang of things by the end. Time and stiffer tests will see improvement. (16/1)

**Auction Hall** is taking time to get right, but showed enough to suggest there is a deal better to come. (16/1)

**2043 Soviet Lady (IRE)**, unsuited by the slow pace, pulled far too hard and this is best ignored. (20/1)

## 2316 GO RACING IN YORKSHIRE MAIDEN H'CAP (0-70) (3-Y.O+) (Class E)

7-15 (7-17) **6f** £3,470.00 (£1,040.00: £500.00: £230.00) Stalls: High GOING: minus 0.10 sec per fur (G)

| | | | | SP | RR | SF |
|---|---|---|---|---|---|---|
| 2162[6] | **Sycamore Lodge (IRE) (67)** (MrsJRRamsden) **5-10-0** KFallon(12) (lw: bhd & pushed along: rapid hdwy 1f out: r.o wl to ld nr fin) | — | **1** | 3/1[1] | 73 | 51 |
| 1781[8] | **Lough Erne (63)** (CFWall) **4-9-10** PatEddery(1) (hld up: hdwy over 2f out: disp ld appr fnl f: no ex nr fin) | nk | **2** | 4/1[2] | 68 | 46 |
| 2026[13] | **Present 'n Correct (43)** (CBBBooth) **3-7-11**ow1 DaleGibson(3) (trckd ldrs: hdwy to disp ld over 1f out: nt qckn towards fin) | s.h | **3** | 33/1 | 48 | 18 |
| 2236[4] | **Camionneur (IRE) (49)** (TDEasterby) **3-8-3b** GDuffield(10) (s.i.s: hdwy & n.m.r 2f out: swtchd & r.o ins fnl f) | 1 | **4** | 10/1 | 51 | 22 |
| *499*[10] | **Jebi (USA) (41)** (CMurray) **6-8-2v[1]**ow3 MFenton(7) (hdwy ½-wy: ch over 1f out: nt qckn) | ½ | **5** | 16/1 | 42 | 17 |
| 2061[10] | **Sea Danzig (65)** (PHowling) **3-9-5** GHind(5) (lw: sn pushed along: hdwy whn nt clr run 2f out: nvr able to chal) | 1¼ | **6** | 12/1 | 63 | 34 |
| 2013[9] | **My Millie (50)** (RBoss) **3-8-4** KDarley(13) (sn outpcd & bhd: hdwy & swtchd 2f out: nvr able to chal) | ¾ | **7** | 11/1 | 46 | 17 |
| 1864[4] | **Lachesis (63)** (RHollinshead) **3-8-12**(5) FLynch(6) (chsd ldrs: rdn over 2f out: r.o one pce) | 1½ | **8** | 7/1 | 55 | 26 |
| 1701[5] | **Midnight Spell (60)** (JWHills) **4-9-7** RHills(4) (lw: cl up: disp ld 3f out tl appr fnl f: wknd) | 1¼ | **9** | 11/2[3] | 48 | 26 |
| 1405[13] | **Lapu-Lapu (52)** (MJCamacho) **3-8-6** JFortune(11) (lw: sme hdwy whn nt clr run appr fnl f: eased) | nk | **10** | 14/1 | 40 | 11 |
| 2162[11] | **Shaa Spin (60)** (JBerry) **4-9-7** JCarroll(2) (prom tl wknd fnl 2f) | 2 | **11** | 16/1 | 42 | 20 |
| 1702[7] | **China Hand (IRE) (39)** (MartynWane) **4-8-0** JFanning(8) (cl up: disp ld 3f tl appr fnl f: wknd) | ½ | **12** | 12/1 | 20 | — |
| 1702[6] | **Blue Lugana (35)** (NBycroft) **4-7-10b** JQuinn(9) (in tch: effrt over 2f out: sn wknd) | 5 | **13** | 16/1 | 3 | — |
| | **Embezzler (40)** (SGollings) **4-8-1b** SSanders(14) (led 3f: hrd drvn & sn wknd) | 5 | **14** | 33/1 | — | — |
| | | | | (SP 135.9%) | **14 Rn** | |

**1m 14.69** (3.69) CSF £16.86 CT £338.96 TOTE £4.50: £2.00 £2.20 £20.90 (£8.00) Trio £461.60; £136.55 to 1/7/96 OWNER Mrs J. R. Ramsden (THIRSK) BRED International Thoroughbred Breeders Inc

LONG HANDICAP Present 'n Correct 7-6 Blue Lugana 7-6

WEIGHT FOR AGE 3yo-7lb

**2162 Sycamore Lodge (IRE)** at last got it right and broke his duck at his thirty-second attempt. He put up an amazing performance, making up an incredible amount of ground to lead where it mattered. (3/1)

**Lough Erne** has always promised to win races and travelled well here but, when it came down to a struggle, she was just touched off. (4/1)

**Present 'n Correct**, who had previously been beaten out of sight in three outings, appreciated the drop in distance and ran well, only to be done for toe late on. (33/1)

**2236 Camionneur (IRE)** appeared unlucky here, but does have his own ideas about the game. If he would fully co-operate, races such as this would be easy meat. (10/1)

**Jebi (USA)**, in a visor for the first time and dropped back four furlongs in distance, ran quite well but was short of speed when it mattered. (16/1)

**1155 Sea Danzig** has run well over this trip in the past, but was short of speed here and that caused him to find trouble and he never got in a blow. (12/1)

## 2317 WESTSIDE MAGAZINE GROUP TENTH ANNIVERSARY CONDITIONS STKS (2-Y.O) (Class D)

7-45 (7-46) **5f** £3,322.00 (£991.00: £473.00: £214.00) Stalls: High GOING: minus 0.10 sec per fur (G)

| | | | | SP | RR | SF |
|---|---|---|---|---|---|---|
| 1308* | **Bayford Thrust** (JBerry) **2-9-1** JCarroll(2) (b: chsd ldrs: led 1½f out: r.o) | — | **1** | 3/1[2] | 87 | 29 |
| 1419[7] | **Foot Battalion (IRE)** (RHollinshead) **2-8-12**(5) FLynch(5) (chsd ldrs: wandered u.p ½-wy: swtchd & hdwy over 1f out: r.o) | ¾ | **2** | 7/1[3] | 87 | 29 |
| 2018* | **Top of The Form (IRE)** (MJohnston) **2-8-10** JWeaver(1) (lw: led tl hdd 1½f out: rdn & fnd nil) | 2½ | **3** | 4/5[1] | 72 | 14 |
| | **Manikato (USA)** (DJSCosgrove) **2-8-11** JFortune(6) (w'like: s.i.s: shkn up & hdwy 2f out: styd on) | 1 | **4** | 7/1[3] | 69 | 11 |
| 1884[3] | **Tickntima** (MDHammond) **2-8-11** KFallon(4) (in tch: effrt 2f out: nt pce to chal) | s.h | **5** | 11/1 | 69 | 11 |
| *1968** | **Calchou** (CWFairhurst) **2-8-10** DeanMcKeown(3) (cl up 3f: sn wknd) | 9 | **6** | 11/1 | 39 | — |
| | | | | (SP 122.2%) | **6 Rn** | |

**62.01 secs** (3.61) CSF £22.63 TOTE £3.10: £1.40 £2.80 (£9.10) OWNER Mrs Jean Turner (COCKERHAM) BRED Mrs J. M. Berry

**1308* Bayford Thrust** has a good attitude and, once he struck the front over a furlong out, he was not going to be passed. (3/1)

**984 Foot Battalion (IRE)** was short of room early on and then wandered about but, once he saw daylight, he did finish to some purpose. (7/1)

**2018* Top of The Form (IRE)** was boiling over in the paddock and, after blasting out of the stalls, she found nothing when tackled over a furlong out. (4/5: Evens-8/11)

**Manikato (USA)**, a reasonable-looking type, was gradually getting the hang of things as the race progressed. (7/1)

**1884 Tickntima** was always short of pace and looks to need further. (11/1)

**1968* Calchou** is her own worst enemy and, after running fast, cried enough with two furlongs left. (11/1)

## 2318 YORKSHIRE-TYNE TEES TELEVISION MAIDEN STKS (3-Y.O+) (Class D)

8-15 (8-16) **1m 2f 60y** £4,012.50 (£1,200.00: £575.00: £262.50) Stalls: Low GOING: minus 0.10 sec per fur (G)

| | | | | SP | RR | SF |
|---|---|---|---|---|---|---|
| 1670[2] | **Three Hills (84)** (BWHills) **3-8-11** PatEddery(4) (lw: mde all: rdn & hld wl fnl f) | — | **1** | 7/4[1] | 91 | 47 |
| 1804[3] | **Berenice (80)** (GWragg) **3-8-6** MHills(2) (trckd ldrs: hdwy to chal 1f out: rdn & r.o: nt pce of wnr) | 1¾ | **2** | 9/4[2] | 83 | 39 |

| | | | | SP | RR | SF |
|---|---|---|---|---|---|---|
| | **Freedom Flame** (MJohnston) **3-8-6** JWeaver(6) (lw: a chsng ldrs: nt qckn appr fnl f) | 3½ | **3** | 9/2 3 | 78 | 34 |
| 1963 3 | **Mallooh** (JHMGosden) **3-8-11** GHind(10) (lw: trckd ldrs tl outpcd fnl 2f) | 8 | **4** | 8/1 | 70 | 26 |
| | **Greenstead (USA)** (JHMGosden) **3-8-11** DaleGibson(3) (w'like: s.i.s: nvr plcd to chal) | 1¾ | **5** | 16/1 | 68 | 24 |
| 1957 4 | **Arktikos (IRE)** (JHMGosden) **3-8-11** JCarroll(8) (b.hind: s.i.s: nvr nr to chal) | ½ | **6** | 12/1 | 67 | 23 |
| | **Candrika** (LMCumani) **3-8-6** OUrbina(1) (in tch tl outpcd fnl 2f) | 2 | **7** | 12/1 | 59 | 15 |
| 1855 10 | **Soufriere (IRE)** (LMCumani) **3-8-6** KFallon(7) (nvr nr ldrs) | 8 | **8** | 16/1 | 46 | 2 |
| 2080 7 | **Lomond Lassie (USA)** (TKersey) **3-8-6** GDuffield(5) (b: cl up tl wknd qckly fnl 4f) | 10 | **9** | 66/1 | 31 | — |

(SP 125.1%) **9 Rn**

**2m 12.05** (5.05) CSF £6.58 TOTE £2.80: £1.30 £1.30 £1.10 (£4.10) Trio £3.00 OWNER Mr K. Abdulla (LAMBOURN) BRED Juddmonte Farms

**1670 Three Hills**, given a really good ride, set a moderate pace and had a bit up his sleeve when challenged. (7/4)

**1804 Berenice** sat waiting to pounce but, when she did entering the final furlong, the winner quickened again and she was well held at the finish. (9/4: 7/2-2/1)

**Freedom Flame** looked fit for this seasonal debut and ran a fine race, and was not knocked about when beaten. (9/2)

**1963 Mallooh** continued his education here and was sympathetically handled once beaten. He is now qualified for handicaps. (8/1: op 5/1)

**Greenstead (USA)** put up a decent first run and was certainly not over-punished. In due course, he will pay back the kindness. (16/1)

**1957 Arktikos (IRE)** had a quiet run and is now qualified for handicaps. (12/1: op 8/1)

## 2319 COLIN GODDARD MEMORIAL STAYERS H'CAP (0-80) (4-Y.O+) (Class D)

8-45 (8-47) **1m 6f 132y** £3,850.00 (£1,150.00: £550.00: £250.00) Stalls: Low GOING: minus 0.10 sec per fur (G)

| | | | | SP | RR | SF |
|---|---|---|---|---|---|---|
| *38** | **Ballynakelly (51)** (RAkehurst) **4-8-1** SSanders(3) (a.p: effrt 3f out: styd on u.p to ld wl ins fnl f) | — | **1** | 9/4 1 | 65 | 48 |
| 1792 10 | **Toy Princess (USA) (71)** (CEBrittain) **4-9-7** GHind(9) (cl up: led 4f out & qcknd: ct wl ins fnl f) | ¾ | **2** | 11/1 | 84 | 67 |
| 2165 7 | **Salska (46)** (AStreeter) **5-7-7**(3) NVarley(5) (lw: bhd tl styd on fnl 4f: nrst fin) | 2½ | **3** | 14/1 | 56 | 39 |
| 1802 6 | **Satin Lover (75)** (MrsMReveley) **8-9-11** KDarley(10) (lw: in tch: effrt over 4f out: rdn & nt pce to chal) | 12 | **4** | 6/1 3 | 72 | 55 |
| 1826 3 | **Blazon of Troy (52)** (TThomsonJones) **7-8-2**ow1 GDuffield(8) (b: chsd ldrs tl outpcd fnl 3f) | hd | **5** | 9/1 | 49 | 31 |
| 2183 3 | **Augustan (49)** (SGollings) **5-7-8**(5) MBaird(4) (s.s: styd on fnl 3f: n.d) | 1½ | **6** | 12/1 | 45 | 28 |
| 1640 9 | **Slapy Dam (56)** (JMackie) **4-8-6** JQuinn(7) (sme hdwy appr st: sn rdn & no imp) | 1¼ | **7** | 25/1 | 50 | 33 |
| *196 7* | **Non Vintage (IRE) (55)** (MCChapman) **5-8-5** KFallon(2) (outpcd & lost pl ½-wy: sme hdwy 3f out: eased whn no ch fnl f) | 7 | **8** | 13/2 | 42 | 25 |
| 1784 5 | **Amiarge (47)** (MBrittain) **6-7-11**ow1 DaleGibson(1) (lw: in tch tl outpcd appr st: n.d.after) | 7 | **9** | 16/1 | 26 | 8 |
| 2042 12 | **Achilles Heel (55)** (CNAllen) **5-8-5** GBardwell(11) (bhd: effrt ent st: sn rdn & btn) | 6 | **10** | 15/2 | 27 | 10 |
| 2002* | **Farringdon Hill (78)** (MajorWRHern) **5-10-0b** RHills(6) (b.hind: led tl hdd 4f out: sn wknd) | 2½ | **11** | 11/2 2 | 48 | 31 |

(SP 128.0%) **11 Rn**

**3m 9.1** (5.50) CSF £27.92 CT £280.42 TOTE £3.20: £1.70 £3.00 £4.90 (£18.90) Trio £359.10 OWNER Y Y Partnership (EPSOM) BRED Crest Stud Ltd

LONG HANDICAP Salska 7-9

**Ballynakelly**, well handicapped on his All-Weather form, had to struggle to win this, but showed he really stays, and he will do better over further. (9/4)

**1194 Toy Princess (USA)**, from a yard that is flying at present, put up a brave display but was worried out of it late on. She is on a decent mark just now. (11/1)

**1826 Salska**, ridden with restraint this time, made up ground all the way up the straight, but could never quite get there. This appeared a decent effort. (14/1)

**1802 Satin Lover** was always close enough if good enough, but the struggle proved too much in the final half-mile. (6/1)

**1826 Blazon of Troy** likes plenty of give in the ground and the jumps game, and was well tapped for toe here once the pace was on in the straight. (9/1)

**2183 Augustan**, trying a longer trip, again gave ground away at the start and failed to get into it. (12/1)

## 2320 STOCKIL H'CAP (0-70) (3-Y.O+ F & M) (Class E)

9-15 (9-19) **7f** £3,903.75 (£1,170.00: £562.50: £258.75) Stalls: High GOING: minus 0.10 sec per fur (G)

| | | | | SP | RR | SF |
|---|---|---|---|---|---|---|
| *1083 8* | **Tael of Silver (59)** (ABailey) **4-9-8** GDuffield(1) (bhd: stdy hdwy over 2f out: led over 1f out: r.o u.p) | — | **1** | 25/1 | 72 | 45 |
| 1991 4 | **It's Academic (60)** (MrsJRRamsden) **4-9-9** KFallon(13) (lw: bhd: hdwy 2f out: rdn & r.o fnl f: nrst fin) | 1½ | **2** | 2/1 1 | 70 | 43 |
| 2130 W | **Sylvan Princess (45)** (CNAllen) **3-7-13b** GBardwell(4) (lw: in tch: rdn ½-wy: styd on & ev ch appr fnl f: nt qkcn) | 1 | **3** | 8/1 | 52 | 16 |
| *111 3* | **Summer Villa (40)** (JHetherton) **4-8-3** JQuinn(3) (hdwy over 2f out: sn chsng ldrs: kpt on one pce fnl f) | 2 | **4** | 20/1 | 43 | 16 |
| 1888 8 | **Katie Komaite (51)** (CaptJWilson) **3-8-5** KDarley(6) (styd on fnl 2f: nvr nr ldrs) | 1¾ | **5** | 16/1 | 50 | 14 |
| 2016* | **Gentle Irony (61)** (MJRyan) **4-9-10** JWeaver(9) (cl up: led wl over 2f out tl over 1f out: wknd) | s.h | **6** | 4/1 2 | 60 | 33 |
| 1528 4 | **So Amazing (60)** (JLEyre) **4-9-9** RLappin(5) (led tl hdd & wknd wl over 2f out) | 1¾ | **7** | 12/1 | 55 | 28 |
| | **Butterwick Belle (IRE) (70)** (RAFahey) **3-9-10** ACulhane(7) (nvr trbld ldrs) | 6 | **8** | 33/1 | 51 | 15 |
| 1805 6 | **Jubilee Place (IRE) (64)** (TThomsonJones) **3-9-4** SSanders(8) (b: chsd ldrs 5f: wknd) | 1¼ | **9** | 14/1 | 42 | 6 |
| *1721 3* | **Down The Yard (42)** (MCChapman) **3-7-10** NKennedy(12) (nvr wnt pce) | 2½ | **10** | 33/1 | 14 | — |
| 1908 3 | **Badger Bay (IRE) (64)** (CADwyer) **3-9-1**(3) NVarley(10) (lw: prom: rdn after 3f: sn wknd) | 1¾ | **11** | 7/1 | 32 | — |
| 1820 11 | **Iceni (IRE) (66)** (HCandy) **3-9-6** AMcGlone(11) (lw: in tch: rdn & btn over 2f out) | s.h | **12** | 9/2 3 | 34 | — |
| | **Lady Ploy (44)** (MissLCSiddall) **4-8-7** GHind(2) (stdd s: sn outpcd & wl bhd) | 10 | **13** | 33/1 | — | — |

(SP 132.8%) **13 Rn**

**1m 27.99** (4.39) CSF £78.36 CT £448.25 TOTE £40.40: £4.60 £1.70 £3.10 (£48.70) Trio £274.40 OWNER Mr Peter Freeman (TARPORLEY) BRED Mrs V. O'Brien

LONG HANDICAP Down The Yard 7-8

WEIGHT FOR AGE 3yo-9lb

**601 Tael of Silver** has changed stables and, as often happens, she changed her outlook and won this convincingly. (25/1)

**1991 It's Academic** let the winner get first run and, despite flying at the end, it was all too late. She looks magnificent at present. (2/1: 3/1-7/4)

**1908 Sylvan Princess** was never on the bridle, but did keep battling on, and would seem to need further. (8/1)

**Summer Villa**, having her first run since January after changing stables, showed enough to suggest that she retains all her ability. (20/1)

**1610 Katie Komaite** was keeping on in the closing stages, suggesting that even further might help. (16/1)

**2016* Gentle Irony** was always being taken on here and finally cried enough approaching the final furlong. (4/1)

**1805 Jubilee Place (IRE)** (14/1: 10/1-16/1)

**1908 Badger Bay (IRE)** (7/1: 5/1-8/1)

T/Plpt: £58.00 (259.08 Tckts). T/Qdpt: £21.60 (42.4 Tckts). AA

## 2198-LINGFIELD (L-H) (Turf Firm, AWT Standard)

### Saturday June 29th

Race 6: hand-timed & flag start
WEATHER: overcast WIND: almost nil

### 2321 SAFFRON APPRENTICE H'CAP (0-70) (3-Y.O+) (Class F)

6-30 (6-35) **1m 3f 106y** £2,469.50 (£702.00: £348.50) Stalls: High GOING minus 0.41 sec per fur (F)

| | | | | SP | RR | SF |
|---|---|---|---|---|---|---|
| 1477$^{8}$ | **Meltemison (66)** (CEBrittain) **3-8-3**(8) JGotobed(5) (mde all: r.o wl) | — | 1 | 3/1$^{2}$ | 73 | 30 |
| *2086$^{3}$* | **Princely Affair (51)** (MBell) **3-7-4**(6) RMullen(1) (a.p: swtchd lft 3f out: rdn over 2f out: r.o one pce) | 1¾ | 2 | 13/8$^{1}$ | 56 | 13 |
| *499$^{2}$* | **Northern Trial (USA) (49)** (KRBurke) **8-8-7v** DSweeney(2) (a.p: rdn over 2f out: one pce) | 4 | 3 | 5/1 | 48 | 18 |
| 1640$^{7}$ | **Admirals Secret (USA) (61)** (CFWall) **7-8-11**(8) PClarke(3) (hdwy over 2f out: rdn over 1f out: one pce) | 1½ | 4 | 7/2$^{3}$ | 58 | 28 |
| *1970$^{2}$* | **Palacegate Jo (IRE) (40)** (DWChapman) **5-7-12** JoHunnam(6) (lw: bolted bef s: prom 9f: b.b.v) | 12 | 5 | 10/1 | 20 | — |
| *2155** | ***Lalindi (IRE) (72)*** (DRCElsworth) **5-9-11b**(5) DavidO'Neill(4) (Withdrawn not under Starter's orders: jockey did not arrive in time) | | W | | — | — |
| | | | | (SP 111.1%) | | **5 Rn** |

**2m 28.93** (4.73) CSF £8.02 TOTE £4.90: £2.40 £1.20 (£2.70) OWNER The Dayspring Company Ltd (NEWMARKET) BRED Dayspring Co Ltd
LONG HANDICAP Princely Affair 7-9
WEIGHT FOR AGE 3yo-13lb

**1047 Meltemison** took the field along and, keeping up the gallop in the straight, was not going to be caught. (3/1)
**2086 Princely Affair**, always close up, was bustled along over quarter of a mile from home and unable to get on terms with the winner. (13/8)
**499 Northern Trial (USA)**, hunting up the winner, could only go up and down in the same place in the straight. (5/1: tchd 8/1)
**771 Admirals Secret (USA)** looked a huge boat of a horse in the paddock. He began an effort from the rear over a quarter of a mile from home, but showed a very high knee-action and could only go up and down in the same place. (7/2)
**1970 Palacegate Jo (IRE)**, who bolted before the start and dropped her rider a couple of times, was close up until her earlier antics told running down the hill. (10/1: op 5/1)

### 2322 LYDD (S) H'CAP (0-60) (3-Y.O+) (Class G)

7-00 (7-04) **1m 5f (Equitrack)** £2,427.00 (£672.00: £321.00) Stalls: Low GOING minus 0.55 sec per fur (FST)

| | | | | SP | RR | SF |
|---|---|---|---|---|---|---|
| 1981$^{3}$ | **Chakalak (54)** (SDow) **8-9-13** TQuinn(10) (lw: rdn over 9f out: hdwy over 3f out: chsd ldr over 2f out: led wl ins fnl f: r.o wl) | — | 1 | 7/2$^{2}$ | 65 | 37 |
| 2060* | **Durham (47)** (RSimpson) **5-9-6b** AClark(8) (lw: a.p: led over 3f out: clr over 2f out: hdd wl ins fnl f: unable qckn) | 1¾ | 2 | 7/2$^{2}$ | 56 | 28 |
| 1534$^{2}$ | **Watch Me Go (IRE) (45)** (BobJones) **7-9-4** WRyan(7) (b: lw: led 5f: rdn over 4f out: one pce) | 10 | 3 | 3/1$^{1}$ | 42 | 14 |
| 2204$^{5}$ | **Pearl Anniversary (IRE) (56)** (MJohnston) **3-9-0** TWilliams(9) (lw: a.p: led 8f out: rdn 5f out: hdd over 3f out: nt r.o) | 4 | 4 | 11/2$^{3}$ | 48 | 5 |
| 1907$^{5}$ | **Lahik (IRE) (38)** (KTIvory) **3-7-10** NAdams(11) (a.p: rdn over 4f out: wknd over 2f out) | 2½ | 5 | 50/1 | 27 | — |
| 1338$^{5}$ | **Ela Agapi Mou (USA) (52)** (GLewis) **3-8-7**(3) AWhelan(5) (prom over 8f) | 2 | 6 | 14/1 | 38 | — |
| 2155$^{9}$ | **Kenyatta (USA) (37)** (AMoore) **7-8-10** CandyMorris(4) (b: prom over 3f) | 3 | 7 | 25/1 | 19 | — |
| *2086$^{7}$* | **Yellow Dragon (IRE) (51)** (BAPearce) **3-8-9v**$^{1}$ NCarlisle(1) (b: s.s: nvr nr to chal) | 1¾ | 8 | 8/1 | 31 | — |
| *2082$^{8}$* | **Kismetim (37)** (DWChapman) **6-8-7**(3) DWright(3) (sme hdwy over 2f out: sn wknd) | 8 | 9 | 33/1 | 7 | — |
| | **Nushka Babushka (33)** (BobJones) **4-8-6** FNorton(6) (s.s: a bhd: t.o fnl 6f) | 12 | 10 | 25/1 | — | — |
| *83$^{13}$* | **Lady Poly (23)** (JRPoulton) **8-7-3b**(7) RMullen(12) (b: bit bkwd: s.s: hdwy over 10f out: wknd over 9f: t.o fnl 5f) | 8 | 11 | 50/1 | — | — |
| 2182$^{3}$ | **Genesis Four (40)** (MrsLStubbs) **6-8-13** JFEgan(2) (a bhd: t.o fnl 6f) | dist | 12 | 8/1 | — | — |
| | | | | (SP 128.3%) | | **12 Rn** |

**2m 48.14** (4.94) CSF £16.80 CT £39.36 TOTE £4.50: £1.70 £1.50 £1.60 (£7.20) Trio £5.80 OWNER Mr P. F. Chakko (EPSOM) BRED Seend Stud
LONG HANDICAP Lady Poly 7-9 Lahik (IRE) 7-9
WEIGHT FOR AGE 3yo-15lb
No bid
OFFICIAL EXPLANATION **Genesis Four: finished distressed**

**1981 Chakalak** was running over what must be his minimum trip these days. Pushed along with fully a circuit to go, he picked up ground over three furlongs from home and soon moved into second place. Still with many lengths to make up on the clear leader, he eventually reeled in that rival in the closing stages. (7/2)
**2060* Durham** was sent on over three furlongs from home and had soon opened up a substantial lead. The winner eventually whittled him down though and he was overhauled in the closing stages. (7/2)
**1534 Watch Me Go (IRE)**, the early leader, was made to look very one-paced in the final half-mile. (3/1)
**1814 Pearl Anniversary (IRE)** may have won twice on the Fibresand at Wolverhampton but he appeared to hate the Equitrack. Going on a mile from home, he was being bustled along five furlongs out, and did not look at all keen. Collared over three furlongs from home, he then threw in the towel. (11/2: 4/1-6/1)
**Lahik (IRE)** had given his all two furlongs out. (50/1)
**Ela Agapi Mou (USA)** (14/1: op 7/1)
**2182 Genesis Four** (8/1: 5/1-9/1)

### 2323 E.B.F. CRAWLEY MAIDEN STKS (2-Y.O) (Class D)

7-30 (7-32) **5f** £3,322.00 (£991.00: £473.00: £214.00) Stalls: High GOING minus 0.41 sec per fur (F)

| | | | | SP | RR | SF |
|---|---|---|---|---|---|---|
| 2073$^{9}$ | **Barrier King (USA)** (PFICole) **2-9-0** TQuinn(1) (mde all: edgd lft wl over 1f out: rdn out) | — | 1 | Evens$^{1}$ | 74 | 37 |
| 1453$^{5}$ | **Double-J (IRE)** (KMcAuliffe) **2-9-0** WJO'Connor(8) (s.s: hdwy over 3f out: rdn wl over 1f out: r.o one pce) | 1¾ | 2 | 12/1 | 68 | 31 |
| 1822$^{3}$ | **Castle Ashby Jack** (PHowling) **2-9-0b** FNorton(4) (b.hind: bmpd s: chsd wnr: rdn wl over 1f out: one pce) | 1¼ | 3 | 12/1 | 64 | 27 |
| 2059$^{3}$ | **Aybeegirl** (MrsJCecil) **2-8-9v**$^{1}$ AClark(5) (bmpd s: a.p: rdn 3f out: one pce) | 2 | 4 | 6/1$^{3}$ | 53 | 16 |
| 1622$^{6}$ | **Trading Aces** (MBell) **2-8-9** WRyan(7) (b.hind: nvr nr to chal) | 2½ | 5 | 10/1 | 45 | 8 |
| 1959$^{4}$ | **Swift Refusal** (MJHaynes) **2-8-9** CRutter(6) (lw: prom 2f) | 3½ | 6 | 8/1 | 34 | — |
| | **Fastnet** (RFJohnsonHoughton) **2-8-9** RPerham(3) (lt-f: s.s: a bhd) | 1½ | 7 | 4/1$^{2}$ | 29 | — |
| | | | | (SP 119.9%) | | **7 Rn** |

**58.44 secs** (1.44) CSF £13.32 TOTE £1.90: £1.30 £2.70 (£10.10) OWNER Allsport Barrier Systems Ltd (WHATCOMBE) BRED Colin Bothway

**1892 Barrier King (USA)**, out of his depth at Royal Ascot last time, opened his account in this small race. Making every post a winning one, he was ridden along to make sure of it. (Evens)
**1453 Double-J (IRE)** lost ground at the start, but soon recovered. Pushed along in the final quarter-mile, he stayed on for second prize, but was unable to peg back the winner. A return to six may help. (12/1: op 8/1)
**1822 Castle Ashby Jack** chased the winner but failed to reel him in, and was overhauled for the runner-up berth inside the final furlong. (12/1: op 8/1)
**2059 Aybeegirl** could only struggle on at one pace from halfway. (6/1)
**1622 Trading Aces** was not given a hard time. Well off the pace at halfway, she did make some late headway under gentle handling and is now qualified for nurseries and, if stepped up in distance, looks one to bear in mind for a small race. (10/1)
**1959 Swift Refusal** (8/1: 6/1-10/1)
**Fastnet** (4/1: 3/1-5/1)

## 2324 WIMPEY HOMES H'CAP (0-70) (3-Y.O+) (Class E)

8-00 (8-00) **5f** £2,906.40 (£865.20: £411.60: £184.80) Stalls: High GOING minus 0.41 sec per fur (F)

| | | | | SP | RR | SF |
|---|---|---|---|---|---|---|
| $2034^{7}$ | **Walk the Beat (59)** (MartynMeade) **6-8-12**(5) RHavlin(2) (s.s: hdwy over 2f out: hrd rdn over 1f out: led last stride) | — | **1** | $11/2^{3}$ | 67 | 46 |
| $1853^{11}$ | **Spender (70)** (PWHarris) **7-9-11**(3) JStack(1) (a.p: rdn over 1f out: led wl ins fnl f: hdd last stride) | s.h | **2** | $3/1^{2}$ | 78 | 57 |
| 2156* | **Bowcliffe Grange (IRE) (43)** (DWChapman) **4-7-10b**(5) CAdamson(4) (lw: led: clr over 2f out: rdn over 1f out: edgd rt: hdd wl ins fnl f: r.o) | nk | **3** | $13/8^{1}$ | 50 | 29 |
| $2156^{3}$ | **Superlao (BEL) (41)** (JJBridger) **4-7-10**(3) DarrenMoffatt(7) (b.nr hind: outpcd: hdwy fnl f: swtchd lft: r.o wl) | ¾ | **4** | 6/1 | 46 | 25 |
| $2156^{6}$ | **Tommy Tempest (43)** (REPeacock) **7-7-10**(5)ow1 ADaly(5) (lost pl over 2f out: rallied fnl f: r.o) | ½ | **5** | 9/1 | 46 | 24 |
| $2156^{10}$ | **Halliard (62)** (TMJones) **5-9-6** RPerham(3) (b: lost pl 2f out: r.o one pce fnl f) | 1 | **6** | 7/1 | 62 | 41 |
| $1776^{12}$ | **Lincon Twenty One (44)** (MJHaynes) **3-7-10b** NCarlisle(6) (lw: a bhd) | 6 | **7** | 33/1 | 25 | — |

(SP 118.2%) **7 Rn**

**58.1 secs** (1.10) CSF £22.04 TOTE £7.80: £3.60 £2.00 (£14.30) OWNER The Country Life Partnership (MALMESBURY) BRED R. B. Warren
LONG HANDICAP Lincon Twenty One 7-6
WEIGHT FOR AGE 3yo-6lb
**1777 Walk the Beat** gained his first win on turf in over three years. Taking closer order at halfway, he responded to pressure from below the distance and eventually managed to get up right on the line. (11/2)
**407* Spender** bounced back to form. Always close up, he managed to get to the front in the closing stages, but was caught by the winner right on the line. He is a winner without a penalty. (3/1)
**2156* Bowcliffe Grange (IRE)** bowled along in front and had established a clear advantage by halfway, but his rivals gradually reeled him in from below the distance and he was worried out of it in the closing stages (13/8)
**2156 Superlao (BEL)** was unable to go the pace, but stayed on well in the final furlong, if finding the line always coming too soon. (6/1)
**2156 Tommy Tempest** got outpaced at halfway but did stay on again in the final furlong. (9/1: op 6/1)

## 2325 DAILY STAR CLAIMING STKS (3-Y.O) (Class F)

8-30 (8-30) **7f (Equitrack)** £2,880.80 (£798.80: £382.40) Stalls: Low GOING minus 0.55 sec per fur (FST)

| | | | | SP | RR | SF |
|---|---|---|---|---|---|---|
| $2013^{5}$ | **Amber Fort (67)** (PFICole) **3-9-4b** CRutter(11) (hdwy over 3f out: led over 1f out: rdn out) | — | **1** | $7/1^{3}$ | 66 | 24 |
| $1776^{8}$ | **Mystical Maid** (HThomsonJones) **3-8-13** WRyan(12) (lw: stdy hdwy 2f out: rdn over 1f out: r.o) | 1¾ | **2** | 8/1 | 57 | 15 |
| *$2158^{9}$* | **Prime Partner (48)** (WRMuir) **3-8-12** WJO'Connor(1) (a.p: led over 3f out tl over 1f out: unable qckn) | 1½ | **3** | 16/1 | 53 | 11 |
| $1185^{10}$ | **Double-O-Seven (78)** (MJohnston) **3-9-6** TWilliams(3) (rdn thrght: a.p: one pce fnl 3f) | 2½ | **4** | $9/4^{1}$ | 55 | 13 |
| $2049^{8}$ | **Ewar Sunrise (67)** (CEBrittain) **3-8-7** SWhitworth(9) (swtg: a.p: ev ch wl over 1f out: sn wknd) | 1¼ | **5** | $7/1^{3}$ | 39 | — |
| $1995^{7}$ | **Patrio (IRE) (55)** (SCWilliams) **3-8-0**(3) MHenry(4) (hdwy over 1f out: r.o) | 1¾ | **6** | 16/1 | 31 | — |
| $1956^{7}$ | **Areish (IRE)** (JFfitch-Heyes) **3-8-8**(3) AWhelan(7) (s.s: hdwy over 1f out: r.o) | hd | **7** | 33/1 | 39 | — |
| $1516^{2}$ | **Scathebury (60)** (KRBurke) **3-9-3v**(3) PMcCabe(8) (lw: hdwy over 3f out: wknd 2f out) | 1½ | **8** | $7/1^{3}$ | 44 | 2 |
| $1429^{8}$ | **Sotonian (HOL)** (MrsLStubbs) **3-8-6** JFEgan(5) (bhd fnl 5f) | 2½ | **9** | 25/1 | 25 | — |
| $1956^{3}$ | **Condor Ridge (47)** (BJMeehan) **3-8-8b**[1] MTebbutt(2) (led over 3f: 4th & wkng whn n.m.r on ins 2f out) | 1½ | **10** | 14/1 | 23 | — |
| $1152^{11}$ | **Cebwob (82)** (PFICole) **3-9-5** TQuinn(10) (b.hind: bhd fnl 3f) | ¾ | **11** | $4/1^{2}$ | 33 | — |
| *$1969^{6}$* | **New Technique (FR)** (KMcAuliffe) **3-8-2v**[1](3) JStack(6) (prom 4f) | 9 | **12** | 20/1 | — | — |

(SP 129.4%) **12 Rn**

**1m 26.76** (2.76) CSF £62.03 TOTE £9.00: £2.40 £2.10 £6.30 (£28.20) Trio £285.50; £365.95 to 1/7/96 OWNER Lord Portman (WHATCOMBE) BRED Campbell Stud
Amber Fort clmd AJHunt £11,000
**2013 Amber Fort** at last lost his maiden tag. Moving up at halfway, he grabbed the initiative below the distance and was ridden along to secure victory. (7/1)
**1122 Mystical Maid**, who spoilt her chances last time by hanging badly, looked very well here. Steadily working her way into the action in the second half of the race, she ran on inside the final furlong, but failed get to the winner in time. She can will a small claimer. (8/1)
**Prime Partner** ran his best race for a long time. Sent on at halfway, he was collared below the distance and failed to find another gear. (16/1)
**Double-O-Seven** gave his rider a very hard time. Ridden along throughout, he was never far away but was made to look very pedestrian in the final three furlongs. (9/4: 2/1-3/1)
**1692 Ewar Sunrise** had every chance entering the short straight before tiring. (7/1: op 4/1)

## 2326 STIRLING COOKE INTERNATIONAL MEDIAN AUCTION MAIDEN STKS (3-Y.O) (Class F)

9-00 (9-06) **1m 1f** £2,785.60 (£771.60: £368.80) Stalls: Low GOING minus 0.41 sec per fur (F)

| | | | | SP | RR | SF |
|---|---|---|---|---|---|---|
| $2004^{5}$ | **Double Bluff (IRE) (85)** (IABalding) **3-9-0** TQuinn(4) (lw: mde all: clr over 2f out: eased ins fnl f) | — | **1** | $4/6^{1}$ | 70+ | 35 |
| $1470^{2}$ | **Amadour (IRE)** (PhilipMitchell) **3-9-0** AClark(6) (lw: hdwy 7f out: chsd wnr fnl 4f: unable qckn) | 3 | **2** | 8/1 | 65 | 30 |
| $2062^{4}$ | **South Wind** (MrsJCecil) **3-8-9** TIves(3) (wl bhd 5f: r.o one pce fnl 3f) | 3 | **3** | $9/2^{3}$ | 54 | 19 |
| | **Fairly Sure (IRE) (40)** (NEBerry) **3-8-4**(5) CAdamson(2) (a.p: slipped bnd over 7f out: one pce fnl 4f) | 3 | **4** | 50/1 | 49 | 14 |
| $1535^{9}$ | **Challenger (IRE)** (JJSheehan) **3-9-0** AMorris(8) (wl bhd 6f: nvr nrr) | 2½ | **5** | 50/1 | 50 | 15 |
| $2015^{2}$ | **Bath Knight (55)** (DJSffrenchDavis) **3-9-0** WJO'Connor(7) (chsd wnr 5f: wknd 3f out: t.o) | 19 | **6** | 11/1 | 16 | — |
| | **Agdistis** (HThomsonJones) **3-8-9** WRyan(1) (unf: scope: s.s: a wl bhd: t.o fnl 7f) | 2 | **7** | $100/30^{2}$ | 7 | — |
| $1972^{8}$ | **Happy Venturer (IRE)** (CMurray) **3-9-0** MTebbutt(5) (Withdrawn not under Starter's orders: bolted bef s) | | **W** | 50/1 | — | — |

(SP 126.6%) **7 Rn**

**1m 53.8** (3.30) CSF £7.68 TOTE £1.80: £1.40 £2.80 (£4.90) OWNER Mr J. C. Smith (KINGSCLERE) BRED Littleton Stud

**2004 Double Bluff (IRE)** once again bowled along in front but, unlike at Sandown last time out, did not set a suicidal pace. Shaking off his only serious rival early in the straight, he was eased right down inside the final furlong and the winning margin is no true reflection of his superiority. (4/6: op Evens)
**1470 Amadour (IRE)** looked very well beforehand. Taking second place turning into the straight, he was unable to contain the winner in the last three furlongs. (8/1: op 12/1)
**2062 South Wind** was soon well adrift of her rivals, but she did stay on in the straight past beaten horses to finish a moderate third. (9/2)
**Fairly Sure (IRE)**, making her seasonal bow, was made to look extremely slow in the final half-mile. (50/1)
**Agdistis** (100/30: 5/2-4/1)

T/Plpt: £96.80 (133.99 Tckts). T/Qdpt: £43.40 (18.94 Tckts). AK

## 2291-NEWCASTLE (L-H) (Firm, Good to firm patches)
## Saturday June 29th

Race 7: hand-timed
WEATHER: overcast & dry WIND: fresh half against

### 2327 E.B.F. JOHN WATSON CONSERVATORIES MAIDEN STKS (2-Y.O) (Class D)
2-05 (2-06) **5f** £3,403.75 (£1,030.00: £502.50: £238.75) Stalls: High GOING: 0.06 sec per fur (G)

| | Horse / details | Dist | Pos | SP | RR | SF |
|---|---|---|---|---|---|---|
| | **China Girl (IRE)** (PWChapple-Hyam) **2-8-9** JReid(3) (leggy: scope: trckd ldrs gng wl: led over 1f out: pushed clr) | — | 1 | 8/13 1 | 66++ | 39 |
| 1537 7 | **Plan For Profit (IRE)** (MJohnston) **2-9-0** JWeaver(6) (led tl over 1f out: no ch w wnr) | 5 | 2 | 3/1 2 | 55 | 28 |
| | **Soda** (TDBarron) **2-9-0** JFortune(4) (leggy: unf: s.i.s: sn pushed along: bhd tl styd on appr fnl f) | ½ | 3 | 16/1 | 53+ | 26 |
| | **No Extradition** (MrsJRRamsden) **2-9-0** KFallon(1) (str: cmpt: sn outpcd: hdwy over 1f out: styd on) | ½ | 4 | 13/2 3 | 52+ | 25 |
| 958 7 | **Changed To Baileys (IRE)** (JBerry) **2-9-0** JCarroll(5) (w ldrs: hung lft & wknd fnl f) | 2 | 5 | 10/1 | 45 | 18 |
| | **Sparkling Harry** (MissLCSiddall) **2-9-0** GHind(2) (neat: bit bkwd: dwlt s: sn drvn along & a outpcd) | 3 | 6 | 25/1 | 36 | 9 |
| | | | | (SP 119.1%) | | **6 Rn** |

**61.87 secs** (3.47) CSF £3.25 TOTE £1.70: £1.30 £1.40 (£2.00) OWNER Mr Ivan Allan (MARLBOROUGH) BRED Ivan W. Allan
**China Girl (IRE)**, on the leg at present, was found a simple opportunity on her debut and she did it with the minimum of fuss. She will be even better suited by six. (8/13)
**1537 Plan For Profit (IRE)**, who has run up a fraction light, was dropped back to five. After making the running, he proved no match whatsoever. (3/1)
**Soda**, a short-backed, unfurnished individual, showed promise on this debut. (16/1)
**No Extradition**, a good-bodied, backward newcomer, did just enough to finish fourth which, significantly with two other runs under his belt, qualifies him for nurseries. (13/2: 4/1-7/1)
**Changed To Baileys (IRE)**, last of seven on his debut, looked very fit. (10/1)

### 2328 JOURNAL 'GOOD MORNING' H'CAP (0-100) (3-Y.O+) (Class C)
2-40 (2-41) **7f** £14,135.00 (£4,280.00: £2,090.00: £995.00) Stalls: High GOING: 0.06 sec per fur (G)

| | Horse / details | Dist | Pos | SP | RR | SF |
|---|---|---|---|---|---|---|
| 2134* | **Almuhimm (USA) (82)** (EALDunlop) **4-8-11** KDarley(8) (swtchd rt s: racd stands' side: effrt & swtchd lft over 2f out: r.o to ld ins fnl f: readily) | — | 1 | 11/4 1 | 93 | 73 |
| 1898 4 | **Primo Lara (82)** (PWHarris) **4-8-11** GHind(12) (lw: mde most stands' side: edgd lft & hdd ins fnl f) | 1 | 2 | 12/1 | 91 | 71 |
| 1785 4 | **Jo Mell (82)** (TDEasterby) **3-8-2** GDuffield(11) (chsd ldrs stands' side: rdn 2f out: edgd rt & kpt on ins fnl f) | hd | 3 | 14/1 | 91 | 62 |
| 1609 13 | **Tawafij (USA) (77)** (MDHammond) **7-8-6**ow1 JWeaver(9) (racd stands' side: hld up & bhd: hdwy over 1f out: styd on wl towards fin) | 1¼ | 4 | 11/1 | 83 | 62 |
| 1824 4 | **Options Open (92)** (MrsJRRamsden) **4-9-7** KFallon(14) (racd stands' side: effrt over 2f out: styng on same pce whn nt clr run ins fnl f) | nk | 5 | 5/1 2 | 97 | 77 |
| 2149* | **Somerton Boy (IRE) (71)** (PCalver) **6-8-0** JQuinn(5) (b.hind: racd far side: sn outpcd: styd on fnl 2f) | 1¼ | 6 | 11/1 | 73 | 53 |
| 2053 23 | **Akil (IRE) (87)** (RWArmstrong) **4-9-2** WCarson(13) (w ldr stands' side: rdn over 2f out: wknd 1f out) | 2½ | 7 | 15/2 | 83 | 63 |
| 1975 3 | **Double Blue (99)** (MJohnston) **7-9-9**(5) KMChin(7) (lw: led far side tl wknd ins fnl f) | nk | 8 | 14/1 | 95 | 75 |
| 1800 9 | **Dovebrace (100)** (ABailey) **3-9-6** JFortune(6) (chsd ldrs far side tl wknd over 1f out) | 3½ | 9 | 20/1 | 88 | 59 |
| 2134 2 | **Mountgate (72)** (MPBielby) **4-8-1** DRMcCabe(1) (dwlt s: racd far side: hdwy ½-wy: sn chsng ldrs: hung lft & wknd over 1f out) | 1¼ | 10 | 8/1 | 57 | 37 |
| 987 3 | **Pharmacy (80)** (JWWatts) **3-8-0**ow1 SSanders(2) (racd far side: chsd ldrs tl wknd over 1f out) | 3½ | 11 | 6/1 3 | 57 | 27 |
| 1885 3 | **Masafah (USA) (77)** (MrsMReveley) **4-8-6** ACulhane(3) (lw: trckd ldrs far side: lost pl over 2f out) | 5 | 12 | 25/1 | 42 | 22 |
| 2007 6 | **Promptly (IRE) (85)** (MRStoute) **3-8-0**(5) FLynch(10) (w ldr stands' side: rdn over 2f out: sn lost pl) | 2 | 13 | 8/1 | 46 | 17 |
| | | | | (SP 137.9%) | | **13 Rn** |

**1m 26.85** (2.35) CSF £38.90 CT £402.17 TOTE £4.30: £1.90 £4.70 £5.00 (£35.80) Trio £178.50 OWNER Maktoum Al Maktoum (NEWMARKET) BRED Gainsborough Farm Inc.
WEIGHT FOR AGE 3yo-9lb
**2134* Almuhimm (USA)**, an edgy type, was racing from a 3lb higher mark. Switched to race with the main body of the field on the stands' side, he scored in good style in the end. (11/4)
**1898 Primo Lara**, who has shot up in the weights since winning at Beverley and Thirsk, tried hard to make all but, in the end, the winner proved much too good. (12/1)
**1785 Jo Mell**, given a more patient ride, stuck on well all the way to the line. (14/1)
**1609 Tawafij (USA)**, who has taken this prize twice in the last four years, sat a long way off the pace. Only asked for an effort over a furlong out, he put in some fine work but had been set an impossible task. (11/1)
**1824 Options Open**, dropped 8lb after his unlucky run at Nottingham, had to search for an opening. He was only staying on at the same pace when denied a run inside the last, but would only have finished second at best. There will be other opportunities. (5/1)
**2149* Somerton Boy (IRE)** came out best of the six who elected to race on the far side. (11/1)

### 2329 TOTE BOOKMAKERS SPRINT TROPHY H'CAP (0-95) (3-Y.O+) (Class C)
3-15 (3-15) **6f** £10,601.25 (£3,210.00: £1,567.50: £746.25) Stalls: High GOING: 0.06 sec per fur (G)

| | Horse / details | Dist | Pos | SP | RR | SF |
|---|---|---|---|---|---|---|
| 2114 3 | **Double Bounce (84)** (PJMakin) **6-9-13** MRoberts(7) (lw: trckd ldrs: n.m.r 2f out: r.o strly to ld wl ins fnl f) | — | 1 | 3/1 1 | 91 | 74 |
| 1442 2 | **Double Splendour (IRE) (80)** (PSFelgate) **6-9-9** KDarley(1) (trckd ldrs: qcknd to ld over 1f out: hdd nr fin) | nk | 2 | 13/2 2 | 86 | 69 |

1853[2] **Bayin (USA) (71)** (MDIUsher) **7-9-0** RStreet(13) (hld up & bhd: gd hdwy on ins over 1f out: styd on towards fin) ....½ **3** 8/1 76 59
1974[5] **Stuffed (70)** (MWEasterby) **4-8-8**(5) GParkin(12) (lw: sn trckng ldrs: effrt & ev ch over 1f out: kpt on same pce) ....nk **4** 7/1[3] 74 57
1829[6] **Fame Again (78)** (MrsJRRamsden) **4-9-7** KFallon(10) (lw: hld up: hdwy over 1f out: n.m.r ins fnl f: kpt on same pce) ....1 **5** 9/1 79 62
1848[9] **Captain Carat (68)** (MrsJRRamsden) **5-8-4**(7) ClaireWest(4) (b.nr fore: s.i.s: hld up & plld hrd: styd on appr fnl f: nvr nr ldrs) ....1¾ **6** 20/1 65 48
2029* **Barato (65)** (MrsJRRamsden) **5-8-8** GCarter(6) (lw: b.nr hind: hld up: hdwy over 2f out: sn chsng ldrs: wknd ins fnl f) ....nk **7** 8/1 61 44
1829[3] **Castlerea Lad (81)** (RHollinshead) **7-9-5**(5) FLynch(5) (trckd ldrs: wknd fnl f) ....2 **8** 10/1 72 55
1790[13] **Thatcherella (75)** (MajorDNChappell) **5-9-4** JReid(3) (w ldrs tl wknd 1f out) ....nk **9** 12/1 65 48
2007* **Mallia (85)** (TDBarron) **3-9-7** JFortune(8) (w ldrs: rdn 2f out: wknd over 1f out) ....1¼ **10** 8/1 72 48
2005[15] **Plum First (63)** (LRLloyd-James) **6-8-6** DHarrison(9) (b: b.hind: led tl over 1f out: sn lost pl) ....1 **11** 20/1 47 30
2005[16] **Amron (62)** (JBerry) **9-8-5** WCarson(2) (mid div: effrt ½-wy: sn wknd) ....2½ **12** 14/1 39 22
1885[4] **Flashy's Son (60)** (FMurphy) **8-8-3** JTate(11) (b: b.hind: w ldrs tl wknd over 1f out) ....3 **13** 20/1 29 12
(SP 131.9%) **13 Rn**

**1m 14.47** (2.97) CSF £24.17 CT £138.74 TOTE £4.00: £2.00 £2.10 £2.50 (£7.00) Trio £64.50 OWNER Mrs P. Scott-Dunn (MARLBOROUGH) BRED Mrs P. Scott-Dunn
WEIGHT FOR AGE 3yo-7lb
STEWARDS' ENQUIRY Street susp. 8-9/7/96 (incorrect use of whip)
**2114 Double Bounce,** 2lb higher in the weights, had to wait for an opening before beginning his final effort. Showing a good turn of foot, he got up near the line. (3/1)
**1442 Double Splendour (IRE),** as usual, travelled strongly. He looked to have stolen it when quickening over a length clear over a furlong out, but was worn down near the line. He has a useful turn of foot and other opportunities will be found. (13/2)
**1853 Bayin (USA),** as usual, sat off the pace. Under an ineffective ride, he was pulling back the first two at the line. It would be interesting to see how he would fare with a stronger jockey on his back. (8/1)
**1974 Stuffed,** as usual, travelled strongly. Short of room at a crucial stage, when the gap came he could only stick on at the same pace. (7/1)
**1829 Fame Again** came from off the pace. Tightened up inside the last, even with a clear run, it is doubtful if she would have finished any better than fifth. (9/1)
**1588 Captain Carat,** who missed the break, ran keenly for the girl. (20/1)

## 2330 'NEWCASTLE BROWN ALE' NORTHUMBERLAND PLATE H'CAP (3-Y.O+) (Class B)
3-50 (3-51) **2m 19y** £57,350.00 (£21,350.00: £10,350.00: £4,350.00: £1,850.00: £850.00) Stalls: High GOING minus 0.18 sec (GF)

SP RR SF

1976[2] **Celeric (96)** (DMorley) **4-9-4** WCarson(7) (hld up: hdwy 6f out: n.m.r over 2f out: qcknd to ld ins fnl f: drvn out) ....— **1** 2/1[1] 106 79
1428* **Snow Princess (IRE) (88)** (LordHuntingdon) **4-8-10** DHarrison(2) (trckd ldrs: led 2f out tl ins fnl f: r.o) ....¾ **2** 5/2[2] 97 70
1875[3] **Secret Service (IRE) (74)** (CWThornton) **4-7-10** JQuinn(3) (a.p: nt clr run over 2f out: styd on u.p fnl f) ....1¼ **3** 25/1 82 55
1802[8] **Embryonic (IRE) (76)** (RFFisher) **4-7-12**ow1 GCarter(1) (hld up: hdwy whn nt clr run over 2f out: styd on wl ins fnl f) ....s.h **4** 25/1 84 56
2042[18] **Noufari (FR) (80)** (RHollinshead) **5-7-11**(5)ow3 FLynch(4) (bhd: hdwy u.p over 3f out: styd on wl fnl f) ....hd **5** 25/1 88 58
2054[5] **Backdrop (IRE) (106)** (PWChapple-Hyam) **3-8-8** JReid(10) (lw: b.off fore: chsd ldrs: drvn along 4f out: hung lft 2f out: one pce) ....2 **6** 8/1 112 65
**Foundry Lane (79)** (MrsMReveley) **5-8-1** MRoberts(9) (plld hrd: led 1f: trckd ldrs: ev ch over 2f out: wknd fnl f) ....2 **7** 7/1[3] 83 56
1976[4] **Invest Wisely (85)** (JMPEustace) **4-8-7** NKennedy(5) (lw: bhd & pushed along 10f out: sme hdwy 2f out: n.d) ....3½ **8** 25/1 85 58
2008[13] **Highflying (81)** (GMMoore) **10-8-3** JTate(12) (trckd ldrs: led over 3f out to 2f out: sn wknd) ....2½ **9** 25/1 79 52
1752a[8] **Daraydan (IRE) (102)** (LadyHerries) **4-9-10** KDarley(6) (a bhd: rdn ½-wy) ....2½ **10** 12/1 97 70
2042[4] **Sea Victor (77)** (JLHarris) **4-7-13**ow1 3x SSanders(13) (led after 1f tl over 3f out: wknd over 2f out) ....8 **11** 10/1 65 37
2042[9] **Fujiyama Crest (IRE) (88)** (MRStoute) **4-8-10v** KFallon(11) (b.nr hind: prom: drvn along 6f out: lost pl over 3f out: t.o) ....20 **12** 9/1 56 29
2055[6] **Remaadi Sun (79)** (MDIUsher) **4-8-1** RStreet(8) (hld up & bhd: effrt on outside whn stumbled ent st: nt rcvr: t.o) ....2½ **13** 12/1 44 17
(SP 139.2%) **13 Rn**

**3m 27.33** (1.83) CSF £8.30 CT £90.77 TOTE £3.40: £1.90 £2.10 £3.10 (£5.00) Trio £70.50 OWNER Mr Christopher Spence (NEWMARKET) BRED Chieveley Manor Enterprises
LONG HANDICAP Secret Service (IRE) 7-9
WEIGHT FOR AGE 3yo-20lb
**1976 Celeric,** who looked very fit, is best when coming from off the pace. Short of room halfway up the straight, when he did see daylight, he showed a nice turn of foot to settle it near the line. A son of Mtoto, he still seems to be on the upgrade. (2/1: op 7/2)
**1428* Snow Princess (IRE),** from a 7lb higher mark, kicked on two furlongs from home but, in the end, she could not match the winner's turn of foot. (5/2)
**1875 Secret Service (IRE),** who looked very fit, ran his best ever race over this extended trip. Though he was short of room halfway up the straight, he would not have troubled the first two in any case. (25/1)
**1529 Embryonic (IRE),** held up to get the trip, was another to meet trouble. Staying on strongly at the finish, he can find another prize when his sights are set lower. (25/1)
**1428 Noufari (FR),** rousted along early in the straight, was staying on when it was all over. All his five wins so far have come on Wolverhampton's All-Weather track. (25/1)
**2054 Backdrop (IRE),** an incredible 26lb higher in the weights compared with when he won at Chester in May, seemed to run a bit flat after his Ascot exertions. (8/1)
**Foundry Lane,** very keen, ran out of stamina entering the final furlong. (7/1)
**2055 Remaadi Sun,** held up to get the trip, was just making an effort on the outside when he lost his back legs turning in. (12/1)

## 2331 UK LAND ESTATES TROPHY H'CAP (0-90) (3-Y.O+) (Class C)
4-20 (4-26) **1m 4f 93y** £6,807.50 (£2,060.00: £1,005.00: £477.50) GOING minus 0.18 sec per fur (GF)

SP RR SF

2221[2] **Canton Venture (60)** (SPCWoods) **4-7-12** WCarson(6) (lw: mde all: drvn along & styd on wl fnl f) ....— **1** 6/5[1] 69 51

2008[6] **Bardon Hill Boy (IRE) (86)** (BHanbury) **4-9-10** JReid(1) (trckd wnr gng wl: effrt over 1f out: rdn & nt qckn ins fnl f)........¾ **2** 15/8[2] 94 76
2164[9] **Nigel's Lad (IRE) (76)** (PCHaslam) **4-8-9**(5) MBaird(4) (hdwy 6f out: styd on one pce u.p fnl 2f)........10 **3** 7/1 71 53
2120[4] **Fanadiyr (IRE) (58)** (WStorey) **4-7-3**(7) IonaWands(7) (bhd & pushed along 6f out: kpt on fnl 2f: n.d)........¾ **4** 16/1 52 34
1341[15] **Forgotten Empress (58)** (AHarrison) **4-7-3**(7) JennyBenson(3) (stumbled s: racd wd: chsd ldrs: effrt over 2f out: sn wknd)........1¼ **5** 33/1 51 33
1867[4] **Ten Past Six (90)** (MartynWane) **4-10-0** DeanMcKeown(5) (lw: hld up: effrt over 3f out: rdn & wknd over 2f out)........8 **6** 11/2[3] 72 54
(SP 116.9%) **6 Rn**

**2m 40.3** (2.80) CSF £4.01 TOTE £1.80: £1.10 £1.40 (£1.60) OWNER Dr Frank Chao (NEWMARKET) BRED High Point B/stock Ltd & Chao Racing & B/stock Ltd
LONG HANDICAP Fanadiyr (IRE) 7-1 Forgotten Empress 7-0
**2221 Canton Venture**, having his second outing in three days, made it five out of six. Given a canny ride from the front, he picked up the pace entering the final furlong and was always just going to withstand the runner-up's challenge. (6/5: Evens-10/11)
**1700 Bardon Hill Boy (IRE)**, who did not shine when ridden by a lady last time, tracked the winner travelling strongly and looked as though he could pick him up at any stage but, with Carson stepping up the gas in front, he could never quite get on level terms. (15/8)
**913 Nigel's Lad (IRE)** has yet to recapture the form that saw him win six times last year. (7/1)
**2120 Fanadiyr (IRE)**, 9lb out of the handicap, struggled to go the pace but was staying on when it was all over. (16/1)
**Forgotten Empress** ran as well as could be expected as she was 10lb wrong at the weights. (33/1)

## 2332 WHITLEY BAY HOLIDAY PARK CHIPCHASE STKS (Listed) (3-Y.O+) (Class A)

4-50 (4-52) **6f** £12,544.00 (£4,696.00: £2,298.00: £990.00: £445.00: £227.00) Stalls: High GOING: 0.06 sec per fur (G)

SP RR SF

727[8] **Sea Dane (100)** (PWHarris) **3-8-8** GHind(4) (hld up: hdwy & ev ch whn bmpd over 1f out: kpt on wl: fin 2nd, 1¼l: awrdd r)........— **1** 16/1 110 63
2072[7] **Venture Capitalist (112)** (DNicholls) **7-9-7** AlexGreaves(6) (lw: hld up: hdwy over 2f out: styd on u.p fnl f: fin 3rd, nk: plcd 2nd)........ **2** 8/1 115 75
1879* **Warning Star (98)** (BWHills) **4-8-10** WCarson(10) (trckd ldrs: n.m.r & lost pl 2f out: styd on ins fnl f: fin 4th, 1½l: plcd 3rd)........ **3** 6/1[3] 100 60
1800[3] **Carranita (IRE) (105)** (BPalling) **6-9-0** TSprake(7) (w ldrs: sltly hmpd over 1f out: kpt on one pce: fin 5th, 1¼l: plcd 4th)........ **4** 8/1 101 61
2072[5] **Iktamal (USA) (110)** (EALDunlop) **4-9-1** PaulEddery(9) (lw: dwlt s: hld up: hdwy on ins & swtchd lft 2f out: squeezed thro: qcknd to ld over 1f out: drvn out: fin 1st: disq: plcd 5th)........ **5** 6/4[1] 113 73
2072[15] **Branston Abby (IRE) (108)** (MJohnston) **7-9-0** MRoberts(8) (lw: hld up: hdwy over 2f out: kpt on fnl f: nvr nr to chal)........1¼ **6** 2/1[2] 97 57
2114[18] **Madly Sharp (102)** (JWWatts) **5-9-1** GDuffield(3) (lw: sn outpcd & pushed along: sme hdwy over 2f out: nvr rchd ldrs)........1½ **7** 12/1 94 54
1129[10] **Westcourt Magic (109)** (MWEasterby) **3-8-12** JReid(1) (swtchd rt after s: led & sn clr: hdd & wknd over 1f out)........1¼ **8** 12/1 95 48
1867[5] **Kissel** (AHarrison) **4-8-10** DeanMcKeown(5) (chsd ldrs tl lost pl over 2f out: sn bhd)........9 **9** 66/1 62 22
1790[3] **Tropical Dance (USA) (91)** (MrsJCecil) **3-8-3** GCarter(2) (lw: chsd ldrs tl lost pl over 2f out: sn bhd)........7 **10** 16/1 43 —
(SP 138.5%) **10 Rn**

**1m 13.72** (2.22) CSF £143.67 TOTE £40.50: £6.00 £2.90 £1.90 (£147.80) Trio £258.60 OWNER Carat Gold Connections (BERKHAMSTED) BRED Miss K. Rausing
WEIGHT FOR AGE 3yo-7lb
STEWARDS' ENQUIRY Eddery susp. 8-11/7/96 (irresponsible riding).
**Sea Dane**, absent since running poorly on soft ground in the Greenham, was pushed sideways in a domino effect started by the winner. (16/1)
**1129* Venture Capitalist**, who loves to come from off the pace, ran right up to his best. (8/1)
**1879* Warning Star**, who is not very robust, had a rough time of it but, to her credit, recovered to be staying on at the line. (6/1)
**1800 Carranita (IRE)** was pushed sideways by the Iktamal over a furlong out. (8/1)
**2072 Iktamal (USA)** has to be covered up, but his rider took his life in his hands, nudging his way out of a pocket on the rail. After winning on merit, the decision to stand him down was just. (6/4)
**1800 Branston Abby (IRE)** ran one of her flat races. No doubt she will bounce back before long. (2/1)
**1107 Madly Sharp** (12/1: op 8/1)

## 2333 SENDRIG CONSTRUCTION AND NEWCASTLE FLOORING MAIDEN STKS (3-Y.O+) (Class D)

5-20 (5-22) **1m** £5,295.00 (£1,605.00: £785.00: £375.00) Stalls: Low GOING minus 0.18 sec per fur (GF)

SP RR SF

**Balladur (USA)** (HRACecil) **3-8-12** AMcGlone(3) (lw: chsd ldr: chal over 2f out: sn rdn: styd on to ld last strides)........— **1** 11/8[1] 82 54
1797[5] **Unitus (IRE)** (MRStoute) **3-8-12** KFallon(2) (lw: chsd ldrs: hdwy u.p & ev ch over 1f out: nt qckn cl home)........nk **2** 2/1[2] 81 53
1662[2] **Hismagicmoment (USA) (85)** (PWChapple-Hyam) **3-8-12** JReid(6) (lw: led tl nr fin)........s.h **3** 5/2[3] 81 53
**Milford Sound** (JRFanshawe) **3-8-12** DHarrison(4) (outpcd over 3f out: kpt on one pce fnl 2f)........6 **4** 8/1 69 41
1797[6] **Berlin Blue** (JWWatts) **3-8-12** NConnorton(7) (lw: hld up: sme hdwy over 2f out: nvr nr ldrs)........½ **5** 16/1 68 40
**Shamokin** (FWatson) **4-9-5**(3) CTeague(1) (bkwd: dwlt s: a bhd & sn drvn along)........18 **6** 50/1 32 14
2048[6] **Messalina (IRE)** (BMactaggart) **3-8-7** MRoberts(8) (plld hrd: trckd ldrs tl lost pl over 3f out: sn bhd)........2½ **7** 50/1 22 —
2150[5] **Blazing Imp (USA)** (WSCunningham) **3-8-12** ACulhane(5) (plld hrd: lost tch over 3f out)........5 **8** 50/1 17 —
(SP 126.9%) **8 Rn**

**1m 41.7** (2.70) CSF £5.12 TOTE £2.40: £1.40 £1.30 £1.10 (£2.90) OWNER Mr K. Abdulla (NEWMARKET) BRED Juddmonte Farms
WEIGHT FOR AGE 3yo-10lb
**Balladur (USA)** answered his rider's every call to get up near the line. (11/8)
**1797 Unitus (IRE)** stuck on under strong pressure, but was edged out near the finish. He will appreciate better ground. (2/1)
**1662 Hismagicmoment (USA)** tried hard to make all and was only worn down near the line. Though no great shakes, his turn will surely come. (5/2)
**Milford Sound**, settled off the pace, needs one more run to qualify for a handicap mark. (8/1)
**1530 Berlin Blue**, having his third outing, is not without ability. His future lies in the hands of the Official Assessor. (16/1)

T/Jkpt: £7,100.00 (0.1 Tckts); £5,986.08 to Doncaster 30/6/96. T/Plpt: £56.70 (591.84 Tckts). T/Qdpt: £23.30 (79.85 Tckts). WG

## 2297-NEWMARKET (R-H) (Good)
## Saturday June 29th
WEATHER: overcast & showers WIND: mod bhd

### 2334 DOM RUINART CHAMPAGNE H'CAP (0-90) (3-Y.O) (Class C)
2-30 (2-30) **1m (July)** £5,900.00 (£1,760.00: £840.00: £380.00) Stalls: Low GOING: minus 0.31 sec per fur (GF)

| | | | | SP | RR | SF |
|---|---|---|---|---|---|---|
| 1807* | **Mawingo (IRE) (75)** (GWragg) **3-7-13**(7) GMilligan(3) (lw: sn pushed along & bhd: hdwy over 2f out: qcknd to ld over 1f out: rdn & r.o) | — | **1** | 2/1$^{2}$ | 86 | 33 |
| 2041* | **North Song (91)** (JHMGosden) **3-9-8** PatEddery(2) (lw: w ldr: led over 2f out tl over 1f out: unable qckn) | 2 | **2** | 7/4$^{1}$ | 98 | 45 |
| 678$^{11}$ | **Polish Widow (70)** (GWragg) **3-8-1** RHills(4) (trckd ldrs: rdn 2f out: styd on fnl f) | nk | **3** | 8/1$^{3}$ | 76 | 23 |
| 1798$^{10}$ | **Salmis (77)** (JRFanshawe) **3-8-5**(3) NVarley(6) (chsd ldrs: rdn & ev ch over 2f out: wknd fnl f) | 5 | **4** | 16/1 | 73 | 20 |
| 2146$^{5}$ | **Quality (IRE) (79)** (WAO'Gorman) **3-8-10v** EmmaO'Gorman(1) (trckd ldrs: no imp fnl 2f) | ¾ | **5** | 9/1 | 74 | 21 |
| 1861$^{5}$ | **Galapino (67)** (CEBrittain) **3-7-5**(7) PDoe(5) (swtg: lw: led over 5f: wknd over 1f out) | 5 | **6** | 16/1 | 52 | — |
| 2041$^{19}$ | **Paint It Black (82)** (RHannon) **3-8-13** RHughes(7) (a bhd) | 2 | **7** | 16/1 | 63 | 10 |
| | | | | (SP 108.5%) | **7 Rn** | |

**1m 39.86** (2.66) CSF £5.41 TOTE £2.60: £1.60 £1.50 (£1.50) OWNER Mrs Claude Lilley (NEWMARKET) BRED Miss Geraldine Browne

**1807* Mawingo (IRE)** ran an extraordinary race as he was detached from the bunch and being pushed along at halfway. Pulled to the centre of the course, he picked up well as those who set the fast pace were beginning to flag and won in the style of an improving horse. (2/1)

**2041* North Song** found being taken on for the lead by Galapino his undoing, as he shook off that rival approaching the final furlong, but had nothing left to respond to the winner. It must be remembered that those who raced by either rail at Royal Ascot enjoyed a considerable advantage, and that the second and third home on the far side in the Brittania, Double Diamond and Alhawa respectively, had subsequently let the form down. (7/4)

**Polish Widow**, who had run poorly in two maidens this year, returned to form on her first effort in a handicap. (8/1)

**611 Salmis**, dropped in trip and taken down steadily, still failed to get home. He beat Missile in a maiden on his only try over seven furlongs. (16/1)

**2146 Quality (IRE)** was easily left behind in the last quarter-mile and needs to return to ten furlongs. (9/1: 10/1-16/1)

**1507 Galapino** made all when winning twice on the All-Weather, and did not relish being taken on for the lead. He looked in good shape and is capable of better. (16/1)

### 2335 KRIS MAIDEN STKS (2-Y.O) (Class D)
3-00 (3-01) **7f (July)** £4,503.00 (£1,344.00: £642.00: £291.00) Stalls: Low GOING: minus 0.31 sec per fur (GF)

| | | | | SP | RR | SF |
|---|---|---|---|---|---|---|
| 1960$^{2}$ | **Benny The Dip (USA)** (JHMGosden) **2-9-0** AGarth(7) (mde all: clr over 2f out: pushed out) | — | **1** | 100/30$^{2}$ | 99+ | 54 |
| 1191$^{11}$ | **Sturgeon (IRE)** (PFICole) **2-9-0** TQuinn(1) (hld up: hdwy over 2f out: r.o wl fnl f: nt trble wnr) | 2½ | **2** | 7/2$^{3}$ | 93 | 48 |
| | **Mithak (USA)** (BWHills) **2-9-0** RHills(6) (w'like: s.i.s: hdwy 2f out: r.o fnl f) | 4 | **3** | 13/2 | 84+ | 39 |
| 2073$^{4}$ | **Party Romance (USA)** (BHanbury) **2-9-0** WRyan(10) (w wnr tl rdn & btn over 2f out) | ¾ | **4** | 3/1$^{1}$ | 82 | 37 |
| | **Supremism** (CEBrittain) **2-9-0** DThomson(8) (chsd ldrs: rdn over 3f out: no imp) | 1½ | **5** | 33/1 | 79 | 34 |
| | **Dawam Allail** (MAJarvis) **2-9-0** PRobinson(9) (cmpt: scope: prom: rdn over 2f out: btn appr fnl f) | hd | **6** | 9/1 | 79 | 34 |
| | **Beryllium** (RHannon) **2-9-0** RHughes(2) (leggy: scope: sn bhd & pushed along: r.o appr fnl f) | 3 | **7** | 20/1 | 72 | 27 |
| | **Belmontee** (HRACecil) **2-9-0** PatEddery(5) (cmpt: scope: bit bkwd: prom: pushed along & lost pl after 2f: n.d after) | 2 | **8** | 10/1 | 67 | 22 |
| 1774$^{7}$ | **Castles Burning (USA)** (CACyzer) **2-9-0** WJO'Connor(3) (a bhd) | 5 | **9** | 40/1 | 56 | 11 |
| | **Maradi (IRE)** (DMorley) **2-9-0** MHills(4) (gd sort: bhd fnl 2f) | 1 | **10** | 20/1 | 54 | 9 |
| | | | | (SP 117.6%) | **10 Rn** | |

**1m 26.01** (1.01) CSF £14.84 TOTE £3.30: £1.30 £1.70 £2.10 (£7.30) Trio £12.90 OWNER Mr Landon Knight (NEWMARKET) BRED Landon Knight

**1960 Benny The Dip (USA)** moved to post really well and has a knee-action which suggests that the rain can only have been in his favour. Getting out well this time, he had burnt these off a long way from home and looks very useful indeed. (100/30)

**1191 Sturgeon (IRE)**, intent to get a lead, was restrained in the early stages. By the time he made his move, the winner had flown, but he ran on strongly and should soon be winning. (7/2)

**Mithak (USA)** moved down too freely and looked to need the experience as he then missed the break. Running on steadily in the final furlong to snatch third place, he showed enough to suggest he will not be too hard to place. (13/2)

**2073 Party Romance (USA)**, running just nine days after his highflying Ascot debut, jumped out with the winner, but had been burnt off some way from home and folded up in the final furlong. (3/1: 6/4-100/30)

**Supremism**, an attractive but backward newcomer, could not live with these at the business end. (33/1)

**Dawam Allail** took a good hold going to post and shaped well until lack of a race found him out. (9/1)

**Belmontee** (10/1: 6/1-11/1)

**Maradi (IRE)** was coltish beforehand. (20/1)

### 2336 HEATH COURT HOTEL FRED ARCHER STKS (Listed) (4-Y.O+) (Class A)
3-30 (3-32) **1m 4f (July)** £11,318.60 (£3,906.60: £1,868.30: £756.50) Stalls: High GOING: minus 0.31 sec per fur (GF)

| | | | | SP | RR | SF |
|---|---|---|---|---|---|---|
| 1863* | **Bequeath (102)** (HRACecil) **4-8-11** PatEddery(1) (lw: trckd ldr: led over 1f out: shkn up & sn qcknd clr) | — | **1** | 7/4$^{1}$ | 120+ | 73 |
| 1509$^{6}$ | **Commoner (USA) (108)** (RHannon) **4-8-11** RHughes(3) (hld up: hdwy over 2f out: r.o fnl f: no ch w wnr) | 4 | **2** | 7/1 | 115 | 68 |
| 2113$^{6}$ | **Dance a Dream (116)** (MRStoute) **4-8-9** TQuinn(2) (b.nr hind: chsd ldrs: pushed along & dropped rr over 2f out: kpt on fnl f) | 1 | **3** | 100/30$^{3}$ | 111 | 64 |
| 1988* | **Midnight Legend (113)** (LMCumani) **5-9-0** WRyan(4) (led: rdn 2f out: hdd over 1f out: wknd ins fnl f) | ¾ | **4** | 15/8$^{2}$ | 115 | 68 |
| | | | | (SP 106.7%) | **4 Rn** | |

**2m 28.93** (-1.07) CSF £10.41 TOTE £2.30: (£6.60) OWNER Mr K. Abdulla (NEWMARKET) BRED Juddmonte Farms

**1863* Bequeath**, having only his fourth race, took this considerable step up in class in great style, travelling best and then quickening away from the field as if they were a class below him. He looks set to make up for lost time. (7/4)

**1509 Commoner (USA)** stuck on well in the last quarter-mile to go second inside the final furlong, but was no match for the winner. (7/1: 5/1-15/2)

**2113 Dance a Dream**, the first off the bridle, looked booked for last place but stuck to her task and managed to get third place on the line. (100/30)

**1988* Midnight Legend**, undoubtedly hindered by the rain that fell earlier in the day, was a spent force once headed by the winner. (15/8)

## 2337 VAN GEEST CRITERION STKS (Gp 3) (3-Y.O+) (Class A)

4-05 (4-06) **7f (July)** £20,928.00 (£7,752.00: £3,726.00: £1,530.00: £615.00: £249.00) Stalls: Low GOING: minus 0.31 sec per fur (GF)

| Form | Horse | Dist | Pos | SP | RR | SF |
|---|---|---|---|---|---|---|
| 2037$^{9}$ | **Gabr (113)** (RWArmstrong) **6-9-10** RHills(6) (lw: trckd ldr: led over 1f out: edgd rt & sn drvn clr) | — | 1 | 14/1 | 129 | 88 |
| 1800* | **Inzar (USA) (112)** (PFICole) **4-9-7** TQuinn(4) (led stands' side: hdd & rdn over 1f out: unable qckn) | 3 | 2 | 9/2$^{2}$ | 119 | 78 |
| 818$^{4}$ | **Bin Rosie (104)** (DRLoder) **4-9-2b** RHughes(8) (hld up: hdwy over 2f out: no imp appr fnl f) | 1¼ | 3 | 10/1 | 111 | 70 |
| 2039$^{9}$ | **World Premier (111)** (CEBrittain) **3-8-7** MWigham(2) (lw: racd far side: led 5f: sn btn) | 3½ | 4 | 12/1 | 103 | 53 |
| 2050$^{2}$ | **Ramooz (USA) (106)** (BHanbury) **3-8-7** WRyan(7) (hld up: rdn & hung lft over 2f out: sn btn) | 1 | 5 | 11/4$^{1}$ | 101 | 51 |
| 2072$^{8}$ | **Dance Sequence (USA) (110)** (MRStoute) **3-8-4** PRobinson(9) (swtg: in tch: outpcd over 2f out: n.d after) | ½ | 6 | 8/1$^{3}$ | 97 | 47 |
| 2037$^{7}$ | **Prince of India (107)** (LordHuntingdon) **4-9-2** MHills(5) (chsd ldrs over 4f) | 7 | 7 | 12/1 | 84 | 43 |
| 1770$^{4}$ | **Tereshkova (USA)** (SbinSuroor) **4-8-13** WJO'Connor(3) (lw: racd far side: sn bhd) | 1¾ | 8 | 9/2$^{2}$ | 77 | 36 |
| 1129$^{8}$ | **Diffident (FR) (113)** (SbinSuroor) **4-9-7** BThomson(1) (swtg: chsd ldr far side: ev ch 2f out: sn btn & eased) | 4 | 9 | 8/1$^{3}$ | 76 | 35 |

(SP 116.4%) **9 Rn**

**1m 24.04** (-0.96) CSF £70.83 TOTE £18.80: £3.60 £1.70 £1.90 (£35.70) Trio £55.30 OWNER Mr Hamdan Al Maktoum (NEWMARKET) BRED Shadwell Estate Company Limited

WEIGHT FOR AGE 3yo-9lb

OFFICIAL EXPLANATION **Gabr: his trainer put the horse's apparent improvement down to the fact that the horse had run too freely in his last race, whereas here they were able to settle Gabr to run his own race.**

**1177 Gabr**, running over seven furlongs in this country for the first time since winning the 1994 Beeswing, left his two recent flops behind him and outclassed these in the final quarter-mile, despite his penalty. (14/1)

**1800* Inzar (USA)** set the pace in the centre of the course and definitely had the overall advantage with two furlongs left, but had no answer to the kick of the winner. (9/2)

**818 Bin Rosie**, probably slightly better over a mile, does run the course well and ran to his best. (10/1)

**1151 World Premier** set the pace under the far rail for the two Godolphin horses, but was flagging in the Dip. (12/1: op 8/1)

**2050 Ramooz (USA)** had been set a near-impossible task by the time he was asked to pick up. In the event, he hung to the far side where the ground may have been slightly slower, and his effort came to nothing. (11/4)

**939 Dance Sequence (USA)** again got too warm on a cool day and did not run up to form. She could prove hard to place. (8/1: 6/1-9/1)

**Prince of India** (12/1: 10/1-16/1)

## 2338 ANTEC VIRKON EMPRESS STKS (Listed) (2-Y.O F) (Class A)

4-35 (4-36) **6f (July)** £9,333.00 (£3,447.00: £1,648.50: £667.50: £258.75: £95.25) Stalls: Low GOING: minus 0.31 sec per fur (GF)

| Form | Horse | Dist | Pos | SP | RR | SF |
|---|---|---|---|---|---|---|
| 1954* | **Moonlight Paradise (USA)** (JLDunlop) **2-8-11** PatEddery(5) (lw: dwlt: sn trckng ldrs: led over 1f out: drvn out) | — | 1 | 8/11$^{1}$ | 85 | 56 |
| 2035* | **Queen Sceptre (IRE)** (BWHills) **2-8-13** MHills(6) (lw: chsd ldrs: ev ch ins fnl f: r.o) | 1 | 2 | 15/2 | 84 | 55 |
| 2059* | **Eye Shadow** (BJMeehan) **2-8-8** MTebbutt(4) (led: c stands' side after 3f: hdd over 1f out: ev ch ins fnl f: no ex) | s.h | 3 | 20/1 | 79 | 50 |
| 1352$^{2}$ | **Natalia Bay (IRE)** (PFICole) **2-8-13** TQuinn(1) (in tch: carried lft over 2f out: rdn & kpt on appr fnl f) | 1½ | 4 | 11/2$^{2}$ | 80 | 51 |
| 1878$^{2}$ | **Halowing (USA)** (PAKelleway) **2-8-8** MWigham(2) (w ldr: rdn & ducked lft over 2f out: sn btn) | 1¾ | 5 | 12/1 | 71 | 42 |
| 1352* | **Naked Poser (IRE)** (RHannon) **2-8-13** RHughes(3) (a bhd) | 2½ | 6 | 6/1$^{3}$ | 69 | 40 |

(SP 111.8%) **6 Rn**

**1m 12.58** (0.58) CSF £6.42 TOTE £1.70: £1.20 £2.70 (£4.00) OWNER Sir Eric Parker (ARUNDEL) BRED Allen E. Paulson

**1954* Moonlight Paradise (USA)** moved to post well but, after looking likely to win well, had to be kept right up to her work. (8/11)

**2035* Queen Sceptre (IRE)**, always in the firing-line, stuck to her task well and was coming back for more at the end. (15/2: 5/1-8/1)

**2059* Eye Shadow** tacked over to the stands' side, bringing the whole field with her. Headed in the Dip, she did not go down without a fight and only gave best in the last 100 yards. (20/1)

**1352 Natalia Bay (IRE)** reversed form with Naked Poser on these better terms and might have got a little closer but for meeting interference at a vital stage. (11/2)

**1878 Halowing (USA)** disputed the lead, but came off a true line once pressure was applied and soon surrendered. (12/1: 8/1-14/1)

**1352* Naked Poser (IRE)** was always towards the rear and never posed a threat. (6/1)

## 2339 NEWMARKET HOSPITAL CLAIMING STKS (3-Y.O) (Class E)

5-05 (5-05) **1m (July)** £3,525.00 (£1,050.00: £500.00: £225.00) Stalls: Low GOING: minus 0.31 sec per fur (GF)

| Form | Horse | Dist | Pos | SP | RR | SF |
|---|---|---|---|---|---|---|
| 2133$^{6}$ | **Princess Pamgaddy (50)** (CNAllen) **3-7-6**(7) PDoe(8) (bhd: hdwy over 3f out: led ins fnl f: rdn clr) | — | 1 | 10/1 | 62 | 22 |
| 1469$^{5}$ | **Uncle George (65)** (MHTompkins) **3-9-8v$^{1}$** PRobinson(3) (led: rdn over 2f out: hdd & wknd ins fnl f) | 2½ | 2 | 9/1 | 80 | 40 |
| 1523$^{6}$ | **Half An Inch (IRE) (67)** (BJMeehan) **3-8-8b** MTebbutt(1) (chsd ldrs: rdn & no ex appr fnl f) | 3½ | 3 | 7/1$^{3}$ | 59 | 19 |
| 2135$^{9}$ | **Soaked** (JRFanshawe) **3-9-2** NDay(5) (prom tl rdn & no imp appr fnl f) | 2½ | 4 | 7/1$^{3}$ | 62 | 22 |
| 2006$^{6}$ | **Truancy (81)** (MBell) **3-8-13v**(7) GFaulkner(6) (chsd ldr: rdn over 2f out: wknd over 1f out) | 4 | 5 | 7/4$^{1}$ | 58 | 18 |
| *245$^{4}$* | **Sovereign Prince (IRE) (50)** (NACallaghan) **3-8-1**(3) PMcCabe(4) (lw: dwlt: sn wl bhd: shkn up 4f out: nvr nrr) | 1¾ | 6 | 16/1 | 39++ | — |
| 1691$^{9}$ | **Farfeste (43)** (DMorris) **3-8-0**(3) JStack(2) (in tch tl wknd 3f out) | 1¼ | 7 | 40/1 | 35 | — |
| 2032$^{6}$ | **Honorable Estate (IRE) (70)** (RHannon) **3-8-11** RHughes(7) (chsd ldrs 6f: eased whn btn) | 8 | 8 | 4/1$^{2}$ | 27 | — |

(SP 108.8%) **8 Rn**

**1m 40.23** (3.03) CSF £79.51 TOTE £13.80: £2.60 £1.40 £1.90 (£48.80) OWNER Theobalds Stud (NEWMARKET) BRED K. Panos

Princess Pamgaddy clmd CMcMillan £6,000

**2133 Princess Pamgaddy**, suited by the rain that fell early in the meeting, raced hard against the rail, and found it easier to peg her rivals back on this occasion. (10/1)

**Uncle George** all but bolted to post in the first-time visor and made the running once the stalls opened, only tying up late in the day. This was a big improvement on his recent efforts and he should soon be winning. (9/1)

**1104 Half An Inch (IRE)**, dropped in trip, proved short of speed at the business end. (7/1)

**Soaked**, dropped in class, was in trouble by the Dip. (7/1: op 9/2)

**2006 Truancy**, dropped in trip, still proved a weak finisher and looks one to treat with caution. (7/4)

**Sovereign Prince (IRE)**, having only his second race on turf, was busy on the All-Weather through the winter but had not run since February. Missing a beat at the stalls, by the time his jockey sent him about his business, he was fully ten lengths behind his rivals. These were strange tactics for a horse who has run well over a mile and a quarter, and he looks worth keeping an eye on. (16/1)

**2340** NGK SPARK PLUGS APPRENTICE H'CAP (0-70) (3-Y.O+) (Class E)
5-35 (5-36) **7f (July)** £3,663.75 (£1,110.00: £542.50: £258.75) Stalls: Low GOING: minus 0.31 sec per fur (GF)

| | | | SP | RR | SF |
|---|---|---|---|---|---|
| 2134[5] | **Wild Palm (64)** (WAO'Gorman) **4-9-3v**(5) SCopp(6) (dwlt: sn in tch: rdn & r.o to ld ins fnl f: sn clr)—— | **1** | 5/1[2] | 78 | 60 |
| 1872[10] | **Rise Up Singing (48)** (WJMusson) **8-8-6b** PMcCabe(11) (dwlt: c towards stands' side: hdwy 3f out: r.o fnl f) ..3 | **2** | 6/1 | 55 | 37 |
| 1807[8] | **Cim Bom Bom (IRE) (67)** (MBell) **4-9-6v**[1](5) GFaulkner(10) (led & sn clr: wknd & hdd ins fnl f)hd | **3** | 9/1 | 74 | 56 |
| 862[16] | **Alakhluki (47)** (GLewis) **3-7-10** NVarley(13) (chsd ldrs: rdn & no imp appr fnl f)½ | **4** | 11/2[3] | 53 | 26 |
| 1625[3] | **Talathath (FR) (60)** (CADwyer) **4-9-4** JStack(12) (chsd ldrs: rdn 3f out: kpt on appr fnl f)¾ | **5** | 3/1[1] | 64 | 46 |
| 1840[7] | **Time For Tea (IRE) (67)** (CACyzer) **3-8-9**(7) PGoode(8) (chsd ldrs: styd on appr fnl f: nt pce to chal)hd | **6** | 10/1 | 71 | 44 |
| 2045[4] | **Ballard Lady (IRE) (38)** (JSWainwright) **4-7-5**(5) PDoe(1) (lw: sn prom: rdn 2f out: wknd fnl f)2 | **7** | 20/1 | 37 | 19 |
| 2130[2] | **Persephone (47)** (ICampbell) **3-7-10v** DarrenMoffatt(2) (in tch: effrt over 2f out: no imp fnl f)3 | **8** | 10/1 | 39 | 12 |
| 2156[11] | **Squire Corrie (60)** (GHarwood) **4-8-13b**(5) GayeHarwood(7) (lw: chsd clr ldr over 4f)½ | **9** | 20/1 | 51 | 33 |
| 2193[6] | **Merrie le Bow (49)** (PatMitchell) **4-8-2**(5) AmandaSanders(9) (trckd ldrs tl rdn & wknd 2f out)3½ | **10** | 12/1 | 32 | 14 |
| 2185[3] | **Martinosky (53)** (GCBravery) **10-8-8**(3) LNewton(4) (dwlt: a bhd)1 | **11** | 10/1 | 34 | 16 |
| 1838[7] | **Last Spin (42)** (JRJenkins) **4-7-11b**(3) ADaly(3) (in tch over 3f: sn rdn & bhd)9 | **12** | 33/1 | 2 | — |
| 2130[17] | **Elraas (USA) (40)** (HJCollingridge) **4-7-7**(5) CAdamson(5) (in tch tl wknd over 2f out)1 | **13** | 33/1 | — | — |

(SP 131.7%) **13 Rn**

**1m 26.16** (1.16) CSF £36.34 CT £252.44 TOTE £6.30: £2.40 £2.80 £2.50 (£27.70) Trio £43.80 OWNER Mr S. Fustok (NEWMARKET) BRED Deerfield Farm

LONG HANDICAP Persephone 7-2 Alakhluki 7-9 Ballard Lady (IRE) 7-5

WEIGHT FOR AGE 3yo-9lb

**2134 Wild Palm**, at last with a bit of cut in the ground, raced by the far rail and ran on strongly from the Dip to quickly draw clear once in front. (5/1)

**Rise Up Singing**, playing at home for the first time this year, was unable to adopt his front-running role after missing the break, but stayed on at the end to snatch second place, and is still capable of winning another race at one of the Newmarket courses, where seven of his eight career wins have been gained. (6/1)

**1506 Cim Bom Bom (IRE)** moved poorly to post but bounced back to something like his best in the first-time visor. Well clear with the race apparently won from halfway, it was only in the last furlong that his stride shortened. (9/1)

**Alakhluki** has developed into a decent-looking filly and shapes as if she will stay further than this, despite her recent efforts over five furlongs. (11/2: op 12/1)

**1625 Talathath (FR)** tried hard to get to the leaders in the last quarter-mile but really needed another furlong. (3/1: 9/2-11/4)

**1013 Time For Tea (IRE)** has spent most of her life sprinting, but looks likely to stay a mile. (10/1)

T/Plpt: £156.10 (158.59 Tckts). T/Qdpt: £52.10 (19.12 Tckts). Dk

# 1890-CHEPSTOW (L-H) (Good to firm, Firm patches)

## Sunday June 30th

WEATHER: overcast WIND: slt against

**2341** DAY OUT H'CAP (0-70) (3-Y.O+) (Class E)
2-15 (2-18) **1m 4f 23y** £3,207.00 (£966.00: £468.00: £219.00) Stalls: Low GOING minus 0.52 sec per fur (F)

| | | | SP | RR | SF |
|---|---|---|---|---|---|
| 2191* | **Reaganesque (USA) (47)** (PGMurphy) **4-8-2**(3) 5x SDrowne(1) (lw: mde all: rdn 2f out: r.o wl)—— | **1** | 3/1[1] | 56 | 13 |
| 1874[7] | **Tappeto (68)** (HCandy) **4-9-12** CRutter(5) (lw: hld up: stdy hdwy over 4f out: chsd wnr over 1f out: one pce) 1¼ | **2** | 4/1[2] | 75 | 32 |
| *1458** | **Premier Dance (46)** (DHaydnJones) **9-8-4** AMackay(4) (hld up: hdwy 8f out: hrd rdn over 2f out: one pce)...1¼ | **3** | 6/1 | 52 | 9 |
| 1773[P] | **Royal Expose (USA) (61)** (RHannon) **3-8-2**(3)ow1 DaneO'Neill(6) (a.p: rdn over 2f out: one pce)2½ | **4** | 10/1 | 63 | 5 |
| 1874[9] | **Duty Sergeant (IRE) (41)** (PhilipMitchell) **7-7-8**(5) CAdamson(9) (hld up & bhd: hdwy 4f out: wknd over 1f out)1¼ | **5** | 8/1 | 42 | — |
| *108[11]* | **Missed the Boat (IRE) (41)** (AGNewcombe) **6-7-13** FNorton(8) (hld up & bhd: stdy hdwy on ins 4f out: rdn 3f out: nvr nr to chal)s.h | **6** | 20/1 | 42 | — |
| | **Monty Royale (IRE) (39)** (NoelChance) **7-7-6**(5)ow1 MartinDwyer(3) (hld up & plld hrd: wknd over 2f out)......1¼ | **7** | 33/1 | 38 | — |
| 1816[5] | **Amlah (USA) (64)** (PJHobbs) **4-9-3**(5) RHavlin(10) (prom: rdn 3f out: sn wknd)½ | **8** | 9/2[3] | 62 | 19 |
| *108[12]* | **Strat's Legacy (44)** (DWPArbuthnot) **9-8-2**ow1 SSanders(2) (b: bit bkwd: hld up: a bhd)½ | **9** | 11/1 | 42 | — |
| | **Mylordmayor (38)** (PBowen) **9-7-3**(7) RFfrench(7) (prom tl wknd qckly over 3f out: t.o)16 | **10** | 50/1 | 15 | — |

(SP 115.7%) **10 Rn**

**2m 37.9** (5.50) CSF £14.54 CT £61.00 TOTE £3.90: £1.40 £1.80 £2.20 (£7.90) Trio £21.10 OWNER Mrs John Spielman (BRISTOL) BRED Gainsborough Farm Inc

LONG HANDICAP Monty Royale (IRE) 7-8 Mylordmayor 6-11

WEIGHT FOR AGE 3yo-14lb

**2191* Reaganesque (USA)** does seem to be well suited by forcing tactics and again made all to defy his penalty. (3/1: op 2/1)

**Tappeto**, who stepped up to this trip last time, seems to stay well enough but could not peg back the winner. (4/1)

**1458* Premier Dance** ran his best race on grass for a long time off a mark 22lb lower than when successful at Wolverhampton last month. (6/1)

**Royal Expose (USA)** was taking on older horses after his misfortune last time. (10/1)

**1472* Duty Sergeant (IRE)** was 4lb higher than when winning at Leicester and may need some cut in the ground nowadays. (8/1)

**Missed the Boat (IRE)**, 4lb higher than when winning at Bath last September, should have found this run blowing the cobwebs away. (20/1)

**2342** FAMILY H'CAP (0-85) (3-Y.O+) (Class D)
2-45 (2-49) **1m 2f 36y** £5,540.00 (£1,670.00: £810.00: £380.00) Stalls: Low GOING minus 0.52 sec per fur (F)

| | | | SP | RR | SF |
|---|---|---|---|---|---|
| 1894* | **Roufontaine (68)** (WRMuir) **5-8-13**(5) RHavlin(3) (lw: a.p: led over 2f out: drvn out)—— | **1** | 3/1[2] | 79 | 31 |
| 1872[3] | **Sharp Consul (IRE) (74)** (HCandy) **4-9-10** CRutter(7) (lw: hld up & bhd: hdwy over 3f out: hrd rdn 2f out: r.o ins fnl f)¾ | **2** | 2/1[1] | 84 | 36 |
| 1870[2] | **Askern (66)** (DHaydnJones) **5-9-2** AMackay(5) (chsd ldr: led over 5f out tl over 2f out: hrd rdn: unable qckn fnl f)nk | **3** | 11/2[3] | 75 | 27 |
| 2155[5] | **Set the Fashion (53)** (DLWilliams) **7-8-3v** TSprake(2) (hld up: hdwy over 5f out: rdn over 2f out: r.o ins fnl f) hd | **4** | 11/1 | 62 | 14 |
| 1900[9] | **Muhtadi (IRE) (71)** (JLDunlop) **3-8-9** GDuffield(4) (lw: hld up: bhd fnl 3f)7 | **5** | 8/1 | 69 | 9 |

2203$^{5}$ **Dormy Three (63)** (RJHodges) **6-8-10**$^{(3)}$ SDrowne(8) (hld up: a bhd) ....1 **6** 12/1 60 12
2312$^{7}$ **Cats Bottom (55)** (AGNewcombe) **4-8-5** FNorton(9) (hld up: hdwy over 4f out: rdn & wknd over 2f out) ....½ **7** 11/1 51 3
1981$^{6}$ **Dtoto (70)** (RJBaker) **4-9-6** NAdams(6) (lw: led over 4f: rdn 4f out: wknd 3f out: t.o) ....18 **8** 50/1 38 —
(SP 111.1%) **8 Rn**

**2m 8.9** (3.60) CSF £8.77 CT £25.55 TOTE £3.20: £1.40 £1.20 £1.80 (£2.40) Trio £4.80 OWNER Mr D. J. Deer (LAMBOURN) BRED D. J. and Mrs Deer
WEIGHT FOR AGE 3yo-12lb

**1894* Roufontaine**, raised a further 4lb, had faster ground to contend with this time but held on well to complete the hat-trick. (3/1: op 2/1)
**1872 Sharp Consul (IRE)** appreciated this return to ten furlongs and came up against a course specialist in good form. (2/1)
**1870 Askern** was dropping back to what is probably his most effective trip. (11/2)
**2155 Set the Fashion** looked more at home over this distance. (11/1: 8/1-12/1)
**803 Muhtadi (IRE)** had been tried in blinkers last time. (8/1)
**2203 Dormy Three** is struggling to return a sub-par round. (12/1: op 7/1)

## 2343 SUNDAY MEDIAN AUCTION MAIDEN STKS (2-Y.O F) (Class E)
3-15 (3-21) **5f 16y** £2,992.50 (£900.00: £435.00: £202.50) Stalls: High GOING minus 0.52 sec per fur (F)

SP RR SF
1842$^{8}$ **Miss Stamper (IRE)** (RHannon) **2-8-8**$^{(3)}$ DaneO'Neill(3) (w ldrs: rdn to ld last strides) ....— **1** 12/1 63 20
**Farewell My Love (IRE)** (PFICole) **2-8-11** CRutter(1) (lt-f: dwlt: hdwy over 2f out: led wl over 1f out: hdd last strides) ....hd **2** 11/4$^{1}$ 63 20
1118$^{7}$ **Bramble Bear** (MBlanshard) **2-8-11** AClark(7) (a.p: ev ch over 1f out: one pce fnl f) ....3 **3** 8/1 53 10
2076$^{8}$ **Perpetual** (SirMarkPrescott) **2-8-11** GDuffield(2) (led over 3f: one pce fnl f) ....1¼ **4** 5/1$^{3}$ 49 6
**Scarlet Lake** (DRLoder) **2-8-8**$^{(3)}$ PMcCabe(4) (leggy: w'like: lw: hld up: no hdwy fnl 2f) ....2½ **5** 11/4$^{1}$ 41 —
**Strat's Quest** (DWPArbuthnot) **2-8-11** RPrice(8) (small: lt-f: nvr trbld ldrs) ....4 **6** 33/1 29 —
**April In Paris** (CJames) **2-8-11** SSanders(6) (small: bit bkwd: rdn 3f out: a bhd) ....2 **7** 25/1 23 —
2031$^{2}$ **Charlton Spring (IRE)** (RJHodges) **2-8-8**$^{(3)}$ SDrowne(5) (bhd fnl 2f) ....nk **8** 4/1$^{2}$ 22 —
(SP 115.6%) **8 Rn**

**58.7 secs** (1.70) CSF £43.11 TOTE £14.90: £3.20 £1.30 £1.40 (£26.30) OWNER J B R Leisure Ltd (MARLBOROUGH) BRED Eamon O'Mahony

**Miss Stamper (IRE)**, a half-sister to four winners abroad, stepped up considerably on her debut to touch off a fancied rival. (12/1: op 8/1)
**Farewell My Love (IRE)**, a half-sister to a couple of smart winners in France, was well touted here and should soon go one better in similar company. (11/4: op 6/4)
**Bramble Bear**, a half-sister to Rambling Bear and Bajan Rose, ran by far her best race to date. (8/1: 7/1-11/1)
**2076 Perpetual**, a half-sister to Watch the Clock, had obviously learnt something from her disappointing debut. (5/1)
**Scarlet Lake**, a half-sister to Maid For the Hills and Maid For Walking, comes from a stable suffering from the ups and downs of racing. (11/4: op 6/4)
**Strat's Quest** is a half-sister to David James' Girl and Quest Again. (33/1)
**2031 Charlton Spring (IRE)** (4/1: op 8/1)

## 2344 MADEMOISELLE LADIES' H'CAP (0-70) (3-Y.O+) (Class G)
3-45 (4-04) **1m 14y** £2,416.00 (£676.00: £328.00) Stalls: Low GOING minus 0.52 sec per fur (F)

SP RR SF
2185$^{5}$ **Asterix (39)** (JMBradley) **8-8-11b$^{1}$**$^{(7)}$ MissLKerr(1) (dwlt: plld hrd & sn rcvrd: led wl over 1f out: r.o wl) ....— **1** 6/1 48 35
1661* **Roman Reel (USA) (70)** (GLMoore) **5-11-2**$^{(5)}$ MrsJMoore(5) (w ldr: ev ch wl over 1f out: no imp) ....4 **2** 11/4$^{1}$ 71 58
1468$^{12}$ **Nabjelsedr (41)** (AGNewcombe) **6-9-1**$^{(5)ow6}$ MissMCarson(10) (lw: hld up: hdwy on stands' side over 2f out: r.o ins fnl f) ....¾ **3** 25/1 41 22
2032$^{3}$ **Irrepressible (IRE) (49)** (RJHodges) **5-9-7**$^{(7)}$ MissTDare(6) (lw: led over 6f: one pce) ....1 **4** 4/1$^{3}$ 47 34
2016$^{6}$ **Miss Iron Heart (USA) (35)** (DJSCosgrove) **4-8-7**$^{(7)}$ MissOCosgrove(3) (swtg: prom tl wknd over 1f out) ....1¾ **5** 25/1 29 16
1689$^{11}$ **Bullpen Belle (55)** (PTWalwyn) **3-9-5**$^{(5)}$ MarchionessBlandford(4) (prom over 5f) ....2 **6** 14/1 45 22
2047$^{9}$ **Fighter Squadron (45)** (REPeacock) **7-9-3**$^{(7)ow10}$ MrsCPeacock(2) (lw: dwlt: racd alone centre: bhd fnl 3f) ..2½ **7** 33/1 30 7
1893$^{2}$ **Queen of Shannon (IRE) (47)** (AWCarroll) **8-9-12** MissJAllison(9) (unruly & uns rdr bef s: s.s: hdwy over 2f out: wknd over 1f out) ....5 **8** 8/1 22 9
1893$^{3}$ **Tony's Mist (43)** (JMBradley) **6-9-8** MrsLPearce(8) (prom: rdn 3f out: sn wknd) ....1¼ **9** 3/1$^{2}$ 16 3
**Relatively High (50)** (PBowen) **5-9-10**$^{(5)}$ MrsKBowen(7) (b.nr hind: a bhd: t.o fnl 3f) ....dist **10** 50/1 — —
(SP 116.3%) **10 Rn**

**1m 34.5** (2.00) CSF £21.67 CT £363.26 TOTE £5.90: £2.10 £1.40 £6.70 (£12.60) Trio £87.40 OWNER Mr Clifton Hunt (CHEPSTOW) BRED Sexton Enterprises
LONG HANDICAP Fighter Squadron 8-11 Miss Iron Heart (USA) 8-9
WEIGHT FOR AGE 3yo-10lb

**2185 Asterix**, tried in blinkers for this return to a mile, took a strong hold and soon reached a handy position after another poor start. Running on strongly after striking the front, his rider had quite a job pulling him up. (6/1)
**1661* Roman Reel (USA)**, raised 5lb for his two wins, was trying to repeat last year's victory in this event off an 8lb higher mark. (11/4)
**Nabjelsedr** showed distinct signs of a long overdue return to form. (25/1)
**2032 Irrepressible (IRE)** is suffering from being put up no less than 16lb for his easy Yarmouth selling win. (4/1)
**1682 Miss Iron Heart (USA)** continues to struggle. (25/1)
**Bullpen Belle** was having her first run in a handicap. (14/1)

## 2345 SUNDAY MARKET (S) STKS (3-Y.O+) (Class G)
4-30 (4-33) **7f 16y** £2,458.00 (£688.00: £334.00) Stalls: High GOING minus 0.52 sec per fur (F)

SP RR SF
2229$^{10}$ **Indrapura (IRE) (60)** (PFICole) **4-9-3b** CRutter(7) (mde virtually all: hrd rdn over 2f out: drvn out) ....— **1** 5/1$^{3}$ 59 28
1689$^{4}$ **Jareer Do (IRE) (60)** (BPalling) **4-8-12** TSprake(3) (chsd wnr: ev ch over 1f out: hrd rdn: r.o) ....hd **2** 11/4$^{1}$ 54 23
1819$^{16}$ **Mislemani (IRE) (54)** (AGNewcombe) **6-8-12**$^{(5)}$ DGriffiths(4) (a.p: rdn 3f out: r.o one pce fnl 2f) ....1¾ **3** 7/1 55 24
1473$^{7}$ **Multan (54)** (GLMoore) **4-9-3** SWhitworth(5) (b: a.p: hrd rdn & one pce fnl 2f) ....½ **4** 9/2$^{2}$ 54 23
1497$^{8}$ **Apartments Abroad (47)** (KMcAuliffe) **3-8-0**$^{(3)}$ AWhelan(12) (b.hind: dwlt: hdwy on stands' side over 4f out: rdn over 2f out: one pce) ....3½ **5** 12/1 41 1
1638$^{6}$ **Daring Ryde (45)** (JPSmith) **5-9-3** SSanders(6) (hld up & bhd: hdwy over 1f out: r.o) ....s.h **6** 9/1 46 15
**Pytchley Dawn (40)** (OO'Neill) **6-8-12** VSlattery(11) (prom 5f) ....3 **7** 25/1 34 3
2075$^{12}$ **Pusey Street Boy (45)** (JRBosley) **9-8-10v**$^{(7)}$ AimeeCook(1) (prom 6f) ....2½ **8** 10/1 33 2
2159$^{11}$ **Sobeloved (40)** (NEBerry) **4-8-12**$^{(5)}$ CAdamson(2) (dwlt: a bhd) ....1¾ **9** 25/1 29 —

**Athenian Alliance** (JMBradley) **7-8-9**(3) SDrowne(10) (prom 3f)....2½ **10** 25/1 19 —
**Masimara Music** (JMBradley) **5-8-12** AMackay(8) (v.rel to rce: a wl t.o)....dist **11** 25/1 — —
(SP 116.2%) **11 Rn**

**1m 22.2** (2.20) CSF £17.53 TOTE £6.00: £2.40 £1.90 £2.60 (£7.90) Trio £31.30 OWNER H R H Sultan Ahmad Shah (WHATCOMBE) BRED John Burns
WEIGHT FOR AGE 3yo-9lb
Sold MPipe 3,000gns
**Indrapura (IRE)**, dropped in class, had the blinkers back on and was running over his best trip. (5/1)
**1689 Jareer Do (IRE)** seems perfectly capable of winning a similar event. (11/4)
**Mislemani (IRE)** appreciated the drop into selling company. (7/1)
**1473 Multan** was another running better in the lower grade. (9/2: 8/1-4/1)
**1312 Apartments Abroad** was without the visor this time. (12/1: op 7/1)
**1638 Daring Ryde** kept on in the closing stages without being knocked about, and needs at least a mile. (9/1: op 5/1)

## 2346 DAY AT THE RACES MAIDEN STKS (3-Y.O+) (Class D)
5-05 (5-06) **7f 16y** £3,962.50 (£1,195.00: £580.00: £272.50) Stalls: High GOING minus 0.52 sec per fur (F)

| | | | | SP | RR | SF |
|---|---|---|---|---|---|---|
| | **Lonely Leader (IRE)** (RHannon) **3-8-9**(3) DaneO'Neill(3) (lw: chsd ldr: led over 2f out: rdn out) | — | **1** | 9/4 2 | 84 | 37 |
| 1438 2 | **Present Generation** (RGuest) **3-8-12** SSanders(4) (trckd ldrs: rdn & wnt 2nd 2f out: unable qckn fnl f) | 2½ | **2** | 9/2 3 | 78 | 31 |
| | **New Spain (USA)** (JHMGosden) **4-9-7** AGarth(6) (b: w'like: lengthy: lw: dwlt: rdn & styd on one pce fnl 2f) | 9 | **3** | 10/1 | 58 | 20 |
| | **Itkan (IRE)** (CJBenstead) **3-8-7** MWigham(7) (str: scope: bkwd: s.s: wl bhd tl gd hdwy over 1f out: nrst fin) | 1¾ | **4** | 33/1 | 49 | 2 |
| 1452 6 | **Irish Kinsman (74)** (PTWalwyn) **3-8-12** TSprake(2) (lw: prom 5f) | hd | **5** | 20/1 | 54 | 7 |
| 1994 8 | **Doth Protest (IRE)** (NoelChance) **4-9-2** NAdams(1) (prom: rdn over 3f out: wknd over 2f out) | 3 | **6** | 100/1 | 42 | 4 |
| 1857 7 | **Snowpoles** (MrsJCecil) **3-8-7** GDuffield(9) (dwlt: a bhd) | ¾ | **7** | 12/1 | 40 | — |
| 1901 2 | **Highland Rhapsody (IRE)** (IABalding) **3-8-2**(5) MartinDwyer(8) (led over 4f: wknd qckly) | hd | **8** | 13/8 1 | 40 | — |

(SP 112.5%) **8 Rn**

**1m 21.1** (1.10) CSF £11.93 TOTE £3.40: £1.10 £1.80 £1.90 (£6.10) Trio £31.70 OWNER Mr Salem Suhail (MARLBOROUGH) BRED Barronstown Bloodstock
WEIGHT FOR AGE 3yo-9lb
**Lonely Leader (IRE)**, a well-bred colt, confirmed the promise shown on his one run last season and looks capable of going on to better things. (9/4)
**1438 Present Generation** again finished runner-up, beating the others easily enough, and should not always come up against one so smart. (9/2)
**New Spain (USA)**, a $125,000 yearling, was making a belated racecourse debut and shaped as though he will need at least another furlong. (10/1: op 5/1)
**Itkan (IRE)**, a half-sister to a couple of winners, seemed likely to finish tailed off until picking up well in the closing stages. She should come on considerably for the outing and will benefit from a longer trip. (33/1)
**1452 Irish Kinsman** is not progressing on this evidence. (20/1)
**1901 Highland Rhapsody (IRE)** was bitterly disappointing and may need better ground. (13/8)

## 2347 SUNDAY SPECIAL H'CAP (0-75) (3-Y.O+) (Class D)
5-35 (5-37) **6f 16y** £3,621.25 (£1,090.00: £527.50: £246.25) Stalls: High GOING minus 0.52 sec per fur (F)

| | | | | SP | RR | SF |
|---|---|---|---|---|---|---|
| 2129 4 | **Denbrae (IRE) (68)** (DJGMurraySmith) **4-9-8** GDuffield(2) (lw: swtg: hld up: hdwy & swtchd lft over 1f out: led nr fin: r.o) | — | **1** | 5/1 2 | 75 | 43 |
| *2084** | **Wardara (64)** (CADwyer) **4-9-4v** CDwyer(5) (a.p: led over 1f out tl ins fnl f: r.o wl) | s.h | **2** | 11/4 1 | 71 | 39 |
| 1684 2 | **How's Yer Father (73)** (RJHodges) **10-9-10**(3) SDrowne(3) (lw: prom: rdn & outpcd over 3f out: rallied over 1f out: led ins fnl f: hdd nr fin) | ½ | **3** | 11/4 1 | 79 | 47 |
| 1615 5 | **Silver Harrow (62)** (AGNewcombe) **3-8-4**(5) DGriffiths(6) (a.p: r.o ins fnl f) | 1¾ | **4** | 8/1 3 | 63 | 24 |
| 2000 8 | **Jolto (74)** (KMcAuliffe) **7-10-0** SSanders(8) (lw: b: w ldr: led 3f out tl over 1f out: wknd fnl f) | 6 | **5** | 14/1 | 59 | 27 |
| 1985 8 | **Colston-C (66)** (RJBaker) **4-9-6** SWhitworth(9) (led 3f: hrd rdn 2f out: sn wknd) | 4 | **6** | 8/1 3 | 41 | 9 |
| 840 8 | **Natal Ridge (63)** (DHaydnJones) **3-8-10** AClark(7) (lw: s.i.s: a bhd) | 6 | **7** | 25/1 | 22 | — |
| 1855 12 | **Daydream Island (49)** (RJBaker) **3-7-10** NAdams(4) (swtg: s.i.s: hld up & bhd: t.o fnl 2f) | 14 | **8** | 25/1 | — | — |
| *155 5* | **Warm Hearted (USA) (55)** (AGNewcombe) **4-8-9** AMackay(1) (a bhd: t.o fnl 3f) | 20 | **9** | 20/1 | — | — |

(SP 111.3%) **9 Rn**

**1m 10.4** (1.20) CSF £17.52 CT £39.18 TOTE £5.30: £1.50 £1.50 £1.50 (£6.80) Trio £2.70 OWNER Mr Michael Mellersh (LAMBOURN) BRED Mellon Stud
LONG HANDICAP Daydream Island 7-6
WEIGHT FOR AGE 3yo-7lb
**2129 Denbrae (IRE)** gained due reward for some consistent efforts. (5/1)
**2084* Wardara** continues in good form and only just failed to defy a 6lb higher rating than when winning at Leicester. (11/4: op 7/4)
**1684 How's Yer Father** ran a fine race off a mark 8lb lower than when he last won back in October 1994. (11/4)
**1615 Silver Harrow** found this trip on the sharp side. (8/1)
**Jolto** seems at his best over Salisbury's stiff seven. (14/1)

T/Plpt: £29.00 (500.11 Tckts). T/Qdpt: £19.60 (43.21 Tckts) KH

# 2315-DONCASTER (L-H) (Good to firm, Good patches)
## Sunday June 30th
WEATHER: unsettled WIND: str half against

## 2348 JOBS GALORE 1996 EURO-AMERICAN CHALLENGE AMATEUR H'CAP (0-65) (3-Y.O+) (Class F)
2-00 (2-02) **1m 2f 60y** £3,631.25 (£1,100.00: £537.50: £256.25) Stalls: Low GOING minus 0.20 sec per fur (GF)

| | | | | SP | RR | SF |
|---|---|---|---|---|---|---|
| 2066 W | **Arabian Heights (49)** (MrsJRRamsden) **3-10-5** MrTMcCarthy(7) (lw: hld up: stdy hdwy 3f out: led appr fnl f: styd on wl) | — | **1** | 5/1 3 | 58 | 28 |
| 1496 9 | **Hawkish (USA) (51)** (DMorley) **7-11-5** MrsDArbuthnot(8) (lw: trckd ldrs: led over 2f out tl appr fnl f: kpt on) | 1¾ | **2** | 11/4 1 | 57 | 39 |
| 2206 6 | **Sea God (44)** (MCChapman) **5-10-12** MrAndiWyss(3) (bhd: hdwy 4f out: ev ch 2f out: kpt on same pce) | ½ | **3** | 12/1 | 50 | 32 |

| | | | SP | RR | SF |
|---|---|---|---|---|---|
| 1778[3] | **Rasayel (USA) (56)** (PDEvans) **6-11-10** RevShawnKennedy(4) (lw: trckd ldrs: effrt & ev ch 3f out: one pce)....4 | **4** | 4/1[2] | 55 | 37 |
| 1665[7] | **Glenvally (30)** (BWMurray) **5-9-12v** MrGordonSmith(10) (cl up: led 7f out tl over 2f out: grad wknd)..............1¾ | **5** | 25/1 | 27 | 9 |
| 2162[10] | **Intrepid Fort (32)** (BWMurray) **7-10-0b**ow2 MrTedMaher(1) (hld up: hdwy on ins ent st: ch 3f out: wknd fnl 2f)....½ | **6** | 20/1 | 28 | 8 |
| 2183[8] | **Gallardini (IRE) (39)** (BSRothwell) **7-10-7** MissKathyNeilson(2) (hld up: effrt 4f out: rdn & nvr able to chal)......5 | **7** | 11/1 | 27 | 9 |
| 1828[4] | **Elite Bliss (IRE) (45)** (MJCamacho) **4-10-13** MissSeverineBottani(6) (s.i.s: jnd ldrs after 3f: wknd 3f out).........6 | **8** | 6/1 | 24 | 6 |
| 2163[5] | **Dispol Conqueror (IRE) (40)** (GROldroyd) **3-9-10** MrMichaelFigge(5) (led 2f: chsd ldrs tl wknd over 4f out)....5 | **9** | 20/1 | 11 | — |
| 1821[17] | **Oxgang (IRE) (44)** (JGFitzGerald) **3-10-0** MrChristianGervai(9) (led after 2f to 7f out: ev ch tl wknd over 3f out)....10 | **10** | 11/1 | — | — |

(SP 115.3%) **10 Rn**

**2m 16.32** (9.32) CSF £18.00 CT £142.10 TOTE £5.80: £1.70 £1.40 £3.20 (£8.10) Trio £23.50 OWNER Mr P. A. Leonard (THIRSK) BRED Stud-On-The-Chart
LONG HANDICAP Dispol Conqueror (IRE) 9-6
WEIGHT FOR AGE 3yo-12lb
**1042 Arabian Heights,** staying on strongly, won his first race here and there are plenty more in the pipe-line. (5/1)
**1496 Hawkish (USA)** ran well but, despite keeping on, found the winner too strong. His turn will come again. (11/4)
**Sea God** was having his seventeenth race this year and gave a game account of himself, but failed to quicken enough in the last quarter-mile. (12/1)
**1778 Rasayel (USA)** looked very well and had her chances, but she is high enough in the weights at present and was going nowhere in the last two furlongs. (4/1)
**Glenvally** has won only one race on the All-Weather, and has shown very little else, but she did put up a reasonable performance this time. (25/1)
**Intrepid Fort,** having his thirty-third race, was given a fine ride by sticking to the rail as the remainder spread out, but was still never good enough. (20/1)

## 2349 GREAT YORKSHIRE GOLD H'CAP (0-90) (3-Y.O+) (Class C)

2-30 (2-31) **5f** £5,343.75 (£1,620.00: £792.50: £378.75) Stalls: High GOING minus 0.20 sec per fur (GF)

| | | | SP | RR | SF |
|---|---|---|---|---|---|
| 2137[4] | **Lago Di Varano (83)** (RMWhitaker) **4-9-7v**(3) FLynch(5) (lw: a chsng ldrs: kpt on wl to ld nr fin)....— | **1** | 10/1 | 90 | 50 |
| 1786[3] | **Premium Gift (58)** (CBBBooth) **4-7-13** GCarter(9) (lw: hld up & bhd: nt clr run & swtchd 2f out: qcknd fnl f: hmpd wl ins fnl f: jst failed)....hd | **2** | 13/2[2] | 65+ | 25 |
| 1630[9] | **Laurel Delight (81)** (JBerry) **6-9-3**(5) PRoberts(11) (b: lw: led: rdn 2f out: edgd lft: r.o: jst ct)....s.h | **3** | 14/1 | 88 | 48 |
| 2137[5] | **Bolshoi (IRE) (73)** (JBerry) **4-9-0b** JCarroll(2) (hld up & bhd: hdwy 2f out: squeezed thro: kpt on fnl f)....¾ | **4** | 10/1 | 77 | 37 |
| 2064[7] | **Shadow Jury (60)** (DWChapman) **6-7-12b**(3) DWright(3) (a chsng ldrs: kpt on fnl f)....hd | **5** | 9/1 | 64 | 24 |
| 2064[4] | **Here Comes a Star (77)** (JMCarr) **8-9-4** ACulhane(10) (a in tch: rdn 2f out: nvr able to chal)....1¼ | **6** | 9/1 | 77 | 37 |
| *1492[2]* | **Perfect Brave (58)** (JBalding) **5-7-13** NCarlisle(8) (lw: in tch: rdn ½-wy: no imp)....½ | **7** | 10/1 | 56 | 16 |
| 1974[3] | **Surprise Mission (76)** (MrsJRRamsden) **4-9-3** KFallon(1) (lw: bhd: effrt 2f out: sltly hmpd & no imp)....¾ | **8** | 5/2[1] | 72 | 32 |
| 2119[4] | **Royal Dome (IRE) (71)** (MartynWane) **4-8-12** MHills(6) (chsd ldrs over 3f)....3½ | **9** | 8/1 | 56 | 16 |
| 2064* | **Insider Trader (77)** (MrsJRRamsden) **5-8-11**(7) TFinn(4) (cl up tl wknd over 1f out)....½ | **10** | 7/1[3] | 60 | 20 |

(SP 119.5%) **10 Rn**

**60.75 secs** (2.35) CSF £68.91 CT £858.84 TOTE £12.20: £3.30 £2.30 £3.20 (£49.10) Trio £234.50 OWNER The PBT Group (LEEDS) BRED Miss S. E. Hall
**2137 Lago Di Varano** was fortunate to win this, but did battle in good style to get his head in front near the line. (10/1)
**1786 Premium Gift** should have won this with ease, but she met with mass traffic problems and still only just failed. (13/2)
**864 Laurel Delight,** who missed all last season, is certainly coming back to form and should pick up a race or two. (14/1)
**1829 Bolshoi (IRE)** tried to come from behind this time and had a bit of a barging match to get a run, and failed to land a blow. He is in really good form. (10/1)
**2064 Shadow Jury** normally likes to blast off in front, but was ridden with restraint this time and was keeping on at the finish. He is on a good mark at present. (9/1)
**2064 Here Comes a Star** wasted a lot of energy in the preliminaries and, at present, is not really taking hold of his bit in the race. (9/1)

## 2350 HOME OF SUNDAY RACING H'CAP (0-105) (3-Y.O+) (Class B)

3-00 (3-02) **1m 2f 60y** £9,321.00 (£3,489.00: £1,707.00: £735.00: £330.00: £168.00) Stalls: Low GOING minus 0.20 sec per fur (GF)

| | | | SP | RR | SF |
|---|---|---|---|---|---|
| 1668* | **Ambassador (USA) (85)** (BWHills) **3-8-4** MHills(9) (trckd ldr: rdn to ld ins fnl f: styd on)....— | **1** | 3/1[2] | 100+ | 36 |
| 1530* | **Arctiid (USA) (85)** (JHMGosden) **3-8-4** GHind(7) (lw: led: qcknd 4f out: hdd & no ex ins fnl f)....1¼ | **2** | 6/4[1] | 98+ | 34 |
| 2008[2] | **Celestial Choir (82)** (JLEyre) **6-8-13** RLappin(4) (hld up & bhd: styd on fnl 3f: too much to do)....5 | **3** | 10/1 | 87 | 35 |
| | **Mellottie (94)** (MrsMReveley) **11-9-6**(5) GLee(3) (bit bkwd: trckd ldrs tl lost pl over 3f out: stdy late hdwy)....2½ | **4** | 16/1 | 95 | 43 |
| 2164[7] | **Sarmatian (USA) (74)** (MDHammond) **5-8-5** JQuinn(8) (lw: hld up: nvr nr to chal)....5 | **5** | 20/1 | 68 | 16 |
| 2164[2] | **Hazard a Guess (IRE) (84)** (DNicholls) **6-9-1** AlexGreaves(1) (lw: trckd ldrs: shkn up 3f out: sn lost pl)....4 | **6** | 15/2 | 71 | 19 |
| 728[20] | **Daunt (90)** (JHMGosden) **4-9-7** JCarroll(6) (chsd ldrs tl wknd fnl 4f)....nk | **7** | 20/1 | 77 | 25 |
| 2164[4] | **Carlito Brigante (79)** (MrsJRRamsden) **4-8-10** KFallon(2) (hld up: hdwy whn nt clr run over 2f out: nvr plcd to chal)....nk | **8** | 7/1[3] | 65 | 13 |
| 694[10] | **Prospector's Cove (94)** (JPearce) **3-8-13** GBardwell(5) (a bhd)....1 | **9** | 10/1 | 79 | 15 |

(SP 122.9%) **9 Rn**

**2m 11.6** (4.60) CSF £8.19 CT £35.47 TOTE £4.40: £2.00 £1.20 £2.30 (£3.50) Trio £23.30 OWNER Maktoum Al Maktoum (LAMBOURN) BRED John R. Gaines
WEIGHT FOR AGE 3yo-12lb
**1668* Ambassador (USA)** certainly stays well and, answering his rider's calls, got on top in the final furlong. Longer trips are likely to suit and further success looks likely. (3/1)
**1530* Arctiid (USA)** tried hard to make all but was outstayed. This was still a useful performance and plenty more opportunities will be found. (6/4)
**2008 Celestial Choir** is in really good form at present, but was given an impossible task here, and did well to finish so close. (10/1)
**Mellottie** needed this and just had a quiet run. He looks likely to be a deal better for this. (16/1)
**1585* Sarmatian (USA)** looks very well and trained to the minute, but never got into this and, if caught in the right mood, will do a deal better. (20/1)
**2164 Hazard a Guess (IRE)** did not give his running here and this is best ignored. (15/2)
**2164 Carlito Brigante,** held up in this moderately-run event, found trouble in the straight, and the form here is best forgotten. (7/1)

## 2351 MAIL ON SUNDAY MILE H'CAP (Qualifier) (0-90) (3-Y.O+) (Class C)

3-35 (3-35) **1m (round)** £7,132.50 (£2,160.00: £1,055.00: £502.50) Stalls: High GOING: minus 0.20 sec per fur (GF)

| | | | | SP | RR | SF |
|---|---|---|---|---|---|---|
| 2053[16] | **New Century (USA) (89)** (DNicholls) **4-10-0** JCarroll(10) (in tch: qcknd to ld wl over 1f out: hdd ins fnl f: rallied to ld post) | — | **1** | 6/1[3] | 100 | 47 |
| 2164[8] | **Mbulwa (60)** (RAFahey) **10-7-13** DaleGibson(4) (trckd ldrs: chal 2f out: led ins fnl f: jst ct) | s.h | **2** | 12/1 | 71 | 18 |
| 2045[2] | **Cashmere Lady (74)** (JLEyre) **4-8-13** KFallon(2) (bhd: hdwy whn nt clr run 2f out: styd on wl fnl f: fin 4th, 2½l: plcd 3rd) | | **3** | 100/30[1] | 77 | 24 |
| 2134[12] | **Ninia (USA) (77)** (MJohnston) **4-9-2** TWilliams(7) (chsd ldrs: n.m.r 2f out: styd on wl fnl f: fin 3rd, 1¼l: disq: plcd 4th) | | **4** | 11/1 | 85 | 32 |
| 1832[4] | **Karinska (61)** (MCChapman) **6-8-0** DRMcCabe(6) (bhd: effrt over 3f out: nvr rchd ldrs) | 1¼ | **5** | 9/1 | 62 | 9 |
| 2145[6] | **The Stager (IRE) (74)** (JRJenkins) **4-8-8**(5) ADaly(8) (lw: cl up: led wl over 3f out tl hdd & outpcd over 2f out: nt clr run wl over 1f out: n.d after) | s.h | **6** | 16/1 | 75 | 22 |
| 2134[8] | **Daryabad (IRE) (80)** (TJNaughton) **4-9-5** MHills(11) (lw: in tch tl outpcd fnl 2f) | 2 | **7** | 16/1 | 77 | 24 |
| *2084*[2] | **Keston Pond (IRE) (72)** (MrsVAAconley) **6-8-11** GCarter(9) (lw: cl up: led over 2f out tl wl over 1f out: wknd fnl f) | 1¼ | **8** | 7/1 | 66 | 13 |
| 2010[7] | **Up in Flames (IRE) (71)** (MDHammond) **5-8-10** JQuinn(1) (hld up: effrt on ins whn nt clr run 2f out: nt rcvr) | nk | **9** | 9/2[2] | 65 | 12 |
| 2010[6] | **Queens Consul (IRE) (84)** (BSRothwell) **6-9-9** MFenton(5) (led tl hdd wl over 3f out: btn whn hmpd wl over 1f out) | 27 | **10** | 10/1 | 24 | — |
| 1890[2] | **Wentbridge Lad (IRE) (66)** (PDEvans) **6-8-5v** GHind(3) (lw: b.off hind: s.s: hdwy ½-wy: hmpd & fell wl over 1f out) | | **F** | 7/1 | — | — |

(SP 127.4%) **11 Rn**

**1m 41.2** (4.70) CSF £72.81 CT £267.01 TOTE £7.40: £2.90 £5.50 £1.30 (£76.20) Trio £150.10 OWNER Mr W. J. Kelly (THIRSK) BRED Sterlingbrook Farm

STEWARDS' ENQUIRY Williams susp. 9-12/7/96 (irresponsible riding)

**1703 New Century (USA)**, in a messy race, was one of the few to get a clear run and, after looking beaten, fought back well. (6/1)
**1819* Mbulwa** did what appeared impossible in this rough race and got a run up the inner but, after leading, was just outbattled. (12/1)
**2045 Cashmere Lady** keeps running well, but met with trouble in the race and did well to finish so close. (100/30)
**1528* Ninia (USA)**, who could never get to the front on this occasion, was short of room two furlongs out and, then after finishing third, was demoted a place. (11/1)
**1832 Karinska** was never really in the race and was off the bit from halfway, but she did stay on when it was all too late. Racing on the outside of the field, she did miss all the trouble. (9/1)
**1505 The Stager (IRE)** probably caused a lot of the trouble in the race as he was short of pace halfway up the straight and seemed to get in everybody's way. (16/1)
**2084 Keston Pond (IRE)** had a hard race last time on the Sand and this time tried too long a trip. (7/1)
**2010 Up in Flames (IRE)** got a shade warm beforehand and never saw daylight in the race. This should be completely forgotten. (9/2)

## 2352 'BOBS RETURN' CUP CONDITIONS STKS (3-Y.O+) (Class B)

4-15 (4-18) **1m 6f 132y** £8,031.00 (£2,811.00: £1,375.50: £592.50) Stalls: Low GOING minus 0.20 sec per fur (GF)

| | | | | SP | RR | SF |
|---|---|---|---|---|---|---|
| 1976* | **Corradini (97)** (HRACecil) **4-9-4** KFallon(4) (lw: hld up: hdwy to ld 2f out: styd on wl fnl f) | — | **1** | 7/4[1] | 109 | 49 |
| 1336* | **Prussian Blue (USA) (100)** (HRACecil) **4-9-8** AMcGlone(2) (led: qcknd 4f out: hdd 2f out: no ex) | 3 | **2** | 5/2[3] | 110 | 50 |
| 1017[6] | **Further Flight (110)** (BWHills) **10-10-0** MHills(1) (hld up: effrt over 4f out: outpcd over 2f out: kpt on fnl f) | 2½ | **3** | 15/8[2] | 113 | 53 |
| 929[4] | **Tinashaan (IRE) (97)** (JRFanshawe) **4-9-3** NDay(3) (lw: b: trckd ldr: chal over 2f out: outpcd fnl 2f) | 1¼ | **4** | 8/1 | 101 | 41 |

(SP 110.8%) **4 Rn**

**3m 10.42** (6.82) CSF £6.09 TOTE £2.40 (£3.60) OWNER Mr K. Abdulla (NEWMARKET) BRED Juddmonte Farms

**1976* Corradini** got a lovely run between the two leaders to take it up two furlongs out and, as he certainly stays, the race was soon his. (7/4)
**1336* Prussian Blue (USA)** tried to set a steady pace and then step on the gas early in the straight, but he could never shake off his opponents and was short of toe in the last couple of furlongs. (5/2)
**1017 Further Flight** won this last year, but his customary turn of foot was never there this time and he failed to make a serious impression, despite keeping on. (15/8)
**929 Tinashaan (IRE)** looked fit enough, despite a couple of months off but, stepping up in trip here, found it all too much in the last two furlongs. (8/1: 5/1-9/1)

## 2353 E.B.F. SUNDAY SPECIAL MAIDEN STKS (2-Y.O) (Class D)

4-50 (4-52) **6f** £3,550.00 (£1,075.00: £525.00: £250.00) Stalls: High GOING minus 0.20 sec per fur (GF)

| | | | | SP | RR | SF |
|---|---|---|---|---|---|---|
| 1959[3] | **Sinecure (USA)** (JHMGosden) **2-9-0** JCarroll(3) (mde all: hrd rdn 1f out: r.o) | — | **1** | 11/8[1] | 65 | 20 |
| | **Amid Albadu (USA)** (JLDunlop) **2-9-0** RHills(4) (gd sort: b.hind: trckd ldrs: effrt & rn green 2f out: chal 1f out: eased whn btn cl home) | 1 | **2** | 7/4[2] | 62+ | 17 |
| | **White Hot** (EALDunlop) **2-9-0** MHills(5) (sturdy: s.i.s: bhd tl styd on fnl 2f: nvr nr to chal) | 3½ | **3** | 4/1[3] | 53+ | 8 |
| | **Highway Robber (IRE)** (JMPEustace) **2-9-0** JTate(1) (w'like: bit bkwd: prom: chal over 2f out: wknd over 1f out) | 2 | **4** | 16/1 | 48 | 3 |
| | **Tom Mi Dah** (MDHammond) **2-9-0** KFallon(2) (w'like: outpcd after 2f: n.d after) | nk | **5** | 16/1 | 47 | 2 |

(SP 110.2%) **5 Rn**

**1m 15.44** (4.44) CSF £4.04 TOTE £2.40: £2.60 £1.10 (£2.20) OWNER Mr K. Abdulla (NEWMARKET) BRED Juddmonte Farms

**1959 Sinecure (USA)**, an excitable sort, needed two lads in the paddock and gave trouble at the start but, in the race, he did things well enough. (11/8: 4/5-6/4)
**Amid Albadu (USA)**, a useful sort, ran well, but was very green and will improve a ton for this. (7/4)
**White Hot**, a well-made sort, was clueless early on, but did pick up as the race progressed. (4/1)
**Highway Robber (IRE)**, skittish in the paddock, needed the race here and blew up in the last two furlongs. (16/1)
**Tom Mi Dah**, after getting left behind early on, finished reasonably well to show there is something left to work on. (16/1)

## 2354 DONCASTER 'SUPER SUNDAY MARKET' CONDITIONS STKS (3-Y.O) (Class C)

5-20 (5-21) **1m (straight)** £5,418.80 (£1,755.80: £860.40: £372.00) Stalls: High GOING: minus 0.20 sec per fur (GF)

| | | | | SP | RR | SF |
|---|---|---|---|---|---|---|
| 1824[5] | **Jarah (USA) (102)** (SbinSuroor) **3-9-0** RHills(1) (trckd ldrs: rdn to ld ins fnl f: hdd & nt qckn towards fin: fin 2nd, ½l: awrdd race) | — | **1** | 9/4[2] | 103 | 45 |

| | | | | SP | RR | SF |
|---|---|---|---|---|---|---|
| 1573a[5] | **Polar Eclipse (100)** (MJohnston) **3-9-0** PRobinson(2) (cl up: led over 2f out tl ins fnl f: kpt on: fin 3rd, ½l: plcd 2nd) | | 2 | 8/1[3] | 102 | 44 |
| 1768[5] | **Rio Duvida (105)** (DRLoder) **3-9-4** DRMcCabe(4) (led tl hdd over 2f out: btn whn sltly hmpd over 2f out: fin 4th, 4l: plcd 3rd) | | 3 | 9/4[2] | 98 | 40 |
| 1770[P] | **Aunty Jane** (BWHills) **3-8-9** MHills(3) (lw: hld up: squeezed thro wl over 1f out: r.o to ld wl ins fnl f: fin 1st: disq: plcd 4th) | | D | 7/4[1] | 99 | 41 |

(SP 109.0%) **4 Rn**

**1m 40.51** (3.51) CSF £14.02 TOTE £3.10: (£9.20) OWNER Mr Hamdan Al Maktoum (NEWMARKET) BRED Shadwell Farm Inc

STEWARDS' ENQUIRY M.Hills susp. 9-13/7/96 (irresponsible riding).

**1824 Jarah (USA)** was soundly beaten here and was very fortunate to get the race in the Stewards' Room. (9/4)

**1573a Polar Eclipse** ran reasonably and kept staying on under pressure, but was tapped for toe in the closing stages. (8/1)

**1768 Rio Duvida** looks none too happy with things this year, and was well beaten when being chopped for room approaching the final furlong. (9/4: 5/4-5/2)

**1007* Aunty Jane**, given a dreadful ride, won this narrowly but should have trotted up. She hampered a no-hoper and was then thrown out, which must be hard to bear for her supporters. (7/4)

T/Jkpt: £7,142.90 (0.7 Tckts); £3,018.17 to Pontefract 1/7/96. T/Plpt: £108.60 (210.76 Tckts). T/Qdpt: £6.80 (204.99 Tckts). AA

## 2174-MUSSELBURGH (R-H) (Good)

## Monday July 1st

WEATHER: fine WIND: almost nil

### 2355 COCKLES APPRENTICE H'CAP (0-65) (3-Y.O+) (Class G)

6-45 (6-45) **1m 4f 31y** £2,144.00 (£609.00: £302.00) Stalls: High GOING minus 0.24 sec per fur (GF)

| | | | | SP | RR | SF |
|---|---|---|---|---|---|---|
| 1977[2] | **Bobanlyn (IRE) (52)** (JSWainwright) **4-9-12** RMullen(1) (hld up: hdwy ent st: led wl over 2f out: r.o) | — | 1 | 4/5[1] | 69 | 35 |
| 1640[11] | **Lawful Love (IRE) (32)** (TWDonnelly) **6-8-6** CLowther(4) (hdwy 5f out: chal 3f out: hung rt & one pce fnl 2f) | 9 | 2 | 16/1 | 37 | 3 |
| 2165[14] | **Red Spectacle (IRE) (53)** (PCHaslam) **4-9-13** CarolDavison(2) (lw: led tl hdd wl over 2f out: sn outpcd) | ¾ | 3 | 15/2[3] | 57 | 23 |
| 738[6] | **Balios (IRE) (64)** (MJohnston) **3-9-11** KSked(5) (chsd ldr: ev ch 4f out: hung lft & nt run on fnl 2f) | 7 | 4 | 2/1[2] | 59 | 12 |
| 2056[19] | **Pillow Talk (IRE) (38)** (SWCampion) **5-8-12** VictoriaAppleby(3) (b: prom tl wknd over 3f out) | 27 | 5 | 25/1 | — | — |

(SP 110.4%) **5 Rn**

**2m 41.6** (8.60) CSF £10.71 TOTE £1.40: £1.00 £6.60 (£8.20) OWNER Mrs Sheila Walker (MALTON) BRED Mrs S. A. Pfeiffer and Partners in Ireland

WEIGHT FOR AGE 3yo-13lb

**1977 Bobanlyn (IRE)** found an easy race and won it in good style. (4/5)

**Lawful Love (IRE)**, who had shown nothing previously, looked to be going quite well early in the straight, but had no answer when the winner stepped up the pace. (16/1)

**1870 Red Spectacle (IRE)**, from a yard that is having a bad season so far, looked well, but was easily picked off in the home straight. (15/2: 5/1-8/1)

**738 Balios (IRE)** has been gelded since he last ran, but his attitude to racing left a lot to be desired when pressure was applied. (2/1)

**Pillow Talk (IRE)** showed nothing here once the pace was on early in the straight. (25/1)

### 2356 EVENING NEWS LIMITED STKS (0-50) (3-Y.O+) (Class F)

7-15 (7-16) **1m 3f 32y** £2,577.00 (£722.00: £351.00) Stalls: High GOING minus 0.24 sec per fur (GF)

| | | | | SP | RR | SF |
|---|---|---|---|---|---|---|
| 1850[4] | **Blenheim Terrace (50)** (CBBBooth) **3-8-8** JWeaver(6) (lw: bhd: hdwy 3f out: led wl over 1f out: drvn out) | — | 1 | 9/4[2] | 56 | 22 |
| 2177* | **Ambidextrous (IRE) (49)** (EJAlston) **4-9-8** KFallon(4) (lw: bhd: effrt 3f out: w wnr wl over 1f out: hrd rdn fnl f: r.o) | nk | 2 | 15/8[1] | 58 | 36 |
| 1850[8] | **Contract Bridge (IRE) (48)** (CWThornton) **3-8-7** DeanMcKeown(1) (lw: hdwy 4f out: ev ch 2f out: hung rt appr fnl f: kpt on) | 2 | 3 | 9/2[3] | 52 | 18 |
| 2165[10] | **Diamond Crown (IRE) (42)** (MartynWane) **5-9-6** JFortune(8) (in tch: hdwy 3f out: chsng ldrs over 1f out: kpt on one pce) | 1¾ | 4 | 16/1 | 50 | 28 |
| 2216[2] | **Uplift (50)** (SirMarkPrescott) **3-8-5** CNutter(7) (disp ld tl hdd over 3f out: sn outcpd) | 10 | 5 | 7/1 | 33 | — |
| 2023[11] | **Rapid Mover (30)** (DANolan) **9-9-6b** JCarroll(5) (lw: chsd ldrs: effrt 4f out: outpcd fnl 3f) | 1¾ | 6 | 66/1 | 33 | 11 |
| 2214[9] | **Ihtimaam (FR) (45)** (MrsASwinbank) **4-9-6** JFanning(3) (disp ld tl led over 3f out: hdd wl over 1f out: wknd) | 5 | 7 | 50/1 | 26 | 4 |
| 991[16] | **Ragazzo (IRE) (30)** (JSWainwright) **6-9-6b** LCharnock(2) (chsd clr ldrs tl wknd 4f out) | 28 | 8 | 66/1 | — | — |

(SP 107.1%) **8 Rn**

**2m 27.0** (7.30) CSF £6.10 TOTE £4.30: £1.40 £1.10 £1.50 (£5.00) OWNER Mr A. Lyons (FLAXTON) BRED A. Lyons

WEIGHT FOR AGE 3yo-12lb

**1850 Blenheim Terrace**, from a yard whose charges are all running well, needed to fight to win this, and did it in most determined style. (9/4)

**2177* Ambidextrous (IRE)** ran his usual race, coming from off the pace. Despite trying hard, he was always second best in the last furlong. (15/8)

**1850 Contract Bridge (IRE)** ran well but was inclined to hang right when the pressure was on and just failed to quicken enough inside the last furlong. (9/2: 3/1-5/1)

**1411 Diamond Crown (IRE)** seems to be coming to form, but was always short of a turn of foot over this trip. (16/1)

**2216 Uplift** found this trip too sharp and was left behind in the last three furlongs. (7/1: op 7/2)

### 2357 EVENING NEWS H'CAP (0-70) (3-Y.O+) (Class E)

7-45 (7-45) **1m 16y** £3,420.00 (£1,035.00: £505.00: £240.00) Stalls: High GOING minus 0.24 sec per fur (GF)

| | | | | SP | RR | SF |
|---|---|---|---|---|---|---|
| *2170[9]* | **Maple Bay (IRE) (68)** (ABailey) **7-9-11**(3) DWright(3) (lw: bhd: hdwy 3f out: led appr fnl f: styd on u.p) | — | 1 | 5/1[2] | 77 | 48 |
| 2240* | **Tinklers Folly (63)** (DenysSmith) **4-9-9** 5x KFallon(5) (lw: in tch: hdwy 3f out: ch 1f out: hrd rdn & kpt on) | 1¼ | 2 | 5/1[2] | 70 | 41 |
| 2214[5] | **Thatched (IRE) (44)** (REBarr) **6-8-4** DeanMcKeown(4) (chsd ldrs: hdwy to ld 2f out: hdd appr fnl f: no ex) | 1½ | 3 | 9/2[1] | 48 | 19 |
| 2149[7] | **Allinson's Mate (IRE) (55)** (TDBarron) **8-9-1** JFortune(2) (lw: bhd: hdwy over 2f out: rdn & nvr able to chal) | 5 | 4 | 12/1 | 49 | 20 |
| 2152[4] | **Dr Edgar (61)** (MDods) **4-9-7** JCarroll(9) (lw: led after 1f tl hdd 2f out: sn btn) | 6 | 5 | 8/1[3] | 43 | 14 |
| 1665[10] | **Mary Macblain (36)** (JLHarris) **7-7-3**(7) RMullen(7) (s.i.s: nvr trbld ldrs) | 1¾ | 6 | 66/1 | 14 | — |
| 2023[3] | **Grey Kingdom (41)** (MBrittain) **5-8-1** DaleGibson(8) (led 1f: chsd ldrs tl wknd & eased fnl 2f) | hd | 7 | 9/2[1] | 19 | — |

| | | | | SP | RR | SF |
|---|---|---|---|---|---|---|
| 2120[6] | **Teejay'n'aitch (IRE) (39)** (JSGoldie) **4-7-13b**ow1 JFanning(1) (prom 5f) | 1¼ | **8** | 25/1 | 15 | — |
| 2188[7] | **Three Arch Bridge (68)** (MJohnston) **4-10-0b** JWeaver(6) (cl up: chal 4f out: wknd fnl 2f) | s.h | **9** | 5/1[2] | 44 | 15 |
| | | | | (SP 110.5%) | **9 Rn** | |

**1m 42.9** (4.30) CSF £26.85 CT £102.60 TOTE £8.20: £2.30 £2.30 £1.70 (£33.50) Trio £54.80 OWNER Mr Roy Matthews (TARPORLEY) BRED Berkshire Equestrian Services Ltd
LONG HANDICAP Mary Macblain 7-2
**2170 Maple Bay (IRE)** bounced back to form after a disappointing effort on Sand last time. He does look particularly well at present. (5/1)
**2240* Tinklers Folly** is in the form of his life but, despite a determined effort, could never peg back the winner. (5/1: 7/2-11/2)
**2214 Thatched (IRE)** is running reasonably well, but is not quite doing the business when it matters. (9/2)
**2149 Allinson's Mate (IRE)**, without the blinkers this time, never looked likely to make an impression, despite staying on in the last three furlongs. He gives the impression he is not giving it his best shot. (12/1: op 8/1)
**2152 Dr Edgar**, dropped back in trip, found things happening too quickly in the last couple of furlongs. (8/1)
**Mary Macblain** runs when in the mood and was not doing much here. (66/1)

## 2358 KIDLAW RATING RELATED MAIDEN STKS (0-65) (3-Y.O+) (Class F)
8-15 (8-15) **1m 16y** £2,507.00 (£702.00: £341.00) Stalls: High GOING: 0.24 sec per fur (G)

| | | | | SP | RR | SF |
|---|---|---|---|---|---|---|
| 2123[4] | **Termon (60)** (MissLAPerratt) **3-8-9** JWeaver(3) (lw: led 1f: cl up: led 3f out: rdn & r.o) | — | **1** | 4/1[3] | 66 | 19 |
| 2019[3] | **Fairy Highlands (IRE) (56)** (SCWilliams) **3-8-9** LCharnock(6) (lw: prom: swtchd & effrt over 2f out: sn chsng wnr: nt qckn) | 2½ | **2** | 7/2[2] | 61 | 14 |
| *2158*[4] | **Bright Eclipse (USA) (55)** (JWHills) **3-8-12** KFallon(2) (chsd ldrs: effrt 3f out: rdn & nt r.o) | 4 | **3** | 3/1[1] | 56 | 9 |
| 2167[4] | **Backhander (IRE) (51)** (MartynWane) **4-9-7** JFortune(1) (bhd: hmpd appr st: styd on fnl 2f: n.d) | 3½ | **4** | 11/1 | 49 | 11 |
| 2048[3] | **Madrina (65)** (JBerry) **3-8-9** JCarroll(4) (bhd & hmpd appr st: efft 3f out: sn btn) | 8 | **5** | 4/1[3] | 30 | — |
| 2242[2] | **Creeking (60)** (SirMarkPrescott) **3-8-9** CNutter(5) (led after 1f to 3f out: sn wknd) | 1¼ | **6** | 5/1 | 28 | — |
| | | | | (SP 112.2%) | **6 Rn** | |

**1m 44.1** (5.50) CSF £17.04 TOTE £4.30: £1.20 £3.40 (£14.20) OWNER Miss L. A. Perratt (AYR) BRED Midhurst Farm Inc and Partners
WEIGHT FOR AGE 3yo-9lb
**2123 Termon** has run consistently well all season and did all that was required here for a most convincing victory. (4/1: op 5/2)
**2019 Fairy Highlands (IRE)** had her chances in the last two furlongs, but always found the winner too strong. (7/2)
**2158 Bright Eclipse (USA)** raced up with the pace but, when pressure was applied, did not seem to relish the struggle. (3/1)
**2167 Backhander (IRE)** did not impress on looks and, after getting messed about on the home turn, was never doing enough to get into it. (11/1: 8/1-12/1)
**2048 Madrina**, stepped up in distance again, did not seem to get it. (4/1)
**2242 Creeking** was a big disappointment, dropping out tamely early in the straight. (5/1)

## 2359 TRAPRAIN LAW (S) H'CAP (0-60) (3-Y.O) (Class F)
8-45 (8-45) **5f** £2,535.00 (£710.00: £345.00) Stalls: High GOING minus 0.24 sec per fur (GF)

| | | | | SP | RR | SF |
|---|---|---|---|---|---|---|
| 1859[9] | **Penny Parkes (44)** (JBerry) **3-8-6b[1]** JCarroll(1) (lw: cl up: led 2f out: rdn & r.o) | — | **1** | 6/1[3] | 60 | 40 |
| 2238[4] | **Good To Talk (43)** (TDEasterby) **3-8-5** JFanning(2) (a chsng ldrs: ev ch 2f out: nt qckn) | 3 | **2** | 6/1[3] | 49 | 29 |
| 2176[2] | **Ready Teddy (IRE) (45)** (MissLAPerratt) **3-8-7** KFallon(10) (lw: swtchd lft after s: gd hdwy 2f out: sn chsng ldrs: nt qckn fnl f) | 1¼ | **3** | 11/8[1] | 47 | 27 |
| 1859[10] | **Marjorie Rose (IRE) (59)** (ABailey) **3-9-4b**(3) DWright(3) (lw: in tch: hmpd over 1f out: put hd in air & run on) | 6 | **4** | 8/1 | 42 | 22 |
| 2123[8] | **Distinctly Swingin (IRE) (45)** (MissLAPerratt) **3-8-7** DaleGibson(4) (s.i.s: wl bhd tl sme late hdwy) | nk | **5** | 66/1 | 27 | 7 |
| 2176[5] | **Snitch (39)** (CSmith) **3-8-1v** CNutter(7) (b: w ldr 3f: grad wknd) | 1¾ | **6** | 12/1 | 16 | — |
| 2156[9] | **Kiwud (43)** (TWDonnelly) **3-7-12b**(7) RMullen(6) (led: hung lft ½-wy: hdd 2f out: sn btn) | 1¾ | **7** | 10/1 | 14 | — |
| 1964[5] | **Double Impression (IRE) (57)** (JLHarris) **3-9-5** JWeaver(8) (lw: chsd ldrs tl outpcd fnl 2f) | 1 | **8** | 5/1[2] | 25 | 5 |
| 2238[8] | **Dancing Rainbow (50)** (MJCamacho) **3-8-12** LCharnock(5) (swtg: prom 3f: sn btn) | 1¾ | **9** | 33/1 | 12 | — |
| *404*[6] | **Sporting Fantasy (52)** (JBalding) **3-9-0** DeanMcKeown(9) (spd 3f: sn lost pl) | 1½ | **10** | 33/1 | 9 | — |
| | | | | (SP 122.6%) | **10 Rn** | |

**59.4 secs** (1.70) CSF £40.76 CT £73.01 TOTE £8.40: £2.30 £2.00 £1.50 (£21.50) Trio £15.30 OWNER Mr Joseph Heler (COCKERHAM) BRED Joseph Heler
Bt in 3,500gns
**1634 Penny Parkes** got the favoured stands' side and won really well. (6/1)
**2238 Good To Talk** always held a good enough position, but lacked a turn of foot to do anything about it. (6/1)
**2176 Ready Teddy (IRE)** tried to cross behind the field to get to the stands' side, but the task was always impossible. (11/8)
**524 Marjorie Rose (IRE)** looks to have plenty of ability, but seems none too keen to use it fully. (8/1: op 5/1)
**Distinctly Swingin (IRE)**, a lightly-made filly, was soon a long way behind, but did finish quite well to show there is ability there. (66/1)
**2176 Snitch** did his usual and failed to see the trip out. (12/1: op 8/1)

## 2360 WHITELAW H'CAP (0-65) (3-Y.O+) (Class F)
9-15 (9-15) **1m 7f 16y** £2,703.00 (£758.00: £369.00) Stalls: High GOING minus 0.24 sec per fur (GF)

| | | | | SP | RR | SF |
|---|---|---|---|---|---|---|
| 2165* | **Bold Elect (45)** (EJAlston) **8-9-4** KFallon(3) (hld up: hdwy to ld 2f out: qcknd: comf) | — | **1** | Evens[1] | 60+ | 15 |
| 2175[3] | **Sharp Sensation (37)** (DWBarker) **6-8-10** JCarroll(2) (prom: ev ch over 2f out: styd on: nt pce of wnr) | 2½ | **2** | 7/1[3] | 49 | 4 |
| 2175[2] | **Mister Aspecto (IRE) (63)** (MJohnston) **3-9-5** JWeaver(5) (prom tl lost pl appr st: hdwy 3f out: no imp) | 3½ | **3** | 2/1[2] | 72 | 10 |
| 2175[6] | **Vain Prince (51)** (NTinkler) **9-9-10b** LCharnock(4) (lw: cl up: led 5f out to 2f out: hung rt & sn wknd) | 11 | **4** | 8/1 | 48 | 3 |
| 2165[12] | **Paronomasia (27)** (JLHarris) **4-8-0b** JFanning(1) (lw: led tl hdd 5f out: wknd 3f out) | nk | **5** | 50/1 | 24 | — |
| | | | | (SP 108.9%) | **5 Rn** | |

**3m 23.7** (13.20) CSF £7.37 TOTE £1.70: £1.30 £1.70 (£6.60) OWNER Mr G. Lowe (PRESTON) BRED Home Stud Ltd
WEIGHT FOR AGE 3yo-17lb
**2165* Bold Elect** is in tremendous form and won with something to spare. (Evens)
**2175 Sharp Sensation** keeps running well and should pick up a modest event in due course. (7/1)
**2175 Mister Aspecto (IRE)** did not impress on looks and his attitude left something to be desired in the race. (2/1)
**2175 Vain Prince** has lost his way for the time being. (8/1: op 5/1)
**Paronomasia** has made the first three once in seventeen starts and never looked likely to improve on that. (50/1)

T/Plpt: £8.80 (1377.42 Tckts). T/Qdpt: £8.90 (106.49 Tckts). AA

# 2025-PONTEFRACT (L-H) (Good to firm)

## Monday July 1st

WEATHER: unsettled WIND: almost nil

### 2361 PADDOCK MAIDEN AUCTION STKS (2-Y.O) (Class D)

2-45 (2-48) **5f** £3,403.75 (£1,030.00: £502.50: £238.75) Stalls: Low GOING minus 0.17 sec per fur (GF)

| | | | | SP | RR | SF |
|---|---|---|---|---|---|---|
| 1842[2] | **Largesse** (JohnBerry) **2-8-7** MFenton(10) (w ldr: led 2f out: r.o wl) | — | 1 | 7/2[3] | 84+ | 24 |
| 1801[2] | **Swino** (PDEvans) **2-8-6**[ow3] RPrice(6) (led to 2f out: kpt on same pce) | 3 | 2 | 3/1[2] | 73 | 10 |
| 823[8] | **Melbourne Princess** (RMWhitaker) **2-8-0** FNorton(8) (a chsng ldrs: drvn along ½-wy: kpt on fnl f) | 1¼ | 3 | 25/1 | 63 | 3 |
| 2059[2] | **Suite Factors** (JAGlover) **2-8-3** PRobinson(7) (chsd ldrs: kpt on one pce fnl 2f) | 1½ | 4 | 11/4[1] | 62 | 2 |
| 1858[4] | **Five Live** (MDHammond) **2-7-12** JQuinn(5) (chsd ldrs: outpcd fnl 2f) | ½ | 5 | 9/1 | 55 | — |
| 2138[5] | **Eastern Firedragon (IRE)** (TDEasterby) **2-7-13**[ow1] JFanning(9) (sn pushed along & outpcd: styd on fnl 2f: nvr nr to chal) | 1½ | 6 | 9/1 | 51 | — |
| *1489[5]* | **Court House** (BAMcMahon) **2-8-3** GCarter(2) (in tch: rdn ½-wy: sn outpcd) | ½ | 7 | 20/1 | 54 | — |
| | **Donna's Dancer (IRE)** (TDBarron) **2-8-3** LCharnock(4) (s.i.s: bhd & rdn along: sme hdwy over 1f out: n.d) | nk | 8 | 25/1 | 53 | — |
| 2076[9] | **Strelitza (IRE)** (MWEasterby) **2-8-0** DaleGibson(1) (s.i.s: outpcd & bhd tl sme late hdwy) | 4 | 9 | 33/1 | 37 | — |
| | **The Wyandotte Inn** (RHollinshead) **2-8-0**(3) FLynch(3) (s.i.s: a bhd) | 2 | 10 | 33/1 | 33 | — |
| | **Southerly Wind** (MrsJRRamsden) **2-8-6**[ow1] KFallon(11) (s.s: a wl bhd) | 1¼ | 11 | 14/1 | 32 | — |
| | | | | (SP 118.9%) | **11 Rn** | |

**64.1 secs** (3.30) CSF £13.91 TOTE £2.90: £1.50 £1.40 £4.80 (£6.70) Trio £91.10 OWNER Mrs Rosemary Moszkowicz (NEWMARKET) BRED Snowdrop Stud Co Ltd

**1842 Largesse**, who did not look sharp enough for five furlongs beforehand, showed a round action going down. Showing plenty of speed, he scored in decisive fashion and should go on to better things. (7/2: op 9/4)

**1801 Swino**, fresh and well after a three-month break, tended to hand away from the rail. Carrying 3lb overweight, in the end the winner proved much too good and he had to settle for second spot for the fifth time. (3/1)

**Melbourne Princess**, who did not take the eye in the paddock and showed a poor action going down, ran creditably. (25/1)

**2059 Suite Factors** looked very fit. In trouble turning in, she is obviously flattered by her Nottingham second to the useful Eye Shadow. (11/4)

**1858 Five Live**, keen going to post, should win a claimer or seller. (9/1: op 6/1)

**2138 Eastern Firedragon (IRE)** is not very big and showed signs of inexperience. (9/1: 5/1-10/1)

**Southerly Wind** (14/1: op 6/1)

### 2362 SMEATON (S) H'CAP (0-60) (3-Y.O) (Class G)

3-15 (3-16) **1m 4f 8y** £2,448.00 (£678.00: £324.00) Stalls: Low GOING minus 0.17 sec per fur (GF)

| | | | | SP | RR | SF |
|---|---|---|---|---|---|---|
| *2168[3]* | **Ragtime Cowgirl (35)** (CWThornton) **3-8-8** JFortune(3) (chsd ldrs: shkn up to ld over 1f out: sn wl clr) | — | 1 | 9/4[1] | 43 | 11 |
| 1887[6] | **Ginger Hodg..s (37)** (RMWhitaker) **3-8-10v** FNorton(2) (led tl over 1f out: no ch w wnr) | 9 | 2 | 4/1[3] | 33 | 1 |
| 1762[8] | **Irish Oasis (IRE) (45)** (BSRothwell) **3-9-4v[1]** MFenton(5) (trckd ldrs: rdn & hung rt 2f out: one pce) | 1 | 3 | 5/2[2] | 40 | 8 |
| 1600[6] | **The Fullbangladesh (48)** (JLEyre) **3-9-4**(3) OPears(6) (w ldrs tl wknd over 2f out) | 2 | 4 | 5/1 | 40 | 8 |
| 2180[11] | **Needwood Fantasy (42)** (BCMorgan) **3-9-1v** CHodgson(1) (b.nr hind: pushed along 5f out: sn wl outpcd: sme hdwy over 1f out: n.d) | 3½ | 5 | 12/1 | 29 | — |
| 2060[10] | **Friendly Dreams (IRE) (30)** (PTDalton) **3-7-12b**(5) CAdamson(4) (lost tch over 3f out) | 19 | 6 | 25/1 | — | — |
| | **Mill House Boy (IRE) (25)** (BSRothwell) **3-7-12** JQuinn(7) (sn pushed along: lost tch 4f out: t.o) | dist | 7 | 14/1 | — | — |
| | | | | (SP 114.2%) | **7 Rn** | |

**2m 45.1** (10.80) CSF £11.19 CT £21.00 TOTE £2.90: £2.10 £2.10 (£6.10) OWNER Mr Guy Reed (MIDDLEHAM) BRED D. G. Mason

No bid

**2168 Ragtime Cowgirl**, despite her pedigree, certainly relished the longer trip, and took this bad race even by seller standards by a wide margin. (9/4)

**1887 Ginger Hodgers**, with the visor back on, set out to make it all, but it was obvious turning in that the winner had her measure. (4/1: op 8/1)

**1477 Irish Oasis (IRE)** raced keenly in a visor for the first time. (5/2: op 6/4)

**658 The Fullbangladesh** dropped back beaten before the home turn. (5/1)

**Needwood Fantasy** (12/1: op 8/1)

### 2363 ACTIVE BUSINESS SERVICES H'CAP (0-90) (3-Y.O+) (Class C)

3-45 (3-48) **6f** £7,700.00 (£2,300.00: £1,100.00: £500.00) Stalls: Low GOING minus 0.17 sec per fur (GF)

| | | | | SP | RR | SF |
|---|---|---|---|---|---|---|
| 2114[11] | **Saseedo (USA) (86)** (WAO'Gorman) **6-9-12** EmmaO'Gorman(5) (s.i.s: bhd & pushed along: hdwy on outside 2f out: r.o to ld post) | — | 1 | 11/2[2] | 96 | 71 |
| 2064[8] | **Formidable Liz (56)** (MDHammond) **6-7-10** JQuinn(12) (sn trckng ldrs: led over 1f out: jst ct) | s.h | 2 | 20/1 | 66 | 41 |
| 1786[2] | **Palo Blanco (79)** (TDBarron) **5-9-5** JFortune(13) (hld up & bhd: hdwy on outside over 1f out: styd on wl towards fin) | 2 | 3 | 6/1[3] | 84 | 59 |
| 2213[3] | **Halmanerror (69)** (MrsJRRamsden) **6-8-9** BThomson(7) (chsd ldrs: effrt & outpcd 2f out: kpt on fnl f) | ½ | 4 | 9/1 | 72 | 47 |
| 1829* | **Bollin Harry (81)** (TDEasterby) **4-9-7** MBirch(11) (lw: trckd ldrs: led over 2f out tl over 1f out: kpt on same pce) | ½ | 5 | 8/1 | 83 | 58 |
| 2329[5] | **Fame Again (78)** (MrsJRRamsden) **4-9-4** KFallon(1) (sn outpcd & pushed along on ins: swtchd outside over 1f out: kpt on: nt rch ldrs) | nk | 6 | 7/2[1] | 79 | 54 |
| 2220[7] | **Rock Symphony (84)** (WJHaggas) **6-9-10** TQuinn(3) (s.i.s: bhd tl sme hdwy over 2f out: n.d) | 4 | 7 | 9/1 | 74 | 49 |
| 2114[12] | **Latching (IRE) (84)** (RFJohnsonHoughton) **4-9-10** JReid(4) (trckd ldrs: effrt over 1f out: sn wknd) | 1 | 8 | 12/1 | 72 | 47 |
| 2311[2] | **Prima Silk (70)** (MJRyan) **5-8-10v[1]** TIves(2) (prom tl lost pl 2f out) | nk | 9 | 14/1 | 57 | 32 |
| 2114[22] | **The Happy Fox (IRE) (82)** (BAMcMahon) **4-9-8** GCarter(10) (led tl over 2f out: hung lft & wknd over 1f out) | 3½ | 10 | 20/1 | 60 | 35 |
| 2030* | **Encore M'Lady (IRE) (60)** (FHLee) **5-8-0** DBiggs(9) (swtg: w ldrs tl wknd over 1f out) | 4 | 11 | 12/1 | 27 | 2 |
| 1505[6] | **Miss Waterline (74)** (PDEvans) **3-8-8** LCharnock(8) (w ldrs: sn rdn along: lost pl 2f out) | 1¼ | 12 | 20/1 | 38 | 7 |
| 2329[8] | **Castlerea Lad (81)** (RHollinshead) **7-9-4**(3) FLynch(6) (a in rr: virtually p.u over 1f out: lame) | dist | 13 | 10/1 | — | — |
| | | | | (SP 128.4%) | **13 Rn** | |

**1m 16.1** (1.80) CSF £102.35 CT £644.50 TOTE £6.90: £2.90 £6.10 £2.90 (£109.30) Trio £759.50 OWNER Mr S. Fustok (NEWMARKET) BRED Audley Farm Incorporated

LONG HANDICAP Formidable Liz 7-8

WEIGHT FOR AGE 3yo-6lb

**1149* Saseedo (USA)**, racing from the same mark from which he won at Newmarket, missed the break and struggled to go the pace. Having to make his effort on the outside, he did well to get up on the line. (11/2)
**2064 Formidable Liz** bounced right back to her best and was only collared in the final stride. (20/1)
**1786 Palo Blanco**, raised 5lb, was dropped in at the start and given a lot to do. Making her effort on the outer, she did well to finish so close. (6/1)
**2213 Halmanerror** was chopped for foot at a vital stage and is definitely better suited by seven. (9/1)
**1829* Bollin Harry** travelled strongly but, from a 3lb higher mark, could find no extra in the final furlong. (8/1)
**2329 Fame Again**, making her second outing in three days, had to switch to the outside to get a run. Staying on at the finish, she is much better suited by seven. (7/2)

## 2364 SPINDRIFTER CONDITIONS STKS (2-Y.O) (Class C)

4-15 (4-15) **6f** £4,660.10 (£1,745.90: £855.45: £369.75: £167.38: £86.42) Stalls: Low GOING minus 0.17 sec per fur (GF)

| | | | SP | RR | SF |
|---|---|---|---|---|---|
| 1849* | **Nigrasine** (JLEyre) **2-9-2** JFortune(1) (chsd ldrs: led over 1f out: rdn & hung rt: styd on wl) — | **1** | 8/1$^{3}$ | 98 | 52 |
| 1795$^{2}$ | **Premier Bay** (PWHarris) **2-9-2** JReid(2) (lw: dwlt: effrt over 2f out: sn rdn: styd on ins fnl f) 1¾ | **2** | 11/8$^{2}$ | 93 | 47 |
| 1980$^{2}$ | **Ride Sally Ride (IRE)** (JBerry) **2-9-0** GCarter(5) (led tl over 1f out: nt qckn ins fnl f) hd | **3** | 12/1 | 91 | 45 |
| 2040$^{7}$ | **Fletcher** (PFICole) **2-9-2** TQuinn(6) (chsd ldrs: rdn & outpcd 2f out: kpt on fnl f) 1½ | **4** | 11/10$^{1}$ | 89 | 43 |
| | **Perfect Bear** (MrsSJSmith) **2-8-7** PBloomfield(3) (unf: sn outpcd) 17 | **5** | 66/1 | 35 | — |
| 2118* | **Bold Brief** (DenysSmith) **2-8-12** LCharnock(4) (w ldrs tl lost pl over 2f out) 1 | **6** | 25/1 | 37 | — |
| 1989* | **Magic Blue (IRE)** (RHollinshead) **2-8-13**(3) FLynch(7) (wl outpcd fr ½-wy) 1¾ | **7** | 25/1 | 38 | — |

(SP 117.7%) **7 Rn**

**1m 16.8** (2.50) CSF £19.62 TOTE £7.70: £2.50 £1.50 (£7.90) OWNER Mr M. Gleason (HAMBLETON) BRED Lady Jennifer Green
**1849* Nigrasine**, a grand type, showed tremendous improvement on his initial winning debut at Redcar. Tending to hang right, his rider had to get serious with him inside the last. (8/1)
**1795 Premier Bay** missed the break slightly and stuck on under pressure inside the last, but was never going to seriously trouble the winner, and probably needs seven now. (11/8)
**1980 Ride Sally Ride (IRE)** showed bags of toe and a drop back to five will not bother him. (12/1)
**697* Fletcher** came under strong pressure after halfway. Only keeping on at the same pace, he definitely now needs seven. (11/10: Evens-10/11)

## 2365 WRAGBY MAIDEN STKS (3-Y.O) (Class D)

4-45 (4-47) **1m 2f 6y** £3,598.75 (£1,090.00: £532.50: £253.75) Stalls: Low GOING minus 0.17 sec per fur (GF)

| | | | SP | RR | SF |
|---|---|---|---|---|---|
| 1668$^{3}$ | **Fitzwilliam (USA)** (IABalding) **3-9-0** TQuinn(7) (lw: mde virtually all: rdn clr over 1f out: eased towards fin).. — | **1** | 1/2$^{1}$ | 83+ | 39 |
| | **Taharqa (IRE)** (JHMGosden) **3-9-0** JReid(2) (w'like: chsd ldrs: drvn 4f out: hung lft & one pce appr fnl f) 2 | **2** | 7/1$^{3}$ | 80 | 36 |
| 2140$^{3}$ | **Secret Gift** (BHanbury) **3-8-6**(3) JStack(4) (b: w wnr: rdn & hung lft over 1f out: sn wknd) 3½ | **3** | 5/1$^{2}$ | 69 | 25 |
| 894$^{11}$ | **Devil's Dance (FR)** (MRStoute) **3-9-0** MBirch(3) (hld up & plld hrd: shkn up over 3f out: nvr nr to chal) 8 | **4** | 20/1 | 62 | 18 |
| | **Quinella** (LordHuntingdon) **3-8-9** BThomson(5) (cmpt: bit bkwd: in tch: drvn along 6f out: sn wl outpcd: sme hdwy over 1f out: n.d) 3 | **5** | 14/1 | 52 | 8 |
| 1675$^{4}$ | **The Great Flood** (NTinkler) **3-9-0** DeanMcKeown(1) (sn bhd: sme hdwy 2f out: n.d) 6 | **6** | 50/1 | 47 | 3 |
| 705$^{14}$ | **Latin Lover (GER)** (MJCamacho) **3-9-0** LCharnock(6) (bit bkwd: hld up: effrt 4f out: sn wknd) 5 | **7** | 50/1 | 39 | — |
| 2062$^{9}$ | **Countess of Cadiz (USA)** (TKersey) **3-8-9** TIves(8) (b: sn bhd: t.o 4f out) dist | **8** | 150/1 | — | — |

(SP 111.8%) **8 Rn**

**2m 14.2** (5.90) CSF £4.51 TOTE £1.40: £1.10 £1.10 £1.30 (£3.10) OWNER Mr Paul Mellon (KINGSCLERE)
**1668 Fitzwilliam (USA)** looked a good thing on paper, as the two who finished ahead of him on his debut had both scored since. A long-striding type, he was ridden clear and able to win easing up. This probably took little winning. (1/2)
**Taharqa (IRE)**, who kept swishing his tail in the paddock, showed a fair bit of knee-action. Hanging left, he kept on at the same pace and proved no match. (7/1)
**2140 Secret Gift**, dropped back half a mile, matched strides with the winner but, hanging left under pressure once in line for home, soon called it a day. (5/1)
**Devil's Dance (FR)** is very keen. Having his third run, he is now in the hands of the Handicapper. (20/1)
**Quinella**, an unimpressive mover, looked backward. Soon flat out to keep up, she stayed on late in the day. (14/1: 10/1-20/1)

## 2366 PONTEFRACT SERIES (ROUND 3) APPRENTICE H'CAP (0-70) (3-Y.O+) (Class F)

5-15 (5-18) **1m 2f 6y** £2,566.00 (£726.00: £358.00) Stalls: Low GOING minus 0.17 sec per fur (GF)

| | | | SP | RR | SF |
|---|---|---|---|---|---|
| 2177$^{2}$ | **Kernof (IRE) (47)** (MDHammond) **3-8-0v$^{1}$** FLynch(9) (chsd ldrs: led over 3f out: sn clr: drvn out) — | **1** | 7/2$^{1}$ | 55 | 19 |
| 2058$^{9}$ | **Commander Glen (IRE) (60)** (MrsJRRamsden) **4-9-5b**(5) TFinn(13) (swtchd lft s: hld up & bhd: hmpd over 4f out: gd hdwy over 2f out: styd on fnl f: nt rch wnr) 3 | **2** | 12/1 | 63 | 38 |
| 1887$^{7}$ | **Lawn Order (43)** (MrsJRRamsden) **3-7-5**(5) PDoe(14) (bhd: hdwy over 2f out: styd on fnl f) 2 | **3** | 7/1 | 43 | 7 |
| 2056* | **Mazilla (41)** (AStreeter) **4-8-5** DDenby(10) (lw: hld up: hdwy over 2f out: sn chsng wnr: hung lft & wknd fnl f) 1¾ | **4** | 8/1 | 38 | 13 |
| 2189$^{7}$ | **Hunza Story (32)** (NPLittmoden) **4-7-10** JoHunnam(6) (gd hdwy 3f out: sn chsng ldrs: styd on same pce appr fnl f) s.h | **5** | 33/1 | 29 | 4 |
| 2077$^{7}$ | **Indonesian (IRE) (64)** (PCalver) **4-9-7**(7) KPrendergast(4) (bhd: hmpd over 4f out: styd on fnl 2f) 3½ | **6** | 20/1 | 56 | 31 |
| 2060$^{9}$ | **Leap in the Dark (IRE) (50)** (MissLCSiddall) **7-8-7**(7)ow18 TSiddall(3) (a in tch: no hdwy fnl 3f) 2 | **7** | 33/1 | 38 | — |
| 2027$^{8}$ | **D'naan (IRE) (64)** (WJHaggas) **3-9-3b** CWebb(7) (hld up: hdwy on ins whn n.m.r over 2f out: n.d) 3 | **8** | 16/1 | 48 | 12 |
| 1863$^{3}$ | **Baraqueta (63)** (JLEyre) **4-9-13** DSweeney(2) (mid div: effrt over 3f out: n.d) 1 | **9** | 6/1$^{3}$ | 45 | 20 |
| 2062$^{3}$ | **Secondment (67)** (LMCumani) **3-9-1**(5) RFfrench(15) (cl up: outpcd 4f out: sn lost pl) 7 | **10** | 13/2 | 38 | 2 |
| 2079$^{6}$ | **Old Roma (IRE) (67)** (JohnBerry) **3-9-6** GFaulkner(8) (hld up: effrt 4f out: sn wknd) 13 | **11** | 11/1 | 17 | — |
| 2183$^{15}$ | **Irie Mon (IRE) (53)** (MPBielby) **4-9-3** JWilkinson(11) (prom: effrt over 3f out: sn wknd) 3 | **12** | 20/1 | — | — |
| 2185$^{9}$ | **Just Dissident (IRE) (54)** (RMWhitaker) **4-8-13**(5) PFredericks(5) (led & sn clr: hdd over 3f out: wknd qckly: t.o 2f out) dist | **13** | 25/1 | — | — |
| 1644$^{6}$ | **State Circus (63)** (LordHuntingdon) **3-9-2** AimeeCook(12) (chsd ldrs tl eased & lost pl over 2f out: p.u ins fnl f: lame) | **P** | 11/2$^{2}$ | — | — |
| *1487*$^{5}$ | **Milltown Classic (IRE) (32)** (JParkes) **4-7-5**(5) CCogan(1) (prom: hmpd after 2f: lost pl & uns rdr over 4f out) ... | **U** | 33/1 | — | — |

(SP 132.9%) **15 Rn**

**2m 15.1** (6.80) CSF £46.17 CT £268.32 TOTE £5.20: £2.20 £3.40 £2.70 (£18.50) Trio £70.70 OWNER Mr J. M. Gahan (MIDDLEHAM) BRED David Wallace
LONG HANDICAP Hunza Story 7-3 Lawn Order 7-9 Leap in the Dark (IRE) 7-7 Milltown Classic (IRE) 7-6
WEIGHT FOR AGE 3yo-11lb

**2177 Kernof (IRE)**, fitted with a visor for the first time, was pushed clear and had his race won in a few strides going into the final turn. (7/2)
**1886 Commander Glen (IRE)** was switched left at the start to overcome his high draw. Meeting trouble when Milltown Classic parted company just over half a mile out, he stayed on in good style in the final furlong, but too late to trouble the winner. He clearly appreciates this extended trip. (12/1: op 7/1)
**1887 Lawn Order** sat off the pace. Staying on at the finish, it was hard to know what trip suits her best. (7/1)
**2056* Mazilla** hung left and weakened inside the last. Her rider gets one out of ten for style. (8/1)
**Hunza Story** ran respectably considering she was racing from 7lb out of the handicap. (33/1)
**Indonesian (IRE)** was staying on when it was all over (20/1)

T/Jkpt: Not won; £6,993.03 to Musselburgh 2/7/96. T/Plpt: £52.40 (352.49 Tckts). T/Qdpt: £16.50 (73.43 Tckts). WG

# 2081-SOUTHWELL (L-H) (Standard)
## Monday July 1st
WEATHER: showery WIND: slt half bhd

### 2367 FULHAM H'CAP (0-60) (3-Y.O+) (Class F)
2-30 (2-31) **6f (Fibresand)** £2,381.00 (£656.00: £311.00) Stalls: Low GOING: 0.03 sec per fur (STD)

| | | | | SP | RR | SF |
|---|---|---|---|---|---|---|
| *$2081^{9}$* | **Lady Silk (43)** (MissJFCraze) **5-8-13** NConnorton(2) (lw: hld up: swtchd centre ent st: hdwy to ld ins fnl f: drvn clr) | — | 1 | $6/1^{2}$ | 50 | 17 |
| $2154^{3}$ | **Most Uppitty (48)** (JBerry) **4-9-4** SDWilliams(5) (lw: hdwy u.p 2f out: kpt on ins fnl f: no ch w wnr) | 2½ | 2 | $5/1^{1}$ | 48 | 15 |
| *$1966^{5}$* | **Orange And Blue (40)** (MissJFCraze) **3-8-4c** AMackay(9) (chsd ldr: rdn & hung lft 2f out: kpt on ins fnl f) | ½ | 3 | 10/1 | 39 | — |
| *$1029^{5}$* | **Monis (IRE) (54)** (JBalding) **5-9-10v** GDuffield(1) (sn led: clr ent st: wknd & hdd ins fnl f) | hd | 4 | $6/1^{2}$ | 53 | 20 |
| $1890^{16}$ | **Verro (USA) (26)** (KBishop) **9-7-10e** NCarlisle(7) (bhd: shkn up over 2f out: r.o appr fnl f: nvr nrr) | ¾ | 5 | 40/1 | 23 | — |
| *$2085^{3}$* | **Valiant Man (38)** (JWharton) **5-8-1v**(7) PDoe(8) (hdwy on outside 2f out: nvr nrr) | s.h | 6 | $6/1^{2}$ | 35 | 2 |
| $973^{16}$ | **Forecast (35)** (JWharton) **3-7-13** GBardwell(10) (bit bkwd: sme hdwy fnl 2f: nvr nrr) | 1¼ | 7 | $8/1^{3}$ | 28 | — |
| $2209^{7}$ | **Spanish Stripper (USA) (40)** (MCChapman) **5-8-7**(3) PMcCabe(4) (swtg: hmpd after 2f: effrt wl over 2f out: nvr nr ldrs) | nk | 8 | $6/1^{2}$ | 33 | — |
| | **Dauntless Fort (28)** (MrsVAAconley) **5-7-7**(5)ow2 MBaird(13) (bit bkwd: trckd ldrs: rdn over 2f out: sn outpcd) | s.h | 9 | 33/1 | 20 | — |
| $2061^{11}$ | **Ebony Boy (50)** (JWharton) **3-8-9**(5) RHavlin(3) (lw: rdn along after 2f: nvr plcd to chal) | 1¼ | 10 | 14/1 | 39 | — |
| $1761^{8}$ | **Gormire (60)** (JHetherton) **3-9-10** NKennedy(6) (prom: rdn over 2f out: sn lost tch) | 4 | 11 | 10/1 | 38 | — |
| $1848^{10}$ | **Rankaidade (26)** (DonEnricoIncisa) **5-7-10** KimTinkler(12) (prom over 4f: sn wknd) | ½ | 12 | 40/1 | 3 | — |
| | **Young Rose (46)** (PatMitchell) **4-9-2** DRMcCabe(11) (bkwd: outpcd & a in rr) | 4 | 13 | 14/1 | 12 | — |

(SP 124.3%) **13 Rn**

**1m 19.7** (6.20) CSF £35.19 CT £284.73 TOTE £5.30: £3.10 £1.40 £3.60 (£12.10) Trio £89.90 OWNER Mr Mel Jackson (YORK) BRED Hesmonds Stud Ltd
LONG HANDICAP Verro (USA) 6-13
WEIGHT FOR AGE 3yo-6lb
**1866 Lady Silk** relished this return to her ideal trip with a comfortably-gained success and, as she usually does come good at this time of year, she should be able to defy a penalty. (6/1)
**1492 Most Uppitty** did not find top gear until far too late and, by then, the winner was virtually home and dry. (5/1: op 3/1)
**1966 Orange And Blue**, a stable-companion of the winner, is another who has been competing over the wrong trips in her previous races this term, but she showed here she will not be long in finding another race. (10/1)
**Monis (IRE)**, returning to sprinting, set out to make all, but he had it all to do with topweight, and had shot his bolt when headed inside the final furlong. (6/1)
**Verro (USA)** has not troubled the Judge for many years, but he did show a glimpse of promise on this return to sprinting, and a seller at this trip could be within his reach. (40/1)
**2085 Valiant Man**, pulled to the centre of the track to make his run, kept on willingly under pressure without ever looking likely to reach the principals. (6/1)

### 2368 HAMPSTEAD CLAIMING STKS (3-Y.O) (Class F)
3-00 (3-00) **1m 3f (Fibresand)** £2,381.00 (£656.00: £311.00) GOING: 0.03 sec per fur (STD)

| | | | | SP | RR | SF |
|---|---|---|---|---|---|---|
| $1900^{7}$ | **Nikita's Star (IRE) (73)** (DJGMurraySmith) **3-9-3** DHolland(7) (plld hrd: a.p: led over 2f out: rdn out fnl ) | — | 1 | $11/10^{1}$ | 70 | 26 |
| $1023^{2}$ | **Los Alamos (65)** (CWThornton) **3-9-0** DeanMcKeown(3) (lw: led tl over 2f out: rdn & ev ch 1f out: one pce) | 1¼ | 2 | $9/4^{2}$ | 65 | 21 |
| *$1993^{8}$* | **Classic Affair (USA) (50)** (RHarris) **3-9-2** AMackay(1) (hld up in rr: rdn over 2f out: nvr nr to chal) | dist | 3 | $9/1^{3}$ | — | — |
| $2180^{8}$ | **Danico (52)** (SCWilliams) **3-8-2**(5) ADaly(2) (trckd ldrs: hrd rdn 3f out: sn outpcd) | hd | 4 | $9/1^{3}$ | — | — |
| $2026^{8}$ | **Domusky (28)** (ABMulholland) **3-7-12b**[1] NCarlisle(4) (chsd ldrs: hrd drvn over 3f out: sn wknd) | 1½ | 5 | 33/1 | — | — |
| $1850^{17}$ | **Oare Budgie (35)** (DonEnricoIncisa) **3-7-12** KimTinkler(6) (hld up: effrt & pushed along 7f out: lost tch fnl 4f: t.o) | 12 | 6 | 33/1 | — | — |
| $2062^{8}$ | **Landfall** (JGFitzGerald) **3-9-7** WRyan(5) (bkwd: w ldrs tl wknd 4f out: sn t.o) | 16 | 7 | $9/1^{3}$ | — | — |

(SP 114.3%) **7 Rn**

**2m 30.9** (10.90) CSF £3.96 TOTE £2.00: £1.20 £1.60 (£1.70) OWNER Nikita's Partners (LAMBOURN) BRED D. Twomey
**Nikita's Star (IRE)** did have to work hard to shake off a persistent runner-up, but he always looked to hold the upper hand and had control in the last 100 yards. (11/10)
**1023 Los Alamos** does not fail for the want of trying, but she is finding it increasingly difficult to get off the mark. Her consistency deserves reward. (9/4: op 6/4)

### 2369 DON NOBLE BOOKMAKER H'CAP (0-60) (3-Y.O+) (Class F)
3-30 (3-34) **1m (Fibresand)** £2,381.00 (£656.00: £311.00) GOING: 0.03 sec per fur (STD)

| | | | | SP | RR | SF |
|---|---|---|---|---|---|---|
| $2075^{13}$ | **Roar on Tour (58)** (MrsMReveley) **7-9-12b** ACulhane(14) (lw: a.p: led 4f out: drvn clr 2f out: r.o strly) | — | 1 | 10/1 | 68 | 46 |
| $2023^{9}$ | **Fatehalkhair (IRE) (40)** (BEllison) **4-8-8** JTate(12) (hld up in tch: effrt 3f out: rdn & r.o wl ins fnl f) | 1 | 2 | 12/1 | 48 | 26 |
| *$1966^{4}$* | **Pc's Cruiser (IRE) (43)** (JLEyre) **4-8-11** DHolland(2) (bhd: rdn over 2f out: gd hdwy appr fnl f: fin wl) | 1¼ | 3 | $5/1^{2}$ | 49 | 27 |
| *$2085^{4}$* | **Tame Deer (54)** (MCChapman) **4-9-5**(3) PMcCabe(5) (hld up: hdwy on ins over 2f out: nvr nrr) | 1½ | 4 | 14/1 | 57 | 35 |
| *$1969^{5}$* | **Hadadabble (44)** (PatMitchell) **3-8-3** NCarlisle(16) (trckd ldrs: rdn wl over 1f out: one pce) | s.h | 5 | 16/1 | 46 | 15 |
| $2192^{10}$ | **Shuttlecock (45)** (MrsNMacauley) **5-8-10**(3) CTeague(8) (rdn ½-wy: styd on appr fnl f: nvr nrr) | s.h | 6 | 12/1 | 47 | 25 |

| | | | | SP | RR | SF |
|---|---|---|---|---|---|---|
| *2168$^{2}$* | **Sis Garden (50)** (TDEasterby) **3-8-9b** GDuffield(11) (trckd ldrs: rdn 2f out: kpt on same pce) | nk | **7** | 7/1 | 52 | 21 |
| *2085** | **David James' Girl (53)** (ABailey) **4-9-0**$^{(7)}$ IonaWands(7) (in tch: rdn & outpcd 5f out: effrt 2f out: nt rch ldrs) | 1 | **8** | 7/2$^{1}$ | 53 | 31 |
| 1633$^{7}$ | **Nobby Barnes (45)** (DonEnricoIncisa) **7-8-13** KimTinkler(10) (a in rr) | 4 | **9** | 16/1 | 37 | 15 |
| 2032$^{5}$ | **Ripsnorter (IRE) (37)** (KBishop) **7-8-5** RPerham(1) (s.s: a in rr) | 1 | **10** | 14/1 | 27 | 5 |
| *2081$^{13}$* | **First Gold (50)** (JWharton) **7-9-4** SDWilliams(13) (hld up: hdwy u.p 2f out: wknd qckly fnl f) | hd | **11** | 10/1 | 40 | 18 |
| 760$^{12}$ | **Ruth's Gamble (40)** (MrsLCJewell) **8-8-8v** NDay(15) (s.s: sn drvn along: a bhd) | ¾ | **12** | 20/1 | 28 | 6 |
| 2027$^{6}$ | **Seeking Destiny (IRE) (51)** (MCChapman) **3-8-10b** DRMcCabe(6) (led to ½-wy: wknd over 3f out) | 2 | **13** | 10/1 | 35 | 4 |
| 1411$^{5}$ | **Mezzoramio (45)** (KAMorgan) **4-8-8v**$^{(5)}$ ADaly(3) (b: disp ld: rdn after 2f: wknd over 3f out: t.o) | 7 | **14** | 12/1 | 15 | — |
| *2085$^{12}$* | **Rainbows Rhapsody (33)** (DWChapman) **5-8-1** CRutter(9) (s.s: a bhd: t.o) | 1½ | **15** | 33/1 | — | — |
| 1830$^{5}$ | **Java Red (IRE) (51)** (JGFitzGerald) **4-9-5** WRyan(4) (lw: dwlt: a bhd: t.o) | 18 | **16** | 13/2$^{3}$ | — | — |

(SP 147.9%) **16 Rn**

**1m 46.6** (6.60) CSF £134.84 CT £669.11 TOTE £16.00: £3.40 £1.90 £1.40 £9.30 (£595.20) Trio £450.00; £316.92 to Musselburgh 2/7/96 OWNER Mrs S. D. Murray (SALTBURN) BRED Pitts Farm Stud

WEIGHT FOR AGE 3yo-9lb

**884 Roar on Tour**, back on his favourite hunting ground, was always travelling best, and the narrowness of his success gives no indication of his superiority. (10/1)

**Fatehalkhair (IRE)** has shown no signs of ability in his previous races, but he must have taken an instant liking to this surface and, staying on particularly well in the latter stages, must have given connections a big uplift. (12/1: op 20/1)

**1966 Pc's Cruiser (IRE)** had the headgear left off this time and, though he did not decide to put his best foot forward until far too late, he finished strongly, despite showing a tendency to hang left. (5/1)

**2085 Tame Deer** kept staying on up the inside rail in the last quarter-mile, but he was never going well enough to get himself into serious contention. (14/1)

**1969 Hadadabble** got slightly outpaced when the winner quickened the tempo soon after turning in and, though she did attempt to rally inside the distance, could not produce the speed to deliver a challenge. (16/1)

**2056 Shuttlecock**, struggling with the pace turning out of the back straight, was gradually getting to terms at the finish, but the line was always going to arrive far too soon. (12/1)

**2085* David James' Girl** ran a very lack-lustre race and gave the impression that three quick races in the past month had taken their toll. (7/2)

## 2370 E.B.F. PUTNEY MAIDEN STKS (2-Y.O) (Class D)

4-00 (4-01) **7f (Fibresand)** £4,306.90 (£1,289.20: £618.60: £283.30) Stalls: Low GOING: 0.03 sec per fur (STD)

| | | | | SP | RR | SF |
|---|---|---|---|---|---|---|
| 2132$^{5}$ | **Shimazu (IRE)** (JHMGosden) **2-9-0** WRyan(8) (a.p: led over 1f out: pushed clr fnl f) | — | **1** | 2/1$^{1}$ | 78 | 25 |
| 1197$^{7}$ | **Hurgill Dancer** (JWWatts) **2-9-0** NConnorton(7) (b: in tch: hdwy wl over 1f out: styd on ins fnl f) | 8 | **2** | 16/1 | 60 | 7 |
| | **Rudimental** (SirMarkPrescott) **2-9-0** GDuffield(6) (leggy: scope: bkwd: led after 1f out tl over 1f out: wknd fnl f) | hd | **3** | 9/2$^{2}$ | 60 | 7 |
| 2122$^{7}$ | **Fast Spin** (TDBarron) **2-9-0** ACulhane(10) (lw: hdwy over 2f out: nt rch ldrs) | 5 | **4** | 33/1 | 48 | — |
| 1849$^{4}$ | **Floating Devon** (TDEasterby) **2-9-0** CRutter(9) (dwlt: sn chsng ldrs: rdn & no hdwy fnl 2f) | 1¼ | **5** | 8/1$^{3}$ | 45 | — |
| 1779$^{3}$ | **General's Star** (MRStoute) **2-9-0** TSprake(3) (b.nr hind: prom tl wknd over 2f out: t.o) | 15 | **6** | 2/1$^{1}$ | 11 | — |
| *1489$^{7}$* | **Petula Boy** (MMcCormack) **2-9-0** NDay(1) (a bhd & outpcd) | 3 | **7** | 33/1 | 4 | — |
| | **Union Town (IRE)** (SirMarkPrescott) **2-8-7**$^{(7)}$ TPengkerego(4) (w'like: leggy: bkwd: a bhd: t.o) | 3 | **8** | 16/1 | — | — |
| 1360$^{2}$ | **Going For Broke** (PCHaslam) **2-9-0** TWilliams(11) (led 1f: prom tl wknd qckly over 2f out: t.o) | 5 | **9** | 12/1 | — | — |
| | **Silent Wells** (JJQuinn) **2-8-9** SDWilliams(2) (lt-f: unf: a bhd: t.o) | 8 | **10** | 33/1 | — | — |

(SP 124.2%) **10 Rn**

**1m 33.4** (6.60) CSF £32.63 TOTE £3.30: £1.20 £4.30 £1.50 (£30.10) Trio £92.00 OWNER Sheikh Mohammed (NEWMARKET) BRED Sheikh Mohammed Bin Rashid Al Maktoum

OFFICIAL EXPLANATION **General's Star: had gurgled.**

**2132 Shimazu (IRE)**, always cruising on the heels of the leaders, took command below the distance and did not need to be extended to win in a canter. This easy success will do his confidence no end of good. (2/1)

**1197 Hurgill Dancer** got better the further he went and, though the useful winner proved much too good for him, this was a step in the right direction. (16/1)

**Rudimental**, a newcomer with plenty of scope, looked as though the run was needed and had met his match entering the final furlong. He is bred to stay and time will improve him. (9/2)

**848 Fast Spin** had a quiet introduction to the All-Weather and was never nearer than at the finish. (33/1)

**1849 Floating Devon**, soon in the chasing group after losing ground at the start, should have no trouble improving on this, but he may be better on turf. (8/1)

**1779 General's Star** did not take to this surface and was back-pedalling before reaching the turn into the home straight. This poor effort can be ignored. (2/1)

## 2371 STABLES AND RESTAURANT CONFERENCE & BANQUETING SUITES (S) STKS (2-Y.O F) (Class G)

4-30 (4-31) **5f (Fibresand)** £2,070.00 (£570.00: £270.00) Stalls: High GOING: 0.03 sec per fur (STD)

| | | | | SP | RR | SF |
|---|---|---|---|---|---|---|
| *1968$^{6}$* | **Make Ready** (JNeville) **2-8-8** AMackay(6) (swvd rt s: made virtually all: rdn & edgd lft fnl f: hld on) | — | **1** | 8/1 | 51 | 24 |
| 1645$^{6}$ | **Loch Dibidale** (JEBanks) **2-8-8** NDay(5) (a.p: rdn & carried lft ins fnl f: r.o) | ¾ | **2** | 9/2$^{2}$ | 49 | 22 |
| 2031$^{3}$ | **Come Too Mamma's** (JBerry) **2-9-0** SDWilliams(1) (a.p: rdn & ev ch over 1f out: no ex fnl f) | 1¼ | **3** | 3/1$^{1}$ | 51 | 24 |
| *2083$^{4}$* | **Little Blue (IRE)** (TDEasterby) **2-8-8** TWilliams(3) (lw: trckd ldrs: effrt & hmpd ins fnl f: swtchd rt: nt rcvr) | ½ | **4** | 13/2 | 43 | 16 |
| *1491$^{4}$* | **Sharp But Fair** (SirMarkPrescott) **2-8-8** GDuffield(11) (prom: rdn over 1f out: unable qckn) | s.h | **5** | 7/1 | 43 | 16 |
| | **Assumpta** (CBBBooth) **2-8-8** ACulhane(7) (small: cmpt: bkwd: hmpd s: effrt ½-wy: nt pce to chal) | 1¼ | **6** | 6/1$^{3}$ | 39 | 12 |
| 1858$^{5}$ | **Superboots** (WWHaigh) **2-8-8** RLappin(10) (trckd ldrs stands' side over 3f) | 1¾ | **7** | 8/1 | 33 | 6 |
| | **Poppy Dancer** (BPalling) **2-8-8** TSprake(8) (small: lt-f: unf: b: s.s: a outpcd) | 6 | **8** | 16/1 | 14 | — |
| | **Bonsiel** (JGFitzGerald) **2-8-3**$^{(5)}$ RHavlin(2) (lt-f: unf: s.s: effrt ½-wy: wknd wl over 1f out) | 2 | **9** | 12/1 | 8 | — |
| *1968$^{4}$* | **Shotley Princess** (NBycroft) **2-8-8** DRMcCabe(9) (prom 3f: sn rdn & outpcd) | 1¾ | **10** | 10/1 | 2 | — |
| *2172$^{8}$* | **Ditty Box** (MDIUsher) **2-8-8** MWigham(4) (b: outpcd) | d.h | **10** | 20/1 | 8 | — |

(SP 133.0%) **11 Rn**

**61.1 secs** (4.10) CSF £46.47 TOTE £12.10: £4.00 £1.90 £1.50 (£41.80) Trio £49.00 OWNER Mr J. Neville (NEWPORT, GWENT) BRED J. Neville

No bid

STEWARDS' ENQUIRY Day susp. 10 & 12/7/96 (excessive use of whip).

**1968 Make Ready** swerved left as she left the stalls, but soon had her head in front and, though she was being strongly pressed all the way, she kept pulling out more, despite edging left and slightly impeding the runner-up in the last 100 yards. (8/1)
**1315 Loch Dibidale** ran over six furlongs in her previous race and the way she was staying on at the finish here could suggest that that trip would suit her style of racing. (9/2)
**2031 Come Too Mamma's** had the disadvantage of being drawn in the centre of the track and, though she broke well to share the pace, found an extra effort beyond her inside the final furlong. (3/1)
**2083 Little Blue (IRE)**, staying on when forced to check and switch inside the last furlong, may not have won but she would have gone very close. (13/2: 9/2-7/1)
**1491 Sharp But Fair**, very much on her toes in the paddock, disputed the lead and only lost out in the sprint to the finish. She will get it right one of these days. (7/1)
**Assumpta**, a small, compact filly, was impeded when the winner came across her as the stalls were released. Reaching the heels of the leaders at halfway, she did not shape badly and she will be all the wiser for the experience. (6/1)
**1968 Shotley Princess** (10/1: op 5/1)

## 2372 WESTMINSTER H'CAP (0-65) (3-Y.O+) (Class F)
5-00 (5-10) **1m 4f (Fibresand)** £2,381.00 (£656.00: £311.00) Stalls: Low GOING: 0.03 sec per fur (STD)

| | | | | SP | RR | SF |
|---|---|---|---|---|---|---|
| $1772^{7}$ | **Flow Back (55)** (GPEnright) **4-9-0**(5) ADaly(9) (hld up in tch: rdn 3f out: led 2f out: all out) | — | 1 | 14/1 | 65 | 9 |
| *$2086^{*}$* | **Harbet House (FR) (57)** (CACyzer) **3-8-8** MFenton(6) (lw: hld up: hdwy over 3f out: rdn & styd on towards fin) | ¾ | 2 | $2/1^{1}$ | 66 | — |
| $1862^{5}$ | **Mansur (IRE) (64)** (DRLoder) **4-10-0** DRMcCabe(4) (w ldr: led over 5f out: rdn & hdd 2f out: kpt on fnl f) | 1½ | 3 | $11/2^{3}$ | 71 | 15 |
| *$2304^{8}$* | **Penmar (60)** (TJEtherington) **4-9-7b**(3) OPears(7) (s.i.s: hmpd after 4f: hdwy over 4f out: rdn 2f out: r.o one pce) | 1 | 4 | 12/1 | 66 | 10 |
| $1478^{8}$ | **Top Prize (33)** (MBrittain) **8-7-11v** GBardwell(11) (hdwy 8f out: rdn 5f out: sn outpcd: n.d afterwards) | 6 | 5 | 10/1 | 31 | — |
| $1874^{16}$ | **Nothing Doing (IRE) (37)** (WJMusson) **7-8-1** AMcGlone(3) (trckd ldrs: effrt ½-wy: rdn & wknd over 2f out) | 4 | 6 | 12/1 | 29 | — |
| *$2173^{3}$* | **Charlie Bigtime (50)** (RHarris) **6-9-0** AMackay(8) (b.hind: sn drvn along in rr: nvr nr to chal) | ¾ | 7 | 8/1 | 41 | — |
| *$2082^{U}$* | **Jalmaid (56)** (BAMcMahon) **4-9-1**(5) LNewton(1) (trckd ldrs: rdn 4f out: sn btn) | 2½ | 8 | 10/1 | 44 | — |
| $558^{13}$ | **Inovar (33)** (CBBBooth) **6-7-11** NCarlisle(5) (led 2f: wknd 5f out: t.o) | 8 | 9 | 12/1 | 10 | — |
| *$1031^{3}$* | **Tempering (57)** (DWChapman) **10-9-7** GDuffield(10) (b: led after 2f tl over 5f out: wknd ent st: t.o) | 6 | 10 | $9/2^{2}$ | 26 | — |
| $1697^{5}$ | **Island Cascade (32)** (DonEnricoIncisa) **4-7-10** KimTinkler(2) (uns rdr bef s: a bhd: t.o fnl 4f) | dist | 11 | 33/1 | — | — |
| | | | | (SP 128.9%) | **11 Rn** | |

**2m 47.5** (15.00) CSF £43.99 CT £173.94 TOTE £26.60: £5.90 £1.70 £2.80 (£67.10) Trio £241.90 OWNER Mr D. Leon (LEWES) BRED Sir Eric Parker
LONG HANDICAP Island Cascade 7-6
WEIGHT FOR AGE 3yo-13lb
**Flow Back** has shown little of note since he came from Ireland, but he was a revelation here and had the prize under safe-keeping from some way out. (14/1)
**2086* Harbet House (FR)**, taking on older rivals for the first time, stayed on relentlessly inside the distance, but the winner had taken first run and was not going to be denied. (2/1)
**1862 Mansur (IRE)**, having his first run on the All-Weather, shared the lead and stuck on grimly in the latter stages, but the concession of a stone plus to the principals was more than he could cope with. His turn is near. (11/2: op 7/2)
**1457* Penmar** ran well after getting stopped in his stride and forced to take a pull a mile out. Recovering to track the leaders, he kept staying on under pressure, but had met his match inside the distance. (12/1)
**Nothing Doing (IRE)**, still not fully wound up, did his best to keep tabs on the leaders, but he was throwing out distress signals on the home turn and called enough passing the quarter-mile pole. (12/1)

T/Plpt: £183.00 (58.31 Tckts). T/Qdpt: £55.70 (13.32 Tckts). IM

# 2192-WINDSOR (Fig. 8) (Good to firm, Good in st becoming Good, Soft in st) Monday July 1st
WEATHER: showers WIND: almost nil

## 2373 CADOGAN GROUP (S) STKS (3-Y.O+) (Class G)
6-30 (6-31) **1m 67y** £2,402.00 (£672.00: £326.00) Stalls: High GOING minus 0.09 sec per fur (G)

| | | | | SP | RR | SF |
|---|---|---|---|---|---|---|
| $1893^{5}$ | **Total Rach (IRE) (45)** (RIngram) **4-8-11b** WWoods(10) (hld up: rdn over 2f out: led ins fnl f: r.o wl) | — | 1 | 9/1 | 57 | 37 |
| $1651^{5}$ | **Cape Pigeon (USA) (63)** (LGCottrell) **11-9-7v** PaulEddery(12) (lw: led 7f: rdn & r.o wl) | s.h | 2 | $6/1^{3}$ | 67 | 47 |
| $1890^{3}$ | **Noeprob (USA) (60)** (RJHodges) **6-8-13**(3) SDrowne(9) (lw: a.p: rdn over 2f out: led over 1f out tl ins fnl f: r.o wl) | s.h | 3 | $15/8^{1}$ | 62 | 42 |
| $2130^{9}$ | **Action Jackson (60)** (BJMcMath) **4-9-2** MRimmer(14) (a.p: rdn over 3f out: r.o one pce) | 2 | 4 | 12/1 | 58 | 38 |
| $2189^{3}$ | **Siesta Time (USA)** (RJO'Sullivan) **6-8-11** AProcter(7) (lw: hdwy over 3f out: rdn over 2f out: one pce) | ¾ | 5 | 9/1 | 52 | 32 |
| $2209^{3}$ | **Balpare (50)** (NACallaghan) **3-8-2** WCarson(8) (hld up: rdn over 3f out: one pce) | 2 | 6 | $5/1^{2}$ | 48 | 19 |
| $2192^{19}$ | **Tauten (IRE) (55)** (PBurgoyne) **6-8-11v**[1] NAdams(4) (rdn & hdwy over 1f out: swtchd rt: r.o one pce) | hd | 7 | 25/1 | 48 | 28 |
| $1515^{15}$ | **Our Little Lady (50)** (JRPoulton) **4-8-11** AMorris(5) (a mid div) | 3½ | 8 | 25/1 | 41 | 21 |
| $1099^{11}$ | **Kama Simba (52)** (JWhite) **4-9-2** RHughes(6) (nvr nrr) | s.h | 9 | 25/1 | 46 | 26 |
| | **Northern Saga (IRE) (49)** (CJDrewe) **3-8-4**(3) MHenry(15) (nvr nrr) | 2½ | 10 | 33/1 | 41 | 12 |
| $2180^{14}$ | **Natatarl (IRE) (45)** (BPalling) **3-8-2b**[1] SSanders(3) (lw: a bhd) | 1¼ | 11 | 25/1 | 33 | 4 |
| *$1602^{7}$* | **Kerrier (IRE)** (RHarris) **4-9-2** JHBrown(11) (prom 5f) | s.h | 12 | 25/1 | 38 | 18 |
| $1470^{4}$ | **Spencer Stallone** (LordHuntingdon) **3-8-4**(3) AWhelan(2) (a bhd) | 2 | 13 | 11/1 | 34 | 5 |
| $2253^{6}$ | **Current Leader (51)** (RHannon) **3-8-4**(3) DaneO'Neill(1) (a bhd) | 2 | 14 | 11/1 | 31 | 2 |
| $748^{19}$ | **Longhill Boy (42)** (BJMeehan) **3-8-7b** BDoyle(13) (chsd ldr over 7f out tl over 3f out: sn wknd: t.o) | dist | 15 | 33/1 | — | — |
| | | | | (SP 135.2%) | **15 Rn** | |

**1m 47.4** (5.20) CSF £64.31 TOTE £8.70: £2.30 £1.90 £1.10 (£37.50) Trio £16.20 OWNER Mrs A. V. Cappuccini (EPSOM) BRED Oldtown Stud
WEIGHT FOR AGE 3yo-9lb
Bt in 4,400 gns
**1893 Total Rach (IRE)** eventually managed to get on top inside the final furlong and just held off her very persistent rivals. (9/1: 6/1-10/1)
**1651 Cape Pigeon (USA)** goes well in this grade round here. Merrily bowling along in front, he was collared over a furlong out but, refusing to give way, went down by only a whisker. (6/1: op 4/1)

**1890 Noeprob (USA)** only just failed to gain her third selling victory here, and lost absolutely nothing in defeat. (15/8)
**Action Jackson** stayed on in the final quarter-mile without posing a serious threat. He is still a maiden. (12/1: op 6/1)
**2189 Siesta Time (USA)** was only treading water in the final quarter-mile. (9/1)
**2209 Balpare** was made to look very pedestrian in the last three furlongs. (5/1)

## 2374 SUNLEY MAIDEN AUCTION STKS (2-Y.O) (Class D)

7-00 (7-02) **5f 10y** £3,387.50 (£1,025.00: £500.00: £237.50) Stalls: High GOING minus 0.09 sec per fur (G)

| | | | | SP | RR | SF |
|---|---|---|---|---|---|---|
| 2195[6] | **Rudi's Pet (IRE)** (RHannon) **2-8-10** JReid(11) (mde virtually all: rdn out) | — | **1** | 5/2[1] | 74 | 31 |
| | **Sous Le Nez** (RGuest) **2-7-11**(3) MHenry(3) (neat: a.p: rdn over 2f out: unable qckn) | 2½ | **2** | 13/2 | 56 | 13 |
| | **Levelled** (MRChannon) **2-8-0**(5) PPMurphy(8) (unf: bit bkwd: a.p: ev ch 2f out: one pce) | 1¾ | **3** | 5/1[3] | 56 | 13 |
| 1842[5] | **Threeplay (IRE)** (JAkehurst) **2-8-5** SWhitworth(7) (rdn thrght: hdwy over 1f out: r.o) | ¾ | **4** | 7/2[2] | 53 | 10 |
| | **Broughtons Error** (WJMusson) **2-8-3** BDoyle(4) (unf: bit bkwd: s.s: rdn thrght: hdwy over 1f out: nvr nrr) | ¾ | **5** | 33/1 | 49 | 6 |
| 2059[6] | **The Four Isles** (DHaydnJones) **2-8-3** FNorton(2) (nvr nr to chal) | 1¼ | **6** | 14/1 | 45 | 2 |
| 1982[6] | **Tailwind** (WRMuir) **2-8-4**ow1 WWoods(1) (a.p: rdn over 2f out: wknd over 1f out) | ¾ | **7** | 12/1 | 43 | — |
| 569[8] | **Countless Times** (WRMuir) **2-8-10** RHughes(6) (bit bkwd: a mid div) | 3 | **8** | 16/1 | 40 | — |
| 2059[7] | **Hever Golf Stormer (IRE)** (TJNaughton) **2-8-7** PaulEddery(9) (bhd fnl 2f) | 3½ | **9** | 20/1 | 26 | — |
| 1834[3] | **Life On The Street** (RHannon) **2-8-5** DHolland(5) (spd over 2f) | 8 | **10** | 6/1 | — | — |
| | **Rotherfield Queen (IRE)** (GMMcCourt) **2-8-0** JFEgan(10) (w'like: bit bkwd: s.s: a bhd) | 4 | **11** | 12/1 | — | — |
| | **Leg Beforum (IRE)** (GLMoore) **2-8-3** SSanders(12) (w'like: bit bkwd: s.s: a bhd) | 3½ | **12** | 33/1 | — | — |
| | | | | (SP 133.7%) | **12 Rn** | |

**62.5 secs** (3.30) CSF £20.97 TOTE £2.70: £1.30 £2.20 £1.90 (£21.10) Trio £74.60 OWNER The Broadgate Partnership (MARLBOROUGH) BRED Declan MacPartlin

OFFICIAL EXPLANATION **Life On The Street: the rider reported that his instructions were to jump the filly out and ride the race as he found it, but she had lost her place and failed to handle the soft ground.**

**2195 Rudi's Pet (IRE)**, who disappointed here last Monday, made no mistake on this occasion and was ridden to assert his superiority from below the distance. (5/2)
**Sous Le Nez**, a neatly-made filly, failed to contain the winner from below the distance. (13/2: op 3/1)
**Levelled**, quite a lengthy gelding, threatened to take the lead a quarter of a mile out, but lack of a previous run took its toll, and he could only keep on at one pace. Sure to strip a lot fitter for this, he should soon find a race. (5/1: 4/1-6/1)
**1842 Threeplay (IRE)**, ridden along from start to finish, was doing all his best work in the last furlong and a half. (7/2: tchd 89/2)
**Broughtons Error**, who looked as though the run would do him good, lost ground at the start and was quickly being bustled along. He stayed on from below the distance, but never threatened to get into the argument. (33/1)
**Rotherfield Queen (IRE)** (12/1: 6/1-14/1)

## 2375 CORAL S.I.A. BILL SHAND-KYDD CONDITIONS STKS (2-Y.O F) (Class C)

7-30 (7-30) **5f 217y** £4,624.80 (£1,684.80: £822.40: £352.00: £156.00) Stalls: High GOING minus 0.09 sec per fur (G)

| | | | | SP | RR | SF |
|---|---|---|---|---|---|---|
| 1998[3] | **Fanny's Choice (IRE)** (RHannon) **2-8-5**(3) DaneO'Neill(1) (lw: hld up: led over 2f out: rdn out) | — | **1** | 6/1 | 84 | 28 |
| 1678* | **Passiflora** (JLDunlop) **2-8-12** TQuinn(5) (hld up: chsd wnr over 1f out: unable qckn) | 1¾ | **2** | 7/4[1] | 83 | 27 |
| 2051[11] | **Saunders Wren** (MRChannon) **2-8-12** RHughes(4) (led over 3f: wknd fnl f) | 3½ | **3** | 7/2[3] | 74 | 18 |
| 1980[4] | **Mirror Four Life (IRE)** (MHTompkins) **2-8-8** PRobinson(2) (stumbled s: hld up: rdn wl over 1f out: wknd fnl f) | ½ | **4** | 14/1 | 69 | 13 |
| 1590* | **Red Embers** (RHannon) **2-8-12** JReid(3) (w ldr over 2f: wknd over 2f out) | 12 | **5** | 9/4[2] | 41 | — |
| | | | | (SP 110.3%) | **5 Rn** | |

**1m 14.5** (4.00) CSF £16.05 TOTE £5.50: £1.90 £1.60 (£6.40) OWNER Mr N. Ahamad (MARLBOROUGH) BRED Peter Magnier

OFFICIAL EXPLANATION **Red Embers: the jockey stated that the filly was never travelling.**

**1998 Fanny's Choice (IRE)**, tucked in behind the front two, went on over a quarter of a mile from home and, ridden along, asserted from below the distance. (6/1)
**1678* Passiflora**, held up but well in touch, moved into second place approaching the final furlong but failed to reel in the winner. She will do better over further. (7/4)
**1315* Saunders Wren** faded in the last 200 yards. (7/2)
**869* Mirror Four Life (IRE)** had nothing more to offer inside the distance. (14/1)
**1590* Red Embers** was very disappointing. Racing with the leader until nearly halfway, she then dropped tamely away. (9/4: op 6/4)

## 2376 CREDIT LYONNAIS LAING H'CAP (0-70) (3-Y.O+) (Class E)

8-00 (8-00) **5f 217y** £2,981.25 (£900.00: £437.50: £103.13: £103.13) Stalls: High GOING minus 0.09 sec per fur (G)

| | | | | SP | RR | SF |
|---|---|---|---|---|---|---|
| 1642[6] | **Blushing Grenadier (IRE) (47)** (MJFetherston-Godley) **4-8-5v**ow1 DHolland(2) (racd far side: mde all: eased ins fnl f) | — | **1** | 14/1 | 63? | 45 |
| 2229[7] | **Victory Team (IRE) (65)** (GBBalding) **4-9-9** TQuinn(11) (a.p: rdn over 2f out: unable qckn) | 4 | **2** | 8/1 | 70 | 53 |
| 2185* | **Cheeky Chappy (52)** (DWChapman) **5-8-10b** 7x JQuinn(8) (a.p: rdn over 1f out: one pce) | 1 | **3** | 9/2[2] | 55 | 38 |
| 1985[12] | **Tinker Osmaston (67)** (MSSaunders) **5-9-11** RPrice(12) (a.p: rdn over 2f out: one pce) | 4 | **4** | 14/1 | 59 | 42 |
| *2171** | **Cretan Gift (68)** (NPLittmoden) **5-9-9b**(3) DaneO'Neill(9) (rdn 4f out: hdwy 2f out: one pce) | d.h | **4** | 4/1[1] | 60 | 43 |
| 2193[3] | **Louisville Belle (IRE) (44)** (MDIUsher) **7-8-2** SSanders(4) (racd far side: hld up: swtchd rt over 3f out: rdn over 1f out: wknd fnl f) | 2½ | **6** | 6/1 | 29 | 12 |
| 2034[5] | **Persian Butterfly (65)** (ICampbell) **4-9-9** AClark(7) (lw: dwlt: nvr nrr) | 1¾ | **7** | 5/1[3] | 46 | 29 |
| 2228[4] | **Be Warned (70)** (NACallaghan) **5-10-0** PaulEddery(3) (lw: rdn over 2f out: sme hdwy 1f out: sn wknd) | 4 | **8** | 6/1 | 40 | 23 |
| 1013[7] | **Nomadic Dancer (IRE) (38)** (MSSaunders) **4-7-10** NAdams(6) (hdwy over 2f out: wknd over 1f out) | 3 | **9** | 33/1 | — | — |
| 1844[10] | **Speedy Classic (USA) (58)** (MJHeaton-Ellis) **7-8-13**(3) SDrowne(5) (prom 4f) | 3 | **10** | 16/1 | 12 | — |
| 2032[11] | **Ism (55)** (MajorWRHern) **4-8-13b** RHills(10) (bhd fnl 2f) | ½ | **11** | 14/1 | 8 | — |
| 1594[12] | **Beauchamp Kate (63)** (HCandy) **3-9-1b**1 CRutter(1) (b.hind: racd far side: swtchd rt over 3f out: bhd fnl 3f) | 2 | **12** | 20/1 | 10 | — |
| | | | | (SP 128.1%) | **12 Rn** | |

**1m 13.1** (2.60) CSF £118.82 CT £557.08 TOTE £22.10: £4.50 £2.70 £1.70 (£100.50) Trio £118.70 OWNER The Pavilion Enders (EAST ILSLEY) BRED James M. Egan

LONG HANDICAP Nomadic Dancer (IRE) 7-9

WEIGHT FOR AGE 3yo-6lb

IN-FOCUS: **Three runners set off to race on the far side in search of better ground, but two came back to join the stands'-side group, leaving the winner to race alone. This was an astute piece of riding by Holland.**

**1642 Blushing Grenadier (IRE)** was given a very enterprising ride by Holland. Making all the running, he had things nicely sewn up inside the final furlong. (14/1)
**1121 Victory Team (IRE)**, always close up on the stands' side, had a ding-dong battle with the third in the last two furlongs, but was unable to get to the winner who was racing on the opposite side of the track. (8/1)
**2185* Cheeky Chappy**, in the firing-line on the stands' side, had a ding-dong battle with Victory Team, but was unable to get to the winner on the opposite side of the course. (9/2: 3/1-5/1)
**1466 Tinker Osmaston** could only plod on at one pace in the last two furlongs. (14/1)
**2171* Cretan Gift**, soon being bustled along, made an effort a quarter of a mile out but could then make no further impression. (4/1: 5/2-9/2)
**2193 Louisville Belle (IRE)** started off by racing on the far rail but her jockey decided to switch her over to the stands'-side group before halfway. (6/1)

## 2377 FAUCETS FOR SHOWERING AND HANDWASHING EQUIPMENT H'CAP (0-75) (3-Y.O+) (Class D)

8-30 (8-30) **1m 3f 135y** £3,870.00 (£1,170.00: £570.00: £270.00) Stalls: High GOING minus 0.09 sec per fur (G)

| Form | Horse | Dist | Pos | SP | RR | SF |
|---|---|---|---|---|---|---|
| 1965[12] | **Newport Knight (61)** (RAkehurst) **5-9-1** TQuinn(9) (b.off hind: hdwy over 2f out: led ins fnl f: rdn out) | — | **1** | 7/1[3] | 73 | 35 |
| 2159[7] | **Labudd (USA) (43)** (RIngram) **6-7-11** NAdams(3) (b: hdwy 5f out: led over 1f out tl ins fnl f: unable qckn) | ¾ | **2** | 11/1 | 54 | 16 |
| 2066[7] | **Bayrak (USA) (65)** (MJRyan) **6-9-5** BDoyle(7) (lw: led: styd stands' s side: hdd over 1f out: one pce) | 2½ | **3** | 7/1[3] | 73 | 35 |
| 2196[2] | **High Desire (IRE) (56)** (JRArnold) **3-7-8**(3) MHenry(5) (hdwy 5f out: ev ch over 1f out: sn wknd) | 3 | **4** | 4/1[2] | 59 | 8 |
| 1655[16] | **Braydon Forest (53)** (CJDrewe) **4-8-7** DHolland(13) (lw: a.p: rdn over 3f out: wknd over 2f out) | 2½ | **5** | 25/1 | 53 | 15 |
| 1841[10] | **Prague Spring (65)** (LadyHerries) **4-9-5** PaulEddery(1) (prom 9f) | 1½ | **6** | 10/1 | 63 | 25 |
| 2056[7] | **Trumble (42)** (MrsNMacauley) **4-7-10** JQuinn(4) (nvr nr to chal) | nk | **7** | 12/1 | 40 | 2 |
| | **Dawn Flight (47)** (JRJenkins) **7-7-10**(5)ow1 ADaly(8) (nvr nrr) | hd | **8** | 33/1 | 44 | 5 |
| 1900[6] | **Sally's Twins (60)** (JSMoore) **3-8-1** JFEgan(10) (a bhd) | hd | **9** | 16/1 | 57 | 6 |
| 1793[13] | **Zermatt (IRE) (74)** (MDIUsher) **6-10-0** SSanders(12) (swtg: prom over 8f) | 1¾ | **10** | 8/1 | 69 | 31 |
| 1894[3] | **Atlantic Mist (63)** (BRMillman) **3-8-1**(3) SDrowne(6) (hld up: rdn over 3f out: wknd over 2f out) | 1 | **11** | 7/2[1] | 56 | 5 |
| | **Without a Flag (USA) (58)** (JWhite) **6-8-9**(3) AWhelan(2) (a bhd) | 17 | **12** | 20/1 | 28 | — |
| | | | | (SP 120.9%) | | **12 Rn** |

**2m 32.2** (8.20) CSF £74.96 CT £517.33 TOTE £8.20: £2.60 £4.50 £2.60 (£60.50) Trio £462.10 OWNER James Thorburn-Muirh Lomax (EPSOM) BRED Pendley Farm
WEIGHT FOR AGE 3yo-13lb
**Newport Knight** began his effort over a quarter of a mile from home and managed to get on top inside the final furlong. (7/1: op 9/2)
**1533 Labudd (USA)** moved up early in the long home straight. Gaining control below the distance, he found the winner too good inside the final furlong. (11/1: 8/1-12/1)
**1839 Bayrak (USA)** took the field along and was the only runner who elected to stay on the stands' side in the straight. With a very useful advantage, he was only collared below the distance. (7/1)
**2196 High Desire (IRE)** began a forward move early in the straight. With every chance below the distance, she had soon come to the end of her tether. (4/1)
**Braydon Forest** played an active role until forced to concede over two furlongs from home. (25/1)
**Prague Spring** was in the thick of the action until giving best over two furlongs out. (10/1)

## 2378 COURAGE BEST LIMITED STKS (0-65) (3-Y.O+) (Class F)

9-00 (9-01) **1m 2f 7y** £2,829.00 (£794.00: £387.00) Stalls: High GOING minus 0.09 sec per fur (G)

| Form | Horse | Dist | Pos | SP | RR | SF |
|---|---|---|---|---|---|---|
| 1894[4] | **Game Ploy (POL) (60)** (DHaydnJones) **4-9-4** PaulEddery(7) (hdwy over 2f out: led ins fnl f: drvn out) | — | **1** | 12/1 | 74 | 47 |
| 1996[9] | **Premier League (IRE) (59)** (JELong) **6-9-4** RPrice(4) (led: styd centre st: rdn over 2f out: hung lft & hdd ins fnl f: r.o) | 1 | **2** | 16/1 | 72 | 45 |
| 1625[15] | **Voila Premiere (IRE) (64)** (MHTompkins) **4-9-4** PRobinson(14) (lw: a.p: rdn over 2f out: ev ch ins fnl f: unable qckn) | hd | **3** | 3/1[1] | 72 | 45 |
| 2141[2] | **Ragsak Jameel (USA) (67)** (MajorWRHern) **3-8-7b** RHills(9) (rdn & hdwy over 2f out: r.o one pce) | 1½ | **4** | 9/2[2] | 70 | 32 |
| 2159[3] | **Allstars Express (62)** (TJNaughton) **3-8-9** AMcGlone(5) (hld up: rdn over 2f out: one pce) | 2 | **5** | 15/2 | 69 | 31 |
| 1833[2] | **Shalateeno (65)** (MRChannon) **3-7-13**(5) PPMurphy(3) (chsd ldr over 8f) | ½ | **6** | 12/1 | 63 | 25 |
| 2203[4] | **Almuhtaram (64)** (MissGayKelleway) **4-9-1**(3) DaneO'Neill(13) (lw: no hdwy fnl 2f) | hd | **7** | 8/1 | 66 | 39 |
| 1965[6] | **Flight Master (63)** (PJMakin) **4-9-4** SSanders(12) (lw: hdwy over 2f out: wknd over 1f out) | ¾ | **8** | 15/2 | 65 | 38 |
| 2014[4] | **Wet Patch (IRE) (64)** (RHannon) **4-9-4** RHughes(8) (lw: prom over 8f) | 4 | **9** | 11/2[3] | 58 | 31 |
| | **Rookery Girl (54)** (HJCollingridge) **4-9-1** JQuinn(1) (nvr nrr) | 4 | **10** | 33/1 | 49 | 22 |
| 1690[6] | **Lucky Begonia (IRE) (63)** (CNAllen) **3-8-4** CHodgson(11) (s.s: bhd fnl 2f) | 2 | **11** | 6/1 | 46 | 8 |
| | **Tony's Delight (IRE) (60)** (JRJenkins) **8-9-4** SWhitworth(10) (a bhd) | 3½ | **12** | 33/1 | 43 | 16 |
| 1414[15] | **Bellateena (50)** (HJCollingridge) **4-9-1** MRimmer(6) (bhd fnl 8f) | 1½ | **13** | 33/1 | 38 | 11 |
| 2129[12] | **Barranak (IRE) (58)** (GMMcCourt) **4-9-4** JFEgan(2) (plld hrd: a bhd) | 25 | **14** | 33/1 | 1 | — |
| | | | | (SP 140.5%) | | **14 Rn** |

**2m 10.8** (5.90) CSF £187.67 TOTE £22.40: £3.90 £5.00 £1.90 (£129.50) Trio £640.20 OWNER Mr Kevan Kynaston (PONTYPRIDD) BRED C. Olsen Ltd
WEIGHT FOR AGE 3yo-11lb
**1894 Game Ploy (POL)**, responding to pressure, got on top inside the final furlong. (12/1)
**1655 Premier League (IRE)** bowled along in front and was the only runner who elected to stay in the centre of the course in the straight. Hanging left in the final furlong, he was soon collared but, to his credit, stuck on well to the line. (16/1)
**Voila Premiere (IRE)**, always close up, was battling hard for the advantage inside the final furlong before tapped for toe. (3/1: op 5/1)
**2141 Ragsak Jameel (USA)**, ridden along to pick up ground over two furlongs from home, stayed on, but never threatened to get there in time. (9/2)
**2159 Allstars Express** could only go up and down in the same place in the last two furlongs. (15/2: 5/1-8/1)
**1833 Shalateeno** raced in second place but, collared for that position over a furlong out, soon had bellows to mend. (12/1: op 8/1)
**2203 Almuhtaram** (8/1: op 5/1)
**Flight Master** (15/2: 4/1-8/1)
**1690 Lucky Begonia (IRE)** (6/1: 7/1-11/1)

T/Plpt: £1,504.30 (12.11 Tckts). T/Qdpt: £1,032.20 (0.57 Tckts); £599.80 to 3/7/96. AK

# 2341-CHEPSTOW (L-H) (Good to firm)
## Tuesday July 2nd
WEATHER: overcast WIND: slt across

## 2379 BOLLINGER CHAMPAGNE CHALLENGE SERIES GENTLEMENS' H'CAP (0-70) (3-Y.O+) (Class G)
2-00 (2-02) **1m 14y** £2,206.00 (£616.00: £298.00) Stalls: High GOING minus 0.41 sec per fur (F)

| Form | Horse | Dist | Pos | SP | RR | SF |
|---|---|---|---|---|---|---|
| 2284[4] | **Super Serenade (52)** (GBBalding) **7-10-7**(4) MrJThatcher(8) (hld up: hdwy over 2f out: swtchd lft wl over 1f out: led ins fnl f: edgd rt: r.o wl) | — | 1 | 6/1[3] | 65 | 47 |
| 2344* | **Asterix (44)** (JMBradley) **8-9-13b**(4) 5x DrMMannish(1) (plld hrd: led over 6f out tl hdd & edgd lft ins fnl f) | 1½ | 2 | 9/4[2] | 54 | 36 |
| 1638* | **Scottish Park (46)** (MCPipe) **7-10-5b** MrTMcCarthy(5) (a.p: ev ch over 2f out: hrd rdn over 1f out: unable qckn ins fnl f) | 1¼ | 3 | 2/1[1] | 54 | 36 |
| 2162[4] | **Haido'hart (46)** (BSRothwell) **4-10-1**(4) MrRBarrett(6) (prom tl wknd over 1f out) | 3½ | 4 | 10/1 | 47 | 29 |
| 1992[5] | **Almapa (48)** (RJHodges) **4-10-3**(4) MrKGoble(4) (plld hrd: rdn over 3f out: sn bhd) | 8 | 5 | 8/1 | 33 | 15 |
| 1841[7] | **Delight of Dawn (69)** (RMStronge) **4-11-10**(4) MrJDewhurst(7) (b: lw: hld up & plld hrd: bhd fnl 3f) | 1¾ | 6 | 11/1 | 50 | 32 |
| 2284[6] | **Royal Acclaim (54)** (JMBradley) **11-10-9v**(4)ow20 MrDPrice(2) (led over 1f: wknd 4f out) | ¾ | 7 | 100/1 | 34 | — |

(SP 107.9%) **7 Rn**

**1m 36.1** (3.60) CSF £18.09 CT £28.07 TOTE £7.40: £2.50 £1.80 (£7.00) OWNER Mr J. G. Thatcher (ANDOVER) BRED J. Maxwell
LONG HANDICAP Royal Acclaim 9-2

**2284 Super Serenade**, over his best trip, was well handled by an amateur riding his first winner. (6/1: op 4/1)
**2344* Asterix**, attempting a quick follow up, took such a strong hold going to post that his rider barely maintained control. Repeating the dose in the race, he proved a difficult ride for a relatively inexperienced pilot. (9/4)
**1638* Scottish Park**, claimed for 4,000 guineas after her Leicester win, was 7lb higher than when running in a selling handicap the time before. (2/1)
**2162 Haido'hart** has come down a stone in the Ratings this season. (10/1)
**1685 Almapa** seems to need more cut in the ground. (8/1)

## 2380 SUMMER (S) STKS (3-Y.O) (Class G)
2-30 (2-31) **1m 14y** £2,346.00 (£656.00: £318.00) Stalls: High GOING minus 0.41 sec per fur (F)

| Form | Horse | Dist | Pos | SP | RR | SF |
|---|---|---|---|---|---|---|
| 2033[8] | **Charlton Imp (USA) (58)** (RJHodges) **3-8-6**(3) SDrowne(8) (lw: w ldrs: led over 2f out: r.o wl) | — | 1 | 11/4[2] | 62 | 28 |
| 2197[14] | **On The Wildside** (MRChannon) **3-8-4**(5) PPMurphy(4) (hld up: hdwy 3f out: rdn over 1f out: r.o ins fnl f) | 1 | 2 | 7/2[3] | 60 | 26 |
| 2162[9] | **Home Cookin' (57)** (MCPipe) **3-8-6**(3) MHenry(7) (swtg: led over 5f: hrd rdn & ev ch over 1f out: nt qckn) | 1¼ | 3 | 2/1[1] | 58 | 24 |
| 2019[6] | **Miletrian City (50)** (JBerry) **3-9-0b[1]** GCarter(2) (lw: hld up: hrd rdn over 2f out: one pce) | 1½ | 4 | 9/2 | 60 | 26 |
| | **Mrs Keen** (RSimpson) **3-8-9** SWhitworth(6) (bit bkwd: hld up: hrd rdn over 2f out: wknd wl over 1f out) | 7 | 5 | 20/1 | 41 | 7 |
| 1644[13] | **Precious Island** (PTDalton) **3-8-9** SSanders(3) (bit bkwd: hrd rdn 4f out: sn bhd) | 2 | 6 | 50/1 | 37 | 3 |
| | **Peggy Ess** (APJames) **3-8-9** NAdams(1) (bit bkwd: sn t.o) | 17 | 7 | 50/1 | 3 | — |
| 1311[11] | **Rebounder** (KMcAuliffe) **3-9-0v[1]** JFEgan(5) (lw: w ldrs 4f: rdn & wknd 3f out: t.o) | 3½ | 8 | 33/1 | 1 | — |

(SP 112.0%) **8 Rn**

**1m 35.3** (2.80) CSF £11.91 TOTE £3.50: £1.20 £1.10 £1.10 (£4.20) OWNER Mr R. J. Hodges (SOMERTON) BRED Brereton C. Jones
Bt in 5,000gns

**1654 Charlton Imp (USA)** found the combination of a mile in selling company enabling her to lose her maiden tag. (11/4: op 7/4)
**On The Wildside**, looking inexperienced, did not seem to know what to do on the first time she has been involved in the business end of a race. (7/2)
**2162 Home Cookin'**, back into a seller, could not quite find enough when brought to the boil. (2/1)
**2019 Miletrian City** was lowered in grade and tried in blinkers. (9/2)

## 2381 STEWARDS TRIAL H'CAP (0-100) (3-Y.O+) (Class C)
3-00 (3-01) **5f 16y** £5,215.00 (£1,570.00: £760.00: £355.00) Stalls: High GOING minus 0.41 sec per fur (F)

| Form | Horse | Dist | Pos | SP | RR | SF |
|---|---|---|---|---|---|---|
| 1473[8] | **Ansellman (75)** (JBerry) **6-8-6v[1]** GCarter(3) (chsd ldr: rdn over 1f out: led ins fnl f: r.o wl) | — | 1 | 10/1 | 83 | 43 |
| 2232[4] | **Bowden Rose (84)** (MBlanshard) **4-9-1b** JQuinn(2) (lw: led tl rdn & hdd ins fnl f) | ¾ | 2 | 9/2[2] | 90 | 50 |
| 2114[5] | **Sir Joey (USA) (87)** (PGMurphy) **7-9-1**(3) SDrowne(5) (hld up: hdwy 2f out: hrd rdn 1f out: r.o one pce) | nk | 3 | 6/4[1] | 92 | 52 |
| 1974[7] | **Crofters Ceilidh (85)** (BAMcMahon) **4-9-2** SSanders(1) (a.p: one pce fnl 2f) | 2 | 4 | 12/1 | 83 | 43 |
| 2114[19] | **Mr Bergerac (IRE) (82)** (BPalling) **5-8-13** TSprake(4) (lw: rdn over 2f out: no hdwy) | ¾ | 5 | 10/1 | 78 | 38 |
| 1829[8] | **Jucea (73)** (JLSpearing) **7-8-4** PaulEddery(6) (lw: hld up & plld hrd: rdn over 2f out: no imp) | s.h | 6 | 7/1 | 69 | 29 |
| 2115[13] | **Wavian (95)** (RHannon) **4-9-9**(3) DaneO'Neill(7) (lw: hld up: bhd fnl 2f) | ¾ | 7 | 6/1[3] | 89 | 49 |

(SP 110.8%) **7 Rn**

**57.6 secs** (0.60) CSF £48.60 TOTE £14.10: £5.30 £2.60 (£21.30) OWNER Ansells of Watford (COCKERHAM) BRED W. L. Caley

**1064 Ansellman** had the headgear refitted but was in a visor for the first time. Off a 6lb higher mark than when winning at Bath in April, he was subsequently described as a bit of a character who needs everything to go his way. (10/1)
**2232 Bowden Rose** seemed in control approaching the final furlong, but is still 5lb higher than the best mark off which she has won. (9/2)
**2114 Sir Joey (USA)**, 6lb higher than when successful at Salisbury, won this race last season off a mark 3lb lower. (6/4)
**Crofters Ceilidh**, lightly-raced, is still 10lb higher than when winning a couple of nurseries at grade one courses two years ago. (12/1: op 8/1)
**Mr Bergerac (IRE)** looked in fine fettle but needs a stiffer five, or six furlongs. (10/1)
**1829 Jucea** seems to have gone off the boil and has never won off a mark as high as this. (7/1: op 4/1)

## 2382 BREAM CLAIMING STKS (2-Y.O) (Class F)
3-30 (3-31) **6f 16y** £2,670.00 (£745.00: £360.00) Stalls: High GOING minus 0.41 sec per fur (F)

| Form | Horse | Dist | Pos | SP | RR | SF |
|---|---|---|---|---|---|---|
| 1713[D] | **Without Friends (IRE)** (MrsLStubbs) **2-9-0** JFEgan(1) (plld hrd early: a.p: rdn to ld wl over 1f out: r.o) | — | 1 | 5/2[1] | 71 | 23 |
| 683[4] | **Dowry** (RHannon) **2-8-9**(3) DaneO'Neill(5) (hld up: hdwy over 1f out: r.o ins fnl f) | 1 | 2 | 11/4[2] | 66 | 18 |
| 1892[8] | **Surprise Event** (WGMTurner) **2-8-2**(5) RHavlin(4) (w ldr: ev ch 2f out: one pce fnl f) | ½ | 3 | 20/1 | 60 | 12 |
| *1813** | **Enchanting Eve** (CNAllen) **2-8-2**(5) LNewton(6) (led over 4f: one pce) | 1 | 4 | 5/1 | 57 | 9 |
| 2254[3] | **Russian Sable** (MRChannon) **2-7-13**(5) PPMurphy(2) (s.i.s: hld up: hdwy 3f out: ev ch 2f out: wknd ins fnl f) | hd | 5 | 100/30[3] | 54 | 6 |
| *2172[2]* | **Our Kevin** (KMcAuliffe) **2-8-8b** DRMcCabe(3) (hld up & bhd: sme hdwy whn nt clr run ins fnl f) | 2 | 6 | 10/1 | 53 | 5 |

(SP 108.8%) **6 Rn**

**1m 12.0** (2.80) CSF £9.02 TOTE £3.80: £1.80 £2.00 (£5.60) OWNER Consultco Ltd (WARTHILL) BRED Churchtown House Stud

**1713 Without Friends (IRE)** is in his element in this sort of company. (5/2)
**683 Dowry** shaped as though she should stay further. (11/4: 2/1-3/1)
**Surprise Event** is bred to want a longer trip. (20/1)
**1813* Enchanting Eve**, reverting to grass, was not disgraced on ground plenty fast enough for her. (5/1)
**2254 Russian Sable**, back to six, surprisingly tied up in the closing stages, and may require good ground. (100/30)
**2172 Our Kevin** seems to need seven on turf. (10/1)

## 2383 MANSION MAIDEN STKS (3-Y.O) (Class D)
4-00 (4-03) **1m 2f 36y** £3,871.50 (£1,167.00: £566.00: £265.50) Stalls: Low GOING minus 0.41 sec per fur (F)

| Form | Horse / details | Dist | Pos | SP | RR | SF |
|---|---|---|---|---|---|---|
| 1873$^{9}$ | **Oops Pettie** (MrsJCecil) **3-8-9** TIves(4) (hld up: hdwy over 3f out: led wl over 1f out: r.o wl) | — | 1 | 8/1 | 78 | 35 |
| 576$^{4}$ | **Renzo (IRE)** (GHarwood) **3-9-0** AClark(7) (lw: s.s: sn rcvrd & hld up: hdwy on ins 4f out: swtchd rt over 1f out: r.o ins fnl f) | 2 | 2 | 11/4$^{1}$ | 80 | 37 |
| 2135$^{2}$ | **Classic Parisian (IRE) (79)** (RHarris) **3-8-9** AMackay(3) (a.p: hrd rdn over 3f out: ev ch over 2f out: one pce) | 1 | 3 | 7/2$^{2}$ | 73 | 30 |
| | **Milton** (PFICole) **3-9-0** TQuinn(5) (a.p: one pce fnl 2f) | 1 | 4 | 5/1 | 77 | 34 |
| | **Mountain Holly** (DRLoder) **3-8-9** RHughes(9) (lw: hld up: rdn over 2f out: hdwy over 1f out: one pce fnl f) | ¾ | 5 | 4/1$^{3}$ | 71 | 28 |
| 2183$^{9}$ | **Spring Campaign (IRE) (69)** (MCPipe) **3-8-11**(3) MHenry(1) (led over 8f: wknd ins fnl f) | 1¼ | 6 | 10/1 | 74 | 31 |
| 1895$^{6}$ | **Lady Magnum (IRE)** (JNeville) **3-8-6**(3) SDrowne(10) (a bhd) | 5 | 7 | 66/1 | 61 | 18 |
| 1656$^{9}$ | **El Presidente** (GPEnright) **3-9-0** BDoyle(8) (hld up: wknd over 2f out) | 1¾ | 8 | 50/1 | 63 | 20 |
| | **Our Adventure** (MPMuggeridge) **3-8-6**(3) DaneO'Neill(2) (lengthy: bit bkwd: sn wl bhd: t.o) | 20 | 9 | 100/1 | 26 | — |
| 2181$^{13}$ | **Myfanwy Bethesda** (BJLlewellyn) **3-8-9** VSlattery(6) (prom over 5f: t.o) | 9 | 10 | 100/1 | 12 | — |

(SP 111.2%) **10 Rn**

**2m 8.4** (3.10) CSF £27.37 TOTE £8.40: £1.90 £1.70 £1.60 (£14.30) Trio £15.10 OWNER Mrs D. MacRae (NEWMARKET) BRED D. Macrae
**1508 Oops Pettie** may not have stayed the mile and a half last time, but fulfilled the promise shown on her debut with a win in clear-cut fashion. (8/1)
**576 Renzo (IRE)**, a half-brother to Cesarewitch winner Captain's Guest, stayed on to secure the runner-up spot, despite carrying his head high. (11/4: 2/1-3/1)
**2135 Classic Parisian (IRE)** may find a longer trip offsetting her lack of finishing speed. (7/2: op 9/4)
**Milton**, out of a sister to Nisnas, should stay further. (5/1)
**Mountain Holly**, a half-sister to Foyer, is out of a Lowther and Nassau Stakes winner and should improve when tackling a mile and a half. (4/1)
**Spring Campaign (IRE)** ran over this trip as a two-year-old, so one could expect he needs a stiffer test of stamina. (10/1)

## 2384 MIDDLE LODGE H'CAP (0-85) (3-Y.O F) (Class D)
4-30 (4-31) **1m 2f 36y** £3,712.25 (£1,118.00: £541.50: £253.25) Stalls: Low GOING minus 0.41 sec per fur (F)

| Form | Horse / details | Dist | Pos | SP | RR | SF |
|---|---|---|---|---|---|---|
| 1407$^{5}$ | **Overruled (IRE) (82)** (DRLoder) **3-9-7** RHughes(2) (lw: a.p: led over 3f out: rdn & hdd 2f out: led over 1f out: r.o wl) | — | 1 | 100/30$^{3}$ | 86 | 48 |
| 2202$^{5}$ | **Classic Romance (73)** (RHarris) **3-8-12** AMackay(4) (hld up: hdwy 4f out: rdn & ev ch over 1f out: unable qckn) | ¾ | 2 | 12/1 | 76 | 38 |
| 2246$^{5}$ | **Trilby (65)** (PFICole) **3-8-4** TQuinn(6) (b.off hind: led over 4f: rdn over 3f out: led 2f out: sn hdd: unable qckn ins fnl f) | s.h | 3 | 3/1$^{2}$ | 68 | 30 |
| 1857$^{3}$ | **Mua-Tab (70)** (PTWalwyn) **3-8-9** WCarson(5) (hld up & plld hrd: hdwy 4f out: hrd rdn & ev ch over 1f out: unable qckn) | s.h | 4 | 5/2$^{1}$ | 73 | 35 |
| 1641$^{14}$ | **Double Up (66)** (LadyHerries) **3-8-5** DeclanO'Shea(1) (hld up: a bhd) | 7 | 5 | 13/2 | 58 | 20 |
| 1775$^{10}$ | **Little Black Dress (USA) (69)** (RCharlton) **3-8-8** TSprake(3) (chsd ldr: led over 5f out tl over 3f out: wknd over 2f out) | 3 | 6 | 6/1 | 56 | 18 |

(SP 112.0%) **6 Rn**

**2m 8.2** (2.90) CSF £32.54 TOTE £4.80: £2.30 £3.50 (£30.20) OWNER Mr E. J. Loder (NEWMARKET) BRED E. J. Loder
**1407 Overruled (IRE)** may well have found the right trip. (100/30)
**Classic Romance** ran her best race of the season. (12/1)
**2246 Trilby** needs a stiffer stamina test. (3/1)
**1857 Mua-Tab** was by no means disgraced considering she ran too freely over this longer trip. (5/2)
**1447* Double Up** settled much better than at Leicester, but does not seem suited to waiting tactics. (13/2: 4/1-7/1)
**888 Little Black Dress (USA)** (6/1: op 4/1)

## 2385 LIONS LODGE H'CAP (0-70) (3-Y.O+) (Class E)
5-00 (5-00) **2m 2f** £3,090.00 (£930.00: £450.00: £210.00) Stalls: Low GOING minus 0.41 sec per fur (F)

| Form | Horse / details | Dist | Pos | SP | RR | SF |
|---|---|---|---|---|---|---|
| 2042$^{2}$ | **Mirador (56)** (RCurtis) **5-9-6** GBardwell(2) (lw: hld up: rdn & hdwy over 3f out: led over 1f out: r.o wl) | — | 1 | 5/2$^{1}$ | 67 | 43 |
| 1981$^{2}$ | **Castle Secret (56)** (DBurchell) **10-9-1**(5) RHavlin(7) (lw: a.p: led over 4f out: hrd rdn over 3f out: hdd over 1f out: unable qckn) | 1½ | 2 | 4/1$^{2}$ | 66 | 42 |
| 2190$^{4}$ | **Mr Copyforce (46)** (MissBSanders) **6-8-10** SSanders(6) (hld up: stdy hdwy 7f out: ev ch 2f out: one pce) | 2½ | 3 | 9/2$^{3}$ | 53 | 29 |
| 2148$^{5}$ | **Witney-de-Bergerac (IRE) (60)** (JSMoore) **4-9-10** JFEgan(3) (hld up: stdy hdwy 7f out: wknd wl over 1f out) | 7 | 4 | 6/1 | 61 | 37 |
| | **Elite Reg (38)** (MCPipe) **7-7-13v**(3) MHenry(8) (lw: led: hrd rdn 9f out: hdd over 6f out: wknd over 4f out) | 2 | 5 | 6/1 | 37 | 13 |
| 2148$^{11}$ | **Gentleman Sid (43)** (PGMurphy) **6-8-7** NAdams(4) (lw: prom: led over 6f out tl over 4f out: wknd over 3f out: t.o) | 27 | 6 | 8/1 | 18 | — |
| | **Bravo Star (USA) (34)** (PaddyFarrell) **11-7-12** JQuinn(5) (prom 11f: t.o fnl 5f) | 29 | 7 | 50/1 | — | — |

(SP 108.4%) **7 Rn**

**3m 56.7** (6.70) CSF £11.58 CT £32.27 TOTE £2.90: £1.50 £2.30 (£6.40) OWNER Mrs J Whitehead,J McGivern & Two Kates (LAMBOURN) BRED Miss T. P. Pile
**2042 Mirador** showed her run at Royal Ascot to be no fluke and now seems likely to go for the Goodwood Stakes. (5/2)
**1981 Castle Secret** had been raised 3lb for his narrow defeat by the third at Bath. (4/1)
**2190 Mr Copyforce** could not confirm the Bath form with the runner-up on 3lb worse terms. (9/2)
**2148 Witney-de-Bergerac (IRE)** was still 3lb higher than when winning a strongly-run Ladies' race over a mile and a half last September, and may have not stayed this trip. (6/1: op 4/1)
**Elite Reg** (6/1: 7/2-13/2)
**Gentleman Sid** (8/1: op 12/1)

T/Plpt: £98.10 (150.23 Tckts). T/Qdpt: £36.40 (30.37 Tckts). KH

## 2355-MUSSELBURGH (R-H) (Good)
### Tuesday July 2nd
WEATHER: overcast WIND: almost nil

### 2386 RAMBLING RIVER AMATEUR H'CAP (0-65) (3-Y.O+) (Class F)
2-15 (2-24) **5f** £2,591.00 (£726.00: £353.00) Stalls: High GOING minus 0.64 sec per fur (F)

| Form | Horse | Dist | Pos | SP | RR | SF |
|---|---|---|---|---|---|---|
| 1889[2] | **Swan At Whalley (60)** (MartynWane) **4-11-9** MrSSwiers(4) (mde most: r.o wl fnl 2f) | — | 1 | 4/1[2] | 73 | 55 |
| 2064[2] | **Kalar (48)** (DWChapman) **7-10-11** MissRClark(7) (w wnr tl rdn & btn appr fnl f) | 4 | 2 | 6/1 | 48 | 30 |
| 2215[7] | **Tropical Beach (59)** (JBerry) **3-11-3** MrsLPearce(1) (hdwy ½-wy: kpt on: nt pce to chal) | 1 | 3 | 3/1[1] | 56 | 33 |
| 1781[2] | **Bold Street (IRE) (65)** (ABailey) **6-12-0** MrVLukaniuk(6) (lw: b: effrt ½-wy: styd on: nvr able to chal) | ¾ | 4 | 3/1[1] | 60 | 42 |
| 1865[9] | **Six for Luck (54)** (DANolan) **4-10-12**(5)ow3 MissSCassels(11) (gd spd 3f: grad wknd) | 3½ | 5 | 100/1 | 37 | 16 |
| | **Supreme Desire (30)** (MissJFCraze) **8-9-2**(5) MrWWenyon(8) (rdn ½-wy: nvr trbld ldrs) | s.h | 6 | 100/1 | 13 | — |
| 2154[9] | **Pallium (IRE) (53)** (MrsAMNaughton) **8-11-2** MissPRobson(9) (lw: wl outpcd fr ½-wy) | hd | 7 | 5/1[3] | 36 | 18 |
| 1765[10] | **Lochon (51)** (JLEyre) **5-11-0b**[1] MissDianaJones(3) (b: in tch tl outpcd fr ½-wy) | 1¼ | 8 | 8/1 | 30 | 12 |
| 2119[8] | **Another Episode (IRE) (55)** (MissLAPerratt) **7-11-4** MrJWeymes(5) (lw: dwlt: nvr trbld ldrs) | ½ | 9 | 50/1 | 32 | 14 |
| 2359[7] | **Kiwud (43)** (TWDonnelly) **3-10-1b** MrMHNaughton(12) (spd 3f: wknd) | 4 | 10 | 25/1 | 8 | — |
| *2154[7]* | ***Leading Princess (IRE) (48)*** (MissLAPerratt) **5-10-11b** MrsSBosley(2) (Withdrawn not under Starter's orders: uns rdr & bolted bef s) | | W | 5/1[3] | — | — |

(SP 136.5%) **10 Rn**

**59.0 secs** (1.30) CSF £27.12 CT £77.40 TOTE £5.30: £1.60 £2.60 £1.90 (£10.10) Trio £19.70 OWNER Capt H. H. Barlow (RICHMOND)
LONG HANDICAP Supreme Desire 9-0
WEIGHT FOR AGE 3yo-5lb

**1889 Swan At Whalley**, getting the favoured stands' side and given a fine ride, made no mistake this time and strode right away in the last furlong and a half. (4/1)
**2064 Kalar** could never get the better of the winner despite trying hard, and finally cried enough in the final furlong. His stable is in really good form at present. (6/1)
**1865* Tropical Beach** takes time to get going and, on this sharper track, the effort was always too late. (3/1)
**1781 Bold Street (IRE)** found this track far too sharp and lacked the speed to get into it, despite staying on at the end. (3/1: op 5/1)
**659 Six for Luck** has plenty of speed but, from his high draw, had little chance. (100/1)
**2154 Pallium (IRE)** won this last year, but showed nothing here. (5/1)

### 2387 LONG NEWTON (S) STKS (2-Y.O) (Class F)
2-45 (2-46) **7f 15y** £2,521.00 (£706.00: £343.00) Stalls: High GOING minus 0.31 sec per fur (GF)

| Form | Horse | Dist | Pos | SP | RR | SF |
|---|---|---|---|---|---|---|
| 2161* | **Stride** (MartynMeade) **2-8-11** KFallon(2) (lw: trckd ldrs: lft in ld ent st: r.o wl) | — | 1 | 1/2[1] | 67 | — |
| 2161[8] | **Apiculate (IRE)** (WTKemp) **2-8-11** JFanning(4) (hdwy & c wd st: rdn & no imp fnl 2f) | 6 | 2 | 33/1 | 53 | — |
| 2174[4] | **Back In The Ussr (IRE)** (MJohnston) **2-8-11** JWeaver(3) (lw: plld hrd: cl up: lft in ld 5f out: rn wd appr st: sn hdd: no imp fnl 3f) | 3½ | 3 | 2/1[2] | 46 | — |
| 2153[4] | **Sweeping Statement** (JBerry) **2-8-6** JCarroll(1) (hdwy to chse wnr ent st: wl outpcd fnl 2½f) | nk | 4 | 14/1[3] | 40 | — |
| 2174[6] | **Chloe's Mark** (RMMcKellar) **2-8-6** TWilliams(5) (led tl rn wd 5f out: bhd fnl 3f) | 23 | 5 | 66/1 | — | — |

(SP 111.1%) **5 Rn**

**1m 32.6** (7.10) CSF £11.77 TOTE £1.20: £1.60 £6.80 (£12.60) OWNER Ladyswood Racing Club (MALMESBURY) BRED Side Hill Stud
Bt in 10,500gns

**2161* Stride**, one of the few to handle the bend, then found herself in front and there were no dangers thereafter. (1/2)
**1543 Apiculate (IRE)**, going wide, crossed over to the stands' side early in the straight, and was never anything like good enough to trouble the winner. (33/1)
**2174 Back In The Ussr (IRE)** gave all sorts of problems by pulling hard and failed to handle the home turn. (2/1)
**2153 Sweeping Statement** blew up in the last couple of furlongs. (14/1: 6/1-16/1)
**Chloe's Mark** has yet to show anything. (66/1)

### 2388 LUFTNESS CLAIMING STKS (3-Y.O) (Class F)
3-15 (3-15) **1m 4f 31y** £2,493.00 (£698.00: £339.00) Stalls: High GOING minus 0.31 sec per fur (GF)

| Form | Horse | Dist | Pos | SP | RR | SF |
|---|---|---|---|---|---|---|
| 2141[3] | **Rossel (USA) (66)** (MRStoute) **3-9-1** KFallon(4) (trckd ldr: led over 3f out: sn clr) | — | 1 | 1/3[1] | 69 | 7 |
| 1850[16] | **Stoleamarch (45)** (MrsMReveley) **3-8-9** ACulhane(2) (bhd: styd on fnl 2f: no ch w wnr) | 8 | 2 | 25/1 | 53 | — |
| 1828[5] | **Cry Baby (46)** (NTinkler) **3-8-7b** JCarroll(5) (trckd ldrs: effrt 3f out: rdn & no rspnse) | 2½ | 3 | 7/1[2] | 47 | — |
| *2168[7]* | **Salsian (50)** (SCWilliams) **3-7-9b**(3) DWright(3) (led tl hdd over 3f out: sn btn) | 2½ | 4 | 11/1[3] | 35 | — |
| 1636[3] | **Phar Closer (50)** (WTKemp) **3-8-4** JFanning(1) (nvr nr to chal) | 6 | 5 | 12/1 | 33 | — |

(SP 107.4%) **5 Rn**

**2m 43.7** (10.70) CSF £7.44 TOTE £1.20: £1.10 £9.00 (£7.70) OWNER Sheikh Mohammed (NEWMARKET) BRED Allen E. Paulson
Rossel (USA) clmd PMonteith 8,000gns

**2141 Rossel (USA)** proved in a different class to this lot. (1/3)
**Stoleamarch** had to be led to post and then brought up the rear until struggling on in the straight, but had no chance at all with the winner. (25/1)
**1828 Cry Baby** looked most ungenerous when ridden early in the straight. (7/1)
**Salsian** looked very moderate once the pace was on early in the straight. (11/1)
**1636 Phar Closer** got a bit warm beforehand and was not overpunished when going nowhere early in the straight. (12/1)

### 2389 JOAN SMITH IS 40 TODAY CLAIMING STKS (2-Y.O) (Class F)
3-45 (3-48) **5f** £2,736.00 (£828.00: £404.00: £192.00) Stalls: High GOING minus 0.64 sec per fur (F)

| Form | Horse | Dist | Pos | SP | RR | SF |
|---|---|---|---|---|---|---|
| 2174* | **Fonzy** (MrsLStubbs) **2-8-11b** KFallon(4) (reard & s.s: hdwy ½-wy: r.o to ld wl ins fnl f) | — | 1 | 4/5[1] | 70 | — |
| 1849[7] | **Not A Lot** (MWEasterby) **2-9-3** DaleGibson(1) (chsd ldr: led over 1f out tl wl ins fnl f) | 1½ | 2 | 7/4[2] | 71? | — |
| | **Marsh Marigold** (MartynMeade) **2-8-2** FNorton(2) (neat: bit bkwd: prom: effrt & ch 2f out: wknd fnl f) | 5 | 3 | 33/1 | 40 | — |
| 2237[3] | **No Rush** (JBerry) **2-8-3b**[1] JCarroll(3) (led over 3f: sn btn) | 4 | 4 | 4/1[3] | 28 | — |

(SP 114.9%) **4 Rn**

**62.4 secs** (4.70) CSF £2.72 TOTE £1.80 (£2.00) OWNER The West Riding Partnership (WARTHILL) BRED J. and Mrs Rose

**2174* Fonzy** gave the others a big start and then picked them off in the final furlong. (4/5)
**Not A Lot** is looking well named at present. (7/4: op 3/1)
**Marsh Marigold** needed this and ran out of petrol approaching the final furlong. (33/1)
**2237 No Rush**, very much on his toes with the blinkers on for the first time, ran worse than ever. (4/1: op 5/2)

## 2390 MUIRFIELD H'CAP (0-80) (3-Y.O+) (Class D)
4-15 (4-15) **1m 3f 32y** £3,501.25 (£1,060.00: £517.50: £246.25) Stalls: High GOING minus 0.31 sec per fur (GF)

| | | | | SP | RR | SF |
|---|---|---|---|---|---|---|
| 2355* | **Bobanlyn (IRE) (52)** (JSWainwright) **4-8-5**$^{(7)}$ RMullen(6) (hld up: hdwy over 3f out: rdn to ld ins fnl f: r.o) | — | **1** | 9/4$^{1}$ | 63 | 30 |
| 2068$^{2}$ | **Break the Rules (68)** (MrsMReveley) **4-10-0** JFortune(3) (a.p: led over 2f out tl ins fnl f: no ex) | ¾ | **2** | 5/1$^{3}$ | 78 | 45 |
| 2356$^{2}$ | **Ambidextrous (IRE) (54)** (EJAlston) **4-9-0** $^{5x}$ KFallon(2) (lw: hld up: hdwy over 3f out: chsng ldrs appr fnl f: nt qckn) | 2½ | **3** | 4/1$^{2}$ | 60 | 27 |
| 2183$^{6}$ | **Pendolino (IRE) (41)** (MBrittain) **5-8-1b** LCharnock(1) (trckd ldrs: led over 4f out tl over 2f out: one pce) | 4 | **4** | 20/1 | 42 | 9 |
| 2020$^{2}$ | **Lord Advocate (53)** (DANolan) **8-8-10b**$^{(3)}$ NVarley(5) (lw: chsd ldrs tl outpcd fnl 3f) | ½ | **5** | 11/2 | 53 | 20 |
| 2177$^{4}$ | **Steadfast Elite (IRE) (45)** (JJO'Neill) **5-8-5** JCarroll(4) (prom tl wknd fnl 3f) | 9 | **6** | 5/1$^{3}$ | 32 | — |
| 1870$^{8}$ | **Victor Laszlo (41)** (RAllan) **4-8-1** JFanning(7) (led tl hdd over 4f out: wknd over 2f out) | 5 | **7** | 14/1 | 21 | — |

(SP 110.9%) **7 Rn**

**2m 25.6** (5.90) CSF £12.69 TOTE £3.40: £1.80 £2.50 (£13.80) OWNER Mrs Sheila Walker (MALTON) BRED Mrs S. A. Pfeiffer and Partners in Ireland

**2355* Bobanlyn (IRE)**, winning her second race in as many days, needed to struggle but did it well in the end. (9/4)
**2068 Break the Rules** appreciated the trip and was given a most forceful ride, but was well outbattled in the closing stages. (5/1)
**2356 Ambidextrous (IRE)**, like the winner, was having his second run in consecutive days. The Handicapper seems to just have his measure. (4/1)
**2183 Pendolino (IRE)** ran reasonably, but was well tapped for toe in the last couple of furlongs. (20/1)
**2020 Lord Advocate** is high enough in the weights at present. (11/2)

## 2391 GULLANE H'CAP (0-60) (3-Y.O+) (Class F)
4-45 (4-47) **7f 15y** £2,766.00 (£776.00: £378.00) Stalls: High GOING minus 0.31 sec per fur (GF)

| | | | | SP | RR | SF |
|---|---|---|---|---|---|---|
| 2357$^{4}$ | **Allinson's Mate (IRE) (55)** (TDBarron) **8-9-11** JFortune(7) (lw: a in tch: hdwy u.p 2f out: hrd rdn to ld wl ins fnl f: edgd lft) | — | **1** | 8/1$^{3}$ | 63 | 36 |
| 1609$^{2}$ | **Zain Dancer (55)** (DNicholls) **4-9-11** AlexGreaves(2) (lw: hdwy 3f out: led jst ins fnl f: hdd & nt qckn wl ins fnl f) | ½ | **2** | 9/2$^{1}$ | 62 | 35 |
| 2154$^{6}$ | **Seconds Away (29)** (JSGoldie) **5-7-10**$^{(3)}$ NVarley(4) (in tch: kpt on u.p fnl 2f: no imp) | 3 | **3** | 9/1 | 29 | 2 |
| *2369*$^{15}$ | **Rainbows Rhapsody (35)** (DWChapman) **5-8-5** LCharnock(14) (chsd ldrs: led over 2f out tl jst ins fnl f: nt qckn) | nk | **4** | 100/1 | 34 | 7 |
| *1966*$^{11}$ | **Blow Dry (IRE) (50)** (MartynWane) **6-9-6** KFallon(12) (hdwy 3f out: sn chsng ldrs: nt qckn fnl f) | ¾ | **5** | 10/1 | 48 | 21 |
| *2085*$^{2}$ | **Have a Nightcap (30)** (NPLittmoden) **7-7-7b**$^{(7)}$ RMullen(9) (hdwy over 3f out: nvr rchd ldrs) | 1¼ | **6** | 12/1 | 25 | — |
| 1889$^{10}$ | **Another Nightmare (IRE) (33)** (RMMcKellar) **4-8-3** TWilliams(8) (hmpd appr st: hdwy over 2f out: n.d) | hd | **7** | 33/1 | 28 | 1 |
| 1665$^{11}$ | **Langtonian (33)** (JLEyre) **7-8-3** FNorton(13) (b.nr hind: s.i.s: n.d) | 6 | **8** | 10/1 | 14 | — |
| 2030$^{4}$ | **Blue Grit (53)** (MDods) **10-9-9b** JCarroll(1) (s.i.s: n.d) | 1½ | **9** | 9/1 | 31 | 4 |
| 1765$^{8}$ | **Taurean Fire (39)** (MrsMReveley) **3-7-12**$^{(3)}$ DWright(6) (cl up: sltly hmpd over 2f out: sn wknd) | ¾ | **10** | 9/1 | 15 | — |
| 2026$^{15}$ | **Madonna da Rossi (44)** (MDods) **3-8-6** DeanMcKeown(5) (lw: plld hrd: a bhd) | 1½ | **11** | 25/1 | 17 | — |
| 2023$^{2}$ | **Miss Pigalle (43)** (MissLAPerratt) **5-8-13b** JFanning(11) (led tl hdd over 2f out: hung lft & sn wknd) | nk | **12** | 13/2$^{2}$ | 15 | — |
| 976$^{10}$ | **Domoor (53)** (MJohnston) **3-9-1** JWeaver(3) (prom over 4f) | 1½ | **13** | 10/1 | 22 | — |
| 2178$^{2}$ | **Diet (52)** (MissLAPerratt) **10-9-8v** NConnorton(10) (nvr wnt pce) | 1 | **14** | 12/1 | 18 | — |

(SP 123.1%) **14 Rn**

**1m 29.5** (4.00) CSF £41.98 CT £311.79 TOTE £12.10: £3.70 £1.10 £4.90 (£16.30) Trio £138.30 OWNER Mr Peter Jones (THIRSK) BRED Gay O'Callaghan

WEIGHT FOR AGE 3yo-8lb

**2357 Allinson's Mate (IRE)** was given a terrific ride here and did just enough to gain the advantage late on, despite edging into the runner-up. (8/1)
**1609 Zain Dancer** had a lot to do from his low draw and did very well to get there, only to be outbattled in the closing stages. (9/2: op 5/2)
**2154 Seconds Away** ran pretty well and has the ability to win a race, but it is anybody's guess when and if it will happen. (9/1)
**Rainbows Rhapsody** showed her first signs of form for the new stable here, and may well be worth keeping an eye on. (100/1)
**882 Blow Dry (IRE)** is edgy and ran quite well, but was short of room and certainly short of pace in the final furlong. (10/1)
**2085 Have a Nightcap** stayed on in the home straight, but lacked the pace to get on terms, and may well be better suited by the All-Weather. (12/1: op 8/1)

T/Jkpt: £1,017.50 (13.14 Tckts). T/Plpt: £23.30 (579.06 Tckts). T/Qdpt: £8.30 (106.6 Tckts). AA

# 1760-CATTERICK (L-H) (Good to soft, Good patches)
## Wednesday July 3rd
WEATHER: Raining WIND: fresh half against

## 2392 5TH REGIMENT ROYAL ARTILLERY CHAMPAGNE POL ROGER (S) STKS (3-Y.O+) (Class G)
2-20 (2-23) **5f 212y** £2,469.00 (£684.00: £327.00) Stalls: High GOING: minus 0.12 sec per fur (G)

| | | | | SP | RR | SF |
|---|---|---|---|---|---|---|
| 2005$^{18}$ | **Blue Bomber (71)** (TDBarron) **5-9-0** JFortune(9) (chsd ldr: racd stands' side & led over 1f out: styd on) | — | **1** | 2/1$^{1}$ | 69 | 51 |
| 2212* | **Sense of Priority (56)** (DNicholls) **7-9-7** AlexGreaves(2) (a chsng ldrs: racd stands' side: kpt on one pce fnl f) | 1½ | **2** | 4/1$^{3}$ | 72 | 54 |
| 2212$^{3}$ | **Best Kept Secret (52)** (PDEvans) **5-9-0v** DHolland(4) (bhd: hdwy over 2f out: styd on towards fin) | 1¼ | **3** | 7/1 | 62 | 44 |
| *2171*$^{8}$ | **Palacegate Touch (75)** (JBerry) **6-9-2b**$^{(5)}$ PRoberts(6) (led tl hdd over 1f out: wknd) | 1 | **4** | 7/2$^{2}$ | 66 | 48 |
| 1707$^{5}$ | **The Frisky Farmer (69)** (WGMTurner) **3-8-8**$^{(7)}$ GHannon(3) (in tch: outpcd ent st: no imp after) | 8 | **5** | 5/1 | 45 | 21 |
| 2212$^{12}$ | **Respectable Jones (45)** (RHollinshead) **10-8-7b**$^{(7)}$ SCrawford(1) (in tch: effrt ent st: no imp) | 5 | **6** | 50/1 | 24 | 6 |
| 1033$^{11}$ | **Manolo (FR)** (JBerry) **3-8-8** JCarroll(7) (nvr wnt pce) | 2 | **7** | 20/1 | 19 | — |
| 1864$^{9}$ | **Dancing Jazztime (20)** (JSWainwright) **5-8-9** NKennedy(8) (s.i.s: n.d) | 15 | **8** | 100/1 | — | — |

**Time Ticks On** (MWEllerby) **3-8-5**(3) CTeague(5) (bkwd: s.s: a wl bhd)....5 **9** 100/1 — —
(SP 113.4%) **9 Rn**

**1m 15.0** (4.10) CSF £9.81 TOTE £3.40: £1.90 £1.80 £1.20 (£5.80) Trio £11.30 OWNER Mr Geoffrey Martin (THIRSK) BRED R. H. Cowell and Mrs R. B. Collie
WEIGHT FOR AGE 3yo-6lb
No bid

**1609 Blue Bomber** acted really well on this softish ground and, getting the favoured stands' rail, saw it out most determinedly. (2/1)
**2212* Sense of Priority**, not really suited by this ground, ran well, but failed to pick up approaching the last furlong. (4/1)
**2212 Best Kept Secret** finished best of the main body of the field racing on the far side of the track and made up a fair amount of ground to do so, but he never looked likely to trouble the winner. (7/1)
**1810 Palacegate Touch**, who loves soft ground, could never get away from his field and, staying on the far side, was comfortably picked off approaching the final furlong. (7/2)
**1707 The Frisky Farmer** goes well in the soft but, on this occasion, was left struggling from halfway for a most disappointing display. (5/1)
**Respectable Jones** is not in a going mood at present. (50/1)

## 2393 FRAGGLES MEDIAN AUCTION MAIDEN STKS (3-Y.O F) (Class F)
2-50 (2-52) **7f** £2,679.00 (£744.00: £357.00) Stalls: Low GOING: minus 0.12 sec per fur (G)

| | Horse / details | | SP | RR | SF |
|---|---|---|---|---|---|
| 1527[14] | **Bollin Dorothy (67)** (TDEasterby) **3-8-11** MBirch(5) (lw: mde all: kpt on wl fnl 2f)....— | **1** | 11/8[2] | 58 | 21 |
| | **Cruz Santa** (TDBarron) **3-8-11** JFortune(2) (w'like: unf: scope: a.p: rn green 2f out: kpt on wl towards fin)....2 | **2** | 25/1 | 53 | 16 |
| 2004[4] | **Divine** (ACStewart) **3-8-11** JWeaver(9) (lw: chsd wnr tl outpcd fnl 2f)....2 | **3** | 10/11[1] | 49 | 12 |
| 867[9] | **Dispol Duchess (35)** (GROldroyd) **3-8-11** KFallon(3) (in tch: effrt 3f out: no imp)....3 | **4** | 66/1 | 42 | 5 |
| 2236[3] | **Marino Street** (PDEvans) **3-8-11v** DHolland(4) (effrt over 2f out: n.d)....2 | **5** | 7/1[3] | 37 | — |
| 2075[17] | **Chilly Looks (47)** (DWBarker) **3-8-11** TWilliams(6) (swtg: chsd ldrs tl outpcd fnl 2f)....s.h | **6** | 50/1 | 37 | — |
| | **Balinsky (IRE)** (JBerry) **3-8-11** JCarroll(7) (w'like: sn outpcd & bhd)....3 | **7** | 25/1 | 31 | — |
| | **Finestatetobein** (FWatson) **3-8-8**(3) CTeague(8) (w'like: bkwd: dwlt: sn t.o)....30 | **8** | 66/1 | — | — |

(SP 119.6%) **8 Rn**

**1m 30.8** (7.20) CSF £29.93 TOTE £2.90: £1.40 £5.20 £1.00 (£32.80) Trio £15.90 OWNER Lady Westbrook (MALTON) BRED Sir Neil and Lady Westbrook

**1527 Bollin Dorothy** looked particularly well and, jumping out first, settled well in front. She won with something in hand and, now she has broken her duck, she should progress. (11/8)
**Cruz Santa** put up a most promising first effort, staying on well after running very green early in the straight. Better should be seen before long. (25/1)
**2004 Divine** looked really well, but is obviously nothing special and was left struggling once the pace increased early in the straight. (10/11: 4/7-Evens)
**Dispol Duchess**, stepping up in trip, showed her first signs of form, but she failed to make any impression on the principals. (66/1)
**2236 Marino Street** had little chance at these weights. Settled off the pace, she never looked likely to get into it, and was wisely not knocked about. (7/1)
**Chilly Looks** had no chance at the weights here, and this sweaty individual was going nowhere in the home straight. (50/1)
**Balinsky (IRE)**, a decent-looking newcomer, moved poorly to post and never showed in the race. (25/1)

## 2394 HONDEGHEM CLAIMING STKS (3-Y.O+) (Class F)
3-20 (3-21) **1m 3f 214y** £2,763.00 (£768.00: £369.00) Stalls: Low GOING: minus 0.12 sec per fur (G)

| | Horse / details | | SP | RR | SF |
|---|---|---|---|---|---|
| *1967** | **Pharly Dancer (55)** (WWHaigh) **7-9-5**(5) LNewton(10) (lw: a.p: led over 1f out: styd on strly)....— | **1** | 5/2[2] | 69 | 30 |
| 2136[2] | **Mithraic (IRE) (53)** (WSCunningham) **4-9-8** ACulhane(9) (lw: led tl hdd over 1f out: sn btn)....5 | **2** | 8/1 | 60 | 21 |
| 2189[6] | **Nosey Native (67)** (JPearce) **3-8-9v** NDay(2) (cl up: chal over 4f out: sn rdn: one pce fnl 2f)....hd | **3** | 6/1[3] | 60 | 8 |
| 2178[3] | **Simand (50)** (GMMoore) **4-8-13** JFortune(3) (lw: a.p: rdn over 4f out: one pce)....9 | **4** | 10/1 | 39 | — |
| 2321[3] | **Northern Trial (USA) (49)** (KRBurke) **8-9-7v**(5) GParkin(8) (in tch: outpcd 5f out: n.d after)....1¼ | **5** | 14/1 | 51 | 12 |
| 2066[8] | **Heathyards Magic (IRE) (52)** (MDods) **4-9-8** JCarroll(13) (in tch: pushed along 7f out: no imp)....12 | **6** | 14/1 | 31 | — |
| 1763[5] | **Cross Talk (IRE) (68)** (RHollinshead) **4-9-9**(3) FLynch(4) (lw: hdwy & prom ½-wy: rdn 4f out: sn btn)....¾ | **7** | 2/1[1] | 33 | — |
| 2056[5] | **Greek Gold (IRE) (41)** (DWBarker) **7-9-4** LCharnock(1) (lw: a bhd)....14 | **8** | 20/1 | 7 | — |
| | **Never so True (40)** (MartynWane) **5-9-1** BThomson(6) (chsd ldrs tl wknd 5f out)....4 | **9** | 20/1 | — | — |
| 2136[5] | **Anorak (USA) (44)** (GMMoore) **6-9-8v** JWeaver(12) (a outpcd & bhd: t.o fnl 4f)....22 | **10** | 10/1 | — | — |
| 1697[7] | **Venture Fourth (20)** (MissMKMilligan) **7-9-2b** MBirch(11) (s.s: a bhd: p.u ent st).... | **P** | 100/1 | — | — |

(SP 129.3%) **11 Rn**

**2m 44.8** (13.40) CSF £23.99 TOTE £3.50: £1.90 £2.20 £2.40 (£16.80) Trio £63.10 OWNER Mr A. Marucci (MALTON) BRED Stud-On-The-Chart
WEIGHT FOR AGE 3yo-13lb
OFFICIAL EXPLANATION **Cross Talk (IRE): the jockey reported that the colt lost his action entering the straight. The trainer stated that the colt had an history of back problems.**

**1967* Pharly Dancer** took the eye in the paddock, and this All-Weather specialist showed what tremendous heart he is in by winning easily. (5/2)
**2136 Mithraic (IRE)** is still a maiden but looks really well and is in good form at present, although he was well outclassed by the winner here. (8/1)
**2189 Nosey Native** had his chances but, after looking to be going best approaching the home turn, he failed to respond when ridden. (6/1: 4/1-7/1)
**2178 Simand**, trying a longer trip here, was off the bit with fully half a mile left and making no impression thereafter. (10/1)
**2321 Northern Trial (USA)** had plenty to do at these weights and was flat out and going nowhere in the final five furlongs. (14/1)
**1866 Heathyards Magic (IRE)** is an in-and-out performer and this was not one of his going days. (14/1)
**1763 Cross Talk (IRE)** apparently has training problems and, although he loves this track, he was obviously not at his best on this occasion, and was left way behind in the last half-mile. (2/1)

## 2395 DRAGON TROOP H'CAP (0-75) (3-Y.O+) (Class D)
3-50 (3-53) **5f** £3,850.00 (£1,150.00: £550.00: £250.00) Stalls: Low GOING: minus 0.12 sec per fur (G)

| | Horse / details | | SP | RR | SF |
|---|---|---|---|---|---|
| 1844[7] | **Ninety-Five (60)** (JGFitzGerald) **4-9-8** KFallon(6) (cl up: led after 2f: r.o: comf)....— | **1** | 9/4[2] | 73+ | 37 |
| 2316[12] | **China Hand (IRE) (39)** (MartynWane) **4-8-1** JFanning(2) (a chsng ldrs: nt pce of wnr fnl 2f)....5 | **2** | 8/1 | 36 | — |
| 1859[12] | **Double Glow (34)** (NBycroft) **4-7-10b** NCarlisle(3) (s.i.s: styd on fnl 2f: n.d)....2½ | **3** | 25/1 | 23 | — |
| 2021* | **Chemcast (67)** (DNicholls) **3-9-10b** AlexGreaves(4) (led 2f: wknd 2f out)....5 | **4** | 11/4[3] | 40 | — |
| | **Kabcast (44)** (DWChapman) **11-8-6b** LCharnock(1) (bit bkwd: spd to ½-wy: sn wknd)....1½ | **5** | 12/1 | 12 | — |

| | | | | SP | RR | SF |
|---|---|---|---|---|---|---|
| *2386** | ***Swan At Whalley (60)*** (MartynWane) **4-9-3**[(5)] PRoberts(5) (Withdrawn not under Starter's orders: ref to ent stalls) | | W | 2/1[1] | — | — |
| | | | | (SP 113.4%) | | **5 Rn** |

**62.1 secs** (4.60) CSF £8.86 TOTE £1.90: £1.10 £2.10 (£3.00) OWNER Mr N. H. T. Wrigley (MALTON) BRED M. H. Wrigley
LONG HANDICAP Double Glow 7-9
WEIGHT FOR AGE 3yo-5lb
**OFFICIAL EXPLANATION Chemcast: pulled off his off-fore shoe.**
**1844 Ninety-Five** was up against some unfancied opponents and beat them most convincingly. She obviously loves this easy ground. (9/4)
**1547 China Hand (IRE)** was no match once the winner stepped up the pace from halfway. (8/1)
**Double Glow**, who did her usual and gave ground away at the start, could never recover. (25/1)
**2021* Chemcast**, easy in the market, did not like the soft ground and was left struggling from halfway. (11/4)
**Kabcast** needed this, his first run of the season, and blew up soon after halfway. (12/1: 7/1-14/1)

## 2396 SANNA'S POST MEDIAN AUCTION MAIDEN STKS (2-Y.O) (Class F)
4-20 (4-21) **7f** £2,763.00 (£768.00: £369.00) Stalls: Low GOING: minus 0.12 sec per fur (G)

| | | | | SP | RR | SF |
|---|---|---|---|---|---|---|
| 2044[3] | **Grate Times** (EWeymes) **2-9-0** KFallon(8) (cl up: led wl over 1f out: r.o) | — | **1** | 8/1 | 67 | 29 |
| 1664[5] | **Mystic Circle (IRE)** (JWWatts) **2-8-9** BThomson(9) (lw: cl up: led over 2f out tl wl over 1f out: kpt on) | 2 | **2** | 5/2[1] | 57 | 19 |
| 2132[8] | **Fancy A Fortune (IRE)** (JPearce) **2-9-0** NDay(4) (bhd: hdwy 2f out: styd on wl) | ¾ | **3** | 14/1 | 61 | 23 |
| 1086[7] | **Mill End Boy** (MWEasterby) **2-8-9**[(5)] GParkin(10) (lw: bhd: hdwy 2f out: nvr able to rch ldrs) | 2 | **4** | 15/2[3] | 56 | 18 |
| 1525[8] | **Sandbaggedagain** (MWEasterby) **2-9-0** DaleGibson(6) (bhd tl styd on wl fnl 2f) | hd | **5** | 40/1 | 56 | 18 |
| 2044[6] | **Imperial Or Metric (IRE)** (JBerry) **2-9-0** JCarroll(7) (lw: hdwy & prom after 3f: rdn & btn appr fnl f) | 1¼ | **6** | 10/1 | 53 | 15 |
| *1489[3]* | **Mystic Quest (IRE)** (KMcAuliffe) **2-9-0** JWeaver(5) (prom tl outpcd fnl 2½f) | 1½ | **7** | 8/1 | 50 | 12 |
| 2044[9] | **Cajun Sunset (IRE)** (TDEasterby) **2-9-0** JFortune(2) (in tch tl wknd fnl 2f) | 2 | **8** | 20/1 | 45 | 7 |
| 1499[2] | **Falls O'Moness (IRE)** (KRBurke) **2-8-9** DHolland(3) (led 2f: w ldrs tl wknd wl over 1f out) | ½ | **9** | 5/2[1] | 39 | 1 |
| *2083[2]* | **Jack Says** (TDEasterby) **2-9-0** MBirch(1) (led after 2f: hdd over 2f out: sn btn & eased: lame) | 26 | **10** | 4/1[2] | — | — |
| | | | | (SP 134.1%) | | **10 Rn** |

**1m 30.3** (6.70) CSF £31.06 TOTE £5.20: £1.30 £2.00 £2.80 (£8.00) Trio £197.70; £222.81 to Catterick 4/7/96 OWNER Mrs M. Ashby (MIDDLEHAM) BRED J. E. Jackson
**OFFICIAL EXPLANATION Falls O' Moness (IRE): his jockey reported that the horse failed to get the trip on the soft ground.**
**2044 Grate Times**, well suited by the easier ground, won really well. (8/1)
**1664 Mystic Circle (IRE)** has a good action more suited to faster ground, but still ran well and will surely find a race in due course. (5/2: op 6/4)
**Fancy A Fortune (IRE)**, although not all that big, is built like a tank and showed plenty here. He looks to be improving fast. (14/1: op 8/1)
**1086 Mill End Boy**, stepped up in trip, ran well and was putting in all his best work at the finish. (15/2: 5/1-8/1)
**1525 Sandbaggedagain**, trying a longer trip, made ground all the way up the straight and there would seem to be a race in him. (40/1)
**2044 Imperial Or Metric (IRE)** does not look the type to be suited by these soft conditions and was left struggling approaching the final furlong. (10/1)
**1489 Mystic Quest (IRE)** did not impress on looks this time and dropped out tamely early in the straight. (8/1)
**2083 Jack Says** (4/1: 3/1-9/2)

## 2397 LILLIBULERO H'CAP (0-70) (3-Y.O) (Class E)
4-50 (4-50) **1m 3f 214y** £3,028.00 (£904.00: £432.00: £196.00) Stalls: Low GOING: minus 0.12 sec per fur (G)

| | | | | SP | RR | SF |
|---|---|---|---|---|---|---|
| 2067[3] | **Etterby Park (USA) (51)** (MJohnston) **3-8-8** JWeaver(1) (lw: cl up: led 7f out: clr over 3f out: eased ins fnl f) | — | **1** | 4/1[3] | 66+ | 16 |
| *2086[4]* | **Champagne Warrior (IRE) (47)** (MJCamacho) **3-8-4** LCharnock(8) (bhd: hdwy & in tch 4f out: styd on: no ch w wnr) | 6 | **2** | 11/1 | 54 | 4 |
| 2027[2] | **Phantom Haze (64)** (MissSEHall) **3-9-4**[(3)] FLynch(7) (lw: bhd: hdwy 7f out: sn rdn & prom: no imp fnl f) | 2½ | **3** | 9/2 | 68 | 18 |
| 1850[5] | **Northern Falcon (40)** (MWEasterby) **3-7-11b**[ow1] DaleGibson(9) (prom: effrt 5f out: one pce) | 3½ | **4** | 16/1 | 39 | — |
| 1821[13] | **The Jolly Barmaid (IRE) (42)** (PCalver) **3-7-13** NCarlisle(10) (effrt ½-wy: no imp) | 3 | **5** | 16/1 | 37 | — |
| 1418[7] | **Alzotic (IRE) (45)** (JNorton) **3-8-2** JFanning(4) (lw: mid div: rdn 5f out: no imp) | 5 | **6** | 5/2[1] | 33 | — |
| *1970[7]* | **Hannahs Bay (39)** (MGMeagher) **3-7-10b** NKennedy(2) (chsd ldrs tl rdn & wknd 7f out) | 5 | **7** | 16/1 | 21 | — |
| 2067[11] | **Jackson Park (59)** (TDEasterby) **3-9-2b**[1] MBirch(3) (chsd ldrs: rdn 4f out: wknd over 2f out) | 11 | **8** | 8/1 | 26 | — |
| 2348* | **Arabian Heights (53)** (MrsJRRamsden) **3-8-10** [4x] KFallon(5) (bhd: pushed along 7f out: hmpd 5f out: n.d) | 8 | **9** | 3/1[2] | 9 | — |
| 2348[9] | **Dispol Conqueror (IRE) (41)** (GROldroyd) **3-7-12v**[ow2] TWilliams(6) (led tl hdd 7f out: sn rdn & wknd: t.o) | 24 | **10** | 50/1 | — | — |
| | | | | (SP 130.8%) | | **10 Rn** |

**2m 44.7** (13.30) CSF £47.65 CT £199.10 TOTE £4.70: £2.60 £2.80 £2.00 (£31.90) Trio £28.30 OWNER Crowther Homes Ltd (MIDDLEHAM) BRED Jayeff "B" Stables
LONG HANDICAP Northern Falcon 7-8 Dispol Conqueror (IRE) 7-7
**2067 Etterby Park (USA)** relished these soft conditions and, quickening clear turning for home, won pulling up. (4/1)
**2086 Champagne Warrior (IRE)** struggled on well in the last half-mile but could never get within sniffing distance of the winner. (11/1: 8/1-12/1)
**2027 Phantom Haze** was ridden to improve from halfway but was never up to the task. (9/2)
**1850 Northern Falcon**, trying a longer trip on softer ground, was going nowhere in the final half-mile. (16/1)
**The Jolly Barmaid (IRE)** failed to show her assets when things got serious in the last five furlongs. (16/1)
**Alzotic (IRE)** was backed with confidence, but he failed to justify it at any stage, and may be better on Sand. (5/2: op 5/1)
**2348* Arabian Heights**, easy to back, ran inexplicably badly and also found trouble. This is best forgotten. (3/1: op 2/1)

T/Jkpt: £1,394.80 (5.09 Tckts). T/Plpt: £23.30 (571.19 Tckts). T/Qdpt: £10.60 (65.66 Tckts). AA

# 1815-EPSOM (L-H) (Good to firm)
## Wednesday July 3rd
WEATHER: overcast WIND: fresh half bhd

## 2398 E.B.F. TATTENHAM MAIDEN STKS (2-Y.O) (Class D)
6-20 (6-21) **6f** £3,420.00 (£1,035.00: £505.00: £240.00) Stalls: High GOING minus 0.31 sec per fur (GF)

| | | | | SP | RR | SF |
|---|---|---|---|---|---|---|
| 1960[3] | **Powder River** (RHannon) **2-8-11b**[(3)] DaneO'Neill(5) (lw: mde all: j.path over 3f out: pushed out ins fnl f) | — | **1** | 5/6[1] | 77 | 26 |

| Form | Horse | Dist | Pos | SP | RR | SF |
|---|---|---|---|---|---|---|
| 2230$^{3}$ | **Rise 'n Shine** (CACyzer) **2-8-9** TQuinn(1) (chsd wnr: rdn & edgd lft ins fnl f: one pce) | 4 | **2** | 5/2$^{2}$ | 61 | 10 |
| 1118$^{9}$ | **Salty Jack (IRE)** (SDow) **2-9-0** JFEgan(4) (rr: rdn & sme hdwy 2f out: kpt on one pce ins fnl f) | 2 | **3** | 12/1 | 61 | 10 |
| | **Signs And Wonders** (CACyzer) **2-8-9** WJO'Connor(6) (unf: bit bkwd: dwlt: sn rdn along: nvr on terms) | 1¾ | **4** | 10/1$^{3}$ | 51 | — |
| 1766$^{5}$ | **Talisman (IRE)** (SDow) **2-8-9**$^{(5)}$ ADaly(2) (chsd ldrs: rdn 3f out: wknd 2f out) | hd | **5** | 10/1$^{3}$ | 56 | 5 |

(SP 109.0%) **5 Rn**

**1m 11.09** (3.09) CSF £3.17 TOTE £1.70: £1.20 £1.40 (£1.30) OWNER Lord Carnarvon (MARLBOROUGH) BRED Highclere Stud Ltd

**1960 Powder River** made all the running and his only worry came when he jumped a path over three furlongs out. Soon back on an even keel, he was quickly back in control. (5/6)

**2230 Rise 'n Shine** did not look very keen when asked to challenge entering the final furlong. (5/2)

**Salty Jack (IRE)** kept on for a modest third without ever posing a threat. (12/1)

**Signs And Wonders** was too green to do herself justice. (10/1)

**1169 Talisman (IRE)** (10/1: 7/1-12/1)

## 2399 CHANTILLY MAIDEN STKS (3-Y.O F) (Class D)

6-50 (6-53) **1m 2f 18y** £3,663.75 (£1,110.00: £542.50: £258.75) Stalls: Centre GOING minus 0.31 sec per fur (GF)

| Form | Horse | Dist | Pos | SP | RR | SF |
|---|---|---|---|---|---|---|
| 1201$^{2}$ | **Nanda** (DRLoder) **3-8-8**$^{(3)}$ JStack(2) (a.p: rdn to ld ent fnl f: r.o wl) | — | **1** | 11/2$^{2}$ | 84 | 36 |
| 1901$^{4}$ | **Supamova (USA) (85)** (PFICole) **3-8-11** TQuinn(4) (hld up mid div: hdwy on ins to ld over 2f out: hdd ent fnl f: unable qckn) | 1¾ | **2** | 100/30$^{1}$ | 81 | 33 |
| 2208$^{4}$ | **Omara (USA) (78)** (HRACecil) **3-8-11** AMcGlone(10) (lw: hld up: hdwy 3f out: ev ch 1f out: one pce) | 2½ | **3** | 12/1 | 77 | 29 |
| 1963$^{2}$ | **Russian Request (IRE)** (MRStoute) **3-8-11** PaulEddery(3) (led: hdd over 2f out: hrd rdn over 1f out: one pce) | 3 | **4** | 100/30$^{1}$ | 73 | 25 |
| 2001$^{3}$ | **Disallowed (IRE) (72)** (MBell) **3-8-11** MFenton(5) (chsd ldr tl over 2f out: wknd over 1f out) | 3½ | **5** | 6/1$^{3}$ | 67 | 19 |
| 2197$^{7}$ | **Love Bateta (IRE) (70)** (RHannon) **3-8-8**$^{(3)}$ DaneO'Neill(6) (chsd ldrs: rdn 5f out: wknd over 2f out) | ½ | **6** | 20/1 | 66 | 18 |
| | **Lucky Hoof** (CEBrittain) **3-8-11** BDoyle(9) (unf: bit bkwd: dwlt: sn in tch: wknd ½-wy) | 5 | **7** | 16/1 | 58 | 10 |
| 1614$^{4}$ | **Tea Party (USA)** (KOCunningham-Brown) **3-8-11** WCarson(7) (mid div tl wknd 4f out) | 4 | **8** | 10/1 | 52 | 4 |
| | **Aravinda (IRE)** (LadyHerries) **3-8-11** DeclanO'Shea(1) (w'like: bit bkwd: a bhd) | ¾ | **9** | 16/1 | 51 | 3 |

(SP 109.1%) **9 Rn**

**2m 8.74** (4.34) CSF £21.53 TOTE £6.30: £2.40 £1.70 £3.20 (£5.90) Trio £22.90 OWNER Sheikh Mohammed (NEWMARKET) BRED Darley Stud Management Co Ltd

**1201 Nanda** was never far away. Asked to go and win her race entering the final furlong, she responded gamely and won going away. (11/2: 7/2-6/1)

**1901 Supamova (USA)** came through to take it up over two furlongs out and, though doing nothing wrong, was unable to repel the winner's late challenge. (100/30: 9/4-7/2)

**2208 Omara (USA)** travelled really well and looked like scoring when coming to challenge below the distance. Not for the first time though, he proved to be one-paced. (12/1: op 8/1)

**1963 Russian Request (IRE)** looked very one-paced here, and is worth a try over further. (100/30)

**2001 Disallowed (IRE)** dropped away disappointingly in the last two furlongs. (6/1)

## 2400 NABS H'CAP (0-95) (3-Y.O+) (Class C)

7-20 (7-23) **7f** £5,420.00 (£1,640.00: £800.00: £380.00) Stalls: Centre GOING minus 0.31 sec per fur (GF)

| Form | Horse | Dist | Pos | SP | RR | SF |
|---|---|---|---|---|---|---|
| 2053$^{19}$ | **Chickawicka (IRE) (82)** (BPalling) **5-9-7** TSprake(2) (mde all: rdn over 2f out: r.o wl) | — | **1** | 10/1 | 91 | 56 |
| 1790$^{2}$ | **My Best Valentine (89)** (JWhite) **6-9-11**$^{(3)}$ AWhelan(5) (lw: hld up in tch: chsd wnr over 1f out: rdn & edgd lft ins fnl f: unable qckn) | 2½ | **2** | 9/2$^{1}$ | 92 | 57 |
| 1790$^{4}$ | **Shamanic (88)** (RHannon) **4-9-10**$^{(3)}$ DaneO'Neill(1) (hld up in tch: chsd wnr 3f out tl over 1f out: n.m.r ins fnl f: one pce) | ½ | **3** | 6/1$^{2}$ | 90 | 55 |
| 2134$^{9}$ | **Rakis (IRE) (78)** (MrsLStubbs) **6-9-3** JFEgan(6) (hld up: hdwy 2f out: rdn & hung lft over 1f out: one pce) | 3 | **4** | 9/2$^{1}$ | 73 | 38 |
| *2170*$^{10}$ | **Worldwide Elsie (USA) (80)** (RHarris) **3-8-11** AMackay(8) (nvr nrr) | 1¾ | **5** | 20/1 | 71 | 28 |
| 2134$^{10}$ | **Toujours Riviera (80)** (JPearce) **6-9-5** GBardwell(4) (wl bhd & outpcd to ½-wy: styd on ins fnl f: nvr nrr) | 1 | **6** | 11/1 | 69 | 34 |
| *854*$^{6}$ | **Comanche Companion (83)** (TJNaughton) **6-9-8** PaulEddery(3) (rr: rdn over 2f out: no hdwy) | 3 | **7** | 13/2$^{3}$ | 65 | 30 |
| 1790$^{5}$ | **Jo Maximus (75)** (SDow) **4-9-0** TQuinn(9) (w wnr over 3f: wknd over 2f out) | 2 | **8** | 9/2$^{1}$ | 53 | 18 |
| 1425$^{7}$ | **Night Wink (USA) (76)** (GLMoore) **4-9-1** SWhitworth(7) (w wnr 3f: wknd over 2f out) | ¾ | **9** | 8/1 | 52 | 17 |

(SP 115.5%) **9 Rn**

**1m 22.1** (1.80) CSF £50.71 CT £272.69 TOTE £12.00: £2.20 £1.70 £2.20 (£34.20) Trio £24.40 OWNER Merthyr Motor Auctions (COWBRIDGE) BRED Charlton Down Stud

WEIGHT FOR AGE 3yo-8lb

STEWARDS' ENQUIRY Whelan susp. 12-13/7/96 (careless riding)

**1018 Chickawicka (IRE)** made all the running. He shook off his two closest pursuers by halfway, and had more than enough in reserve to see off the rest. (10/1)

**1790 My Best Valentine** was the paddock pick and ran well too. Never far away, he was asked to quicken from below the distance, but found his weight anchoring him. (9/2: op 3/1)

**1790 Shamanic** moved into second place going well early in the straight, but found a burst of speed beyond him. (6/1)

**1962* Rakis (IRE)** hung to his left when asked to challenge below the distance and appeared unsuited by the course. (9/2: op 3/1)

**1172 Worldwide Elsie (USA)** was never closer than at the finish. (20/1)

**Toujours Riviera** was well behind until staying on through beaten horses late on. (11/1: op 7/1)

## 2401 UNION BANK OF SWITZERLAND H'CAP (0-90) (3-Y.O+) (Class C)

7-50 (8-02) **1m 4f 10y** £5,602.00 (£1,696.00: £828.00: £394.00) Stalls: Centre GOING: 0.31 sec per fur (G)

| Form | Horse | Dist | Pos | SP | RR | SF |
|---|---|---|---|---|---|---|
| 1792$^{4}$ | **Artic Courier (80)** (DJSCosgrove) **5-9-6**$^{(3)}$ JStack(7) (hld up: hdwy to chse ldr 3f out: led over 2f out: r.o wl) | — | **1** | 9/1 | 91 | 61 |
| 1961$^{6}$ | **Silently (78)** (IABalding) **4-9-7** TQuinn(1) (lw: hld up: hdwy 3f out: rdn 2f out: fin 3rd, 1 3/4l: plcd 2nd) | | **2** | 8/1 | 85 | 55 |
| 2046$^{2}$ | **Chatham Island (70)** (CEBrittain) **8-8-6**$^{(7)}$ JGotobed(10) (chsd clr ldr: led over 5f out: hdd over 2f out: one pce: fin 4th, nk: plcd 3rd) | | **3** | 7/1 | 76 | 46 |
| 1816* | **Rising Dough (IRE) (71)** (GLMoore) **4-8-11**$^{(3)}$ DaneO'Neill(2) (rr: hdwy 4f out: rdn over 2f out: one pce: fin 5th, 3½l: plcd 4th) | | **4** | 6/1$^{3}$ | 73 | 43 |
| 2164* | **Faateq (89)** (JLDunlop) **3-9-5** WCarson(5) (lw: hld up: hdwy 3f out: rdn & hmpd 2f out: nt rcvr: fin 6th, 10l: plcd 5th) | | **5** | 4/1$^{1}$ | 77 | 34 |

| | | | Pos | SP | RR | SF |
|---|---|---|---|---|---|---|
| 2002[5] | **Prince Danzig (IRE) (66)** (DJGMurraySmith) **5-8-9** PaulEddery(6) (a bhd) | 5 | **7** | 12/1 | 48 | 18 |
| 1802[3] | **Riparius (USA) (81)** (HCandy) **5-9-10** CRutter(8) (a bhd) | nk | **8** | 10/1 | 62 | 32 |
| 666[11] | **Aude la Belle (FR) (53)** (SGKnight) **8-7-10** AMackay(4) (a bhd) | 12 | **9** | 50/1 | 18 | — |
| 1792[11] | **Global Dancer (71)** (SDow) **5-8-9**(5) ADaly(11) (led: sn clr: hdd over 5f out: wknd over 3f out) | 9 | **10** | 9/1 | 24 | — |
| 1874[6] | **General Mouktar (57)** (BJMeehan) **6-8-0** JFEgan(9) (hld up: hdwy 3f out: n.m.r over 2f out: swtchd sharply rt 2f out: sn rdn: unable qckn: fin 2nd, 1½l: disq: plcd last) | | **D** | 12/1 | 66 | 36 |
| *2173*[2] | **Lidhama (USA) (59)** (GLewis) **4-7-13**(3) AWhelan(3) (rr: rdn 7f out: bhd whn fell over 3f out: dead) | | **F** | 5/1[2] | — | — |
| | | | | (SP 121.0%) | **11 Rn** | |

**2n. .8.38** (3.38) CSF £74.01 CT £495.01 TOTE £13.60: £3.30 £2.90 £2.00 (£48.00) Trio £119.40 OWNER Britam Promotions Ltd (NEWMARKET) BRED Stud-On-The-Chart
WEIGHT FOR AGE 3yo-13lb
STEWARDS' ENQUIRY Egan susp. 12-13 & 15-17/7/96 (careless riding)
**1792 Artic Courier** normally runs well but, in twenty-seven previous starts, had only won twice. He did everything right here, leading over two furlongs out and seeing it out well. (9/1)
**1686 Silently** moved up dangerously two furlongs out but, not for the first time, found disappointingly little for pressure. (8/1)
**2046 Chatham Island** chased the clear leader and probably went too fast himself, for he had not too much in reserve in the closing stages. He must have gone close ridden with more restraint. (7/1)
**1816* Rising Dough (IRE)** proved one-paced in the final two furlongs. (6/1)
**2164* Faateq** was probably just getting the worst of the argument when badly hampered two furlongs out. (4/1: op 5/2)
**1874 General Mouktar** made good headway on the inside from the three-furlong marker. He ran out of room shortly afterwards and his rider panicked and switched him sharply to his right, badly hampering Faateq. The five-day ban was well justified. (12/1)
**2173 Lidhama (USA)** (5/1: 3/1-11/2)

## 2402 BURGH HEATH CLAIMING STKS (3-Y.O) (Class D)

8-20 (8-42) **1m 114y** £3,598.75 (£1,090.00: £532.50: £253.75) Stalls: Centre GOING minus 0.31 sec per fur (GF)

| | | | Pos | SP | RR | SF |
|---|---|---|---|---|---|---|
| 2339[3] | **Half An Inch (IRE) (67)** (BJMeehan) **3-8-9b** BDoyle(2) (lw: mde all: hrd rdn fnl 2f: all out) | — | **1** | 100/30[2] | 62 | 26 |
| 1661[8] | **Wingnut (IRE) (40)** (MJHaynes) **3-8-0b** WCarson(7) (sn pushed along in rr: wl bhd 3f out: hrd rdn 2f out: str run ins fnl f: fin wl) | hd | **2** | 14/1 | 53 | 17 |
| 2253[3] | **Sunley Secure (55)** (MRChannon) **3-8-11** TQuinn(6) (w wnr: rdn & edgd lft 2f out: ev ch wl ins fnl f: r.o) | hd | **3** | 3/1[1] | 64 | 28 |
| 2180[6] | **Cherry Garden (IRE) (49)** (TJNaughton) **3-8-7** PaulEddery(1) (chsd ldrs: rdn 4f out: ev ch wl ins fnl f: r.o) | nk | **4** | 13/2[3] | 59 | 23 |
| 1956[2] | **Coastguards Hero (57)** (MDIUsher) **3-8-9** SSanders(8) (lw: hld up: hdwy 3f out: hrd rdn 2f out: r.o ins fnl f) | ½ | **5** | 100/30[2] | 60 | 24 |
| *1993*[7] | **People Direct (58)** (KMcAuliffe) **3-8-3**(3) DaneO'Neill(3) (hld up: rdn 4f out: wknd 3f out) | 16 | **6** | 8/1 | 27 | — |
| 1498[14] | **Kuwam (IRE) (47)** (BHanbury) **3-8-4**(3) JStack(4) (chsd ldrs tl wknd 3f out) | 4 | **7** | 14/1 | 21 | — |
| | | | | (SP 108.9%) | **7 Rn** | |

**1m 46.34** (4.34) CSF £37.45 TOTE £3.70: £2.20 £1.90 (£10.30) OWNER Mr T Dale & Mr C Mills (UPPER LAMBOURN) BRED Stonethorn Stud Farms Ltd
**2339 Half An Inch (IRE)** made all the running but was strongly challenged throughout by the third. To his credit, he stuck to his task well and saw it out gamely. (100/30)
**1451 Wingnut (IRE)** was outpaced and behind until producing a storming finish in the final furlong which would have succeeded in a few more strides. (14/1)
**2253 Sunley Secure** disputed the lead for the whole way, but could never quite force his head in front. (3/1)
**2180 Cherry Garden (IRE)** raced in third place. He moved up to challenge entering the final furlong and looked likely to score, but could never quite hit the front. (13/2)
**1956 Coastguards Hero** stayed on in the final two furlongs and was closing strongly at the finish. (100/30)
**1168 Kuwam (IRE)** (14/1: op 8/1)

## 2403 BANSTEAD H'CAP (0-85) (3-Y.O+) (Class D)

8-50 (9-10) **6f** £3,615.00 (£1,095.00: £535.00: £255.00) Stalls: High GOING minus 0.31 sec per fur (GF)

| | | | Pos | SP | RR | SF |
|---|---|---|---|---|---|---|
| 2232[3] | **Golden Pound (USA) (77)** (MissGayKelleway) **4-9-4**(3) DaneO'Neill(7) (lw: hld up in tch: rdn over 1f out: led ins fnl f: r.o wl) | — | **1** | 7/2[1] | 89 | 59 |
| 2376[3] | **Cheeky Chappy (52)** (DWChapman) **5-7-10b** 6x JQuinn(5) (chsd ldrs: rdn over 1f out: ev ch wl ins fnl f: r.o) | 1 | **2** | 4/1[2] | 61 | 31 |
| *2308*[2] | **Yo Kiri-B (52)** (TJNaughton) **5-7-7**(3) MHenry(1) (chsd ldrs: rdn & outpcd 2f out: styd on again ins fnl f) | 1½ | **3** | 6/1[3] | 57 | 27 |
| 2311[5] | **Pearl Dawn (IRE) (68)** (GLMoore) **6-8-12** SWhitworth(4) (lw: rr: rdn over 2f out: styd on ins fnl f) | ¾ | **4** | 9/1 | 71 | 41 |
| 2114[25] | **Shikari's Son (84)** (JCullinan) **9-10-0** TQuinn(8) (rr: rdn 3f out: nvr nrr) | 2 | **5** | 10/1 | 82 | 52 |
| 2017[4] | **Tafahhus (70)** (MJPolglase) **4-8-11**(3) JStack(6) (chsd ldr: rdn over 1f out: wknd ins fnl f) | s.h | **6** | 13/2 | 68 | 38 |
| 2280[2] | **Another Batchworth (56)** (EAWheeler) **4-8-0**ow1 TSprake(3) (led: clr over 2f out: hdd ins fnl f: sn wknd) | hd | **7** | 8/1 | 54 | 23 |
| 2058[7] | **Castel Rosselo (62)** (RHarris) **6-8-6** AMackay(10) (a bhd) | 5 | **8** | 14/1 | 46 | 16 |
| 2286[18] | **Spectacle Jim (52)** (MJHaynes) **7-7-10b** NAdams(9) (a bhd) | s.h | **9** | 20/1 | 36 | 6 |
| 2143[11] | **Sharp Pearl (78)** (JWhite) **3-8-11b**(5) ADaly(2) (a bhd) | 5 | **10** | 7/1 | 49 | 13 |
| | | | | (SP 124.0%) | **10 Rn** | |

**1m 9.3** (1.30) CSF £18.21 CT £79.36 TOTE £4.60: £2.50 £1.40 £1.90 (£7.20) Trio £15.30 OWNER Mr A. P. Griffin (WHITCOMBE) BRED Builder's Mart Inc
LONG HANDICAP Yo Kiri-B 7-8 Spectacle Jim 7-8 Cheeky Chappy 7-3
WEIGHT FOR AGE 3yo-6lb
**2232 Golden Pound (USA)** raced just behind the leaders until produced with a perfectly-timed challenge to score and keep up his trainer's fine run. (7/2)
**2376 Cheeky Chappy** ran a really sound race. Unable to lead as he usually does, he was content to sit just off the pace. Brought to challenge entering the final furlong, no sooner had he collared the leader than he was grabbed himself by the winner. (4/1)
**2308 Yo Kiri-B** stayed on in the final furlong, having been outpaced two furlongs out. Seven is probably her best trip. (6/1)
**2311 Pearl Dawn (IRE)** kept on inside the final furlong to be nearest at the finish. She looks a difficult ride. (9/1)
**631 Shikari's Son** is out of form and was in arrears until staying on late. (10/1)
**2017 Tafahhus** showed good pace to hunt up the leader, but was done with by the furlong pole. (13/2)

T/Plpt: £165.50 (116.4 Tckts). T/Qdpt: £93.40 (33.69 Tckts). SM

# 2279-FOLKESTONE (R-H) (Good to firm, Firm patches becoming Good, Good to firm patches)

## Wednesday July 3rd

WEATHER: raining WIND: str half bhd

## 2404 E.B.F. ROMNEY MARSH MAIDEN STKS (2-Y.O F) (Class D)

2-30 (2-32) **6f 189y** £3,682.05 (£1,100.40: £526.70: £239.85) Stalls: Low GOING minus 0.41 sec per fur (F)

| | Horse | | | SP | RR | SF |
|---|---|---|---|---|---|---|
| 1808[2] | **Hen Harrier** (JLDunlop) **2-8-11** TSprake(4) (chsd ldr: hrd rdn & hung lft 1f out: led last stride) | — | 1 | 7/2[2] | 68 | 35 |
| 2035[4] | **Song Mist (IRE)** (PFICole) **2-8-11** TQuinn(8) (led: rdn over 1f out: edgd lft fnl f: hdd last stride) | s.h | 2 | 4/1[3] | 68 | 35 |
| 1980[3] | **Dayville (USA)** (RCharlton) **2-8-11** SSanders(1) (b: a.p: rdn wl over 1f out: one pce) | 7 | 3 | 3/1[1] | 52 | 19 |
| 1590[8] | **Calamander (IRE)** (PFICole) **2-8-11** JQuinn(3) (a.p: rdn over 2f out: one pce) | 1½ | 4 | 16/1 | 48 | 15 |
| | **Mudflap** (SirMarkPrescott) **2-8-11** GDuffield(7) (neat: lw: s.i.s: hdwy 5f out: lost pl over 3f out: no hdwy fnl 2f) | 5 | 5 | 6/1 | 36 | 3 |
| | **My Girl Lucy** (PhilipMitchell) **2-8-11** AClark(5) (neat: s.s: hdwy 6f out: wknd wl over 1f out) | 3 | 6 | 33/1 | 29 | — |
| 1683[8] | **Watercolour (IRE)** (PFICole) **2-8-11** CRutter(9) (lw: nvr nrr) | 2 | 7 | 33/1 | 25 | — |
| | **Golden Melody** (RHannon) **2-8-8**(3) DaneO'Neill(6) (leggy: bit bkwd: a bhd) | 1 | 8 | 9/1 | 22 | — |
| | **Soden (IRE)** (TGMills) **2-8-11** MarkLynch(2) (str: bit bkwd: prom over 4f) | 1¼ | 9 | 11/1 | 20 | — |
| | **Swallow Breeze** (DrJDScargill) **2-8-11** MFenton(10) (neat: s.s: a bhd) | 1 | 10 | 33/1 | 17 | — |
| 1989[10] | **Singforyoursupper** (GGMargarson) **2-8-11** PBloomfield(11) (bhd fnl 2f) | 3 | 11 | 20/1 | 10 | — |
| | | | | (SP 119.3%) | **11 Rn** | |

**1m 23.7** (0.40 under 2y best) (2.10) CSF £17.27 TOTE £3.80: £1.20 £1.90 £1.80 (£6.40) Trio £3.50 OWNER Sir Thomas Pilkington (ARUNDEL) BRED Mrs Rebecca Philipps

**1808 Hen Harrier** raced in second place. Despite drifting into the centre of the track a furlong out as she threw down her challenge, she managed to get up right on the line. (7/2)

**2035 Song Mist (IRE)** attempted to make all the running. Grimly trying to fend off her rival in the final furlong, she was caught right on the line. Compensation awaits. (4/1)

**1980 Dayville (USA)** was left for dead by the front two from below the distance. (3/1)

**Calamander (IRE)** could only keep on in her own time in the last two furlongs. (16/1)

**Mudflap**, who looked in good shape for this debut, soon recovered from a tardy start, only to lose her pitch at halfway. (6/1)

**My Girl Lucy** is not very big. Soon recovering from a poor start, she had shot her bolt early in the home straight. (33/1)

**Golden Melody** (9/1: op 6/1)

**Soden (IRE)** (11/1: 8/1-12/1)

## 2405 WOODCHURCH H'CAP (0-65) (3-Y.O+) (Class F)

3-00 (3-00) **6f 189y** £2,381.00 (£656.00: £311.00) Stalls: Low GOING minus 0.41 sec per fur (F)

| | Horse | | | SP | RR | SF |
|---|---|---|---|---|---|---|
| *1966*[9] | **Star of Gold (60)** (CREgerton) **4-9-12** PaulEddery(1) (mde all: clr over 1f out: comf) | — | 1 | 6/1[3] | 72+ | 54 |
| *2081*[4] | **Sapphire Son (IRE) (53)** (DMorris) **4-9-5** PBloomfield(7) (lw: chsd wnr: rdn 2f out: unable qckn) | 3½ | 2 | 7/1 | 57 | 39 |
| *502*[7] | **Rubbiyati (48)** (CEBrittain) **4-9-0** BDoyle(5) (hld up: rdn over 2f out: one pce) | 1 | 3 | 8/1 | 50 | 32 |
| 2286[10] | **Pair of Jacks (IRE) (30)** (TJNaughton) **6-7-10** JQuinn(3) (lw: a.p: rdn over 2f out: one pce) | hd | 4 | 14/1 | 31 | 13 |
| 2188[3] | **Mr Cube (IRE) (58)** (JMBradley) **6-9-10v** TQuinn(10) (lw: nvr nr to chal) | 4 | 5 | 100/30[1] | 50 | 32 |
| 2379[5] | **Almapa (48)** (RJHodges) **4-8-9**(5) PPMurphy(11) (hld up: rdn over 3f out: wknd over 2f out) | 2½ | 6 | 13/2 | 34 | 16 |
| 1691[10] | **Arlington Lady (38)** (NACallaghan) **3-7-10** AMackay(9) (s.s: hdwy 6f out: wknd over 2f out) | 5 | 7 | 14/1 | 12 | — |
| 2017* | **Sharp Imp (52)** (RMFlower) **6-9-4b** DBiggs(6) (a bhd) | 7 | 8 | 7/2[2] | 10 | — |
| 1995[10] | **Embroidered (38)** (RMFlower) **3-7-7**(3) NVarley(8) (a bhd) | ½ | 9 | 33/1 | — | — |
| *2201*[8] | **Indian Serenade (44)** (THind) **5-8-10** AClark(4) (lw: hdwy over 3f out: wknd over 2f out) | 7 | 10 | 20/1 | — | — |
| 1994[9] | **Governor's Bid (41)** (MrsLCJewell) **3-7-13**ow3 JFEgan(2) (bhd fnl 2f) | 9 | 11 | 33/1 | — | — |
| | | | | (SP 120.5%) | **11 Rn** | |

**1m 23.3** (1.70) CSF £45.05 CT £316.84 TOTE £11.00: £3.10 £1.90 £2.20 (£15.50) Trio £49.60 OWNER Mr A Allison & Mr A Hayes Partnership (CHADDLEWORTH) BRED Normanby Stud Ltd and C. Shaw

LONG HANDICAP Pair of Jacks (IRE) 7-7 Embroidered 7-7 Arlington Lady 7-8 Governor's Bid 7-7

WEIGHT FOR AGE 3yo-8lb

OFFICIAL EXPLANATION **Sharp Imp: was unsuited by the good ground, and runs best on a firmer surface.**

**Star of Gold** made every post a winning one and forged clear from below the distance for a comfortable success. (6/1)

**2081 Sapphire Son (IRE)**, in pursuit of the winner throughout, failed to peg back that rival in the final quarter-mile. (7/1)

**Rubbiyati**, given a three-month break, could only go up and down in the same place in the home straight. (8/1)

**Pair of Jacks (IRE)**, never far away, was made to look very one-paced in the last two furlongs. (14/1)

**2188 Mr Cube (IRE)** never looked like threatening the leaders. (100/30)

**2379 Almapa**, who ran at Chepstow the day before, chased the leaders but had come to the end of his tether over two furlongs from home. (13/2)

## 2406 HAMSTREET (S) STKS (2-Y.O) (Class G)

3-30 (3-30) **5f** £2,070.00 (£570.00: £270.00) Stalls: Low GOING minus 0.41 sec per fur (F)

| | Horse | | | SP | RR | SF |
|---|---|---|---|---|---|---|
| 2031[10] | **Leitrim Lodge (IRE)** (NACallaghan) **2-8-3**(3) SDrowne(1) (lw: stdy hdwy 2f out: led over 1f out: easily) | — | 1 | 15/8[1] | 64 | 13 |
| 1590[10] | **Windborn** (KMcAuliffe) **2-8-6** JFEgan(2) (lw: led over 3f: unable qckn) | 5 | 2 | 2/1[2] | 48 | — |
| 2199[3] | **Emma's Risk** (RJRWilliams) **2-8-6** JQuinn(3) (hrd rdn & hdwy over 1f out: one pce) | 1¾ | 3 | 10/1 | 42 | — |
| *2172*[7] | **Dancing Star (IRE)** (PDEvans) **2-8-6v** GDuffield(5) (racd centre: a.p: rdn over 2f out: wknd over 1f out) | 4 | 4 | 8/1 | 30 | — |
| 2279[5] | **Tinker's Surprise (IRE)** (BJMeehan) **2-9-3b** TQuinn(4) (racd centre: a.p: rdn & wandered over 1f out: eased whn btn fnl f) | 3½ | 5 | 5/2[3] | 29 | — |
| | | | | (SP 116.9%) | **5 Rn** | |

**60.08 secs** (2.48) CSF £6.22 TOTE £2.60: £3.00 £1.10 (£3.10) OWNER Gallagher Materials Ltd (NEWMARKET) BRED Miss Louise Fitzgerald
No bid

**2031 Leitrim Lodge (IRE)** looked extremely well beforehand and made amends for her Windsor flop. Cruising into the action a quarter of a mile out, she breezed into the lead below the distance and pulled away to win with plenty in hand. (15/8)

**1346 Windborn** attempted to make all the running, but was firmly put in her place when collared by the winner below the distance. (2/1)

**Emma's Risk** was unable to go the early pace. She made up some headway below the distance, but was then only treading water. (10/1)

**838 Dancing Star (IRE)**, who elected to race in the centre of the track, was close up until tiring approaching the final furlong. (8/1: 11/2-9/1)
**2279 Tinker's Surprise (IRE)**, another who elected to race in the centre of the track, was close up but he looked unco-operative as he wandered about below the distance. Finding little, he was eased down in the final furlong. He looks a far from easy ride and is one to avoid. (5/2)

## 2407 ROBYNNE GHENT 1ST BIRTHDAY H'CAP (0-70) (3-Y.O) (Class E)

4-00 (4-00) **1m 7f 92y** £3,206.70 (£957.60: £457.80: £207.90) GOING minus 0.41 sec per fur (F)

| | | | | SP | RR | SF |
|---|---|---|---|---|---|---|
| 2205* | **Hal Hoo Yaroom (71)** (MajorWRHern) **3-9-10** 4x TSprake(5) (mde all: pushed out) | — | **1** | 9/4[2] | 88 | 47 |
| 2204* | **Influence Pedler (56)** (CEBrittain) **3-8-9** 4x BDoyle(4) (chsd wnr fnl 9f: rdn over 2f out: unable qckn) | 4 | **2** | 4/5[1] | 69 | 28 |
| *1997** | **Mighty Phantom (USA) (68)** (JWHills) **3-9-4**(3) MHenry(1) (chsd wnr over 6f: wknd over 3f out) | 12 | **3** | 9/2[3] | 68 | 27 |
| 2282[7] | **Colour Counsellor (47)** (RMFlower) **3-8-0b** DBiggs(3) (lw: bhd fnl 4f) | 4 | **4** | 25/1 | 43 | 2 |
| 2032[14] | **Ben Bowden (57)** (MBlanshard) **3-8-10** JQuinn(2) (a in rr: t.o) | 27 | **5** | 33/1 | 25 | — |
| | | | | (SP 111.3%) | **5 Rn** | |

**3m 23.7** (5.70) CSF £4.38 TOTE £3.10: £1.10 £1.10 (£1.90) OWNER Sheikh Ahmed Al Maktoum (LAMBOURN) BRED Sheikh Ahmed Bin Rashid Al Maktoum

**2205* Hal Hoo Yaroom** put up a polished display. Making all the running, he quickened up the tempo running down the hill and had only the runner-up to worry about. Pushed along, he always had the measure of that rival. (9/4: 6/4-5/2)
**2204* Influence Pedler** moved into second place setting out on the final circuit. Ridden along over a quarter of a mile from home, he failed to get on terms with the winner. (4/5: 6/4-8/11)
**1997* Mighty Phantom (USA)**, in second place in the early stages, had shot her bolt over three furlongs from home. (9/2: 3/1-6/1)

## 2408 SHADDOXHURST H'CAP (0-65) (3-Y.O+) (Class F)

4-30 (4-31) **1m 4f** £2,381.00 (£656.00: £311.00) Stalls: Low GOING minus 0.41 sec per fur (F)

| | | | | SP | RR | SF |
|---|---|---|---|---|---|---|
| 1984[6] | **Minnisam (65)** (JLDunlop) **3-9-5b**[1] TSprake(5) (lw: chsd ldr: led 7f out: clr 5f out: rdn over 2f out: r.o wl) | — | **1** | 6/1 | 77 | 25 |
| 2282* | **Sacred Mirror (IRE) (55)** (CEBrittain) **5-9-8** 5x BDoyle(2) (b: lw: led 5f: rdn over 2f out: unable qckn) | 3 | **2** | 4/1[3] | 63 | 24 |
| 2251[8] | **Seven Crowns (USA) (65)** (RHannon) **3-9-2**(3) DaneO'Neill(8) (hld up: rdn over 3f out: one pce) | 3 | **3** | 11/1 | 69 | 17 |
| 2148[9] | **Uncharted Waters (55)** (CACyzer) **5-9-8** GDuffield(6) (rdn & hdwy 3f out: one pce) | 1¾ | **4** | 7/2[2] | 57 | 18 |
| 2183[5] | **Marchman (49)** (JSKing) **11-9-2** PaulEddery(1) (nvr nr to chal) | 7 | **5** | 6/1 | 41 | 2 |
| | **Wanstead (IRE) (53)** (JRJenkins) **4-9-6v** JQuinn(7) (lw: prom 7f) | 5 | **6** | 33/1 | 39 | — |
| 2183[10] | **Elpida (USA) (61)** (JPearce) **4-10-0** GBardwell(3) (lw: prom over 8f) | 7 | **7** | 12/1 | 37 | — |
| 866[5] | **Damarita (34)** (LadyHerries) **5-8-1** DeclanO'Shea(9) (lw: s.s: a bhd) | 2½ | **8** | 3/1[1] | 7 | — |
| 1838[8] | **Well Suited (29)** (THind) **6-7-7**(3) NVarley(4) (lw: bhd fnl 6f) | nk | **9** | 33/1 | 2 | — |
| | | | | (SP 117.7%) | **9 Rn** | |

**2m 38.2** (7.00) CSF £28.94 CT £234.43 TOTE £8.20: £3.00 £1.20 £3.30 (£16.80) Trio £35.20 OWNER Mrs C. Forrester (ARUNDEL)
WEIGHT FOR AGE 3yo-13lb
IN-FOCUS: **Success in this race gave Tim Sprake his first ever hat-trick.**

**1984 Minnisam** found the application of blinkers helping him to break his duck. Racing in second place, he went on entering the back straight and, soon forging clear, was not going to be caught. (6/1: 4/1-7/1)
**2282* Sacred Mirror (IRE)**, in front until entering the back straight, failed to reel in the winner after that rival had shot clear running down the hill. (4/1: 5/2-9/2)
**1714 Seven Crowns (USA)**, taking a step up in distance, chased the leaders but was made to look very pedestrian in the last three and a half furlongs. (11/1: 6/1-12/1)
**1852 Uncharted Waters**, pushed along to make some headway three furlongs out, was then only treading water. (7/2)
**2014* Elpida (USA)** (12/1: 8/1-14/1)
**866 Damarita** (3/1: 4/1-5/2)

## 2409 TENTERDEN H'CAP (0-60) (3-Y.O+) (Class F)

5-00 (5-01) **1m 1f 149y** £3,047.40 (£846.40: £406.20) Stalls: Low GOING minus 0.41 sec per fur (F)

| | | | | SP | RR | SF |
|---|---|---|---|---|---|---|
| 1996[2] | **Pistol (IRE) (59)** (CAHorgan) **6-9-13** PaulEddery(8) (b.hind: hdwy over 2f out: hrd rdn over 1f out: led nr fin) | — | **1** | 4/1[2] | 70 | 34 |
| 1841[9] | **South Eastern Fred (46)** (HJCollingridge) **5-9-0** JQuinn(15) (chsd ldr over 6f out: led over 2f out: hrd rdn fnl f: hdd nr fin) | nk | **2** | 14/1 | 57 | 21 |
| 2192[3] | **Sinclair Lad (IRE) (35)** (RJHodges) **8-7-12b**(5) PPMurphy(12) (lw: hld up: chsd ldr 2f out tl over 1f out: one pce) | 1¾ | **3** | 14/1 | 43 | 7 |
| 2183[2] | **Zahran (IRE) (39)** (JMBradley) **5-8-4**(3) SDrowne(9) (lw: rdn & hdwy over 2f out: r.o ins fnl f) | 1 | **4** | 7/1[3] | 45 | 9 |
| 2013[7] | **Pride of Kashmir (54)** (PWHarris) **3-8-11** FNorton(1) (a.p: rdn over 2f out: wknd over 1f out) | 1¾ | **5** | 14/1 | 57 | 10 |
| 2226[5] | **Bronze Maquette (IRE) (37)** (THind) **6-8-5** AClark(6) (lw: nvr nr to chal) | 7 | **6** | 16/1 | 29 | — |
| 2130[13] | **Western Horizon (USA) (30)** (CEBrittain) **4-7-5**(7) PDoe(2) (hld up: rdn 3f out: sn wknd) | 5 | **7** | 16/1 | 13 | — |
| 2203[2] | **Chieftain's Crown (USA) (37)** (MissKMGeorge) **5-8-2b**(3) DarrenMoffatt(3) (lw: nvr nrr) | 1¾ | **8** | 100/30[1] | 17 | — |
| 1172[7] | **Nakhal (57)** (DJGMurraySmith) **3-9-0** GDuffield(5) (lw: nvr nrr) | hd | **9** | 14/1 | 37 | — |
| 2203[3] | **Sheilana (IRE) (60)** (TGMills) **3-8-10**(7) JCornally(14) (bhd fnl 2f) | 1 | **10** | 14/1 | 39 | — |
| 2058[5] | **Coven Moon (33)** (DMorris) **6-8-1v** SSanders(13) (led 7f) | 3 | **11** | 12/1 | 7 | — |
| 2189* | **Yet Again (45)** (BHanbury) **4-8-10b**(3) 5x JStack(4) (hdwy over 3f out: wknd over 2f out) | 3 | **12** | 7/1[3] | 14 | — |
| 1857[10] | **Burning Flame (53)** (RMFlower) **3-8-10** AMackay(11) (a bhd) | ½ | **13** | 33/1 | 21 | — |
| 2159[2] | **Conic Hill (IRE) (49)** (JPearce) **5-9-3** GBardwell(7) (lw: bhd fnl 3f) | 1 | **14** | 8/1 | 15 | — |
| 2191[6] | **Efficacious (IRE) (48)** (CJBenstead) **3-8-5** DBiggs(10) (b.hind: lw: prom 4f) | 22 | **15** | 16/1 | — | — |
| | | | | (SP 140.8%) | **15 Rn** | |

**2m 2.8** (5.10) CSF £62.97 CT £709.00 TOTE £5.70: £3.10 £3.50 £4.90 (£29.30) Trio £209.80 OWNER Mrs B. Sumner (PULBOROUGH) BRED David Brogan
WEIGHT FOR AGE 3yo-11lb
OFFICIAL EXPLANATION **Chieftain's Crown (USA): was unsuited by the good ground.**

**1996 Pistol (IRE)** began to weave his way through the pack over a quarter of a mile from home. Coming under pressure below the distance, he managed to get up near the line. He has yet to win anywhere else but here. (4/1)
**1515 South Eastern Fred** moved into second place early in the back straight. Gaining control over two furlongs from home, he grimly tried to hold on but was worried out of it near the line. (14/1)
**2192 Sinclair Lad (IRE)** chased the leaders. Briefly taking second place a quarter of a mile out, he was then only treading water. (14/1)
**2183 Zahran (IRE)**, ridden along to pick up ground turning for home, ran on inside the final furlong but failed to get there in time. (7/1)

**1594 Pride of Kashmir** played an active role until coming to the end of his tether below the distance. (14/1)
**2203 Chieftain's Crown (USA)** (100/30: 9/2-11/4)

T/Plpt: £78.30 (125.09 Tckts). T/Qdpt: £15.40 (35.62 Tckts). AK

# 2204-YARMOUTH (L-H) (Good to firm, Good in st, Firm patches)
## Wednesday July 3rd

WEATHER: overcast, heavy shower after race 1 WIND: fresh half against

### 2410 E.D.P. SPORT ON MONDAY APPRENTICE LIMITED STKS (0-70) (3-Y.O+) (Class G)
6-35 (6-36) **5f 43y** £2,301.00 (£636.00: £303.00) Stalls: Low GOING: minus 0.37 sec per fur (F)

| Form | Horse | Dist | Pos | SP | RR | SF |
|---|---|---|---|---|---|---|
| 1985[11] | **Times of Times (IRE) (70)** (MJRyan) **3-7-12**(7) AMcCarthy(3) (chsd ldrs: shkn up & led ins fnl f: pushed out) | — | 1 | 9/1[3] | 61 | 3 |
| 1985[5] | **Songsheet (68)** (MartynMeade) **3-8-5**(3) RHavlin(2) (w ldr: ev ch 1f out: no ex ins fnl f) | 1¼ | 2 | 7/4[1] | 60 | 2 |
| *1492*[6] | **Super Rocky (70)** (RBastiman) **7-8-13**(3) HBastiman(1) (lw: led over 4f: wknd nr fin) | ¾ | 3 | 7/4[1] | 61 | 8 |
| | **Statistician (69)** (JohnBerry) **4-8-6**(7) AmyQuirk(5) (bit bkwd: outpcd: rdn 2f out: r.o fnl f) | s.h | 4 | 4/1[2] | 58 | 5 |
| 664[7] | **Waders Dream (IRE) (41)** (PatMitchell) **7-8-13v** PMcCabe(4) (lw: hld up: effrt over 2f out: nvr nrr) | ¾ | 5 | 20/1 | 55 | 2 |

(SP 107.5%) **5 Rn**

**64.0 secs** (3.50) CSF £23.20 TOTE £7.50: £2.50 £1.20 (£6.70) OWNER Mr A. S. Reid (NEWMARKET) BRED E. Moloney
WEIGHT FOR AGE 3yo-5lb
**IN-FOCUS: This was McCarthy's first career win.**
**Times of Times (IRE)**, well below-par on her first two starts this year, bounced back to form, despite idling once in front. (9/1: 6/1-10/1)
**1985 Songsheet**, upsides the leader from the off, had run her race in the last half-furlong. (7/4)
**1492 Super Rocky** set the pace against the far rail, but failed to last home. (7/4)
**Statistician**, off for a year, needed this and looked booked for last place when coming under pressure with two furlongs left. Stamina really came to his aid in the last furlong and he finished strongly having proven that he stays six furlongs well last year. (4/1: op 5/2)
**Waders Dream (IRE)** was rather unruly in the stalls but, despite finishing last, did some good work in the final furlong. This was his best run for some time, but his career record now stands at one win in forty-seven outings. (20/1)

### 2411 E.D.P. JOB SEARCH (S) STKS (3-Y.O) (Class G)
7-05 (7-06) **7f 3y** £2,532.00 (£702.00: £336.00) Stalls: Low GOING: minus 0.37 sec per fur (F)

| Form | Horse | Dist | Pos | SP | RR | SF |
|---|---|---|---|---|---|---|
| 2133[2] | **Cointosser (IRE) (63)** (SPCWoods) **3-8-9** WWoods(9) (hmpd after s: hdwy to ld wl over 1f out: edgd lft & hdd ins fnl f: nt qckn: fin 2nd, 1¼l: awrdd r) | — | 1 | 6/5[1] | 53 | 24 |
| 2026[6] | **Bag And A Bit (55)** (BJMeehan) **3-8-7**(7) DSweeney(7) (chsd ldrs: led over 2f out tl wl over 1f out: one pce: fin 3rd, 4l: plcd 2nd) | | 2 | 7/1[3] | 49 | 29 |
| 2034[10] | **Never Think Twice (52)** (KTIvory) **3-8-7b[1]**(7) CScally(1) (lw: racd alone far side: lost pl 3f out: r.o wl fnl f: fin 4th, ½l: plcd 3rd) | | 3 | 12/1 | 48 | 29 |
| 2017[6] | **Shermood (47)** (KTIvory) **3-8-4**(5) MartinDwyer(10) (in tch: lost pl 3f out: r.o fnl f: fin 5th, 5l: plcd 4th) | | 4 | 33/1 | 32 | 24 |
| 2286[22] | **Capture The Moment (50)** (RJRWilliams) **3-8-9b** WRyan(4) (b.nr hind: chsd ldrs: no hdwy fnl 2f: fin 6th, nk: plcd 5th) | | 5 | 20/1 | 31 | 24 |
| 1883[6] | **On The Home Run (50)** (JRJenkins) **3-8-9b[1]** PRobinson(8) (chsd ldrs over 4f) | 1½ | 7 | 33/1 | 27 | 24 |
| | **Reno's Treasure (USA)** (JAHarris) **3-8-9** SDWilliams(6) (w'like: a bhd) | nk | 8 | 20/1 | 27 | 24 |
| *2325*[6] | **Patrio (IRE) (51)** (SCWilliams) **3-8-9** JTate(11) (bdly hmpd sn after s: nt rcvr) | 22 | 9 | 9/1 | — | 24 |
| *2325*[10] | **Condor Ridge (47)** (BJMeehan) **3-9-0b** MTebbutt(3) (taken rt s: led over 4f: eased whn btn) | 10 | 10 | 12/1 | — | 29 |
| 2255[3] | **Corniche Quest (IRE) (52)** (MRChannon) **3-9-0** RHughes(5) (lw: taken rt s: trckd ldrs: led ins fnl f: r.o: fin 1st: disq: plcd last) | | D | 7/2[2] | 61 | 29 |

(SP 121.0%) **10 Rn**

**1m 27.5** (3.30) CSF £10.46 TOTE £1.90: £1.10 £2.20 £3.00 (£7.20) Trio £32.70 OWNER Mr Arashan Ali (NEWMARKET) BRED Mellon Stud
No bid
STEWARDS' ENQUIRY Hughes susp. 12, 13 & 15-20/7/96 (careless riding).
**2133 Cointosser (IRE)**, hampered by Corniche Quest soon after the stalls opened, did not look too keen in a driving finish, edging out to his left. She inevitably got the race in the Stewards' Room. (6/5)
**2026 Bag And A Bit**, back at what appears to be her best trip, struck for home early but could find nothing extra once headed. (7/1)
**Never Think Twice** stuck to the far rail and finished best of all after looking well held. (12/1)
**516 Shermood**, trying a fourth different trip in four turf outings this year, was taken down steadily. Hard at work in the last quarter-mile, she just stayed on past beaten horses. (33/1)
**2133 Capture The Moment** does not seem in love with fast ground and was never travelling on this occasion. (20/1)
**1612 Patrio (IRE)** (9/1: 6/1-10/1)
**1956 Condor Ridge**, a good mover, was drawn one from the far rail but, along with the first past the post, led all bar one of the field over to the far rail in the first furlong and a half, and was fortunate to have been found blameless at the subsequent enquiry. He weakened once headed as he had done at Goodwood, and was eased once his chance had gone. (12/1: 6/1-14/1)
**2255 Corniche Quest (IRE)** caused considerable interference with a rash manoeuvre to get to the stands' rail soon after the start and, although she won on merit, she had to lose the race. (7/2)

### 2412 EASTERN DAILY PRESS H'CAP (0-75) (3-Y.O+) (Class D)
7-35 (7-40) **1m 3y** £3,860.70 (£1,152.60: £550.80: £249.90) Stalls: Low GOING: minus 0.37 sec per fur (F)

| Form | Horse | Dist | Pos | SP | RR | SF |
|---|---|---|---|---|---|---|
| 2340* | **Wild Palm (64)** (WAO'Gorman) **4-9-4v** EmmaO'Gorman(9) (lw: hld up: hdwy 3f out: led ins fnl f: drvn out) | — | 1 | 4/1[1] | 74 | 23 |
| 2130[3] | **Mr Rough (59)** (DMorris) **5-8-6**(7) AEddery(11) (chsd ldrs: ev ch ins fnl f: unable qckn nr fin) | s.h | 2 | 9/1 | 69 | 18 |
| 2340[5] | **Talathath (FR) (60)** (CADwyer) **4-9-0v** MHills(5) (trckd ldrs: led wl over 1f out tl ins fnl f: rallied nr fin) | s.h | 3 | 10/1 | 70 | 19 |
| 2047[5] | **Awesome Venture (50)** (MCChapman) **6-8-1**(3) PMcCabe(7) (hld up: plld out over 1f out: rdn & no imp fnl f) | 4 | 4 | 10/1 | 52 | 1 |
| 1983[4] | **Emily-Mou (IRE) (67)** (MJRyan) **4-9-7** RHughes(2) (led 1f: hdd & c stands' side: led over 3f out: hdd wl over 1f out: sn btn) | 1¾ | 5 | 12/1 | 65 | 14 |
| 1986[2] | **Passage Creeping (IRE) (71)** (LMCumani) **3-9-2** OUrbina(6) (hld up: rdn over 2f out: sn btn) | 6 | 6 | 4/1[1] | 57 | — |
| 1868[6] | **Tatika (68)** (GWragg) **6-9-1**(7) GMilligan(1) (swtg: chsd ldrs: rdn over 2f out: sn btn) | nk | 7 | 13/2[3] | 54 | 3 |
| 2209[6] | **Ahjay (44)** (TJNaughton) **6-7-7**(5) MartinDwyer(4) (chsd ldrs 5f) | 7 | 8 | 25/1 | 16 | — |

| | | | | SP | RR | SF |
|---|---|---|---|---|---|---|
| 2339[2] | **Uncle George (65)** (MHTompkins) **3-8-10v** PRobinson(10) (c stands' side: led after 1f tl over 3f out: sn btn & eased) | 13 | **9** | 8/1 | 11 | — |
| 1198[11] | **Fakih (USA) (74)** (ACStewart) **4-10-0** RHills(8) (lw: a bhd: eased fnl 2f) | 6 | **10** | 6/1[2] | 8 | — |
| 2032[7] | **Kalao Tua (IRE) (65)** (JRFanshawe) **3-8-10** WRyan(3) (wl bhd fnl 4f) | 9 | **11** | 20/1 | — | — |
| | | | | (SP 123.2%) | **11 Rn** | |

**1m 40.0** (4.70) CSF £38.43 CT £322.22 TOTE £5.30: £1.70 £3.70 £3.30 (£36.10) Trio £119.20 OWNER Mr S. Fustok (NEWMARKET) BRED Deerfield Farm
WEIGHT FOR AGE 3yo-9lb
**2340* Wild Palm**, on faster ground than four days earlier, may have been a winner without a penalty but barely scrambled home. (4/1)
**2130 Mr Rough** threw down the gauntlet from the distance, but never quite got his head in front. (9/1)
**2340 Talathath (FR)** got an awful lot closer to the winner than he had done four days earlier. Appearing to travel as well as any for most of the race, he was coming back for more at the finish. (10/1)
**2047 Awesome Venture** looked a big danger when pulled off the stands' rail approaching the final furlong, but could not do enough. (10/1)
**1983 Emily-Mou (IRE)** moved to post well, but could not dominate and would appear to be slightly better over ten furlongs. (12/1: op 8/1)
**1986 Passage Creeping (IRE)**, pulled to the centre of the track to mount a challenge, found little. She is proving hard to place. (4/1)

## 2413 E.D.P. BIG NEWS MAIDEN STKS (2-Y.O) (Class D)
8-05 (8-06) **6f 3y** £3,346.00 (£997.00: £475.00: £214.00) Stalls: Low GOING: minus 0.37 sec per fur (F)

| | | | | SP | RR | SF |
|---|---|---|---|---|---|---|
| 1954[3] | **Sambac (USA)** (HRACecil) **2-8-9** WRyan(4) (mde all: pushed clr appr fnl f) | — | **1** | 4/5[1] | 81 | 13 |
| | **Blue Goblin (USA)** (LMCumani) **2-9-0** OUrbina(8) (unf: scope: hdwy 2f out: r.o fnl f: nt trble wnr) | 2 | **2** | 2/1[2] | 81 | 13 |
| | **Chynna** (MHTompkins) **2-8-9** PRobinson(3) (leggy: unf: chsd ldrs: rdn over 2f out: wknd fnl f) | 7 | **3** | 16/1 | 57 | — |
| 2219[7] | **Princess of Hearts** (WJHaggas) **2-8-9** RMcGhin(6) (hld up: rdn 2f out: kpt on: nt pce to chal) | 4 | **4** | 25/1 | 46 | — |
| | **Wobble** (WJHaggas) **2-9-0** RHills(1) (leggy: scope: chsd ldrs over 3f) | nk | **5** | 7/1[3] | 51 | — |
| | **Anokato** (KTIvory) **2-8-7(7)** CScally(7) (leggy: bit bkwd: hld up: rdn over 3f out: hung lft & no imp) | ¾ | **6** | 33/1 | 49 | — |
| 1467[6] | **Salabatni** (EALDunlop) **2-8-9** MHills(5) (prom 4f) | hd | **7** | 12/1 | 43 | — |
| *2083[8]* | **Frandickbob** (JAHarris) **2-9-0** SDWilliams(2) (reard s: plld hrd: rdn over 3f out: sn wl bhd: t.o) | dist | **8** | 25/1 | — | — |
| | | | | (SP 125.6%) | **8 Rn** | |

**1m 14.5** (3.60) CSF £3.24 TOTE £1.70: £1.40 £1.10 £3.70 (£1.60) OWNER Mr K. Abdulla (NEWMARKET) BRED Juddmonte Farms
**1954 Sambac (USA)** gave no trouble at the start this time and pulled away in style once asked to do the job of outclassing the opposition. (4/5: op Evens)
**Blue Goblin (USA)** stayed on strongly in the last couple of furlongs and will come into his own over further. (2/1: 5/4-9/4)
**Chynna** showed good speed to the distance, but tied up in the run to the line. (16/1)
**Princess of Hearts** reared once installed and was never going the pace of the leaders, although she did stay on late in the day. (25/1)
**Wobble**, outpaced in the last quarter-mile, needs time and a little further. (7/1)
**Anokato** is an ungainly mover and has an awkward head carriage. (33/1)

## 2414 E.B.F. LOWESTOFT JOURNAL MAIDEN STKS (2-Y.O) (Class D)
8-35 (8-36) **7f 3y** £3,765.00 (£1,040.00: £495.00) Stalls: Low GOING: minus 0.37 sec per fur (F)

| | | | | SP | RR | SF |
|---|---|---|---|---|---|---|
| | **Great Ovation (IRE)** (LMCumani) **2-9-0** OUrbina(1) (leggy: unf: trckd ldr: led over 1f out: rdn out) | — | **1** | 15/8[2] | 73 t | 17 |
| | **Mount Kamet** (DRLoder) **2-9-0** RHughes(3) (tall: scope: bit bkwd: hld up: chal over 1f out: rdn & nt qckn ins fnl f) | nk | **2** | 4/7[1] | 72 t | 16 |
| 1424[7] | **Mac's Delight** (EALDunlop) **2-9-0** MHills(2) (led over 5f: sn btn) | 8 | **3** | 8/1[3] | 54 t | — |
| | | | | (SP 109.5%) | **3 Rn** | |

**1m 28.6** (4.40) CSF £3.27 TOTE £3.50: (£1.50) OWNER Mrs E. H. Vestey (NEWMARKET) BRED Swettenham Stud
**Great Ovation (IRE)**, a lean newcomer, proved tenacious in a battle, despite a tendency to edge right and carry his head a shade high. (15/8)
**Mount Kamet**, a half-brother to Kalabo, was settled last. He appeared to be travelling best when challenging, but did not find very much in the last 100 yards and was worried out of it. By far the most scopey of these, he should come on considerably for the outing. (4/7)
**Mac's Delight** set a sedate pace, which he quickened at halfway. Outpaced once the chips were down, time will probably show that there was no disgrace in this. (8/1: 6/1-10/1)

## 2415 E.D.P. FIRST FOR CLASSIFIEDS H'CAP (0-75) (3-Y.O+) (Class D)
9-05 (9-05) **1m 6f 17y** £4,464.00 (£1,332.00: £636.00: £288.00) Stalls: Low GOING: minus 0.37 sec per fur (F)

| | | | | SP | RR | SF |
|---|---|---|---|---|---|---|
| | **Moonlight Quest (75)** (BHanbury) **8-10-0** WRyan(3) (b: hld up: hdwy to ld over 1f out: sn qcknd clr: comf) | — | **1** | 9/4[2] | 86+ | 49 |
| 2002[8] | **Lucky Coin (60)** (PHowling) **4-8-13** SDWilliams(1) (led: qcknd 5f out: hdd over 1f out: one pce) | 6 | **2** | 11/2 | 64 | 27 |
| 2177[3] | **Silver Hunter (USA) (51)** (GCBravery) **5-7-13(5)ow2** LNewton(4) (lw: hld up: hdwy 4f out: ev ch 2f out: edgd lft & fnd nil) | 1½ | **3** | 7/4[1] | 54 | 15 |
| 1011[3] | **Risky Tu (45)** (PAKelleway) **5-7-12** GCarter(2) (plld hrd: chsd ldr 11f: sn btn) | ½ | **4** | 11/4[3] | 47 | 10 |
| | | | | (SP 109.2%) | **4 Rn** | |

**3m 5.4** (6.00) CSF £11.56 TOTE £2.40: (£7.70) OWNER Mrs John Lamb (NEWMARKET) BRED Raintree Stud
**Moonlight Quest** often runs well with welter burdens and beat these with a superior turn of foot. (9/4)
**1695 Lucky Coin**, allowed to dictate the pace, tried to stretch the field from the home turn, but could not respond to the winner. (11/2: op 7/2)
**2177 Silver Hunter (USA)**, supported to atone for his unlucky effort last time, found nothing off the bridle. (7/4)
**1011 Risky Tu** pulled far too hard and was the first beaten. (11/4)

T/Plpt: £119.70 (97.85 Tckts). T/Qdpt: £38.40 (23.5 Tckts). Dk

# 2149-AYR (L-H) (Good to soft)
## Thursday July 4th
WEATHER: overcast WIND: fresh against

## 2416 E.B.F. OCHILTREE MAIDEN STKS (2-Y.O) (Class D)
6-35 (6-36) **7f** £3,452.50 (£1,045.00: £510.00: £242.50) Stalls: Low GOING: 0.37 sec per fur (GS)

| | | | | SP | RR | SF |
|---|---|---|---|---|---|---|
| | **Brave Act** (SirMarkPrescott) **2-9-0** GDuffield(5) (w'like: leggy: scope: hld up: smooth hdwy to ld appr fnl f: shkn up & r.o wl) | — | **1** | 11/8[2] | 60+ | 23 |

**Musheer (USA)** (MissGayKelleway) **2-9-0** KFallon(6) (wl grwn: lw: plld hrd early: effrt ½-wy: led 1½f out: sn hdd & one pce) ....4 **2** 5/4[1] 51+ 14
2153[2] **Brave Montgomerie** (MissLAPerratt) **2-9-0** WJO'Connor(2) (led tl hdd 1½f out: sn outpcd) ....3 **3** 10/1[3] 44 7
1525[10] **Hong Kong Express (IRE)** (JBerry) **2-8-4**(5) PRoberts(1) (b.hind: chsd ldrs tl outpcd fnl 2f) ....2½ **4** 33/1 33 —
**Paldost** (MDHammond) **2-9-0** JWeaver(3) (leggy: s.i.s: a bhd) ....10 **5** 10/1[3] 15 —
2018[4] **Cantsaynowt** (RMMcKellar) **2-8-6**(3) NVarley(4) (cl up: chal 3f out: wknd wl over 1f out) ....1¼ **6** 250/1 8 —
(SP 108.1%) **6 Rn**

**1m 32.96** (8.96) CSF £3.20 TOTE £2.80: £1.20 £1.60 (£1.50) OWNER Mr W. E. Sturt (NEWMARKET) BRED Side Hill Stud and Floors Farming

**Brave Act**, quite an attractive sort, did the job well and was comfortably on top by the finish. There looks to be improvement in him yet. (11/8)
**Musheer (USA)**, a big, strong individual, did not help his chances by pulling hard early on and was then well outpointed in the last furlong and a half. He will find a race or two once he learns to settle. (5/4: 4/5-6/4)
**2153 Brave Montgomerie** showed he is learning here, but the first two were far too good for him in the last furlong and a half. (10/1: op 5/1)
**Hong Kong Express (IRE)** improved on her debut and there is more to come as she gains experience. (33/1)
**Paldost**, an angular colt, needed this experience quite badly and never showed in the race. (10/1: 8/1-16/1)

## 2417 SCANIA 4-SERIES 'HORSEPOWER' TROPHY H'CAP (0-70) (3-Y.O) (Class E)
7-05 (7-05) **7f** £2,957.00 (£896.00: £438.00: £209.00) Stalls: Low GOING: 0.37 sec per fur (GS)

SP RR SF
2139[4] **Oriole (46)** (NTinkler) **3-7-11** KimTinkler(6) (rr div: hdwy 2f out: str run fnl f to ld last strides) ....— **1** 10/1 55 5
2241[2] **Napoleon's Return (47)** (AHarrison) **3-7-5v**(7) JennyBenson(8) (lw: led after 2f: clr over 2f out: no ex towards fin) ....hd **2** 5/2[1] 56 6
2061[7] **Rocky Stream (45)** (RMWhitaker) **3-7-10** AMackay(5) (lw: in tch: nt clr run & swtchd over 1f out: styd on) ....1½ **3** 12/1 50 —
1773[15] **Lazali (USA) (70)** (EALDunlop) **3-9-7** GDuffield(3) (lw: trckd ldrs: effrt 3f out: one pce fnl 2f) ....½ **4** 6/1[3] 74 24
873[15] **Duo Master (70)** (MrsMReveley) **3-9-7** WJO'Connor(7) (lw: s.i.s: bhd tl styd on appr fnl f) ....2½ **5** 14/1 69 19
2139[3] **Shontaine (62)** (MJohnston) **3-8-13** JWeaver(9) (in tch: effrt 3f out: no imp) ....nk **6** 7/2[2] 60 10
*1809*[10] **Polish Saga (51)** (MDods) **3-8-2** LCharnock(4) (chsd ldrs tl wknd fnl 2f) ....1½ **7** 14/1 45 —
2179[8] **Aye Ready (45)** (MissLAPerratt) **3-7-7b**(3) NVarley(1) (dwlt: a bhd) ....2½ **8** 50/1 34 —
*1721*[8] **Efipetite (46)** (NBycroft) **3-7-8**(3)ow1 DarrenMoffatt(10) (s.i.s: a bhd) ....11 **9** 25/1 10 —
2236* **Craignairn (72)** (JBerry) **3-9-4**(5) 6x PRoberts(2) (led 2f: cl up tl wknd over 2f out) ....1½ **10** 10/1 32 —
(SP 110.1%) **10 Rn**

**1m 33.19** (9.19) CSF £31.61 CT £260.86 TOTE £9.90: £1.70 £1.10 £4.10 (£12.60) Trio £57.80 OWNER Don Enrico Incisa (MALTON) BRED Red House Stud
LONG HANDICAP Rocky Stream 7-7 Aye Ready 6-9 Efipetite 7-8

**2139 Oriole**, a very edgy individual, was dropped out and then produced a terrific late burst to snatch it on the line. (10/1)
**2241 Napoleon's Return** put up another good performance but again was just touched off, despite this being a shorter trip. He still looks remarkably well. (5/2)
**1702 Rocky Stream** looks well and is now coming to hand. With a clear run here, he would have been a fair bit closer. (12/1)
**705 Lazali (USA)** had his chances but, when the pressure was really on, he tended to hang left and failed to come up with the goods. (6/1: 4/1-7/1)
**Duo Master**, a useful-looking sort, has shown little since injuring himself as a two-year-old, but he did give an indication this time that he is gradually getting it together. (14/1: op 6/1)
**2139 Shontaine** ran moderately this time which can perhaps be put down to the softish ground. (7/2)
**2236* Craignairn** (10/1: op 6/1)

## 2418 SCANIA 1996 TRUCK OF THE YEAR TROPHY H'CAP (0-85) (3-Y.O+) (Class D)
7-35 (7-35) **1m 5f 13y** £4,182.00 (£1,266.00: £618.00: £294.00) Stalls: Low GOING: 0.37 sec per fur (GS)

SP RR SF
2239* **Desert Frolic (IRE) (70)** (MJohnston) **3-8-13** 4x JWeaver(5) (lw: mde all: clr ent st: styd on strly) ....— **1** 4/5[1] 79 34
2056[4] **Northern Motto (53)** (WStorey) **3-7-7**(3) NVarley(2) (rdn appr st: styd on wl fnl 3f: nvr able to chal) ....3½ **2** 6/1[3] 58 13
2390[5] **Lord Advocate (53)** (DANolan) **8-8-7b**(3) SDrowne(6) (chsd wnr tl outpcd fnl 3f) ....8 **3** 14/1 48 17
1977[5] **Redstella (USA) (63)** (RMWhitaker) **7-9-6** DeanMcKeown(1) (dwlt: sn prom: rdn 8f out: hung lft & no imp fnl 3f) ....2 **4** 7/1 56 25
2164[6] **Cheerful Aspect (IRE) (78)** (EALDunlop) **3-9-7** KFallon(3) (chsd ldrs: rdn 4f out: sn btn) ....5 **5** 9/2[2] 64 19
1585[6] **Home Counties (IRE) (67)** (DMoffatt) **7-9-7**(3) DarrenMoffatt(4) (bhd: rdn 5f out: n.d) ....6 **6** 10/1 46 15
(SP 116.3%) **6 Rn**

**3m 0.1** (15.30) CSF £6.27 TOTE £1.60: £1.10 £2.10 (£4.90) OWNER Maktoum Al Maktoum (MIDDLEHAM) BRED Gainsborough Stud Management Ltd
LONG HANDICAP Northern Motto 7-7
WEIGHT FOR AGE 3yo-14lb

**2239* Desert Frolic (IRE)**, a grand sort who apparently goes on any ground, never looked in danger of defeat here. (4/5)
**2056 Northern Motto** has changes stables and is certainly on the upgrade, especially over this longer trip as, the further he went, the better he got. (6/1)
**2390 Lord Advocate** ran another sound race, but he was off the bit approaching the straight and no danger thereafter. (14/1: op 8/1)
**1977 Redstella (USA)** seems to have his own ideas about the game these days. (7/1)
**2164 Cheerful Aspect (IRE)**, trying his longest trip to date, was found out by the home turn. (9/2)
**Home Counties (IRE)** showed no signs of encouragement here. (10/1: op 6/1)

## 2419 RELIABLE VEHICLES FOR SCANIA CLAIMING STKS (3-Y.O) (Class E)
8-05 (8-08) **1m 2f** £2,827.00 (£856.00: £418.00: £199.00) Stalls: Low GOING: 0.37 sec per fur (GS)

SP RR SF
2241[4] **Society Girl (59)** (CWThornton) **3-9-2** DeanMcKeown(5) (lw: b.nr hind: trckd ldr: led 2½f out: pushed out) ...— **1** 4/6[1] 66 27
2212[10] **Time For A Glass** (DMoffatt) **3-7-11**(3) DarrenMoffatt(2) (in tch: hdwy 2f out: r.o wl fnl f) ....¾ **2** 10/1[3] 49 10
2014[9] **Silent Guest (IRE) (50)** (SirMarkPrescott) **3-8-9b**[1] GDuffield(4) (lw: led tl hdd 2½f out: rdn & fnd nil) ....12 **3** 5/2[2] 39 —
*1972*[6] **The Oddfellow** (NBycroft) **3-8-10**(5) PRoberts(1) (b.off hind: in tch: outpcd ent st: sn wknd) ....14 **4** 14/1 22 —
**Another Picea** (NTinkler) **3-8-9** LCharnock(6) (rdn appr st: a bhd) ....25 **5** 10/1[3] — —
(SP 113.4%) **5 Rn**

**2m 17.5** (12.90) CSF £7.25 TOTE £1.40: £1.30 £1.70 (£6.00) OWNER Mr Guy Reed (MIDDLEHAM) BRED G. Reed

**2241 Society Girl** got the trip well enough but had to be kept up to her work to hold off a very determined runner-up. (4/6)
**Time For A Glass**, taking a big step up in trip, was a revelation as she really picked up in the last two furlongs to give the winner quite a fright. (10/1)

**Silent Guest (IRE)** had blinkers on for the first time but, once pressure was applied over two furlongs out, he soon decided it was not for him. (5/2)
**1972 The Oddfellow** has yet to show any signs of improvement. (14/1)
**Another Picea** kept his record and was last yet again. (10/1: 8/1-12/1)

## 2420 LOGANSWELL MAIDEN STKS (3-Y.O+) (Class D)
8-35 (8-37) **1m** £3,598.75 (£1,090.00: £532.50: £253.75) Stalls: Low GOING: 0.37 sec per fur (GS)

| | | | | SP | RR | SF |
|---|---|---|---|---|---|---|
| 2011[4] | **Sabrak (IRE) (80)** (MAJarvis) **3-8-12** PRobinson(5) (lw: trckd ldrs: smooth hdwy to ld wl over 2f out: rdn & r.o strly) | — | **1** | 9/4[2] | 96 | 51 |
| 2079[2] | **Tarneem (USA) (83)** (MRStoute) **3-8-7** WJO'Connor(4) (lw: trckd ldrs: chal 3f out: r.o: nt pce of wnr) | 7 | **2** | 7/4[1] | 77 | 32 |
| 1090[8] | **Respecting** (DenysSmith) **3-8-12** DeanMcKeown(1) (in tch: hdwy 3f out: wl outpcd fnl 2f) | 6 | **3** | 66/1 | 70 | 25 |
| 2181[2] | **Mubariz (IRE)** (EALDunlop) **4-9-7** KFallon(9) (b: in tch: effrt 3f out: rdn & no imp) | 11 | **4** | 7/2[3] | 48 | 12 |
| | **Serious Sensation** (SirMarkPrescott) **3-8-12** GDuffield(10) (w'like: str: bkwd: dwlt: styd on fnl 3f: n.d) | 1½ | **5** | 8/1 | 45 | — |
| 1649[2] | **Knotty Hill** (RCraggs) **4-9-7** LCharnock(3) (bhd: sme hdwy 3f out: n.d) | nk | **6** | 10/1 | 44 | 8 |
| | **Barbara's Jewel** (ABailey) **4-9-7** JWeaver(7) (cl up tl wknd & eased fnl 3f) | 5 | **7** | 50/1 | 34 | — |
| 2150[4] | **Nordic Gift (DEN) (50)** (MrsDThomson) **3-8-9**(3) DarrenMoffatt(8) (led tl hdd & wknd wl over 2f out) | 8 | **8** | 100/1 | 18 | — |
| | **Midas Man** (DANolan) **5-9-4**(3) SDrowne(2) (bkwd: s.i.s: a bhd) | 23 | **9** | 100/1 | — | — |

(SP 115.0%) **9 Rn**

**1m 44.75** (7.35) CSF £6.31 TOTE £3.40: £1.50 £1.10 £4.80 (£4.70) Trio £190.90 OWNER Sheikh Ahmed Al Maktoum (NEWMARKET) BRED J. M. Lyons
WEIGHT FOR AGE 3yo-9lb
**2011 Sabrak (IRE)** has really come to himself now and won this in tremendous style. Further successes looks likely and he should stay further. (9/4)
**2079 Tarneem (USA)** looked to be going as well as the winner early in the straight but, once the tap was turned on, she was quickly put in her place. (7/4)
**Respecting**, who bolted on the way to post last time, was taken down early here and ran much better. On this showing, he can pick up a small race. (66/1)
**2181 Mubariz (IRE)** found this far too competitive once off the bit early in the straight. (7/2: 9/4-4/1)
**Serious Sensation** has the build of a three-mile chaser and obviously needs time to get his act together. (8/1)
**1649 Knotty Hill**, held up this time, failed to get into it and this is best ignored. (10/1)
**Barbara's Jewel** went very freely to post and needs to learn to settle. (50/1)

## 2421 SCANIA 4-SERIES 'KING OF THE ROAD' TROPHY H'CAP (0-70) (3-Y.O+) (Class E)
9-05 (9-07) **5f** £3,113.00 (£944.00: £462.00: £221.00) Stalls: High GOING: 0.37 sec per fur (GS)

| | | | | SP | RR | SF |
|---|---|---|---|---|---|---|
| 2119[3] | **Rich Glow (53)** (NBycroft) **5-8-12** KFallon(6) (hld up: hdwy 2f out: r.o u.p to ld wl ins fnl f) | — | **1** | 3/1[2] | 60 | 43 |
| *2305*[2] | **Silk Cottage (54)** (RMWhitaker) **4-8-13** DeanMcKeown(7) (lw: led: hrd rdn fnl f: hdd & no ex towards fin) | 1¾ | **2** | 11/4[1] | 55 | 38 |
| 2329[12] | **Amron (62)** (JBerry) **9-9-7** JWeaver(8) (lw: hld up & bhd: hdwy 2f out: styd on towards fin) | 1½ | **3** | 7/2[3] | 59 | 42 |
| 2391[7] | **Another Nightmare (IRE) (37)** (RMMcKellar) **4-7-7**(3) NVarley(2) (w ldr tl rdn & btn ent fnl f) | hd | **4** | 16/1 | 33 | 16 |
| 2316[13] | **Blue Lugana (37)** (NBycroft) **4-7-10** AMackay(1) (chsd ldrs: pushed along thrght: outpcd fnl 2f) | 5 | **5** | 16/1 | 17 | — |
| 2023[5] | **River Garnock (46)** (DNicholls) **4-8-5b**[1] GDuffield(4) (plld hrd: effrt ½-wy: no rspnse) | hd | **6** | 6/1 | 26 | 9 |
| 1541[11] | **Nordisk Legend (38)** (MrsDThomson) **4-7-8b**[1](3)ow1 DarrenMoffatt(9) (spd 3f: wknd) | 3½ | **7** | 66/1 | 7 | — |
| | ***Rhythmic Dancer (69)*** (DANolan) **8-9-11**(3) SDrowne(3) (Withdrawn not under Starter's orders: ref to ent stalls) | | **W** | 11/2 | — | — |

(SP 116.8%) **7 Rn**

**61.89 secs** (4.89) CSF £8.79 CT £16.03 TOTE £2.60: £2.20 £2.00 (£3.60) Trio £3.10 OWNER Mr M. J. Bateson (BRANDSBY) BRED P. Young
LONG HANDICAP Another Nightmare (IRE) 7-6 Nordisk Legend 7-3 Blue Lugana 7-4
**2119 Rich Glow** again showed his liking for this track and distance, but this time he was on softer ground, and he did it really well. (3/1)
**2305 Silk Cottage** ran another fine race but, yet again, was found wanting in the closing stages. He is in tremendous form at present. (11/4)
**1781 Amron** has not won for over two years but is showing signs at present that he should not be written off. (7/2)
**1545 Another Nightmare (IRE)** ran her best race for a long time. (16/1)
**1702 Blue Lugana**, a stable-companion of the winner, was never on the bridle at any stage. (16/1)
**2023 River Garnock**, in blinkers for the first time, was surprisingly held up and just pulled his rider's arms out. (6/1)

T/Plpt: £5.80 (1,881.88 Tckts). T/Qdpt: £2.80 (340.58 Tckts). AA

# 2392-CATTERICK (L-H) (Good to soft, Good patches)
## Thursday July 4th
WEATHER: unsettled WIND: str half against

## 2422 TREATY OF PARIS (S) STKS (2-Y.O) (Class G)
2-15 (2-16) **5f** £2,469.00 (£684.00: £327.00) Stalls: Low GOING: 0.29 sec per fur (G)

| | | | | SP | RR | SF |
|---|---|---|---|---|---|---|
| 770[10] | **I Can't Remember** (PDEvans) **2-8-11** JFortune(3) (lw: chsd ldrs: rdn & hung rt ½-wy: led over 1f out: sn clr) | — | **1** | 6/4[1] | 46 | 3 |
| 2043[8] | **Where's Wally (IRE)** (JBerry) **2-8-11b**[1] JCarroll(4) (chsd ldr: led ½-wy: hung lft & hdd over 1f out: no ch w wnr) | 6 | **2** | 7/2[3] | 27 | — |
| 2237[4] | **Timely Touch** (MWEllerby) **2-8-3**(3) CTeague(5) (swvd rt s: sn bhd & hung rt: hdwy over 1f out: wnt bdly lft & styd on ins fnl f) | 2½ | **3** | 25/1 | 14 | — |
| 1858[7] | **Abstone Again (IRE)** (PDEvans) **2-8-11v** GDuffield(2) (lw: led to ½-wy: hrd rdn & nt r.o) | 4 | **4** | 9/4[2] | 6 | — |
| | **Captain Flint** (ASmith) **2-8-11** MBirch(6) (cmpt: s.i.s: a wl bhd) | 8 | **5** | 15/2 | — | — |
| | **Tooele** (JNorton) **2-8-11** DaleGibson(1) (small: unf: s.i.s: a wl outpcd) | hd | **6** | 9/2 | — | — |

(SP 126.8%) **6 Rn**

**64.4 secs** (6.90) CSF £8.10 TOTE £2.10: £1.30 £2.10 (£6.10) OWNER Peter Graham Racing (WELSHPOOL) BRED C. G. Reid
No bid
**770 I Can't Remember**, having his first run since changing stables and being gelded, behaved himself in the stalls this time and took one of the worst races of the whole season by a wide margin. (6/4)

**Where's Wally (IRE)**, in blinkers for the first time, hung left under pressure and was left behind by the winner. (7/2)
**2237 Timely Touch**, who is only small, covered almost every blade of grass on the track. (25/1)
**1607 Abstone Again (IRE)** almost ran away going to the start. After setting the pace to halfway, he soon called it a day. (9/4: 6/4-5/2)

## 2423 'TURMERIC' H'CAP (0-70) (3-Y.O+) (Class E)

2-45 (2-47) **1m 7f 177y** £3,236.00 (£968.00: £464.00: £212.00) Stalls: Low GOING: 0.29 sec per fur (G)

| | Horse | Dist | Pos | SP | RR | SF |
|---|---|---|---|---|---|---|
| 2165$^{6}$ | **Iota (50)** (JLHarris) **7-9-0** PRobinson(5) (chsd ldrs: styd on to ld nr fin) | — | **1** | 4/1$^{2}$ | 59 | 27 |
| *1488*$^{3}$ | **Cutthroat Kid (IRE) (61)** (MrsMReveley) **6-9-11v** JFortune(4) (lw: a in tch: pushed along 6f out: led stands' side over 1f out: hdd nr fin) | nk | **2** | 11/2$^{3}$ | 70 | 38 |
| 2028* | **Great Oration (IRE) (48)** (FWatson) **7-8-12** KFallon(3) (hld up: hdwy & pushed along over 3f out: nt clr run & swtchd ins fnl f: r.o) | ¾ | **3** | 9/4$^{1}$ | 56 | 24 |
| 1611$^{5}$ | **Hasta la Vista (53)** (MWEasterby) **6-9-3b** DaleGibson(9) (b.off hind: led: styd far side: hdd & nt qckn fnl f) | 4 | **4** | 8/1 | 57 | 25 |
| 2175$^{5}$ | **Little Redwing (36)** (MDHammond) **4-8-0**ow1 JFanning(1) (a chsng ldrs: one pce fnl 2f) | nk | **5** | 10/1 | 40 | 7 |
| 2226$^{6}$ | **Double Echo (IRE) (54)** (JDBethell) **8-9-4** JWeaver(2) (hld up & bhd: hdwy over 5f out: styd on fnl 2f: nvr nr to chal) | 2½ | **6** | 8/1 | 55 | 23 |
| 1803$^{15}$ | **Superhoo (32)** (RCraggs) **5-7-10** LCharnock(6) (lw: chsd ldrs: drvn along 4f out: lost pl over 2f out) | 6 | **7** | 8/1 | 27 | — |
| *1967*$^{7}$ | **Never Time (IRE) (35)** (MrsVAAconley) **4-7-13** NCarlisle(10) (chsd ldrs: pushed along 7f out: styd far side: lost pl over 1f out) | 1½ | **8** | 25/1 | 29 | — |
| 1341$^{14}$ | **Kashana (IRE) (47)** (WStorey) **4-8-8**(3) CTeague(8) (s.s: a bhd) | 12 | **9** | 12/1 | 28 | — |
| 1847$^{8}$ | **Don't Cry (32)** (DonEnricoIncisa) **8-7-10** KimTinkler(7) (sn bhd: t.o 3f out) | 3 | **10** | 50/1 | 10 | — |
| 2175$^{8}$ | **Yaakum (32)** (SEKettlewell) **7-7-10** NKennedy(11) (racd wd: plld hrd: trckd ldrs tl wknd qckly 6f out: t.o 3f out) | 20 | **11** | 25/1 | — | — |
| | | | | (SP 125.9%) | **11 Rn** | |

**3m 40.6** (19.10) CSF £26.59 CT £58.12 TOTE £3.00: £1.40 £1.60 £1.50 (£11.90) Trio £9.10 OWNER Lavender Hill Leisure Ltd (MELTON MOWBRAY) BRED Sheikh Mohammed bin Rashid al Maktoum
LONG HANDICAP Don't Cry 7-1 Yaakum 7-8

**1826 Iota**, hitherto regarded as an All-Weather performer, was suited by the step up in distance and stuck on bravely to show ahead near the line. (4/1: 11/2-7/2)
**1488 Cutthroat Kid (IRE)**, turned out in particularly good shape, pinched the favoured stands'-side rail but, even so, had to give best near the line. (11/2: 4/1-6/1)
**2028* Great Oration (IRE)**, as usual put in the stalls last, was racing off a 7lb higher mark than which he had won off at Pontefract. Not suited by the recent rain, he was pushed along leaving the back straight. Even so, but for being squeezed out between the first two inside the last furlong, he would have gone very close. (9/4)
**1611 Hasta la Vista**, who won here off a 2lb lower mark four runs ago, again stuck to the far side in the final straight but, this time, it seemed to backfire on him. (8/1)
**2175 Little Redwing** ran another sound race. (10/1: 8/1-12/1)
**2226 Double Echo (IRE)**, who is slipping down the weights, shaped as if on the way back. (8/1)
**Kashana (IRE)** (12/1: 8/1-14/1)

## 2424 GEORGE WASHINGTON RATING RELATED MAIDEN STKS (0-60) (3-Y.O) (Class F)

3-15 (3-16) **1m 5f 175y** £2,574.00 (£714.00: £342.00) Stalls: Low GOING: 0.29 sec per fur (G)

| | Horse | Dist | Pos | SP | RR | SF |
|---|---|---|---|---|---|---|
| 2217$^{2}$ | **Grey Galava (57)** (BWHills) **3-8-11** KFallon(3) (chsd ldr: led 7f out: drvn clr over 2f out: eased towards fin) | — | **1** | 13/8$^{2}$ | 65 | 14 |
| 1656$^{10}$ | **Parrot's Hill (IRE) (56)** (MHTompkins) **3-9-0** PRobinson(1) (hdwy to chse wnr over 4f out: rdn & one pce fnl 2f: eased ins fnl f) | 16 | **2** | 6/1$^{3}$ | 49 | — |
| 1600$^{5}$ | **Atienza (USA) (58)** (SCWilliams) **3-8-11** JWeaver(2) (led to 7f out: one pce fnl 4f) | 2½ | **3** | 8/1 | 44 | — |
| 1503$^{3}$ | **What Jim Wants (IRE) (40)** (JJO'Neill) **3-9-0** JFanning(4) (chsd ldrs: pushed along 6f out: lost tch 4f out) | 3½ | **4** | 14/1 | 43 | — |
| 1600$^{2}$ | **Perfect Gift (60)** (PFICole) **3-8-11** CRutter(5) (b.nr hind: chsd ldrs: rdn 6f out: hung rt over 2f out: nt run on: eased fnl f) | 6 | **5** | Evens$^{1}$ | 33 | — |
| | | | | (SP 120.2%) | **5 Rn** | |

**3m 14.0** (18.50) CSF £11.21 TOTE £2.10: £1.10 £2.40 (£6.50) OWNER Maktoum Al Maktoum (LAMBOURN) BRED GAINSBOROUGH STUD MANAGEMENT LTD
**OFFICIAL EXPLANATION Perfect Gift: was unsuited by the easy ground and hung right throughout.**

**2217 Grey Galava**, stepping up in distance, took the race by the scruff of the neck and was out on her own in the final two furlongs. (13/8)
**Parrot's Hill (IRE)**, stepping up in distance, went in pursuit of the winner rounding the home turn but it was soon clear his task was a hopeless one. (6/1: 8/1-5/1)
**Atienza (USA)**, a keen-going sort, was left behind in the final half-mile. (8/1)
**1503 What Jim Wants (IRE)** is only selling plate class. (14/1)
**1600 Perfect Gift** ran an ungenerous race. Hanging right under pressure, she wanted no part of it and her rider eventually gave up. Connections reckoned she was unsuited by the soft ground. (Evens)

## 2425 AMERICAN REVOLUTION H'CAP (0-75) (3-Y.O) (Class D)

3-45 (3-47) **7f** £3,947.50 (£1,180.00: £565.00: £257.50) Stalls: Low GOING: 0.29 sec per fur (G)

| | Horse | Dist | Pos | SP | RR | SF |
|---|---|---|---|---|---|---|
| 2240$^{3}$ | **Silver Welcome (55)** (TDEasterby) **3-7-12**(3) FLynch(3) (mde all: styd on fnl f: hld on wl) | — | **1** | 11/2$^{3}$ | 67 | 39 |
| 2162$^{2}$ | **Mels Baby (IRE) (56)** (JLEyre) **3-7-13**(3) DWright(6) (hld up: effrt over 3f out: hdwy over 1f out: nt qckn ins fnl f) | 1¼ | **2** | 9/2$^{1}$ | 65 | 37 |
| 1780$^{5}$ | **Riccarton (50)** (PCalver) **3-7-10** NCarlisle(10) (hld up: hdwy & swtchd lft over 1f out: kpt on wl) | 3 | **3** | 9/1 | 52 | 24 |
| 2049$^{9}$ | **The Wad (66)** (DNicholls) **3-8-12** KFallon(9) (lw: chsd ldrs: n.m.r over 1f out: kpt on) | ¾ | **4** | 8/1 | 67 | 39 |
| 2151$^{3}$ | **Comic Fantasy (AUS) (75)** (MartynWane) **3-9-7** JCarroll(2) (chsd ldrs: edgd rt & wknd over 1f out) | 3 | **5** | 12/1 | 69 | 41 |
| 1608$^{2}$ | **Blessed Spirit (71)** (CFWall) **3-9-3** PRobinson(8) (b.off hind: chsd ldrs tl wknd fnl f) | ½ | **6** | 9/2$^{1}$ | 64 | 36 |
| 2179* | **Ned's Contessa (IRE) (51)** (MDods) **3-7-11**ow1 6x DaleGibson(1) (dwlt: bhd tl styd on fnl 2f: nvr nr ldrs) | 1¾ | **7** | 10/1 | 40 | 11 |
| 2078$^{5}$ | **Krystal Max (IRE) (75)** (TDBarron) **3-9-7** JFortune(4) (swtg: chsd ldrs: wkng whn n.m.r over 1f out) | ½ | **8** | 5/1$^{2}$ | 62 | 34 |
| 2139$^{2}$ | **Oriel Lad (67)** (PDEvans) **3-8-13b** WJO'Connor(5) (s.i.s: sn drvn along: nvr nr ldrs) | 3 | **9** | 9/2$^{1}$ | 48 | 20 |
| *387*$^{5}$ | **Young Frederick (IRE) (60)** (KRBurke) **3-8-6** SWhitworth(7) (sn bhd) | 5 | **10** | 16/1 | 29 | 1 |
| | | | | (SP 130.4%) | **10 Rn** | |

**1m 29.5** (5.90) CSF £32.10 CT £217.58 TOTE £6.10: £1.10 £2.00 £3.30 (£12.10) Trio £59.50 OWNER Mr Peter Hurst (MALTON) BRED Ahmed M. Foustok

**2240 Silver Welcome**, a keen-going sort, had everything his own way here and, getting the prize stands'-side pitch, in truth, was never going to be overhauled. (11/2)
**2162 Mels Baby (IRE)**, settled off the pace, made ground up the inner to chase the winner in the final furlong. He really needs the mile. (9/2)
**1780 Riccarton**, a keen-going sort, has been dropped 5lb. Shut in on the inner over a furlong out, when switched to the outside, he kept on all the way to the line. He is still learning the ropes. (9/1)
**1707 The Wad** seemed to stay the seven alright, sticking on after being tightened up. (8/1)
**2151 Comic Fantasy (AUS)** came off a true line as her stamina gave out, posing a problem or two. (12/1)

## 2426 BATTLE OF BUNKER HILL LIMITED STKS (0-65) (4-Y.O+) (Class F)
4-15 (4-15) **7f** £2,637.00 (£732.00: £351.00) Stalls: Low GOING: 0.29 sec per fur (G)

| | | | | SP | RR | SF |
|---|---|---|---|---|---|---|
| 1789* | **Legal Issue (IRE) (61)** (WWHaigh) **4-9-0** RLappin(6) (lw: chsd ldr: led over 1f out: jst hld on) | — | 1 | 7/1 | 74 | 56 |
| 2320[2] | **It's Academic (60)** (MrsJRRamsden) **4-8-8** KFallon(7) (lw: hld up: effrt & nt clr run over 2f out: ev ch ins fnl f: hrd rdn & r.o) | hd | 2 | Evens[1] | 68 | 50 |
| 2047[3] | **Kid Ory (64)** (PCalver) **5-8-11** MBirch(2) (hdwy to chse ldrs over 4f out: kpt on same pce appr fnl f) | 2½ | 3 | 11/2[3] | 65 | 47 |
| 2047[8] | **Anonym (IRE) (63)** (DNicholls) **4-8-11** AlexGreaves(1) (lw: hld up: effrt & swtchd lft over 1f out: one pce) | 1 | 4 | 8/1 | 63 | 45 |
| 2022* | **Broctune Gold (65)** (MrsMReveley) **5-9-3** ACulhane(3) (chsd ldrs: drvn along over 2f out: wknd over 1f out) | 1¾ | 5 | 12/1 | 65 | 47 |
| 1041[4] | **Proud Image (60)** (KRBurke) **4-9-0v** SWhitworth(4) (led tl over 1f out: sn wknd) | 3½ | 6 | 16/1 | 54 | 36 |
| 2058[2] | **Yoxall Lodge (64)** (HJCollingridge) **6-8-11** MRimmer(8) (lw: s.i.s: sn chsng ldrs & drvn along: outpcd fnl 2f) | s.h | 7 | 9/2[2] | 51 | 33 |
| 1781[9] | **Bargash (62)** (PDEvans) **4-9-0v**[1] JFortune(5) (trckd ldrs: effrt 2f out: n.m.r & wknd over 1f out) | 3 | 8 | 9/1 | 47 | 29 |
| | | | | (SP 130.8%) | **8 Rn** | |

**1m 29.1** (5.50) CSF £16.11 TOTE £6.60: £2.10 £1.10 £1.80 (£6.50) OWNER Mr B. Valentine (MALTON) BRED Naver Enterprises Ltd
**1789* Legal Issue (IRE)** got the favoured stands' side and held on by the skin of his teeth. (7/1)
**2320 It's Academic** met trouble when trying to improve early in the straight. Under severe pressure, she drew upsides inside the last but could not quite get her head in front. (Evens)
**2047 Kid Ory** ran his usual sound race. (11/2: 4/1-6/1)
**1650 Anonym (IRE)**, held up off the pace, had to switch to get a run but, on this easy ground, could do no more than stay on at the same pace. (8/1: op 9/2)
**2022* Broctune Gold** was as usual taken to post early. (12/1: op 8/1)

## 2427 BOSTON TEA PARTY H'CAP (0-70) (3-Y.O) (Class E)
4-45 (4-46) **5f 212y** £3,444.00 (£1,032.00: £496.00: £228.00) Stalls: High GOING: 0.29 sec per fur (G)

| | | | | SP | RR | SF |
|---|---|---|---|---|---|---|
| 1527[11] | **Bee Health Boy (57)** (MWEasterby) **3-8-8b** NConnorton(8) (led to ½-wy: styd on to ld last strides) | — | 1 | 14/1 | 66 | 34 |
| *2084*[10] | **No Monkey Nuts (68)** (JBerry) **3-9-5** JCarroll(6) (chsd ldrs: led ½-wy tl last strides) | hd | 2 | 10/1 | 77 | 45 |
| 1340[9] | **Desert Lynx (IRE) (70)** (TRWatson) **3-9-4**(3) OPears(12) (bhd: gd hdwy on outside to chse ldrs whn hmpd over 2f out: swtchd & styd on wl fnl f) | 2½ | 3 | 8/1 | 72 | 40 |
| 2316[4] | **Camionneur (IRE) (49)** (TDEasterby) **3-8-0b** TWilliams(2) (dwlt: hdwy to chse ldrs ½-wy: edgd rt over 2f out: kpt on same pce) | s.h | 4 | 4/1[1] | 51 | 19 |
| 2151[5] | **Mister Joel (62)** (MWEasterby) **3-8-13b** DaleGibson(10) (chsd ldrs: edgd rt & wknd 2f out) | 7 | 5 | 11/2[3] | 45 | 13 |
| 2029[6] | **Hickleton Miss (50)** (MrsVAAconley) **3-8-1** NCarlisle(1) (s.i.s: sn chsng ldrs: lost pl ½-wy: n.d after) | 3 | 6 | 10/1 | 25 | — |
| 2238[2] | **Ramsey Hope (67)** (CWFairhurst) **3-9-4b** NKennedy(9) (lw: chsd ldrs tl wknd over 1f out) | ½ | 7 | 4/1[1] | 41 | 9 |
| *264*[4] | **Jemsilverthorn (IRE) (49)** (RCSpicer) **3-8-0** JLowe(4) (outpcd fr ½-wy) | 5 | 8 | 20/1 | 9 | — |
| 1709[11] | **Play The Tune (60)** (KRBurke) **3-8-11** SWhitworth(5) (s.i.s: a bhd) | 7 | 9 | 25/1 | 2 | — |
| 2238[3] | **Katy-Q (IRE) (53)** (PCalver) **3-8-4b** MBirch(3) (w ldrs tl lost pl over 2f out: sn bhd) | 9 | 10 | 5/1[2] | — | — |
| | | | | (SP 116.6%) | **10 Rn** | |

**1m 16.8** (5.90) CSF £129.03 CT £1,095.99 TOTE £14.70: £3.70 £1.70 £2.30 (£68.70) Trio £266.60 OWNER Bee Health Ltd (SHERIFF HUTTON) BRED Roger and Mrs Margaret Lightfoot
**Bee Health Boy** proved well suited by the give underfoot. Coming widest of all off the bend, he played a part in the third being hampered. Sticking on under strong pressure, he put his head in front almost on the line. (14/1: op 8/1)
**1707 No Monkey Nuts**, a winner of three at two, bounced back to his best, showing ahead at halfway and only just being caught. (10/1)
**973* Desert Lynx (IRE)** came from off the pace on the wide outside once in line for home. Running out of room, she had to be switched. Sticking on in the final furlong, she would have gone close but for the trouble. (8/1)
**2316 Camionneur (IRE)**, a frustrating individual, missed the break slightly. Edging right once in line for home, he contributed to Desert Lynx's downfall. (4/1)
**2151 Mister Joel** edged right under pressure over two furlongs out, helping to block Desert Lynx's path. (11/2)

T/Jkpt: Not won; £3,320.73 to Sandown 5/7/96. T/Plpt: £236.70 (54.17 Tckts). T/Qdpt: £58.60 (19.93 Tckts). WG

# 1797-HAYDOCK (L-H) (Good to soft)
## Thursday July 4th
WEATHER: overcast WIND: str half against

## 2428 CLYNOL APPRENTICE H'CAP (0-70) (3-Y.O+) (Class E)
6-50 (6-51) **7f 30y** £3,095.00 (£935.00: £455.00: £215.00) Stalls: Low GOING: 0.37 sec per fur (GS)

| | | | | SP | RR | SF |
|---|---|---|---|---|---|---|
| 2340[7] | **Ballard Lady (IRE) (35)** (JSWainwright) **4-7-5**(5) PDoe(2) (lw: hld up: hdwy 2f out: led ins fnl f: sn clr) | — | 1 | 9/1 | 46 | 26 |
| 2047[7] | **Royal Comedian (39)** (BWMurray) **7-7-7**(7)ow1 RCody-Boutcher(4) (a.p: led over 2f out tl hdd & no ex ins fnl f) | 2 | 2 | 20/1 | 46 | 25 |
| 2240[2] | **My Gallery (IRE) (62)** (ABailey) **5-9-6**(3) AngelaGallimore(5) (hld up: hdwy 2f out: fin wl) | nk | 3 | 100/30[1] | 68 | 48 |
| 2149[8] | **Best of All (IRE) (67)** (JBerry) **4-9-9**(5) CLowther(9) (lw: trckd ldrs: rdn 2f out: edgd rt: one pce) | 1¼ | 4 | 14/1 | 70 | 50 |
| *1993*[6] | **Sheraz (IRE) (61)** (NTinkler) **4-9-5**(3) JoHunnam(6) (hld up: styd on appr fnl f: nvr nrr) | 1½ | 5 | 11/1 | 61 | 41 |
| 2075[14] | **Percy Parrot (43)** (RMWhitaker) **4-7-13**(5)ow3 PFredericks(7) (bhd tl sme late hdwy) | 1¼ | 6 | 12/1 | 40 | 17 |
| *1718** | **Sea Spouse (44)** (MBlanshard) **5-8-5** CAdamson(12) (lw: led tl hdd over 2f out: wknd appr fnl f) | 2½ | 7 | 9/2[2] | 35 | 15 |
| *836*[6] | **Hill Farm Katie (35)** (WMBrisbourne) **5-7-5**(5) JBramhill(3) (a in rr) | 3½ | 8 | 25/1 | 18 | — |
| 1888* | **Wire Act (USA) (60)** (MartynMeade) **3-8-6**(7) ClaireAngell(8) (a in rr) | ¾ | 9 | 13/2 | 42 | 14 |
| 2213[4] | **Winter Scout (USA) (60)** (CPEBrooks) **8-9-7b** SCopp(1) (s.i.s: bhd & rdn 3f out: no imp) | 2½ | 10 | 10/1 | 36 | 16 |

1538[2] **Spanish Steps (IRE) (58)** (MWEasterby) **4-9-5b** GParkin(11) (lw: chsd ldng pair: c stands' side st: racd alone: sn lost tch) ....½ **11** 11/2[3] 33 13
1986[9] **Magic Lake (49)** (EJAlston) **3-8-2** IonaWands(10) (lw: trckd ldrs 5f: sn wknd) ....nk **12** 8/1 23 —
**Maurangi (49)** (BWMurray) **5-8-5**(5) GHannon(13) (s.s: sn chsng ldrs: wknd over 3f out: t.o) ....5 **13** 20/1 12 —
(SP 136.2%) **13 Rn**

**1m 34.98** (7.48) CSF £168.84 CT £536.64 TOTE £10.10: £2.60 £7.10 £2.10 (£55.50) Trio £227.90 OWNER Mrs P. Wake (MALTON) BRED Airlie Stud
LONG HANDICAP Ballard Lady (IRE) 7-8
WEIGHT FOR AGE 3yo-8lb
**2045 Ballard Lady (IRE)** scored her only success here just over twelve months ago. Relishing the easier ground, she won going away and is at the right end of the handicap to follow up. (9/1)
**2047 Royal Comedian** is just coming to herself and, as she needs a sounder surface, she should be able to make amends in the coming weeks. (20/1)
**2240 My Gallery (IRE)** rarely runs a bad race and, with all her weight, performed with credit here. She had allowed the leading pair to get away and was never going to reach them. (100/30)
**1585 Best of All (IRE)** ran well, attempting to concede weight all round, and would seem to be about to find her form. (14/1)
**1719* Sheraz (IRE)** finds this trip inadequate and was only getting into his stride when the race was as good as over. (11/1)
**1830 Percy Parrot** needs a mile and a much sounder surface than he had here and just could not muster the speed to get into it. (12/1)
**1718* Sea Spouse**, who does most of his racing on the All-Weather, tried to make every post a winning one. He was hard at work below the distance and had to admit he had met his match. (9/2)

## 2429 SCANIA 4-SERIES 'HORSEPOWER' (S) STKS (2-Y.O) (Class F)
7-20 (7-23) **6f** £2,577.00 (£722.00: £351.00) Stalls: High GOING: 0.37 sec per fur (GS)

| | | | SP | RR | SF |
|---|---|---|---|---|---|
| 2309[6] **Victoria's Dream (IRE)** (MRChannon) **2-8-6** WCarson(4) (mde all: hrd drvn fnl f: r.o wl) | — | **1** | 13/2 | 63 | 15 |
| 1858[6] **Veerapong (IRE)** (MWEasterby) **2-8-1**(5) GParkin(6) (hdwy 2f out: chal ins fnl f: unable qckn) | 1 | **2** | 14/1 | 60 | 12 |
| *1603*[6] **Suave Star** (PDEvans) **2-8-6** TQuinn(2) (dwlt: hdwy ½-wy: rdn over 1f out: one pce) | 2½ | **3** | 4/1[3] | 54 | 6 |
| 2161[2] **Woodetto (IRE)** (EWeymes) **2-8-11** JFortune(7) (lw: prom tl rdn & btn over 1f out) | 4 | **4** | 7/4[1] | 48 | — |
| 1851[5] **Jilly Woo** (DRCElsworth) **2-8-6** BDoyle(1) (lw: s.i.s: hdwy ½-wy: wknd over 1f out) | 3 | **5** | 11/4[2] | 35 | — |
| 2043[10] **Billycan (IRE)** (BPJBaugh) **2-8-11** WLord(5) (lw: outpcd: a bhd: t.o) | 10 | **6** | 33/1 | 13 | — |
| 2043[9] **Joyful Joy** (BPJBaugh) **2-8-6** ACulhane(3) (chsd wnr: wkng whn n.m.r over 2f out: sn t.o) | 13 | **7** | 25/1 | — | — |
| 2174[2] **Full Traceability (IRE)** (JBerry) **2-8-11** JCarroll(8) (dwlt: a bhd: t.o) | 3 | **8** | 5/1 | — | — |
| | | | (SP 126.5%) | **8 Rn** | |

**1m 19.39** (7.69) CSF £81.98 TOTE £5.60: £1.30 £4.90 £1.30 (£39.40) OWNER Mr Alec Tuckerman (UPPER LAMBOURN) BRED Tullamaine Castle Stud and Robert Clay
Bt in 6,800 gns
**2309 Victoria's Dream (IRE)**, smartly into her stride, was able to cross over to the favoured stands' rail and, driven out firmly, was always holding the persistent runner-up. (13/2)
**1858 Veerapong (IRE)**, having her first run beyond the minimum trip, looked to be going best when putting in her bid 200 yards out, but the winner was not stopping and she was unable to get to terms. (14/1)
**1603 Suave Star**, a bit of a madam at the start, promised to get into the race below the distance but she appeared to find the sixth furlong just too much of a test in the prevailing conditions. (4/1: op 5/2)
**2161 Woodetto (IRE)**, a very bad mover even on this easier ground, sat in behind the leaders going well. He was being made to work passing the quarter-mile marker and was unable to pick up. (7/4)
**1851 Jilly Woo**, sluggish leaving the start, took closer order three furlongs out, but she was finding the ground softer than she cares for and was never able to land a blow. (11/4: 2/1-3/1)

## 2430 SCANIA 1996 TRUCK OF THE YEAR TROPHY H'CAP (0-80) (3-Y.O+ F & M) (Class D)
7-50 (7-51) **1m 3f 200y** £3,575.75 (£1,076.00: £520.50: £242.75) Stalls: High GOING: 0.37 sec per fur (GS)

| | | | SP | RR | SF |
|---|---|---|---|---|---|
| 2321[W] **Lalindi (IRE) (72)** (DRCElsworth) **5-10-0b** TQuinn(3) (lw: chsd ldr: led 6f out: hrd rdn appr fnl f: hld on gamely) | — | **1** | 7/2[1] | 78 | 66 |
| 1123[4] **Alicia (IRE) (70)** (JLDunlop) **3-8-13** WCarson(1) (trckd ldrs: effrt & ev ch appr fnl f: hrd drvn & r.o wl nr fin) | nk | **2** | 4/1[2] | 76 | 51 |
| 766[4] **Naval Gazer (IRE) (76)** (DRLoder) **3-9-5** RHughes(5) (lw: hld up: hdwy over 3f out: rdn & one pce appr fnl f) | 10 | **3** | 9/2[3] | 68 | 43 |
| 1873[4] **Turia (69)** (MajorDNChappell) **3-8-12** BThomson(7) (plld hrd: hld up: rdn & one pce fnl 2f) | 1¼ | **4** | 9/2[3] | 60 | 35 |
| 2390[6] **Steadfast Elite (IRE) (45)** (JJO'Neill) **5-7-12b**(3) FLynch(6) (hld up: effrt & rdn 3f out: grad wknd) | 3 | **5** | 12/1 | 32 | 20 |
| 1900* **Temptress (64)** (PTWalwyn) **3-8-7** SSanders(4) (lw: led to ½-wy: rdn 4f out: wkng whn swvd lft 2f out: sn bhd) | 2½ | **6** | 7/2[1] | 47 | 22 |
| 1361[5] **Ladykirk (75)** (JWWatts) **3-9-4** NConnorton(2) (lw: hld up & bhd: rdn & lost tch over 3f out) | nk | **7** | 13/2 | 58 | 33 |
| | | | (SP 121.8%) | **7 Rn** | |

**2m 40.57** (11.17) CSF £18.08 TOTE £4.80: £1.80 £2.00 (£8.90) OWNER White Horse Racing Ltd (WHITCOMBE) BRED Hascombe and Valiant Studs
WEIGHT FOR AGE 3yo-13lb
**OFFICIAL EXPLANATION Temptress: was unable to stay the trip on the rain-softened ground.**
**2155* Lalindi (IRE)**, a very versatile performer, had rivals queueing up to deliver their challenges for the final three furlongs, but she put her head down and defied them to pass her. (7/2)
**1123 Alicia (IRE)**, taking on handicappers for the first time and stepping down in distance, ran a brave race in defeat and should not be long in finding an opening. (4/1)
**766 Naval Gazer (IRE)**, a very lightly-raced filly trying a mile and a half for the first time, tried to make her presence felt early in the straight but, with the pace not dropping, had burnt her boats before reaching the final furlong. (9/2)
**1873 Turia** raced keenly in behind the leaders, but found very little when let down and she did not seem at all happy on this more testing ground. (9/2)
**1900* Temptress**, off the bridle early in the straight, kept battling away, but she was already in deep trouble when she ducked left two furlongs out and, from then on, could only gallop on the spot. (7/2)

## 2431 FAMOUS GROUSE H'CAP (0-80) (3-Y.O+) (Class D)
8-20 (8-20) **6f** £3,735.00 (£1,125.00: £545.00: £255.00) Stalls: High GOING: 0.37 sec per fur (GS)

| | | | SP | RR | SF |
|---|---|---|---|---|---|
| 1501[8] **Maid O'Cannie (57)** (MWEasterby) **5-8-6b** TQuinn(7) (hld up: swtchd lft appr fnl f: str run to ld post) | — | **1** | 9/2[2] | 62 | 36 |

| | | | | SP | RR | SF |
|---|---|---|---|---|---|---|
| 646[5] | **Nilgiri Hills (IRE) (80)** (JLDunlop) **3-9-9** WCarson(9) (b: hld up: hdwy 2f out: effrt & n.m.r whn hit over hd 100yds out: rallied nr fin: fin 3rd, s.h: plcd 2nd) | | **2** | 9/2[2] | 83 | 51 |
| 2200* | **U-No-Harry (IRE) (72)** (RHollinshead) **3-8-12**(3) 7x FLynch(5) (lw: a.p: led over 2f out: hrd rdn & edgd rt fnl f: ct nr fin: fin 2nd, hd: disq: plcd 3rd) | | **3** | 7/1 | 77 | 45 |
| 1991[3] | **Almasi (IRE) (68)** (CFWall) **4-9-3** WWoods(2) (lw: hld up & bhd: swtchd rt over 2f out: effrt u.p whn nt clr run & eased ins fnl f) | 3 | **4** | 4/1[1] | 63 | 37 |
| 1775[13] | **Flag Fen (USA) (59)** (MartynMeade) **5-8-3b**[1](5) RHavlin(6) (outpcd tl hdwy over 1f out: nvr nrr) | 2½ | **5** | 25/1 | 48 | 22 |
| 1848[6] | **Colway Rake (67)** (JWWatts) **5-9-2b** NConnorton(1) (lw: prom: rdn & wknd appr fnl f) | 1½ | **6** | 14/1 | 52 | 26 |
| 2386[4] | **Bold Street (IRE) (65)** (ABailey) **6-8-11b**(3) DWright(3) (hld up: effrt 2f out: sn rdn no imp) | 2 | **7** | 5/1[3] | 44 | 18 |
| 2005[13] | **Brecongill Lad (71)** (MissSEHall) **4-9-3b**(3) DaneO'Neill(4) (lw: prom: ev ch tl wknd wl over 1f out) | 5 | **8** | 8/1 | 37 | 11 |
| 2220[3] | **Tiler (IRE) (78)** (MJohnston) **4-9-13b**[1] DHolland(8) (led tl over 2f out: sn rdn & wknd) | 3 | **9** | 5/1[3] | 36 | 10 |
| | | | | (SP 123.8%) | | **9 Rn** |

**1m 17.81** (6.11) CSF £25.30 CT £133.06 TOTE £5.90: £1.80 £1.50 £2.00 (£12.90) Trio £18.70 OWNER Mrs E. Rhind (SHERIFF HUTTON) BRED E. Landi

WEIGHT FOR AGE 3yo-6lb

**1501 Maid O'Cannie** had the race run to suit her and, with rivals getting in one another's way, timed her effort to perfection. (9/2)

**646 Nilgiri Hills (IRE)**, brought back to sprinting in an attempt to get off the mark, was a very unlucky loser indeed and it says much for his courage that he was able to figure in such a close encounter. Compensation awaits. (9/2)

**2200* U-No-Harry (IRE)**, an improving colt who was on a roll, just failed to defy a 7lb penalty but this was, without doubt, his best performance yet. (7/1)

**1991 Almasi (IRE)** worked her way over to the stands' side to deliver her challenge and, though she was under pressure, she would have gone very close with a trouble-free run inside the last furlong. (4/1: 5/2-9/2)

**843 Flag Fen (USA)**, twice a winner in Ireland over ten furlongs, was having his first try at sprinting. Blinkered for the first time, he could not go the early pace, but he was staying on well in the latter stages and is capable of better. (25/1)

**1848 Colway Rake** was in with a live chance until the quickening tempo caught him out approaching the final furlong. He is no back-number yet. (14/1)

**2220 Tiler (IRE)** ran much too freely in his first-time blinkers and had burnt himself out entering the last quarter-mile. (5/1)

## 2432 HAYDOCK COMMERCIALS FOR SCANIA MAIDEN STKS (3-Y.O) (Class D)

8-50 (8-54) **7f 30y** £4,008.00 (£1,209.00: £587.00: £276.00) Stalls: Low GOING: 0.37 sec per fur (GS)

| | | | | SP | RR | SF |
|---|---|---|---|---|---|---|
| 1901[10] | **Rivers Magic** (MajorDNChappell) **3-9-0** BThomson(1) (mde all: rdn over 1f out: styd on strly) | — | **1** | 20/1 | 88 | 42 |
| 1855[4] | **Saleemah (USA) (78)** (JLDunlop) **3-8-9** WCarson(6) (a.p: stumbled bnd over 4f out: chsd wnr fnl 2f: kpt on u.p nr fin) | 1 | **2** | 6/4[1] | 81 | 35 |
| 2150[2] | **Woodbury Lad (USA) (81)** (WRMuir) **3-9-0** TQuinn(8) (lw: chsd wnr: ev ch 2f out: wknd appr fnl f) | 4 | **3** | 11/2[3] | 77 | 31 |
| 2139[6] | **Surf City (65)** (WWHaigh) **3-9-0** RLappin(7) (lw: trckd ldrs tl wknd over 1f out) | 3½ | **4** | 25/1 | 69 | 23 |
| 1857[9] | **Redskin Lady** (DRCElsworth) **3-8-6**(3) DaneO'Neill(9) (trckd ldrs: no hdwy fnl 2f) | 3 | **5** | 20/1 | 57 | 11 |
| | **Ruby Angel** (HCandy) **3-8-9** CRutter(10) (lengthy: unf: bit bkwd: hdwy over 1f out: nt rch ldrs) | ¾ | **6** | 20/1 | 56 | 10 |
| 1475[3] | **Willie Miles** (JWWatts) **3-9-0** NConnorton(4) (mid div: effrt over 2f out: no imp) | 8 | **7** | 11/2[3] | 43 | — |
| | **Magic Solution (IRE)** (HCandy) **3-8-9** TWilliams(11) (b.hind: scope: bkwd: trckd ldrs over 4f) | hd | **8** | 20/1 | 37 | — |
| *1972*[2] | **Moonraking** (TJEtherington) **3-9-0** DaleGibson(2) (a in rr) | 1¼ | **9** | 25/1 | 40 | — |
| 2150[3] | **Truly Bay** (TDBarron) **3-9-0** JFortune(5) (dwlt: a bhd) | 1½ | **10** | 20/1 | 36 | — |
| | **Kabalevsky (USA)** (JHMGosden) **3-9-0** JCarroll(3) (w'like: leggy: s.i.s: rn green: a bhd: t.o) | 5 | **11** | 4/1[2] | 25 | — |
| | **Haysong (IRE)** (JPLeigh) **3-8-9** ACulhane(13) (bit bkwd: a bhd: t.o) | 4 | **12** | 33/1 | 11 | — |
| | **Topup** (JWHills) **3-9-0** DHolland(12) (s.i.s: a bhd: t.o) | s.h | **13** | 20/1 | 16 | — |
| | | | | (SP 130.0%) | | **13 Rn** |

**1m 35.05** (7.55) CSF £51.77 TOTE £37.90: £5.60 £1.30 £1.70 (£33.10) Trio £170.20 OWNER Mr Rex Mead (WHITSBURY) BRED Mrs C. F. Van Straubenzee and R. Mead

**Rivers Magic**, a brother to Nomination and much the wiser for his outing last month, adopted catch me if you can tactics and proved much too tough for the hard-ridden favourite. (20/1)

**1855 Saleemah (USA)**, returning to seven furlongs, almost lost her footing a couple of times on the home turn. Driven along to chase the winner for the last quarter-mile, she stuck on willingly but could not find that bit extra to wear him down. (6/4)

**2150 Woodbury Lad (USA)**, taken to post early, stalked the winner and looked to have the edge two furlongs out, but that rival saw the trip out better in this testing ground, and he had shot his bolt approaching the final furlong. (11/2)

**1435 Surf City** was never too far away, but he was hard at work inside the last quarter-mile and could do little more than gallop on the spot. (25/1)

**Redskin Lady**, in more or less the same position throughout, had met her match some way out, but she is gaining valuable experience and her turn will come. (20/1)

**Ruby Angel**, an unfurnished filly whose dam won at middle distances, was the only one staying on at the finish, and she should pay her way in time. (20/1)

**Kabalevsky (USA)**, a very costly yearling, did not show much on this racecourse debut but he did run very green, and a sounder surface will suit him much better than this tiring ground. (4/1)

## 2433 SCANIA 4-SERIES 'KING OF THE ROAD' TROPHY H'CAP (0-80) (3-Y.O) (Class D)

9-20 (9-20) **1m 6f** £3,780.50 (£1,139.00: £552.00: £258.50) Stalls: Centre GOING: 0.37 sec per fur (GS)

| | | | | SP | RR | SF |
|---|---|---|---|---|---|---|
| 1507[4] | **The Swan (68)** (JLDunlop) **3-9-7** WCarson(3) (lw: led after 3f tl over 3f out: rallied u.p to ld nr fin) | — | **1** | 5/6[1] | 78 | 30 |
| 2120[3] | **Charming Admiral (IRE) (62)** (CFWall) **3-9-1** WWoods(2) (lw: hld up in tch: hdwy to ld over 3f out: rdn & edgd lft fnl f: hdd fnl strides) | hd | **2** | 11/4[2] | 72 | 24 |
| 1415[6] | **Dancing Cavalier (67)** (RHollinshead) **3-9-3**(3) FLynch(5) (hld up & bhd: effrt 3f out: sn rdn & outpcd) | 14 | **3** | 9/2[3] | 61 | 13 |
| 2196[3] | **Manoy (61)** (JHetherton) **3-9-0b** BThomson(4) (led 3f: wknd over 2f out) | 7 | **4** | 8/1 | 47 | — |
| 1434[10] | **Gold Lining (IRE) (52)** (EJAlston) **3-8-2**(3) DWright(1) (hld up: gd hdwy ent st: rdn 3f out: sn btn) | ¾ | **5** | 20/1 | 37 | — |
| | | | | (SP 115.3%) | | **5 Rn** |

**3m 16.72** (18.52) CSF £3.70 TOTE £1.70: £1.50 £1.90 (£2.00) OWNER Mr R. J. McAulay (ARUNDEL) BRED Oak Bloodstock Ltd

**1507 The Swan** came into her own over this extended trip, but needed all the help she could get to poke her head in front right on the line. (5/6)

**2120 Charming Admiral (IRE)** got the better of the winner early in the straight and looked to have the prize in safe-keeping, but he was treading ground inside the final furlong and was worn down in the shadow of the post. (11/4)

**594 Dancing Cavalier**, asked for an effort three furlongs out, failed to sustain his run and was never close enough to cause concern. (9/2)

T/Plpt: £109.20 (168.7 Tckts). T/Qdpt: £12.70 (132.6 Tckts). IM

## 2410-YARMOUTH (L-H) (Good to firm, Firm bk st)
### Thursday July 4th
WEATHER: overcast, showers WIND: fresh against

### 2434 FRED ARMSTRONG H'CAP (0-70) (3-Y.O+) (Class E)
2-00 (2-01) **6f 3y** £2,961.00 (£882.00: £420.00: £189.00) Stalls: Low GOING minus 0.19 sec per fur (GF)

| | Horse / Details | Dist | Pos | SP | RR | SF |
|---|---|---|---|---|---|---|
| 2403² | **Cheeky Chappy (52)** (DWChapman) **5-9-0b** 7x JQuinn(6) (mde all: pushed clr fnl f) | — | 1 | 7/2² | 66 | 48 |
| 2280⁴ | **Red Admiral (62)** (CMurray) **6-9-10** MTebbutt(5) (a.p: rdn & ev ch over 2f out: kpt on ins fnl f) | 3½ | 2 | 7/1³ | 67 | 49 |
| 2255* | **Faraway Lass (74)** (LordHuntingdon) **3-9-9**(7) 7x AimeeCook(4) (lw: chsd ldrs: ev ch over 1f out: sn rdn & no ex) | ½ | 3 | 6/4¹ | 77 | 53 |
| 2047¹⁰ | **Super Park (62)** (JPearce) **4-9-10** GBardwell(3) (lw: sn rdn & outpcd: styd on wl fnl f) | 1½ | 4 | 25/1 | 61 | 43 |
| 2185¹⁶ | **Christian Flight (IRE) (46)** (SGollings) **7-8-8b¹** VHalliday(1) (chsd ldrs 3f: sn rdn & btn) | 2½ | 5 | 25/1 | 39 | 21 |
| 1986⁶ | **Snow Falcon (62)** (MBell) **3-9-4b** MFenton(2) (nvr nr to chal) | ¾ | 6 | 8/1 | 53 | 29 |
| 2156⁵ | **Judgement Call (51)** (PHowling) **9-8-13** FNorton(7) (b: lw: w wnr over 3f) | 5 | 7 | 7/1³ | 28 | 10 |

(SP 106.0%) **7 Rn**

**1m 13.3** (2.40) CSF £23.33 TOTE £4.00: £1.70 £2.80 (£10.80) OWNER Mrs Jeanne Chapman (YORK) BRED Ian W. Glenton
WEIGHT FOR AGE 3yo-6lb

**2403 Cheeky Chappy** led the field over to the stands' side and grabbed the favoured rail, winning with a little left in the tank. Having run last evening, he clearly thrives on racing and has gained all but one of his wins within fifteen days of a previous run. (7/2)
**2280 Red Admiral** chased the winner throughout and ran well, but could not make much impression in the last furlong. (7/1)
**2255* Faraway Lass** seemed to run below form, but probably paid the penalty for not getting close to the rail. (6/4)
**1677 Super Park**, who has been running over further, was taken completely off his feet until making late progress. (25/1)
**Christian Flight (IRE)**, blinkered for the first time, was taken to post last, but raced towards the centre of the course, and was beaten by halfway. (25/1)
**1986 Snow Falcon** moved scratchily to post and was never a factor. (8/1)

### 2435 DUNSTON (S) STKS (2-Y.O) (Class G)
2-30 (2-31) **6f 3y** £2,301.00 (£636.00: £303.00) Stalls: High GOING minus 0.19 sec per fur (GF)

| | Horse / Details | Dist | Pos | SP | RR | SF |
|---|---|---|---|---|---|---|
| 2043² | **Retoto** (BJMcMath) **2-8-6** TQuinn(4) (a.p: led 1f out: rdn out) | — | 1 | 15/8¹ | 58 | — |
| 1346¹³ | **Grovefair Maiden (IRE)** (BJMeehan) **2-8-6b¹** BDoyle(3) (hld up: hdwy 3f out: ev ch 1f out: one pce) | 1¼ | 2 | 7/1 | 55 | — |
| 2125³ | **Senate Swings** (WRMuir) **2-8-11** RHughes(5) (w ldr: led over 2f out to 1f out: btn whn n.m.r ins fnl f) | 2 | 3 | 100/30² | 54 | — |
| 2125⁴ | **Caviar And Candy** (DJSCosgrove) **2-8-1**(5) LNewton(6) (lw: led over 3f: one pce fnl f) | ½ | 4 | 7/1 | 48 | — |
| 2059⁸ | **Sharazamataz** (WJHaggas) **2-8-6** MHills(1) (hld up: rdn over 1f out: no imp) | ½ | 5 | 13/2³ | 47 | — |
| 1880⁴ | **Victory At Hart** (ICampbell) **2-8-4**(7) GFaulkner(2) (chsd ldrs: rdn 3f out: sn btn) | 4 | 6 | 8/1 | 41 | — |

(SP 107.3%) **6 Rn**

**1m 16.6** (5.70) CSF £12.97 TOTE £3.20: £2.10 £2.70 (£14.50) OWNER The Likely Bunch (NEWMARKET) BRED M. J. Rozenbroek
Bt in 6,500 gns

**2043 Retoto** moved well to post, but had to work hard to win this poor seller. The clock says it all. (15/8)
**Grovefair Maiden (IRE)** got worked up in the stalls, but lost little ground once they opened. The blinkers seemed to improve her but she looks a handful. (7/1: 4/1-9/1)
**2125 Senate Swings** has a little scope for improvement and would have almost been second had his pilot not had to stop riding when the runner-up edged slightly across him. (100/30)
**2125 Caviar And Candy** seems fated never to win, as she again looked weak in a finish. (7/1: 4/1-8/1)
**Sharazamataz** found nothing once off the bridle but probably needs a lot further. (13/2: 3/1-7/1)
**Victory At Hart**, gambled on, raced nearest the centre and was the first beaten. (8/1)

### 2436 HEMSBY CONDITIONS STKS (3-Y.O+) (Class C)
3-00 (3-00) **7f 3y** £5,463.00 (£2,025.00: £974.50: £401.50: £162.75: £67.25) Stalls: High GOING minus 0.19 sec per fur (GF)

| | Horse / Details | Dist | Pos | SP | RR | SF |
|---|---|---|---|---|---|---|
| 2332⁶ | **Branston Abby (IRE) (108)** (MJohnston) **7-9-3** DHolland(3) (sn pushed along & bhd: hdwy 2f out: edgd rt & led ins fnl f: rdn out) | — | 1 | 100/30¹ | 110 | 79 |
| 2114⁸ | **Monaassib (102)** (EALDunlop) **5-9-0** TQuinn(6) (led over 6f: unable qckn) | ½ | 2 | 100/30¹ | 106 | 75 |
| 694⁷ | **Mawwal (USA) (110)** (RWArmstrong) **3-8-6** RHills(1) (lw: prom: ev ch 2f out: btn whn n.m.r ins fnl f: broke leg nr fin: dead) | 2 | 3 | 100/30¹ | 101 | 62 |
| 2072¹⁰ | **April The Eighth (100)** (BWHills) **3-8-6** MHills(5) (prom tl rdn & btn 2f out) | 3 | 4 | 11/2² | 95 | 56 |
| *321** | **Cornish Snow (USA)** (DRLoder) **3-8-8** RHughes(4) (lw: wl bhd fnl 2f) | 22 | 5 | 6/1³ | 46 | 7 |
| 1441⁷ | **Brighstone (100)** (HRACecil) **3-8-6** WRyan(7) (w ldr 4f: eased whn btn appr fnl f) | 16 | 6 | 14/1 | 8 | — |

(SP 105.6%) **6 Rn**

**1m 24.7** (0.50) CSF £13.00 TOTE £3.10: £1.90 £1.60 (£5.10) OWNER Mr David Abell (MIDDLEHAM) BRED John David Abell
WEIGHT FOR AGE 3yo-8lb

**2332 Branston Abby (IRE)**, taken down early, was off the bridle within a furlong but was her normal tenacious self once she started to pick up. (100/30: op 2/1)
**1623 Monaassib** tried to nick this from the front and it took a good one to pick him up. (100/30)
**Mawwal (USA)** had to check slightly inside the final furlong, but there was no rival nearby when he tragically broke a foreleg a stride from the line. (100/30)
**1431 April The Eighth** ran well but is not quite in this league. He is high enough in the handicap and is going to prove hard to place unless he can find further improvement. (11/2)
**Cornish Snow (USA)**, highly tried back on turf, was the first in trouble. (6/1)
**Brighstone** was upside the leader until folding tamely and being eased. He would appear to have not trained on. (14/1)

### 2437 RADIO NORFOLK H'CAP (0-80) (3-Y.O+ F & M) (Class D)
3-30 (3-30) **7f 3y** £3,761.25 (£1,122.00: £535.50: £242.25) Stalls: High GOING minus 0.19 sec per fur (GF)

| | Horse / Details | Dist | Pos | SP | RR | SF |
|---|---|---|---|---|---|---|
| 1853⁵ | **Patsy Grimes (76)** (JSMoore) **6-9-4**(7) AimeeCook(3) (lw: hld up: hdwy 3f out: led ins fnl f: pushed out) | — | 1 | 8/1 | 90 | 71 |
| 2208* | **Hippy (72)** (CEBrittain) **3-8-13** 6x BDoyle(5) (lw: a.p: rdn over 2f out: led over 1f out tl ins fnl f: unable qckn) | 1¼ | 2 | 6/4¹ | 83 | 56 |

| | | | | SP | RR | SF |
|---|---|---|---|---|---|---|
| 2134[4] | **Zelda Zonk (79)** (BJMeehan) **4-9-7**(7) DSweeney(1) (lw: chsd ldrs: led over 2f out tl over 1f out: wknd ins fnl f) | 5 | **3** | 7/2[2] | 79 | 60 |
| 2134[7] | **Rumba Rhythm (CAN) (73)** (RWArmstrong) **3-9-0** MHills(6) (hld up: rdn over 1f out: r.o: nt rch ldrs) | 2½ | **4** | 6/1[3] | 67 | 40 |
| 2130[11] | **College Night (IRE) (51)** (CADwyer) **4-7-11v**[1](3) MHenry(2) (lw: led over 4f: sn wknd) | 7 | **5** | 12/1 | 29 | 10 |
| | **Euphyllia (66)** (BobJones) **4-9-1** NDay(4) (bkwd: chsd ldr 4f: sn wknd) | 1 | **6** | 12/1 | 42 | 23 |
| 2124[5] | **Fresh Fruit Daily (70)** (PAKelleway) **4-9-5** RHughes(7) (rdn 3f out: a bhd) | 4 | **7** | 14/1 | 37 | 18 |

(SP 109.7%) **7 Rn**

**1m 26.0** (1.80) CSF £19.14 TOTE £7.90: £3.70 £2.00 (£7.80) OWNER Mr J. K. Grimes (HUNGERFORD) BRED J. C. Fox

WEIGHT FOR AGE 3yo-8lb

**1853 Patsy Grimes**, scoring for the first time beyond six furlongs, was held up to get the trip and produced to perfection to win without realising she was in a race. (8/1: 6/1-9/1)

**2208* Hippy** was outpaced by the winner inside the final furlong and needs to return to a mile. (6/4)

**2134 Zelda Zonk** looked to be going best when hitting the front, but edged out to the centre of the course and her stride shortened as the weight told. (7/2)

**2134 Rumba Rhythm (CAN)**, given a totally different ride to last time, could never land a blow. (6/1)

**1533 College Night (IRE)**, a poor mover, set a steady pace in a first-time visor but was beaten a long way from home. (12/1)

**Euphyllia** looked as if the race was much needed and showed up well towards the centre of the course until lack of fitness found her out. She took two runs to strike form last year. (12/1: op 8/1)

**2124 Fresh Fruit Daily** (14/1: 10/1-16/1)

## 2438 CATFIELD CLAIMING STKS (3-Y.O+) (Class F)

4-00 (4-01) **1m 3y** £2,571.40 (£710.40: £338.20) Stalls: High GOING minus 0.19 sec per fur (GF)

| | | | | SP | RR | SF |
|---|---|---|---|---|---|---|
| 2234[3] | **Blockade (USA) (67)** (MBell) **7-9-0** MFenton(3) (t: mde all: rdn out) | — | **1** | 7/4[1] | 67 | 33 |
| 2373[4] | **Action Jackson (60)** (BJMcMath) **4-8-8**(7) DSweeney(4) (chsd wnr: rdn & no ex appr fnl f) | 1¼ | **2** | 9/1 | 66 | 32 |
| 2178* | **Perilous Plight (68)** (WRMuir) **5-9-4** TQuinn(1) (lw: hld up: swtchd ins over 2f out: n.m.r over 1f out tl squeezed thro ins fnl f: no imp nr fin) | hd | **3** | 11/4[3] | 68 | 34 |
| 1615[9] | **Star And Garter (75)** (GWragg) **3-8-9** MHills(2) (hld up: hdwy over 2f out: nvr rchd ldrs) | 1¾ | **4** | 2/1[2] | 65 | 22 |
| 2409[11] | **Coven Moon (33)** (DMorris) **6-8-1v**(7) AEddery(5) (chsd ldrs: rdn over 3f out: sn bhd) | 9 | **5** | 33/1 | 37 | 3 |

(SP 109.3%) **5 Rn**

**1m 40.0** (4.70) CSF £13.91 TOTE £2.50: £1.40 £2.40 (£8.20) OWNER Mr A. M. Warrender (NEWMARKET) BRED Patricia C. Warrender

WEIGHT FOR AGE 3yo-9lb

**2234 Blockade (USA)**, in what was a strong wind for a tubed horse, made light of these disadvantages to gamely make all. (7/4)

**2373 Action Jackson** had come to hand this week but was outbattled by the winner and remains a maiden. (9/1: 5/1-10/1)

**2178* Perilous Plight**, with the fastest strip of ground appearing to be by the stands' rail, was switched to track the winner soon after halfway. However, he never saw daylight and his best chance of victory would have been to jump the two in front. This can be ignored. (11/4)

**Star And Garter**, taking a big drop in class, never looked like winning, and is one to be wary of. (2/1)

**2058 Coven Moon**, rated a couple of stone behind these by the Official Handicapper and having had a hard race the previous day, was unsurprisingly the first beaten. (33/1)

## 2439 HAPPISBURGH MAIDEN STKS (3-Y.O+) (Class D)

4-30 (4-30) **1m 3f 101y** £3,960.15 (£1,183.20: £566.10: £257.55) Stalls: Low GOING minus 0.29 sec per fur (GF)

| | | | | SP | RR | SF |
|---|---|---|---|---|---|---|
| 2054[12] | **Qasida (IRE) (86)** (CEBrittain) **3-8-11** BDoyle(2) (mde all: rdn out) | — | **1** | 3/1[3] | 84 | 54 |
| 2135[4] | **Lear Express (USA)** (HRACecil) **3-8-11** WRyan(9) (a.p: rdn 3f out: unable qckn ins fnl f) | nk | **2** | 15/8[1] | 84 | 54 |
| 1711[3] | **Serenus (USA)** (LordHuntingdon) **3-8-11** MHills(6) (lw: hld up: hdwy 3f out: no imp appr fnl f) | 4 | **3** | 11/4[2] | 78 | 48 |
| 2181[4] | **Blatant Outburst** (GCBravery) **6-9-10** TIves(4) (lw: plld hrd: trckd ldrs: effrt 3f out: styd on one pce) | nk | **4** | 11/1 | 79 | 61 |
| 2036[5] | **Alisura** (JRFanshawe) **3-8-6** NDay(8) (r.o fnl 3f: nvr able to chal) | 5 | **5** | 25/1 | 66 | 36 |
| 2198[3] | **St Adele (USA)** (DRLoder) **3-8-6** DRMcCabe(7) (prom: rdn 3f out: sn wknd) | ¾ | **6** | 14/1 | 65 | 35 |
| | **Antonia Bin (IRE)** (MBell) **3-8-6** MFenton(5) (unf: bhd fnl 6f) | 6 | **7** | 16/1 | 56 | 26 |
| *1717*[10] | **Comedie Arrete (FR)** (MCChapman) **4-9-2**(3) PMcCabe(1) (swtg: plld hrd: chsd wnr 8f: sn wknd: t.o) | dist | **8** | 100/1 | — | — |

(SP 112.2%) **8 Rn**

**2m 25.5** (2.50) CSF £8.52 TOTE £3.90: £1.10 £1.20 £1.70 (£5.70) Trio £3.10 OWNER Sheikh Mohammed Obaid Al Maktoum (NEWMARKET) BRED Sheikh Mohammed Obaid al Maktoum

WEIGHT FOR AGE 3yo-12lb

**1305 Qasida (IRE)**, dropped in class and distance and from a stable in great form, enjoyed setting the pace and battled on well when the chance was there to duck the issue. (3/1)

**2135 Lear Express (USA)** went hammer and tongs at it with the winner through the last quarter-mile, but found his rival too tough a not to crack. His knee-action suggests softer ground might suit him, and he looks sure to stay further. (15/8)

**1711 Serenus (USA)** ran on nicely in the straight but, by the time he went third, the first two had flown. (11/4)

**2181 Blatant Outburst** took a bit of settling but, when pulled out and asked to mount a challenge early in the straight, he showed a tendency to edge in behind his rivals. (11/1)

**2036 Alisura** again stayed on too late in the day to pose the leaders a problem. (25/1)

**2198 St Adele (USA)**, a sister to Irish Derby winner St Jovite, is nothing to look at and again ran moderately. She will have to be well placed to gain the win that would enhance her stud value. (14/1: op 6/1)

## 2440 HICKLING LADIES' H'CAP (0-70) (3-Y.O+) (Class G)

5-00 (5-00) **1m 2f 21y** £2,364.00 (£654.00: £312.00) Stalls: Low GOING minus 0.29 sec per fur (GF)

| | | | | SP | RR | SF |
|---|---|---|---|---|---|---|
| 2284[2] | **Don't Drop Bombs (USA) (35)** (DTThom) **7-9-0v** MissJFeilden(2) (mde all: rdn & hld on wl fnl f) | — | **1** | 100/30[2] | 40 | 22 |
| 2162* | **Squared Away (48)** (JWPayne) **4-9-8b**(5) MissCLake(6) (lw: bhd: gd hdwy over 1f out: nt rch wnr) | hd | **2** | 6/1 | 53 | 35 |
| *1444*[7] | **Hever Golf Diamond (50)** (TJNaughton) **3-8-13**(5)ow4 MrsJNaughton(3) (hdwy over 2f out: r.o wl nr fin) | ½ | **3** | 14/1 | 54 | 21 |
| 2251[7] | **Docklands Courier (45)** (BJMcMath) **4-9-5**(5) MissVMarshall(1) (chsd wnr: ev ch over 2f out tl no ex ins fnl f) | nk | **4** | 33/1 | 49 | 31 |
| 1803[10] | **Ajdar (48)** (MissGayKelleway) **5-9-13** MissDianaJones(5) (lw: hld up: hdwy 2f out: r.o fnl f) | ¾ | **5** | 10/1 | 50 | 32 |
| 2321[2] | **Princely Affair (50)** (MBell) **3-9-4** MrsAPerrett(8) (chsd ldrs: rdn & no ex fnl f) | ½ | **6** | 5/2[1] | 52 | 23 |
| 1953[11] | **Bellas Gate Boy (61)** (JPearce) **4-10-12** MrsLPearce(7) (chsd ldrs: rdn & btn wl over 1f out) | 5 | **7** | 15/2 | 55 | 37 |
| 2344[2] | **Roman Reel (USA) (70)** (GLMoore) **5-11-2**(5) MrsJMoore(9) (lw: hld up: hdwy 3f out: wknd over 1f out) | 2 | **8** | 11/2[3] | 61 | 43 |

| | | | | SP | RR | SF |
|---|---|---|---|---|---|---|
| 2066[12] | **Dancing Destiny (48)** (RBastiman) **4-9-8**(5) MissRBastiman(4) (stdd s: hld up: c centre st: sn bhd) | 13 | **9** | 25/1 | 18 | — |
| | | | | (SP 115.6%) | | **9 Rn** |

**2m 11.1** (6.70) CSF £22.03 CT £224.13 TOTE £4.30: £1.20 £2.10 £3.10 (£14.30) Trio £100.30 OWNER Miss J. Feilden (NEWMARKET) BRED Hurstland Farm Incorporated
LONG HANDICAP Hever Golf Diamond 8-13
WEIGHT FOR AGE 3yo-11lb

**2284 Don't Drop Bombs (USA)**, off the same mark as when touched off last week, was third in this race two years ago but made all this time, just lasting home. (100/30)
**2162* Squared Away** looked to have plenty to do when set alight, but finished so well that she would have prevailed in another couple of strides. (6/1: op 4/1)
**899 Hever Golf Diamond**, outpaced when the winner and Docklands Courier kicked clear on the home turn, was running on strongly as the line approached. (14/1)
**Docklands Courier** fought the winner hard all the way up the home straight, but had to admit defeat entering the final furlong. (33/1)
**1019 Ajdar**, coming down in trip, did not get going until too late but finished with a flourish. (10/1)
**2321 Princely Affair** proved one-paced in the last quarter-mile but the margin of his defeat, under three lengths in finishing sixth, will have put a smile on the Handicapper's face. (5/2)

T/Plpt: £38.50 (332.11 Tckts). T/Qdpt: £4.50 (250.73 Tckts). Dk

## 2441a-2458a (Irish Racing) - See Computer Raceform

## 1935a-CURRAGH (Newbridge, Ireland) (R-H) (Good)
## Friday June 28th

### 2459a CHAPMANS (KILDARE) VOLVO H'CAP (0-105) (3-Y.O+)
8-15 (8-16) **1m** £13,000.00 (£3,800.00: £1,800.00: £600.00)

| | | | | SP | RR | SF |
|---|---|---|---|---|---|---|
| 1573a[2] | **Harghar (USA)** (JOxx,Ireland) **3-8-12** JPMurtagh (prom: 3rd ½-wy: chal over 2f out: rdn to ld wl ins fnl f: r.o) | — | **1** | 6/1[2] | 108 | 41 |
| | **Flaunt (IRE)** (MJGrassick,Ireland) **4-7-4**(6)ow2 EAhern (disp ld tl led after ½-wy: jnd 1f out: hdd u.p wl ins fnl f: no ex) | ½ | **2** | 8/1[3] | 81 | 22 |
| | **Meglio Che Posso (IRE)** (WPMullins,Ireland) **5-8-2** WJSmith (hld up: chsd ldrs fr ½-wy: 6th 2f out: 5th u.p over 1f out: kpt on fnl f: nt trble ldrs) | 4½ | **3** | 5/1[1] | 78 | 21 |
| | **Dr Beat (IRE)** (DHanley,Ireland) **3-8-1**ow1 RMBurke (hld up towards rr: hdwy after ½-wy: 3rd & effrt over 1f out: nt trble ldrs) | nk | **4** | 6/1[2] | 86 | 18 |
| | **Nayil** (KPrendergast,Ireland) **4-9-0** WJSupple (hld up towards rr: sme hdwy 3f out: 7th over 1f out: kpt on) | 7 | **5** | 12/1 | 75 | 18 |
| 2041[5] | **Double Diamond (IRE)** (MJohnston) **3-8-2** TWilliams (led & disp ld to ½-wy: sn rdn & hdd: wknd u.p 2f out) | 1 | **6** | 6/1[2] | 71 | 4 |
| | **Irish Academy (IRE)** (CO'Brien,Ireland) **4-8-6** NGMcCullagh (hld up: 7th ½-wy: rdn & chsd ldrs 2f out: no imp fr wl over 1f out) | s.h | **7** | 10/1 | 65 | 8 |
| 1912a[2] | **Free To Speak (IRE)** (DKWeld,Ireland) **4-9-10** MJKinane (in tch: chsd ldrs 3f out: no imp fr 1½f out) | 3 | **8** | 5/1[1] | 77 | 20 |
| 2053[29] | **Ger's Royale (IRE)** (PJFlynn,Ireland) **5-9-7** MDuffy (cl up: 4th ½-wy: no ex u.p 1½f out) | ½ | **9** | 8/1[3] | 73 | 16 |
| | **Faydini (IRE)** (NMeade,Ireland) **7-7-7** JMorgan (in tch: 5th & chsd ldrs over 3f out: btn & wknd 2f out) | 1½ | **10** | 14/1 | 42 | — |
| | | | | (SP 121.9%) | | **10 Rn** |

**1m 37.7** (2.70) OWNER H H Aga Khan (CURRABEG) BRED H.H. Aga Khan Studs S.C.
**1573a Harghar (USA)**, third at halfway, challenged over two furlongs out and, ridden to get in front 100 yards out, he battled on well. (6/1: op 4/1)
**2041 Double Diamond (IRE)** led and disputed the lead to halfway. Weakening when under pressure two furlongs out, he could only plug on at the one pace over the last furlong. (6/1: op 7/2)
NR

## 2460a-2464a (Irish Racing) - See Computer Raceform

## 2455a-CURRAGH (Newbridge, Ireland) (R-H) (Good)
## Saturday June 29th

### 2465a INDEPENDENT PRETTY POLLY STKS (Gp 2) (3-Y.O+ F & M)
4-00 (4-01) **1m 2f** £30,000.00 (£9,500.00: £4,500.00: £1,500.00)

| | | | | SP | RR | SF |
|---|---|---|---|---|---|---|
| 2052[3] | **Dance Design (IRE)** (DKWeld,Ireland) **3-8-8** MJKinane (hld up in tch: trckd ldrs st: chal 2f out: sn qcknd clr: rdn & r.o) | — | **1** | Evens[1] | 111+ | 51 |
| 1567a[6] | **Zafzala (IRE)** (JOxx,Ireland) **3-8-8** JPMurtagh (hld up: 5th ½-wy: 3rd & hdwy wl over 1f out: rdn & kpt on ins fnl f: nt rch wnr) | 1½ | **2** | 8/1 | 109 | 49 |
| | **Theano (IRE)** (APO'Brien,Ireland) **3-8-8** CRoche (hld up: trckd ldrs st: chal 2f out: 2nd, u.p & no ex wl over 1f out: kpt on same pce) | 3½ | **3** | 9/4[2] | 103 | 43 |
| 1193[13] | **Autumn Affair** (CEBrittain) **4-9-6** SCraine (towards rr: mod 6th st: rdn & kpt on: no imp) | 12 | **4** | 25/1 | 84 | 36 |
| 1770[2] | **Hagwah (USA)** (BHanbury) **4-9-6** MRimmer (led & disp ld: hdd 2f out: dropped away qckly) | 5 | **5** | 12/1 | 76 | 28 |
| 2069[8] | **Ceirseach (IRE)** (JSBolger,Ireland) **3-8-8b** KJManning (sn disp ld: rdn over 2f out: sn hdd & wknd) | hd | **6** | 12/1 | 76 | 16 |
| 1108[3] | **Obsessive (USA)** (MRStoute) **3-8-8** PShanahan (a bhd) | 3 | **7** | 6/1[3] | 71 | 11 |
| | | | | (SP 125.4%) | | **7 Rn** |

**2m 4.2** (0.20) OWNER Moyglare Stud Farm (CURRAGH)
**2052 Dance Design (IRE)**, held up in second place, tracked the leaders. Going supremely well into the straight, she quickened clear after leading two furlongs out, and the extra quarter-mile of the Irish Oaks will not be a problem judged on this display. (Evens)
**1567a Zafzala (IRE)** closed up into third place with over a furlong and a half to race. After going second inside the last 200 yards, she could only keep on at one pace. (8/1)
**Theano (IRE)**, fourth into the straight, challenged from two furlongs out and was in second place but under strong pressure over a furlong out, and found little inside the last 200 yards. (9/4)

**Autumn Affair**, only a moderate sixth into the straight, stayed on over the last two furlongs without ever looking a remote danger. (25/1)
**1770 Hagwah (USA)** made the running until the winner went on, and then dropping away quickly when headed. (12/1: op 8/1)
**2102a Ceirseach (IRE)** disputed the lead until weakening two furlongs out. (12/1: op 7/1)
**1108 Obsessive (USA)** was always towards the rear and presented absolutely no danger over the last two furlongs. (6/1)
NR

## 2466a-2469a (Irish Racing) - See Computer Raceform

## 2462a-CURRAGH (Newbridge, Ireland) (R-H) (Good)
## Sunday June 30th

### 2470a P. V. DOYLE MEMORIAL RAILWAY STKS (Gp 3) (2-Y.O)
2-10 (2-11) **6f** £15,500.00 (£4,750.00: £2,250.00: £750.00)

| | | | | SP | RR | SF |
|---|---|---|---|---|---|---|
| 2040² | **Daylight In Dubai (USA)** (PWChapple-Hyam) **2-8-10** JReid (hld up: last ½-wy: rdn & hdwy 2f out: chal over 1f out: led wl ins fnl f: rdn & kpt on wl) | — | 1 | 9/10 1 | 104 | 49 |
| | **Check The Band (USA)** (APO'Brien,Ireland) **2-8-13** CRoche (hld up: 3rd & chal fr 2f out: led u.p early fnl f: hdd wl ins fnl f: kpt on) | ½ | 2 | 7/2 3 | 106 | 51 |
| | **Quws** (KPrendergast,Ireland) **2-8-13** WJSupple (led over 1f: chsd ldr: rdn & ev ch over 1f out: 3rd 1f out: no ex ins fnl f) | 2½ | 3 | 3/1 2 | 99 | 44 |
| 1565a⁴ | **Mosconi (IRE)** (JSBolger,Ireland) **2-8-10b** TEDurcan (led over 4f out: rdn over 1f out: hdd u.p early ins fnl f: no ex) | 1½ | 4 | 12/1 | 92 | 37 |
| 1910a⁴ | **Via Verbano (IRE)** (JSBolger,Ireland) **2-8-7** KJManning (cl up: 3rd early: 4th & rdn ½-wy: rdn & btn over 2f out: eased) | 6 | 5 | 6/1 | 73 | 18 |
| | | | | (SP 121.8%) | | **5 Rn** |

**1m 12.0** (1.50) OWNER P. D. Savill (MARLBOROUGH) BRED Hargus Sexton & Sandra Ellsworth
**2040 Daylight In Dubai (USA)**, held up in last place and hardly outpaced as was suggested, was being ridden along with over two furlongs to race. Challenging over a furlong out, he led well inside last 200 yards after squeezing through, and always held the upper hand. An extra furlong would certainly be to his advantage, and the Champagne Stakes at Doncaster is a target. (9/10)
**Check The Band (USA)**, held up in the early stages, was challenging in third two furlongs out. He led under pressure early inside the last 200 yards, but the winner was always carrying too many guns for him. (7/2)
**Quws** led early and soon settled in third place. He held every chance a furlong and a half out, but looked one-paced inside the last. He needs further. (3/1)
**1565a Mosconi (IRE)** took them along after a furlong and a half, but was outpaced once headed inside the last. (12/1: op 8/1)
**1910a Via Verbano (IRE)** again failed to give her running, being pushed along at halfway and eased when beaten over two furlongs out. (6/1: op 4/1)

### 2471a SEA WORLD INTERNATIONAL STKS (Gp 2) (3-Y.O+)
2-45 (2-45) **1m** **(New)** £30,000.00 (£9,500.00: £4,500.00: £1,500.00)

| | | | | SP | RR | SF |
|---|---|---|---|---|---|---|
| 2271a³ | **Gothenberg (IRE)** (MJohnston) **3-8-9** JWeaver (sn led: qcknd 2f out: rdn & r.o) | — | 1 | 6/1 | 119 | 72 |
| 2037⁸ | **Timarida (IRE)** (JOxx,Ireland) **4-9-7** JPMurtagh (hld up towards rr: hdwy ½-wy: 5th over 2f out: 3rd on ins 1f out: kpt on wl ins last: nt rch wnr) | 1 | 2 | 6/4 1 | 119 | 82 |
| 2038³ | **Tamayaz (CAN)** (SbinSuroor) **4-9-4** MJKinane (led early: chsd wnr: chal 3f out: ev ch fr 2f out: no ex u.p ins fnl f) | 1 | 3 | 2/1 2 | 114 | 77 |
| 2092a* | **Idris (IRE)** (JSBolger,Ireland) **6-9-8** KJManning (hld up: 3rd & chal over 2f out: rdn & no ex over 1f out) | 2 | 4 | 4/1 3 | 114 | 77 |
| 2092a² | **Burden Of Proof (IRE)** (CO'Brien,Ireland) **4-9-4** CRoche (hld up: 4th ½-wy: effrt over 2f out: btn over 1f out) | 4 | 5 | 7/1 | 102 | 65 |
| 2053¹⁷ | **Tarawa (IRE)** (NACallaghan) **4-9-4** WCarson (sn towards rr: rdn over 3f out: n.d) | 5½ | 6 | 10/1 | 91 | 54 |
| *1768⁴* | ***Silca Blanka (IRE)*** (MRChannon) **4-9-4** PatEddery (Withdrawn not under Starter's orders: lame at s) | | W | 12/1 | — | — |
| | | | | (SP 136.9%) | | **6 Rn** |

**1m 34.8** (-0.20) OWNER Brian Yeardley Continental Ltd (MIDDLEHAM) BRED Brownstown Stud Farm
**2271a Gothenberg (IRE)** popped out in front and made all the running. He visibly quickened two furlongs out, and ran on really well without being subjected to too much pressure. (6/1)
**2037 Timarida (IRE)** put her Ascot experience well behind her. Settled in the rear, she only had one behind her with over two furlongs to run and found little room on the inside with just over a furlong to race. She got the opening well inside the final furlong and ran on strongly. She could hardly be called unlucky, but certainly did not get the run of the race. (6/4)
**2038 Tamayaz (CAN)** ran in second place and came under pressure two furlongs out. He had every chance, but just could not quicken inside the last. (2/1)
**2092a* Idris (IRE)** ran his usual brave race, but this company was a little too hot. In third place early in the straight, his challenge was never going to be successful. (4/1)
**2092a Burden Of Proof (IRE)**, fourth at halfway, made his effort two furlongs out and was soon beaten. (7/1)
**1112 Tarawa (IRE)** was always towards the rear and was not a factor over the last three furlongs. (10/1)

### 2472a JOHN ROARTY MEMORIAL SCURRY H'CAP (0-110) (3-Y.O+)
3-20 (3-22) **6f** £26,000.00 (£7,600.00: £3,600.00: £1,200.00)

| | | | | SP | RR | SF |
|---|---|---|---|---|---|---|
| 1911a³ | **Sunset Reigns (IRE)** (APO'Brien,Ireland) **3-9-2** SCraine (prom: led wl over 1f out: r.o) | — | 1 | 8/1 2 | 108 | 73 |
| | **Nakayama Express (IRE)** (JGCoogan,Ireland) **3-7-4b**(6) EAhern (mid div: rdn & chsd ldrs ½-wy: 7th over 1f out: r.o ins fnl f: wnt 2nd nr fin) | 1½ | 2 | 20/1 | 84 | 49 |
| 1911a⁶ | **Slayjay (IRE)** (JCHayden,Ireland) **3-8-3** NGMcCullagh (in tch: chal over 2f out: 2nd & ev ch over 1f out: no ex ins last) | hd | 3 | 12/1 | 91 | 56 |
| | **Diligent Dodger (IRE)** (KPrendergast,Ireland) **5-9-0** WJSupple (cl up early: chsd ldrs: 9th u.p over 1f out: r.o ins fnl f) | 1 | 4 | 16/1 | 92 | 64 |
| | **Another Sky-Lark (IRE)** (FBerry,Ireland) **8-7-7**(8) FBerry (cl up early: rdn & chsd ldrs fr ½-wy: 7th over 1f out: kpt on ins fnl f) | s.h | 5 | 16/1 | 79 | 51 |
| 2115¹⁴ | **Ailleacht (USA)** (JSBolger,Ireland) **4-9-10** KJManning (prom: 2nd, rdn & ev ch 2f out: 3rd over 1f out: no ex ins fnl f) | ¾ | 6 | 10/1 | 100 | 72 |

**The Bower (IRE)** (CCollins,Ireland) **7-8-6b**(8) JJMullins (in tch: 5th & effrt over 1f out: 4th & no ex over 1f out) ...... ¾ **7** 8/1[2] 88 60
2115[15] **Double Quick (IRE)** (MJohnston) **4-9-8** JWeaver (sn led & clr: hdd wl over 1f out: sn wknd) ...... ¾ **8** 10/1 94 66
**More Risk (IRE)** (JGCoogan,Ireland) **3-7-1b**(8) DPMcDonogh (dwlt: towards rr & rdn: kpt on fnl 2f: nvr nrr) ... hd **9** 14/1 74 39
1235a[5] **America's Cup (IRE)** (CO'Brien,Ireland) **4-9-6** CRoche (in tch: ev ch fr ½-wy: no ex over 1f out) ...... hd **10** 9/1[3] 91 63
2041[16] **Slightly Speedy (IRE)** (JTGorman,Ireland) **3-8-4** PShanahan (towards rr: kpt on fnl 2f: nvr nrr) ...... nk **11** 20/1 82 47
**Krayyalei (IRE)** (JGBurns,Ireland) **5-8-2b** WCarson (cl up: 3rd ½-wy: 6th & no ex 1f out) ...... s.h **12** 12/1 73 45
2114[20] **Sir Silver Sox (USA)** (TStack,Ireland) **4-9-9** JReid (towards rr: sme hdwy ½-wy: no imp over 1f out) ...... 1½ **13** 16/1 90 62
**Diesel Dan (IRE)** (TStack,Ireland) **3-7-7** JMorgan (mid div: rdn & chsd ldrs 2f out: no imp) ...... 1½ **14** 14/1 63 28
1235a[10] **Cossack Count** (MKauntze,Ireland) **3-8-11** WJO'Connor (sn in tch: no imp over 1f out) ...... s.h **15** 10/1 80 45
1253a[5] **Mitch (USA)** (DKWeld,Ireland) **3-8-8b** MJKinane (towards rr: u.p over 2f out: n.d) ...... 2 **16** 9/4[1] 72 37
**Amontillado (IRE)** (JEMulhern,Ireland) **4-7-4**(8) GDPower (n.d) ...... hd **17** 25/1 55 27
(SP 150.0%) **17 Rn**

**1m 10.7** (0.20) OWNER Mrs J. M. Ryan (PILTOWN) BRED Michael Collins
**1911a Sunset Reigns (IRE)**, always prominent, led under two furlongs out and repelled all challengers. (8/1)
**2003* Double Quick (IRE)** showed tremendous early toe and was soon clear. Headed under two furlongs out, she was beaten over a furlong out. (10/1: op 5/1)

## 2473a BUDWEISER IRISH DERBY STKS (Gp 1) (3-Y.O C & F)
4-00 (4-01) **1m 4f** £341,850.00 (£116,350.00: £56,350.00: £20,350.00)

SP RR SF

**Zagreb (USA)** (DKWeld,Ireland) **3-9-0** PShanahan (hld up: 8th ½-wy: hdwy to trck ldrs st: led over 2f out: sn qcknd clr: impressive) ...... — **1** 20/1 126+ 50
1757a[2] **Polaris Flight (USA)** (PWChapple-Hyam) **3-9-0** JReid (mid div: hmpd after 4f: 8th & rdn 5f out: 5th st: sn chal: wnt 2nd u.p over 1f out: kpt on: nt rch wnr) ...... 6 **2** 7/1 118 42
1938a[3] **His Excellence (USA)** (APO'Brien,Ireland) **3-9-0b** WJSupple (towards rr: hdwy 5f out: 5th, rdn & chsd ldrs over 2f out: 5th & no imp over 1f out: styd on: wnt 3rd nr fin) ...... 6 **3** 50/1 110 34
1791[2] **Dushyantor (USA)** (HRACecil) **3-9-0** PatEddery (cl up: 3rd ½-wy: 2nd, rdn & chsd ldr bef st: 3rd, u.p & ev ch over 2f out: one pce) ...... ¾ **4** 5/4[1] 109 33
1574a[2] **Rainbow Blues (IRE)** (APO'Brien,Ireland) **3-9-0** JAHeffernan (in tch: 7th ½-wy: 9th & rdn whn hmpd over 1f out: kpt on: nvr nrr) ...... 2½ **5** 33/1 106 30
1791[14] **Spartan Heartbeat** (CEBrittain) **3-9-0** WJO'Connor (towards rr: 10th over 2f out: styd on: nvr nrr) ...... ½ **6** 100/1 105 29
1125* **Dr Massini (IRE)** (MRStoute) **3-9-0** MJKinane (towards rr: rdn 4f out: kpt on fnl 2f: nvr nrr) ...... nk **7** 9/4[2] 105 29
2074[2] **Private Song (USA)** (RCharlton) **3-9-0** WRyan (sn led: hdd over 2f out: sn wknd) ...... s.h **8** 66/1 105 29
1791[5] **Alhaarth (IRE)** (MajorWRHern) **3-9-0b**[1] WCarson (plld hrd: hld up: last ½-wy: hdwy on outside over 4f out: 7th & effrt 2f out: sn btn) ...... 4½ **9** 13/2[3] 99 23
1757a[4] **Don Micheletto** (SbinSuroor) **3-9-0** TQuinn (in tch: hmpd after 4f: 6th ½-wy: chsd ldrs st: 8th & nt trble ldrs whn sltly hmpd over 1f out: no imp) ...... ½ **10** 14/1 98 22
1873* **Sharaf Kabeer** (SbinSuroor) **3-9-0** JPMurtagh (cl up: 5th ½-wy: 4th & rdn st: no imp whn edgd lft over 1f out: wknd) ...... 2½ **11** 10/1 95 19
1938a[6] **Truth Or Dare** (CO'Brien,Ireland) **3-9-0** CRoche (cl up: 2nd ½-wy: 4th & rdn wl over 3f out: lost pl st: dropped bhd: eased: t.o) ...... dist **12** 33/1 — —
2116* **Amfortas (IRE)** (CEBrittain) **3-9-0** DHolland (in tch: 4th ½-wy: 2nd 5f out: rdn & wknd over 3f out: dropped bhd: eased: t.o) ...... 7 **13** 20/1 — —
(SP 136.7%) **13 Rn**

**2m 30.6** (3.60) OWNER Allen Paulson (CURRAGH) BRED A. E. Paulson
**Zagreb (USA)**, held up, made progress to track the leaders on the inside turning into the straight and took the lead over two furlongs out. He kicked clear and, running on strongly over the last furlong, was value for every inch of the winning distance. The Irish Champion Stakes and a tilt at the Arc are possibilities for the future. (20/1)
**1757a Polaris Flight (USA)** received a check in the first half-mile and was being pushed along five furlongs out. He went in pursuit of the winner, but could make no impression under pressure in the last furlong and a half. (7/1)
**1938a His Excellence (USA)** made headway from the rear five furlongs out and was chasing the leaders in fifth place over two furlongs out. He was never going to get on terms over the last furlong and a half, but stayed on to go third close home. (50/1)
**1791 Dushyantor (USA)**, third at halfway, was in second place and being niggled along before the straight. Third and under pressure over two furlongs out, he was soon left behind. (5/4)
**1574a Rainbow Blues (IRE)** found trouble in running a furlong and a half out when in the latter half of the field, but kept on with some purpose over the last furlong. (33/1)
**1361 Spartan Heartbeat**, always towards the rear, had only three behind him with two furlongs to race, but stayed on over the last furlong and a half to be never nearer. (100/1)
**1125* Dr Massini (IRE)** looked uncomfortable from a long way out. Ridden with half a mile to race, he kept on inside the last 200 yards, but was never a contender. (9/4)
**2074 Private Song (USA)** led until headed by the winner, and then dropped away. (66/1)
**1791 Alhaarth (IRE)** pulled hard early on and was in last place at halfway. He made some headway on the outer on the descent to the straight, but never really got on terms. (13/2: op 7/2)
**1757a Don Micheletto** had some traffic problems early on, but was in sixth place at halfway. He chased the leaders into the straight, but was beaten when slightly hampered a furlong and a half out. (14/1)
**1873* Sharaf Kabeer**, fifth at halfway, was fourth into the straight. Ridden and making no impression when edging left a furlong and a half out, he dropped right out. (10/1)
**1938a Truth Or Dare**, second at halfway, lost his place completely before the straight and, eased down, finished tailed off. (33/1)
**2116* Amfortas (IRE)** went second after halfway but weakened quickly over three furlongs out and was eased right down in the straight. (20/1)

## 2474a BUDWEISER GUINNESS CURRAGH CUP STKS (Gp 3) (3-Y.O+)
4-45 (4-48) **1m 6f** £18,000.00 (£5,700.00: £2,700.00: £900.00)

SP RR SF

1988[4] **Blushing Flame (USA)** (MRStoute) **5-9-10** JReid (mde all: rdn clr over 1f out: styd on strly) ...... — **1** 7/1 114 41
**Fill the Bill (IRE)** (APO'Brien,Ireland) **4-9-10** JAHeffernan (hld up: towards rr early: hdwy & 7th 4f out: 5th & chsd ldrs early st: 2nd & nt trble wnr wl over 1f out: styd on) ...... 4 **2** 16/1 109 36
**Damancher** (PMullins,Ireland) **4-9-10** NGMcCullagh (hld up in tch: 3rd 4f out: 2nd & chal over 2f out: no ex wl over 1f out: kpt on same pce) ...... ¾ **3** 3/1[2] 109 36

| | | | | SP | RR | SF |
|---|---|---|---|---|---|---|
| 1580a[14] | **Touch Judge (USA)** (DKWeld,Ireland) **3-8-7** TQuinn (towards rr: hdwy 4f out: 6th & rdn over 2f out: styd on: nt trble ldrs) | 4 | **4** | 10/1 | 104 | 14 |
| 2102a[3] | **Sun Ballet (IRE)** (JOxx,Ireland) **3-8-4b[1]** WCarson (cl up: wnt 2nd bef ½-wy: rdn & effrt st: 3rd u.p over 2f out: sn wknd) | ½ | **5** | 9/1 | 100 | 10 |
| 726* | **Spout** (RCharlton) **4-9-10** PatEddery (hld up towards rr: rdn & sme hdwy bef st: mod 7th 2f out: kpt on: nt trble ldrs) | s.h | **6** | 2/1[1] | 103 | 30 |
| | **Catalyst (IRE)** (JSBolger,Ireland) **3-8-4** TEDurcan (chsd ldr tl appr ½-wy: 4th & rdn 4f out: wknd st: sn no imp) | 12 | **7** | 12/1 | 87 | — |
| 1791[12] | **Tasdid** (KPrendergast,Ireland) **3-8-7b** WJSupple (in tch: 5th ½-wy: 4th, rdn & chsd ldrs early st: 4th u.p whn swrvd rt, hit rail, stumbled & almost fell over 1f out: nt rcvr) | 2½ | **8** | 20/1 | 87 | — |
| 1938a[8] | **Humbel (USA)** (DKWeld,Ireland) **4-10-3** MJKinane (hld up: 6th ½-wy: chsd ldrs st: 7th & no imp over 2f out) | 1½ | **9** | 6/1[3] | 92 | 19 |
| | **Alisidora (IRE)** (CO'Brien,Ireland) **4-9-7** CRoche (towards rr: lost tch 4f out: n.d) | 8 | **10** | 10/1 | 73 | — |
| | | | | (SP 131.6%) | | **10 Rn** |

**3m 0.6** (7.60) OWNER Cheveley Park Stud (NEWMARKET) BRED Cheveley Park Stud
**1988 Blushing Flame (USA)** made all and, ridden clear under two furlongs out, kept on really well. (7/1: op 4/1)
**Fill the Bill (IRE)** showed signs of a return to form, chasing the leaders early in the straight and keeping on well in second place from over a furlong out. (16/1)
**Damancher**, in third place four furlongs out, challenged over two furlongs out but did not find a lot when let down. (3/1)
**1580a Touch Judge (USA)**, sixth over two furlongs out, stayed on without threatening. (10/1)
**726* Spout**, held up towards the rear, was being ridden along and making real progress before the straight. Seventh with two furlongs to race, she could make no impression. (2/1)

# LYON PARILLY (Lyon, France) (Good)
## Monday June 24th

## 2476a GRAND PRIX DE LYON (Listed) (3-Y.O+)
6-10 (6-10) **1m 4f** £28,986.00 (£10,540.00: £5,270.00)

| | | | | SP | RR | SF |
|---|---|---|---|---|---|---|
| 1353* | **Taipan (IRE)** (JLDunlop) **4-9-2** SGuillot | — | **1** | | 112 | — |
| | **Leeds (IRE)** (HVandePoele,France) **4-9-5** OPeslier | ¾ | **2** | | 114 | — |
| 289a* | **Megaron (FR)** (MPimbonnet,France) **3-8-8** FBlondel | 1½ | **3** | | 115 | — |
| | | | | | | **11 Rn** |

**No Time Taken** P-M 6.80F: 2.50F 1.50F 2.00F (19.00F) OWNER Lord Swaythling (ARUNDEL) BRED C. H. Wacker III
**1353* Taipan (IRE)** tracked the leader before quickening up to take the lead a furlong out, and ran on well to score comfortably. This improving sort needs a bit of cut to show his best, and future plans could see him contest the Grand Prix de Vichy or Grand Prix Anjou Bretagne at Nantes.
DS

# 2269a-EVRY (France) (R-H) (Good)
## Wednesday June 26th

## 2477a PRIX LOVELACE (Listed) (4-Y.O+)
3-25 (3-21) **1m** £18,445.00 (£6,324.00: £3,953.00: £2,055.00)

| | | | | SP | RR | SF |
|---|---|---|---|---|---|---|
| 1484[2] | **Royal Philosopher** (JWHills) **4-8-11** OPeslier | — | **1** | | 105 | — |
| | **Super Gascon** (TLallie,France) **4-9-2** DRegnard | ¾ | **2** | | 109 | — |
| 925[13] | **Verzen (IRE)** (DRLoder) **4-8-11** RHughes | hd | **3** | | 103 | — |
| 2053[8] | **Serious** (LadyHerries) **6-8-11** PaulEddery | hd | **4** | | 103 | — |
| 1770[3] | **Nagnagnag (IRE)** (SDow) **4-8-8** CAsmussen | s.h | **5** | | 100 | — |
| | | | | | | **8 Rn** |

**1m 39.62** (2.62) P-M 6.30F: 2.30F 1.90F 4.50F (31.20F) OWNER Mr A. Miller (LAMBOURN) BRED A. N. Miller
**1484 Royal Philosopher**, whose trainer reported the horse in such fine fettle that he felt he had to run him, was given an inspired ride. Dictating the pace from the start, his jockey quickened things up over two furlongs out and stole an advantage which he kept to the line. Ideally suited by cut in the ground, his next target, dependent on cut in the ground, could be the Minstrel Stakes at the Curragh or the Prix Messidor at Maisons-Laffitte.
**Verzen (IRE)** tracked the leader early on, but was tapped for speed when the winner quickened two furlongs out. Battling on well inside the final furlong to just hold on to third place, this was a good performance, but he lacks a bit of pace in the closing stages.
**1775 Serious** raced in fourth early on, but was outpaced when the pace quickened into the home straight. He did make some late progress and was touched off for third, but he either needs a stronger pace over this distance, or a bit further.
**1770 Nagnagnag (IRE)** did not have the best of runs. Slowly into her stride, she was held up in the rear and was blocked behind a wall of horses coming into the straight. Extricated a furlong out, she made up some ground in the final furlong and is capable of finding a listed race one day.
DS

# HAMBURG (Germany) (R-H) (Soft)
## Saturday June 29th

## 2478a DEUTSCHER HEROLD-PREIS (Gp 3) (3-Y.O+ F & M)
3-43 (4-23) **1m 3f** £38,739.00 (£16,216.00: £8,108.00)

| | | | | SP | RR | SF |
|---|---|---|---|---|---|---|
| | **Wurftaube (GER)** (HRemmert,Germany) **3-8-5** PSchiergen | — | **1** | | 108 | — |
| 1750a[3] | **Anno Luce** (UOstmann,Germany) **3-8-5b[1]** PVanDeKeere | 1½ | **2** | | 106 | — |
| | **Nataliana** (BSchutz,Germany) **3-8-5** NGrant | 1¼ | **3** | | 104 | — |
| 1750a* | **Night Petticoat (GER)** (BSchutz,Germany) **3-8-11** AStarke | 2 | **6** | | 107 | — |
| | | | | | | **9 Rn** |

**2m 22.8** (7.30) TOTE 46DM: 19DM 22DM 39DM (383DM) OWNER Gestut Ravensberg BRED Gestut Ravensberg

## 2478a-HAMBURG (Germany) (R-H) (Soft)
### Sunday June 30th

**2479a** IDEE HANSA PREIS (Gp 2) (3-Y.O+)
3-40 (3-45) **1m 3f** £63,063.00 (£24,775.00: £13,514.00: £4,505.00)

| | | | | SP | RR | SF |
|---|---|---|---|---|---|---|
| 1138a[2] | **Protektor (GER)** (ALowe,Germany) **7-9-2** NGrant (a in tch: 4th st: r.o strly to ld ins fnl f) | — | **1** | | 120 | — |
| 1948a* | **Germany (USA)** (BSchutz,Germany) **5-9-8** AStarke (led tl ins fnl f: kpt on) | 1½ | **2** | | 124 | — |
| 1948a[4] | **Artan (IRE)** (MRolke,Germany) **4-9-2** JTandari (mid div: hdwy ½-wy: ev ch 2f out: no ex) | 5 | **3** | | 111 | — |
| 1948a[5] | **Hollywood Dream (GER)** (UOstmann,Germany) **5-9-4** GBocskai (hld up: last st: sme late hdwy) | 1½ | **4** | | 110 | — |
| 1948a[2] | **Oxalagu (GER)** (Germany) **4-9-4** THellier (in tch: 5th st: no ex fr 2f out) | nk | **5** | | 110 | — |
| | **Kenzo (GER)** (Germany) **5-9-2** LMader (a rr) | 1¼ | **6** | | 106 | — |
| 1948a[6] | **Hondero (GER)** (Germany) **6-9-4** JohnFortune (a bhd) | nk | **7** | | 108 | — |
| 1135a[4] | **Concepcion (GER)** (Germany) **6-9-8** PSchiergen (prom early: wknd fr 4f out) | 3½ | **8** | | 107 | — |
| | | | | | | **8 Rn** |

**2m 20.84** (5.34) TOTE 113DM: 16DM 11DM 16DM (257DM) OWNER D. Joswich BRED Frau H. Liesten
**Protektor (GER)** made strong progress along the stands' rail to take this from the favourite. He had conditions in his favour as he prefers the soft and was receiving weight from the odds-on runner-up. He could now go for the Group One Deutschland-Preis-50 Jahre Nordrhein-Westfalen on July 28th.
**1948a* Germany (USA)** was the second disappointment for trainer Bruno Schutz over the weekend. He was allowed to set his own pace, but had no answer to the winner in the last 150 yards.

## 2273a-SAINT-CLOUD (France) (L-H) (Good)
### Sunday June 30th

**2480a** GRAND PRIX DE SAINT-CLOUD (Gp 1) (3-Y.O+ C & F)
2-15 (2-13) **1m 4f** £158,103.00 (£63,241.00: £31,621.00: £15,810.00)

| | | | | SP | RR | SF |
|---|---|---|---|---|---|---|
| 1757a[5] | **Helissio (FR)** (ELellouche,France) **3-8-8** OPeslier (trckd ldr: hdwy to disp ld ent st: led over 2f out: comf) | — | **1** | 27/10[2] | 126 | — |
| 1794* | **Swain (IRE)** (AFabre,France) **4-9-8** TJarnet (mid div early: 3rd st: rdn 2f out: kpt on fnl f) | 1 | **2** | 9/10[1] | 125 | — |
| 1947a* | **Poliglote** (MmeCHead,France) **4-9-8** FHead (led: jnd 3f out: hdd over 2f out: styd on one pce) | 4 | **3** | 116/10 | 119 | — |
| 2113[4] | **Lear White (USA)** (PAKelleway) **4-9-8** GGuignard (sn prom: 4th & rdn st: r.o fnl f) | ½ | **4** | 487/10 | 119 | — |
| 2276a[7] | **Oliviero (FR)** (PDemercastel,France) **3-8-8** ESaint-Martin (in rr tl rdn 2f out: styd on) | ½ | **5** | 182/10 | 118 | — |
| 1794[3] | **De Quest** (AFabre,France) **4-9-8** DBoeuf (hld up & bhd: sme late hdwy) | 3 | **6** | 22/1 | 114 | — |
| 1757a* | **Ragmar (FR)** (PBary,France) **3-8-8** GMosse (a mid div: nt qckn st) | ¾ | **7** | 57/10[3] | 113 | — |
| 1580a* | **Bahamian Knight (CAN)** (DRLoder) **3-8-8** RHughes (rr early: rdn & hdwy st: wknd) | 1½ | **8** | 204/10 | 111 | — |
| 906a[9] | **Carling (FR)** (MmePBarbe,France) **4-9-5** TThulliez (a bhd) | 2½ | **9** | 117/10 | 105 | — |
| | | | | (SP 126.6%) | | **9 Rn** |

**2m 27.4** (-1.90) P-M 3.70F: 1.30F 1.10F 1.50F (4.40F) OWNER E. Sarasola BRED Ecurie Skymarc Farm
**1139a* Helissio (FR)** put up arguably the best performance by a three-year-old in Europe so far this season. Settled in behind the leader, he strode out without pulling like he had done in the Prix du Jockey-Club. After joining the leader into the home straight, he soon took the lead and quickly stamped his authority on the race. He won comfortably enough and will now have a rest before returning in the Prix Niel in September, en route to the Prix de l'Arc de Triomphe. (27/10)
**1794* Swain (IRE)** ran his usual good race, but was just tapped for speed in the final furlong. After tracking the winner, he came through with a dangerous-looking challenge over a furlong out, but could never peg back the winner. He lacks a change of gear in top company, but is still on course for the King George VI and Queen Elizabeth Diamond Stakes. (9/10)
**1947a* Poliglote** ran his usual tough race. Setting a fast pace from the off, he kept on bravely when headed in the straight. His trainer now wants him to avoid the first two so he could well be seen next in Germany for either the Aral-Pokal at Gelsenkirchen-Horst or the Grosser Preis von Baden at Baden-Baden. (116/10)
**2113 Lear White (USA)** ran a cracking race and seems to be on the upgrade. After racing with the pace for the early part of the race, he was then a little outpaced when the winner kicked for home, but he battled on gamely and secured fourth place on the line. His trainer believes he is getting better with every race and he could go over a longer distance next time. (487/10)
**1580a* Bahamian Knight (CAN)** was under pressure from over three furlongs out and, although he did not have the best of runs in the straight, he would never have troubled the leaders. He could go for the Europachampionat at Hoppegarten. (204/10)
DS

## 1858-BEVERLEY (R-H) (Good to firm)
### Friday July 5th
WEATHER: overcast WIND: mod half against

**2481** FERGUSON FAWSITT ARMS (S) H'CAP (0-60) (3-Y.O+) (Class F)
6-45 (6-47) **7f 100y** £2,868.00 (£798.00: £384.00) Stalls: High GOING minus 0.59 sec per fur (F)

| | | | | SP | RR | SF |
|---|---|---|---|---|---|---|
| 1474[14] | **My Godson (47)** (JLEyre) **6-8-12b**(3) CTeague(14) (sn bhd: gd hdwy on ins & nt clr run 2f out: fin strly to ld nr fin) | — | **1** | 11/2[3] | 60 | 34 |
| 2313[6] | **Bedazzle (38)** (MBrittain) **5-8-6** JLowe(11) (chsd ldrs: led over 1f out tl nr fin) | 1 | **2** | 5/1[2] | 49 | 23 |
| 2212[2] | **Sakharov (58)** (MJohnston) **7-9-12** TWilliams(9) (lw: trckd ldrs: ev ch & rdn over 2f out: kpt on same pce fnl f) | 1 | **3** | 9/4[1] | 67 | 41 |
| 2284[12] | **Pinkerton Polka (44)** (CEBrittain) **4-8-12** KRutter(12) (a chsng ldrs: ev ch over 1f out: one pce) | ½ | **4** | 10/1 | 52 | 26 |
| 2391[8] | **Langtonian (37)** (JLEyre) **7-8-5b**ow4 MFenton(4) (s.s: bhd: hung rt & styd on wl appr fnl f: nt rch ldrs) | 1¼ | **5** | 12/1 | 42 | 12 |
| *427*[8] | **Harsh Times (51)** (TDEasterby) **3-8-11b** WRyan(2) (sn bhd: styd on fnl 2f: nvr nr to chal) | 1¼ | **6** | 10/1 | 53 | 19 |
| 1526[12] | **Mill End Lady (46)** (MWEasterby) **3-8-1**(5)ow1 GParkin(5) (s.i.s: bhd: hdwy over 2f out: edgd lft & wknd fnl f) | hd | **7** | 25/1 | 48 | 13 |
| 2049[12] | **Catwalk Girl (45)** (MissJFCraze) **3-8-5v** NConnorton(1) (swtchd rt s: chsd ldr: led over 4f out tl over 1f out: sn wknd) | ¾ | **8** | 16/1 | 45 | 11 |

*2084*[6] **Hannah's Usher (60)** (CMurray) **4-10-0** MTebbutt(3) (trckd ldrs: effrt on outside over 2f out: no imp)............1½ **9** 16/1 57 31
1538[11] **Cheerful Groom (IRE) (43)** (SRBowring) **5-8-11** NKennedy(6) (s.i.s: a in rr)....................s.h **10** 5/1[2] 40 14
1889[9] **Thick as Thieves (48)** (RonaldThompson) **4-8-11**(5) PRoberts(7) (hld up & plld hrd: hung rt & lost pl over 2f out)..........1 **11** 20/1 43 17
2185[10] **Mystic Times (48)** (MissJFCraze) **3-8-8b[1]** NCarlisle(10) (sn bhd)..........½ **12** 20/1 42 8
1702[9] **Young Ben (IRE) (40)** (JSWainwright) **4-8-1**(7) JBramhill(8) (in tch: effrt on outside over 2f out: sn wknd).........3 **13** 33/1 28 2
1789[11] **Northgate Chief (45)** (MBrittain) **4-8-13** MWigham(15) (swtg: led tl over 4f out: lost pl over 2f out)................13 **14** 33/1 5 —
(SP 136.4%) **14 Rn**

**1m 33.6** (1.60) CSF £35.39 CT £77.51 TOTE £10.50: £2.70 £1.80 £1.70 (£17.20) Trio £32.40 OWNER Linkchallenge Ltd (HAMBLETON) BRED Mrs M. Russell
WEIGHT FOR AGE 3yo-8lb
No bid

**1162 My Godson**, on good terms with himself after an absence of thirty-nine days, came from last to first in a race run at a furious pace. After running completely out of room two furlongs out, he finished with a real flourish to show ahead near the line. (11/2)
**2313 Bedazzle** raced up with the pace. After going ahead, he had no answer to the winner's late rattle. (5/1)
**2212 Sakharov** raced up with the furious pace and, to his credit, kept on all the way to the line. (9/4: op 7/2)
**636 Pinkerton Polka** gave the impression she was never putting everything into her work. (10/1)
**1311 Langtonian**, a frustrating individual who has won just two of his previous sixty-eight outings, gave away more ground at the start than he was eventually beaten. He hung violently right up the straight and gave his jockey no help. (12/1)
**Harsh Times**, who moved to post very short, is probably being aimed at an All-Weather campaign. (10/1)

## 2482 BOLLINGER CHAMPAGNE CHALLENGE SERIES GENTLEMENS' H'CAP (0-70) (3-Y.O+) (Class E)

7-15 (7-15) **1m 3f 216y** £3,119.00 (£932.00: £446.00: £203.00) Stalls: High GOING minus 0.59 sec per fur (F)

SP RR SF

1676[5] **Abalene (36)** (TWDonnelly) **7-9-12** MrMHNaughton(7) (lw: trckd ldrs: led over 4f out: clr over 2f out: kpt on u.p: all out)..........— **1** 2/1[1] 41 34
2120[11] **Go With The Wind (64)** (MBell) **3-10-9**(4) MrRWakley(1) (hld up: hdwy over 2f out: kpt on ins fnl f)..............1½ **2** 5/1[3] 67 47
**Sharkashka (IRE) (52)** (TDEasterby) **6-11-0** MrSSwiers(5) (sn chsng ldrs: wnt 2nd over 3f out: sn rdn: styd on ins fnl f)..........s.h **3** 9/4[2] 55 48
1977[7] **Pepitist (42)** (MDHammond) **5-10-4** MrCBonner(3) (outpcd & drvn along 5f out: one pce fnl 3f)..................5 **4** 12/1 38 31
2130[14] **Dance King (66)** (RHarris) **4-11-10**(4) MrVLukaniuk(2) (trckd ldrs: rn wd & lost pl over 3f out: hrd rdn & hung rt)..........8 **5** 5/1[3] 52 45
**Golden Hadeer (44)** (MJRyan) **5-10-2**(4) MrSLavallin(4) (chsd ldrs: sn pushed along: lost pl over 3f out)..........5 **6** 20/1 23 16
2284[8] **Pennine Wind (IRE) (52)** (SDow) **4-10-10**(4) MrSFetherstonhaugh(6) (led tl over 4f out: lost pl 3f out)..............9 **7** 9/1 19 12
(SP 119.9%) **7 Rn**

**2m 36.9** (4.50) CSF £12.52 TOTE £2.60: £1.90 £2.30 (£5.30) OWNER Mr S. Taberner (SWADLINCOTE) BRED Mr S. Taberner
WEIGHT FOR AGE 3yo-13lb
STEWARDS' ENQUIRY Lukaniuk susp. 15-18/7/96 (excessive use of whip)

**1676 Abalene** won this race a year ago from a 4lb lower mark. Ridden with plenty of enterprise, he was dashed into a four-length lead once in line for home and that was sufficient to see him home. (2/1)
**1877 Go With The Wind**, with the headgear left off, was given a patient ride. Thrashing his tail inside the last furlong, he got up to claim second spot in the last stride. (5/1)
**Sharkashka (IRE)**, a winner twice over hurdles last season, did not impress with her action to post. After hitting her head in the stalls, she made hard work in pursuit of the winner, racing with her tongue hanging out. Staying on inside the last 200 yards, she was never going to summon the pace to get in a blow. She probably needs more use making of her over further. (9/4)
**1977 Pepitist**, lightly-raced both over hurdles and on the Flat of late, lacks anything in the way of finishing speed. (12/1)
**1965* Dance King** forfeited ground running wide off the home turn. With all chance gone and displaying a marked tendency to hang right, his rider disgracefully did not spare the stick. (5/1)

## 2483 WILLIAM JACKSON'S H'CAP (0-85) (4-Y.O+) (Class D)

7-45 (7-45) **1m 100y** £5,824.25 (£1,754.00: £849.50: £397.25) Stalls: High GOING minus 0.59 sec per fur (F)

SP RR SF

2128[3] **Bend Wavy (IRE) (80)** (LMCumani) **4-9-10** PatEddery(9) (b.off hind: sn trckng ldrs: led over 1f out: r.o)........— **1** 9/4[1] 88 52
2293[2] **Sandmoor Chambray (79)** (TDEasterby) **5-9-9** MBirch(3) (lw: chsd ldrs: drvn along 4f out: sn outpcd: hdwy over 1f out: styd on same pce)..........1¼ **2** 9/2[3] 85 49
2218[2] **Second Colours (USA) (66)** (MrsMReveley) **6-8-10** ACulhane(7) (bhd: hdwy over 1f out: styd on same pce).¾ **3** 14/1 70 34
1322[2] **Clifton Fox (81)** (JAGlover) **4-9-11** SDWilliams(5) (s.i.s: hdwy u.p 2f out: hung rt. styd on ins fnl f)................s.h **4** 4/1[2] 85 49
2145[5] **Percy Braithwaite (IRE) (80)** (MJohnston) **4-9-10** TWilliams(4) (led tl over 1f out: grad wknd)..........1¼ **5** 10/1 82 46
2351[9] **Up in Flames (IRE) (71)** (MDHammond) **5-8-12**(3) FLynch(6) (sn chsng ldrs: one pce fnl 2f)..........1½ **6** 11/2 70 34
2351[10] **Queens Consul (IRE) (84)** (BSRothwell) **6-10-0** MFenton(1) (chsd ldrs on outside tl wknd wl over 1f out)........4 **7** 25/1 75 39
1650[2] **Intendant (61)** (JGFitzGerald) **4-8-5** WRyan(8) (hld up: hdwy 4f out: rdn over 2f out: wknd over 1f out)..........nk **8** 8/1 52 16
2000* **Autumn Cover (61)** (PRHedger) **4-8-5** DBiggs(2) (w ldrs: rdn 2f out: sn wknd)..........4 **9** 11/2 44 8
(SP 130.4%) **9 Rn**

**1m 44.8** (0.80) CSF £14.19 CT £116.95 TOTE £4.00: £1.50 £1.80 £2.10 (£7.50) Trio £68.60 OWNER Lord Portsmouth (NEWMARKET) BRED D. Grenfell and R. Hesketh

**2128 Bend Wavy (IRE)**, dropped back in distance and making his debut in handicap company, came in for substantial market support. A shell of a horse and not the best of movers, he scored in decisive fashion in the end and further improvement looks likely. (9/4)
**2293 Sandmoor Chambray**, tapped for foot soon after halfway, stayed on in determined fashion in the final furlong. He is running right up to his best at present. (9/2)
**2218 Second Colours (USA)** still looked in need of the outing. Staying on in good style, he is much better suited to All-Weather surfaces. (14/1)
**1322 Clifton Fox**, who missed the break slightly, gave his rider all sorts of problems. Persisting in hanging right, he was staying on at the finish. (4/1)
**2145 Percy Braithwaite (IRE)** set a very strong pace. (10/1: 7/1-11/1)

## 2484 WELLBEING CONDITIONS STKS (2-Y.O) (Class C)

8-15 (8-15) **5f** £4,234.00 (£1,534.00: £742.00: £310.00: £130.00) Stalls: High GOING minus 0.59 sec per fur (F)

SP RR SF

1699[5] **For Old Times Sake** (JBerry) **2-9-2** GCarter(5) (lw: led early: led 2f out: edgd lft u.p ins fnl f: all out)..........— **1** 10/1 77 28

| | | | | | | |
|---|---|---|---|---|---|---|
| 1815[2] | **Magical Times** (RBoss) **2-9-0** WRyan(2) (trckd ldrs: effrt 2f out: sn rdn & edgd lft: nt qckn ins fnl f) | nk | **2** | 3/1 2 | 74 | 25 |
| 1998* | **Conspiracy** (JLDunlop) **2-8-9** PatEddery(3) (hld up: effrt & swtchd outside 2f out: rdn & ev ch ins fnl f: no ex) | hd | **3** | 4/5 1 | 69 | 20 |
| 1673[3] | **Skyers Flyer (IRE)** (RonaldThompson) **2-8-6** NConnorton(4) (plld hrd: trckd ldrs: effrt 2f out: no imp fnl f) | 1¾ | **4** | 33/1 | 60 | 11 |
| 996* | **Express Girl** (DMoffatt) **2-8-6**(3) DarrenMoffatt(1) (sn led: hdd 2f out: wknd fnl f) | 1½ | **5** | 7/2 3 | 58 | 9 |

(SP 114.8%) **5 Rn**

**63.0 secs** (1.50) CSF £36.97 TOTE £10.10: £4.80 £2.10 (£11.10) OWNER Mrs Bridget Blum (COCKERHAM) BRED Shutford Stud

**1699 For Old Times Sake**, who ran a stale race here last time, looked in good trim after a month's rest. Again showing a scratchy action going down, he capitalised on the best draw and, despite edging left under pressure, showed the right sort of spirit. (10/1: op 6/1)

**1815 Magical Times**, dropped back to five, ran his heart out. (3/1)

**1998* Conspiracy**, dropped in behind, has to switch to the outside to get a run soon after halfway. Almost upsides just inside the last, she showed a very poor action and was never going to do enough. She almost certainly found the ground too lively. (4/5)

**1673 Skyers Flyer (IRE)**, a very keen sort, ran a similar race to last time. (33/1)

**996* Express Girl**, on her toes beforehand, showed bags of toe on this totally different ground, but she had bellows to mend with a furlong left to run. (7/2)

## 2485 JACKSONS FAMILY FOODSTORE MAIDEN STKS (2-Y.O) (Class D)

8-45 (8-46) **5f** £3,760.75 (£1,126.00: £540.50: £247.75) Stalls: High GOING minus 0.59 sec per fur (F)

| | | | | SP | RR | SF |
|---|---|---|---|---|---|---|
| *1603*[4] | **Blazing Castle** (WGMTurner) **2-8-7**(7) DSweeney(4) (mde all: clr & edgd lft over 1f out: unchal) | — | **1** | 4/1 2 | 60 | 10 |
| | **Marylebone (IRE)** (JBerry) **2-9-0** GCarter(3) (leggy: scope: dwlt: sn chsng ldrs & rdn along: wnt 2nd ½-wy: kpt on fnl f) | 3 | **2** | 4/5 1 | 50 | — |
| 2353[5] | **Tom Mi Dah** (MDHammond) **2-8-11**(3) FLynch(1) (hdwy 2f out: kpt on same pce) | 1¾ | **3** | 9/1 | 45 | — |
| | **Cherokee Flight** (MrsJRRamsden) **2-9-0** WRyan(5) (w'like: str: bit bkwd: s.i.s: hdwy to chse ldrs ½-wy: wknd fnl f) | 4 | **4** | 6/1 | 32 | — |
| | **Mazil** (TDEasterby) **2-9-0** MBirch(6) (cmpt: bit bkwd: hld up: hdwy ½-wy: rdn & wknd over 1f out) | 5 | **5** | 11/2 3 | 16 | — |
| 452[12] | **Risky Flight** (ASmith) **2-9-0** JLowe(2) (bit bkwd: chsd wnr to ½-wy: sn lost pl) | 9 | **6** | 20/1 | — | — |

(SP 120.0%) **6 Rn**

**64.1 secs** (2.60) CSF £8.07 TOTE £6.00: £2.10 £1.50 (£3.90) OWNER Mrs D. A. Wetherall (SHERBORNE) BRED Mrs D. A. Wetherall

**1603 Blazing Castle**, a plain sort, always had the legs of his moderate rivals. (4/1)

**Marylebone (IRE)**, bred exclusively for speed on his dam's side, missed the break and had to be ridden along throughout. Keeping on in pursuit of the winner, connections will hope for improvement. (4/5)

**2353 Tom Mi Dah** improved on his first effort and will be suited by a step up to six furlongs. (9/1: 5/1-10/1)

**Cherokee Flight**, a stocky, backward newcomer, is not without ability. He looks more of a long-term prospect. (6/1: op 4/1)

**Mazil** (11/2: 3/1-6/1)

## 2486 SANCTON H'CAP (0-70) (3-Y.O) (Class E)

9-15 (9-15) **1m 1f 207y** £3,132.00 (£936.00: £448.00: £204.00) Stalls: High GOING minus 0.59 sec per fur (F)

| | | | | SP | RR | SF |
|---|---|---|---|---|---|---|
| 2246[2] | **Alreeh (IRE) (70)** (JHMGosden) **3-9-7** RHills(11) (lw: chsd ldrs: styd on to ld ins fnl f: hld on towards fin) | — | **1** | 5/1 3 | 83 | 39 |
| 1883[2] | **Parsa (USA) (61)** (JLDunlop) **3-8-12** PatEddery(5) (hld up: effrt & swtchd outside over 2f out: ev ch 1f out: hung rt & kpt on) | ½ | **2** | 15/8 1 | 73 | 29 |
| 2123[2] | **Sing And Dance (45)** (EWeymes) **3-7-10** JLowe(10) (led early: chsd ldrs: led over 1f out tl ins fnl f: r.o same pce) | hd | **3** | 7/1 | 57 | 13 |
| 2203* | **White Plains (IRE) (68)** (MBell) **3-9-5** MFenton(2) (trckd ldrs: styng on same pce whn n.m.r & swtchd rt ins fnl f) | 1 | **4** | 4/1 2 | 78 | 34 |
| 2366* | **Kernof (IRE) (49)** (MDHammond) **3-7-11b**[1](3)ow2 FLynch(3) (trckd ldrs: led over 2f out tl over 1f out: sn wknd) | 3 | **5** | 4/1 2 | 55 | 9 |
| 1955[3] | **Get Tough (62)** (SDow) **3-8-13** JFEgan(9) (s.i.s: bhd: sme hdwy over 2f out: n.d) | 5 | **6** | 8/1 | 60 | 16 |
| *2081** | **Perpetual Light (65)** (JJQuinn) **3-9-2** WRyan(1) (bhd: effrt on outside & bmpd over 2f out: n.d) | hd | **7** | 8/1 | 62 | 18 |
| 2061[9] | **Falcon's Flame (USA) (51)** (MrsJRRamsden) **3-8-2** GCarter(7) (sn led: hdd over 2f out: sn wknd) | 2½ | **8** | 20/1 | 44 | — |
| *859*[11] | **La Fandango (IRE) (46)** (MWEasterby) **3-7-11**ow1 DaleGibson(8) (s.i.s: a bhd & sn rdn along) | 6 | **9** | 50/1 | 30 | — |
| 2139[8] | **South Pagoda (IRE) (46)** (DNicholls) **3-7-11b**[1] NKennedy(6) (plld hrd: trckd ldrs tl lost pl over 2f out) | 6 | **10** | 25/1 | 20 | — |

(SP 136.7%) **10 Rn**

**2m 4.7** (2.20) CSF £16.81 CT £68.76 TOTE £6.20: £1.60 £1.70 £2.00 (£7.00) Trio £28.20 OWNER Mr Hamdan Al Maktoum (NEWMARKET) BRED Oldtown Stud

LONG HANDICAP Sing And Dance 7-7 La Fandango (IRE) 7-5

**2246 Alreeh (IRE)**, who looked in tremendous trim, showed the right sort of spirit in a tight finish. (5/1)

**1883 Parsa (USA)** showed plenty on knee-action going down. In behind a wall of horses once in line for home, Eddery made his way to the outside, barging Perpetual Light on his outer out of the way. After having every chance, his mount hung right as if feeling the ground and was never going to do quite enough. The Stewards must have been in a lenient mood to deem the interference accidental. (15/8: op 3/1)

**2123 Sing And Dance**, 3lb out of the handicap, is going the right way. (7/1: 10/1-6/1)

**2203* White Plains (IRE)** was within a length of the lead when the runner-up hung across him inside the last. Forced to switch, he could only keep on at the same pace but, even with a clear run, he would still have finished fourth. (4/1)

**2366* Kernof (IRE)**, stewed up beforehand, escaped a penalty for his Pontefract success. With the blinkers on this time, he dropped away coming to the final furlong having been kicked on. (4/1: op 5/2)

T/Plpt: £33.20 (402.25 Tckts). T/Qdpt: £14.60 (66.42 Tckts). WG

# 1865-HAMILTON (R-H) (Good)

## Friday July 5th

WEATHER: overcast WIND: almost nil

## 2487 PIONEER AT STEPEK LADIES' H'CAP (0-75) (3-Y.O+) (Class F)

6-30 (6-30) **1m 3f 16y** £2,766.00 (£776.00: £378.00) Stalls: High GOING minus 0.51 sec per fur (F)

| | | | | SP | RR | SF |
|---|---|---|---|---|---|---|
| 2239[2] | **Kings Cay (IRE) (56)** (THCaldwell) **5-10-0**(4) 5x MrsPWharfe(6) (lw: hdwy 5f out: led 2f out: hld on wl) | — | **1** | 5/2 1 | 65 | 47 |
| 2152[3] | **Far Ahead (73)** (JLEyre) **4-11-7** MissDianaJones(3) (lw: bhd: hdwy over 2f out: styd on wl towards fin) | ½ | **2** | 6/1 2 | 81 | 63 |

| | | | | | |
|---|---|---|---|---|---|
| 2066[4] **Gold Blade (49)** (JPearce) **7-9-11** MrsLPearce(1) (lw: hdwy 5f out: chal 2f out: nt qckn ins fnl f) ....hd | 3 | 5/2[1] | 57 | 39 |
| 2294[2] **Nose No Bounds (IRE) (74)** (MJohnston) **3-10-3b**(7) MrsCWilliams(2) (led tl hdd 2f out: grad wknd) ....2½ | 4 | 6/1[2] | 79 | 49 |
| 2418[3] **Lord Advocate (53)** (DANolan) **8-10-1b** MissPRobson(7) (prom: chal 3f out: wknd over 1f out) ....¾ | 5 | 8/1[3] | 56 | 38 |
| 2008[7] **Philgun (55)** (CWCElsey) **7-10-3v** MissAElsey(4) (lw: cl up tl wknd fnl 2½f) ....2 | 6 | 12/1 | 56 | 38 |
| 1866[10] **Jabaroot (IRE) (44)** (RMMcKellar) **5-9-2**(4)ow6 MissMCarson(5) (dwlt: a bhd) ....24 | 7 | 50/1 | 10 | — |

(SP 106.5%) **7 Rn**

**2m 23.3** (3.90) CSF £15.24 TOTE £4.10: £1.70 £3.10 (£10.00) OWNER Mr R. S. G. Jones (WARRINGTON) BRED The Woodhaven Stud in Ireland
WEIGHT FOR AGE 3yo-12lb
**2239 Kings Cay (IRE)** continued his tremendous run of late and, looking as well as ever, won in game style, despite his rider dropping her whip. (5/2)
**2152 Far Ahead** took time to get going, but certainly finished well and, by the looks of things, will get further. (6/1)
**2066 Gold Blade**, who won this last year, tried hard to repeat the performance, but he is just high enough in the weights at present. (5/2)
**2294 Nose No Bounds (IRE)** did his best out in front, but failed to see this trip out. (6/1: op 7/2)
**2418 Lord Advocate**, having his third run of the week, ran pretty well in the circumstances. (8/1)
**Philgun** would really prefer a bit further and is gradually coming to hand. (12/1: op 7/1)

## 2488 LEBUS FURNITURE/STEPEK SUITE CLAIMING STKS (3-Y.O+) (Class F)
7-00 (7-00) **1m 1f 36y** £2,633.00 (£738.00: £359.00) Stalls: High GOING minus 0.51 sec per fur (F)

| | | SP | RR | SF |
|---|---|---|---|---|
| 2121* **Sir Arthur Hobbs (54)** (JLEyre) **9-9-2** RLappin(2) (chsd ldrs: led 2f out: drifted lft: all out) ....— | 1 | Evens[1] | 60 | 27 |
| 2136[3] **Willy Star (BEL)** (MrsSJSmith) **6-9-4** PBloomfield(9) (prom: chal 2f out: kpt on u.p) ....s.h | 2 | 7/2[2] | 62 | 29 |
| 2296[5] **Northern Spark (50)** (MissLAPerratt) **8-9-0** DeanMcKeown(8) (led tl hdd 4½f out: rallied appr fnl f: sn ev ch: kpt on towards fin) ....nk | 3 | 6/1 | 57 | 24 |
| 1516[7] **The Atheling (IRE) (48)** (MHTompkins) **6-8-11**(3) HKYim(4) (lw: bhd: effrt 4f out: styd on: nvr able to chal) ...1¾ | 4 | 33/1 | 54 | 21 |
| 1637[4] **Forzair (60)** (JJO'Neill) **4-9-5**(3) OPears(6) (lw: in tch: hdwy 3f out: carried lft appr fnl f: swtchd & nt qckn).....s.h | 5 | 5/1[3] | 62 | 29 |
| 2409[12] **Yet Again (40)** (BHanbury) **4-9-8b** JTate(1) (dwlt: sn cl up: led 4½f out to 2f out: wknd) ....3 | 6 | 10/1 | 57 | 24 |

(SP 115.2%) **6 Rn**

**1m 58.0** (3.70) CSF £5.04 TOTE £2.00: £1.00 £3.70 (£3.20) Trio £10.40 OWNER Miss Donna-Marie Lappin (HAMBLETON) BRED A. Tarry
**2121* Sir Arthur Hobbs**, on his favourite track, needed all his courage to get home. (Evens)
**2136 Willy Star (BEL)**, on edge beforehand, ran well and should pick up a race before long. (7/2)
**2296 Northern Spark**, who seems to like this track, ran a decent race and was keeping on at the finish. (6/1)
**The Atheling (IRE)** looked well and showed his first signs of form, staying on in the closing stages. (33/1)
**1637 Forzair** never looked happy at this shorter trip and being slightly messed about by the winner made no real difference. (5/1)
**2189* Yet Again**, a headstrong individual, missed the break. Making up ground too quickly, he shot his bolt a good way out. (10/1: 8/1-16/1)

## 2489 OCEAN DOMESTIC APPLIANCES AT STEPEK LIMITED STKS (0-55) (3-Y.O+) (Class F)
7-30 (7-30) **1m 65y** £2,717.00 (£762.00: £371.00) Stalls: High GOING minus 0.51 sec per fur (F)

| | | SP | RR | SF |
|---|---|---|---|---|
| 2282[3] **Giftbox (USA) (54)** (SirMarkPrescott) **4-9-6** RPerham(4) (lw: trckd ldrs: led 4f out: sn clr) ....— | 1 | 5/4[1] | 65 | 40 |
| 2139[5] **Hobbs Choice (50)** (GMMoore) **3-8-8** JTate(3) (lw: led tl hdd 4f out: sn outpcd) ....6 | 2 | 11/2[3] | 50 | 16 |
| 2320[4] **Summer Villa (40)** (JHetherton) **4-9-1** DeanMcKeown(6) (hdwy 4f out: swtchd over 3f out: nvr able rch ldrs) ....1¼ | 3 | 10/1 | 46 | 21 |
| 2058[8] **Zaaleff (USA) (50)** (BHanbury) **4-9-4b** PBloomfield(2) (outpcd & lost pl 4f out: hung rt: sn btn) ....4 | 4 | 8/1 | 41 | 16 |
| 2358[3] **Bright Eclipse (USA) (55)** (JWHills) **3-8-9b[1]** JFortune(1) (trckd ldrs: effrt & hung lft over 3f out: nt r.o) .........1¾ | 5 | 5/1[2] | 38 | 4 |
| 1518[4] **Cowboy Dreams (IRE) (50)** (MHTompkins) **3-8-6v[1]**(3) HKYim(5) (cl up tl wknd over 3f out) ....5 | 6 | 15/2 | 28 | — |

(SP 108.5%) **6 Rn**

**1m 46.5** (2.40) CSF £7.70 TOTE £2.30: £1.20 £3.10 (£7.10) OWNER Mr Charles Walker (NEWMARKET) BRED Juddmonte Farms
WEIGHT FOR AGE 3yo-9lb
**2282 Giftbox (USA)**, back on the track where he had previously won, came back to form in style. Now he will surely show what he can do. (5/4: Evens-11/8)
**638 Hobbs Choice**, trying a longer trip, was well outclassed in the last three furlongs. (11/2)
**2320 Summer Villa** failed to make any impression, but this came a bit quick after her first run for a while less than a week ago. (10/1)
**1821 Zaaleff (USA)** looks to have his own ideas about the game. (8/1: op 5/1)
**2358 Bright Eclipse (USA)**, tried in blinkers, still did not want any part of it once pressure was applied. (5/1: op 3/1)
**1518 Cowboy Dreams (IRE)** had the visor on for the first time and called it a day once pressure was applied in the last half-mile. (15/2: 5/1-8/1)

## 2490 TOSHIBA AT STEPEK H'CAP (0-70) (3-Y.O+) (Class E)
8-00 (8-00) **6f 5y** £3,345.60 (£1,012.80: £494.40: £235.20) Stalls: High GOING minus 0.51 sec per fur (F)

| | | SP | RR | SF |
|---|---|---|---|---|
| *2171[5]* **Stand Tall (56)** (CWThornton) **4-9-1** DeanMcKeown(2) (lw: trckd ldrs: led & qcknd wl over 1f out: jst hld on) — | 1 | 2/1[1] | 66 | 30 |
| *2367[2]* **Most Uppitty (43)** (JBerry) **4-7-13**(3)ow3 HKYim(7) (cl up: led ½-wy tl wl over 1f out: hung rt: swtchd ins fnl f: fin wl) ....hd | 2 | 11/2[3] | 53 | 14 |
| 2154* **Thwaab (52)** (FWatson) **4-8-11v** JFanning(5) (lw: in tch: hdwy & ev ch 2f out: hmpd over 1f out: nt qckn) ........2 | 3 | 4/1[2] | 56 | 20 |
| 2154[2] **Sunday Mail Too (IRE) (44)** (MissLAPerratt) **4-8-3** LCharnock(3) (a chsng ldrs: rdn 2f out: nt qckn)..............3½ | 4 | 11/1 | 39 | 3 |
| 2215[4] **Opening Chorus (53)** (DNicholls) **3-8-6** JFortune(4) (led to ½-wy: wknd 2f out) ....2 | 5 | 6/1 | 43 | 1 |
| 1634[2] **Craigie Boy (55)** (NBycroft) **6-9-0b** JTate(1) (lw: nvr wnt pce) ....3½ | 6 | 4/1[2] | 36 | — |

(SP 111.3%) **6 Rn**

**1m 11.8** (1.80) CSF £12.12 TOTE £3.00: £2.00 £2.60 (£10.70) OWNER Mr Guy Reed (MIDDLEHAM) BRED Mrs E. Longton
WEIGHT FOR AGE 3yo-6lb
**2171 Stand Tall** travelled well and looked likely to win comfortably when sent on over a furlong from home, but he found little in front and only just managed to last out. (2/1)
**2367 Most Uppitty** has plenty of ability but is inclined to run in snatches and, after hanging right, then finished too late. (11/2)
**2154* Thwaab** ran reasonably in a visor for the second time here, but he was never doing enough when the pressure was seriously on in the last two furlongs. (4/1: 3/1-9/2)
**2154 Sunday Mail Too (IRE)** had her chances, but was never giving it her best shot from halfway. (11/1: 6/1-12/1)
**2215 Opening Chorus** was again disappointing. (6/1: 4/1-13/2)
**1634 Craigie Boy**, who prefers softer ground, was always finding things happening too quickly and never got into it. (4/1: 3/1-9/2)

## 2491 CREATIVE UPHOLSTERY/STEPEK SUITE COLLECTION E.B.F. MEDIAN AUCTION MAIDEN STKS (2-Y.O)
(Class E) 8-30 (8-31) **5f 4y** £3,225.00 (£975.00: £475.00: £225.00) Stalls: High GOING minus 0.51 sec per fur (F)

| | | | | SP | RR | SF |
|---|---|---|---|---|---|---|
| $2219^{4}$ | **Nomore Mr Niceguy** (EJAlston) **2-9-0** JFortune(5) (trckd ldrs: effrt 2f out: r.o u.p fnl f to ld cl home) | — | 1 | $7/4^{2}$ | 67 | 16 |
| $1849^{6}$ | **Fruitana (IRE)** (JBerry) **2-9-0** JCarroll(3) (disp ld tl led ½-wy: sn rdn: hdd & nt qckn towards fin) | hd | 2 | $6/4^{1}$ | 67 | 16 |
| $2343^{4}$ | **Perpetual** (SirMarkPrescott) **2-8-9** RPerham(6) (lw: disp ld to ½-wy: sn rdn & kpt on wl) | ¾ | 3 | $7/2^{3}$ | 59 | 8 |
| | **Mirror Four Sport** (MJohnston) **2-8-9** JFanning(2) (w'like: chsd ldrs: rdn ½-wy: sn outpcd) | 8 | 4 | 12/1 | 34 | — |
| | **Scotmail Lass** (GMMoore) **2-8-9** JTate(4) (w'like: scope: bit bkwd: s.s: sme late hdwy) | 6 | 5 | 33/1 | 15 | — |
| $2118^{3}$ | **Chanson d'Amour (IRE)** (MissLAPerratt) **2-8-9** LCharnock(1) (spd to ½-wy: sn wknd) | 2½ | 6 | 20/1 | 7 | — |
| | | | | (SP 114.0%) | **6 Rn** | |

**60.6 secs** (2.30) CSF £4.76 TOTE £2.60: £1.60 £1.30 (£3.10) OWNER Mrs Carol McPhail (PRESTON) BRED Brick Kiln Stud and Lariston Apartments Ltd

**2219 Nomore Mr Niceguy**, who travelled particularly well, got some strong assistance when it mattered and responded in game style. He should get further. (7/4)

**1849 Fruitana (IRE)**, who ran a decent race last time, for most of the trip looked the likely winner, but was then just touched off. He is a good mover who will go one better before long. (6/4: Evens-7/4)

**2343 Perpetual** is certainly improving and, after looking well beaten just after halfway, battled on bravely. Her winning turn is not far away. (7/2)

**Mirror Four Sport** showed some ability and will no doubt do better in time, especially over further. (12/1: op 7/1)

**Scotmail Lass**, a decent type, needed this and was clueless early on, but did show something at the end. Time is the key. (33/1)

**2118 Chanson d'Amour (IRE)** found this company far too hot. (20/1)

## 2492 ZANUSSI AT STEPEK (S) STKS (3-Y.O+) (Class G)
9-00 (9-03) **5f 4y** £2,276.00 (£636.00: £308.00) Stalls: High GOING minus 0.51 sec per fur (F)

| | | | | SP | RR | SF |
|---|---|---|---|---|---|---|
| 2359* | **Penny Parkes (44)** (JBerry) **3-8-13b** 6x JCarroll(4) (s.i.s: hdwy ½-wy: no ch w wnr: fin 2nd, 1 3/4l: awrdd r) .. | — | 1 | $3/1^{3}$ | 59 | — |
| | **Amylou** (RAllan) **3-8-7** JFanning(3) (w'like: bit bkwd: unruly s: dwlt: n.d: fin 3rd, 7l: plcd 2nd) | | 2 | 25/1 | 31? | — |
| $1964^{3}$ | **La Suquet (67)** (NTinkler) **4-8-12** LCharnock(1) (swtchd rt after s: mde all: easily: fin 1st: disq: plcd last) | | 3 | Evens $^{1}$ | 59+ | 2 |
| $2392^{2}$ | **Sense of Priority (56)** (DNicholls) **7-9-9** AlexGreaves(2) (b.d after 100y) | | B | $9/4^{2}$ | — | — |
| | | | | (SP 109.6%) | **4 Rn** | |

**61.4 secs** (3.10) CSF £27.73 TOTE £3.20: (£11.50) OWNER Mr Joseph Heler (COCKERHAM) BRED Joseph Heler

WEIGHT FOR AGE 3yo-5lb

No bid

STEWARDS' ENQUIRY Charnock susp. 15-24/7/96 (irresponsible riding).

**2359* Penny Parkes** was certainly outclassed, but was given the race in the Stewards' Room. (3/1)

**Amylou** needed this and, after giving problems at the start, was never in the race. (25/1)

**1964 La Suquet** made a manouevre after the start which put her only serious rival on the floor and, after trotting up, she had to be disqualified for what was quite rightly called irresponsible riding. (Evens)

**2392 Sense of Priority** was badly hampered by the favourite after leaving the stalls and finished up on the floor. (9/4)

## 2493 SHARP AT STEPEK MAIDEN H'CAP (0-65) (3-Y.O+) (Class F)
9-30 (9-35) **1m 5f 9y** £2,962.00 (£832.00: £406.00) Stalls: High GOING minus 0.51 sec per fur (F)

| | | | | SP | RR | SF |
|---|---|---|---|---|---|---|
| $2191^{10}$ | **Shirley Sue (52)** (MJohnston) **3-8-13** JFanning(9) (bhd & pushed along 6f out: hdwy to ld over 3f out: styd on strly) | — | 1 | 14/1 | 70 | 31 |
| $2077^{5}$ | **Maftun (USA) (53)** (GMMoore) **4-10-0** JTate(6) (hld up: hdwy 5f out: ev ch 3f out: one pce fnl f) | 5 | 2 | $6/1^{3}$ | 65 | 40 |
| $1514^{6}$ | **Breydon (47)** (MHTompkins) **3-8-5**(3) HKYim(2) (in tch: effrt 4f out: one pce) | 12 | 3 | $3/1^{1}$ | 44 | 5 |
| $1526^{14}$ | **Fiasco (47)** (MJCamacho) **3-8-8** LCharnock(5) (chsd ldrs after 4f: led 4f out tl over 3f out: sn outpcd) | 2½ | 4 | 16/1 | 41 | 2 |
| *$1814^{9}$* | **Rattle (50)** (JJO'Neill) **3-8-11b** JFortune(8) (lw: bhd: effrt 5f out: no imp) | 2 | 5 | 8/1 | 42 | 3 |
| *$2173^{8}$* | **Me Cherokee (43)** (CWThornton) **4-9-4** DeanMcKeown(1) (lw: trckd ldrs: led over 4f out: sn hdd: wknd 3f out) | 7 | 6 | $4/1^{2}$ | 26 | 1 |
| $1544^{6}$ | **School of Science (28)** (DANolan) **6-7-10b**(7) KSked(7) (led: clr after 5f: hdd over 4f out: sn wknd) | 4 | 7 | 33/1 | 6 | — |
| $2036^{10}$ | **Lead Story (IRE) (63)** (EALDunlop) **3-9-10** JCarroll(4) (hld up: effrt over 4f out: sn btn) | 7 | 8 | $3/1^{1}$ | 33 | — |
| | | | | (SP 110.9%) | **8 Rn** | |

**2m 50.1** (4.40) CSF £83.29 CT £282.46 TOTE £18.60: £6.50 £3.00 £2.80 (£52.90) Trio £52.70 OWNER Greenland Park Ltd (MIDDLEHAM) BRED Lahama Ltd

WEIGHT FOR AGE 3yo-14lb

**Shirley Sue** looked none too happy at halfway but, once she got into the straight, she soon showed how good she is to win going away. Galloping tracks look a must. (14/1: 12/1-20/1)

**2077 Maftun (USA)**, stepped back up in trip, was made to look very one-paced by the winner. (6/1)

**Breydon** looked very slow when the pressure was on in the last half-mile. (3/1: op 6/4)

**974 Fiasco**, trying a longer trip, was found out in the final three furlongs. (16/1)

**1637 Me Cherokee** looked well enough, but ran poorly, and seems to have lost her way for the time being. (4/1)

T/Plpt: £131.30 (82.64 Tckts). T/Qdpt: £42.80 (15.3 Tckts). AA

# 2428-HAYDOCK (L-H) (Good)
## Friday July 5th
WEATHER: sunny WIND: str against

## 2494 JOHNNY OSBORNE CLAIMING STKS (3-Y.O+) (Class E)
2-20 (2-24) **1m 3f 200y** £3,030.00 (£915.00: £445.00: £210.00) Stalls: High GOING: 0.21 sec per fur (G)

| | | | | SP | RR | SF |
|---|---|---|---|---|---|---|
| 2394* | **Pharly Dancer (55)** (WWHaigh) **7-9-6** RLappin(3) (chsd ldr: led 4f out: rdn & styd on gamely) | — | 1 | $5/4^{1}$ | 63 | 52 |
| $2189^{4}$ | **Trade Wind (70)** (JGMO'Shea) **5-9-8v**$^{1}$ VSlattery(5) (hld up: hdwy 5f out: jnd wnr 3f out: rdn & one pce fnl f) | 2½ | 2 | 15/2 | 62 | 51 |

2152[6] **Shabanaz (58)** (WRMuir) **11-9-6** JFortune(6) (hld up: hdwy 3f out: kpt on u.p fnl f: nt pce to chal)..................1¼ **3** 7/2[2] 58 47
**Diamond Cut (FR)** (MCPipe) **8-9-8** BThomson(2) (trckd ldrs: effrt & rdn 3f out: kpt on one pce) .......................1 **4** 8/1 59 48
2182[2] **Akiymann (USA)** (MCPipe) **6-10-0** GCarter(7) (hld up & bhd: outpcd 5f out: hdwy 3f out: sn rdn: one pce) ..1¼ **5** 11/1 63 52
2140[6] **Precedency** (KMcAuliffe) **4-9-12v¹** WJO'Connor(1) (led tl hdd 4f out: wknd over 2f out: t.o)...........................11 **6** 33/1 46 35
**Fearless Wonder (51)** (MrsMReveley) **5-8-13b(5)** SCopp(4) (bit bkwd: hld up & bhd: rdn over 3f out: sn lost tch: t.o) ..............................................................................................................................1½ **7** 7/1[3] 36 25
(SP 113.3%) **7 Rn**

**2m 39.56** (10.16) CSF £10.42 TOTE £2.00: £1.30 £3.10 (£9.40) OWNER Mr A. Marucci (MALTON) BRED Stud-On-The-Chart
**2394* Pharly Dancer**, winning his second race in three days, took over soon after entering the straight and, shaking off the runner-up inside the distance, was well on top at the finish. (5/4)
**2189 Trade Wind**, still to win at this trip, gave supporters of the favourite a worrying time until lack of stamina began to take its toll on the approach to the final furlong. (15/2)
**2152 Shabanaz** tried hard to deliver his challenge inside the distance but, over a trip that could be stretching his stamina, was always being held. (7/2)
**Diamond Cut (FR)**, fit from hurdling, waited on the leaders but could not muster the pace to mount a challenge when the pressure was on. (8/1)
**2182 Akiymann (USA)**, taking a step down in distance, needed to be nudged along when the tempo picked up on the home turn. Galvanized into action three furlongs out, he kept staying on but was short of the necessary speed to land a blow. (11/1)

## 2495 HEUBACH MAIDEN AUCTION STKS (2-Y.O) (Class D)

2-50 (2-52) **6f** £3,746.50 (£1,132.00: £551.00: £260.50) Stalls: High GOING: 0.21 sec per fur (G)

SP RR SF
1344[4] **Demolition Man** (JWWatts) **2-8-6** JCarroll(2) (lw: s.i.s: hld up gng wl: hdwy 2f out: led ins fnl f: sn clr)..........— **1** 11/2[3] 84 21
1774[6] **Myrmidon** (JLDunlop) **2-8-11** GCarter(8) (a.p: led over 2f out tl hdd & no ex ins fnl f)...........................................2 **2** 9/4[1] 84 21
**Foxes Tail** (MissSEHall) **2-8-3** NCarlisle(9) (lt-f: unf: s.s: wl bhd tl r.o appr fnl f)..............................................2 **3** 20/1 70 7
1978[4] **Heathyards Pearl (USA)** (RHollinshead) **2-8-0(3)** FLynch(7) (hld up in tch: hdwy 2f out: one pce appr fnl f)..s.h **4** 7/1 70 7
**Monarch's Pursuit** (TDEasterby) **2-8-3** JLowe(4) (tall: s.s: bhd & outpcd tl styd on appr fnl f).........................6 **5** 16/1 54 —
2195[2] **Lamarita** (JMPEustace) **2-8-1** JTate(10) (lw: chsd ldr: led over 3f out tl over 2f out: grad wknd)....................hd **6** 5/2[2] 52 —
**Sandmoor Zoe** (TDEasterby) **2-8-1** LCharnock(12) (lt-f: in tch: rdn & outpcd ½-wy: n.d after).........................nk **7** 20/1 51 —
1827[8] **Ultra Boy** (PCHaslam) **2-8-6** JFortune(11) (led over 2f: wknd 2f out)....................................................¾ **8** 16/1 54 —
*1603*[7] **Presentiment** (JBerry) **2-8-11** DaleGibson(5) (lw: trckd ldrs: rdn 2f out: sn btn) .......................................hd **9** 20/1 59 —
**Good Day** (CWThornton) **2-8-8** DeanMcKeown(1) (leggy: unf: dwlt: effrt ½-wy: wknd wl over 1f out).............¾ **10** 20/1 54 —
**Madison Welcome (IRE)** (MrsJRRamsden) **2-8-11** WJO'Connor(6) (cmpt: bkwd: sn pushed along: a bhd & outpcd) ..............................................................................................................................3½ **11** 14/1 48 —
1705[5] **Manhattan Diamond** (ABailey) **2-8-3** AMackay(3) (prom on outside tl rdn & wknd 2f out) ................................4 **12** 12/1 29 —
(SP 132.4%) **12 Rn**

**1m 18.01** (6.31) CSF £19.02 TOTE £6.00: £1.70 £1.40 £5.50 (£9.00) Trio £233.70; £131.70 to Sandown 6/7/96 OWNER Mrs Kim Fritz (RICHMOND) BRED Southcourt Stud
**1344 Demolition Man**, always travelling comfortably, quickened up well when given the office and ran out a very easy winner. (11/2)
**1774 Myrmidon** gained command over two furlongs out and tried his best to slip the field, but the winner had far too much pace for him when the chips were down. (9/4)
**Foxes Tail**, a lightly-made newcomer, did extremely well to finish so close after missing a beat at the start, and will have no trouble in winning races. (20/1)
**1978 Heathyards Pearl (USA)** put in her bid two furlongs out, but could not raise her pace when the leading pair took one another on. She could be an ideal type for a mile nursery. (7/1)
**Monarch's Pursuit**, a tall colt, was flat-footed as the stalls opened and off the bridle all the way. He was beginning to realise what was needed in the latter stages though, and the experience will not be lost. (16/1)
**2195 Lamarita** helped share the pace, but did not find a lot when the pressure was on, and she may fare better if not so much use is made of her. (5/2)

## 2496 WEATHERBYS GROUP H'CAP (0-70) (3-Y.O+) (Class E)

3-25 (3-28) **5f** £3,013.75 (£910.00: £442.50: £208.75) Stalls: High GOING: 0.21 sec per fur (G)

SP RR SF
2151[7] **Gwespyr (58)** (JBerry) **3-9-1** JCarroll(10) (rdn ½-wy: hdwy to ld wl over 1f out: drvn out)...............................— **1** 8/1 67 41
1642* **Sharp Monty (60)** (RHollinshead) **3-9-0(3)** FLynch(7) (hdwy & hmpd 2f out: swtchd lft: r.o strly fnl f)..............1¾ **2** 9/1 63 37
*2084*[8] **Malibu Man (62)** (EAWheeler) **4-9-10** BThomson(12) (lw: s.i.s: hld up & bhd: swtchd lft 2f out: rdn & r.o wl fnl f) ..............................................................................................................................nk **3** 11/2[2] 64 43
2244[4] **Featherstone Lane (50)** (MissLCSiddall) **5-8-12v** WJO'Connor(11) (lw: hld up: stdy hdwy appr fnl f: nvr nrr)..¾ **4** 6/1[3] 50 29
1708[8] **Gondo (43)** (EJAlston) **9-8-5** JLowe(1) (hdwy centre wl over 1f out: hrd rdn: nvr nrr) .........................................¾ **5** 12/1 41 20
2186* **Sing With the Band (65)** (BAMcMahon) **5-9-13** 7x GCarter(3) (w ldrs: rdn wl over 1f out: one pce)..................½ **6** 7/2[1] 61 40
1859[7] **Prime Property (IRE) (35)** (MWEasterby) **4-7-11bow1** DaleGibson(4) (gd hdwy over 1f out: nt rch ldrs)..........nk **7** 16/1 30 8
2030[7] **Souperficial (48)** (JAGlover) **5-8-10b¹** JFortune(9) (prom: jnd ldrs 2f out: rdn & wknd appr fnl f)......................½ **8** 11/1 42 21
*1716*[7] **Ivy Lilian (IRE) (34)** (WMBrisbourne) **4-7-3(7)** JBramhill(8) (trckd ldrs over 3f) ..................................................1 **9** 16/1 24 3
2049[10] **Maysimp (IRE) (44)** (BPJBaugh) **3-8-1** NCarlisle(6) (outpcd)...............................................................................5 **10** 20/1 18 —
2324[3] **Bowcliffe Grange (IRE) (43)** (DWChapman) **4-8-5b** DeanMcKeown(5) (lw: sn led: rdn & hdd wl over 1f out: wknd qckly) ..............................................................................................................................3 **11** 11/2[2] 8 —
648[13] **Ashik (IRE) (45)** (LJBarratt) **3-8-2** LCharnock(2) (disp ld 2f: outpcd ½-wy: t.o)..................................................6 **12** 33/1 — —
(SP 123.9%) **12 Rn**

**63.7 secs** (4.50) CSF £74.17 CT £406.10 TOTE £9.40: £2.70 £2.90 £2.20 (£55.70) Trio £86.10 OWNER Lord Mostyn (COCKERHAM) BRED R. and Mrs Heathcote
LONG HANDICAP Prime Property (IRE) 7-8 Ivy Lilian (IRE) 7-8
WEIGHT FOR AGE 3yo-5lb
**2151 Gwespyr** has been a long time getting back to winning ways but, when she did strike the front, there was only going to be one winner. (8/1)
**1642* Sharp Monty** looked to be an unlucky loser on this step up in class, for he was forced to check and switch inside the last quarter-mile, and his determined late challenge would suggest he is very much on the upgrade. (9/1)
**1844 Malibu Man**, attempting to make progress up the rail after losing ground at the start, did not enjoy a trouble-free passage, but he fairly sprouted wings after being switched and there is more success beckoning. (11/2)
**2244 Featherstone Lane** runs best when produced from off the pace and that was the way he was ridden here. Doing all his best work inside the last furlong, he is due a change of luck. (6/1)

**Gondo** had been out of sorts so far this term, but he showed he still retains some ability, and he is usually at his best in the second part of the year. (12/1)
**2186* Sing With the Band** disputed the lead but could never get things her own way and was fighting a lost cause approaching the final furlong. (7/2)
**Prime Property (IRE)** needs a stiffer test of stamina and was out with the washing until running on when it was all but over. (16/1)

## 2497 SCOTTISH EQUITABLE/JOCKEYS ASSOCIATION RATED STKS H'CAP (0-95) (3-Y.O+) (Class C)

3-55 (3-55) **7f 30y** £7,758.12 (£2,893.08: £1,406.54: £595.70: £257.85: £122.71) Stalls: Low GOING: 0.21 sec per fur (G)

| | | | | SP | RR | SF |
|---|---|---|---|---|---|---|
| 2363* | **Saseedo (USA) (89)** (WAO'Gorman) **6-9-1** 3x EmmaO'Gorman(8) (lw: hld up & bhd: gd hdwy wl over 1f out: led appr fnl f: pushed clr) | — | **1** | 7/2[1] | 96 | 59 |
| 1800[4] | **Band on the Run (95)** (BAMcMahon) **9-9-7** GCarter(1) (lw: prom: outpcd ½-wy: rallied u.p over 1f out: r.o) | 2 | **2** | 5/1[3] | 98 | 61 |
| 2011[2] | **Bollin Joanne (81)** (TDEasterby) **3-7-13** LCharnock(7) (b: stdd s: hdwy on bit 2f out: squeezed thro appr fnl f: r.o) | 1½ | **3** | 6/1 | 80 | 35 |
| 2053[9] | **Czarna (IRE) (81)** (CEBrittain) **5-8-7** MBirch(6) (lw: chsd ldrs: hrd drvn 2f out: outpcd appr fnl f) | 3½ | **4** | 9/2[2] | 72 | 35 |
| 2114[7] | **Astrac (IRE) (92)** (RAkehurst) **5-8-11**(7) DDenby(3) (lw: trckd ldrs: effrt & rdn 2f out: btn whn hmpd appr fnl f) | ¾ | **5** | 7/2[1] | 82 | 45 |
| 2114[29] | **Bold Effort (FR) (90)** (KOCunningham-Brown) **4-9-2b[1]** JFortune(5) (prom: led over 3f out tl ent fnl f: sn wknd) | ¾ | **6** | 20/1 | 78 | 41 |
| 1432[10] | **Some Horse (IRE) (93)** (MGMeagher) **3-8-11** JCarroll(2) (lw: bhd: effrt & rdn over 2f out: no imp) | 1 | **7** | 14/1 | 79 | 34 |
| 633[9] | **Champagne Grandy (84)** (MRChannon) **6-8-10** AMackay(4) (lw: led tl over 3f out: btn whn hmpd over 1f out) | 3 | **8** | 6/1 | 63 | 26 |

(SP 119.3%) **8 Rn**

**1m 32.45** (4.95) CSF £20.81 CT £94.70 TOTE £4.80: £1.80 £1.60 £1.30 (£10.50) OWNER Mr S. Fustok (NEWMARKET) BRED Audley Farm Incorporated
LONG HANDICAP Bollin Joanne 7-12
WEIGHT FOR AGE 3yo-8lb
**2363* Saseedo (USA)** defied a 3lb penalty for winning earlier in the week with a runaway success over this more suitable trip and, in this form, makes winning look easy. (7/2)
**1800 Band on the Run** won this race last year, but he has risen in the weights since then and this pleasing performance gives every indication that he is no back-number yet. (5/1)
**2011 Bollin Joanne**, running away with nowhere to go two furlongs out, did eventually force her way through a narrow gap, doing several of her rivals no favours at all. Though she did finish well, the winner was by then beyond recall, and it hard to believe that she is still a maiden. (6/1)
**1898 Czarna (IRE)** was still doing battle, but under extreme pressure, when nudged out of the way below the distance, and his chance quickly disappeared. (9/2)
**1107 Astrac (IRE)** sat on the bridle waiting to pounce approaching the quarter-mile marker, but Bold Effort kicked clear, and he was at full stretch and looking held when knocked out of his stride over a furlong out. He does look to need stronger handling. (7/2)
**Bold Effort (FR)** barely stays seven furlongs and, with the first-time blinkers, did far too much too soon, and had cooked his goose when collared entering the last furlong. (20/1)

## 2498 ST HELENS STAR CONDITIONS STKS (3-Y.O+) (Class C)

4-30 (4-32) **6f** £4,909.00 (£1,831.00: £890.50: £377.50: £163.75: £78.25) Stalls: High GOING: 0.21 sec per fur (G)

| | | | | SP | RR | SF |
|---|---|---|---|---|---|---|
| 2114W | **Averti (IRE) (100)** (WRMuir) **5-9-1** BThomson(6) (lw: led 1f: qcknd to ld ent fnl f: r.o wl) | — | **1** | 6/1 | 108 | 66 |
| 2072[13] | **Montendre (100)** (MMcCormack) **9-9-1** MBirch(3) (lw: hld up: swtchd lft & effrt over 1f out: unable qckn fnl f) | 1½ | **2** | 7/2[2] | 104 | 62 |
| | **Lacryma Cristi (IRE)** (RCharlton) **3-8-9** GCarter(1) (bit bkwd: a.p: rdn over 1f out: wknd ins fnl f) | 4 | **3** | 4/1[3] | 93 | 45 |
| 2072[9] | **My Melody Parkes (103)** (JBerry) **3-8-4** JCarroll(5) (lw: led 1f: hdd & wknd appr fnl f) | ½ | **4** | 6/5[1] | 87 | 39 |
| 1753a[9] | **Greek Icon (92)** (MRChannon) **3-8-4** AMackay(4) (s.s: sn chsng ldrs: pushed along over 2f out: sn wknd: t.o) | 12 | **5** | 14/1 | 55 | 7 |
| 1787[7] | **Chelwood** (LRLloyd-James) **4-8-10b[1]** DaleGibson(2) (lw: dwlt: a outpcd: t.o) | 2½ | **6** | 100/1 | 48? | 6 |

(SP 109.6%) **6 Rn**

**1m 15.31** (3.61) CSF £24.50 TOTE £6.80: £2.70 £2.10 (£12.70) OWNER Mr D. J. Deer (LAMBOURN) BRED D. J. and Mrs Deer
WEIGHT FOR AGE 3yo-6lb
**1621 Averti (IRE)** showed he can handle this more yielding ground with a readily-gained first success in almost three years, and there is no reason when he should not follow up. (6/1)
**1332 Montendre** could not match the winner for toe in the sprint to the finish, but he is running well enough to suggest there is another race in the pipe-line. (7/2)
**Lacryma Cristi (IRE)**, having his first outing since changing stables, looked short of peak-fitness and had shot his bolt soon after entering the final furlong. He should not be difficult to place. (4/1)
**1629 My Melody Parkes** should have made short work of this opposition, but she was one of the first beaten and the only possible excuse could have been her inability to handle the ground. (6/5)

## 2499 FRANK WOOTTON H'CAP (0-85) (4-Y.O+) (Class D)

5-00 (5-00) **1m 6f** £3,666.75 (£1,104.00: £534.50: £249.75) Stalls: Centre GOING: 0.21 sec per fur (G)

| | | | | SP | RR | SF |
|---|---|---|---|---|---|---|
| 1870[4] | **Welsh Mill (IRE) (73)** (MrsMReveley) **7-9-5** ACulhane(4) (lw: a.p: led over 2f out: hrd rdn fnl f: hld on gamely) | — | **1** | 6/1 | 82 | 59 |
| 1802* | **Turgenev (IRE) (64)** (RBastiman) **7-8-10b** DaleGibson(1) (hld up & bhd: hdwy over 2f out: str run fnl f: jst failed) | s.h | **2** | 2/1[1] | 73 | 50 |
| 1426[4] | **Raffles Rooster (58)** (AGNewcombe) **4-8-4** AMackay(7) (lw: hld up: hdwy on ins 2f out: ev ch ins fnl f: hrd rdn: r.o) | ½ | **3** | 7/1 | 66 | 43 |
| 2002[3] | **Midyan Blue (IRE) (75)** (JMPEustace) **6-9-4**(3) FLynch(2) (led 1f: led over 3f out: hdd over 2f out: sn rdn & btn) | 4 | **4** | 7/2[2] | 79 | 56 |
| 2042[15] | **Seasonal Splendour (IRE) (78)** (MCPipe) **6-9-10** GCarter(6) (hld up in tch: rdn 2f out: one pce) | ½ | **5** | 5/1[3] | 81 | 58 |
| | **Sugar Mill (68)** (MrsMReveley) **6-9-0** WJO'Connor(3) (bit bkwd: trckd ldrs tl wknd over 2f out) | 7 | **6** | 8/1 | 63 | 40 |
| 2182[13] | **Faugeron (54)** (NTinkler) **7-8-0** KimTinkler(5) (s.s: led after 1f tl over 3f out: rdn & btn 2f out) | 3 | **7** | 25/1 | 46 | 23 |

(SP 114.0%) **7 Rn**

**3m 8.91** (10.71) CSF £17.80 TOTE £7.90: £2.50 £1.90 (£8.00) OWNER Mr D. S. Hall (SALTBURN) BRED Ballymacoll Stud Farm Ltd
STEWARDS' ENQUIRY Mackay susp. 15-16/7/96 (excessive use of whip).

**1870 Welsh Mill (IRE)** kicked for home plenty soon enough and had to work hard to hold on in the end, but he always looked likely to do so. (6/1)
**1802* Turgenev (IRE)** made relentless progress inside the last quarter-mile and gave his all, but the line arrived a stride too soon. (2/1)
**1426 Raffles Rooster**, taken to post early, tackled extended trips when he was trained in France as a three-year old. Delaying his challenge, he battled long and hard inside the final furlong but the winner would not be denied. He will find a staying event in the near future. (7/1)
**2002 Midyan Blue (IRE)**, taking a keen hold and travelling strongly for most of the way, soon threw in the towel when the winner appeared on the scene, and proved a bit disappointing. (7/2)
**573 Seasonal Splendour (IRE)** has not been firing on the Flat this term and, though she did keep plugging away, she was never really in a position to pose a serious threat. (5/1)

T/Plpt: £140.90 (82.17 Tckts). T/Qdpt: £17.80 (46.91 Tckts). IM

# 1998-SANDOWN (R-H) (Good to firm, Good patches becoming Good)
## Friday July 5th
WEATHER: heavy rain races 3-4 WIND: almost nil

## 2500 TIN TIN DAILY NEWS TROPHY H'CAP (0-70) (3-Y.O) (Class E)
2-00 (2-05) **5f 6y** £3,468.75 (£1,050.00: £512.50: £243.75) Stalls: Low GOING minus 0.44 sec per fur (F)

| | Horse / details | Dist | Pos | SP | RR | SF |
|---|---|---|---|---|---|---|
| 2244² | **Clan Chief (58)** (JRArnold) **3-9-0** TQuinn(2) (b.hind: a.p: led 1f out: rdn out) | — | 1 | 2/1 1 | 66 | 42 |
| 2215* | **Fairy Prince (IRE) (60)** (MrsALMKing) **3-8-13**(3) 6x DaneO'Neill(9) (hrd rdn & hdwy over 1f out: r.o wl ins fnl f) | 1½ | 2 | 9/2 2 | 63 | 39 |
| 1840¹³ | **Sunset Harbour (IRE) (45)** (TJNaughton) **3-8-1b** JQuinn(8) (led to 1f out: unable qckn) | ½ | 3 | 16/1 | 47 | 23 |
| 1995⁴ | **Mindrace (60)** (KTIvory) **3-9-2** BDoyle(6) (a.p: rdn over 2f out: one pce) | s.h | 4 | 10/1 | 62 | 38 |
| 2176³ | **Need You Badly (59)** (SPCWoods) **3-9-1** WWoods(3) (no hdwy fnl 2f) | 1½ | 5 | 11/2 3 | 56 | 32 |
| 2193⁴ | **Mystery Matthias (51)** (MissBSanders) **3-8-7v¹** SSanders(7) (swtg: hld up: rdn over 2f out: one pce) | s.h | 6 | 15/2 | 48 | 24 |
| 2301⁵ | **Pleasure Time (65)** (CSmith) **3-9-7** AClark(5) (lw: rdn & hdwy over 2f out: eased whn btn ins fnl f) | 4 | 7 | 12/1 | 49 | 25 |
| 2215⁵ | **Ciserano (IRE) (62)** (MRChannon) **3-8-11**(7) AEddery(4) (s.s: a bhd) | ¾ | 8 | 10/1 | 43 | 19 |
| 2200⁶ | **Dancing Jack (52)** (JJBridger) **3-8-8**ow2 KFallon(10) (lw: prom over 3f) | 3 | 9 | 20/1 | 24 | — |
| 1170¹⁵ | **Music Mistress (IRE) (48)** (JSMoore) **3-8-4b¹** JFEgan(11) (lw: a bhd) | ¾ | 10 | 25/1 | 18 | — |
| *1693⁹* | ***Rififi (60)*** (RIngram) **3-9-2** SWhitworth(1) (Withdrawn not under Starter's orders: lame) | | W | 8/1 | — | — |
| | | | | (SP 130.1%) | **10 Rn** | |

**60.94 secs** (1.14) CSF £11.31 CT £106.37 TOTE £2.20: £1.10 £1.80 £5.70 (£3.40) Trio £72.90 OWNER Mr P. G. Lowe (UPPER LAMBOURN) BRED D. Gill

IN-FOCUS: **This was a very moderate race by Sandown standards.**
**2244 Clan Chief** gained a richly-deserved success after a couple of really good efforts. (2/1)
**2215* Fairy Prince (IRE)**, soon outpaced, began to find his feet from below the distance and ran on really strongly to take second prize. A return to six furlongs would be in his favour. (9/2)
**Sunset Harbour (IRE)** ran her best race on turf this year. (16/1)
**832 Mindrace** was tapped for toe from below the distance. (10/1)
**2176 Need You Badly** raced in midfield and was making little impression on the principals in the last two furlongs. This trip is too sharp for her but, over further, she may be capable of lifting a small handicap, especially as she is due to fall 4lb in future handicaps. (11/2)
**2193 Mystery Matthias**, tried in a visor, raced in midfield, but was treading water in the last two furlongs. (15/2)

## 2501 SING TAO TROPHY H'CAP (0-95) (3-Y.O) (Class C)
2-35 (2-37) **7f 16y** £8,832.00 (£2,676.00: £1,308.00: £624.00) Stalls: High GOING minus 0.25 sec per fur (GF)

| | Horse / details | Dist | Pos | SP | RR | SF |
|---|---|---|---|---|---|---|
| 2137² | **Green Barries (81)** (MJohnston) **3-9-2** JWeaver(10) (a.p: led over 2f out: rdn out) | — | 1 | 9/1 | 89 | 63 |
| 2065* | **Dancing Image (78)** (IABalding) **3-8-13** TQuinn(6) (hmpd 6f out: hrd rdn & hdwy over 1f out: r.o wl ins fnl f) | nk | 2 | 9/2 1 | 85 | 59 |
| 2041⁶ | **Alamein (USA) (85)** (WJHaggas) **3-9-6b** KFallon(4) (lw: rdn over 2f out: hdwy over 1f out: r.o) | 1¼ | 3 | 6/1 3 | 90 | 64 |
| 1864* | **Polar Prospect (75)** (BHanbury) **3-8-7**(3) JStack(1) (b: lw: a.p: rdn over 2f out: r.o) | nk | 4 | 8/1 | 79 | 53 |
| 2041¹⁵ | **Don Bosio (USA) (86)** (MRStoute) **3-9-4**(3) DaneO'Neill(9) (hld up: bmpd 6f out: rdn over 2f out: unable qckn fnl f) | ¾ | 5 | 14/1 | 88 | 62 |
| 978¹¹ | **Ameer Alfayaafi (IRE) (63)** (RAkehurst) **3-7-12** SSanders(8) (hmpd 6f out: nt clr run over 2f out: hdwy & n.m.r over 1f out: nvr nrr) | 3 | 6 | 9/1 | 58 | 32 |
| 2253⁴ | **Sound Check (61)** (BJMeehan) **3-7-10b** JQuinn(3) (nvr nr to chal) | ½ | 7 | 14/1 | 55 | 29 |
| *1809²* | **La Tansani (IRE) (70)** (RHannon) **3-8-5** JFEgan(2) (led over 4f: 6th & btn whn hmpd ins fnl f) | ½ | 8 | 25/1 | 63 | 37 |
| 1983² | **Navigate (USA) (80)** (RHannon) **3-9-1** PatEddery(7) (a.p: bmpd 6f out: ev ch wl over 1f out: btn whn hmpd ins fnl f) | 1½ | 9 | 11/2 2 | 70 | 44 |
| 1648⁶ | **Safio (80)** (CSmith) **3-9-1** AClark(5) (lw: squeezed out s: a bhd) | 1¾ | 10 | 33/1 | 66 | 40 |
| 1422* | **Mutadarra (IRE) (85)** (RWArmstrong) **3-9-6** WCarson(11) (lw: hld up: hmpd on ins 6f out: rdn over 2f out: sn wknd) | 3½ | 11 | 14/1 | 63 | 37 |
| 2209² | **Dubai College (IRE) (67)** (CEBrittain) **3-8-2** BDoyle(12) (hmpd on ins 6f out: bhd fnl 2f) | nk | 12 | 11/2 2 | 44 | 18 |
| | | | | (SP 121.1%) | **12 Rn** | |

**1m 28.78** (0.18) CSF £47.11 CT £249.92 TOTE £9.80: £2.80 £1.80 £1.90 (£16.90) Trio £26.40 OWNER Maktoum Al Maktoum (MIDDLEHAM) BRED Gainsborough Stud Management Ltd
LONG HANDICAP Sound Check 7-6
STEWARDS' ENQUIRY Weaver. susp 15-18/7/96 (careless riding).
**2137 Green Barries** was pushed into the lead over a quarter of a mile from home and, ridden along, proved too strong for his rivals. His jockey was later suspended for four days for careless riding after causing interference in the early stages of the race. (9/1)
**2065* Dancing Image**, done no favours by the scrimmaging in the early part of the contest, really found his feet from below the distance and, responding in tremendous style to pressure, only just failed to get there. Compensation awaits. (9/2: op 3/1)
**2041 Alamein (USA)** began to find his feet from below the distance but, despite running on for third prize, never looked like getting there in time. (6/1: op 4/1)
**1864* Polar Prospect**, in a handy position throughout, was pushed along over two furlongs from home. He stayed on well from below the distance and only just failed to take third prize. (8/1)
**1593 Don Bosio (USA)** was one of several horses fighting for second place entering the final furlong before tapped for toe. (14/1)
**Ameer Alfayaafi (IRE)**, who had shown nothing on the racecourse, had reportedly been working nicely at home of late and gave signs of encouragement here, despite traffic problems. A small handicap may well be found for him. (9/1)

## 2502 HONG KONG JOCKEY CLUB TROPHY H'CAP (3-Y.O+) (Class B)

3-10 (3-20) **1m 2f 7y** £51,750.00 (£19,350.00: £9,450.00: £4,050.00: £1,800.00: £900.00) Stalls: High GOING minus 0.25 sec (GF)

| | | | | SP | RR | SF |
|---|---|---|---|---|---|---|
| 1961[3] | **Sheer Danzig (IRE) (85)** (RWArmstrong) **4-8-7** WWoods(5) (lw: hdwy over 2f out: hrd rdn over 1f out: led nr fin) | — | **1** | 10/1 | 100 | 53 |
| 2052[5] | **Miss Universal (IRE) (99)** (CEBrittain) **3-8-10** BDoyle(4) (a.p: rdn over 3f out: edgd lft & led over 1f out: hrd rdn: hdd nr fin) | s.h | **2** | 25/1 | 114 | 56 |
| 2001[4] | **Spirito Libro (USA) (87)** (CNAllen) **3-7-7**(5)ow2 MBaird(11) (rdn over 3f out: hdwy over 1f out: r.o ins fnl f) | 3 | **3** | 50/1 | 97 | 37 |
| 2299[5] | **Silver Groom (IRE) (75)** (RAkehurst) **6-7-11** JQuinn(1) (rdn over 3f out: hdwy over 1f out: one pce fnl f) | 1¾ | **4** | 12/1 | 82 | 35 |
| 1484[5] | **Wilcuma (89)** (PJMakin) **5-8-11** DHolland(15) (rdn over 3f out: hdwy over 1f out: r.o one pce) | ¾ | **5** | 16/1 | 95 | 48 |
| 2299[3] | **Komreyev Dancer (75)** (ABailey) **4-7-8**(3) DWright(8) (a.p: hrd rdn 3f out: wknd fnl f) | nk | **6** | 50/1 | 81 | 34 |
| 2350[6] | **Hazard a Guess (IRE) (82)** (DNicholls) **6-8-4** JFEgan(17) (rdn over 3f out: hdwy over 1f out: one pce fnl f) | 1¾ | **7** | 20/1 | 85 | 38 |
| 1126* | **Missile (88)** (WJHaggas) **3-7-13** WCarson(12) (rdn over 3f out: hdwy over 1f out: one pce fnl f) | 1¼ | **8** | 9/2[1] | 89 | 31 |
| 2041[22] | **Believe Me (97)** (RHannon) **3-8-8** RPerham(19) (lw: a mid div) | 2½ | **9** | 20/1 | 94 | 36 |
| 2145* | **Salmon Ladder (USA) (104)** (PFICole) **4-9-12** 4x TQuinn(13) (lw: a.p: hrd rdn over 3f out: eased whn btn fnl f) | ½ | **10** | 6/1[3] | 100 | 53 |
| 2053* | **Yeast (91)** (WJHaggas) **4-8-13** 4x KFallon(20) (led over 8f out: rdn over 3f out: hdd over 1f out: wknd fnl f) | d.h | **10** | 11/2[2] | 87 | 40 |
| 2145[8] | **Ball Gown (92)** (DTThom) **6-8-9**(5) LNewton(10) (nvr nrr) | ¾ | **12** | 33/1 | 87 | 40 |
| 925[5] | **Special Dawn (IRE) (90)** (JLDunlop) **6-8-12** PaulEddery(16) (hdwy over 1f out: eased whn btn fnl f) | ¾ | **13** | 20/1 | 84 | 37 |
| 2041[13] | **Winter Romance (102)** (EALDunlop) **3-8-13** MHills(2) (bhd fnl 3f) | ¾ | **14** | 14/1 | 95 | 37 |
| 2055[7] | **Major Change (91)** (RHannon) **4-8-10**(3) 4x DaneO'Neill(14) (b: hdwy over 2f out: wknd over 1f out) | 2 | **15** | 16/1 | 80 | 33 |
| 2006[2] | **Skillington (USA) (90)** (IABalding) **3-7-10**(5) MartinDwyer(7) (lw: bhd fnl 3f) | nk | **16** | 10/1 | 79 | 21 |
| 2074[4] | **Pleasant Surprise (96)** (MJohnston) **3-8-7** JWeaver(9) (led over 1f: wknd over 2f out) | 1½ | **17** | 20/1 | 83 | 25 |
| 2127[6] | **Fieldridge (76)** (MPMuggeridge) **7-7-12** NAdams(18) (prom 4f) | 5 | **18** | 66/1 | 55 | 8 |
| 1484[3] | **Chief Burundi (USA) (102)** (LMCumani) **4-9-10** PatEddery(3) (prom over 5f) | 1½ | **19** | 10/1 | 78 | 31 |
| 2055[13] | **Hardy Dancer (91)** (GLMoore) **4-8-13** SWhitworth(6) (a bhd) | 1¾ | **20** | 33/1 | 64 | 17 |

(SP 135.4%) **20 Rn**

**2m 9.06** (2.36) CSF £224.48 CT £10,426.20 TOTE £13.90: £2.60 £6.60 £7.30 £1.90 (£336.70) Trio £3,833.40; £3,779.44 to Sandown 6/7/96
OWNER Mr R. J. Arculli (NEWMARKET) BRED Mrs Max Morris
LONG HANDICAP Spirito Libro (USA) 7-2
WEIGHT FOR AGE 3yo-11lb

**1961 Sheer Danzig (IRE)** began to pick up ground over a quarter of a mile from home. Throwing down his challenge in the final furlong, he had a real set-to with the runner-up and just managed to prevail with little left in the locker. (10/1)

**2052 Miss Universal (IRE)** failed by only a whisker to lose her maiden tag in this very valuable handicap. Pushed along entering the straight, she drifted into the centre of the track below the distance, but still managed to strike the front. Soon tackled by the winner, she was collared near the line but, refusing to give way, only just failed to get back up. She is a winner without a penalty. (25/1)

**2001 Spirito Libro (USA)**, going nowhere early in the straight, found her feet from below the distance but, despite running on, was never going to get to the front two in time. (50/1)

**2299 Silver Groom (IRE)** began to pick up ground below the distance, but was making no further impression in the final furlong. (12/1)

**1484 Wilcuma**, ridden along early in the straight, was doing all his best work in the last furlong and a half. (16/1)

**2299 Komreyev Dancer**, a leading light from the off, was under pressure for the majority of the straight and finally called it a day inside the last 200 yards. (50/1)

**1126* Missile**, who had an infection in his leg the day before he was due to run in the Britannia Handicap at Royal Ascot, was being pushed along early in the straight. Weaving his way through the pack below the distance, he failed to find another gear in the final furlong.(9/2: 3/1-5/1)

**2053* Yeast** has been in tremendous form this season, but found this longer trip his undoing. A return to a mile is needed. (11/2)

## 2503 HSBC TROPHY CONDITIONS STKS (2-Y.O) (Class B)

3-40 (3-59) **7f 16y** £6,156.00 (£2,304.00: £1,127.00: £485.00: £217.50: £110.50) Stalls: High GOING minus 0.25 sec per fur (GF)

| | | | | SP | RR | SF |
|---|---|---|---|---|---|---|
| 2184* | **Groom's Gordon (FR)** (JLDunlop) **2-9-0** PatEddery(3) (lw: chsd ldr: rdn over 2f out: led ins fnl f: r.o wl) | — | **1** | 5/2[2] | 100 | 32 |
| 2073[5] | **Dalmeny Dancer** (BJMeehan) **2-8-10** BDoyle(6) (led: rdn over 2f out: hdd ins fnl f: unable qckn) | 1¾ | **2** | 8/1[3] | 92 | 24 |
| 2195* | **Maladerie (IRE)** (MRChannon) **2-9-0** RHughes(1) (a.p: rdn over 2f out: one pce) | 1½ | **3** | 8/1[3] | 93 | 25 |
| 2073[3] | **Belgravia** (PFICole) **2-9-0** TQuinn(5) (a.p: rdn over 2f out: sn wknd) | 2 | **4** | Evens[1] | 88 | 20 |
| 2132[7] | **Multitone** (JMPEustace) **2-8-10** WWoods(2) (plld hrd: nvr nr to chal) | nk | **5** | 33/1 | 83? | 15 |
| | **Lady Mail (IRE)** (JMPEustace) **2-8-5** MHills(4) (w'like: bit bkwd: s.s: a wl bhd) | 11 | **6** | 25/1 | 54 | — |

(SP 107.6%) **6 Rn**

**1m 32.71** (4.11) CSF £18.52 TOTE £3.50: £1.50 £2.10 (£14.20) OWNER Mrs H. Focke (ARUNDEL) BRED Haras d'Etreham

**2184* Groom's Gordon (FR)** raced in second place. Woken up over a quarter of a mile from home, he shot into the lead inside the final furlong for a decisive victory. He is certainly going the right way and can complete the hat-trick. (5/2)

**2073 Dalmeny Dancer** attempted to make all the running and brought the field over to the stands' rail in the straight in search of the better ground. Grimly trying to hold off the winner, he was eventually forced to concede defeat inside the final furlong. (8/1: op 9/2)

**2195* Maladerie (IRE)**, never far away, was rousted along over two furlongs from home, but failed to find the necessary turn of foot. (8/1)

**2073 Belgravia**, described by his trainer as 'a bit of a playboy', was never far away but, when asked for his effort over a quarter of a mile from home, tamely folded up. He does not look one to place a great deal of faith in. (Evens)

## 2504 SINO GROUP DRAGON TROPHY STKS (Listed) (2-Y.O) (Class A)

4-10 (4-27) **5f 6y** £11,987.00 (£3,626.00: £1,768.00: £839.00) Stalls: High GOING minus 0.25 sec per fur (GF)

| | | | | SP | RR | SF |
|---|---|---|---|---|---|---|
| 2112[2] | **Vax Star** (JLSpearing) **2-8-10** JWeaver(1) (lw: w ldr: led over 1f out: all out) | — | **1** | 9/4[1] | 89 | 59 |
| 1980* | **Compton Place** (JARToller) **2-9-1** SSanders(5) (lw: led over 3f: hrd rdn: r.o wl) | hd | **2** | 5/2[2] | 94 | 64 |
| 2051[9] | **Dancing Drop** (RHannon) **2-8-7** PatEddery(2) (hld up: rdn over 1f out: r.o) | ¾ | **3** | 9/4[1] | 83 | 53 |
| 2070[8] | **Granny's Pet** (PFICole) **2-9-3** TQuinn(3) (lw: hld up: rdn over 1f out: swtchd rt: unable qckn) | 1¼ | **4** | 5/1[3] | 89 | 59 |
| 1815[3] | **Bettynouche** (RHannon) **2-8-10** RHughes(4) (lw: hld up: rdn over 2f out: wknd wl over 1f out) | 8 | **5** | 25/1 | 57 | 27 |

(SP 110.6%) **5 Rn**

**60.65 secs** (0.85) CSF £7.83 TOTE £2.40: £1.10 £2.00 (£3.00) OWNER Vax Ltd (ALCESTER) BRED A. Brazier

**2112 Vax Star** raced with the leader and looked to have things nicely in hand as she edged her way to the front below the distance. However, she had met a real tartar in the runner-up and held on with not an ounce to spare. She certainly has the right attitude, and the ability to match. (9/4: 6/4-5/2)

**1980* Compton Place** ran a tremendous race and lost absolutely nothing in defeat. Bowling along in front, he was collared below the distance but, showing a tremendous attitude, gave his all, and failed by only a whisker. He is certainly up to landing a listed event. (5/2)
**1480 Dancing Drop**, nicely tucked in behind the front two, was asked for her effort below the distance but, despite running on, was unable to overhaul the front two. (9/4)
**1766* Granny's Pet**, nicely placed behind the front two, was asked for his effort below the distance, but failed to find the necessary foot. (5/1)

## 2505 SUN HUNG KAI SECURITIES MAIDEN STKS (3 & 4-Y.O) (Class D)

4-40 (4-55) **1m 6f** £3,582.50 (£1,085.00: £530.00: £252.50) Stalls: High GOING minus 0.25 sec per fur (GF)

| | | | | SP | RR | SF |
|---|---|---|---|---|---|---|
| 2054[7] | **Clerkenwell (USA) (91)** (MRStoute) **3-8-11** PatEddery(2) (lw: a.p: led on bit over 2f out: easily) | — | **1** | 8/11[1] | 81+ | 38 |
| 2314[2] | **Warning Reef (83)** (MRChannon) **3-8-11** RHughes(8) (lw: hdwy 6f out: ev ch over 2f out: hrd rdn over 1f out: unable qckn) | 6 | **2** | 9/2[2] | 74 | 31 |
| 1875[4] | **Belmarita (IRE) (73)** (MHTompkins) **3-8-6** PRobinson(10) (a.p: rdn over 2f out: one pce) | 2½ | **3** | 6/1[3] | 66 | 23 |
| *1997*[6] | **Rivercare (IRE) (61)** (MJPolglase) **3-8-11** JWeaver(5) (led tl over 2f out: sn wknd) | 4 | **4** | 33/1 | 67 | 24 |
| 1769[10] | **Shirley Venture (76)** (SPCWoods) **3-8-6** WWoods(4) (hld up: rdn over 3f out: sn wknd) | 4 | **5** | 13/2 | 57 | 14 |
| 811[10] | **Cypress Avenue (IRE) (74)** (RHannon) **4-9-9**(3) DaneO'Neill(6) (nvr nr to chal) | 16 | **6** | 33/1 | 44 | 16 |
| 2036[8] | **Melomania (USA)** (TJNaughton) **4-9-12** NAdams(7) (lw: sme hdwy 5f out: wknd) | 9 | **7** | 50/1 | 34 | 6 |
| 1147[10] | **Spread The Word (57)** (LGCottrell) **4-9-7** DHolland(1) (chsd ldr over 7f) | 3½ | **8** | 50/1 | 25 | — |
| 1963[5] | **Hever Golf Classic** (TJNaughton) **3-8-11** PaulEddery(9) (a bhd) | 15 | **9** | 20/1 | 12 | — |
| 2205[3] | **Anchor Venture (60)** (SPCWoods) **3-8-11** KFallon(11) (lw: sme hdwy 5f out: sn wknd) | 1¾ | **10** | 25/1 | 10 | — |
| | **Sliparis** (KOCunningham-Brown) **3-7-13**(7) CMunday(3) (sddle slipped s: a bhd) | 8 | **11** | 66/1 | — | — |
| | | | | (SP 123.6%) | **11 Rn** | |

**3m 5.57** (6.67) CSF £5.00 TOTE £1.80: £1.90 £1.70 £1.60 (£3.60) Trio £7.70 OWNER Sheikh Mohammed (NEWMARKET) BRED Camelot Thoroughbreds and Michael J. Ryan
WEIGHT FOR AGE 3yo-15lb
**IN-FOCUS: Take out the winner and second, and this was a very bad maiden by Sandown standards.**
**1712 Clerkenwell (USA)** proved to be in a different class to this rivals. Breezing into the lead on the bridle over two furlongs from home, he won with a ton in hand. (8/11)
**2314 Warning Reef** moved smoothly into contention at the end of the back straight. He appeared to be going just as well as the winner over a quarter of a mile from home, but he was soon under pressure and put in his place. (9/2: op 5/2)
**1875 Belmarita (IRE)** was made to look very pedestrian in the last two furlongs. (6/1)
**1655 Rivercare (IRE)** took the field along but, collared over two furlongs from home, had soon shot his bolt. (33/1)
**1189 Shirley Venture** chased the leaders, but was a spent force early in the straight. (13/2)

T/Jkpt: £4,107.90 (1.88 Tckts). T/Plpt: £124.10 (243.78 Tckts). T/Qdpt: £27.50 (69.81 Tckts). AK

# 2186-WARWICK (L-H) (Good to firm, Good last 8f)

## Friday July 5th

WEATHER: heavy showers WIND: almost nil

## 2506 ANIL KUMBLE MAIDEN H'CAP (0-65) (3-Y.O+) (Class F)

2-10 (2-22) **1m 2f 169y** £3,356.80 (£934.80: £450.40) Stalls: Low GOING minus 0.36 sec per fur (F)

| | | | | SP | RR | SF |
|---|---|---|---|---|---|---|
| 1689[12] | **Baranov (IRE) (55)** (DJGMurraySmith) **3-8-9** DHarrison(19) (hld up: led over 3f out: clr 2f out: r.o wl) | — | **1** | 25/1 | 72 | 27 |
| 2067[10] | **Jean Pierre (51)** (JPearce) **3-8-5**[ow1] NDay(8) (hdwy 3f out: chsd wnr fnl f: edgd lft: r.o: nt rch wnr) | 1½ | **2** | 12/1 | 66 | 20 |
| 2135[13] | **Full Throttle (60)** (MHTompkins) **3-9-0** PRobinson(14) (dwlt: hdwy 5f out: chsd wnr over 2f out tl wknd fnl f) | 9 | **3** | 5/1[1] | 61 | 16 |
| 2046[4] | **Victoria's Secret (IRE) (51)** (MRChannon) **4-8-12**(5) PPMurphy(9) (pushed along 7f out: hdwy on ins whn n.m.r over 1f out: one pce) | ¾ | **4** | 12/1 | 51 | 18 |
| *1809*[8] | **Taniyar (FR) (42)** (RHollinshead) **4-8-3**(5) DGriffiths(16) (hdwy 6f out: one pce fnl 2f) | 1¼ | **5** | 25/1 | 40 | 7 |
| 2048[5] | **Red Tie Affair (USA) (59)** (MBell) **3-8-13** MFenton(10) (b.nr fore: prom 8f) | 1 | **6** | 10/1 | 56 | 11 |
| 1839[11] | **Amber Ring (44)** (MissKMGeorge) **3-7-12** DeclanO'Shea(12) (nvr nrr) | hd | **7** | 40/1 | 41 | — |
| 1873[7] | **Vendetta (65)** (IABalding) **3-9-5** AMcGlone(7) (lw: prom tl wknd 2f out) | 1 | **8** | 12/1 | 60 | 15 |
| 2062[5] | **Sandicliffe (USA) (58)** (BWHills) **3-8-12** WRyan(6) (dwlt: hdwy whn c wd over 3f out: n.d after) | ½ | **9** | 12/1 | 53 | 8 |
| 1641[18] | **Needwood Epic (60)** (BCMorgan) **3-9-0** CHodgson(11) (hdwy 3f out: wknd wl over 1f out) | 1¾ | **10** | 33/1 | 52 | 7 |
| | **Clued Up (46)** (PDEvans) **3-8-0** DBiggs(5) (prom over 7f) | 5 | **11** | 40/1 | 31 | — |
| 2196[5] | **Tsarskaya (USA) (63)** (MrsJCecil) **3-9-3** TIves(1) (hdwy 8f out: wknd 3f out) | 6 | **12** | 10/1 | 39 | — |
| 2251[2] | **Tarian (USA) (49)** (GBBalding) **4-8-12**(3) SDrowne(15) (prom: rdn whn hmpd over 3f out: sn wknd) | 2½ | **13** | 11/2[2] | 21 | — |
| 1965[5] | **Rising Spray (49)** (CAHorgan) **5-8-10**(5) AmandaSanders(3) (a bhd) | 1½ | **14** | 10/1 | 19 | — |
| 2033[5] | **Nelly's Cousin (56)** (NACallaghan) **3-8-7**(3) PMcCabe(20) (lw: prom: led 6f out tl over 3f out: wknd 2f out) | ½ | **15** | 7/1[3] | 25 | — |
| 2124[7] | **Followthe Allstars (57)** (TJNaughton) **3-8-11** TSprake(17) (dwlt: a bhd) | 1¾ | **16** | 33/1 | 23 | — |
| 1506[3] | **Denomination (USA) (62)** (MCPipe) **4-10-0** DBridgwater(18) (prom 6f) | hd | **17** | 10/1 | 28 | — |
| 2163[8] | **Lagan (45)** (PSFelgate) **3-7-13** FNorton(2) (prom tl wknd qckly over 2f out) | s.h | **18** | 33/1 | 11 | — |
| 1894[8] | **Morning Sir (56)** (CRBarwell) **3-8-10** DRMcCabe(4) (led over 4f: wknd qckly: t.o) | 30 | **19** | 33/1 | — | — |
| | | | | (SP 136.0%) | **19 Rn** | |

**2m 18.5** (5.00) CSF £291.05 CT £1,622.14 TOTE £35.70: £4.40 £3.50 £1.60 £3.10 (£488.60) Trio £272.10; £314.29 to Sandown 6/7/96 OWNER Mrs Susan Nash (LAMBOURN) BRED Shadwell Estate Company Limited
WEIGHT FOR AGE 3yo-12lb
**Baranov (IRE)**, who has been running over seven, showed considerable improvement over this longer trip. (25/1)
**Jean Pierre**, dropped 13lb this season, came away from the others but could not catch the winner. (12/1)
**Full Throttle** may have found this trip just beyond him. (5/1: op 14/1)
**2046 Victoria's Secret (IRE)**, still without the headgear, had been dropped 4lb and should not be considered unlucky. (12/1)
**Taniyar (FR)** was reverting to a longer trip for this first run on grass. (25/1)
**2048 Red Tie Affair (USA)** could well be more effective at shorter distances. (10/1)

## 2507 SANJAY MANJREKAR (S) H'CAP (0-60) (3-Y.O+) (Class G)

2-40 (2-51) **1m** £2,070.00 (£570.00: £270.00) Stalls: Low GOING minus 0.36 sec per fur (F)

| | | | | SP | RR | SF |
|---|---|---|---|---|---|---|
| 2192[12] | **Orchard Gold (42)** (JPearce) **5-9-0** GBardwell(10) (s.s: hdwy 4f out: led over 1f out: edgd lft: drvn out) | — | **1** | 25/1 | 55 | 36 |

| Form | Horse / Details | Dist | Pos | SP | RR | SF |
|---|---|---|---|---|---|---|
| $1992^{2}$ | **Thatchmaster (IRE) (46)** (CAHorgan) **5-9-4** DHarrison(11) (a.p: rdn to ld 2f out: edgd rt & hdd over 1f out: one pce) | 2 | **2** | 6/1 $^{1}$ | 55 | 36 |
| $2180^{3}$ | **Born A Lady (49)** (SRBowring) **3-8-9b**$^{(3)}$ CTeague(14) (led 6f: one pce fnl f) | ½ | **3** | 8/1 $^{3}$ | 57 | 29 |
| $1665^{12}$ | **Elite Racing (38)** (NTinkler) **4-8-10** CRutter(9) (prom: rdn & outpcd 3f out: styd on fnl 2f) | 1½ | **4** | 12/1 | 43 | 24 |
| $2180^{2}$ | **Lila Pedigo (IRE) (51)** (MissJFCraze) **3-9-0** NConnorton(15) (rdn 4f out: hdwy fnl 2f: nt rch ldrs) | nk | **5** | 15/2 $^{2}$ | 55 | 27 |
| $2075^{6}$ | **Buddy's Friend (IRE) (40)** (RJRWilliams) **8-8-5**$^{(7)}$ AimeeCook(16) (nvr nr to chal) | 6 | **6** | 10/1 | 32 | 13 |
| $2179^{6}$ | **Dil Dil (54)** (WJHaggas) **3-8-10**$^{(7)}$ CWebb(13) (no hdwy fnl 2f) | 1 | **7** | 16/1 | 44 | 16 |
| $2185^{12}$ | **Bella Coola (38)** (MartynMeade) **4-8-5**$^{(5)}$ RHavlin(12) (lw: prom tl rdn & wknd over 2f out) | 4 | **8** | 25/1 | 20 | 1 |
| $1979^{9}$ | **Burnt Sienna (IRE) (36)** (JSMoore) **4-8-8** DeclanO'Shea(17) (nvr nrr) | 2½ | **9** | 20/1 | 13 | — |
| $2075^{15}$ | **Prince Rudolf (IRE) (48)** (WGMTurner) **4-9-1v**$^{(5)}$ AmandaSanders(18) (n.d) | nk | **10** | 33/1 | 25 | 6 |
| $2075^{7}$ | **Chief's Lady (37)** (JMBradley) **4-8-9** WRyan(7) (s.s: nvr nr ldrs) | 2½ | **11** | 16/1 | 9 | — |
| $2373^{6}$ | **Balpare (50)** (NACallaghan) **3-8-13** DRMcCabe(8) (a bhd) | s.h | **12** | 14/1 | 22 | — |
| $2373^{*}$ | **Total Rach (IRE) (50)** (RIngram) **4-9-8b** $^{5x}$ AMcGlone(4) (hdwy 5f out: rdn & wknd 2f out) | nk | **13** | 15/2 $^{2}$ | 21 | 2 |
| $2313^{10}$ | **Doodies Pool (IRE) (40)** (PBurgoyne) **6-8-9v**$^{(3)}$ PMcCabe(2) (lw: s.s: a bhd) | 5 | **14** | 25/1 | 1 | — |
| *$2303^{11}$* | **Causley (45)** (DMHyde) **11-8-10**$^{(7)}$ RBrisland(3) (rdn 3f out: a bhd) | 1 | **15** | 33/1 | 4 | — |
| $2344^{9}$ | **Tony's Mist (43)** (JMBradley) **6-8-12**$^{(3)}$ SDrowne(6) (lw: prom over 4f) | ½ | **16** | 11/1 | 1 | — |
| $2180^{4}$ | **Tallulah Belle (45)** (NPLittmoden) **3-8-3**$^{(5)}$ ADaly(5) (prom 5f: t.o) | 14 | **17** | 10/1 | — | — |
| $2380^{3}$ | **Home Cookin' (57)** (MCPipe) **3-9-3**$^{(3)}$ MHenry(19) (bhd fnl 4f: t.o) | 2½ | **18** | 9/1 | — | — |
| $1992^{14}$ | **Rockville Pike (IRE) (52)** (JohnBerry) **4-9-10v** DBiggs(1) (prom 5f: t.o) | 8 | **19** | 16/1 | — | — |

(SP 139.6%) **19 Rn**

**1m 39.5** (3.10) CSF £172.47 CT £1,247.22 TOTE £73.90: £10.20 £1.60 £2.80 £3.50 (£245.00) Trio Not won; £290.38 to Sandown 6/7/96
OWNER Mr S. G. Pitt (NEWMARKET) BRED The Sussex Stud
WEIGHT FOR AGE 3yo-9lb
No bid
**Orchard Gold** appreciated this drop back to a mile on a left-handed course. (25/1)
**1992 Thatchmaster (IRE)** was 1lb higher than at Lingfield and again met one too good. (6/1)
**2180 Born A Lady**, 2lb lower than last time, was due to go back up in future handicaps. (8/1)
**1311* Elite Racing** had disappointed when tried in blinkers on his latest outing. (12/1)
**2180 Lila Pedigo (IRE)** gives the impression she might stay further. (15/2)
**2075 Buddy's Friend (IRE)** has dropped 15lb in the Ratings this season. (10/1)
**2180 Tallulah Belle** (10/1: 8/1-12/1)

## 2508 EAGLE STAR ENGINEERING H'CAP (0-80) (3-Y.O+) (Class D)

3-15 (3-18) **5f** £3,562.35 (£1,060.80: £504.90: £226.95) Stalls: Low GOING minus 0.36 sec per fur (F)

| Form | Horse / Details | Dist | Pos | SP | RR | SF |
|---|---|---|---|---|---|---|
| $2005^{4}$ | **Chadwell Hall (67)** (SRBowring) **5-8-12b**$^{(3)}$ CTeague(2) (mde virtually all: c centre: all out) | — | **1** | 5/1 $^{3}$ | 74 | 52 |
| $2349^{5}$ | **Shadow Jury (60)** (DWChapman) **6-8-8b** DRMcCabe(1) (lw: a.p: styd alone far side 2f out: ev ch fnl f: r.o) | s.h | **2** | 6/1 | 67 | 45 |
| $1708^{3}$ | **Palacegate Jack (IRE) (80)** (JBerry) **5-9-9**$^{(5)}$ PRoberts(7) (w wnr: c centre & rdn 2f out: ev ch 1f out: unable qckn) | 1½ | **3** | 9/2 $^{2}$ | 82 | 60 |
| $2137^{7}$ | **High Domain (IRE) (73)** (JLSpearing) **5-9-4**$^{(3)}$ SDrowne(3) (bhd: c stands' side: hdwy over 1f out: r.o ins fnl f) | 1¼ | **4** | 5/1 $^{3}$ | 71 | 49 |
| $2232^{2}$ | **Tart and a Half (78)** (BJMeehan) **4-9-5b**$^{(7)}$ DSweeney(4) (lw: prom: c stands' side 2f out: wknd over 1f out) | 1¼ | **5** | 7/2 $^{1}$ | 72 | 50 |
| $744^{4}$ | **Fantasy Racing (IRE) (78)** (MRChannon) **4-9-7**$^{(5)}$ PPMurphy(5) (rdn over 3f out: c stands' side: nvr trbld ldrs) | 1¾ | **6** | 8/1 | 66 | 44 |
| $2017^{3}$ | **Bashful Brave (72)** (JWPayne) **5-9-6** AMcGlone(6) (lw: chsd ldrs: c stands' side: wknd over 1f out) | ½ | **7** | 5/1 $^{3}$ | 59 | 37 |

(SP 115.8%) **7 Rn**

**58.9 secs** (0.90) CSF £31.92 TOTE £7.60: £1.90 £2.90 (£36.00) OWNER Mr D. H. Bowring (EDWINSTOWE) BRED J. C. and Mrs C. L. Owen
**2005 Chadwell Hall**, up 2lb for his good fourth over six at York, was 7lb higher than when winning at Ripon. (5/1)
**2349 Shadow Jury**, from a stable in fine form, is knocking at the door. (6/1)
**1708 Palacegate Jack (IRE)** could not raise his game from the furlong pole. (9/2)
**1853 High Domain (IRE)**, reverting to the minimum trip, was unable to dominate from the front. (5/1)
**2232 Tart and a Half** was not helped by the heavy rain before racing. (7/2)
**744 Fantasy Racing (IRE)** (8/1: 5/1-9/1)

## 2509 PYMENTS CLAIMING STKS (2-Y.O) (Class F)

3-45 (3-47) **7f** £2,690.40 (£744.40: £355.20) Stalls: Low GOING minus 0.36 sec per fur (F)

| Form | Horse / Details | Dist | Pos | SP | RR | SF |
|---|---|---|---|---|---|---|
| *$1813^{5}$* | **Ginny Wossername** (WGMTurner) **2-8-2b$^{1}$** TSprake(4) (prom: led 4f out: rdn over 1f out: r.o) | — | **1** | 11/4 $^{2}$ | 47 | 1 |
| $1904^{*}$ | **Irish Fiction (IRE)** (DJSCosgrove) **2-9-2**$^{(3)}$ PMcCabe(3) (s.s: hdwy 3f out: ev ch 1f out: unable qckn) | ½ | **2** | 11/4 $^{2}$ | 63 | 17 |
| *$2307^{3}$* | **Abstone Queen** (PDEvans) **2-8-0** DBiggs(6) (prom: ev ch whn rn wd bnd over 2f out: rdn over 1f out: one pce) | 2½ | **3** | 10/1 | 38 | — |
| $1980^{5}$ | **Dashing Rocksville** (MRChannon) **2-8-7**$^{(5)}$ PPMurphy(5) (led 3f: hrd rdn 2f out: one pce) | s.h | **4** | 5/2 $^{1}$ | 50 | 4 |
| $1980^{6}$ | **Folly Foot Fred** (BRMillman) **2-8-12**$^{(3)}$ SDrowne(7) (lw: w ldrs: rdn & wknd over 3f out) | 5 | **5** | 9/1 $^{3}$ | 42 | — |
| *$2172^{6}$* | **Moor Hall Princess** (KRBurke) **2-8-2** DRMcCabe(1) (a bhd) | 7 | **6** | 20/1 | 13 | — |
| $2031^{9}$ | **Classic Services** (BPalling) **2-8-2**$^{(3)}$ MHenry(2) (b: chsd ldrs tl rdn & wknd over 2f out) | 3 | **7** | 25/1 | 9 | — |

(SP 109.6%) **7 Rn**

**1m 29.5** (4.90) CSF £9.90 TOTE £4.10: £2.30 £2.50 (£4.50) OWNER Mr R. A. Cary (SHERBORNE) BRED G. Corbett
**1494 Ginny Wossername**, a half-sister to Goodbye Millie, did not act on the Sand last time and appreciated this extra furlong. (11/4)
**1904* Irish Fiction (IRE)**, having lost ground at the start, could not dictate from the front this time and lost nothing in defeat in trying to concede so much weight to the winner. (11/4: 9/4-7/2)
**2307 Abstone Queen** did not handle the home turn at all well. (10/1)
**1980 Dashing Rocksville** was back to a more suitable trip. (5/2)

## 2510 SACHIN TENDULKAR MAIDEN STKS (3-Y.O+) (Class D)

4-20 (4-21) **1m** £4,391.10 (£1,315.80: £632.40: £290.70) Stalls: Low GOING minus 0.36 sec per fur (F)

| Form | Horse / Details | Dist | Pos | SP | RR | SF |
|---|---|---|---|---|---|---|
| $2004^{2}$ | **Go Britannia** (DRLoder) **3-8-12** DRMcCabe(4) (a.p: led 3f out: comf) | — | **1** | 5/6 $^{1}$ | 86+ | 46 |
| $1901^{5}$ | **Melt The Clouds (CAN) (80)** (PWHarris) **3-8-12** FNorton(8) (plld hrd: a.p: rdn over 2f out: r.o ins fnl f: nt trble wnr) | 5 | **2** | 4/1 $^{2}$ | 76 | 36 |

| | | | | | | |
|---|---|---|---|---|---|---|
| 2080[6] | **Accondy (IRE)** (CEBrittain) **4-9-4**(3) MHenry(11) (lw: hdwy over 4f out: chsd wnr over 2f out: rdn & edgd rt over 1f out: no imp) | nk | **3** | 5/1[3] | 75 | 44 |
| | **Alfredo Alfredo (USA)** (JLDunlop) **4-9-7** TSprake(5) (lengthy: b: s.s: hld up & wl bhd: stdy hdwy fnl 2f: nvr plcd to chal) | 4 | **4** | 8/1 | 67 | 36 |
| 1855[6] | **Wolf Cleugh (IRE)** (AHide) **3-8-7** AMcGlone(12) (prom: no hdwy fnl 3f) | nk | **5** | 16/1 | 62 | 22 |
| 2011[6] | **Memphis Beau (IRE)** (JARToller) **3-8-12b[1]** DHarrison(9) (led 5f: wknd over 1f out) | 3½ | **6** | 33/1 | 60 | 20 |
| 2198[5] | **Soldier's Song** (RJHodges) **3-8-2**(5) PPMurphy(7) (a bhd) | 14 | **7** | 25/1 | 27 | — |
| | **Tashkent** (MissKMGeorge) **4-9-7** TIves(3) (leggy: unf: prom tl wknd 2f out) | ¾ | **8** | 50/1 | 30 | — |
| 2194[8] | **Red Viper** (NMLampard) **4-9-0**(7) RBrisland(1) (prom 4f) | 8 | **9** | 50/1 | 14 | — |
| 1434[14] | **Kulshi Momken** (RTPhillips) **3-8-12b[1]** CRutter(6) (prom tl wknd qckly 4f out) | 3½ | **10** | 50/1 | 7 | — |
| | **Time Goes On** (RJHodges) **4-8-13**(3) NVarley(2) (w'like: bit bkwd: s.s: a bhd: t.o) | 18 | **11** | 33/1 | — | — |

(SP 123.8%) **11 Rn**

**1m 38.3** (1.90) CSF £5.09 TOTE £1.90: £1.20 £1.40 £1.50 (£4.30) Trio £5.70 OWNER Mr Wafic Said (NEWMARKET) BRED Cheveley Park Stud Ltd

WEIGHT FOR AGE 3yo-9lb

**2004 Go Britannia**, reverting to a mile, proved too sharp for his rivals, and should go on from here. (5/6)
**1901 Melt The Clouds (CAN)** proved a handful to settle, but seemed suited to this return to a mile. (4/1)
**2080 Accondy (IRE)**, reverting to a more suitable trip, tried to make a race of it, but all to no avail. (5/1)
**Alfredo Alfredo (USA)** caught the eye running on nicely in the latter stages. Out of an unraced daughter of Alleged, he is likely to benefit from a stiffer test of stamina. (8/1: 9/4-9/1)
**1855 Wolf Cleugh (IRE)**, now qualified for handicaps, is still worth a try over further. (16/1)
**2011 Memphis Beau (IRE)** did the donkey work in the first-time blinkers. (33/1)

## 2511 MOHAMMAD AZHARUDDIN H'CAP (0-70) (3-Y.O+) (Class E)

4-50 (4-52) **1m 6f 194y** £3,452.40 (£1,033.20: £495.60: £226.80) Stalls: Low GOING minus 0.36 sec per fur (F)

| | | | | SP | RR | SF |
|---|---|---|---|---|---|---|
| 2191[5] | **Mr Speculator (56)** (PAKelleway) **3-8-6v[1]** GBardwell(1) (a.p: pushed along 9f out: led over 3f out: r.o wl) | — | **1** | 16/1 | 66 | 31 |
| 1984* | **Labeed (USA) (69)** (MajorWRHern) **3-9-5** RHills(5) (lw: a.p: rdn & ev ch whn edgd lft over 1f out: one pce) | 3 | **2** | 11/4[1] | 76 | 41 |
| 2042[20] | **Coleridge (54)** (JJSheehan) **8-9-7b** AMorris(4) (hld up: hdwy 7f out: outpcd 3f out: styd on fnl f) | 2½ | **3** | 6/1[3] | 58 | 40 |
| 1124[5] | **Blanchland (43)** (PCRitchens) **7-8-10** DHarrison(2) (hld up: hdwy 7f out: rdn 3f out: one pce) | 3 | **4** | 14/1 | 44 | 26 |
| 2042[16] | **Hever Golf Lady (57)** (TJNaughton) **4-9-10** TSprake(8) (hld up: hdwy 6f out: wknd 5f out) | 2 | **5** | 15/2 | 56 | 38 |
| 2239[3] | **Royal Circus (40)** (PRWebber) **7-8-4**(3) SDrowne(6) (led: hdd over 3f out: wknd over 2f out) | 3½ | **6** | 5/1[2] | 35 | 17 |
| 1874[14] | **Dashing Invader (USA) (46)** (PWHarris) **3-7-10** FNorton(7) (plld hrd: prom over 9f) | 12 | **7** | 20/1 | 28 | — |
| 1454[7] | **Hatta River (USA) (40)** (PTDalton) **6-8-7** DRMcCabe(10) (hld up & bhd: hdwy on ins 7f out: wknd 3f out) | 1 | **8** | 25/1 | 21 | 3 |
| 1877[4] | **Uoni (54)** (CEBrittain) **3-8-1**(3) MHenry(3) (sme hdwy 8f out: wknd 6f out) | 3 | **9** | 6/1[3] | 32 | — |
| 1826[7] | **Persian Smoke (42)** (AHide) **5-8-4**(5) RHavlin(11) (lw: s.s: hdwy 8f out: wknd over 6f out) | 2½ | **10** | 8/1 | 17 | — |
| 2360[5] | **Paronomasia (29)** (JLHarris) **4-7-7b**(3) NVarley(9) (lw: prom 8f) | 3½ | **11** | 33/1 | — | — |

(SP 118.9%) **11 Rn**

**3m 16.0** (6.00) CSF £57.19 CT £280.00 TOTE £20.60: £2.90 £1.90 £2.30 (£22.30) Trio £84.40 OWNER The Speculators (NEWMARKET) BRED Fittocks Stud

LONG HANDICAP Dashing Invader (USA) 7-9 Paronomasia 7-8
WEIGHT FOR AGE 3yo-17lb

**2191 Mr Speculator**, sharpened up by the visor, was stepping up even further in distance and showed stamina is not a problem. (16/1)
**1984* Labeed (USA)**, trying an even longer trip, was fighting a losing battle after being inclined to hang into the winner. (11/4)
**1063* Coleridge** was 7lb higher than when winning at Bath in May. (6/1)
**1124 Blanchland** was trying his luck over a longer trip. (14/1)
**1816 Hever Golf Lady** was 10lb lower in the Ratings than when she last ran on the All-Weather. (15/2: 5/1-8/1)
**1150 Persian Smoke** (8/1: 6/1-9/1)

T/Plpt: £386.60 (22.86 Tckts). T/Qdpt: £17.40 (33.01 Tckts). KH

# 2481-BEVERLEY (R-H) (Good to firm)

## Saturday July 6th

WEATHER: changeable WIND: fresh half against

## 2512 PAUL TEAGUE AND DONNA LARSEN (S) STKS (2-Y.O) (Class F)

2-05 (2-06) **7f 100y** £2,700.00 (£750.00: £360.00) Stalls: High GOING minus 0.51 sec per fur (F)

| | | | | SP | RR | SF |
|---|---|---|---|---|---|---|
| *1720*[3] | **Rons Revenge** (MJRyan) **2-8-11** GBardwell(5) (mde virtually all: rdn over 2f out: jst hld on) | — | **1** | 12/1 | 59 | 11 |
| 2161[3] | **Clonavon Girl (IRE)** (MJCamacho) **2-8-6** ACulhane(9) (a in tch: styd on wl ins fnl f) | nk | **2** | 5/1[3] | 53 | 5 |
| 2224[11] | **Silca's My Key (IRE)** (MRChannon) **2-8-11** JStack(7) (chsd ldrs: rdn & outpcd 2f out: swtchd & styd on ins fnl f) | 1 | **3** | 6/1 | 56 | 8 |
| 1183[5] | **Petrine Gray** (TDEasterby) **2-8-6** MBirch(2) (trckd ldrs: kpt on same pce fnl f) | hd | **4** | 4/1[2] | 51 | 3 |
| *1720*[2] | **Impala** (WGMTurner) **2-8-6**(5) RHavlin(1) (chsd wnr: rdn & hung rt over 2f out: wknd ins fnl f) | 1¼ | **5** | 9/4[1] | 53 | 5 |
| 2161[11] | **Madam Lucy** (WWHaigh) **2-8-6** DeanMcKeown(6) (sn outpcd & bhd: styd on fnl 2f) | nk | **6** | 25/1 | 48 | — |
| | **Dulas Bay** (MWEasterby) **2-8-6**(5) GParkin(11) (rangy: unf: bit bkwd: s.s: bhd & pushed along: styd on appr fnl f) | ½ | **7** | 10/1 | 52 | 4 |
| *2083*[7] | **Super Scravels** (DrJDScargill) **2-8-6** MFenton(3) (s.i.s: sme hdwy over 2f out: nvr nr ldrs) | nk | **8** | 20/1 | 46 | — |
| 2295[7] | **Kingdom Emperor** (MJCamacho) **2-8-11** LCharnock(4) (trckd ldrs: effrt 2f out: hung rt: sn wknd) | 1½ | **9** | 11/2 | 48 | — |
| 1197[12] | **Foolish Flutter (IRE)** (GROldroyd) **2-8-6** DaleGibson(12) (hld up: effrt over 3f out: sn rdn & wknd) | 2½ | **10** | 25/1 | 37 | — |
| | **Sendmetomary** (TDEasterby) **2-8-6** JLowe(10) (cmpt: bit bkwd: s.s: a bhd & sn drvn along) | 4 | **11** | 16/1 | 29 | — |

(SP 132.2%) **11 Rn**

**1m 36.1** (4.10) CSF £73.83 TOTE £11.20: £3.40 £1.90 £2.10 (£34.70) Trio £54.10 OWNER Mr A. S. Reid (NEWMARKET) BRED A. S. Reid

No bid

**1463 Rons Revenge**, well beaten by the favourite last time, turned the tables in decisive fashion, making all the running and just lasting home. (12/1)
**2161 Clonavon Girl (IRE)** only really found her stride inside the last. She needs a mile already. (5/1)

**Silca's My Key (IRE)**, who looked to be carrying plenty of condition, was dropped in class after showing little on his debut. Tapped for foot halfway up the straight, he ran out of room inside the last 200 yards and had to be switched. Staying on when it was all over, he can improve and win a similar event. (6/1)
**1183 Petrine Gray**, stepping up in distance, had every chance. (4/1)
**1720 Impala** chased the winner but wanted to do nothing but hang in behind him, and his stride shortened inside the last. (9/4: op 7/2)
**Madam Lucy**, whose dam stayed all day, was putting in her best work at the finish. (25/1)
**Dulas Bay**, a tall, unfurnished newcomer, showed ability after a slow start and running green. (10/1)

## 2513 HULL MITSUBISHI CENTRE LADIES' H'CAP (0-70) (4-Y.O+) (Class F)
2-35 (2-35) **1m 1f 207y** £2,693.00 (£748.00: £359.00) Stalls: High GOING minus 0.51 sec per fur (F)

| | | | | SP | RR | SF |
|---|---|---|---|---|---|---|
| 1418[8] | **Darling Clover (60)** (DMorley) **4-11-5** MissDianaJones(1) (chsd ldrs: rdn to ld over 1f out: styd on wl) | — | 1 | 7/4[1] | 71 | 45 |
| 2342[4] | **Set the Fashion (53)** (DLWilliams) **7-10-8v**(4) MissSHiggins(8) (chsd ldrs: effrt on outside over 3f out: edgd rt & styd on same pce fnl f) | 3½ | 2 | 3/1[2] | 58 | 32 |
| 2159* | **Sporting Risk (48)** (PWHarris) **4-10-7** MissAElsey(2) (led tl over 1f out: one pce) | 2 | 3 | 100/30[3] | 50 | 24 |
| *1966*[8] | **Public Way (IRE) (43)** (NChamberlain) **6-9-12**(4) MissCMetcalfe(9) (s.i.s: bhd: hdwy on outside over 2f out: styd on one pce fnl f) | hd | 4 | 14/1 | 45 | 19 |
| 2008[11] | **Cante Chico (62)** (OBrennan) **4-11-3**(4) MissMCarson(3) (trckd ldrs: ev ch over 3f out: sn wknd) | ¾ | 5 | 7/1 | 63 | 37 |
| 2348[6] | **Intrepid Fort (30)** (BWMurray) **7-8-10b**(7) MrsCWilliams(5) (hld up & plld hrd: styd on fnl 2f: nvr nr ldrs) | ½ | 6 | 25/1 | 30 | 4 |
| 2348[5] | **Glenvally (28)** (BWMurray) **5-9-1v** MissPRobson(7) (effrt & hung rt over 2f out: n.d) | ½ | 7 | 14/1 | 27 | 1 |
| 1979[8] | **Nord Lys (IRE) (30)** (BJLlewellyn) **5-8-13**(4)ow3 MissEJJones(4) (chsd ldrs: ev ch over 3f out: wknd over 2f out) | 2½ | 8 | 20/1 | 25 | — |

(SP 118.9%) **8 Rn**

**2m 7.8** (5.30) CSF £7.58 CT £14.57 TOTE £2.40: £1.30 £1.30 £1.30 (£5.20) Trio £3.20 OWNER Mr K. Craddock (NEWMARKET) BRED Astalon Ltd
LONG HANDICAP Nord Lys (IRE) 8-9
**1072 Darling Clover**, on good terms with herself after a forty-three day break, was given a fine ride and scored decisively. (7/4)
**2342 Set the Fashion**, with the visor back on, gave away ground coming wide off the turn. Tending to edge right under pressure, he was never going to trouble the winner. (3/1)
**2159* Sporting Risk** raced keenly in front. Wandering off a straight line, he could do no more in the final furlong and a half. (100/30)
**1763 Public Way (IRE)**, who sat off the pace, was staying on when it was all over. (14/1)

## 2514 B.B.C. RADIO HUMBERSIDE H'CAP (0-85) (3-Y.O) (Class D)
3-05 (3-06) **1m 100y** £3,814.50 (£1,146.00: £553.00: £256.50) Stalls: High GOING minus 0.51 sec per fur (F)

| | | | | SP | RR | SF |
|---|---|---|---|---|---|---|
| *2201*[2] | **Give Me A Ring (IRE) (70)** (CWThornton) **3-8-13** DeanMcKeown(5) (mde virtually all: styd on u.p fnl 2f) | — | 1 | 8/1 | 76 | 42 |
| 2188[6] | **Eric's Bett (63)** (FMurphy) **3-8-6b[1]** JTate(10) (hld up: smooth hdwy over 3f out: ev ch over 1f out: wandered: kpt on same pce) | 1½ | 2 | 12/1 | 66 | 32 |
| 2293[6] | **Smarter Charter (68)** (MrsJRRamsden) **3-8-11** MFenton(4) (s.i.s: bhd: hdwy over 2f out: r.o wl fnl f: too much to do) | s.h | 3 | 4/1[3] | 71 | 37 |
| 2065[4] | **Kazimiera (IRE) (72)** (CWCElsey) **3-8-8**(7) GMilligan(1) (swvd lft s: hdwy 4f out: hung rt over 1f out: nvr rchd ldrs) | 4 | 4 | 8/1 | 68 | 34 |
| 2065[5] | **Russian Rascal (IRE) (67)** (TDEasterby) **3-8-10** LCharnock(8) (trckd ldrs: rdn over 2f out: wknd over 1f out) | 3 | 5 | 12/1 | 57 | 23 |
| 2061[2] | **Tissue of Lies (USA) (70)** (MJohnston) **3-8-13** TWilliams(3) (sn chsng ldrs: wknd 2f out) | 1 | 6 | 5/1 | 58 | 24 |
| 2299[4] | **Albaha (USA) (78)** (RWArmstrong) **3-9-7** WRyan(2) (hld up: lost pl 4f out: hdwy over 2f out: nvr nr to chal) | 1½ | 7 | 7/2[2] | 63 | 29 |
| 2079[4] | **Dispol Diamond (74)** (GROldroyd) **3-9-3** JStack(7) (sn chsng ldrs: rdn & lost pl over 2f out) | 7 | 8 | 16/1 | 46 | 12 |
| *1969** | **Mercury (IRE) (72)** (JAGlover) **3-9-1** MBirch(6) (w ldrs: rdn along over 3f out: wknd qckly over 1f out) | 5 | 9 | 100/30[1] | 34 | — |
| 1798[7] | **Misky Bay (75)** (JHMGosden) **3-9-4** DaleGibson(9) (lw: sn bhd & drvn along: hrd rdn over 3f out: no rspnse) | 17 | 10 | 9/1 | 5 | — |

(SP 135.5%) **10 Rn**

**1m 45.4** (1.40) CSF £99.43 CT £428.23 TOTE £9.70: £2.60 £1.90 £2.00 (£72.50) Trio £183.20 OWNER Mr Guy Reed (MIDDLEHAM) BRED W. Maxwell Ervine
**2201 Give Me A Ring (IRE)**, much happier on grass, showed the right sort of spirit to hang on. (8/1)
**2188 Eric's Bett**, tried in blinkers, wandered under pressure and was never really giving his all. (12/1)
**2293 Smarter Charter** looked much better in the paddock this time. After missing the break, his rider was happy to sit off the pace. Making great strides in the final furlong, he had been set an impossible task. (4/1)
**2065 Kazimiera (IRE)**, who ducked left at the start, hung right under pressure at the business end. (8/1)
**2065 Russian Rascal (IRE)**, who looked on the light side, raced keenly and did not find much under pressure. (12/1: op 8/1)
**1969* Mercury (IRE)** still carried plenty of condition. Racing upsides but showing signs of inexperience, he dropped right out over a furlong out. Even allowing for the change of surface, he can surely do better than this. (100/30)

## 2515 MILLERS MILE MAIDEN STKS (3-Y.O+) (Class D)
3-35 (3-35) **1m 100y** £3,918.50 (£1,178.00: £569.00: £264.50) Stalls: High GOING minus 0.51 sec per fur (F)

| | | | | SP | RR | SF |
|---|---|---|---|---|---|---|
| 550[2] | **Papaha (FR) (100)** (HRACecil) **3-8-7** WRyan(6) (mde all: clr 5f out: easily) | — | 1 | 1/16[1] | 51+ | 2 |
| | **With The Tempo (IRE)** (DrJDScargill) **3-8-7** MFenton(1) (cmpt: trckd ldrs: one pce fnl 2f: fin 3rd,1 3/4l: plcd 2nd) | | 2 | 16/1[3] | 38 | — |
| 2136[4] | **Toulston Lady (IRE)** (MJCamacho) **4-9-2** LCharnock(4) (bit bkwd: hld up: effrt & bmpd 2f out: kpt on one pce: fin 4th, 1½l: plcd 3rd) | | 3 | 12/1[2] | 35 | — |
| | **Isit Izzy** (BAMcMahon) **4-8-9**(7) KYu(2) (unf: edgd lft & hdwy 2f out: styd on ins fnl f: no ch w wnr: fin 2nd, 5l: disq: plcd 4th) | | 4 | 25/1 | 42 | 2 |
| 1864[6] | **Shalta Chief (46)** (EHOwenjun) **4-9-2**(5) RHavlin(5) (chsd wnr tl wknd over 1f out) | ½ | 5 | 66/1 | 39 | — |
| | **Petit Flora** (GHolmes) **4-9-2** DeanMcKeown(3) (b.hind: dwlt: a bhd) | 7 | 6 | 25/1 | 21? | — |

(SP 116.9%) **6 Rn**

**1m 49.2** (5.20) CSF £3.42 TOTE £1.10: £1.00 £5.80 (£3.00) OWNER Mr T. F. Harris (NEWMARKET) BRED Robert-James McCreery
WEIGHT FOR AGE 3yo-9lb
STEWARDS' ENQUIRY Yu susp. 15-18/7/96 (irresponsible riding).
**550 Papaha (FR)**, who lacks substance, turns both her fore-feet out. She had a simple task here and had only to gallop round. (1/16: op 1/10)
**With The Tempo (IRE)**, a close-coupled newcomer, raced keenly. (16/1)

**2136 Toulston Lady (IRE)** still looked on the big side. Bumped by the runner-up when trying to improve two furlongs out, she could only keep on in her own time. (12/1)
**Isit Izzy** got into a bumping match with the fourth when trying to improve two furlongs out. She stayed on inside the last 200 yards, but the winner was in a totally different gear. Her Hong Kong-based apprentice was found guilty of irresponsible riding and stood down for four days. (25/1)

## 2516 PETER ADAMSON H'CAP (0-70) (3-Y.O+) (Class E)

4-05 (4-05) **2m 35y** £3,036.25 (£910.00: £437.50: £201.25) Stalls: High GOING minus 0.51 sec per fur (F)

| Form | Runner | Dist | Pos | SP | RR | SF |
|---|---|---|---|---|---|---|
| 2148$^{3}$ | **French Ivy (USA) (57)** (FMurphy) **9-9-10** TWilliams(5) (b: hld up: smooth hdwy over 3f out: led on ins over 1f out: sn qcknd clr) | — | 1 | 13/8$^{1}$ | 67 | 24 |
| 2165$^{5}$ | **Hullbank (55)** (WWHaigh) **6-9-8** JTate(1) (b: chsd ldrs: ev ch over 1f out: nt pce of wnr) | 3 | 2 | 4/1$^{2}$ | 62 | 19 |
| 2060$^{3}$ | **Atherton Green (IRE) (52)** (JAGlover) **6-9-5** MBirch(6) (led to 9f out: one pce fnl 2f) | 1 | 3 | 13/2 | 58 | 15 |
| 852$^{9}$ | **Hit the Canvas (USA) (61)** (MrsMReveley) **5-10-0** ACulhane(4) (chsd ldrs: pushed along 8f out: kpt on fnl 2f) | ¾ | 4 | 8/1 | 66 | 23 |
| 2028$^{4}$ | **Izza (46)** (WStorey) **5-8-6**$^{(7)}$ IonaWands(7) (hld up: hdwy to ld over 3f out: edgd lft: hdd & wknd over 1f out) | 1½ | 5 | 5/1$^{3}$ | 50 | 7 |
| 2175* | **Sarasota Storm (49)** (MBell) **4-9-2** MFenton(3) (hld up: hdwy on outside over 2f out: sn wknd) | 4 | 6 | 5/1$^{3}$ | 49 | 6 |
| *2372*$^{5}$ | **Top Prize (36)** (MBrittain) **8-8-3v** JLowe(8) (shkn up & qcknd to ld 9f out: hdd over 3f out: lost pl & eased over 2f out) | 10 | 7 | 10/1 | 26 | — |

(SP 125.0%) **7 Rn**

**3m 40.0** (9.50) CSF £9.36 CT £33.32 TOTE £2.50: £1.90 £2.20 (£5.40) OWNER Mr K. Flood (MIDDLEHAM) BRED John A. Nerud Revocable Trust

**2148 French Ivy (USA)**, given a confident ride, came through travelling strongly on the inside to lead over a furlong out and, quickening clear, scored in good style. (13/8: op 5/2)
**2165 Hullbank** drew upsides almost over a furlong out, but could not match the winner's turn of finishing speed. (4/1)
**2060 Atherton Green (IRE)**, who raced keenly, helped force the pace but was going up and down in the same place in the last two furlongs. (13/2)
**Hit the Canvas (USA)**, caught out when the pace increased at halfway, stayed on in the final quarter-mile. (8/1)
**2028 Izza**, who raced keenly, edged off the rail over a furlong out, leaving the door open for the winner. (5/1)
**1095* Top Prize** (10/1: 8/1-12/1)

## 2517 JEREMY BUXTON CONDITIONS STKS (2-Y.O) (Class D)

4-35 (4-35) **7f 100y** £3,444.00 (£1,032.00: £496.00: £228.00) Stalls: High GOING minus 0.51 sec per fur (F)

| Form | Runner | Dist | Pos | SP | RR | SF |
|---|---|---|---|---|---|---|
| 1892$^{3}$ | **Imperial President** (HRACecil) **2-8-10** WRyan(3) (lw: hld up: shkn up over 2f out: qcknd to ld over 1f out: sn clr) | — | 1 | 4/6$^{1}$ | 72+ | — |
| 2396* | **Grate Times** (EWeymes) **2-8-9**$^{(5)}$ 4x DGriffiths(4) (led tl over 1f out: kpt on: no ch w wnr) | 4 | 2 | 13/2$^{3}$ | 67 | — |
| 2044* | **Tough Leader** (BHanbury) **2-9-0** JStack(1) (lw: trckd ldr: effrt & hung rt 2f out: kpt on one pce) | ¾ | 3 | 2/1$^{2}$ | 66 | — |
| 2138$^{6}$ | **Lord Discord** (TDEasterby) **2-8-10** MBirch(2) (bit bkwd: trckd ldrs: hmpd 6f out: wl outpcd over 1f out: eased) | 7 | 4 | 16/1 | 47 | — |

(SP 112.5%) **4 Rn**

**1m 38.4** (6.40) CSF £5.00 TOTE £1.40: (£2.50) OWNER Mr K. Abdulla (NEWMARKET) BRED Juddmonte Farms

**1892 Imperial President** had clearly learnt a lot from his first outing. A different proposition on this different ground, he did it in good style. (4/6)
**2396* Grate Times**, allowed to set his own pace, was swept aside by the winner. He has a very choppy action and will appreciate being back on soft ground. (13/2)
**2044* Tough Leader** was inclined to hang right under pressure and his attitude must be questioned. (2/1)
**2138 Lord Discord**, who still looks far from the finished article, was, in the end, allowed to come home in his own time. (16/1)

## 2518 SEARCHERS H'CAP (0-80) (3-Y.O+) (Class D)

5-05 (5-05) **5f** £3,665.00 (£1,100.00: £530.00: £245.00) Stalls: High GOING minus 0.51 sec per fur (F)

| Form | Runner | Dist | Pos | SP | RR | SF |
|---|---|---|---|---|---|---|
| 2349$^{4}$ | **Bolshoi (IRE) (73)** (JBerry) **4-9-11b** EmmaO'Gorman(9) (hld up: gd hdwy ½-wy: rdn to ld over 1f out: sn clr) | — | 1 | 100/30$^{1}$ | 86 | 69 |
| 2366$^{13}$ | **Just Dissident (IRE) (53)** (RMWhitaker) **4-8-5** WRyan(8) (led tl over 1f out: no ch w wnr) | 4 | 2 | 14/1 | 53 | 36 |
| 2186$^{2}$ | **Dominelle (52)** (TDEasterby) **4-8-4**$^{ow1}$ MBirch(6) (hld up: effrt ½-wy: hdwy over 1f out: kpt on ins fnl f) | 1½ | 3 | 100/30$^{1}$ | 47 | 29 |
| 2349$^{6}$ | **Here Comes a Star (76)** (JMCarr) **8-10-0** ACulhane(5) (lw: hld up: hdwy on ins over 1f out: kpt on same pce) | nk | 4 | 7/1$^{3}$ | 70 | 53 |
| 2185$^{7}$ | **Aquado (58)** (SRBowring) **7-8-10b** JQuinn(2) (lw: sn outpcd & bhd: styd on appr fnl f) | s.h | 5 | 7/1$^{3}$ | 52 | 35 |
| 2395$^{5}$ | **Kabcast (44)** (DWChapman) **11-7-10b** LCharnock(7) (a chsng ldrs: one pce fnl 2f) | hd | 6 | 20/1 | 38 | 21 |
| 2329$^{11}$ | **Plum First (61)** (LRLloyd-James) **6-8-8v**$^{(5)}$ AmandaSanders(1) (b.hind: s.i.s: bhd & racd wd: rdn ½-wy: sme hdwy over 1f out) | 1¼ | 7 | 14/1 | 51 | 34 |
| 2017$^{7}$ | **Akalim (73)** (DMorley) **3-9-6b**$^{1}$ MFenton(11) (swtg: w ldrs tl wknd over 1f out) | 1½ | 8 | 6/1$^{2}$ | 58 | 36 |
| *2084*$^{3}$ | **Klipspinger (53)** (BSRothwell) **3-8-0v**$^{ow1}$ JStack(4) (chsd ldrs tl wknd over 1f out) | 1½ | 9 | 6/1$^{2}$ | 33 | 10 |
| 1646$^{7}$ | **Clincher Club (72)** (MJohnston) **3-9-5** TWilliams(10) (sn drvn along: chsd ldrs tl lost pl ½-wy: sn bhd) | 4 | 10 | 9/1 | 40 | 18 |

(SP 127.8%) **10 Rn**

**61.4 secs** (-0.10) CSF £47.55 CT £161.06 TOTE £4.20: £1.80 £2.60 £1.70 (£43.80) Trio £112.30 OWNER Mrs David Brown (COCKERHAM) BRED David John Brown

WEIGHT FOR AGE 3yo-5lb

**2349 Bolshoi (IRE)** was given a confident ride and, after being shaken up to hit the front, did it in good style. (100/30)
**1161 Just Dissident (IRE)**, who ran over ten furlongs last time, led them a merry dance but, at the business end, the winner proved much too good. (14/1)
**2186 Dominelle**, ridden from off the pace, was putting in her best work inside the last. (100/30)
**2349 Here Comes a Star** ran his usual sort of race. (7/1)
**2005 Aquado** did not get going until it was all over, and is much happier over six. (7/1)
**2395 Kabcast**, dropped back in distance and with the blinkers on, did not take the eye in the paddock and, after showing speed, dropped out over a furlong out. He seems to be going the wrong way. (20/1)
**2084 Klipspinger** (6/1: op 4/1)

T/Plpt: £34.70 (245.73 Tckts). T/Qdpt: £7.10 (57.34 Tckts). WG

## 2236-CARLISLE (R-H) (Firm, Good to firm patches)

### Saturday July 6th

WEATHER: overcast WIND: fresh across

### 2519 C.F.M. SOUND OF SUMMER MAIDEN AUCTION STKS (2-Y.O) (Class F)

7-10 (7-12) **5f 207y** £2,633.00 (£738.00: £359.00) Stalls: High GOING minus 0.71 sec per fur (HD)

| Form | Horse | Dist | Pos | SP | RR | SF |
|---|---|---|---|---|---|---|
| 2211$^{4}$ | **Can Can Lady** (MJohnston) **2-8-1** JFanning(4) (unruly s: mde all: kpt on wl fnl 2f) | — | 1 | 7/2$^{2}$ | 63 | — |
| 2044$^{2}$ | **The Deejay (IRE)** (MBrittain) **2-8-0e**$^{(5)ow2}$ GParkin(3) (a chsng wnr: rdn over 2f out: kpt on one pce) | 3½ | 2 | 7/4$^{1}$ | 58 | — |
| 2043$^{5}$ | **Kitty Galore (IRE)** (MDods) **2-8-1** JFEgan(5) (chsd ldrs: one pce fnl 2f) | 2 | 3 | 5/1$^{3}$ | 48 | — |
| 1537$^{14}$ | **Ballydinero (IRE)** (CaptJWilson) **2-8-3** JCarroll(1) (cl up: outpcd & hung lft over 1f out: sn btn) | 2½ | 4 | 14/1 | 44 | — |
| 2025$^{7}$ | **Bloomsy Babe** (JJQuinn) **2-8-1** MDeering(2) (sn outpcd & bhd: sme hdwy 2f out: n.d) | 1¾ | 5 | 16/1 | 37 | — |
| | **Zydecho Queen** (PCalver) **2-7-9**$^{(3)}$ DarrenMoffatt(7) (w'like: bit bkwd: s.i.s: n.d) | 3½ | 6 | 33/1 | 24 | — |
| | **Broctune Line** (MrsMReveley) **2-8-6** OUrbina(6) (w'like: bit bkwd: dwlt: a wl bhd) | 3½ | 7 | 5/1$^{3}$ | 23 | — |

(SP 107.4%) **7 Rn**

**1m 14.9** (2.40) CSF £9.13 TOTE £4.10: £1.60 £1.10 (£3.00) OWNER Mr A. W. Robinson (MIDDLEHAM) BRED Godolphin Management Co Ltd

**2211 Can Can Lady** found a moderate event here and won it well. (7/2)

**2044 The Deejay (IRE)** was always in a good enough position, but lacked a change of gear to do anything about it. He might be worth a chance on the All-Weather. (7/4)

**2043 Kitty Galore (IRE)** ran reasonably in this company, but was well held in the last couple of furlongs. (5/1: op 3/1)

**Ballydinero (IRE)**, despite having had two previous runs, still proved green under pressure. (14/1: 10/1-16/1)

**Bloomsy Babe**, left behind early on, did pick up a little, but has still some way to go and may need further. (16/1)

**Zydecho Queen** needed this and was clueless. (33/1)

### 2520 MACMILLAN NURSES CLAIMING STKS (3-Y.O+) (Class E)

7-40 (7-41) **6f 206y** £2,968.35 (£898.80: £438.90: £208.95) Stalls: High GOING minus 0.71 sec per fur (HD)

| Form | Horse | Dist | Pos | SP | RR | SF |
|---|---|---|---|---|---|---|
| 1532$^{6}$ | **Move With Edes (62)** (WGMTurner) **4-9-1**$^{(7)}$ DSweeney(10) (lw: trckd ldrs: led 2f out: styd on wl & sn clr) | — | 1 | 11/4$^{2}$ | 73 | 52 |
| | **Tibbi Blues** (WStorey) **9-8-10**$^{(7)}$ IonaWands(7) (chsd ldrs: styd on fnl 2f: no ch w wnr) | 9 | 2 | 8/1 | 47 | 26 |
| 2022$^{3}$ | **Double Oscar (IRE) (70)** (MJohnston) **3-8-13b**$^{(5)}$ KMChin(8) (bhd tl styd on u.p fnl 2f: nrst fin) | 2½ | 3 | 9/4$^{1}$ | 51 | 22 |
| 2212$^{8}$ | **Steel Sovereign (32)** (MDods) **5-8-12** JFEgan(3) (bhd tl styd on fnl 3f: nvr nrr) | ½ | 4 | 25/1 | 35 | 14 |
| | **Venus Victorious (IRE) (48)** (RBastiman) **5-9-0**$^{(5)}$ HBastiman(6) (a.p: effrt 3f out: no imp) | s.h | 5 | 33/1 | 42 | 21 |
| 2240$^{5}$ | **Wasblest (57)** (JBerry) **4-8-8**$^{(5)}$ PRoberts(1) (w ldr tl wknd 2f out) | 1½ | 6 | 5/1$^{3}$ | 33 | 12 |
| 2358$^{4}$ | **Backhander (IRE) (51)** (MartynWane) **4-9-0** JCarroll(2) (led tl hdd & wknd 2f out) | 2 | 7 | 5/1$^{3}$ | 29 | 8 |
| *2081*$^{14}$ | **Battle Colours (IRE) (35)** (DonEnricoIncisa) **7-8-12** KimTinkler(9) (a bhd) | ½ | 8 | 20/1 | 26 | 5 |
| 1830$^{13}$ | **Kummel King (48)** (EJAlston) **8-8-10v**$^{1}$ JFanning(4) (a outpcd & bhd) | 7 | 9 | 16/1 | 8 | — |

(SP 119.3%) **9 Rn**

**1m 25.4** (0.20 under best) (-0.30) CSF £23.86 TOTE £4.40: £1.90 £1.10 £1.70 (£28.80) Trio £19.90 OWNER W Ede & Co Partnership (SHERBORNE) BRED Tony J. Smith

WEIGHT FOR AGE 3yo-8lb

**1099 Move With Edes**, a big, awkward-looking individual, certainly took to this galloping track and won a poor event with a deal of ease.(11/4)

**Tibbi Blues** last ran six years ago and has been to stud in the meantime, but she did run quite well here, and there should be a modest event in the pipe-line. (8/1: op 33/1)

**2022 Double Oscar (IRE)** does not impress on looks and is certainly not in love with the game, but he does have ability if caught in the mood. (9/4)

**Steel Sovereign**, after looking disinterested, was kidded along up the straight to make a fair bit of late headway. (25/1)

**Venus Victorious (IRE)** had not been out for almost two years, but ran reasonably here and should benefit a little from it. (33/1)

**2022 Wasblest** either is not doing it or just does not stay. (5/1)

### 2521 STARBIRD H'CAP (0-60) (3-Y.O+) (Class F)

8-10 (8-13) **7f 214y** £2,857.00 (£802.00: £391.00) Stalls: High GOING minus 0.71 sec per fur (HD)

| Form | Horse | Dist | Pos | SP | RR | SF |
|---|---|---|---|---|---|---|
| 2162$^{7}$ | **Gilling Dancer (IRE) (55)** (PCalver) **3-9-3** MBirch(5) (trckd ldrs: led over 3f out: hld on wl) | — | 1 | 11/1 | 62 | 36 |
| 2214$^{7}$ | **Cee-Jay-Ay (46)** (JBerry) **9-8-12**$^{(5)}$ PRoberts(8) (s.i.s: hdwy over 2f out: ch ins fnl f: nt qckn) | 1¼ | 2 | 5/1$^{3}$ | 51 | 34 |
| 2391$^{2}$ | **Zain Dancer (55)** (DNicholls) **4-9-12** JFEgan(7) (trckd ldrs: hdwy & ev ch 2f out: hrd rdn & nt qckn) | nk | 3 | 3/1$^{1}$ | 59 | 42 |
| *2369*$^{9}$ | **Nobby Barnes (42)** (DonEnricoIncisa) **7-8-13** KimTinkler(2) (s.i.s: hdwy 4f out: styd on wl towards fin) | ½ | 4 | 16/1 | 45 | 28 |
| 2489$^{3}$ | **Summer Villa (40)** (JHetherton) **4-8-6**$^{(5)}$ GParkin(6) (chsd ldrs: rdn over 2f out: no imp) | ¾ | 5 | 10/1 | 41 | 24 |
| 2163$^{6}$ | **Sandblaster (54)** (MrsJRRamsden) **3-9-2** OUrbina(11) (in tch: effrt over 2f out: no imp) | 3 | 6 | 5/1$^{3}$ | 49 | 23 |
| 2241$^{3}$ | **Jimjareer (IRE) (49)** (CaptJWilson) **3-8-11** JCarroll(12) (lw: prom: effrt over 3f out: outpcd fnl 2f) | 2½ | 7 | 4/1$^{2}$ | 39 | 13 |
| *2304*$^{9}$ | **Hawwam (43)** (EJAlston) **10-8-7**$^{(7)}$ IonaWands(1) (a rr div) | 1 | 8 | 25/1 | 31 | 14 |
| *1969*$^{3}$ | **Tonto (37)** (CWThornton) **3-7-13** TWilliams(4) (a bhd) | 8 | 9 | 8/1 | 9 | — |
| 2026$^{12}$ | **Mr Titch (34)** (DenysSmith) **3-7-10** NKennedy(3) (prom tl wknd over 3f out) | 5 | 10 | 50/1 | — | — |
| 2136$^{11}$ | **Little Red (30)** (RCraggs) **5-8-1b**$^{1}$ JFanning(9) (set str pce tl hdd & wknd qckly 3f out: t.o) | dist | 11 | 33/1 | — | — |
| | ***Warwick Mist (IRE) (34)*** (BMactaggart) **4-8-5** NConnorton(10) (Withdrawn not under Starter's orders: veterinary advice) | | W | 33/1 | — | — |

(SP 124.4%) **11 Rn**

**1m 39.6** (1.00) CSF £62.63 CT £193.73 TOTE £13.80: £3.30 £2.60 £1.60 (£68.70) Trio £61.20 OWNER Lord Zetland (RIPON) BRED Irish National Stud Co Ltd

LONG HANDICAP Mr Titch 7-6

WEIGHT FOR AGE 3yo-9lb

**2019 Gilling Dancer (IRE)** proved most determined and would not give in after kicking on early in the straight. (11/1)

**1704 Cee-Jay-Ay** did his usual and, after a slow start, came sailing through from behind, but was not quite doing enough at the end. (5/1)

**2391 Zain Dancer** had his chances in the last three furlongs but, despite some strong driving, failed to produce the goods. (3/1)

**1341 Nobby Barnes** ran his usual race, coming from behind, but the task set was too much. (16/1)

**2489 Summer Villa**, having another quick run, did much better this time but was well short of a turn of foot in the last couple of furlongs. (10/1)

**2163 Sandblaster** has temperament problems and was taken to post early, but she never looked likely to peg the others back. (5/1)

**2241 Jimjareer (IRE)** was not made enough use of and was left struggling from two furlongs out. (4/1)

## 2522 RAVE RUNNERS H'CAP (0-70) (3-Y.O+) (Class E)
8-40 (8-40) **1m 4f** £2,859.15 (£865.20: £422.10: £200.55) Stalls: Low GOING minus 0.71 sec per fur (HD)

| | | | | SP | RR | SF |
|---|---|---|---|---|---|---|
| 2418* | **Desert Frolic (IRE) (78)** (MJohnston) **3-10-0**(5) 5x KMChin(2) (mde all: r.o strly fnl 3f) | — | **1** | 1/2 1 | 93 | 48 |
| 1977 4 | **Here Comes Herbie (40)** (WStorey) **4-8-1**(7) IonaWands(1) (hld up: styd on fnl 3f: no ch w wnr) | 6 | **2** | 5/2 2 | 47 | 15 |
| *2372 11* | **Island Cascade (28)** (DonEnricoIncisa) **4-7-10** KimTinkler(4) (outpcd 4f out: styd on fnl 2f: n.d) | 3½ | **3** | 50/1 | 30 | — |
| 2394 9 | **Never so True (40)** (MartynWane) **5-8-8** JCarroll(3) (chsd wnr tl wl outpcd fnl 2f) | 2½ | **4** | 10/1 3 | 39 | 7 |
| 2162 12 | **Bowland Park (36)** (EJAlston) **5-8-4** OUrbina(5) (prom tl wknd fnl 3f) | 9 | **5** | 33/1 | 23 | — |

(SP 109.2%) **5 Rn**

**2m 32.8** (1.80) CSF £2.07 TOTE £1.40: £1.30 £1.10 (£1.50) OWNER Maktoum Al Maktoum (MIDDLEHAM) BRED Gainsborough Stud Management Ltd
WEIGHT FOR AGE 3yo-13lb
**2418* Desert Frolic (IRE)**, ridden with confidence, had a fairly simple task and this smashing filly did it really well. (1/2)
**1977 Here Comes Herbie** let the others try to take the favourite on and then comfortably picked them off for second place. (5/2)
**Island Cascade** lost a place or two on the turn and then stayed on when it was too late. (50/1)
**Never so True** tried her best to take the winner on, but it all proved too much in the last three furlongs. (10/1)
**Bowland Park** has yet to show any real encouragement. (33/1)

## 2523 STARFORM SPRINT H'CAP (0-70) (3-Y.O+) (Class E)
9-10 (9-11) **5f** £2,913.75 (£882.00: £430.50: £204.75) Stalls: High GOING minus 0.71 sec per fur (HD)

| | | | | SP | RR | SF |
|---|---|---|---|---|---|---|
| 2176* | **Time To Tango (65)** (GMMoore) **3-9-8** JFEgan(4) (chsd ldr: led over 1f out: r.o wl) | — | **1** | 9/2 2 | 74 | 52 |
| 2329 6 | **Captain Carat (66)** (MrsJRRamsden) **5-10-0** OUrbina(3) (b.nr fore: hld up: effrt 2f out: styd on wl nr fin) | 2 | **2** | 5/1 3 | 69 | 52 |
| 2154 4 | **Ned's Bonanza (57)** (MDods) **7-9-5** JCarroll(10) (trckd ldrs: effrt 2f out: nt qckn fnl f) | hd | **3** | 5/2 1 | 59 | 42 |
| 2386 7 | **Pallium (IRE) (53)** (MrsAMNaughton) **8-9-1** NConnorton(11) (in tch: effrt 2f out: kpt on: no imp) | 3½ | **4** | 8/1 | 44 | 27 |
| 2154 11 | **Invigilate (54)** (MartynWane) **7-9-2** RLappin(5) (mid div: effrt ½-wy: nvr able to chal) | hd | **5** | 9/1 | 45 | 28 |
| 1859 4 | **Tutu Sixtysix (34)** (DonEnricoIncisa) **5-7-10b** KimTinkler(2) (lw: s.i.s: styd on fnl 2f: nrst fin) | 1½ | **6** | 14/1 | 20 | 3 |
| 2212 6 | **First Option (41)** (RBastiman) **6-8-3** JFanning(8) (t: hmpd s: nvr trbld ldrs) | 1½ | **7** | 16/1 | 22 | 5 |
| 2496 5 | **Gondo (43)** (EJAlston) **9-7-12**(7) IonaWands(1) (nvr trbld ldrs) | s.h | **8** | 14/1 | 24 | 7 |
| 1889 4 | **Serious Hurry (48)** (RMMcKellar) **8-8-3b**(7) KSked(6) (led over 3f: sn wknd) | nk | **9** | 5/1 3 | 28 | 11 |
| 2386 9 | **Another Episode (IRE) (55)** (MissLAPerratt) **7-9-3** MBirch(9) (hung lft & lost tch ½-wy: eased fin 2f) | 19 | **10** | 20/1 | — | — |

(SP 125.2%) **10 Rn**

**59.9 secs** (-0.30) CSF £27.57 CT £66.16 TOTE £4.50: £1.90 £1.70 £1.20 (£12.10) Trio £7.70 OWNER Mrs D. N. B. Pearson (MIDDLEHAM) BRED Mrs D. N. B. Pearson
LONG HANDICAP Tutu Sixtysix 7-7
WEIGHT FOR AGE 3yo-5lb
OFFICIAL EXPLANATION **Another Episode (IRE): appeared to have a back problem, this was confirmed by the trainer.**
**Serious Hurry: finished in a distressed state.**
**2176* Time To Tango** won this in good style and is obviously improving. (9/2)
**2329 Captain Carat** looked to be going well at halfway, but took time to react when ridden and, by the time he did, it was all over. (5/1)
**2154 Ned's Bonanza** looked to be going quite well in behind the leaders but, asked for an effort, was never giving it his best shot. (5/2)
**2386 Pallium (IRE)** is running a bit in and out, but this was one of his better efforts. (8/1)
**1848* Invigilate** ideally needs a bit further than this these days. (9/1)
**1859 Tutu Sixtysix** tried to come from another parish and had no chance of making it. (14/1)
**2212 First Option** took a hefty knock at the start which put paid to all chance. (16/1)
**1889 Serious Hurry** seems to be coming to hand. (5/1)

## 2524 DENTON HOLME CLUB LIMITED STKS (0-65) (3-Y.O+) (Class F)
9-40 (9-41) **5f 207y** £2,577.00 (£722.00: £351.00) Stalls: High GOING minus 0.71 sec per fur (HD)

| | | | | SP | RR | SF |
|---|---|---|---|---|---|---|
| 2137 6 | **Shashi (IRE) (64)** (WWHaigh) **4-8-13b** RLappin(1) (lw: trckd ldrs: hdwy to ld 1f out: edgd rt: jst hld on) | — | **1** | 7/4 1 | 67 | 26 |
| 2329 7 | **Barato (65)** (MrsJRRamsden) **5-9-5** OUrbina(5) (lw: b.nr hind: hld up: stdy hdwy ½-wy: disp ld 1f out: sn hdd: rallied towards fin) | s.h | **2** | 2/1 2 | 73 | 32 |
| 1629 7 | **Regal Fanfare (IRE) (62)** (MrsLStubbs) **4-8-13b** JFEgan(4) (w ldr: slt ld 2f out: hdd 1f out: no ex) | 3 | **3** | 9/1 | 59 | 18 |
| 2154 10 | **Superpride (60)** (MrsMReveley) **4-9-2b** MBirch(6) (led 4f: wknd appr fnl f) | 4 | **4** | 7/2 3 | 51 | 10 |
| | **Dark Shot (IRE) (65)** (RAFahey) **4-9-2** JCarroll(3) (chsd ldrs tl wknd wl over 1f out) | nk | **5** | 8/1 | 50 | 9 |
| *2308 12* | **Globe Runner (53)** (JJO'Neill) **3-8-10** TWilliams(7) (a outpcd & bhd) | 15 | **6** | 33/1 | 10 | — |

(SP 116.0%) **6 Rn**

**1m 13.5** (1.00) CSF £5.76 TOTE £2.90: £1.20 £1.60 (£3.00) OWNER Mr B. Valentine (MALTON) BRED Mohammed bin Rashid al Maktoum
WEIGHT FOR AGE 3yo-6lb
**1786 Shashi (IRE)** managed to scrape home, but did not help her chances by hanging right in the final furlong. (7/4)
**2029* Barato** is not the easiest of rides, but did keep trying and would have made it in another stride. (2/1)
**Regal Fanfare (IRE)** was always in a good position, but her limitations were exposed in the final furlong. (9/1: op 6/1)
**1848 Superpride** was given a good ride here, but it all proved too much approaching the final furlong. (7/2)
**Dark Shot (IRE)** has only ever won on the Sand and this was also his first outing of the season. (8/1: op 12/1)

T/Plpt: £4.40 (2,111.32 Tckts). T/Qdpt: £3.00 (148.12 Tckts). AA

# 2379-CHEPSTOW (L-H) (Good to firm)
## Saturday July 6th
WEATHER: overcast WIND: almost nil

## 2525 WOODPECKER H'CAP (0-80) (3-Y.O+) (Class D)
2-25 (2-27) **1m 2f 36y** £3,780.50 (£1,139.00: £552.00: £258.50) Stalls: Low GOING minus 0.42 sec per fur (F)

| | | | | SP | RR | SF |
|---|---|---|---|---|---|---|
| 1894 2 | **Alaflak (IRE) (78)** (MajorWRHern) **5-9-13** SWhitworth(2) (lw: hld up & bhd: rdn over 3f out: swtchd rt & gd hdwy over 2f out: edgd lft fnl f: hrd rdn to ld last strides) | — | **1** | 11/4 1 | 88 | 51 |

| | | | | SP | RR | SF |
|---|---|---|---|---|---|---|
| $2378^{3}$ | **Voila Premiere (IRE) (64)** (MHTompkins) **4-8-10**$^{(3)}$ HKYim(3) (led: rdn ins fnl f: hdd last strides) | hd | **2** | 7/1$^{3}$ | 74 | 37 |
| $2312^{5}$ | **Pay Homage (73)** (IABalding) **8-9-3**$^{(5)}$ MartinDwyer(7) (lw: hld up & plld hrd: rdn & outpcd over 1f out: rallied ins fnl f) | nk | **3** | 15/2 | 82 | 45 |
| | **Mister O'Grady (IRE) (52)** (RAkehurst) **5-8-1**$^{ow4}$ SSanders(9) (hld up: hdwy 3f out: ev ch over 1f out: one pce) | 2 | **4** | 11/1 | 58 | 17 |
| $1619^{6}$ | **Major Dundee (IRE) (78)** (RHannon) **3-8-13**$^{(3)}$ DaneO'Neill(1) (lw: s.i.s: sn prom: wknd 2f out) | 4 | **5** | 7/1$^{3}$ | 78 | 30 |
| $2344^{4}$ | **Irrepressible (IRE) (49)** (RJHodges) **5-7-9**$^{(3)}$ DWright(6) (w ldr tl wknd wl over 1f out) | 2½ | **6** | 14/1 | 45 | 8 |
| 2234* | **Monument (65)** (JSKing) **4-8-11**$^{(3)}$ SDrowne(5) (lw: hld up & bhd: hrd rdn 4f out: no rspnse) | 6 | **7** | 8/1 | 52 | 15 |
| $1655^{19}$ | **Prince of Spades (55)** (FJordan) **4-8-4** AClark(8) (prom tl wknd 2f out) | 7 | **8** | 33/1 | 31 | — |
| 2206* | **Sovereign Page (USA) (79)** (BHanbury) **7-10-0** WJO'Connor(4) (b: lw: prom tl hrd rdn & wknd over 2f out: virtually p.u fnl f) | 23 | **9** | 5/1$^{2}$ | 18 | — |
| | | | | (SP 109.2%) | | **9 Rn** |

**2m 8.4** (3.10) CSF £19.41 CT £104.03 TOTE £3.30: £1.70 £3.20 £1.60 (£14.30) Trio £50.20 OWNER Mr Hamdan Al Maktoum (LAMBOURN) BRED R. A. Collins
WEIGHT FOR AGE 3yo-11lb
**OFFICIAL EXPLANATION Sovereign Page (USA): lost his action in the final furlong and a half.**
**1894 Alaflak (IRE)**, raised 3lb, needed every yard of this trip to wear down the front-runner. (11/4)
**2378 Voila Premiere (IRE)** ran well for the second time within a week and has clearly come to hand. (7/1: 6/1-9/1)
**2312 Pay Homage**, down a further 2lb, has never won beyond nine furlongs, but fought back well towards the finish. (15/2)
**Mister O'Grady (IRE)** likes fast ground and made a highly respectable reappearance, carrying 4lb overweight. (11/1: 6/1-12/1)
**1619 Major Dundee (IRE)** has yet to prove he gets this trip. (7/1)
**2344 Irrepressible (IRE)** was another who had his stamina limitations exposed. (14/1)
**2206* Sovereign Page (USA)** (5/1: op 3/1)

## 2526 ROTHMANS ROYALS NORTH SOUTH CHALLENGE SERIES H'CAP (0-85) (3-Y.O+) (Class D)

2-55 (3-01) **1m 14y** £4,328.00 (£1,304.00: £632.00: £296.00) Stalls: High GOING minus 0.42 sec per fur (F)

| | | | | SP | RR | SF |
|---|---|---|---|---|---|---|
| $2126^{4}$ | **Catch The Lights (69)** (RHannon) **3-8-3**$^{(3)ow5}$ DaneO'Neill(12) (hld up: hdwy to ld 2f out: r.o wl) | — | **1** | 8/1 | 78 | 52 |
| $496^{5}$ | **Bon Luck (IRE) (70)** (JRFanshawe) **4-9-2** NDay(6) (a.p: ev ch 2f out: no imp) | 2½ | **2** | 14/1 | 74 | 62 |
| $2033^{6}$ | **Attarikh (IRE) (72)** (JHMGosden) **3-8-9v**$^{1}$ AGarth(10) (led 6f: r.o one pce fnl f) | nk | **3** | 12/1 | 75 | 54 |
| 2357* | **Maple Bay (IRE) (73)** (ABailey) **7-9-2**$^{(3)}$ $^{5x}$ DWright(1) (lw: a.p: one pce fnl 2f) | ½ | **4** | 11/2$^{3}$ | 76 | 64 |
| 2058* | **Q Factor (66)** (DHaydnJones) **4-8-9**$^{(3)}$ SDrowne(9) (lw: chsd ldr tl wknd 2f out) | 7 | **5** | 9/1 | 55 | 43 |
| $1190^{9}$ | **Zajko (USA) (77)** (LadyHerries) **6-9-2**$^{(7)}$ PDoe(7) (hld up: no hdwy fnl 2f) | ½ | **6** | 7/1 | 65 | 53 |
| $2058^{3}$ | **Roi de la Mer (IRE) (65)** (JAkehurst) **5-8-11** SWhitworth(5) (hld up & plld hrd: wknd 2f out) | 3½ | **7** | 5/1$^{2}$ | 46 | 34 |
| *$2170^{7}$* | **Artful Dane (IRE) (66)** (MJHeaton-Ellis) **4-8-12** AClark(3) (prom 6f) | 1 | **8** | 12/1 | 45 | 33 |
| $2188^{2}$ | **Bernard Seven (IRE) (80)** (CEBrittain) **4-9-9b**$^{(3)}$ HKYim(8) (lw: prom over 5f) | 1¾ | **9** | 9/1 | 55 | 43 |
| $2311^{3}$ | **Master Millfield (IRE) (69)** (RJBaker) **4-9-1** DBiggs(11) (hld up & plld hrd: rdn 4f out: a bhd) | 4 | **10** | 14/1 | 36 | 24 |
| $1485^{2}$ | **Brighton Road (IRE) (77)** (GBBalding) **3-9-0** SSanders(2) (a bhd) | 1¾ | **11** | 9/2$^{1}$ | 41 | 20 |
| | | | | (SP 122.6%) | | **11 Rn** |

**1m 32.7** (0.20) CSF £103.54 CT £1,252.50 TOTE £10.20: £3.10 £3.20 £2.80 (£162.30) Trio £212.90; £215.97 to Windsor 8/7/96 OWNER Mr T. A. Johnsey (MARLBOROUGH) BRED T. A. Johnsey
WEIGHT FOR AGE 3yo-9lb
**2126 Catch The Lights** had given notice of a return to form last time and can follow up if not heavily punished by the Handicapper. (8/1)
**496 Bon Luck (IRE)**, stepping up to a mile, did nothing wrong, but simply met one too good. (14/1)
**2033 Attarikh (IRE)**, dropped 2lb, was back to a mile and tried in a visor. (12/1)
**2357* Maple Bay (IRE)**, racing on the outside from his low draw, was by no means disgraced under a penalty. (11/2)
**2058* Q Factor**, 4lb higher for her win last time, did not handle fast ground twice in succession. (9/1)
**Zajko (USA)** had ground conditions in his favour, but was 7lb higher than when he last won. (7/1)
**1485 Brighton Road (IRE)** never looked likely to justify market support and seems to need give underfoot. (9/2: op 7/1)

## 2527 E.B.F. MEDIAN AUCTION MAIDEN STKS (2-Y.O) (Class F)

3-30 (3-31) **6f 16y** £2,882.00 (£866.00: £418.00: £194.00) Stalls: High GOING minus 0.42 sec per fur (F)

| | | | | SP | RR | SF |
|---|---|---|---|---|---|---|
| $1896^{5}$ | **Mr Bombastique (IRE)** (BWHills) **2-8-9**$^{(5)}$ JDSmith(2) (a.p: hrd rdn over 1f out: led ins fnl f: r.o wl) | — | **1** | 7/4$^{1}$ | 71 | 29 |
| $2323^{2}$ | **Double-J (IRE)** (KMcAuliffe) **2-9-0** WJO'Connor(1) (lw: a.p: led 1f out tl ins fnl f: r.o) | ½ | **2** | 5/1$^{3}$ | 70 | 28 |
| $1892^{4}$ | **Bold Spring (IRE)** (RHannon) **2-8-11**$^{(3)}$ DaneO'Neill(5) (a.p: led 2f out to 1f out: one pce) | 3½ | **3** | 4/1$^{2}$ | 61 | 19 |
| $2343^{6}$ | **Strat's Quest** (DWPArbuthnot) **2-8-9** RPrice(4) (hdwy 2f out: one pce fnl f) | 2½ | **4** | 25/1 | 49 | 7 |
| $807^{3}$ | **Royal Emblem** (AGFoster) **2-8-9** SSanders(7) (led 4f: wknd over 1f out) | ½ | **5** | 8/1 | 48 | 6 |
| $1590^{2}$ | **Chilling** (PGMurphy) **2-8-6**$^{(3)}$ SDrowne(6) (w ldr tl wknd over 2f out) | 5 | **6** | 4/1$^{2}$ | 34 | — |
| | **Priory Gardens (IRE)** (JMBradley) **2-9-0** NAdams(3) (leggy: bhd whn hung lft over 3f out) | 6 | **7** | 33/1 | 24 | — |
| | | | | (SP 110.9%) | | **7 Rn** |

**1m 11.5** (2.30) CSF £10.08 TOTE £1.90: £1.40 £2.30 (£5.00) OWNER K. Al-Said (LAMBOURN) BRED Charlton Down Stud
**1896 Mr Bombastique (IRE)**, a half-brother to The Deep and Zingibar, had to work hard to land the spoils. (7/4: op Evens)
**2323 Double-J (IRE)** seemed better suited by this return to six. (5/1)
**1892 Bold Spring (IRE)** may be worth a try at the minimum trip. (4/1)
**2343 Strat's Quest** stepped up on her recent debut here. (25/1)
**807 Royal Emblem**, a half-sister to Great Hall, was trying an extra furlong. (8/1)

## 2528 CHAFFINCH MAIDEN H'CAP (0-65) (3-Y.O) (Class F)

4-00 (4-01) **6f 16y** £2,845.00 (£795.00: £385.00) Stalls: High GOING minus 0.42 sec per fur (F)

| | | | | SP | RR | SF |
|---|---|---|---|---|---|---|
| $1654^{18}$ | **Mr Speaker (IRE) (60)** (CFWall) **3-9-3** NCarlisle(10) (hdwy to ld 2f out: edgd lft 1f out: r.o wl) | — | **1** | 14/1 | 66 | 37 |
| $2255^{4}$ | **Lillibella (63)** (IABalding) **3-9-1**$^{(5)}$ MartinDwyer(12) (lw: hdwy 2f out: n.m.r 1f out: ev ch ins fnl f: unable qckn) | ½ | **2** | 9/2$^{1}$ | 68 | 39 |
| | **Real Gem (57)** (PJMakin) **3-9-0** SSanders(15) (swtg: a.p: led over 2f out: sn hdd: unable qckn ins fnl f) | 1 | **3** | 16/1 | 59 | 30 |
| | **Impetuous Lady (USA) (50)** (NEBerry) **3-8-7** DBiggs(14) (lw: a.p: rdn over 2f out: one pce) | 1¾ | **4** | 25/1 | 47 | 18 |
| $2156^{13}$ | **Double Or Bust (39)** (AGNewcombe) **3-7-10** FNorton(9) (swtg: chsd ldrs: ev ch 2f out: wknd over 1f out) | 1¾ | **5** | 20/1 | 32 | 3 |
| $2231^{5}$ | **Mishaweer (60)** (JRFanshawe) **3-9-3v**$^{1}$ DRMcCabe(13) (nvr nr to chal) | ½ | **6** | 5/1$^{2}$ | 52 | 23 |
| *$1719^{8}$* | **Careful (IRE) (64)** (BWHills) **3-9-2**$^{(5)}$ JDSmith(7) (nvr nr to chal) | ¾ | **7** | 12/1 | 54 | 25 |

| | | | | | |
|---|---|---|---|---|---|
| 2255[6] **Ameliajill (52)** (RHannon) **3-8-6**(3) DaneO'Neill(11) (lw: dwlt: nrst fin) | 1½ | **8** | 7/1[3] | 38 | 9 |
| 2151[4] **Man of Wit (IRE) (63)** (APJarvis) **3-9-6v** WJO'Connor(16) (led over 3f: sn wknd) | 1¼ | **9** | 15/2 | 45 | 16 |
| 2235[7] **Extra Hour (IRE) (62)** (WRMuir) **3-9-2b**[1](3) PMcCabe(6) (s.i.s: sn chsng ldrs: wknd 2f out) | 1¾ | **10** | 12/1 | 40 | 11 |
| *131*[11] **Gracious Gretclo (52)** (RJBaker) **3-8-9** SWhitworth(8) (spd centre over 4f: eased whn btn fnl f) | s.h | **11** | 20/1 | 30 | 1 |
| 2049[17] **No Hiding Place (60)** (BHanbury) **3-9-0**(3) MHenry(5) (lw: spd centre 4f) | 1¾ | **12** | 16/1 | 33 | 4 |
| **Golden Silver (45)** (JSMoore) **3-7-11**(5) MBaird(4) (a bhd) | 1 | **13** | 20/1 | 15 | — |
| 1840[16] **Volare (48)** (BJMeehan) **3-8-5b**[1] AClark(3) (prom centre 3f) | ¾ | **14** | 20/1 | 16 | — |
| 2347[7] **Natal Ridge (60)** (DHaydnJones) **3-9-0b**[1](3) SDrowne(1) (s.s: a bhd) | 2½ | **15** | 16/1 | 22 | — |

(SP 121.7%) **15 Rn**

**1m 11.1** (1.90) CSF £71.04 CT £955.48 TOTE £14.80: £3.30 £1.70 £4.40 (£53.80) Trio £182.70 OWNER Hintlesham Racing (NEWMARKET) BRED Miss Anne Marie Burns

LONG HANDICAP Double Or Bust 7-8

**Mr Speaker (IRE)**, down 6lb in the Ratings this season, had been running over a mile. (14/1)

**2255 Lillibella** did not get the best of runs entering the final furlong, but should still have won had she been good enough. (9/2)

**Real Gem** also ran well on her debut at two, but did not progress afterwards. (16/1)

**Impetuous Lady (USA)** is another who went the wrong way after a reasonable racecourse debut last year. (25/1)

**Double Or Bust**, 2lb out of the handicap for this try at an extra furlong, was awash with sweat leaving the paddock. (20/1)

**768 Mishaweer** had a visor fitted for this handicap debut. (5/1)

**2255 Ameliajill** still seems worth a try over further. (7/1)

## 2529 STARLING MAIDEN STKS (3-Y.O F) (Class D)

4-30 (4-33) **7f 16y** £3,939.75 (£1,188.00: £576.50: £270.75) Stalls: High GOING minus 0.42 sec per fur (F)

| | | | SP | RR | SF |
|---|---|---|---|---|---|
| 1593[5] **Shadow Casting** (BWHills) **3-8-6**(5) JDSmith(8) (a.p: led over 3f out: r.o wl) | — | **1** | 11/2[3] | 74 | 23 |
| 1901[6] **Santella Katie** (MajorDNChappell) **3-8-11** AClark(5) (hdwy over 2f out: r.o wl ins fnl f) | nk | **2** | 8/1 | 73 | 22 |
| 2004[3] **Jumairah Sunset** (ACStewart) **3-8-11** SWhitworth(10) (bit bkwd: dwlt: hdwy 3f out: hrd rdn & chsd wnr 2f out: one pce fnl f) | 2 | **3** | 9/4[1] | 69 | 18 |
| 962[4] **Azwah (USA)** (PTWalwyn) **3-8-11** RPrice(4) (a.p: one pce fnl 2f) | 1 | **4** | 6/1 | 67 | 16 |
| 1994[6] **First Law** (MissGayKelleway) **3-8-11** WJO'Connor(6) (b.hind: led 1f: wknd over 1f out) | 3 | **5** | 33/1 | 60 | 9 |
| 1857[6] **Amelanchier (62)** (GBBalding) **3-8-8**(3) SDrowne(3) (nvr nr to chal) | 1¾ | **6** | 25/1 | 56 | 5 |
| **Green Bentley (IRE) (75)** (RHannon) **3-8-8**(3) DaneO'Neill(2) (prom over 4f) | 1½ | **7** | 7/1 | 52 | 1 |
| 1855[11] **Early Warning** (CREgerton) **3-8-4**(7) AimeeCook(7) (sn wl bhd: nvr nrr) | 5 | **8** | 40/1 | 41 | — |
| 2197[9] **Chesteine** (PJMakin) **3-8-11** SSanders(9) (lw: rdn 3f out: a bhd) | 1 | **9** | 33/1 | 39 | — |
| **Partita** (CEBrittain) **3-8-8**(3) MHenry(12) (lw: a bhd) | 4 | **10** | 16/1 | 30 | — |
| **Kentford Conquista** (JWMullins) **3-8-11** FNorton(1) (s.s: hdwy 4f out: wknd over 2f out) | 4 | **11** | 100/1 | 21 | — |
| **Easy Number (USA)** (JHMGosden) **3-8-11** AGarth(11) (w'like: dwlt: plld hrd: led after 1f out tl over 3f out: sn wknd & eased) | 18 | **12** | 5/1[2] | — | — |

(SP 119.8%) **12 Rn**

**1m 22.9** (2.90) CSF £45.68 TOTE £6.20: £1.70 £2.80 £1.40 (£27.20) Trio £22.80 OWNER Mr K. Abdulla (LAMBOURN) BRED Juddmonte Farms

**1593 Shadow Casting**, nicely backed, has clearly come to herself, and won more decisively than the margin suggests. (11/2)

**1901 Santella Katie**, a half-sister to Mild Rebuke, stuck on well in the closing stages, but was never going to get there in time. She can win a similar event, and a mile should not be a problem. (8/1)

**2004 Jumairah Sunset** still looks short of peak-fitness, but might be the type who carries condition. (9/4)

**962 Azwah (USA)** may need a mile to offset her lack of finishing speed. (6/1)

**Green Bentley (IRE)** (7/1: 9/2-8/1)

**Easy Number (USA)** (5/1: op 2/1)

## 2530 SWALLOW MAIDEN H'CAP (0-65) (3-Y.O+) (Class F)

5-00 (5-01) **2m 2f** £2,792.50 (£780.00: £377.50) Stalls: Low GOING minus 0.42 sec per fur (F)

| | | | SP | RR | SF |
|---|---|---|---|---|---|
| 1462[9] **Fortunes Course (IRE) (44)** (JSKing) **7-8-6**(3) SDrowne(10) (led over 11f: led over 1f out: all out) | — | **1** | 9/1 | 55 | 27 |
| 2216[3] **Washington Reef (USA) (52)** (JHMGosden) **3-7-7v**(3) MHenry(2) (hld up: rdn 9f out: hdwy over 5f out: ev ch fnl f: r.o) | hd | **2** | 6/1 | 63 | 14 |
| 2028[2] **Lostris (IRE) (33)** (MDods) **5-7-12** FNorton(4) (chsd ldr: led over 6f out: rdn 4f out: hdd over 1f out: wknd fnl f) | 5 | **3** | 9/2[2] | 40 | 12 |
| **Bellroi (IRE) (43)** (MHTompkins) **5-8-5**(3) HKYim(6) (a.p: ev ch 2f out: wknd fnl f) | 1¼ | **4** | 14/1 | 48 | 20 |
| 2042[11] **Sea Freedom (63)** (GBBalding) **5-10-0v** SSanders(3) (a.p: pushed along 10f out: wknd over 1f out) | s.h | **5** | 4/1[1] | 68 | 40 |
| 2182[8] **Kymin (IRE) (55)** (DJGMurraySmith) **4-9-1b**[1](5) RPainter(1) (hld up & bhd: stdy hdwy 8f out: lost pl 4f out: rallied over 1f out: one pce) | ½ | **6** | 20/1 | 60 | 32 |
| 2204[2] **Glowing Reeds (52)** (CNAllen) **3-7-5**(5) MartinDwyer(5) (hld up & bhd: hdwy 6f out: wknd 3f out) | 10 | **7** | 12/1 | 48 | — |
| 2310[2] **Solatium (IRE) (58)** (MCPipe) **4-9-9v** WJO'Connor(8) (hld up: rdn 9f out: hdwy 7f out: wknd over 2f out) | ½ | **8** | 5/1[3] | 54 | 26 |
| 2028[3] **Gunmaker (33)** (BJLlewellyn) **7-7-7**(5)ow2 MBaird(7) (a bhd) | 1¾ | **9** | 8/1 | 27 | — |
| **Playful Juliet (CAN) (32)** (ABailey) **8-7-8**(3) DWright(12) (a bhd: t.o) | 15 | **10** | 25/1 | 13 | — |
| 2191[11] **Lorcanjo (32)** (AJChamberlain) **5-7-4**(7) JFowle(9) (b: swtg: prom 9f: t.o) | 22 | **11** | 50/1 | — | — |
| 2155[3] **Prince de Berry (43)** (BJMeehan) **5-8-8** SWhitworth(11) (hld up: hdwy over 5f out: wknd 3f out: t.o) | 8 | **12** | 25/1 | — | — |

(SP 119.0%) **12 Rn**

**3m 57.7** (7.70) CSF £57.88 CT £255.16 TOTE £10.50: £2.40 £2.10 £2.00 (£77.60) Trio £40.90 OWNER Mrs A. J. Garrett (SWINDON) BRED Mrs Patricia Conway

LONG HANDICAP Glowing Reeds 7-3 Washington Reef (USA) 7-6 Gunmaker 7-3

WEIGHT FOR AGE 3yo-21lb

**Fortunes Course (IRE)**, successful over both fences and hurdles, was dropped 5lb following her run over an inadequate trip here last time. Relishing this real test of stamina, she gave a very game performance. (9/1)

**2216 Washington Reef (USA)**, back to a visor, is by no means an easy ride, but very nearly pulled this off from out of the handicap. (6/1)

**2028 Lostris (IRE)** could not keep tabs on the two principals in the final 200 yards. (9/2)

**Bellroi (IRE)**, who lost his way after a win over hurdles last winter, was 12lb lower than when he last ran on the Flat. (14/1: op 8/1)

**1782 Sea Freedom** is not one to have the rent money on and remains a maiden after twenty-two starts. (4/1)

**1454 Kymin (IRE)** was blinkered for the first time. (20/1)

T/Plpt: £219.80 (54.85 Tckts). T/Qdpt: £6.90 (85.32 Tckts). KH

# 2494-HAYDOCK (L-H) (Good)

## Saturday July 6th

WEATHER: sunny intervals WIND: fresh against

### 2531 E.B.F. JULY MAIDEN STKS (2-Y.O F) (Class D)

2-00 (2-00) **6f** £3,601.75 (£1,084.00: £524.50: £244.75) Stalls: High GOING: 0.26 sec per fur (G)

| | | | | SP | RR | SF |
|---|---|---|---|---|---|---|
| | **Colombia (IRE)** (MRStoute) **2-8-11** DHarrison(2) (small: lt-f: hld up: hdwy 2f out: led ins fnl f: pushed out) | — | 1 | 5/1[2] | 77+ | 34 |
| | **Ghayyur (USA)** (JLDunlop) **2-8-11** WCarson(4) (unf: scope: rn green: sn bhd & pushed along: swtchd lft 2f out: r.o wl ins fnl f) | ½ | 2 | 8/11[1] | 76+ | 33 |
| 2211[2] | **Danehill Princess (IRE)** (RHollinshead) **2-8-8**(3) FLynch(1) (a.p: ev ch 1f out: one pce ins fnl f) | 3 | 3 | 5/1[2] | 68 | 25 |
| | **Expectation (IRE)** (PRWebber) **2-8-11** BThomson(6) (w'like: scope: bkwd: led tl hdd & wknd ins fnl f) | 2½ | 4 | 12/1 | 61 | 18 |
| | **Eponine** (MRChannon) **2-8-11** RHughes(5) (lt-f: trckd ldrs over 3f: sn outpcd) | 3 | 5 | 8/1[3] | 53 | 10 |
| 2025[9] | **My Dear Watson** (JBerry) **2-8-11** JCarroll(3) (bit bkwd: prom 3f: sn lost tch: t.o) | 11 | 6 | 16/1 | 24 | — |
| | | | | (SP 115.9%) | | **6 Rn** |

**1m 17.67** (5.97) CSF £9.25 TOTE £6.30: £2.80 £1.30 (£3.00) OWNER Sultan Al Kabeer (NEWMARKET) BRED Rathbarry Stud

**Colombia (IRE)**, bred for stamina, was always travelling smoothly and, after leading 200 yards out, did not need to get serious to withstand the challenge of the favourite. (5/1)

**Ghayyur (USA)**, an unfurnished filly, broke well enough, but ran green and soon got outpaced. Driven along, she was gaining with every stride inside the final furlong, but the line was always going to arrive too soon. Sure to benefit from the experience, she can only improve on this. (8/11)

**2211 Danehill Princess (IRE)** did look to have a live chance a furlong out, but she found nothing at all when asked for a final effort and she is proving costly to follow. (5/1)

**Expectation (IRE)**, very much in need of the run, showed plenty of speed to lead her rivals a merry dance until blowing up just inside the last furlong. (12/1)

**Eponine**, a lightly-made half-sister to a winner, was always being taken along faster than she wanted and was flagging from below the distance. (8/1)

### 2532 EDWARD SYMMONS & PARTNERS COCK O' THE NORTH H'CAP (0-100) (3-Y.O) (Class C)

2-35 (2-36) **6f** £5,374.50 (£1,626.00: £793.00: £376.50) Stalls: High GOING: 0.26 sec per fur (G)

| | | | | SP | RR | SF |
|---|---|---|---|---|---|---|
| 1975[6] | **Babsy Babe (89)** (JJQuinn) **3-9-7** JQuinn(8) (hld up & bhd: hdwy 2f out: r.o to ld fnl 50 yrds) | — | 1 | 6/1 | 100 | 66 |
| *2171[11]* | **Splicing (80)** (WJHaggas) **3-8-12** BThomson(2) (led: clr 2f out: wknd & ct wl ins fnl f) | 1 | 2 | 6/1 | 88 | 54 |
| 1901[13] | **Alpine Hideaway (IRE) (80)** (BHanbury) **3-8-12** PatEddery(7) (chsd ldrs: effrt & rdn wl over 1f out: eased whn btn fnl f) | 5 | 3 | 11/2[3] | 75 | 41 |
| 2007[14] | **Blessingindisguise (83)** (MWEasterby) **3-9-1** WCarson(6) (prom: hrd drvn 2f out: r.o one pce) | 2½ | 4 | 7/2[1] | 71 | 37 |
| *2170[5]* | **Sualtach (IRE) (84)** (RHollinshead) **3-8-13**(3) FLynch(3) (lw: hdwy ½-wy: rdn & wknd over 1f out) | 1½ | 5 | 7/1 | 68 | 34 |
| 2078* | **Whittle Rock (84)** (EJAlston) **3-9-2** JFanning(5) (lw: prom: rdn wl over 1f out: sn btn) | nk | 6 | 9/2[2] | 68 | 34 |
| 2007[U] | **Spotted Eagle (84)** (RHannon) **3-9-2** JCarroll(4) (trckd ldrs: drvn along over 2f out: sn outpcd) | 7 | 7 | 13/2 | 49 | 15 |
| | | | | (SP 110.2%) | | **7 Rn** |

**1m 16.01** (4.31) CSF £36.20 CT £177.84 TOTE £6.20: £3.00 £2.80 (£24.90) OWNER Mrs Carol Bloom (MALTON) BRED John Gaines

**1975 Babsy Babe**, stepping down in class, won this with the minimum of fuss and, if kept in her own class, more success should follow. (6/1)

**897 Splicing** looked to have stolen a march when forging clear entering the last quarter-mile, but her stride shortened inside the distance and she was gobbled up towards the finish. (6/1)

**1171 Alpine Hideaway (IRE)**, in pursuit of the leader, never looked likely to reel her in and had begun to tread ground when the winner appeared on the scene. (11/2)

**1340 Blessingindisguise**, a poor mover in his slower paces, held his pitch behind the leaders until finding the pace too hot to handle once the race began in earnest. (7/2: 5/2-4/1)

**2170 Sualtach (IRE)** seems to find this trip inadequate and his short-lived effort had come to an end some way before reaching the final furlong. (7/1)

**2078* Whittle Rock** could not get to the front on this occasion, but she did push the pace until fading under pressure below the distance. (9/2)

### 2533 LETHEBY & CHRISTOPHER LANCASHIRE OAKS STKS (Gp 3) (3-Y.O+ F & M) (Class A)

3-10 (3-15) **1m 3f 200y** £20,920.00 (£7,896.00: £3,848.00: £1,736.00) Stalls: High GOING minus 0.01 sec per fur (G)

| | | | | SP | RR | SF |
|---|---|---|---|---|---|---|
| 2474a[6] | **Spout (109)** (RCharlton) **4-9-6** TSprake(6) (lw: dwlt: hld up & bhd: rapid hdwy over 1f out: str run to ld nr fin) | — | 1 | 13/2 | 114 | 75 |
| 2113[5] | **Phantom Gold (112)** (LordHuntingdon) **4-9-8** DHarrison(1) (hld up in tch: lost pl ent st: hdwy on ins 3f out: led wl ins fnl f tl ct cl home) | ¾ | 2 | 11/2[3] | 115 | 76 |
| 2069[9] | **Ninotchka (USA) (98)** (JLDunlop) **3-8-4** GCarter(5) (trckd ldrs: hdwy 2f out: rdn to ld ins fnl f: sn hdd: no ex) | 1½ | 3 | 9/1 | 108 | 56 |
| 2069[3] | **Shemozzle (IRE) (107)** (JHMGosden) **3-8-4** PatEddery(3) (b.hind: a.p: nt clr run over 2f out: swtchd ins fnl f: fin wl) | nk | 4 | 2/1[1] | 108 | 56 |
| | **My Emma** (RGuest) **3-8-4** FLynch(2) (h.d.w: bkwd: hld up: hdwy 3f out: slt ld 1f out tl ins fnl f: no ex) | 1¼ | 5 | 50/1 | 106 | 54 |
| 1899[2] | **Min Alhawa (USA) (103)** (MajorWRHern) **3-8-4** WCarson(7) (trckd ldrs: nt clr run 2f out: rdn & one pce fnl f) | 2½ | 6 | 9/2[2] | 103 | 51 |
| 1899[4] | **Cabaret (IRE)** (PWChapple-Hyam) **3-8-4** JCarroll(4) (led 5f: led over 3f out to 2f out: one pce) | 2 | 7 | 12/1 | 100 | 48 |
| 2145[2] | **Ellie Ardensky (98)** (JRFanshawe) **4-9-3** BDoyle(10) (hld up: hdwy to chal 3f out: wknd wl over 1f out) | 2 | 8 | 8/1 | 97 | 58 |
| 1988[6] | **Asterita (102)** (RHannon) **4-9-3** RHughes(9) (hld up: hdwy ½-wy: effrt over 3f out: wknd 2f out: eased whn btn) | 8 | 9 | 20/1 | 86 | 47 |
| 2080[3] | **Classic Colleen (IRE) (73)** (RHarris) **3-8-4** AMackay(8) (dwlt: hdwy to ld 7f out: hdd over 3f out: sn wknd: t.o) | 1½ | 10 | 50/1 | 84 | 32 |
| | | | | (SP 117.7%) | | **10 Rn** |

**2m 33.61** (4.21) CSF £39.50 TOTE £6.70: £2.10 £2.00 £3.20 (£20.40) Trio £40.30 OWNER Lady Rothschild (BECKHAMPTON) BRED Exors of the late Mrs D. M. de Rothschild

WEIGHT FOR AGE 3yo-13lb

**2474a Spout**, reported to have been in season when she disappointed in Ireland seven days ago, showed what a useful filly she is on her day and, with her style of racing, does not need to be at full stretch until the latter stages are reached. (13/2)

**2113 Phantom Gold** got outpaced on the home turn but, sticking to the inside, obtained a clear run and nosed ahead 75 yards out before the winner pounced to spoil the party. (11/2)
**1409* Ninotchka (USA)** showed signs of being in season in the paddock, but she ran by far her best race yet and would appear to be very much on the upgrade. (9/1: op 6/1)
**2069 Shemozzle (IRE)**, very edgy after being mounted, found all the trouble going in the race and, though she may have caused a lot of the problems herself, she would and should have won this with anything like a clear run. This was definitely one that got away for Pat Eddery. (2/1)
**My Emma**, a half-sister to St Leger winner Classic Cliche, has done well physically since last year, but she did look to need the run. Moving up from the rear to strike the front two furlongs out, she only faded late on and looks a ready-made winner. (50/1)
**1899 Min Alhawa (USA)**, denied a clear run when poised to challenge entering the last quarter-mile, was unable to pick up again after being switched, but it is doubtful if it cost her the race. (9/2)
**1899 Cabaret (IRE)** does not really extend herself, but she did her share of the pacemaking on this first attempt at the trip until weakening inside the distance. (12/1: op 8/1)

## 2534 LETHEBY & CHRISTOPHER OLD NEWTON CUP H'CAP (0-110) (3-Y.O+) (Class B)
3-40 (3-43) **1m 3f 200y** £17,993.75 (£5,450.00: £2,662.50: £1,268.75) Stalls: High GOING minus 0.01 sec per fur (G)

| | | | | SP | RR | SF |
|---|---|---|---|---|---|---|
| 1706[2] | **Key to My Heart (IRE) (110)** (MissSEHall) **6-10-0** RHughes(2) (b: lw: led 3f: led ins fnl f: hrd rdn: all out) | — | 1 | 9/2[2] | 119 | 94 |
| 1976[3] | **Royal Scimitar (USA) (92)** (PFICole) **4-8-7**(3) FLynch(3) (led after 3f tl ins fnl f: rallied gamely cl home) | nk | 2 | 9/2[2] | 101 | 76 |
| 1712[6] | **Nabhaan (IRE) (92)** (DMorley) **3-7-11**ow1 WCarson(5) (trckd ldrs tl dropped rr 3f out: nt clr run appr fnl f: fin strly: unlucky) | 2 | 3 | 7/4[1] | 98 | 59 |
| 2055[9] | **Ionio (USA) (97)** (CEBrittain) **5-9-1** BDoyle(1) (trckd ldrs: rdn over 2f out: one pce ins fnl f) | 1¼ | 4 | 10/1 | 101 | 76 |
| | **Kaitak (IRE) (78)** (JMCarr) **5-7-10** NKennedy(6) (chsd ldrs: drvn along over 3f out: wknd over 1f out) | 2½ | 5 | 33/1 | 79 | 54 |
| 2300[7] | **Casual Water (IRE) (78)** (AGNewcombe) **5-7-10** AMackay(4) (a in rr: rdn 4f out: no imp on ldrs) | 4 | 6 | 12/1 | 74 | 49 |
| 1767[7] | **Source of Light (100)** (RCharlton) **7-9-4** PatEddery(7) (lw: s.i.s: bhd: effrt 2f out: sn rdn: no imp) | 3 | 7 | 9/2[2] | 92 | 67 |
| 2055[3] | **At Liberty (IRE) (86)** (RHannon) **4-8-4** JFEgan(8) (lw: hld up & bhd: rdn over 3f out: no imp) | 2½ | 8 | 5/1[3] | 74 | 49 |

(SP 127.3%) **8 Rn**

**2m 31.98** (2.58) CSF £26.07 CT £46.35 TOTE £5.50: £1.50 £2.00 £1.20 (£17.70) OWNER Mrs Maureen Pickering (MIDDLEHAM) BRED Miss Fiona Meehan
LONG HANDICAP Kaitak (IRE) 7-0 Casual Water (IRE) 7-3 Nabhaan (IRE) 7-6
WEIGHT FOR AGE 3yo-13lb
**1706 Key to My Heart (IRE)**, who turned in another impressive display in conceding 21lb to a younger rival, showed his true grit and answered his rider's every call. (9/2)
**1976 Royal Scimitar (USA)**, taking a big step up in class, had a running battle with the winner from the start, the pair being clear of their rivals, but he was forced to give best inside the final furlong and his determined late rally was to no avail. (9/2)
**1712 Nabhaan (IRE)**, stopped in his stride when making progress approaching the last furlong, must have made up six to eight lengths when he found room and was without doubt a most unlucky loser. This was not the first time he has suffered from being short of room in a race, but he did look something to bet on with only 7-11 to carry. (7/4)
**1620 Ionio (USA)** showed a return to form with a pleasing display and, as two of his successes have been gained in July, this is the time of year he is at his best. (10/1)
**Kaitak (IRE)**, 10lb out of the handicap, was far from disgraced in this company but his stamina looked to give out in the closing stages. (33/1)

## 2535 ROBERT SICE MEMORIAL JULY TROPHY STKS (Listed) (3-Y.O C & G) (Class A)
4-15 (4-16) **1m 3f 200y** £12,445.00 (£3,760.00: £1,830.00: £865.00) Stalls: High GOING minus 0.01 sec per fur (G)

| | | | | SP | RR | SF |
|---|---|---|---|---|---|---|
| 1461* | **Royal Court (IRE)** (PWChapple-Hyam) **3-8-10** DHarrison(4) (b.nr fore: hld up: effrt & rdn 3f out: chal ent fnl f: sn led: r.o wl) | — | 1 | 15/8[2] | 113 | 78 |
| 2116[3] | **Shantou (USA) (118)** (JHMGosden) **3-8-10** PatEddery(5) (lw: dwlt: sn chsng ldr: disp ld over 1f out tl outpcd ins fnl f) | 3½ | 2 | 7/4[1] | 108 | 73 |
| 2144[4] | **Weet-A-Minute (IRE) (106)** (RHollinshead) **3-8-10** FLynch(3) (led tl ins fnl f: kpt on u.p) | ¾ | 3 | 10/1 | 107 | 72 |
| 2074* | **Samraan (USA) (100)** (JLDunlop) **3-8-10** WCarson(2) (lw: hld up: outpcd & reminders over 2f out: sn btn) | 1½ | 4 | 3/1[3] | 105 | 70 |
| 2194[4] | **Kings Witness (USA) (109)** (WJHaggas) **3-8-10** BThomson(1) (chsd ldng pair: rdn 2f out: sn outpcd & eased) | 7 | 5 | 10/1 | 96 | 61 |

(SP 114.3%) **5 Rn**

**2m 31.71** (2.31) CSF £5.61 TOTE £2.90: £1.90 £1.30 (£3.00) OWNER Mr R. E. Sangster (MARLBOROUGH) BRED Swettenham Stud And Ron Con Ltd.
**1461* Royal Court (IRE)** was the first to feel the effect of the whip and looked to be struggling three furlongs out, but he got stronger the further he went and won going away. He does look to be something special. (15/8)
**2116 Shantou (USA)** let the Derby form down somewhat, for he was fighting for the lead passing the furlong marker but then easily got put in his place. (7/4)
**2144 Weet-A-Minute (IRE)** adopted new front-running tactics and proved a tough nut to crack. These forceful tactics look sure to bring him more success. (10/1)
**2074* Samraan (USA)** probably had a harder race than was thought when winning at Royal Ascot, for he ran a bit flat here, though it must be said he was stepping up from handicap company. (3/1)
**2194 Kings Witness (USA)** had to admit the trip finding him out after chasing the leading pair for over a mile, and he was tenderly handled when all chance had gone. (10/1: op 6/1)

## 2536 SHADWELL STUD SERIES APPRENTICE H'CAP (0-80) (3-Y.O+) (Class E)
4-50 (4-50) **1m 2f 120y** £3,382.50 (£1,020.00: £495.00: £232.50) Stalls: High GOING minus 0.01 sec per fur (G)

| | | | | SP | RR | SF |
|---|---|---|---|---|---|---|
| 2127[4] | **Noble Sprinter (IRE) (72)** (WJHaggas) **4-9-1**(5) ElizabethTurner(10) (lw: dwlt: hld up: hdwy over 3f out: led over 1f out: hld on wl towards fin) | — | 1 | 9/1 | 83 | 67 |
| 2312[6] | **Danegold (IRE) (78)** (MRChannon) **4-9-12v** AEddery(2) (s.i.s: hld up: hdwy over 2f out: chal ins fnl f: no ex nr fin) | nk | 2 | 9/1 | 89 | 73 |
| 2010[11] | **Leif the Lucky (USA) (70)** (MissSEHall) **7-9-4** PRoberts(6) (prom: hmpd & lost pl 3f out: effrt & nt clr run over 1f out: styd on wl ins fnl f) | 6 | 3 | 10/1 | 71 | 55 |
| 2027[10] | **Kingfisher Brave (68)** (MGMeagher) **3-7-13**(5)ow1 RStudholme(9) (a.p: ev ch 2f out: rdn over 1f out: one pce) | 2½ | 4 | 25/1 | 66 | 37 |
| 2246* | **Bakheta (62)** (MissGayKelleway) **4-8-10** FLynch(1) (lw: chsd ldr: led 4f out tl over 1f out: eased whn btn fnl f) | 2 | 5 | 7/4[1] | 57 | 41 |

2218* **Rebel County (IRE) (71)** (ABailey) **3-8-7** LNewton(7) (hdwy ½-wy: rdn & edgd lft 3f out: hung bdly lft over 1f out: sn btn) ....3 **6** 9/2[3] 61 33
1670[4] **Amusing Aside (IRE) (68)** (JWWatts) **3-8-4** CTeague(4) (hld up: c wd & hdwy 3f out: nt rch ldrs) ....s.h **7** 11/4[2] 58 30
1666[6] **Baileys First (IRE) (72)** (MJohnston) **3-8-8** KMChin(3) (lw: led over 6f: wknd wl over 1f out)....½ **8** 12/1 61 33
2428[5] **Sheraz (IRE) (61)** (NTinkler) **4-8-6**(3) JoHunnam(8) (mid div tl rdn & wknd over 2f out) ....1½ **9** 14/1 48 32
*2173*[6] **Locorotondo (IRE) (66)** (MBell) **5-9-0** GFaulkner(5) (hld up & bhd: effrt on ins over 3f out: wknd over 2f out) ....7 **10** 11/1 42 26
(SP 136.8%) **10 Rn**

**2m 16.27** (4.77) CSF £90.37 CT £788.54 TOTE £13.60: £3.60 £2.70 £2.40 (£74.50) Trio £46.50 OWNER Khanmaher (NEWMARKET) BRED T. J. Hurley
WEIGHT FOR AGE 3yo-12lb

**2127 Noble Sprinter (IRE)**, a grand-looking colt, came back to form with the blinkers disposed of and, given a very competent ride, won with more in hand than the margin suggests. (9/1)
**2312 Danegold (IRE)** threw down a determined challenge inside the last furlong, but the winner had kept a bit up his sleeve, and he was unable to wear him down. (9/1)
**211 Leif the Lucky (USA)**, impeded twice by the antics of Rebel County when the race was hotting up, battled back willingly to make the frame and looks to be finding his way again. (10/1)
**Kingfisher Brave**, a poor mover who is struggling to find his form, joined issue two furlongs out and remained in the action until feeling the strain approaching the final furlong. (25/1)
**2246* Bakheta**, failing to run into the prizes for the first time this term, could be feeling the effects of a busy schedule last month and she was tenderly handled when beaten. She will be back. (7/4)
**2218* Rebel County (IRE)**, having her first outing for her new stable, was not far away when she edged left three furlongs out. Making a beeline for the inside rail below the distance, she did Leif the Lucky no favours at all and, in the process, did not help her cause. (9/2)
**1666 Baileys First (IRE)** (12/1: op 8/1)
**2173 Locorotondo (IRE)** (11/1: 8/1-12/1)

T/Plpt: £194.30 (117.05 Tckts). T/Qdpt: £42.50 (35.67 Tckts). IM

# 2180-NOTTINGHAM (L-H) (Firm, Good to firm st)
## Saturday July 6th
WEATHER: fine WIND: mod across

## 2537 'FAMILY NIGHT' (S) H'CAP (0-60) (3-Y.O+) (Class G)
6-50 (6-51) **1m 6f 15y** £1,865.00 (£515.00: £245.00) Stalls: Low GOING minus 0.64 sec per fur (F)

SP RR SF
2189[2] **Risky Rose (35)** (RHollinshead) **4-8-12**(5) DGriffiths(7) (hld up: hdwy to ld over 2f out: sn clr: rdn out)....— **1** 7/2[1] 47 37
2282[5] **Bresil (USA) (27)** (KRBurke) **7-8-9** JQuinn(4) (lw: trckd ldrs: n.m.r 6f out: r.o fnl 2f: nt rch wnr) ....3 **2** 8/1[3] 36 26
2218[3] **Ttyfran (35)** (BPJBaugh) **6-9-3** WLord(8) (in tch: styd on fnl 3f: nt pce to chal)....3 **3** 12/1 40 30
2310[11] **Club Elite (21)** (MFBarraclough) **4-7-12**(5) PPMurphy(6) (lw: chsd ldrs: rdn over 2f out: one pce)....2 **4** 25/1 24 14
2189[8] **Fijon (IRE) (55)** (BWHills) **3-9-8** JFortune(1) (swtg: led: hdd 3f out: wknd fnl f)....1¼ **5** 9/1 57 32
**Teoroma (23)** (DrJDScargill) **6-8-5** NAdams(16) (bit bkwd: hld up: hdwy 7f out: led 3f out: sn hdd & wknd)....5 **6** 14/1 19 9
2159[13] **Tout de Val (27)** (KBishop) **7-8-9** TSprake(3) (lw: nvr nrr)....2 **7** 16/1 21 11
609[15] **High Flown (USA) (42)** (RonaldThompson) **4-9-5**(5) RHavlin(2) (chsd ldrs tl wknd 3f out)....nk **8** 14/1 35 25
2362[6] **Friendly Dreams (IRE) (31)** (PTDalton) **3-7-5b**(7)ow1 RCody-Boutcher(5) (trckd ldr: ev ch 3f out: sn wknd)....hd **9** 33/1 24 —
2366[7] **Leap in the Dark (IRE) (29)** (MissLCSiddall) **7-8-11** DRMcCabe(10) (lw: prom: pushed along 6f out: wknd 4f out) ....¾ **10** 5/1[2] 21 11
2183[12] **Bold Joker (25)** (GROldroyd) **5-8-7** DaleGibson(13) (lw: nvr trbld ldrs) ....2½ **11** 25/1 14 4
1472[10] **Rose Chime (IRE) (30)** (JLHarris) **4-8-12** DBiggs(9) (nvr nr to chal)....1¼ **12** 14/1 18 8
**Bud's Bet (IRE) (29)** (MissJFCraze) **8-8-11** JLowe(11) (a bhd) ....2½ **13** 14/1 14 4
1907[3] **Shamand (USA) (43)** (BJMeehan) **3-8-10** JTate(14) (chsd ldrs tl wknd over 3f out)....8 **14** 9/1 19 —
2192[16] **John Tufty (38)** (JPearce) **5-9-6** GBardwell(12) (lw: in tch: lost pl & rdn 5f out: no ch after)....2 **15** 12/1 12 2
2165[16] **Salutation (IRE) (26)** (TKersey) **5-8-8v** NCarlisle(15) (b: chsd ldrs 7f: t.o fnl 3f) ....dist **16** 50/1 — —
(SP 130.5%) **16 Rn**

**3m 1.0** (2.50) CSF £31.96 CT £295.59 TOTE £3.70: £1.10 £1.60 £3.60 £6.80 (£15.40) Trio £39.80 OWNER Mr M. Johnson (UPPER LONGDON) BRED Miss Sarah Hollinshead
WEIGHT FOR AGE 3yo-15lb
No bid
Fijon (IRE) sld JPearce 800 gns

**2189 Risky Rose**, back over a more suitable trip, was running all over her rivals in the final two furlongs. (7/2)
**642 Bresil (USA)**, just beaten over this course and distance last August, has run poorly since but loves to hear his hooves rattle, and stayed on well in the closing stages after running too freely had got him into trouble in the back straight. He has the ability to pick up a similar race, but his career record of one win from forty-three Flat appearances hardly inspires confidence. (8/1)
**2218 Ttyfran** was only given ten days to recover from his first run in some time and ran a different race in this bigger field, staying on to the end. He retains the ability to win a race, but has a career record of one win and nine places, and one refusal to start over hurdles. (12/1)
**Club Elite**, yet to break her duck, looked short of speed where it matters. (25/1)
**1589 Fijon (IRE)** did not appear to quite get the trip, but has tumbled a long way since finishing fifth to Sil Sila last October, and was sold for 800 guineas after the race. (9/1: op 6/1)
**Teoroma**, returning after a year off, is lightly-raced and ran well enough to suggest he would have made the frame if fully fit. (14/1)
**High Flown (USA)** (14/1: 10/1-16/1)

## 2538 PLAYQUEST MAIDEN AUCTION STKS (2-Y.O) (Class E)
7-20 (7-21) **6f 15y** £3,131.90 (£868.40: £415.70) Stalls: High GOING minus 0.29 sec per fur (GF)

SP RR SF
*2370*[8] **Union Town (IRE)** (SirMarkPrescott) **2-8-10** CNutter(10) (bit bkwd: hdwy 2f out: led ins fnl f: pushed out)....— **1** 25/1 74 5
1851[2] **Smugurs (IRE)** (RJRWilliams) **2-7-12** JQuinn(6) (hdwy over 1f out: r.o fnl f) ....1¼ **2** 2/1[1] 59 —
2044[4] **Jack Flush (IRE)** (BSRothwell) **2-8-3** MFenton(1) (led over 5f: no ex nr fin)....s.h **3** 8/1 64 —
1842[12] **Hever Golf Dancer** (TJNaughton) **2-8-11**ow1 RHughes(8) (hdwy & hung lft 2f out: no imp fnl f)....2½ **4** 20/1 65 —

2157[2] **Pat Said No (IRE)** (DJSCosgrove) **2-8-5** JStack(9) (lw: chsd ldrs: ev ch over 1f out: wknd ins fnl f)................½ **5** 9/4[2] 58 —
**Havago** (RHannon) **2-8-3**(3) DaneO'Neill(5) (unf: scope: w ldrs 3f) ....................................................................½ **6** 7/1[3] 57 —
**Two Bills** (AStreeter) **2-8-3** TSprake(7) (leggy: hld up: nvr trbld ldrs) ..................................................................4 **7** 20/1 44 —
**Moccasin (IRE)** (PRWebber) **2-8-5** BThomson(2) (neat: scope: prom tl wknd 2f out) ...................................1¼ **8** 9/1 43 —
1664[10] **April Jackson** (PTDalton) **2-8-1** NAdams(3) (dwlt: hdwy 4f out: wknd over 2f out)............................................5 **9** 25/1 25 —
**Drift** (SirMarkPrescott) **2-8-10** WWoods(4) (leggy: bkwd: in tch: rdn over 2f out: sn wknd)............................1¼ **10** 9/1 31 —
(SP 124.9%) **10 Rn**

**1m 15.2** (4.70) CSF £76.22 TOTE £28.20: £6.80 £1.10 £2.10 (£47.40) Trio £70.90 OWNER H R H Prince Fahd Salman (NEWMARKET) BRED Newgate Stud Co
No bid
OFFICIAL EXPLANATION **Union Town (IRE): had not liked the kick-back at Southwell, and appreciated the faster going against the stands' rail here.**
**Union Town (IRE)** broke the old adage 'never back a two-year-old within a week of its debut' but resented the kickback at Southwell and probably took little out of himself. Sticking to the advantageous stands' rail and getting a dream run through, he won a shade cosily in the end. (25/1)
**1851 Smugurs (IRE)** ran a similar race to her debut, running on fast and late. (2/1)
**2044 Jack Flush (IRE)** took these along, despite the worst of the draw, but could never get to the stands' rail. He looks close to opening his account. (8/1)
**Hever Golf Dancer**, as poor a mover as his sire, was behind to halfway, but looked to be quickening in dangerous style until ruining his chance by hanging. (20/1)
**2157 Pat Said No (IRE)** looked to have bagged the coveted rails berth until letting the winner up her inside. (9/4)
**Havago** showed early speed but gradually faded in the last quarter-mile. (7/1)
**Moccasin (IRE)** (9/1: 5/1-10/1)
**Drift**, a stable-companion of the winner and apparently the more fancied of the two, cut little ice from a poor draw but will do better in time. (9/1: 5/1-10/1)

## 2539 TALES OF ROBIN HOOD CLAIMING STKS (2-Y.O) (Class F)
7-50 (7-50) **6f 15y** £1,932.00 (£532.00: £252.00) Stalls: High GOING minus 0.29 sec per fur (GF)

SP RR SF
2012[4] **Summer Risotto** (DJSffrenchDavis) **2-8-1** NCarlisle(3) (hld up & plld hrd: qcknd to ld over 1f out: rdn out)...— **1** 3/1[3] 58 —
2254[2] **Maria di Castiglia** (RHannon) **2-8-8**(3) DaneO'Neill(1) (w ldr: led & stumbled 2f out: sn hdd & one pce) .......1¾ **2** 5/4[1] 63 2
2237* **Taome (IRE)** (PDEvans) **2-8-9** JFortune(2) (led 4f: eased whn btn fnl f) ...........................................................4 **3** 13/8[2] 51 —
(SP 107.5%) **3 Rn**

**1m 15.2** (4.70) CSF £6.34 TOTE £4.20: (£3.10) OWNER Hargood Ltd (UPPER LAMBOURN) BRED N. and L. Warburton
**2012 Summer Risotto**, a bitter disappointment last time, put that behind her with a fluent win, although it took Carlisle nearly a furlong to get her to settle in behind the other two. (3/1)
**2254 Maria di Castiglia**, coming down in trip, was beaten for finishing pace in a few strides going to the furlong pole. (5/4: op Evens)
**2237* Taome (IRE)** led up the stands' rail but found little when shaken up and the situation was soon accepted. (13/8)

## 2540 NOTTINGHAM EVENING POST MAIDEN H'CAP (0-70) (3-Y.O+) (Class E)
8-20 (8-21) **1m 1f 213y** £3,857.10 (£1,075.60: £519.30) Stalls: Low GOING minus 0.64 sec per fur (F)

SP RR SF
2251[3] **Racing Hawk (USA) (48)** (MSSaunders) **4-8-10**(5) PPMurphy(4) (led: hdd over 3f out: led again 2f out: rdn out) ..........................................— **1** 13/2[2] 56 15
2036[11] **Rex Mundi (55)** (PDEvans) **4-9-8** JFortune(3) (prom: rdn 3f out: chsd wnr appr fnl f: r.o) ...............................½ **2** 12/1 62 21
2130[5] **Soviet King (IRE) (56)** (PhilipMitchell) **3-8-12** RHughes(1) (b: lw: chsd ldrs: rdn over 1f out: kpt on)..................2 **3** 9/2[1] 60 8
955[5] **Fikra (USA) (62)** (SPCWoods) **3-9-4** WWoods(8) (a.p: one pce fnl 2f) ................................................................4 **4** 9/1 60 8
2196[4] **Zdenka (55)** (MBlanshard) **3-8-11** JQuinn(13) (hdwy 6f out: wknd 2f out)...............................................................2½ **5** 8/1[3] 49 —
**Della Casa (IRE) (68)** (JLDunlop) **3-9-10** WCarson(6) (lw: prom: led over 3f out: sn rdn: hdd & wknd 2f out).1¼ **6** 9/2[1] 60 8
**Infantry Dancer (58)** (GCBravery) **3-9-0** CHodgson(12) (b.hind: chsd ldrs: no hdwy fnl 3f) ............................1¼ **7** 12/1 48 —
*2082*[6] **Forget Paris (IRE) (45)** (BSRothwell) **3-8-1** JStack(7) (dwlt: bhd tl sme hdwy fnl 3f).........................................2½ **8** 16/1 31 —
2197[13] **Isla Glen (55)** (MMcCormack) **3-8-11** TSprake(10) (n.d) ..............................................................................4 **9** 20/1 34 —
2320[13] **Lady Ploy (39)** (MissLCSiddall) **4-8-6** DRMcCabe(11) (a bhd) ....................................................................27 **10** 33/1 — —
2506[13] **Tarian (USA) (50)** (GBBalding) **4-9-3** KFallon(2) (lw: in tch 7f: eased whn btn) ....................................................6 **11** 13/2[2] — —
1864[8] **Totally Different (41)** (GROldroyd) **3-7-11**ow1 DaleGibson(9) (lw: a bhd) ..............................................................3 **12** 33/1 — —
*2168*[4] **Shouldbegrey (49)** (WRMuir) **3-8-2**(3)ow4 DaneO'Neill(5) (chsd ldrs tl stumbled & uns rdr wl over 3f out) ........... **U** 13/2[2] — —
(SP 129.4%) **13 Rn**

**2m 6.6** (4.10) CSF £80.04 CT £363.31 TOTE £6.40: £2.40 £2.80 £2.00 (£90.70) Trio £129.80 OWNER Mr T. Leigh (WELLS) BRED Buckram Oak Farm
LONG HANDICAP Totally Different 7-2
WEIGHT FOR AGE 3yo-11lb
**2251 Racing Hawk (USA)** got off the mark with a battling front-running effort and may be value for a little more than the winning margin. (13/2)
**Rex Mundi**, making his handicap debut, is a good mover but looked none too easy a ride, although he stayed on strongly at the finish, despite carrying his head rather high. (12/1)
**2130 Soviet King (IRE)** appeared to stay well enough and did not look unduly flattered, although this race was dominated by those drawn low. (9/2)
**955 Fikra (USA)**, off for two months, may have just needed this, but looked short of gears in the straight. (9/1)
**2196 Zdenka**, a poor mover, is struggling to find a trip. (8/1: op 12/1)
**Della Casa (IRE)** cruised to the front early in the straight, but was soon sending out distress signals and faded quickly once headed. She did not appear to need the race and a mile may be her trip. (9/2)

## 2541 BBC RADIO NOTTINGHAM H'CAP (0-70) (3-Y.O) (Class E)
8-50 (8-50) **1m 54y** £3,572.20 (£994.20: £478.60) Stalls: Low GOING minus 0.64 sec per fur (F)

SP RR SF
1418[2] **Hawksley Hill (IRE) (62)** (MrsJRRamsden) **3-9-3** KFallon(9) (bhd: hdwy over 3f out: hung lft & led over 1f out: sn clr: comf).............................................................— **1** 2/1[1] 75 33
2180* **How Could-I (IRE) (44)** (MrsNMacauley) **3-7-13b** JQuinn(3) (lw: led: clr over 2f out: hdd over 1f out: unable qckn) ..............................................................2½ **2** 3/1[2] 52 10
2159[4] **Flame of Hope (57)** (JLDunlop) **3-8-12** TSprake(4) (prom: outpcd over 2f out: styd on fnl f)..............................2½ **3** 5/1[3] 60 18
1908[6] **Cerise (IRE) (51)** (CWCElsey) **3-8-1b**(5) MartinDwyer(5) (dwlt: hdwy 2f out: nrst fin)............................................5 **4** 9/1 45 3

| | | | | | | |
|---|---|---|---|---|---|---|
| *1993*3 | **Red Rusty (USA) (63)** (DMorris) **3-8-11**(7) AEddery(1) (chsd ldr: rdn 4f out: wknd over 2f out) | 6 | **5** | 9/1 | 45 | 3 |
| 15946 | **Lady Dignity (IRE) (66)** (PJMakin) **3-9-2**(5) RHavlin(7) (bhd: effrt 4f out: no imp) | 5 | **6** | 8/1 | 38 | — |
| | **Sizzling Serenade (41)** (JAHarris) **3-7-10** JLowe(2) (chsd ldrs tl wknd over 3f out) | 3½ | **7** | 33/1 | 7 | — |
| 19945 | **In The Highlands (52)** (DJSCosgrove) **3-8-7** DaleGibson(6) (b: chsd ldrs 5f) | 1¼ | **8** | 20/1 | 15 | — |
| 19847 | **Dyanko (43)** (MSSaunders) **3-7-9**(3) NVarley(8) (lw: in tch: rn wd after 3f: sn bhd) | 1½ | **9** | 12/1 | 3 | — |
| | | | | (SP 121.5%) | **9 Rn** | |

**1m 42.9** (1.60) CSF £8.70 CT £24.82 TOTE £2.90: £1.40 £1.30 £1.30 (£3.30) Trio £4.40 OWNER Mr Hamish Alexander (THIRSK) BRED The Wickfield Stud Ltd

LONG HANDICAP Sizzling Serenade 7-7

**1418 Hawksley Hill (IRE)**, dropping down in trip, was taken off his feet by the good early pace but this played into his hands as stamina proved his trump as he burst through in the straight. He is still on the upgrade. (2/1)

**2180* How Could-I (IRE)** moved well to post and did her best to stretch her rivals from the gun, kicking again early in the straight. Once headed, there was nothing left in reserve. (3/1)

**2159 Flame of Hope** had looked just the type for handicaps earlier in the season but has failed to progress and did not shape like a miler here, getting outpaced early in the straight before staying on well. (5/1)

**1908 Cerise (IRE)** does not have an ideal temperament, being reluctant to come onto the course and giving away ground at the start. (9/1: op 6/1)

**1993 Red Rusty (USA)**, having only his second race on turf, could not get to the front and tended to race with his head up, as if feeling the ground. (9/1)

**1594 Lady Dignity (IRE)** tried to close in the straight but never got near the leaders. (8/1)

## 2542 'FUN FOR ALL THE FAMILY' LIMITED STKS (0-55) (3-Y.O) (Class F)

9-20 (9-22) **1m 1f 213y** £1,932.00 (£532.00: £252.00) Stalls: Low GOING minus 0.64 sec per fur (F)

| | | | | SP | RR | SF |
|---|---|---|---|---|---|---|
| | **Frog (55)** (SirMarkPrescott) **3-8-11** WWoods(8) (in tch: hdwy to ld over 1f out: sn pushed clr) | — | **1** | 9/4 1 | 64 | 11 |
| 21912 | **Two Socks (57)** (MMcCormack) **3-9-0** RHughes(4) (hdwy 5f out: led over 1f out: sn hdd & one pce) | 3½ | **2** | 11/2 3 | 61 | 8 |
| 5954 | **Fiona Shann (USA) (53)** (JLDunlop) **3-8-11** WCarson(2) (prom: rdn over 3f out: swtchd & r.o fnl f) | ¾ | **3** | 7/2 2 | 57 | 4 |
| 1821* | **Spa Lane (54)** (PJMakin) **3-8-9**(5) RHavlin(11) (chsd ldrs: rdn & ev ch over 3f out: one pce appr fnl f) | s.h | **4** | 6/1 | 60 | 7 |
| 19085 | **Sylvella (53)** (MAJarvis) **3-8-11** PRobinson(3) (bhd: hdwy 4f out: one pce fnl 2f) | 3 | **5** | 6/1 | 52 | — |
| 20145 | **Miss Pravda (53)** (PTWalwyn) **3-8-6**(5) MartinDwyer(7) (a.p: led 3f out tl over 1f out: wknd fnl f) | 1¼ | **6** | 16/1 | 50 | — |
| 20279 | **Islay Brown (IRE) (49)** (CWCElsey) **3-8-11b** KFallon(5) (led 7f) | s.h | **7** | 14/1 | 50 | — |
| 19956 | **Crimson Rosella (55)** (WJHaggas) **3-8-11** RMcGhin(10) (chsd ldrs over 7f) | ½ | **8** | 14/1 | 49 | — |
| 165413 | **Prince Zizim (53)** (CADwyer) **3-8-11**(3) NVarley(1) (s.i.s: hdwy 6f out: wknd 3f out) | ½ | **9** | 33/1 | 52 | — |
| 225111 | **Hank-a-chief (46)** (BSmart) **3-9-0b1** JStack(9) (rn wd over 4f out: a bhd) | 9 | **10** | 40/1 | 37 | — |
| *2158*11 | **Realms of Glory (IRE) (52)** (PhilipMitchell) **3-9-0** JQuinn(6) (bhd fnl 4f) | 16 | **11** | 25/1 | 12 | — |
| | | | | (SP 125.4%) | **11 Rn** | |

**2m 6.6** (4.10) CSF £15.58 TOTE £3.70: £1.30 £1.80 £2.00 (£9.90) Trio £72.80 OWNER Mr B. Haggas (NEWMARKET) BRED Mrs P. A. Clark

**Frog** cut little ice last year but looked ready and the improvement she found was clearly expected. She looks the type to continue to progress in this type of race, and her trainer has no peers when it comes to placing horses of this sort. (9/4: 3/1-2/1)

**2191 Two Socks**, dropping back in trip, looked likely to score when quickening in the centre of the track but was no match for the winner at this trip. (11/2)

**595 Fiona Shann (USA)** looked fit, despite three months off and stayed on well in the last furlong after getting chopped for speed. She may stay further. (7/2)

**1821* Spa Lane**, produced earlier on this occasion, had been shaken off by the furlong pole. (6/1)

**1908 Sylvella** appeared to jump a path in the early stages and lost her action for a few strides. (6/1)

**2014 Miss Pravda** had already been shaken off when her stride shortened in the last furlong. (16/1)

T/Plpt: £149.00 (65.14 Tckts). T/Qdpt: £36.90 (14.34 Tckts). Dk

# 2500-SANDOWN (R-H) (Good to soft)

## Saturday July 6th

WEATHER: unsettled WIND: almost nil

## 2543 E.B.F. PADDOCK MAIDEN STKS (2-Y.O) (Class D)

2-15 (2-15) **7f 16y** £4,182.00 (£1,266.00: £618.00: £294.00) Stalls: High GOING minus 0.20 sec per fur (GF)

| | | | | SP | RR | SF |
|---|---|---|---|---|---|---|
| | **Gretel** (MRStoute) **2-8-9** JReid(6) (leggy: scope: lw: hld up: rdn over 1f out: led ins fnl f: r.o wl) | — | **1** | 7/2 3 | 76+ | 47 |
| | **Medaaly** (SbinSuroor) **2-9-0** MJKinane(1) (w'like: bit bkwd: hld up: swtchd rt over 3f out: led over 1f out tl ins fnl f: unable qckn) | ¾ | **2** | 3/1 2 | 79+ | 50 |
| | **Dark Green (USA)** (PFICole) **2-9-0** TQuinn(7) (w'like: scope: lw: led over 5f: hrd rdn: one pce) | 2 | **3** | 5/2 1 | 75 | 46 |
| 13394 | **Ikatania** (JLDunlop) **2-9-0** JWeaver(3) (nvr nr to chal) | 5 | **4** | 4/1 | 64 | 35 |
| | **Blue River (IRE)** (TGMills) **2-9-0** RHills(4) (wl grwn: lw: a bhd) | 3½ | **5** | 16/1 | 56 | 27 |
| | **Love Has No Pride (USA)** (RHannon) **2-9-0** RPerham(5) (unf: bit bkwd: chsd ldr over 4f) | nk | **6** | 20/1 | 55 | 26 |
| | | | | (SP 106.4%) | **6 Rn** | |

**1m 31.28** (2.68) CSF £12.81 TOTE £4.80: £2.00 £1.70 (£5.40) OWNER Sheikh Mohammed (NEWMARKET) BRED Sheikh Mohammed

**Gretel**, a tall, attractive filly with plenty of scope, was pitched in against the colts on this debut but was certainly up to the task. Nicely tucked in behind the leaders, she delivered her challenge from below the distance and found a nice turn of foot inside the final furlong to settle the issue. Further success awaits her. (7/2)

**Medaaly**, whose dam is a sister to Grand Prix de Paris winner Fort Wood and a half-sister to July Cup winner Hamas and Goodwood Cup winner Mazzacano, is himself a half-brother to the top class miler Charnwood Forest. A very ordinary-looking individual who is not that big, he looked as though the run was needed but nevertheless showed a great deal of promise. Never far away, he moved to the front below the distance but found the winner just too good inside the final furlong. He looks a ready-made winner. (3/1: op 5/4)

**Dark Green (USA)**, an attractive colt with plenty of scope, showed a lot of promise. Bowling along in front, he was collared below the distance and then tapped for toe. He should not be difficult to win with. (5/2: 7/2-9/4)

**1339 Ikatania**, the only runner with experience on his side, was held up at the back of the field but could never get in a serious blow. (4/1)

**Blue River (IRE)**, a half-brother to numerous winners of whom most were best at a round a mile, is an attractive, well-grown colt with plenty of strength and scope. However, on this debut, he was always at the back of the field. (16/1)

**Love Has No Pride (USA)** did not look fully fit for this debut and so it proved for, after racing in second place, he was collared for that pitch over two furlongs from home and soon capitulated. (20/1)

## 2544 KINGSTON RATED STKS H'CAP (0-100) (3-Y.O+) (Class B)

2-50 (2-51) **1m 14y** £12,718.00 (£4,762.00: £2,331.00: £1,005.00: £452.50: £231.50) Stalls: High GOING minus 0.20 sec per fur (GF)

| | | | | SP | RR | SF |
|---|---|---|---|---|---|---|
| 2312* | **Concer Un (87)** (SCWilliams) **4-8-8** MHills(1) (b.nr fore: lw: hdwy over 6f out: hrd rdn fnl f: led last stride) | — | 1 | 6/1 1 | 95 | 61 |
| 2146* | **Golden Pond (IRE) (87)** (RFJohnsonHoughton) **3-7-13** DeclanO'Shea(12) (led: hrd rdn over 1f out: hdd last stride) | hd | 2 | 8/1 3 | 95 | 52 |
| 2053 18 | **Green Green Desert (FR) (100)** (LadyHerries) **5-9-7** TQuinn(9) (lw: s.s: gd hdwy over 1f out: r.o wl ins fnl f) | s.h | 3 | 12/1 | 108 | 74 |
| 2053 12 | **Kayvee (92)** (GHarwood) **7-8-13** RHills(10) (gd hdwy over 1f out: unable qckn ins fnl f) | 1¾ | 4 | 10/1 | 96 | 62 |
| 2041 9 | **Brandon Magic (98)** (IABalding) **3-8-10** JReid(4) (a.p: rdn 2f out: one pce) | 1½ | 5 | 8/1 3 | 99 | 56 |
| 1785 7 | **Murheb (88)** (RWArmstrong) **3-8-0** CRutter(8) (hld up: rdn over 2f out: one pce) | nk | 6 | 14/1 | 89 | 46 |
| 2053 22 | **Moving Arrow (94)** (MissSEHall) **5-9-1** JWeaver(2) (plld hrd: nvr nr to chal) | ½ | 7 | 10/1 | 94 | 60 |
| 1476 14 | **Blue Zulu (IRE) (88)** (JRFanshawe) **4-8-9** WWoods(6) (hld up: rdn over 3f out: wknd over 1f out) | ½ | 8 | 20/1 | 87 | 53 |
| 2053 7 | **Beauchamp Jazz (96)** (JLDunlop) **4-9-3** MJKinane(5) (swtg: hdwy over 1f out: sn wknd) | 2½ | 9 | 13/2 2 | 90 | 56 |
| 2400 7 | **Comanche Companion (86)** (TJNaughton) **6-8-4**(3) NVarley(13) (prom 6f) | 5 | 10 | 16/1 | 70 | 36 |
| 2328 5 | **Options Open (92)** (MrsJRRamsden) **4-8-13** KFallon(3) (lw: hdwy over 2f out: wknd over 1f out) | 1¼ | 11 | 6/1 1 | 73 | 39 |
| 2041 27 | **Oberons Boy (IRE) (98)** (BJMeehan) **3-8-10** MTebbutt(11) (hdwy over 2f out: sn wknd) | 2½ | 12 | 50/1 | 74 | 31 |
| 2053 20 | **Moments of Fortune (USA) (95)** (BHanbury) **4-9-2b** MRimmer(7) (prom over 5f) | 1¾ | 13 | 20/1 | 68 | 34 |
| | | | | (SP 114.0%) | **13 Rn** | |

**1m 42.79** (1.59) CSF £46.98 CT £520.77 TOTE £6.60: £2.90 £2.30 £3.00 (£17.60) Trio £49.80 OWNER Miss L. J. Ward (NEWMARKET) BRED Lloyd Bros

LONG HANDICAP Comanche Companion 8-4

WEIGHT FOR AGE 3yo-9lb

**2312* Concer Un**, soon in a handy position, responded to pressure in the final furlong and managed to get up right on the line in a desperate finish. (6/1)

**2146* Golden Pond (IRE)** continues in tremendous form despite a rise of 15lb since her Nottingham victory. Bowling along in front, she grimly tried to hold off her rivals but was eventually caught right on the line. She is a winner without a penalty. (8/1)

**1112 Green Green Desert (FR)**, put to sleep at the back of the field, began to make giant strides from below the distance but, as so often in the past, just failed to get there. With just one win to his name nearly three years ago and a string of placed efforts, it speaks volumes for his attitude. (12/1)

**Kayvee** made significant progress from below the distance but, after almost getting on terms, was tapped for toe in the last 150 yards. (10/1: 13/2-11/1)

**1395a Brandon Magic**, never far away, failed to find the necessary turn of foot from below the distance. (8/1)

**1785 Murheb** chased the leaders, but could only go up and down in the same place in the last two furlongs. (14/1: 10/1-16/1)

**2328 Options Open** (6/1: 9/2-7/1)

## 2545 SANDOWN PARK SPRINT STKS (Listed) (3-Y.O+) (Class A)

3-25 (3-27) **5f 6y** £12,014.75 (£3,638.00: £1,776.50: £845.75) Stalls: Low GOING minus 0.20 sec per fur (GF)

| | | | | SP | RR | SF |
|---|---|---|---|---|---|---|
| 2115 10 | **Eveningperformance (110)** (HCandy) **5-9-2** CRutter(13) (racd far side: mde all: comf) | — | 1 | 7/1 3 | 113+ | 85 |
| 2332 2 | **Venture Capitalist (112)** (DNicholls) **7-9-10** KFallon(8) (racd far side: s.s: nt clr run 2f out: hdwy over 1f out: r.o wl ins fnl f) | ½ | 2 | 11/1 | 119 | 91 |
| 2270a 2 | **Croft Pool (102)** (JAGlover) **5-9-3** SDWilliams(9) (racd far side: hld up: rdn over 2f out: r.o one pce) | 3 | 3 | 8/1 | 103 | 75 |
| 2115 7 | **Loch Patrick (105)** (MMadgwick) **6-9-3** JReid(7) (lw: racd far side: hld up: rdn over 2f out: r.o one pce) | nk | 4 | 13/2 2 | 102 | 74 |
| 2115 11 | **Mubhij (IRE) (108)** (BWHills) **3-8-12** RHills(12) (lw: racd far side: chsd wnr tl ins fnl f: one pce) | nk | 5 | 6/1 1 | 101 | 68 |
| 1818 4 | **Marl (89)** (RAkehurst) **3-8-7** TQuinn(11) (racd far side: prom 3f) | 3½ | 6 | 10/1 | 85 | 52 |
| 2292 10 | **Takadou (IRE) (94)** (MissLCSiddall) **5-9-3** WWoods(6) (nvr nr to chal) | 4 | 7 | 40/1 | 77 | 49 |
| 2114 24 | **Brave Edge (107)** (RHannon) **5-9-7** RPerham(4) (outpcd) | ¾ | 8 | 11/1 | 79 | 51 |
| 2114 6 | **To the Roof (IRE) (99)** (PWHarris) **4-9-7** MHills(5) (lw: outpcd) | 3½ | 9 | 13/2 2 | 68 | 40 |
| 2472a 8 | **Double Quick (IRE) (102)** (MJohnston) **4-9-2** JWeaver(3) (lw: prom over 3f) | nk | 10 | 8/1 | 62 | 34 |
| 2381 7 | **Wavian (95)** (RHannon) **4-9-3** MTebbutt(1) (lw: bhd fnl 2f) | 7 | 11 | 40/1 | 40 | 12 |
| 2050 9 | **King of The East (IRE) (104)** (MRStoute) **3-8-12** MJKinane(2) (lw: bhd fnl 2f) | ¾ | 12 | 9/1 | 38 | 5 |
| | | | | (SP 116.3%) | **12 Rn** | |

**59.74 secs** (-0.06) CSF £72.23 TOTE £7.30: £2.50 £4.10 £2.10 (£46.70) Trio £149.90 OWNER Mrs David Blackburn (WANTAGE) BRED Mrs R. D. Peacock

WEIGHT FOR AGE 3yo-5lb

**IN-FOCUS: This race was very much a farce as the six horses who elected to tack over and race on the far side, where the ground was much better, were always miles clear of the stands'-side group, and consequently filled the first six places home.**

**927 Eveningperformance** has tremendous early speed and that is exactly what she showed here. Storming off in front on the far side, one would have expected her to tie up on this stiff five furlongs on soft ground but that was not the case on this occasion and, with all her other rivals struggling, she comfortably had things in control in the final furlong. (7/1: op 9/2)

**2332 Venture Capitalist** found this stiff five furlongs a little too sharp. Slowly away, he was at the back the field on the far side until picking up ground from below the distance. He ran on really strongly inside the final furlong but was not going to get there in time. All seven of his career wins have come over six furlongs and a return to that trip is required. (11/1)

**2270a Croft Pool** chased the leaders on the far side but, despite staying on, could never get in a blow. (8/1)

**1621 Loch Patrick** ran well enough up the far side, and continues to leave the impression that there is a decent prize in the pipe-line. (13/2)

**Mubhij (IRE)** chased the winner on the far side, but he was collared for that position inside the final furlong and could only struggle on at one pace. (6/1)

**1818 Marl** was close up on the far side until tiring two furlongs from home. (10/1)

## 2546 CORAL-ECLIPSE STKS (Gp 1) (3-Y.O+) (Class A)

4-10 (4-11) **1m 2f 7y** £147,600.00 (£55,100.00: £26,350.00: £11,350.00) Stalls: High GOING minus 0.20 sec per fur (GF)

| | | | | SP | RR | SF |
|---|---|---|---|---|---|---|
| 1749a* | **Halling (USA) (120)** (SbinSuroor) **5-9-7** JReid(1) (lw: mde all: rdn out) | — | 1 | 100/30 2 | 129 | 78 |
| 2039* | **Bijou d'Inde (120)** (MJohnston) **3-8-10** JWeaver(2) (lw: a.p: rdn over 1f out: ev ch ins fnl f: r.o) | nk | 2 | 12/1 | 129 | 67 |
| *536a* 4 | **Pentire (120)** (GWragg) **4-9-7** MHills(5) (hld up: rdn over 1f out: unable qckn ins fnl f) | 1¾ | 3 | 2/1 1 | 126 | 75 |
| 1793* | **Ela-Aristokrati (IRE) (113)** (LMCumani) **4-9-7** KFallon(6) (lw: rdn over 2f out: nvr nr to chal) | 5 | 4 | 16/1 | 118 | 67 |
| 1575a* | **Definite Article** (DKWeld,Ireland) **4-9-7v1** MJKinane(7) (a.p: rdn over 3f out: wknd over 1f out) | nk | 5 | 7/2 3 | 117 | 66 |

| | | | Pos | SP | RR | SF |
|---|---|---|---|---|---|---|
| 906a* | **Valanour (IRE)** (AdeRoyerDupre,France) **4-9-7** GMosse(4) (lw: hld up: rdn over 2f out: sn wknd) | 2 | **6** | 7/1 | 114 | 63 |
| $2039^{4}$ | **Beauchamp King (115)** (JLDunlop) **3-8-10** TQuinn(3) (hld up: rdn over 2f out: wknd over 1f out) | 6 | **7** | 16/1 | 105 | 43 |
| | | | | (SP 110.6%) | | **7 Rn** |

**2m 8.05** (1.35) CSF £34.18 TOTE £3.80: £2.20 £3.00 (£28.00) OWNER Godolphin (NEWMARKET) BRED Cyril Humphries
WEIGHT FOR AGE 3yo-11lb

**1749a* Halling (USA)** followed up last year's victory with another brilliant display. Making every post a winning one, he looked in serious trouble as the runner-up and third threw down their challenges from below the distance but, refusing to give way, held on in tremendous style. He has now won seven of his last eight races on turf and will now head to York to try and follow up last year's victory in the Juddmonte International. (100/30)

**2039* Bijou d'Inde** has the heart of a lion and any worries that he may not have stayed this longer trip were certainly dispelled, especially when one considers the soft ground and stiffness of this track putting even more emphasis on stamina. Never far away, he threw down a determined challenge from below the distance and looked likely to get up inside the final furlong. He did absolutely nothing wrong and only just failed to succeed. A return clash with the winner in the Juddmonte International at York looks on the cards and that mouth-watering prospect could well see him turning the tables if the ground rides fast. (12/1: 8/1-14/1)

**536a Pentire**, given a rest since his fine fourth in the Dubai World Cup back in March, was nicely tucked in behind his rivals. Delivering his challenge from below the distance, he was almost on terms, but was tapped for toe in the last 100 yards. He is sure to benefit a great deal from this and, on a sounder surface which he can really bounce off, he is going to be a major player in the King George VI and Queen Elizabeth Diamond Stakes. (2/1)

**1793* Ela-Aristokrati (IRE)**, held up at the back of the field, was being pushed along over a quarter of a mile from home and, although slightly short of room, it made little difference as he could never get in a blow. (16/1)

**1575a* Definite Article**, who has gained all bar one of his victories with some cut in the ground, found this company too hot. A leading player from the outset, he had shot his bolt below the distance. (7/2)

**906a* Valanour (IRE)** found the heavy showers of the last few days all against him here. Chasing the leaders, he was bustled along over two furlongs from home but the writing was soon on the wall. (7/1: 5/1-8/1)

**2039 Beauchamp King**, well backed in the morning, was a spent force below the distance. (16/1)

## 2547 COMMONWEALTH H'CAP (0-85) (3-Y.O+) (Class D)

4-45 (4-45) **2m 78y** £7,165.00 (£2,170.00: £1,060.00: £505.00) Stalls: High GOING minus 0.20 sec per fur (GF)

| | | | Pos | SP | RR | SF |
|---|---|---|---|---|---|---|
| $2190^{2}$ | **Pearl Venture (75)** (SPCWoods) **4-9-5** WWoods(6) (stdy hdwy over 2f out: rdn ins fnl f: led nr fin) | — | **1** | 12/1 | 85 | 56 |
| $1611^{2}$ | **Bowcliffe Court (IRE) (64)** (BWHills) **4-8-8** JReid(13) (hdwy over 4f out: led over 1f out tl ins fnl: r.o) | ½ | **2** | 9/1 | 74 | 45 |
| | **Danjing (IRE) (83)** (MCPipe) **4-9-13** DBridgwater(5) (hrd rdn over 6f out: hdwy over 3f out: led ins fnl f: hdd nr fin) | s.h | **3** | 14/1 | 93 | 64 |
| $1407^{3}$ | **Sharaf (IRE) (83)** (JLDunlop) **3-8-8b$^{1}$** RHills(3) (lw: a.p: led 4f out tl over 1f out: one pce) | 2½ | **4** | $7/2^{1}$ | 90 | 42 |
| $2131^{5}$ | **Pine Needle (82)** (DMorley) **3-8-7** MHills(14) (lw: rdn & hdwy over 3f out: one pce fnl 2f) | 3 | **5** | $7/1^{2}$ | 86 | 38 |
| $1981^{5}$ | **World Express (IRE) (56)** (BRMillman) **6-8-0** CRutter(9) (hdwy over 2f out: wknd over 1f out) | 8 | **6** | $8/1^{3}$ | 52 | 23 |
| | **Top Cees (84)** (MrsJRRamsden) **6-10-0** KFallon(4) (nvr nr to chal) | 2½ | **7** | 11/1 | 78 | 49 |
| $2042^{8}$ | **Shadirwan (IRE) (80)** (RAkehurst) **5-9-10** TQuinn(12) (prom 12f) | 1¾ | **8** | $7/1^{2}$ | 72 | 43 |
| $2190^{3}$ | **Deano's Beeno (75)** (MJohnston) **4-9-5** JWeaver(7) (lw: prom 14f) | 1¾ | **9** | 12/1 | 65 | 36 |
| | **Durshan (USA) (52)** (JRJenkins) **7-7-10** DeclanO'Shea(10) (bhd fnl 4f) | 1¼ | **10** | 40/1 | 41 | 12 |
| 1803* | **Soojama (IRE) (53)** (RMFlower) **6-7-11b** RStreet(1) (s.s: a bhd) | 2½ | **11** | $8/1^{3}$ | 40 | 11 |
| $1710^{7}$ | **Supreme Star (USA) (65)** (PRHedger) **5-8-6**(3) NVarley(2) (hld up: rdn over 3f out: wknd over 2f) | 2 | **12** | 40/1 | 50 | 21 |
| $2148^{4}$ | **Paradise Navy (65)** (CREgerton) **7-8-4b**(5) ADaly(8) (swtg: led over 12f) | 11 | **13** | 14/1 | 39 | 10 |
| | | | | (SP 121.4%) | | **13 Rn** |

**3m 38.68** (6.68) CSF £106.89 CT £1,402.54 TOTE £14.00: £3.10 £4.10 £4.90 (£66.90) Trio £297.90 OWNER Dr Frank Chao (NEWMARKET)
BRED Dr Frank Chao and High Point Bloodstock Ltd
LONG HANDICAP Durshan (USA) 7-3
WEIGHT FOR AGE 3yo-19lb

**2190 Pearl Venture** was given a very cool ride. Creeping into the action over a quarter of a mile from home, her jockey sat confidently on her and only asked her for her effort inside the final furlong. She responded well and got up near the line. (12/1)

**1611 Bowcliffe Court (IRE)** moved into contention turning for home. Sent on below the distance, he was collared inside the final furlong but kept on well. (9/1)

**Danjing (IRE)**, bought out of Simon Sherwood's stable for 28,000 guineas, had been off the track since finishing third at Aintree back in March. He certainly knew he had a race here and was being given reminders soon after halfway. Moving into contention in the straight, his jump jockey was busy bustling him along, but the gelding responded and managed to get on top inside the final furlong. However, he was just worried out of it near the line. (14/1)

**1407 Sharaf (IRE)** went on entering the straight appearing to be travelling well. However, collared below the distance, he failed to find another gear. (7/2)

**2131 Pine Needle** moved up early in the straight but was only treading water in the last two furlongs. (7/1)

**1981 World Express (IRE)** made an effort down the centre of the track over a quarter of a mile from home but had come to the end of his tether below the distance. (8/1)

## 2548 VICTORIA AMATEUR TURF CLUB H'CAP (0-95) (3-Y.O+) (Class C)

5-15 (5-17) **5f 6y** £5,602.00 (£1,696.00: £828.00: £394.00) Stalls: Low GOING minus 0.20 sec per fur (GF)

| | | | Pos | SP | RR | SF |
|---|---|---|---|---|---|---|
| $2292^{3}$ | **Lord High Admiral (CAN) (82)** (MJHeaton-Ellis) **8-9-1** JReid(6) (mde all: clr over 1f out: pushed out) | — | **1** | $7/2^{1}$ | 92 | 75 |
| $2156^{4}$ | **Beau Venture (USA) (72)** (BPalling) **8-8-5** CRutter(8) (lw: a.p: rdn over 1f out: r.o one pce) | 2½ | **2** | 7/1 | 74 | 57 |
| $2381^{6}$ | **Jucea (73)** (JLSpearing) **7-8-6** KFallon(4) (lw: rdn over 2f out: hdwy over 1f out: r.o wl ins fnl f) | hd | **3** | 10/1 | 75 | 58 |
| $2017^{5}$ | **Chewit (80)** (AMoore) **4-8-13** CandyMorris(7) (a.p: rdn over 1f out: one pce) | 1¼ | **4** | 14/1 | 78 | 61 |
| $2244^{9}$ | **Magic Mail (68)** (JMPEustace) **3-7-7**(3) NVarley(11) (lw: a.p: rdn over 2f out: one pce) | nk | **5** | 20/1 | 65 | 43 |
| *$2171^{6}$* | **Portend (90)** (SRBowring) **4-9-9b** SDWilliams(10) (no hdwy fnl 2f) | hd | **6** | $5/1^{2}$ | 87 | 70 |
| 1974* | **Canovas Heart (76)** (BobJones) **7-8-9** NDay(5) (prom over 3f) | 2½ | **7** | $5/1^{2}$ | 65 | 48 |
| $2114^{9}$ | **Master of Passion (82)** (JMPEustace) **7-9-1** MTebbutt(2) (outpcd) | nk | **8** | $6/1^{3}$ | 70 | 53 |
| $1962^{10}$ | **Forentia (85)** (JRFanshawe) **3-8-13v$^{1}$** RHills(3) (swtg: outpcd) | 1¾ | **9** | 20/1 | 67 | 45 |
| | | | | (SP 107.6%) | | **9 Rn** |

**60.25 secs** (0.45) CSF £24.01 CT £173.10 TOTE £3.10: £1.40 £2.00 £2.50 (£12.40) Trio £35.90 OWNER Elite Racing Club (WROUGHTON)
BRED Windfields Farm
LONG HANDICAP Magic Mail 7-9
WEIGHT FOR AGE 3yo-5lb

**2292 Lord High Admiral (CAN)** goes well over this stiff five furlongs and, making all the running, surged clear from below the distance to record his fourth course and distance victory. (7/2)
**2156 Beau Venture (USA)**, a leading light from the off, stayed on for second prize but never threatened the winner. (7/1)
**2381 Jucea**, making a quick reappearance, was unable to go the early lick. Finding her feet from below the distance, she ran on strongly and only just failed to take second prize. (10/1)
**2017 Chewit**, a leading light from the off, failed to quicken from below the distance. (14/1)
**783 Magic Mail**, never far away, was only treading water in the last two furlongs. (20/1)
**2171 Portend** chased the leaders but failed to make any impression in the last two furlongs. (5/1)

## 2549 SPINAL INJURIES ASSOCIATION H'CAP (0-80) (3-Y.O+) (Class D)
5-45 (5-46) **1m 3f 91y** £3,870.00 (£1,170.00: £570.00: £270.00) Stalls: High GOING minus 0.20 sec per fur (GF)

| | | | | SP | RR | SF |
|---|---|---|---|---|---|---|
| 2226[8] | **Edan Heights (65)** (SDow) **4-8-8**(5) ADaly(7) (hld up: led over 1f out: rdn out) | — | 1 | 16/1 | 77 | 50 |
| 2067* | **Eagle Canyon (IRE) (77)** (BHanbury) **3-8-13** MRimmer(9) (a.p: led over 2f out tl over 1f out: unable qckn) | 2½ | 2 | 5/1[3] | 86 | 47 |
| 1477[4] | **Shu Gaa (IRE) (72)** (WJHaggas) **3-8-8** KFallon(5) (lw: a.p: rdn 5f out: one pce fnl 2f) | 3 | 3 | 9/2[2] | 76 | 37 |
| 1669[4] | **The Boozing Brief (USA) (64)** (MAJarvis) **3-8-0** RHills(8) (hdwy over 2f out: wknd over 1f out) | 1 | 4 | 4/1[1] | 67 | 28 |
| | **Brandon Court (IRE) (80)** (IABalding) **5-10-0** MHills(2) (lw: hdwy over 1f out: wknd fnl f) | ½ | 5 | 20/1 | 82 | 55 |
| 2191[7] | **Junior Ben (IRE) (50)** (PHowling) **4-7-12** CRutter(6) (nvr nr to chal) | 2 | 6 | 20/1 | 49 | 22 |
| 2074[14] | **Get Away With It (IRE) (78)** (MRStoute) **3-9-0v** JReid(10) (lw: bhd fnl 2f) | nk | 7 | 6/1 | 77 | 38 |
| 1872[6] | **Apache Len (USA) (74)** (RHannon) **3-8-10** RPerham(3) (rdn over 3f out: hdwy over 1f out: sn wknd) | 3 | 8 | 12/1 | 69 | 30 |
| 2377[3] | **Bayrak (USA) (65)** (MJRyan) **6-8-13** NDay(4) (lw: a.p: chsd ldr over 9f out tl over 2f out: sn wknd) | 7 | 9 | 7/1 | 50 | 23 |
| | **Mr Browning (USA) (70)** (RAkehurst) **5-9-4b** TQuinn(1) (led 9f) | 1¾ | 10 | 6/1 | 53 | 26 |
| | | | | (SP 119.0%) | **10 Rn** | |

**2m 27.8** (4.40) CSF £88.68 CT £388.05 TOTE £21.50: £4.00 £1.70 £2.10 (£50.30) Trio £144.60 OWNER Mr T. R. Mountain (EPSOM) BRED T. R. Mountain
WEIGHT FOR AGE 3yo-12lb
**Edan Heights** appreciated the cut in the ground. Chasing the leaders, he went on below the distance and, ridden along, soon asserted. (16/1)
**2067* Eagle Canyon (IRE)** made his bid for glory over two furlongs from home. Collared below the distance, he found the winner too strong. (5/1)
**1477 Shu Gaa (IRE)** was never far away but looked in serious trouble as he was being bustled along turning for home. Nevertheless, he kept plodding on without looking likely to find the necessary turn of foot. (9/2)
**1669 The Boozing Brief (USA)** made an effort over a quarter of a mile from home but was a spent force below the distance. (4/1)
**Brandon Court (IRE)** tried to make up ground along the hedge below the distance, but was soon in trouble. (20/1)
**1872 Apache Len (USA)** (12/1: 7/1-14/1)

T/Jkpt: Not won; £8,289.98 to Windsor 8/7/96. T/Plpt: £895.40 (48.93 Tckts). T/Qdpt: £92.70 (27.89 Tckts). AK

# 2303-WOLVERHAMPTON (L-H) (Standard)
## Saturday July 6th
WEATHER: fine WIND: slt across

## 2550 BLUE SILK LIMITED STKS (0-55) (4-Y.O+) (Class F)
7-00 (7-01) **7f (Fibresand)** £2,450.00 (£675.00: £320.00) Stalls: Low GOING minus 0.15 sec per fur (FST)

| | | | | SP | RR | SF |
|---|---|---|---|---|---|---|
| *2303** | **Mister Rm (61)** (RGuest) **4-9-0** PBloomfield(11) (a.p: chsd wnr over 2f out: led ins fnl f: pushed out) | — | 1 | 11/8[1] | 56 | 41 |
| 2075[10] | **Komlucky (37)** (ABMulholland) **4-8-1b**(7) GFaulkner(7) (chsd ldrs: led over 3f out: rdn & hdd ins fnl f: unable qckn) | 2 | 2 | 50/1 | 45 | 30 |
| *2369[8]* | **David James' Girl (53)** (ABailey) **4-8-4**(7) AngelaGallimore(6) (outpcd: hdwy over 1f out: r.o wl) | 2 | 3 | 3/1[2] | 44 | 29 |
| 2303[6] | **Quinzii Martin (54)** (DHaydnJones) **8-8-11v** AMackay(10) (sn pushed along: effrt over 1f out: no imp) | 1¾ | 4 | 9/2[3] | 40 | 25 |
| | **Best of Bold (48)** (NAGraham) **4-8-11b** BDoyle(12) (s.i.s: bhd tl r.o appr fnl f: nrst fin) | hd | 5 | 14/1 | 40 | 25 |
| *1098[9]* | **Mr Moriarty (IRE) (40)** (SRBowring) **5-9-0** DeanMcKeown(3) (b: swtg: sn outpcd: styd on appr fnl f: nvr nrr) | 1½ | 6 | 33/1 | 39 | 24 |
| *367[7]* | **Runforaction (IRE) (37)** (LRLloyd-James) **4-8-1**(7) CWebb(4) (s.i.s: nvr nrr) | ¾ | 7 | 50/1 | 32 | 17 |
| *2305[7]* | **Sharp Holly (IRE) (41)** (JABennett) **4-8-8b** AClark(2) (chsd ldrs: rdn 2f out: btn appr fnl f) | 1 | 8 | 50/1 | 29 | 14 |
| 2212[5] | **Brookhead Lady (52)** (PDEvans) **5-8-8** SSanders(9) (b.nr fore: w ldrs: rdn 2f out: btn whn n.m.r ins fnl f) | 1 | 9 | 12/1 | 27 | 12 |
| 2075[9] | **Peacefull Reply (USA) (46)** (FHLee) **6-8-11** GCarter(1) (lw: led: hdd over 3f out: eased whn btn fnl f) | 1¼ | 10 | 25/1 | 27 | 12 |
| *2085[10]* | **Jon's Choice (40)** (BPreece) **8-8-11** VSlattery(5) (lw: a outpcd & bhd) | 3 | 11 | 25/1 | 20 | 5 |
| 2428[8] | **Hill Farm Katie (33)** (WMBrisbourne) **5-8-1b**(7) JBramhill(8) (w ldrs tl wknd over 2f out) | 2½ | 12 | 50/1 | 12 | — |
| | | | | (SP 118.1%) | **12 Rn** | |

**1m 28.5** (3.80) CSF £60.82 TOTE £2.30: £1.00 £12.20 £3.40 (£24.60) Trio £129.20: £109.19 to Windsor 8/7/96 OWNER Mr J. W. Biswell (NEWMARKET) BRED Major and Mrs R. B. Kennard
**2303* Mister Rm**, not inconvenienced by this shorter trip, proved far too good for his rivals. (11/8: op Evens)
**1642 Komlucky** may well need to be kept hold of a little longer over this trip. (50/1)
**2369 David James' Girl** was doing her best work in the closing stages. (3/1)
**2303 Quinzii Martin** (9/2: 6/1-4/1)
**Best of Bold** will be all the sharper for this. (14/1: 8/1-16/1)
**2212 Brookhead Lady** (12/1: op 8/1)

## 2551 MAVERICK CLAIMING STKS (3-Y.O+) (Class F)
7-30 (7-33) **1m 100y (Fibresand)** £2,415.00 (£665.00: £315.00) Stalls: Low GOING minus 0.15 sec per fur (FST)

| | | | | SP | RR | SF |
|---|---|---|---|---|---|---|
| *2169[3]* | **Ethbaat (USA) (70)** (WRMuir) **5-9-12** JOsborne(12) (a.p: chsd ldr 2f out: led ins fnl f: rdn out) | — | 1 | 9/2[3] | 82 | 56 |
| *2169[6]* | **Northern Celadon (IRE) (55)** (MJHeaton-Ellis) **5-9-2v[1]** AClark(4) (led: clr over 3f out: hdd & no ex ins fnl f) | 3 | 2 | 12/1 | 66 | 40 |
| *2169[8]* | **Sandmoor Denim (64)** (SRBowring) **9-9-2** DeanMcKeown(9) (a.p: chsd ldr over 3f out: no ex fnl f) | s.h | 3 | 5/1 | 66 | 40 |
| 1872[9] | **Rocky Waters (USA) (70)** (PBurgoyne) **7-8-13**(3) PMcCabe(6) (b.hind: mid div: hdwy over 3f out: no imp fnl f) | ¾ | 4 | 10/1 | 65 | 39 |
| *2169** | **Dragonjoy (65)** (NPLittmoden) **3-8-10b**(3) FLynch(11) (hld up: hdwy over 2f out: nvr trbld ldrs) | 7 | 5 | 9/4[1] | 58 | 23 |
| 2181[11] | **Safa Dancer** (BAMcMahon) **3-8-0**(7)ow3 KYu(2) (prom: rdn ½-wy: wknd 3f out) | 2 | 6 | 33/1 | 48 | 10 |
| *2169[7]* | **Fiaba (34)** (MrsNMacauley) **8-8-2v[1]**(3) CTeague(8) (b: lw: prom: drvn along 3f out: sn btn) | 1¼ | 7 | 33/1 | 34 | 8 |

| | | | | | | |
|---|---|---|---|---|---|---|
| 2303[5] | **My Handsome Prince (40)** (PJBevan) **4-9-2b** GCarter(3) (hld up: n.d) | 9 | **8** | 33/1 | 28 | 2 |
| 2325[4] | **Double-O-Seven (78)** (MJohnston) **3-9-3** JWeaver(5) (chsd ldrs tl rdn & wknd 4f out) | 1¾ | **9** | 4/1 [2] | 35 | — |
| | **Hangoninthere** (NMBabbage) **5-9-4** SSanders(1) (bkwd: chsd ldrs over 4f) | 5 | **10** | 33/1 | 18 | — |
| 1651[14] | **Mannagar (IRE) (30)** (JRPoulton) **4-9-2** AMorris(10) (b: a in rr) | 5 | **11** | 33/1 | 6 | — |
| | **Credit Controller (IRE)** (JFfitch-Heyes) **7-8-11**(3) SDrowne(7) (a in rr) | 1¾ | **12** | 50/1 | 1 | — |
| | | | | (SP 119.1%) | **12 Rn** | |

**1m 49.3** (4.30) CSF £52.25 TOTE £5.70: £1.80 £4.20 £1.80 (£33.00) Trio £41.30 OWNER Fayzad Thoroughbred Ltd (LAMBOURN) BRED Shadwell Farm Inc., & Shadwell Estate Co Ltd
WEIGHT FOR AGE 3yo-9lb
**2169 Ethbaat (USA)**, who gave trouble at the start, handles this sharp track well for a big horse. (9/2: 3/1-5/1)
**836 Northern Celadon (IRE)** is at his best when allowed to dominate, but was easily brushed aside in the latter stages. (12/1: op 7/1)
**1602* Sandmoor Denim**, nearing the veteran stage, still races with enthusiasm. (5/1: op 3/1)
**1533 Rocky Waters (USA)** has yet to win beyond seven furlongs, but he seemed to last this trip. (10/1)
**2169* Dragonjoy** was given far too much to do. (9/4)
**2325 Double-O-Seven** (4/1: 3/1-9/2)

## 2552 PAT LONG BIRTHDAY H'CAP (0-80) (3-Y.O+) (Class D)

8-00 (8-03) **1m 1f 79y (Fibresand)** £4,240.60 (£1,268.80: £608.40: £278.20) Stalls: Low GOING minus 0.15 sec per fur (FST)

| | | | | SP | RR | SF |
|---|---|---|---|---|---|---|
| 1811* | **Mr Teigh (74)** (BSmart) **4-9-10** MTebbutt(4) (mde all: clr 3f out: all out) | — | **1** | 5/1 [2] | 82 | 50 |
| 2306* | **Johnnie the Joker (72)** (JPLeigh) **5-9-8b** DeanMcKeown(8) (a.p: rdn over 1f out: r.o wl) | s.h | **2** | 12/1 | 80 | 48 |
| 1955[6] | **Taufan Boy (73)** (PWHarris) **3-8-13v[1]** BDoyle(11) (mid div: hdwy over 3f out: styd on ins fnl f) | 2½ | **3** | 6/1 [3] | 77 | 35 |
| 2170[2] | **Law Dancer (IRE) (78)** (TGMills) **3-9-4** MarkLynch(5) (swtg: a.p: rdn 2f out: styd on same pce) | 1 | **4** | 14/1 | 80 | 38 |
| 2171[4] | **Desert Invader (IRE) (70)** (DWChapman) **5-9-6** ACulhane(2) (hld up: hdwy over 3f out: no imp appr fnl f) | ½ | **5** | 25/1 | 71 | 39 |
| 2170* | **Bentico (73)** (MrsNMacauley) **7-9-6**(3) CTeague(3) (hld up: hdwy over 3f out: one pce fnl 2f) | 3 | **6** | 12/1 | 69 | 37 |
| 2293* | **Equerry (66)** (MJohnston) **5-9-2** JWeaver(12) (hld up in tch: outpcd 2f out: n.d after) | 1½ | **7** | 7/4 [1] | 59 | 27 |
| 2086[6] | **Domino Flyer (62)** (MrsASwinbank) **3-8-2** GCarter(9) (prom tl rdn & wknd over 2f out) | nk | **8** | 16/1 | 55 | 13 |
| 1811[4] | **Field of Vision (IRE) (74)** (MrsASwinbank) **6-9-5**(5)ow4 JSupple(6) (a outpcd) | ½ | **9** | 9/1 | 66 | 30 |
| 1496[14] | **Kintwyn (71)** (WRMuir) **6-9-4**(3) FLynch(7) (b.hind: outpcd: hdwy over 1f out: eased ins fnl f) | 1½ | **10** | 16/1 | 61 | 29 |
| 2124[4] | **Battle Spark (USA) (74)** (CACyzer) **3-9-0** SSanders(1) (trckd ldrs tl wknd over 2f out: t.o) | 16 | **11** | 16/1 | 36 | — |
| | | | | (SP 120.9%) | **11 Rn** | |

**2m 1.3** (5.30) CSF £58.39 CT £341.48 TOTE £7.70: £1.80 £2.60 £2.00 (£30.60) Trio £65.80 OWNER Mrs Hannah McAuliffe (LAMBOURN) BRED K. G. Bridges
WEIGHT FOR AGE 3yo-10lb
**1811* Mr Teigh**, upped 7lb for his course and distance win here, set a fast pace and just held on in a driving finish. (5/1)
**2306* Johnnie the Joker**, who has done all his winning over shorter trips, stayed this well. (12/1)
**701 Taufan Boy**, in a first-time visor, is gradually coming to hand. (6/1)
**2170 Law Dancer (IRE)** may need to drop a few pounds. (14/1: 10/1-16/1)
**2171 Desert Invader (IRE)** is gradually finding his form. (25/1)

## 2553 DICK GREENHALGH H'CAP (0-70) (3-Y.O+) (Class E)

8-30 (8-31) **1m 4f (Fibresand)** £3,261.30 (£974.40: £466.20: £212.10) Stalls: Low GOING minus 0.15 sec per fur (FST)

| | | | | SP | RR | SF |
|---|---|---|---|---|---|---|
| 2397* | **Etterby Park (USA) (56)** (MJohnston) **3-8-6** 5x JWeaver(7) (led after 1f: pushed out) | — | **1** | 7/4 [1] | 71 | 40 |
| 2173* | **Claque (65)** (DWChapman) **4-10-0b** ACulhane(4) (a.p: rdn to chse wnr 5f out: outpcd appr fnl f) | 5 | **2** | 8/1 | 73 | 55 |
| 2173[5] | **In the Money (IRE) (61)** (RHollinshead) **7-9-7**(3) FLynch(10) (hld up: hdwy over 4f out: rdn over 2f out: styd on same pce) | 2½ | **3** | 5/1 [3] | 66 | 48 |
| 2304[4] | **Chevalier (USA) (65)** (ICampbell) **4-9-7**(7) GFaulkner(9) (trckd ldrs: rdn 2f out: sn btn) | nk | **4** | 20/1 | 70 | 52 |
| 2183[7] | **Rival Bid (USA) (62)** (MrsNMacauley) **8-9-8**(3) CTeague(6) (hld up: effrt over 4f out: n.d) | 5 | **5** | 12/1 | 60 | 42 |
| 2372[2] | **Harbet House (FR) (57)** (CACyzer) **3-8-7** BDoyle(1) (lw: prom tl rdn & wknd over 3f out) | 2½ | **6** | 6/1 | 52 | 21 |
| 2304[7] | **Stevie's Wonder (IRE) (62)** (BJLlewellyn) **6-9-6**(5) MBaird(2) (sn pushed along: a in rr) | s.h | **7** | 20/1 | 57 | 39 |
| 980* | **Tintara (IRE) (61)** (BWHills) **3-8-6**(5) JDSmith(3) (hld up in tch: rdn & wknd 3f out) | 4 | **8** | 5/2 [2] | 50 | 19 |
| 2180[17] | **Pulga Circo (48)** (BAMcMahon) **3-7-5**(7)ow2 JBramhill(5) (led 1f: wknd 4f out) | 8 | **9** | 50/1 | 27 | — |
| 2181[10] | **Dragon Rose (48)** (TPTate) **4-8-11** DeanMcKeown(8) (b.hind: s.i.s: a outpcd & bhd: t.o) | 17 | **10** | 40/1 | 4 | — |
| | | | | (SP 128.6%) | **10 Rn** | |

**2m 38.4** (5.90) CSF £17.46 CT £61.14 TOTE £2.80: £1.40 £2.70 £1.30 (£10.20) Trio £7.60 OWNER Mr G. Middlebrook (MIDDLEHAM) BRED Jayeff "B" Stables
LONG HANDICAP Pulga Circo 6-13
WEIGHT FOR AGE 3yo-13lb
**2397* Etterby Park (USA)**, like most of his stablemates, thrives on racing. (7/4)
**2173* Claque**, under topweight, lost nothing in defeat. (8/1: 6/1-9/1)
**2173 In the Money (IRE)** was as his name suggests, but never looked likely to play a major role. (5/1: op 8/1)
**2304 Chevalier (USA)**, still a maiden, is gradually receding in the weights. (20/1)

## 2554 FIGARO (S) STKS (Qualifier) (2-Y.O) (Class F)

9-00 (9-01) **7f (Fibresand)** £2,415.00 (£665.00: £315.00) Stalls: Low GOING minus 0.15 sec per fur (FST)

| | | | | SP | RR | SF |
|---|---|---|---|---|---|---|
| 1892[6] | **Tinkerbell** (LordHuntingdon) **2-8-6v[1]** DHarrison(6) (prom: led on bit over 2f out: pushed clr fnl f: eased nr fin) | — | **1** | 2/1 [1] | 54+ | — |
| 2307* | **Grovefair Dancer (IRE)** (MissSJWilton) **2-8-10** SWhitworth(1) (w ldr: led over 3f out: hdd over 2f out: no ch w wnr) | 1½ | **2** | 7/2 [2] | 55 | — |
| 2509[3] | **Abstone Queen** (PDEvans) **2-8-6** SSanders(5) (trckd ldrs: rdn over 1f out: r.o one pce) | 2½ | **3** | 13/2 [3] | 45 | — |
| 2307[2] | **Riscatto (USA)** (WRMuir) **2-8-11** JWeaver(4) (led: hdd over 3f out: r.o one pce fnl 2f) | 3½ | **4** | 2/1 [1] | 42 | — |
| | **Sibor Star** (DBurchell) **2-8-8**(3) SDrowne(3) (leggy: lt-f: s.i.s: outpcd tl r.o appr fnl f) | 1¼ | **5** | 33/1 | 39 | — |
| 2122[10] | **Read Your Contract (IRE)** (JBerry) **2-8-11v[1]** GCarter(2) (outpcd fr ½-wy: t.o) | 23 | **6** | 14/1 | — | — |
| | | | | (SP 111.8%) | **6 Rn** | |

**1m 32.0** (1.20 under 2y best) (7.30) CSF £8.91 TOTE £3.00: £1.80 £2.00 (£8.20) OWNER Lord Carnarvon (WEST ILSLEY) BRED Highclere Stud Ltd
Bt in 5,800 gns

**1046 Tinkerbell**, dropped in class, made no mistake. (2/1)
**2307* Grovefair Dancer (IRE)** kept on in fine style and may well stay further. (7/2: op 2/1)
**2509 Abstone Queen** is consistent if nothing else at this level. (13/2: op 4/1)

## 2555 MONTEGO BAY H'CAP (0-60) (3-Y.O+) (Class F)
9-30 (9-33) **5f (Fibresand)** £2,519.00 (£694.00: £329.00) Stalls: Low GOING minus 0.15 sec per fur (FST)

| | | | SP | RR | SF |
|---|---|---|---|---|---|
| *2084*[9] | **Napier Star (51)** (MrsNMacauley) **3-8-13**(3) CTeague(6) (a.p: rdn & hung lft over 1f out: led ins fnl f: r.o wl) ..— | 1 | 9/2 [2] | 57 | 30 |
| *2308** | **Delrob (48)** (DHaydnJones) **5-9-4v** AMackay(8) (outpcd: hdwy over 1f out: fin wl)....1¼ | 2 | 9/4 [1] | 50 | 28 |
| 1512[12] | **Lloc (52)** (CADwyer) **4-9-5**(3) FLynch(1) (trckd ldrs: led over 1f out: hdd & unable qckn ins fnl f)....nk | 3 | 6/1 | 53 | 31 |
| 2244[6] | **Miami Banker (40)** (WRMuir) **10-8-10b** GBardwell(4) (chsd ldrs: ev ch 2f out: no ex fnl f)....¾ | 4 | 7/1 | 39 | 17 |
| *1812*[7] | **Scored Again (58)** (MJHeaton-Ellis) **6-9-9**(5) AmandaSanders(5) (chsd ldrs: rdn over 1f out: r.o one pce).....1¾ | 5 | 11/2 | 51 | 29 |
| | **Steal 'Em (56)** (ABailey) **3-9-0**(7) AngelaGallimore(2) (bit bkwd: outpcd: hdwy 2f out: no ex fnl f)....¾ | 6 | 5/1 [3] | 47 | 20 |
| *1028*[16] | **Bajan Frontier (IRE) (44)** (FHLee) **4-9-0** GCarter(3) (led: hdd over 1f out: sn btn)....5 | 7 | 12/1 | 19 | — |
| 2186[7] | **Highland Fawn (45)** (BAMcMahon) **3-8-10** SSanders(9) (a outpcd)....4 | 8 | 10/1 | 7 | — |
| 2058[12] | **Ballysokerry (IRE) (28)** (JParkes) **5-7-7b**(5)ow2 MBaird(7) (s.i.s: a outpcd: t.o)....dist | 9 | 50/1 | — | — |

(SP 126.5%) **9 Rn**

**62.1 secs** (3.40) CSF £15.91 CT £60.09 TOTE £8.00: £1.90 £1.10 £1.90 (£10.40) Trio £17.20 OWNER Mr P. M. Heaton (MELTON MOWBRAY) BRED P. M. Heaton
LONG HANDICAP Ballysokerry (IRE) 7-4
WEIGHT FOR AGE 3yo-5lb
**1716 Napier Star** proved well suited by a strongly-run race at this minimum trip. (9/2)
**2308* Delrob**, although a winner here over five furlongs, finds this trip plenty sharp enough. (9/4)
**1049 Lloc** showed plenty of dash and is ready to strike. (6/1: op 3/1)
**2244 Miami Banker** is coming to hand. (7/1)
**Steal 'Em** will be all the sharper for this. (5/1)
**1859 Highland Fawn** (10/1: 8/1-12/1)

T/Plpt: £55.20 (167.02 Tckts). T/Qdpt: £13.00 (43.68 Tckts). CR

# 2309-BATH (L-H) (Good to firm)
## Monday July 8th
WEATHER: fine but cloudy WIND: fresh half against

## 2556 KNOCKDOWN (S) H'CAP (0-60) (3-Y.O+) (Class G)
2-00 (2-00) **1m 5f 22y** £2,360.00 (£660.00: £320.00) Stalls: Low GOING minus 0.47 sec per fur (F)

| | | | SP | RR | SF |
|---|---|---|---|---|---|
| 2284[9] | **Dots Dee (28)** (JMBradley) **7-7-8**(3)ow1 MHenry(11) (plld hrd: a.p: led wl over 2f out tl wl over 1f out: led wl ins fnl f: r.o)....— | 1 | 10/1 | 37 | 7 |
| *2322*[2] | **Durham (54)** (RSimpson) **5-9-2b**(7) AimeeCook(13) (a.p: led wl over 1f out tl wl ins fnl f)....¾ | 2 | 9/2 [1] | 62 | 33 |
| 2251[8] | **Supermick (30)** (WRMuir) **5-7-13** CRutter(14) (lw: hld up: hdwy over 3f out: r.o fnl f)....nk | 3 | 6/1 [3] | 38 | 9 |
| 2313[11] | **La Belle Shyanne (28)** (RJBaker) **5-7-11**ow1 JQuinn(8) (hld up: hdwy 7f out: nt clr run over 1f out: r.o ins fnl f)....s.h | 4 | 9/1 | 36 | 6 |
| 2537[2] | **Bresil (USA) (36)** (KRBurke) **7-8-0**(5)ow9 PPMurphy(5) (a.p: ev ch over 2f out: one pce)....2½ | 5 | 5/1 [2] | 41 | 3 |
| 2056[18] | **Naseer (USA) (37)** (KBishop) **7-8-6** RPerham(4) (b: hld up & bhd: hdwy fnl 2f: nvr nrr)....s.h | 6 | 50/1 | 42 | 13 |
| 2192[6] | **Bronze Runner (34)** (EAWheeler) **12-8-3b** TSprake(12) (hld up & bhd: hdwy over 1f out: nt rch ldrs)....¾ | 7 | 6/1 [3] | 38 | 9 |
| 2192[11] | **Beyond Our Reach (46)** (RJHodges) **8-9-1** PatEddery(7) (lw: led over 10f: wknd over 1f out)....1¼ | 8 | 5/1 [2] | 48 | 19 |
| 2282[U] | **Heretical Miss (36)** (JFfitch-Heyes) **6-8-2**(3)ow1 SDrowne(3) (lw: prom 7f)....1¼ | 9 | 33/1 | 37 | 7 |
| 2310[6] | **Coochie (27)** (RJBaker) **7-7-10b** NAdams(6) (s.s: a bhd)....hd | 10 | 12/1 | 28 | — |
| *1444*[6] | **Brick Court (IRE) (37)** (RFJohnsonHoughton) **4-7-13b**1(7) BarrySmith(10) (plld hrd: prom tl wknd over 2f out)....2½ | 11 | 20/1 | 34 | 5 |
| 2385[7] | **Bravo Star (USA) (34)** (PaddyFarrell) **11-8-3b** SSanders(1) (prom tl rdn & wknd over 2f out)....1 | 12 | 50/1 | 30 | 1 |
| | **Woodlands Energy (37)** (PAPritchard) **5-7-13**(7) JoHunnam(9) (bhd fnl 5f)....7 | 13 | 50/1 | 25 | — |
| 2180[16] | **Formentiere (41)** (JMBradley) **3-7-10** AMackay(2) (a bhd: t.o)....13 | 14 | 33/1 | 13 | — |
| *136*[11] | **Orchestral Designs (IRE) (59)** (GAHam) **5-10-0** WJO'Connor(15) (dropped rr 7f out: t.o fnl 4f)....dist | 15 | 50/1 | — | — |

(SP 125.4%) **15 Rn**

**2m 52.3** (6.60) CSF £52.50 CT £274.46 TOTE £13.60: £4.20 £1.10 £3.70 (£20.50) Trio £70.40 OWNER Mr J. M. Kearney (CHEPSTOW) BRED F. Baldwin
LONG HANDICAP La Belle Shyanne 7-8 Coochie 7-5 Formentiere 7-5 Dots Dee 7-5
WEIGHT FOR AGE 3yo-14lb
No bid
**609 Dots Dee**, with her rider unable to claim his full allowance, was carrying 3lb more than her long-handicap mark. Subsequently described by her trainer as a madam who is not one to trust, she certainly had one of her going days and put up a game performance. (10/1: 8/1-12/1)
**2322 Durham**, 6lb higher than when winning at Nottingham, does go well for Miss Cook, but strength from the saddle may have proved the significant factor. (9/2: 3/1-5/1)
**Supermick** has slipped down the Ratings and showed improved form over this longer trip. (6/1: 4/1-7/1)
**La Belle Shyanne** had to be checked briefly at a vital stage, but certainly got the distance and finished with a flourish. (9/1)
**2537 Bresil (USA)**, now only 1lb higher than when winning a similar event here a year ago, may have found this coming too soon after his second on Saturday evening. (5/1)
**Naseer (USA)** has obviously had his training problems, but finished in a style which suggests the patience shown may at long last be paying off. (50/1)
**2192 Bronze Runner** (6/1: op 4/1)
**Coochie** (12/1: op 25/1)

## 2557 LIMPLEY STOKE MAIDEN STKS (3-Y.O) (Class D)
2-30 (2-32) **1m 2f 46y** £3,803.25 (£1,146.00: £555.50: £260.25) Stalls: Low GOING minus 0.47 sec per fur (F)

| | | | SP | RR | SF |
|---|---|---|---|---|---|
| | **Flying Green (FR) (85)** (RCharlton) **3-9-0** TSprake(8) (mde all: rdn over 1f out: r.o wl)....— | 1 | 8/1 [3] | 90 | 51 |

1973$^{2}$ **King of Sparta (80)** (LMCumani) **3-9-0** PatEddery(15) (lw: chsd wnr: rdn over 1f out: no imp) ..........6 **2** 10/11$^{1}$ 81 42
1117$^{4}$ **Kidston Lass (IRE)** (JARToller) **3-8-9** SSanders(11) (hld up: hdwy over 4f out: r.o one pce fnl f) ..........s.h **3** 4/1$^{2}$ 76 37
2198$^{2}$ **Typhoon Lad** (SDow) **3-9-0** TQuinn(4) (prom tl wknd 2f out) ..........7 **4** 8/1$^{3}$ 70 31
1438$^{3}$ **Phonetic** (GBBalding) **3-9-0** AClark(10) (trckd ldrs: wknd over 2f out) ..........s.h **5** 8/1$^{3}$ 70 31
576$^{11}$ **Nereus** (BWHills) **3-8-9**$^{(7)ow2}$ GBrace(9) (nvr trbld ldrs) ..........1½ **6** 25/1 69 28
2036$^{6}$ **Decision Maker (IRE) (72)** (RHannon) **3-8-11v$^{1(3)}$** DaneO'Neill(12) (lw: lost pl over 6f out: sme hdwy 3f out: no imp) ..........3½ **7** 12/1 62 23
1104$^{13}$ **Tathmin** (JRBosley) **3-9-0** CRutter(3) (nvr nr ldrs) ..........3 **8** 50/1 57 18
2383$^{7}$ **Lady Magnum (IRE)** (JNeville) **3-8-9** FNorton(5) (bhd fnl 4f) ..........7 **9** 50/1 41 2
**Freddie's Recall** (MJHeaton-Ellis) **3-8-6**$^{(3)}$ SDrowne(2) (lengthy: unf: a bhd) ..........5 **10** 50/1 33 —
1709$^{10}$ **Governance (IRE)** (KMcAuliffe) **3-8-9** WJO'Connor(7) (a bhd) ..........4 **11** 50/1 27 —
2197$^{12}$ **Allstars Rocket** (TJNaughton) **3-9-0** DHolland(13) (prom 5f) ..........4 **12** 50/1 26 —
**Kealbra Lady** (MSSaunders) **3-8-4**$^{(5)}$ PPMurphy(6) (prom over 6f) ..........3 **13** 50/1 16 —
2383$^{10}$ **Myfanwy Bethesda** (BJLlewellyn) **3-8-9** VSlattery(14) (a bhd: t.o) ..........10 **14** 100/1 — —
(SP 130.0%) **14 Rn**

**2m 7.5** (0.00) CSF £15.98 TOTE £6.50: £2.00 £1.10 £1.70 (£5.30) Trio £7.70 OWNER Mr S M De Zoete (BECKHAMPTON) BRED COZZI

**Flying Green (FR)**, gelded since last year, has been a bit slow to come to hand, but ran on strongly when put to the test. (8/1)
**1973 King of Sparta** was reported to have choked at York last time. Reverting to ten furlongs, he does seem to lack a real turn of foot and only just managed to hold on to the runner-up spot. (10/11: Evens-4/5)
**1117 Kidston Lass (IRE)** confirmed the promise shown on her debut and only just lost out in the battle for second. (4/1)
**2198 Typhoon Lad** found the wind taken out of his sails at the quarter-mile marker. (8/1: 6/1-9/1)
**1438 Phonetic** should have been suited by this longer distance. (8/1)

## 2558 RACING CHANNEL H'CAP (0-80) (3-Y.O+) (Class D)

3-00 (3-01) **1m 2f 46y** £3,848.75 (£1,160.00: £562.50: £263.75) Stalls: Low GOING minus 0.47 sec per fur (F)

SP RR SF

1838$^{3}$ **Florentino (IRE) (68)** (BWHills) **3-9-1** PatEddery(2) (lw: sn chsng ldrs: rdn over 3f out: led ins fnl f: r.o) ..........— **1** 2/1$^{1}$ 80 51
1955* **Classic Defence (IRE) (72)** (JWHills) **3-9-2**$^{(3)}$ MHenry(5) (led: clr 4f out: hrd rdn over 2f out: hdd ins fnl f) ....1¼ **2** 3/1$^{2}$ 82 53
2342$^{3}$ **Askern (66)** (DHaydnJones) **5-9-10** AMackay(1) (hld up: hrd rdn 4f out: edgd rt over 2f out: one pce) ..........2½ **3** 4/1$^{3}$ 72 54
2226$^{4}$ **Fabulous Mtoto (49)** (MSSaunders) **6-8-7** JQuinn(4) (s.s: hrd rdn 4f out: hdwy over 2f out: nvr nr to chal) .....nk **4** 4/1$^{3}$ 55 37
2133$^{7}$ **Meg's Memory (IRE) (58)** (JohnBerry) **3-8-2**$^{(3)}$ NVarley(3) (hrd rdn 4f out: no hdwy) ..........2 **5** 10/1 61 32
*1490*$^{12}$ **Dhulikhel (60)** (DMarks) **3-8-7** DHarrison(6) (lw: prom: hrd rdn 4f out: btn whn carried rt 2f out: sn eased) .......9 **6** 20/1 48 19
(SP 112.2%) **6 Rn**

**2m 8.8** (1.30) CSF £8.06 TOTE £2.50: £1.40 £2.10 (£3.40) OWNER Lady Harrison (LAMBOURN) BRED Fluorocarbon Bloodstock
WEIGHT FOR AGE 3yo-11lb

**1838 Florentino (IRE)**, raised 3lb after his Folkestone win, was up a further 3lb here. Taking a long time to wear down the leader, he will now try a mile and a half at Glorious Goodwood. (2/1)
**1955* Classic Defence (IRE)** again tried to make all, but a 3lb hike in the weights proved too much. (3/1: op 2/1)
**2342 Askern** could not concede the weight to younger rivals. (4/1: 3/1-9/2)
**2226 Fabulous Mtoto**, 8lb higher than when winning at Windsor, was not suited by this drop back in distance. (4/1)
**1883 Meg's Memory (IRE)**, only 3lb higher than when winning on her reappearance over course and distance in April, could be the type who is best when fresh. (10/1)

## 2559 E.B.F. EVERSHOT MAIDEN STKS (2-Y.O) (Class D)

3-30 (3-31) **5f 161y** £3,624.50 (£1,091.00: £528.00: £246.50) Stalls: High GOING minus 0.47 sec per fur (F)

SP RR SF

**Silver Purse** (APJones) **2-8-9** TSprake(11) (w'like: hdwy over 2f out: nt clr run & swtchd rt over 1f out: led ins fnl f: r.o) ..........— **1** 33/1 61 13
**Irtifa** (PTWalwyn) **2-8-9** WCarson(10) (unf: scope: rdn & swtchd rt over 2f out: gd hdwy fnl f: fin wl) ..........s.h **2** 7/2$^{2}$ 61 13
2245$^{7}$ **Oneknight With You** (MJFetherston-Godley) **2-8-9** DHolland(9) (hdwy over 2f out: led & edgd lft over 1f out: hdd ins fnl f) ..........nk **3** 25/1 60 12
2243$^{6}$ **Effervescence** (RHannon) **2-9-0** RHughes(7) (lw: w ldrs: ev ch over 1f out: unable qckn) ..........1½ **4** 100/30$^{1}$ 61 13
2184$^{3}$ **Impulsif (USA)** (DJSffrenchDavis) **2-8-11**$^{(3)}$ DaneO'Neill(2) (lw: w ldrs tl wknd over 1f out) ..........3½ **5** 5/1 51 3
**Flamma Vestalis (IRE)** (JLDunlop) **2-8-9** SWhitworth(4) (rangy: s.s: nvr nrr) ..........¾ **6** 8/1 44 —
2219$^{3}$ **Commander Jones (IRE)** (BJMeehan) **2-9-0** BDoyle(8) (led tl over 1f out: wknd fnl f) ..........s.h **7** 9/2$^{3}$ 49 1
**Happy Go Lucky** (RJO'Sullivan) **2-8-9** SSanders(1) (unf: a bhd) ..........1¼ **8** 20/1 40 —
**Muscatana** (BWHills) **2-8-9** PatEddery(5) (neat: bit bkwd: chsd ldrs: ev ch 2f out: btn whn hmpd over 1f out: eased fnl f) ..........½ **9** 6/1 39 —
**Topps Trio** (KOCunningham-Brown) **2-8-9** DRMcCabe(6) (lt-f: s.s: a bhd) ..........4 **10** 33/1 28 —
**Cryhavoc** (JRArnold) **2-9-0** TQuinn(3) (w'like: bit bkwd: s.s: stumbled 4f out: a bhd) ..........8 **11** 25/1 11 —
(SP 123.9%) **11 Rn**

**1m 12.5** (3.00) CSF £142.52 TOTE £27.60: £3.00 £1.80 £6.20 (£138.20) Trio £276.30; £315.22 to Newmarket 9/7/96 OWNER Mr A. P. Jones (EASTBURY) BRED Home Stud Ltd

**Silver Purse** is a half-sister to Aldwick Colonnade and Credit Squeeze. Working well at home having previously been difficult to train, she became the first juvenile to win for her trainer. (33/1)
**Irtifa**, a half-sister to Mawayed and Tawaaded, finished in great style but the post came a stride too soon. She will not be long in going one better. (7/2: op 2/1)
**1643 Oneknight With You** ran her best race to date and did not help her cause by coming off a true line. (25/1)
**2243 Effervescence,** a brother to mile winner Efipetite, may not be one of his stable's leading lights but is going the right way. (100/30: 6/1-3/1)
**2184 Impulsif (USA)** was a bit disappointing. (5/1: 4/1-6/1)
**Flamma Vestalis (IRE)**, a half-sister to Mill Reef Stakes winner Luqman, is bred to need further and should do better in due course. (8/1: 4/1-10/1)
**2219 Commander Jones (IRE)** seems better suited to the bare minimum at the moment. (9/2)
**Muscatana** (6/1: op 5/2)

## 2560 ACTON TURVILLE MAIDEN H'CAP (0-75) (3-Y.O+) (Class D)

4-00 (4-00) **2m 1f 34y** £3,666.75 (£1,104.00: £534.50: £249.75) Stalls: High GOING minus 0.47 sec per fur (F)

SP RR SF

1977$^{9}$ **Special Beat (52)** (PFICole) **4-8-6** TQuinn(2) (a.p: wnt 2nd 9f out: led on bit 2f out: rdn over 1f out: drvn out) ..........— **1** 4/1$^{3}$ 66 32

| | | | | SP | RR | SF |
|---|---|---|---|---|---|---|
| 1981[4] | **Pedaltothemetal (IRE) (42)** (PhilipMitchell) **4-7-10** JQuinn(4) (lw: hld up: stdy hdwy 8f out: rdn to ld 3f out: hdd 2f out: r.o) | 1 | **2** | 100/30[2] | 55 | 21 |
| 2310[3] | **Sophism (USA) (43)** (MCPipe) **7-7-8**(3)ow1 MHenry(1) (hld up: reminders 8f out: hdwy over 5f out: rdn 4f out: one pce fnl 3f) | 12 | **3** | 11/4[1] | 45 | 10 |
| 2505[6] | **Cypress Avenue (IRE) (74)** (RHannon) **4-10-0** RHughes(3) (lw: led tl hdd 3f out: sn hrd rdn & wknd) | 24 | **4** | 6/1 | 54 | 20 |
| 1587[4] | **Double Dash (IRE) (70)** (MJohnston) **3-8-5** DHolland(7) (prom: rdn 6f out: wknd over 4f out: t.o) | dist | **5** | 11/4[1] | — | — |
| 1685[13] | **Bite the Bullet (42)** (AJChamberlain) **5-7-10** NAdams(6) (reminders after 4f: rdn & dropped rr 9f out: t.o) | 28 | **6** | 50/1 | — | — |
| 1618[13] | **Printers Quill (50)** (MajorDNChappell) **4-8-4** AClark(5) (plld hrd: chsd ldr 8f: wknd 7f out: t.o) | 5 | **7** | 12/1 | — | — |

(SP 120.3%) **7 Rn**

**3m 46.0** (5.00) CSF £17.83 TOTE £5.10: £3.20 £1.70 (£8.70) OWNER Mr C. Marner (WHATCOMBE) BRED Christian Marner
LONG HANDICAP Sophism (USA) 7-9 Pedaltothemetal (IRE) 7-9 Bite the Bullet 6-7
WEIGHT FOR AGE 3yo-19lb

**Special Beat**, a Bustino filly, was suited by this stamina test in what can only be described as a weak contest. (4/1)
**1981 Pedaltothemetal (IRE)**, who lacks finishing speed, proved she gets the trip but could never shake off the winner after making her bid for glory. (100/30: 9/2-3/1)
**2310 Sophism (USA)** could only plod on at one pace. (11/4: 2/1-3/1)
**1587 Double Dash (IRE)** was making heavy weather of it leaving the back straight. (11/4)
**Printers Quill** (12/1: 8/1-14/1)

## 2561 SALTFORD APPRENTICE H'CAP (0-65) (3-Y.O+) (Class G)

4-30 (4-30) **5f 11y** £2,140.50 (£608.00: £301.50) Stalls: High GOING minus 0.47 sec per fur (F)

| | | | | SP | RR | SF |
|---|---|---|---|---|---|---|
| 2324* | **Walk the Beat (61)** (MartynMeade) **6-9-13** DSweeney(7) (hdwy over 2f out: led ins fnl f: r.o) | — | **1** | 7/2[2] | 67 | 30 |
| 2286[9] | **Deardaw (35)** (MDIUsher) **4-7-8**(7) RBrisland(1) (lw: w ldr: led wl over 1f out tl ins fnl f: r.o) | s.h | **2** | 33/1 | 41 | 4 |
| 2286[12] | **Astral Invader (IRE) (51)** (MSSaunders) **4-8-10**(7) RCody-Boutcher(6) (b: s.i.s: gd hdwy fnl f: fin wl) | nk | **3** | 10/1 | 56 | 19 |
| 2244[7] | **Bangles (62)** (LordHuntingdon) **6-9-9**(5) RFfrench(3) (lw: led over 3f: unable qckn fnl f) | ¾ | **4** | 7/4[1] | 65 | 28 |
| 2324[5] | **Tommy Tempest (42)** (REPeacock) **7-8-5**(3) PDoe(4) (no hdwy fnl 2f) | 2 | **5** | 13/2[3] | 38 | 1 |
| 2496[9] | **Ivy Lilian (IRE) (32)** (WMBrisbourne) **4-7-7**(5) JFowle(5) (prom: rdn over 2f out: wknd over 1f out) | ½ | **6** | 12/1 | 27 | — |
| *44*[9] | **Woodlands Electric (30)** (PAPritchard) **6-7-10** JoHunnam(9) (nvr trbld ldrs) | 1½ | **7** | 50/1 | 20 | — |
| 1823[9] | **Johayro (65)** (WGMTurner) **3-9-7**(5) GHannon(11) (prom over 3f) | s.h | **8** | 10/1 | 55 | 13 |
| 1592[7] | **Duet (40)** (JSKing) **3-7-8**(7) KSalt(2) (lw: a bhd) | ¾ | **9** | 20/1 | 27 | — |
| | **Grand Time (31)** (RJBaker) **7-7-11v**ow1 JWilkinson(8) (prom 3f) | ½ | **10** | 14/1 | 17 | — |
| 2186[6] | **Secret Miss (49)** (APJones) **4-9-1** DDenby(10) (hung rt 2f out: a bhd) | 1¼ | **11** | 10/1 | 31 | — |

(SP 123.2%) **11 Rn**

**63.1 secs** (2.60) CSF £92.18 CT £1,011.57 TOTE £4.40: £1.30 £2.90 £2.80 (£63.30) Trio £324.30; £13.71 to Newmarket 9/7/96 OWNER The Country Life Partnership (MALMESBURY) BRED R. B. Warren
LONG HANDICAP Woodlands Electric 6-9
WEIGHT FOR AGE 3yo-5lb

**2324* Walk the Beat**, raised 2lb for his win last time, again got the better of a three-way photo. (7/2: op 9/4)
**Deardaw** has been slipping down the Ratings but took the eye in the paddock and has clearly come to hand. (33/1)
**1536 Astral Invader (IRE)** really needs more than the bare minimum on ground as fast as this. (10/1: 8/1-12/1)
**2244 Bangles** had dropped to a mark 2lb lower than when winning at Salisbury last August. (7/4)
**2324 Tommy Tempest** could never quite make his presence felt. (13/2: 5/1-10/1)
**1598 Ivy Lilian (IRE)** remains a maiden after twenty-seven attempts. (12/1: 10/1-16/1)
**Grand Time** (14/1: op 6/1)

T/Plpt: £164.40 (77.29 Tckts). T/Qdpt: £68.80 (12.06 Tckts). KH

# 2386-MUSSELBURGH (R-H) (Good, Good to firm patches)

## Monday July 8th

WEATHER: sunny WIND: almost nil

## 2562 E.B.F. PRESTONPANS MEDIAN AUCTION MAIDEN STKS (2-Y.O) (Class E)

2-15 (2-15) **5f** £3,046.00 (£856.00: £418.00) Stalls: High GOING minus 0.69 sec per fur (HD)

| | | | | SP | RR | SF |
|---|---|---|---|---|---|---|
| 2343[2] | **Farewell My Love (IRE)** (PFICole) **2-8-9** KDarley(1) (lw: cl up: led wl over 1f out: rdn & r.o) | — | **1** | 1/4[1] | 52+ | — |
| 2076[7] | **Colonel's Pride** (RMWhitaker) **2-9-0** DeanMcKeown(3) (led over 3f: kpt on wl) | 1¾ | **2** | 33/1[3] | 51? | — |
| 2327[3] | **Soda** (TDBarron) **2-9-0** JFortune(2) (lw: a chsng ldrs: shkn up 1f out: kpt on) | nk | **3** | 3/1[2] | 50 | — |

(SP 107.9%) **3 Rn**

**60.3 secs** (2.60) CSF £4.40 TOTE £1.10 (£3.10) OWNER Mr W. H. Ponsonby (WHATCOMBE) BRED Rathbarry Stud

**2343 Farewell My Love (IRE)** always looked likely to win, but it was never easy and she had to be kept up to her work all the way home. (1/4)
**Colonel's Pride**, very much on his toes beforehand, ran by far his best race and seems to be getting it together. (33/1)
**2327 Soda** ran well and was not given a hard time, and looks likely to do better in due course. (3/1)

## 2563 NEWBATTLE (S) H'CAP (0-60) (3-Y.O+) (Class G)

2-45 (2-45) **1m 3f 32y** £2,388.00 (£668.00: £324.00) Stalls: High GOING minus 0.38 sec per fur (F)

| | | | | SP | RR | SF |
|---|---|---|---|---|---|---|
| 2366[U] | **Milltown Classic (IRE) (28)** (JParkes) **4-8-3** JFanning(7) (chsd ldrs: chal over 1f out: styd on to ld nr fin) | — | **1** | 40/1 | 35 | 6 |
| 2394[2] | **Mithraic (IRE) (53)** (WSCunningham) **4-10-0** ACulhane(3) (lw: led: hung lft fnl 2f: jst ct) | hd | **2** | 4/1[1] | 60 | 31 |
| 2175[7] | **Trumped (IRE) (40)** (PMonteith) **4-9-1** SDWilliams(9) (chsd ldrs: chal 2f out: carried lft fnl f: kpt on) | hd | **3** | 6/1[2] | 47 | 18 |
| 2024[9] | **Portite Sophie (26)** (MBrittain) **5-8-1** JLowe(8) (b: w ldrs: rdn 3f out: hmpd over 1f out: nt qckn) | 3½ | **4** | 20/1 | 28 | — |
| *2168*[9] | **Belacqua (USA) (33)** (DWChapman) **3-7-10b** NKennedy(13) (a chsng ldrs: rdn 3f out: one pce) | nk | **5** | 33/1 | 34 | — |
| 1468* | **Kristal Breeze (42)** (WRMuir) **4-9-3** KFallon(11) (pushed along after 3f: hdwy & in tch ent st: nvr able to chal) | ½ | **6** | 4/1[1] | 43 | 14 |
| 2027[7] | **Crystal Warrior (54)** (DNicholls) **3-9-3** KDarley(5) (sme hdwy fnl 2f: nvr nr to chal) | s.h | **7** | 8/1[3] | 55 | 14 |
| 2241[9] | **No More Hassle (IRE) (36)** (MrsMReveley) **3-7-10**(3) DWright(4) (lw: hld up & bhd: rdn & styd on fnl 3f: n.d) | 1 | **8** | 20/1 | 35 | — |
| 1544[8] | **Kalko (21)** (JSGoldie) **7-7-3**(7) IonaWands(2) (bhd: sme hdwy fnl 2f: n.d) | ½ | **9** | 50/1 | 19 | — |

| | | | SP | RR | SF |
|---|---|---|---|---|---|
| 1160$^{8}$ **Bright Pet (45)** (MrsSJSmith) **3-8-8** NConnorton(12) (mid div: drvn along appr st: no imp) | 5 | **10** | 12/1 | 36 | — |
| 2394$^{8}$ **Greek Gold (IRE) (41)** (DWBarker) **7-8-9**(7) JBramhill(6) (in tch to st) | s.h | **11** | 12/1 | 32 | 3 |
| 2357$^{8}$ **Teejay'n'aitch (IRE) (38)** (JSGoldie) **4-8-13** JWeaver(1) (a bhd) | 1½ | **12** | 8/1$^{3}$ | 27 | — |
| 1830$^{11}$ **Cottage Prince (IRE) (42)** (JJQuinn) **3-8-5** TWilliams(10) (hld up: effrt 3f out: sn btn) | 5 | **13** | 4/1$^{1}$ | 24 | — |

(SP 128.8%) **13 Rn**

**2m 27.1** (7.40) CSF £192.70 CT £1,052.22 TOTE £21.20: £4.80 £2.50 £2.80 (£133.80) Trio £230.80 OWNER Mrs Lynn Parkes (MALTON) BRED Noel Finegan
LONG HANDICAP Kalko 7-8 Belacqua (USA) 7-5
WEIGHT FOR AGE 3yo-12lb
No bid
STEWARDS' ENQUIRY Culhane susp. 17-18/7/96 (careless riding).

**1487 Milltown Classic (IRE)**, who has spent most of the season on the All-Weather, put in a much-improved performance and gained her first ever win. (40/1)
**2394 Mithraic (IRE)** was the pick on looks, but he then threw his chances away by hanging left in the last two furlongs and was just caught. (4/1)
**2020 Trumped (IRE)** did not impress on looks, but ran well. Holding every chance up the straight, she was not helped by the runner-up hanging into her. (6/1)
**609 Portite Sophie** has yet to win a race and looked in trouble when being hampered approaching the final furlong. She has the ability if ever caught in the mood. (20/1)
**522 Belacqua (USA)**, from a yard going well, ran reasonably, but she was well short of toe in the last three furlongs. (33/1)
**1468* Kristal Breeze**, off the track for six weeks, never looked happy here and failed to make any impression. (4/1)
**763 Crystal Warrior** failed to get into this, but was not given a hard time and should be all the better for it. (8/1: op 4/1)
**2056 Greek Gold (IRE)** (12/1: 8/1-14/1)
**Cottage Prince (IRE)** (4/1: op 10/1)

## 2564 LE GARCON D'OR H'CAP (0-60) (3-Y.O+) (Class F)

3-15 (3-22) **5f** £2,775.00 (£840.00: £410.00: £195.00) Stalls: High GOING minus 0.69 sec per fur (HD)

| | | | SP | RR | SF |
|---|---|---|---|---|---|
| 2421$^{2}$ **Silk Cottage (54)** (RMWhitaker) **4-9-8v** DeanMcKeown(1) (hld up: hdwy 2f out: rdn to ld ins fnl f) | — | **1** | 2/1$^{1}$ | 63 | 46 |
| 2395$^{W}$ **Swan At Whalley (67)** (MartynWane) **4-10-2**(5) 7x PRoberts(3) (lw: unruly s: led tl hdd ins fnl f: kpt on) | 1 | **2** | 3/1$^{2}$ | 73 | 56 |
| 2523$^{8}$ **Gondo (43)** (EJAlston) **9-8-11v** KFallon(2) (lw: bhd tl hdwy 2f out: styd on wl u.p fnl f) | 1¾ | **3** | 14/1 | 43 | 26 |
| 2395$^{3}$ **Double Glow (33)** (NBycroft) **4-7-8b**(7) IonaWands(4) (s.i.s: sn drvn along: sme late hdwy) | 2½ | **4** | 50/1 | 25 | 8 |
| 2386$^{5}$ **Six for Luck (51)** (DANolan) **4-9-5** KDarley(5) (chsd ldrs: rdn ½-wy. no imp after) | hd | **5** | 20/1 | 43 | 26 |
| 2386$^{2}$ **Kalar (48)** (DWChapman) **7-9-2** JFortune(6) (lw: spd over 3f) | hd | **6** | 9/2$^{3}$ | 40 | 23 |
| 1765$^{7}$ **The Institute Boy (44)** (MissJFCraze) **6-8-12** NConnorton(8) (cl up tl wknd appr fnl f) | 1¼ | **7** | 14/1 | 32 | 15 |
| 2386$^{W}$ **Leading Princess (IRE) (48)** (MissLAPerratt) **5-9-2b** JWeaver(7) (outpcd & bhd fr ½-wy) | hd | **8** | 3/1$^{2}$ | 35 | 18 |

(SP 121.6%) **8 Rn**

**57.7 secs** (0.00) CSF £8.80 CT £61.83 TOTE £3.60: £1.30 £1.10 £2.30 (£5.10) OWNER Mr Christopher Cooke (LEEDS) BRED G. G. Senior D. Lodge and L. Carver

**2421 Silk Cottage**, ridden with restraint this time, finally broke his duck and had too much toe for the runner-up in the final furlong. (2/1)
**2386* Swan At Whalley** gave problems when being loaded. He tried to run his rivals into the ground, but the winner was too good for him in the closing stages. (3/1)
**2496 Gondo** last won almost two years ago, but he does look well at present and put in a sound effort here. (14/1)
**2395 Double Glow** was never going the pace until suddenly picking up in the closing stages. Two of her three wins were on the All-Weather and a return to that surface might help. (50/1)
**2386 Six for Luck** was finding this happening too quickly from halfway. (20/1)
**2386 Kalar**, well held by the favourite on the previous week's form, ran as well as could be expected. (9/2)

## 2565 MUSSELBURGH H'CAP (0-65) (3-Y.O+ F & M) (Class F)

3-45 (3-45) **1m 4f 31y** £2,814.00 (£852.00: £416.00: £198.00) Stalls: High GOING minus 0.38 sec per fur (F)

| | | | SP | RR | SF |
|---|---|---|---|---|---|
| 2390* **Bobanlyn (IRE) (57)** (JSWainwright) **4-9-11**(7) 5x JBramhill(5) (in tch: qcknd to ld wl over 1f out: r.o wl) | — | **1** | 9/4$^{1}$ | 71 | 53 |
| 2066$^{5}$ **Philmist (47)** (CWCElsey) **4-9-8b** NKennedy(9) (lw: a cl up: led over 3f out tl wl over 1f out: kpt on) | 5 | **2** | 3/1$^{2}$ | 54 | 36 |
| 2362* **Ragtime Cowgirl (40)** (CWThornton) **3-7-13**(3) 5x DWright(2) (sn bhd: styd on u.p fnl 3f: n.d) | 7 | **3** | 9/4$^{1}$ | 38 | 7 |
| 2331$^{5}$ **Forgotten Empress (48)** (AHarrison) **4-9-9** DeanMcKeown(4) (lw: in tch: effrt over 3f out: nvr trbld ldrs) | 5 | **4** | 12/1 | 40 | 22 |
| **Persian Symphony (IRE) (48)** (MrsAMNaughton) **5-9-6**(3) OPears(3) (bhd tl sme late hdwy) | 2½ | **5** | 16/1 | 36 | 18 |
| 1600$^{11}$ **Carmenoura (IRE) (28)** (EJAlston) **4-8-3** JFanning(6) (led tl hdd over 3f out: sn btn) | 3½ | **6** | 33/1 | 12 | — |
| 2378$^{6}$ **Shalateeno (65)** (MRChannon) **3-9-13** JFortune(1) (cl up: rn wd paddock bnd & lost pl: n.d after) | 5 | **7** | 6/1$^{3}$ | 42 | 11 |
| 2024$^{6}$ **Funny Rose (27)** (PMonteith) **6-8-2** TWilliams(8) (chsd ldrs tl wknd fnl 3f) | 3 | **8** | 25/1 | — | — |
| 1665$^{18}$ **Hats of to Hilda (30)** (MrsMReveley) **4-8-5** KDarley(7) (a bhd) | 9 | **9** | 20/1 | — | — |

(SP 125.9%) **9 Rn**

**2m 37.9** (4.90) CSF £10.12 CT £16.19 TOTE £4.00: £1.10 £1.20 £1.20 (£6.40) Trio £4.70 OWNER Mrs Sheila Walker (MALTON) BRED Mrs S. A. Pfeiffer and Partners in Ireland
WEIGHT FOR AGE 3yo-13lb

**2390* Bobanlyn (IRE)**, like many in foal, has improved tremendously and this was a particularly good performance. (9/4)
**2066 Philmist** put in a sound effort but was firmly put in her place by the winner in the last two furlongs. (3/1)
**2362* Ragtime Cowgirl** is a funny customer and only decided to stay on when it was all over. (9/4)
**2331 Forgotten Empress** looks well and has plenty of ability, but fails to put it to anything like full use. (12/1)
**Persian Symphony (IRE)**, having her first run on the Flat for some time, ran reasonably but failed to get into it, despite staying on. (16/1)
**Carmenoura (IRE)** ran her best race so far but was still beaten some way out. (33/1)
**2378 Shalateeno** failed to handle the first bend and that was it for her. (6/1)

## 2566 DUNBAR CLAIMING STKS (3-Y.O+) (Class F)

4-15 (4-15) **7f 15y** £2,605.00 (£730.00: £355.00) Stalls: High GOING minus 0.38 sec per fur (F)

| | | | SP | RR | SF |
|---|---|---|---|---|---|
| 2426$^{4}$ **Anonym (IRE) (63)** (DNicholls) **4-9-3**(7) JBramhill(2) (lw: chsd ldr: led 2f out: hld on wl) | — | **1** | 5/2$^{2}$ | 61 | 36 |
| 2391$^{14}$ **Diet (50)** (MissLAPerratt) **10-9-1v** KDarley(5) (led tl hdd 2f out: rallied 1f out: kpt on) | ¾ | **2** | 9/1 | 50 | 25 |
| 2391* **Allinson's Mate (IRE) (55)** (TDBarron) **8-9-5** JFortune(3) (lw: a.p: rdn 3f out: hdwy over 1f out: nvr able chal) | ½ | **3** | 4/5$^{1}$ | 53 | 28 |
| 2316$^{5}$ **Jebi (USA) (40)** (CMurray) **6-9-3v** JWeaver(1) (hld up: effrt over 3f out: n.d) | 4 | **4** | 11/2$^{3}$ | 42 | 17 |

| | Horse | Dist | Pos | SP | RR | SF |
|---|---|---|---|---|---|---|
| | **King of Show (IRE) (44)** (RAllan) **5-8-13** KFallon(4) (chsd ldrs: racd alone far side st: wknd fnl 3f) | 5 | **5** | 33/1 | 27 | 2 |

(SP 112.5%) **5 Rn**

**1m 29.0** (3.50) CSF £19.41 TOTE £3.00: £2.60 £3.90 (£8.50) OWNER Wetherby Racing Bureau Ltd (THIRSK) BRED T. G. Mooney

**2426 Anonym (IRE)**, who at last got it right here, hit the front in the last two furlongs, but could never relax. (5/2)

**2178 Diet** was able to dominate this time and, when passed, kept battling back. (9/1: op 6/1)

**2391* Allinson's Mate (IRE)** was a crazy price for an unreliable horse and, despite keeping on in the last two furlongs, was never doing enough to get there. (4/5)

**2316 Jebi (USA)** did not look the type for this type of track and failed to get into it. (11/2)

## 2567 MILL HILL H'CAP (0-65) (3-Y.O+) (Class F)

4-45 (4-45) **1m 16y** £2,736.00 (£828.00: £404.00: £192.00) Stalls: High GOING minus 0.38 sec per fur (F)

| | Horse | Dist | Pos | SP | RR | SF |
|---|---|---|---|---|---|---|
| 1885[8] | **Jambo (50)** (JLEyre) **3-8-13** RLappin(8) (a.p: led over 2f out: r.o wl) | — | **1** | 11/2[2] | 63 | 35 |
| 2391[4] | **Rainbows Rhapsody (35)** (DWChapman) **5-8-7** TWilliams(2) (lw: bhd: hdwy 3f out: sn chsng ldrs: kpt on wl fnl f) | 3 | **2** | 8/1 | 42 | 23 |
| 2521[8] | **Hawwam (43)** (EJAlston) **10-9-1** KFallon(4) (bhd: hdwy 3f out: styd on: nrst fin) | 1¼ | **3** | 33/1 | 48 | 29 |
| 2019* | **Dungeon Princess (IRE) (62)** (CMurray) **3-9-11** KDarley(7) (lw: hld up: effrt & nt clr run over 1f out: swtchd & styd on one pce) | 1 | **4** | 2/1[1] | 65 | 37 |
| 2428[6] | **Percy Parrot (40)** (RMWhitaker) **4-8-12** SDWilliams(5) (b.hind: led tl over 2f out: grad wknd) | 2½ | **5** | 12/1 | 38 | 19 |
| 2075[8] | **Roseate Lodge (40)** (SEKettlewell) **10-8-12** JFortune(10) (lw: in tch: hdwy u.p 2f out: nvr able to chal) | s.h | **6** | 6/1[3] | 38 | 19 |
| | **Celebration Cake (IRE) (56)** (MissLAPerratt) **4-10-0** JWeaver(1) (prom tl wknd fnl 2f) | 1½ | **7** | 12/1 | 51 | 32 |
| 2242[3] | **Tirols Tyrant (IRE) (55)** (MrsASwinbank) **3-8-13**(5) PRoberts(6) (bhd: rdn 3f out: n.d) | 1¾ | **8** | 10/1 | 46 | 18 |
| 2130[7] | **Monte Cavo (30)** (MBrittain) **5-8-2b[1]** JLowe(3) (cl up tl wknd 3f out: eased whn btn) | 2 | **9** | 8/1 | 17 | — |
| 2023[7] | **Bowcliffe (49)** (MrsAMNaughton) **5-9-7** NConnorton(9) (lw: chsd ldrs tl wknd fnl 3f) | 2½ | **10** | 10/1 | 31 | 12 |

(SP 121.7%) **10 Rn**

**1m 41.7** (3.10) CSF £46.59 CT £1,252.62 TOTE £6.30: £1.90 £3.40 £4.20 (£28.00) Trio £300.70 OWNER Mr A. H. Jackson (HAMBLETON) BRED R. S. A. Urquhart

WEIGHT FOR AGE 3yo-9lb

**Jambo**, who won on this track last year, had shown little since, but she bounced back to form here and did it in style. (11/2)

**2391 Rainbows Rhapsody** put in another good run and will surely find her mark before long. (8/1)

**1468 Hawwam**, from a yard that has now really come to form, ran well but was never doing quite enough to get into it. (33/1)

**2019* Dungeon Princess (IRE)**, who likes to do things on the bridle, was short of a clear run here and, never happy, failed to offer a threat. (2/1)

**2428 Percy Parrot** has to dominate to give his best and, once headed two furlongs out, was then fighting a lost cause. (12/1: 8/1-14/1)

**Roseate Lodge**, who looked well, tried to peg the leaders back early in the straight but, despite staying on, could never get into it. He has certainly slipped to a useful mark in the handicap. (6/1)

**Celebration Cake (IRE)** (12/1: op 8/1)

**2242 Tirols Tyrant (IRE)** (10/1: 12/1-20/1)

**2023 Bowcliffe** (10/1: op 6/1)

T/Plpt: £96.10 (103.74 Tckts). T/Qdpt: £26.50 (34.94 Tckts). AA

# 2075-RIPON (R-H) (Good)
## Monday July 8th

WEATHER: fine WIND: almost nil

## 2568 FISHERGATE (S) STKS (3-Y.O+) (Class F)

7-00 (7-02) **1m 2f** £2,706.70 (£761.20: £372.10) Stalls: High GOING minus 0.31 sec per fur (GF)

| | Horse | Dist | Pos | SP | RR | SF |
|---|---|---|---|---|---|---|
| 2136* | **North Ardar (58)** (MrsMReveley) **6-9-7**(5) SCopp(13) (hld up: hdwy 4f out: led over 1f out: styd on u.p to ld post) | — | **1** | 100/30[2] | 63 | 43 |
| 2068[5] | **Guesstimation (USA) (62)** (JPearce) **7-9-7** GBardwell(3) (effrt over 4f out: styd on u.p to ld ins fnl f: jst ct) | s.h | **2** | 7/4[1] | 58 | 38 |
| 2356[4] | **Diamond Crown (IRE) (42)** (MartynWane) **5-9-7** KFallon(11) (hld up: effrt over 4f out: gd hdwy & nt clr run over 1f out: swtchd: styd on wl towards fin) | 2½ | **3** | 11/1 | 54 | 34 |
| 2180[13] | **Veshca Lady (IRE) (42)** (EWeymes) **3-8-2v[1]**(3) FLynch(5) (bhd: hdwy 3f out: styd on fnl f: nt rch ldrs) | nk | **4** | 9/1 | 48 | 17 |
| 1451[7] | **Lebedinski (IRE)** (MrsPSly) **3-8-5** ACulhane(2) (bhd: hdwy over 3f out: styd on fnl f) | ½ | **5** | 20/1 | 48 | 17 |
| 2488[2] | **Willy Star (BEL)** (MrsSJSmith) **6-9-7** KDarley(8) (dwlt s: sn chsng ldrs: one pce fnl 2f) | 4 | **6** | 6/1[3] | 46 | 26 |
| 2183[14] | **Acquittal (IRE) (52)** (AStreeter) **4-9-2v**(5) RHavlin(6) (chsd ldr tl wknd over 1f out) | 7 | **7** | 20/1 | 35 | 15 |
| 2488[5] | **Forzair (60)** (JJO'Neill) **4-9-12b** JWeaver(9) (lw: bit bkwd: led tl over 1f out: sn wknd) | 3 | **8** | 8/1 | 35 | 15 |
| 2297[4] | **Boy Blakeney** (MrsSJSmith) **3-8-10** DaleGibson(10) (chsd ldrs: sn drvn along: lost pl 3f out) | ½ | **9** | 25/1 | 29 | — |
| 2133[8] | **Princesse Lyphard** (MJPolglase) **3-8-5** WHollick(12) (effrt on outside over 3f out: sn wknd) | 5 | **10** | 25/1 | 16 | — |
| 2348[7] | **Gallardini (IRE) (36)** (BSRothwell) **7-9-7b** JStack(4) (nvr nr ldrs) | 1½ | **11** | 14/1 | 19 | — |
| 2481[6] | **Harsh Times (51)** (TDEasterby) **3-8-5b** MBirch(7) (chsd ldrs: rdn over 5f out: nt run on: virtually p.u 2f out) | dist | **12** | 6/1[3] | — | — |
| | **Sleepy Boy** (WStorey) **3-8-10** JCarroll(1) (s.i.s: a wl bhd: t.o 3f out) | 11 | **13** | 25/1 | — | — |

(SP 145.2%) **13 Rn**

**2m 8.7** (5.20) CSF £11.36 TOTE £4.60: £1.40 £1.60 £3.00 (£7.40) Trio £55.10 OWNER Laurel (Leisure) Ltd (SALTBURN) BRED Mrs H.Seddington

WEIGHT FOR AGE 3yo-11lb

Bt in 5,600gns

**OFFICIAL EXPLANATION Harsh Times: swallowed her tongue at the halfway stage.**

**2136* North Ardar** made it four out of four this year, but it was a very tight thing in the end. (100/30: 2/1-7/2)

**2068 Guesstimation (USA)**, backed to turn over North Ardar, failed by the skin of his teeth. (7/4)

**2356 Diamond Crown (IRE)**, a scratchy mover, had a poor run on the inner and, even after being switched over a furlong out, he still met trouble. Staying on strongly at the finish, he is even better over one and a half miles. (11/1)

**2026 Veshca Lady (IRE)**, in a visor for the first time, looked to have run up a bit light. Given plenty to do, she was putting in her best work at the finish. (9/1)

**1067 Lebedinski (IRE)**, a lazy walker, sat well off the pace this time. Staying on in good style in the final furlong, she should improve and win a seller at least. (20/1)

**2488 Willy Star (BEL)**, closely matched with the winner on Redcar running, tended to wander about under pressure. (6/1: op 4/1)
**2481 Harsh Times**, stepping up in distance, stopped in two strides going into the home turn. She reportedly swallowed her tongue. (6/1)

## 2569 SKELLGATE MAIDEN AUCTION STKS (2-Y.O F) (Class F)

7-25 (7-25) **5f** £2,575.80 (£723.80: £353.40) Stalls: Low GOING minus 0.31 sec per fur (GF)

| | | | SP | RR | SF |
|---|---|---|---|---|---|
| $2025^{4}$ | **Under Pressure** (TDEasterby) **2-8-4** MBirch(6) (lw: mde all: rdn ½-wy: styd on wl fnl f)......— | **1** | 5/1 $^{3}$ | 67 | 17 |
| $2361^{5}$ | **Five Live** (MDHammond) **2-8-7**$^{ow3}$ KFallon(4) (a.p: styd on u.p fnl f)......2 | **2** | 5/1 $^{3}$ | 64 | 11 |
| $1308^{5}$ | **Sheraton Girl** (MJohnston) **2-8-5** MHills(1) (w ldrs: rdn & nt qckn appr fnl f)......1½ | **3** | 10/1 | 57 | 7 |
| $2076^{5}$ | **Teddy's Bow (IRE)** (MWEasterby) **2-8-2** DaleGibson(5) (sn outpcd & drvn along: styd on appr fnl f)......1 | **4** | 7/2 $^{2}$ | 51 | 1 |
| $1595^{2}$ | **Hoh Surprise (IRE)** (MBell) **2-8-2** PRobinson(3) (chsd ldrs tl wknd over 1f out)......1 | **5** | 13/8 $^{1}$ | 47 | — |
| $1595^{6}$ | **Casual Cottage (IRE)** (CMurray) **2-8-7v¹** JWeaver(7) (b.nr hind: w ldrs tl wknd over 1f out)......s.h | **6** | 7/1 | 52 | 2 |
| $2018^{3}$ | **My Girl** (JBerry) **2-8-2** JCarroll(2) (dwlt s: bhd & drvn along: sme hdwy ½-wy: sn wknd)......6 | **7** | 7/1 | 28 | — |
| | | | (SP 127.7%) | **7 Rn** | |

**61.1 secs** (2.70) CSF £30.85 TOTE £7.50: £2.70 £3.00 (£20.50) OWNER Ryedale Associates (MALTON) BRED James Thom and Sons

**2025 Under Pressure** looked particularly well and put two modest efforts behind her, staying on strongly to score in decisive fashion in the end. This looked no better than a claimer though. (5/1)
**2361 Five Live** stuck on in the final furlong and is crying out for six. (5/1)
**1308 Sheraton Girl**, a keen-going type, ran much better than on her debut. (10/1)
**2076 Teddy's Bow (IRE)** has a round action and struggled to go the pace, but was staying on at the finish. She needs six. (7/2)
**1595 Hoh Surprise (IRE)**, absent for thirty-eight days, went down keenly and, after showing plenty of toe, stopped in two strides over a furlong out. (13/8)
**1595 Casual Cottage (IRE)** raced very keenly in a visor for the first time on the wide outside. (7/1)

## 2570 BONDGATE H'CAP (0-80) (3-Y.O) (Class D)

7-50 (7-51) **1m 4f 60y** £4,458.00 (£1,344.00: £652.00: £306.00) Stalls: Low GOING minus 0.31 sec per fur (GF)

| | | | SP | RR | SF |
|---|---|---|---|---|---|
| $2333^{5}$ | **Berlin Blue (72)** (JWWatts) **3-9-1** JCarroll(11) (sn chsng ldrs: led over 1f out: hld on wl towards fin)......— | **1** | 10/1 | 82 | 47 |
| $2140^{2}$ | **Mental Pressure (78)** (MrsMReveley) **3-9-7** KDarley(9) (led tl over 1f out: styd on wl u.p)......½ | **2** | 15/2 | 87 | 52 |
| 2233* | **Village King (IRE) (77)** (RHannon) **3-9-6** JFEgan(1) (lw: s.i.s: sn pushed along: hdwy 4f out: nt qckn fnl 2f)....3 | **3** | 5/1 $^{2}$ | 82 | 47 |
| $2067^{9}$ | **Karisma (IRE) (70)** (DenysSmith) **3-8-13** KFallon(10) (lw: hld up & plld hrd: outpcd over 3f out: kpt on fnl 2f)...7 | **4** | 14/1 | 66 | 31 |
| $1850^{12}$ | **Clash of Swords (60)** (PCalver) **3-8-3** MBirch(7) (sn bhd: rdn over 4f out: styd on fnl 2f)......s.h | **5** | 25/1 | 56 | 21 |
| $1470^{6}$ | **Blurred (IRE) (73)** (MHTompkins) **3-9-2** PRobinson(8) (a chsng ldrs: pushed along 5f out: one pce)......nk | **6** | 12/1 | 69 | 34 |
| $2080^{4}$ | **Mukeed (73)** (JHMGosden) **3-9-2** DaleGibson(3) (bhd & pushed along: sme hdwy 2f out: n.d)......1½ | **7** | 7/1 $^{3}$ | 67 | 32 |
| $2505^{4}$ | **Rivercare (IRE) (61)** (MJPolglase) **3-8-4** NCarlisle(5) (chsd ldrs: sn drvn along: lost pl over 2f out)......1 | **8** | 20/1 | 54 | 19 |
| $1669^{6}$ | **Exactly (IRE) (72)** (JLEyre) **3-9-1** TWilliams(12) (bhd: effrt u.p over 3f out: n.d)......1¾ | **9** | 11/1 | 62 | 27 |
| $2067^{2}$ | **One Pound (70)** (BWHills) **3-8-13** MHills(2) (hld up: effrt 6f out: hdwy to chse ldrs over 3f out: sn rdn & wknd).7 | **10** | 5/4 $^{1}$ | 51 | 16 |
| $2148^{10}$ | **Diego (68)** (CEBrittain) **3-8-11** WRyan(6) (chsd ldrs tl lost pl over 6f out: sn bhd)......7 | **11** | 14/1 | 40 | 5 |
| $1669^{11}$ | **Lord of The Manor (74)** (MJohnston) **3-9-3** JWeaver(4) (plld hrd: racd wd: trckd ldrs tl lost pl over 4f out: virtually p.u 2f out)......14 | **12** | 16/1 | 28 | — |
| | | | (SP 138.3%) | **12 Rn** | |

**2m 38.3** (4.30) CSF £88.06 CT £404.13 TOTE £15.10: £2.70 £2.50 £2.40 (£98.40) Trio £354.20; £204.57 to Newmarket 9/7/96 OWNER Sheikh Mohammed (RICHMOND) BRED Darley Stud Management Co Ltd

OFFICIAL EXPLANATION **One Pound: was in a distressed state.**

**2333 Berlin Blue**, on his handicap bow, showed the right sort of spirit in a tight finish. He should have further improvement in him and will be suited by a step up to a mile and six. (10/1: 7/1-11/1)
**2140 Mental Pressure**, with the rail to help him, stuck on in most determined fashion, but had to give best near the line. He too will appreciate a bit further. (15/2)
**2233* Village King (IRE)**, who is thriving, had been raised 5lb for his Salisbury success. (5/1)
**1361 Karisma (IRE)**, who ran badly on her previous start, is a keen-going type. Taken to post early and settled towards the rear, she was staying on when it was all over. (14/1)
**1359 Clash of Swords** showed his first worthwhile form and looks a potential stayer. (25/1)
**1035 Blurred (IRE)** looked to have been given plenty of weight on his handicap debut. (12/1: op 7/1)
**2080 Mukeed** looked and moved well, but was never going. Flat out from start to finish, if he has a future, it is as a stayer. (7/1)
**2067 One Pound** was in trouble some way from home. The Vet reported him to be in a distressed state afterwards. (5/4)

## 2571 SINGER & FRIEDLANDER H'CAP (0-80) (3-Y.O) (Class D)

8-20 (8-21) **6f** £4,302.00 (£1,296.00: £628.00: £294.00) Stalls: Low GOING minus 0.31 sec per fur (GF)

| | | | SP | RR | SF |
|---|---|---|---|---|---|
| $2425^{4}$ | **The Wad (66)** (DNicholls) **3-8-12** WRyan(5) (chsd ldr: styd on u.p to ld ins fnl f)......— | **1** | 9/1 $^{3}$ | 73 | 38 |
| $1823^{2}$ | **Maiteamia (70)** (SRBowring) **3-9-2b** JWeaver(8) (led: clr ½-wy: sn rdn: hdd ins fnl f: r.o)......nk | **2** | 11/4 $^{1}$ | 76 | 41 |
| $2427^{4}$ | **Camionneur (IRE) (50)** (TDEasterby) **3-7-10b** JLowe(7) (dwlt s: sn drvn along: n.m.r ½-wy: styd on appr fnl f)......2 | **3** | 12/1 | 51 | 16 |
| $2215^{2}$ | **Pathaze (53)** (NBycroft) **3-7-13** DaleGibson(9) (chsd ldrs: rdn & outpcd ½-wy: styd on fnl 2f)......1 | **4** | 10/1 | 51 | 16 |
| 2238* | **Pharaoh's Joy (56)** (JWPayne) **3-8-2** PRobinson(1) (lw: prom: effrt over 2f out: kpt on one pce)......¾ | **5** | 7/2 $^{2}$ | 52 | 17 |
| $2078^{6}$ | **Limerick Princess (IRE) (70)** (JBerry) **3-8-9**(7) JoanneWebster(2) (trckd ldrs: effrt 2f out: grad wknd)......3 | **6** | 9/1 $^{3}$ | 58 | 23 |
| $2137^{8}$ | **Branston Danni (75)** (MrsJRRamsden) **3-9-7** KFallon(4) (b.off hind: dwlt: a in rr: eased fnl f)......11 | **7** | 10/1 | 34 | — |
| 2311* | **Indian Relative (75)** (RGuest) **3-9-2**(5) DGriffiths(3) (lw: prom: sn pushed along: lost pl ½-wy: eased)......12 | **8** | 11/4 $^{1}$ | 2 | — |
| | | | (SP 121.4%) | **8 Rn** | |

**1m 12.8** (2.30) CSF £34.18 CT £283.83 TOTE £6.90: £2.10 £1.80 £1.60 (£12.20) Trio £32.70 OWNER Mr W. J. Kelly (THIRSK) BRED C. R. and V. M. Withers

LONG HANDICAP Camionneur (IRE) 7-9

OFFICIAL EXPLANATION **Indian Relative: was found to have an irregular heart beat.**

**2425 The Wad** was given no chance to duck the issue. Six is definitely his best trip. (9/1)
**1823 Maiteamia**, who carries plenty of condition, had his rivals in trouble at halfway. Just denied in the end, a drop back to five will suit. (11/4)
**2427 Camionneur (IRE)**, still a maiden after nineteen outings, on the face of it did not have the run of the race. After losing ground at the start and being short of room at halfway, he was staying on at the line. (12/1: op 8/1)
**2215 Pathaze**, off a 4lb higher mark, lacks anything in the way of finishing speed. (10/1)

**2238* Pharaoh's Joy** found it tough after being raised 4lb. (7/2)
**1599* Limerick Princess (IRE)** carries plenty of condition and travelled strongly but, from a mark 12lb higher than she won off at Catterick three runs ago, she had no answer in the final two furlongs. (9/1)
**Branston Danni**, in a stew beforehand, lost ground at the start and his rider gave up. (10/1)
**2311* Indian Relative** dropped right out at halfway and was virtually pulled up. Something was clearly amiss. (11/4)

## 2572 KIRKGATE MAIDEN STKS (3-Y.O+) (Class D)
8-50 (8-54) **1m** £3,680.00 (£1,115.00: £545.00: £260.00) Stalls: Low GOING minus 0.31 sec per fur (GF)

| | | | SP | RR | SF |
|---|---|---|---|---|---|
| 2135⁵ | **King's Academy (IRE) (81)** (HRACecil) **3-8-12** WRyan(5) (lw: chsd ldrs: led over 1f out: styd on u.p) .........— | **1** | 10/11 1 | 85 | 31 |
| 2124³ | **Golden Thunderbolt (FR) (78)** (JHMGosden) **3-8-12** JLowe(6) (trckd ldrs: styd on u.p fnl f)........½ | **2** | 9/2 3 | 84 | 30 |
| 1470⁸ | **Dispol Gem (72)** (GROldroyd) **3-8-7** KFallon(14) (a chsng ldrs: styd on same pce fnl 2f)........1 | **3** | 9/1 | 77 | 23 |
| 746⁴ | **Stellar Line (USA) (84)** (BWHills) **3-8-12** MHills(10) (trckd ldrs: led over 3f out tl over 1f out: sn wknd)........2½ | **4** | 4/1 2 | 77 | 23 |
| | **Jeopardize** (CEBrittain) **3-8-7** MBirch(1) (lengthy: unf: sn outpcd: styd on fnl 4f: nvr nr ldrs)........8 | **5** | 11/1 | 56 | 2 |
| | **Sicarian** (MJHeaton-Ellis) **4-9-7** AProcter(7) (sn trckg ldrs: wknd over 2f out)........3 | **6** | 25/1 | 55 | 10 |
| | **Cameron Edge** (ABMulholland) **3-8-7** JStack(2) (bit bkwd: b: s.s: bhd: sme hdwy 2f out: n.d)........5 | **7** | 50/1 | 40 | — |
| 2181⁸ | **Road Racer (IRE)** (MrsJRRamsden) **3-8-12** MDeering(4) (bit bkwd: bhd & rn wd ent st: n.d)........1 | **8** | 25/1 | 43 | — |
| 2515³ | **Toulston Lady (IRE)** (MJCamacho) **4-9-2** DaleGibson(3) (unruly in stalls: bhd fnl 5f)........½ | **9** | 33/1 | 37 | — |
| 2432¹² | **Haysong (IRE)** (JPLeigh) **3-8-7** ACulhane(12) (chsd ldrs: sn drvn along: lost pl over 3f out)........1½ | **10** | 50/1 | 34 | — |
| 1787⁵ | **Petarina** (MissJFCraze) **3-8-7** NConnorton(13) (led tl over 3f out: wknd qckly over 2f out)........5 | **11** | 50/1 | 24 | — |
| 2515⁶ | **Petit Flora** (GHolmes) **4-9-2** JFanning(9) (b.hind: dwlt: a in rr)........hd | **12** | 50/1 | 24 | — |
| 2079⁷ | **Mustard** (ABMulholland) **3-8-7** TWilliams(8) (hld up & plld hrd: a bhd: virtually p.u 2f out)........dist | **13** | 50/1 | — | — |
| | | | (SP 129.3%) | | **13 Rn** |

**1m 41.7** (4.00) CSF £6.15 TOTE £2.20: £2.20 £1.30 £1.70 (£3.60) Trio £15.50 OWNER Mr Michael Poland (NEWMARKET) BRED Michael Poland
WEIGHT FOR AGE 3yo-9lb
**2135 King's Academy (IRE)** has plenty of size and scope and appreciated the drop back to a mile. He made hard work of winning what looked an ordinary maiden though. (10/11: 5/4-4/5)
**2124 Golden Thunderbolt (FR)**, a keen-going sort, is getting better with every outing and gave the winner a good tussle. (9/2)
**1470 Dispol Gem**, unsuited by the soft last time, ran right up to her best. She will struggle in handicap company off 72. (9/1)
**746 Stellar Line (USA)** looked very fit and showed plenty of knee-action going to post. Giving a fair bit of trouble at the start, he did not look very genuine. (4/1)
**Jeopardize**, a poor mover, has had her shins pin-fired. Very green and struggling to go the pace, she did show a glimmer, staying on in the last half-mile. (11/1: 7/1-12/1)
**Sicarian**, having his third run, is a very keen-going sort. Taken to post quietly, he dropped right out halfway up the straight. (25/1)

## 2573 WESTGATE H'CAP (0-70) (3-Y.O+) (Class E)
9-20 (9-21) **1m** £3,096.40 (£938.20: £458.60: £218.80) Stalls: High GOING minus 0.31 sec per fur (GF)

| | | | SP | RR | SF |
|---|---|---|---|---|---|
| 1955⁵ | **Chinensis (IRE) (70)** (LMCumani) **3-9-7** OUrbina(8) (lw: mde virtually all: edgd lft & styd on wl fnl f) ........— | **1** | 9/2 2 | 82 | 49 |
| 2293⁴ | **Scaraben (68)** (SEKettlewell) **8-10-0** JStack(10) (lw: trckd ldrs: ev ch over 1f out: edgd lft & nt qckn ins fnl f)........nk | **2** | 5/2 1 | 79 | 55 |
| 2152⁷ | **Lucky Bea (60)** (MWEasterby) **3-8-11** DaleGibson(11) (trckd ldrs: styd on fnl 2f: nvr nr to chal)........2 | **3** | 8/1 | 67 | 34 |
| 2159⁵ | **Benjamins Law (48)** (JAPickering) **5-8-8** RLappin(12) (a chsng ldrs: kpt on same pce fnl 2f)........¾ | **4** | 12/1 | 54 | 30 |
| 2481³ | **Sakharov (58)** (MJohnston) **7-9-4** JWeaver(9) (chsd ldrs: rdn & hung lft over 2f out: outpcd over 1f out) ........½ | **5** | 9/1 | 63 | 39 |
| 2296⁴ | **Euro Sceptic (IRE) (47)** (TDEasterby) **4-8-4b(3)** FLynch(7) (a in tch: rdn & no imp fnl 3f)........3½ | **6** | 7/1 3 | 45 | 21 |
| 2481² | **Bedazzle (38)** (MBrittain) **5-7-12** JLowe(1) (lw: b: rr div: hdwy over 3f out: nvr nr ldrs)........1¾ | **7** | 11/1 | 32 | 8 |
| 1860⁷ | **Pleasure Trick (USA) (55)** (DonEnricoIncisa) **5-9-1** KimTinkler(4) (s.i.s: sn wl bhd: styd on fnl 3f) ........s.h | **8** | 50/1 | 49 | 25 |
| 508⁷ | **Larn Fort (53)** (CWFairhurst) **6-8-13v** TWilliams(3) (b: hmpd s: a bhd)........½ | **9** | 16/1 | 46 | 22 |
| 2045³ | **Champagne N Dreams (47)** (DNicholls) **4-8-7** KDarley(2) (trckd ldrs: ev ch tl wknd over 2f out)........5 | **10** | 7/1 3 | 30 | 6 |
| 2283⁸ | **Northern Judge (60)** (BHanbury) **3-8-11b** WRyan(6) (swvd lft s: effrt 4f out: sn wknd)........12 | **11** | 12/1 | 19 | — |
| 995¹⁸ | **Oakbury (IRE) (53)** (MissLCSiddall) **4-8-13** KFallon(5) (hmpd s: a wl bhd)........3 | **12** | 33/1 | 6 | — |
| | | | (SP 127.4%) | | **12 Rn** |

**1m 40.7** (3.00) CSF £16.59 CT £85.51 TOTE £5.40: £1.90 £1.70 £3.40 (£7.10) Trio £37.10 OWNER Sheikh Mohammed (NEWMARKET) BRED Sheikh Mohammed bin Rashid al Maktoum
WEIGHT FOR AGE 3yo-9lb
**1955 Chinensis (IRE)** looked particularly well and appreciated the drop back to a mile. His young rider continues to impress. (9/2: 11/4-5/1)
**2293 Scaraben**, a fast-ground mile specialist, gave his all but could not quite peg back the winner. (5/2: 7/2-9/4)
**2123 Lucky Bea**, as usual taken to post early, was racing off a mark 6lb higher than when winning at Newcastle earlier in the year. (8/1)
**2159 Benjamins Law** ran well on the face of it, but he is about 20lb worse off on the All-Weather. (12/1)
**2481 Sakharov** drifted out towards the centre, and is possibly better over seven. (9/1)
**2296 Euro Sceptic (IRE)**, a scratchy mover, seems to reserve his best for Beverley these days. (7/1)
**2481 Bedazzle** (11/1: 8/1-12/1)

T/Plpt: £318.30 (50.95 Tckts). T/Qdpt: £24.70 (57.15 Tckts). WG

# 2373-WINDSOR (Fig. 8) (Good)
## Monday July 8th
WEATHER: fine WIND: almost nil

## 2574 BARRY AND SHEILA NOAKES H'CAP (0-70) (3-Y.O+) (Class E)
6-40 (6-44) **1m 2f 7y** £3,452.50 (£1,045.00: £510.00: £242.50) Stalls: High GOING minus 0.21 sec per fur (GF)

| | | | SP | RR | SF |
|---|---|---|---|---|---|
| 2378* | **Game Ploy (POL) (65)** (DHaydnJones) **4-9-11** 5x PatEddery(16) (lw: gd hdwy 3f out: led over 1f out: r.o wl) .— | **1** | 9/1 3 | 80 | 52 |
| 2183* | **Runic Symbol (39)** (MBlanshard) **5-7-13** JQuinn(7) (hdwy 3f out: ev ch over 1f out: r.o)........2½ | **2** | 16/1 | 50 | 22 |
| *2303*³ | **Ring the Chief (36)** (MDIUsher) **4-7-5(5)** MartinDwyer(2) (b: hdwy 3f out: ev ch over 1f out: nt qckn)........1½ | **3** | 33/1 | 45 | 17 |
| 2378² | **Premier League (IRE) (59)** (JELong) **6-9-5** RPrice(14) (a.p: led wl over 1f out: sn hdd: nt qckn)........2½ | **4** | 7/1 1 | 64 | 36 |
| 2127⁷ | **Princess Danielle (58)** (WRMuir) **4-9-4** CRutter(19) (nvr nrr)........4 | **5** | 20/1 | 56 | 28 |

| | Horse | | Pos | SP | RR | SF |
|---|---|---|---|---|---|---|
| 2192[9] | **Fastini Gold (47)** (MDIUsher) **4-8-7** TSprake(25) (nrst fin) | nk | **6** | 33/1 | 45 | 17 |
| 1965[9] | **Koathary (USA) (55)** (LGCottrell) **5-8-12**(3) SDrowne(22) (lw: led tl wknd wl over 1f out) | 1¼ | **7** | 8/1[2] | 51 | 23 |
| 2214[6] | **Course Fishing (42)** (BAMcMahon) **5-8-2** GCarter(6) (mid div tl r.o fnl 2f) | hd | **8** | 12/1 | 38 | 10 |
| 2226[12] | **Warspite (51)** (RJO'Sullivan) **6-8-11** SSanders(15) (hdwy 3f out: wknd over 1f out) | ½ | **9** | 33/1 | 46 | 18 |
| 1618[10] | **Typhoon Eight (IRE) (68)** (BWHills) **4-10-0b** DHolland(4) (a mid div) | 2 | **10** | 25/1 | 60 | 32 |
| 2377[2] | **Labudd (USA) (43)** (RIngram) **6-8-3** NAdams(17) (b: wl bhd tl r.o fnl 2f) | ½ | **11** | 10/1 | 34 | 6 |
| 2000[4] | **Ashby Hill (IRE) (53)** (RRowe) **5-8-13** AClark(11) (prom tl wknd over 1f out) | 1¾ | **12** | 10/1 | 41 | 13 |
| 2409[4] | **Zahran (IRE) (40)** (JMBradley) **5-8-0** AMackay(21) (lw: a mid div) | 1½ | **13** | 16/1 | 26 | — |
| 1841[4] | **Myfontaine (68)** (KTIvory) **9-10-0** BDoyle(10) (lw: b: nvr bttr than mid div) | 2½ | **14** | 20/1 | 50 | 22 |
| 2203[7] | **Lady Sabina (38)** (WJMusson) **6-7-12** DeclanO'Shea(12) (s.s: nvr on terms) | 7 | **15** | 25/1 | 9 | — |
| *2170[3]* | **Super High (58)** (PHowling) **4-9-4b** FNorton(24) (prom tl wknd over 3f out) | hd | **16** | 14/1 | 28 | — |
| *353[4]* | **General Shirley (IRE) (49)** (PRHedger) **5-8-9** AMcGlone(3) (nvr plcd to chal) | 3 | **17** | 25/1 | 15 | — |
| | **Plinth (56)** (NAGraham) **5-9-2v** DHarrison(20) (w ldr: hrd rdn 4f out: wknd 3f out) | 1¼ | **18** | 14/1 | 20 | — |
| 2000[2] | **Ballpoint (68)** (RHannon) **3-9-0**(3) DaneO'Neill(1) (lw: mid div tl wknd over 2f out) | 1¼ | **19** | 12/1 | 30 | — |
| 2326[5] | **Challenger (IRE) (48)** (JJSheehan) **3-7-8**(3) MHenry(23) (a bhd) | 3 | **20** | 33/1 | 5 | — |
| 1996[4] | **It'sthebusiness (59)** (SDow) **4-9-5v** TQuinn(5) (chsd ldrs tl wknd over 2f out) | 2½ | **21** | 14/1 | 12 | — |
| 2341[5] | **Duty Sergeant (IRE) (39)** (PhilipMitchell) **7-7-13** WCarson(18) (a bhd) | s.h | **22** | 16/1 | — | — |
| 1669[9] | **Skram (58)** (RDickin) **3-8-7** DeanMcKeown(9) (prom tl wknd over 3f out) | 8 | **23** | 33/1 | — | — |
| 2192[5] | **Johns Joy (38)** (JJBridger) **11-7-9**(3)ow1 DarrenMoffatt(13) (b: a bhd) | 5 | **24** | 25/1 | — | — |
| | | | | (SP 144.4%) | **24 Rn** | |

**2m 8.6** (3.70) CSF £143.83 CT £4,169.50 TOTE £10.90: £3.60 £3.00 £9.10 £2.30 (£64.80) Trio £556.30 OWNER Mr Kevan Kynaston (PONTYPRIDD) BRED C. Olsen Ltd
LONG HANDICAP Ring the Chief 7-9
WEIGHT FOR AGE 3yo-11lb
**2378* Game Ploy (POL)** found a good run on the inside at the three-furlong marker. He quickened to the front approaching the final furlong and stayed on strongly. (9/1: 6/1-10/1)
**2183* Runic Symbol** came with the winner and had every chance approaching the final furlong, but lacked the turn of foot. (16/1)
**2303 Ring the Chief** came with a run in the centre of the course to challenge at the distance, but could not quicken in the last furlong. (33/1)
**2378 Premier League (IRE)** travelled strongly on the heels of the leaders but, after striking the front momentarily below the distance, was soon headed and outpaced. (7/1)
**641 Princess Danielle** stayed on through beaten horses. (20/1)
**1522 Fastini Gold** was running on at the finish, but too late to trouble the leaders. (33/1)
**2377 Labudd (USA)** (10/1: 8/1-12/1)

## 2575 MACKESON CONDITIONS STKS (2-Y.O) (Class D)

7-10 (7-11) **5f 217y** £3,338.75 (£1,010.00: £492.50: £233.75) Stalls: High GOING minus 0.21 sec per fur (GF)

| | Horse | | Pos | SP | RR | SF |
|---|---|---|---|---|---|---|
| 2157* | **Victory Dancer** (BJMeehan) **2-9-2** BDoyle(1) (w ldrs: led over 2f out: all out) | — | **1** | 4/1[2] | 87 | 27 |
| 2073[6] | **Green Jewel** (RHannon) **2-8-6**(3) DaneO'Neill(2) (hdwy 2f out: hrd rdn over 1f out: r.o) | nk | **2** | 4/1[2] | 79 | 19 |
| 1897[3] | **Hil Rhapsody** (BPalling) **2-8-9** TSprake(3) (led over 3f: r.o wl ins fnl f) | s.h | **3** | 14/1 | 79 | 19 |
| 2153* | **Peartree House (IRE)** (BWHills) **2-9-0** PatEddery(6) (a.p: hrd rdn fnl 2f: one pce) | 1½ | **4** | 13/8[1] | 80 | 20 |
| 2112[7] | **Meliksah (IRE)** (MBell) **2-8-9**(7) GFaulkner(7) (w ldrs tl wknd over 1f out) | 2 | **5** | 11/2[3] | 77 | 17 |
| 2057[6] | **Lily Jaques** (PFICole) **2-8-5** TQuinn(4) (outpcd) | 9 | **6** | 20/1 | 42 | — |
| | **Dickie Bird (IRE)** (RHannon) **2-8-10** RHughes(5) (w'like: s.s: a bhd) | 1½ | **7** | 14/1 | 43 | — |
| | | | | (SP 111.6%) | **7 Rn** | |

**1m 14.5** (4.00) CSF £18.67 TOTE £5.20: £2.50 £2.30 (£17.20) OWNER Mr Alan Cunliffe (UPPER LAMBOURN) BRED D. J. Simpson
STEWARDS' ENQUIRY Doyle susp. 17-19/7/96 (excessive use of whip).
**2157* Victory Dancer** disputed the lead from the start. He went to the front over two furlongs from home and held on in a driving finish. (4/1)
**2073 Green Jewel** made ground steadily in the centre of the course under a strong ride but, though staying on, could not quite find enough. (4/1)
**1897 Hil Rhapsody** made the running for over three furlongs and, after looking beaten, rallied bravely inside the final furlong. (14/1)
**2153* Peartree House (IRE)**, although not far behind the leaders, did not travel particularly well and, under the hardest driving in the last two furlongs, could stay on only at one pace. (13/8)
**1479* Meliksah (IRE)** went with the leaders until weakening under strong pressure approaching the final furlong. (11/2)
**Dickie Bird (IRE)** (14/1: op 6/1)

## 2576 WHITBREAD LIMITED STKS (0-80) (3-Y.O) (Class D)

7-35 (7-35) **1m 3f 135y** £3,558.00 (£1,074.00: £522.00: £246.00) Stalls: High GOING minus 0.21 sec per fur (GF)

| | Horse | | Pos | SP | RR | SF |
|---|---|---|---|---|---|---|
| 689[2] | **Arabian Story (80)** (LordHuntingdon) **3-8-11** JReid(8) (b: a.p: led on bit 2f out: cheekily) | — | **1** | 9/2[3] | 88+ | 33 |
| 2041[18] | **Infamous (USA) (79)** (PFICole) **3-8-13** TQuinn(9) (lw: hld up: jnd wnr & ev ch over 1f out: hrd rdn: r.o) | ½ | **2** | 12/1 | 89 | 34 |
| 2015* | **Jazz King (75)** (MissGayKelleway) **3-8-13** WJO'Connor(5) (a.p: ev ch 2f out: r.o one pce) | 3½ | **3** | 4/1[2] | 85 | 30 |
| 948[3] | **Northern Fleet (80)** (GHarwood) **3-8-11** PatEddery(4) (a.p: ev ch 2f out: one pce) | 3 | **4** | 8/1 | 78 | 23 |
| 2124* | **Iberian Dancer (CAN) (79)** (JWHills) **3-8-7**(3) MHenry(7) (hdwy over 2f out: hrd rdn over 1f out: nt qckn) | nk | **5** | 5/1 | 77 | 22 |
| 772[2] | **Swan Hunter (80)** (DJSCosgrove) **3-8-13** DeanMcKeown(3) (nvr nr to chal) | 2½ | **6** | 12/1 | 77 | 22 |
| 2314* | **Hayaain (85)** (MajorWRHern) **3-8-13** WCarson(6) (lw: led: hrd rdn over 2f out: sn hdd & wknd) | ½ | **7** | 5/2[1] | 76 | 21 |
| 833[12] | **Baltic Dream (USA) (73)** (KRBurke) **3-8-8** SWhitworth(1) (in tch tl wknd 3f out) | 8 | **8** | 25/1 | 60 | 5 |
| | **Leith Academy (USA) (75)** (BWHills) **3-8-8** DHolland(2) (a bhd: t.o) | 15 | **9** | 14/1 | 39 | — |
| | | | | (SP 120.4%) | **9 Rn** | |

**2m 30.6** (6.60) CSF £51.69 TOTE £5.20: £1.60 £2.60 £1.50 (£21.20) Trio £103.40 OWNER The Queen (WEST ILSLEY) BRED The Queen
**689 Arabian Story**, always close up and going well, was still on the bridle when leading two furlongs out. His rider appeared intent to win by as short a distance as possible. (9/2)
**1407 Infamous (USA)** tracked the leaders and quickened to join the winner approaching the final furlong. However, he was being hard ridden as his rival was cruising, and he is flattered by restricting the winning distance to half a length. (12/1: op 8/1)
**2015* Jazz King** raced in second or third place throughout. He had every chance at the two-furlong marker, but could not quicken with the first two. (4/1)
**948 Northern Fleet** was soon driven up to dispute second place but, after still having every chance two furlongs out, could not quicken under hard driving. (8/1: 6/1-9/1)

**2124* Iberian Dancer (CAN)** came with a run on the inside approaching the two-furlong marker, but could not sustain the effort below the distance. (5/1)
**772 Swan Hunter**, always in the back four, never held out any hope. (12/1)
**2314* Hayaain** proved very disappointing. He made the running but, when coming under hard driving over two furlongs from home, was soon headed and beaten. (5/2)

## 2577 FRENCH HORN AT SONNING H'CAP (0-70) (3-Y.O+) (Class E)

8-05 (8-06) **1m 67y** £3,273.75 (£990.00: £482.50: £228.75) Stalls: High GOING minus 0.21 sec per fur (GF)

| Form | Horse | Dist | Pos | SP | RR | SF |
|---|---|---|---|---|---|---|
| $2253^{5}$ | **General Haven (63)** (TJNaughton) **3-9-2** PatEddery(6) (gd hdwy on ins 3f out: led ins fnl f: all out) | — | 1 | 10/1 | 75 | 37 |
| $1902^{3}$ | **Flying Pennant (IRE) (66)** (RHannon) **3-9-2**(3) DaneO'Neill(14) (gd hdwy on ins 2f out: ev ch ins fnl f: r.o) | hd | 2 | 8/1$^{2}$ | 78 | 40 |
| $2320^{6}$ | **Gentle Irony (58)** (MJRyan) **4-9-6** BDoyle(11) (a.p: led over 2f out tl ins fnl f) | 3 | 3 | 8/1$^{2}$ | 64 | 35 |
| $2234^{5}$ | **Desert Calm (IRE) (50)** (MrsPNDutfield) **7-8-5b**(7) JoHunnam(13) (hdwy fnl 2f: nvr nrr) | 3 | 4 | 25/1 | 50 | 21 |
| *1972** | **Barrack Yard (60)** (ACStewart) **3-8-13** SWhitworth(10) (hdwy 3f out: ev ch over 1f out: one pce) | ½ | 5 | 11/2$^{1}$ | 59 | 21 |
| $1953^{16}$ | **Digpast (IRE) (57)** (RJO'Sullivan) **6-9-5b** SSanders(7) (hdwy 2f out: nvr nr to chal) | 1½ | 6 | 25/1 | 53 | 24 |
| | **Just Harry (61)** (MJRyan) **5-9-2**(7) AMcCarthy(15) (bit bkwd: stdy hdwy 3f out: one pce fnl 2f) | s.h | 7 | 25/1 | 57 | 28 |
| $1515^{13}$ | **Noble Neptune (46)** (WJMusson) **4-8-8** GCarter(12) (stdy hdwy fnl 2f: nvr nrr) | ½ | 8 | 25/1 | 41 | 12 |
| $2229^{4}$ | **Winsome Wooster (59)** (PGMurphy) **5-9-4**(3) SDrowne(17) (hdwy 4f out: wknd over 1f out) | 3 | 9 | 16/1 | 49 | 20 |
| $1613^{5}$ | **African-Pard (IRE) (61)** (DHaydnJones) **4-9-9** TQuinn(3) (hdwy 4f out: wknd 2f out) | 6 | 10 | 14/1 | 39 | 10 |
| $1839^{6}$ | **Sister Kit (IRE) (60)** (BPalling) **3-8-13** TSprake(8) (w ldr: ev ch over 2f out: sn wknd) | ¾ | 11 | 25/1 | 37 | — |
| $2379^{2}$ | **Asterix (47)** (JMBradley) **8-8-6b**(3) MHenry(16) (mid div tl hrd rdn & wknd 2f out) | nk | 12 | 8/1$^{2}$ | 23 | — |
| $2127^{9}$ | **Persian Affair (IRE) (59)** (MRChannon) **5-9-7** RHughes(4) (t.o fnl 4f: dead) | 20 | 13 | 14/1 | — | — |
| $2286^{15}$ | **Justinianus (IRE) (45)** (JJBridger) **4-8-4**(3) DarrenMoffatt(5) (lw: prom tl wknd over 3f out: t.o) | ½ | 14 | 33/1 | — | — |
| $2378^{13}$ | **Bellateena (50)** (HJCollingridge) **4-8-12v$^{1}$** MRimmer(9) (a bhd: t.o) | 3 | 15 | 25/1 | — | — |
| *$2170^{11}$* | **Bellacardia (65)** (GLewis) **3-8-11**(7) AEddery(1) (a bhd: t.o) | ½ | 16 | 16/1 | — | — |
| 2313* | **Indian Jockey (63)** (MCPipe) **4-9-11** DBridgwater(2) (w ldrs: hrd rdn 4f out: wknd 3f out: t.o) | 6 | 17 | 9/1$^{3}$ | — | — |
| $2339^{4}$ | **Soaked (64)** (JRFanshawe) **3-9-3v$^{1}$** NDay(18) (lw: led: jinked rt over 3f out: hdd & wknd qckly over 2f out: t.o) | 6 | 18 | 11/1 | — | — |
| | | | | (SP 127.3%) | **18 Rn** | |

**1m 47.0** (4.80) CSF £83.10 CT £648.06 TOTE £12.80: £3.00 £2.00 £2.40 £7.60 (£64.40) Trio £165.70 OWNER Mr A. Callard (EPSOM) BRED Stetchworth Park Stud Ltd
WEIGHT FOR AGE 3yo-9lb
STEWARDS' ENQUIRY Pat Eddery susp.17-20/7/96 (excessive use of whip).
**2253 General Haven** came with a strong run on the inside from three furlongs out. He led in the last 150 yards and held on all out. (10/1: 8/1-12/1)
**1902 Flying Pennant (IRE)**, well behind until coming with a strong run on the inside at the two-furlong marker, looked set for victory 100 yards from home but could not quite force his head in front. (8/1)
**2320 Gentle Irony**, close up from the start, set sail for home approaching the two-furlong marker, but was collared in the last 150 yards. (8/1)
**2234 Desert Calm (IRE)** came late to snatch fourth place, but was never in the race with a chance. (25/1)
**1972* Barrack Yard** improved from midfield onto the heels of the leaders approaching the final furlong, but could make no further progress. (11/2)
**1173 Digpast (IRE)** improved at the two-furlong marker and ran on to suggest he is about to return to form. (25/1)
**Just Harry**, who looked in need of the race, came with a steady run on the outside three furlongs out and kept on to the finish. He is one to note. (25/1)
**2339 Soaked** (11/1: 8/1-12/1)

## 2578 CHAMPAGNE RUINART H'CAP (0-70) (3-Y.O) (Class E)

8-35 (8-37) **5f 217y** £3,127.50 (£945.00: £460.00: £217.50) Stalls: High GOING minus 0.21 sec per fur (GF)

| Form | Horse | Dist | Pos | SP | RR | SF |
|---|---|---|---|---|---|---|
| $2186^{4}$ | **Croeso Cynnes (56)** (BPalling) **3-8-7** TSprake(17) (w ldr: led over 2f out: qcknd clr over 1f out: r.o) | — | 1 | 8/1$^{2}$ | 66 | 28 |
| $1823^{8}$ | **Kings Harmony (IRE) (64)** (PJMakin) **3-9-1** PatEddery(10) (a.p: r.o ins fnl f) | ¾ | 2 | 8/1$^{2}$ | 72 | 34 |
| $2228^{10}$ | **Dummer Golf Time (60)** (LordHuntingdon) **3-8-11v$^{1}$** DHarrison(12) (lw: hld up: hdwy 2f out: r.o ins fnl f) | nk | 3 | 12/1 | 67 | 29 |
| *$2325^{8}$* | **Scathebury (57)** (KRBurke) **3-8-8** DRMcCabe(15) (swtg: hdwy on ins 2f out: nrst fin) | 2½ | 4 | 16/1 | 58 | 20 |
| $2034^{4}$ | **Ivory's Grab Hire (60)** (KTIvory) **3-8-6b**(5) MartinDwyer(16) (swtg: hdwy 2f out: r.o ins fnl f) | 1½ | 5 | 14/1 | 57 | 19 |
| $2215^{6}$ | **Mullagh Hill Lad (IRE) (48)** (BAMcMahon) **3-7-13b$^{1ow1}$** GCarter(11) (nrst fin) | ¾ | 6 | 13/2$^{1}$ | 43 | 4 |
| $2500^{3}$ | **Sunset Harbour (IRE) (45)** (TJNaughton) **3-7-10b** JQuinn(8) (lw: plld hrd: prom tl wknd over 1f out) | 2½ | 7 | 12/1 | 33 | — |
| $1891^{4}$ | **Members Welcome (IRE) (54)** (JMBradley) **3-8-2**(3) SDrowne(7) (rdn along: nvr bttr than mid div) | 2½ | 8 | 20/1 | 35 | — |
| $2501^{8}$ | **La Tansani (IRE) (70)** (RHannon) **3-9-4**(3) DaneO'Neill(9) (lw: nvr nr to chal) | 1¾ | 9 | 16/1 | 47 | 9 |
| $1891^{3}$ | **Hever Golf Express (65)** (TJNaughton) **3-9-2** DHolland(18) (led tl wknd over 2f out) | ½ | 10 | 10/1 | 40 | 2 |
| $1466^{11}$ | **Itsinthepost (63)** (VSoane) **3-9-0** AMcGlone(14) (nvr trbld ldrs) | 2 | 11 | 20/1 | 33 | — |
| 2410* | **Times of Times (IRE) (70)** (MJRyan) **3-9-0**(7) AMcCarthy(1) (racd alone far side: prom 4f) | hd | 12 | 9/1$^{3}$ | 40 | 2 |
| $2528^{14}$ | **Volare (48)** (BJMeehan) **3-7-13** CRutter(13) (prom 3f) | 1¼ | 13 | 25/1 | 14 | — |
| $2286^{7}$ | **Bella's Legacy (45)** (RJHodges) **3-7-10** FNorton(5) (outpcd) | 3 | 14 | 25/1 | 3 | — |
| $2316^{6}$ | **Sea Danzig (64)** (PHowling) **3-9-1** JReid(3) (outpcd) | ½ | 15 | 11/1 | 21 | — |
| *$194^{3}$* | **Kind of Light (67)** (RGuest) **3-9-4** SSanders(6) (spd 3f) | 8 | 16 | 14/1 | 2 | — |
| $2200^{4}$ | **Meranti (57)** (SDow) **3-8-8** TQuinn(2) (lw: spd 3f) | 4 | 17 | 8/1$^{2}$ | — | — |
| $1412^{17}$ | **Daring Venture (54)** (TJNaughton) **3-8-5** AClark(4) (outpcd) | ¾ | 18 | 25/1 | — | — |
| | | | | (SP 135.6%) | **18 Rn** | |

**1m 13.8** (3.30) CSF £71.40 CT £739.42 TOTE £8.60: £2.10 £2.20 £3.20 £8.20 (£24.90) Trio £194.40 OWNER Davies and Bridgeman (COWBRIDGE) BRED Taplin, Lee and Cain Ltd
LONG HANDICAP Bella's Legacy 7-8
**2186 Croeso Cynnes** disputed the lead. She went to the front over two furlongs from home and, after quickening clear below the distance, was always in command. (8/1)
**1412 Kings Harmony (IRE)**, though always close up, could not quicken with the winner approaching the final furlong, but ran on well in the last 100 yards. (8/1)
**824 Dummer Golf Time**, visored for the first time, was held up on the heels of the leaders. He moved up to challenge approaching the final furlong but, though running on, could not catch the winner. (12/1)
**1516 Scathebury** came with a good run on the inside two furlongs out but, though staying on, could not reach the leading three. (16/1)
**2034 Ivory's Grab Hire** ran on in the last two furlongs, but too late to trouble the leaders. (14/1: 10/1-16/1)
**2215 Mullagh Hill Lad (IRE)**, though blinkered for the first time, failed to go the pace, but ran on strongly in the latter stages. (13/2)
**2500 Sunset Harbour (IRE)** ruined her chance by pulling too hard and did well to hold on for seventh place in the circumstances. (12/1)

## 2579 BONUSPRINT MAIDEN STKS (3-Y.O) (Class D)

9-05 (9-07) **1m 67y** £3,948.00 (£1,194.00: £582.00: £276.00) Stalls: High GOING minus 0.21 sec per fur (GF)

| | | | | SP | RR | SF |
|---|---|---|---|---|---|---|
| 1644[2] | **Questonia** (HRACecil) **3-8-9** PatEddery(8) (lw: w ldr: led over 2f out: rdn clr over 1f out: r.o) | — | **1** | 11/10[1] | 82 | 20 |
| | **Yalta (IRE)** (RCharlton) **3-9-0** SSanders(11) (unf: scope: mid div tl hdwy 2f out: r.o: nt rch wnr) | 1½ | **2** | 7/1[3] | 84 | 22 |
| 2333[4] | **Milford Sound** (JRFanshawe) **3-9-0** DHarrison(15) (lw: mid div tl hdwy 2f out: r.o ins fnl f) | hd | **3** | 20/1 | 84 | 22 |
| | **Bear Hug** (LadyHerries) **3-9-0** JReid(16) (w'like: bit bkwd: a.p: r.o one pce fnl 2f) | 6 | **4** | 20/1 | 72 | 10 |
| | **Chalk Dust (USA)** (PFICole) **3-8-9** TQuinn(2) (lw: led tl over 2f out: wknd over 1f out) | 1¾ | **5** | 4/1[2] | 64 | 2 |
| 1142[14] | **Glen Parker (IRE)** (HRACecil) **3-9-0** AMcGlone(18) (a.p: ev ch 3f out: wknd over 1f out) | ½ | **6** | 12/1 | 68 | 6 |
| | **Miss Romance (IRE)** (MissGayKelleway) **3-8-6**(3) DaneO'Neill(9) (w'like: bit bkwd: hdwy 3f out: nvr nr to chal) | ¾ | **7** | 20/1 | 62 | — |
| | **Nezool Almatar (IRE)** (MAJarvis) **3-8-9** PBloomfield(12) (lw: hdwy 2f out: styd on: nt rch ldrs) | ¾ | **8** | 20/1 | 60 | — |
| 2011[5] | **Veridian** (PWHarris) **3-9-0** BDoyle(13) (prom tl wknd 2f out) | ½ | **9** | 12/1 | 64 | 2 |
| 2420[5] | **Serious Sensation** (SirMarkPrescott) **3-9-0** WWoods(17) (stdd s: hdwy over 2f out: nvr plcd to chal) | hd | **10** | 25/1 | 64 | 2 |
| 2004[7] | **Double March** (PRWebber) **3-9-0** BThomson(14) (hdwy 3f out: wknd 2f out) | 3 | **11** | 33/1 | 58 | — |
| | **Private Percival** (JRPoulton) **3-9-0** AMorris(4) (unf: bit bkwd: s.s: a bhd) | 2½ | **12** | 50/1 | 53 | — |
| | **Stackattack (IRE)** (PRWebber) **3-9-0** WJO'Connor(1) (w'like: bit bkwd: hdwy 3f out: wknd over 1f out) | hd | **13** | 50/1 | 53 | — |
| 1711[15] | **Sylvan Heights** (RTPhillips) **3-9-0** RPerham(7) (prom tl wknd qckly over 3f out) | 2 | **14** | 50/1 | 49 | — |
| 763[12] | **Lady Benson (IRE)** (DJSCosgrove) **3-8-9** MRimmer(10) (a bhd) | ¾ | **15** | 50/1 | 43 | — |
| | **Chant d'Alouette** (RJHodges) **3-8-6**(3) SDrowne(3) (unf: bit bkwd: dwlt: a bhd) | 9 | **16** | 50/1 | 26 | — |
| | **Endaxi Sam** (RIngram) **3-9-0** DHolland(5) (w'like: bkwd: bhd whn rn v.wd 5f out: t.o whn p.u over 3f out) | | **P** | 50/1 | — | — |
| | | | | (SP 133.1%) | **17 Rn** | |

**1m 48.1** (5.90) CSF £10.23 TOTE £1.90: £1.40 £2.80 £3.40 (£6.90) Trio £58.30 OWNER Mr K. Abdulla (NEWMARKET) BRED Juddmonte Farms

**1644 Questonia,** dropped in distance, was able to lie up with the leader without being driven along. She went to the front over two furlongs from home and quickly drew clear when asked for an effort below the distance. (11/10: Evens-11/10)

**Yalta (IRE)** made a promising first appearance. He raced in mid-division until staying on well in the final quarter-mile. He will certainly stay further and win races. (7/1)

**2333 Milford Sound,** racing in the mid-division, began to pick up ground from the two-furlong marker but, though staying on, was never on terms with the leaders, and stayed on at one pace in the final quarter-mile. (20/1)

**Chalk Dust (USA)** made the running but could never shake off the winner. Headed two furlongs from home, her chance had gone below the distance. She will be better for the race. (4/1: 3/1-9/2)

**Glen Parker (IRE)** raced in third place for much of the way but gradually weakened from two and a half furlongs out. (12/1)

**Nezool Almatar (IRE)** looked in need of this, but was staying on at the finish. (20/1)

**2420 Serious Sensation** can do much better than this. (25/1)

T/Jkpt: Not won; £11,879.66 to Newmarket 9/7/96. T/Plpt: £187.60 (121.81 Tckts). T/Qdpt: £15.90 (97.01 Tckts).. Hn

# 2334-NEWMARKET (R-H) (Good)

## Tuesday July 9th

WEATHER: fine WIND: slt half bhd

## 2580 STRUTT & PARKER MAIDEN STKS (2-Y.O) (Class D)

2-05 (2-05) **7f (July)** £5,481.00 (£1,638.00: £784.00: £357.00) Stalls: Low GOING minus 0.48 sec per fur (F)

| | | | | SP | RR | SF |
|---|---|---|---|---|---|---|
| | **Bahhare (USA)** (JLDunlop) **2-9-0** WCarson(9) (gd sort: scope: hdwy centre 3f out: led over 1f out: shkn up & qcknd clr fnl f) | — | **1** | 15/8[1] | 97++ | 46 |
| | **Equal Rights (IRE)** (PWChapple-Hyam) **2-9-0** JReid(2) (cmpt: scope: w ldr far side: led over 2f out: sn hdd: unable qckn fnl f) | 3½ | **2** | 100/30[2] | 89+ | 38 |
| | **Royal Amaretto (IRE)** (BJMeehan) **2-9-0** BDoyle(5) (w'like: scope: bkwd: trckd ldrs far side: r.o wl fnl f) | 1½ | **3** | 25/1 | 86 | 35 |
| | **Mrs Miniver (USA)** (PAKelleway) **2-8-9** KFallon(4) (w'like: scope: sn pushed along & bhd: hdwy over 2f out: r.o wl fnl f) | ¾ | **4** | 33/1 | 79 | 28 |
| | **Musical Dancer (USA)** (EALDunlop) **2-9-0** MJKinane(6) (cmpt: scope: prom far side: led 2f out: sn hdd: wknd fnl f) | 1½ | **5** | 10/1 | 80 | 29 |
| 2335[10] | **Maradi (IRE)** (DMorley) **2-9-0** RHills(8) (in tch centre: effrt 3f out: no imp) | 5 | **6** | 33/1 | 69 | 18 |
| | **The Fly** (BWHills) **2-9-0** PatEddery(11) (cmpt: dwlt: sn disp ld centre: wknd 2f out) | 2 | **7** | 10/1 | 64 | 13 |
| 2009[4] | **Zugudi** (BHanbury) **2-9-0** MRimmer(1) (lw: led far side over 4f) | ½ | **8** | 33/1 | 63 | 12 |
| 2243[3] | **Rehearsal (IRE)** (CACyzer) **2-9-0** MRoberts(10) (prom centre: rdn 4f out: sn btn) | 4 | **9** | 8/1[3] | 54 | 3 |
| 1339[8] | **Generous Gift** (EALDunlop) **2-9-0** RHughes(7) (disp ld centre over 4f) | 1½ | **10** | 12/1 | 51 | — |
| | **Penlop** (BJMeehan) **2-9-0** MTebbutt(3) (neat: racd far side: a bhd) | 2 | **11** | 33/1 | 46 | — |
| | | | | (SP 110.5%) | **11 Rn** | |

**1m 26.03** (1.03) CSF £7.43 TOTE £2.70: £1.10 £1.60 £5.20 (£3.80) Trio £248.70 OWNER Mr Hamdan Al Maktoum (ARUNDEL) BRED Shadwell Farm Inc

**Bahhare (USA),** a well-made half-brother to Bahri, made a tremendous impression here, despite looking a little green both before and during the race. Drifting from the centre of the course to the stands' rail as he made his move, he quickened in marvellous style and looks one to follow, although he is not sure to stay further than this on pedigree. (15/8)

**Equal Rights (IRE),** both keen and inexperienced on the way to post, ran a fine race but was comprehensively outpaced in the final furlong. (100/30: 7/4-7/2)

**Royal Amaretto (IRE),** a tall, good bodied newcomer, was on his toes in the parade ring and took a very good hold going to post. He looked too backward to do himself justice but his late work showed great promise for the future. (25/1)

**Mrs Miniver (USA),** a sparely made filly, was hopelessly left behind in the early stages but made significant ground in the last furlong, as she was persevered with longer than some of her beaten opponents. (33/1)

**Musical Dancer (USA),** a good walker and mover, is well made and attractive. The first to commit for home, he did not last very long once headed but should be all the better for the experience. (10/1: 5/1-12/1)

**2335 Maradi (IRE)** was more settled than on his debut and ran better as a consequence. (33/1)

**The Fly,** bred to stay well, showed a good action on the way to post and some promise in having the speed to recover from a tardy start. (10/1)

**2243 Rehearsal (IRE)** (8/1: 4/1-9/1)

## 2581 H & K COMMISSIONS H'CAP (0-80) (3-Y.O+) (Class D)

2-35 (2-37) **1m (July)** £8,415.00 (£2,520.00: £1,210.00: £555.00) Stalls: Low GOING minus 0.48 sec per fur (F)

| | | | | SP | RR | SF |
|---|---|---|---|---|---|---|
| 1701[3] | **Crown Court (USA) (70)** (LMCumani) **3-8-9** PatEddery(3) (b: a.p: led 3f out: r.o wl) | — | **1** | 6/1[1] | 91+ | 41 |
| 2412[5] | **Emily-Mou (IRE) (67)** (MJRyan) **4-9-1** BDoyle(18) (b: led stands' side: hdd 3f out: rdn 2f out: no ch w wnr) | 5 | **2** | 25/1 | 78 | 37 |
| 843[8] | **Aeroking (USA) (75)** (GHarwood) **5-9-9** TQuinn(6) (disp ld far side: rdn 2f out: kpt on same pce) | 1 | **3** | 20/1 | 84 | 43 |
| 1464[8] | **Moscow Mist (IRE) (70)** (LadyHerries) **5-9-4** TSprake(17) (racd stands' side: rdn & hdwy over 3f out: r.o fnl f) | nk | **4** | 25/1 | 78 | 37 |
| 879[26] | **Nordinex (IRE) (76)** (RWArmstrong) **4-9-10** RPrice(1) (trckd ldrs: one pce fnl 2f) | ½ | **5** | 25/1 | 83 | 42 |
| 2351[5] | **Karinska (60)** (MCChapman) **6-8-8** DRMcCabe(4) (hdwy 2f out: nrst fin) | nk | **6** | 25/1 | 67 | 26 |
| 2328[4] | **Tawafij (USA) (75)** (MDHammond) **7-9-9** JFortune(7) (trckd ldrs: effrt & hung lft 2f out: no imp) | s.h | **7** | 8/1[2] | 82 | 41 |
| 2053[10] | **Mo-Addab (IRE) (77)** (ACStewart) **6-9-11** MRoberts(16) (chsd ldrs stands' side: no hdwy fnl 3f) | hd | **8** | 11/1 | 84 | 43 |
| 2249[3] | **Samba Sharply (75)** (AHide) **5-9-9b** WWoods(2) (swtg: trckd ldrs over 5f) | 1¾ | **9** | 16/1 | 78 | 37 |
| 2351[4] | **Ninia (USA) (79)** (MJohnston) **4-9-13** JWeaver(9) (prom tl rdn & btn 3f out) | 1¼ | **10** | 12/1 | 80 | 39 |
| 2400[6] | **Toujours Riviera (80)** (JPearce) **6-10-0** GBardwell(8) (nvr nr to chal) | 2 | **11** | 16/1 | 77 | 36 |
| 1819[12] | **Deevee (66)** (CJBenstead) **7-9-0** PRobinson(19) (lw: racd stands' side: nvr rchd ldrs) | ½ | **12** | 10/1[3] | 62 | 21 |
| 2283[5] | **Fort Knox (IRE) (58)** (RMFlower) **5-8-6b** DBiggs(10) (swtg: n.d) | s.h | **13** | 25/1 | 53 | 12 |
| 2234[4] | **Reinhardt (IRE) (77)** (PWChapple-Hyam) **3-9-2** JReid(13) (lw: swtchd lft after s: bhd fnl 4f) | 3½ | **14** | 33/1 | 65 | 15 |
| 1337[5] | **Charlie Chang (IRE) (72)** (RHannon) **3-8-11b[1]** MJKinane(5) (lw: nvr trbld ldrs) | 3½ | **15** | 8/1[2] | 53 | 3 |
| 2074[10] | **A Chef Too Far (75)** (RRowe) **3-9-0** WCarson(12) (swtg: chsd ldrs 4f) | hd | **16** | 16/1 | 56 | 6 |
| 2426[7] | **Yoxall Lodge (64)** (HJCollingridge) **6-8-12** MRimmer(15) (chsd ldr stands' side 5f) | ½ | **17** | 25/1 | 44 | 3 |
| 1074[13] | **Bold Habit (61)** (JPearce) **11-8-2**(7) SGaillard(20) (b.nr hind: racd stands' side: a bhd) | 14 | **18** | 40/1 | 13 | — |
| 2134[6] | **Saifan (77)** (DMorris) **7-9-4b**(7) AEddery(14) (lw: s.s: a t.o: virtually p.u appr fnl f) | 22 | **19** | 14/1 | — | — |
| | | | | (SP 119.2%) | | **19 Rn** |

**1m 38.44** (1.24) CSF £125.30 CT £2,619.44 TOTE £5.40: £1.80 £3.90 £6.10 £4.30 (£83.50) Trio £834.60 OWNER Lord De La Warr & Mr Michael Kerr-Dineen (NEWMARKET) BRED Mrs Donna Arnold

WEIGHT FOR AGE 3yo-9lb

**1701 Crown Court (USA)** probably appreciated the slightly easier ground more than last time but, even so, turned his first handicap into a cakewalk, quickening away from his rivals against the far rail once given his head. It is hard to believe that he has been beaten three times and he must be improving quickly. Something needs to be done to prevent these lightly raced horses humiliating exposed handicappers who are doing their best and making the handicap compilers look stupid. (6/1)

**2412 Emily-Mou (IRE)** enjoyed leading the stands' side group throughout, and battled her heart out, but was laughed at by the winner. (25/1)

**Aeroking (USA),** taken down steadily, was right in the firing line until the winner made his move. (20/1)

**Moscow Mist (IRE)** failed dismally twice on soft ground but, on a faster surface here, recaptured something like his best form. (25/1)

**308* Nordinex (IRE),** who won at this meeting last year, was the paddock pick and raced with the leaders until failing to quicken in the last quarter-mile. (25/1)

**2351 Karinska** was doing her best work when the race was over. (25/1)

## 2582 HILLSDOWN CHERRY HINTON STKS (Gp 2) (2-Y.O F) (Class A)

3-05 (3-05) **6f (July)** £22,792.00 (£8,428.00: £4,039.00: £1,645.00: £647.50: £248.50) Stalls: Low GOING minus 0.48 sec per fur (F)

| | | | | SP | RR | SF |
|---|---|---|---|---|---|---|
| 2112* | **Dazzle** (MRStoute) **2-8-9** KFallon(3) (lw: trckd ldrs: qcknd to ld 2f out: r.o strly: eased nr fin) | — | **1** | 2/1[1] | 112+ | 67 |
| 1896* | **Ocean Ridge (USA)** (PWChapple-Hyam) **2-8-9** JReid(2) (a.p: rdn 2f out: r.o: no ch w wnr) | 5 | **2** | 4/1[3] | 99 | 54 |
| 2147[2] | **Well Warned** (BWHills) **2-8-9** PatEddery(6) (trckd ldrs: rdn & ev ch 2f out: one pce) | 3½ | **3** | 9/1 | 89 | 44 |
| 2338[3] | **Eye Shadow** (BJMeehan) **2-8-9** MJKinane(4) (w ldrs: no ex appr fnl f) | 4 | **4** | 25/1 | 79 | 34 |
| 2063* | **Rich In Love (IRE)** (CACyzer) **2-8-9** MRoberts(9) (sn pushed along & bhd: r.o fnl f) | 1¼ | **5** | 25/1 | 75 | 30 |
| 2147* | **Khassah** (JHMGosden) **2-8-9** WCarson(7) (lw: in tch: swtchd rt 2f out: sn rdn & no imp) | s.h | **6** | 7/2[2] | 75 | 30 |
| 2051[10] | **Lycility (IRE)** (CEBrittain) **2-8-9** BDoyle(5) (lw: sn rdn along: bhd fnl 4f) | hd | **7** | 50/1 | 75 | 30 |
| 2051[2] | **Dame Laura (IRE)** (PFICole) **2-8-9** TQuinn(8) (chsd ldrs: ev ch 2f out: sn wknd) | 1¾ | **8** | 13/2 | 70 | 25 |
| 2051[4] | **Connemara (IRE)** (CADwyer) **2-8-9** JWeaver(1) (lw: led 4f: sn wknd) | 1¼ | **9** | 12/1 | 67 | 22 |
| | | | | (SP 116.2%) | | **9 Rn** |

**1m 11.02** (-0.98) CSF £10.13 TOTE £2.50: £1.30 £1.70 £2.80 (£5.40) Trio £21.70 OWNER Cheveley Park Stud (NEWMARKET) BRED Cheveley Park Stud Ltd

**OFFICIAL EXPLANATION Khassah: the jockey reported that the filly had become unbalanced in the final furlong and he felt it prudent to ease her as he was concerned that there was something wrong. She was later found to be lame on her off-hind.**

**2112* Dazzle** showed a little knee action going to post but scotched the negative rumours circulating with a most emphatic display. Showing both courage and speed to nip through a narrow gap between Connemara and the rails, she quickly put daylight between herself and her rivals, living up to her name. She has already been installed favourite for the 1997 1,000 Guineas. (2/1)

**1896* Ocean Ridge (USA)** followed the winner through but, try as she might, it was at an ever more respectful distance. This was, nevertheless, a very useful effort in its own right. (4/1: 3/1-9/2)

**2147 Well Warned,** a maiden stepping up in class, reversed the form with her Ascot conqueror Khassah but was made to look rather onepaced in the latter stages although she stuck to her task. There are races to be won with her. (9/1)

**2338 Eye Shadow** probably ran to her form but, after challenging for the lead going into the Dip, was left standing. (25/1)

**2063* Rich In Love (IRE)** pushed along at the back of the field for most of the race, began to stay on past beaten horses late in the day but was still beaten a long way. (25/1)

**2147* Khassah,** well touted, never looked happy in behind other horses and, by the time she was pulled to the outside at the two furlong pole, her chance was already slipping. (7/2: 5/2-4/1)

**2051 Dame Laura (IRE),** one of five in a line at the two furlong pole, soon began to struggle. This does nothing for the Queen Mary form but she folded so quickly that she cannot have given her true running. (13/2: 9/2-7/1)

**2051 Connemara (IRE)** tried front running again but could not burn these off and was weakening too far from home to blame the trip alone. (12/1)

## 2583 PRINCESS OF WALES'S STKS (Gp 2) (3-Y.O+) (Class A)

3-40 (3-41) **1m 4f (July)** £36,504.00 (£13,536.00: £6,518.00: £2,690.00: £1,095.00: £457.00) Stalls: High GOING minus 0.48 sec per fur (F)

| | | | | SP | RR | SF |
|---|---|---|---|---|---|---|
| 2113[3] | **Posidonas (116)** (PFICole) **4-9-7** TQuinn(6) (hld up & plld hrd: hdwy 4f out: led over 1f out: drvn out) | — | **1** | 20/1 | 129 | 74 |
| 1794[2] | **Singspiel (IRE) (120)** (MRStoute) **4-9-2** MJKinane(3) (lw: hld up: hdwy 3f out: ev ch 1f out: no ex ins fnl f) | 1¼ | **2** | 7/4[2] | 122 | 67 |

2113[2] **Annus Mirabilis (FR) (119)** (SbinSuroor) **4-9-2** JReid(1) (lw: trckd ldr: led 4f out: rdn over 1f out: sn hdd & nt qckn)........2½ **3** 9/2[3] 119 64
2480a[4] **Lear White (USA) (106)** (PAKelleway) **5-9-2** KFallon(2) (lw: hld up: effrt 4f out: r.o wl fnl f)........2½ **4** 25/1 116 61
2336* **Bequeath (102)** (HRACecil) **4-9-2** PatEddery(5) (trckd ldrs: rdn 4f out: no imp fnl 2f)........2 **5** 13/8[1] 113 58
2113[7] **Punishment** (CEBrittain) **5-9-2** BDoyle(4) (bhd: effrt 3f out: btn over 1f out)........3½ **6** 40/1 108 53
1817[6] **Wayne County (IRE) (107)** (RAkehurst) **6-9-2** SSanders(7) (lw: prom tl wknd over 3f out)........14 **7** 50/1 90 35
2336[4] **Midnight Legend (113)** (LMCumani) **5-9-2** JWeaver(9) (led tl hdd & wknd 4f out)........6 **8** 20/1 82 27
(SP 110.4%) **8 Rn**

**2m 28.92** (-1.08) CSF £51.27 TOTE £23.10: £2.60 £1.10 £1.10 (£22.20) Trio £19.70 OWNER Mr Athos Christodoulou (WHATCOMBE) BRED A. Christodoulou

**2113 Posidonas** caused an upset by successfully carrying a Group One penalty for a win at San Siro last September. A poor mover, he took a bit of settling early on but proved most resolute in a driving finish despite his awkward head carriage. (20/1)

**1794 Singspiel (IRE)** is a horse who has been knocking on the door in Group One races, and to lose to a penalised horse in a Group Two race must be a disappointment. He went down fighting over a trip a couple of furlongs beyond that over which he has run most of his best races, and the decision to miss the Eclipse, whilst understandable, has hardly been made to pay. (7/4)

**2113 Annus Mirabilis (FR)** looked to curl up in front at Ascot and the solution to this problem in the eyes involved with the horse, seemed to be to lead even further from home. His stride shortened once again as soon as the pressure was applied. He does need holding up until the last minute but is becoming frustrating. (9/2)

**2480a Lear White (USA)** did not look as if he would ever land a blow until staying on really strongly on meeting the rising ground. He has definitely improved and his soft ground form in Italy is going to make him an interesting prospect come the Autumn. (25/1)

**2336* Bequeath**, so impressive over course and distance ten days ago, was taking a big step up in class and, under pressure to quicken some way from home, never landed a blow. (13/8)

**1794 Punishment**, a good mover who was colty in the preliminaries, made a forward move on the inside rail as the race developed, but finished behind the three of these who had beaten him in the Hardwicke at Ascot. (40/1)

**2336 Midnight Legend** does need to hear his hooves rattle and the watering was against him. He was beaten so badly on ground surely still a little faster than good, that it would be unwise to use this as a complete excuse. (20/1)

## 2584 TYPHOO TEA RATED STKS H'CAP (0-100) (3-Y.O) (Class B)

4-10 (4-12) **6f (July)** £8,183.50 (£3,026.50: £1,450.75: £591.25: £233.13: £89.87) Stalls: Low GOING minus 0.48 sec per fur (F)

SP RR SF

2007[3] **Wildwood Flower (87)** (RHannon) **3-8-5**(3) DaneO'Neill(8) (a.p: led 1f out: rdn out)........— **1** 7/1 95 54
2143[5] **White Emir (86)** (BJMeehan) **3-8-7b[1]** JFEgan(9) (swtg: a.p: rdn 2f out: unable qckn fnl f)........1¼ **2** 25/1 91 50
2041[17] **Royal Mark (IRE) (89)** (JWWatts) **3-8-10** TQuinn(7) (sn pushed along: rdn over 2f out: styd on wl fnl f)........nk **3** 15/2 93 52
1994* **Duel At Dawn (90)** (JHMGosden) **3-8-11** MJKinane(4) (b: b.hind: led 5f: sn btn)........½ **4** 5/1[3] 93 52
2301* **Galine (87)** (WAO'Gorman) **3-8-8** EmmaO'Gorman(2) (bhd: dropped rr 2f out: r.o wl fnl f: gng on fin)........½ **5** 9/2[2] 88 47
2007[7] **Dashing Blue (100)** (IABalding) **3-9-2**(5) MartinDwyer(5) (bhd: effrt & n.m.r 2f out: swtchd over 1f out: sn btn)........1¼ **6** 13/2 98 57
2007[2] **Pleading (92)** (HCandy) **3-8-13** CRutter(3) (lw: s.i.s: hdwy over 2f out: no imp appr fnl f)........1¼ **7** 4/1[1] 87 46
2004[6] **Lucky Archer (90)** (CEBrittain) **3-8-11** BDoyle(6) (chsd ldrs: rdn 2f out: sn wknd)........2½ **8** 25/1 78 37
1667* **Dark Deed (USA) (87)** (BWHills) **3-8-8** PatEddery(1) (w ldr over 3f: eased whn btn fnl f)........nk **9** 13/2 74 33
(SP 113.5%) **9 Rn**

**1m 11.86** (-0.14) CSF £123.68 CT £873.24 TOTE £8.00: £1.40 £4.50 £2.10 (£91.10) Trio £170.80 OWNER Mr G. Howard-Spink (MARLBOROUGH) BRED Sir Stephen Hastings and G. Howard-Spink

LONG HANDICAP White Emir 8-2

OFFICIAL EXPLANATION **Pleading: the trainer reported that the horse got left three lengths at the start, and the rider added that when asked a question three out, Pleading failed to respond.**

**2007 Wildwood Flower**, well handicapped with Galine on their running at the Craven meeting, was the only one of the leading players to get the run of the race and ran out a decisive winner. (7/1)

**2143 White Emir**, who went keenly to post, was always a leading player but could not quicken with the winner at the business end. (25/1)

**1127 Royal Mark (IRE)**, back sprinting for the first time since his two year old debut, found difficulty going the pace but was staying on strongly in the final furlong. (15/2)

**1994* Duel At Dawn** set a decent pace but had not kept enough in reserve for the final sprint. (5/1)

**2301* Galine**, whose waiting tactics worked so well over the minimum trip at the last meeting, backfired here as she was still being restrained at the back two furlongs out. She eventually threaded her way through to be closest at the line. The stable are on the crest of a wave at present. (9/2)

**1431 Dashing Blue** found trouble getting a run and, once clear, could make little impact. (13/2)

**2007 Pleading** lost an awful lot of ground at the start but his jockey seemed content to set him a Herculean task once again. Pulled towards the centre to make his effort where the ground seemed to be riding a little slower, he was soon a spent force. (4/1)

## 2585 HARTLEYS JAM RATED STAKES H'CAP (0-100) (3-Y.O F) (Class B)

4-45 (4-46) **7f (July)** £8,169.00 (£3,021.00: £1,448.00: £590.00: £232.50: £89.50) Stalls: Low GOING minus 0.48 sec per fur (F)

SP RR SF

2126[2] **Lilli Claire (85)** (AGFoster) **3-8-1** TSprake(1) (hld up far side: hdwy to ld 1f out: sn rdn clr)........— **1** 13/2 93 46
2142[2] **Miss Riviera (92)** (GWragg) **3-8-8** MJKinane(5) (prom: led over 1f out: sn rdn & hdd: no ex ins fnl f)........1¼ **2** 3/1[1] 97 50
945[2] **Unconditional Love (IRE) (98)** (MJohnston) **3-9-0** JWeaver(2) (prom far side: led wl over 1f out: sn hdd: no ex fnl f)........½ **3** 9/1 102 55
2142[5] **Prends Ca (IRE) (93)** (RHannon) **3-8-9** JReid(6) (lw: hld up: hdwy over 2f out: r.o ins fnl f)........1¾ **4** 10/1 93 46
2160* **Poetry (IRE) (84)** (MHTompkins) **3-8-0** PRobinson(9) (led over 5f: sn btn)........¾ **5** 6/1[3] 82 35
**Jezyah (USA) (84)** (RWArmstrong) **3-8-0** WCarson(3) (racd far side: dwlt: sn prom: wknd over 1f out)........½ **6** 14/1 81 34
2437[2] **Hippy (84)** (CEBrittain) **3-7-7**(7) PDoe(7) (lw: swtg: prom over 4f)........1¼ **7** 14/1 78 31
1898[5] **Ocean Grove (IRE) (84)** (PWChapple-Hyam) **3-8-0** FNorton(8) (lw: hld up: effrt 3f out: nvr rchd ldrs)........3 **8** 14/1 71 24
2142[6] **Roses In The Snow (IRE) (89)** (JWHills) **3-8-5** RHills(4) (swtg: prom: wknd & eased over 1f out)........2 **9** 20/1 72 25
2354[D] **Aunty Jane (97)** (BWHills) **3-8-13** PatEddery(10) (chsd ldr over 3f)........8 **10** 4/1[2] 62 15
(SP 116.5%) **10 Rn**

**1m 25.04** (0.04) CSF £24.93 CT £162.09 TOTE £8.40: £2.40 £1.70 £2.30 (£18.00) Trio £43.90 OWNER Mr C. Leafe (LAMBOURN) BRED Roger C. Denton

LONG HANDICAP Hippy 7-12 Jezyah (USA) 7-12

**2126 Lilli Claire**, one of only three who elected to race on the far rail, burst clear in the final furlong to win in emphatic style. She had appeared flattered by her run in Listed company at Epsom last month, but this does not seem to be the case. (13/2)

**2142 Miss Riviera**, raised 6lb for her Ascot defeat, again ran well, scoring decisively from the majority of the field who raced on the stands' rails, only to lose to an opponent on the other side of the track. (3/1)
**945 Unconditional Love (IRE)**, quite keen to post, took an overall lead on the far side below the distance, but could not maintain it for long, and was easily left behind by the winner. This should not be taken as conclusive proof that she stays seven. (9/1)
**2142 Prends Ca (IRE)**, restrained at the back of the main stands'-side group, did good late work and should find other opportunities. (10/1: 8/1-12/1)
**2160* Poetry (IRE)**, followed by the majority of the field towards the stands' rail, had lost the lead in the Dip and could do no more. The stable horses are running well without winning at present. (6/1)
**Jezyah (USA)** was difficult at the start as usual, half rearing and losing a couple of lengths. Soon at the head of the far side trio, she was the first to fold. (14/1)
**1898 Ocean Grove (IRE)** (14/1: 10/1-16/1)

## 2586 NGK SPARK PLUGS SOHAM H'CAP (0-80) (3-Y.O+) (Class D)
5-15 (5-16) **5f (July)** £5,208.00 (£1,554.00: £742.00: £336.00) Stalls: Low GOING minus 0.48 sec per fur (F)

| | | | | SP | RR | SF |
|---|---|---|---|---|---|---|
| 2508$^{2}$ | **Shadow Jury (60)** (DWChapman) **6-8-12b** JFortune(10) (lw: w ldrs: rdn fnl f: led nr fin) | — | **1** | 6/1$^{2}$ | 67 | 50 |
| 2324$^{2}$ | **Spender (72)** (PWHarris) **7-9-10** PatEddery(4) (led tl ct nr fin) | s.h | **2** | 11/2$^{1}$ | 79 | 62 |
| 2280* | **Friendly Brave (USA) (72)** (MissGayKelleway) **6-9-10** RHughes(2) (b.hind: wnt rt s: chsd ldrs: swtchd over 1f out: styd on fnl f) | 1¼ | **3** | 7/1$^{3}$ | 75 | 58 |
| 2280$^{3}$ | **Half Tone (47)** (RMFlower) **4-7-10b**(3) NVarley(3) (lw: chsd ldrs: rdn & n.m.r over 1f out: no imp ins fnl f) | hd | **4** | 10/1 | 50 | 33 |
| *117$^{5}$* | **Pageboy (60)** (PCHaslam) **7-8-12b** JWeaver(1) (chsd ldrs: ev ch 3f out: one pce appr fnl f) | s.h | **5** | 10/1 | 62 | 45 |
| 2421* | **Rich Glow (60)** (NBycroft) **5-8-12** 7x KFallon(6) (stdd s: nt clr run 2f out & ins fnl f: nrst fin) | ½ | **6** | 8/1 | 61 | 44 |
| 2193$^{8}$ | **Gone Savage (57)** (WJMusson) **8-8-9** MJKinane(5) (effrt & n.m.r 2f out: nt clr run 1f out: r.o ins fnl f) | nk | **7** | 6/1$^{2}$ | 57 | 40 |
| 2578$^{12}$ | **Times of Times (IRE) (70)** (MJRyan) **3-8-10**(7) AMcCarthy(7) (hdwy over 1f out: nrst fin) | nk | **8** | 16/1 | 69 | 47 |
| 2496$^{4}$ | **Featherstone Lane (49)** (MissLCSiddall) **5-8-1v** PRobinson(9) (hmpd after s: sn chsd ldrs & pushed along: wknd ins fnl f) | 1¾ | **9** | 12/1 | 42 | 25 |
| 2244* | **John O'Dreams (52)** (MrsALMKing) **11-8-4** MRoberts(11) (b: chsd ldrs 3f) | 3 | **10** | 7/1$^{3}$ | 36 | 19 |
| 1199$^{10}$ | **Broadstairs Beauty (IRE) (70)** (PHowling) **6-9-8b** SDWilliams(8) (b: b.hind: w ldrs over 2f) | 3 | **11** | 10/1 | 44 | 27 |
| | | | | (SP 120.9%) | **11 Rn** | |

**58.81 secs** (0.31) CSF £37.40 CT £223.81 TOTE £7.00: £2.10 £2.00 £2.90 (£16.90) Trio £29.70 OWNER Mrs Jeanne Chapman (YORK) BRED J. S. Bell
WEIGHT FOR AGE 3yo-5lb
**2508 Shadow Jury**, touched off at Warwick the previous Friday, ran a similar race but this time got the best of the photo. (6/1)
**2324 Spender**, soon at the head of affairs, ran on well when challenged but could not quite last home. (11/2)
**2280* Friendly Brave (USA)** seemed to spend much of the race hanging and took some pulling out from behind Spender to mount his challenge, running on well once clear. (7/1)
**2280 Half Tone** did not see much daylight at a vital stage. (10/1)
**55 Pageboy**, left to race alone on the far rail in the first couple of furlongs, took hold and was disputing the lead by halfway. He probably did too much too soon but is on the way back. (10/1)
**2421* Rich Glow** got murdered at least twice when looking for a run and has to be considered an unlucky loser. (8/1)
**1844 Gone Savage** moved well to post but was just beginning his move when stopped in his tracks. There is probably still a race in him. (6/1)

T/Jkpt: Not won; £21,921.83 to Newmarket 10/7/96. T/Plpt: £187.90 (213.22 Tckts). T/Qdpt: £23.10 (112 Tckts). Dk

# 2361-PONTEFRACT (L-H) (Good to firm)
## Tuesday July 9th
WEATHER: overcast WIND: fresh half bhd

## 2587 HYDE SPORTING PROMOTIONS LADIES' H'CAP (0-60) (3-Y.O+) (Class F)
2-20 (2-23) **1m 2f 6y** £3,132.00 (£936.00: £448.00: £204.00) Stalls: Low GOING minus 0.27 sec per fur (GF)

| | | | | SP | RR | SF |
|---|---|---|---|---|---|---|
| 2487$^{3}$ | **Gold Blade (49)** (JPearce) **7-10-10** MrsLPearce(8) (trckd ldrs: led 2f out: sn wl clr: eased nr fin) | — | **1** | 11/4$^{1}$ | 67+ | 48 |
| 1830$^{4}$ | **Raindeer Quest (45)** (JLEyre) **4-10-6** MissDianaJones(4) (a chsng ldrs: kpt on same pce appr fnl f) | 10 | **2** | 6/1$^{2}$ | 47 | 28 |
| 2066$^{15}$ | **Never so Brave (35)** (JDBethell) **6-9-3**(7) MrsDWilkinson(6) (s.i.s: hdwy u.p over 3f out: styd on fnl f) | 1¾ | **3** | 50/1 | 34 | 15 |
| 2440* | **Don't Drop Bombs (USA) (43)** (DTThom) **7-10-4v** 5x MissJFeilden(13) (led to 2f out: wknd fnl f) | 1¾ | **4** | 6/1$^{2}$ | 40 | 21 |
| 2155$^{6}$ | **Canary Falcon (50)** (HJCollingridge) **5-10-11** MissJAllison(17) (b: hdwy on outside 3f out: edgd lft & styd on same pce fnl f) | ¾ | **5** | 16/1 | 45 | 26 |
| 2366$^{2}$ | **Commander Glen (IRE) (60)** (MrsJRRamsden) **4-11-0b**(7) MissAJSmith(3) (lw: hld up & wl bhd: swtchd outside 2f out: styd on wl) | s.h | **6** | 8/1 | 55 | 36 |
| 2192$^{2}$ | **Zeliba (32)** (MrsNMacauley) **4-9-7** MissAElsey(10) (hld up: styd on fnl 3f: nt rch ldrs) | 1¼ | **7** | 10/1 | 25 | 6 |
| 2513$^{6}$ | **Intrepid Fort (30)** (BWMurray) **7-8-12b**(7) MrsCWilliams(9) (hld up: hdwy over 2f out: nvr nr to chal) | ½ | **8** | 33/1 | 22 | 3 |
| 1803$^{4}$ | **Cheveley Dancer (USA) (29)** (TJNaughton) **8-9-4** MissPRobson(2) (b: hdwy on outside 3f out: n.d) | 3 | **9** | 13/2$^{3}$ | 17 | — |
| 2130$^{12}$ | **Dauphin (IRE) (36)** (WJMusson) **3-8-9**(5) MrsJMoore(7) (hld up: hmpd after 2f: nvr nr ldrs) | hd | **10** | 14/1 | 23 | — |
| 2155$^{12}$ | **Written Agreement (34)** (REPeacock) **8-9-2**(7)ow9 MrsCPeacock(12) (chsd ldrs: sn pushed along: lost pl 3f out) | ½ | **11** | 100/1 | 21 | — |
| 2032$^{15}$ | **Mediate (IRE) (43)** (AHide) **4-10-4b** MissEJohnsonHoughton(14) (nvr nr to chal) | hd | **12** | 11/1 | 30 | 11 |
| 2066$^{10}$ | **Ice Magic (25)** (FJYardley) **9-8-7v**(7) MissSYardley(1) (b.nr hind: a in rr) | 4 | **13** | 33/1 | 5 | — |
| 2540$^{8}$ | **Forget Paris (IRE) (45)** (BSRothwell) **3-9-9** MrsDKettlewell(15) (sme hdwy over 3f out: sn wknd) | ½ | **14** | 33/1 | 24 | — |
| 1037$^{16}$ | **Newgate Hush (33)** (BWMurray) **4-9-3**(5)ow8 MissMCarson(16) (a bhd) | 7 | **15** | 50/1 | 1 | — |
| 2513$^{4}$ | **Public Way (IRE) (43)** (NChamberlain) **6-9-13**(5) MissCMetcalfe(11) (prom tl rdn & lost pl 3f out) | 2 | **16** | 16/1 | 8 | — |
| 2123$^{7}$ | **Yuppy Girl (IRE) (50)** (CaptJWilson) **3-9-11**(3) MrsSBosley(18) (chsd ldrs tl wknd qckly over 2f out) | 15 | **17** | 25/1 | — | — |
| 1435$^{11}$ | **Paper Maze (48)** (EHOwenjun) **3-9-5**(7) MrsFWilliams(5) (racd wd: wl bhd fnl 3f: t.o) | dist | **18** | 100/1 | — | — |
| | | | | (SP 134.1%) | **18 Rn** | |

**2m 14.9** (6.60) CSF £20.44 CT £672.27 TOTE £3.20: £1.10 £2.30 £36.50 £2.20 (£8.20) Trio £473.30; £226.70 to Newmarket 10/7/96 OWNER Mr Jeff Pearce (NEWMARKET) BRED Ballymacoll Stud Co
LONG HANDICAP Dauphin (IRE) 8-13 Written Agreement 8-6 Ice Magic 8-3
WEIGHT FOR AGE 3yo-11lb
**2487 Gold Blade** and Lydia Pearce, both regulars in this type of event, turned this uncompetitive race into a procession. (11/4)

**1830 Raindeer Quest**, 5lb higher than when winning a seller here earlier in the year, stuck on under her experienced pilot to finish clear second best. (6/1)
**Never so Brave**, tailed off on his reappearance after being fired, came through from off the pace to be staying on at the finish. He has slipped a long way down the weights. (50/1)
**2440* Don't Drop Bombs (USA)**, 8lb higher in the weights than at Yarmouth, made the running but his stride shortened in the final furlong. (6/1)
**2155 Canary Falcon**, who is probably better suited by the All Weather, rolled off a straight line under pressure. (16/1)
**2366 Commander Glen (IRE)** was set an impossible task. Making headway on the wide outside once in line for home, he was putting in some good work at the line. (8/1)

## 2588 DIANNE NURSERY H'CAP (2-Y.O) (Class E)

2-50 (2-51) **6f** £3,874.50 (£1,161.00: £558.00: £256.50) Stalls: Low GOING minus 0.27 sec per fur (GF)

| | | | | SP | RR | SF |
|---|---|---|---|---|---|---|
| 2043* | **Docklands Carriage (IRE)** (NTinkler) **2-9-3b** KDarley(1) (lw: mde all: styd on u.p appr fnl f: all out) | — | 1 | 4/1[3] | 70 | 34 |
| 2076[4] | **Rum Lad** (JJQuinn) **2-9-0**(3) SDrowne(6) (chsd ldrs: rdn & outpcd over 2f out: hdwy & ev ch ins fnl f: nt qckn nr fin) | nk | 2 | 6/1 | 69 | 33 |
| 1583[7] | **Our Future (IRE)** (MJohnston) **2-9-0** JFanning(5) (lw: w ldrs: kpt on same pce fnl f) | ¾ | 3 | 16/1 | 64 | 28 |
| 2025* | **Nostalgic Air (USA)** (EWeymes) **2-9-7** JQuinn(2) (trckd ldrs: effrt & hung lft over 1f out: n.m.r & sn rdn: styd on same pce) | 2 | 4 | 5/4[1] | 66 | 30 |
| 1779[2] | **Ninth Symphony** (PCHaslam) **2-9-4** GCarter(4) (dwlt s: outpcd ½-wy: styd on fnl f) | ½ | 5 | 7/2[2] | 62 | 26 |
| 1595[4] | **Gipsy Princess** (MWEasterby) **2-8-10**(5) GParkin(3) (lw: sn outpcd & drvn along) | 2½ | 6 | 12/1 | 52 | 16 |
| | | | | (SP 114.5%) | **6 Rn** | |

**1m 17.7** (3.40) CSF £24.96 TOTE £4.20: £2.40 £2.20 (£18.00) OWNER Mrs Lisa Olley (MALTON) BRED Topazio Est Vaduz
**2043* Docklands Carriage (IRE)**, with the blinkers on again, had the benefit of the plum number one draw and scraped home. (4/1)
**2076 Rum Lad**, stepping up to six, was keen going to post. Tapped for foot turning in, he drew almost level inside the last but could not find quite enough to force his head in front. (6/1)
**618 Our Future (IRE)** looked particularly well and ran easily his best race so far. (16/1)
**2025* Nostalgic Air (USA)**, carrying plenty of condition, gave her rider problems. Hanging left, though short of room the trouble was of her own making and she can not be counted unlucky. (5/4)
**1779 Ninth Symphony**, restless in the stalls, missed the break and was outpaced and behind until staying on in the final furlong. (7/2)
**1595 Gipsy Princess**, very warm beforehand, seems to be going the wrong way. (12/1)

## 2589 BRADLEY MAIDEN STKS (3-Y.O+) (Class D)

3-20 (3-21) **1m 2f 6y** £3,663.75 (£1,110.00: £542.50: £258.75) Stalls: Low GOING minus 0.27 sec per fur (GF)

| | | | | SP | RR | SF |
|---|---|---|---|---|---|---|
| 2124[2] | **Puce** (LMCumani) **3-7-12**(7) JoHunnam(4) (lw: hld up: effrt 3f out: qcknd to ld ins fnl f: sn clr) | — | 1 | 5/2[3] | 78 | 23 |
| 894[3] | **Degree** (HRACecil) **3-8-5** WRyan(1) (led: rdn along 3f out: hdd & nt qckn ins fnl f) | 3 | 2 | 9/4[2] | 73 | 18 |
| 2197[6] | **Mezzanotte (IRE)** (LMCumani) **3-8-10** KDarley(5) (lw: trckd ldrs: rdn to chal 2f out: hung lft: nt qckn ins fnl f) | ½ | 3 | 5/4[1] | 77 | 22 |
| | **Jungle Fresh** (JDBethell) **3-8-7**(3) SDrowne(2) (rangy: unf: bkwd: chsd ldrs: drvn along & outpcd over 3f out: sn wknd) | 20 | 4 | 66/1 | 46 | — |
| 1159[13] | **Sly Lady** (CWCElsey) **4-9-2** ACulhane(3) (drvn along & outpcd over 3f out: sn wl bhd) | 4 | 5 | 100/1 | 34 | — |
| | **Meadow Blue** (MissLCSiddall) **3-8-5** JCarroll(6) (unf: s.i.s: plld hrd: rn wd bnd after 2f: rdn & lost tch over 3f out) | 5 | 6 | 100/1 | 26 | — |
| | | | | (SP 107.3%) | **6 Rn** | |

**2m 14.2** (5.90) CSF £7.80 TOTE £4.20: £1.50 £1.30 (£3.30) OWNER Fittocks Stud (NEWMARKET) BRED Fittocks Stud
WEIGHT FOR AGE 3yo-11lb
**2124 Puce** was given a confident ride. Quickening ahead to show inside the last furlong, she could be an interesting proposition in handicaps over a mile and a half. (5/2)
**894 Degree**, a moderate mover, tried to make her stamina tell. After fighting off the favorite, she was left for dead by the winner inside the last. She lacks anything in the way of finishing speed and will be suited by a mile and a half. (9/4)
**2197 Mezzanotte (IRE)**, a bonny colt, is not the best of movers. Driven up to challenge once in line for home, he hung left under pressure and faded near the line. This trip must be stretching his stamina to the limit. (5/4)
**Jungle Fresh** showed a poor action and could not keep with the first two in the final three furlongs. (66/1)

## 2590 ACC DAIRYMEN MILK H'CAP (0-80) (3-Y.O+) (Class D)

3-55 (3-55) **6f** £5,344.50 (£1,596.00: £763.00: £346.50) Stalls: Low GOING minus 0.27 sec per fur (GF)

| | | | | SP | RR | SF |
|---|---|---|---|---|---|---|
| 2340[3] | **Cim Bom Bom (IRE) (67)** (MBell) **4-8-12v**(7) GFaulkner(4) (lw: chsd ldr: led over 2f out: rdn clr over 1f out) | — | 1 | 7/1[3] | 79 | 57 |
| 2149[3] | **Murray's Mazda (IRE) (52)** (JLEyre) **7-8-4** RLappin(5) (trckd ldrs: plld hrd: outpcd over 2f out: styd on ins fnl f) | 2 | 2 | 7/1[3] | 59 | 37 |
| 2347[2] | **Wardara (65)** (CADwyer) **4-9-0v**(3) FLynch(7) (lw: chsd ldrs: effrt over 2f out: styd on same pce) | ½ | 3 | 11/4[2] | 70 | 48 |
| 2363[2] | **Formidable Liz (54)** (MDHammond) **6-8-6** JQuinn(6) (lw: hld up: effrt over 2f out: styd on fnl f) | 2 | 4 | 2/1[1] | 54 | 32 |
| 2363[4] | **Halmanerror (69)** (MrsJRRamsden) **6-9-7** DHolland(1) (hld up: effrt over 2f out: no imp) | ¾ | 5 | 7/1[3] | 67 | 45 |
| 2523[2] | **Captain Carat (66)** (MrsJRRamsden) **5-9-4** OUrbina(2) (lw: hld up: effrt over 2f out: n.d) | 6 | 6 | 7/1[3] | 48 | 26 |
| 2005[W] | **Call Me I'm Blue (IRE) (72)** (NTinkler) **6-9-10** MBirch(3) (led tl over 2f out: wknd over 1f out) | hd | 7 | 25/1 | 54 | 32 |
| | | | | (SP 113.8%) | **7 Rn** | |

**1m 16.1** (1.80) CSF £48.16 TOTE £7.50: £2.00 £2.60 (£20.20) OWNER Mr Yucel Birol (NEWMARKET) BRED Tarworth Bloodstock Investments Ltd and J.J. Melk
**2340 Cim Bom Bom (IRE)**, a winner three times as a two year old, has slipped a long way down the weights. Dropped back in distance, he kicked clear off the bend and was soon in no danger. (7/1)
**2149 Murray's Mazda (IRE)** took a keen grip. Tapped for foot turning in, he stayed on inside the last and is better suited coming off the pace over seven. (7/1)
**2347 Wardara** went in pursuit of the winner on the home turn but could do no more than keep on at the one pace. (11/4)
**2363 Formidable Liz**, racing from a 2lb lower mark, was held up off the pace. Sticking on in the final furlong, she was never a threat. (2/1)
**2363 Halmanerror** was another happy to sit off the pace in a race that was basically a two and a half furlong dash. (7/1)
**2523 Captain Carat** had little chance the way the race was run, being held up in last place. (7/1)

## 2591 TANSHELF MAIDEN STKS (3-Y.O+) (Class D)

4-25 (4-26) **1m 4f 8y** £3,647.50 (£1,105.00: £540.00: £257.50) Stalls: Low GOING minus 0.27 sec per fur (GF)

| | | | SP | RR | SF |
|---|---|---|---|---|---|
| 2036[2] | **Dacha (IRE) (89)** (HRACecil) **4-9-7** WRyan(5) (lw: led after 2f: hung rt most of wy: styd on u.p fnl f) .............— | **1** | 2/5[1] | 81 | 52 |
| | **Step Aloft (78)** (LordHuntingdon) **4-9-2** DHarrison(1) (swtg: trckd ldrs: ev ch 1f out: nt qckn)........................1¼ | **2** | 11/4[2] | 74 | 45 |
| | **Totem Dancer** (JLEyre) **3-8-3** RLappin(4) (bit bkwd: pushed along 5f out: sn chsng ldrs: kpt on fnl 3f)...........6 | **3** | 33/1 | 66 | 24 |
| 1973[4] | **Aren't We Lucky (IRE)** (JJO'Neill) **3-8-8** JCarroll(2) (s.i.s: sn prom: outpcd fnl 3f) ........................................14 | **4** | 100/1 | 53 | 11 |
| 2062[7] | **Ballet de Cour** (CWCElsey) **3-8-8** ACulhane(8) (sn bhd & pushed along: n.d) ...................................................6 | **5** | 150/1 | 45 | 3 |
| 2318[7] | **Candrika** (LMCumani) **3-8-4**ow1 OUrbina(6) (hld up: sme hdwy on outside 3f out: sn wknd) ...........................¾ | **6** | 16/1[3] | 40 | — |
| | **Russian Roulette** (MJohnston) **3-8-3** JFanning(9) (lt-f: unf: sn w ldrs: wknd 3f out).......................................12 | **7** | 20/1 | 23 | — |
| 2318[9] | **Lomond Lassie (USA)** (TKersey) **3-8-3** NCarlisle(3) (b: led 2f: chsd ldrs tl lost pl over 3f out) ..........................2 | **8** | 500/1 | 20 | — |
| | **Mineral Water** (JDBethell) **3-8-5**(3) SDrowne(7) (unf: sn wl outpcd & drvn along: t.o 2f out)...........................19 | **9** | 50/1 | — | — |
| | | | (SP 115.5%) | | **9 Rn** |

**2m 39.2** (4.90) CSF £1.96 TOTE £1.40: £1.00 £2.60 £3.50 (£1.30) Trio £8.90 OWNER Cliveden Stud (NEWMARKET) BRED Cliveden Stud
WEIGHT FOR AGE 3yo-13lb

**2036 Dacha (IRE)**, colty in the paddock, soon showed ahead. Hanging away from the rail, he never looked happy and seemed to lose his action inside the last but was still good enough to hold the runner-up. It remains to be seen if all stays well with him. (2/5)
**Step Aloft**, warm beforehand, drew almost upsides entering the final furlong, but even though the winner looked far from happy, he had to give best. (11/4: 2/1-3/1)
**Totem Dancer** showed a poor action going down but ran with credit, keeping on in pursuit of the first two. In the long term this will not have done her handicap mark any good. (33/1)
**1973 Aren't We Lucky (IRE)**, who showed a fair bit of knee action going down, was left behind in the final three furlongs but is now qualified for handicaps. (100/1)

## 2592 KING RICHARD III H'CAP (0-70) (3-Y.O+ F & M) (Class E)

5-00 (5-01) **1m 4y** £3,757.50 (£1,125.00: £540.00: £247.50) Stalls: Low GOING minus 0.27 sec per fur (GF)

| | | | SP | RR | SF |
|---|---|---|---|---|---|
| 1825[5] | **Bubble Wings (FR) (62)** (SPCWoods) **4-9-10** WWoods(8) (lw: hld up & bhd: gd hdwy 2f out: qcknd to ld 1f out: pushed out) ...........— | **1** | 5/1[2] | 75 | 56 |
| 2241[7] | **She's Simply Great (IRE) (51)** (JJO'Neill) **3-8-4**ow1 KDarley(1) (hld up: hdwy over 2f out: kpt on wl fnl f: no imp)...........2 | **2** | 33/1 | 60 | 31 |
| 2133[3] | **Just Millie (USA) (65)** (JEBanks) **3-8-11**(7) GFaulkner(6) (hdwy on outside 3f out: styd on one pce appr fnl f)..4 | **3** | 8/1 | 66 | 38 |
| *2158*[2] | **Hot Dogging (43)** (MrsPSly) **3-7-10** NCarlisle(9) (chsd ldr: led over 2f out to 1f out: sn wknd)..........................2 | **4** | 14/1 | 40 | 12 |
| 2541[2] | **How Could-I (IRE) (44)** (MrsNMacauley) **3-7-11b** JQuinn(5) (led tl over 2f out: wknd over 1f out).......................3 | **5** | 4/1[1] | 35 | 7 |
| 2045[5] | **Prudent Pet (50)** (CWFairhurst) **4-8-12v**[1] JTate(4) (chsd ldrs: drvn along over 3f out: sn outpcd) ..................2½ | **6** | 12/1 | 36 | 17 |
| 2240[4] | **Phase One (IRE) (50)** (JLEyre) **6-8-12** RLappin(2) (mid div: drvn along ½-wy: kpt on)......................................1 | **7** | 7/1 | 34 | 15 |
| 1825[7] | **Racing Brenda (57)** (BCMorgan) **5-9-5** GCarter(3) (chsd ldrs: drvn along over 3f out: sn lost pl) ..................1¾ | **8** | 14/1 | 38 | 19 |
| *2158*[7] | **Voodoo Rocket (63)** (JHMGosden) **3-9-2** JCarroll(11) (b: chsd ldrs: drvn along over 3f out: n.m.r & lost pl 2f out) ..........½ | **9** | 5/1[2] | 43 | 15 |
| 2241[6] | **Alfayza (52)** (JDBethell) **3-8-2**(3) SDrowne(13) (hdwy on outside ½-wy: lost pl over 2f out)...........................1¾ | **10** | 16/1 | 28 | — |
| 2366[5] | **Hunza Story (38)** (NPLittmoden) **4-7-7**(7)ow4 JoHunnam(10) (b.hind: a bhd: pushed along ½-wy) ...................hd | **11** | 25/1 | 14 | — |
| 769[7] | **Oatey (53)** (MrsJRRamsden) **3-8-6** DHolland(7) (hld up & plld hrd: effrt over 3f out: n.d: eased) .......................7 | **12** | 11/2[3] | 15 | — |
| 2192[17] | **Dolly Dolittle (34)** (HJCollingridge) **5-7-10** NAdams(14) (swtg: a bhd) ...............................................1¼ | **13** | 66/1 | — | — |
| | | | (SP 127.5%) | | **13 Rn** |

**1m 44.5** (3.00) CSF £136.28 CT £1,262.58 TOTE £6.30: £2.50 £6.80 £3.10 (£74.10) Trio £305.00 OWNER Dr Frank Chao (NEWMARKET)
BRED H. S. Verrerie, Gue Foulon and Florent Couturier
LONG HANDICAP Hot Dogging 7-9 Hunza Story 7-6 Dolly Dolittle 6-5
WEIGHT FOR AGE 3yo-9lb

**1825 Bubble Wings (FR)**, who apparently has a history of foot trouble, was given a confident ride. Only eighth at the two furlong from home marker, in the end she won with something in hand and can follow up in better company. (5/1)
**1636 She's Simply Great (IRE)** showed a round action and went to post keenly. Sticking on from off the pace, she was a clear second. (33/1)
**2133 Just Millie (USA)**, a poor mover, has slipped down the weights. (8/1)
**2158 Hot Dogging** shows plenty of knee action. He kicked for home off the bend but was left for dead by the winner in the final furlong. (14/1)
**2541 How Could-I (IRE)**, who gets no respite, made the running. Her chance had already evaporated when she was tightened up over a furlong out. (4/1)
**2158 Voodoo Rocket** (5/1: 7/2-11/2)

## 2593 MONKHILL LIMITED STKS (0-70) (3-Y.O+) (Class E)

5-30 (5-30) **1m 2f 6y** £2,944.00 (£892.00: £436.00: £208.00) Stalls: Low GOING minus 0.27 sec per fur (GF)

| | | | SP | RR | SF |
|---|---|---|---|---|---|
| 1671[2] | **Lady Bankes (IRE) (66)** (WGMTurner) **3-8-0**(7) DSweeney(5) (mde all: qcknd over 2f out: hld on wl towards fin) ..........— | **1** | 9/1 | 73 | 7 |
| 2068[3] | **Sharpical (70)** (SirMarkPrescott) **4-9-9** DHarrison(4) (hld up: gd hdwy over 1f out: ev ch ins fnl f: nt qckn nr fin) ..........nk | **2** | 4/1[3] | 78 | 23 |
| 1771[6] | **Call Me (70)** (CWThornton) **3-8-11** DeanMcKeown(2) (chsd ldr: ev ch over 1f out: unable qckn)...................1¼ | **3** | 4/1[3] | 75 | 9 |
| 2214[U] | **Red Valerian (70)** (GMMoore) **5-9-7b** JTate(1) (trckd ldrs: effrt & outpcd over 2f out: kpt on one pce) ...........2½ | **4** | 12/1 | 70 | 15 |
| 2068* | **Another Time (70)** (SPCWoods) **4-9-9** WWoods(6) (hld up: effrt over 2f out: nvr nr to chal)...........................1 | **5** | 2/1[1] | 70 | 15 |
| 2514[3] | **Smarter Charter (68)** (MrsJRRamsden) **3-8-12** DHolland(3) (hld up: effrt over 2f out: eased whn no ch fnl f)...5 | **6** | 3/1[2] | 62 | — |
| | | | (SP 116.0%) | | **6 Rn** |

**2m 16.7** (8.40) CSF £41.58 TOTE £9.60: £3.80 £1.50 (£14.10) OWNER Mr T. Lightbowne (SHERBORNE) BRED Ben Sangster
WEIGHT FOR AGE 3yo-11lb

**1671 Lady Bankes (IRE)** was given a fine tactical ride by the boy. Setting her own pace, she quickened it up off the bend, and did just enough, (9/1: 6/1-10/1)
**2068 Sharpical** sat off the pace. Making up a deal of ground once in line for home, he was almost level inside the last but could then find no more. (4/1)
**1771 Call Me** was the only one to keep tabs on the winner. Almost upsides over a furlong out, she could then only stay on at the same pace. (4/1)

**Red Valerian**, a winning hurdler, was tapped for toe going into the turn. (12/1)
**2068* Another Time** could never have won this the way he was ridden. (2/1)
**2514 Smarter Charter**, stepping up in distance, sat off the pace. He needs a true run race and, with all chance gone a furlong out, he was allowed to coast home. (3/1: 9/4-7/2)

T/Plpt: £191.30 (75.65 Tckts). T/Qdpt: £33.40 (30.77 Tckts) WG

# 2404-FOLKESTONE (R-H) (Good, Good to firm patches)
## Wednesday July 10th
WEATHER: warm WIND: almost nil

### 2594 BRIDGE (S) H'CAP (0-60) (3-Y.O+) (Class G)
2-20 (2-22) **1m 1f 149y** £2,070.00 (£570.00: £270.00) Stalls: Low GOING minus 0.33 sec per fur (GF)

| Form | Horse / details | Dist | Pos | SP | RR | SF |
|---|---|---|---|---|---|---|
| $1534^{6}$ | **Harlequin Walk (IRE) (32)** (RJO'Sullivan) **5-8-9b** SSanders(12) (mde virtually all: clr over 3f out: r.o wl) | — | **1** | 11/2 | 48 | 29 |
| $1314^{15}$ | **Tocco Jewel (19)** (MJRyan) **6-7-10** GBardwell(14) (rdn over 3f out: hdwy over 1f out: chsd wnr ins fnl f: no imp) | 8 | **2** | 20/1 | 22 | 3 |
| $2282^{4}$ | **Kirov Protege (IRE) (31)** (HJCollingridge) **4-8-8** NCarlisle(4) (swtg: hld up: rdn over 3f out: chsd wnr over 1f out tl ins fnl f: one pce) | 3 | **3** | 16/1 | 29 | 10 |
| $2297^{2}$ | **Another Quarter (IRE) (52)** (SPCWoods) **3-9-4b** DBiggs(15) (a.p: rdn over 3f out: one pce) | ½ | **4** | 7/2 $^{1}$ | 49 | 19 |
| *$2158^{3}$* | **Nivasha (33)** (JFfitch-Heyes) **4-8-10** RPerham(1) (rdn over 3f out: hdwy over 1f out: nvr nrr) | hd | **5** | 10/1 | 30 | 11 |
| $1996^{11}$ | **Allez Pablo (28)** (RRowe) **6-8-5** KFallon(5) (rdn over 3f out: hdwy over 1f out: nvr nrr) | ½ | **6** | 20/1 | 24 | 5 |
| $2192^{14}$ | **Moving Up (IRE) (54)** (GLMoore) **3-9-6** SWhitworth(8) (b.hind: lw: nvr plcd to chal) | hd | **7** | 20/1 | 50 | 20 |
| $2402^{4}$ | **Cherry Garden (IRE) (48)** (TJNaughton) **3-9-0** GDuffield(11) (swtg: nvr gng wl: chsd ldrs 8f) | 1½ | **8** | 4/1 $^{2}$ | 41 | 11 |
| $1903^{8}$ | **Fortuitious (IRE) (35)** (JRJenkins) **3-7-10**(5) ADaly(10) (hld up: rdn over 4f out: sn wknd) | ¾ | **9** | 33/1 | 27 | — |
| $1979^{4}$ | **Multi Franchise (56)** (BGubby) **3-9-8** JQuinn(2) (swtg: hld up: rdn over 3f out: wknd over 1f out) | nk | **10** | 11/2 | 48 | 18 |
| *$2322^{5}$* | **Lahik (IRE) (37)** (KTIvory) **3-8-3v$^{1}$** NAdams(13) (lw: chsd wnr 8f) | s.h | **11** | 20/1 | 29 | — |
| $2409^{3}$ | **Sinclair Lad (IRE) (35)** (RJHodges) **8-8-7b**(5) PPMurphy(9) (lw: s.s: a bhd) | 1¼ | **12** | 9/2 $^{3}$ | 25 | 6 |
| *$2322^{8}$* | **Yellow Dragon (IRE) (51)** (BAPearce) **3-9-3** DeanMcKeown(6) (b: s.s: a bhd) | 19 | **13** | 14/1 | 9 | — |

(SP 134.8%) **13 Rn**

**2m 2.1** (4.40) CSF £106.93 CT £1,576.09 TOTE £5.60: £3.40 £7.10 £2.70 (£92.60) Trio £280.90; £79.15 to Newmarket 11/7/96 OWNER Mr R. J. O'Sullivan (WHITCOMBE) BRED Ronnie Boland in Ireland
LONG HANDICAP Tocco Jewel 7-6
WEIGHT FOR AGE 3yo-11lb
No bid
**OFFICIAL EXPLANATION Sinclair Lad (IRE): had tried to sit down in the stalls, and was then slowly away.**
**1534 Harlequin Walk (IRE)** gained her first victory on Turf in this appalling race. Making virtually all the running, she surged clear running down the hill and never looked like being caught. (11/2)
**Tocco Jewel**, racing well off the pace, eventually found her feet in the short home straight but, despite coming through for second prize inside the final furlong, never had a hope of getting near the winner. (20/1)
**Kirov Protege (IRE)** chased the leaders. Struggling into second place below the distance, he never looked like getting on terms with the winner and was collared for that position inside the final furlong. (16/1)
**2297 Another Quarter (IRE)** was never far away but was made to look very pedestrian in the final two furlongs. (7/2)
**2158 Nivasha** stayed on from the rear in the home straight without ever posing a threat. (10/1: 7/1-12/1)
**Allez Pablo**, still out with the washing entering the home straight, made some late headway past beaten horses. (20/1)
**1443 Moving Up (IRE)** was given considerate handling but caught the eye, as she stayed on past beaten rivals to be nearest at the line. (20/1)
**1979 Multi Franchise** (11/2: op 7/2)
**2409 Sinclair Lad (IRE)** (9/2: 3/1-5/1)

### 2595 COWDREY NURSERY H'CAP (2-Y.O) (Class E)
2-50 (2-54) **5f** £3,179.40 (£949.20: £453.60: £205.80) Stalls: Low GOING minus 0.33 sec per fur (GF)

| Form | Horse / details | Dist | Pos | SP | RR | SF |
|---|---|---|---|---|---|---|
| $2051^{12}$ | **Jennelle** (CADwyer) **2-9-0**(7) JoHunnam(6) (a.p: led 1f out: r.o wl) | — | **1** | 6/1 | 89 | 23 |
| $2398^{2}$ | **Rise 'n Shine** (CACyzer) **2-8-9** GDuffield(1) (lw: led to 1f out: unable qckn) | 2 | **2** | 9/2 $^{3}$ | 71 | 5 |
| 2031* | **Whizz Kid** (JJBridger) **2-7-11**(3) DarrenMoffatt(8) (rdn over 2f out: hdwy over 1f out: r.o one pce) | ½ | **3** | 12/1 | 60 | — |
| $685^{4}$ | **Nervous Rex** (WRMuir) **2-8-9** KFallon(5) (a.p: rdn over 2f out: one pce) | 1½ | **4** | 11/2 | 64 | — |
| $2375^{4}$ | **Mirror Four Life (IRE)** (MHTompkins) **2-8-2**(3) HKYim(7) (a.p: rdn over 1f out: one pce) | ½ | **5** | 10/1 | 59 | — |
| $2063^{5}$ | **Aztec Traveller** (MJRyan) **2-8-2** GBardwell(2) (outpcd: nvr nrr) | ¾ | **6** | 4/1 $^{2}$ | 53 | — |
| $2375^{3}$ | **Saunders Wren** (MRChannon) **2-8-4**(5) PPMurphy(4) (hld up: rdn 2f out: wknd 1f out) | s.h | **7** | 3/1 $^{1}$ | 60 | — |
| $1653^{6}$ | **Sweet Emmaline** (WGMTurner) **2-8-4**(7) DSweeney(9) (lw: prom over 2f) | 18 | **8** | 7/1 | 4 | — |

(SP 122.1%) **8 Rn**

**60.7 secs** (3.10) CSF £32.81 CT £296.82 TOTE £5.30: £1.80 £1.10 £3.60 (£16.70) Trio £110.30 OWNER Mrs J. A. Cornwell (NEWMARKET) BRED Mrs A. J. Owen
**715* Jennelle**, out of her depth in the Queen Mary last time, regained the winning thread here. A leading player from the outset, she struck the front a furlong from home and proved too strong for the runner-up. (6/1: 7/2-13/2)
**2398 Rise 'n Shine** looked in good shape here. Attempting to make all the running, she was collared a furlong from home and then put in her place. There is a race waiting for her. (9/2)
**2031* Whizz Kid** moved up below the distance and struggled on for third. (12/1: op 7/1)
**685 Nervous Rex**, after a three month break, was never far away but could only keep on at one pace in the last two furlongs. (11/2)
**2375 Mirror Four Life (IRE)**, a leading player from the outset, could only go up and down in the same place in the last two furlongs.(10/1: 6/1-12/1)
**2063 Aztec Traveller** was unable to go the pace. (4/1)
**2375 Saunders Wren** (3/1: 9/4-7/2)

### 2596 ST LAWRENCE MAIDEN AUCTION STKS (2-Y.O) (Class F)
3-25 (3-27) **6f** £2,381.00 (£656.00: £311.00) Stalls: Low GOING minus 0.33 sec per fur (GF)

| Form | Horse / details | Dist | Pos | SP | RR | SF |
|---|---|---|---|---|---|---|
| $2309^{2}$ | **Secret Combe (IRE)** (PJMakin) **2-8-1** SSanders(1) (lw: mde virtually all: shkn up over 1f out: qcknd fnl f: comf) | — | **1** | 6/5 $^{1}$ | 84+ | 27 |

2187[3] **River of Fortune (IRE)** (MHTompkins) **2-8-2**(3) HKYim(6) (hld up: rdn over 2f out: unable qckn) ....8 **2** 7/1[3] 67 10
2279[2] **Miss Barcelona (IRE)** (MJPolglase) **2-8-1** NCarlisle(5) (hdwy over 2f out: hrd rdn over 1f out: one pce) ....½ **3** 14/1 61 4
*2083[6]* **Tom Pladdey** (RBastiman) **2-8-3** DeanMcKeown(4) (lw: a.p: rdn over 2f out: one pce) ....hd **4** 25/1 63 6
2374[4] **Threeplay (IRE)** (JAkehurst) **2-8-10** KFallon(7) (b.hind: lw: hdwy 2f out: swtchd rt: nt clr run over 1f out: one pce) ....3 **5** 7/2[2] 62 5
2343[8] **Charlton Spring (IRE)** (RJHodges) **2-8-1**(3)ow3 SDrowne(10) (nvr nr to chal) ....s.h **6** 20/1 56 —
2230[8] **Lucy of Arabia (IRE)** (JJSheehan) **2-8-5** AMorris(9) (hdwy 3f out: wknd over 1f out) ....nk **7** 33/1 56 —
1871[7] **Shaken Up** (MrsDHaine) **2-8-6** AGarth(2) (a.p: edgd rt & stumbled 5f out: wknd over 1f out) ....1½ **8** 15/2 53 —
**Mendoza** (DJGMurraySmith) **2-8-10** GDuffield(3) (w'like: bit bkwd: bmpd 5f out: prom over 2f) ....5 **9** 16/1 44 —
**Flower Hill Lad (IRE)** (DJSCosgrove) **2-8-3** JQuinn(8) (w'like: bit bkwd: s.s: a bhd) ....s.h **10** 20/1 37 —
(SP 120.8%) **10 Rn**

**1m 12.4** (2.20) CSF £10.44 TOTE £2.00: £1.30 £1.60 £2.10 (£8.30) Trio £11.00 OWNER Bakewell Bloodstock Ltd (MARLBOROUGH) BRED Rathasker Stud

**2309 Secret Combe (IRE)** simply outclassed this field with a pillar to post victory, and showed a good turn of foot to quicken right away from the opposition in the final furlong. (6/5: 4/5-5/4)

**1871 River of Fortune (IRE)** chased the leaders. She managed to struggle into second place in the closing stages but never threatened the winner. (7/1: 5/1-8/1)

**2279 Miss Barcelona (IRE)** picked up ground soon after halfway, but was only treading water from below the distance. (14/1: 8/1-16/1)

**Tom Pladdey**, never far away, was made to look very pedestrian in the last two furlongs. (25/1)

**2374 Threeplay (IRE)** did not have the best of runs. Picking up ground a quarter of a mile out, he had to be switched right to find a clear passage, but then met some interference approaching the final furlong. From that point on, he could only struggle on at one pace. (7/2: 3/1-5/1)

## 2597 GODFREY EVENS MEDIAN AUCTION MAIDEN STKS (3 & 4-Y.O) (Class E)

3-55 (3-57) **6f** £3,097.50 (£924.00: £441.00: £199.50) Stalls: Low GOING minus 0.33 sec per fur (GF)

SP RR SF

758[2] **Watch The Fire** (JEBanks) **3-8-7** JStack(6) (hdwy over 1f out: hrd rdn: led nr fin) ....— **1** 5/2[2] 68 28
*2158[8]* **Shavinsky (60)** (PHowling) **3-8-12** KFallon(4) (s.s: hdwy over 4f out: chsd ldr over 3f out: led 1f out: hrd rdn: hdd nr fin) ....hd **2** 12/1 73 33
1475[4] **Domak Amaam (IRE) (80)** (JHMGosden) **3-8-12** AGarth(7) (led to 1f out: one pce) ....2 **3** 6/4[1] 67 27
**Paojiunic (IRE)** (LMCumani) **3-8-12** OUrbina(5) (bit bkwd: a.p: rdn 2f out: one pce) ....3 **4** 11/4[3] 59 19
**Charisse Dancer** (CFWall) **3-8-7** GDuffield(8) (s.s: swtchd rt 1f out: nvr plcd to chal) ....2 **5** 12/1 49 9
**Designer Lines** (CJames) **3-8-12** AMcGlone(2) (leggy: chsd ldr over 2f: wknd over 1f out) ....s.h **6** 33/1 54 14
**Fancy Design (IRE)** (PhilipMitchell) **3-8-7** AClark(1) (b.hind: hld up: rdn 3f out: wknd over 1f out) ....3 **7** 20/1 41 1
**Baron Hrabovsky** (PFICole) **3-8-5**(7) JBosley(9) (a bhd) ....s.h **8** 25/1 46 6
(SP 122.2%) **8 Rn**

**1m 12.7** (2.50) CSF £30.14 TOTE £3.70: £1.40 £2.60 £1.10 (£22.20) Trio £4.20 OWNER Mr E. Carter (NEWMARKET) BRED Red House Stud

**758 Watch The Fire** began her effort on the outside below the distance and, rousted along, managed to get on top near the line. (5/2: 6/4-11/4)

**1627 Shavinsky** left previous form well behind. In second place by halfway, he went on below the distance but despite doing little wrong, was worried out of it near the line. (12/1: 8/1-16/1)

**1475 Domak Amaam (IRE)** merrily bowled along in front, but collared a furlong from home, disappointingly found little. (6/4)

**Paojiunic (IRE)**, not looking fully wound up for this first run in over thirteen months, was never far away but failed to find another gear in the last furlongs. (11/4)

**Charisse Dancer** was given sympathetic handling on this seasonal debut. Losing ground at the start, she raced at the back of the field and, although her jockey did wiggle his arms around a bit, she never looked like getting into it. She looks one to keep an eye on. (12/1)

**Designer Lines** shot his bolt below the distance after racing close up. (33/1)

## 2598 SANDGATE MOTORS SKODA FELICIA H'CAP (0-70) (3-Y.O+) (Class E)

4-30 (4-30) **5f** £2,933.70 (£873.60: £415.80: £186.90) Stalls: Low GOING minus 0.33 sec per fur (GF)

SP RR SF

2434* **Cheeky Chappy (60)** (DWChapman) **5-9-4b** 7x JQuinn(6) (lw: a.p: led over 2f out: drvn out) ....— **1** 2/1[1] 65 44
2586[4] **Half Tone (47)** (RMFlower) **4-8-5b** DBiggs(5) (lw: a.p: ev ch over 1f out: r.o wl ins fnl f) ....nk **2** 4/1[2] 51 30
2410[3] **Super Rocky (70)** (RBastiman) **7-9-9**(5) HBastiman(2) (lw: hdwy 2f out: rdn over 1f out: unable qckn) ....1½ **3** 6/1 69 48
1715[13] **The Noble Oak (IRE) (38)** (MJBolton) **8-7-10** GBardwell(4) (b.off hind: lost pl over 2f out: r.o one pce fnl f) ....4 **4** 20/1 24 3
*2555[3]* **Lloc (56)** (CADwyer) **4-9-0** KFallon(8) (led over 2f: wknd over 1f out) ....2½ **5** 9/2[3] 34 13
2500[5] **Need You Badly (55)** (SPCWoods) **3-8-3**(5) MBaird(3) (lw: s.s: nvr nr to chal) ....1½ **6** 6/1 29 3
*278[9]* **Cedar Girl (44)** (RJHodges) **4-7-11**(5)ow4 AmandaSanders(7) (prom 3f) ....¾ **7** 16/1 15 —
2200[8] **Missile Toe (IRE) (66)** (JEBanks) **3-9-5v**[1] JStack(1) (lw: bhd fnl 2f) ....2½ **8** 6/1 29 3
(SP 125.0%) **8 Rn**

**59.3 secs** (1.70) CSF £11.20 CT £40.34 TOTE £3.30: £1.10 £1.30 £3.30 (£6.30) OWNER Mrs Jeanne Chapman (YORK) BRED Ian W. Glenton

LONG HANDICAP The Noble Oak (IRE) 7-6

WEIGHT FOR AGE 3yo-5lb

**2434* Cheeky Chappy** continues in tremendous form despite his hectic schedule. Disputing the lead from the outset, he went on over quarter of a mile from home and, responding to pressure, held on well. (2/1)

**2586 Half Tone** finished fourth at Newmarket on the previous day. He usually gets outpaced but on this occasion he raced right up with the pace. With every chance below the distance, he stuck to his guns in style and only just failed. (4/1: op 5/2)

**2410 Super Rocky** moved up over quarter of a mile from home but was unable to match the first two from below the distance. (6/1)

**The Noble Oak (IRE)** got outpaced at halfway but did struggle on again in the closing stages. It is three years since he has won. (20/1)

**2555 Lloc** held a slender advantage on the outside until halfway. Grimly trying to hold on, she had come to the end of her tether approaching the final furlong. (9/2)

**2500 Need You Badly** was again running over an inadequate trip. It was no surprise to see her failing to get into it, especially after a slow start. She can win a small handicap over further. (6/1)

## 2599 LESLIE AMES MEMORIAL H'CAP (0-70) (3-Y.O+ F & M) (Class E)

5-00 (5-00) **1m 4f** £3,315.90 (£991.20: £474.60: £216.30) Stalls: Low GOING minus 0.33 sec per fur (GF)

SP RR SF

2066[9] **All the Joys (39)** (CACyzer) **5-8-6** GCarter(7) (gd hdwy over 1f out: led ins fnl f: r.o wl) ....— **1** 25/1 47 29
2511[5] **Hever Golf Lady (57)** (TJNaughton) **4-9-5**(5) JDSmith(8) (led over 10f out tl ins fnl f: unable qckn) ....1½ **2** 10/1 63 45
2036[14] **Star Anise (42)** (MrsDHaine) **4-8-9** AGarth(11) (hdwy over 5f out: rdn over 1f out: one pce) ....1¾ **3** 40/1 46 28

2226[W] **Rocquaine Bay (41)** (MJBolton) **9-8-8** JQuinn(9) (lost pl over 4f out: rallied over 1f out: r.o one pce) ..............½ **4** 9/2[3] 44 26
2408[2] **Sacred Mirror (IRE) (56)** (CEBrittain) **5-9-9** SSanders(4) (b: hdwy 6f out: rdn over 2f out: wknd over 1f out) ..........2 **5** 100/30[1] 56 38
2408[4] **Uncharted Waters (55)** (CACyzer) **5-9-8** KFallon(2) (nt clr run over 2f out: nvr nrr) ..........nk **6** 7/1 55 37
2246[3] **Ailesbury Hill (USA) (67)** (PWChapple-Hyam) **3-9-2**(5) RHavlin(3) (lw: a.p: rdn over 2f out: wknd 1f out)......1¼ **7** 4/1[2] 65 34
2297[3] **Native Song (42)** (MJHaynes) **3-7-10** NCarlisle(10) (lw: led over 1f: wknd over 3f out)..........4 **8** 8/1 35 4
1875[5] **Viridis (USA) (64)** (HRACecil) **3-9-4** AMcGlone(5) (hld up: rdn 4f out: sn wknd) ..........6 **9** 6/1 49 18
2340[12] **Last Spin (37)** (JRJenkins) **4-7-13**(5) ADaly(6) (bhd fnl 3f) ..........3½ **10** 40/1 17 —
2284[3] **Owdbetts (IRE) (57)** (GLMoore) **4-9-10** SWhitworth(1) (hdwy over 3f out: wknd over 2f out)..........½ **11** 8/1 37 19
(SP 128.1%) **11 Rn**

**2m 36.6** (5.40) CSF £242.04 CT £8,785.05 TOTE £12.10: £2.90 £3.20 £8.40 (£60.30) Trio £334.40; £235.56 to Newmarket 11/7/96 OWNER Mrs G. M. Gooderham (HORSHAM) BRED Mrs G. Gooderham
WEIGHT FOR AGE 3yo-13lb

**1953 All the Joys**, racing at the back of the field, made giant strides in the short home straight and came swooping through to grab the initiative inside the last 100 yards. (25/1)
**2511 Hever Golf Lady** was soon at the head of affairs. Grimly trying to fend off her rivals, she was eventually overhauled inside the last 100 yards. (10/1: 7/1-12/1)
**Star Anise** moved up at the top of the hill. Grimly trying to get in a challenge in the short home straight, she failed to find that vital turn of foot. (40/1)
**1852 Rocquaine Bay** got outpaced as the runners began the downhill descent. Trying to get back into it below the distance, she did stay on but could never threaten the principals. (9/2)
**2408 Sacred Mirror (IRE)** moved up halfway down the back straight. Rousted along turning for home, she had shot her bolt below the distance. (100/30)
**2408 Uncharted Waters** raced at the back of the field. She did not have the best of runs turning for home, but struggled on through the pack from below the distance to be nearest at the line. (7/1)
**2246 Ailesbury Hill (USA)** (4/1: 5/2-9/2)
**1090 Viridis (USA)** (6/1: 4/1-7/1)

T/Plpt: £1,112.70 (11.12 Tckts). T/Qdpt: £45.30 (27.12 Tckts). AK

## 2224-KEMPTON (R-H) (Good to firm, Firm patches)
## Wednesday July 10th

Race 5 & 6: hand-timed. Race 5: flag start
WEATHER: fine WIND: almost nil

### 2600 E.B.F. CHUBB FIRE MEDIAN AUCTION MAIDEN STKS (2-Y.O) (Class E)
6-30 (6-37) **6f** £3,436.25 (£1,040.00: £507.50: £241.25) Stalls: High GOING minus 0.33 sec per fur (GF)

SP RR SF
1954[2] **Raindancing (IRE)** (RHannon) **2-8-9** PatEddery(13) (lw: a.p: led 2f out: r.o wl)..........— **1** 11/4[2] 79 43
**Isle of Man (USA)** (PFICole) **2-9-0** TQuinn(16) (w'like: scope: lw: a.p: chsd wnr fnl f: one pce)..........3½ **2** Evens[1] 75+ 39
2195[3] **Marsad (IRE)** (CJBenstead) **2-9-0** RHills(10) (a.p: led over 2f out: hdd 2f out: one pce)..........s.h **3** 11/1 75 39
**Mara River** (IABalding) **2-8-4**(5) MartinDwyer(5) (unf: bit bkwd: hld up: rdn 3f out: hdwy over 1f out: styd on ins fnl f)..........4 **4** 33/1 59 23
2195[7] **Palisander (IRE)** (SDow) **2-9-0** MRoberts(8) (chsd ldrs: rdn 2f out: one pce)..........1½ **5** 25/1 60 24
**The Green Grey** (LordHuntingdon) **2-9-0** JReid(15) (unf: scope: bit bkwd: mid div: j.path over 3f out: kpt on one pce fnl 2f) ..........1 **6** 16/1 57 21
**Sherzetto** (JRFanshawe) **2-8-9** DHarrison(14) (nvr nrr) ..........¾ **7** 16/1 50 1
**Ivory Dawn** (KTIvory) **2-8-2**(7) CScally(11) (w'like: bit bkwd: dwlt: hdwy 4f out: j.path over 3f out: n.m.r 2f out: one pce)..........1 **8** 50/1 48 12
2323[3] **Castle Ashby Jack** (PHowling) **2-9-0v**[1] FNorton(9) (b.hind: prom over 4f)..........nk **9** 50/1 52 16
2374[8] **Countless Times** (WRMuir) **2-9-0** DHolland(7) (led over 3f: sn wknd)..........¾ **10** 50/1 50 14
**Aurelian** (MBell) **2-9-0** MFenton(1) (leggy: unf: swtg: dwlt: swtchd rt: a bhd)..........2 **11** 33/1 44 8
2057[4] **Chingachgook** (PWHarris) **2-9-0** GDuffield(6) (lw: mid div: j.path over 3f out: sn rdn & btn) ..........s.h **12** 5/1[3] 44 8
**Grovefair Venture** (BJMeehan) **2-9-0** MTebbutt(12) (cmpt: bit bkwd: bhd fnl 3f)..........½ **13** 33/1 43 7
1424[8] **Protaras Bay** (TTClement) **2-9-0** DeanMcKeown(3) (bhd fnl 3f)..........½ **14** 50/1 42 19
**Linden's Lad (IRE)** (JRJenkins) **2-9-0** PRobinson(2) (unf: bit bkwd: wnt lft s: bhd fnl 3f) ..........2 **15** 50/1 36 —
**Running Free (IRE)** (MJFetherston-Godley) **2-9-0** WJO'Connor(4) (w'like: bit bkwd: a bhd) ..........2 **16** 50/1 31 —
(SP 137.9%) **16 Rn**

**1m 12.26** (0.96) CSF £6.30 TOTE £3.50: £1.50 £1.40 £3.20 (£3.10) Trio £8.00 OWNER Mr N. Hayes (MARLBOROUGH) BRED Mrs R. D. Peacock
OFFICIAL EXPLANATION **Sherzetto: the jockey reported that the gates of the stalls sprung back onto his filly after opening.**

**1954 Raindancing (IRE)** made her previous experience tell and ran out a comfortable winner. (11/4: 2/1-3/1)
**Isle of Man (USA)** looked short of a turn of foot in the closing stages and will improve over further. (Evens)
**2195 Marsad (IRE)** ran another sound race here and can pick up a small race soon. (11/1: 6/1-12/1)
**Mara River**, an attractive filly, was just in need of the race and ran very green in the early stages. Finally getting the hang of things on the final two furlongs, she stayed on in promising style. (33/1)
**1437 Palisander (IRE)** ran a nice race here and is now qualified for nurseries. (25/1)
**The Green Grey** will be better for the experience and stayed on in the closing stages. He can improve. (16/1)

### 2601 CHUBB LOCKS & SAFES MAIDEN STKS (3-Y.O) (Class D)
7-00 (7-17) **1m 4f** £3,615.00 (£1,095.00: £535.00: £255.00) Stalls: High GOING: minus 0.33 sec per fur (GF)

SP RR SF
1873[2] **Time Allowed** (MRStoute) **3-8-9** JReid(13) (a.p: chsd ldr 3f out: led gng wl over 2f out: rdn out ins fnl f).......— **1** 2/1[1] 83 49
1461[2] **Jiyush (86)** (HThomsonJones) **3-9-0** RHills(7) (swtg: hld up: hdwy over 2f out: nt clr run over 1f out: chsd wnr ins fnl f: r.o)..........1¾ **2** 6/1[3] 86 52
2383[2] **Renzo (IRE)** (GHarwood) **3-9-0** AClark(2) (hld up mid div: hdwy 3f out: swtchd lft over 2f out: sn rdn: chsd wnr over 1f out tl ins fnl f: one pce)..........2 **3** 9/1 83 49
2036[3] **Canon Can (USA) (78)** (HRACecil) **3-9-0** WJO'Connor(8) (chsd ldrs: rdn 3f out: kpt on one pce fnl f)..........¾ **4** 25/1 82 48

| | | | | | | |
|---|---|---|---|---|---|---|
| 1711[2] | **Palamon (USA) (84)** (RCharlton) **3-9-0** PatEddery(10) (hld up: hdwy 3f out: hmpd over 2f out: kpt on one pce ins fnl f) | 1¼ | **5** | 9/2[2] | 80 | 46 |
| 2383[3] | **Classic Parisian (IRE) (79)** (RHarris) **3-8-9** AMackay(11) (led: hdd over 2f out: wknd fnl f) | 1½ | **6** | 16/1 | 73 | 39 |
| 1434[3] | **Annecy (USA) (80)** (HRACecil) **3-8-9** WRyan(14) (swtg: chsd ldrs: rdn 3f out: wknd over 1f out) | 4 | **7** | 7/1 | 68 | 34 |
| | **National Treasure** (MRStoute) **3-8-9** PRobinson(4) (w'like: scope: bit bkwd: chsd ldr: rdn over 2f out: sn wknd) | 2 | **8** | 16/1 | 65 | 31 |
| 1656[2] | **Kitty Kitty Cancan** (LadyHerries) **3-8-9** DHarrison(1) (mid div: rdn 3f out: sn btn) | ½ | **9** | 10/1 | 65 | 31 |
| 1711[9] | **Queen Bee** (JLDunlop) **3-8-9** TQuinn(6) (swtg: chsd ldr 7f: wknd over 2f out) | 6 | **10** | 20/1 | 57 | 23 |
| 2080[2] | **Random Kindness (75)** (PWHarris) **3-9-0** GDuffield(3) (prom: chsd ldr 5f to 3f out: sn wknd) | 15 | **11** | 33/1 | 42 | 8 |
| 2314[4] | **Notaire (IRE)** (IABalding) **3-8-9**(5) MartinDwyer(12) (a bhd) | 9 | **12** | 33/1 | 30 | — |
| 2197[19] | **Desert Scout** (KMcAuliffe) **3-9-0v** MTebbutt(9) (a bhd: t.o) | dist | **13** | 100/1 | — | — |
| *1957[3]* | ***Caballus (USA)*** (LordHuntingdon) **3-9-0** BDoyle(5) (Withdrawn not under Starter's orders: veterinary advice) | | **W** | 20/1 | — | — |

(SP 129.4%) **13 Rn**

**2m 32.13** (1.43) CSF £14.66 TOTE £3.30: £1.60 £1.90 £2.30 (£7.90) Trio £14.30 OWNER Mr R. Barnett (NEWMARKET) BRED W. and R. Barnett Ltd

**1873 Time Allowed** was always travelling well and looked like scoring easily when taking it up early in the straight. In the end she had to be ridden out to score. (2/1)
**1461 Jiyush** was settled nicely in the rear here. He did not get the best of runs when starting his challenge below the distance, and would certainly have been closer. (6/1: 9/2-7/1)
**2383 Renzo (IRE)** caused trouble when switching off the rails over two furlongs out and then could only plug on at the one pace. (9/1: 6/1-10/1)
**2036 Canon Can (USA)** had every chance and this is as good as he is. (25/1)
**1711 Palamon (USA)** was closing up when hampered over two furlongs out, but once clear could only plug on at the one speed. (9/2)
**2383 Classic Parisian (IRE)** tried different tactics here but they did not really work. (16/1)
**1656 Kitty Kitty Cancan** (10/1: 8/1-12/1)

## 2602 CHUBB ALARMS H'CAP (0-70) (3-Y.O+) (Class E)

7-30 (7-43) **7f (Jubilee)** £3,842.50 (£1,165.00: £570.00: £272.50) Stalls: High GOING: minus 0.33 sec per fur (GF)

| | | | | SP | RR | SF |
|---|---|---|---|---|---|---|
| 1856[9] | **Soaking (47)** (PBurgoyne) **6-8-5** DRMcCabe(5) (hld up in rr: hdwy on outside over 1f out: str run fnl f: led last stride) | — | **1** | 10/1 | 57 | 24 |
| 2376[2] | **Victory Team (IRE) (65)** (GBBalding) **4-9-9** TQuinn(2) (lw: hmpd s: sn prom: led ½-wy: hrd rdn ins fnl f: hdd last stride) | s.h | **2** | 11/2[3] | 75 | 42 |
| 2013* | **Castan (IRE) (69)** (JLDunlop) **3-9-5** PatEddery(8) (hld up mid div: hdwy 3f out: chsd ldr over 1f out tl wl ins fnl f: r.o) | ¾ | **3** | 4/1[1] | 77 | 36 |
| 1905[6] | **Our Shadee (USA) (50)** (KTIvory) **6-8-1v**(7)ow2 CScally(14) (hld up: hdwy 2f out: styd on ins fnl f) | ½ | **4** | 16/1 | 57 | 22 |
| 2285[9] | **Paddy's Rice (60)** (MMcCormack) **5-9-4** JReid(3) (hmpd s: sn in tch: rdn over 2f out: kpt on ins fnl f) | 3 | **5** | 16/1 | 60 | 27 |
| 2200[7] | **Village Native (FR) (65)** (KOCunningham-Brown) **3-9-1** PRobinson(12) (a.p: chsd ldr 3f out tl over 1f out: sn rdn: one pce) | hd | **6** | 16/1 | 65 | 24 |
| 2376* | **Blushing Grenadier (IRE) (51)** (MJFetherston-Godley) **4-8-9v** 5x DHolland(1) (wnt rt s: prom: rdn 2f out: wknd over 1f out) | 2 | **7** | 8/1 | 46 | 13 |
| 2405* | **Star of Gold (65)** (CREgerton) **4-9-9** 5x RHughes(13) (prom: rdn over 2f out: grad wknd) | nk | **8** | 5/1[2] | 60 | 27 |
| 2405[2] | **Sapphire Son (IRE) (53)** (DMorris) **4-8-11v** PBloomfield(10) (chsd ldrs: rdn over 2f out: grad wknd) | nk | **9** | 11/1 | 47 | 14 |
| *2168[8]* | **Classic Beauty (IRE) (62)** (RHarris) **3-8-12** AMackay(15) (dwlt: nvr nrr) | 2½ | **10** | 20/1 | 50 | 9 |
| 2340[9] | **Squire Corrie (57)** (GHarwood) **4-8-8**(7) GayeHarwood(6) (rr: rdn over 2f out: no hdwy) | ¾ | **11** | 33/1 | 44 | 11 |
| *2081[6]* | **Le Bam Bam (58)** (HAkbary) **4-8-9**(7) CWebb(17) (hld up: hdwy 3f out: wknd 2f out) | ¾ | **12** | 40/1 | 43 | 10 |
| 1010[13] | **Trapper Norman (47)** (RIngram) **4-8-5** NAdams(4) (sltly hmpd s: sn rcvrd into mid div: wknd over 2f out) | 4 | **13** | 40/1 | 23 | — |
| 1658[11] | **Courting Newmarket (42)** (NMBabbage) **8-7-7**(7) RFfrench(7) (prom 4f) | 4 | **14** | 40/1 | 9 | — |
| 2228[7] | **Dancing Heart (67)** (BJMeehan) **4-9-4**(7) DSweeney(11) (led to ½-wy: wknd 3f out) | 5 | **15** | 14/1 | 22 | — |

(SP 119.9%) **15 Rn**

**1m 27.0** (2.50) CSF £59.02 CT £240.59 TOTE £10.50: £2.50 £2.20 £1.90 (£48.60) Trio £116.00 OWNER Mr Philip Saunders (LAMBOURN) BRED David John Brown
WEIGHT FOR AGE 3yo-8lb

**1302 Soaking** was held up in the rear and brought with a beautifully timed run to lead in the shadow of the post. This was a fine piece of riding. (10/1)
**2376 Victory Team (IRE)**, although hampered at the start, soon raced to the fore and got in front by halfway. He looked sure to score entering the final furlong, but was grabbed by the winner's late swoop. (11/2: 9/1-6/1)
**2013* Castan (IRE)** ran a sound race, throwing down a strong challenge in the final two furlongs, but never quite looked like getting there.(4/1)
**1905 Our Shadee (USA)** staged his usual late rally and was running on at the finish. (16/1)
**1689* Paddy's Rice** was another to be hampered at the start and never really got in the race. (16/1)
**2405 Sapphire Son (IRE)** (11/1: 8/1-12/1)

## 2603 CHUBB SECURITY PLC H'CAP (0-90) (3-Y.O+) (Class C)

8-00 (8-15) **1m 2f (Jubilee)** £5,738.50 (£1,738.00: £849.00: £404.50) Stalls: High GOING: minus 0.33 sec per fur (GF)

| | | | | SP | RR | SF |
|---|---|---|---|---|---|---|
| 2128[6] | **Grand Selection (IRE) (77)** (MBell) **4-9-5** MFenton(1) (hld up in rr: hdwy 2f out: str run to ld wl ins fnl f: r.o wl) | — | **1** | 25/1 | 87 | 53 |
| 1066[3] | **Easy Listening (USA) (84)** (RCharlton) **4-9-12** SSanders(14) (hld up in mid div: hdwy to ld over 2f out: hdd wl ins fnl f: r.o) | ¾ | **2** | 12/1 | 93 | 59 |
| 2000[5] | **Formidable Partner (68)** (RWArmstrong) **3-7-13b**[1] GCarter(9) (a.p: rdn 3f out: ev ch wl ins fnl f: r.o) | nk | **3** | 20/1 | 76 | 31 |
| *2306[10]* | **Kriscliffe (82)** (MissGayKelleway) **3-8-13** JReid(18) (a.p: hrd rdn over 1f out: r.o) | nk | **4** | 20/1 | 90 | 45 |
| 2536[2] | **Danegold (IRE) (78)** (MRChannon) **4-9-6v** RHughes(6) (hld up in rr: hdwy over 1f out: hrd rdn ins fnl f: r.o one pce) | 1¼ | **5** | 5/1[2] | 84 | 50 |
| 2377[10] | **Zermatt (IRE) (74)** (MDIUsher) **6-9-2** DHarrison(7) (hld up: hdwy 2f out: wknd ins fnl f) | 5 | **6** | 20/1 | 72 | 38 |
| 2055[20] | **Bob's Ploy (79)** (MHTompkins) **4-9-7** PRobinson(13) (mid div: rdn 2f out: one pce) | 2 | **7** | 33/1 | 74 | 40 |
| 847[7] | **Dolliver (USA) (63)** (SDow) **4-8-5** MRoberts(11) (nvr nrr) | s.h | **8** | 25/1 | 58 | 24 |
| 1961[2] | **Fahs (USA) (68)** (RAkehurst) **4-8-10** TQuinn(2) (swtg: chsd ldr: ev ch over 2f out: sn wknd) | 1¾ | **9** | 9/4[1] | 60 | 26 |
| 2077* | **Rory (75)** (MrsJCecil) **5-8-12**(5) AmandaSanders(5) (chsd ldrs tl wknd 2f out) | ½ | **10** | 11/1 | 66 | 32 |
| 2055[18] | **Burning (USA) (86)** (GHarwood) **4-10-0** RHills(3) (lw: hld up mid div: rdn over 2f out: sn btn) | nk | **11** | 14/1 | 77 | 43 |
| 2053[26] | **Blaze of Song (80)** (RHannon) **4-9-8** WJO'Connor(16) (mid div: rdn over 2f out: sn btn) | 2 | **12** | 25/1 | 67 | 33 |

| | | | | SP | RR | SF |
|---|---|---|---|---|---|---|
| 2249[4] | **Above the Cut (USA) (82)** (PWHarris) **4-9-10b** GDuffield(12) (bhd fnl 3f) | nk | **13** | 25/1 | 69 | 35 |
| 1874[11] | **Fighting Times (63)** (CASmith) **4-8-5** CRutter(17) (a bhd) | ½ | **14** | 20/1 | 49 | 15 |
| 2074[8] | **Serendipity (FR) (84)** (JLDunlop) **3-9-1** PatEddery(8) (led: hdd over 2f out: sn wknd) | 1¾ | **15** | 11/2[3] | 67 | 22 |
| 2384[2] | **Classic Romance (71)** (RHarris) **3-8-2** AMackay(4) (chsd ldrs tl wknd over 2f out) | 3 | **16** | 16/1 | 49 | 4 |
| 1841[8] | **Ron's Secret (75)** (JWPayne) **4-9-3** KFallon(15) (a bhd) | 9 | **17** | 20/1 | 39 | 5 |
| 1662[5] | **Classy Chief (74)** (RBoss) **3-8-5** WRyan(10) (wnt violently lft s: virtually ref to r) | dist | **18** | 25/1 | — | — |
| | | | | (SP 137.4%) | **18 Rn** | |

**2m 4.17** (0.67) CSF £294.36 CT £5,539.09 TOTE £33.20: £5.80 £2.60 £3.90 £4.60 (£237.00) Trio £551.40 OWNER Mr M. B. Hawtin (NEWMARKET) BRED Mount Coote Stud in Ireland

WEIGHT FOR AGE 3yo-11lb

**988 Grand Selection (IRE)** was drawn low, so connections thought it wise to change tactics today and held him up for a late run. This worked a treat. (25/1)

**1066 Easy Listening (USA)** looked like scoring when leading early in the straight, but he could not withstand the winner's late burst. (12/1)

**2000 Formidable Partner** was always to the fore and stayed on most gamely in the closing stages. (20/1)

**2306 Kriscliffe** was never far away and ran a sound race. (20/1)

**2536 Danegold (IRE)** looked dangerous when improving fast below the distance but this challenge petered out late on. (5/1: op 8/1)

**1440* Zermatt (IRE)** never really threatened. (20/1)

## 2604 BRUNSWICK CLAIMING STKS (3-Y.O+) (Class E)

8-30 (8-47) **6f** £3,046.25 (£920.00: £447.50: £211.25) Stalls: High GOING: minus 0.33 sec per fur (GF)

| | | | | SP | RR | SF |
|---|---|---|---|---|---|---|
| 2114[14] | **Law Commission (82)** (DRCElsworth) **6-9-8** TQuinn(2) (hld up: hdwy 2f out: led ins fnl f: r.o wl) | — | **1** | 4/1[3] | 87 | 63 |
| 1964[2] | **Spaniards Close (96)** (PJMakin) **8-9-3** PatEddery(4) (a.p: chsd ldr 3f out: ev ch ins fnl f: one pce) | 2½ | **2** | 6/5[1] | 75 | 51 |
| 1853[4] | **Sing Up (59)** (MMcCormack) **4-8-10** JReid(8) (led: hdd ins fnl f: one pce) | ¾ | **3** | 10/1 | 66 | 42 |
| 2411[3] | **Never Think Twice (52)** (KTIvory) **3-8-1b** NAdams(9) (rr: rdn 2f out: kpt on one pce ins fnl f) | 2½ | **4** | 50/1 | 57 | 27 |
| 2285[2] | **Jaazim (54)** (MMadgwick) **6-9-1**(7) AEddery(5) (dwlt: rr: rdn over 2f out: one pce) | 2 | **5** | 16/1 | 66 | 42 |
| 2228[5] | **Dashing Dancer (IRE) (57)** (RAkehurst) **5-8-7** SSanders(6) (chsd ldr to ½-wy: wknd over 1f out) | 2 | **6** | 25/1 | 46 | 22 |
| 1356* | **Ortolan (85)** (RHannon) **3-8-5**(3) DaneO'Neill(7) (dwlt: a bhd) | 2 | **7** | 7/2[2] | 48 | 18 |
| 2197[18] | **Fig Tree Bay** (TTClement) **3-8-11** DeanMcKeown(3) (prom over 2f) | 21 | **8** | 100/1 | — | — |
| | **Firm Contract (IRE)** (CNAllen) **4-8-7**(5) MartinDwyer(1) (s.s: a wl bhd) | 1¼ | **9** | 33/1 | — | — |
| | | | | (SP 112.4%) | **9 Rn** | |

**1m 11.2** (-0.10) CSF £8.57 TOTE £4.60: £1.90 £1.50 £1.70 (£4.30) Trio £15.90 OWNER Mr Raymond Tooth (WHITCOMBE) BRED Airlie Stud

WEIGHT FOR AGE 3yo-6lb

**1680* Law Commission** was held up under a confident ride and, brought to challenge entering the final furlong, he ran out a ready winner. (4/1)

**1964 Spaniards Close**, although always to the fore, never looked at ease on the ground. (6/5)

**1853 Sing Up** showed the way but was put in his place in the closing stages. (10/1: op 20/1)

**2411 Never Think Twice** made late headway but never threatened to take a hand. (50/1)

**2285 Jaazim** missed the break and never posed a threat. (16/1)

## 2605 CHUBB CITY H'CAP (0-80) (3-Y.O+) (Class D)

9-00 (9-09) **1m (round)** £3,694.50 (£1,116.00: £543.00: £256.50) Stalls: High GOING: minus 0.33 sec per fur (GF)

| | | | | SP | RR | SF |
|---|---|---|---|---|---|---|
| 2229[2] | **Sharp Rebuff (74)** (PJMakin) **5-9-10** PatEddery(1) (lw: hld up mid div: gd hdwy on ins to ld wl over 1f out: r.o wl) | — | **1** | 3/1[1] | 87 | 56 |
| 1953[4] | **Thames Side (60)** (MMadgwick) **5-8-3**(7) AEddery(8) (bhd & outpcd: hdwy over 1f out: squeezed thro on ins wl ins fnl f: wnt 2nd nr line) | 2 | **2** | 7/1 | 69 | 38 |
| 2016[3] | **Mystic Dawn (57)** (SDow) **3-7-12** JQuinn(5) (hld up: rdn & hdwy 2f out: hrd rdn ins fnl f: one pce) | ½ | **3** | 11/2[3] | 65 | 25 |
| 1872[4] | **Admirals Flame (IRE) (74)** (CFWall) **5-9-10** GDuffield(7) (lw: hld up in mid div: hdwy over 2f out: ev ch wl over 1f out: sn rdn: one pce) | s.h | **4** | 9/2[2] | 82 | 51 |
| 2285[5] | **Audrey Grace (47)** (MissGayKelleway) **5-7-11** NAdams(4) (prom: rdn over 2f out: wknd over 1f out) | 5 | **5** | 10/1 | 45 | 14 |
| 2206[4] | **Classic Ballet (FR) (68)** (RHarris) **3-8-9** AMackay(3) (hld up: rdn over 2f out: no hdwy) | 2½ | **6** | 7/1 | 61 | 21 |
| 2285[8] | **Fionn de Cool (IRE) (72)** (RAkehurst) **5-9-8** SSanders(6) (lw: chsd ldrs: rdn 3f out: wknd over 1f out) | 1¾ | **7** | 12/1 | 61 | 30 |
| 2188[4] | **Pab's Choice (56)** (MMcCormack) **5-8-6** RPerham(9) (led: hdd wl over 1f out: sn wknd) | 1¾ | **8** | 14/1 | 42 | 11 |
| *177*[8] | **Flirty Gertie (67)** (RBoss) **4-9-3** WRyan(2) (plld hrd: w ldr 4f: wknd over 2f out) | 12 | **9** | 12/1 | 29 | — |
| | | | | (SP 114.7%) | **9 Rn** | |

**1m 38.7** (1.50) CSF £22.30 CT £100.11 TOTE £3.70: £1.90 £1.80 £1.90 (£12.80) Trio £18.40 OWNER Mr D. M. Ahier (MARLBOROUGH) BRED Farmers Hill and Fitzroy Studs

WEIGHT FOR AGE 3yo-9lb

STEWARDS' ENQUIRY Duffield susp. 19-20/7/96 (careless riding).

**2229 Sharp Rebuff** gained due reward for his consistent efforts this season and ran out a ready winner. (3/1)

**1953 Thames Side** was totally unable to go with the pace early on and was well behind until staying on in the closing stages. (7/1)

**2016 Mystic Dawn** started her challenge at the same time as the winner but lacked the pace to go with him. (11/2)

**1872 Admirals Flame (IRE)** ran a good race here under his weight but was beaten by it in the closing stages. (9/2)

**Audrey Grace** raced prominently but was a beaten horse in the final two furlongs. (10/1)

**1908* Classic Ballet (FR)** was held up but, under pressure early in the straight, had little to give. (7/1: op 98/1)

**2188 Pab's Choice** (14/1: 10/1-16/1)

T/Plpt: £45.20 (399.35 Tckts). T/Qdpt: £24.70 (50.67 Tckts). SM

# 2580-NEWMARKET (R-H) (Good)

## Wednesday July 10th

WEATHER: sunny & warm WIND: mod bhd

## 2606 ELLESMERE (S) STKS (2-Y.O) (Class E)

2-05 (2-06) **7f (July)** £4,659.00 (£1,392.00: £666.00: £303.00) Stalls: Low GOING minus 0.48 sec per fur (F)

| | | | | SP | RR | SF |
|---|---|---|---|---|---|---|
| 1959[8] | **Buzzby** (AGFoster) **2-9-3** TSprake(8) (outpcd tl hdwy over 2f out: led 1f out: r.o) | — | **1** | 9/1 | 71 | 43 |

2382[6] **Our Kevin** (KMcAuliffe) **2-8-13v** DRMcCabe(4) (swtg: led tl hdd 1f out: kpt on) ....1¾ **2** 14/1 63 35
2512[3] **Silca's My Key (IRE)** (MRChannon) **2-8-13** RHughes(7) (lw: cl up: rdn 3f out: styd on wl) ....hd **3** 12/1 63 35
1904[3] **Fan of Vent-Axia** (CNAllen) **2-9-2**(5) MartinDwyer(11) (chsd ldrs tl wknd fnl f)....4 **4** 33/1 62 34
2406* **Leitrim Lodge (IRE)** (NACallaghan) **2-8-8** PatEddery(9) (hld up: effrt over 2f out: edgd lft: styd on one pce: lame) ....2 **5** 2/1[1] 44 16
2254[4] **Spondulicks (IRE)** (RHannon) **2-9-0**(3) DaneO'Neill(12) (lw: bhd: rdn 3f out: styd on wl fnl f) ....nk **6** 13/2[2] 52 24
2396[8] **Cajun Sunset (IRE)** (TDEasterby) **2-8-13** KDarley(10) (chsd ldrs: effrt 2f out: edgd lft & grad wknd)....1¼ **7** 16/1 46 18
2374[5] **Broughtons Error** (WJMusson) **2-8-13** BDoyle(6) (plld hrd: bhd: hdwy whn nt clr run appr fnl f: nt rcvr)....2 **8** 9/1 41 13
2161[4] **Emily-Jayne** (MrsMReveley) **2-8-12** ACulhane(3) (lw: prom: outpcd 3f out: wknd fnl 2f)....s.h **9** 20/1 40 12
1713[7] **Grovefair Flyer (IRE)** (BJMeehan) **2-8-13** MJKinane(1) (chsd ldrs: rdn 3f out: wknd fnl 2f) ....½ **10** 8/1[3] 40 12
2309[8] **Silver Spell** (DrJDScargill) **2-8-8v**[1] MFenton(2) (spd over 5f: wknd qckly)....3½ **11** 12/1 27 —
**Bold Motion** (CMurray) **2-8-8** MTebbutt(5) (w'like: dwlt: pushed along most of wy: a bhd) ....1½ **12** 8/1[3] 23 —
(SP 124.5%) **12 Rn**

**1m 26.53** (1.53) CSF £118.10 TOTE £12.90: £2.80 £2.70 £3.80 (£184.30) Trio £566.40 OWNER Mr P. Carter (LAMBOURN) BRED Miss Juliet Reed
Sld TStafford 11,000gns

**1519 Buzzby** is not very big but certainly appreciated this step up in trip and won in useful style. (9/1)
**2382 Our Kevin** got very warm beforehand, but still ran a useful race and, although well held in the final furlong, he kept staying on. (14/1: 8/1-16/1)
**2512 Silca's My Key (IRE)** was off the bit a long way out but all he does is stay and he kept galloping all the way to the line. (12/1: op 8/1)
**1904 Fan of Vent-Axia**, without the blinkers this time, had every chance until things proved too tough in the final furlong. (33/1)
**2406* Leitrim Lodge (IRE)** was never happy. Although making some ground two furlongs out, she was always tending to hang left and was later officially reported to be lame. (2/1)
**2254 Spondulicks (IRE)** took an age to get into his stride and although finishing well, it was always too late. Some headgear might help sharpen him up. (13/2)
**2374 Broughtons Error** still looked as though this was needed and just when he began to get into the race, he ran into a dead-end. He might well have been in the places but for this, and he looks one to keep in mind. (9/1: 11/2-10/1)
**1103 Grovefair Flyer (IRE)** (8/1: 5/1-9/1)
**Bold Motion** (8/1: 5/1-12/1)

## 2607 TNT INTERNATIONAL AVIATION JULY STKS (Gp 3) (2-Y.O C & G) (Class A)

2-35 (2-36) **6f (July)** £16,272.00 (£6,048.00: £2,924.00: £1,220.00: £510.00: £226.00) Stalls: Low GOING minus 0.48 sec per fur (F)

SP RR SF

2295* **Rich Ground** (JDBethell) **2-8-10** JReid(7) (hdwy over 2f out: r.o u.p to ld nr fin)....— **1** 40/1 104? 54
2243* **Juwwi** (MajorWRHern) **2-8-10** WCarson(4) (lw: hmpd s: outpcd & bhd tl gd hdwy 2f out: r.o wl towards fin) ..hd **2** 5/1[3] 104? 54
1694[2] **Air Express (IRE)** (CEBrittain) **2-8-10** BDoyle(5) (hmpd s: hdwy over 2f out: led ins fnl f: hung lft: no ex nr fin) ....hd **3** 25/1 104? 54
2057* **Close Relative (IRE)** (RCharlton) **2-8-10** PatEddery(6) (lw: s.i.s: hdwy u.p 2f out: nvr able to chal)....2½ **4** 8/1 97 47
2470a[2] **Check The Band (USA)** (APO'Brien,Ireland) **2-8-10** CRoche(2) (gd srt: lw: w ldrs: led over 2f out tl ins fnl f: btn whn hmpd towards fin) ....s.h **5** 3/1[2] 64 47
1694* **Quest Express** (MBell) **2-8-10** MFenton(3) (trckd ldrs: effrt 2f out: sn outpcd: styd on towards fin) ....1 **6** 7/1 94 44
2040[4] **Hula Prince (IRE)** (MJohnston) **2-8-10** JWeaver(9) (slt ld tl hdd over 2f out: wknd over 1f out)....1 **7** 7/1 91 41
2040[3] **Deadly Dudley (IRE)** (RHannon) **2-8-13** MJKinane(8) (b: b.hind: trckd ldrs: rdn 2f out: sn btn) ....hd **8** 11/4[1] 94 44
*2083** **Jupiter (IRE)** (GCBravery) **2-8-10** TQuinn(1) (w ldrs tl wknd qckly wl over 2f out)....28 **9** 20/1 16 —
(SP 115.5%) **9 Rn**

**1m 12.04** (0.04) CSF £208.26 TOTE £51.30: £7.00 £1.50 £4.40 (£123.90) Trio £173.20 OWNER Mrs J. E. Vickers (MIDDLEHAM) BRED C. J. Hill

**2295* Rich Ground** is obviously improving fast, and given some strong assistance, he produced a terrific run in the final furlong to snatch it near the line. (40/1)
**2243* Juwwi** got messed about early on and then picked up in tremendous style from the two furlong marker but the effort was just too late. He has bags of ability when things go his way. (5/1: 7/2-11/2)
**1694 Air Express (IRE)**, stepping up in class, improved a good bit from his debut, but was inclined to hang left under pressure in the closing stages and was just touched off. (25/1)
**2057* Close Relative (IRE)**, last away, took a long time to find his stride and finished as though further is a must. (8/1)
**2470a Check The Band (USA)** was always up with the strong pace and this found him out in the closing stages. His being hampered made no difference. (3/1: op 2/1)
**1694* Quest Express** looked to be going very well when tracking the leaders, but then got outpaced two furlongs out, and, although picking up at the finish, could never get into it and looks likely to appreciate further. (7/1)
**2040 Hula Prince (IRE)** was always being taken on in the lead, but had galloped himself into the ground approaching the last furlong. (7/1: 5/1-15/2)
**2040 Deadly Dudley (IRE)** has lost his edge for the time being and, once off the bit two furlongs out, soon cried enough. (11/4)

## 2608 INFLITE ENGINEERING DUKE OF CAMBRIDGE H'CAP (0-105) (3-Y.O) (Class B)

3-10 (3-11) **1m 2f (July)** £20,875.00 (£6,250.00: £3,000.00: £1,375.00) Stalls: High GOING minus 0.48 sec per fur (F)

SP RR SF

2318[3] **Freedom Flame (78)** (MJohnston) **3-8-5** MRoberts(12) (cl up: rdn to ld over 2f out: r.o wl) ....— **1** 9/1 87 54
2001* **Al Shafa (94)** (JLDunlop) **3-9-7** KDarley(10) (bhd: effrt & nt clr run 2f out: gd hdwy 1f out: hung lft: r.o) ....1 **2** 14/1 101 68
947[2] **Frezeliere (87)** (JLDunlop) **3-9-0** JReid(15) (lw: chsd ldrs: ev ch 2f out: nt qckn ins fnl f) ....2 **3** 14/1 91 58
1857* **Charlotte Corday (85)** (GWragg) **3-8-12** PRobinson(8) (lw: hdwy over 3f out: ch 2f out: rdn & nt qckn)....hd **4** 4/1[1] 89 56
2041[21] **Henry Island (IRE) (90)** (GWragg) **3-8-10**(7) GMilligan(13) (chsd ldrs: effrt over 3f out: btn appr fnl f) ....½ **5** 33/1 93 60
1771[8] **Freequent (92)** (LMCumani) **3-9-5** JWeaver(11) (chsd ldrs: effrt over 3f out: one pce fnl 2f)....1¼ **6** 15/2[3] 93 60
2294* **Hamlet (IRE) (83)** (MBell) **3-8-10** MFenton(3) (hld up & bhd: gd hdwy & ch 2f out: wknd 1f out) ....1¾ **7** 11/1 81 48
2074[9] **Male-Ana-Mou (IRE) (87)** (DRCElsworth) **3-9-0** TQuinn(1) (lw: hdwy 4f out: ch 2f out: btn whn sltly hmpd ins fnl f) ....½ **8** 8/1 85 52
1771[3] **Vola Via (USA) (85)** (IABalding) **3-8-7**(5) MartinDwyer(9) (in tch: rdn over 3f out: no imp) ....2 **9** 14/1 79 46
1771[5] **Burnt Offering (73)** (CEBrittain) **3-7-11**(3) MHenry(14) (b.off hind: rdn 5f out: nvr nr ldrs) ....½ **10** 16/1 67 34
2074[11] **Gold Disc (USA) (90)** (BWHills) **3-9-3** PatEddery(5) (swtg: hld up & bhd: hdwy 4f out: rdn & btn over 1f out)..¾ **11** 12/1 82 49
1955[2] **Daunting Destiny (BEL) (78)** (RHannon) **3-8-2**(3)ow3 DaneO'Neill(4) (chsd ldrs tl wknd fnl 2f) ....1 **12** 14/1 69 33

| | | | | SP | RR | SF |
|---|---|---|---|---|---|---|
| 2333* | **Balladur (USA) (86)** (HRACecil) **3-8-13** WRyan(6) (plld hrd: led tl hdd & wknd qckly over 2f out) | 9 | **13** | $11/2^{2}$ | 62 | 29 |
| | | | | (SP 119.8%) | **13 Rn** | |

**2m 4.57** (-0.43) CSF £114.44 CT £1,601.73 TOTE £7.70: £2.40 £4.40 £6.20 (£52.20) Trio £291.50 OWNER Sheikh Mohammed (MIDDLEHAM) BRED Sheikh Mohammed bin Rashid al Maktoum

**2318 Freedom Flame** went freely to post but settled well in the race and obviously benefited no end from her pipe opener last time. She got first run on the runner-up and was never going to stop. (9/1)

**2001* Al Shafa** seemingly has to come from behind and in doing this, found trouble on this occasion. When he finally got through, the winner had flown. (14/1)

**947 Frezeliere** has not been out for two months but was always in a good position here, but when the pressure was really on in the last two furlongs, she was never then finding enough. (14/1)

**1857* Charlotte Corday**, who got very warm beforehand, was stepping up in trip and had her chance two furlongs out, but was never good enough to take it. (4/1)

**1470* Henry Island (IRE)**, trying a longer trip, looks high enough in the handicap, and seemed a big danger until running out of petrol approaching the last furlong. (33/1)

**1771 Freequent** was always in a good enough position, but he never seemed to fire when ridden, and at the moment it's proving a bit of a mystery as to what trip and going he really wants. (15/2)

**2294* Hamlet (IRE)** produced a useful looking run to have a chance two furlongs out, but, soon under pressure, quickly cried enough. (11/1)

**1711* Male-Ana-Mou (IRE)**, dropping back in trip, was already found out when being squeezed for room inside the last furlong. (8/1)

**1666* Gold Disc (USA)** (12/1: 8/1-14/1)

## 2609 FALMOUTH STKS (Gp 2) (3-Y.O+ F & M) (Class A)

3-40 (3-43) **1m (July)** £34,358.00 (£12,722.00: £6,111.00: £2,505.00: £1,002.50: £401.50) Stalls: Low GOING minus 0.48 sec per fur (F)

| | | | | SP | RR | SF |
|---|---|---|---|---|---|---|
| 1758a* | **Sensation** (MmeCHead,France) **3-8-6** MJKinane(7) (lw: trckd ldrs: led over 2f out: rdn & r.o wl) | — | **1** | $10/11^{1}$ | 112+ | 47 |
| $2052^{4}$ | **Ta Rib (USA) (113)** (EALDunlop) **3-8-12** WCarson(5) (prom: effrt over 2f out: kpt on wl: nt pce of wnr) | 1¾ | **2** | $15/2^{3}$ | 115 | 50 |
| $2053^{4}$ | **Donna Viola (97)** (CFWall) **4-9-1** WWoods(4) (hld up & bhd: effrt over 2f out: r.o wl fnl f: nrst fin) | 1½ | **3** | 14/1 | 106 | 50 |
| 2142* | **Dawna (90)** (HRACecil) **3-8-6** PatEddery(2) (a chsng ldrs: rdn 3f out: one pce appr fnl f) | nk | **4** | $5/1^{2}$ | 105 | 40 |
| $1582a^{2}$ | **Myself (111)** (PWChapple-Hyam) **4-9-1** DHarrison(6) (b: hld up: rdn 3f out: styd on fnl f) | hd | **5** | 12/1 | 105 | 49 |
| 1899* | **Sardonic** (HRACecil) **3-8-6** WRyan(3) (lw: led: edgd rt fr ½-wy: hdd & wknd over 2f out) | 1¼ | **6** | 12/1 | 102 | 37 |
| $1629^{6}$ | **Brief Glimpse (IRE) (102)** (MajorDNChappell) **4-9-1** BThomson(1) (hld up: hdwy to chse ldrs over 2f out: rdn & btn 1f out) | 1¾ | **7** | 40/1 | 99 | 43 |
| $1567a^{9}$ | **Tossup (USA)** (JGBurns,Ireland) **3-8-6** JReid(8) (gd srt: neat: in tch: rdn 3f out: btn wl over 1f out) | 1 | **8** | 20/1 | 97 | 32 |
| $1769^{8}$ | **Honest Guest (IRE) (110)** (MHTompkins) **3-8-6v¹** PRobinson(9) (lw: plld hrd: effrt 3f out: btn over 2f out) | nk | **9** | 14/1 | 96 | 31 |
| | | | | (SP 116.7%) | **9 Rn** | |

**1m 37.53** (0.33) CSF £8.34 TOTE £1.90: £1.30 £2.00 £3.10 (£5.10) Trio £30.80 OWNER Sheikh Mohammed (CHANTILLY) BRED Sheikh Mohammed

WEIGHT FOR AGE 3yo-9lb

**1758a* Sensation** goes on any ground, likes to be up with the pace, has a turn of foot and should stay further. She is going to take a lot of beating. (10/11: tchd Evens)

**2052 Ta Rib (USA)** again got herself worked up beforehand, but still ran a good race only to find the winner too good. (15/2: 5/1-8/1)

**2053 Donna Viola** likes to come from behind but, on this occasion, the pace really hotted up from halfway, and, despite finishing really well, she always had too much on. (14/1)

**2142* Dawna**, stepped up in class, ran a decent race but her limitations were exposed in the last couple of furlongs. (5/1)

**1582a Myself**, having her fourth run at this trip, was staying on after being held up and does seem better over seven. (12/1)

**1899* Sardonic**, dropping back in trip, tried to make her stamina tell, but when ridden, she hung right from halfway and was well-outpointed in the final two furlongs. (12/1)

**1629 Brief Glimpse (IRE)** flattered for a moment two furlongs out but once pressure was applied, she soon gave up. (40/1)

**1769 Honest Guest (IRE)** pulled far too hard in the first time visor. (14/1)

## 2610 MORE O'FERRALL PLC MAIDEN STKS (3-Y.O) (Class D)

4-15 (4-16) **1m 2f (July)** £5,162.50 (£1,540.00: £735.00: £332.50) Stalls: High GOING minus 0.48 sec per fur (F)

| | | | | SP | RR | SF |
|---|---|---|---|---|---|---|
| $2318^{5}$ | **Greenstead (USA)** (JHMGosden) **3-9-0** JCarroll(3) (hld up: hdwy 3f out: rdn to ld ins fnl f: r.o wl) | — | **1** | 16/1 | 85 | 56 |
| | **Lady Joshua (IRE)** (JLDunlop) **3-8-9** WCarson(8) (lw: prom: rdn over 3f out: kpt on strly fnl f) | 2½ | **2** | $5/1^{3}$ | 76 | 47 |
| $2135^{3}$ | **Radiant Star (83)** (GWragg) **3-9-0** MJKinane(13) (chsd ldrs: rdn to ld 1f out: sn hdd & no ex) | nk | **3** | $7/2^{1}$ | 81 | 52 |
| $1189^{2}$ | **Sunset Wells (USA)** (DRLoder) **3-8-9** PatEddery(11) (chsd ldrs tl led wl over 3f out: hdd 1f out: wknd) | 1¼ | **4** | $4/1^{2}$ | 74 | 45 |
| | **Liefling (USA)** (JHMGosden) **3-8-9** BThomson(4) (hdwy & nt clr run 3f out: kpt on wl fnl 2f) | nk | **5** | 33/1 | 73+ | 44 |
| $892^{5}$ | **Moon Mischief** (LadyHerries) **3-9-0** JReid(10) (bkwd: a in tch: effrt over 2f out: hung lft & one pce) | 2 | **6** | $7/2^{1}$ | 75 | 46 |
| | **Mourne Mountains** (HCandy) **3-9-0** CRutter(9) (h.d.w: bhd: hdwy u.p 3f out: nvr rchd ldrs) | 1¼ | **7** | 50/1 | 73 | 44 |
| $2198^{4}$ | **Polar Champ (75)** (SPCWoods) **3-9-0** WWoods(2) (chsd ldrs: rdn over 4f out: no imp fnl 2f) | hd | **8** | 16/1 | 73 | 44 |
| $1614^{17}$ | **Love And Kisses** (CACyzer) **3-8-9** WJO'Connor(7) (bhd: rdn over 3f out: n.d) | 2 | **9** | 50/1 | 65 | 36 |
| | **Trick (IRE)** (LMCumani) **3-8-9** JWeaver(5) (hld up & bhd: sme hdwy u.p 3f out: n.d) | hd | **10** | 12/1 | 64 | 35 |
| $1530^{11}$ | **Filly Mignonne (IRE)** (BWHills) **3-8-9** RHills(12) (in tch: rdn 4f out: hung lft 2f out: sn wknd) | 5 | **11** | 33/1 | 56 | 27 |
| $2208^{6}$ | **Square Mile Miss (IRE)** (PHowling) **3-8-9** MRoberts(1) (led tl hdd & wknd wl over 3f out) | 12 | **12** | 50/1 | 37 | 8 |
| | **What A Fuss** (BHanbury) **3-9-0** WRyan(6) (w'like: hld up & bhd: t.o fnl 3f) | 22 | **13** | 20/1 | 7 | — |
| | | | | (SP 117.1%) | **13 Rn** | |

**2m 5.49** (0.49) CSF £85.88 TOTE £17.70: £3.40 £1.60 £1.70 (£43.30) Trio £38.40 OWNER Sheikh Mohammed (NEWMARKET) BRED Darley Stud Management Inc

**2318 Greenstead (USA)**, all the better for his educational last time out, won this well and should progress. (16/1)

**Lady Joshua (IRE)** was short of toe at a vital stage but did stay on particularly well to suggest that, over further, she will improve. (5/1)

**2135 Radiant Star** was always in the thick of things but was lacking in speed in the final furlong. (7/2)

**1189 Sunset Wells (USA)** tried to make her stamina tell but, in the end, she was well tapped for toe in the last furlong and a half. (4/1: 3/1-9/2)

**Liefling (USA)** put in a most eye-catching run and is one to watch from now on. (33/1)

**892 Moon Mischief** moved down well but may have needed this and failed to quicken in the final two furlongs. (7/2)

**Mourne Mountains** stayed on in the last half-mile. With experience and over further, better will probably be seen. (50/1)

**Trick (IRE)** needed this experience but looks sure to come on for it. (12/1: op 6/1)

## 2611 EQUITY FINANCIAL COLLECTIONS MAIDEN STKS (2-Y.O F) (Class D)

4-45 (4-49) **6f (July)** £5,708.50 (£1,708.00: £819.00: £374.50) Stalls: Low GOING minus 0.48 sec per fur (F)

| | | | | SP | RR | SF |
|---|---|---|---|---|---|---|
| | **Imroz (USA)** (HRACecil) **2-8-11** PatEddery(9) (gd srt: neat: w ldr: led 1f out: qcknd comf) | — | 1 | 2/1 $^{1}$ | 84 | 52 |
| $2051^{8}$ | **Rihan (USA)** (SbinSuroor) **2-8-11** RHills(5) (led tl hdd 1f out: kpt on) | 2½ | 2 | 11/2 $^{2}$ | 77 | 45 |
| | **Quintellina** (LMCumani) **2-8-11** KDarley(10) (w'like: unf: prom: styd on wl fnl f: promising) | 1½ | 3 | 14/1 | 73 | 41 |
| | **Indihash (USA)** (RWArmstrong) **2-8-11** WCarson(6) (w'like: a chsng ldrs: effrt 2f out: nt qckn fnl f) | hd | 4 | 11/2 $^{2}$ | 73 | 41 |
| $1513^{6}$ | **Senorita Matilda (USA)** (RHannon) **2-8-8**(3) DaneO'Neill(15) (lw: chsd ldrs: effrt 2f out: nt qckn ins fnl f) | 1¼ | 5 | 25/1 | 70 | 38 |
| | **Literary** (JHMGosden) **2-8-11** JCarroll(4) (w'like: scope: lw: s.s: stdy hdwy 2f out: r.o towards fin) | 4 | 6 | 14/1 | 59 | 27 |
| | **Blue Lamp (USA)** (MAJarvis) **2-8-8**(3) FLynch(12) (neat: chsd ldrs tl rdn & wknd appr fnl f) | nk | 7 | 10/1 | 58 | 26 |
| | **Right Tune** (BHanbury) **2-8-11** WRyan(3) (hld up: hdwy 2f out: nvr nr to chal) | 2½ | 8 | 16/1 | 52 | 20 |
| | **Etoile (FR)** (PWChapple-Hyam) **2-8-11** JReid(13) (leggy: scope: w ldrs tl wknd fnl 2f) | hd | 9 | 8/1 $^{3}$ | 51 | 19 |
| $2147^{9}$ | **French Mist** (CEBrittain) **2-8-11** BDoyle(7) (in tch: drvn along most of wy: no imp) | hd | 10 | 33/1 | 51 | 19 |
| | **Julietta Mia (USA)** (BWHills) **2-8-11** BThomson(17) (lt-f: unf: nvr wnt pce) | 1¼ | 11 | 33/1 | 48 | 16 |
| | **Sugar Plum** (RHannon) **2-8-11** RHughes(1) (w'like: s.s: nvr nrr) | 1¾ | 12 | 40/1 | 43 | 11 |
| | **West River (USA)** (PAKelleway) **2-8-11** JWeaver(2) (w'like: n.d) | ¾ | 13 | 40/1 | 41 | 9 |
| | **Charm The Stars** (MHTompkins) **2-8-11** PRobinson(8) (w'like: bit bkwd: s.i.s: a bhd) | 1½ | 14 | 66/1 | 37 | 5 |
| | **Breffni (IRE)** (CNAllen) **2-8-11** TGMcLaughlin(14) (leggy: scope: s.i.s: a bhd) | 1½ | 15 | 66/1 | 33 | 1 |
| | **Sally Green (IRE)** (CFWall) **2-8-11** WWoods(16) (cmpt: bkwd: sn pushed along: bhd fr ½-wy) | hd | 16 | 33/1 | 33 | 1 |
| | **Ms Ziman** (MBell) **2-8-11** MFenton(11) (dwlt: a bhd) | 1¼ | 17 | 33/1 | 30 | — |
| | | | | (SP 127.0%) | **17 Rn** | |

**1m 12.19** (0.19) CSF £13.47 TOTE £2.90: £1.70 £1.80 £5.90 (£5.90) Trio £62.50 OWNER Mr K. Abdulla (NEWMARKET) BRED Juddmonte Farms

**Imroz (USA)** looks a useful filly, winning this in style, but she did have the edge on fitness over several of her rivals, and the third especially might give her a race once they try further. (2/1: op 5/4)
**Rihan (USA)** benefited from her Ascot experience but she found the winner here too classy in the final furlong. She could do with having her sights lowered and having a confidence booster. (11/2: 3/1-6/1)
**Quintellina** looks one to get excited about and was learning fast as the race progressed. She should be followed from now on. (14/1: 7/1-16/1)
**Indihash (USA)** ran a useful first race but just failed to pick up in the final furlong. Improvement looks likely. (11/2)
**1513 Senorita Matilda (USA)** did not impress with her action going to post but she ran reasonably and should improve with time. (25/1)
**Literary** fell out of the stalls but then showed plenty, without getting knocked about. She looks one to watch from now on. (14/1: 10/1-16/1)
**Blue Lamp (USA)** showed plenty of toe until blowing up in the last couple of furlongs. (10/1: 12/1-8/1)
**Right Tune** needed this but was not given a hard time. Plenty of improvement should be forthcoming. (16/1)
**Etoile (FR)** should have benefited a good deal from the outing. (8/1: op 3/1)

## 2612 REG DAY MEMORIAL H'CAP (0-95) (3-Y.O+) (Class C)

5-20 (5-21) **2m 24y (July)** £6,108.00 (£1,824.00: £872.00: £396.00) Stalls: High GOING minus 0.48 sec per fur (F)

| | | | | SP | RR | SF |
|---|---|---|---|---|---|---|
| $2054^{9}$ | **Benatom (USA) (85)** (HRACecil) **3-8-7** PatEddery(10) (trckd ldrs: rdn to ld over 1f out: styd on strly) | — | 1 | 6/1 $^{3}$ | 96 | 45 |
| $2042^{14}$ | **Great Easeby (IRE) (59)** (WStorey) **6-8-0** JFanning(8) (bhd: hdwy over 4f out: rdn to chal ins fnl f: no ex towards fin) | 1¼ | 2 | 10/1 | 69 | 37 |
| 2042* | **Southern Power (IRE) (83)** (RAkehurst) **5-9-10** TQuinn(12) (lw: b.nr hind: trckd ldrs: effrt 3f out: n.m.r: styd on wl towards fin) | 1 | 3 | 4/1 $^{1}$ | 92 | 60 |
| $2330^{8}$ | **Invest Wisely (82)** (JMPEustace) **4-9-9** JTate(7) (a cl up: chal 4f out: one pce appr fnl f) | 1½ | 4 | 14/1 | 89 | 57 |
| $1854^{2}$ | **Old Irish (85)** (LMCumani) **3-8-7** MJKinane(9) (stdy hdwy ½-wy: sn prom: effrt & hung lft 2f out: one pce) | nk | 5 | 5/1 $^{2}$ | 92 | 41 |
| $2165^{2}$ | **Uncle Doug (55)** (MrsMReveley) **5-7-10** JLowe(4) (hld up & bhd: smooth hdwy 4f out: rdn & bmpd 2f out: btn 1f out) | 1¼ | 6 | 12/1 | 61 | 29 |
| 2430* | **Lalindi (IRE) (76)** (DRCElsworth) **5-9-3b** 4x RHughes(5) (led tl hdd & wknd over 1f out) | 3½ | 7 | 8/1 | 78 | 46 |
| $2330^{5}$ | **Noufari (FR) (80)** (RHollinshead) **5-9-4**(3) FLynch(6) (lw: hld up & bhd: effrt 4f out: nvr rchd ldrs) | ¾ | 8 | 12/1 | 82 | 50 |
| $2331^{2}$ | **Bardon Hill Boy (IRE) (87)** (BHanbury) **4-9-7**(7) AimeeCook(1) (trckd ldrs: chal over 3f out: wknd appr fnl f) | ¾ | 9 | 14/1 | 88 | 56 |
| 2140* | **Nuzu (IRE) (79)** (BWHills) **3-8-1** WCarson(3) (in tch: drvn along 4f out: btn over 2f out) | 7 | 10 | 13/2 | 73 | 22 |
| *$2304^{2}$* | **Princely Gait (68)** (MJPolglase) **5-8-9** WHollick(11) (b: a bhd) | 7 | 11 | 33/1 | 55 | 23 |
| | | | | (SP 116.1%) | **11 Rn** | |

**3m 27.35** (1.85) CSF £57.68 CT £245.18 TOTE £8.80: £2.90 £3.30 £1.90 (£41.80) Trio £104.10 OWNER Mr T. F. Harris (NEWMARKET) BRED J. S. Meredith

LONG HANDICAP Uncle Doug 7-9
WEIGHT FOR AGE 3yo-19lb

**1407 Benatom (USA)** proved he stays here and needed all his courage to hold on in the final furlong. (6/1)
**1343 Great Easeby (IRE)**, after a disappointing effort last time, came back to form here but found the winner too tough. (10/1)
**2042* Southern Power (IRE)** ran a sound race, but was short of toe and pace at a vital stage, and that made all the difference. (4/1)
**1976 Invest Wisely** seems to be coming right but is one-paced and needs plenty of use made of him. (14/1)
**1854 Old Irish** showed he is still a character when ridden two furlongs out but, to his credit, he did keep on well. (5/1)
**2165 Uncle Doug** travelled well for much of the trip but was already off the bit when bumped two furlongs out, and soon cried enough. (12/1)
**2331 Bardon Hill Boy (IRE)** found this step up in trip too much and stopped approaching the final furlong. (14/1)
**2140* Nuzu (IRE)** disappointingly dropped tamely away in the final two furlongs. (13/2)

T/Jkpt: Not won; £37,187.16 to Newmarket 11/7/96. T/Plpt: £723.20 (53.71 Tckts). T/Qdpt: £18.90 (165.69 Tckts). AA/Dk

# 2525-CHEPSTOW (L-H) (Good to firm, Firm patches)

## Thursday July 11th

WEATHER: fine WIND: almost nil

## 2613 EVENING APPRENTICE H'CAP (0-70) (3-Y.O+) (Class G)

6-30 (6-31) **1m 4f 23y** £2,262.00 (£632.00: £306.00) Stalls: Low GOING minus 0.44 sec per fur (F)

| | | | | SP | RR | SF |
|---|---|---|---|---|---|---|
| $1063^{4}$ | **The Lad (44)** (LMontagueHall) **7-8-4**(3) DDenby(6) (hld up & bhd: hdwy over 4f out: led over 3f out: clr over 2f out: r.o wl) | — | 1 | 7/1 $^{3}$ | 58 | 42 |

2506$^{4}$ **Victoria's Secret (IRE) (51)** (MRChannon) **4-9-0** AEddery(4) (lw: hld up & bhd: hdwy over 4f out: chsd wnr over 2f out: no imp) ....5 **2** 7/1$^{3}$ 58 42
1900$^{10}$ **Four Weddings (USA) (48)** (MCPipe) **3-7-12b$^{1}$** CMunday(1) (w ldrs: rdn over 4f out: wknd 2f out) ....11 **3** 13/2$^{2}$ 41 12
2378$^{7}$ **Almuhtaram (62)** (MissGayKelleway) **4-9-4**(7) BFord(5) (lw: b: w ldrs tl wknd over 3f out) ....hd **4** 8/1 55 39
2408$^{3}$ **Seven Crowns (USA) (63)** (RHannon) **3-8-6**(7) KSalt(8) (swtg: led over 8f: sn wknd) ....1¾ **5** 7/1$^{3}$ 53 24
2331* **Canton Venture (64)** (SPCWoods) **4-9-8**(5) JMoon(7) (lw: w ldrs tl wknd over 4f out) ....2½ **6** 6/5$^{1}$ 51 35
2342$^{8}$ **Dtoto (64)** (RJBaker) **4-9-10**(3) JWilkinson(2) (lw: sn bhd: t.o fnl 5f) ....dist **7** 50/1 — —
(SP 109.4%) **7 Rn**

**2m 34.6** (2.20) CSF £46.46 CT £277.52 TOTE £6.80: £2.50 £2.90 (£18.40) OWNER Treberth Partnership (EPSOM) BRED W. R. and M. E. Scale
WEIGHT FOR AGE 3yo-13lb
**1063 The Lad** stays well and bided his time while the four leaders cut their own throats. (7/1)
**2506 Victoria's Secret (IRE)**, due to drop 2lb in future handicaps, was another sensibly ridden. (7/1)
**849* Four Weddings (USA)**, switching to blinkers this time, was the last of the leading quartet to crack. (13/2)
**2203 Almuhtaram**, reverting to a mile and a half, was hardly ridden to get the trip. (8/1: op 5/1)
**2408 Seven Crowns (USA)** will need more patient tactics to stay this trip. (7/1)
**2331* Canton Venture** was taken on for the lead by three others and this run is best forgotten. (6/5: Evens-11/8)

## 2614 FLEUR DE LYS MAIDEN STKS (2-Y.O) (Class D)
7-00 (7-02) **5f 16y** £3,348.25 (£1,006.00: £485.50: £225.25) Stalls: High GOING minus 0.44 sec per fur (F)

SP RR SF
2230$^{5}$ **Head Over Heels (IRE)** (JHMGosden) **2-8-9** JCarroll(3) (mde all: qcknd over 1f out: comf) ....— **1** 5/2$^{1}$ 61+ 13
**Bold Tina (IRE)** (RHannon) **2-8-6**(3) DaneO'Neill(7) (lt-f: unf: hld up: hdwy over 1f out: r.o ins fnl f: nt trble wnr) ....1¼ **2** 5/2$^{1}$ 57 9
**Jeffrey Anotherred** (KMcAuliffe) **2-9-0** JFEgan(1) (cmpt: lw: a.p: rdn over 1f out: one pce) ....2½ **3** 20/1 54 6
**Pow Wow** (MRChannon) **2-9-0** RHughes(2) (unf: chsd wnr: rdn & ev ch over 1f out: wknd ins fnl f) ....2 **4** 5/1$^{2}$ 48 —
**Corncrake (IRE)** (BJMeehan) **2-8-9** BDoyle(5) (unf: hld up: no hdwy fnl 2f) ....2 **5** 20/1 37 —
**Jonfy (IRE)** (BWHills) **2-8-9**(5) JDSmith(4) (w'like: s.s: a bhd) ....2½ **6** 13/2$^{3}$ 34 —
**Circle of Magic** (PJMakin) **2-8-9** SSanders(6) (leggy: unf: bit bkwd: s.v.s: a bhd) ....s.h **7** 13/2$^{3}$ 29 —
(SP 110.0%) **7 Rn**

**59.4 secs** (2.40) CSF £8.52 TOTE £2.60: £1.80 £1.60 (£3.70) OWNER Ms Rachel Hood (NEWMARKET) BRED Milton Park Stud Partnership
**2230 Head Over Heels (IRE)** had the advantage of previous experience and put it to good use with the aid of the stands' rail. (5/2: op 11/8)
**Bold Tina (IRE)**, a sparely made filly who is a half-sister to Indian Fly amongst others, looks capable of going one better and should not be inconvenienced by a longer trip. (5/2)
**Jeffrey Anotherred** made a reasonable enough start to his career. (20/1)
**Pow Wow** pressed the front-running winner until fading in the closing stages. (5/1: 5/2-11/2)
**Corncrake (IRE)** was given a nice introduction and will be better for the experience. (20/1)
**Jonfy (IRE)** (13/2: op 4/1)

## 2615 MAPLE LIMITED STKS (0-75) (3-Y.O+) (Class D)
7-30 (7-31) **6f 16y** £3,666.75 (£1,104.00: £534.50: £249.75) Stalls: High GOING minus 0.44 sec per fur (F)

SP RR SF
2228$^{3}$ **La Petite Fusee (72)** (RJO'Sullivan) **5-8-11** RHughes(5) (lw: mde all: drvn out) ....— **1** 7/2$^{1}$ 80 58
2381* **Ansellman (75)** (JBerry) **6-9-6v** JCarroll(7) (chsd wnr: ev ch 1f out: unable qckn) ....¾ **2** 6/1 87 65
1853$^{6}$ **Purple Fling (73)** (LGCottrell) **5-9-0** JQuinn(6) (a.p: unable qckn fnl f) ....1¼ **3** 4/1$^{2}$ 78 56
2200$^{5}$ **Thordis (73)** (PJMakin) **3-8-8** SSanders(8) (bhd: rdn over 3f out: hdwy over 1f out: r.o) ....1¾ **4** 12/1 73 45
*2306*$^{4}$ **Intiaash (IRE) (72)** (DHaydnJones) **4-9-0v** PatEddery(4) (b.off hind: swtg: hld up: hdwy over 2f out: rdn over 1f out: one pce) ....¾ **5** 11/2 71 49
2329$^{9}$ **Thatcherella (73)** (MajorDNChappell) **5-9-0** BThomson(2) (prom tl wknd over 1f out) ....s.h **6** 7/1 71 49
2347$^{3}$ **How's Yer Father (73)** (RJHodges) **10-9-0** BDoyle(1) (hdwy 3f out: wknd 2f out) ....½ **7** 5/1$^{3}$ 70 48
1652$^{7}$ **Smithereens (74)** (PTWalwyn) **3-8-5** DHolland(3) (outpcd: t.o) ....12 **8** 16/1 35 7
(SP 114.6%) **8 Rn**

**1m 9.1** (-0.10) CSF £22.83 TOTE £4.10: £1.30 £1.90 £1.50 (£12.90) OWNER Mr M. T. Bevan (WHITCOMBE) BRED H. Powis
WEIGHT FOR AGE 3yo-6lb
**2228 La Petite Fusee** adopted her usual front-running tactics and held on well under pressure with the help of the stands' rail. (7/2)
**2381* Ansellman**, trying to register his first win over six, does seem to find the minimum his optimum trip. (6/1: op 4/1)
**1853 Purple Fling** could never quite get to grips with the winner, but should now be approaching his peak. (4/1)
**2200 Thordis** is crying out for a longer trip. (12/1)
**2306 Intiaash (IRE)** had the visor on for the first time in a year. (11/2)
**1178* Thatcherella** has won on this ground but her last two wins have been on the soft. (7/1)

## 2616 REGAL RATED STKS H'CAP (0-95) (3-Y.O) (Class C)
8-00 (8-01) **1m 4f 23y** £6,915.80 (£2,086.40: £1,013.20: £476.60) Stalls: Low GOING minus 0.44 sec per fur (F)

SP RR SF
2074$^{5}$ **Nador (91)** (DRLoder) **3-9-7** RHughes(4) (lw: hld up & bhd: stdy hdwy on bit over 1f out: rdn to ld last stride) ....— **1** 9/4$^{2}$ 100 46
2006$^{3}$ **Spillo (87)** (LMCumani) **3-9-3** PatEddery(3) (swtg: chsd ldr: led wl over 1f out: hdd last stride) ....hd **2** 2/1$^{1}$ 96 42
1798$^{6}$ **Prince Kinsky (77)** (LordHuntingdon) **3-8-7** DHarrison(5) (swtg: a.p: hrd rdn over 2f out: ev ch ins fnl f: r.o) ..nk **3** 9/1 86 32
1900$^{4}$ **Gumair (USA) (77)** (RHannon) **3-8-4**(3) DaneO'Neill(2) (led over 10f: one pce fnl f) ....3½ **4** 15/2 81 27
1619$^{3}$ **Forza Figlio (87)** (MissGayKelleway) **3-9-3** JReid(1) (b.hind: lw: hld up: rdn over 3f out: hdwy on ins 2f out: wknd over 1f out) ....3 **5** 3/1$^{3}$ 87 33
(SP 110.9%) **5 Rn**

**2m 36.0** (3.60) CSF £6.88 TOTE £2.60: £1.10 £1.70 (£2.60) OWNER Sheikh Mohammed (NEWMARKET) BRED Sheikh Mohammed Bin Rashid Al Maktoum
LONG HANDICAP Gumair (USA) 8-3
**2074 Nador** likes fast ground and was very confidently ridden, but very nearly ended up with egg on his face. Keen under restraint, he may have been better suited by a stronger run race. (9/4)
**2006 Spillo**, back to a mile and a half, only got touched off right on the line. (2/1)
**1798 Prince Kinsky**, dropped 3lb, appreciated this step up in trip. (9/1)

**1900 Gumair (USA)** was not disgraced considering he was 4lb out of the handicap. (15/2)
**1619 Forza Figlio**, who has shown his best form on good ground, did not prove he gets this trip. (3/1)

## 2617 ALVESTON MAIDEN H'CAP (0-70) (3-Y.O+) (Class E)

8-30 (8-35) **7f 16y** £3,343.50 (£1,008.00: £489.00: £229.50) Stalls: High GOING minus 0.44 sec per fur (F)

| | | | | SP | RR | SF |
|---|---|---|---|---|---|---|
| $2235^{3}$ | **White Settler (64)** (RJHodges) **3-9-0** TSprake(15) (gd hdwy stands' side over 1f out: str run to ld last stride) | — | **1** | 9/1 | 73 | 44 |
| $2013^{6}$ | **School Boy (68)** (TJNaughton) **3-9-4** DHolland(17) (led: clr wl over 1f out: ct last stride) | s.h | **2** | 10/1 | 77 | 48 |
| $1613^{11}$ | **Sharp Shuffle (IRE) (65)** (RHannon) **3-8-12**(3) DaneO'Neill(4) (lw: hdwy far side over 1f out: r.o ins fnl f) | 2½ | **3** | 12/1 | 68 | 39 |
| $1649^{3}$ | **Time of Night (USA) (70)** (RGuest) **3-9-1**(5) DGriffiths(13) (hdwy stands' side over 1f out: r.o one pce fnl f) | 3 | **4** | 7/1 2 | 66 | 37 |
| $2197^{15}$ | **Chirico (USA) (68)** (JHMGosden) **3-9-4** PatEddery(16) (lw: prom stands' side: wknd over 1f out) | s.h | **5** | 4/1 1 | 64 | 35 |
| $2123^{5}$ | **Eurobox Boy (59)** (APJarvis) **3-8-9** WJO'Connor(14) (hdwy centre over 1f out: one pce fnl f) | ¾ | **6** | 20/1 | 54 | 25 |
| $2286^{14}$ | **Dantean (38)** (RJO'Sullivan) **4-7-10b** FNorton(8) (prom far side over 5f) | ¾ | **7** | 50/1 | 31 | 10 |
| $549^{9}$ | **Super Hero (38)** (AGNewcombe) **4-7-10** AMackay(1) (nvr trbld ldrs) | ½ | **8** | 8/1 | 30 | 9 |
| $1061^{5}$ | **Kowtow (64)** (MDIUsher) **3-9-0** RStreet(18) (lw: nvr nrr) | 1¾ | **9** | 33/1 | 52 | 23 |
| *$2325^{3}$* | **Prime Partner (46)** (WRMuir) **3-7-10** JQuinn(11) (hdwy centre 2f out: eased whn btn ins fnl f) | hd | **10** | 10/1 | 34 | 5 |
| $2235^{6}$ | **Flying Harold (53)** (MRChannon) **3-8-3** JFEgan(6) (lw: chsd ldr far side: wknd over 1f out) | 3 | **11** | 20/1 | 34 | 5 |
| $2286^{2}$ | **Twice Purple (IRE) (60)** (BJMeehan) **4-9-4b** BDoyle(9) (prom stands' side 5f) | ½ | **12** | 7/1 2 | 40 | 19 |
| $2529^{6}$ | **Amelanchier (62)** (GBBalding) **3-8-12** SSanders(10) (n.d) | 2 | **13** | 9/1 | 37 | 8 |
| *$2158^{6}$* | **Rawi (64)** (MissGayKelleway) **3-9-0b** RHughes(5) (led far side over 5f: wknd qckly) | 1 | **14** | 14/1 | 37 | 8 |
| $2181^{5}$ | **Severn Mill (70)** (JMBradley) **5-10-0** VSlattery(12) (s.s: a bhd) | 5 | **15** | 20/1 | 32 | 11 |
| | **Sandra Dee (IRE) (43)** (EAWheeler) **4-7-10**(5)ow1 ADaly(7) (prom far side 5f) | ½ | **16** | 33/1 | 4 | — |
| $2345^{7}$ | **Pytchley Dawn (40)** (OO'Neill) **6-7-12** NAdams(3) (a bhd) | nk | **17** | 50/1 | — | — |
| $2376^{7}$ | **Persian Butterfly (65)** (ICampbell) **4-9-9** AClark(2) (swtg: a bhd) | 5 | **18** | 15/2 3 | — | — |

(SP 144.5%) **18 Rn**

**1m 21.2** (1.20) CSF £102.15 CT £1,065.51 TOTE £8.10: £2.00 £2.50 £3.00 £2.40 (£31.90) Trio £216.40 OWNER Mr J. Newsome (SOMERTON) BRED Mrs K. Sellers
LONG HANDICAP Dantean 7-3 Prime Partner 7-8
WEIGHT FOR AGE 3yo-8lb
**2235 White Settler** confirmed this as his best distance and surged through for a last gasp win. (9/1)
**2013 School Boy** looked to have this in the satchel but got pipped on the post. (10/1)
**Sharp Shuffle (IRE)** is one to bear in mind when he reverts to a mile. (12/1)
**1649 Time of Night (USA)** has previously given the impression that this drop back from a mile might be the answer. (7/1)
**1797 Chirico (USA)**, reverting back to seven, ran a lot better than last time. (4/1)
**2123 Eurobox Boy**, without the visor this time, was coming back from a mile. (20/1)
**1857 Amelanchier** (9/1: 6/1-10/1)

## 2618 STRAIGHT MILE H'CAP (0-80) (3-Y.O) (Class D)

9-00 (9-01) **1m 14y** £3,712.25 (£1,118.00: £541.50: £253.25) Stalls: High GOING minus 0.44 sec per fur (F)

| | | | | SP | RR | SF |
|---|---|---|---|---|---|---|
| 1692* | **Panata (IRE) (75)** (LMCumani) **3-9-5** PatEddery(2) (mde all: r.o wl) | — | **1** | 8/13 1 | 79 | 51 |
| $2334^{7}$ | **Paint It Black (77)** (RHannon) **3-9-4b1**(3) DaneO'Neill(4) (hld up: hdwy 3f out: ev ch over 1f out: unable qckn ins fnl f) | 1¾ | **2** | 11/2 3 | 78 | 50 |
| $2231^{4}$ | **Finsbury Flyer (IRE) (75)** (RJHodges) **3-9-0**(5) PPMurphy(5) (a.p: one pce fnl 2f) | 3½ | **3** | 7/1 | 69 | 41 |
| $2213^{2}$ | **Power Game (68)** (JBerry) **3-8-12v** JCarroll(1) (chsd wnr tl wknd over 1f out) | ½ | **4** | 3/1 2 | 61 | 33 |

(SP 114.8%) **4 Rn**

**1m 33.7** (1.20) CSF £4.40 TOTE £1.60: (£3.60) OWNER Mrs Angie Silver (NEWMARKET) BRED Dr J. J. Ryan
**1692* Panata (IRE)** dictated matters against the stands' rails and scored readily enough in the end. (8/13)
**917 Paint It Black**, tried in blinkers, had come down 8lb after being highly tried on his three previous runs this season. (11/2: 7/2-6/1)
**2231 Finsbury Flyer (IRE)** was trying an extra furlong. (7/1)
**2213 Power Game** might be more effective over shorter distances. (3/1)

T/Plpt: £73.30 (195.48 Tckts). T/Qdpt: £5.80 (221.09 Tckts). KH

# 2606-NEWMARKET (R-H) (Good to firm)

## Thursday July 11th

WEATHER: sunny periods WIND: slt bhd

## 2619 WEATHERBYS SUPERLATIVE STKS (Listed) (2-Y.O) (Class A)

2-05 (2-05) **7f (July)** £8,792.00 (£3,248.00: £1,554.00: £630.00: £245.00: £91.00) Stalls: Low GOING: minus 0.51 sec per fur (F)

| | | | | SP | RR | SF |
|---|---|---|---|---|---|---|
| $1419^{3}$ | **Recondite (IRE)** (MRChannon) **2-9-0** KDarley(6) (cl up: led 3f out: rdn & hld on wl fnl f) | — | **1** | 14/1 | 92 | 37 |
| 2184* | **Boojum** (BWHills) **2-8-9** PatEddery(3) (hld up: hdwy 2f out: chal ins fnl f: rdn & nt qckn) | 1¼ | **2** | 5/1 2 | 84 | 29 |
| 1871* | **Simple Logic** (AGFoster) **2-8-6** TSprake(2) (b.hind: plld hrd: cl up: rdn 3f out: one pce fnl 2f) | 6 | **3** | 7/1 | 67 | 12 |
| *2370** | **Shimazu (IRE)** (JHMGosden) **2-9-0** MJKinane(5) (lw: stdd s: hdwy ½-wy: rdn & btn 2f out) | 3 | **4** | 11/2 3 | 69 | 14 |
| 2132* | **Makhbar** (RWArmstrong) **2-9-0** WCarson(1) (lw: led tl hdd 3f out: wknd fnl 2f) | 1¾ | **5** | Evens 1 | 65 | 10 |
| $2132^{3}$ | **Millroy (USA)** (PAKelleway) **2-8-11** JWeaver(4) (lw: cl up over 3f: wknd qckly) | 5 | **6** | 20/1 | 50 | — |

(SP 106.0%) **6 Rn**

**1m 26.64** (1.64) CSF £68.13 TOTE £16.10: £3.30 £2.20 (£32.80) OWNER Mr P. D. Savill (UPPER LAMBOURN) BRED P. D. Savill
**1419 Recondite (IRE)** enjoyed this longer trip and, although idling in front, he found all that was required when challenged. (14/1: 10/1-16/1)
**2184* Boojum**, particularly warm beforehand, was patiently ridden and worked hard to get to the winner but was well held by the finish. (5/1: 3/1-11/2)
**1871* Simple Logic** got quite warm beforehand and then raced too freely for her own good. (7/1)
**2370* Shimazu (IRE)**, dropped out early on, tried to improve from halfway but was always finding this company too hot. (11/2: 7/2-6/1)
**2132* Makhbar** took the eye in the paddock and on the way down but, in the race, went far too freely and packed in once headed in the final three furlongs. (Evens)
**2132 Millroy (USA)** ran poorly and dropped tamely away from the halfway point. (20/1)

## 2620 BAHRAIN TROPHY STKS (Listed) (3-Y.O) (Class A)

2-35 (2-35) **1m 6f 175y (July)** £10,577.40 (£3,906.60: £1,868.30: £756.50: £293.25: £107.95) Stalls: High GOING: minus 0.51 sec per fur (F)

| | | | | SP | RR | SF |
|---|---|---|---|---|---|---|
| 2054[3] | **Persian Punch (IRE) (96)** (DRCElsworth) **3-8-10** TQuinn(6) (hld up: hdwy to jn ldrs over 3f out: led ins fnl f: styd on wl) | — | **1** | 3/1[2] | 112 | 66 |
| 2054[2] | **Athenry (97)** (JPearce) **3-8-10** GBardwell(2) (lw: chsd ldrs: led 4f out: hrd rdn appr fnl f: sn hdd: kpt on) | 1¼ | **2** | 3/1[2] | 111 | 65 |
| 2054[8] | **Arnhem (85)** (CEBrittain) **3-8-10** BDoyle(3) (prom tl outpcd 4f out: kpt on appr fnl f) | 9 | **3** | 20/1 | 101 | 55 |
| 2054[6] | **Valedictory (92)** (HRACecil) **3-8-10** PatEddery(5) (b: hld up: effrt 4f out: sn rdn: no imp fnl 2f) | 5 | **4** | 11/4[1] | 96 | 50 |
| 1990[2] | **Mattawan** (MJohnston) **3-8-10** JWeaver(1) (lw: disp ld tl hdd 10f out: cl up tl wknd 4f out) | 2 | **5** | 5/1[3] | 93 | 47 |
| 2227[3] | **Flyfisher (IRE) (103)** (GLewis) **3-8-10** MJKinane(4) (swtg: disp ld tl led 10f out: hdd 4f out: sn wknd) | 5 | **6** | 10/1 | 88 | 42 |
| | | | | (SP 107.2%) | | **6 Rn** |

**3m 6.32** (-2.18) CSF £11.15 TOTE £3.70: £1.80 £1.90 (£3.90) OWNER Mr J. C. Smith (WHITCOMBE) BRED Adstock Manor Stud

**2054 Persian Punch (IRE)** is a real stayer and was well suited by the strong pace and, once he got his head in front inside the final furlong, he just kept powering on. (3/1)

**2054 Athenry,** because of his style of running, never has an easy race but is as game as they come and also gives the impression that easier ground might well suit. (3/1)

**1153* Arnhem** looked slow once the pace was on half a mile out but he did make a little late headway, albeit in vain. (20/1)

**1631* Valedictory,** patiently ridden this time, looked to be going well until coming off the bit over three furlongs out, from which point his response was most disappointing. (11/4)

**1990 Mattawan** ran poorly, dropping tamely away when the race began in earnest in the final half mile. (5/1)

**2227 Flyfisher (IRE),** trying a longer trip, sweated up and raced far too freely out in front, and then stopped in the last four furlongs. (10/1: 8/1-12/1)

## 2621 HARE PARK H'CAP (0-95) (3-Y.O) (Class C)

3-05 (3-07) **1m (July)** £8,415.00 (£2,520.00: £1,210.00: £555.00) Stalls: Low GOING: minus 0.51 sec per fur (F)

| | | | | SP | RR | SF |
|---|---|---|---|---|---|---|
| 1701* | **Fahim (83)** (ACStewart) **3-8-9** WCarson(3) (hld up far side: qcknd to ld wl over 1f out: r.o) | — | **1** | 2/1[1] | 98+ | 46 |
| 2294[3] | **Winston (70)** (JDBethell) **3-7-5**(5) MartinDwyer(5) (bhd far side: hdwy over 1f out: r.o) | 3 | **2** | 33/1 | 79 | 27 |
| 1193[6] | **Censor (87)** (HRACecil) **3-8-13** WRyan(12) (lw: disp ld far side over 5f out: hdd wl over 1f out: kpt on one pce) | 1¼ | **3** | 14/1 | 94 | 42 |
| 2041[11] | **Al Abraq (IRE) (94)** (JWHills) **3-9-6** DHolland(11) (lw: disp ld far side over 5f out: hdd wl over 1f out: one pce) | 1½ | **4** | 25/1 | 98 | 46 |
| 2146[7] | **She's My Love (76)** (JEBanks) **3-7-13**(3)ow1 FLynch(9) (chsd ldrs far side: rdn 3f out: kpt on same pce) | ½ | **5** | 12/1 | 79 | 26 |
| 2041[23] | **Kala Sunrise (86)** (CSmith) **3-8-12** WWoods(4) (s.s: hdwy far side 2f out: nrst fin) | nk | **6** | 33/1 | 88 | 36 |
| 1126[7] | **Sky Dome (IRE) (78)** (MHTompkins) **3-8-1**(3) HKYim(14) (led stands' side: rdn 3f out: sn outpcd) | ¾ | **7** | 14/1 | 78+ | 26 |
| 2532[5] | **Sualtach (IRE) (84)** (RHollinshead) **3-8-10** KDarley(7) (dwlt: hdwy far side 3f out: sn rdn: no imp) | nk | **8** | 33/1 | 84 | 32 |
| 2006[9] | **The Dilettanti (USA) (88)** (JARToller) **3-9-0** SSanders(2) (chsd ldrs far side: rdn over 3f out: no imp) | nk | **9** | 20/1 | 87 | 35 |
| 2231* | **Strazo (IRE) (95)** (JHMGosden) **3-9-7** PatEddery(19) (w ldr stands' side: rdn over 2f out: no imp) | 3½ | **10** | 9/1[3] | 87 | 35 |
| 2299[6] | **Alhawa (USA) (83)** (CJBenstead) **3-8-9** RHills(6) (racd far side: n.d) | s.h | **11** | 20/1 | 75 | 23 |
| 2231[3] | **Slip Jig (IRE) (85)** (RHannon) **3-8-8**(3) DaneO'Neill(13) (b.nr fore: chsd ldrs far side 6f) | ½ | **12** | 16/1 | 76 | 24 |
| *2325** | **Amber Fort (71)** (DRCElsworth) **3-7-8**(3)ow1 MHenry(15) (bhd stands' side: hdwy 3f out: sn wknd) | ½ | **13** | 33/1 | 61 | 8 |
| 2501[4] | **Polar Prospect (75)** (BHanbury) **3-8-1** JStack(17) (b: racd stands' side: prom 4f) | s.h | **14** | 14/1 | 65 | 13 |
| 2420* | **Sabrak (IRE) (85)** (MAJarvis) **3-8-11** 5x PRobinson(20) (prom stands' side: rdn 3f out: sn wknd) | hd | **15** | 8/1[2] | 75 | 23 |
| 2146[9] | **Mancini (76)** (MBell) **3-8-2**ow1 MFenton(1) (lw: led far side over 2f: wknd qckly over 3f out) | hd | **16** | 33/1 | 66 | 13 |
| 2188* | **Al Shadeedah (USA) (84)** (LMCumani) **3-8-10** JWeaver(10) (s.i.s: racd far side: n.d) | nk | **17** | 12/1 | 73 | 21 |
| 2293[5] | **Final Stab (IRE) (80)** (PWHarris) **3-8-6** GDuffield(16) (b: chsd ldrs stands' side over 4f) | 5 | **18** | 20/1 | 59 | 7 |
| 2241[5] | **Sistar Act (70)** (MRChannon) **3-7-10** GBardwell(18) (a bhd stands' side) | 2 | **19** | 33/1 | 45 | — |
| 2079* | **Nasrudin (USA) (89)** (DRLoder) **3-9-1** RHughes(8) (lw: chsd ldrs far side 5f: sn rdn & btn) | 8 | **20** | 12/1 | 48 | — |
| | | | | (SP 139.2%) | | **20 Rn** |

**1m 37.73** (0.53) CSF £76.85 CT £732.61 TOTE £3.40: £1.70 £4.80 £3.30 £7.10 (£70.90) Trio £379.50 OWNER Mr Hamdan Al Maktoum (NEWMARKET) BRED Shadwell Estate Company Limited

LONG HANDICAP Amber Fort 7-7 Winston 7-4

**1701* Fahim** was the winner of what has turned out to be a hot Beverley maiden last time. Put in on a generous mark here, he won in useful style. (2/1)

**2294 Winston,** although 6lb wrong in the handicap, is from a yard that is going well and made up a lot of ground in the last two furlongs, but never looked likely to get to the winner. (33/1)

**1193 Censor,** guaranteed to get the trip, tried to force the pace but was done for speed late on. (14/1)

**808 Al Abraq (IRE),** ridden up with the pace this time, ran better but was just short of toe in the closing stages. (25/1)

**1324 She's My Love** was in good form and ran pretty well but just lacks a real turn of foot. (12/1)

**1432 Kala Sunrise** ran a fine race after a poor start to show he still has the ability if in the mood. (33/1)

**917 Sky Dome (IRE),** after two months off, ran a grand race, winning on the stands' side. (14/1)

**2231* Strazo (IRE)** was hampered by top weight and a bad draw and his rider eventually had to give up. (9/1)

**2325* Amber Fort** was 3lb wrong in the handicap and, coupled with his bad draw, had no chance. (33/1)

## 2622 DARLEY JULY CUP STKS (Gp 1) (3-Y.O+) (Class A)

3-40 (3-41) **6f (July)** £90,588.00 (£33,492.00: £16,046.00: £6,530.00: £2,565.00: £979.00) Stalls: Low GOING: minus 0.51 sec per fur (F)

| | | | | SP | RR | SF |
|---|---|---|---|---|---|---|
| 1581a* | **Anabaa (USA)** (MmeCHead,France) **4-9-5** FHead(2) (nice colt: lw: sn led: r.o strly fnl 2f) | — | **1** | 11/4[2] | 133+ | 80 |
| 2050* | **Lucayan Prince (USA) (111)** (DRLoder) **3-8-13b** RHughes(1) (trckd ldrs: effrt 2f out: r.o) | 1¾ | **2** | 9/1 | 128 | 69 |
| 2115[4] | **Hever Golf Rose (119)** (TJNaughton) **5-9-2** PatEddery(6) (b.hind: led early: cl up tl outpcd over 1f out: styd on wl towards fin) | 3 | **3** | 14/1 | 117 | 64 |
| 2332[5] | **Iktamal (USA) (110)** (EALDunlop) **4-9-5** RHills(3) (lw: trckd ldrs tl outpcd 2f out: styd on u.p ins fnl f) | s.h | **4** | 16/1 | 120 | 67 |
| 1141a[9] | **Danehill Dancer (IRE) (118)** (NACallaghan) **3-8-13** MJKinane(5) (bhd: drvn along ½-wy: hdwy 2f out: styd on wl: nrst fin) | s.h | **5** | 7/1[3] | 120 | 61 |
| 2115* | **Pivotal (104)** (SirMarkPrescott) **3-8-13** GDuffield(8) (hld up: rdn & hdwy ½-wy: ch 2f out: one pce fnl f) | hd | **6** | 9/4[1] | 120 | 61 |
| 2115[2] | **Mind Games (117)** (JBerry) **4-9-5** JCarroll(10) (trckd ldrs: effrt & ev ch 2f out: wknd ins fnl f) | hd | **7** | 15/2 | 120 | 67 |

2115[12] **Lucky Lionel (USA) (115)** (RHannon) **3-8-13** OPeslier(4) (sn outpcd & bhd)........3 **8** 25/1 112 53
2072[12] **Cool Jazz (114)** (CEBrittain) **5-9-5** KDarley(7) (lw: bhd: rdn ½-wy: hdwy over 1f out: no imp)........nk **9** 40/1 111 58
2471a* **Gothenberg (IRE) (108)** (MJohnston) **3-8-13** JWeaver(9) (pushed along & sn w ldrs: wknd over 2f out)........½ **10** 20/1 109 50
(SP 115.3%) **10 Rn**

**1m 10.63** (-1.37) CSF £25.24 TOTE £3.60: £1.80 £2.50 £2.40 (£23.10) Trio £100.60 OWNER Mrs A. Head (CHANTILLY) BRED Gainsborough Farm Inc
WEIGHT FOR AGE 3yo-6lb

**1581a* Anabaa (USA)** handled this fastish ground well and did the right thing, by setting not to fast a pace and always had far too much speed for the opposition. It is beginning to look as though the home team may have a real chance of winning the Prix de l'Abbaye. (11/4)
**2050* Lucayan Prince (USA)** would have preferred a stronger pace and was tapped for speed by the winner in the closing stages. He is really firing at present. (9/1)
**2663a Hever Golf Rose** ran a sound race but just found this ground too fast and got outpaced at a vital stage, but was running on well at the death. (14/1)
**2332 Iktamal (USA)** needs a stronger pace and got left behind when things hotted up two furlongs out. Although responding to pressure in great style late on, his chance had gone. (16/1)
**1141a Danehill Dancer (IRE)**, back to sprinting, found things happening too quickly from halfway but did struggle on determinedly. Given some easier ground, he will give a much better account of himself. (7/1: 10/1-6/1)
**2115* Pivotal** was a shade disappointing here, never really travelling from halfway. He still had his chances, only to cry enough inside the final furlong. This was not his true form. (9/4)
**2115 Mind Games**, held up, looked dangerous two furlongs out but then failed to see it out and would not seem to get the trip. (15/2)
**1129 Lucky Lionel (USA)** never fired at any stage. (25/1)
**1483 Cool Jazz** needs everything in his favour and had none of that in this classy event. (40/1)
**2471a* Gothenberg (IRE)** found things happening far too quickly over this shorter trip, and cried enough some way from home. (20/1)

## 2623 LADBROKE BUNBURY CUP H'CAP (0-105) (3-Y.O+) (Class B)

4-10 (4-11) **7f** **(July)** £24,660.00 (£7,380.00: £3,540.00: £1,620.00) Stalls: Low GOING:minus 0.51 sec per fur (F)

SP RR SF

2053[3] **Crumpton Hill (IRE) (86)** (NAGraham) **4-8-12** MRoberts(3) (bhd: hdwy 2f out: r.o wl to ld wl ins fnl f)........— **1** 7/1[2] 99 61
1151[2] **Rabican (IRE) (100)** (MHTompkins) **3-9-4** PRobinson(13) (lw: prom: rdn to ld ins fnl f: hdd & nt qckn towards fin)........½ **2** 11/1 112 66
**Mullitover (86)** (MJHeaton-Ellis) **6-8-12** WWoods(12) (chsd ldrs: led wl over 1f out tl ins fnl f: kpt on)........½ **3** 20/1 97 59
2328* **Almuhimm (USA) (86)** (EALDunlop) **4-8-12** RHills(1) (hld up & bhd: nt clr run & hmpd 2f out: swtchd & fin wl: too much to do)........hd **4** 4/1[1] 97+ 59
2248[3] **How Long (97)** (LMCumani) **3-9-1** OUrbina(16) (hdwy over 2f out: ev ch over 1f out: no ex)........1 **5** 16/1 105 59
2298[2] **Silent Expression (86)** (BJMeehan) **6-8-12** RHughes(10) (a.p: effrt over 2f out: r.o one pce)........1¼ **6** 33/1 91 53
1820* **Polar Prince (IRE) (98)** (MAJarvis) **3-8-13**(3) FLynch(6) (hld up: effrt & nt clr run over 2f out & over 1f out: nt rcvr)........nk **7** 15/2[3] 103+ 57
2283* **Neuwest (USA) (83)** (NJHWalker) **4-8-9** JStack(5) (trckd ldrs: rdn over 2f out: wknd over 1f out)........nk **8** 14/1 87 49
2437* **Patsy Grimes (81)** (JSMoore) **6-8-0**(7) 5x AimeeCook(14) (hld up: nvr nrr)........s.h **9** 16/1 85 47
2497[4] **Czarna (IRE) (81)** (CEBrittain) **5-8-7b[1]** BDoyle(2) (led after 1f tl wl over 1f out: wknd)........1 **10** 16/1 83 45
2114* **Emerging Market (100)** (JLDunlop) **4-9-12** KDarley(4) (hld up: nt clr run fnl 2f: nt rcvr)........hd **11** 12/1 101+ 63
1962[9] **Scharnhorst (78)** (SDow) **4-7-13**(5) ADaly(9) (led 1f: cl up tl outpcd ½-wy: hdwy u.p 2f out: wknd over 1f out)........4 **12** 33/1 70 32
2497* **Saseedo (USA) (91)** (WAO'Gorman) **6-9-3** 5x EmmaO'Gorman(8) (swtg: s.i.s: n.d)........1¼ **13** 8/1 80 42
2328[7] **Akil (IRE) (85)** (RWArmstrong) **4-8-11b[1]** WCarson(17) (lw: racd centre: bhd fr ½-wy)........½ **14** 14/1 73 35
2436[2] **Monaassib (102)** (EALDunlop) **5-10-0** TQuinn(15) (racd centre: in tch over 5f)........5 **15** 14/1 79 41
1898* **Everglades (IRE) (98)** (RCharlton) **8-9-10** PatEddery(7) (bhd: rdn ½-wy: n.d)........2½ **16** 14/1 69 31
(SP 126.4%) **16 Rn**

**1m 24.43** (-0.57) CSF £77.42 CT £1,409.27 TOTE £8.80: £2.30 £3.30 £3.40 £1.80 (£85.40) Trio £481.50 OWNER Mr T. H. Chadney (NEWMARKET) BRED Michael Doyle
WEIGHT FOR AGE 3yo-8lb

**2053 Crumpton Hill (IRE)**, dropped back in trip, got a tremendous run and showed a terrific turn of foot in the last two furlongs, to come from way behind and win well. (7/1)
**1151 Rabican (IRE)** has shot up the weights from last year but showed he is pretty useful, only just getting touched off. (11/1)
**Mullitover** likes the trip, the track and the going and although 3lb higher than he has ever won off, he still had every chance throughout but was just done for toe in the closing stages. (20/1)
**2328* Almuhimm (USA)** needs to come from behind and met with all sorts of traffic problems, and would undoubtedly have won had he seen daylight sooner. (4/1: 3/1-9/2)
**2248 How Long** ran well from a high draw but, when the race was on in the final furlong, he was found wanting. (16/1)
**2298 Silent Expression** seems high enough in the weights but ran a decent race and is obviously in good form. (33/1)
**1820* Polar Prince (IRE)** never had any luck in running and this effort is best ignored. (15/2)
**2283* Neuwest (USA)** ran as well as could be expected off his present mark. (14/1)
**2437* Patsy Grimes** ran well from a poor draw and is in good heart at present. (16/1)
**2114* Emerging Market** might well have been in the shake up had he ever seen daylight. (12/1)

## 2624 E.B.F. NGK SPARK PLUGS MAIDEN STKS (2-Y.O) (Class D)

4-45 (4-48) **6f** **(July)** £5,435.50 (£1,624.00: £777.00: £353.50) Stalls: Low GOING: minus 0.51 sec per fur (F)

SP RR SF

2302[3] **Grapeshot (USA)** (LMCumani) **2-9-0** JWeaver(11) (mde most: kpt on gamely fnl f)........— **1** 9/2[2] 96 46
**Bahamian Bounty** (DRLoder) **2-9-0** OPeslier(13) (gd sort: w ldr: slt ld over 1f out tl ins fnl f: nt qckn towards fin)........nk **2** 8/1[3] 95 45
2040[8] **Kumait (USA)** (SbinSuroor) **2-9-0** MJKinane(3) (lw: trckd ldrs: chal 2f out: no ex fnl f)........1¾ **3** Evens[1] 91 41
**Shadow Lead** (LMCumani) **2-9-0** OUrbina(2) (w'like: scope: in tch: styd on wl fnl 2f: nvr nr to chal)........3½ **4** 33/1 81 31
**Musical Pursuit** (MHTompkins) **2-9-0** PRobinson(9) (w'like: scope: hdwy over 2f out: styd on steadily)........2½ **5** 33/1 75 25
**Shuwaikh** (RHannon) **2-9-0** RHughes(7) (w'like: in tch: rdn 3f out: r.o one pce)........1½ **6** 20/1 71 21
1694[6] **A Breeze** (DMorris) **2-9-0** DHarrison(12) (trckd ldrs tl grad wknd fnl 2f)........2½ **7** 50/1 64 14
**Compatibility (IRE)** (JHMGosden) **2-9-0** JCarroll(5) (str: cmpt: bkwd: rn wl over 4f)........1¼ **8** 14/1 61 11
**Test The Water (IRE)** (RHannon) **2-8-11**(3) DaneO'Neill(8) (w'like: scope: bit bkwd: s.i.s: n.d)........1 **9** 33/1 58 8
1878[3] **Bold Oriental (IRE)** (NACallaghan) **2-9-0** PatEddery(10) (lw: a bhd)........1 **10** 10/1 55 5

| | Horse | Dist | Pos | SP | RR | SF |
|---|---|---|---|---|---|---|
| | **Shaddad (USA)** (JLDunlop) **2-9-0** WCarson(4) (w'like: leggy: s.i.s: a outpcd & bhd) | 1¼ | **11** | 8/1[3] | 52 | 2 |
| 2353[3] | **White Hot** (EALDunlop) **2-9-0** KDarley(1) (bhd & hmpd 3f out: n.d) | ¾ | **12** | 20/1 | 50 | — |
| | **Feel A Line** (BJMeehan) **2-9-0** BDoyle(6) (cmpt: bkwd: s.i.s: sn drvn along: a bhd) | 4 | **13** | 33/1 | 39 | — |

(SP 129.4%) **13 Rn**

**1m 12.66** (0.66) CSF £40.78 TOTE £6.90: £2.00 £2.60 £1.30 (£29.40) Trio £14.70 OWNER Mrs Timothy von Halle (NEWMARKET) BRED Jody Huckabay and Dr Stuart Brown

**2302 Grapeshot (USA)** has certainly come on for his initial outing, and showed fine courage to gain the day after looking beaten. He should appreciate further. (9/2)

**Bahamian Bounty**, a useful sort, ran a super race and will no doubt be all the better for it. Plenty of improvement can be expected. (8/1: 5/1-9/1)

**2040 Kumait (USA)**, on edge in the paddock, went freely to post and, after holding every chance, failed to see it out. (Evens)

**Shadow Lead** showed a deal of promise and should be a different proposition next time. (33/1)

**Musical Pursuit**, an angular sort, gradually realised what was required as the race progressed and there would seem to be plenty to come. (33/1)

**Shuwaikh** needed this and, off the bit some way out, should have learnt plenty. (20/1)

**A Breeze** still looked likely to benefit from this and ran reasonably well, until stopping in the last couple of furlongs. (50/1)

**Compatibility (IRE)** needed this and showed plenty. There would seem to be a lot of improvement in him. (14/1: 8/1-16/1)

**Shaddad (USA)** never took the slightest interest. (8/1: op 4/1)

T/Jkpt: £48,703.50 (0.5 Tckts); £34,298.24 to York 12/7/96. T/Plpt: £101.50 (423.44 Tckts). T/Qdpt: £15.70 (208.54 Tckts). AA

# 2161-REDCAR (L-H) (Good to firm)

## Thursday July 11th

WEATHER: overcast, rain last race WIND: mod half bhd

## 2625 WESTERDALE MAIDEN AUCTION STKS (2-Y.O) (Class E)

6-45 (6-46) **5f** £3,172.75 (£952.00: £458.50: £211.75) Stalls: Centre GOING minus 0.70 sec per fur (HD)

| | Horse | Dist | Pos | SP | RR | SF |
|---|---|---|---|---|---|---|
| 1827[12] | **Pension Fund** (MWEasterby) **2-8-4** DaleGibson(3) (s.i.s: outpcd & rdn along: hdwy over 1f out: hung rt & led nr fin) | — | **1** | 8/1 | 63 | 30 |
| 2361[4] | **Suite Factors** (JAGlover) **2-8-6** SDWilliams(1) (led: edgd rt 2f out: hdd nr fin) | 1 | **2** | 5/1[3] | 62 | 29 |
| 1537[4] | **Two On The Bridge** (DenysSmith) **2-8-5** LCharnock(7) (a chsng ldrs: rdn ½-wy: styd on wl towards fin) | 1¼ | **3** | 3/1[2] | 57 | 24 |
| 2361[8] | **Donna's Dancer (IRE)** (TDBarron) **2-8-6** JFortune(9) (chsd ldrs: rdn ½-wy: kpt on one pce) | 1½ | **4** | 14/1 | 53 | 20 |
| 2429[4] | **Woodetto (IRE)** (EWeymes) **2-8-4** JFanning(2) (lw: sn in tch & rdn along: outpcd over 1f out) | 4 | **5** | 14/1 | 38 | 5 |
| 1849[12] | **Smoke'n'jo (IRE)** (MWEasterby) **2-8-3**(5)ow2 GParkin(4) (s.i.s: outpcd & bhd tl styd on fnl f) | ½ | **6** | 50/1 | 41 | 6 |
| 2118[2] | **Nifty Norman** (JBerry) **2-8-5** KDarley(6) (w ldrs tl wknd over 1f out) | hd | **7** | 11/4[1] | 37 | 4 |
| | **Why O Six** (RAFahey) **2-8-8** GDuffield(8) (small: bkwd: str: s.s: wl outpcd & sn wl bhd: sme late hdwy) | 1 | **8** | 12/1 | 37 | 4 |
| 2361[3] | **Melbourne Princess** (RMWhitaker) **2-8-0**(3) DWright(5) (chsd ldrs tl wknd over 1f out) | 1¾ | **9** | 5/1[3] | 27 | — |

(SP 119.1%) **9 Rn**

**57.4 secs** (-0.10) CSF £45.53 TOTE £13.60: £3.90 £2.10 £2.20 (£74.00) Trio £77.70 OWNER Mr Stephen Curtis (SHERIFF HUTTON) BRED Pitts Farm Stud

**1344 Pension Fund**, who looked light in the paddock, stepped up considerably on his three previous efforts. After missing the break slightly and struggling to go the pace, he stayed on strongly coming to the final furlong and, despite hanging right, led and went clear near the line. (8/1)

**2361 Suite Factors**, who looked very fit, did not impress with his action going down. Making the running, he edged right soon after halfway but was only collared near the line. (5/1)

**1537 Two On The Bridge**, who has a scratchy action, was dropping back to five. Staying on in determined fashion near the line, he needs a stiffer test. (3/1)

**Donna's Dancer (IRE)**, a poor mover, was outpaced on this ground coming to the final furlong. (14/1: op 6/1)

**2429 Woodetto (IRE)**, dropping back to five, showed a poor action going down and was never really going the pace. (14/1)

**Smoke'n'jo (IRE)**, the paddock pick, lost ground at the start but was staying on when it was all over. He is capable of better in time. (50/1)

**2118 Nifty Norman** looked very fit and was put into the stalls last. He turned in a moderate effort, dropping right out over a furlong out. He is one to have reservations about. (11/4)

**Why O Six** (12/1: op 7/1)

## 2626 RUNSWICK BAY (S) STKS (3-Y.O+) (Class F)

7-15 (7-15) **1m 6f 19y** £2,742.00 (£762.00: £366.00) Stalls: Low GOING minus 0.70 sec per fur (HD)

| | Horse | Dist | Pos | SP | RR | SF |
|---|---|---|---|---|---|---|
| 2499[7] | **Faugeron (51)** (NTinkler) **7-9-8** LCharnock(4) (chsd ldrs: led over 3f out: hld on wl fnl f) | — | **1** | 9/1[3] | 68 | 22 |
| 2182* | **Brodessa (60)** (MrsMReveley) **10-9-13** KDarley(6) (lw: trckd ldr: led on bit over 4f out: hdd over 3f out: swtchd over 2f out: ev ch & hung lft over 1f out: sn rdn & nt qckn) | 1 | **2** | 1/5[1] | 72 | 26 |
| 2494[7] | **Fearless Wonder (51)** (MrsMReveley) **5-9-3b**(5) SCopp(3) (lw: led tl over 4f out: wknd over 2f out) | 5 | **3** | 7/1[2] | 61 | 15 |
| 2189[11] | **Miss Express (BEL)** (MrsSJSmith) **3-8-4**ow2 PBloomfield(2) (hld up: effrt over 4f out: sn rdn & one pce) | 8 | **4** | 66/1 | 49 | — |
| 2182[7] | **Kindred Greeting (29)** (JAHarris) **4-9-8b** JO'Reilly(5) (jnd ldrs 7f out: drvn along 5f out: lost pl over 3f out) | 7 | **5** | 33/1 | 44 | — |
| | **Just A Guess (IRE)** (JJO'Neill) **5-9-8** KFallon(1) (swtg: in tch: rdn & outpcd 6f out: bhd fnl 4f) | 26 | **6** | 50/1 | 15 | — |

(SP 112.2%) **6 Rn**

**3m 4.7** (5.40) CSF £11.26 TOTE £13.90: £2.00 £1.10 (£3.10) OWNER Elite Racing Club (MALTON) BRED J. L. C. Pearce

WEIGHT FOR AGE 3yo-15lb

No bid

**Faugeron**, who had run badly on his two previous outings when ridden by another jockey, caused an upset here. (9/1)

**2182* Brodessa** took it up on the bridle once in line for home and it looked plain sailing. However, when headed by the winner, he persisted in hanging left and for some reason would not let himself down in the final furlong. (1/5)

**Fearless Wonder**, who finished last on his first outing of the season six days ago, made the running but looked anything but keen when headed. (7/1)

**Miss Express (BEL)**, who showed a glimmer of form in Belgium last year, was made to look woefully one-paced in the final half-mile. (66/1)

## 2627 LINGDALE H'CAP (0-70) (3-Y.O) (Class E)

7-45 (7-45) **1m 6f 19y** £3,458.75 (£1,040.00: £502.50: £233.75) Stalls: Low GOING minus 0.70 sec per fur (HD)

| | Horse | Dist | Pos | SP | RR | SF |
|---|---|---|---|---|---|---|
| 2067[6] | **Dirab (62)** (TDBarron) **3-8-13** JFortune(2) (lw: hld up: sn trckng ldrs: outpcd over 4f out: swtchd outside & styd on: hrd rdn to ld post) | — | **1** | 7/4[1] | 75 | 28 |

2356* **Blenheim Terrace (54)** (CBBBooth) **3-8-5** 4x ACulhane(11) (hld up: sn trckng ldrs: led 2f out tl last stride)....s.h **2** 14/1 67 20
2024[4] **Serious Trust (57)** (SirMarkPrescott) **3-8-8** GDuffield(5) (trckd ldrs: led over 3f out: hdd 2f out: kpt on same pce)....1¾ **3** 7/2[2] 68 21
2175[4] **Marsayas (IRE) (50)** (MJCamacho) **3-8-1** LCharnock(8) (hld up: hdwy 8f out: n.m.r 3f out: edgd rt over 1f out: styd on u.p)....s.h **4** 12/1 61 14
1907* **Sedbergh (USA) (70)** (MrsMReveley) **3-9-7** KDarley(6) (lw: hld up gng wl: hdwy on ins whn hmpd over 3f out: swtchd & styd on: nt rch ldrs)....1½ **5** 12/1 79 32
2493* **Shirley Sue (52)** (MJohnston) **3-8-3** 4x JFanning(10) (a chsng ldrs: one pce fnl 3f)....nk **6** 11/2[3] 61 14
2506[18] **Lagan (45)** (PSFelgate) **3-7-7**(3) DWright(12) (hld up: effrt 3f out: one pce whn n.m.r over 1f out)....3½ **7** 66/1 50 3
2424[4] **What Jim Wants (IRE) (45)** (JJO'Neill) **3-7-10** JLowe(9) (unruly stalls: chsd ldrs: pushed along 6f out: wknd 2f out)....2½ **8** 50/1 47 —
2067[5] **Umberston (IRE) (54)** (LMCumani) **3-8-5b**1ow2 KFallon(3) (lw: trckd ldrs: rdn whn hmpd 3f out: eased over 1f out)....7 **9** 8/1 48 —
2397[6] **Alzotic (IRE) (45)** (JNorton) **3-7-10v**1 NKennedy(4) (led tl over 3f out: sn wknd)....1½ **10** 25/1 37 —
2433[4] **Manoy (59)** (JHetherton) **3-8-10b** SDWilliams(7) (lw: trckd ldrs: wkng whn n.m.r 3f out)....3 **11** 40/1 48 1
2318[6] **Arktikos (IRE) (68)** (JHMGosden) **3-9-5** DaleGibson(1) (b.hind: s.i.s: hld up & plld hrd: bhd: drvn over 5f out: no rspnse)....7 **12** 11/2[3] 49 2
(SP 132.3%) **12 Rn**

**3m 2.0** (2.70) CSF £28.50 CT £82.60 TOTE £2.90: £1.80 £3.70 £2.10 (£22.90) Trio £90.00 OWNER Mr Alex Gorrie (THIRSK) BRED Nawara Stud Co Ltd
LONG HANDICAP What Jim Wants (IRE) 7-5
OFFICIAL EXPLANATION **Dirab: explaining the improvement in form, the trainer reported that the gelding has to be held up in his races in order to prevent him from running too freely, and that he had been unable to quicken off a slow pace over a two-furlong shorter trip at Ripon.**
**2067 Dirab**, dropped 3lb in the weights after three quiet runs and taking a step up in distance, landed a Morning Line gamble. Tapped for toe turning in, he stuck on under severe pressure to lead right on the line. Connections obviously expected him to improve and deliver the goods on the day. (7/4)
**2356* Blenheim Terrace** proved suited by the step up in distance. After setting sail for home, he was just caught. (14/1)
**2024 Serious Trust**, 5lb higher in the weights than when winning on his reappearance at Salisbury, kicked on early in the straight and, to his credit, stayed on all the way to the line after being headed. (7/2: tchd 11/2)
**2175 Marsayas (IRE)** is not an easy ride. Dropped in in the early stages, he possibly contributed to his own trouble three furlongs out. Edging right over a furlong out, he was staying on in determined fashion at the line. He will be suited by a step up to two miles. (12/1)
**1907* Sedbergh (USA)** looked to have plenty to do under topweight. Meeting plenty of trouble when going for an ambitious run up the inside, after being switched, he stayed on steadily. (12/1: op 8/1)
**2493* Shirley Sue**, under a 4lb penalty, proved very one-paced. (11/2: 4/1-6/1)
**2318 Arktikos (IRE)** wore a tongue-strap. Refusing to settle, he would not buckle down when driven along turning in. (11/2)

## 2628 BOLLINGER CHAMPAGNE CHALLENGE SERIES GENTLEMENS' H'CAP (0-70) (3-Y.O+) (Class F)
8-15 (8-15) **1m 3f** £2,714.00 (£754.00: £362.00) Stalls: Low GOING minus 0.70 sec per fur (HD)

SP RR SF

2066[14] **Ring of Vision (IRE) (51)** (MrsMReveley) **4-11-1** MrSSwiers(5) (chsd ldrs: led on ins 3f out: r.o u.p)....— **1** 9/2[2] 60 48
2319[6] **Augustan (50)** (SGollings) **5-11-0** JCulloty(8) (effrt over 4f out: ev ch & rdn 3f out: kpt on same pce)....1 **2** 4/1[1] 58 46
2284* **Montone (IRE) (64)** (JRJenkins) **6-11-10v**(4) DrMMannish(9) (led: edgd rt & hdd 3f out: edgd lft & styd on fnl f)....1 **3** 4/1[1] 70 58
2482[4] **Pepitist (42)** (MDHammond) **5-10-6** MrCBonner(2) (bhd: pushed along 6f out: hdwy over 2f out: one pce)....nk **4** 14/1[3] 48 36
2296[3] **Essayeffsee (58)** (MrsMReveley) **7-11-8** MrMHNaughton(7) (lw: trckd ldrs: ev ch 3f out: sn rdn: kpt on same pce)....¾ **5** 9/2[2] 63 51
2587[5] **Canary Falcon (50)** (HJCollingridge) **5-10-10v**(4) MrPClose(1) (hmpd early: sn chsng ldrs: edgd rt & outpcd over 2f out: kpt on)....1¾ **6** 20/1 52 40
**Sylvan Sabre (IRE) (47)** (KAMorgan) **7-10-7**(4) MrRThornton(6) (b: chsd ldrs: rdn & outpcd over 2f out)....3½ **7** 14/1[3] 44 32
2440[3] **Hever Golf Diamond (45)** (TJNaughton) **3-9-7**(4) MrKSantana(4) (bhd: sme hdwy 2f out: n.d)....1¼ **8** 9/2[2] 40 16
*2082*[9] **Highfield Fizz (48)** (CWFairhurst) **4-10-8**(4) MrJWeymes(3) (hld up & bhd: effrt on outside over 4f out: sn wknd & eased)....14 **9** 14/1[3] 23 11
(SP 119.3%) **9 Rn**

**2m 21.0** (3.00) CSF £22.30 CT £72.10 TOTE £6.90: £1.90 £2.00 £1.50 (£10.00) Trio £40.60 OWNER Mr P. D. Savill (SALTBURN) BRED Amberush Investments
WEIGHT FOR AGE 3yo-12lb
**1821 Ring of Vision (IRE)** was given a fine ride, unlike last time. Sticking to the inner, he showed ahead three furlongs out and displayed the right sort of spirit under pressure. (9/2)
**2319 Augustan**, another ridden by a professional in all but name, stuck on under pressure but was never going to get upsides. (4/1)
**2284* Montone (IRE)** set a strong pace. Edging first right and then left, to his credit he kept on all the way to the line. The extended trip proved no problem. (4/1: op 5/2)
**2482 Pepitist**, thanks to the strong early pace, stuck on under pressure but again never looked like quickening to take a hand. (14/1)
**2296 Essayeffsee**, one of half a dozen almost upsides three furlongs out, was only able to stay on at the same pace. The Handicapper looks to have his measure at the moment. (9/2: op 5/2)
**2587 Canary Falcon** lost ground at the start. Given an ineffective ride, he tended to edge right under pressure but to his credit he kept on. The trip did not seem to be a problem. (20/1)

## 2629 WHITBY CONDITIONS STKS (2-Y.O) (Class C)
8-45 (8-45) **7f** £5,917.00 (£1,633.00) Stalls: Centre GOING minus 0.70 sec per fur (HD)

SP RR SF

2416* **Brave Act** (SirMarkPrescott) **2-9-1** GDuffield(1) (hld up: effrt 3f out: shkn up to ld over 1f out: styd on wl)....— **1** 4/11[1] 87+ —
1419[4] **Iechyd-Da (IRE)** (MBell) **2-8-8**(7) GFaulkner(2) (w ldr: rdn to ld ½-wy: edgd lft & hdd over 1f out: nt qckn fnl f)....1¼ **2** 9/4[2] 84 —
2063[6] **Pandiculation** (EWeymes) **2-9-1** JFortune(3) (led to ½-wy: cl up & rdn whn broke leg & p.u appr fnl f: dead).... **P** 20/1[3] — —
(SP 108.9%) **3 Rn**

**1m 26.7** (3.70) CSF £1.53 TOTE £1.20: (£1.10) OWNER Mr W. E. Sturt (NEWMARKET) BRED Side Hill Stud and Floors Farming
**2416* Brave Act**, happy to get a lead, found this much faster ground no problem and scored decisively. A mile will be well within his compass. (4/11)

**1419 Iechyd-Da (IRE)**, driven to the front at halfway, looked to edge left. Changing his legs, he never seemed 100% happy on the ground. (9/4)
**2063 Pandiculation** was running a credible race when he unfortunately broke a leg over a furlong out. (20/1)

## 2630 BEDALE H'CAP (0-80) (3-Y.O+) (Class D)

9-15 (9-17) **7f** £3,918.50 (£1,178.00: £569.00: £264.50) Stalls: Centre GOING minus 0.70 sec per fur (HD)

| | | | SP | RR | SF |
|---|---|---|---|---|---|
| 2242* | **Gymcrak Flyer (58)** (GHolmes) **5-8-12** KFallon(9) (b.hind: sn pushed along: edgd lft & hdwy ½-wy: led ins fnl f: jst hld on)— | **1** | 5/1$^3$ | 66 | 37 |
| 2160$^2$ | **Arterxerxes (78)** (MJHeaton-Ellis) **3-9-7**(3) SDrowne(1) (lw: mde most tl ins fnl f: styd on wl)s.h | **2** | 10/1 | 86 | 49 |
| 2149$^2$ | **Quilling (68)** (MDods) **4-9-8** DeanMcKeown(6) (w ldr to ½-wy: sn rdn & outpcd: kpt on u.p fnl f)3 | **3** | 5/2$^1$ | 69 | 40 |
| 2521$^3$ | **Zain Dancer (55)** (DNicholls) **4-8-9b** GDuffield(2) (trckd ldrs: rdn over 2f out: one pce)½ | **4** | 6/1 | 55 | 26 |
| 1301$^8$ | **Brandonville (60)** (NTinkler) **3-8-6** KimTinkler(8) (sn pushed along: outpcd ½-wy: kpt on fnl 2f)2 | **5** | 25/1 | 55 | 18 |
| 2566$^3$ | **Allinson's Mate (IRE) (61)** (TDBarron) **8-9-1b** 6x JFortune(5) (sn pushed along: nvr rchd ldrs)2 | **6** | 14/1 | 52 | 23 |
| 1546$^9$ | **Great Bear (51)** (DWChapman) **4-8-5** LCharnock(3) (swtchd lft s: chsd ldrs to ½-wy: sn wl outpcd)¾ | **7** | 25/1 | 40 | 11 |
| 2426* | **Legal Issue (IRE) (67)** (WWHaigh) **4-9-7** 6x RLappin(7) (lw: hld up: effrt over 2f out: no imp)hd | **8** | 6/1 | 56 | 27 |
| 2357$^2$ | **Tinklers Folly (58)** (DenysSmith) **4-8-12** KDarley(4) (trckd ldrs: effrt u.p over 2f out: sn wknd)1 | **9** | 4/1$^2$ | 45 | 16 |
| | | | (SP 117.3%) | | **9 Rn** |

**1m 23.0** (0.00) CSF £48.45 CT £139.62 TOTE £6.60: £1.30 £3.20 £1.30 (£63.30) Trio £40.80 OWNER The Gymcrak Thoroughbred Racing Club (PICKERING) BRED D. G. Mason
WEIGHT FOR AGE 3yo-8lb
**2242* Gymcrak Flyer**, who likes this fast ground, held on by the skin of her teeth. (5/1)
**2160 Arterxerxes**, at his best when forcing the pace, battled on strongly and just failed to get back up. (10/1)
**2149 Quilling**, who is now undeniably well handicapped, was unable to dominate. Not enjoying this at halfway, he was persuaded to stick on in the final furlong. (5/2)
**2521 Zain Dancer** had the blinkers back on but they did not have a lot of effect. (6/1)
**714 Brandonville**, rested for fifty-two days after a poor effort last time, was outpaced at halfway but was sticking on at the finish. He will appreciate a step up in distance. (25/1)
**2566 Allinson's Mate (IRE)** (14/1: op 8/1)
**2426* Legal Issue (IRE)**, seeking a hat-trick under a 6lb penalty, showed a poor action going to post. Never happy on the fast ground, he was handled with consideration. (6/1)

T/Plpt: £74.20 (176.96 Tckts). T/Qdpt: £7.90 (109.84 Tckts). WG

# 2550-WOLVERHAMPTON (L-H) (Standard)

## Thursday July 11th

WEATHER: cloudy WIND: almost nil

## 2631 ARLINGTON H'CAP (0-60) (3-Y.O+) (Class F)

2-20 (2-21) **1m 6f 166y (Fibresand)** £2,381.00 (£656.00: £311.00) Stalls: High GOING minus 0.06 sec per fur (STD)

| | | | SP | RR | SF |
|---|---|---|---|---|---|
| *2553** | **Etterby Park (USA) (55)** (MJohnston) **3-8-6** 4x JFanning(1) (mde all: drvn clr 3f out: eased fnl f)— | **1** | 1/3$^1$ | 73+ | 25 |
| *2304$^3$* | **Heighth of Fame (55)** (AJWilson) **5-9-9** JFortune(5) (chsd wnr: rdn over 3f out: kpt on one pce)2½ | **2** | 16/1 | 70 | 39 |
| *1967$^2$* | **Ready to Draw (IRE) (49)** (RJO'Sullivan) **7-9-3** DBiggs(2) (b: hld up: outpcd & rdn ½-wy: n.d after)17 | **3** | 10/1$^2$ | 46 | 15 |
| 1496$^7$ | **Great Tern (41)** (NMBabbage) **4-8-9** KFallon(7) (hld up: effrt 6f out: sn drvn along: outpcd)1¼ | **4** | 12/1$^3$ | 37 | 6 |
| *2372$^4$* | **Penmar (58)** (TJEtherington) **4-9-9b**(3) OPears(3) (lw: plld hrd: trckd ldrs tl lost pl 7f out: sn rdn & btn)6 | **5** | 16/1 | 47 | 16 |
| *2173$^7$* | **Sommersby (IRE) (56)** (MrsNMacauley) **5-9-7**(3) CTeague(8) (lw: hld up & bhd: hdwy 5f out: wknd over 3f out)6 | **6** | 16/1 | 39 | 8 |
| *415$^5$* | **Image Maker (IRE) (47)** (BPreece) **3-7-7b**(5)ow2 MBaird(6) (b: bit bkwd: hdwy after 5f: rdn ½-wy: sn wknd: t.o)dist | **7** | 40/1 | — | — |
| *364$^4$* | **Righteous Gent (54)** (KMcAuliffe) **3-8-5e**ow2 WJO'Connor(4) (bit bkwd: prom tl wknd qckly over 5f out: t.o)26 | **8** | 40/1 | — | — |
| | | | (SP 114.3%) | | **8 Rn** |

**3m 18.9** (11.50) CSF £6.99 CT £20.82 TOTE £2.00: £1.10 £1.80 £1.40 (£4.40) OWNER Mr G. Middlebrook (MIDDLEHAM) BRED Jayeff "B" Stables
LONG HANDICAP Image Maker (IRE) 7-7
WEIGHT FOR AGE 3yo-17lb
**2553* Etterby Park (USA)** had less to do here than when successful at this venue last week, and though he was stepping into the unknown as far as stamina was concerned, had galloped the opposition into submission before reaching the home straight. (1/3: op 1/2)
**2304 Heighth of Fame** did his best to stay within striking distance of the winner, but he was labouring on the turn out of the back straight, and second place was all he could hope for. (16/1)

## 2632 LULLINGTON CLAIMING STKS (I) (3-Y.O+) (Class F)

2-50 (2-51) **7f (Fibresand)** £2,031.00 (£556.00: £261.00) Stalls: High GOING minus 0.06 sec per fur (STD)

| | | | SP | RR | SF |
|---|---|---|---|---|---|
| | **Mirani (IRE)** (DJGMurraySmith) **3-8-11** KFallon(8) (lt-f: unf: bhd & outpcd: hdwy ½-wy: led over 1f out: hld on gamely)— | **1** | 14/1$^3$ | 73 | 30 |
| *2551** | **Ethbaat (USA) (70)** (WRMuir) **5-9-10** MRichards(9) (lw: outpcd & bhd: hdwy over 3f out: jnd wnr ins fnl f: hrd rdn: unable qckn)nk | **2** | 4/11$^1$ | 77 | 42 |
| 2391$^6$ | **Have a Nightcap (30)** (NPLittmoden) **7-9-2v** TGMcLaughlin(3) (a.p: led 4f out tl hdd & wknd over 1f out)8 | **3** | 16/1 | 51 | 16 |
| *2306$^6$* | **What a Nightmare (IRE) (54)** (PHowling) **4-9-2v** FNorton(7) (prom: hrd drvn 2f out: sn lost tch)1¾ | **4** | 13/2$^2$ | 47 | 12 |
| *2367$^6$* | **Valiant Man (38)** (JWharton) **5-8-5v**(7) PDoe(2) (prom: ev ch over 2f out: sn hrd rdn & wknd)3 | **5** | 14/1$^3$ | 36 | 1 |
| *2367$^5$* | **Verro (USA) (15)** (KBishop) **9-8-9e** NCarlisle(4) (a bhd & outpcd)6 | **6** | 100/1 | 20 | — |
| *2550$^{11}$* | **Jon's Choice (40)** (BPreece) **8-8-9** VSlattery(1) (led 3f: hrd drvn & wknd wl over 1f out)2 | **7** | 20/1 | 15 | — |
| *2325$^{12}$* | **New Technique (FR) (30)** (KMcAuliffe) **3-8-5** WJO'Connor(5) (prom over 4f: sn wknd: t.o)5 | **8** | 66/1 | 8 | — |
| | **Brin-Lodge (IRE)** (KSBridgwater) **3-7-13** CRutter(6) (lt-f: unf: s.i.s: a bhd: outpcd: t.o)7 | **9** | 50/1 | — | — |
| | | | (SP 115.1%) | | **9 Rn** |

**1m 29.8** (5.10) CSF £18.96 TOTE £12.80: £2.90 £1.10 £1.70 (£4.50) Trio £25.00 OWNER The Fort Partnership (LAMBOURN) BRED Ballymacarney Stud
WEIGHT FOR AGE 3yo-8lb

**Mirani (IRE)**, a lightly-made debutante, showed the right commitment when strongly pressed inside the final furlong and should go on to better things in time. (14/1)
**2551* Ethbaat (USA)** was certainly not helped by the drop back in trip and, though he may have poked his head in front briefly inside the final furlong, was tapped for toe in the duel to the finish. (4/11)
**2391 Have a Nightcap** helped force the pace, but was a spent force after being headed on the approach to the final furlong, and is much more at home over hurdles. (16/1)
**331 What a Nightmare (IRE)** is finding it difficult to get back to winning ways this season and he may have to descend to selling company to do so. (13/2)
**2367 Valiant Man** pushed the pace but was hard at work entering the straight, and it would seem this trip is too far for him on this surface. (14/1: 10/1-16/1)

## 2633 WORTHINGTON DRAUGHT BITTER MAIDEN STKS (2-Y.O) (Class D)
3-25 (3-25) **6f (Fibresand)** £3,743.15 (£1,119.20: £536.10: £244.55) Stalls: Low GOING minus 0.06 sec per fur (STD)

| | | | | SP | RR | SF |
|---|---|---|---|---|---|---|
| *2370$^{3}$* | **Rudimental** (SirMarkPrescott) **2-9-0** RPerham(5) (sn drvn along: hdwy 2f out: str run to ld wl ins fnl f) | — | 1 | 5/2$^{2}$ | 70 | 34 |
| | **Ricasso** (DRLoder) **2-9-0** DRMcCabe(8) (cmpt: bit bkwd: trckd ldrs: rdn to ld ins fnl f: hdd & no ex nr fin) | ½ | 2 | 9/4$^{1}$ | 69 | 33 |
| 1590$^{5}$ | **Summer Queen** (SPCWoods) **2-8-9** KFallon(10) (plld hrd: hld up: hdwy over 2f out: ev ch fnl f: kpt on) | ¾ | 3 | 100/30$^{3}$ | 62 | 26 |
| 1622$^{5}$ | **Mangus (IRE)** (KOCunningham-Brown) **2-9-0** SWhitworth(3) (a.p: led over 2f out tl ins fnl f) | 2½ | 4 | 16/1 | 60 | 24 |
| 2361$^{10}$ | **The Wyandotte Inn** (RHollinshead) **2-8-9**(5) DGriffiths(4) (bit bkwd: led tl over 2f out: rdn & one pce fnl f) | 1 | 5 | 33/1 | 57 | 21 |
| 1989$^{9}$ | **Pretty Sally (IRE)** (DJGMurraySmith) **2-8-6**(3) SDrowne(9) (bit bkwd: prom: wkng whn n.m.r appr fnl f) | 4 | 6 | 33/1 | 42 | 6 |
| *2370$^{5}$* | **Floating Devon** (TDEasterby) **2-9-0** MBirch(6) (outpcd: a bhd) | 1½ | 7 | 12/1 | 43 | 7 |
| 2211$^{5}$ | **Nant Y Gamer (FR)** (JBerry) **2-9-0** GCarter(2) (s.s: a wl bhd) | ½ | 8 | 20/1 | 41 | 5 |
| 2031$^{6}$ | **Princess Ferdinand (IRE)** (MMcCormack) **2-8-9** WJO'Connor(12) (spd over 3f) | 1 | 9 | 33/1 | 34 | — |
| 916$^{12}$ | **Neon Deion (IRE)** (SCWilliams) **2-9-0** JTate(7) (bit bkwd: outpcd: a bhd) | 2½ | 10 | 40/1 | 32 | — |
| 1774$^{9}$ | **Littlestone Rocket** (WRMuir) **2-9-0** JFortune(11) (bit bkwd: a outpcd) | 5 | 11 | 40/1 | 19 | — |
| 1989$^{5}$ | **Heggies (IRE)** (CREgerton) **2-9-0** CRutter(1) (outpcd: a bhd) | 2 | 12 | 20/1 | 13 | — |

(SP 119.2%) **12 Rn**

**1m 15.6** (4.20) CSF £8.21 TOTE £4.20: £1.40 £1.10 £1.50 (£5.80) Trio £2.20 OWNER Cheveley Park Stud (NEWMARKET) BRED Cheveley Park Stud Ltd

**2370 Rudimental**, taken off his legs on this step down to sprinting, was flat to the boards all the way but did begin to motor once in line for home, and nosed ahead in this dying strides. (5/2)
**Ricasso**, a son of useful Chicarica, ran exceptionally well considering he needed the run and will be the one to beat from now on. (9/4: 5/4-5/2)
**1590 Summer Queen**, restrained just off the pace, put in a determined bid inside the distance and, though she was being held close home, should not be long in finding an opening. (100/30)
**1622 Mangus (IRE)** got to the front on the home turn and made the principals fight to wear him down, but stamina appeared to desert him inside the final furlong, and he tied up quickly once headed. (16/1)
**The Wyandotte Inn** still has something left to work on, but he ran so much better than he did on his debut and is getting the hang of things. (33/1)
**Pretty Sally (IRE)**, a poor mover, pressed the leaders but looked to be at the end of her tether when squeezed for room approaching the final furlong. (33/1)

## 2634 AMEC CIVIL ENGINEERING H'CAP (0-85) (3-Y.O) (Class D)
3-55 (3-55) **6f (Fibresand)** £4,020.50 (£1,199.00: £572.00: £258.50) Stalls: Low GOING minus 0.06 sec per fur (STD)

| | | | | SP | RR | SF |
|---|---|---|---|---|---|---|
| *2305** | **Princess Efisio (57)** (BAMcMahon) **3-7-7**(3) NVarley(2) (trckd ldrs: shkn up 2f out: led fnl 100y: sn clr) | — | 1 | 9/2 | 69 | 39 |
| *2306$^{7}$* | **Vax New Way (74)** (JLSpearing) **3-8-10b**(3) SDrowne(4) (set str pce: sn clr: wknd & hdd ins fnl f) | 5 | 2 | 2/1$^{2}$ | 73 | 43 |
| 2532$^{2}$ | **Splicing (82)** (WJHaggas) **3-9-7** KFallon(5) (prom tl hrd drvn & outpcd wl over 1f out) | 2½ | 3 | 7/4$^{1}$ | 74 | 44 |
| 2428$^{12}$ | **Magic Lake (57)** (EJAlston) **3-7-3**(7) IonaWands(3) (a.p: rdn over 1f out: wknd ins fnl f) | ½ | 4 | 14/1 | 48 | 18 |
| 2200$^{3}$ | **Standown (75)** (JBerry) **3-9-0** GCarter(7) (outpcd & bhd tl sme late hdwy) | 4 | 5 | 4/1$^{3}$ | 55 | 25 |
| *2171$^{10}$* | **Boffy (IRE) (74)** (BPJBaugh) **3-8-13** NCarlisle(8) (sn drvn along: nvr nr ldrs) | 2½ | 6 | 25/1 | 47 | 17 |
| 2528$^{10}$ | **Extra Hour (IRE) (62)** (WRMuir) **3-8-1b** CRutter(6) (lw: s.i.s: outpcd: a bhd) | 5 | 7 | 25/1 | 22 | — |
| 2064$^{11}$ | **Kustom Kit (IRE) (60)** (BAMcMahon) **3-7-13** FNorton(1) (spd to ½-wy: sn lost tch: t.o) | 7 | 8 | 25/1 | 1 | — |

(SP 126.1%) **8 Rn**

**1m 14.0** (2.60) CSF £14.88 CT £19.74 TOTE £8.20: £2.90 £2.80 £1.10 (£25.20) OWNER Mr J. D. Graham (TAMWORTH) BRED J. D. Graham
LONG HANDICAP Princess Efisio 7-6 Magic Lake 7-5

**2305* Princess Efisio** found the sixth furlong made to measure for she would not have caught the long time leader over anything less. The way she stormed clear after striking the front, would suggest this is what she needs. (9/2: 3/1-5/1)
**2306 Vax New Way** returning to his ideal distance, possibly raced too freely in a clear lead for he looked like coming home alone, until his stride shortened and he was worn down inside the last half furlong. (2/1: 6/4-3/1)
**2532 Splicing** fails to produce her best on this surface and she was never really traveling like a winner. (7/4: op 3/1)
**Magic Lake** carries plenty of condition despite having had three outings, but she was in pursuit of the clear leader until finding demands too great for her approaching the final furlong. She has been running over a longer trip and there is much better to come than she has shown so far this term. (14/1: 10/1-16/1)
**2200 Standown**, taken along faster than he wished, did claw back a little of the lee-way in the latter stages but was never a factor. (4/1: 5/2-9/2)

## 2635 SELMESTON (S) STKS (2-Y.O) (Class G)
4-30 (4-30) **5f (Fibresand)** £2,070.00 (£570.00: £270.00) Stalls: Low GOING minus 0.06 sec per fur (STD)

| | | | | SP | RR | SF |
|---|---|---|---|---|---|---|
| *2371$^{3}$* | **Come Too Mamma's** (JBerry) **2-8-11** GCarter(7) (b.nr hind: hdwy over 2f out: r.o to ld nr fin) | — | 1 | 2/1$^{2}$ | 58 | 5 |
| 2279* | **Advance Repro** (JAkehurst) **2-8-11b** KFallon(2) (lw: a.p: rdn to ld ins fnl f: ct cl home) | hd | 2 | 5/1$^{3}$ | 58 | 5 |
| 2406$^{4}$ | **Dancing Star (IRE)** (PDEvans) **2-8-6v** JFortune(9) (dwlt: bhd & outpcd tl r.o wl ins fnl f) | 2½ | 3 | 16/1 | 45 | — |
| 2406$^{5}$ | **Tinker's Surprise (IRE)** (BJMeehan) **2-9-2b** MTebbutt(4) (led tl hrd rdn & hdd ins fnl f) | nk | 4 | 6/1 | 54 | 1 |
| *1093$^{7}$* | **Wedding Music** (PCHaslam) **2-8-1**(5) MBaird(5) (bit bkwd: outpcd: a in rr) | 6 | 5 | 16/1 | 25 | — |
| 2174$^{5}$ | **Whittle Times** (EJAlston) **2-8-6v$^{1}$** JFanning(8) (swtg: outpcd) | ½ | 6 | 25/1 | 23 | — |
| 465$^{W}$ | **Sylvania Lights** (WRMuir) **2-8-6** CRutter(6) (lt-f: prom 3f) | 2½ | 7 | 12/1 | 15 | — |
| 2509$^{7}$ | **Classic Services** (BPalling) **2-8-6b**(5) AmandaSanders(1) (swtg: outpcd: t.o) | 9 | 8 | 20/1 | — | — |
| 2174$^{3}$ | **Just Loui** (WGMTurner) **2-8-9**(7) DSweeney(3) (prom tl stumbled & uns rdr over 3f out) | | U | 6/4$^{1}$ | — | — |

(SP 132.4%) **9 Rn**

**63.8 secs** (5.10) CSF £14.10 TOTE £3.50: £1.00 £3.40 £7.90 (£6.50) Trio £41.40 OWNER Mr J. K. Brown (COCKERHAM) BRED D. Walker
No bid

**2371 Come Too Mamma's**, produced from off the pace, got the better of a hard fought set-to in the final furlong and proved just the stronger. Ridden this way, she will win again. (2/1)
**2279* Advance Repro** looked set to follow up her Folkestone success when gaining control 200 yards out, but despite a game effort, just failed to hang on. (5/1: 7/2-11/2)
**2406 Dancing Star (IRE)**, a shade slow from an outside stall, did not begin to make progress until approaching the last furlong and she could have been involved in the outcome with a level break. (16/1)
**2406 Tinker's Surprise (IRE)** tried for another all the way success but he had given his all just inside the final furlong. (6/1: 5/1-8/1)
**Sylvania Lights** (12/1: 5/1-14/1)
**2174 Just Loui** was swinging along in third place when he struck into the heels of a rival after almost a quarter of a mile, and deposited his rider into the sand head first. (6/4)

## 2636 ALFRISTON MAIDEN H'CAP (0-65) (3-Y.O+ F & M) (Class F)

5-00 (5-00) **1m 100y (Fibresand)** £2,381.00 (£656.00: £311.00) Stalls: Low GOING minus 0.06 sec per fur (STD)

| Form | Horse | Dist | Pos | SP | RR | SF |
|---|---|---|---|---|---|---|
| $2563^{4}$ | **Portite Sophie (29)** (MBrittain) **5-7-11** NCarlisle(7) (b: b.hind: a.p: rdn over 2f out: styd on to ld wl ins fnl f) | — | 1 | 14/1 | 38 | 20 |
| *$2369^{7}$* | **Sis Garden (50)** (TDEasterby) **3-8-9b** MBirch(2) (a.p: led over 4f out: sn clr: hrd rdn & hdd wl ins fnl f) | 1¾ | 2 | $5/2^{2}$ | 56 | 29 |
| *$2325^{2}$* | **Mystical Maid (58)** (HThomsonJones) **3-9-3** GCarter(11) (lw: hld up: effrt 3f out: sn rdn: nvr able to chal) | 3½ | 3 | $2/1^{1}$ | 57 | 30 |
| $1594^{5}$ | **Little Kenny (43)** (MJFetherston-Godley) **3-8-2v¹** FNorton(5) (b.off hind: a.p: hrd drvn over 2f out: one pce) | 2 | 4 | 10/1 | 38 | 11 |
| *$2308^{10}$* | **Nicola's Princess (53)** (BAMcMahon) **3-8-5**(7) KYu(8) (sddle slipped: sn chsng ldrs: wknd over 2f out) | 5 | 5 | 14/1 | 39 | 12 |
| $2507^{8}$ | **Bella Coola (35)** (MartynMeade) **4-8-3** NAdams(10) (nvr trbld ldrs) | 4 | 6 | 14/1 | 13 | — |
| $2058^{11}$ | **Lucy's Gold (28)** (MJRyan) **5-7-3**(7) AMcCarthy(6) (bit bkwd: a in rr) | ¾ | 7 | 33/1 | 5 | — |
| $1608^{7}$ | **Welcome Brief (49)** (EJAlston) **3-8-1**(7) IonaWands(12) (lw: a in rr) | 4 | 8 | 14/1 | 18 | — |
| *$1966^{12}$* | **Caherass Court (IRE) (30)** (BPreece) **5-7-7**(5)ow2 MBaird(9) (dwlt: a bhd) | 5 | 9 | 33/1 | — | — |
| $1876^{10}$ | **Fayre Holly (IRE) (65)** (MJHeaton-Ellis) **3-9-7**(3) SDrowne(4) (bkwd: led tl over 4f out: sn wknd: t.o) | 9 | 10 | 12/1 | 8 | — |
| $2079^{5}$ | **Esquiline (USA) (63)** (JHMGosden) **3-9-8** AMcGlone(1) (lw: s.i.s: hdwy 5f out: rdn & wknd over 2f out: t.o) | 3 | 11 | $4/1^{3}$ | — | — |
| *$1809^{4}$* | **Rustic Song (IRE) (37)** (JWharton) **3-7-10** AMackay(3) (lw: chsd ldrs tl rdn & lost tch 3f out: t.o) | 2½ | 12 | 8/1 | — | — |

(SP 142.3%) **12 Rn**

**1m 51.1** (6.10) CSF £55.49 CT £102.67 TOTE £13.70: £4.30 £1.60 £1.30 (£49.10) Trio £19.40 OWNER Ms Maureen Hanlon (WARTHILL)
BRED Mr and Mrs R. W. Lycett Green
LONG HANDICAP Lucy's Gold 7-2
WEIGHT FOR AGE 3yo-9lb
**2563 Portite Sophie**, having her second outing of the week, appreciated the step down to a shorter trip and battled on gamely to open her account nearing the line. (14/1)
**2168 Sis Garden** made her pursuers work hard to get to her in the closing stages, and there is no doubt she is knocking at the door. (5/2)
**2325 Mystical Maid**, attempting a slightly longer trip, took time to quicken when asked to quicken, and her one pace was just not good enough to get her into the action. (2/1)
**1594 Little Kenny** looked sure to figure in the prizes until fading quickly on the approach to the final furlong. (10/1: op 6/1)
**768 Nicola's Princess** did well to finish where she did after having a slipping saddle to contend with, and this performance can safely be disregarded. (14/1: op 8/1)
**2079 Esquiline (USA)** did not appear to take to the surface and ran no sort of race at all. (4/1: 5/2-9/2)

## 2637 LULLINGTON CLAIMING STKS (II) (3-Y.O+) (Class F)

5-30 (5-30) **7f (Fibresand)** £2,031.00 (£556.00: £261.00) Stalls: High GOING minus 0.06 sec per fur (STD)

| Form | Horse | Dist | Pos | SP | RR | SF |
|---|---|---|---|---|---|---|
| $592^{14}$ | **Berge (IRE) (79)** (WAO'Gorman) **5-9-4b** TIves(6) (trckd ldrs: led on bit wl over 1f out: comf) | — | 1 | $1/2^{1}$ | 67+ | 40 |
| *$2308^{7}$* | **Mustn't Grumble (IRE) (62)** (MissSJWilton) **6-8-13** SWhitworth(4) (hdwy 4f out: chsd wnr appr fnl f: r.o) | 1½ | 2 | 10/1 | 59 | 32 |
| $2496^{8}$ | **Souperficial (63)** (JAGlover) **5-9-2v** GCarter(2) (s.i.s: wl bhd tl gd hdwy 2f out: kpt on wl ins fnl f) | hd | 3 | $9/1^{3}$ | 61 | 34 |
| $1836^{5}$ | **Samara Song (55)** (WGMTurner) **3-8-8b** RPerham(5) (led: clr ½-wy: hdd wl over 1f out: kpt on same pce) | 3 | 4 | 20/1 | 55 | 20 |
| *$2551^{5}$* | **Dragonjoy (65)** (NPLittmoden) **3-8-12b** AMcGlone(3) (outpcd: nvr nrr) | 5 | 5 | $4/1^{2}$ | 47 | 12 |
| *$1719^{5}$* | **Royal Rapport (40)** (BAMcMahon) **3-8-1**(5) LNewton(7) (prom tl wknd fnl 2f) | s.h | 6 | 20/1 | 41 | 6 |
| *$781^{8}$* | **Shanoora (IRE) (40)** (MrsNMacauley) **3-8-2**(3)ow8 CTeague(1) (prom tl rdn & outpcd over 2f out) | 3 | 7 | 40/1 | 33 | — |
| | **Coeur Francais (FR)** (WJMusson) **4-9-6** WHollick(8) (s.i.s: a bhd & outpcd) | 3½ | 8 | 20/1 | 32 | 5 |
| $2193^{11}$ | **Manderella (60)** (JAkehurst) **3-8-3** DBiggs(9) (broke down & p.u over 4f out) | | P | 20/1 | — | — |

(SP 127.2%) **9 Rn**

**1m 29.5** (4.80) CSF £7.84 TOTE £1.80: £1.10 £1.80 £2.70 (£7.30) Trio £13.30 OWNER Mr S. Fustok (NEWMARKET) BRED S. Fustok
WEIGHT FOR AGE 3yo-8lb
**500* Berge (IRE)** is a class apart in claimers and although he had three and a half months' absence from the racecourse to overcome, he won without much trouble though it must be said, he probably hit the front plenty soon enough. (1/2)
**2308 Mustn't Grumble (IRE)** delayed his challenge and went after the winner inside the distance, but the runner-up prize was the only one at stake for him. (10/1: 8/1-12/1)
**Souperficial** was attempting the impossible after giving the principals so much of a start, for he made up an enormous amount of ground in the last quarter-mile, and it would seem he is about to strike form. (9/1: op 6/1)
**1836 Samara Song** set a brisk pace and tried to match strides when challenged, but the leading pair soon took his measure and he had no answer. (20/1)
**2551 Dragonjoy** looked ill at ease cantering to post and, never taking hold of his bit, would seem to be going the wrong way. (4/1)

T/Plpt: £3.50 (2,952.92 Tckts). T/Qdpt: £2.80 (186.55 Tckts). IM

## 2638a-2662a (Irish Racing) - See Computer Raceform

# 2479a-HAMBURG (Germany) (R-H) (Heavy)

## Saturday July 6th

## 2663a HOLSTEN TROPHY (Gp 3) (3-Y.O+)

3-43 (3-58) **6f** £54,054.00 (£21,622.00)

| Form | Horse | Dist | Pos | SP | RR | SF |
|---|---|---|---|---|---|---|
| 1753a* | **Waky Nao** (HBlume,Germany) **3-8-9** ASuborics | — | 1 | | 110 | — |
| $2115^{4}$ | **Hever Golf Rose** (TJNaughton) **5-9-5** DHolland | ½ | 2 | | 113 | — |

| | | | | SP | RR | SF |
|---|---|---|---|---|---|---|
| 1136a2 | **Macanal (USA)** (HJentzsch,Germany) **4-9-3** PSchiergen | 1¼ | **3** | | 107 | — |
| 2271a6 | **Passion For Life** (GLewis) **3-8-11** PaulEddery (btn over 5½l) | | **12** | | — | — |

**13 Rn**

**1m 15.74** (6.24) TOTE 48DM: 19DM 17DM 17DM (205DM) OWNER Mr H. von Finck BRED H. von Finck
**2115 Hever Golf Rose** put up yet another tough and genuine display. Always close up and third into the straight, she took up the running two furlongs out and looked to have the race won, but was just collared on the line.
**2271a Passion For Life** hated the heavy ground and this performance can be disregarded. He showed some good early toe and led the field for three furlongs before weakening, and his jockey eased him down inside the final furlong.

## 2276a-LONGCHAMP (Paris, France) (R-H) (Very Soft)
## Saturday July 6th

### 2664a PRIX DU BOIS (Gp 3) (2-Y.O)
2-00 (1-56) **5f** £28,986.00 (£10,540.00: £5,270.00)

| | | | | SP | RR | SF |
|---|---|---|---|---|---|---|
| 2269a* | **Deep Finesse** (WJarvis) **2-8-11** PRobinson | — | **1** | | 88+ | — |
| 2269a3 | **Nombre Premier** (AdeRoyerDupre,France) **2-8-11** TGillet | ¾ | **2** | | 86 | — |
| | **Alberelle** (MmeMBollack-Badel,France) **2-8-8** ABadel | 3 | **3** | | 73 | — |

**6 Rn**

**59.2 secs** (4.70) P-M 3.30F: 1.90F 3.00F (18.50F) OWNER J. E. Sims (NEWMARKET) BRED D. A. and Mrs Hicks
**2269a* Deep Finesse** pinged out of the stalls for a pillar-to-post victory in France's first two-year-old Group event. This well-developed colt coped particularly well with the soft ground, and looks to have a future in juvenile sprints. His next target could be either the Newbury Super Sprint, or the Prix Robert Papin at Maisons-Laffitte, with the long-term aim, the Flying Childers at Doncaster.
**Nombre Premier**, last early on, came out of the pack to chase the winner in the final furlong.
**Alberelle**, who finished well to take third place having been outpaced at halfway, will probably be suited by a bit further and will come on for this experience. Her next target is either a listed event at Maisons-Laffitte, or the Prix Robert Papin.

### 2665a PRIX HUBERT DE CHAUDENAY (Gp 2) (3-Y.O)
3-35 (3-27) **1m 7f** £39,526.00 (£15,810.00: £7,905.00: £3,953.00)

| | | | | SP | RR | SF |
|---|---|---|---|---|---|---|
| | **Tarator (USA)** (ELellouche,France) **3-8-11** OPeslier (bhd: hdwy to ld 3f out: rdn & wnt clr wl over 1f out: easily) | — | **1** | | 107+ | — |
| 2108a3 | **Irish Woman (FR)** (MmeMBollack-Badel,France) **3-8-8** ABadel (bhd: 4th & rdn st: styd on one pce ins fnl f) | 10 | **2** | | 93 | — |
| 2108a* | **Cachet Noir (USA)** (PBary,France) **3-8-11** FGrenet (mid div: rdn ent st: one pce) | 3 | **3** | | 93 | — |
| 2247* | **Steamroller Stanly** (CACyzer) **3-8-11** FHead (trckd ldr: rdn ½-wy: btn st) | 5 | **4** | | 88 | — |
| 22333 | **Bowled Over** (CACyzer) **3-8-11** PRobinson (led to 3f out: 2nd & rdn st: sn wknd) | 5 | **5** | | 83 | — |

**5 Rn**

**3m 16.1** (10.10) P-M 2.40F: 1.70F 1.90F (11.40F) OWNER Mr Wafic Said BRED Clovelly Farms
**Tarator (USA)** could not have been more impressive. Held up in fourth position early on, he took much closer order coming into the straight and, after leading as they swung for home, simply powered clear to increase the daylight between himself and the second the further they went. This son of Green Dancer made the step up from handicaps without difficulty, and his next target is either the Prix Kergorlay or the Grand Prix de Deauville, both during August.
**2108a Irish Woman (FR)**, outstaying Cachet Noir in the closing stages to secure the runner-up spot, obviously appreciated this trip, but was totally outclassed by the winner.
**2108a* Cachet Noir (USA)** did not seem to stay, being outbattled for second late on. He is a decent listed to Group Three-class horse over a shorter distance, and his limitations in both stamina and class were found out here.
**2247* Steamroller Stanly** was outpaced at halfway and last into the straight. He plugged on for fourth position, but was not up to this class.
**2233 Bowled Over** made the majority of the running, but was back-pedalling as soon as he was headed coming into the straight. Like his stable-companion, he was simply outclassed.
DS

## 2278a-SAN SIRO (Milan, Italy) (R-H) (Soft)
## Saturday July 6th

### 2666a PREMIO CINGOLINA MAIDEN (2-Y.O F)
4-30 (4-43) **7f** £6,902.00

| | | | | SP | RR | SF |
|---|---|---|---|---|---|---|
| | **Folgore (USA)** (JLDunlop) **2-9-0** FJovine | — | **1** | | — | — |
| | **Swith Water (IRE)** (VOriani,Italy) **2-9-0** LPanici | 5¾ | **2** | | — | — |
| | **Standing Ovation (ITY)** (BGrizzetti,Italy) **2-9-0** LSorrentino | hd | **3** | | — | — |

**11 Rn**

**1m 30.5** (11.60) TOTE 16L: 13L 20L 21L (96L) OWNER Allevamento Annarosa (ARUNDEL) BRED Allevamento Annarosa
**Folgore (USA)** put up a gallant display on this debut. Despite missing the break, she was soon on terms and hit the front inside the final two furlongs. Running on strongly all the way to the line, she never looked like being caught and, as she will definitely come on from this run, she is one to keep an eye on.

### 2667a PREMIO BIELMONTE MAIDEN (2-Y.O)
5-00 (5-11) **7f** £6,902.00

| | | | | SP | RR | SF |
|---|---|---|---|---|---|---|
| | **Honey Colour (IRE)** (AColella,Italy) **2-9-0** GBietolini | — | **1** | | — | — |
| | **Minarello (USA)** (GVerricelli,Italy) **2-9-0** LSorrentino | 4½ | **2** | | — | — |
| | **Beton Lucky (USA)** (NBerni,Italy) **2-9-0** ETasende | s.h | **3** | | — | — |
| | **Passi d'Orlando (IRE)** (JLDunlop) **2-9-0** GForte (btn approx 5½l) | | **5** | | — | — |

**10 Rn**

**1m 30.1** (11.20) TOTE 59L: 21L 47L 18L (726L) OWNER San Paolo Agri Stud BRED Azienda Agricola San Paolo
**Passi d'Orlando (IRE)** was disappointing. Soon outpaced and last until halfway, his effort well over a furlong out was short-lived, and he ran on at one pace in the final furlong. He should have benefitted from the race, and will be expected to run better next time.

# 2663a-HAMBURG (Germany) (R-H) (Heavy)
## Sunday July 7th

### 2668a DEUTSCHES DERBY (Gp 1) (3-Y.O C & F)
3-45 (3-49) **1m 4f** £227,477.00

| | Horse | Dist | Pos | SP | RR | SF |
|---|---|---|---|---|---|---|
| 2109a* | **Lavirco (GER)** (PRau,Germany) **3-9-2** TMundry (a.p: 5th st: led over 2f out: r.o wl) | — | 1 | | 114 | — |
| 2109a2 | **Surako (GER)** (HJentzsch,Germany) **3-9-2** PSchiergen (a.p: 4th st: ev ch 2f out: one pce) | 4 | 2 | | 109 | — |
| | **Albaran (GER)** (HHorwart,Germany) **3-9-2** MRimmer (mid div to st: swtchd & gd hdwy over 1f out: no ex) | ½ | 3 | | 108 | — |
| 2109a6 | **Ocean Sea (USA)** (BSchutz,Germany) **3-9-2** LMader (hdwy ½-wy: 6th st: styd on one pce fnl 2f) | 3 | 4 | | 104 | — |
| 2109a4 | **Zero Problemo (IRE)** (BSchutz,Germany) **3-9-2** AStarke (7th st: one pce fr 2f out) | 4 | 5 | | 99 | — |
| | **Master Blade (GER)** (HRemmert,Germany) **3-9-2** KWoodburn (8th st: swtchd & styd on fnl 2f: nvr nrr) | nk | 6 | | 98 | — |
| | **Wind Of Chance (GER)** (BSchutz,Germany) **3-9-2** THellier (a mid div) | 3 | 7 | | 94 | — |
| | **Silver Sign** (HJentzsch,Germany) **3-9-2b1** ATylicki (trckd ldr: 2nd st: sn wknd) | 4½ | 8 | | 88 | — |
| | **Kavin (GER)** (RSuerland,Germany) **3-9-2** AHelfenbein (nvr rchd ldrs) | nk | 9 | | 88 | — |
| 2109a5 | **My Happy Guest (IRE)** (ALowe,Germany) **3-9-2** WMongil (nt rch ldrs) | ½ | 10 | | 87 | — |
| 1751a9 | **Bad Bertrich Again (IRE)** (ALowe,Germany) **3-9-2** NGrant (wl bhd to st: no hdwy) | ½ | 11 | | 87 | — |
| 2109a3 | **Bon Jovi (GER)** (HJentzsch,Germany) **3-9-2** WRyan (prom: 3rd & rdn st: wknd qckly) | ¾ | 12 | | 86 | — |
| | **Val Di Taro (GER)** (HBlume,Germany) **3-9-2** JReid (last st: no imp) | 1 | 13 | | 84 | — |
| 1751a3 | **Flamingo Garden (GER)** (HBlume,Germany) **3-9-2** ASuborics (nvr bttr than mid div) | 1¼ | 14 | | 83 | — |
| 1751a2 | **Agnelli** (HJentzsch,Germany) **3-9-2** LHammer-Hansen (led tl over 2f out: sn wknd) | 1½ | 15 | | 81 | — |
| 1751a4 | **Sir Warren (IRE)** (HBlume,Germany) **3-9-2** MLarsen (a bhd) | 3 | 16 | | 77 | — |
| | **Lucky Power (IRE)** (ALowe,Germany) **3-9-2** CAsmussen (a bhd) | 1½ | 17 | | 75 | — |
| 21164 | **Germano** (GWragg) **3-9-2** MHills (prom over 8f: wknd qckly) | 1¼ | 18 | | 73 | — |

**18 Rn**

**2m 41.7** (13.70) TOTE 29DM: 16DM 18DM 43DM (107DM) OWNER Gestut Fahrhof BRED Gestut Fahrhof Stiftung

**2109a* Lavirco (GER)** justified favouritism with a clear victory to add to his German 2000 Guineas and Union-Rennen successes. He looks better over this distance than a mile.

**2116 Germano** has run much better than this in the past but was unable to handle the conditions. Prominent and travelling well for the first mile, he weakened with four furlongs to go. He should be able to pick up a smaller race on better ground.

# NANTES (France) (L-H) (Very Soft)
## Sunday July 7th

### 2669a GRAND PRIX DE LA REGION DES PAYS DE LA LOIRE (DERBY DE L'OUEST) (Listed) (3-Y.O)
2-25 (2-27) **1m 4f** £21,080.00 (£7,378.00: £3,689.00)

| | Horse | Dist | Pos | SP | RR | SF |
|---|---|---|---|---|---|---|
| 17919 | **Chief Contender (IRE)** (PWChapple-Hyam) **3-8-9** DHarrison | — | 1 | | 103 | — |
| | **Faucon Royal (FR)** (J-CRouget,France) **3-9-2** OPeslier | 1½ | 2 | | 108 | — |
| | **Fly For Fame** (H-APantall,France) **3-8-6** TGillet | nk | 3 | | 98 | — |

**10 Rn**

**2m 48.0** P-M 3.80F: 2.20F 2.30F 8.20F (24.90F) OWNER Mrs S. Magnier (MARLBOROUGH) BRED Jayeff 'B' Stables & Calogo Bloodstock A G

**1791 Chief Contender (IRE)** became the first horse that ran in the Derby to win since. After breaking well, he raced second until about halfway where he took up the running. Lengthening his lead in the straight without being too hard pressed, his trainer believes he learnt a lot from his run at Epsom and is on the upgrade. He will now be aimed at a Group Three race at Deauville.
DS

# AGNANO (Naples, Italy) (R-H) (Good)
## Sunday July 7th

### 2670a GRAN PREMIO CITTA DI NAPOLI (Gp 3) (3-Y.O+)
10-15 **1m 2f** £26,552.00 (£12,363.00: £6,943.00)

| | Horse | Dist | Pos | SP | RR | SF |
|---|---|---|---|---|---|---|
| | **Snake Snap** (VCaruso,Italy) **3-8-2** MEsposito | — | 1 | | 114 | — |
| 2278a2 | **Scribano** (GBotti,Italy) **6-8-13** EBotti | 3½ | 2 | | 108 | — |
| | **Speed Rahy (USA)** (RTibiletti,Italy) **5-8-13** SDettori | 1½ | 3 | | 106 | — |

**13 Rn**

**2m 2.3** TOTE 42L: 18L 17L 41L (69L) OWNER Curtasse Srl BRED Major General Sir G. Burns

# 2666a-SAN SIRO (Milan, Italy) (R-H) (Good)
## Sunday July 7th

### 2671a PREMIO PRIMI PASSI (Gp 3) (2-Y.O)
5-00 (5-30) **6f** £25,895.00

| | Horse | Dist | Pos | SP | RR | SF |
|---|---|---|---|---|---|---|
| 1565a2 | **Kingsinger (IRE)** (MRChannon) **2-8-11** RHughes | — | 1 | | 95 | — |
| | **Doctor Leckter (USA)** (APeraino,Italy) **2-8-11** FJovine | 2 | 2 | | 90 | — |
| | **Miliardaire (IRE)** (GColleo,Italy) **2-8-11** MLatorre | ½ | 3 | | 88 | — |
| 207010 | **Raven Master (USA)** (PWChapple-Hyam) **2-8-11** BThomson | | 5 | | — | — |

**6 Rn**

**1m 11.0** (3.00) TOTE 21L: 13L 14L (26L) OWNER Scuderia Gianni Daniele (UPPER LAMBOURN) BRED Bernard Eivers

**1565a Kingsinger (IRE)** proved a good purchase for his new owners with a comfortable win in this Group Three event. Always prominent, this son of Fairy King went to the fore approaching the final furlong and ran on well to the line. He will now be trained in Italy.

**1519* Raven Master (USA)** disappointed connections with a relatively poor run. Last to halfway, he never got into a challenging position. He is capable of better.

# 2218-CHESTER (L-H) (Good to firm)

## Friday July 12th

Race 4: No Time Taken - Technical Failure, Race 6: hand-timed.
WEATHER: sunny & warm WIND: slt against

### 2672 TARPORLEY APPRENTICE H'CAP (0-70) (3-Y.O+) (Class E)

6-30 (6-31) **7f 122y** £3,114.75 (£948.00: £466.50: £225.75) Stalls: Low GOING minus 0.75 sec per fur (HD)

| Form | Horse | Dist | Pos | SP | RR | SF |
|---|---|---|---|---|---|---|
| $713^{7}$ | **Pine Ridge Lad (IRE) (57)** (JLEyre) **6-9-5** OPears(5) (mde all: drvn clr 2f out: unchal) | — | 1 | $3/1^{1}$ | 71 | 27 |
| $2428^{3}$ | **My Gallery (IRE) (62)** (ABailey) **5-9-5**$^{(5)}$ AngelaGallimore(3) (mid div: effrt over 2f out: r.o fnl f: nt rch wnr) | 2½ | 2 | $9/2^{2}$ | 71 | 27 |
| $2521^{2}$ | **Cee-Jay-Ay (46)** (JBerry) **9-8-1**$^{(7)}$ CLowther(8) (s.i.s: bhd tl r.o wl appr fnl f) | 1 | 3 | 7/1 | 53 | 9 |
| 2428* | **Ballard Lady (IRE) (40)** (JSWainwright) **4-7-9**$^{(7)\ 7x}$ PDoe(11) (lw: chsd wnr tl wknd ins fnl f) | 1¼ | 4 | 7/1 | 44 | — |
| $2428^{2}$ | **Royal Comedian (38)** (BWMurray) **7-7-7**$^{(7)}$ RCody-Boutcher(4) (lw: trckd ldng pair: rdn over 2f out: wknd appr fnl f) | 1¾ | 5 | $11/2^{3}$ | 38 | — |
| *$2303^{4}$* | **Angus McCoatup (IRE) (54)** (BAMcMahon) **3-8-2**$^{(5)}$ KYu(6) (lw: trckd ldrs: rdn 2f out: sn btn) | 2 | 6 | 11/1 | 50 | — |
| $2392^{3}$ | **Best Kept Secret (52)** (PDEvans) **5-8-11v**$^{(3)}$ ADaly(2) (sn drvn along: a bhd) | 2½ | 7 | 14/1 | 43 | — |
| $2222^{3}$ | **Scenicris (IRE) (57)** (RHollinshead) **3-8-7**$^{(3)}$ DGriffiths(10) (bhd & outpcd: rdn over 2f out: no imp) | s.h | 8 | 11/1 | 48 | — |
| *$2550^{3}$* | **David James' Girl (59)** (ABailey) **4-9-2**$^{(5)}$ IonaWands(7) (swtg: a bhd & outpcd) | 6 | 9 | 15/2 | 37 | — |
| | **Dona Filipa (43)** (MissLCSiddall) **3-7-7**$^{(3)}$ CAdamson(1) (bit bkwd: in tch 4f: sn wknd: t.o) | 18 | 10 | 33/1 | — | — |

(SP 121.6%) **10 Rn**

**1m 33.36** (1.36) CSF £16.86 CT £84.01 TOTE £3.60: £1.20 £2.50 £2.20 (£5.60) Trio £26.60 OWNER Whitestonecliffe Racing Partnership (HAMBLETON) BRED Whitechurch Stud in Ireland
LONG HANDICAP Dona Filipa 7-7
WEIGHT FOR AGE 3yo-9lb

**713 Pine Ridge Lad (IRE)**, produced fresh and well after a three-month break, soon established a clear lead and proved far too good for these rivals. (3/1)

**2428 My Gallery (IRE)** turned in another good effort from the top of the handicap, but never looked capable of getting to terms with the winner. (9/2: 6/1-4/1)

**2521 Cee-Jay-Ay** weaved his way through inside the distance and ran on strongly towards the finish, but had set himself too big a task. (7/1)

**2428* Ballard Lady (IRE)**, not quite so effective on this livelier ground, was always at full stretch in an attempt to keep tabs on the winner, and she had shot her bolt approaching the final furlong. (7/1)

**2428 Royal Comedian** came off the bridle before reaching the straight, and was down to a walk inside the last furlong. (11/2)

**2303 Angus McCoatup (IRE)** is still struggling to make his mark and, feeling the strain from some way out, had to accept the inevitable. (11/1)

### 2673 TARVIN LIMITED STKS (0-70) (3-Y.O+) (Class D)

7-00 (7-01) **1m 4f 66y** £3,972.25 (£1,198.00: £581.50: £273.25) Stalls: Low GOING minus 0.75 sec per fur (HD)

| Form | Horse | Dist | Pos | SP | RR | SF |
|---|---|---|---|---|---|---|
| $2390^{2}$ | **Break the Rules (68)** (MrsMReveley) **4-9-6** PaulEddery(3) (hld up in rr: stdy hdwy 3f out: qcknd to ld appr fnl f: comf) | — | 1 | $2/1^{2}$ | 74+ | — |
| *228** | **Seattle Saga (USA) (70)** (DRLoder) **3-8-9** PatEddery(1) (bit bkwd: led: pushed along & qcknd 3f out: rdn whn hdd over 1f out: one pce) | 1¼ | 2 | $5/4^{1}$ | 74 | — |
| $2067^{7}$ | **Chocolate Ice (70)** (CACyzer) **3-8-7** JFortune(4) (chsd ldr: effrt over 2f out: unable qckn ins fnl f) | hd | 3 | $7/2^{3}$ | 72 | — |
| $2482^{5}$ | **Dance King (66)** (RHarris) **4-9-3**$^{(5)}$ ADaly(2) (hld up: effrt over 2f out: rdn & outpcd appr fnl f) | 1½ | 4 | 8/1 | 72 | — |

(SP 111.1%) **4 Rn**

**2m 44.15** (7.55) CSF £4.82 TOTE £2.60 (£1.80) OWNER Mr P. D. Savill (SALTBURN) BRED Cleaboy Farms Co
WEIGHT FOR AGE 3yo-13lb

**2390 Break the Rules**, winning his first race beyond a mile, was always travelling best and, set alight to lead approaching the final furlong, soon had the prize sewn up. (2/1)

**228* Seattle Saga (USA)**, successful on the All-Weather on his only previous run just over five months ago, looked as if the race was needed. Adopting the ideal tactics for this track, he found the far more experienced winner too smart for him in the closing stages. (5/4)

**1631 Chocolate Ice**, the only maiden in the field, tried his best to make a race of it, and it was only his inability to quicken that was beating him in the battle to the finish. He is running well enough to win a race in the none too distant future. (7/2)

**2482 Dance King** delivered his challenge on the approach to the straight, and momentarily looked a danger but, once the winner said go, he was tapped for toe. (8/1)

### 2674 BREITLING WATCHES AND WALTONS OF CHESTER H'CAP (0-90) (3-Y.O+) (Class C)

7-30 (7-31) **1m 4f 66y** £6,167.00 (£1,856.00: £898.00: £419.00) Stalls: Low GOING minus 0.75 sec per fur (HD)

| Form | Horse | Dist | Pos | SP | RR | SF |
|---|---|---|---|---|---|---|
| 2522* | **Desert Frolic (IRE) (78)** (MJohnston) **3-8-6** $^{5x}$ JWeaver(3) (set str pce: clr fnl 2f: unchal) | — | 1 | $7/4^{1}$ | 95 | 34 |
| $2350^{3}$ | **Celestial Choir (82)** (JLEyre) **6-9-6**$^{(3)}$ OPears(7) (lw: hld up: gd hdwy over 3f out: chsd wnr fnl 2f: no imp) | 6 | 2 | 7/1 | 91 | 43 |
| *$2553^{3}$* | **In the Money (IRE) (59)** (RHollinshead) **7-7-11**$^{(3)}$ FLynch(1) (trckd ldrs: rdn over 2f out: styd on fnl f) | 3½ | 3 | 10/1 | 64 | 16 |
| 1618* | **Leading Spirit (IRE) (83)** (CFWall) **4-9-10** PatEddery(6) (lw: hld up & bhd: drvn along & hdwy 3f out: one pce appr fnl f) | 1¼ | 4 | $11/4^{2}$ | 86 | 38 |
| $2006^{5}$ | **Exalted (IRE) (84)** (SirMarkPrescott) **3-8-12** KDarley(4) (lw: chsd wnr: pushed along 5f out: wknd over 2f out) | 6 | 5 | $6/1^{3}$ | 79 | 18 |
| $1793^{11}$ | **Pinkerton's Pal (80)** (CEBrittain) **5-9-7** BDoyle(5) (hld up: a bhd) | 8 | 6 | 20/1 | 65 | 17 |
| $2494^{2}$ | **Trade Wind (67)** (JGMO'Shea) **5-8-8b** VSlattery(2) (trckd ldrs: rdn ½-wy: grad wknd) | s.h | 7 | 14/1 | 52 | 4 |
| $2074^{17}$ | **Shenango (IRE) (78)** (GWragg) **3-8-6** PaulEddery(8) (trckd ldrs tl hrd drvn & wknd over 4f out: t.o) | 11 | 8 | 14/1 | 48 | — |

(SP 117.0%) **8 Rn**

**2m 36.2** (-0.40) CSF £13.94 CT £88.36 TOTE £2.70: £1.50 £1.90 £1.70 (£8.80) OWNER Maktoum Al Maktoum (MIDDLEHAM) BRED Gainsborough Stud Management Ltd
WEIGHT FOR AGE 3yo-13lb

**2522* Desert Frolic (IRE)**, continuing her step up in class, was not afraid to force a strong gallop and, piling on the pressure turning in, was able to saunter home at her leisure. She is still some way ahead of the Handicapper. (7/4: op Evens)

**2350 Celestial Choir** found this strongly-run race testing her stamina to the full, and may have been trying the impossible in attempting to concede 14lb to the still-improving winner. (7/1)

**2553 In the Money (IRE)** was struggling to hold on three furlongs out but, with his undoubted stamina coming into play, battled on in the latter stages to make the frame. (10/1: op 16/1)

**1618* Leading Spirit (IRE)** tried hard to get himself into contention three furlongs out but, with the tempo being maintained, was forced to call enough below the distance. (11/4)
**2006 Exalted (IRE)**, taking on older horses for the first time, found the relentless gallop and the lively ground taking its toll half a mile out, and gradually faded out of contention. (6/1)

## 2675 RETAIL ADVERTISING SERVICES MAIDEN STKS (3-Y.O+ F & M) (Class D)

8-00 (8-01) **7f 122y** £4,276.00 (£1,288.00: £624.00: £292.00) Stalls: Low GOING: 0.00 sec per fur (G)

| | | | | SP | RR | SF |
|---|---|---|---|---|---|---|
| *2555*$^{6}$ | **Steal 'Em (56)** (ABailey) **3-8-12** JFortune(3) (led 6f out: rdn & hld on gamely fnl f) | — | 1 | 6/1$^{3}$ | 67 | — |
| 1882$^{5}$ | **Misrule (USA)** (JHMGosden) **3-8-12** PatEddery(4) (lw: sn chsng wnr: effrt ent st: edgd lft over 1f out: hrd rdn & r.o) | ½ | 2 | 8/13$^{1}$ | 66 | — |
| 2316$^{8}$ | **Lachesis (63)** (RHollinshead) **3-8-9**$^{(3)}$ FLynch(1) (led early: a.p: swtchd rt & rdn appr fnl f: sn outpcd) | 5 | 3 | 11/4$^{2}$ | 55 | — |
| | **Angel Face (USA)** (BPreece) **3-8-12** VSlattery(2) (bit bkwd: unruly s: hld up: hdwy 3f out: outpcd fnl 2f) | 3½ | 4 | 10/1 | 48 | — |
| | | | | (SP 111.9%) | | **4 Rn** |

**No Time Taken** CSF £10.29 TOTE £5.90 (£2.60) OWNER Mr Stephen Hassett (TARPORLEY) BRED Mrs V. E. Hughes
**2555 Steal 'Em**, who made her seasonal debut on the All-Weather seven days ago, proved the stronger of the principals when the pressure was on, and opened her account most unexpectedly. (6/1)
**1882 Misrule (USA)** was pulling double in behind the winner for most of the way but, when push came to shove, she dropped everything, and it was only her jockey's perseverance that enabled her to make a race of it. (8/13)
**1160 Lachesis** failed to find anything extra when the whips were cracking inside the distance, and was brushed aside with ease. (11/4)
**Angel Face (USA)**, very unruly in the preliminaries and in the stalls, closed up three furlongs out, but did not last for long as lack of a recent outing began to take its toll. (10/1)

## 2676 KIDSONS IMPEY H'CAP (0-95) (3-Y.O) (Class C)

8-30 (8-31) **5f 16y** £5,777.00 (£1,736.00: £838.00: £389.00) Stalls: Low GOING minus 0.75 sec per fur (HD)

| | | | | SP | RR | SF |
|---|---|---|---|---|---|---|
| 2431$^{3}$ | **U-No-Harry (IRE) (68)** (RHollinshead) **3-7-10**$^{(3)}$ FLynch(2) (lw: a.p: qcknd to ld 100y out: r.o wl) | — | 1 | 9/4$^{1}$ | 75 | 5 |
| 2292$^{5}$ | **Tadeo (90)** (MJohnston) **3-9-7** JWeaver(1) (led tl ins fnl f: rallied cl home) | nk | 2 | 7/2$^{3}$ | 96 | 26 |
| 2496* | **Gwespyr (65)** (JBerry) **3-7-10**$^{7x}$ JQuinn(5) (s.i.s: hdwy ½-wy: led jst ins fnl f: sn hdd: r.o) | nk | 3 | 3/1$^{2}$ | 70 | — |
| 2222$^{5}$ | **Myttons Mistake (73)** (ABailey) **3-7-11**$^{(7)}$ IonaWands(4) (s.i.s: gd hdwy 2f out: sltly hmpd & swtchd ent fnl f: unable qckn) | 1¼ | 4 | 15/2 | 74 | 4 |
| 1599$^{5}$ | **Princely Sound (71)** (MBell) **3-8-2**$^{ow1}$ MFenton(3) (lw: chsd ldr 3f: sn rdn: outpcd appr fnl f) | 6 | 5 | 3/1$^{2}$ | 53 | — |
| | | | | (SP 114.8%) | | **5 Rn** |

**61.05 secs** (1.05) CSF £10.05 TOTE £2.60: £1.40 £1.90 (£4.40) OWNER Mr D. Coppenhall (UPPER LONGDON) BRED A. J. Poulton (Epping) Ltd
**2431 U-No-Harry (IRE)** had no trouble in reverting to the minimum trip and won this with far more in hand than the verdict might suggest. (9/4)
**2292 Tadeo** appears to be in the hands of the Handicapper at present, but he ran up to his mark here and, when given half a chance, will get back to winning ways. (7/2)
**2496* Gwespyr**, making a quick reappearance, had more on his plate this time, but he came to win his race 200 yards out, before getting tapped for speed in the dash to the line. (3/1)
**2222 Myttons Mistake** made his move between horses entering the straight, but was forced to switch when a rival took his ground passing the furlong marker, and that manoeuvre ended what slight hope remained. (15/2: 5/1-8/1)
**1599 Princely Sound** dropped away very quickly once in line for home, and it is possible he finds the minimum trip on such a tight track too sharp for him. (3/1)

## 2677 FARNDON CONDITIONS STKS (3-Y.O+) (Class B)

9-00 (9-01) **1m 2f 75y** £8,417.50 (£3,152.50: £1,543.75: £666.25: £300.63: £154.37) Stalls: High GOING minus 0.75 sec per fur (HD)

| | | | | SP | RR | SF |
|---|---|---|---|---|---|---|
| 2273a$^{4}$ | **Prince of Andros (USA) (111)** (DRLoder) **6-9-2v**$^{1}$ PatEddery(5) (lw: hld up in tch: led over 1f out: drvn out) | — | 1 | 3/1$^{2}$ | 113 | 34 |
| 2116$^{6}$ | **Don Vito** (RCharlton) **3-8-7** TSprake(3) (dwlt: hld up & bhd: hdwy over 2f out: swtchd rt appr fnl f: fin wl) | 1½ | 2 | 4/1$^{3}$ | 113 | 23 |
| 1949a$^{8}$ | **Solar Crystal (IRE) (110)** (HRACecil) **3-8-0** AMcGlone(1) (hld up: hdwy to ld 3f out: hdd over 1f out: one pce) | 1½ | 3 | 5/2$^{1}$ | 103 | 13 |
| 1963* | **Shanaladee** (MRStoute) **3-8-7** TQuinn(7) (dwlt: hdwy 5f out: hrd drvn ent st: one pce) | 1½ | 4 | 9/2 | 108 | 18 |
| 2274a$^{7}$ | **Quakers Field (102)** (GLMoore) **3-8-6**$^{ow1}$ JWeaver(8) (prom: carried wd after 2f: sn chsng ldrs: rdn & btn 2f out) | 4 | 5 | 20/1 | 101 | 10 |
| 2535$^{3}$ | **Weet-A-Minute (IRE) (106)** (RHollinshead) **3-8-5** FLynch(6) (led tl rn wd & hdd after 2f: led 6f out to 3f out: sn rdn & wknd ent st) | 1½ | 6 | 5/1 | 98 | 8 |
| | **Sayeh (IRE) (95)** (MajorWRHern) **4-9-2** PaulEddery(4) (bit bkwd: hld up in tch: effrt & rdn over 4f out: grad wknd) | 3 | 7 | 14/1 | 93 | 14 |
| 2536$^{6}$ | **Rebel County (IRE) (71)** (ABailey) **3-8-2** MFenton(2) (lw: lft in ld after 2f: hdd 6f out: wknd over 3f out: t.o) | 10 | 8 | 33/1 | 74 | — |
| | | | | (SP 122.8%) | | **8 Rn** |

**2m 9.5** (0.80) CSF £15.82 TOTE £3.80: £1.40 £2.20 £1.70 (£12.40) OWNER Dr Sinn Dung Wing (NEWMARKET) BRED Spendthrift Farm
WEIGHT FOR AGE 3yo-11lb
**2273a Prince of Andros (USA)**, the class act on show, delivered the goods without too much difficulty and supplied his jockey with his hundredth winner of the season. (3/1)
**2116 Don Vito** lacks the experience of the winner and, given a very patient ride on such a fast track, did extremely well to get so close. He looks the type to make the grade. (4/1)
**1004 Solar Crystal (IRE)** adopted more patient tactics on this occasion and, though she did strike the front, she was swamped for speed when the race to the finish really developed. (5/2)
**1963* Shanaladee**, a very poor mover, showed signs of greenness when the pressure was on, but he did not fare badly in this company, and will be all the wiser for the experience. (9/2)
**2274a Quakers Field** could have found this ground plenty fast enough, but he held his pitch until getting left behind when the race began in earnest. He has been highly tried and would appreciate a step down in class. (20/1)
**2535 Weet-A-Minute (IRE)**, in and out of the lead for almost a mile, then had to admit this company was too hot for him. (5/1)

T/Plpt: £261.10 (60.24 Tckts). T/Qdpt: £39.20 (22.73 Tckts). IM

# 2487-HAMILTON (R-H) (Good to firm)
## Friday July 12th

WEATHER: sunny periods WIND: almost nil

## 2678 SUNDAY MAIL AMATEUR H'CAP (0-65) (3-Y.O+) (Class F)

6-45 (6-45) **1m 1f 36y** £2,766.00 (£776.00: £378.00) Stalls: High GOING minus 0.70 sec per fur (HD)

| | | | Pos | SP | RR | SF |
|---|---|---|---|---|---|---|
| 2587* | **Gold Blade (54)** (JPearce) **7-11-8** 5x MrsLPearce(2) (lw: sn prom: effrt 4f out: led over 1f out: styd on wl) | — | 1 | 9/4[1] | 66 | 47 |
| 2214[8] | **New Albion (USA) (57)** (MissZAGreen) **5-11-11** MrABalding(7) (chsd ldrs: lft in ld over 2f out: hdd over 1f out: sn btn) | 2½ | 2 | 20/1 | 65 | 46 |
| 2481[5] | **Langtonian (33)** (JLEyre) **7-10-1b** MissDianaJones(6) (b.nr hind: s.i.s: hdwy ½-wy: hmpd over 2f out: kpt on fnl f: nvr able to chal) | 1 | 3 | 16/1 | 39 | 20 |
| *2303[8]* | **Hutchies Lady (38)** (RMMcKellar) **4-9-13**(7) MrsCWilliams(8) (b.hind: in tch: effrt 4f out: no imp) | 2½ | 4 | 50/1 | 40 | 21 |
| 2014[2] | **Talented Ting (IRE) (60)** (PCHaslam) **7-12-0v** MrCBonner(5) (led tl hdd over 4f out: lft w ev ch 2f out: sn wknd) | 3 | 5 | 5/2[2] | 56 | 37 |
| 2587[6] | **Commander Glen (IRE) (60)** (MrsJRRamsden) **4-11-9**(5) MissERamsden(9) (bhd: effrt ½-wy: n.d) | 3½ | 6 | 14/1 | 50 | 31 |
| | **Black and Blues (30)** (JSGoldie) **10-9-12** MissPRobson(4) (prom tl wknd fnl 4f) | s.h | 7 | 50/1 | 20 | 1 |
| 2379* | **Super Serenade (56)** (GBBalding) **7-11-5**(5) 5x MrJThatcher(3) (bhd: rdn 4f out: n.d) | 3½ | 8 | 9/1 | 40 | 21 |
| 2489* | **Giftbox (USA) (57)** (SirMarkPrescott) **4-11-8**(3) 5x MrPScott(1) (lw: cl up: led over 4f out tl sddle slipped & uns rdr over 2f out) | | U | 11/4[3] | — | — |

(SP 117.2%) **9 Rn**

**1m 57.6** (3.30) CSF £39.37 CT £534.29 TOTE £2.80: £1.50 £3.60 £2.00 (£66.20) Trio £94.40 OWNER Mr Jeff Pearce (NEWMARKET) BRED Ballymacoll Stud Co

**2587* Gold Blade**, despite the shorter trip, won well, but was probably lucky that Giftbox came to grief. (9/4)
**308 New Albion (USA)** won a couple of seasons ago and shaped quite well on his second run for his new stable. (20/1)
**2481 Langtonian** still has the ability, but only runs when he is in the mood and, after a slow start and then being hampered by a faller, ran reasonably. (16/1)
**1633 Hutchies Lady** was never doing enough to make any impression. (50/1)
**2014 Talented Ting (IRE)** has had plenty of outings this season, but still carries a lot of condition and was left struggling in the last couple of furlongs. (5/2)
**2587 Commander Glen (IRE)** was never fully co-operating with his rider. (14/1: op 8/1)
**2489* Giftbox (USA)** was in front and looked to have his rivals in trouble when his saddle slipped and he unshipped his pilot over two furlongs out. (11/4)

## 2679 SCOTTISHPOWER TROPHY H'CAP (0-80) (3-Y.O+) (Class D)

7-15 (7-15) **1m 65y** £3,965.60 (£1,200.80: £586.40: £279.20) Stalls: High GOING minus 0.70 sec per fur (HD)

| | | | Pos | SP | RR | SF |
|---|---|---|---|---|---|---|
| 2241* | **Generous Present (56)** (JWPayne) **3-7-7**(3) DWright(5) (hld up: effrt over 2f out: r.o fnl f to ld cl home) | — | 1 | 5/1[2] | 65 | 15 |
| 2567[7] | **Celebration Cake (IRE) (56)** (MissLAPerratt) **4-8-5** DeanMcKeown(4) (trkcd ldrs: hdwy ½-wy: led over 1f out tl ct cl home) | nk | 2 | 12/1 | 64 | 23 |
| 2428[4] | **Best of All (IRE) (67)** (JBerry) **4-9-2** JCarroll(8) (chsd ldrs: led over 2f out tl over 1f out: ev ch tl wknd towards fin) | 1 | 3 | 6/1[3] | 74 | 33 |
| 2351[3] | **Cashmere Lady (76)** (JLEyre) **4-9-11** RLappin(6) (lw: hld up & bhd: effrt over 2f out: styd on: nrst fin) | 1 | 4 | 7/2[1] | 81 | 40 |
| 2213* | **Impulsive Air (IRE) (60)** (EWeymes) **4-8-9** MTebbutt(7) (swtg: bhd: nt clr run & swtchd over 2f out: styd on towards fin) | 2 | 5 | 9/1 | 61 | 20 |
| 1868[7] | **King Curan (USA) (52)** (DHaydnJones) **5-8-1** AMackay(2) (lw: effrt ½-wy: styd on one pce & no imp) | ½ | 6 | 7/2[1] | 52 | 11 |
| 2357[9] | **Three Arch Bridge (68)** (MJohnston) **4-9-3b** JFanning(1) (w ldr: led over 4f out tl over 2f out: sn wknd) | 5 | 7 | 7/1 | 58 | 17 |
| | **Rood Music (55)** (MGMeagher) **5-8-4** KFallon(9) (led tl hdd over 4f out: sn rdn & btn) | 22 | 8 | 8/1 | 3 | — |
| 1168[5] | **Raise A Ripple (56)** (MrsDThomson) **3-7-7**(3) DarrenMoffatt(3) (lost tch 5f out: sn t.o) | 17 | 9 | 25/1 | — | — |

(SP 120.5%) **9 Rn**

**1m 45.2** (1.10) CSF £57.03 CT £343.25 TOTE £8.40: £2.00 £2.20 £2.40 (£42.40) Trio £141.90 OWNER Mr Alex Penman (NEWMARKET) BRED Snowdrop Stud Co Ltd

LONG HANDICAP Generous Present 7-4 Raise A Ripple 7-3

WEIGHT FOR AGE 3yo-9lb

**2241* Generous Present**, 6lb out of the handicap, so effectively 10lb higher than when winning last time, this rather edgy individual produced a great run in the final furlong to snatch it. (5/1)
**Celebration Cake (IRE)** is coming to hand fast, but just failed to last out this time. (12/1)
**2428 Best of All (IRE)** ran a fine race, being in contention until running out of stamina in the closing stages. (6/1)
**2351 Cashmere Lady**, given plenty to do, was caught flat-footed when things hotted up halfway up the straight and could never peg the leaders back. (7/2)
**2213* Impulsive Air (IRE)**, who made all last time, was ridden from behind on this occasion, and never got going until too late. (9/1)
**King Curan (USA)** was never fully co-operating once the pressure was applied in the last half-mile. (7/2)
**2188 Three Arch Bridge** has had a busy season which seems to have caught up with her for the time being. (7/1)

## 2680 FIELD & LAWN (MARQUEES) LTD (S) STKS (3-Y.O+) (Class G)

7-45 (7-48) **6f 5y** £2,500.00 (£700.00: £340.00) Stalls: High GOING minus 0.70 sec per fur (HD)

| | | | Pos | SP | RR | SF |
|---|---|---|---|---|---|---|
| 1865[10] | **Natural Key (55)** (DHaydnJones) **3-8-9** AMackay(2) (lw: chsd ldrs: slt ld ins fnl f: styd on) | — | 1 | 11/2[3] | 55 | 24 |
| 1474[6] | **Ultra Beet (60)** (PCHaslam) **4-9-6b** DeanMcKeown(9) (led tl hdd ins fnl f: kpt on) | ½ | 2 | 6/1 | 59 | 34 |
| 2030[6] | **Densben (45)** (DenysSmith) **12-9-6** KFallon(1) (lw: outpcd & bhd: hdwy u.p 2f out: nvr rchd ldrs) | 3 | 3 | 11/2[3] | 51 | 26 |
| 2386[3] | **Tropical Beach (58)** (JBerry) **3-8-13**(7) JoanneWebster(4) (chsd ldrs: one pce fnl 2f) | 1 | 4 | 9/2[2] | 54 | 23 |
| 2421[4] | **Another Nightmare (IRE) (33)** (RMMcKellar) **4-9-1** RLappin(6) (a.p: one pce fnl 2f) | 3 | 5 | 25/1 | 35 | 10 |
| 2566[2] | **Diet (50)** (MissLAPerratt) **10-9-6v** JCarroll(3) (chsd ldrs: outpcd ½-wy: sn bhd) | 10 | 6 | 11/2[3] | 14 | — |
| 2328[12] | **Masafah (USA) (77)** (MrsMReveley) **4-8-10**(5) SCopp(7) (prom: rdn ½-wy: sn wknd) | ¾ | 7 | 2/1[1] | 7 | — |
| 2523[10] | **Another Episode (IRE) (55)** (MissLAPerratt) **7-9-6** MTebbutt(8) (s.s: a wl bhd) | 18 | 8 | 100/1 | — | — |
| *2333[7]* | ***Messalina (IRE)*** (BMactaggart) **3-8-4**(5) GLee(10) (Withdrawn not under Starter's orders: unruly & damaged the stalls) | | W | 50/1 | — | — |

2492[2] ***Amylou*** (RAllan) **3-8-9** JFanning(5) (Withdrawn not under Starter's orders: ref to ent stalls) .............................. **W** 20/1 — —
(SP 123.5%) **8 Rn**

**1m 10.7** (0.70) CSF £35.65 TOTE £10.40: £2.10 £2.00 £2.30 (£29.70) Trio £45.30 OWNER Mr Hugh O'Donnell (PONTYPRIDD) BRED Cheveley Park Stud Ltd
WEIGHT FOR AGE 3yo-6lb
Bt in 3,100 gns
**1163 Natural Key** showed she still retains her ability here and, although she does not do anything quickly, she stayed on stoutly once in front. (11/2)
**1474 Ultra Beet**, from a yard that is bang out of form, ran a fine race and would seem to be coming right. (6/1)
**1848 Densben** looks well, and will no doubt pick up a race, but he probably needs seven furlongs these days. (11/2)
**2386 Tropical Beach** was never doing enough when the pressure was applied from halfway. (9/2)
**2421 Another Nightmare (IRE)** had plenty to do at these weights and was going nowhere in the last three furlongs. (25/1)
**1885 Masafah (USA)** disappointed yet again, and this was a very moderate event. (2/1)

## 2681 SCOTTISHPOWER CLASSIC NURSERY H'CAP (2-Y.O) (Class E)
8-15 (8-16) **5f 4y** £3,171.10 (£959.80: £468.40: £222.70) Stalls: High GOING minus 0.70 sec per fur (HD)

| | | | | SP | RR | SF |
|---|---|---|---|---|---|---|
| 2327[2] | **Plan For Profit (IRE)** (MJohnston) **2-8-11** JFanning(2) (lw: mde most: kpt on strly fnl f) | — | **1** | 2/1[1] | 63 | 9 |
| 1869[7] | **Red Romance** (DenysSmith) **2-9-2** KFallon(3) (disp ld 3f: r.o one pce) | 3 | **2** | 5/1 | 58 | 4 |
| 2035[2] | **Robec Girl (IRE)** (JBerry) **2-9-7** JCarroll(6) (trckd ldrs: swtchd & effrt 2f out: nt qckn fnl f) | s.h | **3** | 9/4[2] | 63 | 9 |
| 2374[6] | **The Four Isles** (DHaydnJones) **2-8-11** AMackay(4) (lw: s.s: hdwy ½-wy: nvr able to chal) | 2 | **4** | 9/2[3] | 47 | — |
| 910* | **Tazibari** (DMoffatt) **2-9-0**(3) DarrenMoffatt(1) (prom tl outpcd fnl 2f) | 7 | **5** | 5/1 | 31 | — |
| 2416[6] | **Cantsaynowt** (RMMcKellar) **2-7-11**ow1 DaleGibson(5) (plld hrd early: lost tch fr ½-wy) | nk | **6** | 25/1 | 10 | — |
| | | | | (SP 119.5%) | **6 Rn** | |

**59.9 secs** (1.60) CSF £12.30 TOTE £3.50: £2.00 £2.00 (£8.60) OWNER Professional Racing Partnership (MIDDLEHAM) BRED P. D. Savill
**2327 Plan For Profit (IRE)**, a big, good-looking individual, was turned out particularly well and won this in useful style. Over further, better will be seen. (2/1)
**1308 Red Romance** took the winner on, but found him far too good in the last couple of furlongs. (5/1)
**2035 Robec Girl (IRE)** failed to impress on looks, but travelled well in the race until coming off the bit in the last two furlongs when her response was a shade disappointing. She is better than this. (9/4)
**2059 The Four Isles** threw all chances away with a very slow start, and did well to finish so close. (9/2)
**910* Tazibari**, having her first run for a while, found this going far too fast, and was left behind in the last couple of furlongs. (5/1)
**2018 Cantsaynowt**, who took a fierce hold in the early stages, stopped quickly from halfway, and is basically not very good. (25/1)

## 2682 'JUDGE' CLAIMING STKS (3-Y.O+) (Class F)
8-45 (8-46) **1m 3f 16y** £2,535.00 (£710.00: £345.00) Stalls: High GOING minus 0.70 sec per fur (HD)

| | | | | SP | RR | SF |
|---|---|---|---|---|---|---|
| 2563[2] | **Mithraic (IRE) (53)** (WSCunningham) **4-9-1**(5) RHavlin(2) (t: lw: mde all: kpt on wl fnl 3f) | — | **1** | 11/8[1] | 65 | 34 |
| 2239[6] | **Latvian (63)** (RAllan) **9-9-12** KFallon(1) (chsd ldrs tl outpcd over 6f out: put hd in air & styd on fnl 2f: nrst fin) | 2 | **2** | 9/4[2] | 68 | 37 |
| | **North Bear** (MrsSJSmith) **4-9-10** PBloomfield(3) (hld up: effrt over 2f out: nvr rchd ldrs) | 2 | **3** | 10/1[3] | 63 | 32 |
| 2488[3] | **Northern Spark (48)** (MissLAPerratt) **8-9-2** JCarroll(5) (chsd wnr: efft over 3f out: wknd fnl 2f) | nk | **4** | 9/4[2] | 55 | 24 |
| 2565[8] | **Funny Rose (27)** (PMonteith) **6-8-9** SDWilliams(6) (lw: prom tl wknd fnl 4f) | 28 | **5** | 25/1 | 7 | — |
| 2487[7] | **Jabaroot (IRE) (38)** (RMMcKellar) **5-8-13**(7) DMcGaffin(4) (b.hind: prom tl wknd fnl 5f) | 7 | **6** | 50/1 | 8 | — |
| | | | | (SP 118.5%) | **6 Rn** | |

**2m 21.5** (2.10) CSF £5.15 TOTE £2.70: £1.40 £1.90 (£3.20) OWNER C P M Racing (YARM) BRED J. P. and Miss M. Mangan
**2563 Mithraic (IRE)**, who was tubed earlier this season, gave problems by hanging last time at Musselburgh, but was found to have a back problem. With this having being cured, he made all the running and won nicely. (11/8)
**1544 Latvian** was in one of his non-going moods for much of the trip here but, despite sticking his head high in the air, did run on when it was all too late. (9/4)
**North Bear**, who has been racing in Belgium, ran reasonably and should pick up a modest event. (10/1: 12/1-7/1)
**2488 Northern Spark**, in pursuit of the winner, was the only danger early in the straight but, once pressure was applied, he decided it was not for him in the last two furlongs. (9/4)
**2024 Funny Rose** again looked well enough, but wanted no part of it once the question was asked early in the straight. (25/1)

## 2683 JOE PUNTER MAIDEN H'CAP (0-60) (3-Y.O+) (Class F)
9-15 (9-16) **1m 4f 17y** £2,878.00 (£808.00: £394.00) Stalls: High GOING minus 0.70 sec per fur (HD)

| | | | | SP | RR | SF |
|---|---|---|---|---|---|---|
| 2366[3] | **Lawn Order (42)** (MrsJRRamsden) **3-8-9** KFallon(2) (lw: hld up: hdwy 3f out: led & hung bdly lft ins fnl f: r.o wl) | — | **1** | 13/8[1] | 50 | — |
| *1969*[2] | **Newbridge Boy (52)** (MGMeagher) **3-9-5** JCarroll(6) (chsd ldrs: led over 3f out tl hdd & carried lft ins fnl f: sn btn) | 2½ | **2** | 3/1[3] | 57 | 5 |
| 2521W | **Warwick Mist (IRE) (34)** (BMactaggart) **4-8-9**(5) GLee(3) (chsd ldrs: ev ch 4f out: one pce appr fnl f) | 2½ | **3** | 20/1 | 35 | — |
| 2423[8] | **Never Time (IRE) (35)** (MrsVAAconley) **4-9-1** MDeering(8) (lw: a chsng ldrs: effrt 4f out: one pce appr fnl f) | hd | **4** | 20/1 | 36 | — |
| 2397[2] | **Champagne Warrior (IRE) (47)** (MJCamacho) **3-9-0** LCharnock(9) (lw: prom: rdn 4f out: one pce) | 1 | **5** | 15/8[2] | 47 | — |
| | **Tryph (44)** (MDHammond) **4-9-10** DaleGibson(5) (lw: bhd: drvn along over 3f out: sme late hdwy) | 2½ | **6** | 33/1 | 41 | 2 |
| 537[11] | **All In Good Time (34)** (CWThornton) **3-8-1** AMackay(4) (a in tch: effrt 4f out: outpcd fnl 3f) | ½ | **7** | 25/1 | 30 | — |
| 2567[8] | **Tirols Tyrant (IRE) (55)** (MrsASwinbank) **3-9-8** JFanning(7) (hld up: effrt 4f out: sme hdwy over 2f out: sn wknd) | 2 | **8** | 20/1 | 48 | — |
| 2433[5] | **Gold Lining (IRE) (52)** (EJAlston) **3-9-2**(3) DWright(1) (a rr div) | 6 | **9** | 25/1 | 37 | — |
| 2136[10] | **Mamlouk (35)** (JWPayne) **4-9-1** MTebbutt(10) (led tl hdd & wknd over 3f out) | 6 | **10** | 20/1 | 12 | — |
| | | | | (SP 127.6%) | **10 Rn** | |

**2m 38.5** (6.50) CSF £7.62 CT £71.10 TOTE £2.70: £1.50 £1.10 £7.20 (£3.80) Trio £77.40 OWNER Mrs D. Ridley (THIRSK) BRED Keith Freeman
WEIGHT FOR AGE 3yo-13lb
**2366 Lawn Order**, although very much on her toes in the preliminaries, did look tremendously well. She produced a good run to lead inside the final furlong, despite going badly left. (13/8)
**1969 Newbridge Boy** tried hard here, kicking on almost half a mile from home, but being hampered by the winner inside the final furlong made not the slightest difference. There will be a race to be picked up with him in due course. (3/1)

**Warwick Mist (IRE)** ran a decent race, holding every chance until finding things too tough in the last furlong and a half. (20/1)
**504 Never Time (IRE)**, taken to post early, looked particularly well, and ran reasonably until being short of toe in the last furlong and a half. (20/1)
**2397 Champagne Warrior (IRE)** was off the bit a long way from home and, despite struggling on, never looked likely to take a hand. (15/8)
**Tryph**, who looked pretty fit and did keep on in the closing stages, is one to watch for a return to jumping. (33/1)

T/Plpt: £461.80 (31.18 Tckts). T/Qdpt: £29.30 (36.5 Tckts). AA

## 2321-**LINGFIELD** (L-H) (Turf Good to firm, AWT Standard)
## Friday July 12th
WEATHER: humid WIND: slt half bhd

### 2684 STOCKBROKER CLAIMING STKS (3-Y.O+) (Class F)
2-20 (2-20) **5f (Equitrack)** £2,381.00 (£656.00: £311.00) Stalls: High GOING minus 0.55 sec per fur (FST)

| Form | Horse | Dist | Pos | SP | RR | SF |
|---|---|---|---|---|---|---|
| 2392[4] | **Palacegate Touch (72)** (JBerry) **6-8-12b** GCarter(9) (lw: a.p: led wl over 1f out: sn clr: easily) | — | 1 | 4/1[2] | 72 | 32 |
| 2410[2] | **Songsheet (68)** (MartynMeade) **3-8-5**(5) RHavlin(1) (lw: chsd ldr over 2f: chsd wnr fnl f: r.o one pce) | 5 | 2 | 3/1[1] | 59 | 14 |
| 1657[5] | **Solo Symphony (IRE) (64)** (PWChapple-Hyam) **3-8-10** BThomson(5) (b: a.p: rdn over 1f out: one pce) | 3½ | 3 | 9/2[3] | 48 | 3 |
| 1592[8] | **Astral's Chance (50)** (KRBurke) **3-8-5** SSanders(6) (b.nr fore: lw: no hdwy fnl 3f) | ¾ | 4 | 33/1 | 40 | — |
| 2561[5] | **Tommy Tempest (30)** (REPeacock) **7-8-3v**(3) DaneO'Neill(8) (led over 3f) | 2½ | 5 | 7/1 | 28 | — |
| 2185[17] | **Donington Park (40)** (PTDalton) **3-7-10** NAdams(2) (lw: outpcd: nvr nrr) | 1¾ | 6 | 33/1 | 18 | — |
| 1681[4] | **Little Saboteur (54)** (PJMakin) **7-8-3b** AClark(4) (b.nr hind: lw: hld up: rdn over 2f out: wknd over 1f out) | 1½ | 7 | 4/1[2] | 15 | — |
| 2286[20] | **Jessica's Song (46)** (WGMTurner) **3-7-5**(7) RFfrench(7) (b.hind: swtg: a bhd) | hd | 8 | 12/1 | 15 | — |
| *2308*[13] | **Avant Huit (47)** (MrsNMacauley) **4-8-4v**(3) CTeague(3) (b: hmpd s: a bhd) | 2 | 9 | 20/1 | 12 | — |

(SP 114.0%) **9 Rn**

**58.98 secs** (0.98) CSF £15.41 TOTE £3.70: £1.60 £1.10 £2.00 (£6.80) Trio £5.10 OWNER Laurel (Leisure) Ltd (COCKERHAM) BRED The Woodhaven Stud
WEIGHT FOR AGE 3yo-5lb
**2392 Palacegate Touch** treated this field with contempt. Cruising into the lead entering the straight, he soon pulled clear to win with a ton in hand. (4/1: 5/2-9/2)
**2410 Songsheet**, in second place early, regained that position a furlong out but, by that stage, the winner was already home and dry. (3/1)
**1657 Solo Symphony (IRE)** was asked for effort in the short straight, but failed to find the necessary turn of foot. (9/2)
**Astral's Chance** was made to look very pedestrian in the second half of the race. He is a very poor performer. (33/1)
**2561 Tommy Tempest**, making a quick reappearance, took the field along but, collared entering the short home straight, soon had bellows to mend. (7/1)

### 2685 GRAHAM GROUP PLC (S) STKS (2-Y.O) (Class G)
2-55 (2-56) **6f** £2,469.00 (£684.00: £327.00) Stalls: High GOING minus 0.46 sec per fur (F)

| Form | Horse | Dist | Pos | SP | RR | SF |
|---|---|---|---|---|---|---|
| 2435[2] | **Grovefair Maiden (IRE)** (BJMeehan) **2-8-6b** SSanders(2) (lw: mde virtually all: drvn out) | — | 1 | 5/2[1] | 55 | 20 |
| 1413[6] | **Emilyjill** (RHannon) **2-8-3**(3) DaneO'Neill(5) (rdn over 2f out: hdwy on ins over 1f out: ev ch ins fnl f: r.o) | nk | 2 | 5/1[3] | 54 | 19 |
| 2389[3] | **Marsh Marigold** (MartynMeade) **2-8-6** RPerham(1) (a.p: ev ch over 1f out: unable qckn) | 2 | 3 | 12/1 | 49 | 14 |
| 2199[2] | **Eager To Please** (JBerry) **2-9-2** GCarter(6) (lw: a.p: hrd rdn over 2f out: ev ch over 1f out: wknd ins fnl f) | 2 | 4 | 5/2[1] | 54 | 19 |
| *2307*[7] | **True Vision** (WGMTurner) **2-7-13**(7) GHannon(3) (dwlt: bhd fnl 3f) | 7 | 5 | 20/1 | 25 | — |
| 1463[2] | **Heavenly Miss (IRE)** (BPalling) **2-8-3**(3) SDrowne(4) (prom over 3f) | 1¾ | 6 | 3/1[2] | 20 | — |

(SP 111.3%) **6 Rn**

**1m 11.17** (2.17) CSF £13.88 TOTE £3.40: £1.80 £2.50 (£12.90) OWNER Grovefair Racing Ltd (UPPER LAMBOURN) BRED Rathasker Stud
No bid
**2435 Grovefair Maiden (IRE)**, together with the fourth, were the paddock picks. Making virtually all the running, she had to work very hard indeed to keep the very persistent runner-up at bay. (5/2)
**1413 Emilyjill**, having her first run for her new stable, got into top gear along the inside rail from below the distance. She looked as if she was going to overhaul the winner inside the final furlong, but just failed. (5/1: op 3/1)
**2389 Marsh Marigold**, a leading player from the outset, had every chance below the distance before just tapped for toe. (12/1: 5/1-14/1)
**2199 Eager To Please** looked very well beforehand. A leading light from the outset, he still had every chance under pressure below the distance before tiring inside the last 200 yards. (5/2: op 6/4)

### 2686 AL AMEAD H'CAP (0-70) (3-Y.O+ F & M) (Class E)
3-25 (3-26) **6f** £3,343.20 (£999.60: £478.80: £218.40) Stalls: High GOING minus 0.46 sec per fur (F)

| Form | Horse | Dist | Pos | SP | RR | SF |
|---|---|---|---|---|---|---|
| 2200[2] | **May Queen Megan (52)** (MrsALMKing) **3-8-6** NAdams(9) (a.p: led over 1f out: rdn out) | — | 1 | 7/1[3] | 58 | 39 |
| 2500[6] | **Mystery Matthias (51)** (MissBSanders) **3-8-5v** SSanders(8) (a.p: rdn over 2f out: ev ch wl ins fnl f: r.o) | nk | 2 | 10/1 | 56 | 37 |
| 2255[2] | **Out Line (68)** (MMadgwick) **4-9-11**(3) NVarley(5) (lw: a.p: rdn over 2f out: ev ch wl ins fnl f: r.o) | nk | 3 | 11/1 | 72 | 59 |
| 2255[7] | **Lucky Revenge (64)** (MartynMeade) **3-8-13**(5) RHavlin(10) (hdwy over 1f out: r.o wl ins fnl f) | hd | 4 | 10/1 | 68 | 49 |
| 2156[12] | **Tachycardia (46)** (RJO'Sullivan) **4-8-6** DBiggs(3) (led over 4f: unable qckn ins fnl f) | nk | 5 | 20/1 | 49 | 36 |
| 470[13] | **Secret Pleasure (IRE) (65)** (RHannon) **3-9-2**(3) DaneO'Neill(13) (b.hind: lw: hdwy over 1f out: r.o) | 1¾ | 6 | 10/1 | 64 | 45 |
| 2340[10] | **Merrie le Bow (49)** (PatMitchell) **4-8-4**(5) AmandaSanders(11) (nvr nr to chal) | s.h | 7 | 8/1 | 48 | 35 |
| 2490[2] | **Most Uppitty (40)** (JBerry) **4-8-0** GCarter(7) (s.s: hdwy over 1f out: nvr nrr) | s.h | 8 | 9/2[1] | 38 | 25 |
| 2324[4] | **Superlao (BEL) (41)** (JJBridger) **4-7-12**(3) MHenry(6) (b.nr hind: a.p: ev ch over 1f out: wknd fnl f) | 2 | 9 | 11/1 | 34 | 21 |
| 2340[6] | **Time For Tea (IRE) (65)** (CACyzer) **3-9-5** GDuffield(12) (lw: nvr gng wl: bhd fnl 2f) | s.h | 10 | 9/1 | 58 | 39 |
| 1689[3] | **Always Grace (60)** (MissGayKelleway) **4-9-6** RCochrane(4) (dwlt: outpcd) | 3½ | 11 | 13/2[2] | 44 | 31 |
| 2586[8] | **Times of Times (IRE) (70)** (MJRyan) **3-9-3**(7) AMcCarthy(2) (s.s: outpcd) | 3½ | 12 | 11/1 | 44 | 25 |
| 2193[10] | **Don't Tell Vicki (42)** (JSMoore) **3-7-10** DeclanO'Shea(1) (prom 3f) | 3½ | 13 | 25/1 | 7 | — |

(SP 126.0%) **13 Rn**

**1m 9.82** (0.82) CSF £72.17 CT £714.60 TOTE £7.20: £1.70 £4.90 £5.20 (£22.80) Trio £195.00 OWNER Mr S. J. Harrison (STRATFORD-UPON-AVON) BRED Limestone Stud
LONG HANDICAP Don't Tell Vicki 7-9
WEIGHT FOR AGE 3yo-6lb
**2200 May Queen Megan**, never far away, went on below the distance and, rousted along, just managed to prevail in a very tight finish. (7/1)

**2500 Mystery Matthias,** a leading light from the off, threw down the gauntlet from below the distance. Battling hard to gain the upper hand, she only just failed. (10/1)
**2255 Out Line**, always close up, was another who had every chance in the closing stages and just failed to prevail. (11/1: 8/1-12/1)
**1709 Lucky Revenge** only found her feet from below the distance. She ran on really strongly inside the final furlong, but the line was always beating her. A return to seven furlongs would be in her favour. (10/1)
**Tachycardia** took the field along. Collared below the distance, she failed to find that vital turn of foot inside the last 200 yards. (20/1)
**Secret Pleasure (IRE)** was doing all her best work in the last furlong and a half, and a return to seven furlongs would help her cause. (10/1)
**2193 Merrie le Bow** (8/1: 6/1-9/1)

## 2687 RYDON GROUP LIMITED STKS (0-80) (3-Y.O) (Class D)

3-55 (3-55) **7f 140y** £3,761.25 (£1,122.00: £535.50: £242.25) Stalls: High GOING minus 0.46 sec per fur (F)

| | | | | SP | RR | SF |
|---|---|---|---|---|---|---|
| 2146$^{3}$ | **Divina Luna (80)** (JWHills) **3-8-8**$^{(3)}$ MHenry(5) (led over 2f: led over 3f out: clr over 2f out: comf) | — | 1 | 9/4$^{1}$ | 88+ | 47 |
| 937$^{13}$ | **Tsarnista (80)** (JLDunlop) **3-8-8** GCarter(2) (swtg: a.p: chsd wnr over 2f out: no imp) | 2 | 2 | 9/2 | 81 | 40 |
| 1864$^{2}$ | **Hannalou (FR) (75)** (SPCWoods) **3-8-8** WWoods(7) (hld up: rdn over 3f out: wknd over 1f out) | 10 | 3 | 7/2$^{3}$ | 60 | 19 |
| 1819$^{9}$ | **Philosopher (IRE) (80)** (RHannon) **3-8-8**$^{(3)}$ DaneO'Neill(3) (nvr nr to chal) | 1¾ | 4 | 3/1$^{2}$ | 59 | 18 |
| 2041$^{28}$ | **Detachment (USA) (80)** (PWChapple-Hyam) **3-8-6**$^{(5)}$ RHavlin(4) (lw: a.p: led 5f out tl over 3f out: wknd over 2f out) | ¾ | 5 | 9/1 | 58 | 17 |
| *2369*$^{5}$ | **Hadadabble (42)** (PatMitchell) **3-8-8** NCarlisle(1) (prom 4f) | 3 | 6 | 50/1 | 48 | 7 |
| *391*$^{5}$ | **Carmarthen Bay (78)** (GLMoore) **3-9-0** RCochrane(6) (lw: bhd fnl 3f) | 2 | 7 | 14/1 | 50 | 9 |

(SP 114.8%) **7 Rn**

**1m 29.55** (0.75) CSF £12.25 TOTE £3.10: £1.60 £2.70 (£8.30) OWNER Mr D. J. Deer (LAMBOURN) BRED Azienda Agricola Colle Cardella
**2146 Divina Luna** proved in a different class to these rivals. Regaining the advantage over three furlongs from home, her jockey soon bustled her clear and that was the end of the contest. (9/4)
**Tsarnista** moved into second place over two furlongs from home, but never threatened to get on terms with the winner, despite pulling well clear of the remainder. (9/2)
**1864 Hannalou (FR)**, looking woefully one-paced in the second half of the race, had run out of gas below the distance. (7/2)
**1593 Philosopher (IRE)**, racing at the back of the field, never threatened to get into it. (3/1)
**1667 Detachment (USA)**, fitted with a tongue-strap, stood out in the paddock, but continues to disappoint. (9/1: 7/1-12/1)
**352* Carmarthen Bay** (14/1: 7/1-16/1)

## 2688 AMEC CONSTRUCTION H'CAP (0-80) (3-Y.O) (Class D)

4-25 (4-25) **1m 3f 106y** £3,728.10 (£1,111.80: £530.40: £239.70) Stalls: High GOING minus 0.46 sec per fur (F)

| | | | | SP | RR | SF |
|---|---|---|---|---|---|---|
| 2542* | **Frog (60)** (SirMarkPrescott) **3-8-2** $^{5x}$ GDuffield(4) (lw: mde all: clr over 3f out: easily) | — | 1 | 8/11$^{1}$ | 77+ | 22 |
| 2202* | **Dear Life (USA) (79)** (MrsJCecil) **3-9-7** AClark(3) (hld up: chsd wnr over 6f out: rdn over 3f out: no imp) | 3½ | 2 | 2/1$^{2}$ | 91 | 36 |
| 2247$^{6}$ | **Isitoff (70)** (SCWilliams) **3-8-9**$^{(3)}$ PMcCabe(2) (chsd wnr 5f: rdn over 3f out: one pce) | 2½ | 3 | 11/2$^{3}$ | 79 | 24 |
| 1175$^{9}$ | **Clouds Hill (FR) (72)** (RHannon) **3-8-11**$^{(3)}$ DaneO'Neill(1) (bhd fnl 7f: t.o) | 30 | 4 | 14/1 | 39 | — |

(SP 113.3%) **4 Rn**

**2m 28.38** (4.18) CSF £2.66 TOTE £1.60 (£1.40) OWNER Mr B. Haggas (NEWMARKET) BRED Mrs P. A. Clark
**2542* Frog** jumped off in the lead and towed the field along. Forging clear entering the straight, she won with a ton in hand, and the official distance is certainly no true reflection of her superiority. (8/11)
**2202* Dear Life (USA)** struggled into second place going to the top of the hill, but never looked like posing a threat to the winner in the straight. (2/1)
**2247 Isitoff**, who failed to stay on his last two outings, was back over a more suitable trip here. In second place in the first half of the race, he was made to look extremely one-paced in the straight. (11/2: 4/1-6/1)
**969 Clouds Hill (FR)** (14/1: 6/1-16/1)

## 2689 JIM WALL IS 70 H'CAP (0-70) (3-Y.O+) (Class E)

4-55 (4-56) **1m 2f (Equitrack)** £3,343.20 (£999.60: £478.80: £218.40) Stalls: Low GOING minus 0.55 sec per fur (FST)

| | | | | SP | RR | SF |
|---|---|---|---|---|---|---|
| *2201*$^{5}$ | **Philistar (60)** (JMPEustace) **3-8-11** RCochrane(12) (dwlt: hdwy over 4f out: rdn over 2f out: led wl ins fnl f: drvn out) | — | 1 | 14/1 | 71 | 32 |
| 2487$^{4}$ | **Nose No Bounds (IRE) (62)** (MJohnston) **3-8-13b** WWoods(5) (a.p: led over 5f out: rdn 3f out: hdd wl ins fnl f: unable qckn) | 1½ | 2 | 11/4$^{1}$ | 71 | 32 |
| 2253$^{2}$ | **Superior Force (63)** (MissBSanders) **3-9-0** SSanders(6) (lw: a.p: hrd rdn over 2f out: one pce) | 2½ | 3 | 9/2$^{2}$ | 68 | 29 |
| 2577* | **General Haven (71)** (TJNaughton) **3-9-3**$^{(5)}$ $^{6x}$ JDSmith(14) (b: lw: dwlt: rdn & hdwy over 3f out: r.o one pce) | 1½ | 4 | 8/1$^{3}$ | 73 | 34 |
| *2201*$^{3}$ | **Quiet Arch (IRE) (63)** (CACyzer) **3-9-0** GDuffield(7) (a.p: hrd rdn over 2f out: wknd over 1f out) | 2 | 5 | 10/1 | 62 | 23 |
| 2541$^{5}$ | **Red Rusty (USA) (61)** (DMorris) **3-8-12** TIves(11) (nvr nr to chal) | 3 | 6 | 16/1 | 55 | 16 |
| 2192$^{15}$ | **Still Here (IRE) (55)** (MJHeaton-Ellis) **3-8-3**$^{(3)}$ SDrowne(9) (prom 7f) | s.h | 7 | 25/1 | 49 | 10 |
| *2553*$^{5}$ | **Rival Bid (USA) (62)** (MrsNMacauley) **8-9-7**$^{(3)}$ CTeague(10) (s.s: hdwy 7f out: wknd 3f out) | s.h | 8 | 10/1 | 56 | 28 |
| 2159$^{6}$ | **Double Rush (IRE) (56)** (TGMills) **4-9-4** MarkLynch(3) (prom over 5f) | 12 | 9 | 20/1 | 31 | 3 |
| 2402* | **Half An Inch (IRE) (70)** (BJMeehan) **3-9-2b**$^{(5)}$ $^{6x}$ PPMurphy(8) (bhd fnl 5f) | 2 | 10 | 9/1 | 42 | 3 |
| 1613$^{12}$ | **Oozlem (IRE) (43)** (JRPoulton) **7-8-5b** SWhitworth(2) (b: lw: dwlt: a bhd) | 2 | 11 | 20/1 | 11 | — |
| 1773$^{6}$ | **King Rufus (70)** (JRArnold) **3-9-4**$^{(3)}$ MHenry(1) (lw: a bhd) | 15 | 12 | 9/1 | 14 | — |
| 2326$^{6}$ | **Bath Knight (64)** (DJSffrenchDavis) **3-9-1** GCarter(4) (led over 4f: wknd over 4f out) | 8 | 13 | 16/1 | — | — |

(SP 125.9%) **13 Rn**

**2m 6.67** (2.37) CSF £52.04 CT £195.90 TOTE £17.10: £3.80 £1.70 £1.60 (£35.40) Trio £49.40 OWNER Mr & Mrs A W Hobbs (NEWMARKET) BRED John A. Jones Morgan
WEIGHT FOR AGE 3yo-11lb
**1420 Philistar** moved into contention soon after halfway. Throwing down his challenge in the straight, he did not look over-enthusiastic, but neither did the leader, and he eventually managed to gain the day in the closing stages as his main rival tired. (14/1)
**2487 Nose No Bounds (IRE)** went on just before halfway. He did not look to be enjoying the struggle with the winner in the straight and eventually called it a day in the closing stages. (11/4)
**2253 Superior Force** was under pressure going to the final quarter-mile and could only plod on in his own time. (9/2)
**2577* General Haven**, making a quick reappearance, never posed a serious threat. (8/1)
**2201 Quiet Arch (IRE)** played an active role until his stamina gave out approaching the final furlong. (10/1)

T/Plpt: £62.30 (181.38 Tckts). T/Qdpt: £18.20 (39.44 Tckts). AK

## 2005-YORK (L-H) (Good)
**Friday July 12th**
WEATHER: fine & sunny WIND: slt half against

## 2690 TIM HODGSON KEY OF THE DOOR RATED STKS H'CAP (0-100) (3-Y.O+) (Class B)
2-05 (2-06) **1m 3f 195y** £8,299.50 (£3,070.50: £1,472.75: £601.25: £238.13: £92.87) Stalls: Low GOING minus 0.25 sec per fur (GF)

| | | | SP | RR | SF |
|---|---|---|---|---|---|
| 2055[14] **Son of Sharp Shot (IRE) (100)** (JLDunlop) **6-9-9** PatEddery(7) (lw: hld up gng wl: stdy hdwy over 2f out: effrt 1f out: r.o u.p to ld post) | — | 1 | 5/1[2] | 106 | 68 |
| 2008[3] **Romios (IRE) (86)** (PFICole) **4-8-9** TQuinn(3) (trckd ldrs gng wl: qcknd to ld 1f out: jst ct) | s.h | 2 | 12/1 | 92 | 54 |
| 2055[2] **My Learned Friend (86)** (AHide) **5-8-9** JReid(5) (hld up: hdwy over 3f out: styd on same pce fnl 2f) | 2 | 3 | 11/2[3] | 89 | 51 |
| 2330[13] **Remaadi Sun (86)** (MDIUsher) **4-8-9** RStreet(1) (hld up: hdwy & swtchd ins over 2f out: styd on fnl f) | s.h | 4 | 13/2 | 89 | 51 |
| 2318* **Three Hills (88)** (BWHills) **3-7-12** WCarson(2) (lw: led to 1f out: sn btn: eased nr fin) | 2½ | 5 | 5/2[1] | 88 | 37 |
| 2352[4] **Tinashaan (IRE) (95)** (JRFanshawe) **4-9-4** DHarrison(4) (b: a chsng ldrs: rdn along over 4f out: wl outpcd fnl 2f) | 5 | 6 | 9/1 | 88 | 50 |
| 2074[18] **Count Basie (90)** (HRACecil) **3-8-0**ow2 AMcGlone(9) (in tch: effrt over 4f out: rdn & hung lft 2f out: sn wknd) | hd | 7 | 6/1 | 83 | 30 |
| 1336[6] **English Invader (87)** (RAkehurst) **5-8-10** JWeaver(6) (b.nr hind: w ldr: rdn 4f out: lost pl over 2f out) | 9 | 8 | 20/1 | 68 | 30 |
| 2131[9] **Peter Quince (86)** (MBrittain) **6-8-9** WRyan(8) (chsd ldrs: drvn along 5f out: sn lost pl & bhd) | 24 | 9 | 50/1 | 35 | — |

(SP 112.7%) **9 Rn**

**2m 30.57** (2.77) CSF £53.53 CT £307.73 TOTE £4.30: £1.70 £3.20 £1.60 (£34.20) Trio £48.60 OWNER Windflower Overseas Holdings Inc (ARUNDEL) BRED Windflower Overseas
LONG HANDICAP Romios (IRE) 8-5 Remaadi Sun 8-2 My Learned Friend 8-7 Peter Quince 8-8
WEIGHT FOR AGE 3yo-13lb

**1767 Son of Sharp Shot (IRE)**, as usual, impressed in the paddock. Ridden to perfection by Eddery who knows him so well, he was persuaded to stick his head in front right on the line. (5/1)
**2008 Romios (IRE)**, 4lb out of the handicap, was well suited by the overnight rain. Given a fine tactical ride, he looked to have nicked it when quickening ahead a furlong out, but the post came a stride too late. (12/1)
**2055 My Learned Friend**, from a 5lb higher mark, proved keen and had to be settled. Staying on at the same pace at the business end, a step up to a mile and six should prove no problem. (11/2)
**2330 Remaadi Sun**, 7lb wrong at the weights in this limited handicap, was staying on when it was all over. (13/2)
**2318* Three Hills**, who set his own pace, possibly did not last out the full mile and a half. (5/2)
**2352 Tinashaan (IRE)**, dropping back in distance, was more settled in the preliminaries this time but, under pressure once in line for home, she proved woefully one-paced. (9/1)

## 2691 WWAV NORTH 10TH ANNIVERSARY CONDITIONS STKS (3-Y.O+) (Class B)
2-40 (2-40) **7f 202y** £9,097.50 (£3,147.50: £1,511.25: £618.75) Stalls: Low GOING minus 0.25 sec per fur (GF)

| | | | SP | RR | SF |
|---|---|---|---|---|---|
| 2114[4] **Green Perfume (USA) (106)** (PFICole) **4-9-5** TQuinn(3) (mde all: sn clr: jst lasted) | — | 1 | Evens[1] | 114 | 74 |
| 1898[2] **Hi Nod (99)** (MJCamacho) **6-9-1** LCharnock(4) (hld up: effrt over 3f out: chsd wnr over 1f out: styd on: nt rch wnr) | ½ | 2 | 100/30[2] | 109 | 69 |
| 1768[2] **Behaviour (103)** (MrsJCecil) **4-9-1** JReid(1) (lw: hld up: effrt over 3f out: styd on wl fnl f) | ½ | 3 | 100/30[2] | 108 | 68 |
| 2048* **Sabot (102)** (BWHills) **3-8-8** PatEddery(2) (chsd wnr: rdn over 2f out: wknd over 1f out) | 9 | 4 | 6/1[3] | 92 | 43 |

(SP 110.4%) **4 Rn**

**1m 37.6** (0.80) CSF £4.45 TOTE £2.00 (£2.70) OWNER Lord Sondes (WHATCOMBE) BRED Brereton C. Jones
WEIGHT FOR AGE 3yo-9lb

**2114 Green Perfume (USA)**, suited by this small field, was allowed to set up a useful lead and, with his stamina giving out, it was just sufficient to last home. (Evens)
**1898 Hi Nod**, ridden to get the mile, went in pursuit of the winner coming to the final furlong. Sticking on grimly, he was never quite going to close the gap. (100/30: 9/4-7/2)
**1768 Behaviour** seemed happy to sit last of the four and, like the runner-up, gave the winner plenty of rope. Staying on really well in the final furlong, he was never going to get there. (100/30)
**2048* Sabot**, the only one to keep tabs on the winner, had his limitations exposed. (6/1: 4/1-13/2)

## 2692 MANCHESTER-SINGAPORE SUMMER STKS (Listed) (3-Y.O+ F & M) (Class A)
3-10 (3-10) **6f** £13,041.00 (£3,888.00: £1,854.00: £837.00) Stalls: Low GOING minus 0.09 sec per fur (G)

| | | | SP | RR | SF |
|---|---|---|---|---|---|
| 2332[4] **Carranita (IRE) (105)** (BPalling) **6-9-4** TSprake(1) (lw: trckd ldrs: qcknd to ld over 1f out: sn clr) | — | 1 | 5/1[3] | 113 | 89 |
| 2298* **Daring Destiny (99)** (KRBurke) **5-9-4b** JTate(3) (hld up: stdy hdwy over 1f out: styd on: no ch w wnr) | 4 | 2 | 7/1 | 102 | 78 |
| 2298[3] **Prancing (99)** (DRLoder) **3-8-8** TQuinn(4) (a chsng ldrs: rdn 2f out: kpt on one pce) | 1 | 3 | 13/2 | 96 | 66 |
| 2436* **Branston Abby (IRE) (108)** (MJohnston) **7-9-4** MRoberts(8) (sn outpcd & pushed along: sme hdwy over 2f out: nvr rchd ldrs) | ½ | 4 | 15/8[1] | 98 | 74 |
| 2050[12] **Please Suzanne (99)** (RHannon) **3-8-8** BDoyle(5) (s.i.s: hld up: effrt 2f out: sn rdn & no imp) | 1¼ | 5 | 8/1 | 91 | 61 |
| 2332[3] **Warning Star (98)** (BWHills) **4-9-0** PatEddery(2) (swtg: sn pushed along: sme hdwy ½-wy: wknd over 1f out) | 2½ | 6 | 4/1[2] | 84 | 60 |
| 2298[5] **Welsh Mist (95)** (RBoss) **5-9-0b[1]** WRyan(6) (led & sn clr: hdd & wknd over 1f out) | 2 | 7 | 14/1 | 79 | 55 |
| 1652* **My Cadeaux (85)** (RGuest) **4-9-0** DHarrison(7) (chsd ldrs tl wknd qckly over 1f out) | 7 | 8 | 16/1 | 60 | 36 |

(SP 120.9%) **8 Rn**

**1m 11.42** (0.42) CSF £37.77 TOTE £6.20: £1.60 £2.60 £2.00 (£31.20) OWNER Lamb Lane Associates (COWBRIDGE) BRED Mrs Anita Quinn
WEIGHT FOR AGE 3yo-6lb

**2332 Carranita (IRE)**, who looked in magnificent shape, recorded her thirteenth victory in emphatic fashion, and is in the form of her life. (5/1)
**2298* Daring Destiny** travelled strongly as usual but, when she did make her effort, the winner had flown. (7/1)
**2298 Prancing** gave a good account of herself, but this is probably as good as she is. (13/2)
**2436* Branston Abby (IRE)**, bidding for her twenty-second win, was drawn eight of eight and, with the stalls on the far side, was seeing too much daylight for her own good throughout. She will soon make amends for this. (15/8)
**966* Please Suzanne**, who looked very fit, raced keenly after missing the break slightly. (8/1)
**2332 Warning Star**, stewed up and sweating in the paddock, ran below her best. (4/1)
**2298 Welsh Mist**, in blinkers for the first time, ran much too freely for her own good. (14/1)

## 2693 HEARTHSTEAD HOMES H'CAP (0-90) (3-Y.O+) (Class C)

3-40 (3-42) **7f 202y** £7,895.00 (£2,360.00: £1,130.00: £515.00) Stalls: Low GOING minus 0.25 sec per fur (GF)

| | | | | SP | RR | SF |
|---|---|---|---|---|---|---|
| 2514* | **Give Me A Ring (IRE) (75)** (CWThornton) **3-8-8** 5x DeanMcKeown(2) (chsd ldr: led over 1f out: jst hld on).... | — | **1** | 6/1 3 | 82 | 56 |
| 2483 7 | **Queens Consul (IRE) (82)** (BSRothwell) **6-9-10** MFenton(3) (hld up & bhd: gd hdwy on outside over 1f out: styd on wl) | hd | **2** | 20/1 | 89 | 72 |
| 1860 4 | **Special-K (61)** (EWeymes) **4-8-3**ow1 DHarrison(4) (chsd ldrs: rdn 3f out: styd on wl) | ½ | **3** | 12/1 | 67 | 49 |
| 2351 2 | **Mbulwa (64)** (RAFahey) **10-8-6** LCharnock(6) (a chsng ldrs: kpt on same pce fnl 2f: edgd rt towards fin) | ½ | **4** | 8/1 | 69 | 52 |
| 2166* | **Kamari (USA) (86)** (ACStewart) **3-9-5** WCarson(9) (hld up: effrt over 2f out: kpt on same pce appr fnl f: sltly hmpd & eased nr fin) | 2 | **5** | 13/8 1 | 87+ | 61 |
| 2220 8 | **Courageous Dancer (IRE) (82)** (BHanbury) **4-9-10** JStack(8) (lw: hld up: effrt over 2f out: kpt on: nvr rchd ldrs) | 1½ | **6** | 14/1 | 80 | 63 |
| 2164 5 | **Bollin Frank (69)** (TDEasterby) **4-8-11** MBirch(1) (led tl over 1f out: grad wknd) | 1¼ | **7** | 9/2 2 | 64 | 47 |
| 1819 15 | **Sue's Return (76)** (APJarvis) **4-9-4** WJO'Connor(7) (hld up: effrt over 2f out: sn rdn: no imp) | 1¼ | **8** | 8/1 | 69 | 52 |
| 2246 6 | **Miss Haversham (72)** (CACyzer) **4-9-0** KFallon(5) (chsd ldrs: drvn along 5f out: lost pl over 3f out) | 11 | **9** | 16/1 | 42 | 25 |

(SP 117.8%) **9 Rn**

**1m 38.37** (1.57) CSF £95.34 CT £1,272.83 TOTE £6.50: £1.90 £5.10 £2.20 (£65.70) Trio £178.40 OWNER Mr Guy Reed (MIDDLEHAM) BRED W. Maxwell Ervine

WEIGHT FOR AGE 3yo-9lb

**2514* Give Me A Ring (IRE)** is a progressive sort and scraped home under a 5lb penalty. (6/1)

**2010 Queens Consul (IRE)**, well below her best on her two previous outings, bounced right back here. After being given a lot to do and only making her effort coming to the final furlong, in the end she only just failed to get there. (20/1)

**1860 Special-K**, who won four claimers last year, ran easily her best ever race, proving most persistent under pressure. (12/1)

**2351 Mbulwa**, from a 4lb higher mark, ran really well. (8/1)

**2166* Kamari (USA)**, keen early on, could only stick on at the one pace when the race began in earnest. When he learns to settle, he should be suited by further. (13/8)

**1799 Courageous Dancer (IRE)** is struggling to find his best form this year. (14/1)

**2164 Bollin Frank**, dropping back in distance, set the pace but, much higher in the weights now, could never shrug off the opposition. (9/2)

## 2694 ANTHONY FAWCETT MEMORIAL H'CAP (0-100) (3-Y.O+) (Class C)

4-10 (4-13) **5f** £8,285.00 (£2,480.00: £1,190.00: £545.00) Stalls: Low GOING minus 0.09 sec per fur (G)

| | | | | SP | RR | SF |
|---|---|---|---|---|---|---|
| 2114 13 | **Coastal Bluff (88)** (TDBarron) **4-9-4** JFortune(22) (b.hind: racd stands' side: hdwy & edgd lft 2f out: hrd rdn to ld wl ins fnl f: r.o) | — | **1** | 9/1 | 97+ | 68 |
| 2292 4 | **Tedburrow (85)** (MrsAMNaughton) **4-9-1** ACulhane(6) (swtg: in tch: hdwy over 1f out: ev ch ins fnl f: r.o) | hd | **2** | 12/1 | 94 | 65 |
| 2349 3 | **Laurel Delight (82)** (JBerry) **6-8-7**(5) PRoberts(10) (b: led tl wl ins fnl f: no ex) | ¾ | **3** | 14/1 | 88 | 59 |
| 2220 6 | **Lady Sheriff (83)** (RHollinshead) **5-8-10**(3) FLynch(18) (lw: hdwy ½-wy: styd on fnl f: r.o towards fin) | ½ | **4** | 20/1 | 88 | 59 |
| 2349* | **Lago Di Varano (85)** (RMWhitaker) **4-9-1v** WRyan(17) (bhd: hdwy 2f out: nt qckn ins fnl f) | hd | **5** | 16/1 | 89 | 60 |
| 2228 2 | **Sea-Deer (82)** (CADwyer) **7-8-12** MRoberts(19) (racd stands' side: hdwy & edgd lft over 1f out: styd on wl towards fin) | hd | **6** | 7/1 2 | 86 | 57 |
| 2349 10 | **Insider Trader (77)** (MrsJRRamsden) **5-8-4**(3) HKYim(21) (racd stands' side: in tch: r.o fnl f) | 1½ | **7** | 20/1 | 76 | 47 |
| 1818 12 | **Swynford Dream (84)** (JFBottomley) **3-8-9** JLowe(11) (a.p: nt qckn fnl 2f) | nk | **8** | 33/1 | 82 | 48 |
| 2492 3 | **La Suquet (67)** (NTinkler) **4-7-11** JQuinn(5) (a chsng ldrs: one pce fnl 2f) | ¾ | **9** | 25/1 | 63 | 34 |
| 2381 4 | **Crofters Ceilidh (85)** (BAMcMahon) **4-9-1** JReid(13) (a in tch: effrt 2f out: kpt on same pce) | hd | **10** | 25/1 | 81 | 52 |
| 2586 6 | **Rich Glow (67)** (NBycroft) **5-7-8**(3)ow1 7x DarrenMoffatt(7) (bhd: sme hdwy over 1f out: n.d) | nk | **11** | 25/1 | 62 | 32 |
| 2349 2 | **Premium Gift (66)** (CBBBooth) **4-7-5**(5) MartinDwyer(1) (a wl in tch: rdn 2f out: no imp) | s.h | **12** | 8/1 3 | 60 | 31 |
| 2548 6 | **Portend (90)** (SRBowring) **4-9-6b** DeanMcKeown(15) (in tch: rdn ½-wy: lost pl over 1f out) | 1¼ | **13** | 16/1 | 80 | 51 |
| 2349 8 | **Surprise Mission (75)** (MrsJRRamsden) **4-8-5** KFallon(14) (trckd ldrs: effrt over 2f out: wknd over 1f out) | nk | **14** | 11/1 | 65 | 36 |
| 2137* | **For the Present (83)** (TDBarron) **6-8-13** LCharnock(9) (s.i.s: bhd tl sme hdwy fnl f) | s.h | **15** | 11/1 | 72 | 43 |
| 2586* | **Shadow Jury (67)** (DWChapman) **6-7-11b** 7x DaleGibson(8) (chsd ldrs: btn whn sltly hmpd ins fnl f) | s.h | **16** | 16/1 | 56 | 27 |
| 1186 16 | **Perryston View (88)** (PCalver) **4-9-4v** MBirch(4) (bhd: sme hdwy 2f out: n.d) | ½ | **17** | 14/1 | 76 | 47 |
| 1629 8 | **Femme Savante (95)** (RHannon) **4-9-11** WJO'Connor(16) (s.i.s: a bhd) | 1¼ | **18** | 33/1 | 79 | 50 |
| 2292 8 | **Saint Express (98)** (MrsMReveley) **6-10-0** KDarley(20) (racd stands' side: chsd ldrs over 3f: edgd lft & sn wknd) | hd | **19** | 14/1 | 81 | 52 |
| 1501 5 | **Stolen Kiss (IRE) (76)** (MWEasterby) **4-8-6b** TQuinn(12) (in tch: rdn 2f out: wknd & hung lft ins fnl f) | 1¼ | **20** | 16/1 | 55 | 26 |
| 2548 8 | **Master of Passion (82)** (JMPEustace) **7-8-12** MTebbutt(2) (chsd ldrs to ½-wy: sn lost pl) | 2½ | **21** | 20/1 | 53 | 24 |
| 2292* | **Twice as Sharp (90)** (PWHarris) **4-9-6** PatEddery(3) (s.i.s: rdn ½-wy: sn bhd) | 2½ | **22** | 5/1 1 | 53 | 24 |

(SP 149.9%) **22 Rn**

**59.21 secs** (1.51) CSF £120.55 CT £1,457.75 TOTE £9.90: £2.50 £3.10 £3.40 £6.30 (£54.80) Trio £592.60 OWNER Mrs D. E. Sharp (THIRSK) BRED R. M. West

LONG HANDICAP Premium Gift 7-4 Rich Glow 6-11

WEIGHT FOR AGE 3yo-5lb

**2114 Coastal Bluff**, who made great strides at three, did well to overcome the worst draw. Drifting left to join those on the far side, he made up a fair amount of ground to show ahead near the line. Provided the going is not too firm, he must be on the short list for the Stewards' Cup. (9/1)

**2292 Tedburrow**, as usual, was awash with sweat and showed he is better than ever. (12/1)

**2349 Laurel Delight**, who had a foal last year, won this race two years ago from an 8lb higher mark. Showing that she has retained all her old speed, she led them a merry dance until inside the last. (14/1)

**2220 Lady Sheriff**, back to her best trip, ran her usual race, picking up at halfway and putting her best work in at the line. (20/1)

**2349* Lago Di Varano** for once failed to go the gallop. Picking up ground soon after halfway, he could find no extra inside the last. (16/1)

**2228 Sea-Deer**, one of a handful to race on the stands' side, edged left like the winner to join those on the far side. Sticking on strongly at the death, he is probably better over six. (7/1: op 12/1)

**2064* Insider Trader**, with the visor again left off, was in the end the only one left to race on the stands' side. (20/1)

**2381 Crofters Ceilidh** again hinted at a revival. (25/1)

**2137* For the Present**, from a 4lb higher mark, missed the break and was never a factor over this inadequate trip. He will soon bounce back. (11/1)

**1186 Perryston View** ran better than his finishing position would indicate. (14/1)

**2292* Twice as Sharp** ran badly. After missing the break slightly, he was soon in trouble and his rider sensibly gave up. (5/1: 6/1-4/1)

## 2695 GO RACING IN YORKSHIRE 'MAURITIUS' MILE' MAIDEN STKS (2-Y.O) (Class D)

4-40 (4-42) **6f 214y** £4,581.00 (£1,368.00: £654.00: £297.00) Stalls: High GOING minus 0.25 sec per fur (GF)

| | | | | SP | RR | SF |
|---|---|---|---|---|---|---|
| 2243[2] | **Flaming West (USA)** (HRACecil) **2-9-0** WRyan(4) (lw: trckd ldrs: effrt & hung lft ½-wy: led 1f out: edgd lft & styd on wl) | — | 1 | 5/2[2] | 88? | 40 |
| 2335[2] | **Sturgeon (IRE)** (PFICole) **2-9-0** TQuinn(1) (led to ½-wy: led over 2f out to 1f out: btn whn sltly hmpd ins fnl f) | 2½ | 2 | 8/11[1] | 82 | 34 |
| 2580[9] | **Rehearsal (IRE)** (CACyzer) **2-9-0v[1]** KFallon(3) (lw: w ldr: led ½-wy tl over 2f out: wknd over 1f out) | 2 | 3 | 14/1 | 78 | 30 |
| | **Leviticus (IRE)** (TPTate) **2-9-0** ACulhane(2) (leggy: unf: scope: bit bkwd: dwlt s: sn pushed along: hdwy ½-wy: kpt on wl fnl f) | ¾ | 4 | 33/1 | 76+ | 28 |
| | **Shoumatara (USA)** (MRStoute) **2-9-0** JReid(5) (lengthy: scope: unruly s: sn trckng ldrs: shkn up & lost pl 3f out) | 3½ | 5 | 4/1[3] | 68 | 20 |

(SP 116.1%) **5 Rn**

**1m 26.06** (3.06) CSF £4.90 TOTE £3.10: £1.40 £1.10 (£1.90) OWNER Mr K. Abdulla (NEWMARKET) BRED Juddmonte Farms

**2243 Flaming West (USA)** behaved himself in the stalls this time. Though again showing signs of greenness, in the end he scored in decisive fashion. (5/2)

**2335 Sturgeon (IRE)**, who made no appeal whatsoever in the paddock, showed a very scratchy action going down, and the winner proved much too good in the end. (8/11: 10/11-Evens)

**2243 Rehearsal (IRE)**, a tail-swisher, was making a quick reappearance. Fitted with a visor, he did not look happy under pressure. (14/1)

**Leviticus (IRE)**, who looks as though he needs a fair bit of time, shaped nicely after missing the break. Running green, his final position puts a question mark over the value of the form. (33/1)

**Shoumatara (USA)**, who gave trouble at the stalls, was very green going down, and showed no immediate promise, dropping out soon after halfway. (4/1)

T/Jkpt: £45,452.20 (0.3 Tckts); £44,812.07 to York 13/7/96. T/Plpt: £482.10 (72.12 Tckts). T/Qdpt: £78.30 (33.07 Tckts). WG

# 2672-CHESTER (L-H) (Good to firm, Firm patches)

## Saturday July 13th

WEATHER: warm & sunny WIND: fresh across

## 2696 BROXTON NURSERY H'CAP (2-Y.O) (Class D)

2-10 (2-10) **7f 2y** £3,761.00 (£1,133.00: £549.00: £257.00) Stalls: Low GOING minus 0.56 sec per fur (F)

| | | | | SP | RR | SF |
|---|---|---|---|---|---|---|
| 2387* | **Stride** (MartynMeade) **2-8-9** FNorton(4) (swtg: a.p: qcknd to ld ins fnl f: eased nr fin) | — | 1 | 3/1[2] | 68+ | 18 |
| 2519[2] | **The Deejay (IRE)** (MBrittain) **2-8-3**(5) GParkin(5) (disp ld: rdn over 1f out: one pce) | 1¾ | 2 | 9/1 | 63 | 13 |
| 2112[9] | **Lamorna** (MRChannon) **2-9-7** JCarroll(7) (dwlt: hld up: hdwy 2f out: rdn & r.o fnl f) | ½ | 3 | 4/1[3] | 75 | 25 |
| 2382[2] | **Dowry** (RHannon) **2-8-12** PaulEddery(6) (lw: led tl hdd & no ex ins fnl f) | hd | 4 | 4/1[3] | 66 | 16 |
| 2531[3] | **Danehill Princess (IRE)** (RHollinshead) **2-8-8**(3) FLynch(1) (hld up: effrt & rdn over 2f out: no imp) | ¾ | 5 | 9/4[1] | 63 | 13 |
| 1607[2] | **Bellaf** (MWEasterby) **2-8-0** JQuinn(2) (trckd ldrs tl outpcd fnl 2f) | 6 | 6 | 11/1 | 38 | — |

(SP 114.1%) **6 Rn**

**1m 27.8** (2.60) CSF £25.05 TOTE £3.70: £2.10 £2.80 (£15.40) OWNER Ladyswood Racing Club (MALMESBURY) BRED Side Hill Stud

**2387* Stride** has proved costly to buy in after winning two sellers, but she proved here that she was worth every penny with a very comfortable success on this step up in class, and she has not stopped winning yet. (3/1)

**2519 The Deejay (IRE)** again gave it his best shot and will gain reward before much longer. (9/1)

**1683* Lamorna** is hardly built to carry topweight, but she performed with credit over this longer trip, and will pay her way when she comes down the handicap. (4/1)

**2382 Dowry**, an ideal type for this track, attempted to make all, but she had kept little in reserve, and was made to pay for it inside the last furlong. (4/1)

**2531 Danehill Princess (IRE)** usually races with the pace, but was unable to take advantage of the best of the draw, and was fighting a lost cause from some way out. (9/4)

## 2697 DAVID MCLEAN GROUP H'CAP (0-80) (3-Y.O+) (Class D)

2-45 (2-47) **1m 7f 195y** £6,092.50 (£1,840.00: £895.00: £422.50) Stalls: Low GOING minus 0.56 sec per fur (F)

| | | | | SP | RR | SF |
|---|---|---|---|---|---|---|
| 2423[3] | **Great Oration (IRE) (51)** (FWatson) **7-7-13** JQuinn(5) (hld up in rr: hdwy 3f out: led ins fnl f: drvn clr) | — | 1 | 8/1[3] | 62 | 18 |
| 2183[13] | **Teen Jay (57)** (BJLlewellyn) **6-8-5** WWoods(2) (lw: a.p: rdn 5f out: led appr fnl f: sn hdd: one pce) | 2½ | 2 | 11/1 | 66 | 22 |
| *1082*[6] | **Shakiyr (FR) (52)** (RHollinshead) **5-7-11**(3) FLynch(3) (hld up mid div: rdn & styd on wl appr fnl f) | nk | 3 | 16/1 | 60 | 16 |
| 2330[11] | **Sea Victor (77)** (JLHarris) **4-9-11** PRobinson(4) (lw: a.p: led over 3f out tl appr fnl f: one pce) | 1½ | 4 | 12/1 | 84 | 40 |
| 2401[9] | **Aude la Belle (FR) (48)** (SGKnight) **8-7-10** FNorton(11) (hld up: effrt over 3f out: styd on ins fnl f) | ¾ | 5 | 50/1 | 54 | 10 |
| 1802[7] | **Fabillion (70)** (CASmith) **4-9-4** CRutter(7) (hld up mid div: rdn over 3f out: nvr able to chal) | 3½ | 6 | 10/1 | 72 | 28 |
| 2239[4] | **Floating Line (68)** (EJAlston) **8-9-2** JCarroll(9) (swtg: prom: ev ch wl over 1f out: wknd appr fnl f) | 4 | 7 | 16/1 | 66 | 22 |
| 2042[17] | **Anglesey Sea View (62)** (ABailey) **7-8-7**(3) DWright(6) (trckd ldrs tl rdn & wknd 4f out) | 2 | 8 | 16/1 | 58 | 14 |
| 2221* | **Soba Up (72)** (TJEtherington) **6-9-6** ACulhane(10) (trckd ldrs: rdn 3f out: sn wknd) | 1 | 9 | 4/1[2] | 67 | 23 |
| 2407* | **Hal Hoo Yaroom (82)** (MajorWRHern) **3-8-11** PaulEddery(1) (mde most 12f: wknd qckly) | 2½ | 10 | 2/1[1] | 75 | 12 |
| 2055[16] | **Benfleet (76)** (RWArmstrong) **5-9-10** BThomson(12) (hld up: a in rr) | 3 | 11 | 11/1 | 66 | 22 |
| 2148[6] | **Zamhareer (USA) (55)** (WStorey) **5-7-10**(7) IonaWands(8) (a bhd: t.o fr ½-wy) | 9 | 12 | 8/1[3] | 36 | — |
| *656*[7] | **Twice the Groom (IRE) (60)** (RLee) **6-8-8** JStack(13) (b: a in rr: t.o) | 12 | 13 | 33/1 | 29 | — |

(SP 131.6%) **13 Rn**

**3m 27.48** (4.58) CSF £92.09 CT £1,293.71 TOTE £10.00: £2.40 £2.80 £3.70 (£76.70) Trio £366.00 OWNER M D Hetherington (Packaging) Ltd (SEDGEFIELD) BRED P. F. I. Cole

WEIGHT FOR AGE 3yo-19lb

**2423 Great Oration (IRE)**, at the top of his form at present, took advantage of his lenient handicap mark and won this with the minimum of fuss. When the emphasis is on stamina, he always has to be feared. (8/1)

**Teen Jay**, having his first try at such an extended trip, was being bustled along out in the country and looked set to drop away, but he did respond to strong pressure, and this sort of trip could be what he has been crying out for. (11/1)

**1082 Shakiyr (FR)** has done all his winning on the All-Weather, and he takes time to warm up, but he was into his stride in the latter stages, and is certainly capable of winning on turf. (16/1)

**2042 Sea Victor** kicked for home inside the last half-mile and did not go down without a fight, but the concession of so much weight took its toll in the battle to the line. (12/1)
**Aude la Belle (FR)** has lost the habit of winning but, back over a more suitable trip, was steadily working her way into it inside the last quarter-mile. (50/1)
**1150 Fabillion**, in more or less the same place throughout, was unable to make any further impression when the pressure was on. (10/1)
**2239 Floating Line** ran much better than his finishing position might suggest, for he was fighting for the lead below the distance before having to admit this longer trip proved just that bit too far. (16/1)
**2221* Soba Up** (4/1: op 6/1)
**2407* Hal Hoo Yaroom**, pitted against older, experienced handicappers, this time found his front-running tactics coming to an end just inside the quarter-mile marker. (2/1: op 3/1)
**1792 Benfleet** (11/1: 8/1-12/1)

## 2698 CITY WALL CONDITIONS STKS (3-Y.O+) (Class B)

3-15 (3-17) **5f 16y** £15,317.50 (£5,732.50: £2,803.75: £1,206.25: £540.63: £274.37) Stalls: Low GOING minus 0.56 sec per fur (F)

| | | | | SP | RR | SF |
|---|---|---|---|---|---|---|
| 1818[2] | **Lucky Parkes (100)** (JBerry) **6-8-9** JCarroll(2) (lw: mde all: rdn over 1f out: jst hld on) | — | 1 | 5/4[1] | 93 | 47 |
| 2143[10] | **Amazing Bay (100)** (IABalding) **3-8-4** PaulEddery(3) (lw: swtg: hld up: hdwy 2f out: chal & hung lft appr fnl f: rdn & r.o wl cl home) | s.h | 2 | 8/1 | 93 | 42 |
| 2115[17] | **Ya Malak (105)** (JWPayne) **5-9-0** BThomson(1) (lw: hld up: effrt & n.m.r appr fnl f: nt rcvr) | 1¼ | 3 | 11/2[3] | 94 | 48 |
| 2292[2] | **Ziggy's Dancer (USA) (84)** (EJAlston) **5-9-0** PRobinson(7) (lw: a.p: rdn over 1f out: unable qckn) | s.h | 4 | 6/1 | 94 | 48 |
| | **Bunty Boo** (RHannon) **7-8-9** JQuinn(6) (bit bkwd: hld up & bhd: gd hdwy over 1f out: nrst fin) | s.h | 5 | 4/1[2] | 89 | 43 |
| 1629[5] | **Maid For The Hills (102)** (DRLoder) **3-8-4v** JStack(4) (chsd wnr over 3f: sn rdn & wknd) | 11 | 6 | 13/2 | 54 | 3 |

(SP 118.6%) **6 Rn**

**59.93 secs** (-0.07) CSF £11.34 TOTE £2.00: £1.50 £3.60 (£13.50) OWNER Mr Joseph Heler (COCKERHAM) BRED Joseph Heler
WEIGHT FOR AGE 3yo-5lb

**1818 Lucky Parkes** would probably have been third best on the day but, with the antics going on behind her, she went hell-bent for the line and deservedly held on. (5/4: op 2/1)
**Amazing Bay**, waiting on the winner going extremely well, hung in towards that rival when popped the question entering the final furlong. Straightened up, she was gaining hand over fist at the finish, but was still half a stride down at the line. Had she kept straight, she would have won without any question. (8/1)
**2003 Ya Malak**, restrained taking a very keen hold, was hemmed in on the inside rail by Amazing Bay, and denied any run at all due to that rival continually edging left. He did try to force his way through approaching the final furlong, but was always short of room, and had to sit and suffer. This was a sure indication that he is getting back to something like his best. (11/2)
**2292 Ziggy's Dancer (USA)**, never far away, kept on strongly inside the distance, but could not muster the pace to land a blow. (6/1)
**Bunty Boo** looked just in need of this first run since the autumn. Ridden from off the pace, she finished strongly and will be the one to beat from now on. (4/1)
**1629 Maid For The Hills** showed up behind the winner until past halfway but, when the big guns came on the scene, she stopped as if shot. It would seem this minimum trip is not for her. (13/2)

## 2699 E.B.F. MAIDEN STKS (2-Y.O) (Class D)

3-50 (3-51) **5f 16y** £4,047.00 (£1,221.00: £593.00: £279.00) Stalls: Low GOING minus 0.56 sec per fur (F)

| | | | | SP | RR | SF |
|---|---|---|---|---|---|---|
| 2323[4] | **Aybeegirl** (MrsJCecil) **2-8-9v** PRobinson(5) (trckd ldrs: swvd violently lft & rdr lost iron over 1f out: str run to ld cl home) | — | 1 | 5/1 | 68 | 13 |
| 2559[4] | **Effervescence** (RHannon) **2-9-0** PaulEddery(3) (a.p: led over 1f out tl ct nr fin) | ½ | 2 | 2/1[1] | 71 | 16 |
| 1779[7] | **Midyan Queen** (RHollinshead) **2-8-4**(5) DGriffiths(7) (swtg: s.s: hdwy u.p wl over 1f out: nvr nrr) | 2½ | 3 | 16/1 | 59 | 4 |
| 1760[3] | **Enchantica** (JBerry) **2-8-9** JCarroll(4) (a.p: ev ch 1f out: unable qckn) | nk | 4 | 9/4[2] | 58 | 3 |
| 1713[2] | **Impulsion (IRE)** (RHannon) **2-9-0** JQuinn(2) (led tl hdd appr fnl f: sn outpcd) | 3½ | 5 | 4/1[3] | 52 | — |
| | **Fly-Girl** (BPJBaugh) **2-8-9** ACulhane(1) (small: unf: bkwd: trckd ldrs 3f: sn outpcd) | 4 | 6 | 14/1 | 34 | — |
| 2327[6] | **Sparkling Harry** (MissLCSiddall) **2-9-0** WWoods(6) (outpcd: rn v.wd ent st: t.o) | 6 | 7 | 33/1 | 20 | — |

(SP 116.3%) **7 Rn**

**62.05 secs** (2.05) CSF £15.25 TOTE £5.50: £2.60 £2.30 (£8.10) OWNER Mr Stephen Hobson (NEWMARKET) BRED Miss S. M. Rhodes and R. G. Percival

**2323 Aybeegirl** owes this success to a brave display of rodeo riding by Philip Robinson, for how he kept his seat after losing an iron when in full flight approaching the final furlong and then rousted her along to take command near the line, goodness only knows. (5/1)
**2559 Effervescence** did not stride out without any freedom on this second outing of the week, but he was in the firing-line all the way and only just failed to last home. (2/1: 6/4-9/4)
**1779 Midyan Queen** missed the break and did not get going until far too late but, in the circumstances, this must go down as a promising effort. (16/1)
**1760 Enchantica** was unable to dictate this time, but she was fighting for supremacy passing the furlong pole before finding an extra effort beyond her. (9/4)
**1713 Impulsion (IRE)**, smartly away to set a brisk pace, had run himself into the ground on reaching the final furlong. (4/1)

## 2700 RETAIL ADVERTISING SERVICES CONDITIONS STKS (2-Y.O) (Class C)

4-25 (4-26) **6f 18y** £5,025.00 (£1,875.00: £912.50: £387.50: £168.75: £81.25) Stalls: Low GOING minus 0.56 sec per fur (F)

| | | | | SP | RR | SF |
|---|---|---|---|---|---|---|
| 2112[3] | **Olympic Spirit** (JBerry) **2-8-10** JCarroll(2) (mde all: rdn over 1f out: kpt on strly) | — | 1 | 9/4[2] | 85 | 30 |
| 1892* | **Indian Rocket** (JLDunlop) **2-9-1** PaulEddery(1) (hld up on ins: hdwy ent st: chal 1f out: nt pce of wnr) | 1½ | 2 | Evens[1] | 86 | 31 |
| 2317[2] | **Foot Battalion (IRE)** (RHollinshead) **2-8-10**(3) FLynch(3) (bhd & outpcd tl r.o wl appr fnl f) | 1½ | 3 | 8/1 | 80 | 25 |
| 2491* | **Nomore Mr Niceguy** (EJAlston) **2-8-13** PRobinson(5) (trckd ldrs: shkn up & effrt over 1f out: nt pce to chal) | 1½ | 4 | 12/1 | 76 | 21 |
| 984[4] | **Weet Ees Girl (IRE)** (PDEvans) **2-8-5**(5) DGriffiths(4) (w wnr tl wknd wl over 1f out) | hd | 5 | 20/1 | 73 | 18 |
| 2361* | **Largesse** (JohnBerry) **2-9-1** JQuinn(6) (dwlt: hdwy ½-wy: rdn & wandered over 1f out: sn btn) | 1¼ | 6 | 7/1[3] | 75 | 20 |

(SP 116.8%) **6 Rn**

**1m 14.63** (1.33) CSF £5.03 TOTE £3.10: £1.70 £1.30 (£1.80) OWNER William Hill Organization Ltd (COCKERHAM) BRED W. H. Joyce

**2112 Olympic Spirit** had nothing of the calibre of Dazzle to contend with here and, after shaking off the favourite, was able to win going away. (9/4)
**1892* Indian Rocket** looked sure to score when putting in his bid a furlong out but, when the winner found that bit more, he either could not, or would not, go through with his effort. (Evens)

**2317 Foot Battalion (IRE)**, taken off his legs in the early stages, ran on particularly well inside the distance, and it is possible we have not seen the best of him yet. (8/1: op 5/1)
**2491* Nomore Mr Niceguy**, having his first run beyond the minimum trip, could not summon up the pace to deliver a challenge after being in hot pursuit all the way. (12/1)
**984 Weet Ees Girl (IRE)** showed plenty of speed to match strides with the winner for the first half-mile, but then faded rather quickly, and would seem to need less use making of her. (20/1)

## 2701 CHESHIRE YEOMANRY H'CAP (0-80) (3-Y.O+) (Class D)
4-55 (4-56) **1m 2f 75y** £4,510.00 (£1,360.00: £660.00: £310.00) Stalls: High GOING minus 0.56 sec per fur (F)

| | | | | SP | RR | SF |
|---|---|---|---|---|---|---|
| 2574* | **Game Ploy (POL) (71)** (DHaydnJones) **4-9-8** 5x PaulEddery(8) (hld up gng wl: hdwy 3f out: led appr fnl f: pushed out) | — | **1** | 7/2[1] | 82 | 56 |
| 2552[3] | **Taufan Boy (73)** (PWHarris) **3-8-13v** FNorton(4) (a.p: rdn 3f out: styd on wl ins fnl f) | 1¾ | **2** | 10/1 | 81 | 44 |
| 2552* | **Mr Teigh (67)** (BSmart) **4-9-4** DeanMcKeown(6) (swtg: led: clr ½-wy: hdd ent fnl f: one pce) | 1 | **3** | 4/1[2] | 74 | 48 |
| 2296* | **Alabang (60)** (MJCamacho) **5-8-11** LCharnock(3) (hld up & bhd: hdwy over 3f out: one pce fnl f) | 2½ | **4** | 4/1[2] | 63 | 37 |
| 2041[24] | **Diminutive (USA) (80)** (JWHills) **3-9-6** BThomson(10) (s.i.s: hdwy ½-wy: rdn 2f out: sn btn) | 5 | **5** | 12/1 | 75 | 38 |
| 2351[F] | **Wentbridge Lad (IRE) (66)** (PDEvans) **6-9-3v** WWoods(9) (hld up: hdwy over 3f out: nt rch ldrs) | 2 | **6** | 10/1 | 58 | 32 |
| 2010[15] | **Maradata (IRE) (62)** (RHollinshead) **4-8-8**(5) DGriffiths(1) (hld up in rr: effrt 3f out: sn rdn: no imp) | 3 | **7** | 12/1 | 49 | 23 |
| 2357[5] | **Dr Edgar (60)** (MDods) **4-8-11** PRobinson(5) (trckd ldrs over 6f: sn wknd: t.o) | 8 | **8** | 16/1 | 35 | 9 |
| 2677[8] | **Rebel County (IRE) (70)** (ABailey) **3-8-7**(3) DWright(2) (trckd ldrs tl wknd over 3f out: t.o) | 2½ | **9** | 7/1[3] | 41 | 4 |
| 2128[5] | **Bakers' Gate (USA) (76)** (JHMGosden) **4-9-13v[1]** JCarroll(11) (dwlt: plld hrd: sn wnt prom: wknd qckly over 3f out: sn t.o) | dist | **10** | 8/1 | — | — |

(SP 125.3%) **10 Rn**

**2m 9.34** (0.64) CSF £37.50 CT £138.89 TOTE £4.00: £2.20 £2.50 £1.70 (£41.90) Trio £13.90 OWNER Mr Kevan Kynaston (PONTYPRIDD) BRED C. Olsen Ltd
WEIGHT FOR AGE 3yo-11lb
**2574* Game Ploy (POL)**, completing his hat-trick inside a fortnight, could have been named the winner from some way out and, in this unstoppable form, must be followed until beaten. (7/2)
**2552 Taufan Boy** did not look happy on this fast ground, but he did turn the tables on Mr Teigh and there was not a lot wrong with the form. (10/1)
**2552* Mr Teigh**, an All-Weather specialist, is not quite so effective when he can not get his toe in, but to his credit he gave his supporters a run for their money, and will return to form when conditions suit. (4/1)
**2296* Alabang** needs to come late and he looked to be on cue when reaching a challenging position below the distance but, when the go button was pushed, he was unable to respond, and was never a threat. (4/1)
**2536 Rebel County (IRE)** (7/1: op 12/1)
**2128 Bakers' Gate (USA)**, a maiden carrying topweight in his first handicap, raced much too freely in his visor and was going in reverse at a rate of knots inside the last half-mile. (8/1)

T/Plpt: £159.20 (129.12 Tckts). T/Qdpt: £5.50 (204.09 Tckts). IM

# 2684-LINGFIELD (L-H) (Good to firm, Firm patches)
## Saturday July 13th
WEATHER: warm WIND: slt half against

## 2702 SURREY CONDITIONS STKS (2-Y.O) (Class D)
2-20 (2-20) **7f** £3,773.70 (£1,128.60: £540.80: £246.90) Stalls: High GOING minus 0.43 sec per fur (F)

| | | | | SP | RR | SF |
|---|---|---|---|---|---|---|
| 1896[4] | **Papua** (IABalding) **2-8-11** JReid(2) (lw: a.p: rdn 3f out: led over 1f out: r.o wl) | — | **1** | 7/4[1] | 84 | 44 |
| 2147[8] | **Logica (IRE)** (PAKelleway) **2-8-6** MRoberts(6) (lw: a.p: rdn over 3f out: ev ch ins fnl f: unable qckn) | 2 | **2** | 20/1 | 74 | 34 |
| | **Tasik Chini (USA)** (PFICole) **2-8-11** SSanders(10) (w'like: scope: hld up: rdn over 2f out: r.o one pce) | ¾ | **3** | 6/1 | 78 | 38 |
| 1519[4] | **Golden Fact (USA)** (RHannon) **2-8-11** RPerham(9) (s.s: nt clr run over 3f out & 2f out: hdwy & nt clr run 1f out: r.o) | ½ | **4** | 11/1 | 77+ | 37 |
| 2503[2] | **Dalmeny Dancer** (BJMeehan) **2-9-3** MTebbutt(3) (w ldr: led over 4f out tl over 1f out: wknd fnl f) | ¾ | **5** | 7/2[2] | 81 | 41 |
| 2122[5] | **Ivan Luis (FR)** (MBell) **2-8-11** MFenton(5) (bit bkwd: s.s: hld up: rdn over 2f out: one pce) | nk | **6** | 20/1 | 74 | 34 |
| 2538[10] | **Drift** (SirMarkPrescott) **2-8-11** GDuffield(1) (bit bkwd: a bhd) | 8 | **7** | 33/1 | 56 | 16 |
| 2224[4] | **Head Gardener (IRE)** (JLDunlop) **2-8-11** DHarrison(7) (hld up: rdn over 3f out: wknd over 2f out) | nk | **8** | 11/2[3] | 55 | 15 |
| 1622[10] | **Be True** (AMoore) **2-8-11** CandyMorris(8) (led over 2f: wknd over 2f out) | 1 | **9** | 100/1 | 53 | 13 |
| 1897[6] | **Ihtiyati (USA)** (JLDunlop) **2-8-11** JWeaver(4) (a bhd: t.o fnl 4f) | 10 | **10** | 20/1 | 30 | — |

(SP 114.8%) **10 Rn**

**1m 22.75** (1.15) CSF £31.59 TOTE £2.70: £1.50 £3.30 £2.10 (£38.00) Trio £128.10 OWNER Robert & Elizabeth Hitchins (KINGSCLERE) BRED Exors of the late D. Macrae
**OFFICIAL EXPLANATION Golden Fact (IRE): lost his action and the jockey thought he was lame. On pulling up he was found to have lost a shoe.**
**1896 Papua** confirmed the promise shown at Newbury last month. A leading light from the off, he was one of the first to be shaken up three furlongs from home, but commendably stuck to his task and, leading below the distance, kept on really well. (7/4)
**Logica (IRE)** left her debut run well behind. A leading light from the off, she was being bustled along over three furlongs from home and, sticking to her task really well, still had every chance inside the final furlong, before the winner proved too strong. She can find a race before long. (20/1)
**Tasik Chini (USA)**, quite a tall, well-made individual, chased the leaders. He stayed on for third prize, but never threatened to find that vital turn of foot. The experience will not be lost on him. (6/1: 3/1-13/2)
**1519 Golden Fact (USA)**, who flopped in the mud last time out, had no luck in running here. Continually finding his way blocked, he did extremely well to finish fourth, and it later transpired he had also lost a shoe on his off-fore. He seemed perfectly happy with this longer trip and now may be able to take a small handicap. (11/1: 7/1-12/1)
**2503 Dalmeny Dancer**, the most experienced in the field, disputed the lead until going on half a mile from home. He still appeared to be cruising a quarter of a mile out, but was collared below the distance and tamely dropped away. (7/2)
**2122 Ivan Luis (FR)**, still not looking fully fit, recovered from a tardy start to chase the leaders, but was made to look very pedestrian in the final two furlongs. (20/1)

## 2703 GLOSSBROOK HOMES NURSERY H'CAP (2-Y.O) (Class E)
2-55 (2-55) **6f** £3,097.50 (£924.00: £441.00: £199.50) Stalls: High GOING minus 0.43 sec per fur (F)

| | | | | SP | RR | SF |
|---|---|---|---|---|---|---|
| 2338[5] | **Halowing (USA)** (PAKelleway) **2-9-2** JWeaver(1) (swtg: led 2f: rdn over 2f out: led over 1f out: r.o wl) | — | 1 | 3/1[3] | 75 | 32 |
| 2195[5] | **Kenwood Melody** (MBell) **2-8-10** MFenton(3) (lw: rdn over 2f out: hdwy over 1f out: r.o wl ins fnl f) | ¾ | 2 | 9/1 | 67 | 24 |
| 2230[4] | **Third Party** (SDow) **2-8-4** MRoberts(6) (plld hrd: hld up: rdn over 2f out: r.o one pce) | 1½ | 3 | 11/1 | 57 | 14 |
| 1822* | **Bold Catch (USA)** (RCharlton) **2-9-3** JReid(4) (hld up: ev ch over 1f out: wknd fnl f) | 2 | 4 | 13/8[1] | 65 | 22 |
| 2398* | **Powder River** (RHannon) **2-9-7b** RPerham(2) (lw: w ldr: led 4f out tl over 1f out: sn wknd) | s.h | 5 | 5/2[2] | 69 | 26 |
| | | | | (SP 110.0%) | **5 Rn** | |

**1m 11.11** (2.11) CSF £22.36 TOTE £4.40: £2.00 £3.30 (£31.80) OWNER Mr Richard Trontz (NEWMARKET) BRED Blueberry Hill Farm

**2338 Halowing (USA),** the early leader, regained the advantage below the distance and kept on strongly. (3/1)

**2195 Kenwood Melody,** at the back of the field for the majority of the race, only found his feet on the outside of the field below the distance. He ran on nicely inside the final furlong to snatch second prize, but was unable to overhaul the winner in time. (9/1)

**2230 Third Party,** who took a keen hold early on and chased the leaders, stayed on under pressure, but failed to find a turn of foot. (11/1: op 7/1)

**1822* Bold Catch (USA)** chased the leaders and appeared to be absolutely cruising a quarter of a mile out. Still in with every chance below the distance, he tamely folded up in the final furlong. (13/8)

**2398* Powder River** stood out in the paddock but was very disappointing. Disputing the lead until going on quarter of a mile from home, he was collared below the distance and soon tired. (5/2)

## 2704 DAILY MAIL CLASSIFIED SILVER TROPHY RATED STKS H'CAP (0-105) (Listed) (3-Y.O+) (Class A)
3-25 (3-25) **7f 140y** £10,307.44 (£3,856.96: £1,885.98: £810.90: £362.95: £183.77) Stalls: High GOING minus 0.43 sec per fur (F)

| | | | | SP | RR | SF |
|---|---|---|---|---|---|---|
| 2050[4] | **Almushtarak (IRE) (105)** (MissGayKelleway) **3-9-3** RCochrane(1) (b.hind: lw: hdwy over 2f out: bmpd over 1f out: led wl ins fnl f: all out) | — | 1 | 5/2[1] | 113 | 64 |
| 2328[8] | **Double Blue (99)** (MJohnston) **7-9-6** JWeaver(5) (lw: a.p: rdn over 2f out: led ins fnl f: sn hdd: r.o wl) | s.h | 2 | 6/1 | 107 | 67 |
| 2050[3] | **Bewitching (USA) (102)** (JARToller) **3-9-0** SSanders(6) (lw: hld up: rdn over 2f out: led over 1f out tl ins fnl f: n.m.r: unable qckn) | ½ | 3 | 11/4[2] | 109 | 60 |
| 1327[9] | **Wisam (92)** (RHannon) **3-8-4** MRoberts(2) (led 6f: one pce) | 2 | 4 | 14/1 | 95 | 46 |
| 2544[8] | **Blue Zulu (IRE) (86)** (JRFanshawe) **4-8-7** DHarrison(7) (a.p: rdn over 3f out: one pce) | ½ | 5 | 11/2 | 88 | 48 |
| 889[9] | **Queenfisher (91)** (GLMoore) **4-8-12** GDuffield(4) (s.s: a bhd) | 2½ | 6 | 40/1 | 87 | 47 |
| 2248* | **Louis' Queen (IRE) (100)** (JLDunlop) **4-9-7** JReid(3) (hld up: rdn over 2f out: btn whn bdly hmpd over 1f out) | 2½ | 7 | 4/1[3] | 91+ | 51 |
| | | | | (SP 114.0%) | **7 Rn** | |

**1m 28.8** (0.00) CSF £16.49 TOTE £3.30: £1.80 £2.30 (£6.40) OWNER Mr A. Al-Radi (WHITCOMBE) BRED Stonethorn Stud Farms Ltd

WEIGHT FOR AGE 3yo-9lb

**2050 Almushtarak (IRE),** whose trainer was very confident about his prospects beforehand, despite a rise of 20lb since his Kempton victory, was given a bump below the distance, and Cochrane had to pull out all the stops to get the colt to the front in the closing stages. (5/2)

**1975 Double Blue,** a leading light from the off, managed to poke a whisker in front inside the final furlong and, although soon headed by the winner, kept on really well to only just fail in a really tight finish. (6/1)

**2050 Bewitching (USA)** chased the leaders and showed marginally in front below the distance. Collared inside the final furlong, she was then sandwiched between the front two, but this made little difference to her chances as she was tapped for toe. (11/4)

**1327 Wisam** took the field along but, collared below the distance, could only keep on in his own time. (14/1: 10/1-16/1)

**Blue Zulu (IRE)** was never far away. Rousted along from halfway, she never looked like finding another gear. (11/2: 4/1-6/1)

## 2705 ROTHMANS ROYALS NORTH SOUTH CHALLENGE SERIES H'CAP (0-90) (3-Y.O) (Class C)
4-00 (4-01) **7f** £7,310.00 (£2,180.00: £1,040.00: £470.00) Stalls: High GOING minus 0.43 sec per fur (F)

| | | | | SP | RR | SF |
|---|---|---|---|---|---|---|
| 2126[3] | **Ood Dancer (USA) (82)** (LMCumani) **3-9-3** JWeaver(9) (hdwy 2f out: led over 1f out: rdn out) | — | 1 | 4/1[3] | 91 | 68 |
| 2222* | **Albert The Bear (78)** (JBerry) **3-8-13** SDWilliams(5) (a.p: led over 2f out tl over 1f out: unable qckn) | 2 | 2 | 7/2[2] | 82 | 59 |
| 1820[2] | **Banzhaf (USA) (74)** (GLMoore) **3-8-9** RCochrane(3) (lw: hld up: rdn over 2f out: one pce) | 3 | 3 | 11/2 | 72 | 49 |
| 2301[8] | **Stoney End (USA) (71)** (MRChannon) **3-8-6** RPerham(8) (led over 4f) | 1¼ | 4 | 14/1 | 66 | 43 |
| 2501[6] | **Ameer Alfayaafi (IRE) (63)** (RAkehurst) **3-7-12** SSanders(1) (hld up: rdn over 2f out: wknd over 1f out) | 1 | 5 | 11/4[1] | 55 | 32 |
| 1820[5] | **Ashjar (USA) (86)** (HThomsonJones) **3-9-7** GDuffield(2) (swtg: racd alone centre: prom over 5f) | hd | 6 | 13/2 | 78 | 55 |
| 2225[3] | **La Modiste (80)** (SDow) **3-8-10**(5) ADaly(7) (bhd fnl 2f) | nk | 7 | 20/1 | 72 | 49 |
| 1991[9] | **Petit Point (IRE) (76)** (RHannon) **3-8-11** JReid(6) (hld up: rdn over 2f out: sn wknd) | 2 | 8 | 11/1 | 63 | 40 |
| *2171*[8] | **Mijas (78)** (LMontagueHall) **3-8-13** DHarrison(10) (a bhd: t.o whn p.u over 1f out: dismntd) | | P | 16/1 | — | — |
| | | | | (SP 123.3%) | **9 Rn** | |

**1m 21.24** (-0.36) CSF £18.75 CT £73.60 TOTE £5.10: £1.30 £1.40 £2.10 (£6.30) Trio £5.30 OWNER Sheikh Ahmed Al Maktoum (NEWMARKET) BRED Fares Farms Inc

OFFICIAL EXPLANATION **Mijas: the jockey reported that the bit had slipped through the filly's mouth.**

**2126 Ood Dancer (USA),** put to sleep at the back of the field, moved smoothly through to lead below the distance and, ridden along, soon asserted. (4/1)

**2222* Albert The Bear** went for home over quarter of a mile out but, headed below the distance, found the winner too strong. (7/2)

**1820 Banzhaf (USA)** chased the leaders but, pushed along over two furlongs from home, could only go up and own in the same place. (11/2)

**2021 Stoney End (USA)** took the field along but, collared over two furlongs from home, was soon in trouble. (14/1: 10/1-16/1)

**2501 Ameer Alfayaafi (IRE)** chased the leaders. Almost on terms a quarter of a mile out, he had run out of gas below the distance. (11/4: 7/4-3/1)

**1820 Ashjar (USA)** ploughed a lone furrow down the centre of the course. Nevertheless, he raced up with the pace until tiring below the distance. (13/2)

**1840* Petit Point (IRE)** (11/1: 7/1-12/1)

## 2706 JULY MAIDEN STKS (3-Y.O+) (Class D)
4-35 (4-40) **1m 1f** £3,893.85 (£1,162.80: £555.90: £252.45) Stalls: Low GOING minus 0.43 sec per fur (F)

| | | | | SP | RR | SF |
|---|---|---|---|---|---|---|
| | **Poddington** (RAkehurst) **5-9-7** SSanders(6) (hld up: nt clr run on ins over 3f out tl over 1f out: swtchd rt: squeezed thro to ld ins fnl f: r.o wl) | — | 1 | 4/1[3] | 82 | 41 |
| 2439[4] | **Blatant Outburst** (GCBravery) **6-9-7** JReid(5) (a.p: led over 5f out tl ins fnl f: unable qckn) | 2 | 2 | 3/1[2] | 78 | 37 |
| 1857[2] | **Premier Night (73)** (SDow) **3-8-6** MRoberts(8) (led over 8f out: rel to r & hdd over 5f out: rdn over 2f out: swtchd rt over 1f out: r.o one pce) | nk | 3 | 7/4[1] | 73 | 22 |

| | | | | SP | RR | SF |
|---|---|---|---|---|---|---|
| 1714[4] | **Possessive Artiste (73)** (MRStoute) **3-8-7**ow1 RCochrane(7) (b.nr hind: swtg: hld up: rdn over 1f out: ev ch ins fnl f: one pce) | nk | **4** | 9/2 | 73 | 21 |
| | **Orange Order (IRE)** (GHarwood) **3-8-11** JWeaver(4) (neat: s.s: hdwy 7f out: rdn over 2f out: wknd over 1f out) | 6 | **5** | 5/1 | 67 | 16 |
| 2124[10] | **Bagby Boy (35)** (PRHedger) **4-9-7** DBiggs(2) (led over 1f: wknd over 6f out: t.o fnl 4f) | 15 | **6** | 50/1 | 40 | — |
| 2197[16] | **Colebrook Willie** (JRBosley) **3-8-11** RPerham(3) (a bhd: t.o fnl 3f) | 1¼ | **7** | 50/1 | 38 | — |
| | ***Press Again*** (PHayward) **4-9-2** MFenton(1) (Withdrawn not under Starter's orders: ref to ent stalls) | | **W** | 50/1 | — | — |

(SP 122.1%) **7 Rn**

**1m 53.69** (3.19) CSF £16.57 TOTE £5.60: £1.90 £1.90 (£12.50) OWNER Miss Vivian Pratt (EPSOM) BRED Chesters Stud
WEIGHT FOR AGE 3yo-10lb

**Poddington**, whose only run to date was when finishing third in this race last year, looked fit but dull in his coat. Trapped on the rail in the straight, it looked as if he might not find an opening but he managed to get a run approaching the final furlong and, squeezing through between horses, he hit the front in the last 100 yards and quickly asserted. (4/1)

**2439 Blatant Outburst**, who won a bumper at Southwell just over a year ago, went on at the top of the hill. Grimly trying to hold on, he was eventually overhauled inside the final furlong. (3/1: op 5/1)

**1857 Premier Night** was soon at the head of affairs, but she blatantly downed tools at the top of the hill and virtually came to a standstill, not surprisingly relinquishing the lead. Her pilot managed to get her going again and switched her below the distance to renew her effort. The filly looked far from co-operative but did stay on, only just failing to take second prize. (7/4)

**1714 Possessive Artiste** chased the leaders and appeared to be travelling well in the straight. Rousted along below the distance, she still had every chance inside the final furlong before tapped for toe. (9/2: 3/1-5/1)

**Orange Order (IRE)** soon recovered from a tardy start but, rousted along in the straight, had nothing more to give in the final quarter-mile. (5/1: 5/2-11/2)

## 2707 LADBROKE H'CAP (0-70) (3-Y.O+) (Class E)

5-05 (5-05) **1m 6f** £3,452.40 (£1,033.20: £495.60: £226.80) Stalls: Low GOING: minus 0.43 sec per fur (F)

| | | | | SP | RR | SF |
|---|---|---|---|---|---|---|
| 2319* | **Ballynakelly (56)** (RAkehurst) **4-9-3** SSanders(3) (lw: a.p: led 6f out: clr over 2f out: easily) | — | **1** | 8/11 1 | 69+ | 43 |
| 2385[3] | **Mr Copyforce (46)** (MissBSanders) **6-8-0**(7) JoHunnam(4) (hld up: rdn over 2f out: chsd wnr ins fnl f: unable qckn) | 3 | **2** | 5/1 3 | 56 | 30 |
| 2506[14] | **Rising Spray (48)** (CAHorgan) **5-8-4**(5) AmandaSanders(5) (lw: hdwy 7f out: chsd wnr over 3f out tl ins fnl f: one pce) | 3 | **3** | 20/1 | 54 | 28 |
| 1695* | **Frozen Sea (USA) (67)** (GPEnright) **5-9-9**(5) ADaly(7) (lw: hld up: rdn 3f out: sn wknd: fin 5th, ½l: plcd 4th) | | **4** | 4/1 2 | 65 | 39 |
| 1778[9] | **Cuban Nights (USA) (56)** (BJLlewellyn) **4-9-3** JWeaver(6) (led over 11f out to 8f out: wknd over 6f out: fin 6th, 6l: plcd 5th) | | **5** | 12/1 | 47 | 21 |
| 2415[2] | **Lucky Coin (59)** (PHowling) **4-9-6** RCochrane(2) (led over 2f: led 8f out to 6f out: wknd 3f out) | 11 | **7** | 7/1 | 37 | 11 |
| | **Simply (IRE) (35)** (TPMcGovern) **7-7-3**(7) PDoe(1) (nvr nr to chal: fin 4th, 7l: disq: plcd last) | | **D** | 16/1 | 33 | 7 |

(SP 125.4%) **7 Rn**

**3m 2.7** (0.93 under best) (4.40) CSF £5.79 TOTE £1.70: £1.40 £2.70 (£4.50) OWNER Y Y Partnership (EPSOM) BRED Crest Stud Ltd
LONG HANDICAP Simply (IRE) 7-5
STEWARDS' ENQUIRY Doe susp. 22-23/7/96 (failure to weigh in).

**2319* Ballynakelly** continued his winning sequence in impressive style. Sent to the front at the top of the hill, he forged clear in the straight to win pulling the proverbial bus. (8/11: 4/5-Evens)

**2385 Mr Copyforce** chased the leaders. Having a ding-dong battle for the runner-up prize in the straight, he managed to succeed in the final furlong, but had no hope with the winner. (5/1: 3/1-11/2)

**Simply (IRE)** moved into second place early in the straight, but failed to reel in the winner, and was collared for the runner-up berth inside the final furlong. He was later disqualified when his rider failed to weigh in. (16/1)

T/Plpt: £260.60 (40.52 Tckts). T/Qdpt: £49.50 (13 Tckts). AK

# 2249-SALISBURY (R-H) (Good to firm, Good patches)

## Saturday July 13th

Race 2: Flip start
WEATHER: unsettled WIND: slt half against

## 2708 E.B.F. QUEENPOT MAIDEN STKS (2-Y.O) (Class D)

2-15 (2-18) **6f 212y** £4,207.50 (£1,260.00: £605.00: £277.50) Stalls: High GOING minus 0.46 sec per fur (F)

| | | | | SP | RR | SF |
|---|---|---|---|---|---|---|
| | **Sandstone (IRE)** (JLDunlop) **2-9-0** SWhitworth(9) (unf: hld up: swtchd lft & hdwy over 2f out: led ins fnl f: rdn out) | — | **1** | 9/2 3 | 91+ | 25 |
| 1626[3] | **Silver Widget (USA)** (RCharlton) **2-9-0** TSprake(6) (swtg: a.p: led over 1f out tl ins fnl f) | ¾ | **2** | 7/4 1 | 89 | 23 |
| 2224[3] | **Mister Pink** (RFJohnsonHoughton) **2-9-0** AMcGlone(12) (a.p: ev ch over 1f out: one pce) | 5 | **3** | 8/1 | 78 | 12 |
| 1346[7] | **Lucky Dip** (MajorDNChappell) **2-8-6**(3) MHenry(5) (wnt lft s: a.p: led over 3f out tl over 1f out: wknd fnl f) | 3½ | **4** | 20/1 | 65 | — |
| | **Hidden Meadow** (IABalding) **2-9-0** TIves(3) (leggy: unf: prom on outside: j.path over 3f out: sn edgd lft: no hdwy fnl 2f) | nk | **5** | 11/4 2 | 69 | 3 |
| 2543[6] | **Love Has No Pride (USA)** (RHannon) **2-8-11**(3) DaneO'Neill(10) (prom over 5f) | ½ | **6** | 14/1 | 68 | 2 |
| | **Chief Island** (WGMTurner) **2-8-4**(5) RHavlin(1) (small: lt-f: bkwd: nvr nrr) | ½ | **7** | 33/1 | 62 | — |
| | **Sharp Hat** (RHannon) **2-9-0** NAdams(7) (scope: b.hind: plld hrd: sn prom: ev ch over 1f out: sn wknd) | hd | **8** | 33/1 | 67 | 1 |
| 2224[7] | **Elhafid (USA)** (MajorWRHern) **2-9-0** DeclanO'Shea(2) (nvr trbld ldrs) | nk | **9** | 20/1 | 66 | — |
| | **Kennemara Star (IRE)** (JLDunlop) **2-9-0** WJO'Connor(18) (unf: s.s: sn rcvrd: wknd over 2f out) | hd | **10** | 33/1 | 66 | — |
| 2396[3] | **Fancy A Fortune (IRE)** (JPearce) **2-9-0** GBardwell(8) (a bhd) | 4 | **11** | 25/1 | 56 | — |
| 2243[4] | **Midatlantic** (PTWalwyn) **2-9-0** RPrice(17) (led over 3f: wknd over 2f out) | 1¾ | **12** | 25/1 | 52 | — |
| | **Sunday Market (USA)** (GHarwood) **2-9-0** AClark(4) (w'like: scope: bkwd: hmpd s: sn rdn along: a bhd) | 5 | **13** | 16/1 | 41 | — |
| 2025[8] | **Poly Dancer** (MRChannon) **2-8-9** AGorman(15) (prom 4f) | 5 | **14** | 33/1 | 24 | — |
| | **Poignant (IRE)** (MRChannon) **2-9-0** AMackay(13) (leggy: unf: bkwd: s.s: a bhd: t.o) | 9 | **15** | 33/1 | 9 | — |

(SP 136.8%) **15 Rn**

**1m 29.15** (3.15) CSF £13.45 TOTE £10.40: £2.10 £1.10 £2.30 (£8.40) Trio £28.20 OWNER Mr Peter Winfield (ARUNDEL) BRED Barouche Stud Ltd

**Sandstone (IRE)**, a 90,000 guineas half-brother to the useful Irish three-year-old Truth or Dare, had been reported to have been working well at home. Picking up nicely when sent about his business, it will be a surprise if he does not go on from here. (9/2: op 10/1)
**1626 Silver Widget (USA)**, rather warm in the preliminaries, appreciated this extra furlong and will not always meet one so smart. (7/4: 5/4-9/4)
**2224 Mister Pink**, again without the visor, is nothing if not consistent and seemed to have come up against two above-average sorts for this grade. (8/1: op 4/1)
**1346 Lucky Dip**, a half-sister to Love Returned, appears to be going the right way, but six may be far enough for her at the moment. (20/1)
**Hidden Meadow**, a half-brother to good sprinter Overbrook, looked green and probably saw too much daylight on the outside. He will be better for the experience. (11/4: 5/1-5/2)
**2543 Love Has No Pride (USA)**, not fully wound up for his debut a week ago, may have found this coming too soon. (14/1: op 5/1)
**Chief Island**, a half-sister to several winners including Clare Heights, is out of a Princess Elizabeth Stakes winner. Staying on promisingly in the closing stages, she is sure to come on for the outing. (33/1)
**Sharp Hat**, whose dam is from the same family as Circus Plume, was very free going to post and will do better when he learns to settle. (33/1)

## 2709 FELSTEAD LIMITED STKS (0-65) (3-Y.O+) (Class F)

2-50 (2-52) **1m 6f** £2,847.00 (£792.00: £381.00) Stalls: Low GOING: minus 0.43 sec per fur (F)

SP RR SF

2282$^{2}$ **Silktail (IRE) (65)** (MissGayKelleway) **4-9-3** TSprake(12) (hld up & bhd: swtchd lft & hdwy over 2f out: hung rt over 1f out: rdn to ld nr fin) — **1** 11/4$^{1}$ 72 27
2547$^{12}$ **Supreme Star (USA) (62)** (PRHedger) **5-9-3**$^{(3)}$ DaneO'Neill(10) (a.p: rdn over 2f out: ev ch ins fnl f: r.o) 1 **2** 7/1 74 29
2165$^{3}$ **Tragic Hero (61)** (MCPipe) **4-9-6b** WJO'Connor(8) (plld hrd: a.p: hrd rdn over 2f out: led ins fnl f: hdd nr fin) nk **3** 7/2$^{2}$ 74 29
2547$^{13}$ **Paradise Navy (63)** (CREgerton) **7-9-6** TIves(2) (hld up: hdwy over 4f out: ev ch 1f out: r.o) s.h **4** 7/1 74 29
2202$^{2}$ **Arcady (64)** (PTWalwyn) **3-8-2** DeclanO'Shea(9) (chsd ldr: led over 3f out tl ins fnl f) hd **5** 4/1$^{3}$ 70 10
1100$^{10}$ **Oliver Rock (60)** (MajorDNChappell) **3-8-5** AClark(5) (hld up & bhd: stdy hdwy over 4f out: wknd over 1f out) 10 **6** 16/1 62 2
2251$^{10}$ **Mischief Star (62)** (DRCElsworth) **3-8-2** GBardwell(1) (rdn over 5f out: sn bhd) 3 **7** 14/1 56 —
1807$^{11}$ **Risky Romeo (64)** (GCBravery) **4-9-6** SWhitworth(7) (swtg: hld up & bhd: hdwy over 4f out: eased whn btn over 1f out) 5 **8** 16/1 53 8
1496$^{10}$ **Bronhallow (54)** (MrsBarbaraWaring) **3-8-2**$^{(3)}$ SDrowne(3) (a bhd) 1¼ **9** 50/1 51 —
2155$^{11}$ **Air Command (BAR) (36)** (CTNash) **6-8-13**$^{(7)}$ JWilkinson(11) (lw: led over 10f: wknd qckly over 2f out) 9 **10** 50/1 41 —
2507$^{15}$ **Causley (35)** (DMHyde) **11-9-6** VSlattery(4) (plld hrd: prom tl wknd qckly over 3f out: t.o) 23 **11** 50/1 15 —

(SP 118.2%) **11 Rn**

**3m 5.63** (6.93) CSF £21.15 TOTE £3.20: £1.60 £2.10 £1.60 (£9.90) Trio £22.50 OWNER Pitpersons (WHITCOMBE) BRED Sheikh Mohammed bin Rashid al Maktoum
WEIGHT FOR AGE 3yo-15lb
STEWARDS' ENQUIRY O'Connor susp. 22-23/7/96 (excessive use of the whip).
**2282 Silktail (IRE)**, who is in foal to Mtoto, was suited to this extra quarter-mile. After being inclined to duck in behind Paradise Navy, she stayed on in the closing stages to land the spoils. (11/4)
**Supreme Star (USA)** appreciated this easier company and this drop down to what may well be his best trip. (7/1)
**2165 Tragic Hero** responded willingly to some hard driving against the far rail, and his rider picked up a two-day whip ban. (7/2)
**2148 Paradise Navy** seemed unsuited to front-running tactics on yielding ground at Sandown a week ago. (7/1: op 4/1)
**2202 Arcady** certainly seemed to get this longer trip well enough. (4/1)
**Mischief Star** (14/1: 10/1-16/1)

## 2710 EDWARDS FORD H'CAP (0-80) (3-Y.O) (Class D)

3-20 (3-27) **1m** £4,175.00 (£1,250.00: £600.00: £275.00) Stalls: High GOING minus 0.46 sec per fur (F)

SP RR SF

2526* **Catch The Lights (75)** (RHannon) **3-9-4**$^{(3)}$ DaneO'Neill(7) (lw: prom tl stdd after 2f: hdwy over 2f out: led ins fnl f: r.o wl) — **1** 4/1$^{1}$ 87 50
2402$^{3}$ **Sunley Secure (53)** (MRChannon) **3-7-13** AMackay(5) (led: qcknd over 3f out: clr over 2f out: hdd ins fnl f) 2½ **2** 6/1$^{3}$ 60 23
2347$^{4}$ **Silver Harrow (60)** (AGNewcombe) **3-8-3**$^{(3)}$ SDrowne(6) (hld up & bhd: hdwy over 2f out: rdn over 1f out: one pce) 1¼ **3** 7/1 65 28
2409$^{9}$ **Nakhal (55)** (DJGMurraySmith) **3-8-1b$^{1}$** NAdams(8) (swtg: hrd rdn over 3f out: hdwy over 1f out: styd on fnl f) nk **4** 20/1 59 22
2339$^{8}$ **Honorable Estate (IRE) (65)** (RHannon) **3-8-11** WJO'Connor(1) (prom: rdn over 3f out: wknd 2f out) 5 **5** 16/1 59 22
2501$^{7}$ **Sound Check (55)** (BJMeehan) **3-8-1b** GBardwell(3) (sn chsng ldr: wknd wl over 1f out) 3 **6** 6/1$^{3}$ 43 6
2253* **Mimosa (52)** (SDow) **3-7-9**$^{(3)}$ MHenry(9) (prom: rdn over 3f out: wknd over 2f out) 5 **7** 5/1$^{2}$ 30 —
1711$^{13}$ **Classic Look (IRE) (59)** (MajorDNChappell) **3-8-5** AClark(2) (bhd fnl 3f) nk **8** 12/1 36 —
*2235** ***Bandit Girl (63)*** (IABalding) **3-8-9** TIves(4) (Withdrawn not under Starter's orders: jockey ill) **W** 4/1$^{1}$ — —

(SP 116.1%) **8 Rn**

**1m 42.21** (1.81) CSF £18.01 CT £75.11 TOTE £3.10: £1.70 £1.20 £1.60 (£6.50) Trio £7.30 OWNER Mr T. A. Johnsey (MARLBOROUGH) BRED T. A. Johnsey
**2526* Catch The Lights**, patiently ridden after breaking well, came with a nicely-timed run to defy topweight, and is a filly in good heart at the moment. (4/1: 3/1-9/2)
**2402 Sunley Secure** got most of his rivals in trouble when quickening the tempo at halfway, but the winner had him in her sights in the final quarter-mile. (6/1)
**2347 Silver Harrow**, down 2lb, looked much more at home over this mile than the six last time. (7/1: 5/1-8/1)
**734 Nakhal** had dropped 6lb since his handicap debut and sweated up in the first-time blinkers. (20/1)
**2032 Honorable Estate (IRE)**, a stable-companion of the winner, could not take advantage of a 5lb lower mark. (16/1)
**2253 Sound Check** was back to the mark off which he won over course and distance in May. (6/1)
**1333 Classic Look (IRE)** (12/1: op 8/1)

## 2711 CRESTED LARK AMATEUR H'CAP (0-70) (3-Y.O+) (Class F)

3-55 (3-56) **1m 4f** £2,952.00 (£822.00: £396.00) Stalls: Low GOING minus 0.46 sec per fur (F)

SP RR SF

2124$^{6}$ **Artic Bay (63)** (MrsPNDutfield) **4-11-2**$^{(5)}$ MrLJefford(3) (hld up & bhd: hdwy 4f out: led wl over 1f out: r.o wl) — **1** 14/1 72 56
2401$^{D}$ **General Mouktar (59)** (BJMeehan) **6-11-3** MissJAllison(9) (hld up & bhd: stdy hdwy 4f out: ev ch 2f out: unable qckn ins fnl f) ¾ **2** 4/1$^{2}$ 67 51

2246[8] **Evidence In Chief (57)** (DRCElsworth) **3-9-11**(5)ow3 MrNMoran(13) (lw: hld up & bhd: hdwy & rdr lost iron over 3f out: rdn over 1f out: one pce) ....3½ **3** 16/1 60 28
2587[9] **Cheveley Dancer (USA) (29)** (TJNaughton) **8-8-10**(5) MrsJMoore(12) (b: plld hrd: a.p: led 2f out: sn hdd & btn) ....1 **4** 16/1 31 15
2385[4] **Witney-de-Bergerac (IRE) (58)** (JSMoore) **4-10-11**(5) MrsSMoore(5) (swtg: hld up & bhd: hdwy on ins 4f out: ev ch 2f out: wknd fnl f) ....3 **5** 5/1[3] 56 40
**Paper Cloud (60)** (RTPhillips) **4-10-13**(5) MrsSFaber(4) (prom tl wknd 2f out) ....8 **6** 20/1 47 31
2494[4] **Diamond Cut (FR) (55)** (MCPipe) **8-10-8**(5) MrMFrith(2) (hld up: stdy hdwy 6f out: led over 2f out: sn hdd: wknd over 1f out) ....hd **7** 5/1[3] 42 26
**Haydown (IRE) (39)** (CTNash) **4-9-6**(5) MrPPhillips(10) (prom over 9f) ....12 **8** 50/1 10 —
1655[18] **Mystic Legend (IRE) (32)** (JJSheehan) **4-8-13**(5) MissCHannaford(11) (a.p: led over 3f out tl over 2f out: sn wknd) ....4 **9** 40/1 — —
*2322*[11] **Lady Poly (37)** (JRPoulton) **8-9-4**(5)ow9 MrsCPoulton(1) (b: a bhd: t.o) ....13 **10** 50/1 — —
**Back By Dawn (60)** (DRCElsworth) **3-10-5** PHenley(7) (rdn over 4f out: a bhd: t.o) ....1¼ **11** 10/1 7 —
2394[3] **Nosey Native (60)** (JPearce) **3-10-5v** MrsLPearce(8) (plld hrd: led over 8f: sn wknd: t.o) ....dist **12** 7/2[1] — —
2155[8] **Courbaril (58)** (SDow) **4-10-11**(5) MrSFetherstonhaugh(6) (ref to r: t.n.p) .... **R** 10/1 — —
(SP 123.3%) **13 Rn**

**2m 38.59** (5.99) CSF £66.86 CT £851.95 TOTE £28.10: £4.70 £1.90 £4.40 (£49.30) Trio £240.60; £203.39 to 15/7/96 OWNER Mrs Nerys Dutfield (SEATON) BRED Mrs Nerys Dutfield
LONG HANDICAP Lady Poly 8-8
WEIGHT FOR AGE 3yo-13lb

**Artic Bay**, third in a thirteen furlong bumper at Market Rasen before starting his career on the Flat, settled better than last time in a race run at a furious pace. (14/1: op 7/1)
**2401 General Mouktar**, up 2lb, was another in no hurry to take on the tearaway leaders. (4/1)
**Evidence In Chief**, down 6lb this season, showed improved form over this longer trip and would have finished closer had his rider not lost a pedal. (16/1)
**1803 Cheveley Dancer (USA)**, despite the breakneck pace, was still pulling at halfway, and would have been entitled to have capitulated completely in the final quarter-mile. (16/1)
**2394 Nosey Native**, dropped 12lb since last seen in a handicap, quickly got the better of his experienced rider, and went off at a suicidal pace. (7/2)
**1063 Courbaril** (10/1: op 6/1)

## 2712 MYROBELLA MAIDEN AUCTION STKS (2-Y.O) (Class F)
4-30 (4-31) **6f** £2,910.00 (£810.00: £390.00) Stalls: High GOING minus 0.46 sec per fur (F)

SP RR SF
552[3] **Salty Behaviour (IRE)** (RHannon) **2-8-6**(3) DaneO'Neill(6) (hld up: hdwy over 2f out: led ins fnl f: edgd lft nr fin: r.o) ....— **1** 11/8[1] 76 20
1871[4] **What Happened Was** (MartynMeade) **2-7-9**(3) MHenry(1) (w ldrs: led wl over 1f out tl ins fnl f) ....1¼ **2** 4/1[2] 62 6
2398[3] **Salty Jack (IRE)** (SDow) **2-8-6** SWhitworth(5) (hld up & bhd: hdwy over 2f out: rdn over 1f out: one pce) ....3 **3** 7/1 62 6
2252[5] **Noble Hero** (JJSheehan) **2-8-9** NAdams(7) (a.p: rdn over 2f out: one pce) ....3 **4** 14/1 57 1
2309[7] **Shall We Go (IRE)** (RHannon) **2-8-1** AMcGlone(2) (led over 4f: sn wknd) ....1¼ **5** 16/1 45 —
2531[5] **Eponine** (MRChannon) **2-8-4** AClark(3) (nvr nr to chal) ....nk **6** 6/1[3] 48 —
**Keen Waters** (JRArnold) **2-8-1** TSprake(9) (lengthy: w ldrs over 3f) ....2 **7** 14/1 39 —
**Wee Dram** (RHannon) **2-8-5**ow1 WJO'Connor(4) (w'like: s.i.s: t.o fnl 3f) ....12 **8** 12/1 11 —
**Ela Patricia (IRE)** (DJGMurraySmith) **2-8-1**(3) SDrowne(8) (spd 3f) ....¾ **9** 16/1 8 —
(SP 121.7%) **9 Rn**

**1m 15.69** (2.69) CSF £7.72 TOTE £2.00: £1.30 £1.70 £2.00 (£3.90) Trio £6.60 OWNER Mr J. R. Shannon (MARLBOROUGH) BRED Airlie Stud

**552 Salty Behaviour (IRE)** apparently suffers from an attitude problem which is the reason why he has not been out since his debut three months ago. Showing just what his trainer means after striking the front, perhaps some headgear or a trip to the Vet might help. (11/8)
**1871 What Happened Was** could not hold the winner in the last 150 yards. (4/1)
**2398 Salty Jack (IRE)** is out of a mare who won over seven furlongs in Ireland as a three-year-old. (7/1)
**Noble Hero** is a half-sister to numerous winners in North America, including a Grade Two scorer. (14/1)
**Shall We Go (IRE)** is a half-sister to the sprinter Gorinsky. (16/1)
**2531 Eponine** may do better over seven. (6/1: op 3/1)
**Wee Dram** (12/1: op 7/1)

## 2713 OWEN TUDOR H'CAP (0-70) (3-Y.O+) (Class E)
5-00 (5-01) **6f** £3,392.00 (£1,016.00: £488.00: £224.00) Stalls: High GOING: minus 0.43 sec per fur (F)

SP RR SF
2193* **Pointer (51)** (MrsPNDutfield) **4-8-2**(7) AimeeCook(9) (hld up: swtchd rt & hdwy over 2f out: led over 1f out: rdn & edgd lft ins fnl f: r.o) ....— **1** 4/1[1] 60 24
2283[7] **Robellion (60)** (DWPArbuthnot) **5-9-4v** SWhitworth(4) (lw: hld up & bhd: hdwy 2f out: ev ch whn carried lft & bmpd ins fnl f: r.o) ....½ **2** 14/1 68 32
2285[4] **Scissor Ridge (51)** (JJBridger) **4-8-2**(7) RBrisland(5) (a.p: led wl over 2f out: hrd rdn & hdd over 1f out: ev ch whn carried lft ins fnl f: r.o) ....hd **3** 7/1 58 22
2129[5] **Sizzling (60)** (RHannon) **4-9-1**(3) DaneO'Neill(1) (hld up: hdwy over 1f out: sltly hmpd ins fnl f: r.o wl) ....nk **4** 9/2[2] 67 31
2129[6] **Random (49)** (CJames) **5-8-7** WJO'Connor(3) (hld up & bhd: hdwy over 1f out: one pce ins fnl f) ....¾ **5** 11/1 54 18
2411[D] **Corniche Quest (IRE) (55)** (MRChannon) **3-8-0**(7) AEddery(6) (hdwy over 1f out: one pce fnl f) ....nk **6** 5/1[3] 59 17
2561[3] **Astral Invader (IRE) (51)** (MSSaunders) **4-8-6**(3) SDrowne(7) (no hdwy fnl 2f) ....3½ **7** 7/1 46 10
2340[11] **Martinosky (51)** (GCBravery) **10-8-9b** AMcGlone(2) (lw: a bhd) ....6 **8** 16/1 30 —
**Norling (IRE) (50)** (KOCunningham-Brown) **6-8-1**(7) CMunday(10) (led over 3f: sn hrd rdn & wknd) ....s.h **9** 20/1 28 —
2347* **Denbrae (IRE) (70)** (DJGMurraySmith) **4-9-9**(5) RPainter(8) (swtg: prom: hrd rdn over 2f out: wknd wl over 1f out) ....nk **10** 6/1 48 12
1902[6] **Wilfull Lad (IRE) (60)** (MartynMeade) **3-8-12** VSlattery(11) (lw: w ldr tl wknd over 2f out) ....s.h **11** 14/1 37 —
(SP 126.4%) **11 Rn**

**1m 15.35** (2.35) CSF £56.09 CT £368.39 TOTE £5.20: £1.50 £6.00 £2.40 (£75.40) Trio £224.50; £253.02 to Windsor 15/7/96. OWNER In For The Crack (SEATON) BRED Darley Stud Management Co Ltd
WEIGHT FOR AGE 3yo-6lb
STEWARDS' ENQUIRY Cook susp. 22-23/7/96 (careless riding)

**2193* Pointer**, raised 7lb, edged left on two separate occasions in the final 200 yards, with his rider having her whip in the wrong hand. Miss Cook was suspended for two days for careless riding and it was obviously touch and go as to whether the gelding kept the race. (4/1)
**553 Robellion**, off a mark 8lb lower than when he last scored on turf a year ago, was dropping back to sprinting and very nearly got the race in the Stewards' Room. (14/1)
**2285 Scissor Ridge**, 8lb higher than when winning at Goodwood, probably found seven beyond his best on the same course next time. (7/1)
**2129 Sizzling** found top gear a little too late. (9/2)
**2129 Random**, dropped 2lb, could not sustain a dangerous-looking run in the last half-furlong. (11/1: 8/1-12/1)
**2411 Corniche Quest (IRE)**, up 3lb, was disqualified over seven last time and still looks better suited to that trip. (5/1)
**2347* Denbrae (IRE)** (6/1: op 4/1)
**1119 Wilfull Lad (IRE)** (14/1: 10/1-16/1)

T/Plpt: £13.90 (921.63 Tckts). T/Qdpt: £13.30 (42.7 Tckts). KH

## 2506-WARWICK (L-H) (Good to firm)
## Saturday July 13th
WEATHER: fine & sunny WIND: mod bhd

### 2714 SCANIA 4-SERIES MAIDEN AUCTION STKS (2-Y.O F) (Class F)
6-25 (6-26) **7f** £2,738.00 (£758.00: £362.00) Stalls: Low GOING minus 0.58 sec per fur (F)

| | Horse | Details | Dist | Pos | SP | RR | SF |
|---|---|---|---|---|---|---|---|
| 2147[3] | **Kalinka (IRE)** | (PFICole) **2-8-4** TQuinn(3) (trckd ldrs: led 1f out: comf) | — | **1** | 2/9[1] | 68+ | 26 |
| 1851[11] | **Double Gold** | (BJMeehan) **2-8-7** MTebbutt(4) (led 6f: no ex & eased nr fin) | 3½ | **2** | 33/1 | 63 | 21 |
| | **Blue Hopper** | (MRChannon) **2-8-1** CRutter(6) (w'like: unf: swvd rt s: hdwy 3f out: no imp appr fnl f) | 3 | **3** | 8/1[2] | 50 | 8 |
| 729[7] | **Zanabay** | (MartynMeade) **2-8-2**(5) RHavlin(5) (w ldr tl wknd wl over 1f out) | 4 | **4** | 40/1 | 47 | 5 |
| | **Troia (IRE)** | (BSmart) **2-8-4** JStack(2) (leggy: in tch tl lost pl 3f out: n.d after) | ¾ | **5** | 9/1[3] | 42 | — |
| 2132[9] | **Gibb's Beach (IRE)** | (CADwyer) **2-8-7** MWigham(1) (sn pushed along & bhd) | 4 | **6** | 33/1 | 36 | — |
| | | | | | (SP 111.3%) | | **6 Rn** |

**1m 25.9** (1.30) CSF £8.37 TOTE £1.30: £1.10 £4.10 (£6.50) OWNER Elite Racing Club (WHATCOMBE) BRED John I. O'Byrne
**2147 Kalinka (IRE)** looked a class apart and, despite looking to be feeling the ground when let down, won with plenty in hand. (2/9)
**Double Gold** put up a much-improved display and was not knocked about once her measure was taken. (33/1)
**Blue Hopper**, taken down steadily, lost ground as the stalls opened. She was a cheap purchase, but looks to have a little ability. (8/1: 6/1-9/1)
**Zanabay** went down keenly and raced freely, but she had shot her bolt before the furlong pole. (40/1)
**Troia (IRE)**, a half-sister to Ela Aristokrati, did not show much, but should do better in time. (9/1: 6/1-10/1)
**Gibb's Beach (IRE)** showed little inclination to make a race of it. (33/1)

### 2715 KELTRUCK FOR SCANIA H'CAP (0-80) (3-Y.O F) (Class D)
6-55 (6-56) **7f** £4,092.75 (£1,224.00: £586.50: £267.75) Stalls: Low GOING minus 0.58 sec per fur (F)

| | Horse | Details | Dist | Pos | SP | RR | SF |
|---|---|---|---|---|---|---|---|
| 1662* | **El Opera (IRE) (80)** | (PFICole) **3-9-7** TQuinn(4) (lw: hdwy 3f out: reminder 2f out: led ins fnl f: comf) | — | **1** | 4/5[1] | 90+ | 58 |
| 2255[5] | **Windswept (IRE) (56)** | (DJSffrenchDavis) **3-7-11b[1]** NCarlisle(5) (lw: dwlt: led over 5f out: clr 3f out: hdd & no ex ins fnl f) | 2½ | **2** | 7/1 | 60 | 28 |
| 2222[4] | **Polly Golightly (70)** | (MBlanshard) **3-8-11** JQuinn(1) (hdwy 3f out: rdn 1f out: kpt on) | 1¾ | **3** | 13/2[3] | 70 | 38 |
| 1986[7] | **Maristax (75)** | (PJMakin) **3-9-2** MRoberts(6) (led over 1f: rdn & btn over 1f out) | 1 | **4** | 6/1[2] | 73 | 41 |
| 2320[8] | **Butterwick Belle (IRE) (65)** | (RAFahey) **3-8-6** ACulhane(2) (lw: in tch: effrt 2f out: no imp) | 4 | **5** | 20/1 | 54 | 22 |
| 707[8] | **Age of Reality (USA) (64)** | (HCandy) **3-8-5** CRutter(3) (lost pl after 1f: n.d after) | 1¾ | **6** | 10/1 | 49 | 17 |
| | | | | | (SP 109.5%) | | **6 Rn** |

**1m 24.5** (-0.10) CSF £6.36 TOTE £1.90: £1.40 £1.80 (£3.60) OWNER Mr Faisal Salman (WHATCOMBE) BRED Islanmore Stud
**1662* El Opera (IRE)**, the winner of a poor race last time, looks to be improving fast and put up a good performance. Feeling the ground when hanging in behind the leader momentarily, she quickened nicely to win with something to spare. She can win again. (4/5)
**2255 Windswept (IRE)** strode down well in first-time blinkers, but half-reared and lost a couple of lengths as the stalls opened. Soon pulling her way to the front, she had no more to give once headed. (7/1)
**2222 Polly Golightly**, trying this trip for a second time, looked likely to find more than she did when ridden along in the final furlong. She has yet to prove that she gets this trip. (13/2)
**Maristax** broke well and led early on, but was chasing hard by the home turn. Quite a keen sort, she may be better with different tactics. (6/1: op 4/1)
**Butterwick Belle (IRE)** raced with her head rather high once let down, and has yet to run anywhere near her two-year-old form. (20/1)
**Age of Reality (USA)**, dropping half a mile in trip, was comprehensively outpaced after breaking well. (10/1: op 6/1)

### 2716 KELTRUCK SCANIA 'HORSEPOWER' (S) H'CAP (0-60) (3-Y.O+) (Class G)
7-25 (7-25) **1m 2f 169y** £2,616.00 (£726.00: £348.00) Stalls: Low GOING minus 0.58 sec per fur (F)

| | Horse | Details | Dist | Pos | SP | RR | SF |
|---|---|---|---|---|---|---|---|
| 2366[4] | **Mazilla (40)** | (AStreeter) **4-8-12**(5) RHavlin(14) (hdwy 4f out: led 2f out: sn clr: pushed out) | — | **1** | 13/2[3] | 58 | 39 |
| *2168*[5] | **He's Got Wings (IRE) (48)** | (MBell) **3-8-13v** MFenton(15) (b.hind: chsd ldrs: led 3f out to 2f out: one pce) | 5 | **2** | 14/1 | 59 | 28 |
| 2592[11] | **Hunza Story (30)** | (NPLittmoden) **4-8-0**(7) JoHunnam(10) (trckd ldrs: outpcd 4f out: r.o wl fnl f) | 7 | **3** | 25/1 | 30 | 11 |
| 2379[3] | **Scottish Park (46)** | (MCPipe) **7-9-9b** MRoberts(11) (chsd ldrs: lost pl over 4f out: r.o again fnl 2f) | 1¼ | **4** | 5/1[2] | 44 | 25 |
| 2313[7] | **Clytha Hill Lad (30)** | (JMBradley) **5-8-7** TQuinn(9) (b: prom: no imp fnl 3f) | ¾ | **5** | 10/1 | 27 | 8 |
| 2192[4] | **Eskimo Kiss (IRE) (40)** | (MJFetherston-Godley) **3-8-5b** FNorton(1) (lw: hmpd sn after s: effrt 3f out: styng on whn n.m.r over 2f out) | ½ | **6** | 7/2[1] | 37 | 6 |
| 2594[2] | **Tocco Jewel (19)** | (MJRyan) **6-7-10** GBardwell(8) (sn pushed along & bhd: r.o fnl 3f: nvr rchd ldrs) | ¾ | **7** | 9/1 | 14 | — |
| 2556[7] | **Bronze Runner (34)** | (EAWheeler) **12-8-11b** TSprake(2) (nvr nrr) | 1¼ | **8** | 8/1 | 28 | 9 |
| 1655[11] | **Little Luke (IRE) (35)** | (PButler) **5-8-7**(5) MBaird(5) (lw: prom: led over 4f out to 3f out: sn wknd) | nk | **9** | 20/1 | 28 | 9 |
| 2313[12] | **Bad News (44)** | (JMBradley) **4-9-0**(7) CLowther(13) (plld hrd: chsd ldrs 6f) | 1½ | **10** | 25/1 | 35 | 16 |
| 2192[13] | **Pink Petal (27)** | (RJBaker) **4-8-4** JQuinn(6) (stdd s: sn prom: wknd 4f out) | 1¾ | **11** | 12/1 | 15 | — |
| 2556[13] | **Woodlands Energy (37)** | (PAPritchard) **5-9-0** NAdams(12) (lw: s.i.s: a bhd) | 2½ | **12** | 50/1 | 22 | 3 |
| 2373[10] | **Northern Saga (IRE) (46)** | (CJDrewe) **3-8-11** JStack(7) (chsd ldrs 6f) | 1 | **13** | 33/1 | 29 | — |
| 2507[4] | **Elite Racing (38)** | (NTinkler) **4-9-1** CRutter(17) (swvd rt s: rdn 5f out: a bhd) | 1¾ | **14** | 12/1 | 18 | — |
| 2344[8] | **Queen of Shannon (IRE) (47)** | (AWCarroll) **8-9-10** MTebbutt(16) (b.nr hind: trckd ldrs tl rdn & wknd 3f out) | 3½ | **15** | 16/1 | 22 | 3 |
| | **Soviet Sakti (IRE) (45)** | (PhilipMitchell) **3-8-10** RPerham(4) (led 6f) | 13 | **16** | 16/1 | 1 | — |

*1970*[4] **Gee Gee Tee (46)** (JAkehurst) **3-8-11b**[1] AClark(3) (b: w ldr 4f: t.o fnl 3f)....................18 **17** 16/1 — —
(SP 139.5%) **17 Rn**

**2m 15.6** (2.10) CSF £96.86 CT £2,035.45 TOTE £7.40: £2.10 £4.70 £6.80 £1.70 (£189.70) Trio £373.90; £368.71 to Windsor 15/7/96. OWNER Mr M. Rhodes (UTTOXETER) BRED Mrs H. MacFarlane
LONG HANDICAP Tocco Jewel 7-6
WEIGHT FOR AGE 3yo-12lb
Bt in 3,600gns
**2366 Mazilla**, with her winning pilot of two outings ago back in the plate, was the winner from the moment she began her move, and is in great heart at present. (13/2)
**2168 He's Got Wings (IRE)** has probably now found his trip, but could not match the winner for foot, despite sticking on to the line. (14/1)
**2366 Hunza Story**, soon tracking the leaders towards the inside, was left behind on the home turn but stayed on well enough to secure a distant third place in the last furlong. (25/1)
**2379 Scottish Park**, up with the pace, looked sure to finish nearer last than first when coming under pressure at halfway, but stayed on again in the straight. She needs a more patient ride. (5/1)
**Clytha Hill Lad**, weighted to reverse Nottingham form with the winner, simply got beaten more easily. (10/1)
**2192 Eskimo Kiss (IRE)**, gambled on, was the unlucky horse of the race and seemed to find all the trouble that was going, both at the start, courtesy of her inside draw, and in the home straight. With a clear run, she would probably have made the frame. (7/2: op 10/1)
**2594 Tocco Jewel** (9/1: op 6/1)
**Pink Petal** (12/1: op 20/1)

## 2717 SCANIA 1996 TRUCK OF THE YEAR H'CAP (0-70) (3-Y.O+) (Class E)
7-55 (7-55) **1m 6f 194y** £3,370.50 (£1,008.00: £483.00: £220.50) Stalls: Low GOING minus 0.58 sec per fur (F)

| | Horse / details | Dist | Pos | SP | RR | SF |
|---|---|---|---|---|---|---|
| 2319[3] | **Salska (46)** (AStreeter) **5-8-4** TSprake(6) (trckd ldrs gng wl: led over 1f out: sn clr: comf) | — | **1** | 9/2[1] | 60+ | 44 |
| 2190[5] | **Mizyan (IRE) (58)** (JEBanks) **8-8-9**(7) GFaulkner(1) (hdwy 8f out: led over 5f out tl over 1f out: one pce) | 5 | **2** | 16/1 | 67 | 51 |
| 2190* | **Tonys Gift (72)** (MCPipe) **4-10-2** MRoberts(12) (plld hrd: trckd ldrs: rdn 1f out: kpt on) | 7 | **3** | 11/2[2] | 73 | 57 |
| 2042[21] | **Our Kris (66)** (NJHenderson) **4-9-10** TQuinn(4) (w ldrs: ev ch 2f out: one pce) | 1½ | **4** | 11/2[2] | 66 | 50 |
| *2322** | **Chakalak (48)** (SDow) **8-8-1**(5) ADaly(3) (lw: bhd: rdn 9f out: hdwy 4f out: nrst fin) | 1¾ | **5** | 14/1 | 46 | 30 |
| 1070[12] | **Victoria Day (38)** (BAMcMahon) **4-7-7**(3) NVarley(2) (lw: chsd ldrs: no hdwy fnl 4f) | 6 | **6** | 50/1 | 29 | 13 |
| 2423* | **Iota (55)** (JLHarris) **7-8-13** PRobinson(9) (dwlt: r.o fnl 2f: fin wl) | 2½ | **7** | 8/1 | 44 | 28 |
| 2511* | **Mr Speculator (62)** (PAKelleway) **3-8-3v** GBardwell(10) (lw: prom 12f) | hd | **8** | 6/1[3] | 50 | 17 |
| 2221[4] | **Backview (55)** (BJLlewellyn) **4-8-13** AClark(5) (led over 10f: sn rdn & wknd) | s.h | **9** | 20/1 | 43 | 27 |
| *169*[7] | **La Menorquina (USA) (38)** (DMarks) **6-7-5**(5) CAdamson(8) (a bhd) | ½ | **10** | 20/1 | 26 | 10 |
| 1826[4] | **Mim-Lou-and (45)** (MissHCKnight) **4-8-0**(3) FLynch(11) (lw: chsd ldrs: rdn & btn 3f out) | s.h | **11** | 15/2 | 33 | 17 |
| 2511[4] | **Blanchland (40)** (PCRitchens) **7-7-12** NAdams(7) (hld up: hdwy & rn wd 8f out: wknd over 4f out) | 2½ | **12** | 14/1 | 25 | 9 |
| 2066[3] | **Outstayed Welcome (59)** (MJHaynes) **4-8-12**(5) MBaird(13) (plld hrd: racd wd after 2f: prom tl wknd 6f out) | 8 | **13** | 9/1 | 35 | 19 |

(SP 126.8%) **13 Rn**

**3m 9.9** (-0.10) CSF £70.43 CT £383.15 TOTE £4.60: £2.20 £6.10 £2.20 (£54.80) Trio £65.20 OWNER Mr P. L. Clinton (HEDNESFORD) BRED J. A. Haverhals
LONG HANDICAP La Menorquina (USA) 7-1
WEIGHT FOR AGE 3yo-17lb
**2319 Salska**, winning for only the second time in thirty starts, was always travelling best and showed the merit of her Doncaster third where she finished twelve lengths in front of the rest. (9/2: op 8/1)
**2190 Mizyan (IRE)** ran a fine race and must be close to finding an opening. He may not be quite the force he was and has lost twelve times since his most recent win in May last year. (16/1)
**2190* Tonys Gift**, with a welter-burden, is used to such weights over hurdles and carries them well for quite a small horse. She let the leaders go on the home turn and could never peg them back once the pressure was applied. (11/2)
**Our Kris** looked very one-paced, but will surely stay more than the minimum two miles once put back over hurdles. (11/2)
**2322* Chakalak**, all but tailed off for the first mile, could never get into the race on this easy track. (14/1)
**Victoria Day** is lightly-raced and her future probably lies over hurdles. (50/1)
**2511* Mr Speculator** (6/1: op 4/1)
**1826 Mim-Lou-and** (15/2: 5/1-8/1)

## 2718 KELTRUCK 1996 DEALER OF THE YEAR MAIDEN STKS (3-Y.O+) (Class D)
8-25 (8-30) **7f** £4,225.35 (£1,264.80: £606.90: £277.95) Stalls: Low GOING minus 0.58 sec per fur (F)

| | Horse / details | Dist | Pos | SP | RR | SF |
|---|---|---|---|---|---|---|
| 1901[3] | **High Summer (USA)** (RCharlton) **3-8-8** PatEddery(1) (mde all: clr over 1f out: easily) | — | **1** | 8/13[1] | 73 | 47 |
| 1195[5] | **Cerdan (USA)** (MRStoute) **3-8-13** KFallon(12) (plld hrd: prom: chsd wnr fnl 2f: no imp) | 3½ | **2** | 7/2[2] | 70 | 44 |
| | **Midday Cowboy (USA)** (GHarwood) **3-8-13** AClark(8) (lengthy: unf: bit bkwd: chsd ldrs: rdn 2f out: one pce) | 3 | **3** | 33/1 | 63 | 37 |
| | **Sweet Times** (PFICole) **3-8-8** TQuinn(7) (bit bkwd: chsd wnr 5f: sn btn) | 3 | **4** | 16/1 | 51 | 25 |
| 2281[4] | **Tonic Chord** (JRFanshawe) **3-8-5**(3) NVarley(13) (chsd ldrs: no hdwy fnl 3f) | ½ | **5** | 33/1 | 50 | 24 |
| 2510[4] | **Alfredo Alfredo (USA)** (JLDunlop) **4-9-7** TSprake(14) (b: bit bkwd: s.s: hld up: hdwy fnl 2f: nvr plcd to chal) | 5 | **6** | 6/1[3] | 44+ | 26 |
| 2529[8] | **Early Warning** (CREgerton) **3-8-1**(7) AimeeCook(2) (in tch: eased whn btn appr fnl f) | 1¾ | **7** | 66/1 | 35 | 9 |
| | **Indian Sunset** (CREgerton) **3-8-13** JQuinn(11) (chsd ldrs 4f) | ½ | **8** | 100/1 | 39 | 13 |
| 1452[7] | **Serape** (HCandy) **3-8-8** CRutter(6) (lw: in tch 4f) | hd | **9** | 33/1 | 33 | 7 |
| | **Saving Power** (PWHarris) **3-8-13** BDoyle(15) (unf: scope: bit bkwd: bhd: effrt over 3f out: no imp) | nk | **10** | 33/1 | 38 | 12 |
| | **Enamel Tiger** (KMcAuliffe) **3-8-13** JTate(4) (s.s: bhd: effrt whn rn wd over 2f out: nt rcvr) | ¾ | **11** | 100/1 | 36 | 10 |
| | **Mashmoum** (JHMGosden) **3-8-8** JCarroll(10) (leggy: bit bkwd: s.i.s: nvr plcd to chal) | ½ | **12** | 14/1 | 30+ | 4 |
| | **Passing Strangers (USA)** (PWHarris) **3-8-13** FNorton(3) (lw: hld up: nvr plcd to chal) | ½ | **13** | 50/1 | 34+ | 8 |
| | **Twice Removed** (SDow) **3-8-3**(5) ADaly(9) (s.s: a bhd) | 10 | **14** | 100/1 | 6 | — |
| | **Mr Blue** (GPKelly) **4-9-7** SDWilliams(5) (w'like: swtg: chsd ldrs over 3f) | 11 | **15** | 100/1 | — | — |

(SP 130.1%) **15 Rn**

**1m 24.4** (-0.20) CSF £3.79 TOTE £1.60: £1.10 £1.70 £5.50 (£2.50) Trio £40.30 OWNER Mr K. Abdulla (BECKHAMPTON) BRED Juddmonte Farms
WEIGHT FOR AGE 3yo-8lb
**OFFICIAL EXPLANATION Alfredo Alfredo (USA): was slowly away and outpaced over the insufficient trip, and has had leg trouble in the past and is not probably suited by fast ground.**
**1901 High Summer (USA)** found a moderate race and won with plenty in hand. This will have done her nothing but good. (8/13)
**1195 Cerdan (USA)**, led some of the way to post, pulled hard and tried to give the favourite a race in the straight without success. (7/2)

**Midday Cowboy (USA)**, looking to need the race and sporting a boot on his near-fore, tried his best but could do no more than plug on. He can be made fitter and will no doubt be wiser next time. (33/1)
**Sweet Times** took a good hold and chased the winner until lack of fitness told. A sister to River Deep, she might do better once she settles. (16/1)
**2281 Tonic Chord** is learning, but was easily left behind once in line for home. (33/1)
**2510 Alfredo Alfredo (USA)**, surprisingly dropped in trip, missed the break and only began to stay on when the race was over. He has clearly had his problems, but will set the Handicapper a problem if competing a third time at such an inadequate trip. (6/1: 4/1-7/1)
**Mashmoum** looked highly strung and in need of the experience in the preliminaries. Out the back throughout after missing the break, she looks as if she ought to be capable of better if going the right way. (14/1: op 8/1)
**Passing Strangers (USA)** had two handlers in the paddock and took a good hold going to post, but the emphasis in the race seemed to be on getting him to settle and, possibly as a result, he never took a hand. Now eligible for handicaps, he looks a fair sort who ought to stay middle distances. (50/1)

## 2719 SCANIA 4-SERIES 'KING OF THE ROAD' H'CAP (0-70) (3-Y.O+) (Class E)

8-55 (8-57) **6f** £3,179.40 (£949.20: £453.60: £205.80) Stalls: Low GOING minus 0.58 sec per fur (F)

| | | | | SP | RR | SF |
|---|---|---|---|---|---|---|
| 2209$^{5}$ | **Rockcracker (IRE) (60)** (GGMargarson) **4-9-10b** PRobinson(1) (lw: sn chsng ldrs: qcknd to ld 1f out: rdn out) | — | **1** | 14/1 | 68 | 47 |
| 2500$^{8}$ | **Ciserano (IRE) (60)** (MRChannon) **3-9-4** TQuinn(7) (in tch: hdwy over 1f out: nt trble wnr) | 1½ | **2** | 7/1 | 64 | 37 |
| 2185$^{6}$ | **Sonderise (55)** (NTinkler) **7-9-5** CRutter(3) (lw: dwlt: hdwy 3f out: kpt on fnl f) | 1¼ | **3** | 6/1$^{3}$ | 56 | 35 |
| 2500$^{2}$ | **Fairy Prince (IRE) (61)** (MrsALMKing) **3-9-2**$^{(3)}$ FLynch(6) (lw: chsd ldrs: n.m.r over 1f out: no ex ins fnl f) | ¾ | **4** | 9/4$^{1}$ | 60 | 33 |
| 2376$^{10}$ | **Speedy Classic (USA) (55)** (MJHeaton-Ellis) **7-9-5** MRoberts(4) (dwlt: rdn over 2f out: nvr trbld ldrs) | nk | **5** | 7/1 | 53 | 32 |
| *2171*$^{7}$ | **Little Ibnr (60)** (PDEvans) **5-9-10** KFallon(2) (led 5f: sn btn) | 1½ | **6** | 8/1 | 54 | 33 |
| 2185$^{2}$ | **Rambold (60)** (NEBerry) **5-9-5**$^{(5)}$ CAdamson(5) (lw: w ldr: rdn over 2f out: wknd fnl f) | s.h | **7** | 11/4$^{2}$ | 54 | 33 |
| | | | | (SP 114.5%) | **7 Rn** | |

**1m 12.9** (0.90) CSF £93.72 TOTE £14.20: £5.70 £2.30 (£43.80) OWNER Mr P. E. Axon (NEWMARKET) BRED Mrs Amanda Skiffington
WEIGHT FOR AGE 3yo-6lb
**1039 Rockcracker (IRE)**, scoring his second success over course and distance, found a fine turn of foot when an opening on the rail appeared. (14/1)
**2215 Ciserano (IRE)** had finished behind Fairy Prince on her last two starts, but got a trouble-free run on the outside of the pack to finish best of all. (7/1)
**2030 Sonderise** stayed on in the straight to snatch third place, but did not do Fairy Prince any favours when coming through. This was his third consecutive defeat off this mark. (6/1: op 4/1)
**2500 Fairy Prince (IRE)** could not live with the early pace, but still had hopes at the distance when he found his ground taken and with it his chance. (9/4)
**981 Speedy Classic (USA)** is proving hard to place these days and, surprisingly for a Lingfield All-Weather winner, did not appear to handle the home turn well. (7/1)
**896 Little Ibnr** finally burnt off Rambold early in the straight, but they had cut each other's throats. (8/1)
**2185 Rambold** went into a lot of notebooks when winning on the 'wrong side' at Nottingham last time, but looked to resent being taken on by Little Ibnr and failed to sparkle. She is worth another chance. (11/4)

T/Plpt: £95.00 (122.37 Tckts). T/Qdpt: £88.70 (8.61 Tckts). Dk

# 2690-YORK (L-H) (Good)
## Saturday July 13th
WEATHER: sunny & warm WIND: fresh across

## 2720 JERVAULX MEDIAN AUCTION MAIDEN STKS (2-Y.O) (Class E)

2-00 (2-00) **6f** £3,947.50 (£1,180.00: £565.00: £257.50) Stalls: Low GOING minus 0.36 sec per fur (F)

| | | | | SP | RR | SF |
|---|---|---|---|---|---|---|
| 2132$^{2}$ | **Pun** (DMorley) **2-8-9** WCarson(8) (lw: led after 2f: hld on wl fnl f) | — | **1** | 15/8$^{1}$ | 61 | 19 |
| | **Jackson Falls** (TDEasterby) **2-9-0** MBirch(4) (rangy: bit bkwd: a.p: effrt over 2f out: chal 1f out: kpt on) | hd | **2** | 11/1 | 66 | 24 |
| | **Eurolink Spartacus** (JLDunlop) **2-9-0** PatEddery(1) (w'like: lw: s.i.s: swtchd rt after s: smooth hdwy ½-wy: chal over 1f out: nt qckn towards fin) | hd | **3** | 2/1$^{2}$ | 66 | 24 |
| | **Rock The Casbah** (JHetherton) **2-9-0** TQuinn(2) (w'like: unf: bit bkwd: in tch: effrt ½-wy: kpt on: no imp) | 1½ | **4** | 12/1 | 62 | 20 |
| 1632$^{4}$ | **Wagga Moon (IRE)** (JJO'Neill) **2-9-0** JFortune(3) (hmpd after s: bhd tl hdwy over 2f out: nt qckn fnl f) | 1½ | **5** | 12/1 | 58 | 16 |
| 2211$^{7}$ | **Barresbo** (CWFairhurst) **2-9-0** DeanMcKeown(5) (w ldrs tl rdn & btn appr fnl f) | hd | **6** | 9/1$^{3}$ | 57 | 15 |
| 2224$^{10}$ | **Tirage** (CEBrittain) **2-9-0** BDoyle(6) (led 2f: wknd fnl 2f) | 8 | **7** | 9/1$^{3}$ | 36 | — |
| 2485$^{5}$ | **Mazil** (TDEasterby) **2-9-0** JLowe(7) (bit bkwd: spd to ½-wy: sn outpcd) | 4 | **8** | 20/1 | 25 | — |
| | | | | (SP 116.6%) | **8 Rn** | |

**1m 14.18** (3.18) CSF £20.85 TOTE £2.60: £1.30 £2.40 £1.20 (£14.20) OWNER Lord Hartington (NEWMARKET) BRED Side Hill Stud
**2132 Pun**, who ran in a moderate-looking race at Newmarket last time, likes to be up with the pace and she was always just doing enough when the pressure was on here. (15/8)
**Jackson Falls** put in a useful first effort and, judging by the way he was keeping on, should appreciate further. (11/1)
**Eurolink Spartacus**, after a moderate start, met with trouble and, had he had any experience previously, would probably have won this. (2/1)
**Rock The Casbah** showed a poor action, but ran pretty well and looked likely to benefit from the outing. (12/1)
**1632 Wagga Moon (IRE)**, after almost six weeks off, had a tardy start and was then hampered, but still almost got in a blow. He looks a real nursery type. (12/1)
**2211 Barresbo** ran better this time and is obviously improving with experience. (9/1)

## 2721 ELEPHANT & CASTLE AT WAKEFIELD CONDITIONS STKS (2-Y.O) (Class C)

2-35 (2-35) **6f 214y** £6,360.00 (£1,740.00) Stalls: High GOING minus 0.36 sec per fur (F)

| | | | | SP | RR | SF |
|---|---|---|---|---|---|---|
| 2009* | **Sahm (USA)** (JLDunlop) **2-9-1** WCarson(3) (lw: set slow pce tl qcknd ½-wy: sn clr: eased towards fin) | — | **1** | 1/6$^{1}$ | 98+ | — |
| 2040$^{9}$ | **Tuscany** (PFICole) **2-9-1** TQuinn(1) (lw: trckd wnr: outpcd 3f out: no imp after) | 5 | **2** | 4/1$^{2}$ | 87 | — |
| | | | | (SP 105.7%) | **2 Rn** | |

**1m 30.56** (7.56) TOTE £1.20 OWNER Mr Hamdan Al Maktoum (ARUNDEL) BRED Shadwell Farm Inc
**2009* Sahm (USA)** seems to be going the right way and beat his only rival most convincingly. (1/6: op 2/7)
**1774* Tuscany** tried playing cat and mouse with the winner, but was firmly put in his place from halfway. (4/1: op 2/1)

## 2722 JOHN SMITH'S BITTER H'CAP (0-90) (3-Y.O+) (Class C)

3-05 (3-06) **6f 214y** £6,576.00 (£1,968.00: £944.00: £432.00) Stalls: High GOING: minus 0.36 sec per fur (F)

| | | | | SP | RR | SF |
|---|---|---|---|---|---|---|
| 2351[8] | **Keston Pond (IRE) (70)** (MrsVAAconley) **6-8-10** MDeering(7) (bhd: swtchd 3f out: hdwy u.p 2f out: hung lft: r.o to ld cl home) | — | **1** | 12/1 | 80 | 57 |
| 2220[4] | **Highborn (IRE) (88)** (PSFelgate) **7-10-0** KDarley(6) (lw: chsd ldrs: slt ld 1f out: hdd & nt qckn towards fin) | nk | **2** | 9/1 | 97 | 74 |
| 2293[3] | **Ochos Rios (IRE) (59)** (BSRothwell) **5-7-13**[ow1] JFanning(13) (chsd ldrs: ev ch 2f out: n.m.r & no ex ins fnl f) | 1¾ | **3** | 14/1 | 64 | 40 |
| 2229[3] | **Broughtons Turmoil (63)** (WJMusson) **7-8-3** OUrbina(12) (b: in tch: effrt ½-wy: ch 2f out: btn whn hmpd 1f out) | nk | **4** | 9/2[2] | 68 | 45 |
| 2328[3] | **Jo Mell (82)** (TDEasterby) **3-9-0** MBirch(1) (lw: led tl hdd 1f out: sn btn) | 2 | **5** | 7/2[1] | 82 | 51 |
| 2316* | **Sycamore Lodge (IRE) (70)** (MrsJRRamsden) **5-8-10** KFallon(5) (lw: bhd: hdwy on ins ½-wy: hrd rdn appr fnl f: nvr able to chal) | 3½ | **6** | 7/1 | 62 | 39 |
| | **My Mariam (84)** (CREgerton) **3-9-2** WRyan(8) (bhd & drvn along: n.d) | 3½ | **7** | 25/1 | 68 | 37 |
| | **Dune River (81)** (DRLoder) **7-9-4**(3) PMcCabe(3) (cl up 4f: grad lost pl) | nk | **8** | 6/1[3] | 64 | 41 |
| 1962[6] | **Elite Hope (USA) (75)** (CREgerton) **4-9-1** TQuinn(11) (chsd ldrs: pushed along 3f out: wknd 2f out) | nk | **9** | 9/1 | 58 | 35 |
| | **King Rat (IRE) (82)** (TJEtherington) **5-9-8** GCarter(9) (spd to ½-wy) | 1 | **10** | 16/1 | 62 | 39 |
| 2497[8] | **Champagne Grandy (84)** (MRChannon) **6-9-5**(5) PPMurphy(10) (lw: chsd ldrs 4f: wknd) | 1 | **11** | 14/1 | 62 | 39 |
| 2005[11] | **Grand Chapeau (IRE) (58)** (DNicholls) **4-7-12** DaleGibson(2) (nvr wnt pce) | s.h | **12** | 14/1 | 36 | 13 |

(SP 124.6%) **12 Rn**

**1m 23.56** (0.56) CSF £109.69 CT £1,432.36 TOTE £16.90: £3.70 £2.60 £3.30 (£50.60) Trio £342.20 OWNER Mrs Andrea Mallinson (WEST-OW) BRED John Harrington in Ireland

WEIGHT FOR AGE 3yo-8lb

STEWARDS' ENQUIRY Deering. susp 22-25/7, 26-27/7 & 29/7-3/8/96 (careless riding & excessive use of whip).

**2351 Keston Pond (IRE)** gained his first win of the season here but, in doing so, had a very hard race. (12/1)

**2220 Highborn (IRE)** was always in the right place but, despite a gallant effort under topweight, it just proved beyond him. (9/1)

**2293 Ochos Rios (IRE)** keeps running well, but he looked held when the winner crossed him inside the last furlong. (14/1)

**2229 Broughtons Turmoil** went to post far too fast and, in the circumstances, ran a super race, but he was beaten when being hampered by the winner entering the final furlong. (9/2)

**2328 Jo Mell** raced freely out in front before running out of petrol a furlong from home. (7/2)

**2316* Sycamore Lodge (IRE)** found this more competitive and, despite a determined ride, was never doing enough. (7/1)

**Dune River** looked as though this first run of the season was needed, and blew up in the last two furlongs. (6/1)

## 2723 FOSTER'S SILVER CUP RATED STKS H'CAP (0-105) (Listed) (4-Y.O+) (Class A)

3-40 (3-40) **1m 5f 194y** £11,271.06 (£4,120.56: £1,970.28: £797.40: £308.70) Stalls: Low GOING minus 0.36 sec per fur (F)

| | | | | SP | RR | SF |
|---|---|---|---|---|---|---|
| 2330* | **Celeric (102)** (DMorley) **4-9-7** WCarson(5) (lw: hld up & bhd: hdwy on ins to ld 1f out: qcknd) | — | **1** | Evens[1] | 110 | 71 |
| 1054a[10] | **Kristal's Paradise (IRE) (102)** (JLDunlop) **4-9-7** KDarley(3) (led after 1f tl hdd 1f out: kpt on same pce) | 1½ | **2** | 14/1 | 108 | 69 |
| 2071[5] | **Latahaab (USA) (96)** (RAkehurst) **5-9-1** TQuinn(6) (lw: led 1f: chsd ldr: ev ch & hrd rdn 2f out: nt qckn fnl f) | ¾ | **3** | 3/1[2] | 101 | 62 |
| 2117[4] | **Bahamian Sunshine (USA) (100)** (DRLoder) **5-9-5** DRMcCabe(4) (swtg: chsd ldrs: rdn over 3f out: sn btn) | 8 | **4** | 11/2 | 96 | 57 |
| 1706[4] | **Rainbow Top (96)** (WJHaggas) **4-9-1** KFallon(2) (s.s: sn in tch: rdn 5f out: wknd over 3f out: sn t.o) | dist | **5** | 9/2[3] | — | — |

(SP 115.2%) **5 Rn**

**2m 57.09** (0.89) CSF £12.26 TOTE £1.80: £1.20 £3.90 (£15.10) OWNER Mr Christopher Spence (NEWMARKET) BRED Chieveley Manor Enterprises

**OFFICIAL EXPLANATION Rainbow Top: finished distressed.**

**2330* Celeric** continued his great run with a most emphatic win and was value for a good deal more than the winning margin. (Evens)

**1054a Kristal's Paradise (IRE)**, after over two months off, ran her best race of the season. (14/1: 8/1-16/1)

**2071 Latahaab (USA)** has had some very stiff tasks this season, but keeps running consistently well. (3/1)

**2117 Bahamian Sunshine (USA)** got very warm beforehand and, off the bit early in the straight, was never firing from then on. (11/2)

**1706 Rainbow Top** again gave vital ground away at the start and then ran dismally, stopping in the last half-mile as though something was very wrong. (9/2)

## 2724 JOHN SMITH'S MAGNET CUP H'CAP (0-110) (3-Y.O+) (Class B)

4-15 (4-16) **1m 2f 85y** £58,173.00 (£17,484.00: £8,442.00: £3,921.00) Stalls: Low GOING minus 0.36 sec per fur (F)

| | | | | SP | RR | SF |
|---|---|---|---|---|---|---|
| 2502[5] | **Wilcuma (89)** (PJMakin) **5-9-2** PatEddery(2) (hld up & bhd: hdwy on ins 4f out: rdn to ld 1f out: r.o wl) | — | **1** | 10/1 | 103 | 81 |
| 2502[3] | **Spirito Libro (USA) (80)** (CNAllen) **3-7-5**(5) MartinDwyer(6) (bhd: hdwy on outside 3f out: hrd rdn & hung lft: ev ch ins fnl f: kpt on) | nk | **2** | 11/2[2] | 94 | 61 |
| 2350[2] | **Arctiid (USA) (85)** (JHMGosden) **3-8-1** WRyan(5) (lw: led: hung rt most of wy: hdd 2f out: edgd lft: kpt on wl) | 2½ | **3** | 9/2[1] | 95 | 62 |
| 2350[8] | **Carlito Brigante (79)** (MrsJRRamsden) **4-8-6** KFallon(12) (hld up: effrt 4f out: styd on u.p: nrst fin) | hd | **4** | 16/1 | 89 | 67 |
| 2502[7] | **Hazard a Guess (IRE) (81)** (DNicholls) **6-8-5**(3) PMcCabe(14) (lw: s.i.s: bhd tl gd hdwy over 1f out: fin wl) | ¾ | **5** | 20/1 | 89 | 67 |
| 2502[14] | **Winter Romance (102)** (EALDunlop) **3-9-4** TQuinn(9) (chsd ldr: slt ld 2f out: hdd 1f out: sn btn) | hd | **6** | 20/1 | 110 | 77 |
| 1867[2] | **Billy Bushwacker (93)** (MrsMReveley) **5-9-6** KDarley(11) (in tch: hdwy 3f out: rdn & nvr able to chal) | ½ | **7** | 10/1 | 101 | 79 |
| 2248[5] | **Amrak Ajeeb (IRE) (94)** (BHanbury) **4-9-7** MRimmer(17) (b: in tch: effrt 4f out: no imp) | nk | **8** | 20/1 | 101 | 79 |
| 2145[11] | **Dreams End (80)** (PBowen) **8-8-2**(5) PPMurphy(1) (chsd ldrs: ev ch over 2f out: wknd over 1f out) | ¾ | **9** | 50/1 | 86 | 64 |
| 2300[2] | **Lookingforarainbow (IRE) (72)** (BobJones) **8-7-13** DaleGibson(8) (trckd ldrs: outpcd 3f out: n.d after) | hd | **10** | 20/1 | 78 | 56 |
| 2135* | **Lakeline Legend (IRE) (88)** (MAJarvis) **3-8-4** 5x EmmaO'Gorman(4) (mid div: effrt 4f out: n.m.r over 1f out: nvr rchd ldrs) | 1½ | **11** | 15/2[3] | 91 | 58 |
| 2299[2] | **Secret Aly (CAN) (81)** (CEBrittain) **6-8-8** BDoyle(7) (chsd ldrs tl wknd fnl 2f) | 4 | **12** | 20/1 | 78 | 56 |
| | **Kutta (97)** (RWArmstrong) **4-9-10** WCarson(13) (lw: bhd & rdn over 4f out: n.d) | s.h | **13** | 10/1 | 94 | 72 |
| 2055[19] | **Wafir (IRE) (82)** (PCalver) **4-8-9** MBirch(16) (chsd ldrs: effrt 4f out: sn btn: hmpd over 1f out) | 4 | **14** | 25/1 | 73 | 51 |
| 2010[3] | **Seventeens Lucky (77)** (BobJones) **4-8-4** NDay(3) (chsd ldrs tl wknd 3f out) | 5 | **15** | 20/1 | 60 | 38 |
| 1817[2] | **Yarob (IRE) (98)** (HThomsonJones) **3-9-0** GCarter(15) (bhd: rdn over 4f out: n.d) | 12 | **16** | 20/1 | 63 | 30 |
| 2053[2] | **Tertium (IRE) (87)** (MartynWane) **4-9-0** JFortune(10) (s.i.s: hld up: rdn over 3f out: no rspnse) | 15 | **17** | 9/2[1] | 29 | 7 |

(SP 135.8%) **17 Rn**

**2m 8.53** (-1.17) CSF £65.69 CT £273.34 TOTE £13.50: £3.10 £1.80 £2.20 £4.40 (£61.10) Trio £108.70 OWNER Mr T. G. Warner (MARLBOR-OUGH) BRED Red House Stud

LONG HANDICAP Spirito Libro (USA) 7-7
WEIGHT FOR AGE 3yo-11lb
**OFFICIAL EXPLANATION Tertium (IRE): choked in the race and has suffered wind problems in the past.**
**2502 Wilcuma** obviously just needed his Sandown run last week and, getting a terrific run up the inner here, found all that was necessary under pressure. (10/1)
**2502 Spirito Libro (USA)** tried hard, despite getting unbalanced under pressure in the last three furlongs, but the winner was always holding her in the closing stages. (11/2)
**2350 Arctiid (USA)** is a colt with plenty of ability, but he was always tending to hang away from the rail, giving valuable ground away and, in the end, went to his left. He is certainly off a useful mark if he can be straightened out. (9/2)
**2350 Carlito Brigante**, after his indifferent run last time, was given a ride and a half here and kept staying on, but could never quite get there. (16/1)
**2350 Hazard a Guess (IRE)**, back to more patient tactics, took a long time to find his stride and, although finishing like a train, it was always too late. (20/1)
**2041 Winter Romance** held a good position throughout, but probably did not quite get home. (20/1)
**1867 Billy Bushwacker** did not impress on looks and never got into it, despite struggling on. (10/1)
**2135* Lakeline Legend (IRE)** was short of toe when things got serious early in the straight here and then found a little trouble when staying on. This is best put down to experience. (15/2: 9/2-8/1)

## 2725 NEWCASTLE BROWN ALE H'CAP (0-90) (3-Y.O+) (Class C)

4-45 (4-46) **6f** £6,732.00 (£2,016.00: £968.00: £444.00) Stalls: Low GOING minus 0.36 sec per fur (F)

| | | | | SP | RR | SF |
|---|---|---|---|---|---|---|
| 2329[2] | **Double Splendour (IRE) (82)** (PSFelgate) **6-9-9** KDarley(1) (lw: trckd ldrs: led over 1f out: r.o wl) | — | **1** | 4/1[1] | 93 | 76 |
| 2329[3] | **Bayin (USA) (72)** (MDIUsher) **7-8-13** RStreet(15) (b: hld up & bhd: hdwy 2f out: r.o towards fin) | 3 | **2** | 12/1 | 75 | 58 |
| 2137[3] | **Benzoe (IRE) (77)** (MrsJRRamsden) **6-9-4** KFallon(11) (bhd: hdwy ½-wy: r.o u.p: nrst fin) | ¾ | **3** | 10/1[3] | 78 | 61 |
| 1018[18] | **Samwar (78)** (MissGayKelleway) **4-9-5** WRyan(2) (b: a chsng ldrs: hdwy over 1f out: swtchd rt ins fnl f: styd on wl) | hd | **4** | 10/1[3] | 79 | 62 |
| 2403[5] | **Shikari's Son (81)** (JCullinan) **9-9-3**(5) MartinDwyer(7) (swtchd & hdwy 2½f out: styd on u.p fnl f: nrst fin) | ¾ | **5** | 25/1 | 80 | 63 |
| 2376[4] | **Cretan Gift (68)** (NPLittmoden) **5-8-9v** TGMcLaughlin(17) (bhd: hdwy ½-wy: styd on wl) | nk | **6** | 16/1 | 66 | 49 |
| 2421[3] | **Amron (60)** (JBerry) **9-8-1** GCarter(13) (bhd: hdwy whn hmpd 2½f out: r.o towards fin) | hd | **7** | 25/1 | 58 | 41 |
| 2005* | **Daawe (USA) (68)** (MrsVAAconley) **5-8-9v** MDeering(9) (chsd ldr: ev ch over 1f out: wandered u.p & grad wknd) | ¾ | **8** | 8/1[2] | 64 | 47 |
| 2518[4] | **Here Comes a Star (75)** (JMCarr) **8-9-2** DaleGibson(6) (hdwy whn bdly hmpd 2½f out: nvr nrr) | 2 | **9** | 25/1 | 65 | 48 |
| 2228* | **So Intrepid (IRE) (83)** (JMBradley) **6-9-10** PatEddery(14) (s.i.s & swtchd lft after s: hdwy ½-wy: no imp) | nk | **10** | 8/1[2] | 73 | 56 |
| 2508[6] | **Fantasy Racing (IRE) (77)** (MRChannon) **4-8-13**(5) PPMurphy(19) (in tch: effrt ½-wy: outpcd fnl 2f) | ¾ | **11** | 25/1 | 65 | 48 |
| 2590[2] | **Murray's Mazda (IRE) (55)** (JLEyre) **7-7-7**(3) NVarley(3) (in tch 4f: wknd) | 1 | **12** | 20/1 | 40 | 23 |
| 2508* | **Chadwell Hall (70)** (SRBowring) **5-8-8b**(3) CTeague(4) (led tl hdd & wknd appr fnl f) | ½ | **13** | 11/1 | 54 | 37 |
| 2328[2] | **Primo Lara (82)** (PWHarris) **4-9-9** BDoyle(18) (sn bhd & pushed along: n.d) | nk | **14** | 10/1[3] | 65 | 48 |
| 2363[3] | **Palo Blanco (79)** (TDBarron) **5-9-6** JFortune(8) (hmpd wl over 2f out: n.d) | 4 | **15** | 8/1[2] | 51 | 34 |
| 2425[9] | **Oriel Lad (69)** (PDEvans) **3-8-4b**[ow2] OUrbina(20) (nvr wnt pce) | 3 | **16** | 33/1 | 33 | 8 |
| 2508[4] | **High Domain (IRE) (72)** (JLSpearing) **5-8-13** MBirch(5) (chsd ldrs to ½-wy: sn wknd) | 4 | **17** | 16/1 | 25 | 8 |
| 2490[6] | **Craigie Boy (56)** (NBycroft) **6-7-11b**[ow1] TWilliams(10) (mid div: sn pushed along: lost tch fr ½-wy) | 1½ | **18** | 33/1 | 5 | — |

(SP 134.4%) **18 Rn**

**1m 11.04** (0.04) CSF £52.02 CT £445.53 TOTE £4.40: £1.50 £2.60 £2.20 £3.50 (£24.80) Trio £110.60 OWNER Yorkshire Racing Club Owners Group 1990 (MELTON MOWBRAY) BRED R. McQuillan
LONG HANDICAP Murray's Mazda (IRE) 7-7 Craigie Boy 7-9
WEIGHT FOR AGE 3yo-6lb
**2329 Double Splendour (IRE)** is in tremendous form just now and, once in front, was not going to be caught this time. (4/1)
**2329 Bayin (USA)** did his usual and tried to come from a different county, but the task was always impossible. (12/1)
**2137 Benzoe (IRE)** was always struggling to improve but he did stay on, albeit in vain. He is never one to rely on fully, but is also never one to be left out altogether. (10/1)
**1018 Samwar** ran well after two months off and, judging by the way he finished, a return to seven furlongs should help. (10/1)
**2403 Shikari's Son** looked to cause trouble when switching for room over two furlongs out, but then struggled on to show he still has ability. He is now pretty well handicapped. (25/1)
**2376 Cretan Gift** made up a lot of ground from halfway, and really does deserve to win a race on turf. (16/1)
**2421 Amron** continued his return to form here and looked very unlucky when getting virtually knocked over two and a half furlongs from home. Although finishing fast, the effort was always beyond him from then on. (25/1)
**2005* Daawe (USA)** had his chances, but got unbalanced when the pressure was applied approaching the final furlong and soon cried enough. (8/1)
**2518 Here Comes a Star** is proving difficult to win with this year, but it was not his fault on this occasion, as he was badly hampered over two furlongs out, and had no chance of getting into it. (25/1)
**2363 Palo Blanco** was never really firing this time and being hampered after halfway made little difference. (8/1)

## 2726 FISHERGATE NURSERY H'CAP (2-Y.O) (Class C)

5-15 (5-15) **5f** £5,531.25 (£1,650.00: £787.50: £356.25) Stalls: Low GOING minus 0.36 sec per fur (F)

| | | | | SP | RR | SF |
|---|---|---|---|---|---|---|
| 2317[3] | **Top of The Form (IRE)** (MJohnston) **2-8-5** TWilliams(1) (mde all: qcknd ½-wy: r.o wl) | — | **1** | 7/2[1] | 81 | 15 |
| 2317* | **Bayford Thrust** (JBerry) **2-9-3** GCarter(8) (in tch: hdwy u.p 2f out: hung lft: styd on: nvr able to chal) | 2 | **2** | 7/2[1] | 87 | 21 |
| 2138* | **Burkes Manor** (TDBarron) **2-8-10** JFortune(4) (s.i.s: outpcd & bhd tl styd on appr fnl f) | ¾ | **3** | 7/1 | 77 | 11 |
| 1419[5] | **Exit To Rio (CAN)** (MrsJRRamsden) **2-9-5** KFallon(5) (lw: s.i.s: swtchd outside & hdwy ½-wy: nvr nr to chal) | ¾ | **4** | 7/1 | 84 | 18 |
| 2374* | **Rudi's Pet (IRE)** (RHannon) **2-9-5** PatEddery(7) (lw: chsd ldrs: effrt ½-wy: btn over 1f out) | ¾ | **5** | 5/1[2] | 81 | 15 |
| 2112[6] | **Superior Premium** (RAFahey) **2-9-7** MBirch(3) (chsd wnr over 3f: wknd) | 1½ | **6** | 11/2[3] | 79 | 13 |
| 1673[4] | **Petite Danseuse** (SDow) **2-9-4** WRyan(6) (chsd ldrs tl outpcd 2f out: btn whn hmpd ins fnl f) | 2 | **7** | 7/1 | 69 | 3 |
| 2309[3] | **Bold African** (PDEvans) **2-8-7b** BDoyle(2) (drvn along after 1f: lost tch fr ½-wy) | 2 | **8** | 10/1 | 52 | — |

(SP 123.1%) **8 Rn**

**60.25 secs** (2.55) CSF £16.63 CT £77.53 TOTE £4.40: £1.50 £1.80 £2.30 (£5.10) OWNER Mr R. W. Huggins (MIDDLEHAM) BRED Sean Beston
**2317 Top of The Form (IRE)** behaved himself on this occasion and put his blistering pace to full use to see off all dangers soon after halfway. (7/2)

**2317* Bayford Thrust** could never keep tabs on the winner this time and, when he did stay on, he hung left, causing trouble, and failed to get to grips. (7/2)
**2138* Burkes Manor** found everything happening too quickly and only got going when it was all over. He should appreciate further and probably some cut in the ground. (7/1)
**1419 Exit To Rio (CAN)** has been disappointing in his last two runs and, given an odd ride here, was certainly not knocked about. The ability is there if he can be persuaded. (7/1)
**2374* Rudi's Pet (IRE)** was always struggling with the pace and finally cried enough approaching the last furlong. (5/1)
**2112 Superior Premium** was the only one able to chase the winner early on, and that found him out with a quarter of a mile left. (11/2)
**2309 Bold African** (10/1: 8/1-12/1)

T/Jkpt: £10,904.00 (5.41 Tckts). T/Plpt: £49.10 (873.52 Tckts). T/Qdpt: £44.40 (57.35 Tckts). AA

## 2416-AYR (L-H) (Good to firm)
## Monday July 15th

WEATHER: sunny WIND: mod half against

### 2727 E.B.F. MAIDEN STKS (2-Y.O) (Class D)
2-15 (2-22) **6f** £3,493.00 (£1,054.00: £512.00: £241.00) Stalls: High GOING: minus 0.36 sec per fur (F)

| | | | | SP | RR | SF |
|---|---|---|---|---|---|---|
| 2295[3] | **The Lambton Worm** (DenysSmith) **2-9-0** KFallon(2) (lw: a.p: led over 1f out: rdn & r.o) | — | 1 | 5/4[2] | 77 | 34 |
| 2295[2] | **Canadian Fantasy** (MJohnston) **2-9-0** RHills(3) (lw: w ldr: led over 2f out tl over 1f out: r.o) | 1¼ | 2 | Evens[1] | 74 | 31 |
| 2416[4] | **Hong Kong Express (IRE)** (JBerry) **2-8-9** JCarroll(6) (led tl over 2f out: sn btn) | 6 | 3 | 40/1 | 53 | 10 |
| 2495[11] | **Madison Welcome (IRE)** (MrsJRRamsden) **2-9-0** JFortune(1) (bit bkwd: bhd: pushed along & hdwy ½-wy: nvr nr to chal) | 1¼ | 4 | 33/1[3] | 54 | 11 |
| | **Cairn Dhu** (MrsJRRamsden) **2-9-0** KDarley(4) (cmpt: str: bit bkwd: unruly s: s.i.s: sn trckng ldr: grad wknd fnl 2f) | 1 | 5 | 33/1[3] | 52 | 9 |
| | | | | (SP 102.8%) | **5 Rn** | |

**1m 13.75** (3.95) CSF £2.48 TOTE £2.60: £1.60 £1.10 (£1.10) OWNER Lord Durham (BISHOP AUCKLAND) BRED W. F. Macauley
**2295 The Lambton Worm** turned the tables on the runner-up in style and gained the success this tough and consistent individual deserved. (5/4)
**2295 Canadian Fantasy** raced on what is generally the faster side last time at Newcastle and was nicely second best here, meeting the winner on the same terms. (Evens)
**2416 Hong Kong Express (IRE)** failed to impress on looks this time and, once the pressure was on over two furlongs out, was soon left behind. (40/1)
**Madison Welcome (IRE)** still needed this and, after getting outpaced early on, was learning as the race progressed. He will surely stay further. (33/1)
**Cairn Dhu**, a decent sort, gave problems before the start and then showed some ability until blowing up in the last couple of furlongs. (33/1)

### 2728 GARRY OWEN CUP NURSERY H'CAP (2-Y.O) (Class D)
2-45 (2-48) **5f** £4,162.50 (£1,260.00: £615.00: £292.50) Stalls: High GOING: minus 0.36 sec per fur (F)

| | | | | SP | RR | SF |
|---|---|---|---|---|---|---|
| 1869[2] | **Osomental** (DHaydnJones) **2-9-7b** FNorton(3) (in tch: qcknd to ld ins fnl f: r.o) | — | 1 | 4/1[3] | 73 | 42 |
| 2219[2] | **Maid By The Fire (USA)** (PFICole) **2-9-4** TQuinn(1) (cl up: led over 1f out: hdd & nt qckn ins fnl f) | 1½ | 2 | 3/1[2] | 65 | 34 |
| 2681* | **Plan For Profit (IRE)** (MJohnston) **2-8-13** 7x RHills(6) (lw: trckd ldrs: effrt & n.m.r 2f out: nt pce to chal) | 3 | 3 | 6/4[1] | 51 | 20 |
| *2371*[4] | **Little Blue (IRE)** (TDEasterby) **2-8-0** JLowe(7) (led tl hdd appr fnl f: no ex) | ¾ | 4 | 25/1 | 35 | 4 |
| 2484[5] | **Express Girl** (DMoffatt) **2-9-3**(3) DarrenMoffatt(4) (a chsng ldrs: rdn ½-wy: no imp) | hd | 5 | 6/1 | 55 | 24 |
| 1021* | **Lycius Touch** (MJohnston) **2-9-7** TWilliams(5) (outpcd & bhd: sme hdwy 2f out: n.d) | 3½ | 6 | 20/1 | 45 | 14 |
| 1978[5] | **Molly Drummond** (CWCElsey) **2-9-4** KDarley(2) (cl up tl wknd fnl 2f) | 3½ | 7 | 20/1 | 31 | — |
| | | | | (SP 112.7%) | **7 Rn** | |

**60.15 secs** (3.15) CSF £15.46 TOTE £5.20: £2.20 £2.20 (£8.10) OWNER Mr Hugh O'Donnell (PONTYPRIDD) BRED P. Asquith
**1869 Osomental** has been gelded, which worked the oracle as this previously temperamental customer won authoritatively (4/1)
**2219 Maid By The Fire (USA)** keeps running well but, when it comes down to a struggle, does not seem to have what it takes. (3/1)
**2681* Plan For Profit (IRE)** was not made enough use of this time and was short of toe when asked a question in the last two furlongs. (6/4)
**2371 Little Blue (IRE)** showed fair speed until outpointed in the final furlong, and may well need a bit further. (25/1)
**2484 Express Girl** was at her best early in the season when the ground was soft. (6/1)
**1021* Lycius Touch** looked to have been set a very stiff task by the Handicapper, and was always struggling and behind on this much faster ground. (20/1)

### 2729 DAILY RECORD H'CAP (0-80) (3-Y.O+) (Class D)
3-15 (3-16) **7f** £4,201.50 (£1,272.00: £621.00: £295.50) Stalls: High GOING: minus 0.36 sec per fur (F)

| | | | | SP | RR | SF |
|---|---|---|---|---|---|---|
| 2679[6] | **King Curan (USA) (52)** (DHaydnJones) **5-8-6b** TQuinn(4) (lw: trckd ldrs: led wl over 1f out: sn drvn clr) | — | 1 | 11/1 | 66 | 32 |
| 1648[4] | **Marjaana (IRE) (69)** (PTWalwyn) **3-9-1** RHills(7) (lw: hld up: effrt 3f out: styd on: nt pce to chal) | 3½ | 2 | 8/1 | 75 | 33 |
| 2328[6] | **Somerton Boy (IRE) (71)** (PCalver) **6-9-11** DaleGibson(5) (lw: hld up: nt clr run & swtchd 2f out: nt clr run ins fnl f: nrst fin) | nk | 3 | 3/1[1] | 76 | 42 |
| 2222[2] | **Finisterre (IRE) (63)** (JJO'Neill) **3-8-9** KFallon(9) (lw: bhd: effrt 3f out: nrst fin) | 2 | 4 | 6/1[3] | 64 | 22 |
| 2285[10] | **Don Pepe (60)** (RBoss) **5-9-0** JCarroll(8) (hld up: hdwy on ins whn nt clr run wl over 1f out: nt rcvr) | 2 | 5 | 12/1 | 56 | 22 |
| 2149[5] | **Mister Westsound (70)** (MissLAPerratt) **4-9-10b** KDarley(3) (trckd ldrs: effrt 2f out: sn rdn & btn) | ½ | 6 | 10/1 | 65 | 31 |
| 2630[3] | **Quilling (68)** (MDods) **4-9-8v** JFortune(1) (w ldrs: led wl over 2f out tl wl over 1f out: sn wknd) | 2½ | 7 | 11/2[2] | 57 | 23 |
| 2393* | **Bollin Dorothy (65)** (TDEasterby) **3-8-11** MBirch(6) (lw: led tl hdd & wknd qckly wl over 2f out) | 6 | 8 | 11/2[2] | 41 | — |
| 2283[3] | **Ertlon (74)** (CEBrittain) **6-10-0** BDoyle(2) (w ldrs to ½-wy: sn wknd) | 1½ | 9 | 7/1 | 46 | 12 |
| | | | | (SP 118.8%) | **9 Rn** | |

**1m 28.28** (4.28) CSF £87.50 CT £305.32 TOTE £13.70: £2.70 £2.00 £2.10 (£42.90) Trio £171.90 OWNER Mr Hugh O'Donnell (PONTYPRIDD) BRED Executive Bloodstock & Adstock Manor Stud
WEIGHT FOR AGE 3yo-8lb
**2679 King Curan (USA)** had the blinkers back on and was completely transformed. Despite carrying his head at an angle, he did the business in style in the last couple of furlongs. (11/1)

**1648 Marjaana (IRE)** had to work to improve early in the straight, but all she could do was follow the winner home in the last two furlongs. A pair of blinkers might help. (8/1)
**2328 Somerton Boy (IRE)** met with a fair amount of trouble and was probably second best on merit. He does look particularly well at the moment. (3/1)
**2222 Finisterre (IRE)** looked really well, but took a while to get going and, when he finally did, it was too late. He can win a race at this trip. (6/1)
**2005 Don Pepe** continued his come from behind tactics, but never saw daylight here and this is best forgotten. (12/1)
**2149 Mister Westsound** did not look as well as normal and, after travelling on the bridle, disappointingly found nothing when ridden. (10/1)
**2393* Bollin Dorothy**, who was taken on in the lead, basically went too fast and stopped some way out. (11/2)

## 2730 TENNENT CALEDONIAN BREWERIES SCOTTISH CLASSIC STKS (Gp 3) (3-Y.O+) (Class A)

3-45 (3-45) **1m 2f** £19,636.00 (£7,324.00: £3,562.00: £1,510.00: £655.00: £313.00) Stalls: High GOING: minus 0.36 sec per fur (F)

| | | | | SP | RR | SF |
|---|---|---|---|---|---|---|
| 2038[2] | **Montjoy (USA) (120)** (PFICole) **4-9-7** TQuinn(3) (lw: trckd ldrs gng wl: shkn up to ld wl ins fnl f: pushed out) | — | **1** | 8/11[1] | 115+ | 53 |
| 2194* | **Musetta (IRE) (106)** (CEBrittain) **4-8-13** BDoyle(4) (led: qcknd over 1f out: hdd wl ins fnl f: r.o) | nk | **2** | 10/1 | 107 | 45 |
| 2038[7] | **Desert Shot (115)** (MRStoute) **6-9-5** KFallon(5) (lw: hld up: effrt 3f out: styd on: no imp) | 3½ | **3** | 7/1 | 107 | 45 |
| 1355* | **Captain Horatius (IRE) (110)** (JLDunlop) **7-9-2** KDarley(1) (lw: hld up: effrt 3f out: styd on: nt pce to chal) | s.h | **4** | 13/2[3] | 104 | 42 |
| 2038[6] | **Fahal (USA) (117)** (DMorley) **4-9-5b[1]** RHills(6) (lw: cl up: chal 3f out: rdn & btn over 1f out) | ½ | **5** | 5/1[2] | 106 | 44 |
| 2194[5] | **Leonato (FR)** (PDEvans) **4-9-2** JFortune(2) (lw: cl up tl outcpd fnl 2½f) | 1½ | **6** | 100/1 | 101 | 39 |
| | | | | (SP 110.5%) | | **6 Rn** |

**2m 10.07** (5.47) CSF £7.78 TOTE £1.70: £1.10 £3.10 (£7.10) OWNER Sir George Meyrick (WHATCOMBE) BRED Anthony M. Warrender
**2038 Montjoy (USA)** always looked as though he was going to win this but, in the end, it was not quite as easy as it should have been, as he showed slight signs of temperament. (8/11: 4/5-Evens)
**2194* Musetta (IRE)** loves to be out in front and is game but, despite a valiant effort, was just touched off. (10/1)
**680 Desert Shot** had the conditions he likes here, but was off the bit early in the straight and, although struggling on, was never up to the task. (7/1)
**1355* Captain Horatius (IRE)** has an action these days that looks suited to easier ground and, although struggling on here in the home straight, never looked likely to get into it. (13/2: 4/1-7/1)
**2038 Fahal (USA)**, tried in blinkers this time, raced with the leaders until crying enough approaching the last furlong. (5/1)
**Leonato (FR)** looked to be taking on too much here, but ran reasonably until dropping out in the last two and a half furlongs. (100/1)

## 2731 GLASGOW HOLIDAY (S) STKS (3-Y.O+) (Class F)

4-15 (4-18) **1m 2f** £2,827.00 (£856.00: £418.00: £199.00) Stalls: High GOING: minus 0.36 sec per fur (F)

| | | | | SP | RR | SF |
|---|---|---|---|---|---|---|
| 2567[3] | **Hawwam (43)** (EJAlston) **10-9-5** JLowe(3) (lw: hld up: wnt prom 6f out: led wl over 2f out: styd on) | — | **1** | 25/1 | 59 | 32 |
| 2568* | **North Ardar (58)** (MrsMReveley) **6-9-0**(5) SCopp(11) (hld up: hdwy & prom ent st: rdn to chse wnr ins fnl f: nt qckn) | 1 | **2** | 11/8[1] | 57 | 30 |
| 2568[4] | **Veshca Lady (IRE) (42)** (EWeymes) **3-8-4v**ow1 KDarley(9) (bhd: effrt ent st: styd on wl fnl f: nrst fin) | 2 | **3** | 10/1 | 50 | 11 |
| 2419[2] | **Time For A Glass (39)** (DMoffatt) **3-8-0**(3) DarrenMoffatt(5) (lw: sn prom: ev ch 3f out: sn rdn & one pce) | hd | **4** | 6/1[3] | 49 | 11 |
| 2568[3] | **Diamond Crown (IRE) (44)** (MartynWane) **5-9-5** KFallon(12) (hld up & bhd: hdwy over 3f out: chsng ldrs & rdn whn sltly hmpd over 1f out: one pce after) | 3½ | **5** | 5/2[2] | 48 | 21 |
| 2568[8] | **Forzair (58)** (JJO'Neill) **4-9-5** JFortune(4) (effrt over 3f out: styd on: n.d) | 5 | **6** | 16/1 | 40 | 13 |
| 2379[4] | **Haido'hart (44)** (BSRothwell) **4-9-5** MBirch(1) (lw: nvr nr to chal) | nk | **7** | 10/1 | 40 | 13 |
| 2394[6] | **Heathyards Magic (IRE) (47)** (MDods) **4-9-5v[1]** JCarroll(2) (led tl hdd wl over 2f out: sn rdn & btn) | 2½ | **8** | 33/1 | 36 | 9 |
| 2573[12] | **Oakbury (IRE) (53)** (MissLCSiddall) **4-9-0**(5) PRoberts(6) (chsd ldrs: hmpd & lost pl appr st: n.d after) | ¾ | **9** | 14/1 | 35 | 8 |
| | **Tolepa (IRE)** (JJO'Neill) **3-8-3** DaleGibson(7) (s.i.s: n.d) | 14 | **10** | 66/1 | 7 | — |
| 2420[9] | **Midas Man** (DANolan) **5-9-5** FNorton(8) (chsd ldr tl wknd qckly ent st: virtually p.u) | dist | **11** | 400/1 | — | — |
| | | | | (SP 124.2%) | | **11 Rn** |

**2m 12.53** (7.93) CSF £60.18 TOTE £24.80: £3.60 £1.30 £1.90 (£18.90) Trio £44.60 OWNER North West Racing Club Owners Club (PRESTON) BRED G. Franco
WEIGHT FOR AGE 3yo-11lb
No bid; North Ardar clmd GBernacchi £6,000
**2567 Hawwam** last won a race on turf over six years ago, but he looked extremely well here and, once in front, was always doing just enough. (25/1)
**2568* North Ardar** did not impress on looks, but still ran pretty well, only to find the winner too strong in the closing stages. (11/8)
**2568 Veshca Lady (IRE)** was putting in all her best work at the finish and looks to be coming to hand. (10/1: 7/1-11/1)
**2419 Time For A Glass**, not suited by the conditions of this event, ran pretty well, and is one to look out for in handicaps. (6/1)
**2568 Diamond Crown (IRE)** is only lightly-made and was always finding this trip a bit on the sharp side. When asked the question early in the straight, he failed to get in a blow. (5/2)
**2488 Forzair** has a poor action, and is much happier on the All-Weather. (16/1)
**2379 Haido'hart** (10/1: 8/1-12/1)
**Oakbury (IRE)** got messed about on the home turn and this is best forgotten. (14/1)

## 2732 DASH FOR CASH MAIDEN H'CAP (0-70) (3-Y.O+) (Class E)

4-45 (4-49) **5f** £3,493.00 (£1,054.00: £512.00: £241.00) Stalls: High GOING: minus 0.36 sec per fur (F)

| | | | | SP | RR | SF |
|---|---|---|---|---|---|---|
| 2566[5] | **King of Show (IRE) (44)** (RAllan) **5-8-11v** ACulhane(7) (hld up: qcknd to ld ins fnl f: r.o) | — | **1** | 50/1 | 60 | 43 |
| 2571[3] | **Camionneur (IRE) (49)** (TDEasterby) **3-8-11b** JLowe(11) (lw: s.i.s: hdwy 2f out: led 1f out: sn hdd: nt qckn) | 1¼ | **2** | 4/1[2] | 61 | 39 |
| 2359[3] | **Ready Teddy (IRE) (50)** (MissLAPerratt) **3-8-12** KDarley(3) (w ldrs: led wl over 1f out: hdd 1f out: sn btn) | 3½ | **3** | 11/4[1] | 51 | 29 |
| 2395[2] | **China Hand (IRE) (37)** (MartynWane) **4-8-1**(3) DWright(4) (led over 3f: kpt on one pce) | ½ | **4** | 8/1 | 36 | 19 |
| 2021[7] | **Lord Cornelious (34)** (DANolan) **3-7-10** FNorton(8) (prom: rdn ½-wy: styd on same pce) | 1 | **5** | 25/1 | 30 | 8 |
| 2240[7] | **Rinus Manor (IRE) (50)** (EJAlston) **5-9-3** KFallon(1) (in tch: rdn ½-wy: one pce) | nk | **6** | 9/1 | 45 | 28 |
| *2305[8]* | **Forzara (45)** (JBerry) **3-8-7** JCarroll(9) (b.off hind: bhd: effrt ½-wy: no imp) | 1¾ | **7** | 10/1 | 34 | 12 |
| *1972[7]* | **Hamilton Gold (54)** (MGMeagher) **3-9-2** JFortune(2) (lw: cl up: rdn 2f out: btn 1f out) | 1 | **8** | 9/1 | 40 | 18 |
| 2421[5] | **Blue Lugana (31)** (NBycroft) **4-7-12**ow2 DaleGibson(10) (a outpcd & bhd) | 2 | **9** | 8/1 | 11 | — |
| 2167[2] | **River Tern (66)** (JBerry) **3-9-9**(5) PRoberts(6) (b.nr fore: in tch: effrt 2f out: sn btn) | 1 | **10** | 9/2[3] | 43 | 21 |

2176[6] **Fancy Clancy (46)** (MissLCSiddall) **3-8-3**(5) CAdamson(5) (lw: in tch: effrt & n.m.r ½-wy: sn btn) ..................2½ **11** 25/1 15 —
(SP 125.8%) **11 Rn**

**59.55 secs** (2.55) CSF £236.01 CT £714.50 TOTE £32.20: £5.10 £2.30 £1.50 (£133.20) Trio £80.60 OWNER Mr R. Allan (CORNHILL-ON-TWEED) BRED Gainsborough Stud Management Ltd
LONG HANDICAP Lord Cornelious 7-5
WEIGHT FOR AGE 3yo-5lb
**King of Show (IRE)**, having his first run at this trip, got it right and won most emphatically. (50/1)
**2571 Camionneur (IRE)** is frustrating to say the least and, just when he looked likely to win this poor event, he failed to pick up when ridden. (4/1: op 5/2)
**2359 Ready Teddy (IRE)**, edgy beforehand, had her chances but failed to come up with the goods. (11/4)
**2395 China Hand (IRE)** raced in the front rank but, when an effort was required, it was always beyond him. (8/1)
**Lord Cornelious** is certainly running better, but he never looked likely to get into this, despite staying on. (25/1)
**2240 Rinus Manor (IRE)** has his chances but failed to respond when ridden. (9/1: 6/1-10/1)
**Hamilton Gold** is very lightly-made and never seemed to be galloping on an even keel, despite racing with the leaders for over three furlongs. (9/1)

T/Jkpt: Not won; £5,082.46 to Beverley 16/7/96. T/Plpt: £16.20 (1,025.7 Tckts). T/Qdpt: £5.50 (168.63 Tckts). AA

## 2594-FOLKESTONE (R-H) (Good to firm)
## Monday July 15th

WEATHER: sunny WIND: slt half against

### 2733 HURST GREEN MAIDEN AUCTION STKS (2-Y.O) (Class F)
2-00 (2-00) **6f 189y** £2,381.00 (£656.00: £311.00) Stalls: Low GOING minus 0.28 sec per fur (GF)

| | | | SP | RR | SF |
|---|---|---|---|---|---|
| 2224[8] | **Sun O'Tirol (IRE)** (MRChannon) **2-8-9** PaulEddery(3) (hld up: rdn over 2f out: led wl ins fnl f: r.o wl)............— | 1 | 7/1 | 68 | 24 |
| 2538[2] | **Smugurs (IRE)** (RJRWilliams) **2-8-1** JQuinn(4) (lw: a.p: led wl over 1f out tl wl ins fnl f: r.o) ..........................nk | 2 | 7/4[1] | 59 | 15 |
| 2396[9] | **Falls O'Moness (IRE)** (KRBurke) **2-8-3** DRMcCabe(2) (lw: rdn over 2f out: hdwy over 1f out: r.o wl ins fnl f).nk | 3 | 9/4[2] | 61 | 17 |
| 2396[7] | **Mystic Quest (IRE)** (KMcAuliffe) **2-8-8** JReid(1) (a.p: ev ch wl over 1f out: unable qckn)...............................nk | 4 | 15/2 | 65 | 21 |
| 639[8] | **Scarrots** (SCWilliams) **2-8-9** JTate(7) (bit bkwd: led over 5f) ..........................................................3½ | 5 | 5/1[3] | 58 | 14 |
| 2435[5] | **Sharazamataz** (WJHaggas) **2-8-5** SSanders(5) (hld up: rdn over 2f out: one pce) ..........................................½ | 6 | 14/1 | 53 | 9 |

(SP 114.7%) **6 Rn**

**1m 25.4** (3.80) CSF £19.38 TOTE £9.10: £3.30 £1.50 (£11.00) OWNER Mrs Annette Barwick (UPPER LAMBOURN) BRED J. J. S. Geraghty
**865 Sun O'Tirol (IRE)**, who failed to get a clear run at Kempton last time, had no such problem here. Pushed along turning for home, he eventually managed to get on top in the closing stages. (7/1: 5/1-8/1)
**2538 Smugurs (IRE)**, grimly trying to hold on, was eventually worried out of it in the closing stages and once again had to settle for being the bridesmaid. (7/4)
**1499 Falls O'Moness (IRE)**, who failed to handle the cut in the ground last time, only just failed to get there in time. (9/4)
**2396 Mystic Quest (IRE)** had every chance entering the home straight before failing to find the necessary turn of foot. (15/2: 5/1-8/1)
**639 Scarrots** did not looking fully wound up for this first run in three months. (5/1)
**2435 Sharazamataz** (14/1: op 8/1)

### 2734 E.B.F. ASHFORD MAIDEN STKS (2-Y.O) (Class D)
2-30 (2-30) **6f** £3,437.65 (£1,025.20: £489.10: £221.05) Stalls: Low GOING minus 0.28 sec per fur (GF)

| | | | SP | RR | SF |
|---|---|---|---|---|---|
| | **Lima** (LMCumani) **2-8-9** OUrbina(2) (scope: s.s: hld up: nt clr run over 2f out tl over 1f out: led wl ins fnl f: r.o wl)........— | 1 | 9/4[2] | 75+ | 14 |
| 2398[4] | **Signs And Wonders** (CACyzer) **2-8-9** SSanders(5) (a.p: led 2f out tl wl ins fnl f: unable qckn)...................½ | 2 | 16/1 | 74 | 13 |
| 2112[8] | **Aficionado (IRE)** (RFJohnsonHoughton) **2-9-0** JReid(3) (hld up: rdn over 2f out: one pce fnl f) ....................2 | 3 | Evens[1] | 73 | 12 |
| 1892[5] | **Kewarra** (BRMillman) **2-9-0** WJO'Connor(7) (lw: a.p: ev ch over 1f out: wknd fnl f)........................................2 | 4 | 20/1 | 68 | 7 |
| 2538[4] | **Hever Golf Dancer** (TJNaughton) **2-9-0** DHolland(4) (lw: led 4f) ...........................................................3½ | 5 | 11/2[3] | 59 | — |
| 2195[12] | **Diamond Lil** (CEBrittain) **2-8-9** KRutter(6) (prom 3f) ...........................................................................8 | 6 | 20/1 | 32 | — |

(SP 111.6%) **6 Rn**

**1m 14.2** (4.00) CSF £27.42 TOTE £3.50: £1.80 £3.00 (£23.40) OWNER Sultan Al Kabeer (NEWMARKET) BRED The Sussex Stud
**Lima**, quite a tall filly with scope, made a winning start to her racing career, despite encountering traffic problems. With nowhere to go over a quarter of a mile from home, she eventually got a split approaching the final furlong, and came through to snatch the spoils in the closing stages. (9/4: 7/4-7/2)
**2398 Signs And Wonders**, grimly trying to fend off her rivals, was eventually collared by the winner in the closing stages. (16/1)
**1774 Aficionado (IRE)** was rather disappointing. Almost on terms entering the final furlong, he was then tapped for toe. (Evens)
**1892 Kewarra** had every chance below the distance before running out of gas in the final furlong. A return to five furlongs might help. (20/1)
**2538 Hever Golf Dancer**, collared two furlongs out, had soon shot his bolt. (11/2: 4/1-6/1)

### 2735 WESTERHANGAR H'CAP (0-65) (3-Y.O+) (Class F)
3-00 (3-00) **6f** £2,381.00 (£656.00: £311.00) Stalls: Low GOING minus 0.28 sec per fur (GF)

| | | | SP | RR | SF |
|---|---|---|---|---|---|
| 2286[3] | **Pride of Hayling (IRE) (51)** (PRHedger) **5-9-6**(3) NVarley(7) (lw: a.p: led over 2f out: rdn out).......................— | 1 | 3/1[2] | 62 | 29 |
| 2713[3] | **Scissor Ridge (51)** (JJBridger) **4-9-9** JQuinn(6) (a.p: chsd wnr fnl 2f: r.o one pce) .........................................1½ | 2 | 100/30[3] | 58 | 25 |
| 2344[7] | **Fighter Squadron (32)** (REPeacock) **7-7-13b**(5) ADaly(3) (prom 3f).......................................................3½ | 3 | 16/1 | 30 | — |
| 2228[6] | **Robo Magic (USA) (52)** (LMontagueHall) **4-9-10** SSanders(5) (stumbled over 4f out: hdwy over 2f out: wknd over 1f out).........1½ | 4 | 11/4[1] | 46 | 13 |
| 2286[16] | **Classic Pet (IRE) (42)** (CAHorgan) **4-9-0** NAdams(1) (led over 3f).................................................hd | 5 | 12/1 | 35 | 2 |
| 2410[5] | **Waders Dream (IRE) (41)** (PatMitchell) **7-8-13v** RCochrane(4) (outpcd)...................................................1½ | 6 | 4/1 | 30 | — |
| *2201[11]* | **Hong Kong Dollar (49)** (BAPearce) **4-9-7** DRMcCabe(2) (b: dwlt: outpcd) ..........................................11 | 7 | 25/1 | 9 | — |

(SP 112.2%) **7 Rn**

**1m 14.0** (3.80) CSF £12.59 TOTE £3.70: £2.00 £2.80 (£5.80) OWNER Mr Bill Broomfield (CHICHESTER) BRED Ewar Stud Farm International
**2286 Pride of Hayling (IRE)**, rousted along, asserted her authority from below the distance. (3/1)
**2713 Scissor Ridge**, making a quick reappearance, moved into second place a quarter of a mile out but, despite pulling clear of the rest, failed to cut down the winner. (100/30: 2/1-7/2)

**653 Fighter Squadron** was close up at halfway before made to look very pedestrian. (16/1)
**2228 Robo Magic (USA)** made an effort on the outside of the field over a quarter of a mile from home, but it came to little and he was beaten below the distance. (11/4)
**Classic Pet (IRE)** took the field along but, collared over two furlongs from home, was soon in trouble. (12/1: 8/1-14/1)

## 2736 BROADSTAIRS LIMITED STKS (0-65) (3-Y.O+) (Class F)

3-30 (3-30) **1m 1f 149y** £2,833.20 (£785.20: £375.60) Stalls: Low GOING minus 0.28 sec per fur (GF)

| | | | | SP | RR | SF |
|---|---|---|---|---|---|---|
| 2409* | **Pistol (IRE) (62)** (CAHorgan) **6-9-7** PaulEddery(4) (b.hind: hld up: led over 1f out: drvn out) | — | 1 | 5/2[2] | 73 | 40 |
| 2300[4] | **Kaafih Homm (IRE) (62)** (NACallaghan) **5-9-2**(3) DaneO'Neill(2) (lw: hld up: rdn over 1f out: r.o wl ins fnl f) | hd | 2 | 6/5[1] | 71 | 38 |
| 2506* | **Baranov (IRE) (63)** (DJGMurraySmith) **3-8-10** DHarrison(5) (led 8f: unable qckn) | 2 | 3 | 5/1[3] | 70 | 26 |
| | **Another Fiddle (IRE) (63)** (SDow) **6-9-5** SSanders(3) (chsd ldr over 7f) | 6 | 4 | 9/1 | 58 | 25 |
| 2251[4] | **Forever Noble (IRE) (62)** (MRChannon) **3-8-8** JReid(1) (hld up: rdn 3f out: sn wknd) | 10 | 5 | 10/1 | 41 | — |
| | | | | (SP 109.8%) | **5 Rn** | |

**2m 2.6** (4.90) CSF £5.70 TOTE £2.40: £1.10 £1.60 (£2.50) OWNER Mrs B. Sumner (PULBOROUGH) BRED David Brogan
WEIGHT FOR AGE 3yo-11lb
**2409* Pistol (IRE)** has yet to win anywhere else. Chasing the leaders, he shot into the lead below the distance and, responding to pressure, just had too many guns for the runner-up. This was his fourth course victory. (5/2: 7/4-11/4)
**2300 Kaafih Homm (IRE)**, as usual, was held up at the back of the field. Asked for his effort below the distance, he gradually cut the winner down, but just failed to get there in time. (6/5)
**2506* Baranov (IRE)** took the field along but, collared below the distance, failed to find another gear. (5/1: 7/2-11/2)
**Another Fiddle (IRE)**, having his first run of the season, raced in second place until entering the straight before tiring. (9/1: op 5/1)
**2251 Forever Noble (IRE)** (10/1: 6/1-11/1)

## 2737 SEDLESCOMBE CLAIMING STKS (3-Y.O+) (Class F)

4-00 (4-01) **1m 1f 149y** £2,381.00 (£656.00: £311.00) Stalls: Low GOING minus 0.28 sec per fur (GF)

| | | | | SP | RR | SF |
|---|---|---|---|---|---|---|
| 2506[15] | **Nelly's Cousin (54)** (NACallaghan) **3-8-5**(3) DaneO'Neill(1) (hdwy over 2f out: hrd rdn over 1f out: led ins fnl f: r.o wl) | — | 1 | 12/1 | 69 | 35 |
| 2568[2] | **Guesstimation (USA) (62)** (JPearce) **7-9-10** GBardwell(6) (hdwy over 2f out: hrd rdn over 1f out: edgd rt & ev ch ins fnl f: r.o) | ½ | 2 | 7/2[2] | 73 | 50 |
| *2082*[10] | **Te Amo (IRE) (67)** (RAkehurst) **4-9-10** SSanders(10) (lw: chsd ldr: led 3f out tl ins fnl f: edgd lft: unable qckn) | 1 | 3 | 9/1 | 72 | 49 |
| 2299[7] | **Statajack (IRE) (80)** (DRCElsworth) **8-9-12b** RCochrane(5) (lw: gd hdwy over 1f out: 4th whn hmpd ins fnl f: nt rcvr) | nk | 4 | 15/8[1] | 73 | 50 |
| 2426[6] | **Proud Image (60)** (KRBurke) **4-9-8v** JTate(9) (lw: hld up: rdn over 2f out: wknd fnl f) | 3½ | 5 | 14/1 | 63 | 40 |
| 2401[10] | **Global Dancer (68)** (SDow) **5-9-1**(5) ADaly(11) (led 6f) | 3 | 6 | 13/2[3] | 56 | 33 |
| | **Brass Tacks (60)** (RTPhillips) **4-8-11** RPerham(4) (nvr nr to chal) | 7 | 7 | 16/1 | 36 | 13 |
| 2494[5] | **Akiymann (USA)** (MCPipe) **6-9-12** AMcGlone(7) (a wl bhd) | 13 | 8 | 20/1 | 29 | 6 |
| 2378[10] | **Rookery Girl (54)** (HJCollingridge) **4-8-11** JQuinn(8) (prom 6f) | 1 | 9 | 33/1 | 13 | — |
| 2577[17] | **Indian Jockey (63)** (MCPipe) **4-9-9**(3) MHenry(3) (prom 7f) | 22 | 10 | 12/1 | — | — |
| 2494[6] | **Precedency** (KMcAuliffe) **4-9-12** WJO'Connor(2) (b: lw: a bhd: t.o whn p.u nr fin: dismntd: sddle slipped) | | P | 40/1 | — | — |
| | | | | (SP 118.4%) | **11 Rn** | |

**2m 1.7** (4.00) CSF £50.97 TOTE £19.80: £4.10 £1.10 £3.50 (£23.30) Trio £51.50 OWNER K. Al-Said (NEWMARKET) BRED Charlton Down Stud
WEIGHT FOR AGE 3yo-11lb
**2033 Nelly's Cousin** moved up turning for home. Responding to pressure, she eventually got on top inside the final furlong. (12/1: 6/1-14/1)
**2568 Guesstimation (USA)** moved up from the back of the field turning for home. Under pressure below the distance, she edged slightly to her right in the final furlong, but still had every chance, if just failing to get the better of the winner. (7/2)
**2082 Te Amo (IRE)**, collared inside the final furlong, drifted slightly left and failed to quicken. (9/1: op 4/1)
**2127* Statajack (IRE)** was put to sleep at the back of the field. Making good strides through the field below the distance, he was just about to get on terms when becoming the meat in the sandwich inside the final furlong, from which he could never recover. (15/8)
**1041 Proud Image**, taking a step up in distance, chased the leaders. Rousted along entering the straight, he had run out of stamina in the final furlong. (14/1: 10/1-16/1)
**Global Dancer**, collared three furlongs from home, was soon in trouble. (13/2)
**2313* Indian Jockey** (12/1: op 6/1)

## 2738 ROBERTSBRIDGE H'CAP (0-70) (3-Y.O) (Class E)

4-30 (4-30) **1m 4f** £2,961.00 (£882.00: £420.00: £189.00) Stalls: Low GOING minus 0.28 sec per fur (GF)

| | | | | SP | RR | SF |
|---|---|---|---|---|---|---|
| *2368** | **Nikita's Star (IRE) (60)** (DJGMurraySmith) **3-9-4**(3) DaneO'Neill(5) (rn wd bnd over 9f out: rdn & hdwy 2f out: led ins fnl f: r.o wl) | — | 1 | 3/1[2] | 70 | 39 |
| 2202[4] | **Again Together (55)** (GLMoore) **3-8-13**(3) PMcCabe(1) (led: rdn over 1f out: wknd & hdd ins fnl f) | 2½ | 2 | 7/2[3] | 62 | 31 |
| 2542[8] | **Crimson Rosella (52)** (WJHaggas) **3-8-13** RCochrane(4) (lw: chsd ldr over 10f: one pce) | hd | 3 | 3/1[2] | 59 | 28 |
| 2409[13] | **Burning Flame (48)** (RMFlower) **3-8-9** DBiggs(6) (hld up: rdn over 3f out: wknd over 1f out) | 6 | 4 | 12/1 | 47 | 16 |
| 2511[9] | **Uoni (52)** (CEBrittain) **3-8-13b**[1] KRutter(3) (lw: jinked s: hld up: rdn 4f out: nt r.o) | 2½ | 5 | 2/1[1] | 47 | 16 |
| | | | | (SP 113.2%) | **5 Rn** | |

**2m 37.8** (6.60) CSF £12.87 TOTE £4.60: £1.60 £2.00 (£3.60) OWNER Nikita's Partners (LAMBOURN) BRED D. Twomey
**2368* Nikita's Star (IRE)**, who ran very wide on the bend setting out on the final circuit, was quite some way off the rest of the field for much of the trip. Picking up ground a quarter of a mile from home, he eventually cut down the leader to grab the initiative inside the final furlong. (3/1: 7/4-100/30)
**2016 Again Together** set the pace and looked to have the race under control entering the straight. However, she tied up in the final furlong and was legless when headed. A mile and a quarter may be her trip. (7/2: 5/2-4/1)
**1050 Crimson Rosella**, in second place until below the distance, failed to find another gear. (3/1)
**Burning Flame** chased the leaders until calling it a day below the distance. (12/1: 8/1-16/1)
**1877 Uoni** chased the leaders but, when asked for her effort half a mile from home, she blatantly downed tools, and does not look one to trust at all. (2/1)

## 2739 LEVY BOARD MAIDEN APPRENTICE STKS (3-Y.O+) (Class F)

5-00 (5-00) **1m 4f** £2,619.00 (£724.00: £345.00) Stalls: Low GOING minus 0.28 sec per fur (GF)

| | | | | SP | RR | SF |
|---|---|---|---|---|---|---|
| 668[8] | **Candle Smoke (USA)** (GHarwood) **3-8-3**(5) GayeHarwood(4) (bit bkwd: chsd ldr: led over 2f out: r.o wl)......— | | 1 | 6/1 | 67 | 29 |
| 1305[8] | **Crandon Boulevard** (LordHuntingdon) **3-8-8** AimeeCook(6) (hld up: ev ch over 1f out: unable qckn)...........2½ | | 2 | 10/1 | 64 | 26 |
| 2439[7] | **Antonia Bin (IRE)** (MBell) **3-8-0**(3) RMullen(2) (lw: hld up: rdn over 2f out: one pce)....................................2½ | | 3 | 6/1 | 55 | 17 |
| 2540[3] | **Soviet King (IRE) (56)** (PhilipMitchell) **3-8-8** SophieMitchell(5) (b: lw: hdwy over 3f out: wknd over 1f out)....1¾ | | 4 | 3/1 [2] | 58 | 20 |
| 1826[12] | **Fast Forward Fred (48)** (LMontagueHall) **5-9-7** AEddery(1) (hld up: rdn over 2f out: sn wknd) .........................8 | | 5 | 9/2 [3] | 47 | 22 |
| 2383[6] | **Spring Campaign (IRE) (70)** (MCPipe) **3-8-8** MHumphries(3) (led: rn v.wd bnd 9f out: clr 8f out: hdd over 2f out: wknd qckly) ..........9 | | 6 | 6/4 [1] | 35 | — |
| | | | | (SP 120.8%) | | **6 Rn** |

**2m 37.5** (6.30) CSF £52.72 TOTE £7.10: £3.70 £3.10 (£20.00) OWNER Mr Anthony Speelman (PULBOROUGH) BRED West Star Bloodstock Inc
WEIGHT FOR AGE 3yo-13lb

**Candle Smoke (USA)** looked to be carrying condition for this first run in three months, but still managed to gain the day. (6/1: op 3/1)
**Crandon Boulevard** managed to get on terms with the winner below the distance but then failed to find another gear. (10/1)
**Antonia Bin (IRE)** chased the leaders but, rousted along turning for home, failed to find the necessary turn of foot. (6/1: 4/1-13/2)
**2540 Soviet King (IRE)** moved up nicely over three furlongs from home but had run out of gas below the distance. This trip seemed to be beyond him. (3/1)
**760 Fast Forward Fred** chased the leaders until coming to the end of his tether turning for home. (9/2: 3/1-5/1)
**2383 Spring Campaign (IRE)** set the pace but virtually ran off the course setting out on the final circuit. However, his jockey managed to get him back with the others and he soon strode clear. Headed over two furlongs from home, he folded up very quickly indeed, and does not look one to place a great deal of faith in. (6/4)

T/Plpt: £38.10 (249.02 Tckts). T/Qdpt: £7.20 (108.62 Tckts). AK

# 2574-WINDSOR (Fig. 8) (Good to firm)
## Monday July 15th
WEATHER: fine WIND: nil

## 2740 PICCADILLY (S) STKS (3-Y.O+) (Class G)

6-30 (6-31) **1m 3f 135y** £2,290.00 (£640.00: £310.00) Stalls: High GOING minus 0.22 sec per fur (GF)

| | | | SP | RR | SF |
|---|---|---|---|---|---|
| 2494[3] | **Shabanaz (55)** (WRMuir) **11-9-9** JReid(1) (wnt 2nd 6f out: led over 2f out: r.o) ...............................................— | 1 | 8/11 [1] | 65 | 30 |
| 1979[11] | **Elly Fleetfoot (IRE) (53)** (MJRyan) **4-9-4** WCarson(4) (hdwy 4f out: hrd rdn 2f out: no imp)............................4 | 2 | 4/1 [2] | 55 | 20 |
| 1524[7] | **Monty (50)** (MajorDNChappell) **4-9-9** MRoberts(8) (swtg: led tl over 2f out: one pce) ..................................7 | 3 | 9/1 | 50 | 15 |
| | **Celestial Fire** (JWhite) **4-9-9** WJO'Connor(5) (prom tl wknd over 3f out)...............................................2 | 4 | 33/1 | 47 | 12 |
| 2373[7] | **Tauten (IRE) (47)** (PBurgoyne) **6-9-4v** JStack(6) (stdd s: hdwy 5f out: wknd qckly 2f out) ...........................2½ | 5 | 15/2 [3] | 39 | 4 |
| *2325[7]* | **Areish (IRE)** (JFfitch-Heyes) **3-8-5** AClark(3) (hdwy 5f out: wknd qckly 3f out)...............................................14 | 6 | 12/1 | 19 | — |
| | | | (SP 110.3%) | | **6 Rn** |

**2m 32.5** (8.50) CSF £3.93 TOTE £1.70: £1.20 £1.30 (£2.20) OWNER Fayzad Thoroughbred Ltd (LAMBOURN) BRED The Overbury Stud
WEIGHT FOR AGE 3yo-13lb
No bid

**2494 Shabanaz** had an easy task. He went to the front over two furlongs from home and was in no real danger thereafter. (8/11)
**Elly Fleetfoot (IRE)**, given a patient ride, was hard driven in pursuit of the winner from two furlongs out, but did not show any enthusiasm. (4/1: op 5/2)
**Monty** soon set off in a clear lead but, when collared over two furlongs from home, could find no extra. (9/1: 9/2-10/1)
**Celestial Fire** was close up until weakening quickly over three furlongs from home. (33/1)
**1314 Tauten (IRE)**, steadied into last place in the early stages, came with a promising run three furlongs from home but it soon petered out. (15/2)

## 2741 THUNDER 'THRILL OF IT ALL' MAIDEN STKS (2-Y.O F) (Class D)

7-00 (7-02) **5f 217y** £3,501.25 (£1,060.00: £517.50: £246.25) Stalls: High GOING minus 0.22 sec per fur (GF)

| | | | SP | RR | SF |
|---|---|---|---|---|---|
| 2504[3] | **Dancing Drop** (RHannon) **2-8-11** PatEddery(10) (w ldrs: led 2f out: r.o wl).............................................— | 1 | 5/4 [1] | 83 | 8 |
| | **Princess Topaz** (CACyzer) **2-8-11** MRoberts(8) (leggy: lt-f: wl bhd tl rdn & hdwy over 1f out: fin fast: eased nr fin) ..........1 | 2 | 33/1 | 80 | 5 |
| | **Inflation** (RFJohnsonHoughton) **2-8-11** JReid(9) (leggy: scope: a.p: ev ch over 1f out: edgd bdly lft fnl f).....1¾ | 3 | 4/1 [3] | 76 | 1 |
| | **Nopalea** (CEBrittain) **2-8-11** SSanders(5) (w'like: bit bkwd: led 4f: r.o one pce) ......................................1½ | 4 | 20/1 | 72 | — |
| | **Papita (IRE)** (SDow) **2-8-11** BThomson(3) (w'like: bit bkwd: hdwy 3f out: one pce fnl 2f)..............................1¼ | 5 | 33/1 | 68 | — |
| 2147[7] | **Hadawah (USA)** (JLDunlop) **2-8-11** WCarson(4) (w ldrs: hrd rdn 2f out: sn wknd) ............................................4 | 6 | 7/2 [2] | 58 | — |
| | **Pampasa (FR)** (CJames) **2-8-11** WJO'Connor(6) (lt-f: prom over 3f) .......................................................1 | 7 | 50/1 | 55 | — |
| | **Danish Ayr** (MRChannon) **2-8-11** PaulEddery(1) (bit bkwd: nvr nr to chal) ..................................................7 | 8 | 10/1 | 36 | — |
| 2195[14] | **Sharp Poppet** (MBell) **2-8-4**(7) GFaulkner(7) (outpcd: wl bhd whn hung lft 3f out: no hdwy)...........................2½ | 9 | 50/1 | 30 | — |
| 2374[11] | **Rotherfield Queen (IRE)** (GMMcCourt) **2-8-11** VSlattery(2) (prom tl wknd 3f out) .........................................8 | 10 | 50/1 | 8 | — |
| | | | (SP 112.3%) | | **10 Rn** |

**1m 15.5** (5.00) CSF £33.85 TOTE £2.30: £1.10 £3.50 £1.30 (£22.40) Trio £26.10 OWNER Mr Mohamed Suhail (MARLBOROUGH) BRED Gainsborough Stud Management Ltd

**2504 Dancing Drop**, always disputing the lead on the stands' rail, quickened nicely approaching the final furlong and held on well. (5/4)
**Princess Topaz** ran an astonishing race. Well behind and not travelling, she suddenly began to realise what was required when shaken up in earnest below the distance. She was absolutely flying in the final furlong, and her rider appeared to ease her somewhat prematurely close home when she might still have gained an unlikely win. (33/1)
**Inflation** made an encouraging debut. Travelling strongly on the heels of the leaders for much of the way, she spoiled her chance by edging to her left in the final furlong. She should be better for the experience. (4/1)
**Nopalea** held a narrow lead until approaching the final furlong and kept on under pressure. She should be able to win a race. (20/1)
**Papita (IRE)**, outpaced in the early stages, made ground rapidly at halfway but could find no extra approaching the final furlong. (33/1)
**Hadawah (USA)** went with the leaders but, when hard driven two furlongs from home, soon began to weaken. (7/2: op 6/4)
**Danish Ayr** (10/1: 8/1-25/1)

## 2742 DNB LONDON SILVER JUBILEE RATED STKS H'CAP (0-95) (3-Y.O+) (Class C)

7-30 (7-31) **1m 2f 7y** £4,763.56 (£1,782.04: £871.02: £374.10: £167.05: £84.23) Stalls: High GOING minus 0.22 sec per fur (GF)

| | | | | SP | RR | SF |
|---|---|---|---|---|---|---|
| 2326* | **Double Bluff (IRE) (85)** (IABalding) **3-7-10**(5) MartinDwyer(2) (mde all: r.o wl) | — | **1** | 7/1[3] | 96 | 49 |
| 2502[13] | **Special Dawn (IRE) (88)** (JLDunlop) **6-9-1** PatEddery(8) (rdn & hdwy 4f out: chsd wnr fnl f: r.o) | 2 | **2** | 4/1[2] | 96 | 60 |
| | **Rokeby Bowl (94)** (IABalding) **4-9-7** TQuinn(5) (bit bkwd: hld up in rr: hdwy 3f out: styd on) | 2½ | **3** | 11/1 | 98 | 62 |
| 2608* | **Freedom Flame (81)** (MJohnston) **3-7-11** 3x TWilliams(7) (chsd wnr: hrd rdn 3f out: wknd fnl f) | hd | **4** | 11/8[1] | 85 | 38 |
| 1434* | **Mount Row (85)** (LMCumani) **3-8-1** PRobinson(4) (a.p: ev ch 2f out: one pce) | 1½ | **5** | 4/1[2] | 86 | 39 |
| 674[11] | **Coachella (83)** (MJRyan) **3-7-13** WCarson(1) (reins broke sn after s: prom tl outpcd 5f out: styd on fnl f) | ¾ | **6** | 16/1 | 83 | 36 |
| 1961[8] | **Willie Conquer (80)** (RAkehurst) **4-8-7** SSanders(6) (rdn & outpcd 5f out: no ch after) | 1¾ | **7** | 20/1 | 77 | 41 |

(SP 113.6%) **7 Rn**

**2m 7.2** (2.30) CSF £32.48 CT £277.19 TOTE £6.80: £2.20 £2.80 (£12.00) OWNER Mr J. C. Smith (KINGSCLERE) BRED Littleton Stud

WEIGHT FOR AGE 3yo-11lb

**OFFICIAL EXPLANATION Willie Conquer: lost his action.**

**2326* Double Bluff (IRE)** made all the running. He had his opponents in trouble a long way out and galloped on strongly. (7/1)

**925 Special Dawn (IRE)** had to be ridden to make headway in the straight. Finding a clear run on the inside, he took second place approaching the final furlong but, despite the hardest driving, could not catch the winner. (4/1)

**Rokeby Bowl**, held up in last place, moved up steadily three furlongs from home. It appeared momentarily that he might trouble his stable-companion, but he could not sustain his effort in the last furlong. He will be better for the race. (11/1)

**2608* Freedom Flame**, soon racing in second place, was being hard driven to stay near the winner from three furlongs out and faded in the final furlong. (11/8)

**1434* Mount Row**, close up from the start, still had every chance two furlongs out but soon dropped back beaten. (4/1: 3/1-9/2)

**Coachella**, whose reins broke soon after the start, did well in the circumstances to finish sixth. (16/1)

## 2743 VELO FLEET MANAGEMENT H'CAP (0-70) (3-Y.O+ F & M) (Class E)

8-00 (8-02) **1m 67y** £3,143.75 (£950.00: £462.50: £96.88: £96.88) Stalls: High GOING: minus 0.22 sec per fur (GF)

| | | | | SP | RR | SF |
|---|---|---|---|---|---|---|
| 2405[3] | **Rubbiyati (46)** (CEBrittain) **4-8-9** BDoyle(2) (a.p: led over 1f out: r.o wl) | — | **1** | 16/1 | 60 | 29 |
| 1641[3] | **Budby (62)** (ACStewart) **3-9-2** MRoberts(8) (lw: a.p: hrd rdn & led wl over 1f out: sn hdd: nt qckn) | 1½ | **2** | 4/1[1] | 73 | 33 |
| 2313[3] | **Bakers Daughter (47)** (JRArnold) **4-8-5**(5) MartinDwyer(7) (wl bhd tl gd hdwy fnl 2f: nvr nrr) | 1¼ | **3** | 14/1 | 56 | 25 |
| 2581[2] | **Emily-Mou (IRE) (65)** (MJRyan) **4-10-0** WCarson(11) (w ldr: led over 3f out tl wl over 1f out: nt qckn) | ¾ | **4** | 5/1[2] | 72 | 41 |
| 2567[2] | **Rainbows Rhapsody (34)** (DWChapman) **5-7-11**ow1 TWilliams(4) (gd hdwy & swtchd lft 2f out: nrst fin) | d.h | **4** | 10/1 | 41 | 9 |
| 2246[4] | **Summerhill Special (IRE) (57)** (MrsPNDutfield) **5-8-13b**(7) AimeeCook(9) (hdwy 4f out: styd on ins fnl f) | nk | **6** | 10/1 | 64 | 33 |
| 2032[8] | **Cuban Reef (45)** (WJMusson) **4-8-1**(7) JWilkinson(5) (b: stdy hdwy 3f out: nvr plcd to chal) | 3 | **7** | 20/1 | 46 | 15 |
| *2085*[8] | **Ladybower (IRE) (35)** (LordHuntingdon) **4-7-9**(3) MHenry(16) (lw: nvr bttr than mid div) | ¾ | **8** | 33/1 | 35 | 4 |
| 2339* | **Princess Pamgaddy (50)** (PFICole) **3-8-4**ow1 TQuinn(14) (hdwy & nt clr run over 2f out: wknd over 1f out) | 2 | **9** | 11/2[3] | 46 | 5 |
| 2540[5] | **Zdenka (51)** (MBlanshard) **3-8-5** JQuinn(6) (chsd ldrs: ev ch over 2f out: sn wknd) | 1½ | **10** | 25/1 | 44 | 4 |
| 739[6] | **Pendley Rose (60)** (PWHarris) **3-9-0** PatEddery(13) (rdn over 2f out: nvr nr to chal) | 2 | **11** | 8/1 | 49 | 9 |
| 2286[6] | **Cedar Dancer (33)** (RJHodges) **4-7-10** NAdams(3) (bhd most of wy) | ¾ | **12** | 50/1 | 20 | — |
| 2286[11] | **Hawanafa (51)** (RHannon) **3-8-2**(3)ow1 DaneO'Neill(1) (lw: a bhd) | s.h | **13** | 25/1 | 38 | — |
| 2186[5] | **Nellie North (63)** (GMMcCourt) **3-9-3** JReid(15) (chsd ldrs: wkng whn hmpd over 2f out) | 4 | **14** | 16/1 | 43 | 3 |
| 2373[3] | **Noeprob (USA) (55)** (RJHodges) **6-9-4** PaulEddery(10) (led tl wknd over 3f out) | ½ | **15** | 9/1 | 34 | 3 |
| 2061[5] | **Indira (55)** (HCandy) **3-8-9** CRutter(12) (prom tl wknd 3f out) | hd | **16** | 16/1 | 34 | — |

(SP 133.0%) **16 Rn**

**1m 47.0** (4.80) CSF £79.94 CT £888.78 TOTE £28.00: £4.80 £1.80 £2.90 EM £0.80 RR £1.50 (£57.80) Trio £297.70 OWNER Wyck Hall Stud (NEWMARKET) BRED Gainsborough Stud Management Ltd

LONG HANDICAP Rainbows Rhapsody 7-7

WEIGHT FOR AGE 3yo-9lb

STEWARDS' ENQUIRY Reid susp. 24-25/7/96 (careless riding).

**2405 Rubbiyati**, always close up, was driven along to dispute the lead three furlongs out. She gained a definite advantage approaching the final furlong, and stayed on strongly. (16/1)

**1641 Budby**, close up from the start, had to be hard driven to take a narrow lead below the distance. Soon headed, she kept on, but could not quicken with the winner. (4/1: 3/1-9/2)

**2313 Bakers Daughter** was a long way behind for much of the trip and still looked hopelessly placed at the two-furlong marker, but she finished tremendously fast and would have troubled the first two with a little further to go. (14/1: 10/1-16/1)

**2581 Emily-Mou (IRE)** raced in second place until taking up the running over three furlongs out. She kept on in her usual game style, but was tapped for toe in the final furlong and a half. (5/1)

**2567 Rainbows Rhapsody,** who sat at the back of the field for much of the way, found a good turn of foot when switched to the centre of the course. Although she finished strongly, she could not catch the leaders. (10/1: 7/1-11/1)

**2246 Summerhill Special (IRE)**, dropped in distance, raced in midfield but was struggling to find the pace to challenge from a long way out. He was staying on at the finish and will probably do better when returning to a longer trip. (10/1)

**1613 Cuban Reef** ran a lot better than his final position of seventh would suggest. He was going on in the closing stages and should be able to win a race. (20/1)

**2339* Princess Pamgaddy** (11/2: 4/1-6/1)

**739 Pendley Rose** (8/1: 5/1-10/1)

## 2744 HAMBROS INDEPENDENT MAIDEN STKS (3-Y.O) (Class D)

8-30 (8-35) **1m 2f 7y** £3,753.00 (£1,134.00: £552.00: £261.00) Stalls: High GOING minus 0.22 sec per fur (GF)

| | | | | SP | RR | SF |
|---|---|---|---|---|---|---|
| 2333[2] | **Unitus (IRE)** (MRStoute) **3-9-0** JReid(7) (a gng wl: led over 1f out: easily) | — | **1** | 6/4[1] | 84+ | 50 |
| 1690[2] | **Sea of Stone (USA)** (LMCumani) **3-8-9** PatEddery(3) (a.p: hrd rdn 2f out: r.o ins fnl f: no ch w wnr) | 5 | **2** | 9/4[2] | 71 | 37 |
| 2197[10] | **Llyswen** (JHMGosden) **3-9-0** BThomson(2) (lw: a.p: led over 4f out: hrd rdn 3f out: hdd over 1f out: one pce) | ¾ | **3** | 25/1 | 75 | 41 |
| 2181[3] | **Seeking Fortune (USA)** (JRFanshawe) **3-8-9** TQuinn(10) (unf: led 1f: a.p: ev ch 2f out: one pce) | 1 | **4** | 9/2[3] | 68 | 34 |
| 1319[7] | **Far Dawn (USA)** (GHarwood) **3-9-0** AClark(5) (lw: hdwy 3f out: one pce fnl 2f) | 1¾ | **5** | 33/1 | 70 | 36 |
| 2365[2] | **Taharqa (IRE)** (JHMGosden) **3-9-0** WRyan(4) (lw: hdwy over 3f out: styd on: nt pce to chal) | 1 | **6** | 11/2 | 69 | 35 |
| 2004[8] | **Mr Hacker** (GThorner) **3-8-11**(3) DaneO'Neill(1) (led after 1f tl over 4f out: sn wknd) | 17 | **7** | 66/1 | 42 | 8 |
| | **Golden Fawn** (LadyHerries) **3-8-9e** PaulEddery(12) (a bhd) | 2½ | **8** | 20/1 | 33 | — |

| | | | | SP | RR | SF |
|---|---|---|---|---|---|---|
| 2135[12] | **Foreign Judgement (USA) (64)** (WJMusson) **3-9-0** BDoyle(8) (lw: a bhd) | 2 | **9** | 50/1 | 35 | 1 |
| 2432[13] | **Topup** (JWHills) **3-9-0** MHills(9) (a bhd) | 6 | **10** | 33/1 | 25 | — |
| | **Bolder Still** (RTPhillips) **3-9-0** RPerham(6) (w'like: bit bkwd: prom tl wknd over 3f out) | 12 | **11** | 33/1 | 6 | — |
| 2399[9] | **Aravinda (IRE)** (LadyHerries) **3-8-9** DeclanO'Shea(11) (a bhd) | 10 | **12** | 33/1 | — | — |
| | | | | (SP 128.2%) | **12 Rn** | |

**2m 8.7** (3.80) CSF £5.70 TOTE £3.30: £1.40 £1.20 £3.80 (£3.50) Trio £28.50 OWNER Sheikh Mohammed (NEWMARKET) BRED Sheikh Mohammed bin Rashid al Maktoum

**2333 Unitus (IRE)** was always cruising on the heels of the leaders. He was still on the bridle when taking up the running approaching the final furlong, and needed only a couple of nudges from his rider to go clear. (6/4)

**1690 Sea of Stone (USA)**, close up from the start, was being ridden some way out. She kept staying on and took second place inside the final furlong without being any danger to the winner. (9/4: op 6/4)

**2197 Llyswen** went to the front early in the straight, but was soon under hard driving. When the winner cruised past him approaching the final furlong, he stayed on at one pace. (25/1)

**2181 Seeking Fortune (USA)** disputed the lead from the start and still had every chance two furlongs out, but she then found the winner far too good, and could find no more in the final furlong. (9/2)

**892 Far Dawn (USA)** improved from the rear of the field to the mid-division approaching the three-furlong marker, and kept staying on to the end. An inexperienced sort, she will be better for the outing. (33/1)

**2365 Taharqa (IRE)** tagged onto the back of the leading group three furlongs out and, though unable to quicken in the final quarter-mile, she gave the impression that there is better to come. (11/2: 5/2-6/1)

## 2745 RUDER FINN H'CAP (0-60) (3-Y.O+) (Class F)

9-00 (9-02) **5f 10y** £3,030.00 (£915.00: £445.00: £210.00) Stalls: High GOING minus 0.22 sec per fur (GF)

| | | | | SP | RR | SF |
|---|---|---|---|---|---|---|
| 2496[11] | **Bowcliffe Grange (IRE) (44)** (DWChapman) **4-9-1b** JQuinn(12) (mde all: qcknd clr over 1f out: unchal) | — | **1** | 4/1[1] | 56 | 38 |
| 2564[7] | **The Institute Boy (44)** (MissJFCraze) **6-9-1** NConnorton(9) (a.p: hrd rdn fnl 2f: chsd wnr fnl f: no imp) | 4 | **2** | 10/1 | 43 | 25 |
| 2255[8] | **Oscilights Gift (25)** (PBurgoyne) **4-7-10** NAdams(11) (a.p: r.o ins fnl f) | ¾ | **3** | 33/1 | 22 | 4 |
| 2500[4] | **Mindrace (59)** (KTIvory) **3-9-11** BDoyle(7) (a.p: rdn 2f out: styd on) | ¾ | **4** | 9/1[3] | 54 | 31 |
| | **Runs in the Family (52)** (GMMcCourt) **4-9-9b** JReid(10) (chsd wnr tl wknd fnl f) | ½ | **5** | 10/1 | 45 | 27 |
| 2286[5] | **Petraco (IRE) (57)** (NASmith) **8-10-0** PaulEddery(6) (nvr bttr than mid div) | 3 | **6** | 10/1 | 41 | 23 |
| 2340[13] | **Elraas (USA) (25)** (HJCollingridge) **4-7-3v[1](7)** RMullen(8) (dwlt: sn prom: wknd over 1f out) | 1 | **7** | 33/1 | 5 | — |
| *2555*[2] | **Delrob (44)** (DHaydnJones) **5-9-1v** TQuinn(5) (sn bhd: rdn over 2f out: nvr nrr) | ½ | **8** | 4/1[1] | 23 | 5 |
| *2305*[5] | **Diebiedale (48)** (RBoss) **4-9-5** PatEddery(13) (lw: nvr nr to chal) | s.h | **9** | 10/1 | 27 | 9 |
| 2598[7] | **Cedar Girl (40)** (RJHodges) **4-8-6**(5) AmandaSanders(4) (outpcd) | 1½ | **10** | 20/1 | 14 | — |
| 2186[3] | **Raisa Point (39)** (WRMuir) **5-8-10** MRoberts(1) (nvr bttr than mid div) | 1½ | **11** | 10/1 | 8 | — |
| *273*[5] | **Desert Water (IRE) (38)** (TMJones) **4-8-9** AMcGlone(3) (a bhd) | 2 | **12** | 25/1 | 1 | — |
| 2403[7] | **Another Batchworth (55)** (EAWheeler) **4-9-12** RPerham(14) (a bhd) | 4 | **13** | 5/1[2] | 5 | — |
| 2598[4] | **The Noble Oak (IRE) (34)** (MJBolton) **8-8-5** GBardwell(2) (a bhd) | s.h | **14** | 25/1 | — | — |
| | | | | (SP 130.5%) | **14 Rn** | |

**61.7 secs** (2.50) CSF £44.10 CT £1,101.08 TOTE £6.00: £2.20 £3.70 £17.30 (£32.20) Trio £692.90; £878.45 to 17/7/96 OWNER Mr David Chapman (YORK) BRED Rosemount House Stud

LONG HANDICAP Oscilights Gift 7-5

WEIGHT FOR AGE 3yo-5lb

**2324 Bowcliffe Grange (IRE)**, very fast away, made it all. He quickened clear approaching the final furlong, and can follow up. (4/1)

**1545 The Institute Boy**, never far behind the leaders, was being hard driven soon after halfway. He kept staying on, but had no chance with the winner. (10/1: 8/1-12/1)

**Oscilights Gift**, always in the first half-dozen, was switched to challenge approaching the final furlong. She stayed on, but was never near the winner. (33/1)

**2500 Mindrace**, in midfield to halfway, stayed on under pressure in the last two furlongs without being able to land a blow. (9/1)

**Runs in the Family** raced in second place, albeit at a respectful distance from the winner, until weakening in the final furlong. (10/1)

**2286 Petraco (IRE)**, in midfield for much of the trip, never held out any hope. (10/1)

**2555 Delrob** broke well enough but was soon struggling to go the pace. He was at the back of the field and under pressure at halfway until making a little late headway. (4/1)

T/Plpt: £51.90 (353.02 Tckts). T/Qdpt: £42.80 (26.74 Tckts). Hn

# 2631-WOLVERHAMPTON (L-H) (Standard)

## Monday July 15th

WEATHER: sunny & warm WIND: slt against

## 2746 E.B.F. CARLING PREMIER MAIDEN STKS (2-Y.O) (Class D)

6-45 (6-45) **6f (Fibresand)** £3,477.60 (£1,036.80: £494.40: £223.20) Stalls: Low GOING minus 0.02 sec per fur (STD)

| | | | | SP | RR | SF |
|---|---|---|---|---|---|---|
| 2404[3] | **Dayville (USA)** (RCharlton) **2-8-9** TSprake(6) (b: w ldr: led over 3f out: drvn clr appr fnl f) | — | **1** | 5/2[1] | 69 | 22 |
| 2404[5] | **Mudflap** (SirMarkPrescott) **2-8-9** GDuffield(3) (trckd ldrs: hrd drvn over 2f out: kpt on ins fnl f) | 6 | **2** | 3/1[2] | 53 | 6 |
| *2633*[5] | **The Wyandotte Inn** (RHollinshead) **2-8-9**(5) DGriffiths(4) (led over 2f: rdn wl over 1f out: one pce) | nk | **3** | 9/1 | 57 | 10 |
| 2122[3] | **Ben's Ridge** (PCHaslam) **2-9-0** DeanMcKeown(2) (lw: a.p: rdn over 1f out: sn outpcd) | 1¼ | **4** | 3/1[2] | 54 | 7 |
| 2491[4] | **Mirror Four Sport** (MJohnston) **2-8-9** JFanning(5) (lw: trckd ldrs: rdn & outpcd fnl 2f) | s.h | **5** | 8/1[3] | 49 | 2 |
| *2633*[6] | **Pretty Sally (IRE)** (DJGMurraySmith) **2-8-4**(5) PPMurphy(8) (hdwy ½-wy: rdn & wknd over 1f out) | 1 | **6** | 20/1 | 46 | — |
| | **One Lady** (JLEyre) **2-8-9** RLappin(7) (lt-f: unf: sn pushed along: a bhd) | 3 | **7** | 20/1 | 38 | — |
| 1827[7] | **Real Fire (IRE)** (MGMeagher) **2-9-0** MFenton(1) (a bhd & outpcd: t.o) | 6 | **8** | 16/1 | 27 | — |
| | | | | (SP 115.1%) | **8 Rn** | |

**1m 16.4** (5.00) CSF £10.09 TOTE £2.60: £1.20 £1.90 £2.20 (£3.90) OWNER Mr K. Abdulla (BECKHAMPTON) BRED Juddmonte Farms

**2404 Dayville (USA)**, friendless in the market, showed her true form on this run on Fibresand, but she will have trouble finding such a poor event again. (5/2: 6/4-11/4)

**2404 Mudflap** is not the finished article as yet, but she did stay on to gain the runner-up prize without ever promising to reach the winner. (3/1: op 9/2)

**2633 The Wyandotte Inn**, in the firing-line from the break, was struggling to hold on from the turn into the straight and could do little or nothing about it. (9/1)

**2122 Ben's Ridge**, having his first run on the All-Weather, raced with the pace and had every chance, but the quickening tempo proved too much for him from below the distance. (3/1)
**2491 Mirror Four Sport** held her pitch in the chasing group until failing to pick up when the battle to the finish really got under way. (8/1)

## 2747 WEST MIDLANDS TRAVEL CLAIMING STKS (3 & 4-Y.O) (Class F)

7-15 (7-15) **1m 6f 166y (Fibresand)** £2,381.00 (£656.00: £311.00) Stalls: High GOING minus 0.02 sec per fur (STD)

| Form | Horse | Dist | Pos | SP | RR | SF |
|---|---|---|---|---|---|---|
| *2368*[2] | **Los Alamos (65)** (CWThornton) **3-8-7** DeanMcKeown(5) (lw: a.p: led 5f out: rdn over 3f out: styd on strly) | — | 1 | 4/5[1] | 70 | 18 |
| 2355[4] | **Balios (IRE) (69)** (MJohnston) **3-8-8** JFanning(4) (led to 5f out: hrd rdn & edgd lft 1f out: sn btn) | 3 | 2 | 3/1[2] | 68 | 16 |
| 2577[11] | **Sister Kit (IRE) (60)** (BPalling) **3-8-1** TSprake(3) (hld up & bhd: effrt & pushed along over 3f out: sn lost tch) | 13 | 3 | 8/1 | 47 | — |
| | **Hill Farm Blues** (JLEyre) **3-8-3** RLappin(1) (lt-f: unf: s.s: hdwy 8f out: outpcd over 3f out: sn bhd) | 5 | 4 | 9/2[3] | 43 | — |
| | **Galloping Guns (IRE)** (BJLlewellyn) **4-8-13**(3) FLynch(2) (s.s: plld hrd: sn prom: dropped rr ½-wy: t.o) | dist | 5 | 25/1 | — | — |
| | | | | (SP 113.7%) | | **5 Rn** |

**3m 21.1** (13.70) CSF £3.70 TOTE £1.70: £1.30 £1.80 (£1.60) OWNER Mr Guy Reed (MIDDLEHAM) BRED G. Reed
WEIGHT FOR AGE 3yo-17lb
**2368 Los Alamos** found this extended trip made to measure and finally broke her duck, but she did have to do battle before the prize was hers. (4/5: tchd Evens)
**2355 Balios (IRE)** gave the winner a hard time and only lost out when his stamina gave way inside the final furlong. (3/1: op 2/1)
**1839 Sister Kit (IRE)** did not appear to see the trip out after moving into a challenging position down the back straight. (8/1: 4/1-10/1)
**Hill Farm Blues** looked as fit as a flea on this racecourse debut, but she was in trouble turning out of the back straight and it is hoped she can improve on this. (9/2: op 10/1)

## 2748 RENAULT WOLVERHAMPTON NEW CAR FOR AUGUST LIMITED STKS (0-55) (3-Y.O+) (Class F)

7-45 (7-45) **5f (Fibresand)** £2,381.00 (£656.00: £311.00) Stalls: Low GOING minus 0.02 sec per fur (STD)

| Form | Horse | Dist | Pos | SP | RR | SF |
|---|---|---|---|---|---|---|
| 2598[6] | **Need You Badly (55)** (SPCWoods) **3-8-8** WWoods(8) (a.p: shkn up to ld ins fnl f: r.o) | — | 1 | 8/1 | 58 | 23 |
| 2598[5] | **Lloc (52)** (CADwyer) **4-8-9**(7) JoHunnam(9) (b: a.p: slt ld wl over 1f out tl ins fnl f: no ex) | 1 | 2 | 5/1[2] | 58 | 28 |
| *2367*[4] | **Monis (IRE) (54)** (JBalding) **5-8-9v**(7) JEdmunds(1) (lw: trckd ldrs: rdn & r.o wl ins fnl f) | 1¼ | 3 | 10/1 | 54 | 24 |
| 2240[6] | **Naughty Pistol (USA) (49)** (PDEvans) **4-8-13** MFenton(6) (prom: outpcd 2f out: rallied u.p ins fnl f) | s.h | 4 | 10/1 | 51 | 21 |
| *2555** | **Napier Star (55)** (MrsNMacauley) **3-8-11**(3) CTeague(7) (lw: s.i.s: bhd & outpcd tl r.o ins fnl f) | 1¼ | 5 | 7/2[1] | 53 | 18 |
| *2550*[9] | **Brookhead Lady (52)** (PDEvans) **5-8-13** DBiggs(11) (b.nr fore: sn pushed along: nvr gng pce of ldrs) | 1¼ | 6 | 16/1 | 43 | 13 |
| *122*[12] | **Superbit (47)** (BAMcMahon) **4-9-2** GDuffield(5) (bkwd: sn drvn along: a outpcd) | 1½ | 7 | 7/1[3] | 41 | 11 |
| 2578[4] | **Scathebury (55)** (KRBurke) **3-8-8**(3) FLynch(2) (lw: s.i.s: hdwy on ins ½-wy: wknd over 1f out) | 2 | 8 | 5/1[2] | 34 | — |
| 2386[8] | **Lochon (55)** (JLEyre) **5-9-3**(3)ow1 OPears(4) (outpcd) | 2 | 9 | 16/1 | 32 | 1 |
| | **Super Sonata (52)** (TWall) **4-8-13** JFanning(3) (bkwd: a in rr & outpcd: t.o) | 6 | 10 | 33/1 | 6 | — |
| *2555*[7] | **Bajan Frontier (IRE) (41)** (FHLee) **4-8-13v** GCarter(10) (led: sn clr: wknd & hdd wl over 1f out: t.o) | ¾ | 11 | 16/1 | 3 | — |
| | | | | (SP 117.9%) | | **11 Rn** |

**62.7 secs** (4.00) CSF £44.69 TOTE £8.00: £2.10 £2.10 £3.10 (£17.60) Trio £83.60 OWNER Mr Arashan Ali (NEWMARKET) BRED Sexton Enterprises
WEIGHT FOR AGE 3yo-5lb
**2598 Need You Badly** did well to turn the tables on the runner-up on these worse terms, and needed to pull out all the stops to do so. (8/1)
**2598 Lloc**, who has been kept busy in recent weeks, looked to have the edge when gaining a narrow lead into the straight, but the winner responded to strong pressure and took her measure nearing the line. (5/1)
**2367 Monis (IRE)**, having only his second ever run over this minimum trip, pushed the pace and kept on particularly well in the closing stages. Sprinting would seem to be his game. (10/1)
**Naughty Pistol (USA)**, a winner of three races at sprint distances in the States, got tapped for toe on the home turn, but she came back with all guns blazing inside the last furlong, and may well need a straight track to produce her true form. (10/1)
**2555* Napier Star**, last to exit from the stalls, did a lot of running to finish so close and, if excuses are needed, she was probably the unlucky one of the race. (7/2)
**2212 Brookhead Lady** struggles to go the pace at this trip and she was never in a position to pose a threat. (16/1)
**Superbit** (7/1: op 16/1)

## 2749 BEAZER HOMES H'CAP (0-75) (3-Y.O+) (Class D)

8-15 (8-16) **1m 1f 79y (Fibresand)** £4,426.05 (£1,322.40: £632.70: £287.85) Stalls: Low GOING: minus 0.02 sec per fur (STD)

| Form | Horse | Dist | Pos | SP | RR | SF |
|---|---|---|---|---|---|---|
| *2168** | **Halebid (70)** (SPCWoods) **3-8-13** WWoods(12) (lw: hld up: hdwy 4f out: rdn to ld ins fnl f: jst hld on) | — | 1 | 13/2[3] | 83 | 45 |
| 2678[U] | **Giftbox (USA) (48)** (SirMarkPrescott) **4-8-1** GDuffield(5) (lw: a.p: hrd drvn 2f out: sustained chal fnl f: jst failed) | hd | 2 | 2/1[1] | 61 | 33 |
| *2306*[5] | **Heathyards Lady (USA) (68)** (RHollinshead) **5-9-4**(3) FLynch(11) (hld up: hdwy 4f out: swtchd lft ins fnl f: r.o wl) | 1½ | 3 | 10/1 | 78 | 50 |
| *2169*[2] | **Sweet Supposin (IRE) (70)** (JohnBerry) **5-9-2v**(7) JoHunnam(8) (led over 6f out tl hdd & wknd ins fnl f) | 1¼ | 4 | 12/1 | 78 | 50 |
| *2369*[2] | **Fatehalkhair (IRE) (43)** (BEllison) **4-7-3**(7) IonaWands(9) (hld up: effrt & pushed along ½-wy: wknd over 1f out) | 6 | 5 | 14/1 | 41 | 13 |
| *2689*[2] | **Nose No Bounds (IRE) (62)** (MJohnston) **3-8-5v**[1] JFanning(2) (hld up: hdwy & drvn along 4f out: hrd rdn & wknd over 1f out) | 2 | 6 | 9/2[2] | 57 | 19 |
| *2552*[2] | **Johnnie the Joker (77)** (JPLeigh) **5-10-2b** DeanMcKeown(7) (led 3f: drvn over 2f out: sn btn) | s.h | 7 | 10/1 | 71 | 43 |
| 1983[5] | **Zatopek (55)** (JCullinan) **4-8-8** GCarter(4) (trckd ldrs: rdn along ½-wy: bhd fnl 3f) | ¾ | 8 | 25/1 | 48 | 20 |
| *2551*[3] | **Sandmoor Denim (63)** (SRBowring) **9-8-9**(7) JEdmunds(1) (a bhd: t.o) | 7 | 9 | 14/1 | 44 | 16 |
| 1780[2] | **Yeoman Oliver (73)** (BAMcMahon) **3-8-11**(5) LNewton(6) (lw: trckd ldrs 6f: sn rdn & wknd: t.o) | 11 | 10 | 12/1 | 35 | — |
| 2514[9] | **Mercury (IRE) (72)** (JAGlover) **3-9-1** SDWilliams(10) (a in rr: rdn 4f out: no rspsne: t.o) | 5 | 11 | 8/1 | 26 | — |
| 2251[12] | **Express Routing (51)** (JAkehurst) **4-8-4b**[1] TSprake(3) (b: b.hind: plld hrd: prom tl wknd 5f out: t.o) | dist | 12 | 14/1 | — | — |
| | | | | (SP 133.4%) | | **12 Rn** |

**2m 1.9** (5.90) CSF £21.36 CT £131.71 TOTE £10.50: £3.10 £2.10 £2.40 (£17.40) Trio £79.90 OWNER Mr S. P. C. Woods (NEWMARKET) BRED Top Spin Co Ltd
LONG HANDICAP Fatehalkhair (IRE) 7-7
WEIGHT FOR AGE 3yo-10lb
STEWARDS' ENQUIRY Duffield susp. 24-25/7/96 (excessive use of the whip).
**2168* Halebid** followed up his success over course and distance last month, but had to work much harder in this higher grade to hold off the persistent favourite. (13/2)

**2678 Giftbox (USA)** did not take kindly to the All-Weather at Southwell in the spring and he was at full stretch a long way out here. With the aid of a very determined ride, he only just failed to peg back the winner. (2/1)
**2306 Heathyards Lady (USA)** followed the winner through, but she had to be switched at a crucial time and, losing her momentum, was unable to recover. (10/1: 8/1-12/1)
**2169 Sweet Supposin (IRE)** adopted more forceful tactics and was only forced to give best in the last 200 yards. (12/1: op 8/1)
**2369 Fatehalkhair (IRE)** tried to mount a challenge from midfield on the home turn, but could not muster the pace to get competitive. (14/1)
**2689 Nose No Bounds (IRE)** had reached the heels of the leaders at the end of the back straight, but he had to work hard to get there and his effort petered out once in line for home. (9/2)
**1780 Yeoman Oliver** (12/1: op 6/1)

## 2750 CABLE TV & TELEPHONE (S) STKS (2-Y.O) (Class G)
8-45 (8-46) **7f (Fibresand)** £2,070.00 (£570.00: £270.00) Stalls: High GOING minus 0.02 sec per fur (STD)

| | | | | SP | RR | SF |
|---|---|---|---|---|---|---|
| $2606^{2}$ | **Our Kevin** (KMcAuliffe) **2-9-2v** DRMcCabe(7) (dwlt: hdwy over 3f out: led ins fnl f: edgd lft: r.o) | — | 1 | 5/4 [1] | 64 | 5 |
| *$2307^{6}$* | **Bali-Pet** (WGMTurner) **2-8-5**(5) RHavlin(4) (led after 2f tl ins fnl f: no ex nr fin) | ¾ | 2 | 33/1 | 56 | — |
| $2315^{6}$ | **Soviet Lady (IRE)** (JLEyre) **2-8-5** RLappin(5) (a.p: ev ch fnl f: n.m.r 100y out: r.o nr fin) | nk | 3 | 6/1 | 51 | — |
| *$1813^{3}$* | **Perfect Bliss** (PDEvans) **2-8-5** MFenton(3) (led 2f: ev ch 1f out: wknd ins fnl f) | 3 | 4 | 7/2 [2] | 44 | — |
| $1645^{7}$ | **Ekaterini Paritsi** (WGMTurner) **2-8-5b** TSprake(2) (a bhd: hrd rdn 3f out: t.o) | 6 | 5 | 9/2 [3] | 30 | — |
| $2387^{4}$ | **Sweeping Statement** (JBerry) **2-8-5** GCarter(6) (lw: s.i.s: sn wnt prom: hrd rdn & wknd 2f out: t.o) | 1½ | 6 | 7/1 | 27 | — |
| $2429^{6}$ | **Billycan (IRE)** (BPJBaugh) **2-8-10v**[1] WLord(1) (outpcd: t.o fr ½-wy) | 1½ | 7 | 33/1 | 28 | — |
| | | | | (SP 117.5%) | **7 Rn** | |

**1m 32.8** (0.40 under 2y best) (8.10) CSF £30.15 TOTE £2.00: £1.20 £8.40 (£32.70) OWNER Mr T. Mohan (LAMBOURN) BRED J. Vaughan
Bt in 7,200gns
**2606 Our Kevin** did it the hard way after losing ground at the start and then almost threw it away by drifting off a true line inside the final furlong, but his jockey soon had the situation under control. (5/4)
**Bali-Pet** knew much more this time and, in only being shaken off in the closing stages, gave notice that his turn is near. (33/1)
**2315 Soviet Lady (IRE)** was the one getting tightened up when challenging for the lead inside the final furlong, but she did keep running and it would be wrong to say she was unlucky. (6/1: op 4/1)
**1813 Perfect Bliss,** one of four in line entering the final furlong, was the first to crack, and this initial run at this longer trip could have caught her out. (7/2)
**1459 Ekaterini Paritsi** (9/2: 3/1-5/1)

## 2751 BENHAM BMW MAIDEN H'CAP (0-65) (3-Y.O) (Class F)
9-15 (9-17) **1m 4f (Fibresand)** £2,381.00 (£656.00: £311.00) Stalls: Low GOING minus 0.02 sec per fur (STD)

| | | | | SP | RR | SF |
|---|---|---|---|---|---|---|
| $2683^{2}$ | **Newbridge Boy (52)** (MGMeagher) **3-8-13** DRMcCabe(7) (mde all: hrd drvn 2f out: styd on strly) | — | 1 | 7/2 [2] | 63 | 32 |
| $2432^{9}$ | **Moonraking (49)** (TJEtherington) **3-8-10** GCarter(8) (s.i.s: hdwy over 7f out: hrd drvn 2f out: styd on wl nr fin) | nk | 2 | 3/1 [1] | 60 | 29 |
| $2251^{13}$ | **Pleasureland (IRE) (60)** (PJMakin) **3-9-2**(5) RHavlin(4) (hdwy 8f out: rdn & outpcd over 3f out: kpt on fnl f) | 9 | 3 | 10/1 | 59 | 28 |
| $2120^{10}$ | **Indiphar (46)** (FHLee) **3-8-7** GDuffield(2) (trckd ldrs: rdn along ½-wy: one pce fnl 2f) | 2½ | 4 | 6/1 | 41 | 10 |
| $2540^{4}$ | **Fikra (USA) (59)** (SPCWoods) **3-9-6** WWoods(1) (prom tl rdn & lost tch 3f out) | 9 | 5 | 4/1 [3] | 42 | 11 |
| $2506^{11}$ | **Clued Up (43)** (PDEvans) **3-8-4** DBiggs(5) (hld up: hdwy over 3f out: wknd wl over 1f out) | 5 | 6 | 20/1 | 20 | — |
| *$269^{7}$* | **Bluntswood Hall (35)** (RHollinshead) **3-7-10** NCarlisle(9) (bkwd: a in rr: t.o) | 10 | 7 | 16/1 | — | — |
| $2506^{6}$ | **Red Tie Affair (USA) (57)** (MBell) **3-9-4v**[1] MFenton(10) (b.nr fore: lw: prom: rdn over 3f out: sn wknd: t.o) | 2½ | 8 | 6/1 | 17 | — |
| | **Dino's Mistral (40)** (FHLee) **3-8-1** TSprake(6) (bit bkwd: hld up: gd hdwy over 5f out: rdn & wknd 3f out: t.o) | 7 | 9 | 20/1 | — | — |
| *$1814^{8}$* | **Balmoral Princess (35)** (JHPeacock) **3-7-3b**[1](7) IonaWands(3) (trckd ldrs to ½-wy: sn lost tch: t.o) | 2 | 10 | 33/1 | — | — |
| | | | | (SP 123.2%) | **10 Rn** | |

**2m 42.3** (9.80) CSF £14.66 CT £91.06 TOTE £3.70: £2.00 £1.60 £2.80 (£10.20) Trio £30.00 OWNER Mr Alan Draper (ORMSKIRK) BRED J. R. Wills
LONG HANDICAP Balmoral Princess 7-1
**2683 Newbridge Boy,** not winning out of turn, succeeded in making all, but the line arrived not a stride too soon. (7/2)
**1972 Moonraking,** having his first try at this longer trip, kept on relentlessly inside the distance and only just failed to gain the day. He is not the best of movers and will always need an easy surface. (3/1: op 6/1)
**Pleasureland (IRE)** found the leading pair much too strong for him in the latter stages and he was in trouble before reaching the straight. (10/1)
**1887 Indiphar,** off the bridle from halfway, did keep plugging away, but her measure had been taken on the home turn. (6/1)
**2540 Fikra (USA)** did not get home over this longer trip and she is not built to carry weight. (4/1)

T/Plpt: £29.00 (398.42 Tckts). T/Qdpt: £17.10 (48.5 Tckts). IM

# 2512-BEVERLEY (R-H) (Good to firm)
## Tuesday July 16th
WEATHER: fine WIND: fresh half bhd

## 2752 AST EUROPE APPRENTICE H'CAP (0-65) (3-Y.O) (Class F)
2-00 (2-02) **1m 100y** £2,997.25 (£664.75: £664.75: £198.25) Stalls: High GOING minus 0.57 sec per fur (F)

| | | | | SP | RR | SF |
|---|---|---|---|---|---|---|
| $2486^{8}$ | **Falcon's Flame (USA) (48)** (MrsJRRamsden) **3-8-4** FLynch(14) (lw: trckd ldrs: hdwy to ld 1½f out: hung lft: r.o) | — | 1 | 9/2 [2] | 57 | 13 |
| $2163^{2}$ | **Gulf of Siam (60)** (MissSEHall) **3-8-13**(3) MartinDwyer(9) (hld up: hdwy 3f out: swtchd over 1f out: styd on wl towards fin) | 1¼ | 2 | 9/2 [2] | 67 | 23 |
| $2425^{2}$ | **Mels Baby (IRE) (56)** (JLEyre) **3-8-12** MHenry(10) (chsd ldrs: outpcd over 2f out: kpt on wl towards fin) | d.h | 2 | 3/1 [1] | 63 | 19 |
| $2326^{4}$ | **Fairly Sure (IRE) (48)** (NEBerry) **3-7-13**(5) CAdamson(15) (cl up: chal over 2f out: nt qckn fnl f) | 1¼ | 4 | 12/1 | 52 | 8 |
| $2507^{3}$ | **Born A Lady (51)** (SRBowring) **3-8-2b**(5) JEdmunds(6) (lw: in tch: effrt 3f out: styd on: no imp) | ½ | 5 | 10/1 | 54 | 10 |
| $2356^{3}$ | **Contract Bridge (IRE) (48)** (CWThornton) **3-7-11**(7) GMills(1) (s.s: c wd st: sme late hdwy) | ¾ | 6 | 8/1 | 50 | 6 |
| $2563^{13}$ | **Cottage Prince (IRE) (42)** (JJQuinn) **3-7-12** DWright(8) (w ldr: led ½-wy to 1½f out: wknd) | ¾ | 7 | 16/1 | 43 | — |
| $2573^{3}$ | **Lucky Bea (60)** (MWEasterby) **3-8-11**(5) GParkin(2) (hld up: effrt 3f out: no imp) | 1¾ | 8 | 11/2 [3] | 57 | 13 |
| $1474^{10}$ | **Kudos Blue (43)** (JDBethell) **3-7-6**(7)ow3 NicolaStokes(12) (chsd ldrs: outpcd 3f out: no imp after) | 1½ | 9 | 50/1 | 37 | — |
| $2179^{4}$ | **Fisiostar (40)** (MDods) **3-7-10b** DarrenMoffatt(7) (b.hind: n.d) | 8 | 10 | 20/1 | 19 | — |

| | | | | | | |
|---|---|---|---|---|---|---|
| *2168*[12] | **Animation (50)** (KMcAuliffe) **3-8-1**(5) JBramhill(3) (lw: c wd st: no imp) | 5 | **11** | 33/1 | 20 | — |
| 2541[7] | **Sizzling Serenade (40)** (JAHarris) **3-7-5**(5) RMullen(5) (chsd ldrs 5f: wknd) | 3 | **12** | 33/1 | 4 | — |
| 2540[12] | **Totally Different (40)** (GROldroyd) **3-7-10v**[1] NVarley(4) (s.s: a bhd) | 14 | **13** | 33/1 | — | — |
| 2061[6] | **Rhythmic Ball (48)** (TRWatson) **3-7-13**(5) CWebb(13) (led to ½-wy: sn wknd) | 3 | **14** | 20/1 | — | — |

(SP 130.8%) **14 Rn**

**1m 47.2** (3.20) CSF £12.90 FF, GOS £9.50 FF, MB CT £34.22 FF, GOS, MB £31.75 FF, MB, GOS TOTE £5.80: £2.00 £1.90 GOS £1.40 MB (£11.40 FF, GOS £7.40 FF, MB) Trio £32.00 OWNER Mr Colin Webster (THIRSK) BRED Arthur B. Hancock III

LONG HANDICAP Kudos Blue 6-12 Fisiostar 7-2 Sizzling Serenade 7-0 Totally Different 7-2

**1477 Falcon's Flame (USA)** showed a superb action going to post and won nicely, despite hanging left. (9/2)

**2163 Gulf of Siam** looked dangerous early in the straight, but was then short of both pace and room and, despite keeping on at the finish, never looked likely to make it. (9/2)

**2425 Mels Baby (IRE)** is proving difficult to win with and lost his chance here by getting outpaced in the straight. Despite finishing well, he had set himself too stiff a task. (3/1)

**2326 Fairly Sure (IRE)** showed she is on good terms with herself this season and had every chance throughout, but was just short of toe when it mattered. (12/1)

**2507 Born A Lady** was always in a good enough position, but she lacked a turn of foot to do anything about it. (10/1)

**2356 Contract Bridge (IRE)** threw his chance away by starting slowly, and did well to finish so close after racing very wide in the straight. (8/1)

## 2753 WHIRLPOOL CLAIMING STKS (3-Y.O) (Class E)

2-30 (2-32) **7f 100y** £3,163.00 (£949.00: £457.00: £211.00) Stalls: High GOING minus 0.57 sec per fur (F)

| | | | | SP | RR | SF |
|---|---|---|---|---|---|---|
| 2518[10] | **Clincher Club (66)** (MJohnston) **3-8-0** TWilliams(7) (cl up: led over 3f out: styd on wl fnl f) | — | **1** | 4/1[3] | 49 | 37 |
| | **Miss Impulse (50)** (MissJBower) **3-7-12** JQuinn(4) (chsd ldrs: ch 2f out: r.o one pce) | 3½ | **2** | 25/1 | 40 | 28 |
| 2412[9] | **Uncle George (65)** (MHTompkins) **3-8-9v** PRobinson(6) (led tl rn wd & hdd over 2f out: btn whn hmpd over 2f out & 1f out: fin 4th, 2½l: plcd 3rd) | | **3** | 7/2[2] | 41 | 29 |
| 2544[12] | **Oberons Boy (IRE) (94)** (BJMeehan) **3-9-5b**[1] JReid(1) (lw: cl up: carried wd appr st: ev ch & hung bdly rt fnl 2f: nt r.o: fin 3rd, 2l: disq: plcd 4th) | | **4** | 10/11[1] | 56 | 44 |
| 1311[5] | **Philgem (19)** (JHetherton) **3-7-12** NKennedy(9) (in tch & rdn appr st: nvr able to chal) | 6 | **5** | 33/1 | 17 | 5 |
| 2345[5] | **Apartments Abroad (47)** (KMcAuliffe) **3-8-1v** JLowe(8) (b.hind: nvr wnt pce) | s.h | **6** | 14/1 | 20 | 8 |
| | **Insideout** (FWatson) **3-8-9** JFortune(3) (bit bkwd: nvr trbld ldrs) | 16 | **7** | 50/1 | — | — |
| 1691[18] | **Crystal Fast (USA) (44)** (PAKelleway) **3-8-5** KFallon(5) (a outpcd & bhd) | ½ | **8** | 16/1 | — | — |
| 2180[18] | **Inca Bird (28)** (TWall) **3-7-12**(3)ow3 FLynch(2) (chsd ldrs: carried wd appr st: sn wknd) | 3½ | **9** | 33/1 | — | — |

(SP 118.8%) **9 Rn**

**1m 32.1** (0.10) CSF £77.36 TOTE £7.80: £1.80 £4.40 £1.10 (£197.70) Trio £195.60 OWNER Brian Yeardley Continental Ltd (MIDDLEHAM) BRED Jeremy Green and Sons

**Clincher Club** sat off the pace, pulling her rider's arms out but was soon under control. Well handled, she shot up the inner when the others had problems and, getting this longer trip well, improved as the race progressed. (4/1: 3/1-9/2)

**Miss Impulse** ran a reasonable first race of the season, but found the winner too strong in the final two furlongs. (25/1)

**2339 Uncle George** had problems with the turn and then had plenty more problems, with Oberons Boy hanging into him up the straight. (7/2)

**Oberons Boy (IRE)** had blinkers on for this first time and looked most ungenerous, just wanting to hang right. (10/11)

**1311 Philgem** held her position throughout, but lacked any change of gear to improve. (33/1)

**1067 Crystal Fast (USA)** looked very fit indeed, but was off the bit the whole way, and never looked likely to get anywhere near. (16/1)

## 2754 COMET H'CAP (0-90) (3-Y.O) (Class C)

3-00 (3-03) **7f 100y** £5,247.50 (£1,580.00: £765.00: £357.50) Stalls: High GOING minus 0.57 sec per fur (F)

| | | | | SP | RR | SF |
|---|---|---|---|---|---|---|
| 2501* | **Green Barries (84)** (MJohnston) **3-9-7** MHills(3) (lw: cl up: led 1½f out: hung rt: styd on) | — | **1** | 4/1[2] | 91 | 58 |
| 2065[3] | **Kilvine (83)** (LMCumani) **3-9-6** KDarley(7) (led tl hdd 1½f out: swtchd & rallied towards fin) | ¾ | **2** | 4/1[2] | 88 | 55 |
| 2514[4] | **Kazimiera (IRE) (70)** (CWCElsey) **3-8-2**(5) MartinDwyer(5) (bhd: styd on fnl 2f: no imp) | 3½ | **3** | 10/1 | 68 | 35 |
| 1805[3] | **Jerry Cutrona (IRE) (73)** (NACallaghan) **3-8-10** GCarter(2) (hld up & bhd: effrt 3f out: nvr rchd ldrs) | 1½ | **4** | 5/1[3] | 68 | 35 |
| 2501[10] | **Safio (75)** (CSmith) **3-8-12** AClark(4) (chsd ldrs tl wknd fnl 2f) | hd | **5** | 33/1 | 69 | 36 |
| 2139* | **Mybotye (78)** (GROldroyd) **3-9-1** DaleGibson(6) (lw: prom tl wknd fnl 2f) | 12 | **6** | 6/1 | 47 | 14 |
| *2065*[2] | ***Menoo Hal Batal (USA) (83)*** (MRStoute) **3-9-6** JReid(1) (Withdrawn not under Starter's orders: unruly stalls) | ... | **W** | 9/4[1] | — | — |

(SP 113.8%) **6 Rn**

**1m 32.0** (0.00) CSF £10.37 TOTE £3.90: £1.80 £1.80 (£4.80) OWNER Maktoum Al Maktoum (MIDDLEHAM) BRED Gainsborough Stud Management Ltd

**2501* Green Barries** always looked likely to win this but, once in front, he went to his right, and did not do a lot. There would seem to be more in the tank. (4/1)

**2065 Kilvine** either is not quite giving it his best or may need further, but there is certainly more ability there. (4/1)

**2514 Kazimiera (IRE)** has the ability but only runs when she wants to and, on this occasion, it was always too late. (10/1)

**1805 Jerry Cutrona (IRE)** got kicked about no end in the stalls when her neighbour went down and, not surprisingly, never got into the race. (5/1)

**1648 Safio** showed little, dropping tamely away in the straight. (33/1)

**2139* Mybotye** looked a picture but ran poorly, weakening in the last two furlongs. (6/1)

## 2755 ORANGE MAIDEN AUCTION STKS (2-Y.O) (Class E)

3-30 (3-31) **5f** £3,059.00 (£917.00: £441.00: £203.00) Stalls: High GOING minus 0.68 sec per fur (HD)

| | | | | SP | RR | SF |
|---|---|---|---|---|---|---|
| 2527[2] | **Double-J (IRE)** (KMcAuliffe) **2-8-6** WJO'Connor(4) (lw: chsd ldrs: r.o fnl f to ld cl home) | — | **1** | 7/4[1] | 74 | 23 |
| 2361[2] | **Swino** (PDEvans) **2-8-6** JFortune(6) (led tl ct cl home) | nk | **2** | 11/2[2] | 73 | 22 |
| 2295[5] | **Swiss Coast (IRE)** (MrsJRRamsden) **2-8-6** KFallon(1) (lw: in tch: effrt 2f out: swtchd 1f out: styd on wl towards fin) | ¾ | **3** | 7/4[1] | 71 | 20 |
| 2219[5] | **Mujova (IRE)** (RHollinshead) **2-8-3**(3) FLynch(7) (chsd ldrs: effrt over 1f out: r.o one pce) | nk | **4** | 13/2[3] | 70 | 19 |
| | **Compact Disc (IRE)** (MJohnston) **2-8-1** TWilliams(2) (neat: w ldr tl wknd ins fnl f) | 2 | **5** | 10/1 | 58 | 7 |
| | **Al Ava Consonant** (JDBethell) **2-7-7**(5) MartinDwyer(3) (leggy: unf: scope: a outpcd & bhd) | 3½ | **6** | 13/2[3] | 44 | — |
| | **Juicy Ting** (PCHaslam) **2-8-3** GCarter(5) (cmpt: bit bkwd: s.i.s: hung lft 2f out: nvr nr to chal) | 3 | **7** | 20/1 | 40 | — |

(SP 128.6%) **7 Rn**

**62.3 secs** (0.80) CSF £12.99 TOTE £2.50: £1.50 £2.30 (£5.40) OWNER Mr D. H. Armitage (LAMBOURN) BRED M. and R. Monaghan

**2527 Double-J (IRE)** found this stiff five just right and produced a run to snatch it on the line. (7/4: 5/2-13/8)

**2361 Swino** was finishing second for the sixth time here and perhaps a pair of blinkers might help. (11/2)

**2295 Swiss Coast (IRE)** was always finding this trip a bit too sharp, but was flying at the finish. (7/4)
**2219 Mujova (IRE)** had his chances but was never giving it his best shot when ridden. (13/2)
**Compact Disc (IRE)**, a sharp little filly, showed plenty of toe and should be all the better for this. (10/1: op 6/1)
**Al Ava Consonant** needed this experience and time is the key. (13/2: 10/1-6/1)
**Juicy Ting** is a decent type, but he moves poorly and, hanging in the race, was always out the back. (20/1)

## 2756 SONY H'CAP (0-70) (3-Y.O+) (Class E)

4-00 (4-00) **2m 35y** £3,436.00 (£1,033.00: £499.00: £232.00) Stalls: High GOING minus 0.57 sec per fur (F)

| Form | Horse | Dist | Pos | SP | RR | SF |
|---|---|---|---|---|---|---|
| 2516$^{2}$ | **Hullbank (55)** (WWHaigh) **6-9-3** JTate(11) (b: lw: a.p: led 2f out: r.o) | — | **1** | 11/4$^{1}$ | 66 | 53 |
| 2697$^{2}$ | **Teen Jay (57)** (BJLlewellyn) **6-9-5** TWilliams(6) (cl up: led 6f out to 2f out: one pce) | 3 | **2** | 5/1$^{2}$ | 65 | 52 |
| 2377$^{6}$ | **Prague Spring (62)** (LadyHerries) **4-9-10** KDarley(3) (b.hind: lw: in tch: drvn along appr st: styd on: nt pce to chal) | 1¼ | **3** | 6/1$^{3}$ | 69 | 56 |
| 1847$^{4}$ | **Longcroft (40)** (KWHogg) **4-8-2** NKennedy(4) (bhd: effrt 6f out: styd on fnl 2f: hung rt: nrst fin) | ½ | **4** | 16/1 | 46 | 33 |
| | **All On (41)** (JHetherton) **5-8-3** JLowe(7) (bhd: rdn 5f out: styd on: no imp) | 5 | **5** | 8/1 | 42 | 29 |
| 2360$^{4}$ | **Vain Prince (48)** (NTinkler) **9-8-10** JFortune(9) (lw: prom: chal 5f out: wknd fnl 3f) | 3 | **6** | 12/1 | 46 | 33 |
| 2511$^{6}$ | **Royal Circus (39)** (PRWebber) **7-7-12**$^{(3)}$ MHenry(10) (chsd ldrs: rdn 6f out: outpcd fnl 3f) | 3½ | **7** | 10/1 | 34 | 21 |
| 2516$^{3}$ | **Atherton Green (IRE) (51)** (JAGlover) **6-8-13** MBirch(1) (nvr nr to chal) | 2½ | **8** | 7/1 | 43 | 30 |
| 2506$^{5}$ | **Tanlyar (FR) (39)** (RHollinshead) **4-7-12**$^{(3)}$ FLynch(8) (effrt 6f out: n.d) | 8 | **9** | 25/1 | 24 | 11 |
| 2522$^{3}$ | **Island Cascade (34)** (DonEnricoIncisa) **4-7-10** KimTinkler(2) (a bhd) | 1½ | **10** | 50/1 | 17 | 4 |
| *268*$^{6}$ | **Bourdonner (50)** (MDHammond) **4-8-12** KFallon(5) (lw: led tl hdd 6f out: wknd qckly) | dist | **11** | 10/1 | — | — |

(SP 118.8%) **11 Rn**

**3m 31.3** (0.80) CSF £16.27 CT £70.59 TOTE £3.60: £1.70 £1.90 £2.50 (£8.60) Trio £14.00 OWNER Mrs P. Gibbon (MALTON) BRED D. Gibbon
LONG HANDICAP Island Cascade 7-2
**2516 Hullbank** gained just reward here for his consistency and, always going best, won well. (11/4)
**2697 Teen Jay** improved with the step up in distance at Chester at the weekend and continued that here, but was well second best in the final furlong. (5/1)
**2377 Prague Spring**, stepped up in trip here, was off the bridle a long way out but did struggle on. (6/1)
**1847 Longcroft** ran pretty well, picking up in eyecatching style in the last two furlongs, and should be all the better for this. (16/1)
**All On** has been going well at the jumping game but, stepped up in trip here, looked very slow. (8/1)
**2360 Vain Prince** again failed to sparkle. (12/1)
**2516 Atherton Green (IRE)** was not given a hard race. (7/1)

## 2757 TOSHIBA H'CAP (0-60) (3-Y.O+) (Class F)

4-30 (4-32) **5f** £3,436.00 (£1,033.00: £499.00: £232.00) Stalls: High GOING minus 0.68 sec per fur (HD)

| Form | Horse | Dist | Pos | SP | RR | SF |
|---|---|---|---|---|---|---|
| 2523$^{3}$ | **Ned's Bonanza (57)** (MDods) **7-9-11** AClark(20) (lw: in tch: hdwy over 1f out: r.o wl to ld nr fin) | — | **1** | 11/4$^{1}$ | 62 | 44 |
| 2518$^{3}$ | **Dominelle (51)** (TDEasterby) **4-9-5** MBirch(14) (cl up: led 2f out tl ct cl home) | s.h | **2** | 6/1$^{2}$ | 56 | 38 |
| 2518$^{2}$ | **Just Dissident (IRE) (55)** (RMWhitaker) **4-9-9** DeanMcKeown(3) (lw: led 3f: kpt on u.p fnl f) | ½ | **3** | 14/1 | 58 | 40 |
| 2185$^{4}$ | **Rotherfield Park (IRE) (37)** (CSmith) **4-8-5** KDarley(10) (hdwy 2f out: styd on wl towards fin) | ½ | **4** | 14/1 | 39 | 21 |
| 2518$^{5}$ | **Aquado (57)** (SRBowring) **7-9-11b** JQuinn(1) (racd wd: cl up: kpt on fnl f) | 1 | **5** | 20/1 | 55 | 37 |
| 2021$^{5}$ | **Imp Express (IRE) (48)** (GMMoore) **3-8-12b** JTate(17) (styd on fnl 2f: nrst fin) | nk | **6** | 16/1 | 46 | 24 |
| 2586$^{5}$ | **Pageboy (60)** (PCHaslam) **7-10-0** JFortune(4) (racd wd: a.p: kpt on same pce fnl f) | nk | **7** | 12/1$^{3}$ | 57 | 39 |
| 2434$^{5}$ | **Christian Flight (IRE) (44)** (SGollings) **7-8-12b** VHalliday(16) (prom: rdn 2f out: btn ins fnl f) | ½ | **8** | 25/1 | 39 | 21 |
| 2523$^{4}$ | **Pallium (IRE) (49)** (MrsAMNaughton) **8-9-3** ACulhane(13) (bhd: rdn ½-wy: no imp) | s.h | **9** | 14/1 | 44 | 26 |
| 2286$^{4}$ | **Sound the Trumpet (IRE) (54)** (RCSpicer) **4-9-3**$^{(5)}$ RHavlin(12) (chsd ldrs tl wknd over 1f out) | 1¼ | **10** | 14/1 | 45 | 27 |
| 2238$^{6}$ | **Gagajulu (58)** (PDEvans) **3-9-8** WJO'Connor(19) (lw: chsd ldrs tl wknd appr fnl f) | ½ | **11** | 16/1 | 47 | 25 |
| 1888$^{7}$ | **Time To Fly (52)** (BWMurray) **3-9-2** TWilliams(15) (w ldrs tl wknd fnl f) | hd | **12** | 20/1 | 41 | 19 |
| 2185$^{8}$ | **Mu-Arrik (40)** (GROldroyd) **8-8-8b** DaleGibson(18) (lw: n.d) | s.h | **13** | 20/1 | 29 | 11 |
| 2496$^{7}$ | **Prime Property (IRE) (32)** (MWEasterby) **4-7-9b**$^{(5)}$ MartinDwyer(7) (n.d) | hd | **14** | 25/1 | 20 | 2 |
| *1028*$^{*}$ | **Queens Check (53)** (MissJFCraze) **3-9-3** NConnorton(9) (lw: in tch tl outpcd fr ½-wy) | nk | **15** | 12/1$^{3}$ | 40 | 18 |
| 2523$^{7}$ | **First Option (38)** (RBastiman) **6-8-6** GCarter(8) (t: n.d) | 1 | **16** | 25/1 | 22 | 4 |
| 1039$^{8}$ | **Tenor (55)** (DNicholls) **5-9-9** AlexGreaves(11) (a bhd) | s.h | **17** | 14/1 | 39 | 21 |
| 2523$^{5}$ | **Invigilate (52)** (MartynWane) **7-9-6** KFallon(2) (sn pushed along: bhd fr ½-wy) | hd | **18** | 14/1 | 36 | 18 |
| 1865$^{6}$ | **Coolowen Flash (IRE) (45)** (JLEyre) **5-8-13** RLappin(6) (s.i.s: a bhd) | ½ | **19** | 16/1 | 27 | 9 |
| 1859$^{8}$ | **Branston Kristy (33)** (CSmith) **4-7-8v**$^{(7)}$ IonaWands(5) (nvr wnt pce) | nk | **20** | 25/1 | 14 | — |

(SP 143.7%) **20 Rn**

**62.1 secs** (0.60) CSF £21.32 CT £200.67 TOTE £3.50: £1.40 £1.90 £2.90 £2.40 (£9.40) Trio £42.10 OWNER Mr Ned Jones (DARLINGTON) BRED D. W. McHarg
WEIGHT FOR AGE 3yo-4lb
**2523 Ned's Bonanza** had everything in his favour here, but took a long time to find his stride and got there by the skin of his teeth. (11/4)
**2518 Dominelle** loves this track and tried hard, but just failed to land a blow. (6/1)
**2518 Just Dissident (IRE)** ran a tremendous race from an impossible draw to show just what a frustrating character he is. (14/1)
**2185 Rotherfield Park (IRE)** again finished well but too late to have a chance. (14/1)
**2518 Aquado** had an impossible draw, but he is a law unto himself and ran a fine race. (20/1)
**2021 Imp Express (IRE)** has the ability but does not seem to put it to full use. (16/1)
**2586 Pageboy** is coming to form fast and is one to keep an eye on. (12/1)

T/Jkpt: £7,101.00 (0.5 Tckts); £5,000.72 to Sandown 17/7/96. T/Plpt: £15.80 (1,303.51 Tckts). T/Qdpt: £2.90 (391.1 Tckts). AA

# 2012-BRIGHTON (L-H) (Firm)

## Tuesday July 16th

WEATHER: sunny WIND: str half bhd

## 2758 E.B.F. KEMP TOWN MAIDEN STKS (2-Y.O) (Class D)

2-15 (2-16) **5f 213y** £3,315.45 (£987.60: £470.30: £211.65) Stalls: Low GOING minus 0.52 sec per fur (F)

| Form | Horse | Dist | Pos | SP | RR | SF |
|---|---|---|---|---|---|---|
| 2404$^{2}$ | **Song Mist (IRE)** (PFICole) **2-8-9** TQuinn(2) (lw: mde all: pushed out) | — | **1** | 10/11$^{1}$ | 68 | 34 |

| Form | Horse | Dist | Pos | SP | RR | SF |
|---|---|---|---|---|---|---|
| 2243[7] | **Aim Seven** (RHannon) **2-8-11**(3) DaneO'Neill(3) (lw: hld up: chsd wnr wl over 1f out: no imp) | 1¼ | **2** | 2/1[2] | 70 | 36 |
| | **Beaconscot** (DRLoder) **2-8-9** PatEddery(5) (small: chsd wnr over 4f: eased whn btn ins fnl f) | 5 | **3** | 11/2[3] | 51 | 17 |
| | **Chairmans Daughter** (PFICole) **2-8-9** TSprake(1) (unf: bit bkwd: dwlt: a bhd) | 6 | **4** | 20/1 | 35 | 1 |
| 1632[6] | **Tear White (IRE)** (TGMills) **2-9-0b** MarkLynch(4) (s.s: a bhd) | 2½ | **5** | 33/1 | 34 | — |
| | | | | (SP 108.8%) | | **5 Rn** |

**1m 8.1** (0.40 under 2y best) (0.90) CSF £2.96 TOTE £1.70: £1.10 £1.30 (£2.20) OWNER Mrs Christopher Hanbury (WHATCOMBE) BRED Mrs U.Schwarzenbach and Mrs C. Hanbury

**2404 Song Mist (IRE)**, well backed, never gave her supporters any concern as she made all, needing only to be nudged along to break the juvenile course record. (10/11: op 6/4)

**Aim Seven** looked in good shape in the paddock. Struggling into second place early in the final quarter-mile, he failed to reel in the winner. (2/1)

**Beaconscot** was eased down when all chance had gone inside the last 200 yards. Life is going to be very tough for her. (11/2: 3/1-6/1)

## 2759 STEINE CLAIMING STKS (2-Y.O) (Class F)

2-45 (2-45) **6f 209y** £2,381.00 (£656.00: £311.00) Stalls: Low GOING: minus 0.52 sec per fur (F)

| Form | Horse | Dist | Pos | SP | RR | SF |
|---|---|---|---|---|---|---|
| 1880* | **Barnwood Crackers** (NACallaghan) **2-8-11** PatEddery(3) (lw: hdwy over 2f out: hrd rdn over 1f out: led last stride) | — | **1** | 3/1[2] | 59 | 14 |
| 2606[6] | **Spondulicks (IRE)** (RHannon) **2-8-10**(3) DaneO'Neill(1) (lw: rdn & hdwy over 2f out: hrd rdn: edgd lft & led over 1f out: hdd last stride) | s.h | **2** | 9/2[3] | 61 | 16 |
| 2382[3] | **Surprise Event** (WGMTurner) **2-9-1** TSprake(2) (a.p: swtchd rt over 2f out: nt clr run over 1f out: r.o ins fnl f) | 1¼ | **3** | 11/4[1] | 60 | 15 |
| 990[2] | **Poly Moon** (MRChannon) **2-8-10** TQuinn(5) (a.p: rdn & ev ch 2f out: btn whn hmpd ins fnl f) | 3 | **4** | 5/1 | 48 | 3 |
| 2606[10] | **Grovefair Flyer (IRE)** (BJMeehan) **2-9-0b[1]** MTebbutt(4) (led over 5f: wknd fnl f) | 2 | **5** | 10/1 | 48 | 3 |
| 2512* | **Rons Revenge** (MJRyan) **2-8-11** GBardwell(7) (prom over 4f) | 14 | **6** | 7/1 | 12 | — |
| | **Hot Shot** (GLMoore) **2-8-11** SWhitworth(6) (w'like: bit bkwd: bhd fnl 3f: t.o) | 28 | **7** | 25/1 | — | — |
| | | | | (SP 112.0%) | | **7 Rn** |

**1m 23.0** (3.00) CSF £15.53 TOTE £2.90: £2.20 £2.20 (£8.40) OWNER Mr Yahya Nasib (NEWMARKET) BRED Hamilton Bloodstock (UK) Ltd
Barnwood Crackers clmd GPinchens £7,000
STEWARDS' ENQUIRY O'Neill susp. 25-26/7/96 (careless riding)

**1880* Barnwood Crackers** needed this longer trip to prevail. He moved to the outside and began to pick up ground over two furlongs from home. Under pressure below the distance, he still had it all to do, but eventually managed to reel in the leader right on the line. (3/1)

**2606 Spondulicks (IRE)** picked up ground over two furlongs from home. Drifting to his left as he struck the front below the distance, he grimly tried to hold on but was caught right on the post. His rider was later suspended for two days for careless riding. (9/2: op 11/4)

**2382 Surprise Event** was not really happy on this switch-back track and also encountered traffic problems. Switched right over a quarter of a mile from home, he found his way blocked below the distance but, despite the trouble, ran on strongly in the closing stages. This longer trip is more to his liking and a claimer can be found for him. (11/4)

**990 Poly Moon** had every chance a quarter of a mile from home, but she was soon sending out distress signals, and was held when hampered inside the final furlong. (5/1)

**1103 Grovefair Flyer (IRE)** took the field along. Collared approaching the final furlong, he was soon in trouble. This trip is just beyond him. (10/1: 7/1-11/1)

## 2760 WATERHALL MEDIAN AUCTION MAIDEN STKS (3-Y.O) (Class E)

3-15 (3-16) **6f 209y** £2,961.00 (£882.00: £420.00: £189.00) Stalls: Low GOING minus 0.52 sec per fur (F)

| Form | Horse | Dist | Pos | SP | RR | SF |
|---|---|---|---|---|---|---|
| | **Quinze** (SirMarkPrescott) **3-9-0** GDuffield(1) (w'like: wl bhd over 5f: gd hdwy fnl f: str run to ld nr fin) | — | **1** | 8/1 | 72 | 43 |
| 1301[W] | **Atlantic Storm** (JHMGosden) **3-9-0** WRyan(5) (led 6f out: rdn over 1f out: wknd & hdd nr fin) | ¾ | **2** | 9/4[2] | 70 | 41 |
| 2235[2] | **Anak-Ku (65)** (MissGayKelleway) **3-9-0b[1]** TQuinn(3) (led 1f: hrd rdn over 2f out: r.o ins fnl f) | s.h | **3** | 6/1[3] | 70 | 41 |
| | **Lady Isabell** (SDow) **3-8-9** MRoberts(4) (wl bhd over 5f: nvr nr to chal) | 2½ | **4** | 33/1 | 59 | 30 |
| 2146[2] | **Diamond Beach (84)** (BWHills) **3-9-0** PatEddery(2) (lw: hld up: rdn over 2f out: eased whn btn ins fnl f) | 2 | **5** | 5/6[1] | 60 | 31 |
| | | | | (SP 113.7%) | | **5 Rn** |

**1m 20.8** (0.80) CSF £25.04 TOTE £9.30: £3.40 £1.30 (£18.70) OWNER Lord Fairhaven (NEWMARKET) BRED Lord Fairhaven
**OFFICIAL EXPLANATION Diamond Beach: the jockey reported that the colt was never travelling well on the firm ground and over a distance shorter than last time.**

**Quinze** was taken off his feet and well adrift of the majority of the field for much of the race. Still in last place a furlong from home, he appeared to have no chance whatsoever but, with the leader tying up, he came with a storming run to snatch the spoils in the shadow of the post. (8/1: 5/1-9/1)

**Atlantic Storm** had been gelded after causing trouble in the stalls on his last run back in May. Soon at the head of affairs, he appeared to have the race in control entering the final quarter-mile, but he tied up badly in the closing stages and was caught near the line. (9/4)

**2235 Anak-Ku** broke best of all, but was soon settled in second place. Coming under pressure over a quarter of a mile from home, he did not find a great deal until running on in the closing stages. (6/1: 3/1-13/2)

**Lady Isabell**, who has changed stables since her only run last year, was well adrift until staying on in the final furlong. (33/1)

**2146 Diamond Beach** was very disappointing. Racing in third place, he was pushed along over a quarter of a mile from home, but he failed to find what was expected, and was eased when all chance had gone inside the final furlong. (5/6: 10/11-Evens)

## 2761 ERIC SIMMS MEMORIAL H'CAP (0-80) (3-Y.O+) (Class D)

3-45 (3-45) **7f 214y** £3,728.10 (£1,111.80: £530.40: £239.70) Stalls: Low GOING minus 0.52 sec per fur (F)

| Form | Horse | Dist | Pos | SP | RR | SF |
|---|---|---|---|---|---|---|
| 2400[9] | **Night Wink (USA) (74)** (GLMoore) **4-9-13** SWhitworth(5) (lw: a.p: led over 2f out: rdn out) | — | **1** | 16/1 | 84 | 66 |
| 2581[13] | **Fort Knox (IRE) (58)** (RMFlower) **5-8-11b** DBiggs(6) (s.s: hdwy over 2f out: hrd rdn over 1f out: one pce) | 1¼ | **2** | 12/1 | 66 | 48 |
| 2312[4] | **Confronter (74)** (SDow) **7-9-13** MRoberts(7) (lw: hld up: swtchd rt over 2f out: one pce) | 1½ | **3** | 7/2[2] | 79 | 61 |
| 2710[3] | **Silver Harrow (60)** (AGNewcombe) **3-8-2**(3) DaneO'Neill(2) (hld up: rdn over 2f out: one pce) | 1½ | **4** | 9/1 | 62 | 36 |
| 2312[2] | **Greatest (60)** (RAkehurst) **5-8-13** TQuinn(3) (led over 5f: wknd fnl f) | 2½ | **5** | 10/11[1] | 57 | 39 |
| 2313[2] | **Tomal (48)** (RIngram) **4-7-10**(5)ow4 ADaly(1) (b.hind: w ldr over 5f: wknd fnl f) | 1¼ | **6** | 6/1[3] | 42 | 20 |
| | | | | (SP 112.5%) | | **6 Rn** |

**1m 32.1** (-0.10) CSF £139.02 TOTE £13.70: £5.40 £2.90 (£35.60) OWNER Mrs Dyanne Benjamin (EPSOM) BRED Gainsborough Farm Inc
WEIGHT FOR AGE 3yo-8lb

**1425 Night Wink (USA)** hit the front over quarter of a mile from home and, rousted along, proved too good for his rivals. (16/1)

**1953 Fort Knox (IRE)** lost ground at the start but moved up over a quarter of a mile out. Hard ridden below the distance, he did stay on but never looked like catching the winner. (12/1: op 8/1)

**2312 Confronter**, switched right over a quarter of a mile from home, was then only treading water. (7/2)
**2710 Silver Harrow**, making a quick reappearance, chased the leaders, but was only going up and down in the same place in the last two furlongs. (9/1: 5/1-10/1)
**2312 Greatest** was very disappointing. Setting the pace, he was collared over a quarter of a mile from home, and the writing was soon on the wall. (10/11: 4/5-5/4)
**2313 Tomal**, heavily bandaged behind, raced with the leader until over a quarter of a mile from home. He grimly tried to hold on but was soon in trouble. (6/1: op 7/2)

## 2762 FRIEND-JAMES MEMORIAL LIMITED STKS (0-60) (3-Y.O+) (Class F)
4-15 (4-15) **1m 3f 196y** £2,381.00 (£656.00: £311.00) Stalls: High GOING minus 0.52 sec per fur (F)

| | | | | SP | RR | SF |
|---|---|---|---|---|---|---|
| 2014[6] | **Greenwich Again (53)** (TGMills) **4-9-7** PatEddery(5) (mde all: qcknd 2f out: comf) | — | **1** | 9/1 | 68+ | 41 |
| 2711[2] | **General Mouktar (59)** (BJMeehan) **6-9-5b** MTebbutt(1) (lw: hld up: rdn 3f out: chsd wnr over 1f out: hung lft: unable qckn) | 4 | **2** | 2/1[1] | 61 | 34 |
| 2424[5] | **Perfect Gift (60)** (PFICole) **3-8-4** TQuinn(3) (lw: chsd wnr over 2f out tl over 1f out: r.o ins fnl f) | nk | **3** | 9/4[2] | 57 | 18 |
| 2341[4] | **Royal Expose (USA) (60)** (RHannon) **3-8-4**(3) DaneO'Neill(4) (lw: chsd wnr over 9f: rdn over 2f out: wknd & hung lft over 1f out) | 2 | **4** | 9/2 | 58 | 19 |
| *385*[7] | **In The Band (59)** (LordHuntingdon) **3-8-4** DHarrison(2) (hld up: rdn over 2f out: wknd wl over 1f out) | 8 | **5** | 4/1[3] | 44 | 5 |
| | | | | (SP 112.3%) | **5 Rn** | |

**2m 30.8** (3.20) CSF £25.98 TOTE £6.70: £2.20 £1.20 (£3.60) OWNER John Humphreys (Turf Accountants) Ltd (EPSOM) BRED T. G. Mills Ltd
WEIGHT FOR AGE 3yo-12lb
**1605 Greenwich Again**, the only runner to have won in the last three years, has in fact won four times during that period. Quickening things up a quarter of a mile from home, he came home to win with plenty in hand. (9/1)
**2711 General Mouktar**, making a quick reappearance, continues to prove very expensive to follow. Ridden along three furlongs from home, he struggled into second place below the distance but he hung left and failed to find the necessary turn of foot. (2/1)
**2424 Perfect Gift**, who failed to handle the easy ground last time out, was soon racing in second place. Collared for that position below the distance, he was done no favours by the hanging General Mouktar, but got a second wind in the closing stages. (9/4)
**2341 Royal Expose (USA)** (9/2: op 3/1)
**In The Band** (4/1: 11/4-9/2)

## 2763 PAVILION H'CAP (0-70) (3-Y.O+) (Class E)
4-45 (4-45) **6f 209y** £3,097.50 (£924.00: £441.00: £199.50) Stalls: Low GOING minus 0.52 sec per fur (F)

| | | | | SP | RR | SF |
|---|---|---|---|---|---|---|
| 2229[8] | **Crystal Heights (FR) (59)** (RJO'Sullivan) **8-9-6** SSanders(1) (b: hld up: chsd ldr over 1f out: led ins fnl f: rdn out) | — | **1** | 7/1[3] | 70 | 52 |
| 2577[3] | **Gentle Irony (58)** (MJRyan) **4-9-5** BDoyle(10) (led: rdn over 2f out: hdd ins fnl f: unable qckn) | 1¼ | **2** | 4/1[2] | 66 | 48 |
| 2578[5] | **Ivory's Grab Hire (60)** (KTIvory) **3-9-0b** TQuinn(11) (chsd ldr 5f out tl over 1f out: one pce) | 1¼ | **3** | 9/1 | 65 | 40 |
| 2434[4] | **Super Park (60)** (JPearce) **4-9-7** GBardwell(5) (a.p: rdn over 2f out: one pce) | 1 | **4** | 12/1 | 63 | 45 |
| 2403[4] | **Pearl Dawn (IRE) (67)** (GLMoore) **6-10-0** SWhitworth(3) (nt clr run over 1f out & ins fnl f: nvr nr to chal) | nk | **5** | 10/1 | 69 | 51 |
| 2405[8] | **Sharp Imp (51)** (RMFlower) **6-8-12b** DBiggs(4) (hdwy over 2f out: hrd rdn over 1f out: one pce) | ¾ | **6** | 9/1 | 52 | 34 |
| 1874[10] | **Fairy Knight (67)** (RHannon) **4-9-11**(3) DaneO'Neill(8) (nvr nrr) | 2½ | **7** | 8/1 | 62 | 44 |
| 2438[3] | **Perilous Plight (65)** (WRMuir) **5-9-12** PatEddery(9) (lw: a bhd) | 2½ | **8** | 3/1[1] | 54 | 36 |
| 2345[3] | **Mislemani (IRE) (53)** (AGNewcombe) **6-8-9**(5) DGriffiths(6) (prom over 3f) | ½ | **9** | 15/2 | 41 | 23 |
| 2130[15] | **Hang a Right (41)** (CADwyer) **9-7-9**(7) NicolaCole(7) (s.s: a wl bhd: t.o fnl 5f) | 8 | **10** | 25/1 | 10 | — |
| | | | | (SP 121.0%) | **10 Rn** | |

**1m 20.5** (0.50) CSF £34.31 CT £242.88 TOTE £6.80: £1.70 £2.30 £2.50 (£22.70) Trio £36.00 OWNER Mr Jack Joseph (WHITCOMBE) BRED Ahmad Fustok
WEIGHT FOR AGE 3yo-7lb
OFFICIAL EXPLANATION **Perilous Plight: had sustained an overreach to his off-fore.**
**1532 Crystal Heights (FR)** usually gets outpaced but, on this occasion, tracked the leaders. Coming through to lead early inside the final furlong, he was ridden along to score. (7/1: 5/1-8/1)
**2577 Gentle Irony** ran another solid race. Bowling along in front, she grimly tried to hold on, but was unable to cope with the winner early inside the final furlong. (4/1)
**2578 Ivory's Grab Hire**, soon racing in second place, was collared for that position below the distance and could only struggle on at one pace. (9/1: op 6/1)
**2434 Super Park** failed to find the necessary turn of foot in the last two furlongs. (12/1: 8/1-14/1)
**2403 Pearl Dawn (IRE)** did not get the best of runs in the last two furlongs and could not get in a blow as a result. (10/1: 6/1-11/1)
**2017* Sharp Imp** made his effort on the outside of the field over a quarter of a mile from home, but failed to find another gear from below the distance. (9/1: 6/1-10/1)
**598 Fairy Knight** (8/1: tchd 14/1)
**2345 Mislemani (IRE)** (15/2: 5/1-8/1)

T/Plpt: £1,244.20 (10.49 Tckts). T/Qdpt: £609.00 (1.43 Tckts). AK

# 2758-BRIGHTON (L-H) (Firm)
## Wednesday July 17th
WEATHER: fine WIND: mod half bhd

## 2764 OVINGDEAN MEDIAN AUCTION MAIDEN STKS (2-Y.O F) (Class F)
6-15 (6-15) **5f 59y** £2,381.00 (£656.00: £311.00) Stalls: Low GOING minus 0.56 sec per fur (F)

| | | | | SP | RR | SF |
|---|---|---|---|---|---|---|
| 2606[11] | **Silver Spell** (DrJDScargill) **2-8-11v** DHolland(2) (s.s: hdwy on bit over 2f out: led ins fnl f: all out) | — | **1** | 11/2[3] | 57 | 3 |
| 2527[5] | **Royal Emblem** (AGFoster) **2-8-11** TSprake(3) (prom: rdn 3f out: rallied over 1f out: ev ch ins fnl f: unable qckn) | ¾ | **2** | 8/13[1] | 55 | 1 |
| 2614[5] | **Corncrake (IRE)** (BJMeehan) **2-8-11** TQuinn(1) (w ldr: rdn to ld over 1f out: hdd ins fnl f) | ½ | **3** | 5/2[2] | 53 | — |
| 2279[4] | **Dozen Roses** (TMJones) **2-8-11b**[1] RPerham(4) (led: rdn over 2f out: hdd over 1f out: wknd fnl f) | 5 | **4** | 40/1 | 38 | — |
| | | | | (SP 108.3%) | **4 Rn** | |

**62.7 secs** (2.70) CSF £9.16 TOTE £9.60 (£4.10) OWNER Mrs P. Reditt (NEWMARKET) BRED D. A. and Mrs Hicks

**Silver Spell**, a sister to Argentum, probably failed to get the trip when visored for the first time in a Newmarket seller over seven on her previous outing. (11/2)
**2527 Royal Emblem,** back to the minimum distance, was the first off the bit, but did not go down without a fight. (8/13)
**2614 Corncrake (IRE)** travelled really well for much of the race and may do better over further. (5/2: 13/8-11/4)
**2279 Dozen Roses** did not come on a bunch for the first-time blinkers. (40/1)

## 2765 GO EVENING RACING WITH THE DAILY TELEGRAPH MAIDEN H'CAP (0-70) (3-Y.O+) (Class E)

6-45 (6-45) **5f 213y** £3,015.60 (£898.80: £428.40: £193.20) Stalls: Low GOING minus 0.56 sec per fur (F)

| | | | | SP | RR | SF |
|---|---|---|---|---|---|---|
| 2286[19] | **Dark Menace (45)** (EAWheeler) **4-8-5**(5) ADaly(4) (a.p: swtchd rt over 3f out: hrd rdn to ld last strides) | — | 1 | 25/1 | 53 | 26 |
| 2617[2] | **School Boy (68)** (TJNaughton) **3-10-0** DHolland(2) (lw: led: rdn over 1f out: hdd last strides) | hd | 2 | 3/1[2] | 76 | 44 |
| 2510[6] | **Memphis Beau (IRE) (60)** (JARToller) **3-9-6b** SSanders(1) (chsd ldr over 1f: rdn over 1f out: one pce) | 1¼ | 3 | 12/1[3] | 64 | 32 |
| 2432[5] | **Redskin Lady (55)** (DRCElsworth) **3-8-12**(3) DaneO'Neill(6) (lw: hld up: hung lft over 1f out: swtchd rt & hdwy fnl f: r.o) | ½ | 4 | 3/1[2] | 58 | 26 |
| 2013[2] | **Flagstaff (USA) (54)** (GLMoore) **3-9-0v** MRoberts(3) (plld hrd: chsd ldr over 4f out tl wknd over 1f out) | 11 | 5 | 11/8[1] | 28 | — |
| | **Baroness Blixen (45)** (DJGMurraySmith) **3-8-5** NAdams(5) (dwlt: a bhd) | ½ | 6 | 12/1[3] | 17 | — |
| | | | | (SP 111.3%) | **6 Rn** | |

**1m 8.5** (1.30) CSF £89.83 TOTE £37.60: £7.70 £2.10 (£36.20) OWNER Austin Stroud & Co Ltd (PANGBOURNE) BRED Roger C. Denton
WEIGHT FOR AGE 3yo-5lb
**OFFICIAL EXPLANATION Flagstaff (USA): ran too freely .**
**Dark Menace,** dropped 11lb this season, had set the pace on the unfavourable far side in a big field of platers at Goodwood last time. (25/1)
**2617 School Boy,** coming back to six, was again touched off near the line and deserved a change of luck. (3/1: op 7/4)
**2510 Memphis Beau (IRE)**, a half-brother to the speedy juvenile Cameroun, seemed better suited to sprinting. (12/1: 6/1-14/1)
**2432 Redskin Lady** did not help her cause by hanging into the fence, and finished in a style which suggests she needs to revert to a longer trip. (3/1)
**2013 Flagstaff (USA)** ran much too freely and this explanation was accepted by the Stewards. (11/8)

## 2766 WHITE HAWK (S) STKS (3-Y.O+) (Class G)

7-15 (7-17) **7f 214y** £2,070.00 (£570.00: £270.00) Stalls: Low GOING minus 0.56 sec per fur (F)

| | | | | SP | RR | SF |
|---|---|---|---|---|---|---|
| 2763[5] | **Pearl Dawn (IRE) (67)** (GLMoore) **6-9-0** SWhitworth(1) (hld up: hdwy 2f out: hrd rdn to ld wl ins fnl f: r.o) | — | 1 | 5/2[2] | 53 | 40 |
| *2551*[4] | **Rocky Waters (USA) (56)** (PBurgoyne) **7-9-2**(3) PMcCabe(7) (lw: hld up: hdwy 3f out: hrd rdn & ev ch 1f out: r.o) | ½ | 2 | 5/1[3] | 57 | 44 |
| 2592[3] | **Just Millie (USA) (65)** (JEBanks) **3-8-0b**[1](7)ow1 GFaulkner(4) (plld hrd: led 6f out: rdn over 1f out: hdd wl ins fnl f) | ¾ | 3 | 13/8[1] | 52 | 30 |
| 2507[10] | **Prince Rudolf (IRE) (38)** (WGMTurner) **4-9-0v**(5) AmandaSanders(8) (bhd: rdn over 3f out: hdwy over 1f out: nt rch ldrs) | 3½ | 4 | 40/1 | 49 | 36 |
| *2689*[10] | **Half An Inch (IRE) (60)** (BJMeehan) **3-9-2b** TQuinn(6) (prom: wknd fnl f) | ½ | 5 | 5/1[3] | 53 | 32 |
| 2373[8] | **Our Little Lady (40)** (JRPoulton) **4-9-0** AMorris(5) (lw: led 2f: rdn & wknd 2f out) | 10 | 6 | 40/1 | 22 | 9 |
| 2438[5] | **Coven Moon (33)** (DMorris) **6-8-7v**(7) AEddery(2) (prom: rdn over 3f out: wknd 2f out) | 2½ | 7 | 20/1 | 17 | 4 |
| | | | | (SP 109.6%) | **7 Rn** | |

**1m 33.1** (0.90) CSF £13.80 TOTE £2.80: £1.20 £2.40 (£6.70) OWNER Mrs E. Keep (EPSOM) BRED Niall Creighton
WEIGHT FOR AGE 3yo-8lb
No bid
STEWARDS' ENQUIRY McCabe susp. 26 & 29/7/96 (excessive use of whip).
**2763 Pearl Dawn (IRE),** making amends for her unlucky run over seven here the previous day, was again held up to get this even longer trip. (5/2)
**2551 Rocky Waters (USA)** stuck to his task under strong pressure and his rider picked up a two-day whip ban. (5/1)
**2592 Just Millie (USA)** was too keen for her own good in the first-time blinkers, but only got worn down in the last half-furlong. (13/8)
**2022 Prince Rudolf (IRE)** did finally begin to pick up approaching the final furlong. (40/1)
**2402* Half An Inch (IRE)** had flopped on the Sand at Lingfield over a mile and a quarter the previous week. (5/1)

## 2767 SOUTH DOWNS H'CAP (0-85) (3-Y.O+) (Class D)

7-45 (7-45) **1m 3f 196y** £3,529.20 (£1,050.60: £499.80: £224.40) Stalls: High GOING minus 0.56 sec per fur (F)

| | | | | SP | RR | SF |
|---|---|---|---|---|---|---|
| 2613[6] | **Canton Venture (64)** (SPCWoods) **4-9-5** WWoods(3) (lw: mde all: clr over 5f out: r.o wl) | — | 1 | 2/1[1] | 73 | 53 |
| 2401[4] | **Rising Dough (IRE) (70)** (GLMoore) **4-9-8**(3) DaneO'Neill(2) (lw: chsd wnr: rdn over 3f out: no imp) | 3½ | 2 | 4/1[3] | 74 | 54 |
| 2284[5] | **Norsong (50)** (RAkehurst) **4-8-5** SSanders(1) (lw: hld up: hdwy 6f out: rdn over 3f out: one pce) | 5 | 3 | 5/1 | 48 | 28 |
| 2401[7] | **Prince Danzig (IRE) (64)** (DJGMurraySmith) **5-9-5** PaulEddery(4) (hld up: rdn 6f out: eased whn btn over 1f out) | 17 | 4 | 100/30[2] | 39 | 19 |
| 1782[6] | **St Rita (81)** (JLDunlop) **3-9-10** GDuffield(5) (rdn & lost pl after 4f: t.o fnl 3f) | 13 | 5 | 6/1 | 38 | 6 |
| | | | | (SP 107.4%) | **5 Rn** | |

**2m 28.2** (0.60) CSF £9.13 TOTE £2.80: £1.50 £2.00 (£5.90) OWNER Dr Frank Chao (NEWMARKET) BRED High Point B/stock Ltd & Chao Racing & B/stock Ltd
WEIGHT FOR AGE 3yo-12lb
**2613 Canton Venture** was able to dictate this time and took the race by the scruff of the neck soon after halfway. (2/1)
**2401 Rising Dough (IRE),** 5lb higher than when winning at Epsom, has since stepped up to a mile and half. (4/1: 5/2-9/2)
**2284 Norsong** was trying uncharted waters here and did not really prove he got the trip. (5/1: 7/2-11/2)
**1660 Prince Danzig (IRE),** only 1lb higher than when winning here in May, ran way below that form. (100/30)

## 2768 TELSCOMBE CLIFFS H'CAP (0-65) (3-Y.O) (Class F)

8-15 (8-16) **1m 1f 209y** £2,381.00 (£656.00: £311.00) Stalls: High GOING minus 0.56 sec per fur (F)

| | | | | SP | RR | SF |
|---|---|---|---|---|---|---|
| 2688* | **Frog (67)** (SirMarkPrescott) **3-9-12** 5x GDuffield(2) (mde all: rdn over 3f out: r.o wl) | — | 1 | 1/3[1] | 78+ | 50 |
| 2378[5] | **Allstars Express (62)** (TJNaughton) **3-9-7** DHolland(3) (chsd wnr: rdn & ev ch 2f out: hung lft over 1f out: no imp) | 3 | 2 | 7/1[2] | 68 | 40 |
| 2409[15] | **Efficacious (IRE) (46)** (CJBenstead) **3-8-5** DBiggs(5) (hld up: rdn & hdwy fnl 2f: n.d) | 6 | 3 | 25/1 | 43 | 15 |
| 1613[13] | **Henry Otis (55)** (RAkehurst) **3-9-0** TQuinn(4) (prom: rdn over 4f out: one pce) | nk | 4 | 10/1[3] | 51 | 23 |
| 2738[2] | **Again Together (55)** (GLMoore) **3-8-11**(3) DaneO'Neill(6) (lw: s.i.s: sn rcvrd: rdn over 4f out: wknd over 2f out: eased over 1f out) | 15 | 5 | 7/1[2] | 27 | — |

1682[5] **Tiama (IRE) (53)** (SDow) **3-8-12** SSanders(1) (wl bhd fnl 4f) ....4 6 33/1 19 —
(SP 115.9%) **6 Rn**

**1m 59.7** (1.40) CSF £3.70 TOTE £1.20: £1.20 £2.50 (£2.30) OWNER Mr B. Haggas (NEWMARKET) BRED Mrs P. A. Clark
**2688* Frog** completed a quick hat-trick under a penalty and would have had to carry 3lb more from Saturday. (1/3)
**2378 Allstars Express** posed a real threat until ducking in behind the winner. (7/1: op 4/1)
**2191 Efficacious (IRE)** was never a threat to the leading pair. (25/1)
**Henry Otis**, trying a longer trip, has dropped 10lb since coming over from Ireland. (10/1)

## 2769 LEWES RATING RELATED MAIDEN STKS (0-65) (3-Y.O+) (Class F)
8-45 (8-45) **5f 59y** £2,381.00 (£656.00: £311.00) Stalls: Low GOING minus 0.56 sec per fur (F)

| | | | | SP | RR | SF |
|---|---|---|---|---|---|---|
| 2244[3] | **Literary Society (USA) (64)** (JARToller) **3-8-12** SSanders(3) (lw: led 1f: led over 1f out: drvn out) | — | 1 | 13/8[2] | 67 | 45 |
| 2316[9] | **Midnight Spell (57)** (JWHills) **4-8-10**(3) MHenry(4) (lw: led 4f out tl over 1f out: r.o) | hd | 2 | 5/1[3] | 64 | 46 |
| 2528[2] | **Lillibella (65)** (IABalding) **3-8-9** TQuinn(2) (lw: hld up: rdn over 2f out: wknd over 1f out) | 5 | 3 | 6/5[1] | 49 | 27 |
| 2617[14] | **Rawi (64)** (MissGayKelleway) **3-8-9b**(3) DaneO'Neill(1) (prom early: no hdwy fnl 2f) | s.h | 4 | 12/1 | 51 | 29 |

(SP 107.9%) **4 Rn**

**60.1 secs** (0.10) CSF £8.21 TOTE £2.90 (£4.90) OWNER Duke of Devonshire (WHITSBURY) BRED William R. and Mrs Buster
WEIGHT FOR AGE 3yo-4lb
**2244 Literary Society (USA)** had given notice he was coming to hand at Newbury. (13/8)
**1701 Midnight Spell**, dropping back to the minimum trip, knuckled down well when headed. (5/1)
**2528 Lillibella** was rather disappointing on this return to the minimum distance. (6/5: Evens-6/4)
**949 Rawi**, yet another dropping back in trip, could not hold his good early position. (12/1: op 5/1)

T/Plpt: £442.20 (21.65 Tckts). T/Qdpt: £10.00 (124.54 Tckts). KH

# 2348-DONCASTER (L-H) (Good to firm)
## Wednesday July 17th
WEATHER: sunny WIND: slt half bhd

## 2770 SCANIA 4-SERIES 'HORSEPOWER' CONDITIONS STKS (2-Y.O) (Class C)
6-30 (6-31) **6f** £5,402.25 (£1,723.50: £824.25) Stalls: High GOING minus 0.35 sec per fur (F)

| | | | | SP | RR | SF |
|---|---|---|---|---|---|---|
| 2413* | **Sambac (USA)** (HRACecil) **2-8-10** WRyan(2) (mde all: shkn up 2f out: r.o wl) | — | 1 | 4/11[1] | 81 | 32 |
| 2484[4] | **Skyers Flyer (IRE)** (RonaldThompson) **2-8-6** NConnorton(3) (trckd ldrs: effrt over 2f out: styd on ins fnl f: no ch w wnr) | 2 | 2 | 33/1[3] | 72? | 23 |
| 2230* | **Arruhan (IRE)** (PTWalwyn) **2-8-10** WCarson(1) (unruly in stalls: plld hrd: trckd wnr: effrt 2f out: rdn & wknd over 1f out) | 1¾ | 3 | 5/2[2] | 71 | 22 |

(SP 104.8%) **3 Rn**

**1m 13.36** (2.36) CSF £4.96 TOTE £1.30 (£6.00) OWNER Mr K. Abdulla (NEWMARKET) BRED Juddmonte Farms
**2413* Sambac (USA)** looked considerably more mature than her market rival in the paddock and, sent about her work two furlongs out, was soon in no danger. (4/11)
**2484 Skyers Flyer (IRE)** stayed on inside the last to secure second place prizemoney. (33/1)
**2230* Arruhan (IRE)**, a better walker than the winner, took a keen grip going to post. Playing up in the stalls, she would not settle and found nothing under pressure. (5/2)

## 2771 SHADWELL STUD SERIES APPRENTICE H'CAP (0-70) (3-Y.O+) (Class E)
7-00 (7-01) **5f** £3,160.40 (£957.20: £467.60: £222.80) Stalls: High GOING minus 0.35 sec per fur (F)

| | | | | SP | RR | SF |
|---|---|---|---|---|---|---|
| 2745* | **Bowcliffe Grange (IRE) (51)** (DWChapman) **4-8-4b**(5) 7x KSked(7) (mde all: clr ½-wy: rdn over 1f out: hld on towards fin) | — | 1 | 9/4[1] | 56 | 38 |
| 2119[5] | **Able Sheriff (50)** (MWEasterby) **4-8-8b** GParkin(3) (trckd ldrs: effrt over 1f out: hrd rdn & r.o ins fnl f) | hd | 2 | 6/1 | 55 | 37 |
| 2564* | **Silk Cottage (62)** (RMWhitaker) **4-9-1v**(5) 7x PFredericks(2) (lw: a chsng ldrs: rdn ½-wy: kpt on fnl f) | nk | 3 | 4/1[2] | 66 | 48 |
| 2590[6] | **Captain Carat (66)** (MrsJRRamsden) **5-9-5**(5) ClaireWest(5) (b.nr fore: dwlt: bhd: hdwy over 1f out: styd on wl towards fin) | s.h | 4 | 5/1[3] | 70 | 52 |
| 2745[2] | **The Institute Boy (44)** (MissJFCraze) **6-7-9**(7) CarolynBales(1) (lw: sn chsng ldrs: kpt on wl fnl f) | hd | 5 | 9/1 | 47 | 29 |
| 2395* | **Ninety-Five (67)** (JGFitzGerald) **4-9-11** PRoberts(6) (chsd wnr: outpcd ½-wy: styd on fnl f) | 1½ | 6 | 6/1 | 65 | 47 |
| 2564[4] | **Double Glow (38)** (NBycroft) **4-7-10b** IonaWands(4) (swtg: chsd ldrs: edgd lft ½-wy: n.d after) | 2 | 7 | 20/1 | 30 | 12 |
| 2757[8] | **Christian Flight (IRE) (44)** (SGollings) **7-8-2b** FLynch(8) (sn outpcd) | 4 | 8 | 14/1 | 23 | 5 |

(SP 117.4%) **8 Rn**

**59.87 secs** (1.47) CSF £15.60 CT £47.32 TOTE £3.10: £1.40 £1.80 £1.50 (£19.80) OWNER Mr David Chapman (YORK) BRED Rosemount House Stud
LONG HANDICAP Double Glow 7-3
**2745* Bowcliffe Grange (IRE)**, under a 7lb penalty, made it two wins in three days. In a commanding lead at halfway, he did just enough in the final furlong. (9/4)
**2119 Able Sheriff** bounced back to form here after being pulled up at Carlisle last month. Happy to get a lead, he responded to his rider's urgings and only just failed to get there in the end. (6/1)
**2564* Silk Cottage**, under pressure at halfway, stuck on in the final furlong. (4/1: 3/1-9/2)
**2590 Captain Carat** played up in the stalls and missed the break. Picking up ground over a furlong out, he finished best of all. (5/1)
**2745 The Institute Boy**, beaten four lengths by the winner at Windsor two days earlier, met that rival on 7lb better terms. Worse drawn, his rider proved more of a hindrance than a help. (9/1)
**2395* Ninety-Five**, raised 7lb, was hopelessly outpaced at the halfway mark on this much faster ground. (6/1)

## 2772 E.B.F. WILMINGTON SISTER CITIES CUP MAIDEN STKS (2-Y.O) (Class D)
7-30 (7-34) **5f** £3,557.50 (£1,060.00: £505.00: £227.50) Stalls: High GOING minus 0.35 sec per fur (F)

| | | | | SP | RR | SF |
|---|---|---|---|---|---|---|
| 2374[2] | **Sous Le Nez** (RGuest) **2-8-9** KDarley(5) (w ldr: led ½-wy: r.o wl fnl f) | — | 1 | 7/4[1] | 70 | 33 |
| 1822[5] | **Step N Go (IRE)** (MrsJRRamsden) **2-8-9** KFallon(3) (hld up: shkn up 2f out: styd on wl ins fnl f) | 2½ | 2 | 9/4[2] | 62+ | 25 |
| | **Martine** (ABailey) **2-8-6**(3) DWright(1) (cmpt: dwlt: sn chsng ldr: ev ch 2f out: hung lft & nt qckn appr fnl f) | s.h | 3 | 15/2[3] | 62 | 25 |

| | | | | SP | RR | SF |
|---|---|---|---|---|---|---|
| $2559^{7}$ | **Commander Jones (IRE)** (BJMeehan) **2-9-0b$^{1}$** JCarroll(2) (led to ½-wy: hung rt & lost pl over 1f out) | 5 | **4** | 9/4$^{2}$ | 51d | 14 |
| *$1987^{P}$* | ***Amy*** (CSmith) **2-8-9** NCarlisle(4) (Withdrawn not under Starter's orders: lame) | | **W** | 33/1 | — | — |
| | | | | (SP 112.6%) | **4 Rn** | |

**60.2 secs** (1.80) CSF £5.67 TOTE £2.30: £2.60 (£3.00) OWNER Mr A. P. Davies (NEWMARKET) BRED Jim and Mrs Strange

**2374 Sous Le Nez**, a sharp sort, shrugged off her only serious challenger entering the final furlong. (7/4)

**1822 Step N Go (IRE)** still carries plenty of condition. Patiently ridden, she stayed on in promising fashion inside the last and is sure to improve and win races. Probably a nursery over six, with one more outing under her belt. (9/4)

**Martine** missed the break slightly. Upsides soon after halfway, she drifted towards the centre and soon proved no match. (15/2: 4/1-8/1)

**2559 Commander Jones (IRE)**, with blinkers on for the first time, was very keen beforehand. After breaking smartly and making the running, he hung right and wanted no part of it. (9/4)

## 2773 SCANIA 1996 TRUCK OF THE YEAR TROPHY H'CAP (0-80) (3-Y.O+) (Class D)

8-00 (8-02) **1m (round)** £5,921.25 (£1,770.00: £847.50: £386.25) Stalls: Low GOING minus 0.35 sec per fur (F)

| | | | | SP | RR | SF |
|---|---|---|---|---|---|---|
| $2214^{4}$ | **Ret Frem (IRE) (65)** (MAJarvis) **3-8-6** PRobinson(7) (mde all: rdn over 1f out: hld on wl towards fin) | — | **1** | 11/4$^{1}$ | 76 | 38 |
| $2320^{*}$ | **Tael of Silver (64)** (ABailey) **4-8-13** KDarley(2) (hld up: hdwy on ins 3f out: sn chsng wnr: ev ch fnl f: r.o u.p) | nk | **2** | 5/1$^{3}$ | 74 | 44 |
| $2426^{3}$ | **Kid Ory (62)** (PCalver) **5-8-11** MBirch(5) (trckd ldrs: rdn 3f out: styd on same pce) | 4 | **3** | 7/1 | 64 | 34 |
| $2328^{11}$ | **Pharmacy (79)** (JWWatts) **3-9-6** JCarroll(4) (trckd ldrs: effrt over 2f out: kpt on one pce) | ¾ | **4** | 9/2$^{2}$ | 80 | 42 |
| *$2552^{6}$* | **Bentico (62)** (MrsNMacauley) **7-8-8v$^{(3)}$** CTeague(3) (lw: chsd ldrs: rdn & wandered over 3f out: sn outpcd) | 3 | **5** | 14/1 | 57 | 27 |
| $2581^{7}$ | **Tawafij (USA) (75)** (MDHammond) **7-9-10** JFortune(6) (hld up: effrt over 3f out: sn rdn & no imp) | nk | **6** | 5/1$^{3}$ | 69 | 39 |
| $2294^{5}$ | **Fairywings (74)** (MrsJRRamsden) **3-9-1** KFallon(1) (hld up: effrt over 3f out: nvr nr ldrs) | 1 | **7** | 9/2$^{2}$ | 66 | 28 |
| | | | | (SP 115.5%) | **7 Rn** | |

**1m 38.8** (2.30) CSF £16.00 TOTE £3.30: £1.60 £3.50 (£12.20) OWNER Mrs Anita Green (NEWMARKET) BRED Miss Audrey F. Thompson

WEIGHT FOR AGE 3yo-8lb

**2214 Ret Frem (IRE)**, not suited by the hard ground at Carlisle last time, was able to set his own pace here. Quickening up halfway up the straight, he did just enough to hold his challenger at bay. (11/4)

**2320* Tael of Silver**, raised 5lb and stepping up to a mile, threw down a strong challenge entering the final furlong. Hard as she tried, she was just denied. (5/1)

**2426 Kid Ory** took a keen grip and is possibly better over seven, but he does not win very often. (7/1)

**987 Pharmacy**, who likes to come from behind, would have been suited by a more strongly-run race. (9/2)

**2170* Bentico** hung both ways under pressure. (14/1)

**2328 Tawafij (USA)** was not suited by the modest pace and never looked like picking up. He is best over seven on a straight track in a big field. (5/1)

**2294 Fairywings** almost certainly found the mile too sharp. (9/2)

## 2774 CAMERON 4 SCANIA CONDITIONS STKS (3-Y.O+) (Class C)

8-30 (8-30) **1m (straight)** £5,441.60 (£2,014.40: £967.20: £396.00: £158.00: £62.80) Stalls: High GOING: minus 0.35 sec (F)

| | | | | SP | RR | SF |
|---|---|---|---|---|---|---|
| $2041^{12}$ | **Mushahid (USA) (103)** (JLDunlop) **3-8-10** WCarson(4) (lw: sn trckng ldrs: hrd rdn & styd on fnl f: led post) | — | **1** | 11/4$^{2}$ | 104 | 68 |
| 1574a$^{6}$ | **Phantom Quest** (HRACecil) **3-9-0** WRyan(1) (sn trckng ldr: shkn up to ld 3f out: r.o u.p: jst ct) | hd | **2** | 10/11$^{1}$ | 108 | 72 |
| $1432^{9}$ | **Van Gurp (94)** (BAMcMahon) **3-8-10** KDarley(6) (hld up: bmpd 4f out: swtchd lft over 2f out: styd on fnl f: fin d.h 3rd, 3l: plcd 3rd) | | **3** | 10/1 | 97 | 61 |
| $2248^{2}$ | **Polinesso (99)** (BWHills) **3-9-0** MHills(5) (trckd ldrs: swtchd lft 4f out: ev ch over 1f out: kpt on same pce: fin 3rd, d.h: disq: plcd 4th) | | **4** | 5/1$^{3}$ | 102 | 66 |
| | **Champagne Prince (95)** (PWHarris) **3-8-10** GCarter(2) (led to 3f out: sn lost pl) | 4 | **5** | 14/1 | 89 | 53 |
| $1193^{9}$ | **La Volta (97)** (JGFitzGerald) **3-8-5** KFallon(3) (b: hld up: lost pl over 3f out: sn bhd) | 11 | **6** | 25/1 | 62 | 26 |
| | | | | (SP 115.3%) | **6 Rn** | |

**1m 36.71** (0.47 under best) (-0.29) CSF £5.71 TOTE £3.20: £1.70 £1.30 (£2.00) OWNER Mr Hamdan Al Maktoum (ARUNDEL) BRED Courtney and Congleton

STEWARDS' ENQUIRY Hills susp. 26-27 & 29/7/96 (careless riding).

**1785* Mushahid (USA)**, who had plenty to do at the weights at Royal Ascot, answered his rider's every call. Never flinching under the whip, he poked his head in front right on the line. (11/4)

**1574a Phantom Quest** took it up three furlongs out and stepped up what had been a moderate gallop. Not looking totally happy on the ground, he was pipped on the line. (10/11: 4/5-Evens)

**1125 Van Gurp**, still a maiden, did not have the run of the race. Knocked sideways twice by Polinesso, to his credit he came back for more in the final furlong. When his sights are lowered, he will surely open his account. (10/1)

**2248 Polinesso**, who usually makes the running, was dropped in. Switched violently left at halfway, twice hampering Van Gurp, he was upsides over a furlong out but then could find no more. His stable is struggling to find form at present and he will be better suited by a mile and two. (5/1)

**Champagne Prince** set a modest gallop but, when the race began in earnest, was soon left toiling. (14/1)

## 2775 SCANIA 4-SERIES 'KING OF THE ROAD' TROPHY H'CAP (0-70) (3-Y.O+ F & M) (Class E)

9-00 (9-03) **1m 4f** £3,348.00 (£999.00: £477.00: £216.00) Stalls: Low GOING minus 0.35 sec per fur (F)

| | | | | SP | RR | SF |
|---|---|---|---|---|---|---|
| $2407^{3}$ | **Mighty Phantom (USA) (67)** (JWHills) **3-9-3** MHills(7) (mde all: styd on u.p fnl 2f: jst hld on) | — | **1** | 6/1 | 70 | 44 |
| $1826^{8}$ | **Campaspe (42)** (JGFitzGerald) **4-8-4** DeanMcKeown(3) (trckd ldrs: effrt on ins over 2f out: nt clr run & repeatedly hmpd: swtchd rt & styd on wl towards fin) | nk | **2** | 11/2 | 45 | 31 |
| $2430^{6}$ | **Temptress (64)** (PTWalwyn) **3-9-0** JCarroll(6) (trckd ldrs: effrt 3f out: sn ev ch: nt qckn ins fnl f) | hd | **3** | 3/1$^{1}$ | 67 | 41 |
| $2300^{10}$ | **Strategic Ploy (69)** (MrsJRRamsden) **3-9-5** KFallon(4) (lw: hld up: effrt over 2f out: nt qckn ins fnl f) | 1¼ | **4** | 100/30$^{2}$ | 70 | 44 |
| $2046^{3}$ | **Instantaneous (43)** (TDEasterby) **4-8-5** MBirch(9) (trckd ldrs: effrt over 2f out: wknd over 1f out) | 9 | **5** | 13/2 | 32 | 18 |
| | **Zajira (IRE) (65)** (PEccles) **6-9-13** TIves(5) (sn bhd & pushed along: sme hdwy 3f out: sn wknd) | ½ | **6** | 25/1 | 53 | 39 |
| $2415^{4}$ | **Risky Tu (43)** (PAKelleway) **5-8-5** GBardwell(2) (in tch: sn pushed along: lost pl over 2f out) | 3 | **7** | 9/2$^{3}$ | 27 | 13 |
| $2537^{9}$ | **Friendly Dreams (IRE) (48)** (PTDalton) **3-7-5b$^{(7)ow2}$** RCody-Boutcher(8) (chsd ldrs: drvn along 8f out: rdn 5f out: lost pl over 3f out: sn bhd) | 30 | **8** | 100/1 | — | — |
| | | | | (SP 114.1%) | **8 Rn** | |

**2m 34.33** (4.33) CSF £35.50 CT £107.17 TOTE £6.10: £1.40 £1.90 £1.70 (£19.50) Trio £49.30 OWNER Mr Michael Wauchope (LAMBOURN) BRED Michael S. Anderson and Brick Kiln Stud

LONG HANDICAP Friendly Dreams (IRE) 6-3

WEIGHT FOR AGE 3yo-12lb

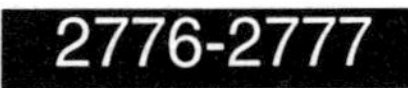


**2407 Mighty Phantom (USA)**, whose only previous success came over two miles on the All-Weather, set out to make her stamina tell. Proving game under pressure, the post came just in time. (6/1)
**1542 Campaspe**, dropped slightly back in distance, looked desperately unlucky. Stuck on the inner with nowhere to go in the final quarter-mile, her rider managed to squeeze her between horses near the line, but she just failed to get up. It is hoped that the buffeting she took here does not affect her confidence. (11/2)
**2430 Temptress**, unsuited by the soft ground last time, had every chance. (3/1)
**1498* Strategic Ploy**, above herself in the paddock, was happy to sit off the pace. Almost upsides inside the last, she could then do no more. (100/30)
**2046 Instantaneous**, who ran over hurdles two weeks ago, dropped out tamely. (13/2)

T/Plpt: £15.50 (798.42 Tckts). T/Qdpt: £10.20 (105.03 Tckts). WG

## 2625-**REDCAR (L-H) (Firm)**
## Wednesday July 17th

WEATHER: sunny WIND: slt half against

### 2776 LANGBAURGH H'CAP (0-70) (3-Y.O+) (Class E)
2-15 (2-19) **1m 3f** £3,195.50 (£959.00: £462.00: £213.50) Stalls: Low GOING minus 0.74 sec per fur (HD)

| Form | Horse | Dist | Pos | SP | RR | SF |
|---|---|---|---|---|---|---|
| 2613[4] | **Almuhtaram (60)** (MissGayKelleway) **4-10-0b** KFallon(10) (b: lost pl appr st: hdwy 3f out: led ins fnl f: r.o) | — | 1 | 5/1[2] | 73 | 55 |
| 2440[9] | **Dancing Destiny (43)** (RBastiman) **4-8-8**(3) DWright(6) (trckd ldrs: smooth hdwy to chal over 3f out: led over 1f out: hdd & one pce ins fnl f) | 3½ | 2 | 7/1[3] | 51 | 33 |
| 2067[8] | **Forest Fantasy (48)** (JWharton) **3-8-5** PRobinson(3) (cl up: led 4f out tl over 1f out: one pce) | 1¾ | 3 | 9/1 | 53 | 24 |
| 2348[2] | **Hawkish (USA) (51)** (DMorley) **7-9-5** MFenton(9) (lw: bhd: effrt 4f out: styd on: nt pce to chal) | ½ | 4 | 3/1[1] | 56 | 38 |
| 1887[5] | **Silverdale Knight (58)** (KWHogg) **3-9-1** DeanMcKeown(5) (trckd ldrs: effrt over 3f out: one pce) | s.h | 5 | 9/1 | 63 | 34 |
| 2628[2] | **Augustan (50)** (SGollings) **5-9-4** VHalliday(7) (s.i.s: bhd tl styd on fnl 3f) | 1¾ | 6 | 5/1[2] | 52 | 34 |
| 2136[6] | **Bardia (32)** (DonEnricoIncisa) **6-8-0** KimTinkler(4) (lw: bhd: effrt 4f out: nvr rchd ldrs) | 5 | 7 | 33/1 | 27 | 9 |
| 2482[3] | **Sharkashka (IRE) (53)** (TDEasterby) **6-9-7** MBirch(2) (in tch tl outpcd fnl 3f) | 1¼ | 8 | 5/1[2] | 46 | 28 |
| 2522[4] | **Never so True (37)** (MartynWane) **5-8-5** JCarroll(1) (led tl hdd 4f out: wknd 3f out) | 3½ | 9 | 33/1 | 25 | 7 |
| 2348[8] | **Elite Bliss (IRE) (42)** (MJCamacho) **4-8-10** JFortune(8) (wnt prom after 2f: outpcd fnl 3f) | nk | 10 | 16/1 | 29 | 11 |
| 2542[7] | **Islay Brown (IRE) (49)** (CWCElsey) **3-8-6b** DaleGibson(11) (s.i.s: plld hrd & hdwy appr st: sn wknd) | 5 | 11 | 25/1 | 29 | — |

(SP 123.1%) **11 Rn**

**2m 17.6** (-0.40) CSF £38.73 CT £284.55 TOTE £6.80: £2.60 £1.40 £2.80 (£35.40) Trio £433.00; £67.09 to Redcar 18/7/96 OWNER Mr A. M. Al-Midani (WHITCOMBE) BRED A. M. Midani
WEIGHT FOR AGE 3yo-11lb
**2613 Almuhtaram**, patiently ridden this time, produced a run to settle it in a few strides inside the last furlong and win with something in hand. (5/1)
**Dancing Destiny**, gambled on, looked dangerous all the way up the straight but, when the pressure was seriously on, she lacked another gear. She should find a race such as this before long. (7/1)
**1477 Forest Fantasy** keeps running well without winning. Her turn will come, and she might well appreciate a bit of cut in the ground. (9/1)
**2348 Hawkish (USA)** likes to come from behind but took forever to get into his stride, and failed to get a blow, despite staying on. A stronger early pace would have suited him. (3/1: op 2/1)
**1887 Silverdale Knight** ran his usual consistent race, but was going nowhere in the last couple of furlongs. (9/1: 6/1-10/1)
**2628 Augustan** again gave ground away at the start, but ran reasonably. He is not doing enough at the business end though. (5/1)
**2482 Sharkashka (IRE)** (5/1: 4/1-6/1)

### 2777 SOUTH SHIELDS CLAIMING STKS (3-Y.O) (Class F)
2-50 (2-52) **6f** £2,868.00 (£798.00: £384.00) Stalls: Centre GOING minus 0.74 sec per fur (HD)

| Form | Horse | Dist | Pos | SP | RR | SF |
|---|---|---|---|---|---|---|
| 2427[2] | **No Monkey Nuts (72)** (JBerry) **3-9-1** JCarroll(1) (mde all: clr 2f out: kpt on wl) | — | 1 | 7/2[2] | 80 | 39 |
| | **Dreams And Schemes (IRE)** (RAFahey) **3-8-6** KFallon(10) (in tch: styd on fnl 2f: no ch w wnr) | 5 | 2 | 7/1 | 58 | 17 |
| 2411[2] | **Bag And A Bit (50)** (BJMeehan) **3-7-13**(3)ow4 FLynch(9) (lw: a.p: kpt on one pce fnl 2f) | 2½ | 3 | 4/1[3] | 47 | 2 |
| 2571* | **The Wad (65)** (DNicholls) **3-9-3** WRyan(13) (lw: chsd ldrs: effrt 3f out: styd on one pce) | hd | 4 | 5/2[1] | 62 | 21 |
| 2359[4] | **Marjorie Rose (IRE) (55)** (ABailey) **3-7-13b**(3) DWright(2) (w wnr tl wknd over 2f out) | ½ | 5 | 8/1 | 45 | 4 |
| *2367*[7] | **Forecast (57)** (JWharton) **3-8-11** PRobinson(6) (a in tch: rdn 3f out: one pce appr fnl f) | 1¾ | 6 | 12/1 | 50 | 9 |
| | **Hotcake** (MissSEHall) **3-8-5** KDarley(12) (b: leggy: scope: hld up: stdy hdwy 3f out: nvr rchd ldrs) | 1 | 7 | 8/1 | 41 | — |
| | **Bataleur** (MissJBower) **3-9-1** DRMcCabe(7) (unf: nvr rchd ldrs) | nk | 8 | 14/1 | 50 | 9 |
| 2391[11] | **Madonna da Rossi (37)** (MDods) **3-8-4** NConnorton(11) (in tch tl outpcd fnl 2½f) | 4 | 9 | 20/1 | 29 | — |
| 1039[11] | **April's Joy (50)** (JNorton) **3-7-12** DaleGibson(15) (outpcd fr ½-wy) | 2½ | 10 | 16/1 | 16 | — |
| 2496[10] | **Maysimp (IRE) (42)** (BPJBaugh) **3-8-4** NCarlisle(5) (lw: n.d) | ¾ | 11 | 25/1 | 20 | — |
| 2392[9] | **Time Ticks On** (MWEllerby) **3-8-6**(3) CTeague(3) (s.s: racd alone far side: n.d) | 5 | 12 | 100/1 | 12 | — |
| 2572[10] | **Haysong (IRE) (40)** (JPLeigh) **3-8-5**ow1 DeanMcKeown(8) (reminders after s: n.d) | 1¾ | 13 | 50/1 | 3 | — |
| 2048[8] | **Clancassie** (EJAlston) **3-8-8** JFortune(4) (lw: sn bhd) | 1½ | 14 | 66/1 | 2 | — |
| | **Packitin** (FWatson) **3-8-7** JFanning(14) (b: bkwd: s.s: a bhd: t.o) | 25 | 15 | 100/1 | — | — |

(SP 139.8%) **15 Rn**

**1m 10.0** (-0.20) CSF £31.07 TOTE £3.40: £1.70 £2.50 £1.40 (£39.30) Trio £28.60 OWNER The Monkey Partnership (COCKERHAM) BRED Miss C. Tagart
**2427 No Monkey Nuts** was most unco-operative in the early part of the season, but he seems to have changed his spots at present. He showed here how much ability he has and fairly scooted up. (7/2: 9/4-4/1)
**Dreams And Schemes (IRE)**, having her first run in this country, was putting in all her best work in the last two furlongs, suggesting that a little further might help. (7/1)
**2411 Bag And A Bit** ideally needs a bit further. Although always well placed, she could never quicken enough when it mattered. (4/1: 9/2-7/1)
**2571* The Wad** ran a decent race, but was well short of toe in the last two furlongs. (5/2)
**2359 Marjorie Rose (IRE)** was the only one able to go with the winner at first, but found it all too much from two furlongs out. (8/1)
**973 Forecast** has been gelded and ran a decent race, but was always short of speed from halfway. He gives the impression that he should get further. (12/1)
**Hotcake**, making his debut, showed ability and, with experience, is likely to pick up similar events. (8/1)
**Bataleur** (14/1: 25/1-10/1)

## 2778 ANDERSONS H'CAP (0-85) (3-Y.O) (Class D)

3-20 (3-21) **6f** £3,814.50 (£1,146.00: £553.00: £256.50) Stalls: Centre GOING minus 0.74 sec per fur (HD)

| | Horse / Details | Dist | Pos | SP | RR | SF |
|---|---|---|---|---|---|---|
| 2049[2] | **Middle East (71)** (TDBarron) **3-9-3** JFortune(6) (swtg: chsd ldrs: led wl over 1f out: r.o u.p) | — | **1** | 9/4[1] | 72 | 35 |
| 2496[2] | **Sharp Monty (62)** (RHollinshead) **3-8-5**(3) FLynch(3) (trckd ldrs: chal 2f out: nt qckn towards fin) | ¾ | **2** | 11/4[3] | 61 | 24 |
| 1667[3] | **Merrily (73)** (MissSEHall) **3-9-5** KFallon(4) (b: hld up: effrt 2f out: ev ch ins fnl f: nt qckn) | nk | **3** | 5/2[2] | 71 | 34 |
| 2425[5] | **Comic Fantasy (AUS) (75)** (MartynWane) **3-9-7** JCarroll(5) (lw: chsd ldrs: ev ch 2f out: btn appr fnl f) | 2 | **4** | 7/1 | 68 | 31 |
| 2427* | **Bee Health Boy (62)** (MWEasterby) **3-8-3b**(5) GParkin(2) (led over 3f: sn outpcd) | 2 | **5** | 9/1 | 50 | 13 |
| 2571[4] | **Pathaze (53)** (NBycroft) **3-7-13** JLowe(1) (cl up over 3f: wknd) | 1¾ | **6** | 10/1 | 36 | — |
| | | | | (SP 117.6%) | **6 Rn** | |

**1m 10.4** (0.20) CSF £8.98 TOTE £2.80: £1.90 £1.60 (£4.00) OWNER Mrs J. Hazell (THIRSK) BRED Miss M. Grantmyre

**2049 Middle East** got pretty warm beforehand but is from a stable flying at present and, responding to pressure, always had the edge in the last furlong and a half. (9/4)

**2496 Sharp Monty** had his chances but, despite keeping on, always found the winner too good. He is on really good terms with himself at present. (11/4)

**1667 Merrily,** held up and behind, looked dangerous when produced approaching the final furlong, but then failed to produce the goods. (5/2)

**2425 Comic Fantasy (AUS),** the pick on looks, had her chances until the weight concession told approaching the final furlong. (7/1)

**2427* Bee Health Boy** found this ground much faster than he prefers. (9/1: op 6/1)

**2571 Pathaze** runs when in the mood. (10/1)

## 2779 RED CROSS H'CAP (0-65) (3-Y.O+) (Class F)

3-50 (3-50) **1m 6f 19y** £3,218.00 (£898.00: £434.00) Stalls: Low GOING minus 0.74 sec per fur (HD)

| | Horse / Details | Dist | Pos | SP | RR | SF |
|---|---|---|---|---|---|---|
| 2717* | **Salska (51)** (AStreeter) **5-8-10**(5) 5x LNewton(5) (lw: hld up: hdwy gng wl 3f out: led wl over 1f out: rdn & styd on) | — | **1** | 2/1[1] | 63+ | 37 |
| 2626[5] | **Kindred Greeting (32)** (JAHarris) **4-7-10b** JO'Reilly(7) (hdwy 4f out: swtchd over 2f out: hung lft & styd on u.p: nrst fin) | 1½ | **2** | 50/1 | 42 | 16 |
| 2487* | **Kings Cay (IRE) (60)** (THCaldwell) **5-9-10** KFallon(6) (lw: hld up: hdwy over 3f out: rdn 2f out: styd on: nvr able to chal) | 1 | **3** | 7/2[2] | 69 | 43 |
| 2120* | **Monaco Gold (IRE) (41)** (MrsMReveley) **4-8-5** KDarley(2) (chsd ldrs: dsip ld over 2f out tl rdn & btn over 1f out) | 4 | **4** | 4/1[3] | 46 | 20 |
| 2226[3] | **Miswaki Dancer (USA) (53)** (LadyHerries) **6-9-3** DeclanO'Shea(3) (b: prom early: lost tch appr st: hdwy over 2f out: nvr nr to chal) | 2½ | **5** | 7/1 | 55 | 29 |
| 2423[11] | **Yaakum (32)** (SEKettlewell) **7-7-7**(3) NVarley(9) (hld up: effrt 4f out: nvr able to chal) | 1¼ | **6** | 50/1 | 32 | 6 |
| 2549[4] | **The Boozing Brief (USA) (62)** (MAJarvis) **3-8-12** PRobinson(1) (led: qcknd 3f out: hdd wl over 1f out: sn btn) | 1¼ | **7** | 5/1 | 61 | 21 |
| 1788[4] | **Ela Man Howa (53)** (ABailey) **5-9-0**(3) DWright(10) (cl up: disp ld over 4f out tl wknd over 2f out) | 3½ | **8** | 16/1 | 48 | 22 |
| 2423[10] | **Don't Cry (32)** (DonEnricoIncisa) **8-7-10** KimTinkler(4) (a bhd: t.o) | 22 | **9** | 50/1 | 2 | — |
| 1478[9] | **Lindisfarne Lady (39)** (MrsMReveley) **4-8-3** JFanning(8) (t: lw: trckd ldrs tl wknd qckly over 4f out: t.o) | 24 | **10** | 33/1 | — | — |
| | | | | (SP 119.4%) | **10 Rn** | |

**3m** (0.70) CSF £70.43 CT £309.23 TOTE £3.30: £1.70 £7.20 £1.50 (£110.30) Trio £158.20 OWNER Mr P. L. Clinton (UTTOXETER) BRED J. A. Haverhals

LONG HANDICAP Yaakum 7-6 Don't Cry 7-1 Kindred Greeting 7-7

WEIGHT FOR AGE 3yo-14lb

**2717* Salska,** who is in tremendous form at present, travelled on the bridle and found all that was necessary when ridden. (2/1)

**Kindred Greeting,** having his twentieth race, put in by far his best performance for a long time and may be getting it together. (50/1)

**2487* Kings Cay (IRE)** ran his usual game race, but it would seem that the combination of the longer distance and the extra weight has found him out. (7/2)

**2120* Monaco Gold (IRE),** up 6lb and in a more competitive race this time, had his limitations exposed. (4/1)

**2226 Miswaki Dancer (USA),** trying a longer trip, was tenderly handled up the straight. Making steady progress in the closing stages suggested that he is coming to hand. (7/1)

**Yaakum** stayed on under pressure in the last half-mile to show that he still has some ability. (50/1)

**2549 The Boozing Brief (USA),** trying a longer trip, did not seem to get it. (5/1)

**Lindisfarne Lady** was tubed for the first time here and ran even worse. (33/1)

## 2780 YORKSHIRE-TYNE TEES TELEVISION H'CAP (0-70) (3-Y.O) (Class E)

4-25 (4-25) **1m 2f** £3,332.00 (£1,001.00: £483.00: £224.00) Stalls: Low GOING minus 0.74 sec per fur (HD)

| | Horse / Details | Dist | Pos | SP | RR | SF |
|---|---|---|---|---|---|---|
| 2163* | **Elashath (USA) (61)** (JHMGosden) **3-9-5** RHills(1) (chsd ldrs: slt ld 2f out: pushed out) | — | **1** | Evens[1] | 72 | 40 |
| 2384[5] | **Double Up (63)** (LadyHerries) **3-9-0**(7) PDoe(8) (lw: led tl hdd 2f out: kpt on wl) | ½ | **2** | 8/1 | 73 | 41 |
| 2294[7] | **Ordained (54)** (EJAlston) **3-8-12** KFallon(11) (lw: hdwy 4f out: chsng ldrs & rdn 2f out: nvr able to chal) | 2½ | **3** | 11/2[3] | 60 | 28 |
| 2133[4] | **Giddy (56)** (JHetherton) **3-9-0** NKennedy(5) (b.hind: chsd ldrs: effrt over 4f out: one pce fnl 3f) | 5 | **4** | 10/1 | 54 | 22 |
| 2524[6] | **Globe Runner (46)** (JJO'Neill) **3-8-4** TWilliams(6) (bhd: hdwy on outside 3f out: nvr rchd ldrs) | 1½ | **5** | 40/1 | 42 | 10 |
| 2419* | **Society Girl (58)** (CWThornton) **3-9-2** DeanMcKeown(3) (b.nr hind: lw: hld up: effrt over 3f out: no imp) | 1 | **6** | 5/1[2] | 52 | 20 |
| 2397[4] | **Northern Falcon (39)** (MWEasterby) **3-7-11b**ow1 DaleGibson(9) (prom tl wknd fnl 3f) | 1¼ | **7** | 10/1 | 31 | — |
| 2541[4] | **Cerise (IRE) (48)** (CWCElsey) **3-8-3b**(3) FLynch(7) (in tch tl outpcd fnl 4f) | 1¾ | **8** | 16/1 | 37 | 5 |
| 1888[10] | **Magical Midnight (38)** (NTinkler) **3-7-10b** KimTinkler(4) (chsd ldr tl wknd over 4f out) | 8 | **9** | 40/1 | 15 | — |
| 2212[11] | **Brownie's Promise (38)** (MBrittain) **3-7-10** JLowe(2) (a bhd) | 7 | **10** | 50/1 | 3 | — |
| 2362[7] | **Mill House Boy (IRE) (38)** (BSRothwell) **3-7-7**(3) NVarley(10) (a bhd) | 3½ | **11** | 66/1 | — | — |
| | | | | (SP 125.6%) | **11 Rn** | |

**2m 4.0** (0.40) CSF £10.54 CT £32.88 TOTE £1.90: £1.20 £2.70 £1.70 (£7.20) Trio £12.00 OWNER Mr Hamdan Al Maktoum (NEWMARKET) BRED Poole Investments and Chris Smith

LONG HANDICAP Northern Falcon 7-9 Magical Midnight 7-7 Brownie's Promise 7-7 Mill House Boy (IRE) 6-6

**2163* Elashath (USA)** certainly does not do anything quickly but he stays well and, once in front approaching the final furlong, just needed to be pushed out to put it beyond doubt. He should get further. (Evens)

**2384 Double Up** ran particularly well out in front and kept rallying gamely in the closing stages to suggest that she is coming back to form. (8/1)

**2163 Ordained** looked ultra-fit and ran a good race, but was inclined to hang left when the pressure was on approaching the final furlong. (11/2: 7/2-6/1)

**2133 Giddy,** having her first run for her new stable, showed up behind the leaders but looked very one-paced in the last three furlongs. (10/1)
**1812 Globe Runner** stayed on from the back of the field in the last three furlongs, albeit without having a chance. (40/1)
**2419* Society Girl** always found this company too hot. (5/1)

## 2781 SIMONSIDE MAIDEN AUCTION STKS (2-Y.O) (Class F)
4-55 (4-58) **5f** £2,805.00 (£780.00: £375.00) Stalls: Centre GOING minus 0.74 sec per fur (HD)

| | | | | SP | RR | SF |
|---|---|---|---|---|---|---|
| 2076[2] | **Ballymote** (JBerry) **2-8-9** JCarroll(7) (mde all: r.o strly fnl 2f) | — | **1** | 5/2[2] | 73 | 13 |
| 2712[2] | **What Happened Was** (MartynMeade) **2-7-12** FNorton(6) (chsd ldrs tl sddle slipped & nt qckn appr fnl f) | 2½ | **2** | 13/8[1] | 54 | — |
| | **Balladoole Bajan** (MJohnston) **2-8-4** TWilliams(9) (neat: chsd ldrs: effrt ½-wy: r.o one pce) | ½ | **3** | 4/1[3] | 58 | — |
| *2083*[5] | **Super Saint** (TDBarron) **2-8-9** JFortune(8) (a.p: kpt on one pce fnl 2f) | 3 | **4** | 14/1 | 54 | — |
| 2122[6] | **Tribal Mischief** (DMoffatt) **2-7-12v**[1](3) DarrenMoffatt(4) (wnt lft s: sn chsng ldrs: hung lft fr ½-wy: btn over 1f out) | 1 | **5** | 8/1 | 43 | — |
| | **Miss Alice** (JNorton) **2-7-12** DaleGibson(1) (leggy: unf: s.i.s: hung lft & bhd tl sme late hdwy) | nk | **6** | 50/1 | 39 | — |
| *2307*[8] | **Stravano** (BPJBaugh) **2-7-12** NCarlisle(2) (outpcd fr ½-wy) | 4 | **7** | 50/1 | 26 | — |
| 2485[6] | **Risky Flight** (ASmith) **2-8-6** JLowe(5) (cl up 3f: wknd) | 2½ | **8** | 25/1 | 26 | — |
| 1827[9] | **Antares** (NTinkler) **2-8-9b**[1] KDarley(3) (lw: bmpd s: outpcd fr ½-wy) | ¾ | **9** | 11/1 | 26 | — |
| | **Petite Risk** (KWHogg) **2-7-12** NKennedy(10) (lt-f: s.i.s: a bhd) | 7 | **10** | 33/1 | — | — |
| | | | | (SP 123.5%) | **10 Rn** | |

**58.5 secs** (1.00) CSF £7.18 TOTE £3.00: £1.60 £1.10 £1.90 (£2.80) Trio £3.50 OWNER Manny Bernstein (Racing) Ltd (COCKERHAM) BRED J. A. and Mrs Duffy
**2076 Ballymote,** from a yard in form, did it well and was well in command in the final furlong. (5/2)
**2712 What Happened Was** had problems with a slipping saddle from halfway and did really well to finish second. (13/8)
**Balladoole Bajan** put in a decent first effort and should be all the sharper for it. (4/1: 5/2-5/1)
**557 Super Saint** kept struggling on from halfway, but lacks any turn of speed to make an impression. (14/1)
**2122 Tribal Mischief** gave problems by hanging left throughout the race, which put paid to any chance. (8/1: 7/1-11/1)
**Miss Alice,** clueless early on, certainly picked up as the race progressed and looks likely to improve with experience. (50/1)

T/Plpt: £51.80 (299.02 Tckts). T/Qdpt: £2.00 (639.36 Tckts). AA

# 2543-SANDOWN (R-H) (Good to firm)
## Wednesday July 17th
WEATHER: v.warm WIND: slt half bhd

## 2782 TIMEFORM RACECARD MAIDEN STKS (2-Y.O) (Class D)
2-00 (2-01) **5f 6y** £3,436.25 (£1,040.00: £507.50: £241.25) Stalls: High GOING minus 0.67 sec per fur (HD)

| | | | | SP | RR | SF |
|---|---|---|---|---|---|---|
| | **Seebe (USA)** (IABalding) **2-8-9** MHills(2) (unf: scope: lw: mde virtually all: shkn up over 1f out: qcknd: easily) | — | **1** | 4/7[1] | 72+ | 22 |
| 1989[2] | **Assume (USA)** (JWHills) **2-9-0** GDuffield(3) (hld up: rdn over 1f out: r.o one pce) | 2½ | **2** | 6/1[3] | 69 | 19 |
| 2614[2] | **Bold Tina (IRE)** (RHannon) **2-8-6**(3) DaneO'Neill(1) (w wnr: rdn over 1f out: one pce) | ½ | **3** | 3/1[2] | 63 | 13 |
| | **Hornbeam** (JRJenkins) **2-9-0** RCochrane(4) (str: scope: lw: hld up: rdn over 1f out: one pce) | 1¼ | **4** | 20/1 | 64 | 14 |
| | | | | (SP 107.7%) | **4 Rn** | |

**60.75 secs** (0.95) CSF £3.95 TOTE £1.60 (£2.70) OWNER Mr George Strawbridge (KINGSCLERE) BRED George Strawbridge
**Seebe (USA),** a sister to Skillington and a half-sister to Selkirk, ran green, but made virtually all. Shaken up below the distance, she quickened right away to win in impressive style. Sure to be a lot wiser for this, she does need time to develop but certainly has the scope to do so, and she can win again. (4/7)
**1989 Assume (USA),** who took quite a keen hold towards the rear of the field, stayed on for second, but had no chance with the winner. (6/1: op 5/2)
**2614 Bold Tina (IRE)** raced with the winner but, when that rival was let loose below the distance, she was left standing. (3/1: op 2/1)
**Hornbeam,** a well-made colt, looked in good shape in the paddock. Held up, he was pushed along below the distance, but failed to find the necessary turn of foot. (20/1)

## 2783 TIMEFORM DAY AT SANDOWN MEDIAN AUCTION MAIDEN STKS (2-Y.O) (Class E)
2-35 (2-38) **7f 16y** £3,550.00 (£1,075.00: £525.00: £250.00) Stalls: High GOING minus 0.67 sec per fur (HD)

| | | | | SP | RR | SF |
|---|---|---|---|---|---|---|
| 2600[2] | **Isle of Man (USA)** (PFICole) **2-9-0** TQuinn(9) (mde all: easily) | — | **1** | 11/10[1] | 75+ | 36 |
| | **Hindsight (IRE)** (WJHaggas) **2-9-0** RCochrane(11) (b.nr fore: unf: scope: bit bkwd: hld up: chsd wnr over 1f out: no imp) | 2 | **2** | 5/1[2] | 71+ | 32 |
| | **Moon Blast** (LadyHerries) **2-9-0** JReid(8) (unf: scope: bit bkwd: rdn 6f out: mid div whn nt clr run on ins over 2f out: hdwy over 1f out: r.o) | 6 | **3** | 12/1[3] | 57 | 18 |
| 2543[5] | **Blue River (IRE)** (TGMills) **2-9-0** PaulEddery(5) (lw: hld up: rdn over 3f out: one pce) | hd | **4** | 33/1 | 57 | 18 |
| 2343[5] | **Scarlet Lake** (DRLoder) **2-8-6**(3) PMcCabe(7) (chsd wnr over 5f: wknd fnl f) | ½ | **5** | 14/1 | 51 | 12 |
| | **Captain William (IRE)** (IABalding) **2-9-0** MHills(1) (str: scope: lw: hdwy over 3f out: wknd over 1f out) | nk | **6** | 5/1[2] | 55 | 16 |
| | **Moonspell** (RCharlton) **2-8-9** TSprake(3) (unf: scope: nvr nr to chal) | 3 | **7** | 12/1[3] | 43 | 4 |
| | **River King** (RHannon) **2-9-0** MRoberts(4) (str: scope: bit bkwd: s.s: a bhd) | 1¼ | **8** | 14/1 | 45 | 6 |
| | **Motcombs Club** (NACallaghan) **2-8-11**(3) DaneO'Neill(6) (unf: scope: bit bkwd: a bhd) | nk | **9** | 33/1 | 45 | 6 |
| 2600[6] | **The Green Grey** (LordHuntingdon) **2-9-0** DHarrison(2) (prom over 4f) | 2 | **10** | 20/1 | 40 | 1 |
| 2224[9] | **Yangtze (IRE)** (BRMillman) **2-9-0** WJO'Connor(10) (hld up: rdn over 3f out: wknd over 2f out) | 3 | **11** | 66/1 | 33 | — |
| | | | | (SP 121.8%) | **11 Rn** | |

**1m 29.41** (0.81) CSF £7.42 TOTE £2.00: £1.10 £1.90 £3.80 (£6.90) Trio £22.40 OWNER H R H Prince Fahd Salman (WHATCOMBE) BRED Newgate Stud Farm Inc.
**2600 Isle of Man (USA)** made no mistake on this occasion. Bowling along merrily in front, his jockey had an armchair ride, and the combination came home to win with a ton in hand. He can progress from here. (11/10: op 4/6)
**Hindsight (IRE),** a plain colt, did not look fully wound up, but still ran well. He will not always meet one so good. (5/1: 4/1-6/1)
**Moon Blast,** a half-brother to high-class middle-distance performers Moon Madness and Sheriff's Star, did not look fully tuned up. Soon being bustled along, he was squeezed for room along the rail over a quarter of a mile from home but, despite this, stayed on well in the last furlong and a half to snatch third. (12/1: op 6/1)

**2543 Blue River (IRE)** failed to find the necessary turn of foot and needs further. (33/1)
**2343 Scarlet Lake** does not possess much substance. (14/1: 6/1-16/1)
**Captain William (IRE)**, an attractive deep-girthed colt, was very well backed for this debut. Taking closer order entering the straight, he found lack of a recent run taking its toll below the distance. He should come on a lot for this and can find a race in due course. (5/1)
**Moonspell** (12/1: op 4/1)

## 2784 COMPUTER TIMEFORM H'CAP (0-80) (3-Y.O+) (Class D)
3-05 (3-08) **1m 2f 7y** £4,201.50 (£1,272.00: £621.00: £295.50) Stalls: High GOING minus 0.67 sec per fur (HD)

| | | | | SP | RR | SF |
|---|---|---|---|---|---|---|
| 2525[4] | **Mister O'Grady (IRE) (49)** (RAkehurst) **5-8-8** TQuinn(8) (a.p: chsd ldr over 3f out: hrd rdn over 2f out: led nr fin) | — | **1** | 7/2[2] | 62 | 21 |
| 2483[9] | **Autumn Cover (61)** (PRHedger) **4-9-6** DBiggs(5) (led: rdn over 2f out: hdd nr fin) | nk | **2** | 12/1 | 74 | 33 |
| 2574[12] | **Ashby Hill (IRE) (53)** (RRowe) **5-8-12** RCochrane(7) (b: stdy hdwy over 2f out: nt clr run on ins over 1f out tl ins fnl f: swtchd lft: nt rcvr) | 1½ | **3** | 10/1 | 63 | 22 |
| 1903[3] | **Harvey White (IRE) (59)** (JPearce) **4-9-4** MHills(2) (rdn over 2f out: hdwy wl over 1f out: r.o one pce) | 3½ | **4** | 13/2 | 64 | 23 |
| 2574[2] | **Runic Symbol (39)** (MBlanshard) **5-7-12** JQuinn(4) (lw: hld up: hrd rdn over 2f out: one pce) | ½ | **5** | 3/1[1] | 43 | 2 |
| 2577[4] | **Desert Calm (IRE) (50)** (MrsPNDutfield) **7-8-2b**(7) JoHunnam(6) (nvr nr to chal) | 2 | **6** | 16/1 | 51 | 10 |
| 2234[2] | **Witherkay (63)** (RHannon) **3-8-12** MRoberts(10) (hld up: rdn over 3f out: eased whn btn over 1f out) | s.h | **7** | 11/2[3] | 64 | 13 |
| 619[2] | **Mentalasanythin (65)** (DHaydnJones) **7-9-10** AMackay(9) (bit bkwd: swtg: a bhd) | hd | **8** | 14/1 | 65 | 24 |
| 2377[5] | **Braydon Forest (50)** (CJDrewe) **4-8-9** DHolland(1) (chsd ldr 5f: wknd 3f out) | 7 | **9** | 25/1 | 39 | — |
| 2574[4] | **Premier League (IRE) (64)** (JELong) **6-9-2**(7) TField(3) (a.p: chsd ldr 5f out tl over 3f out: wknd over 2f out) | 2½ | **10** | 12/1 | 49 | 8 |
| | | | | (SP 116.8%) | **10 Rn** | |

**2m 9.18** (2.48) CSF £40.25 CT £352.22 TOTE £3.80: £2.00 £4.30 £2.40 (£56.70) Trio £63.50 OWNER City Industrial Supplies Ltd (EPSOM) BRED A. Ross
WEIGHT FOR AGE 3yo-10lb
**2525 Mister O'Grady (IRE)** moved into second place early in the straight. Soon under pressure, he eventually managed to get on top in the shadow of the post. (7/2)
**2000* Autumn Cover**, in sparkling form until flopping last time out, bounced back here, if just unable to carry the day. Tackling a longer trip - all three wins have come over a mile - he bowled along in front and grimly held on until collared near the line. (12/1: op 8/1)
**2000 Ashby Hill (IRE)** again met with the traffic problems she had also encountered here last month. Creeping into the action over quarter of a mile from home, she found her way blocked by the front two below the distance and had nowhere to go until her pilot managed to switch her inside the final furlong. By then the damage had been done and she failed to recover, but she should soon be winning on this surface. (10/1)
**1903 Harvey White (IRE)** struggled on in the final quarter-mile for fourth without posing a threat. (13/2)
**2574 Runic Symbol** chased the leaders but, under strong pressure over two furlongs from home, could only go up and down on the spot.(3/1)
**2577 Desert Calm (IRE)**, racing at the back of the field, made a little late headway. (16/1)
**619 Mentalasanythin** (14/1: 8/1-16/1)
**2574 Premier League (IRE)** (12/1: 8/1-14/1)

## 2785 TIMEFORM BLACK BOOK H'CAP (0-70) (3-Y.O+) (Class E)
3-35 (3-37) **7f 16y** £3,501.25 (£1,060.00: £517.50: £246.25) Stalls: High GOING minus 0.67 sec per fur (HD)

| | | | | SP | RR | SF |
|---|---|---|---|---|---|---|
| 2320[3] | **Sylvan Princess (45)** (CNAllen) **3-7-10**(5) MartinDwyer(6) (hdwy over 2f out: led over 1f out: r.o wl) | — | **1** | 5/1[3] | 56 | 28 |
| 2507* | **Orchard Gold (46)** (JPearce) **5-8-9** GBardwell(5) (b.nr fore: hdwy over 2f out: ev ch over 1f out: unable qckn) | 1½ | **2** | 4/1[2] | 54 | 33 |
| 2577[10] | **African-Pard (IRE) (61)** (DHaydnJones) **4-9-10b[1]** TQuinn(8) (hld up: ev ch over 1f out: one pce) | 1½ | **3** | 14/1 | 65 | 44 |
| 2525[6] | **Irrepressible (IRE) (45)** (RJHodges) **5-8-3**(5) ADaly(2) (mid div whn hmpd over 2f out: swtchd lft: hdwy over 1f out: r.o wl ins fnl f) | nk | **4** | 6/1 | 49 | 28 |
| 2578[3] | **Dummer Golf Time (60)** (LordHuntingdon) **3-9-2v** DHarrison(10) (a.p: nt clr run on ins over 2f out: rdn over 1f out: one pce ins fnl f) | ¾ | **5** | 7/4[1] | 62 | 34 |
| 2345[9] | **Sobeloved (33)** (NEBerry) **4-7-5**(5) CAdamson(9) (hld up: n.m.r 2f out: wknd over 1f out) | 5 | **6** | 25/1 | 24 | 3 |
| 2320[9] | **Jubilee Place (IRE) (62)** (TThomsonJones) **3-9-4** SSanders(3) (b: a.p. led over 2f out: edgd rt: hdd over 1f out: eased whn btn ins fnl f) | s.h | **7** | 16/1 | 52 | 24 |
| 2208[7] | **Flying Flowers (64)** (RHannon) **3-9-3**(3) DaneO'Neill(7) (a bhd) | s.h | **8** | 9/1 | 54 | 26 |
| 1956[6] | **Moylough Rebel (43)** (JELong) **3-7-13** NAdams(4) (lw: a bhd) | 2 | **9** | 20/1 | 29 | 1 |
| 2577[14] | **Justinianus (IRE) (45)** (JJBridger) **4-8-8** JQuinn(11) (lw: led over 4f) | 7 | **10** | 33/1 | 15 | — |
| *2367*[13] | **Young Rose (44)** (PatMitchell) **4-8-7** RCochrane(1) (lw: prom over 4f) | ¾ | **11** | 20/1 | 12 | — |
| | | | | (SP 126.2%) | **11 Rn** | |

**1m 28.97** (0.37) CSF £25.75 CT £251.84 TOTE £5.30: £1.30 £2.10 £3.80 (£12.20) Trio £43.00 OWNER Camelot Racing (NEWMARKET) BRED K S P Leisure
WEIGHT FOR AGE 3yo-7lb
**2320 Sylvan Princess** began her effort on the outside of the field over a quarter of a mile from home. Striking the front below the distance, she soon asserted. (5/1)
**2507* Orchard Gold** moved up with the winner over two furlongs out. On level terms with that rival below the distance, he then failed to contain her. (4/1)
**1613 African-Pard (IRE)**, still a maiden and shouldering topweight, was tried in blinkers for the first time. Chasing the leaders, he appeared to be going well a quarter of a mile from home and had every chance below the distance before tapped for toe. (14/1)
**2525 Irrepressible (IRE)**, who failed to stay last time, got hampered at a critical stage over two furlongs from home. Switched left, he ran on really well from below the distance but was never going to get there in time. (6/1)
**2578 Dummer Golf Time**, never far away, was boxed in against the rail over a quarter of a mile from home. He found daylight well over a furlong from home, and grimly tried to peg back the leaders, but was making no further impression in the last 100 yards. (7/4)
**Sobeloved** had come to the end of his tether below the distance. (25/1)

## 2786 TIMEFORM PERSPECTIVE MAIDEN STKS (3-Y.O+) (Class D)
4-10 (4-11) **1m 3f 91y** £3,550.00 (£1,075.00: £525.00: £250.00) Stalls: High GOING minus 0.67 sec per fur (HD)

| | | | | SP | RR | SF |
|---|---|---|---|---|---|---|
| | **Eva Luna (USA)** (HRACecil) **4-9-4** AMcGlone(1) (lw: dwlt: hdwy 10f out: chsd ldr 9f out: led over 3f out: clr over 2f out: wandered: easily) | — | **1** | 4/6[1] | 83+ | 40 |
| 2601[W] | **Caballus (USA)** (LordHuntingdon) **3-8-12** JReid(4) (lw: led 8f: unable qckn) | 10 | **2** | 7/4[2] | 74 | 20 |
| 1508[13] | **Give And Take** (LordHuntingdon) **3-8-12** DHarrison(5) (lw: hld up: rdn over 6f out: wknd 3f out) | 10 | **3** | 8/1[3] | 60 | 6 |

2579[14] **Sylvan Heights** (RTPhillips) **3-8-12** RPerham(3) (chsd ldr over 2f out: wknd over 6f out: t.o)........................15 **4** 66/1 39 —
2579[12] **Private Percival** (JRPoulton) **3-8-12** AMorris(2) (a bhd: t.o).............................................................27 **5** 66/1 1 —
(SP 110.5%) **5 Rn**

**2m 24.58** (1.18) CSF £2.16 TOTE £1.70: £1.10 £1.40 (£1.50) OWNER Mr K. Abdulla (NEWMARKET) BRED Juddmonte Farms
WEIGHT FOR AGE 3yo-11lb

**Eva Luna (USA)**, quite a lean-looking filly who has been plagued with lameness, hence her belated debut, looked fit. Storming into the lead early in the straight, she forged clear with the minimum of fuss to win this bad race. (4/6)
**1957 Caballus (USA)**, collared early in the straight, was left for dead by the winner. (7/4)
**Give And Take** raced in third place but was being shunted along halfway down the back straight, and was a spent force three furlongs from home. (8/1: 6/1-9/1)

## 2787 SURREY RACING H'CAP (0-70) (3-Y.O+) (Class E)
4-40 (4-41) **5f 6y** £3,468.75 (£1,050.00: £512.50: £243.75) Stalls: High GOING minus 0.67 sec per fur (HD)

| | | | | SP | RR | SF |
|---|---|---|---|---|---|---|
| 2548[5] | **Magic Mail (65)** (JMPEustace) **3-9-8**(5) MartinDwyer(10) (lw: a.p: led over 2f out: rdn out) | — | **1** | 14/1 | 71 | 49 |
| 2586[7] | **Gone Savage (57)** (WJMusson) **8-9-9** RCochrane(3) (stdd s: swtchd rt: gd hdwy over 1f out: rt stirrup pin broke ins fnl f: r.o wl) | 1 | **2** | 15/2 | 60 | 42 |
| 2496[3] | **Malibu Man (62)** (EAWheeler) **4-10-0** JReid(8) (lw: led over 2f: rdn over 1f out: unable qckn) | ¾ | **3** | 11/2 [2] | 62 | 44 |
| 2686[9] | **Superlao (BEL) (41)** (JJBridger) **4-8-7** JQuinn(11) (hld up: rdn over 2f out: r.o ins fnl f) | hd | **4** | 13/2 | 41 | 23 |
| 2602[11] | **Squire Corrie (57)** (GHarwood) **4-9-2b**(7) GayeHarwood(9) (lw: a.p: rdn wl over 1f out: one pce) | s.h | **5** | 20/1 | 57 | 39 |
| 2586[10] | **John O'Dreams (53)** (MrsALMKing) **11-9-5** MRoberts(5) (b: lw: nt clr run over 1f out: nvr nr to chal) | 1 | **6** | 12/1 | 50 | 32 |
| 2757* | **Ned's Bonanza (63)** (MDods) **7-10-1** 6x AClark(4) (rdn over 3f out: hdwy over 2f out: one pce) | 1½ | **7** | 5/1 [1] | 55 | 37 |
| 1964[4] | **Metal Boys (56)** (MissLCSiddall) **9-9-1**(7) TSiddall(7) (b.off hind: nvr nrr) | 1½ | **8** | 14/1 | 43 | 25 |
| 2735[5] | **Classic Pet (IRE) (42)** (CAHorgan) **4-8-8** NAdams(2) (a bhd) | 1½ | **9** | 25/1 | 24 | 6 |
| 2434[7] | **Judgement Call (51)** (PHowling) **9-9-3** PaulEddery(12) (b: lw: prom over 2f) | ¾ | **10** | 6/1 [3] | 31 | 13 |
| 2561* | **Walk the Beat (61)** (MartynMeade) **6-9-8**(5) RHavlin(6) (lw: prom 3f) | ½ | **11** | 11/2 [2] | 40 | 22 |
| 2561[2] | **Deardaw (35)** (MDIUsher) **4-8-1** SSanders(1) (prom 3f) | 3½ | **12** | 14/1 | 2 | — |
| | | | | (SP 123.1%) | | **12 Rn** |

**60.11 secs** (0.31) CSF £108.98 CT £613.06 TOTE £14.00: £4.20 £2.70 £2.00 (£69.70) Trio £133.20 OWNER Mr Gary Coull (NEWMARKET) BRED Mrs C. A. Thomson Jones
WEIGHT FOR AGE 3yo-4lb

**2548 Magic Mail**, in the front rank from the outset, went on at halfway and, ridden along, held on well. (14/1: op 8/1)
**2586 Gone Savage** goes well on this course and has gained four of his seven victories here. Steadied in at the start and switched to the favoured far rail, he picked up ground in good style below the distance, but his jockey's stirrup pin broke inside the final furlong, and the combination could only run on to snatch second. (15/2)
**2496 Malibu Man**, in front to halfway, was soon being pushed along, but failed to find another gear. (11/2)
**2324 Superlao (BEL)** chased the leaders. Ridden along from halfway, she ran on inside the final furlong, and only just lost out on third prize. (13/2)
**Squire Corrie** failed to find the necessary turn of foot in the final two furlongs. (20/1)
**2244* John O'Dreams** met with interference early in the final quarter-mile, and could never get on terms with the principals. (12/1)

T/Jkpt: £8,138.90 (0.59 Tckts); £4,699.94 to Leicester 18/7/96. T/Plpt: £78.40 (189.36 Tckts). T/Qdpt: £24.60 (47.94 Tckts). AK

# 2556-BATH (L-H) (Firm)
## Thursday July 18th
WEATHER: fine WIND: nil

## 2788 WHITE HORSE (S) STKS (4-Y.O+) (Class G)
2-00 (2-02) **1m 3f 144y** £2,192.00 (£612.00: £296.00) GOING minus 0.44 sec per fur (F)

| | | | | SP | RR | SF |
|---|---|---|---|---|---|---|
| 2378[8] | **Flight Master (62)** (PJMakin) **4-9-2** SSanders(6) (t: hld up: hdwy over 2f out: hrd rdn over 1f out: led wl ins fnl f: r.o) | — | **1** | 7/4 [1] | 64 | 37 |
| 2373[5] | **Siesta Time (USA)** (CLPopham) **6-8-11** JReid(2) (a.p: wnt 2nd over 3f out: rdn over 2f out: ev ch ins fnl f: r.o) | hd | **2** | 8/1 | 59 | 32 |
| 2556[2] | **Durham (54)** (RSimpson) **5-8-11b**(5) AimeeCook(5) (lw: led tl wl ins fnl f) | 1¾ | **3** | 3/1 [2] | 62 | 35 |
| 2674[7] | **Trade Wind (64)** (JGMO'Shea) **5-9-2v** VSlattery(7) (b.nr hind: lw: chsd ldr tl rdn over 3f out: one pce fnl 2f) | 2 | **4** | 11/2 [3] | 59 | 32 |
| 2373[9] | **Kama Simba (45)** (JWhite) **4-9-2b**[1] TQuinn(3) (prom tl wknd over 1f out) | 3½ | **5** | 16/1 | 54 | 27 |
| 2716[4] | **Scottish Park (46)** (MCPipe) **7-9-2b** MRoberts(4) (hld up: rdn & hdwy on ins 3f out: wknd over 1f out: eased ins fnl f) | 1 | **6** | 11/2 [3] | 53 | 26 |
| | **Lost Realm** (MartynMeade) **4-9-2** RPerham(1) (bkwd: bhd fnl 3f) | 5 | **7** | 40/1 | 46 | 19 |
| | | | | (SP 111.6%) | | **7 Rn** |

**2m 30.8** (4.10) CSF £14.40 TOTE £2.70: £1.80 £2.80 (£13.40) OWNER Mrs P. J. Makin (MARLBOROUGH) BRED P. J. Makin
No bid

**Flight Master**, who has been tubed, had to work hard to take advantage of this drop into selling company. (7/4)
**2373 Siesta Time (USA)**, who has changed stables, was back to a more suitable trip, but could never quite poke her head in front. (8/1: op 5/1)
**2556 Durham**, the reluctant leader, might just as well have set a stronger gallop from the off over this shorter trip. (3/1)
**2494 Trade Wind** lacked the required turn of foot when the race was on in earnest. (11/2)
**Kama Simba** was trying a longer trip for this first run in blinkers. (16/1)
**2716 Scottish Park**, stepping up in distance, could not sustain her run up the inside. (11/2)

## 2789 JAMES & COWPER MAIDEN STKS (3-Y.O) (Class D)
2-30 (2-31) **1m 5y** £3,804.50 (£1,062.00: £513.50) GOING minus 0.44 sec per fur (F)

| | | | | SP | RR | SF |
|---|---|---|---|---|---|---|
| 2432[2] | **Saleemah (USA) (78)** (JLDunlop) **3-8-9** WCarson(2) (mde all: qcknd clr 2f out: easily) | — | **1** | 1/2 [1] | 84 | 47 |
| | **Rehaab** (ACStewart) **3-8-9** MRoberts(3) (unf: chsd wnr: outpcd 2f out: no ch w wnr) | 12 | **2** | 9/4 [2] | 60 | 23 |
| 1670[5] | **Tabl (IRE)** (HThomsonJones) **3-8-9** RHills(1) (hld up: rdn over 2f out: sn outpcd) | 1¾ | **3** | 6/1 [3] | 57 | 20 |
| | | | | (SP 111.7%) | | **3 Rn** |

**1m 39.5** (1.00) CSF £2.01 TOTE £1.30 (£1.50) OWNER Mr Hamdan Al Maktoum (ARUNDEL) BRED Manning Family Trust

**2432 Saleemah (USA)** made short work of her two rivals. (1/2)
**Rehaab** could not go with the winner, but was by no means knocked about. (9/4)
**1670 Tabl (IRE)** lost out in the battle for second with the tenderly-handled runner-up. (6/1)

## 2790 TOTE BOOKMAKERS H'CAP (0-90) (3-Y.O) (Class C)

3-00 (3-04) **5f 11y** £5,502.50 (£1,655.00: £800.00: £372.50) GOING minus 0.44 sec per fur (F)

| Form | Horse | Dist | Pos | SP | RR | SF |
|---|---|---|---|---|---|---|
| 2745[4] | **Mindrace (64)** (KTIvory) **3-7-5**(5) MartinDwyer(4) (a.p: squeezed thro to ld wl ins fnl f: r.o) | — | **1** | 12/1 | 73 | 33 |
| 2584[2] | **White Emir (81)** (BJMeehan) **3-8-13b** JReid(6) (lw: a.p: led over 2f out: edgd lft 1f out: hdd wl ins fnl f) | ½ | **2** | 2/1[1] | 88 | 48 |
| 2403[10] | **Sharp Pearl (76)** (JWhite) **3-8-8b** TQuinn(5) (lw: a.p: r.o one pce fnl f) | 1¾ | **3** | 14/1 | 78 | 38 |
| 2676[3] | **Gwespyr (64)** (JBerry) **3-7-10** GBardwell(7) (s.i.s: hdwy over 2f out: nt clr run over 1f out: r.o ins fnl f) | hd | **4** | 3/1[2] | 66 | 26 |
| 2301[2] | **Rushcutter Bay (89)** (TTClement) **3-9-4v**(3) DaneO'Neill(1) (b: lw: led over 2f: one pce fnl 2f) | nk | **5** | 6/1[3] | 90 | 50 |
| 2719[4] | **Fairy Prince (IRE) (64)** (MrsALMKing) **3-7-7**(3) NVarley(8) (no hdwy fnl 2f) | 2½ | **6** | 12/1 | 57 | 17 |
| 2244[5] | **Step On Degas (67)** (MJFetherston-Godley) **3-7-10v[1]**(3) MHenry(3) (hld up: hmpd 3f out: n.m.r over 2f out: sn bhd) | 5 | **7** | 8/1 | 44 | 4 |
| 2301[3] | **Total Aloof (74)** (WJHaggas) **3-8-6** MHills(2) (lw: prom 3f) | 8 | **8** | 6/1[3] | 26 | — |

(SP 120.1%) **8 Rn**

**61.2 secs** (0.70) CSF £36.47 CT £327.57 TOTE £13.60: £2.60 £1.30 £3.70 (£30.50) OWNER Mr D. F. Abbott (RADLETT) BRED Mrs P. A. Brown
LONG HANDICAP Mindrace 7-5 Fairy Prince (IRE) 7-7 Gwespyr 7-9
**2745 Mindrace**, making a quick reappearance, was only running off his true handicap mark because of his rider's allowance. (12/1)
**2584 White Emir** was due to go up 5lb in future handicaps following his good second in the first-time blinkers at Newmarket. (2/1)
**1663* Sharp Pearl** was still 6lb higher than when scoring at Brighton last month. (14/1)
**2676 Gwespyr**, who played up at the start, was 6lb higher than when winning at Haydock and did not seem to mind this faster ground. (3/1)
**2301 Rushcutter Bay**, up a further 4lb, was 10lb higher than when winning at Nottingham. (6/1)
**2719 Fairy Prince (IRE)**, like the winner, was racing off his correct mark thanks to his rider's allowance. (12/1: 8/1-14/1)

## 2791 LONGLEAT CLAIMING STKS (3-Y.O+) (Class F)

3-30 (3-31) **5f 11y** £2,670.00 (£745.00: £360.00) GOING minus 0.44 sec per fur (F)

| Form | Horse | Dist | Pos | SP | RR | SF |
|---|---|---|---|---|---|---|
| 2403[6] | **Tafahhus (67)** (MJPolglase) **4-9-2b** MRoberts(1) (swtg: a.p: led over 1f out: r.o wl) | — | **1** | 6/4[1] | 57 | 40 |
| 2713[7] | **Astral Invader (IRE) (51)** (MSSaunders) **4-9-3**(5) PPMurphy(5) (bhd: hrd rdn 2f out: gd hdwy fnl f: fin wl) | 1½ | **2** | 8/1 | 58 | 41 |
| 2393[5] | **Marino Street (57)** (PDEvans) **3-8-7v** TQuinn(6) (hld up & bhd: hdwy 2f out: nt clr run 1f out: bdly hmpd ins fnl f: r.o) | s.h | **3** | 6/1[3] | 47 | 26 |
| 2787[12] | **Deardaw (35)** (MDIUsher) **4-8-6** SSanders(7) (b: a.p: hrd rdn & ev ch over 1f out: btn whn edgd lft ins fnl f) | nk | **4** | 8/1 | 41 | 24 |
| 2561[8] | **Johayro (65)** (WGMTurner) **3-8-11b**(7) GHannon(2) (swtg: a.p: btn whn carried lft ins fnl f) | 2 | **5** | 10/1 | 51 | 30 |
| *2684*[5] | **Tommy Tempest (42)** (REPeacock) **7-8-8b**(3) DaneO'Neill(4) (a.p: led over 2f out tl over 1f out: btn whn bmpd ins fnl f) | nk | **6** | 16/1 | 39 | 22 |
| 2347[6] | **Colston-C (65)** (RJBaker) **4-9-2** JReid(3) (led over 2f: rdn & btn whn hmpd on ins over 1f out) | nk | **7** | 11/4[2] | 43 | 26 |
| 2561[7] | **Woodlands Electric (15)** (PAPritchard) **6-8-4**(7) JoHunnam(9) (b.hind: outpcd) | 6 | **8** | 66/1 | 19 | 2 |
| 2347[8] | **Daydream Island (35)** (RJBaker) **3-8-4** NAdams(8) (outpcd) | 4 | **9** | 50/1 | 3 | — |

(SP 121.6%) **9 Rn**

**61.9 secs** (1.40) CSF £14.24 TOTE £2.40: £1.10 £1.90 £2.00 (£14.60) Trio £23.20 OWNER Mr Roger Newton (NEWMARKET) BRED Shadwell Estate Company Limited
WEIGHT FOR AGE 3yo-4lb
Deardaw clmd DPriday £2,500
**2403 Tafahhus**, whose four previous wins have been over six, provided his trainer with his first winner. (6/4)
**2561 Astral Invader (IRE)** ran a carbon copy of his race at Bath two outings ago, and the extended five here might be the answer. (8/1)
**2393 Marino Street**, dropping back to the minimum trip, found traffic problems and was battling for the places when hit for six in the last 200 yards. (6/1)
**2561 Deardaw** was having her second race in less than twenty-four hours. (8/1)
**Johayro** was intimidated into going left-handed by Deardaw. (10/1: 8/1-12/1)
**2684 Tommy Tempest** extended his losing run to eighteen. (16/1)

## 2792 AVEBURY MEDIAN AUCTION MAIDEN STKS (2-Y.O) (Class F)

4-00 (4-03) **5f 161y** £2,722.50 (£760.00: £367.50) GOING minus 0.44 sec per fur (F)

| Form | Horse | Dist | Pos | SP | RR | SF |
|---|---|---|---|---|---|---|
| 2245[4] | **Tumbleweed Pearl** (BJMeehan) **2-8-9** JReid(1) (lw: hld up: hdwy on bit over 2f out: led over 1f out: pushed out) | — | **1** | 4/11[1] | 67+ | 23 |
| 2596[3] | **Miss Barcelona (IRE)** (MJPolglase) **2-8-9** MRoberts(2) (a.p: rdn over 3f out: swtchd rt 2f out: r.o ins fnl f: nt trble wnr) | 2 | **2** | 12/1 | 61 | 17 |
| 2413[6] | **Anokato** (KTIvory) **2-8-7**(7) CScally(5) (s.i.s: sn prom: hrd rdn over 2f out: one pce) | 2½ | **3** | 40/1 | 59 | 15 |
| 1537[6] | **Fine Times** (CWFairhurst) **2-9-0** JTate(6) (hrd rdn over 2f out: no hdwy) | 3½ | **4** | 9/1[2] | 50 | 6 |
| 2527[4] | **Strat's Quest** (DWPArbuthnot) **2-8-9** TQuinn(7) (led over 2f: wknd over 1f out) | 3 | **5** | 11/1[3] | 36 | — |
| | **Poker Princess** (MBell) **2-8-9** MFenton(4) (b.nr hind: small: prom over 3f) | 11 | **6** | 9/1[2] | 6 | — |
| | **Lochlore** (MissKWhitehouse) **2-8-9** SDWilliams(3) (small: dwlt: a bhd) | 9 | **7** | 66/1 | — | — |

(SP 113.3%) **7 Rn**

**1m 11.9** (2.40) CSF £5.70 TOTE £1.40: £1.10 £2.80 (£3.70) OWNER The Tumbleweed Partnership (UPPER LAMBOURN) BRED R. A. Dalton
**2245 Tumbleweed Pearl** proved too sharp for these rivals. (4/11: 1/2-1/3)
**2596 Miss Barcelona (IRE)** deserves credit for the way she battled on, but she was never causing favourite backers any anxiety. (12/1)
**2413 Anokato**, a brother to Mindrace who had scored earlier in the afternoon, fared better than on his debut. (40/1)
**1537 Fine Times** (9/1: 8/1-12/1)
**2527 Strat's Quest** lacks the substance to progress. (11/1: 7/1-12/1)
**Poker Princess** (9/1: 4/1-10/1)

## 2793 WESTONBIRT H'CAP (0-70) (3-Y.O+ F & M) (Class E)

4-30 (4-31) **1m 2f 46y** £3,148.50 (£948.00: £459.00: £214.50) GOING minus 0.44 sec per fur (F)

| Form | Horse | Dist | Pos | SP | RR | SF |
|---|---|---|---|---|---|---|
| 2226[13] | **Royal Thimble (IRE) (50)** (NoelChance) **5-8-3v[1]**(5) MartinDwyer(5) (lw: hld up: led over 1f out: rdn out) | — | **1** | 12/1 | 63 | 44 |

| | | | | | | |
|---|---|---|---|---|---|---|
| 2594* | **Harlequin Walk (IRE) (38)** (RJO'Sullivan) **5-7-7b**(3) 5x NVarley(2) (led tl over 1f out: one pce) | 3 | **2** | 13/8$^{1}$ | 46 | 27 |
| 2348$^{4}$ | **Rasayel (USA) (56)** (PDEvans) **6-9-0** TQuinn(7) (lw: plld hrd: gd hdwy 7f out: wknd over 1f out) | 3½ | **3** | 11/4$^{2}$ | 59 | 40 |
| | **Debutante Days (70)** (CREgerton) **4-10-0** JReid(4) (chsd ldr 6f: rdn & outpcd 3f out: n.d after) | 1 | **4** | 9/2$^{3}$ | 71 | 52 |
| 2592$^{6}$ | **Prudent Pet (50)** (CWFairhurst) **4-8-8** JTate(3) (lw: hdwy 3f out: wknd 2f out) | 2 | **5** | 14/1 | 48 | 29 |
| 2558$^{5}$ | **Meg's Memory (IRE) (58)** (JohnBerry) **3-8-6** MFenton(6) (hrd rdn over 3f out: sn bhd) | 3 | **6** | 8/1 | 51 | 22 |
| 2617$^{9}$ | **Kowtow (64)** (MDIUsher) **3-8-12** RStreet(1) (lw: hld up & plld hrd: a bhd) | 14 | **7** | 16/1 | 36 | 7 |
| | | | | (SP 114.3%) | | **7 Rn** |

**2m 9.1** (1.60) CSF £31.06 TOTE £13.30: £2.60 £2.10 (£18.10) OWNER Mrs M. Chance (LAMBOURN) BRED Somerville Stud
LONG HANDICAP Harlequin Walk (IRE) 7-4
WEIGHT FOR AGE 3yo-10lb
**Royal Thimble (IRE)**, dropped 19lb this season, was apparently in season last time, and found the visor doing the trick. (12/1)
**2594* Harlequin Walk (IRE)**, penalised 5lb for her wide-margin win in poor company last week, was due to go up a further 9lb in future handicaps. (13/8)
**2348 Rasayel (USA)**, whose last two runs have been in amateur races, was still 6lb higher than when successful at Doncaster in May. (11/4)
**Debutante Days**, who got no further than the first when favourite for the Triumph, has since changed stables and was 6lb higher than when winning on her last outing on the Flat. (9/2: 5/2-5/1)
**2045 Prudent Pet** was due to go down 3lb in future handicaps. (14/1)
**2558 Meg's Memory (IRE)**, whose regular pilot deserted her in favour of the favourite, was already set to drop 2lb in the future. (8/1)

T/Plpt: £11.90 (889.92 Tckts). T/Qdpt: £3.70 (218.66 Tckts). KH

## 1986-LEICESTER (R-H) (Good to firm)
## Thursday July 18th
WEATHER: hot & sunny WIND: nil

### 2794 MOUNTSORREL MEDIAN AUCTION MAIDEN STKS (3 & 4-Y.O) (Class F)
2-15 (2-17) **1m 1f 218y** £2,880.80 (£798.80: £382.40) Stalls: High GOING minus 0.39 sec per fur (F)

| | | | | SP | RR | SF |
|---|---|---|---|---|---|---|
| 2601$^{5}$ | **Palamon (USA) (84)** (RCharlton) **3-8-11** TSprake(5) (trckd ldrs: led 2f out: rdn clr fnl f) | — | **1** | 8/15$^{1}$ | 84 | 43 |
| 2326$^{7}$ | **Agdistis** (HThomsonJones) **3-8-6** PRobinson(7) (chsd ldr: ev ch 2f out: rdn & no ex fnl f) | 6 | **2** | 9/1$^{3}$ | 69 | 28 |
| 982$^{6}$ | **Mountain Dream (72)** (LMCumani) **3-8-11** KDarley(3) (hld up: hdwy 4f out: rdn over 2f out: one pce) | 3½ | **3** | 8/1$^{2}$ | 69 | 28 |
| 1826$^{11}$ | **Seventh Edition (57)** (DBurchell) **3-8-8**(3) SDrowne(10) (lw: chsd ldrs: rdn over 2f out: sn btn) | 1¼ | **4** | 20/1 | 67 | 26 |
| *73*$^{2}$ | **Supermodel** (MrsNMacauley) **4-8-13**(3) CTeague(4) (led: clr over 4f out: hdd 2f out: sn wknd) | 5 | **5** | 9/1$^{3}$ | 54 | 23 |
| 2208$^{8}$ | **Blossomville** (MAJarvis) **3-8-6** PBloomfield(9) (trckd ldrs tl rdn & btn 2f out) | hd | **6** | 16/1 | 54 | 13 |
| 1142$^{16}$ | **Beauchamp Knight** (HCandy) **3-8-11** CRutter(1) (lw: chsd ldrs: rdn 3f out: sn btn) | 1¾ | **7** | 9/1$^{3}$ | 56 | 15 |
| 1957$^{5}$ | **Sharp Progress** (APJones) **3-8-11** GCarter(11) (lw: hld up: r.o fnl 2f: nvr rchd ldrs) | 1 | **8** | 16/1 | 54 | 13 |
| 2572$^{12}$ | **Petit Flora** (GHolmes) **4-9-2** DeanMcKeown(13) (b.hind: dwlt: rdn 3f out: nvr trbld ldrs) | 7 | **9** | 33/1 | 38 | 7 |
| | **Queens Fancy** (SDow) **3-8-1**(5) ADaly(6) (lw: in tch 6f) | 1 | **10** | 100/1 | 36 | — |
| 2589$^{6}$ | **Meadow Blue** (MissLCSiddall) **3-8-6** WJO'Connor(2) (bit bkwd: prom tl wknd over 4f out) | 14 | **11** | 100/1 | 14 | — |
| *2325*$^{9}$ | **Sotonian (HOL)** (MrsLStubbs) **3-8-11b1** JFEgan(12) (plld hrd: chsd ldrs 5f) | 11 | **12** | 100/1 | 1 | — |
| | **Psp Lady** (APJones) **3-8-6** MTebbutt(8) (w'like: unf: dwlt: sn wl bhd) | 3½ | **13** | 50/1 | — | — |
| | | | | (SP 130.7%) | | **13 Rn** |

**2m 6.2** (2.50) CSF £7.67 TOTE £1.40: £1.10 £2.50 £1.10 (£11.20) Trio £48.70 OWNER Mr Michael Pescod (BECKHAMPTON) BRED Robert B. Trussell Jr.
WEIGHT FOR AGE 3yo-10lb
**2601 Palamon (USA)** looked a class apart from these on the book and moved to post well. He never looked in serious danger once hitting the front, but had to be bustled up to draw clear of the persistent runner-up. (8/15)
**Agdistis** has plenty of size and certainly did much better than on her debut, giving the winner something to think about in the last couple of furlongs. She should continue to progress. (9/1: 10/1-16/1)
**982 Mountain Dream** looked to get this trip, but was rather one-paced when sent about his business. (8/1: 5/1-9/1)
**1182 Seventh Edition** looked short of gears in the home straight but did stick to his task. (20/1)
**73 Supermodel**, who made all when winning over hurdles in May, tried to stretch these but had done her bit once collared. (9/1: 14/1-8/1)
**Blossomville** ran a little better this time and her future will lie in handicaps. (16/1)

### 2795 SUTTON (S) STKS (2-Y.O) (Class G)
2-45 (2-46) **5f 2y** £2,511.00 (£696.00: £333.00) Stalls: High GOING minus 0.39 sec per fur (F)

| | | | | SP | RR | SF |
|---|---|---|---|---|---|---|
| | **Silver Lining** (APJones) **2-8-11** GCarter(5) (leggy: unf: bhd: hdwy over 1f out: led ins fnl f: comf) | — | **1** | 11/1 | 70+ | 18 |
| 2422* | **I Can't Remember** (PDEvans) **2-9-2** WJO'Connor(7) (chsd ldrs: ev ch fnl f: unable qckn nr fin) | ½ | **2** | 4/1$^{2}$ | 73 | 21 |
| 1851$^{9}$ | **Accountancy Leader (IRE)** (BPalling) **2-8-6** TSprake(4) (chsd ldrs: outpcd 2f out: kpt on ins fnl f) | 3 | **3** | 9/2$^{3}$ | 54 | 2 |
| 2309$^{4}$ | **Nightingale Song** (MartynMeade) **2-8-6** FNorton(9) (swtg: prom: led 2f out: hdd ins fnl f: fnd nil) | s.h | **4** | 2/1$^{1}$ | 54 | 2 |
| 2207$^{2}$ | **Jingoist (IRE)** (JLHarris) **2-8-6b1** PRobinson(8) (lw: hdwy over 2f out: ev ch over 1f out: sn btn) | 2 | **5** | 14/1 | 47 | — |
| 2199$^{4}$ | **Vickys Double** (JSMoore) **2-8-6** JFEgan(10) (sn pushed along & bhd: r.o fnl 2f: nvr able to chal) | ½ | **6** | 12/1 | 46 | — |
| 2207* | **Emmas Breeze** (CADwyer) **2-8-11** DHarrison(1) (chsd ldrs: rdn 2f out: sn btn) | 1¼ | **7** | 11/2 | 47 | — |
| 2422$^{3}$ | **Timely Touch** (MWEllerby) **2-8-3**(3) CTeague(6) (s.i.s: a bhd) | 6 | **8** | 33/1 | 23 | — |
| *2635*$^{7}$ | **Sylvania Lights** (WRMuir) **2-8-6** SWhitworth(3) (swtg: plld hrd: led 3f) | 1¾ | **9** | 16/1 | 17 | — |
| | **Woodland Dove** (KGWingrove) **2-8-3**(3) PMcCabe(2) (lengthy: unf: dwlt: a bhd) | 2 | **10** | 20/1 | 11 | — |
| | | | | (SP 123.2%) | | **10 Rn** |

**61.1 secs** (2.60) CSF £54.05 TOTE £12.90: £2.10 £2.10 £1.60 (£53.50) Trio £128.00 OWNER Mr A. P. Jones (EASTBURY) BRED R. Hutt
Bt in 7,500 gns; Accountancy Leader (IRE) clmd CBjorling £6,000
**Silver Lining**, a decent, angular sort, still has plenty of thickening out to do and has an alarming action. Suddenly realising what was required below the distance, he swept through to lead inside the final furlong and won with a little in hand. (11/1: 8/1-12/1)
**2422* I Can't Remember** has come to hand in no uncertain terms and seemed on good terms with himself, despite the odd flash of the tail. Battling on well in the final furlong, he showed the right qualities, and this seemed an above-average seller. (4/1)
**Accountancy Leader (IRE)** went to post rather freely but was taken off his feet soon after halfway. Sticking on well in the final furlong, he snatched third place on the line. (9/2: op 3/1)
**2309 Nightingale Song**, dropped in grade, looked too good for these on paper and travelled well by the far rail until leading with two furlongs left. When joined and ridden inside the final furlong, she changed her legs and failed to respond. (2/1)

**2207 Jingoist (IRE)**, blinkered for the first time, was on edge in the paddock but settled on the way to post. She flattered briefly by the far rail below the distance, but soon gave in. (14/1)
**Vickys Double**, back to the minimum, was soon taken off her feet. (12/1: op 8/1)
**2207* Emmas Breeze** (11/2: 3/1-6/1)

## 2796 BOLLINGER CHAMPAGNE CHALLENGE SERIES GENTLEMENS' H'CAP (0-70) (3-Y.O+) (Class E)

3-15 (3-16) **7f 9y** £2,988.30 (£890.40: £424.20: £191.10) Stalls: High GOING minus 0.39 sec per fur (F)

| | | | | SP | RR | SF |
|---|---|---|---|---|---|---|
| *2369[14]* | **Mezzoramio (40)** (KAMorgan) **4-9-12v(4)** MrRThornton(5) (b: chsd ldrs: led over 1f out: hld on wl ins fnl f) | — | **1** | 14/1 | 51 | 37 |
| 2577[7] | **Just Harry (61)** (MJRyan) **5-11-5(4)** MrMEmmanuel(3) (hdwy 2f out: nt qckn ins fnl f) | 2 | **2** | 4/1[3] | 68 | 54 |
| *1719[3]* | **Speedy Snaps Pride (37)** (PDCundell) **4-9-13b** MrJRees(1) (lw: chsd ldrs: ev ch over 1f out: rdn & no ex fnl f) | 2½ | **3** | 16/1 | 38 | 24 |
| 2701[6] | **Wentbridge Lad (IRE) (66)** (PDEvans) **6-11-10v(4)** MrWMcLaughlin(6) (chsd ldrs: chal over 1f out: nt qckn fnl f) | ½ | **4** | 4/1[3] | 66 | 52 |
| 2345* | **Indrapura (IRE) (57)** (MCPipe) **4-11-5b** MrMRimell(4) (lw: led over 5f) | 4 | **5** | 100/30[1] | 48 | 34 |
| 2379[6] | **Delight of Dawn (65)** (RMStronge) **4-11-9(4)** MrJDewhurst(2) (b: s.s: hdwy over 2f out: nvr trbld ldrs) | 2 | **6** | 9/1 | 51 | 37 |
| 2577[12] | **Asterix (45)** (JMBradley) **8-10-7b** JCulloty(7) (sn rdn & bhd: hdwy 3f out: wknd over 1f out) | 6 | **7** | 7/2[2] | 17 | 3 |
| | | | | (SP 107.8%) | **7 Rn** | |

**1m 26.6** (3.60) CSF £60.59 TOTE £24.90: £6.10 £1.60 (£13.60) OWNER Mr T. R. Pryke (MELTON MOWBRAY) BRED Saeed Manana
**1411 Mezzoramio** was given a decent ride and, with a good lead, his stamina came into play in the final furlong. (14/1)
**2577 Just Harry** could not go the pace early on, but came with a good looking run approaching the final furlong, although this petered out near the line. He has rather lost his way, but at least he is well handicapped now, and he may soon be winning. (4/1)
**1719 Speedy Snaps Pride**, dropped in trip, found the fast pace bringing his stamina into play, but found his chance had gone when he failed to respond to pressure. (16/1)
**1890 Wentbridge Lad (IRE)** looked to be cruising when challenging below the distance, but found nothing and became unbalanced as the pressure was applied. He is at his best when he can be held up for an even later run. (4/1)
**2345* Indrapura (IRE)** stretched these from the start, but had burnt himself out by the furlong pole, and the situation was quickly accepted. (100/30)
**1099* Delight of Dawn** lost his chance at the start and this run is best forgotten. (9/1: op 6/1)
**2379 Asterix** did not move to post very well and soon found things going against him, as he could not go the early pace and was soon being scrubbed along. He certainly did not pull hard today. (7/2)

## 2797 TATTERSALLS AUCTION NURSERY H'CAP (2-Y.O) (Class E)

3-45 (3-46) **5f 218y** £3,179.40 (£949.20: £453.60: £205.80) Stalls: High GOING minus 0.39 sec per fur (F)

| | | | | SP | RR | SF |
|---|---|---|---|---|---|---|
| 996[6] | **Masterstroke** (BJMeehan) **2-8-7** MTebbutt(2) (chsd ldrs: rdn to ld ins fnl f: sn hdd: r.o to ld post) | — | **1** | 9/2[2] | 65 | — |
| 2012* | **Misty Cay (IRE)** (SDow) **2-8-7** JFEgan(6) (in tch: rdn & hdwy over 2f out: led wl ins fnl f: ct post) | s.h | **2** | 9/2[2] | 65 | — |
| 1471[3] | **Gresatre** (CADwyer) **2-7-10** FNorton(3) (bmpd s: bhd: hdwy over 2f out: r.o wl ins fnl f) | hd | **3** | 8/1 | 54 | — |
| 2519* | **Can Can Lady** (MJohnston) **2-8-9** JFanning(7) (lw: led: stumbled 1f out: hdd & unable qckn ins fnl f) | 1½ | **4** | 3/1[1] | 63 | — |
| 2575[3] | **Hil Rhapsody** (BPalling) **2-9-7** TSprake(4) (sltly hmpd s: in tch: rdn over 2f out: sn btn) | 10 | **5** | 3/1[1] | 48 | — |
| 2696[6] | **Bellaf** (MWEasterby) **2-8-3b[1]** JQuinn(5) (lw: w ldr: rdn over 2f out: wknd over 1f out) | 1¼ | **6** | 14/1 | 27 | — |
| 2539* | **Summer Risotto** (DJSffrenchDavis) **2-7-13** NCarlisle(1) (swtg: hdwy over 3f out: wknd 2f out) | 5 | **7** | 6/1[3] | 9 | — |
| | | | | (SP 118.4%) | **7 Rn** | |

**1m 15.1** (5.10) CSF £24.11 TOTE £5.90: £4.00 £3.50 (£40.60) OWNER Mr N. B. Attenborough (UPPER LAMBOURN) BRED G. C. Morley
STEWARDS' ENQUIRY Egan susp. 27, 29 & 30/7/96 (excessive use of whip).
**996 Masterstroke**, who has been out for ten weeks, looked as if he might just need it, but did not run that way, as he just scraped home in a desperate finish. (9/2: op 3/1)
**2012* Misty Cay (IRE)** set her pilot an all-too-usual dilemma but, responding to the stick, she ran on in the last couple of furlongs and was only just touched off near the line. Her jockey received a ban and she was given a hard race. (9/2)
**1471 Gresatre**, although quickly at the back of the field, began to pick up at halfway and made ground all the way to the line. This was his first run since June and there ought to be a race in him. (8/1)
**2519* Can Can Lady** seemed harshly treated on what she had achieved on the track, but is quite a tall, attractive filly who will probably go the right way. But for losing her action at the furlong pole, she would have gone close to winning. (3/1)
**2575 Hil Rhapsody** received a slight bump at the start and, having not got away too well, could never dominate. (3/1)
**1607 Bellaf** strode down well in first-time blinkers but only ran fast to halfway. (14/1)

## 2798 APPLEBY CLAIMING STKS (3-Y.O+) (Class F)

4-15 (4-16) **1m 3f 183y** £2,785.60 (£771.60: £368.80) Stalls: High GOING minus 0.39 sec per fur (F)

| | | | | SP | RR | SF |
|---|---|---|---|---|---|---|
| 1072[5] | **Rushen Raider (55)** (KWHogg) **4-8-12(5)** ADaly(1) (a.p: ev ch 4f out: outpcd 2f out: r.o wl to ld ins fnl f) | — | **1** | 9/1 | 72 | 45 |
| 2163[7] | **Linda's Joy (IRE) (56)** (MCPipe) **3-8-0b** TSprake(8) (s.i.s: hdwy 5f out: led on bit over 2f out: shkn up over 1f out: nt r.o & hdd ins fnl f) | ½ | **2** | 6/1 | 66 | 27 |
| 2300[8] | **Westminster (IRE) (67)** (MHTompkins) **4-9-7v** PRobinson(7) (chsd ldrs: rdn 3f out: one pce) | 7 | **3** | 7/4[1] | 66 | 39 |
| 2549[9] | **Bayrak (USA) (65)** (MJRyan) **6-9-0(7)** AMcCarthy(2) (lw: prom: led 4f out: hdd over 2f out: sn btn) | 2½ | **4** | 5/1[3] | 63 | 36 |
| 2314[6] | **Song For Jess (IRE)** (FJordan) **3-8-2** AMackay(5) (led over 7f: sn wknd) | 15 | **5** | 33/1 | 35 | — |
| | **Sophie Lockett** (KWHogg) **3-8-4** NKennedy(3) (wl grwn: bit bkwd: a bhd) | 22 | **6** | 33/1 | 7 | — |
| 2008[14] | **Scenic Dancer (46)** (AHide) **8-8-13** DHarrison(6) (lw: s.s: ref to r & sn p.u) | | **P** | 5/1[3] | — | — |
| 2221[3] | **Ciracusa (IRE) (62)** (JMackie) **4-9-1** JQuinn(4) (lw: trckd ldrs tl p.u 5f out) | | **P** | 3/1[2] | — | — |
| | | | | (SP 124.9%) | **8 Rn** | |

**2m 32.7** (3.70) CSF £60.62 TOTE £19.50: £3.00 £2.40 £1.90 (£104.50) OWNER Mrs Thelma White (ISLE OF MAN) BRED M. H. D. Madden and Partners
WEIGHT FOR AGE 3yo-12lb
**1072 Rushen Raider** won this on courage alone, sticking to his guns when all seemed lost. (9/1)
**1806* Linda's Joy (IRE)** seemed in two minds over whether to start but, once racing, was soon travelling well. Pulling her way to the front, Sprake finally called for some effort as Rushen Raider rallied, but she had been in front plenty long enough and the response was very definitely in the negative. She has the ability but is capable of losing any race bar a walkover if in the wrong mood. (6/1: op 7/2)
**2020 Westminster (IRE)** moved down as if hating the ground and has probably had enough of these conditions for the moment. (7/4: 13/8-11/4)
**2377 Bayrak (USA)** seems to move well enough on firm ground, but appears to reserve his best for genuinely good conditions. (5/1)

**Song For Jess (IRE)** did her best to stretch the field but weakened quickly once headed. (33/1)
**Sophie Lockett**, a big filly making a belated debut, showed little and looks more of a hurdler. (33/1)

## 2799 BURTON H'CAP (0-70) (3-Y.O+) (Class E)
4-45 (4-45) **5f 218y** £3,206.70 (£957.60: £457.80: £207.90) Stalls: High GOING minus 0.39 sec per fur (F)

| | | | | SP | RR | SF |
|---|---|---|---|---|---|---|
| 2311[4] | **Kildee Lad (69)** (APJones) **6-10-0** GCarter(3) (lw: chsd ldrs: rdn 2f out: r.o wl to ld ins fnl f) | — | **1** | 7/2[3] | 76 | 34 |
| 2578* | **Croeso Cynnes (63)** (BPalling) **3-9-3**[7x] TSprake(5) (led: clr 2f out: hdd ins fnl f: unable qckn) | nk | **2** | 7/4[1] | 69 | 22 |
| 2431* | **Maid O'Cannie (60)** (MWEasterby) **5-9-5b** JQuinn(7) (dwlt: sn in tch: rdn & one pce fnl 2f) | 6 | **3** | 11/4[2] | 50 | 8 |
| 2376[12] | **Beauchamp Kate (58)** (HCandy) **3-8-12** CRutter(1) (b.hind: outpcd tl rdn & styd on fnl 2f) | ¾ | **4** | 9/1 | 46 | — |
| 2719[6] | **Little Ibnr (60)** (PDEvans) **5-9-5v** WJO'Connor(4) (lw: chsd ldr 4f) | 4 | **5** | 9/1 | 38 | — |
| 1162[5] | **Monkey Zanty (IRE) (46)** (JLHarris) **3-8-0** JFEgan(2) (prom 3f) | 2½ | **6** | 10/1 | 17 | — |
| 2617[16] | **Sandra Dee (IRE) (42)** (EAWheeler) **4-7-10**(5) ADaly(6) (lw: dwlt: sn in tch: wknd 3f out) | 5 | **7** | 20/1 | — | — |
| | | | | (SP 119.1%) | | **7 Rn** |

**1m 13.1** (3.10) CSF £10.29 TOTE £4.20: £2.40 £1.70 (£8.60) OWNER Mr J. F. O'Donovan (EASTBURY) BRED Mrs M. Chubb
WEIGHT FOR AGE 3yo-5lb
**2311 Kildee Lad**, scoring for the first time at very close to six furlongs, has hardly been done any favours by the Handicapper, coming here on a 1lb higher mark than he had ever won off, despite a losing sequence of fourteen. What was in his favour was the opportunity to concede weight to inferior opponents, and this brought out the best in him, although he idled and pricked his ears once in front. (7/2)
**2578* Croeso Cynnes** set a cracking pace and habitual front-runner Little Ibnr could not lay up. She looked in charge at the two-furlong pole but, hard as she tried, she could not peg back the winner once he had taken the lead. She will not be long in regaining winning ways. (7/4)
**2431* Maid O'Cannie** missed a beat as the stalls opened and was always struggling to close on the leader thereafter. (11/4: 2/1-3/1)
**Beauchamp Kate** was hopelessly outpaced for the first half-mile and must be worth a try over a lot further, being by Petoski out of a miler. (9/1: op 6/1)
**2719 Little Ibnr** could not live with the pacemaker and needs a little more freedom to dominate. (9/1)
**606 Monkey Zanty (IRE)** likes to race close to the pace, but was soon being burnt off. (10/1)

T/Jkpt: Not won; £9,513.59 to Newbury 19/7/96. T/Plpt: £335.30 (40.79 Tckts). T/Qdpt: £116.00 (6.97 Tckts). Dk

# 2776-REDCAR (L-H) (Firm)
## Thursday July 18th
WEATHER: sunny WIND: almost nil

## 2800 JOLLY SAILOR (S) H'CAP (0-60) (3-Y.O) (Class G)
6-45 (6-46) **5f** £2,469.00 (£684.00: £327.00) Stalls: Centre GOING minus 0.72 sec per fur (HD)

| | | | | SP | RR | SF |
|---|---|---|---|---|---|---|
| 2578[7] | **Sunset Harbour (IRE) (44)** (SEKettlewell) **3-8-11** JFortune(6) (hdwy ½-wy: led ins fnl f: r.o u.p) | — | **1** | 9/2[2] | 51 | 21 |
| | **L A Touch (49)** (CADwyer) **3-9-2** JStack(3) (chsd ldrs: led over 1f out tl ins fnl f: no ex) | 1¼ | **2** | 7/2[1] | 52 | 22 |
| 2176[8] | **Swifty Nifty (IRE) (35)** (WWHaigh) **3-8-2** DRMcCabe(8) (hld up & bhd: hdwy whn sltly hmpd over 1f out: styd on towards fin) | s.h | **3** | 50/1 | 38 | 8 |
| *2367*[3] | **Orange And Blue (38)** (MissJFCraze) **3-8-5c**[ow1] NConnorton(11) (lw: a cl up: effrt 2f out: nt qckn) | 1¼ | **4** | 16/1 | 37 | 6 |
| 2578[8] | **Members Welcome (IRE) (54)** (JMBradley) **3-9-0v**[1](7) AEddery(10) (hdwy ½-wy: sn chsng ldrs: nt qckn fnl f) | hd | **5** | 20/1 | 53 | 23 |
| 2359[8] | **Double Impression (IRE) (54)** (JLHarris) **3-9-7** DeanMcKeown(5) (lw: led tl hdd over 1f out: sn btn) | ¾ | **6** | 14/1 | 50 | 20 |
| 2732[3] | **Ready Teddy (IRE) (50)** (MissLAPerratt) **3-9-3** KDarley(4) (effrt ½-wy: nvr trbld ldrs) | 2 | **7** | 6/1[3] | 40 | 10 |
| 2359[2] | **Good To Talk (43)** (TDEasterby) **3-8-10** MBirch(2) (w ldrs tl wknd 1f out) | ½ | **8** | 7/2[1] | 31 | 1 |
| 1905[9] | **Welcome Lu (35)** (JLHarris) **3-8-2** TWilliams(12) (effrt ½-wy: no imp) | 1 | **9** | 25/1 | 20 | — |
| 2492* | **Penny Parkes (52)** (JBerry) **3-9-5** JCarroll(7) (bhd: effrt & hung lft 2f out: no imp) | hd | **10** | 9/2[2] | 37 | 7 |
| 2359[6] | **Snitch (39)** (CSmith) **3-8-6v** DaleGibson(9) (b: spd over 3f: wknd) | 1½ | **11** | 25/1 | 19 | — |
| *2555*[8] | **Highland Fawn (37)** (BAMcMahon) **3-8-4** JLowe(1) (hung lft ½-wy: n.d) | 2½ | **12** | 14/1 | 9 | — |
| | | | | (SP 128.7%) | | **12 Rn** |

**58.2 secs** (0.70) CSF £21.35 CT £683.26 TOTE £6.80: £2.00 £1.50 £9.20 (£13.70) Trio £286.20; £366.82 to 20/7/96 OWNER Mr J. Tennant (MIDDLEHAM) BRED Robert J. Thomas
No bid
**2578 Sunset Harbour (IRE)**, having her first run for her new stable, won this moderate event well. This first victory should help boost her confidence. (9/2)
**L A Touch**, having her first outing of the season, put up a decent effort until running out of gas in the closing stages. (7/2)
**Swifty Nifty (IRE)** is a funny customer who does have ability. This was her best effort to date. (50/1)
**2367 Orange And Blue** carries a lot of condition and has speed, but she failed to quicken when the pressure was on. (16/1)
**1891 Members Welcome (IRE)**, dropping back in distance and wearing a visor for the first time, was never quick enough. (20/1)
**1592 Double Impression (IRE)** (14/1: 10/1-16/1)
**2492* Penny Parkes**, one of the last away, never took any interest and just wanted to hang left. (9/2: op 3/1)
**1859 Highland Fawn** (14/1: 10/1-16/1)

## 2801 FURNITURE FACTORS RACING SCHOOLS APPRENTICE H'CAP (0-60) (3-Y.O+) (Class F)
7-15 (7-17) **1m** £3,055.00 (£855.00: £415.00) Stalls: Centre GOING minus 0.72 sec per fur (HD)

| | | | | SP | RR | SF |
|---|---|---|---|---|---|---|
| 2731* | **Hawwam (48)** (EJAlston) **10-9-7**[5x] SDrowne(12) (lw: hdwy 3f out: r.o wl fnl f to ld cl home) | — | **1** | 10/1 | 59 | 36 |
| *2303*[7] | **Miss Zanzibar (49)** (RAFahey) **4-9-3**(5) RFfrench(10) (lw: disp ld tl led 3f out: hdd over 1f out: led ins fnl f: hdd & no ex towards fin) | ½ | **2** | 14/1 | 59 | 36 |
| 2357[3] | **Thatched (IRE) (43)** (REBarr) **6-8-11**(5) KSked(9) (a.p: led over 1f out tl ins fnl f: no ex) | ¾ | **3** | 9/2[1] | 52 | 29 |
| 2568[7] | **Acquittal (IRE) (52)** (AStreeter) **4-9-11v** RHavlin(5) (lw: w ldrs: disp ld ½-wy tl wknd appr fnl f) | 3½ | **4** | 20/1 | 54 | 31 |
| 2313[4] | **Return To Brighton (48)** (JMBradley) **4-9-7** AEddery(3) (chsd ldrs: rdn 3f out: one pce) | ½ | **5** | 11/1 | 49 | 26 |
| 2521[5] | **Summer Villa (37)** (JHetherton) **4-8-10** MBaird(13) (w ldrs: nt qckn fnl 2½f) | 2 | **6** | 10/1 | 34 | 11 |
| 1665[15] | **Brambles Way (42)** (MrsMReveley) **7-9-1** SCopp(11) (effrt ½-wy: no imp) | 3 | **7** | 8/1[3] | 33 | 10 |
| 2513[8] | **Nord Lys (IRE) (23)** (BJLlewellyn) **5-7-3**(7) NPollard(1) (disp ld 4f: rdn & grad wknd) | hd | **8** | 33/1 | 13 | — |
| 2520[4] | **Steel Sovereign (32)** (MDods) **5-8-2**(3) JEdmunds(7) (rdn ½-wy: no imp) | 3½ | **9** | 20/1 | 15 | — |
| 2592[5] | **How Could-I (IRE) (44)** (MrsNMacauley) **3-8-9b** CTeague(17) (racd stands' side: outpcd fr ½-wy) | 1¾ | **10** | 12/1 | 24 | — |

$2428^{13}$ **Maurangi (51)** (BWMurray) **5-9-3**$^{(7)ow2}$ KPrendergast(2) (swtchd rt ½-wy: nvr trbld ldrs) ....................½ **11** 16/1 30 5
*$2085^{9}$* **Ohnonotagain (28)** (BWMurray) **4-7-8**$^{(7)}$ RCody-Boutcher(6) (n.d) ....................1 **12** 50/1 5 —
$2507^{11}$ **Chief's Lady (37)** (JMBradley) **4-8-7**$^{(3)}$ JWilkinson(18) (s.s: n.d) ....................¾ **13** 25/1 12 —
$2130^{4}$ **La Fille de Cirque (44)** (RJRWilliams) **4-9-3** FLynch(8) (in tch 5f) ....................½ **14** 6/1$^{2}$ 18 —
$2521^{*}$ **Gilling Dancer (IRE) (58)** (PCalver) **3-9-9** DGriffiths(14) (disp ld to ½-wy: wknd) ....................½ **15** 9/2$^{1}$ 31 —
$1650^{P}$ **Broughton's Pride (IRE) (50)** (JLEyre) **5-9-9** IonaWands(19) (rdn & outpcd fr ½-wy) ....................1½ **16** 14/1 20 —
$2587^{15}$ **Newgate Hush (27)** (BWMurray) **4-7-11b**$^{1(3)ow2}$ CWebb(4) (n.d) ....................2½ **17** 100/1 — —
$2356^{8}$ **Ragazzo (IRE) (30)** (JSWainwright) **6-8-0**$^{(3)}$ RMullen(15) (chsd ldr 5f) ....................1¼ **18** 33/1 — —
$2056^{22}$ **Legal Brief (35)** (JSWainwright) **4-8-3**$^{(5)}$ PDoe(16) (n.d) ....................7 **19** 100/1 — —
(SP 138.4%) **19 Rn**

**1m 36.5** (0.80) CSF £142.59 CT £680.09 TOTE £14.30: £3.00 £3.40 £1.30 £4.70 (£83.70) Trio £178.70 OWNER North West Racing Club Owners Club (PRESTON) BRED G. Franco
LONG HANDICAP Nord Lys (IRE) 7-9
WEIGHT FOR AGE 3yo-8lb

**2731* Hawwam** continued his tremendous run of form, and produced a terrific burst in the final furlong to settle it close home. (10/1: 8/1-12/1)
**2075 Miss Zanzibar** keeps running well and deserves to find a race. (14/1)
**2357 Thatched (IRE)** looked to have this won when taking it up approaching the final furlong, but then cried enough. Once he really strikes form, he is certainly one to follow. (9/2)
**Acquittal (IRE)**, from a really good yard, is gradually getting it together but just found the struggle too much in the final furlong this time. (20/1)
**2313 Return To Brighton** is running consistently well this year and was just tapped for foot on this occasion. (11/1: 7/1-12/1)
**2521 Summer Villa** ran another fine race and is obviously in good form. She should be kept in mind if returning to the All-Weather. (10/1)
**2592 How Could-I (IRE)** (12/1: op 6/1)

## 2802 E.B.F. MERMAID MAIDEN STKS (2-Y.O) (Class D)

7-45 (7-45) **7f** £3,775.50 (£1,134.00: £547.00: £253.50) Stalls: Centre GOING minus 0.72 sec per fur (HD)

SP RR SF

$2503^{6}$ **Lady Mail (IRE)** (JMPEustace) **2-8-9** RCochrane(1) (hld up: hdwy over 2f out: r.o wl fnl f to ld cl home) .......— **1** 33/1 76 18
**Stories To Tell (USA)** (HRACecil) **2-9-0** WRyan(7) (gd sort: lw: trckd ldrs: chal 2f out: sn rdn: nt qckn towards fin) ....................½ **2** 11/10$^{1}$ 80+ 22
$2335^{6}$ **Dawam Allail** (MAJarvis) **2-9-0** PRobinson(4) (lw: plld hrd: trckd ldrs: rdn to ld ins fnl f: hdd & nt qckn towards fin) ....................nk **3** 2/1$^{2}$ 79 21
**Dream of Nurmi** (DRLoder) **2-9-0** DRMcCabe(5) (w'like: scope: cl up: nt clr run & swtchd over 1f out: styd on) ....................nk **4** 7/2$^{3}$ 79+ 21
**Italian Symphony (IRE)** (MJohnston) **2-9-0** KDarley(3) (cmpt: bit bkwd: led tl hdd & no ex ins fnl f) ....................½ **5** 16/1 77 19
*$2370^{6}$* **General's Star** (MRStoute) **2-9-0** DeanMcKeown(6) (trckd ldrs: outpcd 3f out: n.d after) ....................7 **6** 16/1 61 3
$1849^{10}$ **Mon Performer** (MJCamacho) **2-9-0** JFortune(9) (spd 5f) ....................5 **7** 100/1 50 —
**Kickonsun (IRE)** (RAFahey) **2-9-0** MBirch(8) (unf: bhd: hung lft ½-wy: n.d) ....................2 **8** 100/1 45 —
*$2370^{10}$* **Silent Wells** (JJQuinn) **2-8-9** JLowe(2) (b.hind: bhd & hmpd ½-wy: n.d) ....................11 **9** 100/1 15 —
(SP 120.9%) **9 Rn**

**1m 24.3** (1.30) CSF £70.37 TOTE £18.00: £3.30 £1.10 £1.20 (£18.20) Trio £52.60 OWNER Mr Gary Coull (NEWMARKET) BRED G. Coull

**Lady Mail (IRE)**, after showing nothing on her debut, won this competitive-looking event in good style, and it was certainly no fluke. (33/1)
**Stories To Tell (USA)** ran a fair race. He is not over-blessed with speed and may need time and easier ground, but he will win a race or two. (11/10)
**2335 Dawam Allail**, who raced a bit too freely early on, still ran well and is learning. (2/1: op 7/2)
**Dream of Nurmi** had his chances, but was short of both room and pace and, when switched, it was all too late. He will be all the better for this. (7/2)
**Italian Symphony (IRE)** looked likely to need this, but only ran out of steam in the closing stages, and should improve a fair bit. (16/1)
**2370 General's Star** got outpaced once the tempo increased just after halfway and looked very slow thereafter. (16/1)

## 2803 RYCROFT COMMERCIAL VEHICLE H'CAP (0-80) (3-Y.O+) (Class D)

8-15 (8-16) **1m 2f** £3,736.50 (£1,122.00: £541.00: £250.50) Stalls: Low GOING minus 0.72 sec per fur (HD)

SP RR SF

$2214^{3}$ **Bulsara (55)** (CWFairhurst) **4-8-8** DeanMcKeown(6) (lw: trckd ldrs: led over 2f out: qcknd over 1f out: all out) ....................— **1** 7/2$^{3}$ 65 14
$2701^{4}$ **Alabang (60)** (MJCamacho) **5-8-13** RCochrane(3) (stdd s: hdwy on bit 3f out: effrt over 1f out: r.o: jst failed) ....................hd **2** 7/4$^{1}$ 70 19
*$2552^{9}$* **Field of Vision (IRE) (71)** (MrsASwinbank) **6-9-5**$^{(5)}$ JSupple(1) (led tl hdd over 2f out: rallied fnl f) ....................hd **3** 10/1 81 30
$2628^{5}$ **Essayeffsee (58)** (MrsMReveley) **7-8-11** KDarley(5) (lw: hld up: hdwy on bit to chal 3f out: shkn up 2f out: nt qckn) ....................3 **4** 9/2 63 12
$2206^{5}$ **Villeggiatura (72)** (MrsJRRamsden) **3-9-1** MDeering(4) (dwlt: sn chsng ldr: outpcd fnl 3f) ....................1¾ **5** 16/1 74 13
$1846^{2}$ **Highspeed (IRE) (60)** (SEKettlewell) **4-8-13** JFortune(2) (hld up: hdwy & ch 3f out: wknd fnl 2f) ....................4 **6** 11/4$^{2}$ 56 5
(SP 118.4%) **6 Rn**

**2m 6.2** (2.60) CSF £10.33 TOTE £4.90: £1.60 £1.90 (£4.60) OWNER Twinacre Nurseries Ltd (MIDDLEHAM) BRED P. and Mrs Blacker
WEIGHT FOR AGE 3yo-10lb

**2214 Bulsara**, given a really good ride, went for home over two furlongs out and, getting first run on his opponents, he stole just enough to last home. (7/2)
**2701 Alabang**, held up as he needs to be, looked to be going well halfway up the straight. Ridden along, he took time to react and, despite a tremendous late burst, just failed to make it. (7/4: 5/2-6/4)
**1811 Field of Vision (IRE)** put up a splendid effort and, after looking well beaten two furlongs out, kept fighting back to show he is in really good form. (10/1)
**2628 Essayeffsee** travelled on the bridle but, yet again, when the chips were down, he was found wanting for speed. (9/2)
**1619 Villeggiatura** half-reared at the start, but this free-runner was soon up there, only to get outpaced in the straight. No doubt his new stable will sort him out. (16/1)
**1846 Highspeed (IRE)** had not been out for over a month and ran as if this was needed. (11/4)

## 2804 GO EVENING RACING WITH THE DAILY TELEGRAPH H'CAP (0-75) (3-Y.O+) (Class D)

8-45 (8-46) **2m 4y** £3,743.00 (£1,124.00: £542.00: £251.00) Stalls: Low GOING minus 0.72 sec per fur (HD)

SP RR SF

$2516^{5}$ **Izza (45)** (WStorey) **5-8-8** NKennedy(2) (hld up: nt clr run 3f out: swtchd 2f out: r.o fnl f to ld cl home) ..........— **1** 8/1 58+ 36

| | | | | SP | RR | SF |
|---|---|---|---|---|---|---|
| 2627[4] | **Marsayas (IRE) (50)** (MJCamacho) **3-7-10** JQuinn(6) (lw: a chsng ldrs: led over 2f out: hrd rdn fnl f: r.o: jst ct) | hd | **2** | 3/1[1] | 63 | 24 |
| 2627* | **Dirab (66)** (TDBarron) **3-8-12** 4x JFortune(5) (lw: hld up & bhd: hdwy 4f out: chal 2f out: hrd rdn fnl f: r.o) | nk | **3** | 3/1[1] | 79 | 40 |
| 2423[2] | **Cutthroat Kid (IRE) (65)** (MrsMReveley) **6-10-0v** KDarley(9) (lw: hld up: hdwy 4f out: sn prom: one pce fnl 2f) | 6 | **4** | 7/1 | 72 | 50 |
| 1847[3] | **Jalcanto (55)** (MrsMReveley) **6-8-13**(5) SCopp(4) (hld up: effrt 4f out: sn rdn & no imp) | 1¾ | **5** | 7/2[2] | 60 | 38 |
| 2216* | **Royal Vacation (55)** (GMMoore) **7-9-4** JCarroll(8) (lw: cl up: led wl over 3f out tl over 2f out: sn outpcd) | 11 | **6** | 9/2[3] | 49 | 27 |
| 2560[5] | **Double Dash (IRE) (70)** (MJohnston) **3-9-2b**[1] TWilliams(1) (chsd ldrs tl wknd fnl 4f) | ½ | **7** | 25/1 | 63 | 24 |
| 2423[9] | **Kashana (IRE) (42)** (WStorey) **4-8-5** JFanning(7) (led tl hdd & wknd wl over 3f out) | 3 | **8** | 25/1 | 32 | 10 |
| | **Irish Stamp (IRE) (58)** (FMurphy) **7-9-0**(7) DHayden(3) (prom tl outpcd ½-wy: sn wl bhd) | dist | **9** | 50/1 | — | — |

(SP 123.7%) **9 Rn**

**3m 25.0** (0.00) CSF £32.72 CT £84.42 TOTE £8.90: £2.10 £1.60 £1.50 (£11.80) Trio £23.80 OWNER Mr D. C. Batey (CONSETT) BRED G.W. Mills & Sons

WEIGHT FOR AGE 3yo-17lb

**2516 Izza** put up an incredible performance. She looked to have blown it when running into trouble three furlongs out, but her rider calmly switched her, and she produced a burst in the final furlong to surprise everyone. (8/1)

**2627 Marsayas (IRE)**, up with the pace this time, tried his heart out, but was touched off near the line. He really does deserve to win a race. (3/1)

**2627* Dirab** is game beyond belief when the chips are down, but even his effort could not gain him the day this time. (3/1)

**2423 Cutthroat Kid (IRE)** last won on the Flat two seasons ago and, although looking and travelling well, he never quite seems to come up with the goods these days. (7/1)

**1847 Jalcanto** was asked for an effort early in the straight, but soon decided it was not for him. (7/2)

**2216* Royal Vacation** looked really well, but got outpaced when the tempo increased halfway up the straight. (9/2)

## 2805 FARNDALE LIMITED STKS (0-70) (3-Y.O) (Class E)

9-15 (9-16) **1m** £2,922.50 (£875.00: £420.00: £192.50) Stalls: Centre GOING minus 0.72 sec per fur (HD)

| | | | | SP | RR | SF |
|---|---|---|---|---|---|---|
| 2573* | **Chinensis (IRE) (70)** (LMCumani) **3-9-2** OUrbina(3) (lw: mde all: shkn up 2f out: r.o: comf) | — | **1** | 2/7[1] | 76+ | 28 |
| 2320[11] | **Badger Bay (IRE) (64)** (CADwyer) **3-8-4**(7) JoHunnam(4) (lw: trckd wnr: effrt over 2f out: kpt on: no imp) | 1½ | **2** | 16/1 | 68 | 20 |
| 2514[8] | **Dispol Diamond (70)** (GROldroyd) **3-8-11** KDarley(1) (chsd ldrs: rdn 3f out: edgd lft & nt qckn) | 1¼ | **3** | 7/1[3] | 66 | 18 |
| *237*[3] | **Agent (67)** (JLEyre) **3-9-0** DeanMcKeown(2) (in tch tl outpcd fnl 2½f) | 8 | **4** | 5/1[2] | 53 | 5 |

(SP 112.8%) **4 Rn**

**1m 36.9** (1.20) CSF £5.05 TOTE £1.40 (£4.30) OWNER Sheikh Mohammed (NEWMARKET) BRED Sheikh Mohammed bin Rashid al Maktoum

**2573* Chinensis (IRE)** always had the beating of this bunch and was allowed to take things easy in the final furlong. (2/7)

**1908 Badger Bay (IRE)** looked and ran well, but had no chance with the winner. (16/1)

**2079 Dispol Diamond** was edgy in the paddock and inclined to hang left in the race. (7/1)

**Agent**, having his first run for almost six months, was left struggling in the last three furlongs. (5/1: op 3/1)

T/Plpt: £165.00 (91.3 Tckts). T/Qdpt: £3.40 (336.48 Tckts). AA

## 2806a-2815a (Irish Racing) - See Computer Raceform

# 0151a-TIPPERARY (Ireland) (L-H) (Good to firm)

### Thursday July 11th

## 2816a TIPPERARY DIRECTORS SPRINT (Listed) (3-Y.O+)

6-30 (6-30) **5f** £9,675.00 (£2,775.00: £1,275.00: £375.00)

| | | | | SP | RR | SF |
|---|---|---|---|---|---|---|
| 2472a[6] | **Ailleacht (USA)** (JSBolger,Ireland) **4-8-13** TEDurcan (disp ld: shkn up & led over 1f out: r.o) | — | **1** | 5/4[2] | 105 | — |
| 2472a* | **Sunset Reigns (IRE)** (APO'Brien,Ireland) **3-8-13** SCraine (led & disp ld: hdd over 1f out: no ex ins fnl f) | 1½ | **2** | 9/10[1] | 103 | — |
| 2472a[3] | **Slayjay (IRE)** (JCHayden,Ireland) **3-8-8** WJSupple (a same pl: rdn ½-wy: no imp fnl 1½f) | 6 | **3** | 8/1[3] | 79 | — |
| 2472a[16] | **Mitch (USA)** (DKWeld,Ireland) **3-8-11** PShanahan (dwlt: sn rdn & bhd: u.p ½-wy: n.d) | 4 | **4** | 8/1[3] | 69 | — |

(SP 119.3%) **4 Rn**

**55.9 secs** OWNER Mrs J. S. Bolger (COOLCULLEN)

**1911a Ailleacht (USA)**, meeting her younger rivals on favourable terms, quickened nicely to take control in the final furlong. (5/4)

**2472a* Sunset Reigns (IRE)**, disputing the lead throughout, found the winner carrying too many guns for her well inside the last. (9/10)

**Slayjay (IRE)** came out a bit slowly and, after chasing the leaders to halfway, soon cried enough. (8/1)

**Mitch (USA)** showed no interest, and was struggling throughout. (8/1)

## 2817a-2824a (Irish Racing) - See Computer Raceform

# 1733a-DOWN ROYAL (Lisburn, Ireland) (R-H) (Good)

### Saturday July 13th

## 2825a ULSTER HARP DERBY H'CAP (0-110) (3-Y.O+)

3-30 (3-36) **1m 4f 68y** £32,500.00 (£9,500.00: £4,500.00: £1,500.00)

| | | | | SP | RR | SF |
|---|---|---|---|---|---|---|
| 1912a[3] | **I'm Supposin (IRE)** (KPrendergast,Ireland) **4-9-9** MDuffy (hld up in tch: 4th ½-wy: trckng ldrs 4f out: chal 2f out: led over 1f out: edgd rt jst ins fnl f: r.o) | — | **1** | 6/1 | 111 | — |
| 1247a[2] | **Pro Trader (USA)** (DKWeld,Ireland) **3-8-12b** PShanahan (hld up: hdwy 2f out: fin wl) | 1½ | **2** | 5/1[2] | 111 | — |
| 1938a[5] | **Sheraka (IRE)** (JOxx,Ireland) **3-8-10** DHogan (hld up: 6th 4f out: sn lost pl: hdwy & chsng ledrs over 1f out: sn chal: kpt on) | ½ | **3** | 11/2[3] | 108 | — |
| | **Song Of The Sword** (MKauntze,Ireland) **3-8-0** NGMcCullagh (a.p: chal fr 3f out: led briefly over 1f out: no ex whn hmpd jst ins fnl f) | ½ | **4** | 7/2[1] | 98 | — |
| | **Kates Choice (IRE)** (SJTreacy,Ireland) **4-7-11** JMorgan (sn led: jnd 2f out: hdd over 1f out: 4th & no ex whn sltly hmpd jst ins fnl f) | 2½ | **5** | 16/1 | 79 | — |
| 1066[5] | **Glide Path (USA)** (JWHills) **7-8-7** DHolland (hld up: hdwy 4f out: effrt over 2f out: rdn & no ex ins fnl f) | 1½ | **6** | 9/1 | 87 | — |

2055[17] **Cockney Lad (IRE)** (NMeade,Ireland) **7-8-9**ow1 SCraine (disp ld early: 3rd ½-wy: 4th & chsng ldrs wl over 2f out: 6th & nt trble ldrs over 1f out)....1 **7** 8/1 87 —
**Try For Ever (IRE)** (NMeade,Ireland) **4-8-4**(2) PJSmullen (hld up towards rr: rdn wl over 2f out: kpt on same pce)....½ **8** 8/1 84 —
1567a[8] **Asmara (USA)** (JOxx,Ireland) **3-8-8** WJSmith (hld up: stumbled after 4f: 5th ½-wy: lost pl over 3f out: n.d).....6 **9** 7/1 91 —
(SP 119.2%) **9 Rn**

**No Time Taken** OWNER A. D. Brennan
**1912a I'm Supposin (IRE)** gained due reward for his consistency. Leading a furlong out, despite edging right, he was always in control. (6/1)
**1247a Pro Trader (USA)**, held up in rear, ran on well through horses to have every chance inside the last, but found the winner too strong. (5/1)
**1938a Sheraka (IRE)**, always in touch, did not have the clearest of runs from a furlong and a half out, and was not disgraced. (11/2)
**Song Of The Sword**, in front two furlongs out, appeared to be slightly inconvenienced when the winner went across him, but was beaten at the time. (7/2)
**1066 Glide Path (USA)** appeared to be a slow starter without the stalls and, although making up some ground on the outside in the straight, his intent to jump a path a furlong and a half out did not help his chance. (9/1)

## 2826a-2833a (Irish Racing) - See Computer Raceform

## 2469a-CURRAGH (Newbridge, Ireland) (R-H) (Good to firm) Sunday July 14th

### 2834a OMNI IRISH RACING CLUB CURRAGH STKS (Gp 3) (2-Y.O)
2-50 (2-51) **5f** £19,500.00 (£5,700.00: £2,700.00: £900.00)

SP RR SF
2070[2] **Raphane (USA)** (CCollins,Ireland) **2-9-1b**[1] KDarley (edgd lft s: prom: led 2f out: rdn & r.o)....— **1** 8/11[1] 103 35
**Nevada (IRE)** (APO'Brien,Ireland) **2-8-10** SCraine (dwlt & sltly hmpd s: trckd ldrs: 2nd & effrt over 1f out: kpt on wl: nt rch wnr)....1½ **2** 10/1 93 25
**Petite Princess (USA)** (JSBolger,Ireland) **2-8-7** TEDurcan (outpcd early: towards rr & rdn ½-wy: hdwy & 5th over 1f out: 3rd & drifted rt jst ins fnl f: kpt on wl)....½ **3** 13/2[3] 89 21
2051[6] **Classic Park** (APO'Brien,Ireland) **2-8-7b**[1] CRoche (led: rdn ½-wy: hdd 2f out: btn over 1f out)....4 **4** 7/2[2] 76 8
2040[13] **Future Prospect (IRE)** (MJohnston) **2-8-10** JWeaver (cl up: 4th ½-wy: rdn & no ex 1½f out)....s.h **5** 9/1 79 11
**Classical Risk (IRE)** (JGCoogan,Ireland) **2-8-7** MJKinane (in tch early: 5th ½-wy: btn 2f out)....5½ **6** 16/1 58 —
(SP 118.4%) **6 Rn**

**58.7 secs** (0.70) OWNER Peter Savill (THE CURRAGH)
**2070 Raphane (USA)**, equipped with blinkers for the first time, took over from Classic Park with over two furlongs to race, and came home with Darley doing as little as possible. He will certainly get another furlong and has a choice at Goodwood between the Molecomb and the Richmond Stakes. (8/11)
**Nevada (IRE)** came out a bit slower than the others, but had improved to chase the winner from a furlong and a half out, without ever looking a serious threat. (10/1)
**Petite Princess (USA)** got herself outpaced after a furlong and a half, but made headway from halfway and, despite shying right at the furlong marker, was going on well towards the end. (13/2)
**2051 Classic Park** set a strong pace, but was done with two furlongs out. (7/2)
**1801* Future Prospect (IRE)**, third and under pressure at halfway, was soon beaten. (9/1)

### 2837a KILDANGAN STUD IRISH OAKS (Gp 1) (3-Y.O F)
4-25 (4-26) **1m 4f** £118,700.00 (£38,700.00: £18,700.00: £6,700.00)

SP RR SF
2465a* **Dance Design (IRE)** (DKWeld,Ireland) **3-9-0** MJKinane (hld up: hdwy 3f out: chal over 1f out: led ins fnl f: r.o u.p)....— **1** 9/2[2] 113 31
2277a* **Shamadara (IRE)** (AdeRoyerDupre,France) **3-9-0** GMosse (trckd ldrs: chal 2f out: led 1f out: edgd rt & hdd ins last: kpt on u.p)....s.h **2** 6/1[3] 113 31
2069[2] **Key Change (IRE)** (JOxx,Ireland) **3-9-0** JPMurtagh (chsd ldr: rdn to chal 2f out: ev ch 1f out: one pce ins fnl f)....2 **3** 8/1 110 28
1769* **Lady Carla** (HRACecil) **3-9-0** PatEddery (led: pushed along 4f out: jnd 2f out: hdd 1f out: wknd ins fnl f)......2½ **4** 1/2[1] 107 25
**French Ballerina (IRE)** (PJFlynn,Ireland) **3-9-0** PVGilson (towards rr: rdn 4f out: 5th over 1f out: styd on ins fnl f)....1 **5** 100/1 106 24
2102a* **Tout A Coup (IRE)** (GACusack,Ireland) **3-9-0** RHughes (hld up: 4th 4f out: rdn & no imp fnl 2f: eased).........13 **6** 14/1 88 6
(SP 117.9%) **6 Rn**

**2m 29.7** (2.70) OWNER Moyglare Stud Farm (CURRAGH)
**2465a* Dance Design (IRE)** was heavily backed on the day, despite her trainer's publicised doubts about her stamina, and proved these reservations totally unfounded. She got herself into gear early in the straight, and her sustained run over the last furlong and a half was always going to get her there. However, it was only in the last couple of strides that she mastered the French filly. She is very tough and deserves her break before going for the Vermeille in the autumn. (9/2)
**2277a* Shamadara (IRE)**, after appearing slightly outpaced at the top of the hill, was back chasing the favourite on the turn into the straight, and her measure had been taken when leading a furlong out. She hung right when challenged and did no favours to the third home, but riding infringements of this kind are treated kindly at the Curragh. (6/1)
**2069 Key Change (IRE)** found the ground a bit firm. She battled on to hold every chance a furlong out, and was just galloping on at one pace when Shamadara was allowed to drift across her. She could be a good filly in the autumn when the ground will be more in her favour. (8/1)
**1769* Lady Carla** was quickly sent to the front and did not seem unsuited by the ground. Headed a furlong out, she dropped away quite tamely and was obviously not the filly we saw at Epsom. (1/2)
**French Ballerina (IRE)** is a maiden, and the fact that she had to go up 22lb to justify her finishing position says everything. (100/1)
**2102a* Tout A Coup (IRE)** was in touch until dropping out quickly from two furlongs out, and something was clearly amiss. (14/1)

### 2839a RAGUSA STUD MINSTREL STKS (Gp 3) (3-Y.O+)
5-30 (5-32) **1m** £16,250.00 (£4,750.00: £2,250.00: £750.00)

SP RR SF
2037[2] **Restructure (IRE)** (MrsJCecil) **4-9-4** PatEddery (chsd ldr: chal st: led 2f out: rdn & r.o)....— **1** 6/4[1] 121 25
2337[3] **Bin Rosie** (DRLoder) **4-9-4b** RHughes (hld up: 6th ½-wy: 3rd over 2f out: r.o u.p ins fnl f)....hd **2** 7/1 121 25
2473a[5] **Rainbow Blues (IRE)** (APO'Brien,Ireland) **3-8-10**ow1 CRoche (led: jnd st: hdd 2f out: rdn & rallied: kpt on) ...nk **3** 100/30[2] 121 15

| | | | | SP | RR | SF |
|---|---|---|---|---|---|---|
| 1938a3 | **Al Mohaajir (USA)** (JSBolger,Ireland) **5-9-4b1** KJManning (hld up in tch: 4th ½-wy: rdn & effrt 2f out: kpt on) .2 | **4** | | 5/1 3 | 116 | 20 |
| | **Raiyoun (IRE)** (JOxx,Ireland) **3-8-10**ow1 JPMurtagh (hld up: hdwy over 2f out: rdn over 1f out: kpt on) ..........hd | **5** | | 9/1 | 117 | 11 |
| 1249a5 | **Ahkaam (USA)** (DKWeld,Ireland) **3-8-13b1** MJKinane (hld up: 5th ½-wy: chsd ldrs 2f out: no ex over 1f out)..1 | **6** | | 12/1 | 118 | 13 |
| 1389a5 | **Line Dancer** (GACusack,Ireland) **3-8-9** JReid (chsd ldrs: rdn st: 5th over 2f out: no imp over 1f out) ............1½ | **7** | | 12/1 | 111 | 6 |

(SP 117.6%) **7 Rn**

**1m 37.6** (2.60) OWNER Martin Myers (NEWMARKET) BRED J. H. Stone
**2037 Restructure (IRE)** appeared to have an easy task here but, after going to the front well over a furlong out, had to be ridden out to hold the runner-up. (6/4)
**2337 Bin Rosie** moved into third place with a furlong and a half to race, and kept on strongly. (7/1: op 3/1)
**2473a Rainbow Blues (IRE)** tried to make all and kept on strongly under pressure once headed. (100/30: op 7/4)
**1938a Al Mohaajir (USA)** made a promising move on the home turn, but was one-paced throughout the last furlong. (5/1)

# COMPIEGNE (France) (L-H) (Good)
## Monday July 8th

### 2840a GRAND PRIX DE COMPIEGNE (Listed) (4-Y.O+)
3-25 (3-25) **1m 2f** £18,445.00 (£6,324.00: £3,953.00)

| | | | SP | RR | SF |
|---|---|---|---|---|---|
| *535a11* | **Volochine (IRE)** (RCollet,France) **5-9-2** ESaint-Martin ........— | **1** | | 114 | — |
| | **Zarma (FR)** (ASpanu,France) **4-8-8b1** TThulliez ........nk | **2** | | 106 | — |
| | **Diodeme (FR)** (CRibbe,France) **6-8-11b1** AJunk ........¾ | **3** | | 107 | — |
| 2274a3 | **Maralinga (IRE)** (LadyHerries) **4-9-2** JReid (btn over 9l) ........ | **10** | | — | — |

**14 Rn**

**2m 1.6** P-M 4.50F: 2.20F 6.00F 6.20F (108.70F) OWNER R. McNair (CHANTILLY) BRED R. M. Aubert
**2274a Maralinga (IRE)** finished last in the 1995 Derby, and had been disappointing until finishing third in a Dortmund Group Three event in June. Prominent for most of the way, he was third turning into the straight, but weakened a furlong out.

# 2477a-EVRY (France) (R-H) (Good)
## Friday July 12th

### 2841a PRIX DE RIS ORANGIS (Gp 3) (3-Y.O+)
2-55 (2-54) **6f** £28,986.00 (£10,540.00: £5,270.00)

| | | | SP | RR | SF |
|---|---|---|---|---|---|
| | **Miesque's Son (USA)** (JEHammond,France) **4-9-0** CAsmussen ........— | **1** | | 114 | — |
| 2270a* | **Kistena (FR)** (MmeCHead,France) **3-8-5** ODoleuze ........s.h | **2** | | 111 | — |
| 2270a3 | **Don't Worry Me (IRE)** (GHenrot,France) **4-8-10** AJunk ........½ | **3** | | 109 | — |
| 21155 | **Royale Figurine (IRE)** (MJFetherston-Godley) **5-8-10** DHolland (btn over 5l) ........ | **6** | | — | — |

**13 Rn**

**1m 9.23** (-0.77) P-M 3.70F: 2.00F 2.10F 2.70F (15.80F) OWNER Niarchos Family (CHANTILLY) BRED Flaxman Holdings Ltd
**Miesque's Son (USA)** finally lived up to his breeding. Held up early on, he came with a flying late run to snatch victory on the line. Having justified his connections' decision to keep him in training as a four-year-old, he will now head to Deauville possibly for the Prix Maurice de Gheest.
**Kistena (FR)** got very worked up beforehand and took some time to enter the stalls. Racing in sixth position before making steady progress to take the lead at the furlong pole, she fended off the third's challenge but was pipped in the final stride. This excitable but talented filly could now go to Baden-Baden for the Goldene Peitsch in late August.
**Don't Worry Me (IRE)** ran a much better race this time out. Always prominent, she took the lead a furlong and a half out and, after being headed, she rallied, but could never get on terms with the first two.
**2115 Royale Figurine (IRE)** was travelling well for the first half of the race but, when her jockey asked her to pick up, she found nothing. Connections were disappointed with this below-par performance.
DS

# ARLINGTON PARK (Chicago, USA) (L-H) (Fast)
## Saturday July 13th

### 2842a ARLINGTON CITATION CHALLENGE (INVITATIONAL) (3-Y.O+)
10-42 **1m 1f (Dirt)** £483,871.00 (£96,774.00: 53,226.00)

| | | | SP | RR | SF |
|---|---|---|---|---|---|
| *536a** | **Cigar (USA)** (WMott,USA) **6-9-4** JBailey ........— | **1** | | 135 | — |
| | **Dramatic Gold (USA)** (DHofmans,USA) **3-8-6** CNakatani ........3½ | **2** | | 127 | — |
| | **Eltish (USA)** (RFrankel,USA) **4-8-6** EDelahoussaye ........nk | **3** | | 116 | — |

**10 Rn**

**1m 48.2** P-M 2.60 SF 12.20 (no place or show betting). OWNER A. E. Paulson BRED A. E. Paulson
**536a* Cigar (USA)** entered the record books claiming this, his sixteenth consecutive win, with relative ease. He was settled on the outside in sixth place early on and, with the minimum of effort, came through to take the advantage and stride clear. This success has taken his career earnings to 8.8 million dollars and his trainer confirmed that the Pacific Classic, a $1,000,000 Grade 1 race at Del Mar on August 10th would be his next target.

# HOPPEGARTEN (Berlin, Germany) (R-H) (Good)
## Sunday July 14th

### 2843a BERLIN-BRANDENBURG-TROPHY DER LANDESBANK BERLIN (Gp 2) (3-Y.O+)
4-00 (4-26) **1m** £99,099.00 (£42,793.00: £20,270.00: £11,261.00)

| | | | SP | RR | SF |
|---|---|---|---|---|---|
| 1950a2 | **Manzoni (GER)** (AWohler,Germany) **4-9-6b** ABoschert (a.p: 2nd st: led 2f out: r.o wl)........— | **1** | | 118 | — |
| 2274a* | **Devil River Peek (USA)** (BSchutz,Germany) **4-9-6** AStarke (hld up: 6th st: r.o wl fr 2f out: nt rch wnr) .........1½ | **2** | | 115 | — |
| | **Mill King (GER)** (HBlume,Germany) **3-8-9** ASuborics (unruly s: mid div: r.o strly fnl f: nvr nrr)........nk | **3** | | 112 | — |
| 2479a3 | **Artan (IRE)** (MRolke,Germany) **4-9-6** JTandari (a cl up: kpt on one pce 2f out)........2 | **4** | | 110 | — |

| | Horse | | SP | RR | SF |
|---|---|---|---|---|---|
| | **Federico (USA)** (Germany) **4-9-6** MLarsen (set gd pce: hdd & one pce 2f out) .....nk **5** | | | 110 | — |
| | **Kill the Crab (IRE)** (Germany) **4-9-2** FJohansson (3rd st: no ex fr 2f out) .....1¼ **6** | | | 103 | — |
| 1755a* | **Sinyar** (BSchutz,Germany) **4-9-6** WRyan (mid div: rdn & one pce fr 2f out) .....s.h **7** | | | 107 | — |
| 2271a* | **A Magicman (FR)** (HSteguweit,Germany) **4-9-6** NGrant (hld up: effrt 2f out: sn btn) .....1 **8** | | | 105 | — |
| 1951a² | **Lara (GER)** (BSchutz,Germany) **4-9-2** LPyritz (a in rr) .....1½ **9** | | | 98 | — |
| 1759a³ | **Tres Heureux (GER)** (FrauEMader,Germany) **6-9-6** LMader (a bhd) .....nk **10** | | | 102 | — |
| | **Fiello (GER)** (Germany) **6-9-6** MTrinker (a in rr) .....1½ **11** | | | 99 | — |
| | **Fifire (GER)** (Germany) **4-9-6** CZschache (a in rr) .....1¼ **12** | | | 96 | — |
| | | | | | **12 Rn** |

**1m 36.1** TOTE 58DM: 21DM 21DM 30DM (413DM) OWNER Gestut Hof Heidendom BRED Gestut Hof Heidendom
**1950a Manzoni (GER)** seemed unaffected by spreading a plate at the start, and won a shade comfortably. He collared the long-time leader Federico passing the quarter-mile pole, and was never going to be beaten thereafter.
**Devil River Peek (USA)** is a consistent sort, but met one too good here.
**2271a* A Magicman (FR)** was a disappointing favourite and was one of the first beaten. It would seem that a mile on a stiff track such as this is just too far.

## 2480a-SAINT-CLOUD (France) (L-H) (Good)
### Sunday July 14th

### 2844a PRIX EUGENE ADAM (Gp 2) (3-Y.O)
3-10 (3-11) **1m 2f** £39,526.00 (£15,810.00: £7,905.00: £3,953.00)

| | Horse | Pos | SP | RR | SF |
|---|---|---|---|---|---|
| 1757a¹³ | **Radevore** (AFabre,France) **3-8-11** TJarnet (hld up in rr: rdn over 2f out: outpcd: r.o strly fnl f: fin 2nd, ½l: awrdd r) .....— | **1** | | 116 | — |
| 2144² | **Acharne** (CEBrittain) **3-8-11** BDoyle (a.p: hmpd over 1f out: swtchd rt & hmpd nr line: fin 3rd, ½l: plcd 2nd) ..... | **2** | | 115 | — |
| 2116² | **Desert Boy (IRE)** (PWChapple-Hyam) **3-8-11** SGuillot (mde all: rdn 2f out: wnt lft u.p: eased cl home: fin 1st: disq: plcd 3rd) ..... | **3** | | 117 | — |
| 2116⁵ | **Prize Giving** (GWragg) **3-8-11** MHills (racd 4th tl st: rdn 2f out: kpt on one pce) .....3 | **4** | | 111 | — |
| | **Night Watch (USA)** (AFabre,France) **3-8-11** OPeslier (racd 3rd: rdn wl over 2f out: unable qckn) .....1½ | **5** | | 108 | — |
| 1057a⁷ | **Supreme Commander (FR)** (PBary,France) **3-8-11** CAsmussen (racd 6th: rdn & btn 2f out) .....hd | **6** | | 108 | — |
| 2050⁶ | **General Academy (IRE)** (PAKelleway) **3-8-11** KFallon (a bhd) .....6 | **7** | | 98 | — |
| | | | | | **7 Rn** |

**2m 5.3** (1.80) P-M 4.90F: 3.30F 6.20F (70.40F) OWNER Mr K. Abdullah (CHANTILLY) BRED Juddmonte Farms
**1389a* Radevore** had the luck to be awarded this after finishing second. Held up early on, he was outpaced turning into the straight, but he found his stride and came with a strong run from a furlong and a half out. Even though he hung left inside the final furlong, he did not cause any interference. He is a tough colt who looks likely to be effective over further.
**2144 Acharne**, having tracked the leader on the rail during the early part of the race, was hampered as he tried to come through on the inside early in the straight. His jockey then switched round the leader but was stopped in his tracks close home as the leader slowed before the line. This was a good effort, and he would have been a lot closer without traffic problems. He is on the upgrade and should land a Group Two event in the near future.
**2116 Desert Boy (IRE)** quickened up in the straight but, as he came under pressure, he drifted into the rail, impeding Acharne. He ran on well and had his race won entering the final 50 yards, where his jockey dropped his hands, which had the effect of again hampering Acharne. He is obviously on the upgrade but was just unfortunate on this occasion as his jockey did not change his whip-hand early in the straight.
**2116 Prize Giving** was always in mid-division. Coming into the straight, he looked fairly dangerous but, after being ridden two furlongs out, he could only run on at the one pace. This step back in distance seemed to suit and he pleased connections with his performance.
**2050 General Academy (IRE)** was always in the rear and never mounted a challenge. He is an imposing colt but not up to this grade.

### 2845a PRIX NIMBUS (Listed) (3-Y.O C & G)
2-40 (2-39) **1m 4f 110y** £18,445.00 (£6,324.00: £3,953.00)

| | Horse | Pos | SP | RR | SF |
|---|---|---|---|---|---|
| 1757a¹² | **Water Poet (IRE)** (AFabre,France) **3-9-2** TJarnet .....— | **1** | | 106 | — |
| | **Grisellito (FR)** (ELellouche,France) **3-9-2** OPeslier .....hd | **2** | | 106 | — |
| 323a³ | **Grenadier (FR)** (GCollet,France) **3-9-2** DBoeuf .....1½ | **3** | | 104 | — |
| 2116⁷ | **Legal Right (USA)** (PWChapple-Hyam) **3-9-2** SGuillot (btn approx 4¼l) ..... | **5** | | — | — |
| | | | | | **6 Rn** |

**2m 40.7** P-M 1.80F: 1.20F 1.40F OWNER Sheikh Mohammed (CHANTILLY) BRED Sheikh Mohammed
**1329 Legal Right (USA)** should have been expected to put in a decent effort here, but proved disappointing.

## 2562-MUSSELBURGH (R-H) (Good to firm, Firm patches)
### Friday July 19th
WEATHER: fine WIND: almost nil

### 2846 BRUNTON SHAW CLAIMING STKS (2-Y.O) (Class F)
2-10 (2-19) **5f** £2,605.00 (£730.00: £355.00) Stalls: High GOING minus 0.45 sec per fur (F)

| | Horse | Pos | SP | RR | SF |
|---|---|---|---|---|---|
| 2726⁸ | **Bold African** (PDEvans) **2-9-3b** ACulhane(2) (lw: mde all: easily) .....— | **1** | 2/5 1 | 77? | 40 |
| 2374⁹ | **Hever Golf Stormer (IRE)** (TJNaughton) **2-9-3** JWeaver(4) (lw: sn chsng wnr: hrd rdn appr fnl f: no imp) .....5 | **2** | 9/4 3 | 61 | 24 |
| *2635⁶* | **Whittle Times** (EJAlston) **2-8-4v** JLowe(3) (wl outpcd fr ½-wy: sddle slipped) .....11 | **3** | 16/1 | 13 | — |
| *2389** | ***Fonzy*** (MrsLStubbs) **2-9-3b** KFallon(6) (Withdrawn not under Starter's orders: v.unruly in stalls) ..... | **W** | 5/4 2 | — | — |
| *1645⁹* | ***Thewrightone (IRE)*** (GROldroyd) **2-8-0b¹** DaleGibson(5) (Withdrawn not under Starter's orders: kicked in stalls & broke loose) ..... | **W** | 50/1 | — | — |
| | | | (SP 154.5%) | | **3 Rn** |

**59.0 secs** (1.30) CSF £1.61 TOTE £1.10: £1.70 (£1.10) OWNER Mr D. Maloney (WELSHPOOL) BRED G. Dickinson
**2309 Bold African** had nothing to beat this time and won very easily indeed, gaining a confidence-boosting victory. (2/5: 4/9-5/4)
**Hever Golf Stormer (IRE)**, in pursuit of the winner virtually throughout, was given a hard ride but never looked anything like good enough. (9/4)
**2174 Whittle Times** wears a pricker on her near-side and all she wanted to do was hang. Her saddle then slipped and she was eased a good deal by halfway. (16/1)

## 2847 BERRY BIRCH & NOBLE LIMITED STKS (0-55) (3-Y.O+) (Class F)

2-40 (2-40) **1m 3f 32y** £2,619.00 (£734.00: £357.00) Stalls: High GOING minus 0.45 sec per fur (F)

| | | | | SP | RR | SF |
|---|---|---|---|---|---|---|
| 2682* | **Mithraic (IRE) (53)** (WSCunningham) **4-9-3**(5) RHavlin(8) (lw: t: led: sn wl clr: racd alone stands' side: unchal) | — | 1 | 5/4 1 | 65 | 34 |
| | **Take Two (52)** (MissMKMilligan) **8-9-6** JQuinn(4) (chsd clr ldr: effrt appr st: no imp) | 11 | 2 | 20/1 | 47 | 16 |
| 2390[3] | **Ambidextrous (IRE) (52)** (EJAlston) **4-9-8** KFallon(7) (lw: hld up & bhd: effrt 6f out: hdwy 3f out: no imp) | 3 | 3 | 5/2 2 | 45 | 14 |
| 2487[5] | **Lord Advocate (51)** (DANolan) **8-9-12b** VHalliday(1) (lw: chsd clr ldr: no imp fnl 5f) | 9 | 4 | 10/1 | 36 | 5 |
| 2493[5] | **Rattle (46)** (JJO'Neill) **3-8-9b** TWilliams(6) (rdn 6f out: nvr trbld ldrs) | 2½ | 5 | 14/1 | 26 | — |
| | **Deauville Dancer (IRE) (55)** (DNicholls) **4-9-6** AlexGreaves(3) (bit bkwd: nvr nr to chal) | 8 | 6 | 20/1 | 15 | — |
| 2613[2] | **Victoria's Secret (IRE) (49)** (MRChannon) **4-8-10**(7) AEddery(2) (lw: outpcd ½-wy: a bhd) | 4 | 7 | 4/1 3 | 6 | — |
| 2679[9] | **Raise A Ripple (49)** (MrsDThomson) **3-8-9** JLowe(5) (bhd fr ½-wy) | 23 | 8 | 100/1 | — | — |
| | | | | (SP 119.3%) | **8 Rn** | |

**2m 24.8** (5.10) CSF £23.69 TOTE £2.70: £1.40 £6.70 £1.10 (£72.40) OWNER C P M Racing (YARM) BRED J. P. and Miss M. Mangan
WEIGHT FOR AGE 3yo-11lb

**2682* Mithraic (IRE)** was presented with this when allowed to poach a massive lead by halfway, and there were never going to be any challengers. (5/4: op 2/1)
**Take Two** last won on the Flat four years ago, but he still showed enough here to suggest that there is enough ability there, and this might well sweeten him up for the jumping game. (20/1)
**2390 Ambidextrous (IRE)**, given a lot to do, never had a hope of getting to the winner, and burst himself trying. (5/2)
**2487 Lord Advocate** was the only one to chase the winner early on and had been dealt with before the home turn. (10/1)
**1584 Rattle** never took the slightest interest. (14/1)
**Deauville Dancer (IRE)**, now a useful-looking sort who needed this, looks worth another chance or two. (20/1)

## 2848 WAVERLEY MINING H'CAP (0-60) (3-Y.O+) (Class F)

3-10 (3-11) **1m 7f 16y** £2,931.00 (£888.00: £434.00: £207.00) Stalls: High GOING minus 0.45 sec per fur (F)

| | | | | SP | RR | SF |
|---|---|---|---|---|---|---|
| 2516[6] | **Sarasota Storm (48)** (MBell) **4-9-2** MFenton(1) (hld up & bhd: c wd st: led wl over 1f out: r.o wl) | — | 1 | 5/1 3 | 59 | 15 |
| 2360[2] | **Sharp Sensation (38)** (DWBarker) **6-7-13**(7) JBramhill(7) (hld up: smooth hdwy to ld 3f out: sn rdn: hdd wl over 1f out: nt qckn) | 2½ | 2 | 7/1 | 46 | 2 |
| | **Master Hyde (USA) (56)** (WStorey) **7-9-7**(3) NVarley(4) (trckd ldrs: ev ch 3f out: one pce fnl 2f) | 8 | 3 | 7/2 2 | 56 | 12 |
| 2423[5] | **Little Redwing (35)** (MDHammond) **4-8-3** DaleGibson(6) (cl up: led over 3f out: sn hdd & one pce) | 3 | 4 | 9/1 | 32 | — |
| 2560[2] | **Pedaltothemetal (IRE) (41)** (PhilipMitchell) **4-8-9** JQuinn(8) (lw: chsd ldrs: effrt over 3f out: one pce) | ½ | 5 | 5/2 1 | 37 | — |
| 2627[8] | **What Jim Wants (IRE) (43)** (JJO'Neill) **3-7-10** JLowe(9) (chsd ldrs tl outpcd fnl 3½f) | 5 | 6 | 20/1 | 34 | — |
| 2390[7] | **Victor Laszlo (38)** (RAllan) **4-8-6** KFallon(3) (drvn along appr st: brought wd: sn prom: rdn & btn 2f out) | s.h | 7 | 9/1 | 29 | — |
| 2355[3] | **Red Spectacle (IRE) (51)** (PCHaslam) **4-9-0**(5) MBaird(2) (lw: led tl hdd & wknd over 3f out) | ¾ | 8 | 16/1 | 41 | — |
| 2388[5] | **Phar Closer (45)** (WTKemp) **3-7-12**ow2 TWilliams(10) (lost pl ½wy: n.d afterwards) | 6 | 9 | 20/1 | 29 | — |
| 2537[11] | **Bold Joker (28)** (GROldroyd) **5-7-10** AMackay(5) (a bhd) | 8 | 10 | 100/1 | 3 | — |
| | | | | (SP 116.4%) | **10 Rn** | |

**3m 20.3** (9.80) CSF £36.63 CT £126.13 TOTE £6.50: £1.50 £2.70 £2.10 (£10.30) Trio £22.60 OWNER Mr B. J. Warren (NEWMARKET) BRED B. J. Warren
LONG HANDICAP What Jim Wants (IRE) 7-7 Phar Closer 7-9 Bold Joker 7-4
WEIGHT FOR AGE 3yo-15lb

**2175* Sarasota Storm** loves this track and won really well. (5/1)
**2360 Sharp Sensation** travels well for much of the trip but fails to pick up sufficiently once off the bit. He still carries plenty of condition and will pick up a race in due course. (7/1)
**Master Hyde (USA)**, who won first time out last year, raced closer to the pace and then failed to pick up when ridden. (7/2)
**2423 Little Redwing** keeps showing something, but is basically short of a real turn of foot to do anything serious about it. (9/1)
**2560 Pedaltothemetal (IRE)** had her chances, but was woefully short of toe in the last three furlongs. (5/2)
**1165* Victor Laszlo** (9/1: op 6/1)

## 2849 MONKTONHALL COLLIERY H'CAP (0-70) (3-Y.O+) (Class E)

3-40 (3-41) **5f** £2,918.00 (£884.00: £432.00: £206.00) Stalls: High GOING minus 0.45 sec per fur (F)

| | | | | SP | RR | SF |
|---|---|---|---|---|---|---|
| 2732* | **King of Show (IRE) (51)** (RAllan) **5-8-12v** 7x KFallon(2) (hdwy ½-wy: led ins fnl f: jst hld on) | — | 1 | 9/2 2 | 59 | 33 |
| 2564[8] | **Leading Princess (IRE) (48)** (MissLAPerratt) **5-8-9b** JWeaver(5) (chsd ldrs: led wl over 1f out tl ins fnl f: r.o wl towards fin) | s.h | 2 | 8/1 | 56 | 30 |
| 2771* | **Bowcliffe Grange (IRE) (51)** (DWChapman) **4-8-12** 7x JQuinn(8) (lw: led tl hdd ins fnl f: kpt on) | 1¾ | 3 | 5/4 1 | 53 | 27 |
| 2392[7] | **Manolo (FR) (57)** (JBerry) **3-8-9**(5) PRoberts(7) (hdwy ½-wy: ev ch over 1f out: nt qckn) | ½ | 4 | 33/1 | 58 | 28 |
| 2564[5] | **Six for Luck (50)** (DANolan) **4-8-11b** AMackay(1) (b.off hind: wnt lft s: chsd ldrs: n.m.r over 1f out: nt qckn) | nk | 5 | 11/1 | 50 | 24 |
| 2564[3] | **Gondo (41)** (EJAlston) **9-8-2v** JLowe(4) (bhd: sn drvn along: n.d) | 3½ | 6 | 5/1 3 | 30 | 4 |
| 2395[4] | **Chemcast (67)** (DNicholls) **3-9-10b** AlexGreaves(6) (lw: cl up tl wknd over 1f out) | 1¼ | 7 | 11/2 | 52 | 22 |
| 2421[7] | **Nordisk Legend (37)** (MrsDThomson) **4-7-12**ow2 TWilliams(3) (a bhd) | 3½ | 8 | 100/1 | 10 | — |
| | | | | (SP 118.1%) | **8 Rn** | |

**59.1 secs** (1.40) CSF £36.89 CT £64.91 TOTE £5.40: £1.50 £1.70 £1.10 (£20.30) OWNER Mr R. Allan (CORNHILL-ON-TWEED) BRED Gainsborough Stud Management Ltd
LONG HANDICAP Nordisk Legend 7-5
WEIGHT FOR AGE 3yo-4lb

**2732* King of Show (IRE)** has taken on a new lease of life since being dropped back to sprinting and needed all his determination to hang on this time. (9/2)
**2154 Leading Princess (IRE)**, who had run a couple of indifferent races, showed here that she is not done with yet, and she would have won in another half-stride. (8/1)
**2771* Bowcliffe Grange (IRE)**, without the blinkers and poorly drawn, ran a super race. (5/4)
**Manolo (FR)** is obviously coming to form but, just when he looked dangerous, he failed to prolong the effort. (33/1)
**2564 Six for Luck** did not have the best of runs and would probably have finished a good bit closer. (11/1)
**2564 Gondo** was always finding things happening too quickly for his liking. (5/1)

## 2850 MONKTONHALL COLLIERY (S) STKS (2-Y.O) (Class G)
4-10 (4-10) **7f 15y** £2,263.50 (£636.00: £310.50) Stalls: High GOING minus 0.45 sec per fur (F)

| Form | Horse | Btn | Pos | SP | RR | SF |
|---|---|---|---|---|---|---|
| 2750[6] | **Sweeping Statement** (JBerry) **2-8-6** JQuinn(5) (mde all: qcknd over 2f out: r.o wl) | — | **1** | 12/1 | 52 | — |
| 2512[8] | **Super Scravels** (DrJDScargill) **2-8-6** MFenton(2) (hld up: gd hdwy over 2f out: sn chsng wnr: no ex fnl f) | 2½ | **2** | 7/4[1] | 46 | — |
| 2512[10] | **Foolish Flutter (IRE)** (GROldroyd) **2-8-6v[1]** DaleGibson(4) (prom: effrt 3f out: nt qckn) | 3 | **3** | 10/1 | 40 | — |
| 2387[2] | **Apiculate (IRE)** (WTKemp) **2-8-11** JWeaver(6) (prom: rdn 3f out: one pce) | 3½ | **4** | 9/4[2] | 37 | — |
| 2708[14] | **Poly Dancer** (MRChannon) **2-8-6** KFallon(3) (lost pl & rdn ½-wy: n.d after) | 9 | **5** | 3/1[3] | 11 | — |
| | **Barachois Lad** (JJO'Neill) **2-8-11** TWilliams(1) (unf: bit bkwd: outpcd appr st: n.d after) | ½ | **6** | 12/1 | 15 | — |

(SP 116.6%) **6 Rn**

**1m 32.6** (7.10) CSF £33.24 TOTE £8.30: £3.70 £1.10 (£9.10) OWNER Exors of the late Mrs Caroline Berry (COCKERHAM) BRED Mrs Caroline Berry
No bid
**2387 Sweeping Statement** beat a moderate bunch here, but did it well, and is obviously on the upgrade. (12/1)
**Super Scravels** is only lightly-made, but she has an engine, and she should pick up a similar event. (7/4)
**Foolish Flutter (IRE)** had a visor on for the first time and ran better, but was well held in the last two furlongs. (10/1)
**2387 Apiculate (IRE)** had his chances in a moderate race, and fluffed them. (9/4)
**Poly Dancer** looked fit but ran miserably, and it would seem too bad to be true. (3/1: 6/4-7/2)
**Barachois Lad**, very much in need of this, ran accordingly. (12/1: 8/1-14/1)

## 2851 CALEDONIAN INDUSTRIAL H'CAP (0-60) (3-Y.O+) (Class F)
4-40 (4-40) **1m 16y** £2,857.00 (£802.00: £391.00) Stalls: High GOING minus 0.45 sec per fur (F)

| Form | Horse | Btn | Pos | SP | RR | SF |
|---|---|---|---|---|---|---|
| 2426[5] | **Broctune Gold (60)** (MrsMReveley) **5-10-0** ACulhane(7) (mde all: r.o wl fnl 3f) | — | **1** | 10/1 | 74 | 56 |
| 2391[3] | **Seconds Away (28)** (JSGoldie) **5-7-7**(3) NVarley(1) (bhd: hdwy over 2f out: styd on wl: nrst fin) | 4 | **2** | 14/1 | 34 | 16 |
| 2425[3] | **Riccarton (50)** (PCalver) **3-8-10** MBirch(5) (prom: lost pl & n.m.r 2f out: r.o fnl f) | nk | **3** | 5/1[3] | 56 | 30 |
| 2391[12] | **Miss Pigalle (43)** (MissLAPerratt) **5-8-11b** JWeaver(4) (chsd wnr after 3f: one pce fnl 2f) | s.h | **4** | 9/1 | 48 | 30 |
| 2743[4] | **Rainbows Rhapsody (30)** (DWChapman) **5-7-12** TWilliams(13) (prom: hdwy 2f out: btn appr fnl f) | 2 | **5** | 7/2[1] | 31 | 13 |
| 2678[2] | **New Albion (USA) (57)** (MissZAGreen) **5-9-4**(7) IonaWands(12) (lw: a chsng ldrs: effrt 3f out: r.o one pce) | 3½ | **6** | 11/1 | 52 | 34 |
| 2573[10] | **Champagne N Dreams (47)** (DNicholls) **4-9-1b[1]** AlexGreaves(3) (lw: hld up: effrt over 2f out: rdn & no rspnse) | ½ | **7** | 12/1 | 41 | 23 |
| 2320[5] | **Katie Komaite (48)** (CaptJWilson) **3-8-8** MFenton(8) (swtg: cl up tl wknd fnl 2½f) | nk | **8** | 16/1 | 41 | 15 |
| 2592[2] | **She's Simply Great (IRE) (50)** (JJO'Neill) **3-8-10** KFallon(10) (lw: effrt over 3f out: n.d) | 4 | **9** | 4/1[2] | 35 | 9 |
| 2373[12] | **Kerrier (IRE) (30)** (RHarris) **4-7-12** AMackay(6) (mid div: effrt over 3f out: sn btn) | 3 | **10** | 9/1 | 9 | — |
| 1037[10] | **Silver Sleeve (IRE) (45)** (MDHammond) **4-8-13** DaleGibson(11) (sn bhd) | 1¾ | **11** | 20/1 | 21 | 3 |
| 2678[7] | **Black and Blues (30)** (JSGoldie) **10-7-12** JQuinn(2) (bhd fr ½-wy) | 5 | **12** | 100/1 | — | — |
| 2420[8] | **Nordic Gift (DEN) (45)** (MrsDThomson) **3-8-5** JLowe(9) (a bhd) | ¾ | **13** | 100/1 | 9 | — |

(SP 123.3%) **13 Rn**

**1m 40.4** (1.80) CSF £129.70 CT £745.53 TOTE £10.70: £3.10 £2.70 £3.00 (£72.80) Trio £154.30 OWNER Mrs M. B. Thwaites (SALTBURN) BRED A. J. Poulton (Epping) Ltd
LONG HANDICAP Seconds Away 7-9
WEIGHT FOR AGE 3yo-8lb
**2426 Broctune Gold** likes to have his own way out in front, and got it again this time to gain his second course win in his last two visits. (10/1)
**2391 Seconds Away** runs when in the mood, but the effort here was always too late to trouble the winner. (14/1: 10/1-16/1)
**2425 Riccarton** failed to impress on looks, but ran well after getting messed about, and is worth another chance. (5/1)
**2023 Miss Pigalle**, given a forceful ride, put up a decent performance, but was never doing enough at the business end. (9/1)
**2743 Rainbows Rhapsody** ran reasonably but was short of toe in the last two furlongs. A hard race on Monday might just have taken the edge off her this time. (7/2)
**2678 New Albion (USA)** had his chances, but looked very slow when the pressure was on in the straight. (11/1: 7/1-12/1)
**2045 Champagne N Dreams**, tried in blinkers for the first time, failed to pick up when asked a serious question. (12/1: op 8/1)

T/Plpt: £72.80 (138.86 Tckts). T/Qdpt: £33.70 (14.2 Tckts). AA

# 2243-NEWBURY (L-H) (Good to firm)
## Friday July 19th
WEATHER: hot WIND: almost nil

## 2852 E.B.F. ECCHINSWELL MAIDEN STKS (2-Y.O) (Class D)
2-30 (2-31) **6f 8y** £3,649.00 (£1,102.00: £536.00: £253.00) Stalls: High GOING minus 0.56 sec per fur (F)

| Form | Horse | Btn | Pos | SP | RR | SF |
|---|---|---|---|---|---|---|
| | **Cinema Paradiso** (PFICole) **2-9-0** MHills(11) (leggy: led over 1f: led 2f out: rdn out) | — | **1** | 14/1 | 94+ | 41 |
| | **Jawhari** (JLDunlop) **2-9-0** WCarson(3) (str: scope: bit bkwd: a.p: ev ch over 1f out: unable qckn) | 2½ | **2** | 4/5[1] | 87+ | 34 |
| | **Olivo (IRE)** (PFICole) **2-9-0** TQuinn(1) (str: scope: lw: a.p: led over 4f out to 2f out: one pce) | ¾ | **3** | 7/1[2] | 85 | 32 |
| 2559[11] | **Cryhavoc** (JRArnold) **2-9-0** CRutter(13) (a.p: ev ch over 1f out: wknd fnl f) | ¾ | **4** | 50/1 | 83 | 30 |
| | **Sycamore Boy (USA)** (LordHuntingdon) **2-9-0** DHarrison(4) (w'like: scope: lw: hdwy over 2f out: one pce) | 1¾ | **5** | 8/1[3] | 79 | 26 |
| 2575[7] | **Dickie Bird (IRE)** (RHannon) **2-8-11**(3) DaneO'Neill(5) (b.hind: hld up: rdn over 2f out: sn wknd) | 3½ | **6** | 20/1 | 70 | 17 |
| | **Schisandra** (MJFetherston-Godley) **2-8-9** DHolland(6) (unf: bit bkwd: nvr nr to chal) | 4 | **7** | 50/1 | 54 | 1 |
| 1896[9] | **Abacaxi (IRE)** (RCharlton) **2-9-0** SSanders(9) (hld up: rdn over 2f out: sn wknd) | ½ | **8** | 8/1[3] | 58 | 5 |
| | **Ludo** (RHannon) **2-9-0** JReid(10) (w'like: bit bkwd: dwlt: a bhd) | 1¾ | **9** | 7/1[2] | 53 | — |
| | **Regal Equity** (BJMeehan) **2-9-0** MTebbutt(7) (str: scope: bit bkwd: prom over 3f) | 1¼ | **10** | 50/1 | 50 | — |
| 2614[6] | **Jonfy (IRE)** (BWHills) **2-8-7**(7) GBrace(12) (a bhd) | ½ | **11** | 50/1 | 48 | — |
| | **Perchance To Dream (IRE)** (BRMillman) **2-8-6**(3) SDrowne(8) (wl grwn: bkwd: prom 3f) | ¾ | **12** | 50/1 | 41 | — |

(SP 124.0%) **12 Rn**

**1m 12.55** (0.75) CSF £25.68 TOTE £19.60: £3.30 £1.10 £1.70 (£15.70) Trio £19.80 OWNER Mr Christopher Wright (WHATCOMBE) BRED Barrettstown Stud Farms Ltd
**Cinema Paradiso**, a tall colt with not much substance, was one of the few newcomers who was actually fit. In the lead early, he regained the advantage a quarter of a mile out and, racing under the favoured stands' rail, was ridden along to assert his authority in the final furlong. (14/1)

**Jawhari**, a plain, good-bodied colt, did not look fully tuned up. In the firing-line from the outset, he had every chance below the distance, but he was racing in the centre of the track where the ground was not so fast and failed to quicken. Sure to come on a lot for this, he should soon open his account. (4/5: op 6/4)
**Olivo (IRE)**, an attractive, round-bodied colt, was soon in front. However, he raced down the centre of the track where the ground was not as fast as the stands' side and, collared a quarter of a mile out, failed to find another gear. He should not take long to find a race. (7/1: op 7/2)
**Cryhavoc** stepped up on his initial outing. Keeping the winner company, he had every chance below the distance before tiring inside the last 200 yards. (50/1)
**Sycamore Boy (USA)**, an attractive colt with plenty of substance and scope, began to pick up ground from halfway. He did stay on without threatening to get there in time, and should soon be winning. (8/1)
**Dickie Bird (IRE)** chased the leaders but, rousted along a quarter of a mile out, was soon bowled over. (20/1)
**Abacaxi (IRE)** (8/1: 7/2-9/1)

## 2853 WATERMILL CONDITIONS STKS (3-Y.O+) (Class C)

3-00 (3-00) **7f 64y (round)** £5,025.00 (£1,875.00: £912.50: £387.50: £168.75: £81.25) Stalls: Low GOING minus 0.56 sec per fur (F)

| | | | | SP | RR | SF |
|---|---|---|---|---|---|---|
| 2691* | **Green Perfume (USA) (106)** (PFICole) **4-9-12** TQuinn(2) (lw: mde all: all out) | — | 1 | 15/8 1 | 116 | 86 |
| 2623[16] | **Everglades (IRE) (98)** (RCharlton) **8-9-5** SSanders(1) (chsd wnr: ev ch fnl 2f: r.o) | nk | 2 | 9/1 | 108 | 78 |
| 2114[23] | **Hard to Figure (108)** (RJHodges) **10-9-3** TSprake(3) (rdn over 3f out: hdwy fnl f: r.o one pce) | 5 | 3 | 5/1 3 | 95 | 65 |
| | **Star of Zilzal (USA) (102)** (MRStoute) **4-9-0** JReid(6) (hld up: rdn 2f out: one pce) | ½ | 4 | 7/2 2 | 91 | 61 |
| 2007[8] | **Warning Time (104)** (BJMeehan) **3-8-7** WCarson(7) (a.p: rdn over 2f out: wknd fnl f) | 2½ | 5 | 7/2 2 | 86 | 49 |
| | **Brilliant Red (104)** (PFICole) **3-8-7** CRutter(5) (a bhd) | nk | 6 | 16/1 | 85 | 48 |
| | **Funchal Way** (NMBabbage) **4-8-11** AMcGlone(4) (s.s: a bhd) | 11 | 7 | 100/1 | 58? | 28 |
| | | | | (SP 112.8%) | | **7 Rn** |

**1m 26.13** (0.15 under best) (-1.97) CSF £16.92 TOTE £2.80: £1.70 £3.60 (£8.20) OWNER Lord Sondes (WHATCOMBE) BRED Brereton C. Jones
WEIGHT FOR AGE 3yo-7lb
**2691* Green Perfume (USA)**, uneasy in the market, had no intention of hanging around and set a very strong pace. It looked as if he was going to be passed by the runner-up in the final quarter mile but, sticking to his task really well and responding to severe pressure, held on gamely to break the course record set three years ago. (15/8)
**1898* Everglades (IRE)** raced in second place. Delivering a stern challenge in the final quarter-mile, it looked as if he was going to get up, but he had met a real tartar in the winner and failed to get past. (9/1)
**1332 Hard to Figure**, scrubbed along at the back of the field from halfway, stayed on in the final furlong to finish a moderate third. Only one of his fourteen victories has come over seven furlongs. (5/1: op 3/1)
**Star of Zilzal (USA)**, who has been gelded since last year, chased the leaders but could only go up and down in the same place in the final quarter-mile. (7/2)
**1796 Warning Time** raced in third place, but was being pushed along over a quarter of a mile from home and, failing to find what was required, had nothing more to give in the last 200 yards. (7/2)

## 2854 CHATTIS HILL MAIDEN STKS (2-Y.O F) (Class D)

3-30 (3-31) **5f 34y** £3,493.00 (£1,054.00: £512.00: £241.00) Stalls: High GOING minus 0.56 sec per fur (F)

| | | | | SP | RR | SF |
|---|---|---|---|---|---|---|
| | **Song of Skye** (TJNaughton) **2-8-11** DHolland(4) (leggy: unf: s.s: hdwy 2f out: led over 1f out: r.o wl) | — | 1 | 33/1 | 69 | 30 |
| | **Mayflower** (IABalding) **2-8-11** MHills(5) (leggy: scope: bit bkwd: s.s: swtchd lft & hdwy over 1f out: r.o one pce) | 1¾ | 2 | 7/1 3 | 64 | 25 |
| | **Blues Queen** (MRChannon) **2-8-11** JReid(1) (leggy: unf: w ldr: led 4f out tl over 1f out: one pce) | ¾ | 3 | 9/4 2 | 61 | 22 |
| | **Chloe Nicole (USA)** (PFICole) **2-8-11** TQuinn(2) (leggy: scope: lw: s.s: hld up: rdn over 2f out: one pce) | ½ | 4 | 5/6 1 | 60 | 21 |
| 1834[2] | **Gopi** (RHannon) **2-8-8**(3) DaneO'Neill(3) (b.nr fore: led 1f: wknd over 1f out) | 2½ | 5 | 15/2 | 52 | 13 |
| | | | | (SP 112.5%) | | **5 Rn** |

**61.29 secs** (1.09) CSF £184.60 TOTE £18.80: £3.60 £1.60 (£38.00) OWNER Mr E. J. Fenaroli (EPSOM) BRED Dr and Mrs St J. Collier
**Song of Skye**, quite a leggy individual, caused a real shock here. Rather tardy leaving the stalls, he moved up to snatch the lead below the distance and, ridden along, soon asserted. (33/1)
**Mayflower**, quite a tall, attractive filly, looked big and well in the paddock. Switched left in the final quarter mile, she soon picked up ground but swished her tail every time the whip was applied. Nevertheless, she did stay on to take second prize. (7/1: op 7/2)
**Blues Queen**, quite a tall, plain filly who is yet to develop, was soon at the head of affairs. Collared below the distance, she failed to find another gear. (9/4: 6/4-5/2)
**Chloe Nicole (USA)**, a tall filly with plenty of scope, certainly took the eye in the paddock, but was rather disappointing in the race itself. Recovering from a tardy start to chase the leaders, she was being bustled along from halfway, but failed to find what was required. (5/6: Evens-4/5)
**1834 Gopi** is little more than a rabbit. In the firing-line throughout, she had given her all at the distance. Lack of size is going to make life very difficult for her. (15/2)

## 2855 WHITE HORSE H'CAP (0-80) (3-Y.O F) (Class D)

4-00 (4-01) **1m 2f 6y** £3,655.50 (£1,104.00: £537.00: £253.50) Stalls: Low GOING minus 0.56 sec per fur (F)

| | | | | SP | RR | SF |
|---|---|---|---|---|---|---|
| 2768* | **Frog (67)** (SirMarkPrescott) **3-9-4** 5x WWoods(5) (chsd ldr: led over 4f out: rdn out) | — | 1 | 11/4 2 | 77 | 48 |
| 2251[16] | **Lavender Della (IRE) (58)** (MJFetherston-Godley) **3-8-6**(3) MHenry(1) (lw: hdwy & nt clr run 2f out: chsd wnr fnl f: r.o wl) | ½ | 2 | 33/1 | 67 | 38 |
| 2593[3] | **Call Me (70)** (CWThornton) **3-9-7** DeanMcKeown(4) (hld up: rdn over 3f out: hmpd over 2f out: one pce) | 3½ | 3 | 6/1 | 74 | 45 |
| 2399[8] | **Tea Party (USA) (63)** (KOCunningham-Brown) **3-9-0** JReid(2) (lw: a.p: rdn over 3f out: one pce) | 2 | 4 | 33/1 | 63 | 34 |
| 2251* | **Dramatic Moment (70)** (IABalding) **3-9-2**(5) MartinDwyer(6) (lw: hld up: rdn over 4f out: one pce) | ¾ | 5 | 7/2 3 | 69 | 40 |
| 982[13] | **Budding Annie (55)** (JRBosley) **3-8-6** CRutter(3) (nvr nr to chal) | ¾ | 6 | 50/1 | 53 | 24 |
| 2384[4] | **Mua-Tab (70)** (PTWalwyn) **3-9-7** WCarson(7) (led over 5f: wkng whn hmpd over 2f out) | 2 | 7 | 9/1 | 65 | 36 |
| 2197[11] | **Promissory (70)** (CEBrittain) **3-9-7** MRoberts(8) (a.p: rdn over 3f out: edgd lft over 2f out: wknd over 1f out) | 2½ | 8 | 20/1 | 61 | 32 |
| 2334[3] | **Polish Widow (70)** (GWragg) **3-9-7** MHills(9) (a bhd) | 5 | 9 | 5/2 1 | 53 | 24 |
| | | | | (SP 114.4%) | | **9 Rn** |

**2m 4.83** (1.03) CSF £64.64 CT £460.70 TOTE £4.10: £1.60 £4.80 £2.10 (£63.30) Trio £144.30 OWNER Mr B. Haggas (NEWMARKET) BRED Mrs P. A. Clark
OFFICIAL EXPLANATION **Polish Widow: the jockey stated that the filly was never travelling on the ground.**

**2768* Frog**, who drifted badly in the market, raced in second place. Sent to the front entering the straight, she was ridden along and had poached too much of a lead to be caught. This was her fourth victory of the month and it will surely see the Handicapper raise her dramatically in the weights. (11/4: 11/10-3/1)
**1589 Lavender Della (IRE)** did not have the best of runs. Picking up ground a quarter of a mile out, she found her way blocked and, for a short while, her jockey had to sit and suffer. A gap soon appeared and she soon moved into second place, but the winner had poached too much of lead. (33/1)
**2593 Call Me** chased the leaders. Hampered over a quarter of a mile from home, she failed to find another gear. (6/1)
**1614 Tea Party (USA)** was only treading water in the last three furlongs. (33/1)
**2251* Dramatic Moment**, raised 10lb for her recent victory, chased the leaders but was making little impression in the last half-mile. (7/2)

## 2856 SHRIVENHAM H'CAP (0-90) (3-Y.O+) (Class C)

4-30 (4-31) **6f 8y** £5,540.00 (£1,670.00: £810.00: £380.00) Stalls: High GOING minus 0.56 sec per fur (F)

| | | | | SP | RR | SF |
|---|---|---|---|---|---|---|
| 2725[2] | **Bayin (USA) (72)** (MDIUsher) **7-8-12** RStreet(7) (b: lw: s.s: hdwy over 1f out: led wl ins fnl f: r.o wl) | — | **1** | 11/4[1] | 83 | 51 |
| 2381[5] | **Mr Bergerac (IRE) (79)** (BPalling) **5-9-5** TSprake(4) (hdwy over 2f out: led ins fnl f: sn hdd: unable qckn) | ¾ | **2** | 9/1 | 88 | 56 |
| 2232* | **Mister Jolson (76)** (RJHodges) **7-8-13**(3) SDrowne(6) (hld up: rdn over 2f out: r.o ins fnl f) | nk | **3** | 15/2 | 84 | 52 |
| 2604* | **Law Commission (89)** (DRCElsworth) **6-10-1** 7x TQuinn(10) (nt clr run on ins over 2f out tl over 1f out: gd hdwy fnl f: r.o wl) | nk | **4** | 11/1 | 96 | 64 |
| 2403* | **Golden Pound (USA) (83)** (MissGayKelleway) **4-9-9** RCochrane(5) (swtg: hld up: rdn over 1f out: r.o) | nk | **5** | 9/2[2] | 90 | 58 |
| 2623[6] | **Silent Expression (86)** (BJMeehan) **6-9-12** MTebbutt(2) (a.p: rdn over 2f out: one pce) | ¾ | **6** | 9/1 | 91 | 59 |
| 1790[15] | **Lennox Lewis (85)** (APJarvis) **4-9-11** JTate(3) (lw: led: hrd rdn over 1f out: hdd ins fnl f: one pce) | nk | **7** | 11/1 | 89 | 57 |
| 2400[3] | **Shamanic (88)** (RHannon) **4-9-11**(3) DaneO'Neill(9) (swtg: hld up: nt clr run over 2f out tl wl over 1f out: nt clr run ins fnl f: nt rcvr) | 1 | **8** | 8/1 | 89 | 57 |
| 2497[6] | **Bold Effort (FR) (85)** (KOCunningham-Brown) **4-9-11b** MRoberts(8) (a.p: rdn over 2f out: ev ch ins fnl f: sn wknd) | s.h | **9** | 6/1[3] | 86 | 54 |
| 2722[11] | **Champagne Grandy (84)** (MRChannon) **6-9-5**(5) PPMurphy(1) (lw: spd over 3f) | 8 | **10** | 20/1 | 64 | 32 |
| | | | | (SP 123.4%) | | **10 Rn** |

**1m 11.62** (-0.18) CSF £27.27 CT £159.75 TOTE £4.20: £1.60 £2.90 £2.20 (£18.90) Trio £17.80 OWNER Mr Trevor Barker (SWINDON)
**2725 Bayin (USA)** at last came good after a string of late flourishes failed to succeed. Tardy leaving the stalls, he moved up on the outside of the field below the distance and, with his jockey wiggling his arms, the combination came through to lead in the last 75 yards. (11/4)
**2381 Mr Bergerac (IRE)** moved up soon after halfway. Sent on early inside the final furlong, he found the winner too strong inside the last 75 yards. (9/1)
**2232* Mister Jolson** did run on inside the final furlong to secure third prize. (15/2)
**2604* Law Commission** had no luck in running. Trapped along the inside rail a quarter of a mile from home, he only found daylight a furlong out and, squeezing through between horses, stormed past his opponents to take fourth prize. (11/1: 8/1-12/1)
**2403* Golden Pound (USA)**, ridden along below the distance, ran on but failed to get there in time. (9/2)
**2623 Silent Expression**, in the thick of the action from the outset, failed to increase her work-rate from below the distance. (9/1)
**1334 Lennox Lewis** (11/1: 8/1-12/1)
**2400 Shamanic** (8/1: 6/1-9/1)

## 2857 THAMES VALLEY CHAMBER OF COMMERCE H'CAP (0-85) (3-Y.O+) (Class D)

5-00 (5-00) **2m** £3,597.00 (£1,086.00: £528.00: £249.00) Stalls: Low GOING minus 0.56 sec per fur (F)

| | | | | SP | RR | SF |
|---|---|---|---|---|---|---|
| 2415* | **Moonlight Quest (80)** (BHanbury) **8-9-12** WRyan(2) (b: hdwy 3f out: led over 2f out: all out) | — | **1** | 7/4[1] | 89 | 63 |
| 2612[2] | **Great Easeby (IRE) (59)** (WStorey) **6-8-5** JFanning(5) (rdn over 5f out: hdwy 3f out: n.m.r over 2f out: r.o wl ins fnl f) | hd | **2** | 7/2[2] | 68 | 42 |
| 2511[3] | **Coleridge (53)** (JJSheehan) **8-7-10b**(3) MHenry(4) (lw: rdn over 5f out: lost pl & hmpd on ins over 2f out: rallied fnl f: r.o wl) | s.h | **3** | 14/1 | 62 | 36 |
| 2042[23] | **Unchanged (72)** (CEBrittain) **4-9-4** MRoberts(6) (led over 13f: hrd rdn r.o ins fnl f) | nk | **4** | 8/1 | 81 | 55 |
| 2401[2] | **Silently (78)** (IABalding) **4-9-10** TQuinn(1) (lw: hdwy 3f out: edgd lft over 2f out: hrd rdn over 1f out: r.o) | hd | **5** | 6/1[3] | 86 | 60 |
| 2612[4] | **Invest Wisely (82)** (JMPEustace) **4-10-0** RCochrane(3) (lw: chsd ldr: ev ch over 2f out: sn wknd) | 2½ | **6** | 7/2[2] | 88 | 62 |
| | | | | (SP 112.9%) | | **6 Rn** |

**3m 25.42** (0.99 under best) (0.42) CSF £7.98 TOTE £2.80: £1.40 £2.00 (£3.80) OWNER Mrs John Lamb (NEWMARKET) BRED Raintree Stud
**2415* Moonlight Quest** moved through to grab the initiative over a quarter of a mile from home but, with his rivals refusing to give him any peace, he was all out to hold on. Nevertheless, he smashed the twenty-three-year-old course-record by a second. (7/4)
**2612 Great Easeby (IRE)** was being niggled along turning out of the back straight and the signs certainly did not look good. Moving up three furlongs from home, he really found his feet in the closing stages and may well have prevailed in a few more strides. (7/2: op 2/1)
**2511 Coleridge** raced in a handy position, but he was just getting outpaced when hampered along the inside rail over a quarter of a mile out. That appeared to be the end of his chances, but he came with a renewed effort in the final furlong and finished really strongly. (14/1)
**1306 Unchanged** was not going to hang around and set a really good clip. Collared over a quarter of a mile from home, she ran on commendably to the bitter end. (8/1)
**2401 Silently** moved into the action in the last three furlongs. Under pressure below the distance, he stayed on but just failed to get there in time. (6/1)
**2612 Invest Wisely**, racing in second place, still had every chance approaching the final quarter-mile before tiring. (7/2)

## 2858 LEVY BOARD H'CAP (0-80) (3-Y.O+) (Class D)

5-30 (5-31) **7f (straight)** £3,636.00 (£1,098.00: £534.00: £252.00) Stalls: High GOING minus 0.56 sec per fur (F)

| | | | | SP | RR | SF |
|---|---|---|---|---|---|---|
| 2229* | **Young Duke (IRE) (66)** (MrsSDWilliams) **8-8-12**(3) PMcCabe(6) (hld up: n.m.r over 2f out: led ins fnl f: r.o wl) | — | **1** | 7/2[2] | 76 | 58 |
| 2693[8] | **Sue's Return (76)** (APJarvis) **4-9-11** JTate(2) (hdwy over 2f out: led 1f out tl ins fnl f: unable qckn) | 1¾ | **2** | 12/1 | 82 | 64 |
| 2312[3] | **Easy Jet (POL) (74)** (LordHuntingdon) **4-9-9** DHarrison(5) (a.p: hrd rdn 2f out: one pce) | 2½ | **3** | 2/1[1] | 74 | 56 |
| 2577[9] | **Winsome Wooster (59)** (PGMurphy) **5-8-5**(3) SDrowne(1) (lw: hld up: led over 1f out: sn hdd: one pce) | s.h | **4** | 12/1 | 59 | 41 |
| 2134[15] | **Mister Fire Eyes (IRE) (70)** (CEBrittain) **4-9-5b** MRoberts(8) (hld up: rdn over 1f out: one pce) | 2 | **5** | 15/2 | 66 | 48 |
| | **Chili Heights (55)** (GBBalding) **6-8-4v** TSprake(4) (a bhd) | 5 | **6** | 10/1 | 39 | 21 |
| 2160[3] | **Xenophon of Cunaxa (IRE) (80)** (MJFetherston-Godley) **3-9-8** DHolland(7) (w ldr: led over 3f out to 2f out: wknd fnl f) | 1 | **7** | 6/1[3] | 62 | 37 |

| | | | | | SP | RR | SF |
|---|---|---|---|---|---|---|---|
| *2308[6]* | **Deerly (57)** (CASmith) **3-7-13** CRutter(3) (led over 3f: led 2f out tl over 1f out: cl 3rd whn fell 1f out) | | **F** | | 14/1 | — | — |
| | | | | | (SP 112.7%) | **8 Rn** | |

**1m 24.04** (-0.46) CSF £37.67 CT £95.19 TOTE £3.50: £1.80 £1.50 £1.20 (£27.50) OWNER Mrs Sarah Williams (SOUTH MOLTON) BRED Mrs P. F. McQuillan
WEIGHT FOR AGE 3yo-7lb

**2229* Young Duke (IRE)** showed his Kempton victory to be no fluke. Chasing the leaders, he did not have a great deal of room over a quarter of a mile from home, but he managed to get the split and storm through to lead inside the final furlong. (7/2: op 9/4)
**Sue's Return** made headway over a quarter of a mile out. Striking the front at the distance, she was collared inside the final furlong and failed to find another gear. (12/1)
**2312 Easy Jet (POL)** was under pressure in the final quarter-mile, but failed to quicken. (2/1)
**2229 Winsome Wooster** chased the leaders. Showing in front below the distance, she was soon collared and tapped for toe. (12/1)
**1078 Mister Fire Eyes (IRE)** chased the leaders but failed to quicken from below the distance. (15/2)

T/Jkpt: £11,878.50 (0.1 Tckts); £15,057.32 to Newbury 20/7/96. T/Plpt: £80.60 (217.48 Tckts). T/Qdpt: £32.60 (30.53 Tckts). AK

# 2619-NEWMARKET (R-H) (Good to firm)
## Friday July 19th
WEATHER: warm & sunny WIND: slt against

## 2859 SPORTING INDEX SPREAD BETTING CLAIMING STKS (3-Y.O) (Class E)
6-30 (6-30) **1m (July)** £4,012.50 (£1,200.00: £575.00: £262.50) Stalls: High GOING minus 0.22 sec per fur (GF)

| | | | | SP | RR | SF |
|---|---|---|---|---|---|---|
| 2617[6] | **Eurobox Boy (59)** (APJarvis) **3-8-3**(3) DWright(4) (b.nr hind: led 1f: led 2f out tl over 1f out: led ins fnl f: rdn out) | — | **1** | 9/2 | 61 | 23 |
| 2617[3] | **Sharp Shuffle (IRE) (65)** (RHannon) **3-9-3**(3) DaneO'Neill(8) (lw: hld up: hdwy over 2f out: led over 1f out: rdn & hdd ins fnl f) | 1 | **2** | 9/4[1] | 73 | 35 |
| 2597[8] | **Baron Hrabovsky** (PFICole) **3-9-2** TQuinn(7) (in tch: rdn & outpcd 3f out: kpt on appr fnl f) | 5 | **3** | 25/1 | 59 | 21 |
| 2542[5] | **Sylvella (51)** (MAJarvis) **3-8-3** GCarter(1) (plld hrd: prom: rdn over 2f out: no imp appr fnl f) | 1 | **4** | 100/30[2] | 44 | 6 |
| 2753[3] | **Uncle George (65)** (MHTompkins) **3-9-2** PRobinson(9) (hld up: hdwy 3f out: ev ch 2f out: wknd fnl f) | 1 | **5** | 7/2[3] | 55 | 17 |
| *2303[10]* | **Sweet Amoret (46)** (PHowling) **3-8-7** FNorton(5) (b.off hind: trckd ldrs: rdn 2f out: sn btn) | 3½ | **6** | 20/1 | 39 | 1 |
| | **Koraloona (IRE)** (GBBalding) **3-9-6** MWigham(3) (wl grwn: bhd fnl 3f) | 2 | **7** | 33/1 | 48 | 10 |
| 2411[4] | **Shermood (43)** (KTIvory) **3-8-3** NAdams(2) (b.hind: plld hrd: led after 1f: hdd & wknd 2f out) | 4 | **8** | 25/1 | 23 | — |
| *123[11]* | **Tina Katerina** (RChampion) **3-8-3** GBardwell(6) (rdn 4f out: sn bhd) | 4 | **9** | 33/1 | 15 | — |
| | | | | (SP 112.6%) | **9 Rn** | |

**1m 42.07** (4.87) CSF £13.99 TOTE £6.70: £1.80 £1.30 £2.90 (£7.40) Trio £52.80 OWNER Mr N. Coverdale (ASTON UPTHORPE) BRED G. Revitt

**2617 Eurobox Boy** was always in the front-rank and fought on well when challenged. Up with the pace seems the way to ride him. (9/2)
**2617 Sharp Shuffle (IRE)** got warm and was taken down steadily. Restrained in the early stages, he looked a big danger at the furlong pole, but was soon worried out of it. (9/4)
**Baron Hrabovsky** produced a much-improved display and, despite his pedigree, may stay further still. (25/1)
**2542 Sylvella** proved rather keen, despite the drop in trip, but had no more to give from the Dip. (100/30)
**2753 Uncle George**, who misbehaved in the visor earlier in the week, proved keen going down, despite the aid being dispensed with. A brief effort was all he could muster and he seems to have lost his way, like many from this yard at present. (7/2)
**899 Sweet Amoret**, back on turf for the first time in five outings, probably needs to dominate and resented being held back from the early lead. (20/1)

## 2860 HORSE RACING ABROAD H'CAP (0-80) (3-Y.O+) (Class D)
6-55 (6-55) **6f (July)** £4,230.00 (£1,260.00: £600.00: £270.00) Stalls: High GOING minus 0.22 sec per fur (GF)

| | | | | SP | RR | SF |
|---|---|---|---|---|---|---|
| 2578[16] | **Kind of Light (67)** (RGuest) **3-9-1** JReid(3) (lw: hld up: hdwy to ld over 1f out: drvn out) | — | **1** | 25/1 | 75 | 52 |
| 2431[4] | **Almasi (IRE) (70)** (CFWall) **4-9-9** WWoods(2) (hld up: hdwy 2f out: ev ch over 1f out: sn rdn & no ex) | 2½ | **2** | 11/4[2] | 71 | 53 |
| 2590* | **Cim Bom Bom (IRE) (73)** (MBell) **4-9-5v**(7) 6x GFaulkner(7) (lw: led after 2f: hdd over 1f out: sn btn) | nk | **3** | 5/2[1] | 74 | 56 |
| *2306[3]* | **I'm Your Lady (72)** (BAMcMahon) **5-9-11** GCarter(6) (w ldrs: one pce fnl 2f) | ¾ | **4** | 11/2 | 71 | 53 |
| 2376[8] | **Be Warned (68)** (NACallaghan) **5-9-7** WCarson(1) (bhd: hdwy over 2f out: wknd over 1f out) | 2½ | **5** | 9/2[3] | 60 | 42 |
| 2437[4] | **Rumba Rhythm (CAN) (70)** (RWArmstrong) **3-9-4** MRoberts(4) (led 2f: wknd 2f out) | hd | **6** | 13/2 | 62 | 39 |
| | **Masruf (IRE) (70)** (TThomsonJones) **4-9-9** SSanders(5) (bkwd: w ldrs over 3f) | 3½ | **7** | 25/1 | 52 | 34 |
| | | | | (SP 109.8%) | **7 Rn** | |

**1m 14.02** (2.02) CSF £84.55 TOTE £23.60: £4.00 £2.20 (£26.20) OWNER Mrs B. Mills (NEWMARKET) BRED Theakston Stud
WEIGHT FOR AGE 3yo-5lb

OFFICIAL EXPLANATION **Kind Of Light: connections stated that the filly's last run had been her first for five months, and she had run too freely on what was her first run on turf, when accounting for her apparent improvement.**
**Kind of Light**, having only her second run on turf, was arguably the paddock pick and moved well to post. Despite her starting price, there was no element of fluke about this. (25/1)
**2431 Almasi (IRE)** looked to be feeling the fast ground, but still did her level best. (11/4)
**2590* Cim Bom Bom (IRE)**, rather too free going to post, did not look to enjoy herself on the way back. (5/2)
**2306 I'm Your Lady**, dropping back to a stiff six furlongs, lacked the pace to make a race of it from the Dip. (11/2)
**2228 Be Warned** looks to be taking a long time to come to hand this season, but is certainly on a winning mark now. (9/2)
**2437 Rumba Rhythm (CAN)**, dropping back in trip, tried to take these along, but lacked the basic speed to dominate for long. (13/2)

## 2861 LOUIS ROEDERER CHAMPAGNE MAIDEN STKS (3-Y.O+) (Class D)
7-25 (7-26) **6f (July)** £4,230.00 (£1,260.00: £600.00: £270.00) Stalls: High GOING minus 0.22 sec per fur (GF)

| | | | | SP | RR | SF |
|---|---|---|---|---|---|---|
| 2501[9] | **Navigate (USA) (80)** (RHannon) **3-8-11**(3) DaneO'Neill(4) (lw: hld up: hdwy 2f out: led 1f out: rdn out) | — | **1** | 11/4[2] | 86 | 47 |
| 2346[2] | **Present Generation (85)** (RGuest) **3-9-0** JReid(5) (dwlt: sn trckg ldrs: squeezed thro 1f out: r.o: nt trble wnr) | 1¾ | **2** | 7/4[1] | 81 | 42 |
| | **Disputed** (MAJarvis) **3-9-0** PRobinson(3) (w'like: trckd ldrs: nt clr run over 1f out: swtchd & r.o ins fnl f) | 2 | **3** | 6/1 | 76 | 37 |
| 2597[4] | **Paojiunic (IRE)** (LMCumani) **3-9-0** OUrbina(2) (chsd ldrs: rdn & no ex appr fnl f) | s.h | **4** | 5/1[3] | 76 | 37 |
| 1994[7] | **Cadeau Elegant** (NACallaghan) **3-8-9** SWhitworth(1) (lw: w ldr: led 3f out: hdd 1f out: eased nr fin) | ½ | **5** | 25/1 | 70+ | 31 |

2687[3] **Hannalou (FR) (75)** (SPCWoods) **3-8-9** WWoods(6) (led 3f: wknd over 1f out)....2 **6** 5/1[3] 64 25
(SP 114.5%) **6 Rn**

**1m 14.37** (2.37) CSF £7.93 TOTE £3.90: £2.00 £1.40 (£2.60) OWNER Highclere Thoroughbred Racing Ltd (MARLBOROUGH) BRED David E. Hager II and Lord Howard de Walden

**1983 Navigate (USA)** got warm and did not move to post very well, but found the best turn of foot by far and was always doing enough once in front. (11/4)

**2346 Present Generation**, sprinting for the first time, had difficulty getting a run when it mattered and, by the time he got through, the winner had flown. (7/4)

**Disputed**, a French import, might have given the winner more to think about had he found an opening at the vital moment. (6/1: 4/1-13/2)

**2597 Paojiunic (IRE)**, taken down last, seemed to be beaten on merit but might improve over further. (5/1)

**Cadeau Elegant**, having her third run, certainly was not knocked about once her measure was taken, and is worth keeping an eye on. (25/1)

**2687 Hannalou (FR)** may not have been suited by forcing the pace, but is becoming frustrating. (5/1)

## 2862 SPORTING INDEX H'CAP (0-95) (4-Y.O+) (Class C)

7-55 (7-56) **1m 2f (July)** £7,440.00 (£2,220.00: £1,060.00: £480.00) Stalls: High GOING minus 0.22 sec per fur (GF)

| | | | | SP | RR | SF |
|---|---|---|---|---|---|---|
| 2544[7] | **Moving Arrow (92)** (MissSEHall) **5-9-11** JReid(5) (lw: stdd s: hdwy & nt clr run over 1f out: qcknd to ld ins fnl f) | — | 1 | 10/1 | 104 | 84 |
| 2502[6] | **Komreyev Dancer (75)** (ABailey) **4-8-5**(3) DWright(4) (trckd ldrs: nt clr run fr 2f out: swtchd & r.o wl ins fnl f) | 1 | 2 | 6/1[3] | 85 | 65 |
| 2690[2] | **Romios (IRE) (82)** (PFICole) **4-9-1** TQuinn(2) (lw: trckd ldrs: led 1f out: hung lft: sn hdd & nt qckn) | hd | 3 | 3/1[1] | 92 | 72 |
| 2736[2] | **Kaafih Homm (IRE) (64)** (NACallaghan) **5-7-11**ow1 WCarson(1) (hld up: hdwy 2f out: no ex ins fnl f) | 1½ | 4 | 4/1[2] | 72 | 51 |
| 2206[2] | **Apollono (75)** (JRFanshawe) **4-8-8** NDay(8) (lw: bhd: rdn & hdwy 2f out: edgd lft & r.o fnl f) | hd | 5 | 15/2 | 83 | 63 |
| 2483[4] | **Clifton Fox (81)** (JAGlover) **4-9-0** SDWilliams(3) (hld up: effrt 3f out: nvr nrr) | ¾ | 6 | 7/1 | 88 | 68 |
| 765[16] | **Sveltana (76)** (GWragg) **4-8-9** MHills(6) (plld hrd: a.p: led over 1f out: sn hdd & btn) | 1 | 7 | 12/1 | 81 | 61 |
| | **Missel (95)** (MJohnston) **4-9-9**(5) KMChin(9) (bkwd: plld hrd: trckd ldrs: no imp fnl 3f) | nk | 8 | 25/1 | 99 | 79 |
| 2350[4] | **Mellottie (93)** (MrsMReveley) **11-9-7**(5) GLee(12) (stdd s: rdn 3f out: nvr nr to chal) | 4 | 9 | 10/1 | 91 | 71 |
| 2603[7] | **Bob's Ploy (79)** (MHTompkins) **4-8-12** PRobinson(11) (led over 6f: sn wknd) | ½ | 10 | 16/1 | 76 | 56 |
| | **King Athelstan (USA) (86)** (BAMcMahon) **8-9-5** GCarter(7) (prom: led over 3f out tl over 1f out: sn btn) | 2 | 11 | 33/1 | 80 | 60 |
| | **Northern Law (74)** (JohnBerry) **4-8-4**(3) PMcCabe(10) (b: bhd fnl 5f: virtually p.u 2f out) | dist | 12 | 50/1 | — | — |

(SP 124.1%) **12 Rn**

**2m 5.89** (0.89) CSF £66.71 CT £210.61 TOTE £13.00: £3.30 £2.90 £2.00 (£51.70) Trio £33.60 OWNER Mr G. W. Westgarth (MIDDLEHAM) BRED W. G. Barker

LONG HANDICAP Kaafih Homm (IRE) 7-9

**1799 Moving Arrow**, rejuvenated by waiting tactics, burst through late in the day to win off his highest ever mark. (10/1)

**2502 Komreyev Dancer** has kept his form admirably and might well have won with a clearer run. (6/1)

**2690 Romios (IRE)**, due to rise 5lb in the handicap from Saturday, was rather forced to run here, on ground faster than he had ever won on. Hanging cost him the lead, but it would be charitable to blame the ground alone. (3/1)

**2736 Kaafih Homm (IRE)**, over what is probably his best trip, ran well and is ready to win once his sights are lowered. (4/1)

**2206 Apollono** ruined his chance by hanging as he began to quicken up. (15/2)

**2483 Clifton Fox** does need easier ground to be seen at his best and, in the circumstances, ran well. (7/1)

## 2863 MARK GORSUCH MAIDEN STKS (2-Y.O F) (Class D)

8-25 (8-27) **7f (July)** £4,425.00 (£975.00: £975.00: £285.00) Stalls: High GOING minus 0.22 sec per fur (GF)

| | | | | SP | RR | SF |
|---|---|---|---|---|---|---|
| | **Ovation** (PFICole) **2-8-11** TQuinn(11) (cmpt: scope: trckd ldrs: led over 2f out: sn hdd: rdn & styd on wl to ld nr fin) | — | 1 | 7/1 | 93+ | 42 |
| | **Velour** (DRLoder) **2-8-11** DRMcCabe(9) (neat: trckd ldrs: rdn & r.o ins fnl f) | nk | 2 | 20/1 | 92+ | 41 |
| | **Reams of Verse (USA)** (HRACecil) **2-8-11** WRyan(3) (gd sort: leggy: lw: hld up: hdwy to ld 2f out: rdn fnl f: ct nr fin) | d.h | 2 | 5/4[1] | 92+ | 41 |
| | **Logic** (CEBrittain) **2-8-11** RHills(6) (neat: trckd ldrs: effrt over 2f out: r.o fnl f) | nk | 4 | 20/1 | 92+ | 41 |
| 2531[2] | **Ghayyur (USA)** (JLDunlop) **2-8-11** WCarson(1) (lw: hld up: hdwy over 2f out: no imp & eased fnl f) | 5 | 5 | 100/30[2] | 80 | 29 |
| | **Catwalk** (WJHaggas) **2-8-11** MHills(4) (w'like: hld up: sme hdwy fnl 2f: nvr nr to chal) | ½ | 6 | 25/1 | 79 | 28 |
| | **Manuetti (IRE)** (SbinSuroor) **2-8-11** JReid(10) (gd sort: w ldr: led 3f out: hdd over 2f out: sn wknd) | 1½ | 7 | 4/1[3] | 76 | 25 |
| | **Shouk** (LMCumani) **2-8-11** OUrbina(2) (cmpt: scope: nvr trbld ldrs) | 7 | 8 | 25/1 | 60 | 9 |
| 2315[4] | **Amid The Stars** (RBoss) **2-8-11** MRoberts(5) (lw: led 4f) | 1 | 9 | 50/1 | 57 | 6 |
| 2132[4] | **Rock Fantasy** (CMurray) **2-8-11** MTebbutt(8) (chsd ldrs 4f) | 1 | 10 | 33/1 | 55 | 4 |
| | **Interregnum** (AGFoster) **2-8-8**(3) PMcCabe(7) (w'like: b: in tch 4f: sn bhd) | 11 | 11 | 50/1 | 30 | — |

(SP 124.1%) **11 Rn**

**1m 28.02** (3.02) CSF O&R £8.16 O&V £60.43 TOTE £8.30: £2.00 R £1.40 V £3.70 (O&R £5.80 0&V £32.20) Trio £30.30 OWNER H R H Prince Fahd Salman (WHATCOMBE) BRED Newgate Stud Co

**Ovation**, bred to excel at middle-distances, being by a Derby winner out of a Yorkshire Oaks winner, found this seven furlongs barely far enough, but fought back willingly to win a hot-looking maiden in the final strides. She has a terrific raking stride and is a fine, imposing filly who will surely make a name for herself. (7/1)

**Velour** did not take the eye as much as the winner, but responded gamely to a strong ride in the final furlong and only just failed to get up. (20/1)

**Reams of Verse (USA)**, a half-sister to Elmaamul, looked fit and well, and far more the finished article than the winner. She found a fine turn of foot to establish a lead in the Dip, but could not quite sustain it to the line. She will win races. (5/4: op 2/1)

**Logic**, bred to be suited by a mile and more, shaped really well and should not be difficult to win with. (20/1)

**2531 Ghayyur (USA)** was unlucky to find such an above-average maiden for her second start, and was found wanting for pace when the leading quartet all quickened, but she was not knocked about once her chance had slipped. (100/30)

**Catwalk** flashed her tail like so many of her sire's progeny, but did shape with some promise, and has ability. (25/1)

**Manuetti (IRE)** moved well to post and is well bred, but lack of peak-fitness told in the last couple of furlongs. She will do better in time. (4/1)

**Shouk** looked very highly-strung in the paddock and flashed her tail when popped the question in the race. She looks one to be wary of. (25/1)

## 2864 SPORTING INDEX MATCH BET CONDITIONS STKS (3-Y.O+) (Class C)

8-55 (8-58) **1m 4f (July)** £5,601.60 (£1,785.60: £852.80) Stalls: High GOING minus 0.22 sec per fur (GF)

| | | | | SP | RR | SF |
|---|---|---|---|---|---|---|
| 1706* | **Kalabo (USA) (113)** (SbinSuroor) **4-9-7** JReid(2) (hld up: hdwy 4f out: led wl over 1f out: edgd rt: comf) | — | 1 | 1/3[1] | 113+ | 62 |
| 2144[3] | **Masehaab (IRE) (105)** (JLDunlop) **3-8-4** WCarson(1) (lw: led: clr 8f out: hdd wl over 1f out: unable qckn whn n.m.r ins fnl f) | 2½ | 2 | 3/1[2] | 105 | 42 |

2278a* **Suranom (IRE)** (LMCumani) **4-9-12** FJovine(3) (trckd ldr tl rdn & btn 3f out)....................15 **3** 8/1$^{3}$ 95 44
(SP 111.1%) **3 Rn**

**2m 33.71** (3.71) CSF £1.77 TOTE £1.40: (£1.40) OWNER Godolphin (NEWMARKET) BRED Darley Stud Management Inc
WEIGHT FOR AGE 3yo-12lb

**1706* Kalabo (USA)** has returned from Dubai better than ever and won this well. His action dispelled any lingering doubts about his need for cut in the ground. (1/3)
**2144 Masehaab (IRE)** is not really bred for this trip, but was allowed his head and took some pegging back. (3/1)
**2278a* Suranom (IRE)** has won four times in Italy on much softer ground and was no more a threat to the winner than he had been at Chester. (8/1)

T/Plpt: £37.60 (411.86 Tckts). T/Qdpt: £8.70 (108.34 Tckts). Dk

# 2587-PONTEFRACT (L-H) (Good to firm)
## Friday July 19th
WEATHER: fine WIND: slt half against

## 2865 JACK BERRY APPEAL MAIDEN AUCTION STKS (2-Y.O) (Class D)
6-45 (6-46) **6f** £3,533.75 (£1,070.00: £522.50: £248.75) Stalls: Low GOING minus 0.33 sec per fur (GF)

SP RR SF
2361$^{11}$ **Southerly Wind** (MrsJRRamsden) **2-8-5** JFEgan(10) (hld up: gd hdwy over 1f out: r.o wl to ld nr fin)..........— **1** 16/1 74 26
2696$^{5}$ **Danehill Princess (IRE)** (RHollinshead) **2-7-12v1**(3)ow1 FLynch(8) (led: rdn clr over 1f out: hdd nr fin)............½ **2** 7/2$^{2}$ 69 20
2295$^{4}$ **Hurgill Times** (JWWatts) **2-8-5** JCarroll(3) (lw: b.hind: prom: rdn & outpcd over 2f out: styd on fnl f)..............4 **3** 11/10$^{1}$ 62 14
**Jedi Knight** (MWEasterby) **2-8-3**(5)ow3 GParkin(1) (w'like: unf: bit bkwd: hdwy ½-wy: kpt on fnl 2f: nvr nr to chal)..............................s.h **4** 25/1 65 14
975$^{11}$ **Loch-Hurn Lady** (KWHogg) **2-7-12** NKennedy(2) (chsd ldrs tl wknd fnl f)..............................½ **5** 33/1 54 6
2495$^{9}$ **Presentiment** (JBerry) **2-8-10** KDarley(6) (chsd ldrs tl wknd over 1½f out)..............................1½ **6** 20/1 62 14
2389$^{2}$ **Not A Lot** (MWEasterby) **2-8-2**(3)ow2 CTeague(12) (hung bdly rt: sn bhd: sme hdwy over 1f out: n.d)...........3½ **7** 14/1 47 —
2625$^{8}$ **Why O Six** (RAFahey) **2-8-5** PaulEddery(4) (bit bkwd: bmpd s: outpcd & bhd: sme hdwy over 1f out: n.d).....½ **8** 33/1 46 —
**Sam Peeb** (RAFahey) **2-8-3** JStack(7) (leggy: unf: sn outpcd & bhd)..............................3 **9** 33/1 36 —
2317$^{4}$ **Manikato (USA)** (DJSCosgrove) **2-8-5**(5) LNewton(9) (chsd ldrs: rdn over 2f out: sn wknd)..........................3½ **10** 4/1$^{3}$ 34 —
2157$^{4}$ **Le Shuttle** (MHTompkins) **2-8-0**(7)ow9 JWilkinson(5) (swvd lft s: a bhd)..............................2½ **11** 14/1 24 —
**Wildmoor** (JDBethell) **2-8-5** WJO'Connor(11) (leggy: unf: hdwy to chse ldrs ½-wy: sn lost pl & eased)..........7 **12** 14/1 3 —
(SP 133.2%) **12 Rn**

**1m 17.1** (2.80) CSF £74.93 TOTE £19.70: £3.70 £1.50 £1.30 (£89.40) Trio £22.30 OWNER Mr M. J. Simmonds (THIRSK) BRED M. J. Simmonds

**Southerly Wind**, a well-made son of Slip Anchor, had finished last of eleven on his debut here. Still looking as if the outing would do him good, he seemed to take connections by surprise under his last-minute substitute rider. Making up a lot of ground coming to the final furlong, he ran on with real determination to show ahead near the line. He will be a very interesting proposition in nurseries over seven furlongs or even a mile. (16/1)
**2696 Danehill Princess (IRE)**, in a visor for the first time, was keen to get on with it. Sent clear once in line for home, she had no answer to the winner's late burst. (7/2)
**2295 Hurgill Times**, a promising fourth first time in a race at Newcastle that is working out well, failed completely to go the pace soon after halfway. Getting his second wind in the final furlong, he ought to be capable of better than this. (11/10)
**Jedi Knight**, who looks as though he still needs more time, was keen to get on with it. Dropped out at the start, he showed promise keeping on nicely in the straight. (25/1)
**Loch-Hurn Lady**, who showed plenty of knee-action going down, raced keenly but her stride shortened markedly in the final furlong. (33/1)
**2317 Manikato (USA)**, a tail-swisher, was on edge in the paddock and dropped right back on the turn for home. (4/1)

## 2866 YORKSHIRE-TYNE TEES TELEVISION H'CAP (0-70) (3-Y.O+) (Class E)
7-10 (7-15) **1m 4f 8y** £3,210.00 (£960.00: £460.00: £210.00) Stalls: Low GOING minus 0.33 sec per fur (GF)

SP RR SF
2558$^{4}$ **Fabulous Mtoto (49)** (MSSaunders) **6-8-13** JFEgan(6) (trckd ldrs: led over 1f out: hung lft & styd on wl: hld on wl towards fin)..............................— **1** 4/1$^{2}$ 62 46
1676* **Mock Trial (IRE) (61)** (MrsJRRamsden) **3-8-13** KFallon(8) (hld up: effrt over 3f out: chsd wnr fnl f: styd on u.p)..............................1¼ **2** 11/10$^{1}$ 72 44
2239$^{5}$ **Green Land (BEL) (61)** (SCWilliams) **4-9-11** KDarley(1) (trckd ldrs: effrt 3f out: kpt on same pce appr fnl f).....5 **3** 12/1 66 50
2397$^{9}$ **Arabian Heights (53)** (MrsJRRamsden) **3-8-5** WJO'Connor(2) (led: hdd over 1f out: kpt on one pce).............1 **4** 7/1$^{3}$ 56 28
2321$^{4}$ **Admirals Secret (USA) (59)** (CFWall) **7-9-4**(5) LNewton(3) (hld up: effrt on ins over 2f out: nvr nr to chal)......hd **5** 15/2 62 46
2319$^{7}$ **Slapy Dam (53)** (JMackie) **4-9-0**(3) FLynch(5) (sn chsng ldrs: rdn & wknd over 2f out)..............................15 **6** 16/1 36 20
**Chimanimani (47)** (NTinkler) **5-8-11** JCarroll(4) (swtg: trckd ldr tl rdn & wknd qckly over 1f out)...................nk **7** 25/1 30 14
2226$^{11}$ **Broughtons Formula (46)** (WJMusson) **6-8-3b**(7) JWilkinson(7) (lw: sn wl bhd & pushed along)...................22 **8** 10/1 — —
(SP 118.4%) **8 Rn**

**2m 38.3** (4.00) CSF £8.86 CT £44.27 TOTE £4.70: £1.80 £1.10 £2.90 (£3.80) OWNER Mr N. R. Pike (WELLS)
WEIGHT FOR AGE 3yo-12lb

**2558 Fabulous Mtoto**, a keen-going sort, was back over his optimum trip. Given an enterprising ride, despite tending to hang, he was never going to be reeled in. (4/1)
**1676* Mock Trial (IRE)** looked a handicap certainty as the four who chased him home at Beverley have all won at least one race since. Dropped out in the early stages, he went in pursuit of the winner in the final furlong, but was never going to get in a telling blow. He needs a stronger pace and, as long as the Handicapper does not go back and put his Rating up on the Beverley form, he should enjoy further success. (11/10: Evens-5/4)
**2239 Green Land (BEL)** is not as consistent as her form figures would suggest. (12/1)
**2397 Arabian Heights**, who made no appeal in the paddock, made the running in a race in which his stable-companion started hot favourite. He did not stretch the field, however and, after being headed over a furlong out, stuck on at the same pace. (7/1)
**2321 Admirals Secret (USA)**, tightened up turning in, seems to reserve his best for Catterick these days. (15/2)

## 2867 ANTONIA DEUTERS H'CAP (0-80) (3-Y.O+) (Class D)
7-40 (7-41) **5f** £5,253.50 (£1,568.00: £749.00: £339.50) Stalls: Low GOING minus 0.33 sec per fur (GF)

SP RR SF
2757$^{3}$ **Just Dissident (IRE) (55)** (RMWhitaker) **4-8-6**(3) FLynch(8) (mde all: clr over 1f out: unchal)........................— **1** 5/1$^{3}$ 62 32

2349[9] **Royal Dome (IRE) (70)** (MartynWane) **4-9-10** JCarroll(2) (lw: chsd ldrs: edgd rt & kpt on u.p fnl f: no imp).......2 **2** 9/1 71 41
2771[4] **Captain Carat (66)** (MrsJRRamsden) **5-9-6** KFallon(7) (b.nr fore: hld up: hdwy ½-wy: styd on same pce fnl f)..............s.h **3** 11/4[1] 66 36
*2634*[5] **Standown (72)** (JBerry) **3-9-8** KDarley(4) (sn outpcd & pushed along: styd on appr fnl f)..............¾ **4** 9/1 70 36
2598* **Cheeky Chappy (66)** (DWChapman) **5-9-6b** 7x JQuinn(1) (lw: s.s: effrt on outside 2f out: styd on ins fnl f).....nk **5** 7/2[2] 63 33
2496[6] **Sing With the Band (67)** (BAMcMahon) **5-9-2**(5) LNewton(5) (lw: chsd wnr tl wknd over 1f out)..............2½ **6** 6/1 56 26
1429* **Chalice (72)** (JBalding) **3-9-1**(7) JEdmunds(6) (chsd ldrs tl lost pl over 1f out)..............1½ **7** 16/1 56 22
2787[8] **Metal Boys (56)** (MissLCSiddall) **9-8-10** WJO'Connor(3) (b.off hind: sn outpcd & pushed along)..............1½ **8** 14/1 36 6
(SP 112.4%) **8 Rn**

**62.9 secs** (2.10) CSF £42.37 CT £133.86 TOTE £5.50: £1.70 £1.80 £1.30 (£21.80) OWNER Mrs C. A. Hodgetts (LEEDS) BRED M. Duffy
WEIGHT FOR AGE 3yo-4lb
**2757 Just Dissident (IRE)** ended a losing sequence of seventeen runs. Showing plenty of early pace to overcome the worst draw, he never looked like being overhauled. (5/1)
**2119 Royal Dome (IRE)** showed a return to form after running poorly on his previous four starts. (9/1)
**2771 Captain Carat**, with a senior jockey aboard this time, did nothing wrong in the stalls. (11/4)
**2634 Standown**, inclined to sweat up, seems best suited by claimers these days. (9/1: 6/1-10/1)
**2598* Cheeky Chappy** has shot up 21lb in the weights compared with when he won his first race five outings ago. After missing the break, he had to do it the hard way by making his effort on the wide outside. (7/2)

## 2868 INJURED JOCKEYS FUND HOLIDAY H'CAP (0-70) (3-Y.O+) (Class E)
8-10 (8-11) **1m 4y** £3,465.00 (£1,035.00: £495.00: £225.00) Stalls: Low GOING minus 0.33 sec per fur (GF)

SP RR SF
2573[2] **Scaraben (68)** (SEKettlewell) **8-9-12** JStack(9) (lw: hld up: smooth hdwy over 2f out: wnt 2nd & hung lft over 1f out: styd on to ld ins fnl f)..............— **1** 15/8[1] 82 52
2567[5] **Percy Parrot (38)** (RMWhitaker) **4-7-10** AMackay(1) (b.hind: led tl ins fnl f)..............2½ **2** 16/1 47 17
2412[2] **Mr Rough (62)** (DMorris) **5-8-13**(7) AEddery(4) (a chsng ldrs: kpt on one pce appr fnl f)..............6 **3** 5/1[2] 59 29
2214* **Habeta (USA) (50)** (JWWatts) **10-8-8** JCarroll(8) (rdn 5f out: hdwy 3f out: styd on one pce)..............nk **4** 11/2[3] 46 16
*2551*[8] **My Handsome Prince (40)** (PJBevan) **4-7-12b** NCarlisle(13) (trckd ldrs: effrt 2f out: one pce)..............1½ **5** 33/1 33 3
2573[8] **Pleasure Trick (USA) (55)** (DonEnricoIncisa) **5-8-13** KimTinkler(6) (bhd: pushed along 5f out: sme hdwy fnl 2f)..............hd **6** 33/1 48 18
**Mill Force (75)** (DNicholls) **5-10-0**(5) SCopp(7) (s.s: hdwy u.p over 2f out: n.d)..............1¼ **7** 33/1 66 36
1181[10] **Sharp 'n' Shady (56)** (CFWall) **3-8-6** WLord(10) (in tch tl lost pl over 2f out)..............nk **8** 16/1 46 8
2483[3] **Second Colours (USA) (66)** (MrsMReveley) **6-9-10** KDarley(11) (chsd ldrs: rdn 2f out: sn wknd)..............¾ **9** 5/1[2] 55 25
2672[3] **Cee-Jay-Ay (46)** (JBerry) **9-7-11**(7) CLowther(3) (s.s: hdwy ½-wy: sn chsng ldrs: lost pl 2f out)..............1 **10** 8/1 33 3
2573[9] **Larn Fort (53)** (CWFairhurst) **6-8-11v** DeanMcKeown(14) (b: s.i.s: a bhd)..............3 **11** 33/1 34 4
*2085*[13] **Rasmi (CAN) (38)** (PHowling) **5-7-10** JQuinn(5) (chsd ldrs: drvn along over 2f out: sn wknd)..............nk **12** 33/1 18 —
*2369*[3] **Pc's Cruiser (IRE) (47)** (JLEyre) **4-8-2b**(3) CTeague(2) (s.s: hdwy on outside 5f out: rdn & wknd 3f out)..........7 **13** 10/1 13 —
(SP 130.2%) **13 Rn**

**1m 44.7** (3.20) CSF £31.35 CT £127.00 TOTE £3.00: £1.80 £3.50 £2.00 (£59.40) Trio £170.60 OWNER Mr J. Tennant (MIDDLEHAM) BRED Burton Agnes Stud Co Ltd
LONG HANDICAP Percy Parrot 7-9 Rasmi (CAN) 7-8
WEIGHT FOR AGE 3yo-8lb
**2573 Scaraben**, who won six races last year, opened his account this time, but made hard work of it, showing a marked tendency to hang left under pressure. (15/8: 3/1-7/4)
**2567 Percy Parrot**, just 1lb higher in the weights than when winning an apprentice selling handicap here by five lengths last month, led his rivals a merry dance. Though the winner proved too strong in the closing stages, he still finished a clear second best. (16/1)
**2412 Mr Rough**, a specialist miler, is back to his best. (5/1)
**2214* Habeta (USA)**, raised 2lb, was flat out a long way from home and never going to prove anything like good enough. (11/2)
**Pleasure Trick (USA)**, on his third outing, ran easily his best race. (33/1)

## 2869 ST JOHN AMBULANCE MAIDEN STKS (3-Y.O) (Class D)
8-40 (8-41) **1m 2f 6y** £3,598.75 (£1,090.00: £532.50: £253.75) Stalls: Low GOING minus 0.33 sec per fur (GF)

SP RR SF
2318[2] **Berenice (80)** (GWragg) **3-8-9** PaulEddery(4) (trckd ldrs: shkn up & qcknd to ld ins fnl f: pushed out)............— **1** 1/3[1] 77 18
1117[2] **Tart (FR)** (JRFanshawe) **3-8-9** KDarley(2) (lw: trckd ldr: led over 3f out: sn drvn along: hdd ins fnl f: nt qckn)..............nk **2** 5/2[2] 77 18
*1972*[4] **Snowy Mantle** (JDBethell) **3-8-9** WJO'Connor(1) (led tl over 3f out: wknd over 1f out)..............13 **3** 33/1[3] 24 t —
**Smiling Bess** (RHollinshead) **3-8-6**(3) FLynch(3) (hld up & plld hrd: effrt 2f out: sn wknd)..............6 **4** 40/1 14 t —
(SP 109.0%) **4 Rn**

**2m 14.8** (6.50) CSF £1.53 TOTE £1.40: (£1.20) OWNER Gestut Schlenderhan (NEWMARKET) BRED Biddestone Stud
**2318 Berenice**, given a confident ride, looked in two minds as to whether or not to go through with it, but in the end her rider had the last say. (1/3)
**1117 Tart (FR)**, making the best of her way home, proved willing, but seems to lack anything in the way of a turn of foot. (5/2: 7/4-11/4)
**1972 Snowy Mantle** set a sensible pace but, when the race began in earnest, she was left for dead by the first two. (33/1)
**Smiling Bess**, who had two outings over sprint distances last year, proved very keen but, when pushed along, found nothing at all. (40/1)

## 2870 RED SHIRT NIGHT LIMITED STKS (0-65) (3-Y.O+) (Class F)
9-10 (9-11) **6f** £2,738.00 (£768.00: £374.00) Stalls: Low GOING minus 0.33 sec per fur (GF)

SP RR SF
*2305*[3] **Bowlers Boy (64)** (JJQuinn) **3-8-9** JQuinn(5) (trckd ldrs: effrt over 2f out: styd on to ld wl ins fnl f: drvn out)..............— **1** 5/2[2] 70 33
2729[4] **Finisterre (IRE) (63)** (JJO'Neill) **3-8-12** KFallon(3) (trckd ldrs: led ins fnl f: sn hdd & nt qckn)..............1¼ **2** 6/4[1] 70 33
2193[9] **Samsolom (58)** (PHowling) **8-9-0** KDarley(1) (lw: sn outpcd & pushed along: styd on appr fnl f: nvr nr to chal) 2 **3** 6/1 61 29
2417[10] **Craignairn (65)** (JBerry) **3-8-12b** JCarroll(4) (led tl ins fnl f: sn wknd)..............½ **4** 4/1[3] 63 26
2492[B] **Sense of Priority (63)** (DNicholls) **7-9-9** AlexGreaves(2) (lw: sn trckng ldr: rdn & wknd over 1f out)..............1¼ **5** 11/2 66 34
(SP 118.2%) **5 Rn**

**1m 16.8** (2.50) CSF £6.97 TOTE £3.40: £1.80 £1.40 (£2.70) OWNER Bowlers Racing (MALTON) BRED Roldvale Ltd
WEIGHT FOR AGE 3yo-5lb
**2305 Bowlers Boy** does not lack ability but his attitude has to be questioned. His rider really had to make his mind up for him before he scored in decisive fashion in the end. (5/2)

**2729 Finisterre (IRE)** is running really well at present. (6/4)
**2129 Samsolom** struggled to go the pace. (6/1)
**2236* Craignairn**, with the blinkers back on, waited in front but, when collared inside the last furlong, he soon dropped away. (4/1)
**2492 Sense of Priority**, having his first outing since being brought down two weeks ago, possibly looked too big and well in the paddock. Running out of gas with over a furlong left to run, no doubt other opportunities will be found for him in selling and claiming races. (11/2)

T/Plpt: £8.20 (1,584.22 Tckts). T/Qdpt: £4.70 (124.72 Tckts). WG

## 2727-AYR (L-H) (Good to firm)
## Saturday July 20th

Race 4: hand-timed
WEATHER: fine & sunny WIND: almost nil

### 2871 RONNIE GLENDINNING 60TH BIRTHDAY AMATEUR H'CAP (0-70) (3-Y.O+) (Class E)
6-50 (6-50) **1m 5f 13y** £3,176.25 (£960.00: £467.50: £221.25) Stalls: High GOING minus 0.09 sec per fur (G)

| | | | | SP | RR | SF |
|---|---|---|---|---|---|---|
| 2678* | **Gold Blade (60)** (JPearce) **7-12-0** MrsLPearce(1) (lw: hld up & bhd: hdwy 3f out: str run to ld wl ins fnl f) | — | 1 | 4/1 2 | 67 | 21 |
| 2628 4 | **Pepitist (42)** (MDHammond) **5-10-10** MrCBonner(5) (lw: in tch: effrt 3f out: styd on wl fnl f: nrst fin) | ½ | 2 | 4/1 2 | 48 | 2 |
| 2779 6 | **Yaakum (28)** (SEKettlewell) **7-9-10** MrsDKettlewell(7) (lw: trckd ldrs: chal 3f out: sn hrd drvn: led ins fnl f: sn hdd & nt qckn) | hd | 3 | 10/1 3 | 34 | — |
| 2565 2 | **Philmist (48)** (CWCElsey) **4-11-2b** MissAElsey(9) (led tl hdd & no ex ins fnl f) | 1½ | 4 | 5/2 1 | 52 | 6 |
| 2683* | **Lawn Order (46)** (MrsJRRamsden) **3-9-10**(5) MissERamsden(8) (bhd: effrt 3f out: hdwy over 1f out: styd on) | hd | 5 | 4/1 2 | 50 | — |
| 2779 8 | **Ela Man Howa (53)** (ABailey) **5-11-2**(5) MissBridgetGatehouse(4) (lw: chsd ldrs: effrt ent st: btn wl over 1f out) | 5 | 6 | 20/1 | 51 | 5 |
| 2574 22 | **Duty Sergeant (IRE) (37)** (PhilipMitchell) **7-10-5** MrTMcCarthy(6) (lw: bhd: effrt 3f out: no imp) | 2 | 7 | 14/1 | 33 | — |
| 2563 9 | **Kalko (25)** (JSGoldie) **7-9-7** MissPRobson(2) (chsd ldrs tl outpcd fnl 2½f) | 1½ | 8 | 50/1 | 19 | — |
| 2682 6 | **Jabaroot (IRE) (29)** (RMMcKellar) **5-9-6b**(5) MrsCWilliams(3) (b.hind: chsd ldrs tl wknd fnl 3f) | 2½ | 9 | 100/1 | 20 | — |
| | | | | (SP 112.0%) | **9 Rn** | |

**3m 3.34** (18.54) CSF £18.60 CT £132.13 TOTE £3.30: £1.10 £1.40 £2.40 (£7.00) Trio £65.80 OWNER Mr Jeff Pearce (NEWMARKET) BRED Ballymacoll Stud Co
LONG HANDICAP Kalko 9-1
WEIGHT FOR AGE 3yo-13lb
**OFFICIAL EXPLANATION Lawn Order: the jockey stated that her instructions had been to 'lie mid division and to quicken two furlongs out'. Having been unruly in the stalls and slowly away, as a result the jockey settled the filly towards the rear and when she asked her a question, the filly started to hang.**
**2678* Gold Blade** is proving unstoppable at the moment and, given a super-confident ride, got up where it mattered. (4/1)
**2628 Pepitist** again appreciated the strong pace and kept struggling on, but is short of a real turn of foot to take it. (4/1)
**2779 Yaakum** moved well for much of the trip but, once off the bit early in the straight, had only the one speed. (10/1)
**2565 Philmist** set a good pace and looked likely to hold on for a long way in the home straight, but she was swamped inside the final furlong. (5/2)
**2683* Lawn Order** ran well, but gave the impression that stronger handling would have benefited her. (4/1: 11/4-9/2)
**1788 Ela Man Howa** has changed stables again and is certainly running better, but there is still some way to go. (20/1)

### 2872 HOURSTONS OF AYR CONDITIONS STKS (2-Y.O) (Class D)
7-20 (7-25) **5f** £3,550.00 (£1,075.00: £525.00: £250.00) Stalls: High GOING minus 0.09 sec per fur (G)

| | | | | SP | RR | SF |
|---|---|---|---|---|---|---|
| 2147 6 | **Stone Flower (USA)** (PWChapple-Hyam) **2-8-2**(5) RHavlin(4) (lw: hld up: qcknd to disp ld wl over 1f out: edgd lft: rdn & r.o fnl f) | — | 1 | 6/4 1 | 89 | 9 |
| 2112 10 | **Bride's Reprisal** (MRChannon) **2-8-6**(7) AEddery(5) (trckd ldrs: effrt over 1f out: styd on wl towards fin) | 1¾ | 2 | 3/1 2 | 89 | 9 |
| 1831 2 | **Just Visiting** (CaptJWilson) **2-8-11** JFortune(1) (cl up: disp ld wl over 1f out tl wknd ins fnl f) | 1¾ | 3 | 5/1 | 82? | 2 |
| 2681 3 | **Robec Girl (IRE)** (JBerry) **2-8-11** KDarley(3) (mde most over 3f: rdn & nt qckn) | 2½ | 4 | 100/30 3 | 74 | — |
| 2364 6 | **Bold Brief** (DenysSmith) **2-9-2** DeanMcKeown(2) (lw: in tch: effrt 2f out: sn btn) | 5 | 5 | 40/1 | 63 | — |
| 2681 6 | **Cantsaynowt** (RMMcKellar) **2-8-7** NConnorton(6) (disp ld to ½-wy: hung lft & sn wknd) | 7 | 6 | 150/1 | 31 | — |
| | | | | (SP 107.8%) | **6 Rn** | |

**61.36 secs** (4.36) CSF £5.88 TOTE £1.80: £1.20 £2.10 (£2.70) OWNER Mr R. E. Sangster (MARLBOROUGH) BRED Swettenham Stud
**2147 Stone Flower (USA)** is a wild-eyed filly, but she did the business this time and scored most determinedly. (6/4: 8/11-13/8)
**1884* Bride's Reprisal**, who raced freely in behind the leaders, finished quite well after being short of room, but was never good enough. (3/1)
**1831 Just Visiting** ran a sound race, but she had had some six weeks off and just ran out of petrol inside the last furlong. (5/1)
**2681 Robec Girl (IRE)** was very edgy beforehand and, after leading, dropped out tamely approaching the last furlong. (100/30)
**2118* Bold Brief** improved on his most disappointing effort last time and, looks-wise, seems to be coming back to form. (40/1)

### 2873 E.B.F. FIN ME OOT MILLPORT MEDIAN AUCTION MAIDEN STKS (2-Y.O) (Class D)
7-50 (7-52) **6f** £3,517.50 (£1,065.00: £520.00: £247.50) Stalls: High GOING minus 0.09 sec per fur (G)

| | | | | SP | RR | SF |
|---|---|---|---|---|---|---|
| | **Sugarfoot** (NTinkler) **2-9-0** RCochrane(6) (w'like: scope: bit bkwd: hld up & plld hrd: hdwy 2f out: r.o to ld ins fnl f) | — | 1 | 6/1 3 | 82+ | 24 |
| 1896 7 | **Faringdon Future** (BWHills) **2-9-0** KFallon(5) (trckd ldrs: led wl over 1f tl ins fnl f: kpt on) | 1¼ | 2 | 9/4 2 | 79 | 21 |
| 1849 3 | **Baritone** (JWWatts) **2-9-0** NConnorton(3) (lw: hld up: outpcd & lost tch ½-wy: hdwy 2f out: nt qckn fnl f) | 3 | 3 | 6/4 1 | 71 | 13 |
| 2485 2 | **Marylebone (IRE)** (JBerry) **2-9-0** KDarley(2) (w ldrs tl rdn & btn appr fnl f) | 1¼ | 4 | 8/1 | 67 | 9 |
| 2317 5 | **Tickntima** (MDHammond) **2-9-0** JWeaver(1) (lw: prom tl outpcd fnl 2f) | 2 | 5 | 25/1 | 62 | 4 |
| 1583 5 | **Barnburgh Boy** (TDBarron) **2-9-0** JFortune(4) (led over 4f: btn whn sltly hmpd over 1f out) | ¾ | 6 | 6/1 3 | 60 | 2 |
| | | | | (SP 114.3%) | **6 Rn** | |

**1m 14.49** (4.69) CSF £19.29 TOTE £8.00: £2.50 £1.80 (£27.70) OWNER Mrs D. Wright (MALTON) BRED Whitsbury Manor Stud
**Sugarfoot**, a useful-looking sort, needed this and, after taking a strong hold, won in really good style. He is one to follow. (6/1: 4/1-8/1)
**Faringdon Future**, who has the look of a useful horse, still needed the run and should go on from here. (9/4: 6/4-5/2)
**1849 Baritone**, after almost six weeks off, looked really well, but it seemed as though something was not quite right. This should be forgiven. (6/4)
**2485 Marylebone (IRE)** showed plenty of speed, but was well outpointed in what was probably a decent race. (8/1: 6/1-10/1)
**2317 Tickntima** was outclassed here, but still ran pretty well and does look on really good terms with himself at present. (25/1)

**1583 Barnburgh Boy**, who had been off the track for seven weeks and looked likely to need this, was eased when hampered approaching the final furlong. (6/1: op 4/1)

## 2874 ROTHMANS ROYALS NORTH SOUTH CHALLENGE SERIES H'CAP (0-85) (3-Y.O+) (Class D)
8-20 (8-21) **7f** £5,446.00 (£1,648.00: £804.00: £382.00) Stalls: High GOING minus 0.09 sec per fur (G)

| | | | | SP | RR | SF |
|---|---|---|---|---|---|---|
| 2672[2] | **My Gallery (IRE) (62)** (ABailey) **5-8-5**(3) DWright(4) (hld up: swtchd & qcknd to ld over 1f out: r.o v.wl) | — | 1 | 5/2 [1] | 77 | 20 |
| 2149[4] | **Sagebrush Roller (69)** (JWWatts) **8-9-1** NConnorton(1) (lw: hld up: effrt 2f out: r.o: no ch w wnr) | 5 | 2 | 5/1 [3] | 73 | 16 |
| 2729[7] | **Quilling (68)** (MDods) **4-9-0** DeanMcKeown(5) (lw: led tl hdd over 1f out: sn outpcd) | 2 | 3 | 9/2 [2] | 67 | 10 |
| | **Cavers Yangous (70)** (MJohnston) **5-9-2** JWeaver(7) (lw: cl up: chal 3f out: rdn & btn appr fnl f) | 2 | 4 | 12/1 | 64 | 7 |
| 2679[3] | **Best of All (IRE) (67)** (JBerry) **4-8-13** KDarley(6) (lw: chsd ldrs: effrt & ch 3f out: btn wl over 1f out) | 5 | 5 | 5/1 [3] | 50 | — |
| 2566* | **Anonym (IRE) (61)** (DNicholls) **4-8-0**(7) JBramhill(3) (cl up tl wknd fnl 2f) | ½ | 6 | 5/1 [3] | 43 | — |
| | **Axeman (IRE) (82)** (DNicholls) **4-10-0** JFortune(2) (hld up & bhd: n.d) | 8 | 7 | 16/1 | 46 | — |
| | | | | (SP 110.3%) | | **7 Rn** |

**1m 29.53** (5.53) CSF £13.90 TOTE £2.60: £2.10 £1.10 (£8.10) OWNER Mr Robert Cox (TARPORLEY) BRED East Riding Sack and Paper Co
**2672 My Gallery (IRE)** showed again what a game performer she is. Once she hit the front, her turn of foot was amazing. (5/2)
**2149 Sagebrush Roller** ran a fine race and kept staying on under pressure, but had no answer to the winner's turn of speed. (5/1)
**2630 Quilling** set the race up with his usual front-running tactics and could only wonder at the winner's speed in the final furlong. (9/2)
**Cavers Yangous**, who looked pretty well for this first outing of the season, ran a sound race and should be all the better for it. (12/1)
**2679 Best of All (IRE)** was disappointing, dropping tamely away when the pressure was on. (5/1)
**2566* Anonym (IRE)** found this step up in class too much. (5/1)

## 2875 TICKLY TAP NURSERY H'CAP (2-Y.O) (Class D)
8-50 (8-51) **6f** £3,517.50 (£1,065.00: £520.00: £247.50) Stalls: High GOING minus 0.09 sec per fur (G)

| | | | | SP | RR | SF |
|---|---|---|---|---|---|---|
| 1760[2] | **Double Park (FR)** (MJohnston) **2-9-2** JWeaver(5) (lw: mde most: hld on wl fnl 2f) | — | 1 | 9/4 [1] | 81 | 35 |
| 1105[4] | **Top of The Wind (IRE)** (JJO'Neill) **2-8-6** KFallon(6) (h.d.w: bhd: hdwy & swtchd 2f out: ev ch ins fnl f: nt qckn) | ¾ | 2 | 6/1 | 69 | 23 |
| 2588* | **Docklands Carriage (IRE)** (NTinkler) **2-8-7v[1]** RCochrane(4) (lw: trckd ldrs: nt clr run appr fnl f & ins fnl f: nt rcvr) | 1¼ | 3 | 4/1 [3] | 67+ | 21 |
| 2726[3] | **Burkes Manor** (TDBarron) **2-9-7** JFortune(2) (w wnr: disp ld over 2f out tl rdn & btn ins fnl f) | 1¼ | 4 | 5/1 | 77 | 31 |
| 2122[8] | **Alisadara** (NBycroft) **2-7-8**(3)ow1 DWright(3) (in tch: effrt 2f out: sn rdn & btn) | 6 | 5 | 33/1 | 37 | — |
| 2491[3] | **Perpetual** (SirMarkPrescott) **2-8-8** KDarley(1) (lw: cl up tl rdn & btn appr fnl f) | 2 | 6 | 5/2 [2] | 43 | — |
| | | | | (SP 113.2%) | | **6 Rn** |

**1m 13.84** (4.04) CSF £14.59 TOTE £3.20: £1.80 £2.30 (£7.80) OWNER The 3rd Middleham Partnership (MIDDLEHAM) BRED Gainsborough Stud Management Ltd
**1760 Double Park (FR)** had what appeared the best ground on the stands' rail. In front basically throughout, she got stronger as the race progressed. (9/4)
**1105 Top of The Wind (IRE)** has done well physically, but again showed signs of temperament in the paddock. She put up a fair performance though but not having run for over two months probably made all the difference. (6/1: op 4/1)
**2588* Docklands Carriage (IRE)** is on the upgrade and, with any sort of run, might well have won this. (4/1)
**2726 Burkes Manor** is a very edgy individual indeed and, once the pressure was seriously on, he cried enough entering the final furlong. (5/1)
**1583 Alisadara** ran as well as could be expected from 11lb out of the handicap. (33/1)
**2491 Perpetual** dragged her lass round the paddock throughout the preliminaries and then ran out of energy two thirds of the way through the race. (5/2)

## 2876 GO EVENING RACING WITH THE DAILY TELEGRAPH MAIDEN STKS (3-Y.O+) (Class D)
9-20 (9-22) **1m 2f** £3,517.50 (£1,065.00: £520.00: £247.50) Stalls: High GOING minus 0.09 sec per fur (G)

| | | | | SP | RR | SF |
|---|---|---|---|---|---|---|
| 2557[6] | **Nereus** (BWHills) **3-8-11** KFallon(5) (hld up: qcknd to ld 2f out: sn clr: eased considerably towards fin) | — | 1 | 7/2 [2] | 83+ | 12 |
| 2706[2] | **Blatant Outburst** (GCBravery) **6-9-7** JFortune(2) (lw: led tl hdd 2f out: kpt on: no ch w wnr) | 3 | 2 | 10/11 [1] | 78 | 17 |
| 2326[2] | **Amadour (IRE) (67)** (PhilipMitchell) **3-8-11** KDarley(3) (a chsng ldrs: wl outpcd fnl 2½f) | 16 | 3 | 4/1 [3] | 53 | — |
| 1593[8] | **Crest Wing (USA)** (PWChapple-Hyam) **3-8-6**(5) RHavlin(4) (lw: chsd ldr: rdn appr st: btn wl over 2f out) | hd | 4 | 4/1 [3] | 52 | — |
| | **Thorntoun House (IRE)** (JSGoldie) **3-8-11** DeanMcKeown(1) (w'like: unruly s: dwlt: t.o fnl 7f) | 27 | 5 | 50/1 | 9 | — |
| | | | | (SP 116.6%) | | **5 Rn** |

**2m 14.24** (9.64) CSF £7.38 TOTE £4.10: £1.40 £1.20 (£3.10) OWNER Sheikh Mohammed (LAMBOURN) BRED Sheikh Mohammed bin Rashid al Maktoum
WEIGHT FOR AGE 3yo-10lb
**Nereus** had hardly been sighted previously, but won this in very useful style and had almost stopped to a walk by the line. He is obviously pretty good, but has the look of a bit of a character about him. (7/2: 2/1-4/1)
**2706 Blatant Outburst** set a good pace, but his lack of a change of gear was well exposed in the final two furlongs. (10/11: Evens-6/4)
**2326 Amadour (IRE)** always held a good enough position, but looked very one-paced when the pressure was on early in the straight. (4/1)
**Crest Wing (USA)** has the looks but, as yet, certainly has not got the ability to match. (4/1)
**Thorntoun House (IRE)**, a rangy newcomer, gave problems at the start and showed no ability at all in the race. (50/1)

T/Plpt: £94.90 (116.69 Tckts). T/Qdpt: £47.50 (15.94 Tckts). AA

# 2852-NEWBURY (L-H) (Good to firm)
## Saturday July 20th
WEATHER: hot WIND: almost nil

## 2877 DONCASTER BLOODSTOCK SALES ROSE BOWL STKS (Listed) (2-Y.O) (Class A)
1-30 (1-30) **6f 8y** £9,845.00 (£2,960.00: £1,430.00: £665.00) Stalls: High GOING minus 0.52 sec per fur (F)

| | | | | SP | RR | SF |
|---|---|---|---|---|---|---|
| 2245[2] | **Crystal Crossing (IRE)** (PWChapple-Hyam) **2-8-6** JReid(2) (lw: stdd s: hdwy over 1f out: led ins fnl f: pushed out) | — | 1 | Evens [1] | 95+ | 51 |
| 1705* | **Omaha City (IRE)** (BGubby) **2-8-11** DHolland(4) (b: led: rdn wl over 1f out: hdd ins fnl f: unable qckn) | 2 | 2 | 14/1 | 95 | 51 |
| 2575* | **Victory Dancer** (BJMeehan) **2-8-11** BDoyle(1) (lw: a.p: ev ch over 1f out: wknd ins fnl f) | 3 | 3 | 7/1 [3] | 87 | 43 |

1808* **Hakkaniyah** (DMorley) **2-8-6** WCarson(5) (hld up: rdn over 2f out: one pce)....½ **4** 3/1 2 80 36
2210* **Pelham (IRE)** (RHannon) **2-8-11** TQuinn(6) (lw: w ldr: ev ch over 1f out: wknd fnl f)....s.h **5** 12/1 85 41
1115[7] **Smokey Pete** (RHannon) **2-9-0** MRoberts(3) (lw: bhd fnl 3f)....7 **6** 15/2 70 26
(SP 113.6%) **6 Rn**

**1m 11.49** (0.12 under 2y best) (-0.31) CSF £13.21 TOTE £1.90: £1.30 £4.30 (£13.70) OWNER Mr R. E. Sangster (MARLBOROUGH) BRED Ben Sangster

**2245 Crystal Crossing (IRE)** was well backed and, on this occasion, did not let her supporters down. Put to sleep at the back of the field, she was shaken up in the final quarter-mile and came through to strike the front inside the final furlong, breaking the fourteen-year-old juvenile course-record in convincing style. (Evens)
**1705* Omaha City (IRE)** was taking a step up in class, but ran a race full of promise. Taking the field along, he was still travelling well approaching the final quarter-mile. Eventually overhauled inside the final furlong, he found the winner too strong. He should soon return to the winner's enclosure. (14/1: 8/1-16/1)
**2575* Victory Dancer** held every chance below the distance, but had nothing more to offer inside the last 200 yards. (7/1: 5/1-8/1)
**1808* Hakkaniyah** chased the leaders, but failed to find another gear from below the distance. (3/1)
**2210* Pelham (IRE)** disputed the lead until tiring inside the final furlong. (12/1: op 7/1)
**1115 Smokey Pete** (15/2: 9/2-8/1)

## 2878 MTOTO DONNINGTON CASTLE CONDITIONS STKS (2-Y.O) (Class B)
2-00 (2-00) **7f (straight)** £8,587.00 (£3,112.00: £1,506.00: £630.00: £265.00) Stalls: High GOING minus 0.52 sec per fur (F)

SP RR SF
2517* **Imperial President** (HRACecil) **2-8-13** WRyan(2) (lw: hld up: led over 1f out: all out)....— **1** 9/4 2 99 58
2040[5] **Hello (IRE)** (JLDunlop) **2-8-13** JReid(1) (lw: hld up: rdn over 1f out: r.o wl ins fnl f)....s.h **2** 11/4 3 99 58
1897[2] **Wolf Mountain** (RHannon) **2-8-10** MRoberts(3) (lw: plld hrd: chsd ldr: led over 4f out tl over 1f out: unable qckn ins fnl f)....1¾ **3** 15/8 1 92 51
2364[4] **Fletcher** (PFICole) **2-8-13** TQuinn(5) (lw: led over 2f: hung lft & wknd over 2f out)....3½ **4** 10/1 87 46
**Kinship (IRE)** (PWChapple-Hyam) **2-8-7** WCarson(4) (unf: s.s: a wl bhd)....12 **5** 10/1 54 13
(SP 110.4%) **5 Rn**

**1m 24.13** (1.67 under 2y best) (-0.37) CSF £8.28 TOTE £3.10: £1.20 £1.70 (£5.10) OWNER Mr K. Abdulla (NEWMARKET) BRED Juddmonte Farms

**2517* Imperial President** put up a gutsy display. Held up, he came through to lead below the distance but, with the runner-up finishing with a real flourish, he found the line only just saving him. He beat the course-record by over a second and a half. (9/4)
**2040 Hello (IRE)**, held up, began to get going from below the distance. Running on really strongly inside the final furlong, he would have prevailed in another stride. He should soon gain compensation. (11/4)
**1897 Wolf Mountain** took a very keen hold and had soon pulled himself to the front. Collared below the distance, he grimly tried to hold on, but was tapped for toe inside the last 150 yards. He should make no mistake next time out. (15/8)
**2364 Fletcher**, the early leader, hung left and gave up the fight over two furlongs from home. (10/1: 8/1-12/1)
**Kinship (IRE)** (10/1: 9/2-12/1)

## 2879 WEATHERBYS SUPER SPRINT STKS (2-Y.O) (Class B)
2-30 (2-35) **5f 34y** £57,039.60 (£21,176.40: £10,218.20: £4,241.00: £1,750.50: £754.30) Stalls: High GOING minus 0.52 sec per fur (F)

SP RR SF
2343* **Miss Stamper (IRE)** (RHannon) **2-8-2**ow1 DHarrison(3) (racd centre: hdwy over 2f out: led 1f out: rdn out)...— **1** 14/1 89 36
2063[2] **Young Bigwig (IRE)** (JBerry) **2-8-6** JCarroll(7) (lw: a.p: ev ch ins fnl f: r.o)....½ **2** 9/1 91 39
2614* **Head Over Heels (IRE)** (JHMGosden) **2-8-2** WRyan(10) (lw: led to 1f out: unable qckn)....1¼ **3** 7/1 84 32
2484[2] **Magical Times** (RBoss) **2-8-6** MRoberts(6) (lw: racd centre: hld up: rdn over 2f out: one pce)....¾ **4** 11/2 2 85 33
2375* **Fanny's Choice (IRE)** (RHannon) **2-8-5** DaneO'Neill(4) (lw: swtchd rt s: hdwy over 1f out: nvr nrr)....½ **5** 13/2 3 83 31
2596* **Secret Combe (IRE)** (PJMakin) **2-7-13** SSanders(14) (a.p: rdn over 2f out: one pce)....2 **6** 5/2 1 71 19
2219* **Fredrik The Fierce (IRE)** (JBerry) **2-8-12** JReid(11) (hld up: rdn over 2f out: wknd over 1f out)....nk **7** 16/1 83 31
2252[3] **Class Distinction (IRE)** (RHannon) **2-8-4** RPerham(15) (lw: a mid div)....2 **8** 16/1 68 16
1987[5] **Hangover Square (IRE)** (RHannon) **2-8-8** TQuinn(9) (lw: prom over 3f)....1¼ **9** 20/1 69 17
1362[3] **Seaside (IRE)** (JohnBerry) **2-7-13** AMackay(12) (lw: s.s: outpcd)....nk **10** 16/1 59 7
1645* **Clara Bliss (IRE)** (BJMeehan) **2-8-0** JFEgan(5) (lw: racd centre: hld up: rdn over 2f out: wknd over 1f out)..1¾ **11** 50/1 54 2
**Snap Crackle Pop (IRE)** (RFJohnsonHoughton) **2-8-1** PaulEddery(2) (leggy: racd centre: hdwy over 2f out: wknd over 1f out)....nk **12** 40/1 54 2
**Bewitching Lady** (DWPArbuthnot) **2-8-7** RCochrane(8) (str: scope: bit bkwd: s.s: a wl bhd)....8 **13** 33/1 35 —
2531[4] **Expectation (IRE)** (PRWebber) **2-8-7** BThomson(13) (lw: bhd fnl 2f)....2½ **14** 14/1 28 —
*2595[4]* ***Nervous Rex*** (WRMuir) **2-8-10b1** DHolland(1) (Withdrawn not under Starter's orders: crashed thro rail, uns rdr & bolted bef s).... **W** 33/1 — —
(SP 125.8%) **14 Rn**

**60.59 secs** (0.01 under 2y best) (0.39) CSF £124.86 TOTE £21.50: £5.00 £2.70 £2.80 (£87.50) Trio £311.80 OWNER J B R Leisure Ltd (MARLBOROUGH) BRED Eamon O'Mahony

**2343* Miss Stamper (IRE)**, whose trainer has made this race his own, was one of four who elected to race in the centre of the course. Picking up ground from halfway, she struck the front a furlong out and was ridden along to shade the course-record, set way back in 1969. (14/1: 10/1-16/1)
**2063 Young Bigwig (IRE)** may have got his head in front for a couple of strides around the furlong pole, but found the winner just too strong. (9/1)
**2614* Head Over Heels (IRE)**, collared a furlong out, failed to find another gear. (7/1)
**2484 Magical Times** was a leading light in the centre of the course but several lengths off the stands'-side group. Rousted along from halfway, he failed to find the necessary turn of foot. (11/2)
**2375* Fanny's Choice (IRE)** was unable to cope with the drop in distance. Staying on from below the distance, she was never going to get there in time. A return to six furlongs is required. (13/2)
**2596* Secret Combe (IRE)**, a leading player on the stands' side, failed to quicken in the final quarter-mile. (5/2)

## 2880 HACKWOOD STKS (Listed) (3-Y.O+) (Class A)
3-05 (3-07) **6f 8y** £12,724.00 (£3,832.00: £1,856.00: £868.00) Stalls: High GOING minus 0.52 sec per fur (F)

SP RR SF
2114[10] **Jayannpee (103)** (IABalding) **5-9-3** WRyan(8) (lw: hld up: rdn over 1f out: led ins fnl f: r.o wl)....— **1** 16/1 113 72
1879[3] **Easy Dollar (104)** (BGubby) **4-9-3b** AClark(9) (lw: a.p: rdn over 1f out: ev ch ins fnl f: r.o wl)....nk **2** 20/1 112 71
2545[2] **Venture Capitalist (115)** (DNicholls) **7-9-10** AlexGreaves(10) (lw: nt clr run over 1f out: hdwy 1f out: n.m.r ins fnl f: r.o wl)....¾ **3** 7/1 3 117 76

2114[27] **Espartero (IRE) (102)** (SirMarkPrescott) **4-9-3** SSanders(11) (lw: a.p: rdn over 1f out: edgd rt ins fnl f: r.o)...s.h **4** 16/1 110 69
2072[14] **Rambling Bear (113)** (MBlanshard) **3-9-2** RCochrane(4) (lw: hdwy over 1f out: ev ch ins fnl f: unable qckn)...¾ **5** 6/1[2] 112 66
2692[5] **Please Suzanne (99)** (RHannon) **3-8-7** DaneO'Neill(12) (hdwy over 1f out: nvr nrr) ....½ **6** 16/1 102 56
2498* **Averti (IRE) (107)** (WRMuir) **5-9-3** BThomson(3) (led tl ins fnl f: sn wknd)....¾ **7** 15/2 105 64
2337[2] **Inzar (USA) (112)** (PFICole) **4-9-10** TQuinn(16) (lw: prom over 4f)....½ **8** 5/1[1] 111 70
2498[2] **Montendre (103)** (MMcCormack) **9-9-7** JReid(7) (lw: nvr nr to chal)....½ **9** 33/1 106 65
2332[7] **Madly Sharp (100)** (JWWatts) **5-9-3** JCarroll(6) (lw: hld up: rdn over 2f out: sn wknd) ....1 **10** 20/1 100 59
2545[12] **King of The East (IRE) (104)** (MRStoute) **3-8-12** WCarson(2) (lw: prom over 4f) ....½ **11** 20/1 98 52
2692[2] **Daring Destiny (99)** (KRBurke) **5-9-2b** JTate(5) (hdwy over 1f out: wknd fnl f) ....1¼ **12** 12/1 94 53
2114[28] **Top Banana (95)** (HCandy) **5-9-3** CRutter(14) (a bhd)....1½ **13** 12/1 91 50
2692[4] **Branston Abby (IRE) (108)** (MJohnston) **7-9-2** MRoberts(1) (bhd fnl 3f)....2½ **14** 7/1[3] 83 42
2332* **Sea Dane (107)** (PWHarris) **3-9-2** BDoyle(15) (s.s: a bhd)....hd **15** 10/1 88 42
**No Extras (IRE)** (GLMoore) **6-9-3** CandyMorris(13) (a bhd)....4 **16** 50/1 73 32
(SP 129.0%) **16 Rn**

**1m 10.71** (0.08 under best) (-1.09) CSF £276.62 TOTE £18.70: £5.10 £5.30 £3.00 (£115.50) Trio £603.90 OWNER Mr J. Paniccia (KINGSCLERE) BRED C. H. Bothway
WEIGHT FOR AGE 3yo-5lb
**1818 Jayannpee** chased the leaders. Stoked up from below the distance, he hit the front inside the final furlong and kept on well to beat the seven-year-old course-record. (16/1)
**1879 Easy Dollar** may have got his head in front for a few strides inside the final furlong and kept on really well, but was just unable to master the winner. (20/1)
**2545 Venture Capitalist**, put to sleep at the back of the field, did not get a run at a critical stage below the distance. However, he soon picked up ground and, weaving through the field, finished in fine style. (7/1)
**2114 Espartero (IRE)**, never far away, was rousted along below the distance, and kept on well to the line. (16/1)
**1621* Rambling Bear** made his effort on the outside of the field below the distance. With every chance inside the final furlong, he was then just worried out of it. (6/1)
**2692 Please Suzanne** stayed on from the back of the field in the last furlong and a half without ever posing a threat. (16/1)
**2337 Inzar (USA)** was close up until calling it a day below the distance. Seven furlongs is his trip. (5/1)

## 2881 STEVENTON STKS (Listed) (3-Y.O+) (Class A)
3-35 (3-36) **1m 2f 6y** £12,646.00 (£3,808.00: £1,844.00: £862.00) Stalls: Low GOING minus 0.52 sec per fur (F)

SP RR SF
2039[7] **Wall Street (USA) (105)** (SbinSuroor) **3-8-7** JReid(6) (lw: rdn & hdwy 2f out: led wl ins fnl f: r.o wl)....— **1** 9/2[3] 115 70
2502[10] **Salmon Ladder (USA) (108)** (PFICole) **4-9-3** TQuinn(3) (lw: chsd ldr: rdn over 2f out: led over 1f out tl wl ins fnl f: unable qckn) ....1 **2** 11/4[2] 113 78
**Magellan (USA)** (CEBrittain) **3-8-7** BDoyle(4) (w'like: scope: led over 8f: one pce)....2 **3** 14/1 110 65
2227* **Bal Harbour (109)** (HRACecil) **5-9-6** WRyan(2) (lw: hld up: rdn & ev ch over 2f out: one pce)....1½ **4** 6/4[1] 111 76
2055[10] **Naked Welcome (104)** (MJFetherston-Godley) **4-9-3** JCarroll(7) (lw: s.s: a bhd) ....3 **5** 6/1 103 68
2535[5] **Kings Witness (USA) (107)** (WJHaggas) **3-8-7** RCochrane(5) (b.off fore: hld up: rdn over 3f out: wknd over 2f out) ....10 **6** 14/1 87 42
(SP 112.5%) **6 Rn**

**2m 1.29** (1.47 under best) (-2.51) CSF £16.32 TOTE £4.90: £2.10 £1.70 (£6.00) OWNER Godolphin (NEWMARKET) BRED Darley Stud Management Inc
WEIGHT FOR AGE 3yo-10lb
**1627* Wall Street (USA)**, ridden along to pick up ground a quarter of a mile out, eventually managed to whittle down the leader to get in front inside the final furlong, breaking the course-record in the process. (9/2)
**2145* Salmon Ladder (USA)** raced in second place. Eventually getting in front below the distance, he did little wrong but was just worried out of it near the line. He should soon be winning. (11/4)
**Magellan (USA)**, who has been running in Dubai during the spring, attempted to make all the running. Collared below the distance, he failed to find another gear. (14/1: 25/1-12/1)
**2227* Bal Harbour** has been running so well when dictating matters from the front that it was very surprising to see him held up on this occasion. Moving up in the straight, he still had every chance over a quarter of a mile from home until tapped for toe. He should be given another chance if allowed to make the running. (6/4: 5/4-15/8)

## 2882 HANNINGTON H'CAP (0-90) (3-Y.O+) (Class C)
4-05 (4-06) **1m 5f 61y** £5,702.50 (£1,720.00: £835.00: £392.50) Stalls: Low GOING minus 0.52 sec per fur (F)

SP RR SF
2131[3] **Mystic Hill (87)** (GHarwood) **5-10-0** AClark(9) (hdwy over 2f out: hrd rdn over 1f out: led nr fin)....— **1** 12/1 97 80
2074[16] **Arctic Fancy (USA) (81)** (PWHarris) **3-8-9** PaulEddery(3) (lw: a.p: led over 1f out: hrd rdn: hdd nr fin)....hd **2** 12/1 91 61
2233[2] **Generosa (87)** (HCandy) **3-9-1** TQuinn(10) (rdn & hdwy over 1f out: r.o one pce) ....¾ **3** 8/1 96 66
2319[10] **Achilles Heel (55)** (CNAllen) **5-7-5**(5) MartinDwyer(12) (hdwy over 2f out: wknd fnl f) ....3 **4** 20/1 60 43
2365* **Fitzwilliam (USA) (85)** (IABalding) **3-8-13** WRyan(1) (hdwy over 2f out: rdn over 1f out: one pce)....hd **5** 6/1[2] 90 60
1426[2] **Jermyn Street (USA) (73)** (MrsJCecil) **5-9-0** JReid(6) (rdn over 2f out: hdwy over 1f out: nvr nrr)....½ **6** 12/1 78 61
2591[2] **Step Aloft (78)** (LordHuntingdon) **4-9-5** DHarrison(8) (lw: nvr nr to chal)....2 **7** 7/2[1] 80 63
2055[8] **Shadow Leader (80)** (CREgerton) **5-9-7** RCochrane(2) (hdwy over 5f out: nt clr run over 3f out & over 2f out: wknd over 1f out)....s.h **8** 16/1 82 65
2534[8] **At Liberty (IRE) (86)** (RHannon) **4-9-10**(3) DaneO'Neill(5) (lw: nvr nrr)....3½ **9** 20/1 84 67
2300* **Reimei (70)** (RAkehurst) **7-8-11** SSanders(14) (a.p: led over 2f out tl over 1f out: sn wknd)....3 **10** 7/1 64 47
2226[2] **Make a Stand (75)** (MCPipe) **5-9-2** MRoberts(13) (lw: hdwy over 5f out: wknd over 2f out) ....5 **11** 13/2[3] 63 46
2576[7] **Hayaain (83)** (MajorWRHern) **3-8-11** WCarson(11) (prom 10f) ....4 **12** 12/1 67 37
2226[9] **Horesti (65)** (CEBrittain) **4-8-6** BDoyle(7) (lw: led over 1f: wknd over 3f out)....16 **13** 40/1 29 12
2612[7] **Lalindi (IRE) (76)** (DRCElsworth) **5-9-3b** AProcter(4) (lw: led 12f out tl over 2f out: sn wknd)....14 **14** 20/1 23 6
(SP 126.8%) **14 Rn**

**2m 44.9** (0.25 under best) (-1.60) CSF £139.77 CT £1,135.30 TOTE £17.90: £4.30 £2.40 £2.70 (£162.60) Trio £390.90 OWNER Mrs S. L. Whitehead (PULBOROUGH) BRED Hascombe and Valiant Studs
LONG HANDICAP Achilles Heel 7-8
WEIGHT FOR AGE 3yo-13lb
**2131 Mystic Hill** began to pick up ground over a quarter of a mile from home and, responding to pressure, got up near the line, thus making it the sixth consecutive race of the afternoon in which the course-record was broken. (12/1: op 8/1)

**1782* Arctic Fancy (USA)**, never far away, struck the front below the distance but, despite doing little wrong, was worried out of it near the line. (12/1)
**2233 Generosa** began to pick up ground below the distance but, despite staying on, failed to master the front two in time. (8/1)
**1977* Achilles Heel** made his effort over a quarter of a mile from home, but had run out of gas in the last 200 yards. A mile and a half may well be his best trip. (20/1)
**2365* Fitzwilliam (USA)** picked up ground along the rail over a quarter of a mile from home, but was making no further impression from below the distance. (6/1: 4/1-13/2)
**1426 Jermyn Street (USA)** stayed on in the last furlong and a half to be nearest at the line. (12/1: op 8/1)

## 2883 LEVY BOARD SEVENTH RACE H'CAP (0-90) (3-Y.O+) (Class C)

4-35 (4-36) **1m 1f** £3,711.25 (£3,711.25: £835.00: £392.50) Stalls: Low GOING minus 0.52 sec per fur (F)

| | Horse | Dist | Pos | SP | RR | SF |
|---|---|---|---|---|---|---|
| $2350^{7}$ | **Daunt (88)** (JHMGosden) **4-10-0** JCarroll(2) (mde all: all out) | — | 1 | 25/1 | 98 | 72 |
| $2605^{2}$ | **Thames Side (63)** (MMadgwick) **5-8-3**$^{ow2}$ DHarrison(1) (lw: rdn over 2f out: hdwy over 1f out: str run fnl f: jnd ldr post) | — | 1 | 14/1 | 73 | 45 |
| 2701* | **Game Ploy (POL) (76)** (DHaydnJones) **4-9-2** PaulEddery(3) (rdn over 2f out: hdwy over 1f out: r.o) | 1 | 3 | 6/4$^{1}$ | 84 | 58 |
| 2342* | **Roufontaine (71)** (WRMuir) **5-8-11** BThomson(5) (lw: nt clr run over 3f out: hdwy over 1f out: r.o one pce) | 3½ | 4 | 6/1$^{2}$ | 73 | 47 |
| $2608^{9}$ | **Vola Via (USA) (83)** (IABalding) **3-8-9**$^{(5)}$ MartinDwyer(6) (nvr nr to chal) | 1 | 5 | 12/1 | 83 | 48 |
| $2603^{6}$ | **Zermatt (IRE) (72)** (MDIUsher) **6-8-12** SSanders(9) (swtg: chsd wnr tl ins fnl f: sn wknd) | nk | 6 | 20/1 | 72 | 46 |
| $2010^{8}$ | **Embankment (IRE) (77)** (RHannon) **6-9-0**$^{(3)}$ DaneO'Neill(7) (prom over 7f) | 1¼ | 7 | 12/1 | 75 | 49 |
| $2342^{2}$ | **Sharp Consul (IRE) (75)** (HCandy) **4-9-1** CRutter(10) (hld up: rdn over 3f out: wknd over 1f out) | 1½ | 8 | 13/2$^{3}$ | 70 | 44 |
| $1792^{8}$ | **Country Lover (70)** (LordHuntingdon) **5-8-5v**$^{(5)}$ AimeeCook(4) (lw: hdwy over 5f out: wknd over 1f out) | 2½ | 9 | 11/1 | 60 | 34 |
| $2603^{5}$ | **Danegold (IRE) (80)** (MRChannon) **4-9-6v** JFEgan(8) (swtg: a bhd) | 7 | 10 | 10/1 | 58 | 32 |
| $2497^{7}$ | **Some Horse (IRE) (85)** (MGMeagher) **3-9-2** RPerham(11) (lw: prom 6f) | 1½ | 11 | 20/1 | 60 | 25 |

(SP 120.5%) **11 Rn**

**1m 49.91** (2.34 under best) (-0.39) CSF D&T £146.83 T&D £129.71 CT D,T&G £356.69 T,D&G £348.09 TOTE D£11.30 T£7.20: D£5.00 T£2.30 £1.70 (£299.00) Trio £262.90 OWNER Lord Hartington (NEWMARKET)/Mrs H. Veal (DENMEAD) BRED Side Hill Stud/Miss D. M. Green
WEIGHT FOR AGE 3yo-9lb

**Daunt** took the field along. Rousted along over a quarter of a mile from home, he grimly held on but, with Thames Side finishing in tremendous style, he had to share the spoils in the end. (25/1)
**2605 Thames Side** picked up ground below the distance. Finishing with a real flourish, he managed to force a dead-heat on the line. (14/1)
**2701* Game Ploy (POL)** picked up ground below the distance but, despite running on, failed to get there in time. (6/4)
**2342* Roufontaine** did not have the best of runs early in the straight, but stayed on in the last furlong and a half to be nearest at the finish. (6/1)
**1771 Vola Via (USA)**, racing towards the back of the field, could never get in a blow. (12/1)
**2603 Zermatt (IRE)** raced in second place. With every chance a quarter of a mile from home, he was eventually overhauled for the runner-up berth inside the final furlong, and had nothing more to offer. (20/1)
**1843 Embankment (IRE)** (12/1: 8/1-14/1)
**1338* Country Lover** (11/1: 8/1-12/1)

T/Jkpt: Not won; £24,902.51 to Ayr 21/7/96. T/Plpt: £545.10 (49.46 Tckts). T/Qdpt: £160.90 (8.77 Tckts). AK

# 2859-NEWMARKET (R-H) (Good to firm)

## Saturday July 20th

WEATHER: sunny & hot WIND: almost nil

## 2884 FOOD BROKERS-GLOYSTARNE H'CAP (0-85) (4-Y.O+) (Class D)

2-10 (2-10) **1m 6f 175y (July)** £4,620.00 (£1,380.00: £660.00: £300.00) Stalls: Low GOING minus 0.23 sec per fur (GF)

| | Horse | Dist | Pos | SP | RR | SF |
|---|---|---|---|---|---|---|
| $2547^{7}$ | **Top Cees (82)** (MrsJRRamsden) **6-9-12** KFallon(7) (lw: hld up: hdwy over 2f out: led over 1f out: clr fnl f: easily) | — | 1 | 6/1 | 94+ | 67 |
| $2423^{6}$ | **Double Echo (IRE) (52)** (JDBethell) **8-7-10** GBardwell(4) (led tl hdd over 1f out: kpt on: no ch w wnr) | 1½ | 2 | 10/1 | 62 | 35 |
| $2697^{7}$ | **Floating Line (66)** (EJAlston) **8-8-10** MWigham(2) (swtg: chsd ldr: rdn 2f out: r.o one pce) | ¾ | 3 | 7/1 | 76 | 49 |
| $2534^{6}$ | **Casual Water (IRE) (70)** (AGNewcombe) **5-8-11**$^{(3)}$ SDrowne(6) (plld hrd: hld up: effrt 3f out: nt pce to chal) | nk | 4 | 9/2$^{1}$ | 79 | 52 |
| $2549^{5}$ | **Brandon Court (IRE) (80)** (IABalding) **5-9-10** MHills(5) (plld hrd: hld up in rr: hdwy 3f out: rdn over 1f out: one pce) | 3 | 5 | 11/2$^{3}$ | 86 | 59 |
| $2319^{5}$ | **Blazon of Troy (58)** (TThomsonJones) **7-7-13**$^{(3)ow6}$ FLynch(8) (b: trckd ldrs: rdn over 2f out: eased whn btn fnl f) | 5 | 6 | 14/1 | 59 | 26 |
| $2499^{6}$ | **Sugar Mill (67)** (MrsMReveley) **6-8-11** ACulhane(1) (lw: hld up in rr: rdn & outpcd wl over 2f out: sn btn) | nk | 7 | 6/1 | 67 | 40 |
| *$1458^{6}$* | **Well Arranged (IRE) (62)** (RAkehurst) **5-8-6** JWeaver(3) (lw: prom: rdn 4f out: sn wknd) | 5 | 8 | 5/1$^{2}$ | 57 | 30 |

(SP 107.1%) **8 Rn**

**3m 12.98** (4.48) CSF £52.00 CT £331.23 TOTE £5.90: £2.00 £2.60 £2.00 (£27.50) OWNER Mr R. E. Sangster (THIRSK) BRED Pendley Farm
LONG HANDICAP Blazon of Troy 7-8

**Top Cees**, who looked a million dollars, turned in a performance to match his looks with a clear-cut success that would be value for five or six lengths. The Cesarewitch is again his aim in the autumn. (6/1)
**2423 Double Echo (IRE)** has never won over such an extended trip, but he adopted more forceful tactics on this occasion, and ran by far his best race for quite some time. (10/1)
**2697 Floating Line**, who moved badly to post, had every chance until the winner made his move and then the writing was on the wall. (7/1)
**1792 Casual Water (IRE)** has not really found his true form so far this season and, though he did stay on after being restrained, he lacked the speed to get serious. (9/2)
**2549 Brandon Court (IRE)** does not stride out with any freedom when the ground is lively and, when the tempo picked up running into the Dip, he was left floundering. (11/2)

## 2885 INVESCO H'CAP (0-80) (3-Y.O+) (Class D)

2-45 (2-46) **1m (July)** £4,854.00 (£1,452.00: £696.00: £318.00) Stalls: High GOING minus 0.23 sec per fur (GF)

| | Horse | Dist | Pos | SP | RR | SF |
|---|---|---|---|---|---|---|
| 2541* | **Hawksley Hill (IRE) (69)** (MrsJRRamsden) **3-8-12** KFallon(10) (lw: hld up: smooth hdwy to ld appr fnl f: sn clr: easily) | — | 1 | 7/2$^{1}$ | 82+ | 40 |

| | | | | SP | RR | SF |
|---|---|---|---|---|---|---|
| 2581[11] | **Toujours Riviera (75)** (JPearce) **6-9-12** GBardwell(6) (hld up: gd hdwy appr fnl f: fin wl) ......1¾ | **2** | | 8/1 | 85 | 51 |
| 2605[4] | **Admirals Flame (IRE) (74)** (CFWall) **5-9-4**(7) PClarke(9) (b: hld up in rr: rapid hdwy fnl f: nrst fin)......1¼ | **3** | | 10/1 | 81 | 47 |
| 2581[5] | **Nordinex (IRE) (76)** (RWArmstrong) **4-9-13** MHills(5) (lw: hld up: effrt & swtchd lft wl over 1f out: unable qckn fnl f) ......s.h | **4** | | 7/1[3] | 83 | 49 |
| 1820[6] | **Willisa (65)** (JDBethell) **3-8-8** GCarter(3) (swtg: chsd clr ldr: rdn over 1f out: one pce) ......hd | **5** | | 20/1 | 72 | 30 |
| 2249[2] | **Duello (64)** (MBlanshard) **5-9-1** JQuinn(7) (trckd ldrs: rdn 3f out: kpt on one pce)......½ | **6** | | 9/1 | 70 | 36 |
| 2621[5] | **She's My Love (75)** (JEBanks) **3-9-4** JWeaver(8) (lw: trckd ldrs tl rdn & wknd appr fnl f)......¾ | **7** | | 5/1[2] | 79 | 37 |
| | **Vanborough Lad (54)** (MJBolton) **7-8-2**(3) FLynch(4) (trckd ldrs tl lost pl over 2f out) ......2½ | **8** | | 33/1 | 53 | 19 |
| 2438* | **Blockade (USA) (62)** (MBell) **7-8-13** MFenton(2) (t: swtg: led & sn clr: wknd & hdd over 1f out: eased whn btn) ......nk | **9** | | 11/1 | 61 | 27 |
| 2440[7] | **Bellas Gate Boy (58)** (JPearce) **4-8-2**(7) LisaMoncrieff(1) (s.s: a in rr)......2 | **10** | | 33/1 | 53 | 19 |
| 2340[2] | **Rise Up Singing (48)** (WJMusson) **8-7-13b** DRMcCabe(11) (sn chsng ldrs: effrt over 2f out: bmpd wl over 1f out: wknd qckly appr fnl f: t.o) ......11 | **11** | | 7/1[3] | 21 | — |

(SP 113.1%) **11 Rn**

**1m 40.84** (3.64) CSF £28.09 CT £228.05 TOTE £3.40: £1.50 £3.00 £3.70 (£20.60) Trio £71.20 OWNER Mr Hamish Alexander (THIRSK) BRED The Wickfield Stud Ltd
WEIGHT FOR AGE 3yo-8lb

OFFICIAL EXPLANATION **Admirals Flame (IRE): connections stated that the gelding needs to be settled in his races and, having met trouble in running, was unable to find a clear run until it was too late.**
**Rise Up Singing: had been accidently hit over the nose in the race by a whip, the jockey thought this attributed to it's poor running.**

**2541* Hawksley Hill (IRE)**, a very progressive youngster, burst clear after leading in the Dip and, although he was being reeled in again towards the finish, he won with more in hand than the margin suggests. (7/2: 5/2-4/1)
**2400 Toujours Riviera**, buried in the pack, ran on really well on meeting the rising ground and would seem to be on the way back. (8/1)
**2605 Admirals Flame (IRE)** was one of the backmarkers running into the Dip, but he really found his stride up the hill, and is now ready to strike. (10/1)
**2581 Nordinex (IRE)** did not enjoy a trouble-free passage when mounting his challenge, but he stuck to his work willingly and he is no backnumber yet. (7/1)
**1820 Willisa** had plenty of use made of her here and had nothing more to give when faced with the hill. If kept within her own age group, she is capable of picking up another race. (20/1)
**2249 Duello** ran surprisingly well on ground far from suitable, and he is in the right frame of mind, if only he could get conditions to suit. (9/1)
**2340 Rise Up Singing** (7/1: 5/1-15/2)

## 2886 FOOD BROKERS APHRODITE STKS (Listed) (3-Y.O F) (Class A)

3-15 (3-16) **1m 4f (July)** £11,874.50 (£3,536.00: £1,683.00: £756.50) Stalls: High GOING minus 0.23 sec per fur (GF)

| | | | SP | RR | SF |
|---|---|---|---|---|---|
| 2533[4] | **Shemozzle (IRE) (107)** (JHMGosden) **3-8-4** MHills(1) (hld up gng wl: led over 2f out: edgd rt: pushed out) ...— | **1** | 6/4[1] | 107 | 80 |
| 1899[5] | **Balalaika** (LMCumani) **3-8-6**ow2 JWeaver(4) (lw: hld up: effrt over 1f out: nt pce of wnr)......2 | **2** | 6/1[3] | 106 | 77 |
| 1990* | **Place de L'Opera (102)** (HRACecil) **3-8-4** AMcGlone(3) (lw: a.p: outpcd wl over 1f out: styd on same pce fnl f) ......3½ | **3** | 2/1[2] | 100 | 73 |
| 2069[4] | **Alzabella (IRE)** (JWHills) **3-8-5**ow1 KFallon(5) (lw: trckd ldrs: drvn along over 4f out: wkng whn swtchd lft over 1f out) ......¾ | **4** | 16/1 | 100 | 72 |
| 2227[2] | **Jural (100)** (SbinSuroor) **4-9-2** PRobinson(2) (led tl over 2f out: sn rdn & edgd rt: wknd fnl f) ......s.h | **5** | 7/1 | 99 | 84 |

(SP 106.0%) **5 Rn**

**2m 28.63** (-1.37) CSF £9.07 TOTE £2.10: £1.40 £2.60 (£7.00) OWNER Lord Hartington (NEWMARKET) BRED Side Hill Stud
WEIGHT FOR AGE 3yo-12lb

**2533 Shemozzle (IRE)** hardly needed to be let down to win her first listed race, and she should now go on to better things. She could possibly go to York now for the Galtres Stakes. (6/4)
**1899 Balalaika** turned in a very promising display on this first try at the trip and, though she could not get in a blow at the winner, she did nothing wrong, and the experience will prove beneficial. (6/1)
**1990* Place de L'Opera**, a deep-girthed, impressive-looking filly, sat on the tail of the leader going well, but she got tapped for toe running into the Dip and her chance had gone. (2/1)
**2069 Alzabella (IRE)**, seeing the back-end of the winner for the third time, will do well to avoid her in future races. (16/1)
**2227 Jural** made the running, but could not get the winner off the bridle and stamina appeared to desert her up the final climb. (7/1)

## 2887 PRIMULA MAIDEN STKS (2-Y.O) (Class D)

3-45 (3-46) **6f (July)** £4,503.00 (£1,344.00: £642.00: £291.00) Stalls: High GOING minus 0.23 sec per fur (GF)

| | | | SP | RR | SF |
|---|---|---|---|---|---|
| 2302[2] | **Man Howa (IRE)** (LMCumani) **2-9-0** JWeaver(4) (lw: mde all: drew clr wl over 1f out: comf)......— | **1** | 4/9[1] | 88+ | 40 |
| | **Undercover Agent (IRE)** (JLDunlop) **2-8-9** GCarter(2) (w'like: unf: trckd ldrs: chsd wnr appr fnl f: kpt on wl towards fin) ......1 | **2** | 11/1 | 80+ | 32 |
| 2335[5] | **Supremism** (CEBrittain) **2-9-0** WJO'Connor(3) (gd sort: bit bkwd: a.p: hrd drvn appr fnl f: one pce)......2½ | **3** | 10/1 | 79 | 31 |
| | **China Red (USA)** (JWHills) **2-9-0** MHills(6) (wl grwn: bkwd: hmpd s: hdwy over 2f out: r.o one pce appr fnl f) ......½ | **4** | 7/1[2] | 46 | 29 |
| | **Serenity** (JRFanshawe) **2-8-9** NDay(5) (w'like: prom tl wknd over 1f out)......1¾ | **5** | 15/2[3] | 68 | 20 |
| 2624[13] | **Feel A Line** (BJMeehan) **2-9-0** MTebbutt(8) (bit bkwd: a bhd & outpcd) ......3½ | **6** | 40/1 | 63 | 15 |
| 1626[10] | **Doubly-H (IRE)** (MBell) **2-9-0** MFenton(7) (prom over 3f: sn wknd: t.o) ......10 | **7** | 40/1 | 37 | — |
| | **Ibin St James** (JDBethell) **2-9-0** KFallon(1) (w'like: scope: s.s: a bhd: t.o) ......2 | **8** | 20/1 | 31 | — |

(SP 120.6%) **8 Rn**

**1m 14.79** (2.79) CSF £7.04 TOTE £1.50: £1.20 £1.70 £2.10 (£6.10) OWNER Sheikh Ahmed Al Maktoum (NEWMARKET) BRED Sheikh Ahmed Bin Rashid Al Maktoum

**2302 Man Howa (IRE)** had little to beat and accomplished it with the minimum of fuss, despite the narrowness of the winning margin. (4/9)
**Undercover Agent (IRE)**, a lightly-made debutante, pushed the pace on the far rail and renewed her challenge nearing the finish, but the winner was simply toying with her. She should not be too difficult to place. (11/1: 7/1-12/1)
**2335 Supremism** still looks to need time, but he shaped promisingly and is progressing in the right direction. (10/1: 5/1-11/1)
**China Red (USA)**, very much in need of the run and the experience, was impeded soon after the start, but he recovered well in the latter part of the race, and will be much sharper next time. (7/1: 6/1-9/1)
**Serenity**, a smallish half-sister to a winner, showed plenty of speed to press the leaders for over four furlongs. (15/2: 5/1-8/1)

## 2888 FOOD BROKERS ANIMAL HEALTH TRUST TROPHY RATED STKS H'CAP (0-100) (3-Y.O) (Class B)

4-15 (4-15) **1m (July)** £17,150.00 (£6,350.00: £3,050.00: £1,250.00: £500.00: £200.00) Stalls: High GOING minus 0.23 sec (GF)

| Form | Horse | | Pos | SP | RR | SF |
|---|---|---|---|---|---|---|
| 2502[8] | **Missile (88)** (WJHaggas) **3-8-9** MHills(3) (lw: hld up: swtchd rt 2f out: qcknd to ld wl over 1f out: readily)......— | | 1 | 5/2[1] | 107+ | 54 |
| 1438* | **My Lewicia (IRE) (92)** (PWHarris) **3-8-13** GCarter(7) (b.nr hind: dwlt: hdwy ½-wy: ev ch over 1f out: sn outpcd)......2½ | | 2 | 9/1 | 106 | 53 |
| 2334[2] | **North Song (92)** (JHMGosden) **3-8-13** AMcGlone(4) (lw: led after 2f tl hdd & outpcd wl over 1f out)......4 | | 3 | 6/1[3] | 98 | 45 |
| 2623[5] | **How Long (97)** (LMCumani) **3-9-4** OUrbina(9) (trckd ldrs: n.m.r wl over 1f out: r.o wl fnl f)......hd | | 4 | 8/1 | 103 | 50 |
| 2510* | **Go Britannia (90)** (DRLoder) **3-8-11v[1]** DRMcCabe(10) (hld up: effrt over 2f out: swtchd lft & rdn over 1f out: one pce)......1¼ | | 5 | 9/2[2] | 93 | 40 |
| 2181* | **Iamus (87)** (PTWalwyn) **3-8-8** WJO'Connor(11) (prom: rdn over 2f out: sn btn)......5 | | 6 | 25/1 | 80 | 27 |
| 1329[9] | **Swift Fandango (USA) (95)** (PFICole) **3-9-2** JQuinn(6) (hld up: hdwy 3f out: sn hrd drvn: wknd appr fnl f)......6 | | 7 | 25/1 | 76 | 23 |
| 2354[2] | **Polar Eclipse (100)** (MJohnston) **3-9-7** JWeaver(8) (lw: plld hrd: led 2f: rdn & wknd wl over 1f out)......1½ | | 8 | 20/1 | 78 | 25 |
| 2544[5] | **Brandon Magic (96)** (IABalding) **3-9-3** MFenton(2) (lw: prom: shkn up 3f out: outpcd wl over 1f out)......1¾ | | 9 | 14/1 | 71 | 18 |
| 874[5] | **Really A Dream (IRE) (86)** (MRStoute) **3-8-4(3)** FLynch(1) (prom over 5f)......nk | | 10 | 9/1 | 60 | 7 |
| 2041[4] | **Hidden Oasis (99)** (SbinSuroor) **3-9-6v[1]** KFallon(5) (trckd ldrs: rdn along over 2f out: sn btn)......1¼ | | 11 | 9/1 | 71 | 18 |

(SP 121.3%) **11 Rn**

**1m 39.17** (1.97) CSF £24.49 CT £113.24 TOTE £3.20: £1.80 £2.80 £1.70 (£19.70) Trio £25.00 OWNER Mr J. W. Bogie (NEWMARKET) BRED The Duke of Marlborough

LONG HANDICAP Really A Dream (IRE) 8-4

**2502 Missile** returned to form over this more suitable trip with a breathtaking turn of speed that left his rivals clutching for straws. It is doubtful if he will ever be so well handicapped after this. (5/2)

**1438* My Lewicia (IRE)** put in a good display in this first handicap after being sluggish at the start and, with the winner out of the way, would have scored very easily indeed. She should soon make amends. (9/1)

**2334 North Song**, taken to post early, pulled too hard for his own good and had no answer when the winner appeared on the scene. (6/1)

**2623 How Long** was continually being tightened up when poised to challenge in the Dip and, when he did wriggle free, the race was as good as over. He will not be long in returning to form. (8/1: 6/1-9/1)

**2510* Go Britannia** needed to be switched to find a way through over a furlong out and, in doing so, lost his momentum and never really got going again. This was his first run against handicappers and the experience will not be lost. (9/2)

## 2889 CHEMIST BROKERS H'CAP (0-100) (3-Y.O+) (Class C)

4-45 (4-48) **5f (July)** £6,056.00 (£1,808.00: £864.00: £392.00) Stalls: High GOING minus 0.23 sec per fur (GF)

| Form | Horse | Pos | SP | RR | SF |
|---|---|---|---|---|---|
| 2694[2] | **Tedburrow (88)** (MrsAMNaughton) **4-9-2(5)** DGriffiths(6) (a.p: led ins fnl f: r.o wl)......— | 1 | 11/2[1] | 97 | 74 |
| 2694[5] | **Lago Di Varano (85)** (RMWhitaker) **4-9-1v(3)** FLynch(13) (a.p: ev ch ins fnl f: r.o)......½ | 2 | 9/1 | 92 | 69 |
| 2694[6] | **Sea-Deer (82)** (CADwyer) **7-9-1** AMcGlone(3) (chsd ldr far side tl led over 1f out: kpt on u.p nr fin)......nk | 3 | 6/1[2] | 88 | 65 |
| 2584[5] | **Galine (87)** (WAO'Gorman) **3-9-2** EmmaO'Gorman(5) (hdwy 2f out: ev ch ins fnl f: unable qckn)......s.h | 4 | 6/1[2] | 93 | 66 |
| 2363[10] | **The Happy Fox (IRE) (79)** (BAMcMahon) **4-8-9(3)** PMcCabe(2) (lw: outpcd in rr tl r.o strly ins fnl f)......1¼ | 5 | 33/1 | 81 | 58 |
| 2381[2] | **Bowden Rose (84)** (MBlanshard) **4-9-3b** JQuinn(9) (led centre: clr ldr over 1f out tl ins fnl f)......nk | 6 | 12/1 | 85 | 62 |
| 2518* | **Bolshoi (IRE) (83)** (JBerry) **4-9-2b** GCarter(1) (lw: outpcd tl gd hdwy appr fnl f: nvr nrr)......nk | 7 | 11/2[1] | 83 | 60 |
| 2586[2] | **Spender (76)** (PWHarris) **7-8-9** JStack(7) (hdwy over 1f out: nvr nrr)......½ | 8 | 10/1 | 75 | 52 |
| 2694[19] | **Saint Express (95)** (MrsMReveley) **6-10-0** ACulhane(11) (nvr trbld ldrs)......1½ | 9 | 33/1 | 89 | 66 |
| 2698[4] | **Ziggy's Dancer (USA) (86)** (EJAlston) **5-9-5** KFallon(14) (prom over 3f)......1¾ | 10 | 9/1 | 74 | 51 |
| 2694[18] | **Femme Savante (90)** (RHannon) **4-9-9** WJO'Connor(10) (outpcd)......¾ | 11 | 33/1 | 76 | 53 |
| 2676[2] | **Tadeo (90)** (MJohnston) **3-9-5** JWeaver(8) (prom tl rdn & outpcd over 1f out)......nk | 12 | 7/1[3] | 75 | 48 |
| 2692[7] | **Welsh Mist (93)** (RBoss) **5-9-12b** MHills(12) (spd centre 3f)......nk | 13 | 25/1 | 77 | 54 |
| 2508[5] | **Tart and a Half (78)** (BJMeehan) **4-8-11b** MTebbutt(4) (led tl hdd & wknd over 1f out)......1¼ | 14 | 16/1 | 58 | 35 |

(SP 127.2%) **14 Rn**

**59.17 secs** (0.67) CSF £53.00 CT £292.98 TOTE £6.60: £2.20 £3.50 £2.50 (£27.90) Trio £42.00 OWNER Mr Philip Davies (RICHMOND) BRED Lady Matthews

WEIGHT FOR AGE 3yo-4lb

**2694 Tedburrow**, getting off the mark for the season in this hotly-contested event, followed up a bold display at York on his previous outing and thoroughly deserved this hard-fought success. (11/2)

**2694 Lago Di Varano** finished marginally closer to the winner than he did at York and gave of his best in a thrilling sprint to the line to fail narrowly. He is at the top of his form just now. (9/1)

**2694 Sea-Deer** has had a very busy season, but he retains all of his enthusiasm for the game, and his younger rivals had to work really hard to get the better of him in the shadow of the post. (6/1)

**2584 Galine** was produced to win it entering the final furlong but, on ground plenty firm enough, just could not get her head in front. (6/1)

**1016 The Happy Fox (IRE)** ran up to his best on this return to the minimum trip, but had to weave his way through in the latter stages, and it will be a major surprise if he can not gain just reward in the coming weeks. (33/1)

**2381 Bowden Rose** held the call in the centre of the track and did not give best until well inside the last furlong. She usually comes good at this time of year. (12/1)

**2518* Bolshoi (IRE)**, taken off his legs from the break, put in some sterling work in the latter stages and was still closing fast at the end. (11/2)

## 2890 CHEMIST BROKERS CONDITIONS STKS (2-Y.O) (Class C)

5-20 (5-21) **5f (July)** £5,276.80 (£1,820.80: £870.40: £352.00) Stalls: High GOING minus 0.23 sec per fur (GF)

| Form | Horse | Pos | SP | RR | SF |
|---|---|---|---|---|---|
| 1987* | **Easycall** (BJMeehan) **2-8-10** MTebbutt(1) (lw: a.p: led ½-wy: sn clr: drvn out)......— | 1 | 11/10[1] | 96 | 38 |
| 2595* | **Jennelle** (CADwyer) **2-8-4(7)** JoHunnam(3) (lw: a.p: rdn & kpt on fnl f: nt pce of wnr)......2½ | 2 | 7/4[2] | 89 | 31 |
| 2619[6] | **Millroy (USA)** (PAKelleway) **2-8-10** MWigham(4) (outpcd tl swtchd lft & hdwy over 1f out: fin wl)......s.h | 3 | 16/1 | 88? | 30 |
| 2484* | **For Old Times Sake** (JBerry) **2-9-8** GCarter(2) (slt ld to ½-wy: rdn & outpcd appr fnl f)......1 | 4 | 4/1[3] | 97? | 39 |

(SP 109.9%) **4 Rn**

**60.65 secs** (2.15) CSF £3.31 TOTE £2.00: (£1.80) OWNER Easycall Partnership (UPPER LAMBOURN) BRED Mrs Susan Feddern

**1987* Easycall** confirmed the promise he showed on his debut with another impressive display, and he is beginning to look extremely useful. He has got some interesting dates in mind, notably the Molecomb at Goodwood, followed by the Gimcrack and then the Redcar Gold Trophy. (11/10)

**2595* Jennelle** is no slouch herself, but was out of her depth against the streamlined colt and could do nothing at all about it. (7/4)

**2619 Millroy (USA)**, hopelessly outpaced in his first attempt at the minimum trip, began to find his legs at the death and, finishing with a flourish, only just failed to gain the runner-up prize. (16/1)

**2484* For Old Times Sake,** already a winner of four races, was trying the impossible giving 12lb to the winner and had run his race approaching the final furlong. (4/1)

T/Plpt: £36.70 (728.42 Tckts). T/Qdpt: £6.10 (269.85 Tckts). IM

# 2537-NOTTINGHAM (L-H) (Good to firm, Firm patches)
## Saturday July 20th
WEATHER: fine WIND: nil

## 2891 SCANIA 4-SERIES TROPHY (S) H'CAP (0-60) (3-Y.O+) (Class G)
2-20 (2-20) **1m 6f 15y** £2,658.00 (£738.00: £354.00) Stalls: Low GOING minus 0.62 sec per fur (F)

| | Horse | Dist | Pos | SP | RR | SF |
|---|---|---|---|---|---|---|
| 2556[3] | **Supermick (30)** (WRMuir) **5-8-5** SWhitworth(11) (in tch: hdwy to trck ldrs appr st: led over 3f out: sn rdn clr: jst hld on) | — | 1 | 15/2[3] | 44 | 21 |
| 2779[2] | **Kindred Greeting (31)** (JAHarris) **4-8-6b** JO'Reilly(3) (mid div: rdn 3f out: hdwy over 1f out: styd on strly ins fnl f: jst failed) | s.h | 2 | 6/1[2] | 45 | 22 |
| 2537[3] | **Ttyfran (34)** (BPJBaugh) **6-8-9** WLord(1) (chsd ldrs: drvn along 3f out: kpt on u.p fnl f) | 1 | 3 | 15/2[3] | 47 | 24 |
| 2537* | **Risky Rose (44)** (RHollinshead) **4-9-0**(5) DGriffiths(7) (lw: hld up & bhd: effrt & gd hdwy on outside 2f out: kpt on: too much to do) | ¾ | 4 | 7/2[1] | 56 | 33 |
| 2556[5] | **Bresil (USA) (33)** (KRBurke) **7-8-8** WWoods(2) (hld up in mid div: smooth hdwy appr st: chsd wnr & rdn 2f out: no ex fnl f) | 1½ | 5 | 11/1 | 43 | 20 |
| 2537[4] | **Club Elite (28)** (MFBarraclough) **4-7-12**(5)ow7 PPMurphy(14) (chsd ldrs: rdn wl over 2f out: one pce fr over 1f out) | 3 | 6 | 16/1 | 35 | 5 |
| *2322*[12] | **Genesis Four (46)** (MrsLStubbs) **6-9-2**(5) GLee(12) (lw: hld up: effrt & hdwy 3f out: nt rch ldrs) | ¾ | 7 | 12/1 | 52 | 29 |
| 2556[4] | **La Belle Shyanne (28)** (RJBaker) **5-7-12**(5) ADaly(17) (mid div: stdy hdwy over 5f out: sn chsng ldrs: one pce fnl 2f) | ½ | 8 | 9/1 | 33 | 10 |
| | **Portolano (FR) (24)** (BPJBaugh) **5-7-13** FNorton(16) (b: mde most tl hdd over 3f out: sn rdn & wknd) | s.h | 9 | 40/1 | 29 | 6 |
| 2626[3] | **Fearless Wonder (49)** (MrsMReveley) **5-9-5b**(5) SCopp(5) (mid div tl outpcd appr st: sme hdwy u.p over 2f out: no imp) | 2 | 10 | 9/1 | 52 | 29 |
| | **Patscilla (33)** (RDickin) **5-8-8** TSprake(6) (chsd ldrs: rdn along 4f out: sn wknd) | 4 | 11 | 33/1 | 32 | 9 |
| 2537[6] | **Teoroma (21)** (DrJDScargill) **6-7-10** NAdams(13) (rr div: effrt 6f out: sn outpcd) | 3 | 12 | 16/1 | 16 | — |
| 2341[7] | **Monty Royale (IRE) (36)** (NoelChance) **7-8-11** TIves(9) (b: bhd: effrt over 6f out: sn btn) | 4 | 13 | 9/1 | 27 | 4 |
| *2636*[7] | **Lucy's Gold (21)** (MJRyan) **5-7-3**(7) AMcCarthy(18) (racd keenly: sn w ldr: effrt 4f out: btn 3f out: t.o) | 16 | 14 | 25/1 | — | — |
| 2565[9] | **Hats of to Hilda (26)** (MrsMReveley) **4-8-1** NCarlisle(4) (lw: sn towards rr: rdn & btn appr st: t.o) | 12 | 15 | 33/1 | — | — |
| 2775[8] | **Friendly Dreams (IRE) (39)** (PTDalton) **3-7-7b**(7)ow4 RCody-Boutcher(8) (a bhd: t.o) | 12 | 16 | 50/1 | — | — |
| 2380[7] | **Peggy Ess (35)** (APJames) **3-7-10** DeclanO'Shea(10) (s.s: a bhd: t.o ent st) | 16 | 17 | 50/1 | — | — |

(SP 133.9%) **17 Rn**

**3m 2.2** (3.70) CSF £52.70 CT £335.86 TOTE £6.40: £1.30 £1.90 £2.20 £1.10 (£58.90) Trio £112.60 OWNER Mrs J. M. Muir (LAMBOURN) BRED James Thom and Sons
LONG HANDICAP Lucy's Gold 7-9 Club Elite 7-8 Friendly Dreams (IRE) 7-0 Peggy Ess 6-9
WEIGHT FOR AGE 3yo-14lb
Bt in 5,800 gns

**2556 Supermick**, stepping up a furlong, poached a lead on his rivals in the straight and just held on in a driving finish. (15/2)
**2779 Kindred Greeting** showed his Redcar run to be no fluke and would have won in one more stride. (6/1)
**2537 Ttyfran** ran right up to form and stayed on well in the closing stages. (15/2)
**2537* Risky Rose** ran extremely well, but was set far too stiff a task and did extremely well to finish so close. (7/2)
**2556 Bresil (USA)** had every chance in the straight, but was never quite doing enough in the final two furlongs. (11/1: 8/1-12/1)
**2537 Club Elite** was 2lb out of the handicap and carried 7lb overweight. (16/1)

## 2892 EAST MIDLAND COMMERCIALS FOR SCANIA MAIDEN STKS (2-Y.O F) (Class D)
2-50 (2-50) **6f 15y** £3,743.15 (£1,119.20: £536.10: £244.55) Stalls: High GOING minus 0.62 sec per fur (F)

| | Horse | Dist | Pos | SP | RR | SF |
|---|---|---|---|---|---|---|
| 2245[3] | **Ikdam (USA)** (MajorWRHern) **2-8-11** RHills(5) (lw: mde all: qcknd clr over 1f out: readily) | — | 1 | 1/2[1] | 83+ | 16 |
| | **Catechism (USA)** (JHMGosden) **2-8-11** AGarth(7) (scope: in tch: effrt & nt clr run 2f out: swtchd & sn chsng wnr: nvr able to chal) | 5 | 2 | 12/1 | 70 | 3 |
| 2404[9] | **Soden (IRE)** (TGMills) **2-8-11** MarkLynch(2) (chsd ldrs: rdn over 2f out: one pce fnl f) | 1¾ | 3 | 50/1 | 65 | — |
| | **Telemania (IRE)** (WJHaggas) **2-8-11** WWoods(4) (wl grwn: lengthy: scope: chsd wnr: rdn over 2f out: no ex appr fnl f) | 1½ | 4 | 14/1 | 61 | — |
| | **Zaima (IRE)** (JLDunlop) **2-8-11** SWhitworth(3) (w'like: racd keenly: prom: rn green ½-wy: n.d after) | 1½ | 5 | 10/1[3] | 57 | — |
| | **Icy Guest (USA)** (RCharlton) **2-8-11** TSprake(1) (w'like: scope: s.i.s: hung rt ½-wy: nt pce of ldrs) | ½ | 6 | 9/2[2] | 56 | — |
| | **Classic Line** (JLDunlop) **2-8-11** TIves(6) (unf: scope: sn pushed along: outpcd & bhd fr ½-wy) | ¾ | 7 | 10/1[3] | 54 | — |

(SP 119.4%) **7 Rn**

**1m 12.4** (1.90) CSF £7.94 TOTE £1.40: £1.10 £6.00 (£6.80) OWNER Mr Hamdan Al Maktoum (LAMBOURN) BRED Shadwell Farm Inc
**2245 Ikdam (USA)** fulfilled the promise of her Newbury debut and won in fine style. She can go on from here. (1/2)
**Catechism (USA)** looks a bit of a handful, and was taken down to the start early, but she showed ability, doing some nice work in the closing stages, without ever looking likely to trouble the winner. This experience will not have been wasted on her. (12/1: op 6/1)
**Soden (IRE)** showed up well to the fore, but was tapped for foot in the closing stages. (50/1)
**Telemania (IRE)** showed plenty of dash, but was unable to pull out any extra in the closing stages. (14/1: op 7/1)
**Zaima (IRE)** will be all the better for this experience, having run green. (10/1)
**Icy Guest (USA)**, who holds entries in the Lowther and Cheveley Park Stakes, never looked happy here and, tending to hang right, was not given a hard time. (9/2: 5/2-5/1)

## 2893 SCANIA 4-SERIES 'HORSEPOWER' CLAIMING STKS (3-Y.O) (Class F)
3-25 (3-25) **1m 54y** £2,857.00 (£792.00: £379.00) Stalls: Low GOING minus 0.62 sec per fur (F)

| | Horse | Dist | Pos | SP | RR | SF |
|---|---|---|---|---|---|---|
| 2411* | **Cointosser (IRE) (63)** (SPCWoods) **3-8-10** WWoods(7) (lw: hld up: stdy hdwy 3f out: swtchd to ld over 1f out: hung lft & drvn clr) | — | 1 | 10/11[1] | 65 | 39 |
| 2507[7] | **Dil Dil (45)** (WJHaggas) **3-7-11**(7) CWebb(8) (chsd ldr: led 3f out: sn rdn: hdd over 1f out: no ch w wnr) | 6 | 2 | 8/1[3] | 47 | 21 |

2801[10] **How Could-I (IRE) (44)** (MrsNMacauley) **3-8-10b** TIves(6) (lw: led: rdn & hdd 3f out: kpt on same pce)........1¾ **3** 4/1[2] 50 24
2507[17] **Tallulah Belle (45)** (NPLittmoden) **3-8-6** TGMcLaughlin(4) (chsd ldrs: rdn 3f out: one pce fnl 2f)....................hd **4** 8/1[3] 46 20
2411[8] **Reno's Treasure (USA)** (JAHarris) **3-8-6** TSprake(1) (bhd: effrt & sme hdwy over 3f out: nt pce of ldrs fnl 2f)..........................................................................................................................3½ **5** 50/1 39 13
2393[6] **Chilly Looks (42)** (DWBarker) **3-8-0** NCarlisle(3) (hld up & bhd: hdwy 3f out: btn 2f out).............................1½ **6** 25/1 30 4
*2634*[7] **Extra Hour (IRE) (59)** (WRMuir) **3-8-13** SWhitworth(2) (trckd ldrs: rdn over 3f out: btn 2f out)..........................5 **7** 12/1 33 7
2557[13] **Kealbra Lady** (MSSaunders) **3-8-7**(5) PPMurphy(5) (prom tl rdn & wknd fnl 3f)..............................................21 **8** 50/1 — —
(SP 110.1%) **8 Rn**

**1m 41.8** (0.50) CSF £7.99 TOTE £1.50: £1.10 £1.60 £1.10 (£4.40) OWNER Mr Arashan Ali (NEWMARKET) BRED Mellon Stud
**2411* Cointosser (IRE)** showed a tendency to hang to her left virtually throughout, but was never in any danger of defeat after striking the front. (10/11: Evens-11/10)
**2179 Dil Dil** ran her best race for some time, but was no match for the winner in the closing stages. (8/1)
**2592 How Could-I (IRE)**, making her second appearance in two days, did the donkey work but was well outpaced in the final furlong. (4/1)
**2180 Tallulah Belle** was tapped for foot in the final quarter-mile. (8/1)

## 2894 SCANIA 1996 TRUCK OF THE YEAR TROPHY H'CAP (0-85) (3-Y.O) (Class D)

4-00 (4-00) **1m 54y** £6,347.25 (£1,908.00: £921.50: £428.25) Stalls: Low GOING minus 0.62 sec per fur (F)

SP RR SF

1797* **Victorian Style (84)** (RCharlton) **3-9-7** TSprake(3) (lw: hld up: stdy hdwy over 2f out: led appr fnl f: kpt on wl)...........................................................................................................................— **1** 3/1[3] 92 37
915[5] **Pasternak (75)** (SirMarkPrescott) **3-8-12** WWoods(4) (lw: trckd ldr: effrt & ev ch 2f out: sn rdn: kpt on wl ins fnl f).........................................................................................................................hd **2** 11/8[1] 83 28
937[10] **Flying North (IRE) (79)** (MrsMReveley) **3-8-11**(5) GLee(1) (trckd ldrs: effrt on ins over 2f out: ev ch over 1f out: unable qckn ins fnl f)...........................................................................................2 **3** 7/1 83 28
2001[2] **Alambar (IRE) (78)** (PTWalwyn) **3-9-1** RHills(2) (lw: led: rdn over 2f out: hung rt & strly pressed over 1f out: sn hdd: nt qckn)...........................................................................................................nk **4** 9/4[2] 81 26
(SP 110.4%) **4 Rn**

**1m 43.1** (1.80) CSF £7.25 TOTE £2.50: (£1.90) OWNER Mr K. Abdulla (BECKHAMPTON) BRED Juddmonte Farms
**1797* Victorian Style** fulfilled the promise of her Haydock victory and did so on much faster ground. She is clearly going the right way. (3/1)
**915 Pasternak** was slightly outpaced when the race developed entering the final two furlongs, but rallied in tremendous style. A slightly stiffer test of stamina would suit him and he should soon lose his maiden certificate. (11/8)
**689 Flying North (IRE)**, having his first outing for eleven weeks, ran really well and should not be long in finding winning form. (7/1: 5/1-8/1)
**2001 Alambar (IRE)**, who did the donkey work, proved a hard rival to overhaul and was only mastered entering the final furlong. (9/4)

## 2895 EAST MIDLAND COMMERCIALS-SCANIA KNOW HOW RATING RELATED MAIDEN STKS (0-65) (3-Y.O) (Class F)

4-35 (4-35) **1m 1f 213y** £2,833.20 (£785.20: £375.60) Stalls: Low GOING minus 0.62 sec per fur (F)

SP RR SF

**Circus Star (65)** (SirMarkPrescott) **3-9-0** WWoods(2) (lw: plld hrd: trckd ldrs: shkn up 3f out: styd on u.p to ld wl ins fnl f)..........................................................................................................— **1** 5/4[1] 77 29
2384[3] **Trilby (65)** (PFICole) **3-8-11** TIves(5) (lw: led: rdn & strly pressed over 2f out: rdr dropped whip: hdd wl ins fnl f: no ex)...........................................................................................................½ **2** 3/1[2] 73 25
2397[3] **Phantom Haze (64)** (MissSEHall) **3-8-11**(3) SDrowne(9) (trckd ldrs: effrt & ev ch 2f out: wknd fnl f)..................6 **3** 5/1[3] 67 19
1906[4] **Larissa (IRE) (64)** (GWragg) **3-8-11** RHills(4) (in tch: hdwy & ev ch over 2f out: no ex fr over 1f out)..............¾ **4** 5/1[3] 62 14
2506[8] **Vendetta (62)** (IABalding) **3-8-11** TSprake(8) (trckd ldrs: chal wl over 2f out: wknd wl over 1f out).....................5 **5** 12/1 54 6
**The Legions Pride (56)** (JWHills) **3-9-0** SWhitworth(6) (bhd: drvn along & outpcd appr st: no imp after: t.o) ..10 **6** 20/1 41 —
1641[12] **Tom Swift (IRE) (60)** (RCSpicer) **3-8-9**(5) PPMurphy(3) (chsd ldrs tl lost pl 4f out: sn bhd: t.o).........................12 **7** 33/1 22 —
2189[12] **Crown And Cushion (23)** (KSBridgwater) **3-9-0** VSlattery(1) (cl up tl lost pl qckly over 4f out: sn wl bhd: t.o) 17 **8** 50/1 — —
(SP 120.1%) **8 Rn**

**2m 4.9** (2.40) CSF £5.72 TOTE £2.10: £1.20 £1.50 £1.10 (£3.00) Trio £4.70 OWNER Mr Neil Greig (NEWMARKET) BRED Side Hill Stud and Floors Farming
STEWARDS' ENQUIRY Woods susp. 29-30/7/96 (excessive use of whip).
**Circus Star** looked fit and well for this belated seasonal debut. Taking a very keen hold in the early stages, he stayed on strongly under pressure to wear down the runner-up well inside the final furlong. With this run under his belt, he can go on from here. (5/4)
**2384 Trilby** attempted to lead from pillar-to-post but was collared by the winner well inside the final furlong after her rider had dropped his whip. She would probably have been beaten anyway. (3/1)
**2397 Phantom Haze**, in with every chance two furlongs out, weakened noticeably in the final furlong. (5/1)
**1906 Larissa (IRE)**, stepping up in distance, had every chance approaching the final quarter-mile, but could then do no more. (5/1)
**Vendetta** moved through to have every chance in the straight, but was out on her feet over a furlong from home. (12/1: op 8/1)

## 2896 SCANIA 4-SERIES 'KING OF THE ROAD' H'CAP (0-70) (3-Y.O+) (Class E)

5-05 (5-07) **1m 1f 213y** £3,588.90 (£1,075.20: £516.60: £237.30) Stalls: Low GOING minus 0.62 sec per fur (F)

SP RR SF

2716* **Mazilla (46)** (AStreeter) **4-8-13** SWhitworth(4) (lw: hld up: stdy hdwy on ins fr 3f out: led over 1f out: drvn clr)..........................................................................................................................— **1** 5/2[1] 59+ 29
2378[4] **Ragsak Jameel (USA) (67)** (MajorWRHern) **3-9-10b** RHills(7) (led: rdn 2f out: hdd over 1f out: nt pce of wnr)............................................................................................................................1¾ **2** 7/1[2] 77 37
2563* **Milltown Classic (IRE) (33)** (JParkes) **4-8-0** NCarlisle(5) (chsd ldrs: rdn 3f out: one pce fr wl over 1f out)........1 **3** 10/1 42 12
2776[6] **Augustan (51)** (SGollings) **5-9-4** VHalliday(6) (s.i.s: bhd: effrt over 3f out: kpt on wl fnl 2f: nrst fin)....................2 **4** 16/1 56 26
2574[15] **Lady Sabina (36)** (WJMusson) **6-8-3** DeclanO'Shea(14) (b: dwlt: hld up & bhd: effrt wl over 2f out: styd on wl fnl f)........................................................................................................................½ **5** 20/1 41 11
2540* **Racing Hawk (USA) (53)** (MSSaunders) **4-9-1**(5) PPMurphy(9) (chsd ldrs: rdn 3f out: one pce fnl 2f)............1¼ **6** 9/1[3] 56 26
2793* **Royal Thimble (IRE) (55)** (NoelChance) **5-9-3v**(5) 5x ADaly(15) (in tch: rdn 3f out: nt pce of ldrs fnl 2f).............2 **7** 7/1[2] 54 24
2574[13] **Zahran (IRE) (39)** (JMBradley) **5-8-3**(3) SDrowne(1) (hdwy 3f out: no imp on ldrs fr wl over 1f out)....................½ **8** 12/1 38 8
2574[8] **Course Fishing (40)** (BAMcMahon) **5-8-7** FNorton(10) (racd keenly: trckd ldrs: rdn wl over 2f out: sn btn)....s.h **9** 7/1[2] 39 9
2409[14] **Conic Hill (IRE) (49)** (JPearce) **5-9-2** GBardwell(8) (in tch tl rdn & btn 2f out).............................................4 **10** 16/1 41 11
*12*[7] **Pat's Splendour (43)** (HJCollingridge) **5-8-10** NAdams(11) (nvr nr ldrs).........................................................4 **11** 25/1 29 —
2366[8] **D'naan (IRE) (62)** (WJHaggas) **3-8-12b**(7) ElizabethTurner(2) (nvr trbld ldrs).................................................¾ **12** 25/1 46 6
*2369*[6] **Shuttlecock (38)** (MrsNMacauley) **5-8-2**(3)ow2 CTeague(13) (hdwy on outside to chse ldrs whn rn wd ent st: sn btn)...................................................................................................................½ **13** 20/1 22 —

| | | | | | |
|---|---|---|---|---|---|
| 2573[4] **Benjamins Law (47)** (JAPickering) **5-9-0** TIves(12) (lw: trckd ldrs tl rdn & btn wl over 2f out) .....4 | **14** | 14/1 | 24 | — |
| 1821[3] **Fresh Look (IRE) (44)** (RCSpicer) **4-8-11b** TSprake(3) (a bhd: lost tch over 3f out: t.o) .....12 | **15** | 10/1 | 2 | — |
| | | (SP 137.6%) | **15 Rn** | |

**2m 4.7** (2.20) CSF £22.53 CT £152.62 TOTE £4.50: £2.30 £2.90 £4.80 (£12.60) Trio £90.60 OWNER Mr M. Rhodes (UTTOXETER) BRED Mrs H. MacFarlane
WEIGHT FOR AGE 3yo-10lb
**2716* Mazilla** followed up her recent selling race win at Warwick in tremendous style, and is clearly in great heart at present. (5/2)
**2378 Ragsak Jameel (USA)** attempted to lead from pillar-to-post and ran well under topweight, but was no match for the winner when the chips were down. (7/1: 5/1-8/1)
**2563* Milltown Classic (IRE)**, a shock winner at Musselburgh last time, ran really well again, but could find only one pace in the last quarter-mile. (10/1)
**2776 Augustan** did his best work as usual in the closing stages and was never nearer than at the line. (16/1)
**1696 Lady Sabina**, out the back for most of the race, stayed on really well in the closing stages to be nearest at the finish. (20/1)
**2540* Racing Hawk (USA)** could find only one pace when the chips were down in the final quarter-mile. (9/1)
**2793* Royal Thimble (IRE)** (7/1: op 4/1)

T/Plpt: £9.20 (781.75 Tckts). T/Qdpt: £6.90 (34.55 Tckts). O'R

## 2568-RIPON (R-H) (Good to firm)
## Saturday July 20th
WEATHER: hot & sunny WIND: almost nil

### 2897 E.B.F. ST. GEMMA'S HOSPICE MAIDEN STKS (2-Y.O) (Class D)
2-35 (2-36) **5f** £3,436.25 (£1,040.00: £507.50: £241.25) Stalls: Low GOING minus 0.47 sec per fur (F)

| | | SP | RR | SF |
|---|---|---|---|---|
| 2758[5] **Tear White (IRE)** (TGMills) **2-9-0b** TWilliams(7) (mde all: styd on fnl f) .....— | **1** | 14/1 | 52 | 31 |
| 2720[8] **Mazil** (TDEasterby) **2-9-0b[1]** MBirch(2) (trckd ldrs: rdn 2f out: kpt on ins fnl f) .....2½ | **2** | 14/1 | 44 | 23 |
| 1344[2] **Night Flight** (JJO'Neill) **2-9-0** KDarley(3) (chsd wnr: rdn over 1f out: grad wknd) .....nk | **3** | 7/4[1] | 43 | 22 |
| 2485[4] **Cherokee Flight** (MrsJRRamsden) **2-9-0** MRimmer(6) (bit bkwd: sn outpcd: sme hdwy 2f out: nvr rchd ldrs) .....1½ | **4** | 12/1 | 38 | 17 |
| **Denton Lad** (JWWatts) **2-9-0** NConnorton(5) (cmpt: bit bkwd: sn outpcd & pushed along: hdwy over 1f out: nvr nr to chal) .....1¼ | **5** | 9/2[3] | 34+ | 13 |
| 2327[4] **No Extradition** (MrsJRRamsden) **2-9-0** MDeering(1) (swtg: s.i.s: bhd: sme hdwy over 1f out: nvr nr to chal) .¾ | **6** | 11/2 | 32+ | 11 |
| 2562[3] **Soda** (TDBarron) **2-9-0** JFortune(4) (lw: sn outpcd & rdn along: n.d) .....6 | **7** | 9/4[2] | 13 | — |
| | | (SP 121.7%) | **7 Rn** | |

**60.0 secs** (1.60) CSF £153.12 TOTE £16.90: £3.30 £5.10 (£63.40) OWNER A W Lawson & Co Ltd (EPSOM) BRED A. F. O'Callaghan
OFFICIAL EXPLANATION **Tear White (IRE): had been slowly away and unable to act on the undulating track at Brighton, on his previous run.**
**1632 Tear White (IRE)**, who has shown more temperament than ability in the past, did nothing wrong here. Overcoming the worst draw, he was soon showing them a clean pair of heels but, to be honest, the opposition was weak. (14/1)
**Mazil**, in blinkers, stuck on under pressure to finish second best. (14/1)
**1344 Night Flight**, who had been absent for fifty-nine days after being off colour with a cold and a runny nose, was the only one who looked like making a race of it with the winner but, under pressure over a furlong out, he gradually faded. No doubt the outing will bring him on. (7/4)
**2485 Cherokee Flight** still looked very burly. Soon taken off his legs, he was staying on at the finish and will improve, especially over further. (12/1: op 8/1)
**Denton Lad**, who looked as if the outing would do him good, was staying on late in the day. (9/2)
**2327 No Extradition**, on his toes and sweating beforehand, missed the break slightly and was soon out with the washing. Sticking on at the finish, he has improvement in him in time. (11/2: op 5/2)

### 2898 CENTAUR (S) STKS (3-Y.O+) (Class F)
3-10 (3-10) **1m** £2,600.00 (£725.00: £350.00) Stalls: High GOING minus 0.47 sec per fur (F)

| | | SP | RR | SF |
|---|---|---|---|---|
| 2526[7] **Roi de la Mer (IRE) (65)** (JAkehurst) **5-9-7** KDarley(8) (lw: trckd ldrs: styd on to ld ins fnl f: drvn clr) .....— | **1** | Evens[1] | 53 | 35 |
| *2636[2]* **Sis Garden (48)** (TDEasterby) **3-8-4b**ow1 MBirch(9) (trckd ldr: lft in ld over 4f out: hdd ins fnl f: fnd nil) .....2 | **2** | 6/1[3] | 40 | 13 |
| 1821[14] **Dance of Joy (30)** (JMCarr) **4-9-2** NKennedy(3) (bhd tl hdwy over 1f out: styd on towards fin) .....2½ | **3** | 20/1 | 39 | 21 |
| 2380[4] **Miletrian City (53)** (JBerry) **3-8-8b** SDWilliams(11) (hld up: effrt over 3f out: one pce fnl 2f) .....½ | **4** | 10/1 | 38 | 12 |
| 2520[8] **Battle Colours (IRE) (30)** (DonEnricoIncisa) **7-9-7** KimTinkler(6) (lw: chsd ldrs tl wknd 2f out) .....4 | **5** | 33/1 | 35 | 17 |
| 479[8] **Nukud (USA)** (GROldroyd) **4-9-2** JLowe(7) (bhd: sme hdwy 2f out: n.d) .....1½ | **6** | 33/1 | 27 | 9 |
| 2391[9] **Blue Grit (51)** (MDods) **10-9-7b** JFortune(12) (chsd ldrs tl wknd over 1f out) .....¾ | **7** | 9/1 | 31 | 13 |
| 2366[12] **Irie Mon (IRE) (50)** (MPBielby) **4-9-2**(5) LNewton(5) (in tch: effrt u.p over 3f out: wknd 2f out) .....hd | **8** | 14/1 | 30 | 12 |
| 2520[3] **Double Oscar (IRE) (65)** (MJohnston) **3-8-13v[1]** TWilliams(4) (sn chsng ldrs: wknd 2f out) .....2½ | **9** | 11/4[2] | 25 | — |
| 2801[9] **Steel Sovereign (32)** (MDods) **5-9-7** DaleGibson(10) (a in rr) .....hd | **10** | 33/1 | 25 | 7 |
| 2718[15] **Mr Blue** (GPKelly) **4-8-11**(5) GParkin(1) (led: ran v.wd ent st: bhd & eased fnl 2f) .....22 | **11** | 33/1 | — | — |
| | | (SP 133.2%) | **11 Rn** | |

**1m 40.8** (3.10) CSF £8.71 TOTE £2.10: £1.20 £1.50 £5.60 (£7.10) Trio £235.90; £99.71 to Ayr 21/7/96 OWNER Foundation Developments Ltd (LAMBOURN) BRED Yeomanstown Lodge Stud
WEIGHT FOR AGE 3yo-8lb
Bt in 7,200 gns
**2058 Roi de la Mer (IRE)**, well supported, came with a well-timed run to take it in decisive fashion. He does not always find much off the bridle. (Evens)
**2636 Sis Garden**, tanking along when left in front turning in, found nothing at all when challenged by the winner. (6/1)
**1311 Dance of Joy**, who never runs twice alike, consented to stay on late in the day. (20/1)
**2380 Miletrian City**, with the blinkers on again, stuck on in half-hearted fashion. (10/1: op 5/1)

### 2899 READ HIND STEWART MEDIAN AUCTION MAIDEN STKS (3-Y.O) (Class E)
3-40 (3-41) **1m 1f** £3,047.50 (£910.00: £435.00: £197.50) Stalls: High GOING: minus 0.47 sec per fur (F)

| | | SP | RR | SF |
|---|---|---|---|---|
| 2399[5] **Disallowed (IRE) (71)** (MBell) **3-8-2**(7) GFaulkner(6) (trckd ldrs: effrt over 1f out: hrd rdn & styd on to ld post) .....— | **1** | 5/1[2] | 79 | 26 |

25572 **King of Sparta (80)** (LMCumani) **3-9-0** KDarley(7) (lw: led tl last stride)....s.h **2** 8/11 1 84 31
25723 **Dispol Gem (72)** (GROldroyd) **3-8-9** JFortune(4) (chsd ldrs: effrt & swtchd lft 2f out: kpt on one pce)....4 **3** 6/1 3 72 19
**Sawa-Id** (JHMGosden) **3-9-0** DaleGibson(5) (bit bkwd: stumbled s: sn chsng ldrs: ev ch over 2f out: wknd over 1f out)....7 **4** 5/1 2 64 11
**Swynford Supreme** (JFBottomley) **3-9-0** JLowe(1) (rangy: unf: s.i.s: rn green & bhd: sme hdwy 2f out: nvr nr ldrs)....2½ **5** 20/1 60 7
20484 **Belbay Star** (JLEyre) **3-8-6**(3) MHenry(2) (trckd ldrs: effrt over 3f out: wknd over 1f out)....1¼ **6** 14/1 53 —
258718 **Paper Maze (43)** (EHOwenjun) **3-8-6**(3) DarrenMoffatt(3) (prom early: lost pl 6f out: hung rt & sn bhd)....13 **7** 66/1 30 —
(SP 118.4%) **7 Rn**

**1m 53.4** (3.20) CSF £9.29 TOTE £5.50: £2.20 £1.40 (£3.20) OWNER Mr K. Ratcliffe (NEWMARKET) BRED Dermot Ryan and Partners
STEWARDS' ENQUIRY Faulkner susp. 29-30/7/96 (excessive use of whip)
**2399 Disallowed (IRE)**, who showed a good action going down, responded to her rider's every urging to snatch the race out of the fire right on the line. (5/1)
**2557 King of Sparta** made the running. His rider looked reluctant to pick up his whip and, when he did inside the last, there was not a lot forthcoming, and they were pipped on the line. (8/11: 4/5-Evens)
**2572 Dispol Gem** proved very one-paced. (6/1)
**Sawa-Id**, who had just one outing at two, looked badly in need of the outing. After losing ground by stumbling leaving the stalls, he had every chance, but tied up badly over a furlong out. It will be interesting to see how he fares in handicaps with another outing under his belt. (5/1: op 3/1)
**Swynford Supreme**, who looks badly in need of plenty of time, showed a glimmer of ability, staying on late in the day after running very green. (20/1)
**2048 Belbay Star**, nibbled at in the betting, would not settle and dropped out over a furlong out. (14/1: op 25/1)

## 2900 RIPON BELL-RINGER H'CAP (0-85) (3-Y.O+) (Class D)

4-10 (4-12) **1m 4f 60y** £7,058.75 (£2,120.00: £1,022.50: £473.75) Stalls: Low GOING minus 0.47 sec per fur (F)

SP RR SF

23309 **Highflying (77)** (GMMoore) **10-9-12** KDarley(5) (sn trckng ldrs: effrt over 3f out: r.o to ld ins fnl f: hld on towards fin)....— **1** 7/1 86 58
2631* **Etterby Park (USA) (66)** (MJohnston) **3-8-3** JFanning(7) (led: rdn over 1f out: hdd ins fnl f: r.o)....hd **2** 11/4 1 75 35
24872 **Far Ahead (75)** (JLEyre) **4-9-7**(3) OPears(8) (chsd ldrs: effrt over 3f out: edgd rt & kpt on one pce fnl 2f)....4 **3** 6/1 3 79 51
23006 **Western Sal (70)** (JLHarris) **4-9-5** DaleGibson(3) (sn bhd: pushed along 7f out: sme hdwy 3f out: nvr nr to chal)....3½ **4** 7/1 69 41
27793 **Kings Cay (IRE) (60)** (THCaldwell) **5-8-4**(5) KMChin(10) (trckd ldrs: effrt & swtchd outside 4f out: one pce fnl 2f)....3½ **5** 9/2 2 55 27
24018 **Riparius (USA) (79)** (HCandy) **5-10-0b** JFortune(1) (sn trckng ldrs: rdn over 3f out: hung rt & wknd 2f out) ...hd **6** 15/2 73 45
23003 **Quivira (69)** (HAkbary) **5-9-4** DBiggs(6) (chsd ldrs: drvn along 7f out: outpcd fnl 4f)....4 **7** 6/1 3 58 30
23666 **Indonesian (IRE) (62)** (PCalver) **4-8-11** MBirch(2) (plld hrd: stdd after 2f: effrt on outside 4f out: sn wknd: virtually p.u 2f out)....dist **8** 10/1 — —
(SP 119.3%) **8 Rn**

**2m 36.2** (2.20) CSF £26.33 CT £114.85 TOTE £8.00: £1.80 £1.60 £2.20 (£13.60) Trio £21.80 OWNER Mr B. Batey (MIDDLEHAM) BRED Juddmonte Farms
WEIGHT FOR AGE 3yo-12lb
OFFICIAL EXPLANATION **Indonesian (IRE): suffered an overreach on his near-fore.**
**1428 Highflying**, a grand old stager, recorded his fourteenth victory. Proving as game as ever under pressure, he now tackles the Brown Jack at Ascot, a race he won last year. (7/1)
**2631* Etterby Park (USA)**, raised 9lb, set out to make it all. He battled back when headed and should soon regain the winning thread. (11/4)
**2487 Far Ahead** tended to edge right under pressure and lacked the pace to get near the first two. (6/1)
**2300 Western Sal**, soon behind and off the bit, stayed on at her own speed up the straight. (7/1)
**2779 Kings Cay (IRE)**, who has been very busy, could find no more in the final quarter-mile. (9/2)
**1802 Riparius (USA)** did not look happy under pressure. (15/2)

## 2901 LEEDS HOSPITAL FUND H'CAP (0-80) (3-Y.O+) (Class D)

4-40 (4-41) **1m 2f** £3,850.00 (£1,150.00: £550.00: £250.00) Stalls: High GOING: minus 0.47 sec per fur (F)

SP RR SF

24835 **Percy Braithwaite (IRE) (78)** (MJohnston) **4-9-9**(5) KMChin(3) (trckd ldrs: effrt over 3f out: styd on u.p: hrd rdn & led wl ins fnl f)....— **1** 4/1 3 90 60
25252 **Voila Premiere (IRE) (65)** (MHTompkins) **4-9-1** DaleGibson(5) (lw: w ldr: led over 4f out: hung rt over 2f out: sn clr: hdd wl ins fnl f)....1¼ **2** 9/4 1 75 45
22469 **South Sea Bubble (IRE) (66)** (LMCumani) **4-9-2** KDarley(6) (lw: hld up: outpcd over 4f out: styd on fnl 2f: r.o ins fnl f)....½ **3** 13/2 75 45
25244 **Superpride (59)** (MrsMReveley) **4-8-9** MBirch(7) (led tl over 4f out: edgd lft over 1f out: kpt on one pce)....2½ **4** 8/1 64 34
23184 **Mallooh (70)** (JHMGosden) **3-8-7**(3) MHenry(4) (trckd ldrs: effrt over 3f out: one pce)....½ **5** 11/4 2 74 34
23329 **Kissel (75)** (AHarrison) **4-9-4**(7) GFaulkner(2) (hdwy on outside over 5f out: lost pl over 2f out: eased)....21 **6** 12/1 46 16
26785 **Talented Ting (IRE) (60)** (PCHaslam) **7-8-10** JFortune(1) (chsd ldrs: drvn along over 4f out: sn lost pl & eased: t.o)....dist **7** 7/1 — —
(SP 122.1%) **7 Rn**

**2m 5.1** (1.60) CSF £13.98 TOTE £4.20: £2.40 £2.10 (£5.70) OWNER Brian Yeardley Continental Ltd (MIDDLEHAM) BRED J. G. O'Brien in Ireland
WEIGHT FOR AGE 3yo-10lb
STEWARDS' ENQUIRY Chin susp. 29-30/7/96 (excessive use of whip).
**2483 Percy Braithwaite (IRE)** was given a more patient ride than usual. Capably handled, he stayed on in good style to lead inside the last and give his Hong Kong apprentice his second British winner here on his twenty-second birthday. (4/1)
**2525 Voila Premiere (IRE)** made the best of his way home. Hanging right and ending up on the far rail, he had no answer to the winner's late burst. (9/4)
**South Sea Bubble (IRE)**, who has slipped down the weights, was tapped for foot early in the straight. Staying on in good style inside the last, she just failed to get up for second. (13/2: 4/1-7/1)
**2524 Superpride**, who had never run over seven furlongs before, made the running at his own pace. Keeping on when headed, despite edging out towards the centre, he seemed to stay the trip all right. (8/1)
**2318 Mallooh**, an angular gelding on his debut in handicap company, raced keenly early on. Caught flat-footed just under half a mile from home, he could do no more than keep on at the one pace. He either needs a stronger gallop or further. (11/4)

## 2902 TONY COCKERHAM MEMORIAL MAIDEN H'CAP (0-70) (3-Y.O+) (Class E)
5-10 (5-11) **6f** £3,210.00 (£960.00: £460.00: £210.00) Stalls: Low GOING: minus 0.47 sec per fur (F)

| | | | SP | RR | SF |
|---|---|---|---|---|---|
| 2732[2] | **Camionneur (IRE) (48)** (TDEasterby) **3-8-9b** JLowe(2) (effrt & nt clr run ½-wy: sn chsng ldrs: styd on & hung rt to ld nr fin) —— | **1** | 11/10[1] | 52 | 23 |
| 2286[8] | **Newlands Corner (37)** (JAkehurst) **3-7-12b[1]** TWilliams(9) (a chsng ldrs: hrd rdn & styd on to ld wl ins fnl f: jst ct) s.h | **2** | 12/1 | 41 | 12 |
| 2378[14] | **Barranak (IRE) (58)** (GMMcCourt) **4-9-10** SDWilliams(11) (bmpd s: sn chsng ldrs: led ins fnl f: sn hdd & nt qckn) nk | **3** | 12/1 | 61 | 37 |
| 1888[5] | **Madam Zando (48)** (JBalding) **3-8-2(7)** JEdmunds(5) (a chsng ldrs: nt qckn ins fnl f) nk | **4** | 8/1 | 50 | 21 |
| 2163[9] | **Harriet's Beau (36)** (MWEasterby) **3-7-11bow1** DaleGibson(10) (led tl hdd & wknd ins fnl f) 1¼ | **5** | 12/1 | 35 | 5 |
| 2520[7] | **Backhander (IRE) (51)** (MartynWane) **4-8-12(5)** PRoberts(1) (chsd ldrs: one pce fnl f) 2 | **6** | 6/1[3] | 45 | 21 |
| 2316[10] | **Lapu-Lapu (50)** (MJCamacho) **3-8-11** MBirch(12) (swvd lft s: stdy hdwy ½-wy: nvr plcd to chal) 1½ | **7** | 4/1[2] | 40 | 11 |
| 2236[5] | **Nutcracker Suite (IRE) (42)** (JLEyre) **4-8-5(3)** MHenry(3) (mid div: effrt u.p ½-wy: nvr nr ldrs) s.h | **8** | 16/1 | 32 | 8 |
| 2672[10] | **Dona Filipa (36)** (MissLCSiddall) **3-7-8(3)ow1** DarrenMoffatt(8) (prom over 3f: sn outpcd) s.h | **9** | 25/1 | 25 | — |
| *2368*[6] | **Oare Budgie (35)** (DonEnricoIncisa) **3-7-10v** KimTinkler(4) (s.i.s: a wl outpcd & sn drvn along) hd | **10** | 33/1 | 24 | — |
| 2359[5] | **Distinctly Swingin (IRE) (40)** (MissLAPerratt) **3-8-1** JFanning(7) (in tch to ½-wy: sn lost pl) s.h | **11** | 14/1 | 29 | — |
| 2392[8] | **Dancing Jazztime (30)** (JSWainwright) **5-7-10v[1]** NKennedy(6) (chsd ldrs: hung lft & lost pl ½-wy: sn bhd) 13 | **12** | 50/1 | — | — |
| | | | (SP 137.4%) | | **12 Rn** |

**1m 12.7** (2.20) CSF £18.07 CT £127.07 TOTE £2.20: £1.10 £3.40 £4.30 (£29.30) Trio £69.50 OWNER T E F Freight (Scarborough) Ltd (MALTON) BRED K. Purfield

LONG HANDICAP Dona Filipa 7-5 Harriet's Beau 7-7 Dancing Jazztime 7-0

WEIGHT FOR AGE 3yo-5lb

STEWARDS' ENQUIRY T. Williams susp. 29-30/7/96 (incorrect use of whip).

**2732 Camionneur (IRE)** made it twenty-two lucky. Meeting trouble at halfway, he almost threw it away by hanging violently right near the line. (11/10: 7/4-Evens)

**Newlands Corner**, in blinkers for the first time, stuck on under strong pressure to show ahead in the final 50 yards, but was pipped in the last strides. She had a hard race. (12/1)

**951 Barranak (IRE)** took a bump at the start. Showing ahead halfway through the final furlong, he was edged out near the line. His draw did not help. (12/1: op 8/1)

**1888 Madam Zando** forced her way almost upsides inside the last but could then find no more. (8/1)

**Harriet's Beau**, who ran over nine furlongs last time, showed these rivals a clean pair of heels until running out of petrol inside the last. (12/1: op 8/1)

**857 Lapu-Lapu** went left coming out of the stalls, bumping Barranak. Moving up travelling nicely at halfway, she was by no means knocked about and there is still hope for her. (4/1)

T/Plpt: £616.10 (18.69 Tckts). T/Qdpt: £3.00 (215.97 Tckts). WG

# 2714-**WARWICK (L-H) (Firm)**
## Saturday July 20th
WEATHER: sunny & hot WIND: nil

## 2903 FERNDALE APPRENTICE H'CAP (0-70) (3-Y.O+) (Class F)
6-35 (6-35) **7f** £2,494.00 (£709.00: £352.00) Stalls: Low GOING minus 0.69 sec per fur (HD)

| | | | SP | RR | SF |
|---|---|---|---|---|---|
| 2032[9] | **Whatever's Right (IRE) (60)** (MDIUsher) **7-9-3(7)** RBrisland(7) (a.p: led over 2f out: rdn over 1f out: r.o wl) —— | **1** | 8/1 | 69 | 53 |
| 2757[5] | **Aquado (57)** (SRBowring) **7-9-7b** DDenby(3) (hld up: hdwy over 2f out: rdn & ev ch over 1f out: btn whn hung lft ins fnl f) 3½ | **2** | 3/1[1] | 58 | 42 |
| 2602[5] | **Paddy's Rice (60)** (MMcCormack) **5-9-10** JWilkinson(1) (hld up & bhd: hdwy on ins 2f out: sn rdn: swtchd rt ins fnl f: r.o) hd | **3** | 4/1[3] | 61 | 45 |
| 2431[5] | **Flag Fen (USA) (59)** (MartynMeade) **5-8-13(10)** ClaireAngell(4) (lw: hld up & bhd: hmpd over 2f out: hdwy over 1f out: one pce fnl f) 3 | **4** | 14/1 | 53 | 37 |
| 2405[8] | **Mr Cube (IRE) (54)** (JMBradley) **6-8-13b(5)** CLowther(5) (a.p: 3rd & btn whn bdly hmpd ins fnl f) 2 | **5** | 100/30[2] | 43 | 27 |
| *2550*[8] | **Sharp Holly (IRE) (46)** (JABennett) **4-8-10b** RMullen(2) (lw: hld up: rn wd bnd over 2f out: rdn & edgd rt over 1f out: no hdwy) hd | **6** | 25/1 | 35 | 19 |
| *2632*[3] | **Have a Nightcap (39)** (NPLittmoden) **7-7-12v(5)ow2** DavidO'Neill(9) (lw: prom 5f) 4 | **7** | 10/1 | 19 | 1 |
| *277*[6] | **Hotlips Houlihan (46)** (RJRWilliams) **3-8-3** KSked(8) (led over 3f: wknd wl over 1f out) 3½ | **8** | 13/2 | 18 | — |
| 2392[6] | **Respectable Jones (38)** (RHollinshead) **10-7-6b(10)** SCrawford(6) (w ldr: led over 3f out tl over 2f out: sn wknd) 1 | **9** | 33/1 | 8 | — |
| | | | (SP 115.1%) | | **9 Rn** |

**1m 24.4** (-0.20) CSF £30.42 CT £102.03 TOTE £9.30: £3.10 £1.40 £1.80 (£17.80) Trio £28.20 OWNER Mr M. S. C. Thurgood (SWINDON) BRED Rockville House Stud

WEIGHT FOR AGE 3yo-7lb

**IN-FOCUS: This was a first career winner for Brisland.**

**Whatever's Right (IRE)** took advantage of a 7lb drop in the Ratings since his last run. (8/1: 6/1-10/1)

**2757 Aquado** has yet to win beyond the minimum trip on turf, and the Stewards told his trainer they did not consider the gelding a suitable ride for an apprentice. (3/1)

**2602 Paddy's Rice** was never going to get to grips with the leaders in time. (4/1)

**2431 Flag Fen (USA)**, back to something like a more suitable trip, could well have found this ground too lively. (14/1: op 8/1)

**2405 Mr Cube (IRE)**, blinkered instead of the usual visor, had been dropped to a mark 1lb lower than when he last won. He could have finished third had his rider not been forced to snatch up against the rail. (100/30)

**2632 Have a Nightcap** (10/1: op 6/1)

## 2904 LAMMAS FIELD MAIDEN AUCTION STKS (2-Y.O) (Class F)
7-05 (7-07) **7f** £2,857.00 (£792.00: £379.00) Stalls: Low GOING minus 0.69 sec per fur (HD)

| | | | SP | RR | SF |
|---|---|---|---|---|---|
| 2714[2] | **Double Gold** (BJMeehan) **2-8-4** BDoyle(1) (lw: mde all: qcknd clr 2f out: hrd rdn over 1f out: all out) —— | **1** | 3/1[1] | 63 | 14 |

2309[5] **Kaiser Kache (IRE)** (KMcAuliffe) **2-8-7** WJO'Connor(8) (a.p: chsd wnr over 3f out: outpcd 2f out: r.o ins fnl f) ....1 **2** 8/1 64 15
2600[8] **Ivory Dawn** (KTIvory) **2-8-2** NAdams(11) (hdwy 2f out: rdn & hung lft over 1f out: hung lft ins fnl f: r.o)....1 **3** 10/1 56 7
1884[6] **Skelton Sovereign (IRE)** (RHollinshead) **2-8-2**(3) FLynch(6) (s.s: hdwy over 1f out: nvr nrr) ....½ **4** 33/1 58 9
2254[6] **Herbshan Dancer** (BRMillman) **2-8-0**(3) SDrowne(9) (hdwy over 1f out: r.o ins fnl f) ....s.h **5** 20/1 56 7
2733[2] **Smugurs (IRE)** (RJRWilliams) **2-8-0** JQuinn(10) (prom: rdn & one pce fnl 2f) ....½ **6** 4/1 [2] 52 3
2714[4] **Zanabay** (MartynMeade) **2-8-4** FNorton(5) (hrd rdn over 2f out: no hdwy)....2½ **7** 33/1 50 1
2040[12] **Jack The Lad (IRE)** (CMurray) **2-8-9** MTebbutt(3) (lw: chsd wnr over 3f: wknd wl over 1f out) ....2½ **8** 9/2 [3] 50 1
2187[5] **My Precious** (MMcCormack) **2-8-2** SSanders(2) (hdwy 3f out: wknd wl over 1f out)....2 **9** 16/1 38 —
2712[5] **Shall We Go (IRE)** (RHannon) **2-8-2** JFEgan(4) (nvr gng wl: a bhd)....2½ **10** 12/1 32 —
**Tariff (IRE)** (NAGraham) **2-8-2** TSprake(7) (small: neat: a bhd: t.o fnl 2f)....6 **11** 14/1 19 —
(SP 114.3%) **11 Rn**

**1m 26.2** (1.60) CSF £24.58 TOTE £3.20: £1.40 £2.50 £2.20 (£17.20) Trio £64.30 OWNER Mr Michael Edwards (UPPER LAMBOURN) BRED Catridge Farm Stud Ltd

**2714 Double Gold**, whose rider excels from the front, was at the end of his tether towards the finish, but had poached a big enough lead to last home. (3/1)
**2309 Kaiser Kache (IRE)** was caught a shade flat-footed when the winner went for home, but certainly showed he gets the trip. (8/1)
**Ivory Dawn**, out of a nine-furlong winner, may have given the winner something to think about had her rider pulled his whip through to the left hand. (10/1)
**1884 Skelton Sovereign (IRE)**, a half-brother to Once More For Luck who scored over five furlongs and a mile as a juvenile, found his stamina coming into play late on. (33/1)
**Herbshan Dancer**, a half-brother to ten-furlong winner Slix, ran his best race to date. (20/1)
**2733 Smugurs (IRE)** may have found this coming too soon after Folkestone. (4/1)
**Tariff (IRE)** (14/1: 10/1-16/1)

## 2905 SYD MERCER H'CAP (0-80) (3-Y.O) (Class D)

7-35 (7-35) **1m 2f 169y** £3,694.95 (£1,101.60: £525.30: £237.15) Stalls: Low GOING minus 0.69 sec per fur (HD)

SP RR SF
2768[2] **Allstars Express (62)** (TJNaughton) **3-8-3** TSprake(6) (hld up: hdwy on ins 2f out: led ins fnl f: rdn out) .......— **1** 7/4 [1] 71 16
2576[2] **Infamous (USA) (82)** (PFICole) **3-9-4**(5) DGriffiths(5) (hld up: swtchd rt & ev ch over 1f out: unable qckn).....1½ **2** 9/4 [2] 89 34
2542[4] **Spa Lane (55)** (PJMakin) **3-7-10** JQuinn(1) (swtg: led: qcknd over 2f out: hdd ins fnl f) ....1¼ **3** 7/2 [3] 60 5
2736[3] **Baranov (IRE) (63)** (DJGMurraySmith) **3-8-4** DHarrison(4) (plld hrd: trckd ldr: rn wd bnd over 2f out: ev ch over 1f out: one pce) ....nk **4** 7/2 [3] 68 13
(SP 111.6%) **4 Rn**

**2m 15.8** (2.30) CSF £5.79 TOTE £2.40: (£2.50) OWNER The Allstars Club (EPSOM) BRED P. and Mrs Blacker
**2768 Allstars Express**, making a quick reappearance, had no in-form Frog to contend with this time. (7/4)
**2576 Infamous (USA)**, inclined to run about a bit, gave the impression he was feeling the fast ground. (9/4)
**2542 Spa Lane** was running off a mark 8lb higher than when winning at Nottingham. (7/2)
**2736 Baranov (IRE)**, 8lb higher than when winning over course and distance earlier in the month, refused to settle and swung wide as the tempo increased entering the home straight. (7/2)

## 2906 ASHORNE (S) H'CAP (0-60) (3-Y.O+) (Class G)

8-05 (8-05) **1m 4f 115y** £2,070.00 (£570.00: £270.00) Stalls: Low GOING minus 0.69 sec per fur (HD)

SP RR SF
2587[7] **Zeliba (32)** (MrsNMacauley) **4-8-9** JQuinn(5) (b.hind: lw: dwlt: hdwy 2f out: led over 1f out: hrd rdn: r.o wl) ...— **1** 7/2 [2] 43 21
2408[5] **Marchman (47)** (JSKing) **11-9-10** TQuinn(7) (lw: hld up: hdwy 2f out: rdn over 1f out: unable qckn) ....2 **2** 9/4 [1] 55 33
2556* **Dots Dee (30)** (JMBradley) **7-8-7** TSprake(4) (a.p: led wl over 1f out: sn hdd: one pce)....½ **3** 9/4 [1] 38 16
2189[9] **Spice and Sugar (30)** (BRCambidge) **6-8-4**(3) SDrowne(3) (chsd ldr: ev ch 2f out: wknd over 1f out) ....7 **4** 16/1 29 7
2716[3] **Hunza Story (27)** (NPLittmoden) **4-7-11**(7) JoHunnam(6) (plld hrd: led after 3f: sn clr: hdd wl over 1f out: sn wknd)....6 **5** 11/2 [3] 18 —
2056[17] **Rupiana (IRE) (46)** (CMurray) **4-9-9** MTebbutt(1) (led 3f: rdn 3f out: wknd 2f out)....3½ **6** 20/1 33 11
2716[12] **Woodlands Energy (32)** (PAPritchard) **5-8-9** NAdams(2) (hld up & bhd: stdy hdwy 5f out: rdn 3f out: sn wknd)....5 **7** 40/1 12 —
(SP 112.2%) **7 Rn**

**2m 41.5** (3.00) CSF £11.22 TOTE £4.00: £2.50 £2.00 (£4.70) OWNER Mr G. Wiltshire (MELTON MOWBRAY) BRED Sheikh Mohammed bin Rashid al Maktoum
No bid
**2192 Zeliba** appreciated the return to selling company and responded to pressure to forge clear. (7/2)
**2183 Marchman**, back into a seller, was only 2lb higher than when winning at Nottingham. (9/4)
**2556* Dots Dee** was effectively only 2lb higher than when successful at Bath. (9/4)
**Spice and Sugar** has slipped to a mark 19lb lower than when she last won. (16/1)
**2716 Hunza Story** proved too strong in the battle with her rider over who would gain control. (11/2: op 7/2)

## 2907 WARWICK LIMITED STKS (0-80) (3-Y.O+) (Class D)

8-35 (8-36) **7f** £3,661.80 (£1,091.40: £520.20: £234.60) Stalls: Low GOING minus 0.69 sec per fur (HD)

SP RR SF
2687* **Divina Luna (84)** (JWHills) **3-8-8**(3) MHenry(1) (lw: chsd ldr: rdn to ld 1f out: r.o wl) ....— **1** Evens [1] 88 38
2630[2] **Arterxerxes (82)** (MJHeaton-Ellis) **3-8-7**(3) SDrowne(4) (lw: led: shkn up & qcknd 2f out: hdd 1f out: unable qckn) ....¾ **2** 5/2 [2] 85 35
2437[3] **Zelda Zonk (75)** (BJMeehan) **4-9-4** BDoyle(2) (hld up: rdn over 2f out: one pce appr fnl f) ....3 **3** 4/1 [3] 79 36
2034[11] **Dawalib (USA) (63)** (DHaydnJones) **6-9-3** TQuinn(3) (lw: hld up: bhd fnl 2f)....17 **4** 10/1 40 —
(SP 107.7%) **4 Rn**

**1m 24.6** (0.00) CSF £3.61 TOTE £2.00: (£1.50) OWNER Mr D. J. Deer (LAMBOURN) BRED Azienda Agricola Colle Cardella
WEIGHT FOR AGE 3yo-7lb
**2687* Divina Luna**, who only got into this 0-80 on a technicality - she is now rated 84 - scored more decisively than the margin suggests. (Evens)
**2630 Arterxerxes**, raised 4lb for his narrow defeat last time, was another favoured by race conditions, now being rated 82. (5/2: op 6/4)
**2437 Zelda Zonk** would have been receiving weight from the three-year-olds had this been a handicap. (4/1)
**1522 Dawalib (USA)** would have been much better off in a handicap. (10/1: 14/1-8/1)

## 2908 HENLEY IN ARDEN LIMITED STKS (0-70) (3-Y.O+) (Class E)

9-05 (9-05) **5f** £2,988.30 (£890.40: £424.20: £191.10) Stalls: Low GOING minus 0.69 sec per fur (HD)

| | | | | SP | RR | SF |
|---|---|---|---|---|---|---|
| *2684** | **Palacegate Touch (70)** (JBerry) **6-9-8b** GCarter(1) (a.p: rdn 2f out: led over 1f out: r.o) | — | **1** | 5/2$^{2}$ | 78 | 43 |
| 2598$^{3}$ | **Super Rocky (69)** (RBastiman) **7-8-11b**$^{(5)}$ HBastiman(5) (hld up: hdwy over 1f out: hrd rdn fnl f: r.o) | ½ | **2** | 7/2$^{3}$ | 70 | 35 |
| 2564$^{2}$ | **Swan At Whalley (69)** (MartynWane) **4-9-0**$^{(5)}$ PRoberts(6) (w ldr: ev ch over 1f out: unable qckn) | 1¼ | **3** | 9/4$^{1}$ | 69 | 34 |
| 2410$^{4}$ | **Statistician (69)** (JohnBerry) **4-8-11**$^{(5)}$ KMChin(4) (hrd rdn & no hdwy fnl 2f) | 2½ | **4** | 7/2$^{3}$ | 58 | 23 |
| 1161$^{W}$ | **Windrush Boy (64)** (JRBosley) **6-9-2** RPerham(3) (led over 3f: wknd fnl f) | 1½ | **5** | 14/1 | 54 | 19 |
| | | | | (SP 110.5%) | | **5 Rn** |

**58.2 secs** (0.20) CSF £10.61 TOTE £3.10: £1.80 £1.90 (£5.10) OWNER Laurel (Leisure) Ltd (COCKERHAM) BRED The Woodhaven Stud
STEWARDS' ENQUIRY Chin susp. 1-2/8/96 (excessive use of whip).
**2684* Palacegate Touch** scored for the first time over the minimum trip on the Equitrack last week, and it is most unusual for a horse to be suited by shorter distances as he gets older. (5/2)
**2598 Super Rocky** stuck on well under strong pressure but could not peg back the winner. (7/2)
**2564 Swan At Whalley** continued his streak of consistent performances. (9/4)
**2410 Statistician,** whose rider was in hot water earlier in the afternoon for use of the whip at Ripon, again breached the Rules and collected his second two-day ban of the day. (7/2)

T/Plpt: £143.30 (76.1 Tckts). T/Qdpt: £31.00 (19.5 Tckts). KH

# 2871-AYR (L-H) (Good to firm)
## Sunday July 21st

WEATHER: overcast WIND: almost nil

## 2909 E.B.F. SUNDAY MAIL RACING AHEAD MAIDEN STKS (2-Y.O) (Class D)

2-20 (2-20) **7f** £4,157.50 (£1,170.00: £572.50) Stalls: High GOING minus 0.13 sec per fur (G)

| | | | | SP | RR | SF |
|---|---|---|---|---|---|---|
| 2580$^{2}$ | **Equal Rights (IRE)** (PWChapple-Hyam) **2-8-9**$^{(5)}$ RHavlin(1) (hld up: qcknd to ld 3f out: sn pushed clr: eased fnl f) | — | **1** | 1/5$^{1}$ | 87+ | — |
| | **Happy Minstral (USA)** (MJohnston) **2-9-0** JWeaver(3) (w'like: str: trckd ldr: effrt 3f out: no ch w wnr) | 12 | **2** | 9/2$^{2}$ | 60 | — |
| *2370$^{2}$* | **Hurgill Dancer** (JWWatts) **2-9-0** NConnorton(2) (lw: set slow pce: hdd 3f out: sn btn) | 6 | **3** | 33/1$^{3}$ | 46 | — |
| | | | | (SP 104.5%) | | **3 Rn** |

**1m 32.75** (8.75) CSF £1.35 TOTE £1.20 (£1.10) OWNER Mr R. E. Sangster (MARLBOROUGH) BRED Swettenham Stud
**2580 Equal Rights (IRE)**, in a slowly-run race, showed a tremendous turn of foot from halfway and won pulling up. Much better things look on the cards. (1/5)
**Happy Minstral (USA)**, a well-made newcomer, was full of himself in the paddock and ran quite well, although completely outclassed by the winner. (9/2: op 11/4)
**2370 Hurgill Dancer** was the reluctant early leader and was then left struggling in a few strides three furlongs out. (33/1)

## 2910 JOE PUNTER (S) H'CAP (0-60) (3-Y.O+) (Class F)

2-50 (2-50) **5f** £2,944.00 (£892.00: £436.00: £208.00) Stalls: High GOING minus 0.13 sec per fur (G)

| | | | | SP | RR | SF |
|---|---|---|---|---|---|---|
| 2490$^{4}$ | **Sunday Mail Too (IRE) (44)** (MissLAPerratt) **4-8-13** KDarley(12) (trckd ldrs: nt clr run & swtchd over 1f out: r.o to ld nr fin) | — | **1** | 8/1$^{3}$ | 49 | 31 |
| 2680$^{5}$ | **Another Nightmare (IRE) (33)** (RMMcKellar) **4-8-2** TWilliams(4) (hdwy ½-wy: rdn to ld ins fnl f: nt qckn towards fin) | hd | **2** | 14/1 | 38 | 20 |
| 2757$^{9}$ | **Pallium (IRE) (49)** (MrsAMNaughton) **8-9-4** JWeaver(7) (bhd: hdwy 2f out: styd on: nvr able to chal) | 2½ | **3** | 9/2$^{2}$ | 46 | 28 |
| 2800* | **Sunset Harbour (IRE) (50)** (SEKettlewell) **3-9-1** $^{6x}$ JFortune(11) (mde most tl hdd & no ex ins fnl f) | ¾ | **4** | 2/1$^{1}$ | 44 | 22 |
| *2367$^{12}$* | **Rankaidade (27)** (DonEnricoIncisa) **5-7-10** KimTinkler(1) (lw: a.p: rdn ½-wy: one pce) | 1 | **5** | 66/1 | 18 | — |
| 2849$^{6}$ | **Gondo (41)** (EJAlston) **9-8-10v** KFallon(3) (in tch: drvn along 2f out: one pce) | 1½ | **6** | 10/1 | 27 | 9 |
| 2777$^{5}$ | **Marjorie Rose (IRE) (55)** (ABailey) **3-9-3**$^{(3)}$ DWright(6) (b: bhd tl sme late hdwy) | 1¾ | **7** | 14/1 | 36 | 14 |
| 1642$^{18}$ | **Waverley Star (30)** (JSWainwright) **11-7-13b** JQuinn(10) (w ldrs 3f: wknd) | 2 | **8** | 66/1 | 4 | — |
| 2757$^{17}$ | **Tenor (55)** (DNicholls) **5-9-10** AlexGreaves(2) (lw: a bhd) | nk | **9** | 10/1 | 28 | 10 |
| 2771$^{7}$ | **Double Glow (29)** (NBycroft) **4-7-12b** NCarlisle(9) (s.i.s: a outpcd & bhd) | 1¾ | **10** | 12/1 | — | — |
| 2518$^{6}$ | **Kabcast (42)** (DWChapman) **11-8-11b** JCarroll(5) (disp ld to ½-wy: btn whn hmpd over 1f out) | 2 | **11** | 12/1 | 3 | — |
| | | | | (SP 112.5%) | | **11 Rn** |

**60.13 secs** (3.13) CSF £95.90 CT £520.42 TOTE £6.50: £2.20 £5.70 £1.40 (£96.50) Trio £207.20 OWNER Scottish Daily Record & Sunday Mail Ltd (AYR) BRED Miss Ruth Lonergan in Ireland
LONG HANDICAP Rankaidade 7-9
WEIGHT FOR AGE 3yo-4lb
No bid
**2490 Sunday Mail Too (IRE)**, over a trip that has looked too short in the past, did have the best ground for much of it and, when switched, produced a useful burst to get there. (8/1)
**2680 Another Nightmare (IRE)** has been promising to win a race such as this but, despite a determined effort, was just touched off. (14/1)
**2523 Pallium (IRE)** keeps showing signs of coming to form, but is not quite doing enough as yet. (9/2)
**2800* Sunset Harbour (IRE)** had the best of the draw, but had to use herself too much to take advantage of it, and was done with inside the final furlong. (2/1)
**Rankaidade** looks well and ran her best race of the season, but she has only one win to her credit, and that was three years ago on easy ground. (66/1)
**2849 Gondo** was always struggling to keep in touch and had shot his bolt well over a furlong out. (10/1: 6/1-12/1)
**2777 Marjorie Rose (IRE)** (14/1: op 8/1)
**1039 Tenor** (10/1: op 6/1)

## 2911 SUNDAY MAIL H'CAP (0-85) (3-Y.O+) (Class D)

3-20 (3-25) **6f** £4,318.50 (£1,308.00: £639.00: £304.50) Stalls: High GOING minus 0.13 sec per fur (G)

| | | | | SP | RR | SF |
|---|---|---|---|---|---|---|
| 2490$^{3}$ | **Thwaab (53)** (FWatson) **4-7-10v** NKennedy(9) (bhd: swtchd & gd hdwy over 1f out: led ins fnl f: r.o wl) | — | **1** | 14/1 | 62 | 39 |

| | | | | | |
|---|---|---|---|---|---|
| 2431[9] **Tiler (IRE) (78)** (MJohnston) **4-9-7** JWeaver(1) (lw: a cl up: led appr fnl f: sn hdd & nt qckn) ....1¼ | **2** | 12/1 | 84 | 61 |
| 2867[5] **Cheeky Chappy (64)** (DWChapman) **5-8-7b** JQuinn(12) (led tl hdd appr fnl f: no ex) ....1½ | **3** | 13/2[3] | 66 | 43 |
| 2694[11] **Rich Glow (61)** (NBycroft) **5-8-4** KDarley(10) (trckd ldrs: effrt appr fnl f: r.o one pce) ....nk | **4** | 6/1[2] | 62 | 39 |
| 2119* **Garnock Valley (76)** (JBerry) **6-9-5** JCarroll(5) (bhd: hdwy 2f out: nt cl run & swtchd: nrst fin) ....2½ | **5** | 6/1[2] | 70 | 47 |
| 2431[6] **Colway Rake (65)** (JWWatts) **5-8-8b** NConnorton(11) (lw: cl up tl wknd over 1f out) ....3½ | **6** | 20/1 | 50 | 27 |
| 1652[8] **French Grit (IRE) (77)** (MDods) **4-9-6** DeanMcKeown(2) (nvr bttr than mid div) ....hd | **7** | 25/1 | 62 | 39 |
| 2725[7] **Amron (59)** (JBerry) **9-8-2** NCarlisle(8) (lw: sn outpcd & bhd: sme late hdwy) ....1¼ | **8** | 6/1[2] | 40 | 17 |
| 2729[6] **Mister Westsound (70)** (MissLAPerratt) **4-8-6b**(7) JBramhill(6) (chsd ldrs tl rdn & btn wl over 1f out) ....nk | **9** | 11/1 | 51 | 28 |
| 2524[2] **Barato (67)** (MrsJRRamsden) **5-8-10** KFallon(3) (b.nr hind: bhd: effrt ½-wy: no imp) ....½ | **10** | 6/1[2] | 46 | 23 |
| 2532[6] **Whittle Rock (84)** (EJAlston) **3-9-5b**1(3) SDrowne(7) (chsd ldrs 4f: wknd qckly) ....½ | **11** | 12/1 | 62 | 34 |
| 2694[15] **For the Present (85)** (TDBarron) **6-10-0** JFortune(4) (lw: outpcd fr ½-wy) ....4 | **12** | 11/2[1] | 52 | 29 |

(SP 124.9%) **12 Rn**

**1m 11.95** (2.15) CSF £158.96 CT £1,123.16 TOTE £42.70: £8.90 £2.30 £2.20 (£41.40) Trio £251.10 OWNER Mr J. D. Blythe (SEDGEFIELD) BRED Shadwell Estate Company Limited
LONG HANDICAP Thwaab 7-9
WEIGHT FOR AGE 3yo-5lb

**2490 Thwaab**, taken to post early, was then dropped out and, well suited by this, produced a terrific turn of foot to settle it inside the last furlong. (14/1)
**2431 Tiler (IRE)** ran a super race from an impossible draw and looks in really good form. (12/1)
**2867 Cheeky Chappy** had the best draw and made full use of it, but he is plenty high enough in the weights just now. (13/2)
**2586 Rich Glow** travelled well on this occasion, but his response was disappointing when ridden. (6/1)
**2119* Garnock Valley** met with trouble when making his effort, but he was never doing enough to get into it. (6/1)
**2431 Colway Rake** had his chances but was never giving it his best shot. (20/1)
**2725 Amron** normally likes to come from behind, but he did jump off on terms this time and quickly lost all interest and soon dropped out. This is best ignored. (6/1)

## 2912 TENNENT CALEDONIAN BREWERIES TROPHY RATED STKS H'CAP (0-95) (3-Y.O+) (Class C)
3-50 (3-52) **1m 7f** £6,051.60 (£2,264.40: £1,107.20: £476.00: £213.00: £107.80) Stalls: High GOING minus 0.17 sec per fur (GF)

| | | SP | RR | SF |
|---|---|---|---|---|
| 2570* **Berlin Blue (77)** (JWWatts) **3-8-8** JCarroll(4) (hld up: smooth hdwy over 2f out: led appr fnl f: r.o) ....— | **1** | 100/30[2] | 86 | 23 |
| 2074[15] **Orinoco River (USA) (86)** (PWChapple-Hyam) **3-8-12v**(5) RHavlin(7) (lw: sn trckng ldr: led 3f out tl appr fnl f: r.o) ....1 | **2** | 7/1 | 94 | 31 |
| 2499* **Welsh Mill (IRE) (78)** (MrsMReveley) **7-9-5**(5) GLee(1) (trckd ldrs: n.m.r 3f out: styd on u.p: nt pce to chal) ...1¼ | **3** | 6/1 | 85 | 37 |
| 2330[4] **Embryonic (IRE) (77)** (RFFisher) **4-9-9** KFallon(5) (hld up: effrt 3f out: sn chsng ldrs: one pce appr fnl f) ....1¾ | **4** | 11/4[1] | 82 | 34 |
| 2388* **Rossel (USA) (66)** (PMonteith) **3-7-11** NCarlisle(6) (lw: sn in tch: effrt 3f out: one pce fnl 2f) ....hd | **5** | 25/1 | 71 | 8 |
| 2499[4] **Midyan Blue (IRE) (74)** (JMPEustace) **6-9-6** JTate(3) (led tl hdd 3f out: sn rdn & btn) ....3½ | **6** | 6/1 | 75 | 27 |
| 2330[3] **Secret Service (IRE) (75)** (CWThornton) **4-9-7** DeanMcKeown(2) (chsd ldrs tl rdn & wknd fnl 3f) ....2 | **7** | 4/1[3] | 74 | 26 |

(SP 114.7%) **7 Rn**

**3m 22.21** (11.51) CSF £24.17 TOTE £3.90: £2.20 £3.40 (£13.70) OWNER Sheikh Mohammed (RICHMOND) BRED Darley Stud Management Co Ltd
WEIGHT FOR AGE 3yo-15lb

**2570* Berlin Blue** enjoyed this longer trip and, always travelling best, won with something in hand. He is looking a very useful stayer in the making. (100/30)
**1669* Orinoco River (USA)** stayed this extra distance well enough but, despite trying hard, had met one far too good. (7/1)
**2499* Welsh Mill (IRE)** was short of room when trying to get up the rail early in the straight, and then struggled on, but was always short of the necessary pace. (6/1)
**2330 Embryonic (IRE)** had a hard race last time and that might well have taken the edge off him here. (11/4)
**2388* Rossel (USA)**, stepped up in class, ran pretty well and will no doubt find his mark before long. (25/1)
**2499 Midyan Blue (IRE)** has been disappointing so far this season, but his stable has now struck form, so this was still a moderate effort. (6/1)
**2330 Secret Service (IRE)** was obviously feeling his hard race of last time. (4/1)

## 2913 TAM O'SHANTER GALLOP MAIDEN STKS (3-Y.O+) (Class D)
4-20 (4-20) **1m** £3,582.50 (£1,085.00: £530.00: £252.50) Stalls: High GOING minus 0.13 sec per fur (G)

| | | SP | RR | SF |
|---|---|---|---|---|
| 1617[2] **Elmi Elmak (IRE)** (LMCumani) **3-8-12** OUrbina(1) (lw: trckd ldrs: led appr fnl f: r.o comf) ....— | **1** | 11/10[1] | 75 | 45 |
| 1333[4] **Smooth Asset (IRE)** (PWChapple-Hyam) **3-8-2**(5) RHavlin(2) (trckd ldrs: led 3f out tl appr fnl f: no ex) ....3½ | **2** | 6/4[2] | 63 | 33 |
| **Glen Garnock (IRE)** (DNicholls) **4-9-6** JFortune(3) (bhd: styd on fnl 3f: nvr able to chal) ....10 | **3** | 6/1[3] | 48 | 26 |
| 1649[8] **Lady Seren (IRE)** (SEKettlewell) **4-9-1** NRodgers(5) (cl up: led over 3f out: sn hdd & wl outpcd) ....5 | **4** | 50/1 | 33 | 11 |
| 2333[6] **Shamokin** (FWatson) **4-9-6** JWeaver(7) (b: dwlt: n.d) ....3 | **5** | 50/1 | 32 | 10 |
| 2420[7] **Barbara's Jewel (52)** (ABailey) **4-9-3**(3) DWright(6) (drvn along over 3f out: sn bhd) ....hd | **6** | 50/1 | 32 | 10 |
| 2542[11] **Realms of Glory (IRE) (45)** (PhilipMitchell) **3-8-12b**1 JQuinn(4) (led tl hdd & wknd qckly over 3f out) ....dist | **7** | 33/1 | — | — |

(SP 110.7%) **7 Rn**

**1m 41.36** (3.96) CSF £2.93 TOTE £1.80: £1.10 £1.80 (£1.50) OWNER Sheikh Ahmed Al Maktoum (NEWMARKET) BRED Barnane Partnership
WEIGHT FOR AGE 3yo-8lb

**1617 Elmi Elmak (IRE)** won this modest event pretty well in the end and looks likely to appreciate a bit further. (11/10: 8/11-6/5)
**1333 Smooth Asset (IRE)** has a moderate action, but ran pretty well until running out of steam in the final furlong. Easier ground may be the answer. (6/4)
**Glen Garnock (IRE)** ran reasonably without getting into it, and will obviously benefit from the outing. (6/1: op 14/1)
**Lady Seren (IRE)** showed something this time until crying enough over a furlong out. (50/1)
**Shamokin** made a little late headway, but there is still some way to go. (50/1)

## 2914 ROBERT BURNS BICENTENARY H'CAP (0-60) (3-Y.O) (Class F)
4-50 (4-51) **7f** £3,647.50 (£1,105.00: £540.00: £257.50) Stalls: High GOING minus 0.13 sec per fur (G)

| | | SP | RR | SF |
|---|---|---|---|---|
| *2634*[4] **Magic Lake (40)** (EJAlston) **3-8-4**(3) SDrowne(7) (trckd ldrs gng wl: led wl over 1f out: r.o comf) ....— | **1** | 9/2[3] | 48+ | 22 |
| 2235[9] **Ya Marhaba (35)** (JWPayne) **3-7-13**(3) DWright(10) (lw: cl up: led wl over 2f out tl wl over 1f out: kpt on) ....3 | **2** | 13/2 | 36 | 10 |
| 2778[6] **Pathaze (51)** (NBycroft) **3-9-4** JFortune(9) (bhd: styd on fnl 3f: nrst fin) ....6 | **3** | 11/1 | 38 | 12 |
| 2425[7] **Ned's Contessa (IRE) (45)** (MDods) **3-8-12** JCarroll(3) (lw: bhd tl styd on fnl 3f: nrst fin) ....1 | **4** | 6/1 | 30 | 4 |
| 2597[7] **Fancy Design (IRE) (50)** (PhilipMitchell) **3-9-3** KDarley(8) (b.hind: bhd tl styd on fnl 2f: nvr nrr) ....s.h | **5** | 12/1 | 35 | 9 |

2417* **Oriole (47)** (NTinkler) **3-9-0** KimTinkler(1) (set str pce tl hdd wl over 2f out: wknd over 1f out)........................1¾ **6** 6/1 28 2
2417[8] **Aye Ready (30)** (MissLAPerratt) **3-7-11v[1]** JQuinn(6) (plld hrd: prom tl wknd fnl 3f)........................................6 **7** 50/1 — —
2710[2] **Sunley Secure (54)** (MRChannon) **3-9-7** KFallon(4) (lw: a chsd ldrs: hrd rdn 2f out: wknd wl over 1f out)......1¾ **8** 4/1[2] 17 —
2417[2] **Napoleon's Return (47)** (AHarrison) **3-8-7v(7)** JennyBenson(2) (lw: chsd ldrs: n.m.r appr st: n.d after) ............3 **9** 100/30[1] 4 —
539[12] **Vales Ales (35)** (RMMcKellar) **3-8-2** TWilliams(5) (a bhd: t.o)......................................................dist **10** 100/1 — —
(SP 122.1%) **10 Rn**

**1m 28.94** (4.94) CSF £32.90 CT £232.58 TOTE £7.00: £2.40 £2.20 £2.40 (£24.90) Trio £78.90 OWNER Mr P. D. Ebdon (PRESTON) BRED Cheveley Park Stud Ltd
**2634 Magic Lake** was particularly well suited by this strongly-run event and won with a good deal of ease. (9/2)
**Ya Marhaba** looked well, and this free-runner was always up with the pace, but found the winner far too good in the last two furlongs. (13/2)
**2778 Pathaze** came from off the pace, but never had a hope of getting to the front two. (11/1: 8/1-12/1)
**2179* Ned's Contessa (IRE)** made up a lot of ground in the final two furlongs, but the leaders were then home and dry. (6/1)
**Fancy Design (IRE)** ran quite well, staying on in the last three furlongs, and may well need further. (12/1: 8/1-14/1)
**2417* Oriole** went off at a tremendous pace and had shot his bolt some way out. (6/1: op 4/1)

T/Jkpt: £28,322.60 (1.1 Tckts). T/Plpt: £541.80 (21.61 Tckts). T/Qdpt: £245.30 (2.58 Tckts). AA

## 2434-YARMOUTH (L-H) (Firm)
## Sunday July 21st
WEATHER: warm & sunny WIND: mod across

### 2915 UPTON (S) STKS (3-Y.O) (Class G)
2-00 (2-02) **1m 2f 21y** £2,221.50 (£624.00: £304.50) Stalls: Low GOING minus 0.54 sec per fur (F)

SP RR SF
2434[6] **Snow Falcon (60)** (MBell) **3-8-11** MFenton(6) (hld up & bhd: hdwy over 2f out: led ins fnl f: pushed out).......— **1** 100/30[2] 63 32
2594[4] **Another Quarter (IRE) (50)** (SPCWoods) **3-8-7bow1** WWoods(4) (lw: led: clr 4f out: hdd & unable qckn ins fnl f).......................................................................................................................1¼ **2** 15/8[1] 57 25
2402[7] **Kuwam (IRE) (40)** (BHanbury) **3-8-11** JStack(1) (prom: chsd ldr 3f out tl no ex fnl f)..............................................7 **3** 10/1[3] 50 19
**Nanny-B** (PHowling) **3-8-6** FNorton(2) (leggy: unf: t: chsd ldrs: rdn 3f out: wknd over 1f out)............................8 **4** 33/1 32 1
2388[3] **Cry Baby (43)** (NTinkler) **3-9-3b** MJKinane(3) (swtg: hld up: effrt 5f out: sn rdn & no imp)...................................6 **5** 100/30[2] 34 3
2326[W] **Happy Venturer (IRE)** (CMurray) **3-8-11** MTebbutt(7) (plld hrd: sn chsng ldr: rdn & wknd 3f out)...................10 **6** 14/1 12 —
**Music In Motion** (PHowling) **3-8-6** BThomson(5) (bit bkwd: chsd ldrs 4f: sn bhd: eased appr fnl f) ................11 **7** 25/1 — —
(SP 103.5%) **7 Rn**

**2m 6.8** (2.40) CSF £8.69 TOTE £4.10: £2.10 £1.70 (£3.20) OWNER Mrs G. Rowland-Clark (NEWMARKET) BRED Stratford Place Stud
Bt in 6,500 gns
**2434 Snow Falcon**, stepping up in trip, was dropped out in order to get the trip and, once let down, showed too much speed for his rivals. This ground seems plenty quick enough for him. (100/30)
**2594 Another Quarter (IRE)** did her best to steal this from the front, but found little once challenged. (15/8)
**1168 Kuwam (IRE)** went to post well, but seems to finish weakly whatever trip is tried. (10/1: 6/1-11/1)
**Nanny-B**, tubed for a belated debut, ran quite well but held her head awkwardly when asked for an effort. (33/1)
**2388 Cry Baby** got warm on an admittedly sultry day and took little interest. (100/30: 2/1-7/2)
**1972 Happy Venturer (IRE)**, led to post some time before the off, pulled too hard for his own good once the stalls opened and paid the penalty. (14/1: 6/1-16/1)

### 2916 E.B.F. ACLE MAIDEN STKS (2-Y.O) (Class D)
2-30 (2-30) **6f 3y** £3,650.00 (£1,025.00: £500.00) Stalls: High GOING minus 0.54 sec per fur (F)

SP RR SF
2580[8] **Zugudi** (BHanbury) **2-9-0** MRimmer(4) (lw: mde virtually all: rdn & r.o fnl f)...........................................— **1** 8/1[2] 63 10
1694[5] **Admonish** (MAJarvis) **2-8-9** PBloomfield(3) (hld up: ev ch 1f out: one pce) ...................................................2 **2** 9/1[3] 53 —
2112[4] **Taufan Rookie (IRE)** (RHannon) **2-9-0** PatEddery(2) (lw: w wnr: ev ch 1f out: sn btn & eased)..........................8 **3** 1/7[1] 36 —
(SP 108.6%) **3 Rn**

**1m 14.0** (3.10) CSF £31.60 TOTE £4.40 (£10.50) OWNER Sheik Ahmad Yousuf Al Sabah (NEWMARKET) BRED Cliveden Stud Ltd
**OFFICIAL EXPLANATION Taufan Rookie (IRE): his pilot reported that he did not move well to post and he was concerned about the horse's action during the race. The colt appeared to be lame to the vet.**
**2009 Zugudi** was inconvenienced by the ground, albeit not as much as the favourite, and enjoyed this drop in class. (8/1)
**Admonish** looked just in need of this, but still challenged at the furlong pole before being put in his place. (9/1)
**2112 Taufan Rookie (IRE)**, a big, good-bodied sort, clearly hated the ground, repeatedly changing his legs, losing his action completely and looking likely to pull up after a couple of furlongs. This is not his running as he finished lame on his near-fore. (1/7)

### 2917 SUNDAY H'CAP (0-85) (3-Y.O+) (Class D)
3-00 (3-01) **1m 3y** £3,728.75 (£1,130.00: £552.50: £263.75) GOING minus 0.54 sec per fur (F)

SP RR SF
2581[19] **Saifan (77)** (DMorris) **7-10-0v** CHodgson(4) (dwlt: sn pushed along: hdwy over 2f out: squeezed thro to ld over 1f out: rdn out)..............................................................................................................— **1** 9/1 88 44
2412[3] **Talathath (FR) (63)** (CADwyer) **4-9-0v** MHills(5) (chsd ldrs: ev ch over 1f out: r.o wl ins fnl f)...........................hd **2** 6/1 74 30
2592* **Bubble Wings (FR) (66)** (SPCWoods) **4-9-3** WWoods(2) (swtg: in tch: hdwy over 2f out: ev ch over 1f out: edgd lft & sn btn)..................................................................................................................1¾ **3** 5/2[1] 73 29
1798[5] **A-Aasem (71)** (HThomsonJones) **3-9-0** RHills(3) (stdd s: sn chsng ldrs: led wl over 1f out: sn hdd & nt qckn)hd **4** 9/2[3] 78 26
2514[6] **Tissue of Lies (USA) (68)** (MJohnston) **3-8-11** PRobinson(1) (lw: bhd tl r.o fnl 3f)............................................3 **5** 12/1 69 17
2581[3] **Aeroking (USA) (75)** (GHarwood) **5-9-12** AClark(6) (lw: mde most over 6f: sn btn)........................................1½ **6** 7/2[2] 73 29
2130[6] **Mister Woodstick (IRE) (57)** (MAJarvis) **3-8-0** GBardwell(7) (w ldr: ev ch wl over 1f out: sn wknd) ...............1½ **7** 13/2 52 —
(SP 114.3%) **7 Rn**

**1m 37.4** (2.10) CSF £55.15 TOTE £12.30: £4.20 £2.80 (£31.00) OWNER Mrs L. Brook (NEWMARKET) BRED M. M. Nashar
WEIGHT FOR AGE 3yo-8lb
**OFFICIAL EXPLANATION Saifan: accounting for the horse's apparent improvement, the trainer explained that on his previous run, Saifan had sat down in the stalls and lost several lengths, become detached and thereafter lost interest. This time he was loaded into the stalls and got a much better break, enabling his rider to get him in amongst other horses. He added that the gelding was also suited by the fitting of a visor, instead of the blinkers he wore on his previous run.**

**2134 Saifan**, having his first run in a visor since 1993, bounced back to his best. He likes coming through horses and got his wish this time. (9/1: op 6/1)
**2412 Talathath (FR)** lost a vital length or two when the tempo increased with just over two furlongs left, but stayed on strongly to the line from that point. He remains a maiden, but lacks nothing in courage. (6/1)
**2592* Bubble Wings (FR)** did not move to post well on what was a very firm surface and looked to be feeling the ground throughout. (5/2)
**1798 A-Aasem** still takes an uncomfortably strong hold and saves little for the end of the race. Letting him bowl along might bring the best out of him. (9/2)
**2061 Tissue of Lies (USA)**, ridden with more restraint, could never get to the leaders who were quickening too. (12/1: op 8/1)
**2581 Aeroking (USA)** looked happier on the ground than most of his rivals but folded tamely once headed. (7/2)

## 2918 PLEASURE BEACH MAIDEN STKS (3-Y.O) (Class D)
3-30 (3-33) **7f 3y** £3,696.25 (£1,120.00: £547.50: £261.25) Stalls: High GOING minus 0.54 sec per fur (F)

| | | | | SP | RR | SF |
|---|---|---|---|---|---|---|
| | **Muhandis** (JHMGosden) **3-9-0** RHills(6) (bit bkwd: hdwy 3f out: led & wnt rt ins fnl f: pushed out) | — | 1 | 13/2 | 83 | 45 |
| 2510[2] | **Melt The Clouds (CAN) (77)** (PWHarris) **3-9-0** GHind(3) (lw: hdwy over 2f out: led & edgd lft over 1f out: sn hdd & unable qckn) | 1½ | 2 | 4/1[3] | 80 | 42 |
| 2718[2] | **Cerdan (USA)** (MRStoute) **3-9-0** TQuinn(7) (lw: w ldrs: led wl over 1f out: sn hdd: n.m.r ins fnl f) | ¾ | 3 | 3/1[2] | 78 | 40 |
| | **Yamuna (USA)** (HRACecil) **3-8-9** PatEddery(10) (lw: w ldrs: led 4f out to wl over 1f out: one pce whn hmpd & snatched up ins fnl f) | 2 | 4 | 6/4[1] | 68 | 30 |
| | **With Care** (WJarvis) **3-8-9** BThomson(9) (w'like: unf: bit bkwd: chsd ldrs: rdn 2f out: sn btn) | 5 | 5 | 14/1 | 57 | 19 |
| | **Classic Dame (FR)** (RHarris) **3-8-9** AMackay(4) (leggy: unf: bit bkwd: bhd tl r.o fnl f) | 1½ | 6 | 25/1 | 54 | 16 |
| 2610[12] | **Square Mile Miss (IRE)** (PHowling) **3-8-9** FNorton(1) (swtg: nvr nr to chal) | ½ | 7 | 33/1 | 52 | 14 |
| 2579[P] | **Endaxi Sam** (RIngram) **3-9-0** WWoods(8) (bhd: effrt 3f out: eased whn btn appr fnl f) | 7 | 8 | 66/1 | 41 | 3 |
| 2718[11] | **Enamel Tiger** (KMcAuliffe) **3-9-0** DRMcCabe(2) (b.hind: led 3f: rdn & wknd over 2f out) | 16 | 9 | 66/1 | 5 | — |

(SP 114.8%) **9 Rn**

**1m 24.9** (0.70) CSF £30.47 TOTE £10.70: £2.60 £1.80 £1.30 (£17.30) Trio £11.00 OWNER Mr Hamdan Al Maktoum (NEWMARKET) BRED Lady Juliet de Chair

**Muhandis** looked well in himself but in need of the race, and needed plenty of encouragement to go to post. However, he did little wrong in the race, although he again hung at a vital stage. He looks sure to improve further and more success awaits. (13/2)
**2510 Melt The Clouds (CAN)** moved poorly on this firm surface, but ran a good race, finding a decent turn of speed before being collared by the winner. (4/1)
**2718 Cerdan (USA)** is headstrong and proved rather difficult to get to post, being taken down very steadily. He would not have won even with a clear run but, given his attitude to life, he may be worth a try over six. (3/1)
**Yamuna (USA)**, on her first outing for fourteen months, was loaded late and with a Monty Roberts blanket. It is hoped that the buffeting she received in the last furlong has not put her off as she has the ability to win a small race. (6/4)
**With Care**, very keen going to post, had run herself into the ground by the distance, but will know more next time. (14/1: 10/1-16/1)
**Classic Dame (FR)**, green and left behind early on, was getting the hang of things late in the day and will stay further. (25/1)

## 2919 TUNSTALL CONDITIONS STKS (3-Y.O F) (Class C)
4-00 (4-01) **7f 3y** £4,981.80 (£1,816.80: £888.40: £382.00: £171.00) Stalls: High GOING minus 0.54 sec per fur (F)

| | | | | SP | RR | SF |
|---|---|---|---|---|---|---|
| | **Blue Duster (USA) (119)** (DRLoder) **3-9-2** MJKinane(3) (plld hrd early: trckd ldrs: qcknd to ld 1f out: pushed clr) | — | 1 | 4/5[1] | 102+ | 48 |
| 2585[3] | **Unconditional Love (IRE) (98)** (MJohnston) **3-8-9** MHills(5) (lw: led: qcknd over 2f out: hdd 1f out: sn btn) | 1¾ | 2 | 3/1[2] | 91 | 37 |
| *269[2]* | **Nanshan (IRE)** (DRLoder) **3-8-9** DRMcCabe(4) (w ldr: ev ch 2f out: kpt on ins fnl f) | nk | 3 | 14/1 | 90 | 36 |
| | **Defined Feature (IRE) (96)** (MRStoute) **3-8-9** PatEddery(2) (trckd ldrs: no imp appr fnl f) | 2 | 4 | 4/1[3] | 86 | 32 |
| 2515[2] | **With The Tempo (IRE)** (DrJDScargill) **3-8-9** MFenton(1) (wl bhd fnl 3f) | 11 | 5 | 33/1 | 61 | 7 |

(SP 110.2%) **5 Rn**

**1m 24.8** (0.60) CSF £3.51 TOTE £1.50: £1.20 £1.30 (£2.10) OWNER Sheikh Mohammed (NEWMARKET) BRED Darley Stud Management Inc

**Blue Duster (USA)** has not grown all that much but looked well in herself on this belated reappearance, although still with something to work on. Connections surely took a risk running her on this very firm ground, on which she would not let herself down. However, she was still far too good for these, despite proving rather keen in the first couple of furlongs. (4/5: op 4/9)
**2585 Unconditional Love (IRE)** tried to steal the race by quickening a couple of lengths clear against the stands' rail. The lead was soon pegged back and she was no match for the favourite, despite handling the ground much better than that rival. (3/1)
**Nanshan (IRE)**, in the race to give the winner company both on the way to the start and to give her a lead early on, ran well in her own right and should be able to find a race. (14/1)
**Defined Feature (IRE)** has not been doing much growing over the winter and the jury is still out on whether she has trained on. (4/1)
**2515 With The Tempo (IRE)** was hopelessly outclassed by her rivals. (33/1)

## 2920 BROADLAND 102 RATED STKS H'CAP (0-100) (3-Y.O+) (Class B)
4-30 (4-30) **7f 3y** £8,270.32 (£2,895.92: £1,417.96: £611.80) Stalls: High GOING minus 0.54 sec per fur (F)

| | | | | SP | RR | SF |
|---|---|---|---|---|---|---|
| 2477a[3] | **Verzen (IRE) (97)** (DRLoder) **4-9-4** DRMcCabe(4) (trckd ldr: led over 2f out: rdn clr appr fnl f) | — | 1 | 5/2[3] | 113 | 66 |
| 2007[4] | **Laafee (98)** (HThomsonJones) **3-8-12** RHills(5) (plld hrd early: hld up: chsd wnr 2f out: one pce appr fnl f) | 6 | 2 | 2/1[2] | 100 | 46 |
| 2142[9] | **Tawaaded (IRE) (88)** (PTWalwyn) **3-8-2** BDoyle(2) (led over 4f: sn btn) | 3½ | 3 | 10/1 | 82 | 28 |
| 2704[2] | **Double Blue (100)** (MJohnston) **7-9-7** MHills(3) (lw: chsd ldrs: pushed along over 3f out: wknd over 1f out) | nk | 4 | 6/4[1] | 94 | 47 |

(SP 111.0%) **4 Rn**

**1m 23.4** (-0.80) CSF £7.43 TOTE £4.20 (£5.20) OWNER Mr Saeed Manana (NEWMARKET) BRED Sheikh Mohammed bin Rashid al Maktoum
WEIGHT FOR AGE 3yo-7lb

**2477a Verzen (IRE)** seemed ill-at-ease on the ground, but still turned in a very impressive display, picking up in a manner better than a handicapper, despite racing with his head a shade high. (5/2)
**2007 Laafee**, stepping up in trip, proved hard to settle, but looked a big danger when going second, only to be swamped for speed. (2/1)
**874 Tawaaded (IRE)** had a really hard race at Ascot in May, and this seems to have left its mark as she again quickly gave up once challenged. (10/1: op 6/1)
**2704 Double Blue** tends to find life hard in handicaps as he has won only won one in nineteen attempts since April 1994. This was still a lifeless effort. (6/4)

## 2921 REPPS H'CAP (0-80) (3-Y.O+) (Class D)

5-00 (5-00) **1m 3f 101y** £4,123.50 (£1,248.00: £609.00: £289.50) Stalls: Low GOING minus 0.54 sec per fur (F)

| Form | Horse | Dist | Pos | SP | RR | SF |
|---|---|---|---|---|---|---|
| $2862^{4}$ | **Kaafih Homm (IRE) (62)** (NACallaghan) **5-9-2** MJKinane(1) (hld up: hdwy 4f out: led 1f out: rdn & jst hld on) | — | **1** | $11/4^{3}$ | 72 | 54 |
| $2401^{3}$ | **Chatham Island (70)** (CEBrittain) **8-9-10** BDoyle(2) (dwlt: sn chsng ldrs: n.m.r 2f out tl swtchd ins fnl f: r.o: jst failed) | s.h | **2** | $15/8^{2}$ | 80 | 62 |
| 2767* | **Canton Venture (69)** (SPCWoods) **4-9-9** 5x WWoods(3) (led: rdn over 2f out: hdd 1f out: no ex) | 3 | **3** | $6/4^{1}$ | 75 | 57 |
| $2131^{7}$ | **Petoskin (60)** (JPearce) **4-9-0** GBardwell(4) (lw: chsd ldrs tl rdn & btn 4f out) | dist | **4** | 10/1 | — | — |

(SP 110.5%) **4 Rn**

**2m 23.4** (0.40) CSF £7.81 TOTE £3.20 (£3.20) OWNER Gallagher Materials Ltd (NEWMARKET) BRED Sheikh Ahmed bin Rashid al Maktoum

**2862 Kaafih Homm (IRE)**, given a great ride, got off the mark for the season. Moving to within a neck of the leader, Kinane sat and boxed Chatham Island in until making his move at the furlong pole. The final thrust proved well judged as he just lasted home. (11/4)

**2401 Chatham Island** lost a length at the start but it was a vital length as it meant he could not dictate matters. Blocked in until switching inside the final furlong, he stayed on but the post came just too soon. He should be winning soon if kept to this sort of race. (15/8)

**2767* Canton Venture** tried to steal a clear lead on the home turn, but was gradually pegged back and was a sitting duck once the winner moved upsides. (6/4)

**Petoskin** looked really well but has totally lost his form on the prevailing firm ground. (10/1)

T/Plpt: £706.90 (11.05 Tckts). T/Qdpt: £19.90 (26.45 Tckts). Dk

# 2752-BEVERLEY (R-H) (Good to firm)

## Monday July 22nd

WEATHER: fine WIND: slt half bhd

## 2922 POCKLINGTON (S) STKS (3-Y.O+) (Class G)

6-15 (6-16) **1m 3f 216y** £2,302.50 (£640.00: £307.50) Stalls: High GOING minus 0.38 sec per fur (F)

| Form | Horse | Dist | Pos | SP | RR | SF |
|---|---|---|---|---|---|---|
| $1436^{4}$ | **Pickens (USA) (61)** (NTinkler) **4-9-7** RCochrane(7) (trckd ldrs: effrt over 2f out: rdn to ld over 1f out: jst hld on) | — | **1** | $7/2^{2}$ | 58 | 22 |
| $2682^{3}$ | **North Bear** (MrsSJSmith) **4-9-4**(3) OPears(5) (chsd ldrs: rdn & hung lft over 1f out: styd on towards fin) | ½ | **2** | $7/2^{2}$ | 57 | 21 |
| *$2747^{2}$* | **Balios (IRE) (60)** (MJohnston) **3-8-13** JWeaver(8) (lw: led tl over 1f out: one pce) | nk | **3** | $7/2^{2}$ | 61 | 13 |
| $2731^{3}$ | **Veshca Lady (IRE) (42)** (EWeymes) **3-8-4** KDarley(1) (lw: sn trckng ldrs: effrt 3f out: sltly hmpd over 1f out: kpt on same pce) | 1½ | **4** | $5/2^{1}$ | 50 | 2 |
| $2066^{11}$ | **Master Ofthe House (52)** (MDHammond) **10-9-7** PatEddery(3) (hld up: stdy hdwy over 2f out: rdn over 1f out: nvr nr to chal) | ½ | **5** | $11/2^{3}$ | 54 | 18 |
| | **Penny Peppermint** (REBarr) **4-9-2** DeanMcKeown(2) (bit bkwd: dwlt: bhd: effrt on outside over 3f out: wknd 2f out) | 11 | **6** | 33/1 | 35 | — |
| $1697^{3}$ | **Bold Top (40)** (BSRothwell) **4-9-7v** MFenton(4) (s.i.s: bhd: effrt over 3f out: rdn & wknd 2f out) | 1¾ | **7** | 12/1 | 37 | 1 |

(SP 121.3%) **7 Rn**

**2m 40.6** (8.20) CSF £16.40 TOTE £4.70: £2.00 £3.10 (£20.40) OWNER Mr Philip Grundy (MALTON) BRED Allen E. Paulson

WEIGHT FOR AGE 3yo-12lb

No bid; Balios (IRE) clmd WGMTurner £6,000

**Pickens (USA)**, who has been in action over hurdles, wore a tongue-strap. Well ridden, he was persuaded to do just enough. (7/2)

**2682 North Bear**, who tended to hang in the closing stages, had the winner at full stretch. (7/2)

**2747 Balios (IRE)**, who continually swished his tail in the paddock, made the running. He kept on well when headed and was later claimed. (7/2)

**2731 Veshca Lady (IRE)**, with the visor left off, made hard work of it when forced to switch, and is proving hard to win with. (5/2)

**1196 Master Ofthe House** travelled strongly on the bridle and ran his best race for some time. (11/2)

## 2923 SAILORS' FAMILIES' SOCIETY MAIDEN STKS (2-Y.O) (Class D)

6-40 (6-41) **7f 100y** £3,371.00 (£1,013.00: £489.00: £227.00) Stalls: High GOING: minus 0.38 sec per fur (F)

| Form | Horse | Dist | Pos | SP | RR | SF |
|---|---|---|---|---|---|---|
| $2414^{2}$ | **Mount Kamet** (DRLoder) **2-9-0** RHughes(6) (lw: mde virtually all: clr 2f out: easily) | — | **1** | $8/11^{1}$ | 83+ | 51 |
| $2224^{2}$ | **Eurolink Excaliber (USA)** (JLDunlop) **2-9-0** PatEddery(5) (lw: chsd ldrs: effrt over 3f out: kpt on same pce u.p: no imp) | 5 | **2** | $7/4^{2}$ | 72 | 40 |
| $2580^{6}$ | **Maradi (IRE)** (DMorley) **2-9-0** RCochrane(2) (hld up: bmpd over 2f out: kpt on: nvr nr to chal) | 2 | **3** | $6/1^{3}$ | 68+ | 36 |
| $2122^{4}$ | **Warrlin** (CWFairhurst) **2-9-0** DeanMcKeown(4) (w wnr tl wknd over 2f out: fin 5th, 6l: plcd 4th) | | **4** | 20/1 | 51 | — |
| $2625^{6}$ | **Smoke'n'jo (IRE)** (MWEasterby) **2-8-9**(5) GParkin(9) (chsd ldrs: outpcd over 2f out: n.d after: fin 6th, 1¼l: plcd 5th) | | **5** | 33/1 | 49 | — |
| $2512^{7}$ | **Dulas Bay** (MWEasterby) **2-9-0** DaleGibson(7) (sn bhd) | 3 | **7** | 33/1 | 42 | — |
| $2708^{15}$ | **Poignant (IRE)** (MRChannon) **2-9-0** KDarley(8) (bit bkwd: chsd ldrs: effrt over 3f out: wkng whn hmpd over 2f out: eased) | 10 | **8** | 25/1 | 21 | — |
| *$2746^{4}$* | **Ben's Ridge** (PCHaslam) **2-9-0** JWeaver(3) (bhd: hdwy & swtchd lft over 2f out: kpt on: nvr nr to chal: fin 4th, 1 3/4l: disq: plcd last) | | **D** | 12/1 | 64 | — |

(SP 130.7%) **8 Rn**

**1m 33.5** (1.50) CSF £2.96 TOTE £2.00: £1.40 £1.10 £1.90 (£1.40) Trio £3.00 OWNER Sheikh Mohammed (NEWMARKET) BRED Sheikh Mohammed Bin Rashid Al Maktoum

STEWARDS' ENQUIRY Weaver susp. 31/7-6/8/96 (careless riding).

**2414 Mount Kamet,** the paddock pick, took this with plenty to spare. How good a race this was is open to debate. (8/11)

**2224 Eurolink Excaliber (USA)** had much less use made of him this time, and never looked like finding the speed to get on terms with the winner. (7/4: 5/4-2/1)

**2580 Maradi (IRE)**, having his third run, raced keenly off the pace. Bumped two furlongs out, to say his rider looked after him would be an understatement. Now qualified for nurseries, he is one to keep an eye on. (6/1)

**2746 Ben's Ridge** dived left coming to the final quarter-mile, partially to avoid another runner. This sparked off a set of incidents involving two others. (12/1: tchd 20/1)

## 2924 I. J. BLAKEY HAULAGE H'CAP (0-80) (3-Y.O+ F & M) (Class D)
7-10 (7-11) **1m 1f 207y** £4,206.00 (£1,263.00: £609.00: £282.00) Stalls: High GOING minus 0.38 sec per fur (F)

| | | | | SP | RR | SF |
|---|---|---|---|---|---|---|
| 2513* | **Darling Clover (65)** (DMorley) **4-9-8** RCochrane(5) (trckd ldrs: styd on to ld ins fnl f: drvn out) | — | 1 | 2/1 1 | 74 | 56 |
| | **Maid For Baileys (IRE) (75)** (MJohnston) **3-9-8** JWeaver(6) (led tl ins fnl f: r.o) | ½ | 2 | 13/2 | 83 | 55 |
| 2773[7] | **Fairywings (74)** (MrsJRRamsden) **3-9-7** KFallon(3) (swtg: hld up: hdwy on ins 2f out: nt clr run over 1f out: styd on wl towards fin) | ¾ | 3 | 4/1 2 | 81 | 53 |
| 2593* | **Lady Bankes (IRE) (66)** (WGMTurner) **3-8-8**(5) RHavlin(1) (a chsng ldrs: kpt on same pce appr fnl f) | 2 | 4 | 11/2 3 | 70 | 42 |
| 2521[6] | **Sandblaster (54)** (DNicholls) **3-8-1** NKennedy(7) (dwlt s: plld hrd: sn trckng ldrs: wknd over 1f out) | 4 | 5 | 7/1 | 51 | 23 |
| 1816[9] | **Domitia (USA) (71)** (MBell) **4-10-0** MFenton(2) (hld up: effrt on outside 3f out: rdn & wknd 2f out) | 1¾ | 6 | 8/1 | 66 | 48 |
| 2430[3] | **Naval Gazer (IRE) (73)** (DRLoder) **3-9-6b[1]** RHughes(4) (trckd ldrs: effrt over 3f out: fnd nil & sn wknd) | 10 | 7 | 11/2 3 | 51 | 23 |
| | | | | (SP 121.0%) | | **7 Rn** |

**2m 4.8** (2.30) CSF £15.32 TOTE £3.10: £1.70 £2.00 (£7.90) OWNER Mr K. Craddock (NEWMARKET) BRED Astalon Ltd
WEIGHT FOR AGE 3yo-10lb

**2513* Darling Clover**, 12lb higher in the weights than when winning on her reappearance in April, likes this track and answered her rider's every call in willing fashion to get up near the line. (2/1)
**Maid For Baileys (IRE)**, runner-up on five of her seven outings at two, looked as though the outing may do her good. After making the running, she quickened up on the home turn, but just came off second best. Her luck must change soon. (13/2)
**2773 Fairywings**, awash with sweat in the paddock and back over a more suitable trip, was ridden patiently. Meeting trouble over a furlong out, she was reeling in the first two at the line. Though 10lb higher in the weights than when winning for the first time five outings ago, there should be more success to come. (4/1)
**2593* Lady Bankes (IRE)** did not get her own way this time. (11/2)
**2521 Sandblaster**, who has changed stables, was stepped up in trip and proved too keen for her own good. (7/1)
**2430 Naval Gazer (IRE)** looked far from keen. (11/2)

## 2925 JWE MOBILEPHONE GROUP H'CAP (0-70) (3-Y.O+) (Class E)
7-40 (7-40) **7f 100y** £3,522.00 (£1,056.00: £508.00: £234.00) Stalls: High GOING minus 0.38 sec per fur (F)

| | | | | SP | RR | SF |
|---|---|---|---|---|---|---|
| 2801[3] | **Thatched (IRE) (43)** (REBarr) **6-8-8** DeanMcKeown(5) (trckd ldrs: styd on to ld ins fnl f: drvn out) | — | 1 | 5/1 3 | 52 | 24 |
| 2573[6] | **Euro Sceptic (IRE) (47)** (TDEasterby) **4-8-7b**(5) RHavlin(1) (led tl ins fnl f) | nk | 2 | 7/1 | 55 | 27 |
| 2602[3] | **Castan (IRE) (69)** (JLDunlop) **3-9-13** PatEddery(4) (trckd ldrs: effrt over 2f out: ev ch ins fnl f: kpt on same pce) | ½ | 3 | 7/4 1 | 76 | 41 |
| 1860[2] | **Murphy's Gold (IRE) (52)** (RAFahey) **5-9-3** KFallon(2) (lw: hld up & plld hrd: hdwy & swtchd outside over 1f out: styd on towards fin) | hd | 4 | 2/1 2 | 59 | 31 |
| *2749*[3] | **Heathyards Lady (USA) (57)** (RHollinshead) **5-9-5**(3) FLynch(3) (hld up: swtchd rt after 1f: sn trckng ldrs: nt clr run on ins over 1f out: kpt on one pce) | ¾ | 5 | 15/2 | 63+ | 35 |
| 2763[4] | **Super Park (60)** (JPearce) **4-9-11** GBardwell(6) (swtg: hld up: hmpd after 1f: edgd lft & kpt on fnl 2f: n.d) | 2½ | 6 | 16/1 | 60 | 32 |
| | | | | (SP 116.5%) | | **6 Rn** |

**1m 35.5** (3.50) CSF £34.53 TOTE £6.20: £2.30 £2.60 (£24.70) OWNER Mr C. W. Marwood (MIDDLESBROUGH) BRED D. P. O'Brien
WEIGHT FOR AGE 3yo-7lb
IN-FOCUS: **This was run at a false early pace, and developed into a sprint from halfway.**
**2801 Thatched (IRE)**, ridden to perfection, did just enough. (5/1)
**2573 Euro Sceptic (IRE)**, back on his favourite stamping ground, was given an intelligent ride from the front. Quickening it up from the turn, the winner proved just the stronger. (7/1)
**2602 Castan (IRE)** had every chance but, hard as he tried, he could not quicken inside the last. (7/4)
**1860 Murphy's Gold (IRE)**, fresh and well after a forty-day break, was not suited by the false pace. Refusing to settle early on, after being pulled to the outer over a furlong out, he stayed on in determined fashion. There is no doubt he can win off this mark when everything goes his way. (2/1)
**2749 Heathyards Lady (USA)**, who is about a stone better on the All-Weather, took a keen grip and was short of room over a furlong out. This probably made little difference though. (15/2)

## 2926 SHIPTONTHORPE CLAIMING STKS (2-Y.O) (Class F)
8-10 (8-11) **5f** £2,798.00 (£778.00: £374.00) Stalls: High GOING minus 0.38 sec per fur (F)

| | | | | SP | RR | SF |
|---|---|---|---|---|---|---|
| 2595[7] | **Saunders Wren** (MRChannon) **2-7-11**(5) PPMurphy(9) (mde all: clr over 1f out: pushed out) | — | 1 | 5/4 1 | 64 | 16 |
| 2781[9] | **Antares** (NTinkler) **2-8-9** KimTinkler(10) (chsd ldrs: styd on appr fnl f: no ch w wnr) | 2 | 2 | 16/1 | 65 | 17 |
| 2396[5] | **Sandbaggedagain** (MWEasterby) **2-9-0** DaleGibson(7) (sn pushed along: hdwy & n.m.r 2f out: styd on u.p fnl f) | nk | 3 | 14/1 | 69 | 21 |
| *2307*[4] | **Fearless Cavalier** (RHollinshead) **2-8-2**(3) FLynch(2) (bhd: hdwy on outside ½-wy: hung rt & kpt on one pce) | 1¼ | 4 | 12/1 | 56 | 8 |
| 2846[W] | **Thewrightone (IRE)** (GROldroyd) **2-7-12b** JLowe(13) (bhd: hdwy u.p ½-wy: nvr nr ldrs) | 1½ | 5 | 20/1 | 44 | — |
| 2569[7] | **My Girl** (JBerry) **2-7-10**(3) DWright(8) (s.i.s: sn chsng ldrs: wknd over 1f out) | 1 | 6 | 16/1 | 42 | — |
| *2371*[7] | **Superboots** (WWHaigh) **2-7-13** GBardwell(12) (sn outpcd: hmpd on ins over 3f out: styd on appr fnl f) | s.h | 7 | 10/1 | 42 | — |
| 2728[6] | **Lycius Touch** (MJohnston) **2-8-4** TWilliams(5) (sn pushed along: prom: btn whn n.m.r 2f out) | nk | 8 | 7/1 | 46 | — |
| 2797[6] | **Bellaf** (MWEasterby) **2-8-7** PatEddery(1) (chsd ldrs on outside tl wknd 2f out) | 1½ | 9 | 6/1 3 | 44 | — |
| *1093*[9] | **Imperial Garden (IRE)** (PCHaslam) **2-8-9** JFortune(4) (prom tl lost pl ½-wy: n.d after) | s.h | 10 | 16/1 | 46 | — |
| | **Mint Condition** (MrsLStubbs) **2-8-7** KFallon(11) (leggy: unf: a outpcd & bhd) | 2 | 11 | 3/1 2 | 37 | — |
| 2781[10] | **Petite Risk** (KWHogg) **2-8-1** NKennedy(6) (chsd ldrs tl lost pl ½-wy) | 3 | 12 | 25/1 | 22 | — |
| | | | | (SP 145.9%) | | **12 Rn** |

**64.0 secs** (2.50) CSF £27.33 TOTE £2.50: £1.60 £7.30 £3.40 (£33.20) Trio £166.30 OWNER Charles Saunders Ltd (UPPER LAMBOURN) BRED C. Scott
Saunders Wren clmd Mrs LStubbs £8,000
**2375 Saunders Wren** outclassed her rivals and was in no danger some way from home. (5/4)
**1632 Antares** wore a tongue-strap and bounced back after two poor efforts. (16/1)
**2396 Sandbaggedagain**, on edge beforehand, showed plenty of knee-action going down. Dropped back to five, he struggled to go the pace, but was staying on in resolute fashion near the finish, and needs six or seven. (14/1)
**2307 Fearless Cavalier** hung under pressure as if feeling the ground. (12/1)
**Thewrightone (IRE)**, with the blinkers back on again, showed her first worthwhile form. (20/1)

**2018 My Girl** again lost ground leaving the stalls. (16/1)
**Mint Condition**, very green in the paddock, showed nothing at all on this debut. (3/1: op 5/1)

## 2927 NORWOOD RATING RELATED MAIDEN STKS (0-65) (3-Y.O) (Class F)

8-40 (8-41) **2m 35y** £2,532.00 (£702.00: £336.00) Stalls: High GOING minus 0.38 sec per fur (F)

| | | | | SP | RR | SF |
|---|---|---|---|---|---|---|
| 2141$^{5}$ | **Jamaican Flight (USA) (63)** (JWHills) **3-9-0** JFortune(4) (lw: mde all: styd on u.p fnl 2f: all out) | — | 1 | 2/1$^{2}$ | 63 | 21 |
| 2482$^{2}$ | **Go With The Wind (65)** (MBell) **3-9-0** MFenton(3) (hld up: stdy hdwy to chal 1f out: nt qckn towards fin) | nk | 2 | 6/4$^{1}$ | 63 | 21 |
| 2709$^{7}$ | **Mischief Star (59)** (DRCElsworth) **3-8-11** KFallon(1) (blind off eye: hld up: effrt over 3f out: hrd rdn & styd on same pce fnl 2f: nvr nr to chal) | 1½ | 3 | 5/2$^{3}$ | 58 | 16 |
| 2204$^{6}$ | **Ship's Dancer (53)** (DonEnricoIncisa) **3-8-11v$^{1}$** KimTinkler(2) (chsd wnr: rdn over 3f out: lost pl over 2f out) | 26 | 4 | 12/1 | 33 | — |
| | | | | (SP 109.6%) | | **4 Rn** |

**3m 40.9** (10.40) CSF £5.17 TOTE £2.90 (£2.20) OWNER The Jampot Partnership (LAMBOURN) BRED Foxfield
**2141 Jamaican Flight (USA)** was given a positive ride. Sticking on under strong pressure, he outbattled the runner-up in the end. (2/1)
**2482 Go With The Wind**, produced to challenge a furlong out, again flashed his tail under pressure and would not go past. (6/4)
**Mischief Star**, who is blind in her off-eye, looked to be feeling the ground but stayed on at the finish. She will be better suited by a left-handed track and better ground. (5/2)
**2204 Ship's Dancer**, who has changed stables, was tried in a visor but to no avail. (12/1)

T/Plpt: £178.70 (64.07 Tckts). T/Qdpt: £81.30 (9.48 Tckts). WG

# 2846-MUSSELBURGH (R-H) (Good to soft)

## Monday July 22nd

WEATHER: overcast WIND: almost nil

## 2928 GILLESPIE'S MALT STOUT MAIDEN H'CAP (0-70) (3-Y.O+) (Class E)

2-15 (2-15) **1m 4f 31y** £3,046.25 (£920.00: £447.50: £211.25) Stalls: High GOING minus 0.11 sec per fur (G)

| | | | | SP | RR | SF |
|---|---|---|---|---|---|---|
| 2847$^{7}$ | **Victoria's Secret (IRE) (49)** (MRChannon) **4-9-10** TQuinn(2) (lw: a.p: led over 2f out: r.o: eased ins fnl f) | — | 1 | 5/2$^{2}$ | 56+ | 13 |
| 2424$^{3}$ | **Atienza (USA) (53)** (SCWilliams) **3-9-2** KFallon(4) (lw: cl up: led over 5f out tl over 2f out: sn btn) | 10 | 2 | 9/2$^{3}$ | 47 | — |
| 2848$^{9}$ | **Phar Closer (42)** (WTKemp) **3-8-5** TWilliams(3) (b: led tl hdd over 5f out: wl outpcd fnl 3f) | 2½ | 3 | 14/1 | 33 | — |
| 2365$^{6}$ | **The Great Flood (47)** (NTinkler) **3-8-10** GDuffield(1) (hld up: pushed along 5f out: no imp) | ½ | 4 | 10/11$^{1}$ | 37 | — |
| | | | | (SP 105.8%) | | **4 Rn** |

**2m 46.4** (13.40) CSF £11.04 TOTE £2.70 (£4.20) OWNER Mr Alec Tuckerman (UPPER LAMBOURN)
WEIGHT FOR AGE 3yo-12lb
**2613 Victoria's Secret (IRE)** left her poor run of three days previously well behind and beat this moderate bunch with ease. (5/2: 2/1-3/1)
**2424 Atienza (USA)** looked very lean and fit but, once headed approaching the last two furlongs, she proved to be very slow. (9/2)
**2388 Phar Closer**, warm beforehand, looked very moderate once the race began in earnest approaching the straight. (14/1: 10/1-16/1)
**1675 The Great Flood** never looked happy at any stage from halfway and failed to offer a threat. This was a dismal effort. (10/11: 4/6-Evens)

## 2929 MCEWAN'S 80/- LIMITED STKS (0-60) (3-Y.O+) (Class F)

2-45 (2-45) **7f 15y** £2,633.00 (£548.50: £548.50) Stalls: High GOING minus 0.11 sec per fur (G)

| | | | | SP | RR | SF |
|---|---|---|---|---|---|---|
| 2363$^{11}$ | **Encore M'Lady (IRE) (59)** (FHLee) **5-9-2** JFanning(5) (hld up & bhd: squeezed thro to ld ins fnl f: rdn out) | — | 1 | 14/1 | 59 | 17 |
| 2729$^{5}$ | **Don Pepe (60)** (RBoss) **5-9-2** JCarroll(8) (lw: trckd ldrs: disp ld over 2f out tl ins fnl f: kpt on) | ½ | 2 | 3/1$^{1}$ | 58 | 16 |
| 2417$^{6}$ | **Shontaine (60)** (MJohnston) **3-8-9** TWilliams(7) (led tl hdd ins fnl f: kpt on) | d.h | 2 | 6/1 | 58 | 9 |
| 2483$^{8}$ | **Intendant (59)** (JGFitzGerald) **4-9-2** KFallon(1) (in tch: ch 2f out: btn whn sltly hmpd 1f out) | 2½ | 4 | 3/1$^{1}$ | 52 | 10 |
| 2719$^{2}$ | **Ciserano (IRE) (61)** (MRChannon) **3-8-9** TQuinn(2) (lw: hld up: effrt 3f out: rdn & nvr able to chal) | 1¼ | 5 | 5/1$^{3}$ | 49 | — |
| 1840$^{14}$ | **Truth (60)** (SirMarkPrescott) **3-8-6** GDuffield(6) (hld up: effrt 3f out: no imp) | 1 | 6 | 4/1$^{2}$ | 44 | — |
| 2481$^{9}$ | **Hannah's Usher (60)** (CMurray) **4-9-5** MTebbutt(3) (chsd ldrs tl wknd fnl 2½f) | 6 | 7 | 25/1 | 37 | — |
| *2550*$^{10}$ | **Peacefull Reply (USA) (35)** (FHLee) **6-8-11**(5) MBaird(4) (lw: cl up tl wknd 2f out) | 14 | 8 | 100/1 | 2 | — |
| | | | | (SP 112.5%) | | **8 Rn** |

**1m 31.9** (6.40) CSF EM, DP £25.88 EM, S £42.17 TOTE £14.40: £3.40 DP £1.80 S £2.20 (EM, DP £17.20 EM, S £23.50) OWNER Mr F. H. Lee (WILMSLOW) BRED Irish National Stud Co Ltd in Ireland
WEIGHT FOR AGE 3yo-7lb
STEWARDS' ENQUIRY Fanning susp. 31/7-2/8/96 (careless riding).
**2030* Encore M'Lady (IRE)**, held up to get this trip, barged her way through to settle it inside the final furlong, but was fast running out of stamina as the line approached. (14/1: op 8/1)
**2729 Don Pepe** raced freely, but was restrained and gave the impression that perhaps he should revert to his old front-running tactics. (3/1)
**2417 Shontaine** is coming back to something like his best form and kept battling back when looking beaten here. (6/1)
**1650 Intendant** had his chances, but proved short of toe and getting knocked out of the way by the winner made absolutely no difference. (3/1)
**2719 Ciserano (IRE)**, held up to get the trip, failed to respond when ridden in the last three furlongs. (5/1)
**Truth**, put in the stalls early, tried to come from behind but never fired, and may well have needed this. (4/1)

## 2930 MCEWAN'S 70/- CLASSIC NURSERY H'CAP (2-Y.O) (Class D)

3-15 (3-15) **5f** £3,425.00 (£1,040.00: £510.00: £245.00) Stalls: High GOING minus 0.11 sec per fur (G)

| | | | | SP | RR | SF |
|---|---|---|---|---|---|---|
| 2872$^{2}$ | **Bride's Reprisal** (MRChannon) **2-9-7** TQuinn(4) (trckd ldrs: led over 1f out: r.o: comf) | — | 1 | 8/13$^{1}$ | 88+ | 32 |
| 2569* | **Under Pressure** (TDEasterby) **2-8-12** MBirch(2) (mde most tl hdd over 1f out: no ch w wnr) | 3 | 2 | 3/1$^{2}$ | 69 | 13 |
| 2681$^{2}$ | **Red Romance** (DenysSmith) **2-9-0** KFallon(1) (lw: w ldr: sn drvn along: outpcd fnl 2f) | 3½ | 3 | 5/1$^{3}$ | 60 | 4 |
| 2569$^{6}$ | **Casual Cottage (IRE)** (CMurray) **2-7-13v**(5) MBaird(3) (prom tl rdn & btn over 1f out) | s.h | 4 | 12/1 | 50 | — |
| | | | | (SP 111.3%) | | **4 Rn** |

**61.4 secs** (3.70) CSF £2.87 TOTE £1.30 (£1.90) OWNER Mrs Jean Keegan (UPPER LAMBOURN) BRED J. K. Keegan
**2872 Bride's Reprisal** looked a bit of a character, but had no trouble in dealing with this lot. (8/13)
**2569* Under Pressure** ran as well as could be expected before finding the winner far too good. (3/1: op 2/1)
**2681 Red Romance** is short of speed and, off the bit before halfway, never had a hope. (5/1: 4/1-6/1)
**2569 Casual Cottage (IRE)** tried to get on terms from halfway but, soon ridden for all she was worth, failed to offer a threat. (12/1)

## 2931 MCEWAN'S LAGER RATING RELATED MAIDEN STKS (0-65) (3-Y.O+) (Class F)

3-45 (3-47) **1m 16y** £2,549.00 (£714.00: £347.00) Stalls: High GOING minus 0.11 sec per fur (G)

| Form | Horse | Btn | Pos | SP | RR | SF |
|---|---|---|---|---|---|---|
| 2760[3] | **Anak-Ku (65)** (MissGayKelleway) **3-8-12v[1]** TQuinn(5) (lw: racd wd thrght: mde all: rdn & kpt on fnl 2f) | — | 1 | 8/11[1] | 74 | 48 |
| 2179[2] | **Nkapen Rocks (SPA) (62)** (CaptJWilson) **3-8-12** KFallon(6) (prom: hdwy to chse wnr 2f out: hrd rdn & nt qckn fnl f) | 4 | 2 | 7/4[2] | 66 | 40 |
| 2493[7] | **School of Science (25)** (DANolan) **6-9-6** GDuffield(2) (chsd ldrs: one pce fnl 3f) | 14 | 3 | 50/1 | 38 | 20 |
| 2358[5] | **Madrina (60)** (JBerry) **3-8-9** JCarroll(3) (chsd ldrs tl wknd fnl 2f) | 4 | 4 | 8/1[3] | 27 | 1 |
| | **Corky's Girl (32)** (RMMcKellar) **4-8-10**(7) DMcGaffin(1) (a bhd) | 19 | 5 | 200/1 | — | — |
| *2751[9]* | **Dino's Mistral (40)** (FHLee) **3-8-12** JFanning(7) (a bhd) | 12 | 6 | 33/1 | — | — |
| | | | | (SP 110.8%) | **6 Rn** | |

**1m 42.4** (3.80) CSF £2.28 TOTE £1.40: £1.10 £1.10 (£1.40) OWNER H R H Sultan Ahmad Shah (WHITCOMBE) BRED John Rose
WEIGHT FOR AGE 3yo-8lb

**2760 Anak-Ku**, in a visor for the first time, was given an aggressive ride and was always just doing enough. (8/11)
**2179 Nkapen Rocks (SPA)**, who got pretty warm beforehand, was always having to work hard to get near the winner and finally gave up inside the last furlong. (7/4)
**School of Science**, very much on his toes in the paddock, needed two attendants and then looked pretty slow. (50/1)
**2358 Madrina** again did not seem to see the trip out. (8/1)

## 2932 BEAMISH RED IRISH ALE MAIDEN AUCTION STKS (2-Y.O) (Class F)

4-15 (4-16) **7f 15y** £2,577.00 (£722.00: £351.00) Stalls: High GOING minus 0.11 sec per fur (G)

| Form | Horse | Btn | Pos | SP | RR | SF |
|---|---|---|---|---|---|---|
| 2495[3] | **Foxes Tail** (MissSEHall) **2-8-5** NCarlisle(2) (b: trckd ldrs: chal over 3f out: rdn to ld ins fnl f: r.o) | — | 1 | 1/3[1] | 70 | 4 |
| 2396[6] | **Imperial Or Metric (IRE)** (JBerry) **2-8-8** JCarroll(6) (led tl hdd ins fnl f: kpt on wl) | 1 | 2 | 6/1[2] | 71 | 5 |
| | **Keen To Please** (DenysSmith) **2-8-5**ow2 MBirch(4) (neat: unf: trckd ldrs: effrt & ch over 2f out: btn over 1f out) | 5 | 3 | 9/1 | 56 | — |
| 2025[5] | **Music Express (IRE)** (AHarrison) **2-8-2** GDuffield(3) (plld hrd: hmpd appr st: prom tl outpcd fnl 2f) | 2½ | 4 | 8/1[3] | 48 | — |
| 2519[4] | **Ballydinero (IRE)** (CaptJWilson) **2-7-13**(5) MBaird(1) (bhd: hdwy over 2f out: rdn & no imp) | ½ | 5 | 33/1 | 49 | — |
| 1607[6] | **Silver Raj** (WTKemp) **2-8-3** JFanning(5) (lw: prom tl outpcd fnl 2½f) | 6 | 6 | 40/1 | 34 | — |
| | | | | (SP 115.8%) | **6 Rn** | |

**1m 32.2** (6.70) CSF £3.28 TOTE £1.30: £1.20 £1.50 (£4.30) OWNER Mrs Joan Hodgson (MIDDLEHAM) BRED Miss S. E. Hall

**2495 Foxes Tail** would certainly win no prizes for looks, but the performance was good enough, although never easy. This should have taught him plenty. (1/3)
**2396 Imperial Or Metric (IRE)** is now coming to hand and should be kept on the right side. (6/1)
**Keen To Please**, who is not very big, has ability and was not knocked about when beaten in the last couple of furlongs. (9/1)
**2025 Music Express (IRE)** pulled too hard for her own good and was left struggling in the last two furlongs. (8/1)
**2519 Ballydinero (IRE)** was the only one out of touch approaching the straight and, although keeping on, never looked likely to get anywhere near. (33/1)
**1607 Silver Raj** found this company too good and was left behind once into the home straight. (40/1)

## 2933 MCEWAN'S EXPORT MAIDEN H'CAP (0-70) (3-Y.O+) (Class E)

4-45 (4-46) **5f** £3,078.75 (£930.00: £452.50: £213.75) Stalls: High GOING minus 0.11 sec per fur (G)

| Form | Horse | Btn | Pos | SP | RR | SF |
|---|---|---|---|---|---|---|
| 2732[7] | **Forzara (45)** (JBerry) **3-9-10** JCarroll(5) (chsd ldrs: rdn to ld appr fnl f: styd on) | — | 1 | 3/1[3] | 53 | 31 |
| 2732[4] | **China Hand (IRE) (37)** (MartynWane) **4-9-6** JFanning(2) (led: edgd rt ½-wy: hdd appr fnl f: one pce) | 3 | 2 | 6/4[1] | 35 | 17 |
| 2481[13] | **Young Ben (IRE) (40)** (JSWainwright) **4-9-2v[1]**(7) JBramhill(4) (lw: b: b.hind: cl up: ev ch over 1f out: sn rdn & btn) | ½ | 3 | 20/1 | 37 | 19 |
| 2902[11] | **Distinctly Swingin (IRE) (40)** (MissLAPerratt) **3-9-5** GDuffield(1) (cl up to ½-wy: sn rdn & btn) | 5 | 4 | 12/1 | 21 | — |
| 2566[4] | **Jebi (USA) (40)** (CMurray) **6-9-4v**(5) MBaird(3) (s.i.s: a outpcd & bhd) | hd | 5 | 2/1[2] | 21 | 3 |
| | | | | (SP 110.8%) | **5 Rn** | |

**61.6 secs** (3.90) CSF £7.67 TOTE £4.10: £3.60 £1.10 (£4.00) OWNER Mrs Robert Heathcote (COCKERHAM) BRED R. and Mrs Heathcote
WEIGHT FOR AGE 3yo-4lb

**2176 Forzara** won a bad race by sticking to her task. (3/1: tchd 9/2)
**2732 China Hand (IRE)** made it but, all out from halfway, was never giving it his best shot. (6/4: Evens-7/4)
**Young Ben (IRE)** looked well and had every chance, but ran out of fuel inside the last furlong. (20/1)
**2359 Distinctly Swingin (IRE)** looked very lean and, once off the bit approaching halfway, soon folded up. (12/1)
**2566 Jebi (USA)** ran unbelievably badly in this poor race and never went a yard. To give him a slight excuse, the trip was probably too short. (2/1)

T/Plpt: £9.60 (922.05 Tckts). T/Qdpt: £2.40 (213.66 Tckts). AA

# 2367-SOUTHWELL (L-H) (Standard)

## Monday July 22nd

WEATHER: sunny & hot WIND: fresh across

## 2934 UCCELLO LIMITED STKS (0-65) (3-Y.O+) (Class F)

2-30 (2-31) **1m (Fibresand)** £2,381.00 (£656.00: £311.00) Stalls: Low GOING minus 0.02 sec per fur (STD)

| Form | Horse | Btn | Pos | SP | RR | SF |
|---|---|---|---|---|---|---|
| 1654[12] | **Catherine's Choice (65)** (JDBethell) **3-8-10** JWeaver(15) (lw: hld up in tch: hdwy ent st: led over 1f out: drvn clr) | — | 1 | 20/1 | 74 | 48 |
| 2578[9] | **La Tansani (IRE) (63)** (RHannon) **3-8-10** JFEgan(14) (a.p: led over 2f out tl over 1f out: one pce) | 2½ | 2 | 9/1 | 69 | 43 |
| 1527[21] | **Theatre Magic (64)** (SRBowring) **3-8-10** DeanMcKeown(12) (trckd ldrs: effrt over 2f out: nvr able to chal) | 5 | 3 | 12/1 | 59 | 33 |
| *2552[8]* | **Domino Flyer (60)** (MrsASwinbank) **3-9-2** DHarrison(16) (lw: prom: rdn over 2f out: kpt on same pce) | nk | 4 | 20/1 | 64 | 38 |
| *2170[8]* | **Houghton Venture (USA) (64)** (SPCWoods) **4-9-4** WWoods(7) (trckd ldrs: rdn 2f out: nt pce to chal) | 7 | 5 | 12/1 | 44 | 26 |
| *2689[6]* | **Red Rusty (USA) (59)** (DMorris) **3-8-10** TIves(9) (led after 1f tl over 2f out: sn wknd) | 2½ | 6 | 20/1 | 39 | 13 |
| 1302[14] | **Hawaii Storm (FR) (65)** (DJSffrenchDavis) **8-9-4** RCochrane(5) (s.s: racd wd: kpt on fnl 2f: nvr nrr) | 3½ | 7 | 20/1 | 32 | 14 |
| 2536[9] | **Sheraz (IRE) (63)** (NTinkler) **4-9-7** CRutter(4) (in rr tl sme hdwy fnl 2f) | 1¼ | 8 | 16/1 | 33 | 15 |

| | | | | SP | RR | SF |
|---|---|---|---|---|---|---|
| 1654[19] | **Welcome Royale (IRE) (60)** (MHTompkins) **3-8-10** PRobinson(3) (led 1f: trckd ldrs: rdn over 2f out: grad wknd) | 1½ | **9** | 10/1 | 27 | 1 |
| 2874[5] | **Best of All (IRE) (67)** (JBerry) **4-9-1** JFortune(1) (lw: dropped to mid div ½-wy: rdn over 2f out: no imp) | 1½ | **10** | 6/1[2] | 21 | 3 |
| *836*[4] | **Chadleigh Lane (USA) (64)** (RHollinshead) **4-9-7**(3) FLynch(2) (bit bkwd: nvr nr to chal) | 3 | **11** | 12/1 | 24 | 6 |
| 1780[8] | **Lead Him On (USA) (65)** (PWHarris) **3-8-10** GHind(6) (unruly stalls: dwlt: a in rr) | 2½ | **12** | 7/1 | 13 | — |
| *2637*[5] | **Dragonjoy (65)** (NPLittmoden) **3-9-1b**(7) GFaulkner(11) (a bhd: t.o) | 15 | **13** | 20/1 | — | — |
| *2637*[3] | **Souperficial (60)** (JAGlover) **5-9-4v** GCarter(8) (a in rr: t.o) | 5 | **14** | 13/2[3] | — | — |
| 1617[14] | **Covered Girl (IRE) (63)** (BWHills) **3-8-7** MHills(10) (a in rr: t.o) | ¾ | **15** | 14/1 | — | — |
| *2369** | **Roar on Tour (60)** (MrsMReveley) **7-9-7b** ACulhane(13) (lw: w ldr: rdn ent st: eased whn btn appr fnl f: t.o) | ¾ | **16** | 9/2[1] | — | — |
| | | | | (SP 136.8%) | **16 Rn** | |

**1m 44.5** (4.50) CSF £182.72 TOTE £35.30: £7.70 £3.30 £3.40 (£156.40) Trio £360.50; £462.13 to Worcester 23/7/96 OWNER Chequers Racing Club (MIDDLEHAM) BRED Cheveley Park Stud Ltd

WEIGHT FOR AGE 3yo-8lb

**OFFICIAL EXPLANATION Roar On Tour: was distressed after the race.**

**445 Catherine's Choice** opened his score with a very easily gained success and one would wonder why it has taken him so long. (20/1)

**1809 La Tansani (IRE)**, trying his luck again at this longer trip, did not seem to last it out after being in the firing-line from the start. (9/1)

**701 Theatre Magic** seems to need at least this trip now, though on this occasion he lacked the speed to mount a serious challenge. (12/1)

**1025* Domino Flyer** produces his best when ridden from off the pace and had far too much use made of him. (20/1)

**510 Houghton Venture (USA)**, still struggling to find an opening, failed to pick up when given the office soon after straightening up and was never a threat. (12/1)

**2541 Red Rusty (USA)** adopted more forceful tactics again, but he was in trouble early in the straight and was brushed aside with ease. (20/1)

**2369* Roar on Tour** has produced his best form on this track but he was struggling to hold his pitch from the turn into the straight and the position was accepted when all chance had gone. (9/2)

## 2935 KANDINSKY CLAIMING STKS (I) (3-Y.O+) (Class F)

3-00 (3-01) **1m 3f (Fibresand)** £2,031.00 (£556.00: £261.00) Stalls: Low GOING minus 0.02 sec per fur (STD)

| | | | | SP | RR | SF |
|---|---|---|---|---|---|---|
| 2356[7] | **Ihtimaam (FR) (37)** (MrsASwinbank) **4-9-4** DHarrison(6) (trckd ldrs: rdn to ld ent fnl f: swvd rt: hld on cl home) | — | **1** | 25/1 | 59 | 13 |
| 2737[P] | **Precedency** (KMcAuliffe) **4-9-12** JFEgan(8) (lw: hld up: hdwy 5f out: effrt & rdn 2f out: hmpd & swtchd ins fnl f: fin wl) | ½ | **2** | 33/1 | 66 | 20 |
| | **Uncle Oswald** (RHannon) **5-9-12** RPerham(3) (a.p: jnd ldr ent st: rdn 2f out: r.o one pce) | 1¼ | **3** | 5/4[1] | 65 | 19 |
| *2553*[4] | **Chevalier (USA) (64)** (ICampbell) **4-9-3**(7) GFaulkner(1) (lw: led: rdn 3f out: hdd over 1f out: no ex fnl f) | 1½ | **4** | 5/1[2] | 60 | 14 |
| *1967*[6] | **Broom Isle (57)** (DBurchell) **8-8-8**(3) SDrowne(5) (hdwy ½-wy: rdn wl over 1f out: kpt on one pce) | ½ | **5** | 10/1 | 47 | 1 |
| *2749*[9] | **Sandmoor Denim (63)** (SRBowring) **9-9-2** DeanMcKeown(2) (prom: hrd rdn over 2f out: sn btn) | ¾ | **6** | 5/1[2] | 51 | 5 |
| 2348[10] | **Oxgang (IRE) (55)** (JGFitzGerald) **3-8-7be** JFortune(9) (lw: trckd ldrs: rdn over 2f out: grad wknd) | 1½ | **7** | 16/1 | 50 | — |
| *2551*[9] | **Double-O-Seven (71)** (MJohnston) **3-8-7** JWeaver(7) (hld up in rr: shkn up 5f out: no rspnse: t.o) | dist | **8** | 11/2[3] | — | — |
| 2439[8] | **Comedie Arrete (FR) (40)** (MCChapman) **4-8-4**(7) CScally(4) (stdd s: sn chsng ldrs: wknd ent st: t.o) | 8 | **9** | 33/1 | — | — |
| | | | | (SP 117.9%) | **9 Rn** | |

**2m 32.4** (12.40) CSF £460.41 TOTE £32.30: £4.40 £5.10 £1.30 (£207.80) Trio £203.90; £258.57 to Worcester 23/7/96 OWNER Upex Electrical Distributors Ltd (RICHMOND) BRED Gainsborough Stud Management Ltd

WEIGHT FOR AGE 3yo-11lb

**1474 Ihtimaam (FR)** worked hard to win this, but he did take the runner-up's ground inside the last furlong and may have been a shade fortunate to escape scot-free. (25/1)

**Precedency** responded to pressure from some way out and was still closing when forced to switch 150 yards out. Though he did finish strongly, the Stewards found the interference not worthy of a turn around. (33/1)

**Uncle Oswald**, having his first run in almost a year and taking a step down in class, looked forward enough in condition and appeared likely to take command when he wished. With the leader proving unwilling to give best, he came off the bridle entering the last quarter-mile and was unable to go through with his effort. (5/4: Evens-11/8)

**2553 Chevalier (USA)**, the gamble of the race, proved a tough nut to crack, but he was at the end of his tether approaching the final furlong and forced to accept defeat. (5/1)

**Broom Isle** showed signs of a return to form with a much better display than of late and she could be coming to herself. (10/1)

**2551 Sandmoor Denim**, under the strongest pressure from the turn into the straight, found this trip beyond his best and was never going to take a hand in proceedings. (5/1)

**2325 Double-O-Seven** (11/2: op 7/2)

## 2936 TURNER H'CAP (0-60) (3-Y.O+) (Class F)

3-30 (3-30) **1m 6f (Fibresand)** £2,381.00 (£656.00: £311.00) Stalls: Low GOING minus 0.02 sec per fur (STD)

| | | | | SP | RR | SF |
|---|---|---|---|---|---|---|
| 2627[6] | **Shirley Sue (56)** (MJohnston) **3-8-10** JWeaver(12) (lw: hld up in rr: hdwy 5f out: led 3f out: sn wl clr: unchal) | — | **1** | 3/1[1] | 75 | 16 |
| 2493[3] | **Breydon (48)** (MHTompkins) **3-8-2**ow4 PRobinson(11) (hld up & bhd: hdwy over 3f out: no imp on wnr fnl 2f) | 18 | **2** | 9/1 | 46 | — |
| 2516[7] | **Top Prize (33)** (MBrittain) **8-8-1v** GBardwell(2) (hld up in rr: styd on fnl 3f: nvr nrr) | 2 | **3** | 9/1 | 29 | — |
| | **Drama King (38)** (SRBowring) **4-8-6b** SDWilliams(14) (in tch: hdwy 5f out: rdn ent st: no imp) | nk | **4** | 25/1 | 34 | — |
| 2117[9] | **Jundi (IRE) (47)** (JDBethell) **5-9-1b** RCochrane(9) (hld up: hdwy 8f out: rdn & btn ent st) | 6 | **5** | 16/1 | 36 | — |
| 2418[4] | **Redstella (USA) (60)** (RMWhitaker) **7-10-0v** ACulhane(10) (prom: led 6f out to 3f out: sn rdn & outpcd: fin lame) | 2 | **6** | 11/1 | 47 | 2 |
| 2165[11] | **Jean de Florette (USA) (29)** (RCSpicer) **5-7-11b** FNorton(5) (in tch: rdn 4f out: sn wknd) | 9 | **7** | 16/1 | 5 | — |
| 890[7] | **Belle's Boy (60)** (BPalling) **3-9-0** TSprake(13) (lw: prom: led 7f out to 6f out: wknd over 3f out) | 2 | **8** | 8/1 | 34 | — |
| *1095*[9] | **Dispol Dancer (28)** (MrsVAAconley) **5-7-10** JQuinn(3) (led 1f: wknd over 4f out) | 2 | **9** | 33/1 | — | — |
| 2565[5] | **Persian Symphony (IRE) (45)** (MrsAMNaughton) **5-8-13** NConnorton(4) (trckd ldrs 10f: sn rdn & lost tch) | 4 | **10** | 16/1 | 12 | — |
| *2553*[8] | **Tintara (IRE) (58)** (BWHills) **3-8-12** MHills(7) (lw: hld up in rr: sddle slipped ent st: t.o) | 12 | **11** | 6/1[2] | 12 | — |
| *428*[6] | **Sahhar (60)** (RWArmstrong) **3-9-0** GCarter(6) (hld up mid div: hrd drvn 5f out: sn lost tch: t.o) | hd | **12** | 14/1 | 13 | — |
| 2217[3] | **Anchorena (46)** (MrsASwinbank) **4-9-0** JFortune(1) (swtg: a in rr: t.o) | 3 | **13** | 7/1[3] | — | — |
| 2572[6] | **Sicarian (57)** (MJHeaton-Ellis) **4-9-8**(3) SDrowne(8) (led after 1f to 7f out: wknd 4f out: t.o) | dist | **14** | 16/1 | — | — |
| | | | | (SP 128.2%) | **14 Rn** | |

**3m 12.9** (13.90) CSF £30.41 CT £212.83 TOTE £4.10: £1.40 £2.30 £3.90 (£65.50) Trio £106.70 OWNER Greenland Park Ltd (MIDDLEHAM) BRED Lahama Ltd

LONG HANDICAP Dispol Dancer 7-6

WEIGHT FOR AGE 3yo-14lb

**2627 Shirley Sue**, at the top of her form at present, could be called the winner from a long way out, and these extended trips look made to measure. (3/1)
**2493 Breydon** produced his form almost to the pound with the winner from their previous encounter at Hamilton and never threatened to finish any closer. (9/1)
**1095* Top Prize** finds this trip inadequate and he was only getting into top gear when the winner was already past the post. (9/1)
**Drama King** appeared to find this longer trip testing his stamina to the full and he was fighting a losing battle from the turn into the straight. (25/1)
**2418 Redstella (USA)** helped force the pace even with topweight, but he had been hung out to dry from below the distance and it transpired that he was unsound on pulling up. (11/1)

## 2937 CEZANNE H'CAP (0-70) (3-Y.O+ F & M) (Class E)

4-00 (4-01) **7f (Fibresand)** £3,534.30 (£1,058.40: £508.20: £233.10) Stalls: Low GOING minus 0.02 sec per fur (STD)

| | | | | SP | RR | SF |
|---|---|---|---|---|---|---|
| 942$^{9}$ | **Young Annabel (USA) (58)** (CADwyer) **3-9-1** TIves(9) (hld up: hdwy 4f out: led 2f out: drvn clr) | — | 1 | 9/2$^{3}$ | 69 | 41 |
| *2634** | **Princess Efisio (65)** (BAMcMahon) **3-9-8** GCarter(15) (lw: hld up: hdwy centre over 2f out: nt rch wnr) | 3½ | 2 | 4/1$^{2}$ | 68 | 40 |
| 2745$^{10}$ | **Cedar Girl (38)** (RJHodges) **4-7-11**$^{(5)}$ AmandaSanders(4) (trckd ldrs: effrt ent st: one pce appr fnl f) | 1 | 3 | 25/1 | 39 | 18 |
| 2590$^{4}$ | **Formidable Liz (53)** (MDHammond) **6-9-3** JWeaver(14) (lw: mde most to 2f out: rdn & one pce appr fnl f) | ¾ | 4 | 3/1$^{1}$ | 52 | 31 |
| 2320$^{10}$ | **Down The Yard (43)** (MCChapman) **3-8-0** NKennedy(12) (sn drvn along in rr: styd on fnl 2f: nvr nrr) | 5 | 5 | 14/1 | 31 | 3 |
| 2687$^{6}$ | **Hadadabble (40)** (PatMitchell) **3-7-8**$^{(3)}$ NVarley(5) (lw: trckd ldrs: rdn & no hdwy fnl 2f) | nk | 6 | 20/1 | 27 | — |
| *1719*$^{10}$ | **Prudent Princess (57)** (AHide) **4-9-2b**$^{1(5)}$ RHavlin(8) (dwlt: hdwy after 2f: ev ch 2f out: sn rdn & wknd) | 1 | 7 | 20/1 | 42 | 21 |
| 2316$^{11}$ | **Shaa Spin (55)** (JBerry) **4-9-5** JFortune(10) (lw: disp ld tl rdn & fdd fnl 2f) | 2 | 8 | 20/1 | 35 | 14 |
| 2578$^{11}$ | **Itsinthepost (67)** (VSoane) **3-9-10** AMcGlone(16) (lw: trckd ldrs: hrd rdn over 2f out: sn btn) | hd | 9 | 33/1 | 47 | 19 |
| *2636** | **Portite Sophie (33)** (MBrittain) **5-7-8**$^{(3)ow1}$ DWright(2) (lw: nvr nr ldrs) | 3 | 10 | 12/1 | 6 | — |
| *2550*$^{7}$ | **Runforaction (IRE) (33)** (LRLloyd-James) **4-7-11b**$^{1}$ JLowe(1) (s.s: a bhd & outpcd) | 6 | 11 | 25/1 | — | — |
| 2340$^{8}$ | **Persephone (39)** (ICampbell) **3-7-3v**$^{(7)}$ RMullen(13) (trckd ldrs: rdn along ½-wy: wknd 3f out) | ¾ | 12 | 14/1 | — | — |
| 2851$^{5}$ | **Rainbows Rhapsody (33)** (DWChapman) **5-7-11** JQuinn(3) (prom over 4f: sn wknd: t.o) | ¾ | 13 | 14/1 | — | — |
| 1181$^{5}$ | **Sondos (67)** (JWHills) **3-9-7**$^{(3)}$ MHenry(7) (trckd ldrs over 4f: sn wknd: t.o) | 1 | 14 | 10/1 | 21 | — |
| | **Never Say so (49)** (CSmith) **4-8-10**$^{(3)}$ CTeague(11) (unruly s: a bhd: t.o) | 17 | 15 | 33/1 | — | — |
| 2417$^{3}$ | **Rocky Stream (42)** (RMWhitaker) **3-7-13** AMackay(6) (a bhd: t.o) | 11 | 16 | 10/1 | — | — |
| | | | | (SP 136.9%) | **16 Rn** | |

**1m 31.7** (4.90) CSF £24.27 CT £415.95 TOTE £5.80: £1.10 £2.00 £10.60 £1.50 (£56.90) Trio £311.60 OWNER Trident/Burns (NEWMARKET) BRED Richard S. Trontz
WEIGHT FOR AGE 3yo-7lb
**678 Young Annabel (USA)**, well supported on this big step down in class, was making her All-Weather debut. Delivering her challenge down the centre of the track, she forged clear inside the distance and should have no trouble in winning again. (9/2: op 8/1)
**2634* Princess Efisio**, restrained after breaking well on this first attempt at seven furlongs, stayed on relentlessly inside the distance, but the winner had got away. (4/1: 3/1-9/2)
**Cedar Girl** ran up to her best on this return to seven furlongs and she will hardly need to improve to pick up a small handicap. (25/1)
**2590 Formidable Liz** has been performing well enough to win on turf but her trainer decided to give her another chance on this surface and she shared the lead until early in the straight before the seventh furlong appeared to find her out. (3/1: 4/1-5/2)
**1721 Down The Yard** was off the bridle for most of the way, but did stay on in the latter stages without proving troublesome. (14/1)
**1096 Prudent Princess** did not get the best of the start, but she ran very freely in the first-time blinkers and was fighting for the lead until calling enough approaching the final furlong. She will get it right one of these days. (20/1)
**2636* Portite Sophie** (12/1: op 8/1)

## 2938 MONDRIAN (S) STKS (2-Y.O) (Class G)

4-30 (4-33) **7f (Fibresand)** £2,070.00 (£570.00: £270.00) GOING minus 0.02 sec per fur (STD)

| | | | | SP | RR | SF |
|---|---|---|---|---|---|---|
| 2025$^{11}$ | **Common Rock (IRE)** (JNorton) **2-8-6v**$^{1}$ DaleGibson(6) (trckd ldrs: outpcd over 2f out: styd on u.p to ld nr fin) | — | 1 | 25/1 | 46 | — |
| *2371*$^{9}$ | **Bonsiel** (JGFitzGerald) **2-8-6** JFortune(2) (mde most: hrd rdn over 1f out: wknd & ct cl home) | ½ | 2 | 6/1$^{3}$ | 45 | — |
| | **Hopperetta** (BPalling) **2-8-6** TSprake(3) (w'like: neat: b: s.s: hdwy ½-wy: rdn & rn green 2f out: styng on whn n.m.r nr fin) | nk | 3 | 3/1$^{2}$ | 44 | — |
| 1499$^{6}$ | **Oddfellows Girl** (NBycroft) **2-8-3**$^{(3)}$ CTeague(4) (lw: s.i.s: sn w ldrs: hrd drvn & wandered over 1f out: sn btn) | 2 | 4 | 20/1 | 40 | — |
| 2512$^{2}$ | **Clonavon Girl (IRE)** (MJCamacho) **2-8-6** JQuinn(1) (lw: hld up in tch: rdn along ½-wy: wl bhd fnl 2f) | 21 | 5 | 1/2$^{1}$ | — | — |
| 1537$^{15}$ | **Dissington Times** (JNorton) **2-8-11** FNorton(5) (a bhd: t.o fnl 2f) | 1¾ | 6 | 20/1 | — | — |
| | | | | (SP 119.3%) | **6 Rn** | |

**1m 36.2** (9.40) CSF £146.19 TOTE £29.10: £6.20 £3.40 (£52.20) OWNER Mrs Sylvia Blakeley (BARNSLEY) BRED Ennistown Stud
Bt in 6,400 gns
OFFICIAL EXPLANATION **Clonavaon Girl (IRE): seemed not to face the kick-back.**
**Common Rock (IRE)** finished last on her debut but the application of a visor in this lower-grade event brought about a massive improvement, though she did appear costly to retain. (25/1)
**Bonsiel** tried to make all over this longer trip and certainly looked like doing so, but she wandered about under pressure in the latter stages and was touched off nearing the line. (6/1: op 4/1)
**Hopperetta** soon recovered from a tardy start and was pegging back the leader when becoming the meat in the sandwich inside the last 50 yards. She will be all the sharper for the run. (3/1)
**1499 Oddfellows Girl** had a running battle with Bonsiel, but wandered off a true line when put under pressure on the approach to the final furlong and her measure had been taken. (20/1)
**2512 Clonavon Girl (IRE)**, settled behind the leaders going well, did not relish sand being kicked into her face and she was having none of it long before reaching the home straight. (1/2)

## 2939 KANDINSKY CLAIMING STKS (II) (3-Y.O+) (Class F)

5-00 (5-01) **1m 3f (Fibresand)** £2,031.00 (£556.00: £261.00) Stalls: Low GOING minus 0.02 sec per fur (STD)

| | | | | SP | RR | SF |
|---|---|---|---|---|---|---|
| *2304** | **Troubadour Song (66)** (WWHaigh) **4-9-9**$^{(3)}$ PMcCabe(7) (lw: hld up gng wl: led over 2f out: sn clr: comf) | — | 1 | 13/8$^{1}$ | 79+ | 25 |
| 2737$^{4}$ | **Statajack (IRE) (75)** (DRCElsworth) **8-9-12b** AProcter(4) (hld up in rr: stdy hdwy over 3f out: chsd wnr fnl 2f: no imp) | 4 | 2 | 2/1$^{2}$ | 73 | 19 |
| *2553*$^{7}$ | **Stevie's Wonder (IRE) (60)** (BJLlewellyn) **6-9-2** VSlattery(2) (a.p: hrd drvn over 2f out: one pce) | 8 | 3 | 7/2$^{3}$ | 52 | — |

| | | | Pos | SP | RR | SF |
|---|---|---|---|---|---|---|
| 1417$^{4}$ | **Stone Cross (IRE) (54)** (MartinTodhunter) **4-9-10** NConnorton(8) (hld up: effrt over 3f out: rdn over 2f out: no imp) | 7 | **4** | 8/1 | 49 | — |
| 2756$^{9}$ | **Taniyar (FR) (42)** (RHollinshead) **4-9-1**(3) FLynch(3) (prom: pushed along 6f out: ev ch over 2f out: sn outpcd) | 4 | **5** | 20/1 | 38 | — |
| 2056$^{13}$ | **Undawaterscubadiva (38)** (MPBielby) **4-8-13**(5) LNewton(1) (lw: led: rdn 3f out: sn hdd & wknd: t.o) | 12 | **6** | 33/1 | 20 | — |
| 995$^{20}$ | **Tirlie (IRE) (40)** (JWPayne) **4-8-11**(5) DGriffiths(6) (bkwd: lost tch over 4f out: t.o) | 15 | **7** | 20/1 | — | — |
| *2303$^{13}$* | **Bites (38)** (TTBill) **3-7-10** JQuinn(5) (bhd fnl 5f: t.o) | 2 | **8** | 33/1 | — | — |

(SP 120.2%) **8 Rn**

**2m 31.8** (11.80) CSF £5.49 TOTE £2.60: £1.10 £1.10 £2.40 (£2.00) Trio £5.40 OWNER Spring Cottage Racing Partnership (MALTON) BRED Paul Mellon

WEIGHT FOR AGE 3yo-11lb

**2304* Troubadour Song** landed quite a gamble in completing his hat-trick and the manner in which he won stamps him as a most improved individual since his attention was switched to the Sand. (13/8)

**2737 Statajack (IRE)** played cat and mouse with the winner, but did not possess the speed of that rival when the chips were down and he was unable to land a blow. (2/1: op Evens)

**Stevie's Wonder (IRE)** is only a shadow of his old self and he was under all the aids and beaten soon after entering the straight. (7/2)

**1417 Stone Cross (IRE)** (8/1: op 5/1)

## 2940 PICASSO H'CAP (0-60) (3-Y.O+) (Class F)

5-30 (5-32) **6f (Fibresand)** £2,381.00 (£656.00: £311.00) Stalls: Low GOING: minus 0.02 sec per fur (STD)

| | | | Pos | SP | RR | SF |
|---|---|---|---|---|---|---|
| *2551$^{7}$* | **Fiaba (32)** (MrsNMacauley) **8-8-3v**(3) CTeague(4) (lw: a.p: rdn to ld over 1f out: r.o wl) | — | **1** | 16/1 | 39 | 15 |
| 2185$^{14}$ | **Disco Boy (50)** (PDEvans) **6-9-10** OUrbina(3) (lw: mde most tl hdd over 1f out: unable qckn) | 2 | **2** | 16/1 | 52 | 28 |
| 2735$^{3}$ | **Fighter Squadron (35)** (REPeacock) **7-8-9b** DHarrison(2) (mid div: rdn ½-wy: kpt on ins fnl f) | 3 | **3** | 14/1 | 29 | 5 |
| *2748$^{3}$* | **Monis (IRE) (54)** (JBalding) **5-9-7v**(7) JEdmunds(7) (hdwy u.p 2f out: kpt on fnl f: nvr nr to chal) | hd | **4** | 7/1$^{2}$ | 47 | 23 |
| *2367** | **Lady Silk (50)** (MissJFCraze) **5-9-10** NConnorton(11) (lw: mid div: rdn ent st: nvr able to chal) | 3½ | **5** | 3/1$^{1}$ | 34 | 10 |
| *2369$^{4}$* | **Tame Deer (51)** (MCChapman) **4-9-4**(7) CScally(6) (hdwy on ins fnl 2f: hrd rdn & kpt on ins fnl f) | nk | **6** | 8/1$^{3}$ | 34 | 10 |
| 1902$^{7}$ | **Great Hall (43)** (PDCundell) **7-9-3** GCarter(10) (s.s: bhd tl styd on appr fnl f) | hd | **7** | 12/1 | 26 | 2 |
| *2748$^{4}$* | **Naughty Pistol (USA) (49)** (PDEvans) **4-9-9** JFortune(16) (lw: hdwy on outside over 2f out: nt rch ldrs) | ½ | **8** | 7/1$^{2}$ | 31 | 7 |
| *2636$^{6}$* | **Bella Coola (25)** (MartynMeade) **4-7-13** JQuinn(5) (lw: nvr nrr) | 1½ | **9** | 14/1 | 3 | — |
| 2771$^{8}$ | **Christian Flight (IRE) (39)** (SGollings) **7-8-13b** VHalliday(12) (b.off hind: prom: ev ch 2f out: sn hrd rdn & wknd) | hd | **10** | 14/1 | 16 | — |
| 2763$^{10}$ | **Hang a Right (41)** (CADwyer) **9-8-8**(7) NicolaCole(14) (nvr trbld ldrs) | nk | **11** | 20/1 | 18 | — |
| *2367$^{9}$* | **Dauntless Fort (25)** (MrsVAAconley) **5-7-13** DRMcCabe(8) (in tch tl wknd u.p 2f out: t.o) | 2½ | **12** | 25/1 | — | — |
| *2636$^{12}$* | **Rustic Song (IRE) (27)** (JWharton) **3-7-10** FNorton(1) (lw: in tch 4f: wknd qckly: t.o) | 8 | **13** | 16/1 | — | — |
| *1971$^{9}$* | **General Equation (58)** (JBalding) **3-9-13** SDWilliams(9) (disp ld: rdn over 2f out: sn wknd: t.o) | ¾ | **14** | 14/1 | 5 | — |
| *2632$^{6}$* | **Verro (USA) (24)** (KBishop) **9-7-9e**(3) DWright(13) (a in rr: t.o) | 2 | **15** | 14/1 | — | — |
| 2316$^{3}$ | **Present 'n Correct (45)** (CBBBooth) **3-9-0** ACulhane(15) (sn drvn along on outside: bhd fnl 3f: t.o) | 4 | **16** | 8/1$^{3}$ | — | — |

(SP 139.5%) **16 Rn**

**1m 19.0** (5.50) CSF £248.44 CT £1,948.04 TOTE £26.10: £8.30 £8.80 £4.50 £2.20 (£437.30) Trio £401.40; £508.84 to Worcester 23/7/96 OWNER Mr A. J. Peake (MELTON MOWBRAY) BRED Grange Thoroughbreds

WEIGHT FOR AGE 3yo-5lb

STEWARDS' ENQUIRY Teague susp. 1 & 2/8/96 (excessive & incorrect use of whip).

**Fiaba**, winning her first race in three and a half years, appreciated this return to sprinting and had the prize sewn up entering the final furlong. (16/1)

**653 Disco Boy** tried to win his race from the front and turned in his best display for some time. It would seem he is on the way back. (16/1)

**2735 Fighter Squadron** kept plugging away under strong pressure in the closing stages but his finishing position was as close as he could get. (14/1)

**2748 Monis (IRE)** made progress from off the pace in the last couple of furlongs but could not quicken sufficiently under his welter-weight to threaten the winner. (7/1)

**2367* Lady Silk** kept on from midfield in the latter stages but she was hard at work for quite some way and never going to reach the principals. (3/1)

**2369 Tame Deer** does seem to need a stiffer test of stamina, for he was only just into his stride when the contest was as good as over. (8/1: 6/1-9/1)

**2316 Present 'n Correct** (8/1: op 5/1)

T/Plpt: £1,148.60 (10.61 Tckts). T/Qdpt: £32.40 (32.48 Tckts). IM

# 2740-WINDSOR (Fig. 8) (Good to firm)

## Monday July 22nd

WEATHER: fine & sunny WIND: nil

## 2941 GREAT ORMOND STREET CHILDRENS HOSPITAL CARDIAC UNIT (S) H'CAP (0-60) (3-Y.O+) (Class F)

6-25 (6-34) **1m 3f 135y** £2,773.00 (£778.00: £379.00) Stalls: High GOING minus 0.29 sec per fur (GF)

| | | | Pos | SP | RR | SF |
|---|---|---|---|---|---|---|
| 2563$^{6}$ | **Kristal Breeze (42)** (WRMuir) **4-9-1** JReid(5) (lw: a.p: led ins fnl f: drvn out) | — | **1** | 7/1$^{3}$ | 53 | 35 |
| *2372$^{6}$* | **Nothing Doing (IRE) (35)** (WJMusson) **7-8-8** SWhitworth(6) (hdwy on ins to ld over 3f out: hdd ins fnl f) | 1¾ | **2** | 6/1$^{2}$ | 44 | 26 |
| 2740$^{2}$ | **Elly Fleetfoot (IRE) (53)** (MJRyan) **4-9-12** BDoyle(1) (lw: hdwy 3f out: ev ch over 1f out: nt qckn) | hd | **3** | 8/1 | 62 | 44 |
| 2568$^{6}$ | **Willy Star (BEL) (52)** (MrsSJSmith) **6-9-6**(5) GLee(3) (hdwy 3f out: hrd rdn fnl 2f: r.o ins fnl f) | 1¼ | **4** | 8/1 | 59 | 41 |
| 2906$^{3}$ | **Dots Dee (30)** (JMBradley) **7-8-3** PaulEddery(4) (b.nr fore: a.p: ev ch over 1f out: one pce) | hd | **5** | 6/1$^{2}$ | 37 | 19 |
| 2440$^{5}$ | **Ajdar (48)** (MissGayKelleway) **5-9-4**(3) DaneO'Neill(2) (lw: hdwy fnl 3f: nrst fin) | ½ | **6** | 4/1$^{1}$ | 54 | 36 |
| 2711$^{9}$ | **Mystic Legend (IRE) (28)** (JJSheehan) **4-8-1** CRutter(10) (lw: hdwy 3f out: hrd rdn 2f out: wknd ins fnl f) | s.h | **7** | 33/1 | 34 | 16 |
| 2716$^{7}$ | **Tocco Jewel (23)** (MJRyan) **6-7-3**(7) AMcCarthy(8) (hdwy fnl 2f: nt rch ldrs) | 1¾ | **8** | 33/1 | 26 | 8 |
| 2716$^{8}$ | **Bronze Runner (30)** (EAWheeler) **12-7-12b**(5) ADaly(13) (nvr bttr than mid div) | 6 | **9** | 10/1 | 25 | 7 |
| 2537$^{10}$ | **Leap in the Dark (IRE) (29)** (MissLCSiddall) **7-8-2** GHind(9) (bhd fnl 3f) | 6 | **10** | 14/1 | 16 | — |
| 2203$^{9}$ | **Thorniwama (30)** (JJBridger) **5-8-0**(3) DarrenMoffatt(15) (lw: led 4f out: sn hdd & wknd) | ½ | **11** | 33/1 | 16 | — |
| 2594$^{13}$ | **Yellow Dragon (IRE) (47)** (BAPearce) **3-8-8** LeesaLong(12) (b: s.s: a bhd) | d.h | **11** | 25/1 | 34 | 4 |
| 2310$^{14}$ | **Safety (USA) (33)** (JWhite) **9-8-3b**(3) SDrowne(7) (led 4f: wknd over 3f out) | 4 | **13** | 33/1 | 14 | — |

| | | | | SP | RR | SF |
|---|---|---|---|---|---|---|
| 2592[13] | **Dolly Dolittle (23)** (HJCollingridge) **5-7-10** NAdams(14) (bhd fnl 3f) | 1¼ | **14** | 33/1 | 2 | — |
| | **Last Ambition (IRE) (39)** (RChampion) **4-8-12** AClark(11) (led after 4f tl wknd 4f out: t.o) | dist | **15** | 33/1 | — | — |

(SP 120.5%) **15 Rn**

**2m 29.9** (5.90) CSF £43.00 CT £309.62 TOTE £7.00: £2.00 £2.20 £2.80 (£34.10) Trio £28.40 OWNER Mr S. Lamb (LAMBOURN) BRED R. and Mrs Heathcote

LONG HANDICAP Dolly Dolittle 7-2 Tocco Jewel 7-6

WEIGHT FOR AGE 3yo-12lb

No bid

**2563 Kristal Breeze**, after a long battle, forced her head in front inside the final furlong and held on gamely. (7/1)

**2372 Nothing Doing (IRE)** found a good run through on the inside to strike the front over three furlongs from home. He was flat out from the two-furlong pole and always vulnerable to one with a turn of foot. (6/1)

**2740 Elly Fleetfoot (IRE)** loomed up to challenge in the centre of the course but, after having every chance, could not quicken in the final furlong. (8/1: 6/1-9/1)

**2568 Willy Star (BEL)**, under pressure a long way out, kept staying on but lacked a turn of foot. (8/1)

**2906 Dots Dee** closed up from the start, but could not quicken in the closing stages. (6/1: 9/2-7/1)

**2440 Ajdar** seemed to be set a lot to do and, with a wall of horses in front of him from the two-furlong marker, could do no more. He might be worth another chance in this company. (4/1)

**Mystic Legend (IRE)** came with a run on the outside over two furlongs from home, but the effort petered out in the final furlong. (33/1)

## 2942 E.B.F. NATIONAL CAR PARKS MEDIAN AUCTION MAIDEN STKS (2-Y.O) (Class E)

6-55 (7-00) **5f 10y** £2,997.50 (£905.00: £440.00: £207.50) Stalls: High GOING minus 0.29 sec per fur (GF)

| | | | | SP | RR | SF |
|---|---|---|---|---|---|---|
| | **Gunners Glory** (BJMeehan) **2-9-0** BDoyle(10) (w'like: lw: a.p: qcknd to ld 1f out: drvn out) | — | **1** | 10/1 | 73 | 24 |
| 2699[2] | **Effervescence** (RHannon) **2-8-11**(3) DaneO'Neill(6) (lw: chsd ldr: swtchd lft & qcknd to chal 1f out: r.o) | hd | **2** | 7/4[1] | 73 | 24 |
| | **Incatime** (CJames) **2-9-0** CRutter(8) (w ldr: ev ch over 1f out: nt qckn) | 3 | **3** | 25/1 | 63 | 14 |
| *2633*[4] | **Mangus (IRE)** (KOCunningham-Brown) **2-9-0** SWhitworth(5) (lw: a.p: led 2f out to 1f out: nt qckn) | 1 | **4** | 7/1[3] | 60 | 11 |
| | **V I P Charlie** (JRJenkins) **2-9-0** SSanders(7) (str: scope: hdwy 2f out: styd on fnl f) | nk | **5** | 20/1 | 59 | 10 |
| 2600[10] | **Countless Times** (WRMuir) **2-9-0** PaulEddery(9) (led tl wknd 2f out) | 3 | **6** | 14/1 | 50 | 1 |
| 2044[8] | **Coral Springs (USA)** (PWChapple-Hyam) **2-8-9** JReid(1) (prom tl wknd over 1f out) | ½ | **7** | 7/1[3] | 43 | — |
| 2527[6] | **Chilling** (PGMurphy) **2-8-6**(3) SDrowne(2) (swtg: bhd fnl 2f) | nk | **8** | 7/1[3] | 42 | — |
| | **Ellway Lady (IRE)** (IABalding) **2-8-9** MHills(4) (leggy: unf: s.s: a bhd) | 2 | **9** | 11/2[2] | 36 | — |
| 2852[11] | **Jonfy (IRE)** (BWHills) **2-8-7**(7) GBrace(3) (outpcd) | ¾ | **10** | 25/1 | 38 | — |

(SP 117.5%) **10 Rn**

**62.2 secs** (3.00) CSF £26.85 TOTE £14.70: £3.20 £1.30 £6.20 (£16.20) Trio £213.70; £30.10 to 24/7/96 OWNER Mr Trevor Painting (UPPER LAMBOURN) BRED Trevor Painting and Mrs Christine Painting

**Gunners Glory** travelled well on the heels of the leaders. He gained the upper hand from the furlong pole and held on bravely. (10/1: 8/1-12/1)

**2699 Effervescence** was switched to challenge approaching the final furlong. He quickened readily, but the winner went with him and proved the better. (7/4)

**Incatime** disputed the lead from the start and was not given a hard time when the leading pair quickened away from him in the final furlong. He should certainly be able to win a race. (25/1)

**2633 Mangus (IRE)** was driven into the lead at the two-furlong marker but was outpaced in the final furlong. (7/1)

**V I P Charlie**, badly outpaced in the early stages, responded to pressure in the final two furlongs and will know more about it next time. (20/1)

**Countless Times** made the running until weakening two furlongs out. (14/1)

**1590 Chilling** (7/1: 5/1-8/1)

**Ellway Lady (IRE)** (11/2: op 9/4)

## 2943 MAXIMS CASINO CLUB H'CAP (0-80) (3-Y.O+) (Class D)

7-25 (7-26) **1m 2f 7y** £3,772.50 (£1,140.00: £555.00: £262.50) Stalls: High GOING minus 0.29 sec per fur (GF)

| | | | | SP | RR | SF |
|---|---|---|---|---|---|---|
| 2525[7] | **Monument (65)** (JSKing) **4-9-0** BDoyle(8) (a.p: led wl ins fnl f: all out) | — | **1** | 14/1 | 76 | 55 |
| 1618[8] | **Soviet Bride (IRE) (64)** (SDow) **4-8-8**(5) ADaly(4) (chsd ldr: led over 1f out tl wl ins fnl f: r.o) | s.h | **2** | 11/2[2] | 75 | 54 |
| 2574[5] | **Princess Danielle (56)** (WRMuir) **4-8-5** CRutter(10) (hdwy & hrd rdn 2f out: r.o ins fnl f) | ¾ | **3** | 8/1 | 66 | 45 |
| 1614[11] | **Indian Nectar (61)** (GBBalding) **3-8-0**ow1 SSanders(9) (hdwy 3f out: hrd rdn & r.o one pce fnl 2f) | 1½ | **4** | 12/1 | 68 | 36 |
| 2599[7] | **Ailesbury Hill (USA) (67)** (PWChapple-Hyam) **3-8-6** JReid(5) (lw: led tl wknd over 1f out) | ½ | **5** | 8/1 | 74 | 43 |
| 1618[5] | **Shining Example (75)** (PJMakin) **4-9-10** TQuinn(6) (swtg: hdwy 5f out: hrd rdn 3f out: wknd 2f out) | 8 | **6** | 9/4[1] | 69 | 48 |
| 2576[9] | **Leith Academy (USA) (70)** (BWHills) **3-8-9** DHolland(1) (a bhd: hrd rdn over 2f out: no rspnse) | 1 | **7** | 10/1 | 62 | 31 |
| 2574[14] | **Myfontaine (67)** (KTIvory) **9-8-11**(5) MartinDwyer(7) (b: effrt & rdn 3f out: sn wknd) | ½ | **8** | 14/1 | 58 | 37 |
| 1773[14] | **Sweetness Herself (67)** (MJRyan) **3-8-6** WCarson(2) (lw: prom tl wknd 2f out) | 3 | **9** | 8/1 | 54 | 23 |
| | **Callaloo (65)** (MrsJCecil) **3-8-4** AClark(3) (stdd s: effrt & hrd rdn 3f out: sn wknd) | 1½ | **10** | 6/1[3] | 49 | 18 |

(SP 123.9%) **10 Rn**

**2m 7.3** (2.40) CSF £86.84 CT £619.16 TOTE £22.00: £6.20 £1.70 £2.30 (£54.70) Trio £170.00 OWNER Mrs P. M. King (SWINDON) BRED Exors of the late Mrs D. M. de Rothschild

WEIGHT FOR AGE 3yo-10lb

**OFFICIAL EXPLANATION Shining Example: the gelding was never going, and was hanging right handed in the straight.**

**2234* Monument** was always close up. After a long battle, he forced his head in front well inside the final furlong and held on well. (14/1)

**1124 Soviet Bride (IRE)**, always in the first two, took a long time to master the leader, and had no reserves to hold the winner's determined effort. (11/2)

**2574 Princess Danielle** made ground under pressure two furlongs out but, though staying on, could not catch the leading pair. (8/1: 6/1-9/1)

**1061 Indian Nectar** made a forward move at the junction and kept on at one pace under pressure in the last two furlongs. (12/1)

**2246 Ailesbury Hill (USA)** set a strong pace and had her rivals off the bridle a long way out, but she weakened when headed at the distance. (8/1: 5/1-9/1)

**1618 Shining Example** moved up approaching the straight, but came under strong pressure soon afterwards and all chance had gone. (9/4)

**Leith Academy (USA)** (10/1: 8/1-12/1)

**Callaloo** (6/1: 4/1-13/2)

## 2944 COOLMORE STUD CONDITIONS STKS (2-Y.O F) (Class C)

7-55 (7-56) **5f 217y** £4,771.20 (£1,667.20: £813.60: £348.00) Stalls: High GOING minus 0.29 sec per fur (GF)

| | | | | SP | RR | SF |
|---|---|---|---|---|---|---|
| 2559[2] | **Irtifa** (PTWalwyn) **2-8-9** WCarson(5) (lw: a.p: hrd rdn fnl f: led cl home) | — | **1** | 7/4[2] | 76 | 19 |

2531* **Colombia (IRE)** (MRStoute) **2-8-13** JReid(2) (a.p: hrd rdn to ld wl ins fnl f: hdd cl home)....nk **2** 10/11 1 79 22
2559* **Silver Purse** (APJones) **2-8-13** TSprake(3) (lw: led: hdd wl ins fnl f: btn whn hmpd nr fin)....1¾ **3** 8/1 3 75 18
2595 3 **Whizz Kid** (JJBridger) **2-8-6**(3) DarrenMoffatt(4) (a last: outpcd 3f out: styd on fnl f)....1½ **4** 20/1 67 10
(SP 104.6%) **4 Rn**

**1m 14.1** (3.60) CSF £3.43 TOTE £2.40 (£1.50) OWNER Mr Hamdan Al Maktoum (LAMBOURN) BRED Shadwell Estate Company Limited
**2559 Irtifa** was always close up. She was obviously running lazily as her rider elected to give her a dozen backhanders in the last furlong, and she eventually responded to snatch the race close home. (7/4)
**2531* Colombia (IRE)** disputed second place. She had to be hard driven to master the leader well inside the final furlong, and could find no extra when collared near the line. (10/11: 8/11-5/4)
**2559* Silver Purse** set a slow pace to halfway before quickening. She had both the first two at full stretch, but was caught well inside the final furlong, and was beaten when hampered close home. (8/1: op 4/1)
**2595 Whizz Kid** lost touch when the pace quickened, but did stay on at the finish. (20/1)

## 2945 MASTERS INTERNATIONAL H'CAP (0-80) (3-Y.O+ F & M) (Class D)
8-25 (8-25) **1m 67y** £3,733.50 (£1,128.00: £549.00: £259.50) Stalls: High GOING minus 0.29 sec per fur (GF)

SP RR SF

2526 5 **Q Factor (64)** (DHaydnJones) **4-9-4** AMackay(12) (led tl over 1f out: led ins fnl f: all out)....— **1** 10/1 77 41
2425 6 **Blessed Spirit (71)** (CFWall) **3-9-3** SSanders(10) (lw: a.p: led over 1f out tl ins fnl f: shkn up & nt qckn cl home)....hd **2** 10/1 84 40
2743* **Rubbiyati (51)** (CEBrittain) **4-8-5** 5x BDoyle(6) (hdwy fnl 2f: nvr nrr)....5 **3** 4/1 1 54 18
1792 7 **Ma Petite Anglaise (70)** (WJarvis) **4-9-7**(3) MHenry(1) (a.p: no hdwy fnl 2f)....3 **4** 6/1 2 67 31
1902 8 **La Pellegrina (IRE) (70)** (PWChapple-Hyam) **3-9-2** JReid(7) (a.p: one pce fnl 3f)....nk **5** 15/2 3 67 23
2710 W **Bandit Girl (63)** (IABalding) **3-8-4**(5) MartinDwyer(9) (bhd tl hdwy & hrd rdn 2f out: nvr nrr)....¾ **6** 4/1 1 58 14
*2325 5* **Ewar Sunrise (60)** (KOCunningham-Brown) **3-8-6** TSprake(4) (nvr nr to chal)....1¾ **7** 20/1 52 8
1906* **Lubaba (USA) (72)** (HThomsonJones) **3-9-4** RHills(5) (prom tl wknd qckly 2f out)....3 **8** 6/1 2 58 14
2162 5 **Commin' Up (67)** (JWHills) **3-8-13** MHills(11) (plld hrd: hmpd 6f out: nvr on terms)....1¾ **9** 10/1 50 6
2529 7 **Green Bentley (IRE) (75)** (RHannon) **3-9-4**(3) DaneO'Neill(3) (a bhd)....½ **10** 10/1 57 13
1074 15 **Mam'selle Bergerac (IRE) (59)** (PMitchell) **3-8-5** AClark(2) (a bhd: t.o fnl 2f)....dist **11** 33/1 — —
**Barbrallen (42)** (MrsLCJewell) **4-7-10** DeclanO'Shea(8) (a bhd: t.o fnl 4f)....dist **12** 40/1 — —
(SP 126.8%) **12 Rn**

**1m 46.0** (3.80) CSF £101.87 CT £442.89 TOTE £19.80: £5.00 £3.80 £1.70 (£97.10) Trio £154.10 OWNER Mr H. G. Collis (PONTYPRIDD) BRED A. Sofroniou and H. Collis
LONG HANDICAP Barbrallen 7-7
WEIGHT FOR AGE 3yo-8lb
**2526 Q Factor** set a strong pace. She looked certain to be beaten when headed approaching the final furlong, but rallied to regain the advantage in the last 100 yards. (10/1)
**1608 Blessed Spirit** disputed second place, travelling very well, and appeared set for victory when striking the front approaching the final furlong. When the winner rallied, she had to be shaken up and the response was limited. (10/1: 7/1-11/1)
**2743* Rubbiyati**, in company with six of her rivals, was unable to go the pace. She did stay on, but all too late to trouble the leading pair. (4/1)
**1462 Ma Petite Anglaise**, always in the leading group, could make no headway under pressure in the final quarter-mile. (6/1)
**1117 La Pellegrina (IRE)** was on the heels of the leaders until outpaced approaching the junction. (15/2)
**2235* Bandit Girl** ran most disappointingly. She was behind until making belated headway under pressure two furlongs out, but never promised to take a hand. (4/1)

## 2946 WILLIAMS DE BROE H'CAP (0-70) (3-Y.O) (Class E)
8-55 (8-58) **5f 217y** £3,046.25 (£920.00: £447.50: £211.25) Stalls: High GOING minus 0.29 sec per fur (GF)

SP RR SF

2604 4 **Never Think Twice (47)** (KTIvory) **3-7-7b**(5) MartinDwyer(12) (gd hdwy over 1f out: swvd rt & led ins fnl f: sn clr)....— **1** 10/1 65 34
2686 4 **Lucky Revenge (63)** (MartynMeade) **3-9-0** JReid(11) (a.p: r.o ins fnl f)....5 **2** 7/1 3 68 37
2765 4 **Redskin Lady (55)** (DRCElsworth) **3-8-3**(3) DaneO'Neill(8) (lw: a.p: rdn & styd on one pce fnl 2f)....1½ **3** 12/1 56 25
2799 2 **Croeso Cynnes (60)** (BPalling) **3-8-11** TSprake(9) (led: edgd bdly lft over 1f out: hdd & wknd ins fnl f)....nk **4** 9/4 1 60 29
2501 12 **Dubai College (IRE) (67)** (CEBrittain) **3-9-4** BDoyle(13) (hdwy & hrd rdn fnl 2f: nrst fin)....1¼ **5** 11/2 2 64 33
2686 2 **Mystery Matthias (52)** (MissBSanders) **3-8-3v** SSanders(4) (a.p: one pce fnl 2f)....1½ **6** 10/1 45 14
2528* **Mr Speaker (IRE) (65)** (CFWall) **3-9-2** NCarlisle(3) (nvr nr to chal)....nk **7** 10/1 57 26
2602 6 **Village Native (FR) (62)** (KOCunningham-Brown) **3-8-13** SWhitworth(6) (nvr bttr than mid div)....½ **8** 12/1 52 21
2411 7 **On The Home Run (50)** (JRJenkins) **3-7-10b**(5)ow5 ADaly(7) (nvr trbld ldrs)....5 **9** 33/1 27 —
2528 8 **Ameliajill (50)** (RHannon) **3-8-1** JFEgan(14) (a bhd)....¾ **10** 12/1 25 —
2686 12 **Times of Times (IRE) (68)** (MJRyan) **3-9-5** TQuinn(1) (prom tl wknd over 1f out)....hd **11** 12/1 43 12
2686* **May Queen Megan (54)** (MrsALMKing) **3-8-5** NAdams(5) (prom tl wknd qckly 2f out)....11 **12** 10/1 — —
2597 2 **Shavinsky (77)** (PHowling) **3-10-0** PaulEddery(10) (a bhd)....¾ **13** 14/1 20 —
2405 11 **Governor's Bid (45)** (MrsLCJewell) **3-7-10b**1 DeclanO'Shea(2) (outpcd: t.o)....15 **14** 33/1 — —
(SP 138.3%) **14 Rn**

**1m 12.2** (1.70) CSF £82.76 CT £812.41 TOTE £11.60: £2.30 £2.90 £3.00 (£37.60) Trio £149.20 OWNER Mr K. T. Ivory (RADLETT) BRED Cheveley Park Stud Ltd
LONG HANDICAP On The Home Run 7-8 Governor's Bid 7-0
**2604 Never Think Twice** began a strong run below the distance. Though swerving to the right, he maintained his momentum and burst clear in the last 150 yards. (10/1)
**2686 Lucky Revenge**, always close up, looked held approaching the distance, but stayed on to take second place near the line. (7/1)
**2765 Redskin Lady**, always close up, had every chance and stayed on under pressure in the last two furlongs. (12/1)
**2799 Croeso Cynnes** made the running, apparently travelling well, and quickened approaching the final furlong. In doing so, she edged badly to the left and, when headed in the last 150 yards, quickly tied up. She has astonishing early pace and probably either needs holding up over six, or to make the running over five. (9/4)
**2209 Dubai College (IRE)** stayed on under pressure in the last two furlongs, but was never nearer than at the finish. (11/2)
**2686 Mystery Matthias** could make no real headway under hard driving in the closing stages. (10/1: 6/1-11/1)
**2528* Mr Speaker (IRE)** (10/1: 6/1-11/1)
**2686* May Queen Megan** (10/1: 6/1-11/1)

T/Jkpt: Not won; £3,126.07 to Yarmouth 23/7/96. T/Plpt: £776.20 (23.26 Tckts). T/Qdpt: £124.60 (9.78 Tckts). Hn

# 2915-YARMOUTH (L-H) (Firm)
## Tuesday July 23rd
WEATHER: unsettled WIND: fresh half bhd

### 2947 SCRATBY H'CAP (0-75) (3-Y.O+) (Class D)
2-15 (2-16) **7f 3y** £3,628.65 (£1,081.20: £515.10: £232.05) Stalls: High GOING minus 0.63 sec per fur (F)

| | | | | SP | RR | SF |
|---|---|---|---|---|---|---|
| 2630* | **Gymcrak Flyer (63)** (GHolmes) **5-9-7** DeanMcKeown(5) (lw: hld up gng wl: effrt & n.m.r 2f out: qcknd to ld over 1f out: r.o wl) | — | 1 | 11/4[2] | 72 | 41 |
| 2412[4] | **Awesome Venture (49)** (MCChapman) **6-8-7** DRMcCabe(2) (tk keen hold: prom: drvn & chsd wnr over 1f out: kpt on wl cl home) | ¾ | 2 | 7/1[3] | 56 | 25 |
| 2434[2] | **Red Admiral (62)** (CMurray) **6-9-6** MTebbutt(4) (led tl rdn & hdd over 1f out: one pce) | 1¾ | 3 | 7/1[3] | 65 | 34 |
| 2412* | **Wild Palm (70)** (WAO'Gorman) **4-10-0v** EmmaO'Gorman(3) (dwlt: sn cl up: drvn & ev ch 1½f out: rdr dropped whip 1f out: nt qckn after) | s.h | 4 | 11/4[2] | 73 | 42 |
| 2615[4] | **Thordis (71)** (PJMakin) **3-9-8** SSanders(1) (cl up: pushed along ½-wy: ev ch 1½f out: wknd ins fnl f) | 2 | 5 | 5/2[1] | 70 | 32 |
| | | | | (SP 106.9%) | **5 Rn** | |

**1m 25.2** (1.00) CSF £17.33 TOTE £3.30: £1.50 £2.30 (£9.10) OWNER The Gymcrak Thoroughbred Racing Club (PICKERING) BRED D. G. Mason
WEIGHT FOR AGE 3yo-7lb
**2630* Gymcrak Flyer**, outstanding in the paddock, easily beat these for a turn of speed. (11/4)
**2412 Awesome Venture** will be winning again when he returns to the All-Weather. (7/1)
**2434 Red Admiral**, a sprinter trying a longer trip, did not have his stamina tested in this slowly-run contest. (7/1)
**2412* Wild Palm** looked beaten when the rider dropped her whip. (11/4)
**2615 Thordis** appeared not to stay this longer trip. (5/2)

### 2948 ELIZABETH SIMPSON (S) STKS (2-Y.O) (Class G)
2-45 (2-45) **7f 3y** £2,259.00 (£624.00: £297.00) Stalls: High GOING minus 0.63 sec per fur (F)

| | | | | SP | RR | SF |
|---|---|---|---|---|---|---|
| 2606[3] | **Silca's My Key (IRE)** (MRChannon) **2-8-12**ow1 RHughes(3) (hld up in tch: effrt 2f out: led ins fnl f: sn pushed clr) | — | 1 | 2/1[2] | 63 | 17 |
| 2733[6] | **Sharazamataz** (WJHaggas) **2-8-6** SSanders(1) (chsd ldr: led over 2f out: drvn & hdd ins fnl f: no ex) | 2½ | 2 | 13/2[3] | 51 | 6 |
| 2606[12] | **Bold Motion** (CMurray) **2-8-1**(5) MBaird(4) (cl up: hrd rdn 2f out: wknd over 1f out) | 5 | 3 | 16/1 | 40 | — |
| 2759[3] | **Surprise Event** (WGMTurner) **2-8-6**(5) RHavlin(5) (led tl over 2f out: sn btn) | s.h | 4 | 6/4[1] | 45 | — |
| 2759[6] | **Rons Revenge** (MJRyan) **2-9-2** GBardwell(6) (sn pushed along: struggling after 3f: eased fnl f) | 9 | 5 | 10/1 | 29 | — |
| | **Tirol's Treasure (IRE)** (KTIvory) **2-8-6** BDoyle(2) (dwlt: rdn & bdly outpcd: t.o after 2f) | 22 | 6 | 14/1 | — | — |
| | | | | (SP 108.3%) | **6 Rn** | |

**1m 26.6** (2.40) CSF £13.19 TOTE £2.90: £1.70 £2.20 (£5.80) OWNER Aldridge Racing Ltd (UPPER LAMBOURN) BRED Sheikh Mohammed Bin Rashid Al Maktoum
Bt in 9,300 gns; Sharazamataz clmd DCooper £6,000
**2606 Silca's My Key (IRE)** attracted plenty of excitement at the auction, but there is no reason to suppose he has much scope for improvement. (2/1: 6/4-9/4)
**2435 Sharazamataz**, who is only small, continues to look a very moderate performer. (13/2)
**2759 Surprise Event** proved a disappointment and there seemed to be no excuse. (6/4)
**Tirol's Treasure (IRE)** (14/1: 10/1-16/1)

### 2949 MEDLER MAIDEN STKS (3-Y.O+) (Class D)
3-15 (3-16) **1m 3f 101y** £3,628.65 (£1,081.20: £515.10: £232.05) Stalls: Low GOING minus 0.63 sec per fur (F)

| | | | | SP | RR | SF |
|---|---|---|---|---|---|---|
| 2439[2] | **Lear Express (USA)** (HRACecil) **3-8-12** PatEddery(4) (trckd ldr: rdn to ld wl over 1f out: r.o strly cl home) | — | 1 | 4/9[1] | 74 | 20 |
| 2197[5] | **Royal Action (77)** (JEBanks) **3-8-12** JStack(5) (hld up: hdwy on bit 2f out: jnd wnr ins fnl f: hrd drvn & no ex nr fin) | hd | 2 | 8/1[3] | 74 | 20 |
| | **Welcome Parade** (HRACecil) **3-8-12** WRyan(2) (chsd ldrs: rdn to chal 1f out: ev ch tl no ex cl home) | s.h | 3 | 7/1[2] | 74 | 20 |
| 1504[2] | **Lady of Leisure (USA) (67)** (MrsJCecil) **4-9-4** TIves(3) (plld hrd: sddle slipped early: bhd most of wy: effrt 3f out: rdn & btn 2f out) | 4 | 4 | 7/1[2] | 63 | 20 |
| 2529[10] | **Partita** (CEBrittain) **3-8-7** BDoyle(1) (led: rdn & hdd wl over 1f out: sn btn: eased ins fnl f) | 12 | 5 | 33/1 | 47 | — |
| | | | | (SP 108.3%) | **5 Rn** | |

**2m 26.9** (3.90) CSF £4.22 TOTE £1.30: £1.10 £2.90 (£4.70) OWNER The Thoroughbred Corporation (NEWMARKET)
WEIGHT FOR AGE 3yo-11lb
**2439 Lear Express (USA)** won a touch more cosily than the distances might suggest. (4/9)
**2197 Royal Action** was hacking until he came off the bridle in the final furlong, and is probably flattered by his proximity to the winner. Remember him for hurdling. (8/1)
**Welcome Parade** looked in need of the race and made a spirited bid. He will have benefited from the experience. (7/1: op 5/2)
**1504 Lady of Leisure (USA)** ran a respectable race considering the saddle slipped early on. (7/1: 6/1-9/1)

### 2950 NORTH WALSHAM H'CAP (0-95) (3-Y.O) (Class C)
3-45 (3-45) **6f 3y** £5,796.00 (£1,728.00: £824.00: £372.00) Stalls: High GOING minus 0.63 sec per fur (F)

| | | | | SP | RR | SF |
|---|---|---|---|---|---|---|
| 2143[2] | **Sylva Paradise (IRE) (84)** (CEBrittain) **3-9-1** BDoyle(4) (a gng wl: led 2f out: rdn & qcknd 1f out: comf) | — | 1 | 5/2[2] | 99 | 45 |
| 2281* | **Cross of Valour (80)** (JARToller) **3-8-11** SSanders(3) (cl up: ev ch 2f out: rdn & outpcd fnl f) | 3½ | 2 | 6/1[3] | 86 | 32 |
| 1327[6] | **Mazeed (IRE) (90)** (HThomsonJones) **3-9-7** RHills(6) (w ldr: led 3f out to 2f out: sn btn) | 3½ | 3 | 13/2 | 86 | 32 |
| 2676[5] | **Princely Sound (68)** (MBell) **3-7-6v**1(7) RMullen(5) (plld hrd: slt ld 3f: drvn 2f out: fnd nil) | 2 | 4 | 7/1 | 59 | 5 |
| 2427[7] | **Ramsey Hope (70)** (CWFairhurst) **3-8-1b** NKennedy(1) (sn outpcd) | 2 | 5 | 12/1 | 56 | 2 |
| 2078[2] | **Shanghai Girl (86)** (DRLoder) **3-9-3** RHughes(2) (chsd ldrs: drvn 2f out: sn wknd: virtually p.u ins fnl f) | 8 | 6 | 2/1[1] | 50 | — |
| | | | | (SP 109.7%) | **6 Rn** | |

**1m 11.0** (0.10) CSF £15.50 TOTE £3.70: £1.30 £3.60 (£11.60) OWNER Eddy Grimstead Honda Ltd (NEWMARKET) BRED Mrs J. Costelloe
**OFFICIAL EXPLANATION Shanghai Girl: the trainer reported that the filly could have been unsuited by the firm ground. She also looked reluctant and swished her tail when trying to find a run.**

**2143 Sylva Paradise (IRE)** gained the reward for consistency and completely outpaced the rest. A follow up looks likely. (5/2)
**2281* Cross of Valour** ran a pleasing enough race without extending the winner. (6/1)
**1327 Mazeed (IRE)** was a sharp two-year-old but appears to have gone the wrong way since. (13/2)
**2676 Princely Sound** is becoming rather disappointing and did not appear to relish the application of a visor. (7/1)
**2078 Shanghai Girl** ran well below expectations and connections could only offer the firm ground as a possible tentative excuse. (2/1: 6/4-9/4)

## 2951 E.B.F. SCROBY SANDS MAIDEN STKS (2-Y.O) (Class D)

4-15 (4-15) **5f 43y** £3,460.00 (£1,030.00: £490.00: £220.00) Stalls: High GOING minus 0.63 sec per fur (F)

| | | | | SP | RR | SF |
|---|---|---|---|---|---|---|
| 2624[2] | **Bahamian Bounty** (DRLoder) **2-9-0** RHughes(4) (hrd hld: trckd ldr tl shkn up to ld 2f out: sn clr: canter) | — | 1 | 1/11[1] | 72+ | 9 |
| 2600[9] | **Castle Ashby Jack** (PHowling) **2-9-0v** PaulEddery(5) (racd freely: led 3f: drvn & one pce after) | 2½ | 2 | 25/1[3] | 64 | 1 |
| 2611[15] | **Breffni (IRE)** (CNAllen) **2-8-9** TGMcLaughlin(3) (sn pushed along: chsd ldrs: btn over 1f out) | nk | 3 | 100/1 | 58 | — |
| | **Magyar Titok (IRE)** (BobJones) **2-9-0** NDay(1) (s.i.s: sn rcvrd: btn whn edgd lft fnl f) | hd | 4 | 25/1[3] | 63 | — |
| | **Valentine Fairy** (RBoss) **2-8-9** PatEddery(2) (chsd ldrs: rdn over 2f out: btn whn eased ins fnl f) | 3 | 5 | 11/1[2] | 49 | — |
| | | | | (SP 108.7%) | **5 Rn** | |

**62.8 secs** (2.30) CSF £3.83 TOTE £1.20: £1.10 £2.60 (£3.30) OWNER Lucayan Stud (NEWMARKET) BRED Clarents Racing Ltd
**2624 Bahamian Bounty** could have quadrupled the winning margin if Hughes had released his stranglehold. (1/11)
**2323 Castle Ashby Jack** should win a modest race, but it was never going to be this one. (25/1)
**Valentine Fairy** (11/1: op 5/1)

## 2952 BELTON MAIDEN H'CAP (0-75) (3-Y.O+) (Class D)

4-45 (4-45) **1m 6f 17y** £3,960.15 (£1,183.20: £566.10: £257.55) Stalls: Low GOING minus 0.63 sec per fur (F)

| | | | | SP | RR | SF |
|---|---|---|---|---|---|---|
| 2205[2] | **Bold Classic (IRE) (73)** (JLDunlop) **3-9-8** PatEddery(6) (trckd ldrs: rdn 3f out: led over 2f out: drvn & kpt on wl) | — | 1 | 9/4[1] | 81 | 43 |
| 2533[10] | **Classic Colleen (IRE) (73)** (RHarris) **3-9-8** AMackay(2) (hld up: stdy hdwy 3f out: n.m.r 2f out: squeezed thro to chal & ev ch 1f out: kpt on u.p) | ¾ | 2 | 7/1 | 80 | 42 |
| 2627[12] | **Arktikos (IRE) (68)** (JHMGosden) **3-9-3** GHind(7) (chsd ldrs: ev ch 2f out: drvn & fnd nil fnl f) | 2½ | 3 | 9/1 | 72 | 34 |
| 2549[6] | **Junior Ben (IRE) (46)** (PHowling) **4-8-9** PaulEddery(3) (chsd ldrs: n.m.r 2f out: plld outside & outpcd tl styd on ins fnl f) | nk | 4 | 5/1[2] | 50 | 26 |
| 2120[5] | **Code Red (63)** (JWHills) **3-8-12** RHills(5) (hld up: last & rdn st: n.d after: eased over 1f out) | 5 | 5 | 7/1 | 61 | 23 |
| *2372*[3] | **Mansur (IRE) (64)** (DRLoder) **4-9-13** DRMcCabe(4) (plld hrd: chsd ldr tl led 5f out: hdd over 2f out: btn whn hmpd over 1f out) | nk | 6 | 6/1[3] | 62 | 38 |
| 2738[3] | **Crimson Rosella (52)** (WJHaggas) **3-8-1** SSanders(1) (led 9f: lost pl rapidly over 3f out: t.o) | 25 | 7 | 7/1 | 22 | — |
| | | | | (SP 109.2%) | **7 Rn** | |

**3m 1.9** (2.50) CSF £15.96 TOTE £2.30: £2.00 £3.60 (£6.70) OWNER Mrs H. Focke (ARUNDEL) BRED Mrs Hildegard Focke
WEIGHT FOR AGE 3yo-14lb
**2205 Bold Classic (IRE)** returned to the course where he was a modest second last time and went one better, but this only looked a poor maiden. (9/4)
**2080 Classic Colleen (IRE)** managed to impede a couple of others as she worked her way forward in the last two furlongs and she could not quicken again in the last 100 yards. (7/1: 5/1-8/1)
**2627 Arktikos (IRE)** does not show a very resolute attitude. (9/1: 5/1-10/1)
**2191 Junior Ben (IRE)** got little luck in running and, being so one-paced, he can not afford to suffer such setbacks. (5/1)
**2738 Crimson Rosella** (7/1: op 4/1)

T/Jkpt: £88.60 (116.06 Tckts). T/Plpt: £30.50 (466.5 Tckts). T/Qdpt: £5.60 (157.59 Tckts). Mk

# 2788-BATH (L-H) (Firm)
## Wednesday July 24th

WEATHER: cloudy WIND: fresh half against

## 2953 ORCHARDLEIGH LIMITED STKS (0-65) (3-Y.O+) (Class F)

2-15 (2-15) **1m 3f 144y** £2,705.00 (£755.00: £365.00) Stalls: Low GOING minus 0.37 sec per fur (F)

| | | | | SP | RR | SF |
|---|---|---|---|---|---|---|
| 2736* | **Pistol (IRE) (62)** (CAHorgan) **6-9-8** PaulEddery(3) (b.hind: hld up: stdy hdwy over 3f out: led on bit ins fnl f: cleverly) | — | 1 | 3/1[3] | 79 | 54 |
| 2558[3] | **Askern (65)** (DHaydnJones) **5-9-4** AMackay(8) (led over 4f: led over 2f out: hrd rdn over 1f out: hdd ins fnl f) | 1 | 2 | 13/8[1] | 74 | 49 |
| 2709[5] | **Arcady (64)** (PTWalwyn) **3-8-3** SSanders(2) (chsd ldr: led 7f out tl over 2f out: hrd rdn over 1f out: unable qckn) | ½ | 3 | 5/2[2] | 70 | 33 |
| 2342[6] | **Dormy Three (60)** (RJHodges) **6-9-4** TSprake(1) (bhd tl hdwy on ins fnl 2f: nvr nr ldrs) | 9 | 4 | 14/1 | 61 | 36 |
| | **Colt D'Or (43)** (JWhite) **4-9-4** RHughes(7) (hld up: rdn over 4f out: rdn over 2f out) | 4 | 5 | 66/1 | 55 | 30 |
| *130*[8] | **Landlord (63)** (JARToller) **4-9-4** DHarrison(4) (wl bhd fnl 4f) | 8 | 6 | 25/1 | 44 | 19 |
| 2603[8] | **Dolliver (USA) (61)** (SDow) **4-9-4** TQuinn(5) (prom tl wknd over 2f out) | 1 | 7 | 6/1 | 43 | 18 |
| | | | | (SP 118.0%) | **7 Rn** | |

**2m 29.9** (3.20) CSF £8.43 TOTE £4.10: £1.70 £1.60 (£3.50) OWNER Mrs B. Sumner (PULBOROUGH) BRED David Brogan
WEIGHT FOR AGE 3yo-12lb
**2736* Pistol (IRE)** showed he can do it away from Folkestone, winning cheekily under a confident ride. (3/1: 2/1-100/30)
**2558 Askern** found the winner laughing at him in the final furlong. (13/8)
**2709 Arcady** did little wrong, but is flattered by her proximity to the winner. (5/2: 7/4-11/4)
**2342 Dormy Three** had dropped back to ten furlongs in his two previous outings. (14/1)

## 2954 BE HOPEFUL MEMORIAL H'CAP (0-80) (3-Y.O+) (Class D)

2-45 (2-47) **1m 5y** £3,666.75 (£1,104.00: £534.50: £249.75) Stalls: Low GOING minus 0.37 sec per fur (F)

| | | | | SP | RR | SF |
|---|---|---|---|---|---|---|
| 2602[8] | **Star of Gold (69)** (CREgerton) **4-9-4** RHughes(3) (lw: mde all: hrd rdn over 2f out: r.o wl) | — | 1 | 12/1 | 76 | 50 |
| 2630[7] | **Great Bear (47)** (DWChapman) **4-7-10** JQuinn(2) (a.p: hrd rdn & ev ch over 1f out: unable qckn ins fnl f) | ¾ | 2 | 50/1 | 53 | 27 |
| 2526[4] | **Maple Bay (IRE) (73)** (ABailey) **7-9-3**(5) PRoberts(7) (a.p: hrd rdn over 2f out: r.o ins fnl f) | ½ | 3 | 11/2 | 78 | 52 |

2874* **My Gallery (IRE) (69)** (ABailey) **5-9-1**(3) 7x DWright(5) (lw: a.p: r.o ins fnl f) ... nk **4** 13/8[1] 73 47
2903[5] **Mr Cube (IRE) (54)** (JMBradley) **6-8-3b** TSprake(6) (hld up & bhd: hdwy fnl 2f: nt rch ldrs) ... 1½ **5** 5/1[3] 55 29
2729* **King Curan (USA) (57)** (DHaydnJones) **5-8-6b** 7x AMackay(1) (prom: rdn 3f out: wknd wl over 1f out) ... 10 **6** 100/30[2] 38 12
861[9] **Maple Burl (58)** (MCPipe) **3-7-10**(3) MHenry(8) (a bhd: eased whn no ch 1f out) ... 15 **7** 10/1 9 —
2603[13] **Above the Cut (USA) (79)** (PWHarris) **4-10-0b** GHind(4) (unruly stalls: sn pushed along: chsd ldrs: eased whn btn 2f out) ... 2½ **8** 16/1 25 —
(SP 117.8%) **8 Rn**

**1m 40.6** (2.10) CSF £273.00 CT £3,341.45 TOTE £14.00: £3.70 £5.10 £1.90 (£142.80) OWNER Mr A Allison & Mr A Hayes Partnership (CHADDLEWORTH) BRED Normanby Stud Ltd and C. Shaw
LONG HANDICAP Great Bear 7-4
WEIGHT FOR AGE 3yo-8lb
**2405* Star of Gold**, 9lb higher than when winning at Folkestone, was considered badly handicapped by his trainer. (12/1: 8/1-14/1)
**Great Bear**, 6lb out of the handicap, ran his best race for a long time. (50/1)
**2526 Maple Bay (IRE)**, 5lb higher than when winning at Musselburgh, gave another good account of himself. (11/2)
**2874* My Gallery (IRE)** does not know how to run a bad race, and kept on, despite never having scored beyond seven. (13/8)
**2903 Mr Cube (IRE)**, reverting to a mile, was more patiently ridden. (5/1)
**2729* King Curan (USA)** has never been the most consistent of performers. (100/30: op 7/4)

## 2955 WEST LITTLETON LIMITED STKS (0-80) (3-Y.O) (Class D)
3-15 (3-15) **1m 2f 46y** £3,731.00 (£1,041.00: £503.00) Stalls: Low GOING minus 0.37 sec per fur (F)

SP RR SF
2701[5] **Diminutive (USA) (79)** (JWHills) **3-8-9**(3) MHenry(3) (lw: hld up: led wl over 1f out: r.o wl) ... — **1** 5/6[1] 81 18
2208[5] **Naseem Alsahar (75)** (MajorWRHern) **3-8-7b** TSprake(2) (trckd ldr: rdn & ev ch 2f out: unable qckn) ... 1½ **2** 13/8[2] 74 11
2618[3] **Finsbury Flyer (IRE) (73)** (RJHodges) **3-8-7**(5) PPMurphy(1) (led over 8f: one pce) ... 1 **3** 5/1[3] 77 14
(SP 109.3%) **3 Rn**

**2m 13.8** (6.30) CSF £2.43 TOTE £1.90 (£1.40) OWNER Gainsbury Partnership (LAMBOURN) BRED Mr & Mrs James W. Phillips
**1649* Diminutive (USA)** is not considered well handicapped by his trainer, and found a rather soft 0-80 here. (5/6: Evens-11/10)
**1123 Naseem Alsahar** is not very trustworthy. (13/8)
**2618 Finsbury Flyer (IRE)** would have been better off in a handicap. (5/1)

## 2956 E.B.F. MELKSHAM MAIDEN STKS (2-Y.O) (Class D)
3-45 (3-45) **5f 11y** £3,397.00 (£1,021.00: £493.00: £229.00) Stalls: High GOING minus 0.37 sec per fur (F)

SP RR SF
2343[3] **Bramble Bear** (MBlanshard) **2-8-9** AClark(6) (chsd ldr: led over 2f out: clr over 1f out: r.o wl) ... — **1** 5/2[2] 67 4
1678[5] **Aegean Sound** (RHannon) **2-8-6**(3) DaneO'Neill(2) (lw: a.p: nt clr run 2f out: swtchd rt: r.o fnl f) ... 3 **2** 5/1[3] 58 —
**Dancethenightaway** (BJMeehan) **2-8-9** BDoyle(5) (lt-f: bkwd: a.p: chsd wnr over 1f out: no imp) ... ¾ **3** 13/2 55 —
**Brazilia** (PTWalwyn) **2-8-9** RCochrane(3) (w'like: hld up: rdn & nt clr run 2f out: swtchd rt: no hdwy) ... 1½ **4** 10/11[1] 50 —
1622[11] **Midnight Times** (DCO'Brien) **2-8-9** GBardwell(4) (led: rdn & hdd over 2f out: wknd over 1f out) ... 4 **5** 66/1 38 —
(SP 112.4%) **5 Rn**

**64.2 secs** (3.70) CSF £13.54 TOTE £3.20: £1.40 £2.20 (£4.90) OWNER Mrs Michael Hill & Mrs Heather Chakko (UPPER LAMBOURN) BRED E. A. Badger
**2343 Bramble Bear** put her previous experience to good use and complimented her Chepstow form with Super Sprint winner Miss Stamper. (5/2)
**1678 Aegean Sound** did not get the run of the race, but would not have won in any case. She can win a similar event. (5/1: 7/2-11/2)
**Dancethenightaway** should at least come on for the outing. (13/2: op 3/1)
**Brazilia**, entered in the Lowther and the Cheveley Park, was well touted beforehand, but did not appear to be going anywhere when forced to switch. (10/11: Evens-5/4)

## 2957 DYRHAM SPRINT H'CAP (0-80) (3-Y.O+) (Class D)
4-15 (4-15) **5f 161y** £3,553.00 (£1,069.00: £517.00: £241.00) Stalls: High GOING minus 0.37 sec per fur (F)

SP RR SF
2799* **Kildee Lad (76)** (APJones) **6-10-3** 7x BDoyle(2) (lw: hld up: squeezed thro on ins 1f out: hrd rdn to ld wl ins fnl f: r.o) ... — **1** 6/1 84 48
2694[16] **Shadow Jury (64)** (DWChapman) **6-9-5b** JQuinn(1) (led: hrd rdn & hdd wl ins fnl f) ... nk **2** 3/1[2] 71 35
2719[7] **Rambold (60)** (NEBerry) **5-9-1** RPerham(3) (w wnr: rdn over 2f out: ev ch over 1f out: unable qckn) ... 1½ **3** 15/2 63 27
2713* **Pointer (54)** (MrsPNDutfield) **4-8-9** TQuinn(4) (hld up: hrd rdn 2f out: one pce) ... 1¾ **4** 13/8[1] 52 16
2791[2] **Astral Invader (IRE) (51)** (MSSaunders) **4-8-1**(5) PPMurphy(6) (b: rdn 3f out: sn bhd: fin lame) ... 6 **5** 4/1[3] 32 —
2791* **Tafahhus (74)** (MJPolglase) **4-10-1b** 7x DHarrison(5) (rdn over 3f out: sn bhd: t.o) ... 18 **6** 16/1 5 —
(SP 115.0%) **6 Rn**

**1m 12.0** (2.50) CSF £23.23 TOTE £7.80: £3.20 £1.80 (£13.00) OWNER Mr J. F. O'Donovan (EASTBURY) BRED Mrs M. Chubb
**2799* Kildee Lad** had to work hard to defy a penalty. (6/1: 4/1-7/1)
**2586* Shadow Jury**, 4lb higher than when winning at Newmarket, had only once scored beyond the bare minimum and that was on the Sand. (3/1)
**2719 Rambold**, disappointing last time, had been raised 3lb for his good second at Nottingham. (15/2: 5/1-8/1)
**2713* Pointer**, upped a further 3lb, could not complete his hat-trick over the slightly shorter trip. (13/8)
**2791 Astral Invader (IRE)** was reported by his trainer to have finished lame. (4/1)

## 2958 STAYERS H'CAP (0-70) (3-Y.O+) (Class E)
4-45 (4-45) **2m 1f 34y** £2,895.00 (£870.00: £420.00: £195.00) Stalls: High GOING minus 0.37 sec per fur (F)

SP RR SF
2709[4] **Paradise Navy (64)** (CREgerton) **7-10-0b** RHughes(6) (hld up in rr: stdy hdwy 6f out: led on bit ins fnl f: cleverly) ... — **1** 5/2[2] 75+ 42
2560* **Special Beat (60)** (PFICole) **4-9-10** TQuinn(8) (a.p: hrd rdn & wnt 2nd over 2f out: ev ch ins fnl f: no ch w wnr) ... 1¾ **2** 13/8[1] 69 36
2310* **Wadada (43)** (DBurchell) **5-8-4**(3) SDrowne(4) (lw: w ldr: led 7f out tl over 5f out: led over 3f out tl ins fnl f) ... ½ **3** 100/30[3] 52 19
2310[12] **Chucklestone (32)** (JSKing) **13-7-10** JQuinn(3) (led over 10f: outpcd over 5f out: styd on fnl 2f) ... 1½ **4** 33/1 40 7
2530[6] **Kymin (IRE) (54)** (DJGMurraySmith) **4-8-13b**(5) RPainter(5) (hld up: hdwy 7f out: led over 5f out tl over 3f out: wknd over 1f out) ... 3 **5** 16/1 59 26
2310[4] **King Ubad (USA) (36)** (KOCunningham-Brown) **7-8-0b**ow4 JFEgan(7) (b: wl bhd fnl 3f) ... 8 **6** 16/1 33 —

| | | | | | | |
|---|---|---|---|---|---|---|
| 2506[7] | **Amber Ring (51)** (MissKMGeorge) **3-7-9**(3)ow2 DarrenMoffatt(1) (wl bhd fnl 3f) | 8 | **7** | 50/1 | 41 | — |
| 2182[11] | **Prerogative (55)** (RSimpson) **6-9-0v**(5) AimeeCook(2) (hld up: rdn over 4f out: sn bhd) | ¾ | **8** | 14/1 | 44 | 11 |

(SP 113.1%) **8 Rn**

**3m 50.2** (9.20) CSF £6.64 CT £11.11 TOTE £3.10: £1.10 £1.40 £1.10 (£3.40) OWNER Elite Racing Club (CHADDLEWORTH) BRED Stetchworth Park Stud Ltd
LONG HANDICAP King Ubad (USA) 7-6 Amber Ring 7-3
WEIGHT FOR AGE 3yo-17lb
**2709 Paradise Navy** is the sort who likes to do it all on the bridle, and was certainly able to do it here. (5/2)
**2560* Special Beat**, up 8lb for winning a poor race over course and distance last time, found the winner galloping all over him in the closing stages. (13/8)
**2310* Wadada**, raised 3lb for winning a seller over course and distance last time, did nothing wrong, but the winner is a bit better than a plater. (100/30)
**Chucklestone**, fitter for his debut, stayed on again after looking well held. (33/1)
**2530 Kymin (IRE)** remains a maiden after twelve attempts. (16/1)
**1011 Prerogative** (14/1: op 8/1)

T/Plpt: £96.10 (116.11 Tckts). T/Qdpt: £16.60 (43.71 Tckts). KH

# 2422-CATTERICK (L-H) (Good to soft, Good patches)
## Wednesday July 24th
WEATHER: overcast WIND: fresh half against

## 2959 HUDDERSFIELD (S) STKS (2-Y.O) (Class G)
2-30 (2-31) **7f** £2,427.00 (£672.00: £321.00) Stalls: Low GOING: minus 0.20 sec per fur (GF)

| | | | | SP | RR | SF |
|---|---|---|---|---|---|---|
| 2759[4] | **Poly Moon** (MRChannon) **2-8-6** JCarroll(6) (lw: mde all: qcknd 3f out: r.o) | — | **1** | 7/2 2 | 58 | 1 |
| *2554[3]* | **Abstone Queen** (PDEvans) **2-8-6** JFortune(3) (chsd ldrs: effrt over 2f out: kpt on fnl f) | 1¼ | **2** | 12/1 | 55 | — |
| 2606[7] | **Cajun Sunset (IRE)** (TDEasterby) **2-8-11** KDarley(2) (trckd ldrs: effrt 2f out: r.o one pce) | 1½ | **3** | 4/1 3 | 57 | — |
| 2509* | **Ginny Wossername** (WGMTurner) **2-8-4b**(7) DSweeney(1) (in tch: swtchd & effrt 2f out: styd on wl towards fin) | 1¼ | **4** | 7/2 2 | 54 | — |
| 733[4] | **The Bee Man** (MWEasterby) **2-8-6**(5) GParkin(7) (chsd ldrs tl grad wknd fnl 2f) | 3½ | **5** | 9/2 | 46 | — |
| 2850[4] | **Apiculate (IRE)** (WTKemp) **2-8-11** JWeaver(4) (s.i.s: bhd tl sme hdwy fnl 2f) | 5 | **6** | 33/1 | 34 | — |
| 2850[3] | **Foolish Flutter (IRE)** (GROldroyd) **2-8-6v** DaleGibson(8) (mid div: rdn ent st: no imp) | 1 | **7** | 25/1 | 27 | — |
| | **Who (IRE)** (TDEasterby) **2-8-11** MBirch(12) (leggy: scope: s.i.s: rdn 3f out: nvr rchd ldrs) | 2 | **8** | 16/1 | 28 | — |
| 2685* | **Grovefair Maiden (IRE)** (BJMeehan) **2-8-11b** MTebbutt(5) (rdn ½-wy: nvr trbld ldrs) | 1 | **9** | 3/1 1 | 25 | — |
| *2750[7]* | **Billycan (IRE)** (BPJBaugh) **2-8-11** WLord(9) (prom tl rn wd appr st: sn wl bhd) | 19 | **10** | 50/1 | — | — |
| 2422[6] | **Tooele** (JNorton) **2-8-11v**1 JLowe(10) (s.i.s: a bhd) | 6 | **11** | 100/1 | — | — |
| | **Absolute Charlie** (DWBarker) **2-8-11** NCarlisle(11) (unf: swtg: dwlt: a bhd) | 15 | **12** | 100/1 | — | — |

(SP 131.9%) **12 Rn**

**1m 29.9** (6.30) CSF £46.05 TOTE £4.20: £2.50 £2.90 £1.70 (£22.70) Trio £28.70 OWNER Sheet & Roll Convertors Ltd (UPPER LAMBOURN) BRED Lt-Col and Mrs R. Bromley Gardner
Bt in 6,400 gns
**2759 Poly Moon**, a handy sort well suited to this track and this easy ground, left nothing to chance out in front and won a shade comfortably. (7/2)
**2554 Abstone Queen**, whatever the surface, keeps running a similar race, but is short of a real turn of foot. (12/1)
**Cajun Sunset (IRE)** ran well in a hot seller at Newmarket last time, but this rather weak and edgy individual failed to progress here. Nevertheless, the ability is there if he ever gets it together. (4/1)
**2509* Ginny Wossername** is an edgy sort in the preliminaries and, judging by the way she finished in the race, she will appreciate further yet. (7/2)
**733 The Bee Man**, who has not been out for three months, has done particularly well physically. Stepping up two furlongs in trip here, he should improve as a result of this. (9/2)

## 2960 C.S.S. SDN BHD H'CAP (0-70) (3-Y.O+) (Class E)
3-00 (3-03) **5f** £3,158.00 (£944.00: £452.00: £206.00) Stalls: Low GOING: minus 0.20 sec per fur (GF)

| | | | | SP | RR | SF |
|---|---|---|---|---|---|---|
| 2771[5] | **The Institute Boy (42)** (MissJFCraze) **6-8-1** JLowe(10) (cl up stands' side: led 3f out: clr & eased ins fnl f) | — | **1** | 13/2 | 53 | 20 |
| 2564[6] | **Kalar (48)** (DWChapman) **7-8-7b** JCarroll(8) (led stands' side 2f: cl up tl rdn & btn appr fnl f) | 4 | **2** | 8/1 | 46 | 13 |
| 2771[2] | **Able Sheriff (50)** (MWEasterby) **4-8-4b**(5) GParkin(4) (w ldrs far side: no ch fr ½-wy) | 5 | **3** | 7/2 2 | 32 | — |
| 2523[9] | **Serious Hurry (47)** (RMMcKellar) **8-7-13**(7) KSked(7) (chsd ldrs stands' side: outpcd fr ½-wy) | ¾ | **4** | 16/1 | 27 | — |
| 2771[3] | **Silk Cottage (59)** (RMWhitaker) **4-9-4v** DeanMcKeown(3) (lw: trckd ldrs far side: effrt ½-wy: n.d) | 1¼ | **5** | 9/2 3 | 35 | 2 |
| 2910[10] | **Double Glow (37)** (NBycroft) **4-7-3**(7) IonaWands(5) (swtg: drvn along far side: nvr trbld ldrs) | ½ | **6** | 33/1 | 11 | — |
| 2849[2] | **Leading Princess (IRE) (48)** (MissLAPerratt) **5-8-7b** JWeaver(2) (lw: w ldrs far side tl wknd fnl 2f) | 1½ | **7** | 3/1 1 | 17 | — |
| 2757[6] | **Imp Express (IRE) (48)** (GMMoore) **3-8-3b** NKennedy(1) (lw: w ldrs far side 3f) | 6 | **8** | 8/1 | — | — |
| 591[11] | **Quinta Boy (41)** (JLEyre) **3-7-3**(7) JBramhill(9) (s.s & swtchd far side: a bhd) | 20 | **9** | 25/1 | — | — |
| *2908[3]* | ***Swan At Whalley (69)*** (MartynWane) **4-10-0** JFortune(6) (Withdrawn not under Starter's orders: unruly stalls: veterinary advice) | | **W** | 7/1 | — | — |

(SP 126.1%) **9 Rn**

**60.3 secs** (2.80) CSF £46.17 CT £147.18 TOTE £7.40: £2.50 £1.90 £1.50 (£18.90) Trio £24.60 OWNER Mrs J. Addleshaw (YORK) BRED M. Yiapatos
LONG HANDICAP Double Glow 7-2 Quinta Boy 6-13
WEIGHT FOR AGE 3yo-4lb
**2771 The Institute Boy** had the favoured stands' rail and, once he had shaken off Kalar approaching the final furlong, he gained his first win on turf with a deal of ease. (13/2)
**2564 Kalar**, with the blinkers back on, raced with the winner up the stands' rail but was struggling from halfway and cried enough approaching the last furlong. (8/1)
**2771 Able Sheriff** was always the best of the bunch on the far side in the last couple of furlongs, but never had a hope with the principals on the favoured stands' rail. (7/2)
**2523 Serious Hurry** raced up the favoured stands' side, but never showed his normal blistering early pace, which might well be put down to this easier ground. (16/1)

**2771 Silk Cottage** had no chance racing up the far side, and this is best ignored. (9/2)
**2564 Double Glow**, who got very warm beforehand, again gave ground away at the start and, racing up the unfavoured far side, did well to finish so close. (33/1)
**2849 Leading Princess (IRE)** should be forgiven this because of her draw. (3/1)

## 2961 DEWSBURY MAIDEN STKS (3-Y.O+) (Class D)

3-30 (3-30) **1m 5f 175y** £3,882.50 (£1,160.00: £555.00: £252.50) Stalls: Low GOING: minus 0.20 sec per fur (GF)

| Form | Horse | Dist | Pos | SP | RR | SF |
|---|---|---|---|---|---|---|
| 2054$^{4}$ | **Wilawander (96)** (BWHills) **3-8-7** MHills(5) (lw: mde all: pushed clr 2f out: eased ins fnl f) | — | 1 | 1/5$^{1}$ | 94+ | 23 |
| 2505$^{3}$ | **Belmarita (IRE) (73)** (MHTompkins) **3-8-2** PRobinson(3) (racd wd thrght: a chsng wnr: eased whn no ch ins fnl f) | 9 | 2 | 8/1$^{2}$ | 79 | 8 |
| 2591$^{3}$ | **Totem Dancer** (JLEyre) **3-8-2**$^{(3)ow3}$ CTeague(2) (hld up: hmpd paddock bnd & appr st: nvr trbld ldrs: eased) | 14 | 3 | 8/1$^{2}$ | 65 | — |
| 2591$^{5}$ | **Ballet de Cour** (CWCElsey) **3-8-7** ACulhane(1) (prom: hung rt paddock bnd: outpcd whn hung rt appr st: wl bhd after) | 22 | 4 | 50/1 | 42 | — |
| | **Limyski** (MrsASwinbank) **3-8-7** JWeaver(4) (n.d) | 11 | 5 | 100/1 | 29 | — |
| 2591$^{7}$ | **Russian Roulette** (MJohnston) **3-8-2** TWilliams(6) (chsd ldrs: rdn 6f out: wknd 4f out) | 4 | 6 | 33/1$^{3}$ | 19 | — |

(SP 111.4%) **6 Rn**

**3m 4.8** (9.30) CSF £2.65 TOTE £1.70: £1.10 £1.90 (£1.80) OWNER Maktoum Al Maktoum (LAMBOURN) BRED Gainsborough Stud Management Ltd

**2054 Wilawander** gained his first confidence-boosting win but, despite scoring easily, he had to work early in the straight to shake off a persistent rival. (1/5)
**2505 Belmarita (IRE)**, who looked very lean and fit, ran her heart out, but she had to admit that the winner was too good in the final furlong, and was then eased when well beaten. (8/1)
**2591 Totem Dancer** is not very big and got messed about no end at various stages, but she was certainly not given a hard time, and will do better in due course. (8/1)
**Ballet de Cour** looked quite well, but failed to handle the bends and was left way behind in the last half-mile. (50/1)
**Russian Roulette** looked pretty moderate once the pressure was on in the last three-quarters of a mile. (33/1)

## 2962 LEEDS H'CAP (0-75) (3-Y.O+) (Class D)

4-00 (4-01) **7f** £3,557.50 (£1,060.00: £505.00: £227.50) Stalls: Low GOING: minus 0.20 sec per fur (GF)

| Form | Horse | Dist | Pos | SP | RR | SF |
|---|---|---|---|---|---|---|
| 2209* | **Nashaat (USA) (67)** (MCChapman) **8-9-9**$^{(3)}$ PMcCabe(2) (swtg: hld up: smooth hdwy 2f out: led appr fnl f: all out) | — | 1 | 4/1$^{2}$ | 77 | 44 |
| 2672* | **Pine Ridge Lad (IRE) (64)** (JLEyre) **6-9-6**$^{(3)}$ OPears(6) (mde most tl hdd appr fnl f: rallied) | hd | 2 | 2/1$^{1}$ | 74 | 41 |
| 2910$^{2}$ | **Another Nightmare (IRE) (38)** (RMMcKellar) **4-7-11**$^{ow1}$ TWilliams(7) (a.p: squeezed thro to chal ins fnl f: r.o) | s.h | 3 | 16/1 | 48 | 14 |
| 2536$^{8}$ | **Baileys First (IRE) (70)** (MJohnston) **3-9-8** JWeaver(3) (led 2f: led over 2f out: sn hdd: one pce fnl f) | 2½ | 4 | 11/2$^{3}$ | 74 | 34 |
| 1819$^{8}$ | **Pride of Pendle (69)** (DNicholls) **7-10-0** AlexGreaves(8) (b.nr hind: bhd tl styd on fnl 2f) | ½ | 5 | 6/1 | 72 | 39 |
| 2630$^{4}$ | **Zain Dancer (55)** (DNicholls) **4-9-0** JCarroll(4) (prom tl outpcd appr fnl f) | 1½ | 6 | 6/1 | 54 | 21 |
| *257** | **Prizefighter (62)** (JLEyre) **5-9-4**$^{(3)}$ CTeague(1) (s.i.s: nvr plcd to chal) | 1½ | 7 | 12/1 | 58 | 25 |
| 2358* | **Termon (61)** (MissLAPerratt) **3-8-13** KDarley(5) (chsd ldrs tl rdn & wknd over 1f out) | 2 | 8 | 6/1 | 52 | 12 |

(SP 125.1%) **8 Rn**

**1m 27.7** (4.10) CSF £13.21 CT £112.40 TOTE £5.90: £1.40 £1.40 £3.60 (£6.30) OWNER Mr Tony Satchell (MARKET RASEN) BRED Echo Valley Horse Farm and Swettenham Stud
LONG HANDICAP Another Nightmare (IRE) 7-6
WEIGHT FOR AGE 3yo-7lb

**2209* Nashaat (USA)** travelled particularly well but, if anything, he hit the front too soon and was fast being pegged back as the line approached. (4/1)
**2672* Pine Ridge Lad (IRE)** injured his rider slightly leaving the paddock. In the race, he could never get away from his rivals and, although fighting back, the line came too soon. He remains in tremendous heart. (2/1)
**2910 Another Nightmare (IRE)** is in really good form and this trip might just have been stretching her stamina but, to give her credit, she did keep battling on. (16/1)
**1666 Baileys First (IRE)**, dropped back in trip, could never dominate as she likes too and she was done with approaching the last furlong. (11/2)
**1609 Pride of Pendle** ran well without getting into it, and is now coming back down to a decent handicap mark. (6/1)
**2630 Zain Dancer** was without the blinkers this time and was never doing enough in the last quarter-mile. (6/1)
**Prizefighter**, having his first run for several months, had what can only be described as a pipe-opener. (12/1)

## 2963 LEYBURN CLAIMING STKS (3-Y.O+) (Class F)

4-30 (4-30) **7f** £2,742.00 (£762.00: £366.00) Stalls: Low GOING: minus 0.20 sec per fur (GF)

| Form | Horse | Dist | Pos | SP | RR | SF |
|---|---|---|---|---|---|---|
| 2392* | **Blue Bomber (67)** (TDBarron) **5-8-11** JFortune(2) (cl up: led over 2f out: pushed along: r.o wl) | — | 1 | 2/5$^{1}$ | 60 | 37 |
| 1156* | **Lunch Party** (DNicholls) **4-9-5** JCarroll(1) (led tl hdd over 2f out: sn btn) | 4 | 2 | 9/4$^{2}$ | 59 | 36 |
| 2777$^{9}$ | **Madonna da Rossi (37)** (MDods) **3-8-1** DaleGibson(5) (plld hrd to ½-wy: trckd ldrs: rdn 3f out: styd on: no imp) | hd | 3 | 50/1 | 48 | 18 |
| 2874$^{7}$ | **Axeman (IRE) (82)** (DNicholls) **4-9-8** AlexGreaves(6) (bhd tl sme hdwy fnl 2f) | 15 | 4 | 12/1$^{3}$ | 27 | 4 |
| | **Wacky (IRE)** (WStorey) **5-8-7** NKennedy(4) (t: chsd ldrs: outpcd ½-wy: sn wknd) | 2½ | 5 | 40/1 | 7 | — |
| 2589$^{5}$ | **Sly Lady** (CWCElsey) **4-8-5** ACulhane(3) (a outpcd & bhd) | 7 | 6 | 100/1 | — | — |

(SP 115.3%) **6 Rn**

**1m 27.1** (3.50) CSF £1.81 TOTE £1.40: £1.10 £1.20 (£1.60) OWNER Mr Geoffrey Martin (THIRSK) BRED R. H. Cowell and Mrs R. B. Collie
WEIGHT FOR AGE 3yo-7lb
Blue Bomber clmd GHamilton £4,000

**2392* Blue Bomber**, backed as though defeat was out of the question, was given a determined ride to win decisively. (2/5)
**1156* Lunch Party** was the only one able to match the winner for pace but, after over two months off, he blew up early in the straight. (9/4)
**637 Madonna da Rossi** spent the first half of the race pulling her rider's arms out, and then failed to go any faster when ridden. (50/1)
**Axeman (IRE)** again took the eye in the paddock, but failed to show anything much in the race. (12/1: op 6/1)
**Wacky (IRE)** has been tubed and showed little once under pressure from halfway. (40/1)

## 2964 HALIFAX H'CAP (0-65) (3-Y.O+) (Class F)

5-00 (5-00) **5f 212y** £2,700.00 (£750.00: £360.00) Stalls: High GOING: minus 0.20 sec per fur (GF)

| | | | | SP | RR | SF |
|---|---|---|---|---|---|---|
| $2911^{3}$ | **Cheeky Chappy (64)** (DWChapman) **5-9-13b** KDarley(3) (mde all: qcknd over 1f out: r.o wl) | — | 1 | $4/1^{2}$ | 72 | 60 |
| 2911* | **Thwaab (59)** (FWatson) **4-9-8v** 7x JFortune(1) (lw: trckd ldrs: effrt 2f out: no imp) | 5 | 2 | $3/1^{1}$ | 54 | 42 |
| 2481* | **My Godson (51)** (JLEyre) **6-8-11b**(3) CTeague(4) (bhd: effrt over 2f out: styd on: nrst fin) | ¾ | 3 | $11/2^{3}$ | 44 | 32 |
| $2047^{11}$ | **Henry the Hawk (49)** (MDods) **5-8-5**(7) CWebb(2) (b: swtg: a chsng ldrs: rdn ½-wy: one pce) | 3½ | 4 | $11/2^{3}$ | 32 | 20 |
| 2719* | **Rockcracker (IRE) (65)** (GGMargarson) **4-10-0b** PBloomfield(6) (mid div: effrt ½-wy: nvr able to chal) | 3½ | 5 | 13/2 | 39 | 27 |
| $2757^{18}$ | **Invigilate (52)** (MartynWane) **7-9-1** JCarroll(5) (chsd ldrs: outpcd & wkng whn hmpd over 1f out) | 2½ | 6 | $11/2^{3}$ | 19 | 7 |
| $2777^{10}$ | **April's Joy (50)** (JNorton) **3-8-1v**[1](7) JBramhill(9) (nvr bttr than mid div) | 1¼ | 7 | 66/1 | 14 | — |
| $2427^{6}$ | **Hickleton Miss (50)** (MrsVAAconley) **3-8-8** NCarlisle(7) (a outpcd & bhd) | 1½ | 8 | 33/1 | 10 | — |
| $1635^{7}$ | **Suedoro (43)** (RMMcKellar) **6-7-13**(7) KSked(8) (s.i.s: n.d) | 1 | 9 | 20/1 | — | — |
| $1541^{13}$ | **Brisas (41)** (CWFairhurst) **9-8-4** DeanMcKeown(10) (prom to ½-wy: sn outpcd & bhd) | 9 | 10 | 33/1 | — | — |

(SP 116.6%) **10 Rn**

**1m 13.3** (2.40) CSF £15.63 CT £60.18 TOTE £4.60: £1.80 £1.80 £2.90 (£6.50) Trio £8.20 OWNER Mrs Jeanne Chapman (YORK) BRED Ian W. Glenton

WEIGHT FOR AGE 3yo-5lb

**2911 Cheeky Chappy** enjoyed himself on this easier ground and won with something in hand. This was his first victory on a turning track on turf. (4/1)

**2911* Thwaab**, who likes to be held up, saw too much daylight on this occasion too soon and cried enough approaching the last furlong. (3/1)

**2481* My Godson**, in a race where the going and the best position was paramount, had little chance, trying to come from behind. (11/2)

**1865 Henry the Hawk** got very stirred up beforehand, but still ran reasonably after some five weeks off. (11/2)

**2719* Rockcracker (IRE)** found these soft conditions against him. (13/2)

**2523 Invigilate** is happier on faster ground. (11/2)

T/Plpt: £21.90 (623.44 Tckts). T/Qdpt: £1.90 (507.74 Tckts). AA

# 2794-LEICESTER (R-H) (Good, Good to soft patches)

## Wednesday July 24th

WEATHER: sunny & warm WIND: nil

## 2965 RADIO LEICESTER-CONSTABLES' NURSERY H'CAP (2-Y.O) (Class E)

6-30 (6-30) **5f 2y** £3,179.40 (£949.20: £453.60: £205.80) Stalls: Low GOING: minus 0.18 sec per fur (GF)

| | | | | SP | RR | SF |
|---|---|---|---|---|---|---|
| 2728* | **Osomental** (DHaydnJones) **2-9-8v**[1] 7x AMackay(6) (lw: sn bhd & outpcd: hdwy 2f out: rdn to ld ins fnl f: edgd rt: r.o) | — | 1 | $4/1^{1}$ | 90 | 54 |
| $2795^{2}$ | **I Can't Remember** (PDEvans) **2-7-7**(3) DWright(2) (hdwy ½-wy: rdn over 1f out: ev ch ins fnl f: r.o) | ½ | 2 | $5/1^{2}$ | 62 | 26 |
| $2596^{5}$ | **Threeplay (IRE)** (JAkehurst) **2-8-3v**[1] GCarter(1) (b.off hind: trckd ldrs: rdn & ev ch 1f out: unable qckn) | 2 | 3 | 11/1 | 63 | 27 |
| $2770^{2}$ | **Skyers Flyer (IRE)** (RonaldThompson) **2-8-11** NConnorton(4) (a.p: led over 1f out tl ins fnl f) | s.h | 4 | $7/1^{3}$ | 71 | 35 |
| 2076* | **Divide And Rule** (RHollinshead) **2-8-10**(5) DGriffiths(3) (prom: rdn over 1f out: r.o one pce) | 1¼ | 5 | $7/1^{3}$ | 71 | 35 |
| $2726^{7}$ | **Petite Danseuse** (SDow) **2-8-12**(5) ADaly(5) (lw: bhd & outpcd tl r.o ins fnl f) | ¾ | 6 | 14/1 | 71 | 35 |
| 2485* | **Blazing Castle** (WGMTurner) **2-8-6**(7) DSweeney(8) (trckd ldrs: rdn & wknd appr fnl f) | ½ | 7 | 8/1 | 65 | 29 |
| 2699* | **Aybeegirl** (MrsJCecil) **2-8-10v** PRobinson(9) (drvn along ½-wy: nvr nr ldrs) | 5 | 8 | $7/1^{3}$ | 46 | 10 |
| $1437^{4}$ | **Blue Movie** (MBell) **2-9-4** MFenton(7) (lw: outpcd: a bhd) | 1¼ | 9 | 9/1 | 50 | 14 |
| $1766^{3}$ | **Joint Venture (IRE)** (BJMeehan) **2-9-7b** MTebbutt(10) (lw: led tl hdd & wknd over 1f out) | 3½ | 10 | $7/1^{3}$ | 42 | 6 |

(SP 122.8%) **10 Rn**

**60.6 secs** (2.10) CSF £24.17 CT £196.32 TOTE £5.80: £2.50 £1.90 £3.00 (£11.00) Trio £91.60 OWNER Mr Hugh O'Donnell (PONTYPRIDD) BRED P. Asquith

**2728* Osomental**, taken off his legs and flat to the boards all the way, began to pick up at the distance. Quickening to lead 100 yards out, he did it well in the end. (4/1)

**2795 I Can't Remember** took time to get going, but he responded to pressure and only just failed to match the winner for finishing speed. (5/1)

**2596 Threeplay (IRE)** shows plenty of knee-action and the afternoon rain had come just in time. Running his best race yet, there could be more improvement to follow. (11/1)

**2770 Skyers Flyer (IRE)** took over from the long-time leader below the distance, but could not find anything extra in the sprint to the line. (7/1)

**2076* Divide And Rule** did not impress to post, but did show plenty of speed to push the pace until having to admit his measure taken approaching the final furlong. (7/1)

**1673 Petite Danseuse** has already won twice at this trip, but she struggled with the pace here and was unable to reach a challenging position. (14/1)

## 2966 CWS EXTRA-SUPERINTENDENTS (S) STKS (3-Y.O) (Class G)

7-00 (7-00) **1m 8y** £2,532.00 (£702.00: £336.00) Stalls: Low GOING: minus 0.18 sec per fur (GF)

| | | | | SP | RR | SF |
|---|---|---|---|---|---|---|
| 2893* | **Cointosser (IRE) (63)** (SPCWoods) **3-8-11** WWoods(1) (hld up & bhd: hdwy 2f out: drifted lft & led wl ins fnl f) | — | 1 | $8/11^{1}$ | 66 | 40 |
| *$2158^{10}$* | **Night of Glass (35)** (DMorris) **3-8-11v**[1] NDay(9) (hld up in tch: hdwy to ld over 2f out: sn clr: wknd & hdd nr fin) | 1 | 2 | 14/1 | 64 | 38 |
| $2507^{18}$ | **Home Cookin' (55)** (MCPipe) **3-8-6** MRoberts(10) (a.p: led 4f out tl over 2f out: one pce appr fnl f) | 5 | 3 | $6/1^{2}$ | 49 | 23 |
| $2561^{9}$ | **Duet (35)** (JSKing) **3-8-6** AMackay(11) (prom: rdn 2f out: sn outpcd) | 10 | 4 | 33/1 | 29 | 3 |
| *$2637^{4}$* | **Samara Song (57)** (WGMTurner) **3-8-4v**[1](7) DSweeney(14) (lw: plld hrd: hld up: hdwy 3f out: rdn & outpcd wl over 1f out) | nk | 5 | 12/1 | 34 | 8 |
| $2373^{13}$ | **Spencer Stallone (58)** (LordHuntingdon) **3-8-11** DHarrison(5) (led to ½-wy: rdn & wknd 2f out) | d.h | 5 | 12/1 | 34 | 8 |
| $2061^{8}$ | **Florrie'm (42)** (JLHarris) **3-8-6** PRobinson(3) (hld up: hdwy u.p over 2f out: nt rch ldrs) | 3½ | 7 | 25/1 | 22 | — |
| | **The Black Dubh (IRE) (42)** (JJQuinn) **3-8-11** JFanning(7) (hld up in rr: sme hdwy fnl 2f: nvr nrr) | 2 | 8 | 14/1 | 23 | — |
| $2180^{7}$ | **My Kind (47)** (NTinkler) **3-8-11** KimTinkler(13) (in tch: no hdwy fnl 3f) | 2 | 9 | 20/1 | 19 | — |
| $2425^{10}$ | **Young Frederick (IRE) (55)** (KRBurke) **3-8-11** DBiggs(2) (trckd ldrs: rdn along 3f out: sn btn) | 1 | 10 | $9/1^{3}$ | 17 | — |
| *$2636^{8}$* | **Welcome Brief (49)** (EJAlston) **3-8-6** MFenton(8) (s.s: a in rr) | 2 | 11 | 25/1 | 8 | — |
| $2753^{9}$ | **Inca Bird (28)** (TWall) **3-8-3b**[1](3) DWright(4) (mid div tl wknd 3f out: t.o) | 5 | 12 | 50/1 | — | — |

| | | | Pos | SP | RR | SF |
|---|---|---|---|---|---|---|
| *2632*[9] | **Brin-Lodge (IRE)** (KSBridgwater) **3-8-3**(3) NVarley(12) (bit bkwd: prom over 5f: sn lost tch: t.o) | 6 | **13** | 50/1 | — | — |
| 2166[3] | **Mirus** (RonaldThompson) **3-8-11** NConnorton(6) (bit bkwd: prom 5f: sn wknd: t.o) | 2½ | **14** | 50/1 | — | — |

(SP 132.2%) **14 Rn**

**1m 38.8** (3.80) CSF £14.14 TOTE £1.90: £1.10 £3.10 £2.00 (£16.70) Trio £28.10 OWNER Mr Arashan Ali (NEWMARKET) BRED Mellon Stud
Sold MPipe 7,500 gns
STEWARDS' ENQUIRY Day susp. 2-4/8/96 (excessive use of whip).
**2893* Cointosser (IRE)**, winning her third race this month, had plenty to do approaching the final furlong but she produced a good turn of foot to take command nearing the finish. (8/11)
**Night of Glass**, woken up by the application of a visor, looked to have stolen a march when going clear approaching the last furlong, but the winner, racing wide, proved just too strong close home. There is a similar race to be won with him. (14/1: op 33/1)
**2380 Home Cookin'** helped share the lead and was a main contender until the quickening tempo caught her out approaching the final furlong. (6/1)
**Duet** did not last home over this longer trip and sprinting would appear to be her only hope. (33/1)
**2637 Samara Song**, restrained under a strong hold, did make some headway in the second half of the race, but could not get close enough to cause concern. (12/1)
**856 Spencer Stallone** had run himself out by forcing the pace in the early stages, and he is not yet getting it together. (12/1: op 8/1)

## 2967 INVESCO PRIVATE PORTFOLIO-DETECTIVES' MAIDEN AUCTION STKS (2-Y.O) (Class E)

7-30 (7-31) **7f 9y** £3,370.50 (£1,008.00: £483.00: £220.50) Stalls: Low GOING: minus 0.18 sec per fur (GF)

| | | | Pos | SP | RR | SF |
|---|---|---|---|---|---|---|
| 1339[6] | **Goodwood Lass (IRE)** (JLDunlop) **2-8-6** WCarson(9) (mde virtually all: hrd drvn fnl 2f: r.o wl) | — | **1** | 100/30[2] | 79 | 30 |
| 2714[3] | **Blue Hopper** (MRChannon) **2-7-12** CRutter(8) (hld up in tch: effrt & rdn 2f out: ev ch appr fnl f: no ex nr fin) | 2 | **2** | 8/1 | 67 | 18 |
| | **Love Me Do (USA)** (MJohnston) **2-8-6** JWeaver(13) (w'like: str: bit bkwd: s.i.s: hdwy over 2f out: shkn up & one pce ins fnl f) | ½ | **3** | 8/1 | 73+ | 24 |
| 2596[10] | **Flower Hill Lad (IRE)** (DJSCosgrove) **2-8-3** JStack(2) (dwlt: hdwy & nt clr run 2f out: r.o wl towards fin) | s.h | **4** | 33/1 | 70 | 21 |
| 2404[10] | **Swallow Breeze** (DrJDScargill) **2-8-0** JFanning(6) (w ldrs tl rdn & one pce appr fnl f) | 4 | **5** | 33/1 | 58 | 9 |
| 2224[6] | **William Wallace** (CMurray) **2-8-7** AMackay(11) (a.p: ev ch ent fnl f: wknd last 100y) | ¾ | **6** | 11/2[3] | 63 | 14 |
| 2702[7] | **Drift** (SirMarkPrescott) **2-8-9** WWoods(5) (lw: hld up: effrt & rdn 2f out: nt rch ldrs) | ¾ | **7** | 25/1 | 64 | 15 |
| 2611[14] | **Charm The Stars** (MHTompkins) **2-8-5** PRobinson(7) (trckd ldrs: effrt 2f out: wknd appr fnl f) | 4 | **8** | 12/1 | 51 | 2 |
| 2122[2] | **Select Star (IRE)** (APJarvis) **2-8-0**(3) DWright(1) (plld hrd: hld up: effrt u.p & swvd lft 2f out: sn btn) | ½ | **9** | 5/2[1] | 48 | — |
| *2746*[3] | **The Wyandotte Inn** (RHollinshead) **2-8-1**(3) FLynch(3) (plld hrd: chsd ldrs over 5f: wknd qckly) | 6 | **10** | 12/1 | 35 | — |
| 2600[16] | **Running Free (IRE)** (MJFetherston-Godley) **2-8-10** WJO'Connor(12) (sn pushed along: nvr gng pce of ldrs) | 1¼ | **11** | 50/1 | 38 | — |
| *2370*[7] | **Petula Boy** (MMcCormack) **2-8-10v**[1] AClark(10) (trckd ldrs 4f: sn wknd: t.o) | 6 | **12** | 50/1 | 24 | — |
| | **Dijon** (BobJones) **2-8-5** NDay(4) (outpcd: a bhd: t.o) | 28 | **13** | 12/1 | — | — |

(SP 126.0%) **13 Rn**

**1m 26.8** (3.80) CSF £29.97 TOTE £3.60: £1.10 £2.30 £3.10 (£10.50) Trio £19.70 OWNER Goodwood Racehorse Owners Group (Two) Lt (ARUNDEL) BRED Floors Farming and Side Hill Stud
**OFFICIAL EXPLANATION Select Star (IRE): had become unbalanced on the rain-softened ground.**
**Goodwood Lass (IRE)**, given time to get over her initial outing, forced the pace over this slightly longer trip, and proved a real terrier when the battle to the line got under way. (100/30)
**2714 Blue Hopper** again ran promisingly and, if there is any more to come, she should not be long in getting off the mark. (8/1)
**Love Me Do (USA)**, a late foal from a winning family, looked very much in need of the run, but he ran a fine race in defeat, and should have little trouble in making a name for himself. (8/1: op 5/1)
**Flower Hill Lad (IRE)** has still not mastered the art of trapping, but showed that he does possess ability with a good staying-on effort after finding difficulty in running. (33/1)
**Swallow Breeze** got away on terms this time and was a leading light until fading on the approach to the final furlong. (33/1)
**2224 William Wallace** posed a big threat entering the final furlong, but went out like a light when the pressure was on. (11/2: 4/1-6/1)
**2538 Drift** never got himself into the action, but was doing his best work late on, and is now qualified for handicaps. (25/1)
**Charm The Stars** (12/1: op 8/1)
**2746 The Wyandotte Inn** (12/1: op 8/1)
**Dijon** (12/1: 5/1-14/1)

## 2968 DICKINSON & MORRIS H'CAP (0-80) (3-Y.O) (Class D)

8-00 (8-00) **7f 9y** £3,993.30 (£1,193.40: £571.20: £260.10) Stalls: Low GOING: minus 0.18 sec per fur (GF)

| | | | Pos | SP | RR | SF |
|---|---|---|---|---|---|---|
| 2301[6] | **Angaar (IRE) (79)** (ACStewart) **3-9-7** MRoberts(4) (lw: hld up & plld hrd: swtchd lft appr fnl f: qcknd to ld & edgd rt fnl 50y) | — | **1** | 2/1[2] | 86 | 58 |
| 2785[5] | **Dummer Golf Time (61)** (LordHuntingdon) **3-8-3v** DHarrison(1) (lw: a.p: shkn up to ld ins fnl f: edgd lft briefly: sn hdd: r.o) | s.h | **2** | 7/4[1] | 68 | 40 |
| 2427[5] | **Mister Joel (60)** (MWEasterby) **3-8-2b** DaleGibson(2) (led: hrd rdn 1f out: hdd & no ex ins fnl f) | 2 | **3** | 6/1 | 62 | 34 |
| 2630[5] | **Brandonville (55)** (NTinkler) **3-7-11** KimTinkler(3) (trckd ldrs tl outpcd fnl 2f) | 5 | **4** | 9/2[3] | 46 | 18 |
| *2308*[11] | **Dhes-C (58)** (RHollinshead) **3-7-11**(3)ow4 FLynch(5) (hld up & bhd: effrt & rdn over 2f out: sn outpcd) | 8 | **5** | 16/1 | 31 | — |

(SP 108.0%) **5 Rn**

**1m 25.6** (2.60) CSF £5.54 TOTE £2.30: £1.30 £1.40 (£2.30) OWNER Sheikh Ahmed Al Maktoum (NEWMARKET) BRED Ron Con Ltd
LONG HANDICAP Dhes-C 7-7
**2301 Angaar (IRE)** did not want to see too much daylight on this first attempt at the trip, and he quickened up readily to nose ahead in the final furlong, but he had a fight on his hands all the way to the line. (2/1: 5/4-9/4)
**2785 Dummer Golf Time** was surprisingly preferred in the market to the winner. He renewed his challenge after being collared 100 yards out, and compensation awaits. (7/4)
**2427 Mister Joel** has done the majority of his racing over sprint distances, but he was not afraid to make the running, and was only shaken off in the final furlong. He will not be long in returning to form. (6/1)

## 2969 ALLIANCE & LEICESTER-SERGEANTS' H'CAP (0-90) (3-Y.O+) (Class C)

8-30 (8-30) **1m 3f 183y** £5,744.00 (£1,712.00: £816.00: £368.00) Stalls: Low GOING: minus 0.18 sec per fur (GF)

| | | | Pos | SP | RR | SF |
|---|---|---|---|---|---|---|
| 2055[4] | **Beauchamp Jade (88)** (HCandy) **4-10-0** GCarter(4) (hld up: hdwy on bit to chal ent fnl f: led 100y out: comf) | — | **1** | 11/8[1] | 100 | 69 |

2674* **Desert Frolic (IRE) (89)** (MJohnston) **3-9-3** JWeaver(1) (lw: led: shkn up & hdd ins fnl f: kpt on towards fin)...½ **2** 7/4[2] 100 57
2674[3] **In the Money (IRE) (60)** (RHollinshead) **7-7-11**(3)ow1 FLynch(2) (lw: chsd ldr fr ½-wy: rdn over 3f out: outpcd fnl 2f) ....11 **3** 15/2 56 24
2401* **Artic Courier (85)** (DJSCosgrove) **5-9-11** JStack(5) (lw: hld up in rr: effrt & rdn over 2f out: sn outpcd).........2½ **4** 5/1[3] 78 47
(SP 106.9%) **4 Rn**

**2m 33.1** (4.10) CSF £3.87 TOTE £1.90 (£1.60) OWNER Mr E. Penser (WANTAGE) BRED E. Penser
WEIGHT FOR AGE 3yo-12lb
**2055 Beauchamp Jade** made amends for her unlucky run at Ascot and did it cheekily. She handled this rain-softened ground without too much difficulty. (11/8)
**2674* Desert Frolic (IRE)** could never get away form the winner and, though she did give of her best, she had met one too smart when the chips were down. (7/4)
**2674 In the Money (IRE)** could not reverse placings with the winner even on these better terms. (15/2)
**2401* Artic Courier** never got in a blow and the easing of the ground could have had something to do with it. (5/1)

## 2970 HOVIS-CHIEF CONSTABLES' MEDIAN AUCTION MAIDEN STKS (3-Y.O) (Class F)
9-00 (9-00) **5f 2y** £2,571.40 (£710.40: £338.20) Stalls: Low GOING: minus 0.18 sec per fur (GF)

SP RR SF
2791[3] **Marino Street (57)** (PDEvans) **3-8-9v** JFortune(5) (a.p: led over 1f out: drvn clr) ....— **1** 2/1[1] 54 29
**Failed To Hit** (SirMarkPrescott) **3-9-0** WWoods(4) (gd srt: str: bkwd: s.i.s: sn chsng ldrs: rdn over 1f out: one pce) ....3½ **2** 6/1 48 23
2597[5] **Charisse Dancer** (CFWall) **3-8-9** NCarlisle(2) (swvd lft s: hdwy wl over 1f out: drifted rt: fin wl) ....½ **3** 4/1[2] 41 16
637[14] **John's Law (IRE)** (MJHeaton-Ellis) **3-8-9**(5) AmandaSanders(3) (bit bkwd: hld up: hdwy appr fnl f: nrst fin)..s.h **4** 20/1 46 21
**Poppy My Love** (RHarris) **3-8-9** AMackay(7) (led tl over 1f out: sn rdn & outpcd) ....1¼ **5** 8/1 37 12
2432[8] **Magic Solution (IRE)** (HCandy) **3-8-9** CRutter(8) (prom tl outpcd appr fnl f) ....hd **6** 5/1[3] 37 12
**Sweet Seventeen** (HJCollingridge) **3-8-9** MRimmer(1) (unf: scope: bit bkwd: carried lft s: a in rr) ....1 **7** 14/1 34 9
2732[11] **Fancy Clancy (46)** (MissLCSiddall) **3-8-9** JWeaver(6) (lw: rn v.green: a bhd: t.o) ....12 **8** 9/1 — —
(SP 116.8%) **8 Rn**

**61.4 secs** (2.90) CSF £13.94 TOTE £2.60: £1.10 £2.00 £1.90 (£4.20) OWNER Mr Roy Penton (WELSHPOOL) BRED Mrs B. Thompson
OFFICIAL EXPLANATION **Fancy Clancy: the jockey stated that the horse hung badly to the right, making it impossible for him to ride out properly.**
**2791 Marino Street**, not winning out of turn, did this very easily indeed and may now be allowed a break. (2/1)
**Failed To Hit**, seemingly with something left to work on, got slightly outpaced when the pace lifted below the distance, but was coming back at the finish, and will come into his own over further. (6/1: op 5/2)
**2597 Charisse Dancer** gave away ground by swerving left on leaving the stalls, but she was beginning to peg back the leaders near the finish, and is open to improvement. (4/1)
**John's Law (IRE)** did all his best work in the final furlong, and this was his first sign of ability. (20/1)
**Poppy My Love** impressed to post on this belated seasonal debut and set the pace until running out of steam a furlong out. (8/1: 6/1-10/1)
**Magic Solution (IRE)** found the step down from seven not really in her favour. (5/1)

T/Plpt: £26.60 (444.78 Tckts). T/Qdpt: £6.10 (165.5 Tckts). IM

# 2782-SANDOWN (R-H) (Good to firm, 5f crse Firm patches)
## Wednesday July 24th
WEATHER: fine WIND: mod across

## 2971 HARPERS & QUEEN (S) H'CAP (0-60) (3-Y.O+) (Class E)
6-15 (6-17) **1m 14y** £4,005.00 (£1,215.00: £595.00: £285.00) Stalls: High GOING minus 0.56 sec per fur (F)

SP RR SF
2507[2] **Thatchmaster (IRE) (46)** (CAHorgan) **5-9-0** PaulEddery(10) (lw: mde all: rdn out) ....— **1** 6/1[2] 57 38
2617[8] **Super Hero (33)** (AGNewcombe) **4-8-1** NAdams(11) (lw: a.p: chsd wnr over 2f out: unable qckn) ....1¼ **2** 14/1 42 23
2761[6] **Tomal (44)** (RIngram) **4-8-12** SWhitworth(15) (b.hind: nt clr run over 2f out: hdwy over 1f out: r.o wl ins fnl f) ....½ **3** 9/1[3] 52 33
*2636*[4] **Little Kenny (44)** (MJFetherston-Godley) **3-8-4v**ow1 DHolland(4) (hld up: rdn over 2f out: one pce) ....nk **4** 12/1 51 23
2766[2] **Rocky Waters (USA) (56)** (PBurgoyne) **7-9-10** DRMcCabe(6) (b.hind: rdn over 3f out: hdwy over 1f out: r.o one pce) ....1¾ **5** 10/1 60 41
2313[8] **Only (USA) (47)** (RHannon) **3-8-4**(3) DaneO'Neill(8) (hld up: rdn over 2f out: one pce) ....hd **6** 25/1 50 23
2801[4] **Acquittal (IRE) (45)** (AStreeter) **4-8-8v**(5) RHavlin(16) (hdwy 3f out: nt clr run 2f out: hmpd 1f out: nt rcvr)......nk **7** 11/2[1] 48 29
2344[3] **Nabjelsedr (37)** (AGNewcombe) **6-8-5** BThomson(3) (s.s: nvr nrr) ....2½ **8** 12/1 35 16
2743[15] **Noeprob (USA) (55)** (RJHodges) **6-9-9** TSprake(14) (rdn over 3f out: a mid div) ....¾ **9** 12/1 51 32
2801[5] **Return To Brighton (48)** (JMBradley) **4-8-9**(7) AEddery(9) (s.s: nvr nrr) ....nk **10** 10/1 44 25
2796[3] **Speedy Snaps Pride (37)** (PDCundell) **4-8-5b** GHind(2) (prom over 6f) ....1 **11** 25/1 31 12
2345[6] **Daring Ryde (45)** (JPSmith) **5-8-8**(5) JDSmith(12) (rdn & hdwy 2f out: wknd over 1f out) ....1½ **12** 20/1 36 17
*1027*[8] **Sphinx Levelv (IRE) (47)** (APJarvis) **3-8-7** SSanders(18) (lw: nvr nrr) ....2½ **13** 25/1 33 6
2753[6] **Apartments Abroad (48)** (KMcAuliffe) **3-8-8v**ow1 JReid(13) (b.hind: a.p: rdn over 2f out: wknd 1f out) ....1½ **14** 25/1 31 3
**Corona Gold (42)** (JGFitzGerald) **6-8-10** WRyan(17) (bit bkwd: bhd fnl 5f) ....1½ **15** 12/1 22 3
2507[16] **Tony's Mist (43)** (JMBradley) **6-8-4**(7) JWilkinson(5) (lw: prom over 5f) ....3 **16** 25/1 17 —
2507[14] **Doodies Pool (IRE) (38)** (PBurgoyne) **6-8-6v** CHodgson(1) (hdwy 5f out: wknd over 3f out) ....6 **17** 33/1 — —
2716[16] **Soviet Sakti (IRE) (41)** (PMitchell) **3-8-1** GBardwell(7) (a bhd) ....19 **18** 33/1 — —
(SP 125.2%) **18 Rn**

**1m 42.76** (1.56) CSF £80.55 CT £696.72 TOTE £5.50: £1.40 £5.10 £2.20 £1.90 (£85.40) Trio £148.90 OWNER Mrs B. Sumner (PULBOROUGH) BRED Ballysheehan Stud
WEIGHT FOR AGE 3yo-8lb
No bid
**2507 Thatchmaster (IRE)** at long last lost his maiden tag by making all. (6/1)
**Super Hero**, never far away, struggled into second place over a quarter of a mile from home but, try as he might, failed to get on terms with the winner. (14/1: 10/1-16/1)
**2761 Tomal**, out with the washing entering the straight, ran on really strongly up the hill in the last furlong and a half, but never looked like getting there in time. His only victory to date came as a two-year-old. (9/1: op 6/1)

**2636 Little Kenny,** pushed along over two furlongs from home, could only go up and down in the same place. (12/1: 8/1-14/1)
**2766 Rocky Waters (USA),** at the back of the field entering the straight, stayed on in the last furlong and a half without posing a real threat. (10/1)
**1956 Only (USA)** chased the leaders, but was made to look very pedestrian in the last two furlongs. (25/1)
**2801 Acquittal (IRE)** had no luck in running. Taking closer order, he had nowhere to go a quarter of a mile from home and, every time his jockey looked as if he had found daylight, the horse met with interference. Badly hampered at the furlong pole, he could never recover. (11/2)
**2373 Noeprob (USA)** (12/1: op 8/1)

## 2972 PERCHERON E.B.F. MAIDEN STKS (2-Y.O) (Class D)

6-45 (6-48) **7f 16y** £4,240.50 (£1,284.00: £627.00: £298.50) Stalls: High GOING minus 0.56 sec per fur (F)

| | | | | SP | RR | SF |
|---|---|---|---|---|---|---|
| | **Tarski** (HRACecil) **2-9-0** PatEddery(8) (w'like: scope: lw: rdn over 4f out: hdwy over 2f out: led over 1f out: all out) | — | 1 | 7/2[2] | 88+ | 41 |
| 2695[5] | **Shoumatara (USA)** (MRStoute) **2-9-0** RCochrane(11) (lw: hdwy over 2f out: rdn over 1f out: r.o ins fnl f) | ½ | 2 | 10/1 | 87 | 40 |
| 2335[4] | **Party Romance (USA)** (BHanbury) **2-9-0** WRyan(9) (led 1f: led 3f out tl over 1f out: r.o) | s.h | 3 | 9/2[3] | 87 | 40 |
| 2580[3] | **Royal Amaretto (IRE)** (BJMeehan) **2-9-0** JReid(7) (bit bkwd: a.p: ev ch wl over 1f out: unable qckn) | ½ | 4 | 6/4[1] | 86 | 39 |
| 2758[2] | **Aim Seven** (RHannon) **2-8-11**(3) DaneO'Neill(4) (lw: led 6f out to 3f out: wknd over 1f out) | 8 | 5 | 9/1 | 68 | 21 |
| | **Sudest (IRE)** (IABalding) **2-9-0** PaulEddery(10) (w'like: no hdwy fnl 3f) | 1½ | 6 | 10/1 | 61 | 17 |
| | **Frost King** (MissBSanders) **2-9-0** SSanders(6) (leggy: unf: a bhd) | 1¾ | 7 | 66/1 | 60 | 13 |
| | **Bedouin Honda** (CEBrittain) **2-9-0** BDoyle(1) (unf: s.s: a bhd) | 2 | 8 | 25/1 | 56 | 9 |
| | **Copper Shell** (APJones) **2-9-0** TSprake(3) (leggy: a bhd) | ¾ | 9 | 66/1 | 54 | 7 |
| | **Al Masroor (USA)** (JWPayne) **2-9-0** BThomson(5) (cmpt: bit bkwd: a bhd) | 16 | 10 | 33/1 | 18 | — |

(SP 118.4%) **10 Rn**

**1m 29.66** (1.06) CSF £35.34 TOTE £3.70: £1.80 £2.00 £1.70 (£12.70) Trio £22.00 OWNER Mr K. Abdulla (NEWMARKET) BRED Juddmonte Farms

**Tarski**, an attractive, scopey individual who has reportedly been working well at home, certainly knew he had been in a fight here, but proved up to the task. With Eddery throwing everything he could at the colt, he only just held on, and he will need a rest to get over this very tough race. (7/2: op 2/1)
**2695 Shoumatara (USA)** looked very well in the paddock and left his initial run well behind. Taking closer order over a quarter of a mile from home, he ran on nicely inside the final furlong for second prize, if just failing to peg back the winner. A suitable opportunity should soon be found. (10/1: 6/1-11/1)
**2335 Party Romance (USA)** was not going to hang around and, together with the fifth, set a scorching pace. Eventually overhauled by the winner below the distance, he stuck to his task in tremendous style to finish a very creditable third. There is a race waiting for him. (9/2: 3/1-5/1)
**2580 Royal Amaretto (IRE)**, a strongly-made individual, still did not look fully fit. Racing in third place, he had every chance early in the final quarter-mile before tapped for toe. He should soon be winning. (6/4)
**2758 Aim Seven** looked very well but, together with the third, went off too fast. Not surprisingly, he folded up below the distance. (9/1: 12/1-20/1)
**Sudest (IRE)** failed to live with the tremendous early pace and was making no impression in the straight. (10/1: 6/1-11/1)

## 2973 JENNIFER'S DIARY H'CAP (0-80) (4-Y.O+) (Class D)

7-15 (7-16) **1m 6f** £3,858.75 (£1,170.00: £572.50: £273.75) Stalls: High GOING minus 0.56 sec per fur (F)

| | | | | SP | RR | SF |
|---|---|---|---|---|---|---|
| 2707* | **Ballynakelly (65)** (RAkehurst) **4-8-13** SSanders(8) (a.p: led over 2f out: rdn out) | — | 1 | 5/4[1] | 78+ | 41 |
| 1802[9] | **Tudor Island (80)** (CEBrittain) **7-10-0** BDoyle(7) (hld up: rdn over 3f out: r.o one pce) | 2½ | 2 | 8/1 | 90 | 53 |
| 2709* | **Silktail (IRE) (65)** (MissGayKelleway) **4-8-13** TSprake(4) (rdn over 3f out: hdwy over 1f out: r.o) | nk | 3 | 5/1[2] | 75 | 38 |
| 2697[11] | **Benfleet (74)** (RWArmstrong) **5-9-8** JReid(5) (lw: rdn over 3f out: hdwy fnl f: r.o one pce) | 1¾ | 4 | 10/1 | 82 | 45 |
| 2319[11] | **Farringdon Hill (78)** (MajorWRHern) **5-9-12b** RHills(1) (chsd ldr: led 8f out tl over 2f out: wknd fnl f) | 1 | 5 | 12/1 | 85 | 48 |
| 2709[2] | **Supreme Star (USA) (65)** (PRHedger) **5-8-10**(3) DaneO'Neill(10) (lw: rdn & hdwy over 2f out: one pce) | ¾ | 6 | 7/1[3] | 71 | 34 |
| 2341* | **Reaganesque (USA) (51)** (PGMurphy) **4-7-13** NAdams(3) (lw: a.p: rdn over 3f out: wknd over 1f out) | 10 | 7 | 7/1[3] | 45 | 8 |
| 2848[5] | **Pedaltothemetal (IRE) (48)** (PMitchell) **4-7-10** JQuinn(6) (sme hdwy 5f out: wknd 3f out) | 6 | 8 | 25/1 | 36 | — |
| | **One Voice (USA) (80)** (KBishop) **6-10-0** RPerham(2) (lw: led 6f: wknd over 6f out: t.o) | 30 | 9 | 50/1 | 33 | — |

(SP 119.8%) **9 Rn**

**3m 1.1** (2.20) CSF £11.94 CT £37.30 TOTE £2.60: £1.40 £2.10 £1.60 (£8.10) Trio £9.60 OWNER Y Y Partnership (EPSOM) BRED Crest Stud Ltd

LONG HANDICAP Pedaltothemetal (IRE) 7-9

**2707* Ballynakelly** extended his remarkable winning sequence to six. The Handicapper has been extremely kind on him - he was racing off a mark only 2lb higher than his last All-Weather victory back in January - but surely that will all start to change now. (5/4)
**1802 Tudor Island**, rousted along in the straight, stayed on for second prize without posing a serious threat. (8/1)
**2709* Silktail (IRE)** was doing all her best work in the last furlong and a half. (5/1)
**1792 Benfleet**, out with the washing, was still at the back of the field below the distance. He stayed on in the last 200 yards but, by then, it was all over. (10/1: 8/1-12/1)
**2002* Farringdon Hill** went to the front a mile from home. Collared over two furlongs from home, he tried to hold on, but had nothing more in reserve in the last 200 yards. (12/1: op 8/1)
**2709 Supreme Star (USA)** made an effort over a quarter of a mile from home, but could then make no further impression. (7/1)

## 2974 PANMURE GORDON H'CAP (0-85) (3-Y.O) (Class D)

7-45 (7-45) **7f 16y** £4,357.50 (£1,320.00: £645.00: £307.50) Stalls: High GOING minus 0.56 sec per fur (F)

| | | | | SP | RR | SF |
|---|---|---|---|---|---|---|
| 2710* | **Catch The Lights (81)** (RHannon) **3-9-3**(3) DaneO'Neill(5) (lw: rdn & hdwy over 1f out: led nr fin) | — | 1 | 9/4[1] | 88 | 28 |
| 2229[5] | **Nunsharpa (71)** (JRFanshawe) **3-8-10** JReid(6) (a.p: chsd ldr over 3f out: led over 2f out: rdn over 1f out: hdd nr fin) | nk | 2 | 3/1[3] | 77 | 17 |
| 2578[2] | **Kings Harmony (IRE) (66)** (PJMakin) **3-8-5** PatEddery(3) (lw: chsd ldr over 3f: rdn over 2f out: one pce) | 2½ | 3 | 11/4[2] | 67 | 7 |
| 2529* | **Shadow Casting (77)** (BWHills) **3-8-11**(5) JDSmith(4) (rdn & hdwy over 1f out: one pce) | 1¾ | 4 | 7/2 | 74 | 14 |
| 2687[7] | **Carmarthen Bay (75)** (GLMoore) **3-9-0** RCochrane(2) (lw: a bhd) | 3 | 5 | 14/1 | 65 | 5 |
| 2722[7] | **My Mariam (82)** (CREgerton) **3-9-7** WRyan(1) (led over 4f: wknd over 1f out) | 5 | 6 | 25/1 | 61 | 1 |

(SP 115.2%) **6 Rn**

**1m 31.39** (2.79) CSF £9.27 TOTE £3.30: £1.70 £2.20 (£6.50) OWNER Mr T. A. Johnsey (MARLBOROUGH) BRED T. A. Johnsey

**2710* Catch The Lights**, who has risen 12lb since the first of her two recent victories, almost got caught out by this shorter trip. Only finding her feet below the distance, she threw down her challenge inside the final furlong and managed to get on top in the closing stages. A mile is her ideal distance. (9/4: 5/1-3/1)

**2229 Nunsharpa** made her bid for glory over a quarter of a mile from home, but failed to get away. Bustled along from below the distance, she was just worried out of it near the line. (3/1)
**2578 Kings Harmony (IRE)**, in second place to halfway, could then only keep on at one pace. (11/4)
**2529* Shadow Casting** made her effort below the distance, but was making no further impression inside the last 200 yards. (7/2)
**Carmarthen Bay** was always at the back of the field. (14/1)
**My Mariam**, collared over two furlongs from home, had shot her bolt below the distance. (25/1)

## 2975 'PARTY LINE' CLAIMING STKS (3-Y.O) (Class E)
8-15 (8-17) **1m 2f 7y** £3,485.00 (£1,055.00: £515.00: £245.00) Stalls: High GOING minus 0.56 sec per fur (F)

| | | | | SP | RR | SF |
|---|---|---|---|---|---|---|
| 2711[3] | **Evidence In Chief (55)** (DRCElsworth) **3-8-3v**[1](3) DaneO'Neill(2) (hld up: led over 2f out: rdn out) | — | **1** | 4/1[2] | 70 | 26 |
| 1999[3] | **Domettes (IRE) (58)** (RHannon) **3-8-1** JFEgan(4) (lw: hld up: rdn over 2f out: ev ch 1f out: unable qckn) | 1¾ | **2** | 10/1 | 62 | 18 |
| 2753[4] | **Oberons Boy (IRE) (94)** (BJMeehan) **3-9-3b** JReid(7) (lw: hld up: nt clr run 5f out: rdn over 2f out: ev ch 1f out: nt run on) | s.h | **3** | 8/1[3] | 78 | 34 |
| 2121[3] | **Open Affair** (APJarvis) **3-8-4** JTate(1) (hdwy 4f out: rdn over 2f out: one pce) | 1¾ | **4** | 9/1 | 62 | 18 |
| 1798[9] | **Lear Jet (USA) (90)** (PFICole) **3-9-3** TQuinn(5) (lw: w ldr: led 6f out tl over 2f out: hrd rdn over 1f out: one pce) | ¾ | **5** | 10/11[1] | 74 | 30 |
| 2573[11] | **Northern Judge (55)** (BHanbury) **3-8-5** WRyan(3) (a bhd: t.o: lame) | dist | **6** | 20/1 | — | — |
| 2196[8] | **Poly My Son (IRE) (53)** (MRChannon) **3-8-9** PatEddery(6) (lw: led 4f: t.o whn p.u over 2f out: lame) | | **P** | 12/1 | — | — |

(SP 115.0%) **7 Rn**

**2m 9.29** (2.59) CSF £36.93 TOTE £5.20: £2.60 £5.40 (£37.90) OWNER Mr Raymond Tooth (WHITCOMBE) BRED N. Abbott
**OFFICIAL EXPLANATION Poly My Son (IRE): lost his action on the home turn and was lame when pulled up.**
**Northern Judge: pulled up lame on the near-fore.**
**2711 Evidence In Chief** cruised into the lead over a quarter of a mile from home and, ridden along, kept her rivals at bay. (4/1: op 6/1)
**1999 Domettes (IRE)** chased the leaders. Throwing down her challenge in the final quarter-mile, she was certainly close enough if good enough inside the final furlong before the winner found extra. (10/1: 6/1-12/1)
**2753 Oberons Boy (IRE)**, not for the first time, looked thoroughly ungenuine. With his rider grimly trying to get the gelding on terms, he had every chance entering the final furlong before chucking in the towel in no uncertain terms. He should be avoided at all costs. (8/1)
**2121 Open Affair** took closer order turning for home, but was making little impression in the final quarter-mile. (9/1: 5/1-10/1)
**1619 Lear Jet (USA)**, taking a big drop in class, was very disappointing. Sent on three-quarters of a mile from home, he was headed over two furlongs out. Coming under pressure below the distance, he looked very awkward and could only keep on at one pace. He ran as if there is a problem with him, and he looks one to avoid. (10/11: 4/6-Evens)

## 2976 SURREY RACING H'CAP (0-80) (4-Y.O+) (Class D)
8-45 (8-47) **5f 6y** £4,713.25 (£1,426.00: £695.50: £330.25) Stalls: High GOING minus 0.56 sec per fur (F)

| | | | | SP | RR | SF |
|---|---|---|---|---|---|---|
| 2787[5] | **Squire Corrie (55)** (GHarwood) **4-7-12b**(7) GayeHarwood(7) (lw: a.p: rdn over 1f out: led ins fnl f: r.o wl) | — | **1** | 12/1 | 63 | 15 |
| 2586[3] | **Friendly Brave (USA) (72)** (MissGayKelleway) **6-9-8** PatEddery(2) (b.hind: lw: a.p: hrd rdn over 1f out: r.o ins fnl f: edgd rt nr fin) | nk | **2** | 15/2 | 79 | 31 |
| 2548[3] | **Jucea (73)** (JLSpearing) **7-9-9** JReid(10) (nt clr run 2f out: hdwy over 1f out: r.o wl ins fnl f) | hd | **3** | 11/2[3] | 80 | 32 |
| 2787[2] | **Gone Savage (56)** (WJMusson) **8-8-6** RCochrane(9) (bdly hmpd on ins 2f out: hdwy over 1f out: str run fnl f: hmpd nr fin) | ¾ | **4** | 11/4[1] | 60 | 12 |
| 2713[4] | **Sizzling (60)** (RHannon) **4-8-7**(3) DaneO'Neill(11) (a.p: rdn over 2f out: r.o one pce fnl f) | ¾ | **5** | 9/2[2] | 62 | 14 |
| 2548[2] | **Beau Venture (USA) (73)** (BPalling) **8-9-9** TSprake(6) (lw: a.p: led over 1f out tl ins fnl f: wkng whn hmpd nr fin) | nk | **6** | 8/1 | 74 | 26 |
| 2725[11] | **Fantasy Racing (IRE) (76)** (MRChannon) **4-9-12** RPerham(5) (no hdwy fnl 2f) | 1½ | **7** | 25/1 | 72 | 24 |
| 1958[10] | **Jobie (60)** (BWHills) **6-8-10** RHills(8) (lw: a bhd) | nk | **8** | 9/1 | 55 | 7 |
| 2548[4] | **Chewit (78)** (AMoore) **4-10-0v**[1] CandyMorris(1) (led over 3f) | 3 | **9** | 16/1 | 64 | 16 |
| | **Millesime (IRE) (70)** (BHanbury) **4-9-6** WRyan(4) (b: lw: bhd fnl 2f) | 5 | **10** | 25/1 | 40 | — |
| 2735[4] | **Robo Magic (USA) (52)** (LMontagueHall) **4-8-2b** SSanders(3) (a bhd) | 11 | **11** | 25/1 | — | — |

(SP 118.2%) **11 Rn**

**61.53 secs** (1.73) CSF £90.72 CT £509.41 TOTE £16.60: £3.10 £2.00 £1.90 (£136.30) Trio £344.80 OWNER Mr G. Harwood (PULBOROUGH) BRED Whitsbury Manor Stud
**2787 Squire Corrie**, in the front rank throughout, managed to get on top inside the final furlong and just held on in a desperate finish. (12/1)
**2586 Friendly Brave (USA)** responded well to pressure and, running on strongly, only just failed to get there. (15/2: 6/1-9/1)
**2548 Jucea** did not have much luck. Failing to get a clear run a quarter of a mile from home, she picked up ground below the distance and, running on really strongly, may well have prevailed with a little further to go. Compensation awaits. (11/2)
**2787 Gone Savage**, who loves this course, can be considered very unlucky, as being badly hampered at the back of the field a quarter of a mile from home cost him ground he could ill-afford. Picking up ground below the distance, he produced a storming run in the final furlong but, with some of the others tightening up near the line, he was once again hampered near the finish. His style of racing means that there is always the possibility of meeting with interference and, although he has only won once since 1993, he is in good heart at present and is being given a real chance by the Handicapper. His four wins in handicap company have all come off a mark of 62 or higher, yet he was racing off just 56 here. He goes particularly well at Sandown and should soon gain compensation. (11/4)
**2713 Sizzling** struggled on up the hill without ever threatening to get on terms. (9/2)
**2548 Beau Venture (USA)** poked a whisker in front below the distance, but he was collared inside the final furlong and was squeezed out near the line. (8/1: 6/1-9/1)

T/Jkpt: Not won; £3,533.33 to Brighton 25/7/96. T/Plpt: £237.30 (86.24 Tckts). T/Qdpt: £50.50 (31.1 Tckts). AK

# 2764-BRIGHTON (L-H) (Firm)
## Thursday July 25th
WEATHER: sunny WIND: mod half bhd

## 2977 E.B.F. WOODINGDEAN MEDIAN AUCTION MAIDEN STKS (2-Y.O) (Class E)
2-00 (2-00) **6f 209y** £2,988.30 (£890.40: £424.20: £191.10) Stalls: Low GOING minus 0.43 sec per fur (F)

| | | | | SP | RR | SF |
|---|---|---|---|---|---|---|
| | **Northern Sun** (TGMills) **2-9-0** WWoods(1) (w'like: bit bkwd: hld up in tch: rdn 2f out: led ins fnl f: r.o) | — | **1** | 16/1 | 71 | 12 |

| | Horse / comment | Dist | Pos | SP | RR | SF |
|---|---|---|---|---|---|---|
| $2708^{8}$ | **Sharp Hat** (RHannon) **2-9-0** WJO'Connor(2) (b.off hind: lw: tk keen hold: a.p: led over 3f out: rdn over 1f out: hdd ins fnl f: unable qckn) | ¾ | **2** | Evens $^{1}$ | 69 | 10 |
| $2600^{11}$ | **Aurelian** (MBell) **2-9-0** MFenton(6) (chsd ldr tl rdn & outpcd 4f out: rallied 2f out: styd on strly ins fnl f) | nk | **3** | 5/1 $^{2}$ | 69 | 10 |
| | **Triple Term** (JLDunlop) **2-9-0** SWhitworth(4) (leggy: bit bkwd: dwlt: hld up: hdwy 3f out: rdn 2f out: grad wknd) | 3½ | **4** | 5/1 $^{2}$ | 61 | 2 |
| *$2750^{2}$* | **Bali-Pet** (WGMTurner) **2-8-7**(7) DSweeney(5) (led: rn wd & hdd over 3f out: wknd 2f out) | 5 | **5** | 8/1 | 49 | — |
| $2852^{10}$ | **Regal Equity** (BJMeehan) **2-9-0** MTebbutt(3) (hld up: rdn 3f out: sn wknd) | 6 | **6** | 13/2 $^{3}$ | 35 | — |

(SP 113.7%) **6 Rn**

**1m 24.0** (4.00) CSF £32.34 TOTE £17.90: £6.40 £1.00 (£13.60) OWNER Mr Tony Murray (EPSOM) BRED Broughton Bloodstock
**Northern Sun** belied his burly appearance with a game display here, and can improve. (16/1)
**2708 Sharp Hat** raced a bit freely and, as a consequence, did not have much in reserve when challenged. (Evens)
**Aurelian** ran here as though a mile would suit. (5/1: 3/1-11/2)
**Triple Term** has a middle-distance pedigree and will probably come into his own next year. (5/1: 9/4-11/2)
**Regal Equity** (13/2: 7/2-7/1)

## 2978 KINGSTON (S) H'CAP (0-60) (3-Y.O+) (Class G)

2-35 (2-37) **1m 3f 196y** £2,070.00 (£570.00: £270.00) Stalls: Low GOING minus 0.43 sec per fur (F)

| | Horse / comment | Dist | Pos | SP | RR | SF |
|---|---|---|---|---|---|---|
| $2537^{7}$ | **Tout de Val (26)** (KBishop) **7-7-10** NAdams(1) (chsd ldrs: led over 2f out: rdn & edgd lft over 1f out: r.o) | — | **1** | 14/1 | 33 | 7 |
| $2711^{R}$ | **Courbaril (58)** (SDow) **4-10-0v¹** WWoods(5) (chsd ldr: led 4f out: hdd over 2f out: hrd rdn & swtchd rt over 1f out: unable qckn) | 2 | **2** | 6/1 | 62 | 36 |
| $2556^{6}$ | **Naseer (USA) (34)** (KBishop) **7-8-4** NCarlisle(3) (b: mid div: outpcd 5f out: hrd rdn over 2f out: sltly short of rm over 1f out: r.o one pce ins fnl f) | 3 | **3** | 8/1 | 34 | 8 |
| $2594^{7}$ | **Moving Up (IRE) (50)** (GLMoore) **3-8-8** SWhitworth(7) (hld up: sme hdwy 3f out: rdn 2f out: kpt on one pce ins fnl f) | 2 | **4** | 9/2 $^{2}$ | 48 | 10 |
| $2407^{4}$ | **Colour Counsellor (43)** (RMFlower) **3-8-1b** DBiggs(6) (led: hdd 4f out: wknd over 2f out) | 8 | **5** | 5/1 $^{3}$ | 30 | — |
| $2380^{5}$ | **Mrs Keen (38)** (RSimpson) **3-7-10** FNorton(4) (chsd ldrs: rdn & ev ch 2f out: wknd qckly over 1f out) | 3 | **6** | 33/1 | 21 | — |
| *$1997^{5}$* | **Boston Tea Party (38)** (AMoore) **3-7-7**(3) NVarley(8) (swtg: bhd fnl 4f) | nk | **7** | 25/1 | 20 | — |
| $853^{11}$ | **Taylors Revival (26)** (HJCollingridge) **5-7-10** DeclanO'Shea(2) (swtg: a bhd: t.o fnl 5f) | 30 | **8** | 33/1 | — | — |
| $2798^{2}$ | **Linda's Joy (IRE) (56)** (MCPipe) **3-8-11v¹**(3) MHenry(9) (ref to r) | | **R** | 2/1 $^{1}$ | — | — |

(SP 110.0%) **9 Rn**

**2m 33.6** (6.00) CSF £83.08 CT £617.42 TOTE £14.80: £3.10 £2.00 £2.00 (£60.50) Trio £137.10 OWNER Mr K. Bishop (BRIDGWATER)
LONG HANDICAP Tout de Val 7-8 Taylors Revival 7-7 Mrs Keen 7-6
WEIGHT FOR AGE 3yo-12lb
No bid
**Tout de Val** responded to pressure in the final two furlongs to win a poor contest. (14/1)
**1063 Courbaril** consented to race today but found the 32lb weight concession just too much for him. (6/1)
**2556 Naseer (USA)** is a very big horse who looked ill-at-ease on the track. He stayed on late having floundered coming down the hill. (8/1: 6/1-9/1)
**2594 Moving Up (IRE)** was never nearer than at the finish. (9/2)
**1877 Colour Counsellor** showed the way but had no more to give once headed. (5/1)
**2798 Linda's Joy (IRE)**, who had two handlers in the paddock, looked a mulish customer and, when the stalls opened, she refused to come out. (2/1: 6/4-5/2)

## 2979 WEATHERBYS' BULLETIN MAGAZINE H'CAP (0-60) (3-Y.O) (Class F)

3-10 (3-10) **1m 1f 209y** £2,761.80 (£764.80: £365.40) GOING minus 0.43 sec per fur (F)

| | Horse / comment | Dist | Pos | SP | RR | SF |
|---|---|---|---|---|---|---|
| $2120^{8}$ | **General Glow (40)** (PDEvans) **3-8-1** JFEgan(3) (chsd ldrs: pushed along 3f out: hrd rdn over 1f out: led wl ins fnl f: r.o) | — | **1** | 15/2 | 48+ | 13 |
| $1539^{10}$ | **Khabar (60)** (RBastiman) **3-9-2**(5) HBastiman(8) (a.p: led over 3f out: rdn & edgd lft over 1f out: hdd wl ins fnl f: unable qckn) | ½ | **2** | 9/2 $^{2}$ | 67 | 32 |
| $2409^{5}$ | **Pride of Kashmir (52)** (PWHarris) **3-8-13** FNorton(6) (hld up: hdwy over 2f out: hrd rdn over 1f out: one pce) | 2 | **3** | 5/1 $^{3}$ | 56 | 21 |
| $2358^{6}$ | **Creeking (57)** (SirMarkPrescott) **3-9-4** WWoods(5) (led: hdd over 3f out: swtchd rt over 1f out: rdn & no ex ins fnl f) | 1½ | **4** | 6/1 | 59 | 24 |
| $2716^{2}$ | **He's Got Wings (IRE) (46)** (MBell) **3-8-7v** MFenton(2) (chsd ldrs: lost pl & dropped rr 5f out: rallied 2f out: styd on strly ins fnl f) | s.h | **5** | 4/1 $^{1}$ | 48 | 13 |
| $2768^{3}$ | **Efficacious (IRE) (46)** (CJBenstead) **3-8-7** AMcGlone(4) (rr: sme hdwy 2f out: sn rdn & btn) | 2½ | **6** | 12/1 | 44 | 9 |
| $2409^{10}$ | **Sheilana (IRE) (56)** (TGMills) **3-9-3** MarkLynch(9) (chsd ldrs tl wknd over 2f out) | 4 | **7** | 25/1 | 47 | 12 |
| $2380^{2}$ | **On The Wildside (56)** (MRChannon) **3-8-12**(5) PPMurphy(10) (lw: hld up in rr: rdn 4f out: no hdwy) | 9 | **8** | 11/2 | 33 | — |
| $561^{14}$ | **Polish Lady (IRE) (44)** (CMurray) **3-8-0**(5) MBaird(1) (rr: plld hrd: rapid hdwy 5f out: wknd over 2f out) | 4 | **9** | 40/1 | 14 | — |
| $2506^{16}$ | **Followthe Allstars (54)** (TJNaughton) **3-9-1** PaulEddery(7) (prom to ½-wy) | 9 | **10** | 33/1 | 10 | — |

(SP 113.2%) **10 Rn**

**2m 2.8** (4.50) CSF £37.42 CT £168.12 TOTE £9.70: £1.70 £2.00 £2.40 (£12.60) Trio £60.50 OWNER Mr J. G. White (WELSHPOOL) BRED Messinger Stud Ltd
STEWARDS' ENQUIRY Bastiman susp. 3-4/8/96 (excessive use of whip).
**General Glow**, backed down from 20/1, looked unlikely to land the gamble when pushed along early in the straight but, the more he was ridden, the more he found, and he wore down the runner-up in the last 50 yards. (15/2: 20/1-7/1)
**Khabar** was also well supported in the Ring and looked sure to prevail over a furlong out, but he was worn down late on. (9/2)
**2409 Pride of Kashmir** kept on in the closing stages, but could not go with them when the pace quickened. (5/1)
**2358 Creeking** cut out a lot of the running but had no more to give in the final furlong. She could do with the Handicapper dropping her a few pounds. (6/1: op 7/2)
**2716 He's Got Wings (IRE)** looked a tricky customer here as he lost a prominent position for no good reason five furlongs out, and looked like finishing in the rear. He rallied strongly from the two-furlong pole though and none finished better. (4/1)

## 2980 JOE BLANKS MEMORIAL CHALLENGE CUP H'CAP (0-80) (3-Y.O) (Class D)

3-45 (3-45) **7f 214y** £3,661.80 (£1,091.40: £520.20: £234.60) Stalls: Low GOING minus 0.43 sec per fur (F)

| | Horse / comment | Dist | Pos | SP | RR | SF |
|---|---|---|---|---|---|---|
| *$1718^{2}$* | **Farmost (75)** (SirMarkPrescott) **3-9-5** WWoods(8) (lw: mde all: hrd rdn ins fnl f: r.o wl) | — | **1** | 7/4 $^{1}$ | 85 | 38 |

2412[6] **Passage Creeping (IRE) (70)** (LMCumani) **3-9-0** OUrbina(6) (hld up: brought wd & hdwy 2f out: str run ins fnl f: r.o) ....½ **2** 6/1[3] 79 32
*2552*[4] **Law Dancer (IRE) (70)** (TGMills) **3-9-0** PaulEddery(3) (chsd wnr: rdn 2f out: one pce) ....3 **3** 14/1 73 26
2706[4] **Possessive Artiste (73)** (MRStoute) **3-9-3v[1]** RCochrane(1) (lw: hld up in tch: rdn 2f out: one pce) ....2 **4** 9/2[2] 72 25
2618[2] **Paint It Black (77)** (RHannon) **3-9-7b** WJO'Connor(4) (mid div: rdn 3f out: one pce) ....½ **5** 8/1 75 28
2705[7] **La Modiste (76)** (SDow) **3-9-1**(5) ADaly(2) (prom: rdn over 2f out: sn wknd) ....1¼ **6** 14/1 72 25
2686[10] **Time For Tea (IRE) (64)** (CACyzer) **3-8-8** MHamblett(5) (hld up in tch: rdn over 2f out: sn wknd) ....4 **7** 14/1 51 4
2567[4] **Dungeon Princess (IRE) (62)** (CMurray) **3-8-1**(5) MBaird(7) (hld up: hdwy over 3f out: wknd over 2f out) ....s.h **8** 7/1 49 2
(SP 112.4%) **8 Rn**

**1m 34.8** (2.60) CSF £11.76 CT £98.27 TOTE £2.60: £1.40 £1.60 £2.70 (£10.60) OWNER Mr W. E. Sturt (NEWMARKET) BRED Hesmonds Stud Ltd

**1718 Farmost** looked big and well beforehand, and recorded his fifth victory of the year in the gamest fashion. He made all the running and responded well to pressure in the final furlong. (7/4)
**2412 Passage Creeping (IRE)**, brought wide to challenge early in the straight, took a while to pick up when asked but, finding her stride in the final furlong, she finished to some effect. A stiffer mile would suit. (6/1)
**2552 Law Dancer (IRE)** raced prominently throughout, but could not produce a change of gear. (14/1: op 8/1)
**2706 Possessive Artiste** travelled nicely just behind the leaders, but did not produce much when asked for her effort. (9/2: 6/1-9/1)
**2618 Paint It Black** was hard at work all the way up the straight and just plugged on at the one speed. (8/1: 5/1-9/1)
**2225 La Modiste** (14/1: op 8/1)
**2340 Time For Tea (IRE)** (14/1: op 8/1)

## 2981 ROCK GARDENS CLAIMING STKS (3-Y.O+) (Class F)

4-20 (4-22) **6f 209y** £2,381.00 (£656.00: £311.00) Stalls: Low GOING minus 0.43 sec per fur (F)

SP RR SF

2885[9] **Blockade (USA) (62)** (MBell) **7-9-4** MFenton(5) (t: swtg: chsd ldrs: rdn 2f out: led ins fnl f: r.o) ....— **1** 6/1[3] 67 34
2859[5] **Uncle George (65)** (MHTompkins) **3-8-11b[1]** PRobinson(1) (hld up in rr: hdwy gng wl over 1f out: rdn wl ins fnl f: r.o wl) ....nk **2** 8/1 66 26
2229[11] **Balance of Power (60)** (RAkehurst) **4-8-12** SSanders(6) (chsd ldrs: led over 1f out tl ins fnl f: unable qckn) .1¼ **3** 20/1 57 24
2737[7] **Brass Tacks (60)** (RTPhillips) **4-8-3b** DHarrison(11) (mid div: rdn over 2f out: styd on ins fnl f) ....1¼ **4** 25/1 46 13
2766* **Pearl Dawn (IRE) (67)** (GLMoore) **6-8-7** SWhitworth(2) (hld up: hdwy 2f out: n.m.r 1f out: swtchd rt: r.o one pce) ....s.h **5** 13/8[1] 49 16
2796[5] **Indrapura (IRE) (57)** (MCPipe) **4-8-5v[1]**(3) MHenry(4) (lw: led: hdd over 3f out: led again over 2f out tl over 1f out: wknd ins fnl f) ....1½ **6** 10/1 47 14
2568[10] **Princesse Lyphard** (MJPolglase) **3-8-0** NCarlisle(8) (nvr nrr) ....hd **7** 40/1 46 6
2672[7] **Best Kept Secret (54)** (PDEvans) **5-8-8v** JFEgan(12) (mid div: rdn 3f out: no hdwy) ....¾ **8** 16/1 45 12
2507[9] **Burnt Sienna (IRE) (31)** (JSMoore) **4-7-13v**(5)ow1 AimeeCook(9) (sn outpcd) ....2 **9** 33/1 36 2
2400[8] **Jo Maximus (73)** (SDow) **4-9-3**(5) ADaly(7) (w ldr: led over 3f out: hdd over 2f out: sn wknd) ....s.h **10** 100/30[2] 54 21
2520[5] **Venus Victorious (IRE) (48)** (RBastiman) **5-8-3** AMcGlone(3) (chsd ldrs tl wknd over 2f out) ....7 **11** 25/1 19 —
1839[13] **Little Wobbly** (PCClarke) **6-8-3** NAdams(10) (a bhd) ....13 **12** 40/1 — —
(SP 121.8%) **12 Rn**

**1m 22.5** (2.50) CSF £50.49 TOTE £6.50: £1.60 £2.00 £4.10 (£25.30) Trio £69.90 OWNER Mr A. M. Warrender (NEWMARKET) BRED Patricia C. Warrender
WEIGHT FOR AGE 3yo-7lb

**2438* Blockade (USA)** won this despite being unable to dominate in his usual manner. (6/1)
**2859 Uncle George** appeared to be given too much to do as he was cruising when making headway below the distance, but only late on did his rider shake him up. Although he finished well, he found the post coming too soon. (8/1: 6/1-9/1)
**Balance of Power**, who was never far away, took it up below the distance but, under pressure soon after, had no more to give when challenged. (20/1)
**Brass Tacks** kept on in the closing stages without ever looking dangerous. (25/1)
**2766* Pearl Dawn (IRE)** was making headway when short of room entering the final furlong. Switched shortly afterwards, she had no time to get back in the contest. (13/8)
**2796 Indrapura (IRE)** (10/1: 5/1-12/1)
**1790 Jo Maximus** (100/30: 6/1-3/1)

## 2982 PRESTON PARK LIMITED STKS (0-60) (3-Y.O+) (Class F)

4-55 (4-55) **5f 213y** £2,381.00 (£656.00: £311.00) Stalls: Low GOING minus 0.43 sec per fur (F)

SP RR SF

2763* **Crystal Heights (FR) (59)** (RJO'Sullivan) **8-9-8** DHarrison(1) (rr: hdwy over 1f out: rdn to ld wl ins fnl f: r.o) ..— **1** 9/2[3] 74 39
*2308*[9] **Mellors (IRE) (60)** (JARToller) **3-9-0** SSanders(8) (a.p: led over 2f out: hdd wl ins fnl f: r.o) ....nk **2** 14/1 70 30
2735* **Pride of Hayling (IRE) (51)** (PRHedger) **5-8-13**(3) NVarley(5) (outpcd in rr: hdwy 2f out: styd on one pce ins fnl f) ....4 **3** 3/1[2] 57 22
2236[2] **Nattier (58)** (SirMarkPrescott) **3-8-8** WWoods(6) (led 1f: ev ch over 2f out: wknd over 1f out) ....2 **4** 11/4[1] 48 8
2761[2] **Fort Knox (IRE) (56)** (RMFlower) **5-9-8b** DBiggs(3) (hld up: rdn over 2f out: one pce) ....½ **5** 9/1 56 21
2970* **Marino Street (57)** (PDEvans) **3-8-11v** 3x WJO'Connor(7) (chsd ldrs: rdn 2f out: sn wknd) ....s.h **6** 6/1 50 7
**Royal Carlton (IRE) (58)** (TJNaughton) **4-9-2** PaulEddery(2) (bit bkwd: led 5f out: hdd over 2f out: wknd over 1f out) ....3½ **7** 6/1 40 5
1992[12] **Little Gent (IRE) (25)** (JELong) **5-8-13b[1]**(3) PMcCabe(4) (bhd fnl 4f) .... **8** 66/1 — —
(SP 116.6%) **8 Rn**

**1m 9.1** (1.90) CSF £54.67 TOTE £5.70: £2.10 £3.20 £1.20 (£53.20) OWNER Mr Jack Joseph (WHITCOMBE) BRED Ahmad Fustok
WEIGHT FOR AGE 3yo-5lb

**2763* Crystal Heights (FR)** is in good heart at present and, held up in the rear as usual, was produced with a well-timed challenge to lead in the last 100 yards. (9/2: 5/2-5/1)
**1612* Mellors (IRE)** was always in the van and looked like winning below the distance, but he was worn down late on by the winner's late surge. (14/1: 8/1-16/1)
**2735* Pride of Hayling (IRE)** was outpaced early on and, although staying on in the closing stages, could never really get in the race. (3/1)
**2236 Nattier** raced to the fore until weakening under pressure below the distance. (11/4)
**2761 Fort Knox (IRE)** finds this six furlongs a bit sharp for him nowadays. (9/1: op 5/1)

T/Jkpt: Not won; £7,576.11 to Ascot 26/7/96. T/Plpt: £1,098.10 (11.36 Tckts). T/Qdpt: £31.10 (39.03 Tckts). SM

# 2959-CATTERICK (L-H) (Good to firm, Good patches)
## Thursday July 25th
WEATHER: sunny WIND: slt across

## 2983 NORA BATTY APPRENTICE (S) H'CAP (0-60) (3-Y.O) (Class G)
6-40 (6-41) 7f £2,388.00 (£668.00: £324.00) Stalls: Low GOING: minus 0.30 sec per fur (GF)

| | | | SP | RR | SF |
|---|---|---|---|---|---|
| 2929² | **Shontaine (60)** (MJohnston) **3-9-2**(5) KSked(3) (chsd ldrs: led 2f out: hld on wl)....— | 1 | 6/1 3 | 70 | 45 |
| 2898⁴ | **Miletrian City (53)** (JBerry) **3-8-9b**(5) CLowther(2) (in tch: hdwy 2f out: chsd wnr fnl f: kpt on)....1 | 2 | 12/1 | 61 | 36 |
| 2800⁹ | **Welcome Lu (35)** (JLHarris) **3-7-5**(5) JBramhill(10) (a chsng ldrs: kpt on fnl f)....1¾ | 3 | 25/1 | 39 | 14 |
| 2914⁴ | **Ned's Contessa (IRE) (45)** (MDods) **3-8-3**(3) SCopp(9) (lw: s.i.s: hdwy over 2f out: styd on u.p fnl f)....1 | 4 | 15/2 | 46 | 21 |
| 2859⁸ | **Shermood (44)** (KTIvory) **3-8-2**(3)ow1 CScally(6) (in tch: rdn over 2f out: styd on one pce)....1¼ | 5 | 12/1 | 43 | 17 |
| 1312⁶ | **The Barnsley Belle (IRE) (48)** (JLEyre) **3-8-9** DGriffiths(5) (sn bhd: hdwy fnl 2f: nrst fin)....hd | 6 | 7/2 1 | 46 | 21 |
| 2215³ | **Doug's Folly (46)** (MWEasterby) **3-8-4b**(3) GParkin(1) (in tch: effrt over 2f out: one pce fnl f)....hd | 7 | 9/2 2 | 44 | 19 |
| 2914⁹ | **Napoleon's Return (47)** (AHarrison) **3-8-3v**(5) JennyBenson(8) (w ldr: disp ld 3f out to 2f out: wknd)....¾ | 8 | 10/1 | 43 | 18 |
| 2713⁶ | **Corniche Quest (IRE) (54)** (MRChannon) **3-8-12**(3) AEddery(4) (nvr trbld ldrs)....3 | 9 | 7/2 1 | 44 | 19 |
| 2800⁰ | **Good To Talk (43)** (TDEasterby) **3-8-4** RHavlin(7) (mde most tl hdd & wknd 2f out)....2½ | 10 | 12/1 | 27 | 2 |
| 2594¹¹ | **Lahik (IRE) (35)** (KTIvory) **3-7-7v**(3) CAdamson(11) (s.i.s: n.d)....nk | 11 | 33/1 | 18 | — |
| 2481⁸ | **Catwalk Girl (40)** (MissJFCraze) **3-8-1b¹** LNewton(13) (chsd ldrs tl wknd 2f out)....¾ | 12 | 12/1 | 21 | — |
| 2753² | **Miss Impulse (50)** (MissJBower) **3-8-11** PRoberts(12) (chsd ldrs tl wknd fnl 2f)....8 | 13 | 12/1 | 13 | — |
| | | | (SP 143.0%) | **13 Rn** | |

**1m 26.5** (2.90) CSF £81.71 CT £1,662.09 TOTE £10.00: £3.90 £6.30 £15.60 (£87.10) Trio Not won; £268.56 to 27/7/96 OWNER Mr Paul Dean (MIDDLEHAM) BRED Mark Johnston Racing Ltd
LONG HANDICAP Lahik (IRE) 7-8
Bt in 6,000 gns
**2929 Shontaine** likes to race up with the pace and, once he got his head in front early in the straight, he was not going to stop. (6/1)
**2898 Miletrian City**, dropping back in trip, kept staying on. He gives the impression that, if caught in the mood, he has much more ability. (12/1)
**516 Welcome Lu**, over what looked likely to be her ideal trip, ran her best race for some time. (25/1)
**2914 Ned's Contessa (IRE)** looks extremely well at present and has the ability to do better. (15/2)
**2411 Shermood** was always struggling to find the necessary turn of foot and failed to offer a threat. (12/1: op 8/1)
**1312 The Barnsley Belle (IRE)**, after two months off, got left behind in the early stages, but was making ground up the centre of the track at the end. (7/2: 6/1-3/1)
**2215 Doug's Folly** lacked the pace on this sharp track to take a necessary good position. (9/2)
**2417 Napoleon's Return** (10/1: 8/1-12/1)
**2713 Corniche Quest (IRE)** was never in the mood on this occasion. (7/2)

## 2984 OLIVE OYL NURSERY H'CAP (2-Y.O) (Class E)
7-10 (7-11) 7f £3,470.00 (£1,040.00: £500.00: £230.00) Stalls: Low GOING: minus 0.30 sec per fur (GF)

| | | | SP | RR | SF |
|---|---|---|---|---|---|
| 2595⁵ | **Mirror Four Life (IRE)** (MHTompkins) **2-8-11** NDay(11) (disp ld tl led over 2f out: kpt on wl)....— | 1 | 12/1 | 73 | 26 |
| 1892⁷ | **Flotilla** (SirMarkPrescott) **2-8-12** RPerham(1) (a chsng ldrs: kpt on wl fnl f)....½ | 2 | 10/1 | 73 | 26 |
| 2509⁴ | **Dashing Rocksville** (MRChannon) **2-8-2** AGorman(2) (lw: sn bhd: hdwy on ins 2f out: nvr able to chal)....2½ | 3 | 6/1 3 | 57 | 10 |
| *1459** | **Run Lucy Run** (RGuest) **2-8-4** LCharnock(8) (bhd: hdwy 2f out: nvr rchd ldrs)....3 | 4 | 12/1 | 52 | 5 |
| *2554** | **Tinkerbell** (LordHuntingdon) **2-8-10v** JCarroll(7) (a chsng ldrs: one pce fnl 2f)....½ | 5 | 7/1 | 57 | 10 |
| 2696* | **Stride** (MartynMeade) **2-9-1**(5) RHavlin(10) (chsd ldrs: rdn 2f out: sn btn)....1½ | 6 | 2/1 1 | 64 | 17 |
| 2396⁴ | **Mill End Boy** (MWEasterby) **2-8-8**(5) GParkin(5) (hld up & bhd: nt clr run 2f out: nt rcvr)....½ | 7 | 14/1 | 56 | 9 |
| 2161¹⁰ | **Sparky** (MWEasterby) **2-8-0** DaleGibson(4) (bhd: effrt on ins over 2f out: n.d)....½ | 8 | 12/1 | 41 | — |
| 1164* | **Smokey From Caplaw** (JJO'Neill) **2-9-0** JWeaver(6) (disp ld over 4f: sn wknd)....6 | 9 | 12/1 | 42 | — |
| 2517² | **Grate Times** (EWeymes) **2-9-2**(5) DGriffiths(9) (lw: chsd ldrs 5f: eased whn btn)....2 | 10 | 9/2 2 | 44 | — |
| | | | (SP 124.8%) | **10 Rn** | |

**1m 27.3** (3.70) CSF £118.27 CT £750.81 TOTE £17.00: £2.90 £4.60 £2.90 (£46.40) Trio £196.50 OWNER Mirror 4 Punters Club (NEWMARKET) BRED Dullingham House Stud
**2595 Mirror Four Life (IRE)** appreciated this step up in trip and showed fine determination to make virtually all. (12/1)
**1603 Flotilla**, a strong sort, looked likely to benefit from this and showed a poor action going to post. He ran a cracking race and was keeping on particularly strongly at the end. He obviously has his problems, but there is bags of ability there. (10/1)
**2509 Dashing Rocksville**, never getting the best of runs and soon shuffled back in the field, had to run on the slower ground up the straight, but she did make a fair bit of headway. (6/1: op 4/1)
**1459* Run Lucy Run** has been racing on the All-Weather. This little filly obviously has ability and, trying her longest trip to date, was keeping on well. (12/1)
**2554* Tinkerbell** had her chances but looked very ordinary when off the bit early in the straight. (7/1)
**2696* Stride**, who got warm beforehand, looked very lean and, once off the bridle, failed to fire. (2/1)
**2396 Mill End Boy** ran really well and looks likely to do better in due course. (14/1: op 8/1)
**1164* Smokey From Caplaw** (12/1: op 8/1)
**2517 Grate Times** (9/2: op 3/1)

## 2985 PENELOPE PITSTOP MAIDEN STKS (2-Y.O) (Class D)
7-40 (7-40) 5f 212y £3,281.50 (£982.00: £471.00: £215.50) Stalls: High GOING: minus 0.30 sec per fur (GF)

| | | | SP | RR | SF |
|---|---|---|---|---|---|
| 1344⁷ | **Our Home Land (USA)** (MJohnston) **2-9-0** JWeaver(8) (mde all: rdn & r.o wl fnl 2f)....— | 1 | 6/1 3 | 75 | 40 |
| 1537⁸ | **Ocker (IRE)** (MHTompkins) **2-9-0** NDay(6) (h.d.w: lw: a chsng ldrs: ev ch ins fnl f: nt qckn)....1½ | 2 | 4/1 2 | 71 | 36 |
| *2633²* | **Ricasso** (DRLoder) **2-9-0** DRMcCabe(4) (lw: chsd ldrs: effrt 2f out: nt qckn ins fnl f)....hd | 3 | Evens 1 | 71 | 36 |
| 2611¹¹ | **Julietta Mia (USA)** (BWHills) **2-8-4**(5) JDSmith(1) (s.i.s: hdwy over 2f out: put hd in air: nvr trbld ldrs)....6 | 4 | 7/1 | 19 | 15 |
| 2295⁶ | **Harmony In Red** (JBerry) **2-9-0** JCarroll(3) (lw: cl up tl wknd fnl 2f)....½ | 5 | 8/1 | 53 | 18 |
| 2138⁷ | **Prince Dome (IRE)** (MartynWane) **2-9-0** MBirch(7) (chsd ldrs tl outpcd fnl 2½f)....3 | 6 | 50/1 | 45 | 10 |
| | **William's Well** (MWEasterby) **2-8-9**(5) GParkin(2) (unf: scope: outpcd & lost tch after 2f: n.d after)....6 | 7 | 50/1 | 29 | — |
| 2727⁴ | **Madison Welcome (IRE)** (MrsJRRamsden) **2-9-0** NKennedy(5) (outpcd & lost tch ½-wy: n.d after)....1 | 8 | 25/1 | 26 | — |
| | | | (SP 115.7%) | **8 Rn** | |

**1m 13.2** (2.30) CSF £28.55 TOTE £9.70: £2.30 £1.30 £1.10 (£26.50) OWNER Dr Fuk To Chang (MIDDLEHAM) BRED Antoinette Siegel

**1344 Our Home Land (USA)**, given a typical Weaver ride, was out in front where he likes to be and, once he got the favoured stands' rail, he was not going to stop. (6/1)
**1537 Ocker (IRE)** has done really well physically in the last couple of months, and should not be long in going one better. (4/1)
**2633 Ricasso** took quite a hold to post and, after holding every chance, failed to come up with the goods when the pressure was on. (Evens)
**Julietta Mia (USA)** was very free both to post and in the race and, when asked for an effort, she looked like a real character. (7/1)
**1884 Harmony In Red** is gradually coming to hand but, after showing good speed, stopped in the last couple of furlongs. (8/1)
**Prince Dome (IRE)** showed some speed this time, but still has plenty to learn. (50/1)

## 2986 LILO LILL H'CAP (0-70) (3-Y.O+) (Class E)

8-10 (8-10) **1m 7f 177y** £3,054.00 (£912.00: £436.00: £198.00) Stalls: Low GOING: minus 0.30 sec per fur (GF)

| | | | | SP | RR | SF |
|---|---|---|---|---|---|---|
| 2804* | **Izza (49)** (WStorey) **5-8-10** 4x NKennedy(1) (hld up: smooth hdwy to ld ins fnl f: cleverly) | — | **1** | Evens $^{1}$ | 58+ | — |
| 2682$^{2}$ | **Latvian (63)** (RAllan) **9-9-10** JWeaver(4) (trckd ldr: led & qcknd 2f out: hdd ins fnl f: r.o) | 1 | **2** | 5/1 $^{3}$ | 71 | — |
| 2848$^{4}$ | **Little Redwing (36)** (MDHammond) **4-7-11**ow1 DaleGibson(2) (lw: led tl hdd 2f out: one pce) | 4 | **3** | 11/2 | 40 | — |
| 2697$^{3}$ | **Shakiyr (FR) (53)** (RHollinshead) **5-8-9**(5) DGriffiths(3) (hld up: effrt 3f out: nt pce to chal) | 1½ | **4** | 11/4 $^{2}$ | 55 | — |
| | | | | (SP 108.7%) | | **4 Rn** |

**3m 40.5** (19.00) CSF £5.55 TOTE £1.70 (£3.40) OWNER Mr D. C. Batey (CONSETT) BRED G.W. Mills & Sons
**2804* Izza** was different class to this lot and, despite a very steady pace, she was always on the bridle and won in cheeky fashion. (Evens)
**2682 Latvian** likes this track and ran a fine race to show he is in good heart, but the winner was always toying with him. (5/1)
**2848 Little Redwing** set a very steady pace but, having already shown she has no turn of foot, she got left behind when things got serious. (11/2)

## 2987 EDINA AND PATSY MEDIAN AUCTION MAIDEN STKS (3, 4 & 5-Y.O) (Class F)

8-40 (8-41) **5f 212y** £2,616.00 (£726.00: £348.00) Stalls: High GOING: minus 0.30 sec per fur (GF)

| | | | | SP | RR | SF |
|---|---|---|---|---|---|---|
| 2497$^{3}$ | **Bollin Joanne (80)** (TDEasterby) **3-8-9** MBirch(4) (b: cl up: led & qcknd over 2f out: sn clr) | — | **1** | 10/11 $^{1}$ | 73 | 50 |
| 2760$^{2}$ | **Atlantic Storm** (JHMGosden) **3-9-0** GHind(1) (lw: led tl hdd over 2f out: no ch w wnr) | 8 | **2** | Evens $^{2}$ | 57 | 34 |
| 2333$^{8}$ | **Blazing Imp (USA)** (WSCunningham) **3-8-9**(5) RHavlin(3) (trckd ldrs tl outpcd fnl 3f) | 6 | **3** | 100/1 $^{3}$ | 40 | 17 |
| 2777$^{12}$ | **Time Ticks On** (MWEllerby) **3-8-7**(7) JEdmunds(2) (s.s: n.d) | 3½ | **4** | 200/1 | 31 | 8 |
| 2898$^{11}$ | **Mr Blue** (GPKelly) **4-9-0**(5) GParkin(5) (swtg: outpcd & bhd fr ½-wy) | 7 | **5** | 200/1 | 12 | — |
| | | | | (SP 104.4%) | | **5 Rn** |

**1m 12.2** (1.30) CSF £1.89 TOTE £1.90: £1.00 £1.70 (£1.10) OWNER Lady Westbrook (MALTON) BRED Sir Neil and Lady Westbrook
WEIGHT FOR AGE 3yo-5lb
**2497 Bollin Joanne** did not impress on looks but her performance did all the talking, as she trotted up to gain her first win. (10/11)
**2760 Atlantic Storm** was the paddock pick but was completely outclassed in the race. (Evens)
**2150 Blazing Imp (USA)** ran reasonably but was left struggling once the tap was turned on early in the straight. (100/1)
**Time Ticks On** has been very slow to start on each occasion he has run. (200/1)
**Mr Blue** sweated up and, as yet, has shown next to nothing. (200/1)

## 2988 HINGE AND BRACKET H'CAP (0-70) (3-Y.O+) (Class E)

9-10 (9-11) **1m 3f 214y** £3,210.00 (£960.00: £460.00: £210.00) Stalls: Low GOING: minus 0.30 sec per fur (GF)

| | | | | SP | RR | SF |
|---|---|---|---|---|---|---|
| 1696$^{2}$ | **Contrafire (IRE) (68)** (WJarvis) **4-10-0** JWeaver(1) (lw: mde all: rdn & r.o wl fnl 2f) | — | **1** | 9/2 $^{2}$ | 73 | 29 |
| 2775$^{2}$ | **Campaspe (42)** (JGFitzGerald) **4-8-2** DaleGibson(3) (lw: trckd ldrs: effrt 3f out: swtchd & styd on appr fnl f: nt pce to chal) | 1¾ | **2** | 4/5 $^{1}$ | 45 | 1 |
| 2701$^{8}$ | **Dr Edgar (58)** (MDods) **4-9-4** JCarroll(2) (chsd ldrs: effrt 3f out: kpt on one pce) | nk | **3** | 14/1 | 60 | 16 |
| 2572$^{9}$ | **Toulston Lady (IRE) (49)** (MJCamacho) **4-8-9** LCharnock(4) (in tch: hdwy over 2f out: one pce appr fnl f) | hd | **4** | 10/1 | 51 | 7 |
| *2368*$^{3}$ | **Classic Affair (USA) (58)** (RHarris) **3-8-6** DBatteate(9) (lw: plld hrd: rapid hdwy to jn ldr 7f out: hmpd & hit rails 2f out: one pce after) | ½ | **5** | 25/1 | 60 | 4 |
| 2077$^{9}$ | **Karaylar (IRE) (48)** (WStorey) **4-8-8** JFanning(10) (hld up & bhd: effrt 4f out: no imp) | 4 | **6** | 33/1 | 44 | — |
| *251*$^{9}$ | **Chantry Beath (51)** (CWThornton) **5-8-11** DeanMcKeown(6) (swtg: hld up & bhd: effrt ent st: no imp) | s.h | **7** | 9/1 $^{3}$ | 47 | 3 |
| 2394$^{7}$ | **Cross Talk (IRE) (68)** (RHollinshead) **4-9-9**(5) DGriffiths(7) (lw: hld up: effrt over 2f out: rdn & no imp) | 7 | **8** | 14/1 | 55 | 11 |
| 2366$^{9}$ | **Baraqueta (60)** (JLEyre) **4-9-3**(3) OPears(5) (chsd ldrs tl wknd fnl 3f) | ½ | **9** | 16/1 | 46 | 2 |
| 2731$^{5}$ | **Diamond Crown (IRE) (48)** (MartynWane) **5-8-8** MBirch(8) (hld up & bhd: effrt 3f out: n.d) | 1¾ | **10** | 10/1 | 32 | — |
| | | | | (SP 127.9%) | | **10 Rn** |

**2m 40.4** (9.00) CSF £9.01 CT £49.10 TOTE £5.00: £2.00 £1.40 £2.30 (£3.90) Trio £26.40 OWNER Miss V. R. Jarvis (NEWMARKET) BRED Thoroughbred Trust in Ireland
WEIGHT FOR AGE 3yo-12lb
**1696 Contrafire (IRE)** looked a picture and had the right man on board for this type of ride. Once the tempo increased entering the straight, he was not going to be caught. (9/2)
**2775 Campaspe** needed a stronger pace than was set here and, despite keeping on well, failed to trouble the winner. (4/5)
**2357 Dr Edgar** looked in really good condition and ran a fair race over this longer trip, but was inclined to hang once pressure was on. (14/1)
**2515 Toulston Lady (IRE)**, stepping up in trip, made ground up the unfavoured centre of the track and failed to quicken further in the final furlong. She obviously has the ability and can pick up a race. (10/1)
**1174 Classic Affair (USA)** took charge of her rider early in the race and was then knocked into the rail when making an effort in the straight. In the circumstances, she did pretty well. (25/1)
**1649 Karaylar (IRE)** will probably need further yet and there is certainly more ability there. (33/1)

T/Plpt: £76.70 (150.1 Tckts). T/Qdpt: £2.30 (426.19 Tckts). AA

# 2613-CHEPSTOW (L-H) (Good to firm)

## Thursday July 25th

Race 2: flip start
WEATHER: fine WIND: almost nil

## 2989 LYSAGHT AMATEUR H'CAP (0-70) (3-Y.O+) (Class G)

6-30 (6-33) **1m 4f 23y** £2,500.00 (£700.00: £340.00) Stalls: Low GOING minus 0.59 sec per fur (F)

| | | | | SP | RR | SF |
|---|---|---|---|---|---|---|
| 2896$^{4}$ | **Augustan (51)** (SGollings) **5-11-5** JCulloty(2) (hld up: hdwy over 3f out: led ins fnl f: r.o wl) | — | **1** | 5/1 $^{1}$ | 63 | 48 |

| Form | Horse | Btn | Pos | SP | RR | SF |
|---|---|---|---|---|---|---|
| 2505$^{8}$ | **Spread The Word (53)** (LGCottrell) **4-11-2v$^{1}$**$^{(5)}$ MrLJefford(11) (hld up: hdwy over 5f out: led over 2f out tl ins fnl f) | 1¼ | **2** | 25/1 | 63 | 48 |
| 2717$^{13}$ | **Outstayed Welcome (57)** (MJHaynes) **4-11-11** MissYHaynes(1) (chsd ldr: led 7f out tl over 2f out: r.o) | 1 | **3** | 10/1 | 66 | 51 |
| 2482$^{6}$ | **Golden Hadeer (41)** (MJRyan) **5-10-4**$^{(5)}$ MrSLavallin(18) (hdwy fnl 2f: r.o) | ¾ | **4** | 33/1 | 49 | 34 |
| 2941$^{5}$ | **Dots Dee (30)** (JMBradley) **7-9-7**$^{(5)}$ MissLKerr(15) (b.nr fore: a.p: one pce fnl 2f) | s.h | **5** | 12/1 | 38 | 23 |
| 2711$^{12}$ | **Nosey Native (55)** (JPearce) **3-10-11** MrsLPearce(7) (chsd ldrs: no hdwy fnl 2f) | s.h | **6** | 8/1 | 63 | 36 |
| 2762$^{2}$ | **General Mouktar (60)** (BJMeehan) **6-12-0b** MissJAllison(19) (s.i.s: hdwy over 2f out: nvr nr to chal) | 2 | **7** | 6/1$^{2}$ | 65 | 50 |
| 2711$^{4}$ | **Cheveley Dancer (USA) (27)** (TJNaughton) **8-9-9** MissPRobson(5) (b: swtg: hdwy over 5f out: wknd over 2f out) | 3 | **8** | 20/1 | 28 | 13 |
| 2711$^{6}$ | **Paper Cloud (57)** (RTPhillips) **4-11-6**$^{(5)}$ MrsSFaber(9) (n.d) | hd | **9** | 20/1 | 58 | 43 |
| 2587$^{11}$ | **Written Agreement (28)** (REPeacock) **8-9-5**$^{(5)ow3}$ MrsCPeacock(13) (bhd fnl 3f) | 2½ | **10** | 66/1 | 26 | 8 |
| 2794$^{4}$ | **Seventh Edition (57)** (DBurchell) **3-10-8**$^{(5)}$ MissEJJones(4) (bhd fnl 3f) | 7 | **11** | 12/1 | 46 | 19 |
| 2891$^{4}$ | **Risky Rose (44)** (RHollinshead) **4-10-7**$^{(5)}$ MrCBHills(12) (lw: s.s: a bhd) | 6 | **12** | 13/2$^{3}$ | 25 | 10 |
| 2511$^{8}$ | **Hatta River (USA) (38)** (PTDalton) **6-10-1**$^{(5)}$ MissJWormall(16) (prom 6f) | 1¼ | **13** | 50/1 | 17 | 2 |
| | **Celestial Dollar (38)** (OO'Neill) **5-10-1**$^{(5)}$ MrRThornton(3) (led 5f: wknd over 3f out) | ¾ | **14** | 25/1 | 16 | 1 |
| 1500$^{4}$ | **Northern Clan (40)** (AJChamberlain) **3-9-5**$^{(5)}$ MrVLukaniuk(8) (b: t.o) | 22 | **15** | 33/1 | — | — |
| 1778$^{11}$ | **Florismart (51)** (BPJBaugh) **4-11-0**$^{(5)}$ MrPMiddleton(6) (bhd tl b.d over 1f out) | | **B** | 50/1 | — | — |
| 2487$^{6}$ | **Philgun (51)** (CWCElsey) **7-11-5v** MissAElsey(17) (prom 9f: mid div whn broke leg & fell over 1f out: dead) | | **F** | 14/1 | — | — |
| 2542$^{6}$ | **Miss Pravda (50)** (DJLlewellyn) **3-10-6** MrJLLlewellyn(10) (hdwy after 2f: wknd over 3f out: hmpd & p.u over 1f out) | | **P** | 16/1 | — | — |
| 2234$^{7}$ | **Lilac Rain (42)** (RMStronge) **4-10-5**$^{(5)ow8}$ MrJDewhurst(14) (a bhd: t.o 5f out: hmpd & uns rdr over 1f out) | | **U** | 50/1 | — | — |

(SP 122.9%) **19 Rn**

**2m 37.6** (5.20) CSF £109.03 CT £1,118.04 TOTE £5.30: £1.40 £6.70 £2.70 £15.80 (£105.10) Trio £397.90; £112.10 to 27/7/96 OWNER S K R Racing (LOUTH) BRED Someries Stud

LONG HANDICAP Written Agreement 8-13

WEIGHT FOR AGE 3yo-12lb

**2896 Augustan** likes fast ground and appreciated this return to a mile and a half. (5/1)

**Spread The Word**, dropped 7lb, showed considerable improvement in the first-time visor. (25/1)

**2066 Outstayed Welcome** ran too freely over further last time, and has won over a mile and three-quarters. (10/1)

**Golden Hadeer** gave the impression he would get a longer trip. (33/1)

**2941 Dots Dee** continues to run consistently enough at the moment. (12/1: op 8/1)

**2711 Nosey Native**, down 5lb, settled much better without the visor. (8/1)

**2891 Risky Rose** lost many lengths at the start and this run is best forgotten. (13/2)

## 2990 GO EVENING RACING WITH THE DAILY TELEGRAPH H'CAP (0-80) (3-Y.O) (Class D)

6-55 (6-55) **2m 49y** £3,507.50 (£1,055.00: £510.00: £237.50) GOING minus 0.59 sec per fur (F)

| Form | Horse | Btn | Pos | SP | RR | SF |
|---|---|---|---|---|---|---|
| 2433* | **The Swan (75)** (JLDunlop) **3-9-7** WCarson(3) (mde all: rdn over 1f out: r.o wl) | — | **1** | 13/8$^{1}$ | 82 | 38 |
| 1782$^{4}$ | **Macmorris (USA) (75)** (PFICole) **3-9-7** TQuinn(4) (chsd wnr: rdn & ev ch 2f out: hung lft over 1f out: no imp) | 3 | **2** | 3/1$^{3}$ | 79 | 35 |
| 2673$^{2}$ | **Seattle Saga (USA) (71)** (DRLoder) **3-9-3** RHughes(2) (hld up: hrd rdn over 1f out: no rspnse: eased whn no ch fnl 2f) | 21 | **3** | 2/1$^{2}$ | 54 | 10 |
| *2936$^{11}$* | **Tintara (IRE) (71)** (BWHills) **3-9-3** JReid(1) (hld up & bhd: t.o fnl 4f) | 25 | **4** | 7/1 | 30 | — |

(SP 108.9%) **4 Rn**

**3m 32.4** (4.40) CSF £6.19 TOTE £2.30 (£3.50) OWNER Mr R. J. McAulay (ARUNDEL) BRED Oak Bloodstock Ltd

**2433* The Swan**, raised 7lb, is coming into her own over these longer trips. (13/8)

**1782 Macmorris (USA)**, 5lb higher than when second at Nottingham, was just beginning to get the worst of the argument when ducking in behind the winner. (3/1)

**2673 Seattle Saga (USA)** was very disappointing and there must have been more to it than simply the trip. (2/1)

**980* Tintara (IRE)** ran no race at all on this return to turf. (7/1)

## 2991 GOLDEN DAFFODIL STKS (Listed) (3-Y.O+ F & M) (Class A)

7-25 (7-26) **1m 2f 36y** £10,465.20 (£3,916.80: £1,915.90: £824.50: £369.75: £187.85) Stalls: Low GOING minus 0.59 sec per fur (F)

| Form | Horse | Btn | Pos | SP | RR | SF |
|---|---|---|---|---|---|---|
| 1335$^{3}$ | **Papering (IRE) (101)** (LMCumani) **3-8-5** OUrbina(3) (a gng wl: shkn up to ld ins fnl f: comf) | — | **1** | 100/30$^{1}$ | 107 | 45 |
| 2515* | **Papaha (FR) (100)** (HRACecil) **3-8-5** PatEddery(4) (lw: led tl ins fnl f) | 1½ | **2** | 4/1$^{3}$ | 105 | 43 |
| 2069$^{5}$ | **Bathilde (IRE) (100)** (MRStoute) **3-8-6**$^{ow1}$ JReid(5) (plld hrd: chsd ldr: rdn & ev ch 3f out: one pce fnl 2f) | 2 | **3** | 7/2$^{2}$ | 103 | 40 |
| 2533$^{6}$ | **Min Alhawa (USA) (103)** (MajorWRHern) **3-8-5** WCarson(1) (lw: hld up & plld hrd: hmpd on ins over 5f out: rdn & outpcd over 3f out: rallying on ins whn nt clr run over 2f out: nt rcvr) | ¾ | **4** | 7/2$^{2}$ | 100 | 38 |
| 2225$^{4}$ | **Silk Masque (USA) (90)** (PWChapple-Hyam) **3-8-5** TSprake(2) (hld up & bhd: sme hdwy over 2f out: rdn over 1f out: one pce) | 3 | **5** | 16/1 | 96 | 34 |
| | **Pacific Grove (95)** (PFICole) **3-8-5** TQuinn(7) (hld up & bhd: stdy hdwy over 4f out: wknd over 2f out) | 3½ | **6** | 16/1 | 90 | 28 |
| 1335$^{4}$ | **Scarlet Plume (102)** (JLDunlop) **3-8-5** KDarley(6) (hld up: stdy hdwy over 4f out: wknd over 2f out) | 6 | **7** | 7/1 | 81 | 19 |

(SP 111.8%) **7 Rn**

**2m 4.9** (-0.40) CSF £15.74 TOTE £4.30: £2.00 £1.80 (£6.40) OWNER Sheikh Mohammed (NEWMARKET) BRED Sheikh Mohammed bin Rashid al Maktoum

**1335 Papering (IRE)**, off course since third in the Lupe, showed she has a touch of class about her with a convincing win. (100/30)

**2515* Papaha (FR)** stayed well enough but found the winner too much of a handful. (4/1)

**2069 Bathilde (IRE)**, back to ten furlongs, lacked the required turn of foot. (7/2)

**2533 Min Alhawa (USA)** met more than her fair share of problems in running and deserves a change of luck. (7/2)

**2225 Silk Masque (USA)** could only manage a short-lived effort. (16/1)

**Pacific Grove** was highly tried on this belated seasonal debut. (16/1)

**1335 Scarlet Plume** may well have found the ground too lively. (7/1)

## 2992 JACK BROWN BOOKMAKER H'CAP (0-70) (3-Y.O+) (Class E)

7-55 (7-59) **5f 16y** £2,953.50 (£888.00: £429.00: £199.50) Stalls: High GOING minus 0.59 sec per fur (F)

| Form | Horse | Btn | Pos | SP | RR | SF |
|---|---|---|---|---|---|---|
| 2713$^{2}$ | **Robellion (61)** (DWPArbuthnot) **5-9-10v** TQuinn(1) (b.hind: hld up: hdwy 2f out: led ins fnl f: r.o) | — | **1** | 11/4$^{2}$ | 69 | 31 |
| 2787$^{3}$ | **Malibu Man (62)** (EAWheeler) **4-9-11** TSprake(5) (lw: w ldr: led over 2f out tl ins fnl f) | 1½ | **2** | 9/4$^{1}$ | 65 | 27 |

2787⁶ **John O'Dreams (52)** (MrsALMKing) **11-9-1** RHughes(3) (b: s.i.s: hdwy over 2f out: hrd rdn over 1f out: one pce) ....1½ **3** 9/2 3 51 13
2376⁴ **Tinker Osmaston (65)** (MSSaunders) **5-10-0** JFEgan(7) (lw: outpcd tl hdwy over 1f out: r.o) ....½ **4** 7/1 62 24
*2555⁵* **Scored Again (52)** (MJHeaton-Ellis) **6-8-10**(5) AmandaSanders(4) (prom over 3f) ....1¼ **5** 10/1 45 7
*2940¹⁰* **Christian Flight (IRE) (44)** (SGollings) **7-8-7b** VHalliday(6) (no hdwy fnl 2f) ....1½ **6** 25/1 32 —
2791⁶ **Tommy Tempest (40)** (REPeacock) **7-7-12v**(5) ADaly(2) (led over 2f: wknd over 1f out) ....nk **7** 16/1 27 —
1170⁶ **Rocky Two (42)** (NRMitchell) **5-8-0b**(5)ow1 SophieMitchell(8) (a bhd) ....3 **8** 25/1 20 —
(SP 110.8%) **8 Rn**

**58.4 secs** (1.40) CSF £8.67 CT £21.81 TOTE £2.80: £1.20 £1.30 £1.40 (£2.80) OWNER Mr G. Thompson (COMPTON) BRED Pitts Farm Stud
**2713 Robellion** had given notice of a return to form last time, and was only 1lb higher here. (11/4)
**2787 Malibu Man** could not hold the winner in the closing stages. (9/4)
**2787 John O'Dreams** could not sustain his run off a mark 4lb higher than when scoring at Newbury. (9/2)
**2376 Tinker Osmaston** seems to find the minimum trip on the sharp side on ground as fast as this. (7/1)
**Scored Again** was having his first run on grass for nearly two years. (10/1)

## 2993 WORTHINGTON DRAUGHT BITTER MAIDEN AUCTION STKS (2-Y.O) (Class D)
8-25 (8-28) **6f 16y** £3,311.00 (£998.00: £484.00: £227.00) Stalls: High GOING minus 0.59 sec per fur (F)

SP RR SF
2624⁴ **Shadow Lead** (LMCumani) **2-8-7** PatEddery(2) (w ldr: rdn over 3f out: led 2f out: r.o wl) ....— **1** 1/2 1 84 20
2044⁷ **Gablesea** (BPJBaugh) **2-8-3** WLord(4) (hld up: hdwy & nt clr run over 1f out: swtchd lft: ev ch ins fnl f: rdn & unable qckn) ....1 **2** 40/1 77? 13
**Brandon Jack** (IABalding) **2-8-5** KDarley(5) (w'like: scope: outpcd: hdwy fnl f: r.o) ....4 **3** 8/1 3 69 5
**Mile High** (MRChannon) **2-8-5** TQuinn(3) (str: scope: led 1f: rdn over 2f out: wknd fnl f) ....hd **4** 5/2 2 69 5
**Parijazz (IRE)** (MartynMeade) **2-7-12** NAdams(1) (w'like: bkwd: led after 1f: hdd 2f out: wknd fnl f) ....nk **5** 20/1 61 —
(SP 113.6%) **5 Rn**

**1m 10.6** (1.40) CSF £13.22 TOTE £1.60: £1.10 £3.60 (£7.00) OWNER Mr H. C. Chung (NEWMARKET) BRED Whitsbury Manor Stud
**2624 Shadow Lead** made quite hard work of this, but managed to find more when challenged in the last 200 yards. (1/2: 2/5-8/13)
**Gablesea** certainly gave backers of the hot-pot a fright and seems to be going the right way. (40/1)
**Brandon Jack** only got going late in the day and should do better over a longer trip. (8/1: op 4/1)
**Mile High**, quite well regarded, had been prepared for the Brocklesby at the beginning of the season, but suffered a set-back. With plenty of scope about him, he should do better in due course. (5/2: 3/1-2/1)
**Parijazz (IRE)**, who only cost 1,500 guineas, was by no means disgraced considering she did not look fit enough to do herself justice. (20/1)

## 2994 UNIVERSITY AND LITERARY CLUB H'CAP (0-70) (3-Y.O+) (Class E)
8-55 (8-57) **7f 16y** £3,168.00 (£954.00: £462.00: £216.00) Stalls: High GOING minus 0.59 sec per fur (F)

SP RR SF
1992* **King Parrot (IRE) (51)** (LordHuntingdon) **8-8-9**(5) AimeeCook(12) (lw: hld up: hdwy 2f out: led ins fnl f: edgd lft: r.o) ....— **1** 7/2 1 61 27
2785³ **African-Pard (IRE) (60)** (DHaydnJones) **4-9-9b** TQuinn(3) (hld up: hrd rdn & hdwy 2f out: ev ch ins fnl f: r.o) hd **2** 8/1 70 36
2785⁴ **Irrepressible (IRE) (45)** (RJHodges) **5-8-3**(5) ADaly(2) (prom: rdn to ld 2f out: hdd ins fnl f: r.o) ....nk **3** 8/1 54 20
2925⁵ **Heathyards Lady (USA) (57)** (RHollinshead) **5-9-3**(3) FLynch(10) (hdwy over 2f out: ev ch over 1f out: unable qckn) ....1¼ **4** 13/2 3 63 29
2796⁶ **Delight of Dawn (65)** (RMStronge) **4-10-0** JFEgan(4) (lw: hld up: hdwy 2f out: ev ch over 1f out: one pce) ....hd **5** 11/1 71 37
2581¹⁵ **Charlie Chang (IRE) (70)** (RHannon) **3-9-12** PatEddery(11) (lw: led after 1f: hdd 2f out: wknd over 1f out) ...1½ **6** 4/1 2 73 32
*2937³* **Cedar Girl (39)** (RJHodges) **4-7-11**(5)ow1 AmandaSanders(8) (plld hrd: led 1f: ev ch 2f out: wknd 1f out) ....½ **7** 14/1 41 6
2796⁷ **Asterix (43)** (JMBradley) **8-8-3b**(3) SDrowne(13) (nvr nr to chal) ....s.h **8** 11/1 44 10
**Courageous Knight (50)** (PHayward) **7-8-13**ow1 RHughes(6) (rdn 3f out: a bhd) ....2½ **9** 25/1 46 11
2528⁴ **Impetuous Lady (USA) (48)** (NEBerry) **3-8-4** TSprake(7) (lw: prom 4f) ....1½ **10** 12/1 40 —
2528⁷ **Careful (IRE) (60)** (BWHills) **3-9-2** WCarson(5) (a bhd) ....3 **11** 10/1 46 5
2033¹⁰ **Mac Oates (60)** (DWPArbuthnot) **3-9-2** JReid(9) (a bhd) ....7 **12** 33/1 30 —
(SP 124.7%) **12 Rn**

**1m 21.6** (1.60) CSF £31.16 CT £201.42 TOTE £4.30: £1.90 £2.00 £2.50 (£12.00) Trio £22.60 OWNER Lord Huntingdon (WEST ILSLEY) BRED W. Hastings-Bass in Ireland
WEIGHT FOR AGE 3yo-7lb
**1992* King Parrot (IRE)**, freshened up by a break, continues in good form and completed the hat-trick off a 4lb higher mark. (7/2)
**2785 African-Pard (IRE)**, set to go down 2lb in future handicaps, found the headgear working again. (8/1)
**2785 Irrepressible (IRE)** had also finished a neck behind the runner-up on 1lb worse terms. (8/1)
**2925 Heathyards Lady (USA)** had her excuses earlier in the week at Beverley, but there did not appear to be any here. (13/2)
**2796 Delight of Dawn** ran her best race since being claimed after winning over a mile at Windsor. (11/1)
**1337 Charlie Chang (IRE)** may do better when reverting to a mile. (4/1: 3/1-5/1)

T/Plpt: £23.50 (601.95 Tckts). T/Qdpt: £3.10 (344.7 Tckts). KH

# 2971-SANDOWN (R-H) (Good to firm, 5f crse Firm patches)
## Thursday July 25th
WEATHER: hot WIND: almost nil

## 2995 TATTERSALLS MAIDEN AUCTION STKS (2-Y.O) (Class E)
2-15 (2-18) **5f 6y** £3,533.75 (£1,070.00: £522.50: £248.75) Stalls: High GOING minus 0.46 sec per fur (F)

SP RR SF
1531⁸ **Big Ben** (RHannon) **2-8-6**ow1 PatEddery(6) (lw: mde all: rdn out) ....— **1** 13/2 3 80 12
**Hoh Dancer** (IABalding) **2-8-6** KDarley(5) (leggy: unf: scope: lw: hld up: chsd wnr over 1f out: rn green) ....1¼ **2** 4/6 1 76 9
2712⁷ **Keen Waters** (JRArnold) **2-7-13** CRutter(2) (rdn & hdwy over 1f out: one pce) ....1¾ **3** 25/1 64 —
2792² **Miss Barcelona (IRE)** (MJPolglase) **2-8-1**ow1 MRoberts(1) (swtg: nvr nr to chal) ....1½ **4** 6/1 2 61 —
2764³ **Corncrake (IRE)** (BJMeehan) **2-8-1** BDoyle(3) (prom over 3f) ....½ **5** 10/1 59 —
2741⁸ **Danish Ayr** (MRChannon) **2-8-5** TQuinn(4) (chsd wnr over 3f) ....2 **6** 6/1 2 57 —
(SP 114.8%) **6 Rn**

**62.24 secs** (2.44) CSF £11.43 TOTE £5.20: £2.20 £1.10 (£4.30) OWNER Mrs S. J. Davis (MARLBOROUGH) BRED Mrs M. Lingwood

**Big Ben**, who proved very troublesome going down to the start, was a different proposition on the way back. (13/2: 4/1-7/1)
**Hoh Dancer**, a tall, narrow filly who needs time to develop, looked very well in the paddock, but showed her inexperience in the race. Tracking the leaders, she came through for second place below the distance but, carrying her head very high, did not look entirely sure what was required of her and failed to quicken in the last 100 yards. Sure to be a lot wiser as a result, she should be able to find a race of this nature before long. (4/6)
**Keen Waters** was making no further impression in the final furlong. (25/1)
**2792 Miss Barcelona (IRE)**, having her ninth race of the season, is very exposed as little better than plating company. (6/1)
**2764 Corncrake (IRE)** played an active role until coming to the end of her tether below the distance. (10/1: 5/1-11/1)
**Danish Ayr** raced in second place until tiring approaching the final furlong. (6/1)

## 2996 HEATHROW MAIDEN STKS (3-Y.O+) (Class D)

2-50 (2-53) **1m 14y** £3,907.50 (£1,185.00: £580.00: £277.50) Stalls: High GOING minus 0.46 sec per fur (F)

| | | | | SP | RR | SF |
|---|---|---|---|---|---|---|
| 2579[2] | **Yalta (IRE)** (RCharlton) **3-8-13** PatEddery(7) (lw: a.p: rdn 4f out: led ins fnl f: r.o wl) | — | **1** | 11/10[1] | 89 | 56 |
| 705[5] | **Royal Result (USA)** (MRStoute) **3-8-13** JReid(9) (bit bkwd: chsd ldr: led wl over 1f out tl ins fnl f: r.o) | ½ | **2** | 14/1[3] | 88 | 55 |
| | **Filial (IRE)** (GHarwood) **3-8-13** AClark(4) (w'like: scope: bit bkwd: hld up: rdn over 3f out: r.o one pce) | 3½ | **3** | 16/1 | 81 | 48 |
| 2529[2] | **Santella Katie** (MajorDNChappell) **3-8-8** TQuinn(5) (b.hind: leggy: a.p: rdn over 3f out: r.o one pce fnl f) | 1¾ | **4** | 4/1[2] | 73 | 40 |
| | **Summer Beauty** (JHMGosden) **3-8-8** BThomson(12) (unf: scope: led over 6f) | ½ | **5** | 4/1[2] | 72 | 39 |
| | **Infatuation** (LadyHerries) **3-8-13** MHills(11) (leggy: unf: scope: plld hrd: hdwy over 1f out: nvr nrr: bttr for r) | 5 | **6** | 20/1 | 67 | 34 |
| | **Yipsilanti** (LadyHerries) **3-8-13** KDarley(10) (b.nr hind: w'like: scope: bit bkwd: plld hrd: hld up: rdn over 3f out: wknd over 1f out) | 2½ | **7** | 25/1 | 62 | 29 |
| | **Honeyshan** (DJSffrenchDavis) **4-9-2** MRoberts(2) (b: nvr nrr) | 7 | **8** | 100/1 | 43 | 18 |
| 2572[5] | **Jeopardize** (CEBrittain) **3-8-8** BDoyle(8) (lw: bhd fnl 2f) | 3 | **9** | 25/1 | 37 | 4 |
| 678[10] | **Classic Royale (USA)** (RHarris) **3-8-8** AMackay(6) (a bhd) | s.h | **10** | 25/1 | 37 | 4 |
| 2785[11] | **Young Rose (44)** (PatMitchell) **4-9-2** TSprake(3) (a bhd) | s.h | **11** | 100/1 | 37 | 12 |
| | **Thurstaston (IRE)** (JHMGosden) **3-8-13** RHills(1) (wl grwn: bkwd: s.s: a bhd) | 2 | **12** | 16/1 | 38 | 5 |

(SP 124.3%) **12 Rn**

**1m 41.65** (0.45) CSF £17.87 TOTE £2.00: £1.10 £4.50 £5.00 (£8.50) Trio £46.40 OWNER Lord Weinstock/Exors of late S Weinstock (BECKHAMPTON) BRED Ballymacoll Stud Farm Ltd
WEIGHT FOR AGE 3yo-8lb
**2579 Yalta (IRE)**, an attractive colt, was never far away, but punters looked to be in trouble as he was being ridden along turning into the straight. However, he eventually responded to his rider's urgings and, throwing down his challenge from below the distance, he got on top inside the final furlong. Another quarter of a mile would help him. (11/10: 4/6-6/5)
**705 Royal Result (USA)**, who looked as though this first run in three months would do him good, had been held up on his two previous outings, but he adopted totally different tactics on this occasion and, as a result, ran his best race to date. Racing in second place, he cruised into the lead early in the final quarter-mile, appearing to be going best of all. Eventually collared inside the final furlong, he stuck to his task well, and there is a race waiting for him. (14/1: 8/1-16/1)
**Filial (IRE)**, who looked as though the run would bring him on, chased the leaders. Pushed along early in the straight, he stayed on up the hill for third prize. (16/1)
**2529 Santella Katie** looked in good shape beforehand. Never far away, she was being bustled along early in the straight and failed to quicken with her rivals. She did stay on again in the final furlong but, by then, it was all too late. (4/1)
**Summer Beauty**, a tall, narrow filly, set a good pace but, collared early in the final quarter-mile, was soon in trouble. (4/1: op 6/1)
**Infatuation**, a tall, unfurnished individual, was very green and pulled hard for his head. Given a nice educational ride, he stayed on nicely in the last furlong and a half to be nearest at the line. He should have learnt a lot from this. (20/1)

## 2997 MILCARS STAR STKS (Listed) (2-Y.O F) (Class A)

3-25 (3-27) **7f 16y** £9,758.00 (£2,954.00: £1,442.00: £686.00) Stalls: High GOING minus 0.46 sec per fur (F)

| | | | | SP | RR | SF |
|---|---|---|---|---|---|---|
| 2211* | **Red Camellia** (SirMarkPrescott) **2-8-12** TQuinn(4) (mde all: rdn out) | — | **1** | 8/1 | 94 | 68 |
| 2302* | **Yashmak (USA)** (HRACecil) **2-8-12** PatEddery(5) (a.p: chsd wnr over 2f out: no imp) | 2½ | **2** | 11/10[1] | 88 | 62 |
| 2582[7] | **Lycility (IRE)** (CEBrittain) **2-8-12** BDoyle(2) (lw: chsd wnr over 4f: wknd over 1f out) | 6 | **3** | 50/1 | 75 | 49 |
| 2122* | **Impetuous Air** (EWeymes) **2-8-12** KDarley(3) (swtg: hld up: rdn over 3f out: wknd over 1f out) | 1 | **4** | 33/1 | 73 | 47 |
| 2582[5] | **Rich In Love (IRE)** (CACyzer) **2-9-0** BThomson(1) (nvr nr to chal) | hd | **5** | 25/1 | 74 | 48 |
| 2543* | **Gretel** (MRStoute) **2-8-12** JReid(7) (lw: plld hrd: hld up: rdn over 2f out: sn wknd) | 7 | **6** | 9/4[2] | 56 | 30 |
| 1978* | **Fernanda** (JLDunlop) **2-9-0** WCarson(6) (lw: s.s: a bhd) | 1¾ | **7** | 5/1[3] | 55 | 29 |

(SP 114.9%) **7 Rn**

**1m 27.87** (0.28 under 2y best) (-0.73) CSF £17.07 TOTE £12.70: £2.30 £1.70 (£11.00) OWNER Cheveley Park Stud (NEWMARKET) BRED Cheveley Park Stud Ltd
**2211* Red Camellia** was taking a big step up in class, but annihilated a very useful-looking field. Making all the running, she drew well clear with the runner-up in the final quarter-mile and had that rival well under control in the final furlong, breaking the course record in the process. She looks a high-class filly in the making and may well go for the Group Three Prestige Stakes at Goodwood at the end of August. (8/1)
**2302* Yashmak (USA)**, never far away, moved into second place over a quarter of a mile from home. However, despite pulling well clear of the remainder, she could make little inroads on the winner. Time may tell she lost out to a very talented filly. (11/10: Evens-11/8)
**1664* Lycility (IRE)** was left standing by the front two below the distance. (50/1)
**2122* Impetuous Air** was left for dead in the final quarter-mile. (33/1)
**2582 Rich In Love (IRE)** could never get in a blow. (25/1)
**2543* Gretel** looked in tremendous shape in the paddock, but lost her race by refusing to settle in the first half. Asked for her effort over a quarter of a mile out, she disappointingly found little. The ground was on the easy side when she won here earlier in the month and this fast surface may have been another contributory factor to this poor display. She is worth another chance. (9/4)
**1978* Fernanda** ran no race at all and was always at the back of the field. She is surely better than this. (5/1)

## 2998 PYCRAFT & ARNOLD H'CAP (0-90) (3-Y.O) (Class C)

4-00 (4-00) **1m 6f** £5,550.00 (£1,680.00: £820.00: £390.00) Stalls: High GOING minus 0.46 sec per fur (F)

| | | | | SP | RR | SF |
|---|---|---|---|---|---|---|
| 2547[5] | **Pine Needle (80)** (DMorley) **3-9-7** BThomson(1) (lw: hdwy over 6f out: led 3f out: rdn out) | — | **1** | 4/1[3] | 90 | 48 |
| 2570[11] | **Diego (64)** (CEBrittain) **3-8-5** BDoyle(4) (led over 8f: rdn over 3f out: chsd wnr over 2f out: no imp) | 1¾ | **2** | 12/1 | 72 | 30 |
| 2570[3] | **Village King (IRE) (77)** (RHannon) **3-9-4** JReid(3) (hld up: rdn over 3f out: one pce) | 3½ | **3** | 9/4[1] | 81 | 39 |
| 2549[3] | **Shu Gaa (IRE) (72)** (WJHaggas) **3-8-13** PatEddery(2) (lw: chsd ldr over 7f: lost pl over 5f out: rallied 2f out: wknd over 1f out) | 10 | **4** | 7/2[2] | 65 | 23 |

| | | | | SP | RR | SF |
|---|---|---|---|---|---|---|
| 2738* | **Nikita's Star (IRE) (64)** (DJGMurraySmith) **3-8-5** 4x DHolland(5) (hdwy 5f out: wknd over 2f out) | 9 | **5** | 4/1[3] | 46 | 4 |
| 2377[11] | **Atlantic Mist (63)** (BRMillman) **3-8-4** GBardwell(6) (lw: a.p: led over 5f out to 3f out: sn wknd) | 16 | **6** | 7/1 | 27 | — |
| | | | | (SP 113.2%) | | **6 Rn** |

**3m 2.6** (3.70) CSF £38.69 TOTE £5.10: £2.90 £3.10 (£15.90) OWNER Lord Halifax (NEWMARKET) BRED Lord Halifax
**2547 Pine Needle** took closer order soon after halfway. Hitting the front three furlongs out, she was ridden along to assert her authority. (4/1)
**1788* Diego** took the field along until collared over five furlongs from home. Regaining the runner-up berth approaching the final quarter-mile, he had little chance with the winner. (12/1)
**2570 Village King (IRE)** chased the leaders. Disputing second place over two furlongs from home, he failed to find another gear. (9/4)
**2549 Shu Gaa (IRE)** raced in second place in the first half of the race, but got outpaced turning out of the back straight. Trying to get back into it a quarter of a mile out, he had soon burnt his boats. (7/2)
**2738* Nikita's Star (IRE)** moved up turning out of the back straight, but had shot his bolt over two furlongs from home. (4/1: 3/1-9/2)
**1894 Atlantic Mist** made his bid for glory turning out of the back straight. Collared three furlongs from home, he had soon cooked his goose. (7/1: 5/1-8/1)

## 2999 RAILWAY H'CAP (0-80) (3-Y.O) (Class D)

4-35 (4-37) **5f 6y** £3,680.00 (£1,115.00: £545.00: £260.00) Stalls: High GOING minus 0.46 sec per fur (F)

| | | | | SP | RR | SF |
|---|---|---|---|---|---|---|
| 2500* | **Clan Chief (63)** (JRArnold) **3-8-6** TQuinn(6) (b.hind: mde all: rdn fnl f: r.o wl) | — | **1** | 2/1[1] | 76 | 37 |
| 2790* | **Mindrace (65)** (KTIvory) **3-8-8** 6x BDoyle(7) (a.p: rdn over 1f out: unable qckn) | 2½ | **2** | 7/2[2] | 70 | 31 |
| 2571[5] | **Pharaoh's Joy (56)** (JWPayne) **3-7-10**(3) DWright(5) (hld up: rdn over 1f out: one pce) | s.h | **3** | 6/1[3] | 61 | 22 |
| 2301[4] | **Dande Flyer (78)** (DWPArbuthnot) **3-9-4**(3) DarrenMoffatt(2) (b: hld up: rdn over 1f out: one pce) | 3 | **4** | 7/1 | 73 | 34 |
| 2705[P] | **Mijas (78)** (LMontagueHall) **3-9-7** DHolland(3) (prom 4f) | 1¼ | **5** | 16/1 | 69 | 30 |
| 2787* | **Magic Mail (71)** (JMPEustace) **3-8-7**(7) 6x DSweeney(4) (lw: chsd wnr over 3f) | ½ | **6** | 7/2[2] | 61 | 22 |
| 2705[4] | **Stoney End (USA) (70)** (MRChannon) **3-8-13** KDarley(1) (a bhd) | 1¼ | **7** | 10/1 | 56 | 17 |
| | | | | (SP 119.5%) | | **7 Rn** |

**60.67 secs** (0.87) CSF £9.67 TOTE £2.80: £2.00 £2.30 (£3.80) OWNER Mr P. G. Lowe (UPPER LAMBOURN) BRED D. Gill
OFFICIAL EXPLANATION **Magic Mail: had been struck into about two furlongs out.**
**2500* Clan Chief** followed up his victory earlier in the month. Making all the running, he was woken up in the final furlong to pull away. (2/1)
**2790* Mindrace**, never far away along the inside rail, was rousted along below the distance, but he had no chance with the winner, although he did win the battle for second prize. (7/2)
**2571 Pharaoh's Joy** chased the leaders. Having a ding-dong battle for the runner-up berth in the final furlong, she only just lost out. (6/1)
**2301 Dande Flyer** chased the leaders but failed to quicken from below the distance. (7/1)
**1652 Mijas** was close up until tiring a furlong out. (16/1)
**2787* Magic Mail** raced in second place until collared for that position and tiring approaching the final furlong. (7/2: 3/1-9/2)

## 3000 SURREY RACING APPRENTICE H'CAP (0-70) (3-Y.O+) (Class E)

5-10 (5-10) **1m 2f 7y** £3,313.25 (£1,016.00: £505.50: £250.25) Stalls: High GOING minus 0.46 sec per fur (F)

| | | | | SP | RR | SF |
|---|---|---|---|---|---|---|
| 2737[2] | **Guesstimation (USA) (57)** (JPearce) **7-9-2**(5) RFfrench(6) (stdy hdwy fr over 3f out: led over 1f out: edgd lft fnl f: r.o wl) | — | **1** | 7/4[1] | 62 | 44 |
| 1963[6] | **Windyedge (USA) (60)** (BWHills) **3-8-4**(10) GBrace(3) (lw: led over 7f: ev ch 1f out: unable qckn) | 3 | **2** | 7/1[3] | 60 | 32 |
| *2751[8]* | **Red Tie Affair (USA) (57)** (MBell) **3-8-8v**(3) RMullen(4) (b.nr fore: lw: rdn & hdwy over 1f out: r.o one pce) | 2 | **3** | 20/1 | 54 | 26 |
| 2776* | **Almuhtaram (65)** (MissGayKelleway) **4-9-5b**(10) 5x BFord(5) (b: lw: rdn over 3f out: hdwy over 1f out: r.o one pce) | nk | **4** | 11/4[2] | 62 | 44 |
| 2540[U] | **Shouldbegrey (45)** (WRMuir) **3-7-10**(3) PDoe(7) (lw: hld up: rdn over 2f out: wknd fnl f) | nk | **5** | 10/1 | 41 | 13 |
| 2896[8] | **Zahran (IRE) (39)** (JMBradley) **5-8-3v**[1] JWilkinson(1) (lw: hld up: led over 2f out tl over 1f out: sn wknd) | 1¼ | **6** | 7/1[3] | 33 | 15 |
| 1894[5] | **Master M-E-N (IRE) (54)** (NMBabbage) **4-9-4v** AngelaGallimore(2) (lw: plld hrd: chsd ldr over 7f: t.o) | dist | **7** | 7/1[3] | — | — |
| | | | | (SP 114.4%) | | **7 Rn** |

**2m 9.82** (3.12) CSF £13.45 TOTE £2.60: £1.20 £3.40 (£11.20) OWNER The Exclusive Two Partnership (NEWMARKET) BRED Oak Crest Farm
WEIGHT FOR AGE 3yo-10lb
**2737 Guesstimation (USA)** was given a super-cool ride by his young jockey. Well adrift from the rest of the pack turning out of the back straight, his jockey appeared to have made a serious error, but he had things under control and the combination steadily crept into the action in the straight. Striking the front approaching the final furlong, he drifted left in the closing stages, but had the situation well in hand. (7/4)
**Windyedge (USA)** attempted to make all the running. Collared over a quarter of a mile from home, he refused to give way and still had every chance a furlong from home before failing to quicken. (7/1: op 4/1)
**2506 Red Tie Affair (USA)** stayed on in the final quarter-mile without ever posing a serious threat. (20/1)
**2776* Almuhtaram** was given an interesting ride. With his rider flapping his arms in the straight, the gelding nevertheless struggled on in the last furlong and a half, only just failing to take third prize. (11/4)
**2168 Shouldbegrey** chased the leaders. Ridden along over a quarter of a mile from home, he was less than a length down on the winner entering the final furlong before tiring. (10/1)
**2409 Zahran (IRE)** made his bid for glory over two furlongs from home but, collared below the distance, quickly folded up. (7/1)

T/Plpt: £57.90 (266.28 Tckts). T/Qdpt: £49.80 (19.31 Tckts). AK

## 3001a-3017a (Irish Racing) - See Computer Raceform

# 2652a-LEOPARDSTOWN (Dublin, Ireland) (L-H) (Good to firm)
## Saturday July 20th

## 3018a ROCHESTOWN STKS (Listed) (2-Y.O)

2-30 (2-30) **6f** £9,675.00 (£2,775.00: £1,275.00: £375.00)

| | | | | SP | RR | SF |
|---|---|---|---|---|---|---|
| 1910a* | **Azra (IRE)** (JSBolger,Ireland) **2-8-12** KJManning (led: rdn wl over 1f out: hdd nr fin: rallied to ld last strides) | — | **1** | 2/1[1] | 93 | 41 |
| 2607[5] | **Check The Band (USA)** (APO'Brien,Ireland) **2-8-13b**[1] CRoche (a.p: chal 2f out: led u.p nr fin: no ex & hdd last strides) | ½ | **2** | 2/1[1] | 93 | 41 |

| | | | | SP | RR | SF |
|---|---|---|---|---|---|---|
| 2834a[2] | **Nevada (IRE)** (APO'Brien,Ireland) **2-8-10** SCraine (hld up towards rr: hdwy ½-wy: 3rd over 1f out: kpt on)...4½ | **3** | | 3/1[2] | 78 | 26 |
| 2470a[5] | **Via Verbano (IRE)** (JSBolger,Ireland) **2-8-7** TEDurcan (chsd ldrs: rdn ½-wy: sltly hmpd 2f out: no imp) ..........4 | **4** | | 12/1 | 64 | 12 |
| | **Sharemono (USA)** (APO'Brien,Ireland) **2-8-10** JAHeffernan (dwlt: sn cl up: 3rd ½-wy: no ex 2f out)..............nk | **5** | | 14/1 | 66 | 14 |
| | **Danccini (IRE)** (JGBurns,Ireland) **2-8-7** NGMcCullagh (cl up: 3rd & rdn 2f out: 4th & btn over 1f out)...........1½ | **6** | | 6/1[3] | 59 | 7 |

(SP 120.3%) **6 Rn**

**1m 12.5** (1.80) OWNER D. H. W. Dobson (COOLCULLEN)

**1910a* Azra (IRE)** completed her four-timer but had to work harder this time. She made virtually all the running until headed inside the last half furlong, but fought back bravely and just put her nose in front again on the line. Her dam won the Queen Alexandra Stakes, but she shows extraordinary toe, and the Heinz '57' Stakes will see her bid for her fifth consecutive victory. (2/1)

**2607 Check The Band (USA)** showed no ill-effects from his Newmarket exertions and was wearing blinkers for the first time. He was on terms with the winner through the last furlong and a half, but hung badly left away from the stick and, despite getting his head in front, was pipped on the line. (2/1: op 5/4)

**2834a Nevada (IRE)** moved up promisingly into third pace with less than two furlongs to race, but the run was not sustained in this company. (3/1)

**2470a Via Verbano (IRE)**, fitted with a tongue-strap this time, once again disappointed. (12/1: op 7/1)

## 3021a BALLYROAN STKS (Listed) (3-Y.O+)
4-00 (4-04) **1m 4f** £9,675.00 (£2,775.00: £1,275.00: £375.00)

| | | | SP | RR | SF |
|---|---|---|---|---|---|
| 2465a[2] | **Zafzala (IRE)** (JOxx,Ireland) **3-8-8**ow3 JPMurtagh (hld up: 5th ½-wy: hdwy & 4th st: sn chal: led over 1f out: kpt on wl) ..........— | **1** | Evens[1] | 109 | 45 |
| 2474a[2] | **Fill the Bill (IRE)** (APO'Brien,Ireland) **4-9-6** CRoche (hld up towards rr: hdwy appr st: 5th over 1f out: rdn & styd on fnl f: nt rch wnr) ..........1 | **2** | 6/1[3] | 108 | 59 |
| 2465a[6] | **Ceirseach (IRE)** (JSBolger,Ireland) **3-8-5** TEDurcan (cl up: 3rd & rdn 5f out: led st: hdd & no ex over 1f out)..5 | **3** | 12/1 | 98 | 37 |
| 1938a[7] | **Ashbal (USA)** (KPrendergast,Ireland) **3-8-8** WJSupple (hld up towards rr: 8th ½-wy: hdwy 3f out: 4th & rdn over 1f out: kpt on) ..........1½ | **4** | 12/1 | 99 | 38 |
| | **Lacinia** (JOxx,Ireland) **3-8-5** HUemura (hld up towards rr: chsd ldrs over 3f out: no imp over 1f out)................2 | **5** | 14/1 | 93 | 32 |
| | **Layik (IRE)** (DKWeld,Ireland) **3-8-8** MJKinane (hld up in tch: 4th ½-wy: 3rd & rdn st: one pce over 1f out) ...2½ | **6** | 3/1[2] | 93 | 32 |
| | **Sunless (IRE)** (APO'Brien,Ireland) **3-8-5** JAHeffernan (6th ½-wy: rdn & no imp 2f out)..........7 | **7** | 10/1 | 81 | 20 |
| 2825a[4] | **Song Of The Sword** (MKauntze,Ireland) **3-8-8** NGMcCullagh (cl up: 2nd after 3f: disp ld 5f out: 2nd st: 4th, rdn & nt qckn 2f out)..........1½ | **8** | 12/1 | 82 | 21 |
| 2102a[5] | **Bakiya (USA)** (JOxx,Ireland) **3-8-5** DHogan (sn led: jnd 5f out: hdd over 3f out: wknd bef st)..........15 | **9** | 16/1 | 59 | — |

(SP 134.0%) **9 Rn**

**2m 32.9** (2.90) OWNER H H Aga Khan (CURRABEG)

**2465a Zafzala (IRE)**, well treated by the conditions of this race, justified her short price. Making smooth headway before the straight, she challenged coming off the bend and was in command over a furlong out. She seems to get this trip well and is developing along the right lines. (Evens)

**2474a Fill the Bill (IRE)**, last into the straight, was always going to fill the runner-up position and did not have too hard a time of it once his jockey accepted the situation. (6/1: op 4/1)

**2465a Ceirseach (IRE)** led briefly on the home turn but was soon outpaced. (12/1: op 8/1)

**1938a Ashbal (USA)** moved into fourth place with less than two furlongs to run, but could progress no further. (12/1: op 8/1)

**Lacinia** and her Japanese jockey were travelling smoothly before the turn, but encountered more than their fair share of traffic problems in the straight. (14/1)

## 3022a-3026a (Irish Racing) - See Computer Raceform

# DIEPPE (France) (R-H) (Good)
## Monday July 15th

## 3027a PRIX DE LA VILLE DE ROUXMESNIL-BOUTEILLES CLAIMING (3-Y.O)
**7f** £2,899.00 (£1,449.00)

| | | | SP | RR | SF |
|---|---|---|---|---|---|
| | **Shining Silk (FR)** (FBelmont,France) **3-7-11**(5) NPerret ..........— | **1** | | — | — |
| *2325*[5] | **Ewar Sunrise** (KOCunningham-Brown) **3-8-7** FSanchez ..........s.h | **2** | | — | — |
| | **Stayerka (FR)** (France) **3-8-7** AJunk ..........2 | **3** | | — | — |

**14 Rn**

**No Time Taken** P-M 7.90F: 3.10F 4.00F 1.70F (46.70F) OWNER M. Charlton BRED Laurent Henry & Mme Valerie Rouillere-Henry & Pier

## 3028a PRIX FRANCOIS DE LADOUCETTE (3-Y.O)
**1m 4f** £3,689.00

| | | | SP | RR | SF |
|---|---|---|---|---|---|
| | **Pasi Kali (FR)** (PLamotteD'Argy,France) **3-9-2** DBoeuf ..........— | **1** | | — | — |
| | **Our Highness (FR)** (France) **3-8-12** OPeslier ..........¾ | **2** | | — | — |
| | **Miss Mary Garden (FR)** (France) **3-8-12** GMosse ..........2½ | **3** | | — | — |
| 2196[6] | **Ewar Bold** (KOCunningham-Brown) **3-9-2** FSanchez (btn over 10l) .......... | **8** | | — | — |

**12 Rn**

**No Time Taken** P-M 9.40F: 3.60F 2.70F 2.30F (91.40F) OWNER E. Erculiani BRED Pierre Lepeudry & Guy Agenais

# 2841a-EVRY (France) (R-H) (Good)
## Tuesday July 16th

## 3029a PRIX DE SENART CLAIMING (2-Y.O)
1-50 (1-50) **5f** £9,223.00

| | | | SP | RR | SF |
|---|---|---|---|---|---|
| | **Alips (FR)** (PBary,France) **2-8-6**(5) TCastanheire ..........— | **1** | | 78 | — |
| | **Yosna (FR)** (France) **2-7-7**(5) SCoerette ..........2½ | **2** | | 57 | — |
| | **Roebuck (FR)** (France) **2-8-11** CDehens ..........nk | **3** | | 69 | — |

2382* **Without Friends (IRE)** (MrsLStubbs) **2-9-6** OPeslier (btn over 5l) ........ 8 71 —
**14 Rn**

**58.63 secs** (0.13) P-M 3.20F: 1.60F 7.50F 2.10F (69.20F) OWNER Mr J-L Bouchard (CHANTILLY) BRED Dr Georges Sandor & Mme J. Sandor
**2382* Without Friends (IRE)** has had a successful season in claiming events, bar his disqualification at Goodwood, but found this company just too good.

## 3030a PRIX CHLOE (Gp 3) (3-Y.O F)
2-50 (2-46) **1m 1f** £28,986.00 (£10,540.00: £5,270.00)

| | | | | SP | RR | SF |
|---|---|---|---|---|---|---|
| 1949a6 | **Khalisa (IRE)** (AdeRoyerDupre,France) **3-8-12** GMosse | — | 1 | | 109 | — |
| 1396a3 | **Ecoute (USA)** (MmeCHead,France) **3-8-9** ODoleuze | 1 | 2 | | 104 | — |
| 1140a8 | **Housa Dancer (FR)** (AFabre,France) **3-8-9** TJarnet | hd | 3 | | 104 | — |

**7 Rn**

**1m 48.06** (-1.94) P-M 1.60F: 1.30F 1.60F OWNER Aga Khan (CHANTILLY) BRED H. H. Aga Khan's Studs S.C.
**1388a* Khalisa (IRE)**, who can boil over at the start, bounced back to form here, having disappointed in the Prix de Diane. After being held up early on, she came with a strong challenge over a furlong out, but hung slightly when asked to quicken. Hitting the front inside the final furlong to score comfortably, she is a talented filly, and may now head for the Beverly D Stakes at Arlington Park.
**1396a Ecoute (USA)** led the field at a decent pace until headed by the winner inside the final furlong. A very genuine filly, she sticks to her task, but lacks a turn of foot in the closing stages.
**Housa Dancer (FR)** was slightly outpaced early in the straight, but ran on strongly close home, just failing to get second place. She could need further.

## 3031a PRIX MINERVE (Gp 3) (3-Y.O F)
3-55 (3-56) **1m 4f** £28,986.00 (£10,540.00: £5,270.00)

| | | | | SP | RR | SF |
|---|---|---|---|---|---|---|
| 1396a5 | **L'Annee Folle (FR)** (FDoumen,France) **3-8-9** TGillet | — | 1 | | 110 | — |
| 2277a2 | **Leonila (IRE)** (RCollet,France) **3-8-9** OPeslier | 1 | 2 | | 109 | — |
| | **Daralbayda (IRE)** (AdeRoyerDupre,France) **3-8-9** GMosse | 2½ | 3 | | 105 | — |

**9 Rn**

**2m 28.42** (-1.08) P-M 25.70F: 3.10F 1.20F 1.30F (34.00F) OWNER Mr M. Somerset-Leeke (LAMORLAYE) BRED Simon Steward
**L'Annee Folle (FR)** finally fulfilled her potential by taking this Group Three event. Held up early on, she made smooth progress on the wide outside well over a furlong out and, when asked to quicken, showed her inexperience by swerving sharply left in the final furlong. This classy filly should next be seen out in the Prix de Pomone at Deauville.
**2277a Leonila (IRE)** ran her usual genuine race. She tracked her pacemaker early on and came through to take the lead over a furlong out, but then wandered around a bit under pressure, which she often does, and was tapped for speed when the winner came to challenge. She will probably meet her conqueror again in the Prix de Pomone.
**Daralbayda (IRE)** came off the worst in some scrimmaging that occurred halfway up the straight and, when she was finally extracted, she kept on at one pace to secure third. She would have been closer without interference, but probably would not have had the turn of foot to take the honours, although she should show further improvement next time out.

# MAISONS-LAFFITTE (France) (Good)
**Wednesday July 17th**

## 3032a PRIX SALDI CHOURY (2-Y.O C & G)
1-25 (1-25) **6f** £11,858.00

| | | | | SP | RR | SF |
|---|---|---|---|---|---|---|
| | **Dyhim Diamond (IRE)** (CLaffon-Parias,France) **2-8-13** FSanchez | — | 1 | | 96 | — |
| | **Alpha Plus (USA)** (France) **2-8-9** TJarnet | 1½ | 2 | | 88 | — |
| 23643 | **Ride Sally Ride (IRE)** (JBerry) **2-8-13** CAsmussen | ½ | 3 | | 91 | — |

**7 Rn**

**1m 13.0** (3.30) P-M 7.70F: 2.30F 1.80F OWNER S. Suhail (CHANTILLY) BRED Knocklong House Stud
**2364 Ride Sally Ride (IRE)**, a son of Shalford, will now be trained by Georges Mikhalides.

## 3033a PRIX MESSIDOR (Gp 3) (3-Y.O+)
2-55 (2-58) **1m** £28,986.00 (£10,540.00: £5,270.00)

| | | | | SP | RR | SF |
|---|---|---|---|---|---|---|
| | **Grey Risk (FR)** (PDemercastel,France) **3-8-8** SGuillot | — | 1 | | 110 | — |
| 2271a4 | **Nec Plus Ultra (FR)** (AdeRoyerDupre,France) **5-9-6** TGillet | hd | 2 | | 114 | — |
| 2477a* | **Royal Philosopher** (JWHills) **4-9-2** GMosse | hd | 3 | | 110 | — |

**8 Rn**

**1m 40.5** (4.50) P-M 7.40F: 2.40F 2.20F 2.90F (27.10F) OWNER Ecurie Bader BRED SCEA Ecurie Bader
**Grey Risk (FR)** won this muddling event with a decisive turn of foot. Having raced on the rail, he quickened up well to snatch victory on the line. He has improved from handicaps to Group company since April, and could now take his chance in the Jacques Le Marois, an event for which he would have a lively each-way chance if he carries on going the right way.
**1950a* Nec Plus Ultra (FR)** is as consistent as they come. Having been held up in the rear, he came with a sweeping run on the outside to lead inside the final furlong, but was just pipped by the winner. He is as good as ever at present and will no doubt take another Group race this season.
**2477a* Royal Philosopher** delighted connections by taking third place. He led at a slow pace early on before being asked to quicken over a furlong out, and then battled on gamely to hold third. He would be more suited with a bit of give in the ground, and could next be seen out in the Schweppes Golden Mile.

# 0904a-FRANKFURT (Germany) (L-H) (Good to firm)
**Sunday July 21st**

## 3034a GROSSER PREIS DER LAMPART-EMAILLIERWERKE BUDAPEST-FRANKFURT POKAL (Gp 3) (3-Y.O+)
3-45 (3-53) **1m 2f** £27,027.00 (£10,810.00: £5,405.00)

| | | | | SP | RR | SF |
|---|---|---|---|---|---|---|
| 20384 | **Dankeston (USA)** (MBell) **3-8-3** MRoberts | — | 1 | | 112 | — |

| | Horse | Btn | Pos | SP | RR | SF |
|---|---|---|---|---|---|---|
| 2668a[16] | **Sir Warren (IRE)** (HBlume,Germany) **3-8-3** ASuborics | s.h | **2** | | 112 | — |
| | **Silent Lake (GER)** (HRemmert,Germany) **5-8-13** PSchiergen | nk | **3** | | 111 | — |
| | | | | | | **13 Rn** |

**2m 4.84** TOTE 21DM: 14DM 20DM 23DM OWNER Mr Luciano Gaucci (NEWMARKET) BRED Donald MacRae
**2038 Dankeston (USA)** needs to hit the front at the last possible moment and was given the perfect ride, though victory was only confirmed after the Judge had examined a print of the photo-finish. Close up but short for room turning into the straight, he burst through on the rail passing the furlong pole, but had nothing to spare at the line in a race where less than a length covered the first five home. He will run next in either the Great Voltigeur or the Irish Champion, and would need to improve to cut any ice in that kind of company.

## 3032a-MAISONS-LAFFITTE (France) (Good)
## Sunday July 21st

### 3035a PRIX MAURICE DE NIEUIL (Gp 2) (3-Y.O+)
3-25 (3-25) **1m 4f 110y** £39,526.00 (£15,810.00: £7,905.00: £3,953.00)

| | Horse | Btn | Pos | SP | RR | SF |
|---|---|---|---|---|---|---|
| | **Darazari (IRE)** (AdeRoyerDupre,France) **3-8-7**ow1 GMosse (led 3f: 2nd st: rdn to ld over 1f out: r.o) | — | **1** | | 118 | — |
| 2476a[2] | **Leeds (IRE)** (HVandePoele,France) **4-9-4** OPeslier (mid div: rdn 2f out: r.o cl home) | 2½ | **2** | | 114 | — |
| 2144* | **Astor Place (IRE)** (PWChapple-Hyam) **3-8-5** JReid (led after 3f: qcknd over 3f out: hdd over 1f out: one pce) | ¾ | **3** | | 112 | — |
| 1947a[3] | **Danseur Landais** (JLesbordes,France) **5-9-4** SGuillot (chsd ldrs: rdn over 2f out: one pce) | 2½ | **4** | | 110 | — |
| | **Homme D'Honneur (FR)** (AFabre,France) **4-9-4** TJarnet (chsd ldrs: rdn over 2f out: nt qckn) | ¾ | **5** | | 109 | — |
| 1757a[3] | **Le Destin (FR)** (PDemercastel,France) **3-8-5** TGillet (hld up in rr: rdn 2f out: sn btn) | 1 | **6** | | 106 | — |
| | | | | | | **6 Rn** |

**2m 42.8** (8.30) P-M 2.70F: 2.10F 2.70F OWNER Aga Khan (CHANTILLY) BRED H. H. The Aga Khans Stud S C
**Darazari (IRE)** won this in brilliant style and made the opposition look very ordinary. Always up with the pace, he moved into an attacking position halfway up the straight and then produced top-class acceleration to leave the others cold. A fine-looking colt who must be switched off during the race if he is to show his best, he has enormous scope for improvement and will now be rested until the Prix Niel in September. He has improved so much that he could be a serious force in the Arc de Triomphe in just over two month's time.
**Leeds (IRE)** put up an honourable performance but was just outclassed. He simply did not have the legs to go with the winner, who he tracked for much of the race, but he deserves to win a Group race, and something like the Grand Prix de Vichy might well be on the cards.
**2144* Astor Place (IRE)** was not at all suited by the way the race went, being the reluctant leader as the field cantered early on. He kicked for home early in the straight, but looked very one-paced compared to the winner and, with hindsight, his jockey thought he should have set a faster pace. He could return to France for the Grand Prix de Deauville, but will only run if the ground is on the fast side.
**1947a Danseur Landais** was never better than fourth place, which he held on to gamely after a battle with the fifth. He is not up to this standard, but is a genuine performer.

## 2142-ASCOT (R-H) (Good to firm)
## Friday July 26th
WEATHER: humid WIND: almost nil

### 3036 FOOD BROKERS MAIDEN STKS (Unraced 2-Y.O F) (Class D)
2-15 (2-16) **6f** £6,742.50 (£2,040.00: £995.00: £472.50) Stalls: Low GOING minus 0.31 sec per fur (GF)

| | Horse | Btn | Pos | SP | RR | SF |
|---|---|---|---|---|---|---|
| | **Mayfair** (PFICole) **2-8-11** TQuinn(6) (w'like: scope: lw: mde all: rdn out) | — | **1** | 4/5[1] | 86 t | 26 |
| | **Sleepless** (NAGraham) **2-8-11** DHolland(2) (w'like: scope: lw: hld up: rdn over 3f out: unable qckn) | 1¾ | **2** | 14/1 | 81 t | 21 |
| | **Summerosa (USA)** (PWChapple-Hyam) **2-8-11** JReid(5) (w'like: scope: lw: hld up: rdn over 1f out: one pce) | nk | **3** | 3/1[2] | 81 t | 21 |
| | **Dancing Queen (IRE)** (MBell) **2-8-11** MFenton(1) (w'like: scope: lw: hld up: rdn over 1f out: one pce) | 1¾ | **4** | 5/1[3] | 76 t | 16 |
| | **My Hero (IRE)** (TGMills) **2-8-11** PaulEddery(3) (w'like: scope: lw: chsd wnr 4f) | 4 | **5** | 20/1 | 65 t | 5 |
| | | | | (SP 108.7%) | | **5 Rn** |

**1m 17.27** (3.27) CSF £9.68 TOTE £1.70: £1.20 £2.20 (£6.90) OWNER H R H Prince Fahd Salman (WHATCOMBE) BRED Newgate Stud Co
**Mayfair** had reportedly been working well at home and proved that here. Bowling along in front, she showed her inexperience in the final quarter-mile but, despite that, was rousted along to assert her superiority. (4/5)
**Sleepless**, a half-sister to three winners, chased the leaders but was being nudged along before halfway. She did struggle on to win the battle for second, but had no chance with the winner. She may now take her chance in the Prestige Stakes at Goodwood at the end of August. (14/1: op 5/1)
**Summerosa (USA)** chased the leaders but, ridden along below the distance, failed to find the necessary turn of foot. (3/1: op 2/1)
**Dancing Queen (IRE)** hunted up the front rank. Rousted along below the distance, she failed to find the necessary turn of foot. Well regarded at home, she should soon pick up a race. (5/1: 4/1-6/1)
**My Hero (IRE)** raced in second place until tiring two furlongs out. (20/1)

### 3037 P & O EUROPEAN FERRIES BROWN JACK H'CAP (0-80) (3-Y.O+) (Class D)
2-45 (2-45) **2m 45y** £11,235.00 (£3,405.00: £1,665.00: £795.00) Stalls: High GOING minus 0.31 sec per fur (GF)

| | Horse | Btn | Pos | SP | RR | SF |
|---|---|---|---|---|---|---|
| 2148* | **Bolivar (IRE) (66)** (RAkehurst) **4-9-2b** TQuinn(1) (a.p: led over 1f out: all out) | — | **1** | 6/1[1] | 81 | 59 |
| 2042[5] | **Golden Arrow (IRE) (72)** (MCPipe) **5-9-8** RHughes(20) (hdwy over 4f out: hrd rdn over 2f out: ev ch fnl f: r.o wl) | hd | **2** | 10/1[3] | 87 | 65 |
| 2247[4] | **State Theatre (IRE) (71)** (PWChapple-Hyam) **3-8-4** DHolland(18) (hdwy over 2f out: swtchd lft over 1f out: r.o ins fnl f) | 3½ | **3** | 25/1 | 82 | 43 |
| 1792[3] | **Hattaafeh (IRE) (60)** (MissBSanders) **5-8-10** SSanders(16) (lw: a.p: led over 2f out tl over 1f out: wknd fnl f) | ½ | **4** | 20/1 | 71 | 49 |
| 2697* | **Great Oration (IRE) (56)** (FWatson) **7-8-6** JQuinn(8) (rdn over 3f out: hdwy over 1f out: nvr nrr) | 3 | **5** | 14/1 | 64 | 42 |
| 2516* | **French Ivy (USA) (63)** (FMurphy) **9-8-10**(3) DaneO'Neill(5) (b: swtg: hdwy & n.m.r over 1f out: swtchd rt: nvr nrr) | ¾ | **6** | 6/1[1] | 70 | 48 |
| 2882[6] | **Jermyn Street (USA) (73)** (MrsJCecil) **5-9-9** JReid(11) (swtg: hdwy over 5f out: wknd over 1f out) | 1¾ | **7** | 14/1 | 79 | 57 |
| 2319[2] | **Toy Princess (USA) (77)** (CEBrittain) **4-9-13** BDoyle(10) (lw: led tl over 2f out: sn wknd) | 3½ | **8** | 20/1 | 79 | 57 |
| 2613* | **The Lad (51)** (LMontagueHall) **7-7-10**(5) MartinDwyer(7) (hld up: rdn over 2f out: sn wknd) | ½ | **9** | 20/1 | 53 | 31 |

| | | | | | |
|---|---|---|---|---|---|
| 2499[2] **Turgenev (IRE) (68)** (RBastiman) **7-9-4b** DaleGibson(15) (swtg: nvr nrr) | nk | **10** | 16/1 | 69 | 47 |
| 1063[10] **Shahrani (46)** (MCPipe) **4-7-10** NCarlisle(3) (swtg: prom 9f) | 1 | **11** | 33/1 | 46 | 24 |
| 2848* **Sarasota Storm (52)** (MBell) **4-8-2**ow1 3x MFenton(2) (nvr nrr) | 1½ | **12** | 16/1 | 51 | 28 |
| 2900[2] **Etterby Park (USA) (66)** (MJohnston) **3-7-13** JFanning(13) (chsd ldr tl over 2f out: sn wknd) | 1¼ | **13** | 13/2[2] | 64 | 25 |
| **Argyle Cavalier (IRE) (58)** (BJMeehan) **6-8-8** PatEddery(14) (b: hdwy 3f out: wknd over 1f out) | hd | **14** | 16/1 | 56 | 34 |
| 2148[2] **Requested (51)** (PBurgoyne) **9-8-1** DeclanO'Shea(4) (s.s: a bhd) | 7 | **15** | 20/1 | 42 | 20 |
| 2385[6] **Gentleman Sid (46)** (PGMurphy) **6-7-10** NAdams(17) (b.nr fore: a bhd) | 1¼ | **16** | 66/1 | 35 | 13 |
| 2775[6] **Zajira (IRE) (65)** (PEccles) **6-9-1** TIves(6) (bhd fnl 4f) | 1½ | **17** | 66/1 | 53 | 31 |
| 2547[11] **Soojama (IRE) (50)** (RMFlower) **6-8-0b** DBiggs(9) (swtg: bhd fnl 3f) | 1½ | **18** | 25/1 | 36 | 14 |
| 2697[5] **Aude la Belle (FR) (46)** (SGKnight) **8-7-10** GBardwell(12) (bhd fnl 3f) | 8 | **19** | 50/1 | 25 | 3 |
| 2707[3] **Rising Spray (52)** (CAHorgan) **5-7-11**(5)ow6 AmandaSanders(19) (swtg: s.s: hdwy over 7f out: wknd over 1f out) | 17 | **20** | 50/1 | 14 | — |
| | | | (SP 118.6%) | **20 Rn** | |

**3m 30.61** (3.41) CSF £56.49 CT £1,272.08 TOTE £5.10: £1.80 £2.20 £5.00 £4.10 (£14.80) Trio £361.60 OWNER BEL Leisure Ltd (EPSOM) BRED A. Hanahoe
LONG HANDICAP Gentleman Sid 7-3 Shahrani 7-7
WEIGHT FOR AGE 3yo-17lb
**2148* Bolivar (IRE)**, who has been raised 10lb for his recent victory, put up a gutsy display. In a handy position travelling well, he moved to the front below the distance. Engaged in a tremendous battle with the runner-up, the two of them leant on each other in the closing stages, but Bolivar just held on with not an ounce to spare. (6/1)
**2042 Golden Arrow (IRE)** moved up over half a mile from home. Throwing down his challenge in the final furlong, he and the winner leant badly on each other in the closing stages, but it made little difference to either, and he just lost out. (10/1)
**2247 State Theatre (IRE)** began a forward move early in the straight. He stayed on well for third prize, but was never going to get to the front two. (25/1)
**1792 Hattaafeh (IRE)** made her bid for glory over two furlongs from home but, headed below the distance, had soon run out of gas. (20/1)
**2697* Great Oration (IRE)**, scrubbed along towards the back of the field over three furlongs from home, did all his best work in the final quarter-mile. (14/1)
**2516* French Ivy (USA)** stayed on in the last two furlongs without ever posing a threat. (6/1)

## 3038 JACKMAN'S GARDEN CENTRE RATED STKS H'CAP (0-100) (3-Y.O+) (Class B)
3-15 (3-16) **5f** £15,549.50 (£5,820.50: £2,847.75: £1,226.25: £550.63: £280.37) Stalls: Low GOING minus 0.31 sec per fur (GF)

| | | | SP | RR | SF |
|---|---|---|---|---|---|
| 2889[7] **Bolshoi (IRE) (85)** (JBerry) **4-8-7b** EmmaO'Gorman(9) (hdwy over 1f out: str run fnl f: led last stride) | — | **1** | 6/1[3] | 95 | 46 |
| 2950* **Sylva Paradise (IRE) (87)** (CEBrittain) **3-8-5** 3x BDoyle(4) (lw: a.p: led over 1f out: hrd rdn: hdd last stride) | s.h | **2** | 7/2[2] | 97 | 44 |
| 2889* **Tedburrow (91)** (MrsAMNaughton) **4-8-8**(5) 3x DGriffiths(6) (swtg: hld up: rdn over 1f out: ev ch ins fnl f: one pce) | 1½ | **3** | 11/4[1] | 96 | 47 |
| 2584[6] **Dashing Blue (98)** (IABalding) **3-8-11**(5) MartinDwyer(2) (lw: hld up: rdn 2f out: r.o one pce) | 1¼ | **4** | 10/1 | 99 | 46 |
| 2545[10] **Double Quick (IRE) (99)** (MJohnston) **4-9-7** WCarson(7) (lw: a.p: ev ch over 1f out: one pce) | nk | **5** | 8/1 | 99 | 50 |
| 2725[10] **So Intrepid (IRE) (85)** (JMBradley) **6-8-7** PatEddery(5) (nvr nr to chal) | 1¾ | **6** | 8/1 | 80 | 31 |
| 2545[6] **Marl (89)** (RAkehurst) **3-8-7** TQuinn(1) (led over 3f) | s.h | **7** | 13/2 | 83 | 30 |
| 2694[10] **Crofters Ceilidh (85)** (BAMcMahon) **4-8-7** JReid(8) (hld up: rdn 2f out: sn wknd) | 3½ | **8** | 20/1 | 68 | 19 |
| 1790[16] **Go Hever Golf (87)** (TJNaughton) **4-8-9** PaulEddery(3) (swtg: prom 3f) | ½ | **9** | 20/1 | 69 | 20 |
| | | | (SP 117.3%) | **9 Rn** | |

**61.16 secs** (1.16) CSF £26.19 CT £63.95 TOTE £7.10: £1.80 £1.50 £1.40 (£10.50) Trio £9.90 OWNER Mrs David Brown (COCKERHAM) BRED David John Brown
LONG HANDICAP Bolshoi (IRE) 8-5 Crofters Ceilidh 8-3 So Intrepid (IRE) 8-5
WEIGHT FOR AGE 3yo-4lb
**2889 Bolshoi (IRE)** was given a very cool ride. Put to sleep at the back of the field, he began to weave his way through the pack below the distance and came storming through in the final furlong to snatch the spoils in the last stride. With a penalty for this win, connections are hoping enough horses come out for him to run in the Stewards' Cup next week. (6/1)
**2950* Sylva Paradise (IRE)**, making a quick reappearance, was never far away. Sent on below the distance, he did absolutely nothing wrong, but was caught right on the line. Connections are hopeful for a run in the Stewards' Cup. (7/2)
**2889* Tedburrow** ran another solid race. Throwing down a challenge below the distance, he may well have got his head in front for a few strides, but was just tapped for toe in the last 75 yards. (11/4)
**2584 Dashing Blue** chased the leaders. Pushed along in the final quarter-mile, he stayed on without finding that vital turn of foot. (10/1)
**2472a Double Quick (IRE)**, one of several vying for the lead below the distance, was then tapped for toe. (8/1)

## 3039 HEATHORNS BOOKMAKERS H'CAP (0-90) (3-Y.O) (Class C)
3-50 (3-50) **1m 2f** £8,559.00 (£2,592.00: £1,266.00: £603.00) Stalls: High GOING minus 0.31 sec per fur (GF)

| | | | SP | RR | SF |
|---|---|---|---|---|---|
| 2608[12] **Daunting Destiny (BEL) (74)** (RHannon) **3-8-5**(3) DaneO'Neill(8) (lw: hld up: n.m.r 2f out: swtchd rt: nt clr run over 1f out: swtchd rt: led ins fnl f: rdn out) | — | **1** | 16/1 | 86 | 57 |
| 1843[4] **Crazy Chief (80)** (PFICole) **3-9-0** TQuinn(10) (lw: chsd ldr 1f: rdn over 2f out: ev ch ins fnl f: unable qckn) | 1¾ | **2** | 8/1 | 89 | 60 |
| 2674[5] **Exalted (IRE) (82)** (SirMarkPrescott) **3-9-2** SSanders(9) (lw: chsd ldr 9f out: rdn 3f out: led over 1f out tl ins fnl f: one pce) | ¾ | **3** | 12/1 | 90 | 61 |
| 2486[4] **White Plains (IRE) (70)** (MBell) **3-8-4** MFenton(7) (led: rdn over 2f out: hdd over 1f out: ev ch ins fnl f: one pce) | ½ | **4** | 13/2 | 77 | 48 |
| 2383* **Oops Pettie (78)** (MrsJCecil) **3-8-12** AClark(5) (swtg: rdn over 2f out: hdwy & nt clr run on ins over 1f out: swtchd lft: nt clr run ins fnl f: nt rcvr) | ¾ | **5** | 5/1[2] | 84 | 55 |
| 2608[3] **Frezeliere (87)** (JLDunlop) **3-9-7** JReid(4) (lw: hdwy over 4f out: ev ch over 1f out: one pce) | hd | **6** | 7/2[1] | 93 | 64 |
| 2585[9] **Roses In The Snow (IRE) (85)** (JWHills) **3-9-5** BThomson(3) (lw: hdwy over 3f out: rdn over 2f out: eased whn btn ins fnl f) | 2 | **7** | 25/1 | 88 | 59 |
| 1780* **Le Teteu (FR) (67)** (BobJones) **3-8-1** DaleGibson(2) (lw: prom over 6f) | 10 | **8** | 13/2 | 54 | 25 |
| 2621[6] **Kala Sunrise (85)** (CSmith) **3-9-5** RHughes(1) (swtg: a bhd) | 15 | **9** | 14/1 | 48 | 19 |
| 2300[5] **Firbur (72)** (NAGraham) **3-8-6** PatEddery(6) (7th whn p.u over 7f out: broke leg: dead) | | **P** | 6/1[3] | — | — |
| | | | (SP 115.0%) | **10 Rn** | |

**2m 8.15** (1.35) CSF £122.40 CT £1,453.18 TOTE £17.30: £3.70 £1.70 £4.10 (£28.70) Trio £106.10 OWNER The Gold Buster Syndicate (MARLBOROUGH) BRED Patrick Madelein
**OFFICIAL EXPLANATION Daunting Destiny (BEL): ran a lifeless race last time and was better suited by the turning track here.**

**1955 Daunting Destiny (BEL)** looked absolutely magnificent in the paddock and was given a fine ride. With nowhere to go in the straight, his jockey kept on looking for daylight, only to meet with a dead-end. Luckily a split came on the rail in the final furlong, and he swept into the lead to settle the issue. (16/1)
**1843 Crazy Chief** lacks acceleration, hence the step up in distance. Always handy, he threw down a determined challenge and may well have got his head in front for a few strides around the furlong pole. When the winner struck the front though, he was left standing. (8/1)
**2674 Exalted (IRE)** was soon in second place and poked a nostril in front below the distance. Headed inside the final furlong, he was just tapped for toe. (12/1: 8/1-14/1)
**2486 White Plains (IRE)** attempted to make all. Headed below the distance, he showed real courage and still had every chance in the final furlong, before lacking another gear. (13/2)
**2383* Oops Pettie** had no luck in running. Failing to get a clear run as she tried to pick up ground below the distance, she again found her way blocked in the final furlong. She is worth another chance. (5/1: 7/2-11/2)
**2608 Frezeliere** came there to have every chance below the distance, before tapped for toe. (7/2)

## 3040 DELOITTE & TOUCHE E.B.F. MAIDEN STKS (2-Y.O) (Class D)
4-25 (4-26) **7f** £6,807.50 (£2,060.00: £1,005.00: £477.50) Stalls: Low GOING minus 0.31 sec per fur (GF)

| | Horse | Dist | Pos | SP | RR | SF |
|---|---|---|---|---|---|---|
| 2416[2] | **Musheer (USA)** (MissGayKelleway) **2-9-0** PatEddery(2) (mde all: easily) | — | 1 | 8/1 | 94+ | 46 |
| | **Snow Partridge (USA)** (PFICole) **2-9-0** TQuinn(1) (w'like: scope: lw: chsd wnr: rdn over 2f out: ev ch wl over 1f out: unable qckn) | 1½ | 2 | 9/2[3] | 91 | 43 |
| | **Monza (USA)** (PWChapple-Hyam) **2-9-0** JReid(5) (w'like: scope: lw: hld up: rdn 2f out: r.o ins fnl f) | nk | 3 | 11/10[1] | 90 | 42 |
| 2708[2] | **Silver Widget (USA)** (RCharlton) **2-9-0** SSanders(4) (swtg: hld up: rdn over 3f out: wknd wl over 1f out) | 10 | 4 | 11/4[2] | 67 | 19 |
| | **Norman Conquest (USA)** (IABalding) **2-9-0** PaulEddery(3) (str: scope: bkwd: hld up: rdn over 3f out: sn wknd) | 3½ | 5 | 20/1 | 59 | 11 |

(SP 108.3%) **5 Rn**

**1m 29.6** (2.40) CSF £36.22 TOTE £6.70: £2.40 £2.00 (£12.40) OWNER Bellcoil Ltd (WHITCOMBE) BRED Clovelly Farms, Division of Gnl Agri Services
**2416 Musheer (USA)** put up a highly-impressive performance here to win with a ton in hand. His trainer rates him the best horse she has ever trained, and he works with her three-year-olds. The further he goes, the better he gets. Next on the agenda is a Group race, although this very classy individual will not be over-raced. (8/1: 6/1-10/1)
**Snow Partridge (USA)** was quickly racing in second. On terms with the winner in the final quarter-mile, he was then left for dead by that rival, but will not always meet one so good. (9/2: 3/1-5/1)
**Monza (USA)** was the subject of encouraging home reports. Chasing the leaders, he appeared to be travelling well approaching the final quarter-mile but, soon ridden along, then failed to immediately find another gear. He did run on in the final furlong once he grasped the hang of things, and only just failed to take second. He should soon be winning. (11/10)
**2708 Silver Widget (USA)** was awash with sweat in the paddock, and that is surely where he lost the race. Chasing the leaders, he was being pushed long from halfway and had shot his bolt early in the final quarter-mile. (11/4: 5/4-3/1)
**Norman Conquest (USA)** was far too fat to do himself any justice. (20/1)

## 3041 P & O CRUISES MAIDEN STKS (3-Y.O) (Class D)
5-00 (5-00) **1m 2f** £7,002.50 (£2,120.00: £1,035.00: £492.50) Stalls: High GOING minus 0.31 sec per fur (GF)

| | Horse | Dist | Pos | SP | RR | SF |
|---|---|---|---|---|---|---|
| 1357[2] | **Ta Awun (USA)** (ACStewart) **3-8-9** WCarson(7) (lw: mde all: clr 2f out: easily) | — | 1 | 3/1[2] | 84+ | 56 |
| 2439[3] | **Serenus (USA)** (LordHuntingdon) **3-9-0** BDoyle(8) (hld up: rdn over 2f out: chsd wnr over 1f out: no imp) | 5 | 2 | 7/1[3] | 81 | 53 |
| 2557[3] | **Kidston Lass (IRE)** (JARToller) **3-8-9** SSanders(9) (lw: nt clr run on ins over 7f out: rdn & hdwy over 1f out: r.o one pce) | ¾ | 3 | 14/1 | 75 | 47 |
| 1614[6] | **Namouna (IRE)** (PWChapple-Hyam) **3-8-9** JReid(1) (hld up: rdn over 2f out: wknd over 1f out) | 6 | 4 | 14/1 | 65 | 37 |
| 2744[3] | **Llyswen** (JHMGosden) **3-9-0** BThomson(2) (chsd wnr 8f out tl over 1f out: sn wknd) | s.h | 5 | 9/1 | 70 | 42 |
| 2610[10] | **Trick (IRE)** (LMCumani) **3-8-9** OUrbina(4) (nvr nr to chal) | 3 | 6 | 20/1 | 60 | 32 |
| 1357[4] | **Chabrol (CAN) (75)** (RHarris) **3-8-9**(5) ADaly(5) (bhd fnl 6f) | 3½ | 7 | 50/1 | 60 | 32 |
| | **Triple Leap** (JHMGosden) **3-9-0** PatEddery(6) (str: scope: lw: s.s: a bhd) | ¾ | 8 | 13/8[1] | 59+ | 31 |
| 2579[7] | **Miss Romance (IRE)** (MissGayKelleway) **3-8-6**(3) DaneO'Neill(3) (chsd wnr 2f: wknd over 2f out) | 10 | 9 | 20/1 | 38 | 10 |

(SP 110.4%) **9 Rn**

**2m 8.41** (1.61) CSF £21.35 TOTE £3.40: £1.10 £2.00 £3.30 (£11.30) Trio £20.20 OWNER Mr Hamdan Al Maktoum (NEWMARKET)
**1357 Ta Awun (USA)** destroyed this field in emphatic style. Making all the running, she powered clear a quarter of a mile from home to win doing handsprings. She can progress from here. (3/1)
**2439 Serenus (USA)** chased the leaders. He struggled into second below the distance, but had no hope with the winner. (7/1: 9/2-8/1)
**2557 Kidston Lass (IRE)** struggled on in the final quarter-mile to take third, without having a hope. (14/1: 7/1-16/1)
**1614 Namouna (IRE)** chased the leaders. Given a nudge by a rival over a quarter of a mile from home, it made little difference and she was hung out to dry below the distance. (14/1: 6/1-16/1)
**2744 Llyswen**, soon racing in second place, was collared for that position below the distance and had little left in reserve. (9/1: 7/1-14/1)

T/Jkpt: Not won; £15,883.36 to Ascot 27/7/96. T/Plpt: £215.40 (132.09 Tckts). T/Qdpt: £39.50 (37.94 Tckts). AK

# 2884-NEWMARKET (R-H) (Good to firm)
## Friday July 26th
WEATHER: fine WIND: slt across

## 3042 HUNDON MAIDEN STKS (3-Y.O) (Class D)
6-15 (6-15) **1m 4f (July)** £4,386.00 (£1,308.00: £624.00: £282.00) Stalls: High GOING minus 0.64 sec per fur (F)

| | Horse | Dist | Pos | SP | RR | SF |
|---|---|---|---|---|---|---|
| 2533[5] | **My Emma** (RGuest) **3-8-9** JQuinn(2) (hld up: a gng wl: led on bit over 1f out: shkn up & qcknd clr: easily) | — | 1 | 4/6[1] | 84+ | 40 |
| | **Flamands (IRE)** (LMCumani) **3-8-2**(7) RFfrench(3) (bit bkwd: in tch: pushed along 5f out: r.o wl appr fnl f: no ch w wnr) | 2 | 2 | 40/1 | 81 | 37 |
| 1873[5] | **Ginger Fox (USA)** (HRACecil) **3-9-0** WRyan(1) (swtg: a.p: ev ch whn edgd rt over 1f out: sn btn) | 3 | 3 | 7/2[2] | 82 | 38 |
| | **Kala Noire** (GHarwood) **3-9-0** AClark(4) (leggy: unf: bit bkwd: led 1f: led 4f out tl hdd & hmpd over 1f out) | ¾ | 4 | 20/1 | 81 | 37 |
| | **Congo Man** (MRStoute) **3-9-0** TQuinn(5) (tall: scope: bkwd: chsd ldrs: rdn 6f out: no imp fnl 4f) | 1¼ | 5 | 8/1[3] | 80 | 36 |
| 2744[6] | **Taharqa (IRE)** (JHMGosden) **3-9-0** AMcGlone(6) (swtg: led after 1f to 4f out: wknd 2f out) | 8 | 6 | 12/1 | 69 | 25 |

2365[5] **Quinella** (LordHuntingdon) **3-8-9** RPerham(7) (bhd fnl 4f) ....................16 **7** 25/1 43 —
(SP 112.1%) **7 Rn**

**2m 30.3** (0.30) CSF £20.45 TOTE £1.80: £1.40 £5.20 (£30.80) OWNER Matthews Breeding and Racing (NEWMARKET) BRED Lord Matthews

**2533 My Emma** fairly toyed with this field and looks ready to step back up in class. (4/6)

**Flamands (IRE)**, a tail flasher, needed this race and only began to stay on in the closing stages. (40/1)

**1873 Ginger Fox (USA)** again found little at the business end, but may find a mile and a half too far. He would be interesting in a ten-furlong handicap, if on a decent mark. (7/2: 2/1-4/1)

**Kala Noire** has some growing to do, but showed promise and ought to find a race. (20/1)

**Congo Man** looked a big, backward type and lazy to boot. Whether he has speed enough for this sort of race has still to be seen. (8/1: 6/1-10/1)

**2744 Taharqa (IRE)** got warm and again disappointed, but probably needs the ground to ease before he can show his true colours. (12/1: 8/1-14/1)

## 3043 NGK SPARK PLUGS H'CAP (0-80) (3-Y.O+) (Class D)

6-45 (6-45) **1m 2f** **(July)** £4,581.00 (£1,368.00: £654.00: £148.50: £148.50) Stalls: High GOING minus 0.64 sec per fur (F)

| | | | | SP | RR | SF |
|---|---|---|---|---|---|---|
| 2164[3] | **Angus-G (71)** (MrsMReveley) **4-9-9** JQuinn(2) (lw: trckd ldrs: drvn over 1f out: led ins fnl f: r.o) | — | **1** | 11/4[1] | 80 | 64 |
| 2603[9] | **Fahs (USA) (68)** (RAkehurst) **4-9-6** SSanders(6) (lw: w ldr: led 5f out tl ins fnl f: one pce) | ½ | **2** | 5/1 | 76 | 60 |
| | **Once More for Luck (IRE) (65)** (MrsMReveley) **5-8-12**(5) GLee(7) (lw: hld up: hdwy 2f out: r.o ins fnl f) | s.h | **3** | 16/1 | 73 | 57 |
| 1977[10] | **Advance East (56)** (MrsJRRamsden) **4-8-8** TQuinn(1) (hld up: hdwy 3f out: no ex ins fnl f) | ¾ | **4** | 4/1[2] | 63 | 47 |
| 2737* | **Nelly's Cousin (59)** (NACallaghan) **3-7-10**(5) 5x MartinDwyer(4) (chsd ldrs: nt clr run fr over 1f out: nt rcvr) | d.h | **4** | 5/1 | 66 | 40 |
| 2862[12] | **Northern Law (74)** (JohnBerry) **4-9-12** MFenton(3) (b: bhd fnl 5f) | 16 | **6** | 50/1 | 55 | 39 |
| 2603[3] | **Formidable Partner (69)** (RWArmstrong) **3-8-11** WRyan(8) (lw: chsd ldrs: pushed along 4f out: sn btn) | 1¾ | **7** | 9/2[3] | 48 | 22 |
| 2489[4] | **Zaaleff (USA) (53)** (BHanbury) **4-8-5bow3** MRimmer(5) (lw: led 5f: wknd over 2f out) | 6 | **8** | 20/1 | 22 | 3 |

(SP 110.8%) **8 Rn**

**2m 3.86** (-1.14) CSF £15.28 CT £155.66 TOTE £3.70: £1.70 £2.10 £1.90 (£9.40) OWNER Mr W. Ginzel (SALTBURN) BRED W. Ginzel

WEIGHT FOR AGE 3yo-10lb

**2164 Angus-G** broke his duck and proved well suited to this galloping track. He is lightly-raced and should continue to progress. (11/4)

**1961 Fahs (USA)** seemed suited by this enterprising ride, but was just run out of it in the closing stages. (5/1: op 3/1)

**Once More for Luck (IRE)** looked fit, despite four months off, and responded well to the waiting tactics which have served him well over timber. (16/1)

**1647 Advance East**, brought into the paddock late and last to post, was dropped in trip and well supported. He remains a maiden and has become frustrating. (4/1)

**2737* Nelly's Cousin** was the unlucky horse of the race, being denied room to make her move whilst appearing to travel well. She deserves a chance to atone. (5/1)

## 3044 SNOWDENS' MARQUEES MAIDEN STKS (2-Y.O) (Class D)

7-15 (7-15) **6f** **(July)** £4,464.00 (£1,332.00: £636.00: £288.00) Stalls: Centre GOING minus 0.42 sec per fur (F)

| | | | | SP | RR | SF |
|---|---|---|---|---|---|---|
| | **Hirasah (IRE)** (RWArmstrong) **2-8-9** WCarson(7) (leggy: scope: bit bkwd: led tl wl ins fnl f: led again post) | — | **1** | 9/2[2] | 59 | 16 |
| 2611[6] | **Literary** (JHMGosden) **2-8-9** PatEddery(4) (stdd s: plld hrd & sn chsng ldrs: squeezed thro over 1f out: led wl ins fnl f: ct post) | s.h | **2** | 8/13[1] | 59 | 16 |
| 2495[8] | **Ultra Boy** (PCHaslam) **2-9-0** JFortune(2) (hdwy over 2f out: ev ch 1f out: one pce) | 2 | **3** | 33/1 | 59 | 16 |
| 2852[9] | **Ludo** (RHannon) **2-9-0** RHughes(3) (trckd ldrs: rdn 3f out: ev ch 1f out: sn wknd) | 1¼ | **4** | 8/1[3] | 55 | 12 |
| | **Spaniard's Mount** (MHTompkins) **2-9-0** PRobinson(6) (str: scope: chsd ldrs 4f) | 5 | **5** | 16/1 | 42 | — |
| | **Teraab** (JHMGosden) **2-9-0** AGarth(5) (scope: bkwd: sn pushed along & bhd: nvr rchd ldrs) | 2 | **6** | 10/1 | 37 | — |

(SP 109.1%) **6 Rn**

**1m 15.14** (3.14) CSF £7.34 TOTE £3.40: £1.60 £1.30 (£1.80) OWNER Mr Hamdan Al Maktoum (NEWMARKET) BRED Shadwell Estate Company Limited

IN-FOCUS: **This was a slowly-run event, and it may pay to treat the form with caution.**

**Hirasah (IRE)** looked to need this, but was allowed to dictate from the front. As so often happens in slowly-run races, the horse that sets the pace wins. (9/2: op 5/2)

**2611 Literary** tried to drop in behind but, with no pace on, was pulling hard on the heels of the leaders within a furlong. Quickening to lead inside the last 100 yards, she was denied on the nod. (8/13)

**1827 Ultra Boy** ran much better this time, but his prominent showing may have owed much to the slowly-run nature of the race. (33/1)

**Ludo** did not move to post very fluently, but took a more prominent role than on his debut, only feeling the pinch in the closing stages. (8/1: 4/1-9/1)

**Spaniard's Mount** looked well in his coat but will be better for the run, and should find a race or two. (16/1)

**Teraab**, a brother to First Trump, was too backward to do himself justice, but his demeanour suggests an attitude problem. (10/1: 6/1-12/1)

## 3045 BAILEYS' IRISH CREAM LIQUEUR H'CAP (0-90) (3-Y.O+) (Class C)

7-45 (7-45) **6f** **(July)** £7,440.00 (£2,220.00: £1,060.00: £480.00) Stalls: Centre GOING minus 0.42 sec per fur (F)

| | | | | SP | RR | SF |
|---|---|---|---|---|---|---|
| 2856[2] | **Mr Bergerac (IRE) (79)** (BPalling) **5-9-0**(3) DaneO'Neill(7) (lw: a.p: rdn over 1f out: led nr fin) | — | **1** | 9/2[1] | 89 | 58 |
| 2363[6] | **Fame Again (77)** (MrsJRRamsden) **4-9-1** JFortune(1) (dwlt: hdwy 2f out: rdn to ld ins fnl f: hdd nr fin) | s.h | **2** | 13/2 | 87 | 56 |
| 2856[6] | **Silent Expression (86)** (BJMeehan) **6-9-10** BDoyle(2) (in tch: rdn 2f out: r.o wl fnl f) | 2 | **3** | 14/1 | 91 | 60 |
| 2754[4] | **Jerry Cutrona (IRE) (73)** (NACallaghan) **3-8-6** PatEddery(9) (s.i.s: wl bhd tl swtchd rt & r.o wl appr fnl f) | nk | **4** | 5/1[2] | 77 | 41 |
| 2860[3] | **Cim Bom Bom (IRE) (73)** (MBell) **4-8-4v**(7) GFaulkner(5) (lw: led over 5f) | s.h | **5** | 8/1 | 77 | 46 |
| | **Trafalgar Lady (USA) (80)** (RCharlton) **3-8-13** KDarley(4) (trckd ldrs: rdn & wknd fnl f) | 1 | **6** | 6/1[3] | 81 | 45 |
| 2363[13] | **Castlerea Lad (80)** (RHollinshead) **7-9-4** WRyan(6) (lw: bhd: rdn 2f out: nvr able to chal) | ¾ | **7** | 11/1 | 79 | 48 |
| 2757[7] | **Pageboy (60)** (PCHaslam) **7-7-12** WCarson(3) (racd alone far side: gd spd 4f) | 1¾ | **8** | 6/1[3] | 54 | 23 |
| 2692[8] | **My Cadeaux (85)** (RGuest) **4-9-9** PBloomfield(8) (prom: rdn over 2f out: sn btn) | ½ | **9** | 9/1 | 78 | 47 |

(SP 112.9%) **9 Rn**

**1m 12.53** (0.53) CSF £30.33 CT £341.87 TOTE £4.40: £1.80 £2.80 £4.50 (£21.00) Trio £52.10 OWNER Mr P. R. John (COWBRIDGE) BRED Red House Stud

WEIGHT FOR AGE 3yo-5lb

**2856 Mr Bergerac (IRE)**, back in form and better in on turf than the All-Weather, fought hard to master the runner-up. (9/2)

**2363 Fame Again**, off her lowest mark in the thirteen races since her last win, looked sure to win inside the final furlong but was just denied. (13/2: 4/1-7/1)

**2856 Silent Expression** stayed on so well after looking held that a return to seven should suit. (14/1)
**2754 Jerry Cutrona (IRE)** lost all chance at the start, but the way he flashed home when switched towards the stands' side suggests that he is ahead of the Handicapper. (5/1)
**2860 Cim Bom Bom (IRE)** did not move down well, but at least did not run away this time. Leading until inside the final furlong, he had no more to give. (8/1)
**Trafalgar Lady (USA)**, off since last October, looked a danger until lack of a race took its toll. (6/1)

## 3046 HARGRAVE NURSERY H'CAP (2-Y.O) (Class D)

8-15 (8-16) **7f (July)** £4,854.00 (£1,452.00: £696.00: £318.00) Stalls: Centre GOING minus 0.42 sec per fur (F)

| | | | | SP | RR | SF |
|---|---|---|---|---|---|---|
| 2588[5] | **Ninth Symphony** (PCHaslam) **2-8-4** WCarson(2) (prom tl lost pl over 3f out: rdn 2f out: led 1f out: r.o) | — | **1** | 10/1 | 64 | 23 |
| 2696[4] | **Dowry** (RHannon) **2-8-10** PatEddery(8) (lw: hld up: hdwy 2f out: led & edgd lft over 1f out: sn hdd & unable qckn) | 1 | **2** | 15/2[3] | 68 | 27 |
| 2309* | **My Beloved (IRE)** (RHannon) **2-8-9**(3) DaneO'Neill(10) (lw: hld up: rdn over 1f out: edgd lft & r.o strly fnl f) | ¾ | **3** | 3/1[1] | 68 | 27 |
| 2624[10] | **Bold Oriental (IRE)** (NACallaghan) **2-9-1** RHughes(3) (chsd ldrs: led over 2f out: hdd over 1f out: n.m.r jst ins fnl f: r.o) | s.h | **4** | 11/1 | 71 | 30 |
| 2696[3] | **Lamorna** (MRChannon) **2-9-0**(7) AEddery(5) (prom: ev ch over 1f out: no ex fnl f) | 3 | **5** | 11/1 | 70 | 29 |
| 1878[4] | **Superquest** (WAO'Gorman) **2-8-11** EmmaO'Gorman(6) (led over 4f: wknd ins fnl f) | 1¼ | **6** | 20/1 | 57 | 16 |
| 2509[2] | **Irish Fiction (IRE)** (DJSCosgrove) **2-8-4**(5) LNewton(4) (swtg: prom: rdn over 1f out: no imp) | nk | **7** | 12/1 | 55 | 14 |
| 2606[4] | **Fan of Vent-Axia** (CNAllen) **2-8-0**(5) MartinDwyer(12) (w ldrs 4f) | ¾ | **8** | 9/1 | 49 | 8 |
| 2210[3] | **Smart Boy (IRE)** (PFICole) **2-8-10**(7) DavidO'Neill(1) (prom: led wl over 2f out: sn rdn & hdd: wknd fnl f) | 1¼ | **9** | 11/1 | 58 | 17 |
| *2750** | **Our Kevin** (KMcAuliffe) **2-8-9v** 5x DRMcCabe(11) (swtg: stdd s: a bhd) | 1½ | **10** | 10/1 | 47 | 6 |
| 2435* | **Retoto** (BJMcMath) **2-7-12** JQuinn(9) (b.hind: a bhd) | 7 | **11** | 7/1[2] | 20 | — |
| 1463* | **Don't Forget Shoka (IRE)** (JSMoore) **2-7-12**ow1 JFEgan(7) (plld hrd: prom 3f: sn wl bhd) | 27 | **12** | 25/1 | — | — |

(SP 118.7%) **12 Rn**

**1m 27.7** (2.70) CSF £76.27 CT £261.86 TOTE £11.60: £3.00 £1.90 £1.80 (£33.10) Trio £32.00 OWNER Mr S. A. B. Dinsmore (MIDDLEHAM) BRED Jeremy Green and Sons

**2588 Ninth Symphony** clearly benefited from the step up in trip, although he was flat to the boards in the final furlong. (10/1)
**2696 Dowry**, given a chance in the race having gone too quickly to post, still hit the front briefly in the Dip and plugged on once headed. (15/2)
**2309* My Beloved (IRE)** was settled on the heels of the near-side leaders. Her pilot failed to get an immediate response once he made his move in the Dip, and the situation was made worse by the fact that those on the other side had gone for home. Therefore she was left with far too much to do once into her stride, and she is better than this. (3/1)
**1878 Bold Oriental (IRE)** was squeezed up at a vital stage and would have gone closer with a clear passage. (11/1: 7/1-12/1)
**2696 Lamorna**, a leading light throughout, had had enough by the final furlong. (11/1: 7/1-12/1)
**1878 Superquest** took a good hold going down and forced the pace, but did not last home. (20/1)
**2509 Irish Fiction (IRE)** (12/1: op 8/1)

## 3047 SAWSTON CONDITIONS STKS (3-Y.O+) (Class C)

8-45 (8-45) **5f (July)** £5,394.00 (£1,944.00: £932.00: £380.00: £150.00) Stalls: Centre GOING minus 0.42 sec per fur (F)

| | | | | SP | RR | SF |
|---|---|---|---|---|---|---|
| 2889[3] | **Sea-Deer (82)** (CADwyer) **7-8-10**(3) FLynch(4) (chsd ldrs: n.m.r over 2f out: wnt 2nd fnl f: hmpd & lft in ld wl ins fnl f) | — | **1** | 8/1 | 102 | 53 |
| 2889[4] | **Galine (87)** (WAO'Gorman) **3-8-4** EmmaO'Gorman(2) (hld up: hdwy 2f out: r.o ins fnl f) | nk | **2** | 100/30[2] | 96 | 43 |
| 2698[6] | **Maid For The Hills (100)** (DRLoder) **3-8-4v** PatEddery(5) (lw: led 1f: one pce appr fnl f) | 3 | **3** | 11/2[3] | 86 | 33 |
| 2853[5] | **Warning Time (104)** (BJMeehan) **3-8-9** BDoyle(1) (chsd ldrs over 3f) | ½ | **4** | 6/1 | 90 | 37 |
| 2698[3] | **Ya Malak (105)** (JWPayne) **5-8-13** BThomson(3) (lw: hld up: effrt 2f out: no imp whn hmpd ins fnl f) | 2½ | **5** | 100/30[2] | 82 | 33 |
| 2545[5] | **Mubhij (IRE) (105)** (BWHills) **3-8-9** WCarson(6) (led after 1f: sn clr: broke leg & fell ins fnl f: dead) | | **F** | 3/1[1] | — | — |

(SP 111.9%) **6 Rn**

**58.99 secs** (0.49) CSF £31.94 TOTE £7.30: £2.60 £2.30 (£8.70) OWNER Binding Matters Ltd (NEWMARKET) BRED Stetchworth Park Stud Ltd
WEIGHT FOR AGE 3yo-4lb

**2889 Sea-Deer** is in great form and would have finished a clear second best here but for the incident in the final half-furlong. He would have met all bar the winner on 20lb and more better terms in a handicap, and could have to pass up his winning handicap mark after this. (8/1)
**2889 Galine** was handicapped to beat Sea-Deer on their previous meeting the Saturday before, and may have seen too much daylight. (100/30)
**2698 Maid For The Hills** tried to force the pace, but faded from the Dip and gave best to horses which she would meet on much worse terms in handicaps. (11/2)
**2853 Warning Time**, back over the minimum trip for the first time since a two-year-old, was taken off his feet. (6/1)
**2698 Ya Malak** looked the part when taken steadily to post, but found nothing once asked to pick up, and has lost his form at present. (100/30)

T/Plpt: £39.00 (347.56 Tckts). T/Qdpt: £14.60 (71.57 Tckts). Dk

# 2891-NOTTINGHAM (L-H) (Good to firm, Firm patches)

## Friday July 26th

vis: deteriorating
WEATHER: rain WIND: slt across

## 3048 NOTTINGHAM FOREST EURO '96 (S) STKS (3 & 4-Y.O) (Class G)

6-30 (6-31) **1m 1f 213y** £2,070.00 (£570.00: £270.00) Stalls: Low GOING minus 0.32 sec per fur (GF)

| | | | | SP | RR | SF |
|---|---|---|---|---|---|---|
| 2438[2] | **Action Jackson (50)** (BJMcMath) **4-9-6** GBardwell(5) (swtg: a.p: led over 1f out: hrd rdn: hld on gamely) | — | **1** | 4/1[2] | 61 | 49 |
| 2587[17] | **Yuppy Girl (IRE) (45)** (CaptJWilson) **3-8-2**(3) MHenry(7) (dwlt: hdwy on ins 4f out: jnd wnr 1f out: hrd rdn: kpt on) | hd | **2** | 12/1 | 56 | 34 |
| 1196[6] | **Arcatura (62)** (CJames) **4-9-6** MWigham(4) (lw: a.p: rdn & n.m.r 2f out: r.o one pce) | 5 | **3** | 6/1[3] | 53 | 41 |
| 2394[4] | **Simand (46)** (GMMoore) **4-9-1** DHolland(6) (hld up: hdwy over 2f out: rdn & one pce appr fnl f) | 2½ | **4** | 7/1 | 44 | 32 |
| 2617[11] | **Flying Harold (46)** (MRChannon) **3-8-5**(5) PPMurphy(2) (plld hrd: led tl hdd & wknd over 1f out) | 1 | **5** | 10/1 | 47 | 25 |

| | | | | SP | RR | SF |
|---|---|---|---|---|---|---|
| 2599$^{11}$ | **Owdbetts (IRE) (57)** (GLMoore) **4-9-1** SWhitworth(8) (lw: hld up in rr: effrt & swtchd rt 2f out: sn rdn: nt pce to chal) | ½ | **6** | 2/1$^{1}$ | 41 | 29 |
| 2788$^{5}$ | **Kama Simba (45)** (JWhite) **4-9-3b**$^{(3)}$ SDrowne(3) (lw: swtg: trckd ldrs tl rdn & wknd wl over 1f out) | 1¾ | **7** | 14/1 | 44 | 32 |
| 2563$^{10}$ | **Bright Pet (42)** (MrsSJSmith) **3-8-2**$^{(3)}$ DWright(9) (a in rr) | 2½ | **8** | 25/1 | 35 | 13 |
| 2572$^{7}$ | **Cameron Edge** (ABMulholland) **3-8-2**$^{(3)}$ NVarley(10) (b: bit bkwd: trckd ldrs: effrt 3f out: sn wknd: t.o) | 6 | **9** | 25/1 | 25 | 3 |
| 2568$^{5}$ | **Lebedinski (IRE) (41)** (MrsPSly) **3-8-5** ACulhane(11) (a in rr: t.o) | 7 | **10** | 8/1 | 14 | — |
| | **Farfen** (CADwyer) **4-9-6** TGMcLaughlin(1) (w'like: bkwd: sn pushed along: a bhd: t.o) | dist | **11** | 20/1 | — | — |
| | | | | (SP 127.1%) | | **11 Rn** |

**2m 6.0** (3.50) CSF £49.93 TOTE £5.00: £2.40 £5.20 £2.60 (£19.60) Trio £66.70 OWNER Mr R. G. Levin (NEWMARKET) BRED Stetchworth Park Stud Ltd

WEIGHT FOR AGE 3yo-10lb

No bid

**2438 Action Jackson** had plenty of use made of him over this longer trip, and he showed his battling qualities to just hold the filly at bay. (4/1)

**660 Yuppy Girl (IRE)**, last to leave the stalls, made her move up the inside rail on the turn into the straight. Joining forces entering the final furlong, she just looked to have the edge, but the winner pulled out more and she came off second-best in the photo. (12/1)

**1196 Arcatura**, in the action all the way, was being bustled along when short of room entering the final quarter-mile and could do little more than stay on at the same pace. (6/1)

**2394 Simand** usually finds her form at this time of year and she did get herself into contention at the distance, but she was unable to maintain her effort and was treading water approaching the final furlong. (7/1)

**Flying Harold** raced very freely on this step up to ten furlongs and forced the pace until fading rather quickly after being collared below the distance. (10/1)

**2284 Owdbetts (IRE)** did look something to bet on on this return to selling company, but she took too long to find top gear and was never a factor. (2/1)

## 3049 NOTTINGHAM FOREST SHAREHOLDERS LIMITED STKS (0-65) (3-Y.O+) (Class F)

7-00 (7-02) **5f 13y** £2,381.00 (£656.00: £311.00) Stalls: High GOING minus 0.32 sec per fur (GF)

| | | | | SP | RR | SF |
|---|---|---|---|---|---|---|
| 2790$^{4}$ | **Gwespyr (64)** (JBerry) **3-9-1** JCarroll(1) (hld up: hdwy over 1f out: rdn to ld ins fnl f: r.o wl) | — | **1** | 9/2$^{3}$ | 67 | 49 |
| 2524* | **Shashi (IRE) (62)** (WWHaigh) **4-9-2b** SWhitworth(7) (lw: s.i.s: racd alone stands' side: rdn over 2f out: fin strly) | ½ | **2** | 7/1 | 62 | 48 |
| 2561$^{4}$ | **Bangles (61)** (LordHuntingdon) **6-8-13** DHarrison(9) (a.p: rdn & ev ch ins fnl f: unable qckn) | hd | **3** | 4/1$^{2}$ | 59 | 45 |
| *2634*$^{2}$ | **Vax New Way (62)** (JLSpearing) **3-8-12b**$^{(3)}$ SDrowne(6) (a.p: rdn over 1f out: one pce) | 3 | **4** | 11/1 | 56 | 38 |
| 2500$^{7}$ | **Pleasure Time (63)** (CSmith) **3-8-9b**$^{(3)}$ CTeague(2) (lw: led tl drifted lft & hdd ins fnl) | ½ | **5** | 10/1 | 51 | 33 |
| 2694$^{12}$ | **Premium Gift (61)** (CBBBooth) **4-8-13** MBirch(4) (dwlt: effrt u.p 2f out: nvr nr to chal) | ¾ | **6** | 2/1$^{1}$ | 46 | 32 |
| 2908$^{5}$ | **Windrush Boy (64)** (JRBosley) **6-8-11**$^{(5)}$ AimeeCook(5) (swtg: prom over 3f) | 3½ | **7** | 14/1 | 38 | 24 |
| 2386$^{6}$ | **Supreme Desire (23)** (MissJFCraze) **8-8-13** NConnorton(3) (trckd ldrs 3f: sn outpcd) | s.h | **8** | 50/1 | 34 | 20 |
| 2286* | **Dahiyah (USA) (65)** (DLWilliams) **5-9-8v** DHolland(8) (sn drvn along: a outpcd) | 4 | **9** | 10/1 | 31 | 17 |
| | | | | (SP 119.2%) | | **9 Rn** |

**59.9 secs** (1.30) CSF £33.95 TOTE £6.10: £1.80 £1.50 £2.10 (£18.30) Trio £22.70 OWNER Lord Mostyn (COCKERHAM) BRED R. and Mrs Heathcote

WEIGHT FOR AGE 3yo-4lb

**2790 Gwespyr**, very impressive to post, delivered a sustained challenge going into the final furlong and, showing ahead 150 yards out, was always holding the strong-finishing runner-up. (9/2)

**2524* Shashi (IRE)** finds this trip short of her best, and her determined late challenge was never going to get her there. (7/1: 4/1-8/1)

**2561 Bangles** could not dictate on this occasion, but she pressed the leader and had every chance inside the final furlong without being able to poke her nose in front. (4/1)

**2634 Vax New Way** struggled with the pace over this shorter trip and was never in a position to pose a serious threat. (11/1: 6/1-12/1)

**2301 Pleasure Time** set a scorching pace and may well have held on had he not drifted away to the left in the final furlong. He is overdue another success. (10/1)

**2349 Premium Gift** could not afford to give away ground at the start in a race run in double-quick time and, as such, failed to get in a blow against the principals. (2/1)

**2286* Dahiyah (USA)** (10/1: 6/1-12/1)

## 3050 FRANK CLARK MAIDEN STKS (2-Y.O) (Class D)

7-30 (7-32) **5f 13y** £3,468.20 (£1,034.60: £493.80: £223.40) Stalls: High GOING minus 0.32 sec per fur (GF)

| | | | | SP | RR | SF |
|---|---|---|---|---|---|---|
| 2897$^{4}$ | **Cherokee Flight** (MrsJRRamsden) **2-8-11**$^{(3)}$ SDrowne(2) (lw: a.p: rdn to ld ins fnl f: jst hld on) | — | **1** | 12/1 | 63 | 27 |
| 1779$^{6}$ | **Toronto** (JBerry) **2-9-0** JCarroll(1) (swvd lft s: sn bhd & outpcd: rdn 2f out: str run fnl f: jst failed) | hd | **2** | 16/1 | 63 | 27 |
| 2625$^{2}$ | **Suite Factors** (JAGlover) **2-9-0** SDWilliams(9) (lw: led: sn clr: hdd ins fnl f: rallied nr fin) | nk | **3** | 6/1$^{3}$ | 62 | 26 |
| 2854$^{3}$ | **Blues Queen** (MRChannon) **2-8-4**$^{(5)}$ PPMurphy(8) (a.p: shkn up over 1f out: unable qckn) | 1½ | **4** | 11/10$^{1}$ | 52 | 16 |
| 2138$^{3}$ | **Rivonia (USA)** (MrsJRRamsden) **2-8-9** NKennedy(7) (lw: bhd: pushed along 2f out: kpt on nr fin) | 1¼ | **5** | 15/2 | 48+ | 12 |
| 2562$^{2}$ | **Colonel's Pride** (RMWhitaker) **2-9-0** DeanMcKeown(3) (lw: swtg: trckd ldrs: rdn over 1f out: one pce) | s.h | **6** | 14/1 | 53 | 17 |
| 2755$^{5}$ | **Compact Disc (IRE)** (MJohnston) **2-8-9** JWeaver(5) (a bhd & outpcd) | 1½ | **7** | 4/1$^{2}$ | 43 | 7 |
| 2699$^{6}$ | **Fly-Girl** (BPJBaugh) **2-8-9** ACulhane(10) (bit bkwd: hdwy ½-wy: rdn & swvd bdly lft appr fnl f: sn bhd) | 5 | **8** | 25/1 | 27 | — |
| 2059$^{5}$ | **Trulyfan (IRE)** (RAFahey) **2-8-9** MBirch(4) (sn trckng ldrs: rdn & wknd wl over 1f out: t.o) | 14 | **9** | 10/1 | — | — |
| | | | | (SP 126.8%) | | **9 Rn** |

**61.2 secs** (2.60) CSF £164.08 TOTE £22.80: £3.40 £3.50 £1.90 (£152.60) Trio £149.40; £191.59 to 29/7/96 OWNER Mr P. A. Leonard (THIRSK) BRED Highclere Stud Ltd

**2897 Cherokee Flight**, making a quick reappearance, proved troublesome to load into the stalls. Breaking well to push the pace, he was shaken up to lead inside the final furlong, but needed to pull out all the stops to hold on by the skin of his teeth. (12/1)

**Toronto**, a half-brother to three winners, threw away his chance by swerving badly left as the stalls opened. Soon outpaced and hard at work, he made up a tremendous amount of ground late on and only failed by half a stride. Compensation awaits. (16/1)

**2625 Suite Factors**, smartly into his stride to force the pace on the stands' rail, fought back willingly after being headed inside the distance. His turn will come. (6/1)

**2854 Blues Queen** could have found this race coming just too soon and, though she gave chase to the long-time leader, she was hard at work and held approaching the final furlong. (11/10)

**2138 Rivonia (USA)**, taken off her legs from the start, did keep persevering and was stealthily getting herself into it at the finish. (15/2)

**2562 Colonel's Pride** showed plenty of pace in the centre of the track until feeling the strain at the distance. (14/1: op 8/1)

## 3051 NOTTINGHAM FOREST TRENT END MEDIAN AUCTION MAIDEN STKS (3-Y.O) (Class E)

8-00 (8-01) **1m 54y** £3,234.00 (£966.00: £462.00: £210.00) Stalls: Low GOING minus 0.32 sec per fur (GF)

| | Horse | Dist | Pos | SP | RR | SF |
|---|---|---|---|---|---|---|
| 2579[3] | **Milford Sound (84)** (JRFanshawe) **3-9-0** DHarrison(3) (swtg: hld up: led over 2f out: sn wl clr: eased ins fnl f) | — | **1** | 1/5[1] | 70+ | 37 |
| | **Firle Phantasy** (PCalver) **3-9-0** MBirch(5) (led after 2f: rn v.wd ent st: hrd drvn & hdd over 2f out: rallied nr fin) | nk | **2** | 10/1[2] | 69 | 36 |
| 2744[10] | **Topup** (JWHills) **3-8-11**(3) MHenry(2) (led 2f: rdn over 2f out: kpt on same pce) | 4 | **3** | 20/1 | 62 | 29 |
| 2579[15] | **Lady Benson (IRE)** (DJSCosgrove) **3-8-9** GCarter(6) (lw: hld up: effrt 3f out: rdn & one pce fnl 2f) | 2½ | **4** | 33/1 | 52 | 19 |
| 2718[5] | **Tonic Chord** (JRFanshawe) **3-8-6**(3) NVarley(4) (swtg: b: s.i.s: hld up in rr: drvn along over 3f out: wknd 2f out) | 2 | **5** | 12/1[3] | 48 | 15 |
| | **Longano Bay (IRE)** (JPearce) **3-9-0** GBardwell(1) (w'like: str: bkwd: lost tch ent st: sn t.o) | 25 | **6** | 12/1[3] | 4 | — |

(SP 115.5%) **6 Rn**

**1m 44.9** (3.60) CSF £3.57 TOTE £1.10: £1.10 £2.10 (£1.90) OWNER C I T Racing Ltd (NEWMARKET) BRED Equistock Ltd

**2579 Milford Sound** won this poor race in a canter and would have been value for at least six lengths but for being eased in the last 100 yards. (1/5: 1/4-1/6)

**Firle Phantasy** is sure to strip fitter with this outing under his belt, and was fighting a losing battle from some way out, but rallied gamely when he realised the winner was being eased. He has the ability to win races. (10/1: op 4/1)

**Topup** tried hard to make his presence felt but, when the winner took command, he had to admit he had met his match. (20/1)

**Lady Benson (IRE)** had already finished a long way behind the winner on identical terms, so there was no way she was going to redress the balance. (33/1)

**Longano Bay (IRE)** (12/1: 10/1-16/1)

## 3052 STUART PEARCE H'CAP (0-70) (3-Y.O+) (Class E)

8-30 (8-32) **1m 54y** £3,534.30 (£1,058.40: £508.20: £233.10) Stalls: Low GOING minus 0.32 sec per fur (GF)

| | Horse | Dist | Pos | SP | RR | SF |
|---|---|---|---|---|---|---|
| 2513[2] | **Set the Fashion (53)** (DLWilliams) **7-8-11v** DHolland(9) (hld up: hdwy 4f out: led ins fnl f: r.o strly) | — | **1** | 13/2[3] | 65 | 47 |
| 2785[2] | **Orchard Gold (46)** (JPearce) **5-8-4** GBardwell(8) (b.nr fore: hld up: hdwy & nt clr run 2f out: rdn & r.o wl nr fin) | 1½ | **2** | 9/2[2] | 55 | 37 |
| 2513[3] | **Sporting Risk (48)** (PWHarris) **4-8-6** GHind(7) (led tl ins fnl f) | ¾ | **3** | 12/1 | 56 | 38 |
| 2592[8] | **Racing Brenda (47)** (BCMorgan) **5-8-5** SWhitworth(1) (bit bkwd: hld up: hdwy on ins 3f out: kpt on wl towards fin) | 1 | **4** | 11/1 | 53 | 35 |
| 2796[2] | **Just Harry (60)** (MJRyan) **5-8-13**(5) MBaird(5) (chsd ldrs: effrt & rdn over 2f out: edgd lft: nt pce to chal) | 1¼ | **5** | 7/2[1] | 63 | 45 |
| 2521[4] | **Nobby Barnes (41)** (DonEnricoIncisa) **7-7-13** KimTinkler(4) (dwlt: bhd tl styd on wl appr fnl f) | ¾ | **6** | 20/1 | 43 | 25 |
| 879[25] | **Glowing Jade (68)** (JAGlover) **6-9-12** GCarter(6) (bkwd: nvr trbld ldrs) | 5 | **7** | 7/1 | 60 | 42 |
| 1504[10] | **Gool Lee Shay (USA) (56)** (RMWhitaker) **3-8-6** DeanMcKeown(13) (sn prom: rdn over 3f out: wknd 2f out) | 1 | **8** | 33/1 | 46 | 20 |
| 2773[3] | **Kid Ory (62)** (PCalver) **5-9-6** MBirch(14) (lw: trckd ldrs: rdn over 2f out: sn btn) | ¾ | **9** | 11/1 | 51 | 33 |
| 2235[5] | **Needle Match (59)** (CFWall) **3-8-9** GDuffield(12) (trckd ldrs tl rdn & wknd 2f out) | 1¼ | **10** | 12/1 | 45 | 19 |
| *2201[10]* | **Captain's Day (60)** (TGMills) **4-9-4** JWeaver(10) (nvr bttr than mid div) | ¾ | **11** | 10/1 | 45 | 27 |
| 2528[6] | **Mishaweer (58)** (JRFanshawe) **3-8-8v** DHarrison(2) (prom: rdn & wknd wl over 1f out) | ¾ | **12** | 12/1 | 41 | 15 |
| 2526[8] | **Artful Dane (IRE) (65)** (MJHeaton-Ellis) **4-9-9** JCarroll(3) (lw: a in rr) | 2 | **13** | 20/1 | 45 | 27 |
| 2521[7] | **Jimjareer (IRE) (49)** (CaptJWilson) **3-7-10**(3) MHenry(11) (trckd ldrs: rdn & wknd 3f out: t.o) | 11 | **14** | 20/1 | 7 | — |

(SP 132.3%) **14 Rn**

**1m 43.5** (2.20) CSF £37.02 CT £333.71 TOTE £8.80: £3.30 £2.70 £4.40 (£22.90) Trio £46.80 OWNER Mr R. J. Matthews (NEWBURY) BRED The Queen

WEIGHT FOR AGE 3yo-8lb

OFFICIAL EXPLANATION **Orchard Gold: the jockey reported that his mount had hung left throughout and become unridable in the closing stages.**

**Jimjareer: the jockey reported that his mountn had lost his action from three furlongs out.**

**2513 Set the Fashion**, waiting on the leaders, quickened up readily when set alight inside the final furlong and soon put his stamp on proceedings. The rain had arrived just in time. (13/2)

**2785 Orchard Gold**, denied a clear run when poised to make progress entering the final quarter-mile, did stay on well nearing the finish and should have little trouble in picking up another prize. (9/2)

**2513 Sporting Risk** did not impress to post but he adopted catch-me-if-you-can tactics and was only reeled in inside the last 100 yards. (12/1)

**Racing Brenda** still looked far from fully wound up, but she ran a race full of promise and there is another race beckoning. (11/1)

**2796 Just Harry**, restrained just off the pace, lost his pitch when the tempo lifted just over two furlongs out and, though he attempted to rally, he did his cause no good at all by edging left under pressure entering the final furlong. (7/2)

**2521 Nobby Barnes** is at the right end of the handicap, but he just seems to do as much as he needs, and continues to frustrate. (20/1)

**2773 Kid Ory** (11/1: 8/1-12/1)

## 3053 NOTTINGHAM FOREST BRIDGFORD END H'CAP (0-65) (3-Y.O) (Class F)

9-00 (9-00) **2m 9y** £2,381.00 (£656.00: £311.00) Stalls: Low GOING minus 0.32 sec per fur (GF)

| | Horse | Dist | Pos | SP | RR | SF |
|---|---|---|---|---|---|---|
| 2356[5] | **Uplift (49)** (SirMarkPrescott) **3-8-10** GDuffield(1) (swtg: mde all: hrd rdn fnl f: hld on gamely) | — | **1** | 9/2[3] | 60 | 25 |
| 2804[2] | **Marsayas (IRE) (50)** (MJCamacho) **3-8-11** LCharnock(3) (lw: a.p: jnd wnr 2f out: rdn & no ex ins fnl f: fin 3rd, 2l: plcd 2nd) | | **2** | 2/1[1] | 59 | 24 |
| 2191[4] | **Miss Prism (45)** (JLDunlop) **3-8-6** SWhitworth(5) (a.p: nt clr run 2f out: swtchd rt appr fnl f: fin wl: fin 2nd, hd: disq: plcd 3rd) | | **3** | 5/2[2] | 56 | 21 |
| 2506[9] | **Sandicliffe (USA) (56)** (BWHills) **3-9-3** DHolland(4) (lw: hld up: hdwy 5f out: hrd rdn & one pce fnl 2f) | 7 | **4** | 7/1 | 58 | 23 |
| 2120[2] | **State Approval (60)** (APJarvis) **3-9-7** DHarrison(7) (lw: hld up: pushed along 3f out: grad faded) | 1¼ | **5** | 7/1 | 61 | 26 |
| 763[9] | **Hallikeld (42)** (TJEtherington) **3-8-3** JLowe(2) (chsd wnr: rdn 3f out: sn btn) | 1½ | **6** | 25/1 | 41 | 6 |
| 2627[7] | **Lagan (42)** (PSFelgate) **3-8-0**(3) DWright(8) (swtg: hld up in rr: effrt 3f out: no imp) | nk | **7** | 20/1 | 41 | 6 |
| 2314[5] | **Kings Nightclub (44)** (JWhite) **3-8-2**(3)ow2 SDrowne(6) (trckd ldrs: effrt 3f out: sn rdn & btn) | 1¼ | **8** | 14/1 | 42 | 5 |

(SP 120.4%) **8 Rn**

**3m 32.1** (9.10) CSF £14.15 CT £25.52 TOTE £4.40: £1.70 £1.10 £1.70 (£4.50) OWNER Capt J. Macdonald-Buchanan (NEWMARKET) BRED The Lavington Stud

STEWARDS' ENQUIRY Whitworth susp. 4-7/8/96 (irresponsible riding).

**2356 Uplift** put her stamina to good use, but also needed to show her true grit to hold on with not an ounce to spare. (9/2)

**2804 Marsayas (IRE)**, always in the right place to challenge, looked set to score when moving upsides two furlongs out, but he did not find much when put to the test and was held when forced sideways just inside the final furlong. (2/1: 6/4-9/4)
**2191 Miss Prism**, tackling an extended trip for the first time, did extremely well to run the winner so close after being trapped on the inside rail until barging her way through in the final furlong. She was demoted, but showed enough to suggest that staying could be her game. (5/2: op 4/1)
**2062 Sandicliffe (USA)** failed to see the trip out and is still struggling to get it right. (7/1)
**2120 State Approval**, patiently ridden, came off the bridle when the pace picked up early in the straight, and his stamina gave out soon afterwards. (7/1: op 4/1)
**Hallikeld**, out of action since the spring, settled in behind the winner and called enough halfway up the straight. (25/1)

T/Plpt: £37.00 (306.16 Tckts). T/Qdpt: £8.60 (122.51 Tckts). IM

# 2043-**THIRSK (L-H) (Firm)**
## Friday July 26th
WEATHER: overcast WIND: slt bhd

## 3054 E.B.F. MAIDEN STKS (2-Y.O F) (Class D)
2-05 (2-06) **6f** £3,363.00 (£1,014.00: £492.00: £231.00) Stalls: High GOING minus 0.64 sec per fur (F)

| | Horse | | Dist | Pos | SP | RR | SF |
|---|---|---|---|---|---|---|---|
| 2600$^{7}$ | **Sherzetto** | (JRFanshawe) **2-8-11** DHarrison(5) (disp ld 2f: led 2f out: rdn & r.o) | — | **1** | 4/1$^{3}$ | 78 | 14 |
| 2741$^{2}$ | **Princess Topaz** | (CACyzer) **2-8-11** GDuffield(4) (lw: disp ld 2f: outpcd 2f out: kpt on fnl f) | 1¼ | **2** | Evens$^{1}$ | 75 | 11 |
| 2138$^{4}$ | **Naivasha** | (JBerry) **2-8-11** JCarroll(6) (s.i.s: hdwy to ld after 2f: hung lft: hdd 2f out: nt qckn) | 1¼ | **3** | 9/1 | 71 | 7 |
| 807$^{6}$ | **Show Off** | (WJarvis) **2-8-11** AMcGlone(2) (unruly s: plld hrd early: trckd ldrs: effrt 2f out: nt qckn) | 2 | **4** | 7/1 | 66 | 2 |
| 2559$^{6}$ | **Flamma Vestalis (IRE)** | (JLDunlop) **2-8-11** JWeaver(1) (bhd tl hdwy 2f out: nvr nr to chal) | 3½ | **5** | 7/2$^{2}$ | 57 | — |
| | **Sarteano** | (JMackie) **2-8-11** DeanMcKeown(3) (leggy: unf: lw: sn chsng ldrs: hung lft: outpcd & lost tch ½-wy) | 5 | **6** | 100/1 | 43 | — |
| | | | | | (SP 115.7%) | | **6 Rn** |

**1m 11.6** (1.90) CSF £8.54 TOTE £6.30: £3.10 £1.20 (£4.90) OWNER Car Colston Hall Stud (NEWMARKET) BRED Car Colston Hall Stud
**Sherzetto** really knew her job this time and got nicely on top in the final furlong to show she is progressing. (4/1)
**2741 Princess Topaz** was not really suited by the steady early pace, and may also need a galloping track or a bit further. (Evens)
**2138 Naivasha** is still learning and spent most of the race hanging left. There is certainly more to come once she gets it together. (9/1)
**807 Show Off**, who showed signs of temperament before the start, raced too freely early and failed to pick up later when asked the question. She may still have just needed this. (7/1: op 9/2)
**2559 Flamma Vestalis (IRE)**, outpaced early on, was then educated. She left the impression that, over further, she should improve a good bit.(7/2)
**Sarteano**, a lean, leggy newcomer, was wearing a tongue-strap and looked pretty fit, but lack of experience told from halfway. (100/1)

## 3055 TRANSPENNINE EXPRESS H'CAP (0-80) (3-Y.O+) (Class D)
2-35 (2-36) **6f** £3,782.00 (£1,136.00: £548.00: £254.00) Stalls: High GOING minus 0.64 sec per fur (F)

| | Horse | | Dist | Pos | SP | RR | SF |
|---|---|---|---|---|---|---|---|
| 2911$^{2}$ | **Tiler (IRE) (78)** | (MJohnston) **4-10-0** JWeaver(8) (lw: mde all: all out) | — | **1** | 3/1$^{1}$ | 89 | 60 |
| 2725$^{3}$ | **Benzoe (IRE) (77)** | (MrsJRRamsden) **6-9-13** JFortune(7) (lw: bhd: hdwy 2f out: squeezed thro ins fnl f: r.o u.p cl home) | nk | **2** | 4/1$^{2}$ | 87 | 58 |
| 2964* | **Cheeky Chappy (71)** | (DWChapman) **5-9-7b** 7x GDuffield(6) (chsd wnr: effrt 2f out: nt qckn ins fnl f) | 1½ | **3** | 5/1$^{3}$ | 77 | 48 |
| 2946$^{2}$ | **Lucky Revenge (63)** | (MartynMeade) **3-8-8** DeanMcKeown(11) (chsd ldrs: effrt 2f out: btn whn sltly hmpd ins fnl f) | 1½ | **4** | 10/1 | 65 | 31 |
| 2757$^{2}$ | **Dominelle (51)** | (TDEasterby) **4-8-1** LCharnock(2) (chsd ldrs tl wknd ins fnl f) | 3½ | **5** | 6/1 | 44 | 15 |
| 2301$^{7}$ | **Playmaker (71)** | (DNicholls) **3-9-2** AlexGreaves(10) (bhd tl sme late hdwy) | 1¼ | **6** | 25/1 | 61 | 27 |
| 2725$^{9}$ | **Here Comes a Star (74)** | (JMCarr) **8-9-10** ACulhane(3) (in tch: hdwy 2f out: rdn & btn 1f out) | ½ | **7** | 12/1 | 62 | 33 |
| 2787$^{7}$ | **Ned's Bonanza (64)** | (MDods) **7-9-0** 7x JCarroll(5) (lw: mid div: effrt ½-wy: sn btn) | 7 | **8** | 8/1 | 34 | 5 |
| | **Olifantsfontein (47)** | (DNicholls) **8-7-11** JLowe(4) (bit bkwd: nvr nr to chal) | hd | **9** | 25/1 | 16 | — |
| 2722$^{12}$ | **Grand Chapeau (IRE) (58)** | (DNicholls) **4-8-1**(7) JBramhill(9) (s.s: n.d) | 1 | **10** | 20/1 | 25 | — |
| 2778$^{4}$ | **Comic Fantasy (AUS) (75)** | (MartynWane) **3-9-6** DHarrison(1) (lw: hdwy ½-wy: sn in tch: wknd & eased fnl f) | ¾ | **11** | 20/1 | 40 | 6 |
| | | | | | (SP 121.1%) | | **11 Rn** |

**1m 9.4** (0.20 under best) (-0.30) CSF £15.20 CT £52.92 TOTE £3.70: £1.90 £1.60 £2.10 (£7.30) Trio £11.80 OWNER Mrs C. Robinson (MIDDLEHAM) BRED J. Mamakos
WEIGHT FOR AGE 3yo-5lb
**2911 Tiler (IRE)** made full use of his good draw on the stands' rail, and held on particularly well. (3/1: op 11/2)
**2725 Benzoe (IRE)** produced his usual run from two furlongs out but, despite his rider's valiant efforts, was never doing quite enough. He continues in good form with himself. (4/1)
**2964* Cheeky Chappy** had no chance with Tiler on their running at Ayr at the weekend and, in the circumstances, ran well. (5/1)
**2946 Lucky Revenge** ran pretty well, always chasing the leaders, but was just short of a turn of foot to do anything about it. (10/1)
**2757 Dominelle** had her chances but found this just too competitive in the final two furlongs. (6/1)
**1805 Playmaker**, having his first run for his new stable, showed promise for the future. (25/1)

## 3056 ROYAL ARTILLERY HERITAGE H'CAP (0-80) (3-Y.O+) (Class D)
3-05 (3-05) **1m 4f** £3,678.00 (£1,104.00: £532.00: £246.00) Stalls: High GOING minus 0.64 sec per fur (F)

| | Horse | | Dist | Pos | SP | RR | SF |
|---|---|---|---|---|---|---|---|
| 2855* | **Frog (75)** | (SirMarkPrescott) **3-9-2** 5x GDuffield(2) (lw: mde all: qcknd 4f out: shkn up & r.o wl fnl f) | — | **1** | 1/3$^{1}$ | 88+ | 32 |
| 2803$^{3}$ | **Field of Vision (IRE) (71)** | (MrsASwinbank) **6-9-10** JWeaver(4) (lw: hld up: effrt over 3f out: chal over 1f out: r.o) | 2½ | **2** | 7/2$^{2}$ | 81 | 37 |
| 2204$^{4}$ | **Alwarqa (63)** | (DNicholls) **3-8-4** JLowe(1) (trckd ldr: rdn 4f out: wl outpcd fnl 3f) | 9 | **3** | 8/1$^{3}$ | 61 | 5 |
| 2581$^{14}$ | **Reinhardt (IRE) (72)** | (JSWainwright) **3-8-6**(7) JBramhill(3) (hld up: shkn up ent st: sn btn) | 3 | **4** | 25/1 | 66 | 10 |
| | | | | | (SP 112.2%) | | **4 Rn** |

**2m 32.5** (2.50) CSF £2.06 TOTE £1.40 (£1.80) OWNER Mr B. Haggas (NEWMARKET) BRED Mrs P. A. Clark
WEIGHT FOR AGE 3yo-12lb
**2855* Frog** made it five on the bounce and, although she had to be shaken up to make sure of it, she never looked in any real danger. (1/3)
**2803 Field of Vision (IRE)** is running out of her skin at present and really deserves a change of luck. (7/2)
**2204 Alwarqa**, who has changed stables, was dropped back in distance, which did not seem to suit. (8/1: op 9/2)
**2234 Reinhardt (IRE)**, having his first run for his new yard and stepped up in distance, was beaten once the pressure was on turning for home. (25/1)

## 3057 DUNNINGTON CONDITIONS STKS (2-Y.O) (Class C)

3-40 (3-42) **7f** £4,503.00 (£1,677.00: £813.50: £342.50: £146.25: £67.75) Stalls: Low GOING minus 0.64 sec per fur (F)

| | | | | SP | RR | SF |
|---|---|---|---|---|---|---|
| 2538* | **Union Town (IRE)** (SirMarkPrescott) **2-8-13** GDuffield(3) (reminders after s: cl up: rdn to ld 2f out: r.o) | — | 1 | 11/4[2] | 85 | 19 |
| 2404* | **Hen Harrier** (JLDunlop) **2-8-10** JWeaver(4) (hld up: hdwy to chal over 1f out: hung rt & no ex) | 1 | 2 | 8/15[1] | 80 | 14 |
| 2588[4] | **Nostalgic Air (USA)** (EWeymes) **2-8-8** DHarrison(1) (hld up: hdwy 3f out: rdn & btn appr fnl f) | 5 | 3 | 11/1[3] | 66 | — |
| | **Norbreck House** (JBerry) **2-8-8** JCarroll(6) (w'like: bit bkwd: in tch: effrt 3f out: nt pce to chal) | 2 | 4 | 40/1 | 62 | — |
| 2254* | **Avinalarf** (WGMTurner) **2-8-6** DeanMcKeown(2) (lw: led tl hdd & wknd 2f out) | 1½ | 5 | 11/1[3] | 56 | — |
| 800[5] | **Jib Jab** (DNicholls) **2-8-11** AlexGreaves(5) (prom to st: hmpd 2f out: nvr plcd to chal after) | nk | 6 | 50/1 | 61 | — |

(SP 113.0%) **6 Rn**

**1m 26.4** (2.20) CSF £4.53 TOTE £4.10: £1.70 £1.10 (£1.80) OWNER H R H Prince Fahd Salman (NEWMARKET) BRED Newgate Stud Co

**2538* Union Town (IRE)**, a really nice type, was not entirely suited to this track. Given a most forceful ride, he proved too determined for the runner-up. (11/4)

**2404* Hen Harrier**, who is not much to look at, has plenty of ability, although she threw this away by hanging right. (8/15)

**2588 Nostalgic Air (USA)** gave a glimmer of hope when improving over two furlongs out, but soon found this company too hot. (11/1: 8/1-12/1)

**Norbreck House** needed this and never offered a threat, but should have learnt something. (40/1)

**2254* Avinalarf** raced too freely for her own good and, once headed two furlongs out, soon gave up. (11/1: 6/1-12/1)

**800 Jib Jab** met with a little trouble in running and looks likely to do better in nurseries. (50/1)

## 3058 HUTTON WANDESLEY MAIDEN STKS (3-Y.O) (Class D)

4-10 (4-11) **7f** £3,826.00 (£1,153.00: £559.00: £262.00) Stalls: Low GOING minus 0.64 sec per fur (F)

| | | | | SP | RR | SF |
|---|---|---|---|---|---|---|
| | **Intidab (USA)** (JHMGosden) **3-9-0** RHills(7) (trckd ldr: led 3f out: easily) | — | 1 | 1/10[1] | 52+ | — |
| | **Classic Form (IRE)** (RHarris) **3-8-9** AMackay(2) (w'like: unf: a.p: effrt 2f out: r.o: no ch w wnr) | 2 | 2 | 10/1[2] | 42 | — |
| 2393[7] | **Balinsky (IRE)** (JBerry) **3-8-4**(5) PRoberts(4) (led tl hdd 3f out: wknd over 1f out) | 1¼ | 3 | 20/1[3] | 40 | — |
| 2731[10] | **Tolepa (IRE)** (JJO'Neill) **3-8-9** JWeaver(3) (hld up: sme hdwy 2f out: n.d) | 8 | 4 | 100/1 | 21 | — |
| | **Mystical Mind** (DNicholls) **3-9-0** AlexGreaves(5) (w'like: scope: bit bkwd: nvr trbld ldrs) | hd | 5 | 20/1[3] | 26 | — |
| | **Elle Mac (40)** (MPBielby) **3-8-9** DeanMcKeown(6) (in tch to st: sn outpcd) | 2½ | 6 | 200/1 | 15 | — |

(SP 111.0%) **6 Rn**

**1m 28.9** (4.70) CSF £2.15 TOTE £1.10: £1.10 £3.20 (£2.60) OWNER Mr Hamdan Al Maktoum (NEWMARKET) BRED Shadwell Farm Inc

**Intidab (USA)** only had to run up to form to win this and, although he is a slightly edgy individual, he scored easily. (1/10)

**Classic Form (IRE)** still needs to fill out, but she showed some ability under a vigorous ride, albeit without having a chance with the winner. (10/1)

**2393 Balinsky (IRE)** has improved on her debut but, apart from the winner, this was not a very strong event, and there is still plenty needed. (20/1)

**Tolepa (IRE)**, dropping back in trip, ran a little better, and is obviously learning. (100/1)

**Mystical Mind** needed this. (20/1)

## 3059 HABTON (S) H'CAP (0-60) (3-Y.O) (Class G)

4-40 (4-42) **1m** £2,547.50 (£710.00: £342.50) Stalls: Low GOING minus 0.64 sec per fur (F)

| | | | | SP | RR | SF |
|---|---|---|---|---|---|---|
| 2780[5] | **Globe Runner (46)** (JJO'Neill) **3-9-2** GDuffield(9) (in tch: led over 1f out: all out) | — | 1 | 12/1 | 55 | 29 |
| 2507[5] | **Lila Pedigo (IRE) (51)** (MissJFCraze) **3-9-7** AMackay(2) (bhd: hdwy over 2f out: r.o towards fin) | ¾ | 2 | 7/1 | 59 | 33 |
| 2752[5] | **Born A Lady (51)** (SRBowring) **3-9-7b** DeanMcKeown(3) (lw: led tl hdd 1f out: kpt on) | s.h | 3 | 5/1[2] | 58 | 32 |
| 2893[2] | **Dil Dil (45)** (WJHaggas) **3-8-8**(7) CWebb(4) (a chsng ldrs: effrt 3f out: r.o one pce fnl f) | 2 | 4 | 6/1[3] | 48 | 22 |
| 2417[7] | **Polish Saga (44)** (MDods) **3-9-0** LCharnock(16) (bhd: hdwy 3f out: nvr able to chal) | nk | 5 | 25/1 | 47 | 21 |
| 2486[9] | **La Fandango (IRE) (40)** (MWEasterby) **3-8-10** AlexGreaves(10) (s.i.s: bhd tl styd on fnl 3f) | s.h | 6 | 33/1 | 43 | 17 |
| 2391[13] | **Domoor (46)** (MJohnston) **3-9-2** JWeaver(1) (a chsng ldrs: rdn 3f out: grad wknd fnl 2f) | 1¼ | 7 | 5/1[2] | 46 | 20 |
| 2481[7] | **Mill End Lady (38)** (MWEasterby) **3-8-3b[1]**(5) GParkin(8) (cl up: rdn 3f out: wknd over 1f out) | 1½ | 8 | 8/1 | 35 | 9 |
| 2026[9] | **Eccentric Dancer (30)** (MPBielby) **3-7-11b**(3) DarrenMoffatt(6) (s.i.s: nvr rchd ldrs) | 3 | 9 | 33/1 | 21 | — |
| 2411[9] | **Patrio (IRE) (46)** (SCWilliams) **3-8-11**(5) PRoberts(12) (lw: in tch to st) | 4 | 10 | 16/1 | 29 | 3 |
| 2983[11] | **Lahik (IRE) (33)** (KTIvory) **3-7-12v**(5) CAdamson(5) (in tch: hdwy to chal appr st: wknd wl over 2f out) | 1½ | 11 | 66/1 | 13 | — |
| 2417[9] | **Efipetite (38)** (NBycroft) **3-8-8** JLowe(7) (s.i.s: a bhd) | nk | 12 | 33/1 | 18 | — |
| 2563[5] | **Belacqua (USA) (31)** (DWChapman) **3-8-1b** NKennedy(11) (chsd ldrs tl wknd 3f out) | nk | 13 | 33/1 | 10 | — |
| 2898[2] | **Sis Garden (48)** (TDEasterby) **3-9-4b** MBirch(13) (in tch tl rdn & fnd nil 3f out) | 8 | 14 | 11/4[1] | 11 | — |
| *215*[4] | **Common Divine (IRE) (37)** (CMurray) **3-8-2**(5) MBaird(14) (unruly s: bhd fr ½-wy) | 4 | 15 | 25/1 | — | — |

(SP 132.4%) **15 Rn**

**1m 38.3** (1.80) CSF £93.97 CT £459.71 TOTE £19.50: £3.50 £2.60 £2.80 (£71.70) Trio £80.50 OWNER G & P Barker Ltd/Globe Engineering (PENRITH) BRED Badger Hill Stud

No bid

**2780 Globe Runner** found his right trip and, once in front approaching the final furlong, was always just finding enough. (12/1)

**2507 Lila Pedigo (IRE)** was putting in all her best work in the closing stages, suggesting that further should suit. (7/1)

**2752 Born A Lady** both looked and ran well, and left the impression that she might well stay further. (5/1)

**2893 Dil Dil** is in decent form at present but, after holding every chance, was short of any turn of foot. (6/1)

**638 Polish Saga**, ridden from behind this time, put in a much-improved performance. (25/1)

**La Fandango (IRE)** ran by far her best race of the season. (33/1)

**503 Domoor** had his chances, but proved disappointing, and is better on the All-Weather. (5/1)

**Mill End Lady**, tried in blinkers, had her chances, but failed to respond when ridden. (8/1)

**2898 Sis Garden** (11/4: 3/1-2/1)

## 3060 LEVY BOARD APPRENTICE H'CAP (0-70) (3-Y.O+) (Class E)

5-10 (5-11) **1m** £2,777.00 (£851.00: £423.00: £209.00) Stalls: Low GOING minus 0.64 sec per fur (F)

| | | | | SP | RR | SF |
|---|---|---|---|---|---|---|
| 2488* | **Sir Arthur Hobbs (52)** (JLEyre) **9-8-9**(5) TSiddall(1) (a chsng ldrs: styd on to ld ins fnl f: pushed out) | — | 1 | 9/4[1] | 61 | 39 |
| 2903[4] | **Flag Fen (USA) (59)** (MartynMeade) **5-8-13**(8) ClaireAngell(2) (bhd: hdwy 3f out: styd on wl: nrst fin) | ¾ | 2 | 8/1 | 67 | 45 |
| 2874[6] | **Anonym (IRE) (61)** (DNicholls) **4-9-9** CarolDavison(3) (lw: led: clr 5f out: hdd & no ex ins fnl f) | 1¾ | 3 | 10/1 | 65 | 43 |
| 2520* | **Move With Edes (66)** (WGMTurner) **4-10-0** GHannon(6) (chsd clr ldr: effrt 3f out: one pce appr fnl f) | 2½ | 4 | 11/2[3] | 65 | 43 |
| 2925* | **Thatched (IRE) (49)** (REBarr) **6-8-11** 6x PDoe(5) (lw: hld up & bhd: c wd & effrt 3f out: no imp) | 6 | 5 | 5/2[2] | 36 | 14 |
| 1846[8] | **Upex le Gold Too (35)** (LRLloyd-James) **4-7-11** CLowther(4) (in tch: hdwy to chse ldrs ent st: sn rdn & btn) | 3½ | 6 | 14/1 | 15 | — |

| | | | | SP | RR | SF |
|---|---|---|---|---|---|---|
| 2251$^{14}$ | **Oscar Rose (55)** (LordHuntingdon) **3-8-6**$^{(3)}$ CCogan(8) (prom tl wknd 3f out) | 4 | **7** | 8/1 | 27 | — |
| 2963$^{5}$ | **Wacky (IRE) (34)** (WStorey) **5-7-10** JennyBenson(7) (t: bhd most of wy) | 11 | **8** | 100/1 | — | — |

(SP 113.7%) **8 Rn**

**1m 37.1** (0.60) CSF £18.70 CT £124.36 TOTE £3.10: £1.50 £2.80 £2.10 (£20.80) OWNER Miss Donna-Marie Lappin (HAMBLETON) BRED A. Tarry

LONG HANDICAP Wacky (IRE) 6-12

WEIGHT FOR AGE 3yo-8lb

**2488* Sir Arthur Hobbs**, given a fine ride by Siddall who was partnering his first winner, showed he is in tip-top form at present. (9/4)

**2903 Flag Fen (USA)** stayed on from the back of the field in the straight to suggest that he may need further yet. (8/1)

**2874 Anonym (IRE)** poached a useful lead early on, but had nothing more to give when tackled inside the final furlong. (10/1: op 6/1)

**2520* Move With Edes** had plenty to do at the weights and, after chasing the leaders, was treading water in the last furlong and a half. (11/2)

**2925* Thatched (IRE)** was not in the mood on this occasion. (5/2)

T/Plpt: £12.60 (634.92 Tckts). T/Qdpt: £4.90 (69.57 Tckts). AA

# 2746-WOLVERHAMPTON (L-H) (Standard)

## Friday July 26th

WEATHER: fine but cloudy WIND: almost nil

## 3061 GLADIATEUR H'CAP (0-65) (3-Y.O) (Class F)

2-25 (2-26) **5f (Fibresand)** £2,381.00 (£656.00: £311.00) Stalls: Low GOING: 0.09 sec per fur (STD)

| | | | | SP | RR | SF |
|---|---|---|---|---|---|---|
| 2910$^{7}$ | **Marjorie Rose (IRE) (55)** (ABailey) **3-8-13**$^{(3)}$ DWright(1) (b: sn pushed along: bhd tl hdwy wl over 1f out: r.o wl to ld last strides) | — | **1** | 11/1 | 58 | 36 |
| *2748$^{5}$* | **Napier Star (55)** (MrsNMacauley) **3-8-13**$^{(3)}$ CTeague(2) (lw: chsd ldr: led 3f out: clr 2f out: wknd ins fnl f: hdd last strides) | nk | **2** | 7/4 1 | 57 | 35 |
| 2235$^{10}$ | **Maraschino (40)** (BJMeehan) **3-8-1** JFEgan(8) (w ldrs: outpcd 2f out: r.o ins fnl f) | 4 | **3** | 33/1 | 29 | 7 |
| *2305$^{4}$* | **Bouton d'Or (47)** (PHowling) **3-8-8** FNorton(3) (lw: prom: led over 3f out: sn hdd & outpcd: r.o ins fnl f) | ½ | **4** | 9/1 | 35 | 13 |
| 2800$^{10}$ | **Penny Parkes (52)** (JBerry) **3-8-13b** GCarter(5) (hdwy on ins 2f out: wknd fnl f) | nk | **5** | 5/1 3 | 39 | 17 |
| 2528$^{3}$ | **Real Gem (57)** (PJMakin) **3-9-4** KDarley(7) (no hdwy fnl 2f) | 2 | **6** | 4/1 2 | 37 | 15 |
| *2634$^{8}$* | **Kustom Kit (IRE) (54)** (BAMcMahon) **3-8-12**$^{(3)}$ NVarley(6) (nvr trbld ldrs) | 2 | **7** | 20/1 | 28 | 6 |
| *2684$^{3}$* | **Solo Symphony (IRE) (60)** (PWChapple-Hyam) **3-9-2**$^{(5)}$ RHavlin(4) (led over 1f: wknd 2f out) | ½ | **8** | 13/2 | 32 | 10 |

(SP 112.4%) **8 Rn**

**62.9 secs** (4.20) CSF £28.94 CT £572.85 TOTE £11.70: £2.80 £1.20 £8.00 (£20.40) OWNER Sandy Brow Stables Ltd (TARPORLEY) BRED R. Selby and Partners

**2777 Marjorie Rose (IRE)** came through to collar the leg-weary favourite near the line. (11/1)

**2748 Napier Star** might well have lasted home had she not been in season. (7/4)

**Maraschino** found this trip inadequate. (33/1)

**2305 Bouton d'Or** could not take advantage of a 4lb lower mark. (9/1: 5/1-10/1)

**2800 Penny Parkes** had disappointed when the blinkers were left off last time. (5/1)

**2528 Real Gem** seemed to find this too sharp. (4/1)

## 3062 CARLING BLACK LABEL WELCOME HOME CLAIMING STKS (3-Y.O+) (Class F)

2-55 (2-57) **1m 100y (Fibresand)** £2,381.00 (£656.00: £311.00) Stalls: Low GOING: 0.09 sec per fur (STD)

| | | | | SP | RR | SF |
|---|---|---|---|---|---|---|
| *2632$^{2}$* | **Ethbaat (USA) (71)** (WRMuir) **5-9-12** MRichards(13) (hdwy over 3f out: led 2f out: drvn out) | — | **1** | 3/1 1 | 77 | 57 |
| *2636$^{5}$* | **Nicola's Princess (53)** (BAMcMahon) **3-8-7** GCarter(9) (chsd ldrs: rdn & r.o fnl f: nt trble wnr) | 3 | **2** | 9/1 | 60 | 32 |
| *1970$^{13}$* | **Dome Patrol (41)** (DBurchell) **5-8-7**$^{(5)}$ SCopp(11) (hld up & bhd: rdn & hdwy over 4f out: edgd lft over 1f out: one pce) | 4 | **3** | 16/1 | 50 | 30 |
| 2753* | **Clincher Club (66)** (MJohnston) **3-8-11** TWilliams(6) (plld hrd: prom: rn wd bnd 7f out: led over 3f out: hrd rdn & hdd over 2f out: one pce) | s.h | **4** | 5/1 3 | 57 | 29 |
| *2372$^{8}$* | **Jalmaid (54)** (BAMcMahon) **4-8-2**$^{(5)}$ LNewton(3) (prom: rdn over 4f out: wknd wl over 1f out) | 4 | **5** | 10/1 | 37 | 17 |
| *2637$^{2}$* | **Mustn't Grumble (IRE) (60)** (MissSJWilton) **6-9-2** SWhitworth(5) (lw: hld up & bhd: hdwy fnl 2f: n.d) | ¾ | **6** | 10/1 | 45 | 25 |
| *2551$^{2}$* | **Northern Celadon (IRE) (55)** (MJHeaton-Ellis) **5-8-13v**$^{(3)}$ SDrowne(2) (led 5f: wknd 2f out) | 3½ | **7** | 15/2 | 38 | 18 |
| 2731$^{8}$ | **Heathyards Magic (IRE) (60)** (MDods) **4-8-9**$^{(3)}$ CTeague(1) (dwlt: nvr trbld ldrs) | 6 | **8** | 25/1 | 23 | 3 |
| 2716$^{15}$ | **Queen of Shannon (IRE) (44)** (AWCarroll) **8-8-9** MTebbutt(7) (hld up mid div: bhd fnl 3f) | 1¾ | **9** | 20/1 | 16 | — |
| *2632$^{4}$* | **What a Nightmare (IRE) (50)** (PHowling) **4-9-4v** FNorton(8) (bhd fnl 3f) | 2½ | **10** | 16/1 | 21 | 1 |
| 2430$^{5}$ | **Steadfast Elite (IRE) (42)** (JJO'Neill) **5-8-10b**$^{(3)}$ FLynch(4) (bhd fnl 3f) | 7 | **11** | 14/1 | 2 | — |
| | **Colebrook Leader** (JRBosley) **4-9-12** CRutter(12) (lw: s.s: a bhd: t.o fnl 3f) | dist | **12** | 50/1 | — | — |
| *2632** | **Mirani (IRE)** (DJGMurraySmith) **3-8-13** KDarley(10) (a bhd: virtually p.u fnl f: dismntd: fin lame) | 3 | **13** | 4/1 2 | — | — |

(SP 130.6%) **13 Rn**

**1m 51.2** (6.20) CSF £31.22 TOTE £3.80: £2.00 £4.70 £1.60 (£41.40) Trio £144.80; £108.10 to Ascot 27/6/96 OWNER Fayzad Thoroughbred Ltd (LAMBOURN) BRED Shadwell Farm Inc., & Shadwell Estate Co Ltd

WEIGHT FOR AGE 3yo-8lb

Ethbaat (USA) clmd MDavies £10,000

**2632 Ethbaat (USA)** appreciated this return to an extended mile, and is making a habit of providing jump jockeys with their first winner on the Flat. (3/1)

**2636 Nicola's Princess** appears to get the trip well enough, and stuck on well to secure the runner-up spot. (9/1)

**Dome Patrol** probably failed to stay the eleven furlongs at Southwell last time. (16/1)

**2753* Clincher Club** ran too freely which did not help her cause over this longer trip. (5/1: op 3/1)

**1487 Jalmaid** was dropping back in distance. (10/1)

**2637 Mustn't Grumble (IRE)** was possibly too patiently ridden. (10/1)

## 3063 MILLENNIUM & COPTHORNE HOTELS H'CAP (0-85) (3-Y.O) (Class D)

3-25 (3-26) **1m 1f 79y (Fibresand)** £4,378.00 (£1,309.00: £627.00: £286.00) Stalls: Low GOING: 0.09 sec per fur (STD)

| | | | | SP | RR | SF |
|---|---|---|---|---|---|---|
| 2128$^{2}$ | **Deadline Time (IRE) (82)** (MrsMReveley) **3-9-4** KDarley(4) (hld up: stdy hdwy over 4f out: chal on bit 2f out: rdn over 1f out: led wl ins fnl f: r.o) | — | **1** | 5/1 3 | 91 | 51 |

| | | | | SP | RR | SF |
|---|---|---|---|---|---|---|
| *2749** | **Halebid (75)** (SPCWoods) **3-8-11** [5x] WWoods(7) (a.p: led over 2f out: hrd rdn over 1f out: hdd wl ins fnl f) | nk | **2** | 9/4 [1] | 84 | 44 |
| *2689** | **Philistar (67)** (JMPEustace) **3-8-3** TSprake(12) (a.p: rdn 2f out: r.o ins fnl f) | nk | **3** | 11/1 | 75 | 35 |
| 1359[7] | **Whispered Melody (67)** (PWHarris) **3-8-3**[ow1] GHind(11) (a.p: led 4f out tl over 2f out: wknd over 1f out) | 5 | **4** | 10/1 | 66 | 25 |
| *2749[6]* | **Nose No Bounds (IRE) (66)** (MJohnston) **3-8-2** TWilliams(2) (rdn & hdwy 5f out: one pce fnl 2f) | 1½ | **5** | 11/1 | 63 | 23 |
| *2170[6]* | **Le Sport (85)** (ABailey) **3-9-4**(3) DWright(10) (hld up: stdy hdwy over 4f out: hrd rdn over 2f out: wknd over 1f out) | 2 | **6** | 14/1 | 78 | 38 |
| 1714[6] | **John-T (80)** (JLDunlop) **3-9-2** GCarter(13) (wl bhd tl hdwy fnl 2f: nvr nrr) | 5 | **7** | 8/1 | 65 | 25 |
| 444[16] | **China Castle (73)** (PCHaslam) **3-8-9** MTebbutt(1) (nvr trbld ldrs) | 1¼ | **8** | 16/1 | 56 | 16 |
| 2610[4] | **Sunset Wells (USA) (75)** (DRLoder) **3-8-11** DRMcCabe(5) (led over 5f: eased whn btn over 1f out) | nk | **9** | 4/1 [2] | 57 | 17 |
| 2536[4] | **Kingfisher Brave (68)** (MGMeagher) **3-7-11**(7)[ow1] RStudholme(3) (bhd fnl 3f) | ¾ | **10** | 16/1 | 49 | 8 |
| *2934[13]* | **Dragonjoy (65)** (NPLittmoden) **3-7-12**(3) FLynch(9) (prom 6f: eased whn btn over 1f out) | 3½ | **11** | 25/1 | 40 | — |
| *2749[10]* | **Yeoman Oliver (73)** (BAMcMahon) **3-8-4**(5) LNewton(6) (a bhd) | nk | **12** | 16/1 | 48 | 8 |
| 1631[6] | **Velmez (73)** (RGuest) **3-8-9** PBloomfield(8) (a bhd: t.o) | 13 | **13** | 14/1 | 25 | — |

(SP 139.1%) **13 Rn**

**2m 2.7** (6.70) CSF £18.57 CT £123.46 TOTE £7.60: £2.70 £1.20 £4.90 (£17.10) Trio £20.20 OWNER Mr P. D. Savill (SALTBURN) BRED Johnny Kelly

**2128 Deadline Time (IRE)**, making his debut on the Sand, made hard work of it after appearing to be galloping all over the runner-up. (5/1)
**2749* Halebid** defied a 10lb rise in the weights last time, and proved a tough nut to crack under his penalty. (9/4)
**2689* Philistar**, up 7lb, was fighting back at the end over this slightly shorter trip. (11/1)
**1359 Whispered Melody** may just have needed this first run on the All-Weather. (10/1)
**2749 Nose No Bounds (IRE)** is better suited to forcing the pace. (11/1: 8/1-12/1)
**2170 Le Sport** appeared to find this trip beyond his best. (14/1)
**1714 John-T** seemed likely to finish out with the washing for much of the race. (8/1)
**2610 Sunset Wells (USA)** (4/1: 3/1-9/2)

## 3064 JENNIFER SMART ANNIVERSARY MAIDEN STKS (3-Y.O) (Class D)

4-00 (4-04) **6f (Fibresand)** £4,192.20 (£1,254.60: £601.80: £275.40) Stalls: Low GOING: 0.09 sec per fur (STD)

| | | | | SP | RR | SF |
|---|---|---|---|---|---|---|
| 2011[3] | **Pearl d'Azur (USA)** (DRLoder) **3-9-0** DRMcCabe(4) (sn chsng ldrs: led over 3f out: sn clr: r.o wl) | — | **1** | 11/8 [1] | 82 | 56 |
| 2579[10] | **Serious Sensation** (SirMarkPrescott) **3-9-0** WWoods(6) (hld up: stdy hdwy over 3f out: r.o fnl f: nt trble wnr) | 2½ | **2** | 14/1 | 75 | 49 |
| 2579[13] | **Stackattack (IRE)** (PRWebber) **3-9-0** WJO'Connor(7) (prom: outpcd over 3f out: styd on fnl f) | 2½ | **3** | 33/1 | 69 | 43 |
| 840[3] | **Biscay** (RCharlton) **3-8-9** TSprake(10) (led over 2f: rdn 2f out: wknd over 1f out) | 2 | **4** | 9/2 [3] | 58 | 32 |
| 2597[3] | **Domak Amaam (IRE) (78)** (JHMGosden) **3-9-0** GHind(9) (rdn over 2f out: nvr nr to chal) | ¾ | **5** | 3/1 [2] | 61 | 35 |
| 2255[11] | **Mrs McBadger (59)** (BSmart) **3-8-9b[1]** MTebbutt(12) (prom 3f) | 5 | **6** | 20/1 | 43 | 17 |
| 1614[15] | **Mujtahida (IRE)** (RWArmstrong) **3-8-9** RPrice(1) (nvr nr ldrs) | 5 | **7** | 16/1 | 30 | 4 |
| 1497[11] | **Below The Red Line (35)** (MrsNMacauley) **3-8-11v**(3) CTeague(2) (a bhd) | ¾ | **8** | 50/1 | 33 | 7 |
| *779[5]* | **Tashtaiya** (NPLittmoden) **3-8-9** TGMcLaughlin(13) (bhd fnl 3f) | 1¼ | **9** | 50/1 | 24 | — |
| 2432[7] | **Willie Miles** (JWWatts) **3-9-0** NConnorton(11) (bhd fnl 3f) | 6 | **10** | 10/1 | 13 | — |
| 1864[5] | **Tango Teaser** (ACStewart) **3-8-9** SWhitworth(8) (s.s: a bhd) | 1 | **11** | 8/1 | 6 | — |
| | **Foreverfree** (RFMarvin) **3-8-9** FNorton(5) (unf: b.hind: s.i.s: outpcd: t.o) | 28 | **12** | 50/1 | — | — |
| *1855[8]* | ***Press On Nicky*** (WRMuir) **3-8-6**(3) FLynch(3) (Withdrawn not under Starter's orders: rdr uns & inj s) | | **W** | 10/1 | — | — |

(SP 140.7%) **12 Rn**

**1m 14.9** (3.50) CSF £22.42 TOTE £2.10: £1.40 £2.70 £9.50 (£26.10) Trio £117.40 OWNER Sheikh Mohammed (NEWMARKET) BRED Darley Stud Management Inc

**2011 Pearl d'Azur (USA)** was brought back to sprinting and proved too sharp for these. (11/8)
**2579 Serious Sensation** took the runner-up spot without being knocked about. He is one to bear in mind now qualified for handicaps, and a return to a longer trip could well be on the cards. (14/1: op 8/1)
**Stackattack (IRE)** probably needs further, having made his debut at Windsor over a mile. He seems to be going the right way. (33/1)
**840 Biscay** does not appear to have inherited Unfuwain's stamina. (9/2)
**2597 Domak Amaam (IRE)** continues to disappoint, and could not even make the frame on this occasion. (3/1: 5/2-5/1)
**467 Mrs McBadger** was blinkered for the first time, but showed no signs of improvement. (20/1)

## 3065 GERTRUDE RADCLIFFE (S) STKS (2-Y.O F) (Class G)

4-30 (4-32) **6f (Fibresand)** £2,146.00 (£591.00: £280.00) Stalls: Low GOING: 0.09 sec per fur (STD)

| | | | | SP | RR | SF |
|---|---|---|---|---|---|---|
| *2635[2]* | **Advance Repro** (JAkehurst) **2-9-0b** MTebbutt(4) (mde all: clr wl over 1f out: eased nr fin) | — | **1** | 11/4 [1] | 58+ | 24 |
| 2685[6] | **Heavenly Miss (IRE)** (BPalling) **2-8-8** TSprake(2) (chsd wnr: rdn over 2f out: no imp) | 1¾ | **2** | 9/2 | 47 | 13 |
| 2959[2] | **Abstone Queen** (PDEvans) **2-8-8** WJO'Connor(1) (a.p: rdn over 2f out: r.o one pce) | ¾ | **3** | 100/30 [2] | 45 | 11 |
| 2161[12] | **Shandana** (PCHaslam) **2-8-8** GCarter(6) (dwlt: outpcd tl hdwy on ins 2f out: nt rch ldrs) | 2 | **4** | 7/2 [3] | 40 | 6 |
| | **Simply Blessed** (JNeville) **2-8-8** FNorton(8) (b: w'like: bkwd: prom tl rdn & wknd 3f out) | 6 | **5** | 12/1 | 24 | — |
| *2635[3]* | **Dancing Star (IRE)** (PDEvans) **2-8-8v** GHind(3) (rdn over 3f out: sn bhd) | ¾ | **6** | 6/1 | 22 | — |
| 2792[7] | **Lochlore** (MissKWhitehouse) **2-8-8** SDWilliams(7) (s.i.s: bhd fnl 3f: t.o) | dist | **7** | 20/1 | — | — |

(SP 116.9%) **7 Rn**

**1m 17.3** (5.90) CSF £15.03 TOTE £3.60: £1.30 £2.50 (£9.10) OWNER Advance Reprographic Printers (LAMBOURN) BRED Roldvale Ltd Bt in 6,800 gns

**2635 Advance Repro** found no difficulty staying this extra furlong. (11/4)
**1463 Heavenly Miss (IRE)** is currently finding the turf too firm. (9/2)
**2959 Abstone Queen**, making a quick reappearance, lacked another gear over this shorter trip. (100/30: 2/1-7/2)
**1813 Shandana** comes from a stable that is struggling to find form. (7/2)
**Simply Blessed** is a 12,000 guineas half-sister to modest Gunmaker. (12/1)

## 3066 PERSIMMON AMATEUR H'CAP (0-60) (3-Y.O+) (Class G)

5-00 (5-01) **2m 46y (Fibresand)** £2,070.00 (£570.00: £270.00) Stalls: High GOING: 0.09 sec per fur (STD)

| | | | | SP | RR | SF |
|---|---|---|---|---|---|---|
| *1444[2]* | **Milngavie (IRE) (42)** (BSmart) **6-9-13**(4) MissVMarshall(9) (lw: a.p: led over 7f out: rdn over 2f out: all out) | — | **1** | 7/1 | 53 | 31 |
| 2155[2] | **Old School House (53)** (TJNaughton) **3-9-7**(4) MrsJNaughton(7) (lw: hld up: stdy hdwy over 3f out: rdn & chal over 1f out: r.o) | s.h | **2** | 5/2 [1] | 64 | 25 |

| | | | | SP | RR | SF |
|---|---|---|---|---|---|---|
| 2028[5] | **Greek Night Out (IRE) (50)** (JLEyre) **5-10-11** MissDianaJones(8) (hld up: hdwy over 5f out: rdn & ev ch 2f out: wknd 1f out) | 6 | **3** | 7/2[2] | 55 | 33 |
| 2042[22] | **Chris's Lad (57)** (BJMeehan) **5-11-4** MissJAllison(5) (chsd ldrs tl wknd 4f out) | 11 | **4** | 12/1 | 51 | 29 |
| 2717[7] | **Iota (60)** (JLHarris) **7-11-0**(7) MrGWoodward(2) (lw: hld up mid div: lost pl 9f out: n.d after) | 8 | **5** | 11/2 | 46 | 24 |
| *2631[2]* | **Heighth of Fame (55)** (AJWilson) **5-11-2** JCulloty(1) (led over 8f: wknd over 4f out) | 6 | **6** | 5/1[3] | 35 | 13 |
| 2989[10] | **Written Agreement (35)** (REPeacock) **8-9-3b**[1](7)ow10 MrsCPeacock(10) (a wl bhd) | 5 | **7** | 50/1 | 10 | — |
| *2939[3]* | **Stevie's Wonder (IRE) (60)** (BJLlewellyn) **6-11-7** MrJLLlewellyn(3) (chsd ldr over 8f: wknd 4f out) | 1¼ | **8** | 12/1 | 34 | 12 |
| | **Boogie Bopper (IRE) (38)** (BAPearce) **7-9-6**(7) MrJGoldstein(4) (b: sn wl bhd: t.o fnl 9f) | dist | **9** | 33/1 | — | — |
| *2935[5]* | **Broom Isle (57)** (DBurchell) **8-11-0**(4) MissEJJones(6) (prom tl rdn & wknd 7f out: t.o whn p.u over 2f out) | | **P** | 10/1 | — | — |
| | | | | (SP 124.7%) | **10 Rn** | |

**3m 45.9** (18.90) CSF £25.36 CT £69.18 TOTE £7.70: £1.90 £1.80 £2.50 (£19.70) Trio £12.60 OWNER Mrs Lisa Olley (LAMBOURN) BRED D. Oldrey and D. P. Aykroyd

LONG HANDICAP Written Agreement 8-2

WEIGHT FOR AGE 3yo-17lb

STEWARDS' ENQUIRY Marshall susp. 4-5/8/96 (excessive use of whip).

**1444 Milngavie (IRE)** held on by a whisker in a ding-dong battle up the home straight, and his rider collected a two-day whip-ban. (7/1)

**2155 Old School House,** back to the right sort of distance, looked set to score when joining the winner, but his rival would not be denied. (5/2)

**2028 Greek Night Out (IRE)** was 7lb higher than when winning at Southwell in April. (7/2)

**Chris's Lad** seems to have had his training problems and was having his first outing on the Sand in two years. (12/1: 8/1-14/1)

**2423* Iota** (11/2: 7/2-6/1)

**2935 Broom Isle** (10/1: 8/1-12/1)

T/Plpt: £34.00 (250.06 Tckts). T/Qdpt: £8.20 (77.28 Tckts). KH

## 3036-ASCOT (R-H) (Good to firm)
## Saturday July 27th

WEATHER: fine WIND: almost nil

### 3067 CONDE DIAMOND CONDITIONS LADIES' STKS (3-Y.O+) (Class C)

2-00 (2-03) **1m (round)** £7,360.00 (£2,230.00: £1,090.00: £520.00) Stalls: High GOING minus 0.33 sec per fur (GF)

| | | | | SP | RR | SF |
|---|---|---|---|---|---|---|
| 1484[7] | **Hammerstein (101)** (MRStoute) **3-9-11** MrsSEddery(6) (lw: a.p: led over 2f out tl ins fnl f: hrd rdn: led last strides) | — | **1** | 6/1[3] | 92 | 52 |
| 2544[3] | **Green Green Desert (FR) (103)** (LadyHerries) **5-9-13** MrsMCowdrey(13) (lw: gd hdwy over 1f out: led ins fnl f: edgd rt: nt run on: hdd last strides) | hd | **2** | 7/2[2] | 86 | 54 |
| 2041[3] | **Russian Music (103)** (MissGayKelleway) **3-9-11** MissSKelleway(4) (hld up: nt clr run over 2f out: rdn over 1f out: one pce) | 3½ | **3** | 2/1[1] | 85 | 45 |
| 1769[7] | **Faraway Waters (98)** (DWPArbuthnot) **3-9-0** MrsDArbuthnot(3) (b.hind: hdwy over 4f out: rdn over 1f out: one pce) | 1½ | **4** | 13/2 | 71 | 31 |
| 2853[6] | **Brilliant Red (104)** (PFICole) **3-9-5** MissJAllison(9) (nvr nr to chal) | 3½ | **5** | 9/1 | 69 | 29 |
| 705[2] | **Fourdaned (IRE) (88)** (PWHarris) **3-9-5** MissAElsey(7) (lw: hld up: rdn 2f out: wknd over 1f out) | nk | **6** | 20/1 | 68 | 28 |
| 2760* | **Quinze** (SirMarkPrescott) **3-9-9** MissDianaJones(1) (a.p: rdn over 2f out: wknd over 1f out) | 2 | **7** | 7/1 | 68 | 28 |
| 2440[2] | **Squared Away (49)** (JWPayne) **4-9-13b** MissCLake(5) (nvr nrr) | 2½ | **8** | 66/1 | 59 | 27 |
| 2941[13] | **Safety (USA) (33)** (JWhite) **9-9-10b**(3) MissSBrown(8) (swtg: prom over 5f) | ¾ | **9** | 200/1 | 58 | 26 |
| 2740[5] | **Tauten (IRE) (41)** (PBurgoyne) **6-9-5v**(3) MissMO'Sullivan(2) (s.s: a bhd) | 7 | **10** | 200/1 | 39 | 7 |
| 2709[11] | **Causley (35)** (DMHyde) **11-9-13** MrsSBosley(11) (led over 5f) | ¾ | **11** | 200/1 | 42 | 10 |
| 2420[4] | **Mubariz (IRE) (80)** (CSmith) **4-9-13** MissRClark(12) (bhd fnl 2f) | 5 | **12** | 50/1 | 32 | — |
| 2510[9] | **Red Viper (50)** (NMLampard) **4-9-10**(3) MrsDBlack(10) (swtg: s.s: a bhd) | 1¼ | **13** | 200/1 | 30 | — |
| | | | | (SP 115.9%) | **13 Rn** | |

**1m 43.08** (2.28) CSF £24.89 TOTE £5.30: £1.60 £1.50 £1.30 (£9.20) Trio £5.50 OWNER Sheikh Mohammed (NEWMARKET) BRED Sheikh Mohammed bin Rashid al Maktoum

WEIGHT FOR AGE 3yo-8lb

**1187 Hammerstein,** a leading light from the off, went on early in the short straight. Collared by the reluctant runner-up inside the final furlong, he proved far more resolute than that rival and got back in front again in the last few strides. (6/1)

**2544 Green Green Desert (FR)** once again threw it away. Wisely allowed to run his race at the back of the field, he picked up ground below the distance, but carried his head rather high in the process. Nevertheless, he managed to get into a narrow lead inside the final furlong, only to throw in the towel, losing the race in the last few strides. If he is ever going to win again, he will have to be produced virtually on the line. (7/2)

**2041 Russian Music** chased the leaders. Not getting the best of runs early in the straight, he struggled on for third but failed to find that vital turn of foot. Although he has won on fast ground, his trainer reported that he was not stretching out on the firm ground. He will go for a mile conditions race at Goodwood next Saturday. (2/1)

**1335 Faraway Waters,** taking a drop in distance, picked up ground just before halfway. Rousted along below the distance, she found the shorter trip her undoing as she failed to find the necessary turn of foot. (13/2)

**Brilliant Red** stayed on in the last furlong and a half without ever posing a threat. (9/1)

**705 Fourdaned (IRE),** without a run in three and a half months, chased the leaders until capitulating below the distance. (20/1)

### 3068 PRINCESS MARGARET STKS (Gp 3) (2-Y.O F) (Class A)

2-35 (2-37) **6f** £22,295.00 (£8,438.50: £4,131.75: £1,884.75) Stalls: Low GOING minus 0.33 sec per fur (GF)

| | | | | SP | RR | SF |
|---|---|---|---|---|---|---|
| 2782* | **Seebe (USA)** (IABalding) **2-8-9** MHills(3) (lw: hdwy & nt clr run over 2f out: led over 1f out tl ins fnl f: hrd rdn: led last stride) | — | **1** | 6/1[3] | 99 | 55 |
| 2338* | **Moonlight Paradise (USA)** (JLDunlop) **2-8-12** MJKinane(7) (gd hdwy over 1f out: led ins fnl f: hrd rdn: hdd last stride) | s.h | **2** | 11/2[2] | 102 | 58 |
| 2600* | **Raindancing (IRE)** (RHannon) **2-8-9** TQuinn(6) (a.p: ev ch over 1f out: one pce) | 4 | **3** | 12/1 | 88 | 44 |
| 2338[2] | **Queen Sceptre (IRE)** (BWHills) **2-8-9** RHills(1) (led over 4f: one pce) | 1¾ | **4** | 15/2 | 84 | 40 |
| 2611* | **Imroz (USA)** (HRACecil) **2-8-9** PatEddery(4) (hld up: rdn over 2f out: ev ch over 1f out: sn wknd) | 1¾ | **5** | 11/10[1] | 79 | 35 |
| 2073[7] | **Marathon Maid** (RAFahey) **2-8-9** RCochrane(5) (bhd fnl 3f) | 4 | **6** | 33/1 | 68 | 24 |
| 2582[4] | **Eye Shadow** (BJMeehan) **2-8-9** BDoyle(8) (spd over 4f) | ½ | **7** | 33/1 | 67 | 23 |

2327* **China Girl (IRE)** (PWChapple-Hyam) **2-8-9** JReid(2) (lw: spd over 3f) ....8 **8** 7/1 46 2
(SP 115.1%) **8 Rn**

**1m 14.81** (0.81) CSF £35.82 TOTE £7.30: £1.90 £1.60 £1.90 (£16.90) OWNER Mr George Strawbridge (KINGSCLERE) BRED George Strawbridge

**2782* Seebe (USA)**, who made her racecourse debut only last week, confirmed the promise shown at Sandown with a really gutsy display. Moving through to lead below the distance, she was marginally collared inside the final furlong but, showing a tremendous attitude, managed to get back in front again right on the line. A return match with the runner-up in the Lowther Stakes at York next month is on the cards and, irrespective of who comes out best, these are both very useful fillies. (6/1)

**2338* Moonlight Paradise (USA)** made significant headway below the distance. Poking her head in front inside the final furlong, it looked to be the winning move, but the winner proved a real tartar and she was caught right on the line. She lost nothing in defeat, especially as she was conceding 3lb to the winner, and she may well gain revenge at York. (11/2)

**2600* Raindancing (IRE)**, a leading light from the off, had every chance below the distance before left standing by the front two. (12/1)

**2338 Queen Sceptre (IRE)** had a narrow lead from the off but, collared below the distance, could only go up and down in the same place. (15/2)

**2611* Imroz (USA)** was very disappointing. Chasing the leaders, she moved up to have every chance below the distance before tamely folding up. (11/10)

## 3069 E.B.F. MAIDEN STKS (Unraced 2-Y.O C & G) (Class D)

3-05 (3-07) **6f** £6,840.00 (£2,070.00: £1,010.00: £480.00) Stalls: Low GOING minus 0.33 sec per fur (GF)

| Horse | Dist | Pos | SP | RR | SF |
|---|---|---|---|---|---|
| **Revoque (IRE)** (PWChapple-Hyam) **2-8-11** JReid(4) (b.off hind: w'like: scope: lw: a.p: chsd ldr over 2f out: rdn over 1f out: led ins fnl f: r.o wl) | — | **1** | 7/2 2 | 100 t | 56 |
| **Shii-Take** (RAkehurst) **2-8-11** SSanders(7) (w'like: scope: lw: led: rdn over 1f out: hdd ins fnl f: r.o) | ½ | **2** | 20/1 | 99 t | 55 |
| **Shawaf (USA)** (JLDunlop) **2-8-11** RHills(5) (gd srt: lw: dwlt: rdn over 2f out: hdwy over 1f out: r.o one pce) | 5 | **3** | 11/4 1 | 85t+ | 41 |
| **Beyond Calculation (USA)** (PWHarris) **2-8-11** GHind(8) (w'like: scope: lw: hdwy 2f out: rdn over 1f out: one pce) | nk | **4** | 15/2 | 85 t | 41 |
| **Hattab (IRE)** (PTWalwyn) **2-8-11** MHills(9) (str: scope: lw: a.p: rdn over 2f out: wknd over 1f out) | 4 | **5** | 16/1 | 74 t | 30 |
| **Saltimbanco** (IABalding) **2-8-11** TQuinn(6) (w'like: scope: lw: nvr nr to chal) | 2½ | **6** | 8/1 | 67 t | 23 |
| **Homestead** (RHannon) **2-8-11** PatEddery(2) (w'like: scope: lw: chsd ldr over 3f) | hd | **7** | 10/1 | 67 t | 23 |
| **Gentleman's Word (USA)** (MRStoute) **2-8-11** MJKinane(3) (w'like: bhd fnl 2f) | 3 | **8** | 4/1 3 | 59 t | 15 |
| **The Real McCoy** (MRChannon) **2-8-11** RHughes(1) (unf: scope: lw: s.s: a bhd) | 6 | **9** | 20/1 | 43 t | — |

(SP 116.3%) **9 Rn**

**1m 14.94** (0.94) CSF £57.78 TOTE £5.20: £2.10 £3.60 £1.60 (£52.30) Trio £61.60 OWNER Mr R. E. Sangster (MARLBOROUGH) BRED Minch Bloodstock

**Revoque (IRE)**, an attractive, good-sized colt who stands sixteen hands already, was never far away. On the heels of the leader over a quarter of a mile from home, he was woken up below the distance and eventually managed to get in front inside the final furlong. Connections were worried the ground might be a bit too lively, and he will now have a rest. (7/2: 2/1-4/1)

**Shii-Take**, a good-looking colt, was unruly in the paddock. Nevertheless, he bowled along in front and had all bar the winner beaten below the distance. Eventually collared inside the final furlong, he did stick to his task right to the bitter end, and should have little problem winning. (20/1)

**Shawaf (USA)**, a quality colt who is a half-brother to Bint Shadayid, was rather sluggish leaving the stalls and was being pushed along from halfway. Staying on in the last furlong and a half, he managed to snatch third but had no hope of getting in a serious blow. Over further, he should open his account. (11/4: op 7/4)

**Beyond Calculation (USA)** made his effort on the outside of the field over quarter of a mile from home, but failed to quicken from below the distance. (15/2: 6/1-10/1)

**Hattab (IRE)** played an active role until coming to the end of his tether approaching the final furlong. (16/1)

**Saltimbanco**, who is not quite as big as some of his rivals but still has scope, could never get in a serious blow on this debut. (8/1: op 5/1)

## 3070 KING GEORGE VI AND QUEEN ELIZABETH DIAMOND STKS (Gp 1) (3-Y.O+) (Class A)

3-50 (3-51) **1m 4f** £294,600.00 (£109,600.00: £52,100.00: £22,100.00) Stalls: High GOING minus 0.33 sec per fur (GF)

| | Horse | Dist | Pos | SP | RR | SF |
|---|---|---|---|---|---|---|
| 2546 3 | **Pentire (120)** (GWragg) **4-9-7** MHills(7) (s.s: gd hdwy on bit over 2f out: led over 1f out: shkn up: r.o wl) | — | **1** | 100/30 2 | 132+ | 92 |
| 2071* | **Classic Cliche (IRE) (120)** (SbinSuroor) **4-9-7** MJKinane(5) (a.p: led over 2f out tl over 1f out: unable qckn) | 1¾ | **2** | 5/1 3 | 130 | 90 |
| 1791* | **Shaamit (IRE) (120)** (WJHaggas) **3-8-9** PatEddery(1) (hdwy over 2f out: swtchd rt wl over 1f out: one pce) | nk | **3** | 2/1 1 | 129 | 77 |
| 2113* | **Oscar Schindler (IRE)** (KPrendergast,Ireland) **4-9-7** RHughes(4) (lw: hld up: rdn & n.m.r 2f out: sn wknd) | 10 | **4** | 10/1 | 116 | 76 |
| 2583 3 | **Annus Mirabilis (FR) (116)** (SbinSuroor) **4-9-7v1** RHills(6) (led over 9f) | 11 | **5** | 33/1 | 101 | 61 |
| 2111a 2 | **Luso (120)** (CEBrittain) **4-9-7** JReid(3) (lw: bhd fnl 3f) | 1¾ | **6** | 14/1 | 99 | 59 |
| 2276a 6 | **Farasan (IRE)** (HRACecil) **3-8-9** RCochrane(2) (bhd fnl 3f) | d.h | **6** | 11/1 | 99 | 47 |
| 2111a* | **Strategic Choice (USA) (120)** (PFICole) **5-9-7** TQuinn(8) (lw: chsd ldr over 9f) | 1¾ | **8** | 7/1 | 97 | 57 |

(SP 112.6%) **8 Rn**

**2m 28.11** (-1.89) CSF £18.66 TOTE £3.90: £1.50 £1.90 £1.60 (£7.90) OWNER Mollers Racing (NEWMARKET) BRED Lord Halifax
WEIGHT FOR AGE 3yo-12lb

**2546 Pentire** may have been rather dwarfed by his rivals in the paddock but, as he proved last year, size does not matter when you have the amount of talent that he has, and he put up a breathtaking display here. Losing several lengths at the start, Hills had to roust him along for the first couple of furlongs before he came back on the bridle. Still last half a mile out, he made significant headway on the bit early in the straight and cruised into the lead approaching the final furlong. Shaken up, he soon put the issue beyond doubt. It is going to take something really special to lower his colours, especially on a fast surface. (100/30)

**2071* Classic Cliche (IRE)**, never far away, went on over a quarter of a mile out, but he is susceptible over this shorter trip and, headed by Pentire below the distance, was put in his place. (5/1)

**1791* Shaamit (IRE)**, who missed the Irish Derby and the Eclipse, failed to take this but still acquitted himself well. With only Pentire behind him half a mile from home, he made good progress early in the straight. Switched to the rail early in the final quarter-mile, he then failed to quicken sufficiently. (2/1)

**2113* Oscar Schindler (IRE)** looked superb in the paddock. Chasing the leaders, he was rather tightened up for room a quarter of a mile out, but was going nowhere at the time, and was soon back-pedalling. (10/1)

**2583 Annus Mirabilis (FR)** did a good job of pacemaking but, once headed over two furlongs out, soon curled up. (33/1)

**2111a Luso** dropped to the back of the field three furlongs from home. (14/1)

**2276a Farasan (IRE)** is not up to this class yet. (11/1)

**2111a* Strategic Choice (USA)** was very disappointing and, after racing in second place, lost his position quickly over quarter of a mile from home. (7/1)

## 3071 FIREROSE DIAMOND RATED STKS H'CAP (0-105) (3-Y.O+) (Class B)

4-30 (4-31) **1m 2f** £12,462.80 (£4,665.20: £2,282.60: £983.00: £441.50: £224.90) Stalls: High GOING minus 0.33 sec per fur (GF)

| | | | | SP | RR | SF |
|---|---|---|---|---|---|---|
| 2691$^{3}$ | **Behaviour (100)** (MrsJCecil) **4-9-7** JReid(7) (lw: stdy hdwy 3f out: n.m.r 2f out: rdn over 1f out: led ins fnl f: r.o wl) | — | **1** | 10/1 | 107 | 64 |
| 2145$^{9}$ | **Hoh Express (95)** (IABalding) **4-9-2** TQuinn(10) (lw: hdwy over 2f out: led over 1f out tl ins fnl f: unable qckn) | 1¼ | **2** | 14/1 | 100 | 57 |
| 2502* | **Sheer Danzig (IRE) (93)** (RWArmstrong) **4-9-0** WWoods(2) (rdn over 2f out: hdwy over 1f out: r.o) | 2½ | **3** | 13/2$^{3}$ | 94 | 51 |
| 2862$^{11}$ | **King Athelstan (USA) (86)** (BAMcMahon) **8-8-7** PRobinson(11) (lw: chsd ldr: led over 2f out tl over 1f out: one pce) | ½ | **4** | 66/1 | 86 | 43 |
| 1112$^{3}$ | **Clan Ben (IRE) (97)** (HRACecil) **4-9-4** PatEddery(9) (lw: rdn over 2f out: hdwy fnl f: nvr nrr) | nk | **5** | 4/1$^{1}$ | 97 | 54 |
| 2724$^{7}$ | **Billy Bushwacker (92)** (MrsMReveley) **5-8-13** RCochrane(6) (lw: nvr nr to chal) | hd | **6** | 7/1 | 92 | 49 |
| 2557* | **Flying Green (FR) (90)** (NJHWalker) **3-8-1** TSprake(12) (lw: led over 7f) | ½ | **7** | 11/2$^{2}$ | 89 | 36 |
| 2608$^{5}$ | **Henry Island (IRE) (90)** (GWragg) **3-8-1** JQuinn(3) (swtg: prom over 8f) | ¾ | **8** | 10/1 | 88 | 35 |
| 2354* | **Jarah (USA) (100)** (SbinSuroor) **3-8-11** RHills(8) (swtg: prom over 8f) | 1 | **9** | 8/1 | 96 | 43 |
| 2194$^{7}$ | **Otto E Mezzo (90)** (MJPolglase) **4-8-11** MJKinane(1) (bhd fnl 2f) | 5 | **10** | 33/1 | 78 | 35 |
| | **Bonne Etoile (94)** (DRLoder) **4-9-1** RHughes(5) (hdwy over 3f out: wknd over 1f out) | 1¼ | **11** | 7/1 | 80 | 37 |

(SP 114.1%) **11 Rn**

**2m 8.62** (1.82) CSF £119.90 CT £889.58 TOTE £11.00: £3.40 £4.40 £2.60 (£74.10) Trio £162.50 OWNER Mr James Stone (NEWMARKET) BRED Oceanic Development Co Ltd

LONG HANDICAP King Athelstan (USA) 8-2

WEIGHT FOR AGE 3yo-10lb

**2691 Behaviour** gained his first victory over this trip with a useful display under topweight. Steadily creeping into the action in the last half-mile, he was woken up below the distance and found a good turn of foot to get on top in the final furlong. (10/1)

**1793 Hoh Express** moved through to strike the front below the distance. Collared inside the final furlong, he found the winner too strong. (14/1: 10/1-16/1)

**2502* Sheer Danzig (IRE)**, bustled along early in the straight, was doing all his best work in the last furlong and a half. (13/2: 4/1-7/1)

**King Athelstan (USA)** raced in second place until making his bid for glory early in the straight. Collared below the distance, he could only go up and down in the same place. (66/1)

**1112 Clan Ben (IRE)**, still at the back of the field entering the straight, stayed on in the final furlong but, by then, it was too late. (4/1)

**2724 Billy Bushwacker** tried to make an effort on the outside of the field in the last furlong and a half, but could never get there. (7/1)

## 3072 CROCKER BULTEEL H'CAP (0-105) (3-Y.O+) (Class B)

5-00 (5-05) **1m (straight)** £14,135.00 (£4,280.00: £2,090.00: £995.00) Stalls: Low GOING minus 0.33 sec per fur (GF)

| | | | | SP | RR | SF |
|---|---|---|---|---|---|---|
| 2502$^{10}$ | **Yeast (97)** (WJHaggas) **4-10-0** RCochrane(5) (lw: mde all: rdn 2f out: r.o wl) | — | **1** | 7/2$^{1}$ | 113 | 95 |
| 2299* | **Master Charter (81)** (MrsJRRamsden) **4-8-9**(3) DaneO'Neill(6) (lw: s.s: rdn & hdwy over 1f out: unable qckn) | 3 | **2** | 7/1 | 91 | 73 |
| 1793$^{10}$ | **Wakeel (USA) (82)** (SDow) **4-8-13** TQuinn(2) (hld up: hrd rdn over 2f out: one pce) | nk | **3** | 33/1 | 91 | 73 |
| 2145$^{3}$ | **Conspicuous (IRE) (80)** (LGCottrell) **6-8-11** JQuinn(11) (lw: hdwy over 2f out: rdn over 1f out: wknd fnl f) | 3 | **4** | 13/2$^{3}$ | 83 | 65 |
| 2544$^{9}$ | **Beauchamp Jazz (95)** (JLDunlop) **4-9-12** MJKinane(3) (lw: nt clr run over 2f out: swtchd rt: hdwy 2f out: wknd over 1f out) | 3½ | **5** | 10/1 | 91 | 73 |
| 1520$^{6}$ | **Ki Chi Saga (USA) (84)** (JLDunlop) **4-9-1** RHills(8) (lw: nt clr run over 2f out: hdwy fnl f: nvr nrr) | s.h | **6** | 33/1 | 80 | 62 |
| 2283$^{4}$ | **Mihriz (IRE) (72)** (RAkehurst) **4-8-3** SSanders(1) (prom over 6f) | ¾ | **7** | 10/1 | 67 | 49 |
| 2544$^{4}$ | **Kayvee (92)** (GHarwood) **7-9-9** AClark(4) (nvr nr to chal) | nk | **8** | 6/1$^{2}$ | 86 | 68 |
| 2621$^{20}$ | **Nasrudin (USA) (88)** (DRLoder) **3-8-11**ow1 RHughes(7) (lw: hdwy over 1f out: sn wknd) | 1¾ | **9** | 14/1 | 79 | 52 |
| 2885$^{2}$ | **Toujours Riviera (77)** (JPearce) **6-8-8** GBardwell(10) (prom 6f) | 8 | **10** | 8/1 | 52 | 34 |
| 2544$^{11}$ | **Options Open (92)** (MrsJRRamsden) **4-9-9** WWoods(9) (lw: hld up: rdn over 2f out: sn wknd) | 6 | **11** | 16/1 | 55 | 37 |
| 2544* | **Concer Un (91)** (SCWilliams) **4-9-8** MHills(12) (hld up: rdn over 2f out: sn wknd) | 2½ | **12** | 7/1 | 49 | 31 |

(SP 122.6%) **12 Rn**

**1m 40.32** (-0.88) CSF £27.43 CT £641.82 TOTE £4.10: £1.70 £2.20 £7.10 (£12.80) Trio £347.70 OWNER Mr B. Haggas (NEWMARKET) BRED R. T. and Mrs Watson

WEIGHT FOR AGE 3yo-8lb

**2502 Yeast**, who failed to stay last time, reverted back to his ideal trip. Enjoying himself in front, he increased the tempo a quarter of a mile out and was not going to be caught, as he gained his third win here this season. He may now step up in class and go for a Group Three at Baden-Baden at the end of August. (7/2)

**2299* Master Charter**, rather tardy leaving the stalls, picked up ground below the distance and, although winning the battle for second prize, was not going to get on terms with the winner. (7/1: op 9/2)

**1330 Wakeel (USA)** chased the leaders. Under pressure over a quarter of a mile out, he had a ding-dong battle for second place, and only just lost out. (33/1)

**2145 Conspicuous (IRE)** moved up over a quarter of a mile from home, but had come to the end of his tether in the final furlong. (13/2)

**455 Beauchamp Jazz**, buried in midfield over a quarter of a mile out, was switched right and soon picked up ground. The effort proved short-lived though, and he was beaten below the distance. (10/1: 7/1-11/1)

**1520 Ki Chi Saga (USA)**, who failed to get a clear run at the back of the field over a quarter of a mile from home, stayed on in the final furlong to be nearest at the line. (33/1)

## 3073 BLACKNEST H'CAP (0-95) (3-Y.O+) (Class C)

5-35 (5-36) **1m 4f** £7,197.50 (£2,180.00: £1,065.00: £507.50) Stalls: High GOING minus 0.33 sec per fur (GF)

| | | | | SP | RR | SF |
|---|---|---|---|---|---|---|
| 1336$^{5}$ | **Better Offer (IRE) (93)** (GHarwood) **4-9-12** MJKinane(9) (lw: s.s: hrd rdn & hdwy 2f out: led wl ins fnl f: r.o wl) | — | **1** | 6/1$^{2}$ | 102 | 58 |
| 925$^{7}$ | **Beyond Doubt (80)** (LordHuntingdon) **4-8-13** DHarrison(3) (lw: chsd ldr: rdn over 2f out: ev ch wl ins fnl f: unable qckn) | ½ | **2** | 6/1$^{2}$ | 88 | 44 |
| 2674$^{4}$ | **Leading Spirit (IRE) (82)** (CFWall) **4-9-1** PatEddery(6) (lw: led: rdn over 2f out: hdd wl ins fnl f: one pce) | nk | **3** | 6/1$^{2}$ | 90 | 46 |
| 2549$^{2}$ | **Eagle Canyon (IRE) (80)** (BHanbury) **3-8-1** JStack(11) (hdwy on ins 2f out: rdn over 1f out: r.o) | nk | **4** | 12/1 | 88 | 32 |
| 1486$^{13}$ | **Proton (70)** (RAkehurst) **6-8-3** JQuinn(7) (lw: a.p: rdn over 2f out: one pce) | 1¼ | **5** | 16/1 | 76 | 32 |

| | Horse | Dist | Pos | SP | RR | SF |
|---|---|---|---|---|---|---|
| 2603$^{2}$ | **Easy Listening (USA) (86)** (RCharlton) **4-9-5** SSanders(1) (hdwy over 1f out: nvr nrr) | ¾ | **6** | 9/2$^{1}$ | 91 | 47 |
| 2901* | **Percy Braithwaite (IRE) (81)** (MJohnston) **4-9-0** MHills(2) (prom over 10f) | hd | **7** | 15/2 | 86 | 42 |
| 2921$^{2}$ | **Chatham Island (72)** (CEBrittain) **8-8-5** BDoyle(5) (lw: nvr nr to chal) | 1½ | **8** | 7/1$^{3}$ | 75 | 31 |
| 2603$^{4}$ | **Kriscliffe (85)** (MissGayKelleway) **3-8-6**ow2 RCochrane(4) (b: swtg: prom over 10f) | 1 | **9** | 12/1 | 86 | 28 |
| 2603$^{11}$ | **Burning (USA) (83)** (GHarwood) **4-9-2** AClark(10) (a bhd) | 1½ | **10** | 20/1 | 82 | 38 |
| 2989$^{7}$ | **General Mouktar (63)** (BJMeehan) **6-7-10** GBardwell(8) (swtg: a bhd) | 6 | **11** | 20/1 | 54 | 10 |
| 1792$^{9}$ | **Roisin Clover (72)** (SDow) **5-8-5** TQuinn(12) (plld hrd: a bhd) | 5 | **12** | 14/1 | 57 | 13 |

(SP 122.8%) **12 Rn**

**2m 33.76** (3.76) CSF £40.43 CT £207.74 TOTE £7.70: £2.50 £2.30 £2.30 (£19.40) Trio £51.60 OWNER Mrs Wendy Sainer (PULBOROUGH) BRED John McLoughlin
LONG HANDICAP General Mouktar 7-6
WEIGHT FOR AGE 3yo-12lb
**1336 Better Offer (IRE)**, at the back of the field for the first half of the race, made ground under pressure in the straight and managed to get up in the closing stages. (6/1)
**925 Beyond Doubt** appreciated the return to a longer trip and bounced back to form as a result. Racing in second, she threw down the gauntlet in the straight and was one of three in line in the closing stages, before the winner asserted. (6/1)
**2674 Leading Spirit (IRE)** attempted to make all. Given no peace by the runner-up in the straight, he was eventually overhauled in the closing stages. (6/1)
**2549 Eagle Canyon (IRE)** picked up ground along the inside rail in the final quarter-mile, and only just failed to take third prize. (12/1)
**Proton**, a leading light from the off, failed to find the necessary turn of foot in the last two furlongs. (16/1)
**2603 Easy Listening (USA)** stayed on from below the distance without posing a threat. (9/2)
**2603 Kriscliffe** (12/1: 8/1-14/1)

T/Jkpt: £26,954.90 (0.2 Tckts); £30,371.78 to Windsor 29/7/96. T/Plpt: £58.10 (1,040.24 Tckts). T/Qdpt: £15.50 (172.49 Tckts). AK

# 2702-LINGFIELD (L-H) (Turf Firm, AWT Standard)
## Saturday July 27th
WEATHER: overcast WIND: almost nil

## 3074 DAILY STAR MAIDEN APPRENTICE H'CAP (0-70) (3-Y.O+) (Class F)
6-10 (6-10) **1m 2f (Equitrack)** £2,476.50 (£704.00: £349.50) Stalls: High GOING minus 0.45 sec per fur (FST)

| | Horse | Dist | Pos | SP | RR | SF |
|---|---|---|---|---|---|---|
| 2126$^{6}$ | **Hareb (USA) (70)** (JWHills) **3-9-2**(5) RFfrench(7) (lw: a.p: led over 1f out: rdn & hung rt ins fnl f: sn straightened: r.o) | — | **1** | 7/2$^{2}$ | 80 | 33 |
| 2440$^{4}$ | **Docklands Courier (45)** (BJMcMath) **4-8-6** CWebb(5) (lw: w ldr: hrd rdn 2f out: ev ch wl ins fnl f: r.o) | ½ | **2** | 5/2$^{1}$ | 54 | 17 |
| 2710$^{4}$ | **Nakhal (54)** (DJGMurraySmith) **3-8-0b**(5) RBrisland(6) (hld up mid div: hdwy to ld over 2f out: hdd over 1f out: sn rdn: one pce) | 2½ | **3** | 4/1$^{3}$ | 59 | 12 |
| | **Tablets of Stone (IRE) (45)** (JRBosley) **3-7-3**(7) JBosley(4) (led: hdd over 2f out: hrd rdn over 1f out: one pce) | 2½ | **4** | 33/1 | 46 | — |
| 2481$^{4}$ | **Pinkerton Polka (39)** (JParkes) **4-7-11**(3) PDoe(2) (chsd ldrs: outpcd over 4f out: hrd rdn over 1f out: kpt on one pce ins fnl f) | ½ | **5** | 13/2 | 39 | 2 |
| 2693$^{9}$ | **Miss Haversham (67)** (CACyzer) **4-9-4**(10) PGoode(3) (chsd ldrs: t.k.h: rdn over 3f out: one pce) | ½ | **6** | 10/1 | 67 | 30 |
| *2637*$^{8}$ | **Coeur Francais (FR) (50)** (WJMusson) **4-8-8**(3) JWilkinson(1) (dwlt: hld up: hdwy 3f out: sn rdn & btn) | 5 | **7** | 12/1 | 42 | 5 |
| 2594$^{5}$ | **Nivasha (37)** (JFfitch-Heyes) **4-7-12** RMullen(9) (swtg: hld up: hdwy 5f out: wknd over 3f out) | 3 | **8** | 8/1 | 24 | — |
| 2768$^{6}$ | **Tiama (IRE) (53)** (SDow) **3-7-8**(10)ow6 DSalt(8) (bhd fnl 5f) | ½ | **9** | 16/1 | 39 | — |

(SP 120.8%) **9 Rn**

**2m 8.81** (4.51) CSF £12.79 CT £33.90 TOTE £4.10: £1.80 £1.20 £2.50 (£6.40) Trio £13.40 OWNER Mr Ziad Galadari (LAMBOURN) BRED Nancy Dillman
LONG HANDICAP Tablets of Stone (IRE) 7-5
WEIGHT FOR AGE 3yo-10lb
**1319 Hareb (USA)** had been disappointing since his fifth in the Wood Ditton, but looked magnificent in the paddock here. He looked like scoring easily until hanging badly in the final furlong, but his rider straightened him stylishly, and he saw it out well enough. (7/2)
**2440 Docklands Courier**, to the fore throughout, was almost handed victory by the winner's antics. (5/2)
**2710 Nakhal** tried to steal this with a bold move over two furlongs out, but was soon put in his place. (4/1)
**Tablets of Stone (IRE)** cut out the running and kept on well enough once headed. (33/1)
**2481 Pinkerton Polka** (13/2: 4/1-7/1)
**2246 Miss Haversham** (10/1: op 6/1)
**Coeur Francais (FR)** (12/1: op 6/1)

## 3075 DIGICON GEOPHYSICAL (S) STKS (2-Y.O) (Class G)
6-40 (6-42) **5f** £2,343.00 (£648.00: £309.00) Stalls: High GOING minus 0.37 sec per fur (F)

| | Horse | Dist | Pos | SP | RR | SF |
|---|---|---|---|---|---|---|
| 1320$^{3}$ | **Lunar Music** (MartynMeade) **2-8-6** FNorton(6) (lt-f: a.p: led ½-wy: clr over 1f out: comf) | — | **1** | 7/2$^{3}$ | 65+ | 23 |
| 2569$^{5}$ | **Hoh Surprise (IRE)** (MBell) **2-8-6** MFenton(5) (sn pushed along: hdwy over 2f out: hrd rdn over 1f out: styd on one pce ins fnl f) | 1¾ | **2** | 5/2$^{1}$ | 59 | 17 |
| 2764$^{4}$ | **Dozen Roses** (TMJones) **2-8-6b** RPerham(7) (sn outpcd & pushed along: hdwy over 1f out: styd on one pce ins fnl f) | s.h | **3** | 33/1 | 59 | 17 |
| 2685$^{2}$ | **Emilyjill** (RHannon) **2-8-3**(3) DaneO'Neill(4) (chsd ldrs: stumbled sltly & lost pl over 3f out: hdwy over 1f out: sn hrd rdn: kpt on one pce ins fnl f) | s.h | **4** | 11/4$^{2}$ | 59 | 17 |
| 2846$^{2}$ | **Hever Golf Stormer (IRE)** (TJNaughton) **2-8-11** PaulEddery(3) (a.p: ev ch 2f out: sn rdn: one pce) | s.h | **5** | 6/1 | 64 | 22 |
| | **Miss Darling** (JAkehurst) **2-8-6** MTebbutt(8) (prom over 3f) | 3½ | **6** | 16/1 | 48 | 6 |
| 2279$^{6}$ | **Miss St Kitts** (JRJenkins) **2-7-13**(7) PDoe(1) (led to ½-wy: sn wknd) | 3½ | **7** | 50/1 | 37 | — |
| 1959$^{7}$ | **M T Vessel** (JRJenkins) **2-8-8**(3) PMcCabe(2) (prom: ev ch over 2f out: sn rdn & wknd: eased ins fnl f) | 7 | **8** | 14/1 | 19 | — |

(SP 109.2%) **8 Rn**

**59.04 secs** (2.04) CSF £11.51 TOTE £5.20: £1.90 £1.40 £2.60 (£7.00) OWNER Mrs P. A. Barratt (MALMESBURY) BRED T. Barratt
Bt in 5,600 gns
**1320 Lunar Music** had not run for two months, but showed no sign of ring-rustiness in the race, and ran out an easy winner. (7/2)
**2569 Hoh Surprise (IRE)** ran here as though six would suit. (5/2)

**2764 Dozen Roses** stayed on late having been unable to go the early pace. (33/1)
**2685 Emilyjill** lost her pitch when appearing to clip a rival's heels over three furlongs out. She soon recovered but, when asked to quicken, only had the one speed to offer. (11/4)
**Miss Darling** had little physical scope to improve, but did show some early pace here. (16/1)
**697 M T Vessel** (14/1: 10/1-16/1)

## 3076 EAST GRINSTEAD H'CAP (0-80) (3-Y.O+) (Class D)

7-10 (7-11) **7f 140y** £3,794.40 (£1,132.20: £540.60: £244.80) Stalls: High GOING minus 0.37 sec per fur (F)

| | | | | SP | RR | SF |
|---|---|---|---|---|---|---|
| 2789* | **Saleemah (USA) (78)** (JLDunlop) **3-9-9** RHills(3) (a.p gng wl: led on bit wl over 1f out: pushed clr ins fnl f: comf) | — | 1 | 11/8[2] | 91+ | 51 |
| 2980* | **Farmost (81)** (SirMarkPrescott) **3-9-12** 6x WWoods(5) (lw: a.p: led over 3f out: rdn over 2f out: hdd wl over 1f out: one pce) | 3½ | 2 | 6/5[1] | 87 | 47 |
| 2885[11] | **Rise Up Singing (51)** (WJMusson) **8-8-1b**(3)ow3 PMcCabe(1) (sn wl bhd: sme hdwy 2f out: sn rdn & btn) | 5 | 3 | 7/1[3] | 46 | 11 |
| 2711[8] | **Haydown (IRE) (51)** (CTNash) **4-7-11**(7)ow8 JWilkinson(6) (sn outpcd) | 5 | 4 | 50/1 | 36 | — |
| 2347[5] | **Jolto (72)** (KMcAuliffe) **7-9-11** DHarrison(4) (led: hdd over 3f out: sn wknd) | 11 | 5 | 8/1 | 34 | 2 |
| | | | | (SP 113.1%) | | **5 Rn** |

**1m 30.9** (2.10) CSF £3.43 TOTE £2.00: £1.30 £1.10 (£1.40) OWNER Mr Hamdan Al Maktoum (ARUNDEL) BRED Manning Family Trust
LONG HANDICAP Haydown (IRE) 7-2
WEIGHT FOR AGE 3yo-8lb
**2789* Saleemah (USA)** travelled supremely well throughout and ran out an easy winner. She will hold her own in better company. (11/8)
**2980* Farmost** tried hard under his penalty, but was put very much in his place by the winner. (6/5: Evens-11/8)
**2340 Rise Up Singing** appeared to show little interest in proceedings. (7/1: op 4/1)
**Haydown (IRE)** was soon in arrears. (50/1)
**2347 Jolto** is running poorly at present. (8/1: 5/1-9/1)

## 3077 A. R. DENNIS BOOKMAKERS H'CAP (0-70) (3-Y.O) (Class E)

7-40 (7-40) **2m** £2,988.30 (£890.40: £424.20: £191.10) Stalls: High GOING minus 0.37 sec per fur (F)

| | | | | SP | RR | SF |
|---|---|---|---|---|---|---|
| 2191[3] | **Sterling Fellow (51)** (RHannon) **3-8-1b**(3)ow2 DaneO'Neill(5) (hld up: rdn 4f out: hdwy 2f out: str run fnl f: led nr fin) | — | 1 | 11/2 | 59 | 16 |
| 2407[2] | **Influence Pedler (61)** (CEBrittain) **3-9-0** BDoyle(1) (swtg: a.p: led 6f out: hrd rdn fnl 3f: hdd nr fin) | hd | 2 | 3/1[2] | 69 | 28 |
| 2627[3] | **Serious Trust (58)** (SirMarkPrescott) **3-8-11** WWoods(4) (a.p: rdn over 3f out: hit on face w whip over 2f out: ev ch over 1f out: unable qckn ins fnl f) | 1¼ | 3 | 11/8[1] | 65 | 24 |
| 2673[3] | **Chocolate Ice (68)** (CACyzer) **3-9-7** TQuinn(3) (hld up: hdwy over 3f out: rdn over 2f out: styd on ins fnl f) | nk | 4 | 5/1[3] | 74 | 33 |
| *1997[2]* | **Illegally Yours (43)** (LMontagueHall) **3-7-10** JQuinn(2) (led: hdd 6f out: wknd 4f out) | 19 | 5 | 5/1[3] | 30 | — |
| 2159[12] | **Shoemaker Levy (43)** (RJO'Sullivan) **3-7-7**(3) MHenry(6) (lost tch fr ½-wy) | 17 | 6 | 50/1 | 13 | — |
| | | | | (SP 117.8%) | | **6 Rn** |

**3m 33.05** (9.05) CSF £21.88 TOTE £8.00: £3.40 £2.10 (£11.40) OWNER Mr J. A. Leek (MARLBOROUGH) BRED M. J. Simmonds
LONG HANDICAP Illegally Yours 7-7 Shoemaker Levy 6-13
**2191 Sterling Fellow** looked unlikely to score when being ridden along coming down the hill, but he picked up approaching the final furlong, and came with a strong late run to succeed. (11/2: 4/1-6/1)
**2407 Influence Pedler** led at the top of the hill, but was under pressure a long way from home. To his credit, he never stopped staying on. (3/1: 9/4-7/2)
**2627 Serious Trust** was challenging when the leader's jockey's whip hit his face over two furlongs out, and this appeared to unsettle him slightly. (11/8)
**2673 Chocolate Ice** stayed on under pressure in the final two furlongs without ever quite reaching the leaders. (5/1)

## 3078 VAL FORSTER BIRTHDAY LIMITED STKS (0-65) (3-Y.O+) (Class F)

8-10 (8-12) **7f (Equitrack)** £2,666.60 (£737.60: £351.80) Stalls: High GOING minus 0.45 sec per fur (FST)

| | | | | SP | RR | SF |
|---|---|---|---|---|---|---|
| 2903* | **Whatever's Right (IRE) (64)** (MDIUsher) **7-9-2** BDoyle(2) (w ldr: led over 2f out: hrd rdn ins fnl f: r.o wl) | — | 1 | 6/4[1] | 70 | 42 |
| *2934[2]* | **La Tansani (IRE) (63)** (RHannon) **3-8-6**(3) DaneO'Neill(4) (led: hdd over 2f out: hrd rdn appr fnl f: r.o) | ½ | 2 | 7/2[2] | 69 | 34 |
| *2934[7]* | **Hawaii Storm (FR) (65)** (DJSffrenchDavis) **8-9-2** RCochrane(7) (hld up: sme hdwy 3f out: rdn over 1f out: styd on one pce ins fnl f) | 5 | 3 | 14/1 | 57 | 29 |
| 2982[5] | **Fort Knox (IRE) (61)** (RMFlower) **5-9-8b** DHarrison(1) (hld up: rdn & outpcd over 3f out: kpt on one pce fnl 2f) | 2 | 4 | 9/2[3] | 59 | 31 |
| *2934[5]* | **Houghton Venture (USA) (64)** (SPCWoods) **4-9-2b[1]** WWoods(3) (w ldr: ev ch 2f out: wknd over 1f out) | ½ | 5 | 20/1 | 52 | 24 |
| 2718[4] | **Sweet Times (65)** (PFICole) **3-8-6** TQuinn(5) (bhd fnl 3f) | 9 | 6 | 9/2[3] | 28 | — |
| 2403[9] | **Spectacle Jim (49)** (MJHaynes) **7-9-2b** JQuinn(6) (bhd fnl 3f) | 3 | 7 | 33/1 | 24 | — |
| | | | | (SP 113.0%) | | **7 Rn** |

**1m 25.68** (1.68) CSF £6.93 TOTE £2.30: £1.90 £2.00 (£3.30) OWNER Mr M. S. C. Thurgood (SWINDON) BRED Rockville House Stud
WEIGHT FOR AGE 3yo-7lb
**2903* Whatever's Right (IRE)** was always in the van. He railed well on the final turn and quickened a length or so clear approaching the final furlong. He looked like scoring nicely, but had to be ridden out to secure victory. (6/4)
**2934 La Tansani (IRE)** was caught momentarily flat-footed on the home turn, but rallied well in the closing stages to ensure the winner was put to the test. (7/2: op 2/1)
**177 Hawaii Storm (FR)** was never put in the race but the way he kept on suggests a race can be found for him soon. (14/1)
**2982 Fort Knox (IRE)** was meeting his rivals on worse terms here than he would do in a handicap, but ran a sound enough race in the circumstances. (9/2: 3/1-5/1)
**2934 Houghton Venture (USA)** raced prominently until below the distance. (20/1)
**2718 Sweet Times** looked very moderate. (9/2: 4/1-6/1)

## 3079 H.E.A.T. INSTALLERS JULY H'CAP (0-70) (3-Y.O) (Class E)

8-40 (8-40) **1m 3f 106y** £3,124.80 (£932.40: £445.20: £201.60) Stalls: High GOING minus 0.37 sec per fur (F)

| | | | | SP | RR | SF |
|---|---|---|---|---|---|---|
| 2542[2] | **Two Socks (57)** (MMcCormack) **3-8-8** WWoods(5) (hld up: rdn over 2f out: str run to ld wl ins fnl f) | — | 1 | 9/2 | 65 | 24 |
| 1498[5] | **Spinning Mouse (54)** (DMorley) **3-8-5**ow1 RCochrane(3) (swtg: chsd ldr: led over 2f out: sn hrd rdn: hdd wl ins fnl f: unable qckn) | ¾ | 2 | 11/4[2] | 61 | 19 |

| | | | Pos | SP | RR | SF |
|---|---|---|---|---|---|---|
| 2326[3] | **South Wind (58)** (MrsJCecil) **3-8-9** AClark(2) (hld up in tch: pushed along 4f out: rdn over 2f out: ev ch wl ins fnl f: unable to qckn) | ½ | 3 | 5/1 | 64 | 23 |
| 2905* | **Allstars Express (66)** (TJNaughton) **3-9-3** PaulEddery(4) (hld up: took closer order 3f out: rdn over 2f out: one pce) | 1½ | 4 | 7/4[1] | 70 | 29 |
| 2408* | **Minnisam (70)** (JLDunlop) **3-9-7b** TQuinn(1) (led: hdd over 2f out: ev ch over 1f out: no ex ins fnl f) | 1 | 5 | 4/1[3] | 73 | 32 |
| | | | | (SP 117.9%) | | **5 Rn** |

**2m 29.92** (5.72) CSF £16.83 TOTE £4.00: £1.60 £1.90 (£7.20) OWNER Mrs Satu Marks (WANTAGE) BRED R. J. and Mrs A. R. Wakelam

**2542 Two Socks** was held up in the rear travelling nicely. When asked to quicken two furlongs out, the response was not immediate. Brought wide approaching the final furlong, he found his stride late on and snatched victory in the closing stages. (9/2)

**1498 Spinning Mouse** has not run for two months but ran well here, despite getting warm in the preliminaries. She took up the running early in the straight, but was worn down in the closing stages. A race of this type can be found for her. (11/4)

**2326 South Wind** was being nudged along running down the hill, but kept plugging on all the way up the straight, and still had every chance until the final 100 yards. (5/1)

**2905* Allstars Express** was held up just behind the leaders. Asked to take closer order approaching the two pole, he only had the one pace to give. (7/4)

**2408* Minnisam** cut out the early running and, even though headed early in the straight, was still there with every chance until below the distance. (4/1)

T/Plpt: £26.00 (335.38 Tckts). T/Qdpt: £10.90 (53.01 Tckts). SM

## 2327-NEWCASTLE (L-H) (Good to firm)
## Saturday July 27th

Races 2 & 5: hand-timed
WEATHER: overcast WIND: slt against

### 3080 TATTERSALLS MAIDEN AUCTION STKS (2-Y.O) (Class E)

2-15 (2-18) **6f** £3,152.00 (£956.00: £468.00: £224.00) Stalls: High GOING minus 0.17 sec per fur (GF)

| | | | Pos | SP | RR | SF |
|---|---|---|---|---|---|---|
| 2755[4] | **Mujova (IRE)** (RHollinshead) **2-8-3**(3) FLynch(8) (chsd ldrs stands' side: led ins fnl f: r.o) | — | 1 | 5/1[2] | 76 | 20 |
| | **Pericles** (MJohnston) **2-8-5** JFanning(7) (w'like: scope: bit bkwd: led stands' side tl hdd ins fnl f) | 2 | 2 | 7/1[3] | 70 | 14 |
| | **Head Girl (IRE)** (CWThornton) **2-7-12** AMackay(4) (leggy: s.i.s: wl bhd far side tl r.o fnl 2f) | nk | 3 | 16/1 | 62+ | 6 |
| 1664[3] | **Vagabond Chanteuse** (TJEtherington) **2-8-3** LCharnock(2) (lw: trckd ldrs far side: led 2f out: hrd rdn & fnd nil ins fnl f) | hd | 4 | 3/1[1] | 67 | 11 |
| | **My Betsy** (MissSEHall) **2-7-12** NCarlisle(6) (neat: scope: bit bkwd: hdwy far side over 2f out: ch 1f out: no ex) | 2½ | 5 | 16/1 | 55 | — |
| 2495[5] | **Monarch's Pursuit** (TDEasterby) **2-8-4** MBirch(11) (racd stands' side: nvr trbld ldrs) | 4 | 6 | 9/1 | 50 | — |
| | **Double Espresso (IRE)** (MJohnston) **2-7-12** TWilliams(9) (leggy: unf: bit bkwd: swtchd lft s & racd far side: sn prom: ev ch 2f out: sn wknd) | 1 | 7 | 9/1 | 42 | — |
| 2727[3] | **Hong Kong Express (IRE)** (JBerry) **2-8-3** JCarroll(3) (chsd ldrs far side tl wknd fnl 2f) | ¾ | 8 | 9/1 | 45 | — |
| 2720[4] | **Rock The Casbah** (JHetherton) **2-8-4** KDarley(1) (cl up far side tl rdn & wknd 2f out) | ¾ | 9 | 3/1[1] | 44 | — |
| 1827[10] | **Lady Salome** (JGFitzGerald) **2-8-2** JLowe(12) (s.i.s: racd stands' side: n.d) | ½ | 10 | 16/1 | 40 | — |
| 2865[5] | **Loch-Hurn Lady** (KWHogg) **2-7-12** NKennedy(5) (led far side 4f: wknd) | 1¾ | 11 | 10/1 | 32 | — |
| 2519[6] | **Zydecho Queen** (PCalver) **2-7-9**(3) DarrenMoffatt(10) (racd stands' side: prom to ½-wy: sn wknd) | 6 | 12 | 25/1 | 16 | — |
| | | | | (SP 139.8%) | | **12 Rn** |

**1m 15.55** (4.05) CSF £43.93 TOTE £8.40: £2.00 £3.70 £6.00 (£28.10) Trio £251.30; £247.83 to 29/7/96 OWNER Mr J. D. Graham (UPPER LONGDON) BRED Peter Kelly

**2755 Mujova (IRE)** appreciated this step up in distance. Although he was a bit edgy beforehand, he won well. (5/1)

**Pericles**, a useful type, put in a sound first effort and looks likely to improve a good bit as a result. (7/1)

**Head Girl (IRE)**, clueless early on, was a long way behind until finishing like the proverbial train. Longer trips look the answer. (16/1)

**1664 Vagabond Chanteuse** looked a picture, but her attitude under pressure left something to be desired on this occasion. (3/1)

**My Betsy** looked likely to benefit from this and showed plenty. She will do better before long. (16/1)

**2495 Monarch's Pursuit** raced up what turned out to be the favoured stands' side, but failed to offer a threat. He was not over-pushed and is obviously gaining experience. (9/1)

**Double Espresso (IRE)** was switched to the far side which turned out to be a bad move, but this weak-looking individual still showed plenty. (9/1: 6/1-10/1)

**2720 Rock The Casbah** was disappointing here, dropping tamely away in the final two furlongs. (3/1)

**2865 Loch-Hurn Lady** (10/1: 8/1-12/1)

### 3081 THOMAS LONSDALE GALLAGHER H'CAP (0-85) (3-Y.O+) (Class D)

2-50 (2-51) **1m 2f 32y** £4,240.50 (£1,284.00: £627.00: £298.50) Stalls: Low GOING minus 0.45 sec per fur (F)

| | | | Pos | SP | RR | SF |
|---|---|---|---|---|---|---|
| 2803* | **Bulsara (57)** (CWFairhurst) **4-8-4** DeanMcKeown(3) (lw: in tch: slt ld over 2f out: styd on wl) | — | 1 | 11/2[3] | 68 | 42 |
| 2803[5] | **Villeggiatura (70)** (MrsJRRamsden) **3-8-7** GCooksley(1) (trckd ldrs: effrt over 1f out: edgd lft: styd on) | 1½ | 2 | 14/1 | 79 | 43 |
| 2851[6] | **New Albion (USA) (57)** (MissZAGreen) **5-8-4** JFanning(5) (led tl hdd over 2f out: kpt on) | ¾ | 3 | 25/1 | 65 | 39 |
| 2724[14] | **Wafir (IRE) (81)** (PCalver) **4-10-0** MBirch(7) (lw: chsd ldrs: ev ch 2f out: one pce) | 1½ | 4 | 12/1 | 86 | 60 |
| 2536[3] | **Leif the Lucky (USA) (67)** (MissSEHall) **7-9-0** JFortune(11) (bhd: effrt over 3f out: nvr nr to chal) | 3½ | 5 | 12/1 | 67 | 41 |
| 2862[2] | **Komreyev Dancer (78)** (ABailey) **4-9-8**(3) DWright(8) (lw: hld up: pushed along appr st: nvr rchd ldrs) | 1½ | 6 | 4/1[2] | 75 | 49 |
| 2924[2] | **Maid For Baileys (IRE) (75)** (MJohnston) **3-8-12** JWeaver(9) (lw: chsd ldrs tl wknd fnl 3f) | hd | 7 | 11/4[1] | 72 | 36 |
| 2296[2] | **Manful (69)** (CWCElsey) **4-9-2b** NKennedy(6) (drvn along thrght: a rr div) | 4 | 8 | 11/2[3] | 60 | 34 |
| 2483[2] | **Sandmoor Chambray (80)** (TDEasterby) **5-9-10**(3) FLynch(10) (chsd ldrs tl grad wknd fnl 3f) | 7 | 9 | 6/1 | 60 | 34 |
| 2868[7] | **Mill Force (65)** (DNicholls) **5-8-12** AlexGreaves(4) (rr div whn slipped bdly & uns rdr ent st) | | U | 25/1 | — | — |
| | | | | (SP 121.5%) | | **10 Rn** |

**2m 8.0** (1.30) CSF £71.59 CT £1,615.93 TOTE £6.80: £2.20 £3.20 £8.80 (£68.40) Trio £459.50; £200.64 to 29/7/96 OWNER Twinacre Nurseries Ltd (MIDDLEHAM) BRED P. and Mrs Blacker

WEIGHT FOR AGE 3yo-10lb

**OFFICIAL EXPLANATION Mill Force: the trainer and jockey stated that the gelding lost his action and slipped turning into the home straight, thus unseating his rider.**

**2803* Bulsara**, a tough sort who has really improved for his step up in distance, showed fine determination here. (11/2)

**2803 Villeggiatura** is improving fast and, judging by the way he finished, he should get further. (14/1)
**2851 New Albion (USA)** ran a decent race and kept plugging away when headed, but was basically short of a turn of foot. (25/1)
**1476 Wafir (IRE)** has been in some hot races of late and his confidence may well have been dented. This was a more encouraging effort. (12/1)
**2536 Leif the Lucky (USA)** likes more cut in the ground but, in the circumstances, ran quite well. (12/1: 8/1-14/1)
**2862 Komreyev Dancer** never got the run of the race and lost all interest once ridden early in the straight. (4/1)
**2924 Maid For Baileys (IRE)** was disappointing this time, dropping tamely away in the straight, and may have been feeling the race only five days previously. (11/4)

## 3082 JAMES FLETCHER MARQUEES (S) STKS (2-Y.O) (Class G)

3-25 (3-26) **6f** £2,242.50 (£630.00: £307.50) Stalls: High GOING minus 0.17 sec per fur (GF)

| | | | | SP | RR | SF |
|---|---|---|---|---|---|---|
| *2750[4]* | **Perfect Bliss** (PDEvans) **2-8-7** JFortune(8) (mde all: hld on wl fnl f) | — | **1** | 7/1 | 53 | 17 |
| 2926[4] | **Fearless Cavalier** (RHollinshead) **2-8-9**(3) FLynch(6) (lw: a.p: effrt 2f out: chsd wnr fnl f: kpt on) | ¾ | **2** | 8/1 | 56 | 20 |
| | **Coscoroba (IRE)** (JBerry) **2-8-7** JCarroll(2) (w'like: bit bkwd: bhd: hdwy over 1f out: styd on wl towards fin) | 4 | **3** | 9/1 | 40 | 4 |
| 2495[7] | **Sandmoor Zoe** (TDEasterby) **2-8-7** MBirch(7) (chsd ldrs: rdn 2f out: wknd appr fnl f) | nk | **4** | 5/2[2] | 40 | 4 |
| *2307[5]* | **Samspet** (RAFahey) **2-8-12b[1]** GCooksley(9) (prom tl rdn & wknd wl over 1f out) | 5 | **5** | 12/1 | 31 | — |
| 2875[5] | **Alisadara** (NBycroft) **2-8-2**(5) MartinDwyer(4) (chsd ldrs: effrt ½-wy: wknd 2f out) | 2½ | **6** | 16/1 | 20 | — |
| 2429[2] | **Veerapong (IRE)** (MWEasterby) **2-8-7b[1]** DaleGibson(1) (b.off hind: racd alone far side: rdn ½-wy: eased whn btn appr fnl f) | d.h | **6** | 9/4[1] | 20 | — |
| 2850[6] | **Barachois Lad** (JJO'Neill) **2-8-12** KDarley(10) (a bhd) | 2 | **8** | 20/1 | 19 | — |
| 2519[3] | **Kitty Galore (IRE)** (MDods) **2-8-7** JWeaver(5) (lw: prom: effrt & hung lft ½-wy: sn wknd & eased) | 2 | **9** | 7/2[3] | 9 | — |
| 2926[12] | **Petite Risk** (KWHogg) **2-8-7** NKennedy(3) (a bhd) | 1 | **10** | 33/1 | 6 | — |

(SP 136.5%) **10 Rn**

**1m 15.89** (4.39) CSF £65.18 TOTE £8.50: £2.00 £2.10 £2.20 (£35.10) Trio £148.20 OWNER Mr R. F. F. Mason (WELSHPOOL) BRED Mrs H. B. Raw
No bid
**2750 Perfect Bliss** was given a tremendous ride, and answered all her rider's questions when the pressure was on in the final furlong. (7/1)
**2926 Fearless Cavalier** has always looked good enough to win a race such as this, but he took time to get into it and was never doing things quickly enough. (8/1: 6/1-10/1)
**Coscoroba (IRE)**, a decent type for this sort of event, needed it and showed plenty, running on strongly in the closing stages. (9/1: 5/1-10/1)
**Sandmoor Zoe** had her chances, but failed to respond sufficiently when the pressure was applied. (5/2: 7/4-11/4)
**1845 Samspet** had the blinkers on and they did not seem to help at all. (12/1: op 20/1)
**2875 Alisadara** was always racing on what appeared the slower ground on the outside of the field, and was treading water in the last two furlongs. (16/1)
**2429 Veerapong (IRE)** had the blinkers on and raced on her own up the far side, but this proved an unwise move on this occasion, and she was beaten fully two furlongs out. (9/4)

## 3083 SAAB BRECKENBROUGH BEESWING STKS (Gp 3) (3-Y.O+) (Class A)

4-00 (4-03) **7f** £18,816.00 (£7,044.00: £3,447.00: £1,485.00: £667.50: £340.50) Stalls: High GOING minus 0.17 sec per fur (GF)

| | | | | SP | RR | SF |
|---|---|---|---|---|---|---|
| 2622[4] | **Iktamal (USA) (113)** (EALDunlop) **4-9-0** WRyan(6) (lw: hld up & bhd: hdwy on bit to ld ins fnl f: shkn up: r.o wl) | — | **1** | 3/1[1] | 120 | 80 |
| 2337[6] | **Dance Sequence (USA) (108)** (MRStoute) **3-8-4** FLynch(4) (hld up: hdwy ½-wy: led wl over 1f out tl ins fnl f: no ex) | 3 | **2** | 20/1 | 110 | 63 |
| 2880[14] | **Branston Abby (IRE) (108)** (MJohnston) **7-8-11** DHolland(7) (trckd ldrs: hdwy over 2f out: nt clr run over 1f out: r.o fnl f: nrst fin) | hd | **3** | 7/1 | 110 | 70 |
| 2271a[5] | **Kahir Almaydan (IRE) (115)** (JLDunlop) **3-8-7** KDarley(2) (led tl hdd wl over 1f out: sn rdn & btn) | 5 | **4** | 3/1[1] | 102 | 55 |
| | **Wizard King (114)** (SirMarkPrescott) **5-9-0** GDuffield(1) (cl up tl grad wknd fnl 2f) | ¾ | **5** | 6/1[2] | 100 | 60 |
| 2880[8] | **Inzar (USA) (112)** (PFICole) **4-9-4** CRutter(9) (lw: chsd ldrs: n.m.r 4f out: effrt over 2f out: sn btn) | 10 | **6** | 7/1 | 81 | 41 |
| 2691[2] | **Hi Nod (101)** (MJCamacho) **6-9-0** LCharnock(5) (lw: chsd ldrs: hmpd after 3f: sn rdn: wknd fnl 3f) | 4 | **7** | 12/1 | 68 | 28 |
| 2704* | **Almushtarak (IRE) (107)** (MissGayKelleway) **3-8-7** WJO'Connor(3) (b.hind: effrt ½-wy: sn lost tch) | 3 | **8** | 13/2[3] | 61 | 14 |
| 2072* | **Atraf (112)** (DMorley) **3-8-11** JCarroll(8) (lw: hmpd after 2½f: prom tl wknd fr ½-wy) | 1¾ | **9** | 6/1[2] | 61 | 14 |

(SP 129.4%) **9 Rn**

**1m 24.88** (0.38) CSF £55.51 TOTE £4.10: £1.70 £4.00 £1.80 (£61.00) Trio £125.30 OWNER Maktoum Al Maktoum (NEWMARKET) BRED Green Ireland Properties Ltd
WEIGHT FOR AGE 3yo-7lb
**2622 Iktamal (USA)**, who settles much better these days, enjoyed this longer trip, and proved to be different class. (3/1)
**2337 Dance Sequence (USA)**, brought into the paddock late and with two handlers, behaved herself this time and ran her best race for a while. (20/1)
**2692 Branston Abby (IRE)**, never far off the pace this time, just got messed about at a vital stage and would probably have been second but for that. (7/1)
**2271a Kahir Almaydan (IRE)** was able to dominate this time, but he gave the impression that he is a bit of a character these days, and was well outpointed in the last furlong and a half. (3/1)
**Wizard King** put up a decent first run of the season and was certainly not over-punished. He should improve as a result. (6/1)
**2880 Inzar (USA)**, who got chopped off early on and was then always looking for room, never took an interest when the pressure was applied. He likes things to go his way. (7/1)
**2691 Hi Nod** found this company too hot and was struggling and going nowhere from halfway. (12/1)
**2072* Atraf** got bumped and pushed in the first half of the race, and never ran up to anything like his form. The step up in trip can not be blamed. (6/1)

## 3084 GWEN BUSH FOUNDATION AMATEUR H'CAP (0-80) (3-Y.O+) (Class E)

4-35 (4-36) **1m (round)** £3,891.25 (£1,180.00: £577.50: £276.25) Stalls: High GOING: minus 0.45 sec per fur (F)

| | | | | SP | RR | SF |
|---|---|---|---|---|---|---|
| 2954[2] | **Great Bear (41)** (DWChapman) **4-8-12**(5) MrsCWilliams(10) (trckd ldrs: led ins fnl f: all out) | — | **1** | 13/2[3] | 53 | — |
| 2796* | **Mezzoramio (43)** (KAMorgan) **4-9-5v** MrRThornton(11) (b: led tl hdd ins fnl f: rallied towards fin) | hd | **2** | 10/1 | 55 | — |
| 2868* | **Scaraben (73)** (SEKettlewell) **8-11-7** MrCBonner(7) (lw: hld up: hdwy 3f out: ev ch ins fnl f: hrd rdn & nt qckn) | 1½ | **3** | 13/8[1] | 82 | — |
| 2954[3] | **Maple Bay (IRE) (73)** (ABailey) **7-11-7** MissBridgetGatehouse(2) (lw: w ldrs: effrt over 2f out: r.o one pce) | 1½ | **4** | 10/1 | 79 | — |

| | | | | SP | RR | SF |
|---|---|---|---|---|---|---|
| 2678$^{8}$ | **Super Serenade (57)** (GBBalding) **7-10-5**$^{ow5}$ MrJThatcher(8) (bhd: hdwy over 2f out: styd on: no imp) | s.h | **5** | 12/1 | 63 | — |
| 2593$^{6}$ | **Smarter Charter (70)** (MrsJRRamsden) **3-10-10** MissERamsden(9) (chsd ldrs: rdn 2f out: sn btn) | 4 | **6** | 10/1 | 68 | — |
| 2678$^{6}$ | **Commander Glen (IRE) (59)** (MrsJRRamsden) **4-10-7b** MrPScott(5) (bhd tl sme hdwy fnl 2f) | nk | **7** | 10/1 | 56 | — |
| 2214$^{2}$ | **Spanish Verdict (68)** (DenysSmith) **9-11-2** MissMCarson(4) (lw: w ldrs tl wknd fnl 2f) | 1¾ | **8** | 7/1 | 62 | — |
| 2801* | **Hawwam (52)** (EJAlston) **10-10-0** MrMHNaughton(1) (lw: hld up: effrt 3f out: no imp) | hd | **9** | 6/1$^{2}$ | 45 | — |
| 2780$^{4}$ | **Giddy (53)** (JHetherton) **3-9-7** MissPRobson(6) (cl up tl wknd qckly 2½f out) | 4 | **10** | 25/1 | 38 | — |
| 2581$^{18}$ | **Bold Habit (59)** (JPearce) **11-10-7** MrsLPearce(3) (lw: bhd fr ½-wy) | 2 | **11** | 14/1 | 40 | — |

(SP 132.8%) **11 Rn**

**1m 41.7** (2.70) CSF £70.72 CT £147.26 TOTE £8.60: £2.60 £2.90 £1.60 (£62.40) Trio £39.20 OWNER Mr J. M. Chapman (YORK) BRED Exors of the late Mrs D. M. de Rothschild

WEIGHT FOR AGE 3yo-8lb

**2954 Great Bear** has plummeted down the handicap after some moderate performances over the winter and this year, but he showed earlier in the week that he is coming to form, and he did just enough when in front here. (13/2)
**2796* Mezzoramio** is in top form at the moment, and would probably have got back up with a little further to go. (10/1: 8/1-12/1)
**2868* Scaraben** looked likely to win when challenging entering he final furlong, but his response under pressure was a shade disappointing. (13/8)
**2954 Maple Bay (IRE)** had his chances throughout, but was short of a turn of foot to take them. (10/1: 7/1-11/1)
**2379* Super Serenade** ran poorly last time and took some persuading to get going here, but he did finish quite well. (12/1)
**2593 Smarter Charter** ran a bit flat here, failing to pick up in the last two furlongs. (10/1)
**2678 Commander Glen (IRE)** (10/1: 8/1-12/1)
**Bold Habit** (14/1: op 8/1)

## 3085 ABB POWER H'CAP (0-95) (3-Y.O+) (Class C)

5-05 (5-07) **5f** £5,654.00 (£1,712.00: £836.00: £398.00) Stalls: High GOING minus 0.17 sec per fur (GF)

| | | | | SP | RR | SF |
|---|---|---|---|---|---|---|
| 2694$^{3}$ | **Laurel Delight (83)** (JBerry) **6-9-0**$^{(5)}$ PRoberts(6) (b: hld up: led over 1f out: hld on wl) | — | **1** | 13/2$^{3}$ | 92 | 61 |
| 2694$^{7}$ | **Insider Trader (75)** (MrsJRRamsden) **5-8-11** OUrbina(11) (chsd ldrs: ev ch ins fnl f: r.o) | hd | **2** | 9/1 | 84 | 53 |
| 2911$^{12}$ | **For the Present (84)** (TDBarron) **6-9-6** JFortune(9) (bhd: hdwy over 1f out: r.o wl towards fin) | nk | **3** | 14/1 | 92 | 61 |
| 2889$^{10}$ | **Ziggy's Dancer (USA) (86)** (EJAlston) **5-9-8** JCarroll(13) (lw: hld up: smooth hdwy 2f out: nt qckn fnl f) | 1¼ | **4** | 10/1 | 90 | 59 |
| 2911$^{4}$ | **Rich Glow (60)** (NBycroft) **5-7-5**$^{(5)}$ MartinDwyer(8) (bhd: hdwy over 1f out: nrst fin) | hd | **5** | 12/1 | 63 | 32 |
| 2523* | **Time To Tango (71)** (GMMoore) **3-8-0**$^{(3)}$ FLynch(12) (s.i.s: pushed along & hdwy ½-wy: nvr able to chal) | 2 | **6** | 9/2$^{1}$ | 68 | 33 |
| 2548* | **Lord High Admiral (CAN) (89)** (MJHeaton-Ellis) **8-9-8**$^{(3)}$ SDrowne(10) (w ldrs tl wknd appr fnl f) | ½ | **7** | 7/1 | 84 | 53 |
| 2694$^{14}$ | **Surprise Mission (74)** (MrsJRRamsden) **4-8-10** DeanMcKeown(1) (lw: hld up: hdwy 2f out: nvr nr to chal) | hd | **8** | 16/1 | 69 | 38 |
| 2957$^{2}$ | **Shadow Jury (64)** (DWChapman) **6-8-0v** LCharnock(15) (disp ld tl led ½-wy: hdd over 1f out: wknd) | 2½ | **9** | 6/1$^{2}$ | 51 | 20 |
| 2867* | **Just Dissident (IRE) (60)** (RMWhitaker) **4-7-10** AMackay(3) (lw: cl up tl outpcd appr fnl f) | hd | **10** | 10/1 | 47 | 16 |
| 2889$^{9}$ | **Saint Express (92)** (MrsMReveley) **6-10-0** ACulhane(5) (shkn up ½-wy: a rr div) | hd | **11** | 12/1 | 78 | 47 |
| 2003$^{7}$ | **Cross The Border (93)** (DNicholls) **3-9-11** KDarley(7) (hld up: nvr plcd to chal) | 4 | **12** | 25/1 | 67 | 32 |
| 2950$^{5}$ | **Ramsey Hope (70)** (CWFairhurst) **3-8-2b** NKennedy(2) (drvn along thrght: a bhd) | 2 | **13** | 25/1 | 37 | 2 |
| 2694$^{8}$ | **Swynford Dream (81)** (JFBottomley) **3-8-13** JLowe(14) (disp ld to ½-wy: wknd qckly) | 5 | **14** | 14/1 | 32 | — |
| | **Branston Jewel (IRE) (90)** (MJohnston) **3-9-8** JWeaver(4) (lw: prom tl wknd 2f out) | 4 | **15** | 6/1$^{2}$ | 28 | — |

(SP 143.1%) **15 Rn**

**59.98 secs** (1.58) CSF £69.40 CT £767.00 TOTE £7.40: £2.50 £4.20 £4.10 (£56.60) Trio £526.00 OWNER Laurel (Leisure) Ltd (COCKERHAM) BRED G. Blum and Ridgebarn Farm

LONG HANDICAP Just Dissident (IRE) 7-8

WEIGHT FOR AGE 3yo-4lb

**2694 Laurel Delight** is in really good form just now and showed fine courage to hold on. (13/2)
**2694 Insider Trader**, without the headgear, ran a cracking race but, after looking likely to win, just failed to quicken late on. (9/1)
**2694 For the Present** ran a stinker last weekend, but finished with a tremendous burst and would probably have won in a couple more strides. (14/1)
**2698 Ziggy's Dancer (USA)** has not really been firing this time round but he did travel well on this occasion, only failing to quicken further inside the final furlong. He may well be coming to form. (10/1)
**2911 Rich Glow**, happier back at this trip, only got going when it was all too late. (12/1)
**2523* Time To Tango** was always struggling to recover from a tardy start and never got in a serious blow. (9/2)
**1974 Surprise Mission** ran well from his draw and looks well worth keeping in mind. (16/1)
**2867* Just Dissident (IRE)** was always struggling from a bad draw. (10/1)
**1394a Cross The Border** was not knocked about and looks interesting now that he has changed stables. (25/1)

T/Plpt: £4,663.40 (3.88 Tckts). T/Qdpt: £50.50 (26.97 Tckts). AA

# 2934-SOUTHWELL (L-H) (Standard)

## Saturday July 27th

WEATHER: fine WIND: slt half bhd

## 3086 WHISKY H'CAP (0-60) (3-Y.O+ F & M) (Class F)

6-25 (6-30) **1m 4f (Fibresand)** £2,381.00 (£656.00: £311.00) Stalls: Low GOING: 0.04 sec per fur (STD)

| | | | | SP | RR | SF |
|---|---|---|---|---|---|---|
| 1803$^{9}$ | **Glow Forum (39)** (LMontagueHall) **5-9-3** DHolland(2) (mde virtually all: clr over 2f out: hung rt & styd on u.p fnl f) | — | **1** | 6/1$^{2}$ | 55 | 35 |
| *2936** | **Shirley Sue (61)** (MJohnston) **3-9-13** $^{5x}$ JFanning(9) (unruly in stalls: sn bhd & pushed along: hdwy on outside 7f out: chsd wnr fnl 2f: hung lft & no imp) | 3 | **2** | 8/11$^{1}$ | 73 | 41 |
| 1870$^{6}$ | **Moonlight Calypso (41)** (MGMeagher) **5-9-5** GCarter(1) (sn bhd: hdwy on outside 5f out: one pce fnl 3f) | 13 | **3** | 8/1$^{3}$ | 36 | 16 |
| *2936*$^{13}$ | **Anchorena (46)** (MrsASwinbank) **4-9-10** GDuffield(13) (a chsng ldrs: hung lft over 2f out: one pce) | 5 | **4** | 12/1 | 34 | 14 |
| 2906* | **Zeliba (28)** (MrsNMacauley) **4-8-6** JTate(10) (hdwy 6f out: sn chsng ldrs: rdn & wknd over 2f out) | 14 | **5** | 8/1$^{3}$ | — | — |
| 2683$^{6}$ | **Tryph (42)** (MDHammond) **4-9-1**$^{(5)}$ DGriffiths(12) (hld up: stdy hdwy 5f out: wknd over 2f out) | 1 | **6** | 25/1 | 10 | — |
| 2530$^{7}$ | **Glowing Reeds (39)** (CNAllen) **3-8-5v** NAdams(7) (unruly s: reminders after 1f: chsd ldrs tl lost pl 5f out) | ¾ | **7** | 16/1 | 6 | — |
| 2891$^{14}$ | **Lucy's Gold (20)** (MJRyan) **5-7-7**$^{(5)ow2}$ MBaird(11) (sn wl bhd: sme hdwy 2f out: n.d) | 5 | **8** | 33/1 | — | — |
| 2776$^{7}$ | **Bardia (28)** (DonEnricoIncisa) **6-8-6** KimTinkler(6) (sn bhd & pushed along: sme hdwy 4f out: n.d) | hd | **9** | 33/1 | — | — |
| 2891$^{11}$ | **Patscilla (33)** (RDickin) **5-8-11** TWilliams(3) (in tch: sn rdn along: lost pl 6f out: t.o 4f out) | 14 | **10** | 33/1 | — | — |

| | | | | |
|---|---|---|---|---|
| 2537[12] **Rose Chime (IRE) (34)** (JLHarris) **4-8-12b[1]** DaleGibson(8) (plld hrd: w ldrs tl lost pl 5f out: sn bhd) 1¼ | **11** | 33/1 | — | — |
| 2540[7] **Infantry Dancer (56)** (GCBravery) **3-9-8** SWhitworth(5) (b.hind: sn chsng ldrs: rdn & wknd 5f out) 20 | **12** | 16/1 | — | — |
| **Miss Michelle (24)** (EAWheeler) **6-7-11**(5) ADaly(4) (v.unruly: a wl bhd) ¾ | **13** | 33/1 | — | — |

(SP 132.4%) **13 Rn**

**2m 43.0** (10.50) CSF £11.16 CT £35.07 TOTE £6.20: £2.00 £1.10 £3.00 (£5.20) Trio £30.50 OWNER The Forum Ltd (EPSOM) BRED Forum Bloodstock Ltd

WEIGHT FOR AGE 3yo-12lb

STEWARDS' ENQUIRY Adams susp. 5-6/8/96 (incorrect use of whip).

**1347* Glow Forum**, a winner on soft ground, made the most of her stamina. Kicking clear off the bend, she never looked in any real danger of being caught. (6/1)

**2936* Shirley Sue**, due to the delay at the start, became badly upset in the stalls and had to be let out. Playing up when put back in them, she struggled to go the pace. Though keeping on in the final two furlongs, she was always hanging left and was never going to get on terms. (8/11)

**1870 Moonlight Calypso**, stepping up on her first effort, kept on in her own time. (8/1: op 12/1)

**2217 Anchorena** is by no means consistent. (12/1)

## 3087 BBC RADIO NOTTINGHAM BREAKFAST WITH THE LYNCH'S CLAIMING STKS (2-Y.O) (Class F)

6-55 (6-55) **6f (Fibresand)** £2,381.00 (£656.00: £311.00) Stalls: Low GOING: 0.04 sec per fur (STD)

| | | SP | RR | SF |
|---|---|---|---|---|
| 2875[6] **Perpetual** (SirMarkPrescott) **2-8-12** GDuffield(6) (mde virtually all: styd on u.p appr fnl f: jst hld on) — | **1** | 5/2[2] | 58 | 19 |
| 2795[5] **Jingoist (IRE)** (JLHarris) **2-8-2b** DaleGibson(5) (a chsng ldrs: rdn 2f out: styd on wl ins fnl f) ½ | **2** | 14/1 | 47 | 8 |
| 2685[4] **Eager To Please** (JBerry) **2-8-11** GCarter(4) (w wnr: kpt on same pce appr fnl f) ¾ | **3** | 9/4[1] | 54 | 15 |
| 2926[8] **Lycius Touch** (MJohnston) **2-8-8** TWilliams(3) (sn outpcd & drvn along: lost pl after 2f) 8 | **4** | 100/30[3] | 29 | — |
| *2938[4]* **Oddfellows Girl** (NBycroft) **2-8-5**(3) CTeague(1) (outpcd & bhd after 2f) 3 | **5** | 12/1 | 21 | — |
| *2938[2]* **Bonsiel** (JGFitzGerald) **2-8-0** JFanning(2) (chsd ldrs tl outpcd over 2f out: sn bhd) 18 | **6** | 5/1 | — | — |

(SP 113.4%) **6 Rn**

**1m 19.5** (6.00) CSF £28.09 TOTE £3.30: £1.70 £3.30 (£24.50) OWNER Cheveley Park Stud (NEWMARKET) BRED Cheveley Park Stud Ltd

**2875 Perpetual** was persuaded to do just enough. With her stamina giving out on this testing surface, the line came just in time. (5/2)

**2795 Jingoist (IRE)**, on her toes beforehand, wore blinkers again. Really finding her stride inside the last, she would have got there in another few strides. (14/1)

**2685 Eager To Please**, well supported in the market, appeared to run her best race to date. (9/4: op 4/1)

**2728 Lycius Touch**, very much on her toes beforehand, seems to have lost what speed she had. Soon flat out, she was struggling badly in the last quarter-mile. (100/30)

**2938 Oddfellows Girl** (12/1: 8/1-14/1)

## 3088 MAUN MOTORS MEDIAN AUCTION MAIDEN STKS (2-Y.O F) (Class F)

7-25 (7-26) **7f (Fibresand)** £2,381.00 (£656.00: £311.00) Stalls: Low GOING: 0.04 sec per fur (STD)

| | | SP | RR | SF |
|---|---|---|---|---|
| *1968[8]* **Lucky Oakwood (USA)** (MBell) **2-8-4**(7) GFaulkner(6) (mde all: clr 2f out: rdn out) — | **1** | 9/2[3] | 65 | 32 |
| **Davis Rock** (SirMarkPrescott) **2-8-11** GDuffield(4) (w'like: swvd lft s: sn chsng ldrs: wnt 2nd 2f out: rdn & hung lft: no imp) 7 | **2** | 15/8[1] | 49 | 16 |
| 2187[4] **Dizzy Tilly** (TJNaughton) **2-8-11** DHolland(1) (lw: w wnr: rdn over 2f out: sn wknd) 6 | **3** | 3/1[2] | 35 | 2 |
| 2781[6] **Miss Alice** (JNorton) **2-8-11** DaleGibson(5) (chsd ldrs: outpcd over 2f out: n.d) 2 | **4** | 12/1 | 31 | — |
| **Silver Moon** (BAMcMahon) **2-8-6**(5) LNewton(3) (sltly hmpd s: sn chsng ldrs: wl outpcd fr ½-wy) 9 | **5** | 14/1 | 10 | — |
| *2746[5]* **Mirror Four Sport** (MJohnston) **2-8-11** JFanning(2) (hld up & plld hrd: rdn 4f out: sn bhd) 6 | **6** | 13/2 | — | — |
| 1954[7] **Incandescent** (APJones) **2-8-11** TSprake(7) (hung bdly rt thrght: rn wd & lost pl 4f out: sn t.o) dist | **7** | 6/1 | — | — |

(SP 119.9%) **7 Rn**

**1m 32.6** (5.80) CSF £13.71 TOTE £5.80: £2.20 £1.70 (£6.80) OWNER Sporting Quest (NEWMARKET) BRED Lantern Hill Farm

**OFFICIAL EXPLANATION Incandescent: hung severley right-handed.**

**Lucky Oakwood (USA): on her previous run she had been hanging and unable to let herself down on the surface, but she had returned home with sore shins after that race.**

**1086 Lucky Oakwood (USA)**, who had run very badly here last time, bounced back after a six-week lay-off and was out on her own with her race won soon after passing the two-furlong marker. Showing a very poor action, she had to be kept right up to her work. (9/2: op 5/2)

**Davis Rock**, a desperate mover, went in pursuit of the winner two furlongs out. Tending to hang, she was never going to get near. (15/8)

**2187 Dizzy Tilly** has a powerful action, but was in trouble soon after halfway. (3/1)

**2781 Miss Alice** was under pressure and going nowhere on the home turn. (12/1: 8/1-14/1)

**2746 Mirror Four Sport** gave her rider problems going to post. Dropped in at the start and pulling hard, she wanted nothing to do with it. (13/2)

## 3089 GRANGE FARM BARNBY MOOR H'CAP (0-70) (3-Y.O+) (Class E)

7-55 (7-56) **7f (Fibresand)** £3,425.10 (£1,024.80: £491.40: £224.70) Stalls: Low GOING: 0.04 sec per fur (STD)

| | | SP | RR | SF |
|---|---|---|---|---|
| 2577[5] **Barrack Yard (55)** (ACStewart) **3-8-6** SWhitworth(8) (trckd ldrs: led over 1f out: sn rdn: jst hld on) — | **1** | 7/1[2] | 67 | 42 |
| *2552[5]* **Desert Invader (IRE) (70)** (DWChapman) **5-10-0** ACulhane(5) (lw: chsd ldrs: led over 3f out tl over 1f out: styd on towards fin) hd | **2** | 9/1 | 82 | 64 |
| *2084[4]* **Elton Ledger (IRE) (70)** (MrsNMacauley) **7-10-0v** EmmaO'Gorman(15) (lw: b: trckd ldrs: hung lft & nt qckn fnl 2f) 4 | **3** | 6/1[1] | 73 | 55 |
| *2369[13]* **Seeking Destiny (IRE) (51)** (MCChapman) **3-7-11b**(5) MBaird(16) (sn drvn along: chsd ldrs: outpcd over 2f out: kpt on fnl f) 2½ | **4** | 16/1 | 48 | 23 |
| 2672[6] **Angus McCoatup (IRE) (56)** (BAMcMahon) **3-8-7b** GDuffield(9) (lw: bhd: styd on fnl 2f: nvr nr to chal) ½ | **5** | 10/1 | 52 | 27 |
| *2940[5]* **Lady Silk (50)** (MissJFCraze) **5-8-8** NConnorton(2) (a chsng ldrs: kpt on same pce fnl 2f) s.h | **6** | 8/1[3] | 46 | 28 |
| *2940[7]* **Great Hall (43)** (JAHarris) **7-8-1b** GCarter(14) (b.hind: s.i.s: bhd tl styd on fnl 2f) s.h | **7** | 12/1 | 39 | 21 |
| 2376[11] **Ism (70)** (MajorWRHern) **4-10-0b** TSprake(11) (n.m.r after 1f: sn prom: rdn over 2f out: hung lft & no imp) 1 | **8** | 6/1[1] | 63 | 45 |
| 2868[13] **Pc's Cruiser (IRE) (43)** (JLEyre) **4-8-1** TWilliams(3) (lw: bhd & drvn along: sme hdwy on outside 2f out: hung lft & sn wknd) 2½ | **9** | 6/1[1] | 31 | 13 |
| **Ivan the Terrible (IRE) (44)** (BEllison) **8-8-2** JTate(4) (b: chsd ldrs tl wknd over 2f out) 3 | **10** | 14/1 | 25 | 7 |
| 2918[9] **Enamel Tiger (48)** (KMcAuliffe) **3-7-13** NCarlisle(1) (dwlt s: a rr div) 2½ | **11** | 16/1 | 23 | — |
| *2631[8]* **Righteous Gent (49)** (KMcAuliffe) **3-8-0** CRutter(6) (a bhd) 1¼ | **12** | 25/1 | 21 | — |
| 2524[5] **Dark Shot (IRE) (62)** (RAFahey) **4-9-6** GCooksley(13) (swtchd lft s: led tl over 3f out: sn wknd) 2 | **13** | 14/1 | 30 | 12 |
| **Desert Zone (USA) (65)** (JAHarris) **7-9-9** DHolland(7) (racd wd & a bhd) 5 | **14** | 16/1 | 21 | 3 |
| 2971[15] **Corona Gold (42)** (JGFitzGerald) **6-8-0** JFanning(10) (hmpd after 1f: a bhd) 3½ | **15** | 12/1 | — | — |

| | | | | |
|---|---|---|---|---|
| $2158^{5}$ **Awafeh (48)** (SMellor) **3-7-13b** NAdams(12) (in tch: rdn 4f out: sn bhd: t.o) ....16 | **16** | 14/1 | — | — |

(SP 142.4%) **16 Rn**

**1m 31.3** (4.50) CSF £73.69 CT £404.11 TOTE £10.40: £2.60 £2.40 £1.90 £5.10 (£46.30) Trio £126.30 OWNER Mr Ricky George (NEWMARKET) BRED Britton House Stud
WEIGHT FOR AGE 3yo-7lb

**2577 Barrack Yard**, dropping back in distance and travelling strongly, looked firmly in command when hitting the front but, in the end, the post came just in time. (7/1: 11/2-15/1)
**2552 Desert Invader (IRE)**, dropping back in distance, proved most persistent under pressure and almost got back in front. (9/1: 12/1-8/1)
**2084 Elton Ledger (IRE)**, ridden to conserve his stamina, hung left and could not match strides with the first two at the business end. (6/1)
**1721 Seeking Destiny (IRE)** bounced back to his best, keeping on grimly under pressure. (16/1)
**2672 Angus McCoatup (IRE)**, still a maiden, decided to stay on in good style late in the day. (10/1)
**Ism**, on his favourite stamping ground, was squeezed up after a furlong. (6/1)
**2369 Pc's Cruiser (IRE)**, on a losing run of twenty-five, tried to come with a run on the wide outside two furlongs out. Hanging left, he looked anything but happy in his work. (6/1: op 10/1)
**2524 Dark Shot (IRE)** dived left early to overcome his poor draw. Under pressure once in line for home, he looked far from happy. (14/1)

## 3090 PERNOD MAIDEN (S) STKS (3-Y.O+) (Class G)

8-25 (8-25) **1m 4f (Fibresand)** £2,070.00 (£570.00: £270.00) Stalls: Low GOING: 0.04 sec per fur (STD)

| | | SP | RR | SF |
|---|---|---|---|---|
| $2915^{2}$ **Another Quarter (IRE) (57)** (SPCWoods) **3-8-6** DBiggs(1) (mde virtually all: styd on u.p fnl 2f) ....— | 1 | 4/5 1 | 66 | 11 |
| $1717^{11}$ **Slippery Fin** (WGMTurner) **4-9-4b1** TSprake(8) (trckd ldrs: wnt 2nd over 4f out: rdn & nt qckn fnl 2f) ....5 | 2 | 4/1 2 | 59 | 16 |
| $2935^{9}$ **Comedie Arrete (FR) (40)** (MCChapman) **4-8-11b1(7)** CScally(6) (s.i.s: sn in tch: outpcd over 4f out: kpt on: n.d) ....20 | 3 | 40/1 | 33 | — |
| $2568^{9}$ **Boy Blakeney (37)** (MrsSJSmith) **3-8-11** PBloomfield(9) (in tch: sn drvn along: lost pl over 4f out) ....13 | 4 | 16/1 | 20 | — |
| $2939^{6}$ **Undawaterscubadiva (38)** (MPBielby) **4-9-4(5)** LNewton(4) (chsd ldrs: drvn along 5f out: wknd 3f out) ....3½ | 5 | 20/1 | 16 | — |
| **Cromaboo Crown** (PJBevan) **5-9-4** NCarlisle(2) (sn bhd & drvn along: t.o 3f out) ....10 | 6 | 25/1 | — | — |
| **Clover Girl** (BEllison) **5-9-4** JTate(5) (b: bhd: sme hdwy 5f out: sn wknd: t.o 3f out) ....12 | 7 | 14/1 3 | — | — |
| $2628^{8}$ **Hever Golf Diamond (50)** (TJNaughton) **3-8-11** DHolland(3) (chsd ldrs: sn drvn along: rdn 6f out: sn wknd).s.h | 8 | 4/1 2 | — | — |
| $2939^{7}$ **Tirlie (IRE) (40)** (JWPayne) **4-9-4v1(5)** DGriffiths(7) (chsd ldrs tl wknd qckly 5f out: sn t.o) ....dist | 9 | 40/1 | — | — |

(SP 121.6%) **9 Rn**

**2m 45.4** (12.90) CSF £4.90 TOTE £1.80: £1.20 £1.10 £5.30 (£7.30) Trio £64.80 OWNER Mr S. P. C. Woods (NEWMARKET) BRED J. C. Fagan
WEIGHT FOR AGE 3yo-12lb
Bt in 6,000 gns

**2915 Another Quarter (IRE)**, stepping up to a mile and a half, ensured there was no hanging about. Sticking on under pressure, she won a bad seller. (4/5)
**1605 Slippery Fin**, an ex-French filly, had blinkers on for the first time. Moving up within three lengths of the winner turning in, she looked a possible danger but was soon flat out and making no real impression. (4/1)
**Comedie Arrete (FR)**, an ex-French filly, had shown little on her previous four outings here. Flat out a long way from home, she kept on in the final three furlongs to finish a remote third. (40/1)

## 3091 GIN H'CAP (0-60) (3-Y.O+) (Class F)

8-55 (8-55) **5f (Fibresand)** £2,381.00 (£656.00: £311.00) Stalls: Low GOING: 0.04 sec per fur (STD)

| | | SP | RR | SF |
|---|---|---|---|---|
| $2757^{15}$ **Queens Check (58)** (MissJFCraze) **3-9-8b** NConnorton(5) (a.p: swtchd lft over 1f out: r.o wl to ld ins fnl f)....— | 1 | 5/1 2 | 68 | 46 |
| $2748^{*}$ **Need You Badly (55)** (SPCWoods) **3-9-5** DBiggs(7) (a.p: kpt on wl ins fnl f) ....1¼ | 2 | 9/4 1 | 61 | 39 |
| $2745^{5}$ **Runs in the Family (47)** (GMMcCourt) **4-9-1b** GCarter(11) (w ldrs: r.o fnl f) ....nk | 3 | 6/1 3 | 52 | 34 |
| $2934^{14}$ **Souperficial (60)** (JAGlover) **5-10-0v** DHolland(1) (a chsng ldrs: led over 1f out: edgd rt & hdd ins fnl f) ....1¼ | 4 | 10/1 | 61 | 43 |
| $2940^{6}$ **Tame Deer (51)** (MCChapman) **4-8-12(7)** CScally(3) (bhd: hdwy ½-wy: edgd rt & styd on appr fnl f) ....1¼ | 5 | 14/1 | 48 | 30 |
| $2757^{12}$ **Time To Fly (49)** (BWMurray) **3-8-13** VHalliday(9) (mid div: rdn ½-wy: styd on fnl f) ....1¾ | 6 | 16/1 | 40 | 18 |
| $2800^{4}$ **Orange And Blue (41)** (MissJFCraze) **3-8-2c(3)ow1** CTeague(6) (mde most tl over 1f out: sn wknd) ....hd | 7 | 8/1 | 32 | 9 |
| $2427^{8}$ **Jemsilverthorn (IRE) (52)** (RCSpicer) **3-9-2b** TSprake(4) (prom tl wknd over 1f out) ....1¾ | 8 | 12/1 | 38 | 16 |
| $2910^{5}$ **Rankaidade (28)** (DonEnricoIncisa) **5-7-10** KimTinkler(10) (a outpcd) ....2½ | 9 | 33/1 | 6 | — |
| $2572^{11}$ **Petarina (46)** (MissJFCraze) **3-8-10** JLowe(2) (chsd ldrs: rdn & hung lft ½-wy: sn lost pl) ....hd | 10 | 13/2 | 23 | 1 |
| $2960^{6}$ **Double Glow (30)** (NBycroft) **4-7-12ow2** TWilliams(13) (sn bhd) ....1 | 11 | 14/1 | 4 | — |
| $2940^{12}$ **Dauntless Fort (30)** (MrsVAAconley) **5-7-7(5)ow2** MBaird(8) (s.i.s: a in rr) ....2 | 12 | 20/1 | — | — |
| **Sizzling Romp (52)** (DTThom) **4-9-6** JTate(12) (sn wl outpcd) ....9 | 13 | 20/1 | — | — |

(SP 134.6%) **13 Rn**

**60.6 secs** (3.60) CSF £17.93 CT £72.79 TOTE £6.60: £2.10 £1.80 £1.70 (£8.70) Trio £10.00 OWNER Mr W. Cooper (YORK) BRED Mrs Sandra Cooper
LONG HANDICAP Rankaidade 7-4 Double Glow 7-2 Dauntless Fort 7-7
WEIGHT FOR AGE 3yo-4lb

**1028* Queens Check**, who could not handle the firm ground on turf last time, scored decisively in the end. If she returns to grass, she will need give underfoot. (5/1)
**2748* Need You Badly**, slightly tapped for toe when the pace lifted over a furlong out, stuck on strongly inside the last. (9/4)
**2745 Runs in the Family**, who has slipped down the weights, showed a return to form. (6/1)
**2637 Souperficial** has gone a year without a win and his last start here five days earlier was over a mile. He showed surprising speed to show ahead over a furlong out but, once in front, he edged right and was outspeeded in the closing stages. (10/1)

T/Plpt: £12.10 (821.03 Tckts). T/Qdpt: £4.40 (130.13 Tckts). WG

# 2977-BRIGHTON (L-H) (Firm)

## Monday July 29th

WEATHER: overcast WIND: almost nil

## 3092 RAGGETTS (S) STKS (2-Y.O) (Class G)

2-30 (2-31) **6f 209y** £2,070.00 (£570.00: £270.00) Stalls: Low GOING minus 0.35 sec per fur (F)

| | | SP | RR | SF |
|---|---|---|---|---|
| **Jay-Gee-Em** (RGuest) **2-8-6** JReid(1) (b: w'like: scope: lw: mde virtually all: r.o wl) ....— | 1 | 7/2 3 | 57+ | — |

2959[9] **Grovefair Maiden (IRE)** (BJMeehan) **2-8-11b** BDoyle(3) (lw: a.p: rdn over 3f out: chsd wnr over 1f out: unable qckn)....3 **2** 3/1[2] 55 —
2850[2] **Super Scravels** (DrJDScargill) **2-8-6** MFenton(6) (lw: w wnr over 5f: wknd fnl f)....6 **3** 15/2 36 —
3046[12] **Don't Forget Shoka (IRE)** (JSMoore) **2-8-11** WJO'Connor(4) (lw: a.p: rdn over 2f out: wknd over 1f out)....1 **4** 5/1 39 —
2850[5] **Poly Dancer** (MRChannon) **2-8-6** CRutter(5) (lw: a bhd)....1½ **5** 16/1 31 —
2926[9] **Bellaf** (MWEasterby) **2-8-11b** PatEddery(2) (hld up: rdn over 2f out: wknd over 1f out)....2½ **6** 9/4[1] 30 —
(SP 112.3%) **6 Rn**

**1m 25.5** (5.50) CSF £13.58 TOTE £3.60: £1.90 £2.30 (£8.80) OWNER Matthews Breeding and Racing (NEWMARKET) BRED Nidd Park Stud
Bt in 5,600 gns

**Jay-Gee-Em**, an attractive filly who certainly caught the eye in the paddock, needed only to be shaken up from below the distance to forge clear. (7/2)
**2685* Grovefair Maiden (IRE)** never looked like reeling in the winner. (3/1)
**2850 Super Scravels** disputed the lead with the winner for much of the way. (15/2)
**1463* Don't Forget Shoka (IRE)**, making a quick reappearance, chased the leaders until tiring approaching the final furlong. (5/1: op 3/1)
**2850 Poly Dancer** could never get out of the ruck. (16/1)
**2797 Bellaf** failed to make the long journey from North Yorkshire pay off. (9/4)

## 3093 DAILY STAR MAIDEN STKS (3-Y.O+ F & M) (Class D)

3-00 (3-00) **7f 214y** £3,661.80 (£1,091.40: £520.20: £234.60) Stalls: Low GOING minus 0.35 sec per fur (F)

SP RR SF

2420[2] **Tarneem (USA) (79)** (MRStoute) **3-8-11** PatEddery(2) (chsd ldr: led over 2f out: rdn out)....— **1** 15/8[2] 81 19
2208[3] **Hulm (IRE) (79)** (HThomsonJones) **3-8-11** RHills(3) (led over 5f: ev ch ins fnl f: unable qckn)....1 **2** 7/2[3] 79 17
1855[2] **Tillyard (IRE)** (PWChapple-Hyam) **3-8-11** JReid(5) (hld up: rdn 2f out: r.o ins fnl f)....hd **3** 5/4[1] 79 17
**Dazzling** (DCO'Brien) **3-8-11** GBardwell(4) (leggy: unf: bit bkwd: hdwy over 1f out: r.o)....2 **4** 66/1 75? 13
2760[4] **Lady Isabell** (SDow) **3-8-6(5)** ADaly(1) (hld up: rdn over 2f out: sn wknd)....8 **5** 20/1 59? —
(SP 107.7%) **5 Rn**

**1m 36.5** (4.30) CSF £7.93 TOTE £2.60: £1.30 £1.50 (£4.20) OWNER Mr Mana Al Maktoum (NEWMARKET) BRED Randy Coker and Gainsborough Farm

**2420 Tarneem (USA)** had to battle hard to shake off the persistent runner-up, but eventually did so in the last 100 yards. (15/8)
**2208 Hulm (IRE)**, collared over a quarter of a mile from home, refused to give way and was still battling for honours inside the final furlong before tapped for toe. (7/2)
**1855 Tillyard (IRE)**, a tall filly, did not look comfortable on this switch-back track. Chasing the leaders, her jockey did not look particularly happy on her and the filly only really got going inside the final furlong, by which time it was all too late. She probably needs further. (5/4: 8/11-11/8)
**Dazzling**, a tall, plain, weak-looking filly, was at the back of the field until staying on from below the distance. (66/1)
**2760 Lady Isabell** was racing with her tongue tied down. (20/1)

## 3094 BRIGHTON SUMMER CHALLENGE CUP H'CAP (0-70) (3-Y.O+) (Class E)

3-30 (3-30) **1m 3f 196y** £3,206.70 (£957.60: £457.80: £207.90) Stalls: High GOING minus 0.35 sec per fur (F)

SP RR SF

2896[2] **Ragsak Jameel (USA) (69)** (MajorWRHern) **3-9-1v[1]** RHills(4) (lw: chsd ldr: led over 2f out: rdn out)....— **1** 2/1[1] 76 38
2767[4] **Prince Danzig (IRE) (62)** (DJGMurraySmith) **5-9-6** JReid(6) (lw: rdn 4f out: hdwy wl over 1f out: r.o wl ins fnl f)....¾ **2** 13/2 68 42
1066[9] **Sweet Pavlova (USA) (66)** (PFICole) **4-9-7(3)** MHenry(3) (b: a.p: rdn over 4f out: stumbled over 3f out: ev ch wl over 1f out: nt r.o)....8 **3** 11/2[2] 61 35
*2372*[7] **Charlie Bigtime (44)** (RHarris) **6-8-2hb** AMackay(2) (hld up: rdn 4f out: sn wknd)....1¾ **4** 6/1[3] 37 11
**Distant Storm (53)** (MBell) **3-7-13** GBardwell(5) (bit bkwd: a bhd)....4 **5** 25/1 41 3
2762* **Greenwich Again (62)** (TGMills) **4-9-6** PatEddery(1) (led over 9f)....¾ **6** 2/1[1] 49 23
(SP 113.5%) **6 Rn**

**2m 32.4** (4.80) CSF £13.92 TOTE £2.80: £1.80 £2.00 (£7.00) OWNER Sheikh Ahmed Al Maktoum (LAMBOURN) BRED Airlie Stud
WEIGHT FOR AGE 3yo-12lb

**2896 Ragsak Jameel (USA)**, sent on over a quarter of a mile from home, was ridden along to assert his superiority from below the distance. (2/1)
**2767 Prince Danzig (IRE)**, winner of this last year, looked in good shape beforehand. His jockey was niggling along for a lot of the race and he only found his stride inside the final quarter-mile. Running on strongly in the closing stages, the line was always going to beat him. He loves it round here and can find another race on this switch-back track before long. (13/2)
**Sweet Pavlova (USA)**, never far away, clipped the heels of the runner in front of her over three furlongs from home, but this made little difference and she came to have every chance early in the final quarter-mile. However, when pressure was applied, she looked far from enthusiastic and threw in the towel. (11/2)
**2173 Charlie Bigtime** chased the leaders, but was hung out to dry over three furlongs from home. (6/1)
**Distant Storm**, looking big and well for this reappearance, was always at the back. (25/1)
**2762* Greenwich Again** stopped as if shot once headed. (2/1)

## 3095 BEAU BRUMMEL CLAIMING STKS (3-Y.O+) (Class F)

4-00 (4-01) **1m 1f 209y** £2,381.00 (£656.00: £311.00) Stalls: High GOING minus 0.35 sec per fur (F)

SP RR SF

2740* **Shabanaz (62)** (WRMuir) **11-9-5** JReid(5) (hld up: led over 1f out: rdn out)....— **1** 7/4[1] 72 24
2788[2] **Siesta Time (USA) (52)** (CLPopham) **6-8-8** BDoyle(4) (lw: s.s: hld up: chsd ldrs over 2f out: ev ch over 1f out: unable qckn)....5 **2** 7/2[2] 53 5
2737[6] **Global Dancer (64)** (SDow) **5-8-10(5)** ADaly(2) (led over 8f: sn wknd)....3½ **3** 7/2[2] 54 6
2766[4] **Prince Rudolf (IRE) (38)** (WGMTurner) **4-8-10v(5)** AmandaSanders(3) (chsd ldr over 7f)....19 **4** 16/1 24 —
2378[9] **Wet Patch (IRE) (61)** (RHannon) **4-9-13** RHughes(1) (lw: a bhd: t.o)....21 **5** 9/2[3] 2 —
(SP 104.9%) **5 Rn**

**2m 4.3** (6.00) CSF £7.20 TOTE £2.00: £1.40 £2.00 (£2.60) OWNER Fayzad Thoroughbred Ltd (LAMBOURN) BRED The Overbury Stud
OFFICIAL EXPLANATION **Wet Patch (IRE): the jockey reported that the gelding felt all wrong and was hanging throughout the race.**

**2740* Shabanaz** goes really well in this class. Chasing the leaders, he came through to lead approaching the final furlong and was ridden along to win a bad race. (7/4)
**2788 Siesta Time (USA)** moved into second place over a quarter of a mile from home. One of three almost in line below the distance, she carried her head rather high and did not look to be entirely enjoying the experience. (7/2)
**2737 Global Dancer** attempted to make all the running. Collared over a furlong out, he had little more to offer. (7/2)

**2766 Prince Rudolf (IRE)** raced in second place until stopping over two furlongs from home. (16/1)
**2014 Wet Patch (IRE)**, tailed off over hurdles six days ago, ran another lifeless race and was always in rear. (9/2)

## 3096 A. R. DENNIS BOOKMAKERS JULY H'CAP (0-70) (3-Y.O+) (Class E)

4-30 (4-31) **5f 213y** £3,070.20 (£915.60: £436.80: £197.40) Stalls: Low GOING minus 0.35 sec per fur (F)

| | | | SP | RR | SF |
|---|---|---|---|---|---|
| 2686[11] | **Always Grace (59)** (MissGayKelleway) **4-9-7** RCochrane(6) (c stands's side st: hdwy over 1f out: str run fnl f: led nr fin) .......— | 1 | 5/1 | 63 | 27 |
| 2947[3] | **Red Admiral (63)** (CMurray) **6-9-11** MTebbutt(3) (swtg: led over 1f: c stands' side st: led 3f out tl over 1f out: hrd rdn: hung lft ins fnl f: r.o one pce) .......1¼ | 2 | 6/1 | 64 | 28 |
| 2763[6] | **Sharp Imp (51)** (RMFlower) **6-8-13b** DBiggs(4) (hdwy 2f out: led over 1f out: edgd lft: hdd ins fnl f: one pce)..½ | 3 | 7/2[2] | 50 | 14 |
| 2604[5] | **Jaazim (54)** (MMadgwick) **6-9-2** PaulEddery(1) (lw: a.p: ev ch 2f out: wknd over 1f out) .......4 | 4 | 100/30[1] | 43 | 7 |
| 2193[2] | **Lorins Gold (40)** (AndrewTurnell) **6-7-13**(3) MHenry(2) (a.p: led over 4f out to 3f out: ev ch 2f out: wknd over 1f out) .......2 | 5 | 9/2[3] | 23 | — |
| 2765* | **Dark Menace (47)** (EAWheeler) **4-8-4**(5) ADaly(5) (s.s: c stands' side st: hdwy over 3f out: wknd wl over 1f out) .......1¾ | 6 | 5/1 | 26 | — |
| | | | (SP 111.1%) | | **6 Rn** |

**1m 10.4** (3.20) CSF £29.89 TOTE £4.90: £2.60 £1.90 (£15.40) OWNER Easy Going Partnership (WHITCOMBE) BRED Zetland Stud

**1689 Always Grace**, one of three who elected to come over to the stands' side, only found her feet below the distance. Producing a storming run in the final furlong, she got up near the line. (5/1)
**2947 Red Admiral** set the pace. Electing to come over to the stands' side in the straight, he was back in front again at halfway. Headed below the distance, he then drifted badly left, virtually ending up on the far rail but, having dropped back to third place, struggled on again to regain second prize. (6/1: op 4/1)
**2763 Sharp Imp**, winner of this race last year, looked likely to follow up as he moved smoothly through to lead below the distance. However, this might have been a shade early for him and, headed inside the final furlong, he failed to find another gear. (7/2)
**2604 Jaazim** played an active role until tiring approaching the final furlong. (100/30: 5/1-3/1)
**2193 Lorins Gold**, soon at the head of affairs, was collared at halfway. Still in with every chance two furlongs from home, he had given his all approaching the final furlong. (9/2)
**2765* Dark Menace**, another who elected to come over to the stands' side in the straight, moved up just before halfway but was hung out to dry well over a furlong out. (5/1)

## 3097 FITZHERBERT H'CAP (0-60) (3-Y.O+) (Class F)

5-00 (5-00) **5f 59y** £2,381.00 (£656.00: £311.00) Stalls: Low GOING minus 0.35 sec per fur (F)

| | | | SP | RR | SF |
|---|---|---|---|---|---|
| 2769[2] | **Midnight Spell (60)** (JWHills) **4-9-11**(3) MHenry(6) (hdwy over 1f out: hrd rdn: hdd nr fin) .......— | 1 | 9/4[2] | 68 | 46 |
| 2745[13] | **Another Batchworth (54)** (EAWheeler) **4-9-8** SWhitworth(1) (lw: led: hrd rdn fnl f: hdd nr fin) .......1¼ | 2 | 5/1 | 58 | 36 |
| 2902[5] | **Harriet's Beau (33)** (MWEasterby) **3-7-11b** DaleGibson(3) (lw: hld up: hrd rdn over 2f out: one pce) .......1¾ | 3 | 100/30[3] | 32 | 6 |
| 2686[5] | **Tachycardia (45)** (RJO'Sullivan) **4-8-13** DBiggs(4) (chsd ldr 3f out tl over 1f out: sn wknd) .......5 | 4 | 7/4[1] | 29 | 7 |
| 2791[8] | **Woodlands Electric (28)** (PAPritchard) **6-7-10** GBardwell(5) (b.hind: a bhd) .......3½ | 5 | 66/1 | 1 | — |
| 2745[7] | **Elraas (USA) (28)** (HJCollingridge) **4-7-10v** NAdams(2) (lw: chsd ldr 2f: wknd over 1f out) .......s.h | 6 | 14/1 | 1 | — |
| | | | (SP 115.0%) | | **6 Rn** |

**62.1 secs** (2.10) CSF £13.09 TOTE £3.40: £1.70 £2.40 (£10.10) OWNER Wyck Hall Stud (LAMBOURN) BRED Milton Park Stud Partnership
LONG HANDICAP Woodlands Electric 6-11 Elraas (USA) 7-3
WEIGHT FOR AGE 3yo-4lb

**2769 Midnight Spell** began to find her feet below the distance. Gradually reeling in the tearaway leader, she got up near the line to win a very bad race. (9/4)
**2280 Another Batchworth** stormed off in front and brought the field over to the stands' side in the straight. It looked as if she was going to prevail but, with the winner finishing with a flourish, she was collared near the line. (5/1)
**2902 Harriet's Beau**, making the long haul from North Yorkshire, chased the leaders but, under pressure over two furlongs from home, could only go up and down in the same place. (100/30)
**2686 Tachycardia** moved into second place three furlongs from home. Collared for that position below the distance, she had nothing more to offer. (7/4)
**Elraas (USA)**, in second place early, had nothing more to offer below the distance. (14/1: 8/1-16/1)

T/Plpt: £51.40 (207.62 Tckts). T/Qdpt: £14.50 (50.08 Tckts). AK

# 3080-NEWCASTLE (L-H) (St crse Good to firm, Rnd crse Firm, Good to firm patches)

## Monday July 29th

Races 1, 2 & 6 hand-timed
WEATHER: overcast WIND: almost nil

## 3098 SCANIA 4-SERIES 'HORSEPOWER' TROPHY H'CAP (0-80) (3-Y.O+) (Class D)

2-15 (2-15) **1m 4f 93y** £3,566.25 (£1,080.00: £527.50: £251.25) Stalls: Low GOING minus 0.58 sec per fur (F)

| | | | SP | RR | SF |
|---|---|---|---|---|---|
| 2493[2] | **Maftun (USA) (52)** (GMMoore) **4-8-3** JTate(1) (chsd ldrs: led 1½f out: styd on wl) .......— | 1 | 11/4[1] | 63 | 21 |
| 2847[4] | **Lord Advocate (51)** (DANolan) **8-8-2b** GDuffield(5) (lw: led tl hdd 1½f out: one pce) .......3 | 2 | 5/1[3] | 58 | 16 |
| 450[20] | **Ham N'Eggs (77)** (MDHammond) **5-10-0** JFortune(3) (hld up: effrt whn bdly hmpd ent st: nt rcvr) .......5 | 3 | 11/2 | 78 | 36 |
| 2776[8] | **Sharkashka (IRE) (52)** (TDEasterby) **6-8-0b**[1](3) FLynch(2) (lw: chsd ldrs: bmpd appr st: rdn & nt r.o fnl 3f)...1¼ | 4 | 4/1[2] | 51 | 9 |
| 2697[9] | **Soba Up (72)** (TJEtherington) **6-9-9** ACulhane(4) (pushed along 6f out: outpcd & carried wd st: n.d) .......14 | 5 | 11/4[1] | 53 | 11 |
| 2627[11] | **Manoy (57)** (JHetherton) **3-7-10b** NKennedy(6) (chsd ldrs: effrt whn slipped bdly ent st: nt rcvr) .......16 | 6 | 14/1 | 17 | — |
| | | | (SP 112.1%) | | **6 Rn** |

**2m 40.9** (3.40) CSF £15.26 TOTE £3.30: £1.70 £2.30 (£6.20) OWNER Anmaf Partnership (MIDDLEHAM) BRED Steeple Stone Bloodstock Co
LONG HANDICAP Manoy 7-8
WEIGHT FOR AGE 3yo-12lb

**2493 Maftun (USA)**, bang up with the pace, avoided all the trouble on the home turn, and his staying power won him the day in the last furlong and a half. (11/4)
**2847 Lord Advocate**, having one of his rare forays outside Scotland, put up a decent show, but was chopped for speed in the final furlong. (5/1)

**Ham N'Eggs** was just making his move when he got virtually knocked over entering the straight, and his chance had then gone. (11/2)
**2482 Sharkashka (IRE)**, in blinkers for the first time, was bumped approaching the straight, causing her to run wide, and she soon threw in the towel. (4/1)
**2221* Soba Up** never looked happy and having to come wide into the straight to avoid trouble certainly did not help. (11/4)
**2196 Manoy** had every chance until almost falling on a dangerous patch of ground on the home turn. (14/1)

## 3099 ALEX LAWRIE MEDIAN AUCTION MAIDEN STKS (2-Y.O) (Class E)

2-45 (2-46) **7f** £2,983.00 (£904.00: £442.00: £211.00) Stalls: High GOING minus 0.48 sec per fur (F)

| | | | | SP | RR | SF |
|---|---|---|---|---|---|---|
| 2696$^{2}$ | **The Deejay (IRE)** (MBrittain) **2-8-9**(5) GParkin(4) (lw: mde all: rdn & kpt on wl fnl f) | — | **1** | 11/2 | 63 | 27 |
| | **Dargo** (MJohnston) **2-9-0** JWeaver(7) (w'like: bit bkwd: in tch: shkn up 2f out: chsng wnr fnl f: kpt on) | 1¼ | **2** | 7/4$^{1}$ | 60+ | 24 |
| *1489*$^{10}$ | **Zorba** (CWThornton) **2-9-0** DeanMcKeown(3) (chsd wnr: rdn 2f out: r.o one pce) | 3 | **3** | 33/1 | 53 | 17 |
| *2633*$^{7}$ | **Floating Devon** (TDEasterby) **2-9-0** MBirch(1) (prom: effrt 2f out: one pce) | 1¼ | **4** | 3/1$^{3}$ | 50 | 14 |
| 2519$^{7}$ | **Broctune Line** (MrsMReveley) **2-9-0** ACulhane(2) (bhd: hdwy 2f out: nvr nr to chal) | 3½ | **5** | 16/1 | 42 | 6 |
| 1499$^{5}$ | **Northern Princess** (RHollinshead) **2-8-6**(3) FLynch(5) (in tch tl outpcd fnl 2f) | 1¼ | **6** | 16/1 | 35 | — |
| | **Cartouche** (SirMarkPrescott) **2-9-0** GDuffield(6) (wl grwn: chsd ldrs 4f: sn wknd) | 1½ | **7** | 11/4$^{2}$ | 36 | — |
| | | | | (SP 118.1%) | | **7 Rn** |

**1m 27.2** (2.70) CSF £15.69 TOTE £5.10: £1.60 £2.20 (£7.40) OWNER Mr B. Valentine (WARTHILL) BRED Noel Finegan
**2696 The Deejay (IRE)**, given a good ride, had the edge on fitness and experience, and made full use of that. (11/2: 4/1-6/1)
**Dargo** is a useful type but did appear, if anything, in need of this, and that probably made the difference. Better looks likely. (7/4: Evens-2/1)
**Zorba**, who is improving physically, put up a much-improved effort and seems to be going the right way. (33/1)
**2370 Floating Devon** had a cut here for the first time, but did not seem to know what to do when ridden. (3/1)
**Broctune Line** showed something on this occasion, despite never getting into it, and looks likely to do better with experience over further. (16/1)
**1499 Northern Princess** never showed any sparkle. (16/1)
**Cartouche** (11/4: 2/1-3/1)

## 3100 UNION TRUCKS FOR SCANIA MAIDEN STKS (3-Y.O+) (Class D)

3-15 (3-16) **5f** £3,501.25 (£1,060.00: £517.50: £246.25) Stalls: High GOING minus 0.48 sec per fur (F)

| | | | | SP | RR | SF |
|---|---|---|---|---|---|---|
| 1901$^{12}$ | **Sabaah Elfull (80)** (ACStewart) **3-8-9** DHarrison(5) (lw: mde most: qcknd 2f out: r.o wl) | — | **1** | 2/5$^{1}$ | 69 | 14 |
| 2151$^{8}$ | **Superfrills (46)** (MissLCSiddall) **3-8-9** DeanMcKeown(1) (cl up: chsd wnr fr ½-wy: no imp fnl f) | 4 | **2** | 20/1 | 56 | 1 |
| 2777$^{8}$ | **Bataleur** (MissJBower) **3-9-0** DRMcCabe(3) (prom: effrt ½-wy: r.o one pce) | 3½ | **3** | 25/1 | 50 | — |
| | **Funky** (DNicholls) **3-8-9** AlexGreaves(2) (prom tl grad wknd fnl 2f) | 2 | **4** | 11/2$^{2}$ | 39 | — |
| 2732$^{6}$ | **Rinus Manor (IRE) (48)** (EJAlston) **5-9-4v**$^{1}$ JFortune(4) (effrt ½-wy: no imp) | 1¾ | **5** | 9/1$^{3}$ | 38 | — |
| 2933$^{3}$ | **Young Ben (IRE) (40)** (JSWainwright) **4-9-4v** KDarley(8) (lw: b: b.hind: prom 3f: sn btn) | hd | **6** | 14/1 | 38 | — |
| 2913$^{4}$ | **Lady Seren (IRE)** (SEKettlewell) **4-8-13** NRodgers(9) (outpcd & bhd fr ½-wy) | ½ | **7** | 25/1 | 31 | — |
| 2498$^{6}$ | **Chelwood** (LRLloyd-James) **4-8-13b** KFallon(7) (dwlt: swtchd outside & hdwy ½-wy: sn wknd) | hd | **8** | 25/1 | 31 | — |
| 2732$^{5}$ | **Lord Cornelious (29)** (DANolan) **3-9-0** GDuffield(6) (cl up to ½-wy: sn wknd) | 1½ | **9** | 33/1 | 31 | — |
| | | | | (SP 122.7%) | | **9 Rn** |

**60.74 secs** (2.34) CSF £11.16 TOTE £1.40: £1.10 £4.60 £4.00 (£27.10) Trio £48.30 OWNER Sheikh Ahmed Al Maktoum (NEWMARKET) BRED Bloomsbury Stud
WEIGHT FOR AGE 3yo-4lb
**Sabaah Elfull** is not very big but was certainly fit. Against this company, she looked quite useful, but the opposition was moderate to say the least. (2/5)
**1429 Superfrills** was the only one able to anything like match the winner from halfway, but she was firmly put in her place before the finish. (20/1)
**Bataleur** is learning and should pick up a modest event in due course. (25/1)
**Funky**, having her first run for her new stable, showed a fair bit of promise and, in time, will no doubt do a good deal better. (11/2)
**2732 Rinus Manor (IRE)**, wearing a tongue-strap and also in a visor for the first time, was awkward leaving the paddock and never showed any sparkle at any stage. (9/1)

## 3101 SCANIA 1996 TRUCK OF THE YEAR TROPHY H'CAP (0-85) (3-Y.O+) (Class D)

3-45 (3-45) **7f** £3,517.50 (£1,065.00: £520.00: £247.50) Stalls: High GOING minus 0.48 sec per fur (F)

| | | | | SP | RR | SF |
|---|---|---|---|---|---|---|
| *2552*$^{7}$ | **Equerry (81)** (MJohnston) **5-9-13** JWeaver(5) (lw: stumbled s: sn cl up: rdn to ld appr fnl: r.o) | — | **1** | 3/1$^{2}$ | 88 | 40 |
| 2621$^{8}$ | **Sualtach (IRE) (83)** (RHollinshead) **3-9-8** KDarley(3) (trckd ldrs: effrt 2f out: ev ch ins fnl f: kpt on) | nk | **2** | 9/2$^{3}$ | 89 | 34 |
| 2420$^{6}$ | **Knotty Hill (77)** (RCraggs) **4-9-9** JCarroll(1) (led: hung lft most of wy: hdd appr fnl f: nt qckn) | 1¼ | **3** | 12/1 | 81 | 33 |
| 2773$^{6}$ | **Tawafij (USA) (74)** (MDHammond) **7-9-6** JFortune(2) (hld up: effrt over 1f out: nvr able to chal) | 1¼ | **4** | 2/1$^{1}$ | 75 | 27 |
| 2929* | **Encore M'Lady (IRE) (64)** (FHLee) **5-8-10** 5x JFanning(4) (lw: trckd ldrs: effrt 2f out: nt qckn) | 2½ | **5** | 3/1$^{2}$ | 59 | 11 |
| | | | | (SP 109.2%) | | **5 Rn** |

**1m 27.08** (2.58) CSF £14.52 TOTE £3.60: £1.70 £2.30 (£7.00) OWNER Mr J. R. Good (MIDDLEHAM) BRED J. R. and Mrs P. Good
WEIGHT FOR AGE 3yo-7lb
**2293* Equerry**, well suited by this event where most of the opposition needed holding up, would probably have won more easily had he not slipped badly leaving the stalls. (3/1)
**2532 Sualtach (IRE)** got a dream run up the rail in the last two furlongs, but was never finding enough when ridden, and he is probably happier on easier ground. (9/2)
**2420 Knotty Hill** is certainly high enough in the handicap and was probably flattered here by holding the best position in this slowly-run event. (12/1: op 8/1)
**2773 Tawafij (USA)** is beginning to come to himself looks-wise and, although never getting into this, he was not suited by the steady pace, so this was not a bad effort. (2/1)
**2929* Encore M'Lady (IRE)**, held up, never showed any spark at all when the race began in earnest from the two-furlong marker. (3/1)

## 3102 BUCKNALL AUSTIN H'CAP (0-65) (3-Y.O) (Class F)

4-15 (4-19) **7f** £2,704.50 (£762.00: £373.50) Stalls: High GOING minus 0.48 sec per fur (F)

| | | | | SP | RR | SF |
|---|---|---|---|---|---|---|
| 2785* | **Sylvan Princess (48)** (CNAllen) **3-7-13**(5) MartinDwyer(2) (trckd ldrs far side: led over 1f out: r.o) | — | **1** | 4/1$^{2}$ | 60 | 25 |
| 2567* | **Jambo (57)** (JLEyre) **3-8-13** JFortune(15) (led stands' side: rdn 2f out: r.o) | hd | **2** | 10/1 | 69 | 34 |
| 2983* | **Shontaine (60)** (MJohnston) **3-9-2** JWeaver(8) (cl up stands' side: nt qckn appr fnl f) | 2½ | **3** | 6/1$^{3}$ | 66 | 31 |

2752[10] **Fisiostar (40)** (MDods) **3-7-10b** NKennedy(3) (b.hind: disp ld far side tl hdd over 1f out: no ex)......................s.h **4** 33/1 46 11
2049[7] **Too Hasty (57)** (TDEasterby) **3-8-13** MBirch(1) (chsd ldrs far side: nt qckn fnl 2f)..........................................3½ **5** 20/1 55 20
2752* **Falcon's Flame (USA) (51)** (MrsJRRamsden) **3-8-7** KFallon(12) (bhd & drvn along stands' side ½-wy: styd on: nrst fin)..........................................................hd **6** 6/1[3] 49 14
2393[4] **Dispol Duchess (40)** (GROldroyd) **3-7-10** JLowe(16) (lw: outpcd stands' side tl styd on fnl 2f)........................½ **7** 33/1 37 2
2931[2] **Nkapen Rocks (SPA) (62)** (CaptJWilson) **3-9-4** KDarley(13) (chsd ldrs stands' side: rdn 2f out: btn whn stumbled ins fnl f)..........................................................½ **8** 14/1 57 22
1042[17] **Supermister (50)** (TDEasterby) **3-8-6** JFanning(5) (disp ld far side 5f: wknd)..................................hd **9** 25/1 45 10
2672[8] **Scenicris (IRE) (57)** (RHollinshead) **3-8-10**(3) FLynch(11) (hdwy: prom stands' side ½-wy: wknd fnl 2f)........1¼ **10** 16/1 49 14
2914[6] **Oriole (47)** (NTinkler) **3-8-3** KimTinkler(9) (in tch stands' side 5f)..........................................5 **11** 20/1 28 —
2914* **Magic Lake (48)** (EJAlston) **3-8-1**(3)ow3 SDrowne(7) (trckd ldrs stands' side: effrt over 2f out: sn wknd)..........3½ **12** 15/8[1] 21 —
2780[8] **Cerise (IRE) (46)** (CWCElsey) **3-7-13**(3) DWright(6) (racd far side: bhd fnl 2½f)..........................................3½ **13** 20/1 11 —
1761[9] **Jenny's Charmer (45)** (SEKettlewell) **3-8-1** DRMcCabe(14) (chsd ldrs stands' side over 4f)........................3½ **14** 50/1 2 —
2420[3] **Respecting (65)** (DenysSmith) **3-9-4**(3) CTeague(4) (dwlt: jnd ldrs far side ½-wy: sn wknd)..............................11 **15** 20/1 — —
1674[15] **Energy Man (55)** (MDods) **3-8-11** JCarroll(10) (cl up to ½-wy: wknd qckly: sn t.o)......................................dist **16** 33/1 — —
(SP 138.7%) **16 Rn**

**1m 26.54** (2.04) CSF £46.56 CT £246.41 TOTE £5.30: £1.40 £2.10 £2.30 £14.40 (£26.30) Trio £68.70 OWNER Camelot Racing (NEWMARKET) BRED K S P Leisure
LONG HANDICAP Fisiostar 7-2
**2785* Sylvan Princess**, racing up the far side, which proved no help the previous Saturday, sprinted away in the last furlong and a half to gain the overall advantage. (4/1: 3/1-9/2)
**2567* Jambo** made all up the stands' side but, despite battling on, always looked second best in the final furlong. (10/1)
**2983* Shontaine**, up with the pace as usual, was fighting a lost cause in the last furlong and a half and his draw might well have made all the difference. (6/1)
**2179 Fisiostar** is an in-and-out performer, but has ability when in the mood. (33/1)
**1185 Too Hasty** has dropped 23lb in the handicap this season and, although he is showing glimmers of form, he has yet to show anything concrete. (20/1)
**2752* Falcon's Flame (USA)** always seemed to find this trip too sharp, and never got going until too late. (6/1)
**2393 Dispol Duchess** will need further yet judged by the way she finished here. (33/1)
**2914* Magic Lake**, who had a poor draw, had been upped 5lb in the handicap and, with another 3lb overweight, ran miserably. She can be forgiven this. (15/8)

## 3103 SCANIA 4-SERIES 'KING OF THE ROAD' MAIDEN STKS (3-Y.O+) (Class D)
4-45 (4-47) **1m 2f 32y** £3,631.25 (£1,100.00: £537.50: £256.25) Stalls: High GOING minus 0.58 sec per fur (F)

SP RR SF
1900[2] **Present Arms (USA) (75)** (PFICole) **3-8-11** TQuinn(2) (mde all: rdn & r.o fnl 2f)..............................................— **1** 1/4[1] 80 32
**Opal Jewel** (MRStoute) **3-8-6** KDarley(1) (w'like: trckd wnr: chal over 2f out: nt qckn appr fnl f)........................2 **2** 7/2[2] 72? 24
2899[5] **Swynford Supreme** (JFBottomley) **3-8-11** JLowe(3) (stdd s: a bhd)..................................................dist **3** 25/1[3] — —
**Strata Florida** (MrsMReveley) **3-8-11** JCarroll(4) (w'like: s.i.s: a bhd)..................................................14 **4** 25/1[3] — —
(SP 109.9%) **4 Rn**

**2m 8.8** (2.10) CSF £1.61 TOTE £1.20: (£1.30) OWNER H R H Prince Fahd Salman (WHATCOMBE) BRED Tri-Star Stable
**1900 Present Arms (USA)**, backed as though defeat was out of the question, gave supporters quite a scare, but kept answering his rider's calls and was nicely on top by the finish. (1/4: 4/11-2/9)
**Opal Jewel**, easy in the market, gave the winner quite a fright, but was just outbattled in the final furlong. There would seem to be a race or two in her. (7/2: 9/4-4/1)
**2899 Swynford Supreme**, who was unruly in the paddock, looked a difficult ride and was never in it. (25/1)
**Strata Florida** needed the experience and never showed anything. (25/1)

T/Plpt: £31.90 (343.67 Tckts). T/Qdpt: £12.00 (44.65 Tckts). AA

# 3048-NOTTINGHAM (L-H) (Good to firm, Good patches)
## Monday July 29th
WEATHER: overcast WIND: nil

## 3104 PINXTON MINERS (S) H'CAP (0-60) (3-Y.O) (Class G)
6-25 (6-25) **1m 6f 15y** £2,238.00 (£618.00: £294.00) Stalls: Low GOING minus 0.40 sec per fur (F)

SP RR SF
1503[6] **Brighter Byfaah (IRE) (43)** (NAGraham) **3-9-0** KFallon(3) (b: bit bkwd: hld up: hdwy to ld over 3f out: drvn clr appr fnl f)..........................................................— **1** 3/1[1] 49 23
2563[8] **No More Hassle (IRE) (34)** (MrsMReveley) **3-8-5** ACulhane(2) (plld hrd: trckd ldr: hrd rdn 2f out: no imp).....3½ **2** 100/30[2] 36 10
2397[5] **The Jolly Barmaid (IRE) (39)** (PCalver) **3-8-7**(3) NVarley(7) (hld up: rn wd paddock bnd: effrt & hrd drvn ent st: one pce fnl 2f)..........................................................½ **3** 8/1 41 15
2989[P] **Miss Pravda (50)** (BJLlewellyn) **3-9-7** VSlattery(4) (s.s: bhd tl styd on fr 2f out: nt rch ldrs)..............................2 **4** 7/1 49 23
*2322[4]* **Pearl Anniversary (IRE) (48)** (MJohnston) **3-9-5** JWeaver(5) (lw: chsd ldr: rdn 3f out: sn wknd: t.o)...............16 **5** 100/30[2] 29 3
3059[13] **Belacqua (USA) (31)** (DWChapman) **3-8-2b** NKennedy(1) (lw: led tl hdd over 3f out: sn rdn & wknd: t.o)..........................................................½ **6** 10/1 11 —
2683[7] **All In Good Time (32)** (CWThornton) **3-8-3** GDuffield(6) (lw: prom: rn v.wd paddock bnd: sn bhd & rdn: t.o fnl 5f)..........................................................dist **7** 13/2[3] — —
(SP 117.2%) **7 Rn**

**3m 6.4** (7.90) CSF £13.24 TOTE £3.90: £1.90 £2.20 (£5.80) OWNER Mr Paul Jacobs (NEWMARKET) BRED Limestone Stud
Bt in 3,600 gns
**560 Brighter Byfaah (IRE)**, fresh and well after a two-month break, did not wear the blinkers he sported on his previous outing. Always going easily, he won this poor race with the minimum of fuss and was retained rather cheaply. (3/1: 9/4-7/2)
**No More Hassle (IRE)** took a lot of settling over this longer trip, but stuck on willingly in the latter stages, and should be able to pick up a similar event. (100/30: op 5/1)
**2397 The Jolly Barmaid (IRE)** followed a rival who made his way towards the paddock gate after the first quarter-mile, and lost quite a bit of ground. Pulled towards the centre of the track to male progress early in the straight, she did keep staying on, but had to admit the winner in a class of his own. (8/1)

**2542 Miss Pravda**, flat-footed as the stalls opened, remained at the tail end of the field until staying on when it was all too late. (7/1)
**2322 Pearl Anniversary (IRE)** had plenty of use made of him, but he weakened so quickly early in the straight that it would seem lack of stamina is a problem. (100/30: 9/4-7/2)
**All In Good Time** (13/2: op 4/1)

## 3105 GREASLEY MINERS MAIDEN AUCTION STKS (2-Y.O F) (Class F)
6-55 (6-56) **6f 15y** £2,761.80 (£764.80: £365.40) Stalls: High GOING minus 0.40 sec per fur (F)

| | | | | SP | RR | SF |
|---|---|---|---|---|---|---|
| 2147[4] | **Carati** (RBoss) **2-8-5** GDuffield(3) (mde all centre: overall ldr fr ½-wy: r.o wl) | — | 1 | 1/2[1] | 76 | 10 |
| | **Celebrant** (RHannon) **2-8-2**(3) DaneO'Neill(6) (w'like: leggy: s.s: hdwy ½-wy: drvn & rn green appr fnl f: kpt on towards fin) | ¾ | 2 | 11/2[2] | 74+ | 8 |
| | **Scarlet Crescent** (PTWalwyn) **2-8-3** TSprake(8) (lt-f: unf: bit bkwd: chsd ldr stands' side 4f: rdn & r.o wl nr fin) | 2 | 3 | 15/2 | 67 | 1 |
| | **Oakbrook Rose** (BSmart) **2-8-3** LCharnock(1) (b.hind: lt-f: prom: drvn along wl over 1f out: sn btn) | 2 | 4 | 16/1 | 62 | — |
| | **Ciro's Pearl (IRE)** (MHTompkins) **2-8-2**[ow1] PRobinson(5) (unf: scope: bkwd: c stands' side after 2f: rdn 2f out: no imp) | 3 | 5 | 7/1[3] | 53 | — |
| | **Bestelina** (DJSCosgrove) **2-8-1** GCarter(4) (lt-f: trckd ldrs centre 4f) | nk | 6 | 10/1 | 51 | — |
| 1014[7] | **Champagne On Ice** (PDEvans) **2-8-5** OUrbina(7) (overall ldr on stands' side to ½-wy: rdn & wknd over 2f out) | 2½ | 7 | 20/1 | 48 | — |
| 2519[5] | **Bloomsy Babe** (JJQuinn) **2-8-2** GHind(2) (swtg: s.s: a bhd & outpcd) | 11 | 8 | 33/1 | 16 | — |
| | | | | (SP 129.0%) | **8 Rn** | |

**1m 13.8** (3.30) CSF £5.00 TOTE £1.40: £1.10 £1.40 £2.00 (£2.80) OWNER Mrs Joan Root (NEWMARKET) BRED Hesmonds Stud Ltd
**2147 Carati** did not win as easily as she might have done, but she always appeared to hold the call, and the experience alone will not go amiss. (1/2)
**Celebrant**, a well thought of half-sister to a couple of winners, lost ground at the start and also showed signs of greenness when asked to quicken entering the final furlong. She saw her race out to the finish though and will know more next time. (11/2: op 7/2)
**Scarlet Crescent**, a lightly-made, unfurnished filly who can be made fitter, may well have fared better had she raced with the pace in the centre of the track. For the last couple of furlongs she was more or less on her own, and so this performance could be better than it looks. (15/2)
**Oakbrook Rose** spent quite a lot of time on her hind-legs in the pre-parade ring, but she settled when saddled and performed with credit until feeling the strain below the distance. She will benefit from easier ground. (16/1)
**Ciro's Pearl (IRE)**, a backward-looking filly from a winning family, tacked over to the stands' side and chased her two rivals on that side, but she was hard at work two furlongs out and failed to make the slightest impression. (7/1)
**Bestelina**, a choppy mover, showed up in the chasing group for the first half-mile before running out of puff. (10/1)

## 3106 RJB MINING H'CAP (0-85) (3-Y.O+) (Class D)
7-25 (7-25) **6f 15y** £3,794.40 (£1,132.20: £540.60: £244.80) Stalls: High GOING minus 0.40 sec per fur (F)

| | | | | SP | RR | SF |
|---|---|---|---|---|---|---|
| 3055[3] | **Cheeky Chappy (71)** (DWChapman) **5-9-2b**[7x] GDuffield(1) (lw: mde all: drvn out) | — | 1 | 7/2[2] | 79 | 48 |
| 2363[8] | **Latching (IRE) (83)** (RFJohnsonHoughton) **4-10-0** TSprake(4) (a.p: rdn & outpcd 2f out: r.o strly cl home) | ¾ | 2 | 6/1[3] | 89 | 58 |
| 496[11] | **Hawa Al Nasamaat (USA) (80)** (EALDunlop) **4-9-11** WRyan(2) (bit bkwd: a.p: chsd wnr fnl 2f: nt pce to chal) | nk | 3 | 8/1 | 85 | 54 |
| 2860[4] | **I'm Your Lady (71)** (BAMcMahon) **5-9-2** JFortune(5) (prom: drvn whn n.m.r over 2f out: one pce) | 2½ | 4 | 13/2 | 70 | 39 |
| 2867[3] | **Captain Carat (66)** (MrsJRRamsden) **5-8-11** KFallon(3) (b.nr hind: dwlt: hdwy 2f out: sn rdn: nvr nr to chal) | 2½ | 5 | 100/30[1] | 58 | 27 |
| *2171*[12] | **Hinton Rock (IRE) (76)** (ABailey) **4-9-7b** JWeaver(7) (b.hind: hld up in rr: effrt & rdn 2f out: no imp) | 1 | 6 | 10/1 | 65 | 34 |
| 2722[10] | **King Rat (IRE) (82)** (TJEtherington) **5-9-13b** GCarter(8) (bit bkwd: hld up: effrt over 2f out: sn hrd drvn: no imp) | 1¼ | 7 | 12/1 | 68 | 37 |
| 2501[11] | **Mutadarra (IRE) (82)** (RWArmstrong) **3-9-8b**[1] RPrice(6) (plld hrd: prom 4f: rdn & edgd lft over 1f out: sn btn) | 1¾ | 8 | 7/1 | 64 | 28 |
| | | | | (SP 113.3%) | **8 Rn** | |

**1m 11.7** (1.20) CSF £22.55 CT £140.50 TOTE £3.90: £1.10 £2.30 £4.30 (£18.30) OWNER Mrs Jeanne Chapman (YORK) BRED Ian W. Glenton
WEIGHT FOR AGE 3yo-5lb
**3055 Cheeky Chappy,** a real star who was turned out to perfection, obviously thrives on hard work. He ran his rivals ragged and will now call in at Yarmouth and Thirsk later in the week for good measure. (7/2)
**846* Latching (IRE),** stepping down in class here, would have given the winner a race had she been able to hold her pitch when the tempo was stepped up entering the last quarter-mile. She finished strongly and has not finished for the season yet. (6/1)
**Hawa Al Nasamaat (USA),** having his first try at sprinting after four months on the sidelines, ran extremely well and, with this outing under his belt, looks sure to add to his solitary score. (8/1)
**2860 I'm Your Lady,** in the action from the break, was struggling to keep her place when squeezed for room two furlongs out, and that was the beginning of the end. (13/2)
**2867 Captain Carat** tried to get down in the stalls and lost ground when they opened. Always struggling with the pace from then on, he did make some progress, but was never able to get himself in the race with a live chance. (100/30)

## 3107 ALLIED DUNBAR H'CAP (0-80) (3-Y.O) (Class D)
7-55 (7-55) **1m 54y** £3,960.15 (£1,183.20: £566.10: £257.55) Stalls: Low GOING minus 0.40 sec per fur (F)

| | | | | SP | RR | SF |
|---|---|---|---|---|---|---|
| 2334[4] | **Salmis (75)** (JRFanshawe) **3-8-13**(3) NVarley(1) (chsd ldr: led 200y out: hrd drvn & r.o wl) | — | 1 | 5/1[3] | 81 | 12 |
| 2994[6] | **Charlie Chang (IRE) (70)** (RHannon) **3-8-8**(3) DaneO'Neill(6) (led tl jst ins fnl f: rallied u.p towards fin) | hd | 2 | 6/1 | 76 | 7 |
| 1855[9] | **Gooseberry Pie (62)** (RCharlton) **3-8-3** TSprake(3) (lw: hld up: hdwy on ins 3f out: outpcd 2f out: sn rdn & btn) | 3½ | 3 | 13/8[1] | 61 | — |
| 2126* | **Mazcobar (80)** (PJMakin) **3-9-7** WRyan(2) (swtg: hld up in tch: effrt & outpcd over 2f out: n.d after) | ¾ | 4 | 7/4[2] | 78 | 9 |
| 2675[3] | **Lachesis (63)** (RHollinshead) **3-8-1**(3) FLynch(5) (hld up & bhd: effrt over 2f out: sn rdn: nt pce to chal) | 2 | 5 | 12/1 | 57 | — |
| 2801[15] | **Gilling Dancer (IRE) (58)** (PCalver) **3-7-13** NCarlisle(4) (swtg: hld up: stdy hdwy ½-wy: wknd fnl 2f) | s.h | 6 | 9/1 | 52 | — |
| | | | | (SP 123.1%) | **6 Rn** | |

**1m 47.1** (5.80) CSF £32.76 TOTE £7.20: £2.30 £2.80 (£15.40) OWNER Sally Vere Nicoll, Dexa'tex and Partners (NEWMARKET) BRED The Overbury Stud
**2334 Salmis,** stalking the leader from the start, took over just inside the final furlong and, driven out firmly, was always just getting the better of her tussle with the colt. (5/1)
**2994 Charlie Chang (IRE)** quickened the tempo and tried to slip his field entering the last quarter-mile, but the winner covered his every move, and had the legs of him in an all-out thriller to the post. (6/1)

**1614 Gooseberry Pie**, closely related to several winners, was taking on handicappers for the first time. Delaying her challenge, she got tapped for toe when the pace lifted two furlongs out and, from then on, had little hope of getting back. She should not be too difficult to place. (13/8)
**2126* Mazcobar** has been climbing up the handicap and, though he was waiting to pounce from the turn into the straight, he failed to respond when the principals kicked for home, and his hopes of a hat-trick were soon dented. (7/4)
**2675 Lachesis**, who is still to get her act together, found these handicappers were always just going too well for her, and she was unable to pose a serious threat. (12/1)
**2521* Gilling Dancer (IRE)**, taking a step in class, improved from the rear early in the straight, but his effort petered out before he could land a blow. (9/1)

## 3108 CLIPSTONE MINERS MEDIAN AUCTION MAIDEN STKS (3-Y.O F) (Class E)

8-25 (8-26) **1m 1f 213y** £3,042.90 (£907.20: £432.60: £195.30) Stalls: Low GOING minus 0.40 sec per fur (F)

| | Horse | | | SP | RR | SF |
|---|---|---|---|---|---|---|
| 2789[2] | **Rehaab** (ACStewart) **3-8-11** SWhitworth(3) (trckd ldrs: qcknd to ld 1f out: drvn clr) | — | **1** | 2/1[2] | 67 | 6 |
| 2794[2] | **Agdistis** (HThomsonJones) **3-8-11** GCarter(2) (chsd ldr: led over 5f out to 1f out: nt pce of wnr) | 2 | **2** | 6/4[1] | 64 | 3 |
| 2743[13] | **Hawanafa (47)** (RHannon) **3-8-8**(3) DaneO'Neill(9) (hld up: hdwy over 2f out: nvr nrr) | 8 | **3** | 20/1 | 51 | — |
| | **Pioneerhifidelity** (HRACecil) **3-8-11** WRyan(4) (w'like: scope: hld up: hdwy 3f out: chsd ldng pair tl no ex ins fnl f) | ¾ | **4** | 9/4[3] | 50 | — |
| 2893[5] | **Reno's Treasure (USA)** (JAHarris) **3-8-11** TSprake(1) (plld hrd: trckd ldrs tl outpcd over 2f out) | 2½ | **5** | 50/1 | 46 | — |
| 2798[6] | **Sophie Lockett** (KWHogg) **3-8-11** DeanMcKeown(8) (nvr nr to chal) | hd | **6** | 50/1 | 46 | — |
| 2557[10] | **Freddie's Recall** (MJHeaton-Ellis) **3-8-8**(3) SDrowne(7) (swtg: prom tl rdn & outpcd over 3f out: t.o) | 11 | **7** | 50/1 | 28 | — |
| | **West-Hatch-Spirit** (SGKnight) **3-8-11** VSlattery(5) (cmpt: bkwd: a bhd: t.o) | 12 | **8** | 66/1 | 9 | — |
| 2365[8] | **Countess of Cadiz (USA)** (TKersey) **3-8-11** NCarlisle(6) (b: bit bkwd: led over 4f: wknd 3f out: t.o) | 1¾ | **9** | 150/1 | 6 | — |
| | **Locket** (JABennett) **3-8-11** JWeaver(10) (cmpt: str: bkwd: s.s: a bhd & outpcd: t.o) | dist | **10** | 33/1 | — | — |
| | | | | (SP 119.8%) | **10 Rn** | |

**2m 9.7** (7.20) CSF £5.36 TOTE £3.40: £1.10 £1.20 £5.60 (£2.70) Trio £33.20 OWNER Sheikh Ahmed Al Maktoum (NEWMARKET) BRED Sheikh Ahmed bin Rashid al Maktoum

**2789 Rehaab** moved scratchily to post, but won this readily and, as she is sure to benefit from a longer trip, she should go on improving. (2/1)
**2794 Agdistis** took over before halfway and, with the winner, drew clear of her pursuers, but she had no answer to the superior finishing speed of Rehaab. (6/4)
**1689 Hawanafa** came out of the pack and was doing her best work in the closing stages but, by then, the leading pair had long gone. (20/1)
**Pioneerhifidelity**, a plain-looking filly, did her best to close on the principals early in the straight, but she was always being stretched, and was not knocked about when it was obvious that her measure had been taken. (9/4: op 11/8)
**Reno's Treasure (USA)**, keen to get on with it, kept tabs on the leaders until getting left behind when the contest began in earnest. (50/1)
**2798 Sophie Lockett** improved considerably on her initial outing, but still never got within striking range of the principals. (50/1)

## 3109 RAINWORTH MINERS LIMITED STKS (0-60) (3-Y.O+) (Class F)

8-55 (8-55) **1m 1f 213y** £2,381.00 (£656.00: £311.00) Stalls: Low GOING minus 0.40 sec per fur (F)

| | Horse | | | SP | RR | SF |
|---|---|---|---|---|---|---|
| 2803[2] | **Alabang (61)** (MJCamacho) **5-9-8** LCharnock(2) (lw: stdd s: hdwy 4f out: led over 2f out: sn wl clr: eased towards fin) | — | **1** | 5/2[1] | 74+ | 29 |
| 2715[6] | **Age of Reality (USA) (60)** (HCandy) **3-8-5** GDuffield(3) (a.p: rdn & outpcd 2f out: no ch w wnr) | 3½ | **2** | 14/1 | 61 | 6 |
| 2540[2] | **Rex Mundi (58)** (PDEvans) **4-9-4** JFortune(5) (swtg: hld up: hdwy u.p over 2f out: r.o one pce) | s.h | **3** | 10/1 | 64 | 19 |
| 2896[7] | **Royal Thimble (IRE) (57)** (NoelChance) **5-8-12v**(5) MartinDwyer(8) (lw: trckd ldrs: effrt u.p over 2f out: kpt on one pce) | s.h | **4** | 10/1 | 63 | 18 |
| 1324[6] | **Tarry (60)** (AStreeter) **3-8-5** TSprake(9) (lw: hld up: hdwy over 2f out: nt rch ldrs) | 3 | **5** | 7/1 | 56 | 1 |
| 2776[5] | **Silverdale Knight (57)** (KWHogg) **3-8-8** DeanMcKeown(6) (trckd ldrs: rdn 3f out: grad wknd) | 3 | **6** | 8/1 | 55 | — |
| 2851* | **Broctune Gold (69)** (MrsMReveley) **5-9-10** ACulhane(1) (lw: led 2f: chsd ldr tl wknd over 2f out: t.o) | 10 | **7** | 7/2[2] | 45 | — |
| 2762[4] | **Royal Expose (USA) (58)** (RHannon) **3-8-5**(3) DaneO'Neill(4) (a in rr: t.o) | 4 | **8** | 10/1 | 32 | — |
| 3043[8] | **Zaaleff (USA) (50)** (BHanbury) **4-9-4b** MRimmer(11) (lw: s.s: a bhd: t.o) | 2 | **9** | 14/1 | 29 | — |
| 2847* | **Mithraic (IRE) (65)** (WSCunningham) **4-9-3**(5) RHavlin(12) (lw: led after 2f: sn wl clr: wknd & hdd over 2f out: t.o) | 3 | **10** | 5/1[3] | 28 | — |
| | | | | (SP 131.7%) | **10 Rn** | |

**2m 8.0** (5.50) CSF £38.00 TOTE £4.50: £1.50 £2.90 £3.40 (£38.70) Trio £220.90 OWNER Mr H. Roberts (MALTON) BRED Mrs S. Camacho
WEIGHT FOR AGE 3yo-10lb

**2803 Alabang** had far more use made of him this time and, judging by the way he spreadeagled this field, it would seem this is probably the best way to ride him. (5/2)
**2715 Age of Reality (USA)** got the better of a tough tussle for the runner-up prize without having a hope of troubling the winner, and she is certainly open to improvement. (14/1)
**2540 Rex Mundi** is slowly but surely getting it together, and should not be long in striking form. (10/1)
**2793* Royal Thimble (IRE)**, never far away, kept battling on in the latter stages but looked just to lack that extra turn of pace to do anything serious about it. (10/1)
**1324 Tarry** did not begin to pick up until too late and was never able to threaten the leaders. (7/1)
**2851* Broctune Gold** helped share the pace and then remained in pursuit of the clear leader until fading rather quickly below the distance. He is a different proposition when allowed to dictate on his own. (7/2)
**2847* Mithraic (IRE)** had a head-to-head with Broctune Gold early on which he eventually won, but it took its mark in the latter stages and he was down to a walk entering the final quarter-mile. (5/1: 3/1-11/2)

T/Plpt: £60.90 (187.38 Tckts). T/Qdpt: £22.20 (42.59 Tckts). IM

# 2941-WINDSOR (Fig. 8) (Good)

## Monday July 29th

WEATHER: fine WIND: nil

## 3110 SCANIA 4-SERIES 'HORSEPOWER' (S) STKS (2-Y.O) (Class G)

6-15 (6-16) **5f 217y** £2,332.00 (£652.00: £316.00) Stalls: High GOING minus 0.26 sec per fur (GF)

| | Horse | | | SP | RR | SF |
|---|---|---|---|---|---|---|
| 2795[4] | **Nightingale Song** (MartynMeade) **2-8-6** JReid(2) (mde all: edgd lft fnl f: drvn out) | — | **1** | 6/1[2] | 63 | 25 |

| | | | | SP | RR | SF |
|---|---|---|---|---|---|---|
| $2596^{6}$ | **Charlton Spring (IRE)** (RJHodges) **2-8-6** JQuinn(7) (hld up: hdwy 2f out: ev ch ins fnl f: edgd lft: no ex) | nk | **2** | $6/1^{2}$ | 62 | 24 |
| $2854^{5}$ | **Gopi** (RHannon) **2-8-6** PatEddery(6) (b.nr fore: chsd wnr: ev ch 1f out: wknd ins fnl f) | 4 | **3** | $5/6^{1}$ | 52 | 14 |
| *$2635^{5}$* | **Wedding Music** (PCHaslam) **2-8-6** JStack(4) (hdwy 3f out: wknd over 1f out) | 6 | **4** | 20/1 | 36 | — |
| | **Code** (BJMeehan) **2-8-11** BDoyle(8) (unf: bit bkwd: w'like: bkwd: no hdwy fnl 2f) | 3½ | **5** | $6/1^{2}$ | 31 | — |
| $2435^{6}$ | **Victory At Hart** (ICampbell) **2-8-11** TIves(9) (sn bhd: rdn 3f out: one pce) | 1¾ | **6** | 20/1 | 26 | — |
| | **Koordinaite** (WJMusson) **2-8-6** AMcGlone(5) (in tch tl hung lft & wknd over 2f out) | s.h | **7** | 20/1 | 21 | — |
| $2343^{7}$ | **April In Paris** (CJames) **2-8-6** CRutter(3) (prom tl rdn & wknd over 2f out) | nk | **8** | $16/1^{3}$ | 21 | — |
| | **Lake Spring (IRE)** (RJHodges) **2-8-11** AMackay(1) (neat: s.s: a t.o) | 17 | **9** | 20/1 | — | — |

(SP 122.3%) **9 Rn**

**1m 13.6** (3.10) CSF £39.06 TOTE £6.10: £1.70 £1.40 £1.20 (£12.00) Trio £3.40 OWNER Mr Stephen Bayless (MALMESBURY) BRED A. Bromley
Bt in 8,800 gns

**2795 Nightingale Song**, favoured by the less firm ground, made all the running. Despite edging to the left in the final furlong, she held on well. (6/1)

**2031 Charlton Spring (IRE)** travelled well, tracking the leaders, and looked the likely winner when moving up to challenge at the distance. She edged left under pressure in the final furlong, and could find no more. (6/1)

**2854 Gopi**, dropped again in class, ran rather freely to the start and also took a strong tug in the race. She raced in second but, after having every chance a furlong out, weakened. She may do better over five. (5/6: 8/11-11/10)

**Wedding Music** loomed up on the outside at halfway but, after looking dangerous, her effort petered out below the distance. (20/1)

**Code** was always in midfield, and could make no impression on the leaders in the last two furlongs. (6/1)

## 3111 TING H'CAP (0-70) (3-Y.O+) (Class E)

6-40 (6-44) **1m 2f 7y** £3,192.50 (£965.00: £470.00: £222.50) Stalls: High GOING minus 0.26 sec per fur (GF)

| | | | | SP | RR | SF |
|---|---|---|---|---|---|---|
| $2743^{3}$ | **Bakers Daughter (47)** (JRArnold) **4-8-8** AClark(7) (a.p: led ins fnl f: drvn out) | — | **1** | 10/1 | 59 | 39 |
| $2943^{3}$ | **Princess Danielle (56)** (WRMuir) **4-9-3** JReid(11) (gd hdwy 4f out: led over 1f out tl ins fnl f) | 1¼ | **2** | $13/2^{2}$ | 66 | 46 |
| $2784^{5}$ | **Runic Symbol (42)** (MBlanshard) **5-8-3** JQuinn(1) (hdwy fnl 2f: nrst fin) | 3 | **3** | $8/1^{3}$ | 47 | 27 |
| $2896^{5}$ | **Lady Sabina (35)** (WJMusson) **6-7-10** DeclanO'Shea(4) (hld up & bhd: r.o fnl 2f: nrst fin) | 1 | **4** | 16/1 | 39 | 19 |
| $2784^{10}$ | **Premier League (IRE) (60)** (JELong) **6-9-0**(7) TField(6) (lw: led after 2f tl over 2f out: wknd fnl f) | 1½ | **5** | 16/1 | 61 | 41 |
| $2780^{2}$ | **Double Up (67)** (LadyHerries) **3-8-11**(7) PDoe(3) (swtg: led 2f: led over 2f out tl over 1f out: edgd lft: wknd fnl f) | hd | **6** | $8/1^{3}$ | 68 | 38 |
| $2628^{3}$ | **Montone (IRE) (64)** (JRJenkins) **6-9-11v** PatEddery(14) (hdwy 4f out: wknd 2f out) | 13 | **7** | $13/2^{2}$ | 44 | 24 |
| $2603^{14}$ | **Fighting Times (59)** (CASmith) **4-9-6** CRutter(9) (a bhd) | ½ | **8** | 20/1 | 39 | 19 |
| $2574^{6}$ | **Fastini Gold (45)** (MDIUsher) **4-8-6** BDoyle(5) (a bhd) | ½ | **9** | 33/1 | 24 | 4 |
| 1414* | **Absolutelystunning (58)** (MrsBarbaraWaring) **3-8-9** FNorton(2) (b: lw: prom tl rdn & wknd over 3f out) | nk | **10** | 12/1 | 36 | 6 |
| $2486^{6}$ | **Get Tough (62)** (SDow) **3-8-13** BThomson(8) (a bhd) | 1½ | **11** | 14/1 | 38 | 8 |
| 2784* | **Mister O'Grady (IRE) (53)** (RAkehurst) **5-9-0** SSanders(10) (lw: wl bhd fnl 5f: t.o) | 30 | **12** | $7/2^{1}$ | — | — |
| $1666^{3}$ | **Classic Colours (USA) (68)** (RHarris) **3-9-5** AMackay(12) (b: prom tl wknd qckly 4f out: t.o fnl 3f) | dist | **13** | 14/1 | — | — |
| $2901^{7}$ | **Talented Ting (IRE) (58)** (PCHaslam) **7-9-5** RHughes(13) (prom tl wknd 5f out: t.o fnl 3f) | nk | **14** | 14/1 | — | — |

(SP 127.4%) **14 Rn**

**2m 8.9** (4.00) CSF £72.05 CT £515.60 TOTE £13.90: £2.80 £2.20 £2.80 (£23.50) Trio £55.50 OWNER Mr J. R. Arnold (UPPER LAMBOURN) BRED C. C. Bromley and Son and A. O. Nerses
LONG HANDICAP Lady Sabina 7-9
WEIGHT FOR AGE 3yo-10lb

OFFICIAL EXPLANATION **Lady Sabina: connections reported that the filly needs settling in and riding from behind in order to pass horses.**

**2743 Bakers Daughter**, always close up this time, gained a narrow lead inside the final furlong and won going away. (10/1: 8/1-14/1)

**2943 Princess Danielle** made rapid headway soon after the home turn and appeared to be travelling like a winner from that point. After taking up the running approaching the final furlong, she could find no extra in the last 150 yards. (13/2)

**2784 Runic Symbol** stayed on to take a remote third place, but was never on terms with the leading pair. (8/1: op 9/2)

**2896 Lady Sabina**, settled at the back of the field, made good late headway, but never had a hope of reaching the leading trio. (16/1)

**2574 Premier League (IRE)** went to the front after two furlongs before gradually weakening when headed over two furlongs from home. (16/1)

**2780 Double Up** disputed the early running. After leading again over two furlongs out, he weakened when headed below the distance. (8/1: op 4/1)

**1414* Absolutelystunning** (12/1: 8/1-14/1)

**2784* Mister O'Grady (IRE)** ran extremely badly and, well behind from halfway, finished tailed off. (7/2)

**1666 Classic Colours (USA)** (14/1: op 8/1)

## 3112 JP FRUIT DISTRIBUTORS H'CAP (0-80) (3-Y.O+ F & M) (Class D)

7-10 (7-12) **5f 217y** £3,694.50 (£1,116.00: £543.00: £256.50) Stalls: High GOING minus 0.26 sec per fur (GF)

| | | | | SP | RR | SF |
|---|---|---|---|---|---|---|
| 2860* | **Kind of Light (73)** (RGuest) **3-9-6** JReid(4) (a.p: qcknd to ld over 1f out: r.o wl) | — | **1** | $4/1^{1}$ | 80 | 57 |
| $2193^{7}$ | **Spandrel (57)** (HCandy) **4-8-9** CRutter(7) (hrd rdn over 2f out: gd hdwy fnl f: nrst fin) | 2½ | **2** | 7/1 | 57 | 39 |
| $2743^{14}$ | **Nellie North (61)** (GMMcCourt) **3-8-8** BThomson(5) (a.p: hrd rdn over 2f out: r.o) | nk | **3** | 16/1 | 61 | 38 |
| $2715^{3}$ | **Polly Golightly (67)** (MBlanshard) **3-9-0** RCochrane(3) (led over 2f: r.o one pce) | 1½ | **4** | $6/1^{3}$ | 63 | 40 |
| $2705^{8}$ | **Petit Point (IRE) (76)** (RHannon) **3-9-9** PatEddery(2) (lw: w ldrs: led over 3f out tl over 1f out: wknd fnl f) | 1¾ | **5** | 8/1 | 67 | 44 |
| $2976^{7}$ | **Fantasy Racing (IRE) (76)** (MRChannon) **4-10-0** RHughes(1) (w ldrs: hrd rdn 2f out: nt qckn) | ¾ | **6** | 16/1 | 65 | 47 |
| $2793^{7}$ | **Kowtow (55)** (MDIUsher) **3-8-2** RStreet(6) (lw: a abt same pl) | 1¾ | **7** | 33/1 | 39 | 16 |
| $2363^{9}$ | **Prima Silk (69)** (MJRyan) **5-9-7** BDoyle(9) (nvr nr to chal) | 3 | **8** | 8/1 | 45 | 27 |
| | **Primelta (65)** (RAkehurst) **3-8-12** SSanders(10) (lw: a bhd) | 6 | **9** | 11/1 | 25 | 2 |
| $2617^{18}$ | **Persian Butterfly (64)** (ICampbell) **4-9-2** AClark(8) (bhd fnl 3f) | 11 | **10** | 10/1 | — | — |
| 2597* | **Watch The Fire (73)** (JEBanks) **3-9-6** JStack(11) (lw: bhd fnl 3f) | 5 | **11** | $9/2^{2}$ | — | — |

(SP 119.3%) **11 Rn**

**1m 12.2** (1.70) CSF £30.36 CT £374.16 TOTE £4.10: £1.80 £2.20 £2.90 (£20.60) Trio £77.20 OWNER Mrs B. Mills (NEWMARKET) BRED Theakston Stud
WEIGHT FOR AGE 3yo-5lb

**2860* Kind of Light** sat in fourth place full of running and, when asked to quicken below the distance, settled the issue in a few strides. (4/1)

**2193 Spandrel** came under pressure a long way out, but it was not until the final furlong that she made any significant headway. She was flying at the finish and is surely capable of winning a race. (7/1: 9/12-8/1)

**2186 Nellie North**, always on the heels of the leaders, came under hard driving for the final two and a half furlongs. She stuck on well, but never appeared likely to win. (16/1)
**1840* Petit Point (IRE)** could not quicken with the winner approaching the final furlong. (8/1)
**Primelta** (11/1: 7/1-12/1)
**2597* Watch The Fire** (9/2: op 3/1)

## 3113 SCANIA 1996 TRUCK OF THE YEAR H'CAP (0-70) (3-Y.O+) (Class E)

7-40 (7-46) **1m 3f 135y** £3,046.25 (£920.00: £447.50: £211.25) Stalls: High GOING minus 0.26 sec per fur (GF)

| Form | Horse | Dist | Pos | SP | RR | SF |
|---|---|---|---|---|---|---|
| 2377* | **Newport Knight (66)** (RAkehurst) **5-9-13** SSanders(10) (b.nr hind: a.p: led ins fnl f: drvn out) | — | 1 | 13/2$^{2}$ | 76 | 22 |
| 2941$^{3}$ | **Elly Fleetfoot (IRE) (51)** (MJRyan) **4-8-12b** BDoyle(13) (hld up: qcknd to ld over 2f out: hdd ins fnl f: r.o) | hd | 2 | 15/2 | 61 | 7 |
| 2941$^{2}$ | **Nothing Doing (IRE) (35)** (WJMusson) **7-7-10** DeclanO'Shea(14) (plld hrd: prom tl lost pl 3f out: rallied over 1f out: r.o) | ¾ | 3 | 8/1 | 44 | — |
| 2866* | **Fabulous Mtoto (55)** (MSSaunders) **6-9-2** RPerham(7) (b: hdwy 3f out: ev ch over 1f out: one pce) | 1¾ | 4 | 5/1$^{1}$ | 61 | 7 |
| 1173$^{11}$ | **Abtaal (56)** (RJHodges) **6-9-3** JQuinn(11) (hdwy over 2f out: one pce fnl f) | 6 | 5 | 33/1 | 54 | — |
| 2621$^{16}$ | **Mancini (70)** (MBell) **3-9-5** MFenton(2) (lw: bhd tl hdwy 2f out: nvr nr to chal) | 1¼ | 6 | 16/1 | 66 | — |
| 2341$^{3}$ | **Premier Dance (46)** (DHaydnJones) **9-8-7** AMackay(9) (hdwy over 3f out: wknd over 1f out) | nk | 7 | 15/2 | 42 | — |
| 3000$^{4}$ | **Almuhtaram (67)** (MissGayKelleway) **4-10-0b** RCochrane(3) (lw: hdwy 3f out: rdn & wknd over 1f out) | 2½ | 8 | 13/2$^{2}$ | 60 | 6 |
| 2928* | **Victoria's Secret (IRE) (54)** (MRChannon) **4-9-1** 5x RHughes(4) (chsd ldrs: led over 3f out tl wknd over 2f out) | 1 | 9 | 11/1 | 45 | — |
| 1852$^{11}$ | **Reiterate (51)** (GBBalding) **3-8-0** NAdams(12) (led after 4f tl wknd over 3f out) | 5 | 10 | 33/1 | 35 | — |
| 2709$^{9}$ | **Bronhallow (50)** (MrsBarbaraWaring) **3-7-13** FNorton(5) (b.nr hind: lw: prom tl wknd over 3f out) | 2½ | 11 | 33/1 | 31 | — |
| *2552*$^{10}$ | **Kintwyn (45)** (WRMuir) **6-8-6**ow1 JReid(8) (a bhd) | ½ | 12 | 16/1 | 25 | — |
| 2613$^{5}$ | **Seven Crowns (USA) (61)** (RHannon) **3-8-10** PatEddery(6) (lw: led 4f: ev ch 3f out: sn wknd) | nk | 13 | 7/1$^{3}$ | 41 | — |
| 2247$^{9}$ | **Compass Pointer (62)** (JMPEustace) **3-8-11** MTebbutt(1) (bhd fnl 3f) | 1½ | 14 | 14/1 | 40 | — |

(SP 126.1%) **14 Rn**

**2m 33.9** (9.90) CSF £52.99 CT £366.63 TOTE £8.60: £2.80 £1.90 £3.10 (£24.10) Trio £44.00 OWNER James Thorburn-Muirh Lomax (EPSOM) BRED Pendley Farm
WEIGHT FOR AGE 3yo-12lb
**2377* Newport Knight**, always close up, was driven into the lead entering the final furlong, and held on well. (13/2: 4/1-7/1)
**2941 Elly Fleetfoot (IRE)** was travelling extremely strongly when quickening to take the lead over two furlongs from home. Headed inside the final furlong, she was coming back again at the finish. (15/2)
**2941 Nothing Doing (IRE)** pulled hard on the heels of the leaders, but lost his place at the three-furlong marker. He came again to challenge at the distance, and was running on well at the finish. His luck should surely turn soon. (8/1: 6/1-9/1)
**2866* Fabulous Mtoto** made a forward move three furlongs out but, after having every chance, could find no extra in the last furlong. (5/1)
**Abtaal** improved into a prominent position over two furlongs from home, but could make no further headway in the closing stages. (33/1)
**1106 Mancini**, at the back of the field for much of the way, made ground two furlongs out, but too late to trouble the leading group. (16/1)
**3000 Almuhtaram** made promising headway three furlongs out but, when asked to race in earnest below the distance, could find no extra. (13/2)
**2928* Victoria's Secret (IRE)** (11/1: op 7/1)
**1498 Compass Pointer** (14/1: 8/1-16/1)

## 3114 SOUTHWAY FOR SCANIA MAIDEN STKS (2-Y.O) (Class D)

8-10 (8-17) **5f 10y** £3,517.50 (£1,065.00: £520.00: £247.50) Stalls: High GOING minus 0.26 sec per fur (GF)

| Form | Horse | Dist | Pos | SP | RR | SF |
|---|---|---|---|---|---|---|
| 2230$^{2}$ | **Chili Concerto** (PJMakin) **2-8-9** SSanders(14) (racd stands' side: mde all: comf) | — | 1 | 3/1$^{1}$ | 84+ | 33 |
| | **Sylvan Dancer (IRE)** (CFWall) **2-8-9** JReid(13) (lt-f: racd stands' side: chsd wnr: rdn 2f out: no imp) | 3½ | 2 | 10/1 | 73? | 22 |
| 2852$^{4}$ | **Cryhavoc** (JRArnold) **2-9-0** CRutter(10) (led far side: nvr on terms w first two) | ½ | 3 | 8/1 | 76 | 25 |
| 2624$^{7}$ | **A Breeze** (DMorris) **2-9-0** DHarrison(11) (a.p: r.o one pce fnl f) | 3 | 4 | 8/1 | 67 | 16 |
| 683$^{3}$ | **Silca Key Silca** (MRChannon) **2-8-9** DHolland(2) (a.p: nt qckn fnl f) | ½ | 5 | 13/2$^{3}$ | 60 | 9 |
| | **Tomba** (BJMeehan) **2-9-0** BDoyle(1) (scope: nvr nrr) | 1¾ | 6 | 20/1 | 60 | 9 |
| 1896$^{8}$ | **Ellens Lad (IRE)** (RHannon) **2-9-0** PatEddery(9) (lw: gd spd 3f: eased whn btn fnl f) | 2 | 7 | 7/2$^{2}$ | 53 | 2 |
| 2279$^{3}$ | **Summerville Wood** (PMooney) **2-8-7**(7) CScally(6) (nvr nr to chal) | 5 | 8 | 12/1 | 38 | — |
| | **Pininfarina** (MartynMeade) **2-8-9** RPerham(8) (w'like: outpcd) | 3 | 9 | 25/1 | 23 | — |
| | **Wild Nettle** (JCFox) **2-8-9** RCochrane(3) (w'like: outpcd) | ¾ | 10 | 33/1 | 21 | — |
| 2157$^{W}$ | **Hever Golf Charger (IRE)** (TJNaughton) **2-9-0** PaulEddery(5) (lt-f: s.s: a bhd) | 3½ | 11 | 20/1 | 15 | — |
| | **Sarabi** (JPearce) **2-8-9** GBardwell(7) (w'like: outpcd) | ½ | 12 | 20/1 | 8 | — |
| | **Chilli Boom** (TJNaughton) **2-8-9** AClark(4) (lengthy: a bhd) | 8 | 13 | 25/1 | — | — |
| 2614$^{4}$ | **Pow Wow** (MRChannon) **2-9-0** RHughes(12) (prom 3f: wknd qckly) | 8 | 14 | 12/1 | — | — |

(SP 132.2%) **14 Rn**

**61.5 secs** (2.30) CSF £34.37 TOTE £4.20: £2.00 £3.20 £2.10 (£22.10) Trio £56.90 OWNER Ten Horsepower (MARLBOROUGH) BRED Mrs P. J. Makin
**2230 Chili Concerto**, one of only two to race up the stands' side, made all and was in control a long way out. (3/1)
**Sylvan Dancer (IRE)** and the winner were the only ones to race up the stands' side. Gamely as she struggled, she was always held by her rival. (10/1: 7/1-12/1)
**2852 Cryhavoc** was always leading the twelve on the far side, but they were never on terms with the opposite side. (8/1: 6/1-10/1)
**2624 A Breeze**, always chasing the leading group, ran on under pressure in the last two furlongs. (8/1)
**683 Silca Key Silca** might have needed the run after three months off, but ran fast and was keeping on well at the finish. She should be able to win a similar event. (13/2: 9/2-7/1)
**Tomba** ran on at the end. (20/1)
**Ellens Lad (IRE)** ran fast for over three furlongs and was eased when his chance had gone. (7/2: op 7/4)
**2614 Pow Wow** (12/1: op 8/1)

## 3115 SCANIA 4-SERIES 'KING OF THE ROAD' CLAIMING STKS (3-Y.O+) (Class F)

8-40 (8-41) **1m 67y** £2,787.00 (£782.00: £381.00) Stalls: High GOING minus 0.26 sec per fur (GF)

| Form | Horse | Dist | Pos | SP | RR | SF |
|---|---|---|---|---|---|---|
| 2373$^{2}$ | **Cape Pigeon (USA) (57)** (LGCottrell) **11-8-9v** DHolland(1) (lw: mde all: sn clr: drvn out) | — | 1 | 4/1$^{2}$ | 71 | 16 |
| 2862$^{9}$ | **Mellottie (90)** (MrsMReveley) **11-9-12** KDarley(10) (lw: hdwy 4f out: hrd rdn 2f out: r.o: nvr nr wnr) | 7 | 2 | 4/7$^{1}$ | 75 | 20 |
| 2710$^{5}$ | **Honorable Estate (IRE) (62)** (RHannon) **3-8-1** SSanders(4) (hdwy 5f out: wnt 2nd over 1f out: one pce) | nk | 3 | 7/1$^{3}$ | 57 | — |

| | Horse / details | Dist | Pos | SP | RR | SF |
|---|---|---|---|---|---|---|
| *529*³ | **Mogin** (TJNaughton) **3-8-3** PaulEddery(12) (hdwy on ins 3f out: styd on: nt rch ldrs) | 3½ | **4** | 25/1 | 52 | — |
| | **Proud Brigadier (IRE)** (PBurgoyne) **8-8-12** JStack(7) (b: chsd wnr tl wknd over 1f out) | 1½ | **5** | 33/1 | 50 | — |
| 2859⁷ | **Koraloona (IRE)** (GBBalding) **3-8-10** MWigham(5) (nvr plcd to chal) | 3½ | **6** | 33/1 | 50 | — |
| | **Calandrella** (GBBalding) **3-8-3** AMcGlone(13) (lengthy: unf: sme hdwy fnl 2f: nvr nr to chal) | 1 | **7** | 33/1 | 41 | — |
| | **Platinum Plus** (CADwyer) **4-9-12** CDwyer(11) (b: swtg: nvr nr ldrs) | 1¾ | **8** | 14/1 | 52 | — |
| 2785⁹ | **Moylough Rebel (41)** (JELong) **3-8-10** LeesaLong(8) (prom tl wknd 3f out) | 2½ | **9** | 33/1 | 39 | — |
| | **Bryanston Square (IRE)** (CREgerton) **3-8-13** RHughes(6) (w'like: a wl bhd) | 6 | **10** | 33/1 | 31 | — |
| | **Radical Exception (IRE)** (DLWilliams) **6-8-9** DHarrison(14) (s.s: a wl bhd) | 6 | **11** | 33/1 | 7 | — |
| | **Highly Spirited** (NMLampard) **3-8-1**(7) TField(2) (lengthy: unf: a wl bhd: t.o) | dist | **12** | 33/1 | — | — |
| | | | | (SP 127.2%) | **12 Rn** | |

**1m 48.1** (5.90) CSF £6.58 TOTE £4.20: £1.10 £1.10 £1.90 (£2.70) Trio £2.00 OWNER Mr E. J. S. Gadsden (CULLOMPTON) BRED Ashwood Thoroughbreds, Inc.
WEIGHT FOR AGE 3yo-8lb

**2373 Cape Pigeon (USA)** set an extremely fast pace and had only one rival near him to halfway, and none from then on. Galloping on strongly, he was never in any danger. (4/1)
**2350 Mellottie**, held up towards the back of the field, made ground four furlongs out. Hard driven in the last quarter-mile, he ran on to snatch second place but was never in the same parish as the winner. (4/7)
**2710 Honorable Estate (IRE)** took third place approaching the straight, albeit fifteen lengths behind the leading pair. She went second momentarily, but was never near the winner. (7/1)
**529 Mogin** came with a run on the stands' rail three furlongs out but, though staying on, was never near the leading trio. (25/1)
**Proud Brigadier (IRE)**, the only one ever near the winner, raced in second place until weakening approaching the final furlong. (33/1)
**Koraloona (IRE)** ran better than his final placing would suggest and is one to keep on the right side. (33/1)
**Calandrella** was running on steadily from the two-furlong marker, but was never able to go the very strong pace. (33/1)
**Platinum Plus** (14/1: op 25/1)

T/Jkpt: Not won; £40,130.38 to Goodwood 30/7/96. T/Plpt: £51.90 (375.09 Tckts). T/Qdpt: £10.60 (94.12 Tckts). Hn

## 2922-**BEVERLEY** (R-H) (Good to firm)
## Tuesday July 30th
WEATHER: overcast WIND: mod across

### 3116 LADYGATE (S) H'CAP (0-60) (3-Y.O) (Class F)
2-00 (2-01) **1m 3f 216y** £2,595.00 (£720.00: £345.00) Stalls: High GOING minus 0.27 sec per fur (GF)

| | Horse / details | Dist | Pos | SP | RR | SF |
|---|---|---|---|---|---|---|
| 1042¹⁰ | **Tagatay (35)** (MJCamacho) **3-8-11** LCharnock(2) (hld up & bhd: hdwy & swtchd 2f out: led ins fnl f: styd on wl) | — | **1** | 15/2 | 47 | 7 |
| 2922⁴ | **Veshca Lady (IRE) (42)** (EWeymes) **3-9-1**(3) FLynch(5) (chsd ldrs: rdn to ld over 1f out: hdd & one pce ins fnl f) | 4 | **2** | 7/4 1 | 49 | 9 |
| 2565³ | **Ragtime Cowgirl (40)** (CWThornton) **3-9-2** DeanMcKeown(4) (led tl hdd over 1f out: sn btn) | 2½ | **3** | 2/1 2 | 43 | 3 |
| 2388² | **Stoleamarch (45)** (MrsMReveley) **3-9-7** ACulhane(6) (hld up: rdn 5f out: no imp) | 5 | **4** | 9/2 3 | 42 | 2 |
| 2362² | **Ginger Hodgers (34)** (RMWhitaker) **3-8-10** FNorton(1) (lw: cl up tl rdn & wknd over 2f out) | 10 | **5** | 8/1 | 17 | — |
| 2556¹⁴ | **Formentiere (36)** (JMBradley) **3-8-5**(7) CLowther(3) (hld up: effrt appr st: sn btn) | nk | **6** | 20/1 | 19 | — |
| | | | | (SP 115.5%) | **6 Rn** | |

**2m 42.9** (10.50) CSF £20.86 TOTE £13.00: £4.20 £1.30 (£12.40) OWNER Mr M. Gleason (MALTON) BRED Mrs S. Camacho
No bid

**Tagatay** had not been out for almost three months and got a shade warm beforehand, but this step up in trip certainly suited him. The further he went, the better he got. (15/2)
**2922 Veshca Lady (IRE)** keeps running well, but is short of a turn of foot at the business end. (7/4)
**2565 Ragtime Cowgirl** is not very big and had her limitations well exposed here. (2/1)
**2388 Stoleamarch**, taken to post early as usual, showed little when the pressure was on. (9/2)
**2362 Ginger Hodgers**, without the visor here and after a month off, cried enough once into the home straight. (8/1)
**Formentiere** has yet to show anything positive. (20/1)

### 3117 SWINGS AND ROUNDABOUTS H'CAP (0-70) (3-Y.O+) (Class E)
2-30 (2-32) **1m 3f 216y** £3,150.00 (£945.00: £455.00: £210.00) Stalls: High GOING minus 0.27 sec per fur (GF)

| | Horse / details | Dist | Pos | SP | RR | SF |
|---|---|---|---|---|---|---|
| 2360³ | **Mister Aspecto (IRE) (63)** (MJohnston) **3-9-5v** PRobinson(7) (mde all: styd on wl fnl 3f) | — | **1** | 9/2 2 | 75 | 45 |
| 2998⁵ | **Nikita's Star (IRE) (65)** (DJGMurraySmith) **3-9-7** DHolland(1) (in tch: effrt over 3f out: sn chsng ldrs: styd on one pce) | 3 | **2** | 6/1 3 | 73 | 43 |
| 2891³ | **Ttyfran (35)** (BPJBaugh) **6-8-3** WLord(9) (a chsng ldrs: rdn over 2f out: one pce) | nk | **3** | 9/1 | 43 | 25 |
| 2390⁴ | **Pendolino (IRE) (39)** (MBrittain) **5-8-7b** JLowe(6) (lw: a chsng ldrs: one pce fnl 3f) | 2½ | **4** | 12/1 | 43 | 25 |
| 2775⁵ | **Instantaneous (41)** (TDEasterby) **4-8-9** MBirch(5) (lw: trckd ldrs tl grad wknd fnl 3f) | 1½ | **5** | 12/1 | 43 | 25 |
| 2969³ | **In the Money (IRE) (59)** (RHollinshead) **7-9-10**(3) FLynch(3) (hld up: effrt 4f out: no imp) | 4 | **6** | 15/2 | 56 | 38 |
| 3056³ | **Alwarqa (63)** (DNicholls) **3-9-5** AlexGreaves(2) (hdwy after 4f: grad lost pl fnl 3f) | 2½ | **7** | 10/1 | 57 | 27 |
| 2866⁴ | **Arabian Heights (51)** (MrsJRRamsden) **3-8-7** KFallon(4) (bhd: drvn along 4f out: n.d) | 3 | **8** | 5/2 1 | 41 | 11 |
| 2319⁸ | **Non Vintage (IRE) (52)** (MCChapman) **5-9-6** DRMcCabe(8) (a outpcd & bhd) | 1 | **9** | 12/1 | 40 | 22 |
| | | | | (SP 115.0%) | **9 Rn** | |

**2m 38.0** (5.60) CSF £29.08 CT £211.48 TOTE £5.50: £1.60 £2.20 £1.80 (£16.30) Trio £29.70 OWNER Aspecto Clothing Co Ltd (MIDDLEHAM) BRED Petra Bloodstock Agency Ltd
WEIGHT FOR AGE 3yo-12lb
STEWARDS' ENQUIRY Lord susp. 8-9/8/96 (excessive use of whip).
OFFICIAL EXPLANATION **Arabian Heights: the rider reported that the gelding ran too free early on.**

**2360 Mister Aspecto (IRE)**, from a stable that is flying at present, had the visor refitted here. Given his own way out in front, he stepped on the gas entering the straight, and was always too good. (9/2)
**2998 Nikita's Star (IRE)**, who does not have much of an action, keeps running well, but was left wanting for pace in the last two furlongs. (6/1)
**2891 Ttyfran**, dropping back in trip, had his chances, but proved far too slow. (9/1)
**2390 Pendolino (IRE)** keeps running reasonably, but it is now two years since he last won, and he looks well short of a turn of foot. (12/1)
**2775 Instantaneous** always gives the impression that she has more ability than she cares to show. (12/1: op 8/1)

**2969 In the Money (IRE)** has been up against some useful opposition of late and that may have taken the edge off him. (15/2)
**2866 Arabian Heights** ran no sort of race. (5/2)

## 3118 TIMEFORM FOR THE DOROTHY LAIRD TROPHY LADIES' H'CAP (0-80) (3-Y.O+) (Class E)

3-05 (3-05) **1m 1f 207y** £3,208.50 (£963.00: £464.00: £214.50) Stalls: High GOING minus 0.27 sec per fur (GF)

| | | | | SP | RR | SF |
|---|---|---|---|---|---|---|
| 2871* | **Gold Blade (64)** (JPearce) **7-10-13** MrsLPearce(1) (lw: hld up: effrt 5f out: led appr fnl f: styd on) | — | **1** | 7/4[1] | 74 | 47 |
| 2896[3] | **Milltown Classic (IRE) (33)** (JParkes) **4-8-10** SophieMitchell(7) (lw: led tl hdd over 1f out: kpt on wl) | ½ | **2** | 4/1[3] | 42 | 15 |
| 2924[3] | **Fairywings (74)** (MrsJRRamsden) **3-10-8**(5) MissERamsden(2) (hld up: hdwy 4f out: effrt 2f out: nt pce to chal) | 1¼ | **3** | 2/1[2] | 81 | 44 |
| 2994[8] | **Asterix (42)** (JMBradley) **8-9-0b**(5) MissLKerr(6) (chsd ldrs: ev ch 3f out: wknd wl over 1f out) | 7 | **4** | 14/1 | 38 | 11 |
| 2924[5] | **Sandblaster (54)** (DNicholls) **3-9-7** AlexGreaves(3) (lw: w ldr: disp ld over 3f out: wknd over 2f out) | 7 | **5** | 6/1 | 39 | 2 |
| | | | | (SP 110.6%) | | **5 Rn** |

**2m 9.2** (6.70) CSF £8.39 TOTE £2.60: £1.30 £1.90 (£5.00) OWNER Mr Jeff Pearce (NEWMARKET) BRED Ballymacoll Stud Co
WEIGHT FOR AGE 3yo-10lb
**2871* Gold Blade** is proving unbeatable in these events and, but for looking about when in front, would have won a deal easier. (7/4)
**2896 Milltown Classic (IRE)** put up a game display and kept on fighting back when looking well beaten, and would appear to need further. (4/1)
**2924 Fairywings** ran well enough to suggest that she is in good form and, with stronger handling, she should do better. (2/1)
**2796 Asterix** seemed to find this trip beyond him. (14/1)
**2924 Sandblaster** has all his best form over shorter trips and, after being up with the pace here, weakened once into the straight. (6/1)

## 3119 E.B.F. MINSTER MOORGATE MAIDEN STKS (2-Y.O) (Class D)

3-35 (3-35) **7f 100y** £3,824.00 (£1,064.00: £512.00) Stalls: High GOING minus 0.27 sec per fur (GF)

| | | | | SP | RR | SF |
|---|---|---|---|---|---|---|
| 2580[5] | **Musical Dancer (USA)** (EALDunlop) **2-9-0** KFallon(1) (lw: trckd ldr: smooth hdwy to ld appr fnl f: styd on) | — | **1** | 4/6[1] | 77 | 28 |
| 2802[4] | **Dream of Nurmi** (DRLoder) **2-9-0** DRMcCabe(2) (lw: led: qcknd 3f out: hdd appr fnl f: kpt on) | 1 | **2** | 13/8[2] | 75 | 26 |
| | **Beau Roberto** (MJohnston) **2-9-0** PRobinson(3) (str: bit bkwd: s.i.s: prom tl wl outpcd fnl 2f) | 15 | **3** | 15/2[3] | 43 | — |
| | | | | (SP 109.9%) | | **3 Rn** |

**1m 36.5** (4.50) CSF £2.06 TOTE £1.40 (£1.10) OWNER Maktoum Al Maktoum (NEWMARKET) BRED Parrish Hill Farm & W. S. Farish
**2580 Musical Dancer (USA)** was certainly a deal fitter than on his debut and won nicely. He will benefit from the experience. (4/6)
**2802 Dream of Nurmi** tried to pinch this by quickening early in the straight, but the winner proved too good, despite his game attempts. He is going the right way. (13/8)
**Beau Roberto** needed this and was left struggling once the pace lifted. He needs time. (15/2: 6/1-12/1)

## 3120 MALTON H'CAP (0-80) (3-Y.O+) (Class D)

4-10 (4-10) **1m 100y** £3,998.00 (£1,199.00: £577.00: £266.00) Stalls: High GOING minus 0.27 sec per fur (GF)

| | | | | SP | RR | SF |
|---|---|---|---|---|---|---|
| 3084[6] | **Smarter Charter (70)** (MrsJRRamsden) **3-8-13** KFallon(6) (lw: bhd tl hdwy ent st: led 1½f out: sn clr) | — | **1** | 8/1 | 81 | 42 |
| 2526[2] | **Bon Luck (IRE) (71)** (JRFanshawe) **4-9-8** NDay(7) (lw: lost pl appr st: hdwy & swtchd 2f out: nrst fin) | 3 | **2** | 5/2[1] | 76 | 45 |
| 2874[3] | **Quilling (68)** (MDods) **4-9-5** DeanMcKeown(1) (lw: hld up: effrt 3f out: nvr able to chal) | hd | **3** | 14/1 | 73 | 42 |
| 2679[7] | **Three Arch Bridge (66)** (MJohnston) **4-9-3b** PRobinson(3) (chsd ldrs: disp ld 2f out tl wknd appr fnl f) | 1½ | **4** | 12/1 | 68 | 37 |
| 1983[7] | **Sooty Tern (65)** (JMBradley) **9-8-9**(7) CLowther(8) (mde most tl hdd & wknd 1½f out) | 1¼ | **5** | 14/1 | 65 | 34 |
| 2925[2] | **Euro Sceptic (IRE) (47)** (TDEasterby) **4-7-12b** LCharnock(4) (chsd ldrs: ev ch 2f out: wknd over 1f out) | ¾ | **6** | 6/1[3] | 46 | 15 |
| 2868[6] | **Pleasure Trick (USA) (45)** (DonEnricoIncisa) **5-7-10** KimTinkler(9) (bhd: c wd & effrt over 2f out: n.d) | hd | **7** | 20/1 | 43 | 12 |
| 2925[4] | **Murphy's Gold (IRE) (52)** (RAFahey) **5-8-3** GCarter(10) (prom: effrt 3f out: wknd fnl 2f) | 2½ | **8** | 3/1[2] | 46 | 15 |
| 2350[5] | **Sarmatian (USA) (73)** (MDHammond) **5-9-5b[1]**(5) DGriffiths(5) (lw: prom tl wknd fnl 3f) | 2½ | **9** | 12/1 | 62 | 31 |
| 2868[2] | **Percy Parrot (45)** (RMWhitaker) **4-7-10** AMackay(2) (slt ld tl wknd over 2f out) | 5 | **10** | 14/1 | 24 | — |
| | | | | (SP 119.1%) | | **10 Rn** |

**1m 47.4** (3.40) CSF £27.53 CT £264.95 TOTE £8.80: £3.00 £1.50 £3.70 (£26.30) Trio £61.70 OWNER Mrs Alison Iles (THIRSK) BRED Carlton Consultants Ltd
LONG HANDICAP Percy Parrot 7-3
WEIGHT FOR AGE 3yo-8lb
**3084 Smarter Charter**, disappointing in an amateur race at the weekend, won with surprising ease here. (8/1)
**2526 Bon Luck (IRE)** never seemed happy on this track and lost his position altogether on the home turn. When he did decide to run in the last two furlongs, it was always too late. (5/2)
**2874 Quilling**, poorly drawn, was held up for a change and ran pretty well, but was short of speed in the last two furlongs. (14/1)
**2679 Three Arch Bridge**, after three moderate runs, showed signs of returning to form. (12/1)
**1659 Sooty Tern** is well enough handicapped, but he has just lost his way of late. (14/1)
**2925 Euro Sceptic (IRE)** loves this track, but proved disappointing on this occasion. (6/1)
**2925 Murphy's Gold (IRE)** is a difficult customer to work out these days, but he certainly has the ability when things go his way. (3/1)

## 3121 FAMILY DAY MAIDEN AUCTION STKS (2-Y.O F) (Class F)

4-45 (4-46) **5f** £2,693.00 (£748.00: £359.00) Stalls: High GOING minus 0.27 sec per fur (GF)

| | | | | SP | RR | SF |
|---|---|---|---|---|---|---|
| 2781[2] | **What Happened Was** (MartynMeade) **2-7-12** FNorton(10) (chsd ldrs: r.o u.p fnl f to ld last stride) | — | **1** | Evens[1] | 62 | 10 |
| 2879[12] | **Snap Crackle Pop (IRE)** (RFJohnsonHoughton) **2-8-5** ACulhane(2) (lw: cl up: led wl over 1f out: sn rdn: jst ct) | s.h | **2** | 9/2[2] | 69 | 17 |
| 2755[6] | **Al Ava Consonant** (JDBethell) **2-8-1**(3)ow3 SDrowne(4) (bhd: hdwy ½-wy: styd on fnl f: nrst fin) | 2½ | **3** | 10/1 | 60 | 5 |
| 3080[11] | **Loch-Hurn Lady** (KWHogg) **2-7-12** LCharnock(8) (led over 3f: grad wknd) | 3½ | **4** | 10/1 | 43 | — |
| 2491[5] | **Scotmail Lass** (GMMoore) **2-7-12** NKennedy(7) (styd on fnl 2f: nrst fin) | 1½ | **5** | 33/1 | 38 | — |
| | **Rusty (IRE)** (JBerry) **2-8-1** GCarter(3) (neat: bit bkwd: s.i.s: nvr nr to chal) | 1½ | **6** | 10/1 | 36 | — |
| | **Whisper Low (IRE)** (RHollinshead) **2-7-12**(3) FLynch(6) (str: cmpt: bit bkwd: chsd ldrs tl wknd appr fnl f) | ½ | **7** | 20/1 | 34 | — |
| 2429[7] | **Joyful Joy** (BPJBaugh) **2-7-12** NCarlisle(9) (s.i.s: nvr trbld ldrs) | nk | **8** | 50/1 | 31 | — |
| 2728[4] | **Little Blue (IRE)** (TDEasterby) **2-8-1** JLowe(5) (prom to ½-wy) | 3 | **9** | 8/1[3] | 24 | — |
| 2569[3] | **Sheraton Girl** (MJohnston) **2-8-5** PRobinson(1) (outpcd & bhd fr ½-wy) | s.h | **10** | 8/1[3] | 28 | — |
| | | | | (SP 127.3%) | | **10 Rn** |

**64.7 secs** (3.20) CSF £6.84 TOTE £1.90: £1.20 £1.80 £2.70 (£6.50) Trio £20.70 OWNER Beyts Livestock Ltd (MALMESBURY) BRED Grange Thoroughbreds

**2781 What Happened Was** needed all her courage and experience to win this and, in a desperate finish, just made it. (Evens)
**Snap Crackle Pop (IRE)**, who looked and moved well, always looked the likely winner, but greenness probably made the difference in a driving finish. (9/2)
**2755 Al Ava Consonant**, who is learning, was staying on well at the end. (10/1)
**2865 Loch-Hurn Lady** has plenty of speed and ran well over this shorter trip. (10/1)
**2491 Scotmail Lass** is improving and was noted making steady late headway. (33/1)
**Rusty (IRE)** needed this and, after a poor start, was never able to get into it. (10/1)
**Whisper Low (IRE)** should improve a fair bit in time. (20/1)

## 3122 'GO RACING IN YORKSHIRE' LIMITED STKS (0-70) (3-Y.O+) (Class E)

5-15 (5-15) **5f** £3,094.75 (£928.00: £446.50: £205.75) Stalls: High GOING minus 0.27 sec per fur (GF)

| Form | Horse | Dist | Pos | SP | RR | SF |
|---|---|---|---|---|---|---|
| 2867[2] | **Royal Dome (IRE) (70)** (MartynWane) **4-9-2** JFortune(1) (mde all: kpt on wl fnl f) | — | **1** | 9/4[1] | 74 | 44 |
| 2771[6] | **Ninety-Five (66)** (JGFitzGerald) **4-9-5** KFallon(6) (a chsng ldrs: effrt over 1f out: nt qckn) | 2½ | **2** | 9/1 | 69 | 39 |
| 2960[5] | **Silk Cottage (62)** (RMWhitaker) **4-9-5v** DeanMcKeown(5) (lw: trckd ldrs: effrt 2f out: hrd rdn & nt qckn ins fnl f) | ½ | **3** | 10/1 | 67 | 37 |
| 2999[7] | **Stoney End (USA) (70)** (MRChannon) **3-9-1** GCarter(4) (lw: dwlt: styd on fnl 2f: nrst fin) | 1¾ | **4** | 5/1[3] | 62 | 28 |
| 3049[2] | **Shashi (IRE) (62)** (WWHaigh) **4-8-11b**(5) LNewton(7) (chsd ldrs to ½-wy: sn outpcd) | nk | **5** | 7/2[2] | 58 | 28 |
| 2908[2] | **Super Rocky (69)** (RBastiman) **7-8-11b**(5) HBastiman(3) (lw: prom: rdn ½-wy: sn wknd) | 7 | **6** | 5/1[3] | 35 | 5 |
| 3085[13] | **Ramsey Hope (70)** (CWFairhurst) **3-8-12b** NKennedy(2) (cl up to ½-wy: sn btn) | 2 | **7** | 8/1 | 29 | — |
| | | | | (SP 116.5%) | **7 Rn** | |

**63.6 secs** (2.10) CSF £20.63 TOTE £2.80: £2.20 £3.40 (£20.30) OWNER Mr G. W. Jones (RICHMOND) BRED Michael F. Fogarty
WEIGHT FOR AGE 3yo-4lb
**2867 Royal Dome (IRE)** had the form to win this and left nothing to chance, winning authoritatively. (9/4)
**2771 Ninety-Five** ran quite well and is obviously still on pretty good terms with herself. (9/1)
**2960 Silk Cottage** still looks particularly well and ran a decent race, but was never quite up to the task. (10/1)
**2705 Stoney End (USA)** has plenty more ability, but seems to have his own ideas about how to use it. (5/1)
**3049 Shashi (IRE)** found things happening too quickly halfway through the race and her chance had then gone. (7/2)
**2908 Super Rocky** was disappointing on this occasion. (5/1)

T/Plpt: £67.80 (156.57 Tckts). T/Qdpt: £5.00 (147.2 Tckts). AA

# 2285-GOODWOOD (R-H) (Good to firm)
## Tuesday July 30th

WEATHER: fine WIND: mod against

## 3123 CITROEN XANTIA H'CAP (0-85) (3-Y.O+) (Class D)

2-15 (2-16) **1m** £9,786.00 (£2,928.00: £1,404.00: £642.00) Stalls: High GOING minus 0.19 sec per fur (GF)

| Form | Horse | Dist | Pos | SP | RR | SF |
|---|---|---|---|---|---|---|
| 2784[2] | **Autumn Cover (64)** (PRHedger) **4-8-8** DBiggs(16) (s.s: hdwy 6f out: chsd ldr over 2f out: led over 1f out: r.o wl) | — | **1** | 12/1 | 76 | 63 |
| | **Orsay (75)** (WRMuir) **4-9-5** JWeaver(17) (bit bkwd: led over 6f: unable qckn ins fnl f) | 1¼ | **2** | 16/1 | 85 | 72 |
| 2603[15] | **Serendipity (FR) (82)** (JLDunlop) **3-9-4** RCochrane(3) (s.s: stdy hdwy & nt clr run on ins over 2f out: rdn over 1f out: r.o ins fnl f) | nk | **3** | 12/1 | 91 | 70 |
| 2605[7] | **Fionn de Cool (IRE) (70)** (RAkehurst) **5-9-0** TQuinn(15) (hld up: rdn over 3f out: one pce) | 1¾ | **4** | 14/1 | 75 | 62 |
| 2285* | **Present Situation (57)** (LordHuntingdon) **5-7-12**(3) MHenry(4) (rdn over 3f out: n.m.r & swtchd lft over 2f out: hdwy over 1f out: r.o) | 1 | **5** | 6/1[1] | 60 | 47 |
| 2761[3] | **Confronter (73)** (SDow) **7-9-3** RHughes(5) (nt clr run over 2f out: hdwy on ins over 1f out: one pce) | ¾ | **6** | 20/1 | 75 | 62 |
| 2885[4] | **Nordinex (IRE) (76)** (RWArmstrong) **4-9-6** MHills(6) (lw: rdn over 3f out: hdwy over 1f out: nvr nrr) | 1¾ | **7** | 8/1[2] | 74 | 61 |
| 2572[2] | **Golden Thunderbolt (FR) (79)** (JHMGosden) **3-9-1** GHind(14) (hld up: rdn over 2f out: wknd over 1f out) | ½ | **8** | 10/1[3] | 76 | 55 |
| 2913[2] | **Smooth Asset (IRE) (71)** (PWChapple-Hyam) **3-8-7**[ow1] JReid(9) (lw: prom 3f) | nk | **9** | 14/1 | 68 | 46 |
| 2883[7] | **Embankment (IRE) (74)** (RHannon) **6-9-1**(3) DaneO'Neill(8) (prom 2f) | s.h | **10** | 20/1 | 71 | 58 |
| 2724[15] | **Seventeens Lucky (77)** (BobJones) **4-9-7** MWigham(1) (nvr nrr) | 1¼ | **11** | 25/1 | 71 | 58 |
| 2285[3] | **Chairmans Choice (63)** (APJarvis) **6-8-7** KDarley(11) (prom over 6f) | ¾ | **12** | 12/1 | 56 | 43 |
| 2805* | **Chinensis (IRE) (77)** (LMCumani) **3-8-13** PatEddery(12) (plld hrd: mid div whn nt clr run over 2f out: sn wknd) | nk | **13** | 6/1[1] | 69 | 48 |
| 2618[4] | **Power Game (68)** (JBerry) **3-8-4v** JCarroll(2) (swtg: a bhd) | 2½ | **14** | 25/1 | 55 | 34 |
| 2544[10] | **Comanche Companion (80)** (TJNaughton) **6-9-5**(5) JDSmith(13) (prom 5f) | hd | **15** | 33/1 | 67 | 54 |
| 2761* | **Night Wink (USA) (77)** (GLMoore) **4-9-7** SWhitworth(10) (prom over 5f) | hd | **16** | 12/1 | 64 | 51 |
| 2526[9] | **Bernard Seven (IRE) (79)** (CEBrittain) **4-9-9b** BDoyle(7) (bhd fnl 3f) | 5 | **17** | 33/1 | 56 | 43 |
| | | | | (SP 121.9%) | **17 Rn** | |

**1m 38.5** (1.30) CSF £169.35 CT £2,207.82 TOTE £18.00: £3.80 £5.70 £2.20 £4.60 (£541.50) Trio £1037.00 OWNER Mr G. A. Alexander (CHICHESTER) BRED P. and Mrs Venner
WEIGHT FOR AGE 3yo-8lb
**OFFICIAL EXPLANATION Chinensis (IRE): the rider reported that the colt was squeezed up at the start and never going thereafter.**
**IN-FOCUS: This race provided the week's first evidence of the importance of a high draw on the round course.**
**2784 Autumn Cover** continued in sparkling form with his fourth victory of the campaign. Soon recovering from a tardy start to race in a handy position, he poked a nostril in front approaching the final furlong and eventually managed to shake off the runner-up in the last 100 yards. (12/1)
**Orsay**, who sustained a hairline fracture to his pastern when winning at Leicester in April '95, had been off the course since and did not look fully fit. He still ran a tremendous race, and can win if given time to get over this. (16/1)
**1666 Serendipity (FR)** was steadily getting closer when finding his way blocked along the inside rail over a quarter of a mile out. Daylight soon appeared and he ran on inside the final furlong. (12/1)
**Fionn de Cool (IRE)** was being pushed along entering the straight, and could only struggle on at one pace. (14/1)
**2285* Present Situation**, raised a mere 2lb for his victory here last month, had no luck in running. Pushed along entering the straight, he did not have a great deal of room over a quarter of a mile out, and had to be switched. He certainly had it all to do, but he began to pick up ground below the distance and ran on only to find the principals home and dry. He is still extremely well handicapped. (6/1)
**2761 Confronter**, another to encounter traffic problems over a quarter of a mile out, picked up ground on the inside rail below the distance, but could then make no further impression. (20/1)

## 3124 WESTMINSTER TAXI INSURANCE GORDON STKS (Gp 3) (3-Y.O) (Class A)

2-45 (2-49) **1m 4f** £22,792.00 (£8,428.00: £4,039.00: £1,645.00: £647.50: £248.50) Stalls: Low GOING minus 0.19 sec per fur (GF)

| Form | Horse | Dist | Pos | SP | RR | SF |
|---|---|---|---|---|---|---|
| 1791$^{17}$ | **St Mawes (FR) (107)** (JLDunlop) **3-8-10b$^{1}$** KDarley(12) (nt clr run over 3f out: n.m.r over 2f out: hrd rdn & hdwy over 1f out: led last stride) | — | **1** | 12/1 | 115 | 66 |
| 2669a* | **Chief Contender (IRE) (105)** (PWChapple-Hyam) **3-8-10** DHarrison(9) (lw: rdn over 4f out: hdwy over 3f out: ev ch wl ins fnl f: r.o wl) | hd | **2** | 9/1 | 115 | 66 |
| 1791$^{15}$ | **Storm Trooper (USA) (114)** (HRACecil) **3-8-10** PatEddery(6) (lw: chsd ldr: led over 3f out: clr over 2f out: hrd rdn over 1f out: hdd last strides) | nk | **3** | 6/1$^{2}$ | 115 | 66 |
| 830$^{3}$ | **Mons (115)** (LMCumani) **3-8-10** JWeaver(8) (n.m.r 3f out: rdn over 2f out: hdwy over 1f out: fin wl) | ½ | **4** | 6/1$^{2}$ | 114 | 65 |
| 2677$^{5}$ | **Quakers Field (100)** (GLMoore) **3-8-10** DaneO'Neill(3) (lw: rdn & hdwy 3f out: one pce fnl f) | 1 | **5** | 66/1 | 113 | 64 |
| 2535$^{4}$ | **Samraan (USA) (104)** (JLDunlop) **3-8-10** MHills(2) (lw: prom over 9f) | 3 | **6** | 14/1 | 109 | 60 |
| 2844a$^{3}$ | **Desert Boy (IRE) (112)** (PWChapple-Hyam) **3-8-10** JReid(7) (led over 8f: hrd rdn over 2f out: wknd over 1f out) | ¾ | **7** | 4/1$^{1}$ | 108 | 59 |
| 2608$^{8}$ | **Male-Ana-Mou (IRE) (85)** (DRCElsworth) **3-8-10** RCochrane(10) (nvr nrr) | s.h | **8** | 33/1 | 107 | 58 |
| 2480a$^{8}$ | **Bahamian Knight (CAN) (109)** (DRLoder) **3-9-3v$^{1}$** RHughes(5) (lw: hld up: rdn over 3f out: wknd over 2f out) | ¾ | **9** | 16/1 | 113 | 64 |
| 1110$^{2}$ | **Summer Spell (USA)** (RCharlton) **3-8-10** SSanders(11) (prom over 10f) | 6 | **10** | 20/1 | 98 | 49 |
| 2677$^{2}$ | **Don Vito (106)** (RCharlton) **3-8-10** TSprake(4) (a bhd) | 9 | **11** | 6/1$^{2}$ | 86 | 37 |
| 2744* | **Unitus (IRE) (95)** (MRStoute) **3-8-10** TQuinn(1) (hdwy over 4f out: eased whn btn over 2f out: t.o) | 27 | **12** | 13/2$^{3}$ | 50 | 1 |

(SP 115.6%) **12 Rn**

**2m 35.18** (1.98) CSF £102.42 TOTE £17.30: £3.50 £3.00 £2.20 (£88.20) Trio £84.80 OWNER Lord Swaythling (ARUNDEL) BRED Societe Aland

OFFICIAL EXPLANATION **Unitus (IRE): the trainer reported that the colt had returned home lame.**

IN-FOCUS: **This was the biggest-ever field for the Gordon Stakes, first run in 1902, and a timely boost for the Derby form.**

**1329 St Mawes (FR)**, better for the headgear, did not have a clear run in the straight, but found daylight a quarter of a mile out. Under stern pressure to pick up ground below the distance, he responded to his rider's urgings and came through in the last few strides. His eventual target is the St Leger. (12/1)

**2669a* Chief Contender (IRE)** ran a tremendous race in defeat. Although being bustled along running down the hill, he soon picked up ground and threw down his challenge inside the final furlong. One of three battling for honours near the line, he only just failed. He could be an ideal type for the St Leger. (9/1)

**1791 Storm Trooper (USA)**, off the track since flopping in the Derby, bounced back here and looked set for victory as he moved to the front over three furlongs from home and soon stormed clear. The race looked his, but he came under pressure approaching the final furlong and, tying up, was caught in the last few strides. He will now revert to a mile and a quarter, where he should be able to pick up a nice prize. (6/1)

**830 Mons** had been taking it easy after the Classic Trial at Sandown in April, due to his sore shins, but made an encouraging comeback here. Short of room three furlongs out, he found it all happening too quickly for him and only found his feet below the distance. He finished with a real flourish, but the line came too soon. The Great Voltigeur Stakes at York is his next start. (6/1)

**2677 Quakers Field**, facing a step up in distance and class, acquitted himself well. Pushed along as he moved up to the leaders three furlongs from home, he almost got on terms, but was tapped for toe in the last 200 yards. (66/1)

**2535 Samraan (USA)** played an active role until fading over two furlongs out. (14/1)

## 3125 WILLIAM HILL CUP H'CAP (4-Y.O+) (Class B)

3-20 (3-21) **1m 2f** £35,662.50 (£10,800.00: £5,275.00: £2,512.50) Stalls: High GOING minus 0.19 sec per fur (GF)

| Form | Horse | Dist | Pos | SP | RR | SF |
|---|---|---|---|---|---|---|
| 2603* | **Grand Selection (IRE) (81)** (MBell) **4-8-3** MFenton(2) (hdwy over 2f out: led ins fnl f: rdn out) | — | **1** | 12/1 | 93 | 48 |
| 2502$^{4}$ | **Silver Groom (IRE) (75)** (RAkehurst) **6-7-11** JQuinn(6) (hdwy over 3f out: led over 2f out: rdn over 1f out: hdd ins fnl f: r.o) | nk | **2** | 4/1$^{1}$ | 87 | 42 |
| 2883* | **Daunt (92)** (JHMGosden) **4-9-0** JCarroll(9) (chsd ldr: ev ch over 2f out: hrd rdn over 1f out: unable qckn) | 4 | **3** | 10/1 | 97 | 52 |
| 2742$^{3}$ | **Rokeby Bowl (94)** (IABalding) **4-9-2** KDarley(1) (a.p: ev ch over 2f out: one pce) | 1 | **4** | 5/1$^{2}$ | 98 | 53 |
| 2502$^{12}$ | **Ball Gown (90)** (DTThom) **6-8-12** RHughes(8) (lw: hdwy over 2f out: edgd rt over 1f out: one pce) | 1 | **5** | 16/1 | 92 | 47 |
| 2055$^{11}$ | **Dance So Suite (89)** (PFICole) **4-8-11** TQuinn(13) (lw: a.p: rdn over 2f out: wkng whn hmpd over 1f out) | ¾ | **6** | 10/1 | 90 | 45 |
| 2623$^{10}$ | **Czarna (IRE) (80)** (CEBrittain) **5-8-2** BDoyle(12) (nt clr run on ins over 2f out: nvr nr to chal) | ¾ | **7** | 25/1 | 80 | 35 |
| 2796$^{4}$ | **Wentbridge Lad (IRE) (74)** (PDEvans) **6-7-7v**(3) DWright(11) (b.off hind: hmpd over 1f out: nvr nrr) | 1¾ | **8** | 50/1 | 71 | 26 |
| 2742$^{2}$ | **Special Dawn (IRE) (89)** (JLDunlop) **6-8-11** PaulEddery(10) (a bhd) | 2½ | **9** | 9/1 | 82 | 37 |
| | **Jagellon (USA) (90)** (WRMuir) **5-8-12** JReid(3) (lw: sme hdwy over 2f out: wkng whn hmpd over 1f out) | 1½ | **10** | 20/1 | 80 | 35 |
| 2502$^{19}$ | **Chief Burundi (USA) (102)** (LMCumani) **4-9-10** PatEddery(5) (led over 7f) | 1 | **11** | 7/1$^{3}$ | 91 | 46 |
| 2533$^{8}$ | **Ellie Ardensky (98)** (JRFanshawe) **4-9-6** DHarrison(7) (bhd fnl 2f) | 5 | **12** | 10/1 | 79 | 34 |
| 2549* | **Edan Heights (79)** (SDow) **4-7-10**(5)ow5 ADaly(4) (a.p: rdn 2f out: 6th & btn whn stumbled & uns rdr over 1f out) | | **U** | 20/1 | — | — |

(SP 115.3%) **13 Rn**

**2m 8.52** (3.02) CSF £53.87 CT £460.55 TOTE £12.70: £3.10 £1.70 £2.90 (£28.10) Trio £66.40 OWNER Mr M. B. Hawtin (NEWMARKET) BRED Mount Coote Stud in Ireland

LONG HANDICAP Wentbridge Lad (IRE) 7-1 Edan Heights 7-8

**2603* Grand Selection (IRE)** began his effort over a quarter of a mile from home and came through to lead in the final furlong. The Cambridgeshire now looks on the agenda. (12/1: op 8/1)

**2502 Silver Groom (IRE)** looked likely to follow up last year's victory in this race, despite being 10lb higher as he stormed into the lead over quarter of a mile out, but the winner came with a telling flourish. (4/1)

**2883* Daunt** had every chance when the runner-up went for home over a quarter of a mile out but, soon under pressure, failed to find another gear. A valuable handicap at the Ascot Festival is his target. (10/1: 8/1-12/1)

**2742 Rokeby Bowl** had every chance over two furlongs from home before tapped for toe. (5/1)

**1131 Ball Gown** made an effort over quarter of a mile out, but she drifted right and failed to find another gear. (16/1)

**1792* Dance So Suite**, in trouble a quarter of a mile out, was well beaten when hampered below the distance. (10/1)

## 3126 KING GEORGE STKS (Gp 3) (3-Y.O+) (Class A)

3-50 (3-52) **5f** £27,680.00 (£10,364.00: £4,982.00: £2,174.00) Stalls: Low GOING minus 0.19 sec per fur (GF)

| Form | Horse | Dist | Pos | SP | RR | SF |
|---|---|---|---|---|---|---|
| 2880$^{5}$ | **Rambling Bear (113)** (MBlanshard) **3-8-10** RCochrane(6) (lw: nt clr run over 2f out: switchd lft & hdwy over 1f out: str run fnl f: led nr fin) | — | **1** | 10/1 | 113 | 55 |
| 2622$^{3}$ | **Hever Golf Rose (114)** (TJNaughton) **5-9-7** JWeaver(12) (led: rdn over 1f out: hdd nr fin) | 1 | **2** | 7/1$^{3}$ | 117 | 63 |

2545$^{3}$ **Croft Pool (102)** (JAGlover) **5-9-0** SDWilliams(13) (a.p: rdn over 2f out: ev ch ins fnl f: one pce) ....1 **3** 20/1 107 53
2622$^{9}$ **Cool Jazz (113)** (CEBrittain) **5-9-5** TQuinn(11) (lw: rdn over 2f out: hdwy over 1f out: one pce ins fnl f) ....¾ **4** 25/1 109 55
2292$^{9}$ **Crowded Avenue (96)** (PJMakin) **4-9-0** SSanders(3) (hrd rdn & hdwy over 1f out: r.o one pce) ....nk **5** 16/1 103 49
2545* **Eveningperformance (110)** (HCandy) **5-8-11** CRutter(9) (a.p: rdn over 1f out: 4th & btn whn n.m.r ins fnl f) ...½ **6** 11/4$^{1}$ 99 45
2889$^{13}$ **Welsh Mist (91)** (RBoss) **5-8-11** WRyan(4) (outpcd: hdwy fnl f: nvr nrr) ....s.h **7** 50/1 99 45
2698* **Lucky Parkes (100)** (JBerry) **6-8-11** JCarroll(1) (prom over 3f) ....1¼ **8** 12/1 95 41
2545$^{8}$ **Brave Edge (106)** (RHannon) **5-9-0** PatEddery(8) (lw: hld up: rdn over 2f out: btn whn n.m.r ins fnl f) ....nk **9** 20/1 97 43
2622$^{8}$ **Lucky Lionel (USA) (115)** (RHannon) **3-8-10b$^{1}$** RHughes(5) (lw: bhd fnl 2f) ....s.h **10** 11/1 96 38
2115$^{3}$ **Almaty (IRE)** (CCollins,Ireland) **3-8-10v$^{1}$** KDarley(2) (lw: prom over 3f) ....nk **11** 4/1$^{2}$ 95 37
2698$^{2}$ **Amazing Bay (100)** (IABalding) **3-8-7** PaulEddery(10) (prom 3f) ....1½ **12** 25/1 88 30
2698$^{5}$ **Bunty Boo** (RHannon) **7-9-2** JReid(14) (lw: prom over 2f) ....2 **13** 20/1 86 32
1483$^{4}$ **Leap for Joy (103)** (JHMGosden) **4-9-2** GHind(7) (hld up: rdn over 2f out: wknd over 1f out) ....¾ **14** 20/1 84 30
(SP 118.9%) **14 Rn**

**57.98 secs** (1.28) CSF £71.51 TOTE £12.30: £3.50 £2.00 £5.90 (£41.70) Trio £436.20 OWNER Mrs Michael Hill (UPPER LAMBOURN) BRED E. A. Badger
WEIGHT FOR AGE 3yo-4lb

**2880 Rambling Bear** spoilt the party for Hever Golf Rose. With nowhere to go at halfway, he was switched left when with a tremendous amount of ground to make up, but he went into overdrive below the distance, and came storming through to snatch the spoils near the line. The Haydock Park Sprint Cup is his next likely target, and his trainer thinks he may appreciate a softer surface. (10/1: 7/1-11/1)
**2622 Hever Golf Rose**, winner of this race last year, was shouldered with a 10lb penalty but that did not stop her from running an absolute blinder. Storming off in front, she looked to have the measure of her rivals from below the distance, but just failed to withstand the late surge of the winner. She will now go for the Nunthorpe Stakes at York, then on to Baden-Baden, and ending with the Prix de l'Abbaye, which she won last year. (7/1)
**2545 Croft Pool** was certainly close enough if good enough inside the final furlong, before tapped for toe. (20/1)
**2622 Cool Jazz** ran his best race for a while. Picking up ground below the distance, he almost got on terms before tapped for toe inside the final furlong. (25/1)
**2292 Crowded Avenue** picked up ground below the distance but, despite staying on, never looked like getting there in time. (16/1)
**2545* Eveningperformance** as usual showed tremendous early speed but, on this occasion, just failed to get to the front. Battling hard to get on terms with the leader, she was beaten inside the final furlong when slightly tightened up for room. (11/4)
**2622 Lucky Lionel (USA)** (11/1: 8/1-12/1)

## 3127 OAK TREE STKS (Listed) (3-Y.O+ F & M) (Class A)

4-25 (4-28) **7f** £23,295.00 (£6,960.00: £3,330.00: £1,515.00) Stalls: High GOING minus 0.19 sec per fur (GF)

SP RR SF

2052$^{6}$ **Thrilling Day (110)** (NAGraham) **3-8-13** DHarrison(13) (nt clr run over 2f out: swtchd lft & hdwy over 1f out: hrd rdn: led ins fnl f: r.o wl) ....— **1** 12/1 112 66
1800$^{6}$ **Forest Cat (IRE) (91)** (MrsJCecil) **4-9-0** JCarroll(12) (a.p: rdn over 2f out: led over 1f out tl ins fnl f: unable qckn) ....1¾ **2** 20/1 102 63
2225$^{2}$ **Tamnia (102)** (JLDunlop) **3-8-7** TQuinn(14) (hdwy 3f out: rdn 2f out: 3rd whn n.m.r ins fnl f: one pce) ....1 **3** 14/1 100 54
1639$^{4}$ **Najiya (104)** (JLDunlop) **3-8-7** RHills(6) (bdly hmpd over 2f out: n.m.r wl over 1f out: hdwy over 1f out: r.o wl ins fnl f) ....s.h **4** 16/1 100 54
2692$^{3}$ **Prancing (97)** (DRLoder) **3-8-7** KDarley(3) (hld up: rdn & edgd lft over 2f out: one pce) ....2½ **5** 20/1 94 48
874$^{3}$ **Satin Bell** (JLDunlop) **3-8-7** GDuffield(7) (nvr nr to chal) ....s.h **6** 20/1 94 48
2692* **Carranita (IRE) (109)** (BPalling) **6-9-3** TSprake(5) (lw: a.p: led over 2f out: edgd rt: hdd over 1f out: wknd ins fnl f) ....hd **7** 6/1$^{3}$ 97 58
2623$^{9}$ **Patsy Grimes (82)** (JSMoore) **6-9-0** RHughes(10) (hdwy 2f out: wknd fnl f) ....1¼ **8** 66/1 91 52
2609$^{7}$ **Brief Glimpse (IRE) (102)** (MajorDNChappell) **4-9-3** BThomson(8) (rdn over 4f out: sme hdwy wl over 1f out: sn wknd) ....1 **9** 14/1 91 52
2050$^{13}$ **Sandhill (IRE) (90)** (JHMGosden) **3-8-7** GHind(11) (lw: w ldr: ev ch over 2f out: wknd over 1f out) ....1 **10** 33/1 86 40
2704$^{3}$ **Bewitching (USA) (102)** (JARToller) **3-8-7** SSanders(4) (bhd fnl 3f) ....1¾ **11** 8/1 82 36
2609$^{4}$ **Dawna (103)** (HRACecil) **3-8-10** PatEddery(1) (prom over 3f: wkng whn bdly hmpd over 2f out) ....3½ **12** 4/1$^{1}$ 77 31
2050$^{8}$ **My Branch (112)** (BWHills) **3-8-7** MHills(2) (swtg: a bhd) ....½ **13** 9/2$^{2}$ 73 27
2072$^{6}$ **Isla Del Rey (USA)** (SbinSuroor) **4-9-3** JReid(9) (swtg: led over 4f) ....3 **14** 9/1 69 30
(SP 119.2%) **14 Rn**

**1m 26.07** (1.27) CSF £197.95 TOTE £14.20: £3.60 £4.20 £3.50 (£117.20) Trio £156.20 OWNER Bloomsbury Stud (NEWMARKET) BRED Bloomsbury Stud
WEIGHT FOR AGE 3yo-7lb
OFFICIAL EXPLANATION **Bewitching (USA): on returning home the filly was found to be very sore on both hind feet.**

**2052 Thrilling Day** bounced back to form. Failing to get a clear run over quarter of a mile out, she was switched left and, picking up ground below the distance, swept into the lead inside the final furlong. She will now be entered for the Prix de la Foret at Longchamp and the Challenge Stakes at Newmarket, both over seven. (12/1)
**1800 Forest Cat (IRE)** failed to contain the winner inside the final furlong. (20/1)
**2225 Tamnia** took closer order early in the straight. Almost on level terms a furlong out, she was tightened up soon after and failed to find another gear. (14/1: 10/1-16/1)
**1639 Najiya** was unlucky. Badly hampered towards the back of the field over a quarter of a mile out, she then did not have much room a furlong out. Despite this, she soon picked up ground and, running on really strongly inside the final furlong, only just failed to take third prize. Compensation awaits. (16/1)
**2692 Prancing** drifted left over a quarter of mile out, and could only go up and down in the same place. (20/1)
**874 Satin Bell** made some late headway without posing a threat. (20/1)
**2692* Carranita (IRE)** went on over a quarter of a mile out. Drifting right over to the rail, she was headed below the distance and had nothing more to offer inside the final furlong. She is better over six. (6/1)
**2704 Bewitching (USA)** (8/1: 6/1-9/1)

## 3128 EVENING STANDARD NURSERY H'CAP (2-Y.O) (Class C)

5-00 (5-04) **6f** £8,220.00 (£2,460.00: £1,180.00: £540.00) Stalls: Low GOING minus 0.19 sec per fur (GF)

SP RR SF

2879$^{2}$ **Young Bigwig (IRE)** (JBerry) **2-9-7** JCarroll(1) (swtg: hld up: rdn over 2f out: led over 1f out: drvn out) ....— **1** 13/2$^{3}$ 96 43
2112$^{5}$ **Caviar Royale (IRE)** (RHannon) **2-9-6** PatEddery(3) (lw: dwlt: swtchd rt 3f out: rdn & hdwy over 1f out: ev ch fnl f: r.o wl) ....s.h **2** 6/1$^{2}$ 95 42

| | | | SP | RR | SF |
|---|---|---|---|---|---|
| 2930* | **Bride's Reprisal** (MRChannon) **2-9-7** $^{7x}$ RHughes(2) (rdn over 2f out: hdwy over 1f out: r.o) 1¼ | **3** | 12/1 | 93? | 40 |
| 2965$^{2}$ | **I Can't Remember** (PDEvans) **2-7-7**$^{(3)}$ DWright(5) (lost pl over 2f out: rallied fnl f: r.o wl) hd | **4** | 14/1 | 67 | 14 |
| 2942$^{2}$ | **Effervescence** (RHannon) **2-8-0**$^{(3)ow1}$ DaneO'Neill(10) (lw: hld up: rdn over 2f out: r.o ins fnl f) ¾ | **5** | 10/1 | 72 | 18 |
| 2562* | **Farewell My Love (IRE)** (PFICole) **2-8-2**$^{(7)}$ DavidO'Neill(8) (lw: a.p: ev ch over 1f out: wknd ins fnl f) 1 | **6** | 7/1 | 76 | 23 |
| 2797$^{4}$ | **Can Can Lady** (MJohnston) **2-7-8**$^{(3)}$ MHenry(4) (lw: nvr nr to chal) s.h | **7** | 10/1 | 64 | 11 |
| 2734$^{3}$ | **Aficionado (IRE)** (RFJohnsonHoughton) **2-8-7b**$^{1}$ JReid(9) (hld up: rdn over 2f out: one pce) 1 | **8** | 12/1 | 71 | 18 |
| 2619$^{5}$ | **Makhbar** (RWArmstrong) **2-8-9** RHills(6) (led over 4f) 1 | **9** | 3/1$^{1}$ | 70 | 17 |
| 2944$^{4}$ | **Whizz Kid** (JJBridger) **2-7-7**$^{(3)}$ DarrenMoffatt(11) (outpcd: hdwy over 1f out: wknd fnl f) ¾ | **10** | 25/1 | 55 | 2 |
| 2406$^{2}$ | **Windborn** (KMcAuliffe) **2-7-5**$^{(5)}$ MartinDwyer(7) (bhd fnl 2f) 2 | **11** | 33/1 | 50 | — |
| 2965$^{3}$ | **Threeplay (IRE)** (JAkehurst) **2-7-10v** JQuinn(12) (a.p: ev ch over 1f out: wknd qckly fnl f) 2½ | **12** | 16/1 | 43 | — |
| 2157$^{3}$ | **Will To Win** (PGMurphy) **2-7-13** NAdams(13) (b.hind: swvd rt s: hld up: rdn over 2f out: sn wknd) 4 | **13** | 33/1 | 36 | — |
| | | | (SP 121.0%) | | **13 Rn** |

**1m 13.18** (3.18) CSF £42.70 CT £321.36 TOTE £7.40: £2.40 £2.00 £3.00 (£15.90) Trio £56.20 OWNER Mr W. R. Milner (COCKERHAM) BRED Thoroughbred Trust

IN-FOCUS: **The first three home came out of the three lowest stalls, against the stands' rail. They were also the top three in the weights, continuing the good run of topweights in early-season nurseries this season.**

**2879 Young Bigwig (IRE)** was engaged in a tremendous battle with the runner-up in the final furlong, but just prevailed. (13/2)

**2112 Caviar Royale (IRE)**, switched right at halfway, came through to have every chance in the final furlong and only just failed. He is a winner without a penalty. (6/1)

**2930* Bride's Reprisal** began to pick up ground below the distance but, despite running on, failed to get to the front two in time. (12/1)

**2965 I Can't Remember** got outpaced soon after halfway, but finished to good effect in the final furlong, only just failing to take third. (14/1)

**2942 Effervescence**, ridden along a quarter of a mile from home, stayed on inside the final furlong. (10/1)

**2562* Farewell My Love (IRE)** had every chance below the distance, but this extra furlong appeared just beyond her at this stage, and she tired. (7/1: 5/1-8/1)

**2619 Makhbar** again disappointed. Bowling along in front, he was collared below the distance and tamely dropped away. (3/1)

## 3129 FINDON MAIDEN STKS (2-Y.O F) (Class D)

5-35 (5-38) **6f** £7,132.50 (£2,160.00: £1,055.00: £502.50) Stalls: Low GOING minus 0.19 sec per fur (GF)

| | | | SP | RR | SF |
|---|---|---|---|---|---|
| 2741$^{5}$ | **Papita (IRE)** (SDow) **2-8-11** BThomson(7) (mde all: clr 2f out: unchal) — | **1** | 25/1 | 88 | 30 |
| | **Cambridge Ball (IRE)** (MJohnston) **2-8-11** JWeaver(10) (leggy: hld up: rdn over 2f out: unable qckn) 5 | **2** | 10/1 | 75 | 17 |
| | **Caspian Morn** (APJarvis) **2-8-11** JTate(11) (neat: rdn 3f out: hdwy wl over 1f out: one pce) nk | **3** | 33/1 | 74 | 16 |
| 2230$^{6}$ | **Royal Orchid (IRE)** (RHannon) **2-8-8**$^{(3)}$ DaneO'Neill(1) (b.nr hind: rdn over 2f out: hdwy on ins over 1f out: r.o) ½ | **4** | 13/2$^{3}$ | 73 | 15 |
| | **Nawasib (IRE)** (JLDunlop) **2-8-11** TSprake(8) (bit bkwd: outpcd: nt clr run over 1f out: hdwy 1f out: r.o) nk | **5** | 12/1 | 72 | 14 |
| 2734$^{2}$ | **Signs And Wonders** (CACyzer) **2-8-11** SSanders(6) (a.p: rdn over 1f out: wknd fnl f) ¾ | **6** | 10/1 | 70 | 12 |
| 2863$^{4}$ | **Logic** (CEBrittain) **2-8-11** BDoyle(9) (prom 4f) 5 | **7** | 5/2$^{1}$ | 56 | — |
| | **Gee Bee Dream** (APJarvis) **2-8-11** TQuinn(2) (w'like: bit bkwd: prom over 4f) 1 | **8** | 20/1 | 54 | — |
| 2073$^{10}$ | **Soura (USA)** (PAKelleway) **2-8-11** JReid(5) (prom 4f) 1 | **9** | 14/1 | 51 | — |
| | **Stygian (USA)** (BWHills) **2-8-11** PatEddery(4) (neat: bkwd: prom 3f) nk | **10** | 6/1$^{2}$ | 50 | — |
| | **Eurolink Windsong (IRE)** (LMCumani) **2-8-11** KDarley(12) (scope: a bhd) ½ | **11** | 12/1 | 49 | — |
| | **Three Card Trick (IRE)** (RHannon) **2-8-11** JCarroll(3) (small: s.s: a bhd) 1 | **12** | 20/1 | 46 | — |
| 2323$^{6}$ | **Swift Refusal** (MJHaynes) **2-8-11** CRutter(15) (hld up: rdn over 2f out: sn wknd) 1 | **13** | 33/1 | 44 | — |
| | **Racing Carr** (TJNaughton) **2-8-11** PaulEddery(14) (unf: s.s: a bhd) 1¼ | **14** | 33/1 | 40 | — |
| | **Wrong Bride** (MRChannon) **2-8-11** RHughes(13) (unf: s.s: a bhd: t.o fnl 2f) dist | **15** | 16/1 | — | — |
| | | | (SP 124.5%) | | **15 Rn** |

**1m 13.46** (3.46) CSF £237.00 TOTE £31.80: £6.80 £3.30 £11.80 (£130.60) Trio Not won; £1,566.14 to Goodwood 31/7/96 OWNER Mr G. Steinberg (EPSOM) BRED T. Connolly

IN-FOCUS: **Considering the prize money on offer, this looked a poor race.**

**2741 Papita (IRE)** sprung a major shock, especially to her trainer, who reported that she only goes through the motions at home and had made no significant progress. Making all the running, she had forged clear a quarter of a mile out and came home to win unchallenged. (25/1)

**Cambridge Ball (IRE)** was engaged in a battle for second prize, but had no hope with the winner. (10/1)

**Caspian Morn** picked up ground early in the final quarter-mile and, throwing down her challenge for second place, only just lost out. (33/1)

**2230 Royal Orchid (IRE)**, who finished lame last time out, picked up ground along the inside rail below the distance and stayed on for fourth prize. (13/2: 7/2-7/1)

**Nawasib (IRE)**, a half-sister to Azzilfi, Khamaseen and Tamnia, failed to go the early pace. She was just beginning to pick up ground when meeting a dead-end below the distance but, despite this, stayed on in eyecatching style to finish fifth. Sure to strip a lot fitter for this, she will come into her own over further and can find a suitable race. (12/1: 10/1-16/1)

**2734 Signs And Wonders**, one of several hunting up the winner, was rousted along below the distance, but was soon at the end of her tether. (10/1: 8/1-12/1)

**2863 Logic** was rather surprisingly dropped down in distance and was most disappointing. (5/2)

**Soura (USA)** (14/1: 10/1-16/1)

**Stygian (USA)** (6/1: op 7/2)

**Eurolink Windsong (IRE)** (12/1: 6/1-14/1)

T/Jkpt: Not won; £58,145.45 to Goodwood 31/7/96. T/Plpt: £4,968.40 (11.46 Tckts). T/Qdpt: £315.20 (13.93 Tckts). AK

# 2770-DONCASTER (L-H) (Good to firm)

## Wednesday July 31st

WEATHER: overcast WIND: mod against

## 3130 SUNSHINE (S) STKS (3, 4 & 5-Y.O) (Class E)

2-00 (2-00) **1m 4f** £3,260.25 (£972.00: £463.50: £209.25) Stalls: Low GOING minus 0.07 sec per fur (G)

| | | | SP | RR | SF |
|---|---|---|---|---|---|
| 2798* | **Rushen Raider (60)** (KWHogg) **4-9-11** DMcKeown(4) (trckd ldrs: swtchd & qcknd to ld 2f out: r.o) — | **1** | 3/1$^{2}$ | 72 | 54 |
| 2798$^{3}$ | **Westminster (IRE) (65)** (MHTompkins) **4-9-11b**$^{1}$ PRobinson(2) (hld up: hdwy on bit over 2f out: ev ch ins fnl f: rdn & no ex) 1¼ | **2** | 2/1$^{1}$ | 70 | 52 |
| 2922$^{2}$ | **North Bear** (MrsSJSmith) **4-9-4**$^{(3)}$ OPears(5) (hld up: effrt over 3f out: styd on: nt pce to chal) 2 | **3** | 9/2$^{3}$ | 64 | 46 |

2788[3] **Durham (54)** (RSimpson) **5-9-2b**(5) AimeeCook(3) (lw: hdwy to jn ldrs appr st: disp ld 3f out: one pce fnl 2f)....2½ **4** 5/1 60 42
2922* **Pickens (USA) (61)** (NTinkler) **4-9-11** MBirch(1) (lw: hld up & bhd: effrt over 3f out: no imp)....10 **5** 11/2 51 33
*2551*[10] **Hangoninthere** (NMBabbage) **5-9-7** AMcGlone(7) (cl up: led over 3f out tl hdd & wknd 2f out)....1¼ **6** 33/1 45 27
2537[8] **High Flown (USA) (39)** (RonaldThompson) **4-9-7** NConnorton(6) (led tl hdd over 3f out: sn lost pl)....½ **7** 33/1 45 27
(SP 114.4%) **7 Rn**

**2m 37.34** (7.34) CSF £9.21 TOTE £4.40: £2.70 £1.80 (£4.70) OWNER Mrs Thelma White (ISLE OF MAN) BRED M. H. D. Madden and Partners
Bt in 5,600 gns

**2798* Rushen Raider** is in really good heart at present and again his courage won the day. (3/1)
**2798 Westminster (IRE)** was in blinkers instead of a visor this time but, when it came to an effort, he failed to come up with the goods. (2/1)
**2922 North Bear** keeps running consistently well and gives the impression that he might do even better if more use were made of him. (9/2)
**2788 Durham** looks better suited by a bit further and was tapped for toe in the last couple of furlongs. (5/1)
**2922* Pickens (USA),** happy to sit out the back, never fired at all when asked a question early in the straight. (11/2)
**Hangoninthere**, stepped up half a mile in trip, put in a much-improved performance until his stamina gave way with two furlongs left. (33/1)

## 3131 SILVERDALE MAIDEN STKS (2-Y.O) (Class D)

2-30 (2-30) **7f** £3,559.85 (£1,062.80: £507.90: £230.45) Stalls: High GOING minus 0.07 sec per fur (G)

SP RR SF

2543[2] **Medaaly** (SbinSuroor) **2-9-0** DHolland(4) (lw: trckd ldrs: smooth hdwy to ld 3f out: shkn up & r.o wl fnl f)....— **1** 4/5[1] 91+ 38
**Further Outlook (USA)** (MRStoute) **2-9-0** KFallon(3) (b.hind: w'like: in tch: hdwy 3f out: ev ch 2f out: nt pce of wnr)....2½ **2** 15/2 85+ 32
2580[4] **Mrs Miniver (USA)** (PAKelleway) **2-8-9** GDuffield(6) (lw: bmpd s: sn pushed along: hdwy 2f out: kpt on wl)....¾ **3** 9/2[2] 79 26
**Barnum Sands** (JLDunlop) **2-9-0** GCarter(8) (w'like: leggy: s.i.s: hdwy 3f out: chsng ldrs 2f out: nt qckn)....1¾ **4** 8/1 80 27
2695[4] **Leviticus (IRE)** (TPTate) **2-9-0** ACulhane(5) (bhd: styd on fnl 2f: nvr nr to chal)....1½ **5** 12/1 76 23
2702[3] **Tasik Chini (USA)** (PFICole) **2-9-0** CRutter(1) (disp ld 4f: sn rdn & btn)....13 **6** 11/2[3] 46 —
**Bollin Terry** (TDEasterby) **2-9-0** MBirch(7) (w'like: sn pushed along & bhd: n.d)....1¾ **7** 20/1 42 —
2783[8] **River King** (RHannon) **2-9-0** WJO'Connor(2) (disp ld 4f: sn wknd)....12 **8** 20/1 15 —
(SP 129.2%) **8 Rn**

**1m 28.16** (4.56) CSF £8.89 TOTE £1.80: £1.10 £1.80 £1.60 (£4.40) OWNER Godolphin (NEWMARKET) BRED Sheikh Mohammed Bin Rashid Al Maktoum

**2543 Medaaly** won this in useful style and should have learnt plenty. (4/5: Evens-5/4)
**Further Outlook (USA)** put in a decent first effort here but had to accept the winner was too good in the final furlong. No doubt the experience will bring him on. (15/2)
**2580 Mrs Miniver (USA)** was again outpaced for much of the trip and was not overpunished when beaten, but was keeping on particularly well. Her turn will come and she will appreciate stiffer tests. (9/2: op 3/1)
**Barnum Sands**, who has plenty to learn, did show ability and was not given a hard time once beaten. He will be all the better for it. (8/1)
**2695 Leviticus (IRE)** is still learning, but there is plenty of ability there once he gets it fully together. (12/1)
**2702 Tasik Chini (USA)** was very disappointing and obviously something was wrong. (11/2)

## 3132 VAUX SAMSON CONDITIONS STKS (3-Y.O+) (Class C)

3-05 (3-08) **6f** £5,737.50 (£1,987.50: £956.25: £393.75) Stalls: High GOING minus 0.07 sec per fur (G)

SP RR SF

2115[6] **Royal Applause (117)** (BWHills) **3-8-11** KFallon(2) (lw: mde all: qcknd 2f out: pushed out)....— **1** 4/5[1] 112 49
2050[11] **Russian Revival (USA) (110)** (SbinSuroor) **3-8-11** DHolland(4) (lw: chsd wnr most of wy: r.o u.p fnl f: nrst fin)....nk **2** 6/1 111 48
2003[2] **Speed On (101)** (HCandy) **3-9-2** CRutter(1) (lw: plld hrd early: effrt over 2f out: edgd rt & no imp)....5 **3** 5/1[3] 103 40
**Resounder (USA) (108)** (JHMGosden) **3-8-11** GHind(3) (lw: prom: effrt ½-wy: sn rdn & btn)....11 **4** 8/1 69 6
**Sergeyev (IRE) (110)** (RHannon) **4-9-2** WJO'Connor(6) (lw: hld up & bhd whn stumbled bdly & uns rdr over 3f out).... **U** 9/2[2] — —
(SP 115.8%) **5 Rn**

**1m 13.91** (2.91) CSF £6.08 TOTE £1.70: £1.30 £1.80 (£4.60) OWNER Maktoum Al Maktoum (LAMBOURN) BRED Gainsborough Stud Management Ltd
WEIGHT FOR AGE 3yo-5lb

**2115 Royal Applause,** back to what appears his best trip, did what was required and had as easy a race as possible in the circumstances, but it was not entirely convincing. (4/5)
**1574a Russian Revival (USA),** wearing a tongue-strap, always looked to be well second best. To his credit, he kept battling away and, with a little further to go, it would have been interesting. (6/1: 4/1-13/2)
**2003 Speed On,** stepped up a furlong, raced far too freely and, once off the bit, never seemed to be galloping on an even keel. Something may have been wrong on this occasion. (5/1)
**Resounder (USA)** looked pretty fit for this seasonal debut but, once the tempo increased just after halfway, he was quickly put in his place. This was a most disappointing show. (8/1)
**Sergeyev (IRE)** looked ready to run for his life. Settled out the back, he slipped badly before halfway giving his rider no chance of staying aboard. (9/2: op 7/1)

## 3133 DONCASTER SPONSORSHIP CLUB H'CAP (0-85) (3-Y.O F) (Class D)

3-35 (3-37) **1m (round)** £4,235.00 (£1,265.00: £605.00: £275.00) Stalls: Low GOING minus 0.07 sec per fur (G)

SP RR SF

2945[2] **Blessed Spirit (71)** (CFWall) **3-8-8** SSanders(5) (hld up: swtchd wl over 1f out: qcknd to ld ins fnl f: jst hld on)....— **1** 7/2[2] 83 38
1882* **Fatefully (USA) (83)** (SbinSuroor) **3-9-6** DHolland(8) (bhd: hdwy on ins 3f out: nt clr run & swtchd appr fnl f: fin fast: jst failed)....hd **2** 5/2[1] 95 50
2687[2] **Tsarnista (78)** (JLDunlop) **3-9-1** GCarter(7) (hld up: qcknd to ld over 1f out: hdd & no ex ins fnl f)....1½ **3** 9/2[3] 87 42
1785[5] **Singapore Sting (USA) (72)** (HRACecil) **3-8-9** AMcGlone(4) (chsd ldrs: n.m.r over 2f out: one pce)....4 **4** 8/1 73 28
2744[4] **Seeking Fortune (USA) (76)** (JRFanshawe) **3-8-13** KFallon(1) (trckd ldrs: nt clr run & hmpd fr 3f out tl swtchd ins fnl f: nt rcvr)....¾ **5** 5/1 75 30
833[14] **Kirov Lady (IRE) (84)** (RHannon) **3-9-7** WJO'Connor(2) (disp ld tl led 3f out: hdd & wknd over 1f out)....¾ **6** 16/1 82 37
2805[3] **Dispol Diamond (67)** (GROldroyd) **3-8-4** DaleGibson(10) (in tch tl outpcd fnl 3f)....1¼ **7** 16/1 62 17
2754[3] **Kazimiera (IRE) (68)** (CWCElsey) **3-8-5** GDuffield(9) (chsd ldrs 5f: btn whn hmpd appr fnl f)....3 **8** 8/1 57 12

1861[8] **Tabriz (67)** (JDBethell) **3-8-1v**[1](3) FLynch(6) (disp ld 5f: sn rdn & wknd)....6 **9** 14/1 44 —
(SP 126.3%) **9 Rn**

**1m 41.28** (4.78) CSF £13.44 CT £38.83 TOTE £3.30: £1.70 £1.80 £1.70 (£2.40) Trio £9.20 OWNER Sir William Stuttaford (NEWMARKET) BRED Farmers Hill Stud

**2945 Blessed Spirit** won her first race here and it was all down to her rider avoiding trouble, as she was probably about third best on merit. (7/2)

**1882* Fatefully (USA)** should have won this, but her rider kept trying to get a run up the inner and was continually blocked. When switched, it was just too late. (5/2)

**2687 Tsarnista** had all the luck going in the race, but plain and simply was not good enough. (9/2)

**1785 Singapore Sting (USA)** was shut in behind the leaders and lacked the pace to get out of trouble. (8/1)

**2744 Seeking Fortune (USA)** found even more trouble than the runner-up, and would certainly have been in the shake up. She looks one to keep in mind. (5/1)

**Kirov Lady (IRE)** had not been out for some three months and ran out of petrol approaching the final furlong. (16/1)

## 3134 WARDS BEST BITTER H'CAP (0-85) (3-Y.O+) (Class D)

4-10 (4-10) **1m 2f 60y** £3,913.25 (£1,166.00: £555.50: £250.25) Stalls: Low GOING minus 0.07 sec per fur (G)

| | | | SP | RR | SF |
|---|---|---|---|---|---|
| 2674[2] | **Celestial Choir (83)** (JLEyre) **6-9-11**(3) OPears(1) (hld up: hdwy on ins over 2f out: rdn to ld cl home)....— | **1** | 11/2 | 91 | 63 |
| 2570[6] | **Blurred (IRE) (68)** (MHTompkins) **3-8-3** PRobinson(6) (led: qcknd 3f out: hrd rdn fnl f: jst ct)....nk | **2** | 10/1 | 76 | 38 |
| 2603[10] | **Rory (74)** (MrsJCecil) **5-9-0**(5) AmandaSanders(7) (plld hrd: sn cl up: one pce ins fnl f)....1¾ | **3** | 8/1 | 79 | 51 |
| 3043[4] | **Advance East (56)** (MrsJRRamsden) **4-7-12**(3) FLynch(8) (lw: hld up: nt clr run & swtchd wl over 1f out: gd hdwy ent fnl f: nt qckn towards fin)....hd | **4** | 3/1[2] | 61 | 33 |
| 2693[3] | **Special-K (64)** (EWeymes) **4-8-2**(7)ow3 GFaulkner(5) (chsd ldrs tl wknd fnl 2f)....5 | **5** | 5/1[3] | 61 | 30 |
| 2894[3] | **Flying North (IRE) (79)** (MrsMReveley) **3-9-0** ACulhane(3) (hld up & bhd: hdwy 2½f out: nvr able to chal)....½ | **6** | 9/1 | 75 | 37 |
| 2536[7] | **Amusing Aside (IRE) (66)** (JWWatts) **3-8-1** GDuffield(2) (lw: hld up: effrt over 2f out: n.d)....2½ | **7** | 10/1 | 58 | 20 |
| 2384* | **Overruled (IRE) (84)** (DRLoder) **3-9-5v**[1] DRMcCabe(4) (lw: prom tl rdn & wknd 2f out)....5 | **8** | 11/4[1] | 68 | 30 |

(SP 123.0%) **8 Rn**

**2m 11.16** (4.16) CSF £54.35 CT £409.60 TOTE £6.40: £1.80 £2.50 £2.30 (£53.30) OWNER Mrs Carole Sykes (HAMBLETON) BRED J. L. Eyre
WEIGHT FOR AGE 3yo-10lb

**2674 Celestial Choir** had not won on turf for a year but, given a confident ride, she ran on splendidly to take this. (11/2)

**2570 Blurred (IRE)** looked to have done everything right when pinching a useful-looking lead halfway up the straight, but he just failed to find enough under pressure in the closing stages. (10/1)

**2077* Rory** raced too freely and, after holding every chance, was done for speed in the closing stages. (8/1)

**3043 Advance East** was wearing a special bridle and bit to help keep his tongue down, but it would seem that it is his attitude that is the problem. (3/1)

**2693 Special-K**, trying a longer trip, did not seem to get home. (5/1)

**2894 Flying North (IRE)**, waited with, presumably to get the trip, failed to maintain his run in the final furlong. (9/1)

**1670 Amusing Aside (IRE)** looked and moved very well, but ran most disappointingly. (10/1)

**2384* Overruled (IRE)** was in a visor for the first time and soon threw in the towel when the pressure was on. (11/4)

## 3135 DONCASTER DOME H'CAP (0-70) (3-Y.O) (Class E)

4-45 (4-45) **5f** £3,106.00 (£928.00: £444.00: £202.00) Stalls: Low GOING minus 0.07 sec per fur (G)

| | | | SP | RR | SF |
|---|---|---|---|---|---|
| 2592[12] | **Oatey (53)** (MrsJRRamsden) **3-8-6** KFallon(9) (s.i.s: stdy hdwy ½-wy: qcknd to ld wl ins fnl f: comf)....— | **1** | 13/2 | 63 | 33 |
| 2800[2] | **L A Touch (51)** (CADwyer) **3-8-4** JStack(7) (lw: trckd ldrs: led ins fnl f: sn hdd: kpt on)....1 | **2** | 7/2[1] | 58 | 28 |
| 2902* | **Camionneur (IRE) (51)** (TDEasterby) **3-8-4b** JLowe(2) (lw: a.p: effrt over 1f out: nt qckn wl ins fnl f)....1¼ | **3** | 7/2[1] | 54 | 24 |
| 2867[7] | **Chalice (68)** (JBalding) **3-9-0**(7) JEdmunds(1) (lw: chsd ldrs: led appr fnl f: hdd & no ex ins fnl f)....nk | **4** | 14/1 | 70 | 40 |
| 2778[2] | **Sharp Monty (63)** (RHollinshead) **3-8-13**(3) FLynch(8) (lw: bhd tl styd on fnl 2f: nrst fin)....3 | **5** | 4/1[2] | 55 | 25 |
| 2849[7] | **Chemcast (67)** (DNicholls) **3-9-6b** AlexGreaves(10) (lw: cl up tl wknd appr fnl f)....1½ | **6** | 10/1 | 54 | 24 |
| 3049[5] | **Pleasure Time (63)** (CSmith) **3-8-13b**(3) CTeague(4) (lw: unruly s: led tl hdd & wknd appr fnl f)....3 | **7** | 10/1 | 41 | 11 |
| 2970[8] | **Fancy Clancy (43)** (MissLCSiddall) **3-7-7hc**(3) DarrenMoffatt(5) (lw: a outpcd & bhd)....1½ | **8** | 33/1 | 16 | — |
| 2800[3] | **Swifty Nifty (IRE) (44)** (WWHaigh) **3-7-8**(3)ow1 DWright(6) (s.i.s: n.d)....1 | **9** | 12/1 | 14 | — |
| 2757[11] | **Gagajulu (56)** (PDEvans) **3-8-9b**[1] JFortune(3) (sn drvn along: bhd fr ½-wy)....3½ | **10** | 9/2[3] | 15 | — |

(SP 131.4%) **10 Rn**

**61.46 secs** (3.06) CSF £31.53 CT £91.76 TOTE £13.10: £2.60 £1.80 £1.60 (£22.90) Trio £36.20 OWNER Mr R. Barnett (THIRSK) BRED W. and R. Barnett Ltd
LONG HANDICAP Fancy Clancy 7-9 Swifty Nifty (IRE) 7-3

**769 Oatey** found her mark here in some style and looks likely to follow this up. (13/2)

**2800 L A Touch** looked to be going well until the winner arrived on the scene, and then had to be content with second best. This will not always be the case. (7/2)

**2902* Camionneur (IRE)** made his move approaching the final furlong, but was never doing enough to trouble the front two. (7/2)

**1429* Chalice** ran a sound race, but was never quite up to the task in the final furlong. (14/1)

**2778 Sharp Monty** did not get the best of breaks and this trip then proved inadequate. (4/1: 3/1-9/2)

**2395 Chemcast** has plenty of speed but he failed to see it out. (10/1)

T/Plpt: £35.80 (335.58 Tckts). T/Qdpt: £13.10 (51.46 Tckts). AA

# 2398-EPSOM (L-H) (Good, Good to firm patches)
## Wednesday July 31st

WEATHER: overcast WIND: slt half against

## 3136 WARREN APPRENTICE H'CAP (0-75) (3-Y.O+) (Class E)

6-00 (6-07) **1m 2f 18y** £3,403.75 (£1,030.00: £502.50: £238.75) Stalls: Low GOING minus 0.42 sec per fur (F)

| | | | SP | RR | SF |
|---|---|---|---|---|---|
| 2943[2] | **Soviet Bride (IRE) (64)** (SDow) **4-9-8** RHavlin(2) (mde all: rdn out)....— | **1** | 9/4[1] | 74 | 31 |
| 2921* | **Kaafih Homm (IRE) (64)** (NACallaghan) **5-9-8** PPMurphy(5) (lw: hld up: wnt 2nd 7f out: rdn over 2f out: no imp)....3 | **2** | 100/30[2] | 69 | 26 |
| 2767[2] | **Rising Dough (IRE) (70)** (GLMoore) **4-9-9**(5) JDennis(4) (lw: hld up: hdwy 4f out: hung lft over 1f out: r.o one pce)....nk | **3** | 4/1[3] | 75 | 32 |

2192* **Voices in the Sky (46)** (AGNewcombe) **5-7-11**(7)ow4 DSalt(1) (plld hrd: n.m.r on ins & lost pl 7f out: hdwy over 1f out: n.d)....1½ **4** 10/1 48 1
3000* **Guesstimation (USA) (67)** (JPearce) **7-9-11** 5x DGriffiths(6) (nvr trbld ldrs)....4 **5** 6/1 63 20
*2689*[3] **Superior Force (65)** (MissBSanders) **3-8-13** CScally(3) (lw: chsd wnr 3f: wknd 5f out)....5 **6** 11/1 53 —
(SP 105.6%) **6 Rn**

**2m 9.65** (5.25) CSF £8.95 TOTE £2.60: £1.60 £2.80 (£4.20) OWNER Mr Terry Shepherd (EPSOM) BRED Gainsborough Stud Management Ltd
WEIGHT FOR AGE 3yo-10lb

**2943 Soviet Bride (IRE),** 6lb higher than when winning this race last year, was due to go up 2lb following her narrow defeat at Windsor. (9/4)
**2921* Kaafih Homm (IRE),** raised 2lb, was reverting to a mile and a quarter. (100/30)
**2767 Rising Dough (IRE)** did not find the return to ten furlongs enabling him to repeat his course and distance win. (4/1)
**2192* Voices in the Sky** was 12lb higher in the Ratings than when beating a big field of platers at Windsor. (10/1: op 5/1)
**3000* Guesstimation (USA),** up 5lb for his second two outings ago, was effectively 10lb higher than when successful last time. (6/1: op 4/1)

## 3137 E.B.F. MEDIAN AUCTION MAIDEN STKS (2-Y.O F) (Class D)

6-30 (6-30) **6f** £3,650.00 (£1,025.00: £500.00) Stalls: High GOING minus 0.42 sec per fur (F)

SP RR SF
2956[2] **Aegean Sound** (RHannon) **2-8-11** WJO'Connor(1) (lw: mde all: shkn up over 1f out: comf)....— **1** 8/15[1] 58 —
**Gilding The Lily (IRE)** (MJohnston) **2-8-11** DHolland(3) (neat: bit bkwd: w wnr: rdn over 2f out: one pce)....2 **2** 15/8[2] 53? —
**Coal To Diamonds** (RHarris) **2-8-11** MTebbutt(2) (neat: bit bkwd: s.s: sn wl bhd: t.o)....dist **3** 12/1[3] — —
(SP 107.7%) **3 Rn**

**1m 12.55** (4.55) CSF £1.79 TOTE £1.70 (£1.10) OWNER Theobalds Stud (MARLBOROUGH) BRED Theobalds Stud
**2956 Aegean Sound** proved too sharp for the two newcomers. (8/15)
**Gilding The Lily (IRE),** a half-sister to El Cortes and Sao Paulo, should at least come on for the outing. (15/8)
**Coal To Diamonds** will struggle to ever make the prizemoney again on this evidence. (12/1)

## 3138 CONNECT MAIDEN H'CAP (0-70) (3-Y.O) (Class E)

7-00 (7-02) **1m 114y** £4,200.00 (£1,275.00: £625.00: £300.00) Stalls: Low GOING minus 0.42 sec per fur (F)

SP RR SF
2743[2] **Budby (65)** (ACStewart) **3-9-7** SWhitworth(1) (hld up: rdn & hdwy wl over 1f out: r.o wl to ld last strides)....— **1** 9/4[2] 76 14
2859[2] **Sharp Shuffle (IRE) (63)** (RHannon) **3-9-5** RHughes(2) (led over 1f: led over 2f out: clr over 1f out: ct last strides)....½ **2** 2/1[1] 73 11
2761[4] **Silver Harrow (59)** (AGNewcombe) **3-8-10**(5) DGriffiths(4) (hld up: rdn over 2f out: hdwy over 1f out: r.o ins fnl f)....2½ **3** 6/1[3] 64 2
2557[12] **Allstars Rocket (53)** (TJNaughton) **3-8-9** DHolland(7) (lw: led 7f out tl over 2f out: wknd fnl f)....4 **4** 20/1 51 —
2235[4] **Velvet Jones (58)** (GFHCharles-Jones) **3-9-0** BDoyle(5) (hld up: nvr nr to chal)....nk **5** 6/1[3] 55 —
*2937*[12] **Persephone (40)** (ICampbell) **3-7-10v** GBardwell(3) (prom tl rdn & wknd 2f out)....s.h **6** 12/1 37 —
2529[5] **First Law (65)** (MissGayKelleway) **3-9-7** SSanders(6) (b.hind: hld up: hdwy on ins 3f out: hrd rdn & wknd 2f out)....nk **7** 12/1 62 —
(SP 112.8%) **7 Rn**

**1m 47.94** (5.94) CSF £6.91 TOTE £2.80: £1.70 £1.70 (£2.20) OWNER Mr B. H. Farr (NEWMARKET) BRED R. B. Warren
LONG HANDICAP Persephone 7-9
**2743 Budby,** raised 4lb following a couple of good runs since graduating to handicaps, seems well suited to an extended mile. (9/4)
**2859 Sharp Shuffle (IRE)** just got caught out by the uphill finish and deserves a change of luck. (2/1)
**2761 Silver Harrow** may need even further. (6/1)
**Allstars Rocket** showed his first signs of ability on this handicap debut. (20/1)
**2235 Velvet Jones,** ridden to get this longer trip, never appeared likely to take a hand. (6/1)
**2130 Persephone** has failed to reproduce the form of her second in the first-time visor at Newmarket. (12/1: op 8/1)

## 3139 RING & BRYMER H'CAP (0-70) (3-Y.O+) (Class E)

7-30 (7-34) **7f** £5,038.25 (£1,526.00: £745.50: £355.25) Stalls: Low GOING minus 0.42 sec per fur (F)

SP RR SF
2981[3] **Balance of Power (60)** (RAkehurst) **4-9-7** SSanders(7) (hdwy over 2f out: hrd rdn to ld nr fin)....— **1** 9/1 71 32
2403[3] **Yo Kiri-B (52)** (TJNaughton) **5-8-13** DHolland(4) (led: rdn over 1f out: hdd nr fin)....nk **2** 9/2[1] 62 23
2722[4] **Broughtons Turmoil (63)** (WJMusson) **7-9-7**(3) PMcCabe(1) (b: lw: dwlt: hdwy & nt clr run over 2f out: swtchd rt & n.m.r 1f out: r.o)....nk **3** 11/2[2] 73 34
*201*[7] **Racing Telegraph (40)** (CNAllen) **6-7-10**(5) MartinDwyer(2) (a.p: ev ch 2f out: unable qckn ins fnl f)....¾ **4** 12/1 48 9
2994[2] **African-Pard (IRE) (58)** (DHaydnJones) **4-9-5v**[1] TQuinn(11) (swtg: prom: hrd rdn over 2f out: r.o one pce fnl f)....nk **5** 6/1[3] 65 26
2946[6] **Mystery Matthias (52)** (MissBSanders) **3-8-3v**(3) DaneO'Neill(15) (hdwy over 1f out: r.o)....1½ **6** 14/1 56 10
2602[4] **Our Shadee (USA) (49)** (KTIvory) **6-8-3v**(7) CScally(14) (hld up & bhd: hdwy over 1f out: nvr nrr)....1¼ **7** 12/1 50 11
2981[5] **Pearl Dawn (IRE) (67)** (GLMoore) **6-10-0** SWhitworth(3) (nvr nr to chal)....1 **8** 14/1 66 27
2743[10] **Zdenka (49)** (MBlanshard) **3-8-3** JQuinn(12) (w ldr: wkng whn n.m.r over 1f out)....½ **9** 25/1 47 1
2605[8] **Pab's Choice (54)** (MMcCormack) **5-9-1** RCochrane(5) (hdwy on ins over 2f out: wknd over 1f out)....hd **10** 16/1 51 12
2229[9] **Utmost Zeal (USA) (55)** (PWHarris) **3-8-9** GHind(6) (lw: a bhd)....¾ **11** 20/1 51 5
2763[9] **Mislemani (IRE) (53)** (AGNewcombe) **6-8-9**(5) DGriffiths(9) (a bhd)....½ **12** 16/1 47 8
2962[3] **Another Nightmare (IRE) (37)** (RMMcKellar) **4-7-12** TWilliams(10) (plld hrd: prom: hrd rdn over 1f out: wkng whn hmpd ins fnl f)....2½ **13** 15/2 26 —
2578[17] **Meranti (54)** (SDow) **3-8-8** JFEgan(8) (lw: prom tl wknd 3f out)....4 **14** 14/1 34 —
2737[5] **Proud Image (60)** (KRBurke) **4-9-7v** JTate(13) (lw: prom tl wknd over 2f out)....5 **15** 16/1 28 —
(SP 131.3%) **15 Rn**

**1m 23.27** (2.97) CSF £49.78 CT £240.16 TOTE £10.40: £3.10 £1.90 £2.90 (£31.30) Trio £51.20 OWNER Mr John Falvey (EPSOM) BRED M. V. S. and Mrs Aram
WEIGHT FOR AGE 3yo-7lb
**2981 Balance of Power** had given notice of a return to form last time and was much better off at the weights than in that claimer. (9/1)
**2403 Yo Kiri-B** appreciated this return to seven, but could not quite hold the winner. (9/2)
**2722 Broughtons Turmoil** encountered all sorts of traffic problems and looked rather unlucky. (11/2)
**Racing Telegraph** ran a fine race for his new stable and lack of a recent outing may just have told in the closing stages. (12/1: 8/1-14/1)
**2994 African-Pard (IRE),** switching to a visor this time, was due to go up 5lb in future handicaps. (6/1)
**2946 Mystery Matthias,** trying an extra furlong, did her best work in the latter stages. (14/1)

## 3140 WEATHERBYS CLAIMING STKS (3-Y.O+) (Class E)

8-00 (8-04) **6f** £3,485.00 (£1,055.00: £515.00: £245.00) Stalls: High GOING minus 0.42 sec per fur (F)

| | | | SP | RR | SF |
|---|---|---|---|---|---|
| 2220[10] | **Lord Olivier (IRE) (80)** (WJarvis) **6-9-4** MTebbutt(6) (lw: chsd ldr: edgd rt & hrd rdn 2f out: led wl ins fnl f: drvn out) —— | 1 | 6/1 | 71 | 31 |
| 2957[6] | **Tafahhus (66)** (MJPolglase) **4-8-8b** RCochrane(5) (lw: a.p: hrd rdn & r.o ins fnl f) nk | 2 | 6/1 | 60 | 20 |
| 2908* | **Palacegate Touch (76)** (JBerry) **6-9-0b** GCarter(3) (led: clr over 3f out: wknd & hdd wl ins fnl f) 1¼ | 3 | 7/2 3 | 63 | 23 |
| 2604[6] | **Dashing Dancer (IRE) (55)** (RAkehurst) **5-8-6** TQuinn(7) (hdwy 3f out: one pce fnl 2f) 1¾ | 4 | 14/1 | 50 | 10 |
| 2867[4] | **Standown (71)** (JBerry) **3-8-5** KDarley(8) (lw: hld up: swtchd lft wl over 1f out: one pce) s.h | 5 | 11/4 2 | 54 | 9 |
| 2785[10] | **Justinianus (IRE) (40)** (JJBridger) **4-8-6** JQuinn(1) (no hdwy fnl 2f) 2 | 6 | 50/1 | 45 | 5 |
| 2880[16] | **No Extras (IRE) (100)** (GLMoore) **6-9-12** SWhitworth(4) (b.off hind: a bhd) 2½ | 7 | 9/4 1 | 58 | 18 |
| 2718[14] | **Twice Removed** (SDow) **3-9-2** JFEgan(2) (s.i.s: a bhd) 3 | 8 | 50/1 | 45 | — |

(SP 118.8%) **8 Rn**

**1m 10.34** (2.34) CSF £39.37 TOTE £11.10: £2.40 £1.90 £1.20 (£38.00) OWNER Miss V. R. Jarvis (NEWMARKET) BRED Michael Staunton in Ireland

WEIGHT FOR AGE 3yo-5lb

**Lord Olivier (IRE)** had been finding it tough in handicaps and made the most of this drop into a claimer. (6/1)
**2791* Tafahhus** had run no race at all in a Bath handicap last week, but was back in claiming company on a course he likes. (6/1)
**2908* Palacegate Touch**, stepping up from the minimum trip, did not last home after leading the field a merry dance. (7/2)
**2228 Dashing Dancer (IRE)**, still a maiden after thirty starts, had plenty to do at the weights. (14/1)
**2867 Standown** could never get to grips with the principals. (11/4)
**1516 Justinianus (IRE)** would have been much better off in a handicap. (50/1)
**No Extras (IRE)** suffered a leg injury during the winter and was heavily bandaged on his off-hind. (9/4: 5/4-5/2)

## 3141 LONSDALE H'CAP (0-65) (3-Y.O+) (Class F)

8-30 (8-36) **1m 4f 10y** £4,435.50 (£1,344.00: £657.00: £313.50) Stalls: Low GOING minus 0.42 sec per fur (F)

| | | | SP | RR | SF |
|---|---|---|---|---|---|
| 2891* | **Supermick (33)** (WRMuir) **5-7-8**(3) MHenry(5) (hrd rdn & hdwy 3f out: led ins fnl f: r.o) —— | 1 | 8/1 | 44 | 26 |
| 2767[3] | **Norsong (48)** (RAkehurst) **4-8-12** TQuinn(12) (lw: a.p: led over 3f out tl ins fnl f: r.o) 1¼ | 2 | 6/1 2 | 57 | 39 |
| 2246[10] | **Shining Dancer (61)** (SDow) **4-9-11** JFEgan(1) (hld up: rdn & hdwy 2f out: r.o one pce fnl f) 4 | 3 | 10/1 | 65 | 47 |
| 2341[6] | **Missed the Boat (IRE) (41)** (AGNewcombe) **6-8-2**(3) SDrowne(7) (hld up & bhd: hdwy wl over 1f out: one pce fnl f) ¾ | 4 | 12/1 | 44 | 26 |
| 2574[11] | **Labudd (USA) (46)** (RIngram) **6-8-10** NAdams(9) (b: s.i.s: hdwy fnl 2f: r.o) ½ | 5 | 14/1 | 48 | 30 |
| 2952[4] | **Junior Ben (IRE) (46)** (PHowling) **4-8-10b1** RCochrane(4) (led after 2f tl over 3f out: wknd over 1f out) 4 | 6 | 17/2 | 43 | 25 |
| 2599[4] | **Rocquaine Bay (41)** (MJBolton) **9-8-5** JQuinn(13) (lw: prom tl wknd over 1f out) 1½ | 7 | 4/1 1 | 36 | 18 |
| 3113[13] | **Seven Crowns (USA) (61)** (RHannon) **3-8-10b1**(3) DaneO'Neill(6) (lw: prom 6f) nk | 8 | 20/1 | 56 | 26 |
| 2574[9] | **Warspite (49)** (RJO'Sullivan) **6-8-13** TSprake(3) (lw: prom 8f) 1 | 9 | 7/1 3 | 42 | 24 |
| *2689*[9] | **Double Rush (IRE) (40)** (TGMills) **4-8-4** TWilliams(8) (swtg: hdwy over 5f out: wknd over 1f out) 5 | 10 | 16/1 | 27 | 9 |
| *498*[3] | **El Volador (53)** (CNAllen) **9-8-12**(5) MartinDwyer(11) (lw: prom tl wknd 3f out) 1 | 11 | 8/1 | 38 | 20 |
| 1655[13] | **East Sheen (43)** (CJBenstead) **4-8-7** GHind(2) (a bhd) 1½ | 12 | 33/1 | 26 | 8 |
| 2768[4] | **Henry Otis (52)** (RAkehurst) **3-8-4** SSanders(10) (led 2f: wknd 3f out) 5 | 13 | 10/1 | 29 | — |

(SP 125.7%) **13 Rn**

**2m 38.77** (3.77) CSF £54.18 CT £457.63 TOTE £6.30: £1.90 £2.70 £3.80 (£17.90) Trio £98.40 OWNER Mrs J. M. Muir (LAMBOURN) BRED James Thom and Sons

WEIGHT FOR AGE 3yo-12lb

**2891* Supermick**, up 3lb for scraping home in a seller, took a long time to gain the upper hand over this shorter trip. (8/1: 6/1-9/1)
**2767 Norsong** put any stamina doubts to rest, but the weight concession proved too much. (6/1)
**1841* Shining Dancer**, who lost a shoe when finishing lame last time, was 6lb higher than when dead-heating at Windsor. (10/1: 7/1-11/1)
**2341 Missed the Boat (IRE)** should now be approaching his peak. (12/1)
**2377 Labudd (USA)**, who has been reported to have a heart problem, seems to need this trip nowadays. (14/1: op 8/1)
**2952 Junior Ben (IRE)** may have run a bit too freely in the first-time blinkers. (17/2: 6/1-9/1)
**2599 Rocquaine Bay** was 11lb higher than when landing a gamble in this event last year. (4/1)
**2768 Henry Otis** (10/1: op 6/1)

T/Plpt: £37.60 (295.85 Tckts). T/Qdpt: £16.00 (64.94 Tckts). KH

# 3123-GOODWOOD (R-H) (Good to firm)
## Wednesday July 31st

Race 1: flip start
WEATHER: sunny WIND: mod against

## 3142 MARRIOTT HOTELS GOODWOOD H'CAP (0-90) (3-Y.O+) (Class C)

2-15 (2-16) **2m 4f** £15,010.00 (£4,480.00: £2,140.00: £970.00) Stalls: High GOING minus 0.16 sec per fur (GF)

| | | | SP | RR | SF |
|---|---|---|---|---|---|
| 2612[3] | **Southern Power (IRE) (85)** (RAkehurst) **5-10-0** TQuinn(7) (swtg: a.p: led over 1f out: all out) —— | 1 | 7/2 2 | 96 | 79 |
| 2697[4] | **Sea Victor (76)** (JLHarris) **4-9-5** MHills(9) (lw: chsd ldr: led over 2f out tl over 1f out: ev ch fnl f: r.o wl) nk | 2 | 10/1 | 87 | 70 |
| 2857[4] | **Unchanged (72)** (CEBrittain) **4-9-1** BDoyle(3) (rdn over 5f out: hdwy over 2f out: unable qckn fnl f) 1¼ | 3 | 12/1 | 82 | 65 |
| 2958* | **Paradise Navy (67)** (CREgerton) **7-8-10b** 3x RHughes(2) (swtg: stdy hdwy over 2f out: wknd over 1f out) 7 | 4 | 7/1 | 71 | 54 |
| 2148[7] | **Salaman (FR) (79)** (JLDunlop) **4-9-8** PatEddery(6) (hld up: rdn over 5f out: wknd over 1f out) 1 | 5 | 100/30 1 | 82 | 65 |
| 2385* | **Mirador (60)** (RCurtis) **5-8-3** GBardwell(10) (nvr nr to chal) 3½ | 6 | 9/2 3 | 61 | 44 |
| 2560[4] | **Cypress Avenue (IRE) (67)** (RHannon) **4-8-7**(3) DaneO'Neill(4) (bhd fnl 4f) 4 | 7 | 40/1 | 64 | 47 |
| 2857[3] | **Coleridge (54)** (JJSheehan) **8-7-8b**(3) MHenry(8) (hdwy over 6f out: wknd over 2f out) 2 | 8 | 16/1 | 50 | 33 |
| 2857[6] | **Invest Wisely (80)** (JMPEustace) **4-9-9b1** RCochrane(1) (led tl over 2f out: sn wknd) 6 | 9 | 10/1 | 71 | 54 |

(SP 110.2%) **9 Rn**

**4m 20.3** (5.30) CSF £32.56 CT £318.14 TOTE £4.10: £1.80 £2.00 £3.00 (£14.20) Trio £74.10 OWNER Lucayan Stud (EPSOM) BRED Gay O'Callaghan

**2612 Southern Power (IRE)** loves a severe test and that is certainly what he got here. Never far away, he was travelling supremely well in the straight and cruised into the lead approaching the final furlong. However, he had not bargained on such a determined runner-up and, in the end, won with Quinn giving him the full treatment. (7/2: 9/4-4/1)
**2697 Sea Victor** put up a gutsy display. Racing in second place, he made his bid for glory over a quarter of a mile out but was collared by the winner below the distance. However, refusing to give way, he proved a real thorn in the side of that rival and failed by only a neck to get back up. (10/1)
**2857 Unchanged,** scrubbed along at the top of the hill, picked up ground over a quarter of a mile out but she tended to carry her head to one side as she tried to mount a challenge below the distance and was soon tapped for toe. The Tote Cesarewitch is her target. (12/1: 8/1-14/1)
**2958* Paradise Navy** cruised into the action over a quarter of a mile out travelling really well but, once let down, he failed to find what was expected and had shot his bolt below the distance. (7/1)
**Salaman (FR)** chased the leaders, but was being bustled along at the top of the hill and eventually conceded defeat below the distance. (100/30)
**2857 Invest Wisely** (10/1: 7/1-12/1)

## 3143 LANSON CHAMPAGNE VINTAGE STKS (Gp 3) (2-Y.O) (Class A)

2-45 (2-47) **7f** £23,380.00 (£8,746.50: £4,198.25: £1,825.25) Stalls: High GOING minus 0.16 sec per fur (GF)

| | | | | SP | RR | SF |
|---|---|---|---|---|---|---|
| 1960* | **Putra (USA)** (PFICole) **2-8-11** TQuinn(6) (hld up: rdn over 1f out: wandered & led ins fnl f: r.o wl) | — | 1 | 100/30$^{2}$ | 113+ | 53 |
| 2624* | **Grapeshot (USA)** (LMCumani) **2-8-11** KDarley(3) (lw: a.p: led 2f out tl ins fnl f: unable qckn: fin 3rd, 2l: plcd 2nd) | | 2 | 9/1 | 107 | 47 |
| 2909* | **Equal Rights (IRE)** (PWChapple-Hyam) **2-8-11** JReid(7) (a.p: led over 2f out: sn hdd: ev ch ins fnl f: one pce: fin 4th, nk: plcd 3rd) | | 3 | 12/1 | 107 | 47 |
| 2607$^{3}$ | **Air Express (IRE)** (CEBrittain) **2-8-11** BDoyle(2) (lw: bmpd over 2f out: nvr nr to chal: fin 5th, 1¼l: plcd 4th) | | 4 | 12/1 | 104 | 44 |
| 2878* | **Imperial President** (HRACecil) **2-8-11** PatEddery(1) (hld up: rdn over 2f out: wknd over 1f out: fin 6th, 1l: plcd 5th) | | 5 | 13/2$^{3}$ | 102 | 42 |
| 2291* | **Fun Galore (USA)** (BWHills) **2-8-11** MHills(5) (lw: a bhd) | 10 | 7 | 8/1 | 79 | 19 |
| 2503$^{4}$ | **Belgravia** (PFICole) **2-8-11b$^{1}$** MJKinane(4) (led over 4f) | 3½ | 8 | 33/1 | 71 | 11 |
| 2721* | **Sahm (USA)** (JLDunlop) **2-8-11** RHills(8) (eased out over 2f out: rdn & hdwy over 1f out: ev ch ins fnl f: r.o: fin 2nd, ½l: disq: plcd last) | | D | 7/4$^{1}$ | 112+ | 52 |
| | | | | (SP 112.2%) | **8 Rn** | |

**1m 27.32** (2.52) CSF £28.94 TOTE £4.40: £1.60 £2.60 £2.30 (£25.30) OWNER H R H Sultan Ahmad Shah (WHATCOMBE) BRED John Sullivan and Hargus Sexton
STEWARDS' ENQUIRY R.Hills susp 9-16/8/96 (irresponsible riding)
**IN-FOCUS: The previous five winners of this event, Alhaarth, Eltish, Mister Baileys, Maroof and Dr Devious were all top-notch performers, so Putra has plenty to live up to.**
**1960* Putra (USA)** confirmed the highly-promising debut he made at Sandown in this extremely hot race. An athletic individual who tended to race with his neck stuck out, he gave his rider a few problems as he wandered about, but Quinn corrected him extremely well and, leading inside the final furlong, the colt ran on strongly for an impressive victory. He looks very useful and will now head for the Dewhurst at Newmarket. (100/30)
**2624* Grapeshot (USA)** appreciated the step up in distance and again showed improved form in this higher class. Never far away, he went on a quarter of a mile out and was only overhauled inside the final furlong. Later promoted a place, he should soon be winning again. (9/1)
**2909* Equal Rights (IRE)** moved to the front over a quarter of a mile from home but was soon headed. However, refusing to give way, he still had every chance inside the final furlong before tapped for toe. (12/1: op 8/1)
**2607 Air Express (IRE)**, given a hefty bump by the runner-up over a quarter of a mile out, made a little late headway without posing a threat. (12/1)
**2878* Imperial President** chased the leaders, but was hung out to dry below the distance. (13/2: 9/2-7/1)
**2291* Fun Galore (USA)** ran no race at all and is certainly better than this. (8/1: 9/2-9/1)
**2721* Sahm (USA)** suffered his first defeat but went down with all guns blazing. Trapped in with nowhere to go, his jockey eased him out over a quarter of a mile from home but, in the process, gave Air Express a bump. Soon picking up ground, he threw down a very determined challenge to the winner inside the final furlong and only just lost out. Hills was later suspended for seven days for irresponsible riding and, although the side-on view made this decision look very harsh, the head-on showed exactly why the Stewards had come to this decision. Sahm looks very useful and should soon make amends. (7/4)

## 3144 SUSSEX STKS (Gp 1) (3-Y.O+) (Class A)

3-20 (3-22) **1m** £89,770.00 (£33,641.00: £16,195.50: £7,093.50) Stalls: High GOING minus 0.16 sec per fur (GF)

| | | | | SP | RR | SF |
|---|---|---|---|---|---|---|
| 2038* | **First Island (IRE) (119)** (GWragg) **4-9-7** MHills(9) (swtg: stdy hdwy 2f out: squeezed thro over 1f out: led ins fnl f: rdn out) | — | 1 | 5/1$^{2}$ | 128 | 87 |
| 2037* | **Charnwood Forest (IRE) (120)** (SbinSuroor) **4-9-7** MJKinane(7) (hdwy over 2f out: led over 1f out tl ins fnl f: unable qckn) | 1 | 2 | Evens$^{1}$ | 126 | 85 |
| 2473a$^{9}$ | **Alhaarth (IRE) (116)** (MajorWRHern) **3-8-13b** KDarley(8) (swtg: a.p: rdn 2f out: one pce) | 1¾ | 3 | 14/1 | 123 | 74 |
| 2039$^{3}$ | **Sorbie Tower (IRE) (120)** (MissGayKelleway) **3-8-13** RHughes(4) (b.hind: lw: rdn & hdwy over 2f out: one pce fnl f) | ¾ | 4 | 8/1$^{3}$ | 121 | 72 |
| 2839a* | **Restructure (IRE) (114)** (MrsJCecil) **4-9-7** PaulEddery(5) (swtg: a.p: rdn over 2f out: led wl over 1f out: sn hdd: one pce) | s.h | 5 | 25/1 | 121 | 80 |
| 2037$^{3}$ | **Mistle Cat (USA) (117)** (SPCWoods) **6-9-7** WWoods(2) (led over 6f: wknd fnl f) | 5 | 6 | 25/1 | 111 | 70 |
| 2050$^{5}$ | **Ali-Royal (IRE) (114)** (HRACecil) **3-8-13** PatEddery(6) (swtg: hld up: rdn 3f out: wknd over 1f out) | 3½ | 7 | 12/1 | 104 | 55 |
| 2039$^{5}$ | **Cayman Kai (IRE) (116)** (RHannon) **3-8-13** TQuinn(3) (lw: a bhd) | 7 | 8 | 25/1 | 90 | 41 |
| 1952a$^{12}$ | **Heart Lake** (SbinSuroor) **5-9-7** JReid(1) (bhd fnl 2f) | hd | 9 | 40/1 | 90 | 49 |
| 1949a$^{3}$ | **Matiya (IRE) (119)** (BHanbury) **3-8-10** RHills(10) (b.hind: hld up: rdn 3f out: n.m.r & wknd over 2f out) | s.h | 10 | 8/1$^{3}$ | 87 | 38 |
| | | | | (SP 117.2%) | **10 Rn** | |

**1m 37.75** (0.55) CSF £10.01 TOTE £5.30: £1.90 £1.10 £2.00 (£3.80) Trio £17.30 OWNER Mollers Racing (NEWMARKET) BRED Citadel Stud
WEIGHT FOR AGE 3yo-8lb
**IN-FOCUS: This did not appear to be a vintage renewal of the Sussex.**
**2038* First Island (IRE)**, whose work partner is Pentire, steadily crept closer a quarter of a mile out. Squeezing through a small gap below the distance, he was ridden to lead inside the final furlong and soon asserted. He must be the most-improved horse currently in training. (5/1)
**2037* Charnwood Forest (IRE)** had no excuses, and connections reckon this is as good as he is. Moving into the action over a quarter of a mile from home, he struck the front below the distance but, once passed by the winner inside the final furlong, failed to find another gear. (Evens)

**2473a Alhaarth (IRE)** had no problems with this drop in distance and ran a sound race. Taking a keen hold early, he was always close up, but failed to find the necessary turn of foot in the last two furlongs. Connections believe this is his trip, and the Jacques le Marois could be next, hopefully without the blinds. (14/1)
**2039 Sorbie Tower (IRE)**, in sparkling form this season, made his move on the outside of the field over a quarter of a mile from home. Almost on terms below the distance, he was then tapped for toe. He will now go for the Queen Elizabeth II Stakes at Ascot in September. (8/1)
**2839a* Restructure (IRE)** showed in front early in the final quarter-mile, but was soon passed and failed to find another gear. (25/1)
**2037 Mistle Cat (USA)** took the field along. Collared early in the final quarter-mile, he grimly tried to hold on, but had nothing more to offer inside the distance. (25/1)
**2050 Ali-Royal (IRE)**, who had no luck in running at Royal Ascot, chased the leaders until coming to the end of his tether below the distance.(12/1)

## 3145 TOTE GOLD TROPHY H'CAP (0-105) (3-Y.O) (Class B)

3-50 (3-53) **1m 4f** £36,490.00 (£11,020.00: £5,360.00: £2,530.00) Stalls: Low GOING minus 0.16 sec per fur (GF)

| | | | | SP | RR | SF |
|---|---|---|---|---|---|---|
| $2608^{6}$ | **Freequent (90)** (LMCumani) **3-8-9** PatEddery(4) (rdn over 3f out: hdwy over 2f out: led & edgd rt over 1f out: r.o wl) | — | 1 | 9/1 | 108 | 63 |
| $2601^{*}$ | **Time Allowed (86)** (MRStoute) **3-8-5** RHills(5) (hdwy over 2f out: hrd rdn over 1f out: r.o wl ins fnl f) | ¾ | 2 | $6/1^{2}$ | 103 | 58 |
| $2724^{11}$ | **Lakeline Legend (IRE) (89)** (MAJarvis) **3-8-8** EmmaO'Gorman(2) (a.p: led over 2f out tl over 1f out: unable qckn fnl f) | 1½ | 3 | 14/1 | 104 | 59 |
| $2616^{2}$ | **Spillo (88)** (LMCumani) **3-8-7** OUrbina(10) (swtg: hld up: rdn over 3f out: n.m.r over 1f out: one pce) | 1 | 4 | 16/1 | 102 | 57 |
| $2502^{16}$ | **Skillington (USA) (93)** (IABalding) **3-8-12** TQuinn(3) (lw: led over 7f: led 3f out tl over 2f out: ev ch over 1f out: wknd fnl f) | 1¼ | 5 | 14/1 | 105 | 60 |
| $2576^{*}$ | **Arabian Story (85)** (LordHuntingdon) **3-8-4** DHarrison(11) (s.s: hdwy after 1f: ev ch over 2f out: wknd over 1f out) | ½ | 6 | $4/1^{1}$ | 96 | 51 |
| $2616^{*}$ | **Nador (93)** (DRLoder) **3-8-12** RHughes(1) (s.s: hdwy over 4f out: rdn over 2f out: wknd wl over 1f out) | 4 | 7 | 9/1 | 99 | 54 |
| $1791^{11}$ | **Classic Eagle (97)** (RHarris) **3-9-2** AMackay(6) (lw: nvr nrr) | 1¾ | 8 | 33/1 | 101 | 56 |
| $2350^{*}$ | **Ambassador (USA) (93)** (BWHills) **3-8-12** MHills(8) (a bhd) | ½ | 9 | $7/1^{3}$ | 96 | 51 |
| $2845a^{5}$ | **Legal Right (USA) (102)** (PWChapple-Hyam) **3-9-7** JReid(13) (lw: prom 9f) | s.h | 10 | 20/1 | 105 | 60 |
| $3056^{*}$ | **Frog (78)** (SirMarkPrescott) **3-7-11** 4x JQuinn(7) (chsd ldr: led over 4f out to 3f out: sn wknd) | 4 | 11 | $6/1^{2}$ | 76 | 31 |
| $2608^{2}$ | **Al Shafa (97)** (JLDunlop) **3-9-2** KDarley(12) (lw: s.s: a bhd) | 8 | 12 | 9/1 | 84 | 39 |
| | | | | (SP 118.0%) | **12 Rn** | |

**2m 35.97** (2.77) CSF £57.39 CT £692.22 TOTE £10.60: £3.20 £2.30 £5.40 (£53.60) Trio £354.50 OWNER Fittocks Stud (NEWMARKET) BRED Fittocks Stud

**2608 Freequent** was taking a step up in distance in this very competitive race, but saw it out well. Pushed along as the Bugler called entering the straight, he soon picked up ground and, leading below the distance, despite drifting right, kept on well. (9/1)
**2601* Time Allowed** made her effort over a quarter of a mile from home but, despite running on strongly inside the final furlong, failed to get to the winner in time. She will now go for the Galtres Stakes at York. (6/1)
**2724 Lakeline Legend (IRE)**, taking a step up in trip, went on over a quarter of a mile from home but, headed below the distance, failed to find another gear. (14/1)
**2616 Spillo** chased the leaders. Bustled along as the Bugler called, he did not have a great deal of room in which to manoeuvre below the distance, but was tapped for toe when daylight did appear. (16/1)
**2006 Skillington (USA)** attempted to make all. Collared over half a mile from home, he got back in front three furlongs out only to be headed soon afterwards. Still with every chance below the distance, he then found this longer trip sapping his energy. (14/1)
**2576* Arabian Story** soon recovered from a tardy start. With every chance over a quarter of a mile from home, he had shot his bolt below the distance. (4/1)
**3056* Frog** has been in superb form this month, winning five times, but this was a big step up in class and she at last found the bubble bursting. Racing in second place, she made her bid for glory over half a mile from home but, headed three furlongs out, had soon croaked enough. (6/1)

## 3146 CHARLTON H'CAP (0-80) (4-Y.O+) (Class D)

4-25 (4-26) **5f** £7,570.00 (£2,260.00: £1,080.00: £490.00) Stalls: Low GOING minus 0.16 sec per fur (GF)

| | | | | SP | RR | SF |
|---|---|---|---|---|---|---|
| $2114^{26}$ | **Youdontsay (77)** (TJNaughton) **4-9-9**(3) DaneO'Neill(6) (gd hdwy over 1f out: str run fnl f: led last strides) | — | 1 | 20/1 | 87 | 54 |
| $2598^{2}$ | **Half Tone (48)** (RMFlower) **4-7-8b**(3) NVarley(2) (hdwy 2f out: led 1f out: rdn: hdd last strides) | hd | 2 | 10/1 | 58 | 25 |
| *$3091^{3}$* | **Runs in the Family (50)** (GMMcCourt) **4-7-8v**1(5) MartinDwyer(3) (a.p: led over 1f out: sn hdd: one pce) | ¾ | 3 | 16/1 | 57 | 24 |
| $2129^{8}$ | **Invocation (51)** (AMoore) **9-8-0** TWilliams(1) (b.nr hind: lw: dwlt: rdn over 2f out: hdwy fnl f: r.o) | 1¼ | 4 | 20/1 | 54 | 21 |
| $2508^{7}$ | **Bashful Brave (70)** (JWPayne) **5-9-5** RCochrane(5) (a.p: ev ch over 1f out: wknd fnl f) | 1¼ | 5 | 11/1 | 69 | 36 |
| $2292^{6}$ | **Tuscan Dawn (77)** (JBerry) **6-9-7**(5) PRoberts(10) (swtg: a.p: ev ch 1f out: sn wknd) | nk | 6 | 10/1 | 75 | 42 |
| $2976^{2}$ | **Friendly Brave (USA) (72)** (MissGayKelleway) **6-9-7** PatEddery(9) (b.hind: lw: rdn over 2f out: nvr nr to chal) | hd | 7 | $5/1^{2}$ | 70 | 37 |
| $2902^{3}$ | **Barranak (IRE) (59)** (GMMcCourt) **4-8-8** JReid(13) (prom 3f) | ½ | 8 | 20/1 | 55 | 22 |
| $2856^{3}$ | **Mister Jolson (76)** (RJHodges) **7-9-8**(3) SDrowne(11) (lw: hld up: rdn over 2f out: sn wknd) | 1¾ | 9 | $8/1^{3}$ | 67 | 34 |
| $2992^{4}$ | **Tinker Osmaston (65)** (MSSaunders) **5-9-0** JFEgan(12) (hld up: rdn over 2f out: sn wknd) | 3½ | 10 | 14/1 | 45 | 12 |
| $2286^{24}$ | **Mazzarello (IRE) (47)** (RCurtis) **6-7-5v**(5) MBaird(7) (prom 3f) | nk | 11 | 33/1 | 26 | — |
| $2849^{3}$ | **Bowcliffe Grange (IRE) (53)** (DWChapman) **4-8-2b** JQuinn(4) (led over 3f) | hd | 12 | $3/1^{1}$ | 31 | — |
| $2508^{3}$ | **Palacegate Jack (IRE) (79)** (JBerry) **5-10-0** JCarroll(8) (b.off fore: dwlt: sme hdwy & n.m.r over 1f out: sn wknd) | 2½ | 13 | 11/1 | 49 | 16 |
| | | | | (SP 117.4%) | **13 Rn** | |

**59.05 secs** (2.35) CSF £183.33 CT £2,975.77 TOTE £22.10: £5.30 £3.10 £3.40 (£155.30) Trio £522.20 OWNER Mr Tom Nicholls (EPSOM) BRED Mrs and Exors of the late Col F. R. Hue-Williams
LONG HANDICAP Mazzarello (IRE) 7-3
**OFFICIAL EXPLANATION Bowcliffe Grange (IRE): was found to have damaged muscles in his back.**

**1652 Youdontsay** gained her first victory at five furlongs. In last place a quarter of a mile out with no apparent chance, she came with a storming run from below the distance to snatch victory in the last few strides. (20/1)
**2598 Half Tone** made his effort a quarter of a mile out and came sweeping through to lead entering the final furlong. It looked as if the race was his, but he had not bargained on the fast-finishing winner, and was caught in the last few strides. (10/1)
**3091 Runs in the Family**, making a quick reappearance, was always close up against the stands' rail. Sent on below the distance, she was soon headed and tapped for toe. (16/1)
**1958 Invocation**, racing at the back of the field, was doing all his best work in the final furlong. (20/1)
**2017 Bashful Brave**, a leading player from the outset, had every chance below the distance before tiring. (11/1)
**2292 Tuscan Dawn**, always close up in the centre of the track, still had every chance a furlong out before giving best. (10/1)

**2856 Mister Jolson** (8/1: 6/1-10/1)

## 3147 E.B.F. SELSEY MAIDEN STKS (2-Y.O) (Class D)
5-00 (5-01) **6f** £6,970.00 (£2,110.00: £1,030.00: £490.00) Stalls: Low GOING minus 0.16 sec per fur (GF)

| | | | | SP | RR | SF |
|---|---|---|---|---|---|---|
| | **In Command (IRE)** (BWHills) **2-8-11** MHills(7) (gd sort: hld up: led 1f out: pushed out) | — | 1 | 6/5[1] | 98+ | 45 |
| 2993[4] | **Mile High** (MRChannon) **2-8-11** RHughes(6) (led 5f: hrd rdn: r.o) | ½ | 2 | 10/1 | 97 | 44 |
| | **Orontes (USA)** (RHannon) **2-8-8**(3) DaneO'Neill(8) (scope: rdn over 2f out: hdwy over 1f out: r.o one pce) | 5 | 3 | 20/1 | 83 | 30 |
| 2624[6] | **Shuwaikh** (RHannon) **2-8-11** TQuinn(9) (a.p: rdn 2f out: one pce) | 3½ | 4 | 7/2[2] | 74 | 21 |
| 2600[15] | **Linden's Lad (IRE)** (JRJenkins) **2-8-11** RCochrane(5) (lw: bmpd s: hld up: rdn 2f out: sn wknd) | 3½ | 5 | 50/1 | 65 | 12 |
| | **High Extreme (IRE)** (PWChapple-Hyam) **2-8-11** JReid(3) (str: scope: bmpd s: spd over 4f) | hd | 6 | 13/2[3] | 64 | 11 |
| | **Danka** (PTWalwyn) **2-8-11** PatEddery(1) (w'like: scope: bit bkwd: a bhd) | 1 | 7 | 8/1 | 62 | 9 |
| 1871[5] | **Select Choice (IRE)** (APJarvis) **2-8-11** KDarley(2) (spd over 4f) | 1¼ | 8 | 14/1 | 58 | 5 |

(SP 114.6%) **8 Rn**

**1m 12.58** (2.58) CSF £12.88 TOTE £2.30: £1.30 £1.50 £3.90 (£7.50) Trio £80.80 OWNER Maktoum Al Maktoum (LAMBOURN) BRED Gainsborough Stud Management Ltd

**In Command (IRE)**, an attractive, strongly-made colt who is a half-brother to the top-class Lyric Fantasy and Royal Applause, was very well backed, with major bets standing at £120,000. Held up travelling sweetly, he was shaken up to lead entering the final furlong and needed only to be nudged along to keep the determined runner-up at bay. His trainer believes he needs further, and he can win again. (6/5: Evens-6/4)

**2993 Mile High** left his debut run at Chepstow last week well behind. Bowling along in front, he was collared a furlong out but, to his credit, kept on well to the line. His trainer thinks a lot of him, and he should soon be winning. (10/1)

**Orontes (USA)**, a scopey newcomer, was being pushed along and going nowhere soon after halfway. He did stay on from below the distance, but never threatened the front two. (20/1)

**2624 Shuwaikh** was made to look very pedestrian in the last two furlongs. (7/2)

**Linden's Lad (IRE)**, given a bump at the start, chased the leaders until calling it a day early in the final quarter-mile. (50/1)

**High Extreme (IRE)**, a strongly-made half-brother to Silver Groom, does not have any big race entries but, nevertheless, showed up well until tiring below the distance. (13/2: 3/1-7/1)

## 3148 DRAYTON H'CAP (0-90) (3-Y.O+ F & M) (Class C)
5-35 (5-38) **1m 1f** £8,285.00 (£2,480.00: £1,190.00: £545.00) Stalls: High GOING minus 0.16 sec per fur (GF)

| | | | | SP | RR | SF |
|---|---|---|---|---|---|---|
| 2618* | **Panata (IRE) (80)** (LMCumani) **3-8-12** OUrbina(5) (a.p: led over 2f out: rdn out) | — | 1 | 8/1[3] | 89 | 40 |
| 2576[5] | **Iberian Dancer (CAN) (79)** (JWHills) **3-8-8**(3) MHenry(11) (s.s: nt clr run over 2f out: hdwy over 1f out: r.o wl ins fnl f) | 1 | 2 | 11/1 | 86 | 37 |
| 2704[5] | **Blue Zulu (IRE) (83)** (JRFanshawe) **4-9-10** DHarrison(9) (a.p: rdn over 2f out: unable qckn fnl f) | hd | 3 | 8/1[3] | 90 | 50 |
| 2773[2] | **Tael of Silver (66)** (ABailey) **4-8-7** KDarley(1) (hdwy over 2f out: ev ch over 1f out: one pce) | nk | 4 | 12/1 | 73 | 33 |
| 2603[17] | **Ron's Secret (72)** (JWPayne) **4-8-13** RCochrane(12) (hrd rdn & hdwy over 1f out: eased whn btn wl ins fnl f) | 1¾ | 5 | 16/1 | 75 | 35 |
| 1773[13] | **Royal Diversion (IRE) (70)** (JLDunlop) **3-8-2** TSprake(4) (hdwy over 5f out: rdn over 2f out: one pce) | nk | 6 | 25/1 | 73 | 24 |
| 2894* | **Victorian Style (87)** (RCharlton) **3-9-5** PatEddery(7) (n.m.r & swtchd lft over 2f out: hrd rdn & hdwy over 1f out: one pce) | nk | 7 | 4/1[1] | 89 | 40 |
| 2399[3] | **Omara (USA) (76)** (HRACecil) **3-8-8** WRyan(2) (bhd whn hmpd 3f out: nvr nrr) | 2½ | 8 | 14/1 | 74 | 25 |
| 2974* | **Catch The Lights (86)** (RHannon) **3-9-1**(3) 5x DaneO'Neill(3) (bhd whn bmpd over 2f out) | 1¼ | 9 | 5/1[2] | 82 | 33 |
| 2601[9] | **Kitty Kitty Cancan (75)** (LadyHerries) **3-8-7** PaulEddery(13) (led 2f: wknd over 4f out) | ½ | 10 | 14/1 | 70 | 21 |
| 2862[7] | **Sveltana (74)** (GWragg) **4-9-1** MHills(6) (lw: led 7f out tl over 2f out: eased whn btn over 1f out) | 3½ | 11 | 10/1 | 63 | 23 |
| *2585[6]* | ***Jezyah (USA) (80)*** (RWArmstrong) **3-8-12** RPrice(8) (Withdrawn not under Starter's orders: unruly stalls) | | W | 16/1 | — | — |
| *820[6]* | ***Devon Peasant (72)*** (LGCottrell) **4-8-13** JQuinn(10) (Withdrawn not under Starter's orders: ref to ent stalls) | | W | 16/1 | — | — |

(SP 118.8%) **11 Rn**

**1m 56.28** (4.88) CSF £75.73 CT £565.41 TOTE £7.70: £2.80 £2.50 £2.70 (£36.40) Trio £76.10 OWNER Mrs Angie Silver (NEWMARKET) BRED Dr J. J. Ryan

WEIGHT FOR AGE 3yo-9lb

**2618* Panata (IRE)** completed the hat-trick in this competitive event. Never far away, she went on over a quarter of a mile from home and was ridden along to secure victory. (8/1: 4/1-9/1)

**2576 Iberian Dancer (CAN)** lost ground at the start and then failed to get a clear run over a quarter of a mile from home. She managed to weave her way through the pack from below the distance but, despite running on strongly, found the winner already home and dry. (11/1: 8/1-12/1)

**2704 Blue Zulu (IRE)** desperately tried to get on terms with the winner, but was tapped for toe in the last 200 yards. (8/1)

**2773 Tael of Silver** made her effort on the outside over a quarter of a mile from home and threatened to take the lead below the distance, before tapped for toe. (12/1)

**Ron's Secret** made headway under pressure below the distance, but she was making no further impression inside the final furlong and was eased down when all chance had gone in the closing stages. (16/1)

**1349 Royal Diversion (IRE)** moved up over five furlongs from home, but was only treading water in the final quarter-mile. (25/1)

**2894* Victorian Style** is rather on the small side for carrying big weights like this. Switched left over a quarter of a mile out to get a clear passage, giving Catch the Lights a bad bump, she picked up ground below the distance but could then make no further impression. Eddery can count himself very lucky indeed that the Stewards did not suspend him for that incident. (4/1)

T/Jkpt: £67,352.60 (0.1 Tckts); £85,376.59 to Goodwood 1/8/96. T/Plpt: £565.00 (109.23 Tckts). T/Qdpt: £82.50 (36.86 Tckts). AK

# 3130-DONCASTER (L-H) (Good to firm, Rnd crse Firm patches)
## Thursday August 1st

Race 5: hand-timed

WEATHER: sunny WIND: fresh against

## 3149 DONCASTER RACECOURSE SUNDAY MARKET AMATEUR H'CAP (0-80) (3-Y.O+) (Class F)
6-20 (6-21) **2m 110y** £2,807.00 (£777.00: £371.00) Stalls: Low GOING minus 0.01 sec per fur (G)

| | | | | SP | RR | SF |
|---|---|---|---|---|---|---|
| *3066[2]* | **Old School House (57)** (TJNaughton) **3-8-11**(5)ow2 MrsJNaughton(10) (bhd: hdwy 4f out: led 1½f out: styd on wl) | — | 1 | 13/2 | 68 | 37 |

| | | | | SP | RR | SF |
|---|---|---|---|---|---|---|
| 1478* | **Arian Spirit (IRE) (51)** (JLEyre) **5-9-11** MissDianaJones(3) (trckd ldrs: led 6f out to 1½f out: no ex) | 3½ | **2** | 9/2[3] | 59 | 45 |
| 2739* | **Candle Smoke (USA) (66)** (GHarwood) **3-9-11** MrsAPerrett(11) (lw: in tch: hdwy 6f out: effrt & hung lft over 2f out: styd on one pce) | hd | **3** | 11/4[1] | 74 | 45 |
| 2697[8] | **Anglesey Sea View (60)** (ABailey) **7-10-1**(5) MissBridgetGatehouse(7) (in tch: hdwy to chal appr st: one pce fnl 2f) | 1½ | **4** | 20/1 | 66 | 52 |
| 2804[5] | **Jalcanto (53)** (MrsMReveley) **6-9-13** MrMHNaughton(4) (lw: bhd: effrt 4f out: edgd lft: nvr able to chal) | 2 | **5** | 10/1 | 57 | 43 |
| 2989[6] | **Nosey Native (55)** (JPearce) **3-9-0** MrsLPearce(8) (s.i.s: bhd tl hdwy 6f out: chal over 3f out: wknd over 2f out) | 3 | **6** | 10/1 | 56 | 27 |
| *2173[12]* | **Frontier Flight (USA) (50)** (MissLCSiddall) **6-9-5**(5) MissTCave(1) (in tch: rdn 4f out: no imp after) | nk | **7** | 33/1 | 51 | 37 |
| 2042[25] | **Stompin (75)** (MissHCKnight) **5-11-7** JCulloty(6) (lw: chsd ldrs tl hrd rdn & wknd fnl 3f) | ½ | **8** | 7/2[2] | 75 | 61 |
| 2148[8] | **Good Hand (USA) (69)** (SEKettlewell) **10-11-1** MrCBonner(9) (bhd: effrt 4f out: no imp) | ¾ | **9** | 8/1 | 69 | 55 |
| 2717[5] | **Chakalak (49)** (SDow) **8-9-4**(5)ow1 MrSFetherstonhaugh(2) (cl up tl outpcd appr st: sn bhd) | 23 | **10** | 12/1 | 26 | 11 |
| *279[7]* | **Phanan (48)** (REPeacock) **10-9-3**(5)ow8 MrsCPeacock(5) (plld hrd: led to 6f out: wknd qckly) | 19 | **11** | 33/1 | 7 | — |
| | | | | (SP 128.0%) | **11 Rn** | |

**3m 41.96** (12.96) CSF £36.69 CT £94.05 TOTE £7.00: £2.10 £2.00 £1.60 (£14.00) Trio £23.10 OWNER Just For The Crack Partnership (EPSOM) BRED Miss G. Abbey

LONG HANDICAP Old School House 8-9 Phanan 8-7

WEIGHT FOR AGE 3yo-15lb

**3066 Old School House** is in superb form at present and won this in really good style from 5lb out of the handicap, and also putting up another 2lb overweight. (13/2)

**1478* Arian Spirit (IRE)** ran a fine race after over two months off, and should be all the better for it. (9/2)

**2739* Candle Smoke (USA)** looked to be travelling well but, when an effort was required, he just wanted to hang left and did not help his rider at all. (11/4)

**1802 Anglesey Sea View** had her chances, but proved too slow to take them. (20/1)

**2804 Jalcanto** looked well enough, but he was never doing enough when asked a serious question in the home straight. (10/1)

**2989 Nosey Native** is certainly a bit of a thinker, but has ability and, on this occasion, did not seem to get the trip. (10/1)

**1847* Good Hand (USA)** (8/1: op 5/1)

**2717 Chakalak** (12/1: 8/1-14/1)

## 3150 DONCASTER STALLHOLDERS CONDITIONS STKS (2-Y.O) (Class C)

6-50 (6-51) **7f** £4,726.08 (£1,702.08: £815.04: £331.20: £129.60) Stalls: Low GOING minus 0.01 sec per fur (G)

| | | | | SP | RR | SF |
|---|---|---|---|---|---|---|
| 2702* | **Papua** (IABalding) **2-9-0** KFallon(2) (lw: mde all: qcknd over 2f out: r.o wl) | — | **1** | 3/1[3] | 95 | 32 |
| 2629* | **Brave Act** (SirMarkPrescott) **2-9-5** GDuffield(4) (lw: hld up: effrt over 2f out: r.o: nvr able to chal) | 1½ | **2** | 13/8[2] | 97 | 34 |
| 2700[3] | **Foot Battalion (IRE)** (RHollinshead) **2-8-8**(3) FLynch(1) (lw: hld up: effrt over 2f out: r.o: nt pce to chal) | ¾ | **3** | 14/1 | 87 | 24 |
| 2695* | **Flaming West (USA)** (HRACecil) **2-9-0** WRyan(5) (lw: hld up: hdwy over 2f out: sn rdn & fnd nil) | 6 | **4** | 11/8[1] | 76 | 13 |
| 2291[2] | **Samsung Spirit** (EWeymes) **2-8-6** JFortune(3) (lw: chsd wnr tl wknd fnl 2f) | 8 | **5** | 25/1 | 50 | — |
| | | | | (SP 115.7%) | **5 Rn** | |

**1m 29.09** (5.49) CSF £8.40 TOTE £3.90: £1.80 £1.60 (£5.30) OWNER Robert & Elizabeth Hitchins (KINGSCLERE) BRED Exors of the late D. Macrae

**2702* Papua**, allowed to dictate things, got first run approaching the final two furlongs and the race was always his. He looks a tough sort. (3/1)

**2629* Brave Act** travelled well but, when the pace was really on in the last two and a half furlongs, he had given the winner too much leeway. (13/8)

**2700 Foot Battalion (IRE)**, held up, presumably to get this trip, put in a decent effort, but lacked the pace to get in a real blow. He looks as well as ever. (14/1: 8/1-16/1)

**2695* Flaming West (USA)**, the paddock pick, sailed along on the bridle until an effort was required over two furlongs out, from which point he immediately threw in the towel for a most disappointing effort. (11/8)

**2291 Samsung Spirit** found things happening too quickly when the pace increased in the last three furlongs, and may need easier ground. (25/1)

## 3151 WARD'S THORNE BEST BITTER H'CAP (0-70) (3-Y.O+) (Class E)

7-20 (7-25) **7f** £3,366.00 (£1,008.00: £484.00: £222.00) Stalls: Low GOING minus 0.01 sec per fur (G)

| | | | | SP | RR | SF |
|---|---|---|---|---|---|---|
| 2357[7] | **Grey Kingdom (41)** (MBrittain) **5-8-2** JLowe(10) (mde all: clr over 1f out: drvn out) | — | **1** | 12/1 | 49 | 26 |
| 2870[3] | **Samsolom (57)** (PHowling) **8-9-4** KFallon(2) (lw: hld up: nt clr run 3f out tl over 1f out: r.o wl towards fin) | ¾ | **2** | 10/1 | 63 | 40 |
| 2962[6] | **Zain Dancer (55)** (DNicholls) **4-9-2b** AlexGreaves(5) (s.i.s: hdwy 3f out: chsng ldrs over 1f out: nt qckn) | 1 | **3** | 9/1 | 59 | 36 |
| 2722[3] | **Ochos Rios (IRE) (58)** (BSRothwell) **5-9-0**(5) SCopp(4) (in tch: rdn & n.m.r 3f out: styd on u.p fnl 2f) | nk | **4** | 5/1[2] | 61 | 38 |
| 2907[4] | **Dawalib (USA) (63)** (DHaydnJones) **6-9-10** AMackay(3) (lw: bhd: nt clr run 3f out: hdwy 1f out: nvr rchd ldrs) | 3 | **5** | 11/1 | 60 | 37 |
| 2437[6] | **Euphyllia (65)** (BobJones) **4-9-12v** FNorton(6) (chsd wnr tl wknd 2f out) | ¾ | **6** | 14/1 | 60 | 37 |
| 2630[6] | **Allinson's Mate (IRE) (56)** (TDBarron) **8-9-3** JFortune(1) (lw: chsd ldrs: effrt 3f out: no imp) | nk | **7** | 9/1 | 50 | 27 |
| 2602* | **Soaking (52)** (PBurgoyne) **6-8-13** GDuffield(12) (s.i.s: nvr rchd ldrs) | ½ | **8** | 6/1[3] | 45 | 22 |
| 2163[4] | **Percy Park (USA) (41)** (MWEasterby) **3-7-10** LCharnock(7) (in tch tl wknd fnl 2½f) | 4 | **9** | 14/1 | 25 | — |
| *2940[4]* | **Monis (IRE) (48)** (JBalding) **5-8-2b**[1](7)ow1 JEdmunds(8) (lw: prom tl wknd fnl 2½f) | nk | **10** | 12/1 | 31 | 7 |
| 2523[6] | **Tutu Sixtysix (35)** (DonEnricoIncisa) **5-7-10** KimTinkler(9) (s.i.s: n.d) | ¾ | **11** | 33/1 | 16 | — |
| 3102[3] | **Shontaine (60)** (MJohnston) **3-9-1** PRobinson(11) (lw: spd 4f: sn rdn & wknd) | 3½ | **12** | 7/2[1] | 33 | 4 |
| 2540[10] | **Lady Ploy (35)** (MissLCSiddall) **4-7-7**(3) DarrenMoffatt(15) (s.i.s: n.d) | 1 | **13** | 33/1 | 6 | — |
| 2602[7] | **Blushing Grenadier (IRE) (55)** (MJFetherston-Godley) **4-8-13v**(3) FLynch(13) (s.i.s: a bhd) | 3½ | **14** | 11/1 | 18 | — |
| 2860[7] | **Masruf (IRE) (67)** (TThomsonJones) **4-10-0** WRyan(14) (s.i.s: a bhd) | 20 | **15** | 16/1 | — | — |
| | | | | (SP 139.4%) | **15 Rn** | |

**1m 28.61** (5.01) CSF £131.28 CT £1,087.16 TOTE £19.10: £4.60 £3.00 £3.90 (£47.30) Trio £505.60; £576.89 to 3/8/96 OWNER Mr Mel Brittain (WARTHILL) BRED Northgate Lodge Stud Ltd

LONG HANDICAP Lady Ploy 7-7 Tutu Sixtysix 7-5 Percy Park (USA) 7-9

WEIGHT FOR AGE 3yo-6lb

**2023 Grey Kingdom** was allowed to dominate here which suited him well, and his rider left nothing to chance, keeping him going in good style. (12/1)

**2870 Samsolom** never saw daylight until far too late and, although flying at the end, the task was impossible. (10/1)

**2962 Zain Dancer** showed again he has the ability, but he does not seem to go through with it. (9/1)

**2722 Ochos Rios (IRE)** had another hard race and kept struggling on, but was never doing enough to get there. (5/1)
**2907 Dawalib (USA)** has not really struck form this season, but showed here that he might well be coming to hand. (11/1)
**2437 Euphyllia** ran reasonably and would appear to be improving with each run. (14/1)
**3102 Shontaine** ran poorly, but this was his fourth race in less than two weeks. (7/2)

## 3152 DONCASTER GOOSEHILL MARKET LIMITED STKS (0-70) (3-Y.O+) (Class E)

7-50 (7-52) **6f** £3,132.00 (£936.00: £448.00: £204.00) Stalls: Low GOING minus 0.01 sec per fur (G)

| | | | | SP | RR | SF |
|---|---|---|---|---|---|---|
| 2590$^{5}$ | **Halmanerror (68)** (MrsJRRamsden) **6-9-1** KFallon(6) (lw: trckd ldrs: hdwy to ld over 1f out: rdn & r.o) | — | **1** | 11/2$^{3}$ | 71 | 48 |
| 3122* | **Royal Dome (IRE) (70)** (MartynWane) **4-9-4** 3x JFortune(1) (hld up: hmpd after 1f: hdwy over 1f out: styd on wl fnl f) | 2½ | **2** | 4/1$^{2}$ | 67 | 44 |
| 2725$^{6}$ | **Cretan Gift (67)** (NPLittmoden) **5-9-7b** TGMcLaughlin(9) (bhd: hdwy 2f out: styd on u.p: nrst fin) | ½ | **3** | 10/1 | 69 | 46 |
| 2962$^{4}$ | **Baileys First (IRE) (70)** (MJohnston) **3-8-8** PRobinson(8) (lw: sn outpcd & bhd: styd on wl appr fnl f) | s.h | **4** | 6/1 | 60 | 33 |
| 2431$^{8}$ | **Brecongill Lad (68)** (MissSEHall) **4-9-1** NConnorton(3) (lw: led tl hdd & wknd over 1f out) | ½ | **5** | 11/1 | 62 | 39 |
| 2427$^{3}$ | **Desert Lynx (IRE) (70)** (TRWatson) **3-8-8**(3) FLynch(10) (bhd: hdwy over 1f out: nvr rchd ldrs) | 2½ | **6** | 7/1 | 55 | 28 |
| 2860$^{2}$ | **Almasi (IRE) (70)** (CFWall) **4-9-4** GDuffield(4) (lw: hdwy ½-wy: chal over 1f out: rdn & nt qckn) | nk | **7** | 9/4$^{1}$ | 57 | 34 |
| *2748*$^{7}$ | **Superbit (48)** (BAMcMahon) **4-9-1** WRyan(5) (cl up tl wknd over 1f out) | hd | **8** | 33/1 | 54 | 31 |
| 2590$^{7}$ | **Call Me I'm Blue (IRE) (69)** (NTinkler) **6-9-1** MBirch(7) (spd 4f: wknd) | 3 | **9** | 20/1 | 46 | 23 |
| 2908$^{4}$ | **Statistician (67)** (JohnBerry) **4-8-8**(7) AmyQuirk(2) (cl up tl wknd wl over 1f out) | 5 | **10** | 11/1 | 33 | 10 |
| | | | | (SP 126.4%) | | **10 Rn** |

**1m 14.55** (3.55) CSF £28.48 TOTE £5.90: £1.90 £2.40 £2.90 (£11.70) Trio £59.90 OWNER Mrs Joan Smith (Lincoln) (THIRSK) BRED Ulceby Vale Stud Ltd

WEIGHT FOR AGE 3yo-4lb

**2590 Halmanerror** gained his first win of the season here and was always travelling best, but he did need driving out to put it beyond doubt. (11/2)
**3122* Royal Dome (IRE)**, held up, presumably to get the extra furlong, found trouble, but was still never good enough to get to the winner. (4/1)
**2725 Cretan Gift** ran a fine race, despite looking to have a difficult task at the weights, and is still in top form. (10/1)
**2962 Baileys First (IRE)** seems to have everyone confused as to her trip, but this did seem too short and she was outpaced and behind until finishing well. (6/1)
**1501 Brecongill Lad** looked really well and has plenty of ability, but it is a question of when he is in the mood. (11/1)
**2427 Desert Lynx (IRE)** ran pretty well and should make her mark as the ground eases. (7/1)
**2860 Almasi (IRE)** did not get the best of breaks, but improved at halfway, only to cry enough entering the final furlong. (9/4)

## 3153 'COME TO DONCASTER MARKETS' CONDITIONS STKS (3-Y.O+) (Class C)

8-20 (8-21) **1m (round)** £5,395.20 (£1,996.80: £958.40: £392.00: £156.00: £61.60) Stalls: Low GOING minus 0.01 sec per fur (G)

| | | | | SP | RR | SF |
|---|---|---|---|---|---|---|
| 1108$^{4}$ | **Ruznama (USA) (105)** (BWHills) **3-8-2** RHills(4) (hld up: hdwy over 2f out: slt ld 1f out: r.o wl) | — | **1** | 5/1$^{3}$ | 103 | 63 |
| 810$^{9}$ | **Bishop of Cashel (112)** (JRFanshawe) **4-9-8** KFallon(5) (trckd ldrs: smooth hdwy to ld 2f out: hdd 1f out: hrd rdn & r.o) | hd | **2** | 10/1 | 116 | 83 |
| 2774$^{2}$ | **Phantom Quest (105)** (HRACecil) **3-8-11** PatEddery(2) (hld up & bhd: gd hdwy to chal 1f out: hrd rdn & nt qckn towards fin) | ¾ | **3** | 6/4$^{1}$ | 110 | 70 |
| 2053$^{6}$ | **Cadeaux Tryst (102)** (EALDunlop) **4-9-0** WRyan(10) (lw: b: hld up: hdwy 3f out: ch over 1f out: sn rdn & btn) | 4 | **4** | 4/1$^{2}$ | 98 | 65 |
| 2497$^{2}$ | **Band on the Run (93)** (BAMcMahon) **9-9-0** JFortune(7) (chsd ldrs: hrd rdn over 2f out: r.o one pce) | 3 | **5** | 14/1 | 92 | 59 |
| 2146$^{8}$ | **Capilano Princess (80)** (DHaydnJones) **3-8-2** AMackay(6) (chsd ldrs: rdn ½-wy: no imp) | ¾ | **6** | 66/1 | 86 | 46 |
| 1015$^{5}$ | **Bonarelli (IRE) (100)** (MRStoute) **3-8-7** PRobinson(9) (cl up: led 3f out to 2f out: wknd) | nk | **7** | 11/1 | 90 | 50 |
| 2610* | **Greenstead (USA)** (JHMGosden) **3-8-11** DaleGibson(1) (s.i.s: a bhd) | nk | **8** | 20/1 | 94 | 54 |
| 1623$^{3}$ | **Lap of Luxury (102)** (WJarvis) **7-8-9** BThomson(3) (hld up: hmpd over 4f out: nt clr run over 2f out: nt rcvr) | 7 | **9** | 7/1 | 71 | 38 |
| | **Committal (IRE) (111)** (JHMGosden) **3-8-7** JCarroll(8) (b.hind: led tl hdd 3f out: sn lost pl) | 12 | **10** | 10/1 | 52 | 12 |
| | | | | (SP 128.6%) | | **10 Rn** |

**1m 38.7** (2.20) CSF £53.46 TOTE £6.90: £1.90 £3.80 £1.40 (£59.20) Trio £25.90 OWNER Mr Hamdan Al Maktoum (LAMBOURN) BRED Shadwell Estate Co., Ltd. and Shadwell Farm Inc.

WEIGHT FOR AGE 3yo-7lb

**1108 Ruznama (USA)** looked well here after eleven weeks off and, dropping back in trip, needed all her courage to get home. Judging from this, she should certainly get a bit further. (5/1)
**Bishop of Cashel**, from a yard that is going well at present, ran a super race and kept battling back when all appeared lost. He has always seemed better suited to some give in the ground. (10/1)
**2774 Phantom Quest**, patiently ridden, produced a turn of foot to be envious of to challenge entering the final furlong but, when the chips were really down, he was found wanting. (6/4)
**2053 Cadeaux Tryst** looked on good terms with himself, but he had not been out for six weeks and ran out of steam approaching the final furlong. (4/1)
**2497 Band on the Run** had plenty to do here and, off the bit some way out, did well in the circumstances. (14/1)
**1785 Capilano Princess** was one of the first off the bit but, despite struggling on, was always well short of pace. (66/1)
**1623 Lap of Luxury** never had any luck at all in running and this is best ignored. (7/1)

## 3154 'DAZZLING DONCASTER MARKETS' H'CAP (0-85) (3-Y.O) (Class D)

8-50 (8-50) **6f** £4,235.00 (£1,265.00: £605.00: £275.00) Stalls: Low GOING minus 0.01 sec per fur (G)

| | | | | SP | RR | SF |
|---|---|---|---|---|---|---|
| 2778$^{5}$ | **Bee Health Boy (62)** (MWEasterby) **3-8-1**(5) GParkin(7) (lw: bhd: hdwy ½-wy: styd on u.p to ld wl ins fnl f) | — | **1** | 16/1 | 71 | 30 |
| 2777* | **No Monkey Nuts (76)** (JBerry) **3-9-6** JCarroll(1) (lw: led: rdn 2f out: hdd wl ins fnl f) | nk | **2** | 4/1$^{1}$ | 84 | 43 |
| 2676$^{4}$ | **Myttons Mistake (71)** (ABailey) **3-8-12**(3) DWright(6) (hld up: hdwy over 2f out: n.m.r over 1f out: kpt on) | 1½ | **3** | 15/2 | 75 | 34 |
| 2676* | **U-No-Harry (IRE) (74)** (RHollinshead) **3-9-1**(3) FLynch(4) (lw: trckd ldrs: effrt 2f out: nt qckn ins fnl f) | ¾ | **4** | 5/1$^{2}$ | 76 | 35 |
| 2729$^{8}$ | **Bollin Dorothy (60)** (TDEasterby) **3-8-4** MBirch(2) (lw: cl up: outpcd 2f out: kpt on u.p fnl f) | hd | **5** | 6/1 | 62 | 21 |
| 2778* | **Middle East (74)** (TDBarron) **3-9-4** JFortune(8) (lw: hld up: hdwy over 2f out: rdn & btn over 1f out) | 7 | **6** | 4/1$^{1}$ | 57 | 16 |
| 2773$^{4}$ | **Pharmacy (77)** (JWWatts) **3-9-7** GDuffield(3) (trckd ldrs: chal 2f out: wknd over 1f out) | 1¼ | **7** | 11/2$^{3}$ | 57 | 16 |
| 2778$^{3}$ | **Merrily (73)** (MissSEHall) **3-9-3** KFallon(5) (b: swtg: prom 4f: sn rdn & btn) | 6 | **8** | 4/1$^{1}$ | 37 | — |
| | | | | (SP 124.0%) | | **8 Rn** |

**1m 15.22** (4.22) CSF £78.55 CT £497.85 TOTE £30.40: £5.70 £1.30 £3.30 (£73.80) OWNER Bee Health Ltd (SHERIFF HUTTON) BRED Roger and Mrs Margaret Lightfoot

**2778 Bee Health Boy** proved to be a tough sort, coming from off the pace to snatch it late on. (16/1)
**2777* No Monkey Nuts** is in really good heart at present, but was just outbattled here. (4/1: op 6/1)
**2676 Myttons Mistake** has yet to win this season but he does travel well in the race, and this was a decent effort as he was always a bit short of room. (15/2)
**2676* U-No-Harry (IRE)** ran his usual sound race but had given best entering the final furlong. (5/1)
**2729 Bollin Dorothy** got caught flat-footed approaching the last two furlongs and, despite struggling on, was always fighting a lost cause. She has more ability and is well enough handicapped if she gets it together. (6/1)
**2778* Middle East** sweated up when winning last time, but he was cool as a cucumber here and failed to give his running. (4/1: 3/1-9/2)
**2778 Merrily** is proving disappointing. (4/1)

T/Plpt: £372.70 (43.81 Tckts). T/Qdpt: £73.70 (19.67 Tckts). AA

# 3142-GOODWOOD (R-H) (Good to firm)
## Thursday August 1st
WEATHER: fine WIND: mod against

## 3155 HEYSHOTT RATED STKS H'CAP (0-95) (3-Y.O) (Class C)
2-15 (2-17) **1m 6f** £9,715.80 (£3,592.20: £1,721.10: £700.50: £275.25: £105.15) Stalls: High GOING minus 0.12 sec per fur (G)

| | | | | SP | RR | SF |
|---|---|---|---|---|---|---|
| 2612* | **Benatom (USA) (90)** (HRACecil) **3-9-7** PatEddery(1) (swtg: chsd ldr over 12f out: rdn over 3f out: led over 1f out: r.o wl) | — | 1 | 9/2$^{1}$ | 101 | 74 |
| 2570$^{2}$ | **Mental Pressure (81)** (MrsMReveley) **3-8-12** KDarley(11) (led: rdn over 2f out: hdd over 1f out: unable qckn) | 1¾ | 2 | 7/1$^{3}$ | 90 | 63 |
| 2620$^{3}$ | **Arnhem (88)** (CEBrittain) **3-9-5** BDoyle(3) (swtg: a.p: rdn over 3f out: one pce) | 2½ | 3 | 12/1 | 94 | 67 |
| 2576$^{3}$ | **Jazz King (78)** (MissGayKelleway) **3-8-9** RCochrane(5) (rdn over 3f out: hdwy 2f out: r.o one pce) | nk | 4 | 8/1 | 84 | 57 |
| 2775* | **Mighty Phantom (USA) (73)** (JWHills) **3-8-1**(3) MHenry(6) (a.p: rdn over 3f out: one pce) | s.h | 5 | 20/1 | 79 | 52 |
| 2616$^{4}$ | **Gumair (USA) (73)** (RHannon) **3-8-1**(3) DaneO'Neill(4) (swtg: nvr nr to chal) | 3 | 6 | 12/1 | 75 | 48 |
| 2905$^{2}$ | **Infamous (USA) (82)** (PFICole) **3-8-13** TQuinn(8) (lw: hdwy 7f out: wknd 2f out) | 3 | 7 | 12/1 | 81 | 54 |
| 2233$^{4}$ | **Ela-Yie-Mou (IRE) (80)** (LMCumani) **3-8-11** RHughes(9) (swtg: sme hdwy over 2f out: sn wknd) | 1½ | 8 | 14/1 | 77 | 50 |
| 2547$^{4}$ | **Sharaf (IRE) (83)** (WRMuir) **3-9-0** BThomson(2) (lw: prom 11f) | 6 | 9 | 8/1 | 73 | 46 |
| 2876* | **Nereus (83)** (BWHills) **3-9-0** MHills(7) (lw: a bhd) | 1 | 10 | 13/2$^{2}$ | 72 | 45 |
| 2912$^{2}$ | **Orinoco River (USA) (88)** (PWChapple-Hyam) **3-9-5v** JReid(10) (lw: a bhd: t.o fnl 3f) | 19 | 11 | 11/1 | 56 | 29 |

(SP 109.1%) **11 Rn**

**3m 2.83** (3.83) CSF £30.81 CT £287.64 TOTE £4.60: £2.10 £1.60 £3.00 (£9.70) Trio £100.90 OWNER Mr T. F. Harris (NEWMARKET) BRED J. S. Meredith
LONG HANDICAP Mighty Phantom (USA) 8-2
IN-FOCUS: **Horses that ran well at the Newmarket July Meeting enjoyed a good amount of success at Goodwood this year.**
**2612* Benatom (USA)** overcame a 5lb rise in the handicap thanks, in part, to a typically strong ride from Eddery. (9/2)
**2570 Mental Pressure** is having trouble getting into the winner's enclosure, but ran another gallant race in defeat and deserves a change of luck. (7/1)
**2620 Arnhem** appreciated the drop in class and his handicap mark does not look far wrong. (12/1)
**2576 Jazz King** tried to come from a long way back. He began to pick up nicely early in the straight, but lacked acceleration when put under pressure. (8/1: op 5/1)
**2775* Mighty Phantom (USA)** ran well in this better class, but found her rivals a shade too quick. (20/1)
**2616 Gumair (USA)** has yet to finish in the first three in seven outings, but is no hopeless cause and should find a race one day. (12/1)

## 3156 RICHMOND STKS (Gp 2) (2-Y.O C & G) (Class A)
2-45 (2-46) **6f** £30,296.50 (£11,243.50: £5,421.75: £2,246.25: £923.13: £393.87) Stalls: Low GOING minus 0.12 sec per fur (G)

| | | | | SP | RR | SF |
|---|---|---|---|---|---|---|
| 2890* | **Easycall** (BJMeehan) **2-8-11** BDoyle(2) (w ldr: led over 2f out: hrd rdn 1f out: r.o wl) | — | 1 | 7/2$^{2}$ | 103 | 54 |
| 2834a* | **Raphane (USA)** (CCollins,Ireland) **2-9-0v$^{1}$** KDarley(4) (lw: hld up: rdn & edgd lft over 1f out: unable qckn) | 3 | 2 | 7/4$^{1}$ | 98 | 49 |
| 2070$^{4}$ | **Roman Imp (IRE)** (APJarvis) **2-8-11v$^{1}$** DHolland(3) (lw: a.p: rdn over 2f out: one pce) | ½ | 3 | 11/1 | 94 | 45 |
| 1795* | **Proud Native (IRE)** (APJarvis) **2-8-11** RHughes(6) (hld up: rdn & nt clr run over 1f out: one pce) | 1 | 4 | 5/1$^{3}$ | 91+ | 42 |
| 2782$^{4}$ | **Hornbeam** (JRJenkins) **2-8-11** RCochrane(7) (outpcd: hdwy over 1f out: nvr nrr) | s.h | 5 | 25/1 | 91? | 42 |
| 1959* | **Blue Ridge** (RHannon) **2-8-11** JReid(5) (rdn & hdwy over 1f out: one pce) | hd | 6 | 12/1 | 91 | 42 |
| 2607$^{4}$ | **Close Relative (IRE)** (RCharlton) **2-8-11** PatEddery(1) (lw: led over 3f: wkng whn n.m.r on ins over 1f out) | 5 | 7 | 13/2 | 77 | 28 |

(SP 108.5%) **7 Rn**

**1m 12.13** (2.13) CSF £9.24 TOTE £4.60: £2.20 £1.90 (£4.60) OWNER Easycall Partnership (UPPER LAMBOURN) BRED Mrs Susan Feddern
**2890* Easycall** stayed the extra furlong well and won decisively. It looked a sub-standard Richmond but it is hard to fault his own performance. (7/2)
**2834a* Raphane (USA)**, visored on this occasion and wearing a tongue-strap, has plenty of ability but is not the easiest of rides. It would be no surprise to see him revert to making the running over the minimum trip on his next outing, although the sixth furlong can not be blamed for his defeat here. (7/4)
**2070 Roman Imp (IRE)** ran his race out well in the first-time visor but this is probably as good as he is. (11/1: 8/1-12/1)
**1795* Proud Native (IRE)** is a useful juvenile but these rivals were just too good for him. (5/1)
**2782 Hornbeam**, soon tailed off, made up a lot of ground. He has faced a stiff task in both outings to date but has not been beaten far on either occasion. (25/1)
**1959* Blue Ridge**, unimpressive in appearance, was not quite up to this task. (12/1)

## 3157 GARRARD GOODWOOD CUP STKS (Gp 2) (3-Y.O+) (Class A)
3-20 (3-22) **2m** £38,028.00 (£14,052.00: £6,726.00: £2,730.00: £1,065.00: £399.00) Stalls: High GOING minus 0.12 sec per fur (G)

| | | | | SP | RR | SF |
|---|---|---|---|---|---|---|
| 1752a$^{5}$ | **Grey Shot (110)** (IABalding) **4-9-0** PatEddery(4) (lw: mde all: all out) | — | 1 | 3/1$^{2}$ | 119 | 83 |
| 2583$^{4}$ | **Lear White (USA) (113)** (PAKelleway) **5-9-0** JReid(7) (hdwy 3f out: chsd wnr fnl 2f: ev ch fnl f: r.o wl) | hd | 2 | 13/2 | 119 | 83 |
| 2620* | **Persian Punch (IRE) (99)** (DRCElsworth) **3-7-13** GBardwell(2) (swtg: rdn & hdwy 3f out: unable qckn fnl 2f) | 3½ | 3 | 11/4$^{1}$ | 115 | 64 |
| 2330$^{10}$ | **Daraydan (IRE) (100)** (LadyHerries) **4-9-0** KDarley(1) (a.p: chsd wnr 8f out to 2f out: wknd over 1f out) | 2½ | 4 | 25/1 | 113 | 77 |
| 2473a$^{6}$ | **Spartan Heartbeat (93)** (CEBrittain) **3-7-13** JFEgan(3) (swtg: no hdwy fnl 4f) | s.h | 5 | 20/1 | 113 | 62 |

| | | | | SP | RR | SF |
|---|---|---|---|---|---|---|
| 2864* | **Kalabo (USA) (113)** (SbinSuroor) **4-9-0** JCarroll(6) (hld up: rdn over 3f out: wknd 2f out) | 2½ | **6** | 4/1 [3] | 110 | 74 |
| 2117* | **Admiral's Well (IRE) (108)** (RAkehurst) **6-9-0** TQuinn(5) (lw: chsd wnr 8f: wknd 5f out: t.o) | dist | **7** | 5/1 | — | — |
| | | | | (SP 110.3%) | **7 Rn** | |

**3m 25.17** (1.17) CSF £19.94 TOTE £3.60: £1.80 £2.80 (£9.40) OWNER Mr J. C. Smith (KINGSCLERE) BRED Littleton Stud
WEIGHT FOR AGE 3yo-15lb
OFFICIAL EXPLANATION **Admiral's Well (IRE): the trainer reported that the horse had gurgled.**
**1752a Grey Shot** has taken a while to get over his battle with Double Trigger at Ascot, but he was back to his best here and refused to allow the runner-up to go past him in the last two furlongs. (3/1)
**2583 Lear White (USA)** is worth persevering with over extended trips following this excellent effort against a proven stayer. (13/2: 9/2-7/1)
**2620* Persian Punch (IRE)** stays well, but he was always doing it too slowly to rate a serious threat. (11/4)
**1752a Daraydan (IRE)** ran well for a mile and three-quarters, but he has been short of finishing speed in his races so far this season. (25/1)
**2473a Spartan Heartbeat** never stops staying on, albeit at one pace but, once again, he was a bit out of his depth. (20/1)
**2864* Kalabo (USA)** appeared not to stay this longer trip. (4/1: op 5/2)

## 3158 SCHWEPPES GOLDEN MILE H'CAP (3-Y.O+) (Class B)

3-50 (3-55) **1m** £48,250.00 (£14,500.00: £7,000.00: £3,250.00) Stalls: High GOING minus 0.12 sec per fur (G)

| | | | | SP | RR | SF |
|---|---|---|---|---|---|---|
| 2581[4] | **Moscow Mist (IRE) (75)** (LadyHerries) **5-7-10** DeclanO'Shea(16) (hdwy & squeezed thro over 1f out: hrd rdn: led wl ins fnl f: r.o wl) | — | **1** | 66/1 | 88 | 53 |
| 2888* | **Missile (95)** (WJHaggas) **3-8-9** [7x] MHills(11) (hdwy over 1f out: str run fnl f: fin wl) | s.h | **2** | 9/4 [1] | 108 | 66 |
| 2114[2] | **Prince Babar (89)** (JEBanks) **5-8-3**(7) GFaulkner(18) (a.p: led over 1f out tl wl ins fnl f: unable qckn) | ¾ | **3** | 12/1 | 100 | 65 |
| 3067[2] | **Green Green Desert (FR) (103)** (LadyHerries) **5-9-10** DHarrison(2) (gd hdwy over 1f out: fin wl) | ¾ | **4** | 16/1 | 113 | 78 |
| 2858[2] | **Sue's Return (76)** (APJarvis) **4-7-8**(3) MHenry(17) (a.p: rdn 2f out: r.o ins fnl f) | ¾ | **5** | 12/1 | 84 | 49 |
| 2623[3] | **Mullitover (86)** (MJHeaton-Ellis) **6-8-7** WWoods(9) (lw: a.p: rdn over 2f out: one pce) | 1 | **6** | 14/1 | 92 | 57 |
| 2623[4] | **Almuhimm (USA) (86)** (EALDunlop) **4-8-7** RHills(14) (nt clr run over 3f out & over 1f out: hdwy fnl f: nvr nrr) | 1¼ | **7** | 5/1 [2] | 90 | 55 |
| 2483* | **Bend Wavy (IRE) (84)** (LMCumani) **4-8-5** PatEddery(10) (b.off hind: lw: a.p: ev ch 1f out: wknd fnl f) | ½ | **8** | 8/1 | 87 | 52 |
| 2544[2] | **Golden Pond (IRE) (90)** (RFJohnsonHoughton) **3-8-4** AMcGlone(12) (led over 6f out tl over 1f out: wknd fnl f) | 1 | **9** | 25/1 | 91 | 49 |
| 2053[11] | **Desert Green (FR) (98)** (RHannon) **7-9-2**(3) DaneO'Neill(15) (lw: hdwy on ins over 1f out: one pce) | nk | **10** | 16/1 | 98 | 63 |
| 2581[10] | **Ninia (USA) (79)** (MJohnston) **4-8-0** TWilliams(4) (rdn over 4f out: a mid div) | ¾ | **11** | 50/1 | 78 | 43 |
| 2888[4] | **How Long (97)** (LMCumani) **3-8-11** KDarley(6) (lw: prom over 6f) | s.h | **12** | 20/1 | 96 | 54 |
| 2465a[4] | **Autumn Affair (92)** (CEBrittain) **4-8-13** BDoyle(8) (bhd fnl 2f) | 1½ | **13** | 40/1 | 88 | 53 |
| 2477a[4] | **Serious (97)** (LadyHerries) **6-9-4** PaulEddery(7) (lw: a bhd) | s.h | **14** | 40/1 | 93 | 58 |
| 2249* | **Tregaron (USA) (91)** (RAkehurst) **5-8-12** TQuinn(5) (swtg: prom over 6f) | ½ | **15** | 13/2 [3] | 86 | 51 |
| 2459a[6] | **Double Diamond (IRE) (91)** (MJohnston) **3-8-5** DHolland(1) (led over 1f: wknd over 4f out) | 2½ | **16** | 40/1 | 81 | 39 |
| | **Khayrapour (IRE) (90)** (BJMeehan) **6-8-11b** MTebbutt(13) (lw: a bhd) | 6 | **17** | 25/1 | 68 | 33 |
| 2351* | **New Century (USA) (94)** (DNicholls) **4-9-1** JCarroll(3) (lw: bhd fnl 4f) | 5 | **18** | 40/1 | 62 | 27 |
| | | | | (SP 131.4%) | **18 Rn** | |

**1m 38.95** (1.75) CSF £207.65 CT £1,957.21 TOTE £82.60: £10.50 £1.60 £2.00 £2.50 (£157.70) Trio £516.80 OWNER Merthyr Motor Auctions (LITTLEHAMPTON) BRED Sheikh Mohammed Bin Rashid Al Maktoum
LONG HANDICAP Moscow Mist (IRE) 7-5
WEIGHT FOR AGE 3yo-7lb
**2581 Moscow Mist (IRE)** got first run on the runner-up to foil a major gamble. (66/1)
**2888* Missile** needed only one more stride to justify the mountain of money invested on him. Marginally checked as he made his move below the distance, it probably made the difference between victory and defeat. (9/4)
**2114 Prince Babar**, previously placed in the Victoria Cup and the Wokingham, ran another big race over this longer trip. A versatile sort, he deserves to win a decent handicap at any distance from six furlongs to a mile. (12/1)
**3067 Green Green Desert (FR)** again got his timing wrong on this occasion, rattling home just too late from last place early in the straight. (16/1)
**2858 Sue's Return** is in good form at present and her trainer may attempt to strike while the iron is hot. (12/1)
**2623 Mullitover**, outstanding in the paddock, made a bold bid for victory and looks in good heart at present. (14/1)
**2623 Almuhimm (USA)** tends to meet trouble in running and this is an event notorious for bad luck stories, so it was inevitable that he should get caught in a traffic jam. (5/1)

## 3159 E.B.F. NEW HAM MAIDEN STKS (2-Y.O F) (Class D)

4-25 (4-28) **7f** £7,295.00 (£2,210.00: £1,080.00: £515.00) Stalls: High GOING minus 0.12 sec per fur (G)

| | | | | SP | RR | SF |
|---|---|---|---|---|---|---|
| 2611[3] | **Quintellina** (LMCumani) **2-8-11** KDarley(15) (a.p: nt clr run over 2f out: squeezed thro to ld over 1f out: r.o wl) | — | **1** | 5/4 [1] | 83+ | 27 |
| | **Saabga (USA)** (JHMGosden) **2-8-11** JCarroll(9) (str: scope: bit bkwd: s.s: nt clr run over 3f out, over 2f out & wl over 1f out: swtchd lft: gd hdwy fnl f: fin wl: bttr for r) | 2½ | **2** | 10/1 | 77+ | 21 |
| 2559[8] | **Happy Go Lucky** (RJO'Sullivan) **2-8-11** SSanders(1) (a.p: rdn over 2f out: unable qckn) | ¾ | **3** | 50/1 | 76 | 20 |
| 2315[3] | **Elrayahin** (MajorWRHern) **2-8-11** RHills(14) (lw: hld up: rdn over 2f out: r.o one pce) | s.h | **4** | 9/2 [2] | 76 | 20 |
| 2611[10] | **French Mist** (CEBrittain) **2-8-11** BDoyle(13) (s.s: hdwy on ins over 3f out: ev ch over 1f out: one pce) | s.h | **5** | 50/1 | 75 | 19 |
| 1664[6] | **Dundel (IRE)** (BWHills) **2-8-11** MHills(6) (stdd s: nt clr run on ins over 2f out: stdy hdwy on bit & nt clr run over 1f out: nvr plcd to chal) | 2 | **6** | 14/1 | 71+ | 15 |
| 2892[3] | **Soden (IRE)** (TGMills) **2-8-11** TWilliams(11) (a.p: led over 3f out tl over 1f out: wknd fnl f) | 2½ | **7** | 50/1 | 65 | 9 |
| | **Elegant Dance** (JJSheehan) **2-8-11** AMorris(12) (wl grwn: bit bkwd: a mid div) | ½ | **8** | 50/1 | 64 | 8 |
| 1871[13] | **Amarella (IRE)** (MJHaynes) **2-8-8**(3) DaneO'Neill(10) (nvr nrr) | 1½ | **9** | 50/1 | 61 | 5 |
| | **Laguna Bay (IRE)** (APJarvis) **2-8-11** WJO'Connor(5) (leggy: scope: bit bkwd: nvr nrr) | nk | **10** | 25/1 | 60 | 4 |
| | **Sound Appeal** (AGFoster) **2-8-11** DHolland(4) (leggy: unf: bit bkwd: a bhd) | ¾ | **11** | 50/1 | 58 | 2 |
| | **Ink Pot (USA)** (MRStoute) **2-8-11** JReid(8) (unf: scope: lw: bhd fnl 5f) | 1½ | **12** | 8/1 [3] | 55 | — |
| 2708[4] | **Lucky Dip** (MajorDNChappell) **2-8-11** BThomson(16) (led over 3f: wknd over 1f out) | 1¾ | **13** | 14/1 | 51 | — |
| 2702[2] | **Logica (IRE)** (PAKelleway) **2-8-11** PaulEddery(3) (prom over 4f) | ½ | **14** | 12/1 | 50 | — |
| | **Silver Sands** (TPMcGovern) **2-8-11** JFEgan(2) (w'like: bkwd: bhd fnl 3f) | 9 | **15** | 50/1 | 29 | — |
| | ***Pretty Sharp*** (APJarvis) **2-8-11** RHughes(7) (Withdrawn not under Starter's orders: ref to ent stalls) | | **W** | 33/1 | — | — |
| | | | | (SP 124.4%) | **15 Rn** | |

**1m 29.79** (4.99) CSF £13.34 TOTE £2.30: £1.40 £2.90 £6.00 (£9.10) Trio £387.50 OWNER Mr M. J. Dawson (NEWMARKET) BRED Whitsbury Manor Stud

**OFFICIAL EXPLANATION Dundel (IRE): the jockey reported that he was instructed to move to the inside rail form the start, but from then on could not get a clear run.**
**2611 Quintellina**, combining stamina with a useful turn of foot, responded with authority once the gap appeared. (5/4: 11/10-Evens)
**Saabga (USA)**, a market drifter, was only ninth entering the last furlong after meeting serious trouble in running, and looks a certain future winner. (10/1: 7/1-12/1)
**Happy Go Lucky** stepped up on her debut run and the two fillies in front of her are above-average. (50/1)
**2315 Elrayahin** stays this trip well, but stamina rather than acceleration appears to be her main asset. (9/2)
**French Mist** was better when able to lay up over this extra furlong, and a drop in grade would see her chances improve. (50/1)
**1664 Dundel (IRE)** caught the eye in no uncertain manner and attracted the attention of the Stewards too. It is possible that she does not find much off the bridle, but no one will know unless she is asked a more serious question than she was here. On this occasion, the Stewards accepted that the horse was short of room, but she is still one to keep an eye on in similar company. (14/1: 10/1-16/1)
**2892 Soden (IRE)** may be better over six furlongs than seven at present. (50/1)
**Ink Pot (USA)** (8/1: 5/1-10/1)
**2708 Lucky Dip** (14/1: 20/1-33/1)
**2702 Logica (IRE)** (12/1: op 7/1)

## 3160 EQUITY FINANCIAL COLLECTIONS NURSERY H'CAP (2-Y.O) (Class C)

5-00 (5-01) **5f** £7,830.00 (£2,340.00: £1,120.00: £510.00) Stalls: Low GOING minus 0.12 sec per fur (G)

| | | | | SP | RR | SF |
|---|---|---|---|---|---|---|
| $2879^{7}$ | **Fredrik The Fierce (IRE)** (JBerry) **2-9-7** KDarley(2) (hld up: rdn over 2f out: led ins fnl f: r.o wl) | — | 1 | 8/1 | 94 | 37 |
| 2897* | **Tear White (IRE)** (TGMills) **2-8-1b**(3)ow4 DaneO'Neill(4) (lw: a.p: ev ch over 1f out: unable qckn) | 1 | 2 | $6/1^{2}$ | 74 | 13 |
| 2726* | **Top of The Form (IRE)** (MJohnston) **2-9-0** TWilliams(10) (lw: a.p: led over 1f out tl ins fnl f: one pce) | 1 | 3 | $4/1^{1}$ | 81 | 24 |
| $2726^{5}$ | **Rudi's Pet (IRE)** (RHannon) **2-9-6** JReid(11) (stdy hdwy over 2f out: rdn over 1f out: one pce) | 1¼ | 4 | 14/1 | 83 | 26 |
| $2559^{3}$ | **Oneknight With You** (MJFetherston-Godley) **2-8-1**(3) MHenry(8) (hdwy over 2f out: hrd rdn over 1f out: one pce) | hd | 5 | 9/1 | 66 | 9 |
| $2728^{3}$ | **Plan For Profit (IRE)** (MJohnston) **2-8-4** DHolland(6) (lw: outpcd: hdwy 1f out: nvr nrr) | nk | 6 | 12/1 | 65 | 8 |
| $2965^{6}$ | **Petite Danseuse** (SDow) **2-8-11** BThomson(7) (rdn over 3f out: no hdwy fnl 2f) | 1½ | 7 | 20/1 | 68 | 11 |
| $2872^{4}$ | **Robec Girl (IRE)** (JBerry) **2-8-5** JCarroll(3) (bhd fnl 3f) | 5 | 8 | 11/1 | 46 | — |
| $2965^{10}$ | **Joint Venture (IRE)** (BJMeehan) **2-8-13b** PatEddery(5) (swtg: led over 3f) | nk | 9 | 9/1 | 53 | — |
| 2764* | **Silver Spell** (DrJDScargill) **2-7-10v** GBardwell(1) (a bhd) | 7 | 10 | 16/1 | 13 | — |
| 2956* | **Bramble Bear** (MBlanshard) **2-8-9** 6x AClark(9) (hld up: rdn over 2f out: sn wknd) | 1¼ | 11 | $7/1^{3}$ | 22 | — |
| | | | | (SP 111.2%) | **11 Rn** | |

**59.94 secs** (3.24) CSF £48.56 CT £198.13 TOTE £9.90: £2.60 £2.20 £1.80 (£37.10) Trio £36.10 OWNER Mr Chris Deuters (COCKERHAM) BRED Mrs J. M. Berry

**2219* Fredrik The Fierce (IRE)** was inclined to flash his tail in the finish but, in carrying topweight to victory, he can be excused that peculiarity. (8/1)
**2897* Tear White (IRE)**, with the stands' rail to help him, ran his best race yet. Blinkered juveniles must be treated with caution, but his earlier eccentricities seemed to be under control for the time being, and this was a good effort. (6/1)
**2726* Top of The Form (IRE)** could not dominate this field, but she has plenty of speed, and should continue to use it to good effect. (4/1)
**2726 Rudi's Pet (IRE)**, going well for the first three furlongs, has his share of weight at present. (14/1: 10/1-16/1)
**2559 Oneknight With You** made a satisfactory debut in nursery company. (9/1)
**2728 Plan For Profit (IRE)** found the trip too sharp particularly on this downhill track, and ought to stay further. (12/1: 8/1-14/1)
**2956* Bramble Bear** (7/1: op 9/2)

## 3161 DRAWING ROOM H'CAP (0-80) (3-Y.O+) (Class D)

5-35 (5-36) **1m 1f** £8,805.00 (£2,640.00: £1,270.00: £585.00) Stalls: High GOING minus 0.12 sec per fur (G)

| | | | | SP | RR | SF |
|---|---|---|---|---|---|---|
| $2574^{7}$ | **Koathary (USA) (55)** (LGCottrell) **5-8-4**ow2 KDarley(7) (b.nr fore: hdwy 3f out: led over 2f out: clr over 1f out: r.o wl) | — | 1 | 20/1 | 69 | 43 |
| $754^{8}$ | **Urgent Swift (64)** (APJarvis) **3-8-5**ow1 WJO'Connor(13) (lw: rdn over 3f out: hdwy over 2f out: chsd wnr over 1f out: r.o) | 1¼ | 2 | 25/1 | 76 | 43 |
| $2784^{4}$ | **Harvey White (IRE) (57)** (JPearce) **4-7-13**(7) RFfrench(6) (swtg: nt clr run over 3f out: swtchd lft: hdwy over 1f out: r.o one pce) | 2½ | 3 | 16/1 | 64 | 40 |
| $2763^{7}$ | **Fairy Knight (64)** (RHannon) **4-8-10**(3) DaneO'Neill(9) (rdn over 2f out: hdwy over 1f out: r.o ins fnl f) | ½ | 4 | 20/1 | 70 | 46 |
| $2710^{7}$ | **Mimosa (55)** (SDow) **3-7-10** GBardwell(4) (rdn over 2f out: hdwy over 1f out: nvr nrr) | 1¾ | 5 | 40/1 | 58 | 26 |
| $2724^{10}$ | **Lookingforarainbow (IRE) (74)** (BobJones) **8-9-9** MWigham(10) (lw: hld up: rdn over 2f out: wknd fnl f) | ½ | 6 | 25/1 | 76 | 52 |
| $2899^{2}$ | **King of Sparta (80)** (LMCumani) **3-9-7** PatEddery(8) (nt clr run 3f out: rdn & hdwy over 2f out: n.m.r over 1f out: one pce) | 2½ | 7 | $5/1^{1}$ | 78 | 46 |
| $2894^{2}$ | **Pasternak (77)** (SirMarkPrescott) **3-9-4** WWoods(15) (lw: a.p: ev ch over 2f out: wknd over 1f out) | 2 | 8 | $11/2^{2}$ | 71 | 39 |
| 2883* | **Thames Side (67)** (MMadgwick) **5-8-13**(3) NVarley(16) (rdn thrght: prom over 5f) | ¾ | 9 | 10/1 | 60 | 36 |
| $2744^{5}$ | **Far Dawn (USA) (78)** (GHarwood) **3-9-5** AClark(18) (nvr nr to chal) | 7 | 10 | 16/1 | 59 | 27 |
| 3052* | **Set the Fashion (59)** (DLWilliams) **7-8-8v** 6x DHolland(3) (swtchd lft over 2f out: nvr nrr) | 1½ | 11 | 12/1 | 37 | 13 |
| $3052^{11}$ | **Captain's Day (60)** (TGMills) **4-8-9** JCarroll(2) (rdn over 3f out: nt clr run over 2f out: nvr nrr) | 1 | 12 | 33/1 | 36 | 12 |
| $2525^{3}$ | **Pay Homage (73)** (IABalding) **8-9-3**(5) MartinDwyer(17) (prom 7f) | 5 | 13 | 7/1 | 40 | 16 |
| $2868^{3}$ | **Mr Rough (62)** (DMorris) **5-8-4**(7) AEddery(11) (prom over 5f) | 1¼ | 14 | 16/1 | 27 | 3 |
| $2901^{4}$ | **Superpride (57)** (MrsMReveley) **4-8-6** ACulhane(5) (led over 4f: wknd over 2f out) | 1½ | 15 | 9/1 | 19 | — |
| $2962^{5}$ | **Pride of Pendle (69)** (DNicholls) **7-8-13**(5) PRoberts(12) (b.nr hind: nt clr run on ins over 1f out: a bhd) | 1¾ | 16 | $13/2^{3}$ | 28 | 4 |
| $2917^{6}$ | **Aeroking (USA) (75)** (GHarwood) **5-9-10** TQuinn(14) (w ldr: led over 4f out tl over 2f out: sn wknd) | 6 | 17 | 16/1 | 24 | — |
| $2558^{2}$ | **Classic Defence (IRE) (74)** (JWHills) **3-8-12**(3) MHenry(1) (lw: prom over 3f) | 4 | 18 | 14/1 | 16 | — |
| | | | | (SP 137.5%) | **18 Rn** | |

**1m 55.39** (3.99) CSF £419.99 CT £7,457.89 TOTE £54.00: £7.50 £10.00 £4.20 £4.30 (£586.60) Trio £3,688.76; £2,213.26 to Goodwood 2/8/96 OWNER Mr E. J. S. Gadsden (CULLOMPTON) BRED Calumet Farm
LONG HANDICAP Mimosa 7-7
WEIGHT FOR AGE 3yo-8lb

**1486 Koathary (USA)**, from a stable with a good record on this track, received an excellent ride from Darley, who seized the initiative a long way from home. (20/1)
**575 Urgent Swift** was pegging the winner back at the finish and looks ready to get off the mark. (25/1)
**2784 Harvey White (IRE)** has won only once in twenty-one outings and was 4lb above his winning mark here, but he continues to run with credit. (16/1)

**598 Fairy Knight** showed improved form after being out of form so far this season. He is plummeting down the handicap and capable of winning over a slightly longer trip. (20/1)
**2253* Mimosa** and the word consistent are unlikely ever to appear in the same sentence. Despite Bardwell's efforts, she gave herself far too much to do. (40/1)
**2300 Lookingforarainbow (IRE)** is a grand old warrior who can never be ruled out, but this trip is a bit sharp for him. (25/1)
**2899 King of Sparta** continues to be a punter's nightmare. Such a good-looking horse should be achieving far more than he has done to date. (5/1)

T/Jkpt: Not won; £127,999.75 to Goodwood 2/8/96. T/Plpt: £63.40 (959.88 Tckts). T/Qdpt: £16.50 (180.18 Tckts). LMc

# 2708-SALISBURY (R-H) (Good to firm, Good patches)
## Thursday August 1st

Race 2: flip start
WEATHER: overcast WIND: almost nil

## 3162 NEWNHAM MAIDEN STKS (3-Y.O+) (Class D)
6-05 (6-08) **6f** £4,045.00 (£1,210.00: £580.00: £265.00) Stalls: High GOING minus 0.16 sec per fur (GF)

| | | | | SP | RR | SF |
|---|---|---|---|---|---|---|
| $2346^{8}$ | **Highland Rhapsody (IRE) (75)** (IABalding) **3-8-7** MHills(4) (w ldr stands' side: led 3f out: rdn out) | — | 1 | $5/2^{1}$ | 73 | 36 |
| $2946^{3}$ | **Redskin Lady (55)** (DRCElsworth) **3-8-7** JStack(2) (prom stands' side: ev ch over 1f out: unable qckn) | 2 | 2 | 14/1 | 68 | 31 |
| | **Yukon Hope (USA)** (RCharlton) **3-8-7** TSprake(6) (scope: prom stands' side: swtchd rt over 1f out: r.o ins fnl f) | ¾ | 3 | $5/1^{2}$ | 66 | 29 |
| | **Nakami** (PJMakin) **4-9-2** SSanders(5) (led stands' side 3f: sn hrd rdn: one pce fnl f) | 3 | 4 | 33/1 | 63 | 30 |
| $1429^{2}$ | **Longwick Lad** (WRMuir) **3-8-12** DHarrison(12) (prom: led far side 3f out: r.o one pce fnl 2f) | ½ | 5 | 13/2 | 61 | 24 |
| $2718^{9}$ | **Serape** (HCandy) **3-8-7** CRutter(14) (prom far side: r.o one pce fnl 2f) | hd | 6 | 16/1 | 56 | 19 |
| | **Country Thatch** (CAHorgan) **3-8-12** PaulEddery(1) (racd stands' side: no hdwy fnl 2f) | hd | 7 | 33/1 | 61 | 24 |
| $1856^{5}$ | **Ca'd'oro (53)** (GBBalding) **3-8-12** AProcter(16) (nvr nrr) | ¾ | 8 | 14/1 | 59 | 22 |
| | **Shining Cloud** (LGCottrell) **3-8-7** MFenton(15) (lw: hld up: hdwy centre 2f out: wknd over 1f out) | nk | 9 | 10/1 | 53 | 16 |
| | **One Dream** (BSmart) **3-8-12** MTebbutt(11) (lw: bhd fnl 2f) | 3 | 10 | 25/1 | 50 | 13 |
| $2597^{6}$ | **Designer Lines** (CJames) **3-8-12** AMcGlone(7) (rdn over 4f out: sn bhd) | 3 | 11 | 33/1 | 42 | 5 |
| | **Octavia Hill** (PWHarris) **3-8-7** GHind(13) (lengthy: a bhd) | 1½ | 12 | 16/1 | 33 | — |
| $663^{12}$ | **Cane Them** (TJNaughton) **3-8-5**$^{(7)}$ RachaelMoody(8) (lw: bhd whn swvd lft over 2f out) | 4 | 13 | 66/1 | 27 | — |
| $2510^{11}$ | **Time Goes On** (RJHodges) **4-8-8**$^{(3)}$ SDrowne(10) (bit bkwd: led far side 3f: sn wknd) | 1¾ | 14 | 50/1 | 18 | — |
| $840^{13}$ | **Jades Shadow** (JJBridger) **3-8-5**$^{(7)}$ GFaulkner(9) (bkwd: spd 2f: t.o) | dist | 15 | 66/1 | — | — |
| | **Desert Serenade (USA)** (EALDunlop) **3-8-7** RCochrane(3) (b: unf: scope: prom stands' side: 4th whn stumbled fell over 1f out) | | F | $6/1^{3}$ | — | — |

(SP 124.7%) **16 Rn**

**1m 16.13** (3.13) CSF £35.95 TOTE £3.00: £1.50 £1.90 £2.10 (£8.70) Trio £26.10 OWNER Mrs Christopher Hanbury (KINGSCLERE) BRED Mrs U.Schwarzenbach and Mrs C. Hanbury
WEIGHT FOR AGE 3yo-4lb
**2346 Highland Rhapsody (IRE)**, dropping back to six, appreciated the cut in the ground and put a disappointing run last time behind her. (5/2)
**2946 Redskin Lady** would have been getting 21lb from the winner had this been a handicap. (14/1)
**Yukon Hope (USA)**, out of an unraced half-sister to Reference Point, made a promising debut and is bred to need further. (5/1)
**Nakami** has obviously had his training problems, but showed he still possesses the ability he displayed as a juvenile. (33/1)
**1429 Longwick Lad** was the first home on the far side and ran better than the bare form suggests. (13/2)
**Serape**, another racing on the unfavoured far side, may need a return to seven. (16/1)
**Desert Serenade (USA)**, a sister to Sheikh Albadou, was giving a good account of herself when clipping the heels of the winner with a furlong and a half to go. (6/1: op 3/1)

## 3163 PEMBROKE H'CAP (0-70) (4-Y.O+) (Class E)
6-35 (6-40) **1m 6f** £3,002.00 (£896.00: £428.00: £194.00) Stalls: High GOING minus 0.16 sec per fur (GF)

| | | | | SP | RR | SF |
|---|---|---|---|---|---|---|
| *$3066^{4}$* | **Chris's Lad (57)** (BJMeehan) **5-9-1b**$^{1}$ BDoyle(3) (hld up & bhd: rdn & gd hdwy 2f out: led over 1f out: r.o wl) | — | 1 | 11/1 | 73 | 54 |
| $2530^{5}$ | **Sea Freedom (62)** (GBBalding) **5-9-6v** GHind(7) (chsd ldr 7f out: rdn over 4f out: outpcd over 1f out: styd on fnl f) | 2½ | 2 | 7/1 | 75 | 56 |
| $2717^{4}$ | **Our Kris (64)** (NJHenderson) **4-9-8b** MHills(1) (led: hdd over 1f out: one pce) | 4 | 3 | $9/2^{3}$ | 73 | 54 |
| $2707^{2}$ | **Mr Copyforce (46)** (MissBSanders) **6-8-4** SSanders(5) (prom: jnd ldr 7f out: wknd 2f out) | 3 | 4 | $4/1^{2}$ | 51 | 32 |
| $2973^{3}$ | **Silktail (IRE) (65)** (MissGayKelleway) **4-9-9** TSprake(2) (hld up & bhd: hdwy over 3f out: one pce fnl 2f) | 2 | 5 | $2/1^{1}$ | 68 | 49 |
| $2717^{3}$ | **Tonys Gift (70)** (MCPipe) **4-10-0** RHughes(4) (hld up: stdy hdwy 7f out: eased whn btn over 1f out) | 11 | 6 | $9/2^{3}$ | 60 | 41 |
| $2906^{6}$ | **Rupiana (IRE) (41)** (CMurray) **4-7-13**$^{ow1}$ JFEgan(6) (bhd fnl 3f) | 2 | 7 | 33/1 | 29 | 9 |
| | **Mull House (60)** (GPEnright) **9-8-11**$^{(7)}$ GFaulkner(8) (rdn 6f out: a bhd) | 1½ | 8 | 33/1 | 46 | 27 |

(SP 116.4%) **8 Rn**

**3m 4.53** (5.83) CSF £77.07 CT £362.92 TOTE £13.00: £3.20 £1.70 £1.50 (£33.10) OWNER Mrs Susan McCarthy (UPPER LAMBOURN) BRED Tyrian Breeding
**3066 Chris's Lad**, tried in blinkers, was suited by the ground, which had been watered and then rained upon, making it rather loose. He had been due to drop 5lb in future handicaps. (11/1: 8/1-12/1)
**2530 Sea Freedom** really needs further than this. (7/1)
**2717 Our Kris** has run well in blinkers over hurdles and had them fitted for the first time on the Flat. (9/2)
**2707 Mr Copyforce** did not get the fast ground he likes. (4/1)
**2973 Silktail (IRE)** was another not suited by the rain-affected going. (2/1)

## 3164 TRINITY CONDITIONS STKS (2-Y.O) (Class C)
7-05 (7-05) **6f** £4,724.00 (£1,644.00: £797.00: £335.00) Stalls: High GOING minus 0.16 sec per fur (GF)

| | | | | SP | RR | SF |
|---|---|---|---|---|---|---|
| $2504^{2}$ | **Compton Place** (JARToller) **2-9-0** SSanders(3) (plld hrd: w ldr: led over 3f out: rdn 1f out: r.o wl) | — | 1 | $5/4^{1}$ | 96 | 36 |
| $2702^{5}$ | **Dalmeny Dancer** (BJMeehan) **2-8-12** BDoyle(2) (lw: led over 2f: hrd rdn over 1f out: unable qckn) | 2 | 2 | 16/1 | 89 | 29 |
| $2944^{2}$ | **Colombia (IRE)** (MRStoute) **2-8-9v**$^{1}$ DHarrison(4) (hld up: hrd rdn over 2f out: one pce) | 2½ | 3 | $100/30^{3}$ | 79 | 19 |

| | | | | SP | RR | SF |
|---|---|---|---|---|---|---|
| | **Polish Warrior (IRE)** (PWChapple-Hyam) **2-8-7** JReid(1) (cmpt: hld up: rdn over 1f out: no rspnse) | 2½ | **4** | 13/8[2] | 70 | 10 |

(SP 111.5%) **4 Rn**

**1m 16.56** (3.56) CSF £12.36 TOTE £2.00 (£4.80) OWNER Duke of Devonshire (WHITSBURY) BRED R. J. Turner
**2504 Compton Place**, despite racing keenly, had no problem with the extra furlong and paid Dazzle a compliment through the form. (5/4)
**2702 Dalmeny Dancer** probably found the ground too fast last time. (16/1)
**2944 Colombia (IRE)**, tried in a visor, gave the impression she may not have been 100% committed under strong pressure. (100/30)
**Polish Warrior (IRE)**, reported to have been working well at home, may not have been suited by the rather false ground. (13/8)

## 3165 SPIRE FM H'CAP (0-70) (3-Y.O) (Class E)

7-35 (7-36) **1m** £3,366.00 (£1,008.00: £484.00: £222.00) Stalls: High GOING minus 0.16 sec per fur (GF)

| | | | | SP | RR | SF |
|---|---|---|---|---|---|---|
| 3102* | **Sylvan Princess (53)** (CNAllen) **3-8-1**(5) 5x MartinDwyer(1) (a.p: led wl over 1f out: comf) | — | **1** | 4/1[1] | 64 | 39 |
| 2617* | **White Settler (66)** (RJHodges) **3-9-2**(3) SDrowne(7) (lw: a.p: ev ch over 1f out: no imp) | 2½ | **2** | 11/2[2] | 72 | 47 |
| 2574[19] | **Ballpoint (68)** (RHannon) **3-9-7** RPerham(8) (lw: a.p: rdn over 1f out: one pce) | 1¾ | **3** | 8/1[3] | 71 | 46 |
| *3074[3]* | **Nakhal (54)** (DJGMurraySmith) **3-8-7b** PaulEddery(9) (bhd tl hdwy fnl 2f: r.o) | ½ | **4** | 12/1 | 56 | 31 |
| 3048[5] | **Flying Harold (46)** (MRChannon) **3-7-13** CRutter(10) (lw: led stands' side: overall ld 3f out: hdd wl over 1f out: sn wknd) | 3 | **5** | 20/1 | 42 | 17 |
| 2565[7] | **Shalateeno (60)** (BRMillman) **3-8-13** BDoyle(2) (lw: prom 6f) | 2½ | **6** | 25/1 | 51 | 26 |
| 2855[4] | **Tea Party (USA) (61)** (KOCunningham-Brown) **3-9-0** JReid(12) (lw: racd far side: led 3f: no ch fnl 2f) | 3½ | **7** | 4/1[1] | 45 | 20 |
| 2557[9] | **Lady Magnum (IRE) (55)** (JNeville) **3-8-5**(3) NVarley(5) (n.d) | 2½ | **8** | 33/1 | 34 | 9 |
| 2980[8] | **Dungeon Princess (IRE) (62)** (CMurray) **3-9-1** JFEgan(3) (rdn over 3f out: a bhd) | 6 | **9** | 16/1 | 29 | 4 |
| 2541[3] | **Flame of Hope (57)** (JLDunlop) **3-8-10** TSprake(14) (lw: racd far side: bhd fnl 3f) | 1¼ | **10** | 9/1 | 21 | — |
| 2743[11] | **Pendley Rose (55)** (PWHarris) **3-8-8** GHind(6) (bit bkwd: racd centre: led 5f out to 3f out: eased whn btn over 1f out) | 1¼ | **11** | 20/1 | 17 | — |
| 2506[19] | **Morning Sir (51)** (CRBarwell) **3-8-4** MFenton(13) (racd far side: a bhd) | 1¾ | **12** | 33/1 | 9 | — |
| 3000[5] | **Shouldbegrey (45)** (WRMuir) **3-7-9**(3) MHenry(11) (racd centre: swtchd stands' side & rdn over 3f out: sn bhd: t.o) | 29 | **13** | 14/1 | — | — |
| 2126[5] | **Stone Island (58)** (CACyzer) **3-8-11** SSanders(4) (bhd whn p.u over 3f out) | | **P** | 16/1 | — | — |

(SP 121.9%) **14 Rn**

**1m 44.32** (3.92) CSF £25.04 CT £159.50 TOTE £4.20: £1.90 £2.90 £4.30 (£9.00) Trio £30.90 OWNER Camelot Racing (NEWMARKET) BRED K S P Leisure
OFFICIAL EXPLANATION **Stone Island: the jockey reported that the gelding felt wrong behind.**
**3102* Sylvan Princess** continues in fine form and found the mile no problem, with the low draw turning out to be an advantage. (4/1: 9/4-9/2)
**2617* White Settler**, up 2lb, got the mile well enough but could not concede the weight to a filly in top form. (11/2)
**2000 Ballpoint** was back to a mile in his own age group. (8/1)
**3074 Nakhal** seemed to find this trip inadequate. (12/1)
**3048 Flying Harold**, already due to be dropped 2lb, is having problems finding the right distance. (20/1)
**2565 Shalateeno**, previously trained by Mick Channon, is another struggling to find the right trip. (25/1)
**2855 Tea Party (USA)**, trying her luck at a mile, raced on the wrong side. This run is best forgotten. (4/1: op 10/1)
**2541 Flame of Hope** (9/1: 6/1-10/1)

## 3166 DOWNING CLAIMING STKS (3-Y.O) (Class F)

8-05 (8-07) **6f** £2,868.00 (£798.00: £384.00) Stalls: High GOING minus 0.16 sec per fur (GF)

| | | | | SP | RR | SF |
|---|---|---|---|---|---|---|
| 2604[7] | **Ortolan (80)** (RHannon) **3-9-1**(3) DaneO'Neill(6) (hld up: hdwy 2f out: led ins fnl f: edgd lft: r.o wl) | — | **1** | Evens[1] | 70 | 43 |
| 2528[13] | **Golden Silver (43)** (JSMoore) **3-7-6**(5) CAdamson(3) (hdwy over 1f out: unable qckn ins fnl f) | 3 | **2** | 25/1 | 41 | 14 |
| 2578[14] | **Bella's Legacy (42)** (RJHodges) **3-8-3** BDoyle(5) (hdwy 2f out: ev ch over 1f out: unable qckn) | nk | **3** | 20/1 | 46 | 19 |
| 2180[12] | **Power Princess (35)** (JAPickering) **3-7-6**(5) MartinDwyer(4) (a.p: ev ch over 1f out: one pce) | 2½ | **4** | 33/1 | 34 | 7 |
| 2929[5] | **Ciserano (IRE) (61)** (MRChannon) **3-8-9** RPerham(11) (a.p: led 2f out tl ins fnl f: wknd) | 1 | **5** | 11/2[2] | 43 | 16 |
| 2036[15] | **Royal Intrusion** (RJHodges) **3-8-11**(3) SDrowne(1) (nvr nrr) | 1¼ | **6** | 33/1 | 45 | 18 |
| 2316[7] | **My Millie (49)** (RBoss) **3-8-3v[1]** DHarrison(2) (w ldr tl wknd over 1f out) | s.h | **7** | 16/1[3] | 33 | 6 |
| 2281[5] | **Craven Cottage (52)** (CJames) **3-8-4** CRutter(9) (a bhd) | 1¼ | **8** | 33/1 | 31 | 4 |
| 2971[14] | **Apartments Abroad (43)** (KMcAuliffe) **3-8-3v** JStack(12) (b.hind: s.s: a bhd) | 2½ | **9** | 20/1 | 23 | — |
| 1535[7] | **Red Time (62)** (MSSaunders) **3-9-0** JFEgan(13) (spd 4f) | 1½ | **10** | 20/1 | 30 | 3 |
| 1995[8] | **Farida Seconda (52)** (JLSpearing) **3-8-0**ow3 TSprake(8) (led 4f: sn wknd) | ¾ | **11** | 20/1 | 14 | — |
| 2528[5] | **Double Or Bust (35)** (AGNewcombe) **3-7-8**(3) NVarley(10) (swtg: prom 4f) | 5 | **12** | 33/1 | — | — |
| *3061[6]* | **Real Gem (57)** (PJMakin) **3-8-1** SSanders(14) (swtg: spd 4f) | 1¾ | **13** | 11/2[2] | — | — |

(SP 121.3%) **13 Rn**

**1m 16.33** (3.33) CSF £25.11 TOTE £2.00: £1.40 £4.80 £3.90 (£36.00) Trio £357.90; £171.40 to 3/8/96 OWNER Mr J. A. Lazzari (MARLBOROUGH) BRED Filletts Farm Stud
**1356* Ortolan**, reported to have been hampered at the start last time, had less to do here and was suited by the cut in the ground. (Evens)
**Golden Silver** was another to have previously run well on yielding ground and enjoyed getting her toe in. (25/1)
**Bella's Legacy** appreciated this return to easier company. (20/1)
**Power Princess** probably ran her best race to date. (33/1)
**2929 Ciserano (IRE)** did not get home in the loose ground. (11/2: 4/1-6/1)
**Royal Intrusion**, brought back to sprinting, was also lowered in class. (33/1)

## 3167 MAGDALENE H'CAP (0-80) (3-Y.O+ F & M) (Class D)

8-35 (8-36) **6f 212y** £4,077.50 (£1,220.00: £426.25: £426.25) Stalls: Centre GOING minus 0.16 sec per fur (GF)

| | | | | SP | RR | SF |
|---|---|---|---|---|---|---|
| 2858[4] | **Winsome Wooster (56)** (PGMurphy) **5-8-6**(3) SDrowne(11) (a.p: led over 1f out: r.o wl) | — | **1** | 16/1 | 68 | 36 |
| 2907[3] | **Zelda Zonk (75)** (BJMeehan) **4-10-0** BDoyle(14) (a.p: ev ch over 1f out: one pce) | 3 | **2** | 12/1 | 80 | 48 |
| 2974[2] | **Nunsharpa (71)** (JRFanshawe) **3-9-4** JReid(8) (a.p: rdn over 1f out: one pce) | ½ | **3** | 5/2[1] | 75 | 37 |
| 2605[5] | **Audrey Grace (46)** (MissGayKelleway) **5-7-13** TSprake(10) (hdwy 2f out: r.o ins fnl f) | d.h | **3** | 8/1 | 50 | 18 |
| | **Supreme Thought (61)** (LGCottrell) **4-9-0** MFenton(5) (led over 5f: one pce) | 1¼ | **5** | 20/1 | 62 | 30 |
| 2945[6] | **Bandit Girl (63)** (IABalding) **3-8-5**(5) MartinDwyer(9) (hld up & bhd: swtchd rt & hdwy 3f out: rdn & one pce fnl 2f) | ¾ | **6** | 12/1 | 62 | 24 |
| 2686[6] | **Secret Pleasure (IRE) (62)** (RHannon) **3-8-6**(3) DaneO'Neill(4) (b.nr hind: no hdwy fnl 2f) | ¾ | **7** | 14/1 | 60 | 22 |
| 2729[2] | **Marjaana (IRE) (69)** (PTWalwyn) **3-9-2** PaulEddery(1) (hld up & bhd: nvr nr to chal) | 2 | **8** | 7/1[3] | 62 | 24 |

| | | | | SP | RR | SF |
|---|---|---|---|---|---|---|
| 2605$^{9}$ | **Flirty Gertie (65)** (RBoss) **4-9-4** RPerham(13) (prom 5f) | 1¼ | **9** | 25/1 | 55 | 23 |
| 2983$^{9}$ | **Corniche Quest (IRE) (54)** (MRChannon) **3-8-1** CRutter(6) (hld up: a bhd) | nk | **10** | 12/1 | 44 | 6 |
| 1333$^{2}$ | **Pomona (74)** (PJMakin) **3-9-7** SSanders(2) (a bhd) | 5 | **11** | 7/1$^{3}$ | 52 | 14 |
| 2675$^{2}$ | **Misrule (USA) (69)** (JHMGosden) **3-9-2** GHind(7) (prom 5f) | 1½ | **12** | 6/1$^{2}$ | 44 | 6 |
| 1964$^{8}$ | **Cassimere (56)** (MajorDNChappell) **4-8-9** WJO'Connor(3) (hld up: hdwy 4f out: wknd over 2f out) | ¾ | **13** | 33/1 | 29 | — |
| 2785$^{7}$ | **Jubilee Place (IRE) (60)** (TThomsonJones) **3-8-7** DHarrison(12) (b: bhd fnl 2f) | 3 | **14** | 25/1 | 26 | — |
| | | | | (SP 130.0%) | **14 Rn** | |

**1m 29.85** (3.85) CSF £187.07 CT WW, ZZ, N £308.63 WW, ZZ, AG £501.52 TOTE £15.50: £3.00 £2.40 N £1.10 AG £1.00 (£68.50) Trio N £44.00, AG £50.40 OWNER Miss Amanda Rawding (BRISTOL) BRED Mrs J. A. Rawding and G. C. Greenwood

WEIGHT FOR AGE 3yo-6lb

**2858 Winsome Wooster** did not mind the easier ground and took advantage of a 3lb lower mark. (16/1)
**2907 Zelda Zonk**, 7lb higher than when winning last month, would have preferred genuine good to firm ground. (12/1)
**2974 Nunsharpa** was due to go up 4lb following a good second last week. (5/2: op 5/1)
**2605 Audrey Grace**, reverting to seven, remains a maiden after fifteen attempts. (8/1)
**Supreme Thought** may be better suited by a return to sprinting. (20/1)
**2945 Bandit Girl**, given an awful lot to do last time, did not seem suited to the loose ground here. (12/1)

T/Plpt: £89.20 (121.7 Tckts). T/Qdpt: £9.30 (78.66 Tckts). KH

# 2947-YARMOUTH (L-H) (Good)
## Thursday August 1st

WEATHER: overcast WIND: mod across

## 3168 THURNE H'CAP (0-75) (3-Y.O+) (Class D)

2-00 (2-02) **6f 3y** £3,595.50 (£1,071.00: £510.00: £229.50) Stalls: Low GOING minus 0.24 sec per fur (GF)

| | | | | SP | RR | SF |
|---|---|---|---|---|---|---|
| 2957$^{3}$ | **Rambold (60)** (NEBerry) **5-9-3** RPerham(10) (mde all stands' side: led overall ins fnl f: rdn out) | — | **1** | 7/1 | 71 | 44 |
| 2571$^{8}$ | **Indian Relative (75)** (RGuest) **3-9-9**(5) DGriffiths(8) (lw: chsd ldrs stands' side: ev ch fnl f: unable qckn nr fin) | 1½ | **2** | 12/1 | 82 | 51 |
| 2946* | **Never Think Twice (54)** (KTIvory) **3-8-7b** 7x NAdams(4) (b: lw: hdwy far side over 2f out: ev ch over 1f out: no ex ins fnl f) | 1¼ | **3** | 5/1$^{3}$ | 58 | 27 |
| 3106* | **Cheeky Chappy (71)** (DWChapman) **5-10-0b** 7x JQuinn(5) (lw: led far side: rdn over 1f out: hdd & wknd ins fnl f) | hd | **4** | 3/1$^{1}$ | 74 | 47 |
| *2306*$^{2}$ | **Oberon's Dart (IRE) (72)** (PJMakin) **3-9-6**(5) RHavlin(7) (w wnr stands' side 4f) | 1¼ | **5** | 8/1 | 72 | 41 |
| 3096$^{2}$ | **Red Admiral (63)** (CMurray) **6-9-6** DeanMcKeown(6) (w ldr far side: rdn over 2f out: sn wknd) | 3 | **6** | 4/1$^{2}$ | 55 | 28 |
| 2524$^{3}$ | **Regal Fanfare (IRE) (59)** (MrsLStubbs) **4-8-9b**(7) JoHunnam(2) (nvr trbld ldrs) | nk | **7** | 12/1 | 50 | 23 |
| *2367*$^{8}$ | **Spanish Stripper (USA) (60)** (MCChapman) **5-8-10**(7) CScally(1) (lw: in tch far side 4f) | hd | **8** | 20/1 | 51 | 24 |
| 2757$^{16}$ | **First Option (39)** (RBastiman) **6-7-7**(3) DWright(3) (t: dwlt: rdn & no imp fnl 2f) | 1½ | **9** | 25/1 | 26 | — |
| 3112$^{10}$ | **Persian Butterfly (64)** (ICampbell) **4-9-7v$^{1}$** GCarter(9) (swtg: sn pushed along stands' side: nvr trbld ldrs) | ½ | **10** | 16/1 | 50 | 23 |
| | | | | (SP 115.2%) | **10 Rn** | |

**1m 13.5** (2.60) CSF £75.98 CT £429.32 TOTE £8.50: £2.20 £4.80 £1.90 (£60.90) Trio £184.70 OWNER Mr Ron Collins (UPPER LAMBOURN) BRED Sydney Mason

LONG HANDICAP First Option 7-7

WEIGHT FOR AGE 3yo-4lb

**2957 Rambold**, brought to the stands' side, made all in her group, but only got on top inside the final furlong. (7/1: 4/1-8/1)
**2571 Indian Relative** tried hard to peg back the winner, but could not quite do so. Her wins came on faster ground but she handled this well. (12/1)
**2946* Never Think Twice** moved poorly to post but came through late to win the far-side group, and did not have the benefit of the faster ground this time. (5/1)
**3106* Cheeky Chappy**, off the same mark as when winning last time, tried to make all, but tied up in the closing stages. (3/1)
**2306 Oberon's Dart (IRE)**, back on turf, was unable to dominate, but is worth bearing in mind, particularly over seven furlongs. (8/1)
**3096 Red Admiral** paid the penalty for taking on Cheeky Chappy. (4/1)
**2523 First Option**, who is tubed, also had his tongue tied down. (25/1)
**2034 Persian Butterfly**, visored for the first time, got warm and did not run well. (16/1)

## 3169 BASTWICK (S) STKS (2-Y.O) (Class G)

2-30 (2-31) **6f 3y** £2,364.00 (£654.00: £312.00) Stalls: Low GOING minus 0.24 sec per fur (GF)

| | | | | SP | RR | SF |
|---|---|---|---|---|---|---|
| *3065*$^{3}$ | **Abstone Queen** (PDEvans) **2-8-6b$^{1}$** GCarter(3) (trckd ldrs: led over 1f out: rdn out) | — | **1** | 13/2 | 55 | 11 |
| 2951$^{3}$ | **Breffni (IRE)** (CNAllen) **2-8-6** TGMcLaughlin(8) (trckd ldrs: nt clr run over 1f out: swtchd & r.o wl ins fnl f) | 2½ | **2** | 6/4$^{1}$ | 48+ | 4 |
| 2865$^{11}$ | **Le Shuttle** (MHTompkins) **2-8-6** PRobinson(7) (lw: prom: led 2f out: sn hdd & no ex) | hd | **3** | 6/1$^{3}$ | 48 | 4 |
| 2759$^{5}$ | **Grovefair Flyer (IRE)** (BJMeehan) **2-8-9b**(7) DSweeney(2) (led 4f: one pce) | 2½ | **4** | 11/2$^{2}$ | 51 | 7 |
| 2685$^{3}$ | **Marsh Marigold** (MartynMeade) **2-8-6** RPerham(5) (w ldrs: rdn over 2f out: wkng whn n.m.r wl ins fnl f) | 1½ | **5** | 13/2 | 37 | — |
| 3110$^{6}$ | **Victory At Hart** (ICampbell) **2-8-11v$^{1}$** NDay(4) (lw: hdwy 3f out: wknd over 1f out) | 5 | **6** | 20/1 | 29 | — |
| 2795$^{7}$ | **Emmas Breeze** (CADwyer) **2-8-11** JQuinn(1) (swtg: chsd ldrs over 3f) | 2½ | **7** | 10/1 | 23 | — |
| 2948$^{6}$ | **Tirol's Treasure (IRE)** (KTIvory) **2-8-6** NAdams(6) (a bhd) | 2 | **8** | 20/1 | 12 | — |
| | | | | (SP 115.0%) | **8 Rn** | |

**1m 15.2** (4.30) CSF £16.18 TOTE £7.50: £2.20 £1.20 £1.60 (£8.70) OWNER Mr J. E. Abbey (WELSHPOOL) BRED Ridgebarn Farm

Bt in 3,600 gns

IN-FOCUS: **The entire field tacked over to the stands' rail in the first furlong and a half.**

**3065 Abstone Queen**, on her toes in first-time blinkers, found the little extra she had been needing to get off the mark. (13/2)
**Breffni (IRE)**, taking a big drop in class, travelled well but did not see daylight until near the line. She certainly has the ability to win in this company. (6/4: 2/1-11/2)
**2157 Le Shuttle**, in selling company for the first time, raced keenly but had no more to give in the final furlong. (6/1: 4/1-13/2)
**2759 Grovefair Flyer (IRE)**, dropping back to six, did his best to make all but failed to find extra when challenged. (11/2: 7/2-6/1)
**2685 Marsh Marigold** did not help her cause by pulling hard on the way to post and early in the race. She would have finished a length or so closer but for being hampered. (13/2)

**2435 Victory At Hart**, clearly wound up by the first-time visor, went to post too freely but did show a first sign of ability. (20/1)

## 3170 COTMAN CONDITIONS STKS (2-Y.O) (Class C)
3-05 (3-06) **5f 43y** £4,749.12 (£1,638.72: £783.36: £316.80) Stalls: Low GOING minus 0.24 sec per fur (GF)

| | | | | SP | RR | SF |
|---|---|---|---|---|---|---|
| 2879³ | **Head Over Heels (IRE)** (JHMGosden) **2-8-9** WRyan(2) (trckd ldr: led wl over 1f out: pushed out) | — | 1 | 4/6 1 | 84 | 38 |
| 2854* | **Song of Skye** (TJNaughton) **2-8-9** GCarter(4) (chsd ldrs: pushed along 3f out: hung lft ins fnl f: kpt on) | 2 | 2 | 15/8 2 | 78 | 32 |
| 2772* | **Sous Le Nez** (RGuest) **2-8-4**(5) DGriffiths(3) (hld up: rdn over 1f out: no imp whn carried lft ins fnl f) | 2½ | 3 | 13/2 3 | 70 | 24 |
| 2792³ | **Anokato** (KTIvory) **2-8-4b¹**(7) CScally(1) (led over 3f: btn whn bdly hmpd ins fnl f) | 4 | 4 | 20/1 | 60? | 14 |
| | | | | (SP 112.9%) | | **4 Rn** |

**62.6 secs** (2.10) CSF £2.38 TOTE £1.40 (£1.30) OWNER Ms Rachel Hood (NEWMARKET) BRED Milton Park Stud Partnership
**IN-FOCUS: the field raced by the far rail.**
**2879 Head Over Heels (IRE)** franked the form of the Newbury Super Sprint, taking what looked a tricky race on paper with considerable authority. (4/6)
**2854* Song of Skye**, after looking to be going worst of the four to halfway, moved into a challenging position approaching the final furlong, but hung left, in behind the winner, causing problems for the horses behind. (15/8)
**2772* Sous Le Nez**, on her toes beforehand, could never really go the pace. (13/2)
**2792 Anokato**, blinkered for the first time, was taken down quietly but was soon blazing a trail in the race. He appeared to be forced onto the rail inside the final furlong, but for which he would have finished closer. The Stewards ruled that no interference had occurred. (20/1)

## 3171 TATTERSALLS MAIDEN AUCTION STKS (2-Y.O F) (Class E)
3-35 (3-38) **7f 3y** £3,070.20 (£915.60: £436.80: £197.40) Stalls: Low GOING minus 0.24 sec per fur (GF)

| | | | | SP | RR | SF |
|---|---|---|---|---|---|---|
| 2887² | **Undercover Agent (IRE)** (JLDunlop) **2-8-3** GCarter(2) (hld up: rdn & hdwy over 2f out: edgd lft: led 1f out: rdn out) | — | 1 | 8/15 1 | 76 | 23 |
| 2596² | **River of Fortune (IRE)** (MHTompkins) **2-8-2**ow1 PRobinson(4) (trckd ldrs: led over 1f out: sn hdd: unable qckn) | 1 | 2 | 7/1 3 | 73 | 19 |
| 2252² | **Lady Godiva** (MJPolglase) **2-8-1** NCarlisle(7) (led over 5f: one pce) | 1½ | 3 | 9/2 2 | 68 | 15 |
| 1513¹⁰ | **Janglynyve** (SPCWoods) **2-8-2** DBiggs(1) (w ldr over 4f: sn btn) | 2 | 4 | 33/1 | 65 | 12 |
| | **Fontcaudette (IRE)** (JEBanks) **2-8-0** JQuinn(5) (leggy: unf: chsd ldrs: no hdwy fnl 2f) | hd | 5 | 20/1 | 63 | 10 |
| 2904³ | **Ivory Dawn** (KTIvory) **2-7-13** NAdams(3) (lw: chsd ldrs: rdn over 2f out: wknd over 1f out) | ½ | 6 | 11/1 | 60 | 7 |
| 2611¹⁷ | **Ms Ziman** (MBell) **2-7-11**(7) RMullen(6) (lw: a bhd) | 6 | 7 | 25/1 | 52 | — |
| | | | | (SP 115.8%) | | **7 Rn** |

**1m 28.0** (3.80) CSF £5.14 TOTE £1.30: £1.10 £2.00 (£3.20) OWNER Mr John Rosenheim (ARUNDEL) BRED Castletown Partners
**IN-FOCUS: The field tacked over to the stands' rail in the first furlong and a half.**
**2887 Undercover Agent (IRE)** won cosily enough in the end, but not without giving her supporters a bit of a fright. She was off the bridle by halfway and tended to hang and swish her tail once let down. (8/15)
**2596 River of Fortune (IRE)** is gradually getting her act together and did nothing wrong, only being outpaced close home by the better horse. (7/1)
**2252 Lady Godiva** raced keenly at the head of affairs, keeping nothing in reserve for the closing stages. (9/2)
**1021 Janglynyve** looks a good mover but so far has avoided fast ground. Judging by the way she faded in the final furlong and a half, this trip could be too far. (33/1)
**Fontcaudette (IRE)** never got to grips with the leaders. (20/1)
**2904 Ivory Dawn** ran below her best and may need a left-hand rail to bring out the best in her. (11/1)

## 3172 WROXHAM H'CAP (0-70) (3-Y.O+) (Class E)
4-10 (4-13) **7f 3y** £3,179.40 (£949.20: £453.60: £205.80) GOING minus 0.24 sec per fur (GF)

| | | | | SP | RR | SF |
|---|---|---|---|---|---|---|
| 2962* | **Nashaat (USA) (73)** (MCChapman) **8-10-0**(3) 6x PMcCabe(1) (hld up: hdwy over 1f out: led wl ins fnl f: drvn out) | — | 1 | 6/1 | 81 | 63 |
| 2947² | **Awesome Venture (49)** (MCChapman) **6-8-7** DRMcCabe(5) (led 5f: led ins fnl f: sn hdd & unable qckn) | nk | 2 | 9/2 2 | 56 | 38 |
| 2947⁴ | **Wild Palm (70)** (WAO'Gorman) **4-10-0v** EmmaO'Gorman(3) (lw: trckd ldrs: led 2f out: rdn & hdd ins fnl f: r.o) | s.h | 3 | 9/2 2 | 77 | 59 |
| 3084* | **Great Bear (47)** (DWChapman) **4-8-5** 6x JQuinn(6) (hdwy over 1f out: r.o) | 2 | 4 | 5/1 3 | 50 | 32 |
| *2937** | **Young Annabel (USA) (64)** (CADwyer) **3-9-2** 6x TIves(8) (w ldrs: ev ch 2f out: wknd fnl f) | nk | 5 | 11/4 1 | 66 | 42 |
| 991⁹ | **Thunder River (IRE) (60)** (MJHeaton-Ellis) **6-8-13v**(5) AmandaSanders(2) (racd alone far side: rdn over 3f out: sn bhd) | 6 | 6 | 10/1 | 48 | 30 |
| 2763³ | **Ivory's Grab Hire (60)** (KTIvory) **3-8-5b**(7) CScally(4) (swtg: dwlt: pushed along 3f out: a bhd) | s.h | 7 | 10/1 | 48 | 24 |
| 2868¹² | **Rasmi (CAN) (38)** (PHowling) **5-7-7**(3) DWright(7) (lw: w ldrs over 3f) | 3 | 8 | 50/1 | 19 | 1 |
| | | | | (SP 114.1%) | | **8 Rn** |

**1m 26.8** (2.60) CSF £30.66 CT £121.42 TOTE £7.80: £1.60 £1.80 £1.50 (£12.20) OWNER Mr Tony Satchell (MARKET RASEN) BRED Echo Valley Horse Farm and Swettenham Stud
LONG HANDICAP Rasmi (CAN) 6-12
WEIGHT FOR AGE 3yo-6lb
**2962* Nashaat (USA)** travelled well until let down and defied a welter-burden to clinch his hat-trick. This mark was 5lb higher than he had ever scored off before. (6/1)
**2947 Awesome Venture** looked better weighted than his winning stable-companion, but has always suffered from seconditis, and can never quite last home. (9/2)
**2947 Wild Palm**, with recent rain in his favour, took over towards the centre of the track rather earlier than usual, going down fighting in the last 100 yards. The Handicapper may have his measure at present. (9/2)
**3084* Great Bear**, a poor mover, seemed to find seven on the sharp side. (5/1)
**2937* Young Annabel (USA)** landed a gamble on the All-Weather last time out but, after moving poorly to post, could not repeat the feat on turf. (11/4: 2/1-3/1)
**Thunder River (IRE)** was soon finding racing alone an unwise policy, and this is best ignored. (10/1: 7/1-12/1)

## 3173 DAMGATE H'CAP (0-70) (3-Y.O+ F & M) (Class E)
4-45 (4-47) **1m 2f 21y** £3,261.30 (£974.40: £466.20: £212.10) Stalls: Low GOING minus 0.35 sec per fur (F)

| | | | | SP | RR | SF |
|---|---|---|---|---|---|---|
| 2896* | **Mazilla (52)** (AStreeter) **4-8-5**(5) RHavlin(9) (lw: plld hrd: trckd ldrs: led on bit 4f out: rdn over 1f out: hld on gamely) | — | 1 | 11/4 1 | 65 | 46 |

| | | | Pos | SP | RR | SF |
|---|---|---|---|---|---|---|
| 2393[3] | **Divine (64)** (ACStewart) **3-8-13** SWhitworth(8) (lw: led 3f: chsd wnr over 2f out: r.o wl ins fnl f) | ½ | **2** | 11/2[3] | 76 | 48 |
| 2486[2] | **Parsa (USA) (63)** (JLDunlop) **3-8-12** GCarter(2) (trckd ldrs: rdn over 1f out: no ex ins fnl f) | 1¼ | **3** | 4/1[2] | 73 | 45 |
| 2980[2] | **Passage Creeping (IRE) (70)** (LMCumani) **3-8-12**(7) JoHunnam(5) (hld up: hdwy over 2f out: no ex fnl f) | ½ | **4** | 4/1[2] | 79 | 51 |
| 2896[11] | **Pat's Splendour (43)** (HJCollingridge) **5-8-1** JQuinn(3) (in tch: rdn & kpt on fnl 2f: nt pce to chal) | 2 | **5** | 33/1 | 49 | 30 |
| 2776[2] | **Dancing Destiny (45)** (RBastiman) **4-8-0**(3) DWright(6) (lw: chsd ldrs: rdn 3f out: sn btn) | 1½ | **6** | 6/1 | 49 | 30 |
| 2945[4] | **Ma Petite Anglaise (70)** (WJarvis) **4-9-7**(7) TThomas(7) (s.i.s: bhd tl hdwy 4f out: nt clr run 2f out: rdn & r.o fnl f) | s.h | **7** | 12/1 | 74 | 55 |
| 2297* | **Titchwell Lass (62)** (JEBanks) **3-8-4**(7) RMullen(4) (in tch: rdn over 4f out: sn btn) | 1½ | **8** | 9/1 | 63 | 35 |
| *2751[5]* | **Fikra (USA) (59)** (SPCWoods) **3-8-8** DBiggs(1) (lw: led after 3f to 4f out: wknd over 2f out) | nk | **9** | 20/1 | 60 | 32 |

(SP 121.7%) **9 Rn**

**2m 6.8** (2.40) CSF £18.27 CT £56.68 TOTE £3.90: £1.60 £1.70 £2.00 (£11.80) Trio £26.30 OWNER Mr M. Rhodes (HEDNESFORD) BRED Mrs H. MacFarlane

WEIGHT FOR AGE 3yo-9lb

**2896* Mazilla** is in the form of her life and took this gamely after pulling too hard for her own good. Her run may not be finished yet. (11/4: 2/1-3/1)

**2393 Divine**, stepping up considerably in trip, was coming back for more at the end and should soon find a winning opportunity. (11/2)

**2486 Parsa (USA)**, moving well on the easier ground, proved short of a vital turn of foot where it mattered. (4/1)

**2980 Passage Creeping (IRE)**, stepping up in trip, made a dangerous-looking move in the straight, but this petered out from the distance. (4/1: 5/2-9/2)

**Pat's Splendour** would appear better suited by another half-mile. (33/1)

**2776 Dancing Destiny** could not land a blow off a 2lb higher mark than at Redcar. (6/1: 9/2-8/1)

**2297* Titchwell Lass** (9/1: 6/1-10/1)

T/Plpt: £32.50 (306.96 Tckts). T/Qdpt: £3.80 (179.1 Tckts). Dk

## 3174a-3195a (Irish Racing) - See Computer Raceform

## 2833a-CURRAGH (Newbridge, Ireland) (R-H) (Good to firm)
## Saturday July 27th

### 3196a MELD STKS (Gp 3) (3-Y.O+)
4-35 (4-36) **1m 2f** £16,250.00 (£4,750.00: £2,250.00: £750.00)

| | | | Pos | SP | RR | SF |
|---|---|---|---|---|---|---|
| 2471a[4] | **Idris (IRE)** (JSBolger,Ireland) **6-9-9** KJManning (hld up: 4th st: hdwy on ins over 1f out: led jst ins fnl f: kpt on wl) | — | **1** | 13/2 | 118 | 81 |
| | **Predappio** (JOxx,Ireland) **3-8-8**ow1 JPMurtagh (hld up in tch: wnt 3rd over 7f out: rdn, lost pl & 5th st: hdwy over 1f out: chsd wnr jst ins fnl f: r.o) | ¾ | **2** | 8/1 | 112 | 64 |
| 1509[3] | **Song of Tara (IRE)** (PWChapple-Hyam) **4-9-3** PShanahan (chsd ldr after 1f: rdn appr st: disp ld over 2f out: u.p over 1f out: no ex fnl f) | 2 | **3** | 7/4[1] | 108 | 71 |
| 2677* | **Prince of Andros (USA)** (DRLoder) **6-9-3b**[1] DRMcCabe (hld up: chsd ldrs: effrt to ld over 2f out: sn u.p: hdd & btn ent fnl f) | 2 | **4** | 3/1[2] | 104 | 67 |
| 2474a[8] | **Tasdid** (KPrendergast,Ireland) **3-8-7b** WJSupple (bhd: rdn ent st: kpt on: n.d) | 6 | **5** | 12/1 | 95 | 48 |
| 2473a[3] | **His Excellence (USA)** (APO'Brien,Ireland) **3-8-8b**ow1 CRoche (led: rdn appr st: hdd over 2f out: wknd qckly: eased over 1f out) | hd | **6** | 11/2[3] | 96 | 48 |

(SP 108.9%) **6 Rn**

**2m 2.6** (-1.40) OWNER Michael Keogh (COOLCULLEN)

**2471a Idris (IRE)** landed his third Group Three and his tenth success in all. Effective over seven to ten furlongs, he seemed to have plenty on his plate here but, with his jockey persevering on the inside, he got the opening a furlong out and led 150 yards from home. Now rated 116, he could well find a Group Two contest within his capabilities. (13/2: op 4/1)

**Predappio** was stepping up in class here and, carrying 1lb overweight, ran his best race in defeat. Ridden along in fifth place turning in, he had to be switched to the outer a furlong out and finished well, if always being held by the winner. (8/1: op 5/1)

**1509 Song of Tara (IRE)**, soon in second place, was disputing it from two furlongs out, but the ground was too firm for him. Once under pressure, he was finding no extra. (7/4)

**2677* Prince of Andros (USA)** proved difficult to restrain. He got his head in front over a furlong a half out, but was finding little under pressure and was beaten a furlong out. (3/1)

**1247a Tasdid** never got into contention. (12/1: op 8/1)

**2473a His Excellence (USA)** bowled along in front. He came under pressure early in the straight and, weakening, was soon eased right down. This was not his true running. (11/2: op 7/2)

NR

## 3197a-3198a (Irish Racing) - See Computer Raceform

## 3035a-MAISONS-LAFFITTE (France) (Good)
## Thursday July 25th

### 3199a PRIX JACQUES DE BREMONT (Listed) (4-Y.O+)
2-10 (2-15) **1m** £18,445.00 (£6,324.00: £3,953.00: £2,055.00)

| | | | Pos | SP | RR | SF |
|---|---|---|---|---|---|---|
| 2839a[2] | **Bin Rosie** (DRLoder) **4-8-11** RHughes | — | **1** | | 114 | — |
| | **La Fra Angelico (FR)** (JMartens,Belgium) **5-8-8** TJarnet | 2½ | **2** | | 106 | — |
| 2072[11] | **Bouche Bee (USA)** (JEHammond,France) **4-8-8** ESaint-Martin | ¾ | **3** | | 105 | — |

**6 Rn**

**1m 45.6** (9.60) P-M 2.00F: 1.60F 2.90F (36.20F) OWNER W. Said (NEWMARKET) BRED Addison Racing Ltd Inc

**2839a Bin Rosie** showed his rivals a clean pair of heels to give David Loder his first win in France. He may now go to the Curragh for next month's Desmond Stakes.

# VICHY (France) (R-H) (Good)
## Friday July 26th

### 3200a PRIX LOUIS DESBOUDET (Listed) (4-Y.O+)
2-25 (2-25) **1m 6f** £18,445.00 (£6,324.00: £3,953.00: £2,055.00)

| | | | | SP | RR | SF |
|---|---|---|---|---|---|---|
| | **Ming Dynasty (IRE)** (DSmaga,France) **5-8-11b[1]** FHead | — | 1 | | 123 | — |
| 906a[7] | **Tot Ou Tard (IRE)** (JForesi,France) **6-8-11** TJarnet | 2½ | 2 | | 120 | — |
| | **Droit Divin (FR)** (JGauvain,France) **5-8-11** EAntoinat | hd | 3 | | 120 | — |
| 1988[2] | **Taufan's Melody** (LadyHerries) **5-8-13** ABadel | 1 | 4 | | 121 | — |
| | | | | | | **10 Rn** |

**2m 58.8** P-M 2.80F: 1.40F 1.50F 4.60F (7.40F) OWNER Mme O-A Scemama (LAMORLAYE) BRED Dene Investments NV
**1988 Taufan's Melody** was in midfield turning into the straight and, when asked the question, made some headway over a furlong out. However, he could only keep on at the one pace inside the final furlong.

# 3199a-MAISONS-LAFFITTE (France) (Good)
## Saturday July 27th

### 3201a PRIX ROBERT PAPIN (Gp 2) (2-Y.O C & F)
2-30 (2-30) **5f 110y** £46,113.00 (£18,445.00: £9,223.00: £4,611.00)

| | | | | SP | RR | SF |
|---|---|---|---|---|---|---|
| 2582[2] | **Ocean Ridge (USA)** (PWChapple-Hyam) **2-8-13** TJarnet (mde all: shkn up over 1f out: qcknd clr) | — | 1 | | 90+ | — |
| 2664a[2] | **Nombre Premier** (AdeRoyerDupre,France) **2-9-2** TGillet (hld up: hdwy over 1f out: wnt 2nd cl home) | 2½ | 2 | | 86 | — |
| | **Sheer Reason (USA)** (MmeCHead,France) **2-8-13** FHead (hld up in rr: rdn & r.o one pce fr over 1f out) | hd | 3 | | 82 | — |
| | **Shigeru Summit** (FBoutin,France) **2-8-13** MBoutin (a.p: rdn over 1f out: kpt on) | nk | 4 | | 82 | — |
| 2147[5] | **Hanan (USA)** (PAKelleway) **2-8-13** CAsmussen (mid div: u.p over 2f out: outpcd) | 6 | 5 | | 64 | — |
| | **Winter Brook (FR)** (JBertranDeBalanda,France) **2-8-13** ASanglard (mid div: rdn & no imp over 2f out) | s.h | 6 | | 64 | — |
| | | | | | | **6 Rn** |

**65.9 secs** (2.40) P-M 1.90F: 1.20F 3.30F (4.40F) OWNER Mr R. E. Sangster (MARLBOROUGH) BRED Swettenham Stud
**2582 Ocean Ridge (USA)**, who finished second to Dazzle in the Cherry Hinton Stakes at Newmarket, met slightly easier opposition here and went off odds-on. Setting the pace, she quickened when asked over a furlong out, and did so impressively. It is possible that she could go to York for the Lowther Stakes.
**2664a Nombre Premier** got up close home to win the fight for second prize, but was never going to get to the winner.
**2147 Hanan (USA)** was well supported, but never looked like taking a hand.

### 3202a PRIX BERTEUX (Gp 3) (3-Y.O)
4-00 (4-07) **1m 7f** £28,986.00 (£10,540.00: £5,270.00: £2,635.00)

| | | | | SP | RR | SF |
|---|---|---|---|---|---|---|
| | **Eurynome (GER)** (PBary,France) **3-8-5** TJarnet | — | 1 | | 98 | — |
| | **Kharizmi (FR)** (AdeRoyerDupre,France) **3-8-8** GMosse | nk | 2 | | 101 | — |
| | **Amor's Princess (USA)** (JEHammond,France) **3-8-5** ESaint-Martin | 1½ | 3 | | 96 | — |
| 2277a[U] | **Met Mech Nich (FR)** (J-PPelat,France) **3-8-8** TThulliez | hd | 4 | | 99 | — |
| 2665a[2] | **Irish Woman (FR)** (MmeMBollack-Badel,France) **3-8-8** ABadel | nk | 5 | | 99 | — |
| | | | | | | **5 Rn** |

**3m 18.9** (4.40) P-M 4.70F: 1.50F 1.20F (13.60F) OWNER Exors of the late E Wanke (CHANTILLY) BRED E. Wanke
**Eurynome (GER)** was racing at the back of the field until making progress and hanging right over a furlong out. However, he ran on under pressure and got up to land the spoils on the line.
**Kharizmi (FR)** always held a prominent position. Ridden two furlongs out, he was challenged inside the final furlong and battled on bravely, only to lose it where it mattered.
DS

# 1060a-DUSSELDORF (Germany) (R-H) (Good)
## Sunday July 28th

### 3203a DEUTSCHLANDPREIS-50 JAHRE NORDRHEIN-WESTFALEN (Gp 1) (3-Y.O+)
3-40 (3-47) **1m 4f** £81,081.00 (£31,531.00: £15,766.00: £6,757.00)

| | | | | SP | RR | SF |
|---|---|---|---|---|---|---|
| 2479a[4] | **Hollywood Dream (GER)** (UOstmann,Germany) **5-9-2** JReid (hld up: hdwy over 4f out: 3rd st: qcknd to ld ins fnl f: drvn out) | — | 1 | | 121 | — |
| 2583* | **Posidonas** (PFICole) **4-9-6** TQuinn (a.p: 2nd st: led wl over 1f out tl ins fnl f: rallied cl home) | s.h | 2 | | 125 | — |
| 2479a* | **Protektor (GER)** (ALowe,Germany) **7-9-6** THellier (hld up in rr: 4th st: n.m.r ins fnl f: r.o) | 1¾ | 3 | | 123 | — |
| 2668a[2] | **Surako (GER)** (HJentzsch,Germany) **3-8-6** PSchiergen (a.p: led 5f out tl wl over 1f out: one pce) | 2½ | 4 | | 117 | — |
| 2533[2] | **Phantom Gold** (LordHuntingdon) **4-9-2** DHarrison (a in tch: 5th st: no hdwy) | 2 | 5 | | 113 | — |
| 2478a[6] | **Night Petticoat (GER)** (BSchutz,Germany) **3-8-4**ow1 AStarke (in tch 8f: 6th st: btn 2f out) | 4 | 6 | | 107 | — |
| 1138a[9] | **Caballo (GER)** (HJentzsch,Germany) **5-9-6** SEccles (led 6f: sn wl bhd) | 24 | 7 | | 79 | — |
| | | | | | | **7 Rn** |

**2m 26.35** TOTE 191DM: 32DM 15DM 17DM OWNER Gestut Ittlingen BRED Gestut Hof Ittlingen
**1135a* Hollywood Dream (GER)** was held up until making good headway to take the lead inside the final furlong. This was the combination's second success at the highest level.
**2583* Posidonas** lost nothing in defeat and put up a gallant performance. Always prominent, he took up the running over a furlong out and, when headed inside the final furlong, battled gamely back to go down only by a short-head. He is sure to pick up another Pattern race soon.
**2533 Phantom Gold** just found these too good. Always prominent, she was unable to go with the pace when it quickened soon after entering the straight, but was by no means disgraced.

# 3067-ASCOT (R-H) (Good to firm)
## Friday August 2nd

All races hand-timed
WEATHER: overcast WIND: almost nil

## 3204 BUCKINGHAM PALACE APPRENTICE H'CAP (0-70) (3-Y.O+) (Class E)
6-00 (6-01) **1m 4f** £4,060.50 (£1,239.00: £612.00: £298.50) Stalls: High GOING minus 0.31 sec per fur (GF)

| Form | Horse | Dist | Pos | SP | RR | SF |
|---|---|---|---|---|---|---|
| 3136[4] | **Voices in the Sky (42)** (AGNewcombe) **5-8-10** GParkin(3) (hld up: hdwy 3f out: nt clr run 2f out: led ins fnl f: r.o wl) | — | **1** | 5/1[2] | 49 | 15 |
| 3037[18] | **Soojama (IRE) (50)** (RMFlower) **6-9-4b** CAdamson(6) (s.i.s: hdwy over 3f out: ev ch ins fnl f: unable qckn) | 1¾ | **2** | 7/1[3] | 55 | 21 |
| 2530[12] | **Prince de Berry (38)** (BJMeehan) **5-8-6** DSweeney(5) (hld up: hdwy & swtchd lft 2f out: nt clr run over 1f out: r.o ins fnl f) | ½ | **3** | 25/1 | 42 | 8 |
| 1306[7] | **Tirolette (IRE) (57)** (RJRWilliams) **4-9-11b** AimeeCook(8) (lw: a.p: ev ch whn edgd lft over 1f out: one pce) | ½ | **4** | 8/1 | 60 | 26 |
| 2627[9] | **Umberston (IRE) (51)** (LMCumani) **3-8-3**(5) RFfrench(9) (led after 3f to 6f out: led over 3f out tl ins fnl f) | ½ | **5** | 7/2[1] | 54 | 9 |
| 3037[20] | **Rising Spray (46)** (CAHorgan) **5-9-0** AmandaSanders(11) (stdd s: hdwy over 1f out: nt rch ldrs) | ¾ | **6** | 7/1[3] | 48 | 14 |
| 2547[10] | **Durshan (USA) (45)** (JRJenkins) **7-8-8**(5) PDoe(7) (w ldrs tl wknd over 3f out) | 3 | **7** | 12/1 | 43 | 9 |
| 2941[9] | **Bronze Runner (30)** (EAWheeler) **12-7-12b** IonaWands(10) (plld hrd: sn prom: ev ch over 2f out: wknd wl over 1f out) | 7 | **8** | 20/1 | 18 | — |
| 3048* | **Action Jackson (58)** (BJMcMath) **4-9-9**(3) 4x CWebb(2) (hld up: ev ch over 2f out: sn wknd) | 1 | **9** | 5/1[2] | 45 | 11 |
| 2941[10] | **Leap in the Dark (IRE) (41)** (MissLCSiddall) **7-8-4**(5)ow12 TSiddall(4) (lw: led 3f: wknd 4f out) | 4 | **10** | 25/1 | 23 | — |
| 2794[8] | **Sharp Progress (60)** (APJones) **3-9-3** SophieMitchell(1) (prom: led 6f out tl over 3f out: sn wknd: t.o) | 13 | **11** | 16/1 | 24 | — |

(SP 117.7%) **11 Rn**

**2m 38.4** (8.40) CSF £36.96 CT £718.77 TOTE £3.90: £1.40 £3.10 £7.00 (£26.90) Trio £85.80 OWNER Mr J. A. F. Cairns (BARNSTAPLE) BRED Kiplingcotes Stud
WEIGHT FOR AGE 3yo-11lb

**3136 Voices in the Sky**, making a quick reappearance, settled much better this time and did not seem inconvenienced by the longer trip. (5/1)
**1803* Soojama (IRE)**, 8lb higher than when winning at Newmarket, was due to go down 3lb and would have preferred a stronger gallop than he got here over a trip as short as this. (7/1)
**2155 Prince de Berry**, dropped 13lb in his last three outings, has been trying all sorts of trips and did not get the run of the race. (25/1)
**Tirolette (IRE)** ran well on ground lively enough for her. (8/1)
**2067 Umberston (IRE)**, without the blinkers this time, may have been better off setting a stronger pace. (7/2)
**1965 Rising Spray**, dropped 6lb, was due to go down another 1lb and, with no pace on, found this an insufficient test of stamina. (7/1)

## 3205 INVOSHIRE GROUP H'CAP (0-80) (3-Y.O+) (Class D)
6-30 (6-31) **1m 2f** £5,680.00 (£1,720.00: £840.00: £400.00) Stalls: High GOING minus 0.31 sec per fur (GF)

| Form | Horse | Dist | Pos | SP | RR | SF |
|---|---|---|---|---|---|---|
| 2593[2] | **Sharpical (70)** (SirMarkPrescott) **4-9-4** GDuffield(11) (plld hrd: a.p: led wl over 1f out: drvn out) | — | **1** | 7/1 | 80 | 62 |
| 2953* | **Pistol (IRE) (71)** (CAHorgan) **6-9-5** 5x PaulEddery(8) (b.hind: hld up in rr: plld out 2f out: hdwy & edgd rt over 1f out: r.o ins fnl f) | ¾ | **2** | 11/2[2] | 80 | 62 |
| 2784[3] | **Ashby Hill (IRE) (54)** (RRowe) **5-8-2** AClark(6) (hld up mid div: hdwy 2f out: ev ch fnl f: unable qckn) | s.h | **3** | 8/1 | 63 | 45 |
| 2980[3] | **Law Dancer (IRE) (70)** (TGMills) **3-8-9** DHolland(12) (hld up & bhd: hdwy whn n.m.r over 1f out: nvr nr to chal) | 2 | **4** | 20/1 | 76 | 49 |
| 2525* | **Alaflak (IRE) (80)** (MajorWRHern) **5-10-0** PatEddery(1) (hld up mid div: hdwy whn n.m.r over 1f out: one pce) | 2 | **5** | 6/1[3] | 82 | 64 |
| 2883[4] | **Roufontaine (71)** (WRMuir) **5-9-0**(5) RHavlin(7) (hld up: stdy hdwy 5f out: led over 2f out tl wl over 1f out: wknd fnl f) | 3½ | **6** | 8/1 | 68 | 50 |
| 2701[2] | **Taufan Boy (75)** (PWHarris) **3-9-0b**[1] GHind(9) (prom tl rdn & wknd over 2f out) | nk | **7** | 6/1[3] | 71 | 44 |
| 1687[5] | **Claire's Dancer (IRE) (72)** (AndrewTurnell) **3-8-11** TIves(2) (a.p: ev ch 2f out: wknd over 1f out) | ½ | **8** | 33/1 | 67 | 40 |
| 3043[2] | **Fahs (USA) (68)** (RAkehurst) **4-9-2** SSanders(3) (hld up: sme hdwy over 2f out: wknd over 1f out) | 1 | **9** | 5/1[1] | 62 | 44 |
| 2898* | **Roi de la Mer (IRE) (60)** (JAkehurst) **5-8-8** KFallon(4) (hld up: hdwy whn hmpd over 1f out: sn wknd) | 4 | **10** | 10/1 | 47 | 29 |
| 2801[14] | **La Fille de Cirque (50)** (RJRWilliams) **4-7-7**(5)ow2 MBaird(10) (led over 7f: wknd qckly: t.o) | 22 | **11** | 33/1 | 2 | — |
| 1508[7] | **Charter (75)** (MajorDNChappell) **5-9-9** WJO'Connor(5) (w ldr: reminders 5f out: wknd qckly over 2f out: t.o) | 3½ | **12** | 10/1 | 22 | 4 |

(SP 124.2%) **12 Rn**

**2m 8.73** (1.93) CSF £44.26 CT £293.72 TOTE £9.90: £2.70 £2.20 £2.70 (£35.40) Trio £90.00 OWNER Mr A. S. Reid (NEWMARKET) BRED E. R. W. Stanley and New England Stud Farm Ltd
LONG HANDICAP La Fille de Cirque 7-6
WEIGHT FOR AGE 3yo-9lb

**2593 Sharpical**, in his first handicap since changing stables, proved a real handful under restraint and got a dream of a run through on the inside in the home straight. (7/1)
**2953* Pistol (IRE)**, 12lb higher than before his hat-trick, was set to go up a further 1lb the next day. Drifting across to the far side after beginning his run up the centre, he snatched second place on the line. (11/2)
**2784 Ashby Hill (IRE)** had no excuses this time but ran another sound race. (8/1)
**2980 Law Dancer (IRE)**, ridden to get the trip, was probably a shade unlucky not to have finished closer, and more positive tactics can now be employed. (20/1)
**2525* Alaflak (IRE)**, up 2lb, should not be considered unlucky. (6/1)
**2883 Roufontaine** was 9lb higher in the Ratings following her Chepstow hat-trick. (8/1)
**3043 Fahs (USA)**, set to be raised 1lb the next day, could only manage a token effort. (5/1)
**1065 Charter** (10/1: op 20/1)

## 3206 INVOSHIRE MAIDEN STKS (2-Y.O F) (Class D)
7-00 (7-01) **6f** £5,472.00 (£1,656.00: £808.00: £384.00) Stalls: Low GOING minus 0.31 sec per fur (GF)

| Form | Horse | Dist | Pos | SP | RR | SF |
|---|---|---|---|---|---|---|
| | **Caerfilly Dancer** (RAkehurst) **2-8-11** TQuinn(1) (cmpt: hld up: shkn up to ld ins fnl f: pushed out) | — | **1** | 9/4[1] | 77+ | 25 |
| 2892[2] | **Catechism (USA)** (JHMGosden) **2-8-11** GHind(2) (led tl ins fnl f: r.o) | ½ | **2** | 3/1[3] | 76 | 24 |
| | **Elbaaha** (MAJarvis) **2-8-11** PRobinson(5) (cmpt: hld up: hdwy over 2f out: ev ch 1f out: unable qckn) | hd | **3** | 11/4[2] | 75 | 23 |
| 2892[5] | **Zaima (IRE)** (JLDunlop) **2-8-11** GDuffield(4) (hld up: rdn over 1f out: no hdwy) | 2½ | **4** | 14/1 | 69 | 17 |

Etna (LMCumani) 2-8-11 PatEddery(6) (gd sort: chsd ldr over 3f: wknd over 1f out) ....... 1½ 5 3/1[3] 65 13
(SP 114.1%) 5 Rn

**1m 17.36** (3.36) CSF £9.07 TOTE £3.30: £1.70 £1.80 (£6.00) OWNER Fernray Ltd (EPSOM) BRED Juddmonte Farms
**Caerfilly Dancer**, a half-sister to a winner abroad, scored more decisively than the margin suggests. (9/4)
**2892 Catechism (USA)**, from the first crop of St Jovite, was very much the reluctant leader and shaped as though she will be suited by an extra furlong. (3/1: 2/1-100/30)
**Elbaaha** was the first runner sired by Arazi to go in this country. She will enhance her paddock value in due course. (11/4)
**2892 Zaima (IRE)** finished a fair bit closer to the runner-up than at Nottingham. (14/1: op 6/1)
**Etna** failed to erupt, but doubtless her time will come, probably over further. (3/1: 2/1-100/30)

## 3207 SCOTTISH EQUITABLE/JOCKEYS ASSOCIATION RATED STKS H'CAP (0-95) (3-Y.O+) (Class C)

7-30 (7-31) **7f** £6,318.40 (£2,365.60: £1,157.80: £499.00: £224.50: £114.70) Stalls: Low GOING minus 0.31 sec per fur (GF)

| | Horse / details | Dist | Pos | SP | RR | SF |
|---|---|---|---|---|---|---|
| 2856[4] | **Law Commission (88)** (DRCElsworth) **6-9-3** TQuinn(1) (hld up: nt clr run & swtchd rt over 1f out: rdn to ld nr fin) | — | 1 | 4/1[2] | 97 | 67 |
| 3072[8] | **Kayvee (92)** (GHarwood) **7-9-7** AClark(6) (lw: hld up: stdy hdwy over 3f out: rdn to ld ins fnl f: hdd nr fin) | nk | 2 | 11/2[3] | 100 | 70 |
| 3045[3] | **Silent Expression (84)** (BJMeehan) **6-8-13** BDoyle(2) (lw: w ldr: led over 3f out tl ins fnl f) | 5 | 3 | 7/1 | 81 | 51 |
| 2053[28] | **Star Talent (USA) (84)** (MissGayKelleway) **5-8-13** RHughes(3) (b.hind: lw: hld up: hdwy & swtchd rt over 1f out: wknd ins fnl f) | nk | 4 | 8/1 | 80 | 50 |
| 2774[5] | **Champagne Prince (95)** (PWHarris) **3-9-4** GHind(7) (prom: rdn over 2f out: sn wknd) | 5 | 5 | 6/1 | 80 | 44 |
| 2754[2] | **Kilvine (83)** (LMCumani) **3-8-6** PatEddery(4) (swtg: led over 3f: hrd rdn & wknd 2f out) | ¾ | 6 | 13/8[1] | 66 | 30 |
| 2889[11] | **Femme Savante (86)** (RHannon) **4-9-1** WJO'Connor(5) (lw: hld up: reminders 5f out: wknd wl over 1f out) | 6 | 7 | 20/1 | 55 | 25 |

(SP 116.1%) 7 Rn

**1m 27.94** (0.74) CSF £24.40 TOTE £4.90: £2.50 £2.40 (£14.30) OWNER Mr Raymond Tooth (WHITCOMBE) BRED Airlie Stud
WEIGHT FOR AGE 3yo-6lb
OFFICIAL EXPLANATION **Kilvine: the trainer's representative stated that the colt likes to dominate his race and was unable to do so here.**
**2856 Law Commission**, 9lb higher than when winning at Folkestone in June, was not inconvenienced by this return to seven and outbattled the runner-up. (4/1)
**2544 Kayvee**, 6lb lower than when he last won, was due to go down a further 2lb. Never one to find much off the bridle, he could not resist the winner's late challenge. (11/2)
**3045 Silent Expression**, stepping up in distance, has won up to a mile, but did not seem to last home on this occasion. (7/1)
**1819 Star Talent (USA)** seems better suited to a round course nowadays. (8/1)
**2774 Champagne Prince** was 6lb higher than when winning the second of two nurseries last August. (6/1)
**2754 Kilvine** looked a good thing after Green Barries, his Beverley conqueror, had won so easily at Goodwood earlier in the day. However, he likes to dictate from the front, and is not one to rely on. (13/8)

## 3208 PEREGRINE SECURITIES NURSERY H'CAP (2-Y.O) (Class C)

8-00 (8-01) **7f** £5,576.00 (£1,688.00: £824.00: £392.00) Stalls: Low GOING minus 0.31 sec per fur (GF)

| | Horse / details | Dist | Pos | SP | RR | SF |
|---|---|---|---|---|---|---|
| 3057* | **Union Town (IRE) (86)** (SirMarkPrescott) **2-9-7** 5x GDuffield(7) (lw: hld up: hdwy over 2f out: led wl over 1f out: rdn clr fnl f) | — | 1 | 13/8[1] | 91+ | 49 |
| 2948* | **Silca's My Key (IRE) (73)** (MRChannon) **2-8-8** 5x RPerham(2) (lw: hld up & bhd: outpcd over 3f out: hrd rdn over 2f out: hdwy over 1f out: r.o: no ch w wnr) | 6 | 2 | 11/2[3] | 64 | 22 |
| 3099* | **The Deejay (IRE) (78)** (MBrittain) **2-8-8**(5) 5x GParkin(8) (chsd ldr: led over 2f out tl wl over 1f out: one pce) | 2 | 3 | 11/2[3] | 65 | 23 |
| 2797* | **Masterstroke (74)** (BJMeehan) **2-8-9** BDoyle(4) (prom: rdn over 2f out: wknd over 1f out) | 3 | 4 | 5/1[2] | 54 | 12 |
| 3046[6] | **Superquest (76)** (WAO'Gorman) **2-8-11** EmmaO'Gorman(1) (lw: hld up: rdn over 2f out: wknd over 1f out) | 6 | 5 | 20/1 | 42 | — |
| 2187* | **Briska (IRE) (86)** (RHannon) **2-9-7** RHughes(3) (lw: hld up: hrd rdn & wknd over 1f out) | 5 | 6 | 8/1 | 41 | — |
| 1103[5] | **Sabotini (77)** (BWHills) **2-8-12** PatEddery(6) (led over 4f: wknd over 1f out) | ¾ | 7 | 8/1 | 30 | — |

(SP 112.5%) 7 Rn

**1m 29.91** (2.71) CSF £10.30 CT £35.02 TOTE £2.40: £1.50 £2.80 (£5.80) OWNER H R H Prince Fahd Salman (NEWMARKET) BRED Newgate Stud Co
**3057* Union Town (IRE)**, despite his penalty, would have been 5lb higher in the Ratings in future handicaps. The type who has to be kept right up to his work, unfortunately the win will not go unnoticed by the Handicapper. (13/8)
**2948* Silca's My Key (IRE)**, penalised for winning a seller, is already crying out for a mile. (11/2)
**3099* The Deejay (IRE)**, making a quick reappearance, could not go with the winner under a penalty. (11/2)
**2797* Masterstroke**, stepping up in distance, was due to be raised a further 1lb in future handicaps. (5/1)
**3046 Superquest**, a brother to Oaks third Pearl Angel, is bred for stamina. (20/1)
**2187* Briska (IRE)** had plenty of weight for winning a small Auction race, but this was still disappointing. (8/1)

## 3209 CRANBOURNE CHASE MAIDEN STKS (3-Y.O) (Class D)

8-30 (8-31) **1m 4f** £5,394.00 (£1,632.00: £796.00: £378.00) Stalls: High GOING minus 0.31 sec per fur (GF)

| | Horse / details | Dist | Pos | SP | RR | SF |
|---|---|---|---|---|---|---|
| 2610[5] | **Liefling (USA)** (JHMGosden) **3-8-9** PatEddery(3) (chsd ldr: rdn to ld over 2f out: r.o) | — | 1 | 1/2[1] | 79+ | 34 |
| 2610[6] | **Moon Mischief** (LadyHerries) **3-9-0** PaulEddery(2) (hld up: rdn to chse wnr over 1f out: no imp) | 3 | 2 | 11/2[2] | 80 | 35 |
| | **Ballet High (IRE)** (IABalding) **3-9-0** TQuinn(1) (unf: scope: hld up: rdn 5f out: hrd rdn & one pce fnl 2f) | 3½ | 3 | 13/2 | 75 | 30 |
| 2786[2] | **Caballus (USA)** (LordHuntingdon) **3-9-0** BDoyle(4) (lw: led: hdd over 2f out: wknd over 1f out) | 4 | 4 | 6/1[3] | 70 | 25 |

(SP 109.7%) 4 Rn

**2m 35.25** (5.25) CSF £3.51 TOTE £1.60: (£2.90) OWNER Sheikh Mohammed (NEWMARKET) BRED Darley Stud Management Inc
**2610 Liefling (USA)** was nothing more than a workmanlike winner, but staying does look her game. (1/2)
**2610 Moon Mischief** had finished a length nearer to the winner at Newmarket. Not overblessed with finishing speed, he should stay even further. (11/2: 3/1-6/1)
**Ballet High (IRE)**, a 150,000 guinea half-brother to Polar Falcon, can apparently be very coltish at home. (13/2: op 4/1)
**2786 Caballus (USA)** could well be destined for the winter game. (6/1: 3/1-13/2)

T/Plpt: £83.60 (146.41 Tckts). T/Qdpt: £9.40 (110.99 Tckts). KH

## 3155-GOODWOOD (R-H) (Good to firm)

**Friday August 2nd**
WEATHER: fine WIND: almost nil

### 3210 SEEBOARD H'CAP (0-100) (3-Y.O) (Class C)
2-15 (2-19) **7f** £21,705.00 (£6,540.00: £3,170.00: £1,485.00) Stalls: High GOING minus 0.11 sec per fur (G)

| | Horse / details | Dist | Pos | SP | RR | SF |
|---|---|---|---|---|---|---|
| 2754* | **Green Barries (86)** (MJohnston) **3-8-9** RHills(7) (a.p: led 2f out: clr over 1f out: r.o wl) | — | **1** | 10/1 | 97 | 72 |
| 2501[2] | **Dancing Image (81)** (IABalding) **3-7-13**(5) MartinDwyer(9) (hdwy over 2f out: chsd wnr over 1f out: no imp) | 3 | **2** | 6/1 [1] | 85 | 60 |
| 2585[2] | **Miss Riviera (92)** (GWragg) **3-9-1** MHills(12) (lw: swtchd lft over 3f out: rdn over 2f out: hdwy over 1f out: r.o one pce) | 1¾ | **3** | 11/1 | 92 | 67 |
| 2919[2] | **Unconditional Love (IRE) (98)** (MJohnston) **3-9-7** DHolland(2) (a.p: rdn over 2f out: one pce) | ½ | **4** | 20/1 | 97 | 72 |
| 2705[2] | **Albert The Bear (79)** (JBerry) **3-8-2**ow1 KDarley(10) (rdn & hdwy 2f out: one pce) | ½ | **5** | 16/1 | 77 | 51 |
| 2705[3] | **Banzhaf (USA) (73)** (GLMoore) **3-7-10** JQuinn(14) (led 5f: wknd fnl f) | hd | **6** | 20/1 | 71 | 46 |
| 2704[4] | **Wisam (90)** (RHannon) **3-8-10**(3) DaneO'Neill(18) (prom over 5f) | 1¼ | **7** | 25/1 | 85 | 60 |
| 1820[9] | **Caricature (IRE) (85)** (GLewis) **3-8-8v[1]** PaulEddery(13) (w ldr over 4f: wknd over 1f out) | nk | **8** | 20/1 | 79 | 54 |
| 2675* | **Steal 'Em (73)** (ABailey) **3-7-7**(3) DWright(16) (prom over 5f) | 1¾ | **9** | 33/1 | 63 | 38 |
| 2584[8] | **Lucky Archer (87)** (CEBrittain) **3-8-10** BDoyle(8) (rdn over 3f out: nvr nrr) | 1¼ | **10** | 40/1 | 74 | 49 |
| 2585* | **Lilli Claire (88)** (AGFoster) **3-8-11** TSprake(1) (nvr nrr) | ½ | **11** | 14/1 | 74 | 49 |
| 2585[4] | **Prends Ca (IRE) (90)** (RHannon) **3-8-13** JReid(4) (nvr nrr) | 1¼ | **12** | 25/1 | 73 | 48 |
| 2718* | **High Summer (USA) (86)** (RCharlton) **3-8-9**ow1 RHughes(5) (lw: hdwy over 2f out: wknd over 1f out) | hd | **13** | 15/2 [3] | 69 | 43 |
| 2041[8] | **Royal Canaska (90)** (MJHeaton-Ellis) **3-8-13** AClark(15) (lw: a bhd) | 1¾ | **14** | 25/1 | 69 | 44 |
| 2950[2] | **Cross of Valour (80)** (JARToller) **3-8-3** SSanders(11) (bhd fnl 5f) | nk | **15** | 20/1 | 58 | 33 |
| 2584[3] | **Royal Mark (IRE) (89)** (JWWatts) **3-8-12** TQuinn(17) (s.s: hdwy on ins 5f out: nt clr run over 2f out: swtchd lft: rdn whn hmpd over 1f out: nt rcvr) | 1 | **16** | 10/1 | 65 | 40 |
| 2765[2] | **School Boy (73)** (TJNaughton) **3-7-7b[1]**(3) MHenry(6) (a bhd) | 2 | **17** | 20/1 | 45 | 20 |
| 2705* | **Ood Dancer (USA) (86)** (LMCumani) **3-8-9** PatEddery(3) (hdwy over 2f out: eased whn btn over 1f out) | 2½ | **18** | 13/2 [2] | 52 | 27 |
| | | | | (SP 119.2%) | **18 Rn** | |

**1m 25.85** (1.05) CSF £61.51 CT £622.48 TOTE £9.00: £2.50 £1.70 £2.30 £3.10 (£20.90) Trio £101.30 OWNER Maktoum Al Maktoum (MIDDLEHAM) BRED Gainsborough Stud Management Ltd

LONG HANDICAP Banzhaf (USA) 7-9 School Boy 7-6 Steal 'Em 7-7

**OFFICIAL EXPLANATION High Summer (USA): the jockey reported that he eased the filly up at the furlong marker as she began to gurgle.**

**IN-FOCUS: Unusually for this week, the finish was dominated by horses drawn low to middle. Those drawn high again held good pitches, but failed to take advantage.**

**2754* Green Barries** was highly impressive as he completed the hat-trick in what seemed an extremely competitive race. Sent on a quarter of a mile out, he tore the opposition to shreds as he stormed clear to win in grand style. (10/1)

**2501 Dancing Image**, racing in midfield, began to pick up ground over a quarter of a mile from home. Struggling into second place approaching the final furlong, he never looked like getting to the winner. (6/1)

**2585 Miss Riviera**, who had to be switched left to get a clear run at the back of the field early in the straight, stayed on well in the final quarter-mile for third prize, but never threatened to get there. (11/1)

**2919 Unconditional Love (IRE)** ran a solid race under topweight. Never far away, she got rather outpaced a quarter of a mile from home but, to her credit, did stay on again in the final furlong. (20/1)

**2705 Albert The Bear**, pushed along to pick up ground a quarter of a mile from home, could then make no further impression. (16/1)

**2705 Banzhaf (USA)** took the field along. Collared a quarter of a mile out, he grimly held on to the place position until tiring in the final furlong. (20/1)

**2584 Royal Mark (IRE)** had no luck in running. Recovering from a tardy start to race in midfield, he found his way blocked over a quarter of a mile from home. Switched left to find daylight, he was grimly trying to stay on when hampered below the distance, from which point his jockey allowed him to coast in. This run is best ignored and he has done enough this season to suggest there is a race waiting for him over seven furlongs - the distance at which his two wins as a juvenile came. (10/1)

### 3211 VOLVO TRUCK FINANCE GLOBETROTTER H'CAP (0-110) (3-Y.O) (Class B)
2-45 (2-57) **1m 2f** £34,020.00 (£10,260.00: £4,980.00: £2,340.00) Stalls: High GOING minus 0.11 sec per fur (G)

| | Horse / details | Dist | Pos | SP | RR | SF |
|---|---|---|---|---|---|---|
| 2621* | **Fahim (94)** (ACStewart) **3-8-13** RHills(14) (lw: nt clr run over 2f out: swtchd lft: gd hdwy over 1f out: str run fnl f: led nr fin) | — | **1** | 5/2 [1] | 103+ | 74 |
| 2544[6] | **Murheb (87)** (RWArmstrong) **3-8-6** MHills(1) (a.p: led over 2f out: hrd rdn 1f out: hdd nr fin) | ¾ | **2** | 33/1 | 95 | 66 |
| 2581* | **Crown Court (USA) (85)** (LMCumani) **3-8-4**ow1 PatEddery(4) (lw: hdwy over 2f out: hrd rdn over 1f out: r.o) | nk | **3** | 4/1 [2] | 92 | 62 |
| 2621[9] | **The Dilettanti (USA) (86)** (JARToller) **3-8-5** SSanders(7) (a.p: rdn over 2f out: unable qckn) | ¾ | **4** | 50/1 | 92 | 63 |
| 2334* | **Mawingo (IRE) (81)** (GWragg) **3-8-0** JQuinn(5) (lw: rdn & hdwy 2f out: r.o one pce) | ½ | **5** | 5/1 [3] | 86 | 57 |
| 2011* | **Kuala Lipis (USA) (88)** (PFICole) **3-8-7** TQuinn(3) (hld up: rdn over 3f out: one pce) | 4 | **6** | 14/1 | 87 | 58 |
| 2774* | **Mushahid (USA) (102)** (JLDunlop) **3-9-7** JReid(9) (n.m.r & lost pl over 2f out: r.o one pce fnl f) | 2 | **7** | 25/1 | 98 | 69 |
| 2194[6] | **Wot No Fax (95)** (SDow) **3-9-0** BThomson(8) (lw: hdwy over 2f out: wknd over 1f out) | ¾ | **8** | 25/1 | 90 | 61 |
| 2502[9] | **Believe Me (95)** (RHannon) **3-8-11**(3) DaneO'Neill(11) (w ldr: led over 4f out tl over 2f out: wknd over 1f out) | 1¼ | **9** | 25/1 | 88 | 59 |
| 2742* | **Double Bluff (IRE) (90)** (IABalding) **3-8-4**(5) MartinDwyer(13) (hld up: rdn over 2f out: sn wknd) | ¾ | **10** | 9/1 | 81 | 52 |
| 3039[3] | **Exalted (IRE) (82)** (SirMarkPrescott) **3-8-1** GDuffield(6) (prom 7f) | 4 | **11** | 16/1 | 67 | 38 |
| 2888[6] | **Iamus (85)** (PTWalwyn) **3-8-4** TSprake(2) (lw: sme hdwy over 2f out: sn wknd) | ½ | **12** | 50/1 | 69 | 40 |
| 2621[4] | **Al Abraq (IRE) (94)** (JWHills) **3-8-13** DHolland(12) (bhd fnl 2f) | nk | **13** | 25/1 | 78 | 49 |
| 2742[4] | **Freedom Flame (83)** (MJohnston) **3-8-2** KDarley(10) (led over 5f: wknd 3f out) | 6 | **14** | 16/1 | 57 | 28 |
| | | | | (SP 115.9%) | **14 Rn** | |

**2m 7.27** (1.77) CSF £68.08 CT £293.21 TOTE £4.10: £2.00 £10.00 £2.30 (£113.30) Trio £131.70 OWNER Mr Hamdan Al Maktoum (NEWMARKET) BRED Shadwell Estate Company Limited

**IN-FOCUS: This event saw the much-publicised rematch between Fahim and Crown Court, two of those who competed in the Beverley maiden that has caused such interest.**

**2621* Fahim** put up an amazing performance to land this very valuable handicap. With nowhere to go at a critical stage at the back of the field over a quarter of a mile from home, he appeared to have absolutely no chance of success. However, he went into turbo-drive from below the distance and, sprouting wings, came storming through to snatch the spoils near the line. Unbeaten in three outings this season, he looks very useful and can certainly win a listed event. (5/2)

**2544 Murheb** was much better suited by this mile and a quarter and ran a fine race. Making his bid for glory over a quarter of a mile from home, it looked as if he was going to succeed but he had not bargained on the strong late finish of the winner and was worried out of it near the line. (33/1)
**2581* Crown Court (USA)**, who has been raised a stone for his recent Newmarket victory, began to pick up ground over a quarter of a mile out. He stayed on well under pressure from below the distance and only just failed to take second prize. (4/1)
**1593* The Dilettanti (USA)**, never far away, failed to find that vital turn of foot in the last two furlongs. (50/1)
**2334* Mawingo (IRE)**, scrubbed along to pick up ground a quarter of a mile out, stayed on without ever threatening to get there in time. (5/1)
**2011* Kuala Lipis (USA)** chased the leaders, but was only treading water in the last two furlongs. (14/1: 10/1-16/1)

## 3212 SCHRODERS GLORIOUS RATED STKS H'CAP (0-110) (Listed) (4-Y.O+) (Class A)

3-20 (3-26) **1m 4f** £30,579.20 (£11,412.80: £5,556.40: £2,362.00: £1,031.00: £498.60) Stalls: Low GOING minus 0.11 sec (G)

| | | | | SP | RR | SF |
|---|---|---|---|---|---|---|
| 2881[2] | **Salmon Ladder (USA) (108)** (PFICole) **4-9-5** TQuinn(8) (lw: a.p: rdn over 3f out: led over 1f out: r.o wl) | — | 1 | 7/2[1] | 119 | 92 |
| 2583[8] | **Midnight Legend (110)** (LMCumani) **5-9-7** JReid(6) (lw: chsd ldr: led over 3f out tl over 1f out: unable qckn ins fnl f) | 1¼ | 2 | 5/1[2] | 119 | 92 |
| 3073* | **Better Offer (IRE) (96)** (GHarwood) **4-8-7** MHills(4) (lw: rdn & hdwy 2f out: r.o wl) | ¾ | 3 | 5/1[2] | 104 | 77 |
| 2055[5] | **Sanmartino (IRE) (101)** (BWHills) **4-8-12** PatEddery(3) (lw: rdn & no hdwy fnl 3f) | 6 | 4 | 13/2[3] | 101 | 74 |
| 3125[4] | **Rokeby Bowl (96)** (IABalding) **4-8-7** KFallon(1) (lw: nvr nr to chal) | ½ | 5 | 9/1 | 96 | 69 |
| 2690* | **Son of Sharp Shot (IRE) (102)** (JLDunlop) **6-8-13** PaulEddery(2) (a bhd) | 2½ | 6 | 13/2[3] | 98 | 71 |
| 2534[2] | **Royal Scimitar (USA) (96)** (PFICole) **4-8-7** RHills(9) (led over 8f: wknd 2f out) | 3½ | 7 | 12/1 | 88 | 61 |
| 2534[4] | **Ionio (USA) (96)** (CEBrittain) **5-8-7** BDoyle(5) (b: lw: bhd fnl 3f) | 19 | 8 | 14/1 | 62 | 35 |
| 2194[3] | **River North (IRE) (107)** (LadyHerries) **6-9-4** KDarley(7) (b: bhd fnl 2f) | nk | 9 | 14/1 | 73 | 46 |
| | | | | (SP 113.2%) | | **9 Rn** |

**2m 33.65** (0.45) CSF £19.60 CT £77.78 TOTE £4.00: £1.50 £2.30 £2.00 (£9.20) Trio £10.50 OWNER Mr M. Arbib (WHATCOMBE) BRED Robert N. Clay and Michael J. & Mrs Ryan
LONG HANDICAP Rokeby Bowl 8-5 Royal Scimitar (USA) 8-6 Ionio (USA) 8-6 Better Offer (IRE) 8-4
**OFFICIAL EXPLANATION River North (IRE): lost his action coming down the hill.**
**2881 Salmon Ladder (USA)** appreciated this longer trip and saw it out in fine style to land his first listed handicap. Racing in third place, he was being bustled along as the Bugler called entering the straight, but he gradually reeled in the front two and, striking the front below the distance, eventually disposed of the runner-up in the last 100 yards. He will now be campaigned in Listed or Group Three events. (7/2)
**2583 Midnight Legend** bounced back to form on his favourite track, but suffered his first defeat here - he had won on all three previous visits. Racing in second place, he moved to the front over three furlongs from home. Headed below the distance, he grimly tried to stay with the winner, but was brushed aside in the last 100 yards. (5/1)
**3073* Better Offer (IRE)**, ridden along to pick up ground over a quarter of a mile from home, carried his head rather awkwardly but, despite that, was closing on the front two all the way to the line. He will now head for the Ebor at York. (5/1)
**2055 Sanmartino (IRE)** was making little impression on the leaders in the straight. A mile and three-quarters is his trip. (13/2)

## 3213 JOCKEY CLUB OF KENYA MOLECOMB STKS (Gp 3) (2-Y.O) (Class A)

3-50 (3-55) **5f** £23,400.00 (£8,785.00: £4,242.50: £1,872.50) Stalls: Low GOING minus 0.11 sec per fur (G)

| | | | | SP | RR | SF |
|---|---|---|---|---|---|---|
| 984[3] | **Carmine Lake (IRE)** (PWChapple-Hyam) **2-8-7** JReid(2) (lw: hld up: led 1f out: drvn out) | — | 1 | 6/1[3] | 96 | 53 |
| 2582[9] | **Connemara (IRE) (100)** (CADwyer) **2-8-7** KFallon(1) (hdwy on ins over 2f out: rdn over 1f out: ev ch ins fnl f: r.o) | nk | 2 | 10/1 | 95 | 52 |
| 2664a* | **Deep Finesse** (MAJarvis) **2-9-3** PRobinson(7) (a.p: ev ch 1f out: edgd lft: unable qckn) | 1½ | 3 | 11/2[2] | 100 | 57 |
| 2877[2] | **Omaha City (IRE)** (BGubby) **2-8-12** DHolland(3) (b: hld up: rdn over 1f out: one pce) | 1½ | 4 | 25/1 | 90 | 47 |
| 2700* | **Olympic Spirit (98)** (JBerry) **2-8-7** JCarroll(6) (b.hind: w ldr: led over 2f out to 1f out: 3rd & rdn whn squeezed out ins fnl f) | nk | 5 | 10/1 | 85 | 42 |
| 2070* | **Tipsy Creek (USA)** (BHanbury) **2-9-3** RHills(4) (b.hind: hld up: rdn over 1f out: sn wknd) | 5 | 6 | 11/10[1] | 79 | 36 |
| 2504* | **Vax Star (100)** (JLSpearing) **2-8-10** KDarley(5) (lw: led over 2f: wknd over 1f out) | 3½ | 7 | 7/1 | 60 | 17 |
| | | | | (SP 111.8%) | | **7 Rn** |

**58.32 secs** (1.62) CSF £52.49 TOTE £6.80: £2.80 £3.20 (£36.70) OWNER Mr R. E. Sangster (MARLBOROUGH) BRED Swettenham Stud
**IN-FOCUS: Fillies have now won five of the last six renewals of the Molecomb.**
**984 Carmine Lake (IRE)**, who was pretty lame and pulled muscles behind after her race at Chester back in May, has been off the course since, but bounced back in fine style in this very hot race. Held up travelling sweetly, she was ridden along to lead a furlong out and, responding to pressure, proved just too strong for the runner-up. The Lowther Stakes at York is her next likely target. (6/1)
**2582 Connemara (IRE)** appreciated the return to five furlongs and ran a fine race. Picking up ground along the inside rail at halfway, she threw down her challenge in the final furlong but, despite giving her all, found the winner a bit too strong. A crack at the Nunthorpe Stakes at York looks on the cards. (10/1)
**2664a* Deep Finesse**, a leading light from the off, had every chance a furlong from home. Drifting to his left, doing Olympic Spirit no favours, he failed to find another gear. (11/2: op 7/2)
**2877 Omaha City (IRE)**, taking another step up in class, chased the leaders but failed to quicken from below the distance. (25/1)
**2700* Olympic Spirit** disputed the lead until going on at halfway. Headed a furlong out, she was still close up in third, although just beginning to feel the pinch, when squeezed out with 150 yards to go. (10/1)
**2070* Tipsy Creek (USA)**, sold to Hamdan Al Maktoum after his impressive Royal Ascot victory, ran appallingly and tamely dropped away from below the distance. This downhill track was one theory for his defeat but, even allowing for that, that would not be enough to explain this dreadful performance. He is certainly a great deal better than he showed here and this run in best ignored. (11/10)
**2504* Vax Star** found the opposition too hot and, after showing with a narrow advantage to halfway, capitulated below the distance. (7/1)

## 3214 E.B.F. FOXHALL MAIDEN STKS (2-Y.O C & G) (Class D)

4-25 (4-25) **7f** £6,970.00 (£2,110.00: £1,030.00: £490.00) Stalls: High GOING minus 0.11 sec per fur (G)

| | | | | SP | RR | SF |
|---|---|---|---|---|---|---|
| 2852[6] | **Dickie Bird (IRE)** (RHannon) **2-8-11** PatEddery(5) (lw: w ldr: led over 1f out: hrd rdn: r.o wl) | — | 1 | 7/2[2] | 74 | 45 |
| 2302[4] | **Zaretski (80)** (CEBrittain) **2-8-11** BDoyle(2) (led over 5f: unable qckn) | 1¼ | 2 | 2/1[1] | 71 | 42 |
| | **Prairie Falcon (IRE)** (BWHills) **2-8-11** MHills(1) (w'like: scope: bit bkwd: hld up: rdn over 2f out: sn wknd) | 3½ | 3 | 2/1[1] | 63 | 34 |
| | **Quertier (IRE)** (MRChannon) **2-8-11** RHughes(4) (str: scope: bit bkwd: s.s: a wl bhd) | 18 | 4 | 7/1[3] | 22 | — |
| | **Unknown Territory (IRE)** (MRChannon) **2-8-11** TQuinn(3) (unf: scope: bhd fnl 4f) | 2 | 5 | 10/1 | 17 | — |
| | | | | (SP 110.5%) | | **5 Rn** |

**1m 28.3** (3.50) CSF £10.35 TOTE £3.60: £1.40 £1.70 (£5.40) OWNER Mr George Teo (MARLBOROUGH) BRED John Malone
**2852 Dickie Bird (IRE)** disputed the lead. Forging ahead below the distance, he responded to pressure to win what was a very poor race considering the money on offer. (7/2)

**2302 Zaretski** disputed the lead from the start. However, when the winner began to assert from below the distance, he was tapped for toe. (2/1: 6/4-9/4)
**Prairie Falcon (IRE)**, an attractive, good-bodied half-brother to Hill Hopper, did not look fully fit and so it proved. Racing in third place, it looked as if he was going to get on terms with the front two a quarter of a mile out, but he soon tired as lack of race fitness took its toll. (2/1: tchd 3/1)

## 3215 CHICHESTER CITY H'CAP (0-90) (3-Y.O) (Class C)

5-00 (5-02) **5f** £7,050.00 (£2,100.00: £1,000.00: £450.00) Stalls: Low GOING minus 0.11 sec per fur (G)

| | | | | SP | RR | SF |
|---|---|---|---|---|---|---|
| 2999* | **Clan Chief (70)** (JRArnold) **3-8-5** [7x] TQuinn(2) (b.hind: a.p: n.m.r on ins 3f out: swtchd rt: led 1f out: rdn out) | — | **1** | 9/4 [1] | 81 | 38 |
| 2769* | **Literary Society (USA) (64)** (JARToller) **3-7-13** JQuinn(3) (hld up: rdn over 2f out: nt clr run over 1f out: r.o one pce) | 1¾ | **2** | 4/1 [2] | 69 | 26 |
| 2790[2] | **White Emir (86)** (BJMeehan) **3-9-7b** BDoyle(4) (led 4f: one pce) | ½ | **3** | 9/1 | 90 | 47 |
| 3135[6] | **Chemcast (67)** (DNicholls) **3-8-2b** JFEgan(9) (a.p: ev ch 1f out: one pce) | 1¾ | **4** | 20/1 | 65 | 22 |
| 2999[4] | **Dande Flyer (78)** (DWPArbuthnot) **3-8-13** DHolland(5) (b: hld up: rdn over 1f out: one pce) | nk | **5** | 12/1 | 75 | 32 |
| 3049* | **Gwespyr (71)** (JBerry) **3-8-6** [7x] JCarroll(8) (lw: hdwy over 2f out: rdn over 1f out: eased whn btn ins fnl f) | 4 | **6** | 8/1 | 55 | 12 |
| 2790[7] | **Step On Degas (65)** (MJFetherston-Godley) **3-7-11v**(3) MHenry(7) (lost pl over 3f out: rallied 2f out: wknd 1f out) | 1 | **7** | 14/1 | 46 | 3 |
| 2861[4] | **Paojiunic (IRE) (70)** (LMCumani) **3-8-5** PatEddery(6) (lw: prom 3f) | ¾ | **8** | 6/1 [3] | 49 | 6 |
| 2790[3] | **Sharp Pearl (75)** (JWhite) **3-8-10b** RHughes(1) (lw: bhd fnl 3f) | 12 | **9** | 12/1 | 15 | — |
| | | | | (SP 113.0%) | **9 Rn** | |

**59.05 secs** (2.35) CSF £10.89 CT £59.24 TOTE £2.90: £1.40 £1.60 £2.20 (£5.00) Trio £9.80 OWNER Mr P. G. Lowe (UPPER LAMBOURN) BRED D. Gill
**2999* Clan Chief** continues in sparkling form and completed the hat-trick. Never far away, he showed in front a furlong out and, ridden along, soon asserted. (9/4)
**2769* Literary Society (USA)** chased the leaders. He did not have the best of runs below the distance, but it made little difference to his chances and he stayed on for second prize. (4/1)
**2790 White Emir** attempted to make all the running. Collared a furlong out, he was then tapped for toe. (9/1)
**3135 Chemcast** had every chance entering the final furlong before quicker rivals had his measure. (20/1)
**2999 Dande Flyer** chased the leaders. He appeared to be going well below the distance but, once ridden, failed to find what was required. (12/1)
**3049* Gwespyr** moved up at halfway but, ridden along below the distance, was soon in trouble, and was eased when beaten in the last 150 yards. (8/1)

## 3216 KINRARA APPRENTICE LIMITED STKS (0-80) (4-Y.O+) (Class D)

5-35 (5-35) **6f** £6,807.50 (£2,060.00: £1,005.00: £238.75: £238.75) Stalls: Low GOING minus 0.11 sec per fur (G)

| | | | | SP | RR | SF |
|---|---|---|---|---|---|---|
| 3106[3] | **Hawa Al Nasamaat (USA) (80)** (EALDunlop) **4-8-12** DaneO'Neill(1) (lw: w ldr: led over 1f out: hrd rdn: r.o wl) | — | **1** | 11/4 [1] | 82 | 59 |
| 3055* | **Tiler (IRE) (80)** (MJohnston) **4-9-1** MHenry(10) (lw: led over 4f: hrd rdn & hung lft: edgd rt ins fnl f: unable qckn) | 2½ | **2** | 3/1 [2] | 78 | 55 |
| 3106[6] | **Hinton Rock (IRE) (76)** (ABailey) **4-8-12v**[1] DWright(9) (a.p: hrd rdn over 1f out: one pce fnl f: fin 4th, nk: plcd 3rd) | | **3** | 25/1 | 74 | 51 |
| 2363[7] | **Rock Symphony (80)** (WJHaggas) **6-8-7**(5) ElizabethTurner(2) (s.s: swtchd rt 2f out: hdwy & bmpd over 1f out: bmpd ins fnl f: nvr nrr: fin d.h 5th, hd: plcd 4th) | | **4** | 6/1 [3] | 74 | 51 |
| 2713[5] | **Random (48)** (CJames) **5-8-9** MartinDwyer(3) (swtg: bmpd over 2f out: hdwy 2f out: hrd rdn over 1f out: one pce fnl f: fin 5th, d.h: plcd 4th) | | **4** | 20/1 | 71 | 48 |
| 3112[6] | **Fantasy Racing (IRE) (76)** (MRChannon) **4-8-6**(3) AEddery(5) (hdwy over 3f out: rdn over 2f out: sn wknd) | 4 | **7** | 12/1 | 60 | 37 |
| 2735[2] | **Scissor Ridge (52)** (JJBridger) **4-8-10**(5) RBrisland(4) (prom 3f) | 1½ | **8** | 16/1 | 62 | 39 |
| 2745[6] | **Petraco (IRE) (56)** (NASmith) **8-8-7**(5) JBramhill(7) (prom 4f) | 1¼ | **9** | 50/1 | 56 | 33 |
| 2623[12] | **Scharnhorst (78)** (SDow) **4-9-0**(7) DSalt(8) (lw: prom over 3f) | 1½ | **10** | 12/1 | 61 | 38 |
| 2615[2] | **Ansellman (80)** (JBerry) **6-9-4** PRoberts(6) (s.s: hdwy 2f out: hrd rdn & edgd lft over 1f out: edgd lft ins fnl f: r.o: fin 3rd, nk: disq: plcd last) | | **D** | 13/2 | 81 | 58 |
| | | | | (SP 111.1%) | **10 Rn** | |

**1m 11.95** (1.95) CSF £10.32 TOTE £3.20: £1.80 £1.80 £7.00 (£3.80) Trio £82.10 OWNER Maktoum Al Maktoum (NEWMARKET) BRED Bud Boschert's Stables Inc
STEWARDS' ENQUIRY Roberts susp. 12-14/8/96 (careless riding).
**3106 Hawa Al Nasamaat (USA)** disputed the lead from the start. Showing with a definite advantage below the distance, he was given a few reminders to wake him up, but soon asserted for a cosy success. (11/4)
**3055* Tiler (IRE)** held a slender advantage in the centre of the track. Collared below the distance, he then hung left under pressure. Drifting right again inside the final furlong, giving his rider problems, he failed to find the necessary turn of foot. (3/1)
**1708 Hinton Rock (IRE)** was tapped for toe inside the final furlong. (25/1)
**2220 Rock Symphony** was given little assistance from the saddle. Picking up ground below the distance, he was given a nudge by Ansellman on three occasions, but it made little difference to his chances as he stayed on to be nearest at the line. (6/1: op 4/1)
**2713 Random**, given a bump by Ansellman soon after halfway, then picked up ground. Under pressure below the distance, she grimly tried to get on terms but was tapped for toe inside the final furlong. (20/1)
**2615 Ansellman** began to pick up ground a quarter of a mile out, but he drifted left under pressure and, with his jockey failing to bring his whip through at a critical stage, gave Rock Symphony a couple of bumps. He again nudged that rival inside the final furlong but ran on for third prize. Not surprisingly, his jockey was suspended for careless riding and the gelding demoted to last place. (13/2)

T/Jkpt: £146,029.90 (0.79 Tckts); £43,191.97 to Goodwood 3/8/96. T/Plpt: £207.30 (277.13 Tckts). T/Qdpt: £39.00 (54.59 Tckts). AK

# 3042-NEWMARKET (R-H) (Good to firm)

## Friday August 2nd

WEATHER: overcast WIND: slt half bhd

## 3217 RO-TRUCK FOR SCANIA (S) STKS (3-Y.O+) (Class E)

6-15 (6-18) **1m (July)** £3,720.00 (£1,110.00: £530.00: £240.00) Stalls: High GOING minus 0.45 sec per fur (F)

| | | | | SP | RR | SF |
|---|---|---|---|---|---|---|
| 2121[5] | **Indian Rhapsody (47)** (ABailey) **4-8-13** PBloomfield(2) (hdwy over 3f out: led over 2f out: rdn out) | — | **1** | 12/1 | 60 | 42 |

| | | | SP | RR | SF |
|---|---|---|---|---|---|
| $2763^{8}$ | **Perilous Plight (65)** (WRMuir) **5-9-9** JReid(6) (lw: hld up: hdwy 2f out: chsd wnr appr fnl f: r.o) ....................2½ | **2** | $7/2^{2}$ | 65 | 47 |
| $3084^{9}$ | **Hawwam (52)** (EJAlston) **10-9-9** JLowe(7) (lw: hld up: hdwy over 3f out: rdn 2f out: kpt on) ....................3 | **3** | $15/2^{3}$ | 59 | 41 |
| $2587^{12}$ | **Mediate (IRE) (39)** (AHide) **4-9-4b** DBiggs(10) (lw: a.p: one pce fnl 2f) ....................1¾ | **4** | 25/1 | 51 | 33 |
| $2971^{6}$ | **Only (USA) (47)** (RHannon) **3-8-11** DHarrison(5) (a.p: no imp appr fnl f) ....................½ | **5** | 10/1 | 50 | 25 |
| $2313^{13}$ | **Miss Laughter (53)** (JWHills) **4-9-4** OUrbina(3) (swtg: led 1f: wknd over 2f out) ....................6 | **6** | 12/1 | 38 | 20 |
| $2915^{3}$ | **Kuwam (IRE) (40)** (BHanbury) **3-8-11** JStack(1) (trckd ldrs tl wknd appr fnl f) ....................1¼ | **7** | 12/1 | 35 | 10 |
| $2753^{8}$ | **Crystal Fast (USA) (41)** (PAKelleway) **3-8-4b**$^{1(7)}$ CDomergue(8) (led after 1f tl hdd & wknd over 2f out) ....................8 | **8** | 33/1 | 19 | — |
| $2981^{2}$ | **Uncle George (63)** (MHTompkins) **3-8-11b** WWoods(4) (lw: hld up: effrt 3f out: sn rdn & nt r.o) ....................¾ | **9** | $11/8^{1}$ | 18 | — |
| | | | (SP 115.0%) | | **9 Rn** |

**1m 38.96** (1.76) CSF £50.34 TOTE £12.50: £2.60 £1.50 £1.60 (£19.20) Trio £27.40 OWNER Mr G. G. Ashton (TARPORLEY) BRED Mrs P. Good

WEIGHT FOR AGE 3yo-7lb

No bid

**2121 Indian Rhapsody** is inconsistent but has now won on both her appearances on the July Course. (12/1: op 8/1)

**2438 Perilous Plight** tried hard as usual, but was no match for the winner in the final furlong. (7/2: op 9/4)

**2801* Hawwam** had a stiff task at the weights, but came home really well and is obviously in great heart at present. (15/2: 5/1-8/1)

**Mediate (IRE)** looked to have no chance at the weights, but ran his best race in a long time. He has not won on turf since his two-year-old days, but would be interesting off his current handicap mark. (25/1)

**2971 Only (USA)** took a good hold going down, but proved short of a turn of speed as the race developed. He has yet to make the frame in nine attempts. (10/1: 7/1-11/1)

**1893* Miss Laughter**, edgy and warm beforehand, was unable to dominate and was one of the first beaten. (12/1: op 7/1)

**2981 Uncle George** flashed his tail and looked none too enthusiastic once pressure was applied. (11/8)

## 3218 LUCINDA STOPFORD SACKVILLE LADIES' H'CAP (0-80) (3-Y.O+) (Class E)

6-40 (6-43) **1m 4f (July)** £3,720.00 (£1,110.00: £530.00: £240.00) Stalls: High GOING minus 0.45 sec per fur (F)

| | | | SP | RR | SF |
|---|---|---|---|---|---|
| $2570^{7}$ | **Mukeed (70)** (JHMGosden) **3-11-4v**$^{1}$ MrsCDurkan(2) (mde virtually all: drvn out) ....................— | **1** | $5/1^{2}$ | 77 | 38 |
| $2961^{2}$ | **Belmarita (IRE) (73)** (MHTompkins) **3-11-7** MrsLPearce(7) (w wnr: ev ch fr 3f out tl unable qckn ins fnl f).......½ | **2** | $9/4^{1}$ | 79 | 40 |
| $2599^{3}$ | **Star Anise (42)** (MrsDHaine) **4-9-10**$^{(5)}$ MissKEllis(6) (hld up: hdwy over 5f out: ev ch 3f out: no ex appr fnl f)...2 | **3** | $13/2^{3}$ | 46 | 18 |
| $2341^{9}$ | **Strat's Legacy (43)** (DWPArbuthnot) **9-10-2** MrsDArbuthnot(1) (plld hrd: trckd ldrs: outpcd 3f out: r.o appr fnl f) ....................½ | **4** | 15/2 | 46 | 18 |
| *$309^{11}$* | **Children's Choice (IRE) (53)** (CNAllen) **5-10-12** MrsDKettlewell(5) (trckd ldrs: outpcd 3f out: r.o fnl f) ............½ | **5** | $13/2^{3}$ | 55 | 27 |
| $2927^{2}$ | **Go With The Wind (65)** (MBell) **3-10-13** MrsAPerrett(3) (lw: hld up: effrt 3f out: nvr able to chal)....................¾ | **6** | $13/2^{3}$ | 66 | 27 |
| $2871^{6}$ | **Ela Man Howa (50)** (ABailey) **5-10-4**$^{(5)}$ MissBridgetGatehouse(4) (lw: hld up: lost tch 3f out: r.o wl fnl f)..........½ | **7** | 14/1 | 51 | 23 |
| | | | (SP 105.9%) | | **7 Rn** |

**2m 38.47** (8.47) CSF £14.84 TOTE £6.70: £3.10 £2.00 (£6.10) OWNER Sheikh Ahmed Al Maktoum (NEWMARKET) BRED P. T. Tellwright

WEIGHT FOR AGE 3yo-11lb

**2570 Mukeed**, clearly suited by being able to lead, would not be denied and proved resolute once challenged, despite some forceful reminders. (5/1)

**2961 Belmarita (IRE)**, dropped in trip, was upsides the winner throughout and looked likely to get on top in the Dip, but was worried out of it in the last 100 yards. (9/4)

**2599 Star Anise** poached a clear lead with the two principals with three furlongs left, but was the first to crack. (13/2)

**Strat's Legacy** took some settling at the steady early pace, but was caught out of his ground as the pace suddenly quickened three furlongs out. Despite staying on, he could never get back to the leaders. (15/2)

**Children's Choice (IRE)** could never get back to the leaders after being outpaced with three furlongs left. (13/2)

**2927 Go With The Wind**, who stays further, was not suited by the slow early pace and never looked like making progress in the closing stages. (13/2)

## 3219 VARDY CONTINENTAL H'CAP (0-90) (3-Y.O+) (Class C)

7-10 (7-11) **6f (July)** £6,004.00 (£1,792.00: £856.00: £194.00: £194.00) Stalls: High GOING minus 0.45 sec per fur (F)

| | | | SP | RR | SF |
|---|---|---|---|---|---|
| $2992^{*}$ | **Robellion (68)** (DWPArbuthnot) **5-8-8v** $^{7x}$ SWhitworth(3) (b.hind: chsd ldrs: rdn to ld ins fnl f: hld on wl)........— | **1** | 8/1 | 75 | 54 |
| $2856^{5}$ | **Golden Pound (USA) (83)** (MissGayKelleway) **4-9-9** JReid(6) (trckd ldrs: n.m.r over 1f out: squeezed thro 1f out: ev ch ins fnl f: r.o)....................hd | **2** | $5/1^{3}$ | 90 | 69 |
| $2790^{5}$ | **Rushcutter Bay (88)** (TTClement) **3-9-3**$^{(7)}$ GFaulkner(8) (lw: led tl hdd & no ex ins fnl f)....................½ | **3** | 12/1 | 93 | 68 |
| $2856^{*}$ | **Bayin (USA) (75)** (MDIUsher) **7-9-1** RStreet(7) (b: lw: stdd s: bhd tl hdwy over 1f out: nt rch ldrs)....................2 | **4** | $4/1^{2}$ | 75 | 54 |
| $3045^{2}$ | **Fame Again (77)** (MrsJRRamsden) **4-9-3** JFortune(2) (lw: hld up: r.o appr fnl f: nt pce to chal)....................d.h | **4** | $5/2^{1}$ | 82 | 61 |
| $2034^{3}$ | **Mousehole (75)** (RGuest) **4-9-1b** KDarley(1) (chsd ldrs: ev ch over 1f out: one pce) ....................nk | **6** | 13/2 | 74 | 53 |
| $2584^{9}$ | **Dark Deed (USA) (85)** (BWHills) **3-9-7** MHills(4) (w ldr: ev ch over 2f out: wkng whn hmpd 1f out) ................2½ | **7** | 10/1 | 78 | 53 |
| $2285^{6}$ | **Safey Ana (USA) (65)** (BHanbury) **5-8-5** JStack(5) (b: swtg: in tch 4f: sn bhd)....................¾ | **8** | 16/1 | 56 | 35 |
| | | | (SP 112.3%) | | **8 Rn** |

**1m 12.06** (0.06) CSF £43.01 CT £434.63 TOTE £9.10: £2.60 £1.80 £3.80 (£34.70) OWNER Mr George Thompson (COMPTON) BRED Pitts Farm Stud

WEIGHT FOR AGE 3yo-4lb

OFFICIAL EXPLANATION **Dark Deed (USA): the jockey explained that when the field came to take him on, the filly had no more to give.**

**2992* Robellion** is back to his best and was beaten only a short-head off a 3lb higher mark than this here last year. (8/1)

**2856 Golden Pound (USA)** had no luck in running and this probably made the difference between victory and defeat. (5/1)

**2790 Rushcutter Bay**, kept to front-running with the headgear left off, ran well but was collared late in the day. (12/1)

**2856* Bayin (USA)** did not start his move until the race was all but over. (4/1)

**3045 Fame Again** has yet to win over six and was never doing enough in the last couple of furlongs. (5/2)

**2034 Mousehole**, off for over six weeks since disappointing last time, was in the thick of things until the rising ground took its toll. (13/2)

## 3220 SCANIA 1996 TRUCK OF THE YEAR TROPHY H'CAP (0-70) (3-Y.O+) (Class E)

7-40 (7-41) **1m 2f (July)** £5,754.00 (£1,722.00: £826.00: £378.00) Stalls: High GOING minus 0.45 sec per fur (F)

| | | | SP | RR | SF |
|---|---|---|---|---|---|
| $2020^{6}$ | **Gold Desire (38)** (MBrittain) **6-7-10** JLowe(14) (lw: hdwy 3f out: led 1f out: rdn & r.o wl fnl f)....................— | **1** | 25/1 | 47 | 35 |
| $2628^{*}$ | **Ring of Vision (IRE) (54)** (MrsMReveley) **4-8-12** KDarley(11) (lw: chsd ldrs: ev ch 2f out tl unable qckn ins fnl f) ....................1½ | **2** | $13/2^{2}$ | 61 | 49 |
| $2183^{4}$ | **Fern's Governor (41)** (WJMusson) **4-7-13**$^{ow1}$ DRMcCabe(2) (hdwy 4f out: r.o u.p fnl f)....................3 | **3** | 10/1 | 43 | 30 |

| | | | | SP | RR | SF |
|---|---|---|---|---|---|---|
| 2780* | **Elashath (USA) (66)** (JHMGosden) **3-9-1** RHills(7) (lw: chsd ldrs: rdn over 2f out: sn ev ch: no ex ins fnl f)... | 1½ | **4** | 15/8 [1] | 65 | 44 |
| 2673[4] | **Dance King (66)** (RHarris) **4-9-10** DHarrison(1) (lw: trckd ldrs: led 2f out: sn hdd & no ex)... | 1½ | **5** | 16/1 | 63 | 51 |
| 2032[12] | **Fairelaine (50)** (KCBailey) **4-8-8** BThomson(13) (lw: r.o fnl 3f: nvr able to chal)... | 3 | **6** | 33/1 | 42 | 30 |
| 1890[14] | **Mazirah (50)** (PJMakin) **5-8-8** MHills(9) (bhd tl rdn & sme hdwy fnl 2f)... | 2½ | **7** | 16/1 | 38 | 26 |
| 2896[10] | **Conic Hill (IRE) (47)** (JPearce) **5-8-5** GBardwell(12) (chsd ldrs 7f)... | nk | **8** | 25/1 | 35 | 23 |
| *2081*[7] | **Saltando (IRE) (47)** (PatMitchell) **5-8-5** MTebbutt(3) (lw: hdwy over 3f out: wknd over 1f out)... | 1 | **9** | 25/1 | 33 | 21 |
| 2847[3] | **Ambidextrous (IRE) (52)** (EJAlston) **4-8-10** JFortune(8) (lw: bhd: rdn 5f out: nvr rchd ldrs)... | ¾ | **10** | 12/1 | 37 | 25 |
| 3117[8] | **Arabian Heights (51)** (MrsJRRamsden) **3-7-11**(3) FLynch(5) (led 8f)... | 1¾ | **11** | 10/1 | 33 | 12 |
| 2409[2] | **South Eastern Fred (48)** (HJCollingridge) **5-8-6** JQuinn(4) (lw: chsd ldr 8f)... | nk | **12** | 7/1 [3] | 30 | 18 |
| 2334[6] | **Galapino (64)** (CEBrittain) **3-8-6**(7) JGotobed(10) (dwlt: c wd st: nvr nr ldrs)... | ¾ | **13** | 12/1 | 44 | 23 |
| 2744[9] | **Foreign Judgement (USA) (57)** (WJMusson) **3-7-13**(7) JWilkinson(6) (b.off hind: swtg: a bhd: t.o fnl 3f)... | 15 | **14** | 14/1 | 13 | — |
| | | | | (SP 127.1%) | **14 Rn** | |

**2m 6.27** (1.27) CSF £173.44 CT £1,622.30 TOTE £21.80: £5.00 £2.40 £3.50 (£52.00) Trio £184.90 OWNER Northgate Lodge Racing Club (WARTHILL) BRED Northgate Lodge Stud Ltd

LONG HANDICAP Gold Desire 7-5

WEIGHT FOR AGE 3yo-9lb

**2020 Gold Desire** looked in terrific shape, despite a short lay-off, and proved tenacious once in front. He won this race two years ago, but had only scored once subsequently before now. (25/1)

**2628* Ring of Vision (IRE)** got the worse of a ding-dong battle with the winner, but looks capable of finding another opportunity. (13/2)

**2183 Fern's Governor** was ridden with more restraint this time but, by the time she made her move, the first two had got away. (10/1: op 7/1)

**2780* Elashath (USA)** looked short of speed off his new mark, and needs a step up in trip. (15/8: op 3/1)

**2673 Dance King** possesses only a short burst of speed and it was not enough to see him home on this occasion. (16/1)

**Mazirah**, still a maiden, was very free to post. Returning to a more suitable trip, he showed some promise. (16/1)

## 3221 E.B.F. BEACON MAIDEN STKS (2-Y.O) (Class D)

8-10 (8-10) **7f (July)** £4,581.00 (£1,368.00: £654.00: £297.00) Stalls: High GOING minus 0.45 sec per fur (F)

| | | | | SP | RR | SF |
|---|---|---|---|---|---|---|
| 2611[8] | **Right Tune** (BHanbury) **2-8-9** WRyan(6) (lw: mde all: edgd lft & hld on wl fnl f)... | — | **1** | 16/1 | 78 | 35 |
| 2863[8] | **Shouk** (LMCumani) **2-8-9** OUrbina(8) (chsd ldrs: rdn 3f out: ev ch over 1f out: r.o ins fnl f)... | nk | **2** | 16/1 | 77 | 34 |
| | **Redwing** (JLDunlop) **2-9-0** KDarley(2) (leggy: unf: hld up: hdwy 3f out: ev ch ins fnl f: no ex nr fin)... | hd | **3** | 16/1 | 82 | 39 |
| | **Entrepreneur** (MRStoute) **2-9-0** JReid(9) (gd sort: hld up: effrt over 2f out: rapid hdwy fnl f: fin fast)... | 1½ | **4** | 4/9 [1] | 79+ | 36 |
| 1896[11] | **Maftool** (JHMGosden) **2-9-0** RHills(5) (lw: hld up: hdwy & nt clr run over 2f out: ev ch over 1f out: wknd wl ins fnl f)... | nk | **5** | 16/1 | 78 | 35 |
| | **Social Pillar (USA)** (JHMGosden) **2-9-0** MHills(7) (hdwy 3f out: no imp fnl 2f)... | 3½ | **6** | 9/1 [3] | 70 | 27 |
| | **Indifferent Guy** (CEBrittain) **2-9-0** DHarrison(3) (neat: bit bkwd: chsd ldrs: rdn over 2f out: sn btn)... | 5 | **7** | 33/1 | 59 | 16 |
| | **Pennys From Heaven** (HCandy) **2-9-0** CRutter(4) (leggy: scope: chsd ldr tl rdn & wknd 3f out)... | s.h | **8** | 8/1 [2] | 58 | 15 |
| | **Dixie Jamboree (USA)** (LMCumani) **2-9-0** GCarter(1) (w'like: scope: lw: chsd ldrs 4f)... | 3 | **9** | 25/1 | 52 | 9 |
| | | | | (SP 120.7%) | **9 Rn** | |

**1m 26.86** (1.86) CSF £205.95 TOTE £17.40: £2.50 £3.10 £2.50 (£87.70) Trio £148.30 OWNER Mr Abdullah Ali (NEWMARKET) BRED Gainsborough Stud Management Ltd

**2611 Right Tune** showed how important a previous outing can be, making all in good style. (16/1)

**2863 Shouk**, although still using her tail, was a different kettle of fish this time and battled on right to the line. (16/1)

**Redwing** made a promising debut, only finding things too tough in the last 100 yards, and looks sure to be suited by further. (16/1)

**Entrepreneur**, a fine, imposing colt, was the subject of rave reviews from the gallops and showed a grand action on the way to post. However, once the stalls opened, he looked green and the penny only dropped late in the day. A brother to Dance A Dream, more will be heard of him. (4/9)

**Maftool** was not knocked about as his measure was taken inside the final furlong, and should continue to progress. (16/1)

**Social Pillar (USA)** took a good hold going down and showed some promise, although whether this is his trip remains to be seen. (9/1: op 5/1)

## 3222 DEREK JONES COMMERCIALS FOR SCANIA CONDITIONS STKS (3-Y.O+ F & M) (Class C)

8-40 (8-40) **6f (July)** £5,394.00 (£1,944.00: £932.00: £380.00: £150.00) Stalls: High GOING minus 0.45 sec per fur (F)

| | | | | SP | RR | SF |
|---|---|---|---|---|---|---|
| 2841a[6] | **Royale Figurine (IRE) (107)** (MJFetherston-Godley) **5-8-12** JReid(5) (w ldr: led 2f out: pushed clr fnl f)... | — | **1** | 5/4 [1] | 105+ | 56 |
| 2332[10] | **Tropical Dance (USA) (90)** (MrsJCecil) **3-8-8** KDarley(2) (a.p: chsd wnr fnl f: no imp)... | 4 | **2** | 20/1 | 94 | 41 |
| 3047[3] | **Maid For The Hills (100)** (DRLoder) **3-8-5**(3) PMcCabe(4) (lw: hld up: rdn over 2f out: r.o fnl f)... | 2 | **3** | 11/2 [3] | 89 | 36 |
| 2007[16] | **Red Nymph (93)** (WJarvis) **3-8-8** BThomson(3) (lw: led 4f: edgd lft & sn wknd)... | 2 | **4** | 14/1 | 84 | 31 |
| 2072[3] | **Watch Me (IRE) (105)** (RHannon) **3-8-12** MHills(1) (trckd ldrs: effrt 2f out: btn & eased appr fnl f)... | 9 | **5** | 7/4 [2] | 64 | 11 |
| | | | | (SP 107.6%) | **5 Rn** | |

**1m 12.15** (0.15) CSF £16.45 TOTE £2.20: £1.30 £2.60 (£10.30) OWNER Mr Craig Pearman (EAST ILSLEY) BRED Craig Pearman

WEIGHT FOR AGE 3yo-4lb

**OFFICIAL EXPLANATION Watch Me (IRE): was found to be coughing on returning home.**

**2841a Royale Figurine (IRE)**, with Watch Me running no race at all, had far too much class for the rest and will have done her confidence a deal of good. (5/4: Evens-11/8)

**1790 Tropical Dance (USA)** was again doing her best work at the end and lost nothing in defeat. (20/1)

**3047 Maid For The Hills** continues to prove hard to place. (11/2)

**1493 Red Nymph**, given seven weeks off after her unfortunate experience at York, came through this well and should be kept in mind. (14/1)

**2072 Watch Me (IRE)** may have needed this more than it appeared, for she was the first beaten. (7/4)

T/Plpt: £821.30 (16.1 Tckts). T/Qdpt: £771.10 (1.19 Tckts). Dk

# 3054-THIRSK (L-H) (Good to firm)

## Friday August 2nd

WEATHER: sunny periods WIND: mod bhd

## 3223 GO RACING IN YORKSHIRE H'CAP (0-80) (3-Y.O+) (Class D)

2-00 (2-01) **6f** £3,873.00 (£1,164.00: £562.00: £261.00) Stalls: High GOING minus 0.48 sec per fur (F)

| | | | | SP | RR | SF |
|---|---|---|---|---|---|---|
| 3055[2] | **Benzoe (IRE) (77)** (MrsJRRamsden) **6-10-0** JFortune(6) (lw: hld up: hdwy 2f out: shkn up to ld ins fnl f: sn clr)... | — | **1** | 11/10 [1] | 87 | 70 |

| | Horse | | Pos | SP | RR | SF |
|---|---|---|---|---|---|---|
| $868^{8}$ | **Kira (58)** (JLEyre) **6-8-6**(3) NVarley(9) (b.off hind: led tl hdd ins fnl f: no ch w wnr) | 1¾ | **2** | 9/1 | 63 | 46 |
| $3168^{4}$ | **Cheeky Chappy (71)** (DWChapman) **5-9-8b** 7x LCharnock(2) (a cl up: nt qckn fnl f) | nk | **3** | 5/1 2 | 76 | 59 |
| $3055^{7}$ | **Here Comes a Star (74)** (JMCarr) **8-9-11** ACulhane(4) (hld up & bhd: hdwy 2f out: nrst fin) | 1¼ | **4** | 20/1 | 75 | 58 |
| $2725^{8}$ | **Daawe (USA) (68)** (MrsVAAconley) **5-9-5v** NCarlisle(7) (chsd ldrs: effrt 2f out: btn 1f out) | 1 | **5** | 8/1 | 67 | 50 |
| $2870^{5}$ | **Sense of Priority (63)** (DNicholls) **7-9-0** DaleGibson(3) (bhd tl styd on fnl 2f) | 1½ | **6** | 12/1 | 58 | 41 |
| $3055^{6}$ | **Playmaker (71)** (DNicholls) **3-9-4** AlexGreaves(8) (a abt sme plce) | hd | **7** | 25/1 | 65 | 44 |
| *$2937^{4}$* | **Formidable Liz (58)** (MDHammond) **6-8-6**(3) SDrowne(5) (chsd ldrs tl rdn & wknd wl over 1f out) | 1¼ | **8** | 11/2 3 | 49 | 32 |
| $2586^{9}$ | **Featherstone Lane (48)** (MissLCSiddall) **5-7-13v** TWilliams(1) (hld up: effrt ½-wy: sn btn) | 9 | **9** | 20/1 | 15 | — |
| | | | | (SP 121.8%) | | **9 Rn** |

**1m 9.7** (0.00) CSF £12.08 CT £37.14 TOTE £2.00: £1.10 £2.90 £1.90 (£14.60) Trio £34.00 OWNER Mr Tony Fawcett (THIRSK) BRED Mrs P. Grubb

WEIGHT FOR AGE 3yo-4lb

**3055 Benzoe (IRE)**, who did everything right this time, won in style and is obviously in top form. (11/10)
**762 Kira** has done most of her winning over the minimum trip, but did little wrong here, only to find the winner too strong. (9/1)
**3168 Cheeky Chappy** was having his fifth run in ten days and looked as well as ever. He ran as well as could be expected at the weights, as he was well held by the winner on the previous week's running. (5/1)
**2725 Here Comes a Star** showed something this time and may at last be coming right. (20/1)
**2725 Daawe (USA)** has had some hard races and was fighting a lost cause in the last two furlongs. (8/1)
**2870 Sense of Priority** ran pretty well, staying on from the back of the field, and was not over-punished. (12/1)
**3055 Playmaker** again showed something and should improve in due course. (25/1)

## 3224 LEWIS GEIPEL MEMORIAL CHALLENGE CUP NURSERY H'CAP (2-Y.O) (Class D)

2-30 (2-31) **5f** £3,624.50 (£1,091.00: £528.00: £246.50) Stalls: High GOING minus 0.48 sec per fur (F)

| | Horse | | Pos | SP | RR | SF |
|---|---|---|---|---|---|---|
| 2846* | **Bold African (74)** (PDEvans) **2-8-9b** ACulhane(9) (mde most: kpt on wl fnl f) | — | **1** | 5/1 2 | 78 | 45 |
| $2930^{2}$ | **Under Pressure (72)** (TDEasterby) **2-8-7** MBirch(4) (lw: cl up: rdn 2f out: kpt on towards fin) | 1 | **2** | 13/2 | 73 | 40 |
| $2755^{3}$ | **Swiss Coast (IRE) (81)** (MrsJRRamsden) **2-9-2** MFenton(3) (hld up: hdwy 2f out: styd on towards fin) | ½ | **3** | 7/1 | 80 | 47 |
| $2875^{4}$ | **Burkes Manor (86)** (TDBarron) **2-9-7** JFortune(2) (hld up & bhd: hdwy 2f out: nt qckn ins fnl f) | 1¼ | **4** | 12/1 | 81 | 48 |
| 2781* | **Ballymote (78)** (JBerry) **2-8-13** GCarter(5) (cl up tl wknd appr fnl f) | 1¼ | **5** | 2/1 1 | 69 | 36 |
| $2625^{9}$ | **Melbourne Princess (73)** (RMWhitaker) **2-8-8** DeanMcKeown(6) (lw: in tch: effrt 2f out: nt qckn) | 1½ | **6** | 25/1 | 59 | 26 |
| $2792^{4}$ | **Fine Times (62)** (CWFairhurst) **2-7-11** DaleGibson(8) (nvr wnt pce) | 1¾ | **7** | 6/1 3 | 43 | 10 |
| $2965^{5}$ | **Divide And Rule (82)** (RHollinshead) **2-9-0**(3) FLynch(1) (outpcd & no imp fr ½-wy) | ¾ | **8** | 12/1 | 60 | 27 |
| $2926^{2}$ | **Antares (68)** (NTinkler) **2-8-3** KimTinkler(7) (cl up: edgd lft ½-wy: wknd wl over 1f out) | 4 | **9** | 12/1 | 34 | 1 |
| | | | | (SP 117.0%) | | **9 Rn** |

**58.4 secs** (0.40) CSF £34.80 CT £210.27 TOTE £6.00: £1.40 £1.60 £1.80 (£16.40) Trio £60.90 OWNER Mr D. Maloney (WELSHPOOL) BRED G. Dickinson

**2846* Bold African**, whose win at Musselburgh has obviously done him good, showed fine courage to make virtually all this time. (5/1)
**2930 Under Pressure** looked well and is off a mark that should see her win a similar event. (13/2)
**2755 Swiss Coast (IRE)**, patiently ridden, was keeping on again at the end, suggesting that his turn will come in due course. (7/1: op 9/2)
**2875 Burkes Manor** seems to have his own ideas about the game, but this incessant tooth-grinder has plenty of ability. (12/1: op 8/1)
**2781* Ballymote** had his chances but, when the pressure was on, he was a shade disappointing. (2/1)
**2361 Melbourne Princess** never made her presence felt, but she did look particularly well, and may still be learning. (25/1)

## 3225 PETER BELL MEMORIAL H'CAP (0-70) (3-Y.O F) (Class E)

3-00 (3-00) **1m 4f** £3,187.50 (£960.00: £465.00: £217.50) Stalls: High GOING minus 0.48 sec per fur (F)

| | Horse | | Pos | SP | RR | SF |
|---|---|---|---|---|---|---|
| $2895^{2}$ | **Trilby (65)** (PFICole) **3-9-7** ACulhane(5) (led 3f: cl up: led 3f out tl ins fnl f: sn led again & styd on wl) | — | **1** | 5/2 1 | 74 | 39 |
| $2067^{12}$ | **Daira (62)** (JDBethell) **3-9-1**(3) SDrowne(3) (hld up: swtchd & hdwy over 2f out: slt ld ins fnl f: sn hdd: r.o) | hd | **2** | 20/1 | 71 | 36 |
| $2439^{5}$ | **Alisura (63)** (JRFanshawe) **3-9-2**(3) NVarley(2) (lw: trckd ldrs: pushed along 5f out: n.m.r over 2f out: r.o one pce) | 4 | **3** | 4/1 2 | 67 | 32 |
| $2542^{3}$ | **Fiona Shann (USA) (53)** (JLDunlop) **3-8-9** JFortune(6) (a chsng ldrs: rdn to chal 3f out: outpcd fnl 2f) | ¾ | **4** | 5/2 1 | 56 | 21 |
| $2731^{4}$ | **Time For A Glass (40)** (DMoffatt) **3-7-7**(3) DarrenMoffatt(9) (nvr nr to chal) | 6 | **5** | 7/1 | 35 | — |
| $2927^{4}$ | **Ship's Dancer (53)** (DonEnricoIncisa) **3-8-9** KimTinkler(4) (bhd: sme hdwy appr st: n.d) | 3½ | **6** | 66/1 | 43 | 8 |
| $3059^{6}$ | **La Fandango (IRE) (41)** (MWEasterby) **3-7-11**ow1 DaleGibson(1) (in tch tl outpcd fnl 3½f) | 1½ | **7** | 14/1 | 29 | — |
| $2346^{7}$ | **Snowpoles (54)** (MrsJCecil) **3-8-10** GCarter(8) (lw: sn cl up: led after 3f to 3f out: sn wknd) | 1¼ | **8** | 5/1 3 | 40 | 5 |
| $2019^{7}$ | **Carmosa (USA) (57)** (DNicholls) **3-8-13** AlexGreaves(7) (bhd: effrt appr st: sn btn) | 12 | **9** | 33/1 | 27 | — |
| | | | | (SP 122.2%) | | **9 Rn** |

**2m 34.1** (4.10) CSF £44.95 CT £186.18 TOTE £3.50: £1.20 £3.00 £2.00 (£18.90) Trio £11.70 OWNER H R H Prince Fahd Salman (WHATCOMBE) BRED Newgate Stud Co

STEWARDS' ENQUIRY Culhane susp. 12-13/8/96 (incorrect use of whip)

**2895 Trilby** enjoyed the step back up in distance and, after looking in trouble, fought back bravely. (5/2)
**1600* Daira**, after a poor effort last time, was back to form, but lack of a recent run probably just made the difference. (20/1)
**2439 Alisura**, looking particularly well, had her chances but she is basically short of toe and, because of that, was always struggling for room in which to manoeuvre. She will win a race before long, probably over a bit further. (4/1)
**2542 Fiona Shann (USA)**, stepped up in trip, had her chances but found the last two furlongs just beyond her. (5/2: op 6/4)
**2731 Time For A Glass** ran reasonably without getting into it, and does deserve a change of luck. (7/1: 10/1-11/2)
**Snowpoles** is a very lean individual indeed and, after making much of the running, she folded up double-quick when challenged. (5/1: 4/1-6/1)

## 3226 GROSVENOR CASINOS MAIDEN STKS (3-Y.O+) (Class D)

3-30 (3-31) **1m** £4,107.00 (£1,236.00: £598.00: £279.00) Stalls: Low GOING minus 0.48 sec per fur (F)

| | Horse | | Pos | SP | RR | SF |
|---|---|---|---|---|---|---|
| $2996^{2}$ | **Royal Result (USA)** (MRStoute) **3-8-12** MFenton(5) (lw: mde most: shkn up & r.o fnl f) | — | **1** | 1/5 1 | 62 | 30 |
| | **Vanadium Ore** (JLEyre) **3-8-12** JFortune(3) (leggy: scope: trckd ldrs: hdwy to chal over 1f out: r.o) | ¾ | **2** | 100/1 | 61 | 29 |
| $1690^{5}$ | **Alrayyih (USA)** (JHMGosden) **3-8-12** AMcGlone(7) (disp ld tl wl outpcd fnl 2½f) | 6 | **3** | 4/1 2 | 49 | 17 |
| $2572^{8}$ | **Road Racer (IRE)** (MrsJRRamsden) **3-8-12** NKennedy(1) (hld up: effrt 3f out: nvr nr to chal) | 8 | **4** | 25/1 3 | 33 | 1 |
| | **Rasin Charge** (RCraggs) **5-9-5** DeanMcKeown(4) (wl grwn: bkwd: s.s: nvr nr ldrs) | ¾ | **5** | 200/1 | 31 | 6 |
| $2794^{11}$ | **Meadow Blue** (MissLCSiddall) **3-8-7** GCarter(2) (nvr nr to chal) | s.h | **6** | 300/1 | 26 | — |

| | | | | SP | RR | SF |
|---|---|---|---|---|---|---|
| 3058$^{5}$ | **Mystical Mind** (DNicholls) **3-8-12** AlexGreaves(8) (in tch tl lost pl 3f out) | 9 | **7** | 66/1 | 13 | — |

(SP 110.5%) **7 Rn**

**1m 39.1** (2.60) CSF £17.12 TOTE £1.30: £1.10 £5.80 (£15.10) OWNER Mr Mana Al Maktoum (NEWMARKET) BRED Dr. J. Fred Miller III
WEIGHT FOR AGE 3yo-7lb

**2996 Royal Result (USA)** did what was required, but he was inclined to look about in the last two furlongs and needed waking up.(1/5: op 1/3)
**Vanadium Ore**, a rather leggy colt who really uses himself well, gave the winner quite a fright. Although rather flattered by his proximity to the winner, he should have little difficulty in finding a race. (100/1)
**1690 Alrayyih (USA)** raced with the winner, but the effort proved too much some way out. This was a shade disappointing. (4/1)
**Road Racer (IRE)**, who failed to get into it, left the impression that he is learning, and will do better in time. (25/1)
**Rasin Charge**, a big, strong sort, needed this to gain both fitness and experience, but did show a little. (200/1)

## 3227 GOLDEN FLEECE CLAIMING STKS (2-Y.O) (Class F)
4-05 (4-07) **7f** £2,827.50 (£790.00: £382.50) Stalls: Low GOING minus 0.48 sec per fur (F)

| | | | | SP | RR | SF |
|---|---|---|---|---|---|---|
| 2984$^{3}$ | **Dashing Rocksville (62)** (MRChannon) **2-8-5**ow1 JFortune(5) (hld up: effrt 2f out: qcknd to ld ins fnl f: jst hld on) | — | **1** | 3/1$^{1}$ | 61 | 14 |
| 2926$^{3}$ | **Sandbaggedagain (72)** (MWEasterby) **2-8-11** DaleGibson(6) (sn pushed along: hdwy whn nt clr run 2f out tl ins fnl f: fin fast) | s.h | **2** | 9/2$^{2}$ | 67+ | 21 |
| | **Pirate's Girl** (SirMarkPrescott) **2-8-6** CNutter(10) (cmpt: bit bkwd: sn chsng ldrs: rn green 3f out: styd on wl towards fin) | ¾ | **3** | 6/1$^{3}$ | 60+ | 14 |
| 3046$^{7}$ | **Irish Fiction (IRE) (74)** (DJSCosgrove) **2-8-9** MRimmer(4) (chsd ldrs: swtchd rt 2f out: styd on: nt qckn towards fin) | nk | **4** | 3/1$^{1}$ | 63 | 17 |
| *2750$^{3}$* | **Soviet Lady (IRE) (55)** (JLEyre) **2-8-0** TWilliams(3) (b.off hind: cl up: led over 1f out tl ins fnl f: no ex) | ½ | **5** | 9/1 | 52 | 6 |
| 2850* | **Sweeping Statement (55)** (JBerry) **2-8-0**ow1 GCarter(1) (led tl hdd over 1f out: sn btn) | 2 | **6** | 10/1 | 48 | 1 |
| 3057$^{6}$ | **Jib Jab** (DNicholls) **2-8-11** AlexGreaves(7) (nvr plcd to chal) | 4 | **7** | 15/2 | 50 | 4 |
| 2733$^{5}$ | **Scarrots** (SCWilliams) **2-8-13** JTate(9) (hdwy & prom appr st: wknd 3f out) | 1 | **8** | 10/1 | 49 | 3 |
| 2923$^{8}$ | **Poignant (IRE)** (MRChannon) **2-8-5** AMackay(8) (dwlt: a bhd) | 5 | **9** | 33/1 | 30 | — |
| 1183$^{8}$ | **Classic Partygoer** (MWEasterby) **2-8-9** MBirch(2) (lost tch fnl 3f) | 1½ | **10** | 25/1 | 31 | — |

(SP 129.2%) **10 Rn**

**1m 27.3** (3.10) CSF £18.08 TOTE £4.20: £1.40 £1.90 £2.90 (£11.20) Trio £31.20 OWNER The Crews Missile Syndicate (UPPER LAMBOURN) BRED B. D. Cantle

**2984 Dashing Rocksville**, produced from off the pace, showed a good turn of foot to lead inside the final furlong and stole just enough to hang on. (3/1)
**2926 Sandbaggedagain**, never on the bridle, got messed about no end in the last two furlongs and, with any luck at all, would certainly have won. (9/2)
**Pirate's Girl**, who looked likely to be all the better for this, spoiled his chances by running very green early in the straight. She should be a different proposition next time. (6/1)
**2509 Irish Fiction (IRE)** ran pretty well, having his chances in the straight, but was always short of a bit of room and a turn of foot to do anything about it. (3/1)
**2750 Soviet Lady (IRE)** ran well, but just failed to see the trip out on this occasion. (9/1)
**2850* Sweeping Statement** ran a fair race until running out of petrol approaching the final furlong. She might be the type for nurseries. (10/1)

## 3228 COWESBY MAIDEN APPRENTICE H'CAP (0-70) (3-Y.O+) (Class F)
4-35 (4-35) **7f** £2,595.50 (£738.00: £366.50) Stalls: Low GOING minus 0.48 sec per fur (F)

| | | | | SP | RR | SF |
|---|---|---|---|---|---|---|
| 3055$^{4}$ | **Lucky Revenge (63)** (MartynMeade) **3-9-3**(5) ClaireAngell(4) (a.p: hdwy to ld over 1f out: styd on) | — | **1** | 5/2$^{1}$ | 67 | 38 |
| 3052$^{8}$ | **Gool Lee Shay (USA) (56)** (RMWhitaker) **3-9-1** PFredericks(3) (sn outpcd & bhd: hdwy 3f out: styd on wl: nrst fin) | 1½ | **2** | 16/1 | 57 | 28 |
| 3102$^{4}$ | **Fisiostar (37)** (MDods) **3-7-10b** CLowther(7) (b.hind: a chsng ldrs: one pce fnl 2f) | nk | **3** | 9/2$^{3}$ | 37 | 8 |
| 2902$^{6}$ | **Backhander (IRE) (48)** (MartynWane) **4-8-8**(5) GWright(1) (led tl hdd over 1f out: sn btn) | 4 | **4** | 7/1 | 39 | 16 |
| *2751$^{6}$* | **Clued Up (43)** (PDEvans) **3-8-2b$^{1}$** TFinn(2) (in tch: hrd rdn over 2f out: one pce) | nk | **5** | 16/1 | 33 | 4 |
| 2617$^{4}$ | **Time of Night (USA) (69)** (RGuest) **3-10-0** CScudder(8) (lw: a cl up: effrt 3f out: wknd over 1f out) | s.h | **6** | 3/1$^{2}$ | 59 | 30 |
| | **Arc of The Diver (IRE) (56)** (JBerry) **3-8-10**(5) GMills(6) (in tch tl outpcd fnl 3f) | 1½ | **7** | 16/1 | 43 | 14 |
| 3059$^{14}$ | **Sis Garden (43)** (TDEasterby) **3-7-11b**(5) SCrawford(5) (bhd: effrt 3f out: n.d) | ¾ | **8** | 5/1 | 28 | — |

(SP 118.6%) **8 Rn**

**1m 26.6** (2.40) CSF £35.97 CT £161.87 TOTE £3.40: £1.50 £5.10 £1.30 (£26.40) OWNER Mr Stephen Bayless (MALMESBURY) BRED T. Barratt
LONG HANDICAP Fisiostar 7-5
WEIGHT FOR AGE 3yo-6lb
STEWARDS' ENQUIRY Finn susp. 12-16/8/96 (excessive use of whip).

**3055 Lucky Revenge**, given a fine ride by her inexperienced apprentice, appreciated this slightly longer trip and won nicely. (5/2)
**Gool Lee Shay (USA)**, dropping back in trip once again, ran a fine race but, judging from the way he finished, a mile might be the answer. (16/1)
**3102 Fisiostar** had his chances, but lacked the pace to ever take them. (9/2)
**2358 Backhander (IRE)**, the most experienced of these, found little when the pressure was on in the straight. (7/1)
**Clued Up**, in blinkers for the first time, was given a hard ride and failed to respond. (16/1)
**2617 Time of Night (USA)** raced freely up with the pace and then found nothing when ridden. (3/1)

T/Plpt: £20.70 (505.29 Tckts). T/Qdpt: £7.80 (80.29 Tckts). AA

# 3210-GOODWOOD (R-H) (Good to firm)
## Saturday August 3rd
WEATHER: sunny WIND: almost nil

## 3229 VODAPAGE CONDITIONS STKS (3-Y.O) (Class B)
2-00 (2-03) **1m** £14,300.00 (£5,300.00: £2,550.00: £1,050.00: £425.00: £175.00) Stalls: High GOING minus 0.20 sec per fur (GF)

| | | | | SP | RR | SF |
|---|---|---|---|---|---|---|
| 3067* | **Hammerstein (101)** (MRStoute) **3-9-2** PatEddery(7) (lw: a.p: led over 2f out: rdn out) | — | **1** | 5/1 | 112 | 87 |

3067[3] **Russian Music (103)** (MissGayKelleway) **3-8-12** RCochrane(3) (lw: hld up: rdn & swtchd lft over 2f out: r.o ins fnl f)....1½ **2** 7/2[2] 105 80
2197* **Kammtarra (USA) (100)** (SbinSuroor) **3-8-12** JReid(2) (lw: led 1f: ev ch over 2f out: unable qckn) ....¾ **3** 9/2[3] 104 79
2888[7] **Swift Fandango (USA) (90)** (PFICole) **3-8-12** TQuinn(9) (wl bhd 6f: hdwy over 1f out: r.o wl ins fnl f) ....3½ **4** 33/1 97 72
2621[3] **Censor (89)** (HRACecil) **3-8-12** WRyan(8) (led 7f out tl over 2f out: sn wknd) ....1 **5** 14/1 95 70
2888[2] **My Lewicia (IRE) (99)** (PWHarris) **3-8-7** GHind(5) (dwlt: hdwy 7f out: hrd rdn 3f out: wknd over 2f out) ....½ **6** 3/1[1] 89 64
2888[8] **Polar Eclipse (97)** (MJohnston) **3-8-12** MHills(6) (a bhd) ....2 **7** 33/1 90 65
2774[3] **Van Gurp (95)** (BAMcMahon) **3-8-10** SSanders(4) (prom over 5f) ....9 **8** 16/1 70 45
445* **Insiyabi (USA) (92)** (JLDunlop) **3-8-12** KDarley(1) (lw: hld up: hmpd over 5f out: sn wknd) ....1 **9** 9/1 70 45
(SP 110.5%) **9 Rn**

**1m 36.89** (-0.31) CSF £20.61 TOTE £4.40: £1.70 £1.60 £1.40 (£7.70) Trio £9.10 OWNER Sheikh Mohammed (NEWMARKET) BRED Sheikh Mohammed bin Rashid al Maktoum
**3067* Hammerstein** followed up his win of the previous Saturday at Ascot, and only needed to be ridden along to make sure. (5/1)
**3067 Russian Music**, 4lb better off with the winner for a three-and-a-half-length beating at Ascot, took some time to get going, but did run on inside the final furlong. His trainer believes the colt could win a Group race by the end of the year. (7/2)
**2197* Kammtarra (USA)**, always handy, had every chance over two furlongs out before tapped for toe. (9/2)
**Swift Fandango (USA)**, soon miles off the leaders with apparently no hope, found his feet from below the distance, but it was all too late. (33/1)
**2621 Censor** was soon in trouble once collared. (14/1)
**2888 My Lewicia (IRE)** was very disappointing. She came under pressure three furlongs out and soon capitulated. (3/1)

## 3230 VODATA NURSERY H'CAP (2-Y.O) (Class C)

2-30 (2-31) **7f** £10,690.00 (£3,220.00: £1,560.00: £730.00) Stalls: High GOING minus 0.20 sec per fur (GF)

SP RR SF

2875* **Double Park (FR) (88)** (MJohnston) **2-9-7** JReid(7) (lw: mde all: rdn over 2f out: r.o wl) ....— **1** 4/1[2] 94 55
2733[3] **Falls O'Moness (IRE) (67)** (KRBurke) **2-7-9**(5) MartinDwyer(1) (chsd wnr: ev ch over 1f out: unable qckn)....2 **2** 11/2[3] 68 29
2797[2] **Misty Cay (IRE) (74)** (SDow) **2-8-7** JFEgan(4) (bmpd & nt clr run over 5f out: hdwy over 2f out: hrd rdn over 1f out: one pce) ....4 **3** 7/1 66 27
2733* **Sun O'Tirol (IRE) (75)** (MRChannon) **2-8-8** TQuinn(5) (carried wd over 5f out: nt clr run 3f out: rdn over 2f out: hdwy over 1f out: one pce)....1¼ **4** 7/1 64 25
2702[4] **Golden Fact (USA) (88)** (RHannon) **2-9-7** PatEddery(6) (carried wd over 5f out: rn wd st: hdwy over 2f out: wknd over 1f out)....½ **5** 11/4[1] 76 37
2708[12] **Midatlantic (79)** (PTWalwyn) **2-8-12** SSanders(8) (lw: s.s: slipped on ins over 5f out: bhd fnl 3f) ....1½ **6** 25/1 64 25
2323[5] **Trading Aces (70)** (MBell) **2-8-0**(3) FLynch(3) (b.hind: prom over 4f)....3½ **7** 7/1 47 8
*2371*[2] **Loch Dibidale (63)** (JEBanks) **2-7-7**(3) NVarley(2) (prom over 4f)....2 **8** 16/1 35 —
(SP 109.3%) **8 Rn**

**1m 27.61** (2.81) CSF £23.05 CT £122.30 TOTE £3.20: £1.30 £1.30 £1.80 (£7.80) OWNER The 3rd Middleham Partnership (MIDDLEHAM) BRED Gainsborough Stud Management Ltd
IN-FOCUS: **The three nurseries run at this meeting were all won by horses shouldering 9-7, two of them trained by Jack Berry, who should always be followed here.**
**2875* Double Park (FR)** was much better suited by this longer trip, and was on top from below the distance. (4/1)
**2733 Falls O'Moness (IRE)** was always second. She looked to be going better than the winner when throwing down her challenge in the straight, but that one found another gear below the distance. She will probably run in the Tattersalls Ireland Bonus Race, an event with IR£100,000 on offer, at the Curragh. (11/2)
**2797 Misty Cay (IRE)** met with interference in the early part of the race, and could only go up and down in the same place once under pressure. (7/1)
**2733* Sun O'Tirol (IRE)**, who did not have the best of runs in the first half of the race, picked up below the distance, but could then make no further impression. (7/1)
**2702 Golden Fact (USA)**, who took a very wide course into the straight, moved up over a quarter of a mile out, but had nothing more to give below the distance. (11/4)

## 3231 VODAFONE NASSAU STKS (Gp 2) (3-Y.O+ F & M) (Class A)

3-10 (3-11) **1m 2f** £50,593.00 (£18,787.00: £9,068.50: £3,767.50: £1,558.75: £675.25) Stalls: High GOING minus 0.20 sec per fur (GF)

SP RR SF

2052[2] **Last Second (IRE)** (SirMarkPrescott) **3-8-6** GDuffield(1) (rdn & hdwy 2f out: led ins fnl f: r.o wl) ....— **1** 7/4[1] 116 59
2991* **Papering (IRE) (101)** (LMCumani) **3-8-6** KDarley(5) (swtg: hld up: led over 1f out tl ins fnl f: unable qckn) ....2 **2** 6/1[3] 113 56
2036* **Annaba (IRE) (85)** (JHMGosden) **3-8-6** GHind(3) (hld up: led over 2f out tl over 1f out: ev ch ins fnl f: one pce)....½ **3** 16/1 112 55
1769[6] **Whitewater Affair (105)** (MRStoute) **3-8-6** RCochrane(7) (b: swtg: rdn over 3f out: hdwy over 1f out: r.o)....1¼ **4** 11/2[2] 110 53
2277a[5] **Mezzogiorno (108)** (GWragg) **3-8-6** MHills(2) (stdy hdwy over 4f out: rdn over 2f out: wknd over 1f out)....1½ **5** 13/2 108 51
2609[6] **Sardonic (104)** (HRACecil) **3-8-6** WRyan(8) (lw: a.p: chsd ldr 6f out tl over 4f out: wknd 3f out)....1 **6** 14/1 106 49
2502[2] **Miss Universal (IRE) (106)** (CEBrittain) **3-8-6** BDoyle(4) (led over 6f: wknd over 2f out) ....2 **7** 10/1 103 46
2677[3] **Solar Crystal (IRE) (107)** (HRACecil) **3-8-6** PatEddery(6) (chsd ldr 4f: chsd ldr over 4f out: led over 3f out tl over 2f out: sn wknd)....10 **8** 8/1 87 30
(SP 112.1%) **8 Rn**

**2m 7.45** (1.95) CSF £11.72 TOTE £2.40: £1.50 £1.60 £3.00 (£6.40) OWNER Mr Faisal Salman (NEWMARKET) BRED Miss K. Rausing and Mrs S. M. Rogers
**2052 Last Second (IRE)** is a fragile filly who can not run very often as she takes her races very hard. Off since her tremendous second in the Coronation Stakes at Royal Ascot, she put up another breathtaking display and swooped through to lead inside the final furlong. A high-class filly, she will now have a rest before going for either the Champion Stakes or the Sun Chariot. (7/4: 5/4-15/8)
**2991* Papering (IRE)**, rather edgy in the parade, was unable to cope with the winner inside the final furlong. Her trainer believes she will be better over a mile and a half. (6/1)
**2036* Annaba (IRE)**, taking a big step up in class, ran a tremendous race. Sent on over two furlongs out, she was headed below the distance and tapped for toe. She will be even better over further and can find a nice prize this season. (16/1)
**1335* Whitewater Affair** stayed on from below the distance, but found it all over bar the shouting. (11/2)
**2277a Mezzogiorno** appears to have run up a bit light. Cruising into the action entering the straight, she failed to find what was required when asked. (13/2)
**2609 Sardonic** had shot her bolt three furlongs out. (14/1)

## 3232 VODAC STEWARDS' CUP H'CAP (3-Y.O+) (Class B)

3-45 (3-46) **6f** £49,062.50 (£14,750.00: £7,125.00: £3,312.50) Stalls: Low GOING minus 0.20 sec per fur (GF)

| | Horse | Dist | Pos | SP | RR | SF |
|---|---|---|---|---|---|---|
| 2694* | **Coastal Bluff (91)** (TDBarron) **4-8-5** 3x JFortune(29) (b.hind: a.p: led 2f out: clr over 1f out: r.o wl) | — | **1** | 10/1[1] | 107+ | 71 |
| 2329* | **Double Bounce (87)** (PJMakin) **6-8-1** DHolland(23) (hdwy over 1f out: hrd rdn: r.o wl ins fnl f) | 3 | **2** | 10/1[1] | 95 | 59 |
| 2381[3] | **Sir Joey (USA) (89)** (PGMurphy) **7-8-0**(3)ow2 SDrowne(28) (hld up: rdn over 2f out: chsd wnr 1f out tl ins fnl f: unable qckn) | 1¼ | **3** | 20/1 | 94 | 56 |
| 3038* | **Bolshoi (IRE) (82)** (JBerry) **4-7-10b** 7x NAdams(15) (dwlt: rdn over 2f out: hdwy over 1f out: r.o) | hd | **4** | 14/1 | 86 | 50 |
| 2584* | **Wildwood Flower (93)** (RHannon) **3-8-0**(3)ow3 3x DaneO'Neill(7) (racd stands' side: hrd rdn & hdwy over 1f out: r.o wl ins fnl f) | 1 | **5** | 16/1 | 95 | 52 |
| 2400[2] | **My Best Valentine (89)** (JWhite) **6-8-3** WWoods(30) (lw: hld up: hrd rdn over 1f out: one pce) | hd | **6** | 22/1 | 91 | 55 |
| 2880[3] | **Venture Capitalist (112)** (DNicholls) **7-9-12** RCochrane(3) (racd stands' side: hdwy over 1f out: r.o) | hd | **7** | 16/1 | 113 | 77 |
| 2545[4] | **Loch Patrick (105)** (MMadgwick) **6-9-5** JReid(6) (lw: racd stand side: nt clr run 2f out: hdwy over 1f out: r.o) | hd | **8** | 33/1 | 106 | 70 |
| 2880* | **Jayannpee (110)** (IABalding) **5-9-5**(5) 7x MartinDwyer(11) (lw: a.p: led over 2f out: sn hdd: wknd fnl f) | hd | **9** | 20/1 | 111 | 75 |
| 2545[9] | **To the Roof (IRE) (99)** (PWHarris) **4-8-13** GHind(2) (lw: racd stands' side: prom over 4f) | nk | **10** | 16/1 | 99 | 63 |
| 2856[8] | **Shamanic (88)** (RHannon) **4-8-2** CRutter(17) (outpcd: hdwy 1f out: nvr nrr) | hd | **11** | 50/1 | 88 | 52 |
| 2889[2] | **Lago Di Varano (87)** (RMWhitaker) **4-7-12v**(3)ow2 FLynch(12) (lw: no hdwy fnl 2f) | ¾ | **12** | 40/1 | 85 | 47 |
| 2584[4] | **Duel At Dawn (90)** (JHMGosden) **3-8-0** AGarth(4) (b: b.hind: racd stands' side: prom over 4f) | hd | **13** | 40/1 | 87 | 47 |
| 2725[5] | **Shikari's Son (84)** (JCullinan) **9-7-12** GBardwell(24) (nt clr run on ins 2f out: hdwy over 1f out: one pce) | hd | **14** | 25/1 | 81 | 45 |
| 3038[2] | **Sylva Paradise (IRE) (86)** (CEBrittain) **3-7-10** JQuinn(25) (prom 4f) | ½ | **15** | 12/1[3] | 82 | 42 |
| 2623[11] | **Emerging Market (100)** (JLDunlop) **4-9-0** KDarley(13) (lw: prom over 4f) | s.h | **16** | 25/1 | 96 | 60 |
| 2220[2] | **Selhurstpark Flyer (IRE) (92)** (JBerry) **5-8-1**(5)ow3 PRoberts(21) (w ldr over 3f) | nk | **17** | 22/1 | 87 | 48 |
| 2880[4] | **Espartero (IRE) (102)** (SirMarkPrescott) **4-9-2** GDuffield(20) (nvr nrr) | nk | **18** | 11/1[2] | 96 | 60 |
| 2497[5] | **Astrac (IRE) (92)** (RAkehurst) **5-8-6** SSanders(14) (lw: prom 4f) | hd | **19** | 20/1 | 86 | 50 |
| 2856[7] | **Lennox Lewis (85)** (APJarvis) **4-7-13** JFEgan(5) (racd stands' side: hld up: rdn over 2f out: sn wknd) | 1¼ | **20** | 20/1 | 75 | 39 |
| 2694[21] | **Master of Passion (82)** (JMPEustace) **7-7-10** NKennedy(9) (lw: racd stands' side: rdn over 2f out: hdwy over 1f out: wknd fnl f) | ¾ | **21** | 50/1 | 70 | 34 |
| 2856[9] | **Bold Effort (FR) (90)** (KOCunningham-Brown) **4-8-4v**[1] BDoyle(26) (a mid div) | s.h | **22** | 50/1 | 78 | 42 |
| 3085[3] | **For the Present (83)** (TDBarron) **6-7-11** LCharnock(1) (racd stands' side: prom over 3f) | s.h | **23** | 20/1 | 71 | 35 |
| 3126[9] | **Brave Edge (107)** (RHannon) **5-9-7** PatEddery(22) (bhd fnl 2f) | ¾ | **24** | 33/1 | 93 | 57 |
| 3038[4] | **Dashing Blue (100)** (IABalding) **3-8-10** TQuinn(19) (hld up: rdn over 2f out: sn wknd) | nk | **25** | 25/1 | 85 | 45 |
| 2853[3] | **Hard to Figure (108)** (RJHodges) **10-9-8** TSprake(18) (a bhd) | hd | **26** | 50/1 | 93 | 57 |
| 2889[5] | **The Happy Fox (IRE) (82)** (BAMcMahon) **4-7-10b** DeclanO'Shea(16) (bhd fnl 3f) | 1 | **27** | 50/1 | 64 | 28 |
| 2007[9] | **Norwegian Blue (IRE) (88)** (APJarvis) **3-7-9v**[1](3) DWright(8) (racd stands' side: a.p: ev ch over 2f out: wknd over 1f out) | 1¼ | **28** | 50/1 | 67 | 27 |
| 2220* | **Cyrano's Lad (IRE) (96)** (CADwyer) **7-8-10** KFallon(27) (led over 3f: wknd wl over 1f out) | 2½ | **29** | 11/1[2] | 68 | 32 |
| 2150* | **Statoyork (86)** (BWHills) **3-7-7**(3) MHenry(10) (racd stands' side: hld up: rdn over 2f out: sn wknd) | 1¾ | **30** | 25/1 | 54 | 14 |

(SP 137.3%) **30 Rn**

**1m 10.14** (0.14) CSF £99.32 CT £1,821.83 TOTE £9.40: £3.50 £2.80 £5.00 £3.70 (£35.70) Trio £215.50 OWNER Mrs D. E. Sharp (THIRSK) BRED R. M. West

LONG HANDICAP Bolshoi (IRE) 7-1 Sylva Paradise (IRE) 7-8 Statoyork 7-9

WEIGHT FOR AGE 3yo-4lb

IN-FOCUS: **The temporary running rail, which had been on the far side, was removed for the final day, giving those drawn high a fresh strip of ground to race on.**

**2694* Coastal Bluff** made the most of his plum draw and turned it into something of a procession. He has never had the best of luck with the draw in the past and showed here exactly how good he is. (10/1)

**2329* Double Bounce**, who pulled muscles in his quarters after winning at Newcastle, only began to get going below the distance. Threading his way through the field, he ran on strongly, but the winner had flown. He now goes for the Ayr Gold Cup. (10/1)

**2381 Sir Joey (USA)**, who finished in front on the far side in the Wokingham, ran another fine race, from a better draw this time, and remains in cracking form. (20/1)

**3038* Bolshoi (IRE)**, set to rise 9lb in future handicaps, was doing all his best work in the final furlong and a half. (14/1)

**2584* Wildwood Flower**, with a poor draw, did best of the stands'-side group. She looks to be improving fast. (16/1)

**2400 My Best Valentine**, high in the weights at present, was unable to make his good draw count. (22/1)

**2880 Venture Capitalist** ran a solid race considering he had topweight and a bad draw, staying on nicely from the rear below the distance. (16/1)

## 3233 TURF CLUB CLAIMING STKS (3-Y.O+) (Class D)

4-15 (4-17) **1m** £7,570.00 (£2,260.00: £1,080.00: £490.00) Stalls: High GOING minus 0.20 sec per fur (GF)

| | Horse | Dist | Pos | SP | RR | SF |
|---|---|---|---|---|---|---|
| 2882[9] | **At Liberty (IRE) (84)** (RHannon) **4-9-4**(3) DaneO'Neill(3) (a.p: chsd ldr 5f out: led over 1f out: rdn out) | — | **1** | 5/2[2] | 82 | 64 |
| | **Loki (IRE) (80)** (GLewis) **8-8-8** PatEddery(5) (hld up: rdn over 2f out: r.o wl ins fnl f) | 1¼ | **2** | 15/8[1] | 67 | 49 |
| 2975[4] | **Open Affair** (APJarvis) **3-7-11**(3) DWright(4) (chsd ldr 3f: rdn over 2f out: r.o ins fnl f) | ½ | **3** | 15/2 | 65 | 40 |
| 2128[8] | **Ultimate Warrior (65)** (CACyzer) **6-8-10** RCochrane(2) (lw: led over 6f: wknd ins fnl f) | 1¼ | **4** | 10/1 | 65 | 47 |
| 3071[10] | **Otto E Mezzo (90)** (MJPolglase) **4-9-6** JReid(1) (hld up: rdn over 2f out: sn wknd) | 2½ | **5** | 11/4[3] | 70 | 52 |

(SP 110.9%) **5 Rn**

**1m 39.53** (2.33) CSF £7.31 TOTE £4.10: £2.00 £1.20 (£3.30) OWNER Mr Bruce Adams (MARLBOROUGH) BRED Pegasus Farm

WEIGHT FOR AGE 3yo-7lb

**2055 At Liberty (IRE)** was given a confidence-booster by his trainer, who admitted it was very difficult to know where to place him. Hannon believes him to be better at a mile and a half. (5/2)

**Loki (IRE)**, making a belated reappearance, found this trip too sharp. Covered up, it was not until the final furlong that he really started to pick up. He needs at least a mile and a quarter. (15/8)

**2975 Open Affair** stuck well to her task in the straight. (15/2)

**1772 Ultimate Warrior** would have been much better off in a handicap. (10/1)

**1867 Otto E Mezzo** was hung out to dry a quarter of a mile out. (11/4)

## 3234 RICHARD BAERLEIN MAIDEN STKS (Unraced 2-Y.O) (Class D)

4-45 (4-46) **6f** £7,067.50 (£2,140.00: £1,045.00: £497.50) Stalls: Low GOING minus 0.20 sec per fur (GF)

| | Horse | Dist | Pos | SP | RR | SF |
|---|---|---|---|---|---|---|
| | **The West (USA)** (PFICole) **2-9-0** TQuinn(5) (str: scope: lw: chsd ldr: led over 1f out: comf) | — | **1** | 4/7[1] | 89t+ | 60 |

| | | | Pos | SP | RR | SF |
|---|---|---|---|---|---|---|
| | **Elegant Warning (IRE)** (BWHills) **2-8-9** PatEddery(2) (leggy: hdwy over 2f out: ev ch over 1f out: nt qckn) | 1½ | 2 | 11/2$^{2}$ | 80 t | 51 |
| | **Marengo** (JAkehurst) **2-9-0v$^{1}$** SSanders(3) (unf: led over 4f: wknd fnl f) | 3½ | 3 | 25/1 | 76 t | 47 |
| | **Shifting Time** (IABalding) **2-8-9** KDarley(4) (w'like: scope: a.p: rdn 3f out: wknd wl over 1f out) | 2½ | 4 | 9/1 | 64 t | 35 |
| | **Miss Riviera Rose** (GWragg) **2-8-9** MHills(6) (unf: scope: dwlt: rdn over 2f out: hdwy over 1f out: wknd) | 1¼ | 5 | 7/1$^{3}$ | 61 t | 32 |
| | **Hallmark (IRE)** (RHannon) **2-8-11**$^{(3)}$ DaneO'Neill(7) (leggy: rdn over 3f out: bhd fnl 2f) | 3 | 6 | 16/1 | 58 t | 29 |
| | **Mister Jay** (PTWalwyn) **2-9-0** JReid(1) (lengthy: dipped: a bhd) | 2½ | 7 | 25/1 | 51 t | 22 |

(SP 115.1%) **7 Rn**

**1m 11.45** (1.45) CSF £4.43 TOTE £1.60: £1.30 £2.00 (£2.60) OWNER H R H Prince Fahd Salman (WHATCOMBE) BRED Mr and Mrs John C. Mabee

**The West (USA)**, an attractive, good-bodied individual who cost $140,000, is extremely well regarded and was even entered at the five-day stage for Thursday's Richmond Stakes. He looked absolutely superb in the paddock and, always travelling supremely well, won as he liked. He looks a high-class colt in the making, and may go straight for a Group race. (4/7)
**Elegant Warning (IRE)**, a tall half-sister to three winners, will not always meet one so good. (11/2: 3/1-6/1)
**Marengo**, an unfurnished newcomer, was rather worryingly fitted with a visor for this debut, but still showed ability. (25/1)
**Shifting Time**, a half-sister to Poker Chip and Double Bluff, was close up until calling enough entering the final quarter-mile. (9/1: op 5/1)
**Miss Riviera Rose**, a half-sister to Toujours Riviera, made a brief effort below the distance. (7/1: op 5/2)

## 3235 TRUNDLE H'CAP (0-85) (3-Y.O+) (Class D)

5-20 (5-23) **1m 4f** £7,960.00 (£2,380.00: £1,140.00: £520.00) Stalls: Low GOING minus 0.20 sec per fur (GF)

| | | | Pos | SP | RR | SF |
|---|---|---|---|---|---|---|
| 2884$^{4}$ | **Casual Water (IRE) (70)** (AGNewcombe) **5-8-13**$^{(3)}$ SDrowne(4) (hld up: rdn 3f out: led last stride) | — | 1 | 6/1$^{2}$ | 74 | 60 |
| 2549$^{10}$ | **Mr Browning (USA) (70)** (RAkehurst) **5-9-2b** SSanders(1) (led: hrd rdn 2f out: hdd last stride) | s.h | 2 | 15/2 | 74 | 60 |
| 2589* | **Puce (80)** (LMCumani) **3-9-1** PatEddery(2) (a.p: rdn over 3f out: ev ch over 1f out: one pce) | 2½ | 3 | 13/8$^{1}$ | 81 | 56 |
| 2196* | **Shaha (72)** (RHannon) **3-8-4b**$^{(3)}$ DaneO'Neill(6) (chsd ldr: rdn over 3f out: wknd 1f out) | 3½ | 4 | 7/1$^{3}$ | 68 | 43 |
| 3073$^{12}$ | **Roisin Clover (70)** (SDow) **5-9-2** KFallon(9) (lw: hld up: rdn over 4f out: wknd 2f out) | 2½ | 5 | 14/1 | 63 | 49 |
| 2900$^{5}$ | **Kings Cay (IRE) (60)** (THCaldwell) **5-7-13**$^{(7)}$ JoHunnam(5) (lw: a bhd) | 1¾ | 6 | 10/1 | 50 | 36 |
| 2857$^{5}$ | **Silently (78)** (IABalding) **4-9-10b$^{1}$** KDarley(7) (lw: a bhd) | 3½ | 7 | 8/1 | 64 | 50 |
| *2202$^{3}$* | ***White Sea (IRE) (77)*** (PFICole) **3-8-12** TQuinn(8) (Withdrawn not under Starter's orders: ref to ent stalls & uns rdr) | | W | 7/1$^{3}$ | — | — |

(SP 116.0%) **7 Rn**

**2m 36.96** (3.76) CSF £36.27 CT £71.39 TOTE £7.30: £3.00 £2.90 (£24.50) Trio £19.40 OWNER Mr G. H. Leatham (BARNSTAPLE) BRED Dunderry Stud
WEIGHT FOR AGE 3yo-11lb

**2884 Casual Water (IRE)** bounced back to form, and always looked likely to just get there once starting his challenge. (6/1)
**Mr Browning (USA)** set out to make it all and did nothing wrong, but was collared right on the line. He is a winner without a penalty. (15/2)
**2589* Puce**, settled in third, was rousted along as the Bugler called entering the straight, and failed to contain the front two from below the distance. (13/8)
**2196* Shaha** conceded the inevitable a furlong out. (7/1)
**844* Roisin Clover** was hung out to dry two furlongs out. (14/1)

T/Jkpt: £1,122.60 (49.34 Tckts). T/Plpt: £13.00 (3,818.08 Tckts). T/Qdpt: £5.80 (363.28 Tckts). AK

# 2678-HAMILTON (R-H) (Good to firm)

## Saturday August 3rd

WEATHER: fine WIND: almost nil

## 3236 VARIETY CLUB CHARITY AMATEUR H'CAP (0-65) (3-Y.O+) (Class F)

5-50 (5-51) **6f 5y** £2,484.00 (£684.00: £324.00) Stalls: Low GOING minus 0.51 sec per fur (F)

| | | | Pos | SP | RR | SF |
|---|---|---|---|---|---|---|
| 2567$^{6}$ | **Roseate Lodge (37)** (SEKettlewell) **10-10-3** MrSKettlewell(3) (lw: outpcd stands' side tl swtchd lft & hdwy ½-wy: r.o to ld ins fnl f) | — | 1 | 15/2 | 40 | 14 |
| *2940$^{9}$* | **Bella Coola (29)** (MartynMeade) **4-9-9** MrSRutherford(2) (chsd ldrs stands' side: kpt on wl fnl f) | 1 | 2 | 12/1 | 29 | 3 |
| 2849$^{5}$ | **Six for Luck (65)** (DANolan) **4-12-3**$^{ow18}$ MrDNolan(5) (cl up stands' side: led 2f out tl ins fnl f) | hd | 3 | 25/1 | 65 | 21 |
| 2851$^{2}$ | **Seconds Away (30)** (JSGoldie) **5-9-10** MissPRobson(8) (w ldrs far side: nt qckn ins fnl f) | ½ | 4 | 5/1$^{3}$ | 29 | 3 |
| 2910* | **Sunday Mail Too (IRE) (50)** (MissLAPerratt) **4-11-2** MrJWeymes(7) (lw: led far side over 3f: kpt on one pce) | s.h | 5 | 7/2$^{1}$ | 49 | 23 |
| *2937$^{8}$* | **Shaa Spin (51)** (JBerry) **4-11-3** MrRHale(4) (racd stands' side: nvr trbld ldrs) | 2½ | 6 | 14/1 | 43 | 17 |
| 1846$^{5}$ | **Sallyoreally (IRE) (38)** (WStorey) **5-10-4** MissMCarson(10) (lw: cl up far side: led over 2f out tl wknd ins fnl f) | s.h | 7 | 5/1$^{3}$ | 30 | 4 |
| 2964$^{4}$ | **Henry the Hawk (48)** (MDods) **5-11-0** MrSSwiers(6) (b: lw: w ldrs far side tl wknd appr fnl f) | 1 | 8 | 9/2$^{2}$ | 37 | 11 |
| 2914$^{7}$ | **Aye Ready (33)** (MissLAPerratt) **3-9-9v**$^{ow2}$ MrGWoodward(9) (racd far side: s.i.s: a outpcd & bhd) | 4 | 9 | 50/1 | 12 | — |
| 2324$^{6}$ | **Halliard (63)** (RMMcKellar) **5-12-1**$^{ow1}$ MrRMcKellar(1) (led stands' side 4f: wknd qckly: dead) | 17 | 10 | 10/1 | — | — |

(SP 114.8%) **10 Rn**

**1m 14.1** (4.10) CSF £80.84 CT £1,929.69 TOTE £10.20: £2.00 £6.20 £2.10 (£126.00) Trio £123.80; £158.71 to Ripon 5/8/96 OWNER Mr Jon Firth (MIDDLEHAM) BRED Barrettstown Stud Farms Ltd
LONG HANDICAP Aye Ready 9-1
WEIGHT FOR AGE 3yo-4lb

**2567 Roseate Lodge**, who last won over this trip three years ago, found his staying power winning him the day this time. This ended a long losing run. (15/2)
**Bella Coola**, who had shown little previously, finished in a style which suggested that there is probably a race in her, perhaps over further. (12/1)
**2849 Six for Luck** ran a tremendous race considering he was putting up 18lb overweight, and this was by far his best effort for some time. (25/1)
**2851 Seconds Away** again had his chances, but failed to respond to pressure. (5/1)
**2910* Sunday Mail Too (IRE)** is never one to fully rely on. (7/2)
**1846 Sallyoreally (IRE)**, who looked particularly well, had her chances, but again failed to take them. (5/1)
**2964 Henry the Hawk** would have preferred the minimum trip and soft ground. He is beginning to show signs of a return to form though. (9/2)

## 3237 GLENGOYNE SINGLE HIGHLAND MALT SCOTCH WHISKY MAIDEN STKS (2-Y.O) (Class D)
6-20 (6-21) **6f 5y** £3,517.50 (£1,065.00: £520.00: £247.50) Stalls: Low GOING minus 0.51 sec per fur (F)

| Form | Horse | Dist | Pos | SP | RR | SF |
|---|---|---|---|---|---|---|
| *2633[8]* | **Nant Y Gamer (FR)** (JBerry) **2-9-0** JFanning(2) (mde all: styd on wl u.p fnl 2f) | — | **1** | 25/1 | 72 | 28 |
| 2904[2] | **Kaiser Kache (IRE) (77)** (KMcAuliffe) **2-8-9**[(5)] RHavlin(3) (w wnr: rdn over 2f out: kpt on one pce) | 1½ | **2** | 4/1[3] | 68 | 24 |
| 2967[6] | **William Wallace** (CMurray) **2-9-0** AMackay(1) (lw: trckd ldrs: effrt 2f out: ev ch over 1f out: sn rdn & btn) | 1¾ | **3** | 3/1[2] | 63 | 19 |
| 2727[2] | **Canadian Fantasy (93)** (MJohnston) **2-9-0** TWilliams(4) (chsd ldrs: outpcd after 2f: eased whn wl btn fnl f) | 7 | **4** | 1/2[1] | 45 | 1 |
| | | | | (SP 115.5%) | **4 Rn** | |

**1m 11.9** (1.90) CSF £95.52 TOTE £14.00: (£22.80) OWNER Lord Mostyn (COCKERHAM) BRED Mrs Carolyn Elwes
**2211 Nant Y Gamer (FR)** won this in good style and it was certainly no fluke. (25/1)
**2904 Kaiser Kache (IRE)** is in good form. He stays well and should pick up a run-of-the-mill event. (4/1: 3/1-9/2)
**2967 William Wallace**, dropped in trip, looked dangerous, but failed to pick up when asked. (3/1)
**2727 Canadian Fantasy** proved very disappointing and was never going the pace from halfway. He is doing so well physically that he probably needs a bit more time to come to himself. (1/2)

## 3238 ROTHMANS ROYALS NORTH SOUTH CHALLENGE SERIES H'CAP (0-80) (3-Y.O) (Class D)
6-50 (6-50) **1m 1f 36y** £7,067.50 (£2,140.00: £1,045.00: £497.50) Stalls: High GOING minus 0.51 sec per fur (F)

| Form | Horse | Dist | Pos | SP | RR | SF |
|---|---|---|---|---|---|---|
| 2855[3] | **Call Me (70)** (CWThornton) **3-9-1** DeanMcKeown(4) (lw: trckd ldr: led & qcknd 3f out: pushed out) | — | **1** | Evens[1] | 75 | 30 |
| *3063[5]* | **Nose No Bounds (IRE) (76)** (MJohnston) **3-9-7b** TWilliams(3) (led tl hdd 3f out: kpt on one pce) | 2 | **2** | 9/2[3] | 78 | 33 |
| 2752[2] | **Gulf of Siam (62)** (MissSEHall) **3-8-7** AMackay(1) (hld up: effrt over 3f out: no ex u.p appr fnl f) | 2 | **3** | 5/2[2] | 60 | 15 |
| 2962[8] | **Termon (61)** (MissLAPerratt) **3-8-6** JFanning(2) (hld up: hdwy 4f out: rdn & btn wl over 2f out) | 12 | **4** | 7/1 | 38 | — |
| | | | | (SP 109.3%) | **4 Rn** | |

**1m 57.6** (3.30) CSF £5.24 TOTE £1.90: (£2.30) OWNER Mr Guy Reed (MIDDLEHAM) BRED J. M. Greetham
**2855 Call Me** has been running consistently well all year. Once she struck the front three furlongs out, she was not going to be beaten. (Evens)
**3063 Nose No Bounds (IRE)** keeps trying hard, but he just set the race up for the winner and was always second best. (9/2)
**2752 Gulf of Siam**, looking lean and edgy, had his chances, but failed to go through with the effort. (5/2)
**2358* Termon**, who did not impress on looks, went out like a light once the pressure was on. (7/1: op 9/2)

## 3239 BURNBANK (S) STKS (3-Y.O+) (Class G)
7-20 (7-21) **1m 65y** £2,402.00 (£672.00: £326.00) Stalls: High GOING minus 0.51 sec per fur (F)

| Form | Horse | Dist | Pos | SP | RR | SF |
|---|---|---|---|---|---|---|
| 2731[2] | **North Ardar (62)** (JJO'Neill) **6-9-4**[(5)] SCopp(3) (hld up: hdwy to ld wl over 2f out: rdn & styd on strly) | — | **1** | 4/6[1] | 66 | 32 |
| 2520[2] | **Tibbi Blues** (WStorey) **9-8-7**[(7)] IonaWands(4) (mde most tl hdd wl over 2f out: sn outpcd) | 9 | **2** | 11/8[2] | 40 | 6 |
| 2931[3] | **School of Science (25)** (DANolan) **6-9-5** VHalliday(2) (disp ld 2f: cl up tl rdn & wknd 4f out) | 12 | **3** | 20/1[3] | 22 | — |
| 2931[5] | **Corky's Girl (32)** (RMMcKellar) **4-8-7**[(7)] DMcGaffin(1) (w ldrs tl rdn & wknd qckly 4f out: t.o) | dist | **4** | 66/1 | — | — |
| | | | | (SP 108.4%) | **4 Rn** | |

**1m 47.7** (3.60) CSF £1.86 TOTE £2.00: (£1.20) OWNER Mr A. K. Collins (PENRITH) BRED Mrs H.Seddington
Bt in 6,800 gns
**2731 North Ardar**, dropped in distance, had a simple task here and did it well enough. (4/6)
**2520 Tibbi Blues** would not settle early on and was well outclassed by the winner in the final three furlongs. (11/8)
**2931 School of Science** seems to use up all his energy in the paddock. (20/1)
**Corky's Girl** looked very moderate once the race began in earnest. (66/1)

## 3240 EVENING TIMES H'CAP (0-70) (3-Y.O F) (Class E)
7-50 (7-51) **6f 5y** £3,631.25 (£1,100.00: £537.50: £256.25) Stalls: Low GOING minus 0.51 sec per fur (F)

| Form | Horse | Dist | Pos | SP | RR | SF |
|---|---|---|---|---|---|---|
| 2680* | **Natural Key (56)** (DHaydnJones) **3-8-7** AMackay(2) (lw: hld up: effrt over 1f out: led ins fnl f: r.o wl) | — | **1** | 5/4[1] | 61 | 23 |
| 2914[3] | **Pathaze (49)** (NBycroft) **3-8-0** JFanning(3) (hld up: stdy hdwy to ld over 1f out: hdd ins fnl f: r.o) | 1¼ | **2** | 5/1[3] | 51 | 13 |
| 1666[8] | **Naissant (70)** (RMMcKellar) **3-9-7** TWilliams(4) (led tl hdd over 1f out: sn outpcd) | 6 | **3** | 20/1 | 56 | 18 |
| 3228* | **Lucky Revenge (63)** (MartynMeade) **3-9-0** DeanMcKeown(1) (cl up: effrt 2½f out: sn btn) | 2½ | **4** | 11/8[2] | 42 | 4 |
| | | | | (SP 108.0%) | **4 Rn** | |

**1m 11.8** (1.80) CSF £6.60 TOTE £2.20: (£3.40) OWNER Mr Hugh O'Donnell (PONTYPRIDD) BRED Cheveley Park Stud Ltd
**OFFICIAL EXPLANATION Lucky Revenge: the jockey reported that the filly had lost her action at the two furlong marker.**
**2680* Natural Key** is really firing at present and won in most authoritative fashion. (5/4)
**2914 Pathaze** is showing more consistency at present and there could be a race in her. (5/1)
**1323 Naissant**, who changed stables recently, was dropped back in trip and showed plenty of speed. (20/1)
**3228* Lucky Revenge**, a winner the previous day, may just have been feeling that race, as she failed to fire at all. (11/8: op 4/5)

## 3241 EAGLE TAVERN TAM PARKS MAIDEN AUCTION STKS (2-Y.O) (Class F)
8-20 (8-21) **5f 4y** £2,619.00 (£734.00: £357.00) Stalls: Low GOING minus 0.51 sec per fur (F)

| Form | Horse | Dist | Pos | SP | RR | SF |
|---|---|---|---|---|---|---|
| 2614[3] | **Jeffrey Anotherred** (KMcAuliffe) **2-8-3**[(5)ow1] RHavlin(6) (chsd ldrs: rdn to ld wl ins fnl f) | — | **1** | 2/1[2] | 69 | 15 |
| 2781[3] | **Balladoole Bajan** (MJohnston) **2-8-6** TWilliams(2) (disp ld tl led appr fnl f: hdd & nt qckn towards fin) | ½ | **2** | 11/8[1] | 65 | 12 |
| 2932[3] | **Keen To Please** (DenysSmith) **2-8-2** JFanning(7) (disp ld tl hdd appr fnl f: no ex) | 2 | **3** | 100/30[3] | 55 | 2 |
| 3169[5] | **Marsh Marigold** (MartynMeade) **2-7-7**[(7)] KSked(3) (lw: hung rt most of wy: nvr trbld ldrs) | 5 | **4** | 14/1 | 37 | — |
| 2926[6] | **My Girl (51)** (JBerry) **2-8-0** AMackay(5) (chsd ldrs: sn drvn along: wknd fnl 2f) | 3½ | **5** | 20/1 | 26 | — |
| 3082[6] | **Alisadara (50)** (NBycroft) **2-7-5b**[1(7)] IonaWands(1) (prom tl outpcd fr ½-wy) | 1¼ | **6** | 50/1 | 20 | — |
| | | | | (SP 111.9%) | **6 Rn** | |

**60.3 secs** (2.00) CSF £5.01 TOTE £3.40: £2.40 £1.40 (£2.30) OWNER Highgrove Developments Ltd (LAMBOURN) BRED John Rose
**2614 Jeffrey Anotherred**, all the sharper for his first run, settled it in determined style late on. (2/1)
**2781 Balladoole Bajan** was in the thick of things all the way and kept plugging away, but was just tapped for foot. Her turn will come. (11/8)
**2932 Keen To Please** showed plenty of speed, but this lightly-made sort failed to last home. (100/30)
**3169 Marsh Marigold** gave her rider problems by hanging right for much of the way, and certainly did not give her running. (14/1)
**2926 My Girl** failed to impress on looks and showed little in the race. (20/1)
**3082 Alisadara**, blinkered for the first time, found them having absolutely no effect. (50/1)

**3242** LINN MOTOR GROUP 'V40' H'CAP (0-70) (3-Y.O+) (Class E)
8-50 (8-50) **1m 3f 16y** £3,647.50 (£1,105.00: £540.00: £257.50) Stalls: High GOING minus 0.51 sec per fur (F)

| Form | Horse | Dist | Pos | SP | RR | SF |
|---|---|---|---|---|---|---|
| 2953$^{2}$ | **Askern (65)** (DHaydnJones) **5-10-0** AMackay(1) (lw: chsd ldrs: led over 2f out: r.o strly) | — | 1 | 7/4$^{1}$ | 76 | 58 |
| 2917$^{5}$ | **Tissue of Lies (USA) (68)** (MJohnston) **3-9-7** TWilliams(2) (lw: cl up: led wl over 3f out tl over 2f out: kpt on wl) | 2 | 2 | 6/1$^{3}$ | 76 | 48 |
| 3098$^{2}$ | **Lord Advocate (51)** (DANolan) **8-8-9b**$^{(5)}$ RHavlin(8) (a chsng ldrs: effrt 4f out: r.o one pce) | 3 | 3 | 5/1$^{2}$ | 55 | 37 |
| 2356$^{6}$ | **Rapid Mover (37)** (DANolan) **9-7-7b**$^{(7)ow4}$ KSked(3) (led tl hdd wl over 3f out: sn outpcd) | 5 | 4 | 20/1 | 34 | 12 |
| 2988$^{3}$ | **Dr Edgar (58)** (MDods) **4-9-7** JFanning(7) (bhd: hdwy 4f out: sn chsng ldrs: one pce fnl 2f) | 2½ | 5 | 6/1$^{3}$ | 51 | 33 |
| 2682$^{5}$ | **Funny Rose (33)** (PMonteith) **6-7-3**$^{(7)}$ JBramhill(4) (lw: effrt ½-wy: rdn & no imp) | ½ | 6 | 33/1 | 25 | 7 |
| 2683$^{3}$ | **Warwick Mist (IRE) (33)** (BMactaggart) **4-7-3**$^{(7)}$ IonaWands(5) (prom tl outpcd fnl 3f) | 4 | 7 | 8/1 | 19 | 1 |
| 2418$^{2}$ | **Northern Motto (53)** (WStorey) **3-8-6** DeanMcKeown(6) (bit bkwd: a bhd) | hd | 8 | 6/1$^{3}$ | 39 | 11 |

(SP 114.7%) **8 Rn**

**2m 21.2** (1.80) CSF £12.08 CT £40.08 TOTE £3.20: £1.80 £1.70 £2.00 (£17.70) OWNER Mr Hugh O'Donnell (PONTYPRIDD) BRED Highclere Stud Ltd
LONG HANDICAP Rapid Mover 7-7 Funny Rose 7-0
WEIGHT FOR AGE 3yo-10lb

**2953 Askern** has two ways of running, but is in top form at present, and won in tremendous style. (7/4: op 3/1)
**2917 Tissue of Lies (USA)** is running well and, now that his stable has really struck form, he can find a race. (6/1)
**3098 Lord Advocate** could never summon the speed to get to the front this time, and failed to make any serious impression. (5/1)
**1309 Rapid Mover** last won three years ago, but this was his best effort for a while. (20/1)
**2988 Dr Edgar** was never doing enough once off the bit in the last half-mile. (6/1: op 4/1)
**2418 Northern Motto**, who had had a month off, needed the outing. Dropped in distance, he never showed. (6/1: op 3/1)

T/Plpt: Not won; £5,968.81 to Ripon 5/8/96. T/Qdpt: £13.10 (27.97 Tckts). AA

## 3217-NEWMARKET (R-H) (Good to firm)
## Saturday August 3rd
WEATHER: fine WIND: almost nil

**3243** HERO CONDITIONS STKS (2-Y.O) (Class C)
2-05 (2-06) **7f (July)** £5,376.00 (£1,856.00: £888.00: £360.00) Stalls: Centre GOING minus 0.55 sec per fur (F)

| Form | Horse | Dist | Pos | SP | RR | SF |
|---|---|---|---|---|---|---|
| 2580* | **Bahhare (USA)** (JLDunlop) **2-9-1** RHills(2) (lw: sn trckng ldr: led 2f out: qcknd clr: easily) | — | 1 | 1/3$^{1}$ | 111++ | 59 |
| 2997$^{5}$ | **Rich In Love (IRE) (96)** (CACyzer) **2-8-12** RHughes(4) (led: rdn & hdd 2f out: unable qckn) | 6 | 2 | 16/1 | 94? | 42 |
| 2607$^{6}$ | **Quest Express** (MBell) **2-9-1** MFenton(1) (swvd lft s: hld up: rdn 2f out: edgd lft & no imp) | 1½ | 3 | 11/2$^{2}$ | 94 | 42 |
| 2527* | **Mr Bombastique (IRE)** (BWHills) **2-8-6**$^{(5)}$ JDSmith(3) (lw: chsd ldrs: rdn 3f out: sn btn) | 7 | 4 | 12/1$^{3}$ | 74 | 22 |

(SP 104.0%) **4 Rn**

**1m 24.55** (0.38 under 2y best) (-0.45) CSF £4.65 TOTE £1.20: (£3.40) OWNER Mr Hamdan Al Maktoum (ARUNDEL) BRED Shadwell Farm Inc
**2580* Bahhare (USA)** always had matters under control. Showing fine acceleration to win impressively in a decent time, he is clearly ready to step up to Group company. (1/3)
**2997 Rich In Love (IRE)** beat Young Bigwig at Ripon and is clearly useful in her own right, but she was comprehensively outpaced by the winner. (16/1)
**2607 Quest Express** was another to let down the form of the July Stakes, ducking to his left when the stalls were opened and then hanging as pressure was applied. (11/2: 4/1-6/1)
**2527* Mr Bombastique (IRE)**, stepping up in class, was finding the pace too hot soon after halfway. (12/1: op 8/1)

**3244** YE OLDE OAK HAM CLAIMING STKS (3-Y.O) (Class D)
2-35 (2-36) **7f (July)** £4,425.00 (£1,320.00: £630.00: £285.00) Stalls: Centre GOING minus 0.55 sec per fur (F)

| Form | Horse | Dist | Pos | SP | RR | SF |
|---|---|---|---|---|---|---|
| 3166* | **Ortolan (80)** (RHannon) **3-9-5** RHughes(5) (chsd ldrs: led over 2f out: sn clr: rdn out) | — | 1 | 5/4$^{1}$ | 86 | 55 |
| 3217$^{9}$ | **Uncle George (63)** (MHTompkins) **3-8-5b** PRobinson(3) (hld up: hdwy fnl 2f: nt rch wnr) | 2 | 2 | 9/2$^{2}$ | 67 | 36 |
| 3172$^{7}$ | **Ivory's Grab Hire (60)** (KTIvory) **3-8-8b**$^{(7)}$ CScally(1) (swtg: hdwy over 3f out: hmpd over 2f out: r.o) | 7 | 3 | 10/1 | 61 | 30 |
| *2325*$^{11}$ | **Cebwob (75)** (PFICole) **3-8-10** RHills(7) (b.hind: lw: hld up: r.o fnl 2f: nvr able to chal) | 2½ | 4 | 10/1 | 51 | 20 |
| 2943$^{7}$ | **Leith Academy (USA) (70)** (BWHills) **3-8-6** PaulEddery(8) (chsd ldrs: rdn 3f out: sn btn) | 1 | 5 | 10/1 | 44 | 13 |
| 2859$^{6}$ | **Sweet Amoret (46)** (PHowling) **3-8-2** FNorton(4) (rdn 3f out: sn bhd) | hd | 6 | 33/1 | 40 | 9 |
| 2903$^{8}$ | **Hotlips Houlihan (42)** (RJRWilliams) **3-7-7**$^{(5)}$ MBaird(9) (disp ld over 4f: wnt lft & sn bhd) | ¾ | 7 | 20/1 | 35 | 4 |
| *2636*$^{3}$ | **Mystical Maid (58)** (HThomsonJones) **3-8-3**$^{(3)}$ PMcCabe(2) (lw: hdwy & carried lft over 2f out: rdn & wknd over 1f out) | 2½ | 8 | 7/1$^{3}$ | 37 | 6 |
| 2946$^{9}$ | **On The Home Run (43)** (JRJenkins) **3-7-3b**$^{(7)}$ PDoe(6) (disp ld tl hmpd & wknd over 2f out) | 7 | 9 | 33/1 | 11 | — |

(SP 113.0%) **9 Rn**

**1m 25.16** (0.16) CSF £6.96 TOTE £2.00: £1.20 £1.30 £2.70 (£3.80) Trio £12.90 OWNER Mr J. A. Lazzari (MARLBOROUGH) BRED Filletts Farm Stud
**3166* Ortolan** outclassed these when forging clear, but was struggling to maintain the advantage in the final furlong, and may be better suited to six. (5/4: 4/5-6/4)
**3217 Uncle George**, who ran deplorably here the night before, bounced back to form as if nothing had happened. Consistency would not be his strong suit. (9/2)
**2763 Ivory's Grab Hire**, warm and on his toes, was stopped in his run and could never get near the leaders thereafter. (10/1)
**Cebwob**, who has not grown much and was dwarfed by some of her rivals, looked fit and moved to post well. She tried hard in the last couple of furlongs, but this is probably as good as she is now. (10/1)
**Leith Academy (USA)**, dropped in distance, took a keen hold on the way down, and could do nothing once the race got under way. (10/1)
**2859 Sweet Amoret**, dropped in trip, again failed to dominate. This is best ignored. (33/1)

**3245** E.B.F. CLEARLY CANADIAN MAIDEN STKS (2-Y.O) (Class D)
3-05 (3-07) **6f (July)** £4,464.00 (£1,332.00: £636.00: £288.00) Stalls: Centre GOING minus 0.55 sec per fur (F)

| Form | Horse | Dist | Pos | SP | RR | SF |
|---|---|---|---|---|---|---|
| 2624$^{5}$ | **Musical Pursuit** (MHTompkins) **2-9-0** PRobinson(10) (mde all: rdn & r.o wl appr fnl f) | — | 1 | 11/4$^{1}$ | 96+ | 56 |

**Bachelors Pad** (WJarvis) **2-9-0** BThomson(8) (leggy: unf: bit bkwd: hdwy 2f out: r.o wl fnl f) ....4 **2** 20/1 85 45

$2852^{3}$ **Olivo (IRE)** (PFICole) **2-9-0** AClark(11) (chsd ldrs: rdn 2f out: kpt on) ....nk **3** $3/1^{2}$ 85 45

**Rejoicing (IRE)** (WAO'Gorman) **2-8-9** EmmaO'Gorman(6) (leggy: scope: bit bkwd: sn pushed along & bhd: gd hdwy over 1f out: r.o) ....½ **4** 33/1 78 38

$2624^{11}$ **Shaddad (USA)** (JLDunlop) **2-9-0** RHills(4) (w wnr 4f: wknd fnl f) ....1 **5** 10/1 81 41

**Jalb (IRE)** (ACStewart) **2-9-0** DHarrison(5) (scope: bkwd: chsd ldrs: rdn & outpcd 3f out: r.o again appr fnl f) ....1¾ **6** 14/1 76 36

$1344^{6}$ **Return of Amin** (JDBethell) **2-9-0** PaulEddery(9) (hld up: effrt 2f out: nvr rchd ldrs) ....5 **7** 33/1 63 23

**Mowjood (USA)** (MRStoute) **2-9-0** RHughes(7) (w'like: scope: bhd: effrt 2f out: nvr trbld ldrs) ....2 **8** $9/2^{3}$ 57 17

$2892^{7}$ **Classic Line** (JLDunlop) **2-8-9** WJO'Connor(2) (in tch 4f) ....2½ **9** 33/1 46 6

**Moonshiner (USA)** (GWragg) **2-9-0** FNorton(3) (w'like: bit bkwd: dwlt: nvr nr to chal) ....1 **10** 9/1 48 8

**Home Alone** (JHMGosden) **2-9-0** AMcGlone(1) (b.hind: w'like: unf: hld up: a bhd) ....5 **11** 20/1 35 —

(SP 114.0%) **11 Rn**

**1m 11.74** (-0.26) CSF £47.50 TOTE £3.50: £1.60 £4.10 £1.40 (£26.90) Trio £22.00 OWNER Mr B. Schmidt-Bodner (NEWMARKET) BRED Theakston Stud

**2624 Musical Pursuit** knew more this time and put his experience to good use, stretching the field from halfway. He has a good action, which together with his equally good attitude, should enable him to win more races. (11/4: 4/1-2/1)

**Bachelors Pad** is splendidly named. Rather keen on the way to post, he settled well in the race and came home strongly. He should not be hard to place. (20/1)

**2852 Olivo (IRE)** was very free going to post. Bred to need further, he will have to learn to settle if he is to fulfil his potential. (3/1)

**Rejoicing (IRE)**, very green early on, got the message late in the race and showed plenty of promise. (33/1)

**2624 Shaddad (USA)** looked calm in the paddock this time and ran much better, only fading late on. Even so, it is still hard to see this brother to Shadayid living up to his pedigree. (10/1)

**Jalb (IRE)**, far from fully wound up, showed some promise over a trip that is likely to prove a long way short of his best. (14/1: op 8/1)

**Mowjood (USA)**, an attractive, well-bred newcomer, did not show much, but will come into his own a longer trip. (9/2)

**Moonshiner (USA)**, the first foal of Marling, looked well in himself but in need of the race. A poor start cost him his chance, but he is a very good mover, and ought to pay his way. (9/1)

## 3246 YE OLDE OAK H'CAP (0-80) (3-Y.O) (Class D)

3-35 (3-36) **1m (July)** £4,581.00 (£1,368.00: £654.00: £297.00) Stalls: Centre GOING minus 0.55 sec per fur (F)

SP RR SF

$2621^{7}$ **Sky Dome (IRE) (78)** (MHTompkins) **3-9-7** PRobinson(8) (mde all: qcknd over 2f out: rdn & r.o wl fnl f) ....— **1** $9/2^{3}$ 92 36

$1662^{4}$ **Divine Quest (65)** (HRACecil) **3-8-8** AMcGlone(3) (a.p: rdn over 1f out: r.o) ....1½ **2** 11/2 76 20

$2334^{5}$ **Quality (IRE) (77)** (WAO'Gorman) **3-9-6** EmmaO'Gorman(6) (lw: hld up: hdwy over 1f out: nrst fin) ....1¾ **3** 14/1 85 29

3165* **Sylvan Princess (56)** (CNAllen) **3-7-6**(7) 6x PDoe(5) (trckd ldrs: rdn 2f out: one pce) ....¾ **4** $2/1^{1}$ 62 6

3120* **Smarter Charter (74)** (MrsJRRamsden) **3-9-3** 6x OUrbina(4) (lw: hld up: r.o fnl 2f: nvr able to chal) ....1½ **5** $7/2^{2}$ 77 21

2899* **Disallowed (IRE) (75)** (MBell) **3-8-11**(7) GFaulkner(2) (trckd wnr: rdn over 2f out: sn btn) ....nk **6** 8/1 77 21

*$3063^{8}$* **China Castle (58)** (PCHaslam) **3-7-10**(5) MBaird(7) (hld up: rdn over 2f out: no imp) ....5 **7** 20/1 50 —

$1119^{6}$ **Premier Generation (IRE) (64)** (DWPArbuthnot) **3-8-7** SWhitworth(1) (b: in tch 5f: sn bhd) ....5 **8** 9/1 46 —

(SP 121.7%) **8 Rn**

**1m 39.48** (2.28) CSF £28.82 CT £303.62 TOTE £5.50: £1.70 £1.60 £3.30 (£18.30) OWNER Miss D. J. Merson (NEWMARKET) BRED Andrew Bradley

**2621 Sky Dome (IRE)**, as with many from this yard, was returning from a spell in the doldrums, although he did win on the wrong side in Fahim's race at the July Meeting. Making it all, he had his rivals at full stretch by the time they reached the rising ground. (9/2)

**1662 Divine Quest** led early on in her first couple of races, but could never get the better of the winner here. She did keep trying though and deserves to lose her maiden tag before long. (11/2)

**2334 Quality (IRE)** again stayed on late in the day and would have got closer but for meeting traffic problems. He did best of those coming from behind. (14/1)

**3165* Sylvan Princess**, bidding for a quick four-timer, was flat out and finding no more in the final quarter-mile. (2/1)

**3120* Smarter Charter** was set plenty to do off this fast pace and could never get to grips with the leaders. (7/2: 5/2-4/1)

**2899* Disallowed (IRE)**, dropping in trip, took the winner on, but went too fast, and was a spent force some way out. (8/1)

## 3247 HERO LITE NURSERY H'CAP (2-Y.O) (Class C)

4-10 (4-10) **6f (July)** £18,437.50 (£5,500.00: £2,625.00: £1,187.50) Stalls: Centre GOING minus 0.55 sec per fur (F)

SP RR SF

2879* **Miss Stamper (IRE) (95)** (RHannon) **2-9-2** DHarrison(4) (lw: trckd ldrs: led over 1f out: hung lft & sn rdn clr) ....— **1** $5/2^{1}$ 102 58

2495* **Demolition Man (84)** (JWWatts) **2-8-5** BThomson(7) (lw: hdwy over 2f out: rdn over 1f out: r.o ins fnl f) ....2½ **2** $11/4^{2}$ 84 40

$3044^{3}$ **Ultra Boy (75)** (PCHaslam) **2-7-3**(7) RMullen(3) (led 1f: rdn over 1f out: r.o) ....¾ **3** 8/1 73 29

$2726^{4}$ **Exit To Rio (CAN) (93)** (MrsJRRamsden) **2-9-0** OUrbina(1) (hdwy 2f out: r.o fnl f) ....½ **4** 10/1 90 46

$2890^{4}$ **For Old Times Sake (97)** (JBerry) **2-8-13**(5) MBaird(2) (led after 1f: hdd over 1f out: wknd ins fnl f) ....1½ **5** 10/1 90 46

$2070^{9}$ **For Your Eyes Only (100)** (TDEasterby) **2-9-7** MBirch(9) (b: prom over 4f) ....½ **6** 11/2 92 48

$2985^{2}$ **Ocker (IRE) (81)** (MHTompkins) **2-8-2** PRobinson(5) (lw: w ldr: wknd appr fnl f) ....6 **7** $5/1^{3}$ 57 13

$2700^{4}$ **Nomore Mr Niceguy (91)** (EJAlston) **2-8-12** JLowe(6) (in tch: rdn 2f out: no imp) ....1 **8** 16/1 64 20

(SP 122.5%) **8 Rn**

**1m 11.72** (-0.28) CSF £10.25 CT £45.65 TOTE £3.00: £1.30 £1.40 £2.50 (£4.20) Trio £23.10 OWNER J B R Leisure Ltd (MARLBOROUGH) BRED Eamon O'Mahony

LONG HANDICAP Ultra Boy 7-9

**2879* Miss Stamper (IRE)**, whose Newbury form has been franked aplenty, fairly skated in once given her head, and would have won by further but for hanging violently to the far rail. (5/2)

**2495* Demolition Man** proved rather too free going down, but came back really well, staying on strongly in the final quarter-mile. Another furlong looks within his compass. (11/4: 7/4-3/1)

**3044 Ultra Boy** looked very harshly treated with the runner-up on their Haydock meeting, but got very much closer this time and is obviously going the right way. (8/1)

**2726 Exit To Rio (CAN)**, one of the best movers in the race, looked a tricky ride as he raced with his head rather high when making his move. (10/1: 7/1-11/1)

**2890 For Old Times Sake**, whose four wins have come at the minimum trip, certainly found the sixth furlong too far in this company. (10/1)

**1699* For Your Eyes Only** could not dominate in this company, and tended to edge behind rivals as pressure was applied. (11/2: 10/1-5/1)

## 3248 NGK SPARK PLUGS H'CAP (0-90) (3-Y.O+) (Class C)

4-40 (4-40) **1m 2f (July)** £6,004.00 (£1,792.00: £856.00: £388.00) Stalls: High GOING minus 0.55 sec per fur (F)

| | | | | SP | RR | SF |
|---|---|---|---|---|---|---|
| 2612[9] | **Bardon Hill Boy (IRE) (87)** (BHanbury) **4-9-11** JStack(11) (b.off hind: lw: a.p: led over 1f out: rdn out) | — | **1** | 12/1 | 97 | 63 |
| 2742[7] | **Willie Conquer (76)** (RAkehurst) **4-9-0** PaulEddery(6) (a.p: led 2f out: sn hdd: rdn & r.o wl fnl f) | nk | **2** | 16/1 | 86 | 52 |
| 2862[6] | **Clifton Fox (81)** (JAGlover) **4-9-5** MBirch(2) (hld up: hdwy 3f out: r.o fnl f) | 3 | **3** | 6/1[3] | 86 | 52 |
| 3125[5] | **Ball Gown (90)** (DTThom) **6-10-0** PRobinson(1) (b.hind: hld up: hdwy 3f out: r.o ins fnl f) | 1 | **4** | 6/1[3] | 93 | 59 |
| 3039[5] | **Oops Pettie (78)** (MrsJCecil) **3-8-7** AClark(5) (swtg: in tch: pushed along 5f out: hdwy over 2f out: no ex fnl f) | 1¾ | **5** | 5/2[1] | 78 | 35 |
| 2621[12] | **Slip Jig (IRE) (83)** (RHannon) **3-8-12** RHughes(9) (b.nr fore: lw: chsd ldrs: no hdwy fnl 3f) | s.h | **6** | 16/1 | 83 | 40 |
| 2924[6] | **Domitia (USA) (69)** (MBell) **4-8-7** MFenton(3) (led 8f: sn btn) | 8 | **7** | 16/1 | 56 | 22 |
| 2536* | **Noble Sprinter (IRE) (76)** (WJHaggas) **4-9-0** BThomson(12) (lw: hld up: hdwy 4f out: wknd over 1f out) | 2 | **8** | 7/1 | 60 | 26 |
| 1824[7] | **Keltoi (88)** (LMCumani) **3-9-3** OUrbina(4) (lw: chsd ldrs over 7f) | 2 | **9** | 4/1[2] | 69 | 26 |
| 1852[10] | **Stately Dancer (72)** (GWragg) **3-8-1** FNorton(7) (sddle slipped sn after s: prom over 7f) | ¾ | **10** | 16/1 | 52 | 9 |
| 2608[11] | **Gold Disc (USA) (88)** (BWHills) **3-8-12**(5) JDSmith(8) (swtg: hld up: effrt 5f out: eased whn btn appr fnl f) | 1 | **11** | 12/1 | 66 | 23 |
| 2742[6] | **Coachella (83)** (MJRyan) **3-8-12** SWhitworth(10) (prom: wknd over 4f out: p.u lame over 2f out) | | **P** | 20/1 | — | — |

(SP 133.3%) **12 Rn**

**2m 5.22** (0.22) CSF £180.92 CT £1,183.30 TOTE £14.10: £3.50 £4.60 £2.10 (£105.70) Trio £232.20 OWNER Ms Mary Breslin (NEWMARKET) BRED John McNamee in Ireland

WEIGHT FOR AGE 3yo-9lb

**2612 Bardon Hill Boy (IRE)**, dropped right back to the trip over which he had previously won, was suited by the fast pace as it made his stamina tell. (12/1)

**Willie Conquer**, a lightly-raced maiden, showed improved form and gave the winner a real fright in the final furlong. (16/1)

**2862 Clifton Fox** continues to run well, but could not quicken with the first two approaching the final furlong. (6/1)

**3125 Ball Gown** did not have much room to make her move, but came home well nevertheless. (6/1)

**3039 Oops Pettie** ran a touch below-par, and this race may have come too soon after Ascot. (5/2)

**2231 Slip Jig (IRE)**, stepping up in trip, seemed to stay well enough and will bounce back once the ground eases. (16/1)

## 3249 YE OLDE OAK 'TOP DOG' H'CAP (0-70) (3-Y.O) (Class E)

5-15 (5-17) **1m 4f (July)** £5,049.00 (£1,512.00: £726.00: £333.00) Stalls: High GOING minus 0.55 sec per fur (F)

| | | | | SP | RR | SF |
|---|---|---|---|---|---|---|
| 2915* | **Snow Falcon (60)** (MBell) **3-8-12** MFenton(14) (dwlt: hdwy 4f out: carried lft fnl f: rdn to ld nr fin) | — | **1** | 10/1 | 76 | 42 |
| 2627[2] | **Blenheim Terrace (58)** (CBBBooth) **3-8-10** ACulhane(15) (chsd ldrs: rdn to ld 1f out: hung lft & ct nr fin) | s.h | **2** | 9/2[1] | 74 | 40 |
| *2936*[2] | **Breydon (44)** (MHTompkins) **3-7-3**(7) RMullen(10) (in tch: rdn to ld over 2f out: hdd 1f out: edgd lft & no ex) | 1¼ | **3** | 14/1 | 58 | 24 |
| 2511[7] | **Dashing Invader (USA) (48)** (PWHarris) **3-8-0**ow4 JTate(8) (swtg: led 3f: one pce fnl 2f) | 4 | **4** | 33/1 | 57 | 19 |
| | **Roseberry Avenue (IRE) (69)** (LadyHerries) **3-9-7** RHughes(3) (hdwy 3f out: nvr rchd ldrs) | 1¾ | **5** | 9/2[1] | 76 | 42 |
| 2780[3] | **Ordained (54)** (EJAlston) **3-8-6** JLowe(7) (hld up: rdn 2f out: nvr rchd ldrs) | ½ | **6** | 7/1[3] | 60 | 26 |
| 2775[3] | **Temptress (67)** (PTWalwyn) **3-9-5** PaulEddery(16) (lw: w ldr tl led 9f out: rdn over 3f out: hdd over 2f out: one pce) | ¾ | **7** | 11/2[2] | 72 | 38 |
| 2067[4] | **Batoutoftheblue (60)** (WWHaigh) **3-8-12** MRimmer(5) (prom tl wknd 2f out) | ½ | **8** | 12/1 | 64 | 30 |
| 2610[9] | **Love And Kisses (65)** (CACyzer) **3-9-3** WJO'Connor(9) (lw: bhd: hdwy over 2f out: nvr rchd ldrs) | ½ | **9** | 20/1 | 69 | 35 |
| 2952[3] | **Arktikos (IRE) (68)** (JHMGosden) **3-9-6** BThomson(13) (b.hind: lw: prom: rdn 4f out: sn btn) | 5 | **10** | 8/1 | 65 | 31 |
| 1641[8] | **Induna Mkubwa (55)** (CFWall) **3-8-0**(7) PClarke(6) (nvr trbld ldrs) | 4 | **11** | 33/1 | 47 | 13 |
| 2587[10] | **Dauphin (IRE) (45)** (WJMusson) **3-7-6**(5)ow1 MBaird(1) (lw: dwlt: nvr nr to chal) | 2 | **12** | 33/1 | 34 | — |
| 2205[4] | **Scottish Hero (59)** (JRFanshawe) **3-8-11** JStack(2) (in tch: rdn 3f out: no rspnse) | 2 | **13** | 20/1 | 45 | 11 |
| 2540[6] | **Della Casa (IRE) (66)** (JLDunlop) **3-9-4** SWhitworth(12) (prom 7f) | 13 | **14** | 12/1 | 35 | 1 |
| 2542[9] | **Prince Zizim (50)** (RCSpicer) **3-8-2** FNorton(11) (lw: chsd ldrs tl wknd over 3f out) | hd | **15** | 33/1 | 19 | — |
| 1711[11] | **Future's Trader (62)** (RHannon) **3-9-0** AClark(4) (bhd fnl 3f) | 2 | **16** | 12/1 | 28 | — |

(SP 135.5%) **16 Rn**

**2m 31.6** (1.60) CSF £55.84 CT £599.66 TOTE £11.30: £1.90 £1.70 £3.40 £8.90 (£23.50) Trio £87.50 OWNER Mrs G. Rowland-Clark (NEWMARKET) BRED Stratford Place Stud

LONG HANDICAP Dauphin (IRE) 6-12

STEWARDS' ENQUIRY Culhane susp. 14-15/8/96 (careless riding).

**2915* Snow Falcon** was upped in trip again. He responds well to waiting tactics and did well to put his head in front where it mattered, as the runner-up was carrying him ever closer to the far rail. (10/1)

**2627 Blenheim Terrace**, dropped back to twelve furlongs, looked sure to win until hanging to the far rail late on. (9/2)

**2936 Breydon**, back over what is probably his best trip, does look short of gears, but should be able to win a race. (14/1: 20/1-33/1)

**Dashing Invader (USA)** got warm, but ran his best race to be in the thick of it until lack of pace told. (33/1)

**Roseberry Avenue (IRE)** looked just in need of this belated seasonal debut, but really well in his coat. Staying on to the line, he may need further still. (9/2)

**2780 Ordained**, stepping up in trip, was never doing enough in the last couple of furlongs, having given the leaders a start. (7/1)

T/Plpt: £59.80 (320.03 Tckts). T/Qdpt: £47.50 (23.13 Tckts). Dk

# 3223-THIRSK (L-H) (Firm)

## Saturday August 3rd

WEATHER: cloudy WIND: slt half bhd

## 3250 E.B.F. SUTTON MAIDEN STKS (2-Y.O) (Class D)

2-20 (2-21) **5f** £3,977.00 (£1,196.00: £578.00: £269.00) Stalls: High GOING minus 0.65 sec per fur (HD)

| | | | | SP | RR | SF |
|---|---|---|---|---|---|---|
| 958[4] | **Janib (USA)** (HThomsonJones) **2-9-0** GCarter(8) (bit bkwd: mde all: qcknd clr wl ins fnl f) | — | **1** | 11/4[2] | 79 | 35 |
| 2491[2] | **Fruitana (IRE)** (JBerry) **2-9-0** JCarroll(7) (chsd wnr: effrt & ev ch 1f out: unable qckn) | 2 | **2** | 11/8[1] | 73 | 29 |
| 2865[4] | **Jedi Knight** (MWEasterby) **2-8-9**(5) GParkin(4) (a.p: hrd rdn over 1f out: one pce) | 1¾ | **3** | 8/1 | 67 | 23 |
| 2873[6] | **Barnburgh Boy** (TDBarron) **2-9-0** DeanMcKeown(3) (stdd s: outpcd tl r.o ins fnl f) | hd | **4** | 9/1 | 67 | 23 |
| 2897[6] | **No Extradition** (MrsJRRamsden) **2-9-0** SDWilliams(1) (swtg: lw: trckd ldrs tl rdn & outpcd appr fnl f) | 3½ | **5** | 14/1 | 56+ | 12 |

| | | | | SP | RR | SF |
|---|---|---|---|---|---|---|
| 2772[2] | **Step N Go (IRE)** (MrsJRRamsden) **2-8-9** JFanning(6) (lw: hdwy 2f out: sn rdn: nt rch ldrs) | ¾ | **6** | 5/1[3] | 48+ | 4 |
| 2485[3] | **Tom Mi Dah** (MDHammond) **2-9-0** DaleGibson(2) (outpcd) | 5 | **7** | 16/1 | 37 | — |
| | **Skyers Tryer** (RonaldThompson) **2-8-9** NConnorton(9) (lt-f: unf: dwlt: a outpcd) | ½ | **8** | 40/1 | 31 | — |
| 2772[W] | **Amy** (CSmith) **2-8-6**(3) CTeague(5) (s.s: a bhd & outpcd: t.o) | 20 | **9** | 50/1 | — | — |
| | | | | (SP 123.5%) | **9 Rn** | |

**58.4 secs** (0.40) CSF £7.23 TOTE £2.90: £1.40 £1.20 £2.30 (£3.30) Trio £15.60 OWNER Mr Hamdan Al Maktoum (NEWMARKET) BRED Shadwell Farm Inc. and Shadwell Estate Co. Ltd.

**958 Janib (USA)** had enjoyed a long break since making his racecourse debut in May, and still looked to need this, but racing up the stands' rail saw him home. (11/4)
**2491 Fruitana (IRE)** could be a short-runner on the evidence we have seen so far. (11/8)
**2865 Jedi Knight**, stepping down to the minimum trip, was struggling to stay in touch going to the furlong pole, but his stamina was coming into play at the finish. (8/1)
**2873 Barnburgh Boy** had run much too freely in his previous races and was restrained in the rear this time. After being well adrift, he was doing all his best work in the closing stages. (9/1)
**2897 No Extradition** showed up until fading on the approach to the final furlong. (14/1)
**2772 Step N Go (IRE)**, unable to go the early pace, did improve in the final quarter-mile. (5/1)

## 3251 COOPERS & LYBRAND CONDITIONS STKS (2-Y.O) (Class D)

2-50 (2-53) **6f** £4,055.00 (£1,220.00: £590.00: £275.00) Stalls: High GOING minus 0.65 sec per fur (HD)

| | | | | SP | RR | SF |
|---|---|---|---|---|---|---|
| 2792* | **Tumbleweed Pearl** (BJMeehan) **2-8-10** MTebbutt(2) (trckd ldrs: effrt wl over 1f out: hrd rdn to ld cl home) | — | **1** | 5/6[1] | 83 | 23 |
| 2872[3] | **Just Visiting (84)** (CaptJWilson) **2-8-5**(5) CAdamson(6) (lw: led: rdn fnl f: ct nr fin) | hd | **2** | 10/1[3] | 83 | 23 |
| 2965[4] | **Skyers Flyer (IRE) (81)** (RonaldThompson) **2-8-10** NConnorton(3) (trckd ldrs: shkn up wl over 1f out: one pce) | 4 | **3** | 33/1 | 72 | 12 |
| 1878* | **Isle of Corregidor (USA)** (MrsJCecil) **2-9-3** JCarroll(1) (unruly s: trckd ldrs: hrd drvn 2f out: one pce) | 2 | **4** | 7/4[2] | 74 | 14 |
| 2795* | **Silver Lining** (APJones) **2-9-1** GCarter(4) (lw: chsd ldr: rdn wl over 1f out: sn btn) | 1½ | **5** | 20/1 | 68 | 8 |
| 1845* | **Dee Pee Tee Cee (IRE)** (MWEasterby) **2-8-10**(5) GParkin(5) (s.i.s: sn pushed along: a outpcd) | 6 | **6** | 20/1 | 52 | — |
| | | | | (SP 112.5%) | **6 Rn** | |

**1m 10.8** (1.10) CSF £8.92 TOTE £1.80: £1.10 £3.60 (£13.20) OWNER The Tumbleweed Partnership (UPPER LAMBOURN) BRED R. A. Dalton
**2792* Tumbleweed Pearl** had more on her plate this time and needed to get serious to get up. (5/6)
**2872 Just Visiting**, very much on her toes in the preliminaries, made the running from her stands'-side stall and only just failed to last home. (10/1)
**2965 Skyers Flyer (IRE)** looked in trouble going to the final furlong, but kept plugging away. (33/1)
**1878* Isle of Corregidor (USA)**, very worked up before consenting to be loaded into the stalls, pressed the leaders but was never giving his all. This was a big disappointment after his promising display on his debut. (7/4)
**2795* Silver Lining**, going well within himself for half a mile, was unable to respond when shown the whip and will need much more yielding ground to produce his best. (20/1)
**1845* Dee Pee Tee Cee (IRE)**, flat-footed as the stalls opened, was always last. (20/1)

## 3252 ROCOM LADIES' (S) H'CAP (0-60) (3-Y.O+) (Class E)

3-20 (3-21) **6f** £3,545.00 (£1,070.00: £520.00: £245.00) Stalls: High GOING minus 0.65 sec per fur (HD)

| | | | | SP | RR | SF |
|---|---|---|---|---|---|---|
| 2680[4] | **Tropical Beach (57)** (JBerry) **3-11-7** MrsLPearce(12) (hdwy ½-wy: rdn over 1f out: r.o to ld fnl 100y) | — | **1** | 4/1[1] | 67 | 45 |
| 2960[2] | **Kalar (48)** (DWChapman) **7-10-12b**(4) MissRClark(9) (lw: led tl wl ins fnl f) | 1 | **2** | 7/1[3] | 55 | 37 |
| 3055[5] | **Dominelle (53)** (TDEasterby) **4-11-3**(4) MissADeniel(8) (a.p: drvn over 1f out: kpt on wl nr fin) | ½ | **3** | 11/2[2] | 59 | 41 |
| 2964[3] | **My Godson (51)** (JLEyre) **6-11-1b**(4) MrsCWilliams(13) (s.i.s: hdwy 2f out: nrst fin) | 1 | **4** | 4/1[1] | 54 | 36 |
| *2940[3]* | **Fighter Squadron (30)** (REPeacock) **7-9-5b**(7) MrsCPeacock(11) (hdwy 3f out: kpt on appr fnl f: nt pce to chal) | 1 | **5** | 10/1 | 31 | 13 |
| 2964[6] | **Invigilate (49)** (MartynWane) **7-11-3** MrsDKettlewell(10) (lw: rdn 3f out: kpt on appr fnl f: nvr nrr) | 1¾ | **6** | 8/1 | 45 | 27 |
| *2748[6]* | **Brookhead Lady (50)** (PDEvans) **5-11-0**(4) MrsCFord(14) (prom tl no ex ins fnl f) | 1¼ | **7** | 12/1 | 43 | 25 |
| *2632[7]* | **Jon's Choice (27)** (BPreece) **8-9-2**(7) MissLBoswell(4) (racd alone centre: prom tl wknd appr fnl f) | nk | **8** | 20/1 | 19 | 1 |
| 2678[3] | **Langtonian (33)** (JLEyre) **7-10-1v** MissDianaJones(1) (prom tl outpcd appr fnl f) | 2 | **9** | 10/1 | 20 | 2 |
| 2801[6] | **Summer Villa (37)** (JHetherton) **4-10-5b** MissJFeilden(5) (trckd ldrs 4f: sn wknd) | ¾ | **10** | 11/1 | 22 | 4 |
| 3055[9] | **Olifantsfontein (43)** (DNicholls) **8-10-7**(4) MissERamsden(7) (mid div: drvn along 2f out: sn wknd) | 4 | **11** | 25/1 | 17 | — |
| 2757[14] | **Prime Property (IRE) (32)** (MWEasterby) **4-9-10b**(4) MissVMarshall(2) (a bhd & outpcd) | 3½ | **12** | 20/1 | — | — |
| 2981[11] | **Venus Victorious (IRE) (40)** (RBastiman) **5-10-1b**[1](7) MissRBastiman(6) (swtg: ref to r: t.n.p) | | **R** | 25/1 | — | — |
| *2964[10]* | ***Brisas (38)*** *(CWFairhurst)* ***9-10-2**(4) MrsSBosley(3) (Withdrawn not under Starter's orders: veterinary advice)* | | **W** | 20/1 | — | — |
| | | | | (SP 135.2%) | **13 Rn** | |

**1m 11.8** (2.10) CSF £33.05 CT £147.97 TOTE £4.90: £2.10 £2.20 £2.60 (£16.50) Trio £39.40 OWNER Mr Jim Unsworth (COCKERHAM) BRED P. Balding
WEIGHT FOR AGE 3yo-4lb
Bt in 7,600 gns
STEWARDS' ENQUIRY Bastiman susp. 12-15/8/96 (improper use of whip).
**2680 Tropical Beach** was able to turn the tables on the runner-up over this slightly longer trip, but it took a long time to wear him down. (4/1: 6/1-7/2)
**2960 Kalar** tried his hardest to add a win over six furlongs to his impressive score, but it was not to be. He will have to concentrate on galloping the opposition into the ground at the minimum trip. (7/1)
**3055 Dominelle** is running consistently well, but she does lack a turn of finishing speed. However, a return to the minimum trip in this grade could see her getting back to winning ways. (11/2)
**2964 My Godson** finds this trip a bit on the sharp side these days. (4/1)
**2940 Fighter Squadron**, not at all happy on such fast ground, ran a race full of promise and looks up to winning a similar race when conditions favour him, especially with stronger handling. (10/1)
**2964 Invigilate** has run all his best races on firm ground, but he did not stride out to post, and was reluctant to let himself down on the way back until it was far too late. (8/1)

## 3253 BARCLAYS BANK H'CAP (0-80) (3-Y.O+) (Class D)

3-55 (3-55) **1m 4f** £5,117.50 (£1,540.00: £745.00: £347.50) Stalls: High GOING minus 0.65 sec per fur (HD)

| | | | | SP | RR | SF |
|---|---|---|---|---|---|---|
| 2900[3] | **Far Ahead (74)** (JLEyre) **4-9-8**(3) OPears(2) (hld up: reminders after 4f: hdwy 3f out: led over 1f out: r.o wl) | — | **1** | 7/2[3] | 83 | 34 |

| | | | | SP | RR | SF |
|---|---|---|---|---|---|---|
| 3081[2] | **Villeggiatura (72)** (MrsJRRamsden) **3-8-12** JCarroll(6) (lw: stdd s: hld up: hdwy u.p over 2f out: styd on fnl f) | 1¾ | **2** | 5/2[2] | 79 | 19 |
| 2851[7] | **Champagne N Dreams (45)** (DNicholls) **4-7-3**(7) JBramhill(1) (lw: a.p: led 3f out tl over 1f out: kpt on same pce) | 1½ | **3** | 20/1 | 50 | 1 |
| 2399[4] | **Russian Request (IRE) (73)** (MRStoute) **3-8-13** DeanMcKeown(4) (led to 3f out: rdn & wknd over 1f out) | 4 | **4** | 2/1[1] | 72 | 12 |
| 3098[3] | **Ham N'Eggs (77)** (MDHammond) **5-10-0** GCarter(3) (hld up & bhd: rdn ent st: no imp) | 5 | **5** | 9/2 | 70 | 21 |
| 2866[7] | **Chimanimani (45)** (NTinkler) **5-7-10** KimTinkler(5) (swtg: chsd ldr tl wknd over 3f out: t.o) | 12 | **6** | 33/1 | 22 | — |
| | | | | (SP 110.0%) | **6 Rn** | |

**2m 33.4** (3.40) CSF £11.81 TOTE £4.80: £2.00 £1.70 (£5.00) OWNER Sunpak Potatoes (HAMBLETON) BRED Sir John Astor
LONG HANDICAP Champagne N Dreams 7-9 Chimanimani 7-9
WEIGHT FOR AGE 3yo-11lb

**2900 Far Ahead**, winning for the first time at the trip, took it a shade comfortably. (7/2)
**3081 Villeggiatura**, attempting this extended trip for the first time, was ridden with restraint. He stayed on willingly under a forceful ride in the latter stages, but was never doing things fast enough to pose a threat. (5/2: op 13/8)
**2851 Champagne N Dreams** did not fare badly over this longer trip. (20/1)
**2399 Russian Request (IRE)** seemed to lack the stamina for such an extended trip and was going in reverse before reaching the final furlong. (2/1: 3/1-7/4)
**3098 Ham N'Eggs** did not relish running twice in six days and never took a hold of his bit. (9/2)

## 3254 LORDS TAVERNERS H'CAP (0-80) (3-Y.O+) (Class D)

4-25 (4-25) **1m** £4,987.50 (£1,500.00: £725.00: £337.50) Stalls: Low GOING minus 0.95 sec per fur (HD)

| | | | | SP | RR | SF |
|---|---|---|---|---|---|---|
| 2328[10] | **Mountgate (72)** (MPBielby) **4-9-10** DRMcCabe(1) (lw: hld up & bhd: hdwy 3f out: rdn to ld over 1f out: r.o wl) | — | **1** | 6/1[3] | 83 | 38 |
| 2483[6] | **Up in Flames (IRE) (69)** (MDHammond) **5-9-7** GCarter(2) (hld up in tch: hdwy over 2f out: ev ch over 1f out: unable qckn) | 1¼ | **2** | 6/1[3] | 78 | 33 |
| 2729[3] | **Somerton Boy (IRE) (71)** (PCalver) **6-9-9** JCarroll(4) (lw: hld up: effrt over 2f out: kpt on towards fin) | 1½ | **3** | 11/4[2] | 77 | 32 |
| 3059[3] | **Born A Lady (53)** (SRBowring) **3-7-12b** DaleGibson(5) (lw: a.p: rdn 2f out: r.o one pce) | nk | **4** | 10/1 | 58 | 6 |
| 2962[2] | **Pine Ridge Lad (IRE) (65)** (JLEyre) **6-9-3** SDWilliams(6) (set str pce: rdn & hdd over 1f out: no ex fnl f) | ½ | **5** | 11/8[1] | 69 | 24 |
| 3060[3] | **Anonym (IRE) (60)** (DNicholls) **4-8-12** AlexGreaves(7) (chsd ldng pair tl rdn & wknd 2f out: t.o) | 14 | **6** | 8/1 | 36 | — |
| 2963[4] | **Axeman (IRE) (70)** (DNicholls) **4-9-8** MTebbutt(3) (lw: a bhd: t.o fr ½-wy) | 1¼ | **7** | 25/1 | 43 | — |
| | | | | (SP 121.4%) | **7 Rn** | |

**1m 38.2** (1.70) CSF £39.61 TOTE £6.80: £2.80 £3.80 (£35.50) OWNER Mr J. F. Coupland (GRIMSBY) BRED Llety Stud
WEIGHT FOR AGE 3yo-7lb
**OFFICIAL EXPLANATION Axeman (IRE): had gurgled.**

**2134 Mountgate** had the race run to suit with the hectic early pace, and had little trouble in conceding weight all round. (6/1)
**2351 Up in Flames (IRE)** let the leaders cut their own throats and looked the likely winner when joining issue going to the last furlong, but the winner, racing wide of him, beat him to the punch. (6/1)
**2729 Somerton Boy (IRE)** handles the firm ground surprisingly well for such a heavy-topped individual, but he takes time to find top gear, and it might pay to step him up to a mile again. (11/4)
**3059 Born A Lady** does like to force the pace, but could not lead these older rivals. It is to her credit then that she was able to finish so close in such a strongly-run race. (10/1)
**2962 Pine Ridge Lad (IRE)** was the subject of quite a gamble, but he was being made to work to stay ahead, and had run himself into the ground when collared. (11/8: 2/1-5/4)

## 3255 TONY WHITING PUBLIC RELATIONS MAIDEN STKS (3-Y.O F) (Class D)

4-55 (4-55) **7f** £4,003.00 (£1,204.00: £582.00: £271.00) Stalls: Low GOING minus 0.65 sec per fur (HD)

| | | | | SP | RR | SF |
|---|---|---|---|---|---|---|
| 2918[5] | **With Care** (WJarvis) **3-8-11** MTebbutt(6) (trckd ldrs: shkn up over 1f out: led ins fnl f: drvn clr) | — | **1** | 10/1 | 72 | 22 |
| | **Chalk Dust (USA) (78)** (PFICole) **3-8-11** DRMcCabe(4) (chsd ldr: led over 2f out tl hdd & no ex ins fnl f) | 2 | **2** | 8/13[1] | 67 | 17 |
| 1791[20] | **Portuguese Lil (78)** (DNicholls) **3-8-11** AlexGreaves(2) (bit bkwd: hld up in tch: hdwy over 2f out: nt pce to chal) | 1¼ | **3** | 8/1[3] | 65 | 15 |
| 2718[12] | **Mashmoum** (JHMGosden) **3-8-11** JCarroll(5) (bit bkwd: hld up: hdwy & nt clr run over 1f out: kpt on ins fnl f) | 1½ | **4** | 9/1 | 61 | 11 |
| | **Meznh (IRE)** (HThomsonJones) **3-8-11** GCarter(3) (lengthy: unf: s.s: bhd: hdwy 2f out: nrst fin) | nk | **5** | 7/1[2] | 61 | 11 |
| 2393[2] | **Cruz Santa** (TDBarron) **3-8-11** SDWilliams(7) (swtg: led tl over 2f out: sn rdn & wknd) | 5 | **6** | 7/1[2] | 49 | — |
| 2899[6] | **Belbay Star** (JLEyre) **3-8-4**(7) JBramhill(1) (collided w rails after 1f: trckd ldrs: hrd drvn & wknd 3f out) | s.h | **7** | 33/1 | 49 | — |
| 2675[4] | **Angel Face (USA)** (BPreece) **3-8-11** VSlattery(8) (prom tl wknd over 2f out) | 2½ | **8** | 33/1 | 43 | — |
| | | | | (SP 123.0%) | **8 Rn** | |

**1m 25.9** (1.70) CSF £17.45 TOTE £12.10: £1.60 £1.30 £1.50 (£5.50) OWNER Mr J. M. Greetham (NEWMARKET) BRED J. M. Greetham

**2918 With Care**, from a stable in form, settled much better on this occasion. Sent about her work below the distance, she had the legs of the favourite in the last 100 yards, and won going away. She can improve further on this. (10/1)
**Chalk Dust (USA)**, all the rage, kicked for home entering the last quarter-mile. When push came to shove, it was she who cracked first. (8/13)
**1324 Portuguese Lil**, absent since finishing last in the Derby, did not look fully wound up, but she performed well enough, and should be able to find an opening. (8/1)
**2718 Mashmoum** cut no ice on her debut and never really got into it here, but she should now be beginning to realise what it is all about. (9/1)
**Meznh (IRE)**, a sparely-made debutante who was very green, stayed on pleasingly after losing many lengths at the start. She will be all the wiser with this under her belt. (7/1)
**2393 Cruz Santa** was not quite up to this class, and dropped away tamely after setting the pace for over half a mile. (7/1)

## 3256 LORDS TAVERNERS MAIDEN H'CAP (0-70) (3-Y.O+) (Class E)

5-30 (5-31) **6f** £3,744.75 (£1,128.00: £546.50: £255.75) Stalls: High GOING minus 0.65 sec per fur (HD)

| | | | | SP | RR | SF |
|---|---|---|---|---|---|---|
| 3059[8] | **Mill End Lady (39)** (MWEasterby) **3-7-11b**ow1 DaleGibson(11) (unruly s: dwlt: hdwy u.p 2f out: kpt on strly to ld nr fin) | — | **1** | 6/1 | 50 | 5 |
| 2902[2] | **Newlands Corner (42)** (JAkehurst) **3-8-0b**ow3 DBiggs(5) (swvd lft s: a.p: led 2f out: rdn & edgd rt fnl f: ct cl home) | nk | **2** | 9/2[3] | 52 | 5 |
| 3135[9] | **Swifty Nifty (IRE) (48)** (WWHaigh) **3-8-3**(3)ow10 CTeague(9) (rdn ½-wy: hdwy over 2f out: nt clr run appr fnl f: kpt on) | 3 | **3** | 14/1 | 50 | — |

| | | | | SP | RR | SF |
|---|---|---|---|---|---|---|
| 2902⁴ | **Madam Zando (50)** (JBalding) **3-8-1**(7)ow2 JEdmunds(13) (lw: trckd ldrs: effrt 2f out: one pce ins fnl f) | ¾ | **4** | 4/1 2 | 50 | 4 |
| | **La Finale (57)** (DNicholls) **3-9-1** AlexGreaves(10) (h.d.w: bkwd: prom: rdn 2f out: r.o fnl f) | 2 | **5** | 12/1 | 52 | 8 |
| 2902⁹ | **Dona Filipa (38)** (MissLCSiddall) **3-7-7**(3) DarrenMoffatt(6) (hld up in tch: effrt over 1f out: edgd lft u.p: sn btn) | ¾ | **6** | 50/1 | 31 | — |
| *248⁷* | **Pushka Fair (34)** (TRWatson) **5-7-5**(5) CAdamson(12) (b: bkwd: mde most 4f: eased whn btn fnl f) | hd | **7** | 25/1 | 27 | — |
| 2391¹⁰ | **Taurean Fire (39)** (MrsMReveley) **3-7-11** NCarlisle(8) (prom tl wknd over 1f out) | 2½ | **8** | 11/1 | 25 | — |
| 3152⁴ | **Baileys First (IRE) (68)** (MJohnston) **3-9-12b¹** JCarroll(3) (hmpd s: nvr nr ldrs) | hd | **9** | 11/4 1 | 54 | 10 |
| 2983¹⁰ | **Good To Talk (43)** (TDEasterby) **3-8-1**ow1 GCarter(2) (lw: prom: ev ch over 1f out: sn wknd & eased) | 2½ | **10** | 10/1 | 22 | — |
| 3102¹⁴ | **Jenny's Charmer (45)** (SEKettlewell) **3-8-3b¹** DRMcCabe(1) (a bhd & outpcd) | nk | **11** | 20/1 | 23 | — |
| 2902⁸ | **Nutcracker Suite (IRE) (39)** (JLEyre) **4-7-8**(7) JBramhill(4) (prom over 4f) | 2 | **12** | 20/1 | 12 | — |
| 2902¹⁰ | **Oare Budgie (38)** (DonEnricoIncisa) **3-7-10v** KimTinkler(7) (lw: outpcd: a bhd) | nk | **13** | 50/1 | 10 | — |

(SP 128.2%) **13 Rn**

**1m 11.3** (1.60) CSF £33.49 CT £354.17 TOTE £9.60: £2.70 £1.80 £3.20 (£25.20) Trio £110.80 OWNER Mr W. T. Allgood (SHERIFF HUTTON) BRED Mrs Helen Plumbly

LONG HANDICAP Pushka Fair 7-6 Swifty Nifty (IRE) 7-8 Dona Filipa 7-2 Oare Budgie 7-2

WEIGHT FOR AGE 3yo-4lb

**3059 Mill End Lady**, brought back to sprinting, was very unruly in the stalls and eventually missed a beat when they opened. Driven along but with the stands' rail to assist, she stayed on doggedly to poke her nose in front in the dying strides. (6/1)

**2902 Newlands Corner** nosed ahead two furlongs out but, after looking in control, was worried out of it right on the line. (9/2)

**2800 Swifty Nifty (IRE)**, off the bridle for most of the way, was short of room when trying to mount a challenge going to the final furlong, so did well in the circumstances to run into the prizes. (14/1)

**2902 Madam Zando** had the perfect draw and is beginning to prove very frustrating. (4/1)

**La Finale** has done well physically since last year, but did look to need this first race since the autumn. Stepping down in distance, she remained in the action until finding demands too great inside the final furlong and a half. (12/1)

**Dona Filipa** is performing well enough to win a race, but she does look to need stronger handling. (50/1)

**Pushka Fair** looked quite burly after six months off, but ran a fine race in defeat and is one to bear in mind for a similar event. (25/1)

**3152 Baileys First (IRE)**, impeded by a swerving rival at the start, never really recovered and this is best ignored. (11/4)

T/Plpt: £54.10 (194.32 Tckts). T/Qdpt: £17.50 (22.3 Tckts). IM

## 3110-WINDSOR (Fig. 8) (Good to firm, Good in st)
## Saturday August 3rd

WEATHER: fine WIND: nil

### 3257 FRIENDLY FLAME APPRENTICE (S) H'CAP (0-60) (3-Y.O+) (Class G)

6-00 (6-07) **1m 67y** £2,210.50 (£628.00: £311.50) Stalls: High GOING minus 0.21 sec per fur (GF)

| | | | | SP | RR | SF |
|---|---|---|---|---|---|---|
| *3062⁹* | **Queen of Shannon (IRE) (44)** (AWCarroll) **8-9-3v** RStudholme(16) (hdwy 3f out: led over 1f out: easily) | — | **1** | 25/1 | 58+ | 38 |
| *2689¹¹* | **Oozlem (IRE) (39)** (JRPoulton) **7-8-12b** TField(14) (a.p: hrd rdn & r.o one pce fnl 3f) | 2½ | **2** | 14/1 | 48 | 28 |
| 2971⁴ | **Little Kenny (43)** (MJFetherston-Godley) **3-8-9v** RFfrench(11) (hdwy 3f out: hrd rdn over 1f out: one pce) | s.h | **3** | 7/1 3 | 52 | 25 |
| 2507¹² | **Balpare (42)** (NACallaghan) **3-8-8** JGotobed(10) (hdwy 3f out: ev ch over 1f out: nt qckn) | 1½ | **4** | 14/1 | 48 | 21 |
| 2971¹⁰ | **Return To Brighton (45)** (JMBradley) **4-9-4** CLowther(18) (led tl wknd over 1f out) | nk | **5** | 9/1 | 51 | 31 |
| 3067¹⁰ | **Tauten (IRE) (41)** (PBurgoyne) **6-8-9v**(5) JBosley(2) (nvr nrr) | 1½ | **6** | 14/1 | 44 | 24 |
| 3111⁹ | **Fastini Gold (45)** (MDIUsher) **4-9-4v¹** RBrisland(13) (nrst fin) | nk | **7** | 14/1 | 47 | 27 |
| *155¹³* | **Grey Charmer (IRE) (49)** (RHBuckler) **7-9-3**(5) SCrawford(12) (nvr nr to chal) | 3 | **8** | 20/1 | 45 | 25 |
| 2893⁴ | **Tallulah Belle (45)** (NPLittmoden) **3-8-11** DavidO'Neill(17) (lw: prom tl hrd rdn & wknd over 1f out) | 1 | **9** | 14/1 | 39 | 12 |
| 2989ᵁ | **Lilac Rain (34)** (RMStronge) **4-8-7** CScudder(8) (hrd rdn & swvd bdly lft over 3f out: hdwy 2f out: nt rch ldrs) | 1½ | **10** | 33/1 | 26 | 6 |
| *2689⁷* | **Still Here (IRE) (40)** (MJHeaton-Ellis) **3-8-3v¹**(3) JFowle(6) (lw: a mid div) | 3½ | **11** | 20/1 | 25 | — |
| 2801¹³ | **Chief's Lady (34)** (JMBradley) **4-8-7** AMcCarthy(3) (prom tl wknd 2f out) | nk | **12** | 33/1 | 18 | — |
| 2716¹⁴ | **Elite Racing (36)** (NTinkler) **4-8-9** TSiddall(15) (prom tl wknd 3f out) | ¾ | **13** | 16/1 | 19 | — |
| 2380* | **Charlton Imp (USA) (56)** (RJHodges) **3-9-3**(5) DSalt(4) (lw: nvr nr ldrs) | 1¾ | **14** | 6/1 2 | 35 | 8 |
| 2971⁷ | **Acquittal (IRE) (45)** (AStreeter) **4-9-4v** GHannon(1) (nvr trbld ldrs) | hd | **15** | 9/2 1 | 24 | 4 |
| 2716¹⁰ | **Bad News (40)** (JMBradley) **4-8-8**(5) GMills(5) (outpcd) | hd | **16** | 33/1 | 19 | — |
| *105¹¹* | **Flair Lady (44)** (WGMTurner) **5-8-12**(5) RCody-Boutcher(9) (outpcd) | 1¼ | **17** | 33/1 | 21 | 1 |
| 1667¹⁰ | **Arch Enemy (IRE) (58)** (MissKMGeorge) **3-9-10** PDoe(7) (chsd ldrs tl wknd 4f out: t.o) | 20 | **18** | 33/1 | — | — |

(SP 122.3%) **18 Rn**

**1m 46.9** (4.70) CSF £292.77 CT £2,454.54 TOTE £25.70: £4.30 £2.90 £1.70 £3.30 (£163.70) Trio £212.90; £149.97 to Ripon 5/8/96 OWNER Mr J. Wigmore (WORCESTER) BRED George Killoughery

WEIGHT FOR AGE 3yo-7lb

No bid

**1893 Queen of Shannon (IRE)**, an enigmatic character, found the refitting of a visor doing the trick in no uncertain manner. (25/1)

**200* Oozlem (IRE)** caught the winner on a real going day, but kept on to win the battle for the runner-up spot. (14/1)

**2971 Little Kenny** has now shown consistency in all three starts in the visor. (7/1)

**2373 Balpare** was dropped 8lb after disappointing last time at Warwick. (14/1: 10/1-16/1)

**2801 Return To Brighton** was back down to the mark off which she won a similar event at Ripon. (9/1)

**2740 Tauten (IRE)** had been like a fish out of water in the Ladies Race at Ascot a week ago. (14/1)

**2971 Acquittal (IRE)**, unlucky last time, did not appear to have a defence for being let off here. (9/2)

### 3258 AMERADA COSTS LESS MAIDEN STKS (3-Y.O+) (Class D)

6-30 (6-32) **1m 2f 7y** £3,811.50 (£1,152.00: £561.00: £265.50) Stalls: High GOING minus 0.21 sec per fur (GF)

| | | | | SP | RR | SF |
|---|---|---|---|---|---|---|
| 1899¹⁰ | **Flame Valley (USA) (93)** (MRStoute) **3-8-7** DHarrison(8) (led to 2f out: led ins fnl f: all out) | — | **1** | 7/4 2 | 95 | 68 |
| | **Turning Wheel (USA)** (HRACecil) **3-8-7** WRyan(5) (w'like: smooth hdwy 4f out: led 2f out tl ins fnl f: r.o) | ½ | **2** | 5/4 1 | 94 | 67 |
| 1668⁴ | **Upper Gallery (IRE)** (PWChapple-Hyam) **3-8-12** JReid(9) (lw: hdwy 4f out: one pce fnl 2f) | 16 | **3** | 10/1 3 | 74 | 47 |
| 3093⁴ | **Dazzling** (DCO'Brien) **3-8-7** GBardwell(10) (nrst fin) | 6 | **4** | 16/1 | 59 | 32 |
| 2899⁴ | **Sawa-Id** (JHMGosden) **3-8-12** RHills(4) (lw: hdwy over 3f out: styd on: nvr nr to chal) | s.h | **5** | 10/1 3 | 64 | 37 |
| 2579⁹ | **Veridian (78)** (PWHarris) **3-8-12** GHind(7) (lw: nvr nr to chal) | 2 | **6** | 20/1 | 61 | 34 |

| Form | Horse / Trainer / Age-Wt / Jockey / Comment | Dist | Pos | SP | RR | SF |
|---|---|---|---|---|---|---|
| 1895[7] | **Coh Sho No** (IABalding) **3-8-2**(5) MartinDwyer(13) (lw: mid div whn hmpd 6f out: nt rcvr) | 2½ | **7** | 25/1 | 52 | 25 |
| 2610[13] | **What A Fuss** (BHanbury) **3-8-5**(7) GFaulkner(14) (dwlt: sn w ldrs: hrd rdn & wknd over 2f out) | 1¾ | **8** | 40/1 | 54 | 27 |
| 1857[12] | **Persian Dawn** (MajorDNChappell) **3-8-7** TSprake(1) (nvr on terms) | 9 | **9** | 50/1 | 35 | 8 |
| 2141[7] | **Suitor (57)** (WJarvis) **3-8-12** AMcGlone(2) (lw: nvr bttr than mid div) | ¾ | **10** | 33/1 | 39 | 12 |
| 1891[11] | **Indian Wolf (40)** (BJLlewellyn) **3-8-12** RPrice(6) (prom tl hrd rdn & wknd over 2f out) | 1¾ | **11** | 100/1 | 36 | 9 |
| | **Monte Felice (IRE)** (GHarwood) **3-8-12** JQuinn(12) (w'like: bkwd: dwlt: hmpd 6f out: nt rcvr) | ½ | **12** | 20/1 | 35 | 8 |
| 2794[10] | **Queens Fancy** (SDow) **3-8-7** JFEgan(11) (prom tl wknd 4f out: t.o) | 15 | **13** | 50/1 | 6 | — |
| 2345[10] | **Athenian Alliance** (JMBradley) **7-8-9**(7) CLowther(3) (prom tl wknd qckly over 3f out: t.o) | 1½ | **14** | 100/1 | 4 | — |
| | | | | (SP 129.5%) | | **14 Rn** |

**2m 5.7** (0.80) CSF £4.49 TOTE £3.00: £1.70 £1.60 £1.90 (£2.40) Trio £5.40 OWNER Cheveley Park Stud (NEWMARKET) BRED Flaxman Holdings Ltd
WEIGHT FOR AGE 3yo-9lb

**1077 Flame Valley (USA)**, taking a big drop in class, found her previous experience tipping the scales in her favour. (7/4)
**Turning Wheel (USA)**, a well-bred filly, just got outbattled by the more experienced winner, but will be hard to beat next time. (5/4)
**1668 Upper Gallery (IRE)** is out of a mile and a half winner who was a half-sister to Sun Princess and Saddlers' Hall. She may do better over further. (10/1)
**3093 Dazzling** was running a bit too soon after her debut earlier in the week. (16/1)
**2899 Sawa-Id** is probably capable of better and should get a decent handicap mark. (10/1)
**2011 Veridian**, stepping up in distance, continues to disappoint since a promising debut back in May. (20/1)

## 3259 E.B.F. NORTH SEA MEDIAN AUCTION MAIDEN STKS (2-Y.O) (Class E)

7-00 (7-08) **5f 217y** £3,306.25 (£1,000.00: £487.50: £231.25) Stalls: High GOING minus 0.21 sec per fur (GF)

| Form | Horse / Trainer / Age-Wt / Jockey / Comment | Dist | Pos | SP | RR | SF |
|---|---|---|---|---|---|---|
| | **Mumkin** (TThomsonJones) **2-9-0** JReid(19) (w'like: lw: hdwy 3f out: hmpd over 1f out: led ins fnl f: r.o) | — | **1** | 12/1 | 79 | 32 |
| 2600[3] | **Marsad (IRE) (92)** (CJBenstead) **2-9-0** RHills(17) (lw: w ldrs: led 2f out tl ins fnl f: nt qckn) | 1½ | **2** | 5/2[1] | 75 | 28 |
| 3147[4] | **Shuwaikh** (RHannon) **2-9-0** MHills(13) (lw: chsd ldrs: styd on one pce fnl 2f) | 1¾ | **3** | 8/1 | 70 | 23 |
| 2606[8] | **Broughtons Error** (WJMusson) **2-9-0** JQuinn(20) (hdwy fnl 2f: nrst fin) | ¾ | **4** | 20/1 | 68 | 21 |
| 2580[11] | **Penlop** (BJMeehan) **2-9-0** BDoyle(4) (lw: hdwy fnl 2f: nvr nrr) | s.h | **5** | 33/1 | 68 | 21 |
| 3046[4] | **Bold Oriental (IRE) (80)** (NACallaghan) **2-9-0b[1]** PatEddery(14) (lw: led 4f: edgd rt & bmpd over 1f out: wknd fnl f) | 5 | **6** | 9/2[2] | 55 | 8 |
| 2792[6] | **Poker Princess** (MBell) **2-8-9** WRyan(12) (b: hdwy 2f out: nvr nr to chal) | 1¼ | **7** | 16/1 | 47 | — |
| | **Kalimat** (WJarvis) **2-8-9** TQuinn(16) (leggy: unf: prom tl hmpd over 1f out: no ch after) | ½ | **8** | 6/1 | 45 | — |
| 2942[5] | **V I P Charlie** (JRJenkins) **2-9-0** SWhitworth(2) (nvr plcd to chal) | ½ | **9** | 25/1 | 49 | 2 |
| 2596[7] | **Lucy of Arabia (IRE)** (JJSheehan) **2-8-9** AMorris(21) (spd 4f) | s.h | **10** | 50/1 | 44 | — |
| 2044[5] | **Broadgate Flyer (IRE)** (WJarvis) **2-9-0** AMcGlone(15) (nvr nr to chal) | s.h | **11** | 20/1 | 49 | 2 |
| | **Silver Secret** (MJHeaton-Ellis) **2-8-11**(3) SDrowne(9) (leggy: w'like: s.s: sn mid div: nt rch ldrs) | 2½ | **12** | 33/1 | 42 | — |
| 1453[7] | **Champagne Toast** (RHannon) **2-8-11**(3) DaneO'Neill(11) (lw: a bhd) | nk | **13** | 25/1 | 41 | — |
| 2741[10] | **Rotherfield Queen (IRE)** (GMMcCourt) **2-8-9** CRutter(22) (prom tl wknd wl over 1f out) | 9 | **14** | 50/1 | 12 | — |
| | **Myosotis** (PJMakin) **2-9-0** SSanders(6) (w'like: dwlt: a bhd) | 2½ | **15** | 25/1 | 10 | — |
| 2600[13] | **Grovefair Venture** (BJMeehan) **2-9-0** JFEgan(5) (lw: outpcd) | ¾ | **16** | 50/1 | 8 | — |
| | **Mellwood (IRE)** (MHTompkins) **2-9-0** PRobinson(3) (lengthy: scope: outpcd) | 2 | **17** | 33/1 | 3 | — |
| 2887[7] | **Doubly-H (IRE)** (MBell) **2-8-7b[1]**(7) GFaulkner(8) (w ldrs tl wknd 2f out) | hd | **18** | 50/1 | 3 | — |
| | **Little Progress** (TMJones) **2-9-0** RPerham(7) (w'like: lw: s.s: a wl bhd) | ½ | **19** | 50/1 | 1 | — |
| 2783[5] | **Scarlet Lake** (DRLoder) **2-8-6**(3) PMcCabe(1) (lw: w ldrs: wkng whn bdly hmpd over 1f out: nt rcvr) | s.h | **20** | 16/1 | — | — |
| *1489[8]* | **Biba (IRE)** (RBoss) **2-8-9** GHind(10) (a bhd) | 4 | **21** | 50/1 | — | — |
| *2600[4]* | ***Mara River*** (IABalding) **2-8-4**(5) MartinDwyer(18) (Withdrawn not under Starter's orders: ref to ent stalls) | | **W** | 5/1[3] | — | — |
| | | | | (SP 149.9%) | | **21 Rn** |

**1m 13.9** (3.40) CSF £35.78 TOTE £14.40: £3.50 £2.00 £2.20 (£35.90) Trio £133.80 OWNER Mr Hamdan Al Maktoum (UPPER LAMBOURN) BRED Mrs V. M. Tricks

**Mumkin**, a 35,000 guinea colt, looked well tuned up and had to overcome some trouble in running. (12/1: 8/1-14/1)
**2600 Marsad (IRE)** is continuing to knock on the door. (5/2)
**3147 Shuwaikh**, a half-brother to Femme Sevante, found this easier than Goodwood three days earlier, and can find a suitable opening. (8/1: 6/1-9/1)
**2606 Broughtons Error** might be the type for a nursery when reverting to seven. (20/1)
**Penlop**, a half-brother to four winners, had finished last in a hot maiden at Newmarket. Catching the eye in the closing stages, he is one to note. (33/1)
**3046 Bold Oriental (IRE)**, blinkered for the first time, did the winner no favours, but got plenty in return for his trouble. (9/2)
**Kalimat**, a half-sister to In Excess, ran well on this debut, but may need more time to develop. (6/1)
**2942 V I P Charlie** seems capable of better than this. (25/1)
**2783 Scarlet Lake** gave a much better account of herself than her finishing position suggests. (16/1)

## 3260 AMERADA HESS GAS CHALLENGE H'CAP (0-75) (3-Y.O+) (Class D)

7-30 (7-35) **1m 3f 135y** £3,792.00 (£1,146.00: £558.00: £264.00) Stalls: High GOING minus 0.21 sec per fur (GF)

| Form | Horse / Trainer / Age-Wt / Jockey / Comment | Dist | Pos | SP | RR | SF |
|---|---|---|---|---|---|---|
| | **Wild Rita (71)** (WRMuir) **4-9-10** JReid(6) (led after 2f: drvn out) | — | **1** | 8/1 | 76 | 44 |
| 2737[3] | **Te Amo (IRE) (62)** (RAkehurst) **4-9-1** TQuinn(3) (a.p: r.o ins fnl f) | 1¼ | **2** | 4/1[3] | 65 | 33 |
| 2869[2] | **Tart (FR) (74)** (JRFanshawe) **3-9-2** DHarrison(1) (led 2f: chsd wnr after tl one pce ins fnl f) | ½ | **3** | 7/2[2] | 77 | 34 |
| 2424[2] | **Parrot's Hill (IRE) (54)** (MHTompkins) **3-7-7**(3) MHenry(9) (lw: chsd ldrs: hrd rdn over 2f out: r.o one pce) | nk | **4** | 12/1 | 56 | 13 |
| 2943* | **Monument (68)** (JSKing) **4-9-7** PatEddery(5) (a.p: ev ch 2f out: nt qckn) | s.h | **5** | 2/1[1] | 70 | 38 |
| 2973[6] | **Supreme Star (USA) (64)** (PRHedger) **5-9-0**(3) DaneO'Neill(7) (nvr nr to chal) | 3 | **6** | 8/1 | 62 | 30 |
| 3113[2] | **Elly Fleetfoot (IRE) (54)** (MJRyan) **4-8-7b** BDoyle(10) (hdwy 3f out: hrd rdn 2f out: sn wknd) | ½ | **7** | 13/2 | 51 | 19 |
| 2197[8] | **Noble Lord (72)** (RHBuckler) **3-8-11**(3) SDrowne(2) (a bhd) | 8 | **8** | 16/1 | 58 | 15 |
| 2866[8] | **Broughtons Formula (43)** (WJMusson) **6-7-10b** JQuinn(8) (prom tl wknd over 3f out) | 13 | **9** | 14/1 | 11 | — |
| *2794[3]* | ***Mountain Dream (70)*** (LMCumani) **3-8-12** MHills(4) (Withdrawn not under Starter's orders: ref to ent stalls) | | **W** | 7/1 | — | — |
| | | | | (SP 143.9%) | | **9 Rn** |

**2m 30.7** (6.70) CSF £42.54 CT £128.66 TOTE £9.30: £2.30 £1.50 £1.40 (£24.70) Trio £11.00 OWNER Perspicacious Punters Racing Club (LAMBOURN) BRED Terry Brady
WEIGHT FOR AGE 3yo-11lb

**Wild Rita** held on gamely on this belated seasonal reappearance. (8/1)

**2737 Te Amo (IRE)**, 16lb lower than when last seen in a handicap, was reverting to a longer trip. (4/1)
**2869 Tart (FR)**, on her handicap debut, stayed this longer trip well, but again lacked a turn of finishing speed. (7/2)
**2424 Parrot's Hill (IRE)** kept staying on under pressure, and a return to a longer trip could well be on the cards. (12/1)
**2943* Monument** had to contend with a 3lb hike in the weights over this longer distance. (2/1)
**2973 Supreme Star (USA)** needs further than this nowadays. (8/1)
**3113 Elly Fleetfoot (IRE)** was 3lb higher for a narrow defeat here earlier in the week. (13/2)

## 3261 IT'S A GAS H'CAP (0-70) (3-Y.O+) (Class E)

8-00 (8-05) **5f 10y** £2,932.50 (£885.00: £430.00: £202.50) Stalls: High GOING minus 0.21 sec per fur (GF)

| | | | | SP | RR | SF |
|---|---|---|---|---|---|---|
| 2976[4] | **Gone Savage (58)** (WJMusson) **8-9-5** RCochrane(3) (b: hdwy 2f out: qcknd to ld ins fnl f: r.o) | — | **1** | 9/4[1] | 68 | 36 |
| 1688[8] | **La Belle Dominique (47)** (SGKnight) **4-8-8** BDoyle(6) (a.p: ev ch 1f out: nt qckn) | 2½ | **2** | 33/1 | 49 | 17 |
| 2992[5] | **Scored Again (49)** (MJHeaton-Ellis) **6-8-5**(5) AmandaSanders(5) (b: a.p: r.o ins fnl f) | nk | **3** | 14/1 | 50 | 18 |
| 2960* | **The Institute Boy (50)** (MissJFCraze) **6-8-11** JLowe(10) (b: lw: hdwy 2f out: hrd rdn over 1f out: nt qckn ins fnl f) | ½ | **4** | 4/1[3] | 50 | 18 |
| 2186[8] | **Just Lady (62)** (WGMTurner) **3-8-13**(7) DSweeney(11) (led & sn clr: wknd & hdd ins fnl f) | 3½ | **5** | 25/1 | 50 | 15 |
| | **Imposing Time (65)** (MissGayKelleway) **5-9-12** TQuinn(9) (hld up: effrt & rdn 2f out: sn wknd) | 3 | **6** | 3/1[2] | 44 | 12 |
| 2787[4] | **Superlao (BEL) (40)** (JJBridger) **4-8-1** JQuinn(1) (racd wd: gd spd 3f) | 5 | **7** | 12/1 | 3 | — |
| 2787[9] | **Classic Pet (IRE) (37)** (CAHorgan) **4-7-12v[1]** NAdams(8) (b: a bhd) | 1 | **8** | 25/1 | — | — |
| | **Paley Prince (USA) (62)** (MDIUsher) **10-9-2**(7) RBrisland(7) (lw: a bhd) | 2½ | **9** | 25/1 | 14 | — |
| 2976[10] | **Millesime (IRE) (67)** (BHanbury) **4-10-0** WRyan(4) (b: wl bhd fnl 2f) | 1½ | **10** | 16/1 | 14 | — |
| *2992[2]* | ***Malibu Man (63)*** (EAWheeler) **4-9-10** TSprake(2) (Withdrawn not under Starter's orders: unruly in stalls) | | **W** | 11/2 | — | — |
| | | | | (SP 125.9%) | **10 Rn** | |

**62.1 secs** (2.90) CSF £48.44 CT £503.79 TOTE £2.70: £1.30 £5.30 £2.80 (£71.60) Trio £156.00; £43.97 to Ripon 5/8/96 OWNER The Square Table (NEWMARKET) BRED Mrs C. F. Van Straubenzee and R. Mead
WEIGHT FOR AGE 3yo-3lb
STEWARDS' ENQUIRY Sanders susp. 12/8/96 (improper use of the whip).
**2976 Gone Savage** made amends for a couple of unlucky runs at Sandown. (9/4)
**862 La Belle Dominique**, freshened up by a break, ran her best race for some time. (33/1)
**2992 Scored Again** gave a good account of himself off a 3lb lower mark than at Chepstow. (14/1)
**2960* The Institute Boy** won too easily for his own good at Catterick and was 8lb higher here. (4/1: 3/1-9/2)
**Just Lady**, dropped 8lb, really blazed a trail against the stands' rail. (25/1)
**Imposing Time** has a record of three wins over this trip from twenty-four starts for Tommy Stack in Ireland. (3/1: op 5/1)

## 3262 SOUTH WEST MAIDEN STKS (3-Y.O) (Class D)

8-30 (8-34) **1m 67y** £3,889.50 (£1,176.00: £573.00: £271.50) Stalls: High GOING minus 0.21 sec per fur (GF)

| | | | | SP | RR | SF |
|---|---|---|---|---|---|---|
| 2041[20] | **Civil Liberty (90)** (GLewis) **3-9-0** PatEddery(10) (mde virtually all: rdn over 2f out: r.o wl) | — | **1** | 11/10[1] | 85 | 41 |
| | **Grand Musica** (IABalding) **3-8-9**(5) MartinDwyer(13) (w'like: a.p: chsd wnr fnl 2f: r.o ins fnl f) | 1½ | **2** | 20/1 | 82 | 38 |
| | **Dark Truffle** (MrsJCecil) **3-8-9** BDoyle(6) (a.p: rdn over 2f out: nt qckn) | 6 | **3** | 6/1[3] | 66 | 22 |
| | **Take Notice** (GHarwood) **3-9-0** AClark(2) (w'like: scope: a.p: ev ch 3f out: sn wknd) | 5 | **4** | 13/2 | 61 | 17 |
| | **Dantesque (IRE)** (GWragg) **3-9-0** MHills(12) (w'like: scope: dwlt: hdwy 2f out: nrst fin) | 2½ | **5** | 11/2[2] | 56 | 12 |
| | **Polish Rhythm (IRE)** (MHTompkins) **3-8-9** PRobinson(5) (w'like: scope: prom tl wknd 2f out) | 1¾ | **6** | 16/1 | 48 | 4 |
| 3115[6] | **Koraloona (IRE)** (GBBalding) **3-8-11**(3) SDrowne(15) (nvr nr to chal) | 1 | **7** | 40/1 | 51 | 7 |
| 2181[6] | **The Polymath** (HCandy) **3-9-0** CRutter(3) (plld hrd: prom tl wknd 2f out) | nk | **8** | 10/1 | 50 | 6 |
| | **Samorelle** (MJRyan) **3-8-2**(7) AMcCarthy(8) (w'like: b.hind: nvr nr to chal) | s.h | **9** | 25/1 | 45 | 1 |
| | **Sovereign Crest (IRE)** (CAHorgan) **3-9-0** PaulEddery(9) (scope: nvr bttr than mid div) | ½ | **10** | 40/1 | 49 | 5 |
| 3115[7] | **Calandrella** (GBBalding) **3-8-9** AMcGlone(14) (nvr trbld ldrs) | nk | **11** | 33/1 | 44 | — |
| | **Atomic Shell (CAN)** (CFWall) **3-9-0** GDuffield(7) (scope: lw: wl bhd tl stdy hdwy over 2f out: nvr plcd to chal) | 2½ | **12** | 40/1 | 44 | — |
| 2996[12] | **Thurstaston (IRE)** (JHMGosden) **3-9-0** BThomson(18) (plld hrd: w wnr: grad wknd fnl 3f) | s.h | **13** | 25/1 | 44 | — |
| | **Startingo** (BJLlewellyn) **3-9-0** VSlattery(1) (lengthy: s.s: a bhd) | 9 | **14** | 50/1 | 26 | — |
| | **Theatre's Dream (IRE)** (JEBanks) **3-9-0** JStack(4) (neat: a bhd) | s.h | **15** | 25/1 | 26 | — |
| | **Rapid Retreat (FR)** (EALDunlop) **3-8-9** WRyan(11) (unf: mid div tl wknd 2f out) | nk | **16** | 12/1 | 21 | — |
| | **Bigwig (IRE)** (AMoore) **3-8-11**(3) DaneO'Neill(16) (w'like: s.s: a wl bhd) | 1½ | **17** | 40/1 | 23 | — |
| 3064[W] | **Press On Nicky** (WRMuir) **3-8-9** JReid(17) (Withdrawn not under Starter's orders: ref to ent stalls) | | **W** | 12/1 | — | — |
| | | | | (SP 151.9%) | **17 Rn** | |

**1m 46.3** (4.10) CSF £28.56 TOTE £2.10: £1.30 £5.90 £2.70 (£32.30) Trio £222.40; £140.99 to Ripon 5/8/96 OWNER Midcourts (EPSOM)
**1452 Civil Liberty**, by far the most experienced of the field, proved too good for this bunch. (11/10: 7/4-Evens)
**Grand Musica**, given a nice introduction, beat the others easily enough, and seems capable of finding a race. (20/1)
**Dark Truffle** may do better over further. (6/1: op 10/1)
**Take Notice**, a well-bred newcomer, possesses the physique to progress. (13/2)
**Dantesque (IRE)**, a 115,000 guinea yearling, shaped well enough, and his dam's side suggests he will need a stiffer test of stamina.(11/2: 3/1-6/1)
**Polish Rhythm (IRE)** is a half-sister to Cheveley Park winner Capricciosa and mile juvenile winner Delightful Chime. (16/1)
**3115 Koraloona (IRE)** is now qualified for handicaps. (40/1)
**Atomic Shell (CAN)** was given an educational debut and should do better in due course. (40/1)
**Rapid Retreat (FR)** (12/1: 7/1-14/1)

T/Plpt: £22.10 (560.98 Tckts). T/Qdpt: £6.50 (110.23 Tckts). KH

# 2696-CHESTER (L-H) (Good to firm)

## Sunday August 4th

WEATHER: fine & sunny WIND: mod bhd

## 3263 WEST PENNINE TRUCKS FOR SCANIA CONDITIONS STKS (3-Y.O+) (Class B)

2-30 (2-31) **7f 2y** £9,217.60 (£3,225.60: £1,577.80: £679.00) Stalls: Low GOING minus 0.36 sec per fur (F)

| | | | | SP | RR | SF |
|---|---|---|---|---|---|---|
| 3083[5] | **Wizard King (114)** (SirMarkPrescott) **5-9-2** WWoods(1) (lw: chsd ldr: led over 3f out: sn clr: unchal) | — | **1** | 8/13[1] | 104 | 54 |

| | | | | SP | RR | SF |
|---|---|---|---|---|---|---|
| 2400* | **Chickawicka (IRE) (87)** (BPalling) **5-9-2** DeclanO'Shea(2) (led to ½-wy: rdn & outpcd ent st: kpt on fnl f: no ch w wnr) | 5 | **2** | 13/2$^{3}$ | 93 | 43 |
| 2853$^{4}$ | **Star of Zilzal (USA) (100)** (MRStoute) **4-9-2** KFallon(3) (dwlt: plld hrd in rr: effrt over 2f out: sn rdn & no imp) | 1¼ | **3** | 11/4$^{2}$ | 90 | 40 |
| 2691$^{4}$ | **Sabot (96)** (BWHills) **3-8-13** MHills(4) (trckd ldrs: drvn along & effrt over 2f out: one pce appr fnl f) | 1¼ | **4** | 11/1 | 90 | 34 |
| | | | | (SP 110.2%) | | **4 Rn** |

**1m 26.62** (1.42) CSF £4.57 TOTE £1.70: (£3.20) OWNER Sheikh Ahmed bin Saeed Al Maktoum (NEWMARKET) BRED Sheikh Mohammed bin Rashid al Maktoum
WEIGHT FOR AGE 3yo-6lb

**3083 Wizard King**, let down to lead at halfway, gradually forged clear and outclassed the opposition. From the in-form Prescott stable, he should be able to go on from here. (8/13)
**2400* Chickawicka (IRE)** is hardly up to the class of the winner but his front-running tactics are suited by this track and, though he did drop to the rear on the home turn, he renewed his effort again towards the finish and ran out a worthy runner-up. (13/2)
**2853 Star of Zilzal (USA)** possibly needs a slightly longer trip on such a tight track, for he was hard at work entering the straight and unable to make much impression. (11/4)
**2691 Sabot** followed the winner through, but found him pulling away approaching the final furlong, and had to admit he was a bit out of his class. (11/1)

## 3264 E.B.F. SALTNEY MAIDEN STKS (2-Y.O) (Class D)

3-00 (3-02) **7f 2y** £4,443.00 (£1,248.00: £609.00) Stalls: Low GOING minus 0.36 sec per fur (F)

| | | | | SP | RR | SF |
|---|---|---|---|---|---|---|
| 2073$^{2}$ | **State Fair** (BWHills) **2-9-0** MHills(2) (mde all: qcknd clr 2f out: eased towards fin) | — | **1** | 11/10$^{1}$ | 98+ | 28 |
| 2783$^{2}$ | **Hindsight (IRE)** (WJHaggas) **2-9-0** KFallon(1) (b.nr fore: chsd wnr: hrd drvn 2f out: sn outpcd) | 7 | **2** | 11/10$^{1}$ | 82 | 12 |
| 2865$^{2}$ | **Danehill Princess (IRE) (73)** (RHollinshead) **2-8-6**(3) FLynch(3) (trckd ldrs: ev ch over 2f out: sn rdn & outpcd) | 3½ | **3** | 14/1$^{2}$ | 69 | — |
| | ***Attitre (FR)*** (CEBrittain) **2-8-9** BDoyle(4) (Withdrawn not under Starter's orders: bridle broke at s) | | **W** | 14/1$^{2}$ | — | — |
| | | | | (SP 108.6%) | | **3 Rn** |

**1m 28.74** (3.54) CSF £2.27 TOTE £1.70: (£1.10) OWNER Mr Ray Richards (LAMBOURN) BRED Hesmonds Stud Ltd
OFFICIAL EXPLANATION **Hindsight (IRE): lost his off-fore shoe during the race.**

**2073 State Fair** showed at Royal Ascot that he possesses plenty of ability and, given time, he made mincemeat of this opposition. He looks a class act in the making. (11/10: 4/6-5/4)
**2783 Hindsight (IRE)**, much sharper this time, was always playing second fiddle to the winner and never promised to finish any closer than second. (11/10: op 7/4)
**2865 Danehill Princess (IRE)** tried hard to mount a challenge on the approach to the straight, but the winner only needed to lengthen to draw away, and she found the principals much too good for her. (14/1)

## 3265 MAIL ON SUNDAY MILE H'CAP (Qualifier) (0-85) (3-Y.O+) (Class D)

3-30 (3-30) **7f 122y** £9,525.75 (£2,886.00: £1,410.50: £672.75) Stalls: Low GOING minus 0.36 sec per fur (F)

| | | | | SP | RR | SF |
|---|---|---|---|---|---|---|
| 2954$^{4}$ | **My Gallery (IRE) (70)** (ABailey) **5-8-12**(3) DWright(1) (a.p: qcknd to ld appr fnl f: drvn out) | — | **1** | 100/30$^{1}$ | 79 | 45 |
| 3125$^{8}$ | **Wentbridge Lad (IRE) (65)** (PDEvans) **6-8-10v** SSanders(8) (hld up in rr: hdwy on ins ent st: rdn & r.o wl) | 1¼ | **2** | 7/1 | 71 | 37 |
| 2856$^{10}$ | **Champagne Grandy (80)** (MRChannon) **6-9-6**(5) PPMurphy(2) (trckd ldrs: n.m.r & lost pl over 2f out: rallied u.p fnl f) | 1¾ | **3** | 12/1 | 83 | 49 |
| 2729$^{9}$ | **Ertlon (74)** (CEBrittain) **6-9-5** BDoyle(5) (lw: chsd ldr: hrd rdn wl over 1f out: one pce) | hd | **4** | 12/1 | 76 | 42 |
| 2874$^{2}$ | **Sagebrush Roller (67)** (JWWatts) **8-8-12** NConnorton(9) (lw: hld up: hdwy on outside ent st: styd on wl fnl f) | nk | **5** | 9/2$^{2}$ | 69 | 35 |
| 3152$^{3}$ | **Cretan Gift (67)** (NPLittmoden) **5-8-9b**(3) FLynch(3) (hld up in tch: gd hdwy over 2f out: one pce appr fnl f) | s.h | **6** | 5/1$^{3}$ | 69 | 35 |
| 2693$^{2}$ | **Queens Consul (IRE) (83)** (BSRothwell) **6-9-9**(5) PRoberts(7) (hld up mid div: effrt & rdn 3f out: outpcd ent st) | 2 | **7** | 9/2$^{2}$ | 81 | 47 |
| 2799$^{5}$ | **Little Ibnr (56)** (PDEvans) **5-8-1** JFEgan(4) (lw: led tl rdn & hdd over 1f out: sn btn) | 2 | **8** | 20/1 | 49 | 15 |
| *3063*$^{6}$ | **Le Sport (72)** (ABailey) **3-8-10** GCarter(6) (lw: a bhd: hrd drvn over 2f out: no imp) | 4 | **9** | 16/1 | 57 | 16 |
| | | | | (SP 114.6%) | | **9 Rn** |

**1m 34.27** (2.27) CSF £24.59 CT £226.42 TOTE £3.80: £1.50 £1.90 £2.40 (£11.60) Trio £38.40 OWNER Mr Robert Cox (TARPORLEY) BRED East Riding Sack and Paper Co
WEIGHT FOR AGE 3yo-7lb

**2954 My Gallery (IRE)**, waiting on the leaders, had the gap she had been hoping for soon after entering the straight and, quickening through like a rat up a drainpipe, was soon in control. (100/30)
**2796 Wentbridge Lad (IRE)**, winner of this race last year, had not tasted success since, but he did run a very promising race, and gave the impression that he is approaching his best. (7/1)
**633 Champagne Grandy**, much better when she can get her toe in, was searching for room on the inside over two furlongs out and was forced to check, but she did rally inside the final furlong to go down fighting. (12/1)
**2283 Ertlon** has not won a race for quite some time, but he put in a spirited display here and he is up to winning another race, if the Handicapper will give him a chance. (12/1: op 8/1)
**2874 Sagebrush Roller**, not so effective on such fast ground, produced a sustained run up the centre of the track once in line for home, but could not quite reach the principals. (9/2)
**3152 Cretan Gift** moved into the action entering the straight, but was not able to find anything extra and this longer trip seemed to be stretching his stamina to the limit. (5/1)

## 3266 SCANIA 1996 TRUCK OF THE YEAR RATED STKS H'CAP (0-95) (4-Y.O+) (Class C)

4-00 (4-00) **2m 2f 147y** £15,230.50 (£5,699.50: £2,787.25: £1,198.75: £536.88: £272.12) Stalls: High GOING minus 0.36 sec per fur (F)

| | | | | SP | RR | SF |
|---|---|---|---|---|---|---|
| 3142$^{2}$ | **Sea Victor (76)** (JLHarris) **4-8-2** BDoyle(9) (lw: chsd ldrs: styd on to ld ins fnl f: all out) | — | **1** | 6/1 | 87 | 36 |
| 2547$^{3}$ | **Danjing (IRE) (86)** (MCPipe) **4-8-12** MHills(5) (lost pl ½-wy: hrd rdn 3f out: nt clr run ent st: str run on ins fnl f: jst failed) | nk | **2** | 8/1 | 97 | 46 |
| 2912$^{4}$ | **Embryonic (IRE) (76)** (RFFisher) **4-8-2** GCarter(8) (lw: a.p: led over 1f out tl ins fnl f: rallied gamely nr fin) | hd | **3** | 12/1 | 87 | 36 |
| 2042$^{3}$ | **Candle Smile (USA) (88)** (MRStoute) **4-8-11**(3) FLynch(4) (plld hrd: led & sn clr: rn w paddock bnd: rdn & hdd over 1f out: sn btn) | 5 | **4** | 11/2$^{3}$ | 94 | 43 |

| | Horse / details | Btn | Pos | SP | RR | SF |
|---|---|---|---|---|---|---|
| 2071[6] | **Upper Mount Clair (73)** (CEBrittain) **6-7-13**ow1 JFEgan(6) (hld up in rr: hdwy over 5f out: rdn 2f out: nt rch ldrs) | 1¼ | **5** | 16/1 | 78 | 26 |
| 2547[8] | **Shadirwan (IRE) (78)** (RAkehurst) **5-8-4** SSanders(1) (trckd ldrs: hrd drvn over 2f out: no imp) | 4 | **6** | 12/1 | 80 | 29 |
| 2884* | **Top Cees (87)** (MrsJRRamsden) **6-8-13** KFallon(3) (lw: hld up mid div: drvn along 6f out: effrt 3f out: wknd wl over 1f out & eased) | 9 | **7** | 13/8[1] | 81 | 30 |
| 2690[4] | **Remaadi Sun (84)** (MDIUsher) **4-8-10** RStreet(2) (hld up: a bhd: t.o) | 9 | **8** | 12/1 | 70 | 19 |
| 2547* | **Pearl Venture (80)** (SPCWoods) **4-8-6** WWoods(7) (hld up in rr: t.o fnl 3f) | 6 | **9** | 5/1[2] | 61 | 10 |

(SP 124.5%) **9 Rn**

**4m 5.38** (5.38) CSF £51.42 CT £523.81 TOTE £6.90: £1.90 £2.00 £2.30 (£15.40) Trio £68.90 OWNER Mr David Abell (MELTON MOWBRAY) BRED Juddmonte Farms

OFFICIAL EXPLANATION **Top Cees: the jockey reported that the gelding was under pressure seven furlongs out, felt flat and had no more to give once they turned for home.**

**3142 Sea Victor**, a very tough individual who was narrowly beaten over a marathon trip at Goodwood five days ago, deservedly got back to winning ways with another all-out battle to the line. This time though the photo came out in his favour. (6/1)

**2547 Danjing (IRE)**, hard at work when denied a clear run entering the straight, responded to a forceful ride up the inside rail and only just failed to gain the day. He should not be long in winning for his new connections. (8/1)

**2912 Embryonic (IRE)** does not have the success he deserves, for he never stopped trying and still only came out third best in the photo. At least time is on his side. (12/1)

**2042 Candle Smile (USA)** is not an ideal ride for a boy over such a long trip, for he takes a very keen tug and, as in this case, virtually ran himself into the ground. (11/2)

**1091 Upper Mount Clair** began to stay on six furlongs out, but she was unable to increase her pace under strong pressure and failed to get close enough to land a blow. (16/1)

**449* Shadirwan (IRE)** only does as much as he wants and he was content to stay where he was, despite the strongest encouragement inside the last half-mile. (12/1: op 8/1)

**2884* Top Cees**, nudged along going out on the final circuit, did make a token effort three furlongs out, be he had met his match early in the straight, and the position was accepted. (13/8: op 5/2)

## 3267 SCANIA 4-SERIES 'KING OF THE ROAD' H'CAP (0-70) (3-Y.O+ F & M) (Class E)

4-30 (4-31) **1m 4f 66y** £3,582.50 (£1,085.00: £530.00: £252.50) Stalls: Low GOING minus 0.36 sec per fur (F)

| | Horse / details | Btn | Pos | SP | RR | SF |
|---|---|---|---|---|---|---|
| 2793[3] | **Rasayel (USA) (55)** (PDEvans) **6-9-10** JFEgan(2) (hld up: hdwy 4f out: rdn to ld 2f out: drvn clr) | — | **1** | 5/1 | 68 | 50 |
| 2988[2] | **Campaspe (44)** (JGFitzGerald) **4-8-13** KFallon(5) (lw: hld up: pushed along 7f out: led 4f out to 2f out: hrd rdn: sn btn) | 5 | **2** | 2/1[1] | 51 | 33 |
| 866[4] | **Hill Farm Dancer (50)** (WMBrisbourne) **5-8-12**(7) IonaWands(1) (bit bkwd: s.s: in rr tl styd on fnl 2f) | 3½ | **3** | 8/1 | 52 | 34 |
| 2599[5] | **Sacred Mirror (IRE) (55)** (CEBrittain) **5-9-10** BDoyle(4) (b: prom: drvn along 4f out: one pce fnl 2f) | 4 | **4** | 4/1[3] | 52 | 34 |
| 2941* | **Kristal Breeze (46)** (WRMuir) **4-9-1** MHills(3) (led over 8f: rdn & wknd over 2f out: t.o) | 9 | **5** | 11/4[2] | 31 | 13 |

(SP 107.8%) **5 Rn**

**2m 41.23** (4.63) CSF £14.17 TOTE £6.30: £2.50 £1.40 (£5.70) OWNER Pentons Haulage and Cold Storage Ltd (WELSHPOOL) BRED Gainsborough Farm

OFFICIAL EXPLANATION **Kristal Breeze: was unsuited by having to make the running.**

**2793 Rasayel (USA)**, from a really in-form stable, picked off the favourite very much as she pleased and won this with the minimum of fuss. (5/1)

**2988 Campaspe** has got a bad case of seconditis at the moment and, though she was given every opportunity, she had to admit the winner much too smart for her. (2/1)

**866 Hill Farm Dancer**, not for the first time, lost ground at the start but, on ground as lively as this, was never able to get herself into contention. (8/1)

**2599 Sacred Mirror (IRE)** appears to be in the grasp of the Handicapper, and was struggling to remain in touch in the last three furlongs. (4/1)

**2941* Kristal Breeze** is no more than a selling plater and, after tugging her rivals along for the first mile, gradually faded and tailed off. (11/4)

## 3268 SCANIA 4-SERIES 'HORSEPOWER' NURSERY H'CAP (2-Y.O) (Class D)

5-00 (5-00) **6f 18y** £4,279.50 (£1,296.00: £633.00: £301.50) Stalls: Low GOING minus 0.36 sec per fur (F)

| | Horse / details | Btn | Pos | SP | RR | SF |
|---|---|---|---|---|---|---|
| 3128[4] | **I Can't Remember (70)** (PDEvans) **2-7-7**(3) DWright(3) (hld up: hdwy 2f out: shkn up to ld ins fnl f: r.o wl) | — | **1** | Evens[1] | 67 | 12 |
| 3150[3] | **Foot Battalion (IRE) (95)** (RHollinshead) **2-9-4**(3) FLynch(4) (lw: hld up in rr: effrt wl over 1f out: kpt on wl fnl f) | 1¾ | **2** | 11/4[2] | 87 | 32 |
| 2700[5] | **Weet Ees Girl (IRE) (88)** (PDEvans) **2-8-9**(5) DGriffiths(1) (led: rdn ent st: hdd & no ex ins fnl f) | s.h | **3** | 6/1 | 80 | 25 |
| 1352[3] | **Wait For Rosie (91)** (MRChannon) **2-8-12**(5) PPMurphy(2) (chsd ldr: hrd drvn 2f out: one pce) | nk | **4** | 7/2[3] | 83 | 28 |

(SP 113.2%) **4 Rn**

**1m 16.26** (2.96) CSF £4.11 TOTE £2.00: (£2.10) OWNER Peter Graham Racing (WELSHPOOL) BRED C. G. Reid

**3128 I Can't Remember** is very consistent and took advantage of a lenient handicap mark to win comfortably. (Evens)

**3150 Foot Battalion (IRE)** needs a stiffer test of stamina, and his determined challenge inside the distance was never going to get him there. (11/4)

**2700 Weet Ees Girl (IRE)**, a stable-companion to the winner, adopted more forceful tactics and held the call until tapped for toe inside the final furlong. (6/1)

**1352 Wait For Rosie**, returning after a ten-week break, was always in the action, but she was at full stretch to get the better of the leader, and could not muster the pace to do so. (7/2)

T/Plpt: £126.30 (125.64 Tckts). T/Qdpt: £35.20 (23.86 Tckts). IM

# 3074-LINGFIELD (L-H) (Good to firm, Firm patches)

## Sunday August 4th

WEATHER: hot WIND: almost nil

## 3269 DOM RUINART CHAMPAGNE SUNDAY MAIDEN STKS (2-Y.O) (Class D)

2-20 (2-20) **6f** £3,625.10 (£1,098.80: £537.40: £256.70) Stalls: High GOING minus 0.31 sec per fur (GF)

| | Horse / details | Btn | Pos | SP | RR | SF |
|---|---|---|---|---|---|---|
| 1130[3] | **Hawait (IRE)** (BWHills) **2-9-0** RHills(5) (hld up: chsd ldr over 1f out: led ins fnl f: pushed out) | — | **1** | 2/1[1] | 85+ | 33 |

| Form | Horse | Dist | Pos | SP | RR | SF |
|---|---|---|---|---|---|---|
| | **Curzon Street** (MRStoute) **2-8-9** DHarrison(7) (unf: hld up: nt clr run over 1f out: r.o ins fnl f) | nk | **2** | $5/1^{3}$ | 79+ | 27 |
| $2879^{13}$ | **Bewitching Lady** (DWPArbuthnot) **2-8-9** RPrice(2) (led: rdn over 2f out: hdd ins fnl f: unable qckn) | 1¾ | **3** | 33/1 | 75 | 23 |
| | **Attribute** (RCharlton) **2-8-9** TSprake(9) (unf: scope: hdwy & nt clr run over 1f out: r.o wl ins fnl f) | ½ | **4** | 15/2 | 73+ | 21 |
| $2720^{3}$ | **Eurolink Spartacus** (JLDunlop) **2-9-0** GDuffield(11) (a.p: rdn over 2f out: one pce) | 1½ | **5** | $5/2^{2}$ | 74 | 22 |
| $2702^{9}$ | **Be True** (AMoore) **2-9-0** CandyMorris(8) (swtg: prom over 4f) | 3 | **6** | 100/1 | 66 | 14 |
| | **Greenwich Fore** (TGMills) **2-8-11**(3) DaneO'Neill(10) (str: bkwd: prom over 4f) | s.h | **7** | 33/1 | 66 | 14 |
| | **Heavenly Ray (USA)** (JRFanshawe) **2-8-6**(3) NVarley(4) (leggy: unf: j.path over 4f out: rdn & hdwy over 2f out: wknd over 1f out) | s.h | **8** | 20/1 | 61 | 9 |
| $2852^{8}$ | **Abacaxi (IRE)** (RCharlton) **2-9-0** WRyan(3) (a bhd) | 3½ | **9** | 20/1 | 57 | 5 |
| $2353^{4}$ | **Highway Robber (IRE)** (JMPEustace) **2-9-0** JTate(1) (s.s: a bhd) | 7 | **10** | 20/1 | 38 | — |
| | **Cabcharge Gemini** (GGMargarson) **2-9-0** PBloomfield(6) (leggy: prom over 2f) | 11 | **11** | 50/1 | 9 | — |

(SP 113.5%) **11 Rn**

**1m 11.68** (2.68) CSF £11.42 TOTE £2.90: £1.30 £2.40 £3.90 (£9.30) Trio £80.50 OWNER Maktoum Al Maktoum (LAMBOURN) BRED John R. Gaines

**1130 Hawait (IRE)** looked rather temperamental last time out but has been given an eleven-week break, and did little wrong on this return. Chasing the leaders, he moved into second place below the distance and, shaken up to lead inside the final furlong, won with a little bit in hand. (2/1)

**Curzon Street** chased the leaders. With not a great deal of room in which to manoeuvre below the distance, she then found an opening and ran on nicely inside the final furlong. She should pick up a small race. (5/1: op 5/2)

**Bewitching Lady** attempted to make all. Grimly trying to fend off her rivals, she was eventually overhauled inside the final furlong. (33/1)

**Attribute**, a plain filly, was just picking up ground when meeting traffic problems below the distance. This cost her ground she could ill-afford, but to her credit she did run on inside the final furlong when an opening appeared. A race of this nature is well within her compass. (15/2)

**2720 Eurolink Spartacus**, in the front rank throughout, failed to quicken in the last two furlongs. (5/2)

**Be True** was close up until tiring below the distance. (100/1)

## 3270 WILLIAM HILL H'CAP (0-85) (3-Y.O) (Class D)

2-50 (2-50) **6f** £3,647.50 (£1,105.00: £540.00: £257.50) Stalls: High GOING minus 0.31 sec per fur (GF)

| Form | Horse | Dist | Pos | SP | RR | SF |
|---|---|---|---|---|---|---|
| $2946^{11}$ | **Times of Times (IRE) (66)** (MJRyan) **3-8-9** MTebbutt(6) (rdn over 2f out: nt clr run on ins over 1f out: hdwy fnl f: led nr fin) | — | **1** | 20/1 | 72 | 51 |
| $2578^{15}$ | **Sea Danzig (63)** (JJBridger) **3-8-6** DHarrison(1) (lw: w ldr: rdn over 1f out: led ins fnl f: hdd nr fin) | nk | **2** | 16/1 | 68 | 47 |
| 3112* | **Kind of Light (80)** (RGuest) **3-9-6**(3) 7x DaneO'Neill(3) (hld up: rdn over 1f out: ev ch ins fnl f: one pce) | ½ | **3** | $11/10^{1}$ | 84 | 63 |
| $2946^{12}$ | **May Queen Megan (54)** (MrsALMKing) **3-7-11** NAdams(4) (lw: led: rdn over 1f out: hdd ins fnl f: one pce) | ½ | **4** | 12/1 | 57 | 36 |
| $3168^{3}$ | **Never Think Twice (58)** (KTIvory) **3-7-10b**(5) MartinDwyer(5) (b: reard s: rdn over 2f out: nvr nr to chal) | hd | **5** | $9/2^{3}$ | 60 | 39 |
| $716^{6}$ | **Splinter (IRE) (78)** (RCharlton) **3-9-7** TSprake(2) (hld up: rdn over 1f out: one pce) | nk | **6** | $3/1^{2}$ | 80 | 59 |

(SP 109.1%) **6 Rn**

**1m 10.07** (1.07) CSF £195.88 TOTE £20.70: £5.10 £3.00 (£60.10) OWNER Mr A. S. Reid (NEWMARKET) BRED E. Moloney

**2410* Times of Times (IRE)** bounced back to form. Held up off the pace, she failed to get a clear run along the inside rail below the distance for a while, and her chances did not look good, but she found a nice turn of foot in the final furlong to swoop into the lead near the line. (20/1)

**2316 Sea Danzig** was another to bounce back to form. Disputing the lead, he eventually got on top inside the final furlong, only to be caught near the line. (16/1)

**3112* Kind of Light** chased the leaders. Throwing down her challenge from below the distance, she had every chance inside the final furlong, before tapped for toe. (11/10: Evens-6/5)

**2686* May Queen Megan** attempted to make all. Collared inside the final furlong, she failed to find another gear. (12/1: op 8/1)

**3168 Never Think Twice**, making a quick reappearance, was at the back of the field until making up some late headway without ever threatening the principals. (9/2)

**716 Splinter (IRE)**, after a three and a half month break, chased the leaders and appeared to be going sweetly a quarter of a mile out. Once asked for his effort below the distance, he failed to find what was required. (3/1: 9/4-7/2)

## 3271 TJH GROUP LINGFIELD SUNDAY H'CAP (0-100) (3-Y.O+) (Class C)

3-20 (3-20) **7f** £5,329.70 (£1,613.60: £787.80: £374.90) Stalls: High GOING minus 0.31 sec per fur (GF)

| Form | Horse | Dist | Pos | SP | RR | SF |
|---|---|---|---|---|---|---|
| $3045^{4}$ | **Jerry Cutrona (IRE) (74)** (NACallaghan) **3-7-10** GBardwell(4) (rdn 4f out: hdwy 1f out: led wl ins fnl f: r.o wl) | — | **1** | $11/2^{3}$ | 84 | 60 |
| $2623^{8}$ | **Neuwest (USA) (80)** (NJHWalker) **4-8-8** JStack(3) (lw: hld up: led 2f out: hrd rdn over 1f out: hdd wl ins fnl f: unable qckn) | 1¼ | **2** | $4/1^{1}$ | 87 | 69 |
| $2705^{6}$ | **Ashjar (USA) (85)** (HThomsonJones) **3-8-7** RHills(7) (a.p: led over 2f out: sn hdd: hrd rdn over 1f out: one pce) | nk | **3** | 7/1 | 92 | 68 |
| $3207^{3}$ | **Silent Expression (84)** (BJMeehan) **6-8-12** MTebbutt(8) (rdn over 2f out: hdwy over 1f out: one pce ins fnl f) | ½ | **4** | 13/2 | 89 | 71 |
| $2351^{7}$ | **Daryabad (IRE) (77)** (TJNaughton) **4-8-5** TSprake(9) (rdn over 3f out: nvr nr to chal) | 3 | **5** | 16/1 | 76 | 58 |
| $2880^{6}$ | **Please Suzanne (98)** (RHannon) **3-9-3**(3) DaneO'Neill(6) (hld up: rdn over 1f out: wknd fnl f) | 1¾ | **6** | $5/1^{2}$ | 93 | 69 |
| $2920^{4}$ | **Double Blue (100)** (MJohnston) **7-9-7**(7) NPollard(1) (lw: racd alone centre: led over 4f: wknd over 1f out) | 1 | **7** | 8/1 | 92 | 74 |
| $2602^{2}$ | **Victory Team (IRE) (69)** (GBBalding) **4-7-8**(3) NVarley(2) (prom over 5f) | ½ | **8** | 6/1 | 60 | 42 |

(SP 109.2%) **8 Rn**

**1m 21.13** (-0.47) CSF £24.74 CT £127.14 TOTE £7.40: £2.40 £1.40 £1.80 (£16.20) Trio £36.90 OWNER Mr Michael Hill (NEWMARKET) BRED Dr Paschal Carmody

LONG HANDICAP Jerry Cutrona (IRE) 7-8

WEIGHT FOR AGE 3yo-6lb

**3045 Jerry Cutrona (IRE)**, ridden along and going nowhere in last place at halfway, only found his feet inside the distance. Coming with a wet sail, he got on top in the final stages. (11/2)

**2623 Neuwest (USA)** got to the front a quarter of a mile out but, despite grimly fending off his challengers, was overhauled by the winner in the closing stages. (4/1)

**2705 Ashjar (USA)**, in the front rank throughout, went on over a quarter of a mile out. Soon headed, he failed to find another gear. (7/1)

**3207 Silent Expression** made her effort below the distance, but was tapped for toe in the last 100 yards. (13/2)

**Daryabad (IRE)** could never get in a telling blow. (16/1)

**2880 Please Suzanne** chased the leaders and appeared to be going well a quarter of a mile out but, asked for her effort below the distance, failed to find what was required. (5/1)

**2920 Double Blue** (8/1: 6/1-9/1)

## 3272 SUNDAY EXPRESS BEST FOR SPORT H'CAP (0-80) (3-Y.O+) (Class D)

3-50 (3-50) **1m 2f** £3,501.25 (£1,060.00: £517.50: £246.25) Stalls: Low GOING minus 0.31 sec per fur (GF)

| | | | | SP | RR | SF |
|---|---|---|---|---|---|---|
| $2593^{5}$ | **Another Time (70)** (SPCWoods) **4-9-5** DBiggs(3) (lw: hdwy over 2f out: barged thro over 1f out: led ins fnl f: rdn out) | — | **1** | 13/2 | 83 | 62 |
| | **North Reef (IRE) (70)** (SirMarkPrescott) **5-9-5** GDuffield(5) (swtg: chsd ldrs: led over 2f out tl ins fnl f: unable qckn) | 1 | **2** | 5/2 1 | 81 | 60 |
| $2883^{5}$ | **Vola Via (USA) (80)** (IABalding) **3-9-1**(5) MartinDwyer(4) (lw: s.s: rdn over 3f out: hdwy 1f out: r.o wl ins fnl f) | hd | **3** | 5/1 | 91 | 61 |
| $2918^{3}$ | **Cerdan (USA) (80)** (MRStoute) **3-9-6** TSprake(2) (b.off hind: lw: plld hrd: a.p: hrd rdn over 2f out: ev ch over 1f out: one pce) | 1½ | **4** | 7/1 | 89 | 59 |
| $2862^{5}$ | **Apollono (75)** (JRFanshawe) **4-9-10** RHills(6) (hld up: nt clr run on ins over 1f out: swtchd rt: one pce) | ¾ | **5** | 4/1 3 | 83 | 62 |
| 3136* | **Soviet Bride (IRE) (66)** (SDow) **4-8-10**(5) RHavlin(1) (lw: led over 7f: 4th & btn whn hmpd on ins over 1f out) | 1 | **6** | 7/2 2 | 72 | 51 |
| *$2689^{8}$* | **Rival Bid (USA) (68)** (MrsNMacauley) **8-9-0**(3) CTeague(7) (lw: s.s: a bhd) | 11 | **7** | 20/1 | 56 | 35 |

(SP 118.1%) **7 Rn**

**2m 6.63** (1.93) CSF £22.93 TOTE £9.50: £3.80 £1.70 (£13.50) OWNER Mr D. Sullivan (NEWMARKET) BRED W. G. Barker
WEIGHT FOR AGE 3yo-9lb
STEWARDS' ENQUIRY Biggs susp. 13-14/8/96 (careless riding)

**2593 Another Time** picked up ground in the straight and, pushing his way through a small gap below the distance, got to the front inside the final furlong. His rider was later suspended for this. (13/2)

**North Reef (IRE)**, off the course since disappointing in the William Hill Cup at Goodwood last year, looked fit for this return but sweated up badly. Racing in second place, he moved to the front over quarter of a mile from home, but was unable to contain the winner inside the final furlong. (5/2)

**2883 Vola Via (USA)** was at the back of the field until staying on in the final furlong to be nearest at the line. (5/1)

**2918 Cerdan (USA)** had no problems with this longer trip, but he proved very headstrong. Always close up, he came under pressure over quarter of a mile out and, throwing down his challenge, still had every chance entering the final furlong, before tapped for toe. (7/1: 5/1-8/1)

**2862 Apollono** chased the leaders. He did not have a great deal of room along the inside rail below the distance, but this made little difference to his chances. (4/1)

**3136* Soviet Bride (IRE)** bowled along in front. Collared over two furlongs from home, she was held in fourth when hampered along the inside rail below the distance. (7/2)

## 3273 DISPLAYCRAFT (S) STKS (3-Y.O+) (Class F)

4-20 (4-20) **1m 6f** £2,588.40 (£727.40: £355.20) Stalls: Low GOING minus 0.31 sec per fur (GF)

| | | | | SP | RR | SF |
|---|---|---|---|---|---|---|
| $3130^{4}$ | **Durham (54)** (RSimpson) **5-9-7b** AClark(6) (lw: hdwy over 6f out: chsd ldr over 5f out: led on bit 2f out: easily) | — | **1** | 5/4 2 | 61 | 35 |
| 2626* | **Faugeron (56)** (NTinkler) **7-9-12** GDuffield(3) (lw: led 12f: hrd rdn: unable qckn fnl f) | 3½ | **2** | Evens 1 | 62 | 36 |
| $2788^{7}$ | **Lost Realm** (MartynMeade) **4-9-2**(5) RHavlin(4) (hld up: rdn 7f out: wknd over 3f out) | 10 | **3** | 50/1 | 46 | 20 |
| $2891^{5}$ | **Bresil (USA) (32)** (KRBurke) **7-9-7** DHarrison(2) (lw: chsd ldr 12f out tl over 5f out: wknd over 4f out) | 2½ | **4** | 10/1 3 | 43 | 17 |
| $2794^{13}$ | **Psp Lady** (APJones) **3-8-3** TSprake(1) (swtg: chsd ldr 2f: wknd over 5f out) | 18 | **5** | 50/1 | 17 | — |
| $2579^{16}$ | **Chant d'Alouette** (RJHodges) **3-8-0**(3) NVarley(5) (lw: a bhd: t.o fnl 7f) | 16 | **6** | 25/1 | — | — |

(SP 111.3%) **6 Rn**

**3m 6.37** (8.07) CSF £2.75 TOTE £2.70: £1.80 £1.10 (£1.60) OWNER The Secret Partnership (WELLINGTON) BRED Highclere Stud Ltd
WEIGHT FOR AGE 3yo-13lb
No bid

**3130 Durham**, making a quick reappearance, had little more than a stroll to win this poor race. Cruising up alongside the leader in the straight, he nosed into a narrow advantage a quarter of a mile out and Clark had a very tight rein on the gelding, but the combination always had things in hand and pulled away in the last 100 yards. (5/4)

**2626* Faugeron**, winner of this race last year, attempted to make all. Collared a quarter of a mile out, he remained on level terms with Durham, but it was only on sufferance and, when that one decided to find another gear, he was left standing. (Evens)

**Lost Realm** chased the leaders, but was a spent force entering the straight. (50/1)

**2891 Bresil (USA)**, soon racing in second place, was collared for that position at the top of the hill and soon in trouble. (10/1: 5/1-11/1)

## 3274 TAUBER APPRENTICE H'CAP (0-70) (3-Y.O+) (Class F)

4-50 (4-51) **7f 140y** £2,707.40 (£761.40: £372.20) Stalls: High GOING minus 0.31 sec per fur (GF)

| | | | | SP | RR | SF |
|---|---|---|---|---|---|---|
| $3139^{7}$ | **Our Shadee (USA) (49)** (KTIvory) **6-8-7v**(6) CScally(10) (lw: rdn over 2f out: hdwy over 1f out: str run fnl f: led nr fin) | — | **1** | 8/1 3 | 58 | 43 |
| $3060^{2}$ | **Flag Fen (USA) (59)** (MartynMeade) **5-8-13**(10) ClaireAngell(6) (hld up: rdn over 2f out: led ins fnl f: hdd nr fin) | nk | **2** | 12/1 | 67 | 52 |
| $3139^{3}$ | **Broughtons Turmoil (63)** (WJMusson) **7-9-13** PMcCabe(1) (swtg: hdwy over 4f out: led over 2f out tl ins fnl f: one pce) | 1 | **3** | 7/2 2 | 69 | 54 |
| $2903^{3}$ | **Paddy's Rice (56)** (MMcCormack) **5-9-6** DaneO'Neill(11) (lw: rdn over 2f out: hdwy over 1f out: r.o) | 1 | **4** | 11/4 1 | 60 | 45 |
| $2773^{5}$ | **Bentico (60)** (MrsNMacauley) **7-9-7**(3) CTeague(5) (rdn over 3f out: hdwy & nt clr run over 1f out: swtchd rt: r.o ins fnl f) | 1¾ | **5** | 14/1 | 61 | 46 |
| $3140^{6}$ | **Justinianus (IRE) (40)** (JJBridger) **4-7-13**(5) RBrisland(13) (swtg: led 5f: hrd rdn: sn wknd) | 1½ | **6** | 33/1 | 37 | 22 |
| $2994^{3}$ | **Irrepressible (IRE) (45)** (RJHodges) **5-8-6**(3) AmandaSanders(8) (hdwy over 1f out: one pce) | hd | **7** | 8/1 3 | 42 | 27 |
| $2058^{4}$ | **Helios (64)** (NJHWalker) **8-9-11**(3) GFaulkner(3) (hdwy 3f out: wknd 1f out) | 2 | **8** | 9/1 | 57 | 42 |
| *$2748^{8}$* | **Scathebury (57)** (KRBurke) **3-8-11**(3) DSweeney(2) (hld up: rdn over 2f out: wknd over 1f out) | 1½ | **9** | 12/1 | 47 | 25 |
| $1173^{12}$ | **Sweet Allegiance (46)** (JRPoulton) **6-8-5**(5) TField(12) (b.nr hind: prom over 4f) | 3½ | **10** | 40/1 | 29 | 14 |
| *$2937^{6}$* | **Hadadabble (42)** (PatMitchell) **3-7-13** NVarley(4) (lw: prom over 3f) | 1½ | **11** | 25/1 | 21 | — |
| $2785^{6}$ | **Sobeloved (32)** (NEBerry) **4-7-7**(3) CAdamson(9) (prom over 4f) | 7 | **12** | 40/1 | — | — |
| | **Rockusa (44)** (PRHedger) **4-8-8** MHenry(15) (s.s: a bhd) | ½ | **13** | 33/1 | 8 | — |
| $2706^{6}$ | **Bagby Boy (35)** (PRHedger) **4-7-8**(5) PDoe(16) (a bhd) | 3 | **14** | 50/1 | — | — |
| $1992^{10}$ | **Old Gold N Tan (39)** (JRPoulton) **3-7-10b** MartinDwyer(14) (bhd fnl 5f) | 7 | **15** | 40/1 | — | — |

(SP 122.2%) **15 Rn**

**1m 31.24** (2.44) CSF £91.80 CT £376.66 TOTE £10.40: £2.40 £3.40 £1.70 (£61.70) Trio £72.90 OWNER Mr K. T. Ivory (RADLETT) BRED Overbury Stud
LONG HANDICAP Sobeloved 7-9 Old Gold N Tan 7-4
WEIGHT FOR AGE 3yo-7lb

**2602 Our Shadee (USA)** still had it all to do a quarter of a mile out, but he came with a tremendous rattle from below the distance to sweep into the lead near the line. (8/1: 6/1-9/1)
**3060 Flag Fen (USA)** chased the leaders. He eventually got on top inside the final furlong, only to be worried out of it near the line. (12/1: op 8/1)
**3139 Broughtons Turmoil** moved up before halfway. Sent on over a quarter of a mile out, he grimly tried to fend off his rivals, but was worried out of it inside the final furlong. (7/2: 9/2-3/1)
**2903 Paddy's Rice** began to pick up ground below the distance but, despite staying on, was never going to get there in time. (11/4)
**2773 Bentico** was just picking up ground when failing to get a clear run below the distance. Switched right, he ran on inside the final furlong, but failed to trouble the principals. (14/1)
**3140 Justinianus (IRE)** attempted to make all the running. Collared over a quarter of a mile from home, he was soon in trouble. (33/1)
**2058 Helios** (9/1: op 6/1)

T/Jkpt: Not won; £3,077.37 to Ripon 5/8/96. T/Plpt: £3,057.40 (3.95 Tckts). T/Qdpt: £18.10 (49.72 Tckts). AK

# 3098-NEWCASTLE (L-H) (Good to firm, Firm patches, becoming Firm)
## Sunday August 4th

Race 2: official hand-time. Races 5 & 6: hand timed.
WEATHER: sunny WIND: mod bhd

## 3275 RACING NORTH 'MORE THAN A NEWSPAPER' NURSERY H'CAP (2-Y.O) (Class D)
2-10 (2-11) **6f** £3,533.75 (£1,070.00: £522.50: £248.75) Stalls: High GOING minus 0.57 sec per fur (F)

| | | | | SP | RR | SF |
|---|---|---|---|---|---|---|
| 3082* | **Perfect Bliss (56)** (PDEvans) **2-8-2** DaleGibson(1) (mde all: shkn up & r.o wl appr fnl f) | — | 1 | 3/1 [1] | 52 | 20 |
| *2370*[9] | **Going For Broke (63)** (PCHaslam) **2-8-9** DeanMcKeown(4) (trckd ldrs: hdwy 2f out: styd on: nt pce to chal) | 1¾ | 2 | 14/1 | 54 | 22 |
| 3057[3] | **Nostalgic Air (USA) (73)** (EWeymes) **2-9-5** JQuinn(7) (trckd ldrs: effrt 2f out: r.o one pce fnl f) | 1½ | 3 | 4/1 [2] | 60 | 28 |
| 3050[5] | **Rivonia (USA) (70)** (MrsJRRamsden) **2-9-2** JFortune(6) (lw: in tch: effrt over 2f out: rdn & no imp) | 1 | 4 | 3/1 [1] | 55 | 23 |
| 2984[7] | **Mill End Boy (73)** (MWEasterby) **2-9-0**(5) GParkin(3) (lw: bhd: effrt 2f out: no imp) | 1 | 5 | 12/1 | 55 | 23 |
| 2897[2] | **Mazil (67)** (TDEasterby) **2-8-13b** MBirch(2) (chsd ldrs tl wknd wl over 1f out) | hd | 6 | 6/1 | 49 | 17 |
| 2875[3] | **Docklands Carriage (IRE) (75)** (NTinkler) **2-9-7v** KimTinkler(5) (spd 4f: sn wknd) | 2½ | 7 | 5/1 [3] | 50 | 18 |
| | | | | (SP 115.3%) | | **7 Rn** |

**1m 12.92** (1.42) CSF £35.87 TOTE £3.00: £2.40 £4.00 (£18.70) OWNER Mr R. F. F. Mason (WELSHPOOL) BRED Mrs H. B. Raw
**3082* Perfect Bliss** has not got the best of actions, but she is a game sort and, given another fine, aggressive ride, won well. (3/1)
**1360 Going For Broke** failed to act on the All-Weather last time, but put in another decent performance here, and will surely pick up a race. (14/1)
**3057 Nostalgic Air (USA)** ran better this time, but is short of a real turn of foot to do anything serious about it, and may be better being made more use of. (4/1)
**3050 Rivonia (USA)** never really picked up when asked a question, but still left the impression that there is better to come. (3/1)
**2984 Mill End Boy** is thriving physically and, although never offering a threat here, he showed enough to suggest that there is something more to come. (12/1)
**2897 Mazil** had the blinkers on again, but they failed to have the desired effect this time. (6/1: 3/1-7/1)
**2875 Docklands Carriage (IRE)** moved poorly to post and ran most disappointingly. (5/1)

## 3276 CALDERPRINT LIMITED STKS (0-70) (3-Y.O+) (Class E)
2-40 (2-41) **1m 4f 93y** £2,892.00 (£876.00: £428.00: £204.00) Stalls: Low GOING minus 0.57 sec per fur (F)

| | | | | SP | RR | SF |
|---|---|---|---|---|---|---|
| 2570[9] | **Exactly (IRE) (70)** (JLEyre) **3-8-8** TWilliams(3) (mde all: hld on wl fnl 2f) | — | 1 | 4/1 [3] | 75 | 30 |
| 1900[3] | **Ceilidh Star (IRE) (69)** (BWHills) **3-8-6** JCarroll(4) (lw: trckd wnr: chal 2f out: nt qckn ins fnl f) | ¾ | 2 | 11/10 [1] | 72 | 27 |
| 1700[4] | **Tessajoe (70)** (MJCamacho) **4-9-8** LCharnock(2) (hld up: effrt 5f out: hdwy 3f out: rdn & btn appr fnl f) | 2½ | 3 | 2/1 [2] | 74 | 40 |
| 2912[5] | **Rossel (USA) (65)** (PMonteith) **3-8-11** NCarlisle(1) (lw: chsd ldrs: effrt over 3f out: sn btn) | 2½ | 4 | 15/2 | 71 | 26 |
| | | | | (SP 112.7%) | | **4 Rn** |

**2m 40.33** (2.83) CSF £8.76 TOTE £5.30: (£2.60) OWNER Mr Frank Thornton (HAMBLETON) BRED Asigh Farm Ltd
WEIGHT FOR AGE 3yo-11lb
**1669 Exactly (IRE)** likes to dictate and always had too much courage for the runner-up in the last two furlongs. (4/1)
**1900 Ceilidh Star (IRE)** looked a picture and had her chances, but failed to produce the goods when it mattered. (11/10: 11/8-Evens)
**1700 Tessajoe** ran a fine race after two months off and should be all the better for it. (2/1)
**2912 Rossel (USA)** showed an action that suggests easier ground might well bring improvement. (15/2: 9/2-8/1)

## 3277 E.B.F. MAIDEN STKS (2-Y.O) (Class D)
3-10 (3-11) **7f** £3,452.50 (£1,045.00: £510.00: £242.50) Stalls: High GOING minus 0.57 sec per fur (F)

| | | | | SP | RR | SF |
|---|---|---|---|---|---|---|
| 2503[5] | **Multitone** (JMPEustace) **2-9-0** JCarroll(4) (mde all: qcknd 2f out: r.o wl) | — | 1 | 9/1 | 88 | 44 |
| 2972[2] | **Shoumatara (USA)** (MRStoute) **2-9-0** MBirch(2) (lw: trckd ldrs: outpcd 2f out: hdwy u.p 1f out: nvr able to chal) | 2½ | 2 | 8/11 [1] | 82 | 38 |
| | **Double Flight** (MJohnston) **2-8-9** TWilliams(5) (w'like: leggy: scope: w wnr: effrt 2f out: btn appr fnl f) | 1¾ | 3 | 4/1 [3] | 73 | 29 |
| 2802[3] | **Dawam Allail** (MAJarvis) **2-9-0** PRobinson(1) (lw: trckd ldrs: effrt over 2f out: one pce) | 3½ | 4 | 7/2 [2] | 70 | 26 |
| 2897[3] | **Night Flight** (JJO'Neill) **2-9-0** JFortune(6) (lw: hld up: nvr plcd to chal) | 1¼ | 5 | 12/1 | 67 | 23 |
| 2865[12] | **Wildmoor** (JDBethell) **2-8-11**(3) SDrowne(3) (prom tl outpcd fnl 2f) | 4 | 6 | 50/1 | 58 | 14 |
| | | | | (SP 119.8%) | | **6 Rn** |

**1m 25.1** (0.19 under 2y best) (0.60) CSF £16.93 TOTE £16.20: £4.10 £1.10 (£8.50) OWNER Mr Peter Kan (NEWMARKET) BRED Cheveley Park Stud Ltd
**Multitone**, very much on his toes, was in and out of the paddock like a flash and everything went his way in the race. He won really well and, as long as he does not boil over, he should be quite useful. (9/1: 6/1-10/1)
**2972 Shoumatara (USA)** looked particularly one-paced here, and may do better if more use were made of him. (8/11: 4/5-Evens)
**Double Flight**, quite a nice type, ran really well and will no doubt be all the better for it. (4/1)
**2802 Dawam Allail**, happy to track the leaders, was short of pace when the race really began. (7/2)
**2897 Night Flight** ran quite well and looks one to keep an eye on, especially in nurseries. (12/1: 8/1-14/1)
**Wildmoor**, an edgy sort, was disappointing once off the bit. (50/1)

## 3278 ST. OSWALDS HOSPICE (S) STKS (3-Y.O+) (Class G)
3-40 (3-41) **6f** £2,253.00 (£633.00: £309.00) Stalls: High GOING minus 0.57 sec per fur (F)

| Form | Horse / Details | Dist | Pos | SP | RR | SF |
|---|---|---|---|---|---|---|
| 2963* | **Blue Bomber (67)** (GMMoore) **5-9-9** JFortune(9) (mde most: hld on wl fnl f) | — | 1 | $9/4^{1}$ | 64 | 46 |
| $2910^{3}$ | **Pallium (IRE) (47)** (MrsAMNaughton) **8-9-4** ACulhane(3) (lw: bhd: hdwy 2f out: nt clr run & swtchd ins fnl f: r.o) | s.h | 2 | 25/1 | 59 | 41 |
| $2680^{2}$ | **Ultra Beet (60)** (PCHaslam) **4-9-4v** PRobinson(7) (w ldrs: disp ld appr fnl f: nt qckn towards fin) | s.h | 3 | $9/2^{2}$ | 59 | 41 |
| $2898^{9}$ | **Double Oscar (IRE) (60)** (MJohnston) **3-9-0b** TWilliams(4) (disp ld to ½-wy: sn rdn: btn appr fnl f) | 4 | 4 | 8/1 | 48 | 26 |
| $2123^{6}$ | **Hoh Majestic (IRE) (67)** (MartynWane) **3-9-0v** LCharnock(6) (prom tl outpcd fnl 2f) | 2 | 5 | 6/1 | 43 | 21 |
| $3223^{6}$ | **Sense of Priority (63)** (DNicholls) **7-9-9** AlexGreaves(2) (in tch: sme hdwy 2f out: nvr plcd to chal) | ¾ | 6 | $9/2^{2}$ | 46 | 28 |
| $2976^{8}$ | **Jobie (60)** (BWHills) **6-9-4** JQuinn(8) (in tch tl outpcd fr ½-wy) | 2½ | 7 | $11/2^{3}$ | 34 | 16 |
| $2910^{8}$ | **Waverley Star (26)** (JSWainwright) **11-9-4** DeanMcKeown(1) (sn outpcd & bhd) | 10 | 8 | 50/1 | 7 | — |
| $2870^{4}$ | **Craignairn (64)** (JBerry) **3-9-5b** JCarroll(5) (stumbled bdly s: nt rcvr) | 6 | 9 | 11/1 | — | — |

(SP 122.1%) **9 Rn**

**1m 12.38** (0.88) CSF £47.98 TOTE £3.40: £1.80 £3.50 £1.40 (£28.00) Trio £36.10 OWNER Mr Geoffrey Hamilton (MIDDLEHAM) BRED R. H. Cowell and Mrs R. B. Collie
WEIGHT FOR AGE 3yo-4lb
Sold Scottish Bloodstock 4,600 gns

**2963* Blue Bomber** got the favoured stands' rail and, in a desperate finish, showed fine courage to hold on. (9/4)
**2910 Pallium (IRE)** should have won this, but got messed about entering the final furlong and, when switched, it was just too late. Now he is showing his form, he could be worth following. (25/1)
**2680 Ultra Beet** ran another fine race and really does deserve a change of luck. (9/2: op 7/1)
**2520 Double Oscar (IRE)** ran quite well, racing on the slower ground, wide of the others, but he is an unreliable character. (8/1)
**2123 Hoh Majestic (IRE)** always found the leaders going that stride or so too fast for his liking. (6/1)
**3223 Sense of Priority** had a poor draw and was not given a hard time. (9/2)

## 3279 ROTHMANS ROYALS NORTH SOUTH CHALLENGE SERIES H'CAP (0-85) (3-Y.O+) (Class D)
4-10 (4-12) **1m (round)** £7,197.50 (£2,180.00: £1,065.00: £507.50) Stalls: Low GOING minus 0.57 sec per fur (F)

| Form | Horse / Details | Dist | Pos | SP | RR | SF |
|---|---|---|---|---|---|---|
| $2679^{5}$ | **Impulsive Air (IRE) (60)** (EWeymes) **4-8-7** JQuinn(1) (led 2f: chsd ldrs: hdwy 2f out: r.o to ld cl home) | — | 1 | 14/1 | 70 | 39 |
| 2885* | **Hawksley Hill (IRE) (76)** (MrsJRRamsden) **3-9-2** JFortune(7) (dwlt: hld up: gd hdwy 2f out: ev ch ins fnl f: rdn & r.o) | nk | 2 | $6/4^{1}$ | 85 | 47 |
| $1703^{11}$ | **Persian Fayre (66)** (JBerry) **4-8-13** JCarroll(2) (lw: led after 2f: clr over 1f out: sn rdn: hdd & no ex towards fin) | nk | 3 | 20/1 | 75 | 44 |
| $3084^{3}$ | **Scaraben (73)** (SEKettlewell) **8-9-6** OUrbina(3) (a.p: hdwy 2f out: chsng ldrs ent fnl f: kpt on) | 1 | 4 | $6/1^{3}$ | 80 | 49 |
| $3084^{4}$ | **Maple Bay (IRE) (73)** (ABailey) **7-9-6** PRobinson(4) (lw: hdwy ent st: n.m.r over 1f out: nvr able to chal) | 1¾ | 5 | 9/1 | 76 | 45 |
| $3161^{16}$ | **Pride of Pendle (67)** (DNicholls) **7-9-0** AlexGreaves(5) (lw: hld up: hdwy 2f out: nvr rchd ldrs) | 1¾ | 6 | 8/1 | 67 | 36 |
| $3120^{4}$ | **Three Arch Bridge (66)** (MJohnston) **4-8-13b** TWilliams(8) (cl up tl wknd wl over 1f out) | 2½ | 7 | 16/1 | 61 | 30 |
| $2868^{9}$ | **Second Colours (USA) (65)** (MrsMReveley) **6-8-12** ACulhane(9) (bhd: n.m.r over 2f out & over 1f out: n.d) | s.h | 8 | 20/1 | 60 | 29 |
| $2621^{2}$ | **Winston (74)** (JDBethell) **3-8-11**(3) SDrowne(10) (lw: in tch: rdn over 3f out: sn btn) | 8 | 9 | $9/2^{2}$ | 53 | 15 |
| $3101^{3}$ | **Knotty Hill (77)** (RCraggs) **4-9-10** DeanMcKeown(6) (s.s: nt rcvr) | ½ | 10 | 20/1 | 55 | 24 |

(SP 120.4%) **10 Rn**

**1m 39.6** (0.60) CSF £35.01 CT £400.29 TOTE £22.70: £2.80 £1.70 £4.30 (£38.70) Trio £143.00 OWNER Mr T. A. Scothern (MIDDLEHAM) BRED Rathasker Stud
WEIGHT FOR AGE 3yo-7lb

**2679 Impulsive Air (IRE)**, ridden up with the pace where he likes to be, batted on well in a desperate finish. (14/1)
**2885* Hawksley Hill (IRE)**, given plenty to do, showed a terrific burst of speed two furlongs out, but that sapped all reserves and he just failed to quicken enough late on. (6/4)
**1586 Persian Fayre**, after two months off, looked to have stolen this when going clear over a furlong out, but he was again worried out of it in the closing strides. (20/1)
**3084 Scaraben** always held a good position and kept staying on, but his finishing speed seems to have deserted him. (6/1)
**3084 Maple Bay (IRE)** tried to come from off the pace this time and found trouble in running. (9/1)
**2962 Pride of Pendle** is showing signs of coming back to form. (8/1)
**3120 Three Arch Bridge** could never gain the advantage and packed it in two furlongs out. (16/1)
**2483 Second Colours (USA)** had no sort of run and this is best forgotten. (20/1)
**2621 Winston** ran a stinker and would seem to have a problem. (9/2)

## 3280 NORTHERN ELECTRIC TELECOM H'CAP (0-85) (3-Y.O+) (Class D)
4-40 (4-40) **1m 2f 32y** £3,696.25 (£1,120.00: £547.50: £261.25) Stalls: High GOING minus 0.57 sec per fur (F)

| Form | Horse / Details | Dist | Pos | SP | RR | SF |
|---|---|---|---|---|---|---|
| $2724^{5}$ | **Hazard a Guess (IRE) (82)** (DNicholls) **6-9-13** AlexGreaves(1) (hld up: effrt over 2f out: r.o ins fnl f to ld cl home) | — | 1 | $4/1^{2}$ | 91 | 59 |
| *2939** | **Troubadour Song (51)** (WWHaigh) **4-7-10** JQuinn(4) (hld up & bhd: hdwy 3f out: rdn to ld wl ins fnl f: hdd & nt qckn towards fin) | nk | 2 | $4/1^{2}$ | 60 | 28 |
| $3081^{3}$ | **New Albion (USA) (58)** (MissZAGreen) **5-8-3** JFanning(2) (mde most tl ct wl ins fnl f) | 1¼ | 3 | $8/1^{3}$ | 65 | 33 |
| 3081* | **Bulsara (62)** (CWFairhurst) **4-8-7** DeanMcKeown(3) (trckd ldrs: hdwy & ev ch 2f out: btn & eased ins fnl f) | 5 | 4 | $6/4^{1}$ | 61 | 29 |
| $2430^{7}$ | **Ladykirk (71)** (JWWatts) **3-8-7** JCarroll(7) (disp ld 4f: cl up tl wknd over 2f out) | 2½ | 5 | $8/1^{3}$ | 66 | 25 |
| $2801^{11}$ | **Maurangi (51)** (BWMurray) **5-7-10** LCharnock(5) (b.hind: chsd ldrs tl outpcd fnl 3f) | 1¼ | 6 | 20/1 | 44 | 12 |
| $3056^{4}$ | **Reinhardt (IRE) (67)** (JSWainwright) **3-7-10**(7) JBramhill(6) (a bhd) | ½ | 7 | 25/1 | 59 | 18 |

(SP 110.8%) **7 Rn**

**2m 7.4** (0.70) CSF £18.54 TOTE £4.40: £1.70 £2.50 (£7.70) OWNER Consultco Ltd (THIRSK) BRED A. F. O'Callaghan in Ireland
LONG HANDICAP Troubadour Song 7-7 Maurangi 7-8
WEIGHT FOR AGE 3yo-9lb

**2724 Hazard a Guess (IRE)**, given a fine ride, was produced to take it just where it was needed. (4/1)
**2939* Troubadour Song** has been in tremendous form on Sand and only just failed to land his first turf victory. Being 3lb wrong in the handicap probably made the difference. (4/1)
**3081 New Albion (USA)** ran another sound race, but was tapped for toe in the closing stages. (8/1)
**3081* Bulsara** looked a big danger two furlongs out, but ran out of steam and was eased a fair deal before the finish. (6/4)

**1361 Ladykirk** has been disappointing so far this season and dropped out once the pressure was on. (8/1)
**Maurangi** has not won for two years and is now well enough handicapped if he can regain his form. (20/1)

T/Plpt: £258.40 (35.03 Tckts). T/Qdpt: £11.90 (62.5 Tckts). AA

# 3092-BRIGHTON (L-H) (Firm)
## Monday August 5th
WEATHER: warm WIND: mod half bhd

### 3281 SOUTHERN FM APPRENTICE H'CAP (0-70) (3-Y.O+) (Class F)
5-55 (5-55) **7f 214y** £3,023.60 (£839.60: £402.80) Stalls: Low GOING minus 0.56 sec per fur (F)

| | | | | SP | RR | SF |
|---|---|---|---|---|---|---|
| 2917[2] | **Talathath (FR) (66)** (CADwyer) **4-9-9v**(3) JoHunnam(2) (led over 5f: led 1f out: r.o wl) | — | 1 | 6/4 [1] | 75 | — |
| *3078*[4] | **Fort Knox (IRE) (58)** (RMFlower) **5-9-1b**(3) CAdamson(1) (lw: rdn over 2f out: hdwy over 1f out: ev ch ins fnl f: unable qckn) | 2 | 2 | 5/2 [3] | 63 | — |
| *2940*[11] | **Hang a Right (37)** (CADwyer) **9-7-4**(7)ow1 NicolaCole(3) (b: lw: a.p: led over 2f out to 1f out: one pce) | hd | 3 | 25/1 | 42 | — |
| 2994[5] | **Delight of Dawn (65)** (RMStronge) **4-9-11** DaneO'Neill(4) (lw: hld up: styd far side st: ev ch 1f out: sn wknd) | 2 | 4 | 9/4 [2] | 66 | — |
| 2903[6] | **Sharp Holly (IRE) (43)** (JABennett) **4-8-0b**(3)ow2 SophieMitchell(5) (a.p: rdn over 1f out: wknd fnl f) | ½ | 5 | 20/1 | 43? | — |

(SP 107.9%) **5 Rn**

**1m 38.2** (6.00) CSF £5.25 TOTE £2.00: £1.10 £1.80 (£2.80) OWNER Mrs Christine Rawson (NEWMARKET) BRED Gainsborough Stud Management Ltd

**2917 Talathath (FR)** took the field along and came over to the stands' side in the straight in search of the better ground. Relinquishing the lead over quarter of a mile out, he was back in front again below the distance and kept on really well. (6/4: Evens-13/8)
**3078 Fort Knox (IRE)** made his effort below the distance and looked likely to come through to lead. The winner proved too strong for him though in the last 100 yards. (5/2)
**1658 Hang a Right**, never far away, went on over a quarter of a mile from home but, headed below the distance, failed to find another gear. (25/1)
**2994 Delight of Dawn** was the only runner who elected to stay on the far side in the straight. Throwing down her challenge in the final quarter-mile, she still had every chance entering the final furlong before tiring. (9/4)
**Sharp Holly (IRE)** found this longer trip beyond her and, after playing a leading role, tired in the last 200 yards. (20/1)

### 3282 E.B.F. ALFRISTON MAIDEN STKS (2-Y.O) (Class D)
6-25 (6-25) **5f 59y** £3,407.10 (£1,015.80: £484.40: £218.70) Stalls: Low GOING minus 0.56 sec per fur (F)

| | | | | SP | RR | SF |
|---|---|---|---|---|---|---|
| | **Alumisiyah (USA)** (HThomsonJones) **2-8-9** TQuinn(2) (scope: lw: hld up: swtchd rt 2f out: edgd rt over 1f out: hrd rdn: str run fnl f: led nr fin) | — | 1 | 7/2 [2] | 75 | 23 |
| 2887[6] | **Feel A Line** (BJMeehan) **2-9-0b**[1] MTebbutt(4) (led: hrd rdn over 1f out: hdd nr fin) | ½ | 2 | 15/2 | 79 | 27 |
| 2985[3] | **Ricasso** (DRLoder) **2-9-0** RHughes(6) (a.p: hrd rdn & ev ch 1f out: one pce) | 2½ | 3 | 5/2 [1] | 71 | 19 |
| 2865[10] | **Manikato (USA)** (DJSCosgrove) **2-9-0** WJO'Connor(5) (lw: chsd ldr over 2f: wknd fnl f) | 2½ | 4 | 6/1 [3] | 63 | 11 |
| | **Good News (IRE)** (MMadgwick) **2-8-9** MFenton(1) (leggy: scope: bit bkwd: dwlt: hmpd over 4f out: a bhd) | 2½ | 5 | 16/1 | 51 | — |
| | **Florentine Diamond (IRE)** (SirMarkPrescott) **2-8-9** GDuffield(7) (leggy: scope: bit bkwd: a bhd) | 2 | 6 | 5/2 [1] | 45 | — |
| 2956[5] | **Midnight Times** (DCO'Brien) **2-8-9** GBardwell(3) (a bhd) | 19 | 7 | 66/1 | — | — |

(SP 112.8%) **7 Rn**

**61.3 secs** (1.30) CSF £26.13 TOTE £4.40: £2.10 £3.70 (£17.90) OWNER Mr Hamdan Al Maktoum (NEWMARKET) BRED Shadwell Farm Inc
STEWARDS' ENQUIRY Tebbutt susp. 14-16/8/96 (excessive use of whip)

**Alumisiyah (USA)**, whose stable certainly knows how to get them ready to win first time, chased the leaders. Switched right a quarter of a mile out, her prospects did not look very good below the distance, but she came with a lovely run in the final furlong to get up near the line. (7/2: op 7/4)
**Feel A Line**, fitted with blinkers for the first time, attempted to make all. He came under severe pressure below the distance and held on well until eventually overhauled near the line. It was no surprise to see Tebbutt suspended for his use of the whip. (15/2: 12/1-7/1)
**2985 Ricasso**, a leading light from the off, threatened to take the lead below the distance, but he failed to find what was required and could only plod on at one pace. He is clearly one of the stable's lesser lights. (5/2: op 6/4)
**2865 Manikato (USA)**, in second place to halfway, grimly held on until tiring in the last 200 yards. (6/1)

### 3283 DUKE OF NORFOLK MEMORIAL H'CAP (0-75) (3-Y.O) (Class D)
6-55 (6-55) **1m 3f 196y** £3,694.95 (£1,101.60: £525.30: £237.15) Stalls: High GOING minus 0.56 sec per fur (F)

| | | | | SP | RR | SF |
|---|---|---|---|---|---|---|
| 2979* | **General Glow (50)** (PDEvans) **3-7-12**ow2 JFEgan(3) (hld up: rdn over 4f out: led over 2f out: clr wl over 1f out: r.o wl) | — | 1 | 11/2 | 71+ | 32 |
| 2601[10] | **Queen Bee (66)** (JLDunlop) **3-9-0** GDuffield(5) (lw: chsd ldr: led 5f out tl over 2f out: sn wknd) | 13 | 2 | 9/1 | 70 | 33 |
| 2953[3] | **Arcady (62)** (PTWalwyn) **3-8-10** SSanders(1) (led 7f: wknd over 3f out) | ¾ | 3 | 100/30 [2] | 65 | 28 |
| 3077[4] | **Chocolate Ice (68)** (CACyzer) **3-9-2** WJO'Connor(6) (a.p: rdn over 5f out: wknd over 3f out) | hd | 4 | 15/2 | 70 | 33 |
| 3117[2] | **Nikita's Star (IRE) (65)** (DJGMurraySmith) **3-8-13** TQuinn(4) (lw: nvr gng wl: a wl bhd: virtually p.u ins fnl f) | 14 | 5 | 3/1 [1] | 49 | 12 |
| 2140[4] | **Majdak Jereeb (IRE) (73)** (MajorWRHern) **3-9-7b**[1] TSprake(2) (lw: hung bdly lft 6f out: bhd fnl 4f) | 1½ | 6 | 4/1 [3] | 55 | 18 |

(SP 105.2%) **6 Rn**

**2m 28.5** (0.90) CSF £40.77 TOTE £8.00: £2.90 £3.10 (£32.00) OWNER Mr J. G. White (WELSHPOOL) BRED Messinger Stud Ltd
LONG HANDICAP General Glow 7-6

**2979* General Glow** followed up his recent victory here. Niggled along over half a mile from home, he moved to the front over two furlongs out and soon shot clear to win in decisive style. (11/2: op 3/1)
**1182 Queen Bee** made her bid for glory five furlongs out but, collared over a quarter of a mile out, was soon stung by the winner. (9/1: 4/1-10/1)
**2953 Arcady** had shot her bolt over three furlongs from home. (100/30)
**3077 Chocolate Ice** was close up until calling it a day over three furlongs out. (15/2: 4/1-8/1)
**3117 Nikita's Star (IRE)** ran appallingly and was never travelling. This run is best forgotten. (3/1)

### 3284 A R DENNIS BOOKMAKERS EVENING H'CAP (0-70) (3-Y.O) (Class E)
7-25 (7-25) **1m 1f 209y** £2,933.70 (£873.60: £415.80: £186.90) Stalls: High GOING minus 0.56 sec per fur (F)

| | | | | SP | RR | SF |
|---|---|---|---|---|---|---|
| 3043[4] | **Nelly's Cousin (59)** (NACallaghan) **3-8-9**(3) DaneO'Neill(4) (lw: swvd rt s: hld up: hrd rdn over 1f out: led nr fin) | — | 1 | 13/8 [1] | 69 | 34 |

| | | | | | | |
|---|---|---|---|---|---|---|
| 2931* | **Anak-Ku (68)** (MissGayKelleway) **3-9-7v** TQuinn(3) (lw: led: hrd rdn over 1f out: hdd nr fin) | ½ | **2** | 5/2[2] | 77 | 42 |
| 3079[4] | **Allstars Express (66)** (TJNaughton) **3-9-5** TSprake(1) (lw: hld up: hrd rdn & ev ch over 1f out: wknd ins fnl f) | 3 | **3** | 5/2[2] | 70 | 35 |
| 1644[10] | **Duncombe Hall (46)** (CACyzer) **3-7-10**(3) MHenry(2) (prom over 5f) | 1½ | **4** | 16/1[3] | 48 | 13 |
| 2979[7] | **Sheilana (IRE) (52)** (TGMills) **3-7-12**(7) JCornally(5) (bmpd s: hdwy 7f out: wknd over 2f out) | ½ | **5** | 20/1 | 53 | 18 |

(SP 105.9%) **5 Rn**

**2m 0.1** (1.80) CSF £5.50 TOTE £2.50: £1.10 £1.30 (£2.20) OWNER Mr N. A. Callaghan (NEWMARKET) BRED Charlton Down Stud

**3043 Nelly's Cousin**, held up travelling sweetly, was asked for her effort below the distance and, gradually reeling in the leader, got on top near the line. (13/8)

**2931* Anak-Ku**, under pressure below the distance, gamely held on until overhauled near the finish. (5/2)

**3079 Allstars Express** threw down his challenge a quarter of a mile out, but was in trouble a furlong later. (5/2)

**Duncombe Hall** was close up until losing his pitch over four furlongs from home. (16/1)

## 3285 DOWNS (S) STKS (3-Y.O+) (Class G)

7-55 (7-55) **5f 213y** £2,070.00 (£570.00: £270.00) Stalls: Low GOING minus 0.56 sec per fur (F)

| | | | | SP | RR | SF |
|---|---|---|---|---|---|---|
| 3140[2] | **Tafahhus (66)** (MJPolglase) **4-9-9b** JStack(2) (mde all: clr over 1f out: r.o wl) | — | **1** | 7/4[1] | 70 | 44 |
| 2735[6] | **Waders Dream (IRE) (41)** (PatMitchell) **7-9-4v** MFenton(1) (lw: hld up: chsd wnr over 2f out: no imp) | 3½ | **2** | 20/1 | 56 | 30 |
| 3049[9] | **Dahiyah (USA) (65)** (DLWilliams) **5-9-9** TQuinn(4) (lw: chsd wnr 3f: rdn over 2f out: one pce) | 1¼ | **3** | 100/30[3] | 57 | 31 |
| 3139[8] | **Pearl Dawn (IRE) (65)** (GLMoore) **6-9-1**(3) DaneO'Neill(7) (hdwy over 2f out: one pce) | nk | **4** | 11/4[2] | 52 | 26 |
| 2966[5] | **Samara Song (57)** (WGMTurner) **3-8-7b**(7) DSweeney(5) (lw: sme hdwy over 2f out: wknd over 1f out) | 3 | **5** | 16/1 | 43 | 13 |
| 1009[5] | **Foreman (54)** (RSimpson) **3-8-12**(7) PDoe(6) (bit bkwd: hld up: chsd wnr 3f out tl over 2f out: wknd over 1f out) | 4 | **6** | 12/1 | 38 | 8 |
| 2981[8] | **Best Kept Secret (54)** (PDEvans) **5-9-4b** JFEgan(3) (bhd fnl 3f) | 4 | **7** | 12/1 | 22 | — |

(SP 112.1%) **7 Rn**

**1m 8.1** (0.90) CSF £27.72 TOTE £2.50: £2.00 £3.60 (£22.80) OWNER Mr Roger Newton (NEWMARKET) BRED Shadwell Estate Company Limited

WEIGHT FOR AGE 3yo-4lb

Bt in 5,200 gns

**3140 Tafahhus** made all the running and forged clear in the final quarter-mile, to win in a time only half a second outside the course record. This was a good performance, considering this was only a seller. (7/4: 5/4-2/1)

**2410 Waders Dream (IRE)** moved into second place over two furlongs out, but had no hope of reeling in the winner. (20/1)

**2286* Dahiyah (USA)** looked extremely well in the paddock. In second place to halfway, he was then made to look very pedestrian. (100/30)

**2981 Pearl Dawn (IRE)** began to take closer order over two furlongs out, but was then only treading water. (11/4)

**1009 Foreman** (12/1: op 7/1)

**2392 Best Kept Secret** (12/1: 8/1-14/1)

## 3286 SOUTH COAST RADIO LIMITED STKS (0-50) (3-Y.O) (Class F)

8-25 (8-26) **7f 214y** £2,381.00 (£656.00: £311.00) Stalls: Low GOING minus 0.56 sec per fur (F)

| | | | | SP | RR | SF |
|---|---|---|---|---|---|---|
| 3246[4] | **Sylvan Princess (50)** (CNAllen) **3-8-10**(5) 2x MartinDwyer(5) (dwlt: swtchd rt over 2f out: hdwy over 1f out: led ins fnl f: r.o wl) | — | **1** | 11/10[1] | 61 | 44 |
| 3165[5] | **Flying Harold (44)** (MRChannon) **3-8-12** JFEgan(8) (led: rdn over 2f out: hdd ins fnl f: unable qckn) | 2½ | **2** | 14/1 | 53 | 36 |
| 2743[9] | **Princess Pamgaddy (47)** (PFICole) **3-8-13** TQuinn(1) (b.hind: rdn & hdwy over 2f out: r.o ins fnl f) | s.h | **3** | 3/1[2] | 54 | 37 |
| 2752[4] | **Fairly Sure (IRE) (48)** (NEBerry) **3-8-4**(5) CAdamson(9) (a.p: chsd ldr over 4f out tl over 1f out: one pce) | 1½ | **4** | 7/1[3] | 47 | 30 |
| 3257[9] | **Tallulah Belle (45)** (NPLittmoden) **3-8-9** TGMcLaughlin(2) (lw: nvr nr to chal) | 6 | **5** | 20/1 | 35 | 18 |
| 2981[7] | **Princesse Lyphard (39)** (MJPolglase) **3-8-9** NCarlisle(3) (prom over 3f) | 2½ | **6** | 14/1 | 30 | 13 |
| 2978[6] | **Mrs Keen (34)** (RSimpson) **3-8-2**(7) PDoe(7) (s.s: hdwy 6f out: wknd 3f out) | 2 | **7** | 25/1 | 26 | 9 |
| 2251[17] | **Alajyal (IRE) (47)** (PTWalwyn) **3-8-9** SSanders(4) (lw: prom 6f) | 1½ | **8** | 14/1 | 23 | 6 |
| *102*[8] | **Carwyn's Choice (35)** (PCClarke) **3-8-2**(7) DSweeney(6) (a bhd) | 12 | **9** | 50/1 | — | — |

(SP 115.7%) **9 Rn**

**1m 32.8** (0.60) CSF £15.98 TOTE £2.00: £1.10 £3.30 £1.40 (£12.30) Trio £8.50 OWNER Camelot Racing (NEWMARKET) BRED K S P Leisure

**3246 Sylvan Princess**, given no time off after her Saturday Newmarket defeat, returned to the winner's enclosure here. She was certainly given a lot to do entering the straight, but found a real turn of foot from below the distance and swept into the lead inside the final furlong. (11/10: 4/6-5/4)

**3165 Flying Harold** attempted to make all the running, but failed to cope with the winner inside the final furlong. (14/1: op 8/1)

**2339* Princess Pamgaddy** made an effort over quarter of a mile out and, running on, failed by only a whisker to take second prize. (3/1: tchd 2/1)

**2752 Fairly Sure (IRE)** moved into second place just before halfway but, collared for that position at the distance, was then only treading water. (7/1)

**Alajyal (IRE)** (14/1: op 8/1)

T/Plpt: £137.90 (62.95 Tckts). T/Qdpt: £22.70 (37.53 Tckts). AK

# 2519-CARLISLE (R-H) (Firm)

## Monday August 5th

WEATHER: overcast & v.warm WIND: almost nil

## 3287 SCANIA 4-SERIES 'HORSEPOWER' / CARLISLE CHAMPION APPRENTICE H'CAP (0-70) (3-Y.O+) (Class E)

6-10 (6-10) **7f 214y** £2,968.35 (£898.80: £438.90: £208.95) Stalls: High GOING minus 0.60 sec per fur (F)

| | | | | SP | RR | SF |
|---|---|---|---|---|---|---|
| 2962[7] | **Prizefighter (62)** (JLEyre) **5-9-8** OPears(6) (lw: led 2f: led over 2f out: hld on wl) | — | **1** | 11/8[1] | 70 | 52 |
| 3120[6] | **Euro Sceptic (IRE) (48)** (TDEasterby) **4-8-8b** RHavlin(5) (hdwy ½-wy: chal appr fnl f: no ex towards fin) | nk | **2** | 8/1 | 55 | 37 |
| 2679* | **Generous Present (59)** (JWPayne) **3-8-12** DWright(3) (hld up: effrt over 2f out: rdn & nt qckn) | 6 | **3** | 5/2[2] | 54 | 29 |
| 3084[8] | **Spanish Verdict (68)** (DenysSmith) **9-10-0** CTeague(1) (prom: effrt 3f out: edgd rt & one pce) | 1¼ | **4** | 7/2[3] | 61 | 43 |
| 2776[9] | **Never so True (36)** (MartynWane) **5-7-5**(5) RFfrench(2) (led after 2f tl over 2f out: sn wknd) | 4 | **5** | 25/1 | 21 | 3 |

| | | | | SP | RR | SF |
|---|---|---|---|---|---|---|
| *2168[10]* | **Boundary Bird (IRE) (52)** (MJohnston) **3-8-0b(5)** KSked(4) (lw: chsd ldrs 3f: sn outpcd & bhd) | 12 | **6** | 25/1 | 13 | — |
| | | | | (SP 111.7%) | | **6 Rn** |

**1m 39.1** (0.50) CSF £11.39 TOTE £2.80: £1.50 £3.80 (£12.20) OWNER Diamond Racing Ltd (HAMBLETON) BRED J. K. Bloodstock Ltd
LONG HANDICAP Never so True 7-7
WEIGHT FOR AGE 3yo-7lb
OFFICIAL EXPLANATION **Prizefighter: explaining his apparent improvement, it was reported that the gelding's previous Catterick race was his first for some time, he had started slowly, was not suited by the softer ground or the sharp seven furlongs and he can become disillusioned if not allowed to dominate.**
**2962 Prizefighter** was a different proposition this time and, given a good ride, won convincingly. The money was down here. (11/8)
**3120 Euro Sceptic (IRE)** had his chances in the last two furlongs but, when the pressure was really on, was never doing enough. (8/1)
**2679* Generous Present**, edgy and sweaty as usual, never found as much as looked likely when asked a serious question. (5/2)
**2214 Spanish Verdict** never showed any sparkle on this occasion. (7/2)
**2522 Never so True**, dropping back dramatically on this occasion, was left struggling early in the straight. (25/1)
**Boundary Bird (IRE)** looked fit but gave no signs of encouragement. (25/1)

## 3288 SCANIA 4-SERIES CLAIMING STKS (3-Y.O) (Class F)
6-40 (6-40) **6f 206y** £2,605.00 (£730.00: £355.00) Stalls: High GOING minus 0.60 sec per fur (F)

| | | | | SP | RR | SF |
|---|---|---|---|---|---|---|
| 2983[2] | **Miletrian City (53)** (JBerry) **3-8-7b** JCarroll(4) (lw: hld up: stdy hdwy over 1f out: qcknd to ld wl ins fnl f) | — | **1** | 4/1[3] | 65 | 24 |
| *3062[4]* | **Clincher Club (66)** (MJohnston) **3-8-2** TWilliams(6) (plld hrd: led after 1f tl appr fnl f: no ex) | 5 | **2** | 13/8[1] | 49 | 8 |
| 3256[5] | **La Finale (57)** (DNicholls) **3-7-8(7)** JBramhill(1) (prom: effrt 3f out: wl btn whn hmpd wl ins fnl f) | 3½ | **3** | 2/1[2] | 39 | — |
| 2753[7] | **Insideout** (FWatson) **3-8-11** JFortune(5) (b: prom tl wknd fnl 3f) | 7 | **4** | 66/1 | 33 | — |
| 2777[2] | **Dreams And Schemes (IRE) (65)** (RAFahey) **3-7-8(7)** RFfrench(3) (led 1f: cl up: led over 1f out: hdd & btn whn broke leg & fell wl ins fnl f: dead) | | **F** | 5/1 | — | — |
| | | | | (SP 109.6%) | | **5 Rn** |

**1m 27.4** (1.70) CSF £10.38 TOTE £4.20: £2.80 £1.10 (£3.80) OWNER Miletrian Plc (COCKERHAM) BRED A. and Mrs Griffin
**2983 Miletrian City**, given a super ride, was produced to settle it in the last half-furlong, and hardly knew he had had a race. (4/1)
**3062 Clincher Club** refused to settle, which was her undoing, as she was easily picked off approaching the final furlong. (13/8)
**3256 La Finale** was never giving it her best shot. (2/1)
**Insideout** is s decent type who may yet improve. (66/1)

## 3289 GRAHAM COMMERCIALS FOR SCANIA LIMITED STKS (0-50) (3-Y.O+) (Class F)
7-10 (7-11) **6f 206y** £2,773.00 (£778.00: £379.00) Stalls: High GOING minus 0.60 sec per fur (F)

| | | | | SP | RR | SF |
|---|---|---|---|---|---|---|
| 2868[10] | **Cee-Jay-Ay (46)** (JBerry) **9-8-11(5)** PRoberts(1) (lw: hld up: swtchd & effrt 1½f out: r.o to ld wl ins fnl f) | — | **1** | 9/1 | 59 | 41 |
| 2851[3] | **Riccarton (50)** (PCalver) **3-8-10** MBirch(8) (led: qcknd 3f out: hdd & no ex wl ins fnl f) | 1¼ | **2** | 4/1[2] | 56 | 32 |
| 2988[10] | **Diamond Crown (IRE) (45)** (MartynWane) **5-9-2** JCarroll(4) (hld up: effrt whn hmpd 1½f out: r.o ins fnl f) | 3½ | **3** | 33/1 | 48 | 30 |
| *2550[2]* | **Komlucky (44)** (ABMulholland) **4-8-6b(7)** GFaulkner(9) (a chsng ldrs: rdn 3f out: nt qckn) | 2½ | **4** | 12/1 | 39 | 21 |
| 2983[6] | **The Barnsley Belle (IRE) (48)** (JLEyre) **3-8-7** AClark(3) (lw: cl up: rdn 3f out: one pce) | 1½ | **5** | 9/4[1] | 36 | 12 |
| 2592[10] | **Alfayza (47)** (JDBethell) **3-8-7** SDrowne(2) (chsd ldrs: rdn 3f out: wknd wl over 1f out) | 1 | **6** | 10/1 | 34 | 10 |
| 3059* | **Globe Runner (50)** (JJO'Neill) **3-8-13** TWilliams(5) (in tch: effrt 3f out: one pce) | 1 | **7** | 7/1[3] | 37 | 13 |
| 2680[3] | **Densben (45)** (DenysSmith) **12-9-2** KFallon(10) (hmpd after 1½f: outpcd fnl 3f) | 2 | **8** | 10/1 | 30 | 12 |
| 3252[10] | **Summer Villa (37)** (JHetherton) **4-8-8(5)** GParkin(7) (outpcd & lost pl ½-wy: n.d after) | 1 | **9** | 20/1 | 24 | 6 |
| 3102[9] | **Supermister (50)** (TDEasterby) **3-8-5(5)** RHavlin(12) (mid div: n.m.r 2f out: sn wknd) | hd | **10** | 10/1 | 27 | 3 |
| *2937[11]* | **Runforaction (IRE) (30)** (LRLloyd-James) **4-8-13** VHalliday(6) (lw: a bhd) | 1¼ | **11** | 100/1 | 21 | 3 |
| 3252[11] | **Olifantsfontein (43)** (DNicholls) **8-8-9(7)** JBramhill(11) (chsd ldrs over 4f: wknd) | 2½ | **12** | 100/1 | 18 | — |
| | **Rambo's Rumtime (34)** (FWatson) **4-8-13** JFortune(13) (s.i.s: a wl bhd) | 5 | **13** | 100/1 | 4 | — |
| | | | | (SP 118.9%) | | **13 Rn** |

**1m 26.6** (0.90) CSF £41.91 TOTE £5.30: £2.00 £1.40 £5.10 (£13.30) Trio £129.00 OWNER Mr Richard Jinks (COCKERHAM)
WEIGHT FOR AGE 3yo-6lb
**2672 Cee-Jay-Ay** was having his fiftieth race since his last win here, and there were certainly no doubts about it this time as he won well. (9/1)
**2851 Riccarton**, from a yard out of form, was bathed in sweat. He was always waiting to be picked off. (4/1: op 5/2)
**2731 Diamond Crown (IRE)**, back over his shortest trip for a long time, ran his best race for a while and being bumped by the winner probably helped, rather than hindered, this funny customer. (33/1)
**2550 Komlucky** had her chances but, under pressure some way out, always found the effort too much for her liking. (12/1)
**2983 The Barnsley Belle (IRE)** looked particularly well but, once off the bit turning for home, was never giving it her best. (9/4)
**Alfayza** looked moderate once the pressure was on entering the straight. (10/1)

## 3290 SCANIA 1996 TRUCK OF THE YEAR H'CAP (0-80) (3-Y.O+) (Class D)
7-40 (7-41) **1m 4f** £3,517.50 (£1,065.00: £520.00: £247.50) Stalls: Low GOING minus 0.60 sec per fur (F)

| | | | | SP | RR | SF |
|---|---|---|---|---|---|---|
| 2688[2] | **Dear Life (USA) (79)** (MrsJCecil) **3-9-8** AClark(3) (hld up: effrt 3f out: r.o to ld ins fnl f) | — | **1** | 3/1[2] | 91 | 44 |
| 2848[3] | **Master Hyde (USA) (56)** (WStorey) **7-8-10** DeanMcKeown(2) (trckd ldrs: led 2f out: put hd in air: hdd & nt qckn ins fnl f) | 1 | **2** | 11/4[1] | 67 | 31 |
| 3242[3] | **Lord Advocate (51)** (DANolan) **8-8-2b(3)** NVarley(4) (cl up: led 3f out to 2f out: one pce) | 4 | **3** | 10/1[3] | 56 | 20 |
| 2988* | **Contrafire (IRE) (73)** (WJarvis) **4-9-13** KFallon(5) (lw: led to 3f out: sn outpcd) | 5 | **4** | 11/4[1] | 72 | 36 |
| 3098* | **Maftun (USA) (57)** (GMMoore) **4-8-11** 5x JTate(1) (lw: hld up: effrt 3f out: sn btn) | hd | **5** | 3/1[2] | 56 | 20 |
| | | | | (SP 112.4%) | | **5 Rn** |

**2m 33.1** (2.10) CSF £11.01 TOTE £3.10: £2.30 £1.50 (£7.20) OWNER Lady Howard de Walden (NEWMARKET) BRED Lord Howard de Walden
WEIGHT FOR AGE 3yo-11lb
**2688 Dear Life (USA)** won really well. The further she goes, the better she likes it. (3/1)
**2848 Master Hyde (USA)**, the winner of this race last year, travelled on the bridle but, when an effort was required, he put his head in the air and was never doing enough. (11/4)
**3242 Lord Advocate** had his chances again, but lacked the pace to take them. (10/1)
**2988* Contrafire (IRE)** went to post as though he was feeling this very firm ground. Once taken on turning for home, he was soon left struggling. (11/4)
**3098* Maftun (USA)** was never striding out on this firm ground and failed to offer a threat. (3/1)

## 3291 SCANIA 4-SERIES 'KING OF THE ROAD' MAIDEN AUCTION STKS (2-Y.O) (Class E)
8-10 (8-12) **5f** £2,845.50 (£861.00: £420.00: £199.50) Stalls: High GOING minus 0.60 sec per fur (F)

| | | | | SP | RR | SF |
|---|---|---|---|---|---|---|
| 2755$^{2}$ | **Swino (83)** (PDEvans) **2-8-6** JFortune(4) (lw: mde all: r.o strly appr fnl f) | — | **1** | 8/13$^{1}$ | 73 | 26 |
| 2930$^{3}$ | **Red Romance (70)** (DenysSmith) **2-8-3** LCharnock(2) (w wnr tl rdn & btn over 1f out) | 7 | **2** | 7/2$^{2}$ | 48 | 1 |
| 2926$^{5}$ | **Thewrightone (IRE)** (GROldroyd) **2-7-12b** JLowe(3) (chsd ldrs 3f: sn outpcd) | 4 | **3** | 66/1 | 30 | — |
| 3057$^{4}$ | **Norbreck House** (JBerry) **2-8-3** JCarroll(1) (outpcd ½-wy: sn bhd) | 3 | **4** | 4/1$^{3}$ | 25 | — |
| 2727$^{5}$ | **Cairn Dhu** (MrsJRRamsden) **2-8-13** KFallon(5) (bit bkwd: unruly s: dwlt: n.d) | hd | **5** | 10/1 | 35 | — |

(SP 114.7%) **5 Rn**

**61.1 secs** (0.90) CSF £3.39 TOTE £1.40: £1.20 £2.30 (£1.90) OWNER Swinnerton Transport Ltd (WELSHPOOL) BRED Mrs F. A. Veasey

**2755 Swino**, from a yard that can do little wrong at the moment, won in really good style and will now hopefully get the winning habit. (8/13)
**2930 Red Romance** was the only one to match the winner for speed, but was done with over a furlong out. (7/2)
**2926 Thewrightone (IRE)** showed some speed but, once a real race began from halfway, was soon put in her place. (66/1)
**3057 Norbreck House** was disappointing this time, but can be forgiven on this very firm ground. (4/1: 3/1-9/2)
**2727 Cairn Dhu** again gave problems at the start and then was certainly not in a hurry leaving the stalls. By the time the jockey had adjusted his feet in the irons, the others were almost home. (10/1)

## 3292 GRAHAM COMMERCIALS - SCANIA KNOW HOW H'CAP (0-60) (3-Y.O) (Class F)
8-40 (8-43) **5f 207y** £2,801.00 (£786.00: £383.00) Stalls: High GOING minus 0.60 sec per fur (F)

| | | | | SP | RR | SF |
|---|---|---|---|---|---|---|
| 3256$^{2}$ | **Newlands Corner (39)** (JAkehurst) **3-8-0b** DBiggs(4) (lw: in tch: effrt 2f out: r.o wl fnl f to ld cl home) | — | **1** | 4/1$^{2}$ | 46 | 20 |
| 2790$^{6}$ | **Fairy Prince (IRE) (60)** (MrsALMKing) **3-9-4**(3) FLynch(1) (cl up: led over 2f out tl ct cl home) | ½ | **2** | 8/1$^{3}$ | 66 | 40 |
| 3135* | **Oatey (60)** (MrsJRRamsden) **3-9-7** 7x KFallon(5) (lw: hld up: effrt ½-wy: chal ins fnl f: hrd rdn & nt qckn) | ¾ | **3** | 11/10$^{1}$ | 64 | 38 |
| 2914$^{2}$ | **Ya Marhaba (35)** (JWPayne) **3-7-7**(3) DWright(2) (lw: trckd ldrs: effrt over 1f out: nt qckn) | 1¾ | **4** | 4/1$^{2}$ | 34 | 8 |
| 2982$^{6}$ | **Marino Street (58)** (PDEvans) **3-9-5** JFortune(8) (lw: disp ld early: effrt 2f out: hung rt & nt qckn fnl f) | hd | **5** | 14/1 | 57 | 31 |
| 2983$^{7}$ | **Doug's Folly (45)** (MWEasterby) **3-8-6b** DaleGibson(7) (in tch: drvn along ½-wy: no imp) | 8 | **6** | 8/1$^{3}$ | 22 | — |
| 2427$^{10}$ | **Katy-Q (IRE) (51)** (PCalver) **3-8-12b** MBirch(3) (mde most tl hdd over 2f out: eased whn btn) | 5 | **7** | 25/1 | 15 | — |
| 3100$^{9}$ | **Lord Cornelious (35)** (DANolan) **3-7-7**(3) NVarley(6) (reard s: a bhd) | 8 | **8** | 100/1 | — | — |

(SP 121.3%) **8 Rn**

**1m 13.7** (1.20) CSF £33.97 CT £54.16 TOTE £4.20: £1.10 £2.50 £1.30 (£10.10) OWNER The Jolly Skolars (LAMBOURN) BRED L. A. C. Ashby
LONG HANDICAP Ya Marhaba 7-7 Lord Cornelious 7-4

**3256 Newlands Corner** was beginning to look a bit of a character, but she produced a good run in the final furlong to settle it late on. (4/1)
**2790 Fairy Prince (IRE)** ran another sound race here but, despite battling on, had no answer to the winner's late burst. (8/1)
**3135* Oatey** looked likely to win this when quickening up well approaching the final furlong, but she did not seem to see the trip out. (11/10: 11/8-Evens)
**2914 Ya Marhaba** travelled well but, when off the bit, had only the one speed. Perhaps more use should be made of him over this shorter trip. (4/1)
**2970* Marino Street** had her chances, but was short of courage and room to do anything about it. (14/1)
**2983 Doug's Folly** was going nowhere once off the bit at halfway. (8/1)

T/Plpt: £49.80 (204.12 Tckts). T/Qdpt: £6.70 (139.89 Tckts). AA

# 2897-RIPON (R-H) (Good to firm)
## Monday August 5th
WEATHER: fine WIND: fresh half bhd

## 3293 E.B.F. ROUNDABOUT MAIDEN STKS (2-Y.O) (Class D)
2-30 (2-32) **6f** £3,712.50 (£1,125.00: £550.00: £262.50) Stalls: Low GOING minus 0.69 sec per fur (HD)

| | | | | SP | RR | SF |
|---|---|---|---|---|---|---|
| 2887$^{5}$ | **Serenity** (JRFanshawe) **2-8-9** KFallon(11) (a chsng ldrs: styd on to ld ins fnl f: jst hld on) | — | **1** | 100/30$^{2}$ | 69 | 21 |
| | **Intikhab (USA)** (DMorley) **2-9-0** RHills(8) (str: scope: s.i.s: hdwy ½-wy: swtchd outside over 1f out: ev ch ins fnl f: r.o) | hd | **2** | 8/1$^{3}$ | 74+ | 26 |
| 1525$^{11}$ | **Siouxrouge** (PCHaslam) **2-9-0** JFortune(10) (trckd ldrs: hdwy & n.m.r ins fnl f: kpt on wl) | 1¼ | **3** | 25/1 | 70+ | 22 |
| 2873$^{2}$ | **Faringdon Future** (BWHills) **2-9-0** MHills(2) (lw: trckd ldr: led over 2f out: sn rdn: hdd ins fnl f: nt qckn) | s.h | **4** | 4/7$^{1}$ | 70 | 22 |
| 1404$^{5}$ | **Out of Sight (IRE)** (BAMcMahon) **2-9-0** GCarter(6) (bit bkwd: a chsng ldrs: kpt on one pce fnl 2f) | 2½ | **5** | 20/1 | 64 | 16 |
| 2897$^{5}$ | **Denton Lad** (JWWatts) **2-9-0** NConnorton(1) (led tl over 2f out: hung rt over 1f out: grad wknd) | 1½ | **6** | 16/1 | 60 | 12 |
| 2495$^{10}$ | **Good Day** (CWThornton) **2-9-0** DeanMcKeown(7) (s.i.s: outpcd & bhd tl sme late hdwy) | 2 | **7** | 33/1 | 54 | 6 |
| 2985$^{7}$ | **William's Well** (MWEasterby) **2-8-9**(5) GParkin(9) (bit bkwd: chsd ldrs: drvn along ½-wy: lost pl over 2f out) | 10 | **8** | 50/1 | 28 | — |
| 2315$^{7}$ | **Flo's Choice (IRE)** (JAHarris) **2-8-9** JO'Reilly(3) (w ldrs over 3f: sn wknd) | 1½ | **9** | 50/1 | 19 | — |
| | **Normanton** (MrsPSly) **2-9-0** ACulhane(5) (w'like: scope: bit bkwd: s.s: rn green & a wl bhd) | 1¾ | **10** | 66/1 | 19 | — |
| | **Ohio Royale** (PCHaslam) **2-9-0** LCharnock(4) (scope: bkwd: s.i.s: sn wl outpcd & wl bhd) | 10 | **11** | 33/1 | — | — |

(SP 123.6%) **11 Rn**

**1m 11.5** (1.00) CSF £29.62 TOTE £5.00: £1.40 £2.00 £4.30 (£13.70) Trio £99.60 OWNER Dr Catherine Wills (NEWMARKET) BRED Hyde Stud

**2887 Serenity,** who looked very fit, had raced too keenly for her own good on her debut. Showing the right sort of spirit, she hung on to win an ordinary maiden with nothing to spare. (100/30)
**Intikhab (USA),** a fair sort, showed a bit of knee-action going down. After missing the break slightly, he moved up travelling nicely at halfway and had every chance after being switched before not being given as hard a race as the winner. He is sure to improve on this. (8/1: op 4/1)
**Siouxrouge** certainly caught the eye. Happy to track the leaders, he did not have a lot of room inside the last, but kept on in highly-pleasing fashion. He would probably beat the first two next time. (25/1)
**2873 Faringdon Future,** who looked very fit and had no excuse, is proving expensive to follow. (4/7)
**1404 Out of Sight (IRE),** who showed plenty of knee-action, was far from disgraced and will improve over seven or a mile. (20/1)
**2897 Denton Lad,** much sharper this time, tended to hang under pressure as if feeling the ground. (16/1)

## 3294 SEE-SAW (S) H'CAP (0-60) (3-Y.O+) (Class F)
3-00 (3-00) **5f** £2,718.60 (£764.60: £373.80) Stalls: Low GOING minus 0.69 sec per fur (HD)

| | | | | SP | RR | SF |
|---|---|---|---|---|---|---|
| 2910$^{11}$ | **Kabcast (41)** (DWChapman) **11-8-13b** KDarley(8) (mde all stands' side: r.o wl) | — | **1** | 10/1 | 48 | 30 |

| | | | | SP | RR | SF |
|---|---|---|---|---|---|---|
| 3256$^{10}$ | **Good To Talk (42)** (TDEasterby) **3-8-11v$^{1}$** MBirch(15) (led far side: nt qckn ins fnl f) | ¾ | **2** | 12/1 | 47 | 26 |
| 3100$^{6}$ | **Young Ben (IRE) (37)** (JSWainwright) **4-8-2v$^{(7)}$** JBramhill(16) (b: b.hind: chsd ldrs far side: styd on appr fnl f) | nk | **3** | 20/1 | 41 | 23 |
| 2757$^{4}$ | **Rotherfield Park (IRE) (37)** (CSmith) **4-8-9** WWoods(10) (lw: a chsng ldrs: kpt on same pce fnl 2f) | ½ | **4** | 3/1$^{2}$ | 39 | 21 |
| *3091$^{9}$* | **Rankaidade (24)** (DonEnricoIncisa) **5-7-10** KimTinkler(11) (lw: mid div: rdn ½-wy: kpt on: nvr nr to chal) | 1¾ | **5** | 33/1 | 20 | 2 |
| *3091$^{7}$* | **Orange And Blue (37)** (MissJFCraze) **3-8-6c** NConnorton(14) (chsd ldrs far side: rdn ½-wy: no imp) | nk | **6** | 12/1 | 33 | 12 |
| 2800$^{5}$ | **Members Welcome (IRE) (52)** (JMBradley) **3-9-7v** SDrowne(5) (s.i.s: hdwy 2f out: nvr nr ldrs) | hd | **7** | 12/1 | 47 | 26 |
| 3278$^{8}$ | **Waverley Star (26)** (JSWainwright) **11-7-12b** LCharnock(3) (prom: rdn ½-wy: wknd over 1f out) | 1 | **8** | 33/1 | 18 | — |
| 3278$^{2}$ | **Pallium (IRE) (47)** (MrsAMNaughton) **8-9-5** ACulhane(4) (lw: bhd: rdn ½-wy: n.d) | hd | **9** | 13/8$^{1}$ | 39 | 21 |
| 2910$^{6}$ | **Gondo (39)** (EJAlston) **9-8-11** KFallon(13) (lw: hdwy centre ½-wy: n.d) | hd | **10** | 12/1 | 30 | 12 |
| 3168$^{9}$ | **First Option (36)** (RBastiman) **6-8-8** DeanMcKeown(12) (a bhd) | nk | **11** | 12/1 | 26 | 8 |
| 2185$^{13}$ | **Niteowl Raider (IRE) (45)** (JAHarris) **3-9-0** JO'Reilly(9) (chsd ldrs to ½-wy: sn lost pl) | 2½ | **12** | 16/1 | 27 | 6 |
| 2960$^{8}$ | **Imp Express (IRE) (46)** (GMMoore) **3-9-1v** JFortune(6) (lw: s.i.s: hdwy ½-wy: sn wknd) | ¾ | **13** | 6/1$^{3}$ | 26 | 5 |
| *834$^{7}$* | **Ho Mei Surprise (34)** (BPreece) **4-8-6** VSlattery(2) (a in rr) | 3 | **14** | 25/1 | 4 | — |
| *2748$^{10}$* | **Super Sonata (52)** (TWall) **4-9-7b$^{(3)}$** FLynch(1) (chsd ldrs tl wknd 2f out) | nk | **15** | 33/1 | 21 | 3 |
| 2987$^{4}$ | **Time Ticks On (40)** (MWEllerby) **3-8-2b$^{1(7)}$** JEdmunds(7) (s.v.s: a wl bhd) | dist | **16** | 33/1 | — | — |

(SP 151.2%) **16 Rn**

**58.9 secs** (0.50) CSF £135.64 CT £2,299.94 TOTE £16.60: £3.10 £3.10 £7.80 £1.80 (£58.00) Trio £458.30; £419.65 to Catterick 6/8/96.
OWNER Mrs M. M. Marshall (YORK) BRED D. W. Chapman
LONG HANDICAP Rankaidade 7-9
WEIGHT FOR AGE 3yo-3lb
No bid

**2518 Kabcast**, ending a long losing run, was never headed on the stands' side. (10/1)
**2359 Good To Talk**, tried in a visor, led his two rivals on the far side but, in the closing stages, the winner always just had his measure. (12/1)
**2933 Young Ben (IRE)**, one of three on the far side, stuck on in the final furlong and should be suited by six. (20/1)
**2757 Rotherfield Park (IRE)** is probably better on a stiffer track these days. (3/1)
**2800 Members Welcome (IRE)** (12/1: 8/1-14/1)
**3278 Pallium (IRE)**, who won this race a year ago off an 8lb higher mark, was having his second race in two days and never sparkled at all. (13/8)

## 3295 TOMMY SHEDDEN CHALLENGE TROPHY H'CAP (0-90) (3-Y.O) (Class C)

3-30 (3-52) **1m 1f** £5,679.50 (£1,706.00: £823.00: £381.50) Stalls: High GOING minus 0.49 sec per fur (F)

| | | | | SP | RR | SF |
|---|---|---|---|---|---|---|
| 2693* | **Give Me A Ring (IRE) (77)** (CWThornton) **3-8-10** DeanMcKeown(8) (lw: mde all: shkn up over 1f out: r.o strly) | — | **1** | 11/4$^{1}$ | 86 | 42 |
| 2693$^{5}$ | **Kamari (USA) (84)** (ACStewart) **3-9-3** RHills(6) (trckd ldrs: n.m.r on ins over 2f out: chsd wnr over 1f out: kpt on: no imp) | 1½ | **2** | 11/4$^{1}$ | 90 | 46 |
| *3063$^{2}$* | **Halebid (71)** (SPCWoods) **3-8-4** WWoods(7) (hld up: effrt on ins over 2f out: styd on same pce fnl f) | 3 | **3** | 3/1$^{2}$ | 72 | 28 |
| 952$^{4}$ | **Herodian (USA) (88)** (JHMGosden) **3-9-7v$^{1}$** GHind(3) (plld hrd: sn trckng ldrs: effrt & wandered 2f out: one pce) | s.h | **4** | 8/1$^{3}$ | 89 | 45 |
| 2899$^{3}$ | **Dispol Gem (72)** (GROldroyd) **3-8-5** KFallon(5) (sn outpcd & pushed along: styd on fnl 2f: nvr nr to chal) | 2½ | **5** | 20/1 | 69 | 25 |
| 3238$^{2}$ | **Nose No Bounds (IRE) (76)** (MJohnston) **3-8-9b** PRobinson(4) (lw: chsd ldrs: drvn along over 3f out: wknd 2f out) | 2½ | **6** | 11/1 | 68 | 24 |
| 1687$^{4}$ | **Raed (74)** (PTWalwyn) **3-8-7** MHills(1) (lw: hld up: effrt on outside over 2f out: n.d) | ¾ | **7** | 16/1 | 65 | 21 |
| 3101$^{2}$ | **Sualtach (IRE) (83)** (RHollinshead) **3-9-2** KDarley(2) (lw: hld up: effrt over 2f out: rdn & wknd over 1f out) | 4 | **8** | 11/1 | 67 | 23 |

(SP 116.8%) **8 Rn**

**1m 51.6** (1.40) CSF £10.57 CT £21.45 TOTE £3.70: £1.60 £1.30 £1.30 (£6.30) OWNER Mr Guy Reed (MIDDLEHAM) BRED W. Maxwell Ervine

**2693* Give Me A Ring (IRE)**, raised 2lb, was allowed to set his own pace. Setting sail for home coming to the final furlong, he was never in any danger. His rider deserves ten out of ten for this. (11/4)
**2693 Kamari (USA)** was one of two not dismounted during the long delay to the start. Trapped in on the inner halfway up the straight, he stayed on when he saw daylight, but was never going to trouble the winner. (11/4)
**3063 Halebid**, who is 7lb lower on grass than on the All-Weather, is a poor mover. Tapped for toe and short of room halfway up the straight, he is almost certainly better on the artificial surfaces. (3/1)
**952 Herodian (USA)** finished distressed at Doncaster last time and wore a visor here. Refusing to settle, he ran about under pressure and clearly has a problem. (8/1: op 9/2)
**2899 Dispol Gem** was never able to go the pace. (20/1)
**3238 Nose No Bounds (IRE)** (11/1: 10/1-16/1)

## 3296 ARMSTRONG MEMORIAL CHALLENGE CUP RATED STKS H'CAP (0-95) (3-Y.O+) (Class C)

4-00 (4-21) **6f** £8,623.20 (£3,208.80: £1,554.40: £652.00: £276.00: £125.60) Stalls: Low GOING minus 0.49 sec per fur (F)

| | | | | SP | RR | SF |
|---|---|---|---|---|---|---|
| 2987* | **Bollin Joanne (80)** (TDEasterby) **3-8-5** MBirch(10) (b: b.nr hind: mde all stands' side: r.o strly fnl f) | — | **1** | 11/1 | 95 | 38 |
| 3216$^{2}$ | **Tiler (IRE) (81)** (MJohnston) **4-8-10** RHills(17) (lw: led far side: clr over 1f out: styd on wl) | 1¾ | **2** | 7/2$^{1}$ | 91 | 38 |
| 3085$^{4}$ | **Ziggy's Dancer (USA) (86)** (EJAlston) **5-9-1** KFallon(2) (a in tch: styd on same pce appr fnl f) | 1¼ | **3** | 10/1 | 93 | 40 |
| 2694$^{17}$ | **Perryston View (86)** (PCalver) **4-9-1v** JCarroll(5) (a chsng ldrs: kpt on same pce fnl 2f) | ¾ | **4** | 8/1$^{3}$ | 91 | 38 |
| 2889$^{6}$ | **Bowden Rose (84)** (MBlanshard) **4-8-13b** RCochrane(4) (s.i.s: bhd: hdwy 2f out: nvr rchd ldrs) | 1½ | **5** | 8/1$^{3}$ | 85 | 32 |
| 2911$^{11}$ | **Whittle Rock (83)** (MrsMReveley) **3-8-8** KDarley(9) (hdwy over 2f out: kpt on wl fnl f) | nk | **6** | 16/1 | 83 | 26 |
| 3106$^{4}$ | **I'm Your Lady (78)** (BAMcMahon) **5-8-7** GCarter(16) (lw: chsd ldrs far side: one pce fnl 2f) | hd | **7** | 33/1 | 78 | 25 |
| 3047* | **Sea-Deer (86)** (CADwyer) **7-9-1** JFortune(8) (lw: hld up: effrt over 2f out: nvr nr to chal) | s.h | **8** | 7/1$^{2}$ | 86 | 33 |
| 3038$^{6}$ | **So Intrepid (IRE) (82)** (JMBradley) **6-8-11** SDrowne(13) (swtchd lft s: sn chsng ldrs: one pce fnl 2f) | nk | **9** | 12/1 | 81 | 28 |
| 2694$^{4}$ | **Lady Sheriff (85)** (RHollinshead) **5-8-11$^{(3)}$** FLynch(3) (lw: chsd ldrs centre: rdn & lost pl 2f out) | s.h | **10** | 12/1 | 84 | 31 |
| 2889$^{12}$ | **Tadeo (90)** (MJohnston) **3-9-1** PRobinson(1) (chsd ldrs tl wknd 2f out) | hd | **11** | 16/1 | 89 | 32 |
| 3216$^{4}$ | **Rock Symphony (80)** (WJHaggas) **6-8-9** MHills(6) (sn bhd: sme hdwy 2f out: n.d) | 2 | **12** | 7/1$^{2}$ | 73 | 20 |
| 3085$^{11}$ | **Saint Express (89)** (MrsMReveley) **6-9-4** ACulhane(11) (hld up: effrt ½-wy: n.d) | 2 | **13** | 25/1 | 77 | 24 |
| *2634$^{3}$* | **Splicing (84)** (WJHaggas) **3-8-9** WWoods(12) (s.i.s: swtchd rt s: chsd ldrs far side tl wknd over 2f out) | ½ | **14** | 14/1 | 71 | 14 |
| 2114$^{21}$ | **Stylish Ways (IRE) (92)** (MissSEHall) **4-9-7** NConnorton(14) (b: chsd ldrs far side tl lost pl over 2f out) | 1½ | **15** | 9/1 | 75 | 22 |

| | | | | SP | RR | SF |
|---|---|---|---|---|---|---|
| $2532^{4}$ | **Blessingindisguise (81)** (MWEasterby) **3-8-1**$^{(5)}$ GParkin(15) (chsd ldrs far side tl lost pl ½-wy) | ¾ | **16** | 20/1 | 62 | 5 |
| | | | | (SP 142.2%) | | **16 Rn** |

**1m 10.0** (-0.50) CSF £53.63 CT £412.03 TOTE £12.60: £2.40 £1.60 £1.80 £2.60 (£27.00) Trio £171.30 OWNER Lady Westbrook (MALTON) BRED Sir Neil and Lady Westbrook
LONG HANDICAP I'm Your Lady 8-0
WEIGHT FOR AGE 3yo-4lb

**2987* Bollin Joanne** always dominated the stands' side and, sticking on really strongly, scored in good style in the end. Now she has come to herself, she should enjoy further success. (11/1)
**3216 Tiler (IRE)**, drawn on the far side, dominated that wing. Out on his own on that side two furlongs out, he kept on well, but the winner proved too strong. This was a fine effort. (7/2)
**3085 Ziggy's Dancer (USA)** won six times last season, but he seems to be struggling to get his head in front this time. Sticking on under pressure, he was never going to reach the first two. (10/1)
**2694 Perryston View** has slipped down to a handy mark and there is no doubt that, when he comes right, there is a nice sprint in him. (8/1)
**2889 Bowden Rose** missed the break but came through in good style in the closing stages. She is struggling to overcome the Handicapper this time. (8/1)
**2532 Whittle Rock**, who has changed stables, showed promise, staying on strongly late in the day. (16/1)
**3106 I'm Your Lady** raced on the far side and shaped by no means badly as she is probably better these days over seven. (33/1)

## 3297 BBC RADIO YORK H'CAP (0-70) (3-Y.O+) (Class E)

4-30 (4-51) **1m 4f 60y** £3,014.50 (£913.00: £446.00: £212.50) Stalls: High GOING minus 0.49 sec per fur (F)

| | | | | SP | RR | SF |
|---|---|---|---|---|---|---|
| $2896^{9}$ | **Course Fishing (39)** (BAMcMahon) **5-8-1**$^{ow1}$ GCarter(11) (hld up: effrt over 3f out: styd on wl to ld ins fnl f: readily) | — | **1** | 16/1 | 51 | 27 |
| $2884^{3}$ | **Floating Line (66)** (EJAlston) **8-10-0** KFallon(3) (lw: chsd ldrs: led over 3f out tl ins fnl f: kpt on) | 2 | **2** | 7/2 1 | 75 | 52 |
| | **Cumbrian Rhapsody (58)** (TDEasterby) **6-9-6** MBirch(6) (hdwy to chal over 3f out: styd on same pce fnl 2f) | 1½ | **3** | 14/1 | 65 | 42 |
| $2522^{2}$ | **Here Comes Herbie (39)** (WStorey) **4-7-8**$^{(7)}$ IonaWands(13) (lw: stumbled after 1f: hdwy to trck ldrs 8f out: chal 3f out: kpt on one pce) | ¾ | **4** | 9/1 3 | 46 | 23 |
| $2776^{4}$ | **Hawkish (USA) (51)** (DMorley) **7-8-13** RCochrane(7) (hld up: hdwy over 4f out: sn chsng ldrs: no imp fnl 2f) | 1 | **5** | 7/2 1 | 56 | 33 |
| $2570^{5}$ | **Clash of Swords (55)** (PCalver) **3-8-6** GHind(12) (lw: chsd ldrs tl outpcd fnl 3f) | 3½ | **6** | 13/2 2 | 56 | 22 |
| $2567^{9}$ | **Monte Cavo (34)** (MBrittain) **5-7-10** JLowe(9) (hld up: hdwy over 5f out: sn chsng ldrs: outpcd fnl 2f) | 1¾ | **7** | 25/1 | 32 | 9 |
| $2423^{4}$ | **Hasta la Vista (53)** (MWEasterby) **6-8-10b**$^{(5)}$ GParkin(4) (mde most tl over 3f out: wl outpcd fnl 2f) | 1½ | **8** | 9/1 3 | 49 | 26 |
| $2988^{7}$ | **Chantry Beath (49)** (CWThornton) **5-8-11** DeanMcKeown(15) (chsd ldrs: drvn along over 3f out: sn lost pl) | 1 | **9** | 16/1 | 44 | 21 |
| $2891^{2}$ | **Kindred Greeting (34)** (JAHarris) **4-7-10** JO'Reilly(2) (lw: chsd ldrs: drvn 8f out: lost pl over 3f out) | ¾ | **10** | 10/1 | 28 | 5 |
| *$2322^{9}$* | **Kismetim (34)** (DWChapman) **6-7-10** LCharnock(14) (sn bhd & pushed along: lost tch 3f out) | 12 | **11** | 33/1 | 12 | — |
| *$2936^{4}$* | **Drama King (38)** (SRBowring) **4-8-0b** NKennedy(8) (s.i.s: sn drvn along: a in rr) | hd | **12** | 20/1 | 16 | — |
| $995^{19}$ | **Eden Dancer (55)** (MrsMReveley) **4-9-3** KDarley(5) (sn bhd) | 10 | **13** | 16/1 | 20 | — |
| $2989^{3}$ | **Outstayed Welcome (57)** (MJHaynes) **4-9-0**$^{(5)}$ MBaird(1) (b.off hind: chsd ldrs tl lost pl over 3f out: sn bhd) | 9 | **14** | 13/2 2 | 11 | — |
| $2779^{10}$ | **Lindisfarne Lady (35)** (MrsMReveley) **4-7-11** DaleGibson(10) (a bhd) | 7 | **15** | 33/1 | — | — |
| | | | | (SP 139.0%) | | **15 Rn** |

**2m 37.0** (3.00) CSF £76.13 CT £789.24 TOTE £19.80: £6.50 £1.90 £5.10 (£28.40) Trio £511.20; £439.24 to Catterick 6/8/96 OWNER Mr G. D. Bull (TAMWORTH) BRED Hyde Stud
LONG HANDICAP Kismetim 7-4 Kindred Greeting 7-9 Monte Cavo 7-3
WEIGHT FOR AGE 3yo-11lb

**2214 Course Fishing** bounced right back to his best and, in the end, scored with something in hand. A follow up is very much on the cards. (16/1)
**2884 Floating Line**, making the best of his way home, fought off all but the winner. (7/2)
**Cumbrian Rhapsody**, out of sorts on the Flat last year, had won over hurdles since. She ran a fine race here, especially as this trip is on the short side for her. (14/1)
**2522 Here Comes Herbie** was tightened up and stumbled after a furlong. Challenging early in the straight, the partnership looked tired entering the last. (9/1)
**2776 Hawkish (USA)**, as usual found little off the bridle. The step up in trip did nothing for him. (7/2)

## 3298 'GO RACING IN YORKSHIRE' MAIDEN STKS (3-Y.O+) (Class D)

5-00 (5-22) **1m 2f** £3,745.00 (£1,135.00: £555.00: £265.00) Stalls: High GOING minus 0.49 sec per fur (F)

| | | | | SP | RR | SF |
|---|---|---|---|---|---|---|
| $1359^{3}$ | **Altamura (USA) (84)** (JHMGosden) **3-8-7** GHind(2) (mde all: pushed clr over 3f out: unchal) | — | **1** | Evens 1 | 83 | 32 |
| $1690^{12}$ | **Raise A Prince (FR) (78)** (JWHills) **3-8-12** WWoods(9) (trckd ldrs: effrt over 3f out: styd on: no ch w wnr) | 10 | **2** | 10/1 3 | 72 | 21 |
| $2041^{14}$ | **Forest Robin (86)** (RFJohnsonHoughton) **3-8-12** RCochrane(8) (lw: hld up: hdwy over 3f out: sn rdn: kpt on one pce) | 2½ | **3** | 11/8 2 | 68 | 17 |
| $2961^{3}$ | **Totem Dancer** (JLEyre) **3-8-7** JFanning(7) (hld up: styd on fnl 2f: nvr nr to chal) | 1¾ | **4** | 20/1 | 60 | 9 |
| | **Indiana Princess** (MrsMReveley) **3-8-7** ACulhane(6) (lengthy: unf: bit bkwd: hld up & bhd: hung lft & rn green 3f out: styd on towards fin) | ¾ | **5** | 33/1 | 59 | 8 |
| | **Nirvana Prince** (BPreece) **7-9-7** VSlattery(3) (bit bkwd: chsd ldrs: outpcd over 3f out: sn lost pl) | 10 | **6** | 33/1 | 48 | 6 |
| $3103^{3}$ | **Swynford Supreme** (JFBottomley) **3-8-12** JLowe(1) (trckd wnr: drvn along 4f out: wknd over 2f out) | 3 | **7** | 50/1 | 43 | — |
| | **Chesters Quest** (RHollinshead) **4-9-2**$^{(5)}$ DGriffiths(5) (unf: scope: bit bkwd: a bhd: hung lft over 3f out) | 13 | **8** | 50/1 | 22? | — |
| | | | | (SP 115.8%) | | **8 Rn** |

**2m 6.0** (2.50) CSF £11.22 TOTE £2.10: £1.10 £2.70 £1.10 (£8.50) Trio £5.10 OWNER Sheikh Mohammed (NEWMARKET) BRED Darley Stud Management Inc
WEIGHT FOR AGE 3yo-9lb

**1359 Altamura (USA)** was allowed to set her own pace. Pushed clear halfway up the straight, she thrashed her tail, but was soon out on her own. The opposition was moderate indeed, and hopefully the Handicapper will not overreact. (Evens)
**730 Raise A Prince (FR)**, who has changed stables, had his tongue tied down. Sent in pursuit of the winner, he never looked like getting anywhere near her at all. (10/1: op 5/1)
**969 Forest Robin**, held up to get the trip, proved one-paced. (11/8)
**2961 Totem Dancer**, dropping in distance, fared by no means badly. Now qualified for a handicap mark, she can do better over further. (20/1)
**Indiana Princess** showed plenty of knee-action going down. Nervous at the stalls, she showed definite signs of inexperience, but gave connections some hope for the future, staying on late in the day. (33/1)

T/Jkpt: Not won; £7,327.28 to Catterick 6/8/96. T/Plpt: £143.10 (177.27 Tckts). T/Qdpt: £6.70 (255.52 Tckts). WG

# 3281-BRIGHTON (L-H) (Firm)
## Tuesday August 6th
WEATHER: unsettled WIND: v.str half against

## 3299 JIMMY HEAL MEMORIAL TROPHY NURSERY H'CAP (2-Y.O) (Class D)
2-00 (2-01) **5f 59y** £3,498.75 (£1,044.00: £498.50: £225.75) Stalls: Low GOING minus 0.26 sec per fur (GF)

| Form | Horse | Dist | Pos | SP | RR | SF |
|---|---|---|---|---|---|---|
| 3251[3] | **Skyers Flyer (IRE) (85)** (RonaldThompson) **2-9-7** NConnorton(4) (lw: hdwy over 2f out: led over 1f out: rdn out) | — | 1 | 7/1 | 72 | 17 |
| 2965[7] | **Blazing Castle (82)** (WGMTurner) **2-8-11**[(7)] DSweeney(3) (a.p: rdn over 2f out: r.o wl ins fnl f) | nk | 2 | 10/1 | 68 | 13 |
| 3224* | **Bold African (84)** (PDEvans) **2-9-6b**[7x] ACulhane(2) (lw: led 1f: ev ch over 1f out: unable qckn) | 2 | 3 | 4/1[2] | 64 | 9 |
| 2404[11] | **Singforyoursupper (60)** (GGMargarson) **2-7-10** GBardwell(6) (lw: outpcd: nvr nrr) | 3 | 4 | 33/1 | 31 | — |
| 3169[4] | **Grovefair Flyer (IRE) (61)** (BJMeehan) **2-7-11b**[ow1] CRutter(7) (no hdwy fnl 2f) | ½ | 5 | 10/1 | 30 | — |
| 3160[2] | **Tear White (IRE) (72)** (TGMills) **2-8-8b** TWilliams(8) (lw: led 4f out tl over 1f out: 4th & btn whn n.m.r on ins ins fnl f) | 1 | 6 | 15/8[1] | 38 | — |
| 2012[3] | **Who Told Vicky (IRE) (68)** (JSMoore) **2-8-4** JFEgan(5) (bhd fnl 3f) | 11 | 7 | 20/1 | 1 | — |
| *3110[3]* | ***Gopi (65)*** (RHannon) **2-8-1** JQuinn(1) (Withdrawn not under Starter's orders: veterinary advice) | | W | 11/2[3] | — | — |
| | | | | (SP 108.6%) | **7 Rn** | |

**64.0 secs** (4.00) CSF £44.26 CT £146.75 TOTE £6.90: £2.10 £4.60 (£37.80) OWNER Mrs J. Carney (DONCASTER) BRED Denis Brennan
LONG HANDICAP Grovefair Flyer (IRE) 7-6
**OFFICIAL EXPLANATION Tear White (IRE): did not act on the track.**
**3251 Skyers Flyer (IRE)** moved up from halfway and, striking the front below the distance, was ridden along to score. (7/1)
**2485* Blazing Castle**, never far away, found his feet in the final furlong but, despite running on well, was never going to overhaul the winner in time. (10/1: op 6/1)
**3224* Bold African**, making a quick reappearance, was always prominent. With every chance below the distance, he was then tapped for toe. (4/1)
**1760 Singforyoursupper** was unable to go the pace, but did struggle on in the closing stages to be nearest at the line. (33/1)
**3169 Grovefair Flyer (IRE)** was making little impression on the principals from halfway. (10/1)
**3160 Tear White (IRE)** failed to handle this switch-back track. (15/8: 5/4-2/1)

## 3300 STANMER CLAIMING STKS (3-Y.O) (Class F)
2-30 (2-30) **7f 214y** £2,381.00 (£656.00: £311.00) Stalls: Low GOING minus 0.26 sec per fur (GF)

| Form | Horse | Dist | Pos | SP | RR | SF |
|---|---|---|---|---|---|---|
| 2594[10] | **Multi Franchise (56)** (BGubby) **3-8-5** BDoyle(7) (lw: a.p: led 2f out: drvn out) | — | 1 | 4/1[2] | 60 | 20 |
| 2979[10] | **Followthe Allstars (47)** (TJNaughton) **3-8-11b**[1] SSanders(3) (lw: hdwy over 2f out: edgd lft over 1f out: ev ch wl ins fnl f: r.o) | nk | 2 | 33/1 | 65 | 25 |
| 2558[6] | **Dhulikhel (56)** (DMarks) **3-8-6** GDuffield(2) (a.p: rdn over 1f out: unable qckn) | 2½ | 3 | 11/2[3] | 55 | 15 |
| 3244[2] | **Uncle George (63)** (MHTompkins) **3-8-9b** PRobinson(1) (lw: hld up: rdn over 1f out: nt run on) | nk | 4 | 7/4[1] | 58 | 18 |
| 2893[3] | **How Could-I (IRE) (44)** (MrsNMacauley) **3-8-4b** JQuinn(5) (lw: led 6f: wknd fnl f) | nk | 5 | 11/2[3] | 52 | 12 |
| 2946[14] | **Governor's Bid (35)** (MrsLCJewell) **3-8-1b** JFEgan(4) (lw: bhd fnl 2f) | 16 | 6 | 50/1 | 17 | — |
| 3165[P] | **Stone Island (58)** (CACyzer) **3-9-1b**[1] JReid(6) (lw: bhd fnl 6f) | 2½ | 7 | 7/1 | 26 | — |
| | | | | (SP 104.5%) | **7 Rn** | |

**1m 36.6** (4.40) CSF £71.77 TOTE £5.60: £2.60 £5.20 (£68.30) OWNER Brian Gubby Ltd (BAGSHOT) BRED B. Gubby
**1979 Multi Franchise**, struck the front a quarter of a mile out and, responding to pressure, held on well. (4/1: 3/1-9/2)
**Followthe Allstars** found the drop in class and the first-time blinkers a great help. Moving up over a quarter of a mile out, he drifted left below the distance but, despite this, came to have every chance in the closing stages, if just unable to get the better of the winner. (33/1)
**863 Dhulikhel**, never far away, failed to raised her work-rate from below the distance. (11/2)
**3244 Uncle George** was making a quick reappearance, but looked extremely well in the paddock. Chasing the leaders traveling well, he was asked for his effort in the final quarter-mile, but looked far from enthusiastic and failed to find what was required. He does not look one to place a great deal of faith in. (7/4: 5/4-15/8)
**2893 How Could-I (IRE)** had shot her bolt in the final furlong. (11/2: 7/2-6/1)
**1657 Stone Island** (7/1: op 9/2)

## 3301 HANNINGTONS OF BRIGHTON H'CAP (0-70) (3-Y.O) (Class E)
3-00 (3-00) **6f 209y** £3,206.70 (£957.60: £457.80: £207.90) Stalls: Low GOING minus 0.26 sec per fur (GF)

| Form | Horse | Dist | Pos | SP | RR | SF |
|---|---|---|---|---|---|---|
| 2974[3] | **Kings Harmony (IRE) (66)** (PJMakin) **3-9-6** SSanders(5) (led 6f out: clr over 1f out: r.o wl) | — | 1 | 11/8[1] | 77 | 22 |
| 3244[3] | **Ivory's Grab Hire (60)** (KTIvory) **3-8-9b**[(5)] MartinDwyer(2) (lw: hdwy & bmpd 2f out: chsd wnr ins fnl f: unable qckn) | 3 | 2 | 13/2 | 64 | 9 |
| 3286[6] | **Princesse Lyphard (42)** (MJPolglase) **3-7-10** NCarlisle(4) (lw: hdwy over 1f out: one pce) | 1¾ | 3 | 14/1 | 42 | — |
| 2725[16] | **Oriel Lad (67)** (PDEvans) **3-9-7b** ACulhane(1) (a.p: chsd wnr wl over 1f out tl ins fnl f: sn wknd) | s.h | 4 | 11/2[3] | 67 | 12 |
| *164[4]* | **To The Whire (60)** (GLMoore) **3-9-0** CandyMorris(3) (a.p: hrd rdn & edgd lft 2f out: sn wknd) | 7 | 5 | 15/2 | 44 | — |
| 2929[6] | **Truth (55)** (SirMarkPrescott) **3-8-9** GDuffield(6) (led 1f: rdn over 2f out: wknd over 1f out) | nk | 6 | 5/1[2] | 38 | — |
| | | | | (SP 105.9%) | **6 Rn** | |

**1m 24.8** (4.80) CSF £9.15 TOTE £1.80: £1.30 £2.30 (£4.40) OWNER Ten of Hearts (MARLBOROUGH) BRED Rathasker Stud
LONG HANDICAP Princesse Lyphard 7-7
**2974 Kings Harmony (IRE)** was soon at the head of affairs and, forging clear below the distance, was not going to be denied. (11/8)
**3244 Ivory's Grab Hire** was just beginning to pick up ground when given a bump a quarter of a mile out. He struggled into second inside the final furlong but, by that stage, the winner was already home and dry. (13/2)
**Princesse Lyphard**, who finished sixth here the previous night, made an effort below the distance, but could then make no further impression. (14/1: 12/1-20/1)
**2139 Oriel Lad** moved into second place early in the final quarter-mile but, collared for that position inside the last 200 yards, was soon a spent force. (11/2: 3/1-6/1)
**To The Whire**, given just over six months off, was never far away. Edging left and bumping another rival as she was given a smack a quarter of a mile out, she soon capitulated. (15/2: 5/1-8/1)
**2929 Truth** (5/1: 5/2-11/2)

## 3302 BRIGHTON CHALLENGE CUP H'CAP (0-80) (4-Y.O+) (Class D)
3-30 (3-30) **1m 3f 196y** £3,496.05 (£1,040.40: £494.70: £221.85) Stalls: High GOING minus 0.26 sec per fur (GF)

| | Horse / details | Dist | Pos | SP | RR | SF |
|---|---|---|---|---|---|---|
| $2921^{3}$ | **Canton Venture (70)** (SPCWoods) **4-10-0** WWoods(4) (lw: mde all: clr over 4f out: r.o wl) | — | **1** | $11/4^{3}$ | 79 | 47 |
| 3204* | **Voices in the Sky (42)** (AGNewcombe) **5-8-0** SDrowne(3) (a.p: chsd wnr fnl 4f: r.o ins fnl f) | 1 | **2** | $2/1^{1}$ | 50 | 18 |
| $3113^{4}$ | **Fabulous Mtoto (55)** (MSSaunders) **6-8-13** JFEgan(5) (lw: hld up: rdn over 2f out: r.o one pce) | 1¾ | **3** | 5/1 | 60 | 28 |
| $3094^{2}$ | **Prince Danzig (IRE) (62)** (DJGMurraySmith) **5-9-6** JReid(2) (lw: chsd wnr 8f: wknd fnl f) | 3½ | **4** | $9/4^{2}$ | 63 | 31 |
| $3094^{4}$ | **Charlie Bigtime (44)** (RHarris) **6-8-2** AMackay(1) (b.off hind: bhd fnl 4f) | 13 | **5** | 12/1 | 27 | — |
| | | | | (SP 115.1%) | | **5 Rn** |

**2m 34.0** (6.40) CSF £8.64 TOTE £4.40: £2.20 £1.80 (£4.20) OWNER Dr Frank Chao (NEWMARKET) BRED High Point B/stock Ltd & Chao Racing & B/stock Ltd

**2921 Canton Venture** made every post a winning one. Striding clear at the top of the hill, he was not going to be caught. (11/4: 2/1-3/1)
**3204* Voices in the Sky**, making a quick reappearance, moved into second place half a mile out. She did run on inside the final furlong, but never had a hope of challenging the winner. (2/1)
**3113 Fabulous Mtoto** chased the leaders. Rousted along over a quarter of a mile out, he did stay on, but never threatened to play an active role. (5/1)
**3094 Prince Danzig (IRE)**, in second place for the first mile, grimly tried to hold on for the minor placing, but was hung out to dry in the final furlong. (9/4)

## 3303 GORING (S) H'CAP (0-60) (3-Y.O+) (Class G)
4-00 (4-00) **1m 3f 196y** £2,070.00 (£570.00: £270.00) Stalls: High GOING minus 0.26 sec per fur (GF)

| | Horse / details | Dist | Pos | SP | RR | SF |
|---|---|---|---|---|---|---|
| *$3086^{5}$* | **Zeliba (37)** (MrsNMacauley) **4-8-5** JQuinn(3) (hdwy over 3f out: rdn over 2f out: led wl ins fnl f: r.o wl) | — | **1** | $5/1^{3}$ | 44 | 26 |
| $2979^{6}$ | **Efficacious (IRE) (45)** (CJBenstead) **3-8-2**ow1 PRobinson(5) (b.hind: lw: hdwy over 3f out: rdn over 2f out: r.o wl ins fnl f) | ½ | **2** | 13/2 | 51 | 21 |
| 2788* | **Flight Master (60)** (PJMakin) **4-10-0** SSanders(9) (t: lw: hdwy over 4f out: chsd ldr over 3f out: led over 1f out: hrd rdn: hdd wl ins fnl f: unable qckn) | 1¼ | **3** | $4/1^{2}$ | 65 | 47 |
| $852^{14}$ | **Ever Friends (37)** (RHarris) **4-8-5** AMackay(4) (swtg: lost pl 6f out: rallied over 1f out: r.o wl ins fnl f) | ½ | **4** | 33/1 | 41 | 23 |
| $2978^{5}$ | **Colour Counsellor (43)** (RMFlower) **3-8-0b**ow1 DBiggs(2) (led: clr over 4f out: hdd over 1f out: wknd fnl f) | 1 | **5** | 12/1 | 46 | 16 |
| $3095^{2}$ | **Siesta Time (USA) (52)** (CLPopham) **6-9-6** JReid(6) (lw: hmpd over 4f out: nt clr run & swtchd rt over 3f out: hdwy over 2f out: r.o one pce) | 1¾ | **6** | $7/2^{1}$ | 52 | 34 |
| 2978* | **Tout de Val (30)** (KBishop) **7-7-12** CRutter(7) (lw: hdwy 6f out: chsd ldr 5f out tl over 3f out: sn wknd) | 5 | **7** | $4/1^{2}$ | 24 | 6 |
| $2958^{8}$ | **Prerogative (52)** (RSimpson) **6-9-6v** GDuffield(1) (prom over 7f) | 8 | **8** | 10/1 | 35 | 17 |
| $3130^{7}$ | **High Flown (USA) (39)** (RonaldThompson) **4-8-7v** NConnorton(10) (lw: chsd ldr 7f) | 1¾ | **9** | 12/1 | 19 | 1 |
| $2978^{4}$ | **Moving Up (IRE) (48)** (GLMoore) **3-8-5v$^{1}$** RPerham(8) (lw: bhd fnl 3f) | 1¾ | **10** | 10/1 | 26 | — |
| | | | | (SP 128.7%) | | **10 Rn** |

**2m 34.0** (6.40) CSF £38.34 CT £136.62 TOTE £6.70: £2.90 £2.00 £3.40 (£33.70) Trio £157.50 OWNER Mr G. Wiltshire (MELTON MOWBRAY) BRED Sheikh Mohammed bin Rashid al Maktoum
WEIGHT FOR AGE 3yo-11lb
No bid

**2906* Zeliba** began her effort early in the straight. Rousted along, she eventually managed to get on top in the closing stages. (5/1)
**2768 Efficacious (IRE)** began her effort over three furlongs from home. She ran on well inside the final furlong, but failed to overhaul the winner. (13/2)
**2788* Flight Master** may have been tubed, but he ran well, considering how strong the wind was. Moving up at the top of the hill, he was soon racing in second place. Gaining a narrow advantage below the distance, he was eventually worried out of it in the closing stages. (4/1: 9/4-9/2)
**Ever Friends**, given a three-month break, chased the leaders until losing his pitch at halfway. He ran on nicely from below the distance, but found it all over bar the shouting. (33/1)
**2978 Colour Counsellor** attempted to make all the running. Forging clear at the top of the hill, he was eventually reeled in below the distance. (12/1)
**3095 Siesta Time (USA)** did not have the best of luck. Hampered at the top of the hill, she then failed to get a clear run and had to be switched right over three furlongs from home. By that stage, she had an enormous amount of ground to make up and, although she did stay on, this one-paced mare was never going to get there. (7/2: 9/4-4/1)
**High Flown (USA)** (12/1: 8/1-14/1)
**2978 Moving Up (IRE)** (10/1: 6/1-11/1)

## 3304 BLACK ROCK LIMITED STKS (0-55) (3-Y.O+) (Class F)
4-30 (4-32) **6f 209y** £2,381.00 (£656.00: £311.00) Stalls: Low GOING minus 0.26 sec per fur (GF)

| | Horse / details | Dist | Pos | SP | RR | SF |
|---|---|---|---|---|---|---|
| $3096^{3}$ | **Sharp Imp (51)** (RMFlower) **6-9-6b** DBiggs(3) (hdwy over 1f out: led ins fnl f: hrd rdn & edgd lft: r.o wl) | — | **1** | 13/2 | 66 | 14 |
| $2979^{4}$ | **Creeking (55)** (SirMarkPrescott) **3-8-8b$^{1}$** GDuffield(2) (led: sn clr: hrd rdn over 1f out: hdd ins fnl f: r.o) | ¾ | **2** | $15/8^{1}$ | 58 | — |
| $2957^{5}$ | **Astral Invader (IRE) (52)** (MSSaunders) **4-9-3** RPerham(6) (lw: chsd ldr over 4f: rdn: unable qckn) | 1¼ | **3** | 8/1 | 58 | 6 |
| $2971^{5}$ | **Rocky Waters (USA) (52)** (PBurgoyne) **7-9-0**(3) PMcCabe(4) (b.hind: hdwy over 3f out: chsd ldr over 2f out to 1f out: clr 3rd whn hmpd ins fnl f) | ½ | **4** | $3/1^{2}$ | 57 | 5 |
| $2765^{5}$ | **Flagstaff (USA) (54)** (GLMoore) **3-8-11** SSanders(7) (hld up: rdn over 2f out: sn wknd) | 3½ | **5** | $9/2^{3}$ | 49 | — |
| $3285^{7}$ | **Best Kept Secret (54)** (PDEvans) **5-9-3b** JFEgan(1) (hld up: rdn over 2f out: wknd over 1f out) | 2 | **6** | 10/1 | 45 | — |
| *$2945^{12}$* | ***Barbrallen (39)*** (MrsLCJewell) **4-9-0** TWilliams(5) (Withdrawn not under Starter's orders: jockey ref to ride horse due to unsafe conveyance) | | **W** | 50/1 | — | — |
| | | | | (SP 113.5%) | | **6 Rn** |

**1m 25.5** (5.50) CSF £18.23 TOTE £7.10: £3.40 £1.40 (£7.70) OWNER Mrs G. M. Temmerman (JEVINGTON) BRED James Wigan
WEIGHT FOR AGE 3yo-6lb

**3096 Sharp Imp** may not have been favoured by the weights, but still managed to carry the day. Held up as usual, he came with a flourish on the outside of the field and struck the front inside the final furlong. His jockey gave his a crack and the gelding drifted left, hampering another horse. It was surprising that no suspension was awarded to Biggs. (13/2: op 4/1)
**2979 Creeking**, fitted with blinkers for the first time, scooted off in front and had soon established a clear advantage. She looked certain to be swallowed up below the distance but, to her credit, was only overhauled inside the final furlong. (15/8)
**2957 Astral Invader (IRE)**, in second place until over two furlongs out, could then only tread water. (8/1)
**2971 Rocky Waters (USA)** moved up at halfway. In second place over quarter of a mile out, he was collared for that position entering the final furlong, but was still close up and in third when hampered by the winner in the closing stages. (3/1)

**2765 Flagstaff (USA)** was in trouble early in the final quarter-mile. (9/2: op 5/2)

T/Plpt: £1,308.00 (11.77 Tckts). T/Qdpt: £14.70 (91.34 Tckts). AK

# 2983-CATTERICK (L-H) (Good to firm, Firm patches)
## Tuesday August 6th

WEATHER: rain WIND: almost nil

## 3305 'BEVERLEY WESTWOOD' (S) STKS (3, 4 & 5-Y.O) (Class G)

2-15 (2-15) **1m 7f 177y** £2,238.00 (£618.00: £294.00) Stalls: Low GOING minus 0.25 sec per fur (GF)

| | Dist | Pos | SP | RR | SF |
|---|---|---|---|---|---|
| 2891$^{10}$ **Fearless Wonder (47)** (MrsMReveley) **5-9-8v$^{1}$** KDarley(2) (lw: mde all: qcknd clr 7f out: rdn out) | — | **1** | 5/2$^{2}$ | 57 | 34 |
| 3094$^{5}$ **Distant Storm (53)** (MBell) **3-8-7v$^{1}$** MFenton(4) (lw: outpcd & bhd 7f out: styd on u.p fnl 3f: nrst fin) | 12 | **2** | 5/2$^{2}$ | 45 | 7 |
| 2989$^{12}$ **Risky Rose (44)** (RHollinshead) **4-9-1**$^{(5)}$ DGriffiths(5) (lw: hld up: wnt 2nd 4f out: sn rdn & no imp) | 7 | **3** | 6/5$^{1}$ | 36 | 13 |
| 2876$^{5}$ **Thorntoun House (IRE)** (JSGoldie) **3-8-7** DeanMcKeown(6) (prom tl outpcd over 6f out: n.d after) | 2½ | **4** | 16/1$^{3}$ | 35 | — |
| 2891$^{6}$ **Club Elite (23)** (MFBarraclough) **4-8-12**$^{(5)}$ PPMurphy(1) (chsd wnr tl rdn & btn over 4f out) | 26 | **5** | 100/1 | 4 | — |
| *3090$^{7}$* **Clover Girl** (BEllison) **5-9-3v** JTate(3) (b: outpcd & wl bhd fnl 7f: virtually p.u) | dist | **6** | 20/1 | — | — |
| | | | (SP 114.2%) | | **6 Rn** |

**3m 32.1** (10.60) CSF £8.99 TOTE £2.40: £1.50 £1.60 (£3.00) OWNER Mr William Davies (SALTBURN) BRED W. L. Caley
WEIGHT FOR AGE 3yo-15lb
No bid

**2626 Fearless Wonder**, wearing a tongue-strap for the first time, looked really lit up beforehand and, given an aggressive ride, was never going to be caught. (5/2: 7/2-9/4)
**3094 Distant Storm**, despite wearing a visor for the first time and taking a big step up in distance, looked woefully slow, and only got going when it was all over. (5/2)
**2989 Risky Rose**, held up as she needs to be, was then never doing enough when sent in pursuit of the winner approaching the straight. (6/5: 4/5-5/4)
**2876 Thorntoun House (IRE)** took a big step up in distance here and ran much better, but never looked likely to seriously get into it. (16/1)
**2891 Club Elite** had no chance at these weights. (100/1)

## 3306 'DONCASTER TOWN MOOR' H'CAP (0-60) (3-Y.O+) (Class F)

2-45 (2-49) **7f** £3,204.00 (£894.00: £432.00) Stalls: Low GOING minus 0.25 sec per fur (GF)

| | Dist | Pos | SP | RR | SF |
|---|---|---|---|---|---|
| 3252$^{4}$ **My Godson (51)** (JLEyre) **6-9-5b** KFallon(9) (dwlt: hdwy far side over 2f out: led ins fnl f: r.o) | — | **1** | 11/4$^{1}$ | 63 | 44 |
| 3236* **Roseate Lodge (42)** (SEKettlewell) **10-8-3**$^{(7)}$ $^{6x}$ JennyBenson(10) (bhd: racd far side st & hdwy to ld wl over 1f out: hdd & nt qckn ins fnl f) | 1 | **2** | 10/1 | 52 | 33 |
| 2851$^{4}$ **Miss Pigalle (43)** (MissLAPerratt) **5-8-11b** KDarley(12) (mid div: hdwy to ld stands' side over 1f out: nt qckn ins fnl f) | 1½ | **3** | 16/1 | 49 | 30 |
| 3151$^{7}$ **Allinson's Mate (IRE) (56)** (TDBarron) **8-9-10b** JFortune(4) (lw: in tch: racd far side st: kpt on fnl f) | ½ | **4** | 6/1$^{2}$ | 61 | 42 |
| 3060$^{6}$ **Upex le Gold Too (28)** (LRLloyd-James) **4-7-3**$^{(7)}$ IonaWands(16) (hdwy to jn ldrs stands' side over 2f out: nt qckn ins fnl f) | 1 | **5** | 25/1 | 31 | 12 |
| 2592$^{4}$ **Hot Dogging (37)** (MrsPSly) **3-7-13** DaleGibson(15) (lw: bhd: racd stands' side st: styd on wl fnl 2f) | 1¾ | **6** | 10/1 | 36 | 11 |
| 3102$^{5}$ **Too Hasty (57)** (TDEasterby) **3-9-5** MBirch(11) (lw: sn w ldrs: racd stands' side st: rdn & btn over 1f out) | ½ | **7** | 6/1$^{2}$ | 55 | 30 |
| 2929$^{2}$ **Don Pepe (60)** (RBoss) **5-10-0** JCarroll(17) (lw: in tch: c wd & effrt ent st: no imp) | nk | **8** | 8/1$^{3}$ | 57 | 38 |
| 2898$^{6}$ **Nukud (USA) (40)** (GROldroyd) **4-8-8** JLowe(3) (bhd: racd far side st & hdwy 2f out: n.d) | 1¼ | **9** | 12/1 | 34 | 15 |
| 2994$^{7}$ **Cedar Girl (36)** (RJHodges) **4-7-13**$^{(5)}$ AmandaSanders(1) (disp ld: racd far side st: hdd & wknd wl over 1f out) | nk | **10** | 16/1 | 30 | 11 |
| *2303$^{9}$* **Moneghetti (34)** (RHollinshead) **5-7-13**$^{(3)ow4}$ FLynch(6) (dwlt: racd stands' side st: n.d) | s.h | **11** | 10/1 | 27 | 4 |
| 2568$^{12}$ **Harsh Times (48)** (TDEasterby) **3-8-10b** LCharnock(14) (rr div: racd far side st: n.d) | 2½ | **12** | 33/1 | 36 | 11 |
| *2749$^{5}$* **Fatehalkhair (IRE) (40)** (BEllison) **4-8-8** JTate(18) (prom to st) | ½ | **13** | 20/1 | 27 | 8 |
| 2391$^{5}$ **Blow Dry (IRE) (46)** (MartynWane) **6-9-0** DeanMcKeown(8) (chsd ldrs: racd stands' side st & sn wknd) | 1½ | **14** | 16/1 | 29 | 10 |
| 2801$^{8}$ **Nord Lys (IRE) (29)** (BJLlewellyn) **5-7-4**$^{(7)ow1}$ JBramhill(2) (disp ld: racd far side st: wknd wl over 1f out) | 1½ | **15** | 25/1 | 9 | — |
| 3060$^{8}$ **Wacky (IRE) (28)** (WStorey) **5-7-10** NKennedy(13) (t: prom: racd centre st & sn wknd) | 1½ | **16** | 100/1 | 4 | — |
| *3089$^{15}$* **Corona Gold (40)** (JGFitzGerald) **6-8-8** JFanning(5) (w ldrs: racd stands' side st & sn wknd) | 7 | **17** | 33/1 | — | — |
| *1970$^{11}$* **Thrushwood (28)** (NChamberlain) **4-7-7**$^{(3)}$ NVarley(7) (s.i.s: a bhd) | 2½ | **18** | 100/1 | — | — |
| | | | (SP 139.3%) | | **18 Rn** |

**1m 26.8** (3.20) CSF £32.89 CT £381.12 TOTE £5.00: £1.10 £3.70 £3.10 £2.40 (£39.60) Trio £183.70 OWNER Linkchallenge Ltd (HAMBLETON) BRED Mrs M. Russell
LONG HANDICAP Nord Lys (IRE) 7-4 Wacky (IRE) 7-2 Thrushwood 7-2
WEIGHT FOR AGE 3yo-6lb

**3252 My Godson** likes things to go just right. That was how it worked out here, and he won well. (11/4)
**3236* Roseate Lodge** is obviously on particularly good terms with himself, but the winner was just too strong for him in the closing stages. (10/1)
**2851 Miss Pigalle** came out best of the rest that crossed over to the stands' side, but she was never quite doing enough. (16/1)
**2566 Allinson's Mate (IRE)** kept plugging away up the far side, but lacked the pace to get on terms. He still looks tremendously well, but is proving to be a bit of a character. (6/1: op 4/1)
**Upex le Gold Too** is in good form and, despite pulling hard going to post, ran pretty well. He can pick up a race. (25/1)
**2592 Hot Dogging** keeps showing signs of form and, judging by the way she finished here, there ought to be a race to be found for her. (10/1)
**2929 Don Pepe**, held up again, was never doing enough when ridden. (8/1)

## 3307 'PONTEFRACT PARK' CONDITIONS STKS (2-Y.O) (Class D)

3-15 (3-16) **7f** £3,677.00 (£1,022.00: £491.00) Stalls: Low GOING minus 0.25 sec per fur (GF)

| | Dist | Pos | SP | RR | SF |
|---|---|---|---|---|---|
| 2575$^{4}$ **Peartree House (IRE) (88)** (BWHills) **2-9-1** KFallon(3) (cl up: chal 3f out: slt ld 2f out: styd on strly) | — | **1** | 1/2$^{1}$ | 80 | 36 |
| *3088** **Lucky Oakwood (USA) (80)** (MBell) **2-8-10** MFenton(1) (led tl hdd 2f out: nt qckn) | 3½ | **2** | 5/2$^{2}$ | 67? | 23 |
| 2984$^{10}$ **Grate Times (81)** (EWeymes) **2-9-1** JFortune(2) (chsd ldrs tl outpcd appr st: sn btn) | 19 | **3** | 6/1$^{3}$ | 29 | — |
| | | | (SP 109.5%) | | **3 Rn** |

**1m 27.1** (3.50) CSF £2.05 TOTE £1.30 (£1.70) OWNER Newbyth Stud (LAMBOURN) BRED Cocomo American Thoroughbred Exports Inc

**2575 Peartree House (IRE)**, a big sort, handled this track well and, although having to work hard, won in good style. (1/2)
**3088* Lucky Oakwood (USA)** ran well enough to suggest that she can pick up a race or two on turf. (5/2)
**2517 Grate Times** would probably prefer easier ground and was outclassed in the last three furlongs. (6/1: op 7/2)

## 3308 'REDCAR, RIPON & THIRSK' H'CAP (0-70) (3-Y.O+) (Class E)

3-45 (3-45) **1m 5f 175y** £3,106.00 (£928.00: £444.00: £202.00) Stalls: Low GOING minus 0.25 sec per fur (GF)

| | | | | SP | RR | SF |
|---|---|---|---|---|---|---|
| $3079^{2}$ | **Spinning Mouse (55)** (DMorley) **3-9-3** MFenton(7) (hld up: smooth hdwy 5f out: led 2f out: r.o) | — | **1** | $9/4^{1}$ | 65 | 27 |
| $3109^{6}$ | **Silverdale Knight (57)** (KWHogg) **3-9-5** DeanMcKeown(8) (a.p: effrt 4f out: styd on: nt pce to chal) | 3 | **2** | 20/1 | 64 | 26 |
| $2177^{6}$ | **Punch (37)** (NTinkler) **4-8-12b** JCarroll(6) (led tl hdd 2f out: no ex u.p) | 1½ | **3** | 20/1 | 42 | 17 |
| $3000^{2}$ | **Windyedge (USA) (60)** (BWHills) **3-9-8** KFallon(5) (chsd ldrs: wnt 2nd 5f out: sn rdn & one pce) | 4 | **4** | $9/4^{1}$ | 60 | 22 |
| $2848^{2}$ | **Sharp Sensation (39)** (DWBarker) **6-8-7**(7) JBramhill(9) (lw: hld up: effrt over 5f out: rdn & no imp) | nk | **5** | $5/1^{2}$ | 39 | 14 |
| $1887^{8}$ | **Go-Go-Power-Ranger (62)** (BEllison) **3-9-10** JTate(4) (bhd: effrt 5f out: n.d) | 15 | **6** | 12/1 | 44 | 6 |
| $1070^{4}$ | **Sudden Spin (46)** (JNorton) **6-9-7** NKennedy(2) (s.i.s: hmpd bnd after 5f: n.d after) | 2 | **7** | $13/2^{3}$ | 26 | 1 |
| $2988^{4}$ | **Toulston Lady (IRE) (49)** (MJCamacho) **4-9-10** LCharnock(1) (chsd ldrs: rdn 6f out: sn wknd) | 2½ | **8** | 8/1 | 26 | 1 |
| $2804^{8}$ | **Kashana (IRE) (39)** (WStorey) **4-9-0** JFanning(3) (chsd ldrs tl wknd 5f out) | 3½ | **9** | 25/1 | 12 | — |
| | | | | (SP 123.7%) | **9 Rn** | |

**3m 5.2** (9.70) CSF £41.56 CT £696.21 TOTE £4.00: £1.20 £4.20 £4.20 (£23.20) Trio £136.00 OWNER Lord Hartington (NEWMARKET) BRED Side Hill Stud
WEIGHT FOR AGE 3yo-13lb
**3079 Spinning Mouse** is a narrow, unattractive filly, but she certainly has an engine. Always travelling best here, she won well. (9/4)
**2776 Silverdale Knight**, trying his longest trip to date, ran a smashing race and kept staying on, albeit in vain. (20/1)
**1044 Punch** certainly has the ability and tried different tactics here, but he gave up when headed two furlongs out. (20/1)
**3000 Windyedge (USA)**, trying a longer trip, looked very slow when the pressure was on in the last half-mile. (9/4)
**2848 Sharp Sensation** was off the bit some five furlongs out on this occasion, and was never doing enough from then on. (5/1)
**1325 Go-Go-Power-Ranger**, returning here after almost two months off, failed to impress on looks and needed this. (12/1)
**1070 Sudden Spin**, who missed the break, got carved up on the paddock bend and it was obviously not his day. (13/2: 10/1-5/1)

## 3309 'WETHERBY STEEPLECHASES' CLAIMING STKS (3-Y.O+) (Class F)

4-15 (4-16) **1m 3f 214y** £2,679.00 (£744.00: £357.00) Stalls: Low GOING minus 0.25 sec per fur (GF)

| | | | | SP | RR | SF |
|---|---|---|---|---|---|---|
| 3130* | **Rushen Raider (60)** (KWHogg) **4-9-1**(3) FLynch(6) (trckd ldrs: qckd to ld wl over 1f out: r.o) | — | **1** | $9/4^{2}$ | 71 | 43 |
| *2747** | **Los Alamos (65)** (CWThornton) **3-8-3** DeanMcKeown(2) (lw: trckd ldr: led & qcknd wl over 3f out: hdd wl over 1f out: kpt on) | 1¼ | **2** | $3/1^{3}$ | 65 | 26 |
| 2494* | **Pharly Dancer (62)** (WWHaigh) **7-8-11**(5) LNewton(1) (lw: trckd ldrs: outpcd over 2f out: styd on wl nr fin) | 2½ | **3** | $7/4^{1}$ | 64 | 36 |
| *$2747^{4}$* | **Hill Farm Blues** (JLEyre) **3-7-11**(3) NVarley(8) (rr div: effrt 5f out: styd on: no imp) | 6 | **4** | 16/1 | 51 | 12 |
| $3109^{10}$ | **Mithraic (IRE) (65)** (WSCunningham) **4-9-0**(5) RHavlin(7) (lw: t: chsd ldrs tl outpcd fnl 3f) | 1¾ | **5** | 10/1 | 57 | 29 |
| $2847^{2}$ | **Take Two (52)** (MissMKMilligan) **8-8-12** KDarley(9) (in tch: effrt 5f out: outpcd fnl 3f) | 8 | **6** | 16/1 | 39 | 11 |
| $2393^{8}$ | **Finestatetobein** (FWatson) **3-7-13** NKennedy(3) (in tch tl outpcd fnl 4f) | 4 | **7** | 100/1 | 32 | — |
| $2394^{10}$ | **Anorak (USA) (44)** (GMMoore) **6-9-0v** JTate(4) (led tl hdd wl over 3f out: sn lost pl) | 1½ | **8** | 50/1 | 34 | 6 |
| $2922^{6}$ | **Penny Peppermint** (REBarr) **4-8-10** KFallon(10) (s.i.s: a outpcd & bhd) | 16 | **9** | 100/1 | 8 | — |
| $2780^{11}$ | **Mill House Boy (IRE) (20)** (BSRothwell) **3-8-3v¹** MFenton(5) (outpcd & bhd fnl 7f) | 13 | **10** | 100/1 | — | — |
| | | | | (SP 117.9%) | **10 Rn** | |

**2m 37.3** (5.90) CSF £9.21 TOTE £3.60: £1.10 £1.90 £1.10 (£5.30) Trio £2.60 OWNER Mrs Thelma White (ISLE OF MAN) BRED M. H. D. Madden and Partners
WEIGHT FOR AGE 3yo-11lb
**3130* Rushen Raider**, who travels well and has a good turn of foot, was always too good here. (9/4)
**2747* Los Alamos** ran a cracking race and kept battling on when looking beaten. He will obviously stay further and should soon pick up a race on turf. (3/1)
**2494* Pharly Dancer** just got tapped for toe when the pace increased turning on for home, but was running on splendidly at the end. With slightly easier ground, he would have gone very close. (7/4)
**2747 Hill Farm Blues**, from a yard that is in superb form, showed a much-improved effort. (16/1)
**3109 Mithraic (IRE)** could never gain the initiative and was finally left struggling in the home straight. (10/1: 8/1-12/1)
**2847 Take Two** looked well short of pace once the race began in earnest. (16/1)

## 3310 'YORK KNAVESMIRE' H'CAP (0-65) (3-Y.O+) (Class F)

4-45 (4-46) **5f** £2,658.00 (£738.00: £354.00) Stalls: Low GOING minus 0.25 sec per fur (GF)

| | | | | SP | RR | SF |
|---|---|---|---|---|---|---|
| $3252^{2}$ | **Kalar (48)** (DWChapman) **7-9-8b** KDarley(4) (mde all: kpt on wl fnl f) | — | **1** | $13/8^{1}$ | 55 | 37 |
| $3261^{4}$ | **The Institute Boy (50)** (MissJFCraze) **6-9-10** JLowe(1) (in tch: hdwy ½-wy: chsng wnr fnl f: nt qckn) | 2 | **2** | $11/4^{2}$ | 51 | 33 |
| $2732^{8}$ | **Hamilton Gold (50)** (MGMeagher) **3-9-7** JFortune(8) (chsd ldrs: rdn ½-wy: kpt on one pce) | 1¼ | **3** | 14/1 | 47 | 26 |
| *$331^{8}$* | **Indiahra (47)** (JLEyre) **5-9-7v** KFallon(6) (outpcd: hdwy u.p 2f out: nvr able to chal) | hd | **4** | $7/2^{3}$ | 43 | 25 |
| *$3091^{11}$* | **Double Glow (29)** (NBycroft) **4-7-10b**(7) IonaWands(7) (in tch: effrt whn hmpd appr fnl f: n.d) | 4 | **5** | 25/1 | 13 | — |
| $868^{17}$ | **Samsung Lovelylady (IRE) (42)** (EWeymes) **4-8-13**(3) FLynch(3) (chsd ldrs tl wknd over 1f out) | hd | **6** | 16/1 | 25 | 7 |
| $2933^{2}$ | **China Hand (IRE) (35)** (MartynWane) **4-8-9b¹** JFanning(9) (chsd wnr tl rdn & wknd appr fnl f) | 1¾ | **7** | 11/2 | 13 | — |
| *$2937^{15}$* | **Never Say so (49)** (CSmith) **4-9-6v¹**(3) CTeague(2) (a outpcd & bhd) | 4 | **8** | 50/1 | 14 | — |
| | | | | (SP 120.7%) | **8 Rn** | |

**60.2 secs** (2.70) CSF £6.82 CT £43.17 TOTE £2.80: £1.30 £1.10 £4.70 (£3.20) Trio £28.20 OWNER Mr J. M. Chapman (YORK) BRED C. C. and Mrs Pryor
WEIGHT FOR AGE 3yo-3lb
**3252 Kalar** made no mistake this time. Grabbing the stands' rail, he never looked in danger. (13/8)
**3261 The Institute Boy** always had plenty to do from his draw and, in the end, did well. (11/4: 2/1-3/1)
**2732 Hamilton Gold**, after a poor effort last time, showed here that she can win a race. (14/1)
**166 Indiahra** looked fit after having had almost six months off, but she failed to land a blow, despite a determined effort. (7/2)
**2960 Double Glow** got messed about no end and left the impression that, if she can be persuaded, there is certainly ability there. (25/1)
**617 Samsung Lovelylady (IRE)**, having her first run for over three months, showed plenty of speed until blowing up. (16/1)
**2933 China Hand (IRE)** proved disappointing when ridden in the first-time blinkers. (11/2)

T/Jkpt: £1,265.40 (9.26 Tckts). T/Plpt: £16.80 (930.6 Tckts). T/Qdpt: £4.00 (243.39 Tckts). AA

# 3299-BRIGHTON (L-H) (Firm)
## Wednesday August 7th
WEATHER: sunny WIND: fresh across

## 3311 RINGMER (S) STKS (2-Y.O) (Class G)
2-15 (2-15) **5f 213y** £2,070.00 (£570.00: £270.00) Stalls: Low GOING minus 0.25 sec per fur (GF)

| | Horse / Details | Dist | Pos | SP | RR | SF |
|---|---|---|---|---|---|---|
| 2984[8] | **Sparky (54)** (MWEasterby) **2-8-11b[1]** JFEgan(1) (a.p: led 2f out: drvn out) | — | 1 | 10/1 | 65 | 3 |
| 3169[2] | **Breffni (IRE)** (CNAllen) **2-8-1**(5) MartinDwyer(2) (hld up: hdwy over 1f out: rdn & edgd lft ins fnl f: unable qckn) | 2 | 2 | 10/11 [1] | 55 | — |
| 2161[5] | **Grovefair Lad (IRE)** (BJMeehan) **2-8-11b[1]** BDoyle(4) (led 4f: rdn over 1f out: one pce) | 2½ | 3 | 5/1 [3] | 53 | — |
| 3075[3] | **Dozen Roses (59)** (TMJones) **2-8-6b** RPerham(5) (hld up: rdn 2f out: one pce) | 1 | 4 | 7/2 [2] | 45 | — |
| 2904[9] | **My Precious** (MMcCormack) **2-8-7**ow1 JReid(3) (w ldr: ev ch over 2f out: wknd over 1f out) | 6 | 5 | 10/1 | 30 | — |
| | | | | (SP 109.5%) | | **5 Rn** |

**1m 12.1** (4.90) CSF £19.06 TOTE £7.50: £2.50 £1.10 (£6.20) OWNER Abbots Salford Carav Park (SHERIFF HUTTON) BRED Godolphin Management Co Ltd
No bid
**2043 Sparky**, always to the fore, kicked for home halfway up the straight and never looked like being caught. (10/1: op 9/2)
**3169 Breffni (IRE)** looked ill-at-ease on the course when asked to quicken. (10/11: Evens-6/5)
**2161 Grovefair Lad (IRE)** cut out much of the early running but did not look too keen once headed. (5/1)
**3075 Dozen Roses** was struggling with the pace some way from home. (7/2: 5/2-4/1)
**My Precious** (10/1: op 5/1)

## 3312 MARINA MAIDEN AUCTION STKS (2-Y.O) (Class E)
2-45 (2-45) **6f 209y** £3,261.30 (£974.40: £466.20: £212.10) Stalls: Low GOING minus 0.25 sec per fur (GF)

| | Horse / Details | Dist | Pos | SP | RR | SF |
|---|---|---|---|---|---|---|
| 2224[5] | **Sheer Face** (WRMuir) **2-8-12** JReid(2) (lw: plld hrd: a.p: led ins fnl f: r.o wl) | — | 1 | 5/2 [1] | 81+ | 22 |
| 2733[4] | **Mystic Quest (IRE) (71)** (KMcAuliffe) **2-8-7** JFEgan(6) (led tl hdd ins fnl f: unable qckn) | 2½ | 2 | 4/1 [3] | 70 | 11 |
| 2993[3] | **Brandon Jack** (IABalding) **2-8-11** TQuinn(4) (lw: chsd ldrs: rdn & edgd lft fnl 2f: one pce) | 2½ | 3 | 11/4 [2] | 69 | 10 |
| 2967[5] | **Swallow Breeze** (DrJDScargill) **2-8-2** GBardwell(5) (rr: rdn 3f out: styd on fnl f: nrst fin) | ½ | 4 | 16/1 | 58 | — |
| 3099[7] | **Cartouche** (SirMarkPrescott) **2-8-9** GDuffield(1) (hld up in rr tl styd on fnl f: nvr nrr) | nk | 5 | 5/1 | 65 | 6 |
| 2904[5] | **Herbshan Dancer** (BRMillman) **2-8-4** SDrowne(3) (hld up: rdn over 2f out: sn btn) | 3½ | 6 | 16/1 | 52 | — |
| 741[4] | **Chopin (IRE)** (RFJohnsonHoughton) **2-8-7** AMcGlone(7) (chsd ldr 5f: sn wknd) | 1 | 7 | 10/1 | 52 | — |
| | | | | (SP 112.8%) | | **7 Rn** |

**1m 24.3** (4.30) CSF £12.14 TOTE £2.90: £1.50 £2.90 (£10.20) OWNER Mr A J de V Patrick (LAMBOURN) BRED Mrs C. R. Philipson
**2224 Sheer Face** looked well and moved well to post. He took a while to hit top gear when asked to quicken below the distance but, finding his stride inside the final furlong, won going away. (5/2)
**2733 Mystic Quest (IRE)** ran a sound race, showing the way until getting outpaced inside the final furlong. (4/1: 5/2-5/1)
**2993 Brandon Jack** looked unhappy on the course. (11/4: 7/4-3/1)
**2967 Swallow Breeze** stayed on under pressure from the rear in the final furlong and will come into her own over a longer trip. She is now qualified for nurseries. (16/1)
**Cartouche** ran an eyecatching race, staying on nicely in the closing stages, and will leave this form behind in time. (5/1)
**741 Chopin (IRE)** (10/1: 7/1-12/1)

## 3313 TOTE SPRINT H'CAP (0-80) (3-Y.O+) (Class D)
3-15 (3-15) **5f 213y** £4,308.00 (£1,284.00: £612.00: £276.00) Stalls: Low GOING minus 0.25 sec per fur (GF)

| | Horse / Details | Dist | Pos | SP | RR | SF |
|---|---|---|---|---|---|---|
| 2982* | **Crystal Heights (FR) (67)** (RJO'Sullivan) **8-9-10** DHarrison(8) (b: hld up: hdwy over 1f out: led wl ins fnl f: comf) | — | 1 | 9/2 [1] | 76 | 42 |
| 2982[2] | **Mellors (IRE) (63)** (JARToller) **3-9-2** SSanders(7) (lw: chsd ldrs: led 1f out: hdd wl ins fnl f: unable qckn) | nk | 2 | 13/2 | 71 | 33 |
| 3304* | **Sharp Imp (58)** (RMFlower) **6-9-1b** 7x DBiggs(2) (lw: rr: rdn over 2f out: swtchd rt over 1f out: str run fnl f: fin wl) | nk | 3 | 15/2 | 65 | 31 |
| 2960[3] | **Able Sheriff (52)** (MWEasterby) **4-8-9b** JFEgan(5) (led: hdd 1f out: no ex) | 3 | 4 | 11/2 [3] | 51 | 17 |
| 3096* | **Always Grace (66)** (MissGayKelleway) **4-9-9** 7x RCochrane(3) (stdd s: hld up in rr: rdn 2f out: no hdwy) | 3½ | 5 | 5/1 [2] | 56 | 22 |
| 3168[6] | **Red Admiral (63)** (CMurray) **6-9-6** MTebbutt(4) (prom 4f) | 3½ | 6 | 12/1 | 44 | 10 |
| 3285* | **Tafahhus (73)** (MJPolglase) **4-10-2b** 7x JStack(6) (chsd ldrs: rdn 2f out: sn wknd) | 2½ | 7 | 9/1 | 47 | 13 |
| 3139[2] | **Yo Kiri-B (52)** (TJNaughton) **5-8-9** GDuffield(1) (b: swtg: chsd ldr over 3f: sn wknd) | 1½ | 8 | 9/2 [1] | 22 | — |
| | | | | (SP 111.2%) | | **8 Rn** |

**1m 10.1** (2.90) CSF £29.77 CT £188.37 TOTE £5.10: £2.10 £1.60 £3.40 (£14.70) OWNER Mr Jack Joseph (WHITCOMBE) BRED Ahmad Fustok
WEIGHT FOR AGE 3yo-4lb
**2982* Crystal Heights (FR)** is in great heart at present and, brought with a well-timed challenge, won with more in hand than the winning distance suggests. (9/2)
**2982 Mellors (IRE)** was the paddock pick and ran well too, though is flattered to finish as close to the winner as he did. (13/2)
**3304* Sharp Imp** won the last race here the previous day, and was brought out here looking fresh and well. He could not go the early pace but, finding his stride approaching the final furlong, finished to some effect. (15/2: 5/1-8/1)
**2960 Able Sheriff** showed the way for five furlongs, but had nothing more to give. (11/2)
**3096* Always Grace** never threatened to take a hand. (5/1)
**3168 Red Admiral** (12/1: op 8/1)
**3285* Tafahhus** (9/1: op 6/1)
**3139 Yo Kiri-B** was in trouble some way from home. (9/2)

## 3314 BRIGHTON SUMMER H'CAP (0-60) (3-Y.O+) (Class F)
3-45 (3-45) **1m 1f 209y** £2,381.00 (£656.00: £311.00) Stalls: Low GOING minus 0.25 sec per fur (GF)

| | Horse / Details | Dist | Pos | SP | RR | SF |
|---|---|---|---|---|---|---|
| 3141[10] | **Double Rush (IRE) (40)** (TGMills) **4-8-8** TQuinn(4) (lw: hld up: hdwy over 2f out: led ins fnl f: sn clr: easily) | — | 1 | 8/1 | 54+ | 33 |

2989[8] **Cheveley Dancer (USA) (28)** (GLMoore) **8-7-10** GBardwell(2) (b: lw: rr: hrd rdn & swtchd rt over 2f out: styd on to go 2nd ins fnl f: no ch w wnr) ....4 **2** 14/1 36 15
2979[3] **Pride of Kashmir (52)** (PWHarris) **3-8-11** GHind(6) (chsd ldr: rdn & edgd lft fnl 2f: one pce ins fnl f) ....2½ **3** 6/1[3] 56 26
2793[2] **Harlequin Walk (IRE) (41)** (RJO'Sullivan) **5-8-9b** SSanders(7) (led & sn clr: hdd ins fnl f: no ex) ....1½ **4** 5/2[1] 42 21
2775[7] **Risky Tu (40)** (PAKelleway) **5-8-8** RCochrane(1) (nvr nrr) ....4 **5** 9/1 35 14
2574[21] **It'sthebusiness (57)** (SDow) **4-9-11** JReid(5) (lw: chsd ldr 4f: rdn & lost pl over 3f out: kpt on one pce fnl f) .2½ **6** 6/1[3] 48 27
2971[3] **Tomal (44)** (RIngram) **4-8-12** AMcGlone(11) (b.hind: chsd ldr 6f out tl over 1f out: sn wknd) ....1 **7** 5/1[2] 33 12
2906[5] **Hunza Story (28)** (NPLittmoden) **4-7-10** NCarlisle(8) (b.hind: chsd ldrs over 6f) ....6 **8** 20/1 7 —
2794[6] **Blossomville (55)** (MAJarvis) **3-9-0** PBloomfield(3) (bhd fnl 4f) ....7 **9** 16/1 23 —
2511[11] **Paronomasia (28)** (JLHarris) **4-7-10b** DeclanO'Shea(10) (in tch tl wknd qckly 3f out) ....6 **10** 50/1 — —
**Nita's Choice (28)** (AGNewcombe) **6-7-10** FNorton(9) (bit bkwd: bhd fr ½-wy: t.o) ....16 **11** 25/1 — —
(SP 118.0%) **11 Rn**

**2m 2.9** (4.60) CSF £100.13 CT £659.61 TOTE £7.50: £2.30 £3.20 £2.80 (£93.60) Trio £82.40 OWNER Mr Tony Murray (EPSOM) BRED Dermot Finnegan
LONG HANDICAP Cheveley Dancer (USA) 7-6 Hunza Story 7-7 Paronomasia 7-6 Nita's Choice 7-9
WEIGHT FOR AGE 3yo-9lb
**2159 Double Rush (IRE)** was held up under a confident ride. Brought with a smooth challenge to lead inside the final furlong, he ran out a very easy winner. (8/1)
**2711 Cheveley Dancer (USA)** was under pressure some way out and, though staying on, never looked like getting to the winner. (14/1)
**2979 Pride of Kashmir** was to the fore throughout, but did not help his cause by hanging all the way up the straight. (6/1)
**2793 Harlequin Walk (IRE)** was soon in a clear lead but, collared entering the final furlong, had no more to give. (5/2)
**2415 Risky Tu** was never on terms. (9/1)
**1996 It'sthebusiness** got outpaced coming down the hill and could never recover. (6/1)

## 3315 CLIFTONVILLE MEDIAN AUCTION MAIDEN STKS (3-Y.O) (Class F)
4-15 (4-16) **1m 3f 196y** £2,381.00 (£656.00: £311.00) Stalls: Low GOING minus 0.25 sec per fur (GF)

SP RR SF
**Pike Creek (USA)** (IABalding) **3-8-9** TQuinn(1) (lw: mde all: clr 2f out: v.easily) ....— **1** 15/8[1] 75++ 46
2895[6] **The Legions Pride (56)** (JWHills) **3-9-0** JReid(5) (chsd ldrs: rdn 3f out: kpt on to go mod 2nd ins fnl f: no ch w wnr) ....15 **2** 8/1[3] 60 31
3079[3] **South Wind (58)** (MrsJCecil) **3-8-9** AClark(4) (chsd wnr 5f out to 3f out: sn hrd rdn: one pce) ....2 **3** 2/1[2] 52 23
2557[4] **Typhoon Lad** (SDow) **3-9-0** SSanders(2) (lw: chsd wnr 3f out tl ins fnl f: sn wknd) ....3 **4** 2/1[2] 53 24
2752[11] **Animation (40)** (KMcAuliffe) **3-8-9e** GDuffield(3) (chsd wnr 9f out to 5f out: wknd qckly: t.o) ....dist **5** 66/1 — —
(SP 114.1%) **5 Rn**

**2m 31.6** (4.00) CSF £14.32 TOTE £3.20: £1.20 £2.40 (£7.60) OWNER Mr George Strawbridge (KINGSCLERE) BRED Jeyeff B Stables
**Pike Creek (USA)** looked big and well beforehand and ran out a most impressive winner. Her rivals were modest, but she won with any amount in hand. (15/8)
**The Legions Pride** was hard at work from early in the straight and could make no impression on the very easy winner. (8/1)
**3079 South Wind**, like all his rivals, was ridden to try and close from early in the straight, but only had the one pace to give. (2/1: 6/4-9/4)
**2557 Typhoon Lad** lost a distant second inside the final furlong and appeared not to stay. (2/1)

## 3316 LEVY BOARD MAIDEN H'CAP (0-60) (3-Y.O+) (Class F)
4-45 (4-45) **6f 209y** £2,880.80 (£798.80: £382.40) Stalls: Low GOING minus 0.25 sec per fur (GF)

SP RR SF
2983[3] **Welcome Lu (31)** (JLHarris) **3-7-12** FNorton(1) (a.p: led over 2f out: clr ins fnl f: eased nr fin) ....— **1** 5/1[3] 47+ 20
2014[8] **Office Hours (50)** (CACyzer) **4-9-9** PBloomfield(6) (lw: hld up in tch: ev ch 2f out: sn rdn: one pce) ....3½ **2** 6/1 58 37
2903[7] **Have a Nightcap (32)** (NPLittmoden) **7-8-5b** TGMcLaughlin(9) (mid div: hrd rdn over 2f out: styd on ins fnl f).½ **3** 12/1 39 18
2617[7] **Dantean (28)** (RJO'Sullivan) **4-8-1b** SSanders(7) (chsd ldr: led over 3f out: hdd over 2f out: one pce) ....nk **4** 8/1 34 13
3138[5] **Velvet Jones (58)** (GFHCharles-Jones) **3-9-11** TQuinn(3) (hld up: rdn over 2f out: one pce) ....2 **5** 4/1[2] 60 33
2373[14] **Current Leader (40)** (MissKMGeorge) **3-8-7** RPrice(10) (chsd ldrs 5f) ....3½ **6** 12/1 33 6
3139[6] **Mystery Matthias (51)** (MissBSanders) **3-9-4v** GDuffield(2) (hld up: sme hdwy over 2f out: sn rdn & btn) ....½ **7** 7/2[1] 43 16
3304[5] **Flagstaff (USA) (54)** (GLMoore) **3-9-0v**(7) JDennis(4) (a bhd) ....½ **8** 15/2 45 18
2915[6] **Happy Venturer (IRE) (37)** (CMurray) **3-8-4** DeclanO'Shea(8) (s.i.s: a bhd) ....4 **9** 20/1 19 —
2602[13] **Trapper Norman (42)** (RIngram) **4-9-1** AMcGlone(5) (led to ½-wy) ....1 **10** 33/1 22 1
(SP 119.1%) **10 Rn**

**1m 23.3** (3.30) CSF £33.28 CT £322.08 TOTE £5.50: £1.80 £2.70 £3.70 (£29.60) Trio £81.40 OWNER Mr M. F. Hyman (MELTON MOWBRAY) BRED Red House Stud
WEIGHT FOR AGE 3yo-6lb
**2983 Welcome Lu** ran out an easy winner and is improving. (5/1: op 3/1)
**1532 Office Hours** got outpaced at halfway before staying on late. (6/1)
**2632 Have a Nightcap** travelled nicely but could not quicken when put to the test. (12/1)
**1013 Dantean** ran his best race for some time. (8/1)
**3138 Velvet Jones** was hard at work early in the straight and only had the one pace to give. (4/1)
**3139 Mystery Matthias** made a short-lived effort two furlongs out. (7/2)

## 3317 EDBURTON MAIDEN H'CAP (0-70) (3-Y.O+) (Class E)
5-15 (5-15) **5f 59y** £2,933.70 (£873.60: £415.80: £186.90) Stalls: Low GOING minus 0.25 sec per fur (GF)

SP RR SF
2765[3] **Memphis Beau (IRE) (60)** (JARToller) **3-9-5b** SSanders(2) (lw: w ldr: led over 2f out: hrd rdn & edgd lft ins fnl f: r.o) ....— **1** 11/4[2] 69 27
2994[12] **Mac Oates (50)** (DWPArbuthnot) **3-8-9** RPerham(1) (stdd s: hld up: hdwy to chse wnr over 1f out: hrd rdn ins fnl f: unable qckn) ....1¼ **2** 16/1 55 13
3210[17] **School Boy (69)** (TJNaughton) **3-10-0** AMcGlone(5) (lw: chsd ldrs: sn rdn along: hung bdly fnl 2f: nt r.o) ....3½ **3** 6/4[1] 64 22
2800[6] **Double Impression (IRE) (52)** (JLHarris) **3-8-11** GDuffield(6) (hld up: rdn 2f out: one pce) ....2 **4** 5/1[3] 41 —
3097[3] **Harriet's Beau (37)** (MWEasterby) **3-7-10b** GBardwell(3) (led: hdd over 2f out: wknd over 1f out) ....1 **5** 11/4[2] 23 —
(SP 115.9%) **5 Rn**

**63.3 secs** (3.30) CSF £29.30 TOTE £4.60: £1.20 £3.80 (£26.00) OWNER Blandford Thoroughbreds (WHITSBURY) BRED A. T. Robinson
LONG HANDICAP Harriet's Beau 7-6
**2765 Memphis Beau (IRE)** was always to the fore. He led early in the straight and won this well, despite edging away under pressure. (11/4)

**Mac Oates** threw down a challenge from below the distance and, although keeping on, could never get to the winner. (16/1)
**2765 School Boy** was never going the pace and looked thoroughly unco-operative in the final two furlongs. (6/4)
**1592 Double Impression (IRE)** was under pressure halfway up the straight and could make little headway. (5/1)
**3097 Harriet's Beau** made a lot of the early running but, once headed, soon cried enough. (11/4: 2/1-3/1)

T/Plpt: £401.00 (34.87 Tckts). T/Qdpt: £119.90 (7.43 Tckts). SM

## 2600-KEMPTON (R-H) (Good to firm, Firm patches)
## Wednesday August 7th

WEATHER: fine WIND: almost nil

### 3318 IRISH RACE NIGHT APPRENTICE H'CAP (0-70) (3-Y.O+) (Class E)

5-50 (5-50) **1m 4f** £2,997.50 (£905.00: £440.00: £207.50) Stalls: Low GOING minus 0.39 sec per fur (F)

| | | | | SP | RR | SF |
|---|---|---|---|---|---|---|
| $3053^{5}$ | **State Approval (58)** (APJarvis) **3-8-6**(7) CCarver(7) (sn chsng ldr: led over 1f out: comf) | — | **1** | 12/1 | 67+ | 37 |
| $2973^{7}$ | **Reaganesque (USA) (51)** (PGMurphy) **4-9-3** SDrowne(4) (lw: led after 1f: rdn over 2f out: hdd wl over 1f out: r.o one pce) | 3 | **2** | 7/1 | 56 | 37 |
| 3141* | **Supermick (37)** (WRMuir) **5-8-3** 4x RHavlin(9) (led 1f: r.o one pce fnl 2f) | s.h | **3** | $4/1^{1}$ | 42 | 23 |
| $2882^{4}$ | **Achilles Heel (55)** (CNAllen) **5-9-7** MartinDwyer(3) (lw: hld up: hdwy on ins over 2f out: one pce fnl f) | nk | **4** | $11/2^{2}$ | 60 | 41 |
| 2989* | **Augustan (55)** (SGollings) **5-9-4**(3) AimeeCook(2) (hld up: hdwy over 3f out: r.o one pce fnl f) | 1½ | **5** | $4/1^{1}$ | 58 | 39 |
| $2282^{8}$ | **Wottashambles (39)** (LMontagueHall) **5-8-0**(5) DDenby(1) (lw: nvr nr to chal) | 1 | **6** | 14/1 | 40 | 21 |
| 2975* | **Evidence In Chief (65)** (DRCElsworth) **3-9-6v** DaneO'Neill(5) (lw: bhd fnl 4f) | 8 | **7** | $6/1^{3}$ | 56 | 26 |
| $2762^{5}$ | **In The Band (55)** (LordHuntingdon) **3-8-5**(5) CCogan(10) (prom 9f) | 1¼ | **8** | 20/1 | 44 | 14 |
| | **Lililo (IRE) (60)** (RLee) **4-9-12** OPears(8) (hld up: bhd fnl 3f) | 8 | **9** | 25/1 | 38 | 19 |
| $2377^{4}$ | **High Desire (IRE) (57)** (JRArnold) **3-8-12** MHenry(6) (hld up: rdn 3f out: sn bhd) | 5 | **10** | 8/1 | 29 | — |
| | | | | (SP 116.2%) | **10 Rn** | |

**2m 35.07** (4.37) CSF £84.72 CT £364.58 TOTE £17.40: £2.80 £2.10 £2.10 (£85.50) Trio £287.40; £40.49 to Pontefract 9/8/96 OWNER Mrs Ann Jarvis (ASTON UPTHORPE) BRED Collin Stud and The Pharly Syndicate
WEIGHT FOR AGE 3yo-11lb
IN-FOCUS: **This was a first winner for apprentice Craig Carver.**
**3053 State Approval**, dropped 2lb, was back to a more suitable trip and lost his maiden tag in pretty good style. (12/1: op 8/1)
**2341* Reaganesque (USA)**, raised 9lb for his two wins, had never been able to get to the front over an extra quarter-mile last time. (7/1)
**3141* Supermick**, attempting a hat-trick under a penalty, really finds this distance the bare minimum. (4/1)
**2882 Achilles Heel** is finding it tough off a mark 18lb higher than when winning at York, but had rather given the game away when 18lb out of the handicap on his previous run at Epsom. (11/2)
**2989* Augustan** was 4lb higher for his Chepstow win. (4/1)
**1874 Wottashambles** has scored over two miles on the Sand at Lingfield and gave the impression he needed further here. (14/1: op 8/1)

### 3319 E.B.F. MAIDEN STKS (2-Y.O) (Class D)

6-20 (6-22) **7f (Jubilee)** £3,533.75 (£1,070.00: £522.50: £248.75) Stalls: Low GOING minus 0.39 sec per fur (F)

| | | | | SP | RR | SF |
|---|---|---|---|---|---|---|
| | **Bareeq** (HThomsonJones) **2-9-0** RHills(10) (scope: mde all: rdn over 1f out: edgd lft: rdn out) | — | **1** | $11/4^{1}$ | 89 | 35 |
| | **Al Azhar** (IABalding) **2-9-0** BThomson(13) (str: cmpt: chsd wnr: rdn 3f out: ev ch whn carried lft 1f out: unable qckn) | ½ | **2** | $7/2^{3}$ | 88 | 34 |
| | **Saddlers' Hope** (JRFanshawe) **2-8-9** DHarrison(7) (w'like: hld up & bhd: hdwy whn nt clr run & swtchd rt 2f out: r.o ins fnl f) | 2½ | **3** | 10/1 | 77+ | 23 |
| $3036^{5}$ | **My Hero (IRE)** (TGMills) **2-8-9** BDoyle(9) (hld up: rdn over 1f out: r.o one pce) | 1¾ | **4** | 20/1 | 73 | 19 |
| | **Bubbly** (JLDunlop) **2-9-0** TQuinn(11) (w'like: scope: prom tl wknd over 1f out) | 2 | **5** | 7/1 | 74 | 20 |
| $2543^{4}$ | **Ikatania** (JLDunlop) **2-9-0** TSprake(4) (no hdwy fnl 2f) | s.h | **6** | 12/1 | 74 | 20 |
| | **Kingfisher Mill (USA)** (MrsJCecil) **2-9-0** AClark(6) (str: w'like: s.i.s: bhd: rdn over 4f out: nvr nr to chal) | ½ | **7** | 5/1 | 72 | 18 |
| | **Tom Tailor (GER)** (DRCElsworth) **2-9-0** AProcter(14) (w'like: scope: bit bkwd: prom: rdn 3f out: wknd over 1f out) | 1 | **8** | 20/1 | 70 | 16 |
| | **Klondike Charger (USA)** (BWHills) **2-8-9**(5) JDSmith(5) (w'like: scope: bit bkwd: a bhd) | nk | **9** | 11/1 | 69 | 15 |
| | **As Friendly** (MRStoute) **2-9-0** RCochrane(8) (w'like: scope: sn rdn along: a bhd) | 1½ | **10** | 9/2 | 66 | 12 |
| $1437^{5}$ | **Palaemon** (GBBalding) **2-9-0** SDrowne(1) (a bhd) | ½ | **11** | 20/1 | 65 | 11 |
| | **Indian Blaze** (PWHarris) **2-9-0** GHind(12) (w'like: prom tl rdn & wknd over 2f out) | 2½ | **12** | 12/1 | 59 | 5 |
| *$2783^{3}$* | ***Moon Blast*** (LadyHerries) **2-9-0** JReid(3) (Withdrawn not under Starter's orders: Veterinary advice) | | **W** | $3/1^{2}$ | — | — |
| | | | | (SP 168.3%) | **12 Rn** | |

**1m 27.09** (2.59) CSF £15.30 TOTE £3.50: £1.70 £2.70 £4.00 (£9.10) Trio £82.70 OWNER Mr Hamdan Al Maktoum (NEWMARKET) BRED Shadwell Estate Company Limited
**Bareeq**, a half-brother to ten-furlong winner Dawlah, is out of a daughter of a Kentucky Oaks winner. Drifting across towards the stands' side under pressure in the closing stages, he will be better for the experience. (11/4)
**Al Azhar**, a 100,000 guinea half-brother to mile and quarter winner Shortfall, was reported to have been working well at home. Intimidated by the winner into going left-handed in the last 200 yards, he was second best on merit, but should soon go one better. (7/2)
**Saddlers' Hope**, a half-sister to Never Think Twice, shaped promisingly after meeting traffic problems and will soon step up on this. (10/1: 8/1-12/1)
**3036 My Hero (IRE)**, a half-sister to several winners in Italy, was again highly tried here and was by no means disgraced against some promising newcomers in the first three. (20/1)
**Bubbly**, a 32,000 guinea half-brother to Champagne Prince, ran well until running out of gas below the distance. (7/1: 5/1-8/1)
**2543 Ikatania** is looking the type for a nursery. (12/1)
**Kingfisher Mill (USA)**, a half-brother to Dear Life, is apparently well regarded by his trainer, but is going to need at least a mile on this evidence. (5/1: 7/2-11/2)
**As Friendly** (9/2: 4/1-6/1)

### 3320 'GO RACING IN IRELAND' CLAIMING STKS (3-Y.O) (Class F)

6-50 (6-52) **1m 2f** £2,675.00 (£750.00: £365.00) Stalls: Low GOING minus 0.39 sec per fur (F)

| | | | | SP | RR | SF |
|---|---|---|---|---|---|---|
| $2706^{5}$ | **Orange Order (IRE)** (GHarwood) **3-9-1** PatEddery(4) (chsd ldr: led over 2f out: rdn out) | — | **1** | $3/1^{1}$ | 76 | 42 |

| Form | Horse / details | Dist | Pos | SP | RR | SF |
|---|---|---|---|---|---|---|
| 2975$^{2}$ | **Domettes (IRE) (57)** (RHannon) **3-8-3**$^{(3)}$ DaneO'Neill(1) (a.p: hrd rdn & wnt 2nd over 1f out: no imp) | 1¾ | **2** | 4/1$^{2}$ | 64 | 30 |
| 2975$^{5}$ | **Lear Jet (USA) (82)** (PFICole) **3-9-7b$^{1}$** TQuinn(7) (led tl hrd rdn & hdd over 2f out: wknd over 1f out) | 6 | **3** | 4/1$^{2}$ | 70 | 36 |
| 2975$^{3}$ | **Oberons Boy (IRE) (73)** (BJMeehan) **3-9-7b** JReid(5) (hld up & plld hrd: hdwy 4f out: wknd 2f out) | 10 | **4** | 9/2$^{3}$ | 54 | 20 |
| 2859$^{3}$ | **Baron Hrabovsky (52)** (PFICole) **3-9-1** RCochrane(6) (hld up mid div: bhd fnl 3f) | 5 | **5** | 9/1 | 40 | 6 |
| | **Mrs Drummond (IRE)** (APJarvis) **3-8-8** SDrowne(8) (leggy: prom 7f) | 2½ | **6** | 7/1 | 29 | — |
| 1957$^{7}$ | **Sherna (IRE)** (IABalding) **3-7-12**$^{(5)}$ MartinDwyer(3) (hld up mid div: rdn over 4f out: sn bhd) | 4 | **7** | 25/1 | 17 | — |
| | **Bursul Lady** (MissBSanders) **3-8-10** DHarrison(9) (bhd: reminders 6f out: t.o fnl 3f) | 13 | **8** | 33/1 | 3 | — |
| | **Just Lex** (MrsALMKing) **3-9-4** AClark(2) (neat: s.s: sn rdn: t.o fnl 4f) | 27 | **9** | 33/1 | — | — |

(SP 115.4%) **9 Rn**

**2m 5.62** (3.12) CSF £14.64 TOTE £2.70: £1.40 £1.50 £1.70 (£6.70) Trio £4.90 OWNER Mr K. Abdulla (PULBOROUGH) BRED Juddmonte Farms

Orange Order (IRE) clmd JWhite £12,000

**2706 Orange Order (IRE)**, a half-brother to a listed winner, appreciated this drop in class and saw out the extra furlong well. (3/1)
**2975 Domettes (IRE)** stuck to her guns under strong pressure, but the winner was not for catching. (4/1: op 9/4)
**2975 Lear Jet (USA)**, blinkered after his flop last time, did little more than give the winner a nice lead. (4/1)
**2975 Oberons Boy (IRE)** might just as well revert to last season's front-running tactics. (9/2: 3/1-5/1)
**Mrs Drummond (IRE)** (7/1: 5/1-8/1)

## 3321 LONDON IRISH RUGBY FOOTBALL CLUB NURSERY H'CAP (2-Y.O) (Class D)

7-20 (7-21) **6f** £3,322.50 (£1,005.00: £490.00: £232.50) Stalls: High GOING minus 0.26 sec per fur (GF)

| Form | Horse / details | Dist | Pos | SP | RR | SF |
|---|---|---|---|---|---|---|
| 1626$^{4}$ | **Spaniards Inn (80)** (BJMeehan) **2-8-6** PRobinson(3) (lw: hld up: hrd rdn & swtchd rt 1f out: led wl ins fnl f: r.o) | — | **1** | 7/2$^{2}$ | 70 | 41 |
| 2877$^{5}$ | **Pelham (IRE) (95)** (RHannon) **2-9-7** PatEddery(5) (lw: chsd ldr: led over 1f out: hdd wl ins fnl f: hrd rdn: r.o) | hd | **2** | 11/4$^{1}$ | 85 | 56 |
| 3160$^{7}$ | **Petite Danseuse (83)** (SDow) **2-8-9** BThomson(6) (led: edgd lft over 2f out: hdd over 1f out: wknd ins fnl f) | 6 | **3** | 6/1 | 57 | 28 |
| 3075* | **Lunar Music (74)** (MartynMeade) **2-8-0** FNorton(1) (hld up: rdn whn nt clr run 2f out: hmpd over 1f out: one pce) | 1¾ | **4** | 11/4$^{1}$ | 43 | 14 |
| 996$^{5}$ | **Hit Or Miss (70)** (MRChannon) **2-7-5**$^{(5)}$ MartinDwyer(4) (hld up: rdn over 3f out: wknd over 1f out) | 5 | **5** | 5/1$^{3}$ | 26 | — |

(SP 106.5%) **5 Rn**

**1m 13.26** (1.96) CSF £12.02 TOTE £5.00: £2.20 £1.30 (£4.60) OWNER Mr B. Schmidt-Bodner (UPPER LAMBOURN) BRED J. W. Parker and K. Wills

LONG HANDICAP Hit Or Miss 7-9

**1626 Spaniards Inn**, who may well have been kept with nurseries in mind, had to work hard to see off the runner-up. (7/2)
**2877 Pelham (IRE)**, highly tried last time, lost no caste in defeat under topweight here. (11/4)
**2965 Petite Danseuse** may well need this extra furlong now, but did not last home after adopting front-running tactics. (6/1)
**3075* Lunar Music**, carrying her head towards the stands' rail, did not look an easy ride, but would have finished closer but for being baulked with a furlong and a half to go. (11/4)
**996 Hit Or Miss** seems to need soft ground and has probably been kept for an autumn campaign. (5/1: 5/2-11/2)

## 3322 GUINNESS H'CAP (0-90) (3-Y.O) (Class C)

7-50 (7-50) **7f** £5,374.50 (£1,626.00: £793.00: £376.50) Stalls: Low GOING minus 0.39 sec per fur (F)

| Form | Horse / details | Dist | Pos | SP | RR | SF |
|---|---|---|---|---|---|---|
| 2907* | **Divina Luna (84)** (JWHills) **3-9-4**$^{(3)}$ MHenry(3) (lw: a.p: led wl over 1f out: sn edgd rt: jst hld on) | — | **1** | 4/1$^{2}$ | 92 | 51 |
| 2968* | **Angaar (IRE) (81)** (ACStewart) **3-9-4** DHarrison(9) (lw: hld up: hdwy 2f out: sn rdn: str run ins fnl f: fin wl) | ½ | **2** | 7/2$^{1}$ | 88 | 47 |
| 2907$^{2}$ | **Arterxerxes (82)** (MJHeaton-Ellis) **3-9-5** AClark(4) (led tl wl over 1f out: sn swtchd lft: hrd rdn & rallied wl ins fnl f) | 1 | **3** | 7/1 | 87 | 46 |
| 2946$^{7}$ | **Mr Speaker (IRE) (64)** (CFWall) **3-8-1** NCarlisle(6) (hld up: rdn & hdwy 2f out: one pce fnl f) | 1¼ | **4** | 12/1 | 66 | 25 |
| 2041$^{26}$ | **Lay The Blame (83)** (WJarvis) **3-9-6** TQuinn(1) (hld up: hdwy on ins 3f out: one pce fnl 2f) | 1¾ | **5** | 9/1 | 81 | 40 |
| 3107$^{2}$ | **Charlie Chang (IRE) (70)** (RHannon) **3-8-4**$^{(3)}$ DaneO'Neill(8) (lw: hld up & bhd: nvr nr to chal) | 1½ | **6** | 9/2$^{3}$ | 64 | 23 |
| 2585$^{5}$ | **Poetry (IRE) (84)** (MHTompkins) **3-9-7** PRobinson(7) (lw: prom tl rdn & wknd over 2f out) | 6 | **7** | 9/2$^{3}$ | 65 | 24 |
| 2974$^{6}$ | **My Mariam (75)** (CREgerton) **3-8-12** JReid(5) (prom over 4f) | ¾ | **8** | 20/1 | 54 | 13 |

(SP 113.5%) **8 Rn**

**1m 26.28** (1.78) CSF £17.26 CT £85.09 TOTE £4.40: £1.70 £1.80 £2.20 (£6.70) Trio £20.20 OWNER Mr D. J. Deer (LAMBOURN) BRED Azienda Agricola Colle Cardella

STEWARDS' ENQUIRY Harrison susp. 16-18/8/96 (excessive use of whip).

**2907* Divina Luna** poached a three-length advantage coming to the furlong pole and managed to last home. (4/1)
**2968* Angaar (IRE)**, only 2lb higher than when winning last time, took a long time to find top gear and could not peg back the winner. His rider picked up a three-day whip-ban. (7/2)
**2907 Arterxerxes** was 2lb worse off than when beaten three-quarters of a length by the winner at Warwick. (7/1)
**2528* Mr Speaker (IRE)**, back up to seven, was never going to bring his rivals to order. (12/1: 8/1-14/1)
**1799 Lay The Blame** seems to need to drop a few pounds in the Ratings. (9/1)
**3107 Charlie Chang (IRE)** does seem better suited by a mile. (9/2)

## 3323 IRISH POST H'CAP (0-70) (3-Y.O+) (Class E)

8-20 (8-22) **5f** £2,900.00 (£875.00: £425.00: £200.00) Stalls: High GOING minus 0.26 sec per fur (GF)

| Form | Horse / details | Dist | Pos | SP | RR | SF |
|---|---|---|---|---|---|---|
| 2946$^{4}$ | **Croeso Cynnes (67)** (BPalling) **3-9-3**$^{(5)}$ MartinDwyer(2) (a.p: led over 1f out: jst hld on) | — | **1** | 5/1$^{3}$ | 74 | 37 |
| 1781$^{10}$ | **The Scythian (70)** (BobJones) **4-10-0** NDay(1) (rdn 2f out: str run ins fnl f: jst failed) | s.h | **2** | 14/1 | 77 | 43 |
| 2787$^{11}$ | **Walk the Beat (66)** (MartynMeade) **6-9-5**$^{(5)}$ RHavlin(5) (a.p: ev ch over 1f out: unable qckn ins fnl f) | 1¼ | **3** | 8/1 | 69 | 35 |
| 3219* | **Robellion (72)** (DWPArbuthnot) **5-10-2v** 6x TQuinn(3) (b.hind: rdn & hdwy over 1f out: unable qckn ins fnl f) | 1¼ | **4** | 3/1$^{1}$ | 71 | 37 |
| 2976* | **Squire Corrie (57)** (GHarwood) **4-8-8b**$^{(7)}$ GayeHarwood(4) (a.p: ev ch over 1f out: wknd ins fnl f) | 3 | **5** | 9/2$^{2}$ | 46 | 12 |
| 2992$^{3}$ | **John O'Dreams (51)** (MrsALMKing) **11-8-9** JReid(6) (hld up & bhd: hdwy over 1f out: one pce ins fnl f) | hd | **6** | 5/1$^{3}$ | 40 | 6 |
| 3112$^{4}$ | **Polly Golightly (67)** (MBlanshard) **3-9-8b** RCochrane(8) (racd wd: led over 3f: eased whn btn ins fnl f) | 5 | **7** | 13/2 | 40 | 3 |
| 3261$^{9}$ | **Paley Prince (USA) (62)** (MDIUsher) **10-8-13**$^{(7)}$ RBrisland(9) (b: racd wd: prom over 3f: eased whn btn) | 7 | **8** | 33/1 | 13 | — |
| 3146$^{11}$ | **Mazzarello (IRE) (40)** (RCurtis) **6-7-12v** GBardwell(7) (racd wd: chsd ldr 3f: eased whn btn) | 3½ | **9** | 33/1 | — | — |

(SP 113.5%) **9 Rn**

**60.94 secs** (2.74) CSF £60.50 CT £499.17 TOTE £5.50: £1.80 £3.70 £3.10 (£56.80) Trio £185.60 OWNER Davies and Bridgeman (COWBRIDGE) BRED Taplin, Lee and Cain Ltd

WEIGHT FOR AGE 3yo-3lb

**2946 Croeso Cynnes** seemed to have a stiff task off a 7lb higher mark, but was back to the minimum trip and found the post arriving in the nick of time. (5/1)
**931 The Scythian**, freshened up by a break, fairly flew up the stands' rail in the closing stages, but the post came a stride too soon. His two victories last season both came over six furlongs at Ripon. (14/1)
**2561* Walk the Beat**, disappointing at Sandown last time, was 6lb higher than when scraping home on his previous outing. (8/1)
**3219* Robellion** could not defy what was effectively an 11lb rise in the weights for his two wins. (3/1)
**2976* Squire Corrie** was 2lb higher following his narrow win at Sandown. (9/2)
**2992 John O'Dreams** was 12lb better off with Robellion than when beaten two lengths at Chepstow. (5/1)
**2715 Polly Golightly**, back to what seems her best trip, was switched towards the far side and showed plenty of speed to make the running. She deserves another chance. (13/2)

T/Jkpt: Not won; £3,450.33 to Pontefract 8/8/96. T/Plpt: £66.80 (238.98 Tckts). T/Qdpt: £12.60 (127.45 Tckts). KH

# 3275-NEWCASTLE (L-H) (St crse Good to firm, Rnd crse Firm)
## Wednesday August 7th

Race 2 & 4: hand-timed
WEATHER: overcast & raining WIND: slt against

## 3324 NORTHERN RACING NURSERY H'CAP (2-Y.O) (Class E)
2-30 (2-30) **7f** £2,957.00 (£896.00: £438.00: £209.00) Stalls: High GOING minus 0.07 sec per fur (G)

| | | | | SP | RR | SF |
|---|---|---|---|---|---|---|
| 2875² | **Top of The Wind (IRE) (77)** (JJO'Neill) **2-9-7** KFallon(7) (lw: effrt 3f out: hdwy to ld ins fnl f: styd on u.p) | — | 1 | 7/2 2 | 73 | 37 |
| 2588³ | **Our Future (IRE) (70)** (MJohnston) **2-9-0** JWeaver(8) (lw: led tl ins fnl f: kpt on) | 1 | 2 | 5/1 3 | 64 | 28 |
| 2984⁴ | **Run Lucy Run (62)** (RGuest) **2-8-6** KDarley(6) (lw: w ldr: effrt over 2f out: no ex ins fnl f) | 1 | 3 | 10/1 | 53 | 17 |
| 2904⁴ | **Skelton Sovereign (IRE) (73)** (RHollinshead) **2-9-0**(3) FLynch(5) (effrt ½-wy: sn rdn & no imp) | 3 | 4 | 14/1 | 58 | 22 |
| 2959³ | **Cajun Sunset (IRE) (58)** (TDEasterby) **2-8-2** LCharnock(1) (cl up: effrt 2f out: wknd appr fnl f) | 2½ | 5 | 10/1 | 37 | 1 |
| *2370⁴* | **Fast Spin (59)** (TDBarron) **2-8-3** JFanning(3) (chsd ldrs 5f: sn wknd) | 3 | 6 | 10/1 | 31 | — |
| 3208² | **Silca's My Key (IRE) (68)** (MRChannon) **2-8-12** JFortune(4) (lw: rr div: pushed along 3f out: hrd drvn 2f out: no imp) | ¾ | 7 | 11/8 1 | 38 | 2 |
| 2865⁷ | **Not A Lot (68)** (MWEasterby) **2-8-12** DaleGibson(2) (lost tch fnl 2f) | 4 | 8 | 16/1 | 29 | — |
| | | | | (SP 120.8%) | **8 Rn** | |

**1m 29.74** (5.24) CSF £21.09 CT £134.02 TOTE £4.30: £1.70 £1.90 £2.00 (£10.60) OWNER Mr Jim McGrath (PENRITH) BRED Gay O'Callaghan
**2875 Top of The Wind (IRE)** behaved pretty well this time and did the job in determined style. Hopefully she will continue to go the right way. (7/2)
**2588 Our Future (IRE)**, who is doing well physically, put up another good performance, and is knocking at the door. (5/1: 3/1-11/2)
**2984 Run Lucy Run**, a tough little filly, just found this beyond her, but it was still not a bad effort. (10/1)
**2904 Skelton Sovereign (IRE)** looks on the weak side at present. He is running quite well, even though the Handicapper looks to have given him a stiffish task. (14/1)
**2959 Cajun Sunset (IRE)**, an edgy gelding, had his chances, but cried enough going to the final furlong. (10/1)
**2370 Fast Spin**, who has a moderate action, probably just needed this first run in five weeks. (10/1: 7/1-12/1)
**3208 Silca's My Key (IRE)** apparently clipped the heels of another runner early doors, which would have contributed to what was a poor performance. (11/8)

## 3325 GOSFORTH APPRENTICE (S) STKS (3-Y.O) (Class G)
3-00 (3-00) **1m 4f 93y** £2,169.00 (£609.00: £297.00) Stalls: Low GOING minus 0.67 sec per fur (HD)

| | | | | SP | RR | SF |
|---|---|---|---|---|---|---|
| 2979⁵ | **He's Got Wings (IRE) (46)** (MBell) **3-8-12v** GFaulkner(3) (b.nr hind: sn prom: led wl over 2f out: pushed out) | — | 1 | 8/13 1 | 55 | 26 |
| 2848⁶ | **What Jim Wants (IRE) (39)** (JJO'Neill) **3-8-12** SCopp(4) (hdwy ½-wy: styd on u.p fnl 3f: no ch w wnr) | 9 | 2 | 4/1 3 | 43 | 14 |
| 3116³ | **Ragtime Cowgirl (40)** (CWThornton) **3-8-13** DSweeney(5) (sn cl up: led over 4f out tl wl over 2f out: sn btn) | 10 | 3 | 7/2 2 | 32 | 3 |
| *3090⁴* | **Boy Blakeney (37)** (MrsSJSmith) **3-8-7b¹**(5) CLowther(1) (lw: outpcd & lost tch over 5f out: n.d after) | 5 | 4 | 25/1 | 24 | — |
| 3048⁸ | **Bright Pet (38)** (MrsSJSmith) **3-8-4**(3) AngelaGallimore(2) (outpcd & lost tch 7f out: n.d after) | ¾ | 5 | 25/1 | 18 | — |
| 3048⁹ | **Cameron Edge** (ABMulholland) **3-8-7** CAdamson(6) (b: led tl hdd over 4f out: wknd over 3f out) | 7 | 6 | 20/1 | 9 | — |
| 2568¹³ | **Sleepy Boy** (WStorey) **3-8-12** IonaWands(7) (outpcd & wl bhd fnl 7f) | 17 | 7 | 33/1 | — | — |
| | | | | (SP 119.5%) | **7 Rn** | |

**2m 40.4** (2.90) CSF £3.97 TOTE £2.20: £1.20 £1.80 (£3.80) OWNER Mr Paul Hicks (NEWMARKET) BRED Citadel Stud
Sold JRamsden 6,800 gns
**2979 He's Got Wings (IRE)** travelled well and his rider left nothing to chance, even when there were no challengers in the final furlong. (8/13)
**2424 What Jim Wants (IRE)** is slow but sure. He kept staying on, but never had a hope with the winner. (4/1: 3/1-9/2)
**3116 Ragtime Cowgirl** had her chances again, but looked moderate when passed. (7/2)
**2297 Boy Blakeney**, fitted with a tongue-strap and blinkered for the first time, never showed anything. (25/1)
**Bright Pet** got her best form figure to date, but it was still nothing to shout about. (25/1)

## 3326 UTTOXETER MEDIAN AUCTION MAIDEN STKS (2-Y.O) (Class F)
3-30 (3-30) **6f** £2,589.00 (£729.00: £357.00) Stalls: High GOING minus 0.07 sec per fur (G)

| | | | | SP | RR | SF |
|---|---|---|---|---|---|---|
| 2396² | **Mystic Circle (IRE)** (JWWatts) **2-8-9** NConnorton(1) (cl up: led over 2f out: hld on u.p fnl f) | — | 1 | 7/4 1 | 65 | 18 |
| 3080³ | **Head Girl (IRE)** (CWThornton) **2-8-9** AMackay(2) (s.i.s: sn trckng ldrs: effrt & ev ch ins fnl f: rdn & no ex) | 1 | 2 | 9/4 2 | 62 | 15 |
| | **Sad Mad Bad (USA)** (MJohnston) **2-9-0** KDarley(4) (gd sort: str: bit bkwd: led: rn green & hdd over 2f out: kpt on wl towards fin) | 1¼ | 3 | 3/1 3 | 64+ | 17 |
| 2977³ | **Aurelian** (MBell) **2-9-0** MFenton(3) (lw: cl up tl rdn & wknd over 2f out) | 15 | 4 | 3/1 3 | 24 | — |
| | | | | (SP 117.1%) | **4 Rn** | |

**1m 16.51** (5.01) CSF £6.12 TOTE £2.70: (£3.80) OWNER P T Fenwick & F A P Chapman (RICHMOND) BRED Mrs Elizabeth Wales
**2396 Mystic Circle (IRE)** always looked to be travelling best, but it took some strongish driving to make sure of it inside the last. (7/4)
**3080 Head Girl (IRE)** kept in touch this time but, when a real effort was required, her response left something to be desired. (9/4)
**Sad Mad Bad (USA)**, on a learning mission, looks a power-house. He was not knocked about and is one to keep an eye on. (3/1: op 7/4)
**2977 Aurelian**, a lengthy sort, ran too bad to be true. (3/1)

## 3327 ZANUSSI APPLIANCE OF SCIENCE LIMITED STKS (0-70) (3-Y.O) (Class E)
4-00 (4-00) **1m 1f 9y** £2,814.00 (£852.00: £416.00: £198.00) Stalls: Low GOING minus 0.67 sec per fur (HD)

| Form | Runner | Dist | Pos | SP | RR | SF |
|---|---|---|---|---|---|---|
| 3039[4] | **White Plains (IRE) (70)** (MBell) **3-8-4**(7) RMullen(4) (prom: effrt over 2f out: styd on to ld wl ins fnl f) | — | **1** | 3/1[2] | 78 | — |
| 3242[2] | **Tissue of Lies (USA) (68)** (MJohnston) **3-8-11** JWeaver(1) (lw: led tl hdd over 2f out: led ins fnl f: hdd & nt qckn towards fin) | 1 | **2** | 13/2 | 76 | — |
| 3238* | **Call Me (70)** (CWThornton) **3-9-0** 2x DeanMcKeown(5) (trckd ldr: led & qcknd over 2f out: hdd ins fnl f: no ex) | 1¾ | **3** | 15/8[1] | 76 | — |
| 3246[5] | **Smarter Charter (68)** (MrsJRRamsden) **3-9-1** KFallon(3) (lw: hld up: effrt over 3f out: sn outpcd) | 13 | **4** | 7/2[3] | 54 | — |
| *3074** | **Hareb (USA) (70)** (JWHills) **3-8-11** JFortune(2) (trckd ldrs tl outpcd fnl 3f) | 5 | **5** | 4/1 | 41 | — |

(SP 115.3%) **5 Rn**

**1m 59.1** (6.80) CSF £19.19 TOTE £3.70: £2.30 £2.30 (£10.10) OWNER Deln Ltd (NEWMARKET) BRED Howard Kaskel

**3039 White Plains (IRE)** sat just off the pace this time and produced a steady run up the straight to score in most convincing fashion. (3/1)
**3242 Tissue of Lies (USA)** keeps running well, but looks as though longer trips will bring out the best in him. (13/2: 4/1-7/1)
**3238* Call Me** tried the same tactics as were successful at Hamilton, but could never get away this time, and was outbattled in the final furlong. (15/8)
**3246 Smarter Charter**, given plenty to do off a slowish pace, had little chance when things hotted up. (7/2: 5/2-4/1)
**3074* Hareb (USA)** looked pretty moderate once the pace increased. (4/1: op 5/2)

## 3328 ZANUSSI/NORTHERN ELECTRIC H'CAP (0-85) (3-Y.O+) (Class D)
4-30 (4-30) **7f** £3,533.75 (£1,070.00: £522.50: £248.75) Stalls: High GOING minus 0.07 sec per fur (G)

| Form | Runner | Dist | Pos | SP | RR | SF |
|---|---|---|---|---|---|---|
| 2630[9] | **Tinklers Folly (63)** (DenysSmith) **4-9-0** LCharnock(4) (lw: disp ld tl led ½-wy: hld on wl) | — | **1** | 10/1 | 67 | 33 |
| 2722* | **Keston Pond (IRE) (73)** (MrsVAAconley) **6-9-10** MDeering(1) (lw: trckd ldrs: hdwy to chal 1f out: r.o) | hd | **2** | 3/1[1] | 77 | 43 |
| 2874[4] | **Cavers Yangous (66)** (MJohnston) **5-9-3** JWeaver(5) (lw: disp ld to ½-wy: sn rdn: ev ch tl outpcd ins fnl f) | 1¼ | **3** | 9/2[2] | 67 | 33 |
| 3120[3] | **Quilling (68)** (MDods) **4-9-5** DeanMcKeown(7) (lw: in tch: effrt over 2f out: styd on: nt pce to chal) | hd | **4** | 6/1 | 69 | 35 |
| 3151[2] | **Samsolom (57)** (PHowling) **8-8-8** KDarley(2) (lw: in tch: effrt over 2f out: styd on towards fin: no imp) | hd | **5** | 3/1[1] | 58 | 24 |
| 3052[9] | **Kid Ory (60)** (PCalver) **5-8-11** MBirch(3) (w ldrs tl wknd fnl 2f) | 2½ | **6** | 8/1 | 55 | 21 |
| 2911[10] | **Barato (65)** (MrsJRRamsden) **5-9-2** KFallon(6) (lw: b.nr hind: a bhd: lost tch fnl 2f) | 20 | **7** | 11/2[3] | 14 | — |

(SP 118.1%) **7 Rn**

**1m 29.58** (5.08) CSF £39.15 TOTE £13.60: £4.30 £2.10 (£19.70) OWNER Mr R. O. Manners (BISHOP AUCKLAND) BRED Qualitair Stud Ltd

**2357 Tinklers Folly** bounced back to form after four weeks' rest, and showed courage to hold on. (10/1: op 6/1)
**2722* Keston Pond (IRE)** keeps running his heart out and deserves better. (3/1)
**2874 Cavers Yangous** has never won over this far, but put up a spirited effort. He should get this trip, but seems ideally suited by a stiff six furlongs. (9/2)
**3120 Quilling**, again patiently ridden, did keep on in the last two furlongs to suggest that he may at last be coming to form. (6/1)
**3151 Samsolom** looked magnificent, but never really fired, despite keeping on at the finish. The ability is certainly still there. (3/1)
**2773 Kid Ory** is now on a decent mark and would have been a fair bit closer but for being eased when beaten. (8/1)

## 3329 ST. MODWEN H'CAP (0-70) (3-Y.O+) (Class E)
5-00 (5-00) **2m 19y** £2,879.00 (£872.00: £426.00: £203.00) Stalls: High GOING minus 0.67 sec per fur (HD)

| Form | Runner | Dist | Pos | SP | RR | SF |
|---|---|---|---|---|---|---|
| *3086[2]* | **Shirley Sue (58)** (MJohnston) **3-8-6** JWeaver(5) (lw: hld up: gd hdwy over 2f out: led over 1f out: styd on strly) | — | **1** | 5/2[1] | 72 | — |
| 2165[4] | **Forgie (IRE) (59)** (PCalver) **3-8-7** MBirch(1) (cl up: led over 2f out tl over 1f out: kpt on) | 2 | **2** | 11/2[3] | 71 | — |
| 2927* | **Jamaican Flight (USA) (65)** (JWHills) **3-8-13** JFortune(2) (lw: led tl hdd over 2f out: one pce) | 6 | **3** | 5/1[2] | 71 | — |
| 3037[6] | **French Ivy (USA) (65)** (FMurphy) **9-10-0** TWilliams(3) (b: hld up: effrt over 3f out: nt pce to chal) | ¾ | **4** | 5/2[1] | 70 | 5 |
| 2988[6] | **Karaylar (IRE) (46)** (WStorey) **4-8-9** JFanning(4) (lw: hdwy ½-wy: sn in tch: rdn over 3f out: sn btn) | 12 | **5** | 5/1[2] | 39 | — |
| 2120[9] | **Calcando (33)** (EWeymes) **4-7-10** JLowe(6) (prom tl wknd fnl 3f) | s.h | **6** | 50/1 | 26 | — |
| 2986[2] | **Latvian (64)** (RAllan) **9-9-13** ACulhane(7) (trckd ldrs tl rdn & wknd fnl 3f) | 6 | **7** | 10/1 | 51 | — |

(SP 116.9%) **7 Rn**

**3m 35.98** (10.48) CSF £15.92 TOTE £2.50: £2.00 £3.40 (£8.90) OWNER Greenland Park Ltd (MIDDLEHAM) BRED Lahama Ltd
LONG HANDICAP Calcando 7-9
WEIGHT FOR AGE 3yo-15lb

**3086 Shirley Sue** has been crying out for this trip and put up a super performance. Better looks likely. (5/2: 2/1-3/1)
**2165 Forgie (IRE)**, from an out-of-form yard, ran a sound race but just found one too good. (11/2)
**2927* Jamaican Flight (USA)** tried his front-running tactics again here, but this was a much more competitive event, and he was well outpointed in the final quarter-mile. (5/1)
**3037 French Ivy (USA)** looked to be travelling well but, when the pressure was on in the straight, lacked the required pace. He needs a stronger gallop. (5/2)
**2988 Karaylar (IRE)** is beginning to come to himself looks-wise, but the rain that had fallen during the afternoon probably did not help. (5/1)
**Calcando** showed a little this time but still has a long way to go. (50/1)

T/Plpt: £351.40 (37.22 Tckts). T/Qdpt: £18.90 (51.76 Tckts). AA

# 3104-NOTTINGHAM (L-H) (Good to firm)
## Wednesday August 7th
WEATHER: fine

## 3330 'JAMAICA' (S) STKS (2-Y.O) (Class G)
6-05 (6-06) **6f 15y** £2,070.00 (£570.00: £270.00) Stalls: High GOING minus 0.31 sec per fur (GF)

| Form | Runner | Dist | Pos | SP | RR | SF |
|---|---|---|---|---|---|---|
| 3114[8] | **Summerville Wood** (PMooney) **2-8-4**(7) CScally(3) (b: outpcd ½-wy: hdwy 2f out: r.o to ld wl ins fnl f) | — | **1** | 4/1[3] | 58 | — |
| 3105[7] | **Champagne On Ice** (PDEvans) **2-8-6** JFEgan(8) (a.p: led over 1f out tl hdd nr fin) | hd | **2** | 14/1 | 53 | — |
| 2951[5] | **Valentine Fairy** (RBoss) **2-8-6** JCarroll(5) (lt-f: unf: a.p: ev ch fnl 2f tl no ex wl ins fnl f) | 1¼ | **3** | 3/1[2] | 49 | — |
| 2802[9] | **Silent Wells** (JJQuinn) **2-8-6** JQuinn(6) (b.nr hind: in tch: rdn 3f out: sn lost pl: kpt on u.p fnl f) | 2½ | **4** | 33/1 | 43 | — |

| | | | Pos | SP | RR | SF |
|---|---|---|---|---|---|---|
| *2746$^{7}$* | **One Lady** (JLEyre) **2-8-3**$^{(3)}$ CTeague(1) (mde most over 4f: one pce fnl f) | hd | **5** | 20/1 | 43 | — |
| 3082$^{2}$ | **Fearless Cavalier (60)** (RHollinshead) **2-8-8**$^{(3)}$ FLynch(4) (lw: drvn along ½-wy: nt pce to chal) | hd | **6** | 9/4$^{1}$ | 47 | — |
| *3088$^{5}$* | **Silver Moon** (BAMcMahon) **2-8-1**$^{(5)}$ LNewton(2) (trckd ldrs: rdn & outpcd fnl 2f) | ¾ | **7** | 33/1 | 40 | — |
| 3075$^{4}$ | **Emilyjill (59)** (RHannon) **2-8-6** WJO'Connor(9) (prom tl rdn & wknd 2f out) | nk | **8** | 3/1$^{2}$ | 40 | — |
| 2741$^{9}$ | **Sharp Poppet** (MBell) **2-8-6** PaulEddery(7) (lw: ref to r: p.u sn after s) | | **P** | 16/1 | — | — |

(SP 124.0%) **9 Rn**

**1m 16.9** (6.40) CSF £53.44 TOTE £6.30: £1.30 £3.20 £1.50 (£34.20) Trio £56.70 OWNER Likely Lads Partnership (RADLETT) BRED Sean Kelly Bloodstock

Bt in 8,000 gns

**2279 Summerville Wood**, a May foal, landed quite a touch on this step up to six furlongs, but proved very costly to retain at the auction. (4/1: op 7/1)

**Champagne On Ice**, an improving filly, kicked for home below the distance and was only worn down near the line. She could soon go one better. (14/1)

**Valentine Fairy**, a very sparely-made youngster who was not at all happy on such lively ground, looks capable of winning a race. (3/1)

**Silent Wells**, not much bigger than a pony, struggled with the pace on this step down to a slightly shorter trip, but she was beginning to find her stride inside the distance. (33/1)

**One Lady** held a slight lead down the centre until feeling the strain over a furlong out. (20/1)

**3082 Fearless Cavalier**, a tooth-grinder, is ill-at-ease on such fast ground and was in trouble some way out. (9/4)

## 3331 'BARBADOS' H'CAP (0-60) (3-Y.O+) (Class F)

6-35 (6-36) **5f 13y** £2,381.00 (£656.00: £311.00) Stalls: High GOING minus 0.31 sec per fur (GF)

| | | | Pos | SP | RR | SF |
|---|---|---|---|---|---|---|
| *3091$^{4}$* | **Souperficial (46)** (JAGlover) **5-9-3v** WJO'Connor(4) (trckd ldrs centre: led ent fnl f: drvn out) | — | **1** | 5/1$^{1}$ | 53 | 35 |
| 3152$^{8}$ | **Superbit (48)** (BAMcMahon) **4-9-5** WRyan(1) (lw: a.p: led over 1f out: sn hdd: unable qckn) | 1 | **2** | 7/1$^{3}$ | 52 | 34 |
| 2745$^{3}$ | **Oscilights Gift (25)** (PBurgoyne) **4-7-10** NAdams(3) (a.p: ev ch 1f out: kpt on one pce) | 1 | **3** | 6/1$^{2}$ | 26 | 8 |
| 2941$^{15}$ | **Last Ambition (IRE) (33)** (RChampion) **4-8-4** JQuinn(5) (bhd: hdwy & swtchd rt over 1f out: fin wl) | 1¼ | **4** | 50/1 | 30 | 12 |
| *291$^{7}$* | **Mister Raider (48)** (EAWheeler) **4-9-0b**$^{(5)}$ DGriffiths(13) (swtg: bit bkwd: led stands' side: rdn & no ex ins fnl f) | s.h | **5** | 11/1 | 45 | 27 |
| 3135$^{10}$ | **Gagajulu (56)** (PDEvans) **3-9-10** JFEgan(10) (trckd ldr stands' side 3f) | 5 | **6** | 15/2 | 37 | 16 |
| 3223$^{9}$ | **Featherstone Lane (48)** (MissLCSiddall) **5-9-5v** GCarter(8) (lw: sn rdn along: nvr gng pce of ldrs) | ¾ | **7** | 5/1$^{1}$ | 26 | 8 |
| 2604$^{8}$ | **Fig Tree Bay (35)** (TTClement) **3-8-3** JTate(12) (b.hind: nvr nrr) | 1¾ | **8** | 50/1 | 8 | — |
| *3091$^{10}$* | **Petarina (46)** (MissJFCraze) **3-9-0** DaleGibson(6) (nvr trbld ldrs) | s.h | **9** | 25/1 | 19 | — |
| 3294$^{12}$ | **Niteowl Raider (IRE) (45)** (JAHarris) **3-8-13** JO'Reilly(9) (outpcd) | 1¼ | **10** | 20/1 | 14 | — |
| 2933* | **Forzara (50)** (JBerry) **3-9-4** JCarroll(11) (dwlt: a outpcd) | 1¾ | **11** | 5/1$^{1}$ | 13 | — |
| 2960$^{9}$ | **Quinta Boy (30)** (JLEyre) **3-7-9**$^{(3)}$ NVarley(7) (led: drvn along ½-wy: hdd & wknd over 1f out) | 11 | **12** | 25/1 | — | — |

(SP 113.3%) **12 Rn**

**60.9 secs** (2.30) CSF £35.31 CT £162.43 TOTE £5.50: £2.30 £2.60 £1.60 (£10.80) Trio £34.50 OWNER Mr Noel Wilson (WORKSOP) BRED C. L. Loyd

LONG HANDICAP Oscilights Gift 7-9

WEIGHT FOR AGE 3yo-3lb

**3091 Souperficial** has been doing nearly all his racing on the All-Weather of late, but bounced back to form with a very comfortable success. In this form, he should be able to follow up. (5/1)

**Superbit** would have taken all the beating on easier ground and would seem to be on his way back. (7/1)

**2745 Oscilights Gift** ran well all the way, and that first success can not be far away. (6/1)

**Last Ambition (IRE)**, who has been tried at middle distances without success, came from a long way off the pace, and does possibly need at least another furlong. (50/1)

**203* Mister Raider** ran a fine race after being out of action for over five months, and his front-running tactics did not come to an end until inside the final furlong. (11/1)

**2238 Gagajulu** moved to post worst of all, but tried to keep tabs on the stands'-side leader until left behind inside the final quarter-mile. (15/2)

**2496 Featherstone Lane** was making no impression from halfway. (5/1)

**2933* Forzara** went to post like a crab and, after missing a beat, was always behind. (5/1)

## 3332 'TRINIDAD & TOBAGO' CLAIMING STKS (2-Y.O) (Class F)

7-05 (7-08) **5f 13y** £2,381.00 (£656.00: £311.00) Stalls: High GOING minus 0.31 sec per fur (GF)

| | | | Pos | SP | RR | SF |
|---|---|---|---|---|---|---|
| 3050$^{3}$ | **Suite Factors (80)** (JAGlover) **2-8-13** SDWilliams(4) (lw: mde all: hrd rdn fnl f: jst hld on) | — | **1** | 4/7$^{1}$ | 71 | 3 |
| | **Five-O-Fifty** (JBerry) **2-8-7** JCarroll(5) (lt-f: unf: bhd: rn v.green: swtchd lft appr fnl f: str run u.p: jst failed) | s.h | **2** | 7/1$^{3}$ | 65 | — |
| 3075$^{5}$ | **Hever Golf Stormer (IRE) (64)** (TJNaughton) **2-8-11** PaulEddery(3) (chsd wnr: effrt u.p over 1f out: kpt on) | 1½ | **3** | 6/1$^{2}$ | 64 | — |
| 2926$^{11}$ | **Mint Condition** (MrsLStubbs) **2-9-1** JQuinn(6) (spd 3f: sn rdn & outpcd: t.o) | 13 | **4** | 6/1$^{2}$ | 27 | — |
| | **Geoffreys Gamble** (BPJBaugh) **2-8-11** WLord(2) (b: lt-f: bit bkwd: swvd bdly lft s: t.n.p) | | **R** | 33/1 | — | — |
| | ***Miss Fugit Penance*** (PDEvans) **2-8-6** JFEgan(1) (Withdrawn not under Starter's orders: ref to ent stalls) | | **W** | 8/1 | — | — |

(SP 118.8%) **5 Rn**

**62.7 secs** (4.10) CSF £4.43 TOTE £1.30: £1.10 £1.60 (£2.50) OWNER Mr Kenneth Paul Beecroft (WORKSOP) BRED I and F Yorkshire Holdings

Suite Factors clmd NRShields £8,000; Five-O-Fifty clmd AMorris £5,000.

**3050 Suite Factors** did not appear to have a lot to beat, and was unimpressive in doing it. (4/7)

**Five-O-Fifty**, a very lightly-made late foal who looked as fit as a flea, ran very green throughout and was taken off his legs until producing a late rally. (7/1: op 7/2)

**2846 Hever Golf Stormer (IRE)** ran as if he may well benefit from a longer trip, and there would seem to be a race to be won. (6/1)

## 3333 NOTTINGHAMSHIRE COUNTY CRICKET CLUB H'CAP (0-70) (3-Y.O+) (Class E)

7-35 (7-36) **1m 1f 213y** £3,643.50 (£1,092.00: £525.00: £241.50) Stalls: Low GOING minus 0.31 sec per fur (GF)

| | | | Pos | SP | RR | SF |
|---|---|---|---|---|---|---|
| *460$^{2}$* | **Mattimeo (IRE) (70)** (APJarvis) **3-9-10** WJO'Connor(3) (bit bkwd: hld up: effrt & rdn over 2f out: str run on ins to ld cl home) | — | **1** | 16/1 | 77 | 35 |
| 3094* | **Ragsak Jameel (USA) (74)** (MajorWRHern) **3-10-0v** 5x PaulEddery(6) (swtg: led after 2f: drvn clr appr fnl f: hdd nr fin) | hd | **2** | 6/1$^{2}$ | 81 | 39 |
| 2587$^{2}$ | **Raindeer Quest (45)** (JLEyre) **4-8-8** KFallon(11) (a.p: drvn along 2f out: ev ch ins fnl f: r.o) | nk | **3** | 7/1$^{3}$ | 51 | 18 |

| Form | Horse and details | Dist | Pos | SP | RR | SF |
|---|---|---|---|---|---|---|
| 2866[6] | **Slapy Dam (50)** (JMackie) **4-8-10v[1]**[(3)] FLynch(9) (lw: hld up: hdwy over 3f out: n.m.r & swtchd rt appr fnl f: fin fast) | hd | **4** | 20/1 | 56 | 23 |
| 3059[2] | **Lila Pedigo (IRE) (53)** (MissJFCraze) **3-8-7** NConnorton(2) (trckd ldrs: ev ch ins fnl f: no ex towards fin) | ¾ | **5** | 8/1 | 58 | 16 |
| 3052[6] | **Nobby Barnes (41)** (DonEnricoIncisa) **7-8-4** KimTinkler(4) (hld up: hdwy over 3f out: nt pce to chal) | 1¾ | **6** | 20/1 | 43 | 10 |
| 3111[3] | **Runic Symbol (42)** (MBlanshard) **5-8-5** JQuinn(7) (lw: prom: ev ch over 1f out: unable qckn) | s.h | **7** | 5/1[1] | 44 | 11 |
| 2718[13] | **Passing Strangers (USA) (60)** (PWHarris) **3-9-0** MFenton(15) (lw: hld up & bhd: hdwy on outside 3f out: nvr nrr) | nk | **8** | 7/1[3] | 62 | 20 |
| 2743[16] | **Indira (52)** (HCandy) **3-8-6** CRutter(5) (nvr trbld ldrs) | nk | **9** | 16/1 | 53 | 11 |
| 3109[2] | **Age of Reality (USA) (60)** (HCandy) **3-9-0** JWeaver(8) (led 2f: prom tl wknd wl over 1f out) | hd | **10** | 5/1[1] | 61 | 19 |
| 3000[7] | **Master M-E-N (IRE) (54)** (NMBabbage) **4-9-3v** JCarroll(1) (hld up: hdwy over 3f out: rdn wl over 1f out: sn btn) | 2½ | **11** | 12/1 | 51 | 18 |
| 3113[11] | **Bronhallow (50)** (MrsBarbaraWaring) **3-8-1**[(3)] NVarley(10) (b.nr hind: hdwy ½-wy: wknd over 2f out: t.o) | 9 | **12** | 33/1 | 33 | — |
| *1721*[10] | **Classic Delight (USA) (57)** (RHarris) **3-8-11** AMackay(13) (lw: hld up: hdwy 4f out: sn no imp: t.o) | 2 | **13** | 33/1 | 36 | — |
| 2855[6] | **Budding Annie (50)** (JRBosley) **3-8-4** NAdams(14) (trckd ldrs tl rn wd & lost pl ent st: sn bhd: t.o) | 10 | **14** | 16/1 | 13 | — |
| | **Our Albert (IRE) (60)** (JAGlover) **3-9-0** SDWilliams(12) (bkwd: plld hrd: prom to ½-wy: wknd qckly: t.o) | dist | **15** | 33/1 | — | — |
| | | | | (SP 127.4%) | **15 Rn** | |

**2m 8.3** (5.80) CSF £105.76 CT £685.29 TOTE £18.70: £7.10 £1.90 £3.10 (£46.90) Trio £68.20 OWNER Mrs Monica Keogh (ASTON UPTHORPE) BRED W. J. Byrne

WEIGHT FOR AGE 3yo-9lb

**460 Mattimeo (IRE)**, who has enjoyed a mid-summer break, showed a lot of courage to force his way into the action up the inside rail. With the minimum room in which to manoeuvre and with whips flying in his face, he poked his nose in front a couple of strides from the line. (16/1)

**3094* Ragsak Jameel (USA)** tried to make the most of his proven stamina, but the penalty proved just too much. (6/1)

**2587 Raindeer Quest**, a progressive filly who will benefit from easier ground, battled on willingly when short of room to go down fighting. (7/1)

**512 Slapy Dam**, who has been out of sorts so far this term, was fitted with a visor and returning to a shorter trip. He would have gone close with any run at all inside the distance. He is a winner without a penalty. (20/1)

**3059 Lila Pedigo (IRE)**, taking a step up in class and distance, did not enjoy the smoothest of passages when battling for the lead inside the final furlong, and the position was accepted in the final 50 yards. She should be able to win at this trip. (8/1: op 12/1)

**3052 Nobby Barnes** stayed on relentlessly in the final stages, but was always being tightened up. He does stay this trip and will cause an upset one of these days. (20/1)

**3111 Runic Symbol** sat much closer to the pace than usual. (5/1)

## 3334 'MONSERRAT' H'CAP (0-70) (3-Y.O+ F & M) (Class E)

8-05 (8-12) **1m 54y** £3,479.70 (£1,041.60: £499.80: £228.90) Stalls: Low GOING minus 0.31 sec per fur (GF)

| Form | Horse and details | Dist | Pos | SP | RR | SF |
|---|---|---|---|---|---|---|
| 3102[2] | **Jambo (57)** (JLEyre) **3-8-8** KFallon(9) (lw: a.p: led over 3f out: drvn clr 2f out: r.o wl) | — | **1** | 9/4[1] | 70 | 40 |
| 2743[7] | **Cuban Reef (43)** (WJMusson) **4-8-1** JFEgan(8) (hld up in tch: hdwy to chse wnr over 1f out: kpt on towards fin) | 1¾ | **2** | 14/1 | 53 | 30 |
| 3052[4] | **Racing Brenda (47)** (BCMorgan) **5-8-5** JCarroll(10) (hld up: stdy hdwy 3f out: nvr able to chal) | 4 | **3** | 5/1[2] | 49 | 26 |
| *3086*[12] | **Infantry Dancer (56)** (GCBravery) **3-8-7** DRMcCabe(4) (b.hind: trckd ldrs: hrd drvn over 1f out: kpt on) | ¾ | **4** | 33/1 | 56 | 26 |
| 1965[10] | **Triple Tie (USA) (38)** (MBlanshard) **5-7-10** JQuinn(15) (swtg: unruly s: hdwy over 1f out: nrst fin) | ½ | **5** | 33/1 | 37 | 14 |
| *3062*[5] | **Jalmaid (40)** (BAMcMahon) **4-7-12** AMackay(11) (trckd ldrs: rdn 2f out: one pce) | 2 | **6** | 20/1 | 36 | 13 |
| 3228[6] | **Time of Night (USA) (69)** (RGuest) **3-9-1**[(5)] DGriffiths(5) (hdwy over 2f out: nvr nrr) | 1 | **7** | 20/1 | 63 | 33 |
| 2994[4] | **Heathyards Lady (USA) (57)** (RHollinshead) **5-8-12**[(3)] FLynch(7) (hld up in tch: effrt 2f out: sn drvn along: no imp) | nk | **8** | 10/1 | 50 | 27 |
| 2945[8] | **Lubaba (USA) (70)** (HThomsonJones) **3-9-7b[1]** GCarter(2) (led tl over 3f out: rdn & wknd appr fnl f) | nk | **9** | 14/1 | 62 | 32 |
| 3111[10] | **Absolutelystunning (58)** (MrsBarbaraWaring) **3-8-6**[(3)] NVarley(3) (b: nvr nr to chal) | ½ | **10** | 20/1 | 50 | 20 |
| 3051[4] | **Lady Benson (IRE) (45)** (DJSCosgrove) **3-7-10** NAdams(13) (lw: hld up: hdwy on ins over 2f out: nvr nrr) | 1¼ | **11** | 25/1 | 34 | 4 |
| 3148[4] | **Tael of Silver (66)** (ABailey) **4-9-10** MFenton(1) (lw: a in rr) | nk | **12** | 11/2[3] | 55 | 32 |
| 1042[12] | **Yezza (IRE) (60)** (APJarvis) **3-8-11** WJO'Connor(12) (prom over 4f) | 1¾ | **13** | 16/1 | 45 | 15 |
| 2785[8] | **Flying Flowers (55)** (RHannon) **3-8-6** PaulEddery(14) (lost pl 3f out: sn bhd) | 4 | **14** | 14/1 | 32 | 2 |
| *2303*[2] | **Shanghai Lil (38)** (MJFetherston-Godley) **4-7-3**[(7)] RFfrench(6) (rn wd ent st: a bhd) | ½ | **15** | 16/1 | 14 | — |
| | | | | (SP 127.7%) | **15 Rn** | |

**1m 44.0** (2.70) CSF £33.80 CT £140.27 TOTE £2.50: £1.30 £3.50 £2.00 (£26.30) Trio £60.00 OWNER Mr A. H. Jackson (HAMBLETON) BRED R. S. A. Urquhart

LONG HANDICAP Triple Tie (USA) 7-6 Shanghai Lil 7-0

WEIGHT FOR AGE 3yo-7lb

**OFFICIAL EXPLANATION Time Of Night (USA): the jockey reported that he felt the filly's action go at the four-furlong marker.**

**IN-FOCUS: This win supplied Kieren Fallon with his maiden century.**

**3102 Jambo**, off the same mark as when winning up the stands' side at Newcastle, won readily after kicking clear entering the final quarter-mile. (9/4)

**2743 Cuban Reef** stayed on strongly inside the distance, but her efforts were always in vain this time. She looks to be about to find her way. (14/1)

**3052 Racing Brenda**, carrying 13lb more than when successful in this event twelve months ago, tried her best to double up, but could not summon up the pace to land a blow. She is running well and all is not lost yet. (5/1)

**Infantry Dancer** has not achieved much so far, but performed with credit here, and looks to be heading in the right direction. (33/1)

**Triple Tie (USA)** took a lot of persuading to go into the stalls and then came late on the scene to be nearest at the finish. This trip would seem inadequate. (33/1)

**3062 Jalmaid** needs to get her toe in and, in the circumstances, ran well. She found her form in the autumn of last year. (20/1)

## 3335 'CARIBBEAN' H'CAP (0-65) (3-Y.O+) (Class F)

8-35 (8-39) **2m 9y** £2,381.00 (£656.00: £311.00) Stalls: High GOING minus 0.31 sec per fur (GF)

| Form | Horse and details | Dist | Pos | SP | RR | SF |
|---|---|---|---|---|---|---|
| 2988[5] | **Classic Affair (USA) (58)** (RHarris) **3-8-9** AMackay(14) (lost pl ent st: gd hdwy on ins to ld over 2f out: sn clr: easily) | — | **1** | 25/1 | 69+ | 32 |
| 2756[2] | **Teen Jay (58)** (BJLlewellyn) **6-9-10** VSlattery(16) (hld up: hdwy ent st: chsd wnr appr fnl f: no imp) | 4 | **2** | 7/1[3] | 65 | 43 |
| 2717[2] | **Mizyan (IRE) (58)** (JEBanks) **8-9-3**[(7)] GFaulkner(11) (lw: hld up: hdwy ½-wy: led 4f out tl over 2f out: styd on u.p fnl f) | s.h | **3** | 6/1[2] | 65 | 43 |
| 2717[10] | **La Menorquina (USA) (34)** (DMarks) **6-8-0** NAdams(17) (hld up: hdwy 4f out: ev ch 2f out: sn hrd rdn: one pce) | 1½ | **4** | 20/1 | 40 | 18 |

| | | | | SP | RR | SF |
|---|---|---|---|---|---|---|
| 2319$^{9}$ | **Amiarge (45)** (MBrittain) **6-8-11b** JCarroll(5) (hld up & bhd: hdwy 3f out: rdn & one pce appr fnl f) | ¾ | **5** | 10/1 | 50 | 28 |
| 2958$^{3}$ | **Wadada (43)** (DBurchell) **5-8-9** DeanMcKeown(4) (hld up in tch: effrt over 3f out: rdn & one pce fnl 2f) | 2 | **6** | 9/1 | 46 | 24 |
| 2717$^{6}$ | **Victoria Day (34)** (BAMcMahon) **4-7-11**(3) NVarley(8) (nvr nr to chal) | 1½ | **7** | 25/1 | 35 | 13 |
| | **Inn At the Top (56)** (JNorton) **4-9-8** DaleGibson(1) (bkwd: trckd ldrs over 12f: grad wknd) | 9 | **8** | 16/1 | 48 | 26 |
| 2891$^{7}$ | **Genesis Four (43)** (MrsLStubbs) **6-8-9** JFEgan(7) (in rr: rdn 4f out: sme late hdwy: nvr nrr) | 1 | **9** | 25/1 | 34 | 12 |
| 2182$^{5}$ | **Erlemo (37)** (WClay) **7-8-0v**(3) FLynch(13) (nvr nrr) | hd | **10** | 25/1 | 28 | 6 |
| 3117$^{3}$ | **Ttyfran (35)** (BPJBaugh) **6-8-1** WLord(6) (b: trckd ldrs tl outpcd 3f out) | 1 | **11** | 16/1 | 25 | 3 |
| 3297$^{10}$ | **Kindred Greeting (33)** (JAHarris) **4-7-13b** JO'Reilly(15) (trckd ldrs: rdn over 3f out: sn btn) | 1¼ | **12** | 16/1 | 22 | — |
| 3053$^{7}$ | **Lagan (45)** (PSFelgate) **3-7-7**(3) DWright(10) (lw: prom 12f: wknd qckly: t.o) | 22 | **13** | 33/1 | 12 | — |
| 3053$^{3}$ | **Miss Prism (51)** (JLDunlop) **3-8-2** JQuinn(18) (hld up in rr: effrt & rdn over 3f out: no rspnse: t.o) | 4 | **14** | 5/2 1 | 14 | — |
| 3053$^{4}$ | **Sandicliffe (USA) (54)** (BWHills) **3-8-5** KFallon(3) (prom tl rdn & wknd over 3f out: t.o) | 3 | **15** | 10/1 | 14 | — |
| | **Ozzie Jones (39)** (NMBabbage) **5-8-5v1** DRMcCabe(12) (led after 4f: sn clr: wknd & hdd 4f out: eased whn btn: t.o) | 2 | **16** | 20/1 | — | — |
| | **Masai Man (USA) (41)** (MissJBower) **5-8-7** SDWilliams(2) (bkwd: led 4f: dropped rr ½-wy: sn t.o) | dist | **17** | 25/1 | — | — |
| | | | | (SP 132.9%) | **17 Rn** | |

**3m 30.5** (7.50) CSF £188.26 CT £1,121.23 TOTE £20.30: £2.60 £3.60 £2.40 £2.60 (£200.00) Trio £159.30 OWNER Classic Bloodstock Plc (NEWMARKET) BRED M3 Elevage

LONG HANDICAP Lagan 7-4

WEIGHT FOR AGE 3yo-15lb

OFFICIAL EXPLANATION **Miss Prism: went lame during the race.**

**2988 Classic Affair (USA)** has taken time to win a race but, faced with a true test of stamina, did it well. (25/1)

**2756 Teen Jay** was unable to concede 15lb to his younger rival, but did give of his best, and there is a race waiting. (7/1)

**2717 Mizyan (IRE)** has not yet won at this trip on the Flat, but he did put the pressure on and almost gained the runner-up prize when Teen Jay was prematurely eased. (6/1)

**169 La Menorquina (USA)** ran up to her best on ground much faster than is ideal, and this lightly-raced mare is knocking at the door. (20/1)

**1784 Amiarge**, winner of this event last term, looked likely to follow up when moving in behind the leaders over two furlongs out but, once the winner shot clear, could do little more than stick on at one pace. (10/1)

**2958 Wadada**, always handy, was unable to raise his pace when the race began in earnest. (9/1)

**2717 Victoria Day** kept staying on to finish a respectable seventh and is capable of winning a staying event of this description. (25/1)

**3053 Miss Prism**, most punters' idea of the handicap good thing of the day, was always nearer last than first. (5/2)

T/Plpt: £225.70 (58.31 Tckts). T/Qdpt: £10.10 (135.77 Tckts). IM

## 2953-BATH (L-H) (Good to firm, Firm patches)
## Thursday August 8th

WEATHER: fine WIND: mod across

### 3336 SCANIA 4-SERIES FRANCASAL (S) STKS (2-Y.O) (Class G)

2-30 (2-40) **5f 11y** £2,318.00 (£648.00: £314.00) Stalls: High GOING minus 0.43 sec per fur (F)

| | | | | SP | RR | SF |
|---|---|---|---|---|---|---|
| 1046$^{4}$ | **Statuette** (BPalling) **2-8-6** TSprake(5) (b.nr hind: mde all: sn clr: r.o wl) | — | **1** | 7/2 2 | 61 | 18 |
| 3128$^{13}$ | **Will To Win (75)** (PGMurphy) **2-8-6** SDrowne(7) (b.hind: a.p: chsd wnr over 2f out: no imp) | 5 | **2** | 7/2 2 | 45 | 2 |
| 2252$^{8}$ | **Mujadil Express (IRE)** (JSMoore) **2-8-1**(5) PPMurphy(6) (chsd wnr over 2f: one pce) | 3 | **3** | 20/1 | 36 | — |
| 2153$^{3}$ | **Select Lady** (APJarvis) **2-8-6** WJO'Connor(4) (a.p: one pce fnl 2f) | 1½ | **4** | 7/2 2 | 31 | — |
| 3110$^{9}$ | **Lake Spring (IRE)** (RJHodges) **2-8-11** DeclanO'Shea(9) (swvd bdly rt s: a t.o) | 16 | **5** | 33/1 | — | — |
| 2699$^{5}$ | **Impulsion (IRE) (67)** (RHannon) **2-8-8**(3) DaneO'Neill(1) (lw: bolted to s: nvr gng wl: eased whn btn over 2f out: t.o) | 23 | **6** | 7/4 1 | — | — |
| *2633$^{9}$* | **Princess Ferdinand (IRE)** (MMcCormack) **2-8-6v1** DBiggs(8) (stumbled & rdr lost irons s: sn p.u) | | **P** | 14/1 | — | — |
| *3075$^{6}$* | ***Miss Darling*** (JAkehurst) **2-8-6** MTebbutt(3) (Withdrawn not under Starter's orders: bolted & uns rdr bef s) | | **W** | 12/1 3 | — | — |
| *2795$^{9}$* | ***Sylvania Lights*** (WRMuir) **2-8-6** SWhitworth(2) (Withdrawn not under Starter's orders: uns rdr & bolted) | | **W** | 33/1 | — | — |
| | | | | (SP 128.0%) | **7 Rn** | |

**62.8 secs** (2.30) CSF £15.84 TOTE £4.40: £2.30 £2.10 (£8.70) Trio £107.60 OWNER The Why Delilah Associates (COWBRIDGE) BRED M. C. Collins

Bt in 6,100 gns

OFFICIAL EXPLANATION **Impulsion (IRE): the jockey reported that the colt bolted to post, contributing to the poor performance.**

**1046 Statuette** has had wind problems, but they certainly look behind her now, and she proved much too sharp for these platers. (7/2)

**2157 Will To Win**, dropped into selling company, was playing second fiddle from halfway. (7/2)

**Mujadil Express (IRE)** had been tailed off on her debut in quite a valuable auction race at Salisbury. (20/1)

**2153 Select Lady** could not take advantage of running in this lower grade. (7/2)

**2699 Impulsion (IRE)** bolted to the start, but ought to have had a chance to recover because of the ten-minute delay. (7/4)

### 3337 WESTRUCKS FOR SCANIA H'CAP (0-70) (3-Y.O) (Class E)

3-00 (3-01) **2m 1f 34y** £2,953.50 (£888.00: £429.00: £199.50) Stalls: High GOING minus 0.43 sec per fur (F)

| | | | | SP | RR | SF |
|---|---|---|---|---|---|---|
| 3149* | **Old School House (55)** (TJNaughton) **3-9-3** 5x TSprake(1) (hld up: stdy hdwy 4f out: led over 2f out: clr over 1f out: eased nr fin) | — | **1** | Evens 1 | 62+ | 32 |
| 3077* | **Sterling Fellow (54)** (RHannon) **3-8-13b**(3) DaneO'Neill(5) (hld up: hdwy over 3f out: rdn & chsd wnr over 2f out: no imp) | 2 | **2** | 7/2 2 | 59 | 29 |
| 2793$^{6}$ | **Meg's Memory (IRE) (56)** (JohnBerry) **3-9-1**(3) NVarley(4) (hld up & bhd: hdwy over 2f out: sn rdn: one pce) | s.h | **3** | 20/1 | 61 | 31 |
| 2762$^{3}$ | **Perfect Gift (58)** (PFICole) **3-9-6** JReid(3) (a.p: one pce fnl 2f) | nk | **4** | 11/2 | 63 | 33 |
| 2927$^{3}$ | **Mischief Star (59)** (DRCElsworth) **3-9-7** AProcter(6) (chsd ldr: led over 3f out tl over 2f out: wknd wl over 1f out) | 6 | **5** | 12/1 | 58 | 28 |
| 3053* | **Uplift (56)** (SirMarkPrescott) **3-9-4** GDuffield(2) (led over 13f: eased & p.u lame over 2f out) | | **P** | 4/1 3 | — | — |
| | | | | (SP 120.1%) | **6 Rn** | |

**3m 49.0** (8.00) CSF £5.37 TOTE £1.50: £1.30 £2.10 (£3.50) OWNER Just For The Crack Partnership (EPSOM) BRED Miss G. Abbey

**3149* Old School House**, who, with overweight, was 5lb out of the handicap when winning at Doncaster a week ago, was able to run off the same mark here, despite a penalty. His trainer is hoping he will turn out to be a Cesarewitch horse next year. (Evens)

**3077* Sterling Fellow**, because of overweight last time, was only 1lb higher than when winning at Lingfield. (7/2)
**2793 Meg's Memory (IRE)** was patiently ridden to get this much longer trip. (20/1)
**2762 Perfect Gift**, stepping up in distance, had previously given the impression she would be suited by a stamina test. (11/2: 7/2-6/1)
**2927 Mischief Star**, 6lb lower than when last seen in a handicap, was already due to drop a further pound. (12/1: op 6/1)
**3053* Uplift**, raised 7lb, unfortunately ended up being brought back in a horse ambulance. (4/1: 3/1-9/2)

## 3338 SCANIA 1996 TRUCK OF THE YEAR SPRINT TROPHY H'CAP (0-85) (3-Y.O+) (Class D)

3-30 (3-30) **5f 11y** £4,224.00 (£1,272.00: £616.00: £288.00) Stalls: High GOING minus 0.43 sec per fur (F)

| Form | Horse | Dist | Pos | SP | RR | SF |
|---|---|---|---|---|---|---|
| 3146$^{7}$ | **Friendly Brave (USA) (73)** (MissGayKelleway) **6-9-4** WJO'Connor(1) (a.p: hrd rdn to ld last strides) | — | **1** | 5/1$^{2}$ | 79 | 48 |
| 3085$^{9}$ | **Shadow Jury (66)** (DWChapman) **6-8-11b** SDWilliams(2) (chsd ldr: led 2f out: hrd rdn fnl f: ct last strides) | nk | **2** | 11/2$^{3}$ | 71 | 40 |
| 2889$^{8}$ | **Spender (76)** (PWHarris) **7-9-7** AMcGlone(7) (lw: hdwy over 2f out: ev ch over 1f out: r.o) | s.h | **3** | 7/2$^{1}$ | 81 | 50 |
| 2957* | **Kildee Lad (79)** (APJones) **6-9-10** DBiggs(4) (a.p: one pce fnl 2f) | 1½ | **4** | 7/2$^{1}$ | 79 | 48 |
| 3049$^{7}$ | **Windrush Boy (59)** (JRBosley) **6-8-4** CRutter(3) (stdd s: bhd whn plld out over 1f out: nvr nr to chal) | 1 | **5** | 33/1 | 56 | 25 |
| 2889$^{14}$ | **Tart and a Half (76)** (BJMeehan) **4-9-7b** MTebbutt(8) (hld up: hdwy over 2f out: one pce fnl f) | nk | **6** | 15/2 | 72 | 41 |
| 2976$^{6}$ | **Beau Venture (USA) (72)** (BPalling) **8-9-3** DeclanO'Shea(6) (prom over 3f) | 1¼ | **7** | 5/1$^{2}$ | 64 | 33 |
| 3038$^{9}$ | **Go Hever Golf (83)** (TJNaughton) **4-10-0** SWhitworth(5) (led 3f: eased whn btn fnl f) | 9 | **8** | 14/1 | 47 | 16 |
| | | | | (SP 114.5%) | **8 Rn** | |

**61.6 secs** (1.10) CSF £29.95 CT £98.97 TOTE £5.20: £1.50 £1.90 £1.10 (£16.80) OWNER Grid Thoroughbred Racing Partnership (WHITCOMBE) BRED Foxfield
**2976 Friendly Brave (USA)**, inclined to be lazy, is at his best when coming with a late run. (5/1)
**2957 Shadow Jury** was 6lb higher than when narrowly winning at Newmarket last month. (11/2)
**2586 Spender**, 5lb higher than when winning this race last year, was 2lb worse off with the runner-up when short-headed at Newmarket. (7/2)
**2957* Kildee Lad**, 10lb higher for his two victories, seems to find the bare minimum on the sharp side nowadays. (7/2)
**Windrush Boy**, down 5lb, was dropped out at the start after being very keen to post. (33/1)
**2508 Tart and a Half** has a career record of just one win in twenty-nine attempts. (15/2)

## 3339 SCANIA 4-SERIES 'HORSEPOWER' CLAIMING STKS (3-Y.O+) (Class E)

4-00 (4-01) **5f 161y** £3,031.50 (£912.00: £441.00: £205.50) Stalls: High GOING minus 0.43 sec per fur (F)

| Form | Horse | Dist | Pos | SP | RR | SF |
|---|---|---|---|---|---|---|
| 2578$^{10}$ | **Hever Golf Express (63)** (TJNaughton) **3-9-0** TSprake(5) (mde all: drvn out) | — | **1** | 9/1 | 63 | 50 |
| 3112$^{8}$ | **Prima Silk (69)** (MJRyan) **5-9-1** GBardwell(3) (hrd rdn & hdwy over 2f out: r.o ins fnl f) | nk | **2** | 9/2$^{3}$ | 59 | 50 |
| *2684$^{2}$* | **Songsheet (68)** (MartynMeade) **3-8-11** JReid(9) (a.p: rdn over 2f out: ev ch over 1f out: one pce) | 1¾ | **3** | 11/4$^{2}$ | 54 | 41 |
| 3294$^{7}$ | **Members Welcome (IRE) (52)** (JMBradley) **3-8-5v**(3) DaneO'Neill(1) (a.p: ev ch wl over 1f out: one pce) | ¾ | **4** | 20/1 | 49 | 36 |
| 2615$^{7}$ | **How's Yer Father (73)** (RJHodges) **10-8-8** SDrowne(2) (chsd ldrs: hrd rdn over 2f out: no hdwy) | 1½ | **5** | 6/4$^{1}$ | 41 | 32 |
| 1010$^{B}$ | **Dancing Lawyer (68)** (BJMeehan) **5-9-10** MTebbutt(6) (prom: stdd over 3f out: nvr plcd to chal) | ½ | **6** | 16/1 | 56 | 47 |
| 3162$^{14}$ | **Time Goes On** (RJHodges) **4-8-2**(5) PPMurphy(4) (hld up: a bhd) | 8 | **7** | 66/1 | 16 | 7 |
| 2713$^{9}$ | **Norling (IRE) (47)** (KOCunningham-Brown) **6-8-12** SWhitworth(7) (w wnr tl wknd over 2f out) | 1¼ | **8** | 20/1 | 18 | 9 |
| 3258$^{14}$ | **Athenian Alliance** (JMBradley) **7-8-1** NAdams(8) (s.i.s: a bhd) | nk | **9** | 66/1 | 6 | — |
| | | | | (SP 113.2%) | **9 Rn** | |

**1m 10.4** (0.90) CSF £44.93 TOTE £11.30: £1.70 £2.00 £1.10 (£26.90) Trio £16.30 OWNER Hever Racing Club I (EPSOM) BRED S. Tindall and Stowell Hill Ltd
WEIGHT FOR AGE 3yo-4lb
**1891 Hever Golf Express** seems at his best when dictating matters from the front. (9/1: 6/1-10/1)
**2311 Prima Silk**, tried in a visor two outings ago, appreciated the drop into a claimer but could not peg back the winner. (9/2)
**2684 Songsheet** appeared more effective over the bare five furlongs. (11/4)
**2800 Members Welcome (IRE)** would have been better off at the weights in a handicap. (20/1)
**2347 How's Yer Father** really needs six furlongs and, although well in at the weights, was a short price for a horse who has not scored since October 1994. (6/4)
**1010 Dancing Lawyer** has obviously taken time to recover from his crashing fall at Brighton and this seemed to be a confidence-booster. (16/1)

## 3340 WESTRUCKS - SCANIA KNOW HOW H'CAP (0-75) (3-Y.O+) (Class D)

4-30 (4-30) **1m 5y** £4,276.00 (£1,288.00: £624.00: £292.00) Stalls: Low GOING minus 0.43 sec per fur (F)

| Form | Horse | Dist | Pos | SP | RR | SF |
|---|---|---|---|---|---|---|
| 3052$^{13}$ | **Artful Dane (IRE) (62)** (MJHeaton-Ellis) **4-9-4** SDrowne(8) (hdwy over 2f out: hrd rdn to ld wl ins fnl f: r.o) | — | **1** | 25/1 | 72 | 50 |
| 2954* | **Star of Gold (72)** (CREgerton) **4-9-11**(3) DaneO'Neill(6) (chsd ldr: led over 4f out tl wl ins fnl f) | ¾ | **2** | 5/1$^{3}$ | 81 | 59 |
| 3052$^{2}$ | **Orchard Gold (48)** (JPearce) **5-8-4** GBardwell(5) (stdd s: rdn & hdwy over 2f out: r.o one pce fnl f) | nk | **3** | 5/2$^{1}$ | 56 | 34 |
| 3281$^{4}$ | **Delight of Dawn (65)** (RMStronge) **4-9-7** VSlattery(3) (hld up & bhd: hdwy fnl 2f: r.o) | 1 | **4** | 11/1 | 71 | 49 |
| 2526$^{10}$ | **Master Millfield (IRE) (69)** (RJBaker) **4-9-11** AMcGlone(1) (hld up: hdwy on ins over 3f out: ev ch 2f out: wknd over 1f out) | nk | **5** | 20/1 | 74 | 52 |
| 3109$^{4}$ | **Royal Thimble (IRE) (57)** (NoelChance) **5-8-8v**(5) MartinDwyer(7) (no hdwy fnl 2f) | ¾ | **6** | 10/1 | 61 | 39 |
| 3172$^{4}$ | **Great Bear (48)** (DWChapman) **4-8-4** GDuffield(9) (a.p: ev ch over 1f out: wknd fnl f) | ¾ | **7** | 9/2$^{2}$ | 50 | 28 |
| 3120$^{5}$ | **Sooty Tern (65)** (JMBradley) **9-9-0**(7) AEddery(11) (chsd ldrs over 5f) | ¾ | **8** | 12/1 | 66 | 44 |
| 3139$^{5}$ | **African-Pard (IRE) (63)** (DHaydnJones) **4-9-5v** JReid(10) (led over 3f: wknd over 2f out) | 2½ | **9** | 7/1 | 59 | 37 |
| 2189$^{10}$ | **Reefa's Mill (IRE) (53)** (JNeville) **4-8-6b**1(3) NVarley(4) (bhd fnl 3f) | 8 | **10** | 16/1 | 33 | 11 |
| | | | | (SP 115.5%) | **10 Rn** | |

**1m 40.1** (1.60) CSF £132.85 CT £394.46 TOTE £34.90: £5.50 £2.00 £1.70 (£104.90) Trio £71.80 OWNER S P Lansdown Racing (WROUGHTON) BRED R. A. Keogh
**1856 Artful Dane (IRE)**, dropped 3lb, found more patient tactics enabling him to spring a surprise. (25/1)
**2954* Star of Gold** took a while to get to his favourite pole position, but was only worn down late on. (5/1)
**3052 Orchard Gold**, up 2lb, had quite a lot to do at halfway and could never quite overhaul the front two. (5/2)
**3281 Delight of Dawn** could never get to grips with the principals. (11/1)
**2311 Master Millfield (IRE)**, still 4lb higher than when winning here last September, looked to be cruising on the inside until failing to deliver the goods. (20/1)
**3109 Royal Thimble (IRE)**, 7lb higher than when winning here last month, did not seem to appreciate this drop back to a mile. (10/1)

## 3341 SCANIA 4-SERIES 'KING OF THE ROAD' MAIDEN APPRENTICE H'CAP (0-80) (3-Y.O+) (Class E)

5-00 (5-01) **1m 2f 46y** £2,914.50 (£876.00: £423.00: £196.50) Stalls: Low GOING minus 0.43 sec per fur (F)

| | | | | SP | RR | SF |
|---|---|---|---|---|---|---|
| 2560[7] | **Printers Quill (44)** (MajorDNChappell) **4-8-0**(3)ow2 SophieMitchell(5) (mde all: hrd rdn fnl f: jst hld on) | — | 1 | 25/1 | 50 | 24 |
| 2506[2] | **Jean Pierre (55)** (JPearce) **3-8-0**(5) RFfrench(2) (s.i.s: hdwy over 4f out: chsd wnr over 3f out: hrd rdn & r.o ins fnl f) | s.h | 2 | 100/30[2] | 61 | 28 |
| 2718[8] | **Indian Sunset (55)** (CREgerton) **3-8-5** NVarley(6) (hld up: rdn 4f out: hdwy over 2f out: one pce appr fnl f) | 5 | 3 | 14/1[3] | 53 | 20 |
| 2074[12] | **Illuminate (77)** (MissGayKelleway) **3-9-13** DaneO'Neill(1) (lw: hld up & plld hrd: hdwy over 2f out: hrd rdn over 1f out: sn wknd) | 3½ | 4 | 6/5[1] | 70 | 37 |
| 2996[4] | **Santella Katie (70)** (MajorDNChappell) **3-9-6** SDrowne(7) (chsd wnr 5f: rdn & wknd over 2f out) | 9 | 5 | 100/30[2] | 49 | 16 |
| 2617[15] | **Severn Mill (65)** (JMBradley) **5-9-10** PPMurphy(3) (s.i.s: a bhd) | 10 | 6 | 50/1 | 28 | 4 |
| | **Magic Melody (70)** (PFICole) **3-9-1**(5) DavidO'Neill(4) (plld hrd: jnd wnr 6f out: rdn 4f out: wknd 2f out) | 2 | 7 | 14/1[3] | 30 | — |
| | | | | (SP 110.7%) | | **7 Rn** |

**2m 11.3** (3.80) CSF £96.49 TOTE £16.10: £3.20 £1.80 (£23.70) OWNER Mrs B. Woodford (WHITSBURY) BRED Mrs B. Woodford
WEIGHT FOR AGE 3yo-9lb

**Printers Quill,** who refused to settle when tried over a marathon trip here last time, caused an upset by the skin of his teeth. (25/1)
**2506 Jean Pierre**, raised 4lb, finally began to respond to pressure in the last 200 yards and only just failed to get up. (100/30)
**Indian Sunset**, a 36,000 guinea half-brother to Three Arch Bridge, is presumably destined for a career over hurdles. (14/1: op 7/1)
**1711 Illuminate** was disappointing on his first run for his new stable. (6/5)
**2996 Santella Katie** did not benefit from being stepped up from a mile. (100/30)
**Magic Melody** (14/1: op 8/1)

T/Plpt: £89.10 (161.41 Tckts). T/Qdpt: £17.90 (46.97 Tckts). KH

# 3236-HAMILTON (R-H) (Good to firm)
## Thursday August 8th

WEATHER: overcast WIND: mod bhd

## 3342 SCOTTISH RIFLES APPRENTICE H'CAP (0-70) (3-Y.O+) (Class E)

6-05 (6-05) **5f 4y** £2,968.75 (£910.00: £452.50: £223.75) Stalls: Low GOING minus 0.57 sec per fur (F)

| | | | | SP | RR | SF |
|---|---|---|---|---|---|---|
| 3252* | **Tropical Beach (64)** (JBerry) **3-9-5**(5) 7x CLowther(7) (bhd: hdwy 2f out: styd on to ld wl ins fnl f) | — | 1 | 9/2[3] | 68 | 53 |
| 3122[3] | **Silk Cottage (62)** (RMWhitaker) **4-9-6v**(5) PFredericks(1) (lw: chsd ldrs: rdn to ld 1f out: hdd & nt qckn wl ins fnl f) | ¾ | 2 | 3/1[1] | 64 | 52 |
| 3240[2] | **Pathaze (49)** (NBycroft) **3-8-9** AngelaGallimore(4) (outpcd: hdwy ½-wy: kpt on: nvr able to chal) | 1¾ | 3 | 5/1 | 45 | 30 |
| 3240* | **Natural Key (63)** (DHaydnJones) **3-9-9** 7x RMullen(8) (lw: hdwy ½-wy: ev ch 1f out: nt qckn) | s.h | 4 | 7/2[2] | 59 | 44 |
| 3122[7] | **Ramsey Hope (66)** (CWFairhurst) **3-9-12v[1]** JEdmunds(5) (chsd ldrs: effrt 2f out: sn btn) | 4 | 5 | 20/1 | 49 | 34 |
| 2960[4] | **Serious Hurry (45)** (RMMcKellar) **8-8-8b** KSked(3) (led: hung rt most of wy: wknd & hdd 1f out) | nk | 6 | 5/1 | 27 | 15 |
| 3294[3] | **Young Ben (IRE) (37)** (JSWainwright) **4-8-0v** JBramhill(2) (b: b.hind: lw: sn outpcd & bhd) | 2½ | 7 | 11/1 | 11 | — |
| 3292[8] | **Lord Cornelious (48)** (DANolan) **3-8-1**(7)ow12 DMcGaffin(6) (nvr wnt pce) | 10 | 8 | 100/1 | — | — |
| | | | | (SP 112.8%) | | **8 Rn** |

**58.6 secs** (0.30) CSF £17.22 CT £62.57 TOTE £3.80: £1.60 £1.60 £1.40 (£6.60) OWNER Mr Jim Unsworth (COCKERHAM) BRED P. Balding
LONG HANDICAP Lord Cornelious 7-3
WEIGHT FOR AGE 3yo-3lb
STEWARDS' ENQUIRY Mullen susp. 17-19/8/96 (failure to secure best possible placing).

**3252* Tropical Beach** got the strong pace he needs here and produced a great run from halfway to settle it in useful style late on. (9/2)
**3122 Silk Cottage** had his chances from halfway, but the winner's late surge was just too much for him. (3/1)
**3240 Pathaze** ran well again, but just found this trip a bit on the sharp side. (5/1)
**3240* Natural Key** is certainly better suited by six furlongs. Although holding every chance here, she could never quicken enough. (7/2)
**2238 Ramsey Hope** had the visor on for the first time, but it had little effect once pressure was applied. (20/1)
**2960 Serious Hurry** had speed to burn in the early stages, but spoilt his chances by continually hanging right. (5/1)

## 3343 HYNDFORD CLAIMING STKS (2-Y.O) (Class F)

6-35 (6-35) **6f 5y** £2,619.00 (£734.00: £357.00) Stalls: Low GOING minus 0.57 sec per fur (F)

| | | | | SP | RR | SF |
|---|---|---|---|---|---|---|
| 3092* | **Jay-Gee-Em** (RGuest) **2-8-7** AMackay(5) (cl up: led ½-wy: hung lft: kpt on wl fnl f) | — | 1 | 6/4[1] | 61 | 12 |
| 3057[5] | **Avinalarf (64)** (WGMTurner) **2-8-5**(7) DSweeney(1) (lw: prom tl edgd rt & outpcd ½-wy: styd on wl fnl f) | 1¾ | 2 | 4/1[3] | 61 | 12 |
| 3169* | **Abstone Queen (56)** (PDEvans) **2-8-2b** JFEgan(2) (chsd ldrs: sn drvn along: hung rt fr ½-wy: kpt on one pce fnl f) | ¾ | 3 | 2/1[2] | 49 | — |
| 3121[10] | **Sheraton Girl (60)** (MJohnston) **2-8-8** JWeaver(3) (w ldrs: rdn 2f out: bmpd over 1f out: sn btn) | 1¼ | 4 | 10/1 | 52 | 3 |
| *1459[4]* | **Contravene (IRE) (58)** (JBerry) **2-8-6** JFanning(6) (slt ld to ½-wy: wknd fnl 2f) | 9 | 5 | 8/1 | 26 | — |
| | **Lady Louise (IRE)** (MDHammond) **2-8-5**ow1 ACulhane(4) (angular: sn outpcd & t.o) | 26 | 6 | 66/1 | — | — |
| | | | | (SP 115.0%) | | **6 Rn** |

**1m 12.2** (2.20) CSF £7.82 TOTE £2.30: £1.90 £2.70 (£3.90) OWNER Mr Hugh O'Donnell (NEWMARKET) BRED Nidd Park Stud
Jay-Gee-Em clmd JParkes £7,500

**3092* Jay-Gee-Em** won well, despite showing a tendency to hang left and gave the impression that, on a flatter track, she can improve further. (6/4)
**3057 Avinalarf** got completely outpaced at halfway, but this good-looking filly certainly finished well and would seem to be much better suited by further. (4/1)
**3169* Abstone Queen**, very edgy beforehand, had her chances, but was inclined to hang under pressure and was never doing enough. (2/1)
**2569 Sheraton Girl,** who has a moderate action, did show plenty of speed but she failed to see it out on this occasion. (10/1: 8/1-12/1)
**1459 Contravene (IRE)** did not impress on looks and ran out of petrol soon after halfway. (8/1)

## 3344 WILLIAM HILL SCOTTISH TROPHY H'CAP (0-70) (3-Y.O+) (Class E)

7-05 (7-10) **1m 65y** £7,587.50 (£2,300.00: £1,125.00: £537.50) Stalls: High GOING minus 0.57 sec per fur (F)

| | | | | SP | RR | SF |
|---|---|---|---|---|---|---|
| 2679[2] | **Celebration Cake (IRE) (58)** (MissLAPerratt) **4-9-2** JWeaver(11) (lw: cl up: led over 2f out: r.o wl) | — | 1 | 7/1 | 73 | 50 |

| | | | | SP | RR | SF |
|---|---|---|---|---|---|---|
| $2077^{6}$ | **Bold Amusement (70)** (WSCunningham) **6-9-7b1**(7) DSweeney(4) (bhd: hdwy 3f out: styd on: no ch w wnr) | 4 | **2** | 10/1 | 77 | 54 |
| $3060^{5}$ | **Thatched (IRE) (45)** (REBarr) **6-7-10**(7) KSked(5) (in tch: effrt 4f out: one pce fnl 2½f) | 3 | **3** | 10/1 | 47 | 24 |
| 3151* | **Grey Kingdom (46)** (MBrittain) **5-8-4** 5x JLowe(13) (lw: led tl hdd over 2f out: grad wknd) | ½ | **4** | 10/1 | 47 | 24 |
| $2868^{4}$ | **Habeta (USA) (50)** (JWWatts) **10-8-8b** NConnorton(10) (lw: rr div: hdwy ½-wy: styd on one pce fnl 2f: no imp) | 1½ | **5** | 9/1 | 48 | 25 |
| *$2749^{2}$* | **Giftbox (USA) (57)** (SirMarkPrescott) **4-9-1** RPerham(1) (racd wd: mid div: hdwy u.p ½-wy: rdn & btn 2f out) | ½ | **6** | 11/4$^{1}$ | 54 | 31 |
| $3084^{10}$ | **Giddy (50)** (JHetherton) **3-8-1** NKennedy(12) (chsd ldrs tl wknd fnl 3f) | 3½ | **7** | 25/1 | 40 | 10 |
| $3280^{7}$ | **Reinhardt (IRE) (67)** (JSWainwright) **3-8-11**(7) JBramhill(9) (lw: mid div: sme hdwy 4f out: no imp) | ¾ | **8** | 50/1 | 56 | 26 |
| $2954^{6}$ | **King Curan (USA) (59)** (DHaydnJones) **5-9-3b** AMackay(7) (bhd: swtchd outside & effrt over 3f out: no imp) | 2½ | **9** | 5/1$^{3}$ | 43 | 20 |
| $3236^{4}$ | **Seconds Away (38)** (JSGoldie) **5-7-3**(7) IonaWands(3) (bhd: c wd st: n.d) | 3 | **10** | 20/1 | 16 | — |
| $3254^{2}$ | **Up in Flames (IRE) (69)** (MDHammond) **5-9-13** ACulhane(2) (mid div: effrt 4f out: sn bhd) | 3½ | **11** | 9/2$^{2}$ | 40 | 17 |
| $1866^{3}$ | **Raased (50)** (FWatson) **4-8-8** JFEgan(8) (v.unruly gng to s: s.i.s: n.d) | 5 | **12** | 20/1 | 12 | — |
| $884^{9}$ | **Nizaal (USA) (55)** (RAllan) **5-8-13** JFanning(6) (chsd ldrs tl wknd 4f out) | 1 | **13** | 20/1 | 15 | — |
| | | | | (SP 131.4%) | **13 Rn** | |

**1m 44.6** (0.50) CSF £75.14 CT £682.13 TOTE £7.40: £1.50 £5.20 £3.70 (£53.70) Trio £95.50 OWNER Lightbody of Hamilton Ltd (AYR) BRED John Davison

LONG HANDICAP Seconds Away 7-1

WEIGHT FOR AGE 3yo-7lb

**2679 Celebration Cake (IRE)**, always in the right place, was ridden aggressively in the last two furlongs and quickly left the opposition struggling. (7/1)

**2077 Bold Amusement**, in blinkers for the first time, ran pretty well, but always had too much on his plate to trouble the winner. (10/1)

**3060 Thatched (IRE)** was always close enough if good enough, but he was never giving it enough full co-operation under pressure. (10/1)

**3151* Grey Kingdom** attempted to make all again, but could never shake off the winner. Once passed approaching the last two furlongs, it all proved too much. (10/1)

**2868 Habeta (USA)** still looks on good terms with himself, but he was off the bit too far out on this occasion to seriously get into it. (9/1)

**2749 Giftbox (USA)** had an impossible task from his draw and lacked the early pace to take a good position. This effort is best ignored. (11/4)

## 3345 COURVOISIER CLASSIC LIMITED STKS (0-55) (3-Y.O+) (Class F)

7-35 (7-35) **6f 5y** £2,703.00 (£758.00: £369.00) Stalls: Low GOING minus 0.57 sec per fur (F)

| | | | | SP | RR | SF |
|---|---|---|---|---|---|---|
| $2960^{7}$ | **Leading Princess (IRE) (50)** (MissLAPerratt) **5-8-11b** JWeaver(4) (lw: mde all: all out) | — | **1** | 9/2$^{2}$ | 55 | 28 |
| 2849* | **King of Show (IRE) (54)** (RAllan) **5-9-6v** ACulhane(6) (sn outpcd & bhd: hdwy 2f out: sltly hmpd ins fnl f: fin wl) | nk | **2** | 9/2$^{2}$ | 63 | 36 |
| $3236^{3}$ | **Six for Luck (46)** (DANolan) **4-9-0** VHalliday(5) (chsd ldrs: hung bdly lft ins fnl f: kpt on one pce) | 1¾ | **3** | 8/1$^{3}$ | 53 | 26 |
| $3135^{2}$ | **L A Touch (51)** (CADwyer) **3-8-7** JStack(1) (lw: trckd ldrs: effrt 2f out: btn whn hmpd ins fnl f) | 1¼ | **4** | Evens$^{1}$ | 46 | 15 |
| $3252^{7}$ | **Brookhead Lady (50)** (PDEvans) **5-8-11** JFEgan(2) (chsd ldrs: btn whn hmpd ins fnl f) | hd | **5** | 12/1 | 46 | 19 |
| $3236^{6}$ | **Shaa Spin (50)** (JBerry) **4-8-6**(5) PRoberts(3) (cl up 4f: wknd) | 3 | **6** | 20/1 | 38 | 11 |
| | | | | (SP 109.9%) | **6 Rn** | |

**1m 11.3** (1.30) CSF £22.07 TOTE £4.10: £2.10 £2.10 (£7.40) OWNER Mrs Ruth Wyllie (AYR) BRED Woodford Stud

WEIGHT FOR AGE 3yo-4lb

STEWARDS' ENQUIRY Halliday susp. 17-23/8/96 (careless riding) & 24-26/8/96 (improper riding).

**2960 Leading Princess (IRE)**, well handled, took the race by the scruff of the neck and keeping out of trouble won her the day. (9/2: op 3/1)

**2849* King of Show (IRE)**, who got completely outpaced early on, then met with trouble when making his run and that probably made all the difference. (9/2)

**3236 Six for Luck** showed plenty of speed, but got completely unbalanced under vigorous pressure, causing a fair bit of trouble. His rider received a ban which he thoroughly deserved. (8/1)

**3135 L A Touch** did not travel quite as well this time and being hampered in the closing stages made no difference. The minimum trip may be her best. (Evens)

**2748 Brookhead Lady** is on a long losing run and never really looked likely to rectify that. (12/1: 7/1-14/1)

**Shaa Spin** ran as well as could be expected at these weights. (20/1)

## 3346 BRAVEHEART RACING CLUB H'CAP (0-65) (3-Y.O+) (Class F)

8-05 (8-05) **1m 3f 16y** £3,631.25 (£1,100.00: £537.50: £256.25) Stalls: High GOING minus 0.57 sec per fur (F)

| | | | | SP | RR | SF |
|---|---|---|---|---|---|---|
| 3242* | **Askern (70)** (DHaydnJones) **5-10-5** 5x AMackay(1) (lw: trckd ldrs: led 3f out: r.o wl) | — | **1** | 2/1$^{1}$ | 81 | 46 |
| 2152* | **Stormless (46)** (PMonteith) **5-8-6**(3) DarrenMoffatt(3) (hld up: hdwy 4f out: ev ch 2f out: nt qckn) | 2 | **2** | 11/2$^{3}$ | 54 | 19 |
| $3220^{10}$ | **Ambidextrous (IRE) (52)** (EJAlston) **4-8-12**(3) DWright(4) (lw: hld up & bhd: hdwy whn hmpd 3f out: swtchd outside over 2f out: styd on wl towards fin) | hd | **3** | 12/1 | 60 | 25 |
| $542^{W}$ | **Exclusion (38)** (JHetherton) **7-8-1** NKennedy(7) (led tl hdd & hung lft 3f out: wknd fnl 2f) | 1 | **4** | 12/1 | 45 | 10 |
| 3220* | **Gold Desire (38)** (MBrittain) **6-8-1** 5x JLowe(9) (in tch: effrt & swtchd rt 3f out: no imp) | 1¾ | **5** | 5/2$^{2}$ | 42 | 7 |
| $2563^{3}$ | **Trumped (IRE) (42)** (PMonteith) **4-7-12**(7) JBramhill(8) (chsd ldrs: n.m.r 3f out: wknd 2f out) | 6 | **6** | 9/1 | 37 | 2 |
| $3242^{4}$ | **Rapid Mover (38)** (DANolan) **9-7-8b**(7)ow5 KSked(6) (cl up tl wknd fnl 3f) | 1½ | **7** | 20/1 | 31 | — |
| $3098^{6}$ | **Manoy (55)** (JHetherton) **3-8-8b** JWeaver(5) (prom tl lost pl 4f out) | 6 | **8** | 20/1 | 40 | — |
| $2848^{7}$ | **Victor Laszlo (37)** (RAllan) **4-8-0** JFanning(2) (bhd & rdn 5f out: n.d) | 9 | **9** | 16/1 | 9 | — |
| | | | | (SP 118.1%) | **9 Rn** | |

**2m 22.8** (3.40) CSF £13.18 CT £92.80 TOTE £3.00: £1.60 £1.60 £1.80 (£6.60) Trio £16.50 OWNER Mr Hugh O'Donnell (PONTYPRIDD) BRED Highclere Stud Ltd

LONG HANDICAP Rapid Mover 7-7

WEIGHT FOR AGE 3yo-10lb

OFFICIAL EXPLANATION **Gold Desire: the jockey reported that the gelding did not act down the hill.**

**3242* Askern** is running his heart out at present and, once he stepped up the pace, he was always too strong for the opposition. (2/1)

**2152* Stormless** got warm beforehand but did run quite well after seven weeks off here, and should be all the better for it. (11/2)

**2847 Ambidextrous (IRE)** showed signs of coming back to form, but he had trouble in running and failed to get in a blow. (12/1)

**246 Exclusion** is off a good mark at present if he decides to put his best foot forward but, on this occasion, he just wanted to hang left when ridden. (12/1)

**3220* Gold Desire** is difficult to weigh up and was never doing enough when the pressure was on in the last half-mile. (5/2)

**2563 Trumped (IRE)**, very warm beforehand, soon threw in the towel when slightly squeezed for room three furlongs out. (9/1)

## 3347 CAMERONIANS H'CAP (0-70) (3-Y.O+) (Class E)

8-35 (8-35) **1m 5f 9y** £3,533.75 (£1,070.00: £522.50: £248.75) Stalls: High GOING minus 0.57 sec per fur (F)

| | Horse | Dist | Pos | SP | RR | SF |
|---|---|---|---|---|---|---|
| 2779[4] | **Monaco Gold (IRE) (39)** (MrsMReveley) **4-7-12**(3) DWright(2) (lw: hld up: effrt over 3f out: rdn over 2f out: styd on strly fnl f to ld nr fin) | — | 1 | 9/4[2] | 49 | 11 |
| 2784[8] | **Mentalasanythin (63)** (DHaydnJones) **7-9-11** AMackay(3) (trckd ldr: led & qcknd 2f out: hrd rdn fnl f: hdd & no ex towards fin) | hd | 2 | 7/4[1] | 73 | 35 |
| 2848[8] | **Red Spectacle (IRE) (48)** (PCHaslam) **4-8-3**(7) RMullen(1) (lw: led to 2f out: styd on wl towards fin) | ½ | 3 | 8/1[3] | 57 | 19 |
| 2871[5] | **Lawn Order (46)** (MrsJRRamsden) **3-7-10** NKennedy(5) (lw: trckd ldrs: effrt 3f out: sn btn) | 16 | 4 | 7/4[1] | 36 | — |
| | | | | (SP 114.6%) | | **4 Rn** |

**2m 50.9** (5.20) CSF £6.53 TOTE £2.80: (£2.70) OWNER Mr D. McGonagle (SALTBURN) BRED Miss M. Tucker

WEIGHT FOR AGE 3yo-12lb

STEWARDS' ENQUIRY Wright susp. 17-19/8/96 (excessive use of whip).

**2779 Monaco Gold (IRE)** really had to battle to win this, having looked beaten until suddenly producing a run to settle it late on. (9/4)

**619 Mentalasanythin** looked to have it sewn up when kicking for home two furlongs out, but he just ran out of fuel in the closing stages, and may still have needed this. (7/4)

**2355 Red Spectacle (IRE)** is looking better than ever physically, and rallied in splendid style at the finish to show he is coming to form. (8/1)

**2871 Lawn Order** was a big disappointment here, dropping tamely away in the last three furlongs. (7/4)

T/Plpt: £173.50 (65.13 Tckts). T/Qdpt: £47.20 (17.98 Tckts). AA

# 2865-PONTEFRACT (L-H) (Good to firm)

## Thursday August 8th

WEATHER: overcast WIND: mod half bhd

## 3348 BOLLINGER CHAMPAGNE CHALLENGE SERIES GENTLEMENS' H'CAP (0-70) (3-Y.O+) (Class F)

2-45 (2-46) **1m 2f 6y** £2,950.00 (£880.00: £420.00: £190.00) Stalls: Low GOING minus 0.38 sec per fur (F)

| | Horse | Dist | Pos | SP | RR | SF |
|---|---|---|---|---|---|---|
| 2803[4] | **Essayeffsee (57)** (MrsMReveley) **7-11-7** MrMHNaughton(10) (mid div: hdwy 2f out: swtchd rt 1f out: r.o to ld wl ins fnl f: rdn out) | — | 1 | 5/1[3] | 68 | 57 |
| 2922[7] | **Bold Top (37)** (BSRothwell) **4-9-11**(4) MrRThornton(8) (led: rdn over 1f out: hdd wl ins fnl f: no ex) | 2 | 2 | 20/1 | 45 | 34 |
| 3134[4] | **Advance East (56)** (MrsJRRamsden) **4-11-6** MrSSwiers(7) (mid div: hdwy on ins 2f out: ev ch ins fnl f: nt qckn cl home) | ½ | 3 | 9/4[1] | 63 | 52 |
| 3111[7] | **Montone (IRE) (64)** (JRJenkins) **6-11-10v**(4) DrMMannish(4) (prom: rdn over 2f out: outpcd over 1f out) | 7 | 4 | 9/1 | 60 | 49 |
| 2683[4] | **Never Time (IRE) (38)** (MrsVAAconley) **4-9-12**(4)ow4 MrGMarkham(1) (hld up: hdwy 2f out: kpt on ins fnl f: nt rch ldrs) | ¾ | 5 | 33/1 | 33 | 18 |
| 2896[12] | **D'naan (IRE) (57)** (WJHaggas) **3-10-12b** MrPScott(2) (in rr: late hdwy: nvr nrr) | 1¼ | 6 | 14/1 | 50 | 30 |
| 3134[2] | **Blurred (IRE) (68)** (MHTompkins) **3-11-5**(4) MrMJenkins(3) (in tch: effrt 2f out: sn btn) | hd | 7 | 100/30[2] | 61 | 41 |
| 2989[4] | **Golden Hadeer (41)** (MJRyan) **5-10-1**(4) MrSLavallin(11) (b: w ldr: pushed along over 2f out: wknd over 1f out) | 2 | 8 | 16/1 | 30 | 19 |
| 3084[7] | **Commander Glen (IRE) (57)** (MrsJRRamsden) **4-11-7b** MrCBonner(6) (hld up: pushed along 3f out: n.d) | 1 | 9 | 9/1 | 45 | 34 |
| 2358[2] | **Fairy Highlands (IRE) (56)** (JSHaldane) **3-10-7**(4) MrJAStack(9) (mid div tl wknd qckly 2f out) | 13 | 10 | 20/1 | 23 | 3 |
| 2922[5] | **Master Ofthe House (49)** (MDHammond) **10-10-9**(4) MrTWhitaker(5) (swtg: trckd ldrs: rdn along 2f out: t.o) | 12 | 11 | 12/1 | — | — |
| | | | | (SP 123.2%) | | **11 Rn** |

**2m 14.0** (5.70) CSF £88.30 CT £265.92 TOTE £5.10: £1.60 £9.40 £1.50 (£56.00) Trio £223.80 OWNER Mrs S. D. Murray (SALTBURN) BRED Mrs L. F. Rathbone

WEIGHT FOR AGE 3yo-9lb

**2803 Essayeffsee**, racing off a 9lb higher mark this year, landed this event for the second consecutive season. The seven year old's six wins have all been over ten furlongs. (5/1)

**1697 Bold Top** put in a valiant effort from the front in pursuit of that elusive first victory. (20/1)

**3134 Advance East**, still a maiden, held every chance inside the final furlong. (9/4)

**2628 Montone (IRE)** was taken to post early. This six-year-old gelding was prominent until folding over a furlong out and has had quite a hectic campaign. (9/1)

**2683 Never Time (IRE)** was taken to post early. He is still a maiden after thirty-two attempts, but was noted making late progress without threatening the leaders. (33/1)

## 3349 CORNMILL HOTEL (HULL) MAIDEN STKS (2-Y.O) (Class D)

3-15 (3-17) **6f** £3,327.50 (£1,010.00: £495.00: £237.50) Stalls: Low GOING minus 0.38 sec per fur (F)

| | Horse | Dist | Pos | SP | RR | SF |
|---|---|---|---|---|---|---|
| | **Irish Accord (USA)** (MrsJRRamsden) **2-9-0** KFallon(1) (hld up: hdwy 2f out: led ins fnl f: hung bdly rt cl home: readily) | — | 1 | 16/1 | 80 | 26 |
| 2353[2] | **Amid Albadu (USA)** (JLDunlop) **2-9-0** RHills(5) (lw: in tch: effrt & hdwy 2f out: ev ch ins fnl f: rn green: no ex cl home) | 2 | 2 | Evens[1] | 75 | 21 |
| | **Symonds Inn** (JGFitzGerald) **2-9-0** WRyan(6) (lw: hld up: hdwy over 1f out: styd on: nt rch ldrs) | 5 | 3 | 16/1 | 61 | 7 |
| 2802[5] | **Italian Symphony (IRE)** (MJohnston) **2-9-0** KDarley(7) (led: rdn & hdd ins fnl f: one pce) | hd | 4 | 11/4[2] | 61 | 7 |
| *1489*[6] | **Paddy Lad (IRE)** (RGuest) **2-9-0** PBloomfield(10) (prom: rdn & ev ch ent fnl f: no ex) | ¾ | 5 | 50/1 | 59 | 5 |
| 1433[4] | **Terry's Rose** (RHollinshead) **2-8-6**(3) FLynch(2) (mid div: effrt over 2f out: sn no imp) | 1¾ | 6 | 20/1 | 49 | — |
| | **Coral Strand** (JWWatts) **2-8-9** JCarroll(9) (in rr: sme late hdwy: n.d) | 3 | 7 | 16/1 | 41 | — |
| 3044[5] | **Spaniard's Mount** (MHTompkins) **2-9-0** PRobinson(12) (chsd ldrs: drvn along over 2f out: sn wknd) | 1½ | 8 | 9/1[3] | 42 | — |
| | **Saint Who (USA)** (WAO'Gorman) **2-9-0** TIves(4) (s.i.s: nvr trbld ldrs) | 6 | 9 | 20/1 | 26 | — |
| 568[8] | **Lucybod** (NTinkler) **2-8-9** LCharnock(8) (swtg: mid div: pushed along ½-wy: sn wknd) | 4 | 10 | 50/1 | 11 | — |
| | **Duston Boy** (JWhite) **2-9-0** DaleGibson(3) (bkwd: a bhd) | 1¼ | 11 | 50/1 | 12 | — |
| 2416[5] | **Paldost** (MDHammond) **2-9-0** JFortune(11) (mid div tl wknd 2f out) | 1½ | 12 | 50/1 | 8 | — |
| | **Mysterium** (NPLittmoden) **2-9-0** TGMcLaughlin(13) (lt-f: dwlt: a rr div) | ¾ | 13 | 50/1 | 6 | — |
| | | | | (SP 123.6%) | | **13 Rn** |

**1m 17.4** (3.10) CSF £31.91 TOTE £12.30: £2.70 £1.20 £4.50 (£9.90) Trio £131.50 OWNER Mr P. A. Leonard (THIRSK) BRED Jerome Hyams and Flint S. Schulhofer

**Irish Accord (USA)**, big and American-bred, made a successful racecourse debut, despite hanging badly right in the closing stages. However, this $50,000 son of a juvenile sprint winner in the States was winning with a bit in hand. (16/1)
**2353 Amid Albadu (USA)** held every chance of breaking his maiden tag, but failed to match the winner's extra gear. This son of Sheikh Albadou still has a fair amount to learn about the game, having once again proved fairly green. (Evens)
**Symonds Inn**, a son of Group One winner In the Wings, was putting in his best work towards the end. This half-brother to two winners will certainly appreciate a step up in trip, and is highly regarded as he holds a Derby entry. (16/1)
**2802 Italian Symphony (IRE)** led until inside the final furlong, and this half-brother to a useful juvenile winner in the States is capable of winning in the right grade. (11/4: 4/1-5/2)
**Paddy Lad (IRE)** was returning after a ten-week absence and showed up well until folding inside the final furlong. (50/1)

## 3350 AUGUST CLAIMING STKS (3-Y.O) (Class F)

3-45 (3-47) **5f** £2,666.60 (£737.60: £351.80) Stalls: Low GOING minus 0.38 sec per fur (F)

| | | | | SP | RR | SF |
|---|---|---|---|---|---|---|
| | **Zalotti (IRE)** (TJEtherington) **3-8-11** KDarley(4) (lw: trckd ldrs: effrt over 2f out: qcknd to ld ins fnl f: comf) ... | — | 1 | 3/1[2] | 84+ | 17 |
| 3154[2] | **No Monkey Nuts (76)** (JBerry) **3-8-13** JCarroll(7) (a.p: led jst ins fnl f: sn hdd: nt pce of wnr) ... | 1¼ | 2 | 10/11[1] | 82 | 15 |
| 3215[4] | **Chemcast (67)** (DNicholls) **3-8-13b** AlexGreaves(6) (led: hdd jst ins fnl f: no ex) ... | 2½ | 3 | 9/1 | 74 | 7 |
| 3055[11] | **Comic Fantasy (AUS) (71)** (MartynWane) **3-8-6** JFortune(8) (trckd ldrs: effrt 2f out: one pce fr over 1f out) ... | ¾ | 4 | 9/2[3] | 65 | — |
| *2634[6]* | **Boffy (IRE) (52)** (BPJBaugh) **3-8-9** NCarlisle(3) (in tch: pushed along 2f out: nt pce to chal) ... | hd | 5 | 33/1 | 21 t | — |
| *298[W]* | **Ginas Girl** (MissJBower) **3-8-4** TWilliams(1) (dwlt: towards rr: rdn over 2f out: sn no imp: eased whn btn ins fnl f) ... | 2 | 6 | 40/1 | 10 t | — |
| | **Imperial Red (IRE)** (HJCollingridge) **3-8-7** KFallon(5) (bkwd: a bdly outpcd: wl bhd: t.o) ... | 23 | 7 | 16/1 | — | — |
| | ***My Achates*** (MBrittain) **3-8-1** DaleGibson(2) (Withdrawn not under Starter's orders: unruly s) ... | | W | 33/1 | | |
| | | | | (SP 119.8%) | **7 Rn** | |

**63.7 secs** (2.90) CSF £6.17 TOTE £3.70: £2.20 £1.30 (£2.60) OWNER Mr P. D. Savill (MALTON) BRED Peter Savill
Zalotti (IRE) clmd MTompkins £15,000
**Zalotti (IRE)** is reported to have fractured her off-hind cannon-bone at home since her debut win as a juvenile. This 17,000 guinea yearling showed she was back on song when quickening up to land this claimer cosily. She was the subject of many claims after the race. (3/1)
**3154 No Monkey Nuts** is in good heart with himself, but he failed to match the winner's turn of foot on this occasion. (10/11: 5/4-5/6)
**3215 Chemcast** once again showed plenty of speed, but failed to handle the front two. He possibly needs an easier course. (9/1: 6/1-10/1)
**2778 Comic Fantasy (AUS)** failed to quicken as well as the principals, but this is her trip. (9/2: 3/1-5/1)
**272 Boffy (IRE)** could never reach the leaders. (33/1)
**209 Ginas Girl** was taken to post early, but never figured during the race. (40/1)

## 3351 ROGERTHORPE MANOR HOTEL H'CAP (0-90) (3-Y.O+) (Class C)

4-15 (4-16) **1m 4f 8y** £7,895.00 (£2,360.00: £1,130.00: £515.00) Stalls: Low GOING minus 0.38 sec per fur (F)

| | | | | SP | RR | SF |
|---|---|---|---|---|---|---|
| 2131[8] | **Time for Action (IRE) (78)** (MHTompkins) **4-9-2** PRobinson(5) (mde all: shkn up 2f out: pushed clr fnl f) ... | — | 1 | 13/2[3] | 91 | 35 |
| 2969[4] | **Artic Courier (85)** (DJSCosgrove) **5-9-9** JStack(3) (hld up in rr: hdwy to chse wnr over 2f out: no imp over 1f out) ... | 9 | 2 | 13/2[3] | 86 | 30 |
| 2949* | **Lear Express (USA) (85)** (HRACecil) **3-8-12** WRyan(4) (chsd wnr: pushed along 5f out: lost pl over 2f out: sn btn) ... | ¾ | 3 | 4/5[1] | 85 | 18 |
| 2825a[6] | **Glide Path (USA) (87)** (JWHills) **7-9-11** RHills(2) (hld up: cl up 5f out: wknd 2f out: eased whn btn over 1f out: t.o) ... | dist | 4 | 3/1[2] | — | — |
| | | | | (SP 107.2%) | **4 Rn** | |

**2m 39.8** (5.50) CSF £32.16 TOTE £6.40: (£14.50) OWNER Mrs G. A. E. Smith (NEWMARKET) BRED J. C. Condon
WEIGHT FOR AGE 3yo-11lb
**Time for Action (IRE)** made good use of a lower handicap mark, trouncing his rivals to gain a second career victory. The Tote Ebor is reportedly on the agenda. (13/2)
**2969 Artic Courier** failed to live with the winner inside the final furlong. (13/2)
**2949* Lear Express (USA)** gave supporters little to cheer about, coming under pressure a long way from home. (4/5)
**2825a Glide Path (USA)**, a Group Three winner on the continent, was eased considerably when well held over a furlong out. He has yet to fire this term. (3/1)

## 3352 CHAPLINS CLUB H'CAP (0-70) (3-Y.O+) (Class E)

4-45 (4-49) **5f** £3,752.50 (£1,120.00: £535.00: £242.50) Stalls: Low GOING minus 0.38 sec per fur (F)

| | | | | SP | RR | SF |
|---|---|---|---|---|---|---|
| 3085[5] | **Rich Glow (60)** (NBycroft) **5-9-5** KDarley(10) (mid div: pushed along ½-wy: hdwy over 1f out: r.o to ld cl home) ... | — | 1 | 6/1[3] | 64 | 22 |
| 3055[8] | **Ned's Bonanza (59)** (MDods) **7-9-4** AClark(11) (in tch: effrt & hdwy 2f out: led ins fnl f: hdd & no ex cl home) ... | hd | 2 | 10/1 | 63 | 21 |
| 3106[5] | **Captain Carat (66)** (MrsJRRamsden) **5-9-11** KFallon(2) (mid div: rdn & hdwy over 1f out: styd on) ... | 1½ | 3 | 4/1[1] | 65 | 23 |
| 2719[3] | **Sonderise (54)** (NTinkler) **7-8-13** JCarroll(1) (b: in tch: effrt 2f out: chsd ldrs ins fnl f: kpt on same pce) ... | ½ | 4 | 11/1 | 51 | 9 |
| 3085[10] | **Just Dissident (IRE) (58)** (RMWhitaker) **4-9-0**(3) FLynch(3) (chsd ldr: rdn & ev ch ent fnl f: nt qckn) ... | ½ | 5 | 4/1[1] | 54 | 12 |
| 3294* | **Kabcast (48)** (DWChapman) **11-8-7b** 7x LCharnock(9) (led tl ins fnl f: one pce) ... | s.h | 6 | 11/1 | 44 | 2 |
| 2964[5] | **Rockcracker (IRE) (65)** (GGMargarson) **4-9-10b** PRobinson(8) (in rr: sme late hdwy: nvr trbld ldrs) ... | hd | 7 | 14/1 | 60 | 18 |
| 473[2] | **Polar Refrain (53)** (CADwyer) **3-8-9** TGMcLaughlin(5) (in rr: effrt on ins 2f out: n.d) ... | 2 | 8 | 20/1 | 42 | — |
| 3294[10] | **Gondo (39)** (EJAlston) **9-7-12** DaleGibson(6) (a towards rr & pushed along) ... | 3 | 9 | 20/1 | 18 | — |
| 3252[3] | **Dominelle (53)** (TDEasterby) **4-8-12** MBirch(7) (chsd ldrs: rdn & wknd over 1f out) ... | 2½ | 10 | 11/2[2] | 24 | — |
| *2960[W]* | ***Swan At Whalley (69)*** (MartynWane) **4-10-0** JFortune(4) (Withdrawn not under Starter's orders: ref to ent stalls) ... | | W | 12/1 | — | — |
| | | | | (SP 119.3%) | **10 Rn** | |

**63.9 secs** (3.10) CSF £52.83 CT £216.22 TOTE £6.80: £2.10 £2.40 £1.70 (£45.70) Trio £63.70 OWNER Mr M. J. Bateson (BRANDSBY) BRED P. Young
WEIGHT FOR AGE 3yo-3lb
**OFFICIAL EXPLANATION Dominelle: was unable to act on the track.**
**3085 Rich Glow**, suited by a stiff five furlongs, was winning away from Ayr for the first time, gaining a narrow verdict in the dying strides. (6/1)
**2757* Ned's Bonanza**, a top-of-the-ground performer, was just run out of it close home. (10/1)
**3106 Captain Carat** was once again slow to leave the stalls, but still ran a sound race and is capable of landing a similar event. (4/1)

**2719 Sonderise** failed to shake up the principals. (11/1)
**3085 Just Dissident (IRE)** showed plenty of dash for most of the way. (4/1)
**3294* Kabcast** adopted his usual front-running tactics, but gave way inside the final furlong. (11/1)

## 3353 MATTY BOWN MEMORIAL MAIDEN STKS (3-Y.O+) (Class D)

5-15 (5-16) **1m 4y** £3,712.50 (£1,125.00: £550.00: £262.50) Stalls: Low GOING minus 0.38 sec per fur (F)

| | | | | SP | RR | SF |
|---|---|---|---|---|---|---|
| | **Jamrat Jumairah (IRE)** (EALDunlop) **3-8-9** KFallon(8) (b: lw: a in tch: hdwy 2f out: led over 1f out: sn clr: easily) | — | **1** | 5/4 $^{1}$ | 91+ | 41 |
| 2579$^{6}$ | **Glen Parker (IRE) (76)** (HRACecil) **3-9-0** WRyan(3) (lw: led: rdn & hdd over 1f out: one pce) | 5 | **2** | 11/2 | 86 | 36 |
| 2888$^{10}$ | **Really A Dream (IRE) (83)** (MRStoute) **3-8-9** KDarley(4) (prom: ev ch 2f out: one pce over 1f out) | 2 | **3** | 7/2 $^{2}$ | 77 | 27 |
| | **Silvretta (IRE)** (ACStewart) **3-8-9** DHarrison(2) (hld up: pushed along on ins over 2f out: hdwy wl over 1f out: styd on: nt rch ldrs) | nk | **4** | 16/1 | 76 | 26 |
| 3067$^{6}$ | **Fourdaned (IRE) (88)** (PWHarris) **3-9-0** GHind(1) (trckd ldrs: effrt over 2f out: sn btn) | 7 | **5** | 9/2 $^{3}$ | 68 | 18 |
| | **Roi du Nord (FR)** (SWCampion) **4-9-7** TIves(6) (bkwd: hld up: pushed along over 3f out: nt trble ldrs) | 5 | **6** | 50/1 | 58 | 15 |
| 2718$^{3}$ | **Midday Cowboy (USA)** (GHarwood) **3-9-0** AClark(7) (hld up: hdwy u.p over 2f out: sn no imp: eased whn btn over 1f out) | ¾ | **7** | 11/1 | 56 | 6 |
| 2996$^{10}$ | **Classic Royale (USA)** (RHarris) **3-8-9** DBatteate(5) (cl up tl wknd over 2f out) | ½ | **8** | 50/1 | 50 | — |
| | **Crambella (IRE)** (GPKelly) **4-8-11**(5) GParkin(10) (bkwd: s.s: bhd: sn pushed along: n.d) | 5 | **9** | 200/1 | 40 | — |
| 2515$^{4}$ | **Isit Izzy** (BAMcMahon) **4-9-2** JFortune(9) (cl up tl rdn & wknd qckly over 2f out) | 9 | **10** | 25/1 | 22 | — |
| | **Beano Script** (MissSEHall) **3-9-0** MBirch(12) (bkwd: in tch: wknd qckly over 2f out: eased whn btn ins fnl f) | 15 | **11** | 50/1 | — | — |
| | **Etoile du Nord** (HJCollingridge) **4-9-7** PRobinson(11) (b: bkwd: sn bhd) | 7 | **12** | 100/1 | — | — |

(SP 125.7%) **12 Rn**

**1m 43.8** (2.30) CSF £9.25 TOTE £2.40: £1.60 £1.60 £1.30 (£9.00) Trio £12.50 OWNER Sheikh Ahmed Al Maktoum (NEWMARKET) BRED Roncon and Churchtown House Stud
WEIGHT FOR AGE 3yo-7lb

**Jamrat Jumairah (IRE)** has obviously had her problems, but this half-sister to classy miler Waajib easily brushed aside the opposition. (5/4)
**2579 Glen Parker (IRE)**, a brother to useful miler Clan Ben, tried to make all, but was no match for the winner from the distance. (11/2)
**874 Really A Dream (IRE)** could only plug on at one pace in the closing stages. (7/2: 3/1-5/1)
**Silvretta (IRE)**, by 2000 Guineas winner Tirol and out of a useful seven-furlong and mile performer in Ireland, shaped with promise, staying on without troubling the leaders. (16/1)
**3067 Fourdaned (IRE)** was a spent force from the home turn. (9/2: op 3/1)
**2718 Midday Cowboy (USA)** proved a shade disappointing after his debut run and was eased considerably when his chance had gone over a furlong out. (11/1: 8/1-12/1)

## 3354 TALLY HO H'CAP (0-65) (3-Y.O) (Class F)

5-45 (5-47) **1m 4y** £3,248.00 (£903.00: £434.00) Stalls: Low GOING minus 0.38 sec per fur (F)

| | | | | SP | RR | SF |
|---|---|---|---|---|---|---|
| 2902$^{7}$ | **Lapu-Lapu (47)** (MJCamacho) **3-8-10** LCharnock(8) (in tch: hdwy 2f out: led wl ins fnl f: kpt on gamely) | — | **1** | 8/1 $^{3}$ | 59 | 24 |
| 3102$^{6}$ | **Falcon's Flame (USA) (53)** (MrsJRRamsden) **3-9-2** KFallon(4) (trckd ldrs: effrt over 2f out: led briefly wl ins fnl f: kpt on u.p) | hd | **2** | 11/4 $^{1}$ | 65 | 30 |
| 2752$^{7}$ | **Cottage Prince (IRE) (38)** (JJQuinn) **3-8-1** TWilliams(3) (mid div: hdwy u.p over 2f out: styd on ins fnl f) | 3 | **3** | 14/1 | 44 | 9 |
| 3228$^{2}$ | **Gool Lee Shay (USA) (46)** (RMWhitaker) **3-8-9** WRyan(12) (prom: led over 1f out tl wl ins fnl f: one pce) | ½ | **4** | 100/30 $^{2}$ | 51 | 16 |
| 2752$^{6}$ | **Contract Bridge (IRE) (46)** (CWThornton) **3-8-9** DeanMcKeown(14) (s.i.s: in rr: drvn along ½-wy: hdwy 2f out: styd on) | s.h | **5** | 8/1 $^{3}$ | 51 | 16 |
| 2180$^{5}$ | **Richard House Lad (44)** (RHollinshead) **3-8-4**(3) FLynch(13) (hld up: hdwy 2f out: kpt on u.p ins fnl f: nt rch ldrs) | ½ | **6** | 12/1 | 48 | 13 |
| *2937$^{5}$* | **Down The Yard (35)** (MCChapman) **3-7-5**(7) JFowle(2) (bhd: late hdwy u.p: nvr nrr) | hd | **7** | 20/1 | 39 | 4 |
| *3089$^{5}$* | **Angus McCoatup (IRE) (52)** (BAMcMahon) **3-9-1** JFortune(1) (led tl over 1f out: sn btn) | 3½ | **8** | 12/1 | 49 | 14 |
| 2899$^{7}$ | **Paper Maze (43)** (EHOwenjun) **3-7-13**(7) RCody-Boutcher(6) (trckd ldrs: pushed along over 2f out: sn wknd) | 7 | **9** | 50/1 | 26 | — |
| *3089$^{4}$* | **Seeking Destiny (IRE) (44)** (MCChapman) **3-8-4b**(3) PMcCabe(7) (s.v.s: a bhd) | 4 | **10** | 16/1 | 19 | — |
| 3102$^{7}$ | **Dispol Duchess (40)** (GROldroyd) **3-8-3** DaleGibson(11) (mid div: pushed along ½-wy: wknd over 2f out) | 2½ | **11** | 16/1 | 10 | — |
| 2752$^{13}$ | **Totally Different (34)** (GROldroyd) **3-7-11v**ow1 NCarlisle(9) (s.v.s: a bhd: drvn along over 3f out: no imp) | s.h | **12** | 50/1 | 4 | — |
| 3107$^{6}$ | **Gilling Dancer (IRE) (58)** (PCalver) **3-9-7b**[1] MBirch(5) (s.v.s: mid div after 2f: rdn & wknd over 3f out: t.o) | 18 | **13** | 9/1 | — | — |
| 2683$^{9}$ | **Gold Lining (IRE) (48)** (EJAlston) **3-8-11** JCarroll(10) (cl up tl wknd qckly over 2f out: t.o) | | **14** | 33/1 | — | — |

(SP 127.4%) **14 Rn**

**1m 45.7** (4.20) CSF £30.17 CT £293.05 TOTE £12.30: £3.00 £1.60 £4.90 (£23.90) Trio £267.30 OWNER Mr Dunstan French (MALTON) BRED Mrs S. Camacho
LONG HANDICAP Totally Different 7-2

**2902 Lapu-Lapu** appreciated this step up to a mile with a hard-fought victory. (8/1: op 9/2)
**3102 Falcon's Flame (USA)** managed to get his head in front briefly inside the final furlong, but could not hold the determined efforts of the winner. (11/4)
**Cottage Prince (IRE)** achieved his best placing ever with this effort, and may be capable of landing a seller. (14/1)
**3228 Gool Lee Shay (USA)**, despite running off a mark 10lb lower than when finishing second last time, could not hold onto his lead inside the final furlong. (100/30)

T/Jkpt: Not won; £8,366.34 to Wolverhampton 9/8/96. T/Plpt: £187.80 (101.93 Tckts). T/Qdpt: £211.90 (4.17 Tckts). DO

# 3168-YARMOUTH (L-H) (Good to firm)

## Thursday August 8th

WEATHER: fine WIND: mod against

## 3355 EAST COAST H'CAP (0-80) (3-Y.O+) (Class D)

5-50 (5-50) **1m 6f 17y** £4,053.10 (£1,211.80: £580.40: £264.70) Stalls: High GOING minus 0.42 sec per fur (F)

| | | | | SP | RR | SF |
|---|---|---|---|---|---|---|
| 3073$^{8}$ | **Chatham Island (70)** (CEBrittain) **8-9-7** BDoyle(4) (lw: trckd ldr: rdn over 3f out: led over 1f out: hld on wl) | — | **1** | 6/4 $^{1}$ | 79 | 60 |

| | | | | SP | RR | SF |
|---|---|---|---|---|---|---|
| 2973$^{5}$ | **Farringdon Hill (77)** (MajorWRHern) **5-10-0b** PaulEddery(2) (lw: led tl over 1f out: r.o) | 1¼ | **2** | 4/1$^{2}$ | 85 | 66 |
| 2505$^{5}$ | **Shirley Venture (74)** (SPCWoods) **3-8-12** WWoods(3) (chsd ldrs: rdn over 3f out: ev ch over 1f out: one pce) | 1¾ | **3** | 13/2 | 80 | 48 |
| 3037$^{12}$ | **Sarasota Storm (52)** (MBell) **4-8-3** MFenton(1) (dwlt: hld up: effrt 3f out: no imp appr fnl f) | 3½ | **4** | 9/2$^{3}$ | 54 | 35 |
| 2707$^{4}$ | **Frozen Sea (USA) (65)** (GPEnright) **5-9-2** RCochrane(5) (in tch tl rdn & wknd over 2f out) | 16 | **5** | 13/2 | 48 | 29 |

(SP 104.8%) **5 Rn**

**3m 1.4** (2.00) CSF £6.83 TOTE £1.90: £1.40 £2.60 (£4.60) OWNER Mr B. H. Voak (NEWMARKET) BRED G. C. Hughes
WEIGHT FOR AGE 3yo-13lb

**2921 Chatham Island**, stepping up in trip, looked in trouble for a long time in the straight, but finally managed to get on top. (6/4)
**2973 Farringdon Hill**, able to dictate matters this time, stuck to his task in a drawn-out struggle with the winner. (4/1)
**2505 Shirley Venture** gradually closed on the leaders in the straight, but was under pressure for some time, and the effort took its toll once she reached a challenging position. (13/2)
**2848* Sarasota Storm**, who has never won away from Musselburgh, made only a brief effort in the straight. (9/2)
**1695* Frozen Sea (USA)** was never travelling once in line for home and seems to have gone off the boil. (13/2)

## 3356 MANSHIP MAIDEN STKS (3-Y.O+) (Class D)

6-20 (6-20) **1m 3f 101y** £4,488.50 (£1,343.00: £644.00: £294.50) Stalls: Low GOING minus 0.42 sec per fur (F)

| | | | | SP | RR | SF |
|---|---|---|---|---|---|---|
| 2949$^{3}$ | **Welcome Parade** (HRACecil) **3-8-11** PatEddery(1) (lw: trckd ldr: shkn up 3f out: led 2f out: pushed out) | — | **1** | 1/4$^{1}$ | 83+ | 34 |
| 2399$^{7}$ | **Lucky Hoof** (CEBrittain) **3-8-6** BDoyle(3) (dwlt: in tch: rdn over 2f out: kpt on fnl f: no ch w wnr) | 3½ | **2** | 14/1$^{3}$ | 73 | 24 |
| 2955$^{2}$ | **Naseem Alsahar (72)** (MajorWRHern) **3-8-6b** PaulEddery(4) (lw: led to 2f out: rdn & no rspnse appr fnl f) | 3 | **3** | 4/1$^{2}$ | 69 | 20 |
| 2794$^{5}$ | **Supermodel** (MrsNMacauley) **4-8-13**(3) CTeague(2) (s.i.s: bhd: effrt over 3f out: sn btn) | 6 | **4** | 33/1 | 61 | 22 |

(SP 109.6%) **4 Rn**

**2m 27.0** (4.00) CSF £4.07 TOTE £1.30: (£3.60) OWNER Mr K. Abdulla (NEWMARKET) BRED Juddmonte Farms
WEIGHT FOR AGE 3yo-10lb

**2949 Welcome Parade** hardly moves like a fast-ground horse, but still had too many gears for this opposition after briefly looking in trouble. (1/4)
**Lucky Hoof** is a good mover but, when initially asked for an effort, put her head in the air as if feeling the ground. She did stay on well eventually, and has the ability to find a small race. (14/1: 8/1-16/1)
**2955 Naseem Alsahar** strode along well at the head of affairs and looked to be travelling best but, once battle commenced, she surrendered tamely. (4/1: 3/1-9/2)
**2794 Supermodel**, who is alternating between Flat and hurdles, lost all chance at the start. (33/1)

## 3357 FREETHORPE CLAIMING STKS (3-Y.O) (Class F)

6-50 (6-50) **1m 2f 21y** £2,945.20 (£817.20: £391.60) Stalls: Low GOING minus 0.42 sec per fur (F)

| | | | | SP | RR | SF |
|---|---|---|---|---|---|---|
| 3041$^{7}$ | **Chabrol (CAN) (69)** (RHarris) **3-8-4**(5) RHavlin(7) (set stdy pce tl hdd 5f out: led 2f out: rdn out) | — | **1** | 11/2$^{3}$ | 67 | 31 |
| 2859$^{4}$ | **Sylvella (51)** (MAJarvis) **3-8-4** GCarter(5) (w wnr tl led 5f out: hdd 2f out: kpt on) | 4 | **2** | 3/1$^{2}$ | 56 | 20 |
| 3284* | **Nelly's Cousin (59)** (NACallaghan) **3-8-12** PatEddery(3) (b: lw: trckd ldrs: plld out over 2f out: rdn & nt qckn appr fnl f) | 1½ | **3** | 8/15$^{1}$ | 61 | 25 |
| 2339$^{7}$ | **Farfeste (36)** (DMorris) **3-8-4** NDay(4) (chsd ldrs tl rdn & btn 3f out) | 8 | **4** | 16/1 | 41 | 5 |
| 3108$^{5}$ | **Reno's Treasure (USA)** (JAHarris) **3-8-2** BDoyle(2) (dwlt: rdn over 4f out: a bhd) | 9 | **5** | 20/1 | 24 | — |

(SP 116.2%) **5 Rn**

**2m 8.0** (3.60) CSF £21.13 TOTE £6.10: £2.00 £1.60 (£6.90) OWNER Mr Terry Connors (NEWMARKET) BRED Reade Baker and Ashford Stud

**985 Chabrol (CAN)**, a really classy individual who showed a lot of ability behind his then stable-companion Farasan in the Wood Ditton, had been sold cheaply subsequently and raced here with his tongue tied down. If he has breathing difficulties, the steady pace undoubtedly will have helped, for he was pulling double over these for much of the home straight. (11/2: op 10/1)
**2859 Sylvella** looked likely to draw stumps when headed in the straight but, to her credit, stayed on to retake second place from the favourite. (3/1)
**3284* Nelly's Cousin** moved to post well but, once produced, did not seem to want to let herself down. She had won down the hill on firm ground at Brighton only three days before, and may have needed more time to recover. (8/15)
**Farfeste**, stepping up in trip, hardly has the look of a middle-distance horse and it is surprising that she has never tried a trip below seven furlongs. (16/1)
**3108 Reno's Treasure (USA)**, who moved to post poorly, has run up light and was never going. (20/1)

## 3358 HORSEY (S) H'CAP (0-60) (3 & 4-Y.O) (Class G)

7-20 (7-22) **1m 3y** £2,490.00 (£690.00: £330.00) Stalls: High GOING minus 0.08 sec per fur (G)

| | | | | SP | RR | SF |
|---|---|---|---|---|---|---|
| 3257$^{4}$ | **Balpare (42)** (NACallaghan) **3-8-8** PatEddery(6) (hld up: nt clr run over 3f out: hmpd & snatched up over 1f out: plld out & qcknd: led wl ins fnl f: eased nr fin) | — | **1** | 11/4$^{1}$ | 52 | 27 |
| 3244$^{6}$ | **Sweet Amoret (46)** (PHowling) **3-8-12** FNorton(5) (b.off hind: stdd s: hdwy to ld over 2f out: edgd rt & sn clr: no ex & hdd wl ins fnl f) | ¾ | **2** | 14/1 | 55 | 30 |
| 2013$^{8}$ | **Unspoken Prayer (44)** (JRArnold) **3-8-10** JQuinn(3) (lw: hld up: hdwy over 2f out: one pce fnl f) | 3½ | **3** | 13/2$^{3}$ | 46 | 21 |
| 3217$^{7}$ | **Kuwam (IRE) (40)** (BHanbury) **3-8-6** MRimmer(4) (w ldr: led 3f out: sn hdd & one pce) | 6 | **4** | 9/1 | 30 | 5 |
| *3078$^{5}$* | **Houghton Venture (USA) (55)** (SPCWoods) **4-10-0b** WWoods(8) (lw: in tch 6f) | 4 | **5** | 7/1 | 37 | 19 |
| 2056$^{23}$ | **Boost (35)** (MrsNMacauley) **4-8-5b**(3) CTeague(7) (hld up: rdn over 4f out: nvr trbld ldrs) | s.h | **6** | 20/1 | 16 | — |
| 3095$^{4}$ | **Prince Rudolf (IRE) (38)** (WGMTurner) **4-8-6v**(5) AmandaSanders(2) (lw: chsd ldrs: ev ch over 2f out: sn wknd) | 3½ | **7** | 9/1 | 13 | — |
| *3086$^{11}$* | **Rose Chime (IRE) (29)** (JLHarris) **4-8-2b**ow2 BDoyle(9) (chsd ldrs tl rdn & wknd over 2f out) | 1½ | **8** | 10/1 | 1 | — |
| 3120$^{10}$ | **Percy Parrot (38)** (RMWhitaker) **4-8-11** PaulEddery(1) (b.hind: chsd ldrs over 5f) | nk | **9** | 7/2$^{2}$ | 9 | — |
| 1881$^{8}$ | **Mad About The Girl (IRE) (32)** (DJSCosgrove) **4-8-5** DRMcCabe(11) (lw: chsd ldrs over 4f) | 13 | **10** | 16/1 | — | — |
| *2368$^{5}$* | **Domusky (30)** (RBastiman) **3-7-7**(3) MHenry(10) (led 5f: sn wknd & eased) | 25 | **11** | 10/1 | — | — |

(SP 130.2%) **11 Rn**

**1m 40.9** (5.60) CSF £41.25 CT £226.90 TOTE £4.20: £1.60 £6.30 £2.70 (£41.50) Trio £194.90 OWNER Mrs J. Callaghan (NEWMARKET)
BRED G. R. Smith (Thriplow) Ltd
LONG HANDICAP Domusky 7-8
WEIGHT FOR AGE 3yo-7lb
No bid

**3257 Balpare** got badly messed about in running, but found a good turn of foot once she saw daylight. This may well boost her confidence, and her turn of foot is a useful one in this grade. (11/4)

**3244 Sweet Amoret** has taken time to adapt to the new tactics, but quickly established a three-length lead once let down and was unfortunate to come up against a horse quickening so well in selling company. (14/1: op 8/1)
**1840 Unspoken Prayer** looked really well and moved to post well. Waiting tactics looked likely to bear fruit as she began her move, but she wandered slightly off a true line and did not find as much as was anticipated. This step up in trip looked just beyond her. (13/2)
**2915 Kuwam (IRE)** did not move to post very well and was easily brushed aside once relinquishing the advantage. (9/1)
**3078 Houghton Venture (USA)**, taken to post quietly, has become rather frustrating. (7/1)
**782 Boost** has been hurdling and did not impress with his head carriage once let down on this ground. (20/1)
**2868 Percy Parrot** (7/2: 2/1-4/1)
**Domusky** (10/1: 16/1-8/1)

## 3359 CAISTER CASTLE CONDITIONS STKS (2-Y.O F) (Class C)
7-50 (7-50) **7f 3y** £6,495.60 (£1,780.40) Stalls: High GOING minus 0.08 sec per fur (G)

| | | | SP | RR | SF |
|---|---|---|---|---|---|
| 2863[2] | **Velour** (DRLoder) **2-8-9** PatEddery(1) (trckd ldr: rdn to ld 1f out: eased nr fin) ........—- | **1** | 2/7[1] | 80 | 7 |
| 3245[4] | **Rejoicing (IRE)** (WAO'Gorman) **2-8-9** EmmaO'Gorman(2) (led: qcknd 3f out: hdd 1f out: edgd rt & r.o) ..........1 | **2** | 3/1[2] | 78 | 5 |
| | | | (SP 102.8%) | | **2 Rn** |

**1m 31.1** (6.90) TOTE £1.10 OWNER Sheikh Mohammed (NEWMARKET) BRED Sheikh Mohammed Bin Rashid Al Maktoum
**2863 Velour** confirmed debut promise, but needed to be shaken up for some time to get on top. (2/7)
**3245 Rejoicing (IRE)** did her best to wait in front and quickened soon after halfway. Despite giving the favourite plenty to think about, she had to admit defeat inside the final furlong, and was not knocked about. (3/1)

## 3360 FILBY BRIDGE H'CAP (0-70) (3-Y.O+ F & M) (Class E)
8-20 (8-22) **5f 43y** £3,367.90 (£1,007.20: £482.60: £220.30) Stalls: High GOING minus 0.08 sec per fur (G)

| | | | SP | RR | SF |
|---|---|---|---|---|---|
| 2999[3] | **Pharaoh's Joy (58)** (JWPayne) **3-9-5** RCochrane(6) (hld up: hdwy over 1f out: led ins fnl f: drvn out) ...........—- | **1** | 9/4[1] | 66 | 43 |
| *2748*[2] | **Lloc (54)** (CADwyer) **4-8-11**(7) JoHunnam(5) (lw: w ldrs: led 2f out: hdd & unable qckn ins fnl f)......................1¼ | **2** | 13/2 | 58 | 38 |
| 3049[3] | **Bangles (60)** (LordHuntingdon) **6-9-5**(5) AimeeCook(1) (a.p: ev ch over 1f out: rdn & kpt on fnl f).....................nk | **3** | 11/4[2] | 63 | 43 |
| 3097* | **Midnight Spell (66)** (JWHills) **4-9-13**(3) 6x MHenry(3) (w ldr: led over 2f out: sn hdd: wknd ins fnl f) ...............1¼ | **4** | 9/2[3] | 65 | 45 |
| *3091*[13] | **Sizzling Romp (52)** (DTThom) **4-9-2** JTate(4) (hld up: hdwy & n.m.r over 1f out: swtchd & r.o fnl f) ...............s.h | **5** | 33/1 | 51 | 31 |
| 1761[W] | **Lady Caroline Lamb (IRE) (65)** (RBastiman) **3-9-7**(5) HBastiman(2) (lw: led over 2f: wknd wl over 1f out) .......4 | **6** | 9/2[3] | 52 | 29 |
| | | | (SP 110.1%) | | **6 Rn** |

**63.7 secs** (3.20) CSF £14.94 TOTE £3.00: £1.50 £2.60 (£6.90) OWNER Pyramid Racing Club (NEWMARKET) BRED Mrs L. Popely
WEIGHT FOR AGE 3yo-3lb
**2999 Pharaoh's Joy** found a gap just at the right time and was always finding enough under a strong ride. (9/4)
**2748 Lloc** disputed the lead and never lost the rail berth. Edging towards the winner inside the final furlong, she had to concede that rival had her measure. (13/2)
**3049 Bangles**, possibly not helped by racing towards the centre, was always there, but tended to wander in the strengthening head-wind. (11/4)
**3097* Midnight Spell** appeared not to quite last home in the head-wind. (9/2)
**Sizzling Romp**, unconsidered in the market, ran her best race since her two-year-old days and would have got closer with a clear run. (33/1)
**665* Lady Caroline Lamb (IRE)**, off since being kicked in the stalls in early June, ran fast but could never dominate, and was the first beaten. (9/2)

T/Plpt: £121.20 (56.24 Tckts). T/Qdpt: £36.60 (11.82 Tckts). Dk

## 3361a-3383a (Irish Racing) - See Computer Raceform

# 1132a-LES LANDES (Jersey) (L-H) (Good to firm)
## Sunday July 28th

## 3384a BRENDAN O'CONNOR MEMORIAL SPRINT H'CAP (3-Y.O+)
4-45 (4-47) **5f 110y** £720.00

| | | | SP | RR | SF |
|---|---|---|---|---|---|
| | **Arkady (IRE)** (CMcCready,Jersey) **5-8-7** RMcGhin ........—- | **1** | | 43 | — |
| | **Newbury Coat** (KHarvey,Guernsey) **6-8-10** ATucker ........½ | **2** | | 45 | — |
| | **Jimmy the Skunk (IRE)** (ZJones,Guernsey) **5-10-12** PHolley ........4 | **3** | | 63 | — |
| *2684*[4] | **Astral's Chance** (KRBurke) **3-9-4** RPainter ........ | **4** | | — | — |
| | | | | | **4 Rn** |

**1m 8.0** Tote £6.80 (£6.80) OWNER R A Ltd (JERSEY) BRED Mrs Ian Fox

## 3385a B. B. O'CONNOR LOTTERY H'CAP (3-Y.O+)
5-20 (5-20) **1m 2f** £720.00

| | | | SP | RR | SF |
|---|---|---|---|---|---|
| | **Green's le Sidaner (USA)** (CMcCready,Jersey) **8-10-12** RMcGhin ........—- | **1** | | 47 | — |
| 439[16] | **Sian Wyn** (KRBurke) **6-8-13** RPainter ........2 | **2** | | 17 | — |
| | **Time Lapse** (JSOArthur,Jersey) **7-8-12** ATucker ........12 | **3** | | — | — |
| | | | | | **5 Rn** |

**2m 12.0** Tote £8.40: £2.20 £5.20 (£13.70) OWNER Mrs J. R. Armstrong (JERSEY)

# 3200a-VICHY (France) (R-H) (Good)
## Monday July 29th

## 3386a GRAND PRIX DE VICHY (Gp 3) (3-Y.O+)
9-05 (9-05) **1m 2f** £28,986.00 (£10,540.00: £5,270.00)

| | | | SP | RR | SF |
|---|---|---|---|---|---|
| 2273a[2] | **Bulington (FR)** (H-APantall,France) **4-9-2** CAsmussen ........—- | **1** | | 122 | — |

| | | | | SP | RR | SF |
|---|---|---|---|---|---|---|
| 2273a3 | **Diamond Mix (IRE)** (AFabre,France) **4-9-2** TJarnet | 1½ | 2 | | 120 | — |
| 1389a2 | **Top Glory (FR)** (FDoumen,France) **3-8-6** GMosse | ¾ | 3 | | 118 | — |
| 724a* | **Overbury (IRE)** (SbinSuroor) **5-9-11** SGuillot (btn approx 4¼l) | | 7 | | — | — |
| 2840a10 | **Maralinga (IRE)** (LadyHerries) **4-9-2** FBlondel (btn approx 9¼l) | | 9 | | — | — |
| | | | | | | **10 Rn** |

**2m 4.2** P-M 2.60F: 1.20F 1.50F 1.80F (52.00F) OWNER Mr P. Pierry BRED Blueblood Stud
**2273a Bulington (FR)** finally scored the Group victory he deserved. He was always prominent, despite the strong pace and, after taking the lead over a furlong out, ran on well. He goes next for the Prix Gontaut-Biron at Deauville.
**2273a Diamond Mix (IRE)** had been working well prior to this, and is gradually finding his form on the track. In mid-division until running on to take second place in the closing stages, he is likely to take on the winner again at Deauville.
**1389a Top Glory (FR)** was the victim of some scrimmaging in the straight, but ran on strongly once clear of trouble. He goes for the Prix Guillaume D'Omano next.
**724a* Overbury (IRE)**, having his first race since winning at Sha Tin in April, was well placed until finding nothing extra in the final furlong. He will be better for the run.
**2840a Maralinga (IRE)** was prominent until dropping away in the straight. He may well take on the first two again in the Gontaut-Biron.
DS

# 3201a-MAISONS-LAFFITTE (France) (Good)
## Tuesday July 30th

### 3387a PRIX DAPHNIS (Gp 3) (3-Y.O C & G)
2-15 (2-13) **1m 1f** £28,986.00 (£10,540.00: £5,270.00: £2,635.00)

| | | | | SP | RR | SF |
|---|---|---|---|---|---|---|
| 1756a5 | **Regal Archive (IRE)** (PWChapple-Hyam) **3-8-9** CAsmussen | — | 1 | | 106 | — |
| | **Brindle** (JEHammond,France) **3-8-9** OThirion | 1½ | 2 | | 103 | — |
| 798a4 | **Anziyan (USA)** (AFabre,France) **3-8-9** TJarnet | 1½ | 3 | | 101 | — |
| | **Fort Lamy** (CLaffon-Parias,France) **3-8-9** FHead | 2 | 4 | | 97 | — |
| | | | | | | **4 Rn** |

**1m 52.3** P-M 1.70F: 1.10F 1.90F (SF 7.40F) OWNER Mrs B. V. Sangster (MARLBOROUGH) BRED Studcrown Ltd
**1756a Regal Archive (IRE)** bounced back to form after disappointing in his previous race. He tracked the leader until going on a furlong out, and was always holding the runner-up. He is likely to appear next in the Prix Guillaume D'Ornano at Deauville.
**Brindle** made the running but, after quickening a quarter of a mile from home, had no answer to the winner's challenge. He ran on well though, and looks capable of winning a Group race.
**798a Anziyan (USA)** was in third place throughout, but proved unable to respond when the pace quickened.

### 3388a PRIX DE LIZY H'CAP (5-Y.O+)
2-50 (2-57) **1m 2f** £17,128.00

| | | | | SP | RR | SF |
|---|---|---|---|---|---|---|
| | **Precious Topaze (FR)** (BdeWatrigant,France) **5-8-7** J-BEyquem | — | 1 | | 68 | — |
| | **Celestial Way (USA)** (France) **5-9-1** CAsmussen | nk | 2 | | 76 | — |
| | **Bedfort (FR)** (France) **6-7-11** VVion | nk | 3 | | 57 | — |
| 205327 | **Cedez le Passage (FR)** (KOCunningham-Brown) **5-9-4** FSanchez (btn over 5l) | | 0 | | — | — |
| | | | | | | **18 Rn** |

**2m 4.9** (2.90) P-M 7.70F: 2.10F 1.40F 4.40F (7.50F) OWNER Mr A. Urbano-Roldan BRED Alan Clore
**455 Cedez le Passage (FR)** was always towards the rear, and could make no impression in the straight.

### 3389a PRIX DU LUDE CLAIMING STKS (3-Y.O)
3-50 (3-52) **1m** £7,905.00

| | | | | SP | RR | SF |
|---|---|---|---|---|---|---|
| | **Cent Plaisirs (FR)** (JVanHandenhove,France) **3-8-3b1(5)** SBertin | — | 1 | | 75 | — |
| | **Shycock (FR)** (France) **3-8-9** TGillet | nk | 2 | | 75 | — |
| | **Famous (FR)** (France) **3-8-13b1** MBoutin | 2½ | 3 | | 74 | — |
| 29468 | **Village Native (FR)** (KOCunningham-Brown) **3-9-2** FSanchez (btn approx 14¾l) | | 6 | | — | — |
| | | | | | | **6 Rn** |

**1m 39.3** (3.30) P-M 3.40F: 1.40F 1.40F (SF 8.10F) OWNER Mr H. Vanderdussen BRED Skymarc Farms
**Village Native (FR)** was always in the rear.

# 1581a-DEAUVILLE (France) (R-H) (Good)
## Thursday August 1st

### 3390a PRIX DE CABOURG (Gp 3) (2-Y.O)
3-20 (3-20) **6f** £28,986.00 (£10,540.00: £5,270.00: £2,635.00)

| | | | | SP | RR | SF |
|---|---|---|---|---|---|---|
| | **Zamindar (USA)** (AFabre,France) **2-8-11** TJarnet | — | 1 | | 99 | — |
| 3032a* | **Dyhim Diamond (IRE)** (CLaffon-Parias,France) **2-8-11** FSanchez | 2½ | 2 | | 92 | — |
| | **Elle Est Revenue (IRE)** (DSmaga,France) **2-8-8** DBoeuf | 1½ | 3 | | 85 | — |
| | **Blade Ae (USA)** (MmeCHead,France) **2-8-11** FHead | 1½ | 4 | | 84 | — |
| | | | | | | **4 Rn** |

**1m 12.6** (4.60) P-M 1.40F: 1.10F 1.10F (SF 4.60) OWNER Mr K. Abdullah (CHANTILLY) BRED Juddmonte Farms
**Zamindar (USA)**, like his brother Zafonic, is a very imposing, well-grown individual who possesses a fine action. Taking this race by the scruff of the neck at the start, he dominated throughout and won as he pleased. He is not surprisingly already being quoted as favourite for the 2,000 Guineas, but we should be able to gauge his ability more effectively after his next appearance in the Prix Morny.
**Dyhim Diamond (IRE)** ran on in the final furlong without threatening to catch the winner. He should be capable of winning a listed race.
**Elle Est Revenue (IRE)** challenged on the outside, but her effort petered out in the last furlong. She is useful, and may have more success against her own sex.
DS

## 3390a-DEAUVILLE (France) (R-H) (Good)
### Saturday August 3rd

## 3391a PRIX D'ASTARTE (Gp 2) (3-Y.O+ F & M)
3-35 (3-38) **1m** £39,526.00 (£15,810.00: £7,905.00: £3,953.00)

| | | | | SP | RR | SF |
|---|---|---|---|---|---|---|
| 1952a[15] | **Shaanxi (USA)** (ELellouche,France) **4-9-0** OPeslier (hld up: chal over 1f out: qcknd to ld ins fnl f) | —- | 1 | | 110 | —- |
| | **Zarannda (IRE)** (AdeRoyerDupre,France) **3-8-7** GMosse (hld up in rr: hdwy to ld 1f out: hdd ins fnl f: no ex) | .¾ | 2 | | 109 | —- |
| 3030a[3] | **Housa Dancer (FR)** (AFabre,France) **3-8-7** SGuillot (racd in 3rd: rdn 2f out: one pce) | 1½ | 3 | | 106 | —- |
| 3030a[2] | **Ecoute (USA)** (MmeCHead,France) **3-8-7** FHead (led tl rdn & hdd 1f out: wknd) | 5 | 4 | | 96 | —- |
| | **Proud Fact (USA)** (AFabre,France) **3-8-7** TJarnet (trckd ldr: rdn 2f out: wknd) | 1½ | 5 | | 93 | —- |

**5 Rn**

**1m 39.1** (3.10) P-M 3.10F: 1.60F 1.40F (SF 10.20F) OWNER Mr T. Yoshida BRED Fares Farm Inc

**1952a Shaanxi (USA)**, having her first run since returning from Japan, was held up for a late run, and produced too much acceleration for the favourite. She seems to have held her form well, and will be a threat to all in her next race, the Prix Jacques le Marois.

**Zarannda (IRE)** was heavily backed, and looked likely to justify the support when taking the lead at the furlong marker, but she could not match the winner's turn of foot. Her connections believe she may have found this stiff mile too far, and she will now be brought back in trip for the Prix de la Foret.

**3030a Housa Dancer (FR)** is a consistent performer, and ran another good race, but was out of her depth in this company.

**3030a Ecoute (USA)** tried to make all, but was a spent force when headed a furlong out.

DS

## 3391a-DEAUVILLE (France) (R-H) (Good)
### Sunday August 4th

## 3392a PRIX DE POMONE (Gp 2) (3-Y.O+ F & M)
3-10 (3-22) **1m 5f 110y** £39,526.00 (£15,810.00: £7,905.00: £3,953.00)

| | | | | SP | RR | SF |
|---|---|---|---|---|---|---|
| 902a[3] | **Helen Of Spain** (AFabre,France) **4-9-4** TJarnet (a.p: rdn over 2f out: r.o to ld cl home) | —- | 1 | | 112 | —- |
| 1769[4] | **Camporese (IRE)** (PWChapple-Hyam) **3-8-6** JReid (led: rdn over 2f out: hdd cl home) | s.nk | 2 | | 112 | —- |
| 2533* | **Spout** (RCharlton) **4-9-8** PatEddery (hld up: hdwy & 3rd st: r.o one pce fnl f) | 1½ | 3 | | 114 | —- |
| | **Restiv Star (FR)** (AFabre,France) **4-9-4** SGuillot (hld up early: r.o one pce fnl f) | nk | 4 | | 110 | —- |
| 3031a[2] | **Leonila (IRE)** (RCollet,France) **3-8-6** OPeslier (mid div: no imp st) | s.nk | 5 | | 109 | —- |
| | **Rosi Zambotti (IRE)** (BGrizzetti,Italy) **4-9-4** CAsmussen (mid div tl lost pl st) | 8 | 6 | | 100 | —- |

**6 Rn**

**3m 0.9** (8.90) P-M 4.40F: 1.90F 1.90F (16.10F)
OWNER Sheikh Mohammed (CHANTILLY) BRED Sheikh Mohammed

**902a Helen Of Spain** was produced with a perfectly-timed run by her jockey to hit the front inside the last furlong. She is a thoroughly consistent filly who runs well here, and a return trip is likely for the Grand Prix.

**1769 Camporese (IRE)** was a reluctant leader, but nearly succeeded in making all. She is still improving, and has a number of options open to her, with the most likely targets the Park Hill at Doncaster or the Prix Vermeille.

**2533* Spout** was not suited by the slow early gallop, and could not find the pace to trouble the first two in the last quarter-mile. She is a possible for the Yorkshire Oaks.

**Restiv Star (FR)** was held up, but could not accelerate when required. She is not in this class.

## 3393a PRIX DE CERCLE (Listed) (3-Y.O+)
3-40 (3-53) **5f** £18,445.00 (£6,324.00: £3,953.00)

| | | | | SP | RR | SF |
|---|---|---|---|---|---|---|
| | **Late Parade (IRE)** (ARenzoni,Italy) **5-8-13** JacquelineFreda | —- | 1 | | 116+ | —- |
| 2115[16] | **Struggler** (DRLoder) **4-8-13** RHughes | 2 | 2 | | 110 | —- |
| | **Maggi For Margaret** (DSmaga,France) **3-8-7** DBoeuf | 1½ | 3 | | 102 | —- |

**9 Rn**

**56.9 secs** (0.40) P-M 8.00F: 2.50F 1.30F 2.60F (10.70F) OWNER Scuderia Jerome

**Late Parade (IRE)** made all the running for a comfortable victory. He is likely to return to France for the Prix de l'Abbaye.

**1483 Struggler** found the outside draw against him, but kept on well to be second. He is likely to return for the Prix de Meautry.

## 1751a-MUNICH (Germany) (L-H) (Soft)
### Sunday August 4th

## 3394a DALLMAYR DELIKATESSENHAUSES GROSSER SPRINT PREIS (Listed) (3-Y.O+)
2-35 (2-35) **6f 110y** £10,811.00 (£4,324.00: £2,207.00)

| | | | | SP | RR | SF |
|---|---|---|---|---|---|---|
| 3083[3] | **Branston Abby (IRE)** (MJohnston) **7-9-9** DHolland | —- | 1 | | 113 | —- |
| 1394a[3] | **Sharp Prod (USA)** (HJentzsch,Germany) **6-9-7** SEccles | ½ | 2 | | 110 | —- |
| | **Dorlando** (EPils,Germany) **5-9-2** PPiatowski | 3 | 3 | | 97 | —- |

**9 Rn**

**1m 19.0** Tote 16DM: 11DM 14DM 15DM (36DM) OWNER Mr J. D. Abell (MIDDLEHAM) BRED John David Abell

**3083 Branston Abby (IRE)**, racing on her favoured soft ground, was held up as usual, and came through with a strong challenge to lead half a furlong out. She equalled Laurel Queen's post-war record of twenty-two wins for a mare with this success, and is likely to return to Germany for the Silberne Peitsche on August 18th.

**Sharp Prod (USA)** set a strong pace, but was unable to resist the winner's challenge in the closing stages.

## 3395a GROSSER DALLMAYR PREIS-BAYERISCHES ZUCHTRENNEN (Gp 1) (3-Y.O+)
3-50 (3-52) **1m 2f** £99,099.00 (£42,793.00: £29,720.00: £11,261.00)

| | | | | SP | RR | SF |
|---|---|---|---|---|---|---|
| 2471a[2] | **Timarida (IRE)** (JOxx,Ireland) **4-9-2** JPMurtagh (hld up: gd hdwy appr st: r.o to ld 1f out: hld on wl) | —- | 1 | | 122 | —- |

| | | | | SP | RR | SF |
|---|---|---|---|---|---|---|
| 2479a2 | **Germany (USA)** (BSchutz,Germany) **5-9-6** RCochrane (led to 1f out: rallied cl home) | ½ | 2 | | 125 | — |
| 1750a4 | **La Blue (GER)** (BSchutz,Germany) **3-8-9** DHolland (trckd ldrs: hdwy to chal over 1f out: r.o) | nk | 3 | | 123 | — |
| 2730* | **Montjoy (USA)** (PFICole) **4-9-6** TQuinn (a.p: rdn over 1f out: one pce ins fnl f) | 1 | 4 | | 123 | — |
| 2843a2 | **Devil River Peek (USA)** (BSchutz,Germany) **4-9-6** AStarke (hld up: r.o fnl 2f: nt rch ldrs) | ¾ | 5 | | 122 | — |
| 2843a4 | **Artan (IRE)** (MRolke,Germany) **4-9-6** JTandari (cl up tl r.o one pce fnl 2f) | 2 | 6 | | 119 | — |
| 2038 12 | **Needle Gun (IRE)** (CEBrittain) **6-9-6** MJKinane (trckd ldr: rdn & wknd over 1f out) | 2 | 7 | | 116 | — |
| 2479a7 | **Hondero (GER)** (BoerjeOlsson,Sweden) **4-9-6** PPiatkowski (a bhd) | 1½ | 8 | | 113 | — |

**8 Rn**

**2m 6.6** Tote 37DM: 13DM 12DM 19DM (119DM) OWNER Aga Khan (CURRABEG) BRED H.H. Aga Khan's Studs S.C.
**2471a Timarida (IRE)** was held up early, but moved closer before the straight and, after hitting the front a furlong out, had to dig deep to hold on. She improved rapidly in the second half of last year and, now she has returned to form, she will be a major contender for her next race, the Beverley D Stakes at Arlington.
**2479a Germany (USA)** has returned from stud in good form and, after making most of the running, forced Timarida to pull out all the stops to hold his renewed challenge.
**1060a* La Blue (GER)** may find this trip at the limit of her stamina. She came with a strong challenge, but could find nothing extra inside the last. Nevertheless, this was a good effort against the older generation.
**2730* Montjoy (USA)** was always up with the pace, but was short of room inside the last, and could find nothing extra. His trainer believes the slow early pace was against him.
**1938a* Needle Gun (IRE)** stalked the leader, and had every chance a furlong and a half out, but had nothing left on this ground.

## 2109a-COLOGNE (Germany) (R-H) (Good)
## Sunday August 4th

### 3396a OPPENHEIM RENNEN (Listed) (2-Y.O)
3-25 (3-37) **6f** £13,514.00 (£5,405.00: £2,703.00)

| | | | | SP | RR | SF |
|---|---|---|---|---|---|---|
| | **Shy Lady (FR)** (BSchutz,Germany) **2-8-12** THellier | — | 1 | | 90 | — |
| | **New York (GER)** (BSchutz,Germany) **2-8-12** ASchikora | 3 | 2 | | 82 | — |
| 2040 15 | **Statesman** (MRChannon) **2-9-2** KDarley | 2 | 3 | | 81 | — |

**5 Rn**

**1m 12.5** (2.70) Tote 26DM: 15DM 23DM (212DM) OWNER Mr Jaber Abdullah BRED R. Ades & Haras d'Etreham
**1437* Statesman** was prominent early before losing his place, but stayed on again inside the last.

### 3397a OSTERMANN-POKAL (Gp 3) (3-Y.O+)
4-40 (4-42) **1m** £27,027.00 (£10,811.00: £5,405.00)

| | | | | SP | RR | SF |
|---|---|---|---|---|---|---|
| | **Orfijar (FR)** (PLautner,Germany) **6-9-0** WNewnes | — | 1 | | 110 | — |
| | **Royal Abjar (USA)** (AWohler,Germany) **5-9-2** ABoschert | 1 | 2 | | 110 | — |
| 1755a2 | **Kalatos (GER)** (AWohler,Germany) **4-9-2** PSchiergen | 1½ | 3 | | 107 | — |
| 2471aW | **Silca Blanka (IRE)** (MRChannon) **4-9-0** KDarley (btn 4l) | | 5 | | — | — |

**10 Rn**

**1m 35.9** (5.90) Tote 226DM: 41DM 15DM 25DM (686DM) OWNER Gestut Monchhof
**Orfijar (FR)**, given an excellent ride from the front, quickened two furlongs out and held on well.
**Royal Abjar (USA)** chased the winner throughout the last quarter-mile, but could never get on terms.
**1768 Silca Blanka (IRE)** was held up for a late challenge, but could not peg back the leaders in the last two furlongs.

## 2531-HAYDOCK (L-H) (Good to firm)
## Friday August 9th
WEATHER: overcast WIND: mod across

### 3398 BELLCHARM H'CAP (0-85) (3-Y.O) (Class D)
6-10 (6-10) **1m 3f 200y** £3,689.50 (£1,111.00: £538.00: £251.50) Stalls: High GOING minus 0.30 sec per fur (GF)

| | | | | SP | RR | SF |
|---|---|---|---|---|---|---|
| 2742 5 | **Mount Row (83)** (LMCumani) **3-9-7** JWeaver(5) (led after 1f: qcknd clr 3f out: unchal) | — | 1 | 4/1 1 | 95 | 64 |
| 2525 5 | **Major Dundee (IRE) (76)** (RHannon) **3-9-0** AMcGlone(8) (trckd ldrs: kpt on u.p fnl f: no ch w wnr) | 9 | 2 | 12/1 | 76 | 45 |
| 1990 4 | **Forest Heights (83)** (MrsJCecil) **3-9-7** TIves(2) (bit bkwd: sn chsng ldrs: rdn & outpcd over 2f out) | s.h | 3 | 5/1 3 | 83 | 52 |
| 3155 9 | **Sharaf (IRE) (83)** (WRMuir) **3-9-7** KFallon(3) (lw: hld up: pushed along 6f out: hrd rdn 3f out: nt pce to chal) | ¾ | 4 | 7/1 | 82 | 51 |
| 3308 2 | **Silverdale Knight (58)** (KWHogg) **3-7-7(3)** DWright(4) (led 1f: sn bhd & hld up: hdwy on ins 3f out: nt rch ldrs) | ¾ | 5 | 11/1 | 56 | 25 |
| 2674 8 | **Shenango (IRE) (73)** (GWragg) **3-8-4(7)** GMilligan(6) (lw: hld up: brought wd & effrt 3f out: no imp) | 3½ | 6 | 16/1 | 66 | 35 |
| 1644 8 | **Bechstein (82)** (JLDunlop) **3-9-6** KDarley(1) (lw: sn drvn along: effrt over 2f out: no imp) | 7 | 7 | 9/2 2 | 66 | 35 |
| 2080 5 | **Lepikha (USA) (66)** (BWHills) **3-8-4** JQuinn(10) (hld up: hdwy over 3f out: rdn & wknd wl over 1f out) | 1¾ | 8 | 4/1 1 | 47 | 16 |
| 3042 6 | **Taharqa (IRE) (75)** (JHMGosden) **3-8-13** JCarroll(7) (lw: dropped rr 4f out: sn bhd: t.o) | 3½ | 9 | 10/1 | 52 | 21 |

(SP 118.3%) **9 Rn**

**2m 31.95** (2.55) CSF £45.60 CT £225.71 TOTE £4.30: £2.40 £3.70 £2.10 (£27.40) Trio £31.30 OWNER Lord Hartington (NEWMARKET) BRED Side Hill Stud
LONG HANDICAP Silverdale Knight 7-9
**2742 Mount Row** had little trouble handling this longer trip and had the prize sewn up from a long way out. There is no reason why she can not improve further. (4/1)
**2525 Major Dundee (IRE)** is hardly bred to stay this trip, but he kept plugging on for the runner-up prize and one could not fault his effort. (12/1)
**1990 Forest Heights** did look as if she would strip fitter for this first run in almost two months, and she was treading ground for the last quarter-mile. (5/1)
**2547 Sharaf (IRE)** won his maiden at this trip, but has been tackling longer distances recently and, though he did stay on, he could not get within striking range of the principals. (7/1)
**3308 Silverdale Knight** continues to run well, but his sustained effort up the inside rail was never going to get him there. (11/1)
**2080 Lepikha (USA)**, patiently ridden, could never get herself into contention in this first handicap and proved most disappointing. (4/1)

## 3399 ST. HELENS STAR CLAIMING STKS (3-Y.O+) (Class F)

6-40 (6-41) **6f** £2,675.00 (£750.00: £365.00) Stalls: High GOING minus 0.30 sec per fur (GF)

| | | | SP | RR | SF |
|---|---|---|---|---|---|
| 3140* | **Lord Olivier (IRE) (80)** (WJarvis) **6-9-9** MTebbutt(3) (lw: mde all: shkn up over 1f out: r.o wl) .......................— | 1 | 5/6[1] | 79 | 61 |
| 2034[6] | **Panther (IRE) (65)** (PDEvans) **6-9-1** JFEgan(2) (a.p: rdn over 2f out: ev ch & drifted lft fnl f: unable qckn) ......½ | 2 | 7/2[2] | 70 | 52 |
| 2732[10] | **River Tern (63)** (JBerry) **3-8-11** JCarroll(5) (b: lw: a.p: rdn whn n.m.r appr fnl f: one pce)................................3½ | 3 | 7/1 | 60 | 38 |
| 2946[10] | **Ameliajill (48)** (RHannon) **3-7-13**(3) DWright(7) (b.hind: sn hrd drvn: swtchd lft appr fnl f: r.o) .........................1¼ | 4 | 25/1 | 48 | 26 |
| 3278[5] | **Hoh Majestic (IRE) (67)** (MartynWane) **3-8-7v** KFallon(1) (racd centre: prom tl rdn & outpcd over 1f out) ........3 | 5 | 9/2[3] | 45 | 23 |
| 2777[11] | **Maysimp (IRE) (40)** (BPJBaugh) **3-8-2** NCarlisle(6) (outpcd: a bhd)..................................................................2½ | 6 | 50/1 | 33 | 11 |
| | **Red March Hare** (DMoffatt) **5-7-11**(3) DarrenMoffatt(4) (bkwd: sltly hmpd s: sn pushed along: a outpcd) .......hd | 7 | 50/1 | 27 | 9 |
| | | | (SP 115.2%) | **7 Rn** | |

**1m 13.12** (1.42) CSF £4.29 TOTE £1.80: £1.30 £2.00 (£2.40) OWNER Miss V. R. Jarvis (NEWMARKET) BRED Michael Staunton in Ireland
WEIGHT FOR AGE 3yo-4lb

**3140* Lord Olivier (IRE)** adopted more forceful tactics on this occasion and, though he was inclined to edge right when shaken up, he won with more in hand than the margin would suggest. (5/6)

**2034 Panther (IRE)**, robbed of the opportunity to set the pace, was off the bridle soon after halfway. Though he delivered a determined challenge throughout the final furlong, he did his cause no good at all by drifting away to the left. (7/2)

**2167 River Tern**, slightly impeded when the winner took his ground approaching the final furlong, was struggling to hold on at the time and it was doubtful if the result was effected. (7/1)

**2528 Ameliajill**, still struggling to get off the mark, did run on in the closing stages but was never going well enough to cause concern. (25/1)

**3278 Hoh Majestic (IRE)** has only ever won at the minimum trip and she appears to be something of a short-runner. (9/2)

## 3400 COUNTRYWIDE FREIGHT CONDITIONS STKS (2-Y.O) (Class C)

7-10 (7-12) **6f** £4,706.00 (£1,754.00: £852.00: £360.00: £155.00: £73.00) Stalls: High GOING minus 0.30 sec per fur (GF)

| | | | SP | RR | SF |
|---|---|---|---|---|---|
| 2700[2] | **Indian Rocket (100)** (JLDunlop) **2-9-2** KDarley(7) (lw: hld up: hdwy over 2f out: led ins fnl f: sn clr) ...............— | 1 | 7/4[1] | 91 | 56 |
| 2877[3] | **Victory Dancer (95)** (BJMeehan) **2-9-5b[1]** MTebbutt(5) (lw: led over 3f out tl ins fnl f: eased whn btn nr fin) ..2½ | 2 | 8/1 | 87 | 52 |
| 3128[3] | **Bride's Reprisal (90)** (MRChannon) **2-8-9** JFortune(6) (stdd s: swtchd lft & hdwy 2f out: hung bdly lft: nt pce to chal)..............................................................................................................2½ | 3 | 2/1[2] | 71 | 36 |
| 2727* | **The Lambton Worm (100)** (DenysSmith) **2-9-2** KFallon(2) (lw: hdwy ½-wy: rdn over 1f out: one pce) ............nk | 4 | 8/1 | 77 | 42 |
| 2977* | **Northern Sun** (TGMills) **2-9-0** WWoods(8) (hld up: swtchd lft & effrt 2f out: nt trble ldrs) ..................................4 | 5 | 16/1 | 64 | 29 |
| 2353* | **Sinecure (USA) (84)** (JHMGosden) **2-9-2** AMcGlone(4) (unruly s: trckd ldrs: rdn & n.m.r appr fnl f: sn btn) ......2 | 6 | 11/2[3] | 61 | 26 |
| 1869* | **Bollero (IRE) (78)** (JBerry) **2-8-9** JCarroll(1) (lw: led over 2f: rdn & wknd wl over 1f out)....................................1 | 7 | 14/1 | 51 | 16 |
| 2364[7] | **Magic Blue (IRE) (81)** (RHollinshead) **2-8-13**(3) FLynch(3) (lw: outpcd: rdn 2f out: no imp)...............................7 | 8 | 25/1 | 40 | 5 |
| | | | (SP 123.7%) | **8 Rn** | |

**1m 13.07** (1.37) CSF £16.54 TOTE £3.00: £1.30 £2.30 £1.50 (£14.60) OWNER Mr Khalil Alsayegh (ARUNDEL) BRED Red House Stud

**2700 Indian Rocket** may well need a straight sprint track to produce his best, for he won this very much as he pleased and showed his Chester running to be a bit off the mark. (7/4)

**2877 Victory Dancer** ran up to his best in his first-time blinkers and, though the winner proved much too strong for him at the business end, there was no disgrace in this defeat. (8/1)

**3128 Bride's Reprisal**, steadied leaving the stalls, tried hard to mount a challenge below the distance, but she continually hung left and has yet to prove she really gets the trip. (2/1)

**2727* The Lambton Worm** did his best to get himself into the action below the distance, but he was hard at work to do so and the effort petered out inside the final furlong. (8/1)

**2353* Sinecure (USA)**, very unruly before being loaded into the stalls, showed up just behind the leaders, but he was in trouble when short of room entering the final furlong, and he does appear to have a mental problem. (11/2)

## 3401 GATEHOUSE H'CAP (0-85) (3-Y.O+) (Class D)

7-40 (7-42) **1m 2f 120y** £3,621.25 (£1,090.00: £527.50: £246.25) Stalls: High GOING minus 0.30 sec per fur (GF)

| | | | SP | RR | SF |
|---|---|---|---|---|---|
| 3039* | **Daunting Destiny (BEL) (79)** (RHannon) **3-9-6** WJO'Connor(5) (hld up in tch: effrt over 2f out: led wl ins fnl f: all out)..............................................................................................................— | 1 | 11/4[2] | 86 | 55 |
| 3081[7] | **Maid For Baileys (IRE) (78)** (MJohnston) **3-9-5** JWeaver(3) (led tl wl ins fnl f: rallied cl home) .......................hd | 2 | 5/1 | 85 | 54 |
| 3272[2] | **North Reef (IRE) (70)** (SirMarkPrescott) **5-9-7** GDuffield(2) (chsd ldr: hrd rdn & ev ch over 1f out: unable qckn) ..............................................................................................................1¾ | 3 | 11/10[1] | 74 | 53 |
| 1778* | **Drummer Hicks (50)** (EWeymes) **7-8-1** JQuinn(1) (bit bkwd: trckd ldrs: rdn to chal over 2f out: wknd appr fnl f) ..............................................................................................................4 | 4 | 4/1[3] | 48 | 27 |
| 2418[6] | **Home Counties (IRE) (62)** (DMoffatt) **7-8-10v**(3) DarrenMoffatt(4) (hld up: hrd drvn 4f out: no imp) ..................4 | 5 | 16/1 | 54 | 33 |
| | **Berkeley Bounder (USA) (73)** (MrsMReveley) **4-9-10** KDarley(6) (bit bkwd: a bhd: t.o fnl 3f)........................dist | 6 | 14/1 | — | — |
| | | | (SP 123.5%) | **6 Rn** | |

**2m 14.72** (3.22) CSF £16.90 TOTE £3.80: £1.60 £2.00 (£8.20) OWNER The Gold Buster Syndicate (MARLBOROUGH) BRED Patrick Madelein
WEIGHT FOR AGE 3yo-10lb

**3039* Daunting Destiny (BEL)**, a progressive colt who seems to find his form in the second half of the season, needed to show his battling qualities to get the better of a very willing rival. (11/4: 2/1-3/1)

**3081 Maid For Baileys (IRE)** turned in her only disappointing performance on her previous outing, but she was back on song here and she did not fail for the want of trying. Her turn is near. (5/1)

**3272 North Reef (IRE)** found this race coming far too soon after such a promising effort at the end of last week, and there would seem plenty to look forward to in the coming months. (11/10: op 7/4)

**1778* Drummer Hicks** did not look quite 100% after being out of action for two months. Though he tried to deliver a challenge passing the quarter-mile marker, he had to admit he was not quite up to it. (4/1)

**2418 Home Counties (IRE)** was unable to get himself into the action and is not yet firing. (16/1)

## 3402 HAYDOCK PARK PONY CLUB CLAIMING STKS (3-Y.O+) (Class F)

8-10 (8-12) **1m 2f 120y** £2,647.00 (£742.00: £361.00) Stalls: High GOING minus 0.30 sec per fur (GF)

| | | | SP | RR | SF |
|---|---|---|---|---|---|
| 2723[5] | **Rainbow Top (96)** (WJHaggas) **4-9-12** KFallon(3) (lw: chsd ldr: led over 4f out: clr appr fnl f: comf) ..............— | 1 | 6/4[2] | 80+ | 54 |
| 2744[8] | **Golden Fawn** (LadyHerries) **3-8-1** JQuinn(6) (hld up: hrd drvn & hdwy 2f out: kpt on fnl f: no ch w wnr) .......3½ | 2 | 25/1 | 60 | 24 |
| 3115[2] | **Mellottie (90)** (MrsMReveley) **11-9-12** KDarley(1) (lw: hld up: hdwy 6f out: hrd drvn & one pce fnl 2f)..............3 | 3 | 11/8[1] | 70 | 44 |

| | | | | SP | RR | SF |
|---|---|---|---|---|---|---|
| 3322[6] | **Charlie Chang (IRE) (70)** (RHannon) **3-9-0** WJO'Connor(2) (led 6f: hrd drvn wl over 1f out: sn btn) | 3½ | **4** | 4/1[3] | 63 | 27 |
| 2628[9] | **Highfield Fizz (45)** (CWFairhurst) **4-8-6** DeanMcKeown(4) (trckd ldrs tl rdn & wknd wl over 1f out) | 2½ | **5** | 33/1 | 41 | 15 |
| 2731[9] | **Oakbury (IRE) (42)** (MissLCSiddall) **4-8-11** JWeaver(5) (a bhd: t.o fnl 2f) | 8 | **6** | 33/1 | 34 | 8 |
| 3108[6] | **Sophie Lockett** (KWHogg) **3-8-1** NKennedy(7) (a in rr: lost tch 4f out: t.o) | 14 | **7** | 33/1 | 13 | — |

(SP 114.8%) **7 Rn**

**2m 15.64** (4.14) CSF £28.80 TOTE £2.40: £1.60 £3.80 (£18.90) OWNER Mr B. Haggas (NEWMARKET) BRED Sir Robin McAlpine

WEIGHT FOR AGE 3yo-10lb

**2723 Rainbow Top**, taken to post steadily, won his first race on turf with a clear-cut success and this return to ten furlongs suited him admirably. (6/4)

**Golden Fawn**, a lightly-raced, good-looking filly who can be made fitter, stayed on strongly in the latter stages and should be able to win her share of races. (25/1)

**3115 Mellottie** is having to admit age catching up with him, but he still retains plenty of enthusiasm for the game, and there could still be another race in him. (11/8: Evens-6/4)

**3322 Charlie Chang (IRE)** did not impress to post, but did his share of the pacemaking, and only faded as his stamina ebbed inside the distance. (4/1)

**Highfield Fizz** has not yet found her form this term and, after sitting in behind the leaders for over a mile, found an extra effort beyond her. (33/1)

## 3403 DEAN DAM H'CAP (0-70) (3-Y.O+) (Class E)

8-40 (8-42) **1m 30y** £3,111.25 (£940.00: £457.50: £216.25) Stalls: Low GOING minus 0.30 sec per fur (GF)

| | | | | SP | RR | SF |
|---|---|---|---|---|---|---|
| 1894[7] | **Gloriana (64)** (LadyHerries) **4-9-10** JQuinn(8) (lw: chsd ldr: led over 3f out: clr 2f out: pushed out) | — | **1** | 13/2 | 78 | 42 |
| 1406[10] | **Duke Valentino (57)** (RHollinshead) **4-9-0**(3) FLynch(4) (s.s: bhd: hdwy over 2f out: r.o strly fnl f) | 1¼ | **2** | 10/1 | 69 | 33 |
| 2851[8] | **Katie Komaite (45)** (CaptJWilson) **3-7-12** CRutter(1) (lw: chsd ldng pair: rdn & one pce fnl 2f) | 4 | **3** | 12/1 | 49 | 6 |
| 2701[9] | **Rebel County (IRE) (70)** (ABailey) **3-9-6**(3) DWright(6) (lw: hld up: swtchd ins & effrt over 2f out: nt r.o) | 1½ | **4** | 7/1 | 71 | 28 |
| 2679[8] | **Rood Music (55)** (MGMeagher) **5-9-1** JCarroll(5) (lw: led tl over 3f out: rdn & wknd appr fnl f) | 3½ | **5** | 11/4[1] | 49 | 13 |
| 3217[3] | **Hawwam (52)** (EJAlston) **10-8-12** JLowe(7) (lw: hld up: stumbled home turn: rdn over 2f out: nvr able to chal) | nk | **6** | 7/2[2] | 45 | 9 |
| 2868[5] | **My Handsome Prince (36)** (PJBevan) **4-7-10b** NCarlisle(2) (hld up in rr: plld wd & effrt 3f out: sn rdn: no imp) | nk | **7** | 14/1 | 29 | — |
| 2885[8] | **Vanborough Lad (54)** (MJBolton) **7-9-0** KFallon(3) (hld up in rr: effrt & rdn over 2f out: no imp) | 3 | **8** | 4/1[3] | 41 | 5 |

(SP 118.2%) **8 Rn**

**1m 44.77** (4.17) CSF £61.30 CT £704.83 TOTE £7.90: £1.70 £2.30 £2.20 (£29.80) OWNER Mr D. S. W. Blacker (LITTLEHAMPTON) BRED D. Blacker

LONG HANDICAP My Handsome Prince 7-7

WEIGHT FOR AGE 3yo-7lb

**1515 Gloriana** appreciated this step back to a mile and, after consenting to be given a lead until past halfway, quickly stormed clear for a very easy success. (13/2)

**1048 Duke Valentino**, flat-footed as the stalls opened, lost considerable ground. Making his effort entering the last quarter-mile, he stayed on particularly well inside the final furlong, which would suggest that he is capable of winning on turf. (10/1)

**2320 Katie Komaite**, in the same place virtually throughout, was hard at work below the distance and could do little more than keep on at the one pace. (12/1)

**2536 Rebel County (IRE)**, dropping back to a mile, looked very unwilling indeed when sent about her work over a furlong out and quite simply failed to put her best foot forward. (7/1)

**Rood Music** had only had one previous outing in the past nine months and, though he was fully expected here, he was under strong pressure and in trouble some way before reaching the final furlong. (11/4)

**3217 Hawwam**, who lost his footing on the home turn, could never summon up the pace to mount a serious challenge. (7/2)

**Vanborough Lad** proved to be a damp squib, and was never able to get himself within striking range of the principals. (4/1)

T/Plpt: £84.20 (164.7 Tckts). T/Qdpt: £59.10 (17.67 Tckts). IM

# 3243-NEWMARKET (R-H) (Good to firm)

## Friday August 9th

WEATHER: fine WIND: slt against

## 3404 K & N WAITE CONSTRUCTION H'CAP (0-90) (3-Y.O+) (Class C)

6-00 (6-00) **2m 24y (July)** £5,640.00 (£1,680.00: £800.00: £360.00) GOING minus 0.32 sec per fur (GF)

| | | | | SP | RR | SF |
|---|---|---|---|---|---|---|
| 2601[4] | **Canon Can (USA) (81)** (HRACecil) **3-8-12** PatEddery(4) (lw: in tch: rdn & lost pl over 5f out: styd on to ld 1f out: r.o) | — | **1** | 2/1[1] | 91 | 58 |
| 3117[9] | **Non Vintage (IRE) (52)** (MCChapman) **5-7-12** DeclanO'Shea(5) (lw: hld up: hdwy over 5f out: rdn 2f out: r.o ins fnl f) | 2 | **2** | 12/1 | 60 | 42 |
| 2697[10] | **Hal Hoo Yaroom (82)** (MajorWRHern) **3-8-13** TSprake(1) (lw: led: clr 8f out: rdn 2f out: hdd 1f out: kpt on) | ½ | **3** | 11/2 | 90 | 57 |
| 2912[3] | **Welsh Mill (IRE) (78)** (MrsMReveley) **7-9-5**(5) GLee(3) (swtg: prom: chsd ldr over 3f out: rdn over 2f out: one pce) | ½ | **4** | 7/2[3] | 85 | 67 |
| 2900[4] | **Western Sal (68)** (JLHarris) **4-9-0** TQuinn(6) (chsd ldr: rdn over 3f out: sn wknd) | 17 | **5** | 100/30[2] | 58 | 40 |
| 3043[6] | **Northern Law (70)** (JohnBerry) **4-9-2** MRimmer(2) (b: hld up: rdn & btn 3f out) | 1½ | **6** | 12/1 | 59 | 41 |

(SP 109.4%) **6 Rn**

**3m 28.23** (2.73) CSF £20.29 TOTE £2.70: £1.60 £4.30 (£17.00) OWNER Canon (Anglia) O A Ltd (NEWMARKET) BRED Elkay Stables

WEIGHT FOR AGE 3yo-15lb

**2601 Canon Can (USA)**, stepping up half a mile in trip, looked in big trouble as the tempo quickened, but won this on stamina as, the further they went, the better he got. (2/1: 6/4-9/4)

**Non Vintage (IRE)**, back at the trip over which he made the frame in last year's November Handicap, looked to be travelling well at the three-furlong pole, but he is difficult to win with, and did not help his pilot until hitting the rising ground. (12/1)

**2697 Hal Hoo Yaroom** again blazed the trail, but had been collared by the time the rising ground was reached. (11/2)

**2912 Welsh Mill (IRE)** spent his time trying to peg back the front-runner and could not go the pace in the closing stages. (7/2)

**2900 Western Sal**, stepping up in distance, did not appear to stay. (100/30)

**Northern Law** has shown no signs of returning to form since changing stables over the winter. (12/1)

## 3405 DAVID HEADLAND ASSOCIATES / TUDOR GATE HOTEL (S) STKS (2-Y.O) (Class E)

6-25 (6-25) **7f (July)** £3,850.00 (£1,150.00: £550.00: £250.00) Stalls: Centre GOING minus 0.32 sec per fur (GF)

| | | | | SP | RR | SF |
|---|---|---|---|---|---|---|
| 2904[10] | **Shall We Go (IRE)** (RHannon) **2-8-6** RPerham(6) (w ldrs: led over 1f out: rdn & hld on wl) | — | 1 | 12/1 | 58 | 20 |
| 1871[11] | **Rumbustious** (RHannon) **2-8-3**(3) DaneO'Neill(4) (in tch: pushed along over 3f out: rdn & ev ch ins fnl f: r.o) | hd | 2 | 9/2[3] | 58 | 20 |
| 1960[9] | **Maraud (88)** (RWArmstrong) **2-8-11** MHills(8) (swtg: led tl over 1f out: r.o ins fnl f) | 1¾ | 3 | 5/2[1] | 59 | 21 |
| 2995[4] | **Miss Barcelona (IRE) (66)** (MJPolglase) **2-8-6** PatEddery(3) (lw: hld up: rdn & hdwy over 2f out: no imp appr fnl f) | 4 | 4 | 11/4[2] | 45 | 7 |
| 3259[18] | **Doubly-H (IRE)** (MBell) **2-8-11v¹** TQuinn(5) (b.hind: hld up: rdn over 2f out: nvr trbld ldrs) | nk | 5 | 12/1 | 49 | 11 |
| 2254[5] | **Rebuke (55)** (RFJohnsonHoughton) **2-8-11** JReid(7) (trckd ldrs 5f: sn rdn & btn) | 1¼ | 6 | 6/1 | 46 | 8 |
| 1683[7] | **Fly Down To Rio (IRE)** (DWPArbuthnot) **2-8-6** BDoyle(2) (chsd ldrs over 4f) | 6 | 7 | 25/1 | 27 | — |
| 1513[14] | **Whynotriskme** (RHarris) **2-8-6** JHBrown(1) (spd 4f: wknd qckly) | 25 | 8 | 25/1 | — | — |
| | | | | (SP 110.8%) | **8 Rn** | |

**1m 28.79** (3.79) CSF £58.27 TOTE £19.70: £3.00 £1.60 £1.30 (£38.50) OWNER Kennet Valley Thoroughbreds (MARLBOROUGH) BRED D. Cordell-Lavarack
No bid

**2712 Shall We Go (IRE)** moved well to post and showed dramatic improvement, holding on gamely in a tight finish. (12/1: op 8/1)
**Rumbustious**, dropping in class, fought hammer and tongs with her stable-companion in the last furlong, but could not get by. (9/2: op 3/1)
**1694 Maraud** had run in three hot maidens so this represented a big step down in grade. Cruising in front, he did not impress with his attitude when challenged and seemed to give in tamely, only to rally when the first two were beyond recall. (5/2: 7/4-11/4)
**2995 Miss Barcelona (IRE)**, stepping up in trip and down in grade, did seem to stay the trip, but was not closing on the leaders in the last half-furlong. (11/4)
**Doubly-H (IRE)** looked a tricky ride in the first-time visor and just ran on past beaten horses. (12/1: op 8/1)
**2254 Rebuke** has yet to prove he gets this trip. (6/1)

## 3406 BERNARD LLOYD AND PAUL STANBROOK H'CAP (0-85) (3-Y.O+) (Class D)

6-55 (6-55) **6f (July)** £5,435.50 (£1,624.00: £777.00: £353.50) Stalls: Centre GOING minus 0.32 sec per fur (GF)

| | | | | SP | RR | SF |
|---|---|---|---|---|---|---|
| *3064** | **Pearl d'Azur (USA) (84)** (DRLoder) **3-9-11** PatEddery(1) (lw: trckd ldrs: led 2f out: drvn out) | — | 1 | 9/4[1] | 92 | 48 |
| 3045* | **Mr Bergerac (IRE) (82)** (BPalling) **5-9-13** TSprake(3) (lw: sn pushed along in rr: hdwy over 1f out: r.o wl ins fnl f) | hd | 2 | 5/2[2] | 90 | 50 |
| 3219[2] | **Golden Pound (USA) (83)** (MissGayKelleway) **4-10-0** JReid(4) (lw: in tch: squeezed thro over 2f out: rdn & ev ch fnl f: unable qckn nr fin) | s.h | 3 | 9/4[1] | 91 | 51 |
| 3152[10] | **Statistician (67)** (JohnBerry) **4-8-5**(7) AmyQuirk(6) (w ldrs 4f) | 9 | 4 | 20/1 | 51 | 11 |
| 2999[5] | **Mijas (74)** (LMontagueHall) **3-8-12**(3) DaneO'Neill(2) (swtg: led tl hdd & wknd 2f out) | ½ | 5 | 16/1 | 56 | 12 |
| *1809*[3] | **Beau Bruno (76)** (MBell) **3-9-3** TQuinn(5) (dwlt: rdn & sn chsng ldrs: hmpd over 2f out: sn wknd) | 6 | 6 | 9/1[3] | 42 | — |
| | | | | (SP 110.8%) | **6 Rn** | |

**1m 14.42** (2.42) CSF £7.86 TOTE £2.30: £1.80 £1.50 (£3.90) OWNER Sheikh Mohammed (NEWMARKET) BRED Darley Stud Management Inc
WEIGHT FOR AGE 3yo-4lb

**3064* Pearl d'Azur (USA)** looked in tremendous shape, despite showing some white in his eye, and was brought into the paddock late and immediately mounted and taken to post. He travelled well, but never went clear once sent on and there is more to come. (9/4: 6/4-5/2)
**3045* Mr Bergerac (IRE)** took a long time to get going, but came home to great effect in the final furlong, snatching second place on the line. (5/2)
**3219 Golden Pound (USA)** again ran well but, once more forcing his way through, did Beau Bruno no favours. (9/4)
**2908 Statistician** got a clear run and looks to need some respite from the Handicapper. (20/1)
**2999 Mijas**, taken to post steadily, was soon at the head of affairs, but had run herself out by the Dip. She seems too keen for her own good. (16/1)
**1809 Beau Bruno** looks a hard ride and was already beginning to struggle when knocked completely out of his stride approaching the two-furlong pole. (9/1)

## 3407 CARWIN MAIDEN STKS (2-Y.O) (Class D)

7-25 (7-26) **7f (July)** £4,737.00 (£1,416.00: £678.00: £309.00) GOING minus 0.32 sec per fur (GF)

| | | | | SP | RR | SF |
|---|---|---|---|---|---|---|
| 2783[4] | **Blue River (IRE)** (TGMills) **2-9-0** BDoyle(3) (a.p: rdn to ld ins fnl f) | — | 1 | 20/1 | 72 | 36 |
| | **Elriyadh (USA)** (PFICole) **2-9-0** TSprake(4) (unf: led over 6f: unable qckn) | ¾ | 2 | 10/1 | 70 | 34 |
| | **Stanton Harcourt (USA)** (JLDunlop) **2-9-0** PatEddery(12) (scope: lw: dwlt: hdwy 4f out: rdn & ev ch over 1f out: kpt on) | nk | 3 | 4/1[2] | 70 | 34 |
| | **Yalaietanee** (MRStoute) **2-9-0** JReid(6) (unf: scope: chsd ldrs: ev ch 2f out: no ex ins fnl f) | hd | 4 | 2/1[1] | 69 | 33 |
| 1989[6] | **Silk St John** (MJRyan) **2-9-0** AClark(9) (bit bkwd: r.o fnl 2f: nvr rchd ldrs) | 4 | 5 | 33/1 | 60 | 24 |
| | **Cosmic Prince (IRE)** (MAJarvis) **2-9-0** PRobinson(7) (leggy: scope: lw: stdd s: plld hrd & sn chsng ldrs: ev ch 2f out: sn wknd) | 1¼ | 6 | 33/1 | 57 | 21 |
| 3131[6] | **Tasik Chini (USA)** (PFICole) **2-9-0** TQuinn(10) (in tch: rdn & no hdwy fnl 2f) | ½ | 7 | 12/1 | 56 | 20 |
| | **Conon Falls (IRE)** (JHMGosden) **2-9-0** LDettori(5) (unf: scope: hld up: sme hdwy fnl 2f: nvr nr to chal) | 3 | 8 | 13/2 | 49 | 13 |
| | **Sandystones** (NAGraham) **2-8-9** MHills(8) (leggy: bit bkwd: swvd rt s: nvr nr to chal) | 2½ | 9 | 33/1 | 39 | 3 |
| | **Noble Investment** (JMPEustace) **2-9-0** RCochrane(1) (w'like: scope: bit bkwd: hdwy 3f out: wknd 2f out) | ¾ | 10 | 9/2[3] | 42 | 6 |
| | **Manwal (IRE)** (BHanbury) **2-9-0** WRyan(13) (str: scope: bit bkwd: dwlt: a bhd) | 5 | 11 | 14/1 | 31 | — |
| | **Swift** (MJPolglase) **2-9-0** DHarrison(2) (w'like: unf: bkwd: chsd ldrs 3f: sn bhd) | 1¼ | 12 | 50/1 | 28 | — |
| | **Prince de Loir** (DJSCosgrove) **2-9-0** MRimmer(11) (leggy: scope: bit bkwd: s.i.s: sn prom: rdn & wknd 3f out) | nk | 13 | 50/1 | 27 | — |
| | | | | (SP 125.8%) | **13 Rn** | |

**1m 28.02** (3.02) CSF £194.62 TOTE £23.70: £4.60 £2.80 £2.00 (£84.90) Trio £345.40 OWNER Mr M. J. Legg (EPSOM) BRED J. Hutchinson

**2783 Blue River (IRE)** had experience to call on in a driving finish and this enabled him to spring a surprise. (20/1)
**Elriyadh (USA)**, a lightly-made, athletic newcomer, moved well to post and jumped out. Making the field stretch from halfway, he could never get clear, but shaped well and should not be hard to place. (10/1)
**Stanton Harcourt (USA)**, fractious in the paddock, moved down well and ran well considering he will be better suited by further. (4/1)
**Yalaietanee** took a good hold going to post and looked the likely winner in the Dip, only to find little on the rising ground. Although by Sadler's Wells, his dam is from a very fast family and it may have been the trip rather than lack of condition that found him out. (2/1: 6/4-9/4)

**1989 Silk St John**, off for eight weeks since his debut, looked to need this and never threatened to get into the race proper. (33/1)
**Cosmic Prince (IRE)**, a poor walker who is bred to need much further, pulled very hard in the early stages and had used his energy by the Dip. Quite attractive, he has a future if he can be taught to settle. (33/1)
**Conon Falls (IRE)**, a very good mover, had a fairly quiet introduction and will come on plenty for the run. His pedigree and appearance suggest he will prove useful over middle distances. (13/2)
**Sandystones**, a tail-swisher who had two handlers in the paddock, ducked as the stalls opened and never recovered. She has a decent action if she can be taught to use it. (33/1)
**Noble Investment**, an attractive colt, looked too backward to do himself justice and ran well in the circumstances. Time and a trip should bring improvement. (9/2)
**Manwal (IRE)** (14/1: 10/1-16/1)

## 3408 DR. MARTENS NURSERY H'CAP (2-Y.O) (Class D)

7-55 (7-55) **7f (July)** £4,698.00 (£1,404.00: £672.00: £306.00) GOING minus 0.32 sec per fur (GF)

| | | | | SP | RR | SF |
|---|---|---|---|---|---|---|
| 2708[3] | **Mister Pink (80)** (RFJohnsonHoughton) **2-9-2** JReid(1) (in tch: led 1f out: rdn & r.o wl) | — | **1** | 8/1 | 81 | 32 |
| 3324[7] | **Silca's My Key (IRE) (68)** (MRChannon) **2-8-4** RPerham(10) (lw: wl bhd tl hdwy appr fnl f: fin wl) | 2½ | **2** | 8/1 | 63 | 14 |
| 3057[2] | **Hen Harrier (85)** (JLDunlop) **2-9-7** PatEddery(2) (dwlt: sn chsng ldrs: led over 1f out: sn hdd & no ex) | hd | **3** | 2/1[1] | 80 | 31 |
| 2792[5] | **Strat's Quest (68)** (DWPArbuthnot) **2-8-4** DHarrison(3) (lw: hld up: hdwy 3f out: kpt on fnl f) | s.h | **4** | 25/1 | 63 | 14 |
| 3046* | **Ninth Symphony (78)** (PCHaslam) **2-9-0** GCarter(9) (swtg: chsd ldrs: hung rt & ev ch over 1f out: sn btn) | ¾ | **5** | 13/2[2] | 71 | 22 |
| 3046[10] | **Our Kevin (69)** (KMcAuliffe) **2-8-5b** DRMcCabe(6) (swtg: chsd ldr over 5f: wknd ins fnl f) | 3 | **6** | 12/1 | 55 | 6 |
| 2863[10] | **Rock Fantasy (75)** (CMurray) **2-8-11** TQuinn(8) (swtg: in tch: rdn over 3f out: sn bhd) | 3½ | **7** | 16/1 | 53 | 4 |
| 3307[2] | **Lucky Oakwood (USA) (80)** (MBell) **2-9-2** MFenton(5) (lw: led over 5f: sn btn & eased) | 2 | **8** | 10/1 | 54 | 5 |
| 2595[6] | **Aztec Traveller (67)** (MJRyan) **2-8-3** BDoyle(11) (lw: chsd ldrs 5f) | 1½ | **9** | 8/1 | 37 | — |
| 3046[2] | **Dowry (82)** (RHannon) **2-9-1**(3) DaneO'Neill(7) (lw: hld up: effrt 3f out: nvr trbld ldrs) | ¾ | **10** | 7/1[3] | 51 | 2 |
| | | | | (SP 119.0%) | **10 Rn** | |

**1m 28.61** (3.61) CSF £65.05 CT £166.32 TOTE £7.80: £1.90 £2.20 £1.50 (£33.80) Trio £20.40 OWNER Mr C. W. Sumner (DIDCOT) BRED Southcourt Stud

**2708 Mister Pink** has been gradually improving in decent maidens and is a strong sort, galloping home well once put to work. (8/1)
**3324 Silca's My Key (IRE)** bounced back to form, finishing to great effect after being taken off his feet. An extra furlong will surely help. (8/1)
**3057 Hen Harrier** ran a solid race, but was off the bridle quite a way from home and failed to quicken as well as the first two. She will stay a little further. (2/1)
**2792 Strat's Quest**, stepping up in trip, loomed up dangerously in the Dip before staying on at the same pace. Her pedigree would suggest a shorter trip. (25/1)
**3046* Ninth Symphony** did not help himself by hanging to the stands' rail when asked to mount his challenge, but is still learning. (13/2)
**2750* Our Kevin** got warm and moved to post too freely. As a result, he was a spent force below the distance. (12/1)
**2595 Aztec Traveller** (8/1: 6/1-9/1)

## 3409 RICHARD BOLTON INSURANCE GROUP CONDITIONS STKS (3-Y.O+) (Class C)

8-25 (8-25) **1m 2f (July)** £5,965.20 (£2,155.20: £1,037.60: £428.00: £174.00) Stalls: Low GOING minus 0.32 sec per fur (GF)

| | | | | SP | RR | SF |
|---|---|---|---|---|---|---|
| 1769[11] | **Bint Salsabil (USA) (113)** (JLDunlop) **3-8-2** TSprake(1) (trckd ldr: led on bit 3f out: rdn & hdd 2f out: ev ch fnl f: r.o: fin 2nd, nk: awrdd r) | — | **1** | 3/1[3] | 113 | 74 |
| 2881[3] | **Magellan (USA)** (CEBrittain) **3-8-7** BDoyle(6) (led 7f: wknd over 1f out: fin 3rd, 10l: plcd 2nd) | | **2** | 5/2[2] | 102 | 63 |
| 2730[3] | **Desert Shot (113)** (MRStoute) **6-9-2** TQuinn(3) (hld up: hdwy whn bdly hmpd over 3f out: nt rcvr: fin 4th, 2l: plcd 3rd) | | **3** | 9/4[1] | 98+ | 68 |
| 1988[5] | **Poppy Carew (IRE) (102)** (PWHarris) **4-8-11** GHind(4) (lw: hld up: swtchd over 3f out: led 2f out: rdn out: fin 1st: disq: plcd 4th) | | **4** | 11/2 | 113 | 83 |
| 727[7] | **Lomberto (107)** (RHannon) **3-8-4**(3) DaneO'Neill(5) (lw: chsd ldrs: rdn 5f out: sn bhd) | 3½ | **5** | 10/1 | 93 | 54 |
| | | | | (SP 108.8%) | **5 Rn** | |

**2m 3.43** (-1.57) CSF £10.04 TOTE £3.20: £1.80 £1.40 (£4.20) OWNER Mr Hamdan Al Maktoum (ARUNDEL) BRED Shadwell Estate Company Limited

WEIGHT FOR AGE 3yo-9lb
STEWARDS' ENQUIRY Hind susp. 18-24/8/96 (irresponsible riding).

**1769 Bint Salsabil (USA)** looked eager to get on with things in the preliminaries and cruised to the front at the three-furlong pole. Soon off the bridle, she just got the worst of a protracted duel with Poppy Carew, only to get the race rather fortuitously in the Stewards' Room. (3/1)
**2881 Magellan (USA)**, wearing a net-muzzle, set a break-neck pace and soon established a considerable lead, only to tie up in the last couple of furlongs. (5/2)
**2730 Desert Shot** was almost put over the rail when racing on the winner's inside entering the last half-mile, and he should not be judged on this. (9/4)
**1509 Poppy Carew (IRE)** beat Bint Salsabil on merit, but had to lose this as she had caused serious interference when beginning her move on the stands' rail. This represented a return to her best and, despite not having had a winner for six weeks, the stable's horses are clearly on the way back. (11/2: 5/1-8/1)
**Lomberto** looked out of his league on paper and it proved that way, but he was beaten too far from home to blame a longer trip alone. (10/1)

T/Plpt: £107.10 (136.45 Tckts). T/Qdpt: £20.40 (54.56 Tckts). Dk

# 2800-REDCAR (L-H) (Firm)
## Friday August 9th

WEATHER: fine WIND: slt bhd

## 3410 STAINTONDALE (S) STKS (3-Y.O+) (Class F)

2-40 (2-43) **7f** £2,763.00 (£768.00: £369.00) Stalls: Centre GOING minus 0.83 sec per fur (HD)

| | | | | SP | RR | SF |
|---|---|---|---|---|---|---|
| 3217[2] | **Perilous Plight (65)** (WRMuir) **5-9-9** JWeaver(3) (lw: hld up: hdwy 2f out: rdn to ld 1f out: r.o u.p) | — | **1** | Evens[1] | 65 | 50 |
| 3289[4] | **Komlucky (44)** (ABMulholland) **4-8-6v**[1](7) GFaulkner(5) (a.p: led over 2f out: rdn & hdd 1f out: one pce) | 1¼ | **2** | 8/1 | 52 | 37 |
| 2528[9] | **Man of Wit (IRE) (61)** (APJarvis) **3-8-12** WJO'Connor(6) (lw: hdwy over 2f out: rdn over 1f out: one pce) | 1¼ | **3** | 9/2[3] | 54 | 33 |

| | | | | SP | RR | SF |
|---|---|---|---|---|---|---|
| 2801[2] | **Miss Zanzibar (49)** (RAFahey) **4-8-6**(7) RFfrench(8) (led tl over 2f out: rdn & wknd appr fnl f) | 3 | 4 | 5/2[2] | 42 | 27 |
| 1828[9] | **Mill Dancer (IRE) (36)** (EJAlston) **4-8-13** KFallon(4) (bit bkwd: nvr nr ldrs) | 3 | 5 | 25/1 | 36 | 21 |
| 2898[5] | **Battle Colours (IRE) (30)** (DonEnricoIncisa) **7-9-4** KimTinkler(7) (lw: chsd ldr over 1f: sn rdn & dropped rr) | s.h | 6 | 50/1 | 41 | 26 |
| 2898[7] | **Blue Grit (49)** (MDods) **10-9-4b** LCharnock(2) (prom tl rdn & wknd 3f out) | 5 | 7 | 16/1 | 29 | 14 |
| 2898[10] | **Steel Sovereign (32)** (MDods) **5-9-4** JFEgan(1) (bhd fr ½-wy) | 7 | 8 | 50/1 | 13 | — |
| | **Noble Colours** (JJQuinn) **3-8-12** NConnorton(9) (unruly stalls: sn pushed along: a bhd) | s.h | 9 | 100/1 | 13 | — |
| | | | | (SP 122.5%) | | **9 Rn** |

**1m 21.9** (0.20 under best) (-1.10) CSF £10.25 TOTE £2.10: £1.10 £2.30 £2.20 (£9.10) Trio £16.10 OWNER The Sun Punters Club (LAMBOURN) BRED Crest Stud Ltd
WEIGHT FOR AGE 3yo-6lb
Sold RStubbs 8,200 gns
**3217 Perilous Plight** landed his fourth win of the year. This yard is in good form. (Evens)
**3289 Komlucky**, visored for the first time, had to settle for the runner-up spot for the fourth time this season. (8/1)
**2151 Man of Wit (IRE)**, having his first run in selling company, looked likely to take a hand, but his effort petered out in the closing stages. (9/2)
**2801 Miss Zanzibar**, dropping back in trip after a good second here last month, found the principals too quick where it mattered. (5/2)
**1546 Mill Dancer (IRE)** looked as though she would come on for the run after an eight-week break and ran that way. (25/1)
**776 Battle Colours (IRE)**, with the leader briefly, looked none too keen the way he dropped out so early and so quickly. (50/1)

## 3411 TATTERSALLS AUCTION NURSERY H'CAP (2-Y.O) (Class E)
3-10 (3-11) **6f** £3,276.75 (£984.00: £474.50: £219.75) Stalls: Centre GOING minus 0.83 sec per fur (HD)

| | | | | SP | RR | SF |
|---|---|---|---|---|---|---|
| 3247[3] | **Ultra Boy (75)** (PCHaslam) **2-9-1** GCarter(2) (a.p: rdn appr fnl f: r.o to ld ins fnl f) | — | 1 | 9/4[1] | 76 | 34 |
| 2538[3] | **Jack Flush (IRE) (71)** (BSRothwell) **2-8-11** LCharnock(5) (led: rdn appr fnl f: hdd & no ex ins fnl f) | ½ | 2 | 13/2 | 71 | 29 |
| 2904[8] | **Jack The Lad (IRE) (65)** (CMurray) **2-8-5** JFEgan(6) (chsd ldr: drvn along ½-wy: r.o fnl f) | hd | 3 | 8/1 | 64 | 22 |
| 3224[3] | **Swiss Coast (IRE) (81)** (MrsJRRamsden) **2-9-7** KFallon(4) (lw: bhd: sn pushed along: rdn over 1f out: r.o ins fnl f) | hd | 4 | 3/1[2] | 80 | 38 |
| 2879[10] | **Seaside (IRE) (78)** (JohnBerry) **2-9-4** MFenton(1) (lw: prom: hdwy over 2f out: rdn 1f out: sn wknd) | 3½ | 5 | 7/2[3] | 68 | 26 |
| 3224[2] | **Under Pressure (76)** (TDEasterby) **2-9-2** MBirch(3) (chsd ldr tl wknd over 1f out) | 5 | 6 | 11/2 | 53 | 11 |
| | | | | (SP 117.8%) | | **6 Rn** |

**1m 9.8** (equals 2y best) (-0.40) CSF £16.09 TOTE £3.00: £2.30 £1.90 (£13.30) OWNER Pet Express (W&R) Ltd (MIDDLEHAM) BRED Cheveley Park Stud Ltd
**3247 Ultra Boy** justified market support and equalled the two-year-old record time in doing so. He is still improving. (9/4)
**2538 Jack Flush (IRE)** tried to make all, but was just outpointed in the latter stages. He should pick up a similar contest on this showing. (13/2: 9/2-7/1)
**1842 Jack The Lad (IRE)**, put under pressure some way out to stay in contention, stayed on in the last 100 yards. A step up in trip in this class should pay dividends. (8/1)
**3224 Swiss Coast (IRE)**, niggled along at the back of the field from the outset, was still last when getting a sharp reminder below the distance. He was doing all his best work in the final furlong and may be handicapped to the hilt, but has the ability to win races. (3/1)
**1362 Seaside (IRE)**, never far away, improved to hold every chance over a furlong out, but was soon back-pedalling. (7/2)

## 3412 PAT PHOENIX H'CAP (0-70) (3-Y.O+) (Class E)
3-40 (3-40) **1m 3f** £3,117.50 (£935.00: £450.00: £207.50) Stalls: Low GOING minus 0.83 sec per fur (HD)

| | | | | SP | RR | SF |
|---|---|---|---|---|---|---|
| 3249[6] | **Ordained (54)** (EJAlston) **3-8-5** SDrowne(5) (lw: hld up: stdy hdwy over 3f out: led 2f out: r.o u.p) | — | 1 | 8/1 | 67 | 9 |
| 3113[8] | **Almuhtaram (67)** (MissGayKelleway) **4-10-0b** KFallon(1) (hld up: hdwy 3f out: sn rdn: one pce fnl f) | 1¼ | 2 | 5/1[2] | 78 | 30 |
| 3346[5] | **Gold Desire (38)** (MBrittain) **6-7-13**[5x] JLowe(8) (hld up: pushed along ent st: r.o fr over 1f out: nrst fin) | 1¼ | 3 | 8/1 | 47 | — |
| 3118[2] | **Milltown Classic (IRE) (35)** (JParkes) **4-7-10** NCarlisle(7) (led after 2f tl rdn & hdd 2f out: kpt on same pce) | 2 | 4 | 11/2[3] | 42 | — |
| 3109* | **Alabang (66)** (MJCamacho) **5-9-13**[5x] LCharnock(3) (lw: chsd ldrs: rdn & ev ch 2f out: kpt on one pce) | hd | 5 | 5/4[1] | 72 | 24 |
| *3074*[2] | **Docklands Courier (45)** (BJMcMath) **4-8-6** KDarley(2) (led 2f: styd prom: rdn 3f out: grad wknd) | 1 | 6 | 7/1 | 50 | 2 |
| *3086*[9] | **Bardia (35)** (DonEnricoIncisa) **6-7-10** KimTinkler(4) (in tch: rdn over 3f out: sn btn) | 5 | 7 | 50/1 | 33 | — |
| 3117[5] | **Instantaneous (43)** (TDEasterby) **4-8-4b**[1ow2] MBirch(6) (plld hrd: chsd ldrs tl wknd qckly 2f out: t.o) | 16 | 8 | 14/1 | 17 | — |
| | | | | (SP 119.8%) | | **8 Rn** |

**2m 20.2** (2.20) CSF £45.74 CT £307.83 TOTE £8.60: £1.80 £1.60 £2.00 (£24.30) OWNER Mr P. D. Ebdon (PRESTON) BRED Sheikh Mohammed Bin Rashid Al Maktoum
LONG HANDICAP Milltown Classic (IRE) 7-8 Bardia 7-3
WEIGHT FOR AGE 3yo-10lb
OFFICIAL EXPLANATION **Alabang: the jockey reported that the gelding was shortening his stride on the firm ground and he felt it prudent to hold him together. The trainer also added that he felt the gelding was suffering from the effects of too many races on firm ground.**
**3249 Ordained**, on what is clearly her favourite track and ground, picked up the leaders early in the straight and never looked likely to be denied once she hit the front. (8/1)
**3113 Almuhtaram**, patiently ridden until chased along to take second place below the distance, could make no impression on the winner on the run home. (5/1)
**3346 Gold Desire**, having his second run in less then twenty-four hours, stayed on well in the last quarter-mile. (8/1: op 5/1)
**3118 Milltown Classic (IRE)**, flat to the boards when collared, had no more to give. (11/2)
**3109* Alabang** looked very fit and moved well to post. He appeared the likely winner two furlongs from home, but found little when asked the question. (5/4)
**3074 Docklands Courier**, chased along from some way out, just did not have the pace to get involved. (7/1)

## 3413 SOUTH DURHAM MAIDEN STKS (3-Y.O+) (Class D)
4-10 (4-11) **7f** £3,691.00 (£1,108.00: £534.00: £247.00) Stalls: Centre GOING minus 0.83 sec per fur (HD)

| | | | | SP | RR | SF |
|---|---|---|---|---|---|---|
| 3093[2] | **Hulm (IRE) (79)** (HThomsonJones) **3-8-9b**[1] GCarter(5) (lw: mde all: rdn ent fnl f: r.o) | — | 1 | 13/8[2] | 71 | 41 |
| 1058a[5] | **Robamaset (IRE) (88)** (LMCumani) **3-9-0** FJovine(4) (a.p: chsd wnr fr 2f out: rdn 1f out: unable qckn ins fnl f) | 1 | 2 | 5/4[1] | 74 | 44 |
| | **Mighty Keen** (MJohnston) **3-9-0** JWeaver(2) (str: scope: bit bkwd: chsd ldrs: pushed along ½-wy: rdn & wknd wl over 1f out) | 7 | 3 | 4/1[3] | 58 | 28 |
| 3067[12] | **Mubariz (IRE) (80)** (CSmith) **4-9-6** WJO'Connor(3) (chsd wnr: rdn 2f out: sn btn) | 2½ | 4 | 16/1 | 52 | 28 |
| 3226[5] | **Rasin Charge** (RCraggs) **5-9-6** LCharnock(6) (dwlt: a bhd: t.o) | 22 | 5 | 33/1 | 2 | — |

| | | | | | | |
|---|---|---|---|---|---|---|
| | **Rupert Manners** (EJAlston) **3-9-0** JLowe(1) (wl grwn: bkwd: s.i.s: a bhd: t.o) | 2½ | 6 | 50/1 | — | — |

(SP 113.3%) **6 Rn**

**1m 21.5** (0.60 under best) (-1.50) CSF £4.00 TOTE £2.40: £1.10 £1.30 (£2.60) OWNER Mr Khalil Alsayegh (NEWMARKET) BRED Oldtown Bloodstock Holdings Ltd

WEIGHT FOR AGE 3yo-6lb

**3093 Hulm (IRE)**, blinkered for the first time, was always finding enough to hold off the favourite. (13/8)
**1058a Robamaset (IRE)** lacked the turn of foot necessary to peg back the winner. A return to a longer trip should help. (5/4: op Evens)
**Mighty Keen**, a scopey half-brother to Marina Park, was well outpointed in the second half of the race. This run should do him the power of good. (4/1: op 2/1)
**2420 Mubariz (IRE)** dropped right away in the last two furlongs. (16/1)
**3226 Rasin Charge** was slowly away and never in contention. (33/1)

## 3414 HURWORTH MAIDEN APPRENTICE H'CAP (0-65) (3-Y.O+) (Class F)

4-40 (4-40) **1m 1f** £2,497.50 (£710.00: £352.50) Stalls: Low GOING minus 0.83 sec per fur (HD)

| | | | | SP | RR | SF |
|---|---|---|---|---|---|---|
| 2776[3] | **Forest Fantasy (48)** (JWharton) **3-8-12** RFfrench(2) (in tch: hdwy 3f out: led over 2f out: r.o fnl f) | — | **1** | 11/4[1] | 66 | 19 |
| 3161[2] | **Urgent Swift (63)** (APJarvis) **3-9-10**(3) KHopkins(1) (lw: towards rr: styd on fr over 2f out: rdn over 1f out: r.o) | 6 | **2** | 100/30[2] | 70 | 23 |
| 2752[2] | **Mels Baby (IRE) (58)** (JLEyre) **3-9-3**(5) RCody-Boutcher(9) (lw: a.p: led over 3f out: rdn & hdd over 2f out: sn wknd) | 1 | **3** | 100/30[2] | 64 | 17 |
| | **Whothehellisharry (60)** (JBerry) **3-9-7**(3) CLowther(4) (bkwd: bhd: kpt on fr over 2f out: n.d) | 10 | **4** | 20/1 | 48 | 1 |
| 2587[8] | **Intrepid Fort (26)** (BWMurray) **7-7-12b** TFinn(7) (dwlt: bhd tl kpt on fnl 3f: n.d) | nk | **5** | 20/1 | 13 | — |
| 1526[11] | **Shepherds Dean (IRE) (36)** (PCHaslam) **3-7-6**(8) FBoyle(10) (a bhd) | 2½ | **6** | 16/1 | 19 | — |
| 2565[6] | **Carmenoura (IRE) (25)** (EJAlston) **4-7-11** JFowle(3) (lw: a bhd: t.o) | 1½ | **7** | 50/1 | 5 | — |
| 3228[4] | **Backhander (IRE) (48)** (MartynWane) **4-8-12b**[1](8) GWright(6) (led: sn clr: hdd over 3f out: wknd qckly: t.o) | 4 | **8** | 16/1 | 21 | — |
| 2968[4] | **Brandonville (55)** (NTinkler) **3-9-5** TSiddall(8) (lw: prom tl wknd 3f out: t.o) | 1½ | **9** | 5/1[3] | 25 | — |
| *3074[5]* | **Pinkerton Polka (41)** (JParkes) **4-8-13** PDoe(5) (chsd ldrs tl wknd 4f out: t.o) | 1 | **10** | 12/1 | 10 | — |

(SP 120.4%) **10 Rn**

**1m 50.9** (1.10) CSF £12.29 CT £29.81 TOTE £3.90: £1.10 £1.60 £1.30 (£6.10) Trio £4.70 OWNER Mr G. W. Turner (MELTON MOWBRAY) BRED Mrs Jane Turner

WEIGHT FOR AGE 3yo-8lb

STEWARDS' ENQUIRY Fowle susp. 18-19/8/96 (improper use of whip).

**2776 Forest Fantasy**, given a confident ride, picked up the leaders early in the straight and had the race won at the furlong pole. (11/4)
**3161 Urgent Swift**, who looked ultra-fit, found himself with an awful lot to do turning for home. He did stay on to some effect, but had no chance on catching the winner. (100/30: 9/4-7/2)
**2752 Mels Baby (IRE)** again proved very one-paced in the latter part of the race. (100/30)
**Whothehellisharry** just plugged on through beaten horses. (20/1)

## 3415 CLEVELAND H'CAP (0-80) (3-Y.O+ F & M) (Class D)

5-10 (5-10) **5f** £3,665.00 (£1,100.00: £530.00: £245.00) Stalls: Centre GOING minus 0.83 sec per fur (HD)

| | | | | SP | RR | SF |
|---|---|---|---|---|---|---|
| 3223[2] | **Kira (58)** (JLEyre) **6-8-11**(3) NVarley(3) (b.off hind: lw: mde all: r.o wl fnl f) | — | **1** | 10/11[1] | 66 | 38 |
| 3352[10] | **Dominelle (53)** (TDEasterby) **4-8-9** MBirch(1) (prom: wnt 2nd over 1f out: rdn & no imp fnl f) | 2½ | **2** | 7/1[3] | 53 | 25 |
| 2910[4] | **Sunset Harbour (IRE) (49)** (SEKettlewell) **3-7-9**(7) JennyBenson(4) (chsd ldrs: rdn over 1f out: kpt on same pce) | 1½ | **3** | 12/1 | 44 | 13 |
| 3085[6] | **Time To Tango (71)** (GMMoore) **3-9-10** JFEgan(2) (lw: plld hrd: chsd wnr: rdn over 1f out: sn wknd) | 3 | **4** | 7/4[2] | 57 | 26 |

(SP 108.9%) **4 Rn**

**56.8 secs** (-0.70) CSF £6.29 TOTE £1.70: (£3.70) OWNER Mr J. E. Wilson (HAMBLETON) BRED J. S. Bell

WEIGHT FOR AGE 3yo-3lb

**3223 Kira** won this in good style and may now be stepped up in class. (10/11)
**3252 Dominelle**, having finished plum last twenty-four hours earlier at Pontefract, ran much better here, although clearly second best. (7/1)
**2910 Sunset Harbour (IRE)** looked and ran well without being able to threaten the winner. (12/1: op 8/1)
**3085 Time To Tango** did not settle early and paid the price in the later part of the race. (7/4)

T/Plpt: £37.60 (337.76 Tckts). T/Qdpt: £8.20 (72.27 Tckts). J

# 3061-WOLVERHAMPTON (L-H) (Standard)

## Friday August 9th

WEATHER: fine WIND: almost nil

## 3416 WALES H'CAP (0-65) (3-Y.O+) (Class F)

2-20 (2-22) **5f (Fibresand)** £2,381.00 (£656.00: £311.00) Stalls: Low GOING minus 0.12 sec per fur (FST)

| | | | | SP | RR | SF |
|---|---|---|---|---|---|---|
| *2308[4]* | **Aljaz (42)** (MissGayKelleway) **6-8-9** SSanders(1) (hdwy on ins over 2f out: led over 1f out: drvn out) | — | **1** | 8/1 | 49 | 31 |
| *3061[2]* | **Napier Star (59)** (MrsNMacauley) **3-9-6v**[1](3) CTeague(7) (chsd ldr 3f: ev ch over 1f out: r.o one pce) | 1¼ | **2** | 4/1[2] | 62 | 41 |
| *3091[2]* | **Need You Badly (57)** (SPCWoods) **3-9-7** WWoods(8) (hdwy over 1f out: r.o fnl f) | 3 | **3** | 5/2[1] | 50 | 29 |
| *3061** | **Marjorie Rose (IRE) (60)** (ABailey) **3-9-7**(3) DWright(5) (b: s.i.s: hdwy on ins over 1f out: nt rch ldrs) | hd | **4** | 6/1[3] | 53 | 32 |
| 3146[12] | **Bowcliffe Grange (IRE) (53)** (DWChapman) **4-9-6b** JQuinn(6) (led & sn clr: hdd over 1f out: wknd fnl f) | 1¼ | **5** | 6/1[3] | 42 | 24 |
| 3261[3] | **Scored Again (56)** (MJHeaton-Ellis) **6-9-4v**(5) AmandaSanders(2) (b: prom over 2f) | 2½ | **6** | 7/1 | 45 | 27 |
| *2308[5]* | **Belinda Blue (46)** (RAFahey) **4-8-13** DHarrison(3) (prom over 2f) | d.h | **6** | 7/1 | 27 | 9 |
| 2992[7] | **Tommy Tempest (30)** (REPeacock) **7-7-11v** DeclanO'Shea(4) (bhd fnl 2f) | ½ | **8** | 16/1 | 10 | — |

(SP 119.1%) **8 Rn**

**61.8 secs** (3.10) CSF £38.77 CT £96.48 TOTE £9.40: £2.20 £2.20 £1.10 (£23.60) OWNER Blackham And Gould Partnership (WHITCOMBE) BRED Side Hill Stud

WEIGHT FOR AGE 3yo-3lb

**2308 Aljaz**, rated 22lb lower than on turf, likes give in the ground and was scoring for the first time over the minimum trip. (8/1)
**3061 Napier Star**, tried in a visor, had been raised 4lb after being narrowly beaten when in season here last month. (4/1)

**3091 Need You Badly** was 2lb higher for her good second at Southwell. (5/2)
**3061* Marjorie Rose (IRE)** could not confirm the form of her last-gasp win over Napier Star on 1lb worse terms. (6/1)
**2849 Bowcliffe Grange (IRE)** showed his usual blistering pace, but did not get home on this surface. (6/1: op 4/1)
**3261 Scored Again**, rated 7lb lower on grass, did not seem to benefit from the fitting of a visor. (7/1)

## 3417 ROYAL BANK INVOICE FINANCE NURSERY H'CAP (2-Y.O) (Class E)

2-50 (2-58) **7f (Fibresand)** £3,261.30 (£974.40: £466.20: £212.10) Stalls: High GOING minus 0.12 sec per fur (FST)

| Form | Horse | Dist | Pos | SP | RR | SF |
|---|---|---|---|---|---|---|
| 2923[D] | **Ben's Ridge (62)** (PCHaslam) **2-7-13**[(5)] MartinDwyer(6) (lw: a.p: led over 2f out: clr over 1f out: comf) | — | 1 | 9/1[3] | 65+ | 26 |
| 3275[2] | **Going For Broke (63)** (PCHaslam) **2-8-5** DeanMcKeown(3) (a.p: chsd wnr 2f out: hung lft over 1f out: no imp) | 4 | 2 | 14/1 | 57 | 18 |
| 2984[5] | **Tinkerbell (66)** (LordHuntingdon) **2-8-8v** DHarrison(8) (a.p: ev ch 2f out: wknd over 1f out) | 2½ | 3 | 10/1 | 54 | 15 |
| 2797[3] | **Gresatre (62)** (CADwyer) **2-8-4** FNorton(10) (hdwy over 2f out: wknd over 1f out) | 7 | 4 | 9/1[3] | 34 | — |
| *2633*[3] | **Summer Queen (72)** (SPCWoods) **2-9-0** WWoods(4) (lw: hld up: hdwy over 4f out: wknd over 2f out) | 2½ | 5 | 4/1[2] | 38 | — |
| 3208[5] | **Superquest (73)** (WAO'Gorman) **2-9-1b[1]** SSanders(7) (prom: ev ch over 2f out: wknd over 1f out) | ½ | 6 | 16/1 | 38 | — |
| *3065** | **Advance Repro (66)** (JAkehurst) **2-8-8b** AClark(2) (led over 4f: wknd wl over 1f out) | 3 | 7 | 10/1 | 24 | — |
| 2184[4] | **Classic Mystery (IRE) (70)** (BJMeehan) **2-8-12** MTebbutt(1) (bhd fnl 3f) | 3½ | 8 | 11/1 | 20 | — |
| 2977[5] | **Bali-Pet (61)** (WGMTurner) **2-7-10**[(7)] RMullen(5) (lw: w ldr over 3f: wknd over 2f out) | 4 | 9 | 16/1 | 2 | — |
| *2938** | **Common Rock (IRE) (58)** (JNorton) **2-8-0v** DaleGibson(12) (s.i.s: a t.o) | 12 | 10 | 16/1 | — | — |
| 2984[2] | **Flotilla (79)** (SirMarkPrescott) **2-9-7** GDuffield(11) (sn t.o) | hd | 11 | 7/2[1] | — | — |
| | | | | (SP 113.1%) | **11 Rn** | |

**1m 29.2** (4.00 under 2y best) (4.50) CSF £107.66 CT £1,178.90 TOTE £9.40: £2.50 £3.80 £3.30 (£47.90) Trio £158.80 OWNER Mr S. A. B. Dinsmore (MIDDLEHAM) BRED S. A. B. Dinsmore
OFFICIAL EXPLANATION **Flotilla: the jockey reported that the colt, who had been replated, was never travelling well and pulled up very sore.**
**2923 Ben's Ridge** stepped up considerably on his previous outing here when racing over six. (9/1)
**3275 Going For Broke** showed his previous run on the Sand at Southwell to be all wrong. (14/1)
**2984 Tinkerbell** was racing off a 4lb lower mark than at Catterick. (10/1)
**2797 Gresatre** was 4lb higher than when third at Leicester over six. (9/1: op 6/1)
**2633 Summer Queen**, trying a longer trip, found disappointingly little after travelling well until past halfway. (4/1)
**2984 Flotilla**, replated in the parade ring, was never travelling well. (7/2)

## 3418 STAFFORDSHIRE BUILDING SOCIETY MAIDEN STKS (I) (3-Y.O) (Class D)

3-20 (3-25) **1m 1f 79y (Fibresand)** £3,306.25 (£982.00: £465.50: £207.25) Stalls: Low GOING minus 0.12 sec per fur (FST)

| Form | Horse | Dist | Pos | SP | RR | SF |
|---|---|---|---|---|---|---|
| 937[8] | **Hal's Pal (84)** (DRLoder) **3-9-0** RHughes(3) (lw: plld hrd: led over 7f out: hdd 4f out: led on bit wl over 1f out: rdn & flashed tail: r.o) | — | 1 | 1/3[1] | 92+ | 61 |
| 2610[8] | **Polar Champ (75)** (SPCWoods) **3-9-0** WWoods(1) (w ldr: rdn to ld 4f out: hdd wl over 1f out: hrd rdn: r.o) | ¾ | 2 | 10/1[3] | 91 | 60 |
| 3258[8] | **What A Fuss** (BHanbury) **3-9-0** JStack(9) (a.p: one pce fnl 2f) | 4 | 3 | 33/1 | 84 | 53 |
| 2970[2] | **Failed To Hit** (SirMarkPrescott) **3-9-0** GDuffield(6) (lw: nvr plcd to chal) | 8 | 4 | 5/1[2] | 70 | 39 |
| 2557[8] | **Tathmin** (JRBosley) **3-9-0** CRutter(8) (bhd fnl 4f) | 1¼ | 5 | 50/1 | 68 | 37 |
| 2579[8] | **Nezool Almatar (IRE)** (MAJarvis) **3-8-9** PBloomfield(7) (prom over 4f) | 19 | 6 | 25/1 | 31 | — |
| 932[5] | **Kass Alhawa (82)** (DWChapman) **3-9-0** ACulhane(2) (a bhd: t.o fnl 6f) | 7 | 7 | 10/1[3] | 24 | — |
| | **Charnwood Meg (IRE)** (RHarris) **3-8-9** AMackay(4) (leggy: bkwd: dwlt: a bhd: t.o fnl 6f) | 5 | 8 | 50/1 | 10 | — |
| | **Lovely Morning** (DJGMurraySmith) **3-8-9** DHarrison(5) (bit bkwd: led over 2f: wknd over 4f out) | hd | 9 | 50/1 | 10 | — |
| | | | | (SP 122.5%) | **9 Rn** | |

**1m 59.2** (3.20) CSF £5.59 TOTE £1.20: £1.00 £2.70 £5.50 (£5.50) Trio £34.20 OWNER Mr Wafic Said (NEWMARKET) BRED Cheveley Park Stud Ltd
**937 Hal's Pal** certainly resents the whip and flashed his tail each time he was struck. (1/3: op 1/2)
**2198 Polar Champ** boxed on well when the winner was galloping all over him, and made sure the hot-pot favourite did not have things all his own way. (10/1: 8/1-12/1)
**What A Fuss** showed improved form, switching to the Sand, and is now qualified for handicaps. (33/1)
**2970 Failed To Hit**, a 37,000 guinea colt, had surprisingly made his debut over the minimum trip and gave the impression he can do a lot better than this. (5/1)

## 3419 THORPE VERNON H'CAP (0-85) (3-Y.O+) (Class D)

3-50 (3-54) **1m 100y (Fibresand)** £4,059.60 (£1,213.80: £581.40: £265.20) Stalls: Low GOING minus 0.12 sec per fur (FST)

| Form | Horse | Dist | Pos | SP | RR | SF |
|---|---|---|---|---|---|---|
| 2574[16] | **Super High (76)** (PHowling) **4-9-6b** PaulEddery(12) (lw: a.p: led over 3f out tl over 1f out: led ins fnl f: all out) | — | 1 | 8/1 | 83 | 54 |
| 3274[5] | **Bentico (73)** (MrsNMacauley) **7-9-0**[(3)] CTeague(3) (hld up: stdy hdwy on ins 5f out: led over 1f out tl ins fnl f) | 1¼ | 2 | 9/1 | 78 | 49 |
| 3246[7] | **China Castle (71)** (PCHaslam) **3-8-8** JFortune(7) (hld up & bhd: hdwy fnl 2f: fin wl) | ½ | 3 | 12/1 | 75 | 39 |
| *2201** | **Waikiki Beach (USA) (78)** (GLMoore) **5-9-8** SWhitworth(11) (b: b.hind: a.p: one pce fnl 2f) | 1½ | 4 | 6/1[2] | 79 | 50 |
| *2749*[7] | **Johnnie the Joker (77)** (JPLeigh) **5-9-7b** DeanMcKeown(5) (a.p: rdn 3f out: no hdwy fnl 2f) | 3 | 5 | 9/1 | 72 | 43 |
| *3062** | **Ethbaat (USA) (71)** (MJHeaton-Ellis) **5-9-1** AClark(2) (lw: hdwy over 4f out: rdn over 2f out: one pce) | 1¼ | 6 | 11/2[1] | 64 | 35 |
| 3265[9] | **Le Sport (82)** (ABailey) **3-9-2**[(3)] DWright(6) (nvr nr to chal) | nk | 7 | 20/1 | 74 | 38 |
| 1609[11] | **Dancing Sioux (75)** (DNicholls) **4-9-5** AlexGreaves(10) (lw: prom tl wknd wl over 1f out) | 1¼ | 8 | 10/1 | 65 | 36 |
| *2937*[2] | **Princess Efisio (67)** (BAMcMahon) **3-7-13**[(5)] LNewton(8) (lw: s.s: nvr nr ldrs) | 2½ | 9 | 13/2[3] | 52 | 16 |
| *3089*[2] | **Desert Invader (IRE) (75)** (DWChapman) **5-9-5** ACulhane(1) (lw: a bhd) | 2 | 10 | 10/1 | 56 | 27 |
| | **Takhlid (USA) (80)** (DWChapman) **5-9-10** GDuffield(13) (bit bkwd: led 5f: wknd over 2f out: fin lame) | 1½ | 11 | 16/1 | 59 | 30 |
| *3074*[6] | **Miss Haversham (63)** (CACyzer) **4-8-7** PBloomfield(9) (chsd ldrs 4f: t.o) | dist | 12 | 25/1 | — | — |
| 2228[11] | **Enchanted Guest (IRE) (73)** (PWHarris) **3-8-10** GHind(4) (b.nr fore: prom tl rdn & wknd 3f out: t.o) | 24 | 13 | 16/1 | — | — |
| | | | | (SP 120.4%) | **13 Rn** | |

**1m 49.2** (4.20) CSF £71.96 CT £818.32 TOTE £12.30: £2.60 £2.70 £3.40 (£31.30) Trio £381.20 OWNER Mrs J. M. Khan (NEWMARKET) BRED Nam Seng Yong
WEIGHT FOR AGE 3yo-7lb
OFFICIAL EXPLANATION **Dancing Sioux: the jockey reported that this was the gelding's first run since he suffered a back injury and that in the latter stages of the race he became very tired and she felt it appropriate to ride him sympathetically to the line.**

**2170 Super High** is rated 16lb higher on the artificial surface and again showed his liking for it with a hard-fought win. (8/1)
**3274 Bentico** ran a brave race off a mark 5lb higher than when winning over course and distance in June. (9/1: 6/1-10/1)
**329* China Castle**, from a stable coming out of the doldrums, seems to have come to hand. (12/1)
**2201* Waikiki Beach (USA)** was by no means disgraced considering he was up 9lb for his win last time. (6/1)
**2552 Johnnie the Joker** was 7lb higher than when winning here in June. (9/1)
**3062* Ethbaat (USA)** found it tougher switching to handicap company. (11/2)

## 3420 TSB ASSET FINANCE (S) STKS (3-Y.O+) (Class G)

4-20 (4-23) **6f (Fibresand)** £2,070.00 (£570.00: £270.00) Stalls: Low GOING minus 0.12 sec per fur (FST)

| Form | Horse | Dist | Pos | SP | RR | SF |
|---|---|---|---|---|---|---|
| 3278[3] | **Ultra Beet (65)** (PCHaslam) **4-9-2v** JFortune(1) (s.i.s: sn prom: led over 2f out: drvn out) | — | **1** | 5/2[2] | 63 | 32 |
| 2154[14] | **Efficacy (60)** (APJarvis) **5-8-4**(7) CCarver(11) (w ldr: led over 3f out tl over 2f out: r.o ins fnl f) | ½ | **2** | 7/1[3] | 57 | 26 |
| 3278[6] | **Sense of Priority (73)** (DNicholls) **7-9-7** AlexGreaves(13) (led over 2f: r.o one pce fnl 2f) | 1¾ | **3** | 15/8[1] | 62 | 31 |
| *3089[13]* | **Dark Shot (IRE) (60)** (NTinkler) **4-9-2v** GDuffield(9) (a.p: r.o one pce fnl 2f) | hd | **4** | 9/1 | 57 | 26 |
| *2637[6]* | **Royal Rapport (40)** (BAMcMahon) **3-8-12** SSanders(12) (lw: chsd ldrs: rdn over 3f out: no hdwy fnl 2f) | 1½ | **5** | 16/1 | 53 | 18 |
| 3151[10] | **Monis (IRE) (53)** (JBalding) **5-8-9v**(7) JEdmunds(3) (lw: hdwy over 1f out: nvr nr to chal) | nk | **6** | 10/1 | 52 | 21 |
| 2966[13] | **Brin-Lodge (IRE)** (KSBridgwater) **3-8-2**(5) PPMurphy(4) (prom 4f) | 5 | **7** | 50/1 | 34 | — |
| 3097[6] | **Elraas (USA) (21)** (HJCollingridge) **4-9-2v** NAdams(5) (nvr trbld ldrs) | 2½ | **8** | 50/1 | 32 | 1 |
| 2799[7] | **Sandra Dee (IRE) (38)** (EAWheeler) **4-8-11** SWhitworth(2) (lw: bhd fnl 3f) | nk | **9** | 33/1 | 26 | — |
| *3061[3]* | **Maraschino (37)** (BJMeehan) **3-8-7** MTebbutt(6) (a bhd) | ½ | **10** | 11/1 | 25 | — |
| 2617[17] | **Pytchley Dawn (35)** (OO'Neill) **6-8-11** VSlattery(10) (bhd fnl 3f) | 2 | **11** | 50/1 | 20 | — |
| | **Christian Warrior (21)** (REPeacock) **7-8-13**(3) PMcCabe(7) (bit bkwd: a bhd) | 7 | **12** | 50/1 | 6 | — |
| *2748[11]* | **Bajan Frontier (IRE) (41)** (FHLee) **4-8-11** PaulEddery(8) (lw: sme hdwy over 3f out: wknd over 2f out) | 3½ | **13** | 20/1 | — | — |

(SP 124.7%) **13 Rn**

**1m 15.6** (4.20) CSF £20.20 TOTE £2.90: £1.60 £2.40 £2.20 (£12.50) Trio £9.80 OWNER Pet Express (W&R) Ltd (MIDDLEHAM) BRED Rockhouse Farms Ltd
WEIGHT FOR AGE 3yo-4lb
No bid
**3278 Ultra Beet**, an All-Weather specialist, had been knocking on the door on turf recently. (5/2)
**1715 Efficacy**, whose three wins have been over course and distance, appreciated switching back to this surface. (7/1)
**3278 Sense of Priority** could only keep on at the same pace. (15/8)
**3089 Dark Shot (IRE)** ran better on his first run for Nigel Tinkler. (9/1: op 6/1)
**1719 Royal Rapport** was trying a shorter trip. (16/1)

## 3421 STAFFORDSHIRE BUILDING SOCIETY MAIDEN STKS (II) (3-Y.O) (Class D)

4-50 (4-51) **1m 1f 79y (Fibresand)** £3,273.10 (£971.80: £460.40: £204.70) Stalls: Low GOING minus 0.12 sec per fur (FST)

| Form | Horse | Dist | Pos | SP | RR | SF |
|---|---|---|---|---|---|---|
| *3064[2]* | **Serious Sensation (79)** (SirMarkPrescott) **3-9-0** GDuffield(7) (hld up: stdy hdwy over 4f out: rdn 2f out: led ins fnl f: r.o wl) | — | **1** | 4/7[1] | 82 | 53 |
| 2754[W] | **Menoo Hal Batal (USA) (83)** (MRStoute) **3-9-0** PaulEddery(6) (lw: a.p: led over 3f out tl ins fnl f) | 2½ | **2** | 7/2[2] | 78 | 49 |
| 1994[10] | **Welsh Emblem (IRE) (65)** (GWragg) **3-9-0** WWoods(5) (lw: a.p: rdn 2f out: one pce) | 8 | **3** | 10/1[3] | 64 | 35 |
| *3064[4]* | **Biscay** (RCharlton) **3-8-9** SSanders(3) (no hdwy fnl 2f) | 2½ | **4** | 10/1[3] | 55 | 26 |
| 3258[4] | **Dazzling** (DCO'Brien) **3-8-9** GBardwell(4) (wl bhd fnl 6f) | 10 | **5** | 20/1 | 38 | 9 |
| *3062[2]* | **Nicola's Princess (50)** (BAMcMahon) **3-8-4**(5) LNewton(1) (sddle slipped: led 7f out tl over 3f out: wknd 2f out: eased whn btn) | s.h | **6** | 16/1 | 38 | 9 |
| 2989[11] | **Seventh Edition (57)** (DBurchell) **3-8-9**(5) SCopp(8) (led to 7f out: hrd rdn & wknd over 2f out) | 8 | **7** | 33/1 | 29 | — |
| | **Katie Is My Love (USA)** (RHarris) **3-8-9** AMackay(9) (lengthy: unf: bit bkwd: s.s: t.o fnl 6f) | 9 | **8** | 66/1 | 9 | — |
| *3064[9]* | **Tashtaiya** (NPLittmoden) **3-8-9** TGMcLaughlin(2) (b: a bhd: t.o) | d.h | **8** | 66/1 | 9 | — |

(SP 120.6%) **9 Rn**

**2m 0.1** (4.10) CSF £3.36 TOTE £1.80: £1.10 £1.60 £1.70 (£2.10) Trio £4.40 OWNER Mr G. Moore (NEWMARKET) BRED M. B. Small
**3064 Serious Sensation**, reverting to a more suitable trip, was well backed and delivered the goods. (4/7: op 6/4)
**2065 Menoo Hal Batal (USA)** had no answer to the winner in the final 150 yards. (7/2: op 2/1)
**1667 Welsh Emblem (IRE)** looked really well, but lacked a turn of foot, despite this longer trip on his All-Weather debut. (10/1)
**3064 Biscay** showed little sign of improvement, despite being stepped up in distance. (10/1)

## 3422 SCOTLAND APPRENTICE H'CAP (0-60) (3-Y.O) (Class G)

5-20 (5-21) **1m 4f (Fibresand)** £2,095.00 (£595.00: £295.00) Stalls: Low GOING minus 0.12 sec per fur (FST)

| Form | Horse | Dist | Pos | SP | RR | SF |
|---|---|---|---|---|---|---|
| 3318* | **State Approval (61)** (APJarvis) **3-8-12**(10) 5x CCarver(7) (a.p: rn wd bnd 7f out: led over 4f out: clr over 1f out: easily) | — | **1** | 2/1[1] | 74+ | 45 |
| 3104[5] | **Pearl Anniversary (IRE) (54)** (MJohnston) **3-8-12**(3) KSked(6) (w ldr: led 5f out: sn hdd & rdn: wknd over 1f out) | 9 | **2** | 5/1[3] | 55 | 26 |
| 3249[11] | **Induna Mkubwa (55)** (CFWall) **3-8-8**(8) PClarke(4) (bhd tl hdwy over 4f out: nvr nr ldrs) | 12 | **3** | 20/1 | 40 | 11 |
| *2751** | **Newbridge Boy (60)** (MGMeagher) **3-8-13**(8) RStudholme(3) (led 7f: rdn & wknd over 3f out) | 6 | **4** | 3/1[2] | 37 | 8 |
| *3089[12]* | **Righteous Gent (49)** (KMcAuliffe) **3-8-10be** JBramhill(9) (nvr nr ldrs) | 1¾ | **5** | 25/1 | 24 | — |
| 2717[8] | **Mr Speculator (60)** (PAKelleway) **3-9-7v** ElizabethTurner(10) (hld up & bhd: hdwy 6f out: wknd 3f out) | 9 | **6** | 5/1[3] | 23 | — |
| 2952[7] | **Crimson Rosella (52)** (WJHaggas) **3-8-10**(3) CWebb(1) (a bhd: t.o) | 23 | **7** | 14/1 | — | — |
| 3104[6] | **Belacqua (USA) (35)** (DWChapman) **3-7-10b** AngelaGallimore(8) (prom 5f: t.o) | 1 | **8** | 20/1 | — | — |
| 2989[15] | **Northern Clan (40)** (AJChamberlain) **3-7-10**(5) RBrisland(5) (lw: prom 6f: t.o) | 13 | **9** | 33/1 | — | — |

(SP 114.6%) **9 Rn**

**2m 40.3** (7.80) CSF £11.79 CT £137.50 TOTE £2.60: £1.50 £1.10 £2.80 (£5.90) Trio £41.00 OWNER Mrs Ann Jarvis (ASTON UPTHORPE) BRED Collin Stud and The Pharly Syndicate
LONG HANDICAP Belacqua (USA) 6-11
**3318* State Approval** found no difficulty completing a quick follow-up after his Kempton victory. (2/1)
**3104 Pearl Anniversary (IRE)** won a couple of sellers over course and distance in May, but the winner is much better than a plater. (5/1)
**Induna Mkubwa** was never within hailing distance of the first two. (20/1)
**2751* Newbridge Boy** had been penalised 8lb for winning a maiden handicap here last month. (3/1)

T/Jkpt: Not won; £13,028.12 to Newmarket 10/8/96. T/Plpt: £80.20 (185.24 Tckts). T/Qdpt: £13.40 (63.98 Tckts). KH

## 2909-**AYR** (L-H) (Good)
## Saturday August 10th

Races 1 & 5: hand-timed
WEATHER: sunny periods WIND: almost nil

### 3423 STAR FORM MEDIAN AUCTION MAIDEN STKS (2-Y.O) (Class E)
2-05 (2-06) **7f** £3,148.50 (£948.00: £459.00: £214.50) Stalls: High GOING minus 0.02 sec per fur (G)

| Form | Horse | Dist | Pos | SP | RR | SF |
|---|---|---|---|---|---|---|
| $2580^{7}$ | **The Fly** (BWHills) **2-8-9**(5) JDSmith(6) (lw: bhd: gd hdwy 2f out: r.o wl to ld last stride) | — | 1 | $7/2^{2}$ | 82 | 16 |
| $2783^{6}$ | **Captain William (IRE)** (IABalding) **2-8-9**(5) MartinDwyer(12) (in tch: hdwy 3f out: led ins fnl f: jst ct) | s.h | 2 | $9/2^{3}$ | 82 | 16 |
| | **Palio Sky** (JLDunlop) **2-9-0** TSprake(9) (w'like: lw: s.i.s: sn in tch: hdwy 2f out: n.m.r fnl f: kpt on) | 1 | 3 | 11/2 | 80+ | 14 |
| $3131^{5}$ | **Leviticus (IRE)** (TPTate) **2-8-11**(3) DWright(11) (lw: prom: outpcd ½-wy: styd on wl towards fin) | 1¼ | 4 | 7/1 | 77+ | 11 |
| $3099^{2}$ | **Dargo** (MJohnston) **2-9-0** JWeaver(10) (led tl hdd & wknd ins fnl f) | 1 | 5 | $3/1^{1}$ | 75 | 9 |
| | **Burlesque** (JDBethell) **2-9-0** FNorton(8) (unf: scope: rr div: styd on fnl 3f: n.d) | 3 | 6 | 33/1 | 68 | 2 |
| $2865^{3}$ | **Hurgill Times** (JWWatts) **2-9-0** JCarroll(1) (lw: chsd ldr: effrt over 2f out: wknd appr fnl f) | 1¼ | 7 | 11/1 | 65 | — |
| $2708^{11}$ | **Fancy A Fortune (IRE) (76)** (JPearce) **2-9-0** GBardwell(13) (lw: prom tl wknd fnl 2½f) | 1½ | 8 | 20/1 | 61 | — |
| $1583^{6}$ | **Father Eddie** (JJO'Neill) **2-9-0** SDWilliams(3) (b.nr fore: a rr div) | 8 | 9 | 66/1 | 43 | — |
| $3099^{5}$ | **Broctune Line** (MrsMReveley) **2-8-9**(5) SCopp(7) (s.i.s: a rr div) | nk | 10 | 50/1 | 42 | — |
| $3080^{9}$ | **Rock The Casbah** (JHetherton) **2-9-0** NKennedy(4) (prom tl wknd fnl 3f) | ¾ | 11 | 25/1 | 41 | — |
| $3250^{9}$ | **Amy** (CSmith) **2-8-9** NConnorton(5) (sn drvn along & a bhd) | ½ | 12 | 200/1 | 35 | — |
| $3241^{6}$ | **Alisadara (40)** (NBycroft) **2-8-4**(5) RHavlin(2) (plld hrd: n.d) | 2½ | 13 | 200/1 | 29 | — |

(SP 117.6%) **13 Rn**

**1m 30.9** (6.90) CSF £18.23 TOTE £5.40: £1.40 £2.00 £2.70 (£11.60) Trio £39.80 OWNER Mrs J. M. Corbett (LAMBOURN) BRED S. Wingfield Digby

**2580 The Fly** put in a superb performance as he had a lot of running to do from three furlongs out, but this impressive mover produced an amazing turn of foot to make it. (7/2)

**2783 Captain William (IRE)** always held a good position and kept staying on under pressure but, in the end, was just caught. He does not do anything quickly, but should find a race or two in due course. (9/2)

**Palio Sky** looked fit enough, but it was greenness that cost him his chance here, and he was also short of room in the closing stages. (11/2: 7/2-6/1)

**3131 Leviticus (IRE)** is gradually getting the hang of things, but he does not do anything too quickly and it was always too late when he decided to run. His turn will come before long. (7/1)

**3099 Dargo** had the run of the race out in front, but it would seem he did too much too soon, and he ran out of fuel entering the final furlong. (3/1)

**Burlesque** never really showed in the race, but was keeping on at the end. Some improvement now looks likely. (33/1)

**2865 Hurgill Times** (11/1: 8/1-12/1)

### 3424 HAY & ANDERSON H'CAP (0-75) (3-Y.O+) (Class D)
2-35 (2-38) **6f** £4,131.50 (£1,247.00: £606.00: £285.50) Stalls: Low GOING minus 0.02 sec per fur (G)

| Form | Horse | Dist | Pos | SP | RR | SF |
|---|---|---|---|---|---|---|
| $2672^{4}$ | **Ballard Lady (IRE) (43)** (JSWainwright) **4-7-3**(7) JBramhill(5) (a chsng ldrs: kpt on wl fnl f to ld cl home) | — | 1 | 12/1 | 51 | 33 |
| $3345^{3}$ | **Six for Luck (57)** (DANolan) **4-8-10** VHalliday(9) (mde most tl ct nr fin) | nk | 2 | 16/1 | 64 | 46 |
| $3216^{7}$ | **Fantasy Racing (IRE) (72)** (MRChannon) **4-9-11** TSprake(4) (a w ldrs: nt qckn towards fin) | s.h | 3 | 12/1 | 79 | 61 |
| $3223^{5}$ | **Daawe (USA) (68)** (MrsVAAconley) **5-9-7v** MDeering(13) (a cl up: effrt over 2f out: kpt on one pce) | 1½ | 4 | $6/1^{1}$ | 71 | 53 |
| $2911^{9}$ | **Mister Westsound (68)** (MissLAPerratt) **4-9-7b** JCarroll(11) (bhd: hdwy ½-wy: styd on fnl 2f: nvr able to chal) | ¾ | 5 | $15/2^{3}$ | 69 | 51 |
| $2725^{18}$ | **Craigie Boy (54)** (NBycroft) **6-8-2**(5) MartinDwyer(10) (bhd: hdwy ½-wy: nvr able to chal) | 1¾ | 6 | 16/1 | 50 | 32 |
| $3256^{9}$ | **Baileys First (IRE) (67)** (MJohnston) **3-9-2** JWeaver(1) (in tch: sn drvn along: nvr rchd ldrs) | hd | 7 | $6/1^{1}$ | 63 | 41 |
| $3236^{5}$ | **Sunday Mail Too (IRE) (49)** (MissLAPerratt) **4-8-2** NKennedy(15) (rr div: hdwy over 1f out: nvr nr to chal) | 1¼ | 8 | 12/1 | 42 | 24 |
| $2754^{5}$ | **Safio (70)** (CSmith) **3-9-5** NConnorton(12) (lw: outpcd fr ½-wy) | nk | 9 | 11/1 | 62 | 40 |
| $2805^{4}$ | **Agent (67)** (JLEyre) **3-8-13**(3) DWright(8) (lw: in tch tl wknd fnl 2f) | 2 | 10 | 14/1 | 54 | 32 |
| $2005^{21}$ | **Dictation (USA) (66)** (JJO'Neill) **4-9-5** GBardwell(6) (nvr trbld ldrs) | ½ | 11 | 50/1 | 51 | 33 |
| $3223^{3}$ | **Cheeky Chappy (76)** (DWChapman) **5-9-10b**(5) JDSmith(14) (sn bhd) | ½ | 12 | $7/1^{2}$ | 60 | 42 |
| $3151^{12}$ | **Shontaine (63)** (MJohnston) **3-8-5**(7) KSked(2) (lw: in tch: sn drvn along: wknd fnl 2f) | 1 | 13 | 10/1 | 44 | 22 |
| $2687^{5}$ | **Detachment (USA) (75)** (PWChapple-Hyam) **3-9-5b**[1](5) RHavlin(7) (lw: a outpcd & bhd) | 13 | 14 | 8/1 | 22 | — |
| $3240^{3}$ | **Naissant (65)** (RMMcKellar) **3-9-0** SDWilliams(3) (effrt ½-wy: sddle slipped & eased fnl 2f) | 4 | 15 | 50/1 | 1 | — |

(SP 126.8%) **15 Rn**

**1m 13.02** (3.22) CSF £175.69 CT £2,159.70 TOTE £14.10: £3.30 £10.50 £4.30 (£207.70) Trio Not won; £351.84 to Windsor 12/8/96 OWNER Mrs P. Wake (MALTON) BRED Airlie Stud

LONG HANDICAP Ballard Lady (IRE) 7-7

WEIGHT FOR AGE 3yo-4lb

**2672 Ballard Lady (IRE)** was able to get her toe in here and, though the trip was short of her best, she is game, and she battled on well to lead where it mattered. (12/1)

**3345 Six for Luck** is running particularly well at the moment but, after a gallant effort, was just touched off. (16/1)

**744 Fantasy Racing (IRE)** has been out of form so far this season, but this was a much more encouraging effort and he should now be watched. (12/1)

**3223 Daawe (USA)** is pretty high in the weights at present, but showed he still has the enthusiasm for the job. (6/1)

**2729 Mister Westsound** did a fair amount of running from halfway, but was never doing quite enough and failed to make an impression. (15/2)

**2490 Craigie Boy** likes a bit of cut in the ground and ran reasonably here. Given plenty more rain, he will be back in the winner's enclosure. (16/1)

**3256 Baileys First (IRE)** will be helped by a bit further. (6/1)

**2754 Safio** (11/1: 8/1-12/1)

### 3425 JOHN MAGUIRE EVENING TIMES MAIDEN STKS (3-Y.O+) (Class D)
3-05 (3-16) **1m 2f** £3,735.00 (£1,125.00: £545.00: £255.00) Stalls: High GOING minus 0.02 sec per fur (G)

| Form | Horse | Dist | Pos | SP | RR | SF |
|---|---|---|---|---|---|---|
| $3103^{2}$ | **Opal Jewel** (MRStoute) **3-8-6** JWeaver(11) (lw: in tch: qcknd to ld wl over 1f out: r.o wl) | — | 1 | $5/2^{2}$ | 81 | 38 |

3041[8] **Triple Leap** (JHMGosden) **3-8-11** JCarroll(10) (plld hrd: in tch: effrt over 2f out: kpt on fnl f) ....................2 **2** 7/1 83 40
3258[3] **Upper Gallery (IRE)** (PWChapple-Hyam) **3-8-6**(5) RHavlin(5) (lw: cl up: led 5f out tl wl over 1f out: nt qckn).s.h **3** 6/1[3] 83 40
584[6] **Sinking Sun** (BWHills) **3-8-4v**(5)ow3 JDSmith(8) (b.hind: trckd ldrs: ev ch 2f out: sn rdn & no ex) ....................5 **4** 8/1 73 27
2718[6] **Alfredo Alfredo (USA)** (JLDunlop) **4-9-6** TSprake(1) (b: s.i.s: sn in tch: rdn 3f out: one pce) ....................5 **5** 11/8[1] 67 33
3041[5] **Llyswen (79)** (JHMGosden) **3-8-11** GBardwell(4) (led after 2f tl hdd 5f out: one pce fnl 2½f)....................2½ **6** 10/1 63 20
2913[6] **Barbara's Jewel (48)** (ABailey) **4-9-3**(3) DWright(3) (led 2f: chsd ldrs tl wknd fnl 2½f)....................½ **7** 150/1 62 28
3239[3] **School of Science (25)** (DANolan) **6-9-6** VHalliday(12) (in tch tl wknd fnl 3f)....................15 **8** 150/1 38 4
**Fizzy Boy (IRE)** (PMonteith) **3-8-4**(7) JBramhill(9) (cmpt: bit bkwd: dwlt: t.o fnl 5f) ....................dist **9** 150/1 — —
786[9] **Bright Desert** (RMMcKellar) **3-8-11** SDWilliams(2) (bit bkwd: dwlt: sn t.o) ....................dist **10** 150/1 — —
**Jimmy-S (IRE)** (RMMcKellar) **3-8-11** NConnorton(6) (w'like: bkwd: dwlt: wl t.o fnl 5f) ....................dist **11** 150/1 — —
*2589[4]* ***Jungle Fresh*** (JDBethell) **3-8-11** FNorton(7) (Withdrawn not under Starter's orders: broke out of stalls) .......... **W** 66/1 — —
(SP 122.5%) **11 Rn**

**2m 10.98** (6.38) CSF £19.64 TOTE £2.90: £1.10 £2.40 £1.80 (£6.30) Trio £5.60 OWNER Sheikh Mohammed (NEWMARKET) BRED Sheikh Mohammed Bin Rashid Al Maktoum
WEIGHT FOR AGE 3yo-9lb

**3103 Opal Jewel** was a bit edgy beforehand, but there was nothing wrong with the performance as she won in most emphatic style. (5/2)
**Triple Leap** has obviously come on for his initial outing. Once he learns to settle, there is plenty more ability there. (7/1: op 9/2)
**3258 Upper Gallery (IRE)** has a fair amount of ability, but he may just be a bit of a character, and was worried out of it inside the final furlong. (6/1: op 4/1)
**584 Sinking Sun** took a strong hold going down and, after racing up with the pace, had shot his bolt approaching the final furlong. (8/1)
**2718 Alfredo Alfredo (USA)** is certainly a useful-looking sort, but was just a bit edgy beforehand and then ran disappointingly, failing to quicken in the last two furlongs. (11/8)
**3041 Llyswen** helped force the pace, but he was well short of speed in the last couple of furlongs. (10/1: 8/1-12/1)

## 3426 DAILY STAR OF SCOTLAND H'CAP (0-80) (3-Y.O+) (Class D)

3-35 (3-43) **1m** £4,086.00 (£1,233.00: £599.00: £282.00) Stalls: High GOING minus 0.02 sec per fur (G)

SP RR SF
3265* **My Gallery (IRE) (76)** (ABailey) **5-9-8**(3) DWright(11) (hld up: qcknd over 1f out: r.o strly to ld wl ins fnl f) ....................— **1** 5/1[3] 88 56
3344* **Celebration Cake (IRE) (63)** (MissLAPerratt) **4-8-7**(5) 5x MartinDwyer(5) (lw: chsd ldrs: led & qcknd over 2f out: hdd & no ex wl ins fnl f) ....................1 **2** 3/1[1] 73 41
2188[5] **Knobbleeneeze (79)** (MRChannon) **6-9-7v**(7) AEddery(4) (trckd ldrs: effrt over 2f out: r.o one pce) ....................2½ **3** 7/1 84 52
2803[6] **Highspeed (IRE) (60)** (SEKettlewell) **4-8-2**(7) JennyBenson(3) (lw: mid div: hdwy 3f out: styd on: nvr able to chal) ....................½ **4** 8/1 64 32
2585[8] **Ocean Grove (IRE) (80)** (PWChapple-Hyam) **3-9-3**(5) RHavlin(15) (lw: s.i.s: bhd tl gd hdwy & swtchd 2f out: nvr rchd ldrs) ....................s.h **5** 8/1 84 45
1977[11] **Swandale Flyer (47)** (NBycroft) **4-7-3**(7) JBramhill(7) (chsd ldrs: effrt 3f out: r.o one pce)....................3½ **6** 50/1 44 12
3327[2] **Tissue of Lies (USA) (69)** (MJohnston) **3-8-11** JWeaver(8) (lw: mid div: outpcd ent st: styd on fnl f) ....................hd **7** 4/1[2] 66 27
3346[8] **Manoy (55)** (JHetherton) **3-7-11** NKennedy(9) (chsd ldrs tl wknd fnl 3f)....................2 **8** 50/1 48 9
2587[16] **Public Way (IRE) (47)** (NChamberlain) **6-7-10** GBardwell(10) (nvr trbld ldrs) ....................nk **9** 50/1 39 7
2678[4] **Hutchies Lady (47)** (RMMcKellar) **4-7-3**(7) JMcAuley(13) (b.hind: n.d)....................2½ **10** 50/1 34 2
3344[7] **Giddy (59)** (JHetherton) **3-7-8**(7)ow5 KSked(14) (b.hind: nvr nr ldrs)....................4 **11** 50/1 38 —
*2934[10]* **Best of All (IRE) (67)** (JBerry) **4-9-2** JCarroll(2) (led tl hdd & wknd qckly over 2f out) ....................2 **12** 16/1 42 10
2417[5] **Duo Master (65)** (MrsMReveley) **3-8-7** TSprake(6) (hld up & bhd: n.d)....................½ **13** 10/1 39 —
**In Good Faith (65)** (JJQuinn) **4-8-9**(5) JDSmith(12) (bit bkwd: s.i.s: a bhd)....................3½ **14** 16/1 32 —
*2934** **Catherine's Choice (68)** (JDBethell) **3-8-10** FNorton(1) (lw: chsd ldrs tl wknd over 3f out)....................4 **15** 8/1 27 —
(SP 138.2%) **15 Rn**

**1m 42.36** (4.96) CSF £21.97 CT £105.35 TOTE £6.50: £3.20 £1.50 £3.90 (£7.80) Trio £22.80 OWNER Mr Robert Cox (TARPORLEY) BRED East Riding Sack and Paper Co
LONG HANDICAP Hutchies Lady 7-1 Swandale Flyer 6-11 Giddy 7-6 Public Way (IRE) 7-4
WEIGHT FOR AGE 3yo-7lb

**3265* My Gallery (IRE)** is unbelievable this season and showed an incredible burst of speed to settle this late on. (5/1)
**3344* Celebration Cake (IRE)** is in terrific form and looked to have this sewn up when quickening into a useful lead over two furlongs out, but the winner's late burst was way beyond anything he could muster. (3/1)
**2188 Knobbleeneeze** is on good terms with himself at the moment, but his weight just anchored him in the last two furlongs. (7/1)
**2803 Highspeed (IRE)** is certainly better on this easier ground and, although well up in the weights, he ran a decent race, and is not done with yet. (8/1: 6/1-10/1)
**1898 Ocean Grove (IRE)**, trying her longest trip to date, was given a lot to do and did pretty well to finish so close. (8/1)
**1585 Swandale Flyer** ran a fine race from 13lb out of the handicap. (50/1)
**3327 Tissue of Lies (USA)** found this on the sharp side. (4/1)
**2934* Catherine's Choice** (8/1: 6/1-9/1)

## 3427 AYR FLOWER SHOW (S) H'CAP (0-60) (3-Y.O) (Class F)

4-05 (4-12) **7f** £2,980.00 (£830.00: £400.00) Stalls: High GOING minus 0.02 sec per fur (G)

SP RR SF
3228[8] **Sis Garden (43)** (TDEasterby) **3-8-6b**(5) RHavlin(9) (cl up: chal over 1f out: styd on to ld post) ....................— **1** 14/1 54 21
2963[3] **Madonna da Rossi (37)** (MDods) **3-8-5** TSprake(11) (cl up: led over 2f out: r.o: jst ct) ....................s.h **2** 7/1 48 15
3167[10] **Corniche Quest (IRE) (52)** (MRChannon) **3-8-13**(7) AEddery(7) (lw: in tch tl outpcd 3f out: styd on wl appr fnl f) ....................1¾ **3** 7/1 59 26
3288* **Miletrian City (58)** (JBerry) **3-9-12b** 5x JCarroll(12) (lw: hld up: effrt over 2f out: sn chsng ldrs: nt qckn fnl f) ....................½ **4** 7/2[1] 64 31
3289[7] **Globe Runner (50)** (JJO'Neill) **3-9-4** GBardwell(4) (bhd: hdwy 2f out: styd on wl)....................½ **5** 15/2 55 22
*2937[16]* **Rocky Stream (42)** (RMWhitaker) **3-8-10** FNorton(1) (lw: led tl hdd over 2f out: grad wknd fnl f)....................nk **6** 10/1 46 13
3059[12] **Efipetite (34)** (NBycroft) **3-7-11**(5) MartinDwyer(5) (bhd: hdwy over 2f out: nrst fin)....................¾ **7** 25/1 36 3
2753[5] **Philgem (29)** (CWFairhurst) **3-7-11** NKennedy(8) (chsd ldrs: outpcd 3f out: no imp after)....................nk **8** 16/1 31 —
2983[4] **Ned's Contessa (IRE) (45)** (MDods) **3-8-8**(5) SCopp(3) (bhd: effrt 3f out: nvr rchd ldrs)....................hd **9** 5/1[2] 46 13
2481[12] **Mystic Times (40)** (BMactaggart) **3-8-3**(5)ow2 GLee(2) (prom tl wknd fnl 2f) ....................4 **10** 20/1 32 —
**Braes'O'Shieldhill (30)** (ABailey) **3-7-9**(3) DWright(13) (bhd: effrt over 3f out: n.d) ....................2 **11** 10/1 18 —
3059[7] **Domoor (45)** (MJohnston) **3-8-13** JWeaver(6) (w ldr tl wknd over 2f out) ....................hd **12** 11/2[3] 32 —

| | | | SP | RR | SF |
|---|---|---|---|---|---|
| 3287[6] | **Boundary Bird (IRE) (52)** (MJohnston) **3-9-1b**(5) JDSmith(10) (s.i.s: hdwy appr st: sn wknd)............................4 | **13** | 33/1 | 30 | — |
| | | | (SP 133.3%) | **13 Rn** | |

**1m 30.2** (6.20) CSF £110.72 CT £707.79 TOTE £20.30: £4.00 £2.70 £2.70 (£82.50) Trio £92.10 OWNER Mr Lin Cheng Lee (MALTON) BRED Mrs J. Mackie and Major W. R. Paton Smith
No bid
**2898 Sis Garden** showed here just what he can do when he decides to, but he had to really struggle to make it. (14/1)
**2963 Madonna da Rossi**, a free-runner, looked to have got it right this time, but was just touched off after a gallant effort. (7/1)
**2983 Corniche Quest (IRE)** is coming to hand looks-wise and ran well, finishing strongly after getting outpaced at halfway. (7/1: 6/1-10/1)
**3288* Miletrian City** needs things to go just right and was always seeing too much daylight too soon on this occasion. (7/2)
**3059* Globe Runner** got a good run up the inner in the straight and, although staying on, always had too much to do at this shorter trip. (15/2)
**2417 Rocky Stream**, made a lot of use of this time, had run herself into the ground approaching the final furlong. (10/1)
**Braes'O'Shieldhill** (10/1: tchd 16/1)

## 3428 PORTLAND AMATEUR H'CAP (0-70) (3-Y.O+) (Class E)

4-35 (4-38) **1m 7f** £3,070.50 (£924.00: £447.00: £208.50) Stalls: High GOING minus 0.02 sec per fur (G)

| | | | SP | RR | SF |
|---|---|---|---|---|---|
| 3149[2] | **Arian Spirit (IRE) (51)** (JLEyre) **5-10-13** MissDianaJones(3) (hld up & bhd: gd hdwy 7f out: led over 2f out: drvn out)........— | **1** | 6/4[1] | 63 | 33 |
| 3149[6] | **Nosey Native (53)** (JPearce) **3-10-1** MrsLPearce(2) (hld up & bhd: stdy hdwy ent st: ch 2f out: rdn & styd n)..½ | **2** | 10/1 | 65 | 21 |
| 3163[2] | **Sea Freedom (62)** (GBBalding) **5-11-10v** MrABalding(1) (prom: led 4f out tl over 2f out: one pce)..................hd | **3** | 11/2[3] | 73 | 43 |
| 3149[9] | **Good Hand (USA) (66)** (SEKettlewell) **10-11-10**(4) MissMCarson(10) (lw: hld up & bhd: stdy hdwy fnl 3f: nvr plcd to chal)........7 | **4** | 16/1 | 70 | 40 |
| 2871[2] | **Pepitist (44)** (MDHammond) **5-10-6** MrCBonner(4) (hld up: hdwy appr st: one pce fnl 2f) ..............................2 | **5** | 11/2[3] | 46 | 16 |
| *2553[2]* | **Claque (45)** (DWChapman) **4-10-7b** MissRClark(6) (prom: c wd st: wl outpcd fnl 3f) ..............................6 | **6** | 10/1 | 40 | 10 |
| | **Valiant Dash (31)** (JSGoldie) **10-9-7** MissPRobson(7) (chsd ldrs: led 6f out to 4f out: wknd)...........................3 | **7** | 66/1 | 23 | — |
| 2804[4] | **Cutthroat Kid (IRE) (65)** (MrsMReveley) **6-11-13v** MrSSwiers(8) (in tch: effrt 3f out: one pce) ......................3½ | **8** | 7/2[2] | 53 | 23 |
| | **Kralingen (38)** (NChamberlain) **4-9-10**(4)ow7 MissCMetcalfe(5) (led tl hdd 11f out: wknd appr st: t.o).............27 | **9** | 66/1 | — | — |
| 2871[9] | **Jabaroot (IRE) (31)** (RMMcKellar) **5-9-3b**(4) MrsCWilliams(9) (b.hind: s.s: sn cl up: led 11f to 6f out: sn t.o) .dist | **10** | 66/1 | — | — |
| | | | (SP 121.5%) | **10 Rn** | |

**3m 27.76** (17.06) CSF £17.03 CT £63.13 TOTE £2.00: £1.10 £2.00 £1.60 (£10.50) Trio £11.40 OWNER Mr Martin West (HAMBLETON) BRED M. Ervine in Ireland
LONG HANDICAP Valiant Dash 8-13 Kralingen 8-13 Jabaroot (IRE) 9-2
WEIGHT FOR AGE 3yo-14lb
**3149 Arian Spirit (IRE)**, given a fine ride, was well suited by the strong pace and held on determinedly under pressure. (6/4)
**3149 Nosey Native** had no problems with the trip this time and travelled well but, despite running on, found the winner too determined. (10/1)
**3163 Sea Freedom**, who has yet to win a race, had his chances, but was just tapped for toe in the closing stages, despite staying on. (11/2: op 7/2)
**1847* Good Hand (USA)** ran by far his best race for his new stable. Tenderly handled here, he looks one to keep on the right side. (16/1)
**2871 Pepitist** should be kept in mind if returning to hurdles. (11/2)
**2553 Claque** is much better suited by the All-Weather. (10/1)

T/Plpt: £616.60 (18.1 Tckts). T/Qdpt: £25.10 (25.77 Tckts). AA

# 3398-HAYDOCK (L-H) (Good to firm)
## Saturday August 10th

WEATHER: heavy showers WIND: mod across

## 3429 WRIGHTS OF HORWICH MAIDEN AUCTION STKS (2-Y.O) (Class E)

2-15 (2-15) **5f** £3,046.25 (£920.00: £447.50: £211.25) Stalls: High GOING minus 0.12 sec per fur (G)

| | | | SP | RR | SF |
|---|---|---|---|---|---|
| 3121[2] | **Snap Crackle Pop (IRE)** (RFJohnsonHoughton) **2-8-3**ow1 PaulEddery(6) (a.p: led over 1f out: hld on wl cl home)........— | **1** | 100/30[2] | 68 | 32 |
| 3121[4] | **Loch-Hurn Lady (59)** (KWHogg) **2-7-12** JQuinn(5) (led tl hdd over 1f out: rallied u.p nr fin) ..........................nk | **2** | 20/1 | 62 | 27 |
| 3250[2] | **Fruitana (IRE) (84)** (JBerry) **2-8-10** GCarter(3) (lw: s.i.s: hdwy 2f out: rdn & unable qckn fnl f)......................1¼ | **3** | 11/2[3] | 70 | 35 |
| 2995[2] | **Hoh Dancer** (IABalding) **2-8-5** PatEddery(9) (lw: trckd ldrs: hrd rdn wl over 1f out: sn btn) ...............................2 | **4** | 13/8[1] | 59 | 24 |
| 2879[9] | **Hangover Square (IRE) (87)** (RHannon) **2-8-10** JReid(1) (prom tl rdn & wknd over 1f out) ............................s.h | **5** | 11/2[3] | 64 | 29 |
| 2699[7] | **Sparkling Harry** (MissLCSiddall) **2-8-4**ow1 DeanMcKeown(4) (lw: in tch: pushed along ½-wy: sn outpcd) ....1¾ | **6** | 33/1 | 52 | 16 |
| | **Sandweld** (CADwyer) **2-8-5** SSanders(7) (w'like: bkwd: s.s: bhd & outpcd tl sme late hdwy)..........................nk | **7** | 8/1 | 52 | 17 |
| 3121[7] | **Whisper Low (IRE)** (RHollinshead) **2-7-12**(3)ow3 FLynch(2) (bkwd: prom over 3f: sn lost tch)..........................4 | **8** | 33/1 | 35 | — |
| *2083[10]* | **Impish (IRE)** (TJEtherington) **2-8-4**ow1 MBirch(8) (lw: sn drvn along: a outpcd)..............................................hd | **9** | 33/1 | 38 | 2 |
| | | | (SP 116.6%) | **9 Rn** | |

**61.88 secs** (2.68) CSF £55.47 TOTE £3.90: £1.40 £3.80 £1.50 (£47.50) Trio £46.30 OWNER Short Wills Horn (DIDCOT) BRED A. F. O'Callaghan
**3121 Snap Crackle Pop (IRE)** gained just reward for a narrow defeat on her previous outing, but she had to be put to her best to hold on close home. (100/30)
**3121 Loch-Hurn Lady** ran the winner much closer this time, even on slightly worse terms, and she is just getting the hang of the game. (20/1)
**3250 Fruitana (IRE)**, dropped out at the start in an attempt to get him settled, ran on well inside the distance without ever looking likely to get to terms. (11/2)
**2995 Hoh Dancer** looked very hard-trained and sat in behind the leaders. Never really travelling like a winner, she was unable to respond when shaken up and will need to strengthen before she fulfils her real potential. (13/8)
**1987 Hangover Square (IRE)** is, as yet, failing to see out even this minimum trip, but he is bred to need further, and it could be that he just needs time. (11/2: 4/1-6/1)

## 3430 HARVEY JONES RATED STKS H'CAP (0-90) (3-Y.O+) (Class C)

2-45 (2-46) **1m 30y** £5,158.40 (£1,925.60: £937.80: £399.00: £174.50: £84.70) Stalls: Low GOING minus 0.12 sec per fur (G)

| | | | SP | RR | SF |
|---|---|---|---|---|---|
| 2913* | **Elmi Elmak (IRE) (85)** (LMCumani) **3-8-6** OUrbina(6) (hld up in tch: effrt over 2f out: drvn to ld wl ins fnl f) ...— | **1** | 11/4[2] | 101 | 51 |

3058* **Intidab (USA) (86)** (JHMGosden) **3-8-7** PatEddery(7) (lw: led after 2f tl over 3f out: shkn up to ld over 1f out: hdd fnl 50y)....s.h **2** 9/4[1] 102 52
3072[11] **Options Open (89)** (MrsJRRamsden) **4-9-3** SSanders(4) (lw: led 2f: led over 3f out tl over 1f out: hrd drvn & wknd fnl f)....6 **3** 16/1 93 50
3072[9] **Nasrudin (USA) (84)** (DRLoder) **3-8-5** DRMcCabe(3) (lw: prom tl lost pl 3f out: styd on u.p appr fnl f)....3 **4** 14/1 82 32
2724[17] **Tertium (IRE) (89)** (MartynWane) **4-9-3** KFallon(1) (lw: hld up: effrt over 1f out: sn hrd rdn: no imp)....¾ **5** 9/2[3] 86 43
2603[12] **Blaze of Song (78)** (RHannon) **4-8-6**ow1 JReid(2) (a in rr: rdn 3f out: no rspnse)....2½ **6** 14/1 70 26
3265[7] **Queens Consul (IRE) (82)** (BSRothwell) **6-8-10** MFenton(9) (hld up: hdwy over 4f out: wknd over 2f out)....nk **7** 9/1 73 30
3101* **Equerry (83)** (MJohnston) **5-8-8**(3) FLynch(5) (reard s: hdwy ent st: rdn 3f out: grad wknd)....1 **8** 13/2 72 29
2774[6] **La Volta (89)** (JGFitzGerald) **3-8-10** MBirch(8) (lw: trckd ldrs to ½-wy: sn drvn along & lost pl: t.o fnl 3f)....dist **9** 25/1 — —
(SP 122.0%) **9 Rn**

**1m 43.6** (3.00) CSF £9.62 CT £77.96 TOTE £3.80: £1.60 £1.40 £3.80 (£3.90) Trio £37.40 OWNER Sheikh Ahmed Al Maktoum (NEWMARKET) BRED Barnane Partnership
WEIGHT FOR AGE 3yo-7lb

**2913* Elmi Elmak (IRE),** brought along steadily, had to work hard to win this competitive handicap, but he is very short on experience, and looks to have an interesting future in front of him. (11/4)
**3058* Intidab (USA),** like the winner, was taking on handicappers for the first time. Sharing the lead from the start, he was in no mood to give best and it was only on the nod that the verdict went against him. Losses are only lent. (9/4)
**2328 Options Open** has won on faster ground than this, but he did not stride out with any freedom to post. In and out of the lead, he found his younger rivals galloping all over him entering the last furlong and could do nothing about it. (16/1)
**2079* Nasrudin (USA),** who wore a tongue-strap, ran his race in snatches and was staying on as well as any at the finish. (14/1)
**2053 Tertium (IRE)** again ran as if he has gone off the boil after some promising efforts against top-class opposition early in the season, and a complete break could get him back to what he is capable of. (9/2)
**3101* Equerry** lost all chance when he was on his hind legs as the stalls opened. This effort is best forgotten. (13/2)

## 3431 ROSE OF LANCASTER STKS (Gp 3) (3-Y.O+) (Class A)

3-15 (3-16) **1m 2f 120y** £21,760.00 (£8,218.00: £4,009.00: £1,813.00) Stalls: High GOING minus 0.12 sec per fur (G)

SP RR SF

2471a[3] **Tamayaz (CAN) (116)** (SbinSuroor) **4-9-3** GCarter(7) (lw: a.p: led on bit wl over 1f out: sn clr: impressive)....— **1** 11/2[3] 126+ 79
2546[4] **Ela-Aristokrati (IRE) (116)** (LMCumani) **4-9-3** OUrbina(1) (lw: hld up in rr: hdwy on outside over 2f out: kpt on fnl f: no ch w wnr)....5 **2** 13/2 118 71
2730[4] **Captain Horatius (IRE) (110)** (JLDunlop) **7-9-3** SSanders(3) (dwlt: hdwy over 2f out: styd on wl nr fin)....1¾ **3** 20/1 116 69
2276a[2] **Glory of Dancer (117)** (PAKelleway) **3-9-0** PatEddery(2) (lw: hld up in tch: effrt over 2f out: sn hrd drvn: one pce)....nk **4** 2/1[1] 122 65
2534* **Key to My Heart (IRE) (114)** (MissSEHall) **6-9-3** DeanMcKeown(8) (b: lw: led: clr 3f out: hdd wl over 1f out: sn outpcd)....nk **5** 9/1 115 68
2677[6] **Weet-A-Minute (IRE) (107)** (RHollinshead) **3-8-7** KFallon(4) (trckd ldrs: drvn along 4f out: outpcd fnl 2f)....6 **6** 33/1 106 49
1114[4] **Nash House (IRE)** (PWChapple-Hyam) **3-8-7** JReid(5) (hld up in rr: effrt & reminder 3f out: no imp)....¾ **7** 9/4[2] 105 48
2844a[2] **Acharne (110)** (CEBrittain) **3-8-7** JQuinn(6) (prom: drvn along 3f out: sn lost tch)....7 **8** 14/1 94 37
(SP 117.2%) **8 Rn**

**2m 13.15** (1.65) CSF £37.94 TOTE £7.00: £1.80 £1.90 £5.00 (£13.80) OWNER Godolphin (NEWMARKET) BRED Windfields Farm
WEIGHT FOR AGE 3yo-10lb

**2471a Tamayaz (CAN),** a handsome colt who impressed with his action to post, was always cantering in behind the leaders. Allowed to stride into the lead soon after passing the quarter-mile pole, he lengthened to draw clear readily, and he is going from strength to strength. (11/2)
**2546 Ela-Aristokrati (IRE)** stayed on strongly to gain the runner-up prize in the latter stages but, like the rest, had to concede the winner in a class of his own. (13/2: op 4/1)
**2730 Captain Horatius (IRE)** was once again sluggish leaving the stalls and, after racing in the rear, picked up well in the closing stages to be nearest at the finish. (20/1)
**2276a Glory of Dancer** looked on good terms with himself in the preliminaries and settled well just off the pace but, when the tempo was stepped up three furlongs out, he was soon nudged along, and the response was somewhat limited. (2/1)
**2534* Key to My Heart (IRE)** quickened from the front early in the straight and soon had several rivals in trouble. He was a sitting duck when the winner said go, and he could do little more than plug on at the same pace. (9/1: op 6/1)
**1114 Nash House (IRE),** reappearing after three months on the sidelines, looked well tuned up. Waited with, he was unable to respond when asked for his effort three furlongs out and dropped away tamely. His trainer said it was possible he had again bled internally as he had at York, and he does appear to have a problem. (9/4)

## 3432 CORAL H'CAP (0-100) (3-Y.O+) (Class C)

3-50 (3-53) **5f** £15,305.00 (£4,640.00: £2,270.00: £1,085.00) Stalls: High GOING minus 0.12 sec per fur (G)

SP RR SF

3152[2] **Royal Dome (IRE) (70)** (MartynWane) **4-8-0** GCarter(1) (a.p: centre: rdn to ld wl ins fnl f: r.o)....— **1** 20/1 79 61
2867[6] **Sing With the Band (66)** (BAMcMahon) **5-7-3**(7) AMcCarthy(9) (trckd ldrs: led ins fnl f: sn hdd: r.o)....hd **2** 25/1 75 57
3296[8] **Sea-Deer (86)** (CADwyer) **7-9-2** CDwyer(18) (hld up: rapid hdwy appr fnl f: fin fast)....¾ **3** 16/1 92 74
3219[3] **Rushcutter Bay (88)** (TTClement) **3-8-8**(7) RMullen(10) (in tch centre: rdn over 1f out: r.o wl fnl f)....1 **4** 25/1 91 70
3232[12] **Lago Di Varano (88)** (RMWhitaker) **4-9-4v** OUrbina(2) (in tch centre: hdwy appr fnl f: nvr nrr)....1¼ **5** 20/1 87 69
1630[R] **Sailormaite (85)** (SRBowring) **5-9-1** DeanMcKeown(7) (hdwy over 1f out: nrst fin)....nk **6** 25/1 83 65
2548[7] **Canovas Heart (75)** (BobJones) **7-8-5** NDay(12) (a.p: led over 1f out: sn hdd & one pce)....nk **7** 20/1 72 54
2950[6] **Shanghai Girl (86)** (DRLoder) **3-8-13v**[1] DRMcCabe(3) (in tch: kpt on one pce ins fnl f)....s.h **8** 25/1 83 62
3296[10] **Lady Sheriff (85)** (RHollinshead) **5-8-12**(3) FLynch(14) (lw: trckd ldrs: rdn 2f out: one pce)....d.h **8** 20/1 82 64
2725[13] **Chadwell Hall (70)** (SRBowring) **5-7-9b**(5) MBaird(6) (gd spd 4f)....hd **10** 25/1 67 49
3085[2] **Insider Trader (77)** (MrsJRRamsden) **5-8-7** KFallon(15) (lw: trckd ldrs stands' side 4f)....nk **11** 7/1[2] 73 55
3085[7] **Lord High Admiral (CAN) (89)** (MJHeaton-Ellis) **8-9-5** JReid(11) (lw: mde most over 3f: rdn & outpcd fnl f)....1 **12** 16/1 82 64
3338[2] **Shadow Jury (66)** (DWChapman) **6-7-10b** JQuinn(16) (nvr nr to chal)....½ **13** 25/1 57 39
2976[3] **Jucea (73)** (JLSpearing) **7-7-12**(5) PPMurphy(17) (hld up in tch: effrt & rdn over 1f out: sn btn)....¾ **14** 16/1 62 44
3085* **Laurel Delight (86)** (JBerry) **6-8-11**(5) PRoberts(21) (b: lw: w ldrs stands' side over 3f)....s.h **15** 7/1[2] 74 56
3038[3] **Tedburrow (92)** (MrsAMNaughton) **4-9-8** ACulhane(5) (effrt 2f out: sn rdn & no imp)....nk **16** 11/1[3] 79 61
3219[6] **Mousehole (73)** (RGuest) **4-8-3b** MFenton(20) (prom 3f: sn wknd)....1½ **17** 20/1 56 38
3126[5] **Crowded Avenue (96)** (PJMakin) **4-9-12** SSanders(19) (hmpd sn after s: trckd ldrs stands' side: drvn along ½-wy: sn bhd)....1¾ **18** 7/1[2] 73 55

| | | | | | |
|---|---|---|---|---|---|
| 2363[5] | **Bollin Harry (80)** (TDEasterby) **4-8-10** MBirch(8) (nvr trbld ldrs) ....1 | **19** | 25/1 | 54 | 36 |
| 3146* | **Youdontsay (80)** (TJNaughton) **4-8-10** PatEddery(4) (a outpcd) ....½ | **20** | 11/2[1] | 52 | 34 |
| 3296[11] | **Tadeo (90)** (MJohnston) **3-9-3** JTate(13) (mid div tl wknd fnl 2f) ....3 | **21** | 25/1 | 53 | 32 |
| | | | (SP 133.4%) | | **21 Rn** |

**59.99 secs** (0.79) CSF £415.37 CT £7,286.55 TOTE £22.80: £3.80 £4.90 £4.60 £5.90 (£227.30) Trio £2612.50; £1471.84 to Windsor 12/8/96 OWNER Mr G. W. Jones (RICHMOND) BRED Michael F. Fogarty

WEIGHT FOR AGE 3yo-3lb

STEWARDS' ENQUIRY Fallon susp. 19&23/8/96 (careless riding).

**3152 Royal Dome (IRE)**, a five-furlong specialist who usually finds his form in the late summer, was able to defy the dreaded number-one stall and win rather cleverly. He is at the right end of the handicap to take advantage in the coming weeks. (20/1)

**2496 Sing With the Band** gave the winner a harder race than when they met last month and, in turning in her best performance ever, must have thought she was running loose with only a feather-weight on her back. (25/1)

**3047* Sea-Deer** runs his best races when produced from off the pace, but he was left with too much to do this time and his storming late flourish was always going to be too late. He is back to something like his best this season and connections deserve credit. (16/1)

**3219 Rushcutter Bay** could not get to the front, but he did push the pace and stuck on really well to the finish. (25/1)

**2889 Lago Di Varano** always appeared to be at full stretch in an effort to keep tabs on the leaders, but he found extra inside the final furlong and, as he is possibly better when he can get his toe in, he is worth keeping in mind. (20/1)

**1430* Sailormaite**, with the exception of Sea-Deer, finished best of the remainder, but just mistimed his effort over a trip that, on the prevailing ground, could be short of his ideal. (25/1)

**2548* Lord High Admiral (CAN)** won the battle of the front-runners and held a narrow lead for over three furlongs before the pack pounced and left him standing. (16/1)

## 3433 E.B.F. STRYKE '5' MAIDEN STKS (2-Y.O F) (Class D)

4-20 (4-21) **6f** £3,874.75 (£1,168.00: £566.50: £265.75) Stalls: High GOING minus 0.12 sec per fur (G)

| | | | SP | RR | SF |
|---|---|---|---|---|---|
| 2582[3] | **Well Warned** (BWHills) **2-8-11** PatEddery(1) (mde all: c stands' side sn after s: pushed out) ....— | **1** | 8/13[1] | 77+ | 39 |
| | **Alikhlas** (HThomsonJones) **2-8-11** GCarter(3) (w'like: scope: bit bkwd: a.p: effrt & ev ch appr fnl f: unable qckn) ....2 | **2** | 5/2[2] | 72 | 34 |
| | **All Is Fair** (SirMarkPrescott) **2-8-11** SSanders(5) (wl grwn: bkwd: bhd: hdwy ½-wy: kpt on ins fnl f: improve) ..4 | **3** | 10/1 | 61+ | 23 |
| 3099[6] | **Northern Princess** (RHollinshead) **2-8-8**(3) FLynch(2) (lw: prom: shkn up 2f out: sn wknd) ....7 | **4** | 25/1 | 42 | 4 |
| 3129[4] | **Royal Orchid (IRE) (81)** (RHannon) **2-8-11** JReid(4) (lw: b.nr hind: spd 3f: sn rdn & btn) ....4 | **5** | 7/1[3] | 32 | — |
| | | | (SP 115.9%) | | **5 Rn** |

**1m 15.02** (3.32) CSF £2.77 TOTE £1.60: £1.10 £1.80 (£1.90) OWNER Mr K. Abdulla (LAMBOURN) BRED Juddmonte Farms

**2582 Well Warned** had everything going for her this time and won cosily in the end. She will have trouble confirming the form with the runner-up if they were to clash again. (8/13)

**Alikhlas** did not look fully wound up for this racecourse debut, but she ran a race full of promise and will be the one to beat from now on. (5/2)

**All Is Fair**, who will come into her own when faced with a stiffer test of stamina, will improve considerably with this run under her belt. She looks a good long-term prospect. (10/1)

## 3434 BODDINGTONS GOLD H'CAP (0-85) (3-Y.O+) (Class D)

4-50 (4-50) **1m 6f** £3,894.25 (£1,174.00: £569.50: £267.25) Stalls: Centre GOING minus 0.12 sec per fur (G)

| | | | SP | RR | SF |
|---|---|---|---|---|---|
| 2223[2] | **Fancy Heights (81)** (LadyHerries) **3-9-0** JReid(7) (hld up & bhd: hdwy 3f out: rdn to ld appr fnl f: hld on nr fin) ....— | **1** | 7/2[2] | 90 | 51 |
| 2547[9] | **Deano's Beeno (74)** (MJohnston) **4-9-6** DeanMcKeown(2) (lw: mde most tl hrd rdn & hdd appr fnl f: rallied gamely cl home) ....hd | **2** | 10/1 | 83 | 57 |
| 2998[2] | **Diego (66)** (CEBrittain) **3-7-13** JQuinn(1) (lw: hld up: hdwy to jn ldr 3f out: hrd rdn & one pce appr fnl f) ....2½ | **3** | 7/1 | 72 | 33 |
| 2775[4] | **Strategic Ploy (69)** (MrsJRRamsden) **3-7-13**(3) FLynch(4) (lw: dwlt: hld up: effrt over 3f out: sn hrd drvn: nt rch ldrs) ....10 | **4** | 9/2[3] | 64 | 25 |
| 2430[2] | **Alicia (IRE) (73)** (JLDunlop) **3-8-6** PatEddery(3) (prom: ev ch over 2f out: sn rdn & wknd: t.o) ....17 | **5** | 11/4[1] | 48 | 9 |
| 2900* | **Highflying (82)** (GMMoore) **10-10-0** JTate(5) (chsd ldrs 10f: sn lost tch: t.o) ....dist | **6** | 13/2 | — | — |
| 2884[2] | **Double Echo (IRE) (54)** (JDBethell) **8-8-0**ow1 GCarter(6) (disp ld 10f out to 6f out: sn lost pl: t.o) ....nk | **7** | 11/2 | — | — |
| | | | (SP 117.4%) | | **7 Rn** |

**3m 4.86** (6.66) CSF £33.30 TOTE £4.40: £2.70 £3.10 (£41.30) OWNER Maktoum Al Maktoum (LITTLEHAMPTON) BRED GAINSBOROUGH STUD MANAGEMENT LTD

WEIGHT FOR AGE 3yo-13lb

**2223 Fancy Heights**, given a very patient ride, did eventually manage to open her account, but she had to battle to make sure right to the finish. (7/2)

**2190 Deano's Beeno** did not deserve to be beaten after a brave attempt to make all, and then battled back to fail in a photo-finish. (10/1)

**2998 Diego**, with a considerable weight-advantage, did look the likely winner when moving upsides early in the straight, but the leader just would not give in, and he cried enough inside the last furlong. (7/1)

**2775 Strategic Ploy** tried hard to get serious entering the last quarter-mile, but could not summon up the pace to do so. (9/2)

**2430 Alicia (IRE)** played a leading role until the pressure was on over two furlongs out and then dropped out rather quickly as if lack of stamina was the problem. (11/4)

T/Plpt: £503.20 (54.78 Tckts). T/Qdpt: £127.90 (9.66 Tckts). IM

# 3269-LINGFIELD (L-H) (Turf Good to firm, AWT Standard)
## Saturday August 10th

WEATHER: sunny WIND: fresh half bhd becoming almost nil

## 3435 LADY ELIZABETH (S) H'CAP (0-60) (3-Y.O+) (Class G)

5-40 (5-40) **1m 2f (Equitrack)** £2,070.00 (£570.00: £270.00) Stalls: Low GOING minus 0.45 sec per fur (FST)

| | | | SP | RR | SF |
|---|---|---|---|---|---|
| *1448*[4] | **Our Eddie (57)** (BGubby) **7-9-11v** TIves(1) (a.p: rdn over 3f out: led ins fnl f: r.o wl) ....— | **1** | 8/1 | 69 | 30 |
| *3062*[3] | **Dome Patrol (41)** (DBurchell) **5-8-9** SDrowne(6) (b: led 1f: led 2f out tl ins fnl f: unable qckn) ....1¾ | **2** | 5/1[2] | 50 | 11 |
| 2192[18] | **Awesome Power (51)** (JWHills) **10-9-5** AClark(9) (a.p: rdn over 3f out: r.o ins fnl f) ....nk | **3** | 5/1[2] | 60 | 21 |

| | | | | SP | RR | SF |
|---|---|---|---|---|---|---|
| 2159[10] | **Ketabi (USA) (47)** (RAkehurst) **5-9-1** NGwilliams(3) (swtg: led 9f out to 2f out: wknd fnl f) | 3½ | **4** | 14/1 | 50 | 11 |
| 2034[12] | **Silver Tzar (54)** (RTPhillips) **4-9-8** RPerham(7) (plld hrd: rdn over 3f out: nvr nr to chal) | 4 | **5** | 33/1 | 51 | 12 |
| 3048[6] | **Owdbetts (IRE) (53)** (GLMoore) **4-9-7** SWhitworth(11) (lw: hdwy 4f out: 6th & no ch whn hmpd on ins over 2f out) | 6 | **6** | 5/1[2] | 40 | 1 |
| 3000[6] | **Zahran (IRE) (42)** (JMBradley) **5-8-10v** NAdams(12) (b: lw: hdwy over 4f out: wknd over 2f out) | ½ | **7** | 7/1[3] | 28 | — |
| 2405[9] | **Embroidered (37)** (RMFlower) **3-7-5**(5) CAdamson(5) (bhd fnl 3f) | 1¼ | **8** | 33/1 | 21 | — |
| 3257[10] | **Lilac Rain (47)** (RMStronge) **4-9-1** VSlattery(4) (bhd fnl 4f) | 4 | **9** | 16/1 | 25 | — |
| 3260[7] | **Elly Fleetfoot (IRE) (42)** (MJRyan) **4-8-10b** MTebbutt(10) (lw: hld up: rdn 4f out: sn wknd) | 5 | **10** | 3/1[1] | 12 | — |

(SP 117.0%) **10 Rn**

**2m 9.65** (5.35) CSF £44.61 CT £201.19 TOTE £8.10: £2.30 £1.50 £1.80 (£20.30) Trio £28.70 OWNER Brian Gubby Ltd (BAGSHOT) BRED Brian Gubby Ltd
LONG HANDICAP Embroidered 7-3
WEIGHT FOR AGE 3yo-9lb
No bid

**499 Our Eddie**, whose four previous victories have all come over this course and distance, was never far away and eventually managed to get on top inside the final furlong. (8/1)
**3062 Dome Patrol** was unable to contain the winner inside the final furlong. (5/1)
**499* Awesome Power**, who has won eight times over this course and distance, mainly in low grade races, was always close up. Rousted along over three furlongs from home, he ran on inside the final furlong and only just failed to snatch second prize. (5/1)
**Ketabi (USA)**, tailed off last over hurdles recently, was soon at the head of affairs. Collared a quarter of a mile out, he grimly tried to hold on, but was a spent force in the final furlong. (14/1)
**Silver Tzar**, racing towards the back of the field, could never get into the action. (33/1)
**3048 Owdbetts (IRE)** made her effort half a mile from home, but was already sending out distress signals when hampered along the inside rail over two furlongs out. (5/1)

## 3436 LADY JANE CONDITIONS STKS (2-Y.O) (Class D)

6-10 (6-11) **5f** £3,620.95 (£1,081.60: £517.30: £235.15) Stalls: High GOING minus 0.40 sec per fur (F)

| | | | | SP | RR | SF |
|---|---|---|---|---|---|---|
| 2995* | **Big Ben (80)** (RHannon) **2-9-2** RPerham(3) (lw: a.p: led over 1f out: qcknd: comf) | — | **1** | 5/1 | 93+ | 50 |
| 2741[3] | **Inflation** (RFJohnsonHoughton) **2-8-5** PaulEddery(4) (hld up: rdn over 2f out: r.o one pce) | 3½ | **2** | 2/1[1] | 71 | 28 |
| 2942* | **Gunners Glory** (BJMeehan) **2-9-2** MTebbutt(1) (lw: racd alone far side: led over 3f: wknd fnl f) | 2 | **3** | 4/1[2] | 75 | 32 |
| 2076[3] | **Red Test (USA) (74)** (WAO'Gorman) **2-8-10** TIves(2) (lw: a.p: ev ch over 1f out: wknd fnl f) | ½ | **4** | 14/1 | 68 | 25 |
| 2607[9] | **Jupiter (IRE)** (GCBravery) **2-9-0** CRutter(6) (lw: outpcd) | 1¼ | **5** | 5/1 | 68 | 25 |
| 3114[10] | **Wild Nettle** (JCFox) **2-8-5** AClark(5) (hld up: rdn over 2f out: sn wknd) | 4 | **6** | 50/1 | 46 | 3 |
| 3129[6] | **Signs And Wonders (79)** (CACyzer) **2-8-6**[ow1] SWhitworth(7) (lw: bhd fnl 2f: lame) | 14 | **7** | 9/2[3] | 2 | — |

(SP 113.5%) **7 Rn**

**57.83 secs** (0.83) CSF £14.86 TOTE £5.80: £2.40 £1.90 (£5.50) OWNER Mrs S. J. Davis (MARLBOROUGH) BRED Mrs M. Lingwood

**2995* Big Ben** put up a very polished display. In the firing-line throughout, he was given the office below the distance and quickened right away to win as he pleased. (5/1)
**2741 Inflation** stayed on to take second place inside the final furlong, but had no hope with the winner. (2/1)
**2942* Gunners Glory** tacked over to the far side and held a narrow advantage. Collared below the distance, he was soon in trouble. (4/1)
**2076 Red Test (USA)**, in the firing-line throughout, still had every chance below the distance before tiring. (14/1: op 8/1)
**2083* Jupiter (IRE)** failed to go the pace and could never get in a blow. (5/1)

## 3437 NORMAN HILL GROUP H'CAP (0-70) (3-Y.O+) (Class E)

6-40 (6-41) **2m (Equitrack)** £3,315.90 (£991.20: £474.60: £216.30) Stalls: Low GOING minus 0.45 sec per fur (FST)

| | | | | SP | RR | SF |
|---|---|---|---|---|---|---|
| 3142[4] | **Paradise Navy (65)** (CREgerton) **7-10-0b** TIves(5) (lw: stdy hdwy 7f out: led 1f out: r.o wl) | — | **1** | 7/1 | 72 | 50 |
| 3163* | **Chris's Lad (52)** (BJMeehan) **5-9-1b** MTebbutt(8) (lw: hdwy 7f out: rdn over 4f out: ev ch 1f out: nt qckn) | 3 | **2** | 4/1[2] | 56 | 34 |
| *2751*[3] | **Pleasureland (IRE) (59)** (PJMakin) **3-8-7** AClark(3) (lw: rdn over 5f out: hdwy over 3f out: r.o ins fnl f) | 1¾ | **3** | 20/1 | 61 | 24 |
| 1710[5] | **Sheriff (60)** (JWHills) **5-9-9** DHarrison(6) (lw: a.p: led over 4f out to 1f out: sn wknd) | 3 | **4** | 10/1 | 59 | 37 |
| 3204[2] | **Soojama (IRE) (43)** (RMFlower) **6-8-6b** DBiggs(2) (lw: hld up: rdn over 6f out: one pce) | 5 | **5** | 10/1 | 37 | 15 |
| 3037[9] | **The Lad (42)** (LMontagueHall) **7-8-2**(3)[ow1] DaneO'Neill(1) (lw: a.p: rdn over 4f out: wknd over 2f out) | 1¼ | **6** | 9/2[3] | 35 | 12 |
| 3077[3] | **Serious Trust (58)** (SirMarkPrescott) **3-8-6** GDuffield(7) (led over 11f) | 10 | **7** | 5/2[1] | 41 | 4 |
| 2884[8] | **Well Arranged (IRE) (65)** (MJPolglase) **5-10-0** JStack(4) (hld up: rdn 5f out: sn wknd) | 11 | **8** | 16/1 | 37 | 15 |
| | **Acrow Line (38)** (DBurchell) **11-8-1** SDrowne(9) (b: bit bkwd: a bhd: t.o fnl 12f) | 10 | **9** | 25/1 | — | — |
| 3335[2] | **Teen Jay (58)** (BJLlewellyn) **6-9-7** VSlattery(11) (a bhd: t.o) | 14 | **10** | 12/1 | 6 | — |
| 2738[4] | **Burning Flame (48)** (RMFlower) **3-7-5**(5) CAdamson(12) (swtg: prom 8f: t.o fnl 5f) | 27 | **11** | 33/1 | — | — |
| *3066*[9] | **Boogie Bopper (IRE) (34)** (BAPearce) **7-7-11b**[ow1] NCarlisle(10) (b: bhd fnl 12f: t.o whn p.u over 4f out: dismntd) | | **P** | 50/1 | — | — |

(SP 124.5%) **12 Rn**

**3m 27.23** (5.23) CSF £34.74 CT £506.95 TOTE £7.40: £2.00 £1.60 £4.70 (£14.90) Trio £109.50 OWNER Elite Racing Club (CHADDLEWORTH) BRED Stetchworth Park Stud Ltd
LONG HANDICAP Burning Flame 7-8 Boogie Bopper (IRE) 7-7
WEIGHT FOR AGE 3yo-15lb

**3142 Paradise Navy** is not easy to win with, but had little more than a stroll here. Gradually creeping closer in the second half of the race, he was shaken up to lead a furlong out and soon put the issue beyond doubt. (7/1)
**3163* Chris's Lad** moved up soon after halfway. Rousted along in the last half-mile, he was one of three in line a furlong out before tapped for toe. (4/1: 3/1-9/2)
**2751 Pleasureland (IRE)** moved up over three furlongs from home and did run on inside the final furlong to snatch third prize. (20/1)
**1710 Sheriff** made his bid for glory over half a mile from home. Collared a furlong out, he had shot his bolt. (10/1)
**3204 Soojama (IRE)** chased the leaders, but was made to look extremely one-paced in the last three-quarters of a mile. (10/1)
**2613* The Lad**, never far away, was eventually brushed aside over two furlongs out. (9/2)

## 3438 E.B.F. LADY MARGARET MEDIAN AUCTION MAIDEN STKS (2-Y.O F) (Class F)

7-10 (7-10) **6f** £2,952.20 (£819.20: £392.60) Stalls: High GOING minus 0.40 sec per fur (F)

| | | | | SP | RR | SF |
|---|---|---|---|---|---|---|
| 3129[3] | **Caspian Morn** (APJarvis) **2-8-11** PatEddery(5) (lw: w ldr: led over 2f out: rdn out) | — | **1** | 13/8[1] | 77 | 21 |
| | **Our Way** (CEBrittain) **2-8-11** BDoyle(6) (unf: scope: hdwy 3f out: hrd rdn over 1f out: unable qckn) | 2 | **2** | 8/1 | 72 | 16 |

| | | | | | | |
|---|---|---|---|---|---|---|
| 2956[4] | **Brazilia** (PTWalwyn) **2-8-11** TQuinn(9) (a.p: rdn over 1f out: one pce) | 1 | **3** | 5/1[3] | 69 | 13 |
| 2942[9] | **Ellway Lady (IRE)** (IABalding) **2-8-11** PaulEddery(4) (hld up: rdn over 2f out: one pce) | s.h | **4** | 14/1 | 69 | 13 |
| 2059[9] | **No Class** (RHarris) **2-8-11** AMackay(7) (lw: led over 3f: wknd fnl f) | 1¼ | **5** | 50/1 | 66 | 10 |
| | **Blown-Over** (ACStewart) **2-8-11** DHarrison(8) (neat: bit bkwd: n.m.r over 1f out: nvr nr to chal) | 2½ | **6** | 4/1[2] | 59 | 3 |
| | **Hoh Flyer (USA)** (MBell) **2-8-11** MFenton(3) (unf: scope: bit bkwd: s.s: hdwy 3f out: wknd over 1f out) | 4 | **7** | 5/1[3] | 48 | — |
| 3114[13] | **Chilli Boom** (TJNaughton) **2-8-8**(3) DaneO'Neill(1) (hld up: rdn over 2f out: sn wknd) | ½ | **8** | 50/1 | 47 | — |
| | **Kayzee (IRE)** (SDow) **2-8-11** SWhitworth(2) (b.off hind: w'like: bit bkwd: a bhd) | 3½ | **9** | 20/1 | 38 | — |

(SP 117.9%) **9 Rn**

**1m 11.79** (2.79) CSF £14.66 TOTE £2.90: £1.20 £2.40 £1.70 (£12.30) Trio £12.10 OWNER Mr P. Nabavi (ASTON UPTHORPE) BRED P. Nabavi and Mrs M. Nabavi

**3129 Caspian Morn** disputed the lead until showing in front soon after halfway. Ridden along, she soon asserted her authority from below the distance. (13/8)

**Our Way**, who has quite a nasty scar on her hind-quarter, moved up at halfway. Almost on terms with the winner below the distance, she was then tapped for toe. (8/1: op 4/1)

**2956 Brazilia** was on the winner's quarters below the distance before failing to find another gear. (5/1)

**Ellway Lady (IRE)** chased the leaders but, shaken up soon after halfway, could only go up and down in the same place. (14/1)

**No Class** held a slight advantage until over two furlongs out. She grimly tried to hold on, but had nothing more to offer in the final furlong. (50/1)

**Blown-Over**, who is not that big, looked as though the run would do her good. (4/1: 3/1-5/1)

## 3439 HOLLIWELL SEED & GRAIN CO. H'CAP (0-70) (3-Y.O+) (Class E)

7-40 (7-41) **6f** £3,343.20 (£999.60: £478.80: £218.40) Stalls: High GOING minus 0.40 sec per fur (F)

| | | | | SP | RR | SF |
|---|---|---|---|---|---|---|
| 2316[2] | **Lough Erne (65)** (CFWall) **4-9-9** PatEddery(13) (a.p: led wl over 1f out: pushed out) | — | **1** | 5/1[1] | 79 | 62 |
| 3216[8] | **Scissor Ridge (52)** (JJBridger) **4-8-10** DHarrison(12) (w ldr: led 3f out tl wl over 1f out: unable qckn) | 2 | **2** | 6/1[2] | 61 | 44 |
| 3168* | **Rambold (65)** (NEBerry) **5-9-9** RPerham(5) (led 3f: rdn over 2f out: one pce) | 2 | **3** | 8/1 | 68 | 51 |
| 2686[7] | **Merrie le Bow (48)** (PatMitchell) **4-8-1**(5) AmandaSanders(15) (hld up: rdn over 1f out: r.o one pce) | s.h | **4** | 16/1 | 51 | 34 |
| 3096[5] | **Lorins Gold (40)** (AndrewTurnell) **6-7-9**(3) MHenry(2) (b.nr hind: hld up: rdn 3f out: one pce) | ½ | **5** | 16/1 | 42 | 25 |
| 3270* | **Times of Times (IRE) (68)** (MJRyan) **3-9-8** MTebbutt(6) (hld up: nt clr run over 2f out: one pce) | ¾ | **6** | 7/1[3] | 68 | 47 |
| 3162[6] | **Serape (61)** (HCandy) **3-9-1** CRutter(14) (nvr nr to chal) | 2½ | **7** | 9/1 | 54 | 33 |
| 3146[4] | **Invocation (50)** (AMoore) **9-8-5**(3) DaneO'Neill(4) (b.nr hind: lw: hld up: rdn 3f out: wknd over 1f out) | 1½ | **8** | 10/1 | 39 | 22 |
| 3072[7] | **Mihriz (IRE) (70)** (RAkehurst) **4-10-0** TQuinn(1) (lw: nvr nrr) | 2 | **9** | 8/1 | 54 | 37 |
| 2976[11] | **Robo Magic (USA) (49)** (LMontagueHall) **4-8-7** BDoyle(8) (bmpd s: a bhd) | ¾ | **10** | 12/1 | 31 | 14 |
| 2715[2] | **Windswept (IRE) (56)** (DJSffrenchDavis) **3-8-10b** NCarlisle(7) (bmpd s: a bhd) | ¾ | **11** | 12/1 | 36 | 15 |
| 2719[5] | **Speedy Classic (USA) (53)** (MJHeaton-Ellis) **7-8-11** SDrowne(10) (bmpd s: sme hdwy 2f out: sn wknd) | 2½ | **12** | 14/1 | 26 | 9 |
| 3112[9] | **Primelta (60)** (RAkehurst) **3-9-0** NGwilliams(16) (a bhd) | 1½ | **13** | 20/1 | 29 | 8 |
| 2735[7] | **Hong Kong Dollar (45)** (BAPearce) **4-8-3b** DBiggs(11) (spd over 3f) | 12 | **14** | 33/1 | — | — |

(SP 126.3%) **14 Rn**

**1m 9.67** (0.67) CSF £34.50 CT £230.12 TOTE £4.90: £2.60 £2.00 £2.70 (£11.80) Trio £19.70 OWNER Sir Stanley and Lady Grinstead (NEWMARKET) BRED Sir Stanley Grinstead

WEIGHT FOR AGE 3yo-4lb

**2316 Lough Erne** was sent to the front early in the final quarter-mile and stormed clear to finally lose her maiden tag. (5/1: op 3/1)

**2735 Scissor Ridge** disputed the lead until going on at halfway. Collared well over a furlong from home, he failed to live with the winner. (6/1)

**3168* Rambold**, with a marginal lead to halfway, failed to quicken in the last two furlongs. (8/1)

**2193 Merrie le Bow** chased the leaders. Ridden along below the distance, she stayed on and only just failed to take third prize. (16/1)

**3096 Lorins Gold** chased the leaders. Bustled along from halfway, he failed to find that vital turn of foot. (16/1)

## 3440 COURIER NEWSPAPERS LIMITED STKS (0-80) (3-Y.O+) (Class D)

8-10 (8-10) **7f** £3,761.25 (£1,122.00: £535.50: £242.25) Stalls: High GOING minus 0.40 sec per fur (F)

| | | | | SP | RR | SF |
|---|---|---|---|---|---|---|
| 3271[2] | **Neuwest (USA) (80)** (NJHWalker) **4-9-7** JStack(2) (lw: chsd ldr: led 3f out: hrd rdn over 1f out: r.o wl) | — | **1** | 7/1 | 91 | 66 |
| 3093* | **Tarneem (USA) (79)** (MRStoute) **3-8-10** PatEddery(4) (led 4f: hrd rdn over 1f out: unable qckn) | 2 | **2** | 5/2[2] | 81 | 50 |
| 3216* | **Hawa Al Nasamaat (USA) (85)** (EALDunlop) **4-9-0**(3) DaneO'Neill(6) (lw: a.p: hrd rdn over 1f out: one pce) | 1 | **3** | 6/5[1] | 80 | 55 |
| 2053[25] | **Zygo (USA) (80)** (WJarvis) **4-9-3** TQuinn(3) (lw: bhd fnl 3f) | 3 | **4** | 13/2[3] | 73 | 48 |
| 3265[3] | **Champagne Grandy (80)** (MRChannon) **6-8-11**(5) PPMurphy(5) (lw: a bhd) | 5 | **5** | 10/1 | 61 | 36 |

(SP 109.0%) **5 Rn**

**1m 21.94** (0.34) CSF £22.51 TOTE £7.50: £2.80 £1.60 (£6.30) OWNER Mr Paul Green (WANTAGE) BRED Robert Bloomer and Sharon L. Bloomer

WEIGHT FOR AGE 3yo-6lb

**3271 Neuwest (USA)** looked as tremendous as ever in the paddock. Racing in second place, he went on three furlongs from home and, responding to strong pressure below the distance, kept up the gallop in good style. (7/1)

**3093* Tarneem (USA)** set the pace. Collared three furlongs from home, she came under strong pressure below the distance, but failed to find the necessary turn of foot. (5/2)

**3216* Hawa Al Nasamaat (USA)**, close up in third place, came under pressure below the distance but failed to find the necessary acceleration. (6/5: Evens-5/4)

**1843 Zygo (USA)**, racing in fourth place, was in trouble three furlongs from home. (13/2)

T/Plpt: £70.90 (126.6 Tckts). T/Qdpt: £12.40 (56.18 Tckts). AK

# 3404-NEWMARKET (R-H) (Good to firm)

## Saturday August 10th

Race 6: hand-timed.

WEATHER: fine WIND: almost nil

## 3441 MONTANA WINES MAIDEN STKS (3-Y.O+) (Class D)

2-00 (2-02) **1m 4f (July)** £4,659.00 (£1,392.00: £666.00: £303.00) Stalls: High GOING minus 0.46 sec per fur (F)

| | | | | SP | RR | SF |
|---|---|---|---|---|---|---|
| | **Fine Detail (IRE)** (RCharlton) **3-8-5** WRyan(4) (unf: scope: hld up: hdwy 4f out: led wl over 1f out: hung lft & drvn out) | — | **1** | 15/2 | 81 | 52 |

3042$^{2}$ **Flamands (IRE)** (LMCumani) **3-7-12**(7) RFfrench(2) (trckd ldrs: rdn 2f out: r.o wl & edgd lft fnl f) ....................nk **2** 11/2$^{2}$ 81 52
2610$^{2}$ **Lady Joshua (IRE)** (JLDunlop) **3-8-5** KDarley(3) (prom: led over 3f out: hdd wl over 1f out: hung lft & nt run on) ....................4 **3** 11/10$^{1}$ 75 46
3218$^{2}$ **Belmarita (IRE) (74)** (MHTompkins) **3-8-5** PRobinson(5) (led: hdd over 3f out: wknd over 1f out) ....................3 **4** 6/1$^{3}$ 71 42
2601$^{8}$ **National Treasure** (MRStoute) **3-8-5** MHills(6) (dwlt: sn chsng ldr: ev ch 2f out: sn rdn & btn) ....................2 **5** 8/1 69 40
**Alsahah (IRE)** (DMorley) **3-8-5** RCochrane(7) (leggy: unf: sn trckng ldrs: rdn & btn 3f out) ....................1¼ **6** 16/1 67 38
2591$^{6}$ **Candrika** (LMCumani) **3-7-12**(7) JoHunnam(1) (in tch 9f) ....................2½ **7** 33/1 64 35
**Calendula** (DMorley) **3-8-5** BThomson(8) (leggy: unf: rdn 4f out: a bhd) ....................18 **8** 50/1 40 11
(SP 110.9%) **8 Rn**

**2m 30.12** (0.12) CSF £42.81 TOTE £9.20: £2.10 £1.50 £1.10 (£20.90) OWNER Mr K. Abdulla (BECKHAMPTON) BRED Juddmonte Farms

**Fine Detail (IRE)**, related to a number of useful horses such as Source of Light, clearly has a fair bit of ability but looks highly strung and needed a Monty Roberts blanket for stall entry. She was out on her feet as her tail whirled round, having kicked clear inside the final furlong, but she had enough lead to avoid being pegged back. (15/2: 5/1-9/1)
**3042 Flamands (IRE)** again took an age to get going, but came home strongly, despite swishing her tail and, from a good staying family, looks sure to stay further. (11/2: op 3/1)
**2610 Lady Joshua (IRE)** proved a real let-down over this longer trip for, as battle commenced, she flashed her tail, hung left and did not do a tap. (11/10: 7/4-Evens)
**3218 Belmarita (IRE)** ran a sound race, trying to make all, but finally had to give up the ghost in the Dip. (6/1)
**National Treasure**, a good mover, again finished weakly after travelling quite well. Despite being by Shirley Heights, her dam Brocade was best up to a mile, and it may be that his trip is beyond her. (8/1: 6/1-10/1)
**Alsahah (IRE)** tried to miss a beat at the start, but was soon travelling quite keenly on the heels of the leaders. She was a spent force some way from home, but may be capable of improvement. (16/1)

## 3442 EQUITY FINANCIAL COLLECTIONS CLAIMING STKS (3-Y.O+) (Class E)

2-30 (2-31) **7f (July)** £4,045.00 (£1,210.00: £580.00: £265.00) Stalls: Low GOING minus 0.46 sec per fur (F)

SP RR SF

3244* **Ortolan (80)** (RHannon) **3-8-11**(3) DaneO'Neill(13) (lw: hld up stands' side: hdwy over 3f out: led over 1f out: pushed out) ....................— **1** 2/1$^{2}$ 68 43
2975$^{6}$ **Northern Judge (50)** (BHanbury) **3-8-4b** JStack(6) (chsd ldrs: led far side over 1f out: r.o) ....................2 **2** 33/1 53 28
2971$^{11}$ **Speedy Snaps Pride (30)** (PDCundell) **4-8-5b**(5) DGriffiths(7) (hdwy far side 2f out: r.o wl ins fnl f) ....................hd **3** 50/1 53 34
3288$^{2}$ **Clincher Club (66)** (MJohnston) **3-8-2** PRobinson(8) (led far side over 5f) ....................1 **4** 8/1$^{3}$ 49 24
3271$^{4}$ **Silent Expression (84)** (BJMeehan) **6-9-1** BDoyle(1) (in tch far side: rdn 2f out: nt pce to chal) ....................1 **5** 7/4$^{1}$ 54 35
*3089*$^{7}$ **Great Hall (41)** (PDCundell) **7-8-10b** DHarrison(3) (s.i.s: hdwy far side fnl 2f: nrst fin) ....................1½ **6** 50/1 45 26
2787$^{10}$ **Judgement Call (49)** (PHowling) **9-8-8** KDarley(11) (led stands' side over 5f) ....................1½ **7** 33/1 40 21
3233$^{5}$ **Otto E Mezzo (85)** (MJPolglase) **4-9-6** WHollick(2) (chsd ldrs far over 3f) ....................nk **8** 20/1 51 32
2860$^{5}$ **Be Warned (66)** (NACallaghan) **5-9-3b** LDettori(10) (lw: hdwy far side over 3f out: wknd over 1f out) ....................1¼ **9** 8/1$^{3}$ 45 26
2604$^{9}$ **Firm Contract (IRE)** (CNAllen) **4-8-13** TIves(5) (b: racd far side: bhd fnl 3f) ....................½ **10** 40/1 40 21
3262$^{11}$ **Calandrella** (GBBalding) **3-8-0** NAdams(4) (racd far side: a bhd) ....................¾ **11** 50/1 31 6
2181$^{9}$ **El Bardador (IRE)** (WJarvis) **3-8-11** AMcGlone(9) (s.i.s: a bhd far side) ....................¾ **12** 33/1 41 16
3217* **Indian Rhapsody (47)** (ABailey) **4-8-7** PBloomfield(14) (swtg: hld up stands' side: effrt over 2f out: sn btn) ....................9 **13** 12/1 10 —
**Oh Susannah** (JAHarris) **5-8-8** MHills(12) (chsd ldrs stands' side over 5f) ....................1¾ **14** 33/1 7 —
(SP 124.5%) **14 Rn**

**1m 26.44** (1.44) CSF £60.52 TOTE £3.20: £1.60 £9.30 £10.30 (£143.00) Trio £604.30; £255.34 to Windsor 12/8/96 OWNER Mr J. A. Lazzari (MARLBOROUGH) BRED Filletts Farm Stud
WEIGHT FOR AGE 3yo-6lb

**IN-FOCUS: A group of four including the winner came to the stands' rail and only Silent Expression from stall one stayed hard against the far side fence with the rest racing a few horse widths from the far side.**
**3244* Ortolan** spread-eagled the quartet who raced under the stands' rail, but may not have needed to be at his very best to win the way the race turned out. (2/1)
**1836 Northern Judge**, back to his best trip, returned to form to win the far-side group, but can hardly be described as consistent. (33/1)
**2796 Speedy Snaps Pride**, a maiden consistently beaten in handicaps off marks in the thirties, will give all Handicappers sleepless nights with this performance, beating Silent Expression on 49lb worse terms than they could theoretically meet on in handicaps. This was probably a moderate race but Speedy Snaps Pride could clearly win a little handicap if ever he could be persuaded to put his best foot forward. (50/1)
**3288 Clincher Club**, so keen on the way to post that the saddle appeared to slip, again failed to last out the seven as the brakes failed. (8/1: op 5/1)
**3271 Silent Expression**, without a victory this year, is normally admirably consistent and was dropped in grade to regain the winning habit. Unfortunately, she ran a stinker and looks best avoided at present. (7/4: 5/2-6/4)
**1473 Great Hall**, like his stable-companion who finished third, seemed to run miles above his current handicap mark, but is currently on a losing run of seventeen. (50/1)
**2860 Be Warned** (8/1: op 5/1)
**3217* Indian Rhapsody** (12/1: 8/1-14/1)

## 3443 DANDELION INVITATION LADIES' H'CAP (0-65) (3-Y.O+) (Class F)

3-05 (3-13) **1m (July)** £4,201.50 (£1,272.00: £621.00: £295.50) Stalls: Low GOING minus 0.46 sec per fur (F)

SP RR SF

3084$^{2}$ **Mezzoramio (46)** (KAMorgan) **4-10-9v** BirgitRoesch(2) (b: chsd ldr: led over 2f out: rdn clr ins fnl f) ....................— **1** 5/1$^{1}$ 55 18
2793$^{5}$ **Prudent Pet (47)** (CWFairhurst) **4-10-10** MissEJohnsonHoughton(5) (hld up: hdwy 2f out: r.o wl ins fnl f) ....................1¼ **2** 20/1 54 17
3306$^{2}$ **Roseate Lodge (40)** (SEKettlewell) **10-10-3** MarliesGloor(10) (a.p: ev ch over 2f out tl wknd ins fnl f) ....................½ **3** 7/1$^{3}$ 46 9
3358* **Balpare (47)** (NACallaghan) **3-10-3** 5x MrsDArbuthnot(4) (hld up: hdwy 3f out: no ex fnl f) ....................nk **4** 5/1$^{1}$ 52 8
3281$^{2}$ **Fort Knox (IRE) (58)** (RMFlower) **5-11-7b** OlgaHulinsky(9) (s.i.s: hdwy over 1f out: r.o fnl f) ....................2½ **5** 9/1 58 21
3172$^{2}$ **Awesome Venture (51)** (MCChapman) **6-11-0** MrsSBosley(6) (trckd ldrs: rdn 2f out: wknd fnl f) ....................2½ **6** 11/2$^{2}$ 46 9
2941$^{4}$ **Willy Star (BEL) (52)** (MrsSJSmith) **6-11-1** MrsDKettlewell(3) (prom 5f) ....................¾ **7** 14/1 45 8
3167$^{3}$ **Audrey Grace (46)** (MissGayKelleway) **5-10-9** MrsMMullins(11) (b.hind: in tch: rdn 2f out: sn btn) ....................¾ **8** 7/1$^{3}$ 38 1
2587$^{4}$ **Don't Drop Bombs (USA) (39)** (DTThom) **7-10-2v** MissJFeilden(0) (led over 5f: sn wknd) ....................6 **9** 8/1 19 —
2628$^{7}$ **Sylvan Sabre (IRE) (45)** (KAMorgan) **7-10-8** MissDClerc(7) (b: chsd ldrs tl rdn & wknd 3f out) ....................14 **10** 33/1 — —
*2713*$^{11}$ ***Wilfull Lad (IRE) (60)*** (MartynMeade) **3-11-2** TrineLangvad(12) (Withdrawn not under Starter's orders: bolted bef s) .................... **W** 25/1 — —

*1890[11]* ***Love Legend (41)*** (DWPArbuthnot) **11-10-4** LoneHaugenhaug(8) (Withdrawn not under Starter's orders: bolted bef s) ........ **W** 25/1 — —
(SP 116.9%) **10 Rn**

**1m 43.64** (6.44) CSF £77.73 CT £591.45 TOTE £5.80: £2.30 £3.50 £2.10 (£79.90) Trio £134.60 OWNER Mr T. R. Pryke (MELTON MOWBRAY) BRED Saeed Manana
WEIGHT FOR AGE 3yo-7lb
**IN-FOCUS: This field elected to stick to the far rails.**
**3084 Mezzoramio** seems at home in this type of race and stuck to his guns when taken on in the final furlong. (5/1)
**2793 Prudent Pet**, buried towards the rear, settled better than most and came home well once seeing daylight. (20/1)
**3306 Roseate Lodge** struck for home at the same time as the winner, but was finally worn down by that rival in the last 100 yards. (7/1: 5/1-15/2)
**3358* Balpare** used her speed to get to the heels of the leaders in the Dip and could then find no more. (5/1)
**3281 Fort Knox (IRE)**, the winner of this race twelve months ago, again did his best work at the finish, but too late to take a hand. (9/1: op 6/1)
**3172 Awesome Venture** finds this trip on turf just beyond his best. (11/2)
**2941 Willy Star (BEL)** (14/1: 10/1-16/1)

## 3444 ENZA NEW ZEALAND SWEET SOLERA STKS (Listed) (2-Y.O F) (Class A)
3-35 (3-36) **7f (July)** £10,140.80 (£3,747.20: £1,793.60: £728.00: £284.00: £106.40) Stalls: Low GOING minus 0.46 sec per fur (F)

| | | | SP | RR | SF |
|---|---|---|---|---|---|
| 2863[6] | **Catwalk** (WJHaggas) **2-8-8** MHills(7) (mde all: hld on wl ins fnl f) ........— | **1** | 20/1 | 91 | 28 |
| 2997[7] | **Fernanda (94)** (JLDunlop) **2-8-11b**[1] TQuinn(10) (lw: chsd ldrs: ev ch over 1f out: unable qckn nr fin) ........hd | **2** | 7/1 | 94 | 31 |
| 2741* | **Dancing Drop (95)** (RHannon) **2-8-8** DHarrison(9) (hld up: nt clr run over 1f out: hdwy & edgd rt fnl f: r.o) ....1½ | **3** | 6/1 | 87 | 24 |
| 2802* | **Lady Mail (IRE) (85)** (JMPEustace) **2-8-8** RCochrane(2) (dwlt: swtchd to centre of crse after 1f: hdwy over 1f out: r.o fnl f) ........½ | **4** | 5/1[3] | 86 | 23 |
| 2997[4] | **Impetuous Air (92)** (EWeymes) **2-8-8** KDarley(8) (trckd ldrs: rdn & ev ch over 1f out: sn btn) ........3 | **5** | 12/1 | 79 | 16 |
| 3068[7] | **Eye Shadow (93)** (BJMeehan) **2-8-8** BDoyle(6) (chsd wnr: ev ch 2f out: sn rdn & btn) ........s.h | **6** | 12/1 | 79 | 16 |
| 3044[2] | **Literary** (JHMGosden) **2-8-8** LDettori(5) (dwlt: swtchd to centre of crse after 1f: hdwy 2f out: ev ch over 1f out: sn wknd) ........1 | **7** | 11/4[1] | 77 | 14 |
| 2984[6] | **Stride (78)** (MartynMeade) **2-8-8** WRyan(1) (trckd ldr far side: plld out over 2f out: sn btn) ........3½ | **8** | 25/1 | 69 | 6 |
| 3129* | **Papita (IRE)** (SDow) **2-8-8** BThomson(4) (sn swtchd to centre of crse: w ldrs: ev ch over 1f out: sn wknd) ......4 | **9** | 4/1[2] | 60 | — |
| 2619[3] | **Simple Logic (82)** (AGFoster) **2-8-8** PRobinson(3) (led far side: wl bhd fnl 3f) ........2½ | **10** | 14/1 | 54 | — |

(SP 120.8%) **10 Rn**

**1m 27.26** (2.26) CSF £143.01 TOTE £19.60: £2.90 £2.70 £2.40 (£51.90) Trio £64.80 OWNER Mr Michael Brower (NEWMARKET) BRED Lord Halifax
**IN-FOCUS: Almost the whole field ended up racing centre to stands' side with those drawn high seeming favoured.**
**2863 Catwalk**, stepped up in class and adopting forcing tactics, sprung a surprise and proved a tough nut to crack when challenged on all sides in the last couple of furlongs, although her pilot seemed reluctant to really go for everything. (20/1)
**2997 Fernanda** bounced back to form in first-time blinkers, but her penalty proved decisive. (7/1)
**2741* Dancing Drop**, stepping up in trip, stayed on nicely once she got through, and is knocking at the door in this type of race. (6/1)
**2802* Lady Mail (IRE)** seemed to be left with plenty to do in the last couple of furlongs, but came home well and is worth another chance. (5/1)
**2997 Impetuous Air** showed the strength of Red Camellia's Sandown win, for she ran a similar race and got a good deal closer this time. (12/1)
**2582 Eye Shadow**, stepping up in trip, did not appear to stay. (12/1)
**3044 Literary**, eight lengths in front of Spaniard's Mount here last time, hardly looked an obvious candidate after that horse was beaten considerably further in a Pontefract maiden earlier in the week. Taken to post steadily after the others, she is gradually learning to settle and ought to win a race. (11/4)
**3129* Papita (IRE)** was not helped by her low draw, but could not dominate this time and had her limitations exposed. (4/1: 3/1-9/2)

## 3445 NEW ZEALAND H'CAP (0-105) (3-Y.O+) (Class B)
4-10 (4-12) **7f (July)** £19,737.50 (£5,900.00: £2,825.00: £1,287.50) Stalls: Low GOING minus 0.46 sec per fur (F)

| | | | SP | RR | SF |
|---|---|---|---|---|---|
| 2623[7] | **Polar Prince (IRE) (96)** (MAJarvis) **3-8-13** PRobinson(6) (hld up: hdwy 2f out: n.m.r over 1f out: qcknd to ld ins fnl f) ........— | **1** | 9/1 | 109 | 57 |
| 3158[3] | **Prince Babar (92)** (JEBanks) **5-8-10**(5) DGriffiths(10) (s.i.s: sn prom: led over 1f out: hdd ins fnl f: sn btn) ........¾ | **2** | 11/2[2] | 103 | 57 |
| 2623* | **Crumpton Hill (IRE) (89)** (NAGraham) **4-8-12** TQuinn(9) (hld up: hdwy over 2f out: ev ch over 1f out: unable qckn wl ins fnl f) ........¾ | **3** | 11/2[2] | 99 | 53 |
| 3254* | **Mountgate (78)** (MPBielby) **4-8-1**ow1 BDoyle(8) (lw: hld up: rdn 3f out: hdwy & n.m.r over 1f out: swtchd & r.o ins fnl f) ........2 | **4** | 11/1 | 83 | 36 |
| 2623[13] | **Saseedo (USA) (91)** (WAO'Gorman) **6-9-0** EmmaO'Gorman(11) (swtg: hld up: hdwy over 2f out: nvr able to chal) ........1 | **5** | 12/1 | 94 | 48 |
| 3211[9] | **Believe Me (92)** (RHannon) **3-8-6**(3) DaneO'Neill(4) (lw: w ldrs: led over 2f out tl over 1f out: no ex) ........d.h | **5** | 20/1 | 95 | 43 |
| 3101[4] | **Tawafij (USA) (73)** (MDHammond) **7-7-10** NCarlisle(3) (dwlt: hdwy over 3f out: nt clr run & lost pl over 2f out: r.o wl fnl f) ........½ | **7** | 12/1 | 75+ | 29 |
| 3210* | **Green Barries (98)** (MJohnston) **3-9-1** MHills(7) (lw: a.p: rdn & ev ch over 1f out: wknd ins fnl f) ........1½ | **8** | 7/1[3] | 96 | 44 |
| 3222[3] | **Maid For The Hills (93)** (DRLoder) **3-8-7**(3) PMcCabe(5) (plld hrd: trckd ldrs 5f) ........½ | **9** | 25/1 | 90 | 38 |
| 2920* | **Verzen (IRE) (102)** (DRLoder) **4-9-11** RHughes(2) (led 2f: rdn over 1f out: wkng whn hmpd ins fnl f) ........1½ | **10** | 9/1 | 96 | 50 |
| 3158[7] | **Almuhimm (USA) (89)** (EALDunlop) **4-8-12** KDarley(12) (hld up: hdwy 3f out: rdn & btn appr fnl f) ........1¼ | **11** | 9/2[1] | 80 | 34 |
| 2919[4] | **Defined Feature (IRE) (96)** (MRStoute) **3-8-13** RCochrane(13) (in tch: effrt 3f out: sn btn) ........1½ | **12** | 16/1 | 83 | 31 |
| 3172* | **Nashaat (USA) (76)** (MCChapman) **8-7-6**(7) JFowle(14) (swtg: effrt 3f out: a bhd) ........1¾ | **13** | 20/1 | 59 | 13 |
| 3265[4] | **Ertlon (74)** (CEBrittain) **6-7-8**(3) MHenry(1) (lw: led after 2f tl over 2f out: sn rdn & wknd) ........1 | **14** | 40/1 | 55 | 9 |

(SP 126.9%) **14 Rn**

**1m 25.21** (0.21) CSF £56.77 CT £282.92 TOTE £12.10: £3.90 £2.50 £2.30 (£22.70) Trio £29.70 OWNER Mrs Christine Stevenson (NEWMARKET) BRED Michael Morrin
LONG HANDICAP Tawafij (USA) 7-9
WEIGHT FOR AGE 3yo-6lb
**IN-FOCUS: For some reason the entire field elected to race down the far rails where the slowest ground appeared to be.**
**2623 Polar Prince (IRE)**, who reportedly missed work after his buffeting in the Bunbury Cup, did not impress everyone in his slower paces, but travelled supremely well in the race and found a high-class turn of foot once he saw daylight. He looks hard to beat at this trip. (9/1)
**3158 Prince Babar**, over what may well be his ideal trip, must wonder what he has to do to win a big handicap, for he held off Crumpton Hill in determined fashion, only for the winner to sweep by. (11/2)

**2623* Crumpton Hill (IRE)** moved poorly to post, but ran his best and did not go down without a real fight. (11/2)
**3254* Mountgate** often runs well here and would have got closer but for being momentarily stopped at a vital stage. (11/1)
**2497* Saseedo (USA)** continues in good heart but was never doing quite enough when asked to improve in the last two furlongs. (12/1)
**1771 Believe Me**, dropping in trip, helped force the pace, but could not quicken in the closing stages. (20/1)
**3101 Tawafij (USA)** had no luck in running here and looks set to bounce back to form, for he is very well handicapped now. (12/1: op 20/1)
**3210* Green Barries**, off a 12lb higher mark than last time, could not make the same impact in a stronger-run race and was already beginning to struggle when the winner cut in front of him inside the final furlong. (7/1)
**3158 Almuhimm (USA)** has had some hard races of late and looked edgy and on his toes in the paddock. The fact that the field elected to stick to the far side denied him the opportunity of being covered up, and he ran no race at all. (9/2)

## 3446 SOUTH ISLAND MAIDEN STKS (3-Y.O) (Class D)

4-40 (4-40) **6f (July)** £4,776.00 (£1,428.00: £684.00: £312.00) Stalls: Low GOING minus 0.46 sec per fur (F)

| | | | | SP | RR | SF |
|---|---|---|---|---|---|---|
| 2861[3] | **Disputed** (MAJarvis) **3-9-0** PRobinson(13) (chsd ldrs: rdn over 1f out: r.o to ld nr fin) | — | 1 | 9/2[2] | 84 | 34 |
| 2431[2] | **Nilgiri Hills (IRE) (82)** (JLDunlop) **3-9-0** KDarley(9) (a.p: rdn to ld 1f out: ct nr fin) | hd | 2 | 7/2[1] | 84 | 34 |
| 3210[10] | **Lucky Archer (87)** (CEBrittain) **3-9-0** BDoyle(14) (a.p: led over 1f out: sn hdd & no ex) | ¾ | 3 | 20/1 | 82 | 32 |
| 3162[3] | **Yukon Hope (USA)** (RCharlton) **3-8-9** WRyan(2) (chsd ldrs: ev ch over 1f out: r.o again ins fnl f) | 1 | 4 | 5/1[3] | 74 | 24 |
| | **Danlora** (WJarvis) **3-8-9** BThomson(3) (lengthy: bkwd: led over 4f: kpt on) | hd | 5 | 20/1 | 74 | 24 |
| | **La Mafarr (USA)** (JHMGosden) **3-9-0** LDettori(11) (unf: bit bkwd: hld up: hdwy over 1f out: n.m.r & eased ins fnl f) | 1 | 6 | 9/2[2] | 76 | 26 |
| 3255[2] | **Chalk Dust (USA) (78)** (PFICole) **3-8-9** TQuinn(10) (hld up: effrt 2f out: nvr rchd ldrs) | 1¼ | 7 | 11/2 | 68 | 18 |
| 3262[6] | **Polish Rhythm (IRE)** (MHTompkins) **3-8-6(3)** MHenry(5) (bhd tl r.o fnl 2f) | 1 | 8 | 40/1 | 65 | 15 |
| | **Present Imperfect** (IABalding) **3-8-9** MHills(12) (lengthy: unf: bit bkwd: s.i.s: hld up: hdwy over 1f out: nvr rchd ldrs) | 1½ | 9 | 14/1 | 61 | 11 |
| 3162[5] | **Longwick Lad** (WRMuir) **3-9-0** DHarrison(6) (prom: rdn & ev ch over 1f out: wknd fnl f) | hd | 10 | 33/1 | 66 | 16 |
| 3162[12] | **Octavia Hill** (PWHarris) **3-8-9** AMcGlone(7) (dwlt: nvr plcd to chal) | ½ | 11 | 40/1 | 60 | 10 |
| | **Happy Traveller (IRE)** (CMurray) **3-9-0** RHughes(1) (w ldrs 4f: sn wknd) | 4 | 12 | 40/1 | 54 | 4 |
| | **Hostile Native** (RGuest) **3-9-0** PBloomfield(8) (w'like: bkwd: s.i.s: a bhd) | 5 | 13 | 33/1 | 41 | — |
| | **Classic Warrior** (RHarris) **3-9-0** AMackay(4) (w'like: bkwd: chsd ldrs: rdn 3f out: sn wknd) | 16 | 14 | 33/1 | — | — |
| | | | | (SP 123.0%) | **14 Rn** | |

**1m 13.9** (1.90) CSF £19.80 TOTE £6.50: £2.30 £1.50 £3.60 (£16.80) Trio £87.10 OWNER Sheikh Ahmed Al Maktoum (NEWMARKET) BRED Gallagher Farms

**IN-FOCUS: The field spread right across the middle of the course with those drawn or racing towards the stands' side possibly favoured.**
**2861 Disputed** stepped up on his previous effort, coming late to snatch the race out of the fire. His action suggests more cut in the ground may improve him further. (9/2)
**2431 Nilgiri Hills (IRE)** looked sure to win when hitting the front, but again lost out in the dying strides. Excuses for him are increasingly hard to come by. (7/2)
**1796 Lucky Archer**, back sprinting and with the best of the draw, ran well, but could not hold the advantage for long once he hit the front. (20/1)
**3162 Yukon Hope (USA)**, probably hindered by the draw, looks to need further, for she was outpaced in the Dip before staying on well at the finish. (5/1: 3/1-11/2)
**Danlora**, quite an attractive, good-moving filly, showed plenty of speed on her debut and should not be too hard to place, particularly over a little further. (20/1)
**La Mafarr (USA)**, a deep-bodied, backward-looking newcomer, is a very good mover, but took some time to get the message, running rather green. The situation was accepted in the final furlong and he should come on considerably for the run. (9/2: 5/2-5/1)

## 3447 KFF POTATOES 50TH ANNIVERSARY H'CAP (0-95) (3-Y.O+) (Class C)

5-10 (5-10) **1m 2f (July)** £6,472.00 (£1,936.00: £928.00: £424.00) GOING minus 0.46 sec per fur (F)

| | | | | SP | RR | SF |
|---|---|---|---|---|---|---|
| 3043* | **Angus-G (73)** (MrsMReveley) **4-8-8** KDarley(12) (lw: a.p: rdn over 1f out: styd on to ld wl ins fnl f) | — | 1 | 9/2[1] | 84 | 58 |
| 3125[U] | **Edan Heights (72)** (SDow) **4-8-7** BThomson(4) (lw: chsd ldrs: rdn to ld ins fnl f: sn hdd & no ex) | nk | 2 | 14/1 | 83 | 57 |
| 2901[2] | **Voila Premiere (IRE) (66)** (MHTompkins) **4-7-12(3)** MHenry(7) (led tl ins fnl f: unable qckn) | 1¼ | 3 | 11/2[3] | 75 | 49 |
| 3248[4] | **Ball Gown (89)** (DTThom) **6-9-10** PRobinson(5) (b.hind: hld up: hdwy 2f out: styd on u.p fnl f) | ¾ | 4 | 5/1[2] | 96 | 70 |
| 2888[5] | **Go Britannia (88)** (DRLoder) **3-9-0** RHughes(8) (trckd ldrs: rdn 2f out: nt qckn fnl f) | ¾ | 5 | 13/2 | 94 | 59 |
| 2862[8] | **Missel (93)** (MJohnston) **4-10-0** WWoods(3) (hld up: hdwy 4f out: rdn 3f out: no imp appr fnl f) | 3 | 6 | 20/1 | 94 | 68 |
| 963[3] | **Monarch (87)** (PFICole) **4-9-8** TQuinn(1) (bkwd: hld up: hdwy over 4f out: outpcd appr fnl f) | d.h | 6 | 13/2 | 88 | 62 |
| 3071[6] | **Billy Bushwacker (91)** (MrsMReveley) **5-9-12** RCochrane(6) (stdd s: hld up: n.m.r 4f out: nvr rchd ldrs) | 4 | 8 | 7/1 | 86 | 60 |
| 1476[16] | **Sadler's Walk (77)** (GWragg) **5-8-12** MHills(10) (swtg: hld up: rdn over 2f out: no imp) | 1¾ | 9 | 14/1 | 69 | 43 |
| 2581[6] | **Karinska (61)** (MCChapman) **6-7-3(7)** JFowle(2) (bhd: hdwy 4f out: wknd over 2f out) | 2 | 10 | 20/1 | 50 | 24 |
| 2724[12] | **Secret Aly (CAN) (82)** (CEBrittain) **6-9-3** BDoyle(9) (lw: plld hrd: w ldr: rdn over 3f out: sn btn) | 6 | 11 | 12/1 | 61 | 35 |
| 3125[10] | **Jagellon (USA) (90)** (WRMuir) **5-9-11** WRyan(11) (trckd ldrs 7f: sn wknd & eased) | dist | 12 | 14/1 | — | — |
| | | | | (SP 126.6%) | **12 Rn** | |

**2m 4.69** (-0.31) CSF £62.17 CT £328.18 TOTE £4.20: £1.70 £6.10 £2.00 (£77.50) Trio £123.70 OWNER Mr W. Ginzel (SALTBURN) BRED W. Ginzel

LONG HANDICAP Karinska 7-8
WEIGHT FOR AGE 3yo-9lb

**3043* Angus-G**, raised only 2lb for his recent course and distance success, continues on the upgrade and was suited by the true-run nature of the race, not being one to do anything quickly. (9/2)
**2549* Edan Heights** has won over further and was always close enough to the pace to make his stamina count. He did not go down without a fight and had a hard race. (14/1)
**2901 Voila Premiere (IRE)**, again forcing the pace, lacked that vital little extra in the heat of battle, and looks in the Handicapper's grip unless a softer race can be found. (11/2)
**3248 Ball Gown**, suited by the strong pace, probably ran close to her best, but could not quicken to gain the day when the chance was there. The Handicapper is proving slow to forgive her first-time victory this year. (5/1)
**2888 Go Britannia** was cruising for most of the race, but did not find much off the bridle. He did not seem to benefit from the step up in trip as much as might have been anticipated on his pedigree. (13/2)
**Missel** again ran well on his second run back after a long spell on the sidelines. He is lightly-raced but high in the handicap. (20/1)
**963 Monarch** looked badly in need of the race, but shaped well at a trip some way below his best. (13/2)

T/Jkpt: Not won; £22,387.51 to Windsor 12/8/96. T/Plpt: £212.80 (144.83 Tckts). T/Qdpt: £46.30 (36.18 Tckts). Dk

# 3410-REDCAR (L-H) (Firm, Good to firm patches)
## Saturday August 10th
WEATHER: fine WIND: almost nil

### 3448 BEDALE (S) STKS (2-Y.O) (Class F)
2-10 (2-12) **6f** £2,826.00 (£786.00: £378.00) Stalls: Low GOING minus 0.48 sec per fur (F)

| | | | | SP | RR | SF |
|---|---|---|---|---|---|---|
| $3121^{9}$ | **Little Blue (IRE) (59)** (TDEasterby) **2-8-6** JLowe(6) (mde all: clr over 1f out: rdn out) | — | **1** | 12/1 | 60 | 6 |
| $2118^{4}$ | **Skippy Was A Kiwi (IRE)** (APJarvis) **2-8-6** WJO'Connor(2) (lw: towards rr: hdwy appr fnl f: r.o) | 1 | **2** | 8/1 | 57 | 3 |
| $2959^{5}$ | **The Bee Man (56)** (MWEasterby) **2-8-6**(5) GParkin(10) (lw: a.p: rdn over 1f out: r.o one pce) | 1¼ | **3** | $11/4^{1}$ | 59 | 5 |
| $2512^{4}$ | **Petrine Gray** (TDEasterby) **2-8-6** LCharnock(4) (towards rr: kpt on fr over 1f out: nrst fin) | 1¼ | **4** | 13/2 | 51 | — |
| $3227^{5}$ | **Soviet Lady (IRE) (57)** (JLEyre) **2-8-3**(3) NVarley(1) (lw: b.off hind: dwlt: kpt on fr wl over 1f out: nvr nrr) | nk | **5** | $7/2^{2}$ | 50 | — |
| $1664^{9}$ | **Dance Melody** (GROldroyd) **2-8-6** DaleGibson(7) (lw: bhd: sn rdn along: styd on fr 2f out: nrst fin) | 2½ | **6** | 14/1 | 43 | — |
| *$3065^{6}$* | **Dancing Star (IRE) (50)** (PDEvans) **2-8-6v** JFEgan(13) (lw: led stands' side: wknd appr fnl f) | ½ | **7** | 9/1 | 42 | — |
| $2959^{8}$ | **Who (IRE)** (TDEasterby) **2-8-8**(3) CTeague(5) (a mid div) | ½ | **8** | 20/1 | 46 | — |
| $2795^{8}$ | **Timely Touch (38)** (MWEllerby) **2-8-3**(3) DarrenMoffatt(14) (chsd ldrs stands' side: wknd wl over 1f out) | ½ | **9** | 33/1 | 39 | — |
| $2387^{3}$ | **Back In The Ussr (IRE) (58)** (MJohnston) **2-8-11** TWilliams(12) (swtg: prom tl wknd 2f out) | nk | **10** | $9/2^{3}$ | 43 | — |
| $2926^{7}$ | **Superboots** (WWHaigh) **2-8-2**(5)ow1 LNewton(11) (prom stands' side 4f) | 1¼ | **11** | 12/1 | 36 | — |
| *$3087^{6}$* | **Bonsiel** (JGFitzGerald) **2-8-6** JFanning(9) (in tch tl rdn & wknd wl over 1f out) | hd | **12** | 14/1 | 35 | — |
| $3241^{5}$ | **My Girl (45)** (JBerry) **2-8-6** JFortune(3) (lw: chsd ldrs 4f: sn wknd) | 4 | **13** | 16/1 | 24 | — |
| $3224^{9}$ | **Antares (66)** (NTinkler) **2-8-11** KimTinkler(8) (a bhd) | ½ | **14** | 8/1 | 28 | — |
| | | | | (SP 154.9%) | **14 Rn** | |

**1m 13.4** (3.20) CSF £121.43 TOTE £21.40: £5.90 £3.50 £1.30 (£119.50) Trio £171.90; £157.46 to Windsor 12/8/96 OWNER Ryedale Associates (MALTON) BRED A. T. Robinson
No bid
**2728 Little Blue (IRE)** jumped out and had her rivals in trouble well over a furlong out. This stood her in good stead as she was getting pegged back in the final 100 yards. (12/1: op 8/1)
**2118 Skippy Was A Kiwi (IRE)**, who could not go the early pace, made ground hand over fist in the closing stages, but had given the winner too big a start. (8/1)
**2959 The Bee Man**, always in the firing-line, just lacked the turn of foot required. (11/4)
**2512 Petrine Gray** was again doing her best work in the second half of the race, and another try at a longer trip should help. (13/2)
**3227 Soviet Lady (IRE)** missed the break and did well to finish as close as she did. (7/2)
**Dance Melody** looked likely to be one of the backmarkers, but stayed on very gamely in the final quarter-mile. (14/1)

### 3449 E.B.F. SINNINGTON MAIDEN STKS (2-Y.O F) (Class D)
2-40 (2-41) **7f** £3,704.00 (£1,112.00: £536.00: £248.00) Stalls: Low GOING minus 0.48 sec per fur (F)

| | | | | SP | RR | SF |
|---|---|---|---|---|---|---|
| $3159^{7}$ | **Soden (IRE) (81)** (TGMills) **2-8-11** MarkLynch(3) (trckd ldrs: led wl ins fnl f: jst hld on) | — | **1** | $11/1^{3}$ | 69 | 17 |
| $2315^{2}$ | **Ajayib (USA)** (JLDunlop) **2-8-11** JFortune(2) (lw: led tl hdd 2f out: hrd rdn below dist: r.o wl fnl f) | s.h | **2** | $4/7^{1}$ | 69 | 17 |
| $3036^{4}$ | **Dancing Queen (IRE)** (MBell) **2-8-4**(7) GFaulkner(1) (chsd ldr tl led 2f out: rdn & hdd wl ins fnl f: no ex) | 1 | **3** | $7/4^{2}$ | 67 | 15 |
| $3159^{10}$ | **Laguna Bay (IRE)** (APJarvis) **2-8-11** WJO'Connor(4) (plld hrd: a.p: r.o fnl f) | nk | **4** | 12/1 | 66? | 14 |
| | | | | (SP 116.0%) | **4 Rn** | |

**1m 26.2** (3.20) CSF £18.69 TOTE £9.60: (£6.70) OWNER Albert Soden Ltd (EPSOM) BRED Lodge Park Stud
IN-FOCUS: **Former Irish Champion Apprentice Mark Lynch, rode his first winner for seven years here.**
**3159 Soden (IRE)** became the third leader of the race when taking it up 100 yards from the line and just held off the renewed challenge of the favourite. (11/1)
**2315 Ajayib (USA)** looked really well in the preliminaries but, in this small field, was forced to make her own running. She was briefly left flat-footed once headed, but responded well and would have got back up in one more stride. There is better to come. (4/7)
**3036 Dancing Queen (IRE)** struck for home a quarter of a mile out, only to be caught with 100 yards to go. She should soon be winning. (7/4)
**Laguna Bay (IRE)** took a little while to settle, but stuck on really well in the closing stages. (12/1)

### 3450 ROTHMANS ROYALS NORTH SOUTH CHALLENGE SERIES H'CAP (0-85) (3-Y.O+) (Class D)
3-10 (3-12) **1m** £4,644.75 (£1,398.00: £676.50: £315.75) Stalls: Low GOING minus 0.48 sec per fur (F)

| | | | | SP | RR | SF |
|---|---|---|---|---|---|---|
| $686^{13}$ | **Gladys Althorpe (IRE) (58)** (JLEyre) **3-7-7**(3) NVarley(8) (b.off hind: mid div: drvn along fr ½-wy: styd on fr 2f out: hrd rdn to ld wl ins fnl f) | — | **1** | 25/1 | 68 | 40 |
| 2917* | **Saifan (81)** (DMorris) **7-9-12v** CHodgson(5) (towards rr: rdn 3f out: styd on to ld 1f out: hdd & no ex wl ins fnl f) | ½ | **2** | $10/1^{3}$ | 90 | 69 |
| $3265^{2}$ | **Wentbridge Lad (IRE) (68)** (PDEvans) **6-8-13v** JFEgan(2) (b.off hind: mid div: rdn & hdwy 2f out: ev ch 1f out: one pce) | 2 | **3** | $10/1^{3}$ | 73 | 52 |
| $3279^{5}$ | **Maple Bay (IRE) (71)** (ABailey) **7-8-9**(7) GFaulkner(10) (in tch: rdn 3f out: hdwy below dist: sn ev ch: unable qckn fnl f) | 1 | **4** | 11/1 | 74 | 53 |
| $3123^{16}$ | **Night Wink (USA) (77)** (GLMoore) **4-9-8** JFanning(3) (lw: led tl rdn & hdd 1f out: one pce) | 1½ | **5** | 11/1 | 77 | 56 |
| $3158^{11}$ | **Ninia (USA) (77)** (MJohnston) **4-9-8** TWilliams(6) (chsd ldr: drvn 4f out: wknd appr fnl f) | 1½ | **6** | 12/1 | 74 | 53 |
| $3151^{4}$ | **Ochos Rios (IRE) (58)** (BSRothwell) **5-8-3** LCharnock(1) (prom tl rdn & wknd over 1f out) | 1¼ | **7** | 14/1 | 53 | 32 |
| $3134^{5}$ | **Special-K (60)** (EWeymes) **4-8-5** JLowe(9) (chsd ldrs tl wknd 2f out) | hd | **8** | $10/1^{3}$ | 54 | 33 |
| $3072^{6}$ | **Ki Chi Saga (USA) (82)** (JLDunlop) **4-9-13** JFortune(7) (lw: a rr: btn over 2f out) | 6 | **9** | $15/8^{1}$ | 64 | 43 |
| 3158* | **Moscow Mist (IRE) (80)** (LadyHerries) **5-9-11** DeclanO'Shea(4) (a bhd: lost tch 2f out: t.o) | 24 | **10** | $11/4^{2}$ | 14 | — |
| | | | | (SP 123.6%) | **10 Rn** | |

**1m 35.8** (0.10) CSF £233.32 CT £2,493.45 TOTE £21.80: £2.60 £3.20 £2.00 (£389.60) Trio £222.70; £250.97 to Windsor 12/8/96 OWNER Mr T. S. Ely (HAMBLETON) BRED Mrs R. Kitchin
LONG HANDICAP Gladys Althorpe (IRE) 7-7
WEIGHT FOR AGE 3yo-7lb
STEWARDS' ENQUIRY Varley susp. 19-21/8/96 (excessive use of whip)
**Gladys Althorpe (IRE)** put up a remarkable performance considering she was without a run in nearly four months. This was her first time at the trip and she was 3lb out of the handicap. (25/1)
**2917* Saifan** seemed to have got his come-from-behind tactics bang on again, only to be thwarted at the death. (10/1)
**3265 Wentbridge Lad (IRE)** has not won for a long time, but is certainly running well at present. He could soon get his head in front. (10/1)

**3279 Maple Bay (IRE)**, a very consistent gelding, put in another sound run. (11/1: 8/1-12/1)
**2761* Night Wink (USA)** tried to make all, but had no more to give once headed. (11/1: 8/1-12/1)
**3072 Ki Chi Saga (USA)** was always struggling, but it transpired that he had been struck into during the race. (15/8: 3/1-7/4)
**3158* Moscow Mist (IRE)** (11/4: 2/1-3/1)

## 3451 MARY REVELEY RACING CLUB CLAIMING STKS (3-Y.O) (Class F)

3-40 (3-43) **1m 2f** £2,651.00 (£736.00: £353.00) Stalls: Low GOING minus 0.48 sec per fur (F)

| | | | | SP | RR | SF |
|---|---|---|---|---|---|---|
| 3228$^{5}$ | **Clued Up (43)** (PDEvans) **3-8-4** JFEgan(5) (a.p: led 1f out: r.o) | — | **1** | 14/1 | 49 | 11 |
| 2362$^{3}$ | **Irish Oasis (IRE) (40)** (BSRothwell) **3-8-12** WJO'Connor(3) (led: rdn 2f out: hdd 1f out: r.o one pce) | 3½ | **2** | 10/1 | 51 | 13 |
| 3041$^{9}$ | **Miss Romance (IRE)** (MissGayKelleway) **3-9-2** JFortune(7) (a.p: ev ch 2f out: rdn & r.o one pce) | 1½ | **3** | 5/2$^{2}$ | 53 | 15 |
| 2314$^{3}$ | **Irish Sea (USA) (72)** (DNicholls) **3-9-7** AlexGreaves(2) (hld up: kpt on appr fnl f: nvr able to chal) | nk | **4** | 6/4$^{1}$ | 58 | 20 |
| 3225$^{5}$ | **Time For A Glass (38)** (DMoffatt) **3-7-13**$^{(3)}$ DarrenMoffatt(6) (in tch: rdn & kpt on one pce fnl 2f) | ½ | **5** | 4/1$^{3}$ | 38 | — |
| 2683$^{8}$ | **Tirols Tyrant (IRE) (51)** (MrsASwinbank) **3-8-13** JFanning(8) (chsd ldrs: rdn to chal 3f out: wknd wl over 1f out) | ½ | **6** | 14/1 | 48 | 10 |
| 2966$^{9}$ | **My Kind (44)** (NTinkler) **3-8-0** KimTinkler(1) (a bhd) | 1 | **7** | 14/1 | 33 | — |
| 3058$^{6}$ | **Elle Mac (40)** (MPBielby) **3-8-1**$^{(5)}$ LNewton(4) (towards rr: drvn along 3f out: sn btn) | 5 | **8** | 33/1 | 31? | — |

(SP 120.6%) **8 Rn**

**2m 8.6** (5.00) CSF £128.35 TOTE £13.90: £2.60 £2.60 £1.10 (£45.50) OWNER Mrs E. J. Williams (WELSHPOOL) BRED C. R. and V. M. Withers
OFFICIAL EXPLANATION **Irish Sea (USA): Connections intended making the running, but the gelding missed the break and had his path blocked until the last furlong. He was not suited by the slowly-run race either.**
**3228 Clued Up** continued her stable's good run in getting off the mark with a convincing win. (14/1)
**2362 Irish Oasis (IRE)** ran without the visor here and made the running. He looked very one-paced once the winner went on. (10/1)
**Miss Romance (IRE)**, close up when going as well as any turning for home, lacked that extra gear at the business end. (5/2)
**2314 Irish Sea (USA)**, having his first run for his new yard, sat in behind the leaders below the distance and came outside to pass two rivals inside the final furlong without being knocked about. He is well worth keeping an eye on. (6/4: 4/5-13/8)

## 3452 DRANSFIELD CIU CONVALESCENT HOMES H'CAP (0-75) (3-Y.O+) (Class D)

4-15 (4-15) **1m 2f** £3,855.00 (£1,155.00: £555.00: £255.00) Stalls: Low GOING minus 0.48 sec per fur (F)

| | | | | SP | RR | SF |
|---|---|---|---|---|---|---|
| 2593$^{4}$ | **Red Valerian (69)** (GMMoore) **5-9-10b** JFEgan(4) (lw: chsd ldrs: outpcd 4f out: rdn & hdwy 3f out: styd on to ld nr fin) | — | **1** | 9/1 | 79 | 48 |
| 3111$^{6}$ | **Double Up (66)** (LadyHerries) **3-8-5**$^{(7)}$ PDoe(1) (lw: led: rdn clr over 1f out: wknd ent fnl f: hdd nr fin) | nk | **2** | 3/1$^{2}$ | 76 | 36 |
| 3173* | **Mazilla (56)** (AStreeter) **4-8-11** WJO'Connor(2) (chsd ldr tl rdn & wknd over 1f out) | 12 | **3** | 4/6$^{1}$ | 46 | 15 |
| 3252$^{9}$ | **Langtonian (41)** (JLEyre) **7-7-7v**$^{(3)}$ NVarley(6) (a bhd: effrt over 3f out: rdn & btn over 2f out) | 5 | **4** | 10/1 | 23 | — |
| 2152$^{5}$ | **Efizia (58)** (GMMoore) **6-8-13** JFortune(5) (a bhd: t.o fr 3f out: fin lame) | dist | **5** | 8/1$^{3}$ | — | — |

(SP 115.2%) **5 Rn**

**2m 6.1** (2.50) CSF £33.50 TOTE £9.20: £2.80 £1.60 (£12.30) OWNER Mrs Alurie O'Sullivan (MIDDLEHAM) BRED Mascalls Stud Farm
LONG HANDICAP Langtonian 7-2
WEIGHT FOR AGE 3yo-9lb
**2593 Red Valerian** looked in trouble turning into the straight but, keeping on gamely under pressure, caught the long-time leader in the last few yards. (9/1)
**3111 Double Up** looked to have it sewn up when some five lengths clear at the furlong pole, but her stride shortened and she could not quite hang on. (3/1)
**3173* Mazilla** had her winning run brought to an end, this being her fourth race in less than a month, and she probably needs a break. (4/6)
**2678 Langtonian** could never get in the hunt. (10/1: 8/1-12/1)

## 3453 GO RACING IN YORKSHIRE H'CAP (0-60) (3-Y.O+) (Class F)

4-45 (4-49) **6f** £2,994.00 (£834.00: £402.00) Stalls: Low GOING minus 0.48 sec per fur (F)

| | | | | SP | RR | SF |
|---|---|---|---|---|---|---|
| 2964$^{2}$ | **Thwaab (59)** (FWatson) **4-9-13v** JFortune(11) (hld up: hdwy 2f out: led appr fnl f: r.o) | — | **1** | 5/2$^{1}$ | 67 | 49 |
| 3289$^{8}$ | **Densben (45)** (DenysSmith) **12-8-13** TWilliams(12) (bhd: hdwy over 1f out: r.o fnl f) | 1¼ | **2** | 12/1 | 50 | 32 |
| 3306$^{5}$ | **Upex le Gold Too (28)** (LRLloyd-James) **4-7-3**$^{(7)}$ IonaWands(5) (towards rr: gd hdwy appr fnl f: r.o wl) | ¾ | **3** | 9/1 | 31 | 13 |
| 3135$^{3}$ | **Camionneur (IRE) (51)** (TDEasterby) **3-9-1b** JLowe(4) (lw: mid div: r.o fnl 2f: nrst fin) | 1 | **4** | 6/1$^{3}$ | 51 | 29 |
| *2940$^{8}$* | **Naughty Pistol (USA) (49)** (PDEvans) **4-9-3** JFEgan(14) (lw: a.p: r.o same pce fr over 1f out) | nk | **5** | 12/1 | 48 | 30 |
| 2801$^{18}$ | **Ragazzo (IRE) (28)** (JSWainwright) **6-7-10b** LCharnock(8) (led 2f: styd prom: one pce fr over 1f out) | s.h | **6** | 25/1 | 27 | 9 |
| 2757$^{13}$ | **Mu-Arrik (38)** (GROldroyd) **8-8-1b**$^{(5)}$ GParkin(10) (in tch: & grad wknd fr over 1f out) | 2 | **7** | 20/1 | 32 | 14 |
| 3256$^{3}$ | **Swifty Nifty (IRE) (45)** (WWHaigh) **3-8-6**$^{(3)}$ CTeague(6) (towards rr: kpt on fnl f: nvr nrr) | 1¼ | **8** | 11/1 | 35 | 13 |
| 3151$^{11}$ | **Tutu Sixtysix (30)** (DonEnricoIncisa) **5-7-12b** KimTinkler(7) (swtg: chsd ldr: led after 2f tl rdn & hdd appr fnl f: sn wknd) | hd | **9** | 20/1 | 20 | 2 |
| 3236$^{7}$ | **Sallyoreally (IRE) (36)** (WStorey) **5-8-4** JFanning(2) (swtg: chsd ldrs 4f) | 3 | **10** | 12/1 | 18 | — |
| 3331* | **Souperficial (53)** (JAGlover) **5-9-7v** $^{7x}$ WJO'Connor(13) (towards rr: rdn & btn 2 out: eased) | 5 | **11** | 4/1$^{2}$ | 22 | 4 |
| 2987$^{3}$ | **Blazing Imp (USA) (47)** (WSCunningham) **3-8-4**$^{(7)}$ DSweeney(3) (lw: prom tl rdn & wknd over 1f out) | ¾ | **12** | 20/1 | 14 | — |
| 3256* | **Mill End Lady (43)** (MWEasterby) **3-8-7b** DaleGibson(9) (lw: outpcd) | nk | **13** | 7/1 | 9 | — |
| *2757$^{10}$* | ***Sound the Trumpet (IRE) (53)*** (RCSpicer) **4-9-4**$^{(3)}$ NVarley(1) (Withdrawn not under Starter's orders: unruly in stalls) | | **W** | 20/1 | — | — |

(SP 139.7%) **13 Rn**

**1m 11.6** (1.40) CSF £34.91 CT £244.39 TOTE £3.50: £1.80 £2.90 £3.10 (£10.20) Trio £45.20 OWNER Mr J. D. Blythe (SEDGEFIELD) BRED Shadwell Estate Company Limited
LONG HANDICAP Ragazzo (IRE) 7-7
WEIGHT FOR AGE 3yo-4lb
**2964 Thwaab**, taken to post early, came with a strong run from behind to win well. (5/2: op 11/2)
**2680 Densben**, right out the back as usual until tearing through the field, was only denied by the favourite. (12/1)
**3306 Upex le Gold Too** made rapid progress up the stands' side in the last two furlongs, and a step up in trip might help while he is in this form. (9/1)
**3135 Camionneur (IRE)** ran well enough without ever seriously threatening the principals. (6/1)
**2748 Naughty Pistol (USA)** was always in the firing-line, but lacked of a turn of foot where it mattered. (12/1)

T/Plpt: £7,806.20 (0.45 Tckts); £5,801.96 to Windsor 12/8/96. T/Qdpt: £109.00 (5.08 Tckts). J

# 2965-LEICESTER (R-H) (Good)
## Monday August 12th
WEATHER: fine WIND: slt against

## 3454 E.B.F. MENPHYS MEDIAN AUCTION MAIDEN STKS (2-Y.O F) (Class E)
5-45 (5-50) **7f 9y** £3,370.50 (£1,008.00: £483.00: £220.50) Stalls: Low GOING minus 0.28 sec per fur (GF)

| | | | SP | RR | SF |
|---|---|---|---|---|---|
| | **Crown of Light** (MRStoute) **2-8-11** RCochrane(8) (lt-f: hld up & bhd: hdwy over 2f out: shkn up & r.o strly to ld nr fin) ...— | 1 | 9/2[2] | 72+ | 26 |
| 3105[5] | **Ciro's Pearl (IRE)** (MHTompkins) **2-8-11** PRobinson(7) (led tl ct cl home) ...hd | 2 | 12/1 | 72 | 26 |
| 596[8] | **Northern Girl (IRE)** (BJMeehan) **2-8-11** MTebbutt(6) (hld up in tch: effrt 2f out: outpcd appr fnl f) ...6 | 3 | 20/1 | 58 | 12 |
| | **Arriving** (JWHills) **2-8-11** MHills(10) (w'like: bit bkwd: s.s: hld up: effrt over 2f out: one pce appr fnl f) ...1¼ | 4 | 9/1 | 55 | 9 |
| 1808[4] | **Baby Jane** (RGuest) **2-8-11** MWigham(5) (bit bkwd: hld up: hdwy 2f out: kpt on u.p fnl f) ...1¾ | 5 | 6/1[3] | 51 | 5 |
| 2195[9] | **Petrel** (LordHuntingdon) **2-8-11** DHarrison(14) (prom tl wknd over 1f out) ...nk | 6 | 16/1 | 51 | 5 |
| 2161[7] | **Maremma** (DonEnricoIncisa) **2-8-11** KimTinkler(11) (hld up in tch: effrt 2f out: nt pce to chal) ...nk | 7 | 66/1 | 50 | 4 |
| | **Heavenly Dancer** (SirMarkPrescott) **2-8-11** GDuffield(13) (leggy: lt-f: bit bkwd: trckd ldrs tl wknd 2f out) ...¾ | 8 | 12/1 | 48 | 2 |
| 2852[7] | **Schisandra** (MJFetherston-Godley) **2-8-11** WJO'Connor(12) (bit bkwd: in tch: effrt 2f out: sn btn) ...4 | 9 | 20/1 | 39 | — |
| 3105[6] | **Bestelina** (DJSCosgrove) **2-8-11** MRimmer(9) (prom tl wknd over 2f out) ...s.h | 10 | 20/1 | 39 | — |
| | **Fair Relation** (PFICole) **2-8-11** TQuinn(3) (unf: scope: bit bkwd: prom: drvn along ½-wy: grad wknd) ...½ | 11 | 9/2[2] | 38 | — |
| | **Christmas Rose** (HThomsonJones) **2-8-11** GCarter(4) (neat: bkwd: prom: rdn 2f out: sn wknd) ...1¾ | 12 | 8/1 | 34 | — |
| 2967[2] | **Blue Hopper** (MRChannon) **2-8-11** CRutter(2) (s.s: hdwy ½-wy: wknd qckly 2f out: t.o) ...14 | 13 | 4/1[1] | 2 | — |
| *3264[W]* | ***Attitre (FR)*** (CEBrittain) **2-8-11** BDoyle(1) (Withdrawn not under Starter's orders: ref to ent stalls) ... | W | 14/1 | — | — |

(SP 135.5%) **13 Rn**

**1m 26.8** (3.80) CSF £54.13 TOTE £5.60: £1.60 £5.40 £7.70 (£45.80) Trio Not won; £123.04 to 14/8/96 OWNER Sheikh Mohammed (NEWMARKET) BRED Sheikh Mohammed Bin Rashid Al Maktoum

**Crown of Light**, a lightly-made half-sister to two winners, ran very green and did not begin to make progress until entering the last quarter-mile. Given a reminder, she responded willingly and stayed on strongly to gain control nearing the line. (9/2: op 5/2)

**3105 Ciro's Pearl (IRE)**, still carrying surplus condition, set out to make it all and, for most of the way, looked likely to do so, but the strong, late challenge of the winner proved too much. She should soon be winning. (12/1)

**Northern Girl (IRE)** looked well tuned up having been out of action since the spring and, though she was unable to go with the leading pair inside the distance, gave notice that there is a race in store. (20/1)

**Arriving**, flat-footed as the stalls opened, caught the eye, staying on steadily in the last couple of furlongs, and she will be all the sharper next time. (9/1)

**1808 Baby Jane** still has a bit left to work on, but she was doing all her best work late on, and should not remain a maiden for long. (6/1)

**Petrel**, a daughter of a half-sister to Halling, went with the pace for over five furlongs, and she is getting to know what it is all about. (16/1)

**Fair Relation** (9/2: op 5/2)

**2967 Blue Hopper** never fully recovered after losing ground at the start, but she did finish tailed off in the end, and is definitely not as bad as this. (4/1: op 6/1)

## 3455 LANGHAM NURSERY (S) H'CAP (2-Y.O) (Class G)
6-15 (6-16) **5f 218y** £2,490.00 (£690.00: £330.00) Stalls: Low GOING minus 0.28 sec per fur (GF)

| | | | SP | RR | SF |
|---|---|---|---|---|---|
| *3087[2]* | **Jingoist (IRE) (53)** (JLHarris) **2-9-2b** BDoyle(1) (hld up in tch: hdwy to ld over 2f out: rdn & r.o wl fnl f) ...— | 1 | 5/1[3] | 47 | — |
| 3448[7] | **Dancing Star (IRE) (54)** (PDEvans) **2-9-3** JFEgan(2) (a w ldrs: ev ch tl unable qckn ins fnl f) ...1½ | 2 | 14/1 | 44 | — |
| 3092[4] | **Don't Forget Shoka (IRE) (55)** (JSMoore) **2-9-4** WJO'Connor(6) (trckd ldrs tl rdn & outpcd over 1f out) ...5 | 3 | 9/1 | 32 | — |
| *3065[4]* | **Shandana (51)** (PCHaslam) **2-8-7v[1](7)** RMullen(4) (lw: swvd lft & s.s: hdwy centre ½-wy: one pce appr fnl f) ..¾ | 4 | 4/1[2] | 26 | — |
| 3092[3] | **Super Scravels (50)** (DrJDScargill) **2-8-13** MFenton(5) (in tch: effrt u.p 2f out: wknd appr fnl f) ...1 | 5 | 8/1 | 22 | — |
| *3087[3]* | **Eager To Please (58)** (JBerry) **2-9-7b[1]** GCarter(7) (led over 3f: wknd qckly wl over 1f out) ...10 | 6 | 11/4[1] | 3 | — |
| 2932[6] | **Silver Raj (50)** (WTKemp) **2-8-13b** JQuinn(3) (a bhd & outpcd) ...3 | 7 | 10/1 | — | — |
| 2795[6] | **Vickys Double (48)** (JSMoore) **2-8-8(3)** CTeague(8) (prom tl wknd 2f out) ...3 | 8 | 9/1 | — | — |

(SP 110.2%) **8 Rn**

**1m 16.3** (6.30) CSF £57.34 CT £525.42 TOTE £5.20: £1.40 £2.00 £2.50 (£30.70) OWNER Mr David Abell (MELTON MOWBRAY) BRED Etablissement Equine Investments

No bid

**3087 Jingoist (IRE)**, not winning out of turn, got to the front plenty soon enough and had to work hard enough to shake off her nearest pursuer inside the final furlong. (5/1)

**2635 Dancing Star (IRE)**, pressing the leaders from the start, may have nosed ahead briefly at one stage or another but, hard as she tried, the winner had the legs of her where it mattered. (14/1)

**3092 Don't Forget Shoka (IRE)** did not fare badly but, when the pace lifted approaching the final furlong, she quite simply was not good enough. (9/1: op 6/1)

**3065 Shandana** again lost her chance at the start, but she did rally to put herself into a challenging position below the distance before earlier exertions took their toll. (4/1)

**3092 Super Scravels** could never quite get to terms, but she did stay on, and she will get it right one of these days. (8/1: op 5/1)

**3087 Eager To Please** should have been able to hold his own with the winner on these more favourable terms, but he did too much too soon, and had run himself into the ground. (11/4)

## 3456 INSTITUTE OF INSURANCE BROKERS H'CAP (0-70) (3-Y.O) (Class E)
6-45 (6-46) **1m 8y** £3,397.80 (£1,016.40: £487.20: £222.60) Stalls: Low GOING minus 0.28 sec per fur (GF)

| | | | SP | RR | SF |
|---|---|---|---|---|---|
| 3167[6] | **Bandit Girl (63)** (IABalding) **3-9-2** TQuinn(3) (lw: hld up in tch: hdwy 2f out: rdn to chal ent fnl f: r.o to ld nr fin) ...— | 1 | 9/1 | 76 | 38 |
| 2859* | **Eurobox Boy (51)** (APJarvis) **3-8-4** SDrowne(1) (b.nr hind: a.p: led over 1f out tl hdd nr fin) ...¾ | 2 | 9/2[1] | 63 | 25 |
| 2917[7] | **Mister Woodstick (IRE) (57)** (MAJarvis) **3-8-10** PRobinson(6) (a.p: effrt u.p appr fnl f: unable qckn) ...1¼ | 3 | 8/1[3] | 66 | 28 |
| 3165[3] | **Ballpoint (68)** (RHannon) **3-9-4(3)** DaneO'Neill(10) (led to ½-wy: rdn & btn over 1f out) ...8 | 4 | 15/2[2] | 61 | 23 |
| 2799[4] | **Beauchamp Kate (54)** (HCandy) **3-8-7** CRutter(11) (b.hind: hld up & bhd: hdwy fnl 2f: nvr nrr) ...1 | 5 | 15/2[2] | 45 | 7 |
| 3249[15] | **Prince Zizim (46)** (RCSpicer) **3-7-6b[1](7)** RMullen(9) (swtg: s.i.s: hdwy ½-wy: rdn & drifted lft fnl 2f: nvr nrr) ....nk | 6 | 33/1 | 37 | — |
| 3039[8] | **Le Teteu (FR) (65)** (BobJones) **3-9-4** NDay(5) (lw: prom: led over 2f out tl over 1f out: eased whn btn fnl f) ...hd | 7 | 9/2[1] | 55 | 17 |
| *2934[3]* | **Theatre Magic (56)** (SRBowring) **3-8-9** DeanMcKeown(7) (trckd ldrs over 6f) ...1¾ | 8 | 8/1[3] | 43 | 5 |

| Form | Horse | Dist | Pos | SP | RR | SF |
|---|---|---|---|---|---|---|
| $2918^{7}$ | **Square Mile Miss (IRE) (48)** (PHowling) **3-8-1** FNorton(4) (lw: prom: led ½-wy tl over 2f out: sn rdn & wknd) | 1 | **9** | 16/1 | 33 | — |
| *$2551^{6}$* | **Safa Dancer (43)** (BAMcMahon) **3-7-10** AMackay(13) (lw: hld up: effrt & rdn 3f out: no imp) | 5 | **10** | 25/1 | 18 | — |
| $3138^{6}$ | **Persephone (43)** (ICampbell) **3-7-10v** GBardwell(8) (nvr trbld ldrs) | ½ | **11** | 25/1 | 17 | — |
| $3102^{11}$ | **Oriole (47)** (NTinkler) **3-8-0** KimTinkler(15) (w ldrs far side over 5f: sn wknd: t.o) | 5 | **12** | 20/1 | 11 | — |
| $3139^{9}$ | **Zdenka (46)** (MBlanshard) **3-7-13** JQuinn(12) (chsd ldr far side 5f: t.o) | s.h | **13** | 14/1 | 10 | — |
| $3165^{4}$ | **Nakhal (52)** (DJGMurraySmith) **3-8-5b** DHarrison(14) (lost tch ½-wy: t.o) | ½ | **14** | 10/1 | 15 | — |
| | | | | (SP 129.2%) | **14 Rn** | |

**1m 38.7** (3.70) CSF £49.40 CT £258.55 TOTE £10.50: £2.90 £1.90 £2.80 (£39.70) Trio £156.70; £6.62 to 14/8/96 OWNER Mr J. C. Smith (KINGSCLERE) BRED Littleton Stud

LONG HANDICAP Safa Dancer 7-6 Persephone 7-2

**3167 Bandit Girl**, settled just off the pace, did have to find extra to wear down the leader late on, but she always looked likely to do so, and she was going away at the finish. (9/1)

**2859* Eurobox Boy**, very keen to post, set sail for home approaching the final furlong and gave of his best when challenged, but the winner had delivered her challenge from off the pace, and she proved too tough near the finish. (9/2)

**2130 Mister Woodstick (IRE)**, always poised to challenge, did not fail for the want of trying, but he had to admit his measure taken in the run to the line. (8/1)

**3165 Ballpoint** always seems to have his full quota of weight and, though he usually gives a good account of himself, he has still to get off the mark. (15/2)

**2799 Beauchamp Kate**, running over a more suitable trip, left her effort plenty late enough and her final placing was as close as she got. She is certainly capable of winning races. (15/2: 4/1-8/1)

**Prince Zizim**, stepping back in distance and fitted with blinkers for the first time, tried hard to recover from a sluggish start and, if he had kept straight when mounting his challenge, he would have finished a good deal closer. (33/1)

**1780* Le Teteu (FR)** helped share the pace, but he was under strong pressure approaching the final furlong and had shot his bolt. (9/2)

## 3457 LUMBERS GRANDE CLASSIQUE H'CAP (0-80) (3-Y.O+) (Class D)

7-15 (7-15) **1m 1f 218y** £4,092.75 (£1,224.00: £586.50: £267.75) Stalls: Low GOING minus 0.28 sec per fur (GF)

| Form | Horse | Dist | Pos | SP | RR | SF |
|---|---|---|---|---|---|---|
| $3205^{*}$ | **Sharpical (74)** (SirMarkPrescott) **4-9-11** GDuffield(3) (hld up in rr: hdwy on bit 3f out: qcknd to ld ins fnl f: readily) | — | **1** | 5/2 1 | 85+ | 59 |
| $2917^{4}$ | **A-Aasem (71)** (HThomsonJones) **3-8-13** GCarter(6) (led 1f: led 3f out: hrd rdn & hdd fnl 100y) | 1 | **2** | 6/1 3 | 80 | 45 |
| $2549^{7}$ | **Get Away With It (IRE) (74)** (MRStoute) **3-9-2** RCochrane(7) (lw: hld up & bhd: hdwy over 2f out: nt rch ldrs) | 4 | **3** | 8/1 | 77 | 42 |
| $3272^{7}$ | **Rival Bid (USA) (66)** (MrsNMacauley) **8-9-0**(3) CTeague(10) (lw: dwlt: gd hdwy ent st: jnd ldr 3f out: outpcd appr fnl f) | 4 | **4** | 20/1 | 63 | 37 |
| $2943^{8}$ | **Myfontaine (65)** (KTIvory) **9-8-9**(7) CScally(9) (b: hld up in rr: sme late hdwy: n.d) | 1½ | **5** | 20/1 | 59 | 33 |
| $2900^{6}$ | **Riparius (USA) (77)** (HCandy) **5-10-0b** CRutter(8) (s.i.s: hld up & bhd: effrt over 2f out: nvr plcd to chal) | ½ | **6** | 10/1 | 70 | 44 |
| *$3089^{10}$* | **Ivan the Terrible (IRE) (45)** (BEllison) **8-7-10** JQuinn(1) (b: led after 1f: sn clr: hdd 3f out: sn wknd) | 8 | **7** | 20/1 | 26 | — |
| *$3063^{7}$* | **John-T (80)** (JLDunlop) **3-9-8** TQuinn(4) (lw: trckd ldrs tl wknd over 2f out) | 4 | **8** | 8/1 | 54 | 19 |
| $2589^{2}$ | **Degree (75)** (HRACecil) **3-9-3** PatEddery(2) (chsd ldrs 7f: sn rdn & wknd: t.o) | 7 | **9** | 3/1 2 | 38 | 3 |
| | **Peutetre (76)** (FJordan) **4-9-13** DHarrison(5) (chsd ldrs tl sddle slipped & eased over 2f out: t.o) | 20 | **10** | 33/1 | 7 | — |
| | | | | (SP 116.4%) | **10 Rn** | |

**2m 7.0** (3.30) CSF £16.91 CT £95.62 TOTE £3.60: £1.50 £1.60 £2.20 (£9.60) Trio £17.80 OWNER Mr A. S. Reid (NEWMARKET) BRED E. R. W. Stanley and New England Stud Farm Ltd

LONG HANDICAP Ivan the Terrible (IRE) 7-5

WEIGHT FOR AGE 3yo-9lb

**3205* Sharpical** probably got there too soon, for he was still running away when he reached the heels of the leader below the distance. After getting to the front halfway through the final furlong, he did not find as much as was expected, but did run well, and is in fine form this term. (5/2)

**2917 A-Aasem** put up a game display here. It is hard to believe he has not got off the mark, but it is only a matter of time before he does find an opening. (6/1: op 4/1)

**1090 Get Away With It (IRE)**, returning to possibly what might be his right trip, was never going well enough to trouble the leading pair, but he showed enough to suggest he will win races when he eventually gets it all together. (8/1)

**1838* Rival Bid (USA)** made up ground rather quickly from the turn to the straight after making a sluggish exit from the stalls and, getting the worse of the battle with the runner-up, was forced to admit defeat on the run to the final furlong. (20/1)

**1841 Myfontaine** moved badly to post and was in the rear and going nowhere until staying on when it was all but over. (20/1)

**2900 Riparius (USA)** attempted to get himself into the action entering the last quarter-mile but, over a trip which would appear to be inadequate, was never going to take a hand in proceedings. (10/1)

**2589 Degree**, taking on handicappers for the first time, was in trouble early in the straight and dropped away tamely. (3/1)

## 3458 TRAVELSPHERE CLAIMING STKS (3-Y.O) (Class F)

7-45 (7-47) **7f 9y** £3,071.20 (£853.20: £409.60) Stalls: Low GOING minus 0.28 sec per fur (GF)

| Form | Horse | Dist | Pos | SP | RR | SF |
|---|---|---|---|---|---|---|
| $3115^{3}$ | **Honorable Estate (IRE) (55)** (RHannon) **3-8-10**(3) DaneO'Neill(2) (lw: a.p: led over 1f out: sn drvn clr: easily) | — | **1** | 4/1 1 | 66 | 42 |
| $3274^{9}$ | **Scathebury (57)** (KRBurke) **3-9-1v** TQuinn(5) (lw: plld hrd: hld up: hdwy over 2f out: kpt on: no ch w wnr) | 5 | **2** | 9/1 | 57 | 33 |
| $1041^{7}$ | **Holloway Melody (39)** (BAMcMahon) **3-7-11**(7) AMcCarthy(10) (a.p: led 2f out: sn hdd: kpt on one pce) | ¾ | **3** | 16/1 | 44 | 20 |
| $3166^{3}$ | **Bella's Legacy (48)** (RJHodges) **3-8-7** BDoyle(6) (hld up: hdwy 2f out: nrst fin) | 3 | **4** | 8/1 | 40 | 16 |
| $3166^{4}$ | **Power Princess (35)** (JAPickering) **3-8-1** JFEgan(1) (b: in tch: effrt 2f out: kpt on u.p ins fnl f) | 3½ | **5** | 20/1 | 26 | 2 |
| $3301^{2}$ | **Ivory's Grab Hire (60)** (KTIvory) **3-9-0b**(7) CScally(9) (swtg: plld hrd: led over 3f out to 2f out: eased whn btn fnl f) | 5 | **6** | 11/2 3 | 35 | 11 |
| $3107^{5}$ | **Lachesis (60)** (RHollinshead) **3-8-7** WRyan(4) (w ldrs tl rdn & wknd 2f out) | 3½ | **7** | 5/1 2 | 13 | — |
| $2149^{9}$ | **Morning Surprise (58)** (APJarvis) **3-8-0**(7) CCarver(11) (prom far side: drvn along 2f out: sn outpcd) | 1 | **8** | 4/1 1 | 11 | — |
| $3166^{6}$ | **Royal Intrusion** (RJHodges) **3-9-10** SDrowne(3) (a in rr) | 2½ | **9** | 20/1 | 22 | — |
| $3256^{13}$ | **Oare Budgie (28)** (DonEnricoIncisa) **3-8-1v** KimTinkler(13) (sn bhd & drvn along: n.d) | ½ | **10** | 50/1 | — | — |
| | **Siberian Rose** (JWharton) **3-8-2**(3)ow1 CTeague(7) (lt-f: unf: led to ½-wy: wknd qckly over 2f out: t.o) | 5 | **11** | 33/1 | — | — |
| $2966^{4}$ | **Duet (32)** (JSKing) **3-8-4** AMackay(8) (disp ld 4f: sn lost tch: t.o) | 4 | **12** | 33/1 | — | — |
| $2777^{6}$ | **Forecast (56)** (JWharton) **3-8-12v**1 PRobinson(12) (a in rr: t.o fnl 2f) | 6 | **13** | 14/1 | — | — |
| | | | | (SP 123.1%) | **13 Rn** | |

**1m 25.6** (2.60) CSF £38.15 TOTE £5.60: £2.00 £2.20 £7.30 (£16.30) Trio £113.10 OWNER Mr R. A. Bernard (MARLBOROUGH) BRED James W. Ryan

**3115 Honorable Estate (IRE)** appreciated this return to seven furlongs and left her rivals for dead approaching the final furlong. (4/1)
**2578 Scathebury**, restrained under a very keen hold, did not possess the speed of the winner when set alight and was never going to finish any closer than he did. (9/1)
**834 Holloway Melody**, still struggling to make an impact, was always fighting for the lead but, when the tempo increased, she was unable to respond. (16/1)
**3166 Bella's Legacy** made progress from off the pace in the latter stages, but could not summon the speed to make her presence felt. (8/1)
**3166 Power Princess** did keep staying on in the closing stages, but very much at her one slow pace. (20/1)
**1876 Morning Surprise**, a quick-actioned filly who was very free to post, stalked the leaders and had every chance until feeling the strain from below the distance. (4/1)

## 3459 EVANS OF LEICESTER MERCEDES-BENZ LIMITED STKS (0-65) (3-Y.O) (Class F)

8-15 (8-17) **1m 3f 183y** £2,880.80 (£798.80: £382.40) Stalls: Low GOING minus 0.28 sec per fur (GF)

| | | | SP | RR | SF |
|---|---|---|---|---|---|
| 2943[9] | **Sweetness Herself (64)** (MJRyan) **3-8-3**(5) MBaird(4) (a.p: led over 2f out: hld on wl nr fin) —- | 1 | 16/1 | 71 | 40 |
| 3249[2] | **Blenheim Terrace (60)** (CBBBooth) **3-8-13** JQuinn(6) (hld up: hdwy 3f out: rdn & ev ch fnl f: nt qckn nr fin)...nk | 2 | 6/1 3 | 76 | 45 |
| 2433[3] | **Dancing Cavalier (65)** (RHollinshead) **3-8-8**(5) DGriffiths(7) (lw: hld up in rr: hdwy & swtchd lft 3f out: kpt on u.p) 4 | 3 | 16/1 | 70 | 39 |
| 1498[8] | **Backwoods (57)** (WMBrisbourne) **3-8-11** GDuffield(10) (bkwd: hld up: hdwy u.p 3f out: styd on ins fnl f) 2½ | 4 | 33/1 | 65 | 34 |
| 3173[3] | **Parsa (USA) (63)** (JLDunlop) **3-8-10** PatEddery(3) (hld up in rr: gd hdwy over 2f out: rdn & wknd appr fnl f)..2½ | 5 | 9/4 1 | 60 | 29 |
| 3309[2] | **Los Alamos (65)** (CWThornton) **3-8-10** DeanMcKeown(5) (trckd ldrs: hrd drvn 3f out: sn btn) 1¾ | 6 | 9/2 2 | 58 | 27 |
| 3113[14] | **Compass Pointer (60)** (JMPEustace) **3-8-11** MTebbutt(8) (hld up & bhd: hdwy over 3f out: rdn & one pce appr fnl f) s.h | 7 | 16/1 | 59 | 28 |
| 3308[6] | **Go-Go-Power-Ranger (62)** (BEllison) **3-8-13** JTate(11) (in tch tl wknd wl over 2f out: t.o) 7 | 8 | 14/1 | 52 | 21 |
| 3108[2] | **Agdistis (65)** (HThomsonJones) **3-8-8** GCarter(2) (lw: led tl over 2f out: wknd qckly: t.o) 5 | 9 | 9/2 2 | 40 | 9 |
| 2365[4] | **Devil's Dance (FR) (60)** (MRStoute) **3-8-11** RCochrane(9) (prom: rdn 3f out: sn wknd: t.o) 8 | 10 | 12/1 | 32 | 1 |
| 3109[8] | **Royal Expose (USA) (55)** (RHannon) **3-8-8**(3) DaneO'Neill(1) (chsd ldr: hrd rdn over 2f out: sn lost tch: t.o) .1¾ | 11 | 20/1 | 30 | —- |
| | | | (SP 121.1%) | **11 Rn** | |

**2m 33.5** (4.50) CSF £103.05 TOTE £16.70: £3.40 £1.30 £4.00 (£46.90) Trio £251.00 OWNER Mrs M. J. Lavell (NEWMARKET) BRED Stud-On-The-Chart
**1324 Sweetness Herself** came into her own at this first try at the trip and, though she did have to work in the latter stages, always looked to have the edge. (16/1)
**3249 Blenheim Terrace**, covered up, did not show his usual tendency to hang left when pressure was on, and he gave of his all to go down fighting. (6/1)
**2433 Dancing Cavalier** failed to get himself into the action on this return to twelve furlongs, but he did stay on and once again made sure he ran into the prizes. (16/1)
**Backwoods**, fresh and well after a ten-week break, stuck on promisingly in the closing stages and, with this run to put an edge on him, could be the sort for a three-year-old hurdle. (33/1)
**3173 Parsa (USA)**, held up to get the trip, made significant progress in the straight and, had she been able to maintain the run, would have taken a hand in proceedings, but lack of stamina took its toll over a furlong out. (9/4)
**3309 Los Alamos**, hard driven three furlongs out, did not last much longer and was a spent force well over a furlong out. (9/2)
**3108 Agdistis** had too much use made of her over this longer trip, and she had run herself out when the contest really got under way. (9/2)

T/Plpt: £1,322.30 (9.52 Tckts). T/Qdpt: £53.10 (25.37 Tckts). IM

# 3250-THIRSK (L-H) (Good)
## Monday August 12th

WEATHER: sunny WIND: mod across

## 3460 SCANIA 4-SERIES 'HORSEPOWER' APPRENTICE (S) H'CAP (0-60) (3-Y.O+) (Class F)

6-00 (6-01) **1m** £2,564.00 (£729.00: £362.00) Stalls: Low GOING minus 0.31 sec per fur (GF)

| | | | SP | RR | SF |
|---|---|---|---|---|---|
| 3287[2] | **Euro Sceptic (IRE) (47)** (TDEasterby) **4-8-11b**(4) PDoe(10) (chsd ldrs: led appr fnl f: styd on wl) —- | 1 | 7/4 1 | 65 | 44 |
| 3358[9] | **Percy Parrot (38)** (RMWhitaker) **4-8-2v**(4) PFredericks(12) (b.hind: led: clr after 2f: hdd appr fnl f: no ex) 6 | 2 | 10/1 | 44 | 23 |
| *2937*[13] | **Rainbows Rhapsody (35)** (DWChapman) **5-8-3** KSked(6) (lw: prom early: outpcd appr st: hdwy over 2f out: hung lft: nrst fin) ½ | 3 | 15/2 | 40 | 19 |
| 3306[4] | **Allinson's Mate (IRE) (56)** (TDBarron) **8-9-6b**(4) CScudder(8) (bhd: effrt appr st: styd on: nrst fin) 5 | 4 | 7/2 2 | 51 | 30 |
| 2801[12] | **Ohnonotagain (32)** (BWMurray) **4-8-0**ow4 JDennis(9) (lw: hdwy ½-wy: styd on: nvr rchd ldrs) 1¼ | 5 | 100/1 | 25 | —- |
| 3410[4] | **Miss Zanzibar (49)** (RAFahey) **4-8-13**(4) ClaireWest(7) (bhd: effrt ½-wy: nvr rchd ldrs) 2 | 6 | 6/1 3 | 38 | 17 |
| 2329[13] | **Flashy's Son (58)** (FMurphy) **8-9-6**(6) DHayden(2) (b: hld up & bhd: styd on fnl 3f: n.d) ½ | 7 | 12/1 | 46 | 25 |
| 3306[17] | **Corona Gold (40)** (JGFitzGerald) **6-8-8b** JBramhill(5) (chsd ldrs: wnt 2nd over 3f out: wknd wl over 1f out) ....½ | 8 | 20/1 | 27 | 6 |
| 3310[5] | **Double Glow (29)** (NBycroft) **4-7-11** AngelaGallimore(3) (bhd & n.m.r after 2f: n.d) ½ | 9 | 25/1 | 15 | —- |
| | **Moofaji (39)** (FWatson) **5-8-3**(4) CLowther(11) (chsd ldr to st: sn wknd) 1¾ | 10 | 50/1 | 21 | —- |
| 3151[13] | **Lady Ploy (41)** (MissLCSiddall) **4-8-5**(4)ow13 TSiddall(4) (a bhd) 1¼ | 11 | 100/1 | 21 | —- |
| | | | (SP 114.0%) | **11 Rn** | |

**1m 39.3** (2.80) CSF £17.89 CT £96.88 TOTE £2.50: £1.40 £2.30 £2.60 (£16.70) Trio £20.50 OWNER Mr C. H. Stevens (MALTON) BRED Martyn J. McEnery
LONG HANDICAP Lady Ploy 7-9
Bt in 8,800 gns
**3287 Euro Sceptic (IRE)**, well handled and well suited by the strong pace, made no mistake this time and was far too good in the last furlong. (7/4)
**2868 Percy Parrot** likes to be out in front and set a scorching pace here but, collared approaching the final furlong, was out on his feet. (10/1: 7/1-12/1)
**2851 Rainbows Rhapsody** was always giving her rider problems by hanging left in the straight and, despite keeping on, could never get in a blow. (15/2)
**3306 Allinson's Mate (IRE)** takes some handling and was never doing enough here to get into it. (7/2)
**805 Ohnonotagain** has never won a race, but does look in good trim and, although this was a slightly more encouraging effort, there is still a good way to go. (100/1)
**3410 Miss Zanzibar** ran no sort of a race and this might have come too soon after her effort the previous Friday. (6/1: 7/2-13/2)
**1885 Flashy's Son** had a nice run over the wrong trip and should be all the better for it after six weeks off. (12/1: op 7/1)

## 3461 CHEQUE BOOK H'CAP (0-80) (3-Y.O) (Class D)

6-30 (6-33) **1m** £3,910.25 (£1,172.00: £563.50: £259.25) Stalls: Low GOING minus 0.31 sec per fur (GF)

| | | | | SP | RR | SF |
|---|---|---|---|---|---|---|
| 3271* | **Jerry Cutrona (IRE) (77)** (NACallaghan) **3-9-7** KFallon(5) (lw: in tch: hdwy ent st: styd on to ld wl ins fnl f) | — | **1** | 3/1$^{2}$ | 85 | 51 |
| 2065$^{6}$ | **Royal Ceilidh (IRE) (75)** (DenysSmith) **3-9-5** JFortune(2) (a.p: rdn to ld 1½f out: hdd & no ex wl ins fnl f) | 1½ | **2** | 8/1 | 80 | 46 |
| 3260$^{3}$ | **Tart (FR) (74)** (JRFanshawe) **3-9-1**(3) NVarley(3) (lw: chsd ldr: sn pushed along: led 2f out: sn hdd & one pce) | 3 | **3** | 6/1$^{3}$ | 73 | 39 |
| 3226$^{4}$ | **Road Racer (IRE) (60)** (MrsJRRamsden) **3-8-4** MDeering(1) (lw: bhd: hdwy 2f out: no imp) | 4 | **4** | 16/1 | 51 | 17 |
| 2514$^{2}$ | **Eric's Bett (65)** (FMurphy) **3-8-9b** JWeaver(8) (led tl hdd 2f out: sn btn) | 5 | **5** | 5/2$^{1}$ | 46 | 12 |
| 3100$^{4}$ | **Funky (53)** (DNicholls) **3-7-4**(7) JBramhill(4) (chsd ldrs tl wknd fnl 3f) | ½ | **6** | 10/1 | 33 | — |
| 2979$^{9}$ | **Polish Lady (IRE) (52)** (CMurray) **3-7-10** NCarlisle(6) (a outpcd & bhd) | ½ | **7** | 100/1 | 31 | — |
| 2752$^{8}$ | **Lucky Bea (60)** (MWEasterby) **3-8-4** DaleGibson(7) (sn bhd & pushed along: n.d) | 1¾ | **8** | 10/1 | 36 | 2 |
| *3051$^{2}$* | ***Firle Phantasy (70)*** (PCalver) **3-9-0** MBirch(9) (Withdrawn not under Starter's orders: ref to ent stalls) | | **W** | 9/1 | — | — |
| | | | | (SP 114.0%) | **8 Rn** | |

**1m 39.2** (2.70) CSF £20.30 CT £87.89 TOTE £2.80: £1.50 £1.80 £1.20 (£6.90) Trio £6.20 OWNER Mr Michael Hill (NEWMARKET) BRED Dr Paschal Carmody

LONG HANDICAP Polish Lady (IRE) 6-10

OFFICIAL EXPLANATION **Eric's Bett: was not suited by the front-running tactics which were adopted for the first time.**

**3271* Jerry Cutrona (IRE)** showed a poor action going to post and that, coupled with his rider's histrionics in checking his mount in front of the Stands, caused him to drift in the market, but there were no doubts in the race. (3/1: op 2/1)

**1648 Royal Ceilidh (IRE)** goes well here and ran another fine race after almost eight weeks off, but just found the winner too strong late on. (8/1)

**3260 Tart (FR)**, dropping back in distance, was never on the bridle, but did hold every chance until getting outpaced in the last furlong and a half. (6/1)

**3226 Road Racer (IRE)** is learning and a race can be picked up in due course. (16/1)

**2514 Eric's Bett** needed two attendants in the paddock as he was very edgy indeed, and he had used up all his energy by the two-furlong marker. (5/2: op 9/2)

**3100 Funky**, who took the eye in the paddock, ran reasonably and got messed about in the home straight. (10/1: op 6/1)

## 3462 TATTERSALLS MAIDEN AUCTION STKS (2-Y.O) (Class E)

7-00 (7-01) **7f** £3,317.50 (£1,000.00: £485.00: £227.50) Stalls: Low GOING minus 0.31 sec per fur (GF)

| | | | | SP | RR | SF |
|---|---|---|---|---|---|---|
| 3080$^{4}$ | **Vagabond Chanteuse** (TJEtherington) **2-8-3** LCharnock(6) (lw: a.p: led 1f out: jst hld on) | — | **1** | 10/1 | 77 | 28 |
| | **Blooming Amazing** (JLEyre) **2-8-6**ow1 KFallon(1) (leggy: unf: scope: trckd ldrs: rn green over 2f out: rdn to ld appr fnl f: sn hdd: rallied towards fin) | s.h | **2** | 11/4$^{2}$ | 80+ | 30 |
| 2932$^{2}$ | **Imperial Or Metric (IRE) (69)** (JBerry) **2-8-5** JCarroll(4) (lw: led tl hdd appr fnl f: no ex) | 4 | **3** | 14/1 | 70 | 21 |
| 3129$^{2}$ | **Cambridge Ball (IRE)** (MJohnston) **2-8-1** TWilliams(9) (lw: chsd ldrs: ev ch 2f out: r.o one pce) | nk | **4** | 11/8$^{1}$ | 65 | 16 |
| 3264$^{3}$ | **Danehill Princess (IRE) (73)** (RHollinshead) **2-8-1v**(3) FLynch(8) (s.i.s: styd on fnl 3f: nrst fin) | s.h | **5** | 8/1 | 68 | 19 |
| 2967$^{4}$ | **Flower Hill Lad (IRE)** (DJSCosgrove) **2-8-3** JStack(2) (mid div: shkn up over 2f out: no imp) | ½ | **6** | 6/1$^{3}$ | 66 | 17 |
| 2596$^{8}$ | **Shaken Up** (MrsDHaine) **2-8-5** AGarth(10) (s.i.s: effrt ½-wy: nvr trbld ldrs) | ½ | **7** | 16/1 | 67 | 18 |
| 2517$^{4}$ | **Lord Discord** (TDEasterby) **2-8-8** MBirch(3) (w ldr tl wknd fnl 2f) | 7 | **8** | 16/1 | 54 | 5 |
| 2923$^{5}$ | **Smoke'n'jo (IRE)** (MWEasterby) **2-8-1**(5)ow1 GParkin(7) (prom tl lost pl appr st: n.d after) | 1¼ | **9** | 66/1 | 49 | — |
| 2596$^{4}$ | **Tom Pladdey** (RBastiman) **2-8-3** DaleGibson(5) (s.i.s: n.d) | 4 | **10** | 20/1 | 37 | — |
| 2361$^{6}$ | **Eastern Firedragon (IRE)** (TDEasterby) **2-8-0** JLowe(11) (hld up & a bhd) | ½ | **11** | 25/1 | 33 | — |
| | | | | (SP 131.8%) | **11 Rn** | |

**1m 27.1** (2.90) CSF £40.00 TOTE £11.90: £3.00 £1.70 £2.90 (£30.70) Trio £104.90 OWNER Mr W. R. Green (MALTON) BRED Patrick Eddery Ltd

**3080 Vagabond Chanteuse** again looked magnificent and, after appearing to have it sewn up entering the final furlong, she did just enough. She certainly stays and is learning, but her attitude still leaves a question mark. (10/1)

**Blooming Amazing** came with a big reputation and, but for greenness, would have won. Once he fills to his frame, he should improve a fair bit. (11/4: 13/8-3/1)

**2932 Imperial Or Metric (IRE)** is running progressively better and deserves a change of luck. (14/1)

**3129 Cambridge Ball (IRE)** looked ultra-fit and had her chances, but lacked a change of gear to take them. (11/8)

**3264 Danehill Princess (IRE)** has some useful form, but is disappointing at times and may just need a confidence-boosting win to get her on the right track. (8/1)

**2967 Flower Hill Lad (IRE)**, after a promising effort last time, failed to make an impression here, but is now qualified for nurseries, where he should do better. (6/1: 9/2-7/1)

## 3463 UNION TRUCKS FOR SCANIA H'CAP (0-60) (3-Y.O+) (Class F)

7-30 (7-30) **2m** £3,174.50 (£956.00: £463.00: £216.50) Stalls: Low GOING minus 0.31 sec per fur (GF)

| | | | | SP | RR | SF |
|---|---|---|---|---|---|---|
| 3329* | **Shirley Sue (62)** (MJohnston) **3-9-2** 4x JWeaver(7) (lw: mde most after 3f: hld on wl u.p) | — | **1** | 11/10$^{1}$ | 73 | 38 |
| 2612$^{6}$ | **Uncle Doug (55)** (MrsMReveley) **5-9-10** KDarley(11) (swtg: trckd ldrs: ev ch 2f out: nt qckn ins fnl f) | 2 | **2** | 5/1$^{3}$ | 64 | 44 |
| 3308$^{5}$ | **Sharp Sensation (39)** (DWBarker) **6-8-1**(7) JBramhill(10) (lw: trckd ldrs: disp ld on bit 2f out: rdn & no ex fnl f) | s.h | **3** | 16/1 | 48 | 28 |
| 3218$^{7}$ | **Ela Man Howa (48)** (ABailey) **5-9-3** SSanders(2) (trckd ldr: effrt 3f out: nt clr run 1f out: kpt on) | 1 | **4** | 16/1 | 56 | 36 |
| 3149$^{4}$ | **Anglesey Sea View (59)** (ABailey) **7-10-0** JFortune(6) (a cl up: chal ent st: one pce fnl 2f) | ¾ | **5** | 4/1$^{2}$ | 66 | 46 |
| 3335$^{5}$ | **Amiarge (45)** (MBrittain) **6-8-11b**(3) DWright(5) (bhd: effrt appr st: styd on: nvr able to chal) | 1½ | **6** | 11/1 | 51 | 31 |
| 3308$^{9}$ | **Kashana (IRE) (39)** (WStorey) **4-8-8** JFanning(3) (in tch to st) | 5 | **7** | 50/1 | 40 | 20 |
| 3308$^{7}$ | **Sudden Spin (46)** (JNorton) **6-9-1** KFallon(4) (bhd: pushed along 7f out: n.d) | 6 | **8** | 10/1 | 41 | 21 |
| 3053$^{6}$ | **Hallikeld (42)** (TJEtherington) **3-7-10** LCharnock(8) (lw: led 3f: cl up tl wknd fnl 3f) | hd | **9** | 33/1 | 37 | 2 |
| 3149$^{7}$ | **Frontier Flight (USA) (51)** (MissLCSiddall) **6-9-3**(3)ow3 OPears(1) (lw: hld up & a bhd) | 9 | **10** | 33/1 | 37 | 14 |
| 2847$^{6}$ | **Deauville Dancer (IRE) (50)** (DNicholls) **4-9-5** AlexGreaves(9) (a rr div) | 10 | **11** | 33/1 | 26 | 6 |
| | | | | (SP 124.3%) | **11 Rn** | |

**3m 30.6** (7.60) CSF £7.65 CT £58.02 TOTE £2.30: £1.30 £1.90 £2.60 (£4.60) Trio £24.60 OWNER Greenland Park Ltd (MIDDLEHAM) BRED Laharna Ltd

LONG HANDICAP Hallikeld 7-7

WEIGHT FOR AGE 3yo-15lb

**3329* Shirley Sue** showed she is game here and, although she is not all that big, she also seems to be better suited by a more galloping track than this. (11/10)
**2612 Uncle Doug,** who got very warm beforehand, still ran reasonably, but was never doing enough at the business end. (5/1)
**3308 Sharp Sensation,** as he sometimes does, travelled really well here, but he may have seen too much daylight too soon and was outbattled late on. (16/1)
**2871 Ela Man Howa** is improving fast and, had he got a run entering the final furlong, he may well have been second best. (16/1)
**3149 Anglesey Sea View** had her chances, but lacks any turn of foot to take them. A stronger gallop and probably a more galloping track might be the answer. (4/1)
**3335 Amiarge** just stays, but in his own time, and he was never doing things fast enough to have a chance here. (11/1)

## 3464 SCANIA 1996 TRUCK OF THE YEAR E.B.F. MEDIAN AUCTION MAIDEN STKS (2-Y.O) (Class E)

8-00 (8-01) **5f** £3,226.50 (£972.00: £471.00: £220.50) Stalls: High GOING minus 0.31 sec per fur (GF)

| | | | | SP | RR | SF |
|---|---|---|---|---|---|---|
| 3241$^{2}$ | **Balladoole Bajan** (MJohnston) **2-8-9** JWeaver(6) (bhd: hdwy ½-wy: led ins fnl f: r.o) | — | **1** | 4/1$^{2}$ | 65 | 34 |
| 2985$^{6}$ | **Prince Dome (IRE)** (MartynWane) **2-9-0** JFortune(10) (prom: hdwy over 1f out: styd on wl) | 1½ | **2** | 33/1 | 65 | 34 |
| 3114$^{2}$ | **Sylvan Dancer (IRE)** (CFWall) **2-8-9** WWoods(11) (w ldrs tl hung lft & eased ins fnl f) | 1¾ | **3** | 7/4$^{1}$ | 55 | 24 |
| 3250$^{3}$ | **Jedi Knight** (MWEasterby) **2-8-9**$^{(5)}$ GParkin(3) (cl up: effrt 2f out: r.o one pce) | 1 | **4** | 5/1$^{3}$ | 56 | 25 |
| 3050$^{2}$ | **Toronto** (JBerry) **2-9-0** JCarroll(9) (led: hung bdly lft fr 2f out: hdd & eased ins fnl f) | hd | **5** | 4/1$^{2}$ | 56 | 25 |
| 3275$^{6}$ | **Mazil (65)** (TDEasterby) **2-9-0** MBirch(7) (lw: a chsng ldrs: rdn ½-wy: no imp) | nk | **6** | 16/1 | 55 | 24 |
| 950$^{8}$ | **Style Dancer (IRE)** (RMWhitaker) **2-9-0** JFanning(12) (unruly s: s.i.s: n.d) | 4 | **7** | 50/1 | 42 | 11 |
| 2772$^{3}$ | **Martine** (ABailey) **2-8-6**$^{(3)}$ DWright(2) (cl up over 3f: grad wknd) | 2 | **8** | 7/1 | 31 | — |
| 3293$^{8}$ | **William's Well** (MWEasterby) **2-9-0** DaleGibson(4) (nvr wnt pce) | 1½ | **9** | 50/1 | 31 | — |
| 3291$^{5}$ | **Cairn Dhu** (MrsJRRamsden) **2-9-0** KFallon(8) (s.i.s: nvr nr to chal) | hd | **10** | 50/1 | 31 | — |
| | **Fly Me Home** (BAMcMahon) **2-9-0** KDarley(1) (w'like: s.i.s: sn pushed along: n.d) | s.h | **11** | 50/1 | 31 | — |
| 3259$^{16}$ | **Grovefair Venture** (BJMeehan) **2-9-0** SSanders(5) (s.i.s: nvr wnt pce) | 1½ | **12** | 50/1 | 26 | — |
| | | | | (SP 124.2%) | **12 Rn** | |

**59.9 secs** (1.90) CSF £98.58 TOTE £6.50: £1.80 £9.80 £1.40 (£826.30) Trio £317.00; £53.59 to 14/8/96 OWNER Mr R. H. A. Smith (MIDDLEHAM) BRED Normanby Stud Ltd
**3241 Balladoole Bajan,** ridden from behind this time, was a revelation, producing a tremendous turn of foot to settle it inside the final furlong. (4/1)
**2985 Prince Dome (IRE)** is learning fast and, judging by the way he finished here, it should not be long before he finds a race. (33/1)
**3114 Sylvan Dancer (IRE)** has the speed, but threw her chance away by hanging badly left, and her rider just had to sit and suffer in the closing stages. (7/4)
**3250 Jedi Knight** showed up well and held his position in the last two furlongs, suggesting that further would suit. (5/1)
**3050 Toronto** has the ability, but is proving a difficult ride, and again threw all chances away by hanging violently left in the last couple of furlongs. (4/1)
**3275 Mazil** showed up behind the leaders, but could never really take them on. (16/1)

## 3465 SCANIA 4-SERIES 'KING OF THE ROAD' H'CAP (0-80) (3-Y.O) (Class D)

8-30 (8-31) **5f** £4,027.25 (£1,208.00: £581.50: £268.25) Stalls: High GOING minus 0.31 sec per fur (GF)

| | | | | SP | RR | SF |
|---|---|---|---|---|---|---|
| 3215$^{2}$ | **Literary Society (USA) (66)** (JARToller) **3-8-12** SSanders(5) (a cl up: led 1f out: r.o) | — | **1** | 4/1$^{2}$ | 73+ | 47 |
| 3154* | **Bee Health Boy (66)** (MWEasterby) **3-8-7b**$^{(5)}$ GParkin(8) (mde most tl hdd 1f out: kpt on) | nk | **2** | 10/1$^{3}$ | 72 | 46 |
| 3292$^{3}$ | **Oatey (59)** (MrsJRRamsden) **3-8-5** KFallon(10) (lw: bhd: hdwy 2f out: nt clr run & swtchd ins fnl f: fin fast) | s.h | **3** | 9/4$^{1}$ | 65 | 39 |
| 3350$^{4}$ | **Comic Fantasy (AUS) (71)** (MartynWane) **3-9-3b** NConnorton(9) (cl up: rdn & btn ins fnl f) | 1¾ | **4** | 14/1 | 71 | 45 |
| 1597$^{5}$ | **Miss Bigwig (71)** (JBerry) **3-9-3** JCarroll(11) (sn chsng ldrs: effrt 2f out: nt qckn ins fnl f) | ¾ | **5** | 11/1 | 69 | 43 |
| 3154$^{4}$ | **U-No-Harry (IRE) (73)** (RHollinshead) **3-9-2**$^{(3)}$ FLynch(7) (lw: a.p: effrt 2f out: nt qckn fnl f) | 1 | **6** | 10/1$^{3}$ | 68 | 42 |
| 3453$^{4}$ | **Camionneur (IRE) (51)** (TDEasterby) **3-7-11b** JLowe(6) (bhd: hdwy ½-wy: nvr able to chal) | ½ | **7** | 10/1$^{3}$ | 44 | 18 |
| 3100* | **Sabaah Elfull (74)** (ACStewart) **3-9-6** SWhitworth(2) (lw: outpcd & bhd fr ½-wy) | 7 | **8** | 10/1$^{3}$ | 45 | 19 |
| 3154$^{3}$ | **Myttons Mistake (71)** (ABailey) **3-9-0**$^{(3)}$ DWright(4) (chsd ldrs over 3f) | s.h | **9** | 10/1$^{3}$ | 42 | 16 |
| 3135$^{4}$ | **Chalice (67)** (JBalding) **3-8-6**$^{(7)}$ JEdmunds(1) (hld up: bhd fr ½-wy) | ¾ | **10** | 20/1 | 35 | 9 |
| 3215$^{5}$ | **Dande Flyer (75)** (DWPArbuthnot) **3-9-4b**$^{1(3)}$ DarrenMoffatt(3) (b: sn bhd) | s.h | **11** | 14/1 | 43 | 17 |
| | | | | (SP 122.7%) | **11 Rn** | |

**59.3 secs** (1.30) CSF £41.62 CT £105.63 TOTE £4.10: £2.00 £2.60 £1.80 (£25.00) Trio £53.30 OWNER Duke of Devonshire (WHITSBURY) BRED William R. and Mrs Buster
**3215 Literary Society (USA)** is a game sort with plenty of speed. This helped him overcame his poor draw. (4/1)
**3154* Bee Health Boy,** although taking a step back in trip, had the speed to lay up throughout and, because he stays further, he was keeping on well at the finish. (10/1)
**3292 Oatey,** back to her optimum trip, had the required high draw, but did not get any of the luck needed. She undoubtedly would have won had a gap come sooner. (9/4)
**3350 Comic Fantasy (AUS)** is running consistently well and is now slipping down the handicap. (14/1: 10/1-16/1)
**1597 Miss Bigwig** was a bit short of room at various points but, in the end, just was not good enough. (11/1)
**3154 U-No-Harry (IRE)** still looks amazingly well and ran a fine race. (10/1)
**3453 Camionneur (IRE)** always found this too competitive. (10/1)

T/Plpt: £47.10 (297.04 Tckts). T/Qdpt: £14.70 (80.55 Tckts). AA

# 3257-WINDSOR (Fig. 8) (Good)
## Monday August 12th

WEATHER: fine WIND: almost nil

## 3466 STRATFIELDSAYE (S) STKS (3-Y.O+) (Class G)

2-00 (2-00) **1m 3f 135y** £2,304.00 (£644.00: £312.00) Stalls: High GOING minus 0.05 sec per fur (G)

| | | | | SP | RR | SF |
|---|---|---|---|---|---|---|
| 3095* | **Shabanaz (65)** (WRMuir) **11-9-13** JReid(5) (hdwy 5f out: led over 1f out: r.o wl) | — | **1** | 10/11$^{1}$ | 71 | 48 |
| 2978$^{2}$ | **Courbaril (58)** (SDow) **4-9-7**$^{(3)}$ DaneO'Neill(4) (swtg: a.p: ev ch over 1f out: no imp) | 3 | **2** | 5/1$^{2}$ | 64 | 41 |
| 2953$^{4}$ | **Dormy Three (55)** (RJHodges) **6-9-10** SDrowne(8) (a.p: ev ch over 1f out: nt qckn) | 2½ | **3** | 5/1$^{2}$ | 60 | 37 |

| | | | | SP | RR | SF |
|---|---|---|---|---|---|---|
| 3048[3] | **Arcatura (56)** (CJames) **4-9-10** MWigham(7) (led tl wknd over 1f out) | 1½ | **4** | 11/2[3] | 58 | 35 |
| 3173[5] | **Pat's Splendour (41)** (HJCollingridge) **5-9-5** MRimmer(1) (in tch tl wknd 2f out) | 8 | **5** | 16/1 | 42 | 19 |
| 3320[8] | **Bursul Lady** (MissBSanders) **3-8-8** SSanders(6) (lw: in tch tl wknd over 3f out: t.o) | 22 | **6** | 25/1 | 12 | — |
| 3108[7] | **Freddie's Recall** (MJHeaton-Ellis) **3-8-8** AClark(3) (a bhd: t.o fnl 4f) | 19 | **7** | 33/1 | — | — |
| 3051[6] | **Longano Bay (IRE)** (JPearce) **3-8-13** GBardwell(2) (bit bkwd: prom 4f: t.o fnl 4f) | 4 | **8** | 33/1 | — | — |

(SP 116.7%) **8 Rn**

**2m 32.4** (8.40) CSF £6.09 TOTE £1.80: £1.20 £1.40 £1.80 (£2.70) OWNER Fayzad Thoroughbred Ltd (LAMBOURN) BRED The Overbury Stud
WEIGHT FOR AGE 3yo-11lb
No bid
**3095* Shabanaz**, despite his advancing years, proved much too good for these rivals. He moved up on the home turn and, after taking the lead approaching the final furlong, won decisively. (10/11: 4/5-Evens)
**2978 Courbaril** moved up to challenge approaching the final furlong, but could make no impression on the winner. (5/1)
**2953 Dormy Three**, always on the heels of the leaders, had every chance below the distance, but failed to quicken. (5/1)
**3048 Arcatura** made the running until quickly outpaced approaching the final furlong. (11/2)
**3173 Pat's Splendour**, although in touch with the leaders, was under pressure some way from the finish and all chance had gone two furlongs out. (16/1)

## 3467 SALAMANCA NURSERY H'CAP (2-Y.O F) (Class D)

2-30 (2-32) **5f 217y** £3,485.00 (£1,055.00: £515.00: £245.00) Stalls: High GOING minus 0.05 sec per fur (G)

| | | | | SP | RR | SF |
|---|---|---|---|---|---|---|
| 3110[2] | **Charlton Spring (IRE) (70)** (RJHodges) **2-8-1** SDrowne(10) (hld up: hdwy 2f out: led wl ins fnl f: drvn out) | — | **1** | 16/1 | 64 | 28 |
| 3275* | **Perfect Bliss (65)** (PDEvans) **2-7-3**(7) RFfrench(11) (lw: led tl wl ins fnl f: r.o) | nk | **2** | 4/1[1] | 58 | 22 |
| 3137* | **Aegean Sound (75)** (RHannon) **2-8-3**(3)ow3 DaneO'Neill(6) (a.p: ev ch over 1f out: r.o) | 1¼ | **3** | 6/1[3] | 65 | 26 |
| 3054* | **Sherzetto (78)** (JRFanshawe) **2-8-9** DHarrison(4) (prom tl wknd over 1f out) | 7 | **4** | 5/1[2] | 49 | 13 |
| 2944* | **Irtifa (80)** (PTWalwyn) **2-8-11** WCarson(2) (lw: w ldrs: wknd over 1f out) | nk | **5** | 4/1[1] | 50 | 14 |
| *1093*[4] | **Molly Music (65)** (GGMargarson) **2-7-10** GBardwell(12) (lw: chsd ldr tl wknd 2f out) | 1 | **6** | 33/1 | 33 | — |
| 2995[5] | **Corncrake (IRE) (67)** (BJMeehan) **2-7-12**ow2 CRutter(9) (nvr nr to chal) | nk | **7** | 20/1 | 34 | — |
| 2797[5] | **Hil Rhapsody (86)** (BPalling) **2-9-3** TSprake(3) (swtg: prom tl wknd 2f out) | ½ | **8** | 16/1 | 52 | 16 |
| 2948[2] | **Sharazamataz (66)** (KTIvory) **2-7-6**(5)ow1 MartinDwyer(8) (outpcd) | 8 | **9** | 25/1 | 10 | — |
| 3268[4] | **Wait For Rosie (90)** (MRChannon) **2-9-7** RHughes(7) (outpcd) | 10 | **10** | 14/1 | 7 | — |
| 1331[7] | **Preskidul (IRE) (65)** (DWPArbuthnot) **2-7-10** JQuinn(5) (b.hind: a bhd) | 3 | **11** | 16/1 | — | — |
| 1467* | **Bluebell Miss (85)** (MJRyan) **2-9-2** AClark(1) (a bhd) | 3 | **12** | 11/1 | — | — |

(SP 115.1%) **12 Rn**

**1m 14.3** (3.80) CSF £71.91 CT £402.69 TOTE £17.60: £3.50 £1.70 £2.10 (£33.40) Trio £86.80 OWNER Mr R. J. Hodges (SOMERTON) BRED James M. Egan
LONG HANDICAP Perfect Bliss 6-13 Molly Music 7-9 Preskidul (IRE) 7-8 Sharazamataz 7-0
**3110 Charlton Spring (IRE)**, given a patient ride, moved up from the two-furlong marker and, after quickening to lead well inside the final furlong, held on under pressure. (16/1)
**3275* Perfect Bliss** tried to make all the running on the stands' side and fought back well when headed in the last 100 yards. (4/1)
**3137* Aegean Sound**, the best of those racing on the far side, could find no extra under pressure near the finish. (6/1: 9/2-7/1)
**3054* Sherzetto** travelled well on the heels of the leaders on the far side but, when asked to quicken approaching the final furlong, could find no more. (5/1)
**2944* Irtifa** led the far-side group until past halfway, but all chance had gone approaching the final furlong. (4/1)
**1093 Molly Music** raced in second place until weakening two furlongs from home. (33/1)
**3268 Wait For Rosie** (14/1: 8/1-16/1)
**1467* Bluebell Miss** (11/1: 7/1-14/1)

## 3468 COPENHAGEN CONDITIONS STKS (2-Y.O) (Class C)

3-00 (3-03) **5f 217y** £4,672.40 (£1,702.40: £831.20: £356.00: £158.00) Stalls: High GOING minus 0.05 sec per fur (G)

| | | | | SP | RR | SF |
|---|---|---|---|---|---|---|
| 2892* | **Ikdam (USA)** (MajorWRHern) **2-8-9** WCarson(5) (mde all: r.o wl) | — | **1** | Evens[1] | 95 | 38 |
| 3128[2] | **Caviar Royale (IRE) (98)** (RHannon) **2-9-0** PatEddery(3) (lw: hdwy 2f out: ev ch 1f out: r.o) | 1¾ | **2** | 5/2[2] | 95 | 38 |
| 2872* | **Stone Flower (USA)** (PWChapple-Hyam) **2-8-9** JReid(2) (prom tl wknd 2f out) | 4 | **3** | 11/2[3] | 80 | 23 |
| 2879[6] | **Secret Combe (IRE) (86)** (PJMakin) **2-8-5** SSanders(1) (chsd wnr tl wknd over 1f out) | hd | **4** | 11/2[3] | 75 | 18 |
| | **Bert** (PTWalwyn) **2-8-7** TSprake(4) (w'like: scope: s.s: a bhd: t.o) | 15 | **5** | 20/1 | 37 | — |

(SP 114.1%) **5 Rn**

**1m 14.1** (3.60) CSF £3.99 TOTE £2.00: £1.30 £1.50 (£2.60) OWNER Mr Hamdan Al Maktoum (LAMBOURN) BRED Shadwell Farm Inc
**2892* Ikdam (USA)** made all the running. She had to be rousted up entering the final furlong, but was holding her rivals at the finish. (Evens)
**3128 Caviar Royale (IRE)** had every chance in the last furlong, but was being held near the finish. (5/2)
**2872* Stone Flower (USA)**, well placed to halfway, soon began to lose ground, but stayed on again in the final furlong. (11/2: 2/1-6/1)
**2879 Secret Combe (IRE)** raced in second place until weakening under strong pressure below the distance. (11/2: 5/1-8/1)
**Bert** missed the break and was always well behind, finishing tailed off. (20/1)

## 3469 ROYAL BANK OF SCOTLAND H'CAP (0-70) (3-Y.O+) (Class E)

3-30 (3-30) **1m 67y** £4,502.00 (£1,361.00: £663.00: £314.00) Stalls: High GOING minus 0.05 sec per fur (G)

| | | | | SP | RR | SF |
|---|---|---|---|---|---|---|
| 3281* | **Talathath (FR) (66)** (CADwyer) **4-9-10v** WRSwinburn(5) (a.p: led 1f out: r.o wl) | — | **1** | 5/1[1] | 77 | 56 |
| 3314[7] | **Tomal (44)** (RIngram) **4-8-2** AMcGlone(15) (b.hind: a.p: r.o ins fnl f) | 1½ | **2** | 12/1 | 52 | 31 |
| 3115* | **Cape Pigeon (USA) (65)** (LGCottrell) **11-9-9v** LDettori(14) (lw: led after 2f to 1f out) | s.h | **3** | 13/2[2] | 73 | 52 |
| 3115[5] | **Proud Brigadier (IRE) (55)** (PBurgoyne) **8-8-13** DRMcCabe(13) (b: hdwy fnl 2f: nvr nrr) | 2½ | **4** | 16/1 | 58 | 37 |
| 3096[4] | **Jaazim (53)** (MMadgwick) **6-8-11** JReid(7) (hmpd after 2f: a.p: one pce fnl 2f) | nk | **5** | 10/1 | 56 | 35 |
| 3274* | **Our Shadee (USA) (49)** (KTIvory) **6-8-0v**(7) CScally(11) (lw: nvr nr to chal) | 1 | **6** | 7/1[3] | 50 | 29 |
| 3052[5] | **Just Harry (60)** (MJRyan) **5-9-4** AClark(1) (lw: a mid div) | 3 | **7** | 8/1 | 55 | 34 |
| 2945* | **Q Factor (70)** (DHaydnJones) **4-10-0** AMackay(3) (prom tl wknd over 2f out) | 2½ | **8** | 7/1[3] | 60 | 39 |
| | **Caddy's First (47)** (SMellor) **4-8-2**(3) MHenry(4) (nvr nr ldrs) | 1½ | **9** | 25/1 | 34 | 13 |
| 3161[14] | **Mr Rough (60)** (DMorris) **5-8-11**(7) AEddery(9) (hdwy on ins over 2f out: nt clr run over 1f out: nt rch ldrs) | s.h | **10** | 9/1 | 47 | 26 |
| 2581[12] | **Deevee (64)** (CJBenstead) **7-9-8** TSprake(6) (lw: a bhd) | 1¾ | **11** | 7/1[3] | 48 | 27 |
| 2744[7] | **Mr Hacker (56)** (GThorner) **3-8-4**(3)ow7 DaneO'Neill(2) (bhd fnl 3f) | 1¼ | **12** | 33/1 | 37 | 2 |
| 2159[8] | **Sir Oliver (IRE) (38)** (BAPearce) **7-7-10** DeclanO'Shea(8) (a bhd) | nk | **13** | 50/1 | 19 | — |

| | | | | SP | RR | SF |
|---|---|---|---|---|---|---|
| 2428$^{7}$ | **Sea Spouse (44)** (MBlanshard) **5-8-2** JQuinn(12) (led 2f: wknd over 2f out) | 2½ | **14** | 12/1 | 20 | — |
| 3261$^{8}$ | **Classic Pet (IRE) (38)** (CAHorgan) **4-7-10v** NAdams(10) (s.s: a bhd: t.o fnl 3f) | 13 | **15** | 50/1 | — | — |

(SP 129.7%) **15 Rn**

**1m 47.0** (4.80) CSF £62.53 CT £380.79 TOTE £5.70: £2.00 £5.00 £2.10 (£130.70) Trio £273.20 OWNER Mrs Christine Rawson (NEWMARKET) BRED Gainsborough Stud Management Ltd

LONG HANDICAP Sir Oliver (IRE) 7-2 Classic Pet (IRE) 7-6

WEIGHT FOR AGE 3yo-7lb

**OFFICIAL EXPLANATION Cape Pigeon (USA): became tired in the latter stages and, having made the running in a fast run race, he could not have finished second for more vigorous riding.**

**IN-FOCUS: This was a fairytale return for Swinburn six months after his life-threatening fall in Hong Kong.**

**3281* Talathath (FR)** was always close up. Driven into the lead entering the final furlong, he ran on strongly. (5/1)

**2971 Tomal**, though always close up, did not really find top gear until too late. (12/1)

**3115* Cape Pigeon (USA)**, ridden with considerably less flair than last time, went to the front after two furlongs. He came under pressure once headed but, by then, it was too late. (13/2)

**3115 Proud Brigadier (IRE)** was ridden with far more restraint on this occasion and ran on well in the last two furlongs. He may still be capable of winning a race. (16/1)

**3096 Jaazim**, chopped for room after two furlongs, was nonetheless always close up and kept on at one pace in the final quarter-mile. (10/1)

**3274* Our Shadee (USA)** made a forward move two furlongs out, but could never reach a challenging position. (7/1)

## 3470 SHADWELL STUD SERIES APPRENTICE H'CAP (0-80) (3-Y.O+) (Class E)

4-00 (4-00) **1m 2f 7y** £2,965.00 (£895.00: £435.00: £205.00) Stalls: High GOING minus 0.05 sec per fur (G)

| | | | | SP | RR | SF |
|---|---|---|---|---|---|---|
| 2883$^{8}$ | **Sharp Consul (IRE) (74)** (HCandy) **4-9-3**(7) LJames(8) (gd hdwy to ld over 2f out: pushed out) | — | **1** | 8/1 | 85 | 65 |
| 3272$^{3}$ | **Vola Via (USA) (81)** (IABalding) **3-9-8** MartinDwyer(2) (lost pl 5f out: hdwy over 1f out: r.o wl nr fin) | nk | **2** | 5/1$^{2}$ | 92 | 63 |
| 3111$^{2}$ | **Princess Danielle (59)** (WRMuir) **4-8-9** MHenry(10) (hld up in rr: hdwy 3f out: ev ch fnl f: no ex nr fin) | ¾ | **3** | 7/2$^{1}$ | 68 | 48 |
| 3161$^{3}$ | **Harvey White (IRE) (57)** (JPearce) **4-8-2**(5) RFfrench(3) (swtg: prom tl outpcd 2f out: r.o ins fnl f) | 1½ | **4** | 11/2$^{3}$ | 64 | 44 |
| 2883$^{9}$ | **Country Lover (68)** (LordHuntingdon) **5-9-4v** AimeeCook(11) (lw: hld up: hdwy & ev ch 2f out: nt qckn) | s.h | **5** | 8/1 | 75 | 55 |
| 3246$^{6}$ | **Disallowed (IRE) (73)** (MBell) **3-9-0** GFaulkner(5) (hdwy & ev ch over 2f out: wknd over 1f out) | 7 | **6** | 7/1 | 69 | 40 |
| 3161$^{10}$ | **Far Dawn (USA) (76)** (GHarwood) **3-9-0**(3) GayeHarwood(7) (lw: w ldr tl wknd over 2f out) | 1 | **7** | 20/1 | 70 | 41 |
| 2346$^{5}$ | **Irish Kinsman (70)** (PTWalwyn) **3-8-11** RHavlin(1) (lw: prom tl wknd over 3f out) | 9 | **8** | 20/1 | 50 | 21 |
| 3233$^{2}$ | **Loki (IRE) (78)** (GLewis) **8-10-0** EAhern(6) (lw: dwlt: hdwy & rdn over 2f out: wknd fnl f) | hd | **9** | 6/1 | 58 | 38 |
| 3260$^{8}$ | **Noble Lord (65)** (RHBuckler) **3-7-13**(7) SCrawford(4) (lw: bhd most of wy) | 2 | **10** | 20/1 | 41 | 12 |
| 1618$^{14}$ | **Persian Conquest (IRE) (57)** (RIngram) **4-8-7b** PPMurphy(9) (led tl wknd over 2f out: t.o) | 13 | **11** | 16/1 | 13 | — |

(SP 123.4%) **11 Rn**

**2m 9.7** (4.80) CSF £46.77 CT £150.83 TOTE £9.30: £3.20 £2.10 £1.30 (£31.30) Trio £41.60 OWNER Mrs David Blackburn (WANTAGE) BRED B. Barnwell

WEIGHT FOR AGE 3yo-9lb

**IN-FOCUS: Apprentice Lee James rode his first winner on only his second ride.**

**2342 Sharp Consul (IRE)**, held up at the back of the field, came dashing up on the outside to lead over two furlongs from home. Though hotly challenged on both sides, his rider coolly pushed him out to a narrow win. (8/1)

**3272 Vola Via (USA)** lost his place at halfway, but ran on from two furlongs out. Hard driven, he finished strongly but just too late. (5/1)

**3111 Princess Danielle**, held up in last place, found a good run near the inside from three furlongs out. She had every chance in the last furlong, but was being held near the finish. (7/2)

**3161 Harvey White (IRE)**, close up from the start, was unable to quicken with the leaders two furlongs out, but ran on strongly inside the final furlong. (11/2)

**1338* Country Lover**, patiently ridden, came with a promising run at the two-furlong marker, but could not sustain the effort. (8/1)

**3246 Disallowed (IRE)** moved up to join the winner over two furlongs from home, but beat a retreat from below the distance. (7/1)

**3233 Loki (IRE)** (6/1: 4/1-13/2)

## 3471 BOLLINGER CHAMPAGNE CHALLENGE SERIES GENTLEMENS' H'CAP (0-70) (3-Y.O+) (Class E)

4-30 (4-31) **1m 3f 135y** £3,078.75 (£930.00: £452.50: £213.75) Stalls: High GOING minus 0.05 sec per fur (G)

| | | | | SP | RR | SF |
|---|---|---|---|---|---|---|
| 3220$^{3}$ | **Fern's Governor (40)** (WJMusson) **4-10-2** MrTMcCarthy(3) (a.p: led over 2f out: easily) | — | **1** | 4/1$^{1}$ | 53+ | 35 |
| 2784$^{9}$ | **Braydon Forest (46)** (CJDrewe) **4-10-4**(4) MrRThornton(2) (lw: a.p: hrd rdn over 2f out: styd on: no ch w wnr) | 3 | **2** | 16/1 | 55 | 37 |
| 2989$^{2}$ | **Spread The Word (54)** (LGCottrell) **4-10-12v**(4) MrLJefford(4) (lw: hdwy 4f out: styd on one pce fnl 2f) | 1¾ | **3** | 4/1$^{1}$ | 61 | 43 |
| 3084$^{5}$ | **Super Serenade (52)** (GBBalding) **7-10-10**(4) MrJThatcher(9) (lw: chsd ldr 7f out tl wknd over 1f out) | ½ | **4** | 8/1$^{3}$ | 58 | 40 |
| 3076$^{4}$ | **Haydown (IRE) (35)** (CTNash) **4-9-7**(4) MrPPhillips(10) (hdwy 3f out: r.o one pce fnl 2f) | 2 | **5** | 33/1 | 38 | 20 |
| 2711* | **Artic Bay (66)** (MrsPNDutfield) **4-12-0** MrJDurkan(8) (wl bhd tl hdwy 3f out: nvr nr to chal) | ¾ | **6** | 11/2$^{2}$ | 68 | 50 |
| | **Grand Applause (IRE) (43)** (MDIUsher) **6-10-1**(4) MrMSalaman(11) (nvr nr to chal) | 5 | **7** | 8/1$^{3}$ | 38 | 20 |
| 2716$^{9}$ | **Little Luke (IRE) (31)** (PButler) **5-9-3**(4) MrIMongan(7) (chsd ldr over 4f: wknd over 2f out) | 4 | **8** | 33/1 | 21 | 3 |
| 3095$^{3}$ | **Global Dancer (57)** (SDow) **5-11-1**(4) MrSFetherstonhaugh(6) (plld hrd: led & sn clr: hdd & wknd over 2f out) | 10 | **9** | 14/1 | 33 | 15 |
| 3067$^{13}$ | **Red Viper (50)** (NMLampard) **4-10-8**(4) MrLBaker(13) (lw: prom tl wknd over 2f out) | 1½ | **10** | 25/1 | 24 | 6 |
| 3348$^{8}$ | **Golden Hadeer (41)** (MJRyan) **5-9-13**(4) MrSLavallin(5) (lw: n.d) | 1¾ | **11** | 20/1 | 12 | — |
| | **Misty View (43)** (JWhite) **7-10-1**(4) MrJCrowley(1) (bit bkwd: bhd fnl 4f) | 1¾ | **12** | 33/1 | 12 | — |
| 2247$^{7}$ | **Regal Eagle (70)** (IABalding) **3-11-7** MrABalding(12) (lw: prom tl wknd over 4f out) | ¾ | **13** | 8/1$^{3}$ | 38 | 9 |
| 2192$^{20}$ | **Manabar (55)** (MJPolglase) **4-10-13**(4) DrMMannish(14) (s.v.s: t.o & hrd rdn whn veered bdly lft over 3f out) | 4 | **14** | 16/1 | 17 | — |

(SP 124.6%) **14 Rn**

**2m 34.8** (10.80) CSF £62.17 CT £251.21 TOTE £4.60: £1.70 £6.60 £1.70 (£96.30) Trio £117.20 OWNER Fern Components Ltd (NEWMARKET) BRED E. A. Badger

WEIGHT FOR AGE 3yo-11lb

STEWARDS' ENQUIRY Baker susp. 21-27/8/96 (excessive & incorrect use of whip).

**3220 Fern's Governor**, well suited by the longer trip, quickened to the front over two furlongs from home and was in no danger thereafter. (4/1)

**2377 Braydon Forest**, always chasing the leading group, was under pressure a long way out but, though staying on, had no chance with the winner. (16/1)

**2989 Spread The Word** raced middle to rear until improving early in the straight. She kept staying on, but lacked the pace to ever threaten the winner. (4/1)

**3084 Super Serenade** took second place seven furlongs out, but had shot his bolt below the distance. (8/1: 6/1-10/1)

**3076 Haydown (IRE)** made a forward move three furlongs out but, though staying on, was never on terms. (33/1)
**2711* Artic Bay**, well behind for much of the race, made some headway three furlongs out, but never had any chance of reaching a challenging position. (11/2: 4/1-6/1)

## 3472 WELLINGTON MAIDEN STKS (3-Y.O+) (Class D)
5-00 (5-02) **1m 67y** £3,909.00 (£1,182.00: £576.00: £273.00) Stalls: High GOING minus 0.05 sec per fur (G)

| | | | | SP | RR | SF |
|---|---|---|---|---|---|---|
| 2918$^{4}$ | **Yamuna (USA)** (HRACecil) **3-8-9** WRyan(7) (hld up: hdwy 3f out: led ins fnl f: drvn out) | — | **1** | 8/1 | 94+ | 49 |
| 3262$^{2}$ | **Grand Musica** (IABalding) **3-8-9**(5) MartinDwyer(17) (a.p: led over 1f out tl ins fnl f) | 2 | **2** | 4/1$^{2}$ | 95 | 50 |
| 2501$^{5}$ | **Don Bosio (USA) (84)** (MRStoute) **3-9-0** WRSwinburn(12) (a.p: led over 3f out tl over 1f out: wknd fnl f) | 7 | **3** | 6/5$^{1}$ | 82 | 37 |
| 2918$^{2}$ | **Melt The Clouds (CAN) (77)** (PWHarris) **3-9-0** GHind(9) (lw: a.p: one pce fnl 2f) | 2½ | **4** | 9/1 | 77 | 32 |
| | **Sulawesi (IRE)** (WJarvis) **3-8-9** BThomson(6) (w'like: scope: bit bkwd: stdy hdwy fnl 2f: nvr nr to chal) | 3 | **5** | 25/1 | 66 | 21 |
| | **Galb Alasad (IRE)** (JHMGosden) **3-9-0** LDettori(13) (w'like: scope: lw: hdwy 4f out: eased whn btn over 1f out) | 9 | **6** | 9/1 | 54 | 9 |
| 2706$^{W}$ | **Press Again** (PHayward) **4-9-2** AMcGlone(5) (hdwy 3f out: r.o one pce fnl 2f) | ½ | **7** | 100/1 | 48 | 10 |
| 3262$^{10}$ | **Sovereign Crest (IRE)** (CAHorgan) **3-9-0** PaulEddery(18) (stdy hdwy 3f out: nvr plcd to chal) | 2 | **8** | 50/1 | 49 | 4 |
| 2529$^{9}$ | **Chesteine** (PJMakin) **3-8-4**(5) RHavlin(16) (a mid div) | s.h | **9** | 66/1 | 44 | — |
| 3262$^{4}$ | **Take Notice** (GHarwood) **3-9-0** PatEddery(1) (w ldrs tl wknd over 2f out) | 1¼ | **10** | 5/1$^{3}$ | 46 | 1 |
| 3262$^{9}$ | **Samorelle** (MJRyan) **3-8-2**(7) AMcCarthy(10) (lw: nvr nr ldrs) | ½ | **11** | 33/1 | 40 | — |
| 1326$^{9}$ | **Nawaji (USA)** (WRMuir) **3-8-9** JReid(2) (led tl wknd over 3f out) | 2 | **12** | 33/1 | 37 | — |
| | **Thor's Phantom** (MDIUsher) **3-9-0** RPerham(11) (b: unf: nvr nr ldrs) | 1¾ | **13** | 66/1 | 38 | — |
| 2918$^{8}$ | **Endaxi Sam** (RIngram) **3-8-11**(3) MHenry(8) (lw: a wl bhd) | 4 | **14** | 66/1 | 31 | — |
| 3115$^{11}$ | **Radical Exception (IRE)** (DLWilliams) **6-9-7** NAdams(14) (a bhd) | 4 | **15** | 100/1 | 23 | — |
| | **Bunty Bagshaw** (JLSpearing) **3-8-9** TSprake(15) (a bhd) | 10 | **16** | 66/1 | — | — |
| 3258$^{12}$ | **Monte Felice (IRE)** (GHarwood) **3-9-0** AClark(3) (prom tl wknd over 3f out) | 2½ | **17** | 50/1 | — | — |
| 3162$^{15}$ | **Jades Shadow** (JJBridger) **3-8-7**(7) GFaulkner(4) (a bhd: t.o) | 25 | **18** | 66/1 | — | — |
| | | | | (SP 136.3%) | **18 Rn** | |

**1m 46.3** (4.10) CSF £41.07 TOTE £9.40: £2.30 £1.80 £1.10 (£17.70) Trio £7.10 OWNER Mr K. Abdulla (NEWMARKET) BRED Juddmonte Farms
WEIGHT FOR AGE 3yo-7lb
**2918 Yamuna (USA)**, patiently ridden, moved up steadily three furlongs out. She struck the front just inside the final furlong and quickened readily for a decisive win. (8/1)
**3262 Grand Musica**, going easily on the heels of the leaders from the start, cruised to the front approaching the final furlong but, though going clear of the favourite, could not shake off the winner and could find no extra in the last 100 yards. (4/1: 11/4-9/2)
**2501 Don Bosio (USA)** settled down in third place and moved smoothly to the front over three furlongs from home. When headed approaching the final furlong, he could find no extra and was weakening at the finish. (6/5: 9/4-11/10)
**2918 Melt The Clouds (CAN)**, always chasing the leaders, ran on at one pace in the last two furlongs. (9/1)
**Sulawesi (IRE)** failed to go the pace, but was running on steadily in the final quarter-mile. (25/1)
**Galb Alasad (IRE)** made a satisfactory debut. He moved up three furlongs out and would have finished much closer had he not been eased when his chance had gone below the distance. (9/1)
**Sovereign Crest (IRE)** ran rather better than his position suggests. He moved up steadily three furlongs out but, not being able to reach a challenging position, was not given a hard time. (50/1)

T/Jkpt: £22,984.90 (0.2 Tckts); £25,898.58 to Bath 13/8/96. T/Plpt: £25.50 (905.28 Tckts). T/Qdpt: £8.90 (107.01 Tckts). Hn

# 3336-BATH (L-H) (Good)
## Tuesday August 13th
WEATHER: fine WIND: slt against

## 3473 AUGUST (S) STKS (3-Y.O+) (Class G)
2-00 (2-02) **1m 5y** £2,472.00 (£692.00: £336.00) Stalls: Low GOING minus 0.41 sec per fur (F)

| | | | | SP | RR | SF |
|---|---|---|---|---|---|---|
| 3257$^{14}$ | **Charlton Imp (USA) (56)** (RJHodges) **3-8-5** SDrowne(14) (a.p: led over 2f out tl over 1f out: led last strides) | — | **1** | 13/2 | 46 | 19 |
| 2743$^{12}$ | **Cedar Dancer (30)** (RJHodges) **4-8-2**(5) AmandaSanders(8) (hdwy over 2f out: led over 1f out: hdd last strides) | s.h | **2** | 33/1 | 41 | 21 |
| 2716$^{13}$ | **Northern Saga (IRE) (41)** (CJDrewe) **3-8-7** JQuinn(11) (gd hdwy over 1f out: fin wl) | ½ | **3** | 50/1 | 47 | 20 |
| *3435*$^{4}$ | **Ketabi (USA) (47)** (RAkehurst) **5-9-3** TQuinn(6) (swtg: gd hdwy over 1f out: r.o ins fnl f) | ¾ | **4** | 8/1 | 48 | 28 |
| 2047$^{12}$ | **Morocco (IRE) (58)** (MRChannon) **7-9-3** RHughes(3) (hld up: hdwy on ins over 3f out: n.m.r over 1f out: unable qckn fnl f) | nk | **5** | 5/1$^{3}$ | 48 | 28 |
| 3334$^{15}$ | **Shanghai Lil (28)** (MJFetherston-Godley) **4-8-12** WJO'Connor(7) (nvr nr to chal) | 6 | **6** | 25/1 | 31 | 11 |
| 3165$^{8}$ | **Lady Magnum (IRE) (45)** (JNeville) **3-7-13**(3) NVarley(9) (rdn & hdwy 5f out: ev ch over 1f out: wknd fnl f) | nk | **7** | 5/1$^{3}$ | 27 | — |
| 3138$^{7}$ | **First Law (58)** (MissGayKelleway) **3-8-2** GBardwell(4) (b.hind: chsd ldr tl rdn & wknd over 2f out) | 5 | **8** | 7/2$^{1}$ | 17 | — |
| | **Andy Coin** (WMBrisbourne) **5-8-7** AGarth(1) (b: s.s: nvr nr ldrs) | nk | **9** | 50/1 | 15 | — |
| 3257$^{8}$ | **Grey Charmer (IRE) (49)** (RHBuckler) **7-9-3** JReid(13) (chsd ldrs 4f) | 1¼ | **10** | 14/1 | 22 | 2 |
| 3300$^{2}$ | **Followthe Allstars (47)** (TJNaughton) **3-8-7b** SSanders(15) (a bhd) | nk | **11** | 9/2$^{2}$ | 19 | — |
| *2747*$^{5}$ | **Galloping Guns (IRE)** (BJLlewellyn) **4-8-5**(7) JBramhill(5) (lw: a bhd) | ½ | **12** | 50/1 | 16 | — |
| 2992$^{8}$ | **Rocky Two (37)** (NRMitchell) **5-8-12b**(5) SophieMitchell(12) (prom tl wknd over 2f out) | 7 | **13** | 50/1 | 7 | — |
| 3274$^{12}$ | **Sobeloved (31)** (NEBerry) **4-8-12b**$^{1}$ AMackay(2) (lw: led over 5f: wknd qckly: t.o) | 23 | **14** | 33/1 | — | — |
| | | | | (SP 122.4%) | **14 Rn** | |

**1m 42.2** (3.70) CSF £165.01 TOTE £8.00: £2.20 £7.70 £9.90 (£48.10) Trio Not won; £444.71 to Salisbury 14/8/96 OWNER Mr R. J. Hodges (SOMERTON) BRED Brereton C. Jones
WEIGHT FOR AGE 3yo-7lb
No bid
**2380* Charlton Imp (USA)** disappointed in a selling handicap last time, but bounced back to form to pip her stable-companion. (13/2)
**631 Cedar Dancer**, who would have been better off in a handicap, showed she gets a mile. (33/1)
**Northern Saga (IRE)** ran by far his best race since changing stables in the close-season. (50/1)
**3435 Ketabi (USA)**, with less use made of him, seemed to find the trip inadequate. (8/1: 5/1-9/1)
**1348 Morocco (IRE)**, back into selling company after a break, did not find much off the bridle as usual. (5/1)

**2303 Shanghai Lil** could not take advantage of a drop in class. (25/1)
**First Law**, trying her luck in a seller, has yet to prove she stays a mile. (7/2)
**3300 Followthe Allstars**, descending into a seller, could not reproduce last week's run in the first-time blinkers. (9/2: op 3/1)

## 3474 MILE MAIDEN H'CAP (0-65) (3-Y.O+) (Class F)

2-30 (2-35) **1m 5y** £2,897.50 (£810.00: £392.50) Stalls: Low GOING minus 0.41 sec per fur (F)

| Form | Horse | Dist | Pos | SP | RR | SF |
|---|---|---|---|---|---|---|
| 3162$^{8}$ | **Ca'd'oro (56)** (GBBalding) **3-9-5** SDrowne(13) (hld up: hdwy 3f out: led ins fnl f: jst hld on) | — | **1** | 8/1$^{3}$ | 66 | 41 |
| 3138$^{2}$ | **Sharp Shuffle (IRE) (65)** (RHannon) **3-9-11**(3) DaneO'Neill(11) (hdwy 2f out: r.o wl ins fnl f: jst failed) | s.h | **2** | 7/2$^{2}$ | 75 | 50 |
| 2983$^{5}$ | **Shermood (39)** (KTIvory) **3-7-11**(5) MartinDwyer(7) (b.nr fore: rdn & hdwy 2f out: r.o ins fnl f) | 1½ | **3** | 16/1 | 46 | 21 |
| 3107$^{3}$ | **Gooseberry Pie (62)** (RCharlton) **3-9-11** TSprake(14) (lw: hld up: rdn over 1f out: one pce) | s.h | **4** | 2/1$^{1}$ | 69 | 44 |
| | **Jilly Beveled (40)** (PRWebber) **4-8-10** RPerham(12) (b.hind: led 1f: led over 2f out tl ins fnl f) | hd | **5** | 25/1 | 47 | 29 |
| 3257$^{3}$ | **Little Kenny (43)** (MJFetherston-Godley) **3-7-13v**(7) RFfrench(1) (lw: nvr nrr) | 2½ | **6** | 8/1$^{3}$ | 45 | 20 |
| 3257$^{7}$ | **Fastini Gold (40)** (MDIUsher) **4-8-10** AClark(17) (nvr nr to chal) | 2 | **7** | 25/1 | 38 | 20 |
| 3354$^{6}$ | **Richard House Lad (44)** (RHollinshead) **3-8-4**(3) FLynch(8) (nvr trbld ldrs) | hd | **8** | 16/1 | 41 | 16 |
| *2689*$^{13}$ | **Bath Knight (50)** (DJSffrenchDavis) **3-8-13** TQuinn(2) (prom: btn whn hmpd over 1f out: wknd fnl f) | 1¼ | **9** | 16/1 | 45 | 20 |
| 761$^{10}$ | **Siberian Mystic (37)** (PGMurphy) **3-7-11**(3) NVarley(10) (lw: n.d) | 2½ | **10** | 33/1 | 27 | 2 |
| 3060$^{7}$ | **Oscar Rose (52)** (LordHuntingdon) **3-9-1** DHarrison(4) (lw: sme hdwy over 3f out: wknd over 2f out) | 1 | **11** | 14/1 | 40 | 15 |
| 3258$^{11}$ | **Indian Wolf (40)** (BJLlewellyn) **3-7-10**(7) JBramhill(9) (led after 1f tl over 2f out: sn wknd) | ¾ | **12** | 25/1 | 27 | 2 |
| | **Impending Danger (43)** (KSBridgwater) **3-8-6** KFallon(16) (a bhd) | 1¾ | **13** | 50/1 | 26 | 1 |
| 2989$^{14}$ | **Celestial Dollar (36)** (OO'Neill) **5-8-6** VSlattery(15) (prom: rdn over 3f out: wknd over 2f out) | 1½ | **14** | 20/1 | 16 | — |
| 1979$^{10}$ | **Forliando (38)** (MSSaunders) **3-8-1**ow4 JFEgan(5) (chsd ldrs over 5f) | 1¼ | **15** | 50/1 | 16 | — |
| 3281$^{5}$ | **Sharp Holly (IRE) (41)** (JABennett) **4-8-6b**(5) SophieMitchell(18) (a bhd) | 3½ | **16** | 33/1 | 12 | — |
| | **Fiddles Delight (35)** (MRChannon) **3-7-12** CRutter(6) (lw: a bhd) | 5 | **17** | 33/1 | — | — |

(SP 131.1%) **17 Rn**

**1m 41.3** (2.80) CSF £35.98 CT £423.98 TOTE £9.50: £1.90 £1.20 £5.10 £1.50 (£21.80) Trio £108.60 OWNER Miss B. Swire (ANDOVER) BRED Miss B. Swire
WEIGHT FOR AGE 3yo-7lb
OFFICIAL EXPLANATION **Siberian Music: the rider reported that the filly was bumped and lost her action.**
**1856 Ca'd'oro** appreciated this step up to a mile. (8/1: 6/1-9/1)
**3138 Sharp Shuffle (IRE)**, raised 2lb, only found top gear late on and the post came a stride too soon. (7/2)
**2983 Shermood**, dropped 5lb, might find a drop to selling company over this trip the answer. (16/1)
**3107 Gooseberry Pie** again proved an expensive failure and got a true-run race this time. (2/1: op 7/2)
**Jilly Beveled**, trained by Richard Hannon last year, ran her best race to date and this would have put an edge on her. (25/1)
**3257 Little Kenny** was racing off the same mark as when third in a Windsor seller. (8/1)

## 3475 MENDIP MAIDEN STKS (2-Y.O F) (Class D)

3-00 (3-01) **5f 11y** £3,447.50 (£1,040.00: £505.00: £237.50) Stalls: High GOING minus 0.41 sec per fur (F)

| Form | Horse | Dist | Pos | SP | RR | SF |
|---|---|---|---|---|---|---|
| 2956$^{3}$ | **Dancethenightaway** (BJMeehan) **2-8-11** BDoyle(9) (a.p: led over 1f out: r.o wl) | — | **1** | 10/1 | 74 | 27 |
| 3050$^{4}$ | **Blues Queen** (MRChannon) **2-8-11** RHughes(4) (lw: a.p: rdn over 1f out: swtchd & wnt rt ins fnl f: r.o) | 1½ | **2** | 4/1$^{2}$ | 69 | 22 |
| 2782$^{3}$ | **Bold Tina (IRE)** (RHannon) **2-8-8**(3) DaneO'Neill(1) (lw: led tl over 1f out) | ½ | **3** | 9/4$^{1}$ | 68 | 21 |
| 3160$^{5}$ | **Oneknight With You (76)** (MJFetherston-Godley) **2-8-11** JReid(7) (a.p: rdn over 1f out: btn whn carried rt ins fnl f) | 1 | **4** | 5/1$^{3}$ | 65 | 18 |
| 3114$^{12}$ | **Sarabi** (JPearce) **2-8-11** GBardwell(3) (no hdwy fnl 2f) | 4 | **5** | 40/1 | 52 | 5 |
| 2404$^{4}$ | **Calamander (IRE)** (PFICole) **2-8-11** TQuinn(6) (chsd ldr 3f: wknd over 1f out) | 1 | **6** | 12/1 | 49 | 2 |
| 2559$^{9}$ | **Muscatana** (BWHills) **2-8-11** PatEddery(11) (prom over 2f) | 1¾ | **7** | 7/1 | 43 | — |
| 2611$^{16}$ | **Sally Green (IRE)** (CFWall) **2-8-11** WWoods(8) (a bhd) | 2 | **8** | 40/1 | 37 | — |
| 3282$^{6}$ | **Florentine Diamond (IRE)** (SirMarkPrescott) **2-8-11** GDuffield(5) (a bhd) | s.h | **9** | 7/1 | 37 | — |
| 596$^{9}$ | **Sea Mist (IRE)** (PWChapple-Hyam) **2-8-6**(5) RHavlin(10) (bhd fnl 2f) | 1 | **10** | 16/1 | 33 | — |
| | **Fully Booked** (JWHills) **2-8-8**(3) MHenry(2) (neat: bkwd: a bhd) | ½ | **11** | 20/1 | 32 | — |

(SP 124.7%) **11 Rn**

**62.6 secs** (2.10) CSF £49.55 TOTE £11.10: £2.70 £1.80 £1.30 (£24.60) Trio £24.40 OWNER Mr G. A. Bosley (UPPER LAMBOURN) BRED G. A. Bosley and H. Clarkin
**2956 Dancethenightaway**, fitter this time, appreciated the good ground. (10/1)
**3050 Blues Queen** decided she would keep going in a straight line when switched off the fence at the elbow, and took a while to get back on an even keel. Her turn will come. (4/1: 3/1-9/2)
**2782 Bold Tina (IRE)** may do better when stepped up to six. (9/4)
**3160 Oneknight With You** seems ready for a return to a longer trip. (5/1)
**Sarabi**, out of an unraced three-part sister to Sure Blade and Sure Sharp, is bred to require further than this. (40/1)
**2404 Calamander (IRE)**, out of a half-sister to Middle Park winner Balla Cove, was surprisingly dropped back to the minimum distance. (12/1: op 7/1)
**Muscatana** (7/1: 9/2-8/1)

## 3476 BBC RADIO BRISTOL H'CAP (0-80) (3-Y.O+) (Class D)

3-30 (3-30) **2m 1f 34y** £3,507.50 (£1,055.00: £510.00: £237.50) Stalls: High GOING minus 0.41 sec per fur (F)

| Form | Horse | Dist | Pos | SP | RR | SF |
|---|---|---|---|---|---|---|
| 2958$^{4}$ | **Chucklestone (35)** (JSKing) **13-7-10** JQuinn(3) (led over 10f: hrd rdn & rallied 2f out: led over 1f out: all out) | — | **1** | 11/2$^{3}$ | 43 | 1 |
| 2952* | **Bold Classic (IRE) (78)** (JLDunlop) **3-9-10** PatEddery(4) (chsd ldr: led 3f out: hrd rdn & hdd 2f out: r.o) | nk | **2** | 8/11$^{1}$ | 86 | 29 |
| 3267$^{3}$ | **Hill Farm Dancer (48)** (WMBrisbourne) **5-8-4**(5) MartinDwyer(1) (hld up: led on bit 2f out: rdn & hdd over 1f out: one pce) | 2 | **3** | 4/1$^{2}$ | 54 | 12 |
| 3037$^{19}$ | **Aude la Belle (FR) (43)** (SGKnight) **8-8-4** FNorton(2) (hld up: hdwy to ld 7f out: hdd 3f out: wknd over 1f out) | 2 | **4** | 6/1 | 47 | 5 |

(SP 107.6%) **4 Rn**

**3m 52.0** (11.00) CSF £9.63 TOTE £5.00 (£2.80) OWNER Mrs P. M. King (SWINDON) BRED R. B. Stokes
LONG HANDICAP Chucklestone 7-5
WEIGHT FOR AGE 3yo-15lb
STEWARDS' ENQUIRY Quinn & Eddery susp. 23-24/8/96 (excessive use of whip).
**2958 Chucklestone**, 5lb out of the handicap, has not scored since winning this event two years ago, but put up a real gutsy performance to register his eighth course win. His rider picked up a two-day whip ban. (11/2)

**2952* Bold Classic (IRE)** certainly got the trip well enough, but could not overcome a 5lb hike in the weights. Eddery also collected a two-day whip suspension. (8/11)
**3267 Hill Farm Dancer**, dropped 2lb, seemed sure to score when cruising to the front at the quarter-mile marker and one can only assume she did not see out this extended trip. (4/1)
**2697 Aude la Belle (FR)**, who had a foal last year, is struggling to find her form, despite coming down 15lb in the Ratings this season. (6/1)

## 3477 LUCKINGTON LIMITED STKS (0-70) (3-Y.O+) (Class E)

4-00 (4-04) **5f 11y** £2,856.00 (£858.00: £414.00: £192.00) Stalls: High GOING minus 0.41 sec per fur (F)

| | | | | SP | RR | SF |
|---|---|---|---|---|---|---|
| 3360[4] | **Midnight Spell (64)** (JWHills) **4-9-0**(3) MHenry(7) (hld up: qcknd to ld ins fnl f: pushed out) | — | **1** | 9/2[2] | 72 | 39 |
| 3342[2] | **Silk Cottage (65)** (RMWhitaker) **4-9-6v** DeanMcKeown(1) (lw: led: hrd rdn over 1f out: hdd ins fnl f) | 2½ | **2** | 9/2[2] | 67 | 34 |
| 3152[9] | **Call Me I'm Blue (IRE) (65)** (NTinkler) **6-9-3** KFallon(6) (bhd: rdn 3f out: hdwy & swtchd rt 2f out: edgd lft & r.o ins fnl f) | 1¾ | **3** | 9/1 | 59 | 26 |
| 2999[2] | **Mindrace (68)** (KTIvory) **3-8-12**(5) MartinDwyer(3) (lw: jinked lft s: chsd ldr: wknd fnl f) | ¾ | **4** | 7/4[1] | 59 | 23 |
| 3261[10] | **Millesime (IRE) (64)** (BHanbury) **4-9-3** MRimmer(4) (b: lw: prom: hrd rdn over 2f out: wknd wl over 1f out) | 3 | **5** | 14/1 | 47 | 14 |
| 3166[10] | **Red Time (58)** (MSSaunders) **3-9-0** JFEgan(8) (a bhd) | 2 | **6** | 16/1 | 40 | 4 |
| 3323[3] | **Walk the Beat (66)** (MartynMeade) **6-9-6** TQuinn(2) (hld up: nt clr run on ins & swtchd rt 2f out: n.m.r over 1f out: eased whn btn ins fnl f) | s.h | **7** | 5/1[3] | 43 | 10 |
| *3261[6]* | ***Imposing Time (63)*** (MissGayKelleway) **5-9-3b[1]** JReid(5) (Withdrawn not under Starter's orders: bolted bef s) | | **W** | 7/1 | — | — |

(SP 124.4%) **7 Rn**

**62.2 secs** (1.70) CSF £22.77 TOTE £6.10: £3.10 £2.80 (£10.80) OWNER Wyck Hall Stud (LAMBOURN) BRED Milton Park Stud Partnership
WEIGHT FOR AGE 3yo-3lb

**3360 Midnight Spell**, who has found her best trip, was waiting to pounce on the inside, and did the business when the split came at the furlong pole. (9/2)
**3342 Silk Cottage** had no answer to the winner in the final furlong and would have been a little better off in a handicap. (9/2)
**Call Me I'm Blue (IRE)**, suited by the better ground, ran his best race for a while, and one can only hope he is on the way back. (9/1)
**2999 Mindrace** did not have the ground as fast as when successful here last month. (7/4)
**Millesime (IRE)** is struggling to recapture the form that saw him win twice last summer. (14/1)
**1356 Red Time** needs further than this. (16/1)

## 3478 NUNNEY NURSERY H'CAP (2-Y.O) (Class E)

4-30 (4-30) **5f 161y** £3,090.00 (£930.00: £450.00: £210.00) Stalls: High GOING minus 0.41 sec per fur (F)

| | | | | SP | RR | SF |
|---|---|---|---|---|---|---|
| 2728[2] | **Maid By The Fire (USA) (85)** (PFICole) **2-8-13**(3) DaneO'Neill(6) (lw: a.p: led 1f out: rdn out) | — | **1** | 8/1 | 83 | 45 |
| 2040[10] | **Maserati Monk (90)** (BJMeehan) **2-9-7** JReid(2) (lw: led: edgd rt 2f out tl hdd 1f out: r.o) | s.h | **2** | 3/1[1] | 88 | 50 |
| 3170[4] | **Anokato (66)** (KTIvory) **2-7-6**(5) MartinDwyer(7) (w ldr: ev ch whn carried rt over 1f out: unable qckn fnl f) | 1¼ | **3** | 14/1 | 60 | 22 |
| 3121* | **What Happened Was (71)** (MartynMeade) **2-7-13**(3) FLynch(1) (bhd tl hdwy 2f out: one pce fnl f) | 1½ | **4** | 7/1 | 61 | 23 |
| 3268* | **I Can't Remember (74)** (PDEvans) **2-8-5** JFEgan(10) (lw: bhd tl hdwy over 1f out: nvr nrr) | 1 | **5** | 4/1[2] | 61 | 23 |
| 2527[3] | **Bold Spring (IRE) (77)** (RHannon) **2-8-8** PatEddery(5) (no hdwy fnl 2f) | 2 | **6** | 13/2[3] | 59 | 21 |
| 3046[5] | **Lamorna (85)** (MRChannon) **2-9-2** RHughes(4) (s.s: a bhd) | 2½ | **7** | 16/1 | 60 | 22 |
| 3299[2] | **Blazing Castle (78)** (WGMTurner) **2-8-4**(5) RHavlin(9) (lw: prom over 2f) | 3½ | **8** | 13/2[3] | 43 | 5 |
| 1713[5] | **Castle House (75)** (JAkehurst) **2-8-6** KFallon(3) (prom tl hrd rdn & wknd 2f out: t.o) | 13 | **9** | 20/1 | 4 | — |
| 2942[8] | **Chilling (65)** (PGMurphy) **2-7-7**(3) MHenry(8) (a bhd) | 2½ | **10** | 25/1 | — | — |

(SP 116.4%) **10 Rn**

**1m 11.0** (1.50) CSF £30.50 CT £313.30 TOTE £6.90: £2.50 £1.70 £3.80 (£13.30) Trio £103.70 OWNER Sir Andrew Lloyd Webber (WHATCOMBE) BRED M. I. Farm

**2728 Maid By The Fire (USA)**, up 6lb, was certainly not winning out of turn but it was a case of the runner-up shooting himself in the foot. (8/1)
**1445* Maserati Monk** could not have picked a worse course to drift away from the inside, and can be considered a winner without a penalty. (3/1)
**3170 Anokato**, without the headgear this time, was done no favours by the runner-up and is certainly at the right end of the handicap. (14/1)
**3121* What Happened Was** could not sustain her run in the closing stages. (7/1)
**3268* I Can't Remember**, raised 4lb, was dropping back from six, and only got going in the later stages. (4/1)
**2527 Bold Spring (IRE)** was rather disappointing on this nursery debut. (13/2)

## 3479 ROYAL CRESCENT H'CAP (0-80) (3-Y.O+) (Class D)

5-00 (5-01) **1m 3f 144y** £3,644.00 (£1,097.00: £531.00: £248.00) Stalls: Low GOING minus 0.41 sec per fur (F)

| | | | | SP | RR | SF |
|---|---|---|---|---|---|---|
| 3205[2] | **Pistol (IRE) (73)** (CAHorgan) **6-9-10** PaulEddery(5) (b.hind: hld up & bhd: hdwy 2f out: sn rdn: led ins fnl f: r.o) | — | **1** | 5/2[1] | 81 | 43 |
| 3113* | **Newport Knight (70)** (RAkehurst) **5-9-7** TQuinn(4) (lw: a.p: led over 1f out tl ins fnl f: r.o) | s.h | **2** | 6/1[2] | 78 | 40 |
| 2341[2] | **Tappeto (70)** (HCandy) **4-9-7** CRutter(8) (lw: hld up & bhd: rdn & hdwy over 1f out: r.o ins fnl f) | 1½ | **3** | 6/1[2] | 76 | 38 |
| 3205[7] | **Taufan Boy (74)** (PWHarris) **3-9-0** GHind(6) (lw: chsd ldr: ev ch over 1f out: one pce) | hd | **4** | 15/2[3] | 80 | 31 |
| 3115[8] | **Platinum Plus (60)** (CADwyer) **4-8-11** KFallon(3) (lw: hld up & bhd: hrd rdn & hdwy 2f out: nt rch ldrs) | 2½ | **5** | 5/2[1] | 62 | 24 |
| 2945[5] | **La Pellegrina (IRE) (68)** (PWChapple-Hyam) **3-8-8** JReid(7) (lw: led tl over 1f out: wknd fnl f) | ¾ | **6** | 16/1 | 69 | 20 |
| 3302[3] | **Fabulous Mtoto (55)** (MSSaunders) **6-8-6** JFEgan(1) (plld hrd: prom tl wknd 2f out) | 3 | **7** | 8/1 | 52 | 14 |
| 2855[7] | **Mua-Tab (68)** (PTWalwyn) **3-8-8** WCarson(2) (hld up & plld hrd: bhd fnl 2f) | 1½ | **8** | 10/1 | 63 | 14 |

(SP 123.6%) **8 Rn**

**2m 31.4** (4.70) CSF £18.20 CT £78.34 TOTE £3.50: £1.40 £1.90 £2.20 (£4.60) OWNER Mrs B. Sumner (PULBOROUGH) BRED David Brogan
WEIGHT FOR AGE 3yo-11lb

**3205 Pistol (IRE)**, beaten at Ascot by Sharpical who won again yesterday, defied a 2lb higher mark. (5/2)
**3113* Newport Knight** very nearly pulled off the hat-trick, despite having gone up 9lb for his two successes at Windsor. (6/1: op 4/1)
**2341 Tappeto** was 2lb higher than when second last time. (6/1)
**2701 Taufan Boy**, without the visor this time, may have found this trip just beyond his best. (15/2: 5/1-8/1)
**Platinum Plus** won five of six starts in the Czech Republic last year. Suited by this longer trip, he never appeared likely to justify market support. (5/2)
**2945 La Pellegrina (IRE)** may need more patient tactics if she is to stay this trip. (16/1)
**3302 Fabulous Mtoto** (8/1: 6/1-9/1)

T/Jkpt: Not won; £42,156.81 to Sandown 14/8/96. T/Plpt: £878.10 (23.72 Tckts). T/Qdpt: £68.60 (20.64 Tckts). KH

# 3116-BEVERLEY (R-H) (Good to firm)
## Wednesday August 14th
WEATHER: fine & sunny WIND: fresh half bhd

### 3480 GRAPE LANE (S) STKS (3-Y.O+) (Class F)
2-00 (2-00) **1m 3f 216y** £2,582.50 (£720.00: £347.50) GOING minus 0.61 sec per fur (F)

| | Horse / details | Dist | Pos | SP | RR | SF |
|---|---|---|---|---|---|---|
| 3130³ | **North Bear (56)** (MrsSJSmith) **4-9-2**(3)ow1 OPears(1) (lw: mde all: styd on wl fnl f) | — | 1 | 15/8² | 59 | — |
| 3273* | **Durham (54)** (RSimpson) **5-9-10b** AClark(4) (hld up: hdwy to chse wnr over 4f out: nt qckn ins fnl f) | ¾ | 2 | 100/30³ | 63 | 4 |
| 3239* | **North Ardar (62)** (JJO'Neill) **6-9-5**(5) SCopp(5) (hld up: effrt on ins & nt clr run over 3f out: smooth hdwy & ev ch over 1f out: sn rdn & kpt on same pce) | 1 | 3 | Evens¹ | 62 | 3 |
| 3353⁹ | **Crambella (IRE)** (GPKelly) **4-8-8**(5) GParkin(2) (in tch: rdn & outpcd 3f out: n.d after) | 8 | 4 | 50/1 | 40 | — |
| | **Pimsboy** (GROldroyd) **9-9-4b** DaleGibson(3) (trckd ldrs tl lost pl 3f out) | 4 | 5 | 50/1 | 40 | — |
| 3298⁸ | **Chesters Quest** (RHollinshead) **4-9-4** WRyan(6) (chsd wnr tl over 4f out: lost pl 3f out: sn bhd & eased) | 26 | 6 | 25/1 | 5 | — |

(SP 115.6%) **6 Rn**

**2m 41.5** (9.10) CSF £8.47 TOTE £2.80: £1.30 £1.60 (£3.80) OWNER Mrs S. Smith (BINGLEY) BRED C. Guest
No bid
North Ardar clmd Mrs JL Rogers £6,000

**3130 North Bear** was allowed to set his own pace. His rider never had to get serious with him and he always looked to be holding the upper hand. (15/8)
**3273* Durham**, a desperate mover, made a sharp forward move off the modest pace turning out of the back straight. After getting almost upsides inside the last, he could then do no more. (100/30)
**3239* North Ardar** met trouble on the inner turning for home. Moving up on the bridle, he came under pressure just inside the last and did not seem to get home. (Evens)

### 3481 ALLDERS OF HULL CLAIMING STKS (3-Y.O+) (Class E)
2-30 (2-30) **1m 100y** £2,945.25 (£882.00: £423.50: £194.25) Stalls: High GOING minus 0.61 sec per fur (F)

| | Horse / details | Dist | Pos | SP | RR | SF |
|---|---|---|---|---|---|---|
| 3109⁷ | **Broctune Gold (69)** (MrsMReveley) **5-9-8** KDarley(5) (mde all: styd on wl fnl f) | — | 1 | 11/10¹ | 70 | 42 |
| *781⁷* | **Sheilas Dream (50)** (RSimpson) **3-8-3**ow1 AClark(1) (chsd ldrs: effrt & swtchd outside over 2f out: hung rt & no imp fnl f) | 1¼ | 2 | 14/1 | 56 | 20 |
| 3048⁴ | **Simand (44)** (GMMoore) **4-8-3** JTate(6) (trckd ldrs: effrt on ins 2f out: kpt on same pce) | 1¾ | 3 | 11/2 | 45 | 17 |
| 2075¹⁸ | **Hi Rock (52)** (JNorton) **4-8-2**(5) GParkin(8) (hdwy on ins over 2f out: n.m.r & swtchd ins fnl f: kpt on wl) | ¾ | 4 | 9/1 | 48 | 20 |
| 3451⁴ | **Irish Sea (USA) (72)** (DNicholls) **3-8-10**(7) JBramhill(7) (sn trckng ldrs: rdn 2f out: sn wknd) | ½ | 5 | 9/2³ | 64 | 29 |
| 2313⁵ | **Parliament Piece (63)** (DNicholls) **10-9-10** AlexGreaves(9) (lw: up: effrt over 3f out: wknd over 1f out) | 1¾ | 6 | 4/1² | 61 | 33 |
| 3410⁶ | **Battle Colours (IRE) (30)** (DonEnricoIncisa) **7-8-9** KimTinkler(2) (lw: chsd ldrs: pushed along & lost pl 4f out: n.d after) | 2½ | 7 | 25/1 | 41 | 13 |
| 2587¹⁴ | **Forget Paris (IRE) (38)** (BSRothwell) **3-8-6** MFenton(4) (dwlt: effrt on outside over 3f out: sn lost pl) | 1¼ | 8 | 33/1 | 43 | 8 |
| 2966⁷ | **Florrie'm (37)** (JLHarris) **3-8-2b¹** JFEgan(3) (trckd ldrs: rdn & hung rt over 2f out: sn wknd) | 12 | 9 | 33/1 | 16 | — |

(SP 127.6%) **9 Rn**

**1m 45.5** (1.50) CSF £18.29 TOTE £2.30: £1.20 £2.60 £1.60 (£21.70) Trio £38.90 OWNER Mrs M. B. Thwaites (SALTBURN) BRED A. J. Poulton (Epping) Ltd
WEIGHT FOR AGE 3yo-7lb

**3109 Broctune Gold** seems to be holding his form much longer this time. After making all and running out a decisive winner, he took it into his head to do a lap of honour. (11/10: op 7/4)
**655 Sheilas Dream**, having her first run for four months, hung under pressure and was never giving anything like her all. (14/1)
**3048 Simand**, back at her best trip, showed a return to form. (11/2)
**1196 Hi Rock**, who had run poorly on her two previous starts, would have finished even closer with more luck in running. (9/1)
**3451 Irish Sea (USA)**, after his controversial run at Redcar, showed a poor action and, with an inexperienced boy aboard, dropped out over a furlong out. (9/2)
**2313 Parliament Piece** (4/1: op 5/2)

### 3482 STRUTHERS AND CARTER H'CAP (0-80) (3-Y.O+) (Class D)
3-00 (3-03) **5f** £4,081.00 (£1,228.00: £594.00: £277.00) Stalls: High GOING minus 0.61 sec per fur (F)

| | Horse / details | Dist | Pos | SP | RR | SF |
|---|---|---|---|---|---|---|
| 3152⁵ | **Brecongill Lad (65)** (MissSEHall) **4-9-2** NConnorton(6) (chsd ldr: led over 1f out: hld on wl) | — | 1 | 8/1 | 73 | 55 |
| 3313⁴ | **Able Sheriff (54)** (MWEasterby) **4-8-0b**(5)ow2 GParkin(5) (a chsng ldr: kpt on wl ins fnl f) | ½ | 2 | 11/1 | 60 | 40 |
| 3352⁵ | **Just Dissident (IRE) (58)** (RMWhitaker) **4-8-9** DeanMcKeown(3) (led tl over 1f out: kpt on same pce) | 1¾ | 3 | 8/1 | 59 | 41 |
| 3049⁶ | **Premium Gift (61)** (CBBBooth) **4-8-12** MBirch(7) (mid div: effrt 2f out: styd on same pce appr fnl f) | nk | 4 | 9/1 | 61 | 43 |
| 3432¹⁴ | **Jucea (73)** (JLSpearing) **7-9-10** JFEgan(1) (outpcd: rdn ½-wy: styd on appr fnl f) | 3 | 5 | 7/1³ | 63 | 45 |
| 3352² | **Ned's Bonanza (59)** (MDods) **7-8-10** AClark(8) (lw: in tch: effrt 2f out: grad wknd) | ¾ | 6 | 11/4¹ | 47 | 29 |
| 3294⁴ | **Rotherfield Park (IRE) (45)** (CSmith) **4-7-3**(7) IonaWands(4) (chsd ldrs on outside: wknd over 1f out) | 1½ | 7 | 20/1 | 28 | 10 |
| 3352* | **Rich Glow (67)** (NBycroft) **5-9-4** 7x KDarley(9) (in tch: rdn & outpcd ½-wy: sn wknd) | nk | 8 | 7/1³ | 49 | 31 |
| 3352³ | **Captain Carat (65)** (MrsJRRamsden) **5-9-2** KFallon(10) (b.nr fore: n.d) | 3 | 9 | 4/1² | 38 | 20 |
| 2777⁴ | **The Wad (70)** (DNicholls) **3-9-4** WRyan(2) (lw: s.s: a in rr) | s.h | 10 | 16/1 | 42 | 21 |

(SP 122.9%) **10 Rn**

**61.2 secs** (-0.30) CSF £85.52 CT £674.89 TOTE £9.30: £2.40 £3.60 £2.70 (£37.90) Trio £253.40 OWNER Three Horse Shoes Partnership (MIDDLEHAM) BRED Miss S. E. Hall
LONG HANDICAP Rotherfield Park (IRE) 7-2
WEIGHT FOR AGE 3yo-3lb

**3152 Brecongill Lad**, who has slipped down the weights, was soon racing in the plum spot on the far rail and, in the end, he did more than enough. (8/1)
**3313 Able Sheriff**, back over his best trip, never gave up trying and was closing the gap all the way to the line. (11/1)
**3352 Just Dissident (IRE)** showed bags of toe to overcome his poor draw, but he had no more to give entering the last. (8/1)
**3049 Premium Gift** put her poor effort of last time behind her. Pulled towards the centre to make her effort, she was never doing anything like enough. (9/1)
**2976 Jucea** struggled badly to go the pace, but was making inroads inside the last. She is just below her best at present. (7/1)
**3352 Ned's Bonanza** was struggling at halfway. (11/4)

## 3483 CONTRAC-IMATION NURSERY H'CAP (2-Y.O) (Class D)

3-30 (3-31) **5f** £4,315.00 (£1,300.00: £630.00: £295.00) Stalls: High GOING minus 0.61 sec per fur (F)

| Form | Horse and running | Dist | Pos | SP | RR | SF |
|---|---|---|---|---|---|---|
| $3247^{5}$ | **For Old Times Sake (100)** (JBerry) **2-9-2**$^{(5)}$ MBaird(5) (s.i.s: hdwy on outside ½-wy: led & edgd rt over 1f out: hld on towards fin) | — | 1 | $4/1^{3}$ | 91 | 44 |
| 2755* | **Double-J (IRE) (84)** (KMcAuliffe) **2-8-5**$^{ow1}$ KFallon(4) (lw: sn chsng ldrs: kpt on wl ins fnl f) | nk | 2 | $5/2^{1}$ | 74 | 26 |
| 2625* | **Pension Fund (75)** (MWEasterby) **2-7-10** DaleGibson(6) (chsd ldrs: sn drvn along: styd on wl fnl f) | hd | 3 | $3/1^{2}$ | 65 | 18 |
| $2700^{6}$ | **Largesse (89)** (JohnBerry) **2-8-10** MFenton(1) (swvd rt s: sn chsng ldrs: styng on one pce whn n.m.r 1f out) | ½ | 4 | 5/1 | 77 | 30 |
| 3299* | **Skyers Flyer (IRE) (87)** (RonaldThompson) **2-8-8** 7x NConnorton(3) (sn trckng ldrs: wknd over 1f out) | 1¼ | 5 | 11/2 | 71 | 24 |
| $3268^{3}$ | **Weet Ees Girl (IRE) (87)** (PDEvans) **2-8-8** JFEgan(2) (led tl over 1f out: sn wknd) | 7 | 6 | 9/1 | 49 | 2 |

(SP 115.6%) **6 Rn**

**62.2 secs** (0.70) CSF £14.15 TOTE £5.00: £3.00 £1.60 (£6.70) OWNER Mrs Bridget Blum (COCKERHAM) BRED Shutford Stud
LONG HANDICAP Pension Fund 7-9

**3247 For Old Times Sake** is not very big, but he is all heart and did this the hard way. Missing the break slightly and negating his favourable draw, he had to make his effort on the wide outside but did just enough to become the first two-year-old this season to record five victories. (4/1)

**2755* Double-J (IRE)**, a poor mover, stuck on strongly inside the last, but was never quite going to get there. He will be better suited by six. (5/2)

**2625* Pension Fund**, soon driven along to keep up, put in some solid work in the final furlong. Improving physically all the time, he will be much better suited by six or even seven. (3/1)

**2361* Largesse**, worst drawn, was getting nowhere when the winner went across him. (5/1)

## 3484 HULL DAILY MAIL H'CAP (0-70) (3-Y.O) (Class E)

4-00 (4-01) **1m 1f 207y** £4,003.00 (£1,204.00: £582.00: £271.00) GOING minus 0.61 sec per fur (F)

| Form | Horse and running | Dist | Pos | SP | RR | SF |
|---|---|---|---|---|---|---|
| $1783^{9}$ | **Cumbrian Maestro (52)** (TDEasterby) **3-8-4** KDarley(6) (mde all: qcknd over 3f out: clr over 1f out: unchal) | — | 1 | 16/1 | 66 | — |
| $2688^{3}$ | **Isitoff (69)** (SCWilliams) **3-9-4**$^{(3)}$ PMcCabe(4) (trckd wnr: styd on appr fnl f: no imp) | 2½ | 2 | $7/1^{3}$ | 79 | 4 |
| 3283* | **General Glow (49)** (PDEvans) **3-8-1** 5x JFEgan(2) (trckd ldrs: effrt over 3f out: kpt on one pce fnl 2f) | 2 | 3 | $4/7^{1}$ | 56 | — |
| $3354^{5}$ | **Contract Bridge (IRE) (46)** (CWThornton) **3-7-12** LCharnock(3) (s.s: sn in tch: rdn & outpcd over 2f out: kpt on fnl f) | hd | 4 | $7/2^{2}$ | 53 | — |
| $3220^{13}$ | **Galapino (60)** (CEBrittain) **3-8-5**$^{(7)}$ JGotobed(5) (swtg: chsd ldrs: edgd lft & lost pl 2f out) | 6 | 5 | 12/1 | 57 | — |

(SP 111.9%) **5 Rn**

**2m 8.8** (6.30) CSF £92.85 TOTE £9.40: £2.70 £2.50 (£30.70) OWNER Cumbrian Industrials Ltd (MALTON) BRED Bearstone Stud

**1477 Cumbrian Maestro**, without the headgear, was able to set his own pace. Stepping up the gallop turning in, he was driven clear over a furlong out and was never in any danger. His rider deserves full marks for this and his trainer reports that Cumbrian Maestro jumps well and is a likely juvenile hurdler. (16/1)

**2688 Isitoff**, warm beforehand, gave the winner first run. The drop in distance did nothing for him. (7/1)

**3283* General Glow**, on his toes beforehand, was caught out when the winner stepped up the gallop and had no chance of getting back on terms. Brighton form rarely works out elsewhere. (4/7)

**2752 Contract Bridge (IRE)** walked out of the stalls but, thanks to the pedestrian pace, was soon in touch. Tapped for foot once in line for home, she was staying on when it was all over. She needs a more truly-run race. (7/2)

**2334 Galapino**, short of room on the inside six furlongs out, showed a very poor action and dropped right away in the final two furlongs. (12/1)

## 3485 JOURNAL MAIDEN STKS (2-Y.O) (Class D)

4-30 (4-31) **7f 100y** £3,847.00 (£1,156.00: £558.00: £259.00) GOING minus 0.61 sec per fur (F)

| Form | Horse and running | Dist | Pos | SP | RR | SF |
|---|---|---|---|---|---|---|
| $3131^{2}$ | **Further Outlook (USA)** (MRStoute) **2-9-0** KFallon(1) (b.off hind: mde all: styd on strly fnl 2f: pushed out) | — | 1 | $5/4^{1}$ | 85+ | 51 |
| $2802^{2}$ | **Stories To Tell (USA)** (HRACecil) **2-9-0** WRyan(2) (lw: a chsng wnr: kpt on fnl 2f: no imp) | 2 | 2 | $5/4^{1}$ | 81 | 47 |
| $2923^{3}$ | **Maradi (IRE) (80)** (DMorley) **2-9-0** KDarley(5) (lw: chsd ldrs: ev ch & rdn over 2f out: one pce appr fnl f) | 8 | 3 | $5/1^{2}$ | 64 | 30 |
| $2887^{8}$ | **Ibin St James** (JDBethell) **2-9-0** AClark(4) (dwlt: bhd tl styd on appr fnl f) | hd | 4 | 33/1 | 63 | 29 |
| $2720^{7}$ | **Tirage** (CEBrittain) **2-8-7**$^{(7)}$ JGotobed(7) (hld up & plld hrd: styd on appr fnl f: nvr nr ldrs) | ½ | 5 | 33/1 | 62 | 28 |
| $1445^{5}$ | **Secret Pass (USA)** (EALDunlop) **2-9-0** JTate(6) (trckd ldrs: effrt over 2f out: sn wknd) | 1¾ | 6 | 33/1 | 59 | 25 |
| $2977^{4}$ | **Triple Term** (JLDunlop) **2-9-0** DRMcCabe(3) (unruly stalls: hld up & bhd: sme hdwy 2f out: n.d) | nk | 7 | $20/1^{3}$ | 58 | 24 |
| $2224^{12}$ | **Mutahadeth** (NAGraham) **2-9-0** MFenton(8) (bit bkwd: sn bhd: drvn 4f out: sn lost tch) | 5 | 8 | 33/1 | 47 | 13 |

(SP 122.1%) **8 Rn**

**1m 31.8** (-0.20) CSF £3.34 TOTE £2.20: £1.10 £1.10 £1.10 (£2.00) OWNER Mr Mana Al Maktoum (NEWMARKET) BRED Gainsborough Farm Inc.

**3131 Further Outlook (USA)** has a good attitude and had only to be pushed out. He had clearly learnt a lot from his first run. (5/4: op 4/5)

**2802 Stories To Tell (USA)** never looked like getting in a serious blow at the winner, but he finished well clear of the rest. His turn will surely come. (5/4)

**2923 Maradi (IRE)**, who showed plenty of knee-action going down, was on the heels of the first two early in the straight but was hopelessly outpaced coming to the final furlong. He was beaten a fair way in the end and his future surely lies in handicap company. (5/1)

**Ibin St James**, a tall sort, showed a lot of knee-action going down. Staying on late in the day, stamina will be his strong suit. (33/1)

## 3486 CHARLES ELSEY MEMORIAL CHALLENGE TROPHY H'CAP (0-80) (3-Y.O+) (Class D)

5-00 (5-00) **2m 35y** £4,406.00 (£1,328.00: £644.00: £302.00) GOING minus 0.61 sec per fur (F)

| Form | Horse and running | Dist | Pos | SP | RR | SF |
|---|---|---|---|---|---|---|
| 3309* | **Rushen Raider (68)** (KWHogg) **4-9-2** 5x LCharnock(7) (chsd ldrs: led 2f out: styd on strly fnl f) | — | 1 | 20/1 | 79 | 59 |
| $3266^{3}$ | **Embryonic (IRE) (78)** (RFFisher) **4-9-12** KFallon(5) (lw: hld up: stdy hdwy over 3f out: chsd wnr over 1f out: nt qckn) | 2½ | 2 | $6/1^{3}$ | 87 | 67 |
| $3037^{5}$ | **Great Oration (IRE) (55)** (FWatson) **7-8-3** NKennedy(3) (lw: bhd: pushed along 10f out: hdwy over 2f out: kpt one pce) | 3 | 3 | 8/1 | 61 | 41 |
| $2247^{5}$ | **Double Agent (74)** (MJohnston) **3-8-7** WRyan(1) (lw: hdwy to chse ldrs 10f out: outpcd 4f out: kpt on fnl 2f) | s.h | 4 | $6/1^{3}$ | 80 | 45 |
| $3149^{3}$ | **Candle Smoke (USA) (66)** (GHarwood) **3-7-13** JFEgan(4) (hung lft thrght: w ldr: led over 2f out: sn hdd: wknd over 1f out) | 7 | 5 | $5/1^{2}$ | 65 | 30 |
| 3266* | **Sea Victor (80)** (JLHarris) **4-10-0** MFenton(9) (lw: in tch: rdn 5f out: lost pl 2f out: eased) | 17 | 6 | 13/2 | 62 | 42 |
| 2990* | **The Swan (80)** (JLDunlop) **3-8-13** KDarley(8) (b: mde most tl over 2f out: sn lost pl & eased) | 12 | 7 | $5/2^{1}$ | 50 | 15 |
| $2952^{2}$ | **Classic Colleen (IRE) (75)** (RHarris) **3-8-5**$^{(3)}$ PMcCabe(2) (hdwy 9f out: sn chsng ldrs: edgd lft & lost pl over 2f out: virtually p.u) | 11 | 8 | 11/1 | 34 | — |

**College Don (66)** (MPBielby) **5-9-0** DRMcCabe(6) (b: trckd ldrs tl p.u 7f out).................................................... **P** 25/1 — —
(SP 115.2%) **9 Rn**

**3m 29.3** (0.80 under best) (-1.20) CSF £122.14 CT £959.00 TOTE £14.00: £3.00 £2.20 £2.10 (£41.30) Trio £66.10 OWNER Mrs Thelma White (ISLE OF MAN) BRED M. H. D. Madden and Partners
WEIGHT FOR AGE 3yo-15lb

**3309* Rushen Raider**, who has been making hay in sellers and claimers, proved well suited by the step up in distance. In a race run in record time, he won going away. (20/1)
**3266 Embryonic (IRE)** travelled strongly on the bridle for much of the way but, when the race began in earnest, he lacked the pace to get in a serious blow at the winner. (6/1)
**3037 Great Oration (IRE)**, unusually for him, struggled to go the pace and ran a bit flat. (8/1)
**2247 Double Agent**, who won twice in three days on his first two outings, was reappearing after a month and a half absence. Running flat on the home turn, he was sticking on at the finish and the outing will have blown away the cobwebs. (6/1)
**2990* The Swan**, an habitual tail-swisher, set a strong pace but was given no peace and was harried throughout. After being collared, she tired badly, and her rider allowed her to come home in her own time. (5/2)

T/Plpt: £392.60 (30.23 Tckts). T/Qdpt: £53.70 (19.8 Tckts). WG

# 3342-HAMILTON (R-H) (Good to firm)
## Wednesday August 14th
WEATHER: sunny WIND: almost nil

## 3487 ARIZONA H'CAP (0-80) (3-Y.O+) (Class D)
6-00 (6-01) **1m 5f 9y** £3,820.00 (£1,156.00: £564.00: £268.00) Stalls: High GOING minus 0.51 sec per fur (F)

| | Horse | Dist | Pos | SP | RR | SF |
|---|---|---|---|---|---|---|
| 3117* | **Mister Aspecto (IRE) (68)** (MJohnston) **3-8-13v** JWeaver(4) (mde all: qcknd 1f out: shkn up & kpt on wl fnl f) | — | 1 | 4/1 2 | 77 | 48 |
| 3347 2 | **Mentalasanythin (63)** (DHaydnJones) **7-9-6** AMackay(1) (hld up: effrt 4f out: hdwy 2f out: styd on u.p: nvr able to chal) | 1 | 2 | 3/1 1 | 71 | 54 |
| 3056 2 | **Field of Vision (IRE) (71)** (MrsASwinbank) **6-9-11**(3) FLynch(3) (lw: hld up: effrt over 3f out: chsng ldrs appr fnl f: kpt on) | nk | 3 | 8/1 | 78 | 61 |
| 3347 3 | **Red Spectacle (IRE) (48)** (PCHaslam) **4-7-12**(7) RMullen(7) (lw: dwlt: chsng ldrs after 2f: chal 4f out: hung lft 3f out: sn outpcd) | 2½ | 4 | 7/1 3 | 52 | 35 |
| 3297 2 | **Floating Line (66)** (EJAlston) **8-9-9** MWigham(6) (cl up tl outpcd 4f out: eased whn btn fnl f) | 7 | 5 | 3/1 1 | 62 | 45 |
| 3290 3 | **Lord Advocate (51)** (DANolan) **8-8-5b**(3) NVarley(2) (chsd ldrs tl outpcd fnl 4f) | 4 | 6 | 12/1 | 42 | 25 |
| 3276 4 | **Rossel (USA) (65)** (PMonteith) **3-8-10** NCarlisle(5) (in tch: effrt 4f out: sn btn) | 5 | 7 | 14/1 | 50 | 21 |

(SP 108.0%) **7 Rn**

**2m 47.2** (1.50) CSF £14.76 TOTE £3.80: £2.10 £1.80 (£8.30) OWNER Aspecto Clothing Co Ltd (MIDDLEHAM) BRED Petra Bloodstock Agency Ltd
WEIGHT FOR AGE 3yo-12lb

**3117* Mister Aspecto (IRE)**, who really enjoys being out in front, was again allowed to dictate things and was always finding plenty when challenged. (4/1)
**3347 Mentalasanythin** took time to get going and, despite keeping on well, had always given the winner too much start. (3/1)
**3056 Field of Vision (IRE)** ran another sound race, but was never doing quite enough in the closing stages. (8/1: op 5/1)
**3347 Red Spectacle (IRE)**, after missing the break, was not given such an aggressive ride this time and that was probably his undoing. (7/1)
**3297 Floating Line**, feeling the pace with half a mile to go, gave the impression that this ground was a bit too firm for his liking, and he was not overpunished. (3/1)
**3290 Lord Advocate** was never really firing. (12/1: op 6/1)
**3276 Rossel (USA)** is doing particularly well physically and, given some easier ground, is likely to run better. He is certainly one to watch for the jumping game. (14/1: op 8/1)

## 3488 ARIZONA (S) STKS (2-Y.O) (Class F)
6-30 (6-30) **5f 4y** £2,549.00 (£714.00: £347.00) Stalls: Low GOING minus 0.51 sec per fur (F)

| | Horse | Dist | Pos | SP | RR | SF |
|---|---|---|---|---|---|---|
| 3321 5 | **Hit Or Miss (69)** (MRChannon) **2-8-11** AMackay(1) (hld up: hdwy over 1f out: led wl ins fnl f: all out) | — | 1 | 5/1 3 | 60 | 7 |
| 3110 4 | **Wedding Music (58)** (PCHaslam) **2-8-6** JFortune(3) (led tl wl ins fnl f: rallied) | nk | 2 | 11/1 | 54 | 1 |
| 3332 3 | **Hever Golf Stormer (IRE) (64)** (TJNaughton) **2-8-8**(3) FLynch(4) (in tch: effrt & n.m.r 1f out: styd on towards fin) | 2 | 3 | 100/30 2 | 53 | — |
| 3224 6 | **Melbourne Princess (67)** (RMWhitaker) **2-8-3**(3) NVarley(5) (lw: chsd ldrs: edgd rt over 1f out: nt qckn) | 2 | 4 | 3/1 1 | 41 | — |
| 3343 4 | **Sheraton Girl (60)** (MJohnston) **2-8-6b**1 JWeaver(6) (cl up tl rdn & btn 1f out) | ¾ | 5 | 100/30 2 | 39 | — |
| 2422 2 | **Where's Wally (IRE) (44)** (JBerry) **2-8-11b** JFanning(2) (lw: cl up tl rdn & btn appr fnl f) | 3 | 6 | 13/2 | 34 | — |

(SP 109.5%) **6 Rn**

**61.0 secs** (2.70) CSF £43.79 TOTE £3.80: £1.90 £4.20 (£18.30) OWNER Mr Brian Lovrey (UPPER LAMBOURN) BRED B. Lovrey
Sold ADinsmore 5,400 gns

**3321 Hit Or Miss** has really filled out since the beginning of the season and, given a fine ride, won most determinedly. (5/1: 4/1-6/1)
**3110 Wedding Music**, from a yard that has just struck form, put up a brave attempt to make all and, judging by the way she kept battling back, it suggests that further will suit. (11/1: 8/1-12/1)
**3332 Hever Golf Stormer (IRE)** got slightly messed about when beginning his run approaching the final furlong, but he was basically short of a turn of foot, and may need a slightly longer trip. (100/30)
**3224 Melbourne Princess** has plenty of speed, but got unbalanced when the pressure was on. (3/1)
**3343 Sheraton Girl**, much sharper in the blinkers, finally cried enough when serious pressure was applied approaching the last furlong. (100/30)
**2422 Where's Wally (IRE)**, having his second run in the blinkers, found little when off the bit. (13/2)

## 3489 ARTHUR BALDING H'CAP (0-70) (3-Y.O+) (Class E)
7-00 (7-01) **6f 5y** £3,631.25 (£1,100.00: £537.50: £256.25) Stalls: Low GOING minus 0.51 sec per fur (F)

| | Horse | Dist | Pos | SP | RR | SF |
|---|---|---|---|---|---|---|
| 3045 8 | **Pageboy (58)** (PCHaslam) **7-9-4** JFortune(8) (lw: mde all: qcknd clr appr fnl f: comf) | — | 1 | 9/2 | 72+ | 52 |
| 3342 3 | **Pathaze (48)** (NBycroft) **3-8-4** JFanning(4) (lw: a chsng ldrs: kpt on: no ch w wnr) | 3 | 2 | 8/1 | 54 | 30 |
| 3342 4 | **Natural Key (58)** (DHaydnJones) **3-9-0** AMackay(6) (lw: chsd ldrs: effrt 2f out: nt qckn fnl f) | ¾ | 3 | 3/1 2 | 62 | 38 |

| Form | Horse | Dist | Pos | SP | RR | SF |
|---|---|---|---|---|---|---|
| 3342* | **Tropical Beach (61)** (JBerry) **3-8-10**(7) CLowther(2) (bhd: hdwy ½-wy: sn chsng ldrs: nt qckn fnl f) | s.h | **4** | 9/4[1] | 65 | 41 |
| 3424[15] | **Naissant (65)** (RMMcKellar) **3-9-7** SDWilliams(3) (in tch: outpcd 2f out: n.d after) | 8 | **5** | 100/1 | 48 | 24 |
| 3424[5] | **Mister Westsound (68)** (MissLAPerratt) **4-10-0b** JWeaver(1) (s.i.s: hdwy ½-wy: no imp) | 7 | **6** | 7/2[3] | 32 | 12 |
| 3100[5] | **Rinus Manor (IRE) (48)** (EJAlston) **5-8-8** JLowe(7) (lw: prom to ½-wy: sn rdn & btn) | 3½ | **7** | 50/1 | 3 | — |
| | **Gymcrak Jareer (IRE) (48)** (DANolan) **4-8-8** VHalliday(5) (outpcd & bhd fr ½-wy) | 6 | **8** | 200/1 | — | — |

(SP 110.7%) **8 Rn**

**1m 10.4** (0.40) CSF £34.63 CT £107.48 TOTE £4.60: £1.60 £1.40 £1.50 (£10.60) OWNER Lord Scarsdale (MIDDLEHAM) BRED K. T. Ivory and Partners
WEIGHT FOR AGE 3yo-4lb

**2757 Pageboy** returned to form with a vengeance here. He is well handicapped and further success looks likely. (9/2)
**3342 Pathaze** ran a sound race but, despite keeping on, was never anything like a match for the winner. (8/1)
**3342 Natural Key** looks as well as ever, but always found this well beyond her when the pace was really on in the last couple of furlongs. (3/1)
**3342* Tropical Beach** found this far too competitive and was never doing enough in the last furlong and a half. (9/4)
**3240 Naissant** ran reasonably and is at last beginning to slip down the handicap. (100/1)
**3424 Mister Westsound** never showed any sparkle on this occasion and was obviously not in the mood. (7/2)

## 3490 ARIZONA MAIDEN H'CAP (0-60) (3-Y.O+) (Class F)
7-30 (7-31) **1m 3f 16y** £2,906.00 (£816.00: £398.00) GOING minus 0.51 sec per fur (F)

| Form | Horse | Dist | Pos | SP | RR | SF |
|---|---|---|---|---|---|---|
| 2602[10] | **Classic Beauty (IRE) (60)** (RHarris) **3-9-10** AMackay(6) (lw: hld up: hdwy 3f out: rdn to ld ins fnl f: r.o) | — | **1** | 3/1[2] | 71 | 36 |
| 2851[12] | **Black and Blues (24)** (JSGoldie) **10-7-12**ow2 TWilliams(1) (led tl ins fnl f) | 4 | **2** | 33/1 | 29 | 2 |
| 3238[3] | **Gulf of Siam (60)** (MissSEHall) **3-9-10** MBirch(2) (b: trckd ldrs: effrt 3f out: sn rdn & no rspnse) | 2 | **3** | 6/4[1] | 62 | 27 |
| | **In A Tizzy (35)** (PCHaslam) **3-7-6**(7) RMullen(3) (trckd ldrs: chal 4f out: sn rdn: wknd fnl 2f) | 3 | **4** | 100/30[3] | 33 | — |
| 3425[8] | **School of Science (25)** (DANolan) **6-7-10b**(3) NVarley(5) (chsd ldrs tl outpcd fnl 4f) | 3 | **5** | 10/1 | 19 | — |
| 3289[13] | **Rambo's Rumtime (34)** (FWatson) **4-8-8** DeanMcKeown(4) (bit bkwd: lost tch fnl 4f) | 8 | **6** | 25/1 | 16 | — |

(SP 104.0%) **6 Rn**

**2m 23.8** (4.40) CSF £48.86 TOTE £4.40: £1.90 £9.10 (£88.80) OWNER Classic Bloodstock Plc (NEWMARKET) BRED J. P. McManus
WEIGHT FOR AGE 3yo-10lb

**2168 Classic Beauty (IRE)** has obviously been crying out for this trip and beat this very moderate opposition in good style. (3/1)
**Black and Blues**, stepping up in trip, was trying front-running tactics and it improved him, but he was well outpointed in the last furlong. (33/1)
**3238 Gulf of Siam** either hates racing or more likely this firm ground, as he was never co-operating. (6/4)
**In A Tizzy**, having her first run of the season, ran reasonably until crying enough two furlongs out. (100/30)
**3239 School of Science** is too headstrong for his own good. (10/1)

## 3491 ARIZONA CLAIMING STKS (3-Y.O) (Class F)
8-00 (8-00) **1m 65y** £2,577.00 (£722.00: £351.00) Stalls: High GOING minus 0.51 sec per fur (F)

| Form | Horse | Dist | Pos | SP | RR | SF |
|---|---|---|---|---|---|---|
| 2780[6] | **Society Girl (57)** (CWThornton) **3-8-13** DeanMcKeown(1) (b.nr hind: cl up: led 3f out: kpt on wl fnl f) | — | **1** | 3/1[2] | 66 | 36 |
| 3059[4] | **Dil Dil (43)** (WJHaggas) **3-7-12**(3) FLynch(3) (trckd ldrs: hdwy to disp ld 2f out: sn hdd: kpt on same pce) | 1 | **2** | 100/30[3] | 52 | 22 |
| 3427[4] | **Miletrian City (53)** (JBerry) **3-9-0b** JFortune(5) (lw: trckd ldrs: outpcd 2f out: kpt on u.p fnl f) | hd | **3** | 5/2[1] | 65 | 35 |
| 3116[2] | **Veshca Lady (IRE) (43)** (EWeymes) **3-7-13** JLowe(4) (in tch: effrt over 3f out: sn hrd rdn & one pce) | 2½ | **4** | 5/1 | 45 | 15 |
| 3238[4] | **Termon (58)** (MissLAPerratt) **3-8-13** JWeaver(2) (led to 3f out: sn wknd) | 8 | **5** | 6/1 | 44 | 14 |

(SP 107.6%) **5 Rn**

**1m 46.2** (2.10) CSF £11.84 TOTE £3.50: £1.80 £2.50 (£4.40) OWNER Mr Guy Reed (MIDDLEHAM) BRED G. Reed

**2780 Society Girl** always held a good position and, once in front, gave the impression that there was always a bit more to come. (3/1)
**3059 Dil Dil** had her chances and almost caught the winner by surprise two furlongs out, but she was quickly put in her place. (100/30)
**3427 Miletrian City**, covered up as much as he could be in this small field, had to struggle some way out and the task was beyond him. (5/2)
**3116 Veshca Lady (IRE)** is either very slow or is just not doing it, as she failed to offer a real threat on this occasion. (5/1)
**3238 Termon** is not giving her form at all of late and seems, for the time being, to have lost her way. (6/1)

## 3492 ARIZONA BEVERAGES MAIDEN H'CAP (0-65) (3-Y.O+) (Class F)
8-30 (8-30) **1m 65y** £2,976.00 (£836.00: £408.00) GOING minus 0.51 sec per fur (F)

| Form | Horse | Dist | Pos | SP | RR | SF |
|---|---|---|---|---|---|---|
| 3138[4] | **Allstars Rocket (48)** (TJNaughton) **3-8-13** JFortune(9) (trckd ldrs: rdn to ld ins fnl f: styd on strly) | — | **1** | 3/1[2] | 63 | 34 |
| 3286[2] | **Flying Harold (41)** (MRChannon) **3-8-6** AMackay(4) (lw: led: hrd rdn over 1f out: hdd & no ex ins fnl f) | 3½ | **2** | 9/4[1] | 49 | 20 |
| 3344[10] | **Seconds Away (29)** (JSGoldie) **5-8-1** TWilliams(2) (hld up: hdwy & ev ch 2f out: nt qckn fnl f) | 1¾ | **3** | 10/1 | 34 | 12 |
| 3354[4] | **Gool Lee Shay (USA) (57)** (RMWhitaker) **3-9-1**(7) PFredericks(8) (lw: bhd: hdwy 3f out: hung lft: nvr rchd ldrs) | 4 | **4** | 9/1 | 54 | 25 |
| 2913[5] | **Shamokin (48)** (FWatson) **4-9-6** DeanMcKeown(6) (lw: bhd tl styd on fnl 3f) | ½ | **5** | 20/1 | 44 | 22 |
| 3345[6] | **Shaa Spin (47)** (JBerry) **4-9-5** SDWilliams(10) (chsd ldrs: ev ch 2f out: wknd over 1f out) | 3 | **6** | 25/1 | 37 | 15 |
| 2895[3] | **Phantom Haze (63)** (MissSEHall) **3-10-0** MBirch(1) (hld up: hdwy 4f out: wknd 2f out) | 2 | **7** | 6/1 | 50 | 21 |
| *2935*[7] | **Oxgang (IRE) (41)** (JGFitzGerald) **3-8-6b**[1]ow1 JWeaver(3) (chsd ldrs tl wknd fnl 4f) | 1¾ | **8** | 11/2[3] | 24 | — |
| 2154[12] | **Ballykissangel (32)** (NBycroft) **3-7-8**(3) NVarley(7) (lost tch fnl 4f) | 4 | **9** | 50/1 | 8 | — |
| 3414[7] | **Carmenoura (IRE) (25)** (EJAlston) **4-7-11v**[1] JLowe(5) (lw: prom to ½-wy: sn bhd) | 4 | **10** | 50/1 | — | — |

(SP 117.1%) **10 Rn**

**1m 46.5** (2.40) CSF £9.79 CT £53.38 TOTE £3.90: £2.00 £1.40 £2.40 (£3.70) Trio £37.00 OWNER The Allstars Club (EPSOM) BRED Alvecote Stud
WEIGHT FOR AGE 3yo-7lb

**3138 Allstars Rocket**, an attractive sort, got better as the race progressed and, judging by the manner in which he won, he should have no difficulty in getting further. (3/1)
**3286 Flying Harold**, looking really fit, tried hard to make all but was well and truly outstayed. (9/4: op 6/4)
**3236 Seconds Away**, on his twenty-eighth attempt over various distances, ran one of his better races but was never doing enough at the business end. (10/1: 8/1-12/1)
**3354 Gool Lee Shay (USA)** tried to come from behind this time, but was certainly not helped by continually hanging left. (9/1: 6/1-10/1)
**2913 Shamokin** is getting the hang of things, but he was continually changing his legs on this firm ground, and there would seem to be plenty of improvement in him once he gets it fully together. (20/1)
**3345 Shaa Spin**, an edgy sort, had her chances until her stamina gave out in the last two furlongs. (25/1)

T/Plpt: £296.50 (36.17 Tckts). T/Qdpt: £47.50 (21.47 Tckts). AA

# 3162-SALISBURY (R-H) (Good)
## Wednesday August 14th
WEATHER: fine WIND: almost nil

### 3493 ISLE OF WIGHT MAIDEN STKS (I) (2-Y.O) (Class D)
1-45 (1-49) **6f 212y** £3,216.50 (£962.00: £461.00: £210.50) Stalls: Centre GOING minus 0.46 sec per fur (F)

| | | | SP | RR | SF |
|---|---|---|---|---|---|
| 3147[3] | **Orontes (USA)** (RHannon) **2-8-11**(3) DaneO'Neill(3) (plld hrd early: chsd ldr: rdn to ld wl ins fnl f)................— | **1** | 2/1[1] | 79 | 9 |
| | **Inclination** (MBlanshard) **2-8-9** JQuinn(11) (w'like: scope: led: qcknd clr over 2f out: rdn & hdd wl ins fnl f)....½ | **2** | 25/1 | 73? | 3 |
| 2413[7] | **Salabatni** (EALDunlop) **2-8-9** MHills(6) (lw: hld up & bhd: hdwy 2f out: r.o ins fnl f)........................................1¼ | **3** | 14/1 | 70 | — |
| | **Sword Arm** (RCharlton) **2-9-0** TSprake(7) (scope: lw: hld up & bhd: hdwy over 2f out: rdn over 1f out: r.o ins fnl f)........................................1¼ | **4** | 11/4[2] | 72? | 2 |
| | **Rasmussen (IRE)** (JHMGosden) **2-9-0** RCochrane(8) (unf: scope: lw: hld up & bhd: hdwy over 1f out: r.o)...nk | **5** | 9/2[3] | 71+ | 1 |
| | **Swan Island** (BPalling) **2-8-9** DHarrison(9) (b: leggy: scope: bit bkwd: prom tl wknd over 1f out) ..................nk | **6** | 33/1 | 66 | — |
| 3319[11] | **Palaemon** (GBBalding) **2-9-0** SDrowne(2) (rdn over 3f out: nvr nr to chal) ........................................1¾ | **7** | 16/1 | 67 | — |
| 2985[4] | **Julietta Mia (USA)** (BWHills) **2-8-4**(5) JDSmith(10) (swtg: bhd fnl 2f)........................................1¼ | **8** | 16/1 | 59 | — |
| 3131[8] | **River King** (RHannon) **2-9-0** WJO'Connor(4) (hld up mid div: hmpd over 3f out: bhd fnl 2f)...........................nk | **9** | 33/1 | 63 | — |
| 3044[4] | **Ludo** (RHannon) **2-9-0** JReid(1) (prom over 4f)........................................¾ | **10** | 10/1 | 61 | — |
| | **Fantasy Girl (IRE)** (JLDunlop) **2-8-9** SWhitworth(5) (neat: bit bkwd: s.s: a bhd)........................................2 | **11** | 14/1 | 52 | — |
| | | | (SP 122.1%) | | **11 Rn** |

**1m 30.66** (4.66) CSF £45.92 TOTE £2.90: £1.40 £5.10 £3.80 (£139.90) Trio £172.30; £106.83 to Salisbury 15/8/96 OWNER Mr J. A. Lazzari (MARLBOROUGH) BRED Mrs J. G. Jones Jr

**3147 Orontes (USA)** appreciated the seventh furlong and O'Neill timed his run to perfection. (2/1)
**Inclination** did everything right but win and this good-looking sort looks sure to find a race. (25/1)
**1467 Salabatni** looked better over this trip than she had in previous efforts over six furlongs. (14/1)
**Sword Arm** needed the run and looks likely to improve. (11/4)
**Rasmussen (IRE)**, the pick of the paddock, took a while to get going and is bred to stay further. (9/2)
**Swan Island**, a big, plain filly whose dam won on the Flat and over hurdles, ran surprisingly well for a long way. (33/1)
**3044 Ludo** (10/1: op 6/1)

### 3494 E.B.F. SANDOWN MAIDEN STKS (2-Y.O) (Class D)
2-15 (2-17) **6f** £3,886.00 (£1,168.00: £564.00: £262.00) Stalls: High GOING minus 0.46 sec per fur (F)

| | | | SP | RR | SF |
|---|---|---|---|---|---|
| | **Mukaddar (USA)** (CJBenstead) **2-9-0** RCochrane(1) (unf: lw: hld up: hdwy 3f out: rdn to ld ins fnl f: r.o wl)..— | **1** | 20/1 | 81 | 36 |
| 3164[4] | **Polish Warrior (IRE)** (PWChapple-Hyam) **2-9-0** JReid(2) (lw: a.p: led over 1f out tl ins fnl f)............................2 | **2** | 9/2[2] | 76 | 31 |
| 2302[5] | **Green Power** (JRFanshawe) **2-9-0** DHarrison(4) (a.p: led 2f out tl over 1f out: one pce) ..............................1¾ | **3** | 9/4[1] | 71 | 26 |
| 3069[5] | **Hattab (IRE)** (PTWalwyn) **2-9-0** WCarson(6) (lw: led 4f: one pce) ........................................1¾ | **4** | 6/1[3] | 66 | 21 |
| | **Amyas (IRE)** (BWHills) **2-9-0** MHills(13) (w'like: scope: dwlt: hdwy over 2f out: nvr nr to chal)........................3½ | **5** | 8/1 | 57+ | 12 |
| 2972[6] | **Sudest (IRE)** (IABalding) **2-9-0** WRSwinburn(12) (nvr nrr)........................................1½ | **6** | 6/1[3] | 53 | 8 |
| 1453[3] | **Merciless Cop** (BJMeehan) **2-9-0** BDoyle(3) (stdd s: nvr plcd to chal) ........................................3½ | **7** | 12/1 | 44 | — |
| | **Marytavy** (SirMarkPrescott) **2-8-9** GDuffield(5) (unf: scope: nvr trbld ldrs)........................................s.h | **8** | 14/1 | 39 | — |
| | **Ar Hyd Y Knos** (RCharlton) **2-8-9** TSprake(11) (n.d)........................................1¼ | **9** | 14/1 | 35 | — |
| 2374[10] | **Life On The Street (82)** (RHannon) **2-8-9** WJO'Connor(9) (bhd fnl 2f) ........................................nk | **10** | 25/1 | 34 | — |
| 2977[2] | **Sharp Hat** (RHannon) **2-8-11**(3) DaneO'Neill(10) (swtg: stumbled over 3f out: a bhd) ..............................¾ | **11** | 14/1 | 37 | — |
| 2559[10] | **Topps Trio** (KOCunningham-Brown) **2-8-9** SWhitworth(8) (a bhd) ........................................2½ | **12** | 50/1 | 26 | — |
| 3259[12] | **Silver Secret** (MJHeaton-Ellis) **2-9-0** JCarroll(14) (str: scope: spd over 3f) ........................................4 | **13** | 25/1 | 20 | — |
| | **Arthur's Seat** (LordHuntingdon) **2-9-0** LDettori(7) (unf: scope: w ldrs 3f) ........................................½ | **14** | 12/1 | 19 | — |
| | | | (SP 138.4%) | | **14 Rn** |

**1m 14.78** (1.78) CSF £114.36 TOTE £27.70: £5.70 £2.20 £1.90 (£59.30) Trio £88.70 OWNER Mr Hamdan Al Maktoum (EPSOM) BRED S. Patrick Terry

**Mukaddar (USA)** is a bit lightly-made and not a great mover at a canter, but he did look fit. Running in the owner's second colours, he passed the post in total silence. (20/1)
**3164 Polish Warrior (IRE)** took the eye, both on looks and in condition, and should find a race. (9/2: 3/1-5/1)
**2302 Green Power**, more at home in this sort of company, should stay further. (9/4: 3/1-2/1)
**3069 Hattab (IRE)** only succeeded in setting up the race for his rivals. He has the looks to succeed as long as he is not aimed too high. (6/1)
**Amyas (IRE)**, green and coltish in the paddock, should be better for the experience. (8/1: op 4/1)
**2972 Sudest (IRE)**, still carrying condition, is coming on gradually and needs only one more run to qualify for a handicap mark. (6/1)
**1453 Merciless Cop** seemed to be given a quiet run a could be the type for a Nursery. (12/1: op 8/1)

### 3495 AMESBURY CONDITIONS STKS (3-Y.O+ F & M) (Class C)
2-45 (2-45) **5f** £4,706.00 (£1,754.00: £852.00: £360.00: £155.00: £73.00) Stalls: High GOING minus 0.46 sec per fur (F)

| | | | SP | RR | SF |
|---|---|---|---|---|---|
| 3296[5] | **Bowden Rose (84)** (MBlanshard) **4-9-0b** JQuinn(1) (mde all: rdn out)........................................— | **1** | 9/1 | 95 | 53 |
| 3126[12] | **Amazing Bay (100)** (IABalding) **3-8-11** LDettori(4) (lw: a.p: rdn 2f out: r.o ins fnl f) ..............................½ | **2** | 7/2[2] | 93 | 48 |
| 2498[4] | **My Melody Parkes (103)** (JBerry) **3-8-11** JCarroll(2) (chsd wnr: rdn 2f out: one pce fnl f)..............................nk | **3** | 5/2[1] | 92 | 47 |
| 3126[13] | **Bunty Boo (104)** (RHannon) **7-8-11**(3) DaneO'Neill(6) (hld up: hdwy over 1f out: one pce fnl f) ..................¾ | **4** | 5/2[1] | 90 | 48 |
| 3126[7] | **Welsh Mist (91)** (RBoss) **5-9-0** GDuffield(3) (outpcd: no hdwy fnl 2f) ........................................3 | **5** | 5/1[3] | 80 | 38 |
| | **Lunar Mist (87)** (MartynMeade) **3-8-11** JReid(5) (hld up: rdn 2f out: a bhd) ........................................hd | **6** | 10/1 | 80 | 35 |
| | | | (SP 115.1%) | | **6 Rn** |

**60.37 secs** (0.37) CSF £37.88 TOTE £10.00: £2.80 £2.40 (£13.50) OWNER Mrs C. J. Ward (UPPER LAMBOURN) BRED E. A. Badger
WEIGHT FOR AGE 3yo-3lb

**3296 Bowden Rose** was bottom-rated on official figures, but enjoyed being able to dominate on a track where she had previously scored twice over this trip. (9/1)
**2698 Amazing Bay** looked in outstanding shape in the paddock and is running well enough to find another race. (7/2)
**2498 My Melody Parkes** was favoured by the weights here, but her recent races have been over a furlong further. (5/2)
**2698 Bunty Boo**, best in on official Ratings, was not beaten far but was a shade disappointing. (5/2)
**2692 Welsh Mist** is not running badly at present, despite unimpressive form figures. (5/1)
**Lunar Mist**, looking reasonably fit for this first run of the season, was not disgraced against some useful rivals on unfavourable terms. (10/1)

## 3496 H. S. LESTER MEMORIAL CHALLENGE CUP H'CAP (0-70) (3-Y.O+) (Class E)

3-15 (3-15) **1m 1f 209y** £3,418.00 (£1,024.00: £492.00: £226.00) Stalls: High GOING minus 0.46 sec per fur (F)

| Form | Horse / Trainer / Age-Weight / Jockey (comment) | Dist | Pos | SP | RR | SF |
|---|---|---|---|---|---|---|
| 3205[3] | **Ashby Hill (IRE) (56)** (RRowe) **5-9-2** RCochrane(15) (hld up: hdwy over 2f out: swtchd lft over 1f out: led ins fnl f: all out) | — | **1** | 11/2[1] | 64 | 46 |
| 2971* | **Thatchmaster (IRE) (50)** (CAHorgan) **5-8-10** PaulEddery(14) (lw: chsd ldr: ev ch 1f out: r.o) | nk | **2** | 10/1 | 58 | 40 |
| 3165[6] | **Shalateeno (55)** (BRMillman) **3-8-6** TSprake(6) (lw: led: rdn over 3f out: hdd ins fnl f: r.o) | ½ | **3** | 20/1 | 62 | 35 |
| 3161[4] | **Fairy Knight (64)** (RHannon) **4-9-7**(3) DaneO'Neill(11) (hld up & bhd: hdwy over 2f out: r.o ins fnl f) | ¾ | **4** | 13/2[2] | 70 | 52 |
| 3161[5] | **Mimosa (52)** (SDow) **3-8-3** SSanders(12) (s.i.s: hdwy over 3f out: one pce fnl 2f) | 3½ | **5** | 11/1 | 52 | 25 |
| 3205[4] | **Law Dancer (IRE) (69)** (TGMills) **3-9-6** JReid(3) (lw: no hdwy fnl 3f) | ½ | **6** | 15/2 | 68 | 41 |
| | **Exemption (67)** (HCandy) **5-9-13** GCarter(2) (lw: nvr nrr) | 5 | **7** | 16/1 | 58 | 40 |
| 3141[9] | **Warspite (45)** (RJO'Sullivan) **6-8-5** DHarrison(5) (prom: rdn 3f out: sn wknd) | hd | **8** | 25/1 | 36 | 18 |
| 3094[3] | **Sweet Pavlova (USA) (65)** (PFICole) **4-9-11** TQuinn(9) (prom tl wknd over 2f out) | s.h | **9** | 13/2[2] | 56 | 38 |
| 3333[7] | **Runic Symbol (42)** (MBlanshard) **5-8-2** JQuinn(1) (lw: n.d) | ¾ | **10** | 14/1 | 32 | 14 |
| 2943[4] | **Indian Nectar (60)** (GBBalding) **3-8-11** SDrowne(10) (hld up mid div: wknd over 2f out) | ¾ | **11** | 7/1[3] | 48 | 21 |
| 2896[6] | **Racing Hawk (USA) (52)** (MSSaunders) **4-8-12** RHughes(13) (prom tl hrd rdn & wknd 3f out) | 2½ | **12** | 16/1 | 36 | 18 |
| 3443[W] | **Wilfull Lad (IRE) (60)** (MartynMeade) **3-8-11** JCarroll(4) (plld hrd: prom 7f) | 7 | **13** | 33/1 | 33 | 6 |
| 3260[5] | **Monument (68)** (JSKing) **4-10-0** BDoyle(8) (lw: a bhd) | nk | **14** | 9/1 | 41 | 23 |
| *2369[10]* | **Ripsnorter (IRE) (40)** (KBishop) **7-8-0** NAdams(7) (lw: bhd: rdn 5f out: t.o fnl 3f) | 14 | **15** | 50/1 | — | — |

(SP 125.7%) **15 Rn**

**2m 7.47** (2.17) CSF £56.87 CT £960.68 TOTE £6.50: £2.70 £2.90 £5.70 (£27.60) Trio £448.70 OWNER Miss Meriel Tufnell (PULBOROUGH) BRED Patrick Aspell

WEIGHT FOR AGE 3yo-9lb

OFFICIAL EXPLANATION **Monument: usually prefers to race prominently, but left the stalls awkwardly and thereafter was never travelling. The horse was soon off the bridle and hung to his right in the home straight.**

**3205 Ashby Hill (IRE)** gained her reward for some sound recent performances, but she had to work hard to clinch it. (11/2)
**2971* Thatchmaster (IRE)** stayed the extra two furlongs well and is in good heart at present. (10/1)
**3165 Shalateeno** remains a maiden, despite being tried at a variety of trips, but there was little wrong with this effort. (20/1)
**3161 Fairy Knight** ran another good race this time over a furlong further and is knocking at the door. (13/2)
**3161 Mimosa** gained her only win at a mile and this trip appeared to be stretching her to the limit. (11/1)
**3205 Law Dancer (IRE)** did not reproduce his Ascot running with the winner. (15/2)

## 3497 UPAVON STKS (Listed) (3-Y.O+ F & M) (Class A)

3-45 (3-46) **1m 1f 209y** £10,862.00 (£4,058.00: £1,979.00: £845.00: £372.50: £183.50) Stalls: High GOING minus 0.46 sec (F)

| Form | Horse / Trainer / Age-Weight / Jockey (comment) | Dist | Pos | SP | RR | SF |
|---|---|---|---|---|---|---|
| 3298* | **Altamura (USA) (84)** (JHMGosden) **3-8-5** LDettori(8) (lw: hld up: hdwy 3f out: led wl over 1f out: sn qcknd clr & edgd rt: rdn out) | — | **1** | 5/1 | 111 | 49 |
| 2991[4] | **Min Alhawa (USA) (102)** (MajorWRHern) **3-8-5** WCarson(3) (lw: hld up: carried wd bnd over 6f out: hdwy over 3f out: led over 2f out tl wl over 1f out: r.o one pce) | 2½ | **2** | 5/2[1] | 107 | 45 |
| 3041* | **Ta Awun (USA)** (ACStewart) **3-8-5** SWhitworth(9) (lw: prom: rn wd bnd over 6f out: ev ch over 2f out: one pce) | 2 | **3** | 9/2[3] | 104 | 42 |
| 3258* | **Flame Valley (USA) (93)** (MRStoute) **3-8-5** DHarrison(1) (led 2f: led 4f out tl over 2f out: one pce) | 2½ | **4** | 6/1 | 100 | 38 |
| 1899[8] | **Parrot Jungle (IRE) (100)** (JLDunlop) **3-8-5** TQuinn(4) (nvr nr to chal) | 2 | **5** | 14/1 | 97 | 35 |
| 1144[5] | **Wight (89)** (RHannon) **3-8-5** DaneO'Neill(6) (a bhd) | 13 | **6** | 33/1 | 76 | 14 |
| 3231[6] | **Sardonic (103)** (HRACecil) **3-8-9** PatEddery(5) (lw: led after 2f: rdn 5f out: hdd 4f out: sn wknd) | 1 | **7** | 7/2[2] | 78 | 16 |
| 1004[7] | **Gryada (100)** (WJarvis) **3-8-5** AMcGlone(7) (prom 6f) | ½ | **8** | 33/1 | 73 | 11 |
| 1899[6] | **Caribbean Quest** (BHanbury) **3-8-5** JStack(2) (swtg: sn bhd: hrd rdn 5f out: t.o fnl 3f) | 22 | **9** | 14/1 | 38 | — |

(SP 119.1%) **9 Rn**

**2m 5.77** (0.47) CSF £17.67 TOTE £4.70: £1.50 £1.70 £1.80 (£9.20) Trio £21.20 OWNER Sheikh Mohammed (NEWMARKET) BRED Darley Stud Management Inc

OFFICIAL EXPLANATION **Sardonic: was feeling the effects of two recent hard races.**

**3298* Altamura (USA)**, nicely backed for this step up in class, seemed to idle after crossing over to the fence and had to be kept right up to her work. Nevertheless, this was a good performance and this time one can be sure the Handicapper will take notice. (5/1: op 8/1)
**2991 Min Alhawa (USA)** settled better here, but was playing second fiddle once the winner went for home. (5/2: 7/2-9/4)
**3041* Ta Awun (USA)**, out of a half-sister to Ibn Bey and Roseate Tern, lacked the required turn of foot for this company. (9/2)
**3258* Flame Valley (USA)** was again found wanting on this return to listed company. (6/1: 4/1-13/2)
**794a Parrot Jungle (IRE)** at least showed some signs of a return to form. (14/1)
**3231 Sardonic** was considered by her jockey to be suffering from the effects of two recent hard races. (7/2)

## 3498 BEMBRIDGE CLAIMING STKS (2-Y.O) (Class F)

4-15 (4-16) **6f 212y** £2,805.00 (£780.00: £375.00) Stalls: Centre GOING minus 0.46 sec per fur (F)

| Form | Horse / Trainer / Age-Weight / Jockey (comment) | Dist | Pos | SP | RR | SF |
|---|---|---|---|---|---|---|
| 3230[3] | **Misty Cay (IRE) (74)** (SDow) **2-8-10** TQuinn(13) (a.p: led 3f out tl over 1f out: led ins fnl f: hrd rdn & edgd lft: all out) | — | **1** | 5/2[1] | 66 | 14 |
| 3241[4] | **Marsh Marigold (52)** (MartynMeade) **2-8-0** NAdams(5) (rdn 4f out: hdwy over 2f out: ev ch whn carried lft ins fnl f) | ¾ | **2** | 33/1 | 54 | 2 |
| 3259[11] | **Broadgate Flyer (IRE)** (WJarvis) **2-8-13** AMcGlone(2) (hld up: hdwy 3f out: led over 1f out: hdd & carried lft ins fnl f) | s.h | **3** | 7/1 | 67 | 15 |
| 2967[11] | **Running Free (IRE)** (MJFetherston-Godley) **2-8-11b[1]** JQuinn(6) (s.s: swtchd lft & hdwy 2f out: 4th whn swtchd rt wl ins fnl f) | 1¾ | **4** | 50/1 | 61 | 9 |
| 2759[2] | **Spondulicks (IRE) (62)** (RHannon) **2-8-6**(3) DaneO'Neill(9) (rdn & hdwy 2f out: nvr nr to chal) | 1¾ | **5** | 6/1[3] | 55 | 3 |
| 3227[8] | **Scarrots** (SCWilliams) **2-8-13** GHind(7) (led 4f: wknd 2f out) | 2 | **6** | 40/1 | 55 | 3 |
| 3311[3] | **Grovefair Lad (IRE)** (BJMeehan) **2-8-6b** BDoyle(10) (prom: hmpd over 3f out: sn wknd) | 2½ | **7** | 14/1 | 42 | — |
| 2252[7] | **Fistral Flame** (JSMoore) **2-8-8** JReid(4) (lw: nvr nr ldrs) | ½ | **8** | 16/1 | 43 | — |
| 2254[7] | **Top Titfer** (AGFoster) **2-8-0** TSprake(11) (n.d) | 1¼ | **9** | 66/1 | 32 | — |
| 3269[9] | **Abacaxi (IRE)** (RCharlton) **2-8-9** SSanders(8) (lw: w ldr 4f: wknd 2f out) | 1 | **10** | 7/1 | 39 | — |
| 3227* | **Dashing Rocksville (64)** (MRChannon) **2-8-8** PatEddery(3) (chsd ldrs: rdn 5f out: wknd over 3f out) | s.h | **11** | 3/1[2] | 37 | — |
| | **Silent Valley** (JNeville) **2-8-0** FNorton(12) (scope: bkwd: dwlt: bhd most of wy) | 6 | **12** | 33/1 | 16 | — |

| Form | Horse | Dist | Pos | SP | RR | SF |
|---|---|---|---|---|---|---|
| 3455[8] | **Vickys Double (48)** (JSMoore) **2-7-12** DeclanO'Shea(1) (hld up: a bhd) | 1¾ | **13** | 40/1 | 10 | — |
| | | | | (SP 119.6%) | | **13 Rn** |

**1m 29.8** (3.80) CSF £69.62 TOTE £3.80: £1.60 £4.90 £2.90 (£38.20) Trio £260.10 OWNER Mrs A. M. Upsdell (EPSOM) BRED T. Ward
**3230 Misty Cay (IRE)** took advantage of this lower grade, but had to work hard to land the spoils. (5/2)
**3241 Marsh Marigold** certainly got the longer trip well enough and was intimidated by the winner into going left in the closing stages. (33/1)
**2044 Broadgate Flyer (IRE)** appreciated the combination of good ground and a descent into a claimer. (7/1)
**Running Free (IRE)**, fitted with blinkers, stepped up considerably on his first two efforts. (50/1)
**2759 Spondulicks (IRE)** found this more competitive than when narrowly beaten at Brighton last time. (6/1)

## 3499 ISLE OF WIGHT MAIDEN STKS (II) (2-Y.O) (Class D)

4-45 (4-47) **6f 212y** £3,190.50 (£954.00: £457.00: £208.50) Stalls: Centre GOING minus 0.46 sec per fur (F)

| Form | Horse | Dist | Pos | SP | RR | SF |
|---|---|---|---|---|---|---|
| | **Gonzaga (IRE)** (JLDunlop) **2-9-0** TSprake(3) (unf: scope: hld up & bhd: gd hdwy over 1f out: r.o to ld nr fin) | — | **1** | 10/1 | 78+ | 37 |
| | **Another Night (IRE)** (RHannon) **2-9-0** WJO'Connor(1) (w'like: scope: s.s: hdwy 3f out: led over 1f out tl hdd nr fin) | nk | **2** | 33/1 | 77 | 36 |
| | **American Whisper** (PWHarris) **2-9-0** GHind(6) (leggy: unf: s.s: sn rcvrd: ev ch fnl f: r.o) | ½ | **3** | 25/1 | 76 | 35 |
| 3147[6] | **High Extreme (IRE)** (PWChapple-Hyam) **2-9-0** RHughes(4) (hld up: hdwy over 2f out: hrd rdn & ev ch over 1f out: one pce) | 4 | **4** | 15/2[3] | 67 | 26 |
| 3319[W] | **Moon Blast** (LadyHerries) **2-9-0** JReid(5) (lw: a.p: ev ch 2f out: wknd over 1f out) | s.h | **5** | 11/10[1] | 67 | 26 |
| 3147[7] | **Danka** (PTWalwyn) **2-9-0** JCarroll(9) (led over 5f: wknd fnl f) | 4 | **6** | 20/1 | 58 | 17 |
| | **Kafaf (USA)** (JHMGosden) **2-8-9** WCarson(10) (unf: hdwy 3f out: wknd wl over 1f out) | ½ | **7** | 9/2[2] | 52 | 11 |
| 2335[7] | **Beryllium** (RHannon) **2-8-11**(3) DaneO'Neill(2) (prom over 3f) | 6 | **8** | 10/1 | 43 | 2 |
| 2758[4] | **Chairmans Daughter** (PFICole) **2-8-9** TQuinn(8) (lw: prom 3f) | 1¼ | **9** | 9/1 | 35 | — |
| 3040[5] | **Norman Conquest (USA)** (IABalding) **2-9-0** PaulEddery(11) (prom over 4f) | 2 | **10** | 20/1 | 35 | — |
| | **Smart Prospect** (BJMeehan) **2-9-0** WRSwinburn(7) (w'like: lw: prom tl hmpd over 3f out: sn t.o) | 20 | **11** | 20/1 | — | — |
| | | | | (SP 126.8%) | | **11 Rn** |

**1m 28.06** (2.06) CSF £238.51 TOTE £14.20: £3.10 £5.80 £3.40 (£257.60) Trio £401.70; £396.10 to Salisbury 15/8/96 OWNER Sultan Al Kabeer (ARUNDEL) BRED Prince Sultan Al Kabeer
**Gonzaga (IRE)** is a half-brother to several winners in France and won in a time 2.6 seconds faster than the first division. Entered in the Derby, he seems likely to go on from here. (10/1: op 5/1)
**Another Night (IRE)**, a half-brother to Last Laugh, had to overcome a poor start and will be better for the experience. (33/1)
**American Whisper**, a half-brother to four winners abroad, lost ground at the stalls, but showed plenty of promise for the future. (25/1)
**3147 High Extreme (IRE)**, trying a longer trip, is not one of his stable's leading lights. (15/2: 5/1-8/1)
**2783 Moon Blast** has some big-race entries to his name, but the countdown has been put on hold. (11/10)
**Danka**, a half-brother to juvenile winner Wandering Angel, is out of a mare who won over seven as a juvenile and then scored over hurdles. (20/1)

## 3500 NEWPORT H'CAP (0-70) (3-Y.O+ F & M) (Class E)

5-15 (5-15) **1m 4f** £3,236.00 (£968.00: £464.00: £212.00) Stalls: Centre GOING minus 0.46 sec per fur (F)

| Form | Horse | Dist | Pos | SP | RR | SF |
|---|---|---|---|---|---|---|
| 3267[5] | **Kristal Breeze (46)** (WRMuir) **4-8-8** JReid(9) (hld up: hdwy 2f out: r.o to ld last strides) | — | **1** | 12/1 | 56 | 35 |
| 3267* | **Rasayel (USA) (62)** (PDEvans) **6-9-10** WRSwinburn(14) (hdwy over 2f out: led ins fnl f: hdd last strides) | s.h | **2** | 13/2[2] | 72 | 51 |
| 3141[3] | **Shining Dancer (60)** (SDow) **4-9-8** TQuinn(3) (hld up pllng hrd: hdwy 6f out: led over 1f out tl ins fnl f: r.o) | nk | **3** | 13/2[2] | 70 | 49 |
| 3141[7] | **Rocquaine Bay (40)** (MJBolton) **9-8-2** JQuinn(6) (hld up & bhd: hdwy 3f out: swtchd rt over 1f out: r.o) | 1½ | **4** | 10/1 | 48 | 27 |
| 2300[9] | **Ayunli (66)** (SCWilliams) **5-9-11**(3) MHenry(12) (prom: lost pl 7f out: hrd rdn & hdwy over 1f out: r.o) | 1¼ | **5** | 10/1 | 72 | 51 |
| 3333[10] | **Age of Reality (USA) (55)** (HCandy) **3-8-6** GDuffield(11) (prom: rdn 7f out: styd on one pce fnl 3f) | nk | **6** | 8/1 | 61 | 29 |
| 2430[4] | **Turia (67)** (MajorDNChappell) **3-9-4** TSprake(4) (hdwy 7f out: ev ch over 2f out: wknd over 1f out) | 4 | **7** | 12/1 | 67 | 35 |
| 2855[5] | **Dramatic Moment (68)** (IABalding) **3-9-0**(5) MartinDwyer(15) (no hdwy fnl 3f) | hd | **8** | 5/1[1] | 68 | 36 |
| 3108[3] | **Hawanafa (47)** (RHannon) **3-7-12** DeclanO'Shea(8) (n.d) | ½ | **9** | 10/1 | 46 | 14 |
| 2924[4] | **Lady Bankes (IRE) (66)** (WGMTurner) **3-8-12**(5) PPMurphy(7) (plld hrd: prom: led 4f out tl hdd & wknd over 1f out) | nk | **10** | 12/1 | 65 | 33 |
| 3318[7] | **Evidence In Chief (65)** (DRCElsworth) **3-9-2v** AProcter(1) (a bhd) | ¾ | **11** | 14/1 | 63 | 31 |
| 3113[10] | **Reiterate (48)** (GBBalding) **3-7-13** NAdams(10) (plld hrd: prom 8f) | 9 | **12** | 25/1 | 34 | 2 |
| 2247[3] | **Dalwhinnie (67)** (JWHills) **3-9-4** MHills(5) (led 8f: wkng whn hmpd over 1f out) | nk | **13** | 7/1[3] | 53 | 21 |
| 1123[11] | **Lizium (48)** (JCFox) **4-8-10** WJO'Connor(13) (a bhd) | 5 | **14** | 40/1 | 27 | 6 |
| | | | | (SP 130.2%) | | **14 Rn** |

**2m 35.9** (3.30) CSF £87.72 CT £523.61 TOTE £11.70: £4.60 £1.90 £3.80 (£23.10) Trio £25.10 OWNER Mr S. Lamb (LAMBOURN) BRED R. and Mrs Heathcote
WEIGHT FOR AGE 3yo-11lb
**3267 Kristal Breeze** was 7lb better off with the runner-up than when bitterly disappointing last time. She came through for a last-gasp win, despite having gone up 9lb for winning a couple of selling handicaps. (12/1)
**3267* Rasayel (USA)** had beaten the below-par winner out of sight at Chester, but was 7lb higher here. (13/2)
**3141 Shining Dancer** was very keen to post and it came as no surprise to see her take a strong hold. There was no disgrace in this. (13/2)
**3141 Rocquaine Bay** was on the same mark as when winning this race a year ago. (10/1)
**Ayunli** is still rated 4lb higher than the highest mark off which she has won. (10/1)
**3109 Age of Reality (USA)**, stepping up in distance, kept plugging on without being able to quicken. (8/1)
**2855 Dramatic Moment** was 8lb higher than when winning here over ten furlongs in June. (5/1)

T/Plpt: £221.00 (61.69 Tckts). T/Qdpt: £42.50 (21.57 Tckts). KH

# 2995-SANDOWN (R-H) (Good to firm, Rnd Good patches)
## Wednesday August 14th

WEATHER: dull WIND: almost nil

## 3501 PACEMAKER & THOROUGHBRED BREEDER RACING SCHOOLS APPRENTICE H'CAP (0-80) (3-Y.O+) (Class E)

5-45 (5-46) **1m 14y** £3,371.50 (£1,027.00: £506.00: £245.50) Stalls: High GOING minus 0.48 sec per fur (F)

| Form | Horse | Dist | Pos | SP | RR | SF |
|---|---|---|---|---|---|---|
| 2412[7] | **Tatika (67)** (GWragg) **6-9-3** GMilligan(7) (swtg: n.m.r on ins & lost pl over 5f out: rallied over 3f out: led over 1f out: pushed out) | — | **1** | 8/1 | 77 | 59 |

$3107^{4}$ **Mazcobar (80)** (PJMakin) **3-9-9** RHavlin(8) (swtg: chsd ldr over 1f: led over 2f out tl over 1f out: unable qckn) ....2½ **2** 11/2 $^{2}$ 85 60
$3123^{11}$ **Seventeens Lucky (75)** (BobJones) **4-9-11** RPainter(6) (rdn & hdwy 2f out: r.o ins fnl f) ....s.h **3** 8/1 80 62
$3072^{10}$ **Toujours Riviera (77)** (JPearce) **6-9-10**$^{(3)}$ RFfrench(9) (lw: led over 5f: wknd fnl f) ....2½ **4** 11/2 $^{2}$ 77 59
3287* **Prizefighter (67)** (JLEyre) **5-9-3** $^{5x}$ CTeague(2) (chsd ldr over 6f out tl over 2f out: wknd over 1f out) ....nk **5** 9/4 $^{1}$ 66 48
$3136^{6}$ **Superior Force (65)** (MissBSanders) **3-8-8** DGriffiths(5) (lw: hld up: rdn over 2f out: wknd over 1f out) ....3 **6** 20/1 58 33
$1684^{F}$ **Milos (60)** (TJNaughton) **5-8-10** JWilkinson(4) (lw: a bhd) ....nk **7** 25/1 53 35
3340* **Artful Dane (IRE) (67)** (MJHeaton-Ellis) **4-9-3** $^{5x}$ SDrowne(3) (sme hdwy over 1f out: sn wknd) ....1¾ **8** 15/2 $^{3}$ 56 38
$3257^{2}$ **Oozlem (IRE) (46)** (JRPoulton) **7-7-7b**$^{(3)}$ PDoe(1) (s.s: hdwy over 5f out: wknd over 3f out) ....9 **9** 20/1 18 —
(SP 108.9%) **9 Rn**

**1m 41.54** (0.34) CSF £44.80 CT £298.87 TOTE £9.00: £2.50 £2.00 £1.70 (£35.60) Trio £48.50 OWNER Mr G. Wragg (NEWMARKET) BRED D. J. and Mrs Deer
LONG HANDICAP Oozlem (IRE) 7-3
WEIGHT FOR AGE 3yo-7lb

**1406 Tatika**, a winner of two races on the Fibresand last winter, was gaining his first victory on turf. (8/1: 6/1-9/1)
**3107 Mazcobar** made his bid for glory over two furlongs form home. Collared below the distance, he was unable to cope with the winner. (11/2)
**2010 Seventeens Lucky**, running on inside the final furlong, failed by only a whisker to take second prize. (8/1)
**2885 Toujours Riviera** attempted to make all. Collared over a quarter of a mile out, he commendably stuck to his task, but had given his all entering the final furlong. (11/2)
**3287* Prizefighter**, winner of this race for the last two years, failed in his bid to complete the hat-trick. (9/4)
**2689 Superior Force** chased the leaders but, bustled along over a quarter of a mile out, found the writing was on the wall below the distance. (20/1)
**3340* Artful Dane (IRE)** (15/2: 9/2-8/1)

## 3502 WEYBRIDGE MEDIAN AUCTION MAIDEN STKS (2-Y.O) (Class F)
6-15 (6-18) **5f 6y** £3,566.25 (£1,080.00: £527.50: £251.25) Stalls: High GOING minus 0.48 sec per fur (F)

SP RR SF

$3349^{5}$ **Paddy Lad (IRE)** (RGuest) **2-9-0** PBloomfield(4) (chsd ldr: rdn 2f out: led ins fnl f: r.o wl) ....— **1** 10/1 74 26
$2624^{9}$ **Test The Water (IRE)** (RHannon) **2-9-0** WWoods(5) (lw: rdn over 2f out: hdwy over 1f out: r.o wl ins fnl f) ...1¼ **2** 13/2 $^{2}$ 70 22
$2977^{6}$ **Regal Equity** (BJMeehan) **2-9-0** TIves(6) (a.p: rdn over 2f out: unable qckn) ....1½ **3** 16/1 65 17
$2942^{3}$ **Incatime** (CJames) **2-9-0** CRutter(11) (lw: led: wandered 1f out: hdd ins fnl f: one pce) ....nk **4** 4/1 $^{1}$ 64 16
$1987^{3}$ **Chain Reaction (IRE)** (MAJarvis) **2-8-9** PRobinson(3) (a.p: rdn 2f out: one pce) ....1 **5** 7/1 $^{3}$ 56 8
**Stock Hill Dancer** (KRBurke) **2-8-2**$^{(7)}$ GMilligan(8) (unf: nvr nr to chal) ....¾ **6** 33/1 54 6
**Green Boulevard (USA)** (IABalding) **2-8-9** LDettori(1) (unf: scope: lw: s.s: hdwy 4f out: rdn over 2f out: eased whn btn ins fnl f) ....½ **7** 7/1 $^{3}$ 52 4
**Phylida** (PJMakin) **2-8-7**$^{(5)ow3}$ RHavlin(10) (neat: s.s: outpcd: nvr nrr) ....1¾ **8** 10/1 50 —
**Tukapa** (MrsALMKing) **2-9-0** SDrowne(12) (s.s: a bhd) ....1¼ **9** 16/1 48 —
$2374^{7}$ **Tailwind** (WRMuir) **2-9-0** PatEddery(2) (prom over 3f) ....1¼ **10** 8/1 44 —
**Don Guest (IRE)** (TJNaughton) **2-9-0** GCarter(9) (w'like: blt bkwd: a bhd) ....8 **11** 25/1 18 —
**Merryhill Mariner** (JLHarris) **2-9-0** RCochrane(7) (unf: a bhd) ....3 **12** 10/1 9 —
(SP 115.3%) **12 Rn**

**61.77 secs** (1.97) CSF £66.17 TOTE £13.10: £3.00 £2.40 £9.10 (£37.50) Trio £373.10 OWNER M & G Hill Ltd (Environmental Engineers) (NEWMARKET) BRED Terence McDonald

**3349 Paddy Lad (IRE)** appreciated the drop to five furlongs. Racing in second place, he got on top inside the final furlong and kept on well. (10/1)
**Test The Water (IRE)** was more at home in this company. Bustled along from halfway, he found his feet from below the distance but, despite storming through for second place inside the final furlong, found the winner had got first run and was not for catching. He can find a similar event, probably over six furlongs. (13/2)
**Regal Equity** was being bustled along from halfway, but failed to find that vital turn of foot. (16/1)
**2942 Incatime** attempted to make all the running. Eventually collared inside the final furlong, he failed to find another gear. (4/1)
**1987 Chain Reaction (IRE)**, never far away, was only treading water in the last two furlongs. (7/1: op 4/1)
**Stock Hill Dancer**, an unfurnished newcomer, stayed on up the hill without ever posing a threat. (33/1)
**Green Boulevard (USA)**, a half-sister to Prix Royal-Oak winner El Cuite, has scope for the future, but she was rather green on this debut and had a dreadful draw. She will have learnt a lot from this and can win a similar event in due course. (7/1: op 4/1)
**Phylida** (10/1: 7/1-16/1)
**Tailwind** (8/1: 5/1-10/1)

## 3503 ELMBRIDGE CONDITIONS STKS (3-Y.O+) (Class C)
6-45 (6-47) **1m 14y** £5,296.00 (£1,984.00: £972.00: £420.00: £190.00: £98.00) Stalls: High GOING minus 0.48 sec per fur (F)

SP RR SF

$694^{8}$ **Centre Stalls (IRE) (102)** (RFJohnsonHoughton) **3-8-7** SSanders(2) (lw: rdn & hdwy over 1f out: led ins fnl f: r.o wl) ....— **1** 10/1 106 53
$3153^{3}$ **Phantom Quest (105)** (HRACecil) **3-8-11** PatEddery(3) (lw: hdwy over 1f out: led 1f out tl ins fnl f: unable qckn) ....¾ **2** 7/4 $^{1}$ 109 56
$2050^{14}$ **Tamhid (USA) (104)** (HThomsonJones) **3-8-7** GCarter(4) (hdwy & nt clr run on ins over 2f out: nt clr run on ins & lost pl wl over 1f out: swtchd lft: gd hdwy fnl f: fin wl) ....nk **3** 10/1 104 51
$3153^{9}$ **Lap of Luxury (100)** (WJarvis) **7-8-9** BThomson(7) (a.p: led 1f: led over 2f out to 1f out: one pce) ....¾ **4** 7/2 $^{2}$ 97 51
1495* **Abeyr** (MAJarvis) **3-8-12** PRobinson(6) (swtg: hld up: rdn over 2f out: wknd over 1f out) ....2 **5** 9/2 $^{3}$ 104 51
$3153^{10}$ **Committal (IRE) (105)** (JHMGosden) **3-8-7** LDettori(10) (a.p: n.m.r over 2f out: wknd over 1f out) ....1¾ **6** 9/1 95 42
$3229^{9}$ **Insiyabi (USA) (90)** (JLDunlop) **3-8-11** WCarson(1) (lw: led 6f out tl over 2f out: wknd over 1f out) ....1¾ **7** 14/1 96 43
$2248^{8}$ **Tarte Aux Pommes (USA)** (CEBrittain) **4-8-9** BDoyle(9) (swtg: dwlt: led 7f out to 6f out: wknd wl over 1f out) ....7 **8** 33/1 73? 27
(SP 114.6%) **8 Rn**

**1m 41.17** (-0.03) CSF £26.86 TOTE £12.50: £2.60 £1.30 £2.30 (£17.20) Trio £33.40 OWNER Mr Anthony Pye-Jeary (DIDCOT) BRED Limestone Stud
WEIGHT FOR AGE 3yo-7lb

**574 Centre Stalls (IRE)** looked in good shape, considering he has been off the track for four months. Beginning his run from below the distance, he soon threw down this challenge and eventually got on top in the last 75 yards. (10/1: 8/1-12/1)
**3153 Phantom Quest** has been in good form this season, but once again failed to get his head in front where it mattered. (7/4)

**1187 Tamhid (USA)** was the unlucky horse of the race. His jockey decided to go for a run up the inside rail, but he met a dead-end over a quarter of a mile out and soon found himself back in last place. Switched left, he appeared to have no chance, but he went into turbo-drive in the final furlong and, really flying, would have taken second place in another couple of strides. With a clear run, he could well have won this, and compensation will surely be found. (10/1: 7/1-12/1)
**3153 Lap of Luxury** ran her best race of the season. Sent to the front over a quarter of a mile out, she was headed entering the final furlong and failed to find another gear. (7/2: 9/2-3/1)
**1495* Abeyr**, winner of both her races to date, was returning from an eleven-week absence. Chasing the leaders, she was being bustled along over a quarter of a mile out and was hung out to dry approaching the final furlong. (9/2)
**445* Insiyabi (USA)** (14/1: 10/1-16/1)

## 3504 SURREY RACING H'CAP (0-90) (3-Y.O+) (Class C)

7-15 (7-16) **1m 6f** £5,550.00 (£1,680.00: £820.00: £390.00) Stalls: High GOING minus 0.48 sec per fur (F)

| | | | | SP | RR | SF |
|---|---|---|---|---|---|---|
| 2973* | **Ballynakelly (71)** (RAkehurst) **4-8-12** SSanders(10) (lw: chsd ldr: led over 2f out: rdn out) | — | **1** | 9/4$^{1}$ | 87 | 37 |
| 2601$^{2}$ | **Jiyush (86)** (HThomsonJones) **3-9-0** GCarter(1) (a.p: rdn over 3f out: r.o one pce) | 1½ | **2** | 15/2 | 100 | 37 |
| 2973$^{2}$ | **Tudor Island (80)** (CEBrittain) **7-9-7** BDoyle(2) (led tl over 2f out: one pce fnl f) | 1½ | **3** | 5/1$^{2}$ | 93 | 43 |
| 3337* | **Old School House (68)** (TJNaughton) **3-7-7**(3) 5x MHenry(6) (lw: rdn 3f out: hdwy over 1f out: one pce) | 2½ | **4** | 7/1$^{3}$ | 78 | 15 |
| 3266$^{9}$ | **Pearl Venture (80)** (SPCWoods) **4-9-7** WWoods(7) (nvr nr to chal) | 5 | **5** | 12/1 | 84 | 34 |
| 2665a$^{4}$ | **Steamroller Stanly (86)** (CACyzer) **3-9-0** TQuinn(5) (lw: a.p: rdn over 3f out: wknd over 1f out) | nk | **6** | 10/1 | 90 | 27 |
| 2882$^{2}$ | **Arctic Fancy (USA) (85)** (PWHarris) **3-8-13** GHind(8) (a bhd) | 3 | **7** | 5/1$^{2}$ | 85 | 22 |
| 2973$^{4}$ | **Benfleet (74)** (RWArmstrong) **5-9-1** LDettori(4) (lw: hld up: rdn over 2f out: sn wknd) | 2 | **8** | 8/1 | 72 | 22 |
| | ***Ritto (87)*** (JNeville) **6-10-0** DHarrison(9) (Withdrawn not under Starter's orders: ref to ent stalls) | | **W** | 66/1 | — | — |

(SP 117.8%) **8 Rn**

**3m 2.7** (3.80) CSF £18.27 CT £70.32 TOTE £3.30: £1.70 £1.90 £2.10 (£14.80) Trio £18.40 OWNER Y Y Partnership (EPSOM) BRED Crest Stud Ltd
LONG HANDICAP Old School House 7-4
WEIGHT FOR AGE 3yo-13lb
**2973* Ballynakelly** continues to defy the Handicapper in remarkable fashion with his seventh consecutive success. Racing in second place, he went on over a quarter of a mile from home and, ridden along, eventually asserted in the final furlong. He is sure to rise substantially in the handicap, but will that be enough to stop him? (9/4)
**2601 Jiyush** saw out this longer trip. Never far away, he was being bustled along in the straight, but did stay on well for second prize. (15/2)
**2973 Tudor Island**, 6lb better off with the winner for a two-and-a-half-length beating over course and distance last month, found that rival still too good. Bowling along in front, he was collared over a quarter of a mile out, but grimly held on to his arch-rival until put in his place inside the distance. (5/1)
**3337* Old School House** raced at the back of the field. He did make an effort below the distance, but could then make no further impression. (7/1)
**2547* Pearl Venture**, racing at the back of the field, never posed a threat. (12/1)
**2665a Steamroller Stanly** was close up until calling it a day below the distance. (10/1: 8/1-12/1)
**2882 Arctic Fancy (USA)** (5/1: 9/2-11/4)

## 3505 COBHAM MAIDEN STKS (3-Y.O+) (Class D)

7-45 (7-50) **1m 2f 7y** £3,615.00 (£1,095.00: £535.00: £255.00) Stalls: High GOING minus 0.48 sec per fur (F)

| | | | | SP | RR | SF |
|---|---|---|---|---|---|---|
| 2996$^{3}$ | **Filial (IRE)** (GHarwood) **3-8-12** PatEddery(13) (a.p: chsd ldr 7f out: rdn over 2f out: led nr fin) | — | **1** | 2/1$^{1}$ | 81 | 44 |
| 813$^{5}$ | **Unalloyed (USA)** (DRLoder) **3-8-7** TQuinn(1) (led: rdn over 2f out: hdd nr fin) | hd | **2** | 9/4$^{2}$ | 76 | 39 |
| 845$^{8}$ | **Gulliver** (BWHills) **3-8-12** BThomson(7) (s.s: gd hdwy fnl 2f: nvr plcd to chal) | 5 | **3** | 16/1 | 73 | 36 |
| 3209$^{3}$ | **Ballet High (IRE)** (IABalding) **3-8-12** RCochrane(4) (hld up: rdn over 3f out: one pce) | hd | **4** | 13/2$^{3}$ | 73 | 36 |
| 1906$^{5}$ | **Reticent** (JHMGosden) **3-8-12** LDettori(9) (b.hind: bit bkwd: a.p: rdn over 2f out: one pce) | ¾ | **5** | 9/1 | 72 | 35 |
| | **Prospero** (GHarwood) **3-8-12** WWoods(2) (rdn over 3f out: nvr nr to chal) | 2 | **6** | 50/1 | 68 | 31 |
| 1670$^{9}$ | **Namoodaj** (ACStewart) **3-8-12** DHarrison(15) (lw: s.s: stdy hdwy 2f out: nt clr run on ins over 1f out: nvr plcd to chal) | 7 | **7** | 33/1 | 57 | 20 |
| | **Raheefa (USA)** (JHMGosden) **3-8-7** WCarson(14) (s.s: nvr nrr) | ¾ | **8** | 9/1 | 51 | 14 |
| | **Porlock Castle** (KRBurke) **3-8-12** SSanders(8) (unf: a mid div) | ½ | **9** | 66/1 | 55 | 18 |
| 2711$^{11}$ | **Back By Dawn (56)** (DRCElsworth) **3-8-9**(3) DaneO'Neill(6) (bhd fnl 6f) | 1½ | **10** | 100/1 | 53 | 16 |
| | **Soldier Blue** (PJHobbs) **3-8-12** TIves(3) (w'like: hld up: rdn over 2f out: sn wknd) | 1¾ | **11** | 66/1 | 50 | 13 |
| 2996$^{8}$ | **Honeyshan** (DJSffrenchDavis) **4-9-2** TSprake(5) (b: bhd fnl 2f) | 1½ | **12** | 100/1 | 43 | 15 |
| | **Wybara** (JHMGosden) **3-8-7** GHind(11) (w'like: scope: bit bkwd: prom over 7f) | 5 | **13** | 16/1 | 35 | — |
| 2505$^{11}$ | **Sliparis** (KOCunningham-Brown) **3-8-7** SWhitworth(10) (prom over 4f) | 23 | **14** | 66/1 | — | — |
| | **Solo Volumes** (HGRowsell) **7-9-7** BDoyle(12) (bit bkwd: s.s: a bhd) | 22 | **15** | 100/1 | — | — |

(SP 121.6%) **15 Rn**

**2m 8.43** (1.73) CSF £6.60 TOTE £3.30: £1.70 £1.60 £3.30 (£3.60) Trio £36.20 OWNER Mr K. Abdulla (PULBOROUGH) BRED Juddmonte Farms
WEIGHT FOR AGE 3yo-9lb
**IN-FOCUS: This was not a particularly good maiden by Sandown standards.**
**2996 Filial (IRE)**, in second place halfway down the back straight, was bustled along over a quarter of a mile from home and, throwing down his challenge, eventually got on top near the line. (2/1)
**813 Unalloyed (USA)**, given a three-and-a-half-month break, attempted to make all the running. Desperately trying to stretch them in the straight, she was only worried out of it near the line. She should soon find a race. (9/4)
**684 Gulliver**, a big boat of a horse, was having his first run in three and a half months, but caught the eye in no uncertain fashion. Given a very tender ride, he was out with the washing entering the straight, but he made tremendous strides in the final quarter-mile to snatch third prize on the line. He will surely be better suited by further and, now that he is qualified for handicaps, he could be ready to strike. (16/1)
**3209 Ballet High (IRE)** chased the leaders but, ridden along early in the straight, was made to look very pedestrian. (13/2: 4/1-7/1)
**Reticent**, looking as though this first run in nine weeks would do him good, was never far away, but was made to look very one-paced in the straight. (9/1)
**Prospero**, who looked rather dull in his coat for this belated seasonal debut, raced in midfield. He did struggle on, but never posed a threat. (50/1)
**Namoodaj**, a round-bodied gelding, looked in good shape for this first run in ten weeks. Given considerate handling, he made steady headway from the back of the field a quarter of a mile out, but soon met with interference. He definitely looks one to keep an eye on. (33/1)
**Raheefa (USA)** (9/1: 4/1-10/1)

## 3506 PRINCESS ALICE HOSPICE H'CAP (0-70) (3-Y.O+) (Class E)

8-15 (8-19) **5f 6y** £3,663.75 (£1,110.00: £542.50: £258.75) Stalls: High GOING minus 0.48 sec per fur (F)

| | | | | SP | RR | SF |
|---|---|---|---|---|---|---|
| 3146$^{2}$ | **Half Tone (50)** (RMFlower) **4-8-10b** TQuinn(12) (a.p: led over 1f out: r.o wl) | — | 1 | 5/2$^{2}$ | 60 | 36 |
| 3323$^{5}$ | **Squire Corrie (57)** (GHarwood) **4-8-10b**$^{(7)}$ GayeHarwood(3) (lw: w ldr: ev ch over 1f out: unable qckn) | 2 | 2 | 9/1$^{3}$ | 61 | 37 |
| 3261* | **Gone Savage (64)** (WJMusson) **8-9-10** RCochrane(9) (nt clr run over 2f out: hdwy & hmpd over 1f out: str run fnl f: fin wl) | s.h | 3 | 2/1$^{1}$ | 68+ | 44 |
| 3146$^{8}$ | **Barranak (IRE) (58)** (GMMcCourt) **4-9-4** BThomson(5) (led over 3f: one pce) | 1 | 4 | 14/1 | 58 | 34 |
| 3331$^{3}$ | **Oscilights Gift (36)** (PBurgoyne) **4-7-10** NAdams(2) (a.p: rdn over 2f out: one pce) | s.h | 5 | 33/1 | 36 | 12 |
| 2867$^{8}$ | **Metal Boys (54)** (MissLCSiddall) **9-9-0** DHarrison(11) (rdn 3f out: hdwy 2f out: one pce) | 1 | 6 | 12/1 | 51 | 27 |
| 3097$^{2}$ | **Another Batchworth (54)** (EAWheeler) **4-9-0** TSprake(1) (hld up: rdn 2f out: wknd fnl f) | 2 | 7 | 11/1 | 45 | 21 |
| 3261$^{7}$ | **Superlao (BEL) (40)** (JJBridger) **4-7-7**$^{(7)}$ RBrisland(7) (b.nr hind: nvr nr to chal) | nk | 8 | 16/1 | 30 | 6 |
| 3323$^{8}$ | **Paley Prince (USA) (60)** (MDIUsher) **10-9-6** SWhitworth(4) (b: hdwy over 2f out: wknd over 1f out) | 2½ | 9 | 33/1 | 42 | 18 |
| 2970$^{4}$ | **John's Law (IRE) (54)** (MJHeaton-Ellis) **3-8-11** SSanders(8) (hld up: rdn over 2f out: sn wknd) | 2½ | 10 | 16/1 | 28 | 1 |
| 1101$^{6}$ | **Thai Morning (64)** (PWHarris) **3-9-7** GHind(6) (bit bkwd: a bhd) | 1¼ | 11 | 11/1 | 34 | 7 |
| | **Logie Pert Lad (36)** (JJBridger) **4-7-10** JQuinn(10) (gd spd 3f) | s.h | 12 | 50/1 | 6 | — |
| | | | | (SP 122.5%) | **12 Rn** | |

**60.87 secs** (1.07) CSF £24.70 CT £50.78 TOTE £3.10: £1.40 £2.70 £1.70 (£10.10) Trio £10.10 OWNER Mrs G. M. Temmerman (JEVINGTON) BRED T. M. Jennings

LONG HANDICAP Oscilights Gift 6-12 Logie Pert Lad 7-4

WEIGHT FOR AGE 3yo-3lb

**3146 Half Tone**, whose jockey was an eyecatching booking, finally came good after a string of good efforts. Never far away, he made his bid for glory below the distance and soon had the race in safe-keeping. (5/2)

**3323 Squire Corrie** disputed the lead from the start. He had every chance below the distance before the winner was let loose. (9/1: 6/1-10/1)

**3261* Gone Savage** does love this course, but his style of racing is not ideal for it and, for the third time in the space of a month, he had no luck in running here. Failing to get a clear run at halfway, he was just picking up ground when hampered below the distance. Despite this, he came storming through in the final furlong and just failed to take second prize. (2/1)

**2902 Barranak (IRE)** disputed the lead from the start. Collared below the distance, he was then tapped for toe. (14/1)

**3331 Oscilights Gift**, never far away, never looked like quickening up in the second half of the race. (33/1)

**1964 Metal Boys** made an effort a quarter of a mile from home, but could then only plod on at one pace. (12/1)

**3097 Another Batchworth** (11/1: 7/1-12/1)

T/Jkpt: £48,086.60 (0.1 Tckts); £60,954.89 to Salisbury 15/8/96. T/Plpt: £124.40 (168.63 Tckts). T/Qdpt: £2.60 (778.75 Tckts). AK

# 3480-BEVERLEY (R-H) (Firm)

## Thursday August 15th

WEATHER: sunny & hot WIND: slt bhd

## 3507 TOLL GAVEL (S) H'CAP (0-60) (3-Y.O+) (Class E)

2-00 (2-00) **2m 35y** £3,013.50 (£903.00: £434.00: £199.50) Stalls: High GOING minus 0.74 sec per fur (HD)

| | | | | SP | RR | SF |
|---|---|---|---|---|---|---|
| 2626$^{2}$ | **Brodessa (57)** (MrsMReveley) **10-10-0** KDarley(7) (cl up: led over 6f out: styd on wl) | — | 1 | 11/8$^{1}$ | 71 | 33 |
| 3273$^{2}$ | **Faugeron (54)** (NTinkler) **7-9-11** LCharnock(9) (swtg: a.p: chsd wnr fnl 4f: kpt on) | 1¾ | 2 | 9/2$^{3}$ | 66 | 28 |
| 3335$^{9}$ | **Genesis Four (43)** (MrsLStubbs) **6-9-0** KFallon(3) (lw: hld up: effrt 5f out: chsng ldrs 3f out: one pce fnl 2f) | 5 | 3 | 8/1 | 50 | 12 |
| | **Grey Sonata (36)** (TJEtherington) **9-8-7** MBirch(4) (effrt 6f out: styd on fnl 3f: no imp) | 1¼ | 4 | 50/1 | 42 | 4 |
| 3104$^{2}$ | **No More Hassle (IRE) (40)** (MrsMReveley) **3-7-10** NCarlisle(5) (chsd ldr tl outpcd fnl 4f) | 1¼ | 5 | 10/1 | 45 | — |
| 2989$^{5}$ | **Dots Dee (30)** (JMBradley) **7-7-12**$^{(3)}$ FLynch(6) (b.nr fore: hld up: hdwy 5f out: rdn & wknd wl over 2f out) | 7 | 6 | 7/2$^{2}$ | 28 | — |
| 3303$^{4}$ | **Ever Friends (37)** (RHarris) **4-8-8** AMackay(1) (swtg: led tl hdd over 6f out: sn wknd) | dist | 7 | 9/1 | — | — |
| 2989$^{B}$ | **Florismart (51)** (BPJBaugh) **4-9-1**$^{(7)}$ IonaWands(2) (prom tl outpcd & lost tch 6f out) | 1 | 8 | 33/1 | — | — |
| 1067$^{8}$ | **Chipalata (42)** (TWDonnelly) **3-7-12**$^{ow2}$ DaleGibson(8) (prom tl outpcd 9f out: sn bhd) | 14 | 9 | 25/1 | — | — |
| | | | | (SP 121.5%) | **9 Rn** | |

**3m 35.1** (4.60) CSF £8.41 CT £35.20 TOTE £2.10: £1.30 £1.50 £1.70 (£3.20) Trio £10.00 OWNER Mr R. W. S. Jevon (SALTBURN) BRED B. Fairs

LONG HANDICAP No More Hassle (IRE) 7-4 Chipalata 7-5

WEIGHT FOR AGE 3yo-15lb

No bid

**2626 Brodessa,** winning this for the second year running, was 2lb better in with Faugeron for a length beating last time and that proved just enough. (11/8)

**3273 Faugeron** is in good heart and ran to his form and really made the winner work late on. (9/2)

**2182 Genesis Four** was 8lb better in with the winner for a five length defeat earlier in the season but it made no difference. (8/1)

**Grey Sonata** ran reasonably, staying on in the home straight, but she never looked likely to get anywhere near. (50/1)

**3104 No More Hassle (IRE)** gave the impression that this trip was stretching his stamina somewhat. (10/1)

**2989 Dots Dee** found this trip beyond her. (7/2)

## 3508 E.B.F. WESTWOOD MAIDEN STKS (2-Y.O F) (Class D)

2-30 (2-31) **5f** £3,626.00 (£1,088.00: £524.00: £242.00) Stalls: High GOING minus 0.74 sec per fur (HD)

| | | | | SP | RR | SF |
|---|---|---|---|---|---|---|
| | **Bianca Nera** (DRLoder) **2-8-11** KDarley(2) (neat: str: trckd ldrs: led over 1f out: pushed along & r.o) | — | 1 | 6/4$^{2}$ | 71+ | 27 |
| 1148$^{3}$ | **Solfegietto** (MBell) **2-8-11** MFenton(9) (chsd ldrs: hdwy over 1f out: r.o: nt pce of wnr) | 1¼ | 2 | 8/1$^{3}$ | 67 | 23 |
| 3036$^{2}$ | **Sleepless** (NAGraham) **2-8-11** WRSwinburn(7) (chsd ldrs: effrt 2f out: r.o one pce) | 3 | 3 | 5/4$^{1}$ | 57 | 13 |
| 3429$^{8}$ | **Whisper Low (IRE)** (RHollinshead) **2-8-8**$^{(3)}$ FLynch(5) (led tl hdd & wknd over 1f out) | 1½ | 4 | 33/1 | 53? | 9 |
| 3054$^{3}$ | **Naivasha** (JBerry) **2-8-11** JCarroll(4) (lw: prom tl outpcd fnl 2f) | 1 | 5 | 11/1 | 49 | 5 |
| | **Gymcrak Watermill (IRE)** (GHolmes) **2-8-11** DeanMcKeown(6) (b.hind: cmpt: bkwd: dwlt: rn green & sn t.o) | 12 | 6 | 33/1 | 11 | — |
| | **Something Blue** (TRWatson) **2-8-11** GDuffield(8) (neat: unf: spd to ½-wy: wknd qckly) | hd | 7 | 33/1 | 11 | — |

| | Horse | Dist | Pos | SP | RR | SF |
|---|---|---|---|---|---|---|
| | **Figlia** (CBBBooth) **2-8-11** LCharnock(3) (neat: s.s: rn green & a t.o) | 14 | **8** | 33/1 | — | — |
| | | | | (SP 115.7%) | | **8 Rn** |

**62.0 secs** (0.50) CSF £12.76 TOTE £2.40: £1.20 £1.50 £1.10 (£9.70) Trio £3.20 OWNER Mr S. Frisby (NEWMARKET) BRED Miss S. McCreery and Stowell Hill Ltd

**Bianca Nera**, a very sturdy little filly, was very relaxed in the preliminaries but in the race did all that was required in convincing style and should improve as a result. (6/4)

**1148 Solfegietto**, after three months off, put in an improved performance and would seem to be getting it together. (8/1)

**3036 Sleepless**, a stuffy type of filly, was struggling with the pace from halfway and may need a bit more time. (5/4: Evens-5/6)

**3121 Whisper Low (IRE)** ran her best race to date and is obviously improving. (33/1)

**3054 Naivasha** got outpaced halfway through the race but was keeping on at the end suggesting that further should suit. (11/1: 8/1-12/1)

**Gymcrak Watermill (IRE)**, backward and green, has plenty to learn. (33/1)

## 3509 RAPID LAD H'CAP (0-90) (3-Y.O+) (Class C)

3-00 (3-01) **1m 1f 207y** £5,540.00 (£1,670.00: £810.00: £380.00) Stalls: High GOING minus 0.74 sec per fur (HD)

| | Horse | Dist | Pos | SP | RR | SF |
|---|---|---|---|---|---|---|
| 3118[3] | **Fairywings (76)** (MrsJRRamsden) **3-8-6** KFallon(8) (in tch: effrt over 2f out: rdn to ld wl ins fnl f: all out) | — | **1** | 6/1[3] | 85 | 32 |
| 2924* | **Darling Clover (69)** (DMorley) **4-8-8** KDarley(9) (lw: chsd ldrs: rdn to ld ins fnl f: hdd wl ins fnl f: rallied) | s.h | **2** | 9/2[1] | 78 | 34 |
| 3401[2] | **Maid For Baileys (IRE) (78)** (MJohnston) **3-8-8** TWilliams(1) (led tl hdd & no ex ins fnl f) | 2½ | **3** | 11/2[2] | 83 | 30 |
| 3161[17] | **Aeroking (USA) (73)** (GHarwood) **5-8-12** AClark(6) (trckd ldrs: effrt 3f out: r.o one pce) | 1¾ | **4** | 10/1 | 75 | 31 |
| 3136[2] | **Kaafih Homm (IRE) (64)** (NACallaghan) **5-8-3** GBardwell(7) (lw: in tch: effrt over 2f out: styd on one pce) | hd | **5** | 6/1[3] | 66 | 22 |
| 3430[5] | **Tertium (IRE) (89)** (MartynWane) **4-10-0** JCarroll(3) (bhd: effrt over 3f out: styd on: no imp) | 1 | **6** | 10/1 | 89 | 45 |
| 3248[7] | **Domitia (USA) (66)** (MBell) **4-8-5** MFenton(4) (bhd: c wd over 2f out: no imp) | 3½ | **7** | 16/1 | 61 | 17 |
| 3280* | **Hazard a Guess (IRE) (85)** (DNicholls) **6-9-10** AlexGreaves(5) (hld up: effrt 3f out: sn btn) | 1½ | **8** | 9/2[1] | 77 | 33 |
| | **Vindaloo (89)** (JLHarris) **4-10-0** WRSwinburn(10) (bit bkwd: chsd ldr tl wknd fnl 2f) | 2½ | **9** | 33/1 | 77 | 33 |
| 3071[4] | **King Athelstan (USA) (85)** (BAMcMahon) **8-9-10** GDuffield(2) (mid div tl wknd fnl 3f) | 1¾ | **10** | 10/1 | 70 | 26 |
| | | | | (SP 116.4%) | | **10 Rn** |

**2m 2.3** (-0.20) CSF £31.03 CT £143.99 TOTE £7.10: £2.30 £2.10 £1.70 (£12.20) Trio £10.40 OWNER L C and A E Sigsworth (THIRSK) BRED L. C. and A. E. Sigsworth and The Kris Syndicate

WEIGHT FOR AGE 3yo-9lb

**3118 Fairywings** proved to be a real battler and won here off her highest mark to date. (6/1)

**2924* Darling Clover**, closely handicapped on her running with the winner last time, looked to have done everything right here but, in a desperate finish, just failed. (9/2)

**3401 Maid For Baileys (IRE)**, strictly on her running with the first two here in July, should have been in the shake up but she has had two hard races since and did not quite run up to her form on this occasion. (11/2)

**2917 Aeroking (USA)** normally likes to be forcing the pace but was held up this time and that might have been his undoing as he raced too freely early on. (10/1)

**3136 Kaafih Homm (IRE)** was always close enough if good enough but he could never summon the necessary pace. (6/1)

**3430 Tertium (IRE)** moved moderately to post and never got into the race despite making a little late headway. (10/1)

**3280* Hazard a Guess (IRE)** walked round the paddock as though half asleep and showed no sparkle at all in the race. (9/2)

**Vindaloo** has certainly appreciated the rest and done well physically but did need this and blew up in the home straight. (33/1)

**3071 King Athelstan (USA)** (10/1: 8/1-12/1)

## 3510 EAST RIDING YEOMANRY CHALLENGE TROPHY AMATEUR H'CAP (0-80) (3-Y.O+) (Class E)

3-30 (3-32) **7f 100y** £3,254.00 (£977.00: £471.00: £218.00) Stalls: High GOING minus 0.74 sec per fur (HD)

| | Horse | Dist | Pos | SP | RR | SF |
|---|---|---|---|---|---|---|
| 888[6] | **Polly Peculiar (57)** (BSmart) **5-10-2**(4) MissVMarshall(6) (trckd ldrs: hdwy on ins to ld ins fnl f: r.o) | — | **1** | 12/1 | 65 | 46 |
| 3289* | **Cee-Jay-Ay (51)** (JBerry) **9-10-0** 5x MrsLPearce(5) (s.i.s: hdwy 2f out: r.o wl towards fin) | hd | **2** | 11/4[2] | 59 | 40 |
| 1890[7] | **Breezed Well (44)** (BRCambidge) **10-9-3**(4) MrsHNoonan(7) (led tl ins fnl f: kpt on same pce) | 1¼ | **3** | 33/1 | 49 | 30 |
| 3460* | **Euro Sceptic (IRE) (47)** (TDEasterby) **4-9-6b**(4) MissADeniel(4) (lw: sddle slipped: w ldr: nt qckn appr fnl f) | 2 | **4** | 7/4[1] | 48 | 29 |
| 3219[4] | **Fame Again (79)** (MrsJRRamsden) **4-11-10**(4) MissERamsden(1) (hld up: effrt 2f out: nt qckn) | ¾ | **5** | 9/2[3] | 78 | 59 |
| 3328* | **Tinklers Folly (68)** (DenysSmith) **4-10-13**(4) 5x MissMCarson(2) (trckd ldrs tl outpcd fnl 2f) | 1½ | **6** | 5/1 | 64 | 45 |
| | ***Khattat (USA) (66)*** (JAHarris) **6-10-8**(7) MrGWoodward(3) (Withdrawn not under Starter's orders: ref to ent stalls) | | **W** | 20/1 | — | — |
| | | | | (SP 113.3%) | | **6 Rn** |

**1m 33.0** (1.00) CSF £40.70 TOTE £11.00: £3.20 £1.70 (£18.20) OWNER Miss Victoria Marshall (LAMBOURN) BRED Aston Park Stud

LONG HANDICAP Breezed Well 8-12

**888 Polly Peculiar**, given a fine ride, got a run up the inner to lead inside the final furlong and stole just enough to keep the runner-up at bay. (12/1: 8/1-14/1)

**3289* Cee-Jay-Ay** is in tremendous form and, by the way he finished, he may yet pick up another race or two. (11/4)

**752 Breezed Well** ran a fair race but has only won once in the last seven years and that has been on the All-Weather. (33/1)

**3460* Euro Sceptic (IRE)** was hampered by a slipping saddle from the word go and this can be ignored. (7/4)

**3219 Fame Again** sat in behind the leaders going well but then failed to pick up when asked and is not an easy ride especially for an amateur. (9/2)

**3328* Tinklers Folly** had his chances but was short of speed in the last couple of furlongs. (5/1)

## 3511 HOLDERNESS PONY CLUB CLAIMING STKS (2-Y.O) (Class E)

4-00 (4-03) **5f** £3,241.00 (£973.00: £469.00: £217.00) Stalls: High GOING minus 0.74 sec per fur (HD)

| | Horse | Dist | Pos | SP | RR | SF |
|---|---|---|---|---|---|---|
| 3121[6] | **Rusty (IRE)** (JBerry) **2-8-5** JCarroll(6) (mde all: kpt on wl fnl f) | — | **1** | 10/1[3] | 59 | 4 |
| *3087** | **Perpetual (78)** (SirMarkPrescott) **2-8-11** GDuffield(7) (w wnr: rdn 2f out: nt qckn ins fnl f) | 1½ | **2** | 5/4[1] | 60 | 5 |
| 1858[3] | **In Good Nick** (MWEasterby) **2-8-11** LCharnock(13) (a chsng ldrs: kpt on towards fin) | ½ | **3** | 10/1[3] | 59 | 4 |
| 3324[8] | **Not A Lot (68)** (MWEasterby) **2-8-7**(5) GParkin(8) (mid div: effrt 2f out: nrst fin) | 3½ | **4** | 11/1 | 48 | — |
| 3250[8] | **Skyers Tryer** (RonaldThompson) **2-8-11** NConnorton(10) (chsd ldrs: rdn 2f out: nt qckn) | 1 | **5** | 33/1 | 44 | — |
| | **True Perspective** (JDBethell) **2-8-12** GBardwell(9) (small: unf: bhd: effrt ½-wy: nvr nrr) | ½ | **6** | 16/1 | 44 | — |
| 3291[3] | **Thewrightone (IRE) (57)** (GROldroyd) **2-7-13b** JLowe(3) (mid div: rdn 2f out: n.d) | 1¼ | **7** | 20/1 | 27 | — |
| | **The Dubious Goose** (MWEasterby) **2-9-2** DaleGibson(2) (small: s.i.s: n.d) | 2 | **8** | 25/1 | 37 | — |

2781[7] **Stravano** (BPJBaugh) **2-8-3** NCarlisle(11) (sn outpcd)..........2 **9** 33/1 18 —
2926* **Saunders Wren (74)** (MrsLStubbs) **2-8-11** KFallon(5) (spd 3f: wknd qckly & eased)..........1¾ **10** 2/1[2] 20 —
3293[11] **Ohio Royale** (PCHaslam) **2-9-2** JFortune(4) (rn green ½-wy: a bhd)..........3 **11** 25/1 16 —
3332[R] **Geoffreys Gamble** (BPJBaugh) **2-8-8** WLord(1) (s.i.s: a bhd)..........1¼ **12** 33/1 4 —
(SP 131.5%) **12 Rn**

**63.2 secs** (1.70) CSF £24.20 TOTE £10.20: £2.30 £1.10 £1.80 (£10.10) Trio £16.90 OWNER Mr Norman Jackson (COCKERHAM) BRED T. Ward

**3121 Rusty (IRE)** was a different proposition this time and, jumping off in front, kept up the gallop in game style. (10/1)
**3087* Perpetual** raced with the winner but she was never doing enough when the pressure was on. (5/4)
**1858 In Good Nick** ran well, chasing the leaders, and was keeping on particularly well in the closing stages suggesting that further should suit. (10/1: op 6/1)
**2389 Not A Lot** was gradually getting the hang of things as the race progressed but could never quicken enough to have a chance. (11/1)
**Skyers Tryer** showed plenty of speed but was done with in the last furlong and a half. (33/1)
**True Perspective** is only small but he did show something, staying on when it was all over. (16/1)

## 3512 PUNCH AND JUDY NURSERY H'CAP (2-Y.O) (Class D)

4-30 (4-31) **7f 100y** £3,619.50 (£1,086.00: £523.00: £241.50) Stalls: High GOING minus 0.74 sec per fur (HD)

SP RR SF

3311* **Sparky (59)** (MWEasterby) **2-8-2b** 5x DaleGibson(7) (a.p: rdn to ld appr fnl f: edgd lft & styd on wl)..........— **1** 13/2[3] 65 27
3324[4] **Skelton Sovereign (IRE) (70)** (RHollinshead) **2-8-10**(3) FLynch(6) (s.i.s: hdwy 2f out: styd on wl nr fin)..........1¾ **2** 16/1 72 34
3307[3] **Grate Times (78)** (EWeymes) **2-9-7** GDuffield(4) (a.p: effrt & ch 2f out: edgd rt & one pce fnl f)..........s.h **3** 16/1 80 42
2720* **Pun (78)** (DMorley) **2-9-7** JCarroll(3) (rr div: hdwy on outside 2f out: hung lft: nt qckn ins fnl f)..........s.h **4** 9/2[2] 80 42
2932* **Foxes Tail (77)** (MissSEHall) **2-9-6** NCarlisle(10) (b: b.off hind: lw: bhd: effrt 2f out: nvr able to chal)..........1¼ **5** 9/1 76 38
3099[4] **Floating Devon (62)** (TDEasterby) **2-8-5** MBirch(1) (disp ld tl led over 2f out: hdd appr fnl f: wknd)..........nk **6** 11/1 61 23
*2938*[5] **Clonavon Girl (IRE) (61)** (MJCamacho) **2-8-4** LCharnock(8) (chsd ldrs tl wknd fnl 2f)..........16 **7** 20/1 25 —
3275[4] **Rivonia (USA) (68)** (MrsJRRamsden) **2-8-11** KFallon(5) (lw: hld up: effrt over 2f out: btn & eased fnl f)..........nk **8** 15/8[1] 32 —
2959* **Poly Moon (59)** (MRChannon) **2-8-2** FNorton(9) (disp ld tl wknd over 2f out: bit slipped)..........6 **9** 7/1 10 —
2948[5] **Rons Revenge (58)** (MJRyan) **2-8-1** GBardwell(2) (chsd ldrs tl wknd over 2f out)..........3 **10** 16/1 2 —
(SP 119.5%) **10 Rn**

**1m 32.0** (0.00) CSF £91.07 CT £1,459.59 TOTE £9.70: £2.90 £3.30 £3.00 (£59.50) Trio £349.80; £448.34 to Newbury 16/8/96 OWNER Abbots Salford Carav Park (SHERIFF HUTTON) BRED Godolphin Management Co Ltd

OFFICIAL EXPLANATION **Clonavon Girl (IRE): lost a front shoe during the race.**
**Poly Moon: the bit pulled through the filly's mouth.**

**3311* Sparky** is in great form and, despite hanging to his left in the closing stages, there was nothing wrong with this performance. (13/2)
**3324 Skelton Sovereign (IRE)**, last away, finished fast but was too late to have a chance and obviously has more ability when he gets it together. (16/1)
**3307 Grate Times** has run miserably of late but was back to something like his true form here, just failing to quicken enough late on. (16/1)
**2720* Pun** gave the impression that she likes things to go her way. She was inclined to hang when ridden and may be better suited when out in front. (9/2)
**2932* Foxes Tail** was always a bit short of room and ran well enough to suggest that another race or two can be found. (9/1)
**3099 Floating Devon** helped make this a really strong pace but had run himself into the ground approaching the final furlong. (11/1)
**3275 Rivonia (USA)** was very disappointing, failing to pick up at all in the last two furlongs, and was then eased a good bit when beaten. (15/8)
**2959* Poly Moon** went too fast for her own good and the bit had slipped through her mouth. (7/1)

T/Plpt: £65.30 (192.13 Tckts). T/Qdpt: £35.60 (21.84 Tckts). AA

# 3493-SALISBURY (R-H) (Good to firm)

## Thursday August 15th

Race 2: flip start
WEATHER: fine WIND: almost nil

## 3513 BROAD CHALKE MAIDEN STKS (I) (3-Y.O) (Class D)

2-15 (2-18) **6f 212y** £3,288.00 (£984.00: £472.00: £216.00) Stalls: Centre GOING minus 0.46 sec per fur (F)

SP RR SF

3262[W] **Press On Nicky** (WRMuir) **3-8-6**(3) DaneO'Neill(6) (hld up & bhd: hdwy wl over 1f out: r.o to ld ins fnl f)..........— **1** 16/1 74 39
3353[7] **Midday Cowboy (USA)** (GHarwood) **3-9-0** JQuinn(9) (hld up & bhd: hdwy over 3f out: rdn over 2f out: led over 1f out tl ins fnl f)..........1 **2** 25/1 77 42
1142[9] **Zurs (IRE)** (MissGayKelleway) **3-9-0** RCochrane(3) (b.hind: lw: hld up & bhd: hdwy 2f out: nt clr run 1f out: r.o)..........1¼ **3** 13/2[3] 74 39
1435[2] **High Cut** (IABalding) **3-8-9** TQuinn(2) (swtg: a.p: rdn to ld over 2f out: hdd over 1f out: one pce)..........¾ **4** 100/30[2] 67 32
1901[16] **Sovereigns Court** (MajorDNChappell) **3-9-0** TSprake(4) (hdwy over 2f out: rdn & ev ch over 1f out: sn edgd lft: one pce)..........1½ **5** 25/1 69 34
*3064*[3] **Stackattack (IRE)** (PRWebber) **3-9-0** JFEgan(10) (lw: hld up: swtchd lft over 1f out: nvr nr to chal)..........nk **6** 12/1 68 33
2996[5] **Summer Beauty** (JHMGosden) **3-8-9** JReid(11) (b.hind: hld up & plld hrd: dropped rr over 3f out: late hdwy)..........nk **7** 6/4[1] 62 27
1882[4] **Ruwy (68)** (CJBenstead) **3-8-9** WCarson(8) (bit bkwd: prom: rdn over 2f out: edgd lft over 1f out: nt clr run ins fnl f)..........1¼ **8** 10/1 59 24
3162[2] **Redskin Lady (56)** (DRCElsworth) **3-8-9** PatEddery(7) (led over 4f: wknd wl over 1f out)..........2 **9** 8/1 55 20
3162[7] **Country Thatch (65)** (CAHorgan) **3-9-0** PaulEddery(1) (lw: prom over 4f)..........1¼ **10** 25/1 57 22
2718[10] **Saving Power** (PWHarris) **3-9-0** GHind(5) (prom over 4f)..........6 **11** 50/1 43 8
(SP 123.7%) **11 Rn**

**1m 27.49** (1.49) CSF £297.69 TOTE £16.80: £3.70 £8.40 £2.40 (£78.10) Trio £124.00 OWNER S/M/P Syndicate (LAMBOURN) BRED Sydney Mason

**1333 Press On Nicky**, with her starting-stall problems apparently a thing of the past, seemed to appreciate reverting to seven. (16/1)
**3353 Midday Cowboy (USA)** was another returning to this trip after apparently failing to stay a mile. (25/1)
**1142 Zurs (IRE)** has changed stables since a promising debut. He would have gone very close with an uninterrupted run and should soon pick up a race. (13/2: 4/1-7/1)

**1435 High Cut**, lightly-raced having apparently suffered from a fractured pelvis, was very warm in the preliminaries and is probably better than this. (100/30)
**Sovereigns Court** did the third no favours when coming off a true line and might be worth a try dropping back to six. (25/1)
**3064 Stackattack (IRE)** gives the impression he needs a mile. (12/1: 8/1-14/1)
**2996 Summer Beauty**, a 25,000 guineas half-sister to Uncharted Waters, had made the running on her debut and will do better when she learns to settle. (6/4)
**1882 Ruwy** will be sharper for the outing but may need further. (10/1: op 5/1)

## 3514 VIOLET APPLIN CHALLENGE CUP H'CAP (0-70) (3-Y.O+) (Class E)

2-45 (2-45) **1m 6f** £3,158.00 (£944.00: £452.00: £206.00) Stalls: Low GOING minus 0.46 sec per fur (F)

| Form | Horse | Dist | Pos | SP | RR | SF |
|---|---|---|---|---|---|---|
| 3141[2] | **Norsong (51)** (RAkehurst) **4-9-0** TQuinn(7) (chsd ldr: led over 2f out: all out) | — | 1 | 100/30[1] | 58 | 11 |
| 3337[2] | **Sterling Fellow (55)** (RHannon) **3-8-2b**(3)ow1 DaneO'Neill(2) (lw: a.p: ev ch fnl 2f: r.o) | nk | 2 | 4/1[2] | 62 | 1 |
| 3318[6] | **Wottashambles (39)** (LMontagueHall) **5-8-2** SSanders(3) (hld up: hdwy over 3f out: rdn over 2f out: r.o one pce) | 2 | 3 | 10/1 | 43 | — |
| 3113[6] | **Mancini (67)** (MBell) **3-9-3** RCochrane(4) (prom: rdn over 3f out: r.o one pce) | hd | 4 | 10/1 | 71 | 11 |
| 2739[5] | **Fast Forward Fred (48)** (LMontagueHall) **5-8-11** JFEgan(1) (hld up & bhd: rdn over 3f out: hdwy & edgd rt over 2f out: one pce) | 1½ | 5 | 20/1 | 51 | 4 |
| 3260[6] | **Supreme Star (USA) (62)** (PRHedger) **5-9-4**(7) DavidO'Neill(6) (hld up & plld hrd: nt clr run on ins over 2f out: plld out over 1f out: nvr nr to chal) | 1¼ | 6 | 4/1[2] | 63 | 16 |
| 3079[5] | **Minnisam (69)** (JLDunlop) **3-9-5b** TSprake(8) (led: hrd rdn & hdd over 2f out: wknd over 1f out) | 2½ | 7 | 6/1[3] | 67 | 7 |
| 1618[4] | **Crested Knight (IRE) (54)** (CAHorgan) **4-9-3** PaulEddery(5) (hld up & bhd: rdn over 3f out: no rspnse) | nk | 8 | 8/1 | 52 | 5 |

(SP 111.4%) **8 Rn**

**3m 8.18** (9.48) CSF £15.64 CT £103.80 TOTE £3.30: £1.40 £1.40 £2.60 (£4.80) OWNER The Fairy Story Partnership (EPSOM) BRED Deepwood Farm Stud
WEIGHT FOR AGE 3yo-13lb
**3141 Norsong**, up 3lb, got the extra quarter-mile well and had to dig deep to hold on. (100/30)
**3337 Sterling Fellow** gave a real good account of himself over this shorter trip, but the winner would not be denied. (4/1)
**3318 Wottashambles** seems to need even further to offset his lack of finishing speed. (10/1)
**3113 Mancini**, dropped 3lb, was trying another step up in distance. (10/1)
**2739 Fast Forward Fred** has not reproduced the form of his second to Ashby Hill on his seasonal reappearance. (20/1)
**3260 Supreme Star (USA)**, up to the right sort of trip, was still running off a mark 4lb higher than when registering his third win last season. (4/1)
**3079 Minnisam** should have been suited by the extra quarter-mile, but did not get home on this occasion. (6/1: op 4/1)
**1618 Crested Knight (IRE)** (8/1: 6/1-10/1)

## 3515 TATTERSALLS MAIDEN AUCTION STKS (2-Y.O) (Class E)

3-15 (3-18) **6f** £3,262.00 (£976.00: £468.00: £214.00) GOING minus 0.46 sec per fur (F)

| Form | Horse | Dist | Pos | SP | RR | SF |
|---|---|---|---|---|---|---|
| 2712[3] | **Salty Jack (IRE) (73)** (SDow) **2-8-4** TQuinn(11) (a.p: hrd rdn over 2f out: led last strides) | — | 1 | 10/1 | 75 | 19 |
| 3454[3] | **Northern Girl (IRE)** (BJMeehan) **2-7-8**(5) MartinDwyer(6) (led: hrd rdn & hdd last strides) | hd | 2 | 5/1[2] | 70 | 14 |
| 3105[3] | **Scarlet Crescent** (PTWalwyn) **2-8-0** TSprake(4) (a.p: ev ch 2f out: unable qckn) | 1½ | 3 | 5/1[2] | 67 | 11 |
| 3105[2] | **Celebrant** (RHannon) **2-8-2** JFEgan(13) (a.p: n.m.r over 2f out: sn rdn: one pce) | 1¼ | 4 | 9/4[1] | 65 | 9 |
| 2614[7] | **Circle of Magic** (PJMakin) **2-8-2** SSanders(8) (no hdwy fnl 2f) | 1¾ | 5 | 8/1 | 61 | 5 |
| 3234[6] | **Hallmark (IRE)** (RHannon) **2-8-4**(3) DaneO'Neill(3) (lw: nvr plcd to chal) | hd | 6 | 15/2 | 66 | 10 |
| | **M R Poly** (MRChannon) **2-8-9** CRutter(2) (w'like: bit bkwd: s.s: plld hrd: nvr nrr) | 1¼ | 7 | 16/1 | 64 | 8 |
| | **Saffron Rose** (MBlanshard) **2-7-13** JQuinn(7) (unf: nvr nr ldrs) | ¾ | 8 | 20/1 | 52 | — |
| | **Dom Ruinart (IRE)** (JWHills) **2-8-5** PatEddery(1) (cmpt: bkwd: prom over 4f) | nk | 9 | 7/1[3] | 57 | 1 |
| 3114[11] | **Hever Golf Charger (IRE)** (TJNaughton) **2-8-9** PaulEddery(5) (hld up & plld hrd: bhd fnl 2f) | nk | 10 | 33/1 | 61 | 5 |
| *3088[3]* | **Dizzy Tilly (66)** (TJNaughton) **2-8-1** AMcGlone(12) (lw: w ldr tl rdn & wknd 2f out) | ¾ | 11 | 20/1 | 51 | — |
| | **Ron's Round** (KOCunningham-Brown) **2-8-5** CMunday(9) (leggy: w'like: bit bkwd: s.s: a bhd) | 1¼ | 12 | 33/1 | 51 | — |

(SP 129.9%) **12 Rn**

**1m 15.39** (2.39) CSF £60.55 TOTE £9.40: £2.10 £2.00 £1.70 (£50.90) Trio £62.30 OWNER Salts Of The Earth-Four Seasons Racing (EPSOM) BRED Airlie Stud
**OFFICIAL EXPLANATION Hallmark (IRE): was hanging and rolling around in the final two furlongs, and as a result his rider was unable to ride him out.**
**2712 Salty Jack (IRE)** should stay further and might get in a nursery on a reasonable mark. (10/1)
**3454 Northern Girl (IRE)**, making a quick reappearance, was supported in the ring and very nearly pulled it off. (5/1)
**3105 Scarlet Crescent**, a half-sister to Comeonup, should not be inconvenienced by another furlong. (5/1: op 3/1)
**3105 Celebrant**, an uneasy favourite, should not be considered unlucky. (9/4: op 11/10)
**Circle of Magic**, out of a half-sister to a Prix Lupin winner, fared much better than on her debut. (8/1)
**Hallmark (IRE)**, not surprisingly, caught the eye of the Stewards who considered his running. Having heard from his rider that the colt was hanging and rolling around in the final two furlongs and, as a result, he was unable to ride him out, the Stewards decided not to hold an enquiry. (15/2)
**M R Poly**, a half-brother to seven-furlong winner Chance Report, should come on for this but will need to learn to settle. (16/1)
**Dom Ruinart (IRE)** (7/1: op 7/2)

## 3516 TOTE BOOKMAKERS H'CAP (0-95) (3-Y.O+) (Class C)

3-45 (3-48) **1m** £6,027.50 (£1,820.00: £885.00: £417.50) GOING minus 0.46 sec per fur (F)

| Form | Horse | Dist | Pos | SP | RR | SF |
|---|---|---|---|---|---|---|
| 3076* | **Saleemah (USA) (86)** (JLDunlop) **3-9-1** WCarson(5) (chsd ldr: led on bit over 2f out: pushed out) | — | 1 | 3/1[1] | 98+ | 59 |
| 809[2] | **Almond Rock (88)** (JRFanshawe) **4-9-10** DHarrison(9) (hld up & plld hrd: hdwy over 2f out: ev ch fnl f: unable qckn) | ½ | 2 | 8/1 | 99 | 67 |
| 3123[4] | **Fionn de Cool (IRE) (70)** (RAkehurst) **5-8-6** TQuinn(1) (hld up: hdwy over 2f out: rdn over 1f out: one pce) | 4 | 3 | 7/1[3] | 73 | 41 |
| 2557[5] | **Phonetic (78)** (GBBalding) **3-8-7** SDrowne(7) (hld up & bhd: hdwy fnl 2f: r.o) | nk | 4 | 20/1 | 80 | 41 |
| | **Shamrock Fair (IRE) (70)** (LordHuntingdon) **4-8-6** WWoods(8) (s.s: plld hrd: hdwy over 1f out: nt rch ldrs) | s.h | 5 | 33/1 | 72 | 40 |
| 3148[7] | **Victorian Style (86)** (RCharlton) **3-9-1** TSprake(6) (plld hrd: prom: hrd rdn 2f out: wknd over 1f out) | s.h | 6 | 9/1 | 88 | 49 |
| 2761[5] | **Greatest (60)** (MissGayKelleway) **5-7-5**(5) MartinDwyer(14) (lw: led over 5f: wknd wl over 1f out) | 2 | 7 | 9/1 | 58 | 26 |
| 3123[15] | **Comanche Companion (77)** (TJNaughton) **6-8-13** PaulEddery(3) (prom over 6f) | ½ | 8 | 33/1 | 74 | 42 |

| | Horse / details | Dist | Pos | SP | RR | SF |
|---|---|---|---|---|---|---|
| 2145[4] | **Prize Pupil (IRE) (69)** (CFWall) **4-8-5** PatEddery(2) (hld up: hrd rdn & wknd over 2f out) | nk | **9** | 7/1[3] | 66 | 34 |
| 3072[4] | **Conspicuous (IRE) (79)** (LGCottrell) **6-9-1v[1]** JQuinn(10) (s.s: plld hrd: a bhd) | nk | **10** | 6/1[2] | 75 | 43 |
| 3148[9] | **Catch The Lights (85)** (RHannon) **3-8-11**(3) DaneO'Neill(13) (lw: bhd fnl 2f) | 1¼ | **11** | 12/1 | 79 | 40 |
| 2526[11] | **Brighton Road (IRE) (77)** (GBBalding) **3-8-1**(5) PPMurphy(4) (lw: bhd fnl 2f) | 4 | **12** | 25/1 | 63 | 24 |
| 2743[6] | **Summerhill Special (IRE) (62)** (MrsPNDutfield) **5-7-12**ow2 CRutter(12) (prom over 5f) | 2½ | **13** | 33/1 | 43 | 9 |
| 3210[11] | **Lilli Claire (88)** (AGFoster) **3-9-3** SSanders(11) (plld hrd: bhd fnl 3f) | 8 | **14** | 9/1 | 53 | 14 |
| | | | | (SP 130.5%) | | **14 Rn** |

**1m 40.7** (0.30) CSF £28.13 CT £151.97 TOTE £4.40: £2.60 £2.00 £2.90 (£11.30) Trio £28.30 OWNER Mr Hamdan Al Maktoum (ARUNDEL) BRED Manning Family Trust
LONG HANDICAP Summerhill Special (IRE) 7-7
WEIGHT FOR AGE 3yo-7lb
**3076* Saleemah (USA)** completed the hat-trick off an 8lb higher mark and scored more easily than the margin suggests. (3/1)
**809 Almond Rock**, 4lb higher than when second at Sandown, has probably been waiting for some decent ground and ran a fine race in trying to concede weight to the progressive winner. (8/1: op 5/1)
**3123 Fionn de Cool (IRE)** showed signs of a return to form at Goodwood but could not take advantage of being 19lb better off with the runner-up than when beating him in this race last year. (7/1)
**2557 Phonetic** needs further and perhaps a little more cut in the ground. (20/1)
**Shamrock Fair (IRE)**, taken to post early, may have been slowly away by design because she certainly took a strong hold. This was a pleasing enough comeback. (33/1)
**3148 Victorian Style** could well be at her best with some give underfoot. (9/1)
**2585* Lilli Claire** (9/1: 8/1-12/1)

## 3517 WHITCHURCH CONDITIONS STKS (3-Y.O+) (Class C)

4-15 (4-16) **6f 212y** £5,112.00 (£1,908.00: £929.00: £395.00: £172.50: £83.50) Stalls: Centre GOING minus 0.46 sec per fur (F)

| | Horse / details | Dist | Pos | SP | RR | SF |
|---|---|---|---|---|---|---|
| 3263* | **Wizard King (114)** (SirMarkPrescott) **5-9-10** WWoods(8) (w ldr: led over 5f out: clr over 1f out: r.o wl) | — | **1** | 5/2[1] | 117 | 64 |
| 3229[2] | **Russian Music (103)** (MissGayKelleway) **3-9-0** RCochrane(5) (a.p: chsd wnr over 1f out: no imp) | 2½ | **2** | 11/4[2] | 107 | 48 |
| 3232[8] | **Loch Patrick (105)** (MMadgwick) **6-9-8** JReid(7) (lw: rdn over 3f out: hdwy over 1f out: r.o one pce fnl f) | 1¾ | **3** | 16/1 | 105 | 52 |
| 2346* | **Lonely Leader (IRE)** (RHannon) **3-8-11**(3) DaneO'Neill(3) (lw: a.p: rdn over 2f out: one pce) | s.h | **4** | 9/2[3] | 103 | 44 |
| | **Polska (USA)** (DRLoder) **3-8-5** PatEddery(2) (rdn & hdwy 2f out: nvr nr to chal) | 2 | **5** | 6/1 | 90 | 31 |
| 3127[11] | **Bewitching (USA) (102)** (JARToller) **3-8-11** SSanders(6) (lw: no hdwy fnl 2f) | nk | **6** | 7/1 | 95 | 36 |
| 570[4] | **Tria Kemata (104)** (JLDunlop) **3-8-10** TQuinn(1) (swtg: hld up & plld hrd: a bhd) | ½ | **7** | 16/1 | 93 | 34 |
| 3127[9] | **Brief Glimpse (IRE) (100)** (MajorDNChappell) **4-8-11b[1]** WCarson(4) (led over 1f: w wnr tl rdn & wknd wl over 1f out) | 1¼ | **8** | 15/2 | 85 | 32 |
| | | | | (SP 123.7%) | | **8 Rn** |

**1m 26.5** (0.50) CSF £10.38 TOTE £3.40: £1.90 £1.20 £3.00 (£5.20) OWNER Sheikh Ahmed bin Saeed Al Maktoum (NEWMARKET) BRED Sheikh Mohammed bin Rashid al Maktoum
WEIGHT FOR AGE 3yo-6lb
OFFICIAL EXPLANATION **Brief Glimpse (IRE): was found to be coughing after the race.**
**3263* Wizard King** had more to do here than at Chester, but his style of racing means he finds this type of event easier than conceding lumps of weight in handicaps. (5/2: 7/4-11/4)
**3229 Russian Music** had no excuses, but is probably better at a mile these days. (11/4)
**2545 Loch Patrick** was not disgraced over this longer trip and would have been better off in a handicap. (16/1)
**2346* Lonely Leader (IRE)** had a lot more on his plate here and did not prove up to it. He ran over a mile as a two-year-old so perhaps an extra furlong might help. (9/2)
**Polska (USA)**, making a belated seasonal debut, seems to need a mile. (6/1: op 4/1)
**2704 Bewitching (USA)** was reportedly sore after spreading a plate last time. (7/1)

## 3518 FRESHWATER H'CAP (0-80) (3-Y.O+) (Class D)

4-45 (4-45) **6f** £4,159.00 (£1,252.00: £606.00: £283.00) Stalls: High GOING minus 0.46 sec per fur (F)

| | Horse / details | Dist | Pos | SP | RR | SF |
|---|---|---|---|---|---|---|
| 2615* | **La Petite Fusee (73)** (RJO'Sullivan) **5-9-11** DBiggs(5) (b.nr hind: broke wl: mde all: rdn out) | — | **1** | 8/1 | 85 | 66 |
| 2957[4] | **Pointer (54)** (MrsPNDutfield) **4-8-1**(5) AimeeCook(1) (hld up: hdwy over 2f out: ev ch 1f out: r.o one pce) | ¾ | **2** | 6/1[1] | 64 | 45 |
| 3165[2] | **White Settler (70)** (RJHodges) **3-9-4** TSprake(14) (hld up: swtchd lft & hdwy 2f out: edgd lft ins fnl f: r.o wl) | 2 | **3** | 13/2[2] | 75 | 52 |
| 2615[3] | **Purple Fling (72)** (LGCottrell) **5-9-10** JQuinn(10) (a.p: one pce fnl 2f) | ¾ | **4** | 8/1 | 75 | 56 |
| 819[11] | **Bright Diamond (56)** (JRArnold) **3-8-4** CRutter(7) (hld up & bhd: gd late hdwy: nrst fin) | 1¼ | **5** | 33/1 | 55 | 32 |
| 3167* | **Winsome Wooster (63)** (PGMurphy) **5-9-1** SDrowne(9) (a.p: no hdwy fnl 2f) | nk | **6** | 8/1 | 62 | 43 |
| 2529[4] | **Azwah (USA) (63)** (PTWalwyn) **3-8-11** WCarson(16) (chsd ldrs: rdn 2f out: eased whn btn ins fnl f) | 3 | **7** | 8/1 | 54 | 31 |
| 3340[5] | **Master Millfield (IRE) (69)** (RJBaker) **4-9-7** RCochrane(11) (nvr nr to chal) | hd | **8** | 11/1 | 59 | 40 |
| 2947[5] | **Thordis (70)** (PJMakin) **3-9-4** DHarrison(15) (no hdwy fnl 2f) | ½ | **9** | 12/1 | 59 | 36 |
| 3167[3] | **Nunsharpa (74)** (JRFanshawe) **3-9-8** JReid(8) (a.p: hrd rdn over 2f out: wknd wl over 1f out) | ½ | **10** | 7/1[3] | 62 | 39 |
| 3122[4] | **Stoney End (USA) (66)** (MRChannon) **3-8-7**(7) AEddery(6) (lw: a bhd) | 1¼ | **11** | 16/1 | 50 | 27 |
| 3210[15] | **Cross of Valour (78)** (JARToller) **3-9-12** SSanders(2) (rdn 3f out: a bhd) | ½ | **12** | 20/1 | 61 | 38 |
| 2980[5] | **Paint It Black (75)** (RHannon) **3-9-6b**(3) DaneO'Neill(13) (lw: a bhd) | nk | **13** | 16/1 | 57 | 34 |
| 2858[6] | **Chili Heights (55)** (GBBalding) **6-8-2v**(5) PPMurphy(4) (a bhd) | 1½ | **14** | 20/1 | 33 | 14 |
| 3151[15] | **Masruf (IRE) (64)** (TThomsonJones) **4-9-2** TIves(3) (bhd fnl 2f) | 3 | **15** | 33/1 | 34 | 15 |
| 3151[5] | **Dawalib (USA) (61)** (DHaydnJones) **6-8-13** PaulEddery(12) (prom: hrd rdn over 2f out: wknd qckly) | 2 | **16** | 11/1 | 26 | 7 |
| | | | | (SP 136.1%) | | **16 Rn** |

**1m 13.36** (0.36) CSF £57.41 CT £330.19 TOTE £6.20: £1.80 £1.70 £2.60 £2.10 (£26.80) Trio £88.80 OWNER Mr M. T. Bevan (WHITCOMBE) BRED H. Powis
WEIGHT FOR AGE 3yo-4lb
**2615* La Petite Fusee** quickly got to the far rail and took advantage of being unpenalised by the Handicapper after a win in a Limited Stakes at Chepstow. (8/1)
**2957 Pointer**, challenging up the centre, could never quite peg back the winner. (6/1)
**3165 White Settler**, raised 4lb, found this trip inadequate and finished with a flourish, despite not helping his rider. (13/2)
**2615 Purple Fling** failed to take advantage of being 4lb better off with the winner than at Chepstow. (8/1)
**Bright Diamond**, off the course since the end of April, did not appear suited to this shorter distance and is one to keep an eye on. (33/1)
**3167* Winsome Wooster** had to contend with a 7lb rise in the weights, faster ground and a shorter trip. (8/1)
**2529 Azwah (USA)** was surprisingly trying her luck at sprinting. (8/1)

## 3519 BROAD CHALKE MAIDEN STKS (II) (3-Y.O) (Class D)

5-15 (5-15) **6f 212y** £3,262.00 (£976.00: £468.00: £214.00) Stalls: Centre GOING minus 0.46 sec per fur (F)

| | | | | SP | RR | SF |
|---|---|---|---|---|---|---|
| 669[2] | **Consort** (GHarwood) **3-9-0** TQuinn(6) (lw: plld hrd: a.p: led ins fnl f: pushed out) | — | 1 | 5/6[1] | 80 | 49 |
| 2532[3] | **Alpine Hideaway (IRE) (78)** (BHanbury) **3-9-0** MRimmer(3) (b: b.nr hind: plld hrd: led tl ins fnl f) | 1¾ | 2 | 4/1[2] | 76 | 45 |
| | **Intimation** (JARToller) **3-8-9** SSanders(5) (lt-f: unf: gd hdwy over 2f out: ev ch over 1f out: wknd ins fnl f) | 4 | 3 | 10/1 | 62 | 31 |
| 3226[3] | **Alrayyih (USA)** (JHMGosden) **3-9-0** WCarson(9) (lw: hdwy 3f out: sn rdn: wknd wl over 1f out) | 3 | 4 | 5/1[3] | 60 | 29 |
| 3270[2] | **Sea Danzig (64)** (JJBridger) **3-9-0** DHarrison(7) (w ldrs: rdn over 3f out: wknd over 2f out) | 1¾ | 5 | 12/1 | 56 | 25 |
| 2744[11] | **Bolder Still** (RTPhillips) **3-9-0** CRutter(1) (lw: nvr trbld ldrs) | 3 | 6 | 66/1 | 49 | 18 |
| 3262[16] | **Rapid Retreat (FR)** (EALDunlop) **3-8-9** JReid(8) (b: b.hind: lw: prom over 4f) | 6 | 7 | 10/1 | 30 | — |
| 1319[9] | **Sandpiper** (KOCunningham-Brown) **3-8-9** CMunday(10) (prom over 2f) | ½ | 8 | 50/1 | 29 | — |
| 458[5] | **Riverbourne (USA)** (MRChannon) **3-8-9**(5) PPMurphy(2) (a bhd) | 1¼ | 9 | 9/1 | 31 | — |
| 3115[12] | **Highly Spirited** (NMLampard) **3-8-7**(7) TField(4) (prom 3f: t.o) | 14 | 10 | 66/1 | — | — |
| | | | | (SP 132.0%) | | **10 Rn** |

**1m 26.97** (0.97) CSF £5.74 TOTE £2.40: £1.30 £1.70 £2.80 (£5.90) Trio £32.00 OWNER Mr K. Abdulla (PULBOROUGH) BRED Crest Stud Ltd

**669 Consort** gradually gained control in the final furlong and the time compared favourably with the first division. (5/6)

**2532 Alpine Hideaway (IRE)** has had plenty of chances. (4/1)

**Intimation**, a half-sister to Model Village and several other winners, made a promising enough debut. (10/1: op 7/2)

**3226 Alrayyih (USA)**, dropping back from a mile, does not appear to be progressing but is at least now qualified for handicaps. (5/1: op 3/1)

**3270 Sea Danzig**, coming from handicap company, was stepping up in distance. (12/1: op 8/1)

**Bolder Still** was apparently considered not to have stayed on his ten-furlong debut at Windsor. (66/1)

**Rapid Retreat (FR)** (10/1: op 5/1)

**458 Riverbourne (USA)** (9/1: 6/1-10/1)

T/Jkpt: Not won; £91,244.22 to Newbury 16/8/96. T/Plpt: £349.50 (63.25 Tckts). T/Qdpt: £9.10 (189.41 Tckts). KH

# 3355-YARMOUTH (L-H) (Good to firm)

## Thursday August 15th

WEATHER: fine WIND: mod half bhd

## 3520 24TH RUNNING OF THE BOTTON BROTHERS LADIES' H'CAP (0-70) (3-Y.O+) (Class G)

5-35 (5-35) **1m 6f 17y** £2,385.00 (£660.00: £315.00) Stalls: High GOING minus 0.44 sec per fur (F)

| | | | | SP | RR | SF |
|---|---|---|---|---|---|---|
| 3218[5] | **Children's Choice (IRE) (52)** (CNAllen) **5-11-1** MrsDKettlewell(4) (a.p: rdn over 3f out: led 1f out: styd on wl) | — | 1 | 8/1[3] | 62 | 50 |
| 3308* | **Spinning Mouse (59)** (DMorley) **3-10-9** 4x MissDianaJones(2) (plld hrd: trckd ldrs: rdn 2f out: r.o: nt rch wnr) | 1¼ | 2 | 5/4[1] | 68 | 43 |
| 3141[11] | **El Volador (50)** (CNAllen) **9-10-13** MrsJSaunders(1) (chsd ldrs: rdn 3f out: kpt on appr fnl f) | ¾ | 3 | 14/1 | 58 | 46 |
| 3428[2] | **Nosey Native (53)** (JPearce) **3-10-3** MrsLPearce(3) (stdd s: hdwy 6f out: one pce fnl 2f) | 2 | 4 | 2/1[2] | 59 | 34 |
| 2707[7] | **Lucky Coin (58)** (PHowling) **4-11-7** MissAEmbiricos(5) (led 4f: led 6f out to 1f out: unable qckn) | 1¾ | 5 | 14/1 | 62 | 50 |
| 3348[6] | **D'naan (IRE) (57)** (WJHaggas) **3-10-7b** MissLHide(7) (lw: bhd fnl 7f) | 22 | 6 | 12/1 | 36 | 11 |
| 3273[4] | **Bresil (USA) (42)** (KRBurke) **7-10-2**(3)ow10 MrsHSweeting(8) (lw: rn wd after 2f: led after 4f to 6f out: rn wd & sn bhd) | 1¼ | 7 | 25/1 | 19 | — |
| | | | | (SP 113.8%) | | **7 Rn** |

**3m 6.7** (7.30) CSF £18.02 CT £127.57 TOTE £8.70: £3.20 £1.50 (£6.30) OWNER Mrs A. V. Totman (NEWMARKET) BRED M. J. Cassidy

WEIGHT FOR AGE 3yo-13lb

**3218 Children's Choice (IRE)** fell when clear at the last for this rider at Huntingdon in March and is gradually getting further as she gets older. (8/1: 6/1-10/1)

**3308* Spinning Mouse** looked to travelling best for a long time in the straight but took a long time to pick up once let down and was never doing enough. She is rather light and got warm beforehand but this did not appear to affect her performance. (5/4: Evens-6/4)

**498 El Volador** is an All-Weather specialist who does not seem to win in the summer months but ran well on this occasion despite moving to post as if feeling the ground. (14/1: 10/1-16/1)

**3428 Nosey Native** sulked round the paddock and failed to pick up in the latter stages. (2/1)

**2415 Lucky Coin** seems to prefer fast ground despite a round action and took a fair bit of pegging back. (14/1: op 8/1)

**D'naan (IRE)** looked tremendously well but moved to post dreadfully on the fast surface and was never going. He won his only All-Weather start and looks in need of a return to that surface. (12/1: 7/1-14/1)

**3273 Bresil (USA)** lost many lengths on the bends and this is best ignored. (25/1)

## 3521 DAMGATE LIMITED STKS (0-80) (3-Y.O+) (Class D)

6-05 (6-05) **1m 2f 21y** £3,827.55 (£1,142.40: £545.70: £247.35) GOING minus 0.44 sec per fur (F)

| | | | | SP | RR | SF |
|---|---|---|---|---|---|---|
| 2955* | **Diminutive (USA) (79)** (JWHills) **3-8-9**(3) MHenry(2) (lw: hld up: hdwy whn nt clr run over 2f out: rdn to ld 1f out: r.o wl) | — | 1 | 6/1 | 91 | 54 |
| 2693[6] | **Courageous Dancer (IRE) (79)** (BHanbury) **4-9-0** JStack(1) (swtg: trckd ldrs: led over 1f out: rdn & hdd 1f out: : r.o) | 2 | 2 | 3/1[1] | 81 | 53 |
| 2894[4] | **Alambar (IRE) (78)** (PTWalwyn) **3-8-10** KDarley(3) (lw: led over 8f: unable qckn) | nk | 3 | 4/1[3] | 85 | 48 |
| 3125[7] | **Czarna (IRE) (78)** (CEBrittain) **5-8-10**(7) JGotobed(5) (swtg: hld up: effrt over 1f out: r.o ins fnl f) | ¾ | 4 | 7/2[2] | 82 | 54 |
| 2601[7] | **Annecy (USA) (78)** (HRACecil) **3-8-5** WRyan(4) (w ldr: rdn 3f out: no ex appr fnl f) | s.h | 5 | 4/1[3] | 79 | 42 |
| 2876[2] | **Blatant Outburst (79)** (GCBravery) **6-9-3** WRSwinburn(6) (lw: chsd ldrs: rdn over 2f out: sn btn) | 2½ | 6 | 6/1 | 78 | 50 |
| | | | | (SP 115.8%) | | **6 Rn** |

**2m 5.2** (0.80) CSF £23.38 TOTE £5.80: £3.00 £2.50 (£14.30) OWNER Gainsbury Partnership (LAMBOURN) BRED Mr & Mrs James W. Phillips

WEIGHT FOR AGE 3yo-9lb

**2955* Diminutive (USA)**, the worst in at the weights on Official figures, is at least in form and did these for foot after getting none too clear a run. (6/1)

**2693 Courageous Dancer (IRE)** found an ideal opportunity but still could not break her duck for the season although she ran well, squeezing through towards the inside to head for home only to be outspeeded by the winner. (3/1)

**2894 Alambar (IRE)**, again dictating the pace from the front, tried to steal a march turning for home but could never get clear. (4/1)
**2497 Czarna (IRE)**, stepping up in trip, was held up on this occasion. Pulled wide to challenge, he stayed on late and may be better than this. (7/2)
**1434 Annecy (USA)** took the leader on but cracked early in the straight. (4/1)
**2876 Blatant Outburst**, a good mover, couldn't get to the front and ran rather flat. (6/1)

## 3522 ANGLIAN WATER H'CAP (0-80) (3-Y.O F) (Class D)

6-35 (6-36) **1m 2f 21y** £3,927.00 (£1,173.00: £561.00: £255.00) Stalls: Low GOING minus 0.44 sec per fur (F)

| | | | | SP | RR | SF |
|---|---|---|---|---|---|---|
| 3248[10] | **Stately Dancer (72)** (GWragg) **3-9-5** JStack(2) (prom tl lost pl 7f out: dropped rr over 3f out: str run appr fnl f: led nr fin) | — | **1** | 12/1 | 78 | 40 |
| 3148[8] | **Omara (USA) (74)** (HRACecil) **3-9-7** WRyan(1) (gd hdwy to ld over 1f out: sn rdn & qckn clr: idled & ct nr fin) | hd | **2** | 8/1 | 80 | 42 |
| 2980[4] | **Possessive Artiste (71)** (MRStoute) **3-9-4** WRSwinburn(3) (hld up: hdwy & edgd lft over 3f out: r.o fnl f) | 1 | **3** | 7/1[3] | 75 | 37 |
| 3133[5] | **Seeking Fortune (USA) (74)** (JRFanshawe) **3-9-4**(3) NVarley(8) (prom: led over 3f out tl over 1f out: wknd ins fnl f) | 2 | **4** | 6/1[2] | 75 | 37 |
| 2924[7] | **Naval Gazer (IRE) (70)** (DRLoder) **3-9-3** DRMcCabe(5) (plld hrd: prom: rdn & lost pl over 3f out: styd on fnl f) | ¾ | **5** | 14/1 | 70 | 32 |
| 3249[7] | **Temptress (65)** (PTWalwyn) **3-8-12** KDarley(7) (lw: led tl over 3f out: btn appr fnl f) | hd | **6** | 8/1 | 65 | 27 |
| 3108* | **Rehaab (70)** (ACStewart) **3-9-3** SWhitworth(4) (plld hrd: trckd ldrs: no hdwy fnl 2f) | nk | **7** | 6/4[1] | 69 | 31 |
| 2605[6] | **Classic Ballet (FR) (67)** (RHarris) **3-9-0** AMackay(6) (lw: nvr trbld ldrs) | 4 | **8** | 12/1 | 60 | 22 |
| 2576[8] | **Baltic Dream (USA) (70)** (KRBurke) **3-9-3** GCarter(9) (lw: plld hrd: prom 7f) | 21 | **9** | 20/1 | 30 | — |

(SP 115.8%) **9 Rn**

**2m 7.8** (3.40) CSF £92.97 CT £664.04 TOTE £10.50: £2.40 £2.40 £1.80 (£20.30) Trio £66.20 OWNER Mr A. E. Oppenheimer (NEWMARKET) BRED Hascombe and Valiant Studs

**1117* Stately Dancer**, unlucky last time, made up for it here, but looked all at sea as the pack quickened, and she dropped back last early in the straight. Pulled to the outside, she stayed on very strongly to pull the race out of the fire with a hint of good fortune. (12/1)
**2399 Omara (USA)** is a nightmare ride and on this evidence, needs holding up much longer and putting in front right on the line, for she left these for dead when let down, only to idle and drop everything once a couple of lengths in front. (8/1: 5/1-9/1)
**2980 Possessive Artiste** is a good mover, but again looked short of gears at the business end after travelling well. A longer trip might help. (7/1)
**3133 Seeking Fortune (USA)**, a poor mover who is rather lightly made for top-weight, was in the firing line until her stride shortened dramatically in the final furlong. (6/1)
**2924 Naval Gazer (IRE)** again looked less than fully co-operative, dropping out with her head in the air as the tempo hotted up, only to run on late past beaten horses. (14/1)
**2775 Temptress** didn't seem suited by the drop in trip. (8/1)

## 3523 SIDEGATE PEUGEOT MOTORS NURSERY H'CAP (2-Y.O) (Class D)

7-05 (7-06) **6f 3y** £3,437.65 (£1,025.20: £489.10: £221.05) Stalls: High GOING minus 0.44 sec per fur (F)

| | | | | SP | RR | SF |
|---|---|---|---|---|---|---|
| 3467[2] | **Perfect Bliss (63)** (PDEvans) **2-9-1** JFEgan(3) (lw: chsd ldr tl led over 2f out: sn rdn clr) | — | **1** | 6/4[1] | 68 | 32 |
| 3227[4] | **Irish Fiction (IRE) (66)** (DJSCosgrove) **2-8-13**(5) MartinDwyer(5) (a chsng ldrs: rdn & r.o fnl f) | 3 | **2** | 9/2[2] | 63 | 27 |
| 3408[6] | **Our Kevin (69)** (KMcAuliffe) **2-9-7b** DRMcCabe(6) (hld up: hdwy over 2f out: sn chsng wnr: no ex fnl f) | ¾ | **3** | 13/2 | 64 | 28 |
| 3299[4] | **Singforyoursupper (60)** (GGMargarson) **2-8-12** AMackay(4) (bhd: rdn & hdwy 3f out: wknd 1f out) | 3½ | **4** | 16/1 | 46 | 10 |
| 3408[9] | **Aztec Traveller (67)** (MJRyan) **2-9-5b[1]** WRyan(1) (lw: led over 3f: wknd over 1f out) | 2 | **5** | 13/2 | 47 | 11 |
| *1489[9]* | **Battle Ground (IRE) (62)** (NACallaghan) **2-9-0** RHughes(2) (lw: prom 3f) | 11 | **6** | 11/2[3] | — | — |
| 3160[10] | **Silver Spell (63)** (DrJDScargill) **2-9-1v** MFenton(7) (sn chsng ldrs: rdn over 2f out: sn wknd) | ¾ | **7** | 14/1 | — | — |

(SP 112.8%) **7 Rn**

**1m 13.0** (2.10) CSF £8.30 TOTE £2.20: £1.10 £2.80 (£3.80) OWNER Mr R. F. F. Mason (WELSHPOOL) BRED Mrs H. B. Raw

**3467 Perfect Bliss** quickly grabbed the favoured stands' rail, and soon drew away once his jockey got serious. (6/4)
**3227 Irish Fiction (IRE)**, dropping in trip, stayed on strongly in the closing stages under the stands rail and could be slightly flattered. (9/2)
**3408 Our Kevin** isn't an easy ride, but left the impression that having to make his move in the centre of the track, cost him second place. (13/2)
**3299 Singforyoursupper**, reluctant to go down, made a brief move as she responded to pressure, but could not sustain it in the closing stages. (16/1)
**2595 Aztec Traveller** moved to post safely enough in first time blinkers, but went far too quickly once the stalls opened and was feeling the effects soon after halfway. (13/2)
**1331 Battle Ground (IRE)**, too keen on the way down, took the leaders on and paid the penalty. (11/2: 4/1-6/1)
**2764* Silver Spell** (14/1: 10/1-16/1)

## 3524 GREAT YARMOUTH STEEL CONDITIONS STKS (3-Y.O+) (Class C)

7-35 (7-36) **6f 3y** £5,110.36 (£1,891.24: £907.62: £371.10: £147.55: £58.13) GOING minus 0.44 sec per fur (F)

| | | | | SP | RR | SF |
|---|---|---|---|---|---|---|
| 2623[15] | **Monaassib (102)** (EALDunlop) **5-9-0** WRyan(9) (a.p: led over 1f out: rdn out) | — | **1** | 10/1 | 106 | 56 |
| 3083[2] | **Dance Sequence (USA) (108)** (MRStoute) **3-8-5** PatEddery(4) (sn pushed along: hdwy 3f out: r.o fnl f: nt rch wnr) | nk | **2** | 7/2[1] | 100 | 46 |
| 3132[U] | **Sergeyev (IRE) (110)** (RHannon) **4-9-0** RHughes(2) (lw: hld up: effrt over 1f out: squeezed thro ins fnl f: nrst fin) | hd | **3** | 4/1[2] | 105 | 55 |
| 3232[29] | **Cyrano's Lad (IRE) (96)** (CADwyer) **7-9-7** CDwyer(5) (led tl over 1f out: n.m.r & eased ins fnl f) | 2 | **4** | 10/1 | 107 | 57 |
| 3083[4] | **Kahir Almaydan (IRE) (115)** (JLDunlop) **3-8-10** KDarley(3) (lw: chsd ldrs: rdn & outpcd 2f out: r.o fnl f) | hd | **5** | 7/2[1] | 99 | 45 |
| 3132[4] | **Resounder (USA) (105)** (JHMGosden) **3-8-10** GHind(1) (lw: bhd: effrt 2f out: no imp fnl f) | 1¾ | **6** | 12/1 | 95 | 41 |
| 3126[3] | **Croft Pool (104)** (JAGlover) **5-9-0** SDWilliams(8) (lw: chsd ldrs: rdn 2f out: wknd & eased ins fnl f) | 1¼ | **7** | 7/1[3] | 91 | 41 |
| 966[6] | **Amaniy (USA) (100)** (HThomsonJones) **3-8-5** GCarter(10) (plld hrd: in tch: effrt 2f out: sn btn) | 3 | **8** | 25/1 | 78 | 24 |
| 2248[7] | **King of Peru (105)** (APJarvis) **3-8-10** WJO'Connor(7) (swtg: rdn over 2f out: a bhd) | 4 | **9** | 16/1 | 73 | 19 |

(SP 112.5%) **9 Rn**

**1m 11.2** (0.30) CSF £41.24 TOTE £10.20: £2.40 £1.50 £3.10 (£12.00) Trio £46.20 OWNER Maktoum Al Maktoum (NEWMARKET) BRED Side Hill Stud in Ireland
WEIGHT FOR AGE 3yo-4lb

**2436 Monaassib** made good use of his high draw, and sticking to the stands rail probably made the difference between victory and defeat. (10/1)

**3083 Dance Sequence (USA)**, taken off her feet towards the middle of the track in the early stages, kept responding to pressure and almost got up near the line. She had a hard race but ought to get her head in front soon. (7/2)
**3132 Sergeyev (IRE)** again looked in magnificent shape, but didn't impress on the way to post. The way he threaded his way through, suggests he is no back number. (4/1)
**2220* Cyrano's Lad (IRE)** would have been 13lb and more better off with these in a handicap, but ran a terrific race under his big penalty. Being eased in the final strides appeared to cost him third place. (10/1)
**3083 Kahir Almaydan (IRE)**, coming back to sprinting for the first time this year, could not get to the front and ran as if he does need further these days despite his pedigree. (7/2)
**3132 Resounder (USA)** ran a little better than on his seasonal debut, without making much of an impact. (12/1)
**3126 Croft Pool** ran rather better than his finishing position would suggest. (7/1)

## 3525 WILLIAM YOUNGER EAST ANGLIA H'CAP (0-70) (3-Y.O+ F & M) (Class E)
8-05 (8-06) **7f 3y** £3,425.10 (£1,024.80: £491.40: £224.70) GOING minus 0.44 sec per fur (F)

| | | | | SP | RR | SF |
|---|---|---|---|---|---|---|
| 3246$^{2}$ | **Divine Quest (68)** (HRACecil) **3-9-10** PatEddery(8) (lw: a.p: led over 1f out: pushed out) | — | 1 | 7/4$^{1}$ | 78 | 51 |
| 2048$^{2}$ | **Abir (65)** (HThomsonJones) **3-9-7** GCarter(6) (led over 5f: unable qckn) | 2 | 2 | 5/1$^{2}$ | 70 | 43 |
| 2970$^{3}$ | **Charisse Dancer (55)** (CFWall) **3-8-11** WWoods(5) (dwlt: rdn 3f out: hdwy over 1f out: nrst fin) | 5 | 3 | 9/1$^{3}$ | 49 | 22 |
| 3334$^{13}$ | **Yezza (IRE) (60)** (APJarvis) **3-9-2v$^{1}$** WJO'Connor(10) (lw: hdwy over 1f out: r.o) | s.h | 4 | 25/1 | 54 | 27 |
| 3167$^{12}$ | **Misrule (USA) (67)** (JHMGosden) **3-9-9** GHind(1) (racd alone centre: w ldrs 5f) | 1¼ | 5 | 14/1 | 58 | 31 |
| 2805$^{2}$ | **Badger Bay (IRE) (64)** (CADwyer) **3-8-13**$^{(7)}$ JoHunnam(11) (lw: chsd ldrs: rdn 3f out: one pce appr fnl f) | 1¾ | 6 | 11/1 | 51 | 24 |
| 3352$^{8}$ | **Polar Refrain (53)** (CADwyer) **3-8-9** TGMcLaughlin(2) (bhd: rdn 3f out: nvr rchd ldrs) | nk | 7 | 9/1$^{3}$ | 39 | 12 |
| 3334$^{4}$ | **Infantry Dancer (56)** (GCBravery) **3-8-12** DRMcCabe(7) (b.hind: chsd ldrs: rdn over 2f out: no imp) | 1 | 8 | 14/1 | 40 | 13 |
| 1840$^{4}$ | **Daffodil Express (IRE) (46)** (MJRyan) **3-7-11**$^{(5)}$ MBaird(3) (prom over 4f) | hd | 9 | 12/1 | 30 | 3 |
| 3051$^{5}$ | **Tonic Chord (55)** (JRFanshawe) **3-8-8**$^{(3)}$ NVarley(12) (b: a bhd) | ½ | 10 | 10/1 | 12 | 11 |
| 2992$^{6}$ | **Christian Flight (IRE) (40)** (SGollings) **7-8-2**$^{ow1}$ MFenton(4) (lw: prom tl wknd over 1f out) | 1¼ | 11 | 20/1 | — | — |
| 3360$^{5}$ | **Sizzling Romp (52)** (DTThom) **4-9-0** JTate(9) (s.i.s: hdwy 3f out: sn rdn: no imp) | 29 | 12 | 16/1 | — | — |

(SP 126.0%) **12 Rn**

**1m 25.9** (1.70) CSF £11.51 CT £61.83 TOTE £2.40: £1.30 £2.30 £3.00 (£4.70) Trio £11.20 OWNER Lady Howard de Walden (NEWMARKET) BRED Lord Howard de Walden
WEIGHT FOR AGE 3yo-6lb
**3246 Divine Quest** was content to take the lead from the runner-up until picking up well when popped the question to break her duck. She carried the weight well for one not over-robust, and should continue to progress. (7/4)
**2048 Abir** may have been helped by coming to a right-hand rail, but ran a solid race from the front and looks capable of finding a small race. (5/1)
**2970 Charisse Dancer**, in trouble in the centre of the course some way from home, did stay on late without posing a threat. This trip and further would seem within her compass. (9/1: op 6/1)
**873 Yezza (IRE)** ran better in a first-time visor, but has flattered to deceive before. (25/1)
**2675 Misrule (USA)**, taken to post early, raced alone in the centre of the course. She is being treated as if she is very highly strung. (14/1: 10/1-16/1)
**2805 Badger Bay (IRE)** is not consistent and failed to capitalise on a good draw. (11/1: 8/1-12/1)

T/Plpt: £58.20 (214.67 Tckts). T/Qdpt: £9.00 (106.13 Tckts). Dk

## 3526a-3529a (Irish Racing) - See Computer Raceform

# 0248a-LEOPARDSTOWN (Dublin, Ireland) (L-H) (Good)
## Monday August 5th

## 3530a BROWNSTOWN STUD RACE (Listed) (3-Y.O+)
4-30 (4-32) **1m** £9,675.00 (£2,775.00: £1,275.00: £375.00)

| | | | | SP | RR | SF |
|---|---|---|---|---|---|---|
| 2465a$^{5}$ | **Hagwah (USA)** (BHanbury) **4-9-11** WRyan (mde all: rdn & r.o whn chal) | — | 1 | 6/1 | 113 | 53 |
| 1255a* | **Proud Titania (IRE)** (APO'Brien,Ireland) **3-9-2** CRoche (chsd wnr: disp ld 2f out: no ex u.p ins fnl f) | 1½ | 2 | 11/2$^{3}$ | 108 | 41 |
| | **Charlock (IRE)** (JOxx,Ireland) **3-8-10** JPMurtagh (hld up in tch: 5th ½-wy: hdwy 2f out: rdn & r.o ins fnl f) | hd | 3 | 7/4$^{1}$ | 102 | 35 |
| | **Moonbi Range (IRE)** (APO'Brien,Ireland) **5-9-3** JAHeffernan (mid div: 6th ½-wy: nt clr run wl over 1f out: kpt on) | 4½ | 4 | 16/1 | 93 | 33 |
| 1912a$^{4}$ | **Marqueta (USA)** (CO'Brien,Ireland) **4-9-3** NGMcCullagh (cl up: 4th ½-wy: 3rd & rdn st: 5th & no imp over 1f out) | 2½ | 5 | 10/1 | 88 | 28 |
| 2609$^{8}$ | **Tossup (USA)** (JGBurns,Ireland) **3-9-4** DHarrison (hld up towards rr: hdwy fnl 2f: kpt on: nvr nrr) | ¾ | 6 | 9/2$^{2}$ | 94 | 27 |
| | **Hint Of Humour (USA)** (DKWeld,Ireland) **3-8-10b** MJKinane (cl up: rdn & chsd ldrs st: no imp over 1f out) | ¾ | 7 | 6/1 | 85 | 18 |
| | **Ilanga (IRE)** (JGBurns,Ireland) **3-8-10** RMBurke (towards rr: rdn 3f out: no imp fnl 2f) | 4 | 8 | 16/1 | 77 | 10 |
| | **Night Spell (IRE)** (DKWeld,Ireland) **3-8-10b$^{1}$** WJSupple (towards rr: 7th & rdn st: n.d) | s.h | 9 | 25/1 | 77 | 10 |

(SP 123.2%) **9 Rn**

**1m 40.5** (3.50) OWNER Abdullah Ali (NEWMARKET) BRED Gainsborough Farm Inc
**2465a Hagwah (USA)** kept on well for an all-the-way success, and put her last effort in, the Group Two Pretty Polly Stakes, well behind. Her trainer will now try to find a Group Three event, possibly in Germany. (6/1: op 3/1)
**1255a* Proud Titania (IRE)**, returning after a break, was in second place for most of the race and drew alongside two furlongs out to lay down her challenge. She would have appreciated the rain, and running a good race, should improve from this. (11/2)
**Charlock (IRE)** was favoured to take this after an easy debut win in lesser company. She made her effort on the final bend and went third one and a half furlongs out, keeping on well. This was a decent effort for a relatively inexperienced filly. (7/4)
**Moonbi Range (IRE)** put up a better effort here after being well beaten in a valuable handicap at Galway. In sixth place turning into the straight, she kept on but could not put up a serious challenge. (16/1)
**1255a Marqueta (USA)** tried her best to keep in touch but was being niggled along before the straight and failed to show a turn of speed. (10/1)

## 3531a CHALLENGE RACE (Listed) (3-Y.O+)
5-00 (5-02) **1m 6f** £9,675.00 (£2,775.00: £1,275.00: £375.00)

| | | | | SP | RR | SF |
|---|---|---|---|---|---|---|
| 2250* | **Lord Jim (IRE)** (LordHuntingdon) **4-9-7b$^{1}$** DHarrison (mde all: rdn 3f out: styd on u.p) | — | 1 | 5/1$^{3}$ | 103 | 54 |

| | Horse | Dist | Pos | SP | RR | SF |
|---|---|---|---|---|---|---|
| 2825a* | **I'm Supposin (IRE)** (KPrendergast,Ireland) **4-9-7** WJSupple (hld up: 5th ½-wy: trckd ldrs st: edgd rt & chal over 1f out: rdn & no imp ins fnl f) | 1 | **2** | 7/2 2 | 102 | 53 |
| | **Priolina (IRE)** (JCHayden,Ireland) **3-8-5b** MJKinane (chsd ldrs tl dropped towards rr 5f out: hdwy over 2f out: styd on wl u.p fnl f) | hd | **3** | 11/1 | 99 | 37 |
| 3021a2 | **Fill the Bill (IRE)** (APO'Brien,Ireland) **4-9-7** CRoche (hld up towards rr: hdwy over 3f out: trckng ldrs on ins 2f out: nt clr run & swtchd over 1f out: rdn & kpt on) | 1½ | **4** | 5/4 1 | 100 | 51 |
| 2474a5 | **Sun Ballet (IRE)** (JOxx,Ireland) **3-8-5b** NGMcCullagh (chsd ldrs: rdn & effrt st: no ex over 1f out) | 3½ | **5** | 8/1 | 93 | 31 |
| 3021a3 | **Ceirseach (IRE)** (JSBolger,Ireland) **3-8-5** TEDurcan (chsd wnr tl rdn & no ex over 1f out) | 5 | **6** | 8/1 | 87 | 25 |

(SP 113.9%) **6 Rn**

**3m 2.6** (5.60) OWNER Mrs S. Y. Thomas (WEST ILSLEY) BRED Woodcote Stud Ltd

**2250* Lord Jim (IRE)** made all to gain his second success since joining Lord Huntingdon. Described as a poor worker at home by his trainer, he showed total gameness here. He is a good traveller and may next go to Baden-Baden. (5/1)

**2825a* I'm Supposin (IRE),** winner of the Ulster Harp Derby, ran a sound race but never looked like getting on terms with the winner. (7/2: op 2/1)

**Priolina (IRE),** who was last turning into the straight, ran on very well to make up considerable ground in the closing stages. She seems to have improved well from handicap company. (11/1)

**3021a Fill the Bill (IRE)** met with trouble on the inside in the straight, and lost ground when being switched for daylight. He is better than the placings suggest and can be forgiven on this occasion. (5/4: op 2/1)

**3021a Ceirseach (IRE)** ran in second place for most of the way, and may benefit from a drop in distance. (8/1: op 5/1)

## 3532a-3560a (Irish Racing) - See Computer Raceform

## 0363a-LEOPARDSTOWN (Dublin, Ireland) (L-H) (Good to Yielding)
## Sunday August 11th

### 3561a HEINZ 57 PHOENIX STKS (Gp 1) (2-Y.O C & F)
3-20 (3-23) **6f** £84,500.00 (£29,000.00: £14,000.00: £5,000.00)

| | Horse | Dist | Pos | SP | RR | SF |
|---|---|---|---|---|---|---|
| | **Mantovani (IRE)** (JSBolger,Ireland) **2-9-0** CEverard (chsd ldrs on ins: rdn bef ½-wy: hdwy wl over 1f out: squeezed thro over 1f out: led 1f out: rdn & r.o) | — | **1** | 20/1 | 108 | 65 |
| 20703 | **Muchea** (MRChannon) **2-9-0** RHughes (dwlt: sn in tch: trckd ldrs fr ½-wy: hmpd over 1f out: sn chal: kpt on) | 2 | **2** | 10/1 | 103+ | 60 |
| 2040* | **Verglas (IRE)** (KPrendergast,Ireland) **2-9-0** WJSupple (chsd ldrs: 4th ½-wy: hdwy over 1f out: effrt 1f out: kpt on u.p fnl f) | hd | **3** | 11/8 1 | 102 | 59 |
| 3201a* | **Ocean Ridge (USA)** (PWChapple-Hyam) **2-8-11** JReid (led to 1f out: kpt on) | s.h | **4** | 4/1 2 | 99 | 56 |
| | **Star Profile (IRE)** (DKWeld,Ireland) **2-8-11** MJKinane (dwlt: towards rr: last 2f out: rdn & kpt on fr over 1f out: nrst fin) | 1½ | **5** | 13/2 3 | 95 | 52 |
| 3018a* | **Azra (IRE)** (JSBolger,Ireland) **2-8-11** KJManning (prom: 3rd ½-wy: rdn 2f out: wkng whn edgd lft over 1f out: no imp) | 1 | **6** | 8/1 | 93 | 50 |
| 31562 | **Raphane (USA)** (CCollins,Ireland) **2-9-0** SCraine (prom: 2nd ½-wy: rdn & ev ch over 2f out: wknd over 1f out) | 8 | **7** | 8/1 | 74 | 31 |
| 3018a2 | **Check The Band (USA)** (APO'Brien,Ireland) **2-9-0b** CRoche (chsd ldrs: rdn ½-wy: no imp over 1f out) | ¾ | **8** | 8/1 | 72 | 29 |
| 1910a3 | **Scottish Mist (IRE)** (GMLyons,Ireland) **2-8-11b** LDettori (towards rr: n.d) | 12 | **9** | 50/1 | 37 | — |

(SP 124.6%) **9 Rn**

**1m 13.6** (2.90) OWNER Mrs J. S. Bolger (COOLCULLEN)

**Mantovani (IRE)** provided a major shock here, seeing off some useful opposition. Finding room on the inside over a furlong out, he quickly took control and ran on well. (20/1)

**2070 Muchea** had absolutely no luck in running. He was denied a clear passage two furlongs out and was then hampered by Azra. When he did eventually find an opening, he ran on well but it was too late. (10/1)

**2040* Verglas (IRE)** did not show as much speed as he possesses. However, he did run on well at the finish, but was never going to be near enough to challenge the winner. His trainer admits that he may have been wrong about the going, and insists the horse is a lot better than this. (11/8)

**3201a* Ocean Ridge (USA)** disputed the lead and took the initiative over two furlongs out. However, when tackled by the eventual winner, she failed to quicken. (4/1)

**Star Profile (IRE)** never went the pace on ground her trainer feared would be too slow for her. She will be stepped up in distance in next month's Moyglare Stud Stakes. (13/2)

**3156 Raphane (USA)** showed plenty of speed but dropped out quickly over a furlong out. Five furlongs seems to be his best trip. (8/1)

### 3562a PHOENIX SPRINT (Gp 3) (3-Y.O+)
3-55 (3-58) **6f** £16,250.00 (£4,750.00: £2,250.00: £750.00)

| | Horse | Dist | Pos | SP | RR | SF |
|---|---|---|---|---|---|---|
| 288012 | **Daring Destiny** (KRBurke) **5-8-12b**ow1 RHughes (dwlt: towards rr: hdwy 1½f out: r.o to ld ins fnl f) | — | **1** | 14/1 | 110 | 65 |
| 1431* | **Farhana** (WJarvis) **3-8-7** MJKinane (trckd ldrs pllng hrd: 4th 2f out: chal 1f out: r.o ins fnl f) | hd | **2** | 7/4 1 | 109 | 61 |
| 312614 | **Leap for Joy** (JHMGosden) **4-9-1** LDettori (chsd ldrs: 7th on ins ½-wy: nt clr run & swtchd wl over 1f out: swtchd again jst ins fnl f: r.o: nrst fin) | 1½ | **3** | 15/2 | 109 | 65 |
| 20724 | **Woodborough (USA)** (PWChapple-Hyam) **3-9-0** JReid (trckd ldrs: 3rd ½-wy: sn chal: led wl over 1f out: hdd ins fnl f: kpt on) | ½ | **4** | 7/2 2 | 110 | 62 |
| 20722 | **Catch The Blues (IRE)** (APO'Brien,Ireland) **4-8-11b** CRoche (trckd ldrs: 4th & pushed along ½-wy: 5th & nt clr run over 1f out: nt trble ldrs) | hd | **5** | 4/1 3 | 103 | 59 |
| 2816a2 | **Sunset Reigns (IRE)** (APO'Brien,Ireland) **3-8-8**ow1 SCraine (led tl over 1f out: wknd ins fnl f) | 3½ | **6** | 11/1 | 95 | 46 |
| 2270a4 | **Blue Iris** (MAJarvis) **3-8-7** PRobinson (disp ld over 4f: no ex over 1f out) | 2 | **7** | 15/2 | 89 | 41 |
| | **Peruke (IRE)** (NMeade,Ireland) **5-8-11b**1 PJSmullen (chsd ledrs: 6th ½-wy: btn over 2f out: eased) | 25 | **8** | 33/1 | 22 | — |

(SP 120.1%) **8 Rn**

**1m 13.5** (2.80) OWNER Mrs Ann Wright (WANTAGE) BRED Mrs Ann E. M. Wright

**2692 Daring Destiny** did not have the best of starts and was subsequently held up at the back of the field. Making good headway over a furlong out, she ran on well inside the final furlong. She may need to win another Group race if she is to have a chance of getting into the Hong Kong Invitation Cup, so it is possible she will be sent to Baden-Baden later this month. (14/1)

**1431* Farhana** was produced from off the pace to take the lead but was quickly swallowed up by the winner. (7/4)

**1483 Leap for Joy** has to be considered unlucky. Chasing the leaders, she did not get a clear run on the inside and had to be switched left twice in the final two furlongs for daylight. Once into her stride, she ran on well but it was just too late. (15/2)

**2072 Woodborough (USA)** moved up to dispute the lead over a furlong and a half out. Flat out with a furlong to travel, it appeared that he reached the front just too and failed to quicken. (7/2)
**2270a Blue Iris** led the way but dropped out quickly with a furlong left to travel. (15/2)

## 3563a-3565a (Irish Racing) - See Computer Raceform

## 3392a-DEAUVILLE (France) (R-H) (Good)
### Tuesday August 6th

### 3566a PRIX DES ROCHES (2-Y.O F)
1-59 (1-59) **7f** £11,858.00

| | Horse | | Pos | SP | RR | SF |
|---|---|---|---|---|---|---|
| | **Green Lady (IRE)** (AFabre,France) **2-8-9** TJarnet | — | 1 | | 91 | 60 |
| | **Polykala (FR)** (France) **2-8-9** OPeslier | 2½ | 2 | | 85 | 54 |
| | **Yxenery (IRE)** (France) **2-9-0** FHead | 2 | 3 | | 86 | 55 |
| 2619² | **Boojum** (BWHills) **2-9-0** MHills | ¾ | 4 | | 84 | 53 |

**13 Rn**

**1m 27.5** (3.50) P-M 12.50F: 3.60F 5.40F 3.60F (91.90F) OWNER Maktoum Al Maktoum (CHANTILLY) BRED Gainsborough Stud Management
**2619 Boojum** had a bad draw and the wind in her face throughout this race. She put up a gallant performance and took the lead for a few strides one and a half furlongs out. However, she was soon a spent force and just stayed on to take fourth place in a game manner. She is apparently still growing and a little weak, but she might have been beaten by a horse which will go on to much better things in the future.

### 3567a PRIX DE REUX (Listed) (3-Y.O+)
3-11 (3-11) **1m 4f 110y** £18,445.00 (£6,324.00: £3,953.00)

| | Horse | | Pos | SP | RR | SF |
|---|---|---|---|---|---|---|
| 2845a* | **Water Poet (IRE)** (AFabre,France) **3-8-9** TJarnet | — | 1 | | 111 | 29 |
| | **Sunshack** (AFabre,France) **5-9-4** SGuillot | s.h | 2 | | 109 | 38 |
| | **Running Flame (FR)** (JEHammond,France) **4-9-4** CAsmussen | nk | 3 | | 109 | 38 |

**6 Rn**

**2m 50.0** (11.50) P-M 2.50F: 1.60F 1.60F OWNER Sheikh Mohammed (CHANTILLY) BRED Sheikh Mohammed
**Water Poet (IRE)**, a Sadler's Wells half-brother to Swain, cut down his stable companion in the final strides to make it a one-two for his trainer. He will stay in training as a four year old, and connections say that the St Leger is a possible target.
**Sunshack**, who won the Coronation Cup and Prix Royal-Oak last season, lost nothing in defeat on his seasonal debut. He could now be aimed at the Grosser Preis Von Baden.

## 3566a-DEAUVILLE (France) (R-H) (Good)
### Thursday August 8th

### 3568a PRIX DE LA CALONNE (Listed) (3-Y.O F)
3-30 (3-30) **1m** £18,445.00 (£6,324.00: £3,953.00)

| | Horse | | Pos | SP | RR | SF |
|---|---|---|---|---|---|---|
| | **Hill Silver (USA)** (PBary,France) **3-8-12** GMosse | — | 1 | | 105 | 10 |
| | **Folle Tempete (FR)** (JEHammond,France) **3-8-12** MBoutin | 1½ | 2 | | 102 | 7 |
| | **Contare** (JEPease,France) **3-8-12** FSanchez | nk | 3 | | 101 | 6 |
| 2715* | **El Opera (IRE)** (PFICole) **3-8-12** TQuinn (btn 4½l) | | 5 | | — | — |
| 2585¹⁰ | **Aunty Jane** (BWHills) **3-8-12** MHills (btn 7½l) | | 6 | | — | — |

**9 Rn**

**1m 45.3** (9.30) P-M 5.80F: 2.00F 2.60F 2.30F (37.50F) OWNER Ecurie Skymarc Farm (CHANTILLY) BRED Skymarc Farm Inc
**2715* El Opera (IRE)** raced just behind the leaders and looked extremely dangerous soon after entering the straight, but she did not go through with her effort and stayed at one pace in the final furlong.
**2354 Aunty Jane** raced in mid-division but was never a factor in the straight.

## CLAIREFONTAINE (Deauville, France) (R-H) (Soft)
### Friday August 9th

### 3569a PRIX GERARD DE CHAVAGNAC (4-Y.O+)
3-07 (3-07) **1m** £5,929.00

| | Horse | | Pos | SP | RR | SF |
|---|---|---|---|---|---|---|
| 3232²² | **Bold Effort (FR)** (KOCunningham-Brown) **4-8-9b** FSanchez | — | 1 | | 84 | — |
| | **Mankab (MOR)** (France) **4-8-9** CAsmussen | hd | 2 | | 84 | — |
| | **Time of Trouble (FR)** (France) **4-7-10**(5) VVion | ½ | 3 | | 75 | — |

**14 Rn**

**1m 41.7** P-M 18.80F: 4.20F 4.00F 4.40F (47.50F) OWNER Mr A. J. Richards (STOCKBRIDGE) BRED Ewar Stud Farm
**2497 Bold Effort (FR)** has only previously ever won over six furlongs, and on two occasions on good to firm ground, so taking this event over an extended trip and on much easier going, came somewhat as a surprise. Making his effort two furlongs from home, he took the lead inside the final furlong and ran on well to just hold the persistent runner-up.

## 3568a-DEAUVILLE (France) (R-H) (Good)
### Saturday August 10th

### 3570a PRIX DE PSYCHE (Gp 3) (3-Y.O F)
3-00 (3-01) **1m 2f** £28,986.00 (£10,540.00: £5,270.00)

| | Horse | | Pos | SP | RR | SF |
|---|---|---|---|---|---|---|
| | **Sangria (USA)** (AFabre,France) **3-8-11** OPeslier | — | 1 | | 107 | 35 |
| | **Binary** (AFabre,France) **3-8-11** TJarnet | hd | 2 | | 107 | 35 |

| | | | SP | RR | SF |
|---|---|---|---|---|---|
| 3042* | **My Emma** (RGuest) **3-8-11** CAsmussen ...... ¾ | **3** | | 106 | 34 |
| | | | | | **5 Rn** |

**2m 15.0** (10.00) P-M 4.70F: 1.30F 1.10F OWNER Mr D. Wildenstein (CHANTILLY) BRED Keswick Stables
**Sangria (USA)** was winning for the first time since she made a winning debut over a year ago at this track. She won this race due to her superior finishing speed. There was no early pace and all the fillies bunched up early in the straight. She took the lead inside the final furlong and she ran on well to win in good style. Now that she has hit form, she could go on to better things, and she may be allowed to take her chance in the Prix Vermeille.
**Binary** set a moderate pace and never gave up the fight. She accelerated soon after entering the straight, but could never get away from her rivals and just stayed on in the final furlong.
**3042* My Emma** was totally unsuited by lack of pace in a race which was run in nearly fourteen seconds outside the course record. After settling in fourth place, she made a gallant effort to get on terms early in the straight, but didn't quite have enough acceleration in the final stages. She is a lovely filly and is sure to win a race in this category in the future. Things did not go her way on this occasion, but she could be back for the Prix de la Nonette later in the month.

## 3571a PRIX DE THIBERVILLE (Listed) (3-Y.O F)
3-30 (3-29) **1m 4f 110y** £18,445.00 (£6,324.00: £3,953.00: £2,055.00)

| | | | SP | RR | SF |
|---|---|---|---|---|---|
| | **Vadsa Honor (FR)** (AFabre,France) **3-8-9** TJarnet ...... — | **1** | | 105 | 69 |
| 3202a4 | **Met Mech Nich (FR)** (J-PPelat,France) **3-8-9** TThulliez ...... nk | **2** | | 105 | 69 |
| 1393a4 | **Karlaska** (PBary,France) **3-8-9** DBoeuf ...... 1 | **3** | | 103 | 67 |
| 20697 | **Alessandra** (BWHills) **3-8-9** OPeslier ...... ¾ | **4** | | 102 | 66 |
| | | | | | **10 Rn** |

**2m 45.3** (6.80) P-M 3.20F: 1.70F 3.00F 5.10F (19.00F) OWNER Mr J-L Lagardere (CHANTILLY) BRED J-L Legardere
**1895* Alessandra** was given every chance by her rider. She raced in second place for most of the time and battled on gamely right up to the line. Her trainer thought softer ground would have been an advantage and, though she is a game filly, there are no plans for her at the moment.

# 2843a-HOPPEGARTEN (Berlin, Germany) (R-H) (Good)
## Saturday August 10th

## 3572a GROSSER PREIS VON BERLIN (Gp 3) (3-Y.O+)
3-43 (3-51) **6f 110y** £38,739.00 (£16,216.00: £8,108.00)

| | | | SP | RR | SF |
|---|---|---|---|---|---|
| 2663a3 | **Macanal (USA)** (HJentzsch,Germany) **4-9-6** PSchiergen ...... — | **1** | | 117 | — |
| 2663a* | **Waky Nao** (HBlume,Germany) **3-8-13** ASuborics ...... s.h | **2** | | 114 | — |
| | **Takin (GER)** (FrauEMader,Germany) **5-9-6** LMader ...... 2½ | **3** | | 111 | — |
| | | | | | **10 Rn** |

**1m 16.4** TOTE 51DM: 12DM 11DM 22DM OWNER Gestut Fahrhof BRED Bruce Hundley in USA
**Macanal (USA)** made all and battled on well to hold off the favourite.

# 3570a-DEAUVILLE (France) (R-H) (Good to soft)
## Sunday August 11th

## 3573a PRIX MAURICE DE GHEEST (Gp 1) (3-Y.O+)
2-10 (2-08) **6f 110y** £65,876.00 (£26,350.00: £13,175.00: £6,588.00)

| | | | SP | RR | SF |
|---|---|---|---|---|---|
| 2622* | **Anabaa (USA)** (MmeCHead,France) **4-9-2** FHead (racd in 5th: gd prog to ld 1f out: r.o wl: comf) ...... — | **1** | | 126+ | 87 |
| 2841a* | **Miesque's Son (USA)** (JEHammond,France) **4-9-2** CAsmussen (hld up in rr early: prog on outside 2f out: r.o wl fnl f: nt rch wnr) ...... 1½ | **2** | | 122 | 83 |
| 26225 | **Danehill Dancer (IRE)** (NACallaghan) **3-8-11** RCochrane (hld up in rr early on: u.p fr ½-wy: hdwy over 1f out) ...... hd | **3** | | 121 | 78 |
| 3083* | **Iktamal (USA)** (EALDunlop) **4-9-2** WRyan (in rr early on: prog 2f out: styd on one pce fnl f) ...... 5 | **4** | | 110 | 71 |
| 2919* | **Blue Duster (USA)** (DRLoder) **3-8-8** PatEddery (cl up early on: gng wl over 2f out: rdn & nt qckn) ...... ¾ | **5** | | 104 | 61 |
| 2843a8 | **A Magicman (FR)** (HSteguweit,Germany) **4-9-2** NGrant (racd in 4th early: prog to ld over 3f out: hdd 2f out: no imp) ...... 2 | **6** | | 103 | 64 |
| 20374 | **Young Ern** (SDow) **6-9-2** TQuinn (6th early on: u.p 3f out tl led 2f out: hdd 1f out: fdd) ...... s.h | **7** | | 103 | 64 |
| 28802 | **Easy Dollar** (BGubby) **4-9-2b** TJarnet (racd 2nd early on: wknd fr ½-wy) ...... 2 | **8** | | 98 | 59 |
| | **Poplar Bluff (IRE)** (AFabre,France) **4-9-2** OPeslier (broke wl: led early: hdd ½-wy: dropped out) ...... 8 | **9** | | 78 | 39 |
| | | | | | **9 Rn** |

**1m 19.0** (4.00) P-M 1.50F: 1.10F 1.10F 1.10F (4.50) OWNER Mme A. Head (CHANTILLY) BRED Gainsborough Farm Inc
**2622* Anabaa (USA)** put up one of the finest performances seen in France this year. He cantered throughout this Group One race and reacted immediately once his jockey pressed the button. The race was already won at the furlong pole and Anabaa coasted home in the final stages. He is not only a fine looking colt, but has a good temperament. He settles so well that a mile looks well within his range. There was a temptation to run him four days after this in the Jacques Le Marois but he now goes for the Haydock Park Sprint and the L'Abbaye. This was his sixth consecutive win and he is easily the best sprinter in Europe this year.
**2841a* Miesque's Son (USA)** was held up for a late effort which he produced about one and a half furlongs out. He never looked like catching the winner but ran on gamely to take second place. He is improving with every outing and although he might not beat Anabaa, he is certainly capable of winning a top sprint. He looks likely to take up the challenge again at Haydock Park.
**2622 Danehill Dancer (IRE)** put up an excellent display and certainly appreciated the cut in the ground. Held up early on, he was under pressure three out before running on gamely inside the final furlong.
**3083* Iktamal (USA)** was held up and was putting in his best work at the finish, but never looked like reaching the first three. The soft ground was against him and he will not be taking on Anabaa again in the future.
**2919* Blue Duster (USA)** looked well but had not grown since her two year old days, and was dwarfed by many of her rivals. She was under pressure two out and her stride shortened inside the final furlong. She put up a game display but her connections are not sure where she will go next.
**2037 Young Ern** raced in mid-division and moved up to hit the front at the two furlong marker. He was beaten when the winner went past and gradually dropped out of contention. He does not appear to be the horse he was last season.
**2880 Easy Dollar** was never seen with a chance and was out of his depth in this company.

# 3572a-HOPPEGARTEN (Berlin, Germany) (R-H) (Soft)
## Sunday August 11th

### 3574a BMW EUROPACHAMPIONAT (Gp 2) (3-Y.O)
3-30 (3-33) **1m 4f** £139,640.00 (£58,559.00: £29,279.00: £13,513.00)

| | | | | SP | RR | SF |
|---|---|---|---|---|---|---|
| 2668a[11] | **Bad Bertrich Again (IRE)** (ALowe,Germany) **3-9-2** GBocskai (4th & hdwy st: gd hdwy to ld 1½f out: r.o wl) | — | 1 | | 115 | — |
| 2668a* | **Lavirco (GER)** (PRau,Germany) **3-9-2** TMundry (racd in 3rd to st: swtchd outside to chal 1½f out: sn one pce) | 1¾ | 2 | | 113 | — |
| 2668a[14] | **Flamingo Garden (GER)** (HBlume,Germany) **3-9-2b[1]** ASuborics (led to 2f out: one pce) | 5 | 3 | | 106 | — |
| 2668a[15] | **Agnelli** (HJentzsch,Germany) **3-9-2** PSchiergen (plld hrd: trckd ldr: led 2f out to 1½f out: one pce) | hd | 4 | | 106 | — |
| 2668a[4] | **Ocean Sea (USA)** (Germany) **3-9-2** AStarke (hld up in rr: 5th st: nvr able to chal) | 2½ | 5 | | 103 | — |
| | **Bebeto (IRE)** (Germany) **3-9-2** APietsch (in tch for 8f: last & btn st) | 25 | 6 | | 69 | — |
| | | | | | | **6 Rn** |

**2m 28.6** TOTE 207DM: 17DM 10DM OWNER Rennstall Bad Bertrich BRED Juddmonte Farms

**Bad Bertrich Again (IRE)** took the lead a furlong and a half out and kept on well to beat the short priced favourite.

**2668a* Lavirco (GER)**, the German Derby winner, was a strong odds-on favourite to take this event. Settled in behind the leaders, he challenged over a furlong out but was soon under pressure and, one paced, was not going to get to the winner.

# 3305-CATTERICK (L-H) (Good to firm)
## Friday August 16th
WEATHER: fine WIND: almost nil

### 3575 TATTERSALLS BOOKMAKERS AND INTERNATIONAL RACECOURSE MANAGEMENT AMATEUR H'CAP
(0-70) (3-Y.O+) (Class G) 5-55 (5-55) **1m 3f 214y** £2,343.00 (£648.00: £309.00) Stalls: Low GOING minus 0.13 sec per fur (G)

| | | | | SP | RR | SF |
|---|---|---|---|---|---|---|
| 3118* | **Gold Blade (67)** (JPearce) **7-11-7** MrsLPearce(2) (in tch: nt clr run over 2f out: swtchd: r.o wl to ld ins fnl f: readily) | — | 1 | 10/11[1] | 64+ | 46 |
| 3443[9] | **Don't Drop Bombs (USA) (39)** (DTThom) **7-9-7v** MissJFeilden(4) (led: clr over 2f out: hdd & nt qckn ins fnl f) | 1½ | 2 | 7/2[2] | 34 | 16 |
| 3348[5] | **Never Time (IRE) (48)** (MrsVAAconley) **4-9-11**(5)ow14 MrGMarkham(5) (trckd ldrs: effrt & hung lft over 2f out: kpt on same pce) | 1½ | 3 | 16/1 | 41 | 9 |
| 3348[10] | **Fairy Highlands (IRE) (56)** (JSHaldane) **3-9-9**(5) MrJAStack(6) (bhd: hdwy over 2f out: styd on same pce) | ½ | 4 | 66/1 | 48 | 20 |
| 3428[10] | **Jabaroot (IRE) (32)** (RMMcKellar) **5-9-0** MrsCWilliams(3) (b.hind: dwlt s: bhd: hdwy 2f out: hung lft & kpt on: nvr nr to chal) | ½ | 5 | 100/1 | 24 | 6 |
| 3309[6] | **Take Two (52)** (MissMKMilligan) **8-10-6** MrCBonner(8) (chsd ldrs: one pce fnl 2f) | 1¼ | 6 | 20/1 | 42 | 24 |
| 3242[5] | **Dr Edgar (56)** (MDods) **4-10-10** MrSSwiers(1) (lw: chsd ldrs: pushed along over 3f out: wknd 2f out) | 5 | 7 | 5/1[3] | 39 | 21 |
| 3297[9] | **Chantry Beath (49)** (CWThornton) **5-9-12**(5) MrsDWilkinson(7) (in tch: racd wd: pushed along 6f out: lost pl over 2f out) | ¾ | 8 | 9/1 | 31 | 13 |
| | | | | (SP 114.4%) | | **8 Rn** |

**2m 42.8** (11.40) CSF £4.50 CT £25.06 TOTE £1.70: £1.10 £1.80 £3.30 (£2.60) OWNER Jeff Pearce (NEWMARKET) BRED Ballymacoll Stud Co

LONG HANDICAP Jabaroot (IRE) 8-8

WEIGHT FOR AGE 3yo-10lb

**3118* Gold Blade** completed a five-timer and, in the process, has gone up 18lb in the weights. It was not all plain sailing though, he ran into some trouble on the home turn but in the end, scored in good style. (10/11)

**2587 Don't Drop Bombs (USA)**, 22lb better off with the winner for less than 14 lengths at Pontefract last month, tried to pinch the race, quickening clear on the home turn. In the end the winning partnership proved much too good. (7/2)

**3348 Never Time (IRE)**, carrying a stone overweight, gave his rider problems, contributing to the trouble the winner met. (16/1)

**2358 Fairy Highlands (IRE)** proved well suited by the step up in trip. (66/1)

**Jabaroot (IRE)**, 6lb out of the handicap, came back from a lengthy spell in the doldrums, staying on at the finish after a slow start and giving his rider problems. (100/1)

**152 Chantry Beath** (9/1: op 6/1)

### 3576 PHILLIPS INTERNATIONAL AUCTIONEERS AND VALUERS AUCTION (S) STKS (2-Y.O) (Class G)
6-25 (6-26) **7f** £2,364.00 (£654.00: £312.00) Stalls: Low GOING minus 0.13 sec per fur (G)

| | | | | SP | RR | SF |
|---|---|---|---|---|---|---|
| 3343[3] | **Abstone Queen (65)** (PDEvans) **2-8-6v[1]** JFortune(6) (swtg: trckd ldrs: led over 1f out: sn clr: eased nr fin) | — | 1 | 6/4[2] | 59+ | 2 |
| 3291[4] | **Norbreck House** (JBerry) **2-8-11** JCarroll(1) (trckd ldrs: effrt over 3f out: kpt on fnl f: no ch w wnr) | 4 | 2 | 11/8[1] | 55 | — |
| 3455[7] | **Silver Raj (50)** (WTKemp) **2-8-4b**(7) KSked(3) (s.i.s: hdwy to chse ldr over 3f out: led over 2f out: wandered: hdd over 1f out: one pce) | hd | 3 | 12/1 | 55 | — |
| *3087[5]* | **Oddfellows Girl** (NBycroft) **2-8-6** JLowe(5) (chsd ldr: one pce fnl 2f: sddle slipped) | 2½ | 4 | 33/1 | 44 | — |
| 3105[8] | **Bloomsy Babe** (JJQuinn) **2-7-13**(7) RFfrench(4) (s.i.s: outpcd & pushed along: hdwy on outside over 2f out: hung rt: nvr nr ldrs) | 3 | 5 | 33/1 | 37 | — |
| 3082[8] | **Barachois Lad** (JJO'Neill) **2-8-11** TWilliams(7) (led tl over 2f out: wknd over 1f out) | 5 | 6 | 33/1 | 31 | — |
| 3448[9] | **Timely Touch (38)** (MWEllerby) **2-8-6** JFanning(2) (s.i.s: a wl bhd: hung bdly lft fnl 2f) | 15 | 7 | 10/1 | — | — |
| *3082[9]* | ***Kitty Galore (IRE) (56)*** (MDods) **2-8-6** DaleGibson(8) (Withdrawn not under Starter's orders: v.unruly in stalls) | | W | 6/1[3] | — | — |
| | | | | (SP 122.0%) | | **7 Rn** |

**1m 30.3** (6.70) CSF £3.39 TOTE £2.00: £1.10 £2.10 (£1.30) OWNER Mr J. E. Abbey (WELSHPOOL) BRED Ridgebarn Farm

No bid

OFFICIAL EXPLANATION **Timely Touch: hung left throughout the race, preventing her rider from riding her to any avail.**

**3343 Abstone Queen**, fitted with a visor this time, defeated some moderate rivals with plenty to spare. (6/4: Evens-13/8)

**3291 Norbreck House**, stepping up in distance, struggled to go the pace at halfway. (11/8)

**2932 Silver Raj**, with the blinkers back on, would do anything but keep straight under pressure. (12/1)

**2938 Oddfellows Girl** was not knocked about. It transpired that her saddle had slipped. (33/1)

## 3577 NORTHERN AGGREGATES NURSERY H'CAP (2-Y.O) (Class E)

6-55 (6-56) **5f 212y** £3,158.00 (£944.00: £452.00: £206.00) Stalls: High GOING minus 0.13 sec per fur (G)

| Form | Horse | Dist | Pos | SP | RR | SF |
|---|---|---|---|---|---|---|
| 3523* | **Perfect Bliss (70)** (PDEvans) **2-8-6**$^{(7)}$ $^{7x}$ RFfrench(3) (led: rn wd ent st: hung rt fnl 2f: jst hld on) | — | **1** | 2/1$^{2}$ | 72 | 34 |
| 3237* | **Nant Y Gamer (FR) (77)** (JBerry) **2-9-6** JCarroll(8) (a in tch: hdwy to chal ins fnl f: r.o) | s.h | **2** | 5/1$^{3}$ | 72 | 48 |
| 3241* | **Jeffrey Anotherred (78)** (KMcAuliffe) **2-9-7** TWilliams(7) (sn chsng ldrs: one pce fnl 2f) | 2½ | **3** | 7/4$^{1}$ | 66 | 42 |
| $2781^{4}$ | **Super Saint (66)** (TDBarron) **2-8-9** JFortune(5) (bhd: styd on fnl 2f: nt rch ldrs) | ¾ | **4** | 7/1 | 52 | 28 |
| $2985^{8}$ | **Madison Welcome (IRE) (67)** (MrsJRRamsden) **2-8-10** JFanning(6) (hld up: hdwy 2f out: styd on wl ins fnl f) | ½ | **5** | 40/1 | 52 | 28 |
| $3251^{6}$ | **Dee Pee Tee Cee (IRE) (69)** (MWEasterby) **2-8-7**$^{(5)}$ GParkin(1) (lw: a outpcd & bhd) | 4 | **6** | 33/1 | 43 | 19 |
| $2872^{5}$ | **Bold Brief (75)** (DenysSmith) **2-9-4** LCharnock(4) (chsd ldrs: edgd rt & lost pl 2f out) | 2½ | **7** | 50/1 | 42 | 18 |
| $3448^{3}$ | **The Bee Man (54)** (MWEasterby) **2-7-11** DaleGibson(2) (lw: chsd wnr: rdn over 2f out: sn wknd) | 1 | **8** | 7/1 | 19 | — |

(SP 118.7%) **8 Rn**

**1m 14.6** (3.70) CSF £12.38 CT £18.81 TOTE £2.60: £1.10 £1.80 £1.50 (£7.00) OWNER Mr R. F. F. Mason (WELSHPOOL) BRED Mrs H. B. Raw

**3523* Perfect Bliss**, recorded her second victory in less than 24 hours. Running a shade wide off the bend and hanging right, the post came just in time. (2/1)

**3237* Nant Y Gamer (FR)** showed that his Hamilton win was no fluke. (5/1)

**3241* Jeffrey Anotherred**, who gave a problem or two in the stalls, seemed well suited by the step up to six. (7/4)

**2781 Super Saint** had trouble handling the bends. Staying on when it was all over, he is capable of better on a more orthodox track. (7/1)

**2727 Madison Welcome (IRE)**, stoutly-bred on his dam's side, came from some way off the pace to stay on in good style under a considerate ride. He looks capable of better, especially over seven and a mile. (40/1)

## 3578 CHARLES CLINKARD FINE FOOTWEAR H'CAP (0-70) (3-Y.O+) (Class E)

7-25 (7-27) **7f** £3,392.00 (£1,016.00: £488.00: £224.00) Stalls: Low GOING minus 0.13 sec per fur (G)

| Form | Horse | Dist | Pos | SP | RR | SF |
|---|---|---|---|---|---|---|
| 3316* | **Welcome Lu (40)** (JLHarris) **3-7-10** $^{6x}$ FNorton(2) (s.i.s: bhd & pushed along: hdwy 2f out: styd on wl to ld cl home) | — | **1** | 7/2$^{2}$ | 49 | 23 |
| *$2201^{4}$* | **Four of Spades (51)** (PDEvans) **5-8-7v**$^{(5)}$ AmandaSanders(4) (chsd ldrs: led jst ins fnl f: jst ct) | nk | **2** | 5/1$^{3}$ | 59 | 38 |
| $3461^{7}$ | **Polish Lady (IRE) (40)** (CMurray) **3-7-10** LCharnock(7) (a chsng ldrs: hrd rdn to ld over 1f out: hdd jst ins fnl f: kpt on same pce) | ½ | **3** | 33/1 | 47 | 21 |
| $3168^{7}$ | **Regal Fanfare (IRE) (55)** (MrsLStubbs) **4-8-9b**$^{(7)}$ JoHunnam(10) (hld up: hdwy on outside over 2f out: hung lft: kpt on same pce) | 1 | **4** | 20/1 | 60 | 39 |
| $3424^{13}$ | **Shontaine (63)** (MJohnston) **3-9-5** DeanMcKeown(9) (a chsng ldrs: one pce fnl 2f) | 1¾ | **5** | 8/1 | 64 | 38 |
| $3460^{4}$ | **Allinson's Mate (IRE) (56)** (TDBarron) **8-9-3v** JFortune(3) (sn bhd & drvn along: hdwy over 1f out: nt rch ldrs) | nk | **6** | 11/4$^{1}$ | 56 | 35 |
| $3120^{7}$ | **Pleasure Trick (USA) (42)** (DonEnricoIncisa) **5-8-3** KimTinkler(1) (bhd & drvn along: styd on appr fnl f) | 1 | **7** | 12/1 | 40 | 19 |
| $3255^{7}$ | **Belbay Star (53)** (JLEyre) **3-8-9** TWilliams(5) (b.off hind: sn in tch: effrt over 2f out: no imp) | 2½ | **8** | 8/1 | 45 | 19 |
| 3278* | **Blue Bomber (67)** (VThompson) **5-10-0** JFanning(11) (lw: led tl over 1f out: sn wknd) | ¾ | **9** | 8/1 | 58 | 37 |
| | **Wild Prospect (35)** (ABailey) **8-7-10** JLowe(12) (lost pl after 1f: sn bhd) | 1¼ | **10** | 14/1 | 23 | 2 |
| $775^{19}$ | **Euro Express (50)** (TDEasterby) **3-8-6b** MBirch(8) (chsd ldrs tl lost pl over 2f out) | nk | **11** | 33/1 | 37 | 11 |

(SP 123.9%) **11 Rn**

**1m 27.6** (4.00) CSF £21.39 CT £461.72 TOTE £4.40: £2.00 £1.70 £11.60 (£10.60) Trio £136.60 OWNER Mr M. F. Hyman (MELTON MOWBRAY) BRED Red House Stud

LONG HANDICAP Polish Lady (IRE) 7-8 Wild Prospect 7-8 Welcome Lu 7-1

WEIGHT FOR AGE 3yo-5lb

**3316* Welcome Lu** did it the hard way coming from last to first, but it was a tight thing in the end. (7/2)

**2201 Four of Spades**, who is much better suited by the All-Weather, is from a stable that can do little wrong at present. After edging into the lead, his rider struggled to get to the bottom of him and in the end, they were just shaded out of it. (5/1)

**Polish Lady (IRE)**, who wore a tongue strap, ran easily her best race so far. (33/1)

**2524 Regal Fanfare (IRE)** has lost her way since her promising juvenile career and gave her rider problems, hanging and never giving her all. (20/1)

**3460 Allinson's Mate (IRE)** struggled badly to go the pace. He is something of a character these days. (11/4: op 9/2)

**2868 Pleasure Trick (USA)** (12/1: 16/1-10/1)

## 3579 DAVID MALLABURN MEMORIAL CLAIMING STKS (3-Y.O+) (Class F)

7-55 (7-57) **5f** £2,721.00 (£756.00: £363.00) Stalls: Low GOING minus 0.13 sec per fur (G)

| Form | Horse | Dist | Pos | SP | RR | SF |
|---|---|---|---|---|---|---|
| $3140^{3}$ | **Palacegate Touch (75)** (JBerry) **6-8-13b** JCarroll(8) (a in tch: styd on to ld cl home) | — | **1** | 9/4$^{1}$ | 71 | 34 |
| $3232^{27}$ | **The Happy Fox (IRE) (77)** (BAMcMahon) **4-8-13** JFanning(6) (lw: trckd ldrs: led jst ins fnl f: r.o: hdd cl home) | hd | **2** | 3/1$^{3}$ | 71 | 34 |
| $3223^{4}$ | **Here Comes a Star (73)** (JMCarr) **8-8-11** ACulhane(12) (bhd & nt clr run after 1f: hdwy 2f out: styd on wl towards fin) | 2½ | **3** | 5/2$^{2}$ | 61 | 24 |
| $3261^{5}$ | **Just Lady (57)** (WGMTurner) **3-7-13** LCharnock(2) (led: clr ½-wy: edgd rt: hdd jst ins fnl f: grad wknd) | ½ | **4** | 10/1 | 49 | 10 |
| $3294^{15}$ | **Super Sonata (52)** (TWall) **4-7-7b**$^{(7)}$ AMcCarthy(1) (chsd ldrs tl wknd 1f out) | 2 | **5** | 33/1 | 42 | 5 |
| $3265^{8}$ | **Little Ibnr (54)** (PDEvans) **5-8-8** JFortune(5) (a chsng ldrs: edgd rt & kpt on same pce fnl 2f) | nk | **6** | 25/1 | 49 | 12 |
| $3294^{9}$ | **Pallium (IRE) (52)** (MrsAMNaughton) **8-8-6** WJO'Connor(13) (bhd: rdn ½-wy: nvr nr ldrs) | ¾ | **7** | 33/1 | 44 | 7 |
| $3239^{2}$ | **Tibbi Blues** (WStorey) **9-7-11**$^{(7)}$ IonaWands(11) (bhd: sme hdwy 2f out: n.d) | 1 | **8** | 20/1 | 39 | 2 |
| $3049^{8}$ | **Supreme Desire (23)** (MissJFCraze) **8-8-0** DaleGibson(3) (sn outpcd & drvn along: sme hdwy over 1f out: n.d) | ½ | **9** | 100/1 | 34 | — |
| $3146^{5}$ | **Bashful Brave (69)** (JWPayne) **5-8-9b**$^{1}$ AClark(7) (b: in tch tl lost pl 2f out) | 1½ | **10** | 5/1 | 38 | 1 |
| $3294^{5}$ | **Rankaidade (23)** (DonEnricoIncisa) **5-8-0** KimTinkler(9) (a bhd) | nk | **11** | 100/1 | 28 | — |
| $3288^{4}$ | **Insideout** (FWatson) **3-8-7** DeanMcKeown(4) (s.i.s: a in rr) | 2 | **12** | 100/1 | 30 | — |
| $3294^{6}$ | **Orange And Blue (37)** (MissJFCraze) **3-7-13c** JLowe(10) (a outpcd & bhd) | 1½ | **13** | 100/1 | 18 | — |

(SP 128.5%) **13 Rn**

**60.5 secs** (3.00) CSF £9.92 TOTE £3.30: £1.70 £1.60 £2.10 (£5.70) Trio £3.90 OWNER Laurel (Leisure) Ltd (COCKERHAM) BRED The Woodhaven Stud

WEIGHT FOR AGE 3yo-2lb

**3140 Palacegate Touch**, unable to dominate, never looked happy in his work but still had sufficient ability to show ahead near the line. (9/4)
**2889 The Happy Fox (IRE)**, who looked to have an outstanding chance at the weights, just failed to outbattle the winner. (3/1)
**3223 Here Comes a Star** met trouble early on and was left with a lot to do. In the circumstances, he ran creditably. (5/2)
**3261 Just Lady**, a handful in the paddock, showed tremendous foot but even five on a sharp track seems beyond her. (10/1)
**Super Sonata**, who would have been meeting the winner on a stone better terms in a handicap, ran a respectable race. (33/1)

## 3580 PLANTATION STUD MAIDEN H'CAP (0-70) (3-Y.O+) (Class E)

8-25 (8-27) **1m 7f 177y** £3,366.00 (£1,008.00: £484.00: £222.00) Stalls: Low GOING minus 0.13 sec per fur (G)

| | Runner | Btn | Pos | SP | RR | SF |
|---|---|---|---|---|---|---|
| 3053[2] | **Marsayas (IRE) (54)** (MJCamacho) **3-8-10** LCharnock(2) (trckd ldrs: led over 6f out: styd on wl fnl 2f) | — | **1** | 6/4[1] | 63 | 8 |
| 3297[6] | **Clash of Swords (55)** (PCalver) **3-8-11** MBirch(12) (lw: trckd ldrs: wnt 2nd over 4f out: hrd rdn & ev ch whn swvd bdly rt 1f out: kpt on) | 1 | **2** | 11/1 | 63 | 8 |
| 3258[10] | **Suitor (50)** (WJarvis) **3-8-6** WJO'Connor(3) (chsd ldrs: rdn & outpcd over 4f out: kpt on fnl 2f) | 3 | **3** | 10/1[3] | 55 | — |
| 3109[3] | **Rex Mundi (58)** (PDEvans) **4-10-0** JFortune(1) (in tch: effrt 3f out: one pce) | ½ | **4** | 5/1[2] | 62 | 21 |
| 1826[10] | **Greystyle (35)** (MBrittain) **6-8-5v** JLowe(7) (led tl over 6f out: wknd over 2f out) | 7 | **5** | 25/1 | 32 | — |
| 3329[5] | **Karaylar (IRE) (46)** (WStorey) **4-9-2** JFanning(9) (bhd: hdwy 8f out: sn drvn along: outpcd fnl 4f) | nk | **6** | 5/1[2] | 43 | 2 |
| | **Canary Blue (IRE) (27)** (PRWebber) **5-7-11** DaleGibson(10) (bhd & pushed along 8f out: sme hdwy 2f out: nvr nr ldrs) | 1½ | **7** | 14/1 | 23 | — |
| 3225[6] | **Ship's Dancer (49)** (DonEnricoIncisa) **3-8-5** KimTinkler(11) (sn bhd: sme hdwy 2f out: n.d) | 2 | **8** | 14/1 | 43 | — |
| 3335[7] | **Victoria Day (34)** (BAMcMahon) **4-8-4** AClark(6) (sn bhd: sme hdwy 2f out: nvr nr ldrs) | nk | **9** | 25/1 | 27 | — |
| 2794[9] | **Petit Flora (40)** (GHolmes) **4-8-10** DeanMcKeown(5) (hld up: stdy hdwy 4f out: rdn over 2f out: sn wknd) | 9 | **10** | 12/1 | 24 | — |
| | **Mistroy (37)** (MissMKMilligan) **6-8-7** ACulhane(8) (trckd ldrs tl lost pl over 3f out) | 9 | **11** | 25/1 | 12 | — |
| *2939*[4] | **Stone Cross (IRE) (54)** (MartinTodhunter) **4-9-10** JCarroll(4) (mid div: hmpd 7f out: effrt over 2f out: sn wknd) | 3 | **12** | 16/1 | 26 | — |
| 2591[8] | **Lomond Lassie (USA) (41)** (MissJFCraze) **3-7-11**ow1 TWilliams(13) (bhd: hdwy to chse ldrs 5f out: lost pl over 3f out: sn bhd & eased) | 18 | **13** | 33/1 | — | — |

(SP 132.1%) **13 Rn**

**3m 37.3** (15.80) CSF £20.41 CT £132.74 TOTE £2.40: £1.60 £2.80 £3.20 (£13.40) Trio £156.80 OWNER Mr M. Gleason (MALTON) BRED J. Beckett

WEIGHT FOR AGE 3yo-14lb

**3053 Marsayas (IRE)**, from a 4lb higher mark, took the bull by the horns soon after halfway after a sedate early pace. Staying on under pressure, he was handed the prize by the runner-up's antics, but would probably have prevailed anyway. (6/4: tchd 9/4)
**2570 Clash of Swords**, suited by the step up in distance, was almost on terms when he dived badly right a furlong out away from the whip. (11/1: 8/1-12/1)
**Suitor**, a poor mover, was badly outpaced turning out of the back straight but to his credit, kept on all the way to the line. He shapes like an out and out stayer and will be suited by easier ground. (10/1: 6/1-12/1)
**3109 Rex Mundi**, on paper, seemed to stay the trip all right, but the pace was modest to halfway, and there must still be a question of his stamina. (5/1: op 3/1)
**3329 Karaylar (IRE)** struggled badly to go the pace down the back straight. In effect it was only a seven furlong dash and this staying hurdler needs a true test. (5/1: op 8/1)
**2927 Ship's Dancer** (14/1: 33/1-50/1)
**Petit Flora** (12/1: op 8/1)

T/Plpt: £5.30 (2,001.57 Tckts). T/Qdpt: £4.30 (189.95 Tckts) WG

# 2733-FOLKESTONE (R-H) (Good to firm)

## Friday August 16th

WEATHER: hot WIND: almost nil

## 3581 E.B.F. LE SHUTTLE MAIDEN STKS (2-Y.O) (Class D)

2-00 (2-00) **5f** £3,437.65 (£1,025.20: £489.10: £221.05) Stalls: Low GOING minus 0.40 sec per fur (F)

| | Runner | Btn | Pos | SP | RR | SF |
|---|---|---|---|---|---|---|
| 3129[10] | **Stygian (USA)** (BWHills) **2-8-4**(5) JDSmith(1) (chsd ldr over 3f out: rdn over 1f out: led ins fnl f: r.o wl) | — | **1** | 10/11[1] | 66 | 10 |
| | **Batsman** (WJMusson) **2-9-0** PRobinson(6) (leggy: a.p: rdn over 1f out: swtchd rt ins fnl f: r.o) | 1½ | **2** | 14/1 | 66 | 10 |
| 2942[4] | **Mangus (IRE) (70)** (KOCunningham-Brown) **2-9-0** SWhitworth(2) (led tl ins fnl f: sn wknd) | 1½ | **3** | 9/2[2] | 61 | 5 |
| | **Hever Golf Mover** (TJNaughton) **2-8-9** PaulEddery(4) (leggy: lt-f: bit bkwd: s.s: outpcd: nvr nrr) | 2½ | **4** | 6/1 | 48 | — |
| 2315[5] | **Auction Hall** (MBell) **2-8-9** MFenton(5) (lw: a bhd) | 8 | **5** | 5/1[3] | 23 | — |
| | **Formidable Spirit** (MJHeaton-Ellis) **2-9-0** SSanders(3) (leggy: chsd ldr over 1f: wknd 2f out) | 1¼ | **6** | 8/1 | 24 | — |

(SP 119.3%) **6 Rn**

**60.5 secs** (2.90) CSF £13.08 TOTE £2.10: £1.50 £2.80 (£20.40) OWNER Mr K. Abdulla (LAMBOURN) BRED Juddmonte Farms

**Stygian (USA)** is not very big at all but was still good enough to beat this bad field. Racing in second, she had to be stoked up below the distance and got on top in the last 100 yards as the leader tired. (10/11)
**Batsman** looked far from fit but ran surprisingly well. Never far away, he was switched right early inside the final furlong and kept on well. (14/1: op 5/1)
**2942 Mangus (IRE)** barely stays five. Bowling along in front, he looked to have the measure of his rivals below the distance but, headed inside the final furlong, had nothing left to offer. (9/2: op 2/1)
**Hever Golf Mover**, with no scope whatsoever and not looking fully wound up, was completely taken off her feet but did make some late headway. (6/1: op 9/4)
**2315 Auction Hall** (5/1: 4/1-6/1)
**Formidable Spirit** (8/1: op 5/1)

## 3582 PAT MARSH SHOW (S) STKS (2-Y.O F) (Class G)

2-30 (2-36) **6f** £2,070.00 (£570.00: £270.00) Stalls: Low GOING minus 0.40 sec per fur (F)

| | Runner | Btn | Pos | SP | RR | SF |
|---|---|---|---|---|---|---|
| | **Sparkling Edge** (APJones) **2-8-10** GHind(5) (unf: dwlt: hdwy over 1f out: led ins fnl f: r.o wl) | — | **1** | 16/1 | 64 | 1 |
| 3169[3] | **Le Shuttle (59)** (MHTompkins) **2-8-10** PRobinson(10) (led tl ins fnl f: unable qckn) | 1¼ | **2** | 5/1[3] | 61 | — |
| 3075[2] | **Hoh Surprise (IRE) (59)** (MBell) **2-8-10** MFenton(9) (hld up: hrd rdn over 1f out: ev ch ins fnl f: one pce) | ½ | **3** | 100/30[2] | 59 | — |
| | **Impy Fox (IRE)** (CADwyer) **2-8-10** MWigham(4) (leggy: bit bkwd: rdn & hdwy over 1f out: nvr nrr) | 2½ | **4** | 14/1 | 53 | — |
| 3336[3] | **Mujadil Express (IRE)** (JSMoore) **2-8-10** SWhitworth(8) (hld up: rdn over 2f out: wknd wl over 1f out) | 2 | **5** | 16/1 | 47 | — |

| | | | | | | |
|---|---|---|---|---|---|---|
| | **Hippy Chick** (DJSCosgrove) **2-8-10** NDay(7) (leggy: unf: s.s: nvr nr to chal) | 3½ | **6** | 5/1[3] | 38 | — |
| 2509[6] | **Moor Hall Princess** (KRBurke) **2-8-10** SSanders(2) (spd over 4f) | 1½ | **7** | 20/1 | 34 | — |
| 3455[3] | **Don't Forget Shoka (IRE) (55)** (JSMoore) **2-9-0** WRyan(11) (bhd fnl 2f) | 1½ | **8** | 12/1 | 34 | — |
| 3046[11] | **Retoto (60)** (BJMcMath) **2-9-0** MRimmer(1) (spd over 4f) | 1½ | **9** | 11/4[1] | 30 | — |
| 3293[9] | **Flo's Choice (IRE)** (JAHarris) **2-8-10** JO'Reilly(3) (spd over 3f) | 3½ | **10** | 16/1 | 17 | — |
| 3230[8] | **Loch Dibidale (58)** (JEBanks) **2-8-5b1**(5) DGriffiths(6) (spd over 3f) | 2 | **11** | 7/1 | 11 | — |
| | | | | (SP 132.3%) | **11 Rn** | |

**1m 14.5** (4.30) CSF £97.44 TOTE £35.20: £8.00 £2.10 £1.80 (£155.50) Trio £83.60 OWNER Mr A. P. Jones (EASTBURY) BRED Benham Stud
Sld SRoss 5,000 gns

**Sparkling Edge** may be little more than a rabbit but was certainly good enough to beat this field. Put to sleep at the back of the field, she came through the field in the final quarter-mile and, gaining control in the last 75 yards, ran on strongly. (16/1)
**3169 Le Shuttle** attempted to make all. Collared inside the final furlong, she found the winner too strong. (5/1: 7/2-11/2)
**3075 Hoh Surprise (IRE)**, moving up in distance, chased the leaders. Throwing down her challenge in the final quarter-mile, she still had every chance inside the final furlong, before tapped for toe. (100/30: 7/4-7/2)
**Impy Fox (IRE)**, a very cheap buy, looked as though this initial run would do her good. Making some headway below the distance, she struggled on to finish a remote fourth. (14/1: 10/1-16/1)
**3336 Mujadil Express (IRE)** was hung out to dry early in the final quarter-mile. (16/1)
**Hippy Chick** was heavily backed on this debut, but losing ground at the start, never gave her supporters anything to cheer about. Her trainer later expressed concern that the filly had been got at, as she returned with a badly swollen head and neck and the vet confirmed she had suffered an allergic reaction. (5/1: 12/1-9/2)

## 3583 ROSS & CO. SOLICITORS H'CAP (0-60) (3-Y.O+) (Class F)

3-00 (3-02) **6f** £3,095.00 (£860.00: £413.00) Stalls: Low GOING minus 0.40 sec per fur (F)

| | | | | SP | RR | SF |
|---|---|---|---|---|---|---|
| 3270[5] | **Never Think Twice (57)** (KTIvory) **3-9-2b**(7) CScally(3) (b: dwlt: hdwy over 2f out: led ins fnl f: r.o wl) | — | **1** | 5/1[3] | 73 | 36 |
| 3439[2] | **Scissor Ridge (52)** (JJBridger) **4-9-7** SSanders(10) (a.p: led wl over 1f out tl ins fnl f: unable qckn) | 2½ | **2** | 3/1[1] | 61 | 27 |
| 3292[2] | **Fairy Prince (IRE) (60)** (MrsALMKing) **3-9-12** MWigham(9) (lw: hld up: hrd rdn over 1f out: one pce) | 2 | **3** | 5/1[3] | 64 | 27 |
| 3285[2] | **Waders Dream (IRE) (41)** (PatMitchell) **7-8-10v** MFenton(7) (rdn & hdwy 2f out: one pce) | ¾ | **4** | 4/1[2] | 43 | 9 |
| 3165[11] | **Pendley Rose (50)** (PWHarris) **3-9-2** GHind(4) (a.p: ev ch 2f out: wknd 1f out) | 3 | **5** | 8/1 | 44 | 7 |
| 3339[8] | **Norling (IRE) (47)** (KOCunningham-Brown) **6-9-2** SWhitworth(6) (hdwy over 2f out: wkng whn hmpd 2f out) | 1¾ | **6** | 8/1 | 36 | 2 |
| 3316[2] | **Office Hours (50)** (CACyzer) **4-9-5** PBloomfield(1) (lw: hdwy 2f out: wknd over 1f out) | s.h | **7** | 7/1 | 39 | 5 |
| 2982[7] | **Royal Carlton (IRE) (55)** (TJNaughton) **4-9-10** PaulEddery(2) (swtg: led 5f out tl wl over 1f out: sn wknd) | 3½ | **8** | 8/1 | 35 | 1 |
| *2081*[15] | **Petite Heritiere (54)** (MJRyan) **3-9-1b1**(5) MBaird(8) (outpcd) | 2 | **9** | 16/1 | 29 | — |
| 3331[10] | **Niteowl Raider (IRE) (45)** (JAHarris) **3-8-11b1** JO'Reilly(5) (swtg: led 1f: wknd 3f out) | 8 | **10** | 20/1 | — | — |
| | | | | (SP 134.8%) | **10 Rn** | |

**1m 12.8** (2.60) CSF £22.62 CT £80.43 TOTE £6.70: £1.90 £1.60 £1.70 (£8.80) Trio £16.10 OWNER Mr K. T. Ivory (RADLETT) BRED Cheveley Park Stud Ltd
WEIGHT FOR AGE 3yo-3lb

**3270 Never Think Twice** began to pick up ground soon after halfway and came sweeping into the lead inside the final furlong. (5/1)
**3439 Scissor Ridge** ran another solid race if again failing to get his head in front. Gaining control early in the final quarter-mile, he found the winner too strong inside the final furlong. (3/1)
**3292 Fairy Prince (IRE)**, almost on terms below the distance, began to find top weight anchoring him. (5/1)
**3285 Waders Dream (IRE)** made an effort a quarter of a mile from home, but could then only tread water. (4/1: 3/1-9/2)
**739 Pendley Rose** (8/1: op 12/1)

## 3584 CHERITON MAIDEN H'CAP (0-60) (3-Y.O+) (Class F)

3-30 (3-30) **1m 4f** £2,381.00 (£656.00: £311.00) Stalls: Low GOING minus 0.40 sec per fur (F)

| | | | | SP | RR | SF |
|---|---|---|---|---|---|---|
| 3204[6] | **Rising Spray (44)** (CAHorgan) **5-9-8** PaulEddery(3) (hdwy over 2f out: led over 1f out: r.o wl) | — | **1** | 11/2[2] | 58 | 40 |
| 3249[12] | **Dauphin (IRE) (32)** (WJMusson) **3-7-9**(5) MBaird(4) (hdwy 2f out: rdn over 1f out: r.o) | 3 | **2** | 20/1 | 42 | 14 |
| 3249[4] | **Dashing Invader (USA) (45)** (PWHarris) **3-8-13** GHind(11) (lw: led over 10f: sn wknd) | 3½ | **3** | 13/2 | 50 | 22 |
| 2779[7] | **The Boozing Brief (USA) (60)** (MAJarvis) **3-9-9**(5) DGriffiths(2) (hdwy 5f out: chsd ldr over 2f out tl over 1f out: sn wknd) | 2 | **4** | 6/1[3] | 63 | 35 |
| 3284[4] | **Duncombe Hall (46)** (CACyzer) **3-8-11**(3) MHenry(12) (a.p: rdn over 2f out: wknd over 1f out) | 3½ | **5** | 8/1 | 44 | 16 |
| 2148[12] | **Birthday Boy (IRE) (46)** (JRJenkins) **4-9-10b** SWhitworth(8) (nvr nr to chal) | ¾ | **6** | 10/1 | 43 | 25 |
| *3074*[9] | **Tiama (IRE) (47)** (SDow) **3-9-1** SSanders(10) (prom 8f) | 8 | **7** | 16/1 | 33 | 5 |
| 2996[11] | **Young Rose (37)** (PatMitchell) **4-9-1** MWigham(1) (lw: a bhd) | hd | **8** | 25/1 | 23 | 5 |
| 3260[4] | **Parrot's Hill (IRE) (54)** (MHTompkins) **3-9-8** PRobinson(9) (chsd ldr 9f out tl over 5f out: 3rd whn stumbled 3f out: wknd over 2f out) | 3 | **9** | 3/1[1] | 36 | 8 |
| 3141[6] | **Junior Ben (IRE) (44)** (PHowling) **4-9-8b** WRyan(5) (a.p: chsd ldr over 5f out tl over 2f out: sn wknd) | nk | **10** | 6/1[3] | 26 | 8 |
| 3000[3] | **Red Tie Affair (USA) (56)** (MBell) **3-9-10v** MFenton(6) (lw: b.nr fore: s.s: bhd fnl 3f) | 4 | **11** | 7/1 | 33 | 5 |
| | | | | (SP 129.5%) | **11 Rn** | |

**2m 36.4** (5.20) CSF £100.57 CT £690.67 TOTE £5.80: £2.50 £7.10 £2.00 (£61.60) Trio £143.80; £162.08 to Ripon 17/8/96 OWNER Mr J. T. Heritage (PULBOROUGH) BRED Pendley Farm
WEIGHT FOR AGE 3yo-10lb

**3204 Rising Spray** at long last came good at the 21st attempt. Picking up ground entering the short home straight, he struck the front below the distance and soon pulled away. (11/2)
**Dauphin (IRE)** began his effort early in the straight, but despite running on to finish a clear second best, had no hope with the winner. (20/1)
**3249 Dashing Invader (USA)** attempted to make all but, collared below the distance, had little left in reserve. (13/2)
**2779 The Boozing Brief (USA)**, who failed to stay a mile and three-quarters last time, was returning to a better trip here. Moving up into second over a quarter of a mile from home, he was collared for that position below the distance and was soon in trouble. (6/1)
**3284 Duncombe Hall**, stepping up in distance, was close up until his stamina ran out below the distance. (8/1)

## 3585 DAILY STAR H'CAP (0-65) (3-Y.O+) (Class F)

4-00 (4-00) **6f 189y** £3,309.20 (£921.20: £443.60) Stalls: Low GOING minus 0.40 sec per fur (F)

| | | | | SP | RR | SF |
|---|---|---|---|---|---|---|
| 3139[11] | **Utmost Zeal (USA) (50)** (PWHarris) **3-8-8** GHind(9) (mde all: clr over 1f out: comf) | — | **1** | 14/1 | 64+ | 40 |

*3078** **Whatever's Right (IRE) (65)** (MDIUsher) **7-10-0** WRyan(2) (chsd wnr fnl 5f: hrd rdn over 1f out: unable qckn) 5 **2** 13/8[1] 67 48
3167[7] **Secret Pleasure (IRE) (60)** (RHannon) **3-9-4** PRobinson(3) (lw: b.nr hind: chsd wnr 2f: rdn over 2f out: one pce) ........ 1¾ **3** 5/1[3] 58 34
2602[9] **Sapphire Son (IRE) (53)** (DMorris) **4-9-2** PBloomfield(8) (lw: a.p: rdn over 2f out: one pce) ........ 1 **4** 9/1 49 30
3304[W] **Barbrallen (42)** (MrsLCJewell) **4-8-0**(5)ow3 SophieMitchell(12) (lw: hdwy on ins 2f out: one pce) ........ hd **5** 50/1 38 16
3167[14] **Jubilee Place (IRE) (57)** (TThomsonJones) **3-9-1** SSanders(5) (b: hld up: rdn over 2f out: sn wknd) ........ 4 **6** 20/1 43 19
2713[8] **Martinosky (49)** (GCBravery) **10-8-12** NDay(7) (nvr nrr) ........ nk **7** 14/1 35 16
3278[7] **Jobie (54)** (BWHills) **6-8-12**(5) JDSmith(11) (swtg: hdwy over 3f out: wknd over 2f out) ........ 2 **8** 9/1 35 16
3469[15] **Classic Pet (IRE) (39)** (CAHorgan) **4-7-9**(7)ow5 GayeHarwood(10) (bhd fnl 2f) ........ 2 **9** 16/1 15 —
3328[5] **Samsolom (59)** (PHowling) **8-9-8** PaulEddery(6) (lw: bhd fnl 3f) ........ hd **10** 7/2[2] 35 16
3084[11] **Bold Habit (57)** (JPearce) **11-8-13**(7) LisaMoncrieff(4) (b.nr hind: s.s: a bhd) ........ 1¼ **11** 20/1 30 11
(SP 127.7%) **11 Rn**

**1m 23.1** (1.50) CSF £38.39 CT £134.45 TOTE £23.80: £3.40 £1.10 £1.90 (£43.20) Trio £109.80 OWNER Thanet Leasing Ltd and Mrs P W Harris (BERKHAMSTED) BRED Braeburn Farm Corp
WEIGHT FOR AGE 3yo-5lb
**1693 Utmost Zeal (USA)**, who drifted badly in the market, made every post a winning one and, forging clear in the short home straight, won with plenty to spare. (14/1: op 8/1)
**3078* Whatever's Right (IRE)** was soon racing in second place. The only danger to the winner in the straight, he was soon put in his place. (13/8)
**2686 Secret Pleasure (IRE)**, in second place early on, was made to look very pedestrian in the home straight. (5/1: 4/1-6/1)
**2405 Sapphire Son (IRE)** was made to look very one-paced in the final quarter-mile. (9/1: 6/1-10/1)

## 3586 KENT MESSENGER GROUP NEWSPAPER MAIDEN H'CAP (0-70) (3-Y.O+) (Class E)
4-30 (4-30) **1m 1f 149y** £3,425.10 (£1,024.80: £491.40: £224.70) Stalls: Low GOING minus 0.40 sec per fur (F)

SP RR SF
3258[5] **Sawa-Id (67)** (JHMGosden) **3-9-10** PaulEddery(3) (chsd ldrs over 8f out: led over 3f out: clr whn edgd lft over 1f out: r.o wl) ........ — **1** 11/4[2] 76 42
3258[6] **Veridian (70)** (PWHarris) **3-9-13** GHind(5) (hdwy over 2f out: hrd rdn over 1f out: chsd wnr ins fnl f: r.o) ........ 1½ **2** 6/1 77 43
2408[8] **Damarita (32)** (LadyHerries) **5-7-8**(3) MHenry(9) (hdwy over 2f out: chsd wnr over 1f out tl ins fnl f: unable qckn) ........ 2½ **3** 4/1[3] 34 8
*2934[9]* **Welcome Royale (IRE) (60)** (MHTompkins) **3-9-3** PRobinson(1) (lw: hdwy over 1f out: one pce) ........ 4 **4** 14/1 56 22
3274[11] **Hadadabble (45)** (PatMitchell) **3-8-2**ow3 MFenton(2) (swtg: led 6f) ........ 2½ **5** 20/1 37 —
2482[7] **Pennine Wind (IRE) (48)** (SDow) **4-8-13** WRyan(8) (bhd fnl 7f) ........ 3½ **6** 20/1 34 8
*3074[4]* **Tablets of Stone (IRE) (45)** (JRBosley) **3-7-9v**[1](7) JBosley(7) (lw: prom over 6f) ........ nk **7** 20/1 30 —
*1048[9]* **Yeath (IRE) (57)** (RAkehurst) **4-9-8** SSanders(6) (b.nr hind: prom 7f) ........ 5 **8** 12/1 34 8
3341[2] **Jean Pierre (55)** (JPearce) **3-8-12** NDay(4) (bhd fnl 3f) ........ 15 **9** 2/1[1] 7 —
(SP 122.9%) **9 Rn**

**2m 1.6** (3.90) CSF £19.75 CT £58.35 TOTE £4.50: £1.90 £2.10 £2.10 (£16.20) Trio £15.80 OWNER Mr Hamdan Al Maktoum (NEWMARKET) BRED Mrs W. H. Gibson Fleming
WEIGHT FOR AGE 3yo-8lb
OFFICIAL EXPLANATION **Jean Pierre: hung badly left and was unable to handle the track.**
**3258 Sawa-Id** made a winning debut in handicap company. Soon racing in second place, he went on over three furlongs from home and forged clear in the home straight, despite drifting left below the distance. (11/4: 5/4-3/1)
**3258 Veridian** went on over quarter of a mile from home. He eventually won the battle for second inside the final furlong, but was unable to threaten the winner. (6/1: 7/2-7/1)
**866 Damarita** moved up to take second place below the distance but was worried out of it inside the final furlong. (4/1)
**Welcome Royale (IRE)** made a small effort below the distance. (14/1: 6/1-16/1)
**Yeath (IRE)** (12/1: 8/1-14/1)
**3341 Jean Pierre** (2/1: op 3/1)

T/Plpt: £75.60 (104.48 Tckts). T/Qdpt: £15.20 (36.5 Tckts) AK

# 3429-HAYDOCK (L-H) (Good to firm)
## Friday August 16th
WEATHER: overcast WIND: slt half against

## 3587 SUTTON APPRENTICE H'CAP (0-80) (3-Y.O+) (Class F)
5-40 (5-40) **1m 3f 200y** £2,633.00 (£738.00: £359.00) Stalls: High GOING minus 0.44 sec per fur (F)

SP RR SF
3318[2] **Reaganesque (USA) (51)** (PGMurphy) **4-8-1** SDrowne(2) (lw: mde all: rdn over 1f out: hld on gamely) ........ — **1** 4/1[2] 57 20
3302* **Canton Venture (75)** (SPCWoods) **4-9-11** 5x NVarley(5) (a.p: jnd wnr over 3f out: rdn over 1f out: unable qckn) ........ ½ **2** 3/1[1] 80 43
3253* **Far Ahead (78)** (JLEyre) **4-10-0** OPears(4) (hld up: effrt & rdn over 2f out: styd on wl towards fin) ........ hd **3** 9/2[3] 83 46
3346[3] **Ambidextrous (IRE) (51)** (EJAlston) **4-8-1** DWright(3) (lw: hld up in rr: nt clr run over 2f out: hdwy appr fnl f: no ex nr fin) ........ ½ **4** 4/1[2] 56 19
3476[3] **Hill Farm Dancer (48)** (WMBrisbourne) **5-7-7**(5) JBramhill(6) (hld up: effrt 3f out: sn hrd drvn: kpt on same pce) ........ ½ **5** 9/2[3] 52 15
3401[5] **Home Counties (IRE) (62)** (DMoffatt) **7-8-12v** DarrenMoffatt(1) (trckd ldrs: drvn along over 2f out: one pce ins fnl f) ........ hd **6** 11/1 66 29
(SP 109.7%) **6 Rn**

**2m 33.91** (4.51) CSF £15.03 TOTE £3.80: £2.20 £1.70 (£3.60) OWNER Mrs John Spielman (BRISTOL) BRED Gainsborough Farm Inc
**3318 Reaganesque (USA)** was able to adopt his catch me if you can tactics here but needed to dig deep to hang on close home. (4/1)
**3302* Canton Venture**, denied the opportunity to force the pace, seemed to be going best when ranging upsides early in the straight, but the winner kept pulling out more and the weight concession proved beyond him. (3/1)
**3253* Far Ahead** carries weight well for such a lightly-made horse, but he was hard at work from some way out, and it was only nearing the finish he was able to make any impression. (9/2: op 3/1)
**3346 Ambidextrous (IRE)** was short of room when making progress entering the final quarter-mile. He did eventually get through approaching the last furlong, but lacked the speed to deliver his challenge. (4/1)

**3476 Hill Farm Dancer**, ridden along for all she was worth over two furlongs out, kept staying on without ever promising to get to terms. (9/2)
**3401 Home Counties (IRE)** has not won a race for some time and this was one of his better efforts. (11/1: 8/1-12/1)

## 3588 ECCLES MAIDEN STKS (2-Y.O) (Class D)

6-10 (6-12) **6f** £3,642.50 (£1,100.00: £535.00: £252.50) Stalls: High GOING minus 0.44 sec per fur (F)

| | | | | SP | RR | SF |
|---|---|---|---|---|---|---|
| | **Reliquary (USA)** (DRLoder) **2-9-0** PatEddery(6) (unf: scope: hld up: swtchd lft ½-wy: qcknd to ld appr fnl f: sn clr) | — | **1** | 4/6$^{1}$ | 81+ | 38 |
| $2887^{4}$ | **China Red (USA)** (JWHills) **2-9-0** MHills(8) (hld up: swtchd lft after 2f: led over 1f out: sn hdd & rdn: no ex fnl f) | 2 | **2** | 3/1$^{2}$ | 76 | 33 |
| $3114^{6}$ | **Tomba** (BJMeehan) **2-9-0** JWeaver(3) (swtg: a.p: led wl over 1f out: sn hdd: kpt on one pce) | 2½ | **3** | 16/1 | 69 | 26 |
| | **Bea's Ruby (IRE)** (ABailey) **2-8-6**(3) DWright(2) (lt-f: dwlt: hdwy to ld over 3f out: hdd wl over 1f out: sn btn) | 3 | **4** | 33/1 | 56 | 13 |
| $3349^{4}$ | **Italian Symphony (IRE)** (MJohnston) **2-9-0** KDarley(5) (hld up: effrt 2f out: sn hrd drvn & no imp) | 1¾ | **5** | 9/1$^{3}$ | 56 | 13 |
| $2495^{4}$ | **Heathyards Pearl (USA)** (RHollinshead) **2-8-6**(3) FLynch(1) (prom tl rdn & wknd over 1f out) | ¾ | **6** | 16/1 | 49 | 6 |
| $3293^{6}$ | **Denton Lad** (JWWatts) **2-9-0** NConnorton(9) (lw: led 1f: lost pl over 2f out: sn bhd) | 3 | **7** | 25/1 | 46 | 3 |
| $2122^{9}$ | **Don't Worry Mike** (FHLee) **2-9-0** NCarlisle(4) (bit bkwd: led after 1f tl over 3f out: sn rdn & outpcd) | s.h | **8** | 50/1 | 46 | 3 |
| | **Willskip (USA)** (JBerry) **2-9-0** KFallon(7) (w'like: scope: bkwd: s.s: swvd bdly lft after 2f: sn t.o) | dist | **9** | 16/1 | — | — |

(SP 121.4%) **9 Rn**

**1m 13.37** (1.67) CSF £3.42 TOTE £1.70: £1.10 £1.10 £2.30 (£1.80) Trio £6.80 OWNER Sheikh Mohammed (NEWMARKET) BRED Darley Stud Management Inc

**Reliquary (USA)**, a late foal, came here with a glowing reputation. Quickening to take it up approaching the final furlong, he sprinted clear effortlessly, but whether he beat much, only time will tell. (4/6)
**2887 China Red (USA)** did not look very happy cantering to post but ran up to his mark, only to find the winner much too good for him. (3/1)
**3114 Tomba** helped share the pace and remained in the action, until feeling the strain inside the final furlong. (16/1)
**Bea's Ruby (IRE)** may well need further but did not show up badly after being sluggish leaving the stalls. She may benefit from some give. (33/1)
**3349 Italian Symphony (IRE)**, restrained just behind the leaders, failed to pick up when set alight and is still in the process of learning. (9/1: 6/1-10/1)
**2495 Heathyards Pearl (USA)** pressed the leaders and had every chance until getting left behind approaching the final furlong. (16/1)

## 3589 GO EVENING RACING WITH THE DAILY TELEGRAPH H'CAP (0-70) (3-Y.O+) (Class E)

6-40 (6-40) **1m 2f 120y** £3,030.00 (£915.00: £445.00: £210.00) Stalls: High GOING minus 0.44 sec per fur (F)

| | | | | SP | RR | SF |
|---|---|---|---|---|---|---|
| $3484^{3}$ | **General Glow (49)** (PDEvans) **3-9-3** 5x JFEgan(6) (lw: a.p: led over 3f out: sn drvn clr: comf) | — | **1** | 15/8$^{1}$ | 61 | 38 |
| $3297^{7}$ | **Monte Cavo (27)** (MBrittain) **5-8-4** GBardwell(4) (lw: a.p: hrd drvn 2f out: nt pce of wnr) | 1¾ | **2** | 20/1 | 36 | 22 |
| | **Minster Glory (41)** (MWEasterby) **5-9-4** KDarley(7) (lw: hld up: hdwy ½-wy: shkn up over 3f out: styd on) | 2½ | **3** | 11/1 | 47 | 33 |
| $3333^{3}$ | **Raindeer Quest (45)** (JLEyre) **4-9-8** JWeaver(5) (led tl over 3f out: sn hrd drvn: kpt on one pce) | 1 | **4** | 5/2$^{2}$ | 49 | 35 |
| $3220^{11}$ | **Arabian Heights (49)** (MrsJRRamsden) **3-9-3** KFallon(3) (swtg: hld up in tch: hrd drvn 3f out: no imp) | ¾ | **5** | 9/2$^{3}$ | 52 | 29 |
| $3426^{6}$ | **Swandale Flyer (34)** (NBycroft) **4-8-11** JQuinn(2) (hld up in rr: pushed along & lost tch over 3f out: t.o) | 17 | **6** | 16/1 | 11 | — |
| $3280^{6}$ | **Maurangi (47)** (BWMurray) **5-9-10** SDrowne(1) (b.hind: s.i.s: a bhd: t.o fnl 4f) | 17 | **7** | 16/1 | — | — |

(SP 106.4%) **7 Rn**

**2m 15.2** (3.70) CSF £27.87 TOTE £2.70: £1.50 £6.50 (£36.30) OWNER Mr J. G. White (WELSHPOOL) BRED Messinger Stud Ltd
WEIGHT FOR AGE 3yo-9lb

**3484 General Glow** suffered a setback when beaten at Beverley two days ago, but he was back on song here and stayed on too strongly for his pursuers. (15/8: 11/10-2/1)
**Monte Cavo** ran up to his best and though the winner proved too strong, he would seem to be finding his way. (20/1)
**Minster Glory**, a winner over hurdles but off the track for 16 months, did look as though he had done plenty of work. He found his stride in the closing stages and looks one to keep in mind. (11/1)
**3333 Raindeer Quest**, a well-made filly on short legs, found these weights too much and was galloping on the spot when the race really developed. (5/2)
**3117 Arabian Heights**, waited with just off the pace, could not muster the speed to land a blow and would seem of little account. (9/2)

## 3590 RAINHILL NURSERY H'CAP (2-Y.O) (Class E)

7-10 (7-12) **5f** £3,078.75 (£930.00: £452.50: £213.75) Stalls: High GOING minus 0.44 sec per fur (F)

| | | | | SP | RR | SF |
|---|---|---|---|---|---|---|
| $3299^{3}$ | **Bold African (80)** (PDEvans) **2-8-12b** JFEgan(8) (mde all: sn clr: drvn out) | — | **1** | 11/2$^{3}$ | 82 | 36 |
| $2984^{9}$ | **Smokey From Caplaw (68)** (JJO'Neill) **2-8-0** JQuinn(7) (hld up & plld hrd: hdwy & swtchd lft over 1f out: hung lft fnl f: r.o wl) | 1¼ | **2** | 20/1 | 66 | 20 |
| $3224^{8}$ | **Divide And Rule (82)** (RHollinshead) **2-8-11**(3) FLynch(9) (hld up in tch: effrt 2f out: rdn & r.o wl ins fnl f) | ½ | **3** | 12/1 | 78 | 32 |
| $3170^{3}$ | **Sous Le Nez (76)** (RGuest) **2-8-8** KDarley(5) (prom: pushed along wl over 1f out: sn btn) | 3½ | **4** | 3/1$^{1}$ | 61 | 15 |
| $3321^{4}$ | **Lunar Music (70)** (MartynMeade) **2-7-13**(3) DWright(6) (chsd wnr 3f: rdn & one pce appr fnl f) | hd | **5** | 9/2$^{2}$ | 55 | 9 |
| $3247^{8}$ | **Nomore Mr Niceguy (89)** (EJAlston) **2-9-7** SDrowne(3) (s.i.s: hdwy ½-wy: rdn 2f out: r.o one pce) | 2½ | **6** | 12/1 | 66 | 20 |
| $1989^{7}$ | **Sharp Return (66)** (MJRyan) **2-7-12** GBardwell(1) (nvr gng pce of ldrs) | 1¼ | **7** | 12/1 | 39 | — |
| $2879^{W}$ | **Nervous Rex (76)** (WRMuir) **2-8-8b** KFallon(4) (prom: rdn over 2f out: sn wknd & eased) | 3½ | **8** | 11/2$^{3}$ | 38 | — |
| $3250^{5}$ | **No Extradition (73)** (MrsJRRamsden) **2-8-5** MDeering(2) (s.i.s: a bhd & outpcd) | hd | **9** | 9/1 | 34 | — |

(SP 111.8%) **9 Rn**

**60.56 secs** (1.36) CSF £84.33 CT £809.67 TOTE £4.80: £1.80 £4.20 £3.40 (£87.10) Trio £271.20 OWNER Mr D. Maloney (WELSHPOOL) BRED G. Dickinson

**3299 Bold African** continued the impressive run his stable is enjoying at the moment with a clear-cut, all the way success. Racing with his tongue tied down, he is certainly paying his way. (11/2)
**1164* Smokey From Caplaw** shows plenty of knee action and took a very keen hold on the step back to the minimum trip, and did not find top gear until late on. (20/1)
**2965 Divide And Rule** finished way behind the winner earlier in the month, and was never in the position to offer a serious threat here. (12/1)
**3170 Sous Le Nez** pushed the pace but was never travelling that well, and had met her match before the final furlong. (3/1)
**3321 Lunar Music** tried hard to keep tabs on the winner but was labouring below the distance and her measure had been taken. (9/2)

## 3591 SWAN WITH TWO NECKS (S) STKS (3-Y.O) (Class F)

7-40 (7-45) **1m 30y** £2,675.00 (£750.00: £365.00) Stalls: Low GOING minus 0.44 sec per fur (F)

| | | | SP | RR | SF |
|---|---|---|---|---|---|
| $3123^{14}$ | **Power Game (66)** (JBerry) **3-9-0b** JWeaver(4) (trckd ldrs: rdn to ld wl ins fnl f: all out) ...— | **1** | 7/4 1 | 64 | 27 |
| $3228^{7}$ | **Arc of The Diver (IRE) (55)** (JBerry) **3-9-0b¹** KDarley(10) (lw: a.p: led over 2f out: hrd rdn & hdd wl ins fnl f) ...hd | **2** | 10/1 | 64 | 27 |
| $2766^{3}$ | **Just Millie (USA) (64)** (JEBanks) **3-8-7**(7) GFaulkner(5) (hld up: hdwy over 1f out: hrd rdn & r.o wl cl home) .1¾ | **3** | 3/1 2 | 60 | 23 |
| $3102^{10}$ | **Scenicris (IRE) (57)** (RHollinshead) **3-8-6**(3) FLynch(2) (lw: plld hrd: hld up: swtchd outside over 2f out: kpt on u.p towards fin) ...s.h | **4** | 10/1 | 55 | 18 |
| 3451* | **Clued Up (40)** (PDEvans) **3-9-0** JFEgan(1) (trckd ldrs: rdn 2f out: ev ch ent fnl f: unable qckn) ...1 | **5** | 9/2 3 | 58 | 21 |
| $3458^{3}$ | **Holloway Melody (39)** (BAMcMahon) **3-8-6**(3) DWright(7) (hld up & bhd: hdwy u.p over 1f out: nvr nrr) ...1¼ | **6** | 12/1 | 51 | 14 |
| $3354^{14}$ | **Gold Lining (IRE) (48)** (EJAlston) **3-8-9v¹** SDrowne(9) (led tl hdd & wknd over 2f out) ...9 | **7** | 25/1 | 33 | — |
| $3059^{5}$ | **Polish Saga (44)** (MDods) **3-8-9** KFallon(12) (swtg: hld up: effrt over 2f out: sn no imp) ...2 | **8** | 12/1 | 29 | — |
| $3399^{6}$ | **Maysimp (IRE) (40)** (BPJBaugh) **3-8-9** NCarlisle(3) (mid div tl wknd wl over 2f out: t.o) ...13 | **9** | 25/1 | 4 | — |
| | **Run With Pride** (EWeymes) **3-8-9** JQuinn(11) (w'like: str: bkwd: s.s: a bhd: t.o) ...3 | **10** | 25/1 | — | — |
| | | | (SP 124.7%) | | **10 Rn** |

**1m 44.22** (3.62) CSF £20.09 TOTE £2.90: £1.50 £2.70 £1.60 (£22.30) Trio £25.10 OWNER Countrywide Racing (COCKERHAM) BRED Bearstone Stud

No bid

**2618 Power Game** looked something to bet on in this first time seller, but he had to work very hard indeed to get the better of his stable companion. (7/4)

**Arc of The Diver (IRE)**, blinkered for the first time, proved a tough nut to crack and with form like this, he shouldn't have much trouble in finding a race. (10/1)

**2766 Just Millie (USA)** had the blinkers left off after running too free at Brighton and was settled off the pace. She did not find her stride until the race was almost over. (3/1: op 2/1)

**2222 Scenicris (IRE)** is certainly up to winning in this class but she ran much too freely in the early stages, and though she did stay on well towards the finish, was never going to get there. (10/1: op 6/1)

**3451* Clued Up** failed to keep the Evans bandwagon rolling, but it was not for the want of trying and she will strike again in the coming weeks. (9/2: 7/1-4/1)

**3458 Holloway Melody**, having her second outing of the week, is not certain to get this trip. (12/1)

**3059 Polish Saga** (12/1: op 8/1)

## 3592 CLAUDE HARRISON MEMORIAL CHALLENGE TROPHY H'CAP (0-70) (3-Y.O+) (Class E)

8-10 (8-13) **1m 30y** £3,143.75 (£950.00: £462.50: £218.75) Stalls: Low GOING minus 0.44 sec per fur (F)

| | | | SP | RR | SF |
|---|---|---|---|---|---|
| $3426^{2}$ | **Celebration Cake (IRE) (63)** (MissLAPerratt) **4-10-0** 5x JWeaver(2) (lw: hld up: hdwy to ld over 1f out: sn drvn clr) ...— | **1** | 4/1 2 | 79 | 52 |
| $3354^{2}$ | **Falcon's Flame (USA) (51)** (MrsJRRamsden) **3-8-10** KFallon(1) (hld up in rr: stumbled bnd 5f out: hdwy on ins over 2f out: kpt on wl fnl f) ...3 | **2** | 11/4 1 | 61 | 28 |
| $3403^{2}$ | **Duke Valentino (57)** (RHollinshead) **4-9-5**(3) FLynch(3) (lw: hld up: hdwy 2f out: rdn & edgd lft fnl f: r.o wl) ....hd | **3** | 9/1 | 67 | 40 |
| 2966* | **Cointosser (IRE) (63)** (MCPipe) **3-9-1**(7) GFaulkner(5) (a.p: led over 2f out tl rdn & hdd over 1f out: one pce) ...½ | **4** | 5/1 3 | 72 | 39 |
| $3334^{2}$ | **Cuban Reef (43)** (WJMusson) **4-8-8** JFEgan(11) (lw: hld up & bhd: gd hdwy appr fnl f: nrst fin) ...1¼ | **5** | 5/1 3 | 50 | 23 |
| $2573^{7}$ | **Bedazzle (38)** (MBrittain) **5-8-3** GBardwell(4) (prom: drvn along 4f out: hrd rdn & wknd appr fnl f) ...¾ | **6** | 20/1 | 43 | 16 |
| $3274^{2}$ | **Flag Fen (USA) (59)** (MartynMeade) **5-9-3**(7) ClaireAngell(6) (trckd ldrs: hrd drvn over 2f out: sn lost pl) .......1¾ | **7** | 12/1 | 61 | 34 |
| $3399^{7}$ | **Red March Hare (32)** (DMoffatt) **5-7-8**(3)ow1 DarrenMoffatt(7) (b: bkwd: hld up & bhd: effrt over 2f out: nt rch ldrs) ...s.h | **8** | 50/1 | 33 | 5 |
| $3410^{5}$ | **Mill Dancer (IRE) (36)** (EJAlston) **4-8-1** SDrowne(8) (led tl over 2f out: sn rdn & wknd) ...1½ | **9** | 20/1 | 35 | 8 |
| $2929^{4}$ | **Intendant (58)** (JGFitzGerald) **4-9-9** KDarley(9) (lw: hld up: hdwy 3f out: rdn & wknd 2f out) ...3 | **10** | 14/1 | 51 | 24 |
| $3354^{9}$ | **Paper Maze (43)** (EHOwenjun) **3-8-2** NCarlisle(12) (trckd ldrs over 5f: wknd qckly: t.o) ...11 | **11** | 50/1 | 14 | — |
| $3226^{6}$ | **Meadow Blue (48)** (MissLCSiddall) **3-8-7** JQuinn(10) (trckd ldrs tl past ½-wy: sn wknd: t.o) ...6 | **12** | 33/1 | 7 | — |
| | | | (SP 120.7%) | | **12 Rn** |

**1m 43.01** (2.41) CSF £14.93 CT £83.43 TOTE £5.00: £1.70 £1.60 £2.90 (£5.70) Trio £28.60 OWNER Lightbody of Hamilton Ltd (AYR) BRED John Davison

LONG HANDICAP Red March Hare 7-9

WEIGHT FOR AGE 3yo-6lb

**3426 Celebration Cake (IRE)** gave the impression he was feeling the ground cantering to post, but was always travelling throughout the race, and drew clear at will when sent about his work. (4/1)

**3354 Falcon's Flame (USA)** ran very free in the early stages but was restrained among the back markers. Galvanised into action approaching the quarter-mile marker, he stayed on strongly nearing the finish but the winner had gone beyond recall. (11/4)

**3403 Duke Valentino** is running well enough to get back to winning ways, and leaves the impression that a stiffer test of stamina is needed when the ground rides so fast. (9/1)

**2966* Cointosser (IRE)** had more on her plate on this first outing for new connections, but turned in another good display, and should not take long in repaying some of her purchase price. (5/1)

**3334 Cuban Reef** came from a long way back and it would seem she is crying out for a longer trip. (5/1)

**2481 Bedazzle** is inconsistent but showed he could return to form in selling company. (20/1)

T/Plpt: £35.40 (334.72 Tckts). T/Qdpt: £22.10 (39.17 Tckts) IM

# 2877-NEWBURY (L-H) (Good)
## Friday August 16th

WEATHER: fine WIND: almost nil

## 3593 SPARSHOLT MAIDEN STKS (2-Y.O F) (Class D)

2-10 (2-12) **6f 8y** £4,276.00 (£1,288.00: £624.00: £292.00) Stalls: High GOING minus 0.30 sec per fur (GF)

| | | | SP | RR | SF |
|---|---|---|---|---|---|
| $3206^{2}$ | **Catechism (USA)** (JHMGosden) **2-8-11** LDettori(14) (lw: a.p: rdn over 1f out: r.o to ld nr fin) ...— | **1** | 8/1 3 | 85 | 38 |

| | | | | SP | RR | SF |
|---|---|---|---|---|---|---|
| 2741$^{4}$ | **Nopalea** (CEBrittain) **2-8-11** BDoyle(10) (led over 4f: led wl ins fnl f: hdd nr fin) | ½ | **2** | 33/1 | 84 | 37 |
| 3234$^{2}$ | **Elegant Warning (IRE)** (BWHills) **2-8-11** MHills(17) (lw: a.p: led on bit over 1f out: rdn, edgd rt & hdd wl ins fnl f: nt run on) | nk | **3** | 6/4$^{1}$ | 83 | 36 |
| | **Sahara River (USA)** (RCharlton) **2-8-11** TSprake(7) (small: cmpt: bit bkwd: hld up: hdwy whn swtchd rt over 1f out: fin wl) | ¾ | **4** | 25/1 | 81+ | 34 |
| | **Chorus Song (USA)** (PWChapple-Hyam) **2-8-11** JReid(3) (w'like: a.p: rdn over 2f out: r.o ins fnl f) | 1¼ | **5** | 12/1 | 78 | 31 |
| | **Injazaat (USA)** (MajorWRHern) **2-8-11** WCarson(5) (rangy: scope: hrd rdn & hdwy over 2f out: eased whn btn ins fnl f) | ½ | **6** | 12/1 | 76 | 29 |
| | **Rose Carnival** (DRLoder) **2-8-11** PatEddery(13) (leggy: unf: prom over 4f) | ½ | **7** | 8/1$^{3}$ | 75 | 28 |
| 3269$^{2}$ | **Curzon Street** (MRStoute) **2-8-11** WRSwinburn(6) (prom tl rdn & wknd over 1f out: eased whn btn ins fnl f) | 1½ | **8** | 7/1$^{2}$ | 71 | 24 |
| | **Mawhiba (USA)** (JLDunlop) **2-8-11** GCarter(19) (cmpt: lw: hld up & bhd: stdy hdwy over 1f out: nt clr run ins fnl f: bttr for r) | s.h | **9** | 20/1 | 71+ | 24 |
| 3129$^{8}$ | **Gee Bee Dream** (APJarvis) **2-8-11** WJO'Connor(8) (hld up mid div: sme hdwy over 1f out: nt clr run ins fnl f) | 1 | **10** | 50/1 | 68 | 21 |
| | **Flourishing Way** (RCharlton) **2-8-11** KDarley(4) (cmpt: bkwd: hld up: rdn over 2f out: wknd over 1f out) | 1½ | **11** | 16/1 | 64 | 17 |
| | **Snow Eagle (IRE)** (RHannon) **2-8-8**(3) DaneO'Neill(11) (leggy: unf: bit bkwd: s.s: nvr nrr) | nk | **12** | 33/1 | 63 | 16 |
| | **Karawan** (JHMGosden) **2-8-11** BThomson(16) (scope: nvr bttr than mid div) | hd | **13** | 25/1 | 63 | 16 |
| | **Golden Goddess** (IABalding) **2-8-11** TQuinn(9) (lengthy: scope: a bhd) | 2 | **14** | 20/1 | 58 | 11 |
| 2852$^{12}$ | **Perchance To Dream (IRE)** (BRMillman) **2-8-11** RCochrane(18) (hld up: a bhd) | hd | **15** | 50/1 | 58 | 11 |
| | **Racing Heart** (PJMakin) **2-8-6**(5) RHavlin(2) (w'like: bkwd: a bhd) | 1 | **16** | 50/1 | 55 | 8 |
| | **Push A Venture** (SPCWoods) **2-8-11** WWoods(15) (unf: s.s: a bhd) | 8 | **17** | 50/1 | 34 | — |
| | **Wing And A Prayer (IRE)** (RHannon) **2-8-11** NAdams(1) (rangy: wnt lft s: a bhd) | 1¼ | **18** | 50/1 | 30 | — |
| | **Flood's Hot Stuff** (MRChannon) **2-8-11** AMackay(12) (w'like: scope: bhd fnl 3f) | 1 | **19** | 33/1 | 28 | — |
| | | | | (SP 131.8%) | **19 Rn** | |

**1m 14.07** (2.27) CSF £218.26 TOTE £7.10: £2.80 £9.30 £1.40 (£86.80) Trio £87.00 OWNER Mr Thomas Tatham (NEWMARKET) BRED Oak Cliff Thoroughbred Bloodstock Ltd 1985

**3206 Catechism (USA)**, described by her trainer as quite highly strung, needed every yard of this trip to get on top, and again gave the impression that another furlong would not go amiss. (8/1: op 5/1)

**2741 Nopalea** showed the right sort of attitude, which is more than can be said about the favourite. (33/1)

**3234 Elegant Warning (IRE)** had shown signs of temperament at Goodwood, which could have been attributed to greenness on her debut. She threw in the towel here once coming under pressure and definitely has an attitude problem. (6/4)

**Sahara River (USA)** is not very big. Bred to require further, she finished in good style and looks a ready-made future winner. (25/1)

**Chorus Song (USA)** did shape as if she would benefit from further. (12/1: 5/1-14/1)

**Injazaat (USA)** will be better for the experience. (12/1)

**Rose Carnival** figured prominently over a trip which should have been short of her best. (8/1: op 5/1)

**3269 Curzon Street** found this much more competitive than her debut. (7/1)

**Mawhiba (USA)**, a half-sister to Erhaab and Oumaldaaya, made an eye-catching debut but is likely to need further. (20/1)

## 3594 BONUSPRINT H'CAP (0-100) (3-Y.O) (Class C)

2-40 (2-44) **1m 2f 6y** £9,826.00 (£2,968.00: £1,444.00: £682.00) Stalls: High GOING minus 0.30 sec per fur (GF)

| | | | | SP | RR | SF |
|---|---|---|---|---|---|---|
| 3153$^{8}$ | **Greenstead (USA) (89)** (JHMGosden) **3-8-11** LDettori(6) (swtg: hld up: hdwy on ins 3f out: rdn to ld over 1f out: qcknd clr ins fnl f) | — | **1** | 15/2$^{3}$ | 103 | 60 |
| 2888$^{9}$ | **Brandon Magic (93)** (IABalding) **3-9-1** WRSwinburn(1) (a.p: outpcd over 2f out: styd on fnl f: nt trble wnr) | 3½ | **2** | 20/1 | 101 | 58 |
| 2996* | **Yalta (IRE) (85)** (RCharlton) **3-8-7** PatEddery(14) (lw: a.p: ev ch 2f out: sn rdn: one pce) | ¾ | **3** | 3/1$^{1}$ | 92 | 49 |
| 2621$^{14}$ | **Polar Prospect (74)** (BHanbury) **3-7-5**(5) MartinDwyer(10) (led over 8f: one pce) | 1¼ | **4** | 20/1 | 79 | 36 |
| 3211$^{2}$ | **Murheb (92)** (RWArmstrong) **3-9-0** RPrice(4) (plld hrd: a.p: one pce fnl 2f) | hd | **5** | 13/2$^{2}$ | 97 | 54 |
| 2774$^{4}$ | **Polinesso (99)** (BWHills) **3-9-7** MHills(11) (hld up & bhd: hdwy fnl 2f: nvr nrr) | s.h | **6** | 12/1 | 104 | 61 |
| 2621$^{15}$ | **Sabrak (IRE) (88)** (MAJarvis) **3-8-10** JReid(15) (lw: no hdwy fnl 2f) | nk | **7** | 16/1 | 93 | 50 |
| 3207$^{5}$ | **Champagne Prince (90)** (PWHarris) **3-8-12** BDoyle(5) (hld up & plld hrd: no hdwy fnl 3f) | 1½ | **8** | 33/1 | 92 | 49 |
| 3067$^{5}$ | **Brilliant Red (98)** (PFICole) **3-9-6** TQuinn(7) (plld hrd mid div: rdn & hdwy 3f out: wknd 2f out) | ½ | **9** | 10/1 | 99 | 56 |
| 3211$^{8}$ | **Wot No Fax (92)** (SDow) **3-8-11**(3) DaneO'Neill(3) (nvr nrr) | ¾ | **10** | 20/1 | 92 | 49 |
| 2128* | **Fasil (IRE) (81)** (CJBenstead) **3-8-3** WCarson(13) (bhd fnl 2f) | 5 | **11** | 8/1 | 73 | 30 |
| 2135$^{7}$ | **Ambassadori (USA) (74)** (CEBrittain) **3-7-10** DeclanO'Shea(2) (a bhd) | 6 | **12** | 20/1 | 57 | 14 |
| 2724$^{16}$ | **Yarob (IRE) (95)** (HThomsonJones) **3-9-3** GCarter(12) (hld up: stdy hdwy over 3f out: wknd over 2f out) | 1¾ | **13** | 20/1 | 75 | 32 |
| 3071$^{7}$ | **Flying Green (FR) (89)** (NJHWalker) **3-8-11** JStack(16) (prom tl rdn & wknd over 2f out) | ¾ | **14** | 33/1 | 68 | 25 |
| 3229$^{4}$ | **Swift Fandango (USA) (90)** (PFICole) **3-8-12** KDarley(9) (hld up & plld hrd: bhd fnl 3f) | 7 | **15** | 14/1 | 57 | 14 |
| | | | | (SP 120.2%) | **15 Rn** | |

**2m 5.1** (1.30) CSF £129.40 CT £501.16 TOTE £10.70: £3.40 £5.20 £1.70 (£96.40) Trio £252.50 OWNER Sheikh Mohammed (NEWMARKET) BRED Darley Stud Management Inc

LONG HANDICAP Ambassadori (USA) 7-9

**2610* Greenstead (USA)** was back to a more suitable trip and showed a nice turn of foot to put the issue beyond doubt. (15/2)

**2544 Brandon Magic**, dropped 3lb, appreciated this longer trip but really needs softer ground to offset his lack of a turn of foot. (20/1)

**2996* Yalta (IRE)** was stepping up in trip. He may have got his head in front entering the final quarter-mile, but could not match the winner's finishing speed. (3/1)

**2501 Polar Prospect** did not set too strong a pace but might benefit from more patient tactics over this extra quarter-mile. (20/1)

**3211 Murheb** ran too freely and could not defy a 5lb rise in the weights for his good second at Goodwood. (13/2)

**2774 Polinesso**, patiently ridden, got the trip well and can adopt more aggressive tactics in the future. (12/1)

**3067 Brilliant Red** refused to settle and can do better than this. (10/1)

## 3595 WASHINGTON SINGER STKS (Listed) (2-Y.O) (Class A)

3-10 (3-12) **7f (straight)** £9,384.00 (£2,832.00: £1,376.00: £648.00) Stalls: High GOING minus 0.30 sec per fur (GF)

| | | | | SP | RR | SF |
|---|---|---|---|---|---|---|
| 3264* | **State Fair (100)** (BWHills) **2-9-0** MHills(4) (chsd ldr: led over 2f out: r.o wl) | — | **1** | 4/7$^{1}$ | 95 | 35 |
| | **In Question** (BWHills) **2-8-8** PatEddery(5) (str: bit bkwd: scope: hld up: sn outpcd: rdn & gd hdwy over 1f out: r.o wl ins fnl f: nt rch wnr) | 1¼ | **2** | 12/1 | 86? | 26 |
| | **Davoski** (BWHills) **2-8-8** WCarson(3) (w'like: bit bkwd: scope: outpcd: rdn & gd hdwy over 1f out: r.o ins fnl f) | ¾ | **3** | 25/1 | 84? | 24 |

**Count Roberto (USA)** (PWChapple-Hyam) **2-8-8** JReid(1) (w'like: bit bkwd: a.p: rdn & ev ch 2f out: one pce) ....2 **4** 9/2$^{2}$ 80 20

$2703^{5}$ **Powder River (89)** (RHannon) **2-9-0b** LDettori(2) (lw: racd wd: led: clr over 4f out: hdd over 2f out: wknd over 1f out) ....4 **5** 8/1$^{3}$ 77 17

(SP 104.5%) **5 Rn**

**1m 27.74** (3.24) CSF £6.34 TOTE £1.50: £1.10 £2.70 (£4.00) OWNER Mr Ray Richards (LAMBOURN) BRED Hesmonds Stud Ltd

**3264* State Fair**, bought as a long term Ascot Gold Cup prospect, led the way in a 1-2-3 for his stable and now heads for the Royal Lodge. (4/7)

**In Question**, is a really imposing individual, for him it was a case of the further they went, the better he got. (12/1: 8/1-14/1)

**Davoski**, a half-brother to Marl, should win a race on this showing. (25/1)

**Count Roberto (USA)** should win races but may not live up to his entries including the Royal Lodge and the Dewhurst. (9/2: op 5/2)

**2703 Powder River**, found his trail-blazing tactics did not help him to get the seven. (8/1)

## 3596 HUNGERFORD STKS (Gp 3) (3-Y.O+) (Class A)

3-40 (3-41) **7f 64y (round)** £21,480.00 (£8,049.00: £3,874.50: £1,696.50) Stalls: High GOING minus 0.30 sec per fur (GF)

SP RR SF

3199a* **Bin Rosie (113)** (DRLoder) **4-9-0b** LDettori(8) (hld up: hdwy over 2f out: qcknd to ld ins fnl f: drvn out) ....— **1** 9/2$^{2}$ 121 83

$3144^{6}$ **Mistle Cat (USA) (117)** (SPCWoods) **6-9-3** WWoods(6) (w ldr: led over 3f out tl ins fnl f: r.o one pce) ....1¾ **2** 6/1 120 82

$3409^{2}$ **Magellan (USA)** (CEBrittain) **3-8-9** BDoyle(4) (hld up: rdn & ev ch over 1f out: unable qckn) ....hd **3** 25/1 117 74

$2609^{2}$ **Ta Rib (USA) (113)** (EALDunlop) **3-9-0** WCarson(2) (swtg: hld up: rdn & hdwy on ins over 2f out: one pce fnl f) ....1¾ **4** 5/1$^{3}$ 118 75

3229* **Hammerstein (110)** (MRStoute) **3-8-9** PatEddery(5) (swtg: hld up: rdn over 2f out: ev ch over 1f out: wknd ins fnl f) ....1 **5** 4/1$^{1}$ 111 68

$3126^{10}$ **Lucky Lionel (USA) (115)** (RHannon) **3-8-9** JReid(1) (lw: hld up & bhd: nvr nr to chal) ....hd **6** 14/1 111 68

3127* **Thrilling Day (112)** (NAGraham) **3-8-9** KDarley(3) (rdn over 3f out: a bhd) ....12 **7** 11/2 84 41

2853* **Green Perfume (USA) (106)** (PFICole) **4-9-0** TQuinn(7) (led over 3f: wknd wl over 1f out) ....1 **8** 5/1$^{3}$ 82 44

(SP 111.7%) **8 Rn**

**1m 27.28** (-0.82) CSF £28.17 TOTE £5.70: £1.70 £1.90 £4.00 (£13.60) OWNER Mr Wafic Said (NEWMARKET) BRED Addison Racing Ltd Inc

WEIGHT FOR AGE 3yo-5lb

STEWARDS' ENQUIRY Woods susp. 25-26/8/96 (excessive use of the whip).

**3199a* Bin Rosie** needs to be produced in the closing stages to use his turn of foot, and Dettori timed it to perfection. (9/2)

**3144 Mistle Cat (USA)** fought with Green Perfume for the lead. Having seen that rival off, he stuck on well for second once collared by the winner. (6/1)

**3409 Magellan (USA)**, dropped in distance, sat a few lengths off the two tearaway leaders, but could not get past the runner-up, let alone the winner. (25/1)

**2609 Ta Rib (USA)**, sweated up as usual, and her run up the inner was being held at the distance. (5/1)

**3229* Hammerstein** could not make the transition to Group class. (4/1)

**2622 Lucky Lionel (USA)** never threatened to take a hand. (14/1)

**3127* Thrilling Day** ran no race at all. (11/2)

**2853* Green Perfume (USA)** did not benefit from being taken on in the lead. (5/1)

## 3597 NEWTOWN CONDITIONS STKS (3-Y.O+) (Class C)

4-10 (4-10) **1m 4f 5y** £4,843.60 (£1,812.40: £886.20: £381.00: £170.50: £86.30) Stalls: High GOING minus 0.30 sec per fur (GF)

SP RR SF

$1580a^{11}$ **Heron Island (IRE) (105)** (PWChapple-Hyam) **3-8-9** JReid(6) (lw: hld up: swtchd rt & hdwy over 1f out: qcknd to ld wl ins fnl f: r.o wl) ....— **1** 11/2$^{3}$ 114 66

$1176^{2}$ **Minds Music (USA) (113)** (HRACecil) **4-9-3** PatEddery(3) (chsd ldr: led wl over 1f out: sn hdd: hrd rdn to ld ins fnl f: sn hdd: unable qckn) ....1¼ **2** 6/4$^{1}$ 110 72

$3200a^{4}$ **Taufan's Melody (112)** (LadyHerries) **5-9-5** RCochrane(5) (hld up: led over 1f out tl ins fnl f) ....nk **3** 5/2$^{2}$ 112 74

$1580a^{10}$ **Babinda (101)** (CEBrittain) **3-8-7** BDoyle(1) (a.p: rdn & one pce fnl 2f) ....4 **4** 14/1 105 57

$3212^{9}$ **River North (IRE) (105)** (LadyHerries) **6-9-3** KDarley(4) (b: lw: hld up: rdn over 2f out: no rspnse) ....½ **5** 14/1 104 66

**Poltarf (USA) (103)** (JHMGosden) **5-9-3** LDettori(2) (lw: led: rdn & hdd wl over 1f out: wknd fnl f) ....¾ **6** 7/1 103 65

(SP 109.8%) **6 Rn**

**2m 30.49** (0.49) CSF £13.46 TOTE £6.50: £2.20 £1.50 (£4.80) OWNER Mr R. E. Sangster (MARLBOROUGH) BRED Barronstown Stud and Roncon Ltd

WEIGHT FOR AGE 3yo-10lb

**1580a Heron Island (IRE)**, off course since disappointing in the Italian Derby, may have been waiting for some decent ground, and came with a well-timed run. (11/2)

**1176 Minds Music (USA)**, another not seen out since May, worked hard to get his head in front, but the winner's late run brooked no argument. (6/4)

**3200a Taufan's Melody** could not hold the runner-up let alone the winner in the last 200 yards. (5/2)

**1580a Babinda** had finished a length and a half in front of the winner in the Italian Derby, and like that rival had not been seen out since. (14/1: 10/1-16/1)

**2194 River North (IRE)** is looking a light of other days after a sinus operation. (14/1: op 6/1)

**Poltarf (USA)** made a satisfactory comeback over a trip short of his best. (7/1: 6/1-10/1)

## 3598 LEVY BOARD H'CAP (0-85) (3-Y.O+) (Class D)

4-40 (4-41) **2m** £5,426.50 (£1,642.00: £801.00: £380.50) Stalls: High GOING minus 0.30 sec per fur (GF)

SP RR SF

$2042^{24}$ **En Vacances (IRE) (73)** (AGFoster) **4-9-5** TSprake(1) (hld up: hdwy 4f out: hrd rdn over 2f out: swtchd rt over 1f out: r.o to ld wl ins fnl f) ....— **1** 7/1 85 65

2986* **Izza (52)** (WStorey) **5-7-12** NKennedy(7) (lw: hld up & bhd: hdwy over 3f out: rdn 2f out: ev ch ins fnl f: r.o) ....1 **2** 4/1$^{1}$ 63 43

$3142^{5}$ **Salaman (FR) (78)** (JLDunlop) **4-9-10b$^{1}$** TQuinn(2) (lw: hld up: hdwy over 5f out: wnt 2nd over 3f out: ev ch ins fnl f: unable qckn) ....hd **3** 13/2$^{3}$ 89 69

3463* **Shirley Sue (64)** (MJohnston) **3-7-10** 5x NAdams(4) (lw: a.p: wnt 2nd 9f out: led over 4f out: hrd rdn & hdd wl ins fnl f) ....hd **4** 4/1$^{1}$ 75 41

$2756^{3}$ **Prague Spring (62)** (LadyHerries) **4-8-8** RCochrane(8) (b: chsd ldr after 3f to 9f out: rdn & wknd 4f out) ....7 **5** 9/1 66 46

3335* **Classic Affair (USA) (64)** (RHarris) **3-7-10** 5x AMackay(9) (lw: hld up & bhd: effrt 3f out: sn wknd) ....5 **6** 6/1$^{2}$ 63 29

$2547^{2}$ **Bowcliffe Court (IRE) (67)** (BWHills) **4-8-13** WCarson(6) (swtg: hld up: a bhd) ....12 **7** 7/1 54 34

$3037^{8}$ **Toy Princess (USA) (75)** (CEBrittain) **4-9-7** BDoyle(3) (lw: led 1f: wknd 4f out) ....3½ **8** 12/1 58 38

| | | | Pos | SP | RR | SF |
|---|---|---|---|---|---|---|
| 3209$^{4}$ | **Caballus (USA) (70)** (LordHuntingdon) **3-8-2** GCarter(5) (plld hrd: led after 1f: hdd over 4f out: wknd over 3f out: t.o) | 13 | **9** | 16/1 | 40 | 6 |

(SP 116.2%) **9 Rn**

**3m 27.98** (2.98) CSF £33.14 CT £175.37 TOTE £7.70: £1.60 £1.80 £2.50 (£18.70) Trio £46.00 OWNER Lambourn Valley Racing (LAMBOURN) BRED The Woodhaven Stud

LONG HANDICAP Classic Affair (USA) 7-2 Shirley Sue 7-4

WEIGHT FOR AGE 3yo-14lb

**1710 En Vacances (IRE)**, given a mid-summer break, took advantage of the ease in the going. (7/1)

**2986* Izza** had shot up 20lb thanks to her three wins this season, and continues in good form. (4/1)

**3142 Salaman (FR)**, was blinkered for the first time but, after swinging off the bridle on the heels of the leader, failed to deliver the goods. (13/2)

**3463* Shirley Sue**, in contrast to the third, is as tough as they come and was only worn down late on. (4/1)

**2547 Bowcliffe Court (IRE)** (7/1: 5/1-8/1)

## 3599 JACK COLLING POLAR JEST APPRENTICE H'CAP (0-90) (3-Y.O+) (Class E)

5-10 (5-11) **6f 8y** £3,275.00 (£980.00: £470.00: £215.00) Stalls: High GOING minus 0.30 sec per fur (GF)

| | | | Pos | SP | RR | SF |
|---|---|---|---|---|---|---|
| 3127$^{8}$ | **Patsy Grimes (88)** (JSMoore) **6-10-0** PPMurphy(5) (hld up: hdwy over 1f out: hrd rdn to ld wl ins fnl f: r.o) | — | **1** | 9/1 | 97 | 58 |
| 2434$^{3}$ | **Faraway Lass (75)** (LordHuntingdon) **3-8-9**(3) AimeeCook(1) (a.p: led over 1f out tl wl ins fnl f) | ½ | **2** | 5/1 2 | 83 | 41 |
| 3439$^{3}$ | **Rambold (65)** (NEBerry) **5-8-5** PRoberts(9) (led 4f: r.o one pce fnl f) | 1¼ | **3** | 6/1 | 69 | 30 |
| 3162* | **Highland Rhapsody (IRE) (75)** (IABalding) **3-8-12** MartinDwyer(2) (a.p: led 2f out: sn hdd: one pce fnl f) | ½ | **4** | 9/4 1 | 78 | 36 |
| 3045$^{6}$ | **Trafalgar Lady (USA) (80)** (RCharlton) **3-8-12**(5) RBrisland(7) (s.s: sn rcvrd: rdn over 1f out: one pce) | 1¼ | **5** | 11/2 3 | 80 | 38 |
| 987$^{12}$ | **Elite Force (IRE) (78)** (PWChapple-Hyam) **3-8-8**(7) RCody-Boutcher(8) (prom: rdn 2f out: no hdwy) | ½ | **6** | 16/1 | 76 | 34 |
| 2615$^{6}$ | **Thatcherella (71)** (MajorDNChappell) **5-8-11** RHavlin(3) (prom over 4f) | 1¼ | **7** | 11/2 3 | 66 | 27 |
| 3442$^{6}$ | **Great Hall (56)** (PDCundell) **7-7-5b**(5) PDoe(4) (s.i.s: bhd most of wy) | 2½ | **8** | 12/1 | 45 | 6 |
| 3339$^{6}$ | **Dancing Lawyer (68)** (BJMeehan) **5-8-3**(5) GHannon(6) (hld up: a bhd) | 3½ | **9** | 11/1 | 47 | 8 |

(SP 124.4%) **9 Rn**

**1m 13.84** (2.04) CSF £53.16 CT £276.70 TOTE £10.30: £2.50 £1.70 £2.10 (£22.70) Trio £50.40 OWNER Mr J. K. Grimes (HUNGERFORD) BRED J. C. Fox

LONG HANDICAP Great Hall 6-9

WEIGHT FOR AGE 3yo-3lb

**2623 Patsy Grimes**, not inconvenienced by the shorter trip, defied a 6lb hike in the ratings since winning at Yarmouth in July. (9/1)

**2434 Faraway Lass**, 8lb higher than when successful at Salisbury, had been beaten off a 2lb higher mark last time. (5/1)

**3439 Rambold** was raised 5lb after winning at Yarmouth and it does seem as if the Handicapper has her measure. (6/1)

**3162* Highland Rhapsody (IRE)** could not make a successful transition to handicap company. (9/4)

**3045 Trafalgar Lady (USA)** needs more give underfoot. (11/2: 4/1-6/1)

**774 Elite Force (IRE)**, was dropping back in distance after a break. (16/1)

T/Jkpt: £106,444.40 (0.2 Tckts); £119,937.39 to Newbury 17/8/96. T/Plpt: £53.50 (543.42 Tckts). T/Qdpt: £15.40 (73.93 Tckts) KH

# 3086-SOUTHWELL (L-H) (Standard)

## Friday August 16th

WEATHER: fine WIND: slt across

## 3600 KEN AND NICK BRIGHT PHOTOGRAPHY H'CAP (0-65) (3-Y.O+ F & M) (Class F)

2-20 (2-22) **1m 4f (Fibresand)** £2,381.00 (£656.00: £311.00) Stalls: Low GOING: 0.01 sec per fur (STD)

| | | | Pos | SP | RR | SF |
|---|---|---|---|---|---|---|
| *3086** | **Glow Forum (48)** (LMontagueHall) **5-8-13**(3) FLynch(6) (b: chsd ldrs: led 7f out: pushed clr over 2f out: r.o) | — | **1** | 6/4 1 | 59 | 39 |
| 3133$^{9}$ | **Tabriz (60)** (JDBethell) **3-9-4** SDrowne(2) (lw: chsd ldrs: effrt 6f out: chsd wnr fnl 2½f: no imp) | 9 | **2** | 14/1 | 59 | 29 |
| 3204$^{4}$ | **Tirolette (IRE) (57)** (RJRWilliams) **4-9-11b** DBiggs(5) (bhd: hdwy 4f out: nvr nrr) | 6 | **3** | 12/1 | 48 | 28 |
| 3315$^{3}$ | **South Wind (58)** (MrsJCecil) **3-9-2** AClark(8) (hdwy & prom ½-wy: rdn 4f out: wnt 2nd over 3f out: sn btn) | 4 | **4** | 10/1 | 44 | 14 |
| 3267$^{2}$ | **Campaspe (37)** (JGFitzGerald) **4-8-5** JCarroll(1) (sn outpcd & bhd: styd on fnl 3f: nrst fin) | 4 | **5** | 9/2 2 | 17 | — |
| 3117$^{7}$ | **Alwarqa (60)** (DNicholls) **3-9-4** AlexGreaves(10) (bhd: sme hdwy fnl 3f: n.d) | 3 | **6** | 12/1 | 36 | 6 |
| 2895$^{4}$ | **Larissa (IRE) (59)** (GWragg) **3-9-3** JQuinn(7) (sn chsng ldrs: hrd drvn over 3f out: sn btn) | ½ | **7** | 6/1 3 | 35 | 5 |
| 2738$^{5}$ | **Uoni (54)** (CEBrittain) **3-8-12** MBirch(4) (lw: cl up tl outpcd fnl 4f) | 9 | **8** | 11/1 | 18 | — |
| 2321$^{5}$ | **Palacegate Jo (IRE) (35)** (DWChapman) **5-8-3** GDuffield(9) (led after 2f to 7f out: sn wknd) | 2 | **9** | 11/1 | — | — |
| 1540$^{4}$ | **Winn Caley (55)** (CWFairhurst) **3-8-13** DeanMcKeown(3) (led 2f: lost tch ½-wy: t.o) | dist | **10** | 25/1 | — | — |

(SP 124.1%) **10 Rn**

**2m 42.0** (9.50) CSF £22.96 CT £187.49 TOTE £2.90: £1.30 £3.30 £2.20 (£33.70) Trio £48.80 OWNER Mr Andy Smith (EPSOM) BRED Forum Bloodstock Ltd

WEIGHT FOR AGE 3yo-10lb

**3086* Glow Forum**, despite a 9lb rise in the weights, showed just how good she is on this surface, and spread-eagled the field. (6/4)

**1526 Tabriz** again gave problems and, when mounted on the track, set off in the wrong direction. She ran a fair race though but had no chance with the winner. (14/1)

**3204 Tirolette (IRE)**, at the first attempt on this surface, was getting the hang of things as the race progressed and, should she return, she is worth keeping in mind. (12/1: 8/1-14/1)

**3315 South Wind** took the leader on from halfway, but this slow surface found her out in the home straight. (10/1: 5/1-12/1)

**3267 Campaspe** started her career on the All-Weather and was also disappointing then. (9/2)

**3056 Alwarqa** (12/1: 8/1-14/1)

**2895 Larissa (IRE)** was never happy on this surface. (6/1: op 4/1)

**2738 Uoni** (11/1: op 6/1)

## 3601 ROB AND LYNDSEY'S WEDDING CLAIMING STKS (3-Y.O+) (Class F)

2-50 (2-53) **7f (Fibresand)** £2,381.00 (£656.00: £311.00) Stalls: Low GOING: 0.01 sec per fur (STD)

| | | | Pos | SP | RR | SF |
|---|---|---|---|---|---|---|
| *2637** | **Berge (IRE) (79)** (WAO'Gorman) **5-9-6b** EmmaO'Gorman(1) (sn trckng ldrs: led wl over 2f out: r.o) | — | **1** | 13/8 1 | 82 | 57 |
| 3339$^{2}$ | **Prima Silk (72)** (MJRyan) **5-9-3** AClark(14) (chsd ldrs: hdwy u.p over 2f out: nt qckn ins fnl f) | 1¾ | **2** | 8/1 3 | 75 | 50 |
| *3091$^{5}$* | **Tame Deer (49)** (MCChapman) **4-8-12** DRMcCabe(5) (bhd tl hdwy 2f out: styd on wl towards fin) | nk | **3** | 33/1 | 69 | 44 |

| | | | SP | RR | SF |
|---|---|---|---|---|---|
| 3419[10] | **Desert Invader (IRE) (75)** (DWChapman) **5-9-5** ACulhane(10) (lw: a cl up: nt qckn fnl 2f)..........1 | **4** | 7/1[2] | 74 | 49 |
| 3296[7] | **I'm Your Lady (68)** (BAMcMahon) **5-9-3** GDuffield(7) (w ldrs: rdn 3f out: r.o one pce)..........½ | **5** | 8/1[3] | 71 | 46 |
| 3089[3] | **Elton Ledger (IRE) (70)** (MrsNMacauley) **7-9-1v**(3) FLynch(8) (b: bhd: hdwy ½-wy: nvr rchd ldrs)..........1¾ | **6** | 8/1[3] | 68 | 43 |
| | **Demoiselle** (CWThornton) **4-8-9** DeanMcKeown(2) (in tch tl grad wknd fnl 2f)..........5 | **7** | 33/1 | 48 | 23 |
| 3076[5] | **Jolto (68)** (KMcAuliffe) **7-9-12** JFEgan(4) (b.hind: slt ld over 4f: grad wknd)..........½ | **8** | 20/1 | 63 | 38 |
| | **Power Don (60)** (WGMTurner) **3-8-4b**[1] LCharnock(13) (prom 4f: wknd)..........4 | **9** | 16/1 | 37 | 7 |
| 3419[8] | **Dancing Sioux (75)** (DNicholls) **4-9-12** AlexGreaves(11) (w ldr tl wknd over 2½f out)..........s.h | **10** | 9/1 | 54 | 29 |
| 3167[9] | **Flirty Gertie (68)** (RBoss) **4-9-1** JCarroll(12) (s.i.s: hdwy & in tch ½-wy: sn wknd)..........11 | **11** | 8/1[3] | 18 | — |
| 3086[8] | **Lucy's Gold (14)** (MJRyan) **5-8-5** DBiggs(9) (bhd fr ½-wy)..........8 | **12** | 66/1 | — | — |
| 1828[8] | **Beacon Hill Lady** (BEllison) **3-8-4** JQuinn(3) (sn outpcd & wl bhd)..........16 | **13** | 66/1 | — | — |
| | | | (SP 124.6%) | **13 Rn** | |

**1m 30.9** (4.10) CSF £15.46 TOTE £2.20: £1.20 £2.70 £3.50 (£8.20) Trio £89.60 OWNER Mr S. Fustok (NEWMARKET) BRED S. Fustok
WEIGHT FOR AGE 3yo-5lb
OFFICIAL EXPLANATION **Dancing Sioux: got his tongue over the bit and choked.**
**2637* Berge (IRE)** loves these events and although he had to struggle to make sure of it, he always had the edge. (13/8)
**3339 Prima Silk** has won over course and distance and put in a sound effort here, but just found the winner too tough. (8/1)
**2940 Tame Deer** came from a long way behind to finish best of all. He obviously has bags of ability but as yet, has won only once. (33/1)
**3089 Desert Invader (IRE)** looked and ran well, although he does not win that often, in this mood he should always be considered. (7/1: 5/1-15/2)
**3296 I'm Your Lady** has never won on this surface, but did show enough to suggest a race can be found. (8/1)
**Demoiselle** will be better for this quiet run. (33/1)
**1609 Dancing Sioux** (9/1: 6/1-10/1)

## 3602 LANGLEY MECHANICAL SERVICES H'CAP (0-65) (3-Y.O+) (Class F)

3-20 (3-22) **6f (Fibresand)** £2,381.00 (£656.00: £311.00) Stalls: Low GOING: 0.01 sec per fur (STD)

| | | | SP | RR | SF |
|---|---|---|---|---|---|
| 2745[8] | **Delrob (49)** (DHaydnJones) **5-8-12b**[1] FNorton(9) (chsd ldrs: led ins fnl f: styd on wl)..........— | **1** | 9/1[3] | 55 | 33 |
| 2940[2] | **Disco Boy (53)** (PDEvans) **6-9-2** JFEgan(2) (chsd ldrs: outpcd ½-wy: hdwy & edgd rt 2f out: styd on wl)......1¼ | **2** | 12/1 | 56 | 34 |
| 2937[9] | **Itsinthepost (65)** (VSoane) **3-9-11** AMcGlone(13) (outpcd & bhd tl hdwy 2f out: fin wl)..........1 | **3** | 25/1 | 65 | 40 |
| 3416[2] | **Napier Star (59)** (MrsNMacauley) **3-9-2v**(3) CTeague(8) (mde most tl hdd ins fnl f: wknd towards fin)..........½ | **4** | 9/1[3] | 58 | 33 |
| 3416* | **Aljaz (49)** (MissGayKelleway) **6-8-12** [7x] RHughes(3) (lw: hdwy ½-wy: sn chsng ldrs: one pce appr fnl f)..........1 | **5** | 4/1[1] | 45 | 23 |
| 3432[8] | **Lady Sheriff (65)** (RHollinshead) **5-9-11**(3) FLynch(4) (lw: disp ld to ½-wy: grad wknd fnl 2f)..........hd | **6** | 7/1[2] | 61 | 39 |
| 3254[4] | **Born A Lady (55)** (SRBowring) **3-9-1b** DeanMcKeown(5) (lw: in tch: outpcd ½-wy: sme late hdwy)..........1½ | **7** | 12/1 | 47 | 22 |
| 2308[3] | **Anita's Contessa (IRE) (57)** (BPalling) **4-9-6** CRutter(16) (s.i.s: racd wd: styd on wl fnl 2f)..........1½ | **8** | 12/1 | 45 | 23 |
| 2983[8] | **Napoleon's Return (50)** (JLEyre) **3-8-10** SDrowne(6) (no imp fr ½-wy)..........3½ | **9** | 14/1 | 28 | 3 |
| 3416[3] | **Need You Badly (57)** (SPCWoods) **3-9-3** DBiggs(14) (c wd st: nvr trbld ldrs)..........1 | **10** | 9/1[3] | 33 | 8 |
| 3477[3] | **Call Me I'm Blue (IRE) (65)** (NTinkler) **6-10-0** JCarroll(10) (lw: in tch tl outpcd fnl 2½f)..........hd | **11** | 12/1 | 41 | 19 |
| 3416[6] | **Belinda Blue (46)** (RAFahey) **4-8-9** MBirch(11) (lw: b: prom to ½-wy: sn lost pl)..........2 | **12** | 14/1 | 16 | — |
| 2982[4] | **Nattier (57)** (SirMarkPrescott) **3-9-3** GDuffield(7) (swtg: in tch over 3f: wknd)..........1¾ | **13** | 9/1[3] | 23 | — |
| 3091[8] | **Jemsilverthorn (IRE) (49)** (RCSpicer) **3-8-2b**(7) RMullen(1) (outpcd fr ½-wy)..........½ | **14** | 20/1 | 13 | — |
| 3424[12] | **Cheeky Chappy (65)** (DWChapman) **5-10-0b** JFortune(12) (lw: bhd: hdwy u.p ½-wy: sn btn)..........hd | **15** | 10/1 | 29 | 7 |
| 850[11] | **Dissentor (IRE) (56)** (JAGlover) **4-9-5** SDWilliams(15) (s.i.s: racd wd: a bhd)..........15 | **16** | 16/1 | — | — |
| | | | (SP 140.2%) | **16 Rn** | |

**1m 18.2** (4.70) CSF £116.39 CT £2,544.25 TOTE £12.20: £2.50 £4.50 £4.60 £2.90 (£178.60) Trio Not won; £463.29 to Ripon 17/8/96 OWNER Mrs E. M. HaydnJones (PONTYPRIDD) BRED J. K. S. Cresswell
WEIGHT FOR AGE 3yo-3lb
**2745 Delrob** had the blinkers on for the first time and they worked the oracle. (9/1: op 6/1)
**2940 Disco Boy** was struggling with the pace halfway through the race, and was then never doing enough despite staying on. (12/1)
**Itsinthepost** gave the impression that over a bit further, better should be seen. (25/1)
**3416 Napier Star** is going up the weights and ran another sound race, but just failed to last home. (9/1)
**3416* Aljaz** had his chances but just found his penalty too much. (4/1)
**2694 Lady Sheriff** had her first run back on the All-Weather for some time. Although she is not as good on this surface, she did not run too badly. (7/1)
**3254 Born A Lady** found this a bit on the sharp side. (12/1)
**2982 Nattier** (9/1: op 5/1)

## 3603 SUNLINE DIRECT MAIL H'CAP (0-70) (3-Y.O+) (Class E)

3-50 (3-50) **1m (Fibresand)** £3,452.40 (£1,033.20: £495.60: £226.80) Stalls: Low GOING: 0.01 sec per fur (STD)

| | | | SP | RR | SF |
|---|---|---|---|---|---|
| 3089[9] | **Pc's Cruiser (IRE) (40)** (JLEyre) **4-7-12v** TWilliams(11) (chsd ldrs: rdn to ld appr fnl f: styd on wl)..........— | **1** | 8/1 | 54 | 36 |
| 3456[8] | **Theatre Magic (62)** (SRBowring) **3-9-0** DeanMcKeown(8) (lw: disp ld tl led 3f out: hdd appr fnl f: no ex).......2½ | **2** | 12/1 | 71 | 47 |
| 3426[15] | **Catherine's Choice (68)** (JDBethell) **3-9-6** SDrowne(2) (lw: a chsng ldrs: rdn & one pce fnl 2f)..........2½ | **3** | 12/1 | 72 | 48 |
| 3344[6] | **Giftbox (USA) (52)** (SirMarkPrescott) **4-8-10** GDuffield(9) (hmpd & lost pl after 1½f: hdwy u.p ½-wy: styd on: no imp)..........1¼ | **4** | 13/2[3] | 54 | 36 |
| 3172[3] | **Wild Palm (66)** (WAO'Gorman) **4-9-10v** EmmaO'Gorman(1) (lw: s.i.s: hdwy ½-wy: kpt on: nvr able to chal) .1½ | **5** | 5/1[2] | 65 | 47 |
| 2672[9] | **David James' Girl (53)** (ABailey) **4-8-4**(7) IonaWands(13) (in tch: outpcd ½-wy: styd on fnl 2f)..........1¼ | **6** | 12/1 | 49 | 31 |
| 3172[5] | **Young Annabel (USA) (67)** (CADwyer) **3-9-5** TIves(5) (in tch: rdn over 2f out: no imp)..........½ | **7** | 7/2[1] | 62 | 38 |
| 2689[5] | **Quiet Arch (IRE) (63)** (CACyzer) **3-9-1** RHughes(16) (disp ld 5f: sn hrd rdn & wknd)..........nk | **8** | 12/1 | 57 | 33 |
| 2631[5] | **Penmar (58)** (TJEtherington) **4-9-2b** LCharnock(3) (s.i.s: wnt prom after 2f: wknd fnl 2f)..........8 | **9** | 20/1 | 36 | 18 |
| 2081[11] | **No Submission (USA) (55)** (DWChapman) **10-8-13b** ACulhane(12) (lw: s.i.s: wl bhd tl sme late hdwy)..........3 | **10** | 16/1 | 27 | 9 |
| 2896[13] | **Shuttlecock (47)** (MrsNMacauley) **5-8-2b**(3)ow5 CTeague(14) (in tch tl wknd fnl 3f)..........hd | **11** | 20/1 | 19 | — |
| 3062[7] | **Northern Celadon (IRE) (55)** (MJHeaton-Ellis) **5-8-13** AClark(4) (swtg: prom 5f: wknd)..........15 | **12** | 14/1 | — | — |
| 3306[13] | **Fatehalkhair (IRE) (40)** (BEllison) **4-7-12** JQuinn(6) (prom 5f: wknd)..........1½ | **13** | 14/1 | — | — |
| 2946[5] | **Dubai College (IRE) (67)** (CEBrittain) **3-9-5** MBirch(7) (outpcd & bhd fr ½-wy)..........½ | **14** | 10/1 | 5 | — |
| 713[14] | **Oneoftheoldones (68)** (JNorton) **4-9-12** SDWilliams(15) (outpcd & bhd fr ½-wy)..........6 | **15** | 25/1 | — | — |
| 3443[2] | **Prudent Pet (57)** (CWFairhurst) **4-9-1** JTate(10) (bhd fr ½-wy)..........14 | **16** | 9/1 | — | — |
| | | | (SP 145.8%) | **16 Rn** | |

**1m 44.8** (4.80) CSF £108.15 CT £1,144.47 TOTE £12.10: £2.60 £3.40 £5.10 £2.30 (£106.00) Trio £164.10; £115.63 to Ripon 17/8/96 OWNER PC Racing Partners (HAMBLETON) BRED Mrs Maureen Graham
WEIGHT FOR AGE 3yo-6lb

**3089 Pc's Cruiser (IRE)**, whose yard is in blinding form, is well-handicapped after his recent poor run and won this comfortably. (8/1)
**2934 Theatre Magic** really likes this surface and ran a fine race, looking on particularly good terms with himself. (12/1)
**2934* Catherine's Choice** is certainly better on this surface and ran another sound race, only to be tapped for toe in the closing stages. (12/1: op 8/1)
**3344 Giftbox (USA)** got trapped for room early on and was struggling to regain ground thereafter. (13/2: 9/2-7/1)
**3172 Wild Palm** looks the sort who has more ability when things go his way. (5/1)
**2550 David James' Girl** ran a bit flat halfway through the race and after a month off, may have needed this. (12/1)

## 3604 PLUMBAGO (S) STKS (2-Y.O) (Class G)

4-20 (4-23) **5f (Fibresand)** £2,070.00 (£570.00: £270.00) Stalls: High GOING: 0.01 sec per fur (STD)

| | | | | SP | RR | SF |
|---|---|---|---|---|---|---|
| *$2371^{6}$* | **Assumpta** (CBBBooth) **2-8-6** MBirch(8) (lw: a.p: hrd rdn to ld ins fnl f) | — | 1 | 9/2 $^{2}$ | 60 | 30 |
| *$2635^{U}$* | **Just Loui (68)** (WGMTurner) **2-8-9**$^{(7)}$ DSweeney(5) (cl up: led over 1f out: hdd ins fnl f: no ex) | ¾ | 2 | 11/1 | 68 | 38 |
| *2371** | **Make Ready (64)** (JNeville) **2-8-11** FNorton(7) (lw: a chsng ldrs: kpt on fnl f) | 2½ | 3 | 11/2 $^{3}$ | 55 | 25 |
| $3311^{2}$ | **Breffni (IRE) (60)** (CNAllen) **2-7-13**$^{(7)}$ RMullen(6) (in tch: hdwy over 1f out: styd on) | 2 | 4 | 6/1 | 43 | 13 |
| $2435^{3}$ | **Senate Swings (58)** (WRMuir) **2-8-11** DRMcCabe(3) (chsd ldrs: nt qckn appr fnl f) | 4 | 5 | 10/1 | 35 | 5 |
| $1982^{5}$ | **Municipal Girl (IRE)** (BPalling) **2-8-6** CRutter(9) (s.i.s: nvr nrr) | ½ | 6 | 20/1 | 29 | — |
| | **Jay Tee Ef (IRE)** (BAMcMahon) **2-8-11** GDuffield(10) (cmpt: bit bkwd: in tch: sn drvn along: no ch fr ½-wy) | 4 | 7 | 10/1 | 21 | — |
| $3436^{4}$ | **Red Test (USA) (72)** (WAO'Gorman) **2-8-11b**$^{1}$ EmmaO'Gorman(1) (wnt lft s: racd alone far side: led over 3f: wknd) | 2½ | 8 | 100/30 $^{1}$ | 13 | — |
| $3448^{14}$ | **Antares (66)** (NTinkler) **2-8-11** KimTinkler(11) (prom tl outpcd fnl 2f) | 1 | 9 | 20/1 | 10 | — |
| $3423^{12}$ | **Amy** (CSmith) **2-8-6b**$^{1}$ AClark(2) (sn outpcd) | ¾ | 10 | 33/1 | 2 | — |
| | **Treasured Spirit (IRE)** (CADwyer) **2-7-13**$^{(7)}$ JoHunnam(12) (unf: s.i.s: a bhd) | 2½ | 11 | 16/1 | — | — |
| | **Moonraker (IRE)** (JGFitzGerald) **2-8-13**$^{ow2}$ RHughes(4) (cmpt: dwlt: a bhd) | 13 | 12 | 10/1 | — | — |
| | | | | (SP 124.9%) | **12 Rn** | |

**60.5 secs** (3.50) CSF £51.11 TOTE £5.40: £2.00 £3.10 £2.00 (£33.20) Trio £62.20 OWNER Mr C. B. B. Booth (FLAXTON) BRED Mrs S. O'Donnell
Sold KBjorling 9,000 gns; Breffni (IRE) clmd RDickin £6,000
**2371 Assumpta** had learnt plenty from her initial outing and responded to some vigorous driving to put this beyond doubt inside the last furlong. (9/2)
**2635 Just Loui** has the speed and responded to pressure but just found one too good. (11/1: 7/1-12/1)
**2371* Make Ready** ran a sound race but was not quite up to it in the final furlong. (11/2)
**3311 Breffni (IRE)** is a headstrong individual but did show ability, staying on at the end. (6/1: op 7/2)
**2435 Senate Swings**, at his first attempt on this surface, ran reasonably well but was just short of a turn of foot. (10/1: op 5/1)
**Municipal Girl (IRE)**, having her first run for two months, showed enough to suggest that better is likely. (20/1)
**Moonraker (IRE)** (10/1: 7/1-12/1)

## 3605 HONEYSUCKLE MAIDEN AMATEUR H'CAP (0-65) (3-Y.O+) (Class G)

4-50 (4-50) **1m 6f (Fibresand)** £2,070.00 (£570.00: £270.00) Stalls: High GOING: 0.01 sec per fur (STD)

| | | | | SP | RR | SF |
|---|---|---|---|---|---|---|
| $3249^{9}$ | **Love And Kisses (62)** (CACyzer) **3-10-2**$^{(5)}$ MrRThornton(6) (a.p: led wl over 2f out: styd on strly) | — | 1 | 6/1 $^{2}$ | 70 | 33 |
| *$2935^{2}$* | **Precedency (64)** (KMcAuliffe) **4-11-2**$^{(5)}$ MrKGoble(8) (swtg: b.hind: hdwy 6f out: chsng ldrs over 2f out: one pce) | 3 | 2 | 6/1 $^{2}$ | 69 | 44 |
| $3335^{8}$ | **Inn At the Top (56)** (JNorton) **4-10-8**$^{(5)}$ MrFPCunningham(7) (chsd ldrs: led 3f out: sn hdd & one pce) | s.h | 3 | 7/1 $^{3}$ | 61 | 36 |
| *$210^{3}$* | **Star Performer (IRE) (46)** (MrsMReveley) **5-10-3** MrMHNaughton(1) (trckd ldrs: swtchd & effrt over 2f out: rdn & no ex) | ¾ | 4 | 7/2 $^{1}$ | 50 | 25 |
| *$3090^{8}$* | **Hever Golf Diamond (45)** (TJNaughton) **3-8-13**$^{(5)}$ MrsJNaughton(4) (bhd: hdwy 4f out: no imp) | 11 | 5 | 8/1 | 36 | — |
| $2928^{2}$ | **Atienza (USA) (48)** (SCWilliams) **3-9-2**$^{(5)}$ MissKWright(10) (led & sn clr: hdd 3f out: wknd) | 8 | 6 | 15/2 | 30 | — |
| *$370^{3}$* | **Havana Heights (IRE) (41)** (JLEyre) **3-9-0** MissDianaJones(5) (b.nr hind: bhd: effrt 6f out: nvr trbld ldrs) | s.h | 7 | 6/1 $^{2}$ | 23 | — |
| $3116^{4}$ | **Stoleamarch (49)** (MrsMReveley) **3-9-3**$^{(5)ow6}$ MrVLukaniuk(9) (lost tch fr ½-wy) | 9 | 8 | 7/1 $^{3}$ | 21 | — |
| *$3066^{7}$* | **Written Agreement (36)** (REPeacock) **8-9-2**$^{(5)ow7}$ MrsCPeacock(3) (a outpcd & bhd) | 1 | 9 | 50/1 | 7 | — |
| *$3090^{3}$* | **Comedie Arrete (FR) (32)** (MCChapman) **4-9-3b** MrsSBosley(2) (swtg: chsd ldrs tl wknd qckly over 6f out) | dist | 10 | 9/1 | — | — |
| | | | | (SP 124.9%) | **10 Rn** | |

**3m 14.5** (15.50) CSF £41.53 CT £243.39 TOTE £3.70: £2.00 £2.60 £2.30 (£13.80) Trio £15.30 OWNER Mr R. M. Cyzer (HORSHAM) BRED Mrs M. J. Hills
LONG HANDICAP Written Agreement 7-12 Havana Heights (IRE) 8-13
WEIGHT FOR AGE 3yo-12lb
**Love And Kisses** just gallops and stays and is well-suited to this surface. (6/1)
**2935 Precedency**, trying a longer trip, kept staying on but was never doing enough to trouble the winner. (6/1: 4/1-13/2)
**Inn At the Top** had his chances but he was off the bit a long way out, and lacked any turn of foot. (7/1)
**210 Star Performer (IRE)**, after a long absence, travelled best of all but he failed to respond when ridden in the home straight. (7/2)
**2440 Hever Golf Diamond** (8/1: 6/1-9/1)
**2928 Atienza (USA)** (15/2: 5/1-8/1)
**370 Havana Heights (IRE)** (6/1: op 3/1)

T/Plpt: £355.10 (25.93 Tckts). T/Qdpt: £370.80 (1.5 Tckts) AA

# 3435-LINGFIELD (L-H) (Turf Good to firm, AWT Standard)

## Saturday August 17th

WEATHER: sunny WIND: almost nil

## 3606 BLACKBERRY LANE APPRENTICE H'CAP (0-60) (3-Y.O+) (Class G)

5-15 (5-19) **7f 140y** £2,095.00 (£595.00: £295.00) Stalls: High GOING minus 0.33 sec per fur (GF)

| | | | | SP | RR | SF |
|---|---|---|---|---|---|---|
| $3286^{4}$ | **Fairly Sure (IRE) (46)** (NEBerry) **3-8-8** DDenby(7) (a.p: rdn over 1f out: led wl ins fnl f: r.o) | — | 1 | 9/1 | 45 | 32 |
| $3469^{7}$ | **Just Harry (60)** (MJRyan) **5-9-6**$^{(8)}$ AMcCarthy(8) (chsd ldrs: rdn over 1f out: ev ch wl ins fnl f: r.o) | nk | 2 | 8/1 | 58 | 51 |
| $2925^{6}$ | **Super Park (57)** (JPearce) **4-9-8**$^{(3)}$ RFfrench(1) (a.p: led 2f out: hdd wl ins fnl f: r.o) | s.h | 3 | 14/1 | 55 | 48 |
| $3304^{3}$ | **Astral Invader (IRE) (52)** (MSSaunders) **4-9-6** PDoe(6) (led: hdd 2f out: rdn over 1f out: unable qckn) | 1 | 4 | 7/1 $^{3}$ | 48 | 41 |

| | Horse / details | Dist | Pos | SP | RR | SF |
|---|---|---|---|---|---|---|
| 2954[5] | **Mr Cube (IRE) (52)** (JMBradley) **6-9-1b**(5) CLowther(2) (chsd ldrs: rdn over 1f out: unable qckn) | hd | **5** | 10/1 | 48 | 41 |
| 3469[6] | **Our Shadee (USA) (49)** (KTIvory) **6-9-0v**(3) CScudder(9) (rr: rdn 3f out: hdwy 2f out: kpt on one pce ins fnl f) | ¾ | **6** | 4/1 [1] | 43 | 36 |
| 3052[3] | **Sporting Risk (48)** (PWHarris) **4-8-11**(5) LJames(5) (hld up: hdwy 2f out: sn rdn: wknd ins fnl f) | 1½ | **7** | 6/1 [2] | 39 | 32 |
| 3286[5] | **Tallulah Belle (41)** (NPLittmoden) **3-7-12**(5) DavidO'Neill(4) (prom over 6f) | 1½ | **8** | 20/1 | 29 | 16 |
| *307[4]* | **Allstars Dancer (37)** (TJNaughton) **3-7-3**(10) RachaelMoody(10) (prom 6f) | 1¼ | **9** | 16/1 | 23 | 10 |
| 3274[10] | **Sweet Allegiance (40)** (JRPoulton) **6-8-3**(5) TField(15) (bhd fnl 3f) | 3 | **10** | 50/1 | 19 | 12 |
| 3076[3] | **Rise Up Singing (46)** (WJMusson) **8-8-11b**(3) JWilkinson(13) (a bhd) | ½ | **11** | 7/1 [3] | 24 | 17 |
| 3300[7] | **Stone Island (55)** (CACyzer) **3-8-7**(10) PGoode(11) (bhd fnl 4f) | 4 | **12** | 20/1 | 25 | 12 |
| 3286[9] | **Carwyn's Choice (34)** (PCClarke) **3-7-5**(5) JFowle(14) (dwlt: sn rcvrd into mid div: wknd 4f out) | 2½ | **13** | 50/1 | — | — |
| 2594[3] | **Kirov Protege (IRE) (29)** (MrsLCJewell) **4-7-6**(5) RBrisland(3) (bhd fr ½-wy) | 2 | **14** | 20/1 | — | — |
| *2551[11]* | **Mannagar (IRE) (32)** (JRPoulton) **4-8-0**ow2 JDennis(16) (bhd fr ½-wy) | 2½ | **15** | 50/1 | — | — |
| | | | | (SP 122.2%) | | **15 Rn** |

**1m 31.62** (2.82) CSF £73.54 CT £941.65 TOTE £15.20: £3.00 £2.10 £2.80 (£77.30) Trio £184.60; £182.02 to 19/8/96 OWNER Heavyweight Racing (UPPER LAMBOURN) BRED Mrs P. H. Burns
LONG HANDICAP Carwyn's Choice 7-8
WEIGHT FOR AGE 3yo-6lb

**3286 Fairly Sure (IRE)** was never far away and with the advantage of the rail inside the final furlong, saw it out well. (9/1: 6/1-10/1)
**3052 Just Harry** raced just behind the leaders and was brought to challenge inside the final furlong, but just lost out. (8/1)
**2763 Super Park** was always to the fore and went down fighting. (14/1)
**3304 Astral Invader (IRE)** showed the way but once headed two furlongs out, found quickening beyond him. (7/1)
**2954 Mr Cube (IRE)** raced just behind the leaders. Ridden below the distance, he could not change gear. (10/1)
**3469 Our Shadee (USA)** kept on as usual without threatening the principals. (4/1)

## 3607 SHARON MASSEY 30TH BIRTHDAY (S) STKS (2-Y.O) (Class G)
5-45 (5-45) **6f** £2,301.00 (£636.00: £303.00) Stalls: High GOING minus 0.33 sec per fur (GF)

| | Horse / details | Dist | Pos | SP | RR | SF |
|---|---|---|---|---|---|---|
| 3405[2] | **Rumbustious** (RHannon) **2-8-6** SSanders(3) (a.p: led 2f out: rdn ins fnl f: r.o) | — | **1** | 8/15 [1] | 58 | 30 |
| 3214[5] | **Unknown Territory (IRE)** (MRChannon) **2-8-11** CRutter(1) (a.p: ev ch 1f out: unable qckn) | 1½ | **2** | 6/1 [3] | 59 | 31 |
| 3488[3] | **Hever Golf Stormer (IRE) (65)** (TJNaughton) **2-8-6**(5) JDSmith(2) (led: hdd 2f out: grad wknd) | 3 | **3** | 4/1 [2] | 51 | 23 |
| 3336[P] | **Princess Ferdinand (IRE)** (MMcCormack) **2-8-6** AClark(5) (prom over 3f) | 11 | **4** | 16/1 | 17 | — |
| | | | | (SP 105.4%) | | **4 Rn** |

**1m 11.24** (2.24) CSF £3.60 TOTE £1.60 (£2.40) OWNER Mr Christopher Curtis (MARLBOROUGH) BRED Fulling Mill Stud and C. Curtis
Bt in 6,000 gns

**3405 Rumbustious**, always to the fore, led two furlongs out and had to be ridden to resist the runner-up's challenge entering the final furlong, but was well on top at the finish. (8/15)
**Unknown Territory (IRE)** was always prominent and threw down a challenge approaching the final furlong, but the winner had his measure late on. (6/1)
**3488 Hever Golf Stormer (IRE)** showed the way for four furlongs. (4/1)
**2031 Princess Ferdinand (IRE)** was beaten by halfway. (16/1)

## 3608 O'KEEFE CHALLENGE H'CAP (0-65) (3-Y.O+ F & M) (Class F)
6-15 (6-15) **1m 2f (Equitrack)** £2,809.40 (£778.40: £372.20) Stalls: High GOING minus 0.45 sec per fur (FST)

| | Horse / details | Dist | Pos | SP | RR | SF |
|---|---|---|---|---|---|---|
| 3111* | **Bakers Daughter (48)** (JRArnold) **4-9-2** AClark(10) (lw: hld up: hdwy to chse ldr 4f out: led on bit over 2f out: sn clr: pushed out ins fnl f) | — | **1** | 13/8 [1] | 59 | 33 |
| 3300[3] | **Dhulikhel (42)** (DMarks) **3-8-2** SSanders(8) (chsd ldrs: rdn & lost pl 4f out: rallied over 1f out: styd on one pce ins fnl f) | 5 | **2** | 6/1 [2] | 45 | 11 |
| *3419[12]* | **Miss Haversham (60)** (CACyzer) **4-10-0b**[1] PBloomfield(5) (hld up: hdwy 3f out: sn hrd rdn: one pce) | s.h | **3** | 33/1 | 63 | 37 |
| *3064[7]* | **Mujtahida (IRE) (51)** (RWArmstrong) **3-8-11** RPrice(7) (sn rdn along: hdwy 6f out: led 5f out: hdd over 2f out: wknd over 1f out) | 1 | **4** | 17/2 | 52 | 18 |
| 3244[5] | **Leith Academy (USA) (58)** (BWHills) **3-8-13b**[1](5) JDSmith(4) (chsd ldr 5f: rdn 4f out: wknd over 2f out) | 5 | **5** | 10/1 | 51 | 17 |
| 3474[3] | **Shermood (39)** (KTIvory) **3-7-8**(5) MartinDwyer(9) (b: b.hind: stdd s: hld up: hdwy on outside over 4f out: wknd over 2f out) | 6 | **6** | 7/1 [3] | 23 | — |
| 1468[6] | **She Said No (53)** (AMoore) **4-9-7** CandyMorris(2) (lw: bhd fnl 5f) | 6 | **7** | 25/1 | 27 | 1 |
| *521[12]* | **Zacaroon (50)** (JFfitch-Heyes) **5-9-4** TIves(3) (b.hind: bhd fr ½-wy) | hd | **8** | 14/1 | 24 | — |
| 2718[7] | **Early Warning (52)** (CREgerton) **3-8-9**(3) MHenry(6) (a bhd) | 9 | **9** | 10/1 | 12 | — |
| *2636[11]* | **Esquiline (USA) (60)** (JHMGosden) **3-9-6** CRutter(1) (led to ½-wy: sn wknd) | 7 | **10** | 11/1 | 8 | — |
| | | | | (SP 115.4%) | | **10 Rn** |

**2m 8.2** (3.90) CSF £11.27 CT £207.78 TOTE £2.50: £1.40 £2.20 £4.10 (£5.30) Trio £31.10 OWNER Mr J. R. Arnold (UPPER LAMBOURN) BRED C. C. Bromley and Son and A. O. Nerses
WEIGHT FOR AGE 3yo-8lb

**3111* Bakers Daughter** travelled well throughout and was in no danger in the final two furlongs. (13/8)
**3300 Dhulikhel** lost his place at the top of the hill and although rallying late on for second, was no threat to the winner. (6/1)
**2246 Miss Haversham** made headway under pressure coming down the hill, without ever looking like reaching the winner. (33/1)
**Mujtahida (IRE)** led at the top of the hill but, once headed approaching the two pole, soon cried enough. (17/2)
**Zacaroon** (14/1: 12/1-20/1)
**2636 Esquiline (USA)** (11/1: 8/1-12/1)

## 3609 MALAYA GATWICK MERCEDES MEDIAN AUCTION MAIDEN STKS (3-Y.O) (Class F)
6-45 (6-46) **7f 140y** £2,904.60 (£805.60: £385.80) Stalls: High GOING minus 0.33 sec per fur (GF)

| | Horse / details | Dist | Pos | SP | RR | SF |
|---|---|---|---|---|---|---|
| 3162[11] | **Designer Lines** (CJames) **3-9-0v**[1] CRutter(8) (chsd ldrs: hrd rdn over 2f out: styd on to ld wl ins fnl f) | — | **1** | 25/1 | 81 | 38 |
| 2760[5] | **Diamond Beach (84)** (BWHills) **3-9-0** TQuinn(9) (hld up: hdwy over 2f out: led wl over 1f out: hdd wl ins fnl f: nt r.o) | 1½ | **2** | 13/8 [2] | 78 | 35 |
| 3472[11] | **Samorelle** (MJRyan) **3-8-9** AClark(4) (b.hind: hld up: rdn over 3f out: kpt on one pce fnl 2f) | 8 | **3** | 25/1 | 56 | 13 |
| 3525[6] | **Badger Bay (IRE) (64)** (CADwyer) **3-8-2v**[1](7) JoHunnam(3) (chsd ldr: rdn & hung lft over 2f out: one pce) | 1½ | **4** | 4/1 [3] | 53 | 10 |
| 2987[2] | **Atlantic Storm (65)** (JHMGosden) **3-9-0v**[1] GHind(5) (led: hdd wl over 1f out: sn wknd) | 1¼ | **5** | 6/4 [1] | 55 | 12 |
| 2601[13] | **Desert Scout** (KMcAuliffe) **3-9-0** SSanders(7) (a bhd) | 10 | **6** | 66/1 | 34 | — |

3115[9] **Moylough Rebel (39)** (JELong) **3-9-0** LeesaLong(1) (prom 4f) ....5 **7** 50/1 24 —
1995[9] **The Grey Weaver (35)** (RMFlower) **3-9-0** SDrowne(6) (sn rdn along: bhd fnl 4f) ....10 **8** 50/1 3 —
3350[7] **Imperial Red (IRE)** (HJCollingridge) **3-9-0** VSmith(2) (bhd fnl 4f) ....24 **9** 66/1 — —
(SP 112.7%) **9 Rn**

**1m 31.58** (2.78) CSF £61.68 TOTE £19.20: £3.10 £1.10 £3.90 (£19.60) Trio £281.40; £35.68 to 19/8/96 OWNER Mr Gordon Curzon (NEWBURY) BRED G. E. Curzon

OFFICIAL EXPLANATION **Atlantic Story: finished distressed.**

**2597 Designer Lines** hunted up the leaders. He came under pressure some way from home, but seemed keener on winning than most of his rivals. (25/1)

**2760 Diamond Beach** looked far from keen under pressure. (13/8)

**Samorelle** kept on in the final two furlongs to finish a remote third. (25/1)

**3525 Badger Bay (IRE)** hung badly under pressure. (4/1)

**2987 Atlantic Storm** made the running but showed a disappointing attitude when headed. (6/4)

## 3610 MARITIME SERVICES LIMITED STKS (0-70) (3-Y.O+) (Class E)

7-15 (7-15) **2m (Equitrack)** £2,961.00 (£882.00: £420.00: £189.00) Stalls: High GOING minus 0.45 sec per fur (FST)

SP RR SF

3504[4] **Old School House (59)** (TJNaughton) **3-8-11**(3) DaneO'Neill(6) (b: lw: hld up: hdwy 6f out: rdn over 3f out: led over 1f out: hdd ins fnl f: rallied to ld again nr fin) ....— **1** 4/1 79 37
3155[5] **Mighty Phantom (USA) (65)** (JWHills) **3-8-6**(3) MHenry(3) (chsd ldr: led over 3f out: hdd over 1f out: led again ins fnl f: hdd nr fin) ....nk **2** 7/2 3 74 32
*3437** **Paradise Navy (71)** (CREgerton) **7-9-12b** TIves(4) (hld up: hdwy 4f out: rdn over 2f out: wknd over 1f out) ....5 **3** 2/1 1 72 44
3225* **Trilby (69)** (PFICole) **3-8-7b[1]** TQuinn(5) (led: hdd over 3f out: wknd over 2f out) ....17 **4** 5/2 2 50 8
3283[4] **Chocolate Ice (66)** (CACyzer) **3-8-8** PBloomfield(2) (b: in tch tl wknd 5f out) ....10 **5** 8/1 41 —
1772[5] **Juliasdarkinvader (39)** (AMoore) **6-9-8** AClark(1) (b: chsd ldrs: rdn 6f out: wnt lame 5f out: sn p.u & dismntd) .... **P** 33/1 — —
(SP 118.2%) **6 Rn**

**3m 27.15** (5.15) CSF £17.96 TOTE £5.30: £1.80 £2.20 (£10.50) OWNER Mr T. J. Naughton (EPSOM) BRED Miss G. Abbey

WEIGHT FOR AGE 3yo-14lb

**3504 Old School House** had a ding dong battle with the runner-up over the final two furlongs, and just prevailed. (4/1)

**3155 Mighty Phantom (USA)** ran her heart out but just had to give best. (7/2)

**3437* Paradise Navy** made a move coming down the hill, but was in trouble before the home turn. (2/1)

**3225* Trilby** showed the way but dropped away quickly once headed. (5/2)

**3283 Chocolate Ice** was beaten at the top of the hill. (8/1)

## 3611 MILLCROFT GROUP H'CAP (0-70) (3-Y.O+) (Class E)

7-45 (7-45) **1m 3f 106y** £3,124.80 (£932.40: £445.20: £201.60) Stalls: High GOING minus 0.33 sec per fur (GF)

SP RR SF

3249[10] **Arktikos (IRE) (65)** (JHMGosden) **3-9-10v[1]** BDoyle(1) (lw: mde all: hrd rdn ins fnl f: all out) ....— **1** 8/1 74 26
2506[3] **Full Throttle (59)** (MHTompkins) **3-9-4** PRobinson(3) (a.p: chsd wnr over 1f out: hrd rdn & n.m.r ins fnl f: r.o) ....hd **2** 7/1 68 20
3333[8] **Passing Strangers (USA) (57)** (PWHarris) **3-9-2** GHind(7) (chsd ldrs: rdn over 2f out: styd on ins fnl f) ....½ **3** 3/1 1 65 17
3111[11] **Get Tough (60)** (SDow) **3-9-5** TQuinn(4) (hld up: rdn 2f out: styd on one pce ins fnl f) ....1¼ **4** 9/2 2 66 18
*2081[12]* **Studio Thirty (37)** (CASmith) **4-8-5** CRutter(6) (swtg: hld up: rdn 2f out: styd on one pce ins fnl f) ....hd **5** 25/1 43 4
3479[7] **Fabulous Mtoto (55)** (MSSaunders) **6-9-9** OUrbina(2) (lw: hld up: rdn over 2f out: one pce) ....1¼ **6** 13/2 3 60 21
3079* **Two Socks (63)** (MMcCormack) **3-9-8** AClark(8) (lw: tk keen hld: chsd wnr tl over 1f out: wknd ent fnl f) ....3 **7** 3/1 1 63 15
2941[11] **Yellow Dragon (IRE) (44)** (BAPearce) **3-8-3** LeesaLong(5) (b: dwlt: sn rcvrd into mid div: rn wd turning for home: nt rcvr) ....19 **8** 33/1 18 —
(SP 111.9%) **8 Rn**

**2m 32.36** (8.16) CSF £54.83 CT £185.71 TOTE £10.50: £2.00 £1.90 £1.90 (£20.70) OWNER Sheikh Mohammed (NEWMARKET) BRED Barronstown Stud And Ron Con Ltd

WEIGHT FOR AGE 3yo-9lb

**2952 Arktikos (IRE)** made all under a fine ride from Doyle. He set a steady pace and quickened it up halfway up the straight, to just have enough in reserve to see it out. (8/1: 6/1-10/1)

**2506 Full Throttle** was challenging strongly when short of room inside the final furlong, but for which he would probably have won. (7/1)

**2718 Passing Strangers (USA)**, never far away, was tapped for foot approaching the two furlong pole, and although keeping on inside the final furlong, it was all too late. (3/1)

**1955 Get Tough** was set a lot to do in a slowly run race, and although staying on inside the final furlong, never looked like taking a hand. (9/2)

**1903 Studio Thirty** was another one out the back door. He stayed on strongly inside the final furlong, but had too much to make up. (25/1)

T/Plpt: £187.50 (46.78 Tckts). T/Qdpt: £30.90 (29.88 Tckts) SM

# 3593-NEWBURY (L-H) (Good)
## Saturday August 17th

WEATHER: hot WIND: almost nil

## 3612 ANDOVER RATED STKS H'CAP (0-100) (3-Y.O+) (Class B)

2-00 (2-00) **7f 64y (round)** £8,127.00 (£3,033.00: £1,476.50: £627.50: £273.75: £132.25) Stalls: Low GOING minus 0.24 sec per fur (GF)

SP RR SF

1484[4] **Cool Edge (IRE) (96)** (MHTompkins) **5-9-6** PRobinson(6) (hld up: nt clr run over 2f out tl over 1f out: led ins fnl f: rdn out) ....— **1** 6/1 2 105 87
2623[14] **Akil (IRE) (85)** (RWArmstrong) **4-8-9** WCarson(2) (a.p: led over 2f out: rdn over 1f out: hdd ins fnl f: unable qckn) ....1½ **2** 12/1 91 73
3158[15] **Tregaron (USA) (89)** (RAkehurst) **5-8-13** TQuinn(9) (lw: hdwy 3f out: rdn over 1f out: one pce) ....1½ **3** 6/1 2 91 73
3207[2] **Kayvee (97)** (GHarwood) **7-9-7** AClark(10) (rdn over 2f out: hdwy over 1f out: r.o ins fnl f) ....1¾ **4** 12/1 96 78
3426[3] **Knobbleeneeze (83)** (MRChannon) **6-8-7v** LDettori(13) (lw: rdn over 3f out: hdwy over 1f out: one pce ins fnl f) ....2½ **5** 16/1 76 58

3232[11] **Shamanic (86)** (RHannon) **4-8-7**(3) DaneO'Neill(8) (lw: n.m.r over 1f out: nvr nr to chal).....nk **6** 16/1 78 60
2920[2] **Laafee (98)** (HThomsonJones) **3-9-3** RHills(7) (hdwy 3f out: n.m.r over 2f out: eased whn btn ins fnl f) .........2½ **7** 14/1 85 62
3106[2] **Latching (IRE) (85)** (RFJohnsonHoughton) **4-8-9** JReid(5) (lw: hld up: rdn over 3f out: wknd over 2f out) .....1¼ **8** 12/1 69 51
3440* **Neuwest (USA) (85)** (NJHWalker) **4-8-9** JStack(3) (lw: prom over 5f) .....¾ **9** 17/2[3] 68 50
876[17] **Roderick Hudson (85)** (JARToller) **4-8-9** SSanders(1) (lw: led 5f: wknd wl over 1f out).....nk **10** 33/1 67 49
3210[8] **Caricature (IRE) (85)** (GLewis) **3-8-4b** PaulEddery(11) (a bhd).....hd **11** 20/1 67 44
3153[5] **Band on the Run (93)** (BAMcMahon) **9-9-3** GCarter(12) (lw: rdn over 3f out: bhd fnl 2f) .....1¼ **12** 14/1 72 54
3158[6] **Mullitover (87)** (MJHeaton-Ellis) **6-8-11** SDrowne(4) (prom 5f).....3½ **13** 7/2[1] 58 40
(SP 117.2%) **13 Rn**

**1m 27.85** (-0.25) CSF £67.42 CT £426.10 TOTE £6.60: £2.60 £3.80 £3.80 (£52.70) Trio £160.50 OWNER Mr Henry Chan (NEWMARKET) BRED Hollybank Breeders
LONG HANDICAP Knobbleeneeze 8-3
WEIGHT FOR AGE 3yo-5lb
**1484 Cool Edge (IRE)**, off the course since the end of May, chased the leaders but found himself with nowhere to go halfway up the straight. Luckily, an opening did appear from below the distance, and rousted along, he managed to get on top inside the final furlong. (6/1)
**967 Akil (IRE)** bounced back to form. Never far away, he went on over a quarter of a mile from home, but despite doing little wrong, was worried out of it inside the last 75 yards. (12/1)
**2249* Tregaron (USA)**, 10lb higher than when he last won, took closer order three furlongs out. Rousted along below the distance, he then failed to find another gear. (6/1)
**3207 Kayvee** was at the back of the field until staying on really well in the last furlong and a half, to be nearest at the line. (12/1)
**3426 Knobbleeneeze** made his effort below the distance but was making no further impression inside the final furlong. (16/1)
**2400 Shamanic**, racing in midfield, was rather tightened up for room below the distance, but it made little difference to his chances as he had never looked like getting in a serious challenge. (16/1)

## 3613 SWETTENHAM STUD ST HUGH'S STKS (Listed) (2-Y.O F) (Class A)

2-30 (2-31) **5f 34y** £9,696.00 (£2,928.00: £1,424.00: £672.00) Stalls: High GOING minus 0.24 sec per fur (GF)

SP RR SF

3170* **Head Over Heels (IRE) (96)** (JHMGosden) **2-8-11** LDettori(6) (lw: b.hind: hld up: swtchd lft wl over 1f out: rdn: led last stride).....— **1** 7/2[1] 92 44
3213[5] **Olympic Spirit (98)** (JBerry) **2-8-11** GCarter(3) (b.hind: led: rdn over 2f out: hdd last stride) .....s.h **2** 4/1[2] 92 44
3068[4] **Queen Sceptre (IRE) (99)** (BWHills) **2-8-11** MHills(1) (a.p: rdn over 1f out: one pce fnl f).....2½ **3** 6/1 84 36
3429* **Snap Crackle Pop (IRE)** (RFJohnsonHoughton) **2-8-8** PaulEddery(4) (a.p: rdn 2f out: one pce fnl f) .....nk **4** 20/1 80 32
3400[3] **Bride's Reprisal (100)** (MRChannon) **2-8-8** TQuinn(9) (hdwy over 1f out: nvr nrr).....2 **5** 6/1 74 26
3036[3] **Summerosa (USA)** (PWChapple-Hyam) **2-8-8** JReid(8) (lw: outpcd: nvr nrr) .....s.h **6** 11/2[3] 74 26
2879[5] **Fanny's Choice (IRE) (91)** (RHannon) **2-8-11** PatEddery(5) (prom over 3f).....¾ **7** 6/1 75 27
3128[10] **Whizz Kid (70)** (JJBridger) **2-8-8** JQuinn(2) (bhd fnl 3f) .....7 **8** 50/1 50 2
2944[3] **Silver Purse (83)** (APJones) **2-8-8** TSprake(7) (lw: hld up: rdn over 2f out: sn wknd) .....hd **9** 20/1 49 1
(SP 111.9%) **9 Rn**

**62.07 secs** (1.87) CSF £16.36 TOTE £3.20: £1.30 £1.80 £2.00 (£7.20) Trio £8.10 OWNER Ms Rachel Hood (NEWMARKET) BRED Milton Park Stud Partnership
**3170* Head Over Heels (IRE)** continues in fine form. Switched left early in the final quarter-mile, she was rousted along and managed to get up right on the line. (7/2)
**3213 Olympic Spirit** was not going to hang around and dictated matters from the front. Bustled along from halfway, she gave her all and was only beaten right on the line. She continues in cracking form and can certainly win a Listed race. (4/1)
**3068 Queen Sceptre (IRE)**, never far away, was rousted along below the distance but found the return to five just too sharp. (6/1)
**3429* Snap Crackle Pop (IRE)**, a leading light from the off, was rousted along a quarter of a mile from home. She grimly tried to get on terms but was tapped for toe in the last 200 yards. (20/1)
**3400 Bride's Reprisal** stayed on from below the distance, without ever looking likely to trouble the principals. (6/1: op 4/1)
**3036 Summerosa (USA)** found the drop down to five all against her and could never go the pace. (11/2: 7/2-6/1)
**2879 Fanny's Choice (IRE)** (6/1: op 4/1)

## 3614 TRIPLEPRINT GEOFFREY FREER STKS (Gp 2) (3-Y.O+) (Class A)

3-00 (3-00) **1m 5f 61y** £42,824.00 (£16,030.45: £7,702.73: £3,357.82) Stalls: Low GOING minus 0.24 sec per fur (GF)

SP RR SF

3203a[5] **Phantom Gold (111)** (LordHuntingdon) **4-9-3** LDettori(5) (hdwy over 2f out: led over 1f out: rdn & edgd lft ins fnl f: r.o wl) .....— **1** 6/1[3] 121 84
3203a[2] **Posidonas (120)** (PFICole) **4-9-9** TQuinn(4) (lw: nt clr run & lost pl over 3f out: swtchd rt over 2f out: rallied over 1f out: r.o) .....3½ **2** 10/11[1] 123 86
3196a[3] **Song of Tara (IRE)** (PWChapple-Hyam) **4-9-3** JReid(7) (lw: hdwy 3f out: ev ch over 1f out: unable qckn) .....hd **3** 4/1[2] 117 80
3124[6] **Samraan (USA) (104)** (JLDunlop) **3-8-6** MHills(6) (lw: hld up: led over 3f out tl over 1f out: one pce) .....nk **4** 11/1 116 68
3431[5] **Key to My Heart (IRE) (114)** (MissSEHall) **6-9-3** RHughes(3) (b: lw: hdwy on ins 3f out: wknd over 1f out) ......5 **5** 6/1[3] 110 73
**Whitechapel (USA) (88)** (LordHuntingdon) **8-9-3** TIves(1) (led 5f: wknd over 2f out) .....9 **6** 40/1 99 62
2583[7] **Wayne County (IRE) (105)** (RAkehurst) **6-9-3** SSanders(2) (w ldr: led over 9f out tl over 3f out: sn wknd: t.o) .....dist **7** 50/1 — —
(SP 113.7%) **7 Rn**

**2m 46.18** (-0.32) CSF £11.65 TOTE £6.40: £2.30 £1.50 (£4.50) OWNER The Queen (WEST ILSLEY) BRED The Queen
WEIGHT FOR AGE 3yo-11lb
**3203a Phantom Gold** reversed German form with Posidonas. Moving up nicely over quarter of a mile from home, she struck the front below the distance and although flashing her tail when ridden, soon had the race in safe keeping. (6/1)
**3203a Posidonas** did not have luck on his side. Chasing the leaders, he was shuffled to the back of the field by the weakening Wayne County over three furlongs out, and Quinn had to switch the colt round the field soon after. Picking up ground well below the distance, he found the winner had already flown but just managed to snatch second. The Irish St. Leger is his likely target. (10/11)
**3196a Song of Tara (IRE)** moved into contention three furlongs from home. One of three almost in line below the distance, he then found the fast ground against him. He can open his account for the season with some give. (4/1)
**3124 Samraan (USA)** went to the front over three furlongs out but, collared by the winner below the distance, could then only keep on at one pace. (11/1: 8/1-12/1)
**3431 Key to My Heart (IRE)** made his effort along the inside rail three furlongs from home, but had shot his bolt below the distance. (6/1: 4/1-13/2)
**Whitechapel (USA)** had given his all over two furlongs out after a belated absence. (40/1)

## 3615 E.B.F. EDDIE KING 60TH BIRTHDAY MAIDEN STKS (2-Y.O) (Class D)

3-30 (3-31) **7f** £4,172.00 (£1,256.00: £608.00: £284.00) Stalls: High GOING minus 0.24 sec per fur (GF)

| Form | Horse | Dist | Pos | SP | RR | SF |
|---|---|---|---|---|---|---|
| 3040[3] | **Monza (USA)** (PWChapple-Hyam) **2-9-0** JReid(10) (a.p: led over 1f out: rdn out) | — | **1** | 11/4[1] | 89 | 51 |
| 3069[2] | **Shii-Take** (RAkehurst) **2-9-0** TQuinn(13) (lw: hdwy 4f out: rdn 3f out: chsd wnr over 1f out: unable qckn) | 1½ | **2** | 7/2[2] | 86 | 48 |
| 2335[3] | **Mithak (USA)** (BWHills) **2-9-0** WCarson(14) (hld up: rdn over 2f out: r.o ins fnl f) | ½ | **3** | 9/2[3] | 54 | 46 |
| | **Haydn James (USA)** (PWHarris) **2-9-0** GHind(8) (leggy: scope: bit bkwd: hdwy 2f out: rdn over 1f out: one pce) | ¾ | **4** | 33/1 | 83 | 45 |
| | **Mardi Gras (IRE)** (JLDunlop) **2-9-0** SWhitworth(12) (leggy: s.s: hdwy & n.m.r over 1f out: nt clr run ins fnl f: nt rcvr: bttr for r) | nk | **5** | 33/1 | 82+ | 44 |
| | **Dick Turpin (USA)** (LordHuntingdon) **2-9-0** LDettori(17) (w'like: scope: bit bkwd: rdn over 2f out: hdwy & nt clr run 1f out: one pce) | 2½ | **6** | 9/1 | 76 | 38 |
| | **Fallah** (MajorWRHern) **2-9-0** RHills(4) (w'like: scope: bit bkwd: s.s: rdn over 2f out: hdwy over 1f out: nvr nrr: bttr for r) | ¾ | **7** | 12/1 | 75+ | 37 |
| | **Invermark** (JRFanshawe) **2-9-0** NDay(15) (nvr nrr) | ¾ | **8** | 14/1 | 73 | 35 |
| 3069[7] | **Homestead** (RHannon) **2-8-11**(3) DaneO'Neill(6) (lw: a mid div) | 1¼ | **9** | 33/1 | 70 | 32 |
| 2972[10] | **Al Masroor (USA)** (JWPayne) **2-9-0** BThomson(2) (led over 5f) | 2 | **10** | 66/1 | 66 | 28 |
| | **Tango King** (JLDunlop) **2-9-0** PRobinson(11) (leggy: unf: s.s: nvr nrr) | 1½ | **11** | 50/1 | 62 | 24 |
| 3114[7] | **Ellens Lad (IRE)** (RHannon) **2-9-0** PatEddery(5) (a.p: rdn over 2f out: eased whn btn fnl f) | 3 | **12** | 25/1 | 55 | 17 |
| | **Sir Ricky (USA)** (RCharlton) **2-9-0** TSprake(1) (prom over 4f) | 2½ | **13** | 12/1 | 50 | 12 |
| | **Clear The Air** (PFICole) **2-8-2**(7) JBosley(9) (leggy: prom over 3f) | nk | **14** | 50/1 | 44 | 6 |
| 3259[15] | **Myosotis** (PJMakin) **2-9-0** WRyan(16) (a bhd) | 2½ | **15** | 50/1 | 43 | 5 |
| | **Beauchamp Lion** (JLDunlop) **2-9-0** GCarter(7) (w'like: scope: lw: a bhd) | s.h | **16** | 16/1 | 43 | 5 |
| | **Browbeat** (RCharlton) **2-9-0** SSanders(3) (unf: scope: s.s: bhd fnl 2f) | ½ | **17** | 33/1 | 42 | 4 |

(SP 128.0%) **17 Rn**

**1m 26.8** (2.30) CSF £12.70 TOTE £3.50: £1.50 £1.90 £1.80 (£5.00) Trio £4.20 OWNER Mr R. E. Sangster (MARLBOROUGH) BRED Swettenham Stud

**3040 Monza (USA)**, a leading light throughout, struck the front below the distance and, ridden along, asserted his authority. (11/4)

**3069 Shii-Take**, in a handy position by halfway, was soon being bustled along. Taking second place approaching the final furlong, he was unable to master the winner. (7/2)

**2335 Mithak (USA)** chased the leaders. Ridden along over a quarter of a mile from home, he stayed on for third inside the final furlong. (9/2)

**Haydn James (USA)**, a tall, scopey colt, did not look fully tuned up. Making his effort a quarter of a mile from home, he failed to find another gear from below the distance. (33/1)

**Mardi Gras (IRE)** made a very pleasing debut especially considering the interference he met. Losing ground at the start, he was picking up ground when tightened up for room below the distance. Again meeting interference inside the final furlong, the situation was then accepted. He should not be hard to win with. (33/1)

**Dick Turpin (USA)** looked as though the run would do him good. Bustled along in midfield over a quarter of a mile from home, nevertheless he picked up ground below the distance, but was held up entering the final furlong as he met with trouble. From that point, he could only struggle on at one pace. (9/1)

**Fallah** did not look fully wound up but showed promise for the future, staying on nicely to finish an eye-catching seventh. He would have learnt a lot from this. (12/1: 6/1-14/1)

**Sir Ricky (USA)** (12/1: 7/1-14/1)

## 3616 LEVY BOARD NURSERY H'CAP (2-Y.O) (Class C)

4-00 (4-02) **7f 64y (round)** £5,134.00 (£1,552.00: £756.00: £358.00) Stalls: Low GOING minus 0.24 sec per fur (GF)

| Form | Horse | Dist | Pos | SP | RR | SF |
|---|---|---|---|---|---|---|
| 2904* | **Double Gold (73)** (BJMeehan) **2-7-11**(5) MartinDwyer(5) (plld hrd: mde virtually all: rdn out) | — | **1** | 6/1 | 72 | 42 |
| 3312* | **Sheer Face (81)** (WRMuir) **2-8-10** PatEddery(10) (lw: rdn over 3f out: hdwy over 2f out: chsd wnr over 1f out: unable qckn) | 1½ | **2** | 9/2[2] | 77 | 47 |
| 3408* | **Mister Pink (86)** (RFJohnsonHoughton) **2-9-1** JReid(7) (swtchd rt over 2f out: rapid hdwy fnl f: fin wl) | ½ | **3** | 4/1[1] | 81 | 51 |
| 3230[5] | **Golden Fact (USA) (84)** (RHannon) **2-8-10**(3) DaneO'Neill(11) (a.p: rdn over 2f out: one pce) | 2 | **4** | 9/1 | 74 | 44 |
| 2671a[5] | **Raven Master (USA) (92)** (PWChapple-Hyam) **2-9-7** LDettori(6) (rdn over 3f out: nvr nr to chal) | hd | **5** | 8/1 | 82 | 52 |
| 3444[8] | **Stride (78)** (MartynMeade) **2-8-7** WRyan(8) (swtg: a.p: rdn over 2f out: wknd over 1f out) | 1¾ | **6** | 16/1 | 64 | 34 |
| 3449* | **Soden (IRE) (80)** (TGMills) **2-8-9** RHills(9) (rdn over 3f out: hdwy over 1f out: 4th & no ch whn n.m.r on ins ins fnl f) | s.h | **7** | 12/1 | 66 | 36 |
| 2967* | **Goodwood Lass (IRE) (84)** (JLDunlop) **2-8-13** WCarson(1) (prom 6f) | 4 | **8** | 11/2[3] | 61 | 31 |
| 3230[4] | **Sun O'Tirol (IRE) (75)** (MRChannon) **2-8-4** PaulEddery(2) (hld up: rdn over 3f out: wknd over 1f out) | 4 | **9** | 16/1 | 44 | 14 |
| *3417*[8] | **Classic Mystery (IRE) (72)** (BJMeehan) **2-8-1b**[1ow2] BDoyle(3) (lw: bhd fnl 2f) | ½ | **10** | 16/1 | 39 | 7 |
| *2554*[4] | **Riscatto (USA) (67)** (WRMuir) **2-7-10** JQuinn(12) (lw: bhd fnl 5f) | 7 | **11** | 33/1 | 19 | — |

(SP 117.2%) **11 Rn**

**1m 30.28** (2.18) CSF £31.03 CT £113.24 TOTE £7.40: £1.80 £2.20 £1.50 (£18.00) Trio £18.30 OWNER Mr Michael Edwards (UPPER LAMBOURN) BRED Catridge Farm Stud Ltd

LONG HANDICAP Riscatto (USA) 7-7

**2904* Double Gold** took a keen hold and had soon established herself at the head of affairs. With a useful advantage over quarter of a mile from home, she kept on too well for her rivals. (6/1)

**3312* Sheer Face**, bustled along from halfway, soon picked up ground. He moved into second place below the distance, but failed to get on terms with the winner. (9/2)

**3408* Mister Pink**, unable to go the pace, still only had one rival behind him below the distance. Going into turbo drive in the final furlong, he stormed through to take third. (4/1)

**3230 Golden Fact (USA)**, a leading light from the off, was asked for his effort over a quarter of a mile form home, but he did not look totally co-operative and could only plod on at one pace. (9/1: 6/1-10/1)

**2671a Raven Master (USA)**, bustled along from halfway, could never get in a serious blow. (8/1: op 5/1)

**2984 Stride**, in a handy position from the outset, had shot her bolt below the distance. (16/1)

## 3617 TRIUMVIRATE LIMITED STKS (0-80) (3-Y.O+) (Class D)

4-35 (4-36) **1m 4f 5y** £6,227.25 (£2,271.00: £1,110.50: £477.50: £213.75) Stalls: Low GOING minus 0.24 sec per fur (GF)

| Form | Horse | Dist | Pos | SP | RR | SF |
|---|---|---|---|---|---|---|
| 3248[2] | **Willie Conquer (80)** (RAkehurst) **4-9-5** PaulEddery(4) (lw: hld up: led over 1f out: drvn out) | — | **1** | 9/4[2] | 86 | 58 |

3235[7] **Silently (77)** (IABalding) **4-9-5** PatEddery(2) (lw: led 9f: rdn: r.o ins fnl f)....½ **2** 11/2[3] 85 57
2612[10] **Nuzu (IRE) (78)** (BWHills) **3-8-11** MHills(1) (lw: hld up: rdn 3f out: unable qckn)....2 **3** 6/1 85 47
3073[4] **Eagle Canyon (IRE) (80)** (BHanbury) **3-8-13** WRyan(3) (chsd ldr: led 3f out tl over 1f out: one pce)....nk **4** 7/4[1] 86 48
2998[3] **Village King (IRE) (77)** (RHannon) **3-8-8**(3) DaneO'Neill(5) (lw: hld up: rdn over 2f out: sn wknd)....6 **5** 11/2[3] 76 38
(SP 112.2%) **5 Rn**

**2m 33.75** (3.75) CSF £13.06 TOTE £2.50: £1.50 £2.40 (£6.70) OWNER Mr Raymond Tooth (EPSOM) BRED W. and R. Barnett Ltd
WEIGHT FOR AGE 3yo-10lb

**3248 Willie Conquer**, held up and travelling well, cruised into the lead below the distance, but with the runner-up putting in a renewed effort in the final furlong, his jockey had to get down to some serious work to gain the day. (9/4: op 6/4)
**2857 Silently** dictated matters from the front. Collared three furlongs from home, he was soon being busted along. Renewing his effort in the final furlong, he made sure the winner did not have things all his own way. (11/2: 4/1-6/1)
**2612 Nuzu (IRE)** chased the leaders, but he found this shorter trip against him and was later tapped for toe. (6/1)
**3073 Eagle Canyon (IRE)** raced in second place until going to the front three furlongs from home. Collared below the distance, he failed to find another gear. (7/4)
**2998 Village King (IRE)** (11/2: 3/1-6/1)

## 3618 STRATTON H'CAP (0-95) (3-Y.O+) (Class C)

5-05 (5-06) **5f 34y** £5,556.50 (£1,682.00: £821.00: £390.50) Stalls: High GOING minus 0.24 sec per fur (GF)

SP RR SF

1430[6] **Glorious Aragon (77)** (RFJohnsonHoughton) **4-8-13** TQuinn(2) (swtg: hdwy over 1f out: edgd rt & led ins fnl f: drvn out)....— **1** 14/1 90 50
3432[3] **Sea-Deer (88)** (CADwyer) **7-9-10** LDettori(9) (lw: hdwy over 1f out: squeezed thro on ins ins fnl f: r.o)....2 **2** 2/1[1] 95 55
2220[9] **Bajan Rose (84)** (MBlanshard) **4-9-6** JQuinn(6) (rdn over 2f out: hdwy over 1f out: unable qckn)....s.h **3** 14/1 91 51
3432[5] **Lago Di Varano (87)** (RMWhitaker) **4-9-9b** RHills(3) (hdwy & nt clr run over 1f out: one pce)....hd **4** 6/1[2] 93 53
3232[17] **Selhurstpark Flyer (IRE) (89)** (JBerry) **5-9-6**(5) PRoberts(4) (a.p: rdn over 2f out: n.m.r 1f out: one pce)....1¼ **5** 9/1[3] 91 51
3432[10] **Chadwell Hall (69)** (SRBowring) **5-8-5b** SDWilliams(13) (led tl ins fnl f: sn wknd)....½ **6** 14/1 70 30
3432[12] **Lord High Admiral (CAN) (87)** (MJHeaton-Ellis) **8-9-9** JReid(8) (a.p: rdn 2f out: btn whn n.m.r ins fnl f)....1¼ **7** 10/1 84 44
1113[15] **Portelet (77)** (RGuest) **4-8-10**(3) DaneO'Neill(7) (lw: prom over 3f)....¾ **8** 16/1 72 32
3338[6] **Tart and a Half (74)** (BJMeehan) **4-8-10b** MTebbutt(12) (nvr nrr)....s.h **9** 12/1 69 29
3338[7] **Beau Venture (USA) (71)** (BPalling) **8-8-7** TSprake(11) (lw: a bhd)....1½ **10** 14/1 61 21
3038[8] **Crofters Ceilidh (81)** (BAMcMahon) **4-9-3** GCarter(10) (prom over 2f)....1 **11** 25/1 68 28
3140[7] **No Extras (IRE) (90)** (GLMoore) **6-9-12** SWhitworth(5) (swtg: s.s: a bhd)....2 **12** 16/1 71 31
2694[22] **Twice as Sharp (92)** (PWHarris) **4-10-0** GHind(1) (swtg: hld up: rdn over 2f out: sn wknd)....1¾ **13** 12/1 67 27
(SP 124.4%) **13 Rn**

**61.8 secs** (1.60) CSF £41.53 CT £404.95 TOTE £17.50: £3.60 £1.50 £3.80 (£33.20) Trio £135.00 OWNER Lord Leverhulme (DIDCOT) BRED Viscount Leverhulme

**1430 Glorious Aragon**, given a 12 week break, gained her first win. Picking up ground below the distance, she drifted right as she struck the front inside the final furlong, but responding to pressure, soon asserted. (14/1)
**3432 Sea-Deer**, 15lb higher than when he last won, began an effort along the inside rail below the distance. Squeezing through a narrow gap in the final furlong, he won the battle for second but was unable to get on terms with the winner. (2/1)
**1974 Bajan Rose** made her effort over a furlong from home, but failed to find another gear inside the last 200 yards. (14/1)
**3432 Lago Di Varano** was picking up ground when tightened up for room below the distance. In the final furlong, he failed to find the necessary turn of foot. (6/1)
**2220 Selhurstpark Flyer (IRE)**, a leading light from the off, was looking one-paced when done no favours by the winner entering the final furlong. (9/1)
**2508* Chadwell Hall** attempted to make all. Collared inside the final furlong, he was soon beaten. (14/1: 9/1-16/1)
**3432 Lord High Admiral (CAN)** (10/1: 8/1-12/1)
**2694 Twice as Sharp** (12/1: op 8/1)

T/Jkpt: £48,897.90 (3.07 Tckts). T/Plpt: £24.80 (1,805.08 Tckts). T/Qdpt: £5.30 (243.39 Tckts) AK

# 3293-RIPON (R-H) (Good)
## Saturday August 17th

WEATHER: sunny & hot WIND: almost nil

## 3619 HARROGATE (S) H'CAP (0-60) (3-Y.O) (Class F)

2-15 (2-18) **1m 2f** £2,790.00 (£785.00: £384.00) Stalls: High GOING minus 0.37 sec per fur (F)

SP RR SF

3333[5] **Lila Pedigo (IRE) (53)** (MissJFCraze) **3-9-5** NConnorton(6) (a.p: led 2f out: r.o)....— **1** 13/2[2] 64 27
2851[9] **She's Simply Great (IRE) (50)** (JJO'Neill) **3-9-2** KFallon(19) (hdwy 4f out: hmpd & swtchd over 1f out: r.o towards fin)....3 **2** 9/1 56 19
3325[3] **Ragtime Cowgirl (39)** (CWThornton) **3-8-5** DeanMcKeown(5) (cl up: led over 4f out to 2f out: nt qckn)....¾ **3** 8/1 44 7
3451[6] **Tirols Tyrant (IRE) (46)** (MrsASwinbank) **3-8-12** JWeaver(15) (led tl hdd over 4f out: kpt on wl)....2½ **4** 12/1 47 10
3427[8] **Philgem (30)** (CWFairhurst) **3-7-10** NKennedy(16) (cl up: effrt 4f out: one pce fnl 2f)....2 **5** 16/1 28 —
3474[8] **Richard House Lad (44)** (RHollinshead) **3-8-10** WJO'Connor(8) (in tch: effrt 3f out: one pce fnl 2f)....1½ **6** 7/1[3] 39 2
3048[2] **Yuppy Girl (IRE) (50)** (CaptJWilson) **3-9-2** JFortune(1) (rr div: hdwy 4f out: rdn & no imp fnl 2½f)....3½ **7** 5/2[1] 40 3
3048[10] **Lebedinski (IRE) (41)** (MrsPSly) **3-8-7** ACulhane(17) (lw: bhd: hdwy on ins 4f out: nvr rchd ldrs)....nk **8** 16/1 30 —
2966[8] **The Black Dubh (IRE) (37)** (JJQuinn) **3-8-3** DaleGibson(12) (in tch: effrt 4f out: no imp)....1½ **9** 33/1 24 —
2362[5] **Needwood Fantasy (37)** (BCMorgan) **3-8-3** LCharnock(10) (nvr trbld ldrs)....4 **10** 25/1 18 —
3335[13] **Lagan (39)** (PSFelgate) **3-8-5b[1]** KDarley(18) (bhd & hmpd appr st: n.d after)....1 **11** 10/1 18 —
3414[6] **Shepherds Dean (IRE) (32)** (PCHaslam) **3-7-12** TWilliams(7) (in tch: effrt 4f out: wknd over 2f out)....3 **12** 16/1 6 —
3354[12] **Totally Different (30)** (GROldroyd) **3-7-7v**(3) NVarley(11) (dwlt: n.d)....6 **13** 100/1 — —
3427[7] **Efipetite (30)** (NBycroft) **3-7-10** GBardwell(13) (a bhd)....5 **14** 16/1 — —
3225[7] **La Fandango (IRE) (40)** (MWEasterby) **3-8-1b[1]**(5)ow2 GParkin(14) (a rr div)....1½ **15** 12/1 — —
1539[11] **Bold Future (IRE) (37)** (JWWatts) **3-8-3b[1]** JCarroll(9) (chsd ldrs tl wknd qckly over 4f out)....5 **16** 20/1 — —
3298[7] **Swynford Supreme (55)** (JFBottomley) **3-9-7b[1]** JLowe(3) (hung rt thrght: prom to st: sn wknd & eased)....¾ **17** 33/1 — —

2780[10] **Brownie's Promise (30)** (MBrittain) **3-7-10b[1]** NCarlisle(2) (cl up tl wknd 4f out) ....10 **18** 50/1 — —
(SP 141.0%) **18 Rn**

**2m 9.2** (5.70) CSF £67.23 CT £462.83 TOTE £8.40: £1.90 £1.80 £1.70 £2.50 (£22.10) Trio £32.70 OWNER Mr Geoff Dove (YORK) BRED Miss Corona O'Brien

LONG HANDICAP Philgem 7-7 Totally Different 7-0

No bid

**OFFICIAL EXPLANATION Lagan: the blinkers slipped leaving the stalls and the horse was running blind.**
**Swynford Flyer: his jockey reported that the gelding was hanging badly right-handed throughout the race.**

**3333 Lila Pedigo (IRE)** made no mistake this time and got the trip really well, to score most convincingly. (13/2)
**2592 She's Simply Great (IRE)** got stopped when trying for a run up the rails approaching the final furlong, and when switched, it was all too late. (9/1)
**3325 Ragtime Cowgirl**, dropped back in trip, ran better but was short of toe in the last two furlongs. (8/1)
**2242 Tirols Tyrant (IRE)** had his chances but proved to be very one-paced when the pressure was on. (12/1)
**2753 Philgem** ran reasonably but was never doing enough when pressure was applied in the last half-mile. (16/1)
**2180 Richard House Lad**, trying a longer trip, had his chance to get on terms but was treading water in the last couple of furlongs. (7/1)
**3048 Yuppy Girl (IRE)**, having to race wide from her poor draw, always had too much running to do. (5/2: op 5/1)
**2568 Lebedinski (IRE)**, after a poor run last time, showed ability again here, staying on from last place on the home turn. (16/1)
**Lagan** was unfortunate as his blinkers had slipped. (10/1)

## 3620 KNARESBOROUGH CONDITIONS STKS (2-Y.O) (Class D)

2-45 (2-45) **6f** £3,313.10 (£1,002.80: £489.40: £232.70) Stalls: Low GOING minus 0.37 sec per fur (F)

| | | | | SP | RR | SF |
|---|---|---|---|---|---|---|
| 3251[2] | **Just Visiting (88)** (CaptJWilson) **2-8-10** KFallon(4) (mde all: pushed clr fr ½-wy: eased ins fnl f) | — | **1** | 3/1 2 | 85 | 37 |
| 3080* | **Mujova (IRE) (81)** (RHollinshead) **2-9-0**(3) FLynch(7) (hld up & bhd: gd hdwy 2f out: sn chsng wnr: no imp fnl f) | 4 | **2** | 9/1 | 81 | 33 |
| 3259* | **Mumkin** (TThomsonJones) **2-9-3** KDarley(6) (lw: trckd ldrs: effrt over 2f out: r.o one pce) | 5 | **3** | 5/4 1 | 68 | 20 |
| 3400[7] | **Bollero (IRE) (78)** (JBerry) **2-8-12** JCarroll(2) (lw: a.p: effrt ½-wy: kpt on same pce) | ½ | **4** | 16/1 | 62 | 14 |
| 3131[7] | **Bollin Terry** (TDEasterby) **2-8-11** MBirch(1) (bit bkwd: w wnr to ½-wy: grad wknd fnl 2f) | 2 | **5** | 33/1 | 55 | 7 |
| 3269[3] | **Bewitching Lady** (DWPArbuthnot) **2-8-7**ow1 JFortune(5) (chsd ldrs: rdn ½-wy: grad wknd) | 2 | **6** | 7/1 | 46 | — |
| 3438* | **Caspian Morn** (APJarvis) **2-8-10** WJO'Connor(3) (s.i.s: effrt ½-wy: sn rdn & btn) | 4 | **7** | 4/1 3 | 38 | — |

(SP 120.8%) **7 Rn**

**1m 12.3** (1.80) CSF £27.66 TOTE £4.00: £1.90 £4.70 (£23.50) OWNER Mrs Rosemary Moszkowicz (PRESTON) BRED Henry and Mrs Rosemary Moszkowicz

**3251 Just Visiting** is in tip-top condition and, stepping up the pace from halfway, soon put it beyond doubt. Further success looks likely. (3/1: op 2/1)
**3080* Mujova (IRE)**, dropped out the back, showed a useful turn of foot to chase the winner approaching the final furlong, but was never good enough to trouble her. (9/1)
**3259* Mumkin** is not the best of movers, and once off the bit from halfway, was never doing enough. (5/4)
**1869* Bollero (IRE)** had her chances but once the pace was really on, she was quickly put in her place. (16/1)
**Bollin Terry** still needed this and showed some useful speed for two-thirds of the race. (33/1)
**3269 Bewitching Lady** took a strongish hold going down, but her limitations were well exposed when the pace was really on from halfway. (7/1: 5/1-8/1)
**3438* Caspian Morn** ran no sort of race and there would seem to be something wrong. (4/1)

## 3621 BILLY NEVETT MEMORIAL CHALLENGE CUP H'CAP (0-80) (3-Y.O+) (Class D)

3-15 (3-16) **1m 4f 60y** £3,840.50 (£1,154.00: £557.00: £258.50) Stalls: Low GOING minus 0.37 sec per fur (F)

| | | | | SP | RR | SF |
|---|---|---|---|---|---|---|
| 2884[7] | **Sugar Mill (64)** (MrsMReveley) **6-8-12** ACulhane(4) (hld up: swtchd 2f out: qcknd to ld ins fnl f: r.o wl) | — | **1** | 14/1 | 76 | 33 |
| 3081[4] | **Wafir (IRE) (80)** (PCalver) **4-10-0** JCarroll(8) (led 2f: trckd ldrs: led 2f out: hdd & no ex ins fnl f) | 2 | **2** | 7/1 3 | 89 | 46 |
| 2901[3] | **South Sea Bubble (IRE) (66)** (LMCumani) **4-9-0** KDarley(3) (lw: trckd ldrs: n.m.r over 3f out: swtchd & effrt over 1f out: one pce ins fnl f) | ½ | **3** | 5/4 1 | 75 | 32 |
| 3276* | **Exactly (IRE) (72)** (JLEyre) **3-8-10** TWilliams(7) (led after 2f to 2f out: wandered u.p & r.o one pce) | 2 | **4** | 13/2 2 | 78 | 25 |
| 3297* | **Course Fishing (48)** (BAMcMahon) **5-7-10** GBardwell(1) (hld up: hdwy 4f out: rdn over 2f out: nvr able to chal) | hd | **5** | 7/1 3 | 54 | 11 |
| 3412* | **Ordained (58)** (EJAlston) **3-7-10** JLowe(10) (trckd ldrs: effrt & hmpd 3½f out: nt rcvr) | 3½ | **6** | 9/1 | 59 | 6 |
| 3290[2] | **Master Hyde (USA) (58)** (WStorey) **7-8-3**(3) NVarley(2) (hld up: hdwy on outside 4f out: sn rdn: wknd over 2f out) | hd | **7** | 8/1 | 59 | 16 |
| 3098[5] | **Soba Up (72)** (TJEtherington) **6-9-6** RCochrane(9) (cl up: n.m.r over 3f out: wknd over 2f out) | 5 | **8** | 16/1 | 67 | 24 |
| 3253[3] | **Champagne N Dreams (48)** (DNicholls) **4-7-3**(7) JBramhill(5) (plld hrd: sddle slipped: sme hdwy 4f out: sn btn & eased) | dist | **9** | 25/1 | — | — |

(SP 120.3%) **9 Rn**

**2m 39.2** (5.20) CSF £100.91 CT £194.98 TOTE £26.60: £5.00 £2.20 £1.40 (£49.00) Trio £42.40 OWNER Mr C. C. Buckley (SALTBURN) BRED Snailwell Stud Co Ltd

LONG HANDICAP Ordained 7-8 Course Fishing 7-6 Champagne N Dreams 7-6

WEIGHT FOR AGE 3yo-10lb

**Sugar Mill** has been running over further but returned to form in this messy race in really good style. (14/1)
**3081 Wafir (IRE)**, always in a good position in this slowly run race, was just tapped for toe late on. (7/1)
**2901 South Sea Bubble (IRE)**, well-backed, was not suited by the slow pace and, once she saw daylight approaching the final furlong, she then looked very slow indeed. (5/4)
**3276* Exactly (IRE)** set a moderate pace and then quickened in the last half-mile, but inclined to edge off a true line, she was out-sprinted. (13/2)
**3297* Course Fishing** was 9lb higher this time and this moderate mover was not suited by the slow pace, failing to land a blow. He should not be written off yet. (7/1)

## 3622 WILLIAM HILL GREAT ST WILFRID H'CAP (0-105) (3-Y.O+) (Class B)

3-45 (3-55) **6f** £19,560.00 (£5,880.00: £2,840.00: £1,320.00) Stalls: Low GOING minus 0.37 sec per fur (F)

| | | | | SP | RR | SF |
|---|---|---|---|---|---|---|
| 2725[4] | **Samwar (78)** (MissGayKelleway) **4-8-6** RCochrane(2) (lw: trckd ldrs: led wl over 1f out: qcknd) | — | **1** | 15/2 2 | 95 | 45 |
| 3430[3] | **Options Open (88)** (MrsJRRamsden) **4-9-2** KFallon(3) (lw: in tch: hdwy u.p 2f out: styd on wl: nrst fin) | 2 | **2** | 10/1 | 100 | 50 |

| Form | Horse | Btn | Pos | SP | RR | SF |
|---|---|---|---|---|---|---|
| 3424[3] | **Fantasy Racing (IRE) (73)** (MRChannon) **4-8-1** JFEgan(7) (a chsng ldrs: hdwy 2f out: nt qckn ins fnl f) | 1¼ | **3** | 20/1 | 81 | 31 |
| 3232[4] | **Bolshoi (IRE) (90)** (JBerry) **4-9-4b** EmmaO'Gorman(9) (bhd: hdwy 2f out: nrst fin) | 1¼ | **4** | 9/1[3] | 95 | 45 |
| 3296* | **Bollin Joanne (88)** (TDEasterby) **3-8-13** MBirch(10) (lw: disp ld over 4f: kpt on one pce) | 1¾ | **5** | 100/30[1] | 88 | 35 |
| 3323[2] | **The Scythian (73)** (BobJones) **4-8-1** JFanning(5) (w ldrs: nt qckn appr fnl f) | ½ | **6** | 9/1[3] | 72 | 22 |
| 3296[4] | **Perryston View (85)** (PCalver) **4-8-13v** JCarroll(6) (disp ld over 4f: no ex) | s.h | **7** | 9/1[3] | 84 | 34 |
| 2722[2] | **Highborn (IRE) (90)** (PSFelgate) **7-9-4** KDarley(12) (in tch: rdn ½-wy: no imp) | 2 | **8** | 10/1 | 84 | 34 |
| 3296[3] | **Ziggy's Dancer (USA) (85)** (EJAlston) **5-8-13** JLowe(17) (racd far side: rdn ½-wy: no imp) | s.h | **9** | 16/1 | 78 | 28 |
| 3323[4] | **Robellion (70)** (DWPArbuthnot) **5-7-12v** GBardwell(4) (b.hind: nvr trbld ldrs) | ¾ | **10** | 14/1 | 61 | 11 |
| 2799[3] | **Maid O'Cannie (68)** (MWEasterby) **5-7-7b**(3) NVarley(14) (lw: racd far side: outpcd fr ½-wy) | 1¾ | **11** | 66/1 | 55 | 5 |
| 3424[4] | **Daawe (USA) (68)** (MrsVAAconley) **5-7-10v** NCarlisle(8) (cl up over 3f: wknd) | nk | **12** | 25/1 | 54 | 4 |
| 773[2] | **First Maite (77)** (SRBowring) **3-8-2b** DaleGibson(11) (n.d) | 2 | **13** | 25/1 | 58 | 5 |
| 3232[20] | **Lennox Lewis (82)** (APJarvis) **4-8-10** WJO'Connor(1) (disp ld over 3f: wknd) | 1 | **14** | 16/1 | 60 | 10 |
| 3232[23] | **For the Present (84)** (TDBarron) **6-8-12** JFortune(13) (nvr wnt pce) | 1 | **15** | 14/1 | 59 | 9 |
| 3271[7] | **Double Blue (100)** (MJohnston) **7-10-0** JWeaver(16) (racd far side: hung lft & outpcd fr ½-wy) | 1 | **16** | 14/1 | 73 | 23 |
| 3432[6] | **Sailormaite (85)** (SRBowring) **5-8-13** DeanMcKeown(15) (racd far side: hung lft & outpcd fr ½-wy) | 1½ | **17** | 14/1 | 54 | 4 |
| | | | | (SP 135.4%) | **17 Rn** | |

**1m 11.5** (1.00) CSF £81.24 CT £1,368.84 TOTE £8.60: £2.20 £3.80 £5.10 £3.50 (£52.60) Trio £492.30 OWNER Maygain Ltd (WHITCOMBE) BRED Juddmonte Farms

LONG HANDICAP Maid O'Cannie 7-1 Daawe (USA) 7-9

WEIGHT FOR AGE 3yo-3lb

**2725 Samwar**, travelled really well and it was always a question of when and how far. In this mood he is going to take some beating. (15/2)

**3430 Options Open**, dropped back in trip, stayed on splendidly in the last couple of furlongs but the winner was always too good. His turn will surely come. (10/1)

**3424 Fantasy Racing (IRE)** is in really good form just now and deserves to find a race. (20/1)

**3232 Bolshoi (IRE)** produced his customary run in the last two furlongs but was never doing enough on this occasion to get in to it. (9/1)

**3296* Bollin Joanne** showed plenty of speed from her far-from-ideal draw, but she was fighting a lost cause in the last furlong and a half. (100/30: 5/1-3/1)

**3323 The Scythian** really likes this track, and is in good form at the moment, but he was well held in the final furlong. (9/1)

**3296 Perryston View**, from a yard that can do little right at present, ran reasonably until dropping away approaching the final furlong. When things eventually come right, he is going to be well handicapped. (9/1)

**3296 Ziggy's Dancer (USA)** had next to no chance racing up the far side and always saw too much daylight. (16/1)

## 3623 ROTHMANS ROYALS NORTH SOUTH CHALLENGE SERIES H'CAP (0-80) (3-Y.O+) (Class D)

4-15 (4-27) **1m 1f** £8,033.75 (£2,420.00: £1,172.50: £548.75) Stalls: High GOING minus 0.37 sec per fur (F)

| Form | Horse | Btn | Pos | SP | RR | SF |
|---|---|---|---|---|---|---|
| 3450[6] | **Ninia (USA) (76)** (MJohnston) **4-9-10** JWeaver(3) (lw: sn w ldr: led 3f out: r.o wl fnl 2f) | — | **1** | 12/1 | 86 | 50 |
| 3081[9] | **Sandmoor Chambray (80)** (TDEasterby) **5-10-0** MBirch(15) (a chsng ldrs: kpt on u.p fnl f) | 1½ | **2** | 12/1 | 87 | 51 |
| 2693[7] | **Bollin Frank (67)** (TDEasterby) **4-9-1** LCharnock(5) (mde most tl hdd 3f out: kpt on wl) | hd | **3** | 10/1[3] | 74 | 38 |
| 3148[5] | **Ron's Secret (71)** (JWPayne) **4-9-5** RCochrane(7) (lw: bhd: swtchd & hdwy over 2f out: styd on wl: t.m.t.d) | 2½ | **4** | 7/2[1] | 74 | 38 |
| 3328[4] | **Quilling (68)** (MDods) **4-9-2** JFEgan(16) (hld up: effrt 3f out: styd on towards fin) | ½ | **5** | 14/1 | 70 | 34 |
| 3450[8] | **Special-K (59)** (EWeymes) **4-8-7** KDarley(10) (a chsng ldrs: one pce fnl 3f) | 2 | **6** | 9/1[2] | 57 | 21 |
| 1799[6] | **Nordic Breeze (IRE) (71)** (ABailey) **4-9-5** JFortune(14) (in tch: effrt 3f out: styd on one pce) | ½ | **7** | 12/1 | 68 | 32 |
| 3280[4] | **Bulsara (62)** (CWFairhurst) **4-8-10** DeanMcKeown(12) (chsd ldrs: effrt 3f out: wknd wl over 1f out) | ½ | **8** | 11/1 | 59 | 23 |
| 3287[4] | **Spanish Verdict (68)** (DenysSmith) **9-9-2** KFallon(9) (lw: mid div: rdn 3f out: no imp) | 1½ | **9** | 12/1 | 62 | 26 |
| 2963[2] | **Lunch Party (56)** (DNicholls) **4-8-4** JCarroll(17) (hld up: nvr nr to chal) | nk | **10** | 9/1[2] | 49 | 13 |
| 3403[6] | **Hawwam (51)** (EJAlston) **10-7-13** JLowe(8) (a rr div) | 3½ | **11** | 16/1 | 38 | 2 |
| 3333[6] | **Nobby Barnes (48)** (DonEnricoIncisa) **7-7-10** KimTinkler(6) (bhd: effrt 4f out: n.d) | 1 | **12** | 33/1 | 33 | — |
| 3357* | **Chabrol (CAN) (69)** (TTClement) **3-8-5**(5) RHavlin(11) (in tch tl wknd 3f out) | 2 | **13** | 10/1[3] | 51 | 8 |
| 1069[7] | **Rambo Waltzer (68)** (DNicholls) **4-9-2** AlexGreaves(13) (prom tl wknd wl over 3f out) | 4 | **14** | 12/1 | 43 | 7 |
| 3450[7] | **Ochos Rios (IRE) (58)** (BSRothwell) **5-8-6** MFenton(4) (n.d) | ½ | **15** | 33/1 | 32 | — |
| *3419*[2] | **Bentico (60)** (MrsNMacauley) **7-8-5**(3) CTeague(1) (lw: in tch tl wknd fnl 4f) | 3½ | **16** | 11/1 | 28 | — |
| 3481[5] | **Irish Sea (USA) (72)** (DNicholls) **3-8-6**(7) JBramhill(2) (prom to ½-wy) | 2½ | **17** | 33/1 | 35 | — |
| | | | | (SP 136.9%) | **17 Rn** | |

**1m 53.2** (3.00) CSF £148.65 CT £1,440.19 TOTE £13.80: £2.50 £3.50 £3.00 £1.80 (£84.20) Trio £146.60 OWNER Mrs D. R. Schreiber (MIDDLEHAM) BRED Newgate Stud Farm Inc

LONG HANDICAP Nobby Barnes 7-2

WEIGHT FOR AGE 3yo-7lb

**2351 Ninia (USA)** was winning off her highest mark to date and also from a poor draw which made this a useful performance. (12/1)

**2483 Sandmoor Chambray** rarely runs a bad race and kept battling away, but always in vain as far as winning was concerned. (12/1: op 8/1)

**2693 Bollin Frank** was in the front rank throughout as he likes to be and although struggling some way from home, he did keep staying on, and is certainly not done with yet. (10/1)

**3148 Ron's Secret**, set an impossible task, did well to finish so close and is well worth bearing in mind. (7/2: 7/1-3/1)

**3328 Quilling**, again dropped in behind the leaders, ran reasonably but failed to land a blow and perhaps more positive tactics should be tried. (14/1)

**3134 Special-K** was at her best last year when dropped in class and perhaps this is what she needs again. (9/1)

**2963 Lunch Party**, trying a longer trip, was dropped out and failed to get anywhere near and was not knocked about. (9/1: op 5/1)

## 3624 BOROUGHBRIDGE MAIDEN STKS (3-Y.O+) (Class D)

4-50 (4-59) **5f** £3,598.75 (£1,090.00: £532.50: £253.75) Stalls: Low GOING minus 0.37 sec per fur (F)

| Form | Horse | Btn | Pos | SP | RR | SF |
|---|---|---|---|---|---|---|
| 3506[4] | **Barranak (IRE) (58)** (GMMcCourt) **4-9-2** JWeaver(2) (lw: mde all: shkn up over 1f out: r.o wl) | — | **1** | 9/4[1] | 70 | 60 |
| 3154[8] | **Merrily (72)** (MissSEHall) **3-8-9** KFallon(12) (b: cl up: effrt 2f out: r.o one pce) | 2½ | **2** | 9/4[1] | 57 | 45 |
| 3399[3] | **River Tern (63)** (JBerry) **3-9-0v**[1] JCarroll(4) (b: bmpd s: prom: nt qckn fnl 2f) | 2½ | **3** | 11/2[2] | 54 | 42 |
| | **Foreign Relation (IRE)** (PRWebber) **3-8-9** DaleGibson(7) (cmpt: bit bkwd: outpcd tl hdwy over 1f out: r.o) | 2 | **4** | 14/1 | 43 | 31 |
| 3100[2] | **Superfrills (53)** (MissLCSiddall) **3-8-9** DeanMcKeown(1) (chsd ldrs: effrt ½-wy: nt qckn) | 1¾ | **5** | 16/1 | 37 | 25 |
| 2913[3] | **Glen Garnock (IRE)** (DNicholls) **4-9-2** AlexGreaves(13) (hdwy on outside ½-wy: nvr nr to chal) | nk | **6** | 20/1 | 41 | 31 |
| 3255[6] | **Cruz Santa** (TDBarron) **3-8-9** JFortune(6) (wnt lft s: nvr plcd to chal) | 1½ | **7** | 10/1 | 31 | 19 |
| 3446[12] | **Happy Traveller (IRE)** (CMurray) **3-9-0** JFEgan(9) (chsd ldrs tl wknd fnl 2f) | 2 | **8** | 12/1 | 30 | 18 |
| 3331[9] | **Petarina (46)** (MissJFCraze) **3-8-9** NConnorton(8) (cl up 3f: wknd) | ½ | **9** | 50/1 | 23 | 11 |

| | | | | SP | RR | SF |
|---|---|---|---|---|---|---|
| 2732[9] | **Blue Lugana (26)** (NBycroft) **4-9-2** MWigham(11) (nvr trbld ldrs) | s.h | **10** | 100/1 | 28 | 18 |
| | **Girl of My Dreams (IRE)** (MJHeaton-Ellis) **3-8-9** KDarley(3) (w'like: bit bkwd: s.s: a bhd) | 3½ | **11** | 13/2[3] | 12 | — |
| 3100[3] | **Bataleur** (MissJBower) **3-9-0** DRMcCabe(5) (bmpd s: eased & bhd fr ½-wy) | s.h | **12** | 50/1 | 17 | 5 |
| | **Honeyhall** (NBycroft) **3-8-9** JLowe(10) (small: bkwd: dwlt: a bhd) | 6 | **13** | 66/1 | — | — |
| | | | | (SP 130.8%) | **13 Rn** | |

**58.9 secs** (0.50) CSF £8.27 TOTE £3.80: £1.70 £1.80 £1.80 (£6.60) Trio £7.50 OWNER Mr Mac Carthy (WANTAGE) BRED M. MacCarthy
WEIGHT FOR AGE 3yo-2lb

**3506 Barranak (IRE)** had the required good draw, and all the necessary speed, and scored a shade comfortably. Now he has broken his duck he will hopefully continue. (9/4: op 7/2)
**3154 Merrily** had plenty to do from her draw and showed some useful speed, but then failed to match the winner in the last furlong and a half. (9/4)
**3399 River Tern** was in a visor for the first time and showed up behind the leaders but was never doing enough when the pressure was on. (11/2)
**Foreign Relation (IRE)**, green in the early stages, was picking up particularly well at the finish and should be all the better for this. (14/1)
**3100 Superfrills** had her chances but also had her limitations exposed. (16/1)
**2913 Glen Garnock (IRE)**, dropped back in distance, had another nice run and will come to hand in due course. (20/1)
**3255 Cruz Santa**, having her third run, is now qualified for handicaps and better should be seen before long. (10/1: 6/1-12/1)
**Happy Traveller (IRE)** (12/1: op 8/1)
**3100 Bataleur** never saw daylight and was given a pretty easy time in the circumstances. (50/1)

T/Plpt: £137.40 (143.17 Tckts). T/Qdpt: £16.90 (60.23 Tckts) AA

# 3416-WOLVERHAMPTON (L-H) (Standard)
## Saturday August 17th
WEATHER: cloudy & warm WIND: slt across

## 3625 E.B.F. STARFISH MAIDEN STKS (2-Y.O) (Class D)
7-00 (7-01) **7f (Fibresand)** £3,817.50 (£1,140.00: £545.00: £247.50) Stalls: Low GOING minus 0.27 sec per fur (FST)

| | | | | SP | RR | SF |
|---|---|---|---|---|---|---|
| *2746[2]* | **Mudflap** (SirMarkPrescott) **2-8-9** GDuffield(4) (chsd ldr: led 4f out: clr appr fnl f: eased nr fin) | — | **1** | 100/30[3] | 76+ | 27 |
| 3119[2] | **Dream of Nurmi** (DRLoder) **2-9-0v[1]** RHughes(5) (lw: a.p: rdn wl over 1f out: sn outpcd) | 2½ | **2** | 11/8[1] | 75 | 27 |
| 3293[3] | **Siouxrouge** (PCHaslam) **2-9-0** JStack(7) (swtg: trckd ldrs: effrt 3f out: rdn & one pce fnl 2f) | 7 | **3** | 9/4[2] | 59 | 13 |
| | **Count Tony** (SPCWoods) **2-9-0** DBiggs(1) (w'like: bit bkwd: sn rdn along & outpcd: styd on fnl 2f: nvr nrr) | 1½ | **4** | 14/1 | 56 | 10 |
| 3269[10] | **Highway Robber (IRE)** (JMPEustace) **2-9-0** JTate(2) (swtg: prom over 4f: sn lost tch) | 1 | **5** | 25/1 | 54 | 8 |
| 3349[13] | **Mysterium** (NPLittmoden) **2-9-0** TGMcLaughlin(3) (led 3f: rdn 3f out: sn wknd: t.o) | 18 | **6** | 50/1 | 12 | — |
| | **Le Grand Gousier (USA)** (RJRWilliams) **2-9-0** AMcGlone(8) (w'like: str: bkwd: s.i.s: a outpcd & wl bhd: t.o) | 6 | **7** | 20/1 | — | — |
| | **Carlys Quest** (JNeville) **2-9-0** ACulhane(9) (w'like: str: bkwd: s.s: sn wl bhd & outpcd: t.o) | 1¼ | **8** | 40/1 | — | — |
| | **Ronquista d'Or** (GAHam) **2-9-0** WJO'Connor(6) (w'like: str: bkwd: s.s: a t.o) | 21 | **9** | 40/1 | — | — |
| | | | | (SP 118.1%) | **9 Rn** | |

**1m 28.5** (0.70 under 2y best) (3.80) CSF £8.21 TOTE £3.70: £1.10 £1.40 £1.20 (£2.60) Trio £2.20 OWNER Major Gen George Burns (NEWMARKET) BRED Major-Gen Sir George Burns

**2746 Mudflap** had plenty of use made of her on this return to seven, and she quite simply galloped the opposition into the ground. (100/30: 7/1-3/1)
**3119 Dream of Nurmi**, an impressive easy mover who was blinkered for this first run on Fibresand, pushed the pace and had every chance until the winner proved much too smart for him. (11/8: Evens-6/4)
**3293 Siouxrouge** continuing his step up in distance, was poised to challenge at the end of the back straight, but once the tempo lifted, he was out of his depth. (9/4)
**Count Tony** was always struggling with the pace and he did not begin to find his stride until it was all but over. (14/1: op 8/1)

## 3626 SEA BREEZE CLAIMING STKS (3-Y.O) (Class F)
7-30 (7-31) **1m 1f 79y (Fibresand)** £2,381.00 (£656.00: £311.00) Stalls: Low GOING minus 0.27 sec per fur (FST)

| | | | | SP | RR | SF |
|---|---|---|---|---|---|---|
| *3063[12]* | **Yeoman Oliver (71)** (BAMcMahon) **3-9-1b[1]** GDuffield(4) (lw: mde all: hrd rdn fnl 2f: r.o wl) | — | **1** | 7/4[1] | 70 | 28 |
| 3059[9] | **Eccentric Dancer (42)** (MPBielby) **3-8-0b** JQuinn(9) (hld up: hdwy 5f out: chsd wnr over 3f out: rdn & no ex appr fnl f) | 2½ | **2** | 14/1 | 51 | 11 |
| | **Afon Alwen** (SCWilliams) **3-9-0** JTate(6) (lt-f: unf: s.s: hdwy over 4f out: styd on u.p appr fnl f) | 9 | **3** | 14/1 | 49 | 11 |
| 3320[6] | **Mrs Drummond (IRE)** (APJarvis) **3-8-6** WJO'Connor(1) (lw: trckd ldrs: rdn & outpcd 3f out: styd on appr fnl f) | ¾ | **4** | 11/1 | 40 | 2 |
| | **Theme Arena** (SMellor) **3-9-0** AMcGlone(3) (unf: bkwd: s.s: wl bhd tl sme late hdwy) | 3½ | **5** | 25/1 | 42 | 4 |
| 2859[9] | **Tina Katerina (40)** (RChampion) **3-8-6** RCochrane(8) (b.hind: prom tl outpcd over 2f out) | s.h | **6** | 20/1 | 34 | — |
| *834** | **Lia Fail (IRE) (53)** (RHollinshead) **3-8-1(3)** FLynch(7) (sddle slipped: chsd ldrs: rdn 3f out: grad fdd) | 2½ | **7** | 3/1[2] | 28 | — |
| *3418[7]* | **Kass Alhawa (82)** (DWChapman) **3-8-9b[1]** ACulhane(5) (b: sn chsng wnr: rdn 4f out: wknd over 2f out) | 5 | **8** | 5/1[3] | 24 | — |
| | | | | (SP 108.3%) | **8 Rn** | |

**2m 1.8** (5.80) CSF £21.57 TOTE £2.70: £1.10 £2.70 £5.30 (£11.40) Trio £121.90; £77.28 to 19/8/96 OWNER Mr Michael Stokes (TAMWORTH) BRED M. G. T. Stokes

**1780 Yeoman Oliver** had to work much harder than was expected on this step down in class. He was well on top where it mattered though. (7/4)
**1456 Eccentric Dancer** does seem to produce her best on this surface, and she gave supporters of the favourite a worrying time, until shaken off approaching the final furlong. (14/1)
**Afon Alwen** showed plenty of promise on this debut and should be able to make her mark in time. (14/1: 10/1-16/1)
**Mrs Drummond (IRE)** is just getting to know what the game is all about and stayed on after getting outpaced in the back straight. She should go on improving. (11/1)
**Theme Arena** never got into the race but will be all the wiser for the run. (25/1)

## 3627 FOLEY STEELSTOCK H'CAP (0-85) (3-Y.O+) (Class D)
8-00 (8-04) **1m 1f 79y (Fibresand)** £3,960.15 (£1,183.20: £566.10: £257.55) Stalls: Low GOING minus 0.27 sec per fur (FST)

| | | | | SP | RR | SF |
|---|---|---|---|---|---|---|
| *3418** | **Hal's Pal (84)** (DRLoder) **3-9-7b[1]** RHughes(6) (lw: swtg: plld hrd: led 6f out: shkn up wl over 1 out: drew clr fnl f) | — | **1** | 4/1[2] | 95 | 70 |

| Form | Horse | Dist | Pos | SP | RR | SF |
|---|---|---|---|---|---|---|
| $3421^{*}$ | **Serious Sensation (84)** (SirMarkPrescott) **3-9-7** GDuffield(2) (hld up: gd hdwy 5f out: rdn & ev ch appr fnl f: sn outpcd) | 3½ | 2 | $13/8^{1}$ | 89 | 65 |
| $3419^{*}$ | **Super High (81)** (PHowling) **4-9-11b** PaulEddery(3) (lw: b.hind: led over 3f: rdn over 2f out: one pce) | 7 | 3 | $11/1^{3}$ | 74 | 58 |
| $3220^{12}$ | **South Eastern Fred (77)** (HJCollingridge) **5-9-7** MRimmer(7) (in tch: effrt & rdn 3f out: kpt on sme pce) | 1½ | 4 | 16/1 | 68 | 52 |
| $3450^{4}$ | **Maple Bay (IRE) (84)** (ABailey) **7-9-9**(5) PRoberts(12) (trckd ldrs tl rdn & lost pl over 3f out: rallied appr fnl f) | 1¼ | 5 | 14/1 | 72 | 57 |
| $3601^{4}$ | **Desert Invader (IRE) (75)** (DWChapman) **5-9-5** ACulhane(13) (chsd ldrs: rdn over 3f out: no imp) | nk | 6 | 25/1 | 63 | 48 |
| $1773^{9}$ | **Cool Fire (76)** (SPCWoods) **3-8-13** DBiggs(10) (bit bkwd: nvr nr ldrs) | 1 | 7 | 16/1 | 62 | 41 |
| $3419^{4}$ | **Waikiki Beach (USA) (78)** (GLMoore) **5-9-8** SWhitworth(4) (b: trckd ldrs tl rdn & wknd over 2f out) | ½ | 8 | 12/1 | 63 | 48 |
| $3334^{8}$ | **Heathyards Lady (USA) (69)** (RHollinshead) **5-8-10**(3) FLynch(11) (a in rr) | 2½ | 9 | 14/1 | 50 | 36 |
| $3419^{7}$ | **Le Sport (79)** (ABailey) **3-9-2** JStack(5) (a in rr) | 2½ | 10 | 33/1 | 56 | 35 |
| $3063^{3}$ | **Philistar (69)** (JMPEustace) **3-8-6** RCochrane(1) (trckd ldrs over 6f: sn hrd drvn & wknd) | 1 | 11 | 12/1 | 44 | 24 |
| $3419^{6}$ | **Ethbaat (USA) (70)** (MJHeaton-Ellis) **5-9-0** AMcGlone(8) (a bhd) | 2½ | 12 | 14/1 | 41 | 28 |
| $3340^{9}$ | **African-Pard (IRE) (61)** (DHaydnJones) **4-8-5v** AMackay(9) (lw: a in rr) | 2½ | 13 | 20/1 | 28 | 16 |

(SP 125.1%) **13 Rn**

**1m 57.5** (1.50) CSF £10.86 CT £64.49 TOTE £4.40: £1.90 £1.40 £3.30 (£3.30) Trio £15.90 OWNER Mr Wafic Said (NEWMARKET) BRED Cheveley Park Stud Ltd

WEIGHT FOR AGE 3yo-7lb

**3418* Hal's Pal** proved his worth in the first time blinkers, and won this in useful style. He could well go on to better things. (4/1)

**3421* Serious Sensation** delivered a determined challenge approaching the final furlong, but the winner held all the aces and only needed to lengthen to leave him standing. (13/8)

**3419* Super High** had an impossible task, trying to concede weight to two younger, improving rivals and he was left in no man's land from the turn into the straight. (11/1: op 7/1)

**2409 South Eastern Fred** reserves his best for the All-Weather and though he was outclassed here, did keep persevering and all is not lost yet. (16/1)

**3450 Maple Bay (IRE)** used to be the bee's knees at this venue but the Handicapper has made him pay for it, and his best efforts in recent months have been on the Turf. (14/1: 10/1-16/1)

**3601 Desert Invader (IRE)** battled on under a powerful drive but was never going to get himself into the action and this trip proved beyond his best. (25/1)

**3419 Waikiki Beach (USA)** (12/1: op 8/1)

## 3628 PLYVINE CATERING H'CAP (0-65) (3-Y.O+) (Class F)

8-30 (8-31) **7f (Fibresand)** £2,381.00 (£656.00: £311.00) Stalls: Low GOING minus 0.27 sec per fur (FST)

| Form | Horse | Dist | Pos | SP | RR | SF |
|---|---|---|---|---|---|---|
| $3060^{4}$ | **Move With Edes (64)** (WGMTurner) **4-9-7**(7) DSweeney(8) (trckd ldrs: led wl over 1f out: rdn & drifted rt: jst hld on) | — | 1 | 9/1 | 70 | 37 |
| $854^{11}$ | **Twin Creeks (54)** (VSoane) **5-9-4** RCochrane(9) (hld up: gd hdwy 2f out: swtchd lft appr fnl f: fin fast) | s.h | 2 | 8/1 | 60 | 28 |
| $135^{11}$ | **Shahik (USA) (62)** (DHaydnJones) **6-9-12** FNorton(1) (hld up: hdwy 3f out: styd on strly ins fnl f) | 2½ | 3 | 25/1 | 62 | 30 |
| $3399^{2}$ | **Panther (IRE) (48)** (PDEvans) **6-8-12** JFEgan(6) (mid div: effrt ent st: kpt on fnl f) | 1¾ | 4 | $5/2^{1}$ | 44 | 14 |
| $3063^{11}$ | **Dragonjoy (62)** (NPLittmoden) **3-9-7b** RHughes(2) (trckd ldrs: led 2f out: sn hdd: one pce fnl f) | hd | 5 | 14/1 | 58 | 22 |
| $3442^{2}$ | **Northern Judge (49)** (BHanbury) **3-8-8b** JStack(5) (s.i.s: hdwy 5f out: led over 2f out: sn hdd & wknd over 1f out) | 5 | 6 | $9/2^{2}$ | 34 | — |
| $2550^{4}$ | **Quinzii Martin (54)** (DHaydnJones) **8-9-4b** AMackay(11) (bhd: hdwy 2f out: nvr nrr) | hd | 7 | $6/1^{3}$ | 38 | 9 |
| $3089^{16}$ | **Awafeh (48)** (SMellor) **3-8-7v1** NAdams(3) (led 2f: prom tl wknd 2f out) | ¾ | 8 | 20/1 | 31 | — |
| $3062^{10}$ | **What a Nightmare (IRE) (48)** (PHowling) **4-8-12b** PaulEddery(7) (a in rr) | 3 | 9 | 12/1 | 24 | — |
| $2983^{13}$ | **Miss Impulse (55)** (MissJBower) **3-9-0** JQuinn(12) (lw: disp ld over 4f: sn drvn along & wknd: t.o) | 7 | 10 | 20/1 | 15 | — |
| $3410^{3}$ | **Man of Wit (IRE) (58)** (APJarvis) **3-9-3v** WJO'Connor(10) (lw: slt ld 5f out tl over 2f out: sn rdn & wknd: t.o) | 6 | 11 | 10/1 | 4 | — |

(SP 119.0%) **11 Rn**

**1m 29.2** (4.50) CSF £72.84 CT £1,623.34 TOTE £12.30: £2.90 £2.80 £9.20 (£342.50) Trio £71.20; £90.28 to 19/08/96 OWNER W Ede & Co Partnership (SHERBORNE) BRED Tony J. Smith

WEIGHT FOR AGE 3yo-5lb

STEWARDS' ENQUIRY Obj. to Move With Edes by Cochrane overruled.

**3060 Move With Edes** had no trouble handling this surface, but he did take the runner-up's ground by hanging into the whip in the final furlong, and he was fortunate to keep the race. (9/1)

**345* Twin Creeks,** stepping down to seven furlongs again, needed to switch when stopped in his tracks on the approach to the final furlong, and his spirited late challenge only just failed. (8/1)

**Shahik (USA),** who last won at Abu-Dhabi in 1994, ran a fine race after a long absence. Faced with a stiffer test of stamina, he could soon pick up a race. (25/1)

**3399 Panther (IRE)** has never been quite so effective over these longer trips and, though he did keep on, lacked the speed to deliver a challenge. (5/2)

**2637 Dragonjoy** pressed the leaders from the start. Poking his nose in front on the home turn, he was then tapped for toe in the sprint to the line. (14/1: op 8/1)

**3442 Northern Judge** missed the beat at the start, but recovered to lead briefly on the home turn before fading when the pace increased on straightening up. (9/2)

## 3629 CANDY-FLOSS (S) STKS (2-Y.O) (Class G)

9-00 (9-01) **7f (Fibresand)** £2,070.00 (£570.00: £270.00) Stalls: Low GOING minus 0.27 sec per fur (FST)

| Form | Horse | Dist | Pos | SP | RR | SF |
|---|---|---|---|---|---|---|
| $3417^{3}$ | **Tinkerbell (66)** (LordHuntingdon) **2-8-11v** RHughes(7) (hld up: hdwy on bit over 2f out: shkn up to ld wl ins fnl f) | — | 1 | $4/6^{1}$ | 59 | 8 |
| $3498^{7}$ | **Grovefair Lad (IRE) (52)** (BJMeehan) **2-8-11** MTebbutt(6) (hld up: hdwy 3f out: led 2f out tl wl ins fnl f) | nk | 2 | 8/1 | 58 | 8 |
| $2938^{3}$ | **Hopperetta** (BPalling) **2-8-6** TSprake(1) (a.p: ev ch 2f out: rdn & unable qckn fnl f) | 1¼ | 3 | $7/1^{3}$ | 51 | 1 |
| $2948^{4}$ | **Surprise Event (67)** (WGMTurner) **2-8-4**(7) DSweeney(4) (bhd tl styd on appr fnl f) | 4 | 4 | $11/2^{2}$ | 46 | — |
| $2554^{6}$ | **Read Your Contract (IRE)** (JBerry) **2-8-11v** JQuinn(5) (led to 2f out: sn rdn & wknd) | 8 | 5 | 16/1 | 28 | — |
| $1026^{5}$ | **Candle Light (IRE)** (APJarvis) **2-8-6** WJO'Connor(2) (prom tl rdn & wknd over 2f out) | 3 | 6 | 16/1 | 16 | — |
| | **Rambo Tango** (BRCambidge) **2-8-11** ACulhane(3) (lt-f: outpcd: a t.o) | 3½ | 7 | 66/1 | 13 | — |

(SP 112.3%) **7 Rn**

**1m 30.4** (5.70) CSF £6.39 TOTE £1.70: £1.20 £3.10 (£8.00) OWNER Lord Carnarvon (WEST ILSLEY) BRED Highclere Stud Ltd

Sold MissSWilton 7,000 gns

**3417 Tinkerbell** was going to win this cheekily, but in the end, did need to be shaken up to make sure. It will be interesting to see how far she can go. (4/6: op Evens)
**3311 Grovefair Lad (IRE)** showed improved form at this first attempt on Fibresand, and he will hardly need to step up on this to pick up a similar event. (8/1)
**2938 Hopperetta** ran a race full of promise and her turn cannot be far away. (7/1)
**2948 Surprise Event** was unable to hold his pitch but he did pick up in the closing stages, and his turn will come. (11/2: op 5/2)

## 3630 CHEMIQUE ADHESIVES MAIDEN H'CAP (0-65) (3-Y.O+) (Class F)

9-30 (9-30) **1m 4f (Fibresand)** £2,484.00 (£684.00: £324.00) Stalls: Low GOING minus 0.27 sec per fur (FST)

| | Runner | | | SP | RR | SF |
|---|---|---|---|---|---|---|
| 3297$^{12}$ | **Drama King (36)** (SRBowring) **4-8-0b** JQuinn(5) (a.p: led over 3f to 2f out: rallied u.p & edgd rt to ld wl ins fnl f) | — | **1** | 25/1 | 41 | 13 |
| *2749*$^{8}$ | **Zatopek (52)** (JCullinan) **4-9-2** RHughes(6) (hld up: hdwy & rdn over 3f out: swtchd lft ins fnl f: kpt on) | 1¼ | **2** | 14/1 | 55 | 26 |
| *2935*$^{4}$ | **Chevalier (USA) (62)** (ICampbell) **4-9-12** SWhitworth(4) (lw: led 3f: led 2f out tl wl ins fnl f) | nk | **3** | 10/1 | 65 | 35 |
| 3104$^{4}$ | **Miss Pravda (50)** (BJLlewellyn) **3-7-11**$^{(7)}$ JBramhill(7) (a.p: rdn 2f out: kpt on fnl f) | 1 | **4** | 16/1 | 52 | 14 |
| 3459$^{4}$ | **Backwoods (57)** (WMBrisbourne) **3-8-11** GDuffield(2) (lw: in rr tl styd on fnl 2f: nvr nrr) | 2 | **5** | 7/1$^{3}$ | 56 | 18 |
| *2751*$^{2}$ | **Moonraking (56)** (TJEtherington) **3-8-10** DaleGibson(12) (bhd & hrd drvn ½-wy: styd on wl towards fin) | hd | **6** | 3/1$^{1}$ | 55 | 17 |
| 3220$^{7}$ | **Mazirah (47)** (PJMakin) **5-8-11** PaulEddery(9) (lw: led 9f out tl over 3f out: sn rdn & btn) | 1½ | **7** | 15/2 | 44 | 16 |
| *899*$^{4}$ | **Nordic Hero (IRE) (51)** (APJarvis) **3-8-5**$^{ow1}$ WJO'Connor(3) (prom tl outpcd over 3f out: effrt ent st: no imp) | 1¼ | **8** | 12/1 | 46 | 9 |
| *2939*$^{5}$ | **Taniyar (FR) (40)** (RHollinshead) **4-8-1**$^{(3)}$ FLynch(8) (a in rr) | 4 | **9** | 16/1 | 30 | 4 |
| 3341$^{3}$ | **Indian Sunset (51)** (CREgerton) **3-8-5** TSprake(1) (mid div: rdn over 3f out: sn wknd) | ½ | **10** | 8/1 | 40 | 4 |
| 3320$^{5}$ | **Baron Hrabovsky (52)** (PFICole) **3-8-6b**$^{1}$ JFEgan(10) (trckd ldrs tl rdn & wknd over 3f out: t.o) | 16 | **11** | 10/1 | 20 | — |
| *3421*$^{5}$ | **Dazzling (62)** (DCO'Brien) **3-9-2** GBardwell(11) (lt-f: in tch: drvn along over 4f out: sn btn: t.o) | 2½ | **12** | 11/2$^{2}$ | 27 | — |
| | | | | (SP 123.9%) | **12 Rn** | |

**2m 40.5** (8.00) CSF £302.88 CT £3,394.45 TOTE £40.60: £10.90 £4.00 £3.10 (£637.60) Trio Not won; £174.95 to 19/8/96 OWNER Mrs Zoe Grant (EDWINSTOWE) BRED D. J. Watkins
WEIGHT FOR AGE 3yo-10lb
**2936 Drama King** got off the mark from the bottom of the handicap, but won with authority and could at long last be finding his way. (25/1)
**470 Zatopek** looks a hard ride but he did seem to appreciate this longer trip and should be able to find an opening. (14/1)
**2935 Chevalier (USA)** helped push the pace and was only forced to concede defeat inside the last 100 yards. This was a courageous effort at the weights. (10/1)
**3104 Miss Pravda** proved a real terrier but could never quite get to the front, and was short of the necessary turn of foot on the run to the line. (16/1)
**3459 Backwoods,** having his second outing of the week, was out with the washing going nowhere until staying on past beaten rivals from the turn into the straight. (7/1)
**2751 Moonraking** found stamina coming into play in the closing stages. (3/1)

T/Plpt: £269.20 (47.32 Tckts). T/Qdpt: £280.50 (1.93 Tckts) IM

# 3311-BRIGHTON (L-H) (Firm)

## Sunday August 18th

WEATHER: hot WIND: almost nil

## 3631 DITCHLING BEACON MAIDEN STKS (2-Y.O) (Class D)

2-30 (2-30) **5f 213y** £3,258.85 (£986.80: £481.90: £229.45) Stalls: Low GOING minus 0.31 sec per fur (GF)

| | Runner | | | SP | RR | SF |
|---|---|---|---|---|---|---|
| 2708$^{6}$ | **Love Has No Pride (USA)** (RHannon) **2-8-11**$^{(3)}$ DaneO'Neill(2) (chsd ldr: led over 1f out: pushed out) | — | **1** | 11/4$^{2}$ | 70 | 28 |
| | **Allegro** (DRLoder) **2-9-0** TQuinn(4) (w'like: scope: lw: led over 4f: unable qckn) | 5 | **2** | 10/11$^{1}$ | 57 | 15 |
| 3269$^{6}$ | **Be True** (AMoore) **2-9-0** CandyMorris(1) (no hdwy fnl 3f) | 2 | **3** | 33/1 | 51 | 9 |
| | **Absolute Liberty (USA)** (SPCWoods) **2-9-0** DBiggs(5) (neat: bit bkwd: a bhd) | 10 | **4** | 6/1$^{3}$ | 24 | — |
| 2184$^{5}$ | **Philosophic** (SirMarkPrescott) **2-9-0** GDuffield(3) (s.s: a bhd) | 3 | **5** | 15/2 | 16 | — |
| | | | | (SP 108.0%) | **5 Rn** | |

**1m 10.1** (2.90) CSF £5.39 TOTE £3.40: £1.20 £1.20 (£2.20) OWNER Miss L. Regis (MARLBOROUGH) BRED Ralph C. Wilson Jnr
**2708 Love Has No Pride (USA)** raced in second place. Coming through to lead over a furlong out, he needed only to be shaken up to win this race. (11/4)
**Allegro** was a very uneasy favourite. Storming off in front, he attempted to drive his rivals into the ground but, collared over a furlong out, found the winner too strong. (10/11: 4/7-11/10)
**3269 Be True** raced in third place but was making little impression on the front two from halfway. He is a very poor individual, which says little for those behind him. (33/1)

## 3632 A. R. DENNIS BOOKMAKERS NURSERY H'CAP (2-Y.O) (Class D)

3-00 (3-00) **6f 209y** £4,201.50 (£1,272.00: £621.00: £295.50) Stalls: Low GOING minus 0.31 sec per fur (GF)

| | Runner | | | SP | RR | SF |
|---|---|---|---|---|---|---|
| 3400$^{5}$ | **Northern Sun (83)** (TGMills) **2-9-7** TQuinn(5) (a.p: led over 1f out: rdn & r.o wl) | — | **1** | 2/1$^{1}$ | 77 | 39 |
| 3423$^{8}$ | **Fancy A Fortune (IRE) (73)** (JPearce) **2-8-11** GBardwell(2) (lw: w ldr: rdn over 2f out: ev ch over 1f out: unable qckn) | 2½ | **2** | 12/1 | 61 | 23 |
| 3171$^{4}$ | **Janglynyve (64)** (SPCWoods) **2-8-2** DBiggs(4) (no hdwy fnl 3f) | 2½ | **3** | 4/1$^{3}$ | 47 | 9 |
| 1713$^{4}$ | **Hello Dolly (IRE) (67)** (KRBurke) **2-8-5** SSanders(3) (led over 5f) | s.h | **4** | 4/1$^{3}$ | 49 | 11 |
| 3330* | **Summerville Wood (69)** (PMooney) **2-8-0**$^{(7)ow2}$ CScally(1) (s.s: a bhd) | 2 | **5** | 100/30$^{2}$ | 47 | 7 |
| | | | | (SP 104.1%) | **5 Rn** | |

**1m 23.1** (3.10) CSF £17.67 TOTE £2.40: £1.80 £2.40 (£8.40) OWNER Mr Tony Murray (EPSOM) BRED Broughton Bloodstock
**2977* Northern Sun,** who found six too sharp last time out, was much happier back over the trip he won over on his debut. In a handy position throughout, he was pushed into the lead below the distance and shaken up to assert his authority. (2/1: op 3/1)
**2396 Fancy A Fortune (IRE)** disputed the lead from the start. Still in with every chance below the distance, he was firmly put in his place by the winner. (12/1: op 8/1)
**3171 Janglynyve** was making little impression in the second half of the race. (4/1: op 9/4)
**1713 Hello Dolly (IRE)** was tackling seven for the first time, but failed to see it out. Disputing the lead from the start, she was collared over a furlong out and soon capitulated. A return to six is needed. (4/1)

## 3633 TRULEIGH HILL MEDIAN AUCTION MAIDEN STKS (3-Y.O) (Class F)
3-30 (3-30) **1m 1f 209y** £2,398.00 (£673.00: £328.00) Stalls: High GOING minus 0.31 sec per fur (GF)

| | | | | SP | RR | SF |
|---|---|---|---|---|---|---|
| 3161[7] | **King of Sparta (78)** (LMCumani) **3-9-0** OUrbina(1) (lw: mde all: clr over 3f out: unchal) | — | 1 | 1/7[1] | 71 | 44 |
| 2716[6] | **Eskimo Kiss (IRE) (40)** (MJFetherston-Godley) **3-8-6v[1]**(3) DaneO'Neill(2) (chsd wnr: rdn over 4f out: wknd 3f out) | 11 | 2 | 7/1[2] | 48 | 21 |
| 3166[8] | **Craven Cottage (47)** (CJames) **3-9-0** CRutter(3) (a wl bhd: t.o fnl 4f) | 20 | 3 | 16/1[3] | 21 | — |
| | | | | (SP 105.9%) | | **3 Rn** |

**2m 1.6** (3.30) CSF £1.54 TOTE £1.10 (£1.10) OWNER Sheikh Mohammed (NEWMARKET) BRED Sheikh Mohammed bin Rashid al Maktoum

**3161 King of Sparta** has probably had more work at home, as he strolled round to beat two useless rivals. (1/7: 1/10-1/6)

## 3634 MAIL ON SUNDAY MILE H'CAP (Qualifier) (0-85) (3-Y.O) (Class D)
4-00 (4-00) **7f 214y** £7,002.50 (£2,120.00: £1,035.00: £492.50) Stalls: Low GOING minus 0.31 sec per fur (GF)

| | | | | SP | RR | SF |
|---|---|---|---|---|---|---|
| 3123[13] | **Chinensis (IRE) (77)** (LMCumani) **3-9-4** OUrbina(5) (lw: mde all: drvn out) | — | 1 | 100/30[3] | 85 | 60 |
| 3403[4] | **Rebel County (IRE) (67)** (ABailey) **3-8-8** SSanders(4) (lw: hdwy over 2f out: ev ch fnl f: r.o) | hd | 2 | 9/1 | 75 | 50 |
| 3286* | **Sylvan Princess (62)** (CNAllen) **3-7-12**(5) MartinDwyer(3) (hdwy over 2f out: hrd rdn over 1f out: one pce) | 1½ | 3 | 3/1[2] | 67 | 42 |
| 3284[3] | **Allstars Express (65)** (TJNaughton) **3-8-6** TSprake(6) (a.p: rdn over 2f out: ev ch over 1f out: one pce fnl f) | ¾ | 4 | 10/1 | 68 | 43 |
| 3133[6] | **Kirov Lady (IRE) (80)** (RHannon) **3-9-4**(3) DaneO'Neill(2) (prom over 5f) | 8 | 5 | 16/1 | 67 | 42 |
| 3067[7] | **Quinze (74)** (SirMarkPrescott) **3-9-1** GDuffield(7) (bhd fnl 3f) | 4 | 6 | 9/4[1] | 53 | 28 |
| 2605[3] | **Mystic Dawn (57)** (SDow) **3-7-12** JQuinn(1) (lw: hld up: rdn over 2f out: sn wknd) | ½ | 7 | 13/2 | 35 | 10 |
| | | | | (SP 117.2%) | | **7 Rn** |

**1m 33.6** (1.40) CSF £29.54 TOTE £3.90: £2.20 £4.00 (£34.00) OWNER Sheikh Mohammed (NEWMARKET) BRED Sheikh Mohammed bin Rashid al Maktoum

OFFICIAL EXPLANATION **Quinze: raced too freely in the early stages and thereafter became unbalanced.**

**2805* Chinensis (IRE)** enjoyed the return to a front-running role. Strongly pressed inside the final quarter-mile, he gave his all and just held off the runner-up. (100/30)

**3403 Rebel County (IRE)** moved up over two furlongs out. Soon throwing down her challenge, she had a battle royal with the winner in the final furlong, and only just lost out. (9/1)

**3286* Sylvan Princess** began her effort on the outside of the field over a quarter of a mile from home. Coming under pressure below the distance, she stayed on, if unable to get on terms with the front two. (3/1)

**3284 Allstars Express** ran another sound race. In a handy position throughout, he had every chance below the distance before tapped for toe. (10/1: op 6/1)

**3133 Kirov Lady (IRE)** played an active role until coming to the end of her tether over two furlongs out. (16/1)

**2760* Quinze** gave his rider real steering problems in the straight and was being left behind in the final three furlongs. (9/4)

## 3635 SWEETIE FLO AND JIM ROGERS MEMORIAL H'CAP (0-70) (3-Y.O+) (Class E)
4-30 (4-31) **1m 1f 209y** £2,872.80 (£869.40: £424.20: £201.60) Stalls: High GOING minus 0.31 sec per fur (GF)

| | | | | SP | RR | SF |
|---|---|---|---|---|---|---|
| 3314* | **Double Rush (IRE) (48)** (TGMills) **4-8-6** TQuinn(7) (lw: stdy hdwy 2f out: led ins fnl f: r.o wl) | — | 1 | 9/4[1] | 62 | 44 |
| 3111[12] | **Mister O'Grady (IRE) (53)** (RAkehurst) **5-8-11** SSanders(6) (hdwy over 3f out: led over 1f out tl ins fnl f: r.o) | hd | 2 | 6/1 | 67 | 49 |
| 3173[7] | **Ma Petite Anglaise (68)** (WJarvis) **4-9-9**(3) MHenry(5) (swtchd lft & hdwy over 2f out: ev ch ins fnl f: unable qckn) | ½ | 3 | 5/1[3] | 81 | 63 |
| 3272[6] | **Soviet Bride (IRE) (69)** (SDow) **4-9-10**(3) DaneO'Neill(2) (a.p: ev ch over 1f out: sn wknd) | 5 | 4 | 9/2[2] | 74 | 56 |
| 3136[5] | **Guesstimation (USA) (63)** (JPearce) **7-9-0**(7) RFfrench(1) (a.p: swtchd lft over 1f out: btn whn squeezed thro & hmpd on ins 1f out) | 3 | 5 | 6/1 | 63 | 45 |
| 2440[8] | **Roman Reel (USA) (70)** (GLMoore) **5-10-0** SWhitworth(9) (lw: led over 8f: wkng whn bmpd 1f out) | 1¼ | 6 | 14/1 | 68 | 50 |
| *349** | **One Off the Rail (USA) (40)** (AMoore) **6-7-12** JQuinn(8) (bkwd: swtg: prom 8f) | 2 | 7 | 10/1 | 35 | 17 |
| 3303[5] | **Colour Counsellor (46)** (RMFlower) **3-7-7b**(3) NVarley(4) (bhd fnl 3f) | 13 | 8 | 33/1 | 20 | — |
| | | | | (SP 112.9%) | | **8 Rn** |

**2m 0.7** (2.40) CSF £14.88 CT £54.29 TOTE £3.30: £1.40 £2.10 £1.30 (£8.10) Trio £5.40 OWNER Mr Tony Murray (EPSOM) BRED Dermot Finnegan

LONG HANDICAP Colour Counsellor 7-6

WEIGHT FOR AGE 3yo-8lb

**3314* Double Rush (IRE)** steadily crept into the action travelling sweetly a quarter of a mile from home. With his pilot oozing confidence, he was shaken up to lead inside the final furlong to settle matters. (9/4)

**3111 Mister O'Grady (IRE)**, tailed off at Windsor last time out, bounced back here. Moving into contention over three furlongs from home, he struck the front below the distance but found the winner a little bit too good. (6/1: 4/1-7/1)

**2945 Ma Petite Anglaise**, switched left to pick up ground over a quarter of a mile from home, was certainly close enough if good enough before tapped for toe. (5/1)

**3272 Soviet Bride (IRE)**, in a handy position throughout, had every chance below the distance before giving best. (9/2)

**3136 Guesstimation (USA)**, never far away, was switched to the rails below the distance. Going for a minute gap a furlong out, he caused serious trouble. (6/1: op 4/1)

**2344 Roman Reel (USA)** was done no favours by Guesstimation. (14/1: op 8/1)

## 3636 HANNINGTONS MACMILLAN CHAPEL APPEAL H'CAP (0-70) (3-Y.O+) (Class E)
5-00 (5-00) **5f 59y** £2,872.80 (£869.40: £424.20: £201.60) Stalls: Low GOING minus 0.31 sec per fur (GF)

| | | | | SP | RR | SF |
|---|---|---|---|---|---|---|
| 2982[3] | **Pride of Hayling (IRE) (56)** (PRHedger) **5-9-0** TQuinn(6) (lw: outpcd: hdwy over 1f out: led ins fnl f: r.o wl) | — | 1 | 11/4[3] | 67 | 47 |
| 3313[2] | **Mellors (IRE) (64)** (JARToller) **3-9-6** SSanders(3) (lw: led: rdn over 1f out: hdd ins fnl f: unable qckn) | 3 | 2 | 2/1[1] | 66 | 44 |
| 3339* | **Hever Golf Express (72)** (TJNaughton) **3-10-0** TSprake(4) (b.off hind: w ldr: ev ch over 1f out: one pce) | 1½ | 3 | 5/1 | 69 | 47 |
| 3313[3] | **Sharp Imp (58)** (RMFlower) **6-9-2b** DBiggs(1) (outpcd: hdwy over 1f out: r.o one pce) | s.h | 4 | 5/2[2] | 55 | 35 |
| 1891[12] | **Into Debt (40)** (JRPoulton) **3-7-10** DeclanO'Shea(2) (s.s: outpcd: nvr nr to chal) | 1½ | 5 | 40/1 | 33 | 11 |
| | | | | (SP 107.7%) | | **5 Rn** |

**61.4 secs** (1.40) CSF £8.02 TOTE £3.70: £1.70 £1.10 (£2.40) OWNER Mr Bill Broomfield (CHICHESTER) BRED Ewar Stud Farm International

LONG HANDICAP Into Debt 7-5

WEIGHT FOR AGE 3yo-2lb

**2982 Pride of Hayling (IRE)**, unable to go the early pace, began her effort from below the distance and, swooping into the lead inside the final furlong, soon put daylight between her and her rivals. (11/4)
**3313 Mellors (IRE)** set a blistering pace. Eventually overhauled inside the final furlong, he was left standing by the winner. (2/1)
**3339* Hever Golf Express** disputed the lead from the start. Soon with every chance approaching the final furlong, he was then tapped for toe. (5/1)
**3313 Sharp Imp**, unable to go the early pace, picked up ground along the inside below the distance and, staying on, only just failed to take third. (5/2)

T/Plpt: £24.00 (386.18 Tckts). T/Qdpt: £6.70 (65.36 Tckts) AK

# 3348-PONTEFRACT (L-H) (Good to firm)
## Sunday August 18th
WEATHER: sunny & hot WIND: mod half against

## 3637 E.B.F. SUNDAY PLATE MAIDEN STKS (2-Y.O) (Class D)
2-15 (2-16) **5f** £4,162.50 (£1,260.00: £615.00: £292.50) Stalls: Low GOING minus 0.27 sec per fur (GF)

| | | | | SP | RR | SF |
|---|---|---|---|---|---|---|
| $3114^{4}$ | **A Breeze (79)** (DMorris) **2-9-0** KDarley(1) (lw: trckd ldrs: r.o wl to ld jst ins fnl f) | — | **1** | 4/1$^{2}$ | 82 | 12 |
| $2873^{4}$ | **Marylebone (IRE)** (JBerry) **2-9-0** JCarroll(8) (chsd ldr: rdn to ld over 1f out: sn hdd & nt qckn) | 2½ | **2** | 5/1$^{3}$ | 74 | 4 |
| | **Gaelic Storm** (MJohnston) **2-9-0** TWilliams(7) (w'like: bkwd: led: hung lft & hdd over 1f out: kpt on same pce) | 2 | **3** | 20/1 | 68 | — |
| | **Daring Flight (USA)** (LordHuntingdon) **2-9-0** WRyan(4) (w'like: scope: bit bkwd: trckd ldrs: kpt on wl fnl f) | hd | **4** | 11/4$^{1}$ | 67+ | — |
| $1626^{9}$ | **No Comment** (MBell) **2-9-0** MFenton(2) (s.i.s: bhd tl styd on wl ins fnl f) | 5 | **5** | 14/1 | 51+ | — |
| | **Chaluz** (MJohnston) **2-9-0** JWeaver(5) (cmpt: str: bit bkwd: s.i.s: hdwy ½-wy: wknd over 1f out) | 2½ | **6** | 11/2 | 43 | — |
| $3114^{14}$ | **Pow Wow** (MRChannon) **2-9-0** JFEgan(10) (prom: rdn over 2f out: sn wknd) | 2 | **7** | 16/1 | 37 | — |
| | **King Uno** (MrsJRRamsden) **2-9-0** KFallon(6) (w'like: scope: bit bkwd: s.i.s: a outpcd & bhd) | 1 | **8** | 9/1 | 34 | — |
| $2211^{6}$ | **Epic Stand** (MrsJRRamsden) **2-9-0** JFortune(3) (dwlt s: a bhd) | 1 | **9** | 16/1 | 31 | — |
| $3349^{10}$ | **Lucybod** (NTinkler) **2-8-9** LCharnock(9) (swtg: nvr wnt pce) | hd | **10** | 33/1 | 25 | — |
| | | | | (SP 114.9%) | **10 Rn** | |

**64.8 secs** (4.00) CSF £22.47 TOTE £4.90: £1.50 £1.50 £3.60 (£8.00) Trio £127.00 OWNER Bloomsbury Stud (NEWMARKET) BRED Bloomsbury Stud
**3114 A Breeze** was the paddock pick and tracked the leaders travelling strongly. In the end he did it in good style. (4/1)
**2873 Marylebone (IRE)** looked very fit but in the end, proved no match for the winner. (5/1)
**Gaelic Storm** showed a pronounced knee action going to post. After leading his rivals, he hung left as if feeling the fast ground. (20/1)
**Daring Flight (USA)**, looking in need of the outing, tracked the leaders and was not knocked about at any stage. He should come on a good deal. (11/4)
**No Comment** was carrying plenty of condition and stayed on late in the day. He looks capable of better especially over further. (14/1)
**Chaluz**, who looked badly in need of the outing, can be expected to do better over further. (11/2)

## 3638 MAGIC 828 (S) STKS (3-Y.O+) (Class F)
2-45 (2-48) **1m 4f 8y** £2,654.00 (£744.00: £362.00) Stalls: Low GOING minus 0.27 sec per fur (GF)

| | | | | SP | RR | SF |
|---|---|---|---|---|---|---|
| *3090** | **Another Quarter (IRE) (50)** (SPCWoods) **3-8-7** WRyan(6) (lw: b: mde all: rdn clr 2f out: unchal) | — | **1** | 5/4$^{1}$ | 52 | 23 |
| $2028^{6}$ | **Record Lover (IRE) (28)** (MCChapman) **6-9-8** KFallon(5) (rdn 5f out: n.m.r on ins over 2f out: styd on: no ch w wnr) | 5 | **2** | 6/1 | 50 | 31 |
| $3480^{4}$ | **Crambella (IRE)** (GPKelly) **4-8-7**(5) GParkin(7) (a chsng ldrs: one pce fnl 2f) | ¾ | **3** | 33/1 | 39 | 20 |
| $3412^{7}$ | **Bardia (28)** (DonEnricoIncisa) **6-8-12** KimTinkler(4) (s.i.s: hdwy to chse ldrs ½-wy: hrd rdn 3f out: wknd over 1f out) | 6 | **4** | 33/1 | 31 | 12 |
| $3443^{7}$ | **Willy Star (BEL) (52)** (MrsSJSmith) **6-9-3** PBloomfield(8) (swtg: chsd ldrs tl lost pl over 2f out) | 13 | **5** | 9/2$^{3}$ | 19 | — |
| $3507^{3}$ | **Genesis Four (43)** (MrsLStubbs) **6-9-3** JFEgan(1) (a bhd: lost tch over 3f out) | 25 | **6** | 13/2 | — | — |
| 3305* | **Fearless Wonder (51)** (MrsMReveley) **5-9-8** KDarley(2) (sn drvn along: hung bdly lft & virtually p.u over 1f out) | 7 | **7** | 3/1$^{2}$ | — | — |
| $2510^{10}$ | **Kulshi Momken** (JNorton) **3-8-7** DaleGibson(3) (plld hrd: trckd ldrs tl lost pl ½-wy: t.o 3f out) | 26 | **8** | 25/1 | — | — |
| | | | | (SP 125.0%) | **8 Rn** | |

**2m 41.7** (7.40) CSF £10.12 TOTE £2.50: £1.10 £1.80 £7.00 (£9.90) OWNER Mr S. P. C. Woods (NEWMARKET) BRED J. C. Fagan
WEIGHT FOR AGE 3yo-10lb
Sold AMann 6,100 gns
**OFFICIAL EXPLANATION Fearless Wonder: became disappointed when unable to make the running.**
**3090* Another Quarter (IRE)**, who has not shone over hurdles since her Southwell win, found this a relatively straightforward task. She changed hands at the auction. (5/4: op 2/1)
**208* Record Lover (IRE)**, tailed off in a test of stamina last time, stuck on to finish second best. (6/1)
**Crambella (IRE)** ran easily her best ever race. (33/1)
**1832 Bardia** has won only one of her forty three starts. (33/1)
**2941 Willy Star (BEL)** (9/2: op 3/1)
**3305* Fearless Wonder** was able to dominate at Catterick, but was not happy here and hung badly left as if something was amiss, until being almost pulled up. (3/1)

## 3639 STANLEY LEISURE H'CAP (0-85) (3-Y.O+) (Class D)
3-15 (3-18) **6f** £5,888.00 (£1,784.00: £872.00: £416.00) Stalls: Low GOING minus 0.27 sec per fur (GF)

| | | | | SP | RR | SF |
|---|---|---|---|---|---|---|
| $3223^{8}$ | **Formidable Liz (57)** (MDHammond) **6-8-5** KDarley(3) (trckd ldrs: effrt & swtchd over 1f out: styd on wl to ld ins fnl f) | — | **1** | 9/1 | 69 | 43 |
| 3489* | **Pageboy (64)** (PCHaslam) **7-8-12** 6x JFortune(4) (lw: trckd ldr: led over 1f out tl ins fnl f) | ½ | **2** | 6/1$^{3}$ | 75 | 49 |
| $3045^{5}$ | **Cim Bom Bom (IRE) (72)** (MBell) **4-8-13v**(7) GFaulkner(1) (prom: effrt & n.m.r on ins over 2f out: styd on same pce appr fnl f) | 2½ | **3** | 7/1 | 76 | 50 |
| $2911^{7}$ | **French Grit (IRE) (73)** (MDods) **4-9-7** AClark(2) (led tl over 1f out: one pce) | hd | **4** | 20/1 | 77 | 51 |
| 3152* | **Halmanerror (70)** (MrsJRRamsden) **6-9-4** KFallon(6) (lw: bhd: effrt on ins & hmpd over 2f out: swtchd outside over 1f out: styd on: nt rch ldrs) | 1¾ | **5** | 4/1$^{1}$ | 69 | 43 |

| | | | | SP | RR | SF |
|---|---|---|---|---|---|---|
| $3265^{6}$ | **Cretan Gift (69)** (NPLittmoden) **5-9-3b** TGMcLaughlin(12) (a in tch: kpt on same pce fnl 2f) | hd | **6** | 11/1 | 68 | 42 |
| $3328^{7}$ | **Barato (65)** (MrsJRRamsden) **5-8-6**(7) TFinn(5) (s.i.s: bhd: hdwy on ins whn hmpd over 2f out: kpt on fnl f) | s.h | **7** | 16/1 | 64 | 38 |
| $3106^{7}$ | **King Rat (IRE) (79)** (TJEtherington) **5-9-13b** WCarson(8) (chsd ldrs tl outpcd over 1f out) | 2 | **8** | 25/1 | 72 | 46 |
| $3440^{5}$ | **Champagne Grandy (80)** (MRChannon) **6-10-0** JFEgan(11) (lw: trckd ldrs: plld hrd: edgd lft over 2f out: sn wl outpcd) | 2½ | **9** | 20/1 | 67 | 41 |
| $3328^{3}$ | **Cavers Yangous (66)** (MJohnston) **5-9-0b**[1] JWeaver(13) (racd wd: a in rr) | 3½ | **10** | 8/1 | 43 | 17 |
| $3045^{7}$ | **Castlerea Lad (78)** (RHollinshead) **7-9-9**(3) FLynch(10) (s.i.s: sme hdwy over 2f out: sn wknd) | 3½ | **11** | 10/1 | 46 | 20 |
| *$3602^{15}$* | **Cheeky Chappy (75)** (DWChapman) **5-9-9b** JCarroll(9) (lw: bhd: effrt & sltly hmpd over 2f out: n.d) | 1 | **12** | 16/1 | 40 | 14 |
| 3453* | **Thwaab (65)** (FWatson) **4-8-13v** NKennedy(7) (s.i.s: a bhd) | 1 | **13** | 5/1 [2] | 28 | 2 |
| | | | | (SP 127.1%) | | **13 Rn** |

**1m 16.1** (1.80) CSF £61.37 CT £294.62 TOTE £11.10: £2.30 £2.60 £2.40 (£61.70) Trio £86.40 OWNER Mr J. Johnson (MIDDLEHAM) BRED S. M. Saud

**2937 Formidable Liz** bounced right back to her best and, in the end, did it in good style. (9/1)
**3489* Pageboy**, in peak form, almost made light of a 6lb penalty. (6/1)
**3045 Cim Bom Bom (IRE)**, tightened up by Champagne Grandy, caused a domino effect behind him. (7/1)
**716 French Grit (IRE)** showed bags of toe and ran his best race for some time. (20/1)
**3152* Halmanerror**, knocked back going into the turn, finished well after being switched wide. (4/1)
**3265 Cretan Gift** seemed to run right up to his best, but is more effective on Fibresand. (11/1)
**2524 Barato**, a frustrating individual, stuck on after being hampered. (16/1)
**King Rat (IRE)** ran his best race so far this time. He still looks a trifle high in the weights. (25/1)
**3453* Thwaab** is possibly best on a straight track and missed the break slightly. (5/1)

## 3640 ROTHMANS ROYALS NORTH SOUTH CHALLENGE SERIES H'CAP (0-90) (3-Y.O+) (Class C)

3-45 (3-48) **1m 4y** £7,685.00 (£2,330.00: £1,140.00: £545.00) Stalls: Low GOING minus 0.27 sec per fur (GF)

| | | | | SP | RR | SF |
|---|---|---|---|---|---|---|
| | **Awaamir (85)** (JHMGosden) **3-9-6** WCarson(2) (b: b.hind: trckd ldrs: led over 1f out: drvn out) | — | **1** | 15/8 [1] | 99 | 45 |
| $3279^{2}$ | **Hawksley Hill (IRE) (78)** (MrsJRRamsden) **3-8-13** KFallon(11) (hld up: hdwy over 2f out: ev ch & hung lft over 1f out: nt qckn) | 1¼ | **2** | 5/2 [2] | 90 | 36 |
| *$3627^{5}$* | **Maple Bay (IRE) (70)** (ABailey) **7-8-6**(5) PRoberts(3) (lw: trckd ldrs: n.m.r on ins over 1f out: styd on wl ins fnl f) | 1¼ | **3** | 20/1 | 79 | 31 |
| $3134^{6}$ | **Flying North (IRE) (76)** (MrsMReveley) **3-8-11** KDarley(5) (hld up & plld hrd: effrt over 2f out: kpt on same pce fnl f) | ½ | **4** | 20/1 | 84 | 30 |
| $3072^{2}$ | **Master Charter (83)** (MrsJRRamsden) **4-9-10** JFortune(4) (hld up & bhd: hdwy on ins 2f out: n.m.r & swtchd: styd on wl ins fnl f) | 2½ | **5** | 15/2 [3] | 86 | 38 |
| 3450* | **Gladys Althorpe (IRE) (63)** (JLEyre) **3-7-12** TWilliams(12) (w ldrs: chal over 2f out: rdn & wknd over 1f out) | 5 | **6** | 8/1 | 56 | 2 |
| $2145^{7}$ | **Access Adventurer (IRE) (72)** (RBoss) **5-8-13** JCarroll(9) (led tl over 1f out: sn wknd) | 1¼ | **7** | 16/1 | 63 | 15 |
| $2581^{8}$ | **Mo-Addab (IRE) (75)** (ACStewart) **6-9-2** WRyan(7) (mid div: effrt over 2f out: n.d) | 2 | **8** | 10/1 | 62 | 14 |
| $3255^{3}$ | **Portuguese Lil (76)** (DNicholls) **3-8-11** AlexGreaves(10) (nvr trbld ldrs) | 2 | **9** | 33/1 | 59 | 5 |
| 3051* | **Milford Sound (84)** (JRFanshawe) **3-9-5** NDay(8) (bhd: effrt on outside over 2f out: sn wknd) | hd | **10** | 10/1 | 66 | 12 |
| $3481^{6}$ | **Parliament Piece (63)** (DNicholls) **10-7-11b**(7) JBramhill(6) (in tch tl wknd over 1f out) | 9 | **11** | 33/1 | 27 | — |
| | | | | (SP 125.7%) | | **11 Rn** |

**1m 45.3** (3.80) CSF £7.36 CT £67.53 TOTE £3.00: £1.70 £1.50 £3.10 (£4.30) Trio £24.50 OWNER Mr Hamdan Al Maktoum (NEWMARKET) BRED Shadwell Estate Company Limited

WEIGHT FOR AGE 3yo-6lb

**Awaamir**, who had just two outings as a juvenile, took a keen grip in the early stages. She justified the market support in decisive fashion. (15/8)
**3279 Hawksley Hill (IRE)** ranged upsides looking a real danger going to the final furlong, but under pressure, he tended to hang left and did not do anything like as much as the winner. The Handicapper will have his measure now. (5/2)
**3627 Maple Bay (IRE)**, having his second outing in less than twenty-four hours, stuck on strongly at the finish after being chopped for room on the inner. (20/1)
**3134 Flying North (IRE)**, who needs to be settled, appreciated the drop back in distance but is proving hard to win with. (20/1)
**3072 Master Charter** certainly took the eye, finishing strongly after being switched. He looked third best on merit. (15/2: 5/1-8/1)
**3450* Gladys Althorpe (IRE)**, from a 5lb higher mark, called enough over a furlong out. (8/1)
**1190 Mo-Addab (IRE)** is slipping down the weights and did not shape badly at all. (10/1)

## 3641 'GO RACING IN YORKSHIRE' H'CAP (0-65) (3-Y.O+) (Class F)

4-15 (4-17) **2m 1f 22y** £2,738.00 (£768.00: £374.00) Stalls: Centre GOING minus 0.27 sec per fur (GF)

| | | | | SP | RR | SF |
|---|---|---|---|---|---|---|
| $2530^{4}$ | **Bellroi (IRE) (43)** (MHTompkins) **5-8-6** NDay(1) (chsd ldr: rdn to ld over 1f out: styd on strly) | — | **1** | 9/1 | 56 | 30 |
| $3329^{2}$ | **Forgie (IRE) (63)** (PCalver) **3-8-12** MBirch(2) (lw: sn trckng ldrs: kpt on same pce appr fnl f) | 2½ | **2** | 100/30 [2] | 74 | 34 |
| $2804^{6}$ | **Royal Vacation (53)** (GMMoore) **7-9-2** JFortune(3) (lw: led tl over 1f out: one pce) | 3½ | **3** | 12/1 | 60 | 34 |
| $1611^{4}$ | **Mondragon (65)** (MrsMReveley) **6-10-0** KDarley(4) (hld up: hdwy 7f out: rdn 3f out: sn wknd) | 10 | **4** | 9/2 [3] | 63 | 37 |
| $3335^{12}$ | **Kindred Greeting (33)** (JAHarris) **4-7-10b** JO'Reilly(7) (hdwy to chse ldrs ½-wy: outpcd 5f out: wknd over 2f out) | 1¾ | **5** | 16/1 | 29 | 3 |
| *$169^{8}$* | **Pride of May (IRE) (53)** (CWFairhurst) **5-9-2** WCarson(8) (chsd ldrs: sn drvn along: lost pl ½-wy: t.o 4f out) | 22 | **6** | 14/1 | 29 | 3 |
| $2866^{2}$ | **Mock Trial (IRE) (65)** (MrsJRRamsden) **3-9-0** KFallon(5) (hld up: hdwy 7f out: rdn over 3f out: no rspnse & eased) | 2 | **7** | 5/4 [1] | 39 | — |
| | | | | (SP 115.9%) | | **7 Rn** |

**3m 48.2** (8.70) CSF £37.28 CT £334.33 TOTE £11.10: £3.50 £2.70 (£14.60) OWNER Mrs G. A. E. Smith (NEWMARKET) BRED Mrs K. Twomey and Mrs S. O'Riordan

LONG HANDICAP Kindred Greeting 7-9

WEIGHT FOR AGE 3yo-14lb

OFFICIAL EXPLANATION **Mock Trial (IRE): was having his first race beyond twelve furlongs and his trainer considered he had not stayed.**

**2530 Bellroi (IRE)**, a winning hurdler, just stays and stays. He will now be switched back over timber. (9/1: 6/1-10/1)
**3329 Forgie (IRE)**, raised 4lb, in the end was outstayed by the winner. (100/30)
**2804 Royal Vacation** seemed to set a strong gallop but had to give best with over a furlong left to go. (12/1)
**1611 Mondragon** put in another poor effort. (9/2)
**2866 Mock Trial (IRE)**, as usual, was stewed up beforehand. He moved up travelling strongly at halfway, but came under pressure just under half a mile from home. Finding nothing, he was eased right up. It would be dangerous to say he does not stay on this effort. (5/4: Evens-6/4)

## 3642 KIDS COME FREE MAIDEN STKS (3-Y.O+) (Class D)

4-45 (4-46) **1m 4y** £3,647.50 (£1,105.00: £540.00: £257.50) Stalls: Low GOING minus 0.27 sec per fur (GF)

| | | | SP | RR | SF |
|---|---|---|---|---|---|
| 3353$^{2}$ | **Glen Parker (IRE) (76)** (HRACecil) **3-8-12** WRyan(1) (trckd ldr gng wl: led over 1f out: pushed clr) ............— | **1** | 8/13$^{1}$ | 79 | 21 |
| 3413$^{3}$ | **Mighty Keen** (MJohnston) **3-8-12** JWeaver(9) (led tl over 1f out: no ch w wnr) ............7 | **2** | 5/1$^{3}$ | 65 | 7 |
| 962$^{11}$ | **White Hare** (MrsMReveley) **3-8-7** KDarley(4) (bit bkwd: sn trckng ldrs: kpt on same pce fnl 2f) ............4 | **3** | 50/1 | 52 | — |
| 3226$^{2}$ | **Vanadium Ore** (JLEyre) **3-8-12** JFortune(6) (chsd ldrs: outpcd over 2f out: kpt on appr fnl f) ............1½ | **4** | 100/30$^{2}$ | 54 | — |
| 1670$^{10}$ | **Nexsis Star** (MrsSJSmith) **3-8-12** PBloomfield(2) (dwlt s: hld up: hdwy ½-wy: wknd over 1f out) ............nk | **5** | 50/1 | 54 | — |
| 3298$^{5}$ | **Indiana Princess** (MrsMReveley) **3-8-7** ACulhane(7) (sn trckng ldrs: outpcd over 2f out: n.d after) ............1¼ | **6** | 20/1 | 46 | — |
| 1608$^{14}$ | **Skylight** (MissMKMilligan) **3-8-12** JFanning(5) (s.i.s: hdwy on outside ½-wy: hung lft & lost pl over 1f out)......7 | **7** | 66/1 | 37 | — |
| | **Grand Popo** (SEKettlewell) **3-8-12** NRodgers(3) (leggy: unf: bhd & drvn along 4f out) ............½ | **8** | 33/1 | 36 | — |
| 3413$^{6}$ | **Rupert Manners** (EJAlston) **3-8-12** JLowe(8) (plld hrd: trckd ldrs tl lost pl over 3f out: sn bhd: t.o) ............dist | **9** | 66/1 | — | — |

(SP 116.3%) **9 Rn**

**1m 47.1** (5.60) CSF £4.35 TOTE £1.70: £1.10 £1.50 £3.90 (£2.30) Trio £27.00 OWNER Angus Dundee Plc (NEWMARKET) BRED T. Hillman

**3353 Glen Parker (IRE)** was found an easy opportunity and did it with the minimum of fuss. (8/13)
**3413 Mighty Keen**, stepping up a furlong, made the running but it was obvious some way out that he was only the hare. (5/1)
**White Hare** still looked in need of the outing, and was asked to do just enough to finish third. With another outing, she will be qualified for handicaps. (50/1)
**3226 Vanadium Ore** was another who seemed to be ridden with his long-term future in mind. (100/30)

## 3643 FAMILY DAY H'CAP (0-65) (3-Y.O+) (Class F)

5-15 (5-16) **5f** £2,822.00 (£792.00: £386.00) Stalls: Low GOING minus 0.27 sec per fur (GF)

| | | | SP | RR | SF |
|---|---|---|---|---|---|
| 3415* | **Kira (63)** (JLEyre) **6-9-9**(3) OPears(1) (lw: b.off hind: mde all: qcknd clr over 1f out: hld on wl towards fin) ............— | **1** | 3/1$^{2}$ | 71 | 40 |
| 3465$^{3}$ | **Oatey (60)** (MrsJRRamsden) **3-9-7** KFallon(10) (lw: hld up: hdwy ½-wy: chsd wnr over 1f out: kpt on wl)........¾ | **2** | 2/1$^{1}$ | 66 | 33 |
| 3482$^{6}$ | **Ned's Bonanza (62)** (MDods) **7-9-11** AClark(6) (in tch: outpcd ½-wy: styd on fnl f: fin 4th, 1 3/4l: plcd 3rd)........ | **3** | 8/1 | 52 | 21 |
| 3482$^{3}$ | **Just Dissident (IRE) (57)** (RMWhitaker) **4-9-6** DeanMcKeown(7) (sn chsng ldr: wknd over 1f out: fin 5th, 1l: plcd 4th)............ | **4** | 7/1$^{3}$ | 44 | 13 |
| 3453$^{6}$ | **Ragazzo (IRE) (33)** (JSWainwright) **6-7-10b** LCharnock(3) (lw: bhd: sme hdwy over 1f out: nvr nr to chal: fin 6th, 13/4l: plcd 5th)............ | **5** | 50/1 | 15 | — |
| 3360$^{6}$ | **Lady Caroline Lamb (IRE) (64)** (RBastiman) **3-9-6**(5) HBastiman(8) (hld up: nt clr run on ins 3f out: hdwy over 1f out: nvr nr to chal)............1½ | **7** | 14/1 | 41 | 8 |
| 3292$^{7}$ | **Katy-Q (IRE) (49)** (PCalver) **3-8-3b**(7) JBramhill(4) (lw: chsd ldrs tl wknd over 1f out)............nk | **8** | 25/1 | 25 | — |
| 3294$^{11}$ | **First Option (33)** (RBastiman) **6-7-10** JLowe(2) (t: in tch: wkng whn hmpd 1f out)............¾ | **9** | 33/1 | 6 | — |
| 3352$^{6}$ | **Kabcast (45)** (DWChapman) **11-8-8b** KDarley(12) (chsd ldrs: rdn ½-wy: lost pl over 1f out)............s.h | **10** | 14/1 | 18 | — |
| 3453$^{9}$ | **Tutu Sixtysix (33)** (DonEnricoIncisa) **5-7-10b** KimTinkler(13) (s.i.s: sme hdwy & hrd rdn over 2f out: sn wknd)............1½ | **11** | 50/1 | 2 | — |
| 3310$^{7}$ | **China Hand (IRE) (37)** (MartynWane) **4-8-0**ow2 JFanning(5) (chsd ldrs tl wknd over 2f out) ............2 | **12** | 25/1 | — | — |
| 3453$^{7}$ | **Mu-Arrik (36)** (GROldroyd) **8-7-13v** DaleGibson(11) (a in rr)............6 | **13** | 33/1 | — | — |
| 3352$^{4}$ | **Sonderise (53)** (NTinkler) **7-9-2** JWeaver(9) (hld up: hdwy ½-wy: swtchd lft over 1f out: kpt on: fin 3rd, 3l: disq: plcd last) ............ | **D** | 15/2 | 49 | 18 |

(SP 124.5%) **13 Rn**

**63.7 secs** (2.90) CSF £9.38 CT £42.27 TOTE £3.90: £1.60 £1.70 £2.50 (£3.30) Trio £13.20 OWNER Mr J. E. Wilson (HAMBLETON) BRED J. S. Bell

LONG HANDICAP First Option 7-7 Ragazzo (IRE) 7-2 Tutu Sixtysix 7-3
WEIGHT FOR AGE 3yo-2lb
STEWARDS' ENQUIRY Weaver referred to Portman Square (irresponsible riding).

**3415* Kira**, best drawn, was out of the stalls in a flash and never looked in any real danger of being overhauled. (3/1)
**3465 Oatey** went in pursuit of the winner once in line for home. Sticking on strongly, she finished clear second best. She is likely to go up in the weights now, so hopefully a win is on the cards soon. (2/1)
**3482 Ned's Bonanza** ran with more sparkle than at Beverley last time. (8/1)
**3482 Just Dissident (IRE)** was never able to dominate and called it a day once in line for home. (7/1)
**3352 Sonderise** was switched violently left coming to the final furlong, hampering the weakening First Option. His rider takes chances at times. (15/2)

T/Jkpt: Not won; £2,786.22 to Windsor 19/8/96. T/Plpt: £111.60 (156.17 Tckts). T/Qdpt: £18.40 (55.33 Tckts) WG

# 3487-HAMILTON (R-H) (Good to firm, Firm patches)

## Monday August 19th

WEATHER: overcast & rain later WIND: almost nil

## 3644 STOATER APPRENTICE H'CAP (0-70) (3-Y.O+) (Class E)

2-15 (2-15) **6f 5y** £3,290.70 (£996.60: £486.80: £231.90) Stalls: Low GOING minus 0.62 sec per fur (F)

| | | | SP | RR | SF |
|---|---|---|---|---|---|
| 3139$^{13}$ | **Another Nightmare (IRE) (39)** (RMMcKellar) **4-7-10**(5) KSked(1) (hung rt most of wy: a.p: led wl over 1f out: r.o wl)............— | **1** | 6/1$^{3}$ | 54 | 32 |
| 3489$^{5}$ | **Naissant (65)** (RMMcKellar) **3-9-5**(5) JEdmunds(10) (prom: styd on fnl 2f: no ch w wnr) ............4 | **2** | 66/1 | 69 | 44 |
| 3345* | **Leading Princess (IRE) (52)** (MissLAPerratt) **5-8-9b**(5) AngelaGallimore(11) (lw: led & sn clr: hdd wl over 1f out: no ex)............s.h | **3** | 8/1 | 56 | 34 |
| *3420** | **Ultra Beet (61)** (PCHaslam) **4-9-9v** SDrowne(6) (cl up: rdn 2f out: r.o one pce)............3½ | **4** | 7/2$^{1}$ | 56 | 34 |
| 3489$^{4}$ | **Tropical Beach (66)** (JBerry) **3-9-6**(5) CLowther(8) (sn pushed along: hdwy & prom ½-wy: no imp)............2 | **5** | 13/2 | 56 | 31 |
| 3443$^{3}$ | **Roseate Lodge (46)** (SEKettlewell) **10-8-3**(5) JennyBenson(4) (outpcd & bhd tl styd on appr fnl f)............2 | **6** | 9/1 | 30 | 8 |
| 3339$^{4}$ | **Members Welcome (IRE) (52)** (JMBradley) **3-8-8v**(3) AEddery(7) (nvr trbld ldrs)............1 | **7** | 7/1 | 34 | 9 |
| 3424$^{8}$ | **Sunday Mail Too (IRE) (49)** (MissLAPerratt) **4-8-11** RHavlin(5) (chsd ldrs 4f)............¾ | **8** | 9/1 | 29 | 7 |
| 3301$^{4}$ | **Oriel Lad (65)** (PDEvans) **3-9-10b** CTeague(2) (lw: a outpcd & bhd)............1¼ | **9** | 11/2$^{2}$ | 41 | 16 |
| 3310$^{6}$ | **Samsung Lovelylady (IRE) (38)** (EWeymes) **4-8-0** DarrenMoffatt(9) (swtg: prom to ½-wy: sn outpcd) ............7 | **10** | 9/1 | — | — |

| | | | | SP | RR | SF |
|---|---|---|---|---|---|---|
| $3414^{8}$ | **Backhander (IRE) (44)** (MartynWane) **4-8-6b** PRoberts(3) (chsd ldrs 4f: wknd) | 1¾ | **11** | 20/1 | — | — |

(SP 125.1%) **11 Rn**

**1m 10.0** (0.00) CSF £225.82 CT £2,980.38 TOTE £7.30: £2.60 £8.40 £3.70 (£150.90) Trio £185.50; £209.07 to York 20/8/96 OWNER GM Engineering (LESMAHAGOW) BRED John J. Ryan

WEIGHT FOR AGE 3yo-3lb

**2962 Another Nightmare (IRE)**, although continually hanging right, was given a fine ride and was well on top in the closing stages. This would seem to be her ideal trip. (6/1)

**3489 Naissant** is improving and, by the way she kept staying on, a little further might help. (66/1)

**3345* Leading Princess (IRE)** showed tremendous early speed to lead by several lengths, but she is pretty high in the handicap just now and the effort proved too much approaching the final furlong. (8/1)

**3420* Ultra Beet** had his chances but that spark was never there when the pressure was on. (7/2)

**3489 Tropical Beach** was always having to work to improve and the effort proved too much from halfway. (13/2)

**3443 Roseate Lodge** is in good heart and, after being left way behind and completely outpaced in the early stages, did finish well. Over a bit further, he can win again. (9/1)

**3301 Oriel Lad** (11/2: 4/1-6/1)

## 3645 STARFORM (S) H'CAP (0-60) (3-Y.O+) (Class G)

2-45 (2-46) **1m 1f 36y** £2,458.00 (£688.00: £334.00) Stalls: High GOING minus 0.62 sec per fur (F)

| | | | | SP | RR | SF |
|---|---|---|---|---|---|---|
| $3427^{10}$ | **Mystic Times (31)** (BMactaggart) **3-8-3** JQuinn(8) (prom: styd on u.p to ld ins fnl f) | — | **1** | 14/1 | 43 | 18 |
| $3287^{5}$ | **Never so True (33)** (MartynWane) **5-8-12** JCarroll(13) (led: clr 6f out: hdd & no ex ins fnl f) | 1¼ | **2** | 14/1 | 43 | 25 |
| $3460^{10}$ | **Moofaji (39)** (FWatson) **5-8-13**(5) RHavlin(6) (chsd ldrs: hung rt & outpcd 3f out: styd on fnl f) | 2 | **3** | 50/1 | 45 | 27 |
| $3492^{3}$ | **Seconds Away (29)** (JSGoldie) **5-8-8** TWilliams(2) (hld up: hdwy 4f out: chsng ldrs appr fnl f: sn btn) | hd | **4** | 13/2 3 | 35 | 17 |
| $2801^{7}$ | **Brambles Way (42)** (MrsMReveley) **7-9-7v** KDarley(10) (in tch: hdwy 3f out: one pce fnl 2f) | 1 | **5** | 7/1 | 46 | 28 |
| *$3435^{7}$* | **Zahran (IRE) (38)** (JMBradley) **5-9-3v** JWeaver(7) (b: bhd & rdn 4f out: styd on: n.d) | 5 | **6** | 5/1 1 | 34 | 16 |
| $3257^{13}$ | **Elite Racing (36)** (NTinkler) **4-9-1** LCharnock(11) (lw: chsd ldrs: stumbled 7f out: wknd fnl 3f) | 1 | **7** | 25/1 | 30 | 12 |
| $2056^{8}$ | **Absolute Ruler (IRE) (38)** (JLHarris) **5-9-3b** GDuffield(4) (lw: in tch: rdn over 3f out: sn btn) | 1 | **8** | 7/1 | 30 | 12 |
| $3242^{6}$ | **Funny Rose (23)** (PMonteith) **6-8-2** AMackay(5) (lw: bhd: effrt ½-wy: n.d) | ¾ | **9** | 10/1 | 14 | — |
| $3257^{5}$ | **Return To Brighton (45)** (JMBradley) **4-9-3**(7) AEddery(9) (bhd: rdn 4f out: n.d) | 1¾ | **10** | 11/2 2 | 33 | 15 |
| $3592^{9}$ | **Mill Dancer (IRE) (33)** (EJAlston) **4-8-12** SDrowne(3) (chsd ldrs tl rdn & wknd fnl 4f) | 5 | **11** | 15/2 | 12 | — |
| $1474^{13}$ | **Care And Comfort (44)** (GMMoore) **4-9-9** JFortune(1) (bhd & rdn 5f out: n.d) | 1¾ | **12** | 33/1 | 20 | 2 |
| $2868^{11}$ | **Larn Fort (44)** (CWFairhurst) **6-9-9v** DeanMcKeown(12) (b: s.i.s: a bhd: lame) | 7 | **13** | 14/1 | 8 | — |

(SP 120.0%) **13 Rn**

**1m 56.7** (2.40) CSF £173.60 CT £8,345.35 TOTE £40.70: £8.20 £4.30 £9.30 (£236.50) Trio Not won; £200.35 to York 20/8/96 OWNER Colin Barnfather and Frank Steele (HAWICK) BRED Miss S. E. Hall

WEIGHT FOR AGE 3yo-7lb

No bid

**OFFICIAL EXPLANATION Larn Fort: was found to be lame on his near fore.**

**Mystic Times** appreciated this step up in distance, and the further she went, the stronger she got. (14/1: 12/1-25/1)

**3287 Never so True** goes well on this track and, adopting her usual front-running tactics, had her rivals in trouble until running out of steam inside the last furlong. (14/1)

**Moofaji** was inclined to hang when the pressure was on halfway up the straight, but to his credit, he did stay on at the finish. (50/1)

**3492 Seconds Away** did his usual at this trip and flattered only to deceive entering the last two furlongs. (13/2)

**1538 Brambles Way** has yet to win a race and, once the pressure was on in the last half-mile, there were no positive signs here. (7/1: op 9/2)

**3000 Zahran (IRE)** won this last year, but at present, his attitude seems to have got the better of him. (5/1)

**2682 Funny Rose** (10/1: 8/1-14/1)

**70 Larn Fort** (14/1: op 7/1)

## 3646 CAPTAIN J. C. STEWART MEMORIAL H'CAP (0-75) (3-Y.O+) (Class D)

3-15 (3-20) **1m 65y** £3,838.20 (£1,161.60: £566.80: £269.40) Stalls: High GOING minus 0.62 sec per fur (F)

| | | | | SP | RR | SF |
|---|---|---|---|---|---|---|
| $3340^{8}$ | **Sooty Tern (62)** (JMBradley) **9-9-4** JWeaver(5) (lw: trckd ldrs gng wl: led over 1f out: rdn & r.o) | — | **1** | 7/1 | 80 | 48 |
| $3344^{9}$ | **King Curan (USA) (59)** (DHaydnJones) **5-9-1b** AMackay(6) (lw: led tl hdd over 1f out: kpt on one pce) | 3 | **2** | 7/1 | 71 | 39 |
| 3279* | **Impulsive Air (IRE) (63)** (EWeymes) **4-9-5** JQuinn(1) (hdwy ½-wy: chsng ldrs 2f out: rdn & r.o one pce) | 8 | **3** | 4/1 1 | 60 | 28 |
| $3111^{14}$ | **Talented Ting (IRE) (55)** (PCHaslam) **7-8-11v** JFortune(9) (pushed along after s: hdwy 3f out: nvr able to chal) | 2½ | **4** | 10/1 | 47 | 15 |
| $3346^{7}$ | **Rapid Mover (43)** (DANolan) **9-7-6b**(7)ow3 KSked(2) (outpcd & bhd tl sme late hdwy) | 3½ | **5** | 100/1 | 28 | — |
| $3344^{12}$ | **Raased (42)** (FWatson) **4-7-12** NKennedy(4) (chsd ldrs tl rdn & wknd fnl 3f) | s.h | **6** | 16/1 | 27 | — |
| $3623^{7}$ | **Nordic Breeze (IRE) (71)** (ABailey) **4-9-8v**(5) PRoberts(8) (in tch: effrt over 3f out: wknd over 2f out) | 1 | **7** | 11/2 3 | 54 | 22 |
| $3426^{4}$ | **Highspeed (IRE) (59)** (SEKettlewell) **4-9-1** KDarley(7) (hld up: effrt over 3f out: sn rdn & btn) | ½ | **8** | 5/1 2 | 41 | 9 |
| $3344^{2}$ | **Bold Amusement (72)** (WSCunningham) **6-9-9b**(5) RHavlin(3) (lw: in tch tl rdn & wknd 3f out) | 6 | **9** | 11/2 3 | 43 | 11 |

(SP 108.4%) **9 Rn**

**1m 44.6** (0.50) CSF £47.09 CT £180.62 TOTE £10.80: £2.70 £3.90 £1.10 (£25.20) Trio £59.40 OWNER Mr J. M. Bradley (CHEPSTOW) BRED Sheikh Mohammed bin Rashid al Maktoum

LONG HANDICAP Rapid Mover 7-0

**OFFICIAL EXPLANATION Raased: finished lame.**

**Bold Amusement: lost his action early and was never travelling.**

**3120 Sooty Tern** loves this track and, always travelling particularly well, won with a fair amount of ease to gain his fourth course victory. (7/1)

**2954 King Curan (USA)**, driven into the lead from the start, showed more enthusiasm this time but was completely outclassed in the final furlong. (7/1)

**3279* Impulsive Air (IRE)** was pretty warm beforehand, but still ran reasonably until finding things too tough in the last furlong and a half. (4/1)

**2678 Talented Ting (IRE)**, with the visor back on, never really fired and failed to get the lead as he likes to, but he did show something, making a little progress in the straight, and may be coming back to form. (10/1)

**3242 Rapid Mover** found this trip too sharp and was struggling in behind until making a little late headway. (100/1)

**1866 Raased** again gave problems aplenty before the start and then showed little in the race once pressure was applied. (16/1)

**3426 Highspeed (IRE)** was disappointing here and was probably not suited by the track. (5/1)

## 3647 E.B.F. DAILY STAR OF SCOTLAND MAIDEN STKS (2-Y.O) (Class D)
3-45 (3-46) **6f 5y** £3,468.75 (£1,050.00: £512.50: £243.75) Stalls: Low GOING minus 0.62 sec per fur (F)

| | | | | SP | RR | SF |
|---|---|---|---|---|---|---|
| 3433[3] | **All Is Fair** (SirMarkPrescott) **2-8-9** GDuffield(5) (lw: led after 1f: qcknd ½-wy: pushed along & r.o appr fnl f) | — | **1** | 5/2[3] | 76 | — |
| | **Dazzling Stone** (MRStoute) **2-9-0** KDarley(2) (w'like: scope: trckd ldrs: rdn & rn green 2f out: r.o towards fin) | ¾ | **2** | 2/1[2] | 79+ | 2 |
| 3080[2] | **Pericles** (MJohnston) **2-9-0** JWeaver(4) (lw: led 1f: cl up: rdn 2f out: nt qckn) | 2 | **3** | 13/8[1] | 74 | — |
| 3080[8] | **Hong Kong Express (IRE) (68)** (JBerry) **2-8-9** JCarroll(3) (cl up tl outpcd fnl 2f) | 3½ | **4** | 50/1 | 59 | — |
| 2681[4] | **The Four Isles (66)** (DHaydnJones) **2-9-0** AMackay(1) (bhd: rdn ½-wy: no imp) | 2½ | **5** | 16/1 | 58 | — |
| | | | | (SP 107.8%) | **5 Rn** | |

**1m 13.1** (3.10) CSF £7.34 TOTE £2.80: £1.10 £1.40 (£2.20) OWNER Miss K. Rausing (NEWMARKET) BRED Miss K. RAUSING

**3433 All Is Fair**, a decent type, won this well and should have learnt plenty. Better is likely, especially over further. (5/2: 6/4-11/4)
**Dazzling Stone** stuck his head up and did not know what to do when the pressure was on, but he was certainly getting the hang of things in the closing stages, and should be much the better for this. (2/1)
**3080 Pericles** is still learning what the game is about and this should have brought him on plenty. (13/8)
**2727 Hong Kong Express (IRE)** again failed to impress on looks but she ran well enough to suggest that a race can be found. (50/1)
**2681 The Four Isles** never showed at any stage and may have got his own ideas about the game. (16/1)

## 3648 MAC THE KNIFE CLAIMING STKS (2-Y.O) (Class F)
4-15 (4-15) **6f 5y** £2,549.00 (£714.00: £347.00) Stalls: Low GOING minus 0.62 sec per fur (F)

| | | | | SP | RR | SF |
|---|---|---|---|---|---|---|
| 3343[5] | **Contravene (IRE) (52)** (JBerry) **2-8-6** JCarroll(6) (mde all: kpt on u.p fnl f) | — | **1** | 14/1 | 66 | 2 |
| *1080*[6] | **I'm Still Here** (JBerry) **2-8-6**(5) PRoberts(5) (trckd ldrs: effrt 2f out: nt qckn ins fnl f) | 1¼ | **2** | 16/1 | 68 | 4 |
| *3087*[4] | **Lycius Touch (57)** (MJohnston) **2-8-8** JWeaver(1) (bhd: effrt 2f out: styd on strly towards fin) | s.h | **3** | 12/1[3] | 65 | 1 |
| 3576* | **Abstone Queen (57)** (PDEvans) **2-8-2v** TWilliams(7) (lw: sn pushed along: styd on fnl 2f: nrst fin) | 2 | **4** | 9/4[1] | 53 | — |
| 3455* | **Jingoist (IRE) (53)** (JLHarris) **2-8-4b** KDarley(3) (cl up: effrt 2f out: wknd appr fnl f) | ½ | **5** | 9/4[1] | 54 | — |
| 3121[5] | **Scotmail Lass** (GMMoore) **2-8-0** DaleGibson(2) (chsd ldrs: rdn & edgd rt ½-wy: wknd fnl 2f) | 5 | **6** | 7/2[2] | 37 | — |
| 2872[6] | **Cantsaynowt (40)** (RMMcKellar) **2-8-6** DeanMcKeown(4) (chsd ldrs 4f: sn outpcd) | 1 | **7** | 40/1 | 40 | — |
| 3330[4] | **Silent Wells (53)** (JJQuinn) **2-8-2** JQuinn(8) (b.nr hind: sn bhd) | 6 | **8** | 16/1 | 20 | — |
| | | | | (SP 112.3%) | **8 Rn** | |

**1m 12.6** (2.60) CSF £166.41 TOTE £11.70: £3.20 £3.00 £2.70 (£20.00) OWNER Mr William Burns (COCKERHAM) BRED E. O'Leary

**3343 Contravene (IRE)** got her own way out in front and held on well. (14/1: op 8/1)
**1080 I'm Still Here**, returning from a three month lay-off, ran quite well and should be all the better for it. (16/1)
**3087 Lycius Touch** either needs further, or easier ground as she finished fast but always too late. (12/1: op 6/1)
**3576* Abstone Queen** was never happy on this occasion and failed to land a blow. (9/4)
**3455* Jingoist (IRE)**, looking very lean, ran fast but threw in the towel once real pressure was on over a furlong out. (9/4)
**3121 Scotmail Lass** ran most disappointingly, dropping away tamely in the last couple of furlongs. (7/2)

## 3649 SCOTLAND THE RAVE H'CAP (0-70) (3-Y.O+) (Class E)
4-45 (4-45) **1m 4f 17y** £3,283.20 (£993.60: £484.80: £230.40) Stalls: High GOING minus 0.62 sec per fur (F)

| | | | | SP | RR | SF |
|---|---|---|---|---|---|---|
| 3487[2] | **Mentalasanythin (64)** (DHaydnJones) **7-10-0** AMackay(7) (trckd ldrs: led & qcknd over 3f out: r.o) | — | **1** | 7/4[1] | 75 | 35 |
| 3487[6] | **Lord Advocate (50)** (DANolan) **8-8-7b**(7) KSked(2) (led tl hdd over 3f out: kpt on wl) | 2½ | **2** | 25/1 | 58 | 18 |
| *3419*[3] | **China Castle (53)** (PCHaslam) **3-8-7** JFortune(1) (hld up: hdwy 3f out: sn rdn: styd on: nt pce to chal) | ½ | **3** | 4/1[2] | 60 | 10 |
| 3587[4] | **Ambidextrous (IRE) (54)** (EJAlston) **4-9-4** SDrowne(6) (lw: bhd: hdwy 4f out: chsng ldrs 2f out: nt qckn) | 2½ | **4** | 5/1[3] | 58 | 18 |
| 3113[3] | **Nothing Doing (IRE) (36)** (WJMusson) **7-8-0** TWilliams(8) (trckd ldrs: effrt 3f out: no imp whn hmpd appr fnl f) | 1¾ | **5** | 5/1[3] | 37 | — |
| 3297[4] | **Here Comes Herbie (39)** (WStorey) **4-8-3** NKennedy(5) (in tch: effrt 4f out: btn over 2f out) | 3 | **6** | 9/1 | 36 | — |
| 3487[7] | **Rossel (USA) (65)** (PMonteith) **3-9-0**(5) PRoberts(3) (cl up tl wknd fnl 2½f) | 1¼ | **7** | 33/1 | 61 | 11 |
| 3575[5] | **Jabaroot (IRE) (32)** (RMMcKellar) **5-7-3**(7) JennyBenson(4) (b.hind: a bhd) | 3½ | **8** | 33/1 | 23 | — |
| | | | | (SP 109.4%) | **8 Rn** | |

**2m 36.2** (4.20) CSF £33.22 CT £128.09 TOTE £2.10: £1.30 £3.10 £1.50 (£10.80) OWNER Mr Hugh O'Donnell (PONTYPRIDD) BRED R. B. Warren
LONG HANDICAP Jabaroot (IRE) 6-13
WEIGHT FOR AGE 3yo-10lb

**3487 Mentalasanythin** gained his sixth course win here and, given a most positive ride, did it well. (7/4)
**3487 Lord Advocate** basically did not go fast enough early on and, after being headed, was staying on well at the end. (25/1)
**3419 China Castle** has yet to win on turf but he did show enough to suggest that it can be rectified. (4/1)
**3587 Ambidextrous (IRE)** needed a stronger early pace than was set here. (5/1)
**3113 Nothing Doing (IRE)** has the ability to do better but needs to be in the right mood. (5/1)
**3297 Here Comes Herbie** (9/1: op 11/2)

T/Plpt: £2,100.90 (5.49 Tckts). T/Qdpt: £25.20 (46.5 Tckts) AA

# 3454-LEICESTER (R-H) (Good to firm)
## Monday August 19th
WEATHER: fine & v.warm WIND: slt half bhd

## 3650 POINTON YORK LIMITED STKS (0-65) (3-Y.O+) (Class F)
5-40 (5-41) **7f 9y** £2,809.40 (£778.40: £372.20) Stalls: High GOING minus 0.48 sec per fur (F)

| | | | | SP | RR | SF |
|---|---|---|---|---|---|---|
| 2968[2] | **Dummer Golf Time (63)** (LordHuntingdon) **3-8-11v** DHarrison(2) (trckd ldrs: hdwy to ld ins fnl f: sn clr) | — | **1** | 9/4[1] | 69 | 33 |
| 3219[8] | **Safey Ana (USA) (60)** (BHanbury) **5-9-2** JStack(3) (b: a.p: led 2f out tl hdd & no ex ins fnl f) | 2 | **2** | 4/1[2] | 65 | 34 |
| 3410* | **Perilous Plight (60)** (MrsLStubbs) **5-9-11** JFEgan(4) (trckd ldrs: effrt & hrd drvn 2f out: kpt on one pce) | 1½ | **3** | 11/1 | 70 | 39 |
| *3063*[4] | **Whispered Melody (65)** (PWHarris) **3-8-8** JReid(6) (w ldr: shkn up 2f out: outpcd fnl f) | nk | **4** | 9/2[3] | 57 | 21 |
| 2598[8] | **Missile Toe (IRE) (63)** (JEBanks) **3-8-11** MWigham(1) (lw: hld up: hdwy over 2f out: sn rdn: nt pce to chal) | 1¾ | **5** | 8/1 | 56 | 20 |

| | | SP | RR | SF |
|---|---|---|---|---|
| 3101[5] **Encore M'Lady (IRE) (61)** (FHLee) **5-9-5** RCochrane(9) (stdd s: effrt & hrd drvn 2f out: no imp).......................6 | **6** | 12/1 | 46 | 15 |
| 492[3] **Quinntessa (53)** (BPalling) **3-8-8** TSprake(7) (swtg: mde most for 5f: sn rdn & wknd) ..................................3½ | **7** | 25/1 | 32 | — |
| 2049[15] **Inaminit (62)** (HJCollingridge) **3-8-11** FNorton(5) (dwlt: rdn 3f out: no imp) ..........................................................6 | **8** | 16/1 | 21 | — |
| 3592[3] **Duke Valentino (58)** (RHollinshead) **4-8-13**(3) FLynch(8) (swtg: hld up in tch: reminders over 2f out: sn lost pl) .........................................................................................................................................2½ | **9** | 8/1 | 16 | — |
| | | (SP 116.9%) | **9 Rn** | |

**1m 24.8** (1.80) CSF £11.37 TOTE £3.00: £1.60 £1.10 £2.60 (£6.80) Trio £19.30 OWNER Coriolan Partnership (WEST ILSLEY) BRED R. M. Whitaker

WEIGHT FOR AGE 3yo-5lb

**2968 Dummer Golf Time** made amends for a narrow defeat here a month ago with a smooth victory and he would seem to be thriving. (9/4)

**Safey Ana (USA)**, well supported in the ring, did not relish this lively ground but he gave his followers a good run for their money. (4/1: op 6/1)

**3410* Perilous Plight**, having his first outing since changing stables, ran extremely well in this step up in class and he could prove a good buy. (11/1)

**3063 Whispered Melody**, stepping back in distance, pressed the leaders and had every chance until getting outpaced inside the distance. (9/2: 5/2-5/1)

**1905 Missile Toe (IRE)**, restrained off the pace on this attempt at a longer trip, began a forward move entering the final quarter-mile but could not muster the pace to get serious. (8/1)

**3592 Duke Valentino** (8/1: op 4/1)

## 3651 NEXT CLASSIC (S) STKS (2-Y.O) (Class G)

6-10 (6-11) **5f 218y** £2,385.00 (£660.00: £315.00) Stalls: High GOING minus 0.48 sec per fur (F)

| | | SP | RR | SF |
|---|---|---|---|---|
| *3065*[2] **Heavenly Miss (IRE) (57)** (BPalling) **2-8-6** TSprake(8) (a gng wl: led wl over 1f out: sn clr: easily)................— | **1** | 9/1 | 63+ | 18 |
| 3349[9] **Saint Who (USA)** (WAO'Gorman) **2-8-11** EmmaO'Gorman(1) (trckd ldrs: hdwy over 2f out: kpt on fnl f: nt pce of wnr) .........................................................................................................................2 | **2** | 11/2[3] | 63 | 18 |
| 3330[6] **Fearless Cavalier (58)** (RHollinshead) **2-8-8**(3) FLynch(2) (outpcd: hdwy ½-wy: rdn & edgd rt over 1f out: one pce towards fin)........................................................................................................................2½ | **3** | 11/2[3] | 56 | 11 |
| 3330[2] **Champagne On Ice (61)** (PDEvans) **2-8-6** JFEgan(7) (w ldrs 4f: sn drvn & wknd appr fnl f)...............................6 | **4** | 100/30[1] | 35 | — |
| 3448[2] **Skippy Was A Kiwi (IRE)** (APJarvis) **2-8-6** WJO'Connor(5) (prom tl rdn & wknd 2f out)...............................1¾ | **5** | 100/30[1] | 30 | — |
| **Lady Grovefair (IRE)** (BJMeehan) **2-8-6** MTebbutt(4) (neat: cmpt: bkwd: hmpd s: a in rr & outpcd)...............nk | **6** | 9/2[2] | 30 | — |
| 3330[8] **Emilyjill (53)** (RHannon) **2-8-6** PatEddery(6) (led tl hdd & wknd wl over 1f out) ................................................5 | **7** | 11/2[3] | 16 | — |
| 2959[10] **Billycan (IRE)** (BPJBaugh) **2-8-11** WLord(3) (squeezed out s: a outpcd: t.o) ...................................................9 | **8** | 50/1 | — | — |
| | | (SP 122.5%) | **8 Rn** | |

**1m 12.3** (2.30) CSF £55.95 TOTE £9.60: £2.30 £2.00 £2.10 (£65.90) OWNER Rhiwbina Racing (COWBRIDGE) BRED Edward and Mrs S. Hannigan

Sold TRPearson 9,000 gns

**3065 Heavenly Miss (IRE)**, always pulling double over her rivals, quite simply outclassed the opposition and it came as no great surprise that connections lost her in the auction. (9/1)

**Saint Who (USA)**, quite a well grown youngster, shaped with promise and he could be better than this class in time. (11/2)

**3330 Fearless Cavalier**, taken off his legs in the early stages, did battle on inside the distance but the winner by then had set sail for home. (11/2)

**3330 Champagne On Ice** shared the lead for half a mile but was soon being bustled along for all she was worth and unable to hang on. (100/30)

**3448 Skippy Was A Kiwi (IRE)** faded away rather quickly over two furlongs out and she may fare better when not so much use is made of her. (100/30)

**Lady Grovefair (IRE)**, a poor mover, was very much in need of the race, the run and the experience. She was the meat in the sandwich leaving the stalls, and had little hope of recovery. (9/2)

## 3652 GRAHAME GARDNER H'CAP (0-70) (3-Y.O+) (Class E)

6-40 (6-42) **5f 2y** £3,234.00 (£966.00: £462.00: £210.00) Stalls: High GOING minus 0.48 sec per fur (F)

| | | SP | RR | SF |
|---|---|---|---|---|
| 3360[3] **Bangles (59)** (LordHuntingdon) **6-9-4** DHarrison(4) (a.p: led wl over 1f out: sn drvn clr) ................................— | **1** | 9/2[2] | 68 | 55 |
| 3446[10] **Longwick Lad (67)** (WRMuir) **3-9-10** JReid(6) (chsd ldrs: effrt & ev ch wl over 1f out: unable qckn fnl f) .......1¾ | **2** | 13/2 | 70 | 55 |
| 3323[7] **Polly Golightly (65)** (MBlanshard) **3-9-8b** TQuinn(1) (hdwy 2f out: r.o u.p ins fnl f) ..........................................¾ | **3** | 13/2 | 66 | 51 |
| 3292[5] **Marino Street (57)** (PDEvans) **3-9-0v** JFEgan(5) (swtg: trckd ldrs: drvn along ½-wy: one pce ins fnl f)............½ | **4** | 8/1 | 56 | 41 |
| 3331[7] **Featherstone Lane (43)** (MissLCSiddall) **5-8-2v** NCarlisle(2) (hld up: hdwy over 1f out: nt pce to chal).........s.h | **5** | 12/1 | 42 | 29 |
| *3416*[6] **Scored Again (48)** (MJHeaton-Ellis) **6-8-2**(5) AmandaSanders(10) (b: mde most over 3f: outpcd fnl f)..............2 | **6** | 16/1 | 41 | 28 |
| 3338[5] **Windrush Boy (56)** (JRBosley) **6-9-1** PatEddery(7) (hld up: effrt 2f out: no real imp).........................................nk | **7** | 7/2[1] | 48 | 35 |
| 3310[2] **The Institute Boy (50)** (MissJFCraze) **6-8-9** JLowe(8) (prom: ev ch & rdn wl over 1f out: wknd fnl f) ...............½ | **8** | 6/1[3] | 40 | 27 |
| 3350[5] **Boffy (IRE) (52)** (BPJBaugh) **3-8-2**(7) IonaWands(9) (prom over 3f: sn outpcd).........................................2½ | **9** | 14/1 | 34 | 19 |
| | | (SP 112.7%) | **9 Rn** | |

**58.8 secs** (0.30) CSF £30.28 CT £171.23 TOTE £3.70: £1.60 £2.10 £2.80 (£20.40) Trio £38.00 OWNER Mr J. Rose (WEST ILSLEY) BRED John Rose

WEIGHT FOR AGE 3yo-2lb

**3360 Bangles** usually finds her form at this time of year, and she had put her stamp on proceedings some way out. (9/2: op 3/1)

**3162 Longwick Lad** turned in a tremendous effort under top weight in his first handicap and he is almost sure to have to pay for it. (13/2)

**3323 Polly Golightly**, given a more patient ride, ran on well in the closing stages without being able to hold out much hope for her supporters. (13/2)

**3292 Marino Street** ran on willingly when sent about her business, but she had been hard at work for quite a long way, and could not summon the pace to get at the leaders. (8/1)

**3331 Featherstone Lane** tried to get himself into the action approaching the final furlong but, with the pace not dropping, was unable to do so. (12/1)

**3416 Scored Again**, who only trotted to the start, soon held the call in the centre of the track, but he had been swallowed up below the distance and had nothing more to give. He could be about to return to form. (16/1)

**3338 Windrush Boy**, successful in this event twelve months ago, was always struggling with the pace and was never a threat. (7/2)

**3350 Boffy (IRE)** (14/1: 10/1-16/1)

## 3653 CHOICE DISCOUNT STORES H'CAP (0-80) (3-Y.O+) (Class D)

7-10 (7-12) **1m 3f 183y** £3,960.15 (£1,183.20: £566.10: £257.55) Stalls: High GOING minus 0.48 sec per fur (F)

| | | SP | RR | SF |
|---|---|---|---|---|
| 3333[2] **Ragsak Jameel (USA) (75)** (MajorWRHern) **3-9-2v** TSprake(1) (swg: a.p: shkn up to ld over 1f out: rdn out)— | **1** | 9/2[1] | 85 | 48 |

3457[3] **Get Away With It (IRE) (74)** (MRStoute) **3-9-1** RCochrane(3) (hld up & bhd: gd hdwy over 2f out: str run fnl f)....nk **2** 5/1[2] 84 47
3260[2] **Te Amo (IRE) (63)** (RAkehurst) **4-9-0** TQuinn(5) (lw: a.p: ev ch 2f out: sn rdn & outpcd: styd on towards fin)....2½ **3** 6/1 69 42
3043[7] **Formidable Partner (69)** (RWArmstrong) **3-8-10v[1]** JReid(7) (lw: trckd ldrs: effrt & ev ch 2f out: one pce appr fnl f)....1¾ **4** 8/1 73 36
3333[4] **Slapy Dam (50)** (JMackie) **4-8-1v** GCarter(10) (lw: s.i.s: hld up & bhd: hdwy over 2f out: sn ev ch: unable qckn fnl f)....1¼ **5** 5/1[2] 52 25
3037[13] **Etterby Park (USA) (69)** (MJohnston) **3-8-10** PRobinson(2) (prom tl rdn & wknd over 2f out)....4 **6** 11/2[3] 66 29
3457[6] **Riparius (USA) (77)** (HCandy) **5-10-0b** CRutter(4) (hld up in rr: hdwy over 3f out: hrd drvn 2f out: sn btn)....1¾ **7** 14/1 71 44
2866[3] **Green Land (BEL) (60)** (SCWilliams) **4-8-11** PatEddery(6) (b.nr fore: led tl rdn & hdd over 1f out: sn btn)....nk **8** 8/1 54 27
3117[6] **In the Money (IRE) (57)** (RHollinshead) **7-8-5**(3) FLynch(9) (dwlt: sn in tch: rdn 3f out: grad wknd)....7 **9** 14/1 42 15
3457[10] **Peutetre (76)** (FJordan) **4-9-13** DHarrison(8) (mid div tl lost pl & pushed along 8f out: sn t.o)....20 **10** 50/1 34 7
(SP 118.7%) **10 Rn**

**2m 31.1** (2.10) CSF £26.06 CT £125.69 TOTE £4.80: £2.00 £1.70 £2.60 (£13.20) Trio £22.80 OWNER Sheikh Ahmed Al Maktoum (LAMBOURN) BRED Airlie Stud
WEIGHT FOR AGE 3yo-10lb
STEWARDS' ENQUIRY Sprake susp. 28-29/8/96 (excessive use of whip).

**3333 Ragsak Jameel (USA)** acts surprisingly well for such a powerful individual on this fast ground and, back over a more suitable trip, stole the race coming to the final furlong. (9/2)
**3457 Get Away With It (IRE)**, still to open his account, put in a sustained last furlong challenge that only just failed to succeed. His turn is near at hand. (5/1)
**3260 Te Amo (IRE)** looked to be travelling best passing the quarter-mile marker but he then got slightly outpaced until rallying under pressure towards the finish. He looks a million dollars and is due a change of fortune. (6/1)
**2603 Formidable Partner**, always in the firing line, was unable to match strides when the tempo picked up inside the distance. (8/1)
**3333 Slapy Dam** made smooth progress to put himself in with a live chance two furlongs out, but lacked the necessary speed when the whips were cracking. (5/1)
**2866 Green Land (BEL)**, reluctant to enter the stalls, settled down in front once in action, but she did not have a lot in reserve when taken on and was galloping on the spot approaching the final furlong. (8/1)

## 3654 PEDIGREE PETFOODS CLAIMING STKS (3-Y.O) (Class F)
7-40 (7-41) **1m 1f 218y** £2,690.40 (£744.40: £355.20) Stalls: High GOING minus 0.48 sec per fur (F)

SP RR SF
3320[2] **Domettes (IRE) (57)** (RHannon) **3-9-0** PatEddery(6) (mde all: hrd rdn & fnd ex nr fin)....— **1** 11/10[1] 64 —
3244[4] **Cebwob (67)** (PFICole) **3-8-12** TQuinn(3) (lw: a.p: jnd wnr ent fnl f: hrd rdn & r.o wl)....nk **2** 7/2[2] 62 —
3474[6] **Little Kenny (43)** (MJFetherston-Godley) **3-8-1v**(3) FLynch(8) (prom: effrt u.p over 1f out: nvr able to chal)....3 **3** 8/1[3] 49 —
3451[7] **My Kind (38)** (NTinkler) **3-8-0** KimTinkler(2) (prom: hrd drvn over 2f out: kpt on same pace)....6 **4** 25/1 35 —
3358[2] **Sweet Amoret (51)** (PHowling) **3-8-12** FNorton(4) (b.off hind: lw: hld up: hdwy over 3f out: rdn 2f out: sn btn)....3 **5** 10/1 42 —
3341[7] **Magic Melody (65)** (PFICole) **3-8-12** JReid(5) (s.i.s: bhd: effrt 3f out: sn rdn & outpcd)....2½ **6** 10/1 38 —
3262[15] **Theatre's Dream (IRE)** (JEBanks) **3-9-5** JStack(1) (a in rr: rdn 3f out: sn lost tch)....1¾ **7** 20/1 43 —
2915[4] **Nanny-B** (PHowling) **3-8-6** PaulEddery(7) (b.hind: bit bkwd: a in rr)....¾ **8** 33/1 28 —
(SP 110.7%) **8 Rn**

**2m 12.2** (8.50) CSF £5.03 TOTE £1.60: £1.00 £1.60 £2.00 (£3.10) OWNER Albion Investments (MARLBOROUGH) BRED Sandville Stud
Little Kenny clmd K Warrington £4,000

**3320 Domettes (IRE)**, not winning out of turn, did it all from the front and had enough in hand to thwart the strong-challenging runner-up close home. (11/10: Evens-5/4)
**3244 Cebwob** looked to have the edge when moving upsides entering the last furlong, but she had a real battle on her hands and could not quicken sufficiently to take command. Another success is just around the corner. (7/2)
**3474 Little Kenny** held her pitch and tried her heart out but the leading pair were too smart for her in the sprint to the finish. (8/1)
**1806 My Kind** did not fare badly and, with stronger handling, could soon improve on this. (25/1)
**3358 Sweet Amoret** (10/1: 7/1-11/1)

## 3655 CLECO H'CAP (0-70) (3-Y.O) (Class E)
8-10 (8-11) **1m 8y** £3,234.00 (£966.00: £462.00: £210.00) Stalls: High GOING minus 0.48 sec per fur (F)

SP RR SF
3456[2] **Eurobox Boy (52)** (APJarvis) **3-8-5**ow1 WJO'Connor(9) (b.nr hind: lw: hld up: pushed along 3f out: hdwy to ld over 1f out: sn drvn clr)....— **1** 5/1[3] 65 10
3414* **Forest Fantasy (57)** (JWharton) **3-8-10** PRobinson(6) (a.p: ev ch over 1f out: kpt on u.p)....2 **2** 9/2[2] 66 12
3456* **Bandit Girl (68)** (IABalding) **3-9-7** 5x TQuinn(10) (hld up: hdwy over 2f out: hrd rdn & r.o)....¾ **3** 9/2[2] 76 22
3138* **Budby (68)** (ACStewart) **3-9-7** SWhitworth(2) (hld up: hdwy u.p 3f out: one pce wl ins fnl f)....1 **4** 9/2[2] 74 20
3586[5] **Hadadabble (43)** (PatMitchell) **3-7-10** NCarlisle(4) (lw: led to 2f out: hrd rdn & no ex fin f)....nk **5** 33/1 48 —
3135[5] **Sharp Monty (62)** (RHollinshead) **3-8-12**(3) FLynch(7) (prom: led 2f out tl over 1f out: r.o one pce)....½ **6** 12/1 66 12
3474[2] **Sharp Shuffle (IRE) (65)** (RHannon) **3-9-4** PatEddery(1) (prom tl rdn & wknd over 1f out)....4 **7** 9/4[1] 61 7
3357[4] **Farfeste (45)** (DMorris) **3-7-12**ow2 StephenDavies(3) (prom tl rdn & wknd wl over 1f out: eased whn btn)....5 **8** 50/1 31 —
**Bianca Cappello (IRE) (43)** (PSFelgate) **3-7-3**(7) RBrisland(8) (bkwd: bhd: hdwy over 2f out: wknd wl over 1f out)....2½ **9** 50/1 24 —
3140[8] **Twice Removed (50)** (SDow) **3-8-3** JFEgan(5) (bit bkwd: a in rr: t.o)....7 **10** 25/1 17 —
(SP 120.4%) **10 Rn**

**1m 38.8** (3.80) CSF £26.99 CT £100.12 TOTE £5.90: £1.60 £2.50 £1.30 (£16.90) Trio £24.70 OWNER Mr N. Coverdale (ASTON UPTHORPE) BRED G. Revitt
LONG HANDICAP Farfeste 7-3 Bianca Cappello (IRE) 6-11 Hadadabble 7-9

**3456 Eurobox Boy** gained his revenge over Bandit Girl on these slightly better terms, and won going away. His jockey continues to impress. (5/1)
**3414* Forest Fantasy**, fighting for the lead from the break, did not go down for the want of trying and she would seem very much on the upgrade. (9/2)
**3456* Bandit Girl** tried hard to mount her challenge approaching the last furlong but, with her penalty, just lacked that bit extra when it was most needed. (9/2)
**3138* Budby** stayed on relentlessly inside the last couple of furlongs, but she was at the end of her tether in the final one hundred yards. (9/2)
**2369 Hadadabble** forced the pace for six furlongs but found this company much stronger than she had met in the past. (33/1)

**3135 Sharp Monty** tried to kick clear two furlongs out, but the winner was on to him in next to no time and he was short of finishing speed late on. (12/1)
**3474 Sharp Shuffle (IRE)** sat in behind the leaders travelling smoothly but, when the tempo picked up inside the final quarter-mile, he got brushed aside with ease. (9/4)

T/Plpt: £60.90 (191.53 Tckts). T/Qdpt: £8.80 (128.78 Tckts) IM

# 3466-WINDSOR (Fig. 8) (Good to firm)
## Monday August 19th
WEATHER: fine WIND: nil

## 3656 BAA DUTY AND TAX FREE SHOPPING MAIDEN STKS (3-Y.O) (Class D)
2-30 (2-35) **1m 2f 7y** £4,006.50 (£1,212.00: £591.00: £280.50) Stalls: High GOING minus 0.16 sec per fur (GF)

| | | | | SP | RR | SF |
|---|---|---|---|---|---|---|
| $3258^{2}$ | **Turning Wheel (USA)** (HRACecil) **3-8-9** PatEddery(10) (led after 2f: qcknd 3f out: easily) | — | **1** | $1/3^{1}$ | 91+ | 67 |
| | **Multicoloured (IRE)** (MRStoute) **3-9-0** JReid(5) (unf: bit bkwd: a.p: chsd wnr fnl 3f: no imp) | 5 | **2** | $9/2^{2}$ | 88 | 64 |
| | **Mount Pleasant (IRE)** (PFICole) **3-9-0** TQuinn(2) (leggy: scope: chsd ldrs: r.o one pce fnl 2f) | 3 | **3** | 20/1 | 83 | 59 |
| | **Opalette** (LadyHerries) **3-8-9** RCochrane(6) (chsd ldr to 3f out: one pce) | hd | **4** | 33/1 | 78 | 54 |
| $1895^{4}$ | **Grand Splendour** (LadyHerries) **3-8-9** DHarrison(15) (led 2f: wknd over 2f out) | 4 | **5** | 33/1 | 72 | 48 |
| $2603^{18}$ | **Classy Chief (74)** (RBoss) **3-9-0** RHughes(9) (s.s: hdwy 4f out: one pce fnl 2f) | nk | **6** | 50/1 | 76 | 52 |
| | **Dark Waters (IRE)** (MRStoute) **3-9-0** WRSwinburn(11) (bit bkwd: mid div whn jinked rt over 3f out: nvr nr to chal) | 1 | **7** | $16/1^{3}$ | 75 | 51 |
| $2610^{7}$ | **Mourne Mountains** (HCandy) **3-9-0** CRutter(1) (prom tl wknd 3f out) | 4 | **8** | 33/1 | 68 | 44 |
| | **Galaka** (LMCumani) **3-8-9** OUrbina(14) (bit bkwd: prom tl wknd 4f out) | 7 | **9** | 33/1 | 52 | 28 |
| | **Charcol** (JEBanks) **3-8-2**(7) GFaulkner(7) (w'like: bit bkwd: a bhd) | 8 | **10** | 100/1 | 39 | 15 |
| $1901^{14}$ | **One In The Eye** (JRPoulton) **3-8-11**(3) PMcCabe(13) (a bhd) | nk | **11** | 100/1 | 44 | 20 |
| | **Shoshone** (JHMGosden) **3-8-9** WRyan(8) (w'like: bit bkwd: b.hind: a bhd) | s.h | **12** | 33/1 | 39 | 15 |
| $3262^{17}$ | **Bigwig (IRE)** (AMoore) **3-9-0** AClark(12) (bit bkwd: mid div tl wknd over 3f out) | 10 | **13** | 100/1 | 28 | 4 |
| | **Sterin** (MarkCampion) **3-8-9** RPerham(3) (leggy: lt-f: a bhd) | 3 | **14** | 50/1 | 18 | — |
| $3108^{10}$ | **Locket** (JABennett) **3-8-4**(5) SophieMitchell(4) (bit bkwd: bhd fnl 5f: t.o) | dist | **15** | 50/1 | — | — |

(SP 127.4%) **15 Rn**

**2m 6.6** (1.70) CSF £2.94 TOTE £1.40: £1.10 £1.80 £2.90 (£3.10) Trio £13.30 OWNER Niarchos Family (NEWMARKET) BRED Flaxman Holdings Ltd

**3258 Turning Wheel (USA)** confirmed the good impression she made here recently. Cruising into the lead after two furlongs, she readily quickened clear at the three furlong marker and won in a canter. (1/3)
**Multicoloured (IRE)** made an encouraging debut. Always close up, he took second place at the three furlong marker, and though he had no chance with the winner, he kept on under pressure. (9/2)
**Mount Pleasant (IRE)**, always chasing the leading group, stayed on in the final quarter-mile without causing any concern to the winner. (20/1)
**Opalette** raced in second place until gradually weakening in the last two and a half furlongs. (33/1)
**1895 Grand Splendour** made the early running and remained close up until weakening approaching the two furlong marker. (33/1)
**1662 Classy Chief** did well to reach sixth place after a very slow start. He made good ground four furlongs out, but the effort of making so much headway left him with no reserves for later. (50/1)

## 3657 HIGHLAND QUEEN WHISKEY QUORTINA CHALLENGE CUP H'CAP (0-80) (3-Y.O) (Class D)
3-00 (3-01) **1m 3f 135y** £3,597.00 (£1,086.00: £528.00: £249.00) Stalls: High GOING minus 0.16 sec per fur (GF)

| | | | | SP | RR | SF |
|---|---|---|---|---|---|---|
| 3103* | **Present Arms (USA) (75)** (PFICole) **3-9-7b¹** TQuinn(4) (lw: led 7f out: drvn clr over 3f out: unchal) | — | **1** | $7/2^{2}$ | 86 | 55 |
| $2998^{6}$ | **Atlantic Mist (60)** (BRMillman) **3-8-6** BDoyle(6) (hdwy 4f out: chsd wnr over 2f out: no imp) | 3 | **2** | 8/1 | 67 | 36 |
| $2399^{6}$ | **Love Bateta (IRE) (68)** (JEBanks) **3-8-7**(7) GFaulkner(10) (a.p: chsd wnr over 4f out tl over 2f out: one pce) | ¾ | **3** | 25/1 | 74 | 43 |
| $3357^{3}$ | **Nelly's Cousin (63)** (NACallaghan) **3-8-9** PatEddery(3) (b: hdwy & hrd rdn 3f out: one pce fnl 2f) | ¾ | **4** | $6/1^{3}$ | 68 | 37 |
| $3148^{10}$ | **Kitty Kitty Cancan (72)** (LadyHerries) **3-8-11**(7) RSmith(9) (a mid div: styd on one pce fnl 2f) | ½ | **5** | 12/1 | 76 | 45 |
| $3320^{4}$ | **Oberons Boy (IRE) (70)** (BJMeehan) **3-9-2** WRSwinburn(2) (hld up in rr: hdwy whn hit rails 3f out: nvr nr ldrs) | 9 | **6** | 12/1 | 62 | 31 |
| 3249* | **Snow Falcon (64)** (MBell) **3-8-10** MFenton(5) (a bhd) | 1¾ | **7** | $3/1^{1}$ | 53 | 22 |
| $3425^{6}$ | **Llyswen (74)** (JHMGosden) **3-9-6v¹** LDettori(7) (prom tl wknd 2f out: eased whn btn) | 2½ | **8** | 8/1 | 60 | 29 |
| $3260^{W}$ | **Mountain Dream (70)** (LMCumani) **3-9-2** OUrbina(1) (a bhd: t.o) | 24 | **9** | 8/1 | 23 | — |
| *$3422^{9}$* | **Northern Clan (50)** (AJChamberlain) **3-7-10b** GBardwell(8) (b: led to 7f out: wknd qckly over 4f out: t.o) | dist | **10** | 50/1 | — | — |

(SP 116.0%) **10 Rn**

**2m 29.3** (5.30) CSF £28.97 CT £550.84 TOTE £4.30: £2.00 £1.80 £5.30 (£18.50) Trio £301.10; £84.83 to York 20/8/96 OWNER H R H Prince Fahd Salman (WHATCOMBE) BRED Tri-Star Stable
LONG HANDICAP Northern Clan 7-0

**3103* Present Arms (USA)**, blinkered for the first time, was kept wide of his rivals and went to the front seven furlongs out. Going clear approaching the three furlong marker, there was no danger of defeat. (7/2)
**2998 Atlantic Mist** made smooth headway four furlongs out, but after reaching second place approaching the two furlong marker, could make no impression on the winner. (8/1)
**921 Love Bateta (IRE)** took second place early in the straight, but was finding no more when pressure was applied over two furlongs out. (25/1)
**3357 Nelly's Cousin** made ground under strong pressure two furlongs out, but could make no further progress in the final quarter-mile. (6/1)
**1656 Kitty Kitty Cancan**, always in mid division, was staying on at the finish but lacked the pace to trouble the leaders. (12/1)
**3320 Oberons Boy (IRE)**, held up and last, was improving when hitting the rails over three furlongs out and was never in the race with a chance. (12/1)
**3425 Llyswen** was heavily eased after running prominently until two furlongs out. (8/1)

## 3658 BAA BONUSPOINTS FREQUENT BUYER CONDITIONS STKS (3-Y.O+) (Class C)
3-30 (3-30) **1m 2f 7y** £4,892.55 (£1,783.80: £871.90: £374.50: £167.25) Stalls: High GOING minus 0.16 sec per fur (GF)

| | | | | SP | RR | SF |
|---|---|---|---|---|---|---|
| $3386a^{9}$ | **Maralinga (IRE) (100)** (LadyHerries) **4-9-0** DeclanO'Shea(4) (mde all: r.o wl) | — | **1** | 6/1 | 105 | 78 |
| $1899^{9}$ | **Kinlochewe (98)** (HRACecil) **3-8-4** WRyan(3) (swtg: hdwy on ins 2f out: ev ch fnl f: r.o) | nk | **2** | $5/1^{3}$ | 103 | 68 |

| | | | | SP | RR | SF |
|---|---|---|---|---|---|---|
| 581[6] | **Inquisitor (USA) (107)** (JHMGosden) **4-9-0** LDettori(2) (hld up: hdwy 3f out: ev ch 2f out: hrd rdn: nt qckn) | 4 | **3** | 6/5 [1] | 98 | 71 |
| 3262* | **Civil Liberty (90)** (GLewis) **3-8-9** PatEddery(1) (lw: chsd wnr tl rdn & wknd 2f out) | 4 | **4** | 100/30 [2] | 95 | 60 |
| 3409[5] | **Lomberto (102)** (RHannon) **3-8-3**(3) DaneO'Neill(5) (prom tl wknd 3f out) | 6 | **5** | 12/1 | 82 | 47 |

(SP 107.2%) **5 Rn**

**2m 5.8** (0.90) CSF £29.11 TOTE £8.80: £2.00 £2.80 (£16.80) OWNER Mr D K R & Mrs J B C Oliver (LITTLEHAMPTON) BRED W. H. Elliott
WEIGHT FOR AGE 3yo-8lb

**3386a Maralinga (IRE)** made all the running. Strongly pressed on both sides throughout the final quarter-mile, he held on bravely. (6/1: 4/1-13/2)
**1111 Kinlochewe** sneaked up on the inside two furlongs out, but after having every chance in the final furlong, could not quite peg back the winner. (5/1: 7/2-11/2)
**581 Inquisitor (USA)** moved up smoothly enough to draw almost level at the two furlong marker, but when put to his best, could find no more. (6/5)
**3262* Civil Liberty** raced in second place until weakening under pressure two furlongs out. (100/30)
**3409 Lomberto** was close up for nine furlongs. (12/1: op 8/1)

## 3659 GREENALLS LONDON DRY GIN NURSERY H'CAP (2-Y.O) (Class D)
4-00 (4-05) **5f 217y** £3,306.25 (£1,000.00: £487.50: £231.25) Stalls: High GOING minus 0.16 sec per fur (GF)

| | | | | SP | RR | SF |
|---|---|---|---|---|---|---|
| 3237[2] | **Kaiser Kache (IRE) (74)** (KMcAuliffe) **2-8-13** BDoyle(4) (a.p: led over 1f out: all out) | — | **1** | 9/1 | 73 | 27 |
| 3467[3] | **Aegean Sound (72)** (RHannon) **2-8-8**(3) DaneO'Neill(8) (lw: hdwy over 1f out: r.o wl ins fnl f) | s.h | **2** | 5/2 [1] | 71 | 25 |
| 3110* | **Nightingale Song (71)** (MartynMeade) **2-8-3**(7) DSweeney(6) (led over 4f) | 1¾ | **3** | 4/1 [3] | 65 | 19 |
| 3478[5] | **I Can't Remember (74)** (PDEvans) **2-8-13** LDettori(1) (hrd rdn over 3f out: hdwy 2f out: one pce fnl f) | nk | **4** | 11/4 [2] | 67 | 21 |
| 2797[7] | **Summer Risotto (57)** (DJSffrenchDavis) **2-7-10** NCarlisle(3) (chsd ldrs tl wknd over 1f out) | 7 | **5** | 20/1 | 32 | — |
| 2429* | **Victoria's Dream (IRE) (68)** (MRChannon) **2-8-7** TQuinn(7) (chsd ldr tl wknd over 1f out) | ½ | **6** | 15/2 | 41 | — |
| 2965[9] | **Blue Movie (82)** (MBell) **2-9-7** MFenton(5) (a bhd) | 9 | **7** | 10/1 | 31 | — |
| *3208[4]* | ***Masterstroke (74)*** (BJMeehan) **2-8-13** PatEddery(2) (Withdrawn not under Starter's orders: broke out of stalls) | | **W** | 5/1 | — | — |

(SP 127.5%) **7 Rn**

**1m 14.5** (4.00) CSF £29.54 CT £91.58 TOTE £10.10: £4.90 £2.00 (£15.00) OWNER Mr Peter Barclay (LAMBOURN) BRED St Simon Foundation
LONG HANDICAP Summer Risotto 7-8

**3237 Kaiser Kache (IRE)** was always close up. He led approaching the final furlong and held on all out. (9/1)
**3467 Aegean Sound**, patiently ridden, was switched to challenge in the last furlong. Well as she ran on, she needed one more stride. (5/2)
**3110* Nightingale Song** made the running but could find no extra when headed approaching the final furlong. (4/1)
**3478 I Can't Remember**, though never far behind the leaders, was under pressure a long way out and though staying on to the end, never appeared likely to win. (11/4: 5/2-4/1)
**2539* Summer Risotto** gradually weakened from the two pole. (20/1)
**2429* Victoria's Dream (IRE)** faded quickly approaching the final furlong. (15/2)

## 3660 E.B.F. AIRPORT SHOPPING VALUE GUARANTEE MAIDEN STKS (2-Y.O F) (Class D)
4-30 (4-31) **5f 10y** £3,452.50 (£1,045.00: £510.00: £242.50) Stalls: High GOING minus 0.16 sec per fur (GF)

| | | | | SP | RR | SF |
|---|---|---|---|---|---|---|
| | **Joza** (HCandy) **2-8-11** CRutter(1) (unf: scope: a.p: led on bit 2f out: drvn out fnl f) | — | **1** | 3/1 [2] | 84+ | 39 |
| | **Dark Mile (USA)** (JHMGosden) **2-8-11** LDettori(4) (w'like: bit bkwd: s.s: gd hdwy 2f out: r.o wl ins fnl f) | ¾ | **2** | 5/1 [3] | 82+ | 37 |
| 3464[8] | **Martine** (ABailey) **2-8-11** BDoyle(9) (chsd ldrs: styd on fnl 2f) | 5 | **3** | 33/1 | 66 | 21 |
| | **Noble Story** (RAkehurst) **2-8-11** PaulEddery(11) (unf: dwlt: sn mid div: hdwy over 1f out: r.o) | s.h | **4** | 10/1 | 66 | 21 |
| 3282[5] | **Good News (IRE)** (MMadgwick) **2-8-11** RPerham(8) (b.hind: led 3f: r.o one pce) | hd | **5** | 33/1 | 65 | 20 |
| | **Husun (USA)** (PTWalwyn) **2-8-11** RHills(12) (w'like: scope: bit bkwd: a.p: no hdwy fnl 2f) | ½ | **6** | 6/1 | 64 | 19 |
| 3269[4] | **Attribute** (RCharlton) **2-8-11** PatEddery(7) (rdn along: prom tl wknd 1f out) | nk | **7** | 2/1 [1] | 63 | 18 |
| | **Karen's Hat (USA)** (IABalding) **2-8-6**(5) MartinDwyer(5) (w'like: bit bkwd: outpcd: nrst fin) | 2½ | **8** | 25/1 | 55 | 10 |
| 3259[7] | **Poker Princess** (MBell) **2-8-11** MFenton(13) (a bhd) | ¾ | **9** | 33/1 | 52 | 7 |
| 3330[3] | **Valentine Fairy** (RBoss) **2-8-11** RHughes(2) (prom tl wknd over 1f out: eased fnl f) | 1¼ | **10** | 33/1 | 49 | 4 |
| | **Tsarina** (RHannon) **2-8-8**(3) DaneO'Neill(10) (neat: b.hind: s.s: a bhd) | s.h | **11** | 20/1 | 48 | 3 |
| 3436[6] | **Wild Nettle** (JCFox) **2-8-11** AClark(6) (swtg: w ldrs tl wknd 2f out) | 3½ | **12** | 66/1 | 37 | — |
| 3054[4] | **Show Off** (WJarvis) **2-8-11** AMcGlone(3) (w ldr: wknd qckly 2f out) | 4 | **13** | 10/1 | 25 | — |

(SP 129.3%) **13 Rn**

**61.7 secs** (2.50) CSF £19.14 TOTE £3.60: £1.50 £1.70 £7.30 (£12.00) Trio £383.90; £329.89 to York 20/8/96 OWNER H R H Prince Fahd Salman (WANTAGE) BRED Newgate Stud Co

**Joza** cruised into the lead at the two furlong marker, and had all but the second in trouble immediately. She had to be driven out at the finish but will come on for this sparkling debut. (3/1)
**Dark Mile (USA)** completely missed the break and time may show that she was trying to give start to a very useful rival. She made ground rapidly two furlongs out, and put in a spirited challenge in the last furlong, but racing very wide of her rival. Compensation will follow. (5/1)
**2772 Martine**, always in the group chasing the leaders, stayed on to snatch third place but could not match the pace of the leading pair. (33/1)
**Noble Story**, after a slow start, soon moved into the middle division and was running on steadily in the last furlong and a half. There is plenty of improvement in her. (10/1: 8/1-12/1)
**Good News (IRE)** held a narrow lead for three furlongs and ran on at one pace under pressure. (33/1)
**Husun (USA)**, always chasing the leading group, could make no impression in the final quarter-mile. (6/1)
**3269 Attribute** was being ridden along to hold her place after two furlongs. She found the going too tough late on. (2/1)
**3054 Show Off** (10/1: op 16/1)

## 3661 FREEPHONE AIRPORT SHOPPING LINE APPRENTICE H'CAP (0-70) (3-Y.O+) (Class F)
5-00 (5-02) **5f 10y** £2,487.00 (£707.00: £351.00) Stalls: High GOING minus 0.16 sec per fur (GF)

| | | | | SP | RR | SF |
|---|---|---|---|---|---|---|
| *1455[7]* | **Ashkernazy (IRE) (43)** (NEBerry) **5-8-1**(5) KerryBaker(14) (w ldr: led over 1f out: pushed out) | — | **1** | 20/1 | 47 | 25 |
| 3477[W] | **Imposing Time (63)** (MissGayKelleway) **5-9-4b**(8) BFord(6) (hld up & bhd: gd hdwy fnl 2f: fin wl) | nk | **2** | 5/1 [2] | 66 | 44 |
| 3331[5] | **Mister Raider (47)** (EAWheeler) **4-8-10b** EmilyJoyce(9) (w ldrs: ev ch 1f out: r.o) | hd | **3** | 12/1 | 50 | 28 |
| 3146[3] | **Runs in the Family (51)** (GMMcCourt) **4-9-0v** RStudholme(10) (led: hdd & hrd rdn over 1f out: r.o ins fnl f) | nk | **4** | 7/2 [1] | 53 | 31 |
| 3339[3] | **Songsheet (66)** (MartynMeade) **3-9-10**(3) ClaireAngell(2) (w ldrs: r.o one pce fnl 2f) | ½ | **5** | 9/1 | 66 | 42 |
| 3439[5] | **Lorins Gold (39)** (AndrewTurnell) **6-7-11**(5) KSalt(5) (b.nr hind: hdwy 2f out: r.o ins fnl f) | 1¾ | **6** | 10/1 | 34 | 12 |
| 3477[2] | **Silk Cottage (63)** (RMWhitaker) **4-9-9v**(3) PFredericks(4) (hdwy fnl 2f: nvr nrr) | nk | **7** | 5/1 [2] | 57 | 35 |

| | | | | SP | RR | SF |
|---|---|---|---|---|---|---|
| 3274[6] | **Justinianus (IRE) (40)** (JJBridger) **4-8-3** TField(3) (prom tl wknd over 1f out) | hd | **8** | 33/1 | 33 | 11 |
| 2745[14] | **The Noble Oak (IRE) (33)** (MJBolton) **8-7-10** CCogan(12) (prom 3f) | 1¾ | **9** | 25/1 | 21 | — |
| 3215[7] | **Step On Degas (64)** (MJFetherston-Godley) **3-9-11** RFfrench(7) (wl bhd tl hdwy over 1f out: nvr nr ldrs) | nk | **10** | 7/1[3] | 51 | 27 |
| 2528[11] | **Gracious Gretclo (50)** (RJBaker) **3-8-11** AMcCarthy(13) (chsd ldrs tl wknd over 1f out) | ½ | **11** | 16/1 | 35 | 11 |
| 1806[10] | **Casino Chip (37)** (TTClement) **3-7-12** JGotobed(11) (a bhd) | 6 | **12** | 25/1 | 3 | — |
| 3439[14] | **Hong Kong Dollar (39)** (BAPearce) **4-7-11b**[(5)] DSalt(1) (bhd fnl 3f) | nk | **13** | 33/1 | 4 | — |
| 3506[9] | **Paley Prince (USA) (59)** (MDIUsher) **10-9-8** RBrisland(8) (mid div whn sddle slipped 2f out) | s.h | **14** | 16/1 | 24 | 2 |
| | **Mister Sean (IRE) (50)** (JWPayne) **3-8-6**[(5)] TPengkerego(15) (b.hind: s.s: a last) | ¾ | **15** | 20/1 | 13 | — |
| | | | | (SP 129.7%) | **15 Rn** | |

**62.3 secs** (3.10) CSF £115.80 CT £1,212.36 TOTE £19.80: £4.70 £2.50 £5.20 (£141.70) Trio £565.80 OWNER London Bridge II (UPPER LAMBOURN) BRED G. P. Griffin
LONG HANDICAP The Noble Oak (IRE) 7-6
WEIGHT FOR AGE 3yo-2lb
**IN-FOCUS: The winning jockey was having her first ride.**
**Ashkernazy (IRE)** disputed the lead from the start. Given a very cool ride, she was pushed out after taking a narrow advantage at the distance. (20/1)
**3261 Imposing Time**, who had bolted with a senior jockey before the start and been withdrawn recently, was taken down very slowly on this occasion. Dropped out as the stalls opened, he had a lot to do from two furlongs out but finished in tremendous style. His turn is near at hand. (5/1)
**3331 Mister Raider** went with the leaders but after having every chance, could not find any extra. (12/1)
**3146 Runs in the Family** held a narrow lead from the start until resenting her rider's use of the whip approaching the final furlong. Once he had put it down, she ran on well but too late. (7/2)
**3339 Songsheet**, racing wide in the centre of the course, went with the leaders throughout and kept on well to the end. (9/1)
**3439 Lorins Gold** found this too sharp and, though staying on at the finish, the effort came too late. (10/1: 7/1-11/1)
**2244 Step On Degas** (7/1: 5/1-15/2)

T/Jkpt: Not won; £7,346.09 to York 20/8/96. T/Plpt: £959.00 (17.48 Tckts). T/Qdpt: £628.50 (1.25 Tckts) Hn

## 3581-FOLKESTONE (R-H) (Good to firm, Firm patches)
## Tuesday August 20th

WEATHER: raining WIND: almost nil

### 3662 SMARDEN (S) STKS (2-Y.O) (Class G)
2-20 (2-20) **6f 189y** £2,070.00 (£570.00: £270.00) Stalls: Low GOING minus 0.47 sec per fur (F)

| | | | | SP | RR | SF |
|---|---|---|---|---|---|---|
| 2413[4] | **Princess of Hearts (73)** (WJHaggas) **2-8-6** RMcGhin(9) (dwlt: hdwy over 5f out: led 1f out: rdn out) | — | **1** | 5/1 | 58 | 6 |
| 3454[8] | **Heavenly Dancer** (SirMarkPrescott) **2-8-6** GDuffield(5) (lw: chsd ldr over 5f out: rdn over 3f out: ev ch fnl f: r.o) | ½ | **2** | 5/2[1] | 57 | 5 |
| 2959[4] | **Ginny Wossername (55)** (WGMTurner) **2-8-4b**[(7)] DSweeney(8) (led to 1f out: sn wknd) | 3½ | **3** | 4/1[3] | 54 | 2 |
| *3629*[2] | **Grovefair Lad (IRE) (52)** (BJMeehan) **2-8-11** MTebbutt(4) (lost pl 5f out: no hdwy fnl 2f) | ¾ | **4** | 10/1 | 52 | — |
| 3498[5] | **Spondulicks (IRE) (65)** (RHannon) **2-8-11** DaneO'Neill(7) (lw: nvr nr to chal) | ¾ | **5** | 100/30[2] | 50 | — |
| 3171[7] | **Ms Ziman** (MBell) **2-8-6** MFenton(6) (lw: hdwy over 4f out: wknd over 2f out) | 9 | **6** | 20/1 | 24 | — |
| 3312[7] | **Chopin (IRE) (65)** (RFJohnsonHoughton) **2-8-4**[(7)] BarrySmith(1) (bhd fnl 3f) | hd | **7** | 14/1 | 29 | — |
| | | | | (SP 108.8%) | **7 Rn** | |

**1m 25.4** (3.80) CSF £16.36 TOTE £7.80: £2.90 £1.30 (£9.60) Trio £20.30 OWNER Cheveley Park Stud (NEWMARKET) BRED Cheveley Park Stud Ltd
Sold MissJAllison 6,200 gns; Heavenly Dancer clmd JBates £6,000
**2413 Princess of Hearts** appreciated the drop in class. Soon recovering from a tardy start, she travelled well and, getting a split between rivals to lead a furlong out, was ridden along to keep the persistent runner-up at bay. (5/1: 11/4-11/2)
**Heavenly Dancer**, taking a drop in class, was very well backed in the market. Soon racing in second place, she threw down her challenge in the straight and, having a ding dong battle with the winner in the final furlong, only just lost out. She can win a similar event. (5/2: 5/1-9/4)
**2959 Ginny Wossername** attempted to make all the running. Collared a furlong out, she was soon put in her place by the front two. (4/1: op 5/2)
**3629 Grovefair Lad (IRE)** broke well enough but had completely lost his pitch after a couple of furlongs. He was making little impression on the leaders in the straight. (10/1: 6/1-12/1)
**3498 Spondulicks (IRE)** has had plenty of chances but has still not broken his duck. Unable to go the pace, he never threatened to get into it. (100/30: 2/1-7/2)
**741 Chopin (IRE)** (14/1: 8/1-16/1)

### 3663 JOHN MCCARTHY MAIDEN STKS (2-Y.O F) (Class D)
2-50 (2-52) **6f 189y** £3,743.15 (£1,119.20: £536.10: £244.55) Stalls: Low GOING minus 0.47 sec per fur (F)

| | | | | SP | RR | SF |
|---|---|---|---|---|---|---|
| | **The In-Laws (IRE)** (SirMarkPrescott) **2-8-11** GDuffield(1) (leggy: scope: bit bkwd: a.p: rdn over 2f out: led over 1f out: r.o wl) | — | **1** | 5/2[2] | 64+ | 6 |
| | **Mutribah (USA)** (HThomsonJones) **2-8-11** RHills(8) (neat: hld up: rdn 2f out: ev ch fnl f: r.o) | nk | **2** | 7/4[1] | 63 | 5 |
| | **Cowtharee** (MRStoute) **2-8-11** PaulEddery(4) (neat: lw: led 6f out tl over 1f out: ev ch ins fnl f: unable qckn) | ½ | **3** | 9/2[3] | 62 | 4 |
| 2758[3] | **Beaconscot** (DRLoder) **2-8-11** DRMcCabe(7) (led 1f: rdn over 2f out: one pce) | ½ | **4** | 10/1 | 61 | 3 |
| 2741[6] | **Hadawah (USA)** (JLDunlop) **2-8-11** TSprake(5) (b.hind: hdwy over 1f out: n.m.r ins fnl f: one pce) | ½ | **5** | 10/1 | 60 | 2 |
| | **Epsilon** (CEBrittain) **2-8-11** SSanders(3) (leggy: lt-f: hld up: rdn over 2f out: wknd wl over 1f out) | 5 | **6** | 33/1 | 48 | — |
| 3499[9] | **Chairmans Daughter** (PFICole) **2-8-11** CRutter(2) (prom over 5f) | 1½ | **7** | 50/1 | 45 | — |
| | **Control Freak** (AGFoster) **2-8-6**[(5)] JDSmith(6) (leggy: lt-f: bhd fnl 6f) | 7 | **8** | 50/1 | 28 | — |
| | | | | (SP 108.2%) | **8 Rn** | |

**1m 25.8** (4.20) CSF £6.55 TOTE £3.50: £1.50 £1.10 £1.40 (£4.20) OWNER Mr G. D. Waters (NEWMARKET) BRED G. D. Waters
**IN-FOCUS: Whilst this race was contested by many of the big stables and on paper looked an above average Folkestone maiden, one should not get carried away as, judging on paddock inspection, they looked their trainers' lesser lights.**
**The In-Laws (IRE)**, a tall, attractive filly, had far more scope than her rivals but did look as though this run might just do her good. Always handy, she was rousted along to lead over a furlong out and just held off her very persistent rivals. (5/2: 7/4-11/4)

**Mutribah (USA)** is not very big compared with many of the Thomson Jones inmates. Chasing the leaders, she threw down her challenge from below the distance and may well have got her head in front for a few strides. However, try as she might, she found the winner a little bit too strong. (7/4)
**Cowtharee**, quite a flashy filly, is not very big but nevertheless showed promise. Soon at the head of affairs, she was collared below the distance but still had every chance inside the final furlong, before just failing to cope with the front two. A small maiden can be found. (9/2: op 5/2)
**2758 Beaconscot** is only small. In a handy position throughout, she failed to quicken in the last two furlongs. (10/1: 4/1-12/1)
**2741 Hadawah (USA)** began an effort below the distance but, although she did not have a great deal of room inside the final furlong, she was looking onepaced at the time. (10/1: 4/1-12/1)
**Epsilon**, a lightly-made filly, chased the leaders but was a spent force early in the home straight. (33/1)

## 3664 WEATHERBYS STALLION BOOK H'CAP (0-70) (3-Y.O+) (Class E)

3-25 (3-25) **1m 4f** £3,343.20 (£999.60: £478.80: £218.40) Stalls: Low GOING minus 0.47 sec per fur (F)

| | | | | SP | RR | SF |
|---|---|---|---|---|---|---|
| $3584^{*}$ | **Rising Spray (49)** (CAHorgan) **5-8-13** 5x PaulEddery(6) (hdwy 7f out: chsd ldr 6f out: led wl over 1f out: comf) | — | **1** | 5/2 1 | 59+ | 17 |
| $3094^{6}$ | **Greenwich Again (60)** (TGMills) **4-9-10** RHills(5) (led: sn clr: hdd wl over 1f out: unable qckn) | 2½ | **2** | 9/2 3 | 67 | 25 |
| $3303^{*}$ | **Zeliba (40)** (MrsNMacauley) **4-8-4** TSprake(2) (hld up: hrd rdn over 1f out: one pce) | 1¼ | **3** | 4/1 2 | 45 | 3 |
| $3500^{4}$ | **Rocquaine Bay (40)** (MJBolton) **9-8-4** DaneO'Neill(3) (hdwy over 3f out: hrd rdn over 1f out: one pce) | nk | **4** | 4/1 2 | 45 | 3 |
| | **Aramon (32)** (MJHaynes) **6-7-10** NAdams(4) (chsd ldr 6f) | 9 | **5** | 66/1 | 25 | — |
| $3490^{*}$ | **Classic Beauty (IRE) (65)** (RHarris) **3-9-5** 5x AMackay(1) (lw: bhd fnl 3f) | 10 | **6** | 4/1 2 | 44 | — |

(SP 108.2%) **6 Rn**

**2m 37.8** (6.60) CSF £12.51 TOTE £2.90: £1.70 £2.90 (£4.60) OWNER Mr J. T. Heritage (PULBOROUGH) BRED Pendley Farm
LONG HANDICAP Aramon 7-1
WEIGHT FOR AGE 3yo-10lb

**3584* Rising Spray** followed up his win here last Friday. Moving up to take second place halfway down the back straight, he swept into the lead early in the final quarter-mile and comfortably had the measure of his rivals. (5/2)
**3094 Greenwich Again** was not going to hang around and had soon set up a useful lead. Headed early in the final quarter-mile, he failed to find another gear. (9/2)
**3303* Zeliba** chased the leaders but, under pressure below the distance, could only go up and down in the same place. (4/1: 3/1-9/2)
**3500 Rocquaine Bay** made her effort running down the hill, but failed to quicken in the home straight. (4/1: 3/1-9/2)

## 3665 GRAFTY GREEN MEDIAN AUCTION MAIDEN STKS (3 & 4-Y.O) (Class F)

4-00 (4-00) **6f** £2,381.00 (£656.00: £311.00) Stalls: Low GOING minus 0.47 sec per fur (F)

| | | | | SP | RR | SF |
|---|---|---|---|---|---|---|
| *$3418^{4}$* | **Failed To Hit** (SirMarkPrescott) **3-9-0** GDuffield(5) (chsd ldr: hrd rdn & wandered over 1f out: led nr fin) | — | **1** | 5/6 1 | 73 | 11 |
| $2946^{13}$ | **Shavinsky (75)** (PHowling) **3-9-0** PaulEddery(7) (led: rdn over 2f out: edgd rt ins fnl f: hdd nr fin) | ½ | **2** | 5/2 2 | 72 | 10 |
| | **Il Doria (IRE)** (AHide) **3-8-9** RHills(6) (b.hind: lw: rdn & hdwy 2f out: one pce) | 3 | **3** | 5/1 3 | 59 | — |
| $3162^{10}$ | **One Dream** (BSmart) **3-9-0** MTebbutt(3) (hld up: rdn 3f out: wknd wl over 1f out) | 2 | **4** | 20/1 | 58 | — |
| $2970^{7}$ | **Sweet Seventeen** (HJCollingridge) **3-8-9** MRimmer(1) (hld up: rdn over 2f out: wknd wl over 1f out) | 7 | **5** | 20/1 | 35 | — |
| $3162^{13}$ | **Cane Them** (TJNaughton) **3-9-0** TSprake(2) (lw: outpcd) | 16 | **6** | 40/1 | — | — |

(SP 111.7%) **6 Rn**

**1m 13.6** (3.40) CSF £3.27 TOTE £1.70: £1.10 £1.50 (£2.00) OWNER Hesmonds Stud (NEWMARKET) BRED The Lavington Stud

**3418 Failed To Hit** was more at home over this trip but was still rather green. Racing in second place, he wandered about in the final quarter-mile as his rider got down to work on him, but he eventually managed to get up near the line to win this bad race. (5/6)
**2597 Shavinsky** attempted to make all the running. Rousted along in the second half of the race, he drifted right under pressure inside the final furlong and was collared near the line. (5/2: op 4/5)
**Il Doria (IRE)**, looking in good shape for this first run since last October, moved up a quarter of a mile from home but failed to find another gear from below the distance. (5/1)
**One Dream** chased the leaders but was a spent force early in the final quarter-mile. (20/1)

## 3666 HIGH HALDEN LIMITED STKS (0-60) (3-Y.O+) (Class F)

4-30 (4-30) **6f** £2,381.00 (£656.00: £311.00) Stalls: Low GOING minus 0.47 sec per fur (F)

| | | | | SP | RR | SF |
|---|---|---|---|---|---|---|
| $3583^{4}$ | **Waders Dream (IRE) (41)** (PatMitchell) **7-9-0v** MFenton(1) (lw: hld up: nt clr run over 1f out: squeezed thro to ld ins fnl f: r.o wl) | — | **1** | 20/1 | 59 | 19 |
| $3583^{2}$ | **Scissor Ridge (54)** (JJBridger) **4-9-3** DHarrison(2) (led: rdn over 2f out: hdd wl over 1f out: led 1f out tl ins fnl f: unable qckn) | ¾ | **2** | 2/1 2 | 60 | 20 |
| $3306^{8}$ | **Don Pepe (60)** (RBoss) **5-9-0** GDuffield(3) (a.p: led wl over 1f out to 1f out: sn wknd) | 3 | **3** | 6/4 1 | 49 | 9 |
| $3458^{2}$ | **Scathebury (55)** (KRBurke) **3-8-11v** PaulEddery(4) (b.nr fore: lw: hld up: rdn over 1f out: one pce) | 1¼ | **4** | 6/1 | 46 | 3 |
| $749^{6}$ | **Face the Future (56)** (VSoane) **7-9-0** SSanders(5) (prom over 4f) | 2½ | **5** | 5/1 3 | 39 | — |

(SP 109.0%) **5 Rn**

**1m 13.0** (2.80) CSF £55.10 TOTE £23.90: £4.90 £1.20 (£10.30) OWNER Mr Richard Berenson (NEWMARKET) BRED Yeomanstown Lodge Stud
WEIGHT FOR AGE 3yo-3lb

**3583 Waders Dream (IRE)**, tucked in behind the leaders, did not have much room to manoeuvre below the distance. Luckily, a small gap emerged and, squeezing through, he shot into the lead inside the final furlong to win only his second race in fifty-one starts. (20/1)
**3583 Scissor Ridge**, making a quick reappearance, once again gave his all but had to settle for being the bridesmaid. Dictating matters from the front, he was collared early in the final quarter-mile but, to his credit, got back in front again a furlong out. However, he failed to cope with the turn of foot of the winner inside the last one hundred yards. (2/1)
**3306 Don Pepe** appeared to be travelling well in the front rank and moved into a slender lead early in the final quarter-mile. However, once let down he failed to find what was anticipated and, collared a furlong out, tamely dropped away. (6/4: 11/10-Evens)
**3458 Scathebury** chased the leaders but failed to quicken from below the distance. (6/1: 4/1-13/2)
**749 Face the Future** was close up until tiring over a furlong out. (5/1)

## 3667 PAUL COOK APPRENTICE H'CAP (0-70) (3-Y.O) (Class F)

5-00 (5-03) **2m 93y** £2,761.80 (£764.80: £365.40) GOING minus 0.47 sec per fur (F)

| | | | | SP | RR | SF |
|---|---|---|---|---|---|---|
| $3486^{5}$ | **Candle Smoke (USA) (66)** (GHarwood) **3-8-12**(5) GayeHarwood(2) (a.p: chsd ldr over 2f out: led over 1f out: r.o wl) | — | **1** | 7/2 2 | 78 | 46 |

| | | | | SP | RR | SF |
|---|---|---|---|---|---|---|
| 3329[3] | **Jamaican Flight (USA) (64)** (JWHills) **3-9-1** MHenry(8) (lw: led: rdn over 2f out: hdd over 1f out: unable qckn) | 6 | **2** | 11/2 | 70 | 38 |
| 3337[4] | **Perfect Gift (57)** (PFICole) **3-8-1**(7) DavidO'Neill(3) (lw: gd hdwy 2f out: r.o wl: t.m.t.d) | 1½ | **3** | 9/1 | 62 | 30 |
| 3077[2] | **Influence Pedler (63)** (CEBrittain) **3-8-11**(3) AimeeCook(1) (swtg: chsd ldr tl over 2f out: sn wknd) | 2 | **4** | 3/1[1] | 66 | 34 |
| 2570[10] | **One Pound (70)** (BWHills) **3-9-7** JDSmith(7) (hdwy over 5f out: wknd 3f out) | 11 | **5** | 5/1[3] | 62 | 30 |
| *3086[7]* | **Glowing Reeds (45)** (CNAllen) **3-7-5v**(5) RMullen(6) (bhd fnl 3f) | 9 | **6** | 16/1 | 28 | — |
| 3337[3] | **Meg's Memory (IRE) (56)** (JohnBerry) **3-8-7** PMcCabe(5) (a bhd) | 14 | **7** | 10/1 | 26 | — |
| 3218[6] | **Go With The Wind (63)** (MBell) **3-8-9**(5) GFaulkner(4) (a bhd) | 11 | **8** | 14/1 | 22 | — |

(SP 110.9%) **8 Rn**

**3m 34.9** (3.90) CSF £20.63 CT £136.56 TOTE £3.50: £1.80 £1.80 £2.00 (£14.20) OWNER Mr Anthony Speelman (PULBOROUGH) BRED West Star Bloodstock Inc

LONG HANDICAP Glowing Reeds 7-8

**3149 Candle Smoke (USA)** raced in third place. Moving up turning for home, he gained control below the distance and soon asserted. (7/2)

**3329 Jamaican Flight (USA)** attempted to make all the running. Collared below the distance, he failed to cope with the winner. (11/2)

**3337 Perfect Gift** was given far too much to do. Still out with the washing running down the hill with his jockey still making little attempt to close on the leaders, his inexperienced rider at last got down to work turning for home. However, by then it was too late and, although the filly made up plenty of ground, she never remotely threatened to get near the winner. (9/1: 6/1-10/1)

**3077 Influence Pedler** raced in second place but, collared for that position over two furlongs from home, was soon done with. (3/1)

**2570 One Pound** moved up towards the end of the back straight, but this trip proved beyond him and he was in trouble three furlongs from home. (5/1: 3/1-11/2)

**3337 Meg's Memory (IRE)** (10/1: 6/1-11/1)

**3218 Go With The Wind** (14/1: 7/1-16/1)

T/Plpt: £48.60 (243.9 Tckts). T/Qdpt: £10.60 (68.85 Tckts) AK

# 2720-**YORK (L-H) (Good)**
## Tuesday August 20th

WEATHER: hot & changeable WIND: fresh half against

## 3668 DEPLOY ACOMB CONDITIONS STKS (2-Y.O) (Class B)

2-05 (2-06) **6f 214y** £13,488.00 (£4,992.00: £2,396.00: £980.00: £390.00: £154.00) Stalls: High GOING minus 0.39 sec per fur (F)

| | | | | SP | RR | SF |
|---|---|---|---|---|---|---|
| 3069* | **Revoque (IRE)** (PWChapple-Hyam) **2-9-0** JReid(7) (lw: trckd ldr: led over 1f out: r.o strly) | — | **1** | 5/2[2] | 94+ | 52 |
| 3349[3] | **Symonds Inn** (JGFitzGerald) **2-8-10** KFallon(2) (w'like: leggy: trckd ldrs: outpcd ½-wy: edgd rt & styd on wl fnl f) | 2½ | **2** | 20/1 | 84 | 42 |
| 3147* | **In Command (IRE)** (BWHills) **2-9-0** MHills(3) (hld up: effrt 2f out: hung lft & wknd ins fnl f) | 1¾ | **3** | 8/11[1] | 84 | 42 |
| 2993* | **Shadow Lead** (LMCumani) **2-9-0** LDettori(5) (led: rdn over 2f out: hdd over 1f out: one pce) | s.h | **4** | 11/2[3] | 84 | 42 |
| 3293[5] | **Out of Sight (IRE)** (BAMcMahon) **2-8-10** GCarter(6) (a chsng ldrs: rdn over 2f out: one pce) | 1¾ | **5** | 50/1 | 76 | 34 |
| | **Get The Point** (RHollinshead) **2-8-10** MJKinane(1) (w'like: str: bit bkwd: hld up: effrt 3f out: sn wl outpcd) | 3½ | **6** | 25/1 | 68 | 26 |
| 2132[6] | **Drive Assured** (CEBrittain) **2-8-10** BDoyle(4) (s.i.s: outpcd fnl 3f) | s.h | **7** | 50/1 | 68 | 26 |

(SP 114.4%) **7 Rn**

**1m 24.05** (1.05) CSF £38.24 TOTE £3.30: £1.40 £3.70 (£21.20) OWNER Mr R. E. Sangster (MARLBOROUGH) BRED Minch Bloodstock

**3069* Revoque (IRE)** showed a round action going down. Appreciating the well-watered ground, he stuck on strongly to pull clear in the final furlong. A mile will be no problem. (5/2)

**3349 Symonds Inn** looks as though he needs more time and struggled to keep up at halfway. Sticking on in the final furlong, his effort here gave a boost to the form at Pontefract on his debut. (20/1)

**3147* In Command (IRE)**, bred for stamina on his sire's side, but exclusively for speed on his dam's side, took a strong grip on what was only a three furlong sprint. Tending to hang left under pressure, he was never going to pose a real threat. (8/11: Evens-11/10)

**2993* Shadow Lead**, who is not very big, set a moderate gallop. Quickening up soon after halfway, he was left for dead in the final furlong. (11/2: 7/2-6/1)

**3293 Out of Sight (IRE)**, beaten in two moderate maiden events, was probably flattered in what was only a three furlong sprint. (50/1)

**Get The Point** has plenty of scope and size, but will need more time yet. (25/1)

## 3669 MELROSE RATED STKS H'CAP (0-100) (3-Y.O) (Class B)

2-35 (2-36) **1m 5f 194y** £16,657.00 (£6,163.00: £2,956.50: £1,207.50: £478.75: £187.25) Stalls: Low GOING minus 0.39 sec per fur (F)

| | | | | SP | RR | SF |
|---|---|---|---|---|---|---|
| 1817[4] | **Yom Jameel (IRE) (97)** (MRStoute) **3-9-7** WRSwinburn(8) (effrt over 4f out: led over 2f out: styd on wl) | — | **1** | 11/1 | 112 | 82 |
| 2961* | **Wilawander (97)** (BWHills) **3-9-7** MHills(5) (hld up: effrt & n.m.r 4f out: styd on fnl 2f: nt qckn ins fnl f) | ¾ | **2** | 13/2[3] | 111 | 81 |
| 3155[2] | **Mental Pressure (84)** (MrsMReveley) **3-8-8** KDarley(3) (led 2f: led over 3f out tl over 2f out: styd on same pce) | 1½ | **3** | 7/1 | 96 | 66 |
| 3434* | **Fancy Heights (85)** (LadyHerries) **3-8-9** JReid(9) (lw: hld up: hdwy over 3f out: kpt on same pce fnl 2f) | ½ | **4** | 8/1 | 97 | 67 |
| 3209* | **Liefling (USA) (80)** (JHMGosden) **3-8-4** JCarroll(4) (swtg: chsd ldrs tl wknd over 1f out: eased towards fin) | 5 | **5** | 6/1[2] | 86 | 56 |
| 2074[13] | **Warbrook (88)** (IABalding) **3-8-12** TQuinn(2) (lw: chsd ldrs tl lost pl over 2f out) | 3 | **6** | 20/1 | 91 | 61 |
| 2473a[8] | **Private Song (USA) (92)** (RCharlton) **3-9-2** PatEddery(7) (lw: led after 2f tl over 3f out: wknd 2f out) | hd | **7** | 7/2[1] | 95 | 65 |
| 3155[4] | **Jazz King (80)** (MissGayKelleway) **3-8-4** WCarson(6) (sn bhd & rdn along) | 17 | **8** | 10/1 | 63 | 33 |
| 2912* | **Berlin Blue (83)** (JWWatts) **3-8-7** LDettori(10) (in tch: drvn along & outpcd 5f out: rdn & lost pl over 2f out: eased) | ¾ | **9** | 7/2[1] | 65 | 35 |
| 2665a[5] | **Bowled Over (84)** (CACyzer) **3-8-8v[1]** KFallon(1) (chsd ldrs tl lost pl over 3f out) | 10 | **10** | 16/1 | 55 | 25 |

(SP 123.7%) **10 Rn**

**2m 54.77** (-1.43) CSF £78.03 CT £502.83 TOTE £14.70: £3.00 £2.40 £2.00 (£36.00) Trio £155.10 OWNER Sheikh Ahmed Al Maktoum (NEWMARKET) BRED Mitchelstown Stud

LONG HANDICAP Jazz King 8-2 Liefling (USA) 8-3

**1817 Yom Jameel (IRE)** looked to have been given plenty to do at the weights and took a fair bit of stoking up. Once in front, he showed the right sort of spirit. He is definitely a stayer. (11/1)

**2961* Wilawander** looked to have been given a fair mark on his first outing in handicap company, but had to fight for room to begin his effort. Sticking on under pressure, he was never going to find quite enough to get in a serious blow at the winner. (13/2)

**3155 Mental Pressure** ran another good race. Still a maiden, he is creeping up the weights all the time. (7/1)

**3434* Fancy Heights**, raised 4lb, ran as well as could be expected. (8/1)
**3209* Liefling (USA)** was warm beforehand and seemed to get the trip. She was eased at the line. (6/1)
**2473a Private Song (USA)** was far from disgraced when acting as a pace-maker in the Irish Derby. He was not knocked about here once his measure had been taken. (7/2)
**2912* Berlin Blue** ran badly and his rider sensibly gave up some way from home. (7/2)

## 3670 JUDDMONTE INTERNATIONAL STKS (Gp 1) (3-Y.O+) (Class A)

3-10 (3-12) **1m 2f 85y** £165,548.00 (£60,932.00: £28,966.00: £11,530.00: £4,265.00: £1,359.00) Stalls: Low GOING minus 0.39 sec per fur (F)

| | | | | SP | RR | SF |
|---|---|---|---|---|---|---|
| 2546* | **Halling (USA) (120)** (SbinSuroor) **5-9-5** LDettori(1) (lw: mde all: qcknd over 2f out: edgd rt & r.o strly) | — | **1** | 6/4[1] | 134 | 94 |
| 3144* | **First Island (IRE) (119)** (GWragg) **4-9-5** MHills(4) (lw: hld up: effrt over 3f out: r.o fnl 2f: no ch w wnr) | 3 | **2** | 3/1[2] | 129 | 89 |
| 2546[2] | **Bijou d'Inde (120)** (MJohnston) **3-8-11** JWeaver(5) (lw: trckd wnr: effrt over 2f out: kpt on same pce) | 1½ | **3** | 4/1[3] | 127 | 79 |
| 2276a* | **Grape Tree Road** (AFabre,France) **3-8-11** TJarnet(3) (hld up: effrt 3f out: styd on fnl f) | ¾ | **4** | 9/1 | 126 | 78 |
| 1177[3] | **Spectrum (IRE) (120)** (PWChapple-Hyam) **4-9-5** JReid(6) (trckd ldrs: effrt over 2f out: wknd over 1f out) | nk | **5** | 6/1 | 126 | 86 |
| 2583[6] | **Punishment (109)** (CEBrittain) **5-9-5** BDoyle(2) (lw: hld up: effrt 3f out: nvr nr ldrs) | 1 | **6** | 66/1 | 102 t | 84 |
| | | | | (SP 110.8%) | | **6 Rn** |

**2m 6.88** (-2.82) CSF £6.10 TOTE £2.30: £1.40 £2.00 (£3.70) OWNER Godolphin (NEWMARKET) BRED Cyril Humphries
WEIGHT FOR AGE 3yo-8lb

**2546* Halling (USA)** made it twelve on the bounce on Turf. Repeating last year's victory in most impressive fashion, he made all the running and stepped up the gallop halfway up the straight, and raced with tremendous enthusiasm. (6/4)
**3144* First Island (IRE)** showed a scratchy action going down but stuck on really strongly from off the pace. He has not stopped improving. (3/1: op 2/1)
**2546 Bijou d'Inde**, who has a most placid temperament, tracked the winner, but when that rival stepped on the gas, all he could do was stick on at the same pace. He might be interesting making the running, as he does not do anything in a hurry. (4/1)
**2276a* Grape Tree Road**, who showed a scratchy action going down, stayed on from off the pace late in the day. (9/1)
**1177 Spectrum (IRE)** looked to be carrying a lot of condition and seemed to tire coming to the final furlong. The outing will have blown away the cobwebs. (6/1)
**2583 Punishment**, a French import, was far from disgraced and belied his long odds. (66/1)

## 3671 GREAT VOLTIGEUR STKS (Gp 2) (3-Y.O C & G) (Class A)

3-45 (3-46) **1m 3f 195y** £48,451.40 (£17,912.60: £8,581.30: £3,491.50: £1,370.75: £522.45) Stalls: Low GOING minus 0.39 sec per fur (F)

| | | | | SP | RR | SF |
|---|---|---|---|---|---|---|
| 2473a[4] | **Dushyantor (USA) (120)** (HRACecil) **3-8-9** PatEddery(2) (lw: trckd ldr: led over 2f out: styd on wl fnl f) | — | **1** | 3/1[2] | 122 | 43 |
| 3124[4] | **Mons (115)** (LMCumani) **3-8-9** LDettori(5) (swtg: led tl over 2f out: nt qckn ins fnl f) | ½ | **2** | 7/2[3] | 121 | 42 |
| 2535* | **Royal Court (IRE)** (PWChapple-Hyam) **3-8-9** JReid(6) (swtg: trckd ldrs: effrt & outpcd over 2f out: kpt on wl fnl f) | 1½ | **3** | 11/4[1] | 119 | 40 |
| 3070[6] | **Farasan (IRE) (115)** (HRACecil) **3-8-9** KFallon(3) (hld up: effrt & ev ch over 3f out: sn outpcd: styd on appr fnl f) | 1¼ | **4** | 9/1 | 118 | 39 |
| 1791[13] | **Even Top (IRE) (120)** (MHTompkins) **3-8-9** PRobinson(1) (lw: hld up: effrt over 3f out: edgd lft & grad wknd fnl 2f) | 2 | **5** | 7/2[3] | 115 | 36 |
| 3034a* | **Dankeston (USA) (110)** (MBell) **3-8-9** WCarson(4) (lw: reard s: hld up & plld v.hrd: effrt 2f out: sn bhd) | 7 | **6** | 12/1 | 106 | 27 |
| | | | | (SP 113.8%) | | **6 Rn** |

**2m 30.64** (2.84) CSF £13.21 TOTE £3.10: £1.80 £1.80 (£7.40) OWNER Mr K. Abdulla (NEWMARKET) BRED Juddmonte Farms

**2473a Dushyantor (USA)** put his unlucky run at Epsom and his poor performance at the Curragh behind him. A lazy type, he does just enough. (3/1: 2/1-100/30)
**3124 Mons**, on his toes beforehand, dictated the pace. He fought back when headed but had to give best in the closing stages. (7/2)
**2535* Royal Court (IRE)**, warm beforehand, seemed to be caught out by his inexperience. Staying on in the final furlong, he will be suited by a step up to the St Leger trip. (11/4)
**3070 Farasan (IRE)** was caught flat-footed halfway up the straight. Staying on again at the finish, this is as good as he is. (9/1: 6/1-10/1)
**1791 Even Top (IRE)** took a keen grip going down and also in the race. He did not get home, and would be interesting if dropped back in distance on easier ground. (7/2)
**3034a* Dankeston (USA)** reared up leaving the stalls and gave his rider a wretched time. (12/1)

## 3672 EAGLE LANE H'CAP (0-100) (3-Y.O+) (Class C)

4-15 (4-18) **6f** £14,840.00 (£4,445.00: £2,135.00: £980.00) Stalls: Low GOING minus 0.39 sec per fur (F)

| | | | | SP | RR | SF |
|---|---|---|---|---|---|---|
| 3622[2] | **Options Open (88)** (MrsJRRamsden) **4-9-2** KFallon(17) (lw: in tch: sn drvn: hdwy to ld over 1f out: r.o wl) | — | **1** | 9/1[3] | 101 | 64 |
| 2725* | **Double Splendour (IRE) (92)** (PSFelgate) **6-9-6** KDarley(18) (s.i.s: hdwy ½-wy: styd on fnl f: no ch w wnr) | 2 | **2** | 4/1[1] | 100 | 63 |
| 3038[7] | **Marl (88)** (RAkehurst) **3-8-13** TQuinn(20) (a chsng ldrs: kpt on same pce appr fnl f) | 1¼ | **3** | 20/1 | 92 | 52 |
| 3524[4] | **Cyrano's Lad (IRE) (96)** (CADwyer) **7-9-10** WRSwinburn(16) (led tl over 1f out: kpt on wl) | hd | **4** | 12/1 | 100 | 63 |
| 3399* | **Lord Olivier (IRE) (79)** (WJarvis) **6-8-7** JReid(4) (racd far side: a chsng ldrs: kpt on same pce fnl 2f) | ¾ | **5** | 16/1 | 81 | 44 |
| 3232[2] | **Double Bounce (91)** (PJMakin) **6-9-5** LDettori(7) (b: hld up: effrt over 2f out: kpt on: nvr rchd ldrs) | 1¼ | **6** | 5/1[2] | 90 | 53 |
| 1186[6] | **Seigneurial (89)** (GHarwood) **4-9-3** AClark(9) (bit bkwd: hld up: hdwy 2f out: kpt on fnl f: eased towards fin) | nk | **7** | 16/1 | 87 | 50 |
| 2571[2] | **Maiteamia (73)** (SRBowring) **3-7-12v[1]** JQuinn(3) (trckd ldr far side: edgd rt & kpt on wl fnl 2f) | nk | **8** | 25/1 | 70 | 30 |
| 3406[3] | **Golden Pound (USA) (84)** (MissGayKelleway) **4-8-12** PatEddery(11) (chsd ldrs tl over 1f out: eased) | 1¼ | **9** | 12/1 | 78 | 41 |
| 2329[4] | **Stuffed (72)** (MWEasterby) **4-8-0** DaleGibson(5) (racd far side: hdwy & edgd rt over 2f out: n.d) | hd | **10** | 14/1 | 66 | 29 |
| 3296[13] | **Saint Express (87)** (MrsMReveley) **6-9-1** ACulhane(14) (bhd: sme hdwy over 1f out: n.d) | hd | **11** | 50/1 | 80 | 43 |
| 3350[2] | **No Monkey Nuts (79)** (JBerry) **3-8-4** JCarroll(6) (chsd ldrs tl edgd lft & wknd 2f out) | ½ | **12** | 25/1 | 71 | 31 |
| 3223* | **Benzoe (IRE) (83)** (MrsJRRamsden) **6-8-11** JFortune(13) (s.i.s: a in rr) | hd | **13** | 12/1 | 75 | 38 |
| 3432[19] | **Bollin Harry (80)** (TDEasterby) **4-8-8** MBirch(22) (chsd ldrs tl wknd over 1f out) | hd | **14** | 33/1 | 71 | 34 |
| 2436[4] | **April The Eighth (98)** (BWHills) **3-9-9** MHills(10) (hld up: effrt & hmpd 2f out: eased) | s.h | **15** | 25/1 | 89 | 49 |
| 3146[9] | **Mister Jolson (76)** (RJHodges) **7-8-4** SDrowne(19) (nvr nr ldrs) | ¾ | **16** | 20/1 | 65 | 28 |
| 3219[4] | **Bayin (USA) (75)** (MDIUsher) **7-8-3** RStreet(12) (b: s.i.s: a bhd) | 2 | **17** | 16/1 | 59 | 22 |
| 3296[2] | **Tiler (IRE) (84)** (MJohnston) **4-8-12** JWeaver(21) (lw: chsd ldrs tl lost pl 2f out) | ½ | **18** | 10/1 | 67 | 30 |
| 3482[10] | **The Wad (71)** (DNicholls) **3-7-10** LCharnock(1) (lw: led far side tl wknd over 2f out) | 5 | **19** | 33/1 | 40 | — |
| 3432* | **Royal Dome (IRE) (75)** (MartynWane) **4-8-3** GCarter(15) (lw: chsd ldrs tl lost pl 2f out) | 2½ | **20** | 16/1 | 38 | 1 |
| | **Snipe Hall (91)** (TRWatson) **5-9-2**(3)ow1 OPears(2) (bit bkwd: swtg: s.i.s: racd far side: a bhd) | nk | **21** | 100/1 | 53 | 15 |

| | | | | SP | RR | SF |
|---|---|---|---|---|---|---|
| *$3442^{5}$* | ***Silent Expression (82)*** *(BJMeehan)* ***6-8-10b$^{1}$*** *MJKinane(8) (Withdrawn not under Starter's orders: kicked at s)* | | **W** | 25/1 | — | — |
| | | | | (SP 142.8%) | **21 Rn** | |

**1m 11.23** (0.23) CSF £45.76 CT £507.23 TOTE £10.00: £2.50 £1.90 £5.80 £3.20 (£23.20) Trio £252.40 OWNER Mr Jonathan Ramsden (THIRSK) BRED D. H. Jones

LONG HANDICAP The Wad 7-9

WEIGHT FOR AGE 3yo-3lb

**3622 Options Open** won this in good style, showing plenty of enthusiasm. He certainly has the ability to win more races over six but seven could prove his optimum trip. (9/1)

**2725* Double Splendour (IRE)**, raised 10lb, made things hard for himself, missing the break. He stuck on to finish clear second best and is not done winning yet. (4/1)

**2545 Marl** ran her best race for some time. (20/1)

**3524 Cyrano's Lad (IRE)** ran a tremendous race under top weight. He is a credit to his trainer. (12/1)

**3399* Lord Olivier (IRE)** has not won a handicap now in twenty three attempts. (16/1)

**3232 Double Bounce** ran as if just needing the outing. (5/1)

**1186 Seigneurial**, absent for 94 days, looked as though he needed this and was not knocked about. (16/1)

**2571 Maiteamia** did best of the handful who raced on the far side. (25/1)

**2292 Saint Express**, who is slipping down the weights, showed a choppy action going down to the start but showed a glimmer of promise. (50/1)

## 3673 LONSDALE STKS (Listed) (3-Y.O+) (Class A)

4-45 (4-45) **1m 7f 195y** £19,014.00 (£7,026.00: £3,363.00: £1,365.00: £532.50: £199.50) Stalls: Low GOING minus 0.39 sec per fur (F)

| | | | | SP | RR | SF |
|---|---|---|---|---|---|---|
| 2723* | **Celeric (107)** (DMorley) **4-9-4** WCarson(7) (lw: hld up: effrt over 3f out: qckngd to ld 1f out: pushed out) | — | 1 | 9/4$^{1}$ | 119+ | 76 |
| $2071^{4}$ | **Always Aloof (USA) (106)** (MRStoute) **5-9-1** MJKinane(4) (lw: trckd ldrs: led 2f out to 1f out: nt pce of wnr fnl f) | 2 | 2 | 9/2$^{3}$ | 114 | 71 |
| $3212^{4}$ | **Sanmartino (IRE) (100)** (BWHills) **4-9-1** MHills(1) (lw: hld up: hdwy to chal 2f out: kpt on same pce fnl f) | nk | 3 | 8/1 | 114 | 71 |
| 3157* | **Grey Shot (110)** (IABalding) **4-9-8** LDettori(2) (lw: led to 2f out: sn wknd) | 4 | 4 | 5/2$^{2}$ | 117 | 74 |
| | **Anchor Clever (109)** (PAKelleway) **4-9-1** JReid(5) (bit bkwd: hld up & plld hrd: effrt over 3f out: n.d) | 5 | 5 | 20/1 | 105 | 62 |
| 3155* | **Benatom (USA) (95)** (HRACecil) **3-8-1** AMcGlone(3) (chsd ldrs: pushed along 5f out: hung lft & wknd over 1f out: eased) | 4 | 6 | 6/1 | 101 | 44 |
| $2723^{3}$ | **Latahaab (USA) (96)** (RAkehurst) **5-9-1** TQuinn(6) (lw: chsd ldrs: pushed along over 6f out: lost pl over 4f out: t.o) | dist | 7 | 20/1 | — | — |
| | | | | (SP 112.4%) | **7 Rn** | |

**3m 20.33** (-0.87) CSF £11.95 TOTE £2.70: £1.90 £1.90 (£6.50) OWNER Mr Christopher Spence (NEWMARKET) BRED Chieveley Manor Enterprises

WEIGHT FOR AGE 3yo-14lb

OFFICIAL EXPLANATION **Benatom (USA): became extremely tired in the closing stages and hung badly to the left. Bearing in mind the colt's fatigue, his rider said he felt it prudent to hold his mount together, adding that he would not have finished fifth for more vigorous riding.**

**2723* Celeric** made the step up from handicap company. He possesses a good turn of foot for a stayer and always looked to be going best. (9/4)

**2071 Always Aloof (USA)** ran really well, but as so often in the past, his lack of finishing speed found him out. (9/2)

**3212 Sanmartino (IRE)**, suited by the step up in distance, ran really well. (8/1)

**3157* Grey Shot**, conceding weight all round, could never shake off his rivals. It is possible his Goodwood Cup race has taken the edge off him for the time being. (5/2)

**Anchor Clever**, who has shown good form abroad, looked in need of the outing, his first since last October. (20/1)

**3155* Benatom (USA)**, biting off a lot more, had every chance two furlongs out but tamely dropped out hanging left, and his rider eased him. (6/1)

## 3674 EGLINTON NURSERY H'CAP (2-Y.O) (Class C)

5-15 (5-16) **6f 214y** £11,550.00 (£3,450.00: £1,650.00: £750.00) Stalls: High GOING minus 0.39 sec per fur (F)

| | | | | SP | RR | SF |
|---|---|---|---|---|---|---|
| $3483^{3}$ | **Pension Fund (75)** (MWEasterby) **2-7-10** DaleGibson(10) (lw: drvn along after 1f: hdwy on outside over 2f out: hrd rdn & styd on to ld nr fin) | — | 1 | 8/1 | 72 | 22 |
| $3247^{2}$ | **Demolition Man (87)** (JWWatts) **2-8-8** KDarley(7) (trckd ldrs: led 2f out tl nr fin) | hd | 2 | 11/4$^{1}$ | 84 | 34 |
| $3408^{5}$ | **Ninth Symphony (77)** (PCHaslam) **2-7-12** WCarson(4) (swtg: bhd: swtchd to centre over 2f out: styd on wl fnl f) | nk | 3 | 12/1 | 73 | 23 |
| $2063^{3}$ | **Bolero Boy (100)** (MWEasterby) **2-9-7** LDettori(1) (lw: swtg: hld up: n.m.r & swtchd rt over 2f out: kpt on) | 2 | 4 | 14/1 | 92 | 42 |
| $1795^{5}$ | **Burlington House (USA) (80)** (PFICole) **2-8-1** GCarter(5) (lw: unruly in stalls: led to 2f out: kpt on one pce) | hd | 5 | 11/1 | 71 | 21 |
| 3214* | **Dickie Bird (IRE) (85)** (RHannon) **2-8-6** PatEddery(12) (lw: chsd ldrs: ev ch 2f out: one pce) | hd | 6 | 6/1$^{3}$ | 76 | 26 |
| 3467* | **Charlton Spring (IRE) (76)** (RJHodges) **2-7-11** 6x JQuinn(2) (sn chsng ldrs: outpcd & wandered over 2f out: n.d) | 1¾ | 7 | 12/1 | 63 | 13 |
| 3050* | **Cherokee Flight (77)** (MrsJRRamsden) **2-7-12** JFEgan(6) (effrt ½-wy: sn rdn: nvr nr to chal) | 2 | 8 | 5/1$^{2}$ | 59 | 9 |
| 3269* | **Hawait (IRE) (94)** (BWHills) **2-9-1** MHills(11) (hld up: stdy hdwy ½-wy: rdn & wknd 2f out) | 1½ | 9 | 8/1 | 73 | 23 |
| $3277^{2}$ | **Shoumatara (USA) (88)** (MRStoute) **2-8-9** JReid(9) (lw: prom: drvn along ½-wy: sn lost pl) | 1 | 10 | 13/2 | 65 | 15 |
| | | | | (SP 123.6%) | **10 Rn** | |

**1m 25.2** (2.20) CSF £30.50 CT £258.77 TOTE £10.30: £2.40 £1.50 £3.10 (£13.30) Trio £87.40 OWNER Mr Stephen Curtis (SHERIFF HUTTON) BRED Pitts Farm Stud

STEWARDS' ENQUIRY Gibson susp. 29-30/8/96 (excessive use of whip).

**3483 Pension Fund**, as expected, seemed well suited by the step up in distance. Never flinching under a hard ride, he stuck on to lead near the line. (8/1)

**3247 Demolition Man** looked home and dried when quickening two lengths clear two furlongs out, but being out on his own for some time, he began to tread water inside the last and was just caught. (11/4)

**3408 Ninth Symphony** did not have the run of the race. Switched to the centre, he stuck on strongly in the final furlong and should win another similar event. (12/1)

**2063 Bolero Boy** looks to have been crucified by the Handicapper. (14/1)

**1795 Burlington House (USA)**, upset in the stalls, raced too keenly for his own good. (11/1)

**3214* Dickie Bird (IRE)** had every chance but, under strong pressure, could only stick on at the same pace. (6/1)

T/Jkpt: Not won; £27,210.83 to York 21/8/96. T/Plpt: £132.60 (412.63 Tckts). T/Qdpt: £12.80 (254.66 Tckts) WG

# 3423-AYR (L-H) (Good)
## Wednesday August 21st
WEATHER: overcast WIND: slt against

### 3675 E.B.F. KIRKOSWALD MAIDEN STKS (2-Y.O F) (Class D)
2-15 (2-15) **6f** £3,403.75 (£1,030.00: £502.50: £238.75) Stalls: Low GOING: 0.07 sec per fur (G)

| | | | | SP | RR | SF |
|---|---|---|---|---|---|---|
| $3114^{5}$ | **Silca Key Silca** (MRChannon) **2-8-11** RHughes(3) (lw: mde most: kpt on wl fnl f) | — | **1** | $7/2^{3}$ | 72 | 42 |
| $3259^{8}$ | **Kalimat** (WJarvis) **2-8-11** MTebbutt(4) (lw: chsd ldrs: effrt 2f out: hrd rdn & nt qckn ins fnl f) | 1 | **2** | $5/2^{2}$ | 69 | 39 |
| $3137^{2}$ | **Gilding The Lily (IRE)** (MJohnston) **2-8-11** JCarroll(1) (nvr wnt pce) | 6 | **3** | 10/1 | 53 | 23 |
| | **Thahabyah (USA)** (HThomsonJones) **2-8-11** JFortune(2) (gd sort: str: sn disp ld: rdn & wknd 2f out) | 6 | **4** | $Evens^{1}$ | 37 | 7 |
| | | | | (SP 109.9%) | | **4 Rn** |

**1m 13.92** (4.12) CSF £11.26 TOTE £2.70 (£3.30) OWNER Aldridge Racing Ltd (UPPER LAMBOURN) BRED Alan Gibson
**3114 Silca Key Silca** looked a picture and did this really well. As the easier ground comes, she will find further success. (7/2: op 7/4)
**3259 Kalimat**, although on the lean side, proved to be a tough customer but, despite trying hard, always found the winner too good. Her turn should come. (5/2: op 4/1)
**3137 Gilding The Lily (IRE)** was disappointing and could never get into the race at any stage. (10/1: op 5/1)
**Thahabyah (USA)**, who on looks would have picked this lot up and carried them, proved disappointing in the race, stopping as though shot in the last two furlongs. (Evens)

### 3676 FAILFORD (S) STKS (3-Y.O+) (Class F)
2-45 (2-45) **1m 5f 13y** £2,556.00 (£716.00: £348.00) Stalls: High GOING: 0.07 sec per fur (G)

| | | | | SP | RR | SF |
|---|---|---|---|---|---|---|
| $3346^{6}$ | **Trumped (IRE) (42)** (PMonteith) **4-8-7**(7) JBramhill(5) (swtg: mde all: qcknd ent st: drvn clr fnl 3f) | — | **1** | $7/1^{3}$ | 67? | 19 |
| $3329^{7}$ | **Latvian (62)** (RAllan) **9-9-10** ACulhane(2) (lw: sn chsng wnr: rdn appr st: no rspnse) | 13 | **2** | $7/4^{2}$ | 61 | 13 |
| $3428^{8}$ | **Cutthroat Kid (IRE) (63)** (MrsMReveley) **6-9-5v** JFortune(1) (lw: chsd ldrs: drvn along 4f out: no imp after) | 7 | **3** | $Evens^{1}$ | 48 | — |
| $3242^{7}$ | **Warwick Mist (IRE) (31)** (BMactaggart) **4-8-9**(5) GLee(4) (chsd ldrs tl outpcd appr st: sn lost tch) | 24 | **4** | 33/1 | 13 | — |
| $2966^{11}$ | **Welcome Brief (39)** (EJAlston) **3-8-3** SDrowne(3) (lw: a bhd) | 5 | **5** | 50/1 | 7 | — |
| | | | | (SP 103.8%) | | **5 Rn** |

**2m 58.97** (14.17) CSF £17.56 TOTE £10.70: £2.50 £1.10 (£7.00) OWNER Mr John Pirie (ROSEWELL) BRED R. N. Clay and Airlie Stud
WEIGHT FOR AGE 3yo-11lb
Bt in 4,000 gns
**3346 Trumped (IRE)**, very warm beforehand, nevertheless did nothing wrong in the race and, once she got her iffy opponents off the bit turning for home, the race was hers. (7/1: 5/1-8/1)
**2986 Latvian** looked to be travelling well when sat on the winner's heels but, once an effort was required turning into the straight, he soon decided it was not for him. (7/4)
**2804 Cutthroat Kid (IRE)** has his own ideas about the game and cried enough fully four furlongs out. (Evens)
**2683 Warwick Mist (IRE)** stopped as though shot once off the bit turning for home. (33/1)
**Welcome Brief** has shown nothing in the past and this step up in distance produced the same result. (50/1)

### 3677 AUCHENCRUIVE H'CAP (0-80) (3-Y.O+) (Class E)
3-20 (3-22) **1m 2f** £3,675.00 (£1,110.00: £540.00: £255.00) Stalls: High GOING: 0.07 sec per fur (G)

| | | | | SP | RR | SF |
|---|---|---|---|---|---|---|
| $3346^{2}$ | **Stormless (48)** (PMonteith) **5-7-5**(7) JBramhill(6) (hld up: qcknd to ld over 4f out: sn clr: drvn out) | — | **1** | $3/1^{1}$ | 60 | 38 |
| $3621^{6}$ | **Ordained (58)** (EJAlston) **3-8-0**ow2 SDrowne(1) (in tch: hdwy over 3f out: sn chsng wnr: nvr able to chal) | 2 | **2** | 7/1 | 67 | 35 |
| $1361^{7}$ | **Sadler's Realm (73)** (MRStoute) **3-9-1** NConnorton(8) (lw: trckd ldrs: effrt over 3f out: hung lft & no imp) | 6 | **3** | $100/30^{2}$ | 72 | 42 |
| $3487^{3}$ | **Field of Vision (IRE) (71)** (MrsASwinbank) **6-9-7** JFortune(2) (chsd ldrs: outpcd appr st: no imp after) | 3½ | **4** | $4/1^{3}$ | 65 | 43 |
| $3589^{6}$ | **Swandale Flyer (47)** (NBycroft) **4-7-8**(3)ow1 DWright(7) (disp ld tl hdd over 4f out: sn outpcd) | 2 | **5** | 50/1 | 37 | 14 |
| $3344^{13}$ | **Nizaal (USA) (50)** (RAllan) **5-7-11**(3) DarrenMoffatt(4) (prom tl wknd fnl 3f) | nk | **6** | 33/1 | 40 | 18 |
| $3295^{6}$ | **Nose No Bounds (IRE) (74)** (MJohnston) **3-9-2v** JCarroll(3) (hld up: effrt appr st: sn btn) | 10 | **7** | 9/1 | 48 | 18 |
| $3280^{3}$ | **New Albion (USA) (58)** (MissZAGreen) **5-8-8** JFanning(9) (disp ld tl hdd over 4f out: sn wknd) | 20 | **8** | 9/1 | — | — |
| $3426^{13}$ | **Duo Master (62)** (MrsMReveley) **3-8-4** ACulhane(10) (dwlt: a bhd) | 22 | **9** | 16/1 | — | — |
| | | | | (SP 111.4%) | | **9 Rn** |

**2m 10.89** (6.29) CSF £21.56 CT £63.79 TOTE £3.70: £1.30 £1.80 £1.90 (£9.20) Trio £11.50 OWNER Mr D. St Clair (ROSEWELL) BRED D. V. St Clair
LONG HANDICAP Swandale Flyer 7-3
WEIGHT FOR AGE 3yo-8lb
**3346 Stormless** shot past the field into a clear lead entering the straight and, although needing to be kept going, the race was his from then on. (3/1)
**3412* Ordained** tried to go with the winner early in the straight, but battling on, was never good enough. She may have appreciated a bit further. (7/1)
**1361 Sadler's Realm**, after three months off, travelled really well but, when pressure was applied, he just wanted to hang left. (100/30)
**3487 Field of Vision (IRE)** got tapped for speed when the tempo increased on the home turn and was then always finding this trip a bit too sharp. (4/1)
**3426 Swandale Flyer**, 7lb out of the handicap this time, got hampered in the straight but was already finding this trip beyond him. (50/1)
**Nizaal (USA)** looks a decent type but it is a long time since he showed anything positive. (33/1)

### 3678 MINISHANT NURSERY H'CAP (2-Y.O) (Class E)
3-55 (3-59) **1m** £3,095.00 (£935.00: £455.00: £215.00) Stalls: High GOING: 0.07 sec per fur (G)

| | | | | SP | RR | SF |
|---|---|---|---|---|---|---|
| $2802^{6}$ | **General's Star (70)** (MRStoute) **2-8-13** NConnorton(3) (trckd ldrs: effrt ent st: chal over 1f out: styd on to ld wl ins fnl f) | — | **1** | 5/1 | 72 | 33 |
| *3417** | **Ben's Ridge (78)** (PCHaslam) **2-9-7** JFortune(7) (lw: hld up: hdwy 3f out: led appr fnl f: hrd rdn & hdd wl ins fnl f: kpt on) | hd | **2** | $9/2^{3}$ | 80 | 41 |
| $3324^{5}$ | **Cajun Sunset (IRE) (58)** (TDEasterby) **2-8-1** JFanning(6) (trckd ldrs: led 2f out tl appr fnl f: sn btn) | 4 | **3** | 20/1 | 52 | 13 |
| $3324^{3}$ | **Run Lucy Run (62)** (RGuest) **2-8-2**(3) DWright(5) (lw: led after 1f to 2f out: no ex) | 1¼ | **4** | $9/2^{3}$ | 53 | 14 |
| $3408^{2}$ | **Silca's My Key (IRE) (69)** (MRChannon) **2-8-12** RHughes(4) (lw: hld up: hdwy on ins 3f out: sn rdn & no imp) | 8 | **5** | $3/1^{1}$ | 44 | 5 |

2959[6] **Apiculate (IRE) (54)** (WTKemp) **2-7-4**[(7)ow1] JBramhill(2) (chsd ldrs tl wknd fnl 3f) ....17 **6** 66/1 — —
3324[2] **Our Future (IRE) (72)** (MJohnston) **2-9-1** JCarroll(1) (led 1f: chsd ldrs: rdn over 3f out: sn wknd) ....10 **7** 7/2[2] — —
(SP 106.5%) **7 Rn**

**1m 44.24** (6.84) CSF £23.94 TOTE £7.60: £2.90 £1.70 (£17.10) OWNER Mr Saeed Suhail (NEWMARKET) BRED Meon Valley Stud
LONG HANDICAP Apiculate (IRE) 7-7

**2802 General's Star** was wearing a tongue-strap for the first time. He certainly does not do anything quickly and needed plenty of help from the saddle to lead late on. Even more cut in the ground should suit. (5/1)
**3417* Ben's Ridge**, the pick on looks, showed a useful turn of foot to lead approaching the final furlong only then to be worried out of it. Perhaps more patient tactics are needed. (9/2)
**3324 Cajun Sunset (IRE)** keeps showing a glimmer of form but he was soon dealt with here when the pressure was really on. (20/1)
**3324 Run Lucy Run** left the paddock going far too freely and her rider then had problems in getting her to the start. She probably used up too much energy before the race. (9/2)
**3408 Silca's My Key (IRE)**, trying his longest trip to date, ran miserably for the second time when having to make a particularly long journey in a horsebox. (3/1: 7/4-100/30)
**3324 Our Future (IRE)** ran too bad to be true and obviously something was wrong here. (7/2)

## 3679 ARRAN MEDIAN AUCTION MAIDEN STKS (3-Y.O) (Class E)
4-25 (4-25) **7f** £2,827.00 (£856.00: £418.00: £199.00) Stalls: High GOING: 0.07 sec per fur (G)

SP RR SF
1686[W] **Roushan (73)** (SCWilliams) **3-9-0** JTate(2) (mde all: rdn over 1f out: hld on wl) ....— **1** 8/1[3] 78 30
2589[3] **Mezzanotte (IRE) (79)** (LMCumani) **3-9-0** JFortune(1) (lw: hld up: hdwy on bit to chal appr fnl f: rdn & no rspnse towards fin) ....nk **2** 4/7[1] 77 29
*3064*[5] **Domak Amaam (IRE) (76)** (JHMGosden) **3-9-0** JCarroll(3) (lw: trckd ldr: effrt over 2f out: sn hrd drvn: btn over 1f out) ....4 **3** 2/1[2] 68 20
**Sorara** (DMoffatt) **3-8-6**[(3)] DarrenMoffatt(4) (unf: scope: dwlt: a bhd) ....10 **4** 25/1 40? —
(SP 111.9%) **4 Rn**

**1m 30.24** (6.24) CSF £13.27 TOTE £10.40 (£3.10) OWNER Mr R. J. Cummings (NEWMARKET) BRED Mascalls Stud Farm
**1469 Roushan**, a headstrong individual, was taken early to post and proved to be a tough customer on the way back, refusing to give in. (8/1)
**2589 Mezzanotte (IRE)** looked likely to take this whenever he wanted, but, when it came down to an effort in the closing stages, he failed to come up with the goods. (4/7)
**3064 Domak Amaam (IRE)** had his chances but, yet again, looked very slow. (2/1)
**Sorara**, after a tardy start, always found things happening too quickly. (25/1)

## 3680 AYR SUMMER H'CAP (0-70) (3-Y.O+) (Class E)
4-55 (4-55) **7f** £2,965.00 (£895.00: £435.00: £205.00) Stalls: High GOING: 0.07 sec per fur (G)

SP RR SF
3161[15] **Superpride (55)** (MrsMReveley) **4-9-2** ACulhane(2) (lw: mde all: edgd rt fnl f: all out) ....— **1** 8/1 70 32
3102[12] **Magic Lake (45)** (EJAlston) **3-8-1** SDrowne(5) (lw: trckd ldrs: hdwy & ev ch appr fnl f: rdn & nt qckn) ....3 **2** 9/2[3] 53 10
3306[3] **Miss Pigalle (43)** (MissLAPerratt) **5-8-4b** JCarroll(7) (hdwy to chse ldrs ent st: nt qckn fnl 2f) ....3 **3** 20/1 44 6
3265[5] **Sagebrush Roller (67)** (JWWatts) **8-10-0** JFortune(6) (lw: hld up & bhd: effrt 3f out: styd on: no imp) ....4 **4** 11/2 59 21
3424* **Ballard Lady (IRE) (45)** (JSWainwright) **4-7-13**[(7)] JBramhill(3) (lw: chsd ldrs: rdn 3f out: grad wknd) ....nk **5** 3/1[2] 37 —
3644* **Another Nightmare (IRE) (39)** (RMMcKellar) **4-7-7**[(7)] KSked(4) (cl up tl rdn & wknd fnl 2f: lame) ....1¼ **6** 5/2[1] 28 —
3489[2] **Pathaze (48)** (NBycroft) **3-8-4** JFanning(1) (lw: chsd ldrs tl wknd fnl 3f) ....1½ **7** 12/1 33 —
(SP 110.7%) **7 Rn**

**1m 30.21** (6.21) CSF £39.12 TOTE £13.70: £4.80 £1.80 (£31.40) OWNER Mrs Muriel Ward (SALTBURN) BRED Mrs Muriel Ward
WEIGHT FOR AGE 3yo-5lb
OFFICIAL EXPLANATION **Superpride: was not suited by the extra two furlongs last time, and that seven furlongs appeared his best trip. Another Nightmare (IRE): was lame on her off hind.**
**2901 Superpride** looked particularly well and, out in front all the way, was given some strong assistance. By the way he was hanging in the closing stages, he does not look one to trust entirely. (8/1)
**3102 Magic Lake** was back to something like her form here but could never quite overhaul the winner. (9/2: op 3/1)
**3306 Miss Pigalle** ran another reasonable race but was never doing enough when it mattered. (20/1)
**3265 Sagebrush Roller** runs when he is in the mood and, by the time he did here, it was always too late. (11/2)
**3424* Ballard Lady (IRE)** was a shade disappointing here, dropping tamely away when pressure was on in the last three furlongs. (3/1)
**3644* Another Nightmare (IRE)** has never won at this trip but that was not the reason for this defeat as she was struggling and beaten a long way from home. (5/2: 2/1-3/1)
**3489 Pathaze** (12/1: op 8/1)

T/Plpt: £2,829.10 (2.11 Tckts). T/Qdpt: £400.80 (0.9 Tckts); £54.17 to York 22/8/96 AA

# 3318-KEMPTON (R-H) (St course Good, Rest Good, Good to firm patches) Wednesday August 21st
WEATHER: v.warm WIND: almost nil

## 3681 FORESTER APPRENTICE H'CAP (0-70) (3-Y.O) (Class E)
5-30 (5-32) **1m 2f (Jubilee)** £3,046.25 (£920.00: £447.50: £211.25) Stalls: High GOING minus 0.26 sec per fur (GF)

SP RR SF
3295[3] **Halebid (70)** (SPCWoods) **3-9-4**[(3)] CWebb(10) (mde all: clr over 2f out: r.o wl) ....— **1** 5/1[2] 75 32
3334[10] **Absolutelystunning (55)** (MrsBarbaraWaring) **3-8-6** IonaWands(7) (b: chsd wnr: rdn over 2f out: r.o wl ins fnl f) ....1¼ **2** 16/1 58 15
1821[8] **Laughing Buccaneer (46)** (MJHeaton-Ellis) **3-7-6**[(5)] JFowle(8) (hld up: rdn over 2f out: r.o wl ins fnl f) ....1 **3** 20/1 47 4
2514[10] **Misky Bay (70)** (JHMGosden) **3-9-7v**[1] AEddery(13) (a.p: rdn over 2f out: r.o one pce) ....1¾ **4** 12/1 69 26
3286[3] **Princess Pamgaddy (47)** (PFICole) **3-7-5**[(7)] JBosley(3) (hdwy over 1f out: r.o) ....nk **5** 6/1[3] 45 2
2313[9] **Spiral Flyer (IRE) (45)** (MDIUsher) **3-7-5**[(5)] RBrisland(4) (s.s: hdwy over 1f out: nvr nrr) ....nk **6** 33/1 43 —
3473[3] **Northern Saga (IRE) (45)** (CJDrewe) **3-7-7**[(3)] RMullen(1) (lw: hdwy over 1f out: nvr nrr) ....nk **7** 20/1 42 —
3492* **Allstars Rocket (53)** (TJNaughton) **3-8-1**[(3) 5x] JWilkinson(5) (hld up: rdn over 2f out: wknd over 1f out) ....1½ **8** 7/2[1] 48 5
2253[7] **Scimitar (64)** (PJMakin) **3-9-1** DSweeney(14) (lw: nvr nr to chal) ....1¾ **9** 20/1 56 13
1773[16] **Sam Rockett (58)** (CAHorgan) **3-8-6**[(3)] GayeHarwood(9) (dwlt: a bhd) ....½ **10** 6/1[3] 49 6

| | Horse | Dist | Pl | SP | RR | SF |
|---|---|---|---|---|---|---|
| 2196[7] | **Safecracker (64)** (JWHills) **3-8-10b[1]**(5) RFfrench(6) (lw: prom over 8f) | 3 | **11** | 12/1 | 50 | 7 |
| 3474[11] | **Oscar Rose (52)** (LordHuntingdon) **3-8-3** AimeeCook(2) (a bhd) | 1¼ | **12** | 16/1 | 36 | — |
| 2549[8] | **Apache Len (USA) (70)** (RHannon) **3-9-7** SophieMitchell(12) (bhd fnl 3f) | hd | **13** | 10/1 | 54 | 11 |
| | | | | (SP 120.9%) | **13 Rn** | |

**2m 9.88** (6.38) CSF £74.11 CT £1,357.65 TOTE £6.00: £2.30 £2.20 £3.00 (£30.50) Trio £170.30 OWNER Mr S. P. C. Woods (NEWMARKET) BRED Top Spin Co Ltd

LONG HANDICAP Northern Saga (IRE) 7-6 Spiral Flyer (IRE) 7-5

**3295 Halebid** was given a fine ride. Making all the running, he strode clear early in the straight and, although his rivals closed the gap on him in the final furlong, he was not going to be denied. (5/1)

**1414* Absolutelystunning** ran her best race since her victory back in May. Racing in second place, she had a lot of ground to make up on the winner and, although closing that gap considerably inside the final furlong, never looked like overhauling him in time. (16/1)

**Laughing Buccaneer** chased the leaders. Bustled along over a quarter of a mile from home, he ran on strongly inside the final furlong but was never going to get there. He is still a maiden after seventeen attempts. (20/1)

**786 Misky Bay**, never far away, was pushed along early in the straight but, despite staying on, never seriously threatened. (12/1: 8/1-14/1)

**3286 Princess Pamgaddy** stayed on well from the back of the field in the last furlong and a half and only just missed out on the prize money. (6/1: 4/1-7/1)

**Spiral Flyer (IRE)**, who lost ground at the start, put in her best work from below the distance. (33/1)

**Sam Rockett** (6/1: 5/1-8/1)

**1872 Apache Len (USA)** (10/1: op 6/1)

## 3682 E.B.F. CONFEDERACY MAIDEN STKS (2-Y.O) (Class D)

5-55 (5-56) **7f (Jubilee)** £3,517.50 (£1,065.00: £520.00: £247.50) Stalls: High GOING minus 0.26 sec per fur (GF)

| | Horse | Dist | Pl | SP | RR | SF |
|---|---|---|---|---|---|---|
| 3221[4] | **Entrepreneur** (MRStoute) **2-9-0** JReid(5) (lw: led over 2f: led over 2f out: qcknd clr: easily) | — | **1** | 1/2[1] | 88+ | 43 |
| | **Falak (USA)** (MajorWRHern) **2-9-0** WRSwinburn(6) (w'like: scope: bit bkwd: rdn over 2f out: hdwy over 1f out: r.o) | 5 | **2** | 10/1[3] | 77 | 32 |
| | **Heart of Armor** (PFICole) **2-9-0** DaneO'Neill(3) (leggy: scope: rdn 5f out: hdwy over 1f out: r.o) | ¾ | **3** | 14/1 | 75 | 30 |
| 3221[8] | **Pennys From Heaven** (HCandy) **2-9-0** CRutter(9) (chsd ldrs: rdn over 2f out: unable qckn fnl f) | 1 | **4** | 33/1 | 73 | 28 |
| 3214[3] | **Prairie Falcon (IRE)** (BWHills) **2-8-9**(5) JDSmith(13) (w ldr: led over 4f out tl over 2f out: wknd over 1f out) | 4 | **5** | 8/1[2] | 63 | 18 |
| | **Shalaal (USA)** (EALDunlop) **2-9-0** SWhitworth(4) (w'like: scope: bit bkwd: s.s: rdn over 2f out: nvr nr to chal) | 2½ | **6** | 40/1 | 58 | 13 |
| 2972[7] | **Frost King** (MissBSanders) **2-8-11**(3) AWhelan(10) (a mid div) | nk | **7** | 66/1 | 57 | 12 |
| | **Padauk** (MJHaynes) **2-9-0** DHarrison(8) (a mid div) | ¾ | **8** | 66/1 | 55 | 10 |
| | **Bold Words (CAN)** (EALDunlop) **2-9-0** WRyan(1) (w'like: scope: bkwd: rdn over 2f out: a mid div) | 1 | **9** | 20/1 | 23 | 8 |
| | **Supreme Sound** (PWHarris) **2-9-0** AClark(14) (w'like: scope: s.s: a bhd) | ½ | **10** | 33/1 | 52 | 7 |
| | **Silver Patriarch (IRE)** (JLDunlop) **2-9-0** TSprake(11) (w'like: scope: bit bkwd: a bhd) | ½ | **11** | 12/1 | 51 | 6 |
| | **State of Gold (IRE)** (WJHaggas) **2-9-0** TIves(15) (w'like: scope: s.s: a bhd) | 1¼ | **12** | 33/1 | 48 | 3 |
| | **St Lawrence (CAN)** (CEBrittain) **2-9-0** BDoyle(7) (unf: bit bkwd: s.s: a bhd) | ½ | **13** | 33/1 | 47 | 2 |
| | **Warring** (MRChannon) **2-8-9**(5) PPMurphy(12) (bhd fnl 4f) | 13 | **14** | 33/1 | 17 | — |
| 869[9] | **Always Alight** (KRBurke) **2-8-7**(7) EmilyJoyce(2) (prom 4f) | ¾ | **15** | 66/1 | 15 | — |
| | | | | (SP 127.6%) | **15 Rn** | |

**1m 27.33** (2.83) CSF £7.53 TOTE £1.50: £1.10 £1.60 £3.30 (£4.60) Trio £45.90 OWNER Mr M Tabor & Mrs John Magnier (NEWMARKET) BRED Cheveley Park Stud Ltd

**3221 Entrepreneur** made up for his shock Newmarket defeat in no uncertain fashion. Storming off in front with Prairie Falcon, the two strode well clear of the rest of the field. Quickening up nicely a quarter of a mile out, he soon shot clear to win in tremendous style. A good-looking colt, he has the making of a top-class individual and can certainly go on from here. (1/2)

**Falak (USA)**, an attractive, good-bodied individual, looked as though this run would do him good. Ridden along early in the straight, he ran on nicely in the last furlong and a half to snatch second place in the closing stages. He will have learnt a lot from this and should soon find a race. (10/1: 8/1-12/1)

**Heart of Armor**, a tall newcomer, was soon being bustled along. He ran on in the last furlong and a half and just managed to snatch third prize. (14/1: op 8/1)

**Pennys From Heaven** chased the front two but at some considerable distance. Bustled along over a quarter of a mile from home, he actually managed to get into second place inside the final furlong before being swamped. (33/1)

**3214 Prairie Falcon (IRE)** was the only runner who was able to live with the winner. Disputing the lead, he eventually paid the price and, tiring in the last two furlongs, was collared for second prize inside the last two hundred yards. (8/1)

**Shalaal (USA)**, an attractive newcomer who did not look fully wound up, made some late headway without posing a threat. (40/1)

**Silver Patriarch (IRE)** (12/1: op 8/1)

## 3683 RACING & FOOTBALL OUTLOOK H'CAP (0-90) (3-Y.O+) (Class C)

6-25 (6-25) **1m 4f** £5,374.50 (£1,626.00: £793.00: £376.50) Stalls: High GOING minus 0.26 sec per fur (GF)

| | Horse | Dist | Pl | SP | RR | SF |
|---|---|---|---|---|---|---|
| 3356* | **Welcome Parade (83)** (HRACecil) **3-9-1** WRyan(1) (chsd ldr over 9f: led ins fnl f: drvn out) | — | **1** | 7/2[2] | 95 | 54 |
| 993* | **Haya Ya Kefaah (61)** (NMBabbage) **4-8-3** TSprake(3) (a.p: chsd ldr over 2f out: ev ch ins fnl f: unable qckn) | 1¼ | **2** | 10/1 | 71 | 40 |
| 3073[3] | **Leading Spirit (IRE) (83)** (CFWall) **4-9-11** JReid(8) (lw: led: sn clr: rdn over 1f out: hdd ins fnl f: one pce) | 1¼ | **3** | 11/4[1] | 92 | 61 |
| 3248[8] | **Noble Sprinter (IRE) (74)** (WJHaggas) **4-8-9**(7) ElizabethTurner(4) (hdwy on ins over 2f out: r.o) | 1¾ | **4** | 14/1 | 80 | 49 |
| 3351[2] | **Artic Courier (84)** (DJSCosgrove) **5-9-12** JStack(2) (rdn & hdwy over 2f out: r.o one pce) | s.h | **5** | 8/1 | 90 | 59 |
| 2862[3] | **Romios (IRE) (86)** (PFICole) **4-9-7**(7) DavidO'Neill(9) (lw: hdwy over 2f out: sn wknd) | 3 | **6** | 7/1 | 88 | 57 |
| 3290* | **Dear Life (USA) (84)** (MrsJCecil) **3-9-2** AClark(6) (lw: s.s: hdwy over 2f out: wknd over 1f out) | ¾ | **7** | 6/1[3] | 85 | 44 |
| 3073[11] | **General Mouktar (59)** (BJMeehan) **6-8-1** BDoyle(7) (lw: hdwy over 2f out: sn wknd) | 8 | **8** | 14/1 | 50 | 19 |
| | **Volunteer (IRE) (63)** (RJO'Sullivan) **4-8-5** DBiggs(5) (b: a bhd) | 22 | **9** | 33/1 | 24 | — |
| | | | | (SP 112.2%) | **9 Rn** | |

**2m 34.41** (3.71) CSF £33.18 CT £97.60 TOTE £4.30: £1.60 £3.10 £1.20 (£16.70) Trio £35.70 OWNER Mr K. Abdulla (NEWMARKET) BRED Juddmonte Farms

WEIGHT FOR AGE 3yo-10lb

**3356* Welcome Parade** may have been up against seasoned campaigners, but he still came out best on this handicap debut. Racing in second place, he was collared for that position over a quarter of a mile from home but, refusing to give way, he managed to force his way into the lead inside the final furlong and, responding to pressure, kept on well. (7/2)

**993* Haya Ya Kefaah**, given a fifteen week break, was racing in third place and moved into the runner-up berth early in the straight. Throwing down his challenge from below the distance, he had every chance inside the final furlong before the winner proved a bit too strong. (10/1)
**3073 Leading Spirit (IRE)** stormed off in front and had soon opened up a commanding advantage. Refusing to give way, he was only overhauled inside the final furlong. (11/4)
**2536* Noble Sprinter (IRE)** was given no assistance from the saddle. Nevertheless, he picked up ground along the inside rail over a quarter of a mile from home and stayed on for fourth prize. (14/1)
**3351 Artic Courier**, scrubbed along to take closer order early in the straight, stayed on and only just failed to get into the prize money. (8/1)

## 3684 GO EVENING RACING WITH THE DAILY TELEGRAPH CONDITIONS STKS (2-Y.O) (Class C)

6-55 (6-55) **7f (Jubilee)** £4,884.20 (£1,827.80: £893.90: £384.50: £172.25: £87.35) Stalls: High GOING minus 0.26 sec per fur (GF)

| Form | Horse | Dist | Pos | SP | RR | SF |
|---|---|---|---|---|---|---|
| 2414* | **Great Ovation (IRE)** (LMCumani) **2-9-2** OUrbina(7) (hld up: led over 1f out: pushed out) | — | 1 | 11/2 | 97 | 42 |
| 3119* | **Musical Dancer (USA)** (EALDunlop) **2-9-2** WRyan(4) (lw: swtchd lft & hdwy over 1f out: r.o ins fnl f) | 1 | 2 | 12/1 | 95 | 40 |
| 2721[2] | **Tuscany (98)** (PFICole) **2-9-2** TQuinn(1) (led over 5f: wknd fnl f) | 5 | 3 | 9/1 | 83 | 28 |
| 2972* | **Tarski** (HRACecil) **2-9-2** PatEddery(6) (lw: a.p: ev ch 2f out: wknd fnl f) | 1¼ | 4 | 7/2[2] | 80 | 25 |
| 2708* | **Sandstone (IRE)** (JLDunlop) **2-9-2** JReid(2) (lw: hld up: rdn over 2f out: sn wknd) | ½ | 5 | 100/30[1] | 79 | 24 |
| 1437[3] | **Bali Paradise (USA)** (PFICole) **2-9-2** DaneO'Neill(3) (dwlt: nvr nr to chal) | hd | 6 | 13/2 | 79 | 24 |
| 3319* | **Bareeq** (HThomsonJones) **2-9-2** TSprake(5) (lw: prom over 4f) | 13 | 7 | 5/1[3] | 49 | — |
| | | | | (SP 108.4%) | | 7 Rn |

**1m 27.6** (3.10) CSF £53.34 TOTE £6.20: £3.50 £3.30 (£24.50) OWNER Mrs E. H. Vestey (NEWMARKET) BRED Swettenham Stud
**2414* Great Ovation (IRE)**, tucked in behind the front three, found a gap along the inside rail and, shooting into the lead below the distance, was pushed along to dispose of the persistent runner-up. (11/2: op 7/2)
**3119* Musical Dancer (USA)**, switched left as he began to pick up ground below the distance, pulled well clear of the remainder but found the winner just too strong. He should soon regain the winning thread. (12/1)
**2721 Tuscany** held a slender advantage from the start. Collared over a furlong out, he was left standing by the front two. (9/1)
**2972* Tarski** looked very well beforehand. In the front rank throughout, he had every chance a quarter of a mile from home, but had reached the end of his tether entering the final furlong. (7/2)
**2708* Sandstone (IRE)** chased the leaders but, bustled along early in the straight, was soon done with. (100/30)
**1437 Bali Paradise (USA)**, who has been gelded since his defeat here three months ago, was at the back of the field and never threatened to get in it. (13/2)
**3319* Bareeq**, with less substance than others in the field, was close up until tiring over two furlongs from home. (5/1)

## 3685 E.B.F. WIGAN MEDIAN AUCTION MAIDEN STKS (2-Y.O) (Class F)

7-25 (7-27) **6f** £2,997.00 (£842.00: £411.00) Stalls: High GOING minus 0.26 sec per fur (GF)

| Form | Horse | Dist | Pos | SP | RR | SF |
|---|---|---|---|---|---|---|
| 3438[7] | **Hoh Flyer (USA)** (MBell) **2-8-9** MFenton(8) (lw: a.p: led over 1f out: rdn out) | — | 1 | 14/1 | 66 | 33 |
| 3502[2] | **Test The Water (IRE)** (RHannon) **2-9-0** PatEddery(9) (lw: a.p: ev ch fnl 2f: hrd rdn: r.o) | nk | 2 | 5/2[1] | 70 | 37 |
| 3259[13] | **Champagne Toast** (RHannon) **2-9-0** DaneO'Neill(11) (lw: hdwy over 2f out: rdn over 1f out: r.o) | 1½ | 3 | 25/1 | 66 | 33 |
| 2904[6] | **Smugurs (IRE) (66)** (RJRWilliams) **2-8-9** DRMcCabe(17) (led over 4f: one pce) | nk | 4 | 10/1 | 60 | 27 |
| | **Certain Magic** (WRMuir) **2-9-0** JReid(14) (str: scope: bit bkwd: a.p: rdn over 2f out: wknd over 1f out) | 6 | 5 | 20/1 | 49 | 16 |
| 3221[7] | **Indifferent Guy** (CEBrittain) **2-9-0** BDoyle(7) (nvr nr to chal) | 8 | 6 | 16/1 | 28 | — |
| | **Ejeer (IRE)** (MRChannon) **2-8-9**(5) PPMurphy(12) (unf: s.s: outpcd: hdwy 2f out: nvr nrr) | ½ | 7 | 25/1 | 27 | — |
| 3438[6] | **Blown-Over** (ACStewart) **2-8-9** DHarrison(15) (w'like: scope: prom over 4f) | s.h | 8 | 4/1[2] | 22 | — |
| | **Kingsdown Trix (IRE)** (AMoore) **2-9-0** CRutter(10) (str: bkwd: s.s: outpcd: nvr nrr) | hd | 9 | 50/1 | 26 | — |
| | **Wrn Princess** (BJMeehan) **2-8-9** MTebbutt(6) (prom over 3f) | 1½ | 10 | 20/1 | 17 | — |
| 3438[4] | **Ellway Lady (IRE)** (IABalding) **2-8-9** WRyan(2) (bmpd s: a bhd) | 3 | 11 | 14/1 | 9 | — |
| | **Blood Orange** (GGMargarson) **2-9-0** PBloomfield(13) (w'like: scope: prom over 3f) | 1¼ | 12 | 16/1 | 11 | — |
| 3105[4] | **Oakbrook Rose** (BSmart) **2-8-9** JStack(3) (bmpd s: bhd fnl 2f) | 1¾ | 13 | 14/1 | 1 | — |
| | **Royal Roulette** (SPCWoods) **2-8-9** DBiggs(5) (w'like: bit bkwd: bmpd s: a bhd) | 6 | 14 | 33/1 | — | — |
| | **Spanish Warrior** (JWHills) **2-9-0** AClark(16) (str: bkwd: a bhd) | 1¼ | 15 | 12/1 | — | — |
| 3438[8] | **Chilli Boom** (TJNaughton) **2-8-9** TSprake(1) (a bhd) | ½ | 16 | 50/1 | — | — |
| 3234[3] | **Marengo** (JAkehurst) **2-9-0** TQuinn(4) (b.off hind: jinked s: mid div tl swvd lft & virtually ref to r over 2f out) | 1½ | 17 | 5/1[3] | — | — |
| | | | | (SP 137.9%) | | 17 Rn |

**1m 14.07** (2.77) CSF £51.25 TOTE £44.70: £9.80 £1.60 £5.60 (£82.10) Trio £420.80; £533.52 to 23/8/96 OWNER Mr D. F. Allport (NEWMARKET) BRED R. and Mrs Lyons
**Hoh Flyer (USA)**, all the fitter for her recent debut at Lingfield, was never far away. Striking the front below the distance, she was stoked up to beat the determined runner-up. (14/1)
**3502 Test The Water (IRE)**, never far away, threw down a determined challenge in the final quarter-mile. Giving it his all he only just failed. His turn is near. (5/2)
**Champagne Toast** ran his best race to date. Picking up ground over a quarter of a mile from home, he stuck to his task really well inside the final furlong to snatch third prize close home. Staying is going to be his game and over further, more improvement can be expected. (25/1)
**2904 Smugurs (IRE)** attempted to make all the running. Collared below the distance, she grimly tried to hold on but was worried out of third place near the line. (10/1: op 6/1)
**Certain Magic**, a well-made colt, was close up until lack of race fitness took its toll below the distance. (20/1)
**Indifferent Guy** made some late headway without posing a threat. (16/1)
**Spanish Warrior** (12/1: 8/1-14/1)
**3234 Marengo** ran without the visor this time which was a serious mistake. Jinking as the stalls opened bumping a couple of rivals, he raced in midfield until swerving violently left over a quarter of a mile out and downing tools completely. Despite all his jockey's efforts, he virtually refused to race from that point. He looks one to treat with a great deal of caution. (5/1: 5/2-11/2)

## 3686 CUNLIFFE H'CAP (0-70) (3-Y.O+) (Class E)

7-55 (7-56) **7f (round)** £3,176.25 (£960.00: £467.50: £221.25) Stalls: High GOING minus 0.26 sec per fur (GF)

| Form | Horse | Dist | Pos | SP | RR | SF |
|---|---|---|---|---|---|---|
| 3274[3] | **Broughtons Turmoil (66)** (WJMusson) **7-9-11** PatEddery(13) (stdy hdwy on ins over 2f out: led over 1f out: shkn up: comf) | — | 1 | 4/1[1] | 76 | 60 |
| 3274[4] | **Paddy's Rice (56)** (MMcCormack) **5-9-1** JReid(6) (hdwy over 1f out: r.o ins fnl f) | 2½ | 2 | 7/1[3] | 60 | 44 |
| 3139[4] | **Racing Telegraph (40)** (CNAllen) **6-7-8**(5) MartinDwyer(7) (lw: n.m.r & swtchd lft 2f out: hdwy over 1f out: r.o ins fnl f) | s.h | 3 | 14/1 | 44 | 28 |

| | | | | SP | RR | SF |
|---|---|---|---|---|---|---|
| $3585^{2}$ | **Whatever's Right (IRE) (65)** (MDIUsher) **7-9-10** BDoyle(16) (a.p: rdn over 2f out: unable qckn) | 2 | **4** | 13/2 $^{2}$ | 65 | 49 |
| $3473^{5}$ | **Morocco (IRE) (58)** (MRChannon) **7-8-10**$^{(7)}$ AEddery(10) (lw: s.s: hdwy on ins over 1f out: r.o) | s.h | **5** | 25/1 | 58 | 42 |
| $3518^{2}$ | **Pointer (54)** (MrsPNDutfield) **4-8-8**$^{(5)}$ AimeeCook(5) (hdwy over 1f out: nvr nrr) | s.h | **6** | 13/2 $^{2}$ | 53 | 37 |
| $3115^{4}$ | **Mogin (47)** (TJNaughton) **3-8-1** TSprake(2) (swtg: rdn 2f out: nvr nr to chal) | 1¼ | **7** | 20/1 | 44 | 23 |
| *$2731^{0}$* | **Al Shaati (FR) (37)** (RJO'Sullivan) **6-7-10** NAdams(14) (led over 5f: eased whn btn ins fnl f) | ¾ | **8** | 33/1 | 32 | 16 |
| | **Sharp Move (44)** (MrsJCecil) **4-8-3**$^{ow2}$ AClark(11) (prom over 5f) | 1¾ | **9** | 33/1 | 35 | 17 |
| 3458* | **Honorable Estate (IRE) (60)** (RHannon) **3-9-0** $^{5x}$ DaneO'Neill(12) (lw: a.p: rdn over 2f out: wknd 1f out) | 1 | **10** | 10/1 | 49 | 28 |
| 3139* | **Balance of Power (63)** (RAkehurst) **4-9-8** SSanders(3) (sme hdwy over 1f out: sn wknd) | hd | **11** | 8/1 | 51 | 35 |
| $3093^{5}$ | **Lady Isabell (58)** (SDow) **3-8-12** WRyan(1) (a bhd) | 1½ | **12** | 33/1 | 43 | 22 |
| 3384a$^{4}$ | **Astral's Chance (50)** (KRBurke) **3-8-4** MFenton(9) (lw: prom over 4f) | 1¼ | **13** | 33/1 | 32 | 11 |
| $3151^{14}$ | **Blushing Grenadier (IRE) (55)** (MJFetherston-Godley) **4-9-0** DHarrison(8) (lw: bhd fnl 2f) | 16 | **14** | 25/1 | — | — |
| $3112^{2}$ | **Spandrel (58)** (HCandy) **4-9-3** CRutter(4) (bhd fnl 2f) | nk | **15** | 7/1 $^{3}$ | 3 | — |
| | | | | (SP 122.8%) | **15 Rn** | |

**1m 26.77** (2.27) CSF £30.00 CT £327.30 TOTE £5.80: £2.70 £2.30 £3.90 (£12.70) Trio £185.90 OWNER Broughton & Westwood (NEWMARKET) BRED Tally Ho Stud Co (U.K.) Ltd and Ninevah Ltd

WEIGHT FOR AGE 3yo-5lb

**3274 Broughtons Turmoil** put up a polished display. Steadily creeping closer in the straight, he cruised into the lead below the distance and, shaken up, soon put the race beyond doubt. (4/1)

**3274 Paddy's Rice** weaved his way through the pack from below the distance but, despite running on to snatch second prize, was not going to trouble the winner. (7/1)

**3139 Racing Telegraph** picked up ground after his jockey switched him to get a clear run. Running on inside the final furlong, he only just lost out in the battle for second prize. (14/1)

**3585 Whatever's Right (IRE)**, a leading light from the off, was bustled along early in the straight but failed to find that vital turn of foot. (13/2)

**3473 Morocco (IRE)**, who lost ground at the start, stayed on nicely in the last furlong and a half to be nearest at the line. (25/1)

**3518 Pointer** picked up ground from below the distance without ever posing a threat. (13/2)

**3112 Spandrel** (7/1: 5/1-8/1)

T/Plpt: £197.50 (62.13 Tckts). T/Qdpt: £52.10 (20.99 Tckts) AK

## 3668-YORK (L-H) (Good, Good to firm back st)
## Wednesday August 21st

WEATHER: fine & warm WIND: slt half against

## 3687 ROUS (S) STKS (2-Y.O) (Class E)

2-05 (2-07) **6f** £11,576.25 (£3,510.00: £1,717.50: £821.25) Stalls: Low GOING minus 0.33 sec per fur (GF)

| | | | | SP | RR | SF |
|---|---|---|---|---|---|---|
| $3478^{7}$ | **Lamorna (85)** (MRChannon) **2-8-6** PatEddery(11) (mde virtually all: reminder wl over 1f out: sn clr) | — | **1** | 6/1 $^{2}$ | 77 | 44 |
| $3411^{4}$ | **Swiss Coast (IRE) (82)** (MrsJRRamsden) **2-8-11** KFallon(21) (sn drvn along: hdwy 2f out: styd on wl ins fnl f) | 1¾ | **2** | 3/1 $^{1}$ | 77 | 44 |
| $3321^{3}$ | **Petite Danseuse (79)** (SDow) **2-8-6** JReid(13) (swtg: a.p: ev ch over 1f out: one pce) | ½ | **3** | 9/1 | 71 | 38 |
| $3326^{2}$ | **Head Girl (IRE)** (CWThornton) **2-8-6** AMackay(18) (bhd tl styd on wl appr fnl f) | 2 | **4** | 14/1 | 66 | 33 |
| $3590^{5}$ | **Lunar Music (70)** (MartynMeade) **2-8-5**$^{(5)ow4}$ RHavlin(20) (a chsng ldrs: unable qckn appr fnl f) | ½ | **5** | 16/1 | 68 | 31 |
| $2210^{4}$ | **Supercharmer (78)** (CEBrittain) **2-8-8**$^{(3)}$ FLynch(12) (a chsng ldrs: ev ch 2f out: sn rdn: one pce) | s.h | **6** | 16/1 | 69 | 36 |
| $3282^{2}$ | **Feel A Line (80)** (BJMeehan) **2-8-11b** MJKinane(10) (chsd ldrs far side: rdn 2f out: one pce) | 3 | **7** | 9/1 | 61 | 28 |
| | **Silver Button** (MissSEHall) **2-8-11** MBirch(3) (leggy: styd on fnl 2f: nvr nrr) | 1¾ | **8** | 25/1 | 57 | 24 |
| $3462^{3}$ | **Imperial Or Metric (IRE) (69)** (JBerry) **2-8-11** JPMurtagh(14) (trckd ldrs over 4f) | s.h | **9** | 20/1 | 56 | 23 |
| $3511^{3}$ | **In Good Nick** (MWEasterby) **2-8-6** LDettori(19) (in tch tl rdn & one pce appr fnl f) | 1¼ | **10** | 7/1 $^{3}$ | 48 | 15 |
| $2755^{7}$ | **Juicy Ting** (PCHaslam) **2-8-11** GCarter(6) (chsd ldrs over 4f: grad fdd) | 1 | **11** | 25/1 | 50 | 17 |
| $3082^{6}$ | **Veerapong (IRE) (66)** (MWEasterby) **2-8-6** JFEgan(17) (in tch tl wknd fnl 2f) | 1¼ | **12** | 33/1 | 42 | 9 |
| $3121^{3}$ | **Al Ava Consonant** (JDBethell) **2-8-6** JWeaver(7) (s.s: a in rr) | 1¼ | **13** | 12/1 | 39 | 6 |
| $3511^{8}$ | **The Dubious Goose** (MWEasterby) **2-8-11** DaleGibson(4) (bit bkwd: a outpcd) | nk | **14** | 33/1 | 43 | 10 |
| $3275^{7}$ | **Docklands Carriage (IRE) (72)** (NTinkler) **2-8-11v** RCochrane(15) (lw: trckd ldrs: rdn along ½-wy: eased whn btn over 1f out) | ¾ | **15** | 10/1 | 41 | 8 |
| $3259^{17}$ | **Mellwood (IRE)** (MHTompkins) **2-8-11** PRobinson(5) (bit bkwd: sn outpcd) | 1 | **16** | 20/1 | 38 | 5 |
| $3454^{9}$ | **Schisandra** (MJFetherston-Godley) **2-8-7**$^{ow1}$ MHills(16) (sn outpcd: t.o) | 5 | **17** | 33/1 | 21 | — |
| 3488* | **Hit Or Miss (66)** (PCHaslam) **2-8-6** WCarson(9) (lw: gd spd over 3f: wknd qckly: t.o) | 4 | **18** | 14/1 | 9 | — |
| | **Ocean Breeze** (JSWainwright) **2-8-11** DeanMcKeown(2) (leggy: unf: bit bkwd: s.s: sn t.o) | 5 | **19** | 33/1 | 1 | — |
| 770* | **Mill End Girl (74)** (MWEasterby) **2-8-1**$^{(5)}$ GParkin(8) (trckd ldrs over 3f: sn rdn & lost tch: t.o) | 2½ | **20** | 16/1 | — | — |
| | | | | (SP 148.5%) | **20 Rn** | |

**1m 12.29** (1.29) CSF £26.71 TOTE £6.80: £2.60 £2.00 £2.80 (£11.00) Trio £26.50 OWNER Mr W. H. Ponsonby (UPPER LAMBOURN) BRED E. M. Thornton

Bt in 20,500 gns

Swiss Coast (IRE) clmd GMoscrop £10,000

OFFICIAL EXPLANATION **Docklands Carriage (IRE): the rider reported that the colt was moving so badly that he did not persevere.**

**3046 Lamorna**, given a reminder soon after entering the final quarter-mile, quickened up readily to draw clear and soon had the prize safely under wraps. (6/1)

**3411 Swiss Coast (IRE)** gave the impression that he does need a stiffer test of stamina, for he was off the bridle all the way, and was still staying on to chase up the winner. (3/1)

**3321 Petite Danseuse** has got speed to burn, but as yet she is barely seeing out six. (9/1)

**3326 Head Girl (IRE)**, taken to post steadily, found the early pace something of a problem and she did not strike top gear until far too late. (14/1)

**3590 Lunar Music** sat in behind the leaders and was always poised to challenge. When the button was pushed approaching the final furlong, she could do little more than run on at the same pace. (16/1)

**1989 Supercharmer**, content to be given a lead this time, looked a live threat passing the two furlong marker, but he failed to pick up when popped the question and was soon struggling to hold on. (16/1)

**Silver Button**, a leggy, light-framed gelding, making his racecourse debut, was getting to know what it was all about in the latter stages. He will soon improve on this. (25/1)

## 3688 ASTON UPTHORPE YORKSHIRE OAKS STKS (Gp 1) (3-Y.O+ F & M) (Class A)

2-35 (2-37) **1m 3f 195y** £78,815.50 (£28,964.50: £13,732.25: £5,423.75: £1,961.88: £577.12) Stalls: Low GOING minus 0.33 sec per fur (GF)

| | | | | SP | RR | SF |
|---|---|---|---|---|---|---|
| 2837a$^{3}$ | **Key Change (IRE)** (JOxx,Ireland) **3-8-8** JPMurtagh(1) (a.p: led over 6f out: styd on strly fnl f) | — | 1 | 7/1 | 116 | 67 |
| 3231$^{2}$ | **Papering (IRE) (103)** (LMCumani) **3-8-8** KDarley(6) (hld up: hdwy on ins over 3f out: styd on wl ins fnl f) | 1¾ | 2 | 8/1 | 114 | 65 |
| 3231$^{5}$ | **Mezzogiorno (108)** (GWragg) **3-8-8** MHills(5) (hld up: effrt & drvn along 3f out: styd on fnl f: nvr able to chal: fin 4th, 3l: plcd 3rd) | | 3 | 16/1 | 109 | 60 |
| 2837a$^{2}$ | **Shamadara (IRE)** (AdeRoyerDupre,France) **3-8-8** GMosse(8) (gd sort: hld up: outpcd & lost pl over 5f out: rdn & styd on fnl 2f: fin 5th, nk: plcd 4th) | | 4 | 2/1$^{1}$ | 109 | 60 |
| 3231$^{4}$ | **Whitewater Affair (105)** (MRStoute) **3-8-8** TQuinn(7) (trckd ldrs: rdn 3f out: sltly hmpd wl over 1f out: one pce: fin 6th, nk: plcd 5th) | | 5 | 14/1 | 108 | 59 |
| *395a$^{2}$* | **Russian Snows (IRE)** (SbinSuroor) **4-9-4** LDettori(3) (led 1f: trckd ldrs: hrd drvn 2f out: edgd lft & kpt on fnl f: fin 3rd, nk: disq & plcd 6th) | | 6 | 11/2$^{3}$ | 113 | 74 |
| 2886* | **Shemozzle (IRE) (107)** (JHMGosden) **3-8-8** PatEddery(4) (lw: led 7f out: sn hdd: rdn over 2f out: one pce) | 1 | 7 | 15/2 | 107 | 58 |
| 1144$^{2}$ | **Quota** (HRACecil) **3-8-8** WRyan(2) (led after 1f to 7f out: hung rt over 4f out: wknd over 2f out) | 4 | 8 | 16/1 | 102 | 53 |
| 1949a* | **Sil Sila (IRE) (115)** (BSmart) **3-8-8** RCochrane(9) (hld up: effrt 4f out: lost pl & eased wl over 2f out: t.o) | 24 | 9 | 9/2$^{2}$ | 69 | 20 |
| | | | | (SP 120.7%) | **9 Rn** | |

**2m 27.56** (-0.24) CSF £57.76 TOTE £11.50: £2.30 £2.80 £5.10 (£66.40) Trio £333.40 OWNER Lady Clague (CURRABEG) BRED Collinstown Stud Farm Ltd

WEIGHT FOR AGE 3yo-10lb

STEWARDS' ENQUIRY Dettori susp. 30-31/8 & 2-3/9/96 (irresponsible riding).

**2837a Key Change (IRE)** had it all to do to beat the favourite at levels, but she made sure that this was going to be a true test of stamina, and in the end, the ploy worked a treat. (7/1)

**3231 Papering (IRE)** turned in a very pleasing display at this first attempt at the trip, staying on relentlessly inside the distance. There will be plenty more opportunities coming her way. (8/1)

**3231 Mezzogiorno** tried to come from behind to deliver a challenge, but could not step up her pace under strong driving and was always being comfortably held. (16/1)

**2837a Shamadara (IRE)** adopted the wrong tactics on such fast ground, and though she did try to get herself into the action, was fighting a lost cause from the turn into the straight. (2/1)

**3231 Whitewater Affair**, hard at work and making little impression, was squeezed for room entering the final quarter-mile and always feeling the pace. (14/1)

**395a Russian Snows (IRE)**, produced fresh and well for her first run in this country, pushed the pace and was just beginning to stay on, when she edged left and tightened up a couple of rivals two furlongs out. After finishing third, she was demoted to sixth. In the past, she has found her best form in the autumn. (11/2)

## 3689 TOTE EBOR H'CAP (3-Y.O+) (Class B)

3-10 (3-16) **1m 5f 194y** £94,745.00 (£28,460.00: £13,730.00: £6,365.00) Stalls: Low GOING minus 0.33 sec per fur (GF)

| | | | | SP | RR | SF |
|---|---|---|---|---|---|---|
| 2505* | **Clerkenwell (USA) (98)** (MRStoute) **3-7-11**$^{(3)ow4}$ FLynch(2) (lw: plld hrd: hld up in tch: led over 2f out: sn clr: hld on) | — | 1 | 17/2 | 112 | 75 |
| 2969* | **Beauchamp Jade (92)** (HCandy) **4-8-6**$^{4x}$ GCarter(18) (hld up: effrt over 2f out: styd on strly wl ins fnl f) | ¾ | 2 | 8/1$^{3}$ | 105 | 84 |
| 2352* | **Corradini (99)** (HRACecil) **4-8-13** KFallon(13) (sn drvn along in rr: gd hdwy 2f out: nt clr run appr fnl f: fin wl) | ½ | 3 | 7/1$^{1}$ | 112 | 91 |
| 2074$^{3}$ | **Harbour Dues (94)** (LadyHerries) **3-7-10** JQuinn(22) (lw: hld up in tch: effrt over 2f out: kpt on fnl f) | 1¾ | 4 | 7/1$^{1}$ | 105 | 72 |
| 3266$^{8}$ | **Remaadi Sun (84)** (MDIUsher) **4-7-12** RStreet(19) (hld up & bhd: hdwy on outside 3f out: r.o) | nk | 5 | 33/1 | 94 | 73 |
| 3266$^{7}$ | **Top Cees (87)** (MrsJRRamsden) **6-8-1** DHarrison(21) (bhd & pushed along: styd on wl fnl 3f: nrst fin) | 1¼ | 6 | 16/1 | 96 | 75 |
| 3212$^{3}$ | **Better Offer (IRE) (100)** (GHarwood) **4-9-0**$^{7x}$ MJKinane(3) (bhd: nt clr run over 2f out: styd on strly fnl f) | nk | 7 | 12/1 | 108 | 87 |
| 2352$^{2}$ | **Prussian Blue (USA) (100)** (HRACecil) **4-9-0** PatEddery(15) (a chsng ldrs: rdn & nt qckn fnl 2f) | 1½ | 8 | 20/1 | 107 | 86 |
| 2881$^{5}$ | **Naked Welcome (104)** (MJFetherston-Godley) **4-9-4** JReid(7) (lw: hld up & bhd: effrt over 3f out: nt rch ldrs) | nk | 9 | 33/1 | 110 | 89 |
| 2690$^{3}$ | **My Learned Friend (84)** (AHide) **5-7-12** AMcGlone(20) (lw: hld up: hdwy over 3f out: n.d) | 1¾ | 10 | 33/1 | 88 | 67 |
| 3124$^{8}$ | **Male-Ana-Mou (IRE) (94)** (DRCElsworth) **3-7-10** GBardwell(11) (trckd ldrs: drvn along 5f out: sn lost tch: n.d) | ½ | 11 | 25/1 | 98 | 65 |
| 3145$^{9}$ | **Ambassador (USA) (94)** (BWHills) **3-7-10** WCarson(8) (lw: trckd ldrs tl rdn & wknd over 2f out) | nk | 12 | 10/1 | 97 | 64 |
| 3504$^{8}$ | **Benfleet (82)** (RWArmstrong) **5-7-10** NCarlisle(10) (nvr nrr) | 1¼ | 13 | 66/1 | 84 | 63 |
| 2969$^{2}$ | **Desert Frolic (IRE) (94)** (MJohnston) **3-7-10** TWilliams(1) (chsd ldr: led over 6f out tl over 2f out: sn wknd) | s.h | 14 | 14/1 | 96 | 63 |
| 3351* | **Time for Action (IRE) (85)** (MHTompkins) **4-7-13**$^{7x}$ DaleGibson(9) (chsd ldrs tl wknd over 3f out) | 7 | 15 | 25/1 | 79 | 58 |
| 3145$^{3}$ | **Lakeline Legend (IRE) (94)** (MAJarvis) **3-7-10** FNorton(16) (hld up: hdwy over 3f out: nt clr run over 1f out: sn btn) | s.h | 16 | 16/1 | 88 | 55 |
| 2330$^{2}$ | **Snow Princess (IRE) (92)** (LordHuntingdon) **4-8-6** RHills(14) (in tch: rdn along & lost pl ent st) | 1½ | 17 | 15/2$^{2}$ | 84 | 63 |
| 2724$^{9}$ | **Dreams End (82)** (PBowen) **8-7-10** AMackay(5) (mid div tl wknd over 3f out) | 1 | 18 | 100/1 | 73 | 52 |
| 2330$^{7}$ | **Foundry Lane (82)** (MrsMReveley) **5-7-10** LCharnock(6) (a in rr: rdn over 4f out: no imp) | nk | 19 | 14/1 | 73 | 52 |
| 3447$^{6}$ | **Monarch (89)** (PFICole) **4-8-3**$^{ow2}$ TQuinn(12) (mid div: effrt 3f out: sn no imp: t.o) | 11 | 20 | 14/1 | 67 | 44 |
| 3212$^{2}$ | **Midnight Legend (110)** (LMCumani) **5-9-10** LDettori(4) (lw: led 8f: wknd qckly 3f out: t.o) | dist | 21 | 16/1 | — | — |
| | | | | (SP 136.6%) | **21 Rn** | |

**2m 53.47** (-2.73) CSF £74.69 CT £482.16 TOTE £8.90: £1.90 £2.40 £1.90 £3.10 (£34.60) Trio £84.80 OWNER Sheikh Mohammed (NEWMARKET) BRED Camelot Thoroughbreds and Michael J. Ryan

LONG HANDICAP Clerkenwell (USA) 7-9 Benfleet 7-2 Desert Frolic (IRE) 7-5 Male-Ana-Mou (IRE) 7-1 Ambassador (USA) 7-9 Dreams End 7-6 Foundry Lane 7-7 Harbour Dues 7-8 Lakeline Legend (IRE) 7-5

WEIGHT FOR AGE 3yo-12lb

**OFFICIAL EXPLANATION Midnight Legend: was struck into in the early stages.**

**2505* Clerkenwell (USA)**, a progressive three year old at the right end of the handicap, won this by kicking clear two furlongs out. Though he was being reeled in at the finish, he had given his rivals the slip. (17/2)

**2969* Beauchamp Jade**, settled in the pack on this first run beyond twelve furlongs, still looked full of running when set alight approaching the last quarter-mile, but she had allowed the winner to get away and the task was always beyond her. (8/1)

**2352* Corradini** never took hold of his bit and was nearer last than first for most of the way. He did respond to strong driving though in the latter stages, and it is more than likely he would have won, if he had condescended to race sooner. (7/1)

**2074 Harbour Dues** has had this race in mind for some time, but a two month break may not have been such a good approach to such a big test, and though he did stay on well enough, the race was only for the places once the winner burst clear. (7/1: 5/1-15/2)
**2690 Remaadi Sun**, pulled to the centre of the track to make progress once in line for home, was close enough if good enough two furlongs out, but he was not bred to win at these extended trips, and could do little more than gallop on the spot. (33/1)
**3266 Top Cees**, always struggling with the pace, stayed on relentlessly in the closing stages without being able to gain a challenging position. (16/1)
**3212 Better Offer (IRE)**, short of room when trying to mount a challenge over two furlongs out, always had too much to do when he did manage to wriggle free. This performance was much better than it looks on paper. (12/1)
**2330 Snow Princess (IRE)** lost her pitch before reaching the home straight, and ran very flat. She is happier when she can get her toe in. (15/2)

## 3690 SCOTTISH EQUITABLE GIMCRACK STKS (Gp 2) (2-Y.O C & G) (Class A)

3-45 (3-46) **6f** £65,831.70 (£24,390.30: £11,727.65: £4,820.75: £1,942.88: £791.72) Stalls: Low GOING minus 0.33 sec per fur (GF)

| | | | | SP | RR | SF |
|---|---|---|---|---|---|---|
| 1437[2] | **Abou Zouz (USA)** (DRLoder) **2-8-11** LDettori(7) (lw: hld up gng wl: effrt & rdn over 1f out: led fnl 50y) | — | **1** | 4/1[3] | 112 | 71 |
| 3164* | **Compton Place** (JARToller) **2-8-11** SSanders(9) (mde most tl hrd rdn, edgd lft & hdd wl ins fnl f) | ½ | **2** | 12/1 | 111 | 70 |
| 3234* | **The West (USA)** (PFICole) **2-8-11** TQuinn(5) (lw: a.p: rdn over 1f out: ev ch & rn green: nt qckn fnl f) | 1¼ | **3** | 2/1[1] | 107 | 66 |
| 3156* | **Easycall** (BJMeehan) **2-9-2** MJKinane(2) (dwlt: drvn along ½-wy: kpt on: nvr nr to chal) | 3 | **4** | 9/4[2] | 104 | 63 |
| 2364* | **Nigrasine** (JLEyre) **2-8-11** DeanMcKeown(1) (w ldrs 4f: sn rdn & outpcd) | 1¼ | **5** | 8/1 | 96 | 55 |
| 3247[6] | **For Your Eyes Only (100)** (TDEasterby) **2-8-11** PatEddery(8) (w ldrs: sn drvn along: outpcd fnl 2f) | 1½ | **6** | 16/1 | 92 | 51 |
| 2607[7] | **Hula Prince (IRE) (100)** (MJohnston) **2-8-11** JWeaver(3) (lw: hld up: effrt ½-wy: sn no imp) | ½ | **7** | 12/1 | 91 | 50 |
| 3147[8] | **Select Choice (IRE)** (APJarvis) **2-8-11** KDarley(6) (prom over 3f) | 2½ | **8** | 100/1 | 84 | 43 |
| 3156[4] | **Proud Native (IRE) (100)** (APJarvis) **2-8-11** WJO'Connor(4) (swtg: sn outpcd) | 2 | **9** | 14/1 | 79 | 38 |
| | | | | (SP 124.1%) | | **9 Rn** |

**1m 10.78** (-0.22) CSF £47.75 TOTE £4.80: £1.50 £2.70 £1.40 (£48.90) Trio £32.70 OWNER Mr Wafic Said (NEWMARKET) BRED G. Watts Humphrey Jnr
**1437 Abou Zouz (USA)**, always travelling strongly on the heels of the leaders, needed to be woken up to go about his work, but he won with a bit to spare and there is no doubt he is a useful colt. (4/1)
**3164* Compton Place** is a courageous colt who will always prove difficult to beat as he is game for a fight, and he lost no caste in defeat here. (12/1)
**3234* The West (USA)** put up a brave struggle here to go down fighting. It was probably lack of experience that was the deciding factor, but he looks set to go places. (2/1)
**3156* Easycall** lost his unbeaten record after a tardy start, and in such a class race on lively ground, that was something he could not afford to do. He should soon regain winning ways. (9/4)
**2364* Nigrasine** had the worst of the draw to contend with, but showed that he is not that far behind the best, and there will be plenty more races to be won with him. (8/1)
**3247 For Your Eyes Only** was flat to the boards to stay up with the pace this time, and it was obvious that on this ground, he was out of his class. (16/1)

## 3691 MOTABILITY RATED STKS H'CAP (0-105) (3-Y.O+) (Class B)

4-15 (4-19) **1m 2f 85y** £14,207.20 (£5,264.80: £2,532.40: £1,042.00: £421.00: £172.60) Stalls: Low GOING minus 0.33 sec per fur (GF)

| | | | | SP | RR | SF |
|---|---|---|---|---|---|---|
| 2724[8] | **Amrak Ajeeb (IRE) (92)** (BHanbury) **4-9-0** MRimmer(1) (hld up: hdwy on ins ½-wy: styd on to ld ins fnl f) | — | **1** | 20/1 | 104 | 80 |
| 3211* | **Fahim (102)** (ACStewart) **3-9-2** WCarson(4) (lw: hld up in tch: nt clr run 3f out: led 2f out tl ins fnl f) | ½ | **2** | 7/4[1] | 113 | 81 |
| 3125[6] | **Dance So Suite (88)** (PFICole) **4-8-10** TQuinn(16) (hld up: hdwy fnl 2f) | 3½ | **3** | 14/1 | 94 | 70 |
| 574[7] | **Wood Magic (104)** (DRLoder) **3-9-4** LDettori(2) (trckd ldrs: kpt on one pce fnl 2f) | ¾ | **4** | 20/1 | 109 | 77 |
| 3071[5] | **Clan Ben (IRE) (96)** (HRACecil) **4-9-4** PatEddery(3) (lw: hld up: effrt & outpcd over 3f out: sn rdn: styd on fnl f) | nk | **5** | 11/2[2] | 100 | 76 |
| 3125* | **Grand Selection (IRE) (88)** (MBell) **4-8-10** MFenton(10) (hld up: hdwy on outside over 2f out: nvr able to chal) | 1½ | **6** | 11/1 | 90 | 66 |
| 1817[5] | **Tawkil (USA) (98)** (BWHills) **3-8-12** RHills(9) (led after 1f to 2f out: wknd fnl f) | hd | **7** | 20/1 | 100 | 68 |
| 3071[2] | **Hoh Express (99)** (IABalding) **4-9-7** MHills(7) (hld up: effrt & n.m.r 2f out: styd on fnl f) | nk | **8** | 14/1 | 100 | 76 |
| 3509[8] | **Hazard a Guess (IRE) (85)** (DNicholls) **6-8-7** AlexGreaves(12) (hld up: nt clr run fnl 2f: nvr nr to chal) | ½ | **9** | 20/1 | 86 | 62 |
| 2862* | **Moving Arrow (97)** (MissSEHall) **5-9-5** MJKinane(13) (hld up: plld hrd in rr: n.d) | s.h | **10** | 14/1 | 97 | 73 |
| 2439* | **Qasida (IRE) (87)** (CEBrittain) **3-7-12**(3) FLynch(15) (trckd ldrs over 7f: grad fdd) | nk | **11** | 16/1 | 87 | 55 |
| 3447[8] | **Billy Bushwacker (89)** (MrsMReveley) **5-8-11** RCochrane(6) (hld up in rr: nt clr run on ins fnl 3f: n.d) | s.h | **12** | 10/1[3] | 89 | 65 |
| 3263[3] | **Star of Zilzal (USA) (96)** (MRStoute) **4-9-4** KFallon(8) (swtg: hld up: effrt 3f out: sn no imp) | 1½ | **13** | 16/1 | 94 | 70 |
| 3145[12] | **Al Shafa (97)** (JLDunlop) **3-8-11** KDarley(14) (s.s: a in rr) | nk | **14** | 14/1 | 94 | 62 |
| 3211[4] | **The Dilettanti (USA) (89)** (JARToller) **3-8-3** SSanders(11) (hdwy on outside ½-wy: wknd fnl 3f) | 2 | **15** | 14/1 | 83 | 51 |
| 3509[9] | **Vindaloo (89)** (JLHarris) **4-8-11** JWeaver(5) (led 1f: chsd ldrs tl wknd wl over 2f out: t.o) | 15 | **16** | 33/1 | 60 | 36 |
| | | | | (SP 136.3%) | | **16 Rn** |

**2m 8.71** (-0.99) CSF £57.61 CT £529.77 TOTE £30.70: £5.20 £1.10 £5.50 £3.00 (£39.80) Trio £686.80 OWNER Mr A. Merza (NEWMARKET) BRED Ovidstown Investments Ltd
WEIGHT FOR AGE 3yo-8lb
**2248 Amrak Ajeeb (IRE)** hardly ever runs two races alike, but he is useful on his day and this proved to be one of those days. (20/1)
**3211* Fahim** found the gap that he had been waiting for and, quickening to take charge entering the final quarter-mile, looked all over the winner. In a spirited duel to the line, he was forced to give best. (7/4)
**3125 Dance So Suite** does seem to be better over twelve furlongs these days, but he did nothing wrong here and will be worth keeping in mind when he returns to that trip. (14/1)
**Wood Magic** was thrown in at the deep end in this first handicap over an extended trip, but he adapted well enough, and should be able to go on from here. (20/1)
**3071 Clan Ben (IRE)** did not stride to post with any enthusiasm, and did not find his stride until it was all over. (11/2)
**3125* Grand Selection (IRE)** was unable to go through with his run, after looking to be going really well with two furlongs left. It could be that the Handicapper has got his measure. (11/1)
**3071 Hoh Express** was one of several to suffer in a messy race, but ran much better than his placing suggests. His turn is near. (14/1)
**3509 Hazard a Guess (IRE)** had no run at all when trying to find room up the inside rail throughout the last quarter-mile. This decent effort is a sure sign that he is holding his form. (20/1)
**2608 Al Shafa** (14/1: 10/1-16/1)

## 3692 ROSES STKS (Listed) (2-Y.O C & G) (Class A)

4-45 (4-45) **5f** £12,110.00 (£3,605.00: £1,715.00: £770.00) Stalls: Low GOING minus 0.33 sec per fur (GF)

| | | | SP | RR | SF |
|---|---|---|---|---|---|
| 3250* | **Janib (USA)** (HThomsonJones) **2-8-11** RHills(3) (lw: chsd ldr: shkn up to chal over 1f out: led wl ins fnl f)....— | 1 | 9/2[3] | 105 | 36 |
| 3213[6] | **Tipsy Creek (USA) (100)** (BHanbury) **2-9-5** WCarson(1) (b.hind: awkward leaving stalls: sn led & clr: hdd & no ex wl ins fnl f) ....1¼ | 2 | 6/4[1] | 109 | 40 |
| 3160[4] | **Rudi's Pet (IRE) (92)** (RHannon) **2-8-11** LDettori(5) (outpcd tl kpt on u.p fnl) ....2½ | 3 | 11/1 | 93 | 24 |
| 3436* | **Big Ben (92)** (RHannon) **2-8-11** RPerham(2) (outpcd tl kpt on appr fnl f) ....hd | 4 | 7/2[2] | 93 | 24 |
| 3160* | **Fredrik The Fierce (IRE) (100)** (JBerry) **2-8-11** KDarley(4) (s.i.s: a wl outpcd) ....1¼ | 5 | 7/2[2] | 89 | 20 |
| | | | (SP 111.0%) | | **5 Rn** |

**59.46 secs** (1.76) CSF £11.28 TOTE £6.00: £2.30 £1.40 (£5.00) OWNER Mr Hamdan Al Maktoum (NEWMARKET) BRED Shadwell Farm Inc. and Shadwell Estate Co. Ltd.

**3250* Janib (USA)**, the only one able to keep tabs on the favourite, proved to be most resolute when the sprint to the post developed. (9/2)

**3213 Tipsy Creek (USA)** came out of the stalls at an angle but such is his speed that he was able to blaze a trail. He looked to have the measure of the winner 200 yards out, but his stride shortened and slightly more restraining tactics would probably have been enough to have seen him home. (6/4)

**3160 Rudi's Pet (IRE)** looked ill at ease on the ground and did not begin to pick up until well inside the final furlong. (11/1)

**3436* Big Ben** is hardly up to this class yet and was taken off his legs throughout. (7/2)

## 3693 FALMOUTH H'CAP (0-100) (3-Y.O) (Class C)

5-15 (5-17) **5f** £12,037.50 (£3,600.00: £1,725.00: £787.50) Stalls: Low GOING minus 0.33 sec per fur (GF)

| | | | SP | RR | SF |
|---|---|---|---|---|---|
| 3562a[7] | **Blue Iris (97)** (MAJarvis) **3-9-7** PRobinson(7) (a.p: rdn to ld wl ins fnl f: r.o wl) ....— | 1 | 11/1 | 107 | 66 |
| 3215* | **Clan Chief (77)** (JRArnold) **3-7-12**(3) MHenry(15) (b.hind: hdwy over 2f out: str chal wl ins fnl f)....1¼ | 2 | 11/2[1] | 83 | 42 |
| 3232[25] | **Dashing Blue (96)** (IABalding) **3-9-6** LDettori(17) (hld up: hdwy ½-wy: r.o wl fnl f)....hd | 3 | 11/1 | 102 | 61 |
| 3432[4] | **Rushcutter Bay (88)** (TTClement) **3-8-5v**(7) GFaulkner(8) (a in tch: kpt on u.p fnl f)....hd | 4 | 16/1 | 93 | 52 |
| 1630[7] | **Pride of Brixton (87)** (GLewis) **3-8-11** PaulEddery(14) (lw: led tl hdd & wknd wl ins fnl f)....1½ | 5 | 10/1[3] | 88 | 47 |
| 3085[14] | **Swynford Dream (80)** (JFBottomley) **3-8-4** JLowe(2) (racd far side: w ldrs over 3f)....hd | 6 | 50/1 | 80 | 39 |
| 959* | **Fond Embrace (95)** (HCandy) **3-9-5** GCarter(13) (lw: a.p: ev ch whn nt clr run jst ins fnl f)....s.h | 7 | 12/1 | 95 | 54 |
| 3232[28] | **Norwegian Blue (IRE) (86)** (APJarvis) **3-8-10v** WJO'Connor(10) (nvr rchd ldrs)....1¼ | 8 | 33/1 | 82 | 41 |
| 3465* | **Literary Society (USA) (73)** (JARToller) **3-7-11**[7x] JQuinn(4) (stmbld s: sn chsng ldrs: one pce fnl f)....nk | 9 | 14/1 | 68 | 27 |
| 2143[13] | **Kunucu (IRE) (95)** (TDBarron) **3-9-5** MJKinane(20) (chsd ldrs: rdn 2f out: nt pce to chal)....s.h | 10 | 16/1 | 90 | 49 |
| 3047[2] | **Galine (89)** (WAO'Gorman) **3-8-13** EmmaO'Gorman(6) (hld up & bhd: hmpd & swtchd lft over 1f out: nvr nrr)....s.h | 11 | 9/1[2] | 84 | 43 |
| 2816a[3] | **Slayjay (IRE) (92)** (JCHayden,Ireland) **3-9-2** WJSupple(3) (spd 3f)....½ | 12 | 14/1 | 85 | 44 |
| 3350[3] | **Chemcast (72)** (DNicholls) **3-7-10b** LCharnock(19) (a bhd)....½ | 13 | 33/1 | 64 | 23 |
| 3465[6] | **U-No-Harry (IRE) (77)** (RHollinshead) **3-7-12**(3)ow4 FLynch(9) (s.s: a bhd)....hd | 14 | 25/1 | 68 | 23 |
| 2143* | **Midnight Escape (94)** (CFWall) **3-9-4** NCarlisle(5) (gd spd over 3f)....1¼ | 15 | 9/1[2] | 81 | 40 |
| 3350* | **Zalotti (IRE) (80)** (MHTompkins) **3-8-4** KDarley(18) (in tch over 3f)....hd | 16 | 11/2[1] | 67 | 26 |
| 3477[4] | **Mindrace (72)** (KTIvory) **3-7-5**(5) MartinDwyer(12) (in rr most of wy)....½ | 17 | 25/1 | 57 | 16 |
| 3495[6] | **Lunar Mist (87)** (MartynMeade) **3-8-6**(5) RHavlin(16) (outpcd)....nk | 18 | 16/1 | 71 | 30 |
| 3296[14] | **Splicing (82)** (WJHaggas) **3-8-6** MHills(11) (lw: outpcd)....2 | 19 | 20/1 | 60 | 19 |
| 3270[6] | **Splinter (IRE) (77)** (RCharlton) **3-8-1** SSanders(1) (chsd ldrs to ½-wy: sn lost tch)....4 | 20 | 16/1 | 42 | 1 |
| | | | (SP 141.4%) | | **20 Rn** |

**58.28 secs** (0.58) CSF £73.23 CT £675.65 TOTE £11.90: £3.00 £1.60 £2.50 £3.80 (£45.80) Trio £139.70 OWNER Mr M. A. Jarvis (NEWMARKET) BRED North Cheshire Trading and Storage Ltd

LONG HANDICAP Chemcast 7-6 Mindrace 7-6

**3562a Blue Iris** found the concession of weight to handicappers no problem at all, and she was well on top at the end. (11/1)

**3215* Clan Chief** has been on a roll but all good things come to an end, and the classy winner proved to be just too good. (11/2: 4/1-6/1)

**3038 Dashing Blue** delivered a determined challenge just inside the last furlong, but the pace was not easing and, over this trip, the line was always going to arrive too soon. (11/1: 16/1-10/1)

**3432 Rushcutter Bay** ran another good race and only just failed to make the frame. He deserves to win more races than he does. (16/1)

**1113 Pride of Brixton**, from a stable just coming out of the doldrums, showed the blistering speed he displayed earlier in the year, and this first outing in almost three months is sure to have put an edge on him. (10/1)

**1188 Swynford Dream**, drawn on the slower far side, ran extremely well all the way and, with the autumn rains beckoning, should soon be paying his way again. (50/1)

**959* Fond Embrace**, returning to action after almost four months, could not maintain her winning sequence, but she ran up to her best and only failed as lack of peak fitness took its toll. She will soon be back. (12/1)

**3350* Zalotti (IRE)** found this opposition much tougher than she had met before, and she was feeling the strain soon after halfway. (11/2)

T/Jkpt: Not won; £48,919.77. T/Plpt: £297.10 (212.43 Tckts). T/Qdpt: £9.10 (363.06 Tckts) IM

# 3513-SALISBURY (R-H) (Firm becoming Good to firm)

## Thursday August 22nd

Race 6 - flip start & hand-timed

WEATHER: raining WIND: almost nil

## 3694 WOODFORD APPRENTICE H'CAP (0-70) (3-Y.O+) (Class F)

5-30 (5-32) **1m** £2,487.00 (£707.00: £351.00) Stalls: High GOING minus 0.32 sec per fur (GF)

| | | | SP | RR | SF |
|---|---|---|---|---|---|
| 3274[8] | **Helios (64)** (NJHWalker) **8-9-4**(10) MatthewWilliams(14) (lw: a.p: led 2f out tl ins fnl f: unable qckn: fin 2nd, 1l: awrdd r)....— | 1 | 14/1 | 73 | 54 |
| 3469[5] | **Jaazim (53)** (MMadgwick) **6-9-3** GayeHarwood(12) (lw: a.p: rdn over 1f out: one pce: fin 3rd, 5l: plcd 2nd)........ | 2 | 6/1[3] | 52 | 33 |
| 3257* | **Queen of Shannon (IRE) (50)** (AWCarroll) **8-8-9v**(5) RStudholme(4) (s.s: stdy hdwy on ins over 3f out: bdly hmpd over 2f out: swtchd lft & rallied over 1f out: r.o: fin 4th, 1l: plcd 3rd)........ | 3 | 8/1 | 47+ | 28 |
| 2971[8] | **Nabjelsedr (37)** (AGNewcombe) **6-7-12**(3) RFfrench(15) (s.s: hdwy 7f out: hrd rdn & edgd rt over 2f out: led ins fnl f: r.o wl: fin 1st: disq & plcd 4th)........ | 4 | 9/1 | 48 | 29 |

| | | | SP | RR | SF |
|---|---|---|---|---|---|
| $2784^{6}$ **Desert Calm (IRE) (48)** (MrsPNDutfield) **7-8-7b**$^{(5)}$ RSmith(13) (a.p: hrd rdn over 2f out: one pce) | 1 | **5** | 12/1 | 43 | 24 |
| $3491^{2}$ **Dil Dil (43)** (WJHaggas) **3-7-12**$^{(3)}$ CWebb(8) (lw: s.s: stdy hdwy over 3f out: wknd over 1f out) | 3½ | **6** | 6/1 3 | 31 | 6 |
| $3606^{4}$ **Astral Invader (IRE) (52)** (MSSaunders) **4-9-2** PDoe(3) (b. lw: nvr nr to chal) | ¾ | **7** | 12/1 | 39 | 20 |
| $3471^{10}$ **Red Viper (50)** (NMLampard) **4-8-7**$^{(7)}$ RCody-Boutcher(10) (hld up: rdn 4f out: sn wknd) | ½ | **8** | 33/1 | 36 | 17 |
| *$3420^{9}$* **Sandra Dee (IRE) (36)** (EAWheeler) **4-8-0** JWilkinson(6) (lw: nvr nrr) | hd | **9** | 33/1 | 21 | 2 |
| $3606^{2}$ **Just Harry (60)** (MJRyan) **5-9-2**$^{(8)}$ AMcCarthy(7) (lw: bhd fnl 4f) | nk | **10** | 5/1 1 | 45 | 26 |
| $3599^{8}$ **Great Hall (41)** (PDCundell) **7-8-5b** JDennis(2) (lw: a bhd) | hd | **11** | 20/1 | 26 | 7 |
| $3518^{14}$ **Chili Heights (55)** (GBBalding) **6-9-2v**$^{(3)}$ CScudder(1) (a bhd) | 1¼ | **12** | 14/1 | 37 | 18 |
| $3205^{10}$ **Roi de la Mer (IRE) (59)** (JAkehurst) **5-9-9** DDenby(5) (led 6f) | nk | **13** | 11/2 2 | 40 | 21 |
| $2981^{12}$ **Little Wobbly (37)** (PCClarke) **6-7-5**$^{(10)ow2}$ CherylBone(9) (bhd fnl 5f: t.o) | dist | **14** | 50/1 | — | — |
| | | | (SP 123.1%) | | **14 Rn** |

**1m 43.54** (3.14) CSF £117.40 CT £540.83 TOTE £17.40: £3.80 £4.10 £2.60 (£410.30) Trio £237.60; £150.61 to 24/8/96 OWNER Box 40 Racing (WANTAGE) BRED Sunley Stud

WEIGHT FOR AGE 3yo-6lb

STEWARDS' ENQUIRY Ffrench susp. 31/8 & 2-7/9/96 (irresponsible riding).

**2058 Helios** went on a quarter of a mile from home, but was unable to cope with the winner inside the final furlong. He was later awarded the race in the Stewards' Room, his rider's first winner. (14/1)

**3469 Jaazim** was pushed along below the distance but never looked like finding the required turn of foot. (6/1)

**3257* Queen of Shannon (IRE)** lost ground at the start, but steadily crept closer from halfway. She almost fell a quarter of a mile out as a rival veered in front of her. Switched left and picking up ground below the distance, she did well to finish fourth. (8/1: 6/1-9/1)

**2344 Nabjelsedr** soon recovered form a tardy start. Given a crack of the whip, the gelding edged right, almost causing a rival to fall over a quarter of a mile from home. He got on top inside the final furlong, but was later disqualified and his jockey suspended. (9/1: 5/1-10/1)

**2784 Desert Calm (IRE)**, shown the persuader over two furlongs out, could only plod on at one insufficient pace. (12/1)

**3491 Dil Dil** steadily crept closer in the second half of the race, but was a spent force below the distance. (6/1)

## 3695 NETHERAVON MAIDEN STKS (2-Y.O) (Class D)

6-00 (6-02) **6f 212y** £3,645.50 (£1,094.00: £527.00: £243.50) Stalls: High GOING minus 0.32 sec per fur (GF)

| | | | SP | RR | SF |
|---|---|---|---|---|---|
| **Fahris (IRE)** (HThomsonJones) **2-9-0** GCarter(3) (str: scope: lw: led 1f: led over 2f out: rdn & edgd rt over 1f out: r.o wl) | — | **1** | 5/2 2 | 84 | 35 |
| $3499^{2}$ **Another Night (IRE)** (RHannon) **2-9-0** WJO'Connor(1) (lw: chsd ldrs: rdn over 4f out: chsd wnr over 1f out: unable qckn) | 3 | **2** | 5/4 1 | 77 | 28 |
| $2667a^{5}$ **Passi d'Orlando (IRE)** (JLDunlop) **2-9-0** TSprake(5) (w'like: hdwy over 2f out: rdn over 1f out: one pce) | ¾ | **3** | 11/2 3 | 75 | 26 |
| $3319^{8}$ **Tom Tailor (GER)** (DRCElsworth) **2-9-0** AProcter(6) (hld up: rdn 2f out: wknd over 1f out) | 1¾ | **4** | 8/1 | 71 | 22 |
| **Around Fore Alliss** (TGMills) **2-9-0** MarkLynch(8) (unf: plld hrd: prom over 5f) | 1 | **5** | 40/1 | 69 | 20 |
| **Bold Saint (IRE)** (PWHarris) **2-9-0** FNorton(4) (w'like: bit bkwd: a bhd) | 2½ | **6** | 10/1 | 63 | 14 |
| $3214^{4}$ **Quertier (IRE)** (MRChannon) **2-9-0** AClark(7) (lw: led 6f out tl over 2f out: sn wknd) | 19 | **7** | 33/1 | 20 | — |
| | | | (SP 114.0%) | | **7 Rn** |

**1m 29.22** (3.22) CSF £5.89 TOTE £3.40: £1.90 £1.90 (£2.60) OWNER Mr Hamdan Al Maktoum (NEWMARKET) BRED Shadwell Estate Company Limited

**Fahris (IRE)**, an attractive, good-bodied colt, looked in great shape for this debut. In front for the first furlong, he remained with the leader and regained the advantage over a quarter of a mile out. Despite drifting right below the distance, he soon established a clear advantage and his pilot was able to take things easy in the closing stages. (5/2)

**3499 Another Night (IRE)** chased the leaders, but was being ridden along well before halfway. Nevertheless, he struggled into second place approaching the second furlong, if having no chance with the winner. (5/4)

**2667a Passi d'Orlando (IRE)**, who disappointed in the mud at San Siro on his debut, ran better here. Moving up over a quarter of a mile out, he failed to find that vital turn of foot from below the distance. (11/2: 4/1-6/1)

**Tom Tailor (GER)** chased the leaders, travelling well. Asked for his effort a quarter of a mile from home, he had soon shot his bolt. (8/1)

**Around Fore Alliss** pulled extremely hard in the early stages but played an active role, until coming to the end of his tether below the distance. (40/1)

**Bold Saint (IRE)** (10/1: 8/1-12/1)

## 3696 BODDINGTONS H'CAP (0-85) (3-Y.O+) (Class D)

6-30 (6-31) **6f 212y** £3,743.00 (£1,124.00: £542.00: £251.00) Stalls: High GOING minus 0.32 sec per fur (GF)

| | | | SP | RR | SF |
|---|---|---|---|---|---|
| $1615^{12}$ **Blue Flyer (IRE) (72)** (RIngram) **3-8-10** SWhitworth(6) (a.p: rdn over 2f out: led over 1f out: r.o wl) | — | **1** | 10/1 | 82 | 52 |
| 3442* **Ortolan (80)** (RHannon) **3-9-4** WJO'Connor(5) (lw: hld up: rdn over 1f out: chsd wnr fnl f: r.o) | 1 | **2** | 15/8 1 | 88 | 58 |
| $3518^{6}$ **Winsome Wooster (63)** (PGMurphy) **5-8-6** SDrowne(4) (led over 5f: unable qckn) | 4 | **3** | 5/1 3 | 62 | 37 |
| $3207^{4}$ **Star Talent (USA) (84)** (MissGayKelleway) **5-9-13** GCarter(3) (b.hind: lw: hld up: rdn over 2f out: wknd over 1f out) | 2½ | **4** | 5/1 3 | 77 | 52 |
| $3271^{8}$ **Victory Team (IRE) (69)** (GBBalding) **4-8-12** DHarrison(1) (hld up: rdn over 2f out: sn wknd) | 13 | **5** | 6/1 | 32 | 7 |
| 3301* **Kings Harmony (IRE) (72)** (PJMakin) **3-8-10** SSanders(2) (prom over 4f) | 1½ | **6** | 9/2 2 | 32 | 2 |
| | | | (SP 109.7%) | | **6 Rn** |

**1m 27.42** (1.42) CSF £27.30 TOTE £10.60: £3.50 £1.50 (£12.30) OWNER Mr B. Scott (EPSOM) BRED Matt Carr

WEIGHT FOR AGE 3yo-5lb

**692 Blue Flyer (IRE)** bounced back here after a three month break. In the firing line throughout, he gained control below the distance, and ridden along, proved just too strong for the runner-up. (10/1)

**3442* Ortolan**, successful in three claimers this month, was taking a step up in class. Tucked in behind the front rank, he was asked for his effort below the distance, but despite moving into second place entering the final furlong, was unable to overhaul the winner. (15/8)

**3518 Winsome Wooster** attempted to make all the running. Collared below the distance, she was left standing by the front two. (5/1)

**3207 Star Talent (USA)**, held up and travelling well, was asked for his effort over quarter of a mile from home, but in the rain-softened ground, he tired below the distance. (5/1: 7/2-11/2)

**2602 Victory Team (IRE)** chased the leaders but was hung out to dry a quarter of a mile out. (6/1)

**3301* Kings Harmony (IRE)** played an active role until calling it a day over two furlongs from home. (9/2)

## 3697 NIGHTFALL CONDITIONS STKS (2-Y.O) (Class C)

7-00 (7-02) **5f** £4,597.60 (£1,605.60: £782.80: £334.00) Stalls: High GOING 0.01 sec per fur (G)

| | | | SP | RR | SF |
|---|---|---|---|---|---|
| $3068^{8}$ **China Girl (IRE)** (PWChapple-Hyam) **2-8-3**$^{(5)}$ RHavlin(4) (mde all: clr over 1f out: r.o wl) | — | **1** | 11/8 1 | 87+ | 47 |

| | Horse | | Pos | SP | RR | SF |
|---|---|---|---|---|---|---|
| 3475* | **Dancethenightaway (82)** (BJMeehan) **2-8-8** MTebbutt(3) (bmpd s: hdwy to chse wnr over 1f out: no imp) | 3 | **2** | 9/4[2] | 77 | 37 |
| 3128[9] | **Makhbar (85)** (RWArmstrong) **2-8-13** RPrice(1) (a.p: rdn over 2f out: wknd over 1f out) | 6 | **3** | 3/1[3] | 63 | 23 |
| 2972[5] | **Aim Seven (85)** (RHannon) **2-8-10** WJO'Connor(2) (a.p: rdn over 2f out: wknd over 1f out) | 1¼ | **4** | 6/1 | 56 | 16 |
| | | | | (SP 112.2%) | **4 Rn** | |

**61.12 secs** (1.12) CSF £4.73 TOTE £2.20 (£2.40) OWNER Mr Tony Huang and Mr Ivan Allan (MARLBOROUGH) BRED Ivan W. Allan
STEWARDS' ENQUIRY Obj. to China Girl (IRE) by Tebbutt overruled

**2327* China Girl (IRE)**, who flopped in the Princess Margaret Stakes at Ascot last month, bounced back here. Making all the running in the rain-softened ground, she forged clear below the distance to win with plenty in hand. (11/8)

**3475* Dancethenightaway**, who was given a slight nudge by the winner leaving the stalls, was unable to go the pace. Picking up ground below the distance to take second, she had no hope with the winner. (9/4)

**3128 Makhbar**, dropping down to the minimum trip for the first time, was in the front rank until tiring below the distance. He has become very disappointing following his impressive debut back in June. (3/1)

**2972 Aim Seven**, reverting to the minimum trip, was in a handy position until calling it a day over a furlong out. (6/1: op 4/1)

## 3698 NETTON CLAIMING H'CAP (0-60) (3-Y.O+) (Class F)

7-30 (7-32) **6f** £3,204.00 (£894.00: £432.00) Stalls: High GOING: 0.01 sec per fur (G)

| | Horse | | Pos | SP | RR | SF |
|---|---|---|---|---|---|---|
| 3292* | **Newlands Corner (44)** (JAkehurst) **3-8-12b** DBiggs(6) (racd stands' side: hrd rdn & hdwy over 1f out: led ins fnl f: r.o wl) | — | **1** | 7/2[1] | 53 | 31 |
| 3636[5] | **Into Debt (35)** (JRPoulton) **3-8-3** DeclanO'Shea(4) (racd stands' side: hrd rdn & hdwy over 1f out: unable qckn fnl f) | 3 | **2** | 20/1 | 36 | 14 |
| 3216[9] | **Petraco (IRE) (56)** (NASmith) **8-9-6**(7) JBramhill(5) (racd stands' side: hrd rdn & hdwy over 2f out: ev ch ins fnl f: one pce) | hd | **3** | 12/1 | 57 | 38 |
| 3506[8] | **Superlao (BEL) (40)** (JJBridger) **4-8-4**(7) TField(18) (w ldr: led 3f out: hrd rdn & edgd lft over 1f out: hdd ins fnl f: one pce) | ¾ | **4** | 14/1 | 39 | 20 |
| 3442[11] | **Calandrella (48)** (GBBalding) **3-9-2** AMcGlone(15) (hdwy over 3f out: one pce fnl 2f) | 1¼ | **5** | 14/1 | 43 | 21 |
| 3477[6] | **Red Time (58)** (MSSaunders) **3-9-12** FNorton(13) (a.p: rdn over 2f out: one pce) | hd | **6** | 20/1 | 53 | 31 |
| 3052[10] | **Needle Match (55)** (CFWall) **3-9-9** SSanders(11) (hdwy over 2f out: wknd fnl f) | 2 | **7** | 10/1 | 45 | 23 |
| 3096[6] | **Dark Menace (47)** (EAWheeler) **4-9-4** TSprake(7) (racd stands' side: outpcd: nvr nrr) | ½ | **8** | 10/1 | 36 | 17 |
| 3399[4] | **Ameliajill (48)** (RHannon) **3-9-2** RPerham(2) (b: b.hind: racd stands' side: outpcd: nvr nrr) | nk | **9** | 10/1 | 36 | 14 |
| 3516[13] | **Summerhill Special (IRE) (57)** (MrsPNDutfield) **5-9-9b**(5) AimeeCook(17) (hld up: swtchd lft 2f out: wknd over 1f out) | nk | **10** | 20/1 | 44 | 25 |
| 3166[13] | **Real Gem (54)** (PJMakin) **3-9-8** DHarrison(8) (racd stands' side: a mid div) | 4 | **11** | 12/1 | 30 | 8 |
| 1658[8] | **Forgotten Dancer (IRE) (45)** (RIngram) **5-9-2** SWhitworth(3) (racd stands' side: dwlt: a bhd) | 1¼ | **12** | 20/1 | 18 | — |
| 3525[9] | **Daffodil Express (IRE) (46)** (MJRyan) **3-8-9**(5) MBaird(20) (led 3f: wknd over 1f out) | 1¾ | **13** | 8/1[3] | 14 | — |
| 3458[4] | **Bella's Legacy (48)** (RJHodges) **3-9-2** SDrowne(14) (s.s: a bhd) | 6 | **14** | 9/1 | — | — |
| 3585[9] | **Classic Pet (IRE) (34)** (CAHorgan) **4-7-12**(7) GayeHarwood(12) (bhd fnl 2f) | 4 | **15** | 25/1 | — | — |
| 3473[10] | **Grey Charmer (IRE) (49)** (RHBuckler) **7-9-6** AProcter(9) (racd stands' side: a bhd) | hd | **16** | 16/1 | — | — |
| 3583[6] | **Norling (IRE) (45)** (KOCunningham-Brown) **6-9-2** CMunday(10) (bhd fnl 3f) | 4 | **17** | 13/2[2] | — | — |
| 3217[5] | **Only (USA) (45)** (RHannon) **3-8-13** AClark(16) (s.s: a bhd) | ¾ | **18** | 9/1 | — | — |
| | | | | (SP 151.4%) | **18 Rn** | |

**1m 17.82** (4.82) CSF £80.65 CT £570.61 TOTE £4.70: £1.60 £4.30 £2.80 £5.60 (£208.20) Trio £469.20; £284.17 to 24/8/96 OWNER The Jolly Skolars (LAMBOURN) BRED L. A. C. Ashby
WEIGHT FOR AGE 3yo-3lb

**3292* Newlands Corner**, one of eight who elected to race on the stands' side, looked to be on the worse side, as all those rivals were outpaced and unable to live with the far side group. She got on terms with her rivals though, below the distance and, striking the front inside the final furlong, ran on strongly. (7/2)

**Into Debt**, making a quick reappearance, ran her best race to date. Under pressure as she picked up ground on the stands' side below the distance, she was almost on the winner's quarters entering the final furlong, before tapped for toe. (20/1)

**2745 Petraco (IRE)**, in front on the stands' side, picked up ground to get on terms with the far side group over a quarter of a mile from home. With every chance inside the final furlong, he was then tapped for toe. (12/1: 8/1-14/1)

**2787 Superlao (BEL)** disputed the lead until going on at halfway. Drifting right below the distance, she was collared inside the final furlong and failed to find another gear. (14/1)

**3115 Calandrella** moved up into a handy position before halfway, but failed to find a necessary turn of foot in the last two furlongs. (14/1)

**3477 Red Time**, a leading light from the off, could only go up and down in the same place in the last two furlongs. (20/1)

**3458 Bella's Legacy** (9/1: 14/1-8/1)

## 3699 ODSTOCK MAIDEN STKS (3-Y.O+) (Class D)

8-00 (8-00) **1m 6f** £3,717.00 (£1,116.00: £538.00: £249.00) Stalls: High GOING: 0.01 sec per fur (G)

| | Horse | | Pos | SP | RR | SF |
|---|---|---|---|---|---|---|
| 2882[3] | **Generosa (90)** (HCandy) **3-8-0** CRutter(6) (a.p: chsd ldr over 4f out: led over 2f out: clr over 1f out: eased ins fnl f) | — | **1** | 1/2[1] | 74+ | — |
| 3283[6] | **Majdak Jereeb (IRE) (69)** (MajorWRHern) **3-8-5v**[1] TSprake(1) (led tl over 2f out: hrd rdn: unable qckn) | 4 | **2** | 8/1 | 74 | — |
| 2135[W] | **High Atlas** (BWHills) **3-8-0** AMcGlone(4) (leggy: hld up: rdn 3f out: one pce) | 2 | **3** | 11/2[3] | 67 | — |
| 2739[2] | **Crandon Boulevard** (LordHuntingdon) **3-8-5** DHarrison(5) (chsd ldr over 9f: rdn: one pce) | nk | **4** | 7/2[2] | 72 | — |
| *2551[12]* | **Credit Controller (IRE)** (JFfitch-Heyes) **7-9-3** SWhitworth(2) (hdwy 8f out: wknd over 5f out: t.o fnl 4f) | dist | **5** | 25/1 | — | — |
| 2529[11] | **Kentford Conquista** (JWMullins) **3-8-0** FNorton(3) (a bhd: t.o fnl 3f) | ½ | **6** | 33/1 | — | — |
| | | | | (SP 122.2%) | **6 Rn** | |

**3m 17.45** (18.75) CSF £5.99 TOTE £1.60: £1.10 £2.80 (£4.10) OWNER H R H Prince Fahd Salman (WANTAGE) BRED Newgate Stud Co
WEIGHT FOR AGE 3yo-12lb

**2882 Generosa** at last came good after a string of solid efforts. Moving into second place over half a mile from home, she was bustled along to lead two furlongs later and, forging clear from below the distance, was eased considerably in the closing stages. The winning distance is certainly no true reflection of her superiority. (1/2)

**2140 Majdak Jereeb (IRE)** attempted to make all. Collared over a quarter of a mile from home, he was soon put in his place. (8/1: op 5/1)

**High Atlas**, quite a tall filly who has had stalls trouble in the past, and has had to be withdrawn, at last made her debut. Chasing the leaders, she was bustled along three furlongs out but was made to look very pedestrian. (11/2: 7/2-6/1)

**2739 Crandon Boulevard**, in second place until over four furlongs from home, could then only keep on at one pace. (7/2)

T/Plpt: £51.80 (212.49 Tckts). T/Qdpt: £9.10 (96.91 Tckts). AK

# 3520-YARMOUTH (L-H) (Good to firm, Firm bk st)
## Thursday August 22nd
WEATHER: fine WIND: fresh against

## 3700 BUNGAY H'CAP (0-70) (3-Y.O+ F & M) (Class E)
2-20 (2-22) **6f 3y** £3,097.50 (£682.50: £682.50: £199.50) Stalls: High GOING minus 0.01 sec per fur (G)

| | | | | SP | RR | SF |
|---|---|---|---|---|---|---|
| 2590$^{3}$ | **Wardara (65)** (CADwyer) **4-10-0v** RHills(8) (lw: hld up: hdwy, nt clr run & squeezed thro over 1f out: led ins fnl f: r.o wl) | — | **1** | 11/4$^{1}$ | 77 | 59 |
| 3439$^{4}$ | **Merrie le Bow (47)** (PatMitchell) **4-8-5**$^{(5)}$ AmandaSanders(6) (lw: trckd ldrs gng wl: ev ch ins fnl f: unable qckn) | ¾ | **2** | 11/1 | 57 | 39 |
| 3345$^{4}$ | **L A Touch (53)** (CADwyer) **3-8-6**$^{(7)}$ JoHunnam(9) (swtg: hld up: nt clr run, swtchd lft & hdwy over 1f out: r.o wl ins fnl f) | d.h | **2** | 8/1 | 63 | 42 |
| 3599$^{3}$ | **Rambold (65)** (NEBerry) **5-9-9**$^{(5)}$ DGriffiths(5) (led tl ins fnl f) | 1½ | **4** | 6/1$^{3}$ | 62 | 44 |
| 3439$^{6}$ | **Times of Times (IRE) (68)** (MJRyan) **3-10-0** RCochrane(2) (lw: s.s: hdwy over 2f out: bmpd over 1f out: wknd ins fnl f) | 6 | **5** | 7/1 | 49 | 28 |
| 2769$^{3}$ | **Lillibella (63)** (IABalding) **3-9-4**$^{(5)}$ MartinDwyer(7) (lw: s.s: hdwy 3f out: wknd over 1f out) | 5 | **6** | 9/2$^{2}$ | 30 | 9 |
| 3345$^{5}$ | **Brookhead Lady (45)** (PDEvans) **5-8-8** JFEgan(10) (b.nr fore: w ldr: rdn over 2f out: wknd over 1f out) | ½ | **7** | 20/1 | 11 | — |
| 1422$^{7}$ | **Desert Skimmer (USA) (55)** (MBell) **3-9-1** MFenton(1) (prom 4f) | ¾ | **8** | 16/1 | 19 | — |
| 3256$^{4}$ | **Madam Zando (49)** (JBalding) **3-8-2**$^{(7)ow2}$ JEdmunds(3) (lw: prom over 3f) | 1¼ | **9** | 11/1 | 10 | — |
| *2940** | **Fiaba (43)** (MrsNMacauley) **8-8-3v**$^{(3)ow6}$ CTeague(4) (a bhd: t.o) | 13 | **10** | 14/1 | — | — |
| | | | | (SP 116.7%) | **10 Rn** | |

**1m 14.2** (3.30) CSF LAT & MLB £40.82 MLB & LAT £43.22 CT LAT, MLB & R £258.78 MLB, LAT & R £265.57 TOTE LAT £5.30 MLB £7.10: LAT £1.80 MLB £3.40 £2.90 (£63.10) Trio 87.60 OWNER Binding Matters Ltd (NEWMARKET) BRED G. B. Turnbull Ltd

WEIGHT FOR AGE 3yo-3lb

STEWARDS' ENQUIRY Hills susp. 31/8 & 2-4/9/96 (irresponsible riding).

**IN-FOCUS: Wardara was originally disqualified and placed last, but after appeal, the intereference was considered accidental. Wardara was reinstated to first, and the four-day ban on Hills was lifted.**

**2590 Wardara**, freshened up by a break, was adjudged to have created her own opening when beginning her own run, and Hills was suspended for irresponsible riding. Wardara was later reinstated after appeal and the ban on the jockey lifted. (11/4)

**3439 Merrie le Bow** raced keenly on the heels of the leaders, but failed to match Wardara in the closing stages. (11/1: 8/1-12/1)

**3345 L A Touch** did not get the best of runs and finished with a flourish. (8/1: 5/1-9/1)

**3599 Rambold** continues to find it tough off a mark of 65. (6/1: op 4/1)

**3270* Times of Times (IRE)**, the sufferer in the scrimmaging, had a big weight for a three-year-old, and should not be considered unlucky. (7/1: 5/1-8/1)

**2769 Lillibella**, back to six, was reluctant to go to post and then proceeded to lose a good six lengths at the start. (9/2)

**2940* Fiaba** (14/1: 10/1-16/1)

## 3701 E.B.F. WAXHAM MAIDEN STKS (2-Y.O) (Class D)
2-50 (2-51) **6f 3y** £3,785.00 (£1,130.00: £540.00: £245.00) Stalls: High GOING minus 0.06 sec per fur (G)

| | | | | SP | RR | SF |
|---|---|---|---|---|---|---|
| | **Kharir (IRE)** (HThomsonJones) **2-9-0** RHills(6) (str: scope: mde all: rdn wl over 1f out: r.o wl) | — | **1** | 6/4$^{1}$ | 90 | 30 |
| | **Sky Commander (USA)** (MRStoute) **2-9-0** RCochrane(2) (gd sort: hld up & bhd: gd hdwy over 1f out: r.o wl ins fnl f: bttr for r) | ½ | **2** | 7/2$^{3}$ | 89+ | 29 |
| 3359$^{2}$ | **Rejoicing (IRE)** (WAO'Gorman) **2-8-9** EmmaO'Gorman(3) (a.p: ev ch 2f out: unable qckn) | 2 | **3** | 2/1$^{2}$ | 78 | 18 |
| | **Ferny Hill (IRE)** (SirMarkPrescott) **2-9-0** CNutter(4) (unf: scope: hld up: hdwy fnl f: bttr for r) | 1¼ | **4** | 14/1 | 80 | 20 |
| 3407$^{11}$ | **Manwal (IRE)** (BHanbury) **2-9-0** JStack(5) (lw: w ldr: rdn over 2f out: wknd over 1f out) | hd | **5** | 16/1 | 80 | 20 |
| | **Mujazi (IRE)** (RWArmstrong) **2-9-0** MFenton(1) (str: rangy: scope: wl bhd fnl 4f: t.o) | 13 | **6** | 14/1 | 45 | — |
| | | | | (SP 114.8%) | **6 Rn** | |

**1m 15.4** (4.50) CSF £7.11 TOTE £2.10: £1.40 £1.60 (£3.00) OWNER Mr Hamdan Al Maktoum (NEWMARKET) BRED Shadwell Estate Company Limited

**Kharir (IRE)** is out of a sister to Larrocha and half-sister to Ardross. Bred to need further, he may have benefited from the runner-up being tenderly handled. (6/4)

**Sky Commander (USA)**, a well-bred $160,000 colt, was given a nice introduction and will be hard to beat next time. (7/2)

**3359 Rejoicing (IRE)** came up against a couple of potentially useful types and may fare better in a nursery. (2/1: 6/4-5/2)

**Ferny Hill (IRE)** caught the eye in the closing stages and will soon step up on this. (14/1: op 7/1)

**Manwal (IRE)** fared better than on his debut earlier in the month. (16/1)

**Mujazi (IRE)** (14/1: op 8/1)

## 3702 LIMPENHOE H'CAP (0-80) (3-Y.O+) (Class D)
3-25 (3-28) **7f 3y** £3,761.25 (£1,122.00: £535.50: £242.25) Stalls: High GOING minus 0.06 sec per fur (G)

| | | | | SP | RR | SF |
|---|---|---|---|---|---|---|
| 3246$^{3}$ | **Quality (IRE) (76)** (WAO'Gorman) **3-9-10** EmmaO'Gorman(8) (lw: a.p: rdn over 1f out: led ins fnl f: jst hld on) | — | **1** | 7/1$^{2}$ | 84 | 57 |
| 3445$^{13}$ | **Nashaat (USA) (75)** (MCChapman) **8-9-11**$^{(3)}$ PMcCabe(7) (swtg: hld up & plld hrd: stdy hdwy over 1f out: rdn & r.o wl ins fnl f) | s.h | **2** | 9/2$^{1}$ | 83 | 61 |
| 3585$^{10}$ | **Samsolom (59)** (PHowling) **8-8-12** PaulEddery(1) (lw: hld up: hdwy & nt clr run over 1f out: ev ch fnl f: r.o) | ½ | **3** | 11/1 | 66 | 44 |
| 3650$^{2}$ | **Safey Ana (USA) (60)** (BHanbury) **5-8-13** JStack(3) (b: swtg: chsd ldr: led over 2f out tl ins fnl f) | 1¼ | **4** | 9/2$^{1}$ | 64 | 42 |
| 3443$^{6}$ | **Awesome Venture (51)** (MCChapman) **6-8-4** DRMcCabe(6) (led over 4f: wknd ins fnl f) | nk | **5** | 8/1$^{3}$ | 54 | 32 |
| 3313$^{5}$ | **Always Grace (61)** (MissGayKelleway) **4-9-0** RCochrane(9) (lw: hld up: hdwy 2f out: one pce fnl f) | ½ | **6** | 9/2$^{1}$ | 63 | 41 |
| 2885$^{10}$ | **Bellas Gate Boy (55)** (JPearce) **4-8-8** GBardwell(5) (bhd: rdn over 4f out: nvr nrr) | 1¼ | **7** | 20/1 | 54 | 32 |
| 3518$^{5}$ | **Bright Diamond (56)** (JRArnold) **3-7-13**$^{(5)}$ MartinDwyer(2) (lw: prom over 5f) | ¾ | **8** | 8/1$^{3}$ | 54 | 27 |
| *3603*$^{14}$ | **Dubai College (IRE) (67)** (CEBrittain) **3-9-1** RHills(4) (lw: prom 5f) | 7 | **9** | 8/1$^{3}$ | 49 | 22 |
| | | | | (SP 113.5%) | **9 Rn** | |

**1m 28.0** (3.80) CSF £35.29 CT £312.96 TOTE £8.40: £1.90 £2.50 £1.90 (£11.80) Trio £57.90 OWNER Mr N. S. Yong (NEWMARKET) BRED Major C.R. Philipson

WEIGHT FOR AGE 3yo-5lb

**OFFICIAL EXPLANATION Awesome Venture: ducked away from the whips of two other jockeys over a furlong out.**

**3246 Quality (IRE)** was ridden closer to the pace on this drop back to seven. (7/1)
**3172* Nashaat (USA)**, who found the company too hot at Newmarket last time, very nearly pulled it off, despite being 2lb higher than when completing a hat-trick here at the start of the month. (9/2)
**3328 Samsolom** extended his losing run to twenty-three, but gave it a really good go on this occasion. (11/1)
**3650 Safey Ana (USA)**, making a quick reappearance, was 5lb lower than when last seen in a handicap, and has dropped nearly a stone this season. (9/2)
**3443 Awesome Venture** had been beaten only a neck by the runner-up on identical terms here earlier in the month. (8/1)
**3313 Always Grace**, 2lb higher than the second of her two wins at Brighton, has yet to win beyond six. (9/2)
**3518 Bright Diamond** could easily have found this coming too soon after her comeback run last week. (8/1)
**2946 Dubai College (IRE)** (8/1: op 5/1)

## 3703 CROMER LIMITED STKS (0-65) (3-Y.O+) (Class F)

4-00 (4-01) **1m 3y** £2,976.00 (£888.00: £424.00: £192.00) Stalls: High GOING minus 0.06 sec per fur (G)

| | | | | SP | RR | SF |
|---|---|---|---|---|---|---|
| 3634[3] | **Sylvan Princess (62)** (CNAllen) **3-8-11**(5) MartinDwyer(11) (trckd ldrs gng wl: led wl over 1f out: rdn out) | — | **1** | 4/1[2] | 72 | 20 |
| 3168[8] | **Spanish Stripper (USA) (56)** (MCChapman) **5-9-0**(3) PMcCabe(3) (hld up & bhd: stdy hdwy over 2f out: ev ch over 1f out: unable qckn) | 2 | **2** | 20/1 | 63 | 17 |
| 3469[10] | **Mr Rough (60)** (DMorris) **5-9-3b[1]** NDay(7) (a.p: ev ch over 1f out: one pce) | 1¾ | **3** | 11/2 | 60 | 14 |
| 2198[6] | **Classic Lover (IRE) (63)** (RHarris) **3-8-5**(3) NVarley(8) (rdn over 3f out: hdwy over 2f out: one pce fnl f) | nk | **4** | 7/1 | 56 | 4 |
| 3623[16] | **Bentico (60)** (MrsNMacauley) **7-9-2v**(3) CTeague(5) (lw: a.p: one pce fnl 2f) | 1 | **5** | 12/1 | 59 | 13 |
| 3484[5] | **Galapino (60)** (CEBrittain) **3-8-11** JFEgan(6) (led over 6f: one pce) | nk | **6** | 14/1 | 56 | 4 |
| 1589[4] | **Basood (USA) (60)** (SPCWoods) **3-8-8** DBiggs(2) (nvr nr to chal) | ¾ | **7** | 20/1 | 52 | — |
| *3418*[3] | **What A Fuss (64)** (BHanbury) **3-8-11** MRimmer(10) (lw: w ldr: hrd rdn over 2f out: sn wknd) | 5 | **8** | 5/1[3] | 45 | — |
| 3220[9] | **Saltando (IRE) (44)** (PatMitchell) **5-9-3** RCochrane(9) (lw: hld up: a bhd) | 3 | **9** | 20/1 | 39 | — |
| 2952[6] | **Mansur (IRE) (62)** (DRLoder) **4-9-3** DRMcCabe(4) (lw: racd wd: bhd fnl 2f) | 8 | **10** | 7/1 | 23 | — |
| 3424[7] | **Baileys First (IRE) (65)** (MJohnston) **3-8-8** RHills(1) (racd wd: bhd fnl 3f) | 1¼ | **11** | 3/1[1] | 17 | — |
| | | | | (SP 130.7%) | **11 Rn** | |

**1m 42.6** (7.30) CSF £76.12 TOTE £3.70: £1.50 £11.00 £1.90 (£51.20) Trio £388.90; £328.70 to Newmarket 23/8/96 OWNER Camelot Racing (NEWMARKET) BRED K S P Leisure
WEIGHT FOR AGE 3yo-6lb

**3634 Sylvan Princess** holds her form remarkably well, despite a hectic schedule, and is a credit to all concerned. (4/1)
**Spanish Stripper (USA)**, trying a longer trip, produced by far his best effort of the season. (20/1)
**2868 Mr Rough** showed improved form in the first-time blinkers after a couple of disappointing runs. (11/2)
**447 Classic Lover (IRE)**, a springer in the market, has been struggling to find the right trip. (7/1: op 14/1)
**3419 Bentico** was tried in a visor after his recent flop at Ripon. (12/1: 7/1-14/1)
**3484 Galapino** seems better suited to the artificial surface. (14/1: 10/1-16/1)
**3424 Baileys First (IRE)**, trying her luck at a mile, was struggling soon after halfway. The trainer's representative could offer the Stewards no explanation for this disappointing performance. (3/1)

## 3704 JOHN BECKET MAIDEN STKS (3-Y.O+) (Class D)

4-30 (4-32) **1m 2f 21y** £3,960.15 (£1,183.20: £566.10: £257.55) Stalls: High GOING minus 0.54 sec per fur (F)

| | | | | SP | RR | SF |
|---|---|---|---|---|---|---|
| 3041[6] | **Trick (IRE)** (LMCumani) **3-8-7** OUrbina(2) (hld up: hdwy & nt clr run over 2f out: led ins fnl f: rdn out) | — | **1** | 4/1[3] | 72+ | 27 |
| *3418*[2] | **Polar Champ (75)** (SPCWoods) **3-8-12v[1]** DBiggs(7) (a.p: led over 2f out tl ins fnl f: r.o wl) | s.h | **2** | 4/1[3] | 77 | 32 |
| 3353[6] | **Roi du Nord (FR)** (SWCampion) **4-9-6** TIves(5) (chsd ldr: ev ch 2f out: one pce fnl f) | 3 | **3** | 33/1 | 72 | 35 |
| 2949[2] | **Royal Action (82)** (JEBanks) **3-8-5**(7) GFaulkner(3) (hld up: ev ch over 1f out: one pce) | ½ | **4** | 9/4[1] | 71 | 26 |
| 3472[5] | **Sulawesi (IRE)** (WJarvis) **3-8-7** RCochrane(4) (hld up & plld hrd: rdn & no hdwy fnl 2f) | 1¾ | **5** | 7/2[2] | 64 | 19 |
| | **Mutanassib (IRE)** (ACStewart) **3-8-12** RHills(8) (w'like: scope: s.s: no hdwy fnl 3f) | 1¾ | **6** | 6/1 | 66 | 21 |
| *79*[3] | **Royal Legend** (JPearce) **4-9-6** GBardwell(6) (lw: a bhd) | 2½ | **7** | 20/1 | 62 | 25 |
| 3425[4] | **Sinking Sun (68)** (BWHills) **3-8-7v** PaulEddery(1) (lw: led over 7f: sn wknd) | ¾ | **8** | 9/1 | 56 | 11 |
| | | | | (SP 125.0%) | **8 Rn** | |

**2m 7.0** (2.60) CSF £21.06 TOTE £5.70: £1.70 £2.30 £6.60 (£16.70) OWNER Lady Halifax (NEWMARKET) BRED Lord Halifax
WEIGHT FOR AGE 3yo-8lb

**2610 Trick (IRE)** stepped up on her two previous outings, and put the experience gained to good use. (4/1)
**3418 Polar Champ** had finished in front of the winner when she was making her debut, and went down with all guns blazing in the first-time visor. (4/1: 3/1-9/2)
**Roi du Nord (FR)**, bought after winning a selling hurdle at Nottingham, then went on to win another seller at Fakenham. (33/1)
**2949 Royal Action** could not sustain a dangerous-looking challenge. (9/4)
**3472 Sulawesi (IRE)** did not settle as well as her rider would have liked. (7/2: op 9/4)
**Mutanassib (IRE)** is a half-brother to Cabochon and Sudden Spin. (6/1: 7/2-7/1)

## 3705 MUNDESLEY MAIDEN H'CAP (0-65) (3-Y.O+) (Class F)

5-00 (5-01) **1m 3f 101y** £2,809.40 (£778.40: £372.20) Stalls: High GOING minus 0.54 sec per fur (F)

| | | | | SP | RR | SF |
|---|---|---|---|---|---|---|
| | **Clifton Game (37)** (MRChannon) **6-7-12**(5) PPMurphy(8) (lw: a.p: led over 2f out: clr over 1f out: r.o wl) | — | **1** | 16/1 | 49 | 31 |
| 2204[3] | **Soldier Mak (60)** (AHide) **3-9-3** GBardwell(4) (a.p: chsd wnr wl over 1f out: no imp) | 7 | **2** | 4/1[3] | 62 | 35 |
| 2882[13] | **Horesti (60)** (CEBrittain) **4-9-12** TIves(5) (lw: hld up: rdn 3f out: hdwy on ins 2f out: one pce) | 3½ | **3** | 14/1 | 57 | 39 |
| *2936*[12] | **Sahhar (60)** (RWArmstrong) **3-9-3** MFenton(7) (led after 1f: rdn over 3f out: hdd over 2f out: wknd over 1f out) | ½ | **4** | 14/1 | 57 | 30 |
| 3584[9] | **Parrot's Hill (IRE) (54)** (MHTompkins) **3-8-11** NDay(9) (rdn & no hdwy fnl 3f) | ¾ | **5** | 7/1 | 50 | 23 |
| 3283[2] | **Queen Bee (65)** (JLDunlop) **3-9-8** RCochrane(6) (nvr nr ldrs) | 1¾ | **6** | 100/30[1] | 58 | 31 |
| 3357[2] | **Sylvella (51)** (MAJarvis) **3-8-8** DRMcCabe(10) (a bhd) | 1½ | **7** | 5/1 | 42 | 15 |
| 3315[2] | **The Legions Pride (65)** (JWHills) **3-9-8** PaulEddery(1) (lw: led 1f: chsd ldr tl wknd over 2f out) | 3 | **8** | 10/1 | 52 | 25 |
| *1448*[8] | **Direct Dial (USA) (62)** (MissGayKelleway) **4-10-0** JFEgan(3) (swtg: bhd: rdn 7f out: t.o fnl 3f) | 18 | **9** | 14/1 | 24 | 6 |
| 3308[4] | **Windyedge (USA) (59)** (BWHills) **3-9-2** RHills(2) (hld up: rdn 5f out: t.o fnl 3f) | 1¼ | **10** | 7/2[2] | 19 | — |
| | | | | (SP 129.4%) | **10 Rn** | |

**2m 25.0** (2.00) CSF £81.42 CT £881.90 TOTE £26.30: £3.40 £1.40 £4.80 (£76.10) Trio £273.50; £238.91 to Newmarket 23/8/96 OWNER Mr G. Palmer (UPPER LAMBOURN) BRED Oping Enterprises
WEIGHT FOR AGE 3yo-9lb

**Clifton Game,** looking well prepared, took advantage of a 5lb lower mark than when last seen out in the spring of '95. This was a fine training performance. (16/1)
**2204 Soldier Mak** has run well on yielding ground and had been given a mid-summer break. (4/1)
**668 Horesti** is very much in the shadow of his close relative Petoski. (14/1)
**Sahhar** has yet to prove he gets this sort of trip. (14/1)
**3260 Parrot's Hill (IRE)** was already set to go down 3lb. (7/1)
**3283 Queen Bee** never threatened to take a hand. (100/30)
**3315 The Legions Pride** (10/1: 8/1-12/1)
**Direct Dial (USA)** (14/1: 10/1-16/1)

T/Plpt: £489.80 (25.24 Tckts). T/Qdpt: £36.00 (23.98 Tckts). KH

## 3687-YORK (L-H) (Good to firm)
## Thursday August 22nd
WEATHER: sunny spells WIND: fresh bhd

### 3706 MOORESTYLE CONVIVIAL MAIDEN STKS (2-Y.O) (Class D)
2-05 (2-05) **6f** £10,965.00 (£3,270.00: £1,560.00: £705.00) Stalls: Low GOING minus 0.52 sec per fur (F)

| | Horse | Dist | Pos | SP | RR | SF |
|---|---|---|---|---|---|---|
| | **Indiscreet (CAN)** (DRLoder) **2-9-0** LDettori(7) (gd srt: trckd ldrs: led wl over 1f out: r.o strly) | — | 1 | 4/1$^{3}$ | 101++ | 74 |
| | **Swiss Law** (JGFitzGerald) **2-9-0** KFallon(3) (w'like: scope: chsd ldrs: chal over 2f out: nt qckn appr fnl f) | 3 | 2 | 16/1 | 93 | 66 |
| | **Wasp Ranger (USA)** (PFICole) **2-9-0** TQuinn(4) (tall: cl up: led over 2f out tl wl over 1f out: no ex) | nk | 3 | 7/2$^{2}$ | 92+ | 65 |
| | **Elnadim (USA)** (JLDunlop) **2-9-0** WCarson(2) (w'like: leggy: dwlt: sn rcvrd: chal over 2f out: sn rdn & nt qckn) | 3 | 4 | 11/8$^{1}$ | 84+ | 57 |
| | **Musalsal (IRE)** (BWHills) **2-9-0** MHills(1) (leggy: scope: chsd ldrs tl wknd qckly over 2f out) | 3 | 5 | 9/1 | 76 | 49 |
| 2890$^{3}$ | **Millroy (USA) (87)** (PAKelleway) **2-9-0b$^{1}$** JCarroll(5) (led tl hdd & wknd over 2f out) | s.h | 6 | 16/1 | 76 | 49 |
| 3438$^{2}$ | **Our Way** (CEBrittain) **2-8-9** BDoyle(8) (outpcd after 2f: n.d after) | 6 | 7 | 16/1 | 55 | 28 |
| | **Double Eight (IRE)** (BWHills) **2-8-9** KDarley(6) (neat: scope: bit bkwd: outpcd after 2f: bhd after) | 2 | 8 | 16/1 | 50 | 23 |

(SP 117.9%) **8 Rn**

**1m 9.59** (0.25 under 2y best) (-1.41) CSF £54.38 TOTE £3.90: £1.50 £1.70 £1.60 (£31.00) OWNER Mrs Virginia Kraft Payson (NEWMARKET) BRED Virginia Kraft Payson
**Indiscreet (CAN)**, a most attractive sort, won this in some style and looks the type to improve over further. (4/1: op 5/2)
**Swiss Law**, looking likely to be all the better for this, ran a cracking race and should go on from here. (16/1)
**Wasp Ranger (USA)** is all legs at present and needs time to strengthen, but he showed plenty and ought to improve as a result. (7/2)
**Elnadim (USA)**, a fair sort who was coltish in the paddock, showed a terrific action going to post. Green in the early stages, he still had his chances, only to run out of petrol approaching the final furlong. Better should follow. (11/8)
**Musalsal (IRE)** was one of the best lookers in a decent field but proved a shade disappointing, stopping quickly approaching the final two furlongs. Something may have gone wrong. (9/1: 6/1-10/1)
**2890 Millroy (USA)**, very edgy in the first-time blinkers, soon folded when an effort was required. (16/1)

### 3707 STAKIS CASINOS LOWTHER STKS (Gp 2) (2-Y.O F) (Class A)
2-35 (2-37) **6f** £46,050.50 (£17,079.50: £8,227.25: £3,398.75: £1,386.88: £582.12) Stalls: Low GOING minus 0.52 sec per fur (F)

| | Horse | Dist | Pos | SP | RR | SF |
|---|---|---|---|---|---|---|
| 3508* | **Bianca Nera** (DRLoder) **2-8-11** KDarley(6) (lw: a cl up: led ½-wy: r.o wl) | — | 1 | 6/1 | 98 | 58 |
| 2070$^{7}$ | **Arethusa (95)** (RHannon) **2-8-11** RHughes(9) (trckd ldrs: disp ld 2f out: nt qckn wl ins fnl f) | nk | 2 | 16/1 | 97 | 57 |
| 3068* | **Seebe (USA)** (IABalding) **2-9-0** MHills(1) (lw: trckd ldrs: chal 2f out: nt qckn towards fin) | ½ | 3 | 11/4$^{1}$ | 99 | 59 |
| 3213* | **Carmine Lake (IRE)** (PWChapple-Hyam) **2-9-0** JReid(10) (hld up: swtchd & effrt over 1f out: edgd lft & r.o one pce) | ¾ | 4 | 7/2$^{2}$ | 97 | 57 |
| 2051$^{3}$ | **Moonshine Girl (USA)** (MRStoute) **2-8-11** LDettori(3) (trckd ldrs: hdwy to chal 2f out: wknd ins fnl f) | 1½ | 5 | 7/2$^{2}$ | 90 | 50 |
| 3444$^{6}$ | **Eye Shadow (93)** (BJMeehan) **2-8-11** MTebbutt(7) (outpcd & bhd tl sme late hdwy) | 2½ | 6 | 33/1 | 83? | 43 |
| 823* | **Daylight Dreams** (CACyzer) **2-8-11** KFallon(2) (lw: cl up 4f: wknd) | 3½ | 7 | 33/1 | 74 | 34 |
| 3433* | **Well Warned** (BWHills) **2-8-11** PatEddery(5) (swtg: led to ½-wy: sn btn) | hd | 8 | 11/2$^{3}$ | 74 | 34 |
| 2703* | **Halowing (USA) (92)** (PAKelleway) **2-8-11** JWeaver(8) (lw: cl up tl wknd over 2f out) | 3 | 9 | 33/1 | 66 | 26 |

(SP 115.5%) **9 Rn**

**1m 10.54** (-0.46) CSF £80.23 TOTE £8.30: £1.80 £4.70 £1.20 (£93.20) Trio £77.20 OWNER Mr S. Frisby (NEWMARKET) BRED Miss S. McCreery and Stowell Hill Ltd
**3508* Bianca Nera** has a superb attitude and proved to be a real battler, winning in convincing style. (6/1)
**1143 Arethusa**, trying a longer trip, came back to form but, despite trying really hard, found the winner too tough a nut to crack. (16/1)
**3068* Seebe (USA)** ran well and held every chance throughout. It is quite probable that a low draw made all the difference. (11/4)
**3213* Carmine Lake (IRE)**, edgy before the start, beat herself by failing to co-operate with her rider. (7/2)
**2051 Moonshine Girl (USA)** travelled well, but ran out of fuel when it mattered. Being off the track for over two months may have made the difference. (7/2)
**3444 Eye Shadow** seemed not to stay seven last time, but ran the opposite way over this shorter trip, staying on after getting outpaced. (33/1)
**3433* Well Warned**, who sweated up and looked to have run her race in the paddock, dropped out tamely from halfway. (11/2)

### 3708 NUNTHORPE STKS (Gp 1) (Class A)
3-10 (3-11) **5f** £72,464.50 (£26,555.50: £12,527.75: £4,876.25: £1,688.13: £412.87) Stalls: Low GOING minus 0.52 sec per fur (F)

| | Horse | Dist | Pos | SP | RR | SF |
|---|---|---|---|---|---|---|
| 2622$^{6}$ | **Pivotal (120)** (SirMarkPrescott) **3-9-7** GDuffield(5) (lw: sn pushed along: hdwy ½-wy: r.o wl u.p to ld last stride) | — | 1 | 100/30$^{3}$ | 127 | 80 |
| 3126$^{6}$ | **Eveningperformance (110)** (HCandy) **5-9-6** CRutter(1) (lw: led: rdn over 1f out: r.o: jst ct) | s.h | 2 | 16/1 | 124 | 79 |
| 3126$^{2}$ | **Hever Golf Rose (114)** (TJNaughton) **5-9-6** JWeaver(3) (lw: stmbld s: a chsng ldrs: kpt on wl fnl f) | 1¼ | 3 | 11/4$^{2}$ | 120 | 75 |
| 2622$^{7}$ | **Mind Games (118)** (JBerry) **4-9-9** JCarroll(7) (lw: sn w ldr: rdn 2f out: kpt on same pce) | ¾ | 4 | 7/4$^{1}$ | 120 | 75 |
| 3562a$^{5}$ | **Catch The Blues (IRE)** (APO'Brien,Ireland) **4-9-6v** CRoche(6) (sn outpcd & bhd: hdwy over 1f out: r.o) | ½ | 5 | 20/1 | 116 | 71 |
| 3393a$^{2}$ | **Struggler (111)** (DRLoder) **4-9-9** LDettori(2) (lw: a chsng ldrs: n.m.r ½-wy: r.o one pce) | 1½ | 6 | 10/1 | 114 | 69 |
| 3126$^{4}$ | **Cool Jazz (113)** (CEBrittain) **5-9-9** TQuinn(8) (lw: sn outpcd & nvr trbld ldrs) | 1½ | 7 | 20/1 | 109 | 64 |

1943a* **Windmachine (SWE)** (BjoernOlsen,Norway) **5-9-6** FDiaz(4) (spd to ½-wy: wknd qckly)....4 **8** 33/1 93 48
(SP 113.5%) **8 Rn**

**56.53 secs** (-1.17) CSF £44.60 TOTE £4.00: £1.60 £3.10 £1.10 (£25.70) OWNER Cheveley Park Stud (NEWMARKET) BRED Cheveley Park Stud Ltd

WEIGHT FOR AGE 3yo-2lb

**2622 Pivotal** came back to his best here, but needed all his considerable courage to make it. Both he and his pilot really have the heart for the game. He still gives the impression that six will suit him even better. (100/30: 9/4-7/2)
**3126 Eveningperformance** could not lead at Goodwood last time but was at her very best on this occasion and really blazed a trail, only to be touched off right on the stick. From her draw, this was a tremendous performance, and it deserved better. (16/1)
**3126 Hever Golf Rose** stumbled leaving the stalls, but it made no difference. Once this game mare can get her toe in, she will soon turn the tables. (11/4)
**2622 Mind Games** took the leader on, but was off the bit a long way out, which is unusual for him. Although keeping on, he was never doing quite enough. (7/4)
**2072 Catch The Blues (IRE)** found things happening far too quickly for her liking and was soon well behind. Although finishing to some purpose, six furlongs is needed in this company. (20/1)
**3393a Struggler** was always flat out to chase the leaders, and this poor-actioned colt was a bit short of room at halfway, and never good enough thereafter. (10/1)
**3126 Cool Jazz** was never going the pace at any stage. (20/1)
**Windmachine (SWE)** was back-pedalling from halfway. (33/1)

## 3709 BRADFORD & BINGLEY RATED STKS H'CAP (0-105) (3-Y.O+) (Class B)

3-45 (3-46) **7f 202y** £25,309.20 (£9,382.80: £4,516.40: £1,862.00: £756.00: £313.60) Stalls: Low GOING minus 0.52 sec per fur (F)

| | | | | SP | RR | SF |
|---|---|---|---|---|---|---|
| 3072[12] | **Concer Un (90)** (SCWilliams) **4-8-10** KDarley(8) (b.nr fore: a in tch: pushed along 3f out: hdwy & swtchd over 1f out: r.o wl to ld cl home) | — | **1** | 16/1 | 103 | 85 |
| 2888[3] | **North Song (92)** (JHMGosden) **3-8-6** LDettori(2) (led: rdn over 2f out: hdd & nt qckn towards fin) | 1 | **2** | 11/2[1] | 103 | 79 |
| 2544[13] | **Moments of Fortune (USA) (93)** (BHanbury) **4-8-13** WRyan(3) (lw: a cl up: disp ld 3f out: nt qckn wl ins fnl f) | s.h | **3** | 20/1 | 104 | 86 |
| 3612[3] | **Tregaron (USA) (89)** (RAkehurst) **5-8-9** SSanders(17) (hdwy ½-wy: disp ld over 2f out: nt qckn wl ins fnl f) | ½ | **4** | 8/1[3] | 99 | 81 |
| 2477a[5] | **Nagnagnag (IRE) (94)** (SDow) **4-9-0** RHughes(16) (hld up & bhd: effrt 3f out: r.o wl appr fnl f: nrst fin) | ¾ | **5** | 20/1 | 102 | 84 |
| 2053[5] | **Star Manager (USA) (87)** (PFICole) **6-8-7** TQuinn(10) (bhd: hdwy 4f out: sn prom: drvn along 3f out: r.o one pce) | 2½ | **6** | 12/1 | 90 | 72 |
| 3072[5] | **Beauchamp Jazz (93)** (JLDunlop) **4-8-13** JReid(1) (lw: chsd ldrs: rdn 3f out: r.o one pce) | s.h | **7** | 11/1 | 96 | 78 |
| 3509[6] | **Tertium (IRE) (89)** (MartynWane) **4-8-9** JCarroll(15) (lw: hld up: effrt over 2f out: rdn & no imp) | 1¼ | **8** | 20/1 | 90 | 72 |
| 3083[7] | **Hi Nod (101)** (MJCamacho) **6-9-7** LCharnock(13) (lw: mid div: hdwy to chse ldrs over 2f out: btn over 1f out) | 2 | **9** | 16/1 | 98 | 80 |
| 1617* | **Gold Spats (USA) (88)** (MRStoute) **3-7-13**(3) FLynch(19) (bhd: effrt over 3f out: n.d) | 2½ | **10** | 6/1[2] | 80 | 56 |
| 2053[30] | **Gymcrak Premiere (88)** (GHolmes) **8-8-8** KFallon(7) (b.hind: bhd: rdn over 4f out: no imp) | ½ | **11** | 25/1 | 79 | 61 |
| | **Hunters of Brora (IRE) (91)** (JDBethell) **6-8-11** JWeaver(5) (lw: s.i.s: nvr rchd ldrs) | 1¼ | **12** | 25/1 | 79 | 61 |
| 3158[13] | **Autumn Affair (90)** (CEBrittain) **4-8-10** BDoyle(6) (lw: chsd ldrs tl wknd fnl 3f) | hd | **13** | 33/1 | 78 | 60 |
| 3211[7] | **Mushahid (USA) (102)** (JLDunlop) **3-9-2** MHills(18) (lw: gd hdwy 3f out: sn chsng ldrs: wknd wl over 1f out) | nk | **14** | 20/1 | 89 | 65 |
| 3158[10] | **Desert Green (FR) (96)** (RHannon) **7-9-2** DaneO'Neill(14) (swtg: bhd: effrt ½-wy: n.d) | 2 | **15** | 16/1 | 79 | 61 |
| 3430[2] | **Intidab (USA) (93)** (JHMGosden) **3-8-7** WCarson(11) (in tch: drvn along over 3f out: sn btn) | 1 | **16** | 11/2[1] | 74 | 50 |
| 3158[18] | **New Century (USA) (93)** (DNicholls) **4-8-13** PatEddery(9) (in tch: hdwy over 3f out: sn rdn & btn) | 1¾ | **17** | 16/1 | 71 | 53 |
| 970[3] | **Axford (USA) (90)** (PWChapple-Hyam) **3-8-4** JQuinn(12) (chsd ldrs 5f: wknd) | 8 | **18** | 12/1 | 52 | 28 |

(SP 133.1%) **18 Rn**

**1m 34.81** (0.31 under best) (-1.99) CSF £100.80 CT £1,679.07 TOTE £22.60: £4.20 £1.60 £7.00 £2.20 (£52.10) Trio £899.50 OWNER Miss L. J. Ward (NEWMARKET) BRED Lloyd Bros

LONG HANDICAP Star Manager (USA) 8-6

WEIGHT FOR AGE 3yo-6lb

OFFICIAL EXPLANATION **Concer Un: accounting for the apparent improvement in the gelding's form, his jockey stated that on his previous run he had been drawn wide, could not be covered up and raced keenly in the early stages before fading badly after halfway. The trainer remarked that the horse would appear suited by a round course, rather than a straight mile and here he was able to be covered up and had the race run to his liking.**

**2544* Concer Un**, after a disappointing effort last time, bounced back to form here, but it was never easy, and his jockey really earned his money. (16/1)
**2888 North Song**, a free-runner who likes to be up with the pace, proved determined under pressure and just failed to last out (11/2)
**1131 Moments of Fortune (USA)** has a poor action, but certainly stays well and had every chance throughout. On easier ground, he can do better. (20/1)
**3612 Tregaron (USA)** had plenty of running to do from his draw but he did get there, only to tie up in the closing stages. This was a really good effort. (8/1)
**2477a Nagnagnag (IRE)**, poorly drawn, tried to drop in behind, but always then had too much on her plate, despite finishing fast. She looks one to keep on the right side. (20/1)
**2053 Star Manager (USA)** has won first time out for the last two seasons so could be expected to go well here after two months off. He is high enough in the handicap at present and would also prefer easier ground. (12/1)
**3072 Beauchamp Jazz** is gradually slipping down the handicap and had his chances, but was short of toe in the last couple of furlongs. (11/1)
**3509 Tertium (IRE)** showed signs of coming back to form and travelled well, but failed to pick up when asked a question. (20/1)
**1322 Gymcrak Premiere** should come on for this fitness-wise. (25/1)
**3430 Intidab (USA)** (11/2: op 7/2)

## 3710 LADBROKE KNAVESMIRE H'CAP (0-95) (3-Y.O+) (Class C)

4-15 (4-20) **1m 3f 195y** £17,350.00 (£5,200.00: £2,500.00: £1,150.00) Stalls: Low GOING minus 0.37 sec per fur (F)

| | | | | SP | RR | SF |
|---|---|---|---|---|---|---|
| 3134* | **Celestial Choir (86)** (JLEyre) **6-9-3**(3) OPears(2) (lw: hld up: hdwy ent st: led over 1f out: hrd rdn & r.o) | — | **1** | 14/1 | 99 | 68 |
| 3071[3] | **Sheer Danzig (IRE) (93)** (RWArmstrong) **4-9-13** PRobinson(6) (lw: trckd ldrs: hdwy to chal 3f out: kpt on u.p) | 1¼ | **2** | 10/1[3] | 104 | 73 |
| 1712[5] | **General Macarthur (89)** (JLDunlop) **3-8-13** TQuinn(8) (bhd: rdn 3f out: styd on strly towards fin) | s.h | **3** | 11/1 | 100 | 59 |
| 2591* | **Dacha (IRE) (89)** (HRACecil) **4-9-9** PatEddery(11) (lw: chsd ldrs: led 3f out tl over 1f out: no ex) | ½ | **4** | 11/2[1] | 100 | 69 |
| 3125[3] | **Daunt (92)** (JHMGosden) **4-9-12** LDettori(7) (led 10f out to 3f out: rdn & btn appr fnl f) | 1¼ | **5** | 10/1[3] | 101 | 70 |

| Form | Horse (details) | Dist | Pos | SP | RR | SF |
|---|---|---|---|---|---|---|
| 1637[5] | **Lord Hastie (USA) (66)** (CWThornton) **8-8-0** JQuinn(14) (lw: hld up: hdwy 4f out: ev ch 3f out: one pce fnl 2f) | 1½ | **6** | 25/1 | 73 | 42 |
| 2055[15] | **Lombardic (USA) (90)** (MrsJCecil) **5-9-10** JReid(9) (lw: bhd: rdn 4f out: styd on: nvr rchd ldrs) | 1¼ | **7** | 20/1 | 95 | 64 |
| 3233* | **At Liberty (IRE) (84)** (RHannon) **4-9-4** RHughes(18) (bhd: hdwy 4f out: sn prom: one pce fnl 2f) | ½ | **8** | 16/1 | 89 | 58 |
| 3145[4] | **Spillo (88)** (LMCumani) **3-8-12** JWeaver(16) (mid div: effrt 4f out: no imp) | s.h | **9** | 9/1[2] | 93 | 52 |
| 3205[5] | **Alaflak (IRE) (80)** (MajorWRHern) **5-9-0** WCarson(10) (hdwy ent st: sn chsng ldrs & rdn: eased whn btn over 1f out) | 4 | **10** | 14/1 | 79 | 48 |
| 3039[9] | **Kala Sunrise (84)** (CSmith) **3-8-8** KDarley(15) (hld up: hdwy 4f out: sn rdn & no imp) | 3 | **11** | 33/1 | 79 | 38 |
| 3617[5] | **Village King (IRE) (78)** (RHannon) **3-8-2**ow1 DaneO'Neill(20) (bhd tl sme late hdwy) | nk | **12** | 25/1 | 73 | 31 |
| 3346* | **Askern (76)** (DHaydnJones) **5-8-10** AMackay(1) (chsd ldrs tl wknd fnl 2 ½f) | hd | **13** | 16/1 | 71 | 40 |
| 3487[5] | **Floating Line (70)** (EJAlston) **8-8-4**ow2 JCarroll(5) (led 2f: w ldrs tl wknd 3f out) | ¾ | **14** | 25/1 | 64 | 31 |
| 3333* | **Mattimeo (IRE) (76)** (APJarvis) **3-7-7**(7)ow4 CCarver(21) (racd wd: prom: wkng whn swvd & hit rails 3f out) | nk | **15** | 16/1 | 69 | 24 |
| 3500[5] | **Ayunli (66)** (SCWilliams) **5-7-11**(3) MHenry(4) (lw: nvr trbld ldrs) | 1½ | **16** | 10/1[3] | 57 | 26 |
| 3276[3] | **Tessajoe (70)** (MJCamacho) **4-8-4** LCharnock(12) (mid div: effrt 4f out: wknd fnl 3f) | 2½ | **17** | 16/1 | 58 | 27 |
| 2062[2] | **Rusk (75)** (JPearce) **3-7-13** JLowe(13) (chsd ldrs tl wknd 3f out) | 1½ | **18** | 20/1 | 61 | 20 |
| 3145[5] | **Skillington (USA) (91)** (IABalding) **3-9-1** MHills(17) (lw: chsd ldrs: effrt 4f out: wknd 3f out) | 2 | **19** | 12/1 | 74 | 33 |
| 1476[13] | **Quango (92)** (JGFitzGerald) **4-9-12** KFallon(22) (bit bkwd: a bhd) | 4 | **20** | 25/1 | 70 | 39 |
| 2534[5] | **Kaitak (IRE) (72)** (JMCarr) **5-8-6** GDuffield(3) (mid div: hdwy appr st: rdn & wknd over 3f out) | ½ | **21** | 33/1 | 49 | 18 |
| 2690[5] | **Three Hills (88)** (BWHills) **3-8-12** WRSwinburn(19) (racd wd: prom tl wknd 4f out) | ½ | **22** | 12/1 | 64 | 23 |

(SP 144.0%) **22 Rn**

**2m 28.74** (0.94) CSF £151.34 CT £1,510.13 TOTE £15.50: £3.10 £3.10 £2.80 £2.10 (£61.20) Trio £297.20 OWNER Mrs Carole Sykes (HAMBLETON) BRED J. L. Eyre

WEIGHT FOR AGE 3yo-10lb

**3134* Celestial Choir** is as game as they come. Given a most confident ride, she won really well to gain her first victory over this trip on turf. (14/1)

**3071 Sheer Danzig (IRE)**, on ground plenty fast enough and given a stiffish task by the Handicapper, ran a super race and kept staying on all the way to the line. (10/1)

**1712 General Macarthur** looks a bit of a character, but he has plenty of ability and is improving. By the way he finished, he should stay further. (11/1: 8/1-12/1)

**2591* Dacha (IRE)** had plenty on in his first handicap, but ran a useful race, only to find it too much in the closing stages. (11/2)

**3125 Daunt**, trying his longest trip to date, helped force the pace, but had shot his bolt approaching the final furlong. (10/1)

**1421 Lord Hastie (USA)**, after almost three months off, returned here in great form and is likely to be all the better for it. (25/1)

**564* Lombardic (USA)** usually likes to be out in front, but tried opposite tactics here after some disappointing efforts, and was way behind until running on at the death. (20/1)

**3233* At Liberty (IRE)** has done his winning over shorter trips and is a funny customer. He called it a day on this occasion with two furlongs left. (16/1)

## 3711 GALTRES STKS (Listed) (3-Y.O+ F & M) (Class A)

4-45 (4-50) **1m 3f 195y** £15,140.00 (£4,520.00: £2,160.00: £980.00) Stalls: Low GOING minus 0.52 sec per fur (F)

| Form | Horse (details) | Dist | Pos | SP | RR | SF |
|---|---|---|---|---|---|---|
| 2786* | **Eva Luna (USA)** (HRACecil) **4-9-4** PatEddery(7) (tall: leggy: lw: s.i.s: sn rcvrd & cl up: led 4f out tl wl over 1f out: r.o gamely to ld wl ins fnl f) | — | **1** | 100/30[2] | 110 | 77 |
| 3145[2] | **Time Allowed (91)** (MRStoute) **3-8-8** JReid(3) (b: a.p: led wl over 1f out: hdd & nt qckn towards fin) | hd | **2** | 9/1 | 110 | 67 |
| 3531a[3] | **Priolina (IRE)** (JCHayden,Ireland) **3-8-8b** JFortune(6) (lt-f: unf: hdwy ent st: sn chsng ldrs & rdn: ev ch appr fnl f: no ex) | 1¾ | **3** | 14/1 | 108 | 65 |
| 2991[3] | **Bathilde (IRE) (98)** (MRStoute) **3-8-8** KFallon(4) (trckd ldrs: ev ch 3f out: one pce appr fnl f) | 3½ | **4** | 10/1 | 103 | 60 |
| 3231[3] | **Annaba (IRE) (106)** (JHMGosden) **3-8-8** LDettori(5) (lw: led tl hdd 4f out: ev ch tl btn over 1f out) | 1¼ | **5** | 3/1[1] | 101 | 58 |
| 3409[4] | **Poppy Carew (IRE) (107)** (PWHarris) **4-9-10** WRSwinburn(2) (bhd: hdwy over 4f out: sn rdn & no imp) | 3 | **6** | 9/1 | 103 | 70 |
| 2886[2] | **Balalaika (105)** (LMCumani) **3-8-8** MHills(8) (chsd ldrs: pushed along over 4f out: sn wknd) | 6 | **7** | 4/1[3] | 89 | 46 |
| 2533[3] | **Ninotchka (USA) (101)** (JLDunlop) **3-8-8** KDarley(10) (rr div: pushed along 5f out: btn over 3f out) | 7 | **8** | 8/1 | 80 | 37 |
| 3315* | **Pike Creek (USA)** (IABalding) **3-8-8** TQuinn(1) (swtg: chsd ldrs: rdn over 4f out: sn wknd) | 10 | **9** | 14/1 | 66 | 23 |
| *3608*[3] | **Miss Haversham (60)** (CACyzer) **4-9-4b** PBloomfield(9) (a bhd: t.o fnl 4f) | 11 | **10** | 100/1 | 51 | 18 |

(SP 122.6%) **10 Rn**

**2m 27.14** (-0.66) CSF £32.26 TOTE £3.70: £1.80 £2.30 £2.80 (£20.30) Trio £224.60 OWNER Mr K. Abdulla (NEWMARKET) BRED Juddmonte Farms

WEIGHT FOR AGE 3yo-10lb

STEWARDS' ENQUIRY Eddery susp. 13 & 16/9/96 (excessive use of whip).

**2786* Eva Luna (USA)** is a big, awkward-looking filly, but she is certainly game. After making her usual tardy start, she needed all her courage in the closing stages. She should stay further. (100/30)

**3145 Time Allowed** is still learning and, after striking the front over a furlong out, just found the winner too tough. (9/1)

**3531a Priolina (IRE)** worked hard to have her chance approaching the final furlong, only then finding it beyond her. This was another sound effort in this company. (14/1)

**2991 Bathilde (IRE)** has proved a shade disappointing since winning here in May and, over a trip that should suit, failed to pick up approaching the final furlong. (10/1)

**3231 Annaba (IRE)**, stepping up in trip, may have been flattered last time and ran out of steam approaching the final furlong. (3/1)

**3409 Poppy Carew (IRE)** was always struggling to improve and never really fired. (9/1)

**2886 Balalaika** was most disappointing. Struggling on the home turn, she was soon beaten. (4/1: 3/1-9/2)

## 3712 CITY OF YORK STKS (Listed) (3-Y.O+) (Class A)

5-15 (5-16) **6f 214y** £13,392.00 (£3,996.00: £1,908.00: £864.00) Stalls: High GOING minus 0.37 sec per fur (F)

| Form | Horse (details) | Dist | Pos | SP | RR | SF |
|---|---|---|---|---|---|---|
| 3153* | **Ruznama (USA) (100)** (BWHills) **3-8-4** WCarson(7) (cl up: led ½-wy: hld on wl) | — | **1** | 4/1[2] | 106 | 73 |
| 3144[7] | **Ali-Royal (IRE) (114)** (HRACecil) **3-9-0** WRyan(1) (lw: hld up: effrt 3f out: r.o wl towards fin) | 1 | **2** | 100/30[1] | 114 | 81 |
| 3127[2] | **Forest Cat (IRE) (102)** (MrsJCecil) **4-8-9** KFallon(4) (lw: trckd ldrs: ev ch 3f out: hrd rdn & nt qckn appr fnl f) | hd | **3** | 11/2 | 104 | 76 |
| 2609[5] | **Myself (110)** (PWChapple-Hyam) **4-8-9** JReid(5) (led to ½-wy: hung lft: ev ch tl btn appr fnl f) | ½ | **4** | 9/2[3] | 102 | 74 |
| 3524[3] | **Sergeyev (IRE) (110)** (RHannon) **4-9-8** RHughes(3) (stdd s: plld hrd: effrt 3f out: styd on: nvr able to chal) | nk | **5** | 7/1 | 115 | 87 |
| 3445* | **Polar Prince (IRE) (103)** (MAJarvis) **3-8-9** PRobinson(6) (lw: in tch: effrt ½-wy: kpt on one pce) | ½ | **6** | 9/2[3] | 106 | 73 |
| 3158[12] | **How Long (96)** (LMCumani) **3-8-9** KDarley(8) (chsd ldrs: effrt over 3f out: btn 2f out) | ¾ | **7** | 16/1 | 104 | 71 |

3394a* **Branston Abby (IRE) (108)** (MJohnston) **7-9-0** JWeaver(2) (hld up & bhd: effrt ½-wy: no imp) ..........................1 **8** 13/2 102 74
(SP 126.5%) **8 Rn**

**1m 21.77** (0.05 under best) (-1.23) CSF £18.76 TOTE £6.00: £1.90 £1.90 £1.60 (£11.40) OWNER Mr Hamdan Al Maktoum (LAMBOURN) BRED Shadwell Estate Co., Ltd. and Shadwell Farm Inc.
WEIGHT FOR AGE 3yo-5lb

**3153* Ruznama (USA)**, dropping back in trip again, stamped her authority on the race from halfway and, getting first run, was always going to last out. (4/1)
**3144 Ali-Royal (IRE)** took time to get into his stride, but he did finish well and is one to be suited by much easier ground. (100/30)
**3127 Forest Cat (IRE)** was in an ideal position throughout, but was never good enough to take advantage of it, despite a determined effort. (11/2)
**2609 Myself** tried to come wide into the straight, but spoiled her chances by hanging left, and her rider could never get the best out of her. (9/2)
**3524 Sergeyev (IRE)**, dropped out at the start as usual, took a strong hold and was then never doing enough in the final sprint, despite keeping on. He has the ability if he can get his act together. (7/1)
**3445* Polar Prince (IRE)** got tapped for toe when the pace was really on just after halfway but, to his credit, he was staying on at the end, although the effort was always too late. (9/2)
**3394a* Branston Abby (IRE)** has lost her sparkle for now. (13/2)

T/Jkpt: Not won; £79,070.85 to Newmarket 23/8/96. T/Plpt: £221.60 (264.05 Tckts). T/Qdpt: £44.60 (83.91 Tckts). AA

## 3713a-3727a (Irish Racing) - See Computer Raceform

## 3192a-CURRAGH (Newbridge, Ireland) (R-H) (Good to firm)
### Saturday August 17th

### 3728a ROYAL WHIP STKS (Gp 3) (3-Y.O+)
3-00 (3-01) **1m 2f** £16,250.00 (£4,750.00: £2,250.00: £750.00)

| | | | | SP | RR | SF |
|---|---|---|---|---|---|---|
| 2038[8] | **Pilsudski (IRE)** (MRStoute) **4-9-4** WRSwinburn (chsd ldrs: hdwy appr st: led 2f out: clr 1f out: kpt on) | — | 1 | 5/2[2] | 119 | 72 |
| 3531a[2] | **I'm Supposin (IRE)** (KPrendergast,Ireland) **4-9-1** WJSupple (hld up in tch: wnt 3rd wl over 1f out: r.o u.p ins fnl f) | 1½ | 2 | 6/1 | 114 | 67 |
| 3196a[2] | **Predappio** (JOxx,Ireland) **3-8-7b[1]** MJKinane (chsd ldr: disp ld over 2f out: sn hdd & rdn: no imp) | hd | 3 | 2/1[1] | 113 | 58 |
| 1520* | **Murajja (USA)** (PTWalwyn) **4-9-1** JPMurtagh (led to 2f out: sn wknd) | 5 | 4 | 4/1[3] | 105 | 58 |
| 3531a[4] | **Fill the Bill (IRE)** (APO'Brien,Ireland) **4-9-1** CRoche (hld up in tch: rdn & btn wl over 2f out) | 5 | 5 | 6/1 | 97 | 50 |
| | | | | (SP 110.5%) | | **5 Rn** |

**2m 3.0** (-1.00) OWNER Lord Weinstock/ExorsLate Simon (NEWMARKET) BRED Ballymacoll Stud Co

**2038 Pilsudski (IRE)**, who found the ground a little too fast at Ascot last time, got back to winning ways here. Always going well, he was clear a furlong out, but began to idle in front. However, he did not look like being caught and kept on well. His jockey believes he will have no problem going back up to a mile and a half. (5/2)
**3531a I'm Supposin (IRE)**, up with the pace early on, found himself a little outpaced turning into the straight. However, he stayed on well with a furlong left to travel to get up for second place close home. (6/1)
**3196a Predappio**, blinkered for the first time, led briefly early in the straight. When the winner kicked for home, he could find little under pressure and was caught for second prize close home. (2/1)
**1520* Murajja (USA)**, running for the first time since May, set a moderate pace and, when challenged early in the straight, looked to be struggling. The ground may have been a little fast for him. (4/1)

### 3731a RIDGEWOOD PEARL DESMOND STKS (Gp 3) (3-Y.O+)
4-30 (4-30) **1m** £19,500.00 (£5,700.00: £2,700.00: £900.00)

| | | | | SP | RR | SF |
|---|---|---|---|---|---|---|
| 3196a* | **Idris (IRE)** (JSBolger,Ireland) **6-9-7** KJManning (hld up: swtchd lft & effrt over 1f out: sn led: qcknd clr) | — | 1 | 9/4[1] | 122 | 39 |
| 2839a[5] | **Raiyoun (IRE)** (JOxx,Ireland) **3-8-9**ow1 JPMurtagh (cl up: ev ch 2f out: no ex 1f out: kpt on ins fnl f) | 4 | 2 | 5/1[3] | 108 | 18 |
| | **Peace Prize (IRE)** (DKWeld,Ireland) **3-8-8** MJKinane (led: rdn over 2f out: hdd 1f out: nt qckn) | hd | 3 | 7/1 | 107 | 18 |
| 2053[31] | **Blomberg (IRE)** (JRFanshawe) **4-9-4** WRSwinburn (sn trckng ldr: ev ch fr 2f out: kpt on) | s.h | 4 | 11/2 | 111 | 28 |
| 2465a[3] | **Theano (IRE)** (APO'Brien,Ireland) **3-8-5** JAHeffernan (in tch: rdn over 2f out: wknd qckly over 1f out) | 8 | 5 | 5/2[2] | 88 | — |
| 1574a[10] | **Flame of Athens (IRE)** (MJGrassick,Ireland) **3-8-12** WJSupple (hld up in rr: rdn & sme hdwy 2f out: sn wknd) | 2½ | 6 | 12/1 | 90 | 1 |
| | | | | (SP 111.6%) | | **6 Rn** |

**1m 38.4** (3.40) OWNER Michael Keogh (COOLCULLEN)

**3196a* Idris (IRE)** is a most remarkable and consistent individual, and put up an impressive display to take his fourth Group Three success of the year. Held up towards the rear, he was in last place with two furlongs left to travel, but seemed comfortable. Getting down to work late on, he ran on very well to take the lead and won well. He has improved with racing and it is now hopeful that he will go to Longchamp for the Arc weekend, where possibilities include the Group 2 Prix Dollar and the Group 2 Prix du Rond-Point. (9/4)
**Raiyoun (IRE)** had every chance a furlong from home and kept on well to win the battle for second prize. (5/1)
**Peace Prize (IRE)** set a strong pace. Asked to keep up his effort, he could give no more when headed a furlong out. (7/1)
**1768* Blomberg (IRE)** tracked the leader for most of the way and his effort seemed slightly one-paced. This was his first appearance since the Royal Hunt Cup, and he is sure to come on for the run. (11/2)
NR

## 3732a-3743a (Irish Racing) - See Computer Raceform

## 3573a-DEAUVILLE (France) (R-H) (Good)
### Thursday August 15th

### 3744a HANDICAP DE NORMANDIE (3-Y.O+)
2-25 (2-28) **1m** £22,398.00

| | | | | SP | RR | SF |
|---|---|---|---|---|---|---|
| | **Attune (FR)** (HVandePoele,France) **6-9-2** SGuillot | — | 1 | | 100 | 74 |

325a* **Hunter Field (FR)** (France) **4-8-12** TJarnet ....2 **2** 92 66
**Speransella (FR)** (France) **6-9-0** AJunk ....s.h **3** 94 68
3072[3] **Wakeel (USA)** (SDow) **4-9-4** MJKinane (btn approx 6½l) .... **10** — —
**18 Rn**

**1m 40.0** (4.00) P-M 7.90F: 2.90F 2.40F 3.00F (24.30F) OWNER Mlle M-F Hermans BRED Sir Robin McAlpine
**3072 Wakeel (USA)** never looked like taking a hand in the finish.

## 3745a PRIX DU HARAS DE FRESNAY-LE-BUFFARD JACQUES LE MAROIS (Gp 1) (3-Y.O+ C & F)
3-05 (3-06) **1m** £131,752.00 (£52,701.00: £26,350.00: £13,175.00)

SP RR SF

2039[6] **Spinning World (USA)** (JEPease,France) **3-8-11** CAsmussen (trckd ldrs: gd hdwy over 1f out: led ins fnl f: r.o) ....— **1** 17/10[2] 130 79
1950a[3] **Vetheuil (USA)** (AFabre,France) **4-9-4** OPeslier (hld up: hdwy over 1f out: r.o strly nr fin) ....½ **2** 107/10 129 85
3391a* **Shaanxi (USA)** (ELellouche,France) **4-9-0** MEbina (hld up: gng wl over 1f out: rdn 1f out: kpt on one pce) ....¾ **3** 73/10 124 80
3144[2] **Charnwood Forest (IRE)** (SbinSuroor) **4-9-4** LDettori (cl up early: rdn 2f out: led over 1f out: hdd ins fnl f: no ex) ....¾ **4** 13/10[1] 126 82
3033a* **Grey Risk (FR)** (PDemercastel,France) **3-8-11** SGuillot (hld up & bhd: rdn wl over 1f out: styd on fnl f) ....1 **5** 86/10 124 73
3391a[2] **Zarannda (IRE)** (AdeRoyerDupre,France) **3-8-8** MrCMosse (hld up: hdwy & chal 2f out: wknd fnl f) ....2½ **6** 62/10[3] 116 65
2622[10] **Gothenberg (IRE)** (MJohnston) **3-8-11** JWeaver (set str pce: rdn 2f out: hdd over 1f out: wknd) ....2½ **7** 39/1 114 63
2276a[4] **Le Triton (USA)** (MmeCHead,France) **3-8-11** FHead (trckd ldr early: rdn & outpcd fr 2f out) ....3 **8** 13/10[1] 108 57
2609* **Sensation** (MmeCHead,France) **3-8-8** MJKinane (chsd ldrs: rdn over 2f out: outpcd & eased cl home) ....10 **9** 13/10[1] 85 34
(SP 214.9%) **9 Rn**

**1m 39.1** (3.10) P-M 2.70F: 1.60F 3.10F 2.50F (28.40F) OWNER Niarchos Family (CHANTILLY)
**IN-FOCUS: For betting purposes, Charnwood Forest, Le Triton & Sensation were coupled.**
**2039 Spinning World (USA)** looked a picture in the paddock, and lived up to his appearance by winning with something in hand. His Ascot defeat was blamed on too many races too quickly, although the ground at Ascot was possibly too fast for him, as he is suited by some cut in the ground. His immediate targets are the Prix du Moulin, and the Breeders' Cup Mile. (17/10)
**1950a Vetheuil (USA)** handled the step up in class really well, and was suited by the good pace. He will take on the winner again at Longchamp, and may then go to the Breeders' Cup, where he is sure to get the race run to suit him. (107/10)
**3391a* Shaanxi (USA)** did not have the clearest of runs, but still performed with credit. She will join the first two in the Moulin. (73/10)
**3144 Charnwood Forest (IRE)** was always prominent, and looked the likely winner when hitting the front. He found little extra when asked but, with the ground riding softer than the official good, he may have had his excuses. (13/10)
**2622 Gothenberg (IRE)** set off in front as usual, but had nothing left when challenged. He was out of his depth in this class over this trip. (39/1)

## 3746a PRIX GUILLAUME D'ORNANO (Gp 2) (3-Y.O)
3-35 (3-40) **1m 2f** £39,562.00 (£15,810.00: £7,905.00: £3,953.00)

SP RR SF

2006* **Sasuru** (GWragg) **3-8-11** MHills (mid div pllng hrd: hdwy st: chal over 1f out: led wl ins fnl f: jst hld on) ....— **1** 115 22
2276a[3] **Android (USA)** (AFabre,France) **3-8-11** OPeslier (bhd & plld hrd: hdwy u.p over 1f out: ev ch ins fnl f: jst failed) ....s.h **2** 115 22
2668a[5] **Zero Problemo (IRE)** (BSchutz,Germany) **3-8-11** AStarke (a.p: led st: rdn 2f out: hdd nr line) ....s.h **3** 115 22
2881* **Wall Street (USA)** (SbinSuroor) **3-8-11** LDettori (set slow pce: hdd st: rdn & outpcd 2f out: r.o cl home) ....¾ **4** 114 21
3035a[6] **Le Destin (FR)** (PDemercastel,France) **3-8-11** SGuillot (s.i.s: bhd early: sme late hdwy) ....1½ **5** 111 18
2844a[5] **Night Watch (USA)** (AFabre,France) **3-8-11** TJarnet (mid div pllng hrd: 5th & rdn st: nvr able to chal) ....s.h **6** 111 18
1757a[10] **Arbatax (IRE)** (PBary,France) **3-9-2** CAsmussen (mid div early: 4th st: rdn & outpcd cl home) ....s.h **7** 116 23
2480a[5] **Oliviero (FR)** (AVergeade,France) **3-8-11** ESaint-Martin (mid div: 6th st: kpt on one pce) ....1 **8** 110 17
3386a[3] **Top Glory (FR)** (FDoumen,France) **3-8-11** GMosse (in rr early: last st: nvr nr to chal) ....hd **9** 109 16
**9 Rn**

**2m 16.1** (11.10) P-M 9.30F: 2.90F 1.30F 4.80F (15.30F) OWNER Lady Oppenheimer (NEWMARKET) BRED Hascombe and Valiant Studs
**2006* Sasuru** was brought to challenge early in the straight, and then held off the favouite by the narrowest of margins in a desperate finish. This was a fine effort from a progressive colt who would have preferred better ground. He may be seen in France again in the Prix Dollar.
**2276a Android (USA)** came with a very late challenge, and was in front a stride after the post. He may have been unlucky, but this is probably as good as he is.
**Zero Problemo (IRE)** ran a terrific race, and refused to give in. He was in the first two throughout and lost out by inches in the end.
**2881* Wall Street (USA)** attempted to make all the running but, after being outpaced early in the straight, ran on in the closing stages. He is a nice colt with plenty of scope, and could be a better four-year-old.
DS

# SAN SEBASTIAN (Spain) (R-H) (Good)
## Thursday August 15th

## 3747a COPA DE ORO DE SAN SEBASTIAN (Gp 3) (3-Y.O+)
6-15 (7-00) **1m 4f** £26,545.00 (£10,618.00: £5,309.00)

SP RR SF

**Mdudu** (JCampos,Spain) **5-9-4** SCalle ....— **1** 118 —
**El Ceremonioso (SPA)** (MarquesdeCuellar,Spain) **4-9-4** MBorrego ....1½ **2** 116 —
**Madrileno (IRE)** (RMartin,Spain) **4-9-4** JLMartinez ....2½ **3** 113 —
**10 Rn**

**2m 31.92** TOTE 830SP: 260SP 360SP (2270SP) OWNER Cuadra Laia BRED Mrs E. Longton

# 3386a-VICHY (France) (R-H) (Soft)
## Thursday August 15th

## 3748a PRIX DES JOUVENCEAUX ET DES JOUVENCELLES (Listed) (2-Y.O)
3-25 **7f** £15,810.00 (£5,270.00: £2,635.00: £1,318.00)

SP RR SF

**Ballade Viennoise (FR)** (JGauvain,France) **2-8-8** EAntoinat ....— **1** 93 —

| | | | | SP | RR | SF |
|---|---|---|---|---|---|---|
| | **Fine Fellow (IRE)** (MmeCHead,France) **2-8-11** RLibert | s.h | **2** | | 96 | — |
| | **Queen Maud (IRE)** (JdeRoualle,France) **2-8-8** TGillet | hd | **3** | | 93 | — |
| 3400[2] | **Victory Dancer** (BJMeehan) **2-8-11b** BDoyle | 4 | **4** | | 87 | — |
| | | | | | | **7 Rn** |

**1m 30.4** P-M 4.90F: 2.30F 2.00F OWNER J. Bedel BRED Ecurie Maulepaire

## 3744a-DEAUVILLE (France) (R-H) (Good)
### Saturday August 17th

### 3749a PRIX GONTAUT-BIRON (Gp 3) (4-Y.O+)
3-00 (3-03) **1m 2f** £28,986.00 (£10,540.00: £5,270.00)

| | | | | SP | RR | SF |
|---|---|---|---|---|---|---|
| 2480a[9] | **Carling (FR)** (MmePBarbe,France) **4-8-8** TThulliez | — | **1** | | 114 | — |
| 2881[4] | **Bal Harbour** (HRACecil) **5-8-9** GMosse | 1 | **2** | | 113 | — |
| 1947a[4] | **Percutant** (DSmaga,France) **5-9-0** DBoeuf | 1½ | **3** | | 116 | — |
| | | | | | | **10 Rn** |

**2m 9.3** (4.30) P-M 5.90F: 2.30F 2.90F 3.50F (25.40F) OWNER Mr T. Yoshida BRED Ecurie Delbart in France
**622a Carling (FR)** came back to form after being injured in her box in May. She burst into the lead over a furlong out, and held on well. Her connections believe that ten furlongs is her best trip, and likely targets are the La Coupe de Maisons-Laffitte, and the Champion Stakes. She is also still in the Arc.
**2881 Bal Harbour** ran a fine race against a top-class filly. He tried to make all, and rallied well when headed.
**1947a Percutant** ran well, despite giving weight to the first two. He is a little inconsistent, but well capable of winning again at this level.

## 3749a-DEAUVILLE (France) (R-H) (Good)
### Sunday August 18th

### 3750a PRIX MORNY PIAGET (Gp 1) (2-Y.O C & F)
2-05 (2-05) **6f** £105,402.00 (£42,161.00: £21,080.00: £10,540.00)

| | | | | SP | RR | SF |
|---|---|---|---|---|---|---|
| 2951* | **Bahamian Bounty** (DRLoder) **2-9-0** LDettori (broke wl: cl up: rdn 2f out: led 1f out: kpt on cl home) | — | **1** | 56/10[3] | 110 | 63 |
| 3390a* | **Zamindar (USA)** (AFabre,France) **2-9-0** TJarnet (set gd pce: hdd 1f out: rdn & r.o ins fnl f) | s.nk | **2** | 30/100[1] | 110 | 63 |
| | **Pas De Reponse (USA)** (MmeCHead,France) **2-8-11** FHead (chsd ldrs: rdn over 2f out: kpt on fnl f) | 3 | **3** | 41/10[2] | 99 | 52 |
| 2607* | **Rich Ground** (JDBethell) **2-9-0** PaulEddery (hld up last: rdn 2f out: no imp) | 4 | **4** | 77/10 | 91 | 44 |
| 3156[6] | **Blue Ridge** (RHannon) **2-9-0** RHughes (mid div early: u.p ½-wy: outpcd) | s.nk | **5** | 20/1 | 91 | 44 |
| | | | | (SP 127.9%) | | **5 Rn** |

**1m 11.0** (3.00) P-M 6.60F: 1.10F 1.10F OWNER Lucayan Stud Ltd (NEWMARKET) BRED Clarents Racing Ltd
**2951* Bahamian Bounty**, who looked well in the paddock, was given a superb ride and made the big step from a maiden race at Yarmouth in good style. Likely to finish his season in the Middle Park, he is bred to be a sprinter, and it will be interesting to see if is kept to sprint trips as a three-year-old. (56/10)
**3390a* Zamindar (USA)** should not be written off as a Classic prospect yet, as the race did not go his way, and his trainer was reportedly unhappy with the way he was ridden. Chopped for speed at a vital stage, he did not give up, and was running on well close home. He goes for the Prix de la Salamandre, and the longer distance should be in his favour. (30/100)
**Pas De Reponse (USA)** was not given a hard race when it was clear she could not beat the principals. She will probably go for the Cheveley Park Stakes next, and could be a different proposition against her own sex. (41/10)
**2607* Rich Ground** found this tougher opposition than at Newmarket. However, he had bruised a foot earlier in the week, and then lost a shoe in the race, so he should be given a chance to prove he is better than this. (77/10)
**3156 Blue Ridge** was out of his depth here, and was beaten two furlongs out. (20/1)

### 3751a PRIX KERGORLAY (Gp 2) (3-Y.O+)
3-15 (3-15) **1m 7f** £39,526.00 (£15,810.00: £7,905.00: £3,953.00)

| | | | | SP | RR | SF |
|---|---|---|---|---|---|---|
| | **Kassani (IRE)** (AdeRoyerDupre,France) **4-9-4** GMosse (hld up & bhd: rdn over 2f out: hdwy to ld 1f out: r.o wl) | — | **1** | | 124 | 67 |
| 2071[3] | **Nononito (FR)** (JLesbordes,France) **5-9-4** SGuillot (hld up: hdwy appr st: rdn & outpcd 2f out: r.o fnl f) | 1 | **2** | | 123 | 66 |
| 3124[2] | **Chief Contender (IRE)** (PWChapple-Hyam) **3-8-5** LDettori (trckd ldr early: led 5f out: rdn st: hdd over 2f out: kpt on one pce) | ¾ | **3** | | 122 | 52 |
| 3200a* | **Ming Dynasty (IRE)** (DSmaga,France) **5-9-4b** FHead (set slow pce to 5f out: led over 2f out to 1f out: wknd) | 5 | **4** | | 117 | 60 |
| 2071[7] | **Assessor (IRE)** (RHannon) **7-9-4v[1]** RHughes (chsd ldrs to st: no imp) | 2½ | **5** | | 114 | 57 |
| | | | | | | **5 Rn** |

**3m 16.1** (8.10) P-M 2.40F: 1.30F 1.30F OWNER Aga Khan (CHANTILLY) BRED Aga Khan's Studs S.C.
**Kassani (IRE)** was brought with a well-timed run to win with authority. Best when fresh, he prefers a right-handed track, and is likely to be a major contender in the Prix du Cadran.
**2071 Nononito (FR)**, a good third in the Ascot Gold Cup, ran really well in his first race since. He is likely to meet the winner again in the Cadran, and the extra five furlongs there could well enable him to turn the tables.
**3124 Chief Contender (IRE)** ran with credit against some experienced stayers. Having led into the straight, he kept on well to the line. He is likely to go for the St Leger next, and his proven stamina will be a useful weapon.
**Ming Dynasty (IRE)** took the field along before dropping away in the straight. He was out of his depth here.
**1482 Assessor (IRE)** is not the force he was and, without the testing ground that suits him so well, was never able to get in a blow.

## 0789a-GELSENKIRCHEN-HORST (Gelsenkirchen, Germany) (R-H) (Good)
### Sunday August 18th

### 3752a SILBERNE PEITSCHE PREIS DER SPEILBANK HOHENSYBURG (Listed) (3-Y.O+)
2-35 (2-40) **7f** £9,009.00 (£3,604.00: £1,802.00: £901.00)

| | | | | SP | RR | SF |
|---|---|---|---|---|---|---|
| 1060a[7] | **Personal Love (USA)** (HSteinmetz,Germany) **3-8-5** ABest | — | **1** | | 108 | — |

| | | | | SP | RR | SF |
|---|---|---|---|---|---|---|
| 1753a² | **My King (GER)** (HRemmert,Germany) **3-8-7** KWoodburn | 2½ | 2 | | 104 | — |
| | **Tristano** (ALowe,Germany) **4-9-0** THellier | ¾ | 3 | | 105 | — |
| 3712⁸ | **Branston Abby (IRE)** (MJohnston) **7-9-2** JReid | ½ | 4 | | 105 | — |
| | | | | | | **8 Rn** |

**1m 27.46** TOTE 105DM: 29DM 16DM 20DM OWNER Stall Nizza BRED R. Berger et al

**Personal Love (USA)** made all the running, and ran on strongly in the final furlong.

**3712 Branston Abby (IRE)** did not have the best of runs when trying to mount her challenge and, although she got through to take second place inside the last furlong, she faded close home.

## 3753a ARAL-POKAL (Gp 1) (3-Y.O+)
3-45 (3-53) **1m 4f** £94,595.00 (£40,541.00: £22,523.00: £11,261.00)

| | | | | SP | RR | SF |
|---|---|---|---|---|---|---|
| 3070⁶ | **Luso** (CEBrittain) **4-9-6** MJKinane (mde all: qcknd 2f out: r.o wl) | — | 1 | | 124 | — |
| 3203a* | **Hollywood Dream (GER)** (UOstmann,Germany) **5-9-2** JReid (hld up in rr: hdwy st: ev ch over 1f out: no ex) | 1¾ | 2 | | 118 | — |
| 3157² | **Lear White (USA)** (PAKelleway) **5-9-6** FJovine (mid div: cl up ½-wy: 2nd st: outpcd 2f out: styd on fnl f) | 3 | 3 | | 118 | — |
| | **Lentini** (BSchutz,Germany) **5-9-6** THellier (a cl up: 3rd st: outpcd 2f out: rallied cl home) | 1½ | 4 | | 116 | — |
| 2668a⁷ | **Wind Of Chance (GER)** (BSchutz,Germany) **3-8-8** AStarke (hld up: hdwy st: wnt 3rd over 1f out: wknd cl home) | nk | 5 | | 113 | — |
| 1752a³ | **Little Smart (GER)** (PLautner,Germany) **4-9-6** WNewnes (5th st: sn btn) | 9 | 6 | | 103 | — |
| | **O'Connor (IRE)** (AWohler,Germany) **4-9-6** ABoschert (prom 7f: 4th st: sn btn) | 5 | 7 | | 97 | — |
| 3203a⁷ | **Caballo (GER)** (HJentzsch,Germany) **5-9-6** LHammer-Hansen (last st: a bhd) | 2 | 8 | | 94 | — |
| | | | | | | **8 Rn** |

**2m 32.98** TOTE 20F: 11F 13F 15F OWNER Mr Saeed Manana (NEWMARKET) BRED Saeed Manana

**3070 Luso** dictated the pace and, with his rider giving him a breather before quickening up in the straight, ran out a comfortable winner.

**3203a* Hollywood Dream (GER)** has been running well this season and, although unable to cope with the winner, had the rest well beaten.

**3157 Lear White (USA)** was close enough turning for home, but could not cope with the principals in the last quarter-mile.

# KLAMPENBORG (Copenhagen, Denmark) (R-H) (Firm)
## Sunday August 18th

## 3754a SCANDINAVIAN OPEN CHAMPIONSHIP (3-Y.O+)
2-35 (-) **1m 4f** £69,767.00

| | | | | SP | RR | SF |
|---|---|---|---|---|---|---|
| 2843a⁵ | **Federico (USA)** (SJensen,Denmark) **4-9-2** KAndersen | — | 1 | | 103 | — |
| 1944a³ | **Dulford Lad** (JFretheim,Norway) **5-9-2** MSantos | 3 | 2 | | 99 | — |
| 2479a⁸ | **Concepcion (GER)** (HJentzsch,Germany) **6-9-4** PSchiergen | 2 | 3 | | 98 | — |
| 3351⁴ | **Glide Path (USA)** (JWHills) **7-9-4** MHills (btn over 7 3/4l) | | 6 | | — | — |
| 3442⁸ | **Otto E Mezzo** (MJPolglase) **4-9-2** WHollick (btn over 8l) | | 7 | | — | — |
| 3212⁶ | **Son of Sharp Shot (IRE)** (JLDunlop) **6-9-2** PatEddery (btn over 13½l) | | 9 | | — | — |
| | | | | | | **12 Rn** |

**2m 26.0** TOTE 40.70DKR: 20DKR 24DKR 19DKR (176DKR) OWNER Strecker Brothers

**Federico (USA)**, the Danish Derby winner of last year, stormed to the front two furlongs out for an easy win. He is likely to go for the Prix Dollar at Longchamp in an attempt to record his first victory outside Denmark.

**3351 Glide Path (USA)** was prominent until entering the straight, but then dropped away.

**3233 Otto E Mezzo** was close up until fading over a furlong out.

**2690* Son of Sharp Shot (IRE)** started favourite, but refused to settle early on and, although he moved up to the leaders turning for home, he was beaten soon after.

# 3747a-SAN SEBASTIAN (Spain) (R-H) (Firm)
## Sunday August 18th

## 3755a GOBIERNO VASCO (3-Y.O+)
6-15 (6-27) **1m** £26,545.00

| | | | | SP | RR | SF |
|---|---|---|---|---|---|---|
| | **Okawango (SPA)** (MDelcher,Spain) **3-8-10** SVidal | — | 1 | | 102 | — |
| | **Eneldo (SPA)** (JPAvial,Spain) **3-9-2**ow3 FRodriguez | 3½ | 2 | | 101 | — |
| | **Estragon (SPA)** (RMartin,Spain) **3-8-10** JLMartinez | ½ | 3 | | 94 | — |
| 2337⁷ | **Prince of India** (LordHuntingdon) **4-9-2** TIves (btn over 9l) | | 5 | | — | — |
| | | | | | | **10 Rn** |

**1m 38.48** TOTE 350SP: 150SP 340SP 240SP (5230SP) OWNER Cuadra San Antonio BRED Yeguada Balmoral Sa

**Prince of India**, settled in mid-division, could find no more when asked to quicken two furlongs out.

# 3441-NEWMARKET (R-H) (Good to soft)
## Friday August 23rd
WEATHER: raining WIND: slt against

## 3756 EQUITY FINANCIAL COLLECTIONS MAIDEN STKS (2-Y.O F) (Class D)
2-00 (2-01) **7f (July)** £4,386.00 (£1,308.00: £624.00: £282.00) Stalls: High GOING minus 0.09 sec per fur (G)

| | | | | SP | RR | SF |
|---|---|---|---|---|---|---|
| 2863² | **Reams of Verse (USA)** (HRACecil) **2-8-11** WRyan(3) (lw: a.p: led over 2f out: rdn out) | — | 1 | 4/7 1 | 92 | 40 |
| | **Bint Baladee** (SbinSuroor) **2-8-11** LDettori(4) (gd sort: scope: hdwy 3f out: ev ch whn swvd lft ins fnl f: edgd lft & r.o wl nr fin) | nk | 2 | 12/1 | 91+ | 39 |
| | **Woodsia** (DRLoder) **2-8-11** TQuinn(5) (gd sort: wl grwn: bit bkwd: hld up: hdwy over 2f out: wknd over 1f out) | 14 | 3 | 5/1 2 | 59 | 7 |

Santa Rosa (IRE) (JLDunlop) **2-8-11** TSprake(8) (w'like: scope: hld up: r.o one pce fnl f) ...... ¾ **4** 20/1 58 6
$2611^{4}$ **Indihash (USA)** (RWArmstrong) **2-8-11** WCarson(6) (chsd ldr tl wknd over 2f out) ...... s.h **5** $13/2^{3}$ 58 6
**Gersey** (MRStoute) **2-8-11** JReid(2) (w'like: scope: bit bkwd: dwlt: plld hrd: a bhd) ...... 1 **6** 16/1 55 3
**Ganga (IRE)** (WJarvis) **2-8-11** RCochrane(7) (cmpt: bkwd: b.off hind: dwlt: hld up: bhd fnl 3f) ...... 1½ **7** 33/1 52 —
$3277^{3}$ **Double Flight** (MJohnston) **2-8-11** JWeaver(1) (lw: led over 4f: sn wknd: t.o) ...... 18 **8** 16/1 11 —
(SP 120.8%) **8 Rn**

**1m 29.07** (4.07) CSF £9.02 TOTE £1.60: £1.10 £2.30 £1.70 (£4.80) OWNER Mr K. Abdulla (NEWMARKET) BRED Juddmonte Farms

**2863 Reams of Verse (USA)**, possibly in front soon enough, greatly benefited by the erratic course taken by the runner-up in the closing stages. Her trainer thought there was plenty in the tank, although one can't help but think that Bint Baladee would be the shorter price should the two meet again. (4/7)

**Bint Baladee**, a half-sister to Shanaladee, seemed to be coming to win her race when running very green in the final 200 yards. With hindsight, Dettori would have been better off letting her cross to the far rail, instead of pulling his whip through. She can be considered a winner without a penalty. (12/1: op 8/1)

**Woodsia**, a half-sister to Polka and Millstream, will come on for the run and would possibly have preferred better ground. (5/1: 7/2-11/2)

**Santa Rosa (IRE)**, a half-sister to Decorated Hero and Beneficiary, was steadied leaving the stalls and gave the impression her rider was concentrating on teaching her to settle. (20/1)

**2611 Indihash (USA)**, a half-brother to Mur Taasha and Shujan, did not live up to her promising debut and one can only think it may have been the easier ground. (13/2)

**Gersey**, a half-sister to Jahafil amongst others, will do better when she learns to settle. (16/1)

## 3757 GIRTON MAIDEN STKS (2-Y.O C & G) (Class D)

2-35 (2-40) **7f (July)** £4,659.00 (£1,392.00: £666.00: £303.00) Stalls: High GOING minus 0.09 sec per fur (G)

SP RR SF

$3407^{4}$ **Yalaietanee** (MRStoute) **2-8-11** JReid(1) (lw: trckd ldrs: led over 2f out: rdn clr fnl f) ...... — **1** $2/1^{1}$ 92+ 27
**Flirting Around (USA)** (MRStoute) **2-8-11** KBradshaw(2) (gd sort: hld up: hdwy over 2f out: r.o ins fnl f) ...... 4 **2** 25/1 83+ 18
$2413^{2}$ **Blue Goblin (USA)** (LMCumani) **2-8-11** OUrbina(5) (a.p: ev ch 2f out: one pce) ...... ¾ **3** $3/1^{3}$ 81 16
**Cape Cross (IRE)** (JHMGosden) **2-8-11** RCochrane(12) (wl grwn: bkwd: b: b.hind: dwlt: hdwy over 3f out: r.o fnl f) ...... ¾ **4** 14/1 79+ 14
**Baaheth (USA)** (RWArmstrong) **2-8-11** WCarson(3) (neat: scope: s.s: hdwy over 3f out: sn rdn: one pce fnl 2f) ...... hd **5** 14/1 79 14
$2624^{3}$ **Kumait (USA)** (SbinSuroor) **2-8-11** LDettori(4) (lw: plld hrd: led 1f: wknd fnl f) ...... nk **6** $5/2^{2}$ 79d 14
**Super Monarch** (EALDunlop) **2-8-11** WRyan(7) (leggy: scope: bkwd: s.s: hdwy over 2f out: wknd fnl f) ...... 2½ **7** 20/1 73 8
$3221^{9}$ **Dixie Jamboree (USA)** (LMCumani) **2-8-11** JWeaver(11) (plld hrd early: dropped rr after 2f: rdn & r.o appr fnl f) ...... 3½ **8** 33/1 65 —
$2040^{11}$ **Saratoga Red (USA) (85)** (WAO'Gorman) **2-8-11** EmmaO'Gorman(10) (nvr trbld ldrs) ...... 1¾ **9** 66/1 61 —
$3651^{2}$ **Saint Who (USA)** (WAO'Gorman) **2-8-11** TIves(13) (plld hrd: led after 1f: hdd over 2f out: sn wknd) ...... 3 **10** 66/1 54 —
$2600^{12}$ **Chingachgook** (PWHarris) **2-8-11** AClark(9) (hld up: a bhd) ...... 1¼ **11** 50/1 51 —
**Dawn Summit** (BHanbury) **2-8-11** JStack(6) (str: cmpt: s.s: plld hrd: a bhd) ...... ½ **12** 20/1 50 —
$2951^{4}$ **Magyar Titok (IRE)** (BobJones) **2-8-11** RPerham(8) (lw: swtg: prom over 4f) ...... 1 **13** 50/1 48 —
(SP 123.5%) **13 Rn**

**1m 30.24** (5.24) CSF £47.59 TOTE £3.20: £1.50 £7.20 £1.70 (£71.00) Trio £71.90 OWNER Maktoum Al Maktoum (NEWMARKET) BRED Gainsborough Stud Management Ltd

**IN-FOCUS: The Maktoum family's seven representatives filled the first seven places.**

**3407 Yalaietanee**, a half-brother to Molecomb winner Sahara Star, was well backed. Relishing the cut in the ground, there was a lot to like about this performance, and he can go on from here. (2/1: 7/2-7/4)

**Flirting Around (USA)**, a $275,000 half-brother to a winner in the States, is out of an unraced half-sister to Song of Sixpence. Very much the stable's second-string, he would not have to improve much to get off the mark. (25/1)

**2413 Blue Goblin (USA)**, stepping up in trip, raced more keenly than his rider would have liked, and could not go with winner in the final quarter-mile. There will be other days for him. (3/1: 5/2-4/1)

**Cape Cross (IRE)** is a half-brother to Pastorale and good French middle-distance winner Lord of Appeal. Staying on promisingly in the later stages, he seems sure to improve. (14/1: 7/1-16/1)

**Baaheth (USA)**, a $200,000 first foal, will be better for the experience. (14/1: op 7/1)

**2624 Kumait (USA)**, not knocked about, did not seem to see out the extra furlong in the rain-softened ground. (5/2: 7/4-7/2)

## 3758 NGK SPARK PLUGS APPRENTICE H'CAP (0-80) (3-Y.O+) (Class E)

3-05 (3-06) **6f (July)** £3,615.00 (£1,095.00: £535.00: £255.00) Stalls: High GOING minus 0.09 sec per fur (G)

SP RR SF

$3465^{2}$ **Bee Health Boy (66)** (MWEasterby) **3-9-0** GParkin(1) (lw: w ldr: led wl over 1f out: drvn out) ...... — **1** $11/4^{1}$ 74 33
$3666^{3}$ **Don Pepe (60)** (RBoss) **5-8-8**(3) GFaulkner(4) (lw: hld up: hdwy over 1f out: r.o ins fnl f) ...... nk **2** 8/1 67 29
$3152^{7}$ **Almasi (IRE) (70)** (CFWall) **4-9-2**(5) PClarke(7) (hld up: hdwy 2f out: edgd lft & nt qckn wl ins fnl f) ...... 1 **3** $11/2^{3}$ 75 37
$3639^{2}$ **Pageboy (63)** (PCHaslam) **7-9-0** 5x SDrowne(8) (led over 4f: one pce) ...... 2 **4** $7/2^{2}$ 62 24
$3168^{2}$ **Indian Relative (76)** (RGuest) **3-9-10** DGriffiths(2) (prom: ev ch over 1f out: one pce) ...... ¾ **5** 8/1 73 32
$3240^{4}$ **Lucky Revenge (64)** (MartynMeade) **3-8-9**(3) DSweeney(6) (lw: prom: ev ch over 1f out: n.m.r & sn wknd) ...... 1½ **6** 10/1 57 16
$3406^{4}$ **Statistician (62)** (JohnBerry) **4-8-6**(7) AmyQuirk(5) (bhd fnl 2f) ...... 2 **7** 25/1 50 12
$3639^{3}$ **Cim Bom Bom (IRE) (72)** (MBell) **4-9-4v**(5) RMullen(3) (dwlt: hdwy 4f out: rdn & ev ch 2f out: wknd over 1f out) ...... 6 **8** 15/2 44 6
(SP 111.2%) **8 Rn**

**1m 16.16** (4.16) CSF £21.92 CT £98.53 TOTE £3.30: £1.10 £1.90 £2.40 (£12.50) OWNER Bee Health Ltd (SHERIFF HUTTON) BRED Roger and Mrs Margaret Lightfoot

WEIGHT FOR AGE 3yo-3lb

**3465 Bee Health Boy**, who loves soft ground, was back to his best trip and landed a touch. He was already due to go up 2lb in future handicaps. (11/4)

**3666 Don Pepe** did win over this trip at Goodwood in June, but his other five victories have all come over seven. (8/1)

**3152 Almasi (IRE)** probably had an apprentice aboard because she has gone up 16lb for two wins this season. Unable to sustain a promising-looking run up the stands' rail, she probably would have benefited from stronger handling. (11/2: 4/1-6/1)

**3639 Pageboy**, apparently not suited by the ease in the ground, could not defy a penalty, despite being due to go up to a mark 4lb higher than the one he ran off here. (7/2: op 7/4)

**3168 Indian Relative** had even softer ground to contend with this time. (8/1)

**3240 Lucky Revenge** seems better suited to seven. (10/1)

## 3759 PORTLAND PLACE PROPERTIES HOPEFUL STKS (Listed) (3-Y.O+) (Class A)

3-35 (3-35) **6f (July)** £11,859.20 (£4,392.80: £2,111.40: £867.00: £348.50: £141.10) Stalls: High GOING minus 0.09 sec per fur (G)

| Form | Horse / Details | Dist | Pos | SP | RR | SF |
|---|---|---|---|---|---|---|
| 3127$^{7}$ | **Carranita (IRE) (108)** (BPalling) **6-8-13** TSprake(4) (hld up: hdwy over 2f out: led over 1f out: edgd lft: r.o wl) | — | **1** | 100/30$^{1}$ | 114 | 52 |
| 3083$^{9}$ | **Atraf (112)** (DMorley) **3-9-4** WCarson(6) (lw: a.p: led over 2f out tl over 1f out: r.o) | 1 | **2** | 7/1 | 119 | 54 |
| 3126* | **Rambling Bear (113)** (MBlanshard) **3-9-4** RCochrane(2) (swtg: hld up: hdwy over 2f out: rdn & r.o one pce fnl f) | 1½ | **3** | 6/1$^{3}$ | 115 | 50 |
| 3232$^{9}$ | **Jayannpee (107)** (IABalding) **5-9-4** WRyan(5) (b.off hind: lw: hld up: hdwy over 2f out: ev ch over 1f out: one pce) | hd | **4** | 9/1 | 112 | 50 |
| 2332$^{8}$ | **Westcourt Magic (109)** (MWEasterby) **3-9-1** LCharnock(9) (lw: led over 3f: wknd over 1f out) | 3 | **5** | 25/1 | 104 | 39 |
| 2880$^{11}$ | **King of The East (IRE) (102)** (MRStoute) **3-8-11** FLynch(7) (prom: ev ch wl over 1f out: wknd ins fnl f) | nk | **6** | 9/1 | 99 | 34 |
| 3573a$^{8}$ | **Easy Dollar (106)** (BGubby) **4-9-0b** JWeaver(10) (w ldr: rdn over 2f out: wknd 1f out) | ½ | **7** | 8/1 | 98 | 36 |
| 3132$^{2}$ | **Russian Revival (USA) (110)** (SbinSuroor) **3-8-11** LDettori(13) (prom over 4f) | 5 | **8** | 11/2$^{2}$ | 85 | 20 |
| 579$^{5}$ | **High Priority (IRE) (100)** (MRChannon) **3-8-11** RPerham(12) (h.d.w: prom over 3f) | 4 | **9** | 33/1 | 74 | 9 |
| 3232$^{7}$ | **Venture Capitalist (112)** (DNicholls) **7-9-7** AlexGreaves(1) (a bhd) | nk | **10** | 8/1 | 80 | 18 |
| 2880$^{15}$ | **Sea Dane (107)** (PWHarris) **3-9-1** AClark(11) (b: bhd fnl 2f: t.o) | 14 | **11** | 20/1 | 40 | — |

(SP 119.0%) **11 Rn**

**1m 14.73** (2.73) CSF £25.51 TOTE £4.20: £2.00 £2.60 £2.10 (£18.60) Trio £21.70 OWNER Lamb Lane Associates (COWBRIDGE) BRED Mrs Anita Quinn

WEIGHT FOR AGE 3yo-3lb

**IN-FOCUS: The runners raced up the centre.**

**3127 Carranita (IRE)**, back to her best trip, edged over to the far rail after taking it up, and set the tone for the remainder of the afternoon. (100/30: 9/2-3/1)

**3083 Atraf** never gave up the task in hand and was possibly racing on slower ground up the middle. (7/1)

**3126* Rambling Bear** could not produce the same sort of finish over an extra furlong on slower ground. (6/1)

**2880* Jayannpee** has never scored on ground worse than good and ran another fine race. (9/1)

**1129 Westcourt Magic**, not helped by the rain-softened ground, is far more effective over the minimum trip. (25/1)

**1493* King of The East (IRE)** had ground conditions in his favour, and was accordingly supported in the Ring. (9/1: op 16/1)

**3132 Russian Revival (USA)** (11/2: 4/1-6/1)

## 3760 BREHENY H'CAP (0-95) (3-Y.O+) (Class C)

4-10 (4-11) **1m 6f 175y (July)** £5,900.00 (£1,760.00: £840.00: £380.00) Stalls: High GOING minus 0.09 sec per fur (G)

| Form | Horse / Details | Dist | Pos | SP | RR | SF |
|---|---|---|---|---|---|---|
| 2080* | **Flying Legend (USA) (85)** (HRACecil) **3-8-8** WRyan(6) (lw: hld up: led over 3f out: clr over 2f out: rdn out) | — | **1** | 2/1$^{1}$ | 103+ | 33 |
| 3504$^{3}$ | **Tudor Island (80)** (CEBrittain) **7-9-2** LDettori(5) (led over 10f: r.o one pce) | 5 | **2** | 6/1 | 93 | 36 |
| 3404$^{5}$ | **Western Sal (68)** (JLHarris) **4-8-4** TSprake(2) (lw: hld up: styd on one pce fnl 2f) | 3 | **3** | 20/1 | 77 | 20 |
| 2534$^{3}$ | **Nabhaan (IRE) (93)** (DMorley) **3-9-2** WCarson(3) (hld up: rdn over 6f out: hdwy over 3f out: wknd over 1f out) | 6 | **4** | 5/2$^{2}$ | 96 | 26 |
| 3037* | **Bolivar (IRE) (73)** (RAkehurst) **4-8-9b** TQuinn(4) (lw: chsd ldr: led 4f out: sn hdd: wknd over 2f out) | 16 | **5** | 7/2$^{3}$ | 59 | 2 |
| 2576$^{6}$ | **Swan Hunter (78)** (DJSCosgrove) **3-8-1** JStack(1) (a bhd) | 7 | **6** | 33/1 | 56 | — |
| 2882* | **Mystic Hill (92)** (GHarwood) **5-10-0** AClark(7) (hld up & plld hrd: a bhd: eased whn btn fnl 2f) | 1 | **7** | 9/1 | 69 | 12 |

(SP 116.1%) **7 Rn**

**3m 18.32** (9.82) CSF £13.76 TOTE £3.00: £1.70 £2.30 (£8.10) OWNER Mr Jim Browne (NEWMARKET) BRED Fares Farms Inc

WEIGHT FOR AGE 3yo-13lb

**2080* Flying Legend (USA)** really came into his own given this stamina test and, suited by the give under foot, turned the race into a procession. He may go for the St Leger if he continues to progress to the liking of his trainer. (2/1)

**3504 Tudor Island** did nothing wrong, but it was very much a case of finishing best of the rest. (6/1)

**3404 Western Sal** could not peg back the runner-up, let alone bother the winner. (20/1)

**2534 Nabhaan (IRE)**, trying a longer trip, had no excuses this time. (5/2)

## 3761 FREEDOM FARM STUD (S) H'CAP (0-60) (3 & 4-Y.O) (Class E)

4-40 (4-42) **7f (July)** £4,435.00 (£1,330.00: £640.00: £295.00) Stalls: High GOING minus 0.09 sec per fur (G)

| Form | Horse / Details | Dist | Pos | SP | RR | SF |
|---|---|---|---|---|---|---|
| 3442$^{3}$ | **Speedy Snaps Pride (44)** (PDCundell) **4-8-7b**$^{(5)}$ DGriffiths(18) (a.p: led over 1f out: jst hld on) | — | **1** | 7/1$^{3}$ | 54 | 43 |
| 3410$^{2}$ | **Komlucky (44)** (ABMulholland) **4-8-5v**$^{(7)}$ GFaulkner(5) (trckd ldrs gng wl: ev ch fnl f: r.o) | s.h | **2** | 10/1 | 54 | 43 |
| *3608*$^{6}$ | **Shermood (39)** (KTIvory) **3-8-2** CScally(9) (b.nr fore: b.hind: hld up: hdwy over 1f out: hung lft: r.o) | 1¾ | **3** | 10/1 | 45 | 29 |
| 3427$^{3}$ | **Corniche Quest (IRE) (52)** (MRChannon) **3-9-1** LDettori(8) (lw: hdwy over 2f out: no ex ins fnl f) | s.h | **4** | 4/1$^{1}$ | 58 | 42 |
| 3474$^{5}$ | **Jilly Beveled (40)** (PRWebber) **4-8-8** RPerham(15) (b: b.hind: wnt lft s: sn prom: led over 2f out tl over 1f out: one pce) | ¾ | **5** | 13/2$^{2}$ | 44 | 33 |
| 3456$^{9}$ | **Square Mile Miss (IRE) (48)** (PHowling) **3-8-11** AClark(7) (rdn 3f out: hdwy 2f out: eased whn btn ins fnl f) | 3½ | **6** | 20/1 | 44 | 28 |
| 3619$^{15}$ | **La Fandango (IRE) (38)** (MWEasterby) **3-8-1** LCharnock(14) (hmpd s: nvr nrr) | 6 | **7** | 25/1 | 20 | 4 |
| 3358$^{3}$ | **Unspoken Prayer (44)** (JRArnold) **3-8-7** TQuinn(3) (lw: hld up: effrt & nt clr run 2f out: nt rch ldrs) | ¾ | **8** | 10/1 | 25 | 9 |
| 3481$^{9}$ | **Florrie'm (38)** (JLHarris) **3-8-1b**$^{ow1}$ DBiggs(11) (chsd ldrs over 4f) | nk | **9** | 33/1 | 18 | 1 |
| 3059$^{10}$ | **Patrio (IRE) (41)** (SCWilliams) **3-8-4** SDrowne(1) (prom: edgd lft & wknd 2f out) | 3 | **10** | 33/1 | 14 | — |
| 3585$^{4}$ | **Sapphire Son (IRE) (53)** (DMorris) **4-9-7** JWeaver(12) (prom: rdn & wknd over 2f out) | 4 | **11** | 12/1 | 17 | 6 |
| 1500$^{15}$ | **Harvest Reaper (50)** (JLHarris) **4-9-4** TSprake(19) (w ldrs 4f) | 1¼ | **12** | 14/1 | 11 | — |
| 3151$^{6}$ | **Euphyllia (60)** (BobJones) **4-10-0v** TIves(6) (w ldrs: wknd over 2f out) | s.h | **13** | 8/1 | 21 | 10 |
| 3655$^{8}$ | **Farfeste (36)** (DMorris) **3-7-13v**$^{1}$ StephenDavies(17) (hrd rdn over 3f out: bhd fnl 2f) | s.h | **14** | 25/1 | — | — |
| *3603*$^{6}$ | **David James' Girl (53)** (ABailey) **4-9-4**$^{(3)}$ DWright(13) (n.d) | ¾ | **15** | 14/1 | 12 | 1 |
| 2500$^{10}$ | **Music Mistress (IRE) (45)** (JSMoore) **3-8-3**$^{(5)}$ PPMurphy(10) (a bhd) | 2 | **16** | 20/1 | — | — |
| 3244$^{7}$ | **Hotlips Houlihan (37)** (RJRWilliams) **3-7-9b**$^{1(5)}$ MBaird(2) (lw: led over 4f: wkng whn n.m.r over 2f out) | 1¾ | **17** | 14/1 | — | — |
| *3064*$^{8}$ | **Below The Red Line (42)** (MrsNMacauley) **3-8-2b**$^{1(3)ow7}$ CTeague(16) (swtg: a bhd: t.o fnl 3f) | 13 | **18** | 33/1 | — | — |

(SP 137.9%) **18 Rn**

**1m 28.85** (3.85) CSF £77.09 CT £682.18 TOTE £9.30: £2.30 £2.20 £2.90 £1.40 (£28.20) Trio £197.90 OWNER Mr P. D. Cundell (NEWBURY) BRED Pineapple Clothing Co Ltd

WEIGHT FOR AGE 3yo-5lb

No bid

**IN-FOCUS: The runners raced up the far side.**

**3442 Speedy Snaps Pride**, raised 7lb after his good run in a claimer last time, held on by the skin of his teeth. (7/1)
**3410 Komlucky** only needed another stride and deserves a change of fortune. (10/1)
**3474 Shermood**, who probably failed to stay ten furlongs last time, again gave the impression she needs a mile, but might still have been able to pick up the two leaders had she been more co-operative. (10/1)
**3427 Corniche Quest (IRE)** failed to sustain his effort in the final 200 yards. (4/1)
**3474 Jilly Beveled** may have found this coming plenty soon enough after a reappearance last week. (13/2)
**Square Mile Miss (IRE)** could not take advantage of a drop in class. (20/1)

## 3762 SAXHAM NURSERY H'CAP (2-Y.O) (Class C)
5-10 (5-11) **1m (July)** £6,056.00 (£1,808.00: £864.00: £392.00) Stalls: High GOING minus 0.09 sec per fur (G)

| | | | | SP | RR | SF |
|---|---|---|---|---|---|---|
| 3407* | **Blue River (IRE) (84)** (TGMills) **2-9-7** TQuinn(6) (w ldr: led ins fnl f: rdn out) | — | 1 | 11/4[2] | 88 | 4 |
| 3171[3] | **Lady Godiva (67)** (MJPolglase) **2-8-4** JStack(2) (led: qcknd over 2f out: hdd ins fnl f) | 1¾ | 2 | 8/1 | 68 | — |
| 3312[4] | **Swallow Breeze (63)** (DrJDScargill) **2-8-0** StephenDavies(4) (hld up & plld hrd: swtchd rt over 4f out: hdwy over 1f out: r.o wl ins fnl f) | 1¼ | 3 | 14/1 | 61 | — |
| 3221* | **Right Tune (80)** (BHanbury) **2-9-3** WRyan(3) (hld up: outpcd over 2f out: r.o one pce fnl f) | s.h | 4 | 9/4[1] | 78 | — |
| *3417*[2] | **Going For Broke (66)** (PCHaslam) **2-7-10**(7) RMullen(1) (lw: reard s: plld hrd: outpcd over 2f out: styd on fnl f) | 1¼ | 5 | 12/1 | 61 | — |
| 2759* | **Barnwood Crackers (64)** (MissGayKelleway) **2-7-12**(3)ow1 FLynch(8) (lw: plld hrd: prom over 5f) | 1¾ | 6 | 4/1[3] | 56 | — |
| *2633*[10] | **Neon Deion (IRE) (60)** (SCWilliams) **2-7-8**(3) DWright(5) (hld up: bmpd over 4f out: a bhd: t.o) | 17 | 7 | 25/1 | 18 | — |
| 3616[9] | **Sun O'Tirol (IRE) (75)** (MRChannon) **2-8-12** LDettori(7) (hld up: eased whn btn wl over 1f out) | 16 | 8 | 10/1 | 1 | — |

(SP 115.8%) **8 Rn**

**1m 46.62** (9.42) CSF £22.94 CT £239.52 TOTE £3.90: £1.30 £1.70 £2.40 (£13.40) OWNER Mr M. J. Legg (EPSOM) BRED J. Hutchinson
**IN-FOCUS: Runners raced far side.**
**3407* Blue River (IRE)**, out of a mare who won over two miles, was not inconvenienced by this extra furlong. (11/4)
**3171 Lady Godiva** stepped up the moderate tempo with over a quarter of a mile to go. Never able to shake off the winner, she finally got sent to Coventry in the last 150 yards. (8/1)
**3312 Swallow Breeze**, stepping up to a mile, would seemingly have preferred a stronger gallop. (14/1)
**3221* Right Tune** got caught flat-footed when pace was injected over a quarter of a mile out. (9/4)
**3417 Going For Broke** would have settled better in a stronger-run race. (12/1: 8/1-14/1)
**2759* Barnwood Crackers** was another who pulled because of the lack of early pace. (4/1)

T/Jkpt: £4,437.50 (19.15 Tckts). T/Plpt: £22.00 (1,530.46 Tckts). T/Qdpt: £14.20 (96.48 Tckts). KH

# 3501-SANDOWN (R-H) (Good to soft)
## Friday August 23rd
Race 3: hand-time
WEATHER: sunny WIND: slt half against

## 3763 THAMES DITTON NURSERY (S) H'CAP (2-Y.O) (Class E)
2-15 (2-16) **5f 6y** £3,420.00 (£1,035.00: £505.00: £240.00) Stalls: Low GOING minus 0.02 sec per fur (G)

| | | | | SP | RR | SF |
|---|---|---|---|---|---|---|
| 3523[4] | **Singforyoursupper (50)** (GGMargarson) **2-7-10** GBardwell(1) (rdn thrght: hdwy on ins 2f out: led ins fnl f: r.o wl) | — | 1 | 10/1 | 50 | — |
| 3311[4] | **Dozen Roses (51)** (TMJones) **2-7-11b** NCarlisle(3) (swtg: dwlt: rdn over 2f out: hdwy over 1f out: r.o) | ½ | 2 | 14/1 | 49 | — |
| 3336[2] | **Will To Win (60)** (PGMurphy) **2-8-3**(3) NVarley(6) (rdn & hdwy over 2f out: r.o one pce) | 1¼ | 3 | 6/1[3] | 54 | — |
| 3582[2] | **Le Shuttle (56)** (MHTompkins) **2-8-2** PRobinson(2) (a.p: ev ch over 1f out: wknd ins fnl f) | 4 | 4 | 100/30[1] | 38 | — |
| *2635*[4] | **Tinker's Surprise (IRE) (63)** (BJMeehan) **2-8-9** SSanders(8) (a.p: led 2f out tl ins fnl f: sn wknd) | ½ | 5 | 15/2 | 43 | — |
| 3455[2] | **Dancing Star (IRE) (54)** (PDEvans) **2-8-0**ow1 JFEgan(4) (b.off hind: led 3f: wkng whn n.m.r over 1f out) | 7 | 6 | 6/1[3] | 12 | — |
| 3251[5] | **Silver Lining (75)** (APJones) **2-9-7** WJO'Connor(5) (hld up: rdn over 2f out: sn wknd) | nk | 7 | 4/1[2] | 32 | — |
| 3488[2] | **Wedding Music (60)** (PCHaslam) **2-8-1**(5) MartinDwyer(7) (prom over 2f) | 1¾ | 8 | 4/1[2] | 11 | — |

(SP 119.2%) **8 Rn**

**65.55 secs** (5.75) CSF £116.57 CT £845.37 TOTE £12.20: £2.40 £2.50 £2.30 (£35.90) OWNER Mrs S. M. Martin (NEWMARKET) BRED Mrs L. Martin
No bid
**3523 Singforyoursupper**, dropped 10lb in the handicap, took advantage of it. Bustled along throughout, she picked up ground along the inside rail from halfway and, striking the front inside the final furlong, kept on well. (10/1)
**3311 Dozen Roses** began a forward move below the distance but, despite running on for second, failed to get on terms with the winner. (14/1)
**3336 Will To Win**, 15lb lower than when last appearing in a nursery, picked up ground at halfway and stayed on for third prize. (6/1: 9/2-7/1)
**3582 Le Shuttle**, who had to be mounted on the course, was a leading light from the off. With every chance below the distance, she had run out of petrol inside the final furlong. (100/30)
**2635 Tinker's Surprise (IRE)** went on a quarter of a mile out. Collared inside the final furlong, he had little left in the tank. (15/2)
**3455 Dancing Star (IRE)** set the pace. Collared a quarter of a mile out, she was soon in trouble. (6/1)

## 3764 AUGUST MAIDEN STKS (2-Y.O F) (Class D)
2-45 (2-53) **1m 14y** £3,485.00 (£1,055.00: £515.00: £245.00) Stalls: High GOING minus 0.02 sec per fur (G)

| | | | | SP | RR | SF |
|---|---|---|---|---|---|---|
| 3159[3] | **Happy Go Lucky** (RJO'Sullivan) **2-8-11** SSanders(4) (led 1f: led over 2f out: rdn out) | — | 1 | 7/1 | 78 | 31 |
| 3206[3] | **Elbaaha** (MAJarvis) **2-8-11** PRobinson(3) (hld up: rdn 2f out: chsd wnr over 1f out: unable qckn) | 1¾ | 2 | 2/1[2] | 75 | 28 |
| 3159[4] | **Elrayahin** (MajorWRHern) **2-8-11** RHills(1) (lw: hld up: rdn over 2f out: r.o one pce) | 1 | 3 | 11/2[3] | 73 | 26 |
| 3319[3] | **Saddlers' Hope** (JRFanshawe) **2-8-11** WRSwinburn(6) (hdwy 6f out: led over 4f out tl over 2f out: one pce) | ½ | 4 | 6/4[1] | 72 | 25 |
| 3159[W] | **Pretty Sharp** (APJarvis) **2-8-11** WJO'Connor(2) (neat: swtg: s.s: bhd fnl 2f) | 11 | 5 | 50/1 | 50 | 3 |
| 3159[5] | **French Mist** (CEBrittain) **2-8-8**(3) MHenry(5) (swtg: led 7f out tl over 4f out: wknd over 2f out) | 5 | 6 | 10/1 | 40 | — |

(SP 112.3%) **6 Rn**

**1m 47.62** (6.42) CSF £20.49 TOTE £8.20: £2.40 £1.60 (£13.90) OWNER Whitcombe Manor Racing Stables Ltd (WHITCOMBE) BRED Casterbridge Stud
**3159 Happy Go Lucky** appreciated the longer trip. In front for the first furlong, she regained the initiative over a quarter of a mile out and, ridden along, asserted her superiority. (7/1)

**3206 Elbaaha** appreciated the longer trip, if unable to gain the day. Held up travelling well, she was shaken up a quarter of a mile out when on the heels of the winner. However, she failed to find the necessary turn of foot and had to settle for second prize. (2/1: op 5/4)
**3159 Elrayahin** does lack a turn of foot. Chasing the leaders, she was bustled along a quarter of a mile from home and, despite staying on, never looked like finding the necessary acceleration. Staying is her game. (11/2: op 3/1)
**3319 Saddlers' Hope** was soon in a handy position. Sent on turning for home, she was collared over a quarter of a mile out and was tapped for toe. The soft ground may not have been in her favour and her trainer was obviously slightly concerned, as he was asking some of the jockeys on the walkway whether they thought he might have been better running the filly at Beverley the following day. She is worth another chance on a sounder surface. (6/4)
**Pretty Sharp**, who refused to enter the stalls and had to be withdrawn from her intended start at Goodwood recently, had to be mounted on the course and was taken down very sedately. Losing ground at the start, she was in trouble and losing touch approaching the final quarter-mile. (50/1)

## 3765 RON MILLER BIRTHDAY CELEBRATION H'CAP (0-85) (3-Y.O+) (Class D)

3-20 (3-23) **1m 14y** £4,260.00 (£1,290.00: £630.00: £300.00) Stalls: High GOING minus 0.02 sec per fur (G)

| | | | | SP | RR | SF |
|---|---|---|---|---|---|---|
| 3161* | **Koathary (USA) (63)** (LGCottrell) **5-8-11** JFEgan(9) (lw: nt clr run 3f out: hdwy 2f out: swtchd lft: led over 1f out: r.o wl) | — | 1 | 9/2[2] | 73 | 47 |
| 3501[7] | **Milos (60)** (TJNaughton) **5-8-8** RHills(7) (lw: rdn over 2f out: hdwy over 1f out: r.o one pce) | 3 | 2 | 16/1 | 64 | 38 |
| 3123[7] | **Nordinex (IRE) (75)** (RWArmstrong) **4-9-9** MHills(2) (lw: a.p: led over 2f out tl over 1f out: one pce) | nk | 3 | 7/1 | 79 | 53 |
| 3120[2] | **Bon Luck (IRE) (71)** (JRFanshawe) **4-9-5** NDay(5) (lw: hdwy 3f out: ev ch over 1f out: one pce) | 1 | 4 | 9/2[2] | 73 | 47 |
| 3516[3] | **Fionn de Cool (IRE) (70)** (RAkehurst) **5-9-4** SSanders(4) (lw: a.p: rdn 3f out: one pce fnl 2f) | 2 | 5 | 4/1[1] | 68 | 42 |
| 3430[6] | **Blaze of Song (74)** (RHannon) **4-9-8** DaneO'Neill(8) (lost pl 5f out: rallied & n.m.r on ins over 2f out: nt clr run on ins over 1f out: one pce) | ¾ | 6 | 13/2[3] | 70 | 44 |
| 3123[17] | **Bernard Seven (IRE) (76)** (CEBrittain) **4-9-10b** WJO'Connor(1) (led 2f: wknd over 2f out) | 5 | 7 | 14/1 | 62 | 36 |
| 3516[9] | **Prize Pupil (IRE) (69)** (CFWall) **4-9-3** NCarlisle(6) (hdwy 7f out: led 6f out tl over 2f out: wknd wl over 1f out) | 1¼ | 8 | 8/1 | 53 | 27 |
| 755[3] | **Mansab (USA) (74)** (PGMurphy) **3-9-2** JTate(3) (lw: bhd fnl 3f) | 12 | 9 | 7/1 | 34 | 2 |
| | | | | (SP 118.4%) | **9 Rn** | |

**1m 45.9** (4.70) CSF £62.87 CT £461.19 TOTE £5.40: £1.70 £4.90 £1.90 (£53.90) Trio £157.80 OWNER Mr E. J. S. Gadsden (CULLOMPTON) BRED Calumet Farm
WEIGHT FOR AGE 3yo-6lb
**3161* Koathary (USA)** began to creep closer in the straight and, coming through to lead below the distance, kept on really well. (9/2)
**1516 Milos**, racing at the back of the field, stayed on up the hill in the last furlong and a half to snatch second prize in the last few strides. (16/1)
**2885 Nordinex (IRE)** made his bid for glory over a quarter of a mile out but, collared below the distance, failed to find another gear. (7/1)
**3120 Bon Luck (IRE)** moved into contention early in the straight. Throwing down his challenge, he still had every chance below the distance before tapped for toe. He is still a maiden. (9/2)
**3516 Fionn de Cool (IRE)**, bustled along early in the straight, was made to look very pedestrian in the last two furlongs. (4/1: 3/1-9/2)
**1469 Blaze of Song** met with a lot of traffic problems but, once he found racing room, he failed to pick up from below the distance. (13/2)
**2145 Prize Pupil (IRE)** (8/1: op 5/1)

## 3766 HINCHLEY WOOD LIMITED STKS (0-80) (3-Y.O+) (Class D)

3-50 (3-53) **1m 3f 91y** £3,712.50 (£1,125.00: £550.00: £262.50) Stalls: High GOING minus 0.02 sec per fur (G)

| | | | | SP | RR | SF |
|---|---|---|---|---|---|---|
| 2074[20] | **Traceability (79)** (SCWilliams) **3-8-11** GCarter(5) (lw: chsd ldr: led over 1f out: rdn out) | — | 1 | 3/1[3] | 92 | 32 |
| 2882[7] | **Step Aloft (76)** (LordHuntingdon) **4-9-1** WRSwinburn(1) (lw: led 10f: unable qckn) | 2½ | 2 | 6/5[1] | 84 | 33 |
| 3521* | **Diminutive (USA) (79)** (JWHills) **3-8-12(3)** MHenry(3) (lw: plld hrd: hld up: rdn over 2f out: one pce) | 1¾ | 3 | 13/8[2] | 90 | 30 |
| *3608*[8] | **Zacaroon (65)** (JFfitch-Heyes) **5-9-1** SSanders(4) (lw: a bhd) | 20 | 4 | 16/1 | 53 | 2 |
| | | | | (SP 114.4%) | **4 Rn** | |

**2m 32.31** (8.91) CSF £7.07 TOTE £5.00: (£3.10) OWNER Mr J. W. Lovitt (NEWMARKET) BRED J. S. A. and Mrs Shorthouse
WEIGHT FOR AGE 3yo-9lb
**1687* Traceability** raced in second place. Asked for his effort, he moved to the front approaching the final furlong and, ridden along, kept on well. (3/1)
**2591 Step Aloft** does not seem to know how to win. Setting a moderate pace, she quickened things up in the straight but, collared below the distance, was tapped for toe. She has now finished second in six of her nine outings, a statistic which says it all. (6/5)
**3521* Diminutive (USA)** refused to settle at the back of the field. Asked for his effort over a quarter of a mile from home, he failed to quicken in up in the ground. The soft surface was not in his favour. (13/8: Evens-7/4)

## 3767 WALTON MAIDEN STKS (3-Y.O+ F & M) (Class D)

4-20 (4-24) **7f 16y** £3,598.75 (£1,090.00: £532.50: £253.75) Stalls: High GOING minus 0.02 sec per fur (G)

| | | | | SP | RR | SF |
|---|---|---|---|---|---|---|
| 678[4] | **Kerry Ring** (JHMGosden) **3-8-11** AMcGlone(9) (a.p: rdn over 1f out: led wl ins fnl f: drvn out) | — | 1 | 9/4[1] | 82 | 47 |
| 3255[5] | **Meznh (IRE)** (HThomsonJones) **3-8-11** RHills(6) (lw: a.p: led over 2f out: hrd rdn over 1f out: hdd wl ins fnl f: r.o wl) | nk | 2 | 5/1 | 81 | 46 |
| 2686[3] | **Out Line (68)** (MMadgwick) **4-8-13(3)** NVarley(2) (rdn over 3f out: hdwy over 1f out: r.o) | 3 | 3 | 12/1 | 75 | 45 |
| 3353[3] | **Really A Dream (IRE) (75)** (MRStoute) **3-8-11** WRSwinburn(8) (led over 4f: hrd rdn over 1f out: sn wknd) | 1¾ | 4 | 4/1[2] | 71 | 36 |
| | **Windrush Holly** (JRBosley) **3-8-11** CRutter(1) (unf: rdn & hdwy over 2f out: wknd over 1f out) | 2 | 5 | 33/1 | 66 | 31 |
| | **Scherma** (WJarvis) **3-8-11** WJO'Connor(3) (w'like: scope: bit bkwd: nvr plcd to chal) | 4 | 6 | 16/1 | 57 | 22 |
| 3162[9] | **Shining Cloud (70)** (LGCottrell) **3-8-11** JFEgan(7) (lw: prom over 4f) | ½ | 7 | 16/1 | 56 | 21 |
| 3162[F] | **Desert Serenade (USA)** (EALDunlop) **3-8-11** SWhitworth(4) (b: hld up: rdn over 2f out: sn wknd) | ½ | 8 | 4/1[2] | 55 | 20 |
| 3446[5] | **Danlora** (WJarvis) **3-8-11** MHills(10) (lw: bhd fnl 3f) | 2½ | 9 | 9/2[3] | 49 | 14 |
| | | | | (SP 128.0%) | **9 Rn** | |

**1m 32.76** (4.16) CSF £15.03 TOTE £3.10: £1.50 £1.90 £3.30 (£10.40) Trio £52.30 OWNER Sheikh Mohammed (NEWMARKET) BRED Sheikh Mohammed bin Rashid al Maktoum
WEIGHT FOR AGE 3yo-5lb
**678 Kerry Ring**, given a four-month break, belied her rather burly paddock appearance. Always close up, her jockey had to get down to some serious work in the final furlong to get her up in the closing stages. (9/4: 6/4-5/2)
**3255 Meznh (IRE)**, a lot wiser for her Thirsk debut, moved to the front travelling well over a quarter of a mile from home. Under pressure below the distance, she refused to give way without a struggle and only went down in the closing stages. Despite being only lightly-made, she should soon find a race. (5/1)

**2686 Out Line**, bustled along and going nowhere at the back of the field, stayed on up the hill to snatch third prize. (12/1)
**3353 Really A Dream (IRE)** took the field along. Collared over a quarter of a mile from home, she had nothing left in reserve inside the distance. (4/1)
**Windrush Holly** made an effort over a quarter of a mile from home, but was a spent force below the distance. (33/1)
**Scherma**, a plain, good-bodied filly, looked as though the run was needed and, under considerate handling, never threatened to get into it. She should come on for this. (16/1)

## 3768 SURREY RACING H'CAP (0-80) (3-Y.O) (Class D)
4-50 (4-51) **1m 6f** £3,875.00 (£1,175.00: £575.00: £275.00) Stalls: High GOING minus 0.02 sec per fur (G)

| Form | Horse | Dist | Pos | SP | RR | SF |
|---|---|---|---|---|---|---|
| $3249^{5}$ | **Roseberry Avenue (IRE) (67)** (LadyHerries) **3-8-10** WJO'Connor(3) (lw: a.p: led over 3f out: clr over 1f out: r.o wl) | — | 1 | $2/1^{1}$ | 76 | 45 |
| $2433^{2}$ | **Charming Admiral (IRE) (68)** (CFWall) **3-8-11** SSanders(5) (rdn & hdwy 4f out: chsd wnr over 1f out: no imp) | 5 | 2 | $7/2^{2}$ | 71 | 40 |
| $3398^{2}$ | **Major Dundee (IRE) (76)** (RHannon) **3-9-5** DaneO'Neill(2) (lw: rdn & hdwy over 2f out: one pce) | 1 | 3 | $6/1^{3}$ | 78 | 47 |
| $1854^{3}$ | **Shooting Light (IRE) (78)** (PGMurphy) **3-9-7** MHills(1) (lw: a.p: led 6f out tl over 3f out: one pce fnl 2f) | hd | 4 | $6/1^{3}$ | 80 | 49 |
| *3422** | **State Approval (63)** (APJarvis) **3-7-13**(7) CCarver(6) (bhd fnl 4f) | 10 | 5 | $7/2^{2}$ | 54 | 23 |
| $2570^{8}$ | **Rivercare (IRE) (60)** (MJPolglase) **3-8-3** NCarlisle(4) (lw: led 8f) | 7 | 6 | 8/1 | 43 | 12 |

(SP 117.5%) **6 Rn**

**3m 7.33** (8.43) CSF £9.46 TOTE £2.90: £1.80 £2.50 (£3.60) OWNER Mr P. D. Savill (LITTLEHAMPTON) BRED Lowquest Ltd
**3249 Roseberry Avenue (IRE)** relished the step up in trip and really came into his own. Sent on entering the straight, he forged clear in the final quarter-mile to win in fine style. (2/1)
**2433 Charming Admiral (IRE)** moved up turning for home but, despite struggling into second place at the distance, never threatened to get on terms with the winner. (7/2)
**3398 Major Dundee (IRE)** made an effort over a quarter of a mile from home, but could then only plod on at one pace. (6/1: 4/1-13/2)
**1854 Shooting Light (IRE)**, sold out of Michael Jarvis's stable for 21,000 guineas, went on turning out of the back straight. Collared over three furlongs from home, he was left for dead by the winner below the distance. (6/1: 7/2-13/2)
**3422* State Approval** (7/2: 5/2-4/1)

T/Plpt: £1,742.60 (7.32 Tckts). T/Qdpt: £72.40 (14.46 Tckts). AK

# 3460-THIRSK (L-H) (Good)
## Friday August 23rd
WEATHER: overcast, rain and sunny periods later WIND: almost nil

## 3769 PETER BEAUMONT (S) STKS (2-Y.O) (Class F)
2-25 (2-31) **7f** £2,845.00 (£795.00: £385.00) Stalls: Low GOING minus 0.13 sec per fur (G)

| Form | Horse | Dist | Pos | SP | RR | SF |
|---|---|---|---|---|---|---|
| $3448^{5}$ | **Soviet Lady (IRE) (55)** (JLEyre) **2-8-6** TWilliams(8) (trckd ldrs: led over 1f out: styd on) | — | 1 | $6/1^{3}$ | 59 | 9 |
| $3405^{3}$ | **Maraud (64)** (RWArmstrong) **2-8-11** KDarley(3) (lw: cl up: rdn over 2f out: ev ch over 1f out: styd on one pce) | 1¼ | 2 | $4/5^{1}$ | 61 | 11 |
| $3467^{7}$ | **Corncrake (IRE) (65)** (BJMeehan) **2-8-6** MTebbutt(7) (mde most tl hdd over 1f out: sn btn) | 1 | 3 | $9/2^{2}$ | 54 | 4 |
| $916^{8}$ | **Time Can Tell** (CMurray) **2-8-11** DeanMcKeown(4) (b: bhd: styd on fnl 3f: nrst fin) | 1½ | 4 | 12/1 | 55 | 5 |
| $3576^{2}$ | **Norbreck House** (JBerry) **2-8-11** JCarroll(10) (hdwy appr st: sn chsng ldrs: hung bdly lft 2f out: sn btn) | 6 | 5 | 9/1 | 42 | — |
| $2802^{8}$ | **Kickonsun (IRE)** (RAFahey) **2-8-11** JFortune(6) (nvr trbld ldrs) | 6 | 6 | 20/1 | 28 | — |
| $3448^{8}$ | **Who (IRE)** (TDEasterby) **2-8-6**(5) RHavlin(5) (b.hind: uns rdr & bolted leaving paddock: prom to st) | 8 | 7 | 16/1 | 10 | — |
| $3576^{4}$ | **Oddfellows Girl** (NBycroft) **2-8-6** JLowe(11) (cl up: wkng whn bmpd 2f out) | ¾ | 8 | 20/1 | 3 | — |
| $3576^{3}$ | **Silver Raj (50)** (WTKemp) **2-8-4b**(7) KSked(1) (s.s: a wl bhd) | 1¾ | 9 | 20/1 | 4 | — |
| $3080^{12}$ | **Zydecho Queen** (PCalver) **2-8-6** MBirch(2) (lw: cl up tl lost pl appr st) | 17 | 10 | 20/1 | — | — |
| *$3576^{5}$* | ***Bloomsy Babe*** (JJQuinn) **2-8-6b**[1] DaleGibson(9) (Withdrawn not under Starter's orders: uns rdr & bolted bef s) | | W | 33/1 | — | — |

(SP 133.6%) **10 Rn**

**1m 30.3** (6.10) CSF £11.89 TOTE £7.20: £1.80 £1.20 £1.60 (£5.40) Trio £6.60 OWNER Mrs Patricia Waldron (HAMBLETON) BRED Rathbarry Stud
No bid
**3448 Soviet Lady (IRE)** sat in behind the leaders and, once she struck the front approaching the final furlong, she was then always doing just enough under pressure. (6/1)
**3405 Maraud** is nothing much to look at, but has fair ability. However, he was never finding enough under pressure in the home straight. (4/5)
**2995 Corncrake (IRE)**, at her first attempt over this trip, tried forcing tactics, but had shot her bolt approaching the last furlong. (9/2: 3/1-5/1)
**Time Can Tell** has not been out for over three months and, stepping up in trip, ran a useful race, and looks well worth keeping in mind. (12/1: op 8/1)
**3576 Norbreck House** has plenty of ability, but all he wanted to do was hang left, and his rider had all sorts of problems. (9/1: op 7/2)

## 3770 MICK EASTERBY LIMITED STKS (0-80) (3-Y.O+) (Class D)
2-55 (2-58) **1m** £4,027.25 (£1,208.00: £581.50: £268.25) Stalls: Low GOING minus 0.13 sec per fur (G)

| Form | Horse | Dist | Pos | SP | RR | SF |
|---|---|---|---|---|---|---|
| $3430^{7}$ | **Queens Consul (IRE) (80)** (BSRothwell) **6-9-2** MFenton(6) (mde all: kpt on wl fnl 2f) | — | 1 | $4/1^{2}$ | 88 | 39 |
| $2197^{3}$ | **Dilazar (USA) (79)** (JRFanshawe) **3-8-11** JCarroll(5) (lw: a chsng wnr: effrt over 2f out: nvr able to chal) | 2½ | 2 | 6/1 | 84 | 29 |
| $3461^{2}$ | **Royal Ceilidh (IRE) (75)** (DenysSmith) **3-8-10** JFortune(2) (a.p: hdwy u.p 2f out: nt qckn fnl f) | 3 | 3 | 5/1 | 77 | 22 |
| $2679^{4}$ | **Cashmere Lady (74)** (JLEyre) **4-9-2** TWilliams(1) (hld up: effrt over 2f out: nvr rchd ldrs) | 1¾ | 4 | $9/2^{3}$ | 74 | 25 |
| *$3627^{2}$* | **Serious Sensation (79)** (SirMarkPrescott) **3-8-13** GDuffield(4) (lw: hld up: effrt over 2f out: rdn & no hdwy) | 5 | 5 | $5/4^{1}$ | 67 | 12 |
| $3413^{4}$ | **Mubariz (IRE) (75)** (CSmith) **4-9-3** KDarley(3) (lost tch & eased fnl 3f) | dist | 6 | 50/1 | — | — |

(SP 115.5%) **6 Rn**

**1m 41.4** (4.90) CSF £25.16 TOTE £5.00: £3.00 £1.80 (£10.40) OWNER Miss Heather Davison (MALTON) BRED Mrs Ann Galvin
WEIGHT FOR AGE 3yo-6lb
**2693 Queens Consul (IRE)**, after trying more patient tactics of late, was back to front-running here. Really enjoying herself, she never looked likely to be caught. (4/1)

**2197 Dilazar (USA)** looked particularly fit and always held a good position but, when an effort was required, he wandered about and failed to respond sufficiently. (6/1)
**3461 Royal Ceilidh (IRE)** runs well here, but she was always struggling to improve and, despite a forceful ride, was never up to the task. (5/1)
**2679 Cashmere Lady**, after six weeks off, ran quite well and should be all the better for it. (9/2)
**3627 Serious Sensation** was a big disappointment, failing to respond to pressure in the last two furlongs. It seemed important to be up with the pace on this rain-softened ground, and he never was. (5/4)
**3413 Mubariz (IRE)** obviously had a problem as his rider eased him considerably in the home straight. (50/1)

## 3771 JIMMY FITZGERALD NURSERY H'CAP (2-Y.O) (Class D)

3-25 (3-25) **6f** £4,011.00 (£1,203.00: £579.00: £267.00) Stalls: High GOING minus 0.13 sec per fur (G)

| | | | | SP | RR | SF |
|---|---|---|---|---|---|---|
| 3577* | **Perfect Bliss (71)** (PDEvans) **2-7-7**(7) 7x RFfrench(1) (lw: mde most: wandered u.p & hld on wl) | — | **1** | 5/2$^{2}$ | 72 | 16 |
| 2237$^{2}$ | **Brutal Fantasy (IRE) (71)** (JLEyre) **2-8-0** TWilliams(6) (b.off hind: trckd wnr: chal 2f out: sn rdn: sltly hmpd & swtchd appr fnl f: no ex) | 1½ | **2** | 9/4$^{1}$ | 68 | 12 |
| 3577$^{4}$ | **Super Saint (67)** (TDBarron) **2-7-10** JLowe(5) (in tch: kpt on fnl 2f: nvr nrr) | 1¼ | **3** | 11/2 | 61 | 5 |
| 3275$^{5}$ | **Mill End Boy (69)** (MWEasterby) **2-7-12** DaleGibson(4) (s.i.s: styd on u.p fnl 2f: nrst fin) | nk | **4** | 6/1 | 62 | 6 |
| 2726$^{2}$ | **Bayford Thrust (92)** (JBerry) **2-9-7** JCarroll(3) (b.nr hind: chsd ldrs tl wknd fnl 2f) | 1¾ | **5** | 9/2$^{3}$ | 80 | 24 |
| 2309$^{10}$ | **Red Garter (IRE) (68)** (KMcAuliffe) **2-7-6**(5) CAdamson(2) (reard s: sn prom: outpcd fnl 2f) | nk | **6** | 20/1 | 55 | — |

(SP 112.0%) **6 Rn**

**1m 13.8** (4.10) CSF £8.22 TOTE £2.80: £1.20 £1.70 (£4.00) OWNER Mr R. F. F. Mason (WELSHPOOL) BRED Mrs H. B. Raw
LONG HANDICAP Super Saint 7-9
STEWARDS' ENQUIRY Ffrench susp. 5-6/9/96 (careless riding).
**3577* Perfect Bliss** refuses to be beaten at the moment. She did wander about under pressure slightly, hampering the runner-up, but it made not the slightest difference. (5/2)
**2237 Brutal Fantasy (IRE)** always looked likely to win this, but he failed to come up with the goods. To give him the benefit this time, it was his first run for almost two months. (9/4)
**3577 Super Saint** kept staying on to suggest that a bit further might help. (11/2)
**3275 Mill End Boy** failed to fire on this occasion, despite staying on at the end, and could need a bit further. (6/1)
**2726 Bayford Thrust**, returning here after six weeks off, went fast until running out of fuel approaching the last furlong. (9/2)
**1479 Red Garter (IRE)**, coming back after a rest, ran reasonably until blowing up in the last quarter-mile. (20/1)

## 3772 TIM EASTERBY H'CAP (0-75) (3-Y.O+) (Class D)

3-55 (3-55) **2m** £3,939.50 (£1,181.00: £568.00: £261.50) Stalls: Low GOING minus 0.13 sec per fur (G)

| | | | | SP | RR | SF |
|---|---|---|---|---|---|---|
| 2804$^{3}$ | **Dirab (70)** (TDBarron) **3-9-5** JFortune(3) (lw: mde all: pushed along 3f out: r.o) | — | **1** | 9/4$^{3}$ | 84 | 35 |
| *3437*$^{2}$ | **Chris's Lad (61)** (BJMeehan) **5-9-10b** MTebbutt(2) (chsd ldr to ½-wy: sn outpcd: styd on u.p fnl 2f: no imp) | 2 | **2** | 2/1$^{2}$ | 73 | 38 |
| 3428* | **Arian Spirit (IRE) (53)** (JLEyre) **5-9-2** TWilliams(1) (lw: hdwy to chse wnr ½-wy: rdn 3f out: btn 2f out) | 5 | **3** | 7/4$^{1}$ | 60 | 25 |
| 3463$^{3}$ | **Sharp Sensation (40)** (DWBarker) **6-8-3**ow2 JCarroll(4) (lw: hld up: effrt 3f out: no rspnse) | 6 | **4** | 7/1 | 41 | 4 |

(SP 113.0%) **4 Rn**

**3m 34.7** (11.70) CSF £6.89 TOTE £3.20: (£5.90) OWNER Mr Alex Gorrie (THIRSK) BRED Nawara Stud Co Ltd
WEIGHT FOR AGE 3yo-14lb
**2804 Dirab**, given a fine tactical ride, warmed the pace up once into the straight and never had to be seriously knocked about to hold on. (9/4)
**3437 Chris's Lad** got tapped for toe at halfway and, although staying on in the end, never looked likely to get back on terms. (2/1)
**3428* Arian Spirit (IRE)** had her chances from halfway, but she failed to pick up when pressure was applied early in the straight. (7/4)
**3463 Sharp Sensation** sat just off the pace going well but, once asked, failed to pick up at all. More aggressive tactics might help. (7/1)

## 3773 E.B.F. NIGEL TINKLER MAIDEN STKS (2-Y.O) (Class D)

4-25 (4-25) **6f** £4,186.50 (£1,257.00: £606.00: £280.50) Stalls: High GOING minus 0.13 sec per fur (G)

| | | | | SP | RR | SF |
|---|---|---|---|---|---|---|
| | **Starborough** (DRLoder) **2-9-0** KDarley(11) (w'like: scope: lw: mde all: easily) | — | **1** | 2/5$^{1}$ | 76++ | 34 |
| 3319$^{12}$ | **Indian Blaze** (PWHarris) **2-9-0** ACulhane(5) (lw: in tch: hdwy 2f out: r.o: no ch w wnr) | 3 | **2** | 8/1$^{2}$ | 68 | 26 |
| | **All In Leather** (WJHaggas) **2-8-9** RMcGhin(4) (w'like: str: s.i.s: hld up & bhd: stdy hdwy fnl 2f: nvr plcd to chal) | 7 | **3** | 8/1$^{2}$ | 44+ | 2 |
| | **Splashed** (TDBarron) **2-8-9** JFortune(1) (neat: scope: bit bkwd: chsd ldrs: hung lft 2f out: nt qckn) | 2 | **4** | 25/1 | 39 | — |
| | **Erosion (IRE)** (MJohnston) **2-9-0** JCarroll(7) (angular: bit bkwd: s.i.s: hdwy ½-wy: nvr nr to chal) | 1 | **5** | 14/1$^{3}$ | 41 | — |
| 3494$^{8}$ | **Marytavy** (SirMarkPrescott) **2-8-9** GDuffield(9) (bhd tl sme late hdwy) | 3 | **6** | 8/1$^{2}$ | 28 | — |
| 3464$^{9}$ | **William's Well** (MWEasterby) **2-9-0** DaleGibson(2) (chsd ldrs over 4f) | ¾ | **7** | 100/1 | 31 | — |
| | **Fantasy Flight** (MrsJRRamsden) **2-8-9** MFenton(10) (w'like: outpcd fr ½-wy) | s.h | **8** | 16/1 | 26 | — |
| 3349$^{12}$ | **Paldost** (MDHammond) **2-9-0** MBirch(8) (outpcd & bhd fr ½-wy) | ¾ | **9** | 100/1 | 29 | — |
| | **Onemoretime** (BWMurray) **2-8-9** TWilliams(6) (unf: b.hind: gd spd to ½-wy: wknd qckly) | 6 | **10** | 50/1 | 8 | — |

(SP 125.1%) **10 Rn**

**1m 13.4** (3.70) CSF £5.40 TOTE £1.20: £1.10 £2.20 £2.20 (£6.10) Trio £21.60 OWNER Sheikh Mohammed (NEWMARKET) BRED Sheikh Mohammed Bin Rashid Al Maktoum
OFFICIAL EXPLANATION **All In Leather: the rider reported that the filly became fractious in the stalls, lost ground at the start and ran green. As a result, he had to keep her balanced.**
**Starborough**, a useful type, won as he pleased and can go on to better things. He does have the look of a bit of a character about him, and was declared to wear a tongue-strap, which he refused to have fitted. (2/5)
**Indian Blaze** took the eye in the paddock and ran a fair race, but the winner was in a different league. (8/1)
**All In Leather**, a well-made individual, was given what can only be described as an educational run here, and showed plenty under very tender handling. Yeast, from the same stable, started his career at this track in fairly similar fashion. (8/1)
**Splashed** showed promise aplenty, but the only worrying thing was her tendency to hang left. (25/1)
**Erosion (IRE)** needed this both experience and fitness wise, but has ability, and better will be seen with time. (14/1)
**Marytavy**, a most laid-back filly, showed something and looks a good long-term prospect. (8/1)

## 3774 MAURICE CAMACHO H'CAP (0-70) (3-Y.O+) (Class E)

4-55 (4-56) **5f** £3,549.75 (£1,068.00: £516.50: £240.75) Stalls: High GOING minus 0.13 sec per fur (G)

| | | | | SP | RR | SF |
|---|---|---|---|---|---|---|
| 3643$^{2}$ | **Oatey (60)** (MrsJRRamsden) **3-9-4** JFortune(8) (bhd: hdwy ½-wy: squeezed thro wl over 1f out: r.o u.s.p to ld cl home) | — | **1** | 13/8$^{1}$ | 67 | 47 |

| Form | Horse / details | Dist | Pos | SP | RR | SF |
|---|---|---|---|---|---|---|
| 3310* | **Kalar (53)** (DWChapman) **7-8-13b** KDarley(10) (lw: led: rdn over 1f out: r.o: jst ct) | nk | **2** | 11/4[2] | 59 | 41 |
| 3643* | **Kira (70)** (JLEyre) **6-9-13**(3) 7x OPears(3) (lw: b.off hind: a cl up: kpt on u.p fnl f) | 1½ | **3** | 6/1[3] | 71 | 53 |
| 3294[2] | **Good To Talk (43)** (TDEasterby) **3-8-1b**[1] JFanning(7) (a cl up: no ex appr fnl f) | nk | **4** | 12/1 | 43 | 23 |
| 2571[7] | **Branston Danni (70)** (MrsJRRamsden) **3-10-0** JCarroll(6) (b.nr hind: hld up: hdwy 2f out: n.m.r 1f out: nvr nr to chal) | 1¾ | **5** | 25/1 | 65 | 45 |
| 2968[3] | **Mister Joel (60)** (MWEasterby) **3-9-4b** DaleGibson(11) (pushed along thrght: chsd ldrs: nt qckn appr fnl f) | 1¾ | **6** | 13/2 | 49 | 29 |
| | **Arasong (58)** (EWeymes) **4-9-4** RLappin(12) (prom 3f: sltly hmpd & no imp after) | ½ | **7** | 20/1 | 46 | 28 |
| 3317[5] | **Harriet's Beau (38)** (MWEasterby) **3-7-5b**(5) CAdamson(5) (cl up: rdn ½-wy: wknd over 1f out) | ¾ | **8** | 25/1 | 23 | 3 |
| *3091*[6] | **Time To Fly (46)** (BWMurray) **3-8-4** TWilliams(4) (in tch: effrt ½-wy: no imp) | ½ | **9** | 33/1 | 30 | 10 |
| 3465[4] | **Comic Fantasy (AUS) (69)** (MartynWane) **3-9-13b** NConnorton(2) (lw: prom 3f: sn wknd) | 3½ | **10** | 14/1 | 41 | 21 |
| 2902[12] | **Dancing Jazztime (40)** (JSWainwright) **5-7-7**(7)ow4 RFfrench(9) (spd to ½-wy) | 1¾ | **11** | 100/1 | 7 | — |
| 3460[9] | **Double Glow (36)** (NBycroft) **4-7-10b** JLowe(1) (nvr wnt pce) | 1¼ | **12** | 50/1 | — | — |
| | | | | (SP 125.1%) | | **12 Rn** |

**60.5 secs** (2.50) CSF £6.79 CT £21.34 TOTE £2.40: £1.40 £1.30 £2.20 (£4.00) Trio £5.30 OWNER Mr R. Barnett (THIRSK) BRED W. and R. Barnett Ltd

LONG HANDICAP Harriet's Beau 7-3 Dancing Jazztime 6-4 Double Glow 7-1

WEIGHT FOR AGE 3yo-2lb

**3643 Oatey**, given a brilliant ride, produced a storming run to settle it late on and gain a thoroughly-deserved success. (13/8)

**3310* Kalar** had the draw and the speed to make full use of it, but just found one too good. He looks particularly well at the moment. (11/4)

**3643* Kira** ran another fine race from a virtually impossible draw, but was always fighting a lost cause in the last furlong and a half. (6/1)

**3294 Good To Talk**, previously in a visor, was in blinkers this time and showed plenty of speed, but just failed to quicken enough when it mattered. (12/1: op 8/1)

**2571 Branston Danni** was putting in some useful work in the last two furlongs, but was then short of room at vital stages, and this edgy sort was not knocked about. (25/1)

**2968 Mister Joel** normally likes to blast off in front, but could never go the pace on this occasion and failed to offer a threat. (13/2)

T/Plpt: £30.80 (305.04 Tckts). T/Qdpt: £8.70 (58.24 Tckts). AA

# 3507-**BEVERLEY** (R-H) (Good)

## Saturday August 24th

WEATHER: fine WIND: mod across

## 3775 DRIFFIELD (S) H'CAP (0-60) (3-Y.O+) (Class G)

2-20 (2-21) **2m 35y** £2,322.00 (£642.00: £306.00) Stalls: High GOING minus 0.27 sec per fur (GF)

| Form | Horse / details | Dist | Pos | SP | RR | SF |
|---|---|---|---|---|---|---|
| 3149[5] | **Jalcanto (51)** (MrsMReveley) **6-9-10** ACulhane(3) (rdn along & hdwy 9f out: led wl over 1f out: drvn out) | — | **1** | 7/4[1] | 62 | 23 |
| | **Kesanta (35)** (WGMTurner) **6-8-1**(7)ow1 DSweeney(9) (b: hld up: hdwy 4f out: chsd wnr appr fnl f: one pce) | 2½ | **2** | 9/1 | 44 | 4 |
| *2936*[3] | **Top Prize (34)** (MBrittain) **8-8-7v** JLowe(8) (chsd ldrs tl outpcd 4f out: sn lost pl: sme late hdwy) | 2½ | **3** | 5/2[2] | 40 | 1 |
| *3605*[7] | **Havana Heights (IRE) (40)** (JLEyre) **3-7-13** TWilliams(7) (chsd ldrs: drvn along 4f out: one pce) | 1½ | **4** | 16/1 | 45 | — |
| 3308[3] | **Punch (36)** (NTinkler) **4-8-9b** KDarley(6) (lw: led tl hdd wl over 1f out: sn lost pl) | 5 | **5** | 7/1[3] | 36 | — |
| 2928[3] | **Phar Closer (37)** (WTKemp) **3-7-10** NKennedy(5) (chsd ldrs tl wknd fnl 3f) | 1¼ | **6** | 14/1 | 35 | — |
| 3335[11] | **Ttyfran (34)** (BPJBaugh) **6-8-7** WLord(2) (b: chsd ldrs: rdn 4f out: sn wknd) | 20 | **7** | 8/1 | 13 | — |
| 2626[4] | **Miss Express (BEL) (39)** (MrsSJSmith) **3-7-12**ow2 DaleGibson(4) (outpcd & lost tch fnl 4f) | 30 | **8** | 33/1 | — | — |
| 3507[4] | **Grey Sonata (33)** (TJEtherington) **9-8-6** MBirch(1) (prom tl lost pl 10f out: sn t.o: fin lame) | 18 | **9** | 9/1 | — | — |
| | | | | (SP 124.0%) | | **9 Rn** |

**3m 44.2** (13.70) CSF £18.31 CT £38.76 TOTE £3.00: £1.40 £3.10 £1.70 (£17.30) Trio £13.20 OWNER The Mary Reveley Racing Club (SALTBURN) BRED Southcourt Stud

LONG HANDICAP Miss Express (BEL) 7-9 Phar Closer 7-9

WEIGHT FOR AGE 3yo-14lb

No bid

**3149 Jalcanto** appreciated this drop in class and, well handled, scored in good style. (7/4)

**Kesanta**, having her first run for three years, ran pretty well and will no doubt make her mark over hurdles. (9/1: 8/1-12/1)

**2936 Top Prize** looked woefully slow when getting outpaced approaching the straight and, despite keeping on in the closing stages, had no further chance. (5/2)

**370 Havana Heights (IRE)**, trying her longest trip to date, looked slow in the last half-mile. (16/1)

**3308 Punch** appeared to be going well enough in front until suddenly downing tools altogether entering the last two furlongs. (7/1)

## 3776 SNOWY GRAY MEMORIAL MAIDEN STKS (3-Y.O+) (Class D)

2-50 (2-51) **2m 35y** £3,847.00 (£1,156.00: £558.00: £259.00) Stalls: High GOING minus 0.27 sec per fur (GF)

| Form | Horse / details | Dist | Pos | SP | RR | SF |
|---|---|---|---|---|---|---|
| 2576[4] | **Northern Fleet (77)** (GHarwood) **3-8-7** KDarley(4) (trckd ldrs: effrt 6f out: led 1½f out: hung rt: styd on) | — | **1** | 5/4[1] | 78 | 28 |
| 677[15] | **Safa (USA)** (ACStewart) **3-8-2** TWilliams(2) (pushed along after 6f: in tch: hdwy 4f out: styd on: nvr able to chal) | 2½ | **2** | 8/1[3] | 71 | 21 |
| 3355[3] | **Shirley Venture (72)** (SPCWoods) **3-7-13**(3) MHenry(5) (lw: led tl hdd 1½f out: sn btn) | nk | **3** | 11/8[2] | 70 | 20 |
| 3298[6] | **Nirvana Prince** (BPreece) **7-9-7** VSlattery(1) (prom: rdn ½-wy: one pce) | 11 | **4** | 16/1 | 64? | 28 |
| | **Euphoric Illusion** (MrsSJSmith) **5-9-4**(3) OPears(6) (tall: cl up: rdn 5f out: wknd 3f out) | 29 | **5** | 8/1[3] | 36? | — |
| | **Kaye's Secret** (CSmith) **3-8-2** FNorton(3) (unf: lost tch ½-wy: t.o fnl 6f) | dist | **6** | 50/1 | — | — |
| | | | | (SP 116.6%) | | **6 Rn** |

**3m 39.5** (9.00) CSF £11.11 TOTE £2.00: £1.60 £3.10 (£4.40) OWNER Mr K. Abdulla (PULBOROUGH) BRED Juddmonte Farms

WEIGHT FOR AGE 3yo-14lb

**2576 Northern Fleet** wears a pricker on his off-side and certainly needs it as he was always tending to hang right. He also appreciated this longer trip and won most convincingly. (5/4: op Evens)

**Safa (USA)**, taking a big step up in distance, was flat out before halfway but, to her credit, she did keep staying on, but she would have needed another circuit to get to the winner. (8/1: 6/1-9/1)

**3355 Shirley Venture**, happy to make it, had little more to offer once tackled approaching the final furlong. (11/8)

**Nirvana Prince** looked very one-paced once off the bit from halfway. (16/1)

**Euphoric Illusion** had run reasonably in bumpers last winter, but was disappointing here and this big sort will probably be happier over hurdles. (8/1)

## 3777 ST JOHN AMBULANCE H'CAP (0-70) (3-Y.O+) (Class E)
3-25 (3-27) **7f 100y** £3,158.00 (£944.00: £452.00: £206.00) Stalls: High GOING minus 0.27 sec per fur (GF)

| | | | | SP | RR | SF |
|---|---|---|---|---|---|---|
| 3510[4] | **Euro Sceptic (IRE) (55)** (TDEasterby) **4-9-2b**(5) RHavlin(12) (trckd ldrs: nt clr run 2f out: hdwy 1f out: r.o to ld post) | — | 1 | 7/1[3] | 64 | 46 |
| 3344[3] | **Thatched (IRE) (44)** (REBarr) **6-8-10** DeanMcKeown(10) (lw: a.p: led appr fnl f: sn rdn: jst ct) | s.h | 2 | 8/1 | 53 | 35 |
| 3306* | **My Godson (57)** (JLEyre) **6-9-6**(3) CTeague(3) (bhd: effrt over 2f out: r.o fnl f) | 1¼ | 3 | 13/2[2] | 63 | 45 |
| 3492[4] | **Gool Lee Shay (USA) (51)** (RMWhitaker) **3-8-12** KFallon(2) (in tch: drvn along 4f out: styd on: nt pce to chal) | nk | 4 | 14/1 | 57 | 34 |
| 3344[4] | **Grey Kingdom (43)** (MBrittain) **5-8-9** JLowe(1) (lw: led tl hdd & no ex appr fnl f) | 1 | 5 | 8/1 | 46 | 28 |
| 3510[2] | **Cee-Jay-Ay (53)** (JBerry) **9-9-0**(5) PRoberts(9) (lw: s.i.s: hdwy on outside 2f out: nvr able to chal) | ½ | 6 | 7/2[1] | 55 | 37 |
| 3585* | **Utmost Zeal (USA) (63)** (PWHarris) **3-9-7**(3) MHenry(6) (chsd ldrs: chal 3f out: wknd fnl 2f) | 3 | 7 | 7/1[3] | 59 | 36 |
| 3460[8] | **Corona Gold (30)** (JGFitzGerald) **6-7-10b** LCharnock(4) (chsd ldrs tl wknd fnl 3f) | 3½ | 8 | 33/1 | 18 | — |
| *2632*[5] | **Valiant Man (40)** (JWharton) **5-8-6** KDarley(8) (a rr div) | 5 | 9 | 20/1 | 18 | — |
| 2757[19] | **Coolowen Flash (IRE) (41)** (JLEyre) **5-8-7** TWilliams(7) (plld hrd: a bhd) | ¾ | 10 | 16/1 | 17 | — |
| 3578* | **Welcome Lu (45)** (JLHarris) **3-8-6** FNorton(11) (prom: rdn 4f out: sn wknd) | 1½ | 11 | 7/2[1] | 18 | — |
| 3451[2] | **Irish Oasis (IRE) (45)** (BSRothwell) **3-8-6** MBirch(5) (n.d) | 2 | 12 | 20/1 | 14 | — |
| | | | | (SP 130.0%) | **12 Rn** | |

**1m 35.4** (3.40) CSF £62.33 CT £366.35 TOTE £8.10: £2.50 £2.60 £2.50 (£21.80) Trio £52.90 OWNER Mr C. H. Stevens (MALTON) BRED Martyn J. McEnery
WEIGHT FOR AGE 3yo-5lb

**3510 Euro Sceptic (IRE)** would have been an unlucky loser here, but he got the gap just in time and flew to snatch it on the line. This was a good effort after shooting up 8lb in the handicap. (7/1)
**3344 Thatched (IRE)** is coming to himself looks-wise and ran a fine race, only just to be touched off. Although he can be an unpredictable character, he does look reasonably handicapped. (8/1)
**3306* My Godson,** who likes to come off a strong pace, took time to find a run here and, when he did, it was always too late. (13/2: 9/2-7/1)
**3492 Gool Lee Shay (USA)** keeps running well and kept staying on here, but was short of a real turn of foot. (14/1)
**3344 Grey Kingdom** tried hard to dictate things, but was always being taken on in the home straight, and finally gave up approaching the final furlong. (8/1)
**3510 Cee-Jay-Ay** is in good form but, despite staying on up the straight, was never doing enough to get in a chance. (7/2)
**3585* Utmost Zeal (USA)** could never get to the front this time and, 13lb higher in the handicap, not surprisingly ran out of steam in the last couple of furlongs. (7/1)

## 3778 E.B.F. SHELPHEN RESOURCE MAIDEN STKS (2-Y.O F) (Class D)
4-00 (4-00) **7f 100y** £3,908.00 (£1,088.00: £524.00) Stalls: High GOING minus 0.27 sec per fur (GF)

| | | | | SP | RR | SF |
|---|---|---|---|---|---|---|
| | **Out West (USA)** (HRACecil) **2-8-11** KFallon(2) (leggy: scope: lw: hld up: hdwy to ld wl over 1f out: sn clr: easily) | — | 1 | 2/9[1] | 90+ | 45 |
| 2863[5] | **Ghayyur (USA)** (JLDunlop) **2-8-11** GCarter(3) (cl up: led over 3f out tl wl over 1f out: no ch w wnr: b.b.v) | 10 | 2 | 7/2[2] | 69? | 24 |
| 3054[6] | **Sarteano** (JMackie) **2-8-11** DeanMcKeown(1) (led tl hdd over 3f out: sn btn) | 26 | 3 | 33/1[3] | 13 | — |
| | | | | (SP 107.0%) | **3 Rn** | |

**1m 34.6** (2.60) CSF £1.35 TOTE £1.30 (£1.10) OWNER Buckram Oak Holdings (NEWMARKET) BRED Buckram Oak Farm
OFFICIAL EXPLANATION **Ghayyur (USA): had bled from the nose.**

**Out West (USA),** an athletic type, was fit and won this really well, despite running green, and can obviously go on from here. (2/9)
**2863 Ghayyur (USA)** tried hard to take the winner on, but was firmly put in her place in the last two furlongs. On returning, she was found to have broken a blood-vessel. (7/2: 5/2-4/1)
**3054 Sarteano** was well outclassed, and this was accepted some way out. (33/1)

## 3779 MANOR ROAD MAIDEN STKS (2-Y.O) (Class D)
4-30 (4-30) **1m 100y** £3,333.50 (£998.00: £479.00: £219.50) Stalls: High GOING minus 0.27 sec per fur (GF)

| | | | | SP | RR | SF |
|---|---|---|---|---|---|---|
| | **Besiege** (HRACecil) **2-9-0** KFallon(1) (gd sort: lw: sn chsng ldrs: pushed along ½-wy: led 1½f out: styd on wl) | — | 1 | 8/13[1] | 89+ | 43 |
| 2702[6] | **Ivan Luis (FR)** (MBell) **2-8-7**(7) GFaulkner(4) (cl up: led wl over 2f out: edgd lft: hdd 1½f out: kpt on wl) | 1 | 2 | 11/2[3] | 87? | 41 |
| 3407[2] | **Elriyadh (USA)** (PFICole) **2-9-0** KDarley(2) (led tl hdd wl over 2f out: sn btn) | 9 | 3 | 5/2[2] | 70 | 24 |
| 3277[6] | **Wildmoor** (JDBethell) **2-9-0** GCarter(6) (bhd: hdwy over 2f out: hung bdly lft: nrst fin) | 7 | 4 | 50/1 | 57 | 11 |
| 1869[6] | **Plutarch Angel** (WTKemp) **2-9-0** FNorton(7) (outpcd fr ½-wy) | 4 | 5 | 100/1 | 49 | 3 |
| 3462[9] | **Smoke'n'jo (IRE)** (MWEasterby) **2-8-9**(5) GParkin(5) (b.nr fore: nvr nr ldrs) | 1¼ | 6 | 50/1 | 47 | 1 |
| | **Captain Carparts** (JLEyre) **2-9-0** TWilliams(3) (leggy: scope: hdwy ½-wy: sn chsng ldrs: wknd qckly wl over 2f out) | 11 | 7 | 20/1 | 26 | — |
| | | | | (SP 115.5%) | **7 Rn** | |

**1m 47.4** (3.40) CSF £4.73 TOTE £1.50: £1.20 £2.90 (£3.50) OWNER Mr K. Abdulla (NEWMARKET) BRED Juddmonte Farms

**Besiege,** a brother to Armiger, looked the part here, but was not entirely suited to this track, and took some riding to gain the upper hand. He does not do anything quickly, will probably need further and a more galloping track, and better should then be seen. (8/13)
**2702 Ivan Luis (FR)** is certainly getting the hang of things, and ran a fine race here. He will surely find winning opportunities before long. (11/2)
**3407 Elriyadh (USA)** tried to force the pace, but he suddenly tied up early in the straight and, with his tongue lolling out, stopped quickly. (5/2)
**3277 Wildmoor** only ran on in the home straight but, in doing so, hung badly left, and obviously has plenty to learn. (50/1)
**Plutarch Angel** ran as well as can be expected in this company. (100/1)

## 3780 WOODMANSEY MAIDEN APPRENTICE H'CAP (0-60) (3-Y.O+) (Class F)
5-00 (5-02) **1m 1f 207y** £2,508.00 (£713.00: £354.00) Stalls: High GOING minus 0.27 sec per fur (GF)

| | | | | SP | RR | SF |
|---|---|---|---|---|---|---|
| 3474[10] | **Siberian Mystic (33)** (PGMurphy) **3-7-10** RFfrench(16) (trckd ldrs: hdwy 3f out: led 1f out: styd on) | — | 1 | 5/1[2] | 42 | 3 |
| 3589[3] | **Minster Glory (41)** (MWEasterby) **5-8-12** CLowther(5) (chsd ldrs: led 1½f out: hdd 1f out: nt qckn) | 1¾ | 2 | 9/2[1] | 47 | 16 |
| 3589[2] | **Monte Cavo (31)** (MBrittain) **5-8-2** JFowle(13) (lw: led tl hdd 1½f out: kpt on) | ½ | 3 | 10/1 | 36 | 5 |
| 3442[12] | **El Bardador (IRE) (53)** (WJarvis) **3-8-11**(5) TThomas(14) (lw: s.s: in tch after 3f: kpt on wl fnl 2f: hung lft towards fin) | hd | 4 | 12/1 | 58 | 19 |

3354[3] **Cottage Prince (IRE) (39)** (JJQuinn) **3-8-2** RBrisland(2) (in tch: hdwy u.p 3f out: no imp) ....1¼ **5** 9/1 42 3
**Hee's a Dancer (35)** (MJCamacho) **4-8-6** CScudder(15) (chsd ldrs: effrt 3f out: grad wknd fnl 2f) ....hd **6** 16/1 38 7
3490[4] **In A Tizzy (33)** (PCHaslam) **3-7-5**(5) FBoyle(6) (chsd ldrs tl grad wknd fnl 3f) ....2 **7** 12/1 33 —
3284[5] **Sheilana (IRE) (49)** (TGMills) **3-8-7**(5) JCornally(3) (lw: b.hind: in tch: effrt over 3f out: sn btn) ....5 **8** 10/1 41 2
3348[2] **Bold Top (37)** (BSRothwell) **4-8-8** TSiddall(11) (lw: nvr trbld ldrs) ....3 **9** 6/1[3] 24 —
3427[6] **Rocky Stream (42)** (RMWhitaker) **3-8-5** PFredericks(10) (in tch: effrt over 3f out: no imp) ....3½ **10** 16/1 23 —
2026[5] **Craigmore Magic (USA) (45)** (MissMKMilligan) **3-8-3**(5) MMathers(17) (n.d) ....1¾ **11** 33/1 24 —
**Royal Rigger (37)** (CSmith) **3-8-0**ow1 GHannon(1) (c wd st: n.d) ....s.h **12** 33/1 15 —
3344[8] **Reinhardt (IRE) (56)** (JSWainwright) **3-9-0**(5) RCody-Boutcher(9) (bhd fr ½-wy) ....5 **13** 12/1 26 —
2988[9] **Baraqueta (57)** (JLEyre) **4-10-0** SBuckley(7) (chsd ldrs tl wknd fnl 3f) ....1¼ **14** 14/1 25 —
2162[13] **Fergal (USA) (37)** (MissJFCraze) **3-7-9**(5) CarolynBales(18) (b.hind: n.d) ....1½ **15** 33/1 3 —
3456[6] **Prince Zizim (45)** (RCSpicer) **3-8-3b**(5)ow3 JO'Leary(12) (s.s: a bhd) ....3 **16** 20/1 6 —
3609[3] **Samorelle (55)** (MJRyan) **3-9-4** AMcCarthy(8) (wl bhd fnl 4f) ....14 **17** 14/1 — —
3289[10] **Supermister (45)** (TDEasterby) **3-8-3**(5)ow3 MatthewWilliams(4) (lost tch fnl 4f) ....½ **18** 20/1 — —
(SP 143.8%) **18 Rn**

**2m 9.6** (7.10) CSF £30.41 CT £216.82 TOTE £5.70: £1.30 £1.30 £3.50 £4.20 (£18.30) Trio £93.00 OWNER The Merry Men (BRISTOL) BRED Deerfield Farm
LONG HANDICAP Siberian Mystic 7-7
WEIGHT FOR AGE 3yo-8lb
OFFICIAL EXPLANATION **Siberian Mystic: accounting for her apparent improvement in form, the trainer's wife explained that the filly's two previous bad runs had been due to her being bumped and losing her action and then being replated in the last start, possibly causing soreness. In her only other race, Syberian Mystic ran poorly due to suffering from sinus trouble and had since been operated on.**
**Siberian Mystic**, gambled on, was confidently handled and, responding to pressure, stayed on to settle it in the final furlong. She was apparently hampered at Bath last time. (5/1: 10/1-9/2)
**3589 Minster Glory** is running well but, despite responding to pressure, just found one too good. He deserves a change of luck. (9/2)
**3589 Monte Cavo** looked particularly well and ran a fine race, staying on when headed. (10/1)
**El Bardador (IRE)** missed the break yet again but, trying his longest trip to date here, was putting in some useful work late on. (12/1)
**3354 Cottage Prince (IRE)** had his chances, but was short of a turn of foot to take them. (9/1: 6/1-10/1)
**Hee's a Dancer**, a dual winner over hurdles, was having his first run for over nine months, and showed enough to suggest he is again in good heart. (16/1)
**3056 Reinhardt (IRE)** (12/1: op 20/1)
**3609 Samorelle** (14/1: op 8/1)

T/Plpt: £31.90 (263.87 Tckts). T/Qdpt: £18.10 (19.58 Tckts). AA

# 3229-GOODWOOD (R-H) (Good)
## Saturday August 24th
WEATHER: overcast & unsettled WIND: str half against

## 3781 SPORT ON 5 MARCH STKS (Listed) (3-Y.O) (Class A)
2-15 (2-17) **1m 6f** £12,560.00 (£4,640.00: £2,220.00: £900.00: £350.00: £130.00) Stalls: High GOING: 0.19 sec per fur (G)
SP RR SF

2473a[11] **Sharaf Kabeer** (SbinSuroor) **3-8-11** LDettori(4) (lw: chsd ldrs over 1f: chsd ldr 6f out: led 3f out: rdn over 2f out: clr over 1f out: r.o wl) ....— **1** 11/4[1] 109 68
2864[2] **Masehaab (IRE) (104)** (JLDunlop) **3-8-11** WCarson(3) (led to 3f out: rdn over 3f out: unable qckn) ....2½ **2** 8/1 106 65
3124[10] **Summer Spell (USA) (99)** (RCharlton) **3-8-11** SSanders(2) (hld up: rdn over 3f out: one pce fnl 2f) ....¾ **3** 5/1[3] 105 64
3145* **Freequent (97)** (LMCumani) **3-8-11** JWeaver(6) (lw: dwlt: rdn over 3f out: hdwy over 2f out: one pce) ....nk **4** 100/30[2] 105 64
2054[13] **Zaforum (103)** (LMontagueHall) **3-8-11** DaneO'Neill(8) (hdwy 8f out: chsd ldr 7f out to 6f out: wknd 3f out) ....4 **5** 25/1 100 59
2677[4] **Shanaladee** (MRStoute) **3-8-11** JReid(5) (hdwy over 4f out: wknd over 2f out) ....¾ **6** 5/1[3] 100 59
3431[6] **Weet-A-Minute (IRE) (107)** (RHollinshead) **3-8-11** WRyan(1) (chsd ldr over 12f out to 7f out: wknd 3f out) ....5 **7** 10/1 94 53
(SP 107.1%) **7 Rn**

**3m 6.57** (7.57) CSF £20.74 TOTE £2.40: £2.00 £2.20 (£7.70) OWNER Sheikh Ahmed Al Maktoum (NEWMARKET) BRED Sheikh Ahmed Bin Rashid Al Maktoum
**2473a Sharaf Kabeer**, given plenty of time to recover from his Irish Derby flop, looked extremely well beforehand and is an improving individual. Regaining second place three-quarters of a mile from home, he moved into the lead early in the straight and, bustled along, forged clear below the distance to win in fine style. His trainer believes he could be a Group One horse and, now that he has proved he stays this longer trip, he will now go for the St Leger. (11/4)
**2864 Masehaab (IRE)** attempted to make all the running. Collared three furlongs from home, he had dropped back into fourth place below the distance but, to his credit, struggled on to regain the runner-up berth inside the final furlong. He is not the most straightforward of horses as his trainer later revealed, and he may now be tried in blinkers. The Cumberland Lodge at Ascot is a possibility. (8/1)
**1110 Summer Spell (USA)** chased the leaders. Bustled along early in the straight, he could only plod on at the one pace in the last two furlongs. (5/1)
**3145* Freequent**, ridden along as the Bugler called entering the straight, soon picked up ground, but failed to find another gear from below the distance. His jockey later reported that they did not go fast enough for the colt. (100/30)
**1076 Zaforum** moved up to show in second place briefly at halfway, but was a spent force three furlongs from home. (25/1)
**2677 Shanaladee** (5/1: op 3/1)

## 3782 CAFFREY'S IRISH ALE RATED STKS H'CAP (0-105) (3-Y.O+) (Class B)
2-45 (2-47) **7f** £9,959.40 (£3,684.60: £1,767.30: £721.50: £285.75: £111.45) Stalls: High GOING: 0.19 sec per fur (G)
SP RR SF

3612[2] **Akil (IRE) (91)** (RWArmstrong) **4-8-7** WCarson(8) (mde all: qcknd clr over 1f out: pushed out) ....— **1** 15/2[3] 97 53
3207* **Law Commission (95)** (DRCElsworth) **6-8-11** RCochrane(3) (hdwy over 1f out: chsd wnr ins fnl f: r.o) ....2 **2** 10/1 96 52
3612* **Cool Edge (IRE) (102)** (MHTompkins) **5-9-4** PRobinson(6) (hld up: chsd wnr over 1f out tl ins fnl f: unable qckn) ....¾ **3** 6/4[1] 102 58
3503[5] **Abeyr (100)** (MAJarvis) **3-8-11** LDettori(5) (swtg: chsd wnr 5f: wknd fnl f) ....5 **4** 9/2[2] 88 39
3232[26] **Hard to Figure (105)** (RJHodges) **10-9-7** SDrowne(4) (lw: hld up: rdn over 2f out: sn wknd) ....¾ **5** 20/1 92 48
1484[11] **Jawaal (91)** (LadyHerries) **6-8-7** JReid(2) (lw: a.p: chsd wnr 2f out tl over 1f out: sn wknd) ....nk **6** 14/1 77 33
3445[5] **Saseedo (USA) (91)** (WAO'Gorman) **6-8-7** EmmaO'Gorman(1) (swtg: a bhd) ....8 **7** 8/1 59 15

$3445^{5}$ **Believe Me (91)** (RHannon) **3-8-2** DaneO'Neill(7) (lw: reard s: a wl bhd: t.o 5f out: p.u 1f out: dismntd) ............. **P** 10/1 — —
(SP 110.7%) **8 Rn**

**1m 29.36** (4.56) CSF £66.23 CT £149.84 TOTE £5.20: £1.60 £2.10 £1.10 (£37.90) OWNER Mr Hamdan Al Maktoum (NEWMARKET) BRED Denis Noonan
LONG HANDICAP Akil (IRE) 8-4 Jawaal 8-6 Saseedo (USA) 8-6 Believe Me 8-0
WEIGHT FOR AGE 3yo-5lb
**OFFICIAL EXPLANATION Believe Me: came out of the stalls awkwardly and the jockey felt he had damaged his back.**

**3612 Akil (IRE)** was given a superb ride by Carson who certainly showed up some of the other jockeys in the race. Really enjoying this ground, he made all the running and quickened clear in the last two furlongs to win in emphatic style. (15/2: 5/1-8/1)
**3207* Law Commission** was given far too much to do by his experienced rider. Put to sleep at the back of the field, his jockey still had not shown any urgency on the gelding going to the final quarter-mile, even though they were still at the back of the field. At last picking up ground below the distance, he swept into second place in the last 75 yards but, by then, the winner was already home and dry. Despite this defeat, his trainer is expecting a big run from him in the Ladbroke Ayr Gold Cup next month. (10/1)
**3612* Cool Edge (IRE)**, who beat the winner on the same terms at Newbury last week, was not given a good ride. Held up travelling sweetly, he was only asked for his effort in the final quarter-mile, by which time the winner was beginning to forge clear. Soon in second place, he failed to peg back his rival and was collared for the runner-up berth in the last 75 yards. (6/4)
**3503 Abeyr** raced in second place. Collared for that position a quarter of a mile out, she grimly tried to hold on, but had nothing left to offer inside the distance. (9/2)
**2853 Hard to Figure** chased the leaders but, bustled along over two furlongs from home, was soon in trouble. (20/1)
**876 Jawaal**, a leading player from the start, showed briefly in front a quarter of a mile out before tiring. (14/1)

## 3783 LADBROKE RACING SPRINT H'CAP (0-95) (3-Y.O+) (Class C)

3-15 (3-16) **6f** £14,460.00 (£4,380.00: £2,140.00: £1,020.00) Stalls: Low GOING: 0.19 sec per fur (G)

| | | | | SP | RR | SF |
|---|---|---|---|---|---|---|
| $3232^{5}$ | **Wildwood Flower (92)** (RHannon) **3-9-12** DaneO'Neill(1) (hdwy on ins 2f out: led over 1f out: rdn out) | — | **1** | 8/1$^{2}$ | 102 | 75 |
| 3622* | **Samwar (85)** (MissGayKelleway) **4-9-8** RCochrane(7) (b: s.s: hdwy over 1f out: rdn & r.o) | ¾ | **2** | 3/1$^{1}$ | 93 | 69 |
| $2694^{13}$ | **Portend (88)** (SRBowring) **4-9-11b** SDWilliams(8) (rdn over 2f out: hdwy over 1f out: squeezed thro 1f out: hrd rdn & edgd lft ins fnl f: r.o) | hd | **3** | 25/1 | 96 | 72 |
| $3222^{4}$ | **Red Nymph (90)** (WJarvis) **3-9-10** JReid(2) (lw: hld up: hrd rdn over 1f out: unable qckn) | ½ | **4** | 25/1 | 96 | 69 |
| $3232^{3}$ | **Sir Joey (USA) (88)** (PGMurphy) **7-9-11** SDrowne(11) (lw: hld up: rdn 2f out: ev ch 1f out: one pce) | 1½ | **5** | 8/1$^{2}$ | 90 | 66 |
| $3622^{3}$ | **Fantasy Racing (IRE) (73)** (MRChannon) **4-8-10** PaulEddery(5) (a.p: ev ch over 1f out: one pce) | nk | **6** | 11/1$^{3}$ | 75 | 51 |
| 3313* | **Crystal Heights (FR) (70)** (RJO'Sullivan) **8-8-7** SSanders(6) (b: lw: s.s: rdn over 2f out: hdwy over 1f out: nvr nrr) | 1¼ | **7** | 16/1 | 68 | 44 |
| $3622^{14}$ | **Lennox Lewis (79)** (APJarvis) **4-9-2** WJO'Connor(15) (lw: hld up: rdn over 2f out: bmpd 1f out: wknd ins fnl f) | ½ | **8** | 20/1 | 76 | 52 |
| $3661^{4}$ | **Runs in the Family (59)** (GMMcCourt) **4-7-3v**(7) RMullen(12) (lw: led over 4f) | ¾ | **9** | 33/1 | 54 | 30 |
| $3339^{5}$ | **How's Yer Father (68)** (RJHodges) **10-8-5** CRutter(13) (nvr nrr) | hd | **10** | 33/1 | 63 | 39 |
| $3216^{D}$ | **Ansellman (83)** (JBerry) **6-9-6v** JCarroll(14) (b.hind: a.p: ev ch over 1f out: wknd fnl f) | 1½ | **11** | 14/1 | 74 | 50 |
| $3618^{12}$ | **No Extras (IRE) (85)** (GLMoore) **6-9-8** SWhitworth(16) (b.off hind: a bhd) | s.h | **12** | 20/1 | 76 | 52 |
| $3232^{6}$ | **My Best Valentine (88)** (JWhite) **6-9-8**(3) AWhelan(10) (hld up: rdn over 2f out: wknd over 1f out) | ½ | **13** | 11/1$^{3}$ | 77 | 53 |
| $2232^{5}$ | **Sally Slade (76)** (CACyzer) **4-8-13** LDettori(3) (bhd fnl 2f) | 1 | **14** | 12/1 | 63 | 39 |
| 3518* | **La Petite Fusee (79)** (RJO'Sullivan) **5-9-2** DBiggs(4) (gd spd 4f) | 1¼ | **15** | 8/1$^{2}$ | 62 | 38 |
| $3296^{12}$ | **Rock Symphony (79)** (WJHaggas) **6-9-2** WCarson(9) (lw: s.s: bhd fnl 2f) | 10 | **16** | 20/1 | 36 | 12 |

(SP 123.1%) **16 Rn**

**1m 13.54** (3.54) CSF £30.37 CT £561.82 TOTE £8.90: £2.20 £1.70 £5.60 £6.30 (£12.80) Trio £286.10 OWNER Mr G. Howard-Spink (MARLBOROUGH) BRED Sir Stephen Hastings and G. Howard-Spink
LONG HANDICAP Runs in the Family 7-2
WEIGHT FOR AGE 3yo-3lb

**3232 Wildwood Flower**, who finished fifth here in the Stewards' Cup three weeks ago despite a bad draw, found a lovely run up the inside rail in the final quarter-mile and, sweeping into the lead approaching the final furlong, was ridden along to assert. The Ladbroke Ayr Gold Cup is her next likely target. (8/1)
**3622* Samwar**, whose trainer was extremely confident beforehand, travelled well at the back of the field, but had a difficult task as he threaded his way through the pack below the distance. Running on well, he was never going to overhaul the winner in time. The Ayr Gold Cup is his target and, with luck on his side, he must have a very good chance. (3/1)
**2548 Portend** began to pick up ground below the distance and, squeezing through a narrow gap, ran on, despite drifting left inside the final furlong. (25/1)
**3222 Red Nymph** chased the leaders. Almost on terms below the distance, she was then tapped for toe. (25/1)
**3232 Sir Joey (USA)** chased the leaders, and may even have got his head in front for a few strides around the furlong pole before being tapped for toe. (8/1)
**3622 Fantasy Racing (IRE)**, a leading light from the off, had every chance below the distance before failing to find another gear. (11/1)
**3313* Crystal Heights (FR)**, who has gained all his grass wins at Brighton, stayed on in the last furlong and a half without ever posing a threat. (16/1)

## 3784 TRIPLEPRINT CELEBRATION MILE STKS (Gp 2) (3-Y.O+) (Class A)

3-50 (3-50) **1m** £35,170.00 (£13,030.00: £6,265.00: £2,575.00: £1,037.50: £422.50) Stalls: High GOING: 0.19 sec per fur (G)

| | | | | SP | RR | SF |
|---|---|---|---|---|---|---|
| $2039^{8}$ | **Mark of Esteem (IRE) (120)** (SbinSuroor) **3-9-1** LDettori(7) (lw: hld up: nt clr run, swtchd rt & led over 1f out: qcknd: r.o wl) | — | **1** | 11/4$^{1}$ | 134 | 74 |
| $3153^{2}$ | **Bishop of Cashel (111)** (JRFanshawe) **4-9-1** WRSwinburn(5) (lw: hld up: ev ch over 1f out: r.o one pce) | 3½ | **2** | 5/1$^{3}$ | 121 | 67 |
| $3144^{3}$ | **Alhaarth (IRE) (118)** (MajorWRHern) **3-8-9** WCarson(1) (lw: led over 6f: one pce) | ¾ | **3** | 7/2$^{2}$ | 120 | 60 |
| $3144^{5}$ | **Restructure (IRE) (116)** (MrsJCecil) **4-9-1** PaulEddery(6) (lw: lost pl over 3f out: one pce fnl 2f) | ¾ | **4** | 6/1 | 118 | 64 |
| $1567a^{4}$ | **Distant Oasis (USA)** (HRACecil) **3-8-6** WRyan(4) (nvr nr to chal) | ¾ | **5** | 6/1 | 114 | 54 |
| $3745a^{7}$ | **Gothenberg (IRE) (118)** (MJohnston) **3-8-12** JWeaver(2) (lw: w ldr: rdn over 2f out: wkng whn nt clr run on ins over 1f out) | 5 | **6** | 12/1 | 110 | 50 |
| $2546^{7}$ | **Beauchamp King (118)** (JLDunlop) **3-8-9** JReid(3) (a bhd) | 7 | **7** | 6/1 | 93 | 33 |

(SP 116.1%) **7 Rn**

**1m 41.18** (3.98) CSF £16.09 TOTE £2.50: £2.10 £3.30 (£11.10) OWNER Godolphin (NEWMARKET) BRED Sheikh Mohammed Bin Rashid Al Maktoum
WEIGHT FOR AGE 3yo-6lb

**926* Mark of Esteem (IRE)**, who was forced to miss the Derby because of a temperature and then ran deplorably in the St James's Palace Stakes at Royal Ascot, bounced back in emphatic style with a brilliant display, despite a 6lb Group One penalty. Held up traveling sweetly, he had nowhere to go entering the final quarter-mile but, with Gothenberg weakening, Dettori switched the colt to the rail below the distance and his mount soon swept into the lead. Showing a brilliant turn of foot, he left his rivals for dead to win in tremendous style. The Queen Elizabeth II at Ascot is next on the agenda and, in this sort of form, he could prove very difficult to beat. (11/4)
**3153 Bishop of Cashel** ran a fine race in defeat on ground that was not as easy as many people had first thought, the heavy showers that had fallen in the South in the morning having failed to materialise at Goodwood. Held up travelling sweetly, he appeared to be cruising below the distance but, when the winner was let loose and into the lead, he was then left standing. On really soft ground, there is certainly a Group race waiting for him this season. (5/1)
**3144 Alhaarth (IRE)**, without the blinkers on this occasion, had the conditions of the race in his favour, but was still unable to take advantage. Bowling along in front, he was collared over a furlong out and failed to find another gear. He has been disappointing this season, when one compares it to his scintillating campaign last year, and it is difficult to know where to go with him now. (7/2)
**3144 Restructure (IRE)**, who got rather outpaced at halfway, plodded on at the one pace in the last two furlongs. (6/1)
**1567a Distant Oasis (USA)**, who came back with a lung infection after finishing fourth in the Irish 1000 Guineas, has had a break since. Racing at the back of the field, she never threatened to get into the action. (6/1: 4/1-13/2)
**3745a Gothenberg (IRE)** disputed the lead from the start, but was already tiring and beginning to back-pedal when done no favours by Mark of Esteem below the distance. (12/1)

## 3785 CHICHESTER OBSERVER SERIES CLAIMING H'CAP (0-70) (3-Y.O+) (Class E)

4-20 (4-21) **1m 2f** £4,370.00 (£1,310.00: £630.00: £290.00) Stalls: High GOING: 0.19 sec per fur (G)

| | | | | SP | RR | SF |
|---|---|---|---|---|---|---|
| 3496[2] | **Thatchmaster (IRE) (52)** (CAHorgan) **5-8-12** PaulEddery(1) (lw: chsd ldr: led over 3f out: clr over 1f out: pushed out) | — | **1** | 11/2[2] | 64 | 50 |
| 3466[5] | **Pat's Splendour (40)** (HJCollingridge) **5-7-7**(7)ow1 JoHunnam(4) (hdwy over 3f out: chsd wnr over 2f out: unable qckn) | 1¼ | **2** | 16/1 | 50 | 35 |
| | **War Requiem (IRE) (36)** (RJO'Sullivan) **6-7-7**(3) NVarley(12) (rdn over 4f out: hdwy 2f out: r.o) | 1¾ | **3** | 11/1 | 43 | 29 |
| 3111[4] | **Lady Sabina (36)** (WJMusson) **6-7-10** DeclanO'Shea(2) (lw: hdwy over 3f out: rdn over 2f out: one pce) | 3 | **4** | 9/1 | 38 | 24 |
| 1514[11] | **Todd (USA) (47)** (PMitchell) **5-8-7** JTate(11) (lw: a.p: rdn 3f out: one pce) | 1½ | **5** | 25/1 | 47 | 33 |
| 2701[7] | **Maradata (IRE) (61)** (RHollinshead) **4-9-7** WRSwinburn(14) (lw: stdy hdwy over 2f out: one pce) | ¾ | **6** | 12/1 | 60 | 46 |
| 3457[5] | **Myfontaine (63)** (KTIvory) **9-9-9** JWeaver(9) (b: lw: hld up: chsd wnr 3f out tl over 2f out: wknd over 1f out) | hd | **7** | 16/1 | 62 | 48 |
| 3470[4] | **Harvey White (IRE) (57)** (JPearce) **4-9-3** GBardwell(18) (swtg: rdn over 3f out: nvr nrr) | 5 | **8** | 5/1[1] | 48 | 34 |
| 3233[4] | **Ultimate Warrior (65)** (CACyzer) **6-9-11** JCarroll(6) (hdwy over 3f out: wknd 2f out) | 10 | **9** | 20/1 | 40 | 26 |
| 3473[4] | **Ketabi (USA) (42)** (RAkehurst) **5-8-2** NGwilliams(8) (swtg: a mid div) | 1 | **10** | 8/1[3] | 15 | 1 |
| 3246[8] | **Premier Generation (IRE) (62)** (DWPArbuthnot) **3-9-0** RPrice(19) (b: hld up: rdn over 3f out: wknd over 2f out) | 1 | **11** | 16/1 | 33 | 11 |
| 3233[3] | **Open Affair (64)** (APJarvis) **3-9-2** WJO'Connor(16) (lw: prom 4f) | nk | **12** | 10/1 | 35 | 13 |
| 3217[6] | **Miss Laughter (53)** (JWHills) **4-8-13** RHills(7) (prom over 7f) | ½ | **13** | 16/1 | 23 | 9 |
| 3258[13] | **Queens Fancy (46)** (SDow) **3-7-7**(5)ow2 MBaird(17) (lw: prom over 6f) | hd | **14** | 50/1 | 16 | — |
| 3500[14] | **Lizium (44)** (JCFox) **4-7-11**(7) RMullen(3) (lw: a bhd) | 2½ | **15** | 50/1 | 10 | — |
| 3505[10] | **Back By Dawn (56)** (DRCElsworth) **3-8-8** SDrowne(15) (swtg: bhd fnl 4f) | ½ | **16** | 33/1 | 21 | — |
| 2766[5] | **Half An Inch (IRE) (54)** (TMJones) **3-8-6b** DBiggs(20) (b.hind: led over 6f) | 9 | **17** | 16/1 | 5 | — |
| 2601[12] | **Notaire (IRE) (56)** (IABalding) **3-8-8** WRyan(13) (s.s: a wl bhd) | 15 | **18** | 14/1 | — | — |
| 3470[11] | **Persian Conquest (IRE) (53)** (RIngram) **4-8-13b** SWhitworth(5) (lw: a bhd: t.o fnl 4f) | dist | **19** | 25/1 | — | — |
| | | | | (SP 133.7%) | **19 Rn** | |

**2m 13.15** (7.65) CSF £88.45 CT £889.18 TOTE £4.70: £1.40 £5.70 £3.10 £1.90 (£81.60) Trio £590.10 OWNER Mrs B. Sumner (PULBOROUGH) BRED Ballysheehan Stud
LONG HANDICAP Lady Sabina 7-8 Queens Fancy 7-1
WEIGHT FOR AGE 3yo-8lb
**3496 Thatchmaster (IRE)** gained a very decisive victory. Racing in second place, he went on as the Bugler called entering the straight, and forged clear in the final quarter-mile to win with plenty in hand. (11/2)
**3466 Pat's Splendour** moved up early in the straight. Soon racing in second place, she tried to get on level terms with the winner but found that rival always just too good. (16/1)
**War Requiem (IRE)**, off the track for almost a year, was being bustled along as the runners began the descent, but did stay on well in the straight to take third place. (11/1)
**3111 Lady Sabina** moved up early in the straight but, soon rousted along, failed to find another gear. (9/1)
**670 Todd (USA)**, given a three-month break, was always close up, but was made to look very pedestrian in the last three furlongs. (25/1)
**1704* Maradata (IRE)** steadily threaded her way through the pack over a quarter of a mile from home, but was making no further impression from below the distance. (12/1)
**3470 Harvey White (IRE)**, scrubbed along and going nowhere at the back of the field entering the straight, did make up a little late headway without ever posing a threat. (5/1)

## 3786 RICHMOND-BRISSAC TROPHY GENTLEMENS' H'CAP (0-85) (3-Y.O+) (Class E)

4-50 (4-53) **1m 1f** £3,655.00 (£1,090.00: £520.00: £235.00) Stalls: High GOING: 0.19 sec per fur (G)

| | | | | SP | RR | SF |
|---|---|---|---|---|---|---|
| 3450[5] | **Night Wink (USA) (76)** (GLMoore) **4-11-10** MrKGoble(9) (lw: hdwy to ld over 3f out: clr over 1f out: r.o wl) | — | **1** | 11/1 | 86 | 58 |
| 3161[13] | **Pay Homage (73)** (IABalding) **8-11-7** MrABalding(5) (lw: hdwy on ins over 3f out: chsd wnr 2f out: r.o wl ins fnl f) | ¾ | **2** | 15/2 | 82 | 54 |
| 3123[10] | **Embankment (IRE) (72)** (RHannon) **6-11-6** MrCVigors(7) (hld up: rdn over 2f out: unable qckn) | 3 | **3** | 8/1 | 75 | 47 |
| 3469[3] | **Cape Pigeon (USA) (65)** (LGCottrell) **11-10-13v** MrLJefford(8) (a.p: edgd lft over 3f out: rdn: wknd over 1f out) | 4 | **4** | 11/2[3] | 61 | 33 |
| 3516[12] | **Brighton Road (IRE) (74)** (GBBalding) **3-11-1** MrLMaynard(6) (hdwy over 3f out: hdwy over 1f out: nvr nrr) | 6 | **5** | 10/1 | 60 | 25 |
| 3348[4] | **Montone (IRE) (63)** (JRJenkins) **6-10-11v** DrMMannish(2) (prom over 6f) | 1½ | **6** | 14/1 | 46 | 18 |
| | **Camden's Ransom (USA) (55)** (HGRowsell) **9-10-3** MrTMcCarthy(3) (bhd fnl 2f) | 4 | **7** | 33/1 | 31 | 3 |
| *3435** | **Our Eddie (50)** (BGubby) **7-9-12v** MrAndiWyss(11) (b: lw: hld up: rdn over 3f out: sn wknd) | 4 | **8** | 16/1 | 19 | — |
| 1660* | **Renown (68)** (LordHuntingdon) **4-11-2** MrLAUrbano(1) (mid div whn bdly hmpd over 3f out: nt rcvr) | 1¾ | **9** | 4/1[1] | 34 | 6 |
| 3443* | **Mezzoramio (50)** (KAMorgan) **4-9-12v** MrMHNaughton(10) (b: lw: led over 5f) | 2 | **10** | 9/2[2] | 12 | — |

| | | | | SP | RR | SF |
|---|---|---|---|---|---|---|
| 3161[18] | **Classic Defence (IRE) (74)** (JWHills) **3-11-1** MrFGrasso-Caprioli(4) (lw: prom 5f: wkng whn hmpd & fell over 3f out) | | F | 14/1 | — | — |
| | | | | (SP 116.0%) | | **11 Rn** |

**2m 1.58** (10.18) CSF £82.00 CT £639.16 TOTE £20.10: £4.10 £2.90 £2.90 (£50.90) Trio £29.40 OWNER Mrs Dyanne Benjamin (EPSOM) BRED Gainsborough Farm Inc
WEIGHT FOR AGE 3yo-7lb

**3450 Night Wink (USA)** railed well into the straight and picked up ground to sweep into the lead. Forging clear below the distance, he was not going to be denied. (11/1: 8/1-12/1)
**2525 Pay Homage** sneaked up along the inside rail as the Bugler called entering the straight. Taking second place a quarter of a mile out, he ran on well inside the final furlong, but was never going to seriously threaten the winner. (15/2: 5/1-8/1)
**1843 Embankment (IRE)** chased the leaders but, bustled along over two furlongs from home, never looked like finding that vital turn of foot. He has not won for over two years. (8/1)
**3469 Cape Pigeon (USA)**, a leading light from the off, had eventually come to the end of his tether below the distance. (11/2: 4/1-6/1)
**2526 Brighton Road (IRE)**, racing at the back of the field, did make up a little late headway. (10/1)
**3348 Montone (IRE)** played an active role until calling it a day over two furlongs from home. (14/1)
**2558 Classic Defence (IRE)** (14/1: op 8/1)

## 3787 E.B.F. SOLENT MAIDEN STKS (2-Y.O F) (Class D)

5-25 (5-26) **7f** £4,581.00 (£1,368.00: £654.00: £297.00) Stalls: High GOING: 0.19 sec per fur (G)

| | | | | SP | RR | SF |
|---|---|---|---|---|---|---|
| | **Fleet River (USA)** (HRACecil) **2-8-11** WRyan(5) (cmpt: lw: mde all: qcknd 2f out: clr over 1f out: easily) | — | 1 | 11/8[1] | 87++ | 28 |
| 1954[4] | **Caribbean Star** (MRStoute) **2-8-11** WRSwinburn(4) (hld up: nt clr run & bmpd over 2f out: chsd wnr over 1f out: no imp) | 9 | 2 | 7/2[3] | 66 | 7 |
| | **Siyadah (USA)** (SbinSuroor) **2-8-11** RHills(1) (leggy: unf: scope: lw: hld up: rdn & bmpd over 2f out: one pce) | nk | 3 | 11/4[2] | 66 | 7 |
| 3159[9] | **Amarella (IRE)** (MJHaynes) **2-8-11** JCarroll(2) (lw: chsd wnr over 5f: one pce) | 1½ | 4 | 50/1 | 62 | 3 |
| 2404[8] | **Golden Melody** (RHannon) **2-8-11** WJO'Connor(6) (bit bkwd: a bhd) | 2½ | 5 | 40/1 | 57 | — |
| 3129[5] | **Nawasib (IRE)** (JLDunlop) **2-8-11** JTate(3) (a bhd) | hd | 6 | 15/2 | 56 | — |
| | **Cheek To Cheek** (CACyzer) **2-8-11** SDrowne(7) (unf: scope: bit bkwd: prom over 4f) | 3 | 7 | 20/1 | 50 | — |
| | | | | (SP 111.9%) | | **7 Rn** |

**1m 31.86** (7.06) CSF £6.33 TOTE £2.40: £1.60 £1.70 (£4.20) OWNER Mr K. Abdulla (NEWMARKET) BRED Juddmonte Farms

**Fleet River (USA)**, a close-coupled half-sister to Eltish and the very useful sprinter Forest Gazelle, was the subject of some very encouraging home reports. Making all the running, she showed an impressive turn of foot in the last two furlongs to quicken right away from the opposition to win with a ton in hand. Not surprisingly, she was given an immediate 10/1 second favourite quote for next year's 1000 Guineas. Whilst one should hardly rush out and back her at that price, she does look a very useful filly in the making, and can certainly go on from here. (11/8: Evens-6/4)
**1954 Caribbean Star** chased the leaders, but was boxed in with nowhere to go over quarter of a mile out, and had a bumping match with the third. Moving into second place at the distance, she had no hope of reeling in the winner. (7/2)
**Siyadah (USA)**, whose dam Roseate Tern won the Irish Oaks and was placed in the Epsom Oaks and St Leger, is a tall, rather weak-looking filly but does have plenty of scope. Chasing the leaders, she was given a bump by the runner-up over a quarter of a mile form home, but that made little difference to her chances as she could only struggle on at the one pace. She should not be difficult to win with. (11/4: 2/1-7/2)
**Amarella (IRE)** raced in second place but, collared for that position at the distance, failed to find another gear. (50/1)
**3129 Nawasib (IRE)** (15/2: 3/1-8/1)

T/Plpt: £283.00 (110.5 Tckts). T/Qdpt: £63.00 (19.23 Tckts). AK

# 3756-NEWMARKET (R-H) (Good, Good to soft in Dip becoming Good to soft)
## Saturday August 24th

WEATHER: heavy showers WIND: mod across

## 3788 EQUITY FINANCIAL COLLECTIONS MAIDEN STKS (3-Y.O+) (Class D)

2-00 (2-01) **1m (July)** £4,659.00 (£1,392.00: £666.00: £303.00) Stalls: Low GOING: 0.01 sec per fur (G)

| | | | | SP | RR | SF |
|---|---|---|---|---|---|---|
| | **Province** (GLewis) **3-8-11** RHughes(10) (w'like: leggy: stdd s: hdwy over 3f out: led ins fnl f: pushed out) | — | 1 | 25/1 | 85 | 32 |
| 3229[8] | **Van Gurp (95)** (BAMcMahon) **3-8-11** JFortune(6) (plld hrd: prom: led 2f out tl hdd & no ex ins fnl f) | ½ | 2 | 5/1[2] | 84 | 31 |
| 3472[10] | **Take Notice** (GHarwood) **3-8-11** AClark(11) (hld up: rdn & hdwy over 2f out: r.o fnl f) | 2 | 3 | 16/1 | 80 | 27 |
| 3472[6] | **Galb Alasad (IRE)** (JHMGosden) **3-8-11** AMcGlone(4) (b: b.hind: trckd ldrs: ev ch over 2f out: rdn over 1f out: sn wknd) | 4 | 4 | 10/1 | 72 | 19 |
| 3262[5] | **Dantesque (IRE)** (GWragg) **3-8-11** JStack(8) (lw: chsd ldrs: outpcd over 2f out: r.o fnl f) | s.h | 5 | 5/2[1] | 72 | 19 |
| | **Poetic Dance (USA)** (JLDunlop) **3-8-11** GDuffield(3) (h.d.w: bhd tl r.o fnl 2f) | 1¼ | 6 | 33/1 | 69 | 16 |
| 3353[4] | **Silvretta (IRE)** (ACStewart) **3-8-6** DHarrison(1) (w ldr 4f: n.m.r & sn bhd: styd on again appr fnl f) | 1¾ | 7 | 11/2[3] | 61 | 8 |
| | **Latin Quarter (USA)** (RCharlton) **3-8-11** TSprake(12) (gd sort: chsd ldrs 5f) | ¾ | 8 | 11/2[3] | 64 | 11 |
| 3353[5] | **Fourdaned (IRE) (80)** (PWHarris) **3-8-11** BDoyle(5) (led 6f: wknd ins fnl f) | s.h | 9 | 20/1 | 64 | 11 |
| | **Regal Splendour (CAN)** (PFICole) **3-8-11** TQuinn(2) (w'like: scope: sn rdn & wknd) | 2 | 10 | 9/1 | 60 | 7 |
| 1142[12] | **Bello Carattere** (LordHuntingdon) **3-8-11** OUrbina(7) (lw: chsd ldrs: rdn 4f out: sn wknd) | 2½ | 11 | 33/1 | 55 | 2 |
| 3446[13] | **Hostile Native** (RGuest) **3-8-11** PBloomfield(9) (bkwd: a bhd) | 2 | 12 | 33/1 | 51? | — |
| | | | | (SP 118.4%) | | **12 Rn** |

**1m 43.45** (6.25) CSF £134.69 TOTE £17.00: £3.70 £1.80 £5.60 (£60.90) Trio £325.10; £366.42 to Nottingham 25/8/96 OWNER Highclere Thoroughbred Racing Ltd (EPSOM) BRED Campbell Stud and Partners

**Province**, gelded before this belated racecourse debut, was steadied at the start and switched towards the far rail. Challenging on the rail from the Dip, he got on top readily inside the final furlong. (25/1)
**2774 Van Gurp** has been highly-tried this year and this looks to have left its mark, for he looked sure to win when striking the front, but raced with his head rather high, and did not prove difficult to pass. (5/1: 3/1-11/2)
**3262 Take Notice** showed that his run from a bad draw last time was all wrong, staying on strongly in the latter stages. He appears to get a mile, but his pedigree suggests speed, and he ought to be effective at a lesser trip. (16/1)
**3472 Galb Alasad (IRE)** moved poorly to post and may have found this race coming too quickly after his eyecatching debut, for he folded tamely in the last furlong as the pressure was applied. (10/1: 4/1-11/1)

**3262 Dantesque (IRE)** was taken off his feet at a vital stage, but was staying on stoutly at the finish and should prove well suited by another couple of furlongs. (5/2)
**Poetic Dance (USA)** was rather keen to post, but lost all chance inside the first furlong before running on nicely when the race was over. He could find a small race if he gets his act together. (33/1)
**3353 Silvretta (IRE)** dropped away totally at halfway, only to stay on again in the closing stages. Her pedigree does not suggest a longer trip will suit, although on this evidence that is a possibility. (11/2)
**Regal Splendour (CAN)** (9/1: 5/1-10/1)

## 3789 NGK SPARK PLUGS CLAIMING STKS (3-Y.O) (Class E)

2-35 (2-36) **7f (July)** £3,915.00 (£1,170.00: £560.00: £255.00) Stalls: Low GOING: 0.01 sec per fur (G)

| | Dist | Pos | SP | RR | SF |
|---|---|---|---|---|---|
| *3628*[6] **Northern Judge (49)** (BHanbury) **3-8-3b**(7) GMilligan(9) (hld up: hdwy 3f out: led ins fnl f: pushed out) | — | 1 | 13/2 | 69 | 46 |
| 3300[4] **Uncle George (63)** (MHTompkins) **3-8-7v** NDay(4) (a.p: led over 1f out: hdd ins fnl f: r.o) | nk | 2 | 4/1[2] | 65 | 42 |
| 3591* **Power Game (66)** (JBerry) **3-9-2b** JFortune(10) (hld up: hdwy over 2f out: no imp ins fnl f) | 3 | 3 | 7/2[1] | 68 | 45 |
| 3518[13] **Paint It Black (75)** (RHannon) **3-9-11b** RHughes(12) (lw: in tch: hdwy 3f out: one pce appr fnl f) | 5 | 4 | 6/1[3] | 65 | 42 |
| 3350[6] **Ginas Girl (47)** (MissJBower) **3-8-8** AMcGlone(7) (led over 5f: sn wknd) | s.h | 5 | 25/1 | 48 | 25 |
| 1485[10] **Western Venture (IRE) (64)** (JWPayne) **3-8-4** MFenton(5) (b: trckd ldrs: rdn 2f out: sn btn) | ½ | 6 | 10/1 | 43 | 20 |
| 3458[11] **Siberian Rose** (JWharton) **3-7-10** NAdams(3) (nvr nr to chal) | 9 | 7 | 50/1 | 14 | — |
| 3472[13] **Thor's Phantom** (MDIUsher) **3-8-7** TSprake(1) (chsd ldrs 4f) | 3 | 8 | 50/1 | 18 | — |
| 3458[13] **Forecast (56)** (JWharton) **3-8-4** GDuffield(6) (reminder after 1f: sn pulling hrd & trckd ldrs: rdn & wknd 2f out) | 2 | 9 | 14/1 | 11 | — |
| 2752[12] **Sizzling Serenade (25)** (JAHarris) **3-7-10** AMackay(2) (in tch 4f: sn rdn & bhd) | hd | 10 | 50/1 | 3 | — |
| *3420*[10] **Maraschino (40)** (BJMeehan) **3-8-11** MTebbutt(8) (lw: chsd ldrs over 4f: sn rdn & wknd) | 1½ | 11 | 33/1 | 14 | — |
| 3458[6] **Ivory's Grab Hire (60)** (KTIvory) **3-8-5b**(5) MartinDwyer(11) (reard s & v.slowly away: a t.o) | 16 | 12 | 7/1 | — | — |
| | | | (SP 110.8%) | | **12 Rn** |

**1m 29.15** (4.15) CSF £28.61 TOTE £7.60: £1.50 £2.20 £1.50 (£12.70) Trio £22.90 OWNER Mr B. Hanbury (NEWMARKET) BRED Shutford Stud
**3628 Northern Judge** was the second winner in two days to frank the form of the Claimer here two weeks ago and, despite his head-carriage, he showed just too much enthusiasm for the runner-up. (13/2)
**3300 Uncle George** was probably the pick of this moderate bunch on the way to post, but once again looked less than co-operative in a close finish. (4/1: op 6/1)
**3591* Power Game**, dropped back in trip, was set too stern a task for the final two furlongs. (7/2)
**2980 Paint It Black** may have been disadvantaged by racing centre to stands' side, but can hardly be said to be going the right way. (6/1: op 3/1)
**3350 Ginas Girl**, taken down very early, still nearly ran away and proved very keen in the race. (25/1)
**Western Venture (IRE)**, a fortunate winner at Folkestone a year ago, had beaten just two rivals in three subsequent runs. Therefore, this run, even in this grade, may represent a glimmer of hope. (10/1)

## 3790 CHRIS BLACKWELL MEMORIAL H'CAP (0-90) (3-Y.O) (Class C)

3-10 (3-10) **7f (July)** £6,264.00 (£1,872.00: £896.00: £408.00) Stalls: Low GOING: 0.01 sec per fur (G)

| | Dist | Pos | SP | RR | SF |
|---|---|---|---|---|---|
| 3296[6] **Whittle Rock (82)** (MrsMReveley) **3-9-1** JFortune(15) (a.p: hung lft & led ins fnl f: rdn out) | — | 1 | 12/1 | 91 | 44 |
| 3599[5] **Trafalgar Lady (USA) (77)** (RCharlton) **3-8-10** TSprake(6) (hld up: hdwy 2f out: r.o wl fnl f) | 1 | 2 | 10/1[3] | 84 | 37 |
| 3461* **Jerry Cutrona (IRE) (81)** (NACallaghan) **3-9-0** RHughes(3) (hdwy 2f out: n.m.r & swtchd ins fnl f: r.o nr fin) | ½ | 3 | 8/1[2] | 87+ | 40 |
| 3322[2] **Angaar (IRE) (83)** (ACStewart) **3-9-2** DHarrison(2) (lw: hld up & plld hrd: hdwy over 2f out: led over 1f out: edgd lft & hdd ins fnl f) | s.h | 4 | 5/1[1] | 89 | 42 |
| 3446[3] **Lucky Archer (81)** (CEBrittain) **3-9-0** BDoyle(16) (prom: led after 3f tl over 1f out: one pce) | 2½ | 5 | 14/1 | 81 | 34 |
| 3513* **Press On Nicky (75)** (WRMuir) **3-8-8** OUrbina(8) (trckd ldrs: rdn 3f out: one pce) | ½ | 6 | 14/1 | 74 | 27 |
| 3255* **With Care (80)** (WJarvis) **3-8-13** TQuinn(7) (lw: hld up: squeezed thro wl over 1f out: r.o: nvr able to chal) | hd | 7 | 5/1[1] | 78 | 31 |
| 3215[3] **White Emir (87)** (BJMeehan) **3-9-6b** MTebbutt(11) (hld up: effrt 3f out: no imp appr fnl f) | 1½ | 8 | 25/1 | 82 | 35 |
| 3210[7] **Wisam (88)** (RHannon) **3-9-7** RPerham(12) (stdd s: nvr nr to chal) | ¾ | 9 | 25/1 | 81 | 34 |
| 3432[8] **Shanghai Girl (84)** (DRLoder) **3-9-3v** DRMcCabe(10) (plld hrd: chsd ldrs: rdn 2f out: wknd ins fnl f) | 1¾ | 10 | 12/1 | 73 | 26 |
| 3446* **Disputed (84)** (MAJarvis) **3-9-3** PBloomfield(4) (swtg: prom 5f: sn wknd) | 2 | 11 | 8/1[2] | 69 | 22 |
| 3210[9] **Steal 'Em (68)** (ABailey) **3-7-12**(3) DWright(14) (led 3f: wknd 2f out) | 1¼ | 12 | 25/1 | 50 | 3 |
| 3322[4] **Mr Speaker (IRE) (63)** (CFWall) **3-7-10** NCarlisle(1) (chsd ldrs tl rdn & wknd over 2f out) | 2 | 13 | 14/1 | 40 | — |
| 3322[7] **Poetry (IRE) (84)** (MHTompkins) **3-9-3** NDay(13) (w ldrs tl rdn & wknd 3f out) | 8 | 14 | 16/1 | 43 | — |
| 2885[7] **She's My Love (74)** (JEBanks) **3-8-2**(5) MartinDwyer(5) (prom: rdn 3f out: sn wknd) | 8 | 15 | 11/1 | 15 | — |
| 2950[3] **Mazeed (IRE) (85)** (HThomsonJones) **3-9-4** GDuffield(9) (chsd ldrs: rdn over 2f out: wkng whn hmpd wl over 1f out) | 1¼ | 16 | 20/1 | 23+ | — |
| | | | (SP 130.5%) | | **16 Rn** |

**1m 29.75** (4.75) CSF £123.14 CT £979.03 TOTE £15.60: £4.10 £3.60 £2.00 £2.00 (£118.70) Trio £462.90 OWNER Bay Horse Racing Syndicate (SALTBURN) BRED J. Needham
**3296 Whittle Rock** had looked a doubtful stayer when tried at this trip from her previous yard, but she battled hard in the testing ground, despite steering a slightly erratic course. Cut in the ground looks to suit her. (12/1)
**3599 Trafalgar Lady (USA)** does relish these underfoot conditions. Stepping up to seven furlongs for the first time, he was ridden to get the trip and did not get going until too late. (10/1)
**3461* Jerry Cutrona (IRE)** is in grand shape at present and does love a rail to race against. He made a dangerous move against the far rail, which might have prevailed had it not been halted in full flow. (8/1)
**3322 Angaar (IRE)**, with the field electing to come down the centre of the course in the first part of the race, saw too much daylight, but still took some pegging back once sent for home. He does look capable of winning a race of this type when things go right. (5/1)
**3446 Lucky Archer** takes a very good hold and showed a lot of speed in the centre of the track until finding little at the business end as usual. (14/1)
**3513* Press On Nicky** raced rather closer to the pace this time and, although she was feeling the pace soon after halfway, she kept plugging away to the end. (14/1)

## 3791 DANEPAK CLASSIC RATED STKS H'CAP (0-95) (3-Y.O+) (Class C)

3-40 (3-41) **1m 2f (July)** £10,010.00 (£3,710.00: £1,785.00: £735.00: £297.50: £122.50) Stalls: High GOING: 0.23 sec per fur (G)

| | Dist | Pos | SP | RR | SF |
|---|---|---|---|---|---|
| 3447[4] **Ball Gown (88)** (DTThom) **6-9-1** DRMcCabe(1) (lw: b: b.hind: hdwy 5f out: led 1f out: rdn clr) | — | 1 | 5/1[2] | 100 | 72 |
| 3071[8] **Henry Island (IRE) (89)** (GWragg) **3-8-1**(7) GMilligan(7) (swtg: a.p: led over 1f out: sn hdd & one pce) | 4 | 2 | 12/1 | 95 | 59 |
| 3211[10] **Double Bluff (IRE) (90)** (IABalding) **3-8-4**(5) MartinDwyer(5) (led tl hdd over 1f out: kpt on) | ½ | 3 | 16/1 | 95 | 59 |

| | | | | SP | RR | SF |
|---|---|---|---|---|---|---|
| 3248* | **Bardon Hill Boy (IRE) (92)** (BHanbury) **4-9-5** JStack(4) (chsd ldrs: one pce fnl 2f) | 4 | **4** | 9/1 | 90 | 62 |
| 3447[12] | **Jagellon (USA) (86)** (WRMuir) **5-8-13** JFEgan(2) (trckd ldrs: rdn 2f out: no imp) | hd | **5** | 33/1 | 84 | 56 |
| 772[4] | **House of Riches (86)** (LMCumani) **3-8-5** OUrbina(12) (plld hrd: chsd ldrs 7f: n.d afterwards) | 3 | **6** | 16/1 | 79 | 43 |
| 3509[10] | **King Athelstan (USA) (83)** (BAMcMahon) **8-8-10** JFortune(6) (lw: chsd ldrs: ev ch over 2f out: sn btn) | 6 | **7** | 25/1 | 67 | 39 |
| 2579* | **Questonia (89)** (HRACecil) **3-8-8** AMcGlone(13) (lw: chsd ldrs: rdn 3f out: sn wknd) | 1½ | **8** | 9/4[1] | 70 | 34 |
| 3212[8] | **Ionio (USA) (94)** (CEBrittain) **5-9-7** BDoyle(3) (rdn 6f out: a bhd) | 7 | **9** | 16/1 | 64 | 36 |
| 1961[4] | **Kings Assembly (80)** (PWHarris) **4-8-7** GDuffield(10) (chsd ldrs: rdn 5f out: wknd 3f out) | 7 | **10** | 16/1 | 39 | 11 |
| 3155[7] | **Infamous (USA) (81)** (PFICole) **3-8-0b[1]** TSprake(9) (a bhd) | 8 | **11** | 8/1 | 27 | — |
| 2502[15] | **Major Change (91)** (RHannon) **4-9-4** RHughes(11) (a bhd) | ¾ | **12** | 14/1 | 36 | 8 |
| 3125[2] | **Silver Groom (IRE) (80)** (RAkehurst) **6-8-7** TQuinn(8) (dropped rr & rdn 6f out: sn t.o) | dist | **13** | 6/1[3] | — | — |
| | | | | (SP 127.5%) | **13 Rn** | |

**2m 10.68** (5.68) CSF £61.77 CT £844.72 TOTE £6.70: £2.20 £3.40 £4.30 (£36.40) Trio £177.00 OWNER Mr C. V. Lines (NEWMARKET) BRED J. M. Greetham

LONG HANDICAP Kings Assembly 8-6

WEIGHT FOR AGE 3yo-8lb

**3447 Ball Gown** had conditions to suit, notably Newmarket, ten furlongs, a very strong early pace and cut in the ground. Under these circumstances, her turn of foot becomes a major asset, and she used it to full effect. (5/1)

**2608 Henry Island (IRE)** battled long and hard to get to the front, only for the winner to sweep by the moment he got there. (12/1)

**2742* Double Bluff (IRE)**, reverting to forcing tactics, set a strong pace considering the conditions and certainly did not disgrace himself. (16/1)

**3248* Bardon Hill Boy (IRE)**, never far off the pace, was struggling to quicken at all in the testing conditions. (9/1)

**Jagellon (USA)**, off a 13lb higher mark than from that which he has scored before, handles this ground and looked to be travelling well for almost a mile, but could not pick up once let down. (33/1)

**772 House of Riches** could never get to the front and was brought to the stands' rail, away from his rivals, but this made little difference. (16/1)

**2579* Questonia** hardly looked over-burdened for her handicap debut, but was in trouble a long way from home. Her sire Rainbow Quest's winning percentages drop from sixteen on good and fast ground to eleven when the ground rides softer than good, so Questonia is worth another chance on a faster surface. (9/4)

**1961* Major Change** (14/1: 10/1-16/1)

**3125 Silver Groom (IRE)** was beaten after half a mile and something must have been seriously amiss. (6/1)

## 3792 TOTE MULTIBET NURSERY H'CAP (2-Y.O) (Class C)

4-10 (4-11) **6f (July)** £15,140.00 (£4,520.00: £2,160.00: £980.00) Stalls: Low GOING: 0.23 sec per fur (G)

| | | | | SP | RR | SF |
|---|---|---|---|---|---|---|
| 2879[4] | **Magical Times (98)** (RBoss) **2-9-7** GDuffield(8) (trckd ldrs: str run to ld wl ins fnl f) | — | **1** | 10/1 | 94 | 56 |
| 3247[7] | **Ocker (IRE) (75)** (MHTompkins) **2-7-9**(3) DWright(7) (hld up: hdwy 2f out: led ins fnl f: sn hdd & r.o) | s.h | **2** | 11/1 | 71 | 33 |
| 2703[4] | **Bold Catch (USA) (84)** (RCharlton) **2-8-7** TSprake(5) (hdwy 3f out: led over 1f out: hdd & unable qckn ins fnl f) | ½ | **3** | 12/1 | 79 | 41 |
| 3224[4] | **Burkes Manor (84)** (TDBarron) **2-8-7** JFortune(1) (lw: in tch: rdn 2f out: r.o fnl f) | 3 | **4** | 14/1 | 71 | 33 |
| 3160[6] | **Plan For Profit (IRE) (75)** (MJohnston) **2-7-12** JFanning(2) (chsd ldrs: led 2f out: hdd over 1f out: wknd ins fnl f) | ½ | **5** | 10/1 | 60 | 22 |
| 3478[3] | **Anokato (73)** (KTIvory) **2-7-5**(5) MartinDwyer(4) (led 4f: edgd rt & wknd) | 7 | **6** | 20/1 | 40 | 2 |
| 3291* | **Swino (83)** (PDEvans) **2-8-6** JFEgan(12) (w ldrs over 3f) | 2 | **7** | 10/1 | 44 | 6 |
| 3478[2] | **Maserati Monk (96)** (BJMeehan) **2-9-5** MTebbutt(11) (plld hrd: prom 4f) | 2 | **8** | 11/2[2] | 52 | 14 |
| 2965* | **Osomental (97)** (DHaydnJones) **2-9-6b** AMackay(9) (dwlt: nvr nr to chal) | 3½ | **9** | 7/1 | 44 | 6 |
| 3616[4] | **Golden Fact (USA) (83)** (RHannon) **2-8-6** RPerham(10) (dwlt: sn pushed along: hung lft over 2f out: nvr nr ldrs) | hd | **10** | 12/1 | 29 | — |
| 3282[3] | **Ricasso (75)** (DRLoder) **2-7-12b[1]** DRMcCabe(6) (lw: plld hrd: chsd ldrs: hmpd over 2f out: sn bhd) | 1¼ | **11** | 4/1[1] | 18 | — |
| 2878[4] | **Fletcher (94)** (PFICole) **2-9-3** TQuinn(3) (w ldrs: rdn 3f out: sn bhd) | 6 | **12** | 6/1[3] | 21 | — |
| | | | | (SP 124.6%) | **12 Rn** | |

**1m 16.85** (4.85) CSF £108.02 CT £1,236.75 TOTE £9.90: £2.90 £4.20 £4.70 (£77.10) Trio £321.10 OWNER Ms Lynn Bell (NEWMARKET) BRED White Lodge Farm Stud

LONG HANDICAP Anokato 7-7

**2879 Magical Times** ran well against subsequent Group winner Kingsinger on his only previous attempt on rain-softened ground, and was another to frank the Newbury Super Sprint form by sticking to his guns gamely to defy topweight. (10/1)

**2985 Ocker (IRE)**, ridden with much more restraint this time, did everything right and will surely soon find a race. (11/1: 8/1-12/1)

**2703 Bold Catch (USA)** appears to have one short run which needs to be used at the right moment. (12/1)

**3224 Burkes Manor** might have been expected to find this trip on this ground stretching his stamina, but he kept plugging away. (14/1)

**3160 Plan For Profit (IRE)** has a pedigree which suggests seven furlongs to a mile, but he does not seem to stay six furlongs yet. (10/1)

**3478 Anokato** does appear to have a problem running straight at the business end of a race. (20/1)

**3478 Maserati Monk** ruined his chance by pulling far too hard in this testing ground. (11/2)

**2965* Osomental** (7/1: 5/1-15/2)

**3616 Golden Fact (USA)**, who flopped on soft ground before, hung across the course, flashing his tail once put to work. (12/1)

**3282 Ricasso** seems to be going the wrong way and, although he consented to go down quietly in the first-time blinkers, he was pulling his pilot's arms out once the stalls opened. (4/1)

## 3793 HAMELLS LADIES' H'CAP (0-85) (3-Y.O+) (Class E)

4-40 (4-41) **5f (July)** £4,620.00 (£1,380.00: £660.00: £300.00) Stalls: Low GOING: 0.23 sec per fur (G)

| | | | | SP | RR | SF |
|---|---|---|---|---|---|---|
| 2022[2] | **Moon Strike (FR) (74)** (HAkbary) **6-11-2**(5) MissIFoustok(8) (hld up: hdwy over 1f out: led ins fnl f: pushed clr) | — | **1** | 16/1 | 85 | 75 |
| 3644[5] | **Tropical Beach (66)** (JBerry) **3-10-11** MrsLPearce(1) (lw: outpcd: rdn & hdwy 2f out: nt clr run over 1f out: swtchd & r.o fnl f) | 3 | **2** | 9/1 | 67 | 55 |
| 3506[2] | **Squire Corrie (57)** (GHarwood) **4-10-4b** MrsAPerrett(4) (w ldrs: led over 2f out: hdd ins fnl f: unable qckn) | s.h | **3** | 11/2[3] | 58 | 48 |
| 3624* | **Barranak (IRE) (67)** (GMMcCourt) **4-10-9**(5) MrsSEddery(5) (prom: ev ch over 1f out: sn btn) | 1 | **4** | 13/2 | 65 | 55 |
| 3432[17] | **Mousehole (71)** (RGuest) **4-10-13**(5) MissZBurkett(6) (in tch: rdn 2f out: no imp) | ½ | **5** | 11/1 | 67 | 57 |
| 3639[4] | **French Grit (IRE) (71)** (MDods) **4-11-4** MissDianaJones(2) (led over 2f: no ex fnl f) | s.h | **6** | 8/1 | 67 | 57 |
| 3465[9] | **Myttons Mistake (70)** (ABailey) **3-10-10**(5) MissBridgetGatehouse(11) (outpcd: effrt 2f out: nvr able to chal) | 4 | **7** | 16/1 | 54 | 42 |
| 3432[13] | **Shadow Jury (66)** (DWChapman) **6-10-13b** MissRClark(3) (w ldr 3f: wknd over 1f out) | ½ | **8** | 9/1 | 48 | 38 |

3342[6] **Serious Hurry (42)** (RMMcKellar) **8-8-12b**(5) MrsCWilliams(9) (spd 2f: hung rt & wknd over 1f out) ..............3½ **9** 25/1 13 3
3360[2] **Lloc (54)** (CADwyer) **4-9-10**(5) MrsSDwyer(10) (lw: swtg: chsd ldrs 3f) ..............2½ **10** 5/1 [2] — 7
3700* **Wardara (65)** (CADwyer) **4-10-7v**(5) MissAAnderson(7) (s.i.s: sn t.o) ..............4 **11** 5/2 [1] — 5
(SP 129.0%) **11 Rn**

**62.93 secs** (4.43) CSF £148.37 CT £853.55 TOTE £19.50: £4.90 £2.20 £1.90 (£108.90) Trio £195.40 OWNER Mr A. Foustok (NEWMARKET) BRED Haras de Manneville in France
WEIGHT FOR AGE 3yo-2lb
OFFICIAL EXPLANATION **Wardara: was restless in the stalls and never travelling in the race**
**2022 Moon Strike (FR)** is useful on his day and often runs well after a break. His best trip is probably seven furlongs, but the fast pace on this ground brought his stamina into play, and he ran out a decisive winner. (16/1)
**3644 Tropical Beach** would have got rather closer had his run not been interrupted. (9/1)
**3506 Squire Corrie** did best of those that disputed the early lead, but could not last home. (11/2)
**3624* Barranak (IRE)** could not dominate this time, but still ran another sound race. (13/2: 9/2-7/1)
**3219 Mousehole** was taken off his feet to past halfway and is better over six. (11/1: 7/1-12/1)
**3639 French Grit (IRE)** set a terrific pace on this testing surface and paid the penalty on meeting the rising ground. (8/1: op 5/1)

## 3794 E.B.F. PARK LODGE MAIDEN STKS (2-Y.O) (Class D)
5-15 (5-15) **6f (July)** £4,152.00 (£1,236.00: £588.00: £264.00) Stalls: Low GOING: 0.23 sec per fur (G)

SP RR SF

**Desert Story (IRE)** (MRStoute) **2-9-0** KBradshaw(5) (gd sort: bkwd: hld up: hdwy over 1f out: led ins fnl f: pushed out) ..............— **1** 5/2 [2] 90+ 35
**Imperial Scholar (IRE)** (JMPEustace) **2-8-9** MTebbutt(1) (leggy: scope: trckd ldrs: nt clr run & swtchd 1f out: r.o wl) ..............1¼ **2** 25/1 82 27
**Rapier** (RHannon) **2-9-0** DHarrison(4) (w'like: chsd ldrs: rdn & ev ch 1f out: one pce) ..............½ **3** 4/1 85 30
2852[2] **Jawhari** (JLDunlop) **2-9-0** TQuinn(3) (w ldr: led 1f out: sn hdd & btn) ..............1½ **4** 9/4 [1] 81 26
3245[6] **Jalb (IRE)** (ACStewart) **2-9-0** RHughes(2) (led: rdn 2f out: hdd & wknd 1f out) ..............2 **5** 100/30 [3] 76 21
**Frankie** (MHTompkins) **2-9-0** NDay(6) (str: scope: bkwd: sn pushed along & bhd) ..............10 **6** 12/1 49 —
(SP 114.0%) **6 Rn**

**1m 17.93** (5.93) CSF £38.97 TOTE £3.50: £2.10 £2.70 (£34.10) OWNER Maktoum Al Maktoum (NEWMARKET) BRED Gainsborough Stud Management Ltd
**Desert Story (IRE)**, out of disqualified Oaks winner Aliysa, had apparently given some stalls problems at home, but showed little sign of it here. Waiting for a gap, he quickened readily when it finally came, and he looks sure to come on considerably for the run. (5/2)
**Imperial Scholar (IRE)** looked fit, but is rather lightly-built. She clearly has an engine though, and got no sort of a run at a vital stage, before finishing strongly. (25/1)
**Rapier** probably appreciated the cut in the ground, being by Sharpo, and ran creditably, but had a harder race than the first two. (4/1)
**2852 Jawhari** still looked as if this run was needed, and was a spent force in the final furlong. (9/4)
**3245 Jalb (IRE)** still looked rather green going to post and probably didn't handle the ground, folding tamely in the final furlong. (100/30: 2/1-7/2)
**Frankie** looked a long way short of peak-fitness, and those who backed him down knew their fate after a furlong. (12/1)

T/Jkpt: Not won; £5,928.70 to Goodwood 25/8/96. T/Plpt: £1,132.50 (27.08 Tckts). T/Qdpt: £135.70 (14.40 Tckts). Dk

# 3656-WINDSOR (Fig. 8) (Soft)
## Saturday August 24th
WEATHER: unsettled WIND: almost nil

## 3795 GREAT CHARTER (S) STKS (2-Y.O) (Class F)
5-15 (5-16) **5f 217y** £2,605.00 (£730.00: £355.00) Stalls: High GOING minus 0.19 sec per fur (GF)

SP RR SF

3582[3] **Hoh Surprise (IRE) (56)** (MBell) **2-8-6** MFenton(7) (s.i.s: hdwy 3f out: led over 1f out: r.o wl) ..............— **1** 5/2 [1] 63 23
3512[9] **Poly Moon (59)** (MRChannon) **2-8-11** CRutter(4) (led: hrd rdn & hdd over 1f out: unable qckn) ..............1¼ **2** 5/2 [1] 65 25
*3604*[5] **Senate Swings (56)** (WRMuir) **2-8-8**(3) FLynch(1) (hdwy over 2f out: r.o ins fnl f) ..............1½ **3** 12/1 61 21
2904[7] **Zanabay (62)** (MartynMeade) **2-8-6** NAdams(8) (s.s: hdwy over 2f out: one pce fnl f) ..............2 **4** 7/2 [2] 50 10
3651[6] **Lady Grovefair (IRE)** (BJMeehan) **2-8-6** SSanders(6) (prom 4f) ..............hd **5** 9/1 50 10
*3629*[4] **Surprise Event (67)** (WGMTurner) **2-8-11b**[1] AClark(2) (prom 3f: eased whn btn over 1f out) ..............9 **6** 5/1 [3] 31 —
3169[8] **Tirol's Treasure (IRE)** (KTIvory) **2-8-6b**[1] CScally(5) (b: b.hind: s.s: a t.o) ..............28 **7** 25/1 — —
(SP 117.6%) **7 Rn**

**1m 14.2** (3.70) CSF £9.25 TOTE £2.70: £1.50 £1.60 (£2.70) OWNER Mr D. F. Allport (NEWMARKET) BRED A. F. O'Callaghan
No bid
IN-FOCUS: **A heavy thunder storm before racing changed the ground from good to soft. The runners raced on the far side.**
**3582 Hoh Surprise (IRE)** seemed more at home on the rain-drenched ground. (5/2)
**3512 Poly Moon**, dropping back in distance, had already shown a liking for give underfoot. (5/2)
**3604 Senate Swings** appears to need at least six now. (12/1: 8/1-14/1)
**2714 Zanabay** was dropped in both class and trip. (7/2)
**3651 Lady Grovefair (IRE)** fared better than when hampered at the start on her debut earlier in the week. (9/1: op 5/1)

## 3796 TATTERSALLS MAIDEN AUCTION STKS (2-Y.O) (Class E)
5-45 (5-50) **5f 217y** £3,257.50 (£985.00: £480.00: £227.50) Stalls: High GOINGminus 0.19 sec per fur (GF)

SP RR SF

**Johnny Staccato** (JMPEustace) **2-8-11** RCochrane(15) (small: cmpt: stdd s: gd hdwy over 2f out: led 1f out: easily) ..............— **1** 20/1 89+ 38
2993[5] **Parijazz (IRE)** (MartynMeade) **2-7-12** NAdams(4) (w ldr: ev ch 1f out: unable qckn) ..............2½ **2** 20/1 69 18
3515[2] **Northern Girl (IRE) (70)** (BJMeehan) **2-7-13** WCarson(1) (led 5f: one pce) ..............nk **3** 4/1 [2] 70 19
3411[3] **Jack The Lad (IRE) (66)** (CMurray) **2-8-3**(3) FLynch(11) (a.p: one pce fnl 2f) ..............1¾ **4** 16/1 72 21
3515[4] **Celebrant** (RHannon) **2-8-2** DaneO'Neill(9) (a.p: no hdwy fnl 2f) ..............½ **5** 5/1 [3] 67 16
**For Lara (IRE)** (HCandy) **2-7-13** CRutter(14) (w'like: prom 4f) ..............7 **6** 14/1 45 —
**Righty Ho** (PTWalwyn) **2-8-4** JStack(8) (leggy: nvr nrr) ..............¾ **7** 25/1 48 —
3515[5] **Circle of Magic** (PJMakin) **2-8-3**ow1 SSanders(16) (prom over 3f) ..............1 **8** 14/1 44 —

| | | | | SP | RR | SF |
|---|---|---|---|---|---|---|
| | **Java Bay** (MBlanshard) **2-8-5** AClark(12) (neat: chsd ldrs: hung lft over 2f out: sn wknd) | 2 | **9** | 16/1 | 41 | — |
| | **The Commodore (IRE)** (WJarvis) **2-8-9** StephenDavies(13) (w'like: b: chsd ldrs over 3f) | 1½ | **10** | 16/1 | 41 | — |
| 3515[7] | **M R Poly** (MRChannon) **2-8-4**(5) PPMurphy(10) (prom over 3f) | 1¼ | **11** | 16/1 | 37 | — |
| | **Jack Brown** (TTClement) **2-8-3**(5) LNewton(6) (w'like: prom over 3f) | ¾ | **12** | 33/1 | 34 | — |
| 3259[4] | **Broughtons Error (80)** (WJMusson) **2-8-3** AMcGlone(17) (dwlt: a bhd) | ½ | **13** | 7/1 | 28 | — |
| 3429[4] | **Hoh Dancer** (IABalding) **2-8-7**ow1 LDettori(3) (prom over 3f) | 1¾ | **14** | 7/2[1] | 27 | — |
| | **Star Turn (IRE)** (MBell) **2-8-6** MFenton(18) (w'like : scope: a bhd) | 1 | **15** | 12/1 | 24 | — |
| | **Hype Energy** (GLewis) **2-8-5**(3)ow3 AWhelan(5) (lengthy: a bhd) | hd | **16** | 20/1 | 26 | — |
| 1008[4] | **Mike's Double (IRE)** (GLewis) **2-8-7** CScally(2) (s.s: a bhd) | 3 | **17** | 25/1 | 16 | — |
| | **Major Twist (IRE)** (RHannon) **2-8-6** OUrbina(7) (w'like: s.s: a bhd) | ½ | **18** | 20/1 | 14 | — |

(SP 145.6%) **18 Rn**

**1m 13.4** (2.90) CSF £372.54 TOTE £43.00: £8.80 £7.90 £1.90 (£381.80) Trio £460.50; £324.31 to 26/8/96 OWNER Mr J. C. Smith (NEWMARKET) BRED Bishop's Down Farm

OFFICIAL EXPLANATION **Hoh Dancer: the rider stated that the filly lost her action on the ground and became unbalanced.**

IN-FOCUS: **Runners raced on the far side.**

**Johnny Staccato**, a half-brother to a winner in Scandinavia, is out of an unraced sister to Jester. Given plenty to do, he took to the conditions like a duck to water and can score again on this sort of ground. (20/1)

**2993 Parijazz (IRE)**, fitter this time, was obviously not inconvenienced by the rain-softened ground and confirmed the promise of her debut. (20/1)

**3515 Northern Girl (IRE)** again adopted front-running tactics and handled the change in the going well enough. (4/1)

**3411 Jack The Lad (IRE)** could not do the business, despite underfoot conditions putting more of an emphasis on stamina. (16/1)

**3515 Celebrant** could not raise her game when the chips were down. (5/1)

**For Lara (IRE)** showed signs of ability and may have lasted longer on better ground. (14/1)

**Righty Ho**, a half-brother to Sarasota Storm, is out of a mare who won over seven as a juvenile, and shaped as though he will do better when tackling further. (25/1)

**3515 Circle of Magic** (14/1: 10/1-16/1)

**3429 Hoh Dancer** (7/2: tchd 11/2)

**Star Turn (IRE)** (12/1: 9/2-14/1)

## 3797 WEATHERBYS SPONSORSHIP IN RACING CONDITIONS STKS (3-Y.O+) (Class C)

6-15 (6-17) **1m 3f 135y** £4,791.40 (£1,792.60: £876.30: £376.50: £168.25: £84.95) Stalls: High GOING: 0.19 sec per fur (G)

| | | | | SP | RR | SF |
|---|---|---|---|---|---|---|
| 2535[2] | **Shantou (USA) (115)** (JHMGosden) **3-8-7** LDettori(3) (hld up: hdwy to ld over 2f out: pushed out) | — | **1** | 11/8[1] | 121 | 45 |
| 1791[10] | **Double Leaf (110)** (MRStoute) **3-8-6**ow1 JReid(5) (a.p: rn wd bnd 6f out: chsd wnr over 1f out: no imp) | 3½ | **2** | 11/4[2] | 115 | 38 |
| 1329[6] | **Side Note** (HRACecil) **3-8-7** RCochrane(2) (a.p: rdn to ld over 3f out: hdd over 2f out: wknd over 1f out) | 3½ | **3** | 9/1 | 111 | 35 |
| 2730[5] | **Fahal (USA) (114)** (DMorley) **4-9-1** WCarson(1) (led 8f: eased whn btn over 1f out: t.o) | dist | **4** | 9/2[3] | — | — |
| 3597[4] | **Babinda (101)** (CEBrittain) **3-8-5** BDoyle(4) (prom tl rdn & wknd over 3f out: t.o) | 30 | **5** | 9/1 | — | — |
| | **Captain's Guest (IRE)** (GHarwood) **6-9-1** AClark(6) (sn t.o) | 13 | **6** | 20/1 | — | — |

(SP 111.7%) **6 Rn**

**2m 31.9** (7.90) CSF £5.39 TOTE £2.00: £1.40 £2.00 (£3.10) OWNER Sheikh Mohammed (NEWMARKET) BRED Darley Stud Management Inc

WEIGHT FOR AGE 3yo-10lb

**2535 Shantou (USA)** had won his Sandown maiden on yielding ground and it does seem to bring out the best in him. (11/8)

**1114 Double Leaf** had finished seven lengths behind the winner in the Derby, so at least he halved the deficit. (11/4: 2/1-3/1)

**1329 Side Note**, a galloping-companion of Dushyantor, has presumably been kept on the sidelines during the summer while the fast ground prevailed. (9/1: 6/1-10/1)

**2730 Fahal (USA)**, without the blinkers this time, found the ground coming up all wrong for him. (9/2)

**3597 Babinda** (9/1: 6/1-10/1)

## 3798 WINTER HILL STKS (Gp 3) (3-Y.O+) (Class A)

6-45 (6-46) **1m 2f 7y** £19,290.00 (£7,302.00: £3,576.00: £1,632.00) Stalls: High GOING: 0.19 sec per fur (G)

| | | | | SP | RR | SF |
|---|---|---|---|---|---|---|
| 3070[5] | **Annus Mirabilis (FR) (116)** (SbinSuroor) **4-9-0v** LDettori(3) (lw: hld up: c wd 4f out: r.o to ld wl ins fnl f) | — | **1** | 85/40[2] | 120 | 73 |
| 3212* | **Salmon Ladder (USA) (112)** (PFICole) **4-9-0** TQuinn(4) (led over 7f: hrd rdn to ld 1f out: hdd wl ins fnl f) | ¾ | **2** | 9/4[3] | 119 | 72 |
| 3124[3] | **Storm Trooper (USA) (114)** (HRACecil) **3-8-6** RCochrane(2) (lw: hld up: hdwy over 3f out: led over 2f out to 1f out: unable qckn) | ¾ | **3** | 7/4[1] | 118 | 63 |
| 1791[19] | **Prince of My Heart (103)** (BWHills) **3-8-6** GDuffield(6) (chsd ldr over 6f: sn wknd) | 12 | **4** | 16/1 | 99 | 44 |
| 3071* | **Behaviour (107)** (MrsJCecil) **4-9-0** JReid(1) (hld up: bhd fnl 4f) | 4 | **5** | 9/1 | 92 | 45 |

(SP 115.0%) **5 Rn**

**2m 9.1** (4.20) CSF £7.31 TOTE £3.20: £1.30 £1.60 (£2.30) OWNER Godolphin (NEWMARKET) BRED Darley Stud Management Co Ltd

WEIGHT FOR AGE 3yo-8lb

**3070 Annus Mirabilis (FR)** had won on soft ground as a two-year-old and, nipping through against the far rail, finally managed to win a Group race. (85/40: 3/1-2/1)

**3212* Salmon Ladder (USA)** battled his heart out to get the better of Storm Trooper, but could not withstand the winner's late run. This ground was plenty soft enough for him. (9/4)

**3124 Storm Trooper (USA)**, dropping back in distance, seemed to be going well enough when taking it up, but got outbattled by the runner-up, let alone the winner. (7/4: 5/4-2/1)

**3071* Behaviour** (9/1: 5/1-10/1)

## 3799 SHEET & ROLL CONVERTORS POLY RATED STKS H'CAP (0-90) (3-Y.O+) (Class C)

7-15 (7-16) **1m 67y** £4,874.92 (£1,824.28: £892.14: £383.70: £171.85: £87.11) Stalls: High GOING: 0.19 sec per fur (G)

| | | | | SP | RR | SF |
|---|---|---|---|---|---|---|
| 2885[3] | **Admirals Flame (IRE) (74)** (CFWall) **5-9-1** GDuffield(10) (hld up: hdwy over 2f out: rdn to ld nr fin) | — | **1** | 6/1 | 86 | 63 |
| 2128[4] | **Hilaala (USA) (80)** (PTWalwyn) **3-9-1** WCarson(1) (a.p: led over 1f out: hdd nr fin) | nk | **2** | 13/2 | 91 | 62 |
| 3123[2] | **Orsay (78)** (WRMuir) **4-9-5** JWeaver(9) (led: hrd rdn over 2f out: hdd over 1f out: one pce) | 3 | **3** | 9/4[1] | 84 | 61 |
| 3298[3] | **Forest Robin (80)** (RFJohnsonHoughton) **3-9-1** BDoyle(4) (rdn & hdwy over 1f out: nvr nr to chal) | 1½ | **4** | 9/1 | 83 | 54 |
| 3501[3] | **Seventeens Lucky (75)** (BobJones) **4-8-11**(5) LNewton(11) (lw: plld hrd: a.p: ev ch over 1f out: wknd fnl f) | 1 | **5** | 12/1 | 76 | 53 |
| 3521[2] | **Courageous Dancer (IRE) (74)** (BHanbury) **4-9-1** JStack(6) (hdwy over 3f out: wknd over 1f out) | ¾ | **6** | 4/1[2] | 73 | 50 |
| 2045[6] | **Prima Volta (75)** (RHannon) **3-8-10b** JFEgan(8) (lw: prom over 5f) | 4 | **7** | 20/1 | 67 | 38 |
| 3516[8] | **Comanche Companion (73)** (TJNaughton) **6-9-0** PaulEddery(5) (a bhd) | 1¼ | **8** | 11/2[3] | 62 | 39 |

| | | | | SP | RR | SF |
|---|---|---|---|---|---|---|
| 1127[12] | **Green Bopper (USA) (80)** (MBell) **3-9-1** MFenton(2) (prom over 4f) | 8 | **9** | 20/1 | 54 | 25 |
| 809[15] | **Sejaal (IRE) (78)** (RAkehurst) **4-9-5** TQuinn(7) (plld hrd: prom tl wknd qckly 3f out: t.o) | 13 | **10** | 12/1 | 27 | 4 |
| 2007[13] | **Oh Whataknight (86)** (JWHills) **3-9-7** MHills(3) (bhd: rdn 4f out: sn t.o) | 13 | **11** | 25/1 | 10 | — |

(SP 132.5%) **11 Rn**

**1m 46.7** (4.50) CSF £46.75 CT £111.41 TOTE £7.10: £2.50 £2.00 £1.60 (£15.80) Trio £22.40 OWNER Hintlesham Racing (NEWMARKET) BRED A. Tarry

WEIGHT FOR AGE 3yo-6lb

**2885 Admirals Flame (IRE)** had shown he can handle soft ground when winning a seller as a three-year-old, and benefited from stronger handling than at Newmarket. (6/1: op 4/1)

**2128 Hilaala (USA)**, another not inconvenienced by the ease in the going, went very close on her debut in handicap company. (13/2)

**3123 Orsay** had to contend with softer ground and a 3lb higher mark. (9/4)

**3298 Forest Robin**, dropped 6lb, may benefit from a longer trip on this sort of going. (9/1)

**3501 Seventeens Lucky** needs better ground than he encountered here. (12/1: op 6/1)

**3521 Courageous Dancer (IRE)** had ground conditions in her favour, and was backed accordingly, but could not take advantage of an 8lb lower mark. (4/1)

**455 Comanche Companion** (11/2: 8/1-5/1)

**Sejaal (IRE)** (12/1: 6/1-14/1)

## 3800 RUNNYMEDE H'CAP (0-75) (3-Y.O+ F & M) (Class D)

7-45 (7-46) **1m 67y** £3,733.50 (£1,128.00: £549.00: £259.50) Stalls: High GOING: 0.19 sec per fur (G)

| | | | | SP | RR | SF |
|---|---|---|---|---|---|---|
| 3469[8] | **Q Factor (70)** (DHaydnJones) **4-10-0** SDrowne(7) (lw: a.p: led over 2f out: all out) | — | **1** | 9/1 | 77 | 59 |
| 3167[11] | **Pomona (74)** (PJMakin) **3-9-12** SSanders(3) (lw: hld up & bhd: gd hdwy over 1f out: edgd lft fnl f: r.o) | hd | **2** | 14/1 | 81 | 57 |
| 3334[7] | **Time of Night (USA) (66)** (RGuest) **3-8-13**(5) DGriffiths(6) (hld up: hdwy over 2f out: ev ch over 1f out: hung lft ins fnl f: one pce) | 3 | **3** | 10/1 | 67 | 43 |
| 3525[3] | **Charisse Dancer (55)** (CFWall) **3-8-7** GDuffield(12) (lw: a.p: one pce fnl 2f) | 1¼ | **4** | 9/2[2] | 54 | 30 |
| 3592[5] | **Cuban Reef (47)** (WJMusson) **4-8-5** AMcGlone(2) (gd hdwy 3f out: ev ch 2f out: wknd over 1f out) | nk | **5** | 7/1[3] | 45 | 27 |
| 2722[9] | **Elite Hope (USA) (70)** (CREgerton) **4-9-9**(5) AimeeCook(9) (plld hrd: prom tl wknd over 1f out) | 2 | **6** | 12/1 | 64 | 46 |
| 2603[16] | **Classic Romance (71)** (RHarris) **3-9-9** AMackay(4) (hld up: hdwy over 3f out: wknd over 2f out) | 6 | **7** | 7/1[3] | 54 | 30 |
| 3470[6] | **Disallowed (IRE) (71)** (MBell) **3-9-9** MFenton(5) (a bhd) | ½ | **8** | 10/1 | 53 | 29 |
| 3472[7] | **Press Again (53)** (PHayward) **4-8-11** RPerham(11) (led over 5f: sn wknd) | nk | **9** | 25/1 | 34 | 16 |
| 2945[10] | **Green Bentley (IRE) (70)** (RHannon) **3-9-8** DaneO'Neill(10) (prom over 6f) | 2½ | **10** | 12/1 | 46 | 22 |
| | **Narbonne (55)** (BJMcMath) **5-8-6**(7) DSweeney(8) (bit bkwd: a bhd) | 2 | **11** | 14/1 | 27 | 9 |
| 3173[4] | **Passage Creeping (IRE) (73)** (LMCumani) **3-9-11** JWeaver(1) (hld up: hdwy 3f out: hrd rdn & wknd 2f out) | s.h | **12** | 2/1[1] | 45 | 21 |

(SP 137.3%) **12 Rn**

**1m 48.4** (6.20) CSF £128.62 CT £1,213.98 TOTE £8.90: £2.30 £3.70 £6.60 (£145.30) Triuo £485.90 OWNER Mr H. G. Collis (PONTYPRIDD) BRED A. Sofroniou and H. Collis

WEIGHT FOR AGE 3yo-6lb

OFFICIAL EXPLANATION **Passage Creeping (IRE): appeared unable to handle the soft ground.**

**2945* Q Factor** had scored on the soft as a two-year-old, and defied a 6lb hike in the Ratings after winning over course and distance last month. (9/1)

**1333 Pomona** looks a different animal on soft ground and she may have prevailed had she kept straight. (14/1: op 8/1)

**3228 Time of Night (USA)** seemed to handle the ground well enough, but was inclined to duck in behind the winner in the final 200 yards. (10/1)

**3525 Charisse Dancer** was stepping up to a mile, but had a different surface to contend with. (9/2)

**3592 Cuban Reef**, upped 4lb, may have preferred better ground. (7/1: op 4/1)

**1962 Elite Hope (USA)** took a strong hold to post, and it came as no surprise to see her run freely in the race. This meant that she was never going to stay a mile in this ground. (12/1: op 8/1)

**2384 Classic Romance** (7/1: 6/1-12/1)

**3470 Disallowed (IRE)** (10/1: 7/1-12/1)

**Narbonne** (14/1: op 8/1)

**3173 Passage Creeping (IRE)** gave cause for concern about her soundness, and only ran after being trotted outside the paddock and again under the eye of the Vet at the start. Back to a mile, she may in any case have not handled the soft ground. (2/1)

T/Plpt: £69.80 (129.84 Tckts). T/Qdpt: £22.10 (42.34 Tckts). KH

# 3781-GOODWOOD (R-H) (Good, Good to soft st)

## Sunday August 25th

WEATHER: unsettled WIND: str half against

## 3801 UCELLO II AND UBU III TROPHY (N.H JOCKEYS) H'CAP (0-70) (4-Y.O+) (Class E)

1-45 (1-45) **2m** £3,615.00 (£1,095.00: £535.00: £255.00) Stalls: Low GOING: 0.02 sec per fur (G)

| | | | | SP | RR | SF |
|---|---|---|---|---|---|---|
| 3329[4] | **French Ivy (USA) (63)** (FMurphy) **9-11-4** PCarberry(5) (stdy hdwy over 5f out: led on bit over 2f out: rdn out) | — | **1** | 7/2[1] | 70 | 55 |
| 3428[3] | **Sea Freedom (62)** (GBBalding) **5-11-3v** APMcCoy(8) (a.p: rdn over 7f out: led 3f out tl over 2f out: ev ch over 1f out: r.o) | 1 | **2** | 11/2[3] | 68 | 53 |
| 1347[6] | **Ginka (45)** (JWMullins) **5-10-0** SCurran(2) (rdn over 4f out: hdwy on ins over 1f out: r.o) | 9 | **3** | 100/1 | 42 | 27 |
| 3204[7] | **Durshan (USA) (45)** (JRJenkins) **7-10-0** NWilliamson(1) (lw: rdn over 4f out: hdwy over 3f out: wknd over 1f out) | ½ | **4** | 16/1 | 42 | 27 |
| 3598[5] | **Prague Spring (61)** (LadyHerries) **4-11-2** EMurphy(12) (b: rdn over 4f out: hdwy over 1f out: nvr nrr) | 2½ | **5** | 12/1 | 55 | 40 |
| *3610[3]* | **Paradise Navy (69)** (CREgerton) **7-11-10b** JOsborne(13) (lw: s.s: stdy hdwy over 5f out: hrd rdn over 1f out: sn wknd) | 5 | **6** | 9/2[2] | 58 | 43 |
| | **King William (45)** (NEBerry) **11-10-0** DGallagher(6) (a mid div) | ¾ | **7** | 50/1 | 33 | 18 |
| 2226* | **Nordansk (55)** (MMadgwick) **7-10-10** JRKavanagh(3) (lw: s.s: stdy hdwy 10f out: led over 5f out to 3f out: wknd 2f out) | 2½ | **8** | 6/1 | 41 | 26 |
| 3142[7] | **Cypress Avenue (IRE) (63)** (RHannon) **4-11-4** JAMcCarthy(7) (led 1f: led over 6f out tl over 5f out: wknd over 4f out) | ½ | **9** | 25/1 | 48 | 33 |
| 3641* | **Bellroi (IRE) (48)** (MHTompkins) **5-10-3** AThornton(14) (prom 12f) | 10 | **10** | 9/1 | 23 | 8 |

| | Horse | Dist | Pos | SP | RR | SF |
|---|---|---|---|---|---|---|
| 3476* | **Chucklestone (45)** (JSKing) **13-10-0** CLlewellyn(4) (bhd fnl 7f) | 2½ | **11** | 16/1 | 18 | 3 |
| *3437*[10] | **Teen Jay (59)** (BJLlewellyn) **6-11-0** VSlattery(9) (lw: a bhd) | 16 | **12** | 14/1 | 16 | 1 |
| *3437*[8] | **Well Arranged (IRE) (59)** (MJPolglase) **5-11-0** DBridgwater(11) (led 15f out tl over 6f out: wknd over 5f out) | ½ | **13** | 16/1 | 15 | — |
| 635[13] | **Spumante (56)** (MPMuggeridge) **4-10-11** BPowell(10) (bhd fnl 3f) | 3½ | **14** | 33/1 | 9 | — |
| | | | | (SP 121.8%) | **14 Rn** | |

**3m 39.23** (15.23) CSF £22.06 CT £1,508.94 TOTE £5.00: £1.90 £2.00 £21.70 (£8.50) Trio £402.70 OWNER Mr K. Flood (MIDDLEHAM) BRED John A. Nerud Revocable Trust

LONG HANDICAP Durshan (USA) 9-10 Chucklestone 9-7 Ginka 8-9 King William 9-5

**3329 French Ivy (USA)** gave his brilliant jump jockey a dream ride. Cruising into the lead on the bridle over a quarter of a mile from home, he only needed to be woken up to keep the ever-determined runner-up at bay. He will probably go hurdling this winter - he finished second at Wetherby on his only outing over them last season - and his trainer thinks he can run up a fair tally of low-key races in the North. (7/2)

**3428 Sea Freedom** was being bustled along from halfway, but nevertheless poked a nostril in front early in the straight. Collared over a quarter of a mile from home, he refused to give way and, although unable to get the better of the winner, he stuck to his task in tremendous style. A frustrating individual who is still a maiden after twenty-five attempts, he could soon lose that tag if this race is anything to go by. (11/2)

**1347 Ginka**, off the course for three months, is still a maiden and, racing from 19lb out of the handicap, did well to finish third, running on in the last furlong and a half. (100/1)

**Durshan (USA)** began to pick up ground as the Bugler called entering the straight, but had come to the end of his tether below the distance. (16/1)

**2756 Prague Spring** stayed on in the last furlong and a half without ever posing a threat. (12/1)

**3610 Paradise Navy** steadily crept into the action running down the hill but, when pressure was applied below the distance, soon folded up. (9/2)

**2226* Nordansk** failed to stay this longer trip. Showing in front at the top of the hill, he was collared three furlongs out, and had run out of stamina a furlong later. (6/1)

## 3802 BOLLINGER CHAMPAGNE CHALLENGE SERIES GENTLEMENS' H'CAP (0-70) (3-Y.O+) (Class E)

2-20 (2-21) **1m 4f** £3,452.50 (£1,045.00: £510.00: £242.50) Stalls: Low GOING: 0.02 sec per fur (G)

| | Horse | Dist | Pos | SP | RR | SF |
|---|---|---|---|---|---|---|
| 3509[5] | **Kaafih Homm (IRE) (64)** (NACallaghan) **5-11-10**(4) MrRThornton(3) (hld up: led over 2f out: r.o wl) | — | **1** | 13/2[3] | 78 | 60 |
| 3218[4] | **Strat's Legacy (42)** (DWPArbuthnot) **9-10-2**(4) MrKSantana(5) (hdwy over 1f out: r.o one pce) | 8 | **2** | 12/1 | 45 | 27 |
| 2779[5] | **Miswaki Dancer (USA) (51)** (LadyHerries) **6-11-1** MrPPritchard-Gordon(4) (b: a.p: hrd rdn 3f out: one pce) | ½ | **3** | 7/1 | 54 | 36 |
| | **Euphonic (62)** (IABalding) **6-11-12** MrABalding(2) (bkwd: c stands' side st: hdwy over 1f out: r.o one pce) | ½ | **4** | 14/1 | 64 | 46 |
| 2871[7] | **Duty Sergeant (IRE) (37)** (PMitchell) **7-10-1** MrMHNaughton(1) (lw: rdn over 2f out: nvr nrr to chal) | 6 | **5** | 25/1 | 31 | 13 |
| 3471[3] | **Spread The Word (53)** (LGCottrell) **4-10-13v**(4) MrLJefford(12) (a.p: led over 6f out to 3f out: wknd over 1f out) | nk | **6** | 11/2[2] | 47 | 29 |
| 3471* | **Fern's Governor (48)** (WJMusson) **4-10-12** MrTMcCarthy(10) (a.p: led 3f out tl over 2f out: wknd fnl f) | s.h | **7** | 11/4[1] | 42 | 24 |
| 3471[4] | **Super Serenade (52)** (GBBalding) **7-10-12**(4) MrJThatcher(6) (s.s: bhd fnl 2f) | 8 | **8** | 10/1 | 35 | 17 |
| 3667[5] | **One Pound (70)** (BWHills) **3-11-6**(4) MrCBHills(8) (lw: hdwy on ins over 4f out: wknd 3f out) | 7 | **9** | 10/1 | 44 | 16 |
| 573[18] | **Chief's Song (52)** (SDow) **6-10-12**(4) MrSFetherstonhaugh(9) (lw: bhd fnl 9f: t.o) | 20 | **10** | 10/1 | — | — |
| 3260[9] | **Broughtons Formula (39)** (WJMusson) **6-9-13b**(4) MrKGoble(11) (a bhd: t.o) | nk | **11** | 25/1 | — | — |
| 3520[5] | **Lucky Coin (57)** (PHowling) **4-11-7** MrMRimell(7) (led over 5f: wknd over 4f out: t.o) | | **12** | 16/1 | — | — |
| | | | | (SP 123.1%) | **12 Rn** | |

**2m 45.39** (12.19) CSF £76.24 CT £518.01 TOTE £6.40: £2.40 £3.50 £2.20 (£58.50) Trio £142.30 OWNER Gallagher Materials Ltd (NEWMARKET) BRED Sheikh Ahmed bin Rashid al Maktoum

WEIGHT FOR AGE 3yo-10lb

**3509 Kaafih Homm (IRE)** chased the leaders. Sent on over quarter of a mile from home, he strode clear in the final furlong for a decisive victory. (13/2)

**3218 Strat's Legacy**, whose rider was not a great deal of help, stayed on in the last furlong and a half to snatch second prize. (12/1)

**2779 Miswaki Dancer (USA)** was shown the persuader early in the straight and stayed on to eventually win the battle for third prize. (7/1)

**Euphonic**, off the track since finishing out the back in a novice hurdle back in March '94, was not surprisingly carrying plenty of condition for this return. The only runner to be brought over to the stands' side in search of the better ground, he stayed on in the last furlong and a half to finish fourth. (14/1: 16/1-25/1)

**2341 Duty Sergeant (IRE)** made a little late headway without ever posing a threat. (25/1)

**3471 Spread The Word** went on just before halfway. Collared three furlongs out, she grimly tried to hold on, but had shot her bolt below the distance. (11/2)

## 3803 PAYNE & GUNTER (S) STKS (2-Y.O) (Class E)

2-50 (2-51) **6f** £10,991.25 (£3,330.00: £1,627.50: £776.25) Stalls: High GOING: 0.24 sec per fur (G)

| | Horse | Dist | Pos | SP | RR | SF |
|---|---|---|---|---|---|---|
| 3128[6] | **Farewell My Love (IRE) (82)** (PFICole) **2-8-6** KDarley(2) (lw: mde virtually all: hung rt fnl 2f: rdn out) | — | **1** | 3/1[2] | 76 | 37 |
| 2210[2] | **Last Chance (86)** (GLewis) **2-8-11** PaulEddery(12) (swtg: a.p: rdn 2f out: ev ch 1f out: unable qckn) | 5 | **2** | 11/4[1] | 68 | 29 |
| 3515[10] | **Hever Golf Charger (IRE)** (TJNaughton) **2-8-11** TSprake(4) (lw: s.s: hdwy 2f out: rdn over 1f out: one pce) | 1¼ | **3** | 33/1 | 64 | 25 |
| 3405[4] | **Miss Barcelona (IRE) (53)** (MJPolglase) **2-8-6** JQuinn(7) (swtg: hld up: nt clr run on ins over 2f out: swtchd rt over 1f out: one pce fnl f) | 1½ | **4** | 20/1 | 55 | 16 |
| 1982[4] | **Bapsford (76)** (GLMoore) **2-8-11** RPerham(9) (hld up: rdn over 2f out: sn wknd) | 3 | **5** | 20/1 | 52 | 13 |
| 3475[7] | **Muscatana** (BWHills) **2-8-6** MHills(11) (hdwy 1f out: wknd ins fnl f) | 1¼ | **6** | 11/1 | 44 | 5 |
| 3332* | **Suite Factors (75)** (KRBurke) **2-8-11** SSanders(8) (nvr nr to chal) | s.h | **7** | 10/1 | 49 | 10 |
| 2382[5] | **Russian Sable (60)** (MRChannon) **2-8-1**(5) PPMurphy(10) (hld up: rdn over 2f out: wknd over 1f out) | ½ | **8** | 14/1 | 43 | 4 |
| 3523[2] | **Irish Fiction (IRE) (66)** (DJSCosgrove) **2-8-6**(5) MartinDwyer(5) (prom over 4f) | nk | **9** | 8/1 | 47 | 8 |
| 1954[8] | **Alimerjam (55)** (JWhite) **2-8-3**(3) AWhelan(6) (lw: a bhd) | 1 | **10** | 33/1 | 39 | — |
| 3511* | **Rusty (IRE) (64)** (JBerry) **2-8-6** JCarroll(13) (lw: prom over 4f) | 5 | **11** | 7/1[3] | 26 | — |
| 3129[14] | **Racing Carr** (TJNaughton) **2-8-6** SWhitworth(1) (s.s: a bhd) | ½ | **12** | 33/1 | 24 | — |
| | | | | (SP 117.7%) | **12 Rn** | |

**1m 15.18** (5.18) CSF £11.03 TOTE £3.60: £1.70 £1.60 £10.50 (£3.90) Trio £104.10 OWNER Mr W. H. Ponsonby (WHATCOMBE) BRED Rathbarry Stud

Bt in 30,000 gns; Last Chance clmd DCosgrove £10,000

**IN-FOCUS: This was an extremely valuable seller and the winner was bought in for a new British record price of 30,000 guineas, surpassing the previous record of 23,000 guineas, set at York on May 30th, 1989.**

**3128 Farewell My Love (IRE)**, who appeared to not quite get home over this course and distance last time, made no mistake on this occasion. Making virtually all the running, she gave her rider steering problems in the final quarter-mile as the filly cocked her head to the left and tried hanging to the right. Despite this, she pulled away in the final furlong for a decisive victory. Blinkers would help her. (3/1)

**2210 Last Chance** appeared to be going well over a quarter of a mile from home. Still in with every chance entering the final furlong, he then failed to cope with the winner's turn of foot. He should soon regain the winning thread. (11/4)
**Hever Golf Charger (IRE)** lost ground at the start, but moved up on the outside of the field a quarter of a mile from home, and then failed to find another gear in the last 200 yards. (33/1)
**3405 Miss Barcelona (IRE)** chased the leaders, but failed to get a clear run along the inside rail soon after halfway. Switched right below the distance as she grimly tried to get on terms, she failed to find the necessary turn of foot. (20/1)
**1982 Bapsford** chased the leaders but, bustled along over a quarter of a mile from home, was soon done with. (20/1)
**Muscatana** made an effort on the outside of the field a furlong out, but it proved short-lived and she was soon in trouble. (11/1)

## 3804 CROWSON PRESTIGE STKS (Gp 3) (2-Y.O F) (Class A)
3-20 (3-22) **7f** £21,180.00 (£7,934.00: £3,817.00: £1,669.00) GOING: 0.24 sec per fur (G)

| Form | Horse | Dist | Pos | SP | RR | SF |
|---|---|---|---|---|---|---|
| 2997* | **Red Camellia** (SirMarkPrescott) **2-8-12** GDuffield(1) (lw: mde all: clr 2f out: eased wl ins fnl f: impressive) | — | **1** | 10/11 [1] | 111++ | 38 |
| 3444[2] | **Fernanda (100)** (JLDunlop) **2-8-9b** TSprake(4) (lw: lost pl over 2f out: rallied fnl f: r.o one pce) | 6 | **2** | 10/1 | 94 | 21 |
| 3359* | **Velour** (DRLoder) **2-8-9** KDarley(5) (chsd wnr over 4f: rdn & chsd wnr ins fnl f: unable qckn) | s.h | **3** | 4/1 [2] | 94 | 21 |
| 3613[3] | **Queen Sceptre (IRE) (99)** (BWHills) **2-8-9** MHills(2) (hdwy over 2f out: chsd wnr over 1f out tl ins fnl f: one pce) | 1½ | **4** | 14/1 | 91 | 18 |
| 3036* | **Mayfair** (PFICole) **2-8-9** RHughes(3) (lw: hld up: chsd wnr over 2f out tl over 1f out: sn wknd) | 7 | **5** | 9/2 [3] | 75 | 2 |

(SP 106.3%) **5 Rn**

**1m 31.41** (6.61) CSF £8.36 TOTE £1.70: £1.20 £2.90 (£5.00) OWNER Cheveley Park Stud (NEWMARKET) BRED Cheveley Park Stud Ltd
**2997* Red Camellia**, whose connections were worried about the softish ground as she had been so impressive on a fast surface at Sandown last time, put up a performance that had to be seen to be believed. Making all the running, she forged clear a quarter of a mile out and, with a tremendous advantage inside the final furlong, was eased down considerably in the last 50 yards to win in highly-impressive style. The winning distance is certainly no true reflection of her superiority as she was value for at least fifteen lengths. She is a seriously good filly, and is now around 10/1 second-favourite for next year's 1000 Guineas. (10/11: 4/5-Evens)
**3444 Fernanda**, described as a bit of madam by her pilot, completely lost her pitch as the tempo increased over a quarter of a mile from home. She came with a wet sail in the final furlong and managed to snatch second prize right on the line. (10/1)
**3359* Velour** is only small and did not take the eye in the paddock. Racing in second until over a quarter of a mile from home, she managed to regain that berth inside the final furlong, but had not got a hope of catching the winner, and was caught for second prize right on the line. (4/1)
**3613 Queen Sceptre (IRE)**, tried over a longer trip, moved up over two furlongs out. Taking second place below the distance, she was collared for that place inside the final furlong and could only struggle on at one pace. (14/1)
**3036* Mayfair** was rather disappointing. Looking very well in the paddock, she took second place over a quarter of a mile from home but, collared for that position below the distance, tamely dropped away. (9/2)

## 3805 MAIL ON SUNDAY H'CAP (Qualifier) (0-90) (3-Y.O+) (Class C)
3-50 (3-52) **1m** £14,785.00 (£4,480.00: £2,190.00: £1,045.00) Stalls: High GOING: 0.24 sec per fur (G)

| Form | Horse | Dist | Pos | SP | RR | SF |
|---|---|---|---|---|---|---|
| 3246* | **Sky Dome (IRE) (84)** (MHTompkins) **3-9-6**(3) MHenry(6) (lw: mde all: rdn out) | — | **1** | 12/1 | 95 | 47 |
| 3123[5] | **Present Situation (57)** (LordHuntingdon) **5-8-2** DHarrison(12) (a.p: rdn over 2f out: squeezed thro over 1f out: r.o wl ins fnl f) | hd | **2** | 7/1 [2] | 68 | 26 |
| 3158[5] | **Sue's Return (76)** (APJarvis) **4-9-7** WJO'Connor(10) (a.p: rdn over 2f out: ev ch ins fnl f: unable qckn) | 1½ | **3** | 7/1 [2] | 84 | 42 |
| 3426* | **My Gallery (IRE) (83)** (ABailey) **5-9-11**(3) DWright(13) (hdwy, nt clr run & snatched up on ins over 2f out: hrd rdn over 1f out: r.o ins fnl f) | 1 | **4** | 4/1 [1] | 89 | 47 |
| 3450[3] | **Wentbridge Lad (IRE) (68)** (PDEvans) **6-8-13v** JFEgan(11) (b.off hind: hld up: rdn over 2f out: bmpd over 1f out: one pce) | 2 | **5** | 12/1 | 70 | 28 |
| 1102[9] | **Master Beveled (72)** (PDEvans) **6-8-10**(7) RFfrench(2) (lw: hdwy over 2f out: rdn over 1f out: one pce) | s.h | **6** | 16/1 | 74 | 32 |
| 3445[4] | **Mountgate (77)** (MPBielby) **4-9-8** DRMcCabe(3) (s.s: hdwy 2f out: wknd over 1f out) | 6 | **7** | 11/1 | 67 | 25 |
| 3123[6] | **Confronter (72)** (SDow) **7-9-3** SWhitworth(8) (hld up: rdn 3f out: sn wknd) | ¾ | **8** | 12/1 | 60 | 18 |
| 3123[3] | **Serendipity (FR) (84)** (JLDunlop) **3-9-9** KDarley(4) (nt clr run over 2f out: a mid div) | ½ | **9** | 8/1 [3] | 71 | 23 |
| 2526[6] | **Zajko (USA) (75)** (LadyHerries) **6-9-6** DeclanO'Shea(1) (lw: hld up: rdn over 2f out: wknd over 1f out) | nk | **10** | 20/1 | 62 | 20 |
| 3461[5] | **Eric's Bett (65)** (FMurphy) **3-8-4** JQuinn(14) (a bhd) | 2½ | **11** | 14/1 | 47 | — |
| 3439[9] | **Mihriz (IRE) (68)** (RAkehurst) **4-8-13** SSanders(7) (prom over 6f) | ¾ | **12** | 14/1 | 48 | 6 |
| 3123* | **Autumn Cover (70)** (PRHedger) **4-9-1** DBiggs(9) (lw: prom over 6f) | 7 | **13** | 10/1 | 36 | — |
| 1961[9] | **Menas Gold (82)** (SDow) **4-9-13** RHughes(5) (lw: a bhd) | 4 | **14** | 25/1 | 40 | — |

(SP 124.4%) **14 Rn**

**1m 44.92** (7.72) CSF £89.11 CT £607.37 TOTE £16.10: £4.40 £2.40 £2.30 (£87.80) Trio £83.60 OWNER Miss D. J. Merson (NEWMARKET) BRED Andrew Bradley
WEIGHT FOR AGE 3yo-6lb
**3246* Sky Dome (IRE)** made every post a winning one and, given one or two reminders, kept on well. The Cambridgeshire is the likely target. (12/1: op 8/1)
**3123 Present Situation** again did not have the best of runs. Never far away, he found himself rather boxed in below the distance and had to squeeze through a tiny gap. Running on in good style inside the final furlong, he was never going to overhaul the winner in time. There is a race waiting for him. (7/1: 5/1-15/2)
**3158 Sue's Return** threw down her challenge in the final quarter-mile and may even have got her head in front for a couple of strides inside the final furlong before tapped for toe. (7/1)
**3426* My Gallery (IRE)** has had a remarkable year, winning no fewer than eight times, and has gone up 35lb since the first win. She was having her twenty-second race of the year, but had no luck in running here. (4/1)
**3450 Wentbridge Lad (IRE)** chased the leaders. Given a bump, he could then only plod on at one pace. (12/1)
**843 Master Beveled**, given a three and a half month break, moved up over quarter of a mile from home, but cold then make no further impression. (16/1)
**3445 Mountgate** (11/1: 8/1-12/1)
**3461 Eric's Bett** (14/1: 8/1-16/1)
**3123* Autumn Cover**, who has gained all his victories on firm ground, flopped on this easier surface. (10/1)

## 3806 TOTE TRIO TRIUMVIRATE LIMITED STKS (0-80) (3-Y.O+) (Class D)
4-20 (4-24) **1m 1f** £6,214.00 (£2,326.00: £1,138.00: £490.00: £220.00: £112.00) Stalls: Low GOING: 0.24 sec per fur (G)

| Form | Horse | Dist | Pos | SP | RR | SF |
|---|---|---|---|---|---|---|
| 3516[10] | **Conspicuous (IRE) (77)** (LGCottrell) **6-9-3** JQuinn(3) (stdy hdwy 3f out: shkn up to ld over 1f out: r.o wl) | — | **1** | 11/4 [1] | 90 | 29 |

| | | | | SP | RR | SF |
|---|---|---|---|---|---|---|
| 3509[3] | **Maid For Baileys (IRE) (80)** (MJohnston) **3-8-7** JCarroll(7) (lw: led: rdn over 2f out: hdd over 1f out: unable qckn) | 3 | **2** | 5/1 | 82 | 14 |
| 2146[11] | **Proud Monk (77)** (GLMoore) **3-8-10** SWhitworth(4) (b.off fore: lw: a.p: chsd ldr 4f out: ev ch over 1f out: sn wknd) | 3½ | **3** | 10/1 | 78 | 10 |
| 3440[2] | **Tarneem (USA) (79)** (MRStoute) **3-8-9** MHills(6) (hld up: rdn over 2f out: wknd over 1f out) | 2½ | **4** | 4/1[3] | 73 | 5 |
| 3073[10] | **Burning (USA) (80)** (GHarwood) **4-9-3b[1]** KDarley(5) (lw: chsd ldr 5f) | 3 | **5** | 12/1 | 69 | 8 |
| 3501[4] | **Toujours Riviera (76)** (JPearce) **6-9-3** GBardwell(1) (hdwy over 3f out: wknd over 2f out) | 10 | **6** | 10/1 | 51 | — |
| 3148[2] | **Iberian Dancer (CAN) (80)** (JWHills) **3-8-6**(3) MHenry(2) (hdwy over 3f out: wknd over 2f out) | 1 | **7** | 7/2[2] | 48 | — |

(SP 111.4%) **7 Rn**

**2m 1.61** (10.21) CSF £15.36 TOTE £3.90: £1.80 £2.20 (£10.20) OWNER Mrs Jenny Hopkins (CULLOMPTON) BRED Gerry Canavan
WEIGHT FOR AGE 3yo-7lb

**3072 Conspicuous (IRE)**, always travelling well, was shaken up to lead below the distance and soon put daylight between himself and his rivals. (11/4)

**3509 Maid For Baileys (IRE)** attempted to make all the running but, collared at the distance, failed to find another gear. She has now been second in eight of her twelve races. (5/1: op 3/1)

**1819 Proud Monk** moved into second place soon after halfway, and threatened to take the lead in the straight. Still battling for the advantage below the distance, he soon ran out of steam. (10/1: 8/1-12/1)

**3440 Tarneem (USA)** chased the leaders, but had come to the end of her tether below the distance. (4/1: 3/1-9/2)

**580 Burning (USA)**, fitted with blinkers for the first time, yet again flopped and, after racing in second place, lost that position four furlongs out, and tamely dropped away. (12/1)

**3501 Toujours Riviera** made an effort over three furlongs out, but it came to little. (10/1: 7/1-12/1)

**3148 Iberian Dancer (CAN)** (7/2: 5/2-4/1)

## 3807 SINGLETON MEDIAN AUCTION MAIDEN STKS (2-Y.O) (Class D)

4-50 (4-53) **6f** £4,513.50 (£1,368.00: £669.00: £319.50) Stalls: High GOING: 0.24 sec per fur (G)

| | | | | SP | RR | SF |
|---|---|---|---|---|---|---|
| 1130[2] | **Referendum (IRE)** (GLewis) **2-9-0** PaulEddery(8) (lw: mde all: rdn over 1f out: r.o wl) | — | **1** | 9/4[1] | 94 | 39 |
| 3593[10] | **Gee Bee Dream** (APJarvis) **2-8-9** WJO'Connor(14) (stdy hdwy over 3f out: rdn over 1f out: unable qckn) | 7 | **2** | 20/1 | 70 | 15 |
| | **Hopesay** (JHMGosden) **2-8-9** JCarroll(19) (w'like: scope: s.s: hdwy over 2f out: rdn over 1f out: one pce) | 1¼ | **3** | 5/1[2] | 67 | 12 |
| 3269[5] | **Eurolink Spartacus** (JLDunlop) **2-9-0** TSprake(10) (lost pl over 2f out: rallied fnl f: r.o one pce) | hd | **4** | 12/1 | 72 | 17 |
| 2854[2] | **Mayflower** (IABalding) **2-8-9** KDarley(18) (a.p: rdn over 2f out: one pce) | 1 | **5** | 5/1[2] | 64 | 9 |
| | **Mon Bruce** (WRMuir) **2-9-0** SSanders(1) (unf: hld up: rdn 2f out: one pce) | s.h | **6** | 33/1 | 69 | 14 |
| 1525[7] | **Cauda Equina** (MRChannon) **2-9-0** RHughes(7) (bit bkwd: a.p: hrd rdn over 1f out: sn wknd) | 1 | **7** | 16/1 | 66 | 11 |
| 2783[9] | **Motcombs Club** (NACallaghan) **2-9-0** SWhitworth(9) (rdn over 3f out: hdwy over 1f out: nvr nrr) | ½ | **8** | 33/1 | 65 | 10 |
| | **Contentment (IRE)** (JWHills) **2-9-0** MHills(11) (unf: bit bkwd: a mid div) | nk | **9** | 12/1 | 64 | 9 |
| 3054[2] | **Princess Topaz** (CACyzer) **2-8-9** PBloomfield(5) (nvr nrr) | hd | **10** | 8/1[3] | 59 | 4 |
| | **Distinctive Dream (IRE)** (KTIvory) **2-9-0** CScally(2) (w'like: bit bkwd: s.s: nvr nrr) | hd | **11** | 50/1 | 64 | 9 |
| 3349[11] | **Duston Boy** (JWhite) **2-8-11**(3) AWhelan(3) (lw: prom 4f) | 2 | **12** | 50/1 | 58 | 3 |
| 3069[6] | **Saltimbanco** (IABalding) **2-8-9**(5) MartinDwyer(15) (lw: bhd whn stumbled bdly 4f out: nt rcvr) | 6 | **13** | 16/1 | 42 | — |
| | **Ajnad (IRE)** (CJBenstead) **2-9-0** MWigham(17) (w'like: bkwd: s.s: hdwy over 2f out: wknd over 1f out) | 1 | **14** | 25/1 | 40 | — |
| 3129[12] | **Three Card Trick (IRE)** (RHannon) **2-8-9** DHarrison(6) (bhd fnl 3f) | 1½ | **15** | 33/1 | 31 | — |
| 3475[11] | **Fully Booked** (JWHills) **2-8-6**(3) MHenry(12) (a bhd) | 1¼ | **16** | 33/1 | 27 | — |
| 3475[9] | **Florentine Diamond (IRE)** (SirMarkPrescott) **2-8-9** GDuffield(20) (s.s: hdwy over 2f out: wknd over 1f out) | s.h | **17** | 20/1 | 27 | — |
| 1062[8] | **Rosenkavalier (IRE)** (LGCottrell) **2-9-0** JQuinn(13) (prom over 2f) | s.h | **18** | 33/1 | 32 | — |
| 3259[19] | **Little Progress** (TMJones) **2-9-0** RPerham(16) (bhd fnl 3f) | 7 | **19** | 50/1 | 13 | — |

(SP 136.3%) **19 Rn**

**1m 15.6** (5.60) CSF £48.87 TOTE £2.70: £1.50 £11.80 £2.80 (£124.50) Trio £152.60 OWNER Highclere Thoroughbred Racing Ltd (EPSOM) BRED Deerpark Stud

**1130 Referendum (IRE)**, whose stable has had a wretched time this season with a throat infection, looked in fine fettle for this first run in three and a half months and did not let his supporters down. Making all the running, he was bustled along below the distance and pulled away in the last furlong for a decisive victory. (9/4)

**Gee Bee Dream** steadily crept into the action at halfway. Bustled along below the distance, she failed to contain the winner. (20/1)

**Hopesay** moved up soon after halfway but, ridden along below the distance, failed to find another gear. (5/1: op 3/1)

**3269 Eurolink Spartacus** chased the leaders, but got outpaced soon after halfway. He did stay on again in the final furlong and only just failed to take third prize. He needs further and, with three runs under his belt, he should be watched for in a nursery over further. (12/1: op 8/1)

**2854 Mayflower**, never far away, failed to find the necessary turn of foot in the last two furlongs. (5/1)

**1525 Cauda Equina**, not looking fully fit for this first run in three months, showed plenty of promise, racing in the front-rank until tiring approaching the final furlong. He is a nice-looking individual and a race will surely come his way before long. (16/1)

**Contentment (IRE)** (12/1: op 8/1)

T/Jkpt: £7,108.30 (0.1 Tckts); £9,010.58 to Newcastle 26/8/96. T/Plpt: £81.60 (261 Tckts). T/Qdpt: £11.30 (135.66 Tckts). AK

# 3330-NOTTINGHAM (L-H) (Good to soft)

## Sunday August 25th

WEATHER: overcast & showers WIND: almost nil

## 3808 LETHEBY & CHRISTOPHER (S) H'CAP (0-60) (3-Y.O+) (Class G)

2-00 (2-01) **1m 1f 213y** £3,065.00 (£865.00: £425.00) Stalls: Low GOING: 0.01 sec per fur (G)

| | | | | SP | RR | SF |
|---|---|---|---|---|---|---|
| 1012[5] | **Sharp Gazelle (39)** (BSmart) **6-8-7**ow1 RCochrane(9) (hdwy 6f out: led over 1f out: hld on nr fin) | — | **1** | 14/1 | 48 | 28 |
| 3402[6] | **Oakbury (IRE) (34)** (MissLCSiddall) **4-8-2**ow2 GHind(20) (led 3f: brought centre ent st: str chal fnl f: r.o) | nk | **2** | 33/1 | 43 | 22 |
| 3619[3] | **Ragtime Cowgirl (39)** (CWThornton) **3-7-13** DaleGibson(12) (lw: hld up in tch: hdwy over 3f out: ev ch ins fnl f: r.o) | hd | **3** | 11/1 | 47 | 20 |
| 3204[9] | **Action Jackson (56)** (BJMcMath) **4-9-10** GCarter(18) (led after 3f tl over 3f out: sn hrd drvn: kpt on) | 2½ | **4** | 11/1 | 60 | 41 |
| 3113[5] | **Abtaal (54)** (RJHodges) **6-9-8** SDrowne(6) (trckd ldrs: rdn 2f out: kpt on one pce) | 1¾ | **5** | 14/1 | 56 | 37 |
| 3591[5] | **Clued Up (49)** (PDEvans) **3-8-9** OUrbina(5) (hld up: hdwy over 3f out: sn rdn: nt pce to chal) | nk | **6** | 7/1[3] | 50 | 23 |
| 3412[4] | **Milltown Classic (IRE) (35)** (JParkes) **4-8-3** MFenton(8) (prom: led over 3f out tl over 1f out: sn rdn & btn) | s.h | **7** | 6/1[1] | 36 | 17 |

3645[6] **Zahran (IRE) (38)** (JMBradley) **5-8-6b[1]** DaneO'Neill(15) (lw: b: hld up: hdwy over 2f out: nvr nrr)....................nk **8** 14/1 39 20
3314[11] **Nita's Choice (28)** (AGNewcombe) **6-7-3**(7) IonaWands(4) (hdwy over 2f out: nvr nrr) ....................................hd **9** 33/1 28 9
3474[7] **Fastini Gold (37)** (MDIUsher) **4-8-5** AClark(23) (hdwy centre over 3f out: rdn & one pce appr fnl f) ...............1¾ **10** 25/1 35 16
3645[8] **Absolute Ruler (IRE) (38)** (JLHarris) **5-8-6b** BDoyle(3) (nvr nr to chal)..............................................................nk **11** 20/1 35 16
1468[8] **Wordsmith (IRE) (39)** (JLHarris) **6-8-7** JFortune(7) (bit bkwd: mid div tl lost tch 4f out) ..................................1½ **12** 16/1 34 15
3452[4] **Langtonian (33)** (JLEyre) **7-8-1** TWilliams(22) (lw: b.nr hind: trckd ldrs: rdn over 2f out: grad wknd)..............3½ **13** 20/1 22 3
2891[8] **La Belle Shyanne (28)** (CJHill) **5-7-7**(3) NVarley(10) (nvr nr ldrs) ...................................................................1¾ **14** 12/1 14 —
*3603*[11] **Shuttlecock (37)** (MrsNMacauley) **5-8-2b**(3)ow2 CTeague(19) (trckd ldrs tl rdn & wknd over 3f out) ................1¾ **15** 20/1 20 —
3403[7] **My Handsome Prince (29)** (PJBevan) **4-7-11b** NCarlisle(1) (s.s: a bhd)...............................................................3 **16** 33/1 8 —
*3602*[7] **Born A Lady (53)** (SRBowring) **3-8-13** SDWilliams(13) (hld up: nvr bttr than mid div).......................................s.h **17** 16/1 32 5
3303[7] **Tout de Val (30)** (KBishop) **7-7-12** NAdams(17) (a in rr) .......................................................................................1¾ **18** 20/1 6 —
3357[5] **Reno's Treasure (USA) (40)** (JAHarris) **3-8-0** CRutter(16) (swtg: a in rr).........................................................1¼ **19** 33/1 14 —
1979[7] **In Cahoots (39)** (AGNewcombe) **3-7-13** JLowe(11) (hld up: effrt ent st: sn hrd drvn & wknd)..........................¾ **20** 13/2[2] 12 —
2906[2] **Marchman (49)** (JSKing) **11-9-3** RHills(14) (a in rr)..........................................................................................1¾ **21** 8/1 19 —
3443[10] **Sylvan Sabre (IRE) (45)** (KAMorgan) **7-8-10v**(3) FLynch(21) (b: dwlt: a bhd) ...................................................3 **22** 25/1 10 —
3606[14] **Kirov Protege (IRE) (30)** (MrsLCJewell) **4-7-7**(5)ow1 MBaird(2) (a bhd: t.o) ..........................................................10 **23** 33/1 — —
(SP 148.8%) **23 Rn**

**2m 10.4** (7.90) CSF £405.08 CT £4,772.91 TOTE £14.70: £4.20 £8.30 £2.30 £4.10 (£355.90) Trio Not won; £331.19 to Newcastle 26/8/96
OWNER Mr M. J. Samuel (LAMBOURN) BRED Aston Park Stud
LONG HANDICAP Nita's Choice 7-9
WEIGHT FOR AGE 3yo-8lb
No bid

**1012 Sharp Gazelle**, a lightly-made mare who was fresher than most after a long mid-summer break, struck the front below the distance and hung on grimly to the end. (14/1)
**2731 Oakbury (IRE)** has shown very little sign of ability in the past, but he ran well here, having more use made of him, and that elusive first win could be near at hand. (33/1)
**3619 Ragtime Cowgirl** has only ever won one race, but runs consistently well and does look to need a slightly longer trip. (11/1)
**3048* Action Jackson** failed to last the trip on his previous outing, but remained in the firing-line all the way, only to find the concession of so much weight taking its toll below the distance. (11/1)
**3113 Abtaal** sat a bit closer to the pace on this occasion but, when the pressure was really on, he could do little more than gallop on the spot. (14/1)
**3591 Clued Up** finds it much harder to show her true form against older rivals, and she was unable to get herself close enough to cause concern. (7/1)
**3412 Milltown Classic (IRE)** does like to force the pace and she looked to be going best when nosing ahead early in the straight, but challenges came in thick and fast in the latter stages, and she was unable to maintain the run. (6/1)

## 3809 RAY SLACK FAMILY MAIDEN AUCTION STKS (2-Y.O) (Class E)

2-30 (2-32) **6f 15y** £3,113.00 (£944.00: £462.00: £221.00) Stalls: High GOING: 0.01 sec per fur (G)

SP RR SF

3312[3] **Brandon Jack** (IABalding) **2-8-8** RCochrane(4) (lw: a.p centre: shkn up 2f out: led fnl 100y: r.o wl) ..............— **1** 9/2[3] 75 26
3462[4] **Cambridge Ball (IRE)** (MJohnston) **2-8-2** RHills(5) (led centre tl rdn & hdd wl ins fnl f) ...................................¾ **2** 7/4[1] 67 18
3515[6] **Hallmark (IRE)** (RHannon) **2-8-7** DaneO'Neill(3) (a.p centre: rdn & one pce fnl f)............................................2½ **3** 3/1[2] 65 16
**With A Will** (HCandy) **2-8-5** CRutter(7) (small: unf: bit bkwd: racd stands' side: outpcd fnl 2f)..........................6 **4** 7/1 48 —
**Lightning Rebel** (CWThornton) **2-8-5** SDrowne(10) (lt-f: racd stands' side: styd on appr fnl f: nvr nrr)...........hd **5** 16/1 47 —
2538[7] **Two Bills** (AStreeter) **2-8-4** AClark(11) (racd stands' side: effrt over 2f out: nvr trbld ldrs)..............................nk **6** 14/1 46 —
*3088*[4] **Miss Alice** (JNorton) **2-7-12** DaleGibson(8) (chsd ldr stands' side: no ch fnl 2f).............................................2½ **7** 16/1 33 —
2527[7] **Priory Gardens (IRE)** (JMBradley) **2-8-4** TWilliams(9) (led stands' side over 4f: sn outpcd) ...........................nk **8** 33/1 38 —
**Go For Green** (DrJDScargill) **2-8-4** MFenton(6) (prom stands' side 4f)..................................................................s.h **9** 16/1 38 —
3468[5] **Bert** (PTWalwyn) **2-8-9v[1]** JFortune(1) (swtg: swvd lft s: chsd ldrs centre over 4f) ...............................................½ **10** 16/1 42 —
(SP 125.2%) **10 Rn**

**1m 15.3** (4.80) CSF £13.24 TOTE £5.00: £1.90 £1.50 £1.80 (£5.60) Trio £3.20 OWNER Mr R. P. B. Michaelson (KINGSCLERE) BRED Highclere Stud Ltd

**3312 Brandon Jack**, poised to challenge from the break, responded willingly when shown the whip and, gaining command inside the last furlong, won with a bit to spare. (9/2: op 3/1)
**3462 Cambridge Ball (IRE)** held the overall lead in the centre of the track and gave of her all, but the winner proved too strong for her inside the distance. (7/4)
**3515 Hallmark (IRE)** sat in behind the leader going well, but he did not find much when an extra effort was called for, and had shot his bolt inside the final furlong. (3/1)
**With A Will**, a small colt from a winning family, raced on the slower stands' side and could not get himself into the action, despite staying on. (7/1: op 4/1)
**Lightning Rebel** was beginning to stay on in the closing stages after struggling with the pace in the last half-mile. (16/1)
**Two Bills** performed better than on his debut, but was never a serious factor, and looks to need a stiffer test of stamina. (14/1)

## 3810 TOTE NOTTINGHAM STEWARDS CUP H'CAP (0-85) (3-Y.O+) (Class D)

3-00 (3-02) **6f 15y** £7,620.00 (£2,310.00: £1,130.00: £540.00) Stalls: High GOING: 0.01 sec per fur (G)

SP RR SF

3439* **Lough Erne (72)** (CFWall) **4-9-1** RHills(6) (lw: hld up in rr: hdwy wl over 1f out: led wl ins fnl f: readily)........................................................................................................................— **1** 9/2[1] 82+ 50
3338[4] **Kildee Lad (79)** (APJones) **6-9-8** BDoyle(10) (hld up in rr: gd hdwy appr fnl f: fin wl)..........................................1 **2** 11/1 86 54
3622[15] **For the Present (84)** (TDBarron) **6-9-13** JFortune(4) (lw: a.p: led over 1f out tl wl ins fnl f)..............................½ **3** 10/1 90 58
3639[6] **Cretan Gift (68)** (NPLittmoden) **5-8-8b**(3) FLynch(5) (a.p centre: drvn along over 1f out: r.o)..........................hd **4** 11/1 74 42
3112[3] **Nellie North (61)** (GMMcCourt) **3-8-1v[1]** CRutter(3) (led: wnt rt & lft u.p over 1f out: sn hdd & btn) .................2½ **5** 14/1 60 25
3424[10] **Agent (63)** (JLEyre) **3-8-3** TWilliams(7) (trckd ldrs: pushed along whn n.m.r appr fnl f: one pce) .......................¾ **6** 33/1 60 25
3672[17] **Bayin (USA) (75)** (MDIUsher) **7-9-4** RStreet(2) (dwlt: hdwy 2f out: nvr nr to chal) ..........................................hd **7** 8/1[3] 72 40
3622[10] **Robellion (70)** (DWPArbuthnot) **5-8-13v** RCochrane(1) (b.hind: hld up: effrt over 2f out: one pce appr fnl f)....½ **8** 12/1 66 34
3672[16] **Mister Jolson (76)** (RJHodges) **7-9-5b[1]** SDrowne(11) (lw: trckd ldrs: rdn wl over 2f out: no imp)...................1¼ **9** 10/1 68 36
*3601*[2] **Prima Silk (67)** (MJRyan) **5-8-10** TIves(14) (prom over 4f) ............................................................................nk **10** 11/1 59 27
3622[17] **Sailormaite (83)** (SRBowring) **5-9-12** SDWilliams(8) (prom over 4f)..................................................................hd **11** 7/1[2] 74 42
3352[7] **Rockcracker (IRE) (64)** (GGMargarson) **4-8-7b** GCarter(15) (w ldrs: rdn & n.m.r over 1f out: sn wknd).........s.h **12** 14/1 55 23

| | Horse | Details | Dist | Pos | SP | RR | SF |
|---|---|---|---|---|---|---|---|
| | **Fog City (75)** | (WJarvis) **3-9-1** EmmaO'Gorman(13) (a bhd: rdn over 1f out: no imp) | 3 | **13** | 16/1 | 58 | 23 |
| 3270$^{3}$ | **Kind of Light (80)** | (RGuest) **3-9-1**$^{(5)}$ DGriffiths(12) (trckd ldrs: btn whn n.m.r wl over 1f out) | s.h | **14** | 8/1$^{3}$ | 63 | 28 |

(SP 125.9%) **14 Rn**

**1m 14.0** (3.50) CSF £51.33 CT £445.27 TOTE £5.70: £2.10 £4.90 £6.70 (£29.80) Trio £279.60 OWNER Sir Stanley and Lady Grinstead (NEWMARKET) BRED Sir Stanley Grinstead

WEIGHT FOR AGE 3yo-3lb

**3439* Lough Erne** has really found her form of late and the ease of this success would suggest that this lightly-raced filly has come to herself now. (9/2)

**3338 Kildee Lad** runs best when produced from off a fast pace but he does like to hear his feet rattle, and on this softer ground, had to admit the winner too much of a handful. (11/1)

**3085 For the Present** is at his best on fast ground and the recent rain has put paid to that. He still performed with credit in attempting to concede weight all round, and there was no disgrace in this. (10/1)

**3639 Cretan Gift**, still to win on turf, pressed the leaders all the way in the centre of the track and kept on so well that he only just lost out on third. (11/1)

**3112 Nellie North**, visored for the first time, attempted to make it all but she wandered when strongly challenged approaching the final furlong, and was at the end of her tether once headed. (14/1)

**2805 Agent**, poised to challenge for most of the way, did not enjoy the smoothest of passages when putting in his bid approaching the final furlong, but it may have been his inability to quicken that was the main reason for his downfall. (33/1)

**2856 Mister Jolson** (10/1: 8/1-12/1)

**3601 Prima Silk** (11/1: 8/1-12/1)

**2964 Rockcracker (IRE)** (14/1: op 8/1)

## 3811 HIGHGROVE SUNDAY CONDITIONS STKS (3-Y.O+) (Class C)

3-30 (3-31) **1m 54y** £4,909.50 (£1,840.50: £902.75: £391.25: £213.13) Stalls: Low GOING: 0.01 sec per fur (G)

| | Horse | Details | Dist | Pos | SP | RR | SF |
|---|---|---|---|---|---|---|---|
| 3612$^{4}$ | **Kayvee (97)** | (GHarwood) **7-9-2** AClark(2) (lw: chsd ldng pair: effrt over 1f out: led ins fnl f: r.o) | — | **1** | 2/1$^{1}$ | 100 | 40 |
| 3153$^{7}$ | **Bonarelli (IRE) (98)** | (MRStoute) **3-8-10** BDoyle(6) (swtg: hld up & bhd: hdwy wl over 1f out: hrd drvn & r.o wl towards fin) | nk | **2** | 7/2$^{2}$ | 99 | 33 |
| | **Mawjud** | (HThomsonJones) **3-8-10** RHills(1) (h.d.w: bit bkwd: chsd ldr: led appr fnl f: hdd & no ex fnl 100y) | 1½ | **3** | 9/2$^{3}$ | 97 | 31 |
| 438a$^{9}$ | **Pater Noster (USA) (98)** | (MrsJCecil) **7-9-2** GHind(3) (led: rdn 2f out: hdd & one pce appr fnl f) | 1½ | **4** | 2/1$^{1}$ | 94 | 34 |
| 455$^{24}$ | **Sharp Prospect (82)** | (VSoane) **6-9-2** RCochrane(5) (bkwd: hld up in rr: lost tch over 2f out: t.o) | dist | **5** | 12/1 | — | — |

(SP 114.8%) **5 Rn**

**1m 47.5** (6.20) CSF £9.05 TOTE £2.10: £1.20 £2.50 (£3.90) OWNER Mr J. H. Richmond-Watson (PULBOROUGH) BRED Normanby Stud Ltd

WEIGHT FOR AGE 3yo-6lb

**3612 Kayvee** had not won on such testing ground as this, but he was on his best behaviour here and, though the outcome was close, he never looked likely to relinquish the advantage once he had taken control. (2/1: op 5/4)

**1015 Bonarelli (IRE)** has not really fired this season and there have been doubts as to whether he has trained on. He did put in a determined late challenge and there is every possibility that he needed this ground to show what he is made of. (7/2)

**Mawjud**, successful on his previous appearance in the autumn of last year, has done well physically but looked in need of this. He will be the one to beat from now on. (9/2)

**438a Pater Noster (USA)**, produced fit and well after a break since the early spring, was soon adopting his favoured front-running tactics. Unable to shake off Mawjud, he was forced to give best. (2/1)

## 3812 DOVEBRACE H'CAP (0-70) (3-Y.O+) (Class E)

4-00 (4-01) **1m 54y** £3,048.00 (£924.00: £452.00: £216.00) Stalls: Low GOING: 0.01 sec per fur (G)

| | Horse | Details | Dist | Pos | SP | RR | SF |
|---|---|---|---|---|---|---|---|
| 3640$^{3}$ | **Maple Bay (IRE) (70)** | (ABailey) **7-9-7**$^{(7)}$ GFaulkner(8) (a.p: led 1f out: rdn out) | — | **1** | 4/1$^{1}$ | 84 | 58 |
| 3473* | **Charlton Imp (USA) (54)** | (RJHodges) **3-8-6** SDrowne(11) (led over 2f: led over 3f out tl over 1f out: one pce fnl f) | 2 | **2** | 9/1 | 64 | 32 |
| *839$^{7}$* | **Don't Get Caught (IRE) (46)** | (JLHarris) **4-8-4** BDoyle(14) (bkwd: hld up in tch: hdwy over 2f out: styd on towards fin) | 1½ | **3** | 16/1 | 53 | 27 |
| 3289$^{6}$ | **Alfayza (47)** | (JDBethell) **3-7-6**$^{(7)}$ NicolaStokes(2) (lw: hld up: stdy hdwy on ins 3f out: nt pce to chal) | 1½ | **4** | 33/1 | 51 | 19 |
| 3334$^{3}$ | **Racing Brenda (45)** | (BCMorgan) **5-8-3** GCarter(3) (hld up & bhd: hdwy 2f out: sn rdn: nt rch ldrs) | ¾ | **5** | 4/1$^{1}$ | 48 | 22 |
| 3161$^{11}$ | **Set the Fashion (60)** | (DLWilliams) **7-9-4v** RCochrane(4) (hld up in rr: effrt on ins over 2f out: kpt on u.p nl f) | 2 | **6** | 9/2$^{2}$ | 59 | 33 |
| 3442$^{14}$ | **Oh Susannah (40)** | (JAHarris) **5-7-12** CRutter(6) (hld up: hdwy 3f out: nt rch ldrs) | 1½ | **7** | 33/1 | 36 | 10 |
| 3457$^{4}$ | **Rival Bid (USA) (64)** | (MrsNMacauley) **8-9-5**$^{(3)}$ CTeague(1) (lw: s.s: hdwy on outside 3f out: wknd wl over 1f out) | nk | **8** | 11/1 | 60 | 34 |
| *2550$^{6}$* | **Mr Moriarty (IRE) (38)** | (SRBowring) **5-7-10** NKennedy(15) (b: trckd ldrs: hrd drvn 3f out: sn btn) | ¾ | **9** | 16/1 | 32 | 6 |
| 3592$^{6}$ | **Bedazzle (38)** | (MBrittain) **5-7-10** JLowe(13) (trckd ldrs tl rdn & wknd 2f out) | 1½ | **10** | 10/1 | 29 | 3 |
| 3344$^{5}$ | **Habeta (USA) (50)** | (JWWatts) **10-8-5**$^{(3)}$ RHavlin(7) (mid div tl rdn & wknd wl over 2f out) | 2 | **11** | 9/1 | 37 | 11 |
| 3606$^{5}$ | **Mr Cube (IRE) (51)** | (JMBradley) **6-8-9b** DaneO'Neill(12) (nvr nrr ldrs) | nk | **12** | 7/1$^{3}$ | 38 | 12 |
| 3469$^{9}$ | **Caddy's First (44)** | (SMellor) **4-8-2** DaleGibson(5) (bit bkwd: drvn along 4f out: a in rr) | 4 | **13** | 20/1 | 23 | — |
| 3585$^{5}$ | **Barbrallen (46)** | (MrsLCJewell) **4-7-13**$^{(5)ow8}$ SophieMitchell(9) (led 6f out tl over 3f out: wknd fnl 2f) | ½ | **14** | 20/1 | 24 | — |

(SP 135.3%) **14 Rn**

**1m 46.8** (5.50) CSF £41.99 CT £506.39 TOTE £5.10: £2.50 £3.50 £4.40 (£34.40) Trio £221.10; £218.02 to Newcastle 26/8/96 OWNER Mr Roy Matthews (TARPORLEY) BRED Berkshire Equestrian Services Ltd

LONG HANDICAP Mr Moriarty (IRE) 7-7 Barbrallen 7-8

WEIGHT FOR AGE 3yo-6lb

**3640 Maple Bay (IRE)** got back to winning ways with quite a comfortable success and, for such a consistent individual, it was just reward for some very game performances. (4/1)

**3473* Charlton Imp (USA)**, a poor mover in her slower paces, did her share of the pacemaking, but had to admit the winner much too good in the battle to the line. (9/1)

**217 Don't Get Caught (IRE)**, carrying condition for this first outing on the turf in this country, gave notice of better things to come and stayed on well. (16/1)

**3289 Alfayza**, successful over seven in the autumn last year, runs as though she needs much further than the mile nowadays, and this effort could be a sign that she is on her way back. (33/1)

**3334 Racing Brenda** had everything in her favour, but she did not produce her true running, and this must have been an off-day. (4/1)

**3052* Set the Fashion** made relentless progress up the inside rail from the quarter-mile marker, but could not quicken sufficiently to pose a serious threat. (9/2)

**3813** LETHEBY & CHRISTOPHER LIMITED STKS (0-55) (3-Y.O+) (Class F)
4-30 (4-31) **1m 6f 15y** £2,410.50 (£678.00: £331.50) Stalls: Low GOING: 0.01 sec per fur (G)

| | | | | SP | RR | SF |
|---|---|---|---|---|---|---|
| 2905[3] | **Spa Lane (54)** (PJMakin) **3-8-5**(3) RHavlin(3) (hld up: hdwy 3f out: rdn to ld over 2f out: styd on strly) | — | 1 | 9/1 | 64 | 33 |
| 3520* | **Children's Choice (IRE) (56)** (CNAllen) **5-9-5** RCochrane(1) (hld up in tch: lost pl ent st: hdwy 2f out: styd on fnl f) | 1½ | 2 | 3/1 1 | 61 | 42 |
| *3605*[3] | **Inn At the Top (54)** (JNorton) **4-9-6** DaleGibson(2) (hld up in tch: effrt over 2f out: styd on wl fnl f) | 1¼ | 3 | 10/1 | 61 | 42 |
| 3037[15] | **Requested (51)** (PBurgoyne) **9-9-3**(3) PMcCabe(6) (s.s: in rr tl hdwy 3f out: styd on wl appr fnl f) | 2½ | 4 | 9/1 | 58 | 39 |
| 3514[2] | **Sterling Fellow (57)** (RHannon) **3-8-10b** DaneO'Neill(7) (prom: rdn over 2f out: one pce) | 2½ | 5 | 7/2 2 | 57 | 26 |
| 3434[7] | **Double Echo (IRE) (53)** (JDBethell) **8-9-6** SDrowne(4) (trckd ldrs: rdn & ev ch 2f out: grad fdd) | 1½ | 6 | 11/1 | 54 | 35 |
| 3584[3] | **Dashing Invader (USA) (43)** (PWHarris) **3-8-8** GHind(5) (led tl over 5f out: rdn & wknd 3f out) | 1¾ | 7 | 14/1 | 52 | 21 |
| 3225[4] | **Fiona Shann (USA) (53)** (JLDunlop) **3-8-5** JFortune(8) (lw: hld up: hdwy 4f out: nt rch ldrs) | 1¾ | 8 | 4/1 3 | 47 | 16 |
| | **Tommy Cooper (40)** (MrsBarbaraWaring) **5-9-6** AClark(10) (b: bit bkwd: prom: led over 5f out to 4f out: sn wknd) | 3½ | 9 | 25/1 | 46 | 27 |
| *398*[9] | **Rose of Glenn (42)** (BPalling) **5-9-3** CRutter(11) (hld up: hdwy to ld 4f out: hdd over 3f out: grad wknd) | ¾ | 10 | 25/1 | 42 | 23 |
| 3335[15] | **Sandicliffe (USA) (52)** (BWHills) **3-8-5** RHills(9) (hld up: hdwy 8f out: led over 3f out tl over 2f out: wknd qckly) | 2 | 11 | 16/1 | 39 | 8 |
| | | | | (SP 124.9%) | **11 Rn** | |

**3m 9.2** (10.70) CSF £36.36 TOTE £13.40: £2.50 £1.80 £2.30 (£16.00) Trio £65.20 OWNER Mr R. J. K. Roberts (MARLBOROUGH) BRED R. J. K. Roberts
WEIGHT FOR AGE 3yo-12lb

**2905 Spa Lane**, ridden to get the trip, was in no mood to give best once he had struck the front and won with more ease than the margin suggests. (9/1)
**3520* Children's Choice (IRE)** acts well with cut in the ground, but she did her cause no good at all when losing her place turning in, and her determined late challenge was always being matched with ease. (3/1)
**3605 Inn At the Top** is very high in the weights for a maiden, but he continues to give of his best, and a success would not be coming out of turn. (10/1)
**2148 Requested** lost quite a bit of ground at the start and was content to amble around in the rear until staying on when it was all too late. (9/1)
**3514 Sterling Fellow** held his pitch in the chasing group, but had no answer when the tempo picked up approaching the final quarter-mile, and could only stay on at the one pace. (7/2)
**2884 Double Echo (IRE)**, bustled along but holding every chance two furlongs out, was unable to hang on for long, and has yet to prove that he does really stay this trip. (11/1)

T/Plpt: £60.10 (181.33 Tckts). T/Qdpt: £11.10 (57.98 Tckts). IM

## 3448-REDCAR (L-H) (Good to firm)
## Sunday August 25th
WEATHER: overcast WIND: almost nil

**3814** REDCAR SUNDAY MARKET NURSERY H'CAP (2-Y.O) (Class C)
2-10 (2-10) **6f** £5,158.50 (£1,563.00: £764.00: £364.50) Stalls: Centre GOING minus 0.46 sec per fur (F)

| | | | | SP | RR | SF |
|---|---|---|---|---|---|---|
| 3648[4] | **Abstone Queen (57)** (PDEvans) **2-7-12v** LCharnock(1) (w ldr: led 1f out: drvn out) | — | 1 | 7/2 3 | 49 | — |
| 3250[7] | **Tom Mi Dah (65)** (MDHammond) **2-8-6** JFanning(2) (lw: trckd ldrs: effrt 2f out: ev ch wl ins fnl f: no ex nr fin) | hd | 2 | 12/1 | 57? | — |
| 3326* | **Mystic Circle (IRE) (75)** (JWWatts) **2-9-2** WRyan(5) (lw: led: qcknd 2f out: hdd 1f out: kpt on) | nk | 3 | 13/8 2 | 66 | — |
| 3250[4] | **Barnburgh Boy (77)** (TDBarron) **2-9-4** JWeaver(4) (stdd s: plld hrd: effrt & ev ch over 1f out: kpt on) | nk | 4 | 6/4 1 | 67 | — |
| | | | | (SP 108.0%) | **4 Rn** | |

**1m 14.3** (4.10) CSF £24.37 TOTE £3.10 (£13.60) OWNER Mr J. E. Abbey (WELSHPOOL) BRED Ridgebarn Farm
**3648 Abstone Queen**, in a race that turned out to be a two and a half furlong sprint, had the best turn of foot. (7/2: 9/4-4/1)
**2485 Tom Mi Dah** has an action that suggests softer ground may help. In this messy event, he ran a fine race. (12/1: op 8/1)
**3326* Mystic Circle (IRE)** held the best position in this slowly-run event, but was still outsprinted in the final furlong. (13/8)
**3250 Barnburgh Boy** was not suited by this messy race and this effort is best ignored. (6/4: op Evens)

**3815** RACING NORTH MORE THAN A NEWSAGENT H'CAP (0-85) (3-Y.O+) (Class D)
2-40 (2-41) **1m** £5,158.50 (£1,563.00: £764.00: £364.50) Stalls: Centre GOING minus 0.46 sec per fur (F)

| | | | | SP | RR | SF |
|---|---|---|---|---|---|---|
| 2572* | **King's Academy (IRE) (81)** (HRACecil) **3-9-4** WRyan(5) (lw: hld up: smooth hdwy 3f out: led over 1f out: r.o) | — | 1 | 2/1 1 | 92 | 57 |
| 3509* | **Fairywings (82)** (MrsJRRamsden) **3-9-5** KFallon(6) (hld up: hdwy 3f out: ev ch over 1f out: nt qckn) | 2 | 2 | 11/2 2 | 89 | 54 |
| 3254[5] | **Pine Ridge Lad (IRE) (65)** (JLEyre) **6-8-8** LCharnock(1) (cl up: effrt over 2f out: kpt on fnl f) | s.h | 3 | 6/1 3 | 72 | 43 |
| 3623[5] | **Quilling (67)** (MDods) **4-8-10** DeanMcKeown(8) (lw: trckd ldrs: effrt & nt clr run 2f out: swtchd & styd on one pce) | 1 | 4 | 7/1 | 72 | 43 |
| 3481* | **Broctune Gold (69)** (MrsMReveley) **5-8-12** ACulhane(4) (led tl hdd 1f out: wknd ins fnl f) | 1¾ | 5 | 9/1 | 70 | 41 |
| 3344[11] | **Up in Flames (IRE) (71)** (MDHammond) **5-9-0** JWeaver(7) (chsd ldrs: ev ch 2f out: rdn & no ex) | s.h | 6 | 8/1 | 72 | 43 |
| 3450[2] | **Saifan (85)** (DMorris) **7-10-0v** CHodgson(3) (outpcd & wl bhd fr ½-wy) | 9 | 7 | 6/1 3 | 68 | 39 |
| 1069[10] | **Elpidos (67)** (MDHammond) **4-8-10** JFanning(2) (outpcd & wl bhd fr ½-wy) | 15 | 8 | 25/1 | 20 | — |
| | | | | (SP 114.7%) | **8 Rn** | |

**1m 36.3** (0.60) CSF £12.76 CT £51.24 TOTE £2.60: £1.20 £2.10 £1.30 (£7.40) OWNER Mr Michael Poland (NEWMARKET) BRED Michael Poland
WEIGHT FOR AGE 3yo-6lb

**2572* King's Academy (IRE)**, having his first run in seven weeks, did it nicely and seems to be on the upgrade. (2/1)
**3509* Fairywings**, off her highest mark to date, ran a super race, but found the winner too good in the closing stages. (11/2)
**3254 Pine Ridge Lad (IRE)** does not seem to know how to run a bad race these days and, though he could never get to the front this time, he kept trying all the way to the line. (6/1)
**3623 Quilling** got himself boxed in at a vital stage, otherwise he would have been in the places. He is looking exceptionally well just now. (7/1)

**3481* Broctune Gold** could never fully dictate here and, once passed over a furlong out, he soon packed it in. (9/1)
**3254 Up in Flames (IRE)** had his chances but, when asked to struggle, he was found wanting. He needs things to go all his own way. (8/1)

## 3816 DEREK THOMPSON H'CAP (0-80) (3-Y.O+) (Class D)

3-10 (3-10) **1m 6f 19y** £3,842.50 (£1,165.00: £570.00: £272.50) Stalls: Low GOING minus 0.46 sec per fur (F)

| | | | | SP | RR | SF |
|---|---|---|---|---|---|---|
| 3434$^{6}$ | **Highflying (80)** (GMMoore) **10-10-0** JTate(3) (lw: led after 2f: hld on gamely fnl 3f) | — | 1 | 2/1$^{2}$ | 86 | 51 |
| 3253$^{2}$ | **Villeggiatura (73)** (MrsJRRamsden) **3-8-9** KFallon(1) (lw: hld up: effrt 2f out: gd hdwy 1f out: edgd lft: kpt on) | nk | 2 | 3/1$^{3}$ | 79 | 32 |
| | **Aztec Flyer (USA) (60)** (MrsMReveley) **3-7-10** LCharnock(4) (hld up: pushed along over 3f out: styd on towards fin) | 4 | 3 | 20/1 | 61 | 14 |
| 3487* | **Mister Aspecto (IRE) (72)** (MJohnston) **3-8-8v** JWeaver(2) (lw: led 2f: cl up: chal over 3f out: hung rt & wknd fnl 2f) | ¾ | 4 | 10/11$^{1}$ | 72 | 25 |
| | | | | (SP 115.5%) | | **4 Rn** |

**3m 3.6** (4.30) CSF £7.90 TOTE £3.60 (£5.10) OWNER Mr B. Batey (MIDDLEHAM) BRED Juddmonte Farms
LONG HANDICAP Aztec Flyer (USA) 6-6
WEIGHT FOR AGE 3yo-12lb
OFFICIAL EXPLANATION **Highflying: the improvement in the gelding's performance from his last run was accounted for by the trainer. He stated that the horse prefers faster going and, though it was officially good to firm when he last ran, there had been heavy showers and the going was quite loose on top.**
**2900* Highflying** found the loose ground against him last time and, back to his best here, refused to give in when challenged in the straight. (2/1)
**3253 Villeggiatura**, very edgy in the stalls, looked likely to win this entering the final two furlongs but, inclined to wander under pressure, was never doing enough, despite keeping on. The ability is there if his attitude will allow it. (3/1)
**Aztec Flyer (USA)** has done very well physically and, though never offering a threat here, he showed enough to suggest that better is now likely. (20/1)
**3487* Mister Aspecto (IRE)** was not allowed his own way here and, once the pressure was on approaching the final two furlongs, he wanted nothing more to do with it. (10/11: Evens-5/6)

## 3817 TOTE BOOKMAKERS H'CAP (0-80) (3-Y.O+) (Class D)

3-40 (3-43) **7f** £3,810.00 (£1,155.00: £565.00: £270.00) Stalls: Centre GOING minus 0.46 sec per fur (F)

| | | | | SP | RR | SF |
|---|---|---|---|---|---|---|
| 3271$^{5}$ | **Daryabad (IRE) (72)** (TJNaughton) **4-9-1b$^{1(5)}$** JDSmith(9) (lw: trckd ldrs: effrt 3f out: led 1½f out: r.o u.p.) | — | 1 | 7/1 | 79 | 61 |
| 3639$^{8}$ | **King Rat (IRE) (75)** (TJEtherington) **5-9-9b** JTate(11) (lw: a.p: effrt over 2f out: kpt on wl towards fin) | ½ | 2 | 8/1 | 81 | 63 |
| 3639$^{10}$ | **Cavers Yangous (65)** (MJohnston) **5-8-13v$^{1}$** JWeaver(6) (cl up: led after 2f tl 1½f out: one pce) | 1¾ | 3 | 10/1 | 67 | 49 |
| 3453$^{2}$ | **Densben (51)** (DenysSmith) **12-7-13**$^{ow3}$ JFanning(5) (bhd: hdwy over 2f out: styd on wl towards fin) | ½ | 4 | 11/1 | 52 | 31 |
| 3639$^{5}$ | **Halmanerror (70)** (MrsJRRamsden) **6-9-4** KFallon(1) (hld up & bhd: hdwy over 2f out: nvr able to chal) | ¾ | 5 | 9/4$^{1}$ | 69 | 51 |
| 3680* | **Superpride (61)** (MrsMReveley) **4-8-9** $^{6x}$ ACulhane(10) (cl up: drvn along 3f out: wknd fnl 2f) | 4 | 6 | 13/2$^{3}$ | 51 | 33 |
| | **Mahool (USA) (76)** (JLEyre) **7-9-7**$^{(3)}$ OPears(7) (bhd: effrt 3f out: no imp) | nk | 7 | 16/1 | 65 | 47 |
| 3328$^{6}$ | **Kid Ory (58)** (PCalver) **5-8-6** MBirch(8) (led 2f: sn rdn: wknd ½-wy) | 3 | 8 | 11/1 | 40 | 22 |
| 2947* | **Gymcrak Flyer (67)** (GHolmes) **5-9-1** DeanMcKeown(3) (lw: b.hind: s.i.s: rdn ½-wy: no imp) | ¾ | 9 | 4/1$^{2}$ | 48 | 30 |
| 3578$^{3}$ | **Polish Lady (IRE) (53)** (CMurray) **3-7-10** LCharnock(2) (chsd ldrs 4f: wkng whn bmpd over 2f out) | 4 | 10 | 20/1 | 25 | 2 |
| 2428$^{10}$ | **Winter Scout (USA) (58)** (CPEBrooks) **8-8-6b** WRyan(4) (nvr wnt pce) | 9 | 11 | 12/1 | 9 | — |
| | | | | (SP 131.8%) | | **11 Rn** |

**1m 23.3** (0.30) CSF £63.24 CT £540.33 TOTE £8.50: £2.20 £1.80 £3.10 (£26.00) Trio £104.60 OWNER The C & M Racing Partnership (EPSOM) BRED His Highness the Aga Khans Studs S. C.
LONG HANDICAP Densben 7-9 Polish Lady (IRE) 6-9
WEIGHT FOR AGE 3yo-5lb
**3271 Daryabad (IRE)** won his first race in this country and, though he did knock one opponent out of the way, he did it well under some vigorous driving. (7/1)
**3639 King Rat (IRE)** last won at this meeting a year ago and tried hard to repeat that. He is obviously back to something like his best. (8/1)
**3328 Cavers Yangous**, in a visor for the first time instead of blinkers, ran much better and would seem to be coming to hand. (10/1)
**3453 Densben** showed he still has ability by staying on well, but always too late to have a chance. (11/1)
**3639 Halmanerror** never really fired on this occasion, but still looks in good nick, and should not be written off. (9/4)
**3680* Superpride** had his chances, but wandered when under pressure after halfway, and then cried enough approaching the final furlong. (13/2)
**Mahool (USA)**, having his first run for well over a year, showed enough to suggest he is in good heart. (16/1)

## 3818 PAUL DANIELS MAIDEN STKS (3-Y.O+) (Class D)

4-10 (4-13) **1m 1f** £3,663.75 (£1,110.00: £542.50: £258.75) Stalls: Low GOING minus 0.46 sec per fur (F)

| | | | | SP | RR | SF |
|---|---|---|---|---|---|---|
| *3421$^{2}$* | **Menoo Hal Batal (USA) (83)** (MRStoute) **3-8-12** KFallon(6) (plld hrd early: prom: shkn up to ld 2f out: r.o: eased ins fnl f) | — | 1 | 8/11$^{1}$ | 78+ | 8 |
| 1174$^{3}$ | **Pep Talk (USA)** (HRACecil) **3-8-12** WRyan(1) (lw: led: qcknd 4f out: hdd 2f out: kpt on) | 2½ | 2 | 100/30$^{2}$ | 74 | 4 |
| 2918$^{6}$ | **Classic Dame (FR)** (RHarris) **3-8-7** AMackay(5) (plld hrd: effrt 3f out: sn chsng ldrs: nt qckn appr fnl f) | ¾ | 3 | 14/1 | 67 | — |
| 3513$^{2}$ | **Midday Cowboy (USA)** (GHarwood) **3-8-5**$^{(7)}$ GayeHarwood(4) (a.p: effrt 3f out: one pce fnl 2f) | 1½ | 4 | 13/2$^{3}$ | 70 | — |
| 3341$^{4}$ | **Illuminate (72)** (MissGayKelleway) **3-8-12b$^{1}$** JWeaver(3) (plld hrd: trckd ldr: chal 4f out: wknd 2f out) | 3 | 5 | 13/2$^{3}$ | 64 | — |
| 3642$^{6}$ | **Indiana Princess** (MrsMReveley) **3-8-7** ACulhane(2) (plld hrd: nvr nr ldrs) | 7 | 6 | 25/1 | 47 | — |
| | | | | (SP 118.2%) | | **6 Rn** |

**1m 55.6** (5.80) CSF £3.92 TOTE £1.60: £1.40 £1.50 (£2.00) OWNER Sheikh Ahmed Al Maktoum (NEWMARKET) BRED W. Lazy T. Ltd.
**3421 Menoo Hal Batal (USA)** at last got it right here and, in the end, did it well. If his mind could be fully concentrated on racing, there is certainly more to come. (8/11: Evens-11/10)
**1174 Pep Talk (USA)** set a very steady pace and then kept quickening all the way up the straight, but the winner was far too good for him. (100/30)
**2918 Classic Dame (FR)** pulled too hard for her own good, both going to post and in the race, and was well tapped for toe in the last two furlongs. (14/1)
**3513 Midday Cowboy (USA)** looks short of a turn of foot and was not suited by this messy event. (13/2: 9/2-7/1)
**3341 Illuminate**, lit up in the first-time blinkers, packed it in once asked a serious question over two furlongs out. (13/2)
**3298 Indiana Princess** never showed over this inadequate trip. (25/1)

## 3819 FANGIO'S MASERATI LIMITED STKS (0-70) (3-Y.O+) (Class E)

4-40 (4-41) **1m 3f** £3,061.00 (£928.00: £454.00: £217.00) Stalls: Low GOING minus 0.46 sec per fur (F)

| | | | | SP | RR | SF |
|---|---|---|---|---|---|---|
| 3276[2] | **Ceilidh Star (IRE) (69)** (BWHills) **3-8-3b**[1](5) JDSmith(4) (a.p: led 2f out: styd on wl fnl 2f) | — | 1 | 5/2[1] | 76 | 45 |
| 3298[4] | **Totem Dancer (66)** (JLEyre) **3-8-8** JFanning(1) (hld up: hdwy to disp ld 2f out: no ex fnl f) | 1 | 2 | 5/2[1] | 75 | 44 |
| 3412[2] | **Almuhtaram (67)** (MissGayKelleway) **4-9-8b** KFallon(3) (lw: hld up: swtchd & effrt 2f out: rdn & no imp) | 4 | 3 | 11/4[2] | 74 | 52 |
| 3111[13] | **Classic Colours (USA) (68)** (RHarris) **3-8-11** AMackay(5) (trckd ldrs: slt ld 3f out: put hd in air: hdd & wknd 2f out) | 7 | 4 | 12/1 | 62 | 31 |
| 2949[4] | **Lady of Leisure (USA) (69)** (MrsJCecil) **4-9-3** JWeaver(2) (lw: led tl hdd 3f out: sn btn) | 5 | 5 | 7/2[3] | 51 | 29 |
| | | | | (SP 113.7%) | | **5 Rn** |

**2m 19.5** (1.50) CSF £8.90 TOTE £3.00: £1.20 £4.10 (£4.70) OWNER Mr John Grant (LAMBOURN) BRED Airlie Stud
WEIGHT FOR AGE 3yo-9lb

**3276 Ceilidh Star (IRE)** had the blinkers on for the first time and they certainly worked here. (5/2)
**3298 Totem Dancer** is not the best of movers, but did run well, and may do even better on easier ground. (5/2)
**3412 Almuhtaram** needs things to go just right and, once off the bit, finds little. (11/4)
**1666 Classic Colours (USA)** had his chances, but refused to battle. (12/1: op 8/1)
**2949 Lady of Leisure (USA)** ran badly in the tongue-strap, dropping out badly when tackled in the straight. (7/2: 5/2-4/1)

T/Plpt: £456.60 (21.22 Tckts). T/Qdpt: £98.90 (4.5 Tckts). AA

# 2989-CHEPSTOW (L-H) (Good)
## Monday August 26th
WEATHER: overcast WIND: almost nil

## 3820 E.B.F. JULIET MAIDEN STKS (2-Y.O F) (Class D)

2-15 (2-17) **1m 14y** £3,533.50 (£1,063.00: £514.00: £239.50) Stalls: High GOING minus 0.22 sec per fur (GF)

| | | | | SP | RR | SF |
|---|---|---|---|---|---|---|
| 3449[2] | **Ajayib (USA)** (JLDunlop) **2-8-11** PatEddery(4) (lw: mde all: rdn over 1f out: r.o wl) | — | 1 | 2/1[1] | 75 | 30 |
| | **Nile Valley (IRE)** (PWChapple-Hyam) **2-8-8**(3) RHavlin(5) (neat: a.p: rdn 2f out: ev ch ins fnl f: r.o) | nk | 2 | 7/1 | 74+ | 29 |
| 2783[7] | **Moonspell** (RCharlton) **2-8-11** SSanders(2) (plld hrd early: a.p: rdn over 3f out: styd on fnl f) | 2½ | 3 | 12/1 | 69 | 24 |
| 1346[4] | **Permission** (RHannon) **2-8-11** DaneO'Neill(3) (w wnr: rdn & ev ch over 1f out: one pce) | nk | 4 | 3/1[2] | 69 | 24 |
| 3454[5] | **Baby Jane** (RGuest) **2-8-11** PaulEddery(7) (hld up: hrd rdn over 1f out: r.o one pce ins fnl f) | s.h | 5 | 7/2[3] | 69 | 24 |
| | **Indian Rapture** (RHannon) **2-8-11** WJO'Connor(1) (w'like: dwlt: wl bhd 5f out: nvr nrr) | 3 | 6 | 25/1 | 63 | 18 |
| 3405[7] | **Fly Down To Rio (IRE)** (DWPArbuthnot) **2-8-11** RPrice(6) (bhd fnl 2f) | 3 | 7 | 50/1 | 57 | 12 |
| 3615[14] | **Clear The Air** (PFICole) **2-8-11** CRutter(8) (dwlt: wl bhd fnl 5f) | 7 | 8 | 16/1 | 43 | — |
| | | | | (SP 112.4%) | | **8 Rn** |

**1m 36.8** (4.30) CSF £14.96 TOTE £2.10: £1.40 £1.90 £2.70 (£7.00) OWNER Mr Hamdan Al Maktoum (ARUNDEL) BRED Sugar Maple Farm and Deborah Norton

**3449 Ajayib (USA)**, stepping up to a mile, found her previous experience and the help of the stands' rail enabling her to hold on in the closing stages. (2/1)
**Nile Valley (IRE)** may have prevailed if she could have had the stands' rail to race against. She does seem to lack scope, but a similar event is there for the taking. (7/1: op 3/1)
**Moonspell** still looked as though the run would do her good and stamina was certainly not a problem. (12/1)
**1346 Permission** (3/1: 9/4-7/2)
**3454 Baby Jane** appreciated the longer trip, but never looked likely to score. (7/2)
**Indian Rapture** will benefit from the experience. (25/1)

## 3821 E.B.F. ROMEO MAIDEN STKS (2-Y.O C & G) (Class D)

2-50 (2-55) **1m 14y** £3,533.50 (£1,063.00: £514.00: £239.50) Stalls: High GOING minus 0.22 sec per fur (GF)

| | | | | SP | RR | SF |
|---|---|---|---|---|---|---|
| 3319[2] | **Al Azhar** (IABalding) **2-8-11** PatEddery(2) (lw: mde all: clr over 1f out: easily) | — | 1 | 11/8[1] | 86+ | 31 |
| | **Panama City (USA)** (PWChapple-Hyam) **2-8-8**(3) RHavlin(1) (str: cmpt: bit bkwd: a.p: rdn & chsd wnr fnl 2f: no imp) | 3½ | 2 | 9/2[3] | 79+ | 24 |
| 2967[9] | **Select Star (IRE)** (APJarvis) **2-8-11** WJO'Connor(6) (chsd wnr 3f: rdn 3f out: r.o one pce) | 2½ | 3 | 20/1 | 74 | 19 |
| 3493[5] | **Rasmussen (IRE)** (JHMGosden) **2-8-11** PaulEddery(4) (lw: chsd wnr 5f out: rdn over 2f out: wknd over 1f out) | 1½ | 4 | 2/1[2] | 71 | 16 |
| 3615[9] | **Homestead** (RHannon) **2-8-11** DaneO'Neill(8) (nvr nr ldrs) | 2½ | 5 | 12/1 | 66 | 11 |
| | **Big Bang** (MMcCormack) **2-8-11** SDrowne(3) (w'like: bit bkwd: s.s: a bhd) | nk | 6 | 33/1 | 66 | 11 |
| 2335[9] | **Castles Burning (USA) (75)** (CACyzer) **2-8-11** CRutter(7) (bhd: eased whn no ch over 2f out) | 24 | 7 | 50/1 | 18 | — |
| *2865[6]* | ***Presentiment*** (JBerry) **2-8-11** SDWilliams(5) (Withdrawn not under Starter's orders: Veterinary advice) | | W | 33/1 | — | — |
| | | | | (SP 113.9%) | | **7 Rn** |

**1m 36.7** (4.20) CSF £7.50 TOTE £1.50: £1.50 £2.00 (£3.00) OWNER Al Muallim Partnership (KINGSCLERE) BRED P. D. and Mrs Player

**3319 Al Azhar** won easing up and this impressive winner is definitely going the right way. (11/8)
**Panama City (USA)** looked as though he would come on for the outing and, though no match for the winner, will not always meet one so smart. (9/2: op 3/1)
**2122 Select Star (IRE)** settled better than at Leicester, but found this company much hotter. (20/1)
**3493 Rasmussen (IRE)**, a brother to Jabaroot, should have appreciated this extra furlong and was rather disappointing. (2/1)
**Homestead** (12/1: op 6/1)
**Big Bang** will derive benefit from the run. (33/1)

## 3822 FRANKIE DETTORI TON-UP CONDITIONS STKS (3-Y.O+) (Class C)

3-20 (3-23) **7f 16y** £4,822.00 (£1,798.00: £874.00: £370.00: £160.00: £76.00) Stalls: High GOING minus 0.22 sec per fur (GF)

| | | | | SP | RR | SF |
|---|---|---|---|---|---|---|
| 3517* | **Wizard King (114)** (SirMarkPrescott) **5-9-12** SSanders(5) (lw: w ldr: led over 2f out: rdn out) | — | 1 | 10/11[1] | 119 | 70 |
| 3517[2] | **Russian Music (103)** (MissGayKelleway) **3-8-13** PatEddery(3) (lw: led over 4f: hrd rdn: unable qckn fnl f) | 2 | 2 | 3/1[2] | 107 | 53 |
| 2880[9] | **Montendre (103)** (MMcCormack) **9-9-0** PaulEddery(2) (lw: hld up: rdn over 2f out: one pce) | 5 | 3 | 7/1[3] | 91 | 42 |
| 3524[6] | **Resounder (USA) (100)** (JHMGosden) **3-8-9** CRutter(4) (s.i.s: rdn over 2f out: wknd over 1f out) | 5 | 4 | 10/1 | 80 | 26 |

Dublin River (USA) (104) (HThomsonJones) 3-8-9 SDrowne(1) (hld up: rdn 3f out: sn wknd) ....3½ 5 11/1 72 18
3145[8] **Classic Eagle (95)** (RHarris) **3-8-9** DBatteate(6) (swtg: prom 3f) ....6 6 16/1 58 4
(SP 113.2%) **6 Rn**

**1m 21.6** (1.60) CSF £4.06 TOTE £1.60: £1.40 £1.40 (£1.80) OWNER Sheikh Ahmed bin Saeed Al Maktoum (NEWMARKET) BRED Sheikh Mohammed bin Rashid al Maktoum
WEIGHT FOR AGE 3yo-5lb
**3517* Wizard King**, taken steadily to post, was again expertly placed by her trainer who is in cracking form at the moment. (10/11)
**3517 Russian Music** could not reverse the Salisbury form with the winner, despite being 3lb better off. (3/1)
**2498 Montendre** has never won beyond six. (7/1)
**3524 Resounder (USA)** has yet to hit form. (10/1)

## 3823 BANK HOLIDAY NURSERY H'CAP (2-Y.O) (Class D)

3-50 (3-52) **5f 16y** £3,330.50 (£1,004.00: £487.00: £228.50) Stalls: High GOING minus 0.22 sec per fur (GF)

SP RR SF
3511[2] **Perpetual (69)** (SirMarkPrescott) **2-8-0**ow2 SSanders(2) (mde all: rdn over 1f out: r.o wl) ....— **1** 5/2[2] 71 19
2484[3] **Conspiracy (92)** (JLDunlop) **2-9-9** PatEddery(1) (lw: a.p: rdn & chsd wnr 2f out: unable qckn fnl f) ....2 **2** 15/8[1] 88 38
3494[10] **Life On The Street (66)** (RHannon) **2-7-11**ow1 CRutter(6) (outpcd: hdwy fnl f: r.o) ....1¾ **3** 7/1[3] 56 5
2734[4] **Kewarra (76)** (BRMillman) **2-8-7** WJO'Connor(7) (a.p: one pce fnl 2f) ....½ **4** 7/1[3] 65 15
*3604*[2] **Just Loui (68)** (WGMTurner) **2-7-8**(5) CAdamson(5) (lw: w ldr: rdn & wknd wl over 1f out) ....4 **5** 10/1 44 —
3590[8] **Nervous Rex (70)** (WRMuir) **2-8-1** SDrowne(4) (rdn 3f out: a bhd) ....nk **6** 9/1 45 —
715[4] **Northern Sal (78)** (JBerry) **2-8-6**(3) RHavlin(3) (b.nr hind: dwlt: rdn & sme hdwy 3f out: wknd 2f out) ....2 **7** 9/1 47 —
(SP 117.4%) **7 Rn**

**59.7 secs** (2.70) CSF £7.70 TOTE £3.90: £2.00 £1.70 (£1.90) OWNER Cheveley Park Stud (NEWMARKET) BRED Cheveley Park Stud Ltd
**3511 Perpetual** could have been fancied on her fourth to Miss Stamper back here in July, when two subsequent winners finished second and third. (5/2: 2/1-3/1)
**2484 Conspiracy** probably had a tough task in trying to concede so much weight to the winner, and was by no means disgraced. (15/8)
**1834 Life On The Street** ran over six last time and one could see why on this evidence. (7/1)
**2734 Kewarra** was duly dropped back to the minimum trip, but the run at Folkestone last time might have been misleading. (7/1: op 4/1)
**3604 Just Loui**, returning to turf, found this company too hot. (10/1: op 6/1)
**715 Northern Sal** (9/1: op 6/1)

## 3824 JOHN HYLTON WATTS CLAIMING STKS (3-Y.O+) (Class F)

4-20 (4-23) **1m 4f 23y** £2,600.00 (£725.00: £350.00) Stalls: High GOING minus 0.22 sec per fur (GF)

SP RR SF
3333[9] **Indira (49)** (HCandy) **3-8-0** CRutter(9) (hld up & bhd: hdwy 4f out: led over 2f out: rdn out) ....— **1** 5/1[2] 63 22
3466* **Shabanaz (65)** (WRMuir) **11-9-3** PatEddery(3) (lw: hld up: stdy hdwy 5f out: ev ch over 1f out: unable qckn) ....1¾ **2** 4/7[1] 68 37
3303[6] **Siesta Time (USA) (50)** (CLPopham) **6-8-4**(3) RHavlin(2) (lw: s.i.s: hdwy 4f out: outpcd over 2f out: styd on fnl f) ....4 **3** 10/1 52 21
3785[9] **Ultimate Warrior (65)** (CACyzer) **6-9-11** RPrice(5) (a.p: led 4f out tl over 2f out: wknd wl over 1f out) ....2 **4** 12/1 68 37
3466[3] **Dormy Three (55)** (RJHodges) **6-9-3** SDrowne(8) (prom tl wknd over 2f out) ....10 **5** 9/1[3] 47 16
**Hightown-Princess (IRE)** (PCRitchens) **8-9-0** DaneO'Neill(6) (bkwd: hld up: stdy hdwy 5f out: wknd over 2f out) ....5 **6** 50/1 37 6
2056[20] **Grandes Oreilles (IRE) (38)** (NJHWalker) **4-8-4b**(7)ow4 MatthewWilliams(4) (led & sn clr: hdd 4f out: wknd 3f out) ....1½ **7** 33/1 32 —
761[12] **Madam Marash (IRE) (48)** (AGFoster) **3-7-9**(5) CAdamson(1) (prom tl wknd 3f out) ....6 **8** 50/1 23 —
3273[5] **Psp Lady** (APJones) **3-8-1**ow1 SSanders(7) (a bhd) ....8 **9** 66/1 13 —
(SP 115.4%) **9 Rn**

**2m 39.4** (7.00) CSF £7.92 TOTE £4.80: £1.40 £1.10 £2.10 (£2.70) Trio £6.40 OWNER Mrs J. E. L. Wright (WANTAGE) BRED Wheelersland Stud
WEIGHT FOR AGE 3yo-10lb
Indira clmd MrsLMurphy £4,000
**2061 Indira**, dropped in class, appreciated this longer trip and could make a successful transition back into handicap company over this distance. (5/1: op 3/1)
**3466* Shabanaz** came up against an unexposed three-year-old in the winner over this sort of trip. (4/7)
**3303 Siesta Time (USA)** was 1lb better off than when beaten five lengths by the runner-up over ten furlongs at Brighton last month. (10/1: op 6/1)
**3233 Ultimate Warrior**, reverting to a mile and a half, is possibly more effective over shorter. (12/1: 8/1-14/1)
**3466 Dormy Three** had only been beaten five and a half lengths by the second on 3lb better terms at Windsor. (9/1)

## 3825 SEVERN BRIDGE H'CAP (0-65) (3-Y.O+) (Class F)

4-50 (4-56) **1m 2f 36y** £2,932.50 (£820.00: £397.50) Stalls: High GOING minus 0.22 sec per fur (GF)

SP RR SF
3496[3] **Shalateeno (56)** (BRMillman) **3-8-12** SSanders(4) (mde all: qcknd clr over 2f out: r.o wl) ....— **1** 15/2 69 43
3664* **Rising Spray (55)** (CAHorgan) **5-9-5** 5x PaulEddery(6) (lw: s.s: hdwy 3f out: r.o ins fnl f: no ch w wnr) ....4 **2** 5/2[1] 62 44
3302[2] **Voices in the Sky (45)** (AGNewcombe) **5-8-9** SDrowne(9) (lw: a.p: chsd wnr over 2f out: no imp) ....1¼ **3** 9/2[2] 50 32
3621[5] **Course Fishing (44)** (BAMcMahon) **5-8-8** SDWilliams(13) (s.i.s: gd hdwy & edgd lft over 1f out: one pce fnl f) ....¾ **4** 8/1 48 30
3654* **Domettes (IRE) (62)** (RHannon) **3-9-4** 5x DaneO'Neill(11) (no hdwy fnl 3f) ....7 **5** 7/1 55 29
1338[3] **Battleship Bruce (64)** (MissGayKelleway) **4-10-0** PatEddery(7) (lw: hld up & bhd: hdwy 4f out: wknd over 2f out) ....½ **6** 13/2[3] 56 38
3168[10] **Persian Butterfly (59)** (RMStronge) **4-9-9** VSlattery(14) (lw: hld up: hdwy on bit over 3f out: wknd over 2f out) ....nk **7** 33/1 50 32
1838[4] **Hand of Straw (IRE) (57)** (PGMurphy) **4-9-7v** WJO'Connor(8) (nvr trbld ldrs) ....¾ **8** 16/1 47 29
3341* **Printers Quill (46)** (MajorDNChappell) **4-8-5**(5) SophieMitchell(2) (n.d) ....¾ **9** 14/1 35 17
3500[6] **Age of Reality (USA) (54)** (HCandy) **3-8-10b**[1] CRutter(3) (swtg: prom tl wknd over 2f out) ....nk **10** 10/1 42 16
2540[9] **Isla Glen (50)** (MMcCormack) **3-8-3**(3)ow2 RHavlin(12) (prom tl wknd over 2f out) ....2½ **11** 33/1 35 7
2740[3] **Monty (48)** (GHYardley) **4-8-12** RPrice(10) (mid div: rdn 5f out: bhd fnl 4f) ....1 **12** 25/1 31 13
3611[5] **Studio Thirty (37)** (CASmith) **4-7-8**(7) JFowle(1) (swtg: a bhd) ....½ **13** 33/1 19 1

3420[12] **Christian Warrior (33)** (REPeacock) **7-7-6**(5)ow1 CAdamson(5) (hld up: stdy hdwy over 5f out: rdn & wknd 3f out: t.o) ....11 **14** 50/1 — —
(SP 131.7%) **14 Rn**

**2m 9.7** (4.40) CSF £27.45 CT £94.04 TOTE £9.30: £2.60 £1.80 £1.80 (£20.80) Trio £59.20 OWNER Mr G. Palmer (CULLOMPTON) BRED Mrs M. Palmer and G. Palmer
LONG HANDICAP Christian Warrior 7-1
WEIGHT FOR AGE 3yo-8lb
**3496 Shalateeno** seems well suited to forcing tactics over this trip, and slipped the field going to the quarter-mile marker. (15/2: 5/1-8/1)
**3664* Rising Spray**, 11lb higher than the first of his two recent Folkestone wins, did not appear suited to this shorter trip. (5/2: op 6/1)
**3302 Voices in the Sky** was not so inconvenienced by this shorter distance as the runner-up. (9/2)
**3621 Course Fishing** was 9lb higher than when winning this event last year. (8/1)
**3654* Domettes (IRE)**, 2lb higher than when last in a handicap, may not have been suited by the step up to a mile and a half. (7/1)
**1338 Battleship Bruce**, blinkered last time, had previously been trained by Neville Callaghan. (13/2: 9/2-7/1)

T/Plpt: £4.00 (2,001.64 Tckts). T/Qdpt: £2.20 (126.28 Tckts). KH

## 3136-EPSOM (L-H) (Good, Rnd crse Good to soft patches)
## Monday August 26th

WEATHER: fine WIND: mod half against

### 3826 TADWORTH NURSERY H'CAP (2-Y.O) (Class D)
2-20 (2-20) **7f** £3,468.75 (£1,050.00: £512.50: £243.75) Stalls: Low GOING: 0.04 sec per fur (G)

| | | | SP | RR | SF |
|---|---|---|---|---|---|
| 3405* | **Shall We Go (IRE) (62)** (RHannon) **2-8-0**ow3 DBiggs(5) (lw: led over 3f: led over 2f out: all out) ....— | **1** | 4/1 2 | 68 | 22 |
| 3171 2 | **River of Fortune (IRE) (67)** (MHTompkins) **2-8-5** AClark(3) (hld up: rdn over 2f out: chsd wnr over 1f out: r.o wl ins fnl f) ....s.h | **2** | 4/1 2 | 73 | 30 |
| 3632* | **Northern Sun (83)** (TGMills) **2-9-0**(7) JCornally(7) (rdn & hdwy over 2f out: unable qckn) ....5 | **3** | 5/1 3 | 78 | 35 |
| 3164 3 | **Colombia (IRE) (76)** (MRStoute) **2-8-11**(3) MHenry(2) (lw: rdn & hdwy over 2f out: one pce) ....½ | **4** | 11/4 1 | 69 | 26 |
| 3498* | **Misty Cay (IRE) (70)** (SDow) **2-8-8** GHind(1) (swtg: chsd wnr: led over 3f out tl over 2f out: wknd over 1f out) ....2 | **5** | 11/2 | 59 | 16 |
| 3771 6 | **Red Garter (IRE) (64)** (KMcAuliffe) **2-8-2** JStack(4) (lw: prom over 5f) ....3½ | **6** | 20/1 | 45 | 2 |
| 3498 11 | **Dashing Rocksville (60)** (MRChannon) **2-7-12** AGorman(6) (a bhd) ....7 | **7** | 14/1 | 25 | — |

(SP 110.1%) **7 Rn**

**1m 25.69** (5.39) CSF £18.41 TOTE £3.70: £1.50 £2.60 (£8.90) OWNER Kennet Valley Thoroughbreds (MARLBOROUGH) BRED D. Cordell-Lavarack
**3405* Shall We Go (IRE)** looked in good shape beforehand and made a winning debut in handicap company. Making all the running, she was strongly pressed by the runner-up inside the final furlong and found the line coming just in time. (4/1: 3/1-9/2)
**3171 River of Fortune (IRE)**, bustled along over a quarter of a mile out, went in pursuit of the winner below the distance. Running on strongly in the final furlong, she would have prevailed in a couple more strides. (4/1)
**3632* Northern Sun** began to pick up ground over two furlongs out, but found topweight anchoring him from below the distance. (5/1)
**3164 Colombia (IRE)**, bustled along to take closer order over two furlongs out, was only treading water from below the distance. (11/4)
**3498* Misty Cay (IRE)** raced with the winner and showed briefly in front in the straight, but had come to the end of her tether below the distance. (11/2)
**3771 Red Garter (IRE)** was close up until tiring early in the final two furlongs. (20/1)

### 3827 INDIGENOUS H'CAP (0-95) (3-Y.O+) (Class C)
2-50 (2-51) **5f** £10,308.75 (£3,120.00: £1,522.50: £723.75) Stalls: High GOING: 0.04 sec per fur (G)

| | | | SP | RR | SF |
|---|---|---|---|---|---|
| 3618 8 | **Portelet (75)** (RGuest) **4-8-13** PBloomfield(7) (lw: mde all: rdn out) ....— | **1** | 7/1 | 89 | 70 |
| 3432 20 | **Youdontsay (80)** (TJNaughton) **4-9-4** OUrbina(8) (lw: hld up: rdn 2f out: chsd wnr over 1f out: unable qckn) ....2½ | **2** | 6/1 2 | 86 | 67 |
| 3477* | **Midnight Spell (68)** (JWHills) **4-8-3**(3) MHenry(9) (rdn 2f out: hdwy over 1f out: r.o one pce) ....1¼ | **3** | 5/1 1 | 70 | 51 |
| 3618 9 | **Tart and a Half (72)** (BJMeehan) **4-8-10** MTebbutt(11) (rdn & hdwy over 1f out: r.o) ....1¼ | **4** | 15/2 | 70 | 51 |
| 3146 6 | **Tuscan Dawn (76)** (JBerry) **6-8-9**(5) PRoberts(2) (a.p: rdn 2f out: wknd fnl f) ....1¾ | **5** | 10/1 | 68 | 49 |
| 3432 7 | **Canovas Heart (74)** (BobJones) **7-8-12** NDay(5) (a.p: rdn over 2f out: wknd 1f out) ....1¾ | **6** | 5/1 1 | 61 | 42 |
| 3618 13 | **Twice as Sharp (90)** (PWHarris) **4-10-0** GHind(6) (lw: hld up: rdn over 2f out: hung lft over 1f out: sn wknd) ....½ | **7** | 10/1 | 75 | 56 |
| 3783 14 | **Sally Slade (76)** (CACyzer) **4-9-0** SWhitworth(10) (s.i.s: a bhd) ....4 | **8** | 13/2 3 | 48 | 29 |
| 3652 2 | **Longwick Lad (67)** (WRMuir) **3-8-3** DBiggs(3) (bhd fnl 2f) ....1¾ | **9** | 15/2 | 34 | 13 |
| 3313 7 | **Tafahhus (73)** (MJPolglase) **4-8-11b** JStack(1) (bhd fnl 2f) ....2 | **10** | 25/1 | 33 | 14 |
| 3612 10 | **Roderick Hudson (81)** (JARToller) **4-9-5** AClark(4) (lw: s.i.s: a bhd) ....¾ | **11** | 20/1 | 39 | 20 |

(SP 123.8%) **11 Rn**

**56.17 secs** (1.67) CSF £47.50 CT £215.19 TOTE £9.00: £2.50 £2.60 £1.90 (£51.10) Trio £33.00 OWNER Matthews Breeding and Racing (NEWMARKET) BRED Lord Victor Matthews
WEIGHT FOR AGE 3yo-2lb
**Portelet** bounced back to form with this pillar-to-post victory, needing only to be ridden along with hands and heels to secure victory. (7/1)
**3146* Youdontsay** chased the leaders. Struggling into second place approaching the final furlong, she failed to get on terms with the winner. (6/1)
**3477* Midnight Spell**, racing towards the back of the field, stayed on in the last furlong and a half to take third. (5/1)
**3338 Tart and a Half**, racing at the back of the field, began to pick up ground approaching the final furlong but, despite running on, found it all over bar the shouting. She has now won one race from thirty-three starts. (15/2)
**3146 Tuscan Dawn**, in the firing line throughout, eventually had to give best inside the final furlong. (10/1)
**1974* Canovas Heart**, a leading light from the off, had come to the end of his tether entering the final furlong. (5/1)

### 3828 MOET & CHANDON SILVER MAGNUM GENTLEMENS' H'CAP (0-90) (3-Y.O+) (Class C)
3-25 (3-32) **1m 4f 10y** £10,552.50 (£3,195.00: £1,560.00: £742.50) Stalls: Low GOING minus 0.15 sec per fur (GF)

| | | | SP | RR | SF |
|---|---|---|---|---|---|
| 3145 6 | **Arabian Story (83)** (LordHuntingdon) **3-11-3** MrLAUrbano(4) (b: lw: a.p: led 5f out: clr over 1f out: r.o wl) ....— | **1** | 4/1 2 | 103 | 81 |

| Form | Horse | Dist | Pos | SP | RR | SF |
|---|---|---|---|---|---|---|
| 3496$^{4}$ | **Fairy Knight (64)** (RHannon) **4-10-8** MrCVigors(10) (lw: hld up: chsd wnr over 4f out: hrd rdn & hung lft 2f out: unable qckn) | 11 | **2** | 12/1 | 69 | 57 |
| 3235* | **Casual Water (IRE) (73)** (AGNewcombe) **5-11-3** MrMRimell(11) (hdwy over 5f out: rdn 3f out: one pce) | 3½ | **3** | 7/1$^{3}$ | 74 | 62 |
| 3471$^{6}$ | **Artic Bay (65)** (MrsPNDutfield) **4-10-9** MrLJefford(7) (no hdwy fnl 3f) | 3½ | **4** | 14/1 | 61 | 49 |
| 3290$^{4}$ | **Contrafire (IRE) (71)** (WJarvis) **4-11-1** MrLMaynard(2) (a.p: rdn over 3f out: wknd fnl f) | 1¾ | **5** | 12/1 | 65 | 53 |
| 3470$^{9}$ | **Loki (IRE) (73)** (GLewis) **8-11-3** MrEHennau(6) (wl bhd 10f: nvr nrr) | s.h | **6** | 8/1 | 67 | 55 |
| 3710$^{6}$ | **Lord Hastie (USA) (66)** (CWThornton) **8-10-10** MrMHNaughton(12) (lw: nvr nrr) | 1¼ | **7** | 12/1 | 58 | 46 |
| 3617$^{2}$ | **Silently (78)** (IABalding) **4-11-8** MrABalding(8) (lw: bhd fnl 5f) | 5 | **8** | 12/1 | 63 | 51 |
| 3235$^{5}$ | **Roisin Clover (68)** (SDow) **5-10-12** MrPJarven(1) (lw: chsd ldr over 5f) | 5 | **9** | 25/1 | 47 | 35 |
| 3073$^{5}$ | **Proton (69)** (RAkehurst) **6-10-13** MrTMcCarthy(9) (lw: bhd fnl 2f) | 3½ | **10** | 5/2$^{1}$ | 43 | 31 |
| | **Persian Elite (IRE) (84)** (CREgerton) **5-12-0** MrJDurkan(3) (led 7f: t.o fnl 2f) | dist | **11** | 40/1 | — | — |
| 1506* | **Early Peace (IRE) (70)** (MJPolglase) **4-11-0** MrAndiWyss(5) (lw: s.s: a bhd: t.o fnl 4f) | dist | **12** | 20/1 | — | — |

(SP 120.7%) **12 Rn**

**2m 40.29** (5.29) CSF £47.45 CT £303.76 TOTE £4.90: £1.80 £2.80 £2.30 (£29.80) Trio £51.10 OWNER The Queen (WEST ILSLEY) BRED The Queen

WEIGHT FOR AGE 3yo-10lb

**3145 Arabian Story**, not meeting the calibre of horses such as Freequent and Time Allowed as he had done at Goodwood last time, went to the front running down Tattenham Hill and forged away in the final quarter-mile for a clear-cut win. (4/1)

**3496 Fairy Knight** moved into second place rounding Tattenham Corner. Under pressure and hanging left on the camber a quarter of a mile out, he had no hope with the winner. (12/1)

**3235* Casual Water (IRE)** began to pick up ground running down the hill. Bustled along early in the straight, he could only plod on at one insufficient pace. (7/1: 5/1-15/2)

**3471 Artic Bay** was making no impression on the principals in the straight. (14/1)

**3290 Contrafire (IRE)**, a leading light from the off, was made to look very pedestrian in the straight and had come to the end of his tether in the final furlong. (12/1)

**3233 Loki (IRE)** was given a very strange ride. Racing at the back of the field, he was still out with the washing a quarter of a mile from home, but then stayed on in the final furlong past beaten horses to finish sixth. (8/1)

**3073 Proton** is yet to find his form this season and was getting left behind in the last two furlongs. (5/2)

## 3829 LADAS MAIDEN STKS (2-Y.O) (Class D)

3-55 (3-59) **6f** £3,582.50 (£1,085.00: £530.00: £252.50) Stalls: High GOING: 0.04 sec per fur (G)

| Form | Horse | Dist | Pos | SP | RR | SF |
|---|---|---|---|---|---|---|
| 3588$^{3}$ | **Tomba** (BJMeehan) **2-9-0** MTebbutt(1) (swtg: mde virtually all: rdn over 1f out: r.o wl) | — | **1** | 5/1$^{3}$ | 80 | 42 |
| 3478$^{6}$ | **Bold Spring (IRE) (72)** (RHannon) **2-9-0** RPerham(5) (w wnr: rdn over 2f out: unable qckn) | 1½ | **2** | 14/1 | 76 | 38 |
| 3494$^{2}$ | **Polish Warrior (IRE)** (PWChapple-Hyam) **2-9-0** AClark(3) (lw: a.p: rdn over 2f out: one pce) | hd | **3** | 15/8$^{1}$ | 76 | 38 |
| 3259$^{2}$ | **Marsad (IRE) (82)** (CJBenstead) **2-9-0** GHind(6) (swtg: a.p: hrd rdn over 1f out: one pce) | nk | **4** | 11/4$^{2}$ | 75 | 37 |
| | **Right Man** (GLewis) **2-9-0** SWhitworth(7) (w'like: bkwd: s.s: outpcd: nvr nrr) | 11 | **5** | 6/1 | 46 | 8 |
| 3438$^{9}$ | **Kayzee (IRE)** (SDow) **2-8-9** DBiggs(4) (bhd fnl 4f) | 11 | **6** | 50/1 | 11 | — |
| 3637$^{5}$ | **No Comment** (MBell) **2-9-0** JStack(2) (s.s: a wl bhd) | ½ | **7** | 8/1 | 15 | — |
| | **Hippios** (SDow) **2-8-11**(3) AWhelan(8) (str: bkwd: s.s: a wl bhd: t.o fnl 5f) | 28 | **8** | 20/1 | — | — |

(SP 116.9%) **8 Rn**

**1m 12.08** (4.08) CSF £60.37 TOTE £8.10: £1.90 £3.00 £1.30 (£93.90) OWNER Mr J. R. Good (UPPER LAMBOURN) BRED Mrs P. Good

**3588 Tomba**, awash with sweat in the preliminaries, made virtually all the running. Shaken up below the distance, he ran on strongly for a cosy success. (5/1)

**3478 Bold Spring (IRE)** disputed the lead from the start. Ridden along over a quarter of a mile from home, he failed to cope with the winner. (14/1: 7/1-16/1)

**3494 Polish Warrior (IRE)** looked extremely well in the paddock. Always close up, he was ridden along over a quarter of a mile from home, but may well have not been suited by this course and could only plod on at one pace. (15/8)

**3259 Marsad (IRE)** appeared to be travelling well in the straight. When pressure was applied below the distance, he looked rather unhappy on this tricky course, and could only struggle on at one pace. (11/4: 2/1-3/1)

## 3830 ROTHMANS ROYALS NORTH SOUTH CHALLENGE SERIES H'CAP (0-90) (3-Y.O) (Class C)

4-25 (4-25) **1m 114y** £7,100.00 (£2,150.00: £1,050.00: £500.00) Stalls: Low GOING minus 0.15 sec per fur (GF)

| Form | Horse | Dist | Pos | SP | RR | SF |
|---|---|---|---|---|---|---|
| 3634$^{2}$ | **Rebel County (IRE) (69)** (ABailey) **3-8-0** DBiggs(6) (lw: hmpd 5f out: swtchd rt & stdy hdwy over 2f out: led over 1f out: qcknd: r.o wl) | — | **1** | 5/1$^{1}$ | 81 | 36 |
| 3501$^{2}$ | **Mazcobar (80)** (PJMakin) **3-8-11** AClark(4) (lw: rdn over 3f out: hdwy over 2f out: r.o one pce) | 7 | **2** | 5/1$^{1}$ | 79 | 34 |
| 3248$^{6}$ | **Slip Jig (IRE) (82)** (RHannon) **3-8-13** RPerham(8) (b.nr fore: a.p: rdn over 3f out: led wl over 1f out: sn hdd: one pce) | ¾ | **3** | 12/1 | 79 | 34 |
| 3127$^{10}$ | **Sandhill (IRE) (90)** (JHMGosden) **3-9-7** GHind(9) (swtg: led 7f) | ¾ | **4** | 5/1$^{1}$ | 86 | 41 |
| 3594$^{7}$ | **Sabrak (IRE) (87)** (MAJarvis) **3-9-4** PBloomfield(5) (nvr nr to chal) | ½ | **5** | 11/2$^{2}$ | 82 | 37 |
| 3634$^{4}$ | **Allstars Express (65)** (TJNaughton) **3-7-7**(3) MHenry(10) (a.p: rdn over 3f out: wknd over 1f out) | 3½ | **6** | 12/1 | 54 | 9 |
| 3522$^{8}$ | **Classic Ballet (FR) (66)** (RHarris) **3-7-11** AGorman(1) (lw: bhd whn bdly hmpd 5f out) | 8 | **7** | 16/1 | 40 | — |
| 3594$^{4}$ | **Polar Prospect (74)** (BHanbury) **3-8-5** JStack(2) (prom tl nt clr run on ins & snatched up 5f out: nt rcvr) | 2 | **8** | 11/2$^{2}$ | 44 | — |
| 3640$^{9}$ | **Portuguese Lil (73)** (DNicholls) **3-8-4** OUrbina(11) (lw: hdwy over 5f out: wknd over 3f out) | 2½ | **9** | 33/1 | 38 | — |
| | **Sweet Wilhelmina (75)** (LordHuntingdon) **3-8-3**(3) AWhelan(7) (prom over 4f) | 6 | **10** | 6/1$^{3}$ | 29 | — |

(SP 119.3%) **10 Rn**

**1m 45.73** (3.73) CSF £28.95 CT £263.67 TOTE £6.70: £2.10 £2.00 £3.60 (£12.00) Trio £119.30 OWNER Show Time Ice Cream Concessionaire (TARPORLEY) BRED C. J. Foy

OFFICIAL EXPLANATION **Polar Prospect: had suffered interference at the five-furlong marker due to general bunching.**

**3634 Rebel County (IRE)**, hampered running down the hill, made steady headway travelling well over a quarter of a mile from home. Sent to the front below the distance, she showed a tremendous turn of foot to sprint right away from the opposition. (5/1)

**3501 Mazcobar** began to pick up ground over a quarter of a mile from home but, despite struggling on to win the battle for second, had no hope with the winner. (5/1)

**3248 Slip Jig (IRE)**, a leading light from the off, poked a nostril in front early in the final quarter-mile, but was soon passed by the winner and put in his place. (12/1)

**1435* Sandhill (IRE)** attempted to make all the running. Collared well over a furlong from home, she was soon done with. (5/1)

**2420* Sabrak (IRE)** stayed on in the final quarter-mile without ever posing a threat. (11/2)

**3634 Allstars Express** was close up until tiring below the distance. (12/1)

## 3831 CICERO CLAIMING STKS (3-Y.O) (Class E)

4-55 (4-56) **1m 2f 18y** £3,387.50 (£1,025.00: £500.00: £237.50) Stalls: Low GOING minus 0.15 sec per fur (GF)

| | | | | SP | RR | SF |
|---|---|---|---|---|---|---|
| 3456[4] | **Ballpoint (68)** (RHannon) **3-9-3** RPerham(6) (lw: hld up: rdn over 3f out: chsd ldr over 2f out: led ins fnl f: r.o wl) | — | **1** | 11/2 | 80 | 30 |
| 3657[4] | **Nelly's Cousin (63)** (NACallaghan) **3-8-8** JStack(4) (b: lw: chsd ldr: led 3f out: clr 2f out: hrd rdn & wandered over 1f out: hdd ins fnl f: unable qckn) | 2½ | **2** | 2/1[1] | 67 | 17 |
| 2594[8] | **Cherry Garden (IRE) (48)** (TJNaughton) **3-8-5** AClark(5) (rdn & hdwy 3f out: one pce) | 7 | **3** | 12/1 | 53 | 3 |
| *3610[5]* | **Chocolate Ice (66)** (CACyzer) **3-9-7** SWhitworth(3) (led 7f) | nk | **4** | 20/1 | 68 | 18 |
| 2402[2] | **Wingnut (IRE) (42)** (MJHaynes) **3-7-9b**(3) MHenry(1) (lw: hld up: rdn over 3f out: wknd over 1f out) | 5 | **5** | 11/4[2] | 38 | — |
| 3414[4] | **Whothehellisharry (58)** (JBerry) **3-8-8**(5) PRoberts(7) (lw: prom over 6f) | 9 | **6** | 20/1 | 38 | — |
| 3681[4] | **Misky Bay (70)** (JHMGosden) **3-8-13v** GHind(2) (lw: bhd fnl 3f) | s.h | **7** | 7/2[3] | 38 | — |
| | | | | (SP 114.8%) | | **7 Rn** |

**2m 11.84** (7.44) CSF £16.49 TOTE £6.40: £2.60 £1.90 (£5.30) OWNER Mr A. N. Solomons (MARLBOROUGH) BRED R. D. Sears

**OFFICIAL EXPLANATION Misky Bay: failed to handle the track and had choked.**

**3456 Ballpoint** chased the leaders, but got slightly outpaced entering the straight. Scrubbed along for all he was worth to take second approaching the final quarter-mile, he eventually whittled down the leader and, striking the front inside the final furlong, the writing was quickly on the wall. (11/2: 4/1-6/1)

**3657 Nelly's Cousin** chased the leader until going on three furlongs out. Soon forging clear, the race looked to be hers, but she began to wander under pressure and, with her stride shortening, was collared early inside the final furlong. (2/1: 6/4-9/4)

**2402 Cherry Garden (IRE),** ridden along to pick up ground three furlongs from home, could then only plod on at one insufficient pace. (12/1)

**3610 Chocolate Ice** set the pace but, collared three furlongs from home, was soon in trouble. (20/1)

**2402 Wingnut (IRE)** chased the leaders, but was being bustled along early in the straight, and had come to the end of her tether below the distance. (11/4)

**3681 Misky Bay** (7/2: op 2/1)

## 3832 SHERWOOD MAIDEN STKS (3-Y.O) (Class D)

5-25 (5-26) **7f** £3,745.00 (£1,135.00: £555.00: £265.00) Stalls: Low GOING: 0.04 sec per fur (G)

| | | | | SP | RR | SF |
|---|---|---|---|---|---|---|
| 3472[2] | **Grand Musica** (IABalding) **3-9-0** SWhitworth(6) (chsd ldr: led 2f out: rdn out) | — | **1** | 5/6[1] | 84 | 39 |
| 2861[6] | **Hannalou (FR) (68)** (SPCWoods) **3-8-9** DBiggs(4) (led 5f: unable qckn) | 2½ | **2** | 14/1 | 73 | 28 |
| 1171[5] | **Onefortheditch (USA)** (JHMGosden) **3-8-9** AGarth(11) (bit bkwd: hld up: rdn over 2f out: one pce) | 3½ | **3** | 6/1[3] | 65 | 20 |
| 1986[4] | **Ashanti Dancer (IRE) (65)** (MJHaynes) **3-8-9** RPerham(3) (b.off hind: s.i.s: rdn 3f out: hdwy over 1f out: r.o one pce) | ½ | **4** | 14/1 | 64 | 19 |
| 3519[3] | **Intimation** (JARToller) **3-8-6**(3) MHenry(12) (rdn & hdwy over 2f out: wknd ins fnl f) | ¾ | **5** | 7/2[2] | 62 | 17 |
| 3446[11] | **Octavia Hill** (PWHarris) **3-8-9** GHind(2) (hld up: shkn up over 2f out: one pce) | 1 | **6** | 16/1 | 60 | 15 |
| 3058[3] | **Balinsky (IRE)** (JBerry) **3-8-4**(5) PRoberts(9) (prom over 5f) | ¾ | **7** | 20/1 | 58 | 13 |
| 3624[11] | **Girl of My Dreams (IRE)** (MJHeaton-Ellis) **3-8-9** AClark(1) (s.s: sme hdwy 3f out: wknd over 2f out) | 2½ | **8** | 50/1 | 53 | 8 |
| | **Prove The Point (IRE)** (MrsPNDutfield) **3-8-9** AGorman(8) (w'like: bit bkwd: bhd fnl 3f) | 9 | **9** | 66/1 | 32 | — |
| | **Martindale (IRE)** (BWHills) **3-8-7**(7) GBrace(10) (unf: scope: lw: s.s: a wl bhd) | hd | **10** | 14/1 | 37 | — |
| 3446[14] | **Classic Warrior** (RHarris) **3-9-0** JHBrown(5) (bhd fnl 4f) | 9 | **11** | 66/1 | 16 | — |
| *3315[5]* | ***Animation (37)*** (KMcAuliffe) **3-8-9b[1]** JStack(7) (Withdrawn not under Starter's orders: Veterinary advice) | | **W** | 66/1 | — | — |
| | | | | (SP 128.1%) | | **11 Rn** |

**1m 25.34** (5.04) CSF £14.77 TOTE £1.90: £1.30 £2.80 £1.90 (£12.40) Trio £16.50 OWNER Mach 3 Racing (KINGSCLERE) BRED R. Leah

**3472 Grand Musica** chased the leader until going on a quarter of a mile from home. Ridden along, he soon put his stamp on the race. (5/6: 4/5-Evens)

**2861 Hannalou (FR)** attempted to make all. Collared a quarter of a mile out, she found the winner too strong but, to her credit, kept on well for second. (14/1: 10/1-16/1)

**1171 Onefortheditch (USA),** looking in need of this first run in three and a half months, chased the leaders. Pushed along over a quarter of a mile from home, she came through for third prize. (6/1: 5/1-8/1)

**1986 Ashanti Dancer (IRE),** slow to find her stride, stayed on in the final quarter-mile to be nearest at the line. (14/1)

**3519 Intimation,** ridden along over a quarter of a mile from home, showed in third place below the distance, but had run out of steam inside the final furlong. (7/2: 5/2-4/1)

**Octavia Hill** was given a very quiet ride. Chasing the leaders, her jockey was certainly not hard on her, and she could only struggle on at one pace in the straight. (16/1)

**Martindale (IRE)** (14/1: 10/1-16/1)

T/Plpt: £39.70 (541.21 Tckts). T/Qdpt: £10.10 (97.62 Tckts). AK

# 3324-NEWCASTLE (L-H) (Good, Good to firm patches)

## Monday August 26th

Races 3, 4 & 7: hand-timed

WEATHER: sunny

## 3833 UK LAND ESTATES CUP H'CAP (0-90) (3-Y.O+) (Class C)

2-05 (2-07) **7f** £7,100.00 (£2,150.00: £1,050.00: £500.00) Stalls: High GOING minus 0.43 sec per fur (F)

| | | | | SP | RR | SF |
|---|---|---|---|---|---|---|
| 3279[3] | **Persian Fayre (67)** (JBerry) **4-8-11** KDarley(7) (w ldr: led 3f out: rdn & styd on strly fnl f) | — | **1** | 12/1 | 83 | 63 |
| 3328[2] | **Keston Pond (IRE) (75)** (MrsVAAconley) **6-9-5** LDettori(10) (a chsng ldrs: styd on appr fnl f: no ch w wnr) | 3½ | **2** | 11/2[2] | 83 | 63 |
| 2722[5] | **Jo Mell (82)** (TDEasterby) **3-9-7** JReid(6) (lw: trckd ldrs: nt clr run over 2f out: styd on same pce appr fnl f) | 1½ | **3** | 11/1 | 87 | 62 |
| 3525* | **Divine Quest (76)** (HRACecil) **3-9-1** WRyan(12) (lw: sn outpcd & pushed along: hdwy & nt clr run over 1f out: styd on towards fin) | s.h | **4** | 5/2[1] | 81 | 56 |
| 3334[12] | **Tael of Silver (66)** (ABailey) **4-8-10** GDuffield(8) (sn bhd: gd hdwy over 1f out: styd on wl towards fin) | ¾ | **5** | 20/1 | 69 | 49 |
| 3271[3] | **Ashjar (USA) (85)** (HThomsonJones) **3-9-10** RHills(11) (mde most 4f: wknd over 1f out) | 2 | **6** | 12/1 | 83 | 58 |
| 3322[5] | **Lay The Blame (77)** (WJarvis) **3-9-2** TQuinn(9) (s.i.s: effrt & hung lft ½-wy: nvr nr ldrs) | 3 | **7** | 12/1 | 68 | 43 |

2400[4] **Rakis (IRE) (78)** (MrsLStubbs) **6-9-8** RCochrane(2) (hld up: effrt ½-wy: nvr nr ldrs)....½ **8** 14/1 68 48
3430[8] **Equerry (83)** (MJohnston) **5-9-13** JWeaver(4) (chsd ldrs: rdn ½-wy: wknd over 2f out)....nk **9** 12/1 73 53
3445[14] **Ertlon (72)** (CEBrittain) **6-9-2** BDoyle(1) (chsd ldrs tl wknd 2f out)....1 **10** 25/1 59 39
3510[6] **Tinklers Folly (66)** (DenysSmith) **4-8-10** LCharnock(3) (w ldrs: rdn ½-wy: wknd over 2f out)....1½ **11** 16/1 50 30
3510[5] **Fame Again (78)** (MrsJRRamsden) **4-9-8** KFallon(5) (hld up: racd wd: effrt over 2f out: sn bhd & eased)....12 **12** 6/1[3] 34 14
(SP 118.5%) **12 Rn**

**1m 24.19** (-0.31) CSF £71.15 CT £692.51 TOTE £15.80: £3.90 £1.40 £3.50 (£39.00) Trio £55.20 OWNER Mr Murray Grubb (COCKERHAM) BRED Aramstone Stud Co
WEIGHT FOR AGE 3yo-5lb
**3279 Persian Fayre**, who prefers to dominate, took this in good style. (12/1)
**3328 Keston Pond (IRE)**, 5lb higher in the weights than when winning at York two runs ago, ran up to his best, but found the winner much too strong in the final furlong. (11/2)
**2722 Jo Mell**, a keen-going sort, met some trouble, but would only have finished third at best anyway. He takes some settling and is probably better suited by a round track. (11/1)
**3525* Divine Quest**, raised 8lb, showed plenty of knee-action going down. Struggling to go the pace and meeting trouble, she was staying on at the finish. (5/2)
**3148 Tael of Silver**, who showed a very scratchy action, came through strongly late in the day. (20/1)

## 3834 NEWCASTLE SPORTING CLUB H'CAP (0-100) (3-Y.O+) (Class C)
2-35 (2-35) **2m 19y** £10,503.75 (£3,180.00: £1,552.50: £738.75) Stalls: High GOING minus 0.43 sec per fur (F)
SP RR SF

1194[4] **Orchestra Stall (80)** (JLDunlop) **4-9-0** TQuinn(8) (b: trckd ldr: led over 2f out: sn drvn wl clr: eased towards fin)....— **1** 5/1[3] 93+ 55
3486[2] **Embryonic (IRE) (78)** (RFFisher) **4-8-12** KDarley(4) (hld up & bhd: hdwy on outside over 2f out: styd on fnl f)....5 **2** 7/1 86 48
1976[6] **Harbour Island (82)** (MRStoute) **4-9-2b** KFallon(10) (effrt & drvn along 5f out: styd on one pce fnl 3f)....1¼ **3** 12/1 89 51
2612[8] **Noufari (FR) (77)** (RHollinshead) **5-8-8**(3) FLynch(9) (s.i.s: bhd: hdwy on outside 3f out: kpt on same pce)....½ **4** 20/1 83 45
3404[4] **Welsh Mill (IRE) (78)** (MrsMReveley) **7-8-12** ACulhane(1) (in tch: effrt over 3f out: one pce)....2 **5** 12/1 82 44
2117[2] **Speed to Lead (IRE) (90)** (HRACecil) **4-9-10** WRyan(5) (led tl over 2f out: sn wknd)....1½ **6** 9/2[2] 93 55
3434[2] **Deano's Beeno (77)** (MJohnston) **4-8-11** JWeaver(7) (chsd ldrs tl wknd over 2f out)....hd **7** 14/1 80 42
3266[2] **Danjing (IRE) (89)** (MCPipe) **4-9-9** LDettori(3) (chsd ldrs tl wknd over 2f out)....hd **8** 4/1[1] 92 54
3486[6] **Sea Victor (80)** (JLHarris) **4-9-0** BDoyle(6) (lw: chsd ldrs tl rdn & lost pl 3f out)....½ **9** 12/1 82 44
2857[2] **Great Easeby (IRE) (62)** (WStorey) **6-7-10** NKennedy(2) (lw: sn outpcd & pushed along: a bhd)....¾ **10** 6/1 63 25
(SP 116.1%) **10 Rn**

**3m 27.43** (1.93) CSF £36.56 CT £363.64 TOTE £7.50: £2.50 £2.20 £4.10 (£21.70) Trio £106.20 OWNER Mr D. Sieff (ARUNDEL) BRED Alan Gibson
LONG HANDICAP Great Easeby (IRE) 7-9
**1194 Orchestra Stall** had been absent for over three months whilst waiting for the ground to ease. Racing with plenty of enthusiasm, he took this in tremendous style and the margin would have been doubled but for being eased up. The Handicapper will take a dim view of this performance. (5/1)
**3486 Embryonic (IRE)** came from off the pace as usual, but was never going to get near the winner. (7/1)
**Harbour Island**, who has been dropped 6lb after two inept efforts this year, tended to run in snatches. He probably needs plenty of give underfoot to bring out the best in him. (12/1)
**2330 Noufari (FR)** managed to extend his losing sequence to eighteen. (20/1)
**2117 Speed to Lead (IRE)**, 11lb higher than when winning at Goodwood two outings ago, set a strong pace. (9/2)
**3266 Danjing (IRE)** was in one of his unco-operative moods. (4/1)

## 3835 NEWCASTLE EXHIBITION ALE BLAYDON RACE NURSERY H'CAP (2-Y.O) (Class C)
3-05 (3-09) **1m 3y (straight)** £29,830.00 (£9,040.00: £4,420.00: £2,110.00) Stalls: High GOING minus 0.43 sec per fur (F)
SP RR SF

3423* **The Fly (85)** (BWHills) **2-8-6** RHills(12) (hld up: gd hdwy over 1f out: led ins fnl f: r.o strly)....— **1** 7/1[2] 88+ —
3674[2] **Demolition Man (87)** (JWWatts) **2-8-8** KDarley(5) (sn trckng ldrs: led over 1f out tl ins fnl f: no ch w wnr)....3 **2** 9/2[1] 84 —
3462* **Vagabond Chanteuse (77)** (TJEtherington) **2-7-12** LCharnock(16) (racd stands' side: outpcd: hdwy over 1f out: r.o towards fin)....s.h **3** 20/1 74 —
3243[2] **Rich In Love (IRE) (97)** (CACyzer) **2-9-4** KFallon(20) (led stands' side: kpt on wl fnl f)....hd **4** 25/1 94 —
*3625** **Mudflap (84)** (SirMarkPrescott) **2-8-5** GDuffield(9) (led tl over 1f out: one pce)....hd **5** 7/1[2] 81 —
3674* **Pension Fund (82)** (MWEasterby) **2-8-3** 5x DaleGibson(6) (in tch: sn drvn along: styd on fnl 2f)....1¼ **6** 12/1 76 —
3512[4] **Pun (78)** (DMorley) **2-7-6**(7) PDoe(2) (a chsng ldrs: one pce fnl 2f)....½ **7** 16/1 71 —
2923[2] **Eurolink Excalibur (USA) (83)** (JLDunlop) **2-8-4** TQuinn(13) (swtchd lft s: bhd: styd on fnl 2f: nvr nr ldrs)....2½ **8** 12/1 71 —
3324* **Top of The Wind (IRE) (81)** (JJO'Neill) **2-8-2** JFanning(18) (chsd ldrs stands' side tl wknd over 1f out)....s.h **9** 12/1 69 —
3512[5] **Foxes Tail (75)** (MissSEHall) **2-7-10** NCarlisle(11) (b: in tch: effrt & outpcd over 2f out: n.d after)....½ **10** 20/1 62 —
3678[2] **Ben's Ridge (78)** (PCHaslam) **2-7-6**(7) RMullen(8) (lw: mid div: no ch whn hmpd ins fnl f)....1¼ **11** 10/1 62 —
3674[3] **Ninth Symphony (77)** (PCHaslam) **2-7-12** JLowe(1) (bhd & pushed along: styng on whn hmpd ins fnl f)....½ **12** 12/1 60 —
3616[5] **Raven Master (USA) (91)** (PWChapple-Hyam) **2-8-12v**[1] JReid(3) (chsd ldrs: effrt over 2f out: sn wknd: hmpd ins fnl f)....1¼ **13** 16/1 72 —
3512[2] **Skelton Sovereign (IRE) (82)** (RHollinshead) **2-8-0**(3)ow7 FLynch(10) (s.i.s: sn chsng ldrs: wknd 3f out)....1 **14** 33/1 58 —
3616* **Double Gold (80)** (BJMeehan) **2-7-10**(5) MartinDwyer(15) (lw: racd centre: w ldrs: hung lft & lost pl 2f out)....nk **15** 10/1 58 —
3674[4] **Bolero Boy (100)** (MWEasterby) **2-9-7** LDettori(14) (hld up: racd stands' side: a in rr)....3 **16** 9/1[3] 72 —
3407[7] **Tasik Chini (USA) (75)** (PFICole) **2-7-3b**1(7) RFfrench(7) (trckd ldrs tl lost pl over 2f out)....2½ **17** 10/1 42 —
3275[3] **Nostalgic Air (USA) (75)** (EWeymes) **2-7-10** NKennedy(19) (racd stands' side: a outpcd & bhd)....½ **18** 33/1 41 —
3208[3] **The Deejay (IRE) (75)** (MBrittain) **2-7-10** DeclanO'Shea(17) (chsd ldr stands' side tl lost pl over 2f out)....hd **19** 25/1 41 —
2997[3] **Lycility (IRE) (94)** (CEBrittain) **2-9-1** BDoyle(4) (prom: rdn ½-wy: sn lost pl)....¾ **20** 16/1 59 —
(SP 152.0%) **20 Rn**

**1m 38.8** CSF £43.47 CT £620.51 TOTE £8.10: £2.50 £1.50 £10.50 £4.60 (£23.40) Trio £1,971.90 OWNER Mrs J. M. Corbett (LAMBOURN) BRED S. Wingfield Digby
LONG HANDICAP Skelton Sovereign (IRE) 7-2 Nostalgic Air (USA) 7-8
**IN-FOCUS: Britain's richest nursery, this was the first race run over Newcastle's straight mile since the 1950s.**
**3423* The Fly** did it the hard way, coming from last to first. Showing a good turn of foot, he won going right away and is open to further improvement. (7/1)

**3674 Demolition Man** seemed to stay the mile alright. (9/2)
**3462* Vagabond Chanteuse** did best of the handful who raced on the stands' side. Only getting going late in the day, she needed every inch of the mile. (20/1)
**3243 Rich In Love (IRE)**, who looked to have a lot on at the weights, ran really well on the stands' side. (25/1)
**3625* Mudflap** set out to make her stamina tell, but was swept aside in the final furlong. She looks a one-paced stayer. (7/1)
**3674* Pension Fund**, under a 5lb penalty, takes plenty of riding. Sticking on at the finish, he probably ran right up to his York form with the runner-up. (12/1)
**3324* Top of The Wind (IRE)**, who raced towards the stands' side, seemed not to stay the mile. (12/1)

## 3836 NORTHERN REGIONAL ASSEMBLY UNISON VIRGINIA RATED STKS H'CAP (0-105) (Listed) (3-Y.O+ F & M)

(Class A) 3-40 (3-44) **1m 2f 32y** £12,277.20 (£3,421.10: £3,421.10: £967.00: £433.50: £220.10) Stalls: High GOING minus 0.43 sec per fur (F)

| | | | | SP | RR | SF |
|---|---|---|---|---|---|---|
| 3530a* | **Hagwah (USA) (101)** (BHanbury) **4-9-7** WRyan(8) (mde all: jst hld on) | — | 1 | $6/1^{3}$ | 114 | 61 |
| $3039^{7}$ | **Roses In The Snow (IRE) (87)** (JWHills) **3-7-13** FLynch(3) (hld up: hdwy on outside 2f out: hung lft & kpt on wl ins fnl f) | s.h | 2 | 33/1 | 100 | 39 |
| $3497^{4}$ | **Flame Valley (USA) (93)** (MRStoute) **3-8-5** KFallon(11) (trckd ldrs: styd on wl fnl f) | d.h | 2 | $9/2^{2}$ | 106 | 45 |
| 3497* | **Altamura (USA) (103)** (JHMGosden) **3-9-1** LDettori(9) (trckd ldrs: ev ch fnl 2f: nt qckn ins fnl f) | ½ | 4 | $6/4^{1}$ | 115 | 54 |
| $2533^{7}$ | **Cabaret (IRE) (95)** (PWChapple-Hyam) **3-8-7** JReid(6) (lw: in tch: rdn & outpcd over 2f out: styd on wl ins fnl f) | s.h | 5 | 14/1 | 107 | 46 |
| 3568a$^{5}$ | **El Opera (IRE) (97)** (PFICole) **3-8-9** TQuinn(4) (trckd ldrs: effrt & hung lft over 1f out: no imp) | 1½ | 6 | 11/1 | 107 | 46 |
| $3125^{12}$ | **Ellie Ardensky (96)** (JRFanshawe) **4-9-2** NVarley(5) (chsd ldrs tl wknd ins fnl f) | nk | 7 | 10/1 | 105 | 52 |
| $3709^{12}$ | **Hunters of Brora (IRE) (91)** (JDBethell) **6-8-11** JWeaver(2) (dwlt: bhd: sme hdwy over 2f out: sn wknd) | 6 | 8 | 14/1 | 91 | 38 |
| $2991^{7}$ | **Scarlet Plume (100)** (JLDunlop) **3-8-12** KDarley(1) (trckd ldrs: effrt 2f out: sn wl outpcd) | 2½ | 9 | 16/1 | 96 | 35 |
| $3067^{4}$ | **Faraway Waters (95)** (DWPArbuthnot) **3-8-7** RCochrane(7) (b.hind: hld up & plld hrd: sme hdwy over 2f out: sn wknd) | 5 | 10 | 12/1 | 83 | 22 |
| $3497^{8}$ | **Gryada (92)** (WJarvis) **3-8-4** RHills(10) (hld up & bhd: effrt over 2f out: sn lost pl) | 7 | 11 | 33/1 | 69 | 8 |

(SP 122.7%) **11 Rn**

**2m 7.8** (1.10) CSF H, FV £16.26 H, RITS £73.99 CT H, FV, RITS £380.96 H, RITS, FV £447.21 TOTE £7.50: £2.30 £1.50 £5.40 (H, FV £13.40, H, RITS £36.50) Trio £204.30 OWNER Mr Abdullah Ali (NEWMARKET) BRED Gainsborough Farm Inc
LONG HANDICAP Roses In The Snow (IRE) 7-9
WEIGHT FOR AGE 3yo-8lb
**OFFICIAL EXPLANATION Faraway Waters: lost a front shoe.**
**3530a* Hagwah (USA)** is a tough individual and versatile too. (6/1)
**2142 Roses In The Snow (IRE)**, 4lb out of the handicap, ran easily her best-ever race. (33/1)
**3497 Flame Valley (USA)**, given a much more patient ride, finished with a real flourish. (9/2)
**3497* Altamura (USA)**, almost certainly flattered by her Salisbury success, as at Ripon, flashed her tail under pressure. (6/4)
**2533 Cabaret (IRE)**, who looked a picture, was tapped for foot halfway up the straight. Sticking on strongly at the finish, she is better over a mile and a half. (14/1)
**3568a El Opera (IRE)**, raised 10lb after her fifth in a slowly-run listed event at Deauville, wanted to do nothing but hang left under pressure. (11/1)

## 3837 E.B.F. STANLEY RACING MAIDEN STKS (2-Y.O) (Class D)

4-10 (4-14) **7f** £3,550.00 (£1,075.00: £525.00: £250.00) Stalls: High GOING minus 0.43 sec per fur (F)

| | | | | SP | RR | SF |
|---|---|---|---|---|---|---|
| $3221^{3}$ | **Redwing** (JLDunlop) **2-9-0** KDarley(4) (sn trckng ldrs: styd on appr fnl f: led nr fin) | — | 1 | $9/2^{1}$ | 82 | 45 |
| | **Hurricane State (USA)** (PWChapple-Hyam) **2-9-0** JReid(5) (cmpt: w ldrs: led over 1f out tl nr fin) | hd | 2 | $6/1^{3}$ | 82 | 45 |
| | **Taunt** (DMorley) **2-9-0** RCochrane(6) (w'like: s.i.s: hdwy ½-wy: ev ch fnl f: r.o) | nk | 3 | $5/1^{2}$ | 81 | 44 |
| $3407^{10}$ | **Noble Investment** (JMPEustace) **2-9-0** JTate(12) (led tl hdd & wknd over 1f out) | 6 | 4 | 10/1 | 67 | 30 |
| | **Mount Holly (USA)** (JHMGosden) **2-9-0** LDettori(13) (w'like: bit bkwd: sltly hmpd s: bhd: hdwy over 2f out: rn green: nvr rchd ldrs) | s.h | 5 | $6/1^{3}$ | 67+ | 30 |
| $3462^{2}$ | **Blooming Amazing** (JLEyre) **2-9-0** LCharnock(2) (trckd ldrs: effrt over 2f out: edgd lft & wknd over 1f out) | 2½ | 6 | $6/1^{3}$ | 62 | 25 |
| | **Hachiyah (IRE)** (HThomsonJones) **2-8-9** RHills(3) (leggy: unf: unruly s: w ldrs: hung lft & lost pl over 1f out) | s.h | 7 | 7/1 | 56 | 19 |
| $1191^{5}$ | **Puzzlement** (CEBrittain) **2-9-0** BDoyle(9) (in tch: effrt over 1f out: sn wl outpcd) | 1¾ | 8 | 20/1 | 57 | 20 |
| | **Kippilaw** (MJohnston) **2-8-9** JWeaver(11) (leggy: unf: w ldrs tl wknd over 1f out) | 2½ | 9 | 16/1 | 47 | 10 |
| $3245^{8}$ | **Mowjood (USA)** (MRStoute) **2-9-0** KFallon(7) (sn bhd & drvn along: sme hdwy over 2f out: sn wknd) | 7 | 10 | $5/1^{2}$ | 36 | — |
| $3119^{3}$ | **Beau Roberto** (MJohnston) **2-9-0** JFanning(1) (bit bkwd: in tch to ½-wy: sn lost pl) | 1½ | 11 | 50/1 | 32 | — |
| | **Shaded (IRE)** (JWWatts) **2-9-0** TQuinn(10) (w'like: bit bkwd: outpcd ½-wy: sn bhd) | 6 | 12 | 16/1 | 19 | — |
| $3631^{5}$ | **Philosophic** (SirMarkPrescott) **2-9-0** GDuffield(8) (s.s: a bhd) | 6 | 13 | 50/1 | 5 | — |

(SP 136.4%) **13 Rn**

**1m 25.96** (1.46) CSF £34.16 TOTE £4.00: £1.90 £2.50 £2.60 (£12.10) Trio £161.20 OWNER Sir Thomas Pilkington (ARUNDEL) BRED Sir Thomas Pilkington
**3221 Redwing**, on edge beforehand, did just enough. (9/2)
**Hurricane State (USA)**, a close-coupled colt, will have no difficulty going one better. (6/1: op 4/1)
**Taunt** recovered from a sluggish break to have every chance. He will be better suited by a mile. (5/1: op 8/1)
**3407 Noble Investment** ran better on his debut and there might be more to come. (10/1)
**Mount Holly (USA)**, who showed plenty of knee-action going down, ran very green and should come on a good deal for the outing. (6/1)
**3462 Blooming Amazing** showed a very poor action. Tending to edge left towards the centre, he ran as if feeling the ground. (6/1)
**3245 Mowjood (USA)** (5/1: 3/1-11/2)

## 3838 GMB UNION TROPHY CLAIMING STKS (2-Y.O) (Class F)

4-40 (4-45) **5f** £2,801.00 (£848.00: £414.00: £197.00) Stalls: High GOING minus 0.43 sec per fur (F)

| | | | | SP | RR | SF |
|---|---|---|---|---|---|---|
| $3241^{3}$ | **Keen To Please** (DenysSmith) **2-8-8** JWeaver(2) (w ldr: led over 1f out: hld on wl towards fin) | — | 1 | $9/4^{2}$ | 58 | 30 |
| $3763^{5}$ | **Tinker's Surprise (IRE) (63)** (BJMeehan) **2-8-5** BDoyle(6) (trckd ldrs: effrt & ev ch over 1f out: nt qckn ins fnl f) | 1 | 2 | $13/2^{3}$ | 52 | 24 |
| $3160^{8}$ | **Robec Girl (IRE) (76)** (JBerry) **2-8-10** KDarley(4) (led tl over 1f out: sn wknd) | 7 | 3 | $Evens^{1}$ | 34 | 6 |
| $3511^{4}$ | **Not A Lot (60)** (MWEasterby) **2-8-13b$^{1}$** TQuinn(1) (chsd ldrs: rdn ½-wy: wknd 2f out) | 4 | 4 | $13/2^{3}$ | 25 | — |

3508[8] **Figlia** (CBBBooth) **2-8-10** LCharnock(3) (sn outpcd & pushed along: edgd lft ½-wy)....10 **5** 50/1 — —
2371[10] **Shotley Princess (48)** (NBycroft) **2-8-8** KFallon(5) (Withdrawn not under Starter's orders: uns rdr & unruly gng to s) .... **W** 33/1 — —
(SP 112.3%) **5 Rn**

**59.92 secs** (1.52) CSF £14.14 TOTE £3.10: £1.40 £2.20 (£10.60) OWNER Carlton Appointments (Aberdeen) Ltd (BISHOP AUCKLAND) BRED Woodsway Stud and Nigel Fenner Fownes

**3241 Keen To Please** did just enough. (9/4)
**3763 Tinker's Surprise (IRE)**, on his toes beforehand, again ran with the blinkers left off. After moving up on the heels of the winner looking to be travelling the better a furlong out, in the end, he was outgunned. This is probably as good as he is now. (13/2: 4/1-7/1)
**2872 Robec Girl (IRE)**, who looked on the light side, seems to be going backwards. (Evens)
**3511 Not A Lot** wore blinkers for the first time, but they had no effect. (13/2)

## 3839 TELEWEST COMMUNICATIONS MAIDEN STKS (3-Y.O) (Class D)
5-10 (5-10) **1m (round)** £4,143.00 (£1,254.00: £612.00: £291.00) Stalls: Low GOING minus 0.43 sec per fur (F)

| | | | | SP | RR | SF |
|---|---|---|---|---|---|---|
| 1895[3] | **Lothlorien (USA) (82)** (PWChapple-Hyam) **3-8-9** JReid(4) (led to 2f out: styd on wl to ld 1f out: rdn out)....... | — | **1** | 6/4 1 | 85 | 21 |
| 3513[3] | **Zurs (IRE)** (MissGayKelleway) **3-9-0** RCochrane(1) (b.hind: hld up: effrt over 2f out: sn outpcd: styd on ins fnl f).... | 3 | **2** | 6/4 1 | 84 | 20 |
| 1709[4] | **State of Caution (85)** (JLDunlop) **3-9-0** TQuinn(2) (trckd ldrs: outpcd over 3f out: hdwy to ld 2f out: hdd 1f out: unable qckn).... | nk | **3** | 11/4 2 | 83 | 19 |
| | **Miss Walsh** (CBBBooth) **3-8-9** LCharnock(3) (unf: bit bkwd: chsd ldrs: ev ch tl wknd over 1f out) .... | 4 | **4** | 16/1 3 | 31 t | 6 |

(SP 112.5%) **4 Rn**

**1m 42.8** (3.80) CSF £4.14 TOTE £2.20 (£2.40) OWNER Mr R. E. Sangster (MARLBOROUGH) BRED Swettenham Stud

**1895 Lothlorien (USA)** made her stamina tell. Battling back to regain the lead a furlong out, she won going away. (6/4)
**3513 Zurs (IRE)**, having his third run, looked to be ridden with his handicap mark in mind. His rider never got serious and, after being tapped for toe, asked him to do just enough to take second spot. (6/4)
**1709 State of Caution**, absent for almost two months, was caught flat-footed on the home turn. After taking charge two furlongs out, his stamina seemed to give out entering the last. (11/4)
**Miss Walsh**, who looked backward, seemed to run well, but was probably flattered in what was only a three and half furlong sprint. (16/1)

T/Jkpt: Not won; £14,968.23 to Ripon 27/8/96. T/Plpt: £420.70 (63.28 Tckts). T/Qdpt: £64.70 (14.04 Tckts). WG

# 3619-RIPON (R-H) (Good to soft)
## Monday August 26th
WEATHER: overcast, rain at times WIND: almost nil

## 3840 GLASSHOUSES (S) STKS (2-Y.O) (Class F)
2-10 (2-11) **6f** £2,647.20 (£744.20: £363.60) Stalls: Low GOING: 0.29 sec per fur (G)

| | | | | SP | RR | SF |
|---|---|---|---|---|---|---|
| 3508[5] | **Naivasha (68)** (JBerry) **2-8-6** JCarroll(1) (lw: cl up: led over 2f out: r.o) .... | — | **1** | 9/4 1 | 69 | 26 |
| 3607[2] | **Unknown Territory (IRE)** (MRChannon) **2-8-11** WCarson(11) (lw: a chsng ldrs: rdn over 2f out: kpt on same pce) .... | 2 | **2** | 7/2 3 | 69 | 26 |
| 3687[11] | **Juicy Ting** (PCHaslam) **2-8-11** JFortune(10) (in tch: kpt on wl fnl f) .... | 2½ | **3** | 6/1 | 62 | 19 |
| *3604*[6] | **Municipal Girl (IRE)** (BPalling) **2-8-6** DHarrison(7) (lw: a.p: hdwy u.p 2f out: nvr able to chal) .... | 2½ | **4** | 25/1 | 50 | 7 |
| 3448[4] | **Petrine Gray (56)** (TDEasterby) **2-8-6** MBirch(4) (lw: led over 3f: grad wknd) .... | 1¼ | **5** | 14/1 | 47 | 4 |
| 3511[5] | **Skyers Tryer** (RonaldThompson) **2-8-6** NConnorton(2) (mid div: hdwy 2f out: nvr nr to chal) .... | 1 | **6** | 14/1 | 44 | 1 |
| 3502[12] | **Merryhill Mariner** (JLHarris) **2-8-8**(3) CTeague(6) (hdwy ½-wy: rdn & nvr trbld ldrs) .... | 5 | **7** | 20/1 | 36 | — |
| 3651[3] | **Fearless Cavalier (58)** (RHollinshead) **2-8-11** MFenton(8) (lw: effrt ½-wy: sn btn & eased) .... | 11 | **8** | 10/1 | 7 | — |
| 3080[5] | **My Betsy** (MissSEHall) **2-8-6** MHills(5) (s.i.s: a bhd) .... | 3½ | **9** | 11/4 2 | — | — |
| | **What's That Amy** (NBycroft) **2-8-6** JQuinn(3) (w'like: bit bkwd: dwlt: a bhd) .... | s.h | **10** | 66/1 | — | — |
| 3637[10] | **Lucybod** (NTinkler) **2-8-6** DeanMcKeown(9) (dwlt: a bhd) .... | 6 | **11** | 33/1 | — | — |
| 3648[7] | **Cantsaynowt (40)** (RMMcKellar) **2-8-6** TWilliams(12) (early spd: outpcd & bhd fr ½-wy) .... | 17 | **12** | 66/1 | — | — |

(SP 130.9%) **12 Rn**

**1m 16.8** (6.30) CSF £11.48 TOTE £3.70: £1.60 £1.40 £2.90 (£4.30) Trio £23.70 OWNER Mrs Joy Hobby (COCKERHAM) BRED J. A. E. Hobby
No bid; Unknown Territory (IRE) clmd RonaldThompson £6,000

OFFICIAL EXPLANATION **Cantsaynowt: lost her action at halfway.**
**My Betsy: tried to get down in the stalls and was never going well thereafter.**

**3508 Naivasha** had the best draw and, appreciating this trip on easy ground, won really well. (9/4)
**3607 Unknown Territory (IRE)**, who looked in good heart, keeps trying hard and should find a race or two in due course. (7/2)
**2755 Juicy Ting**, a good-looking sort, is learning fast and worth bearing in mind. (6/1)
**3604 Municipal Girl (IRE)** is coming to hand looks-wise and ran well enough to suggest that a race can be found. (25/1)
**3448 Petrine Gray**, at her first attempt on easy ground, showed plenty of speed this time, but was going nowhere in the last two furlongs. (14/1)
**3511 Skyers Tryer** showed enough to suggest that there is a race to be found. (14/1)
**3080 My Betsy** played up badly in the stalls and this run in best ignored. (11/4)

## 3841 GRASSINGTON MAIDEN STKS (3-Y.O) (Class D)
2-40 (2-40) **1m 4f 60y** £3,566.25 (£1,080.00: £527.50: £251.25) Stalls: Low GOING: 0.29 sec per fur (G)

| | | | | SP | RR | SF |
|---|---|---|---|---|---|---|
| 1791[18] | **Busy Flight (105)** (BWHills) **3-9-0** MHills(1) (lw: mde all: styd on strly fnl 3f: eased ins fnl f) .... | — | **1** | 7/4 2 | 95+ | 64 |
| 3656[2] | **Multicoloured (IRE)** (MRStoute) **3-9-0** WRSwinburn(5) (lw: trckd wnr: chal over 3f out: sn rdn: eased whn btn appr fnl f) .... | 6 | **2** | 10/11 1 | 87 | 56 |
| 3656[3] | **Mount Pleasant (IRE)** (PFICole) **3-9-0** JFortune(2) (hld up: effrt over 4f out: rdn & no imp) .... | 3 | **3** | 13/2 3 | 83 | 52 |
| 2383[5] | **Mountain Holly** (DRLoder) **3-8-9** DRMcCabe(4) (lw: hld up: rdn over 4f out: sn btn) .... | 28 | **4** | 10/1 | 42 | 11 |
| 2786[3] | **Give And Take** (LordHuntingdon) **3-9-0** DHarrison(3) (chsd ldrs: pushed along ½-wy: wknd over 4f out) .... | 22 | **5** | 33/1 | 18 | — |

(SP 114.1%) **5 Rn**

**2m 42.8** (8.80) CSF £3.79 TOTE £2.70: £1.30 £1.10 (£1.70) OWNER Mr S. WingfieldDigby (LAMBOURN) BRED S. Wingfield Digby

**830 Busy Flight**, having his first run since the Derby, certainly appreciated this soft ground and had seen off all challengers entering the last two furlongs. He will stay further and, given similar conditions underfoot, is well worth following. (7/4)

**3656 Multicoloured (IRE)** was the only one able to take the winner on in the home straight, but he was firmly dealt with in the last two furlongs, and was wisely not knocked about when well beaten. (10/11: Evens-4/5)
**3656 Mount Pleasant (IRE)** went in pursuit of the leaders once into the straight but, all out with half a mile left, was never anything like good enough. (13/2)
**2383 Mountain Holly** raced quite keenly early on but, once off the bit early in the straight, there was nothing there. (10/1)
**2786 Give And Take** was struggling by halfway and soon dropped away for a dismal display. (33/1)

## 3842 RIPON ROWELS H'CAP (0-100) (3-Y.O+) (Class C)

3-10 (3-11) **1m** £5,881.00 (£1,768.00: £854.00: £397.00) Stalls: High GOING: 0.44 sec per fur (GS)

| Form | Horse | Dist | Pos | SP | RR | SF |
|---|---|---|---|---|---|---|
| 3516$^{2}$ | **Almond Rock (94)** (JRFanshawe) **4-9-11** DHarrison(5) (lw: a.p: rdn to chal over 1f out: slt ld ins fnl f: r.o) | — | 1 | 5/2$^{1}$ | 105 | 78 |
| 3623$^{3}$ | **Bollin Frank (69)** (TDEasterby) **4-8-0** TWilliams(7) (cl up: led 5f out tl ins fnl f: rallied) | nk | 2 | 4/1$^{2}$ | 79 | 52 |
| 3623$^{9}$ | **Spanish Verdict (67)** (DenysSmith) **9-7-12** JQuinn(2) (hld up: effrt over 3f out: styd on: no imp) | 9 | 3 | 16/1 | 59 | 32 |
| 3516* | **Saleemah (USA) (95)** (JLDunlop) **3-9-6** WCarson(1) (lw: cl up: rdn over 2f out: sn btn) | ½ | 4 | 5/2$^{1}$ | 86 | 53 |
| 3691$^{10}$ | **Moving Arrow (97)** (MissSEHall) **5-10-0** NConnorton(3) (hld up: effrt 4f out: btn over 2f out) | 3 | 5 | 5/1$^{3}$ | 82 | 55 |
| | **Iblis (IRE) (90)** (GWragg) **4-9-7** MHills(6) (lw: hld up: hdwy 3f out: wknd fnl 2f) | 7 | 6 | 9/1 | 61 | 34 |
| 3279$^{10}$ | **Knotty Hill (77)** (RCraggs) **4-8-8** DeanMcKeown(4) (led to 5f out: wknd fnl 3f) | 9 | 7 | 33/1 | 30 | 3 |

(SP 112.6%) **7 Rn**

**1m 44.2** (6.50) CSF £12.13 TOTE £3.10: £1.90 £2.00 (£6.60) OWNER C I T Racing Ltd (NEWMARKET) BRED Lord Halifax
WEIGHT FOR AGE 3yo-6lb

**3516 Almond Rock** looked well, despite getting a bit warm in the preliminaries. Obviously appreciating this easier ground, he scored in determined fashion. (5/2)
**3623 Bollin Frank** loves soft ground and is a real battler, but just found the winner too good, despite a valiant effort. (4/1)
**3287 Spanish Verdict** ran pretty well considering he is at his best on the firm. (16/1)
**3516* Saleemah (USA)** has shot up the weights. That, coupled with the soft ground, anchored her in the last couple of furlongs. (5/2)
**2862* Moving Arrow** should have been wherever Bollin Frank was strictly on form. Ridden with restraint, he did not give his running this time. (5/1)
**Iblis (IRE)**, who trotted up first time out last season, disappointed here and was not knocked about. This moderate-actioned colt should be all the better for it. (9/1)

## 3843 RIPON CHAMPION TROPHY STKS (Listed) (2-Y.O) (Class A)

3-45 (3-45) **6f** £12,755.00 (£4,745.00: £2,297.50: £962.50: £406.25: £183.75) Stalls: Low GOING: 0.44 sec per fur (GS)

| Form | Horse | Dist | Pos | SP | RR | SF |
|---|---|---|---|---|---|---|
| 3400* | **Indian Rocket (100)** (JLDunlop) **2-9-0** WCarson(3) (lw: cl up: rdn to ld over 1f out: r.o wl) | — | 1 | 6/4$^{1}$ | 106 | 67 |
| 3213$^{4}$ | **Omaha City (IRE) (100)** (BGubby) **2-8-11** MHills(6) (hld up: hdwy over 2f out: r.o: no ch w wnr) | 3 | 2 | 9/2$^{3}$ | 95 | 56 |
| 3620* | **Just Visiting (90)** (CaptJWilson) **2-8-6** DHarrison(2) (lw: led tl over 1f out: no ex u.p) | 3 | 3 | 6/1 | 82 | 43 |
| 3690$^{6}$ | **For Your Eyes Only (94)** (TDEasterby) **2-9-2** MBirch(4) (b: lw: hld up: outpcd ½-wy: styd on fnl f: no imp) | 2½ | 4 | 10/1 | 85 | 46 |
| 3128* | **Young Bigwig (IRE) (100)** (JBerry) **2-8-11** JCarroll(7) (lw: chsd ldrs tl wknd fnl 2f) | nk | 5 | 7/2$^{2}$ | 80 | 41 |
| 3400$^{4}$ | **The Lambton Worm (93)** (DenysSmith) **2-8-11** JFortune(5) (lw: in tch tl outpcd ½-wy: sn btn) | 4 | 6 | 25/1 | 69 | 30 |
| 3707$^{7}$ | **Daylight Dreams** (CACyzer) **2-8-6** MFenton(1) (lw: a.p: effrt over 2f out: sn btn) | 1¾ | 7 | 7/1 | 59 | 20 |

(SP 120.1%) **7 Rn**

**1m 15.3** (4.80) CSF £9.03 TOTE £2.60: £1.70 £2.60 (£6.60) OWNER Mr Khalil Alsayegh (ARUNDEL) BRED Red House Stud

**3400* Indian Rocket** acted well on this soft ground, and this good-looking colt won in useful style. He is in top form just now. (6/4)
**3213 Omaha City (IRE)** took a strong hold on the way to post and on the way back, but still ran well, only to find the winner too good. (9/2: 5/1-3/1)
**3620* Just Visiting** tried the same tactics as last time, but could never shake off the favourite, and found she had to cry enough with a furlong left. (6/1: op 4/1)
**3690 For Your Eyes Only** ran as though he will appreciate further. (10/1: 6/1-12/1)
**3128* Young Bigwig (IRE)**, at his first attempt on this ground, was left struggling in the last two furlongs. (7/2)
**3400 The Lambton Worm** was always finding this company and these conditions beyond him. (25/1)
**823* Daylight Dreams** (7/1: 8/1-12/1)

## 3844 SUMMER BRIDGE H'CAP (0-80) (3-Y.O) (Class D)

4-15 (4-16) **6f** £3,728.75 (£1,130.00: £552.50: £263.75) Stalls: Low GOING: 0.44 sec per fur (GS)

| Form | Horse | Dist | Pos | SP | RR | SF |
|---|---|---|---|---|---|---|
| 3644$^{2}$ | **Naissant (60)** (RMMcKellar) **3-7-11**$^{(7)}$ KSked(17) (cl up far side: led over 2f out: styd on strly fnl f) | — | 1 | 10/1 | 77 | 48 |
| 3583* | **Never Think Twice (65)** (KTIvory) **3-8-9b** CScally(18) (b: lw: racd far side: hdwy 2f out: r.o: nt rch wnr) | 6 | 2 | 9/1 | 66 | 37 |
| 3154$^{6}$ | **Middle East (73)** (TDBarron) **3-9-3** JFortune(4) (cl up stands' side: led over 1f out: no ch w ldrs far side) | 2 | 3 | 12/1 | 69 | 40 |
| 3323* | **Croeso Cynnes (71)** (BPalling) **3-9-1** JCarroll(3) (lw: hld up stands' side: hdwy & n.m.r 2f out: r.o) | nk | 4 | 13/2$^{2}$ | 66 | 37 |
| 3622$^{13}$ | **First Maite (75)** (SRBowring) **3-9-5b** DeanMcKeown(7) (lw: in tch stands' side: effrt ½-wy: nt qckn appr fnl f) | 1½ | 5 | 15/2$^{3}$ | 66 | 37 |
| 3700$^{9}$ | **Madam Zando (52)** (JBalding) **3-7-7**$^{(3)}$ DarrenMoffatt(1) (lw: chsd ldrs stands' side: nt qckn fnl 2f) | 2½ | 6 | 25/1 | 36 | 7 |
| 3518$^{7}$ | **Azwah (USA) (61)** (PTWalwyn) **3-8-5** WCarson(13) (led far side over 3f: sn btn) | 2½ | 7 | 11/1 | 39 | 10 |
| 3774$^{6}$ | **Mister Joel (62)** (MWEasterby) **3-8-1b**$^{(5)ow2}$ GParkin(10) (chsd ldrs stands' side: no imp fnl 2f) | 1 | 8 | 12/1 | 37 | 6 |
| 3140$^{5}$ | **Standown (70)** (JBerry) **3-9-0** EmmaO'Gorman(14) (swtchd stands' side: nvr rchd ldrs) | 1 | 9 | 14/1 | 42 | 13 |
| 3774$^{10}$ | **Comic Fantasy (AUS) (69)** (MartynWane) **3-8-13** NConnorton(8) (racd stands' side: nvr trbld ldrs) | 2 | 10 | 20/1 | 36 | 7 |
| 3154$^{5}$ | **Bollin Dorothy (59)** (TDEasterby) **3-8-3** TWilliams(5) (w ldrs stands' side: led over 2f out tl wknd over 1f out) | nk | 11 | 4/1$^{1}$ | 25 | — |
| 2151$^{6}$ | **Goretski (IRE) (72)** (NTinkler) **3-9-2** KimTinkler(2) (led stands' side over 3f: wknd) | ½ | 12 | 20/1 | 37 | 8 |
| 2870* | **Bowlers Boy (64)** (JJQuinn) **3-8-8** JQuinn(11) (racd stands' side: nvr trbld ldrs) | 3 | 13 | 9/1 | 21 | — |
| 3624$^{2}$ | **Merrily (67)** (MissSEHall) **3-8-11** MHills(15) (b: chsd ldrs far side over 3f: wknd) | 1 | 14 | 16/1 | 21 | — |
| 3655$^{6}$ | **Sharp Monty (62)** (RHollinshead) **3-8-6** DHarrison(12) (lw: racd stands' side: n.d) | 2 | 15 | 16/1 | 11 | — |
| 2950$^{4}$ | **Princely Sound (66)** (MBell) **3-8-10** MFenton(6) (lw: racd stands' side: cl up 4f: wknd) | 3½ | 16 | 12/1 | 5 | — |
| 2858$^{F}$ | **Deerly (57)** (CASmith) **3-8-1** DRMcCabe(9) (racd stands' side: n.d) | ½ | 17 | 20/1 | — | — |
| 2281$^{2}$ | **Sihafi (USA) (77)** (JMCarr) **3-9-7** ACulhane(16) (racd far side: wl bhd fr ½-wy) | 6 | 18 | 20/1 | — | — |

(SP 146.9%) **18 Rn**

**1m 16.0** (5.50) CSF £105.05 CT £1,079.80 TOTE £12.80: £3.60 £2.30 £3.40 £1.90 (£22.20) Trio £397.10 OWNER Mr William Graham (LESMAHAGOW) BRED Sheikh Marwan al Maktoum
LONG HANDICAP Madam Zando 7-5

**3644 Naissant** revelled in this soft ground and, one of the few to race up the far rail, fairly shot away in the final two furlongs. (10/1)
**3583* Never Think Twice** chased the winner in the final furlong up the far rail, but had taken too long to get going and never had a hope. (9/1)
**3154 Middle East** seems to run his best races when he gets warm beforehand and he certainly did here. He won the stands'-side race, but had no chance with the opposite side in the closing stages. (12/1)
**3323* Croeso Cynnes**, given plenty to do, did well in the end in this soft ground and should not be written off yet. (13/2)
**773 First Maite** likes this ground and had his chances, but never really fired when the pressure was on soon after halfway. This was still an improvement from his run last time and he is gradually getting back to form. (15/2)
**3256 Madam Zando** had the favoured stands'-side draw, but was never good enough to make full use of it. (25/1)
**3518 Azwah (USA)** (11/1: 8/1-12/1)
**3154 Bollin Dorothy** had the draw and the ground, but proved disappointing. (4/1)

## 3845 PATELEY BRIDGE H'CAP (0-70) (3-Y.O) (Class E)
4-45 (4-46) **1m 2f** £2,927.40 (£886.20: £432.60: £205.80) Stalls: High GOING: 0.44 sec per fur (GS)

| | | | | SP | RR | SF |
|---|---|---|---|---|---|---|
| 3484[4] | **Contract Bridge (IRE) (46)** (CWThornton) **3-7-4**(7) AMcCarthy(2) (hdwy ½-wy: swtchd outside over 2f out: hung rt appr fnl f: r.o to ld cl home) | — | **1** | 10/1 | 54 | 22 |
| 3484* | **Cumbrian Maestro (57)** (TDEasterby) **3-8-8** MBirch(10) (cl up: led over 4f out: hrd rdn fnl f: jst ct) | s.h | **2** | 7/1[3] | 65 | 33 |
| 3619* | **Lila Pedigo (IRE) (60)** (MissJFCraze) **3-8-11** NConnorton(4) (a.p: ev ch over 2f out: nt qckn ins fnl f) | 1¼ | **3** | 8/1 | 66 | 34 |
| 2621[19] | **Sistar Act (68)** (MRChannon) **3-8-12**(7) AEddery(11) (hld up: hdwy 4f out: chsng ldrs over 2f out: nt qckn) | 5 | **4** | 7/1[3] | 66 | 34 |
| | **Gunner B Special (45)** (SRBowring) **3-7-7b[1]**(3) DarrenMoffatt(3) (b: b.hind: bhd tl styd on fnl 3f) | ½ | **5** | 50/1 | 42 | 10 |
| 3314[3] | **Pride of Kashmir (52)** (PWHarris) **3-8-3** MFenton(6) (racd wd: hdwy ½-wy: ev ch 2f out: wknd over 1f out) | 7 | **6** | 13/2[2] | 38 | 6 |
| 3295[5] | **Dispol Gem (70)** (GROldroyd) **3-9-7** JFortune(1) (in tch: effrt ent st: wknd fnl 2f) | nk | **7** | 10/1 | 55 | 23 |
| 2159[9] | **May King Mayhem (50)** (MrsALMKing) **3-8-1** TWilliams(12) (chsd ldr tl wknd over 3f out) | 2 | **8** | 14/1 | 32 | — |
| 2486[7] | **Perpetual Light (62)** (JJQuinn) **3-8-13** JQuinn(8) (in tch: effrt 4f out: wknd 2f out) | 2 | **9** | 13/2[2] | 41 | 9 |
| 3347[4] | **Lawn Order (47)** (MrsJRRamsden) **3-7-12**ow1 DRMcCabe(7) (a rr div) | 4 | **10** | 12/1 | 20 | — |
| 3356[3] | **Naseem Alsahar (69)** (MajorWRHern) **3-9-6b** WCarson(13) (chsd ldrs tl wknd fnl 4f) | 20 | **11** | 6/1[1] | 10 | — |
| 3225[8] | **Snowpoles (51)** (MrsJCecil) **3-8-2**ow1 DHarrison(5) (led tl over 4f out: sn wknd) | 3½ | **12** | 10/1 | — | — |
| 3472[12] | **Nawaji (USA) (53)** (WRMuir) **3-8-4b[1]**ow1 JCarroll(9) (prom tl lost pl appr st) | 10 | **13** | 14/1 | — | — |
| | | | | (SP 127.3%) | **13 Rn** | |

**2m 15.3** (11.80) CSF £76.85 CT £554.17 TOTE £18.70: £3.80 £2.60 £2.00 (£59.70) Trio £93.90 OWNER Racegoers Club Spigot Lodge Owners Group (MIDDLEHAM) BRED E. O'Leary
LONG HANDICAP Gunner B Special 7-5
**3484 Contract Bridge (IRE)** appreciated this easy ground and, despite hanging into the whip in the closing stages, she did enough to make it. (10/1)
**3484* Cumbrian Maestro** is in really good form but, despite a game attempt in the final furlong, was just touched off. (7/1)
**3619* Lila Pedigo (IRE)**, upped 7lb and raised in class, ran well but was just short of a turn of foot to take it. (8/1)
**2241 Sistar Act** ran reasonably after six weeks off and should be all the better for it. (7/1)
**Gunner B Special**, in blinkers for the first time, had shown nothing previously, but did stay on well in the closing stages. (50/1)
**3314 Pride of Kashmir** was always racing wide of the field on the slower ground, and cried enough approaching the final furlong. (13/2)
**3347 Lawn Order** (12/1: op 8/1)
**3225 Snowpoles** (10/1: op 6/1)

T/Plpt: £46.30 (186.34 Tckts). T/Qdpt: £94.10 (2.74 Tckts). AA

# 2903-WARWICK (L-H) (Good, Good to firm patches)
## Monday August 26th
WEATHER: overcast WIND: str bhd

## 3846 ALBERT E. SHARP NURSERY H'CAP (2-Y.O) (Class E)
2-00 (2-01) **6f** £3,261.30 (£974.40: £466.20: £212.10) Stalls: Low GOING minus 0.55 sec per fur (F)

| | | | | SP | RR | SF |
|---|---|---|---|---|---|---|
| 3494[11] | **Sharp Hat (70)** (RHannon) **2-8-6** JFEgan(2) (a.p: led over 2f out: drvn out) | — | **1** | 10/1 | 67 | 26 |
| *3629** | **Tinkerbell (68)** (MissSJWilton) **2-8-4v** TSprake(1) (in tch: hdwy over 2f out: kpt on fnl f) | 1 | **2** | 12/1 | 62 | 21 |
| 3577[2] | **Nant Y Gamer (FR) (82)** (JBerry) **2-9-4** GCarter(6) (lw: sn bhd & pushed along: hmpd over 3f out: styd on u.p appr fnl f) | 1¾ | **3** | 9/2[2] | 72 | 31 |
| 3282[4] | **Manikato (USA) (70)** (DJSCosgrove) **2-8-3**(3) PMcCabe(7) (hld up in rr: hdwy & brought wd ent st: r.o) | 1 | **4** | 12/1 | 57 | 16 |
| 2758* | **Song Mist (IRE) (85)** (PFICole) **2-9-7** RHughes(3) (slt ld over 3f: hrd drvn & wknd wl over 1f out) | 5 | **5** | 7/4[1] | 59 | 18 |
| 3590[7] | **Sharp Return (62)** (MJRyan) **2-7-7**(5)ow2 MBaird(9) (trckd ldrs: rdn & wknd 2f out) | 1¾ | **6** | 12/1 | 31 | — |
| 3763* | **Singforyoursupper (61)** (GGMargarson) **2-7-11** 7x GBardwell(5) (a bhd) | 4 | **7** | 12/1 | 19 | — |
| 3651* | **Heavenly Miss (IRE) (64)** (DBurchell) **2-8-0** 7x AMackay(4) (prom over 3f) | 1½ | **8** | 13/2[3] | 18 | — |
| *1097[5]* | **Face It (60)** (WGMTurner) **2-7-10** NAdams(8) (bkwd: spd over 3f) | 1¼ | **9** | 50/1 | 11 | — |
| | | | | (SP 109.7%) | **9 Rn** | |

**1m 13.4** (1.40) CSF £100.64 CT £524.80 TOTE £16.80: £3.30 £2.10 £1.70 (£84.60) Trio £51.70 OWNER Mr J. C. Smith (MARLBOROUGH) BRED Littleton Stud
LONG HANDICAP Face It 7-0
**2977 Sharp Hat** almost took off on the way to post, but was eventually restrained and then taken down steadily. Keen to get on with it, he took over soon after straightening up and, driven out firmly, was always going to win. (10/1)
**3629* Tinkerbell** needs all of seven furlongs to put her stamina to good use and, though she was closing fast at the finish, the winner had taken first run and was not for catching. (12/1: op 8/1)
**3577 Nant Y Gamer (FR)**, off the bridle all the way, did not enjoy a trouble-free passage when trying to close and, in the circumstances, did well to make the frame. (9/2: op 11/4)
**3282 Manikato (USA)** drifted wide off the home turn and stayed on really well inside the last furlong, but just lacked the pace to mount a challenge. Ridden this way, he will be suited by a slightly longer trip. (12/1)
**2758* Song Mist (IRE)** again tried to make it all, but her big weight on this more yielding ground took its toll and she was down to a walk by the time she had reached the final furlong. (7/4)
**3763* Singforyoursupper** (12/1: op 11/2)

## 3847 B.B.T. FINANCIAL SERVICES MAIDEN STKS (3-Y.O+ F & M) (Class D)

2-30 (2-31) **1m** £3,694.95 (£1,101.60: £525.30: £237.15) Stalls: Low GOING minus 0.55 sec per fur (F)

| | | | | SP | RR | SF |
|---|---|---|---|---|---|---|
| | **Inchyre** (RCharlton) **3-8-11** TSprake(5) (hld up: pushed along & outpcd ent st: led ent fnl f: r.o wl) | — | 1 | 8/15[1] | 66 | — |
| 3108[4] | **Pioneerhifidelity** (HRACecil) **3-8-11** AMcGlone(2) (hld up in rr: outpcd ent st: r.o wl appr fnl f) | 1¾ | 2 | 9/2[2] | 63 | — |
| *3418[9]* | **Lovely Morning** (DJGMurraySmith) **3-8-11** RHughes(4) (lw: led: qcknd over 2f out: hdd ent fnl f: one pce) | 3 | 3 | 20/1 | 57 | — |
| 2346[4] | **Itkan (IRE)** (CJBenstead) **3-8-11** MWigham(6) (bit bkwd: swvd rt s: sn chsng ldr: rdn over 2f out: outpcd) | 4 | 4 | 11/2[3] | 49 | — |
| 2029[9] | **February (42)** (AJChamberlain) **3-8-11** TGMcLaughlin(3) (b: bit bkwd: plld hrd: prom tl outpcd over 2f out: sn t.o) | 9 | 5 | 66/1 | 31 | — |
| | **Soul Sister** (DHaydnJones) **3-8-11** AMackay(1) (unf: bkwd: dwlt: outpcd: a bhd: t.o) | 4 | 6 | 33/1 | 23 | — |

(SP 108.0%) **6 Rn**

**1m 41.5** (5.10) CSF £3.17 TOTE £1.50: £1.10 £1.90 (£2.30) OWNER Mr A. E. Oppenheimer (BECKHAMPTON) BRED Hascombe and Valiant Studs

**Inchyre** has been subject to several set-backs, but was turned out in tip-top condition for this belated seasonal debut. Outclassing the opposition, she put substantial value on her future stud career with this success. (8/15)

**3108 Pioneerhifidelity**, tapped for toe on the turn into the straight, stayed on strongly inside the distance and she should now be experienced enough to go one better. (9/2: op 3/1)

**Lovely Morning**, waiting in front, tried to slip her field turning in, but she did not possess the speed to get away and was worn down with ease when the battle to the line really got under way. (20/1)

**2346 Itkan (IRE)** (11/2: op 7/2)

## 3848 ALVIS VEHICLES MAIDEN AUCTION STKS (2-Y.O) (Class F)

3-00 (3-04) **7f** £3,071.20 (£853.20: £409.60) GOING minus 0.55 sec per fur (F)

| | | | | SP | RR | SF |
|---|---|---|---|---|---|---|
| 3515[3] | **Scarlet Crescent** (PTWalwyn) **2-8-2** TSprake(6) (lw: hld up in tch: rdn over 1f out: r.o strly to ld fnl strides) | — | 1 | 3/1[1] | 67 | 19 |
| 3647[3] | **Pericles** (MJohnston) **2-8-7** FNorton(16) (a.p: led 2f out: clr ent fnl f: ct post) | s.h | 2 | 7/2[2] | 72 | 24 |
| | **Gift Token** (MajorDNChappell) **2-8-1**ow1 GCarter(8) (leggy: scope: lw: hdwy over 1f out: fin wl) | 1 | 3 | 14/1 | 64 | 15 |
| 3312[2] | **Mystic Quest (IRE) (71)** (KMcAuliffe) **2-8-7** JFEgan(17) (chsd ldrs: rdn 3f out: no ex fnl f) | 2 | 4 | 6/1[3] | 65 | 17 |
| 3515[8] | **Saffron Rose** (MBlanshard) **2-8-2** NAdams(12) (hmpd & snatched up after 1f: trckd ldrs: rdn 2f out: r.o fnl f) | ¾ | 5 | 16/1 | 58 | 10 |
| 2361[7] | **Court House** (BAMcMahon) **2-8-2**(5) LNewton(14) (in tch: effrt 2f out: sn rdn: one pce) | ½ | 6 | 33/1 | 62 | 14 |
| | **Jukebox Jive** (CMurray) **2-7-7**(7)ow2 JoHunnam(15) (leggy: trckd ldrs: rn wd ent st: sn hrd rdn & no imp) | 1½ | 7 | 50/1 | 52 | 2 |
| 3438[5] | **No Class** (RHarris) **2-8-0** AMackay(13) (led 5f: sn rdn & wknd) | 2 | 8 | 20/1 | 47 | — |
| 3312[5] | **Cartouche** (SirMarkPrescott) **2-8-10** CNutter(4) (trckd ldrs: effrt 2f out: rdn & nt clr run over 2f out: sn btn) | 3½ | 9 | 7/1 | 49 | 1 |
| 3312[6] | **Herbshan Dancer** (BRMillman) **2-8-3** AMcGlone(2) (dwlt: sn rcvrd to chse ldrs: wknd 2f out) | ½ | 10 | 16/1 | 41 | — |
| | **Hoh Down (IRE)** (KMcAuliffe) **2-7-9**(7) JBramhill(1) (leggy: s.s: nvr nrr) | hd | 11 | 25/1 | 40 | — |
| | **Interdream** (RHannon) **2-8-3** GBardwell(5) (w'like: scope: chsd ldrs 5f: eased whn btn fnl f) | 2½ | 12 | 20/1 | 35 | — |
| | **Bella Daniella** (TTClement) **2-7-7**(5) MBaird(10) (lt-f: unf: s.s: a bhd) | 2½ | 13 | 33/1 | 24 | — |
| 2712[9] | **Ela Patricia (IRE)** (DJGMurraySmith) **2-8-2**(3) DWright(7) (bit bkwd: bhd fnl 3f) | ¾ | 14 | 33/1 | 30 | — |
| 2932[5] | **Ballydinero (IRE) (53)** (CaptJWilson) **2-7-10**(7) AngelaHartley(9) (in tch over 4f) | 2½ | 15 | 33/1 | 22 | — |
| 3499[11] | **Smart Prospect** (BJMeehan) **2-8-2**(3) PMcCabe(11) (bit bkwd: a bhd) | ½ | 16 | 33/1 | 23 | — |
| | **Danehill Prince** (MRChannon) **2-8-0**(5) PPMurphy(3) (scope: bkwd: t.o fnl 3f) | 6 | 17 | 14/1 | 9 | — |

(SP 129.1%) **17 Rn**

**1m 26.5** (1.90) CSF £13.92 TOTE £3.80: £1.80 £1.80 £7.10 (£4.10) Trio £40.50 OWNER Mrs P. T. Walwyn (LAMBOURN) BRED P. J. McCalmont

**3515 Scarlet Crescent**, very impressive going to post, needed all of this extra furlong to enable her to get off the mark. (3/1)

**3647 Pericles** looked to have stolen a march when going clear approaching the final furlong, but the winner stayed on just the better to touch him off on the line. (7/2)

**Gift Token**, a May filly who is a half-sister to a couple of winning sprinters, took time to find top gear but, when she did, she simply flew, and she is definitely one for the notebook. (14/1)

**3312 Mystic Quest (IRE)**, more experienced than most of his rivals, pushed the pace, but he was hard at work on the home turn and lacked the speed to get serious. (6/1)

**Saffron Rose** ran into the back of a rival in the early stages and was forced to check. Running on in pleasing style inside the distance, she should be able to win a race. (16/1)

**1489 Court House**, a tall, lean colt, chased the leaders from the start, but was struggling below the distance and could only stay on at the one pace. (33/1)

## 3849 SSAFA (S) STKS (3-Y.O+) (Class G)

3-30 (3-30) **1m 2f 169y** £2,070.00 (£570.00: £270.00) Stalls: Low GOING minus 0.55 sec per fur (F)

| | | | | SP | RR | SF |
|---|---|---|---|---|---|---|
| 3635[5] | **Guesstimation (USA) (62)** (JPearce) **7-9-7** GBardwell(1) (hld up pllng hrd: gd hdwy over 1f out: str run to ld post) | — | 1 | 3/1[1] | 59 | 26 |
| *1605[4]* | **Dannistar** (PDEvans) **4-9-2** JFEgan(10) (hld up: hdwy 4f out: led wl over 1f out: sn clr: ct fnl strides) | hd | 2 | 6/1 | 54 | 21 |
| 3303[3] | **Flight Master (60)** (PJMakin) **4-9-10** RHughes(9) (bhd: hdwy over 2f out: styd on wl fnl f) | 2½ | 3 | 5/1[3] | 58 | 25 |
| 3586[7] | **Tablets of Stone (IRE) (40)** (JRBosley) **3-8-9**(3) DWright(6) (lw: led: rdn 4f out: hdd wl over 1f out: sn outpcd) | ¾ | 4 | 33/1 | 54 | 12 |
| 3619[7] | **Yuppy Girl (IRE) (50)** (CaptJWilson) **3-8-7** GCarter(15) (hdwy 2f out: r.o fnl f: nvr nrr) | nk | 5 | 15/2 | 49 | 7 |
| *3089[14]* | **Desert Zone (USA)** (JLHarris) **7-9-7** FNorton(12) (plld hrd: prom tl wknd over 1f out) | 2½ | 6 | 5/1[3] | 50 | 17 |
| 3466[4] | **Arcatura (54)** (CJames) **4-9-7** MWigham(7) (trckd ldrs: rdn 2f out: sn outpcd) | 3½ | 7 | 14/1 | 45 | 12 |
| 3314[8] | **Hunza Story (23)** (NPLittmoden) **4-8-9**(7) JoHunnam(2) (hld up: hdwy fnl 2f: nrst fin) | hd | 8 | 33/1 | 40 | 7 |
| 3333[14] | **Budding Annie (47)** (JRBosley) **3-8-2**(5) AimeeCook(5) (nvr trbld ldrs) | 2 | 9 | 14/1 | 37 | — |
| 1468[9] | **Brown Eyed Girl (39)** (BJMcMath) **4-9-2** AMcGlone(14) (nvr nr to chal) | 1¼ | 10 | 40/1 | 35 | 2 |
| 3591[3] | **Just Millie (USA) (60)** (JEBanks) **3-8-3v1**(5)ow1 DGriffiths(4) (plld hrd: trckd ldrs tl wknd 2f out) | 1¼ | 11 | 9/2[2] | 34 | — |
| 3130[6] | **Hangoninthere** (NMBabbage) **5-9-7** TSprake(8) (bit bkwd: plld hrd: prom tl wknd wl over 1f out) | 1½ | 12 | 33/1 | 36 | 3 |
| 3473[9] | **Andy Coin** (WMBrisbourne) **5-8-9**(7) IonaWands(13) (lw: prom: rn wd after 2f: wknd 4f out: t.o) | 9 | 13 | 50/1 | 17 | — |
| | **Charmed Again** (MSSaunders) **3-8-7** NAdams(11) (neat: unf: s.s: a bhd: t.o) | 25 | 14 | 25/1 | — | — |

| Form | Horse / details | Dist | Pos | SP | RR | SF |
|---|---|---|---|---|---|---|
| 2706[7] | **Colebrook Willie** (JRBosley) **3-8-5v[1]**[(7)] GFaulkner(3) (bit bkwd: in tch tl rdn & wknd over 3f out: t.o) | 6 | **15** | 50/1 | — | — |
| | | | | (SP 134.9%) | | **15 Rn** |

**2m 18.2** (4.70) CSF £22.86 TOTE £4.00: £1.70 £2.30 £2.40 (£18.10) Trio £22.80 OWNER The Exclusive Two Partnership (NEWMARKET)
BRED Oak Crest Farm
WEIGHT FOR AGE 3yo-9lb
No bid
STEWARDS' ENQUIRY Hunnam susp. 4-5/9/96 (excessive & improper use of whip).
**3635 Guesstimation (USA)**, returning to selling company, raced freely, but was restrained just off the pace. He got caught out when the runner-up quickened the tempo below the distance and it is to his credit that he was able to make up all of six lengths to get up right on the line. (3/1)
**1605 Dannistar**, having her first outing on turf, looked to have the prize sewn up entering the final furlong, but she was probably a bit ring-rusty after almost three months on the side-lines and, with her stride shortening, was worn down in the final stride. She must be given the chance to make amends. (6/1)
**3303 Flight Master** came late on the scene and found the race over before he could land a blow. He does seem to need a stiffer test of stamina now. (5/1)
**3074 Tablets of Stone (IRE)**, lowered in class, held the call until early in the straight and then kept on to show he does possess some ability. (33/1)
**3619 Yuppy Girl (IRE)** came out of the pack in the latter stages, but had mis-timed her effort and was unable to cause concern. She will get it right one of these days. (15/2: 5/1-8/1)
**Desert Zone (USA)**, very lightly-raced in recent years, has not won since 1992 but he pressed the leaders and held every chance until blowing up inside the last quarter-mile. (5/1: op 12/1)
**3591 Just Millie (USA)** raced freely in behind the leaders until weakening soon after straightening up. She will need to settle to get this trip. (9/2: op 3/1)

## 3850 ROVER CARS H'CAP (0-80) (3-Y.O+) (Class D)

4-00 (4-00) **2m 20y** £3,960.15 (£1,183.20: £566.10: £257.55) Stalls: Low GOING minus 0.55 sec per fur (F)

| Form | Horse / details | Dist | Pos | SP | RR | SF |
|---|---|---|---|---|---|---|
| 3037[2] | **Golden Arrow (IRE) (78)** (MCPipe) **5-9-13** RHughes(6) (hld up & bhd: hdwy over 3f out: led ins fnl f: comf) | — | **1** | 3/1 [1] | 90 | 38 |
| 3425[3] | **Upper Gallery (IRE) (76)** (PWChapple-Hyam) **3-8-11** FNorton(7) (hld up in tch: pushed along 4f out: hdwy 2f out: rdn & wandered ent fnl f: nt rch wnr) | 1½ | **2** | 11/2 [3] | 87 | 21 |
| 3149[8] | **Stompin (73)** (MissHCKnight) **5-9-1**[(7)] GFaulkner(4) (lw: a.p: led over 6f out tl over 1f out: one pce) | 4 | **3** | 5/1 [2] | 80 | 28 |
| 3598[6] | **Classic Affair (USA) (64)** (RHarris) **3-7-13** AMackay(3) (hld up pllng hrd: stdy hdwy 5f out: led over 1f out tl ins fnl f: no ex) | s.h | **4** | 15/2 | 71 | 5 |
| 944* | **Bellara (61)** (NMBabbage) **4-8-10** MRimmer(2) (bit bkwd: chsd ldrs: rdn 3f out: sn btn) | 8 | **5** | 7/1 | 60 | 8 |
| 3335[3] | **Mizyan (IRE) (59)** (JEBanks) **8-8-3**[(5)ow1] DGriffiths(5) (lw: a in rr: t.o) | 6 | **6** | 12/1 | 52 | — |
| 1835[9] | **Allmosa (47)** (TJNaughton) **7-7-10** NAdams(1) (bit bkwd: trckd ldrs 12f: sn wknd: t.o) | ¾ | **7** | 40/1 | 39 | — |
| 3476[2] | **Bold Classic (IRE) (80)** (JLDunlop) **3-9-1** TSprake(9) (led: qcknd ½-wy: hdd over 6f out: wknd 4f out: t.o) | nk | **8** | 11/2 [3] | 72 | 6 |
| 3142[9] | **Invest Wisely (79)** (JMPEustace) **4-10-0** GCarter(8) (lw: prom: outpcd 7f out: sn bhd: t.o) | s.h | **9** | 7/1 | 71 | 19 |
| | | | | (SP 119.3%) | | **9 Rn** |

**3m 32.1** (6.10) CSF £19.35 CT £74.22 TOTE £4.00: £1.50 £2.80 £1.70 (£23.10) Trio £35.20 OWNER Spinach Partnership (WELLINGTON)
BRED Paul Mellon
LONG HANDICAP Allmosa 7-8
WEIGHT FOR AGE 3yo-14lb
**3037 Golden Arrow (IRE)** got back to winning ways on the Flat with the help of a very patient ride, and it is doubtful if he will realise he was in a race. (3/1)
**3425 Upper Gallery (IRE)**, a heavy-topped colt who shows plenty of knee-action, was taking on handicappers for the first time at this initial attempt at such an extended trip. Picking up once in line for home, he ran on well despite edging both right and left inside the distance, and he should not be long in finding an opening. (11/2: op 7/2)
**1835* Stompin** finished much closer to the winner than he did at Royal Ascot, but he was already in trouble before that rival took his measure entering the final furlong. (5/1)
**3335* Classic Affair (USA)** worked hard to poke her nose in front below the distance, but the winner picked her off with ease and she had shot her bolt nearing the finish. (15/2)
**944* Bellara** did not shape badly after a long break, but she was treading ground on the home turn and gradually faded. (7/1)
**3335 Mizyan (IRE)** (12/1: op 8/1)

## 3851 WARWICK PARTNERSHIP (INTERNATIONAL RECRUITMENT) CLAIMING STKS (3-Y.O+) (Class F)

4-30 (4-31) **5f** £2,999.80 (£832.80: £399.40) Stalls: Low GOING minus 0.55 sec per fur (F)

| Form | Horse / details | Dist | Pos | SP | RR | SF |
|---|---|---|---|---|---|---|
| 3652[7] | **Windrush Boy (56)** (JRBosley) **6-8-5**[(5)] AimeeCook(9) (a.p: qcknd to ld wl ins fnl f: edgd rt: hld on nr fin) | — | **1** | 11/1 | 63 | 45 |
| 3579* | **Palacegate Touch (75)** (JBerry) **6-9-6b** GCarter(6) (lw: chsd ldrs: n.m.r & swtchd lft ins fnl f: fin strly) | nk | **2** | 3/1 [1] | 72 | 54 |
| 3331[2] | **Superbit (49)** (BAMcMahon) **4-8-8** AMackay(2) (lw: a.p: led 2f out tl wl ins fnl f) | nk | **3** | 12/1 | 59 | 41 |
| 3579[2] | **The Happy Fox (IRE) (74)** (BAMcMahon) **4-9-1**[(5)] LNewton(5) (lw: hld up: a.p: effrt & n.m.r over 1f out: rdn & hung lft: r.o nr fin) | ¾ | **4** | 5/1 [2] | 69 | 51 |
| 3698[3] | **Petraco (IRE) (56)** (NASmith) **8-8-3**[(7)] JBramhill(13) (sn pushed along & bhd: hdwy 2f out: swtchd lft appr fnl f: r.o wl) | 1¼ | **5** | 14/1 | 55 | 37 |
| 3636[3] | **Hever Golf Express (70)** (TJNaughton) **3-9-2** TSprake(8) (lw: led 3f: rdn & no ex ins fnl f) | ¾ | **6** | 6/1 [3] | 60 | 40 |
| | **Nineacres (51)** (NMBabbage) **5-8-10v** RHughes(1) (bit bkwd: dwlt: hdwy 3f out: sn rdn & outpcd) | 3 | **7** | 33/1 | 43 | 25 |
| 3122[6] | **Super Rocky (69)** (RBastiman) **7-8-13b**[(5)] HBastiman(4) (lw: prom: rdn & ev ch 2f out: sn outpcd) | 2½ | **8** | 8/1 | 43 | 25 |
| 3665[5] | **Sweet Seventeen** (HJCollingridge) **3-8-9** MRimmer(14) (s.i.s: a outpcd) | 1¼ | **9** | 50/1 | 32 | 12 |
| 3661[15] | **Mister Sean (IRE) (50)** (JWPayne) **3-8-6** AMcGlone(10) (b.hind: lw: trckd ldrs 3f) | 2 | **10** | 33/1 | 22 | 2 |
| 3216[3] | **Hinton Rock (IRE) (76)** (ABailey) **4-8-7**[(3)] DWright(3) (b.hind: trckd ldrs: hmpd over 2f out: sn btn: fin lame) | ¾ | **11** | 3/1 [1] | 22 | 4 |
| 2893[8] | **Kealbra Lady (20)** (MSSaunders) **3-8-3** NAdams(7) (bhd fnl 2f) | hd | **12** | 66/1 | 17 | — |
| *3420[7]* | **Brin-Lodge (IRE) (40)** (KSBridgwater) **3-7-12**[(5)ow2] PPMurphy(12) (s.i.s: a bhd & outpcd) | ½ | **13** | 25/1 | 15 | — |
| *388[7]* | **Fiery Footsteps (46)** (SWCampion) **4-8-1** GBardwell(11) (bit bkwd: a bhd & outpcd) | 1¼ | **14** | 66/1 | 7 | — |
| | | | | (SP 129.4%) | | **14 Rn** |

**58.1 secs** (0.10) CSF £44.47 TOTE £17.90: £2.70 £1.40 £3.30 (£26.10) Trio £185.50 OWNER Miss Cynthia Commons (WANTAGE) BRED M. A. Wilkins
WEIGHT FOR AGE 3yo-2lb
**OFFICIAL EXPLANATION Hinton Rock (IRE): finished lame.**

**3652 Windrush Boy** goes well for this jockey and he kept up his record of winning in August for the third year in succession with a powerful late challenge that was timed to perfection. (11/1)
**3579* Palacegate Touch** did not enjoy the run of the race and he needed to be switched at a crucial time, but he still put in a sustained late challenge that only just failed. (3/1)
**3331 Superbit** got to the front once straightened up for home and did his best to kick clear, but he was being tightened up after being headed and was beaten to the punch in the sprint to the post. His turn is near at hand. (12/1)
**3579 The Happy Fox (IRE)** had his chance to gain revenge over the favourite, but he was denied a clear run when poised to challenge and, inclined to hang left, was certainly doing himself no favours. (5/1)
**3698 Petraco (IRE)**, appreciating the easier ground, finds this trip on such an easy track much too sharp nowadays and his erratic late challenge was never quite going to succeed. (14/1)
**3636 Hever Golf Express** blazed a trail, but he may have found this rain-softened ground against him, and he was getting the worst of the argument inside the last furlong. (6/1)
**3216 Hinton Rock (IRE)** would have had trouble winning at this trip on such an easy track, but he held his pitch, albeit at full stretch, until hampered and forced to take a pull soon after halfway. He was reported unsound on his return to be unsaddled. (3/1)

## 3852 WARWICKSHIRE & WORCESTERSHIRE YEOMANRY H'CAP (0-70) (3-Y.O) (Class E)

5-00 (5-01) **1m** £3,670.80 (£1,100.40: £529.20: £243.60) Stalls: Low GOING minus 0.55 sec per fur (F)

| Form | Horse | Dist | Pos | SP | RR | SF |
|---|---|---|---|---|---|---|
| *2306[9]* | **Veni Vidi Vici (IRE) (55)** (MJHeaton-Ellis) **3-8-11** GCarter(7) (lw: dwlt: hld up: hdwy & rdn 2f out: led wl ins fnl f: edgd lft: r.o) | — | **1** | 16/1 | 67 | 30 |
| 3439[11] | **Windswept (IRE) (56)** (DJSffrenchDavis) **3-8-9**(3) PMcCabe(8) (hdwy 3f out: led ins fnl f: sn hdd: unable qckn) | 1½ | **2** | 11/1 | 65 | 28 |
| 3592[4] | **Cointosser (IRE) (63)** (MCPipe) **3-9-5** RHughes(6) (hld up in tch: hdwy 2f out: rdn & r.o ins fnl f) | s.h | **3** | 9/4[1] | 72 | 35 |
| 3650[5] | **Missile Toe (IRE) (63)** (JEBanks) **3-9-5** MWigham(5) (lw: in tch: hdwy 3f out: rdn & one pce fnl f) | 3 | **4** | 20/1 | 66 | 29 |
| 3606* | **Fairly Sure (IRE) (47)** (NEBerry) **3-7-10**(7) DDenby(13) (a.p: led 2f out tl hdd & wknd ins fnl f) | 3½ | **5** | 10/1 | 43 | 6 |
| 3474* | **Ca'd'oro (60)** (GBBalding) **3-9-2** AMcGlone(11) (wnt rt s: chsd ldrs: one pce appr fnl f) | ½ | **6** | 7/1[3] | 55 | 18 |
| 3606[8] | **Tallulah Belle (44)** (NPLittmoden) **3-7-7**(7)ow4 JoHunnam(14) (s.s: r.o fnl 2f: nvr nrr) | s.h | **7** | 25/1 | 39 | — |
| 2033[4] | **Mono Lady (IRE) (55)** (DHaydnJones) **3-8-11** AMackay(3) (nvr nr to chal) | 1¾ | **8** | 16/1 | 46 | 9 |
| 2784[7] | **Witherkay (63)** (RHannon) **3-9-5** JFEgan(12) (hmpd s: sn chsng ldrs: wknd over 2f out) | 6 | **9** | 8/1 | 42 | 5 |
| 3470[8] | **Irish Kinsman (65)** (PTWalwyn) **3-9-7** TSprake(2) (lw: nvr trbld ldrs) | ¾ | **10** | 16/1 | 43 | 6 |
| 3456[5] | **Beauchamp Kate (51)** (HCandy) **3-8-7** NAdams(9) (lw: led 1f: sn drvn along: rdn & outpcd over 1f out) | hd | **11** | 10/1 | 29 | — |
| 3655[9] | **Bianca Cappello (IRE) (41)** (PSFelgate) **3-7-8**(3)ow1 DWright(15) (s.i.s: rdn 3f out: a bhd) | 1¼ | **12** | 40/1 | 16 | — |
| 2541[9] | **Dyanko (40)** (MSSaunders) **3-7-10v1** FNorton(4) (in tch over 5f) | 3 | **13** | 33/1 | 9 | — |
| 3469[12] | **Mr Hacker (42)** (GThorner) **3-7-12** GBardwell(10) (lw: led after 1f tl over 4f out: prom: wkng whn hmpd 3f out) | 2½ | **14** | 40/1 | 6 | — |
| 3492[2] | **Flying Harold (47)** (MRChannon) **3-7-12**(5)ow1 PPMurphy(1) (led over 4f out to 2f out: wknd & eased fnl f) | 6 | **15** | 13/2[2] | — | — |
| | | | | (SP 128.3%) | | **15 Rn** |

**1m 38.4** (2.00) CSF £172.45 CT £509.02 TOTE £19.70: £3.30 £4.20 £1.50 (£89.20) Trio £133.30 OWNER Mr R. A. Bicker (WROUGHTON) BRED Michael Moran

LONG HANDICAP Dyanko 7-8 Tallulah Belle 7-6 Bianca Cappello (IRE) 7-0

**1972 Veni Vidi Vici (IRE)** has had a couple of runs on the All-Weather this season without being about able to trouble the Judge, but he found his form over this longer trip and won going away. (16/1)
**2715 Windswept (IRE)**, a previous winner here at the minimum trip, produced a determined run to nose ahead inside the final furlong, but the winner pounced almost immediately and did her for toe. (11/1)
**3592 Cointosser (IRE)**, supported to the exclusion of the rest, did not respond when shaken up approaching the final furlong, but she did keep on strongly towards the finish and should stay further. (9/4)
**3650 Missile Toe (IRE)** has failed to stay when tried over seven furlongs in the past and this trip was always going to be too far. (20/1)
**3606* Fairly Sure (IRE)**, produced to win her race entering the last quarter-mile, was brushed aside with ease inside the final furlong and she may need holding up as late as possible. (10/1)
**3474* Ca'd'oro**, always in the action, was hard at work soon after entering the straight and could not muster the pace to deliver a challenge. (7/1)
**3456 Beauchamp Kate** is crying out for a longer trip as she has not got the speed to succeed at this trip, and immediate improvement should follow when she is given the opportunity. (10/1)

T/Plpt: £21.40 (305.28 Tckts). T/Qdpt: £6.20 (48.89 Tckts). IM

# 3840-RIPON (R-H) (Soft becoming Heavy)
## Tuesday August 27th

Races 5 & 6 Abandoned - Waterlogged
WEATHER: heavy rain WIND: almost nil

## 3853 CLARO MAIDEN AUCTION STKS (2-Y.O) (Class F)

2-30 (2-31) **5f** £2,587.70 (£727.20: £355.10) Stalls: Low GOING: 0.69 sec per fur (GS)

| Form | Horse | Dist | Pos | SP | RR | SF |
|---|---|---|---|---|---|---|
| 2781[5] | **Tribal Mischief (58)** (DMoffatt) **2-7-12**(3) DarrenMoffatt(6) (hdwy ½-wy: led ins fnl f: styd on wl) | — | **1** | 13/2 | 64 | 27 |
| | **Caution** (MrsJRRamsden) **2-8-6**ow1 KFallon(1) (neat: unf: s.i.s: hdwy 2f out: r.o towards fin) | ¾ | **2** | 6/1[3] | 67+ | 29 |
| 2625[7] | **Nifty Norman (72)** (JBerry) **2-8-6** JCarroll(7) (led tl hdd & no ex ins fnl f) | 1½ | **3** | 9/2[2] | 62 | 25 |
| 3637[3] | **Gaelic Storm** (MJohnston) **2-8-10** JWeaver(9) (chsd ldrs: effrt 2f out: nt qckn) | 2½ | **4** | 9/2[2] | 58 | 21 |
| | **Gold Edge** (MRChannon) **2-8-1** CRutter(5) (neat: str: chsd ldrs: nt qckn appr fnl f) | 3 | **5** | 7/1 | 39 | 2 |
| 2361[9] | **Strelitza (IRE)** (MWEasterby) **2-8-5** DaleGibson(3) (s.i.s: nvr rchd ldrs) | 1 | **6** | 20/1 | 40 | 3 |
| 3429[6] | **Sparkling Harry** (MissLCSiddall) **2-8-4** DeanMcKeown(2) (in tch: outpcd ½-wy: n.d after) | 2 | **7** | 12/1 | 33 | — |
| 3757[13] | **Magyar Titok (IRE)** (BobJones) **2-8-4** JFanning(10) (prom: rdn & hung lft 2f out: sn wknd) | 3 | **8** | 12/1 | 23 | — |
| 3332[2] | **Five-O-Fifty** (JLEyre) **2-8-4** TWilliams(4) (spd to ½-wy: wknd qckly) | 6 | **9** | 11/4[1] | 4 | — |
| | | | | (SP 123.3%) | | **9 Rn** |

**65.3 secs** (6.90) CSF £44.24 TOTE £9.60: £1.90 £1.90 £2.20 (£40.60) Trio £116.00 OWNER Mr G. R. Parrington (CARTMEL) BRED Campbell Stud

**2781 Tribal Mischief** revelled in these very soft conditions and, coming from behind, settled it inside the final furlong. (13/2)
**Caution** is not very big and did not move at all well going to post, but was obviously suited to this ground. Another few strides would have seen her come out on top. (6/1: op 4/1)

**2625 Nifty Norman** acted pretty well in the ground, but just failed to see it out. (9/2: 5/2-5/1)
**3637 Gaelic Storm** put in a decent run, only to find the conditions too testing approaching the final furlong. (9/2)
**Gold Edge**, a sturdy newcomer, ran well and should be all the better for it. (7/1)
**Strelitza (IRE)** was always struggling in the conditions and could never offer a threat. (20/1)
**3332 Five-O-Fifty** stopped quickly from halfway as though hating the ground. (11/4)

## 3854 DEVERELL CLAIMING STKS (3-Y.O+) (Class F)

3-00 (3-11) **1m** £2,647.20 (£744.20: £363.60) Stalls: High GOING: 1.02 sec per fur (S)

| | | | SP | RR | SF |
|---|---|---|---|---|---|
| *3601*[3] **Tame Deer (57)** (MCChapman) **4-8-8** DRMcCabe(1) (bhd: hdwy 3f out: styd on to ld ins fnl f) | — | **1** | 16/1 | 47 | 51 |
| 3402[3] **Mellottie (85)** (MrsMReveley) **11-9-2**(5) GLee(4) (lw: bhd: hdwy over 2f out: styd on wl towards fin) | ¾ | **2** | 6/1[3] | 59 | 63 |
| 3306[12] **Harsh Times (43)** (TDEasterby) **3-7-10b** JLowe(9) (cl up: led over 3f out: hdd ins fnl f: kpt on) | 1 | **3** | 40/1 | 38 | 36 |
| 3133[7] **Dispol Diamond (63)** (GROldroyd) **3-7-13**(3)ow2 FLynch(6) (a.p: ev ch 1f out: nt qckn) | ½ | **4** | 11/2[2] | 43 | 39 |
| 3426[9] **Public Way (IRE) (41)** (NChamberlain) **6-8-9** GBardwell(3) (rr div: effrt 4f out: no imp) | 15 | **5** | 16/1 | 14 | 18 |
| 3402* **Rainbow Top (95)** (WJHaggas) **4-9-9** KFallon(10) (lw: led tl over 3f out: wknd & eased fnl 2f) | 5 | **6** | 4/6[1] | 18 | 22 |
| 3481[7] **Battle Colours (IRE) (36)** (DonEnricoIncisa) **7-8-7** KimTinkler(7) (chsd ldrs tl wknd fnl 3f) | 1 | **7** | 100/1 | — | 4 |
| 3309[4] **Hill Farm Blues** (JLEyre) **3-8-0** TWilliams(5) (prom tl wknd fnl 3½f) | 5 | **8** | 25/1 | — | — |
| 3254[6] **Anonym (IRE) (60)** (DNicholls) **4-8-12** AlexGreaves(2) (a bhd) | 2 | **9** | 25/1 | — | — |

(SP 112.6%) **9 Rn**

**1m 49.9** (12.20) CSF £96.53 TOTE £11.90: £1.90 £1.70 £5.30 (£44.40) Trio £200.10 OWNER Mr Mattie O'Toole (MARKET RASEN) BRED Stetchworth Park Stud Ltd
WEIGHT FOR AGE 3yo-6lb
OFFICIAL EXPLANATION **Rainbow Top: was unable to act on the soft ground and finished distressed.**
**3601 Tame Deer** likes a stiff test, which he got here, and came from behind to settle it late on. (16/1)
**3402 Mellottie**, a top-of-the-ground horse all his life, ran a cracking race, staying on all the way up the straight to be nearest at the finish. (6/1: op 7/2)
**2568 Harsh Times** travelled well here but, after kicking on some way out, was worried out of it inside the last furlong. (40/1)
**2805 Dispol Diamond** was a contender most of the way, but these conditions just found her out in the closing stages. (11/2)
**2513 Public Way (IRE)** likes the soft, but could never get in a blow in these very testing conditions. (16/1)
**3402* Rainbow Top**, who found these testing conditions against him, was very tired in the closing stages and was later reported to be distressed. (4/6)

## 3855 WEATHERBYS/HISCOX HOUSEHOLD INSURANCE H'CAP (0-70) (3-Y.O+) (Class E)

3-30 (3-36) **2m** £2,968.35 (£898.80: £438.90: £208.95) Stalls: Low GOING: 1.02 sec per fur (S)

| | | | SP | RR | SF |
|---|---|---|---|---|---|
| 3463[2] **Uncle Doug (55)** (MrsMReveley) **5-9-4** ACulhane(1) (hld up & bhd: hdwy 4f out: led over 1f out: styd on) | — | **1** | 6/1[3] | 66 | 40 |
| 3598[4] **Shirley Sue (66)** (MJohnston) **3-9-1** JWeaver(6) (led tl over 1f out: kpt on gamely) | 1¼ | **2** | 7/2[1] | 76 | 36 |
| 1498[3] **Ski For Gold (68)** (JLDunlop) **3-9-3** KDarley(9) (lw: hld up: hdwy 7f out: ev ch over 2f out: rdn & no ex) | 8 | **3** | 7/2[1] | 70 | 30 |
| 3459[6] **Los Alamos (61)** (CWThornton) **3-8-10** DeanMcKeown(3) (in tch: hdwy u.p 4f out: swtchd over 2f out: r.o one pce) | 1½ | **4** | 14/1 | 61 | 21 |
| *2936*[5] **Jundi (IRE) (47)** (JDBethell) **5-8-10** GDuffield(2) (bhd: effrt on outside 4f out: nvr nr to chal) | 8 | **5** | 20/1 | 39 | 13 |
| 3598[7] **Bowcliffe Court (IRE) (65)** (BWHills) **4-10-0** MHills(11) (hdwy ½-wy: effrt 4f out: nvr able to chal) | 4 | **6** | 5/1[2] | 53 | 27 |
| 3580[5] **Greystyle (33)** (MBrittain) **6-7-10v** JLowe(5) (chsd ldrs tl wknd fnl 3f) | 3 | **7** | 20/1 | 18 | — |
| 3404[2] **Non Vintage (IRE) (53)** (MCChapman) **5-9-2** KFallon(8) (bhd: effrt 4f out: n.d) | 3½ | **8** | 12/1 | 35 | 9 |
| 3649[8] **Jabaroot (IRE) (33)** (RMMcKellar) **5-7-3**(7) JennyBenson(7) (b.hind: chsd ldrs to ½-wy: n.d after) | 2 | **9** | 100/1 | 13 | — |
| 2397[8] **Jackson Park (57)** (TDEasterby) **3-8-3**(3) RHavlin(12) (prom tl wknd fnl 4f) | 3 | **10** | 11/1 | 34 | — |
| 3283[3] **Arcady (60)** (PTWalwyn) **3-8-9** JCarroll(4) (chsd ldrs: ev ch 4f out: wknd fnl 3f) | 1½ | **11** | 16/1 | 35 | — |
| 2697[12] **Zamhareer (USA) (55)** (WStorey) **5-8-11**(7) IonaWands(13) (outpcd & lost pl 10f out: n.d after) | hd | **12** | 12/1 | 30 | 4 |

(SP 122.2%) **12 Rn**

**3m 54.0** (29.00) CSF £26.57 CT £79.85 TOTE £5.80: £1.30 £1.80 £1.70 (£9.60) Trio £8.80 OWNER Mr D. D. Saul (SALTBURN) BRED Charlton Down Stud
LONG HANDICAP Greystyle 7-8 Jabaroot (IRE) 7-3
WEIGHT FOR AGE 3yo-14lb
**3463 Uncle Doug** stays and acts in the ground, and that was enough to see him home. (6/1)
**3598 Shirley Sue** goes on any ground, stays forever and is as game as they come. With a bit further to go, she might well have got back on terms. (7/2)
**1498 Ski For Gold**, stepping up in trip, would probably have got it in normal conditions, but this was testing beyond belief and it proved too much in the last two furlongs. (7/2)
**3459 Los Alamos** stays well but, in these conditions, it takes something extra. Always tending to hang under pressure, she was never doing enough in the last couple of furlongs. (14/1)
**Jundi (IRE)** put in an interesting run, staying on in the last half-mile, and may be coming to hand. (20/1)
**2547 Bowcliffe Court (IRE)** was close enough from the home turn, but always found the struggle too much. (5/1)
**3404 Non Vintage (IRE)** (12/1: op 8/1)
**2148 Zamhareer (USA)** hated this very heavy ground and was soon struggling and behind. (12/1)

## 3856 STEVE NESBITT CHALLENGE TROPHY H'CAP (0-90) (3-Y.O+) (Class C)

4-00 (4-05) **1m 2f** £5,718.50 (£1,718.00: £829.00: £384.50) Stalls: High GOING: 1.02 sec per fur (S)

| | | | SP | RR | SF |
|---|---|---|---|---|---|
| 3621[2] **Wafir (IRE) (80)** (PCalver) **4-9-12** JCarroll(10) (chsd ldrs: led wl over 1f out: edgd lft ins fnl f: styd on) | — | **1** | 8/1 | 89 | 32 |
| 3452* **Red Valerian (70)** (GMMoore) **5-9-2b** JFEgan(9) (in tch: styd on wl fnl 2f: nrst fin) | ¾ | **2** | 14/1 | 78 | 21 |
| 2418[5] **Cheerful Aspect (IRE) (75)** (EALDunlop) **3-8-13** KFallon(3) (racd wd thrght: a in tch: hdwy 3f out: kpt on wl fnl f) | hd | **3** | 14/1 | 83 | 18 |
| 2673* **Break the Rules (72)** (MrsMReveley) **4-9-4** KDarley(1) (racd wd thrght: chsd ldrs: rdn 4f out: one pce fnl 2f) | 3½ | **4** | 6/1[3] | 74 | 17 |
| 3623[2] **Sandmoor Chambray (82)** (TDEasterby) **5-10-0** MBirch(6) (cl up: led 3f out tl wl over 1f out: wknd) | 6 | **5** | 9/1 | 74 | 17 |
| 3470* **Sharp Consul (IRE) (76)** (HCandy) **4-9-8** CRutter(7) (racd wd thrght: in tch: effrt 4f out: edgd rt & one pce fnl 2f) | nk | **6** | 3/1[1] | 68 | 11 |
| 3272* **Another Time (73)** (SPCWoods) **4-9-5** DBiggs(5) (racd wd fnl 5f: no imp) | 12 | **7** | 7/1 | 46 | — |

3148[11] **Sveltana (72)** (GWragg) **4-9-4** MHills(11) (led tl hdd & wknd 3f out) ....1½ **8** 20/1 42 —
3496[6] **Law Dancer (IRE) (68)** (TGMills) **3-8-6** BDoyle(2) (racd wd to st: sn wknd & t.o) ....dist **9** 11/1 — —
3450[9] **Ki Chi Saga (USA) (82)** (JLDunlop) **4-10-0** JFortune(8) (lost tch fr ½-wy: t.o) ....dist **10** 15/2 — —
3401[3] **North Reef (IRE) (71)** (SirMarkPrescott) **5-9-3** GDuffield(4) (racd wd thrght: chsd ldrs tl wknd 3f out: virtually p.u) ....dist **11** 4/1[2] — —
(SP 131.1%) **11 Rn**

**2m 23.4** (19.90) CSF £109.84 CT £1,445.49 TOTE £12.50: £2.80 £3.00 £3.20 (£56.50) Trio £428.30 OWNER Mr Kenneth MacPherson (RIPON) BRED Ronnie Boland
WEIGHT FOR AGE 3yo-8lb

**3621 Wafir (IRE)** took well to these testing conditions and won his first race in this country, but he needed some strong driving to do so. (8/1)
**3452* Red Valerian**, who has done his winning on fast ground, coped well here and was staying on determinedly at the finish. (14/1)
**2418 Cheerful Aspect (IRE)**, dropped back in trip, handled the ground pretty well. He kept staying on up the straight, but racing wide probably cost him more ground than he was beaten. (14/1)
**2673* Break the Rules** tried the impossible by trying to find some better ground in racing wide, and was fighting a lost cause in the last three furlongs. (6/1)
**3623 Sandmoor Chambray**, even in these diabolical conditions, put in another sound effort, but his stamina gave out approaching the final furlong. (9/1)
**3470* Sharp Consul (IRE)** normally acts in the soft, but this was a different matter. (3/1)
**3401 North Reef (IRE)** was found out in these testing conditions and, extremely tired, only managed to walk the final furlong. (4/1: 3/1-9/2)

## 3857 E.B.F. SAPPER MAIDEN STKS (2-Y.O) (Class D)
**Abandoned** - Waterlogged

## 3858 CURFEW NURSERY H'CAP (2-Y.O) (Class E)
**Abandoned** - Waterlogged

T/Jkpt: Not won; £24,394.40 to Carlisle 28/8/96. T/Plpt: £110.60 (246.4 Tckts). T/Qdpt: £9.50 (205.95 Tckts). AA

# 3631-BRIGHTON (L-H) (Good to firm)
## Wednesday August 28th
WEATHER: sunny WIND: almost nil

## 3859 E.B.F. MEDIAN AUCTION MAIDEN STKS (2-Y.O F) (Class F)
2-20 (2-20) **5f 213y** £2,571.40 (£710.40: £338.20) Stalls: Low GOING minus 0.29 sec per fur (GF)

SP RR SF
3502[5] **Chain Reaction (IRE) (72)** (MAJarvis) **2-8-11** WRSwinburn(1) (lw: chsd ldr: led over 1f out: rdn out) ....— **1** 11/10[1] 72 23
3438[3] **Brazilia** (PTWalwyn) **2-8-11** RCochrane(3) (led over 4f: unable qckn) ....1¼ **2** 9/4[2] 69 20
**City Gambler** (GCBravery) **2-8-11** NDay(2) (w'like: lw: dwlt: hld up: rdn over 2f out: one pce) ....½ **3** 6/1[3] 67 18
3502[8] **Phylida** (PJMakin) **2-8-11** SSanders(4) (hld up: rdn over 2f out: sn wknd) ....4 **4** 8/1 57 8
(SP 103.8%) **4 Rn**

**1m 10.4** (3.20) CSF £3.49 TOTE £1.90: (£1.20) OWNER Mrs Gay Jarvis (NEWMARKET) BRED Martyn J. McEnery

**3502 Chain Reaction (IRE)** did not appear to be going as well as the leader over a quarter of a mile from home. Nevertheless, she gained control approaching the final furlong and, ridden along, proved too strong for her rivals. (11/10: 6/5-Evens)
**3438 Brazilia** brought them over to the stands' side in search of the better ground. Collared below the distance, she found the winner too good. (9/4)
**City Gambler**, a nicely-built filly, looked in good shape for this debut. Sluggish leaving the stalls, she chased the leaders, but was being bustled along soon after halfway. Given a reminder below the distance, she flashed her tail each time she was hit and could only struggle on at one pace. A half-sister to staying handicapper Upper Mount Clair, she needs further. (6/1: 5/1-8/1)
**Phylida** (8/1: 4/1-9/1)

## 3860 DITCHLING CLAIMING STKS (3-Y.O+) (Class F)
2-50 (2-51) **1m 1f 209y** £2,381.00 (£656.00: £311.00) Stalls: High GOING minus 0.29 sec per fur (GF)

SP RR SF
3785[10] **Ketabi (USA) (42)** (RAkehurst) **5-9-4** TQuinn(3) (swtg: hdwy over 4f out: led over 1f out: drvn out) ....— **1** 7/1[3] 66 23
3635[6] **Roman Reel (USA) (68)** (GLMoore) **5-9-6** SWhitworth(6) (lw: hld up: ev ch fnl 3f: r.o wl) ....nk **2** 4/6[1] 68 25
*2322*[6] **Ela Agapi Mou (USA) (52)** (GLewis) **3-8-1**(3) AWhelan(4) (a.p: led 4f out tl over 1f out: unable qckn) ....2 **3** 20/1 56 5
3473[11] **Followthe Allstars (46)** (TJNaughton) **3-8-10b** SSanders(1) (b.hind: lw: hdwy over 3f out: wknd over 1f out) ..7 **4** 14/1 51 —
*3608*[7] **She Said No (49)** (AMoore) **4-8-7** CandyMorris(2) (lw: led 6f: wknd 3f out) ....12 **5** 16/1 21 —
3656[11] **One In The Eye** (JRPoulton) **3-9-0b[1]** DeclanO'Shea(7) (s.s: a bhd) ....1½ **6** 5/1[2] 33 —
3472[15] **Radical Exception (IRE)** (DLWilliams) **6-9-2** NAdams(8) (plld hrd: prom over 5f) ....2 **7** 66/1 24 —
3808[23] **Kirov Protege (IRE) (29)** (MrsLCJewell) **4-9-2** JFEgan(5) (lw: bhd fnl 4f) ....4 **8** 40/1 18 —
(SP 110.4%) **8 Rn**

**2m 4.8** (6.50) CSF £11.32 TOTE £5.50: £1.30 £1.10 £2.50 (£3.50) OWNER Bob and Diana Whitney (EPSOM) BRED Gainsborough Farm Inc
WEIGHT FOR AGE 3yo-8lb

**3473 Ketabi (USA)**, awash with sweat beforehand and making a quick reappearance, would have been the best part of two stone better in with the odds-on favourite had this been a handicap. Moving into the action at the top of the hill, he gained control approaching the final furlong and, in a driving finish, just held off his rival. (7/1: op 9/2)
**3635 Roman Reel (USA)**, with conditions all in his favour, threw down his challenge travelling well in the straight. However, despite giving his all in a ding-dong battle, he just failed to get to the front. He should gain compensation in a similar event. (4/6: op Evens)
**Ela Agapi Mou (USA)** went on half a mile from home but, collared approaching the final furlong, failed to find another gear. (20/1)
**3473 Followthe Allstars**, pushed along to take closer order over three furlongs from home, was hung out to dry below the distance. (14/1: 7/1-16/1)
**1468 She Said No** took the field along. Collared half a mile from home, she was soon done with. (16/1)

## 3861 QUEENS PARK CENTENARY CHALLENGE CUP H'CAP (0-70) (3-Y.O+) (Class E)
3-20 (3-20) **7f 214y** £3,152.10 (£940.80: £449.40: £203.70) Stalls: Low GOING minus 0.29 sec per fur (GF)

SP RR SF
3686[11] **Balance of Power (63)** (RAkehurst) **4-9-7** TQuinn(10) (hld up: led over 1f out: rdn out) ....— **1** 7/1 74 57

3646* **Sooty Tern (67)** (JMBradley) **9-9-11** 5x DaneO'Neill(2) (hld up: ev ch over 1f out: unable qckn) ........................2 **2** 9/2$^{2}$ 74 57
3469* **Talathath (FR) (70)** (CADwyer) **4-10-0v** WRSwinburn(3) (a.p: ev ch over 1f out: one pce) ..............................½ **3** 11/4$^{1}$ 76 59
3443$^{5}$ **Fort Knox (IRE) (58)** (RMFlower) **5-9-2b** DBiggs(8) (swtg: rdn over 2f out: hdwy over 1f out: one pce) ...........¾ **4** 5/1$^{3}$ 63 46
3661$^{6}$ **Lorins Gold (39)** (AndrewTurnell) **6-7-8**(3) MHenry(7) (b.nr hind: led 6f out tl over 1f out: wknd fnl f).............1½ **5** 14/1 41 24
*3628*$^{2}$ **Twin Creeks (53)** (VSoane) **5-8-11** RCochrane(4) (lw: prom tl n.m.r on ins & wknd 2f out)..........................2½ **6** 14/1 50 33
1890$^{12}$ **Mr Nevermind (IRE) (61)** (GLMoore) **6-9-5** SWhitworth(1) (s.s: stdy hdwy over 2f out: shkn up: nvr plcd to chal) .......................................................................................................................1½ **7** 14/1 54 37
3606$^{10}$ **Sweet Allegiance (38)** (JRPoulton) **6-7-10** DeclanO'Shea(6) (a bhd).............................................................16 **8** 50/1 — —
1655$^{17}$ **Park Ridge (41)** (TGMills) **4-7-13** JQuinn(5) (led 2f: wkng whn n.m.r 2f out)...............................................1½ **9** 33/1 — —
3686* **Broughtons Turmoil (71)** (WJMusson) **7-10-1** 5x GHind(9) (stdd s: a bhd).........................................................14 **10** 9/2$^{2}$ 1 —
(SP 117.1%) **10 Rn**

**1m 34.3** (2.10) CSF £36.23 CT £100.54 TOTE £9.80: £2.50 £2.30 £1.70 (£30.20) Trio £22.60 OWNER Mr John Falvey (EPSOM) BRED M. V. S. and Mrs Aram

LONG HANDICAP Sweet Allegiance 7-2

OFFICIAL EXPLANATION **Broughtons Turmoil: the jockey reported that the gelding became upset in the stalls and lost ground at the start and by halfway had begun to race very flat. The trainer added that this run was probably too soon after his win last week. The Vet also reported that the gelding returned with an irregular heartbeat.**

**3139* Balance of Power**, who disappointed at Kempton last week, bounced back here. Chasing the leaders, he gained control below the distance and, ridden along, kept on well. (7/1: 5/1-8/1)

**3646* Sooty Tern** chased the leaders. One of several with every chance below the distance, he then found the winner too strong. (9/2)

**3469* Talathath (FR)** was close enough if good enough below the distance before tapped for toe. (11/4)

**3443 Fort Knox (IRE)** began to pick up ground below the distance, but could make no further impression in the last 200 yards. (5/1)

**3661 Lorins Gold** was soon racing at the head of affairs. Collared below the distance, he had nothing left to offer inside the final furlong. (14/1)

**3628 Twin Creeks** raced up with the pace, but was feeling the pinch when not getting a great deal of room along the inside rail a quarter of a mile from home. (14/1: 10/1-16/1)

**1532 Mr Nevermind (IRE)** caught the eye under considerate handling. Losing ground at the start, he was shaken up as he steadily crept closer over a quarter of a mile from home and was almost on the heels of the leaders when his jockey decided to ease him down in the final furlong. This was his first run in eleven weeks and, sure to be a lot fitter as a result, it would be no surprise to see him pop up in a small race, possibly on the Equitrack at Lingfield where he has gained four of his seven victories to date. (14/1: 10/1-16/1)

## 3862 GORING MEDIAN AUCTION MAIDEN STKS (3-Y.O) (Class F)

3-50 (3-53) **6f 209y** £2,381.00 (£656.00: £311.00) Stalls: Low GOING minus 0.29 sec per fur (GF)

SP RR SF
3686$^{7}$ **Mogin (47)** (TJNaughton) **3-8-9** TQuinn(4) (hld up: led 2f out: rdn out) ..............................................................— **1** 6/4$^{1}$ 57 31
3525$^{10}$ **Tonic Chord (55)** (JRFanshawe) **3-8-9** NDay(3) (b: swtg: a.p: ev ch wl over 1f out: unable qckn).................3½ **2** 5/1$^{3}$ 49 23
3316$^{5}$ **Velvet Jones (56)** (GFHCharles-Jones) **3-9-0** SWhitworth(1) (chsd ldr 3f: dropped rr over 2f out: one pce)...1¾ **3** 4/1$^{2}$ 50 24
**Frutina** (CMurray) **3-8-9** JStack(5) (leggy: lt-f: hdwy over 2f out: ev ch wl over 1f out: wknd fnl f) ..............1¼ **4** 20/1 42 16
3698$^{6}$ **Red Time (56)** (MSSaunders) **3-9-0** JFEgan(6) (led: styd far side st: edgd rt & hdd 2f out: wknd fnl f)..............2 **5** 11/1 42 16
3317$^{2}$ **Mac Oates (51)** (DWPArbuthnot) **3-9-0** RPerham(7) (hld up: chsd ldr 4f out: ev ch wl over 1f out: sn wknd) ..s.h **6** 13/2 42 16
1304$^{8}$ **Heights of Love (45)** (JWHills) **3-8-6**(3) MHenry(2) (plld hrd: hdwy over 3f out: ev ch wl over 1f out: sn wknd)..................................................................................................................................................4 **7** 20/1 28 2
(SP 107.9%) **7 Rn**

**1m 23.0** (3.00) CSF £8.43 TOTE £2.00: £1.30 £3.80 (£9.10) OWNER Miss L. A. Elliott (EPSOM)

**3115 Mogin** chased the leaders. With virtually the whole field in line a quarter of a mile out, she soon moved to the front and was ridden along to win an atrocious race. (6/4: op 5/2)

**2718 Tonic Chord**, never far away, was one of a host of horses with every chance early in the final quarter-mile before tapped for foot. (5/1)

**3316 Velvet Jones**, in second place early, got slightly tapped for toe and was the only runner not to have every chance a quarter of a mile out. He did stay on to take third prize without ever looking likely to find the necessary turn of foot, and remains a maiden after eighteen attempts. (4/1: 11/4-9/2)

**Frutina**, a lightly-made filly, moved up to have every chance early in the final quarter-mile before tiring in the last 200 yards. (20/1)

**3698 Red Time** (11/1: op 6/1)

**3317 Mac Oates**, in second place before halfway, had every chance well over a furlong out before capitulating. (13/2: op 3/1)

## 3863 ARTHUR BORROW KING MEMORIAL H'CAP (0-70) (3-Y.O) (Class E)

4-20 (4-21) **5f 213y** £3,179.40 (£949.20: £453.60: £205.80) Stalls: Low GOING minus 0.29 sec per fur (GF)

SP RR SF
3698* **Newlands Corner (51)** (JAkehurst) **3-8-7b** 7x DBiggs(9) (lw: hdwy 2f out: led ins fnl f: rdn out).......................— **1** 2/1$^{1}$ 60 30
2049$^{6}$ **Tymeera (57)** (BPalling) **3-8-10**(3) MHenry(5) (a.p: led over 1f out tl ins fnl f: unable qckn) ..............................3 **2** 8/1 58 28
3652$^{3}$ **Polly Golightly (65)** (MBlanshard) **3-9-7b** TQuinn(10) (hld up: ev ch 2f out: one pce) ..................................s.h **3** 5/1$^{2}$ 66 36
3583$^{5}$ **Pendley Rose (47)** (PWHarris) **3-8-3** JQuinn(6) (led over 4f: one pce)..........................................................¾ **4** 20/1 46 16
3506$^{11}$ **Thai Morning (61)** (PWHarris) **3-9-3** GHind(4) (s.s: hdwy 5f out: ev ch 2f out: one pce) ................................nk **5** 8/1 59 29
2769$^{4}$ **Rawi (57)** (MissGayKelleway) **3-8-13** DaneO'Neill(2) (lw: hdwy over 2f out: rdn over 1f out: one pce fnl f) .......¾ **6** 14/1 53 23
3317* **Memphis Beau (IRE) (64)** (JARToller) **3-9-6b** SSanders(11) (lw: hld up: ev ch 2f out: wknd over 1f out).......1¼ **7** 7/1$^{3}$ 57 27
3606$^{9}$ **Allstars Dancer (42)** (TJNaughton) **3-7-7**(5)ow2 MBaird(7) (hld up: rdn & n.m.r over 2f out: swtchd lft: one pce) ....................................................................................................................................................2 **8** 14/1 29 —
2253$^{9}$ **No Sympathy (50)** (GLMoore) **3-8-6** SWhitworth(3) (lw: hld up: rdn over 2f out: wknd fnl f)...............................3 **9** 16/1 29 —
3331$^{6}$ **Gagajulu (51)** (PDEvans) **3-8-7** JFEgan(8) (prom over 3f) .................................................................................s.h **10** 16/1 30 —
3698$^{2}$ **Into Debt (40)** (JRPoulton) **3-7-10** DeclanO'Shea(1) (s.s: a bhd)..................................................................2½ **11** 16/1 12 —
(SP 120.5%) **11 Rn**

**1m 9.6** (2.40) CSF £18.03 CT £68.26 TOTE £2.90: £1.90 £4.40 £2.80 (£12.30) Trio £24.30 OWNER The Jolly Skolars (LAMBOURN) BRED L. A. C. Ashby

LONG HANDICAP Allstars Dancer 7-1 Into Debt 7-5

**3698* Newlands Corner** began her effort a quarter of a mile out and, gaining control inside the final furlong, was ridden along to pull away to complete the hat-trick. (2/1)

**2049 Tymeera**, never far away, went on below the distance but, collared inside the final furlong, found the winner too good. (8/1)

**3652 Polly Golightly** chased the leaders. With every chance a quarter of a mile from home, she began to hang and could only struggle on at one pace. (5/1: 4/1-6/1)

**739 Pendley Rose** attempted to make all the running. Collared below the distance, she could only go up and down in the same place. (20/1)

**1101 Thai Morning** soon recovered from a tardy start and had every chance two furlongs from home before lack of acceleration proved his undoing. (8/1)
**2769 Rawi**, racing out the back, picked up ground over a quarter of a mile from home, but failed to make any further impression in the last 150 yards. (14/1)

## 3864 HANNINGTONS OF BRIGHTON H'CAP (0-80) (3-Y.O+) (Class D)

4-50 (4-50) **5f 59y** £3,694.95 (£1,101.60: £525.30: £237.15) Stalls: Low GOING minus 0.29 sec per fur (GF)

| Form | Horse | Btn | Pos | SP | RR | SF |
|---|---|---|---|---|---|---|
| 3261[2] | **La Belle Dominique (50)** (SGKnight) **4-8-1**[ow3] SSanders(1) (hld up: rdn over 1f out: led ins fnl f: r.o wl) | — | **1** | 13/2 | 59 | 35 |
| 3661[2] | **Imposing Time (63)** (MissGayKelleway) **5-9-0v**[1] DaneO'Neill(2) (lw: dwlt: outpcd: hdwy over 1f out: r.o one pce) | 2 | **2** | 9/4[1] | 66 | 45 |
| 3506[7] | **Another Batchworth (54)** (EAWheeler) **4-8-5** SWhitworth(7) (chsd ldr: led 2f out tl ins fnl f: unable qckn) | ½ | **3** | 9/2[3] | 55 | 34 |
| 1992[7] | **Lift Boy (USA) (52)** (AMoore) **7-8-3**[ow2] CandyMorris(5) (outpcd: nvr nrr) | 2½ | **4** | 12/1 | 46 | 23 |
| 3215[9] | **Sharp Pearl (75)** (JWhite) **3-9-10b** TQuinn(4) (lw: outpcd) | ½ | **5** | 8/1 | 67 | 44 |
| *3416*[5] | **Bowcliffe Grange (IRE) (53)** (DWChapman) **4-8-4b** JQuinn(3) (led 3f) | 2½ | **6** | 5/2[2] | 38 | 17 |
| 3506[12] | **Logie Pert Lad (45)** (JJBridger) **4-7-3**(7) RMullen(6) (outpcd) | ½ | **7** | 100/1 | 28 | 7 |

(SP 110.6%) **7 Rn**

**61.5 secs** (1.50) CSF £20.07 TOTE £7.50: £3.80 £2.10 (£6.10) OWNER Mr Richard Withers (TAUNTON) BRED C. R. and V. M. Withers
LONG HANDICAP Logie Pert Lad 6-5
WEIGHT FOR AGE 3yo-2lb
**3261 La Belle Dominique** at last broke her duck at the twenty-fifth attempt. Racing in third place, she gradually reeled in the front two and, snatching the lead inside the final furlong, kept on well. (13/2)
**3661 Imposing Time**, unable to go the early pace, began to pick up ground below the distance but, despite staying on to snatch second prize in the closing stages, never looked like threatening the winner. (9/4)
**3097 Another Batchworth** was certainly not going to hang around and stormed off in second place. Sent to the front a quarter of a mile out, she was eventually reeled in inside the final furlong. (9/2)
**1681* Lift Boy (USA)**, unable to go the pace, made up a little late headway without posing a threat. (12/1)
**2790 Sharp Pearl** was taken off his feet from start to finish. (8/1)
**3416 Bowcliffe Grange (IRE)** went off like a scalded cat and soon had the field well strung out. Collared a quarter of a mile from home, he had little more to offer. (5/2)

T/Plpt: £15.20 (744.15 Tckts). T/Qdpt: £7.30 (135.2 Tckts). AK

# 3287-CARLISLE (R-H) (Good, Good to firm patches)
# Wednesday August 28th

WEATHER: overcast WIND: mod bhd

## 3865 'SAMUEL WHISKERS' CLAIMING STKS (3-Y.O+) (Class F)

2-10 (2-11) **1m 4f** £2,521.00 (£706.00: £343.00) Stalls: Low GOING minus 0.67 sec per fur (HD)

| Form | Horse | Btn | Pos | SP | RR | SF |
|---|---|---|---|---|---|---|
| 3676[2] | **Latvian (60)** (RAllan) **9-9-2v**[1] KFallon(1) (lw: chsd ldrs: styd on to ld over 1f out: pushed out) | — | **1** | 11/4[3] | 69 | 33 |
| 3676* | **Trumped (IRE) (42)** (PMonteith) **4-8-2**(7) JBramhill(3) (led & sn clr: hung lft 3f out: hdd over 1f out: sn btn) | 5 | **2** | 7/4[1] | 55 | 19 |
| 3653[9] | **In the Money (IRE) (57)** (RHollinshead) **7-9-3**(3) FLynch(2) (lw: chsd clr ldr: rdn 4f out: no imp) | 6 | **3** | 9/4[2] | 58 | 22 |
| *3605*[8] | **Stoleamarch (43)** (MrsMReveley) **3-8-4** ACulhane(6) (prom: outpcd 5f out: n.d after) | 10 | **4** | 10/1 | 39 | — |
| 3591[10] | **Run With Pride** (EWeymes) **3-7-11** NCarlisle(7) (s.i.s & wnt rt s: rdn 4f out: a bhd) | 4 | **5** | 100/1 | 27 | — |
| 3309[9] | **Penny Peppermint** (REBarr) **4-8-13** LCharnock(5) (a outpcd & bhd) | ¾ | **6** | 100/1 | 32 | — |

(SP 104.9%) **6 Rn**

**2m 33.1** (2.10) CSF £7.14 TOTE £3.40: £1.50 £1.30 (£2.80) OWNER Mr I. Bell (CORNHILL-ON-TWEED) BRED Fittocks Stud Ltd
WEIGHT FOR AGE 3yo-10lb
**3676 Latvian** is a law unto himself, but the visor was on for the first time and it worked on this occasion. (11/4)
**3676* Trumped (IRE)** tried forcing tactics again, but she has temperament problems and, once into the straight, she hung badly and threw it away. (7/4)
**3117 In the Money (IRE)**, in a field full of characters, chased the pacemaker but, once off the bit approaching the straight, he soon cried enough. (9/4)
**3116 Stoleamarch** was off the bit well before the straight and soon threw in the towel. (10/1)
**Run With Pride** again made a slow start and showed very little thereafter. (100/1)

## 3866 'MRS TIGGYWINKLE' H'CAP (0-70) (3-Y.O+ F) (Class E)

2-40 (2-42) **7f 214y** £3,132.15 (£949.20: £464.10: £221.55) Stalls: High GOING minus 0.67 sec per fur (HD)

| Form | Horse | Btn | Pos | SP | RR | SF |
|---|---|---|---|---|---|---|
| 3640[6] | **Gladys Althorpe (IRE) (63)** (JLEyre) **3-9-5** KFallon(8) (b.off hind: bhd: hdwy over 2f out: led 1f out: r.o) | — | **1** | 9/2[2] | 75 | 35 |
| 3491* | **Society Girl (57)** (CWThornton) **3-8-13** DeanMcKeown(1) (b.nr hind: cl up: led 2f out to 1f out: no ex) | 1 | **2** | 7/1 | 67 | 27 |
| 3591[4] | **Scenicris (IRE) (55)** (RHollinshead) **3-8-8**(3) FLynch(14) (bhd: gd hdwy to chal appr fnl f: nt qckn) | nk | **3** | 14/1 | 64 | 24 |
| 3354* | **Lapu-Lapu (53)** (MJCamacho) **3-8-9** LCharnock(5) (a.p: effrt over 2f out: r.o one pce) | 3 | **4** | 4/1[1] | 56 | 16 |
| 3645* | **Mystic Times (41)** (BMactaggart) **3-7-11**[ow1 5x] DaleGibson(3) (lw: a chsng ldrs: one pce fnl 2f) | ½ | **5** | 12/1 | 43 | 2 |
| 3460[3] | **Rainbows Rhapsody (35)** (DWChapman) **5-7-11** TWilliams(11) (lw: a chsng ldrs: effrt appr st: one pce) | ½ | **6** | 16/1 | 36 | 2 |
| 3580[13] | **Lomond Lassie (USA) (40)** (MissJFCraze) **3-7-10** JLowe(2) (chsd ldrs: effrt 3f out: no imp) | 1½ | **7** | 100/1 | 38 | — |
| 3427* | **Sis Garden (47)** (TDEasterby) **3-8-3b** JFanning(9) (w ldr: effrt 2f out: sn btn) | 1¼ | **8** | 9/1 | 43 | 3 |
| 3845[4] | **Sistar Act (68)** (MRChannon) **3-9-10** KDarley(7) (lw: outpcd & bhd 4f out: n.d) | 1¾ | **9** | 13/2[3] | 60 | 20 |
| 3579[8] | **Tibbi Blues (45)** (WStorey) **9-8-2**(5) GParkin(4) (in tch tl outpcd fnl 2f) | ½ | **10** | 20/1 | 36 | 2 |
| 3645[2] | **Never so True (34)** (MartynWane) **5-7-10** NCarlisle(13) (led tl hdd & wknd 2f out) | 3 | **11** | 9/1 | 19 | — |
| 3619[14] | **Efipetite (40)** (NBycroft) **3-7-3**(7) IonaWands(6) (bhd: hdwy ½-wy: sn wknd) | 1¾ | **12** | 50/1 | 22 | — |
| *3603*[16] | **Prudent Pet (51)** (CWFairhurst) **4-8-8**(5) AimeeCook(10) (a rr div) | 3½ | **13** | 14/1 | 26 | — |

(SP 118.6%) **13 Rn**

**1m 40.0** (1.40) CSF £33.33 CT £389.10 TOTE £3.90: £2.10 £2.20 £4.20 (£12.60) Trio £110.80 OWNER Mr T. S. Ely (HAMBLETON) BRED Mrs R. Kitchin
LONG HANDICAP Mystic Times 7-1 Never so True 7-9 Efipetite 6-12 Lomond Lassie (USA) 7-8
WEIGHT FOR AGE 3yo-6lb

**3640 Gladys Althorpe (IRE)**, ridden with more restraint this time, was back to her best and these are obviously the tactics that suit her best. (9/2)
**3491* Society Girl** had her chances throughout, but just proved short of that vital turn of speed in the closing stages. To her credit, she was keeping on. (7/1)
**3591 Scenicris (IRE)** has plenty of ability and is running pretty well at the moment, but this was her twenty-fourth run without success. (14/1)
**3354* Lapu-Lapu** ran pretty well after going up 6lb in the handicap and is well worth keeping in mind. (4/1)
**3645* Mystic Times** ran a useful race on this step up in class and is obviously on really good terms with herself. (12/1: op 8/1)
**3460 Rainbows Rhapsody** keeps running quite well and gives the impression that there is more to come when she gets it fully together. (16/1)
**3645 Never so True** (9/1: 6/1-10/1)

## 3867 'JEMIMA PUDDLEDUCK' LIMITED STKS (0-60) (3-Y.O+) (Class F)

3-10 (3-11) **6f 206y** £2,605.00 (£730.00: £355.00) Stalls: High GOING minus 0.67 sec per fur (HD)

| | | | | SP | RR | SF |
|---|---|---|---|---|---|---|
| 3844* | **Naissant (60)** (RMMcKellar) **3-8-2**(7) 3x KSked(4) (cl up: led over 3f out: hung rt over 2f out: r.o) | — | **1** | 5/4$^{1}$ | 67 | 19 |
| 3623$^{6}$ | **Special-K (58)** (EWeymes) **4-8-6**(5) DGriffiths(5) (lw: led tl over 3f out: swtchd 2f out: kpt on wl) | 1½ | **2** | 4/1$^{2}$ | 61 | 18 |
| 3650$^{3}$ | **Perilous Plight (60)** (MrsLStubbs) **5-9-9** KFallon(3) (lw: bhd: hdwy u.p 3f out: nt pce to chal) | 2 | **3** | 6/1 | 68 | 25 |
| 3777$^{6}$ | **Cee-Jay-Ay (53)** (JBerry) **9-8-12**(5) PRoberts(7) (lw: prom: effrt 3f out: no imp) | 1½ | **4** | 7/1 | 59 | 16 |
| 3686$^{5}$ | **Morocco (IRE) (57)** (MRChannon) **7-9-3** KDarley(1) (in tch: rdn 3f out: r.o one pce) | hd | **5** | 11/2$^{3}$ | 58 | 15 |
| 3624$^{8}$ | **Happy Traveller (IRE) (51)** (CMurray) **3-8-9** JFortune(6) (lw: chsd ldrs tl wknd fnl 3f) | 8 | **6** | 33/1 | 37 | — |
| *3602*$^{13}$ | **Nattier (57)** (SirMarkPrescott) **3-8-6** GDuffield(2) (lw: stdd s: hld up & bhd: rdn 3f out: n.d) | 3½ | **7** | 14/1 | 26 | — |

(SP 116.2%) **7 Rn**

**1m 27.5** (1.80) CSF £6.77 TOTE £2.00: £1.30 £2.40 (£5.40) OWNER Mr William Graham (LESMAHAGOW) BRED Sheikh Marwan al Maktoum
WEIGHT FOR AGE 3yo-5lb
**3844* Naissant** is in tremendous form and got this trip well. Despite hanging when in front, she did it in good style. (5/4)
**3623 Special-K** ran her best race of the season and being hampered made little difference, but the pleasing thing was that she kept running all the way to the line. (4/1)
**3650 Perilous Plight** responded to some strong driving in the straight and kept staying on, but was never good enough to have a live chance. (6/1)
**3777 Cee-Jay-Ay** jumped off on terms for a change, but his customary run at the end of the race was never there. (7/1)
**3686 Morocco (IRE)** has his own ideas about the game and was never doing enough on this occasion. (11/2: 4/1-6/1)
**2982 Nattier** (14/1: 8/1-16/1)

## 3868 'PETER RABBIT' H'CAP (0-80) (3-Y.O+) (Class D)

3-40 (3-40) **5f** £3,745.30 (£1,134.40: £554.20: £264.10) Stalls: High GOING minus 0.67 sec per fur (HD)

| | | | | SP | RR | SF |
|---|---|---|---|---|---|---|
| 3643$^{4}$ | **Just Dissident (IRE) (57)** (RMWhitaker) **4-8-9** DeanMcKeown(8) (mde all: kpt on wl) | — | **1** | 11/1 | 64 | 46 |
| 3482* | **Brecongill Lad (69)** (MissSEHall) **4-9-7** NConnorton(1) (lw: bhd: hdwy on bit 2f out: effrt & ev ch 1f out: hung rt & nt qckn) | 1½ | **2** | 5/1$^{1}$ | 71 | 53 |
| 3851$^{4}$ | **The Happy Fox (IRE) (74)** (BAMcMahon) **4-9-7**(5) LNewton(6) (bhd: hdwy over 1f out: styd on wl nr fin) | s.h | **3** | 10/1 | 76 | 58 |
| 3415$^{2}$ | **Dominelle (52)** (TDEasterby) **4-8-4** MBirch(11) (a chsng ldrs: nt qckn appr fnl f) | ¾ | **4** | 8/1 | 52 | 34 |
| 3643$^{3}$ | **Ned's Bonanza (59)** (MDods) **7-8-8**(3) FLynch(3) (lw: hdwy 2f out: styd on towards fin) | 1 | **5** | 11/1 | 55 | 37 |
| 3482$^{8}$ | **Rich Glow (63)** (NBycroft) **5-9-1** KDarley(10) (in tch: rdn 2f out: no imp) | s.h | **6** | 12/1 | 59 | 41 |
| 3310$^{4}$ | **Indiahra (46)** (JLEyre) **5-7-12** NCarlisle(4) (bhd: hdwy 2f out: nvr able to chal) | hd | **7** | 16/1 | 42 | 24 |
| 3793$^{9}$ | **Serious Hurry (44)** (RMMcKellar) **8-7-3b**(7) JMcAuley(2) (chsd ldrs to ½-wy: sn lost pl) | 1¾ | **8** | 66/1 | 34 | 16 |
| 3672$^{20}$ | **Royal Dome (IRE) (75)** (MartynWane) **4-9-13** GDuffield(13) (chsd ldrs tl wknd appr fnl f) | hd | **9** | 6/1$^{2}$ | 65 | 47 |
| 3643$^{10}$ | **Kabcast (45)** (DWChapman) **11-7-11b** LCharnock(5) (cl up over 3f: wknd) | 2 | **10** | 25/1 | 29 | 11 |
| 3345$^{2}$ | **King of Show (IRE) (60)** (RAllan) **5-8-12v** JFortune(12) (prom 3f: wknd) | hd | **11** | 8/1 | 43 | 25 |
| 3482$^{9}$ | **Captain Carat (63)** (MrsJRRamsden) **5-9-1** KFallon(9) (b.nr fore: s.i.s: n.d) | 1½ | **12** | 9/1 | 42 | 24 |
| 3579$^{3}$ | **Here Comes a Star (72)** (JMCarr) **8-9-10** ACulhane(7) (lw: bhd: effrt & n.m.r 2f out: sn btn) | ½ | **13** | 7/1$^{3}$ | 49 | 31 |
| 2911$^{5}$ | **Garnock Valley (76)** (JBerry) **6-10-0** JCarroll(14) (bhd: n.m.r ½-wy: n.d) | 1¼ | **14** | 9/1 | 49 | 31 |

(SP 130.3%) **14 Rn**

**59.7 secs** (0.10 under best) (-0.50) CSF £65.67 CT £556.95 TOTE £15.70: £2.20 £2.80 £3.20 (£189.00) Trio £329.70 OWNER Mrs C. A. Hodgetts (LEEDS) BRED M. Duffy
LONG HANDICAP Serious Hurry 7-8
**3643 Just Dissident (IRE)** had speed aplenty. Making it all, he was never going to stop. (11/1)
**3482* Brecongill Lad** is a most frustrating character and he has so much ability, but he plain and simply refused to go through with it on this occasion. If he could ever be straightened out, he would win plenty, and in better company. (5/1)
**3851 The Happy Fox (IRE)** does not win very often, but does seem in sound form at the moment, and may pick up a race. (10/1: 7/1-11/1)
**3415 Dominelle** ran fast, but was always off the bit to do so and the struggle was just beyond her. (8/1)
**3643 Ned's Bonanza** looked particularly well, but only got going when it was too late. (11/1)
**3352* Rich Glow** needs things to go just right, and they never were on this occasion. (12/1)
**3310 Indiahra**, having her second run for her new stable, ran well enough to suggest that she will do better before long. (16/1)
**3342 Serious Hurry**, poorly drawn, did not get the required fast start. (66/1)

## 3869 E.B.F. 'MR TOD' MEDIAN AUCTION MAIDEN STKS (2-Y.O) (Class F)

4-10 (4-10) **5f** £2,759.00 (£774.00: £377.00) Stalls: High GOING minus 0.67 sec per fur (HD)

| | | | | SP | RR | SF |
|---|---|---|---|---|---|---|
| 2374$^{3}$ | **Levelled** (MRChannon) **2-9-0** KDarley(2) (lw: mde all: edgd lft fnl 2f: styd on wl) | — | **1** | 5/4$^{1}$ | 58 | 25 |
| *3088*$^{2}$ | **Davis Rock** (SirMarkPrescott) **2-8-9** GDuffield(1) (lw: s.i.s: sn cl up: rdn appr fnl f: kpt on wl) | ½ | **2** | 5/4$^{1}$ | 51 | 18 |
| 699$^{10}$ | **Mr Fortywinks (IRE)** (JLEyre) **2-8-11**(3) FLynch(4) (a chsng ldrs: drvn along ½-wy: no imp) | 3½ | **3** | 9/1$^{2}$ | 45 | 12 |
| | **My Saltarello (IRE)** (ABMulholland) **2-9-0** DeanMcKeown(5) (w'like: bkwd: sn drvn along: nvr nr ldrs) | 6 | **4** | 25/1 | 26 | — |
| 3588$^{9}$ | **Willskip (USA)** (JBerry) **2-9-0** JCarroll(3) (drvn along after 2f: a bhd) | nk | **5** | 14/1$^{3}$ | 25 | — |

(SP 109.4%) **5 Rn**

**61.3 secs** (1.10) CSF £3.06 TOTE £2.20: £1.10 £1.10 (£1.40) OWNER Maygain Ltd (UPPER LAMBOURN) BRED J. F. Watson
**2374 Levelled** looked a picture and, despite showing a tendency to hang left, always had the runner-up's measure. (5/4)
**3088 Davis Rock** needed shaking up early on to get upsides the winner after a tardy start, and then kept battling throughout, but was always second best. She should have learnt plenty. (5/4)

**441 Mr Fortywinks (IRE)**, off the track for over four months, ran pretty well here, but was never able to trouble the leading pair. (9/1)
**My Saltarello (IRE)**, a decent sort, needed this quite badly and could never offer a threat. (25/1)
**Willskip (USA)** always found the pace too fast. (14/1: 8/1-20/1)

## 3870 'SQUIRREL NUTKIN' MAIDEN H'CAP (0-60) (3-Y.O+) (Class F)

4-40 (4-40) **2m 1f 52y** £2,731.00 (£766.00: £373.00) Stalls: High GOING minus 0.67 sec per fur (HD)

| | | | | SP | RR | SF |
|---|---|---|---|---|---|---|
| *3605$^{4}$* | **Star Performer (IRE) (46)** (MrsMReveley) **5-9-8** KDarley(10) (hld up & bhd: hdwy 3f out: led appr fnl f: r.o) | — | **1** | 11/2$^{3}$ | 59 | — |
| 3580$^{6}$ | **Karaylar (IRE) (42)** (WStorey) **4-9-4** JFanning(6) (a.p: hdwy to chal appr fnl f: kpt on) | ½ | **2** | 16/1 | 55 | — |
| 3507$^{5}$ | **No More Hassle (IRE) (34)** (MrsMReveley) **3-7-7**(3) DWright(8) (plld hrd: hdwy 3f out: chal appr fnl f: no ex) | 2 | **3** | 16/1 | 45 | — |
| 522$^{6}$ | **Onefourseven (37)** (JLEyre) **3-7-13** TWilliams(7) (in tch: hdwy & ev ch 3f out: wknd over 1f out) | 5 | **4** | 20/1 | 43 | — |
| 3580$^{3}$ | **Suitor (48)** (WJarvis) **3-8-10** WJO'Connor(11) (lw: cl up: led 10f out tl appr fnl f: wknd) | 2½ | **5** | 9/4$^{1}$ | 52 | — |
| 3580$^{2}$ | **Clash of Swords (55)** (PCalver) **3-9-3b$^{1}$** MBirch(12) (chsd ldrs: effrt over 3f out: sn btn) | 5 | **6** | 100/30$^{2}$ | 54 | — |
| 3580$^{7}$ | **Canary Blue (IRE) (25)** (PRWebber) **5-8-1b** LCharnock(2) (chsd ldrs: chal 6f out: wknd 3f out) | 2½ | **7** | 10/1 | 22 | — |
| 1343$^{5}$ | **Sujud (IRE) (52)** (MDHammond) **4-9-7**(7) ClaireWest(9) (hld up & bhd: effrt 7f out: n.d) | 1¾ | **8** | 10/1 | 47 | — |
| 3580$^{9}$ | **Victoria Day (30)** (BAMcMahon) **4-8-6** JFortune(13) (led to 10f out: wknd over 4f out) | 8 | **9** | 33/1 | 18 | — |
| 2891$^{12}$ | **Teoroma (20)** (DrJDScargill) **6-7-10** NCarlisle(4) (outpcd & bhd fr ½-wy) | ¾ | **10** | 33/1 | 7 | — |
| 3329$^{6}$ | **Calcando (28)** (EWeymes) **4-8-4** JLowe(5) (outpcd & bhd fnl 4f) | 1¾ | **11** | 33/1 | 13 | — |
| 2223$^{5}$ | **So Keen (60)** (ABailey) **3-9-8** GDuffield(3) (bhd: effrt 8f out: n.d) | 3 | **12** | 12/1 | 43 | — |
| | | | | (SP 120.5%) | **12 Rn** | |

**3m 49.8** CSF £80.34 CT £1,198.26 TOTE £5.20: £1.70 £5.00 £1.70 (£49.60) Trio £81.50 OWNER Mr P. D. Savill (SALTBURN) BRED Stud-On-The-Chart
LONG HANDICAP Teoroma 7-7
WEIGHT FOR AGE 3yo-14lb
OFFICIAL EXPLANATION **Suitor: the rider reported that the colt hung and lost his action.**
**3605 Star Performer (IRE)**, gaining his first Flat win at his eighteenth attempt, did it well and staying is obviously his game. (11/2: op 7/2)
**3580 Karaylar (IRE)** ran his best race to date and kept staying on. Provided the ground remains fast, he should pick up a race. (16/1)
**3507 No More Hassle (IRE)** had his chances in the last two furlongs, but ran out of fuel late on. (16/1)
**522 Onefourseven**, who has changed stables and had a rest, ran really well until blowing up approaching the final furlong. (20/1)
**3580 Suitor** made this a real test, but he had galloped himself into the ground approaching the final furlong and, judging by his action, some give underfoot would certainly help. (9/4)
**3580 Clash of Swords** had the blinkers on this time, but they failed to have the desired effect. (100/30)
**Canary Blue (IRE)** (10/1: op 6/1)
**2062 So Keen** (12/1: op 8/1)

T/Jkpt: £25,718.20 (0.69 Tckts); £11,229.08 to Musselburgh 29/8/96. T/Plpt: £82.50 (206.96 Tckts). T/Qdpt: £29.90 (27.09 Tckts). AA

# 3606-LINGFIELD (L-H) (AWT Standard, Turf Good to soft)
## Thursday August 29th

WEATHER: overcast WIND: fresh half against

## 3871 HEINEKEN CLAIMING STKS (2-Y.O) (Class F)

2-00 (2-00) **6f** £2,642.80 (£730.80: £348.40) Stalls: High GOING: 0.35 sec per fur (G)

| | | | | SP | RR | SF |
|---|---|---|---|---|---|---|
| 3408$^{10}$ | **Dowry (81)** (RHannon) **2-8-6** PatEddery(5) (lw: hld up: led wl over 1f out: rdn out) | — | **1** | 9/4$^{1}$ | 63 | 3 |
| 3436$^{3}$ | **Gunners Glory (81)** (BJMeehan) **2-9-0**(5) MartinDwyer(6) (lw: chsd ldr: rdn & ev ch fnl 2f: r.o) | nk | **2** | 100/30$^{2}$ | 75 | 15 |
| 3803$^{8}$ | **Russian Sable (60)** (MRChannon) **2-8-4** TQuinn(4) (rdn & hdwy wl over 1f out: r.o wl ins fnl f) | nk | **3** | 7/1 | 59 | — |
| 3659$^{5}$ | **Summer Risotto (55)** (DJSffrenchDavis) **2-7-12** NCarlisle(3) (lw: hld up: rdn over 2f out: unable qckn) | 3½ | **4** | 12/1 | 44 | — |
| *3629$^{3}$* | **Hopperetta** (BPalling) **2-8-2** BDoyle(2) (lw: hld up: rdn over 3f out: one pce) | nk | **5** | 12/1 | 47 | — |
| 3582* | **Sparkling Edge** (CADwyer) **2-7-13**(7) JoHunnam(7) (sme hdwy over 1f out: sn wknd) | 2½ | **6** | 4/1$^{3}$ | 45 | — |
| 3478$^{9}$ | **Castle House (65)** (JAkehurst) **2-8-9b$^{1}$** GDuffield(8) (lw: led: clr 4f out: hdd wl over 1f out: sn wknd) | 9 | **7** | 9/1 | 24 | — |
| 3110$^{7}$ | **Koordinaite** (WJMusson) **2-7-13** JQuinn(1) (a bhd) | 3½ | **8** | 33/1 | 4 | — |
| | | | | (SP 114.7%) | **8 Rn** | |

**1m 17.26** (8.26) CSF £9.81 TOTE £2.90: £1.30 £1.40 £1.70 (£6.20) OWNER Cheveley Park Stud (MARLBOROUGH) BRED Cheveley Park Stud Ltd
**3046 Dowry** chased the leaders. Moving into a marginal lead early in the final quarter-mile, she was given no peace by the runner-up but, ridden along, just managed to keep that rival at bay. (9/4)
**3436 Gunners Glory** chased the leader. Throwing down his challenge in the final quarter-mile, he may well have got his head in front for a few strides, but was then unable to cope with the determined winner. (100/30)
**2382 Russian Sable** began to pick up ground early in the final quarter-mile but, despite running on strongly inside the final furlong, found the line always coming too soon. (7/1: 5/1-8/1)
**3659 Summer Risotto** chased the leaders but, pushed along soon after halfway, failed to find the necessary turn of foot. (12/1: 6/1-14/1)
**3629 Hopperetta** tracked the leaders but, bustled along before halfway, could only go up and down in the same place. (12/1)
**3582* Sparkling Edge**, who has changed stables since her initial run, made a very brief effort over a furlong from home, but it came to little. (4/1)
**1713 Castle House** (9/1: 8/1-12/1)

## 3872 LABATTS H'CAP (0-60) (3-Y.O) (Class F)

2-30 (2-36) **2m (Equitrack)** £2,738.00 (£758.00: £362.00) Stalls: Low GOING minus 0.69 sec per fur (FST)

| | | | | SP | RR | SF |
|---|---|---|---|---|---|---|
| 3337$^{5}$ | **Mischief Star (56)** (DRCElsworth) **3-9-5** TQuinn(11) (a.p: led 2f out: clr over 1f out: r.o wl) | — | **1** | 7/1 | 67 | 38 |
| 3335$^{14}$ | **Miss Prism (51)** (JLDunlop) **3-9-0** PatEddery(9) (chsd ldr: led over 4f out to 2f out: unable qckn) | 5 | **2** | 11/2$^{3}$ | 57 | 28 |
| *3422$^{2}$* | **Pearl Anniversary (IRE) (50)** (MJohnston) **3-8-13** JWeaver(2) (lw: hld up: rdn over 4f out: r.o ins fnl f) | 1 | **3** | 9/2$^{2}$ | 55 | 26 |
| 3584$^{5}$ | **Duncombe Hall (42)** (CACyzer) **3-8-5** MFenton(6) (rdn & hdwy over 3f out: one pce) | 9 | **4** | 20/1 | 38 | 9 |
| *3437$^{3}$* | **Pleasureland (IRE) (58)** (PJMakin) **3-9-7** AClark(8) (lw: hld up: rdn 7f out: wknd over 2f out) | ½ | **5** | 3/1$^{1}$ | 54 | 25 |
| 3077$^{5}$ | **Illegally Yours (48)** (LMontagueHall) **3-8-11** DaneO'Neill(7) (prom over 7f) | 17 | **6** | 9/1 | 27 | — |
| *2936$^{8}$* | **Belle's Boy (56)** (BPalling) **3-9-5** DHarrison(1) (led tl over 4f out: sn wknd) | 1 | **7** | 12/1 | 34 | 5 |
| *2553$^{6}$* | **Harbet House (FR) (58)** (CACyzer) **3-9-7** GCarter(10) (bhd fnl 4f) | 1 | **8** | 6/1 | 35 | 6 |

| | | | | SP | RR | SF |
|---|---|---|---|---|---|---|
| 3667$^{7}$ | **Meg's Memory (IRE) (56)** (JohnBerry) **3-9-2**(3) NVarley(5) (bhd fnl 4f) | 4 | **9** | 16/1 | 29 | — |
| 3619$^{11}$ | **Lagan (53)** (PSFelgate) **3-9-2b** GDuffield(4) (a bhd) | 5 | **10** | 33/1 | 21 | — |
| 3474$^{15}$ | **Forliando (33)** (MSSaunders) **3-7-10v** NAdams(3) (bhd fnl 4f) | 12 | **11** | 33/1 | — | — |
| | | | | (SP 119.6%) | **11 Rn** | |

**3m 24.0** (2.00) CSF £42.88 CT £176.69 TOTE £8.90: £2.70 £1.90 £1.60 (£13.40) Trio £35.60 OWNER Mrs P. J. Sheen (WHITCOMBE) BRED Mrs John Trotter

LONG HANDICAP Forliando 7-6

**3337 Mischief Star** made a winning debut on the All-Weather. Sent into the lead turning for home, she shot clear in the short home straight to win in fine style. (7/1)

**3335 Miss Prism** raced in second place until going on over half a mile from home. Collared turning into the straight, she was left standing by the winner. (11/2: 7/2-6/1)

**3422 Pearl Anniversary (IRE)** chased the leaders, but was being bustled along over half a mile from home. He did stay on again inside the final furlong, but never threatened. (9/2)

**3584 Duncombe Hall** began to pick up ground over three furlongs from home, but could then make no further impression. (20/1)

**3437 Pleasureland (IRE)** chased the leaders, but he was being bustled along soon after halfway and had come to the end of his tether over two furlongs from home. (3/1)

## 3873 H. P. BULMERS MAIDEN STKS (I) (2-Y.O) (Class D)

3-00 (3-02) **7f 140y** £3,204.30 (£953.40: £453.20: £203.10) Stalls: High GOING: 0.35 sec per fur (G)

| | | | | SP | RR | SF |
|---|---|---|---|---|---|---|
| 3131$^{4}$ | **Barnum Sands** (JLDunlop) **2-9-0** TQuinn(1) (lw: a gng wl: a.p: led ins fnl f: qcknd: easily) | — | **1** | Evens$^{1}$ | 83+ | 17 |
| | **Go For Salt (USA)** (MRStoute) **2-8-9** JReid(7) (neat: dwlt: rdn over 3f out: hdwy over 2f out: r.o ins fnl f) | 1¾ | **2** | 7/1$^{3}$ | 74 | 8 |
| | **Northern Pass (USA)** (RAkehurst) **2-8-9** SSanders(5) (leggy: a.p: led over 2f out tl ins fnl f: unable qckn) | 3 | **3** | 20/1 | 68 | 2 |
| 3493$^{4}$ | **Sword Arm** (RCharlton) **2-9-0** WRSwinburn(3) (hld up: rdn over 2f out: one pce) | ¾ | **4** | 7/2$^{2}$ | 72 | 6 |
| 3454$^{6}$ | **Petrel** (LordHuntingdon) **2-8-9** DHarrison(8) (hld up: rdn over 3f out: one pce) | s.h | **5** | 20/1 | 66 | — |
| 3159$^{14}$ | **Logica (IRE) (80)** (PAKelleway) **2-8-9** GBardwell(9) (lw: led 5f: wknd over 1f out) | ¾ | **6** | 7/1$^{3}$ | 65 | — |
| 3499$^{6}$ | **Danka** (PTWalwyn) **2-9-0** JCarroll(2) (hld up: rdn over 3f out: wknd fnl f) | 2 | **7** | 20/1 | 66 | — |
| | **Colour Key (USA)** (DRCElsworth) **2-9-0** DaneO'Neill(4) (unf: dwlt: a bhd) | nk | **8** | 20/1 | 65 | — |
| 3631$^{4}$ | **Absolute Liberty (USA)** (SPCWoods) **2-9-0** DBiggs(6) (lw: prom 5f) | 2 | **9** | 40/1 | 61 | — |
| | | | | (SP 118.7%) | **9 Rn** | |

**1m 38.79** (9.99) CSF £8.77 TOTE £2.10: £1.10 £1.90 £2.90 (£6.10) Trio £41.80 OWNER Aylesfield Farms Stud (ARUNDEL) BRED Aylesfield Farms Stud

**3131 Barnum Sands** put up a very polished display. Always travelling supremely well, Quinn toyed with the opposition and only decided to let the colt into the lead inside the final furlong. Showing a tremendous turn of foot, he settled the issue within strides. He can score again. (Evens)

**Go For Salt (USA)**, a very plain, smallish filly with little to recommend her, is certainly one of the stable's lesser lights. Pushed along soon after halfway, she picked up ground over a quarter of a mile from home and did run on inside the final furlong to snatch second prize. (7/1: op 3/1)

**Northern Pass (USA)**, a tall filly who is closely related to Champion USA two-year-old filly Outstandingly, showed in front over a quarter of a mile from home. Collared inside the final furlong, she was left standing. Her trainer in not renowned for his two-year-old winners, but she should be able to find a small race. (20/1)

**3493 Sword Arm** chased the leaders, but could only plod on in his own time in the last two furlongs. (7/2: 5/2-4/1)

**3454 Petrel** chased the leaders, but could only go up and down in the same place in the last three furlongs. (20/1)

**2702 Logica (IRE)** took the field along. Collared over a quarter of a mile from home, she tried to hold on, but had shot her bolt below the distance. (7/1)

## 3874 H. P. BULMERS MAIDEN STKS (II) (2-Y.O) (Class D)

3-30 (3-31) **7f 140y** £3,173.75 (£944.00: £448.50: £200.75) Stalls: High GOING: 0.35 sec per fur (G)

| | | | | SP | RR | SF |
|---|---|---|---|---|---|---|
| 3326$^{3}$ | **Sad Mad Bad (USA)** (MJohnston) **2-9-0** JWeaver(4) (lw: stumbled s: chsd ldr: rdn 4f out: led over 1f out: r.o wl) | — | **1** | 7/2$^{2}$ | 80 | 25 |
| 3493$^{2}$ | **Inclination** (MBlanshard) **2-8-9** JQuinn(8) (led: rdn over 2f out: hdd over 1f out: unable qckn) | 1 | **2** | 2/1$^{1}$ | 73 | 18 |
| | **Quest For Best (USA)** (JHMGosden) **2-8-9** GHind(5) (lt-f: s.s: hdwy over 2f out: shkn up over 1f out: one pce) | hd | **3** | 6/1$^{3}$ | 73 | 18 |
| 3269$^{7}$ | **Greenwich Fore** (TGMills) **2-9-0** BDoyle(3) (hld up: rdn 3f out: swtchd rt 1f out: one pce) | 1½ | **4** | 10/1 | 75 | 20 |
| 2708$^{10}$ | **Kennemara Star (IRE)** (JLDunlop) **2-9-0** GCarter(6) (lw: hdwy over 4f out: rdn over 2f out: ev ch over 1f out: wknd ins fnl f) | 2½ | **5** | 15/2 | 69 | 14 |
| 3234$^{7}$ | **Mister Jay** (PTWalwyn) **2-9-0** JCarroll(7) (prom over 3f) | 8 | **6** | 20/1 | 53 | — |
| | **Euro Superstar (FR)** (SDow) **2-9-0** WJO'Connor(2) (w'like: s.s: a bhd) | 1½ | **7** | 33/1 | 49 | — |
| *3625$^{7}$* | **Le Grand Gousier (USA)** (RJRWilliams) **2-8-9**(5) LNewton(9) (bhd fnl 4f) | s.h | **8** | 33/1 | 49 | — |
| 2708$^{13}$ | **Sunday Market (USA)** (GHarwood) **2-9-0** PatEddery(1) (lw: prom 4f) | 14 | **9** | 8/1 | 20 | — |
| | | | | (SP 112.5%) | **9 Rn** | |

**1m 37.99** (9.19) CSF £10.16 TOTE £3.30: £1.10 £1.20 £1.70 (£3.50) Trio £6.80 OWNER Mr P. D. Savill (MIDDLEHAM) BRED Loch Lea Farm Inc

**3326 Sad Mad Bad (USA)** raced in second place, but Weaver was bustling him along fully half a mile from home. Nevertheless, the colt stuck to his task really well and, showing with a narrow lead below the distance, ran on strongly. (7/2: 7/4-4/1)

**3493 Inclination** dictated matters from the front and appeared to be going far better than the winner. Ridden along over a quarter of a mile from home, she was collared below the distance and failed to quicken. She should soon go one better. (2/1)

**Quest For Best (USA)**, a lightly-made filly with no scope whatsoever, is certainly one of the stable's lesser lights but did show promise under considerate handling. Moving up over a quarter of a mile from home, she threatened to take second place inside the final furlong, but just failed to succeed. A maiden can be found on one of the smaller tracks. (6/1: 3/1-13/2)

**Greenwich Fore** chased the leaders. Bustled along soon after halfway, he was switched right entering the final furlong, but failed to find the necessary turn of foot. (10/1: tchd 20/1)

**Kennemara Star (IRE)**, a half-brother to Dawning Street and Special Dawn, looked very well in the preliminaries and stepped up on his debut. Soon racing in a handy position, he had every chance below the distance before tiring inside the last 150 yards. He looks one to note for a nursery in due course. (15/2: 5/1-8/1)

## 3875 WADWORTH 6X CONDITIONS STKS (3-Y.O+) (Class C)

4-00 (4-00) **5f** £5,066.28 (£1,874.52: £899.26: £367.30: £145.65: £56.99) Stalls: High GOING: 0.35 sec per fur (G)

| | | | | SP | RR | SF |
|---|---|---|---|---|---|---|
| 3126$^{8}$ | **Lucky Parkes (100)** (JBerry) **6-9-2** JCarroll(5) (mde all: drvn out) | — | **1** | 7/1 | 101 | 68 |

| | | | | SP | RR | SF |
|---|---|---|---|---|---|---|
| 3495* | **Bowden Rose (90)** (MBlanshard) **4-9-0b** JQuinn(1) (lw: a.p: rdn over 1f out: ev ch ins fnl f: r.o) | nk | 2 | 11/1 | 98 | 65 |
| 3693[7] | **Fond Embrace (95)** (HCandy) **3-8-12** GCarter(9) (lw: a.p: rdn over 2f out: r.o ins fnl f) | s.h | 3 | 9/4[1] | 98 | 63 |
| 3232[24] | **Brave Edge (103)** (RHannon) **5-9-9** PatEddery(8) (rdn & hdwy over 1f out: r.o wl ins fnl f) | nk | 4 | 5/1[3] | 106 | 73 |
| 3759[6] | **King of The East (IRE) (102)** (MRStoute) **3-9-3** WRSwinburn(7) (lw: rdn over 2f out: hdwy fnl f: nvr nrr) | 1¾ | 5 | 7/1 | 96 | 61 |
| 2292[11] | **That Man Again (96)** (GLewis) **4-9-0b** GDuffield(6) (lw: a.p: rdn over 1f out: wknd fnl f) | hd | 6 | 10/1 | 91 | 58 |
| 3495[2] | **Amazing Bay (100)** (IABalding) **3-8-7** TQuinn(3) (lw: prom over 3f) | 2½ | 7 | 4/1[2] | 78 | 43 |
| | **Princely Hush (IRE)** (MBell) **4-9-0** MFenton(4) (lw: sme hdwy over 1f out: wknd fnl f) | 1¼ | 8 | 16/1 | 79 | 46 |
| 3759[9] | **High Priority (IRE) (100)** (MRChannon) **3-8-12** RPerham(2) (lw: a bhd) | ¾ | 9 | 33/1 | 77 | 42 |
| | | | | (SP 118.7%) | | **9 Rn** |

**60.57 secs** (3.57) CSF £72.18 TOTE £5.50: £1.40 £2.50 £1.30 (£20.00) Trio £26.80 OWNER Mr Joseph Heler (COCKERHAM) BRED Joseph Heler

WEIGHT FOR AGE 3yo-2lb

**2698* Lucky Parkes** excels in these types of races. Making all the running, she was strongly pressed but, responding well to pressure, was not going to be denied as she won her seventeenth conditions race - she is yet to score outside this class. She is a real credit to her trainer who has managed to place her perfectly throughout her career. (7/1: 4/1-8/1)

**3495* Bowden Rose** threw down her challenge in the final quarter-mile, but found she had met a real tartar in the winner. (11/1: 8/1-12/1)

**3693 Fond Embrace**, a leading light from the off, kept on well inside the final furlong and failed by only a whisker to take second prize. (9/4)

**1818 Brave Edge** at last found his feet below the distance but, despite running on really strongly inside the final furlong, found the line always coming too soon. (5/1)

**3759 King of The East (IRE)** stayed on in the final furlong, but found the principals already home and dry. (7/1: 5/1-8/1)

**2003 That Man Again** was bang in contention until weakening entering the final furlong. He only just stays five furlongs and really does need to hear his feet rattle. (10/1: 6/1-12/1)

## 3876 BODDINGTONS H'CAP (0-80) (3-Y.O+) (Class D)

4-30 (4-31) **1m 3f 106y** £4,324.80 (£1,295.40: £622.20: £285.60) Stalls: High GOING: 0.35 sec per fur (G)

| | | | | SP | RR | SF |
|---|---|---|---|---|---|---|
| 3586[2] | **Veridian (70)** (PWHarris) **3-8-12** GHind(2) (a.p: led over 2f out: r.o wl) | — | 1 | 9/1 | 81 | 54 |
| *3600** | **Glow Forum (46)** (LMontagueHall) **5-7-6**(5) MartinDwyer(4) (b: a.p: ev ch over 2f out: unable qckn) | 1½ | 2 | 15/8[1] | 55 | 37 |
| 3500[3] | **Shining Dancer (61)** (SDow) **4-8-12** DHarrison(5) (s.s: rdn 3f out: hdwy over 2f out: r.o one pce) | 1½ | 3 | 10/1 | 68 | 50 |
| 3302[4] | **Prince Danzig (IRE) (63)** (DJGMurraySmith) **5-9-0** JReid(7) (lw: rdn 3f out: hdwy over 1f out: one pce) | 7 | 4 | 14/1 | 60 | 42 |
| 3611* | **Arktikos (IRE) (68)** (JHMGosden) **3-8-10v** BDoyle(9) (b.hind: lw: a.p: rdn 3f out: sn wknd) | 3½ | 5 | 5/1[3] | 60 | 33 |
| 3205[8] | **Claire's Dancer (IRE) (67)** (AndrewTurnell) **3-8-9** TIves(6) (lw: nvr nr to chal) | 1¾ | 6 | 25/1 | 57 | 30 |
| 3235[2] | **Mr Browning (USA) (73)** (RAkehurst) **5-9-10b** SSanders(1) (led 9f) | 1¾ | 7 | 9/2[2] | 60 | 42 |
| 3434[5] | **Alicia (IRE) (73)** (JLDunlop) **3-9-1** WRSwinburn(3) (w ldr 9f) | s.h | 8 | 8/1 | 60 | 33 |
| 3710[12] | **Village King (IRE) (75)** (RHannon) **3-9-3b1** WJO'Connor(10) (hld up: rdn over 3f out: sn wknd) | 1½ | 9 | 14/1 | 60 | 33 |
| 3656[6] | **Classy Chief (74)** (RBoss) **3-9-2** GDuffield(11) (s.s: a bhd) | 3 | 10 | 25/1 | 55 | 28 |
| | | | | (SP 120.9%) | | **10 Rn** |

**2m 34.32** (10.12) CSF £26.01 CT £162.37 TOTE £12.50: £1.80 £1.30 £2.80 (£63.50) Trio £39.60 OWNER Mrs P. W. Harris (BERKHAMSTED) BRED A. L. Penfold and H. Lascelles

WEIGHT FOR AGE 3yo-9lb

**3586 Veridian**, a leading light from the off, went on over a quarter of a mile from home and kept on really well. (9/1)

**3600* Glow Forum**, never far away, had every chance over a quarter of a mile out, but then failed to match the winner's turn of foot. (15/8)

**3500 Shining Dancer** picked up ground over a quarter of a mile from home and stayed on without seriously threatening the front two. (10/1)

**3302 Prince Danzig (IRE)** plodded on from the back of the field in the final quarter-mile without posing a threat. (14/1)

**3611* Arktikos (IRE)** was close up until weakening approaching the final quarter-mile. (5/1: 4/1-6/1)

**3235 Mr Browning (USA)** took the field along but, collared over two furlongs out, soon had bellows to mend. He needs a faster surface. (9/2)

## 3877 MERRYDOWN H'CAP (0-70) (3-Y.O+) (Class E)

5-00 (5-01) **7f (Equitrack)** £3,588.90 (£1,075.20: £516.60: £237.30) Stalls: Low GOING minus 0.69 sec per fur (FST)

| | | | | SP | RR | SF |
|---|---|---|---|---|---|---|
| 3439[12] | **Speedy Classic (USA) (63)** (MJHeaton-Ellis) **7-9-7** AClark(5) (a.p: led 4f out: clr over 1f out: rdn out) | — | 1 | 20/1 | 80 | 50 |
| 3076[2] | **Farmost (66)** (SirMarkPrescott) **3-9-5** GDuffield(15) (lw: a.p: chsd wnr over 1f out: r.o) | 1¼ | 2 | 11/10[1] | 80 | 45 |
| 3304[4] | **Rocky Waters (USA) (60)** (PBurgoyne) **7-9-4v1** TQuinn(14) (b.hind: hdwy over 3f out: wknd over 1f out) | 9 | 3 | 7/1[2] | 54 | 24 |
| 3439[8] | **Invocation (66)** (AMoore) **9-9-10** DaneO'Neill(7) (b.nr hind: lw: a.p: rdn over 2f out: wknd over 1f out) | 1¼ | 4 | 16/1 | 57 | 27 |
| *3078[3]* | **Hawaii Storm (FR) (60)** (DJSffrenchDavis) **8-8-13**(5) RPainter(9) (lw: outpcd: nvr nrr) | 2 | 5 | 16/1 | 46 | 16 |
| 3353[8] | **Classic Royale (USA) (60)** (RHarris) **3-8-13** AMackay(16) (outpcd: nvr nrr) | s.h | 6 | 25/1 | 46 | 11 |
| 3578[2] | **Four of Spades (70)** (RJHodges) **5-9-9v**(5) AmandaSanders(11) (lw: no hdwy fnl 3f) | ½ | 7 | 10/1 | 55 | 25 |
| 3501[6] | **Superior Force (63)** (MissBSanders) **3-9-2** SSanders(4) (lw: outpcd: nvr nrr) | ½ | 8 | 16/1 | 47 | 12 |
| 3711[10] | **Miss Haversham (60)** (CACyzer) **4-9-4b** PBloomfield(8) (outpcd) | ¾ | 9 | 25/1 | 42 | 12 |
| 3661[8] | **Justinianus (IRE) (45)** (JJBridger) **4-8-3** JQuinn(3) (lw: prom over 4f) | ¾ | 10 | 33/1 | 25 | — |
| 3606[6] | **Our Shadee (USA) (69)** (KTIvory) **6-9-13v** CScally(12) (lw: a bhd) | 1 | 11 | 16/1 | 47 | 17 |
| 3636[4] | **Sharp Imp (60)** (RMFlower) **6-9-4b** DBiggs(1) (bhd fnl 2f) | hd | 12 | 8/1[3] | 38 | 8 |
| *3601[8]* | **Jolto (60)** (KMcAuliffe) **7-9-4b1** JWeaver(13) (b.hind: led 3f: wknd 3f out) | 7 | 13 | 25/1 | 22 | — |
| 1599[7] | **Time Clash (67)** (BPalling) **3-9-1**(5) MartinDwyer(2) (a bhd) | 4 | 14 | 25/1 | 20 | — |
| 3285[3] | **Dahiyah (USA) (56)** (DLWilliams) **5-9-0v** DHarrison(6) (lw: prom 3f) | 1 | 15 | 16/1 | 6 | — |
| | **Symmetrical (39)** (MMadgwick) **7-7-8**(3)ow1 NVarley(10) (bhd fnl 5f) | ½ | 16 | 100/1 | — | — |
| | | | | (SP 133.8%) | | **16 Rn** |

**1m 23.76** (-0.24) CSF £43.61 CT £194.46 TOTE £28.80: £3.90 £1.10 £2.00 £4.00 (£26.80) Trio £154.80 OWNER Stainless Design Services (WROUGHTON) BRED Lagrange Chance Partnership & Overbrook Farm

LONG HANDICAP Symmetrical 6-11

WEIGHT FOR AGE 3yo-5lb

**2719 Speedy Classic (USA)** bounced back to form on this his favourite surface. Sent on half a mile from home, he forged clear in the straight and was not going to be caught. (20/1)

**3076 Farmost**, never far away, went in pursuit of the winner early in the home straight but, despite running on, was never going to peg him back in time. (11/10)

**3304 Rocky Waters (USA)** took closer order at halfway, but was left for dead below the distance. (7/1: op 12/1)

**3146 Invocation** was close up until left standing over a furlong out. (16/1)

T/Plpt: £10.70 (1,221.78 Tckts). T/Qdpt: £3.70 (218.78 Tckts) AK

# 2928-MUSSELBURGH (R-H) (Good to firm)

## Thursday August 29th

WEATHER: sunny WIND: almost nil

## 3878 ROYAL SCOTS H'CAP (0-70) (3-Y.O+) (Class E)

2-20 (2-20) **1m 4f 31y** £3,152.00 (£956.00: £468.00: £224.00) Stalls: High GOING minus 0.25 sec per fur (GF)

| Form | Horse | Details | Dist | Pos | SP | RR | SF |
|---|---|---|---|---|---|---|---|
| 3611$^{2}$ | **Full Throttle (61)** | (MHTompkins) **3-8-13**(3) MHenry(8) (lw: in tch: led wl over 2f out: r.o: comf) | — | **1** | 5/1$^{3}$ | 74 | 47 |
| 3459$^{2}$ | **Blenheim Terrace (65)** | (CBBBooth) **3-9-6** ACulhane(3) (hld up & bhd: hdwy over 3f out: chsng ldrs appr fnl f: hrd rdn & nt pce of wnr) | 2 | **2** | 7/2$^{1}$ | 75 | 48 |
| *3600*$^{5}$ | **Campaspe (43)** | (JGFitzGerald) **4-8-8** KFallon(1) (lw: in tch: ev ch over 2f out: hung lft & nt qckn) | 2½ | **3** | 6/1 | 50 | 33 |
| 3649$^{4}$ | **Ambidextrous (IRE) (54)** | (EJAlston) **4-9-5** JFortune(2) (bhd: hdwy 3f out: rdn & no imp) | 5 | **4** | 10/1 | 55 | 38 |
| 3855$^{9}$ | **Jabaroot (IRE) (31)** | (RMMcKellar) **5-7-3**(7) JMcAuley(7) (bhd: hdwy on outside 3f out: nvr rchd ldrs) | 2½ | **5** | 66/1 | 28 | 11 |
| 3575$^{8}$ | **Chantry Beath (45)** | (CWThornton) **5-8-10** DeanMcKeown(4) (chsd ldrs tl wknd fnl 3f) | 2½ | **6** | 20/1 | 39 | 22 |
| 2798$^{4}$ | **Bayrak (USA) (63)** | (MJRyan) **6-10-0** MTebbutt(11) (lw: chsd ldrs: led 3f out: sn hdd & wknd) | ½ | **7** | 12/1 | 56 | 39 |
| 3645$^{4}$ | **Seconds Away (32)** | (JSGoldie) **5-7-11**ow1 TWilliams(5) (hld up & bhd: gd hdwy 3f out: rdn & btn 2f out) | hd | **8** | 25/1 | 25 | 7 |
| 3646$^{5}$ | **Rapid Mover (34)** | (DANolan) **9-7-6b**(7)ow3 KSked(10) (in tch tl grad wknd over 3f out) | ½ | **9** | 33/1 | 26 | 6 |
| 3347* | **Monaco Gold (IRE) (41)** | (MrsMReveley) **4-8-3**(3) DWright(6) (lw: bhd: effrt 3f out: hung rt & no hdwy) | 1¾ | **10** | 4/1$^{2}$ | 31 | 14 |
| 3649$^{2}$ | **Lord Advocate (49)** | (DANolan) **8-9-0b** VHalliday(9) (lw: led tl hdd 3f out: sn wknd) | ½ | **11** | 8/1 | 39 | 22 |
| 1325$^{8}$ | **Noir Esprit (53)** | (JMCarr) **3-8-8** NKennedy(12) (jnd ldr after 4f: wknd qckly fnl 3f) | 1½ | **12** | 50/1 | 41 | 14 |

(SP 116.1%) **12 Rn**

**2m 38.0** (5.00) CSF £21.09 CT £97.91 TOTE £7.30: £3.20 £2.60 £2.60 (£16.50) Trio £13.80 OWNER Pamela, Lady Nelson of Stafford (NEWMARKET) BRED Dullingham House Stud

LONG HANDICAP Rapid Mover 7-9 Seconds Away 7-8 Jabaroot (IRE) 7-5

WEIGHT FOR AGE 3yo-10lb

**OFFICIAL EXPLANATION Monaco Gold (IRE): was found to have a nasal discharge.**

**3611 Full Throttle** has really found his form since being put into handicaps and, staying well, won this with something to spare. (5/1)

**3459 Blenheim Terrace** has thrown chances away of late and has now gone up 7lb. Although staying on here, he was never doing enough to trouble the winner. (7/2)

**3600 Campaspe** had her chances again but, when the pressure was on, she hung left and failed to come up with the goods. (6/1)

**3649 Ambidextrous (IRE)** made ground early in the straight but was soon all out and never doing enough to get there. (10/1)

**3575 Jabaroot (IRE)** ran one of his better races this time, coming from behind, but he still never had a hope. (66/1)

**152 Chantry Beath** is off a useful mark at present, but the spark was never there on this occasion. (20/1)

**3347* Monaco Gold (IRE)** looked uncomfortable when asked a question early in the straight and was later reported to have a nasal discharge. (4/1: op 5/2)

## 3879 SALAMANCA (S) STKS (2-Y.O) (Class F)

2-50 (2-50) **5f** £2,654.00 (£744.00: £362.00) Stalls: High GOING minus 0.25 sec per fur (GF)

| Form | Horse | Details | Dist | Pos | SP | RR | SF |
|---|---|---|---|---|---|---|---|
| 3687$^{5}$ | **Lunar Music (65)** | (MartynMeade) **2-8-4**(7) DSweeney(4) (lw: chsd ldrs: rdn to ld wl over 1f out: sn clr: eased ins fnl f) | — | **1** | 4/5$^{1}$ | 80+ | 14 |
| 3488$^{4}$ | **Melbourne Princess (65)** | (RMWhitaker) **2-8-6** DeanMcKeown(3) (racd stands' side: led over 3f: sn btn) | 5 | **2** | 9/1 | 59 | — |
| 3763$^{4}$ | **Le Shuttle (57)** | (MHTompkins) **2-8-3**(3) MHenry(1) (wnt lft s: chsd ldrs & edgd rt most of wy: kpt on: no imp) | 1 | **3** | 13/2$^{3}$ | 56 | — |
| 3763$^{8}$ | **Wedding Music (60)** | (PCHaslam) **2-8-6** JFortune(2) (racd stands' side: a chsng ldrs: rdn & no imp fnl 2f) | 1¾ | **4** | 9/1 | 50 | — |
| 3648* | **Contravene (IRE) (52)** | (JBerry) **2-8-11** KDarley(6) (cl up to ½-wy: sn outpcd) | 1¾ | **5** | 4/1$^{2}$ | 50 | — |
| 3332$^{W}$ | **Miss Fugit Penance** | (PDEvans) **2-8-6** JFEgan(5) (b.nr fore: leggy: unf: prom to ½-wy: sn btn) | 3 | **6** | 16/1 | 35 | — |
| 3576$^{6}$ | **Barachois Lad** | (JJO'Neill) **2-8-11b**[1] TWilliams(7) (outpcd after 2f) | 3 | **7** | 66/1 | 30 | — |
| 3511$^{6}$ | **True Perspective** | (JDBethell) **2-8-11** SDrowne(8) (sn outpcd) | 4 | **8** | 20/1 | 18 | — |

(SP 121.0%) **8 Rn**

**61.2 secs** (3.50) CSF £9.25 TOTE £1.80: £1.10 £2.00 £1.10 (£21.20) OWNER Mrs P. A. Barratt (MALMESBURY) BRED T. Barratt

Bt in 8,200 gns

**3687 Lunar Music** made short work of some inferior rivals and won really well. (4/5)

**3488 Melbourne Princess**, taken early to post, had the best ground up the stands' side, but was no match for the winner. (9/1)

**3763 Le Shuttle**, after ducking left out of the stalls, should have taken advantage of the stands' rails but her rider, in his wisdom, then worked his way across to the far side. In the circumstances this was not a bad effort. (13/2)

**3488 Wedding Music** had her chances up the stands' rail, but was never good enough. (9/1)

**3648* Contravene (IRE)** showed plenty of speed towards the far side, but could never dominate and finally called it a day some way out. (4/1)

**Miss Fugit Penance** is not much to look at and has plenty to learn. (16/1)

## 3880 STEVE WOOD MEMORIAL NURSERY H'CAP (2-Y.O) (Class E)

3-20 (3-21) **7f 15y** £2,820.00 (£840.00: £400.00: £180.00) Stalls: High GOING minus 0.25 sec per fur (GF)

| Form | Horse | Details | Dist | Pos | SP | RR | SF |
|---|---|---|---|---|---|---|---|
| 3835$^{11}$ | **Ben's Ridge (78)** | (PCHaslam) **2-9-6** JFortune(4) (lw: hld up: hdwy 3f out: carried lft & racd stands' side: led ins fnl f: all out) | — | **1** | 7/2$^{1}$ | 80 | 33 |
| 3632$^{4}$ | **Hello Dolly (IRE) (61)** | (KRBurke) **2-8-3** SDrowne(1) (hdwy ½-wy: racd stands' side: led over 1f out: hdd ins fnl f: no ex nr fin) | nk | **2** | 12/1 | 62 | 15 |
| 3099$^{3}$ | **Zorba (64)** | (CWThornton) **2-8-6** DeanMcKeown(6) (lw: plld hrd: sn cl up: hmpd over 2f out: sn ev ch: nt qckn towards fin) | nk | **3** | 7/1 | 65 | 18 |
| 3616$^{6}$ | **Stride (75)** | (MartynMeade) **2-8-10**(7) DSweeney(3) (hdwy ½-wy: carried lft & hmpd 2f out: nt clr run & swtchd 1f out: nt rcvr) | 1 | **4** | 6/1$^{3}$ | 73+ | 26 |
| 3659$^{4}$ | **I Can't Remember (72)** | (PDEvans) **2-9-0** JFEgan(2) (lw: plld hrd: trckd ldrs: racd stands' side st: ev ch over 1f out: nt qckn) | nk | **5** | 8/1 | 70 | 23 |
| 3588$^{5}$ | **Italian Symphony (IRE) (79)** | (MJohnston) **2-9-7** KDarley(7) (led: hung bdly lft over 2f out: hdd & wknd over 1f out) | 6 | **6** | 4/1$^{2}$ | 63 | 16 |
| 3648$^{2}$ | **I'm Still Here (60)** | (JBerry) **2-8-2** LCharnock(8) (effrt ½-wy: sn rdn & btn) | 6 | **7** | 6/1$^{3}$ | 31 | — |
| 3590$^{2}$ | **Smokey From Caplaw (69)** | (JJO'Neill) **2-8-11** KFallon(5) (bhd: effrt ½-wy: sn btn) | 1½ | **8** | 8/1 | 36 | — |

| | | | | SP | RR | SF |
|---|---|---|---|---|---|---|
| 2491$^{6}$ | **Chanson d'Amour (IRE) (60)** (MissLAPerratt) **2-8-2** TWilliams(9) (prom tl wknd fnl 3f) | 16 | **9** | 50/1 | — | — |

(SP 115.2%) **9 Rn**

**1m 29.8** (4.30) CSF £39.24 CT £255.91 TOTE £4.00: £1.40 £3.20 £2.80 (£41.20) Trio £110.60 OWNER Mr S. A. B. Dinsmore (MIDDLEHAM) BRED S. A. B. Dinsmore

**3678 Ben's Ridge** was messed about no end in the straight, but this probably suited him and he had the required turn of foot when it mattered. (7/2)

**3632 Hello Dolly (IRE)** intentionally raced up the stands' side. She made a real fight of it and, seemed to get the trip well enough this time, but it was a messy race. (12/1)

**3099 Zorba** might well have won this but for being hampered over two furlongs out, which cost him valuable momentum and ground. (7/1)

**3616 Stride** is coming back to form and would have been in the shake-up but for getting messed about throughout the last two and a half furlongs. (6/1)

**3659 I Can't Remember**, who took a strong hold, raced up the stands' side in the straight, but was never good enough when the pressure was on in the last furlong and a half. (8/1)

**3588 Italian Symphony (IRE)** caused all sorts of problems here by hanging violently left in the home straight, and there was nothing his rider could do about it. (4/1)

## 3881 INTER CHRISTMAS TREE H'CAP (0-70) (3-Y.O) (Class E)

3-50 (3-53) **7f 15y** £3,566.25 (£1,080.00: £527.50: £251.25) Stalls: High GOING minus 0.25 sec per fur (GF)

| | | | | SP | RR | SF |
|---|---|---|---|---|---|---|
| 3666$^{4}$ | **Scathebury (55)** (KRBurke) **3-8-13b** KFallon(1) (prom: racd stands' side: led 2f out: r.o) | — | **1** | 10/1 | 64 | 33 |
| 3491$^{3}$ | **Miletrian City (57)** (JBerry) **3-9-1b** KDarley(2) (lw: stdd s: hdwy far side 3f out: styd on: nvr able to chal) | 1¾ | **2** | 5/1$^{3}$ | 62 | 31 |
| 3228$^{3}$ | **Fisiostar (40)** (MDods) **3-7-12b** NKennedy(10) (chsd ldrs: one pce fnl 3f) | 1½ | **3** | 9/1 | 42 | 11 |
| 3304$^{2}$ | **Creeking (54)** (SirMarkPrescott) **3-8-9b**$^{(3)}$ RHavlin(6) (lw: led: racd stands' side: hdd 2f out: sn btn) | ½ | **4** | 9/2$^{2}$ | 55 | 24 |
| 3358$^{11}$ | **Domusky (39)** (RBastiman) **3-7-8**$^{(3)ow1}$ DWright(8) (bhd tl styd on fnl 3f: nrst fin) | nk | **5** | 100/1 | 39 | 7 |
| 3680$^{2}$ | **Magic Lake (45)** (EJAlston) **3-8-3** SDrowne(5) (lw: trckd ldrs: racd stands' side: ev ch 2f out: sn rdn & wknd) | 1 | **6** | 7/2$^{1}$ | 43 | 12 |
| 3427$^{2}$ | **Madonna da Rossi (40)** (MDods) **3-7-12** LCharnock(4) (lw: chsd ldrs: led far side 3f out: sn wknd) | 6 | **7** | 7/1 | 24 | — |
| 3491$^{5}$ | **Termon (55)** (MissLAPerratt) **3-8-13v**$^{1}$ JFortune(7) (chsd ldrs 4f: wknd) | 5 | **8** | 20/1 | 28 | — |
| 3583$^{9}$ | **Petite Heritiere (50)** (MJRyan) **3-8-3**$^{(5)}$ MBaird(9) (lw: cl up to st: sn wknd) | 1¼ | **9** | 33/1 | 20 | — |
| 3789$^{2}$ | **Uncle George (63)** (MHTompkins) **3-9-4v**$^{(3)}$ MHenry(3) (racd stands' side: bhd fnl 3f) | 5 | **10** | 6/1 | 22 | — |

(SP 111.6%) **10 Rn**

**1m 29.2** (3.70) CSF £52.88 CT £432.17 TOTE £12.00: £2.70 £1.40 £3.30 (£32.20) Trio £97.50 OWNER Mr Nigel Shields (WANTAGE) BRED The Duke Of Marlborough

LONG HANDICAP Domusky 6-9

**3666 Scathebury**, with the blinkers back on after trying without them and with a visor of late, came up with the goods this time but it was not much of a race. (10/1)

**3491 Miletrian City**, dropped out, ran pretty well but racing on the opposite side to the winner probably did not help as he had to see too much daylight too soon. He looks in good form. (5/1)

**3228 Fisiostar** had his chances, but lacked a change of gear to do anything about it. (9/1)

**3304 Creeking**, in blinkers for the second time, again blazed off in front but, once tackled two furlongs out, put up little resistance. (9/2)

**Domusky** has proved disappointing when racing up with the pace and came from behind here to put in a better effort. (100/1)

**3680 Magic Lake** showed a moderate action and ran disappointingly, dropping tamely away in the last two furlongs. (7/2)

## 3882 RILEY SCOTLAND GOLD HEART CLAIMING STKS (3-Y.O) (Class F)

4-20 (4-20) **1m 3f 32y** £2,598.00 (£728.00: £354.00) Stalls: High GOING minus 0.25 sec per fur (GF)

| | | | | SP | RR | SF |
|---|---|---|---|---|---|---|
| 3808$^{3}$ | **Ragtime Cowgirl (39)** (CWThornton) **3-8-1** TWilliams(7) (trckd ldrs: smooth hdwy to ld over 2f out: r.o) | — | **1** | 5/2$^{2}$ | 47 | 12 |
| 3249$^{3}$ | **Breydon (44)** (MHTompkins) **3-9-3**$^{(3)}$ MHenry(2) (a.p: ev ch over 2f out: r.o one pce) | 3 | **2** | 7/1 | 62 | 27 |
| 3654$^{2}$ | **Cebwob (67)** (PFICole) **3-9-1** JFortune(1) (hld up: hdwy ent st: chal 2f out: rdn & nt qckn) | ½ | **3** | 9/4$^{1}$ | 56 | 21 |
| *3600*$^{2}$ | **Tabriz (60)** (JDBethell) **3-9-5** SDrowne(3) (cl up tl grad wknd over 2f out) | nk | **4** | 5/1 | 60 | 25 |
| 3591$^{2}$ | **Arc of The Diver (IRE) (55)** (JBerry) **3-9-4b** KDarley(8) (lw: chsd ldrs: outpcd ent st: rdn & no imp after) | 3 | **5** | 9/2$^{3}$ | 54 | 19 |
| 3619$^{5}$ | **Philgem (27)** (CWFairhurst) **3-8-3** NKennedy(6) (lw: led tl hdd & wknd over 2f out) | 6 | **6** | 33/1 | 31 | — |
| 3591$^{8}$ | **Polish Saga (44)** (MDods) **3-8-7** JFEgan(5) (lw: effrt appr st: nvr trbld ldrs) | 15 | **7** | 20/1 | 13 | — |
| 3425$^{11}$ | **Jimmy-S (IRE)** (RMMcKellar) **3-8-3**$^{(7)}$ JMcAuley(4) (prom tl wknd qckly 6f out: sn wl t.o) | dist | **8** | 33/1 | — | — |

(SP 117.3%) **8 Rn**

**2m 27.4** (7.70) CSF £19.28 TOTE £3.60: £1.30 £1.40 £1.20 (£9.30) OWNER Mr Guy Reed (MIDDLEHAM) BRED D. G. Mason

Breydon clmd PMonteith £10,000; Ragtime Cowgirl clmd GMC Racing £3,000

**3808 Ragtime Cowgirl** was always travelling too well for this lot and won most authoritatively. (5/2)

**3249 Breydon**, dropping back in trip again, had his chances, but was woefully short of speed. (7/1: 5/1-8/1)

**3654 Cebwob** is nothing much to look at and probably found this trip just beyond her. (9/4)

**3600 Tabriz** has the ability, but it is anybody's guess as to when she will put it to full use. (5/1: 7/2-11/2)

**3591 Arc of The Diver (IRE)**, stepping up in trip, was never happy from the home turn. (9/2)

**3619 Philgem** set the race up and put up no fight at all when tackled early in the straight. (33/1)

## 3883 PERGODA APPRENTICE H'CAP (0-70) (3-Y.O+) (Class F)

4-50 (4-55) **5f** £2,766.00 (£776.00: £378.00) Stalls: High GOING minus 0.25 sec per fur (GF)

| | | | | SP | RR | SF |
|---|---|---|---|---|---|---|
| 3122$^{2}$ | **Ninety-Five (66)** (JGFitzGerald) **4-9-11** FLynch(6) (mde all stands' side: kpt on wl fnl f) | — | **1** | 13/2$^{2}$ | 72 | 52 |
| 2791$^{5}$ | **Johayro (59)** (JSGoldie) **3-9-2b** GLee(15) (w ldrs far side: led 1f out: ct post) | s.h | **2** | 33/1 | 65 | 43 |
| 3774$^{2}$ | **Kalar (53)** (DWChapman) **7-8-12b** DWright(9) (lw: led far side: hdd 1f out: hung rt & kpt on wl) | hd | **3** | 3/1$^{1}$ | 59 | 39 |
| 3661$^{5}$ | **Songsheet (66)** (MartynMeade) **3-9-6**$^{(3)}$ DSweeney(12) (prom centre: kpt on wl fnl f: nrst fin) | nk | **4** | 14/1 | 71 | 49 |
| 3680$^{6}$ | **Another Nightmare (IRE) (46)** (RMMcKellar) **4-7-12**$^{(7)}$ $^{7x}$ JMcAuley(13) (w ldrs far side: kpt on fnl f) | ¾ | **5** | 7/1$^{3}$ | 48 | 28 |
| 3644$^{3}$ | **Leading Princess (IRE) (52)** (MissLAPerratt) **5-8-6b**$^{(5)}$ JBramhill(4) (cl up stands' side: outpcd 2f out: kpt on towards fin) | ¾ | **6** | 10/1 | 52 | 32 |
| 3643$^{8}$ | **Katy-Q (IRE) (45)** (PCalver) **3-8-2b** DarrenMoffatt(2) (lw: a chsng ldrs stands' side: rdn 2f out: nt qckn) | 1¼ | **7** | 10/1 | 41 | 19 |
| 3415$^{3}$ | **Sunset Harbour (IRE) (48)** (SEKettlewell) **3-8-0**$^{(5)}$ JennyBenson(1) (lw: prom stands' side: wnt rt ½-wy: no imp) | nk | **8** | 7/1$^{3}$ | 43 | 21 |
| 3424$^{2}$ | **Six for Luck (58)** (DANolan) **4-8-12**$^{(5)}$ KSked(14) (b.off hind: cl up far side: nt qckn fnl f) | 1¼ | **9** | 14/1 | 49 | 29 |
| 3643$^{7}$ | **Lady Caroline Lamb (IRE) (62)** (RBastiman) **3-9-5** HBastiman(10) (dwlt: hdwy centre ½-wy: no imp) | 1 | **10** | 20/1 | 50 | 28 |
| 2849$^{4}$ | **Manolo (FR) (54)** (JBerry) **3-8-11** PRoberts(5) (lw: racd stands' side: a outpcd & bhd) | s.h | **11** | 7/1$^{3}$ | 41 | 19 |

3661[7] **Silk Cottage (65)** (RMWhitaker) **4-9-10b** SDrowne(8) (lw: s.i.s: racd stands' side & hdwy ½-wy: wknd fnl f)....½ **12** 12/1 51 31
3698[13] **Daffodil Express (IRE) (46)** (MJRyan) **3-8-3** MBaird(11) (sn outpcd & bhd) ....7 **13** 16/1 9 —
3579[5] **Super Sonata (48)** (TWall) **4-8-2b**(5) AMcCarthy(7) (rdr lost irons & wl bhd fr ½-wy)....4 **14** 10/1 — —
*3579[4] **Just Lady (57)*** (WGMTurner) **3-9-0** RHavlin(3) (Withdrawn not under Starter's orders: bolted bef s) .... **W** 8/1 — —
(SP 148.8%) **14 Rn**

**59.7 secs** (2.00) CSF £186.03 CT £754.23 TOTE £9.20: £4.30 £5.10 £1.30 (£128.80) Trio £260.00 OWNER Mr N. H. T. Wrigley (MALTON) BRED M. H. Wrigley
WEIGHT FOR AGE 3yo-2lb

**3122 Ninety-Five** is improving and always had the edge on the stands' side. Running on gallantly, she got the advantage overall in the very last stride. (13/2)
**2791 Johayro** has dropped down the handicap and this was a better effort. But for a barging match with Kalar, he might have prevailed. (33/1)
**3774 Kalar** looks in tremendous form at the moment, but he got unbalanced under pressure in the final furlong and was just touched off. (3/1)
**3661 Songsheet** ran well and, judging by the way she was staying on, she should find another race before long. (14/1)
**3680 Another Nightmare (IRE)**, who found this trip on this track just a shade too sharp, still ran well up the far side, if always short of toe in the last furlong. (7/1)
**3644 Leading Princess (IRE)** is a bit of a character and was never doing enough here, but still ran reasonably well. (10/1)

T/Jkpt: Not won; £16,749.76 to Sandown 30/8/96. T/Plpt: £123.80 (134.69 Tckts). T/Qdpt: £45.80 (20.37 Tckts). AA

## 3884a-3902a (Irish Racing) - See Computer Raceform

## 3750a-DEAUVILLE (France) (R-H) (Good)
### Tuesday August 20th

### 3903a PRIX DE LA VALLEE D'AUGE (Listed) (2-Y.O C & G)
2-30 **5f** £18,445.00 (£6,324.00: £3,953.00)

| | | | | SP | RR | SF |
|---|---|---|---|---|---|---|
| | **Clever Caption (IRE)** (AFabre,France) **2-8-11** OPeslier | — | **1** | | 97 | — |
| 3613* | **Head Over Heels (IRE)** (JHMGosden) **2-9-0** CAsmussen | ½ | **2** | | 98 | — |
| 2890[2] | **Jennelle** (CADwyer) **2-8-8** JoHunnam | 1 | **3** | | 89 | — |
| | | | | | | **6 Rn** |

**59.3 secs** (2.80) P-M 4.10F:1.80F 1.50F OWNER I. Allan (CHANTILLY) BRED Mrs M. Heffernan
**3613* Head Over Heels (IRE)** took the lead inside the final furlong, but failed to hold off the late challenge of the winner. She was giving 6lb in weight, so it was not a bad effort. She will now be rested until the Ayr Western Meeting.
**2890 Jennelle** was always up with the pace, and led at the furlong marker before her stride shortened. Her jockey lost her whip a furlong and a half from the line, but it didn't make much difference.

## 1948a-BADEN-BADEN (Germany) (L-H) (Good)
### Friday August 23rd

### 3904a KRONIMUS RENNEN (Listed) (2-Y.O)
1-35 (1-37) **7f** £11,261.00 (£4,505.00: £2,793.00: £1,712.00)

| | | | | SP | RR | SF |
|---|---|---|---|---|---|---|
| | **Widar** (ALowe,Germany) **2-8-12** THellier | — | **1** | | 90 | — |
| 3423[2] | **Captain William (IRE)** (IABalding) **2-8-7** WNewnes | 1¼ | **2** | | 82 | — |
| | **Vision Of Spirit (USA)** (HJentzsch,Germany) **2-8-12** PSchiergen | 6 | **3** | | 73 | — |
| 2503[3] | **Maladerie (IRE)** (MRChannon) **2-8-12** RHughes | 1¼ | **4** | | 71 | — |
| | | | | | | **6 Rn** |

**1m 23.65** TOTE 47DM: 22DM 21DM OWNER A & R Ubber BRED Sheikh Ahmed Al Maktoum
**3423 Captain William (IRE)**, held up in the early stages, made headway to take the lead a furlong and a half out. Headed by the winner 100 yards out, he could find no extra.
**2503 Maladerie (IRE)** held a slight lead a furlong and a half out, but was soon beaten.

### 3905a SPRETI-RENNEN (Gp 3) (4-Y.O+)
3-25 (3-29) **1m 2f** £33,784.00 (£13,514.00: £6,757.00: £3,604.00)

| | | | | SP | RR | SF |
|---|---|---|---|---|---|---|
| 3395a[6] | **Artan (IRE)** (MRolke,Germany) **4-8-11** PSchiergen | — | **1** | | 119 | — |
| 3395a[5] | **Devil River Peek (USA)** (BSchutz,Germany) **4-8-13** AStarke | 4 | **2** | | 115 | — |
| 2730[2] | **Musetta (IRE)** (CEBrittain) **4-8-7** BDoyle | 1¾ | **3** | | 106 | — |
| 623a[4] | **Penny Drops** (LordHuntingdon) **7-8-7** ASuborics (btn approx 7½l) | | **6** | | — | — |
| 3397a[5] | **Silca Blanka (IRE)** (MRChannon) **4-8-11** RHughes (btn over 9 3/4l) | | **9** | | — | — |
| | | | | | | **13 Rn** |

**2m 1.55** TOTE 48DM: 15DM 15DM 15DM OWNER Stall Brandenburg BRED J. Brennen
**Artan (IRE)**, always up with the pace, was in third place entering the straight and, soon taking the lead, ran on strongly to the finish.
**2730 Musetta (IRE)**, soon ridden along and tracking the leader, made headway to take the lead over three furlongs out. She was unable to hold the winner's challenge two furlongs out, and could only run on at one pace in the closing stages.
**623a Penny Drops**, prominent in the early stages, was in fourth place as the field turned into the straight, but weakened going to the final furlong.
**3397a Silca Blanka (IRE)** was in touch until three furlongs out and finished the race lame.

## 2842a-ARLINGTON PARK (Chicago, USA) (L-H) (Firm)
### Saturday August 24th

### 3906a NEWBURY H'CAP (Listed) (3-Y.O+)
9-20 (9-20) **1m 110y** £38,710.00 (£12,903.00: £7,097.00: £3,871.00)

| | | | | SP | RR | SF |
|---|---|---|---|---|---|---|
| | **Pennine Ridge (USA)** (DDonk,USA) **5-8-0** JVelasquez | — | **1** | | 108 | — |

| | | | | SP | RR | SF |
|---|---|---|---|---|---|---|
| | **Homing Pigeon (USA)** (HVanier,USA) **6-8-2** RAlbarado | ½ | **2** | | 109 | — |
| | **Joy of Glory (USA)** (RHessJnr,USA) **7-8-4** KDesormeaux | ½ | **3** | | 110 | — |
| 2354[3] | **Rio Duvida** (DRLoder) **3-7-12** SSellers (btn over 27l) | | **9** | | — | — |

**9 Rn**

**1m 41.56** P-M 10.80: (1-2) 4.80 4.60 (1-2-3) 3.20 2.80 2.20 OWNER December Hill Farm BRED A. Brancato & P. Sengupta
**2354 Rio Duvida** was in touch until weakening over three furlongs out.

## 3907a BEVERLY D STKS (Gp 1) (3-Y.O+ F & M)
10-45 (10-46) **1m 1f 110y** £193,548.00 (£64,516.00: £35,484.00: £19,355.00)

| | | | | SP | RR | SF |
|---|---|---|---|---|---|---|
| 3395a* | **Timarida (IRE)** (JOxx,Ireland) **4-8-11** JPMurtagh | — | **1** | | 120 | — |
| | **Perfect Arc (USA)** (APenna,USA) **4-8-11** JVelasquez | 2½ | **2** | | 116 | — |
| | **Alpride (IRE)** (RMcAnally,USA) **5-8-11** CMcCarron | 3½ | **3** | | 110 | — |
| 3030a* | **Khalisa (IRE)** (AdeRoyerDupre,France) **3-8-5** GMosse | 1 | **4** | | 109 | — |

**10 Rn**

**1m 54.06** P-M 5.20 (coupled with Khalisa): (1-2) 3.00 5.00 (1-2-3)2.80 4.20 7.20 OWNER Aga Khan (CURRABEG) BRED H.H. Aga Khan's Studs S.C.
**3395a* Timarida (IRE)** was held up in the early stages and, always travelling well, made good headway, but found little room over two furlongs out. Taking the lead inside the final furlong, she was ridden out to score. This tough filly has now won races in France, Germany, Canada and the United States, but may well return home for the Irish Champion Stakes.
**3030a* Khalisa (IRE)**, always in a prominent position, took third place as the field entered the straight and, ridden along, seemed slightly one-paced inside the final two furlongs.

# 3903a-DEAUVILLE (France) (R-H) (Good)
## Saturday August 24th

## 3908a PRIX DU CALVADOS (Gp 3) (2-Y.O F)
2-20 (2-20) **7f** £28,986.00 (£10,540.00: £5,270.00)

| | | | | SP | RR | SF |
|---|---|---|---|---|---|---|
| 3201a[4] | **Shigeru Summit** (CBoutin,France) **2-8-9** MBoutin | — | **1** | | 102 | 70 |
| | **Dame D'Harvard (USA)** (RCollet,France) **2-8-9** OPeslier | 1½ | **2** | | 99 | 67 |
| 3566a* | **Green Lady (IRE)** (AFabre,France) **2-8-9** TJarnet | hd | **3** | | 98 | 66 |
| 3230* | **Double Park (FR)** (MJohnston) **2-8-9** MHills (btn approx 8l) | | **8** | | — | — |

**10 Rn**

**1m 25.9** (1.90) P-M 17.40F: 4.60F 3.00F 2.00F (93.70F) OWNER R. Tanaka BRED Stud-on-the-Chart
**Shigeru Summit** was held up for a late run and dominated the final stages. The change of tactics seemed to work as she had previously finished fourth to Ocean Ridge in the Robert Papin. She is likely to run next in the Prix d'Aumale.
**Dame D'Harvard (USA)** took the lead a furlong out, but could not hold the winner inside the final furlong.
**Green Lady (IRE)** is a fine-looking filly. She was unlucky in this race as she did not get a run until the furlong marker, and by then it was too late. She looks one to follow in the future.
**3230* Double Park (FR)** was prominent for the first five furlongs, but was a beaten force soon after. This was a below-par performance and this race is best forgotten.

## 3909a PRIX DE LIEUREY (Listed) (3-Y.O F)
2-50 (2-48) **1m** £18,445.00 (£6,324.00: £3,953.00)

| | | | | SP | RR | SF |
|---|---|---|---|---|---|---|
| | **Moon Is Up (USA)** (JEHammond,France) **3-9-0** CAsmussen | — | **1** | | 98 | 12 |
| | **Daneskaya** (AFabre,France) **3-9-0** TJarnet | hd | **2** | | 98 | 12 |
| 3210[3] | **Miss Riviera** (GWragg) **3-9-0** MHills | ½ | **3** | | 97 | 11 |
| 3127[6] | **Satin Bell** (JLDunlop) **3-9-0** TThulliez (btn over 1 3/4l) | | **5** | | — | — |

**8 Rn**

**1m 44.3** (8.30) P-M 2.70F: 1.40F 1.40F 1.90F (5.50F) OWNER Niarchos Family (CHANTILLY)
**3210 Miss Riviera** raced in mid-division and ran on really well in the final stages, but could not get to the first two. A listed race should be within her capabilities.
**3127 Satin Bell** was always prominent, but could not quicken in the final furlong.

## 3910a PRIX MERCEDES-BENZ H'CAP (3-Y.O+)
3-20 (3-23) **5f** £22,398.00

| | | | | SP | RR | SF |
|---|---|---|---|---|---|---|
| | **Owen Meany (FR)** (RCrepon,France) **4-9-6** AJunk | — | **1** | | 89 | 72 |
| | **Arctic Starry (FR)** (France) **4-9-1b[1]** TGillet | 1½ | **2** | | 79 | 62 |
| 3569a* | **Bold Effort (FR)** (KOCunningham-Brown) **4-9-5** FSanchez | s.h | **3** | | 83 | 66 |

**16 Rn**

**58.2 secs** (1.70) P-M 4.40F: 2.30F 3.90F 5.40F (33.30) OWNER Mr H. Honore BRED H. Honore
**3569a* Bold Effort (FR)** was always up with the pace and stuck to his guns to the bitter end in this competitive handicap. He had previously won at Clairefontaine and should have a bright future in this sort of race if he stays in France.

# 3906a-ARLINGTON PARK (Chicago, USA) (L-H) (Firm)
## Sunday August 25th

## 3911a SECRETARIAT STKS (Gp 1) (3-Y.O)
9-45 (9-36) **1m 2f** £193,548.00 (£64,516.00: £35,484.00: £19,355.00)

| | | | | SP | RR | SF |
|---|---|---|---|---|---|---|
| | **Marlin (USA)** (DWLukas,USA) **3-8-2** SSellers | — | **1** | | 118 | — |
| | **Trial City (USA)** (WMott,USA) **3-9-0** PDay | 4 | **2** | | 124 | — |
| 2275a[2] | **Dancing Fred (USA)** (DKWeld,Ireland) **3-8-2** MGuidry | hd | **3** | | 111 | — |
| 2825a[2] | **Pro Trader (USA)** (DKWeld,Ireland) **3-8-2** MJKinane (btn over 4½l) | | **5** | | — | — |

| | | | SP | RR | SF |
|---|---|---|---|---|---|
| 3387a* | **Regal Archive (IRE)** (PWChapple-Hyam) **3-8-5** CMcCarron (btn 7½l) | **8** | | — | — |
| 3124[9] | **Bahamian Knight (CAN)** (DRLoder) **3-8-5** PatEddery (btn 8½l) | **9** | | — | — |
| 3196a[6] | **His Excellence (USA)** (APO'Brien,Ireland) **3-8-2** RAlbarado (btn 13l) | **10** | | — | — |

**10 Rn**

**2m 1.09** P-M 16.40: (1-2) 5.80 3.00 (1-2-3) 4.00 2.40 2.80 OWNER Michael Tabor BRED Gilbert G. Campbell
**Dancing Fred (USA)** raced in last place until well over a furlong out. He was forced to come round the wide outside of the field and stayed on well to the finish.
**2825a Pro Trader (USA)** led the way for the first two furlongs, and disputed it for the following four with the eventual winner. He was in third place entering the straight, but had nothing left in the closing stages.
**3387a* Regal Archive (IRE)** was disappointing here, and could never mount an effective challenge.
**2480a Bahamian Knight (CAN)** never got into the race and was always towards the rear.
**3196a His Excellence (USA)** kept up with the pace for the first mile, but soon faded.

## 3912a ARLINGTON MILLION XVI (Gp 1) (3-Y.O+)
10-45 (10-46) **1m 2f** £387,097.00 (£129,032.00: £70,968.00: £38,710.00)

| | | | | SP | RR | SF |
|---|---|---|---|---|---|---|
| | **Mecke (USA)** (ETortora,USA) **4-9-0** RobbieDavis | — | **1** | | 128 | — |
| | **Awad (USA)** (DDonk,USA) **6-9-0** CMcCarron | 2 | **2** | | 125 | — |
| | **Sandpit (BRA)** (RMandella,USA) **7-9-0** CNakatani | 2¼ | **3** | | 121 | — |
| 3431[4] | **Glory of Dancer** (PAKelleway) **3-8-8** MJKinane | 1¼ | **4** | | 121 | — |
| 3395a[7] | **Needle Gun (IRE)** (CEBrittain) **6-9-0** SSellers (btn approx 11½l) | | **7** | | — | — |
| 2546[6] | **Valanour (IRE)** (AdeRoyerDupre,France) **4-9-0** GMosse (btn approx 26½l) | | **8** | | — | — |
| 3196a[4] | **Prince of Andros (USA)** (DRLoder) **6-9-0** PatEddery (btn approx 35½l) | | **9** | | — | — |

**9 Rn**

**2m 0.49** P-M 33.00: (1-2) 10.20 4.80 (1-2-3)4.60 3.00 2.40 OWNER James Lewis Jnr
**3431 Glory of Dancer** was in sixth place with little room as the field entered the straight. Switched right at the furlong pole, he stayed on well.
**3395a Needle Gun (IRE)**, a well-travelled horse, raced in second place, but could only run on at the one pace from over two furlongs out.
**2546 Valanour (IRE)** was fifth into the straight, but soon weakened.
**3196a Prince of Andros (USA)** was up with the pace in the early stages, but weakened well over three furlongs out.

# 3904a-BADEN-BADEN (Germany) (L-H) (Good)
## Sunday August 25th

## 3913a FURSTENBERG-RENNEN (Gp 3) (3-Y.O)
3-25 (3-27) **1m 3f** £33,784.00 (£13,514.00: £6,757.00)

| | | | | SP | RR | SF |
|---|---|---|---|---|---|---|
| 2478a* | **Wurftaube (GER)** (HRemmert,Germany) **3-8-9** KWoodburn | — | **1** | | 108+ | — |
| | **Narrabeth (IRE)** (HJentzsch,Germany) **3-8-13** THellier (fin 3rd, 1¼l: plcd 2nd) | | **2** | | 108 | — |
| 3203a[4] | **Surako (GER)** (UweStoltefuss,Germany) **3-8-13** PSchiergen (fin 2nd, 3/4l: disq: plcd 3rd) | | **3** | | 111 | — |

**7 Rn**

**2m 16.18** TOTE 27DM: 11DM 12DM 10DM OWNER Gestut Ravensberg BRED Gestut Ravensberg
**Wurftaube (GER)** extended her winning distance to five with this impressive performance. She was always travelling well within herself and moved smoothly past the German Derby second Surako 100 yards from home. She is almost certain to stay in training and connections, who do not want her to race outside Germany, may give her one more race this year, possibly in the Deutsches St Leger.
**Narrabeth (IRE)** was hampered by the hard-ridden Surako, and the Stewards promoted him to second place.
**2109a Surako (GER)** was demoted to third by the Stewards, and his jockey received a one-day ban, despite trying his best to keep the colt straight.

# 3908a-DEAUVILLE (France) (R-H) (Good)
## Sunday August 25th

## 3914a PRIX DE MEAUTRY (Gp 3) (3-Y.O+)
1-55 (1-55) **6f** £28,986.00 (£10,540.00: £5,270.00: £2,635.00)

| | | | | SP | RR | SF |
|---|---|---|---|---|---|---|
| 2841a[2] | **Kistena (FR)** (MmeCHead,France) **3-8-8** RLibert | — | **1** | | 116 | 79 |
| 2115[9] | **Titus Livius (FR)** (JEPease,France) **3-8-11** CAsmussen | 2½ | **2** | | 112 | 75 |
| 2271a[2] | **Bashaayeash (IRE)** (CLaffon-Parias,France) **4-9-0** GGuignard | hd | **3** | | 112 | 78 |
| 3562a[3] | **Leap for Joy** (JHMGosden) **4-8-11** LDettori | s.h | **4** | | 109 | 75 |
| 2692[6] | **Warning Star** (BWHills) **4-8-11** TQuinn (btn approx 5¼l) | | **8** | | — | — |

**9 Rn**

**1m 10.5** (2.50) P-M 3.10F: 1.20F 1.40F 1.80F OWNER Wertheimer Brothers (CHANTILLY) BRED J.Wertheimer & Frere
**2841a Kistena (FR)** won this race with plenty in hand. She burst into the lead just over a furlong out and drew clear to win comfortably. She was given an excellent ride by her young jockey, who was winning his first ever Group event. As connections wish to avoid stablemate Anabaa, she will now be going for the Prix de Seine-et-Oise at Maisons-Laffitte. She looks a very useful sprinter.
**1581a Titus Livius (FR)** has not developed much since he was a two-year-old, but put up his best performance of the year. Held up in the early stages, he ran on really well in the final furlong without troubling the winner. There may well be another Group race in this colt who may take on the winner again in the Prix Seine-et-Oise, but is more likely to go for the Diadem Stakes at Ascot.
**2271a Bashaayeash (IRE)** was slightly hampered when crossed by the winner a furlong and a half out and could only run on at one pace in the final furlong. He may be suited by a slightly longer distance.
**3562a Leap for Joy** was outpaced early on, but stayed on in the final furlong. This was a good effort.
**2692 Warning Star** was kept just in behind the leaders, but could not quicken with her rivals.

## 3915a GRAND PRIX DE DEAUVILLE LANCEL (Gp 2) (3-Y.O+)
2-30 (2-29) **1m 4f 110y** £65,876.00 (£26,350.00: £13,175.00: £6,588.00)

| | | | | SP | RR | SF |
|---|---|---|---|---|---|---|
| 3070[8] | **Strategic Choice (USA)** (PFICole) **5-9-11** TQuinn (racd in 3rd tl led after 7f: wnt wd ent st: rdn 2f out: all out) | — | **1** | | 124 | 93 |

| | Horse | Btn | Pos | SP | RR | SF |
|---|---|---|---|---|---|---|
| 2665a* | **Taratör (USA)** (ELellouche,France) **3-8-10** OPeslier (mid div: rdn & lost pl 3f out: styd on strly fr 2f out: nvr nrr) | nk | **2** | | 119 | 78 |
| 3749a[3] | **Percutant** (DSmaga,France) **5-9-4** DBoeuf (hld up in rr: last st: rdn & r.o strly fr over 1f out: nrst fin) | s.h | **3** | | 117 | 86 |
| 3392a* | **Helen Of Spain** (AFabre,France) **4-9-4** TJarnet (racd in 6th: 5th & rdn st: outpcd tl r.o fnl f) | 1 | **4** | | 115 | 84 |
| 3035a[2] | **Leeds (IRE)** (HVandePoele,France) **4-9-4** SGuillot (hld up: kpt on u.p fnl 2f) | 1½ | **5** | | 113 | 82 |
| 3746a[8] | **Oliviero (FR)** (AVergeade,France) **3-8-7** MBoutin (hld up: rdn over 2f out. one pce fnl f) | hd | **6** | | 112 | 71 |
| 3567a* | **Water Poet (IRE)** (AFabre,France) **3-8-7** LDettori (racd in 4th: rdn over 2f out: one pce) | hd | **7** | | 112 | 71 |
| 1757a[9] | **High Baroque (IRE)** (PWChapple-Hyam) **3-8-7** JReid (set stdy pce 7f: 2nd st: racd on ins: rdn & one pce) | 3 | **8** | | 108 | 67 |
| | **Matarun (IRE)** (HVandePoele,France) **4-9-4** AJunk (prom: 3rd & rdn st: sn wknd) | 3 | **9** | | 105 | 74 |

**9 Rn**

**2m 44.3** (5.80) P-M 8.00F: 2.20F 1.30F 2.30F (11.40F) OWNER Mr M. Arbib (WHATCOMBE) BRED M. Arbib

**3070 Strategic Choice (USA)** put up a top-class performance. Carrying a Group One penalty, he took command five furlongs out and stayed on to the end. It is a mystery as to why he does not always run up to his best, but he did it the hard way on this occasion, and looked thoroughly genuine in the process. A repeat of this performance could see him involved in the finish of the Arc de Triomphe.

**2665a* Tarator (USA)** proved on this occasion that he has considerable class. He was not suited by the lack of pace in the early stages, and was slightly boxed in when eager to challenge soon after entering the straight. He was putting in his best work at the finish where he was catching the winner. He is still an exciting prospect and seems to improve with every race. Now that he has proved he is a force to be reckoned with at around twelve furlongs, he may well be supplemented for the Arc de Triomphe.

**3749a Percutant** has two ways of running, but put up one of his better efforts on this occasion. Having been held up for a late run, he was staying on well at the finish.

**3392a* Helen Of Spain** was given every chance, but found this distance a bit sharp, particularly as there was little early pace. She requires a fast-run twelve furlongs or even longer to be seen at her best. The Prix de Royallieu now looks on the cards for her.

**1757a High Baroque (IRE)** was a reluctant leader as there were no other takers. He set a steady pace until five out and then just stayed on in the straight. He requires softer ground to show his best, and he may well be aimed at the Jockey Club Gold Cup in Milan.

## 3916a PRIX DE LA NONETTE (Gp 3) (3-Y.O F)

3-40 (3-39) **1m 2f** £28,986.00 (£10,540.00: £5,270.00: £2,635.00)

| | Horse | Btn | Pos | SP | RR | SF |
|---|---|---|---|---|---|---|
| 1949a[7] | **Luna Wells (IRE)** (AFabre,France) **3-9-0** TJarnet (fin 3rd, 1¼l: awrdd r) | — | **1** | | 109 | 71 |
| 3409* | **Bint Salsabil (USA)** (JLDunlop) **3-9-0** WCarson (fin 1st: disq: plcd 2nd) | | **2** | | 111 | 73 |
| 1567a[12] | **Bint Shadayid (USA)** (SbinSuroor) **3-9-0** LDettori (fin 2nd, nk: disq: plcd 3rd) | | **3** | | 111 | 73 |
| 2609[9] | **Honest Guest (IRE)** (MHTompkins) **3-9-0** TQuinn | 1½ | **4** | | 106 | 68 |

**6 Rn**

**2m 10.7** (5.70) P-M 1.70F: 1.10F 2.00F OWNER Mr J-L Lagardere (CHANTILLY) BRED S.N.C. Lagardere Elevage et al

STEWARDS' ENQUIRY Dettori susp. 3-6/9/96 (careless riding). Carson susp. 3-6/9/96 (careless riding).

**1396a* Luna Wells (IRE)** was awarded this race by the Stewards. She came to challenge between Bint Salsabil and Bint Shadayid just over a furlong out, but then got hit in the face with a whip and squeezed. This cost her her chance, and she just stayed on in the closing stages. The Stewards' decision was rather controversial, but they thought that the winner and runner-up were at fault for different reasons. This was her comeback after a rest of over two months, and she now heads for the Prix Vermeille.

**3409* Bint Salsabil (USA)** ran out the winner by a neck, but was subsequently placed second as the Stewards thought she edged left in the final stages and hampered Luna Wells. She may well be aimed at the Sun Chariot Stakes.

**1567a Bint Shadayid (USA)** raced in third place until challenging all the way up the straight. She was relegated from second to third by the Stewards. This was a decent effort considering she had been off the track since mid-May. She should improve for this outing and may also go for the Sun Chariot Stakes.

**2609 Honest Guest (IRE)** led until early in the straight, but could only stay on at one pace. She would have preferred softer ground.

DS

# 2671a-SAN SIRO (Milan, Italy) (R-H) (Soft)

## Sunday August 25th

## 3917a PREMIO NICO E VITTORIO CASTELLINI (4-Y.O+)

**1m 2f** £10,150.00 (£4,466.00: £2,436.00)

| | Horse | Btn | Pos | SP | RR | SF |
|---|---|---|---|---|---|---|
| 1135a[8] | **Tarhelm (IRE)** (GColleo,Italy) **4-9-8** MLatorre | — | **1** | | 113 | — |
| 2111a[4] | **Pay Me Back (IRE)** (GVerricelli,Italy) **6-8-11** SDettori | hd | **2** | | 102 | — |
| 1392a[3] | **Baujes (IRE)** (JHeloury,Italy) **6-8-11** GForte | 6½ | **3** | | 91 | — |
| 2864[3] | **Suranom (IRE)** (LMCumani) **4-9-4** FJovine (btn over 9l) | | **5** | | — | — |

**5 Rn**

**2m 5.3** (11.30) TOTE 76L: 22L 16L OWNER No Owner BRED Scuderia Andy Capp in Ireland

**2864 Suranom (IRE)** led and disputed the lead for the majority of the race, but was headed and weakened approaching the final furlong.

# 3263-CHESTER (L-H) (Good to soft)

## Friday August 30th

WEATHER: cloudy WIND: fresh against

## 3918 ARTHUR O'HARE APPRENTICE H'CAP (0-70) (3-Y.O+) (Class E)

2-10 (2-10) **1m 2f 75y** £2,962.25 (£908.00: £451.50: £223.25) Stalls: High GOING: 0.11 sec per fur (G)

| | Horse | Btn | Pos | SP | RR | SF |
|---|---|---|---|---|---|---|
| 3780[2] | **Minster Glory (41)** (MWEasterby) **5-8-2b[1]** CLowther(3) (plld hrd: sn led: rdn over 1f out: hld on gamely) | — | **1** | 11/4[1] | 51 | 32 |
| 3327[5] | **Hareb (USA) (65)** (JWHills) **3-9-4** AMcCarthy(2) (a.p: effrt on ins & ev ch over 1f out: kpt on towards fin) | 1 | **2** | 8/1[3] | 74 | 47 |
| 2980[7] | **Time For Tea (IRE) (62)** (CACyzer) **3-8-7**(8) PGoode(4) (chsd ldrs: effrt & rdn ent st: jnd wnr & hung 1f out: no ex) | 1¼ | **3** | 25/1 | 69 | 42 |
| 3279[8] | **Second Colours (USA) (63)** (MCPipe) **6-9-10** CScudder(6) (dropped rr ½-wy: hdwy 3f out: nt rch ldrs) | 13 | **4** | 6/1[2] | 49 | 30 |
| 3500[2] | **Rasayel (USA) (63)** (PDEvans) **6-9-10** DavidO'Neill(1) (rn in snatches: rdn 3f out: sn lost tch) | ½ | **5** | 11/4[1] | 49 | 30 |
| 2515[5] | **Shalta Chief (46)** (EHOwenjun) **4-8-7** RBrisland(7) (lw: in tch to ½-wy: sn lost pl) | hd | **6** | 25/1 | 32 | 13 |
| 3479[6] | **La Pellegrina (IRE) (66)** (PWChapple-Hyam) **3-8-11**(8) RCody-Boutcher(8) (hld up: effrt & drvn over 3f out: wknd 2f out) | 1 | **7** | 8/1[3] | 50 | 23 |

| | | | | SP | RR | SF |
|---|---|---|---|---|---|---|
| 2001[6] | **Crabbie's Pride (70)** (MGMeagher) **3-9-9** TFinn(9) (a in rr) | ¾ | **8** | 10/1 | 53 | 26 |
| *3063*[10] | **Kingfisher Brave (64)** (MGMeagher) **3-9-0**(3) RStudholme(5) (lw: a in rr: t.o) | 8 | **9** | 10/1 | 34 | 7 |
| | | | | (SP 115.7%) | | **9 Rn** |

**2m 16.86** (8.16) CSF £23.06 CT £402.56 TOTE £3.50: £1.40 £2.00 £4.30 (£14.70) Trio £64.40 OWNER Mr P. A. H. Hartley (SHERIFF HUTTON) BRED A. and M. Scarfe
WEIGHT FOR AGE 3yo-8lb

**3780 Minster Glory** pulled hard in the first-time blinkers and made it all, staying on extremely well to put his lenient handicap mark to full use. (11/4)
**3327 Hareb (USA)**, a winner on the All-Weather, appreciated the rain-softened ground and was staying on best of all inside the final furlong. (8/1)
**2340 Time For Tea (IRE)**, trying a longer trip, looked the likely winner when delivering his challenge into the final furlong, but she hung off a true line when shaken up, and failed to last home. With stronger handling, she is worth another try at this trip. (25/1)
**3279 Second Colours (USA)** began to pick up three furlongs out, but the progress was always too slow. (6/1)
**3500 Rasayel (USA)**, given a very inept ride, was struggling to stay in touch from some way out. (11/4)

## 3919 E.B.F. O'HARE AVENUE MAIDEN STKS (2-Y.O) (Class D)
2-45 (2-46) **7f 2y** £3,548.00 (£1,064.00: £512.00: £236.00) Stalls: Low GOING: 0.11 sec per fur (G)

| | | | | SP | RR | SF |
|---|---|---|---|---|---|---|
| 3349[2] | **Amid Albadu (USA)** (JLDunlop) **2-9-0** WCarson(4) (lw: s.i.s: sn drvn along: hdwy 2f out: swtchd lft & led ins fnl f: pushed out) | — | **1** | 5/4[1] | 75 | 44 |
| 2057[7] | **Nominator Lad** (BAMcMahon) **2-9-0** JFortune(1) (bit bkwd: led over 2f: led over 2f out tl rdn & hdd ins fnl f) | 1¼ | **2** | 33/1 | 72? | 41 |
| 3595[4] | **Count Roberto (USA)** (PWChapple-Hyam) **2-8-11**(3) RHavlin(5) (lw: a.p: led over 4f out tl over 2f out: ev ch ins fnl f: unable qckn) | 1 | **3** | 13/8[2] | 70 | 39 |
| 3069[8] | **Gentleman's Word (USA)** (MRStoute) **2-9-0** KFallon(6) (bit bkwd: hld up: hdwy 3f out: rdn & ev ch appr fnl f: kpt on) | hd | **4** | 9/2[3] | 70 | 39 |
| 2712[6] | **Eponine** (MRChannon) **2-8-9** JFEgan(3) (hld up in tch: effrt & rdn 3f out: wknd appr fnl f) | 2 | **5** | 16/1 | 60 | 29 |
| | **Nesbet** (BRCambidge) **2-9-0** ACulhane(2) (small: lt-f: bit bkwd: s.s: hdwy 4f out: wknd over 2f out: sn t.o) | dist | **6** | 33/1 | — | — |
| | | | | (SP 112.5%) | | **6 Rn** |

**1m 30.59** (5.39) CSF £25.72 TOTE £2.20: £1.30 £6.30 (£25.30) OWNER Mr Hamdan Al Maktoum (ARUNDEL) BRED Airlie Stud

**3349 Amid Albadu (USA)** responded to a forceful ride over this longer trip and proved much the stronger in the battle to the line. (5/4: 11/10-11/)
**Nominator Lad** looked to need this after a ten-week break, but turned in a very pleasing performance. If there is any more improvement to come, he ought to be able to win races. (33/1)
**3595 Count Roberto (USA)** had plenty of use made of him, but was found wanting when the chips were down. He did nothing wrong though and will win his share of races. (13/8)
**Gentleman's Word (USA)**, who made his debut in a hot event at Ascot, is still far from the finished article, but shaped with promise and is heading in the right direction. (9/2)
**2712 Eponine** could never really get herself into the action and had to admit these colts too strong. (16/1)

## 3920 O'HARE CUP RATED STKS H'CAP (0-95) (3-Y.O+) (Class C)
3-15 (3-15) **7f 2y** £7,910.08 (£2,950.72: £1,435.36: £608.80: £264.40: £126.64) Stalls: Low GOING: 0.11 sec per fur (G)

| | | | | SP | RR | SF |
|---|---|---|---|---|---|---|
| 3709* | **Concer Un (93)** (SCWilliams) **4-9-10** 3x JTate(4) (b.nr fore: hld up: hdwy u.p 2f out: swtchd rt appr fnl f: r.o strly to ld post) | — | **1** | 11/2[1] | 104 | 78 |
| 3783[13] | **My Best Valentine (88)** (JWhite) **6-9-5** WJO'Connor(6) (lw: trckd ldrs: rdn to ld 1f out: eased & ct last stride) | s.h | **2** | 14/1 | 99+ | 73 |
| 3210[5] | **Albert The Bear (78)** (JBerry) **3-8-4** JCarroll(5) (chsd ldr: led ent st to 1f out: no ex fnl f) | 1¾ | **3** | 10/1 | 85 | 54 |
| 3322* | **Divina Luna (88)** (JWHills) **3-8-11**(3) MHenry(3) (lw: a.p: rdn & ev ch over 1f out: one pce fnl f) | nk | **4** | 13/2[2] | 94 | 63 |
| 3263[2] | **Chickawicka (IRE) (87)** (BPalling) **5-9-4** TSprake(2) (led: sn drvn along: hdd ent st: one pce fnl f) | 1 | **5** | 11/2[1] | 91 | 65 |
| 3210[12] | **Prends Ca (IRE) (88)** (RHannon) **3-9-0** KFallon(10) (hld up: hdwy over 2f out: sn hrd rdn: nt rch ldrs) | 1¾ | **6** | 10/1 | 88 | 57 |
| 3770* | **Queens Consul (IRE) (83)** (BSRothwell) **6-9-0** 3x MFenton(8) (trckd ldrs on outside: drvn along 3f out: wknd fnl 2f) | 3½ | **7** | 11/1 | 75 | 49 |
| 3639[9] | **Champagne Grandy (79)** (MRChannon) **6-8-10** JFEgan(14) (nvr nr ldrs) | 1¾ | **8** | 16/1 | 67 | 41 |
| 3295[8] | **Sualtach (IRE) (85)** (RHollinshead) **3-8-11** JFortune(1) (hld up: hdwy over 3f out: n.m.r & wknd wl over 1f out) | nk | **9** | 20/1 | 72 | 41 |
| 3622[8] | **Highborn (IRE) (90)** (PSFelgate) **7-9-7** GHind(9) (lw: hld up mid div: hrd drvn & wknd wl over 1f out) | 1½ | **10** | 10/1 | 74 | 48 |
| 3693[18] | **Lunar Mist (87)** (MartynMeade) **3-8-6**(7) DSweeney(7) (a in rr) | s.h | **11** | 20/1 | 71 | 40 |
| 3833[7] | **Lay The Blame (77)** (WJarvis) **3-8-0**(3) FLynch(11) (s.i.s: a bhd) | 1 | **12** | 16/1 | 58 | 27 |
| 3426[5] | **Ocean Grove (IRE) (79)** (PWChapple-Hyam) **3-8-2**(3) RHavlin(13) (a bhd & outpcd) | 1 | **13** | 12/1 | 58 | 27 |
| 3210[16] | **Royal Mark (IRE) (89)** (JWWatts) **3-9-1** WRSwinburn(12) (lw: hld up: effrt over 2f out: sn rdn & no imp) | hd | **14** | 7/1[3] | 68 | 37 |
| | | | | (SP 127.9%) | | **14 Rn** |

**1m 28.51** (3.31) CSF £76.74 CT £698.54 TOTE £6.00: £2.50 £5.00 £2.50 (£132.10) Trio £207.40 OWNER Miss L. J. Ward (NEWMARKET) BRED Lloyd Bros
WEIGHT FOR AGE 3yo-5lb
STEWARDS' ENQUIRY O'Connor susp. 9-14/9/96 (failure to ensure best possible placing).

**3709* Concer Un**, winning for the first time at this slightly shorter trip, defied the penalty incurred for his hard-fought York win, and connections are enjoying a bonanza. (11/2)
**3232 My Best Valentine**, buried in the pack but always within striking distance, responded to pressure to lead into the final furlong. With the race seemingly won, he was eased a few strides too soon and, to the amazement of almost everyone, came out second best in the photo. His jockey admitted that this defeat was down to him. (14/1)
**3210 Albert The Bear** got the better of the leader on the home turn and went hell-bent for the line, but he was unable to hold on. This was another good effort and there could be more success to come. (10/1)
**3322* Divina Luna** was always in the right place but, when the tempo increased early in the straight, she just lacked that bit extra. (13/2)
**3263 Chickawicka (IRE)** had to work hard to keep a determined rival at bay, and it left him with very little in hand. (11/2)
**2585 Prends Ca (IRE)**, successful here in the spring, needed all the help she could get to improve on the approach to the straight, but she was unable to pick up sufficiently to land a blow. (10/1)

## 3921 JANI CHAMPIONSHIP CONDITIONS STKS (2-Y.O F) (Class C)

3-50 (3-50) **6f 18y** £4,938.00 (£1,842.00: £896.00: £380.00: £165.00: £79.00) Stalls: Low GOING: 0.11 sec per fur (G)

| | | | | SP | RR | SF |
|---|---|---|---|---|---|---|
| 2770* | **Sambac (USA) (100)** (HRACecil) **2-9-2** WRyan(1) (trckd ldrs: led wl over 1f out: sn clr: easily) | — | **1** | 6/5[1] | 88+ | 47 |
| 3613[2] | **Olympic Spirit (100)** (JBerry) **2-9-2** JCarroll(3) (b.hind: lw: ½-reard s: hdwy 3f out: rdn & outpcd fnl f) | 5 | **2** | 7/4[2] | 75 | 34 |
| 1433[3] | **Ruby Tuesday** (BAMcMahon) **2-8-8** JFortune(2) (bkwd: slt ld over 4f: outpcd fnl f) | hd | **3** | 20/1 | 67? | 26 |
| 3660[3] | **Martine (70)** (ABailey) **2-8-5**(3) DWright(4) (bhd & outpcd tl r.o wl nr fin) | nk | **4** | 33/1 | 66 | 25 |
| 3468[3] | **Stone Flower (USA)** (PWChapple-Hyam) **2-8-8**(3) RHavlin(6) (hld up: rdn over 3f out: nt clr run ent st: no imp) | ¾ | **5** | 5/1[3] | 67 | 26 |
| 3483[6] | **Weet Ees Girl (IRE) (84)** (PDEvans) **2-8-11** JFEgan(5) (disp ld over 3f: sn rdn & wknd) | 10 | **6** | 20/1 | 41 | — |
| | | | | (SP 110.9%) | | **6 Rn** |

**1m 17.86** (4.56) CSF £3.55 TOTE £2.00: £1.20 £1.70 (£1.70) OWNER Mr K. Abdulla (NEWMARKET) BRED Juddmonte Farms

**2770* Sambac (USA)** had more on her plate here, but she brushed aside her rivals with contempt. She would seem a very progressive filly. (6/5)

**3613 Olympic Spirit**, up in the air as the stalls were released, recovered soon after halfway, but earlier exertions told when the winner quickened. (7/4)

**1433 Ruby Tuesday** looked burly after three months off, but she ran by far her best race yet. She will soon be paying her way. (20/1)

**3660 Martine**, taken along faster than she cared for at this first attempt at the trip, was going nowhere until making progress up the inside rail in the last 200 yards. (33/1)

**3468 Stone Flower (USA)**, driven along to try and reach a challenging position soon after halfway, was making hard work of it when denied a clear passage soon after entering the straight. Forced to check, she was unable to make her presence felt. (5/1)

## 3922 O'HARE SOBRIETY SALVER H'CAP (0-80) (3-Y.O+) (Class D)

4-20 (4-20) **1m 7f 195y** £4,328.00 (£1,304.00: £632.00: £296.00) Stalls: Low GOING: 0.11 sec per fur (G)

| | | | | SP | RR | SF |
|---|---|---|---|---|---|---|
| 3598[2] | **Izza (54)** (WStorey) **5-8-5** NKennedy(1) (hld up & bhd: stdy hdwy 5f out: led ins fnl f: styd on strly) | — | **1** | 4/1[2] | 64 | 42 |
| 3710[14] | **Floating Line (67)** (EJAlston) **8-9-4** KFallon(9) (hld up in tch: led over 2f out: hrd rdn & hdd ins fnl f: kpt on) | nk | **2** | 10/1 | 77 | 55 |
| 3486[7] | **The Swan (80)** (JLDunlop) **3-9-3** TSprake(6) (b: led over 5f: hrd drvn & hmpd over 2f out: rallied towards fin) | 1½ | **3** | 13/2 | 88 | 52 |
| 2986[4] | **Shakiyr (FR) (51)** (RHollinshead) **5-7-13**(3) FLynch(4) (hld up & bhd: hdwy 3f out: styd on ins fnl f) | 4 | **4** | 9/1 | 55 | 33 |
| 3463[5] | **Anglesey Sea View (58)** (ABailey) **7-8-9** JFortune(8) (led over 10f out tl over 2f out: sn rdn: grad wknd) | 1 | **5** | 6/1[3] | 61 | 39 |
| *3605** | **Love And Kisses (62)** (CACyzer) **3-7-13** TWilliams(5) (trckd ldrs: shkn up 3f out: hmpd ent st: no imp) | 1 | **6** | 8/1 | 64 | 28 |
| 3855[2] | **Shirley Sue (66)** (MJohnston) **3-8-3** WCarson(2) (prom: drvn along ½-wy: sn lost tch: n.d after) | 4 | **7** | 2/1[1] | 64 | 28 |
| 2502[18] | **Fieldridge (73)** (MPMuggeridge) **7-9-10** VSlattery(3) (lw: hld up in rr: rdn 6f out: no imp: t.o) | 13 | **8** | 16/1 | 58 | 36 |
| 3587[5] | **Hill Farm Dancer (48)** (WMBrisbourne) **5-7-13** AGarth(7) (hld up & bhd: hdwy 7f out: wknd 3f out: t.o) | 2½ | **9** | 14/1 | 31 | 9 |
| | | | | (SP 123.7%) | | **9 Rn** |

**3m 34.25** (11.35) CSF £41.49 CT £240.42 TOTE £4.10: £1.70 £3.20 £2.70 (£47.10) Trio £56.10 OWNER Mr D. C. Batey (CONSETT) BRED G.W. Mills & Sons

WEIGHT FOR AGE 3yo-14lb

**3598 Izza** got back to winning ways and was in no small way helped by her undoubted stamina. She is always game to the end and this success was well deserved. (4/1)

**3487 Floating Line** struck the front on the home turn and was in no mood to give best, but the 13lb weight-concession swung the issue. He is running consistently well and compensation awaits. (10/1: 8/1-12/1)

**3486 The Swan**, a terrible walker, was in the action all the way. The victim of a knock-on effect entering the straight, she deserves credit for getting so close. Lightly-raced, more will be heard of her. (13/2)

**2697 Shakiyr (FR)** did not decide to put his best foot forward until too late and was only finding his stride when the race was all but over. (9/1)

**3463 Anglesey Sea View**, who has not troubled the Judge since winning her maiden fourteen months ago, did try her best here, but it was not good enough. (6/1)

**3605* Love And Kisses** had little time in which to recover from being hampered, but it is doubtful as to whether it cost her any prizemoney. (8/1)

**3855 Shirley Sue** had a punishing race in the bottomless conditions at Ripon four days ago, and would have needed a constitution of iron to recover so quickly. (2/1: op 3/1)

## 3923 O'HARE LEISURE H'CAP (0-100) (3-Y.O) (Class C)

4-55 (4-55) **1m 2f 75y** £5,540.00 (£1,670.00: £810.00: £380.00) Stalls: High GOING: 0.11 sec per fur (G)

| | | | | SP | RR | SF |
|---|---|---|---|---|---|---|
| 3248[11] | **Gold Disc (USA) (86)** (BWHills) **3-9-5** WRyan(9) (lw: hld up in rr: hdwy over 2f out: str run on ins to ld wl ins fnl f) | — | **1** | 12/1 | 95 | 56 |
| 3225[2] | **Daira (64)** (JDBethell) **3-7-11** FNorton(3) (hld up in tch: effrt 3f out: jnd ldr over 1f out: slt ld ins fnl f: sn hdd: nt qckn) | 1½ | **2** | 7/1 | 71 | 32 |
| 3594[8] | **Champagne Prince (88)** (PWHarris) **3-9-7** GHind(1) (lw: slt ld after 3f: hrd drvn & hdd ins fnl f: r.o) | hd | **3** | 9/1 | 95 | 56 |
| 2294[4] | **Expensive Taste (88)** (MRStoute) **3-9-7** KFallon(6) (a.p: rdn to chal ent fnl f: unable qckn) | hd | **4** | 6/1[3] | 94 | 55 |
| 3298[2] | **Raise A Prince (FR) (76)** (JWHills) **3-8-6**(3) MHenry(2) (led after 2f: sn hdd: prom tl wknd 2f out) | 8 | **5** | 7/1 | 70 | 31 |
| 2233[5] | **Ski Academy (IRE) (87)** (PWChapple-Hyam) **3-9-3**(3) RHavlin(4) (hld up & bhd: rdn over 3f out: nvr nr to chal) | ¾ | **6** | 16/1 | 80 | 41 |
| 3039[2] | **Crazy Chief (82)** (PFICole) **3-9-1** JFortune(8) (prom: rdn 3f out: wknd wl over 1f out) | 3½ | **7** | 3/1[1] | 69 | 30 |
| 3669[10] | **Bowled Over (84)** (CACyzer) **3-9-3** JCarroll(5) (hld up: a bhd: t.o) | 8 | **8** | 12/1 | 59 | 20 |
| 3295[2] | **Kamari (USA) (88)** (ACStewart) **3-9-7** WCarson(7) (lw: led 2f: rdn & dropped rr 3f out: t.o) | 21 | **9** | 7/2[2] | 31 | — |
| | | | | (SP 117.8%) | | **9 Rn** |

**2m 15.89** (7.19) CSF £85.46 CT £730.35 TOTE £18.30: £4.00 £2.10 £2.40 (£68.90) Trio £119.30 OWNER Mr K. Abdulla (LAMBOURN) BRED Juddmonte Farms

**OFFICIAL EXPLANATION Gold Disc (USA): accounting for the horse's apparent in form, the trainer's representative reported that on his previous two outings, Gold Disc (USA) had become very excitable. In this race the colt seemed more settled and appeared suited by the good to soft ground.**

**1666* Gold Disc (USA)** had been very highly tried in recent races, but was back in his own class here. Given a confident ride, he found the better turn of finishing speed to land the spoils. (12/1)

**3225 Daira**, winner of her maiden over a longer trip earlier in the month, ran possibly her best race yet. After battling hard to get the better of one rival, the winner came to spoil the party. (7/1)

**3207 Champagne Prince** has done all his winning on a sound surface, but he was not put out by this much softer ground and did a grand job of pacemaking until forced to give best in the final 200 yards. Lightly-raced this term, his turn is near. (9/1)
**2294 Expensive Taste** could have found this yielding ground a bit of a problem, but she gave her true running and was only done for speed inside the distance. (6/1)
**3298 Raise A Prince (FR)**, still to open his account, was taking on handicappers for the first time. Pushing the pace until weakening once into the home straight, he will find an easier opening before long. (7/1)
**3039 Crazy Chief**, poised to challenge but driven along three furlongs out, did not fade until early in the straight, but this performance would be some way below what he is capable of. (3/1)
**3295 Kamari (USA)**, driven along and struggling out in the country, dropped right away to finish tailed off. The ground could not have been the only reason. (7/2)

T/Plpt: £295.80 (57.9 Tckts). T/Qdpt: £32.10 (43.47 Tckts). IM

## 3763-SANDOWN (R-H) (Good)
## Friday August 30th
WEATHER: overcast WIND: almost nil

### 3924 ORLEANS NURSERY H'CAP (2-Y.O) (Class D)
2-00 (2-00) **5f 6y** £3,598.75 (£1,090.00: £532.50: £253.75) Stalls: High GOING minus 0.21 sec per fur (GF)

| | | | | SP | RR | SF |
|---|---|---|---|---|---|---|
| 3692[3] | **Rudi's Pet (IRE) (92)** (RHannon) **2-9-7** DaneO'Neill(2) (chsd ldrs: rdn over 3f out: n.m.r over 1f out: led wl ins fnl f: r.o wl) | — | **1** | 13/2[3] | 93 | 35 |
| 3823* | **Perpetual (72)** (SirMarkPrescott) **2-8-1** 5x GDuffield(6) (lw: led: rdn over 2f out: hdd wl ins fnl f: unable qckn) | 1 | **2** | 5/2[2] | 70 | 12 |
| 3687[7] | **Feel A Line (80)** (BJMeehan) **2-8-9b** TQuinn(7) (outpcd: hdwy fnl f: r.o) | 1½ | **3** | 9/1 | 73 | 15 |
| 2495[2] | **Myrmidon (86)** (JLDunlop) **2-9-1** PatEddery(3) (swtg: chsd ldrs: rdn over 3f out: 3rd & btn whn hmpd ins fnl f) | 1¼ | **4** | 9/4[1] | 75 | 17 |
| 3299[6] | **Tear White (IRE) (81)** (TGMills) **2-8-10v[1]** JReid(4) (lw: chsd ldr: rdn over 1f out: swvd lft ins fnl f: sn wknd) | ¾ | **5** | 7/1 | 68 | 10 |
| 3436[5] | **Jupiter (IRE) (76)** (GCBravery) **2-8-5** MHills(5) (swtg: dwlt: outpcd) | 3 | **6** | 9/1 | 53 | — |
| 3160[11] | **Bramble Bear (78)** (MBlanshard) **2-8-7** AClark(1) (prom over 3f) | 1¾ | **7** | 12/1 | 50 | — |
| 3662[7] | **Chopin (IRE) (68)** (RFJohnsonHoughton) **2-7-8b[1]**(3)ow1 DarrenMoffatt(8) (s.s: a bhd) | ½ | **8** | 50/1 | 38 | — |
| | | | | (SP 114.8%) | **8 Rn** | |

**62.91 secs** (3.11) CSF £22.13 CT £134.82 TOTE £6.20: £1.70 £1.10 £3.20 (£6.50) OWNER The Broadgate Partnership (MARLBOROUGH) BRED Declan MacPartlin
LONG HANDICAP Chopin (IRE) 7-8
**3692 Rudi's Pet (IRE)**, soon pushed along, did not have much room below the distance as another jockey's whip was flashed accidentally in his face, but came through to lead late on. (13/2)
**3823* Perpetual**, a winner at Chepstow on Monday, again led. Despite looking likely to be swamped, she stuck to her task really well. (5/2)
**3282 Feel A Line**, unable to go the pace, was doing his best work late in the day. (9/1)
**2495 Myrmidon** looked well in himself, but had sweated up by the time they had left the paddock. Chasing the leaders, he was held in third when hampered by Tear White. (9/4)
**3299 Tear White (IRE)** is a very tricky customer. Racing in second, he failed to pick up when asked, and he ducked violently left away from the whip in the final furlong. He looks one to steer clear of. (7/1)
**3436 Jupiter (IRE)**, turned out looking tremendous, spoilt it by sweating up leaving the paddock. He never had the pace to get into it. (9/1)
**2956* Bramble Bear** (12/1: op 8/1)

### 3925 CHARTERHOUSE CONDITIONS STKS (2-Y.O) (Class C)
2-35 (2-36) **1m 14y** £4,588.40 (£1,715.60: £837.80: £359.00: £159.50: £79.70) Stalls: High GOING minus 0.21 sec per fur (GF)

| | | | | SP | RR | SF |
|---|---|---|---|---|---|---|
| 3131* | **Medaaly** (SbinSuroor) **2-9-0** JReid(2) (chsd ldr: led over 2f out: comf) | — | **1** | 4/9[1] | 102+ | 55 |
| 3143[5] | **Imperial President (100)** (HRACecil) **2-9-7** PatEddery(3) (lw: hld up: chsd wnr fnl 2f: no imp) | 3½ | **2** | 4/1[2] | 102 | 55 |
| 3407[8] | **Conon Falls (IRE)** (JHMGosden) **2-8-11** MHills(5) (lw: led over 5f: one pce) | 1½ | **3** | 12/1[3] | 89 | 42 |
| 3904a[4] | **Maladerie (IRE) (96)** (MRChannon) **2-9-0** KDarley(6) (lw: a.p: rdn over 3f out: wknd over 2f out) | 3 | **4** | 25/1 | 86 | 39 |
| 3685[6] | **Indifferent Guy** (CEBrittain) **2-8-11** BDoyle(4) (lw: a bhd) | nk | **5** | 50/1 | 83 | 36 |
| 3493* | **Orontes (USA)** (RHannon) **2-9-0** DaneO'Neill(1) (a bhd) | 1 | **6** | 12/1[3] | 84 | 37 |
| | | | | (SP 110.4%) | **6 Rn** | |

**1m 43.8** (2.60) CSF £2.64 TOTE £1.20: £1.10 £1.50 (£2.00) OWNER Godolphin (NEWMARKET) BRED Sheikh Mohammed Bin Rashid Al Maktoum
**3131* Medaaly** put up a highly-impressive display. Racing in second until sent on over two furlongs out, he was pushed along to have the situation in hand. Connections must be delighted with the way he is improving, and he must have a great chance in the Royal Lodge next month, his next target. (4/9)
**3143 Imperial President**, with a 7lb penalty to contend with, went second two furlongs out, but could never get on terms with the winner. (4/1: 5/2-9/2)
**3407 Conon Falls (IRE)**, once passed over two furlongs out, was soon put in his place. A good-looking colt, he should have no problems picking up a maiden. (12/1: 6/1-14/1)
**3904a Maladerie (IRE)** was hung out to dry over two furlongs out. (25/1)
**3685 Indifferent Guy** was always struggling. (50/1)
**3493* Orontes (USA)** was very disappointing. (12/1: op 5/1)

### 3926 BLOOD DONOR H'CAP (0-90) (3-Y.O) (Class C)
3-05 (3-08) **1m 14y** £5,680.00 (£1,720.00: £840.00: £400.00) Stalls: High GOING minus 0.21 sec per fur (GF)

| | | | | SP | RR | SF |
|---|---|---|---|---|---|---|
| 2146[10] | **Select Few (83)** (LMCumani) **3-9-5** OUrbina(5) (b.off fore: led 6f: led over 1f out: rdn out) | — | **1** | 13/2[2] | 92 | 67 |
| 3133* | **Blessed Spirit (76)** (CFWall) **3-8-12** SSanders(9) (stdy hdwy on bit over 2f out: ev ch ins fnl f: r.o) | hd | **2** | 7/1[3] | 85 | 60 |
| 3519* | **Consort (85)** (GHarwood) **3-9-7** PatEddery(10) (lw: hdwy over 2f out: hrd rdn over 1f out: unable qckn wl ins fnl f) | 1¼ | **3** | 9/2[1] | 91 | 66 |
| 3133[3] | **Tsarnista (79)** (JLDunlop) **3-9-1** JReid(12) (hld up: rdn over 2f out: one pce) | nk | **4** | 9/1 | 85 | 60 |

| | | | | SP | RR | SF |
|---|---|---|---|---|---|---|
| $3612^{11}$ | **Caricature (IRE) (81)** (GLewis) **3-9-0b**(3) AWhelan(3) (a.p: led 2f out tl over 1f out: one pce) | 1½ | **5** | 20/1 | 84 | 59 |
| $3634^{5}$ | **Kirov Lady (IRE) (76)** (RHannon) **3-8-12** DaneO'Neill(11) (rdn over 3f out: n.m.r & swtchd lft over 2f out: hdwy & nt clr run 1f out: r.o) | hd | **6** | 25/1 | 79 | 54 |
| $2621^{11}$ | **Alhawa (USA) (81)** (CJBenstead) **3-9-3** RHills(8) (lw: rdn over 3f out: nvr nr to chal) | ½ | **7** | 14/1 | 83 | 58 |
| 3107* | **Salmis (78)** (JRFanshawe) **3-8-11**(3) NVarley(7) (prom over 6f) | 1¼ | **8** | 8/1 | 77 | 52 |
| $3786^{5}$ | **Brighton Road (IRE) (74)** (GBBalding) **3-8-10** TQuinn(13) (prom 6f) | 3 | **9** | 10/1 | 67 | 42 |
| *3063** | **Deadline Time (IRE) (82)** (MrsMReveley) **3-9-4** KDarley(2) (lw: hdwy over 1f out: wknd ins fnl f) | hd | **10** | 7/1 3 | 75 | 50 |
| $3153^{6}$ | **Capilano Princess (80)** (DHaydnJones) **3-9-2** AMackay(4) (prom 5f) | 1¾ | **11** | 9/1 | 70 | 45 |
| $2974^{5}$ | **Carmarthen Bay (73)** (GLMoore) **3-8-9** RCochrane(1) (lw: a bhd) | 1¾ | **12** | 33/1 | 59 | 34 |
| *$3603^{3}$* | **Catherine's Choice (64)** (JDBethell) **3-8-0** SDrowne(6) (lw: bhd fnl 2f) | 8 | **13** | 33/1 | 34 | 9 |

(SP 117.9%) **13 Rn**

**1m 43.15** (1.95) CSF £47.08 CT £205.63 TOTE £6.80: £2.00 £3.00 £2.40 (£26.60) Trio £33.20 OWNER Sheikh Mohammed (NEWMARKET) BRED Sheikh Mohammed bin Rashid al Maktoum

**1843* Select Few**, given a ten-week break after running no sort of race at Ascot in June, was reported to have been working well at home. Setting the pace, he showed the right sort of spirit to get back in front, and then hold on tenaciously. (13/2)

**3133* Blessed Spirit** was absolutely swinging as she cruised into contention in the straight. It looked a matter of when and how far but, when let down, she failed to find what was expected. (7/1)

**3519* Consort**, with no easy task under topweight having run just twice, put up a bold showing and was only tapped for toe in the final 50 yards. (9/2)

**3133 Tsarnista**, asked for an effort over two furlongs out, failed to find that vital turn of foot. (9/1)

**1127 Caricature (IRE)**, in the firing-line all the way, went on passing the quarter-mile pole. Headed over a furlong out, he failed to find another gear. (20/1)

**3634 Kirov Lady (IRE)**, who raced in rear, was beginning to pick up when failing to get a run a furlong out. She did run on, but the damage was done. (25/1)

**3107* Salmis** (8/1: 6/1-9/1)

## 3927 SOLARIO STKS (Gp 3) (2-Y.O) (Class A)

3-40 (3-40) **7f 16y** £19,380.00 (£7,336.50: £3,593.25: £1,640.25) Stalls: High GOING minus 0.21 sec per fur (GF)

| | | | | SP | RR | SF |
|---|---|---|---|---|---|---|
| $3150^{2}$ | **Brave Act (100)** (SirMarkPrescott) **2-8-11** GDuffield(1) (lw: mde virtually all: all out) | — | **1** | 9/2 | 107 | 63 |
| 2252* | **Falkenham** (PFICole) **2-8-11** TQuinn(5) (hld up: chsd wnr over 2f out: ev ch ins fnl f: r.o wl) | s.h | **2** | 8/1 | 107 | 63 |
| $3143^{4}$ | **Air Express (IRE) (100)** (CEBrittain) **2-8-11** BDoyle(7) (hdwy over 2f out: ev ch over 1f out: unable qckn) | 1¼ | **3** | 10/1 | 104 | 60 |
| $2878^{2}$ | **Hello (IRE) (100)** (JLDunlop) **2-8-11** JReid(2) (lw: plld hrd: hld up: rdn over 2f out: one pce) | 2 | **4** | 4/1 3 | 100 | 56 |
| 2923* | **Mount Kamet** (DRLoder) **2-8-11** PatEddery(4) (lw: chsd wnr over 4f: hrd rdn 2f out: one pce) | s.h | **5** | 9/4 1 | 99 | 55 |
| 3684* | **Great Ovation (IRE)** (LMCumani) **2-8-11** OUrbina(3) (lw: hld up: rdn over 3f out: sn wknd) | 11 | **6** | 7/2 2 | 75 | 31 |
| 3396a$^{3}$ | **Statesman (100)** (MRChannon) **2-8-11** KDarley(6) (swtg: hld up: rdn over 2f out: sn wknd) | 2½ | **7** | 20/1 | 69 | 25 |

(SP 116.1%) **7 Rn**

**1m 29.97** (1.37) CSF £35.54 TOTE £6.40: £2.80 £3.10 (£29.70) OWNER Mr W. E. Sturt (NEWMARKET) BRED Side Hill Stud and Floors Farming

OFFICIAL EXPLANATION **Great Ovation (IRE): was never travelling.**

**3150 Brave Act**, a tall, well-made colt who looked in good shape, put up a really gutsy display. Making most, he held on by the skin of his teeth after a tremendous tussle. (9/2)

**2252* Falkenham**, off the track for nine weeks, went second over two furlongs out. He did carry his head rather high, but lost his unbeaten record by only a whisker. (8/1)

**3143 Air Express (IRE)** moved up travelling sweetly over two furlongs out and looked a serious threat below the distance. Asked for an effort, he failed to find the expected. (10/1: 7/1-11/1)

**2878 Hello (IRE)**, who took a very keen hold early, chased the leaders. Ridden over two furlongs out, he could only go up and down in the same place. (4/1)

**2923* Mount Kamet**, a tall colt, looked very well in the paddock. Second until over two furlongs out, he was soon under the cosh and failed to find another gear. (9/4: 2/1-100/30)

**3684* Great Ovation (IRE)** ran no race at all and was the first beaten. (7/2)

**3396a Statesman** looks to be going the wrong way. (20/1)

## 3928 CLAYGATE STAYERS H'CAP (0-70) (3-Y.O+) (Class E)

4-10 (4-11) **2m 78y** £3,810.00 (£1,155.00: £565.00: £270.00) Stalls: High GOING minus 0.21 sec per fur (GF)

| | | | | SP | RR | SF |
|---|---|---|---|---|---|---|
| $3772^{2}$ | **Chris's Lad (61)** (BJMeehan) **5-9-8b** BDoyle(4) (lw: hdwy 8f out: rdn over 3f out: led last stride) | — | **1** | 10/1 3 | 74 | 56 |
| 3667* | **Candle Smoke (USA) (66)** (GHarwood) **3-8-6**(7) GayeHarwood(1) (plld hrd: a.p: led 3f out: rdn over 2f out: edgd rt wl ins fnl f: hdd last stride) | s.h | **2** | 13/2 2 | 79 | 47 |
| 3768* | **Roseberry Avenue (IRE) (71)** (LadyHerries) **3-9-4** 4x KDarley(5) (lw: lost pl 8f out: rdn over 5f out: rallied & edgd rt over 2f out: ev ch ins fnl f: 3rd & btn whn n.m.r on ins nr fin) | 1½ | **3** | 11/8 1 | 83 | 51 |
| 3705* | **Clifton Game (41)** (MRChannon) **6-7-11**(5) 4x PPMurphy(6) (hld up: rdn over 2f out: ev ch over 1f out: wknd ins fnl f) | 4 | **4** | 13/2 2 | 49 | 31 |
| $3463^{4}$ | **Ela Man Howa (48)** (ABailey) **5-8-9** SSanders(11) (lw: rdn & hdwy over 2f out: one pce) | s.h | **5** | 10/1 3 | 56 | 38 |
| $3801^{2}$ | **Sea Freedom (62)** (GBBalding) **5-9-9v** RCochrane(9) (nvr nr to chal) | 1¼ | **6** | 10/1 3 | 68 | 50 |
| $3463^{6}$ | **Amiarge (43)** (MBrittain) **6-8-4b** GDuffield(8) (lw: nvr nrr) | 1 | **7** | 20/1 | 48 | 30 |
| $3802^{11}$ | **Broughtons Formula (39)** (WJMusson) **6-8-0b** JQuinn(13) (lw: a bhd) | 8 | **8** | 33/1 | 37 | 19 |
| $3768^{6}$ | **Rivercare (IRE) (60)** (MJPolglase) **3-8-7** NCarlisle(7) (lw: led 14f out to 3f out: sn wknd) | 6 | **9** | 33/1 | 52 | 20 |
| $3699^{2}$ | **Majdak Jereeb (IRE) (69)** (MajorWRHern) **3-9-2v** PatEddery(2) (lw: led over 2f: wknd over 3f out) | 2 | **10** | 10/1 3 | 59 | 27 |
| $2952^{5}$ | **Code Red (61)** (JWHills) **3-8-8** MHills(3) (hdwy over 7f out: wknd over 4f out) | 11 | **11** | 25/1 | 40 | 8 |

(SP 119.6%) **11 Rn**

**3m 39.04** (7.04) CSF £68.87 CT £132.76 TOTE £7.90: £1.70 £2.20 £1.40 (£18.90) Trio £12.20 OWNER Mrs Susan McCarthy (UPPER LAMBOURN) BRED Tyrian Breeding

WEIGHT FOR AGE 3yo-14lb

**3772 Chris's Lad** moved up at halfway. Bustled along in the straight, he clawed his way to the front right on the line. (10/1)

**3667* Candle Smoke (USA)** took a very keen hold in a prominent position. Sent on three furlongs out, he drifted right inside the final furlong and was caught on the stick. He is a winner without a penalty. (13/2)

**3768* Roseberry Avenue (IRE)** made his jockey work for his fee. Losing his pitch at halfway and bustled along turning for home, he picked up over two furlongs out and may have led for a few strides in the final 200 yards, but failed to find another gear. (11/8)

**3705* Clifton Game** chased the leaders and had every chance below the distance, but ran out of steam inside the final 150 yards. (13/2)
**3463 Ela Man Howa** picked up over two furlongs out, but could then make no further impression. (10/1)

## 3929 HOGS BACK CLAIMING STKS (3-Y.O) (Class D)

4-45 (4-46) **1m 1f** £3,615.00 (£1,095.00: £535.00: £255.00) Stalls: High GOING minus 0.21 sec per fur (GF)

| | | | | SP | RR | SF |
|---|---|---|---|---|---|---|
| 3799[7] | **Prima Volta (75)** (RHannon) **3-8-7** DaneO'Neill(5) (lw: hdwy 2f out: led over 1f out: drvn out) | — | **1** | 7/2[2] | 71 | 36 |
| 3681[13] | **Apache Len (USA) (70)** (RHannon) **3-8-13b[1]** PatEddery(2) (lw: a.p: rdn over 2f out: ev ch fnl f: r.o wl) | s.h | **2** | 7/2[2] | 77 | 42 |
| 2966[3] | **Home Cookin' (55)** (MCPipe) **3-7-6(5)** MartinDwyer(3) (led: rdn 3f out: hdd over 1f out: one pce) | 5 | **3** | 4/1[3] | 52 | 17 |
| *3603[8]* | **Quiet Arch (IRE) (60)** (CACyzer) **3-8-12** GDuffield(6) (hmpd 8f out: rdn over 4f out: hdwy wl over 1f out: one pce) | 1½ | **4** | 10/1 | 64 | 29 |
| 3655[5] | **Hadadabble (40)** (PatMitchell) **3-8-7** RCochrane(4) (lw: w ldr: ev ch over 2f out: sn wknd) | 5 | **5** | 11/1 | 51 | 16 |
| 3451[3] | **Miss Romance (IRE) (49)** (MissGayKelleway) **3-8-3ow1** SSanders(8) (b.hind: a.p: ev ch over 2f out: wknd over 1f out) | 4 | **6** | 3/1[1] | 39 | 3 |
| 3789[8] | **Thor's Phantom** (MDIUsher) **3-8-3** DHarrison(1) (lw: s.s: a bhd) | 1½ | **7** | 50/1 | 37 | 2 |
| 1963[8] | **Lord Ellangowan (IRE) (41)** (RIngram) **3-8-5b** SWhitworth(7) (lw: hmpd 8f out: a bhd) | hd | **8** | 50/1 | 39 | 4 |

(SP 110.8%) **8 Rn**

**1m 57.49** (4.39) CSF £14.78 TOTE £3.70: £1.50 £1.20 £1.30 (£7.10) OWNER The Boardroom Syndicate (MARLBOROUGH) BRED Bearstone Stud

**2045 Prima Volta** went on below the distance and just got the better of a titanic struggle to win a very bad race. (7/2)
**1872 Apache Len (USA)**, blinkered for the first time and dropped in class, was always handy. He threw down his challenge from below the distance, but was foiled by the narrowest of margins. (7/2)
**2966 Home Cookin'**, collared below the distance, was then left standing. (4/1: op 9/4)
**2689 Quiet Arch (IRE)** improved along the inner just inside the final quarter-mile, but could make no further headway. (10/1: 8/1-12/1)
**3655 Hadadabble** disputed it until coming to the end of her tether two furlongs out. She is still a maiden after seventeen attempts. (11/1: 16/1-10/1)
**3451 Miss Romance (IRE)** had every chance over two furlongs out, but was soon bustled along and punters quickly knew their fate. (3/1)

## 3930 SURREY RACING H'CAP (0-80) (3-Y.O+) (Class D)

5-15 (5-19) **5f 6y** £3,826.25 (£1,160.00: £567.50: £271.25) Stalls: High GOING minus 0.21 sec per fur (GF)

| | | | | SP | RR | SF |
|---|---|---|---|---|---|---|
| 3793[3] | **Squire Corrie (57)** (GHarwood) **4-8-2b(7)** GayeHarwood(14) (lw: mde virtually all: rdn out) | — | **1** | 11/2[2] | 66 | 39 |
| 3506[3] | **Gone Savage (64)** (WJMusson) **8-9-2** RCochrane(2) (hdwy over 1f out: r.o ins fnl f) | ¾ | **2** | 5/1[1] | 71 | 44 |
| 3482[5] | **Jucea (72)** (JLSpearing) **7-9-10** JReid(15) (hdwy 2f out: hrd rdn over 1f out: unable qckn fnl f) | nk | **3** | 13/2 | 78 | 51 |
| 3827[9] | **Longwick Lad (67)** (WRMuir) **3-9-3** TQuinn(3) (hld up: rdn over 2f out: one pce fnl f) | s.h | **4** | 20/1 | 73 | 44 |
| 3518[4] | **Purple Fling (71)** (LGCottrell) **5-9-9** JQuinn(5) (lw: a.p: rdn 2f out: one pce) | ½ | **5** | 14/1 | 75 | 48 |
| 3323[6] | **John O'Dreams (50)** (MrsALMKing) **11-8-2** DaneO'Neill(13) (b.off fore: rdn over 2f out: hdwy fnl f: nvr nrr) | 1¼ | **6** | 10/1 | 50 | 23 |
| 3700[2] | **Merrie le Bow (51)** (PatMitchell) **4-7-12(5)ow4** AmandaSanders(7) (nvr nr to chal) | ½ | **7** | 20/1 | 49 | 18 |
| 3666[5] | **Face the Future (56)** (VSoane) **7-8-8** AMcGlone(9) (a mid div) | s.h | **8** | 25/1 | 54 | 27 |
| *3091** | **Queens Check (51)** (MissJFCraze) **3-8-1b** AMackay(16) (prom over 3f) | 1¼ | **9** | 6/1[3] | 45 | 16 |
| 3506[6] | **Metal Boys (52)** (MissLCSiddall) **9-8-1(3)ow1** PMcCabe(12) (b.off hind: bhd fnl 2f) | ¾ | **10** | 16/1 | 44 | 16 |
| 2999[6] | **Magic Mail (69)** (JMPEustace) **3-9-0(5)** MartinDwyer(11) (lw: w wnr over 3f) | 3½ | **11** | 10/1 | 50 | 21 |
| 3519[5] | **Sea Danzig (64)** (JJBridger) **3-9-0** DHarrison(6) (lw: s.s: a bhd) | ½ | **12** | 33/1 | 43 | 14 |
| 3162[4] | **Nakami (68)** (PJMakin) **4-9-6** SSanders(10) (prom over 3f) | 1 | **13** | 8/1 | 44 | 17 |
| 3827[8] | **Sally Slade (76)** (CACyzer) **4-10-0b[1]** GDuffield(8) (s.s: a bhd) | ½ | **14** | 25/1 | 50 | 23 |
| 3472[18] | **Jades Shadow (47)** (JJBridger) **3-7-8(3)ow1** DarrenMoffatt(17) (lw: s.s: a bhd) | 20 | **15** | 66/1 | — | — |
| *3261[W]* | ***Malibu Man (63)*** (EAWheeler) **4-9-1** SWhitworth(1) (Withdrawn not under Starter's orders: spread plate at s) | ... | **W** | 20/1 | — | — |

(SP 127.9%) **15 Rn**

**62.0 secs** (2.20) CSF £31.52 CT £175.50 TOTE £6.00: £1.80 £1.60 £2.90 (£9.30) Trio £23.80 OWNER Mr G. Harwood (PULBOROUGH) BRED Whitsbury Manor Stud

LONG HANDICAP Jades Shadow 6-8
WEIGHT FOR AGE 3yo-2lb

**3793 Squire Corrie** made most and, ridden along, held on well. He remains in fine form. (11/2)
**3506 Gone Savage** was drawn low, which is usually a major disadvantage when the stalls are on the far side although moves have been made by the course to negate the effect, but he is something of an enigma. Racing down the centre and thus avoiding traffic - something he had encountered on his previous three outings here - he picked up below the distance and snatched second late on. (5/1)
**3482 Jucea** weaved through two furlongs out, but was tapped for toe in the final furlong. (13/2)
**3652 Longwick Lad**, making a quick reappearance, failed to find another gear in the final 200 yards. (20/1)
**3518 Purple Fling** failed to find the necessary turn of foot in the final quarter-mile. (14/1)
**3323 John O'Dreams** was out with the washing until staying on in the final furlong to be nearest at the line. (10/1)
**2999 Magic Mail** (10/1: 8/1-12/1)

T/Jkpt: £21,962.70 (0.1 Tckts); £27,840.15 to Sandown 31/8/96. T/Plpt: £46.20 (598.01 Tckts). T/Qdpt: £19.90 (70.48 Tckts). AK

# 3918-CHESTER (L-H) (Good to soft)

## Saturday August 31st

WEATHER: cloudy WIND: slt against

## 3931 LINENHALL CONDITIONS STKS (2-Y.O C & G) (Class C)

1-55 (1-56) **6f 18y** £4,909.00 (£1,831.00: £890.50: £377.50: £163.75: £78.25) Stalls: Low GOING: 0.10 sec per fur (G)

| | | | | SP | RR | SF |
|---|---|---|---|---|---|---|
| 1653* | **Andreyev (IRE)** (RHannon) **2-8-13** RHughes(3) (lw: hld up: smooth hdwy over 2f out: qcknd to ld over 1f out: sn clr) | — | **1** | 6/5[1] | 104+ | 57 |
| 3156[7] | **Close Relative (IRE) (100)** (RCharlton) **2-8-13** TSprake(4) (swtg: bhd: sn pushed along: hdwy u.p wl over 1f out: nvr nrr) | 4 | **2** | 7/2[2] | 94 | 47 |
| 1362[4] | **Braveheart (IRE) (86)** (MRChannon) **2-8-10** TQuinn(1) (mde most tl hdd & outpcd over 1f out) | s.h | **3** | 6/1 | 90 | 43 |
| 3792[9] | **Osomental (97)** (DHaydnJones) **2-8-10** FNorton(6) (chsd ldrs: hrd drvn ent st: swtchd ins over 1f out: nt pce to chal) | nk | **4** | 6/1 | 90 | 43 |
| 3748a[4] | **Victory Dancer (100)** (BJMeehan) **2-8-13b** MTebbutt(2) (disp ld tl rdn & wknd over 1f out) | 5 | **5** | 4/1[3] | 79 | 32 |

| | | | Pos | SP | RR | SF |
|---|---|---|---|---|---|---|
| 2252⁶ | **Prairie Minstrel (USA)** (RDickin) **2-8-10** JCarroll(5) (bit bkwd: trckd ldrs: rdn ½-wy: wknd wl over 1f out) | 7 | **6** | 33/1 | 58 | 11 |
| | | | | (SP 119.2%) | | **6 Rn** |

**1m 16.87** (3.57) CSF £6.18 TOTE £2.20: £1.30 £2.00 (£3.90) OWNER Mr J. Palmer-Brown (MARLBOROUGH) BRED T. F. Moorhead

**1653* Andreyev (IRE)**, a very attractive colt, was fresh and well after a mid-summer break. He pulverised this opposition and should certainly make a name for himself. (6/5: Evens-6/4)

**2607 Close Relative (IRE)**, never travelling all that well, did stay on to chase up the winner, but could not get within striking range. (7/2)

**1362 Braveheart (IRE)** shook off his nearest rival on the approach to the straight, but the winner cruised past on the bridle and his hopes were soon dashed. (6/1)

**2965* Osomental**, hard at work in an effort to keep tabs on the leaders turning in, had no answer to the superior pace of the winner and was soon put in his place. (6/1)

**3400 Victory Dancer** showed plenty of pace to match strides with the leader, but he was always getting the worst of the argument. (4/1)

## 3932 WEATHERBYS GROUP H'CAP (0-85) (3-Y.O+) (Class D)

2-30 (2-31) **5f 16y** £7,385.50 (£2,224.00: £1,077.00: £503.50) Stalls: Low GOING: 0.10 sec per fur (G)

| | | | Pos | SP | RR | SF |
|---|---|---|---|---|---|---|
| *3628⁴* | **Panther (IRE) (68)** (PDEvans) **6-8-12v** JFEgan(1) (s.i.s: hdwy ½-wy: rdn to ld & edgd lft ins fnl f: r.o) | — | **1** | 14/1 | 75 | 60 |
| 3693⁶ | **Swynford Dream (78)** (JFBottomley) **3-9-6** JLowe(3) (led tl hrd rdn & hdd ins fnl f) | ½ | **2** | 10/1 | 83 | 66 |
| 3432¹¹ | **Insider Trader (76)** (MrsJRRamsden) **5-9-6** KFallon(2) (chsd ldrs: ev ch ins fnl f: rdn & r.o wl cl home) | hd | **3** | 9/2 ¹ | 81 | 66 |
| 3622⁹ | **Ziggy's Dancer (USA) (84)** (EJAlston) **5-10-0** StephenDavies(4) (lw: hld up: hdwy on ins ent st: n.m.r ins fnl f: nt rcvr) | ½ | **4** | 7/1 ² | 88 | 73 |
| 3783⁶ | **Fantasy Racing (IRE) (73)** (MRChannon) **4-9-3** RHughes(10) (sn drvn along: chsd ldrs: kpt on ins fnl f) | 2 | **5** | 12/1 | 70 | 55 |
| 3618* | **Glorious Aragon (82)** (RFJohnsonHoughton) **4-9-12** TQuinn(5) (lw: chsd ldrs: rdn wl over 1f out: nt pce to chal) | hd | **6** | 9/2 ¹ | 79 | 64 |
| 3618⁶ | **Chadwell Hall (68)** (SRBowring) **5-8-9b**(3) CTeague(13) (trckd ldrs: hrd drvn & no ex appr fnl f) | 2 | **7** | 16/1 | 59 | 44 |
| 3793⁷ | **Myttons Mistake (69)** (ABailey) **3-8-8**(3) DWright(9) (chsd ldrs: rdn & one pce appr fnl f) | ½ | **8** | 20/1 | 58 | 41 |
| 3618¹¹ | **Crofters Ceilidh (78)** (BAMcMahon) **4-9-3v¹**(5) LNewton(16) (nvr trbld ldrs) | hd | **9** | 33/1 | 67 | 52 |
| 3810⁴ | **Cretan Gift (68)** (NPLittmoden) **5-8-12b** TGMcLaughlin(15) (dwlt: nvr nr ldrs) | ½ | **10** | 14/1 | 55 | 40 |
| 3827⁵ | **Tuscan Dawn (76)** (JBerry) **6-9-1**(5) PRoberts(8) (prom tl wknd appr fnl f) | 1¼ | **11** | 10/1 | 59 | 44 |
| 3618¹⁰ | **Beau Venture (USA) (70)** (BPalling) **8-9-0** TSprake(14) (swtg: sn drvn along: a outpcd) | nk | **12** | 20/1 | 52 | 37 |
| 3482² | **Able Sheriff (56)** (MWEasterby) **4-8-0b** DaleGibson(11) (outpcd) | 2½ | **13** | 8/1 ³ | 30 | 15 |
| 3883¹² | **Silk Cottage (64)** (RMWhitaker) **4-8-5**(3) FLynch(6) (dwlt: a bhd) | hd | **14** | 20/1 | 38 | 23 |
| 2064⁹ | **Allwight Then (IRE) (64)** (THCaldwell) **5-8-8** JCarroll(7) (spd over 3f) | 2 | **15** | 33/1 | 32 | 17 |
| | | | | (SP 125.2%) | | **15 Rn** |

**62.95 secs** (2.95) CSF £137.78 CT £501.28 TOTE £14.70: £3.10 £3.50 £1.50 (£73.40) Trio £43.20 OWNER Treble Chance Partnership (WELSHPOOL) BRED My Treasure Ltd

WEIGHT FOR AGE 3yo-2lb

OFFICIAL EXPLANATION **Gymcrak Premiere: the jockey explained that his instructions were to settle the gelding and then to ride the race as he found it. He added that the horse started slowly and immediately hung to the right. Initially he thought his saddle had slipped and therefore trying to keep his mount from hanging, he was unable to ride vigorously until the home straight when the gelding ran on under pressure. The trainer added that Gymcrak Premier can be moody was obviously unsuited by the tight track.**

**3628 Panther (IRE)**, back over his correct trip, produced one of his better performances with a very gutsy display. Success at this level was not coming out of turn. (14/1)

**3693 Swynford Dream** had more than his full quota of weight, but he did what he is best at and blazed a trail. He was maybe a shade unfortunate to be worn down inside the final furlong. (10/1)

**3085 Insider Trader** showed he is back to something like his best with a very genuine performance. Although he may be slightly more effective with headgear on, he gave of his all here. (9/2)

**3622 Ziggy's Dancer (USA)** followed the winner through on the inside rail and was in full flight when that rival edged in front of him 200 yards out. Although it only momentarily impeded him, it was enough to prevent him from making the frame. (7/1)

**3783 Fantasy Racing (IRE)**, a previous winner here but without a success since the autumn of last year, kept battling away and all is not lost yet. (12/1)

**3618* Glorious Aragon** gained just reward for some decent efforts earlier in the month, but she was back to her old self here, running well all the way before just missing out when there was a prize up for grabs. (9/2)

## 3933 ROTHMANS ROYALS NORTH SOUTH CHALLENGE SERIES H'CAP (0-100) (3-Y.O+) (Class C)

3-00 (3-03) **7f 122y** £8,022.50 (£2,420.00: £1,175.00: £552.50) Stalls: Low GOING: 0.10 sec per fur (G)

| | | | Pos | SP | RR | SF |
|---|---|---|---|---|---|---|
| 3805⁴ | **My Gallery (IRE) (83)** (ABailey) **5-8-13**(3) DWright(6) (a.p: led 1f out: rdn & r.o wl) | — | **1** | 4/1 ¹ | 92 | 71 |
| 3833³ | **Jo Mell (82)** (TDEasterby) **3-8-9** MBirch(3) (a.p: led 2f out to 1f out: rdn & one pce fnl f) | 1¾ | **2** | 9/1 ³ | 87 | 60 |
| 3830* | **Rebel County (IRE) (75)** (ABailey) **3-8-2** 6x DBiggs(8) (hdwy over 2f out: rdn & r.o wl ins fnl f) | ¾ | **3** | 13/2 ² | 79 | 52 |
| 3812* | **Maple Bay (IRE) (77)** (ABailey) **7-8-3**(7)ow1 GFaulkner(13) (hdwy on outside over 2f out: nrst fin) | 1½ | **4** | 16/1 | 78 | 56 |
| | **Absolute Magic (75)** (WJHaggas) **6-8-5**(3) FLynch(7) (bit bkwd: hld up: hdwy u.p 2f out: nvr nrr) | 1¾ | **5** | 25/1 | 72 | 51 |
| 3254³ | **Somerton Boy (IRE) (71)** (PCalver) **6-8-4** JCarroll(4) (lw: chsd ldrs: rdn over 1f out: one pce) | hd | **6** | 16/1 | 68 | 47 |
| 3783³ | **Portend (90)** (SRBowring) **4-9-6v¹**(3) CTeague(11) (hld up & bhd: hdwy over 1f out: nvr nrr) | 1 | **7** | 12/1 | 85 | 64 |
| 3612⁵ | **Knobbleeneeze (79)** (MRChannon) **6-8-12v** RHughes(5) (chsd ldr: led 3f out to 2f out: rdn & wknd appr fnl f) | ¾ | **8** | 10/1 | 72 | 51 |
| 3521⁶ | **Blatant Outburst (75)** (GCBravery) **6-8-8** RLappin(2) (lw: trckd ldrs: rdn & nt clr run ins fnl f: eased) | ½ | **9** | 25/1 | 67 | 46 |
| *1810** | **High Premium (68)** (RAFahey) **8-8-1** FNorton(16) (bkwd: hld up: sme hdwy fnl 2f: nvr nrr) | ½ | **10** | 20/1 | 59 | 38 |
| 3516⁵ | **Shamrock Fair (IRE) (71)** (LordHuntingdon) **4-8-4**ow1 OUrbina(9) (lw: hld up: hdwy on ins whn nt clr run appr fnl f: nt rcvr) | 2 | **11** | 11/1 | 58 | 36 |
| 3709¹¹ | **Gymcrak Premiere (86)** (GHolmes) **8-9-5** TWilliams(1) (b.hind: bhd tl sme late hdwy) | ¾ | **12** | 25/1 | 71 | 50 |
| 3612¹² | **Band on the Run (91)** (BAMcMahon) **9-9-5**(5) LNewton(17) (trckd ldrs over 4f) | 4 | **13** | 25/1 | 68 | 47 |
| 3790* | **Whittle Rock (87)** (MrsMReveley) **3-8-9**(5) GLee(18) (lw: trckd ldrs 5f: sn wknd) | nk | **14** | 10/1 | 63 | 36 |
| 3623¹⁴ | **Rambo Waltzer (66)** (DNicholls) **4-7-13** DaleGibson(12) (a in rr) | ½ | **15** | 20/1 | 41 | 20 |
| 3612⁷ | **Laafee (98)** (HThomsonJones) **3-9-11** KFallon(10) (trckd ldrs: rdn over 2f out: sn wknd: t.o) | 8 | **16** | 16/1 | 56 | 29 |
| 3817² | **King Rat (IRE) (79)** (TJEtherington) **5-8-12b** WRSwinburn(15) (prom over 4f: sn lost tch: t.o) | nk | **17** | 12/1 | 36 | 15 |
| | **Air Commodore (IRE) (90)** (DWPArbuthnot) **5-9-9** TQuinn(14) (b: bkwd: led over 4f: grad wknd: t.o) | hd | **18** | 33/1 | 39 | 18 |
| | | | | (SP 130.7%) | | **18 Rn** |

**1m 35.4** (3.40) CSF £39.47 CT £222.48 TOTE £4.00: £1.40 £2.00 £2.10 £5.80 (£18.10) Trio £38.90 OWNER Mr Robert Cox (TARPORLEY) BRED East Riding Sack and Paper Co

WEIGHT FOR AGE 3yo-6lb

**OFFICIAL EXPLANATION Gymcrak Premiere: the jockey stated that his instructions were to settle the gelding and ride the race as he found it. He added that the horse started slowly and immediately hung right. He added that initially he thought the saddle slipped and that, in trying to keep his mount from hanging, he was unable to ride vigorously until the straight, when the gelding ran on under pressure. The trainer added that the gelding can be moody and was obviously unsuited by the tight track.**

**3805 My Gallery (IRE)** made it win number nine for the season in a hotly-contested event. It was fairly comfortable in the end and she remains a credit to all concerned. (4/1)

**3833 Jo Mell** looked to have the edge when leading into the straight but, hard as he tried, just could not contain the in-form winner. He is at his best at present and another success is long overdue. (9/1)

**3830* Rebel County (IRE)** looked the pick of her stable's three runners at the weights but, over a trip short of her ideal, could not summon up the pace to deliver a challenge. She has not stopped winning yet. (13/2)

**3812* Maple Bay (IRE)** did not possess the speed to land a blow, but this was a highly-promising run. He, like the rest of his stable, is holding his form particularly well. (16/1)

**Absolute Magic** needed this airing after over a year out of action, but he stuck on willingly in the closing stages and he has not lost any of his ability. (25/1)

**3254 Somerton Boy (IRE)** always looks a million dollars and invariably runs well. Although he does not win as often as he should, he has looked fully committed in recent outings and his turn may be just delayed. (16/1)

**3521 Blatant Outburst** ran extremely well for a maiden and would have finished closer but for being stopped in his stride just inside the final furlong. (25/1)

## 3934 CHESTER RATED STKS H'CAP (0-110) (Listed) (3-Y.O+) (Class A)

3-30 (3-30) **1m 5f 89y** £15,185.20 (£5,666.80: £2,758.40: £1,172.00: £511.00: £246.60) Stalls: Low GOING: 0.10 sec per fur (G)

| Form | Horse | Dist | Pos | SP | RR | SF |
|---|---|---|---|---|---|---|
| 3212[7] | **Royal Scimitar (USA) (94)** (PFICole) **4-8-12** TQuinn(2) (lw: chsd ldrs: qcknd to ld over 2f out: sn clr: r.o) | — | **1** | 8/1 | 105 | 64 |
| 2730[6] | **Leonato (FR) (100)** (PDEvans) **4-9-4** JFEgan(3) (hld up: hdwy over 2f out: kpt on u.p ins fnl f) | 1¾ | **2** | 50/1 | 109 | 68 |
| 3689[17] | **Snow Princess (IRE) (92)** (LordHuntingdon) **4-8-10** WRSwinburn(6) (lw: a.p: ev ch 2f out: rdn & unable qckn fnl f) | nk | **3** | 9/2[3] | 101 | 60 |
| 3398* | **Mount Row (97)** (LMCumani) **3-8-4** OUrbina(1) (hld up: hdwy 5f out: rdn 2f out: sn btn) | 8 | **4** | 5/1 | 96 | 44 |
| 3689[14] | **Desert Frolic (IRE) (93)** (MJohnston) **3-8-0** TWilliams(7) (chsd ldrs: drvn 4f out: wknd 2f out) | 4 | **5** | 9/1 | 87 | 35 |
| 1111[4] | **Wild Rumour (IRE) (90)** (PWChapple-Hyam) **3-7-11** FNorton(9) (bit bkwd: s.s: nvr nr to chal) | 4 | **6** | 20/1 | 80 | 28 |
| 3597[6] | **Poltarf (USA) (103)** (JHMGosden) **5-9-7** JCarroll(4) (swtg: led tl hdd & wknd over 2f out: t.o) | 10 | **7** | 11/1 | 81 | 40 |
| 3669* | **Yom Jameel (IRE) (101)** (MRStoute) **3-8-8** KFallon(5) (lost pl ½-wy: sn hrd drvn: t.o) | 3 | **8** | 5/2[1] | 75 | 23 |
| 3689[8] | **Prussian Blue (USA) (98)** (HRACecil) **4-9-2** RHughes(8) (hld up in tch tl rdn & wknd over 2f out: t.o) | dist | **9** | 4/1[2] | — | — |
| | | | | (SP 119.6%) | **9 Rn** | |

**2m 56.8** (6.80) CSF £213.17 CT £1,839.49 TOTE £10.00: £2.60 £5.40 £1.40 (£171.80) Trio £367.30 OWNER H R H Prince Fahd Salman (WHATCOMBE) BRED Newgate Stud Farm Inc

WEIGHT FOR AGE 3yo-11lb

**OFFICIAL EXPLANATION Yom Jameel (IRE): finished distressed.**

**Russian Blue (USA): made a noise and may have swallowed his tongue.**

**2534 Royal Scimitar (USA)** did not have quite so much use made of him this time and it paid off handsomely with a clear-cut success. This may be the best way to ride him. (8/1)

**2730 Leonato (FR)** seemed well suited by the step up in distance and turned in by far his best effort yet. (50/1)

**3689 Snow Princess (IRE)** got black type against her name through being placed in this listed race and was clawing back the principals at the finish over a trip which would seem inadequate these days. (9/2)

**3398* Mount Row** sat in behind the leaders travelling comfortably but, once the pace picked up, she was soon in trouble. (5/1)

**3597 Poltarf (USA)** again made sure there was no hanging about, but he is not yet quite 100% and had run himself into the ground once collared. (11/1)

**3669* Yom Jameel (IRE)** ran as if he had not fully recovered from his hard race at York, and he was beginning to tail off soon after halfway. (5/2)

## 3935 ROUGE ROSE MAIDEN STKS (3-Y.O F) (Class D)

4-00 (4-01) **1m 4f 66y** £4,608.00 (£1,288.00: £624.00) Stalls: Low GOING: 0.10 sec per fur (G)

| Form | Horse | Dist | Pos | SP | RR | SF |
|---|---|---|---|---|---|---|
| 3441[2] | **Flamands (IRE) (83)** (LMCumani) **3-8-11** OUrbina(3) (lw: s.s: sn chsng ldr: pushed along 4f out: led over 1f out: rdn out) | — | **1** | 8/13[1] | 87 | 51 |
| 1804[5] | **Heart** (MRStoute) **3-8-11** KFallon(2) (hld up: effrt on ins & nt clr run ent st: swtchd outside & str run wl ins fnl f) | ½ | **2** | 5/1[3] | 86 | 50 |
| 2399[2] | **Supamova (USA) (80)** (PFICole) **3-8-11** TQuinn(1) (lw: led: rdn & hdd over 1f out: eased whn btn) | 7 | **3** | 11/4[2] | 77 | 41 |
| | | | | (SP 105.2%) | **3 Rn** | |

**2m 44.75** (8.15) CSF £3.18 TOTE £1.60: (£2.40) OWNER Sultan Al Kabeer (NEWMARKET) BRED Lyonstown Stud, Swettenham Stud and Ron Con Ltd

**3441 Flamands (IRE)**, flat to the boards passing the three-furlong pole, struck the front below the distance and got first run on Heart. (8/13)

**1804 Heart** would have won this with any luck at all, but she was hemmed in on the inside rail turning in. When she did get free, the winner was beyond recall. (5/1: op 3/1)

**2399 Supamova (USA)** made the running but never looked happy on this tight track and was brushed aside with ease. (11/4)

## 3936 PARADISE NURSERY H'CAP (2-Y.O) (Class C)

4-30 (4-32) **7f 2y** £5,475.00 (£1,650.00: £800.00: £375.00) Stalls: Low GOING: 0.10 sec per fur (G)

| Form | Horse | Dist | Pos | SP | RR | SF |
|---|---|---|---|---|---|---|
| 3880[5] | **I Can't Remember (74)** (PDEvans) **2-8-1** JFEgan(10) (a.p: rdn to ld ins fnl f: r.o wl) | — | **1** | 8/1 | 75 | 37 |
| 2575[2] | **Green Jewel (86)** (RHannon) **2-8-13** RHughes(6) (b: lw: a.p: rdn 2f out: ev ch 1f out: kpt on nr fin) | 1½ | **2** | 7/2[1] | 84 | 46 |
| 3400[6] | **Sinecure (USA) (84)** (JHMGosden) **2-8-11** JCarroll(5) (lw: a.p: hrd drvn over 2f out: styd on ins fnl f) | ½ | **3** | 9/2[3] | 80 | 42 |
| 3247[4] | **Exit To Rio (CAN) (94)** (MrsJRRamsden) **2-9-7** KFallon(1) (lw: hld up in tch: snatched up 4f out: sn hrd rdn: kpt on: nt pce to chal) | s.h | **4** | 7/2[1] | 90 | 52 |
| 3687* | **Lamorna (81)** (MRChannon) **2-8-8** TQuinn(7) (led tl hdd & no ex ins fnl f) | 1 | **5** | 4/1[2] | 75 | 37 |
| 3826[3] | **Northern Sun (87)** (TGMills) **2-9-0** WRSwinburn(3) (hld up: effrt & rdn 2f out: no imp) | 1½ | **6** | 11/2 | 78 | 40 |
| 3512[3] | **Grate Times (78)** (EWeymes) **2-8-5** RLappin(4) (lw: hld up: effrt on outside 2f out: sn hrd drvn & wknd) | 3 | **7** | 10/1 | 62 | 24 |
| 3835[14] | **Skelton Sovereign (IRE) (74)** (RHollinshead) **2-7-12**[(3)ow4] FLynch(9) (s.s: a bhd & outpcd) | 11 | **8** | 14/1 | 33 | — |
| | | | | (SP 124.9%) | **8 Rn** | |

**1m 30.5** (5.30) CSF £36.95 CT £136.33 TOTE £9.80: £1.70 £1.50 £2.20 (£30.20) Trio £60.30 OWNER Peter Graham Racing (WELSHPOOL) BRED C. G. Reid

**3880 I Can't Remember**, from a yard in tip-top form, obviously thrives on hard work and this first success over such a trip was well deserved. (8/1)
**2575 Green Jewel** is not yet quite getting home over seven furlongs, but she is bred to need at least this trip and should not be written off yet. (7/2)
**3400 Sinecure (USA)**, always pushing the pace, kept beavering away in the latter stages and we have not seem the best of him yet. (9/2)
**3247 Exit To Rio (CAN)**, a strong colt who does not look to be an easy ride, lacked the pace to get himself among the leaders. (7/2: 5/2-4/1)
**3687* Lamorna** does not appear to be getting home with so much use made of her at this trip. More patient tactics would seem the obvious solution. (4/1)
**3826 Northern Sun** could not get himself into it, despite the firmest of rides, and seems to reserve his best for near-at-home engagements. (11/2)

T/Plpt: £135.50 (139.65 Tckts). T/Qdpt: £27.50 (34.52 Tckts). IM

## 3853-**RIPON** (R-H) (Soft, Heavy patches)
## Saturday August 31st
WEATHER: fine WIND: almost nil

### 3937 STABLE LADS WELFARE TRUST APPRENTICE H'CAP (0-70) (3-Y.O+) (Class F)
2-10 (2-11) **6f** £2,909.00 (£819.00: £401.00) Stalls: Low GOING: 0.26 sec per fur (G)

| Form | Runner | Pos | SP | RR | SF |
|---|---|---|---|---|---|
| 3883[5] | **Another Nightmare (IRE) (47)** (RMMcKellar) **4-7-13**(7) JMcAuley(19) (lw: trckd ldrs: led over 1f out: r.o wl) ..— | 1 | 9/1[3] | 59 | 42 |
| 3793[11] | **Wardara (69)** (CADwyer) **4-10-0v** JoHunnam(7) (s.i.s: racd stands' side: sn chsng ldrs: kpt on wl fnl f) .........2½ | 2 | 8/1[2] | 74 | 57 |
| 3292[6] | **Doug's Folly (42)** (MWEasterby) **3-7-12b** CAdamson(2) (led stands' side tl over 1f out: kpt on same pce)......½ | 3 | 16/1 | 46 | 26 |
| *3602*[2] | **Disco Boy (42)** (PDEvans) **6-8-1** GMilligan(12) (a chsng ldrs: styd on same pce appr fnl f)...............hd | 4 | 9/1[3] | 46 | 29 |
| 2911[8] | **Amron (58)** (JBerry) **9-8-12**(5) CLowther(11) (lw: a chsng ldrs: kpt on same pce fnl 2f).............½ | 5 | 9/1[3] | 60 | 43 |
| 3783[9] | **Runs in the Family (51)** (GMMcCourt) **4-8-5v**(5) RStudholme(14) (led tl over 1f out: kpt on)..........hd | 6 | 7/1[1] | 53 | 36 |
| 3453[13] | **Mill End Lady (43)** (MWEasterby) **3-7-13b**ow1 AEddery(6) (racd stands' side: chsd ldrs: edgd rt & kpt on wl fnl f) .........nk | 7 | 16/1 | 44 | 23 |
| 2578[6] | **Mullagh Hill Lad (IRE) (46)** (BAMcMahon) **3-7-11**(5) AMcCarthy(15) (styd on fnl 2f: nt rch ldrs).........hd | 8 | 14/1 | 47 | 27 |
| 3465[7] | **Camionneur (IRE) (50)** (TDEasterby) **3-8-3b**(3) PDoe(20) (lw: chsd ldrs: styd on same pce fnl 2f)..........¾ | 9 | 9/1[3] | 49 | 29 |
| *2937*[7] | **Prudent Princess (55)** (AHide) **4-8-9**(5)ow1 CScudder(8) (racd stands' side: in tch: effrt over 2f out: no imp) ..nk | 10 | 25/1 | 53 | 35 |
| 3424[6] | **Craigie Boy (52)** (NBycroft) **6-8-8b**(3) JBramhill(3) (racd stands' side: chsd ldrs tl outpcd appr fnl f)..........s.h | 11 | 9/1[3] | 50 | 33 |
| *3602*[10] | **Need You Badly (54)** (SPCWoods) **3-8-7**(3) CWebb(17) (chsd ldrs: rdn & edgd lft over 1f out: sn wknd) ..........2 | 12 | 14/1 | 47 | 27 |
| 3624[10] | **Blue Lugana (37)** (NBycroft) **4-7-10b** IonaWands(1) (racd stands' side: nvr wnt pce)..........nk | 13 | 33/1 | 29 | 12 |
| 3622[11] | **Maid O'Cannie (59)** (MWEasterby) **5-9-1b**(3) JEdmunds(9) (dwlt: sme hdwy 2f out: n.d)..........2½ | 14 | 9/1[3] | 44 | 27 |
| 3644[10] | **Samsung Lovelylady (IRE) (37)** (EWeymes) **4-7-7**(3) KSked(13) (w ldrs tl wknd 2f out)..........s.h | 15 | 33/1 | 22 | 5 |
| 3223[7] | **Playmaker (66)** (DNicholls) **3-9-8** SophieMitchell(4) (lw: racd stands' side: nvr nr ldrs)..........s.h | 16 | 8/1[2] | 51 | 31 |
| 1805[7] | **Beldray Park (IRE) (65)** (MrsALMKing) **3-9-7** DSweeney(5) (racd stands' side: chsd ldrs tl edgd rt & wknd fnl 2f) ..........2 | 17 | 14/1 | 45 | 25 |
| 3506[10] | **John's Law (IRE) (50)** (MJHeaton-Ellis) **3-8-6** AmandaSanders(18) (sn drvn along & outpcd)..........1½ | 18 | 20/1 | 26 | 6 |
| 1893[7] | **Polli Pui (41)** (WMBrisbourne) **4-7-9**(5) JFowle(16) (sn bhd)..........½ | 19 | 25/1 | 15 | — |
| 3815[8] | **Elpidos (62)** (MDHammond) **4-9-0**(7) JO'Leary(10) (sn wl outpcd & bhd)..........5 | 20 | 33/1 | 23 | 6 |
| | | | (SP 147.8%) | | **20 Rn** |

**1m 15.5** (5.00) CSF £85.67 CT £1,113.82 TOTE £13.40: £2.50 £2.30 £4.70 £2.20 (£70.00) Trio £507.20; £514.35 to Hamilton 2/9/96 OWNER GM Engineering (LESMAHAGOW) BRED John J. Ryan
LONG HANDICAP Blue Lugana 6-13 Samsung Lovelylady (IRE) 7-8
WEIGHT FOR AGE 3yo-3lb
**IN-FOCUS: This was the 21-year-old jockey's first success.**
**3883 Another Nightmare (IRE)**, 8lb higher than when winning at Hamilton three runs ago, took this in good style. (9/1)
**3700* Wardara**, one of just eight to race on the stands' side, put a poor run over five furlongs last time behind her. Reluctant to leave the paddock, she missed the break, but seemed to relish the soft ground, staying on strongly in the final furlong. (8/1)
**3292 Doug's Folly** ran her best race so far this term, showing bags of toe to lead on the stands' side. (16/1)
**3602 Disco Boy**, from a stable that can do little wrong at present, ran well, but is better on the All-Weather. (9/1)
**2911 Amron**, who has slipped down the weights, appreciated the give underfoot. With stronger handling, there is another handicap in him. (9/1)
**3661 Runs in the Family**, a keen-going sort, towed them along on the far side, (7/1)

### 3938 MOORLAND POULTRY H'CAP (0-80) (3-Y.O+ F & M) (Class D)
2-40 (2-40) **1m 2f** £3,712.50 (£1,125.00: £550.00: £262.50) Stalls: High GOING: 0.26 sec per fur (G)

| Form | Runner | Pos | SP | RR | SF |
|---|---|---|---|---|---|
| 1669[3] | **Ground Game (78)** (DRLoder) **3-9-12** DRMcCabe(10) (b.hind: mde virtually all: edgd lft & styd on wl u.p fnl 2f: hld on wl towards fin)..........— | 1 | 100/30[1] | 90 | 61 |
| 3470[3] | **Princess Danielle (59)** (WRMuir) **4-9-1** MHills(1) (hld up: effrt 3f out: n.m.r over 1f out: styd on ins fnl f).........¾ | 2 | 9/2[2] | 70 | 49 |
| 3461[3] | **Tart (FR) (74)** (JRFanshawe) **3-9-5**(3) NVarley(9) (lw: a chsng ldrs: one pce fnl 3f)..........5 | 3 | 6/1 | 77 | 48 |
| 3655[2] | **Forest Fantasy (57)** (JWharton) **3-8-5** GHind(6) (trckd ldrs: effrt over 2f out: one pce)..........nk | 4 | 11/2[3] | 59 | 30 |
| 3522[2] | **Omara (USA) (76)** (HRACecil) **3-9-10** AMcGlone(7) (lw: trckd ldrs gng wl: effrt over 1f out: fnd nil)..........s.h | 5 | 9/2[2] | 78 | 49 |
| 3619[2] | **She's Simply Great (IRE) (52)** (JJO'Neill) **3-8-0**ow1 GCarter(2) (lw: hld up: effrt over 3f out: wknd over 2f out: eased)..........12 | 6 | 9/1 | 35 | 5 |
| 3402[5] | **Highfield Fizz (45)** (CWFairhurst) **4-8-1** LCharnock(8) (in tch: rdn over 3f out: sn wknd)..........hd | 7 | 25/1 | 28 | 7 |
| 2489[2] | **Hobbs Choice (48)** (GMMoore) **3-7-10** NKennedy(5) (w wnr: drvn over 3f out: sn lost pl)..........2 | 8 | 11/1 | 28 | — |
| 2062* | **Russian Rose (IRE) (73)** (AHide) **3-9-7** JStack(3) (effrt & hung lft 4f out: sn wknd)..........1½ | 9 | 6/1 | 50 | 21 |
| 1671[6] | **Matam (64)** (MWEasterby) **3-8-7**(5) GParkin(4) (bit bkwd: a in rr)..........4 | 10 | 20/1 | 35 | 6 |
| | | | (SP 130.3%) | | **10 Rn** |

**2m 12.1** (8.60) CSF £20.11 CT £85.36 TOTE £4.40: £2.50 £1.90 £2.20 (£8.30) Trio £28.90 OWNER Mrs P. T. Fenwick (NEWMARKET) BRED Michael Watt and Miss Jemima Johnson
WEIGHT FOR AGE 3yo-8lb
**OFFICIAL EXPLANATION Russian Rose (IRE): was found to have a muscle problem afterwards.**
**1669 Ground Game**, fresh and well after an absence of almost three months, relished the give underfoot. Changing her legs several times, she proved a most willing customer. (100/30)
**3470 Princess Danielle** met trouble for a couple of strides. Moving onto the winner's quarters inside the final furlong, she looked likely to succeed, but was being held at the line. She is a luckless sort, but just seems to lack that finishing punch. (9/2)

**3461 Tart (FR)** is willing but seems to lack anything in the way of finishing speed. (6/1)
**3655 Forest Fantasy** travelled nicely but, off the bit, did not find as much as expected. Perhaps the ground was too soft for her here. (11/2)
**3522 Omara (USA)** travelled strongly as usual. She looked as though she could pick up the winner any time she pleased all the way up the straight but, when her rider asked, she quickly ran up the white flag. (9/2)
**2062* Russian Rose (IRE)** (6/1: op 10/1)

## 3939 CROWTHER HOMES H'CAP (0-80) (3-Y.O+) (Class D)

3-15 (3-17) **1m 4f 60y** £3,840.00 (£1,140.00: £540.00: £240.00) Stalls: Low GOING: 0.26 sec per fur (G)

| | | | | SP | RR | SF |
|---|---|---|---|---|---|---|
| 3621* | **Sugar Mill (67)** (MrsMReveley) **6-9-6** ACulhane(1) (lw: hld up: effrt 4f out: styd on wl u.p to ld ins fnl f) | — | 1 | $11/4^{1}$ | 77 | 47 |
| $2331^{3}$ | **Nigel's Lad (IRE) (72)** (PCHaslam) **4-9-11** GCarter(3) (chsd ldrs: rdn & outpcd over 2f out: swtchd outside & styd on wl fnl f) | nk | 2 | 14/1 | 82 | 52 |
| $3653^{6}$ | **Etterby Park (USA) (68)** (MJohnston) **3-8-11** MHills(11) (a chsng ldrs: swtchd rt over 1f out: styd on wl) | 1¼ | 3 | 9/1 | 76 | 36 |
| $3710^{18}$ | **Rusk (73)** (JPearce) **3-9-2** MWigham(2) (trckd ldrs: led 2f out tl ins fnl f) | nk | 4 | 16/1 | 81 | 41 |
| $1022^{5}$ | **Eau de Cologne (66)** (CWThornton) **4-9-5** DeanMcKeown(9) (bit bkwd: trckd ldrs: ev ch tl wknd over 1f out: eased) | 8 | 5 | $6/1^{2}$ | 63 | 33 |
| $3479^{4}$ | **Taufan Boy (74)** (PWHarris) **3-9-3** GHind(5) (a in tch: outpcd over 3f out: n.d) | 1 | 6 | 8/1 | 70 | 30 |
| $3081^{8}$ | **Manful (68)** (CWCElsey) **4-9-7b** NKennedy(6) (a in tch: effrt over 3f out: outpcd fnl 2f) | nk | 7 | 12/1 | 64 | 34 |
| $3081^{5}$ | **Leif the Lucky (USA) (65)** (MissSEHall) **7-9-4** NConnorton(4) (plld hrd: trckd ldrs: led on bit over 2f out: sn hdd: wknd & eased appr fnl f) | nk | 8 | $7/1^{3}$ | 60 | 30 |
| $3290^{5}$ | **Maftun (USA) (55)** (GMMoore) **4-8-8** JTate(7) (lw: w ldr: led 4f out tl over 2f out: sn wknd) | 3 | 9 | 14/1 | 46 | 16 |
| *$3603^{15}$* | **Oneoftheoldones (55)** (JNorton) **4-8-8** SDWilliams(8) (lw: hld up & plld hrd: a in rr) | 1 | 10 | 33/1 | 45 | 15 |
| | **Marchant Ming (IRE) (58)** (MDHammond) **4-8-11** RCochrane(10) (bit bkwd: led to 4f out: wknd & eased over 2f out) | ½ | 11 | $6/1^{2}$ | 47 | 17 |
| $612^{9}$ | **Ashover (58)** (TDBarron) **6-8-11** JFanning(12) (bit bkwd: s.i.s: a bhd) | ¾ | 12 | 10/1 | 46 | 16 |
| $3401^{6}$ | **Berkeley Bounder (USA) (70)** (MrsMReveley) **4-9-9** LCharnock(13) (lw: hld up: a in rr) | 15 | 13 | 16/1 | 39 | 9 |

(SP 133.7%) **13 Rn**

**2m 45.9** (11.90) CSF £42.71 CT £307.11 TOTE £3.70: £2.00 £3.90 £2.60 (£24.70) Trio £35.50 OWNER Mr C. C. Buckley (SALTBURN) BRED Snailwell Stud Co Ltd

WEIGHT FOR AGE 3yo-10lb

**3621* Sugar Mill,** from a 3lb higher mark, was one of the first to come under pressure. Staying on in resolute fashion, he will be even better suited by a flatter, more galloping track. (11/4)
**2331 Nigel's Lad (IRE),** who won six races last year, bounced right back to his best. Tapped for foot and forced to switch halfway up the straight, he threw down a strong challenge inside the last. (14/1)
**2900 Etterby Park (USA),** who showed a moderate action going down, put two poor efforts behind him, staying on resolutely after being switched. (9/1)
**2062 Rusk,** who had his tongue tied down, was back in his proper class and was only run out of it inside the final furlong. (16/1)
**1022 Eau de Cologne,** absent since early May, proved awkward to load. Looking in need of the outing, he ran really well until blowing up over a furlong out. He will soon be adding to his record. (6/1: op 10/1)
**3081 Leif the Lucky (USA)** saw a lot of daylight on the outside and would not settle. His stamina gave out over a furlong from home, and he was eased up. (7/1)
**Marchant Ming (IRE),** a soft-ground hurdler, ran much better than his finishing position indicates. After making the running, he was eased off once he blew up. From this sort of mark, there is definitely a handicap or two to be won with him this autumn. (6/1)

## 3940 RIPON HORN BLOWER CONDITIONS STKS (2-Y.O) (Class B)

3-50 (3-50) **5f** £6,160.00 (£2,290.00: £1,107.50: £462.50: £193.75: £86.25) Stalls: Low GOING: 0.26 sec per fur (G)

| | | | | SP | RR | SF |
|---|---|---|---|---|---|---|
| 3483* | **For Old Times Sake (100)** (JBerry) **2-9-4** GCarter(5) (lw: s.i.s: sn chsng ldrs: rdn 2f out: edgd lft: led ins fnl f: styd on wl) | — | 1 | $7/2^{2}$ | 96 | 57 |
| 3590* | **Bold African (84)** (PDEvans) **2-8-10b** ACulhane(6) (led: clr ½-wy: hdd ins fnl f: btn whn hmpd nr fin) | 1¾ | 2 | 15/2 | 82 | 43 |
| $3692^{4}$ | **Big Ben (92)** (RHannon) **2-8-12** RPerham(4) (chsd ldrs: rdn ½-wy: kpt on same pce appr fnl f) | 1 | 3 | $7/2^{2}$ | 81 | 42 |
| $958^{2}$ | **The Gay Fox** (BAMcMahon) **2-8-10** RCochrane(3) (bit bkwd: trckd ldrs: effrt over 1f out: edgd lft & kpt on same pace) | hd | 4 | $9/2^{3}$ | 79 | 40 |
| $2575^{5}$ | **Meliksah (IRE) (86)** (MBell) **2-8-10** JTate(2) (lw: trckd ldrs: effrt ½-wy: sn rdn: wknd ins fnl f) | 3 | 5 | 11/2 | 69 | 30 |
| $2834a^{5}$ | **Future Prospect (IRE) (93)** (MJohnston) **2-8-12** MHills(1) (sn outpcd: sme hdwy ½-wy: edgd rt & wknd over 1f out: eased) | 10 | 6 | $100/30^{1}$ | 39 | — |

(SP 112.9%) **6 Rn**

**62.3 secs** (3.90) CSF £25.27 TOTE £4.00: £2.00 £2.60 (£10.00) OWNER Mrs Bridget Blum (COCKERHAM) BRED Shutford Stud

**3483* For Old Times Sake** is as tough as teak. Edging left, despite his rider switching his whip, he had the race won when slightly hampering the runner-up near the line. (7/2)
**3590* Bold African** has speed to burn. Three lengths clear at halfway, he was worn down inside the last and was held when short of room near the line. (15/2)
**3692 Big Ben** never looked truly happy on this soft ground. (7/2)
**958 The Gay Fox,** absent since being disqualified at Haydock in May, looked on the burly side. Travelling keenly, he again showed signs of inexperience. Still learning, there is surely a race or two to be won with him. (9/2)
**2575 Meliksah (IRE),** who hammered Bold African by four lengths at Redcar on his debut, seemed to run out of stamina even over this minimum trip inside the last. (11/2)
**2834a Future Prospect (IRE),** who has been highly tried, was never travelling on the ground, and his rider eventually gave up. (100/30)

## 3941 TATTERSALLS MAIDEN AUCTION STKS (2-Y.O) (Class E)

4-20 (4-21) **6f** £3,009.30 (£911.40: £445.20: £212.10) Stalls: Low GOING: 0.26 sec per fur (G)

| | | | | SP | RR | SF |
|---|---|---|---|---|---|---|
| $3685^{5}$ | **Certain Magic** (WRMuir) **2-8-7**ow1 RCochrane(2) (sn drvn along: hdwy ½-wy: hung rt & styd on to ld wl ins fnl f) | — | 1 | $3/1^{1}$ | 77 | 21 |
| | **Hurgill Lady** (JWWatts) **2-8-1** JFanning(3) (w'like: scope: bit bkwd: trckd ldrs gng wl: smooth hdwy to ld jst ins fnl f: edgd rt & hdd nr fin) | 1 | 2 | 12/1 | 68+ | 13 |
| $1308^{4}$ | **Treasure Touch (IRE)** (GMMoore) **2-8-5** JTate(14) (a.p: styd on same pce appr fnl f) | 1 | 3 | 12/1 | 70 | 15 |
| | **Penprio (IRE)** (BAMcMahon) **2-8-4** AMackay(12) (lt-f: unf: trckd ldrs: n.m.r 2f out: kpt on wl fnl f) | 1¾ | 4 | 16/1 | 64 | 9 |
| $3050^{7}$ | **Compact Disc (IRE)** (MJohnston) **2-8-2** JStack(6) (w ldrs: led over 2f out tl jst ins fnl f: sn wknd) | 1½ | 5 | 13/2 | 58 | 3 |

| | | | | SP | RR | SF |
|---|---|---|---|---|---|---|
| 2865[8] | **Why O Six** (RAFahey) **2-8-8** ACulhane(7) (bit bkwd: unruly gng to s: chsd ldrs: wknd & eased ins fnl f) | 2 | **6** | 20/1 | 59 | 4 |
| | **Coral Island** (JGFitzGerald) **2-8-7** DRMcCabe(1) (rangy: scope: bit bkwd: s.s: bhd tl stdy hdwy 2f out: styd on wl towards fin) | 2 | **7** | 14/1 | 52+ | — |
| 3647[4] | **Hong Kong Express (IRE) (68)** (JBerry) **2-8-3** GCarter(15) (swtg: swvd rt s: sn in tch: rdn & outpcd ½-wy: grad wknd) | ½ | **8** | 9/1 | 47 | — |
| 3687[8] | **Silver Button** (MissSEHall) **2-8-8** AMcGlone(13) (in tch: effrt over 2f out: no imp) | nk | **9** | 7/1 | 51 | — |
| 3462[11] | **Eastern Firedragon (IRE)** (TDEasterby) **2-8-0b[1]** LCharnock(11) (led tl over 2f out: sn wknd) | 2½ | **10** | 16/1 | 37 | — |
| 2538[6] | **Havago** (RHannon) **2-8-6** RPerham(9) (w ldrs tl wknd 2f out) | nk | **11** | 4/1[2] | 42 | — |
| | **Globetrotter (IRE)** (MJohnston) **2-8-7** MHills(4) (w'like: str: bit bkwd: sn bhd) | 1½ | **12** | 6/1[3] | 39 | — |
| 2865[9] | **Sam Peeb** (RAFahey) **2-8-4** DeanMcKeown(10) (bit bkwd: trckd ldrs tl lost pl over 2f out) | hd | **13** | 33/1 | 36 | — |
| *1968[W]* | **Rising Glory** (MissJFCraze) **2-8-9** SDWilliams(5) (w'like: small: bkwd: s.i.s: a outpcd & wl bhd) | 5 | **14** | 33/1 | 27 | — |
| | **Crosby Nod** (EWeymes) **2-8-5** GHind(8) (str: cmpt: bkwd: s.i.s: a wl bhd) | 8 | **15** | 25/1 | 2 | — |
| | | | | (SP 143.4%) | **15 Rn** | |

**1m 17.1** (6.60) CSF £43.61 TOTE £4.20: £1.90 £4.80 £3.50 (£45.60) Trio £240.50; £176.20 to Hamilton 2/9/96 OWNER Delamere Partnership (LAMBOURN) BRED D. J. and Mrs Deer

**3685 Certain Magic** was well backed to step up on his initial effort. Giving his rider a few problems, he was persuaded to stay on and gain the day near the line. He will be suited by a step up to seven. (3/1: op 7/1)

**Hurgill Lady**, who looked as though the outing would do her a power of good, tracked the leaders travelling smoothly. After hitting the front, she made hard work of it and, edging off a true line, was just worried out of it. She should be a different proposition next time. (12/1)

**1308 Treasure Touch (IRE)**, who has changed stables since his Thirsk run, gave a good account of himself and showed what a good thing he would have been in the seller at Doncaster for which he was withdrawn after playing up badly at the start. (12/1)

**Penprio (IRE)** is nothing much to look at but he showed ability, travelling strongly. Messed about, he was putting in some solid work in the final furlong. (16/1)

**2755 Compact Disc (IRE)** lacks size and scope. (13/2)

**Why O Six**, who still looked on the backward side, gave a rodeo display on the way to the start. He shaped by no means badly and was not knocked about. Hopefully he will settle down with racing. (20/1)

**Coral Island**, who has plenty of size and scope, showed promise after a slow start. He looks a fair long-term prospect. (14/1)

## 3942 WENSLEYDALE MAIDEN STKS (3-Y.O+) (Class D)

4-50 (4-50) **1m 2f** £3,810.00 (£1,155.00: £565.00: £270.00) Stalls: High GOING: 0.26 sec per fur (G)

| | | | | SP | RR | SF |
|---|---|---|---|---|---|---|
| 3425[2] | **Triple Leap** (JHMGosden) **3-8-12** GHind(3) (lw: sn trckng ldrs: led over 2f out: pushed clr: eased towards fin) | — | **1** | 11/8[1] | 86+ | 50 |
| 2601[6] | **Classic Parisian (IRE) (76)** (RHarris) **3-8-7** AMackay(10) (lw: w ldr: led over 3f out: hdd over 2f out: kpt on: no ch w wnr) | 3 | **2** | 5/1[3] | 76 | 40 |
| 3818[2] | **Pep Talk (USA)** (HRACecil) **3-8-12** AMcGlone(9) (lw: chsd ldrs: pushed along 6f out: outpcd over 3f out: styd on same pce fnl 2f) | 1¼ | **3** | 11/4[2] | 79 | 43 |
| 3441[5] | **National Treasure** (MRStoute) **3-8-7** MHills(7) (chsd ldrs tl lost pl over 1f out) | 9 | **4** | 5/1[3] | 60 | 24 |
| 3441[8] | **Calendula** (DMorley) **3-8-7** GCarter(2) (hdwy on outside over 3f out: ev ch & wandered 2f out: sn wknd) | hd | **5** | 50/1 | 60 | 24 |
| 3656[12] | **Shoshone** (JHMGosden) **3-8-7** DeanMcKeown(4) (b.hind: bit bkwd: sn outpcd & pushed along: nvr nr ldrs) | 5 | **6** | 20/1 | 52 | 16 |
| | **Koli** (HJCollingridge) **3-8-4**(3) PMcCabe(5) (leggy: scope: sn wl bhd: t.o 4f out: styd on fnl 2f) | s.h | **7** | 33/1 | 52 | 16 |
| 3704[3] | **Roi du Nord (FR)** (SWCampion) **4-9-6** TIves(1) (trckd ldrs: rdn 3f out: sn lost pl) | 10 | **8** | 12/1 | 41 | 13 |
| | **Tilston** (MrsJCecil) **5-9-6** JStack(8) (led tl over 3f out: eased & sn bhd) | nk | **9** | 16/1 | 40 | 12 |
| 578[14] | **Polonaise Prince (USA)** (VSoane) **3-8-12** RCochrane(6) (bit bkwd: hld up: a bhd) | hd | **10** | 20/1 | 40 | 4 |
| | | | | (SP 130.1%) | **10 Rn** | |

**2m 11.8** (8.30) CSF £9.95 TOTE £2.50: £1.40 £1.60 £1.50 (£7.70) Trio £4.90 OWNER Sheikh Mohammed (NEWMARKET) BRED Sheikh Mohammed bin Rashid al Maktoum

WEIGHT FOR AGE 3yo-8lb

**3425 Triple Leap**, who looked outstanding in the paddock, is a moderate mover and was suited by the soft ground. He took it in good style in the end and his future now lies in the hands of the Handicapper. (11/8)

**2601 Classic Parisian (IRE)** stuck on at the one pace and proved no match. She seems to lack anything in the way of finishing speed. (5/1)

**3818 Pep Talk (USA)**, unimpressive in the paddock, gave his rider problems by carrying his head high under pressure. (11/4)

**3441 National Treasure** is not without some ability. Her dam was smart over shorter trips and she might just make it in handicaps, possibly over a mile. (5/1)

**Calendula** shaped much better than on her debut. Still with a lot to learn, further improvement seems on the cards. (50/1)

T/Plpt: £88.00 (162.42 Tckts). T/Qdpt: £23.50 (31.34 Tckts). WG

# 3924-SANDOWN (R-H) (Good)

## Saturday August 31st

WEATHER: fine WIND: almost nil

## 3943 B.D.M. NURSERY (S) H'CAP (2-Y.O) (Class E)

2-00 (2-01) **7f 16y** £3,225.00 (£975.00: £475.00: £225.00) Stalls: High GOING minus 0.38 sec per fur (F)

| | | | | SP | RR | SF |
|---|---|---|---|---|---|---|
| 3678[4] | **Run Lucy Run (60)** (RGuest) **2-9-2** GDuffield(9) (hdwy over 2f out: hrd rdn over 1f out: led nr fin) | — | **1** | 8/1 | 57 | 35 |
| 3769[2] | **Maraud (65)** (RWArmstrong) **2-9-4b[1]**(3) MHenry(13) (lw: led 5f: led over 1f out: rdn & hdd nr fin) | nk | **2** | 9/1 | 61 | 39 |
| 3632[5] | **Summerville Wood (63)** (PMooney) **2-9-0b[1]**(5) MartinDwyer(5) (rdn over 2f out: hdwy over 1f out: r.o wl ins fnl f) | hd | **3** | 14/1 | 59 | 37 |
| 3662[5] | **Spondulicks (IRE) (57)** (RHannon) **2-8-13** DaneO'Neill(7) (lw: hdwy over 2f out: hrd rdn over 1f out: n.m.r on ins ins fnl f: r.o one pce) | 3½ | **4** | 9/1 | 45 | 23 |
| 3498[2] | **Marsh Marigold (55)** (MartynMeade) **2-8-8**(3) RHavlin(12) (a.p: rdn over 2f out: ev ch over 1f out: wknd fnl f) | 1 | **5** | 7/1[3] | 41 | 19 |
| 3762[6] | **Barnwood Crackers (62)** (MissGayKelleway) **2-9-4** PatEddery(11) (swtg: hrd rdn & hdwy over 2f out: 5th whn nt clr run 1f out tl ins fnl f: nt rcvr) | ½ | **6** | 11/2[1] | 47 | 25 |
| 3795[2] | **Poly Moon (59)** (MRChannon) **2-9-1** JFortune(8) (lw: a.p: led 2f out tl over 1f out: wknd fnl f) | 6 | **7** | 13/2[2] | 30 | 8 |
| 3455[5] | **Super Scravels (44)** (DrJDScargill) **2-8-0** NCarlisle(3) (lw: bmpd 6f out: nvr nr to chal) | 2½ | **8** | 25/1 | 10 | — |
| 3662[4] | **Grovefair Lad (IRE) (57)** (BJMeehan) **2-8-13** BDoyle(4) (bhd fnl 2f) | s.h | **9** | 20/1 | 22 | — |

3648[3] **Lycius Touch (57)** (MJohnston) **2-8-13** WCarson(6) (bhd fnl 3f) ....2½ **10** 7/1[3] 17 —
3512[10] **Rons Revenge (51)** (MJRyan) **2-8-7** GBardwell(10) (hld up: rdn over 4f out: wknd 3f out) ....7 **11** 25/1 — —
3582[8] **Don't Forget Shoka (IRE) (47)** (JSMoore) **2-7-12**(5) PPMurphy(2) (bmpd 6f out: bhd fnl 3f) ....3 **12** 25/1 — —
3616[11] **Riscatto (USA) (58)** (WRMuir) **2-9-0** SWhitworth(1) (lw: prom over 4f) ....¾ **13** 20/1 — —
(SP 112.6%) **13 Rn**

**1m 31.73** (3.13) CSF £67.39 CT £926.72 TOTE £9.50: £2.30 £3.90 £7.50 (£22.90) Trio £228.80 OWNER Matthews Breeding and Racing (NEWMARKET) BRED Lord Matthews
Sold CSparrowhawk 5,000gns
**3678 Run Lucy Run** began to pick up over two furlongs out and, responding to pressure, whittled down the leader near the line. (8/1)
**3769 Maraud**, blinkered for the first time, had no intentions of hanging around and set a brisk pace. After being headed, he went on again and, to his credit, was only overhauled near the finish. (9/1)
**3330* Summerville Wood**, blinkered for the first time, ran on really well up the hill but the line was always beating him. (14/1: 10/1-16/1)
**3662 Spondulicks (IRE)** was held when not having a great deal of room along the inside rail inside the final furlong. He is thoroughly exposed. (9/1)
**3498 Marsh Marigold** had every chance below the distance, but soon came to the end of her tether. (7/1)
**3762 Barnwood Crackers** did not have much luck, and all chance had evaporated when he did get free inside the final furlong. He would not have troubled the winner, but may well have reached a place. (11/2)

## 3944 PARAGON AMATEUR LIMITED STKS (0-70) (3-Y.O+) (Class E)
2-35 (2-38) **1m 2f 7y** £3,225.00 (£975.00: £475.00: £225.00) Stalls: High GOING minus 0.38 sec per fur (F)

| | | | | SP | RR | SF |
|---|---|---|---|---|---|---|
| 3205[6] | **Roufontaine (70)** (WRMuir) **5-11-9** MrTMcCarthy(5) (a.p: led over 3f out: clr over 2f out: eased wl ins fnl f) | — | **1** | 6/1[2] | 81+ | 63 |
| 3802* | **Kaafih Homm (IRE) (72)** (NACallaghan) **5-11-10** MrRThornton(15) (lw: nt clr run on ins over 5f out: hdwy over 2f out: rdn over 1f out: unable qckn) | 2½ | **2** | 5/2[1] | 78 | 60 |
| 3148[6] | **Royal Diversion (IRE) (68)** (JLDunlop) **3-10-9** MissEJohnsonHoughton(2) (hdwy over 2f out: one pce) | ½ | **3** | 7/1 | 70 | 44 |
| 3136[3] | **Rising Dough (IRE) (70)** (GLMoore) **4-11-8** MrsJMoore(16) (hdwy over 2f out: rdn over 1f out: one pce) | ½ | **4** | 13/2[3] | 74 | 56 |
| 1420[6] | **Absolute Utopia (USA) (67)** (NEBerry) **3-10-8**(4) MissEFolkes(3) (a.p: one pce fnl 2f) | 1½ | **5** | 50/1 | 70 | 44 |
| 3825[6] | **Battleship Bruce (64)** (MissGayKelleway) **4-11-2**(4) MrNMoran(10) (lw: hld up: hrd rdn wl over 1f out: one pce) | hd | **6** | 10/1 | 70 | 52 |
| 3340[4] | **Delight of Dawn (64)** (RMStronge) **4-11-1**(4) MrJDewhurst(1) (b: hdwy over 2f out: one pce) | 1¼ | **7** | 16/1 | 67 | 49 |
| | **Matamoros (70)** (GHarwood) **4-11-6** MrsAPerrett(14) (mid div whn hmpd on ins & lost pl over 5f out: nvr nrr) | 5 | **8** | 12/1 | 60 | 42 |
| 3149[11] | **Phanan (33)** (REPeacock) **10-11-2**(4) MrsCPeacock(12) (lw: prom over 7f) | 2½ | **9** | 100/1 | 56 | 38 |
| 3471[5] | **Haydown (IRE) (34)** (CTNash) **4-11-6** MrPPhillips(4) (bhd fnl 4f) | 1¼ | **10** | 100/1 | 54 | 36 |
| 3204[8] | **Bronze Runner (25)** (EAWheeler) **12-11-6b** MrEJames(9) (bhd fnl 2f) | 1½ | **11** | 100/1 | 52 | 34 |
| | **Bajan (IRE) (65)** (LadyHerries) **5-11-6** MrPPritchard-Gordon(8) (prom over 7f) | nk | **12** | 8/1 | 51 | 33 |
| 2127[10] | **Zamalek (USA) (68)** (GLMoore) **4-11-6** MrKGoble(11) (swtg: a bhd) | 20 | **13** | 33/1 | 19 | 1 |
| 2284[10] | **Legal Drama (USA) (42)** (JohnBerry) **4-10-13**(4) MrVCoogan(13) (lw: bhd fnl 4f) | 2 | **14** | 100/1 | 13 | — |
| | **Griffin's Girl (30)** (PMooney) **4-10-13**(4) MissLMcIntosh(6) (swtg: led over 6f) | 9 | **15** | 100/1 | — | — |
| 2513[5] | **Cante Chico (60)** (OBrennan) **4-11-8** MissVHaigh(7) (prom 6f) | 5 | **16** | 40/1 | — | — |

(SP 114.8%) **16 Rn**

**2m 11.73** (5.03) CSF £18.78 TOTE £8.20: £2.50 £1.50 £2.10 (£8.00) Trio £16.10 OWNER Piercefield Stables (LAMBOURN) BRED D. J. and Mrs Deer
WEIGHT FOR AGE 3yo-8lb
**3205 Roufontaine** gained her fifth victory of the year in emphatic style. Sent on entering the straight, she soon stormed clear and was able to ease down considerably in the closing stages. The winning distance is no true reflection of her superiority, and she was value for at least twelve lengths. (6/1)
**3802* Kaafih Homm (IRE)** stayed on to win the separate battle for second, but was greatly flattered to have finished so close to the winner. (5/2)
**3148 Royal Diversion (IRE)** never looked like finding another gear. (7/1: op 4/1)
**3136 Rising Dough (IRE)** never looked like winning. (13/2)
**1420 Absolute Utopia (USA)**, bought out of Ed Dunlop's stable for a mere 1,700 guineas, was having his first run in three months. His rider proved of little assistance in the straight, and he could only plod on. (50/1)
**Bajan (IRE)** (8/1: 5/1-9/1)

## 3945 LYCEUM ATALANTA STKS (Listed) (3-Y.O+ F & M) (Class A)
3-10 (3-13) **1m 14y** £11,849.00 (£3,587.00: £1,751.00: £833.00) Stalls: High GOING minus 0.38 sec per fur (F)

| | | | | SP | RR | SF |
|---|---|---|---|---|---|---|
| 2225* | **Wandering Star (USA) (97)** (JRFanshawe) **3-8-8** NDay(7) (lw: rdn over 2f out: hdwy over 1f out: squeezed thro to ld wl ins fnl f: r.o wl) | — | **1** | 12/1 | 108 | 62 |
| 3231[7] | **Miss Universal (IRE) (106)** (CEBrittain) **3-8-8** BDoyle(9) (lw: chsd ldr over 6f out: rdn over 2f out: led ins fnl f: sn hdd: unable qckn) | 1 | **2** | 8/1 | 106 | 60 |
| 3472* | **Yamuna (USA) (88)** (HRACecil) **3-8-8** PatEddery(6) (rdn & n.m.r over 2f out: hdwy & nt clr run over 1f out: squeezed thro ins fnl f: r.o) | 2 | **3** | 7/2[1] | 102 | 56 |
| | **Arabride** (LordHuntingdon) **4-9-4** DaneO'Neill(5) (b: lw: a.p: rdn over 1f out: one pce) | nk | **4** | 25/1 | 106 | 66 |
| 3503[4] | **Lap of Luxury (96)** (WJarvis) **7-9-0** SSanders(2) (rdn & hdwy over 1f out: r.o) | nk | **5** | 15/2 | 101 | 61 |
| 3231[8] | **Solar Crystal (IRE) (107)** (HRACecil) **3-8-8** WRyan(10) (led: rdn over 2f out: hdd ins fnl f: sn wknd) | 1½ | **6** | 8/1 | 98 | 52 |
| 3640* | **Awaamir (90)** (JHMGosden) **3-8-8** RHills(4) (b: b.hind: hld up: rdn over 2f out: wknd over 1f out) | 3 | **7** | 6/1[2] | 92 | 46 |
| 2465a[7] | **Obsessive (USA) (100)** (MRStoute) **3-8-8** GDuffield(8) (swtg: plld hrd: hld up: rdn over 6f out: btn whn nt clr run on ins over 1f out) | 1½ | **8** | 11/1 | 89 | 43 |
| 583* | **Thea (USA)** (JRFanshawe) **3-8-8** JFortune(3) (sme hdwy over 1f out: sn wknd) | 1¼ | **9** | 7/1[3] | 87 | 41 |
| 3127[4] | **Najiya (104)** (JLDunlop) **3-8-8** WCarson(11) (prom over 6f) | nk | **10** | 6/1[2] | 86 | 40 |
| 1493[3] | **Agnella (IRE) (96)** (GLMoore) **3-8-8** JQuinn(1) (lw: a bhd) | ½ | **11** | 40/1 | 85 | 39 |

(SP 119.6%) **11 Rn**

**1m 41.25** (0.05) CSF £96.40 TOTE £16.10: £3.20 £2.60 £1.50 (£104.10) Trio £337.10 OWNER Aylesfield Farms Stud (NEWMARKET) BRED Mr and Mrs R. Lyons
WEIGHT FOR AGE 3yo-6lb
**2225* Wandering Star (USA)** squeezed through a narrow gap inside the final furlong to shoot into the lead. A step up to a mile and a quarter should suit. (12/1)

**2502 Miss Universal (IRE)** remains a maiden, despite some very good efforts. She poked her head in front inside the final furlong, only for the winner to come by. (8/1)
**3472* Yamuna (USA)**, a galloping companion of Bosra Sham, did not have the best of runs. She should soon gain compensation. (7/2)
**Arabride**, sold out of James Toller's stable for 145,000 guineas at the Newmarket December Sales, looked in good shape for this first run in a year, and ran well. (25/1)
**3503 Lap of Luxury**, winner of this race in 1993, stayed on to only just fail to reach the prizes. She has done all her winning in the second half of the season. (15/2)
**2677 Solar Crystal (IRE)** did most of the donkey-work. (8/1: 6/1-9/1)
**3640* Awaamir** (6/1: 7/2-13/2)

## 3946 BISON RATED STKS H'CAP (0-100) (3-Y.O+) (Class B)

3-40 (3-44) **5f 6y** £6,987.00 (£2,613.00: £1,276.50: £547.50: £243.75: £122.25) Stalls: High GOING minus 0.38 sec per fur (F)

| | | | | SP | RR | SF |
|---|---|---|---|---|---|---|
| 3432[18] | **Crowded Avenue (95)** (PJMakin) **4-9-5** SSanders(10) (hld up: rdn over 1f out: led ins fnl f: r.o wl) | — | **1** | 7/1[2] | 108 | 56 |
| 3693[3] | **Dashing Blue (96)** (IABalding) **3-8-13**(5) MartinDwyer(14) (lw: led: rdn over 1f out: hdd ins fnl f: unable qckn) | ¾ | **2** | 7/1[2] | 107 | 53 |
| 2880[13] | **Top Banana (95)** (HCandy) **5-9-5** CRutter(12) (rdn over 2f out: hdwy on ins over 1f out: nt clr run 1f out: r.o) | 2 | **3** | 7/1[2] | 99 | 47 |
| 3618[4] | **Lago Di Varano (87)** (RMWhitaker) **4-8-8v**(3) RHavlin(8) (s.s: outpcd: hdwy over 1f out: r.o) | 2½ | **4** | 11/1[3] | 83 | 31 |
| 3406* | **Pearl d'Azur (USA) (86)** (DRLoder) **3-8-8** PatEddery(11) (lw: w ldr: rdn over 2f out: wknd fnl f) | 2 | **5** | 5/2[1] | 76 | 22 |
| 3672[7] | **Seigneurial (88)** (GHarwood) **4-8-12** AClark(2) (rdn over 3f out: no hdwy fnl 2f) | hd | **6** | 20/1 | 78 | 26 |
| 3432[16] | **Tedburrow (91)** (MrsAMNaughton) **4-8-10**(5) DGriffiths(5) (lw: nvr nr to chal) | hd | **7** | 12/1 | 80 | 28 |
| 3618[3] | **Bajan Rose (84)** (MBlanshard) **4-8-8** JQuinn(6) (hld up: rdn 3f out: wknd over 1f out) | hd | **8** | 16/1 | 73 | 21 |
| 2545[7] | **Takadou (IRE) (92)** (MissLCSiddall) **5-9-2** DaneO'Neill(3) (a bhd) | 1 | **9** | 33/1 | 78 | 26 |
| 3693[5] | **Pride of Brixton (86)** (GLewis) **3-8-8** WRyan(4) (a.p: rdn over 2f out: wknd fnl f) | nk | **10** | 7/1[2] | 71 | 17 |
| 3693[10] | **Kunucu (IRE) (92)** (TDBarron) **3-9-0** JFortune(9) (lw: hld up: rdn over 2f out: sn wknd) | 1¼ | **11** | 25/1 | 73 | 19 |
| 3038[5] | **Double Quick (IRE) (97)** (MJohnston) **4-9-7** BDoyle(7) (lw: spd over 3f) | 2 | **12** | 16/1 | 72 | 20 |
| 3232[13] | **Duel At Dawn (88)** (JHMGosden) **3-8-10** WCarson(1) (b: b.hind: swtg: a bhd) | 4 | **13** | 20/1 | 50 | — |
| | | | | (SP 122.7%) | **13 Rn** | |

**60.66 secs** (0.86) CSF £52.64 CT £260.80 TOTE £8.30: £2.30 £2.20 £1.90 (£16.30) Trio £17.30 OWNER Mr T. W. Wellard (MARLBOROUGH) BRED The Duke of Marlborough
WEIGHT FOR AGE 3yo-2lb
**3126 Crowded Avenue**, in tremendous form last year when he scored five times, got off the mark for 1996. The draw obviously had a lot to do with it though. (7/1)
**3693 Dashing Blue** was only overhauled inside the final furlong having led from his plum draw. (7/1)
**1630* Top Banana** is best at this trip, and this signalled something of a return to form. (7/1)
**3618 Lago Di Varano**, taken off his feet after a slow start, ran on but found it all over bar the shouting. (11/1)
**3406* Pearl d'Azur (USA)**, who disputed the lead for much of the way, called it a day inside the final furlong. (5/2)
**3672 Seigneurial** made no impression from halfway. (20/1)

## 3947 WILLIAM HILL H'CAP (0-90) (3-Y.O+) (Class C)

4-15 (4-22) **1m 2f 7y** £5,160.00 (£1,560.00: £760.00: £360.00) Stalls: High GOING minus 0.38 sec per fur (F)

| | | | | SP | RR | SF |
|---|---|---|---|---|---|---|
| 3623* | **Ninia (USA) (81)** (MJohnston) **4-9-5** BDoyle(10) (lw: a.p: led over 2f out: clr over 1f out: drvn out) | — | **1** | 20/1 | 92 | 71 |
| 3447* | **Angus-G (76)** (MrsMReveley) **4-9-0** JFortune(9) (lw: rdn & hdwy over 2f out: r.o wl ins fnl f) | ½ | **2** | 11/2[2] | 86 | 65 |
| 3248[3] | **Clifton Fox (80)** (JAGlover) **4-9-4** NDay(13) (rdn over 2f out: hdwy over 1f out: r.o wl ins fnl f) | ½ | **3** | 12/1 | 89 | 68 |
| 3457* | **Sharpical (80)** (SirMarkPrescott) **4-9-4** GDuffield(2) (hdwy over 2f out: hrd rdn over 1f out: unable qckn) | 1½ | **4** | 9/2[1] | 87 | 66 |
| *3608** | **Bakers Daughter (58)** (JRArnold) **4-7-5**(5) MartinDwyer(1) (lw: a.p: rdn 3f out: one pce) | 6 | **5** | 20/1 | 55 | 34 |
| 3496* | **Ashby Hill (IRE) (59)** (RRowe) **5-7-11** JQuinn(15) (lw: nt clr run on ins 3f out: hdwy over 1f out: nvr nrr) | ½ | **6** | 10/1 | 56 | 35 |
| 3327* | **White Plains (IRE) (71)** (MBell) **3-7-8**(7) RMullen(14) (nvr nr to chal) | 1¾ | **7** | 20/1 | 65 | 36 |
| 3457[2] | **A-Aasem (74)** (HThomsonJones) **3-8-4** RHills(3) (lw: chsd ldr: led 4f out tl over 2f out: wknd over 1f out) | 2½ | **8** | 16/1 | 64 | 35 |
| 3205[9] | **Fahs (USA) (69)** (RAkehurst) **4-8-7** SSanders(6) (lw: nvr nrr) | ½ | **9** | 16/1 | 58 | 37 |
| 2502[20] | **Hardy Dancer (88)** (GLMoore) **4-9-12** SWhitworth(16) (nvr nrr) | ¾ | **10** | 33/1 | 76 | 55 |
| 2883[3] | **Game Ploy (POL) (78)** (DHaydnJones) **4-9-2** SDrowne(20) (a mid div) | hd | **11** | 9/1 | 66 | 45 |
| 3505* | **Filial (IRE) (84)** (GHarwood) **3-9-0** PatEddery(11) (lw: rdn over 5f out: hdwy over 2f out: sn wknd) | 1½ | **12** | 8/1[3] | 69 | 40 |
| 3447[2] | **Edan Heights (74)** (SDow) **4-8-12** WRyan(17) (lw: prom 8f) | 1½ | **13** | 14/1 | 57 | 36 |
| 879[10] | **Ocean Park (69)** (LadyHerries) **5-8-7** AClark(12) (b: rdn & hdwy 2f out: wknd over 1f out) | ½ | **14** | 20/1 | 51 | 30 |
| 3496[7] | **Exemption (67)** (HCandy) **5-8-5** CRutter(18) (bhd fnl 6f) | ½ | **15** | 25/1 | 48 | 27 |
| 3073[9] | **Kriscliffe (82)** (MissGayKelleway) **3-8-12** DaneO'Neill(7) (b: lw: hld up: rdn over 3f out: wknd over 2f out) | s.h | **16** | 25/1 | 63 | 34 |
| 3039[6] | **Frezeliere (87)** (JLDunlop) **3-9-3** WCarson(5) (a bhd) | hd | **17** | 16/1 | 68 | 39 |
| 3691[16] | **Vindaloo (86)** (JLHarris) **4-9-7**(3) MHenry(4) (lw: hld up: rdn over 3f out: sn wknd) | ½ | **18** | 50/1 | 66 | 45 |
| 3828[12] | **Early Peace (IRE) (70)** (MJPolglase) **4-8-8** MRimmer(19) (lw: s.s: a bhd) | ¾ | **19** | 66/1 | 49 | 28 |
| 2505[7] | **Melomania (USA) (58)** (TJNaughton) **4-7-10** NAdams(8) (lw: led 6f) | 26 | **20** | 50/1 | — | — |
| | | | | (SP 130.9%) | **20 Rn** | |

**2m 6.88** (0.18) CSF £121.62 CT £1,306.76 TOTE £32.90: £5.80 £1.70 £2.90 £1.80 (£91.20) Trio £300.90 OWNER Mrs D. R. Schreiber (MIDDLEHAM) BRED Newgate Stud Farm Inc
LONG HANDICAP Bakers Daughter 7-5 Melomania (USA) 7-8
WEIGHT FOR AGE 3yo-8lb
**3623* Ninia (USA)**, after responding to pressure to go clear below the distance, was never going to be caught. (20/1)
**3447* Angus-G** weaved through from the two-furlong pole but, despite running on up the hill, was never going to get there. (11/2)
**3248 Clifton Fox** picked up below the distance and ran on really strongly up the hill, but had left it too late. (12/1)
**3457* Sharpical** tended to carry his head very high under pressure. (9/2)
**3608* Bakers Daughter** failed to raise her work-rate in the final three furlongs when needed. (20/1)
**3496* Ashby Hill (IRE)** stayed on to be nearest at the finish. (10/1: 8/1-12/1)

## 3948 SUNLEY H'CAP (0-80) (3-Y.O+) (Class D)

4-45 (4-51) **1m 6f** £3,870.00 (£1,170.00: £570.00: £270.00) Stalls: High GOING minus 0.38 sec per fur (F)

| | | | | SP | RR | SF |
|---|---|---|---|---|---|---|
| 2117[6] | **Ivor's Flutter (78)** (DRCElsworth) **7-9-9**(5) DGriffiths(3) (hdwy over 2f out: led over 1f out: rdn out) | — | **1** | 16/1 | 90 | 45 |
| 3459[7] | **Compass Pointer (60)** (JMPEustace) **3-7-7**(5) MartinDwyer(12) (rdn over 3f out: hdwy over 2f out: ev ch over 1f out: r.o) | ½ | **2** | 20/1 | 71 | 14 |

2862[10] **Bob's Ploy (74)** (MHTompkins) **4-9-7**(3) MHenry(6) (hdwy over 6f out: led over 2f out tl over 1f out: unable qckn) ....1¾ **3** 14/1 83 38
1428[6] **Blaze Away (USA) (77)** (IABalding) **5-9-13** PatEddery(11) (lw: hdwy over 1f out: r.o one pce) ....4 **4** 13/2[2] 82 37
1631[4] **Desert Dunes (75)** (NAGraham) **3-8-13** DaneO'Neill(7) (lw: rdn & hdwy over 2f out: one pce) ....½ **5** 12/1 79 22
3653[3] **Te Amo (IRE) (63)** (RAkehurst) **4-8-6**(7) DDenby(1) (hld up: rdn over 3f out: wknd over 1f out) ....nk **6** 13/2[2] 67 22
3785[5] **Todd (USA) (46)** (PMitchell) **5-7-10** JQuinn(8) (a.p: led over 3f out tl over 2f out: wknd over 1f out) ....4 **7** 33/1 45 —
3760[3] **Western Sal (67)** (JLHarris) **4-9-3** BDoyle(4) (lw: nvr nrr) ....1½ **8** 7/1[3] 65 20
3768[4] **Shooting Light (IRE) (78)** (PGMurphy) **3-9-2** WRyan(9) (lw: prom 7f: no ch whn hmpd on ins over 2f out) ....12 **9** 7/1[3] 62 5
**Muntafi (73)** (GHarwood) **5-9-9** AClark(5) (lw: prom over 10f) ....2 **10** 33/1 55 10
3514* **Norsong (55)** (RAkehurst) **4-8-5** SSanders(2) (prom over 11f) ....6 **11** 4/1[1] 30 —
**Polo Kit (IRE) (72)** (RJO'Sullivan) **5-9-8** GDuffield(10) (b: lw: led over 10f) ....8 **12** 13/2[2] 38 —
(SP 115.9%) **12 Rn**

**3m 5.47** (6.57) CSF £247.86 CT £4,093.92 TOTE £21.20: £4.60 £5.80 £4.10 (£198.10) Trio £486.20 OWNER Mr W. I. M. Perry (WHITCOMBE) BRED W. I. M. Perry
LONG HANDICAP Todd (USA) 7-9
WEIGHT FOR AGE 3yo-12lb

**1710 Ivor's Flutter** is a tricky customer, but was in one of his good moods here. He struck the front below the distance and was ridden out to score. (16/1)
**1498 Compass Pointer** moved up early in the straight. He had every chance below the distance and kept on, but was unable to get the better of the winner. (20/1)
**Bob's Ploy** moved into contention towards the end of the back straight. Sent on over two furlongs out, he was headed below the distance and failed to find another gear. (14/1)
**1428 Blaze Away (USA)**, off for three months, stayed on without threatening. (13/2)
**1631 Desert Dunes** had been out of action for three months. (12/1: op 8/1)
**3653 Te Amo (IRE)** had been hung out to dry below the distance. (13/2)
**3760 Western Sal** (7/1: 5/1-8/1)
**3514* Norsong** was very disappointing and stopped as if shot over two furlongs out. (4/1: 3/1-9/2)

## 3949 OASIS FOREST HOLIDAY VILLAGES MAIDEN STKS (3-Y.O F) (Class D)

5-20 (5-25) **1m 14y** £3,387.50 (£1,025.00: £500.00: £237.50) Stalls: High GOING minus 0.38 sec per fur (F)

SP RR SF
3513[8] **Ruwy (68)** (CJBenstead) **3-8-11** WCarson(9) (lw: led 1f: led over 2f out: rdn out) ....— **1** 16/1 75 39
3446[4] **Yukon Hope (USA)** (RCharlton) **3-8-11** PatEddery(12) (rdn over 3f out: hdwy over 2f out: r.o ins fnl f) ....¾ **2** 11/4[1] 74 38
3767[6] **Scherma** (WJarvis) **3-8-11** DaneO'Neill(2) (a.p: ev ch over 2f out: unable qckn) ....2 **3** 25/1 70 34
1857[4] **Kentucky Fall (FR)** (LadyHerries) **3-8-11** DeclanO'Shea(13) (rdn & hdwy over 2f out: r.o one pce) ....1 **4** 9/1 68 32
3446[8] **Polish Rhythm (IRE)** (MHTompkins) **3-8-8**(3) MHenry(14) (lw: rdn over 3f out: hdwy over 1f out: one pce)...s.h **5** 33/1 68 32
**Diamond Dance (IRE)** (JHMGosden) **3-8-8**(3) RHavlin(1) (w'like: scope: lw: hdwy over 1f out: nvr nrr) ....2 **6** 16/1 64 28
3513[7] **Summer Beauty** (JHMGosden) **3-8-11** WRyan(11) (lw: a.p: n.m.r on ins over 1f out: wknd fnl f) ....nk **7** 7/1 63 27
3262[3] **Dark Truffle** (MrsJCecil) **3-8-11** BDoyle(10) (hld up: rdn over 2f out: sn wknd) ....4 **8** 6/1[3] 55 19
**Prima Verde** (LMCumani) **3-8-11** JQuinn(5) (str: scope: bit bkwd: s.s: nvr nrr) ....s.h **9** 20/1 55 19
921[4] **Scarpetta (USA)** (JWHills) **3-8-11** RHills(4) (lw: hdwy over 2f out: wknd over 1f out) ....1½ **10** 9/2[2] 52 16
3513[4] **High Cut (83)** (IABalding) **3-8-6b**[1](5) MartinDwyer(3) (swtg: led 7f out tl over 2f out: wknd over 1f out) ....1 **11** 7/1 50 14
840[9] **Rose Tint (IRE)** (LordHuntingdon) **3-8-11** SSanders(6) (a bhd) ....nk **12** 33/1 49 13
**Ma Belle Poule** (PFICole) **3-8-11** CRutter(8) (bit bkwd: s.s: hdwy 7f out: rdn over 2f out: sn wknd) ....4 **13** 25/1 41 5
**Stolen Music (IRE)** (MajorDNChappell) **3-8-11** AClark(7) (bhd fnl 6f) ....18 **14** 50/1 6 —
(SP 126.2%) **14 Rn**

**1m 43.78** (2.58) CSF £58.87 TOTE £14.00: £2.90 £1.80 £7.90 (£20.70) Trio £386.90 OWNER Mr Hamdan Al Maktoum (EPSOM) BRED Shadwell Estate Company Limited

**3513 Ruwy** led for a second time over two furlongs out and, ridden along, kept the persistent runner-up at bay. (16/1)
**3446 Yukon Hope (USA)** was snapping at the winner's heels all the way through the final furlong and made sure that one did not have it all her own way. (11/4)
**3767 Scherma** stepped up on her gentle introduction here last week and had every chance until just tapped for toe. (25/1)
**1857 Kentucky Fall (FR)**, off the course for eleven weeks, stayed on up the hill for fourth. (9/1)
**3262 Polish Rhythm (IRE)** stayed on in the final furlong and a half and only just failed to reach the prizemoney. (33/1)
**Diamond Dance (IRE)**, a good-bodied filly, was doing all her best work in the final furlong and a half. (16/1)
**3513 Summer Beauty** (7/1: 3/1-15/2)
**3513 High Cut** got very uptight in the paddock upon being mounted. (7/1)

T/Jkpt: Not won; £39,638.62 to Hamilton 2/9/96. T/Plpt: £2,410.80 (17.71 Tckts). T/Qdpt: £633.00 (4.58 Tckts). AK

# 3625-WOLVERHAMPTON (L-H) (Standard)

## Saturday August 31st

WEATHER: fine WIND: slt half bhd

## 3950 BALOO MAIDEN AUCTION STKS (2-Y.O) (Class F)

7-00 (7-02) **5f (Fibresand)** £2,070.00 (£570.00: £270.00) Stalls: Low GOING minus 0.18 sec per fur (FST)

SP RR SF
2926[10] **Imperial Garden (IRE)** (PCHaslam) **2-8-10** JFortune(8) (chsd ldrs: str run appr fnl f: rdn to ld nr fin) ....— **1** 16/1 63 19
2967[10] **The Wyandotte Inn (65)** (RHollinshead) **2-8-3**(3) FLynch(6) (led over 3f out: clr over 1f out: rdn fnl f: ct nr fin) ....s.h **2** 11/8[1] 59 15
3448[13] **My Girl (45)** (JBerry) **2-8-1b**[1] NCarlisle(5) (b.hind: chsd ldrs: one pce fnl 2f) ....3½ **3** 16/1 43 —
3429[7] **Sandweld** (CADwyer) **2-7-13**(7) JoHunnam(1) (lw: in tch: rdn & styd on fnl 2f: nvr trbld ldrs) ....1½ **4** 3/1[2] 43 —
3488[5] **Sheraton Girl (51)** (MJohnston) **2-8-5b** JCarroll(2) (lw: led over 1f: wknd over 1f out) ....1¾ **5** 8/1 36 —
*3604*[7] **Jay Tee Ef (IRE)** (BAMcMahon) **2-8-1**(5) LNewton(7) (prom 2f) ....nk **6** 50/1 36 —
3423[11] **Rock The Casbah (63)** (JHetherton) **2-8-6** MTebbutt(3) (sn outpcd & bhd: btn whn rn wd over 1f out) ....3½ **7** 4/1[3] 25 —
(SP 111.9%) **7 Rn**

**62.3 secs** (1.30 under 2y best) (3.60) CSF £36.84 TOTE £29.20: £7.30 £1.70 (£54.70) OWNER Mr K. E. Williamson (MIDDLEHAM) BRED Mrs C. L. Weld

**Imperial Garden (IRE)** had shown next to nothing on his first couple of starts but, with the yard hitting form, he came good with a fine late burst. He will get further. (16/1)
**2746 The Wyandotte Inn** does seem to prefer this surface to turf and, despite dropping back in trip, had the speed to poach a two-length lead on the home turn. He could not quite hang on to the line, but a similar race ought to come his way. (11/8: op 5/2)
**3241 My Girl** could not confirm the form with the winner. (16/1)
**Sandweld** stuck to his task as the pressure was firmly applied in the home straight, but probably needs another furlong at least. (3/1: 2/1-100/30)
**3488 Sheraton Girl** again moved down poorly and was feeling the strain by the time the field straightened up. (8/1: 11/2-9/1)
**Jay Tee Ef (IRE)** broke well enough but was one of the first in trouble. (50/1)
**3080 Rock The Casbah** looks a hard ride, hanging badly on the home turn, and does not threaten to reproduce his debut effort. (4/1)

## 3951 RAMA CLAIMING STKS (3-Y.O+) (Class F)

7-30 (7-31) **1m 100y (Fibresand)** £2,070.00 (£570.00: £270.00) Stalls: Low GOING minus 0.18 sec per fur (FST)

| | | | | SP | RR | SF |
|---|---|---|---|---|---|---|
| 2402$^{6}$ | **People Direct (62)** (KMcAuliffe) **3-8-6** JFEgan(5) (b.hind: lw: mde all: rdn clr appr fnl f) | — | **1** | 8/1 | 70 | 40 |
| | **Medland (IRE)** (BJMcMath) **6-8-7** DBiggs(7) (b: bkwd: sn chsng wnr: rdn 2f out: edgd rt & one pce) | 5 | **2** | 25/1 | 56 | 32 |
| *3628$^{7}$* | **Quinzii Martin (52)** (DHaydnJones) **8-9-1** AMackay(11) (lw: chsd ldrs: one pce fnl 2f) | 1¼ | **3** | 14/1 | 61 | 37 |
| 3139$^{15}$ | **Proud Image (60)** (KRBurke) **4-8-13v** KFallon(6) (chsd ldrs: rdn 2f out: no imp) | 2 | **4** | 14/1 | 55 | 31 |
| *3626** | **Yeoman Oliver (71)** (BAMcMahon) **3-9-1b** GDuffield(2) (prom tl rdn & btn over 1f out) | 2½ | **5** | 11/4$^{1}$ | 59 | 29 |
| *3628$^{5}$* | **Dragonjoy (58)** (NPLittmoden) **3-8-9b** RHughes(13) (b: chsd ldrs: rdn over 2f out: sn btn) | ½ | **6** | 7/2$^{2}$ | 52 | 22 |
| 3808$^{16}$ | **My Handsome Prince (29)** (PJBevan) **4-8-11b** NCarlisle(3) (lw: s.i.s: hdwy 4f out: nvr trbld ldrs) | 1¼ | **7** | 50/1 | 45 | 21 |
| 3058$^{4}$ | **Tolepa (IRE)** (JJO'Neill) **3-8-10** JFortune(10) (lw: dwlt: nvr rchd ldrs) | 11 | **8** | 25/1 | 30 | — |
| *404$^{8}$* | **Arch Angel (IRE) (44)** (GFHCharles-Jones) **3-8-2** NAdams(12) (chsd ldrs tl wknd 3f out) | 1½ | **9** | 33/1 | 19 | — |
| 3653$^{10}$ | **Peutetre (73)** (FJordan) **4-8-12**(3) FLynch(9) (effrt 5f out: nvr trbld ldrs) | 2 | **10** | 20/1 | 22 | — |
| 3789$^{3}$ | **Power Game (62)** (JBerry) **3-8-11b** JCarroll(1) (lw: a bhd) | 1 | **11** | 4/1$^{3}$ | 22 | — |
| 3854$^{3}$ | **Harsh Times (47)** (TDEasterby) **3-7-10b** JLowe(8) (dwlt: a bhd) | 4 | **12** | 7/1 | — | — |
| | **Flowing Ocean (76)** (DWChapman) **6-8-13** ACulhane(4) (bkwd: a bhd) | 5 | **13** | 16/1 | 1 | — |
| | | | | (SP 129.1%) | | **13 Rn** |

**1m 48.8** (3.80) CSF £171.30 TOTE £12.80: £3.00 £5.90 £5.90 (£167.90) Trio Not won; £133.72 to Hamilton 2/9/96 OWNER Mr Peter Barclay (LAMBOURN) BRED James Thom and Sons and Peter Orr
WEIGHT FOR AGE 3yo-6lb
**1490 People Direct**, scoring for the first time away from Southwell, clearly likes Fibresand and front-running, and had these in trouble the moment she kicked on the home turn. (8/1)
**Medland (IRE)** looked badly in need of this first run in fourteen months, but ran remarkably well, if rather lacking a change of gear in the straight. (25/1)
**2303 Quinzii Martin**, always up with the pace, may have led the winner for the first 100 yards, but could only plug on at the business end. This did represent a return to form after recent poor efforts. (14/1)
**2737 Proud Image**, having only his second run on sand, has yet to find his best turf form on this surface. (14/1)
**3626* Yeoman Oliver** is not very consistent and could not set the pace as she had two weeks ago. Sticking to the inside, he was in trouble early in the straight. (11/4)
**3628 Dragonjoy**, weighted to trouble the winner on their meeting at Southwell in March, has been in two different yards since and has yet to show anything like his best for the current one. (7/2)

## 3952 SHELTON TRENCHING SYSTEMS H'CAP (0-65) (3-Y.O+) (Class F)

8-00 (8-00) **1m 6f 166y (Fibresand)** £2,070.00 (£570.00: £270.00) Stalls: High GOING: 0.18 sec per fur (SLW)

| | | | | SP | RR | SF |
|---|---|---|---|---|---|---|
| *3630$^{5}$* | **Backwoods (56)** (WMBrisbourne) **3-8-6** AGarth(11) (rdn 7f out: hdwy 5f out: hmpd over 1f out: led ins fnl f: pushed out) | — | **1** | 6/1$^{3}$ | 65 | 24 |
| *3630** | **Drama King (40)** (SRBowring) **4-8-3b** JQuinn(1) (hdwy 8f out: ev ch 4f out: led over 1f out: edgd rt & hdd ins fnl f: r.o) | 1¼ | **2** | 7/1 | 48 | 20 |
| 3801$^{13}$ | **Well Arranged (IRE) (63)** (MJPolglase) **5-9-12b$^{1}$** SSanders(12) (b: a.p: led 5f out tl over 1f out: one pce) | 4 | **3** | 20/1 | 66 | 38 |
| 3302$^{5}$ | **Charlie Bigtime (48)** (RHarris) **6-8-11** AMackay(4) (b.hind: hdwy 5f out: rdn 3f out: one pce) | nk | **4** | 8/1 | 51 | 23 |
| 3335$^{6}$ | **Wadada (37)** (DBurchell) **5-8-0** SDrowne(9) (chsd ldr: lft in ld over 6f out: hdd 5f out: rdn & one pce fnl 3f) | 2 | **5** | 4/1$^{1}$ | 38 | 10 |
| *3605$^{2}$* | **Precedency (64)** (KMcAuliffe) **4-9-13** JFEgan(3) (b.hind: hdwy 8f out: wknd 3f out) | 7 | **6** | 7/1 | 57 | 29 |
| 3801$^{12}$ | **Teen Jay (55)** (BJLlewellyn) **6-9-4** VSlattery(2) (lw: dwlt: nvr nr to chal) | 6 | **7** | 8/1 | 42 | 14 |
| 3428$^{6}$ | **Claque (65)** (DWChapman) **4-10-0b** ACulhane(8) (chsd ldrs tl wknd 3f out) | nk | **8** | 7/1 | 51 | 23 |
| 3479$^{5}$ | **Platinum Plus (59)** (CADwyer) **4-9-8** CDwyer(5) (b: lw: chsd ldrs: hmpd 7f out: rdn & wknd over 4f out) | 9 | **9** | 11/2$^{2}$ | 36 | 8 |
| | **Awestruck (35)** (BPreece) **6-7-12** FNorton(10) (bhd fnl 5f) | 2 | **10** | 25/1 | 10 | — |
| 2188$^{8}$ | **Mapengo (65)** (JCullinan) **5-10-0** RHughes(6) (bit bkwd: led: rdn clr 10f out: virtually p.u over 7f out: sn hdd & eased) | dist | **11** | 25/1 | — | — |
| | | | | (SP 121.8%) | | **11 Rn** |

**3m 17.3** (9.90) CSF £45.56 CT £724.59 TOTE £11.50: £2.70 £2.80 £3.10 (£68.20) Trio £74.00; £46.96 to Hamilton 2/9/96 OWNER Mr P. R. Kirk (NESSCLIFFE) BRED Sheikh Mohammed bin Rashid al Maktoum
WEIGHT FOR AGE 3yo-13lb
STEWARDS' ENQUIRY Hughes susp. 9-14/9/96 (irresponsible riding).
**3630 Backwoods** found this step up in trip just what was needed and, after looking in trouble going out on the final circuit, won a shade cosily. (6/1)
**3630* Drama King**, who beat the winner over a mile and a half here last time, was not weighted to confirm the form but ran well enough. However, the bump he gave the winner might have caused his demotion had he won. (7/1)
**1458 Well Arranged (IRE)**, running over the course and distance for the first time since scoring here in May, has changed yards since and ran a sound race off a 2lb higher mark. (20/1)
**3094 Charlie Bigtime** has not won for over a year. Taken wide for much of the race, he only briefly threatened to break that sequence. (8/1)
**3335 Wadada**, a recent hurdle winner, has had plenty of racing in the last four months but is keeping his form well. (4/1)
**3605 Precedency** looks one-paced and seems to have started his handicap career on a high mark. (7/1)
**3479 Platinum Plus**, hardly helped by Mapengo's antics when pulling up a circuit early, did not appear to get this longer trip. (11/2: op 3/1)
**Mapengo** had ironically been running over a mile, for his jockey had a brainstorm and rode a finish a circuit early. Hughes may have been misled by another rider, but surely it ought to be the Starter's responsibility to ensure that the jockeys are made aware of the race distance and the number of circuits of each race. (25/1)

## 3953 SUN PUNTERS CLUB H'CAP (0-80) (3-Y.O+) (Class D)

8-30 (8-31) **6f (Fibresand)** £3,264.00 (£969.00: £459.00: £204.00) Stalls: Low GOING minus 0.18 sec per fur (FST)

| Form | Horse | Dist | Pos | SP | RR | SF |
|---|---|---|---|---|---|---|
| $3618^{2}$ | **Sea-Deer (74)** (CADwyer) **7-9-8** KFallon(6) (rdn & hdwy over 2f out: led ins fnl f: r.o) | — | **1** | $4/5^{1}$ | 83 | 65 |
| $3432^{2}$ | **Sing With the Band (73)** (BAMcMahon) **5-9-7** SSanders(9) (w ldr tl led over 2f out: hdd & unable qckn ins fnl f) | 1½ | **2** | $10/1^{3}$ | 78 | 60 |
| $3168^{5}$ | **Oberon's Dart (IRE) (72)** (PJMakin) **3-9-3** AClark(10) (led over 3f: one pce fnl f) | 2½ | **3** | $10/1^{3}$ | 70 | 49 |
| $3672^{12}$ | **No Monkey Nuts (65)** (JBerry) **3-8-10** JCarroll(2) (b.nr hind: chsd ldrs: no ex appr fnl f) | 1¼ | **4** | $9/1^{2}$ | 60 | 39 |
| $3627^{6}$ | **Desert Invader (IRE) (73)** (DWChapman) **5-9-7** ACulhane(11) (lw: chsd ldrs: rdn along 3f out: kpt on) | 1¾ | **5** | 20/1 | 63 | 45 |
| $2431^{7}$ | **Bold Street (IRE) (67)** (ABailey) **6-8-12b**(3) DWright(8) (b: dwlt: hdwy whn nt clr run over 1f out: r.o fnl f) | 1¾ | **6** | 20/1 | 53 | 35 |
| $3652^{5}$ | **Featherstone Lane (70)** (MissLCSiddall) **5-9-4v** NCarlisle(13) (lw: chsd ldrs: c wd over 1f out: sn btn) | 1 | **7** | 20/1 | 53 | 35 |
| $3644^{4}$ | **Ultra Beet (65)** (PCHaslam) **4-8-13v** JFortune(12) (lw: w ldrs: rdn 2f out: sn btn) | nk | **8** | 12/1 | 47 | 29 |
| $3652^{9}$ | **Boffy (IRE) (70)** (BPJBaugh) **3-8-8**(7) IonaWands(5) (bhd fnl 3f) | ½ | **9** | 33/1 | 51 | 30 |
| $1812^{5}$ | **Jigsaw Boy (67)** (PGMurphy) **7-8-12**(3) NVarley(1) (sn outpcd) | 3 | **10** | 14/1 | 40 | 22 |
| $3602^{6}$ | **Lady Sheriff (65)** (RHollinshead) **5-8-10**(3) FLynch(4) (lost pl after 2f: no ch afterwards) | nk | **11** | 12/1 | 37 | 19 |
| $3049^{4}$ | **Vax New Way (73)** (JLSpearing) **3-9-4b** SDrowne(7) (sn pushed along: in tch 4f) | 1¼ | **12** | $10/1^{3}$ | 42 | 21 |
| $3599^{9}$ | **Dancing Lawyer (78)** (BJMeehan) **5-9-12** MTebbutt(3) (lw: outpcd) | 4 | **13** | 25/1 | 36 | 18 |

(SP 136.0%) **13 Rn**

**1m 13.2** (0.6 under best) (1.80) CSF £11.94 CT £61.46 TOTE £2.20: £1.40 £2.50 £2.70 (£5.30) Trio £26.10 OWNER Binding Matters Ltd (NEWMARKET) BRED Stetchworth Park Stud Ltd

WEIGHT FOR AGE 3yo-3lb

**3618 Sea-Deer** looked very well handicapped on his best. Although he is at his best still on turf, he may not be now on the All-Weather, but he still had sufficient class to see him home. (4/5: Evs/1-6/5)

**3432 Sing With the Band** has made the frame on six of her seven runs here and is overdue a win, but she ran into a handicap snip here, so did well in the circumstances. (10/1)

**3168 Oberon's Dart (IRE)** could not shake off his rivals and is better at seven. (10/1)

**3350 No Monkey Nuts** ran respectably on his second try on the surface without quite reproducing his turf form. (9/1)

**3627 Desert Invader (IRE)** went to post keenly, but was gradually outpaced from halfway. He finds this trip too sharp. (20/1)

**2386 Bold Street (IRE)** has become frustrating to follow, but ran rather better than his finishing position suggests. (20/1)

**3602 Lady Sheriff** (12/1: op 8/1)

## 3954 AKELA (S) STKS (2-Y.O F) (Class F)

9-00 (9-03) **6f (Fibresand)** £2,070.00 (£570.00: £270.00) Stalls: Low GOING minus 0.18 sec per fur (FST)

| Form | Horse | Dist | Pos | SP | RR | SF |
|---|---|---|---|---|---|---|
| $3582^{4}$ | **Impy Fox (IRE)** (CADwyer) **2-8-2**(7) JoHunnam(2) (hdwy over 2f out: led over 1f out: pushed out) | — | **1** | 10/1 | 65 | 19 |
| $3128^{11}$ | **Windborn (53)** (KMcAuliffe) **2-8-9** JFEgan(5) (lw: sn w ldrs: rdn 2f out: r.o fnl f) | 1¾ | **2** | $9/2^{3}$ | 60 | 14 |
| $3582^{5}$ | **Mujadil Express (IRE) (54)** (JSMoore) **2-8-4**(5) PPMurphy(1) (a.p: led 2f out: sn hdd & no ex) | 1 | **3** | 16/1 | 58 | 12 |
| $3769^{3}$ | **Corncrake (IRE) (62)** (BJMeehan) **2-8-9** MTebbutt(6) (lw: led 3f: rdn 2f out: no ex) | 2 | **4** | $5/4^{1}$ | 52 | 6 |
| $3455^{4}$ | **Shandana (48)** (PCHaslam) **2-8-9** JFortune(11) (chsd ldrs tl wknd over 1f out) | 6 | **5** | $7/2^{2}$ | 36 | — |
| $3330^{7}$ | **Silver Moon** (BAMcMahon) **2-8-9** GDuffield(4) (s.i.s: hdwy after 2f: wknd over 1f out) | ½ | **6** | 20/1 | 35 | — |
| $3582^{11}$ | **Loch Dibidale (63)** (JEBanks) **2-8-9** JQuinn(3) (w ldrs: led 3f out: hdd 2f out: sn wknd) | 3 | **7** | 14/1 | 27 | — |
| $3582^{7}$ | **Moor Hall Princess** (KRBurke) **2-8-9** SSanders(8) (nvr nrr to chal) | 2½ | **8** | 16/1 | 20 | — |
| $3498^{12}$ | **Silent Valley** (JNeville) **2-8-9** FNorton(7) (dwlt: nvr trbld ldrs) | nk | **9** | 20/1 | 20 | — |
| $2948^{3}$ | **Bold Motion** (CMurray) **2-8-9** JStack(9) (b.nr hind: lw: outpcd) | 1¾ | **10** | 10/1 | 15 | — |
| $2795^{10}$ | **Woodland Dove** (KGWingrove) **2-8-4**(5) MBaird(10) (unruly bef s: hdwy after 1f: wknd 3f out) | 4 | **11** | 33/1 | 4 | — |

(SP 133.9%) **11 Rn**

**1m 15.7** (4.30) CSF £57.96 TOTE £8.70: £2.40 £2.00 £4.10 (£12.30) Trio Not won; £96.89 to Hamilton 2/9/96 OWNER Mr B. L. Benson (NEWMARKET) BRED J. M. Cusack

Bt in 8,000 gns

**3582 Impy Fox (IRE)** nipped through on the inside on the home turn and soon had matters well in hand. She ought to go on from here. (10/1: op 5/1)

**2406 Windborn** took to the surface well but could never get to the front, despite harrying the leaders throughout. She was coming back for more at the line. (9/2: 4/1-6/1)

**3582 Mujadil Express (IRE)**, just behind the winner at Folkestone, saw that form confirmed on this different surface. (16/1)

**3769 Corncrake (IRE)**, a good mover, was a wholesale gamble, but could not justify the support. Losing the lead at halfway and staying wide, she could never get back, despite her rider's urgings. (5/4: 3/1-11/10)

**3455 Shandana** seems to have gone the wrong way for, with the yard now in form, her performances seem to be getting worse. (7/2)

**Silver Moon** broke well enough but took time to get going. She has the scope to progress and will stay much further in time. (20/1)

**2371 Loch Dibidale** (14/1: op 8/1)

**Bold Motion** (10/1: op 6/1)

## 3955 JACK KENNEDY 80TH BIRTHDAY H'CAP (0-70) (3-Y.O+) (Class E)

9-30 (9-30) **1m 1f 79y (Fibresand)** £2,070.00 (£570.00: £270.00) Stalls: Low GOING minus 0.18 sec per fur (FST)

| Form | Horse | Dist | Pos | SP | RR | SF |
|---|---|---|---|---|---|---|
| $3877^{2}$ | **Farmost (66)** (SirMarkPrescott) **3-9-3** GDuffield(11) (lw: plld hrd: w ldrs: led over 2f out: drvn & hld on wl fnl f) | — | **1** | $11/10^{1}$ | 77 | 48 |
| $3628^{3}$ | **Shahik (USA) (62)** (DHaydnJones) **6-9-6** FNorton(12) (lw: hdwy 5f out: ev ch fnl f: unable qckn) | 1 | **2** | $2/1^{2}$ | 71 | 49 |
| $3627^{9}$ | **Heathyards Lady (USA) (69)** (RHollinshead) **5-9-10**(3) FLynch(10) (a.p: ev ch over 2f out: one pce fnl f) | ½ | **3** | 14/1 | 77 | 55 |
| $2631^{6}$ | **Sommersby (IRE) (53)** (MrsNMacauley) **5-8-8**(3) CTeague(7) (b: dwlt: hdwy 3f out: wknd fnl f) | 4 | **4** | 25/1 | 55 | 33 |
| $3812^{9}$ | **Mr Moriarty (IRE) (40)** (SRBowring) **5-7-12** JQuinn(4) (b: chsd ldrs: rdn 3f out: sn btn) | 2 | **5** | 25/1 | 38 | 16 |
| $3630^{2}$ | **Zatopek (53)** (JCullinan) **4-8-11b**[1] RHughes(6) (led tl hdd & wknd over 2f out) | 6 | **6** | 25/1 | 41 | 19 |
| $3585^{11}$ | **Bold Habit (48)** (JPearce) **11-8-6** GBardwell(1) (b.nr hind: nvr nrr) | 2½ | **7** | 16/1 | 32 | 10 |
| $2749^{4}$ | **Sweet Supposin (IRE) (70)** (JohnBerry) **5-10-0v** SWhitworth(3) (lw: bhd: hdwy over 3f out: wknd 2f out) | 3½ | **8** | $8/1^{3}$ | 48 | 26 |
| $2731^{6}$ | **Forzair (69)** (JJO'Neill) **4-9-6**(7) DJewett(13) (nvr trbld ldrs) | hd | **9** | 33/1 | 47 | 25 |
| $3657^{6}$ | **Oberons Boy (IRE) (66)** (BJMeehan) **3-9-3b** MTebbutt(5) (hdwy 6f out: wknd over 2f out) | 2½ | **10** | 16/1 | 39 | 10 |
| $3412^{6}$ | **Docklands Courier (48)** (BJMcMath) **4-8-6** DBiggs(9) (prom tl rdn & wknd over 4f out) | 7 | **11** | 9/1 | 9 | — |
| $2557^{11}$ | **Governance (IRE) (49)** (KMcAuliffe) **3-8-0v**[1] ow2 JFEgan(8) (chsd ldrs 6f: sn bhd) | dist | **12** | 33/1 | — | — |

| Form | Horse | Dist | Pos | SP | RR | SF |
|---|---|---|---|---|---|---|
| 1597[8] | **Happy Tycoon (IRE) (64)** (CMurray) **3-9-1** JFortune(2) (stumbled & uns rdr s) | | **U** | 25/1 | — | — |
| | | | | (SP 141.8%) | | **13 Rn** |

**2m 0.4** (4.40) CSF £4.65 CT £23.55 TOTE £2.30: £1.70 £1.90 £3.00 (£4.40) Trio £117.00; £32.96 to 2/9/96 OWNER Mr W. E. Sturt (NEWMARKET) BRED Hesmonds Stud Ltd

WEIGHT FOR AGE 3yo-7lb

**3877 Farmost** was sure to go up considerably in the handicap for his recent win, so his astute trainer turned him out again quickly to take full advantage of his lenient All-Weather mark. Pulling hard, he had to battle to score over his longest ever winning trip. (11/10)

**3628 Shahik (USA)**, who took a good hold going to post, is certainly ready to win, and will not always meet one so well handicapped. (2/1)

**2994 Heathyards Lady (USA)**, still on a higher mark than she has ever won off despite a losing run of nine, acquitted herself really well in the circumstances. (14/1)

**Sommersby (IRE)**, taking quite a drop in trip, still tied up inside the final furlong. (25/1)

**367 Mr Moriarty (IRE)** needs further and was readily outpaced as the tempo quickened. (25/1)

**3630 Zatopek**, reverting to a shorter trip, tried to force the pace to make full use of his stamina, but had run himself out by the home turn. (25/1)

**2749 Sweet Supposin (IRE)** moved down poorly, but cruised up to the leaders on the home turn, only to fold tamely. (8/1)

**3412 Docklands Courier** (9/1: op 20/1)

T/Plpt: £1,498.60 (7.92 Tckts). T/Qdpt: £22.80 (20.63 Tckts). Dk

# 3644-HAMILTON (R-H) (Good, Good to firm patches)

## Monday September 2nd

WEATHER: sunny periods WIND: almost nil

## 3956 E.B.F. ALMADA MAIDEN STKS (2-Y.O) (Class D)

2-15 (2-16) **5f 4y** £3,631.25 (£1,100.00: £537.50: £256.25) Stalls: Low GOING minus 0.37 sec per fur (F)

| Form | Horse | Dist | Pos | SP | RR | SF |
|---|---|---|---|---|---|---|
| 3508[2] | **Solfegietto** (MBell) **2-8-9** MFenton(6) (lw: trckd ldrs: led ins fnl f: rdn out cl home) | — | **1** | 4/9 [1] | 67 | 23 |
| 3277[5] | **Night Flight (75)** (JJO'Neill) **2-9-0** JFEgan(5) (lw: led tl ins fnl f: r.o) | hd | **2** | 8/1 [3] | 72 | 28 |
| 2327[5] | **Changed To Baileys (IRE)** (JBerry) **2-9-0** JCarroll(3) (cl up: rdn over 1f out: wknd ins fnl f) | 3½ | **3** | 20/1 | 61 | 17 |
| | **Audencia (IRE)** (MJohnston) **2-8-9** KDarley(4) (w'like: scope: outpcd & bhd tl styd on wl fnl f) | 1 | **4** | 5/1 [2] | 52+ | 8 |
| | **Bold Gayle** (MrsJRRamsden) **2-8-9** KFallon(1) (wl grwn: bhd: hdwy over 1f out: styd on wl towards fin) | nk | **5** | 14/1 | 51+ | 7 |
| | **Murron Wallace** (RMWhitaker) **2-8-9** AMackay(7) (w'like: bit bkwd: s.i.s: nvr wnt pce) | 7 | **6** | 20/1 | 29 | — |
| 3050[9] | **Trulyfan (IRE)** (RAFahey) **2-8-9** ACulhane(2) (nvr nr to chal) | 3 | **7** | 33/1 | 20 | — |
| | | | | (SP 116.1%) | | **7 Rn** |

**60.6 secs** (2.30) CSF £5.03 TOTE £1.30: £1.10 £4.80 (£3.90) OWNER Cheveley Park Stud (NEWMARKET) BRED Miss G. Abbey

**3508 Solfegietto** looked likely to win this smoothly but, in the end, she needed keeping up to her work to hang on. She is probably still learning. (4/9)

**3277 Night Flight** put up a good show and kept fighting back when looking beaten. A race will surely be found before long. (8/1: 4/1-10/1)

**2327 Changed To Baileys (IRE)**, having her first run for over two months, is doing well physically and ran a useful race until blowing up inside the last furlong. (20/1)

**Audencia (IRE)**, a fair sort, should have learnt plenty from this and, judging by the way she finished, further will be appreciated. (5/1: 4/1-6/1)

**Bold Gayle**, a useful type, took time to find her stride but did run on strongly at the end to suggest that there is better to come, especially over longer trips. (14/1: 10/1-20/1)

**Murron Wallace** needed this and could never go the pace. (20/1)

## 3957 STONEFIELD (S) H'CAP (0-60) (3-Y.O+) (Class G)

2-45 (2-45) **5f 4y** £2,346.00 (£656.00: £318.00) Stalls: Low GOING minus 0.37 sec per fur (F)

| Form | Horse | Dist | Pos | SP | RR | SF |
|---|---|---|---|---|---|---|
| *3416*[4] | **Marjorie Rose (IRE) (53)** (ABailey) **3-9-3**(3) DWright(9) (b: lw: trckd ldrs gng wl: led over 2f out: rdn & r.o) | — | **1** | 5/1 [1] | 60 | 41 |
| 3236[8] | **Henry the Hawk (47)** (MDods) **5-8-12**(3) CTeague(6) (b: outpcd tl hdwy 2f out: r.o towards fin) | 1¾ | **2** | 10/1 | 48 | 30 |
| 3643[5] | **Ragazzo (IRE) (28)** (JSWainwright) **6-7-10b** LCharnock(8) (lw: in tch: hdwy u.p over 1f out: styd on wl) | 2 | **3** | 10/1 | 23 | 5 |
| 3644[8] | **Sunday Mail Too (IRE) (48)** (MissLAPerratt) **4-9-2** MFenton(12) (racd far side: a cl up: nt qckn appr fnl f) | 1¼ | **4** | 6/1 [2] | 39 | 21 |
| 3868[10] | **Kabcast (45)** (DWChapman) **11-8-13b** KDarley(5) (a chsng ldrs: kpt on u.p fnl 2f) | s.h | **5** | 9/1 [3] | 36 | 18 |
| 3774[12] | **Double Glow (28)** (NBycroft) **4-7-10b** JQuinn(1) (a chsng ldrs stands' side: kpt on fnl f) | nk | **6** | 40/1 | 18 | — |
| 3579[13] | **Orange And Blue (35)** (MissJFCraze) **3-8-2c** AMackay(3) (a chsng ldrs stands' side: nt qckn fnl 2f) | 1¼ | **7** | 20/1 | 21 | 2 |
| 3643[9] | **First Option (28)** (RBastiman) **6-7-7**(3) MHenry(2) (t: s.i.s: nvr rchd ldrs) | 1¼ | **8** | 16/1 | 10 | — |
| *3602*[14] | **Jemsilverthorn (IRE) (44)** (RCSpicer) **3-8-11b** KFallon(4) (chsd ldrs tl rdn & btn appr fnl f) | s.h | **9** | 20/1 | 26 | 7 |
| 3579[9] | **Supreme Desire (28)** (MissJFCraze) **8-7-10** JLowe(10) (led to ½-wy: sn rdn & btn) | ¾ | **10** | 12/1 | 7 | — |
| 3774[7] | **Arasong (56)** (EWeymes) **4-9-10** RLappin(11) (lw: prom: sn drvn along: wknd fr ½-wy) | ¾ | **11** | 5/1 [1] | 33 | 15 |
| *3061*[5] | **Penny Parkes (52)** (JBerry) **3-9-5b** JCarroll(13) (s.i.s: a outpcd & bhd) | 1 | **12** | 6/1 [2] | 26 | 7 |
| 3294[8] | **Waverley Star (28)** (JSWainwright) **11-7-3v**(7) JBramhill(7) (a outpcd & bhd) | 10 | **13** | 33/1 | — | — |
| | | | | (SP 118.6%) | | **13 Rn** |

**60.1 secs** (1.80) CSF £49.38 CT £443.54 TOTE £6.60: £2.20 £1.80 £2.70 (£19.90) Trio £211.60 OWNER Sandy Brow Stables Ltd (TARPORLEY) BRED R. Selby and Partners

LONG HANDICAP Ragazzo (IRE) 7-7 Supreme Desire 7-5 Double Glow 7-6 Waverley Star 7-4

WEIGHT FOR AGE 3yo-1lb

No bid

**3416 Marjorie Rose (IRE)** travelled on the bridle and, once she hit the front at halfway, the race was always hers, although she did need driving out to make sure of it. She is in top form just now. (5/1)

**3236 Henry the Hawk**, despite getting pretty warm beforehand, ran well, finishing strongly. Once the ground eases further, he is certainly off a useful mark. (10/1)

**Ragazzo (IRE)** is coming to form and, judging by the way he finished, there is a race to be picked up. (10/1)

**3236 Sunday Mail Too (IRE)** had the favoured far rail throughout, but the struggle was always beyond her in the last furlong and a half. (6/1: op 4/1)

**3352 Kabcast** ran fast up the middle of the track, but could never dominate, and was fighting a lost cause from some way out. (9/1)

**3310 Double Glow** ran reasonably well up the stands' rail, but she was always tapped for toe in the last two furlongs. (40/1)

## 3958 SOUTER OF STIRLING H'CAP (0-60) (3-Y.O+) (Class F)

3-15 (3-17) **1m 65y** £2,983.00 (£904.00: £442.00: £211.00) Stalls: High GOING minus 0.37 sec per fur (F)

| | | | | SP | RR | SF |
|---|---|---|---|---|---|---|
| $3646^{2}$ | **King Curan (USA) (60)** (DHaydnJones) **5-10-0v** AMackay(12) (lw: mde all: shkn up 2f out: r.o: eased towards fin) | — | **1** | 4/1$^{1}$ | 76+ | 58 |
| $3812^{5}$ | **Racing Brenda (43)** (BCMorgan) **5-8-11** SWhitworth(14) (lw: trckd ldrs: stdy hdwy 3f out: effrt & chsng wnr 2f out: nt pce to chal) | 3 | **2** | 6/1$^{3}$ | 53 | 35 |
| $3289^{2}$ | **Riccarton (50)** (PCalver) **3-8-13** MBirch(11) (a chsng wnr: effrt 3f out: one pce) | 2 | **3** | 6/1$^{3}$ | 56 | 33 |
| *$2369^{16}$* | **Java Red (IRE) (51)** (JGFitzGerald) **4-9-5** KFallon(9) (lw: hdwy on ins ½-wy: prom 2f out: nt qckn) | 1¾ | **4** | 16/1 | 54 | 36 |
| $3427^{5}$ | **Globe Runner (49)** (JJO'Neill) **3-8-12** GBardwell(13) (chsd ldrs: rdn over 3f out: no imp) | 2½ | **5** | 14/1 | 47 | 24 |
| $3644^{6}$ | **Roseate Lodge (44)** (SEKettlewell) **10-8-5**(7) JennyBenson(5) (lw: mid div: effrt ½-wy: nvr rchd ldrs) | s.h | **6** | 14/1 | 42 | 24 |
| $2075^{3}$ | **Flyaway Blues (49)** (MrsMReveley) **4-9-3b** ACulhane(1) (lw: bhd: rdn over 3f out: nrst fin) | 1¼ | **7** | 14/1 | 45 | 27 |
| $3623^{12}$ | **Nobby Barnes (40)** (DonEnricoIncisa) **7-8-8** KimTinkler(3) (s.i.s: sme hdwy fnl 3f) | nk | **8** | 25/1 | 35 | 17 |
| | **Top Skipper (IRE) (50)** (MartynWane) **4-9-4** RLappin(7) (effrt ½-wy: no imp) | 1½ | **9** | 100/1 | 42 | 24 |
| *3603** | **Pc's Cruiser (IRE) (45)** (JLEyre) **4-8-13v** TWilliams(16) (chsd ldrs tl wknd fnl 3f) | s.h | **10** | 5/1$^{2}$ | 37 | 19 |
| $3677^{6}$ | **Nizaal (USA) (45)** (RAllan) **5-8-10**(3) DarrenMoffatt(15) (bhd: hdwy on ins 3f out: n.d) | s.h | **11** | 40/1 | 37 | 19 |
| $3878^{11}$ | **Lord Advocate (49)** (DANolan) **8-9-3b** VHalliday(10) (sn prom: rdn ½-wy: wknd fnl 2f) | 2½ | **12** | 33/1 | 36 | 18 |
| $3812^{11}$ | **Habeta (USA) (48)** (JWWatts) **10-9-2** LCharnock(4) (lw: bhd: rdn over 3f out: n.d) | 16 | **13** | 12/1 | 4 | — |
| $3340^{7}$ | **Great Bear (47)** (DWChapman) **4-9-1** KDarley(6) (a bhd) | 2½ | **14** | 8/1 | — | — |
| $3646^{4}$ | **Talented Ting (IRE) (53)** (PCHaslam) **7-9-7** JCarroll(8) (lw: prom tl outpcd ½-wy: sn btn & eased) | 3½ | **15** | 14/1 | — | — |

(SP 126.8%) **15 Rn**

**1m 46.6** (2.50) CSF £27.84 CT £136.93 TOTE £5.30: £1.90 £1.10 £2.20 (£16.20) Trio £50.70 OWNER Mr Hugh O'Donnell (PONTYPRIDD) BRED Executive Bloodstock & Adstock Manor Stud
WEIGHT FOR AGE 3yo-5lb
OFFICIAL EXPLANATION **Great Bear: was suffering from muscle spasm.**

**3646 King Curan (USA)**, again ridden from the front, enjoyed himself and was well on top by the finish. (4/1)
**3812 Racing Brenda** is off a very useful handicap mark at present and travelled particularly well but, when asked a serious question, her response was most disappointing. (6/1)
**3289 Riccarton**, a hot individual, had his chances throughout, but failed to quicken when asked. (6/1)
**1830 Java Red (IRE)**, off the track for two months, has ability and ran well enough to suggest that there is better to come. (16/1)
**3427 Globe Runner** showed up well, but was off the bit some way out and never finding enough thereafter. (14/1)
**3644 Roseate Lodge** looks a picture, but does take some riding. Although never seriously getting into it, he should not be written off. (14/1: 10/1-16/1)
**3344 Habeta (USA)** (12/1: op 8/1)
**3646 Talented Ting (IRE)** (14/1: 12/1-20/1)

## 3959 LANGS SUPREME H'CAP (0-75) (3-Y.O) (Class D)

3-45 (3-45) **6f 5y** £4,038.40 (£1,223.20: £597.60: £284.80) Stalls: Low GOING minus 0.37 sec per fur (F)

| | | | | SP | RR | SF |
|---|---|---|---|---|---|---|
| $3489^{3}$ | **Natural Key (60)** (DHaydnJones) **3-9-0** AMackay(7) (trckd ldrs: led 2f out: hld on wl) | — | **1** | 9/2$^{2}$ | 67 | 35 |
| $3844^{13}$ | **Bowlers Boy (64)** (JJQuinn) **3-9-4** JQuinn(8) (trckd wnr: chal over 1f out: hrd rdn & r.o) | hd | **2** | 7/2$^{1}$ | 71 | 39 |
| $1092^{5}$ | **Charming Bride (56)** (SCWilliams) **3-8-10** KDarley(1) (cl up: effrt 2f out: edgd rt & nt qckn: fin 4th, 1½l: plcd 3rd) | | **3** | 6/1$^{3}$ | 48 | 16 |
| $3278^{9}$ | **Craignairn (64)** (JBerry) **3-9-4b** JCarroll(6) (led 4f: edgd lft & grad wknd: fin 5th, 2½l: plcd 4th) | | **4** | 12/1 | 50 | 18 |
| $3680^{7}$ | **Pathaze (49)** (NBycroft) **3-8-3** TWilliams(4) (prom 4f: btn whn bmpd over 1f out: fin 6th, 1 3/4l: plcd 5th) | | **5** | 6/1$^{3}$ | 30 | — |
| $2715^{5}$ | **Butterwick Belle (IRE) (60)** (RAFahey) **3-9-0** ACulhane(3) (prom 4f: wknd) | s.h | **7** | 8/1 | 41 | 9 |
| $3774^{5}$ | **Branston Danni (67)** (MrsJRRamsden) **3-9-7** KFallon(5) (b.nr hind: s.i.s: in tch & rdn ½-wy: sn btn & eased) | 3 | **8** | 7/2$^{1}$ | 40 | 8 |
| $3399^{5}$ | **Hoh Majestic (IRE) (61)** (MartynWane) **3-9-1v** JFEgan(2) (lw: chsd ldrs: outpcd 2f out: swtchd over 1f out: styd on: fin 3rd, 4l: disq: plcd last) | | **D** | 14/1 | 57 | 25 |

(SP 116.7%) **8 Rn**

**1m 12.2** (2.20) CSF £19.89 CT £87.72 TOTE £4.20: £2.20 £1.50 £3.40 (£22.00) OWNER Mr Hugh O'Donnell (PONTYPRIDD) BRED Cheveley Park Stud Ltd
STEWARDS' ENQUIRY Egan susp. 11-14/9/96 (irresponsible riding)

**3489 Natural Key** showed fine determination to hold on, despite drifting right in the closing stages. She ought to stay a bit further. (9/2)
**2870* Bowlers Boy** got a bit warm beforehand, but still ran a sound race, despite drifting right, like the winner, in the final furlong. (7/2)
**1092 Charming Bride** ran well after over three months off, but was inclined to wander when the pressure was on in the last furlong and a half. (6/1: op 4/1)
**2870 Craignairn** ran fast but, when pressure was applied, he edged left and soon cried enough. (12/1)
**3489 Pathaze** ran poorly here and being hampered made little difference to her finishing position. (6/1)
**2715 Butterwick Belle (IRE)** (8/1: op 12/1)
**3774 Branston Danni** (7/2: 9/4-4/1)
**3399 Hoh Majestic (IRE)** was tapped for toe halfway through the race and, when staying on again, blatantly knocked an opponent out of the way. After finishing third, he was disqualified and placed last. (14/1)

## 3960 GAETAN BILLIARD CHAMPAGNE MEDIAN AUCTION MAIDEN STKS (3, 4 & 5-Y.O) (Class E)

4-15 (4-18) **1m 3f 16y** £2,927.40 (£886.20: £432.60: £205.80) Stalls: High GOING minus 0.37 sec per fur (F)

| | | | | SP | RR | SF |
|---|---|---|---|---|---|---|
| $3173^{2}$ | **Divine (67)** (ACStewart) **3-8-8** SWhitworth(2) (lw: mde all: r.o strly fnl 3f: comf) | — | **1** | 1/2$^{1}$ | 64+ | 17 |
| $3642^{4}$ | **Vanadium Ore** (JLEyre) **3-8-13** KFallon(1) (lw: trckd wnr: effrt 4f out: no imp) | 10 | **2** | 5/2$^{2}$ | 55 | 8 |
| | **Dunrowan** (MrsMReveley) **3-8-8** KDarley(6) (neat: bhd: effrt 4f out: n.d) | 9 | **3** | 7/1$^{3}$ | 37 | — |
| $2780^{9}$ | **Magical Midnight (30)** (DonEnricoIncisa) **3-8-8** KimTinkler(4) (bhd: hrd rdn fnl 3½f: n.d) | 1½ | **4** | 33/1 | 34 | — |
| $3425^{9}$ | **Fizzy Boy (IRE)** (PMonteith) **3-8-6**(7) JBramhill(5) (bit bkwd: trckd ldrs: chal 4f out: sn rdn & wknd) | 8 | **5** | 100/1 | 28 | — |
| | **Swift Move** (PMonteith) **4-9-2** AMackay(3) (swtg: prom tl wknd over 4f out) | 20 | **6** | 100/1 | — | — |

(SP 112.7%) **6 Rn**

**2m 26.0** (6.60) CSF £2.18 TOTE £1.50: £1.10 £1.10 (£1.30) OWNER Mrs J. V. Sheffield (NEWMARKET) BRED Normanby Stud Ltd
WEIGHT FOR AGE 3yo-8lb

**3173 Divine**, much better suited by these longer trips, won in useful style and should go on from here. (1/2)

**3642 Vanadium Ore** was always in pursuit of the winner but, off the bit entering the last half-mile, was never anything like good enough. (5/2)
**Dunrowan** was learning as the race progressed, but there is still a long way to go. (7/1)
**867 Magical Midnight** was given some vigorous assistance with the whip in the last half-mile, but still failed to get anywhere near. (33/1)
**Fizzy Boy (IRE)** ran reasonably until blowing up in the last three furlongs. (100/1)

## 3961 HAMILTON HEAVY PLANT EXHIBITION H'CAP (0-70) (3-Y.O) (Class E)
4-45 (4-45) **1m 3f 16y** £3,330.00 (£1,008.00: £492.00: £234.00) Stalls: High GOING minus 0.37 sec per fur (F)

| | | | | SP | RR | SF |
|---|---|---|---|---|---|---|
| 3878* | **Full Throttle (66)** (MHTompkins) **3-9-4**(3) 5x MHenry(8) (lw: hld up & bhd: swtchd & effrt 3f out: r.o wl to ld wl ins fnl f) | — | **1** | 7/4$^{1}$ | 75 | 41 |
| 3819$^{2}$ | **Totem Dancer (66)** (JLEyre) **3-9-4**(3) OPears(3) (lw: prom: rdn over 3f out: hdwy to ld ins fnl f: hdd & nt qckn towards fin) | nk | **2** | 3/1$^{2}$ | 75 | 41 |
| 3780$^{5}$ | **Cottage Prince (IRE) (42)** (JJQuinn) **3-7-11**ow1 TWilliams(5) (swtg: hld up: effrt 4f out: styd on & ch 1f out: no ex) | 2 | **3** | 20/1 | 48 | 13 |
| 3866$^{5}$ | **Mystic Times (41)** (BMactaggart) **3-7-10** JQuinn(9) (a.p: led over 2f out tl ins fnl f: sn btn) | 1¼ | **4** | 16/1 | 45 | 11 |
| 3463$^{9}$ | **Hallikeld (41)** (TJEtherington) **3-7-10** LCharnock(2) (lw: led to 3f out: one pce) | 2 | **5** | 33/1 | 42 | 8 |
| 3852$^{8}$ | **Mono Lady (IRE) (55)** (DHaydnJones) **3-8-10** AMackay(4) (chsd ldrs: led 3f out: sn hdd & grad wknd) | hd | **6** | 7/1 | 56 | 22 |
| 3677$^{2}$ | **Ordained (60)** (EJAlston) **3-9-1** KFallon(1) (lw: hld up & bhd: hdwy on ins over 3f out: wknd fnl 2f) | 8 | **7** | 5/1$^{3}$ | 49 | 15 |
| 3580$^{8}$ | **Ship's Dancer (45)** (DonEnricoIncisa) **3-8-0** KimTinkler(6) (prom tl outpcd fnl 4f) | 1 | **8** | 50/1 | 33 | — |
| 2979$^{2}$ | **Khabar (63)** (RBastiman) **3-8-13**(5) HBastiman(10) (hld up: n.m.r 3f out: outpcd fnl 2f) | 1½ | **9** | 15/2 | 49 | 15 |

(SP 117.8%) **9 Rn**

**2m 24.2** (4.80) CSF £7.40 CT £69.64 TOTE £2.40: £1.50 £1.10 £3.10 (£3.50) Trio £71.40 OWNER Pamela, Lady Nelson of Stafford (NEWMARKET) BRED Dullingham House Stud
LONG HANDICAP Hallikeld 7-6 Cottage Prince (IRE) 7-7 Mystic Times 7-6
**3878* Full Throttle** did this the hard way and had to switch round the field and come up the unfavoured centre of the track. He is certainly much better suited by further. (7/4)
**3819 Totem Dancer** ran another sound race and kept staying on. Her luck will surely change. (3/1)
**3780 Cottage Prince (IRE)** is running well at present but, over this trip, he just found the front pair too strong in the final furlong. (20/1)
**3866 Mystic Times** ran well from 4lb out of the handicap but, in the end, this trip may just have been stretching things too far. (16/1)
**3053 Hallikeld**, taking a big drop back in trip, was found wanting for speed and would seem to need a bit further. (33/1)
**2033 Mono Lady (IRE)** had her chances, but was never doing enough under serious pressure in the last three furlongs. (7/1)
**3677 Ordained** (5/1: 4/1-6/1)

T/Jkpt: £621.10 (82.25 Tckts). T/Plpt: £13.70 (1,726.15 Tckts). T/Qdpt: £4.40 (421.66 Tckts). AA

# 3859-BRIGHTON (L-H) (Firm)
## Tuesday September 3rd
WEATHER: sunny WIND: slt half bhd

## 3962 ALDRINGTON NURSERY H'CAP (0-75) (2-Y.O) (Class E)
2-30 (2-31) **6f 209y** £3,425.10 (£1,024.80: £491.40: £224.70) Stalls: Low GOING minus 0.54 sec per fur (F)

| | | | | SP | RR | SF |
|---|---|---|---|---|---|---|
| 3607* | **Rumbustious (62)** (RHannon) **2-8-8** DaneO'Neill(6) (a.p: rdn over 2f out: led ins fnl f: r.o wl) | — | **1** | 100/30$^{1}$ | 65 | 28 |
| 3757$^{10}$ | **Saint Who (USA) (65)** (WAO'Gorman) **2-8-11** EmmaO'Gorman(4) (hdwy over 4f out: led wl over 1f out tl ins fnl f: unable qckn) | 1¾ | **2** | 20/1 | 64 | 27 |
| 3823$^{3}$ | **Life On The Street (65)** (RHannon) **2-8-11** TSprake(3) (hdwy 5f out: rdn over 2f out: one pce) | ½ | **3** | 12/1 | 63 | 26 |
| 3687$^{6}$ | **Supercharmer (75)** (CEBrittain) **2-9-7** BDoyle(2) (led over 1f: led over 2f out tl wl over 1f out: one pce) | 1½ | **4** | 16/1 | 69 | 32 |
| 3678$^{5}$ | **Silca's My Key (IRE) (69)** (MRChannon) **2-9-1** RPerham(5) (rdn over 3f out: hdwy over 1f out: one pce) | nk | **5** | 10/1 | 63 | 26 |
| 3795* | **Hoh Surprise (IRE) (58)** (MBell) **2-8-4**ow2 MFenton(9) (rdn over 3f out: hdwy over 1f out: one pce) | hd | **6** | 8/1$^{3}$ | 51 | 12 |
| 3663$^{5}$ | **Hadawah (USA) (72)** (JLDunlop) **2-9-4** JReid(8) (b.off hind: rdn over 5f out: nvr nr to chal) | 1¾ | **7** | 4/1$^{2}$ | 61 | 24 |
| 3632$^{2}$ | **Fancy A Fortune (IRE) (72)** (JPearce) **2-9-4** NDay(7) (lw: prom 2f) | 1¾ | **8** | 16/1 | 57 | 20 |
| 3494$^{7}$ | **Merciless Cop (70)** (BJMeehan) **2-9-2** MTebbutt(11) (lw: a bhd) | 3 | **9** | 4/1$^{2}$ | 49 | 12 |
| 3475$^{6}$ | **Calamander (IRE) (68)** (PFICole) **2-9-0** TQuinn(1) (lw: led over 5f out tl over 2f out: wknd over 1f out) | ½ | **10** | 14/1 | 45 | 8 |
| 3631$^{3}$ | **Be True (66)** (AMoore) **2-8-12** CandyMorris(13) (bhd fnl 5f) | nk | **11** | 33/1 | 43 | 6 |
| 3343$^{2}$ | **Avinalarf (68)** (WGMTurner) **2-8-7**(7) DSweeney(10) (lw: bhd fnl 4f) | 2 | **12** | 11/1 | 40 | 3 |
| 3523$^{7}$ | **Silver Spell (55)** (DrJDScargill) **2-8-1** NCarlisle(12) (prom over 3f) | 3 | **13** | 20/1 | 20 | — |

(SP 130.2%) **13 Rn**

**1m 21.4** (1.40) CSF £65.92 CT £693.83 TOTE £4.00: £1.90 £12.00 £5.70 (£172.20) Trio £292.60; £131.90 to York 4/8/96 OWNER Mr Christopher Curtis (MARLBOROUGH) BRED Fulling Mill Stud and C. Curtis
**3607* Rumbustious** produced her effort in the centre of the course in the straight. Vying for the lead in the final quarter-mile, she got on top inside the final furlong and kept on strongly. (100/30)
**3651 Saint Who (USA)**, in a handy position by halfway, gained a slender advantage along the inside rail early in the final quarter-mile. Overhauled by the winner inside the final furlong, he failed to find another gear. (20/1)
**3823 Life On The Street**, soon in a prominent position, was asked for her effort over two furlongs from home, but failed to find that vital turn of foot from below the distance. (12/1: 8/1-14/1)
**3687 Supercharmer** showed in front for a second time over a quarter of a mile out but, soon collared, could then only keep on at one pace. (16/1)
**3678 Silca's My Key (IRE)** made an effort over a furlong out, but could then make no further impression. (10/1: 7/1-12/1)
**3795* Hoh Surprise (IRE)**, ridden along at halfway, took closer order below the distance, but could then only go up and down in the same place. (8/1: 6/1-9/1)
**3494 Merciless Cop** (4/1: 6/1-7/2)
**3475 Calamander (IRE)** (14/1: 10/1-16/1)
**3343 Avinalarf** (11/1: 8/1-12/1)

## 3963 TATTERSALLS MAIDEN AUCTION STKS (2-Y.O) (Class E)
3-00 (3-01) **6f 209y** £3,097.50 (£924.00: £441.00: £199.50) Stalls: Low GOING minus 0.54 sec per fur (F)

| | | | | SP | RR | SF |
|---|---|---|---|---|---|---|
| 3848$^{12}$ | **Interdream** (RHannon) **2-8-3**ow1 DaneO'Neill(5) (b.off hind: rdn & hdwy over 2f out: led 1f out: r.o wl) | — | **1** | 20/1 | 69 | 14 |

3687[2] **Swiss Coast (IRE) (82)** (NTinkler) **2-8-8v[1]** TQuinn(3) (lw: led: rdn over 2f out: hdd 1f out: unable qckn) ....1½ **2** 5/6[1] 71 17
**Here's To Howie (USA)** (RHannon) **2-8-8** JReid(8) (leggy: unf: a.p: rdn over 2f out: one pce) ....1¼ **3** 10/1 68 14
*3625*[8] **Carlys Quest** (JNeville) **2-8-6** AClark(9) (b: lw: a.p: ev ch over 2f out: one pce) ....½ **4** 33/1 65 11
3803[3] **Hever Golf Charger (IRE) (75)** (TJNaughton) **2-8-9** TSprake(2) (hld up: rdn over 2f out: wknd fnl f) ....1¾ **5** 7/2[2] 64 10
3685[9] **Kingsdown Trix (IRE)** (AMoore) **2-8-5** CRutter(6) (bit bkwd: a bhd) ....¾ **6** 33/1 58 4
3171[5] **Fontcaudette (IRE)** (JEBanks) **2-8-0** JQuinn(4) (bhd fnl 3f) ....½ **7** 11/2[3] 52 —
3796[11] **M R Poly** (MRChannon) **2-8-9** BDoyle(7) (lw: prom over 4f) ....9 **8** 20/1 40 —
(SP 116.6%) **8 Rn**

**1m 22.2** (2.20) CSF £36.99 TOTE £23.80: £4.00 £1.10 £3.20 (£10.90) Trio £19.60 OWNER Mr Charles Farr & Mr Mark Heaton (MARLBOROUGH) BRED Mrs G. Kindersley

**Interdream** left his debut run well behind. Picking up ground over two furlongs from home, he struck the front a furlong out and kept on strongly. (20/1)
**3687 Swiss Coast (IRE)** failed to make the long journey from Malton pay off. Dictating matters from the front, he was vigorously pushed along over two furlongs from home, but he failed to get away from his rivals and, collared at the furlong pole, failed to find another gear. (5/6)
**Here's To Howie (USA)**, a tall colt with not much substance at present, was never far away, but failed to find that vital turn of foot in the last two furlongs. (10/1: op 6/1)
**Carlys Quest** had every chance over two furlongs from home before quicker rivals had his measure. (33/1)
**3803 Hever Golf Charger (IRE)** chased the leaders. One of five closely grouped up in the straight, he eventually called it a day in the final furlong. (7/2)
**3171 Fontcaudette (IRE)** (11/2: 6/1-10/1)

## 3964 E.B.F. GARDEN AWARD MAIDEN STKS (2-Y.O) (Class D)

3-30 (3-30) **7f 214y** £3,743.15 (£1,119.20: £536.10: £244.55) Stalls: Low GOING minus 0.54 sec per fur (F)

SP RR SF

3794[3] **Rapier** (RHannon) **2-9-0** DaneO'Neill(7) (lw: a.p: rdn over 2f out: led ins fnl f: r.o wl) ....— **1** 11/8[2] 77 32
3682[13] **St Lawrence (CAN)** (CEBrittain) **2-9-0** BDoyle(3) (bit bkwd: rdn over 5f out: lost pl 4f out: swtchd lft over 2f out: rallied over 1f out: r.o wl) ....¾ **2** 33/1 76 31
3682[3] **Heart of Armor** (PFICole) **2-9-0** TQuinn(4) (lw: led: rdn over 4f out: hdd ins fnl f: unable qckn) ....hd **3** 4/5[1] 75 30
3485[7] **Triple Term** (JLDunlop) **2-9-0** SWhitworth(1) (rdn over 4f out: swtchd rt 3f out: hdwy 2f out: r.o one pce) ....2 **4** 14/1[3] 71 26
3485[8] **Mutahadeth** (NAGraham) **2-9-0** DHarrison(6) (lw: a.p: rdn over 4f out: wknd over 2f out) ....5 **5** 33/1 61 16
3803[10] **Alimerjam (55)** (JWhite) **2-8-9** TSprake(5) (a bhd) ....5 **6** 50/1 46 1
829[9] **Streamline (IRE)** (GLewis) **2-8-11**(3) AWhelan(2) (lw: prom over 4f) ....9 **7** 40/1 33 —
(SP 114.6%) **7 Rn**

**1m 34.0** (1.80) CSF £31.67 TOTE £2.50: £1.40 £7.20 (£29.30) OWNER Noodles Racing (MARLBOROUGH) BRED J. Repard
**3794 Rapier**, always close up, mounted his challenge in the straight and eventually got on top inside the final furlong. (11/8)
**St Lawrence (CAN)**, still carrying condition, stepped up on his debut at Kempton where he finished over thirteen lengths behind Heart of Armor. Losing his pitch at halfway, he looked to be out of it, but he got his second wind below the distance and ran on strongly to snatch second prize in the last couple of strides. (33/1)
**3682 Heart of Armor**, who made an encouraging debut at Kempton recently, was not happy on this switchback track. Setting the pace, Quinn was already niggling at the colt at the top of the hill. Trying to stretch them over a quarter of a mile from home, he failed to get away from the winner and, headed inside the final furlong, failed to quicken. He is worth another chance. (4/5)
**2977 Triple Term**, pushed along at the top of the hill, made an effort a quarter of a mile from home but, despite staying on, never threatened the principals. (14/1)
**Mutahadeth** was close up until weakening over two furlongs out. (33/1)

## 3965 FRIENDS OF QUEEN'S PARK APPRENTICE (S) H'CAP (0-60) (3-Y.O) (Class G)

4-00 (4-03) **1m 3f 196y** £2,070.00 (£570.00: £270.00) Stalls: High GOING minus 0.54 sec per fur (F)

SP RR SF

3635[8] **Colour Counsellor (41)** (RMFlower) **3-8-8b** CAdamson(13) (mde all: clr 5f out: r.o wl) ....— **1** 15/2 53 26
3860[3] **Ela Agapi Mou (USA) (52)** (GLewis) **3-9-2**(3) PDoe(2) (hld up: chsd wnr fnl 3f: no imp) ....3 **2** 6/1[2] 60 33
*3872*[4] **Duncombe Hall (42)** (CACyzer) **3-8-4**(5) CLowther(10) (a.p: rdn over 3f out: one pce) ....2 **3** 10/1 47 20
3633[2] **Eskimo Kiss (IRE) (40)** (MJFetherston-Godley) **3-8-2v**(5) DavidO'Neill(3) (a.p: rdn over 3f out: one pce) ....2½ **4** 7/1[3] 42 15
3053[8] **Kings Nightclub (40)** (JWhite) **3-8-2**(5) JFowle(6) (lw: hdwy over 3f out: one pce) ....2½ **5** 20/1 39 12
*3605*[5] **Hever Golf Diamond (48)** (TJNaughton) **3-8-12**(3) CWebb(4) (hdwy over 5f out: wknd 2f out) ....nk **6** 11/1 46 19
1534[14] **Driftholme (29)** (GLMoore) **3-7-5**(5) AMcCarthy(7) (nvr nr to chal) ....1 **7** 33/1 26 —
3808[20] **In Cahoots (34)** (AGNewcombe) **3-8-1b[1]** AEddery(9) (bhd fnl 8f) ....2 **8** 9/1 28 1
3303[2] **Efficacious (IRE) (46)** (CJBenstead) **3-8-13** DSweeney(8) (lw: hdwy over 5f out: wknd 3f out) ....1 **9** 100/30[1] 39 12
3780[12] **Royal Rigger (36)** (CSmith) **3-8-3** SophieMitchell(1) (a bhd) ....6 **10** 33/1 21 —
3681[10] **Sam Rockett (54)** (CAHorgan) **3-9-4**(3) GayeHarwood(12) (lw: prom over 7f) ....9 **11** 10/1 27 —
*3600*[8] **Uoni (50)** (CEBrittain) **3-8-12**(5) JGotobed(11) (bhd fnl 6f) ....½ **12** 10/1 22 —
3606[13] **Carwyn's Choice (30)** (PCClarke) **3-7-4**(7)ow1 CherylBone(5) (ref to r: t.n.p) .... **R** 33/1 — —
(SP 120.8%) **13 Rn**

**2m 31.1** (3.50) CSF £48.95 CT £412.71 TOTE £8.90: £2.10 £3.20 £2.60 (£23.10) Trio £87.60 OWNER Mrs G. M. Temmerman (JEVINGTON) BRED M. A. Kirby
LONG HANDICAP Driftholme 7-9
No bid
**3303 Colour Counsellor** was given an enterprising ride. Making all the running, he surged clear at the top of the hill and was not going to be caught. (15/2: 6/1-10/1)
**3860 Ela Agapi Mou (USA)** moved into second place three furlongs from home but, try as he might, he failed to reel in the winner. (6/1)
**3872 Duncombe Hall** never looked like quickening up in the straight. (10/1)
**2716 Eskimo Kiss (IRE)** was made to look very pedestrian in the straight. (7/1)
**Kings Nightclub** made an effort over three furlongs from home, but could then only plod on at one very insufficient pace. (20/1)

## 3966 RACE HILL MEDIAN AUCTION MAIDEN STKS (3-Y.O F) (Class F)

4-30 (4-30) **1m 1f 209y** £2,381.00 (£656.00: £311.00) Stalls: High GOING minus 0.54 sec per fur (F)

SP RR SF

*3626*[3] **Afon Alwen** (SCWilliams) **3-8-11** TQuinn(1) (lw: mde all: hrd rdn over 1f out: r.o wl) ....— **1** 7/1 57 15

| | | | | SP | RR | SF |
|---|---|---|---|---|---|---|
| 3402[2] | **Golden Fawn** (LadyHerries) **3-8-11** JQuinn(5) (lw: hld up: rdn over 2f out: unable qckn) | 1½ | **2** | 6/4[1] | 55 | 13 |
| 3852[7] | **Tallulah Belle (36)** (NPLittmoden) **3-8-11** BDoyle(2) (lw: rdn & hdwy over 2f out: one pce) | nk | **3** | 20/1 | 54 | 12 |
| 3800[4] | **Charisse Dancer (53)** (CFWall) **3-8-11** JReid(7) (hld up: rdn over 2f out: one pce) | hd | **4** | 2/1[2] | 54 | 12 |
| 3472[9] | **Chesteine (55)** (PJMakin) **3-8-8**(3) RHavlin(3) (hld up: rdn 3f out: wknd over 2f out) | 8 | **5** | 25/1 | 41 | — |
| 3847[3] | **Lovely Morning** (DJGMurraySmith) **3-8-11** DaneO'Neill(6) (lw: chsd wnr over 6f) | 4 | **6** | 9/2[3] | 35 | — |
| | | | | (SP 112.6%) | **6 Rn** | |

**2m 2.6** (4.30) CSF £17.46 TOTE £8.20: £2.10 £1.60 (£5.30) OWNER Mr J. E. Lloyd (NEWMARKET) BRED Lloyd Bros

**3626 Afon Alwen** dictated matters from the front. Responding to pressure below the distance, she kept on well to win a dreadful race. (7/1: 5/1-8/1)

**3402 Golden Fawn**, tucked in behind the leaders, was asked for her effort over a quarter of a mile from home and, although struggling on to win the battle for second prize, never looked like finding that vital turn of foot. (6/4)

**2893 Tallulah Belle**, pushed along to take closer order over two furlongs from home, was then only treading water. She is still a maiden after twenty attempts. (20/1)

**3800 Charisse Dancer** chased the leaders, but never looked like finding another gear in the last two furlongs. (2/1)

**Chesteine** chased the leaders, but was hung out to dry over two furlongs from home. (25/1)

## 3967 HANNINGTONS OF BRIGHTON H'CAP (0-80) (3-Y.O+) (Class D)

5-00 (5-01) **6f 209y** £3,993.30 (£1,193.40: £571.20: £260.10) Stalls: Low GOING minus 0.54 sec per fur (F)

| | | | | SP | RR | SF |
|---|---|---|---|---|---|---|
| 2981[10] | **Jo Maximus (70)** (SDow) **4-9-6** DaneO'Neill(9) (chsd ldr: led over 2f out: rdn out) | — | **1** | 10/1 | 81 | 55 |
| 3861* | **Balance of Power (69)** (RAkehurst) **4-9-5** 6x TQuinn(5) (hld up: rdn over 1f out: r.o) | ½ | **2** | 5/2[1] | 79 | 53 |
| *3877*[12] | **Sharp Imp (58)** (RMFlower) **6-8-8b** JQuinn(2) (hdwy over 2f out: ev ch ins fnl f: unable qckn) | 1¼ | **3** | 12/1 | 65 | 39 |
| 3702* | **Quality (IRE) (78)** (WAO'Gorman) **3-9-10** EmmaO'Gorman(4) (lw: rdn & hdwy 2f out: one pce) | 1¾ | **4** | 7/2[2] | 81 | 51 |
| 3666* | **Waders Dream (IRE) (53)** (PatMitchell) **7-8-3v** MFenton(1) (lw: rdn over 3f out: hdwy over 1f out: nvr nrr) | 2½ | **5** | 14/1 | 50 | 24 |
| 3636* | **Pride of Hayling (IRE) (62)** (PRHedger) **5-8-9**(3) NVarley(6) (lw: rdn over 3f out: hdwy 2f out: wknd over 1f out) | s.h | **6** | 9/1 | 59 | 33 |
| 3861[4] | **Fort Knox (IRE) (58)** (RMFlower) **5-8-8b** DHarrison(7) (lw: a bhd) | 2 | **7** | 10/1 | 51 | 25 |
| 3606[3] | **Super Park (57)** (JPearce) **4-8-7** NDay(8) (lw: prom over 4f) | 2½ | **8** | 8/1 | 44 | 18 |
| 3474[4] | **Gooseberry Pie (62)** (RCharlton) **3-8-8** JReid(3) (led over 4f: wknd over 1f out) | 2½ | **9** | 6/1[3] | 43 | 13 |
| | | | | (SP 118.7%) | **9 Rn** | |

**1m 20.1** (0.10) CSF £34.48 CT £289.25 TOTE £16.40: £3.60 £2.60 £3.00 (£20.60) Trio £57.80 OWNER J & S Kelly (EPSOM) BRED Capt A. L. Smith-Maxwell

WEIGHT FOR AGE 3yo-4lb

**1790 Jo Maximus**, whose two previous victories have both come here, raced in second place. Sent on over a quarter of a mile out, he was ridden along to hold off the persistent runner-up to complete a memorable four-timer for O'Neill. (10/1: 8/1-12/1)

**3861* Balance of Power** chased the leaders. Vigorously ridden below the distance, he stuck to his task really well, but was unable to overhaul the winner in time. (5/2)

**3636 Sharp Imp** made his effort over quarter of a mile from home and looked a live threat below the distance. Still in with every chance inside the final furlong, he was then tapped for toe. (12/1: op 8/1)

**3702* Quality (IRE)** made his effort two furlongs from home, but then failed to raise his work-rate. (7/2)

**3666* Waders Dream (IRE)**, out with the washing early in the straight, stayed on in the last furlong and a half past beaten horses. (14/1: 10/1-20/1)

**3636* Pride of Hayling (IRE)** failed to last out this longer trip and an effort two furlongs from home had soon burnt out. A return to six furlongs or even five is required. (9/1)

T/Plpt: £101.80 (146.91 Tckts). T/Qdpt: £33.50 (27.38 Tckts). AK

# 3637-PONTEFRACT (L-H) (Good, Good to firm patches)

## Tuesday September 3rd

WEATHER: fine WIND: slt half against

## 3968 PONTEFRACT SERIES (ROUND 4) APPRENTICE LIMITED STKS (0-65) (3-Y.O+) (Class F)

2-45 (2-46) **1m 4f 8y** £2,531.00 (£716.00: £353.00) Stalls: Low GOING: 0.05 sec per fur (G)

| | | | | SP | RR | SF |
|---|---|---|---|---|---|---|
| 3710[16] | **Ayunli (64)** (SCWilliams) **5-9-0** GMilligan(2) (lw: mde all: edgd rt over 1f out: styd on wl) | — | **1** | 13/8[1] | 68 | 49 |
| 3641[7] | **Mock Trial (IRE) (64)** (MrsJRRamsden) **3-8-10** FLynch(3) (trckd ldrs: chal over 2f out: sn rdn: swtchd ins & nt qckn fnl f) | 1¼ | **2** | 5/2[2] | 71 | 43 |
| 3657[7] | **Snow Falcon (64)** (MBell) **3-8-12** RMullen(7) (hld up & plld hrd: sddle slipped: hdwy over 2f out: styd on fnl f) | 10 | **3** | 9/2[3] | 60 | 32 |
| 3586[4] | **Welcome Royale (IRE) (55)** (MHTompkins) **3-8-8** GFaulkner(1) (s.i.s: sn chsng ldrs: wknd over 1f out) | 1¼ | **4** | 10/1 | 54 | 26 |
| 3939[12] | **Ashover (58)** (TDBarron) **6-8-12**(5) PFredericks(8) (sn in tch: lost pl over 2f out) | 6 | **5** | 9/1 | 46 | 27 |
| 3638[2] | **Record Lover (IRE) (34)** (MCChapman) **6-9-3** JEdmunds(6) (prom: drvn along & outpcd 4f out: sn wknd) | ½ | **6** | 33/1 | 46 | 27 |
| 3204[10] | **Leap in the Dark (IRE) (26)** (MissLCSiddall) **7-8-12**(5) TSiddall(4) (chsd ldrs tl wknd 3f out) | 12 | **7** | 66/1 | 30 | 11 |
| 998* | **De-Veers Currie (IRE) (53)** (MartinTodhunter) **4-9-2** KSked(5) (stdd s: plld hrd: sn trckng ldrs on outside: lost pl over 3f out) | 30 | **8** | 16/1 | — | — |
| | **The Cottonwool Kid (37)** (TKersey) **4-8-12**(5) PClarke(9) (chsd ldrs tl wknd qckly ½-wy: sn bhd: t.o 3f out) | dist | **9** | 100/1 | — | — |
| | | | | (SP 115.2%) | **9 Rn** | |

**2m 42.4** (8.10) CSF £5.91 TOTE £2.70: £1.40 £1.20 £1.30 (£3.70) Trio £4.00 OWNER Mr I. A. Southcott (NEWMARKET) BRED I. A. Southcott

WEIGHT FOR AGE 3yo-9lb

**3500 Ayunli**, a winner five times last year, was well favoured by the race conditions. Setting her own pace, she always looked to be in control. (13/8)

**3641 Mock Trial (IRE)**, who had two handlers in the paddock, would have been meeting the winner on 5lb better terms in a handicap. After travelling strongly for much of the way, he went in behind the winner under pressure, and could only keep on at the same pace. Despite his failure over an extended two miles here last time, he still looks basically a stayer. (5/2)

**3249* Snow Falcon**, a poor mover, did as well as could be expected, his saddle having slipped forward at an early stage. (9/2)

**3586 Welcome Royale (IRE)** did as well as could be expected at the weights. (10/1)

**196 Ashover**, who still looked in need of the outing, as usual wore a tongue-strap. He is probably being readied for an All-Weather back-end campaign. (9/1: 6/1-10/1)

## 3969 COMPUTER TIMEFORM NURSERY H'CAP (0-85) (2-Y.O) (Class D)

3-15 (3-18) **6f** £3,978.50 (£1,193.00: £574.00: £264.50) Stalls: Low GOING: 0.05 sec per fur (G)

| Form | Horse / details | Dist | Pos | SP | RR | SF |
|---|---|---|---|---|---|---|
| $3674^{5}$ | **Burlington House (USA) (78)** (PFICole) **2-9-2** PatEddery(2) (lw: mde all: qcknd clr over 1f out: unchal) | — | **1** | $11/4^{1}$ | 87+ | 43 |
| $3792^{4}$ | **Burkes Manor (83)** (TDBarron) **2-9-7** DeanMcKeown(12) (unruly in stalls: swvd lft s: sn chsng ldrs: styd on appr fnl f: no ch w wnr) | 4 | **2** | $8/1^{3}$ | 81 | 37 |
| $3771^{2}$ | **Brutal Fantasy (IRE) (72)** (JLEyre) **2-8-10** KDarley(10) (b.hind: a chsng ldrs: kpt on same pce fnl 2f) | 1¾ | **3** | $13/2^{2}$ | 66 | 22 |
| $3687^{10}$ | **In Good Nick (64)** (MWEasterby) **2-8-2** DaleGibson(11) (lw: sltly hmpd s: hdwy over 2f out: styd on fnl f) | 1¾ | **4** | 14/1 | 53 | 9 |
| 3814* | **Abstone Queen (59)** (PDEvans) **2-7-8v**$^{(3)ow1}$ DWright(15) (a chsng ldrs: one pce fnl 2f) | hd | **5** | 10/1 | 48 | 3 |
| $3637^{9}$ | **Epic Stand (65)** (MrsJRRamsden) **2-8-3** SSanders(8) (trckd ldrs tl grad wknd fnl 2f) | 3½ | **6** | 16/1 | 44 | — |
| $3588^{7}$ | **Denton Lad (72)** (JWWatts) **2-8-10** NConnorton(13) (lw: hld up: stdy hdwy fnl 2f: nvr plcd to chal) | ¾ | **7** | 16/1 | 49+ | 5 |
| $3674^{7}$ | **Charlton Spring (IRE) (82)** (RJHodges) **2-9-6** SDrowne(14) (racd wd: sn bhd: pushed along & hdwy over 2f out: nvr nr ldrs) | 1¾ | **8** | 16/1 | 55 | 11 |
| $3467^{11}$ | **Preskidul (IRE) (58)** (DWPArbuthnot) **2-7-7**$^{(3)}$ DarrenMoffatt(3) (b: b.hind: nvr wnt pce) | 2½ | **9** | 33/1 | 24 | — |
| $3687^{15}$ | **Docklands Carriage (IRE) (70)** (NTinkler) **2-8-8** RCochrane(9) (bhd: sme hdwy over 1f out: n.d) | nk | **10** | 14/1 | 35 | — |
| $3464^{6}$ | **Mazil (65)** (TDEasterby) **2-8-3** JLowe(4) (in tch: effrt over 2f out: sn wknd) | ½ | **11** | 20/1 | 29 | — |
| $3227^{7}$ | **Jib Jab (72)** (DNicholls) **2-8-10** WRyan(5) (w wnr to ½-wy: sn bhd) | 3½ | **12** | 20/1 | 27 | — |
| $3590^{9}$ | **No Extradition (70)** (MrsJRRamsden) **2-8-8** KFallon(7) (sn outpcd & bhd) | hd | **13** | 12/1 | 24 | — |
| $2720^{5}$ | **Wagga Moon (IRE) (76)** (JJO'Neill) **2-9-0** GDuffield(1) (b: in tch: sn drvn along: wknd 2f out) | nk | **14** | 14/1 | 30 | — |
| $3835^{18}$ | **Nostalgic Air (USA) (73)** (EWeymes) **2-8-11** GHind(6) (s.i.s: sme hdwy ½-wy: sn wknd) | 5 | **15** | 10/1 | 13 | — |
| | | | | (SP 127.1%) | **15 Rn** | |

**1m 18.8** (4.50) CSF £25.02 CT £130.41 TOTE £3.40: £1.90 £3.20 £1.80 (£19.70) Trio £19.10 OWNER Richard Green (Fine Paintings) (WHATCOMBE) BRED John A. Bell III & B. B. Williams

LONG HANDICAP Preskidul (IRE) 7-8

**3674 Burlington House (USA)** behaved himself in the stalls this time. A powerful mover, he was well suited by the step back to six and, quickening clear off the bend, he should win again. (11/4)

**3792 Burkes Manor** behaved badly in the stalls. Poorly drawn, he ran well in the race itself despite, like the rest, having no chance with the easy winner. (8/1)

**3771 Brutal Fantasy (IRE)**, a keen-going sort, travelled strongly from a poor draw but, off the bridle, could only stick on at the same pace. (13/2)

**3511 In Good Nick**, tightened up at the start, was putting in her best work at the finish and will be suited by a step up to seven. (14/1)

**3814* Abstone Queen** ran well from a bad draw. Though a fussy type, she is holding her form remarkably well after a tough and rewarding year. (10/1)

**2211 Epic Stand** raced keenly. Dropping away once in line for home, he can be expected to do better over further in due course. (16/1)

**3293 Denton Lad** looked to have been set plenty to do on his handicap debut. Not knocked about at any stage, connections will be hoping for some mercy. (16/1)

## 3970 TIMEFORM RACE CARD (S) STKS (3-Y.O+) (Class G)

3-45 (3-49) **1m 2f 6y** £2,784.00 (£774.00: £372.00) Stalls: Low GOING: 0.05 sec per fur (G)

| Form | Horse / details | Dist | Pos | SP | RR | SF |
|---|---|---|---|---|---|---|
| $3808^{4}$ | **Action Jackson (56)** (BJMcMath) **4-9-0** KDarley(6) (w ldrs: led over 3f out: jst hld on) | — | **1** | $3/1^{2}$ | 51 | 45 |
| $3824^{2}$ | **Shabanaz (65)** (WRMuir) **11-9-7** PatEddery(10) (lw: sn bhd & drvn along: hdwy 2f out: n.m.r ins fnl f: styd on strly towards fin) | nk | **2** | $3/1^{2}$ | 58 | 52 |
| $3780^{9}$ | **Bold Top (37)** (BSRothwell) **4-9-0b** OUrbina(14) (led tl over 3f out: one pce) | 1¾ | **3** | 25/1 | 48 | 42 |
| 3849* | **Guesstimation (USA) (62)** (JPearce) **7-9-0** GBardwell(13) (lw: trckd ldrs: effrt over 2f out: wandered over 1f out: nt qckn) | 1¼ | **4** | $7/4^{1}$ | 46 | 40 |
| $3481^{4}$ | **Hi Rock (45)** (JNorton) **4-8-4**$^{(5)}$ GParkin(17) (hdwy over 2f out: prom whn hung lft over 1f out: nt qckn) | 2½ | **5** | 20/1 | 37 | 31 |
| $3938^{7}$ | **Highfield Fizz (45)** (CWFairhurst) **4-8-9** RCochrane(16) (lw: mid div: hdwy u.p 3f out: no imp) | 3 | **6** | 25/1 | 32 | 26 |
| $3358^{5}$ | **Houghton Venture (USA) (50)** (SPCWoods) **4-9-0** DBiggs(2) (trckd ldrs: effrt 2f out: one pce) | 1½ | **7** | 20/1 | 35 | 29 |
| *$3090^{5}$* | **Undawaterscubadiva (34)** (MPBielby) **4-8-11**$^{(3)}$ PMcCabe(3) (hld up: hdwy on outer over 2f out: nvr nr ldrs) | 5 | **8** | 50/1 | 27 | 21 |
| $3849^{8}$ | **Hunza Story (23)** (NPLittmoden) **4-8-2**$^{(7)}$ JoHunnam(1) (b.hind: lw: bhd: sme hdwy over 1f out: n.d) | ½ | **9** | 50/1 | 21 | 15 |
| $3849^{10}$ | **Brown Eyed Girl (39)** (BJMcMath) **4-8-9** WRyan(18) (racd wd: chsd ldrs tl wknd over 1f out) | 5 | **10** | 50/1 | 13 | 7 |
| $3777^{12}$ | **Irish Oasis (IRE) (43)** (BSRothwell) **3-8-7** JFEgan(4) (w ldrs tl lost pl over 1f out) | 1¾ | **11** | 25/1 | 15 | 2 |
| $3808^{5}$ | **Abtaal (52)** (RJHodges) **6-9-0** SDrowne(9) (lw: chsd ldrs tl wknd fnl 3f) | 3 | **12** | $14/1^{3}$ | 10 | 4 |
| $3456^{10}$ | **Safa Dancer (32)** (BAMcMahon) **3-8-2** AMackay(7) (s.i.s: a bhd) | 7 | **13** | 25/1 | — | — |
| $3306^{9}$ | **Nukud (USA) (35)** (GROldroyd) **4-9-0** KFallon(11) (sn bhd & drvn along: n.d) | 5 | **14** | 33/1 | — | — |
| $3849^{13}$ | **Andy Coin** (WMBrisbourne) **5-8-9** AGarth(8) (s.i.s: a bhd) | 1½ | **15** | 50/1 | — | — |
| $3460^{11}$ | **Lady Ploy (27)** (MissLCSiddall) **4-8-9** GHind(15) (bhd fnl 4f) | 11 | **16** | 50/1 | — | — |
| $3789^{9}$ | **Forecast (50)** (JWharton) **3-8-7** GDuffield(19) (sn bhd & drvn along: nt r.o) | 5 | **17** | 33/1 | — | — |
| *$159^{9}$* | **Aconorace** (RAFahey) **4-9-0** MBirch(5) (in tch tl lost pl 4f out: sn t.o: virtually p.u) | dist | **18** | 50/1 | — | — |
| | | | | (SP 135.6%) | **18 Rn** | |

**2m 15.6** (7.30) CSF £12.86 TOTE £4.60: £1.80 £1.20 £9.30 (£10.00) Trio £171.40 OWNER Mr R. G. Levin (NEWMARKET) BRED Stetchworth Park Stud Ltd

WEIGHT FOR AGE 3yo-7lb

Bt in 6,000 gns

**3808 Action Jackson**, given a positive ride, found the post coming just in time. (3/1)

**3824 Shabanaz** showed a very poor action going down. His rider was soon hard at work and only his perseverance got him so close. But for being tightened up for a couple of strides inside the last, he might well have got there. (3/1)

**3348 Bold Top** looked on bad terms with himself in the paddock but, over a course he likes, ran remarkably well, considering he would have been meeting the winner on 19lb more favourable terms in a handicap. (25/1)

**3849* Guesstimation (USA)** came off a true line under pressure, getting in the way of the runner-up. (7/4)

**3481 Hi Rock**, who wants to do nothing but hang, seemed to stay the trip alright. (20/1)

## 3971 TIMEFORM FUTURITY CONDITIONS STKS (2-Y.O) (Class B)

4-15 (4-17) **6f** £6,214.00 (£2,326.00: £1,138.00: £490.00: £220.00: £112.00) Stalls: Low GOING: 0.05 sec per fur (G)

| Form | Horse / details | Dist | Pos | SP | RR | SF |
|---|---|---|---|---|---|---|
| 2734* | **Lima** (LMCumani) **2-8-10** OUrbina(5) (lw: trckd ldrs: effrt over 2f out: edgd lft over 1f out: r.o wl to ld ins fnl f) | — | **1** | $4/1^{2}$ | 90 | 44 |

3690⁵ **Nigrasine (100)** (JLEyre) **2-9-7** DeanMcKeown(4) (trckd ldrs: led 2f out tl ins fnl f: r.o wl)....1 **2** 4/1 [2] 98 52
3701* **Kharir (IRE)** (HThomsonJones) **2-9-1** RHills(1) (trckd ldrs on ins: n.m.r over 2f out & over 1f out: kpt on same pce fnl f)....2½ **3** 5/1 [3] 86 40
3349* **Irish Accord (USA)** (MrsJRRamsden) **2-9-1** KFallon(6) (unruly s: hld up: effrt over 2f out: sltly hmpd over 1f out: swtchd outside & ducked bdly rt)....2 **4** 13/8 [1] 80 34
3771* **Perfect Bliss (77)** (PDEvans) **2-8-6** JFEgan(2) (led to 2f out: edgd lft & wknd over 1f out)....3 **5** 16/1 63 17
3684² **Musical Dancer (USA) (100)** (EALDunlop) **2-9-1** WRyan(7) (trckd ldrs: effrt over 2f out: sn wknd)....hd **6** 5/1 [3] 72 26
(SP 117.3%) **6 Rn**

**1m 18.3** (4.00) CSF £19.47 TOTE £5.10: £2.80 £2.40 (£13.90) OWNER Sultan Al Kabeer (NEWMARKET) BRED The Sussex Stud
**2734* Lima**, the pick of the paddock, did it nicely in the end and will be suited by a step up to seven. (4/1)
**3690 Nigrasine**, who had missed work before York due to a cough, still did not look at his best. Conceding the winner 11lb, this was a fine effort and connections will now be looking to the Redcar Two-Year-Old Trophy. (4/1)
**3701* Kharir (IRE)**, tucked in on the inner, did not have the best of runs but, when the opening came coming to the final furlong, the first two ran away from him. (5/1)
**3349* Irish Accord (USA)** behaved badly at the start. Taking a keen grip, he was messed about early in the straight but, when switched to the outside, dived violently right and there was nothing his rider could do about it. He clearly has some sort of problem and does not look like a six-furlong horse. Possibly a right-handed track might be needed. (13/8)
**3771* Perfect Bliss**, who gets no respite, made the running, but was hanging off the rail throughout. (16/1)
**3684 Musical Dancer (USA)** was completely tapped for foot when the race began in earnest and he might even need a mile. (5/1)

## 3972 PHIL BULL TROPHY CONDITIONS STKS (3-Y.O+) (Class C)

4-45 (4-46) **2m 1f 216y** £5,341.60 (£1,869.60: £914.80: £394.00) Stalls: Centre GOING: 0.05 sec per fur (G)

SP RR SF

3404* **Canon Can (USA) (84)** (HRACecil) **3-8-6** WRyan(4) (lw: trckd ldrs: effrt over 3f out: led over 1f out: styd on strly)....— **1** 4/1 [2] 115 47
2723² **Kristal's Paradise (IRE) (103)** (JLDunlop) **4-8-11** PatEddery(5) (led tl over 1f out: eased whn btn ins fnl f)....7 **2** 8/11 [1] 100 46
3673⁵ **Anchor Clever (109)** (PAKelleway) **4-9-2** KFallon(3) (swtg: dwlt: hld up & plld hrd: hdwy on outside 5f out: rdn over 2f out: fnd nil)....5 **3** 4/1 [2] 100 46
2723⁴ **Bahamian Sunshine (USA) (98)** (RAkehurst) **5-9-2** SSanders(1) (swtg: trckd ldr: chal over 3f out: rdn & fnd nil 2f out)....½ **4** 6/1 [3] 100 46
(SP 112.2%) **4 Rn**

**4m 2.9** (10.90) CSF £7.41 TOTE £3.60: (£1.90) OWNER Canon (Anglia) O A Ltd (NEWMARKET) BRED Elkay Stables
WEIGHT FOR AGE 3yo-14lb
**3404* Canon Can (USA)**, a progressive stayer, looked outstanding in the paddock. He did this in really good style, especially considering he would have been two stone worse off with the runner-up in a handicap. He is sure to take a stiff rise in the weights after this, but the Cesarewitch is an early-closing race, and he should get in off a low mark with no penalty. He must have an outstanding chance in that. (4/1)
**2723 Kristal's Paradise (IRE)** set out to make this a stamina test and, but for being eased when held, the margin of defeat would have been about three lengths. (8/11)
**3673 Anchor Clever**, warm beforehand, took a keen grip but, when pulled to the outside, he did very little. He is one to have reservations about. (4/1)
**2723 Bahamian Sunshine (USA)**, who has been gelded and has changed stables, was awash with sweat beforehand. Asked to challenge on the run up to the final turn, he wanted nothing to do with it. (6/1)

## 3973 TIMEFORM BLACK BOOK H'CAP (0-70) (3-Y.O+) (Class E)

5-15 (5-23) **6f** £3,808.00 (£1,144.00: £552.00: £256.00) Stalls: Low GOING: 0.05 sec per fur (G)

SP RR SF

3055¹⁰ **Grand Chapeau (IRE) (55)** (DNicholls) **4-8-13** AlexGreaves(13) (mde all: clr over 1f out: hld on towards fin) — **1** 20/1 65 39
3774³ **Kira (70)** (JLEyre) **6-9-11**(3) OPears(11) (b.hind: lw: a chsng ldrs: styd on wl ins fnl f)....¾ **2** 7/1 [2] 78 52
3639⁷ **Barato (63)** (MrsJRRamsden) **5-9-7** KFallon(4) (b.hind: lw: bhd: hdwy on ins 2f out: kpt on same pce fnl f)....2 **3** 15/2 [3] 66 40
3810⁸ **Robellion (69)** (DWPArbuthnot) **5-9-13v** RCochrane(10) (b.hind: swtchd to r wd: hdwy on outside 2f out: styd on wl towards fin)....½ **4** 12/1 70 44
2870² **Finisterre (IRE) (64)** (JJO'Neill) **3-9-6** KDarley(3) (lw: in tch: hmpd over 2f out & over 1f out: styd on wl towards fin)....1¼ **5** 7/1 [2] 62 34
3868¹² **Captain Carat (63)** (MrsJRRamsden) **5-9-7** OUrbina(14) (b.nr fore: a in tch: kpt on ins fnl f: nvr nr to chal)....½ **6** 12/1 60 34
3758⁴ **Pageboy (66)** (PCHaslam) **7-9-10** SDrowne(18) (lw: a chsng ldrs: kpt on same pce fnl 2f)....hd **7** 10/1 62 36
2903² **Aquado (56)** (SRBowring) **7-9-0b** DeanMcKeown(12) (lw: bhd: hmpd over 1f out: kpt on towards fin)....1¾ **8** 12/1 48 22
3424¹¹ **Dictation (USA) (62)** (JJO'Neill) **4-9-6** JFEgan(1) (in tch: effrt over 2f out: one pce)....s.h **9** 33/1 54 28
3783¹⁰ **How's Yer Father (66)** (RJHodges) **10-9-5**(5) AmandaSanders(17) (racd wd: n.d)....½ **10** 20/1 56 30
3817³ **Cavers Yangous (65)** (MJohnston) **5-9-9v** RHills(16) (racd wd: chsd ldrs tl lost pl 1f out: eased)....7 **11** 9/1 37 11
1423⁶ **White Sorrel (57)** (SEKettlewell) **5-9-1** JStack(7) (sn bhd: n.m.r over 2f out: n.d)....s.h **12** 25/1 29 3
3844¹⁷ **Deerly (57)** (CASmith) **3-8-13** SSanders(15) (lw: racd wd: chsd ldrs tl wknd over 2f out)....2 **13** 33/1 23 —
3863⁵ **Thai Morning (61)** (PWHarris) **3-9-3** GHind(2) (lw: rr div whn hmpd over 2f out)....hd **14** 10/1 27 —
3624⁷ **Cruz Santa (57)** (TDBarron) **3-8-13** LCharnock(6) (a bhd)....hd **15** 25/1 23 —
2432⁴ **Surf City (65)** (WWHaigh) **3-9-7** RLappin(5) (sn bhd)....5 **16** 20/1 17 —
3810¹³ **Fog City (70)** (WJarvis) **3-9-12** PatEddery(9) (lw: bhd fr ½-wy)....8 **17** 5/1 [1] 1 —
*3758⁷* ***Statistician (57)*** (JohnBerry) **4-9-1** MRimmer(8) (Withdrawn not under Starter's orders: broke out of stalls).... **W** 33/1 — —
(SP 135.5%) **17 Rn**

**1m 18.9** (4.60) CSF £151.76 CT £1,113.87 TOTE £73.00: £12.70 £1.80 £1.80 £3.20 (£442.90) Trio £954.30 OWNER Mr V. Greaves (THIRSK) BRED Norelands Bloodstock
WEIGHT FOR AGE 3yo-2lb
OFFICIAL EXPLANATION **Grand Chapeau (IRE): regarding the apparent improvement in form, the trainer reported that the gelding started slowly on its last run, at a time when his horses were suffering from the virus.**
**Fog City: was never travelling well and appeared to lose his action.**
**2005 Grand Chapeau (IRE)** flew out of the traps to make light of his high draw. Four lengths clear once in line for home, he did not even have to be ridden out. There was certainly no fluke about this. (20/1)
**3774 Kira** ran her usual game race. Despite being better over five, she stuck on gamely in the closing stages but, in truth, was never going to overhaul the winner. (7/1)

**3639 Barato**, favourably drawn for once, made his effort on the inside off the turn but, when his rider became serious, he could only stick on at the same pace. (15/2)
**3323 Robellion**, switched right to find the faster ground, stayed on strongly at the finish. He has won over much further on the All-Weather. (12/1)
**2870 Finisterre (IRE)**, absent for forty-six days, had no luck at all in running. (7/1)
**Fog City** could never get away from the rear division and, looking to lose his action, his rider sensibly gave up. (5/1)

## 3974 TIMEFORM PERSPECTIVE AND RACE RATINGS H'CAP (0-80) (3-Y.O+) (Class D)

5-45 (5-49) **1m 4y** £4,142.50 (£1,240.00: £595.00: £272.50) Stalls: Low GOING: 0.05 sec per fur (G)

| | | | | SP | RR | SF |
|---|---|---|---|---|---|---|
| $3933^{4}$ | **Maple Bay (IRE) (76)** (ABailey) **7-9-7**(7) GFaulkner(8) (chsd ldrs: led over 1f out: r.o wl) | — | **1** | 3/1 1 | 88 | 69 |
| $3799^{6}$ | **Courageous Dancer (IRE) (73)** (BHanbury) **4-9-11** JStack(14) (lw: hld up: hdwy & nt clr run over 1f out: styd on wl ins fnl f) | ¾ | **2** | 9/1 | 84 | 65 |
| $3348^{3}$ | **Advance East (56)** (MrsJRRamsden) **4-8-8** KFallon(9) (lw: hld up: hdwy 3f out: ch ins fnl f: nt qckn) | 1¾ | **3** | 7/1 3 | 63 | 44 |
| $3777^{2}$ | **Thatched (IRE) (47)** (REBarr) **6-7-6**(7) KSked(11) (hld up: effrt & n.m.r over 2f out: hdwy on outside over 1f out: edgd lft & styd on one pce) | nk | **4** | 10/1 | 53 | 34 |
| $3578^{7}$ | **Pleasure Trick (USA) (44)** (DonEnricoIncisa) **5-7-10** KimTinkler(16) (hdwy on outside ½-wy: sn prom: rdn & one pce fnl 2f) | 2½ | **5** | 50/1 | 45 | 26 |
| | **Wickins (68)** (HJCollingridge) **6-9-6** VSmith(5) (in tch: rdn & outpcd over 2f out: kpt on fnl f) | hd | **6** | 12/1 | 69 | 50 |
| $3133^{4}$ | **Singapore Sting (USA) (70)** (HRACecil) **3-9-3** WRyan(15) (lw: a in tch: effrt 2f out: one pce) | 2½ | **7** | 7/1 3 | 66 | 42 |
| $3640^{4}$ | **Flying North (IRE) (75)** (MrsMReveley) **3-9-8** KDarley(6) (hld up: effrt over 2f out: nvr nr ldrs) | ½ | **8** | 6/1 2 | 70 | 46 |
| $3849^{6}$ | **Desert Zone (USA) (48)** (JLHarris) **7-8-0** FNorton(12) (led tl over 1f out: sn wknd) | hd | **9** | 25/1 | 43 | 24 |
| $3933^{15}$ | **Rambo Waltzer (66)** (DNicholls) **4-9-4** AlexGreaves(3) (trckd ldrs: shkn up over 2f out: wknd over 1f out: eased) | ¾ | **10** | 16/1 | 60 | 41 |
| $3842^{3}$ | **Spanish Verdict (67)** (DenysSmith) **9-9-2**(3) CTeague(7) (chsd ldrs tl wknd over 1f out) | 2 | **11** | 14/1 | 57 | 38 |
| $2581^{9}$ | **Samba Sharply (74)** (AHide) **5-9-7**(5) MartinDwyer(1) (prom: hmpd 6f out: lost pl over 3f out) | 1¼ | **12** | 7/1 3 | 61 | 42 |
| $3704^{7}$ | **Royal Legend (63)** (JPearce) **4-9-1** GBardwell(10) (lw: a in rr) | ¾ | **13** | 20/1 | 49 | 30 |
| $2901^{6}$ | **Kissel (71)** (SEKettlewell) **4-9-9** OUrbina(2) (lw: a bhd) | 1½ | **14** | 25/1 | 54 | 35 |
| $3461^{W}$ | **Firle Phantasy (70)** (PCalver) **3-9-3** MBirch(13) (chsd ldrs tl wknd 3f out: eased) | 10 | **15** | 16/1 | 33 | 9 |
| | | | | (SP 136.4%) | **15 Rn** | |

**1m 46.2** (4.70) CSF £32.41 CT £180.40 TOTE £4.30: £1.40 £3.20 £2.70 (£22.30) Trio £51.80 OWNER Mr Roy Matthews (TARPORLEY) BRED Berkshire Equestrian Services Ltd
LONG HANDICAP Pleasure Trick (USA) 7-5
WEIGHT FOR AGE 3yo-5lb

**3933 Maple Bay (IRE)** is in the form of his life and won his ninth race this year, eight of them handicaps. He races with tremendous enthusiasm. (3/1)
**3799 Courageous Dancer (IRE)** appreciated the well-watered ground and ran easily her best race so far this year. With better luck in running, she would have gone even closer. (9/1)
**3348 Advance East**, dropped considerably in distance, wore a tongue-strap. Travelling strongly when his rider got down to work, he did not look to be giving him full co-operation. (7/1)
**3777 Thatched (IRE)**, who likes to come from off the back in a strongly-run race, found himself short of room and had to switch to the outside. Once out there, he edged back left. (10/1)
**2868 Pleasure Trick (USA)**, 5lb out of the handicap, ran his best race for some time. (50/1)
**Wickins** has been carrying all before him in Jersey this year. (12/1)
**3133 Singapore Sting (USA)** looks in the grip of the Handicapper. (7/1)

T/Jkpt: Not won; £3,838.34 to York 4/9/96. T/Plpt: £152.10 (134.37 Tckts). T/Qdpt: £76.40 (13.29 Tckts). WG

# 3962-BRIGHTON (L-H) (Firm)
## Wednesday September 4th

WEATHER: fine WIND: fresh half bhd

## 3975 NEWHAVEN NURSERY H'CAP (0-85) (2-Y.O) (Class E)

2-20 (2-21) **5f 59y** £3,206.70 (£957.60: £457.80: £207.90) Stalls: Low GOING minus 0.59 sec per fur (F)

| | | | | SP | RR | SF |
|---|---|---|---|---|---|---|
| $3924^{2}$ | **Perpetual (72)** (SirMarkPrescott) **2-8-8** 6x GDuffield(10) (lw: a.p: led over 1f out: drvn out) | — | **1** | 100/30 1 | 71 | 31 |
| $3259^{6}$ | **Bold Oriental (IRE) (73)** (NACallaghan) **2-8-4**(5) DGriffiths(7) (rdn over 2f out: hdwy over 1f out: swtchd lft: r.o wl ins fnl f) | 1¼ | **2** | 7/1 3 | 68 | 28 |
| $2879^{11}$ | **Clara Bliss (IRE) (74)** (BJMeehan) **2-8-10** CRutter(4) (lw: a.p: ev ch over 1f out: unable qckn) | nk | **3** | 16/1 | 68 | 28 |
| $3940^{2}$ | **Bold African (81)** (PDEvans) **2-9-3b** SSanders(12) (lw: a.p: rdn & ev ch 2f out: one pce) | 1 | **4** | 5/1 2 | 72 | 32 |
| $3757^{11}$ | **Chingachgook (69)** (PWHarris) **2-8-5** MFenton(3) (hld up: rdn over 1f out: one pce) | nk | **5** | 7/1 3 | 59 | 19 |
| $2965^{8}$ | **Aybeegirl (71)** (MrsJCecil) **2-8-7v** AClark(5) (rdn over 2f out: nvr nr to chal) | 1¼ | **6** | 16/1 | 58 | 18 |
| $3871^{2}$ | **Gunners Glory (81)** (BJMeehan) **2-9-3** MTebbutt(9) (lw: hld up: rdn over 1f out: btn whn n.m.r ins fnl f) | 1¾ | **7** | 7/1 3 | 62 | 22 |
| $3613^{8}$ | **Whizz Kid (70)** (JJBridger) **2-8-3**(3) DarrenMoffatt(11) (a bhd) | 3 | **8** | 25/1 | 42 | 2 |
| $3871^{7}$ | **Castle House (65)** (JAkehurst) **2-8-1** DBiggs(1) (lw: a.p: ev ch over 1f out: sn wknd) | 3 | **9** | 33/1 | 28 | — |
| 3336* | **Statuette (71)** (BPalling) **2-8-7** TSprake(6) (led over 3f) | 1¼ | **10** | 7/1 3 | 30 | — |
| $3660^{12}$ | **Wild Nettle (60)** (JCFox) **2-7-10** FNorton(8) (a bhd) | 5 | **11** | 33/1 | 4 | — |
| | | | | (SP 111.2%) | **11 Rn** | |

**60.4 secs** (0.40) CSF £23.62 CT £287.95 TOTE £2.90: £1.00 £3.00 £5.10 (£26.00) Trio £165.90; £187.00 to York 5/9/96 OWNER Cheveley Park Stud (NEWMARKET) BRED Cheveley Park Stud Ltd

**3924 Perpetual**, who ran a fine race in defeat at Sandown last Friday, continues in tremendous heart. In the front-line throughout, she gained control over a furlong from home and was kept up to her work to secure victory. (100/30: 9/4-7/2)
**3259 Bold Oriental (IRE)**, having his first run over five furlongs, found it too sharp for him, especially on a course like this. Only finding his feet below the distance, he was switched left and ran on really strongly inside the final furlong, only to find the line always beating him. A return to six or seven furlongs is required. (7/1)
**1645* Clara Bliss (IRE)**, always in a handy position, was one of several with every chance below the distance before tapped for toe. (16/1)
**3940 Bold African**, making a quick reappearance, was having his sixteenth race of the season. Always well placed, he was close enough if good enough a quarter of a mile out before failing to find another turn of foot. (5/1)

**2057 Chingachgook** chased the leaders, but failed to find another gear from below the distance. (7/1: op 9/2)
**2699* Aybeegirl** made some late headway without posing a threat. (16/1)
**3871 Gunners Glory** chased the leaders. Asked for his effort below the distance, he failed to find what was required and was held when not having a great deal of room early inside the final furlong. A return to six furlongs is needed. (7/1)

## 3976 SEAGULLS (S) STKS (2-Y.O) (Class G)

2-50 (2-51) **6f 209y** £2,070.00 (£570.00: £270.00) Stalls: Low GOING minus 0.59 sec per fur (F)

| | | | | SP | RR | SF |
|---|---|---|---|---|---|---|
| $3803^{9}$ | **Irish Fiction (IRE) (66)** (DJSCosgrove) **2-9-2** MRimmer(12) (hld up: hrd rdn over 1f out: led last stride) | — | **1** | 7/2 1 | 63 | 22 |
| *$3954^{9}$* | **Silent Valley** (JNeville) **2-8-6** SDrowne(2) (a.p: led over 1f out: hung lft: hrd rdn: hdd last stride) | s.h | **2** | 33/1 | 53 | 12 |
| $3848^{17}$ | **Danehill Prince** (MRChannon) **2-8-11v¹** CRutter(10) (bit bkwd: outpcd: gd hdwy fnl f: fin wl) | ½ | **3** | 8/1 | 57 | 16 |
| $3662^{3}$ | **Ginny Wossername (58)** (WGMTurner) **2-8-11** TSprake(6) (a.p: rdn over 2f out: ev ch over 1f out: unable qckn) | ½ | **4** | 13/2 2 | 56 | 15 |
| $3763^{2}$ | **Dozen Roses (54)** (TMJones) **2-8-6b** NCarlisle(1) (lw: hdwy 3f out: one pce fnl 2f) | 3 | **5** | 8/1 | 44 | 3 |
| $3762^{7}$ | **Neon Deion (IRE) (55)** (SCWilliams) **2-8-11e** JTate(11) (lw: nvr nr to chal) | nk | **6** | 20/1 | 48 | 7 |
| $3651^{4}$ | **Champagne On Ice (57)** (PDEvans) **2-8-6** SSanders(4) (led over 5f out tl over 1f out: wknd ins fnl f) | hd | **7** | 7/1 3 | 43 | 2 |
| $3820^{7}$ | **Fly Down To Rio (IRE) (63)** (DWPArbuthnot) **2-8-3**(3) DarrenMoffatt(8) (bhd fnl 3f) | 2 | **8** | 10/1 | 38 | — |
| $3807^{15}$ | **Three Card Trick (IRE)** (RHannon) **2-8-6** DaneO'Neill(5) (bhd fnl 3f) | 2½ | **9** | 8/1 | 32 | — |
| $3464^{12}$ | **Grovefair Venture** (BJMeehan) **2-8-11** MTebbutt(7) (lw: led over 1f: wknd over 3f out) | 3 | **10** | 20/1 | 31 | — |
| $3695^{7}$ | **Quertier (IRE)** (MRChannon) **2-8-11** RHughes(9) (lw: hld up: rdn over 3f out: wknd over 2f out) | 14 | **11** | 10/1 | — | — |

(SP 112.0%) **11 Rn**

**1m 22.2** (2.20) CSF £84.78 TOTE £4.60: £1.30 £16.20 £4.20 (£150.30) Trio £124.00; £143.28 to York 5/9/96 OWNER Camelot Racing (NEWMARKET) BRED Miss Peg Farrington
Bt in 7,600 gns; Silent Valley clmd BMeehan £6,000

**3523 Irish Fiction (IRE)**, having his twelfth run of the season, chased the leaders. Coming under pressure below the distance, he conjured up a fine run to snatch the spoils right on the line. (7/2)
**Silent Valley**, never far away, went on below the distance but, despite hanging left, she did little wrong and appeared to have won. However, the photo-finish showed she had been beaten a whisker. (33/1)
**Danehill Prince**, tried in a visor and still not looking fully fit, was soon well adrift and was still in last place below the distance. However, he went into overdrive in the final furlong and, coming with a wet sail, stormed past beaten rivals to snatch third prize. (8/1)
**3662 Ginny Wossername**, never far away, had every chance over a furlong out before lack of acceleration proved her downfall. (13/2)
**3763 Dozen Roses** moved up early in the straight, but could only go up and down in the same place in the final quarter-mile. (8/1)
**657 Neon Deion (IRE)** made a little late headway without posing a threat. (20/1)

## 3977 ROTTINGDEAN LIMITED STKS (0-60) (3-Y.O) (Class F)

3-20 (3-22) **6f 209y** £2,381.00 (£656.00: £311.00) Stalls: Low GOING minus 0.59 sec per fur (F)

| | | | | SP | RR | SF |
|---|---|---|---|---|---|---|
| $3849^{11}$ | **Just Millie (USA) (60)** (JEBanks) **3-8-2v**(7) GFaulkner(9) (lw: hld up: rdn over 2f out: led nr fin) | — | **1** | 8/1 3 | 63 | 35 |
| $3585^{3}$ | **Secret Pleasure (IRE) (60)** (RHannon) **3-8-9** DaneO'Neill(5) (b.nr hind: lw: a.p: led over 1f out: hrd rdn: hdd nr fin) | ½ | **2** | 5/2 1 | 62 | 34 |
| $3863^{6}$ | **Rawi (57)** (MissGayKelleway) **3-8-12** GDuffield(2) (lw: hdwy over 4f out: led 2f out tl over 1f out: one pce) | 1½ | **3** | 9/1 | 61 | 33 |
| $3761^{4}$ | **Corniche Quest (IRE) (52)** (MRChannon) **3-8-12** RHughes(12) (lw: hld up: hrd rdn over 1f out: one pce) | 1½ | **4** | 8/1 3 | 58 | 30 |
| $3681^{8}$ | **Allstars Rocket (56)** (TJNaughton) **3-9-1** DHarrison(11) (lw: lost pl 4f out: one pce fnl 2f) | 1¼ | **5** | 4/1 2 | 58 | 30 |
| $3862^{3}$ | **Velvet Jones (56)** (GFHCharles-Jones) **3-8-12b¹** CRutter(4) (hld up: rdn over 2f out: wknd over 1f out) | 1¾ | **6** | 9/1 | 51 | 23 |
| *$3877^{14}$* | **Time Clash (60)** (BPalling) **3-8-9** TSprake(1) (led over 4f out to 2f out: wknd fnl f) | 1¼ | **7** | 10/1 | 45 | 17 |
| $3301^{5}$ | **To The Whire (60)** (GLMoore) **3-8-9** SWhitworth(10) (prom over 4f) | 2 | **8** | 12/1 | 41 | 13 |
| *$220^{6}$* | **Honestly (60)** (BSmart) **3-8-9** MTebbutt(13) (lw: bhd fnl 4f) | 5 | **9** | 9/1 | 29 | 1 |
| *$3435^{8}$* | **Embroidered (30)** (RMFlower) **3-8-9b¹** DBiggs(3) (a bhd) | s.h | **10** | 33/1 | 29 | 1 |
| $3847^{5}$ | **February (42)** (AJChamberlain) **3-8-9** TGMcLaughlin(7) (a bhd) | 3 | **11** | 33/1 | 22 | — |
| $3851^{12}$ | **Kealbra Lady (20)** (MSSaunders) **3-8-9** NAdams(6) (led over 2f: wknd over 2f out) | s.h | **12** | 33/1 | 22 | — |
| $3862^{7}$ | **Heights of Love (45)** (JWHills) **3-8-9** AClark(8) (s.s: a bhd) | 20 | **13** | 25/1 | — | — |

(SP 130.2%) **13 Rn**

**1m 20.6** (0.60) CSF £29.19 TOTE £10.10: £2.90 £2.80 £3.10 (£10.70) Trio £29.90 OWNER Mr E. Carter (NEWMARKET) BRED Golden Gate Stud

**3849 Just Millie (USA)** chased the leaders. Bustled along over a quarter of a mile from home, she managed to get up near the line. (8/1)
**3585 Secret Pleasure (IRE)**, always well placed, was sent on below the distance but, despite doing little wrong, was eventually worried out of it near the line. (5/2)
**3863 Rawi**, in a handy position by the top of the hill, made his bid for glory a quarter of a mile out. Collared below the distance, he was then tapped for toe. (9/1)
**3761 Corniche Quest (IRE)** chased the leaders but, hard ridden below the distance, failed to find another gear. (8/1)
**3492* Allstars Rocket** got outpaced at the top of the hill and could never get back into it. A mile is more his trip. (4/1: op 8/1)
**3862 Velvet Jones**, fitted with blinkers for the first time, is basically paceless and, after chasing the leaders, was done with in the final quarter-mile. He is very poor and is still a maiden after nineteen attempts. The chances of him winning a race are remote and, if he does, it will need to be an atrocious race. (9/1: 6/1-10/1)
**1121 Time Clash** (10/1: 7/1-11/1)

## 3978 SADDLESCOMBE CLAIMING STKS (3-Y.O+) (Class F)

3-50 (3-50) **7f 214y** £2,381.00 (£656.00: £311.00) Stalls: Low GOING: 0.59 sec per fur (GS)

| | | | | SP | RR | SF |
|---|---|---|---|---|---|---|
| $3861^{7}$ | **Mr Nevermind (IRE) (61)** (GLMoore) **6-9-6** SWhitworth(11) (a.p: led over 2f out: drvn out) | — | **1** | 4/1 2 | 73 | 49 |
| $3789^{6}$ | **Western Venture (IRE) (55)** (JWPayne) **3-8-5** MFenton(1) (b: lw: led over 5f: hrd rdn over 1f out: unable qckn fnl f) | ¾ | **2** | 16/1 | 62 | 33 |
| 3694* | **Helios (64)** (NJHWalker) **8-9-5**(3) AWhelan(7) (a.p: rdn over 2f out: one pce) | 1¼ | **3** | 4/1 2 | 71 | 47 |
| $3583^{7}$ | **Office Hours (52)** (CACyzer) **4-9-4** PBloomfield(12) (lw: rdn & hdwy over 2f out: one pce) | 1¾ | **4** | 14/1 | 64 | 40 |
| 3860* | **Ketabi (USA) (42)** (RAkehurst) **5-8-12** SSanders(9) (rdn over 4f out: hdwy over 2f out: one pce) | 1¼ | **5** | 7/1 3 | 55 | 31 |
| | **Soldier Cove (USA) (62)** (MartynMeade) **6-8-7**(7) DSweeney(3) (rdn & hdwy over 2f out: one pce) | ½ | **6** | 25/1 | 56 | 32 |
| 3300* | **Multi Franchise (55)** (BGubby) **3-8-5** TSprake(4) (lw: prom 6f) | ¾ | **7** | 7/1 3 | 51 | 22 |
| $3789^{4}$ | **Paint It Black (70)** (RHannon) **3-8-13** RHughes(8) (lw: rdn & hdwy over 1f out: eased whn btn fnl f) | 1 | **8** | 7/2 1 | 57 | 28 |
| $3473^{7}$ | **Lady Magnum (IRE) (37)** (JNeville) **3-8-4** SDrowne(10) (bhd fnl 4f) | 3 | **9** | 25/1 | 41 | 12 |

| | | | | SP | RR | SF |
|---|---|---|---|---|---|---|
| $3785^{17}$ | **Half An Inch (IRE) (52)** (TMJones) **3-8-13v$^{1}$** NCarlisle(6) (b.hind: prom over 4f) | nk | **10** | 10/1 | 50 | 21 |
| $3661^{9}$ | **The Noble Oak (IRE) (27)** (MJBolton) **8-8-6** GDuffield(5) (lw: bhd fnl 4f) | 12 | **11** | 50/1 | 14 | — |
| $3852^{13}$ | **Dyanko (38)** (MSSaunders) **3-8-9** AMackay(2) (lw: a wl bhd) | 10 | **12** | 33/1 | 2 | — |

(SP 121.5%) **12 Rn**

**1m 32.5** (0.30) CSF £60.31 TOTE £4.80: £2.70 £3.30 £1.20 (£52.10) Trio £217.80; £190.28 to York 5/9/96 OWNER Pennine Partners (EPSOM) BRED Robert Corridan
WEIGHT FOR AGE 3yo-5lb

**3861 Mr Nevermind (IRE)**, who caught the eye here last week, rewarded followers on this occasion. Racing up with the pace this time, he poked a nostril in front under the stands' rail over a quarter of a mile from home and, driven along, held on well. (4/1)
**3789 Western Venture (IRE)** attempted to make all the running. Collared over a quarter of a mile from home, he refused to give way, but was eventually tapped for toe inside the final furlong. (16/1)
**3694* Helios** failed to find the necessary turn of foot in the last two furlongs. (4/1: op 9/4)
**3316 Office Hours**, bustled along to take closer order over two furlongs out, could then make no further impression. (14/1)
**3860* Ketabi (USA)** did not appreciate the drop in distance. Bustled along at the top of the hill, he made progress over a quarter of a mile from home, but was then only treading water. A return to a mile and a quarter is required. (7/1)
**Soldier Cove (USA)**, off the course since last October, made an effort over two furlongs from home, but could then only plod on in his own time. (25/1)
**2766 Half An Inch (IRE)** (10/1: 8/1-12/1)

## 3979 GEORGE ROBEY CHALLENGE TROPHY H'CAP (0-70) (3-Y.O+ F & M) (Class E)

4-20 (4-22) **1m 3f 196y** £3,315.90 (£991.20: £474.60: £216.30) Stalls: High GOING: 0.59 sec per fur (GS)

| | | | | SP | RR | SF |
|---|---|---|---|---|---|---|
| $3522^{5}$ | **Naval Gazer (IRE) (68)** (DRLoder) **3-9-8** DRMcCabe(4) (hdwy over 2f out: led ins fnl f: rdn out) | — | **1** | 8/1 | 81 | 47 |
| $3825^{3}$ | **Voices in the Sky (45)** (AGNewcombe) **5-8-8** SDrowne(3) (hdwy over 5f out: led wl over 1f out tl ins fnl f: r.o) | ¾ | **2** | 11/2$^{1}$ | 57 | 32 |
| $3163^{5}$ | **Silktail (IRE) (65)** (MissGayKelleway) **4-10-0** DaneO'Neill(8) (lw: rdn over 2f out: hdwy over 1f out: one pce) | 3 | **3** | 6/1$^{2}$ | 73 | 48 |
| $3802^{12}$ | **Lucky Coin (55)** (PHowling) **4-9-4** FNorton(13) (led: hrd rdn over 2f out: hdd wl over 1f out: one pce) | 2 | **4** | 20/1 | 60 | 35 |
| $3522^{7}$ | **Rehaab (69)** (ACStewart) **3-9-9** SWhitworth(11) (hld up: rdn over 3f out: wknd fnl f) | 5 | **5** | 7/1$^{3}$ | 68 | 34 |
| $3314^{5}$ | **Risky Tu (38)** (PAKelleway) **5-8-1** DBiggs(9) (nvr nr to chal) | 2½ | **6** | 16/1 | 33 | 8 |
| $3813^{8}$ | **Fiona Shann (USA) (50)** (JLDunlop) **3-8-4b$^{1}$** GDuffield(6) (lw: prom 10f) | hd | **7** | 11/1 | 45 | 11 |
| $3664^{4}$ | **Rocquaine Bay (40)** (MJBolton) **9-8-3$^{ow1}$** SSanders(1) (bhd fnl 3f) | ¾ | **8** | 11/1 | 34 | 8 |
| $3657^{3}$ | **Love Bateta (IRE) (67)** (JEBanks) **3-9-0$^{(7)}$** GFaulkner(7) (prom over 10f) | 1 | **9** | 8/1 | 60 | 26 |
| $3479^{8}$ | **Mua-Tab (65)** (PTWalwyn) **3-9-5** TSprake(10) (prom 9f) | 7 | **10** | 12/1 | 48 | 14 |
| *$3877^{9}$* | **Miss Haversham (60)** (CACyzer) **4-9-9** PBloomfield(5) (bhd fnl 4f) | 10 | **11** | 25/1 | 30 | 5 |
| $3664^{3}$ | **Zeliba (39)** (MrsNMacauley) **4-8-2** CRutter(12) (a bhd) | 1¼ | **12** | 12/1 | 7 | — |
| *$188^{7}$* | **Note of Caution (USA) (53)** (NAGraham) **3-8-7** DHarrison(2) (prom 8f) | 8 | **13** | 20/1 | 10 | — |

(SP 115.7%) **13 Rn**

**2m 29.2** (1.60) CSF £46.54 CT £259.44 TOTE £9.60: £2.40 £2.10 £3.20 (£18.10) Trio £49.00 OWNER Mr William Fox (NEWMARKET) BRED Barronstown Bloodstock Ltd
WEIGHT FOR AGE 3yo-9lb

**3522 Naval Gazer (IRE)** began her effort over a quarter of a mile from home and, rousted along, came through to lead in the last 100 yards. (8/1)
**3825 Voices in the Sky** moved up soon after halfway. Sent to the front early in the final quarter-mile, she was collared in the last 100 yards but, to her credit, kept on well to the line. (11/2)
**3163 Silktail (IRE)** only began to find her feet from below the distance but, despite staying on for third prize, found the first two already home and dry. (6/1)
**3520 Lucky Coin** attempted to make all the running but, collared early inside the final quarter-mile, could only keep on in her own time. (20/1)
**3108* Rehaab**, bustled along early in the straight, was eventually hung out to dry inside the distance. (7/1)

## 3980 BRIGHTON AMATEUR H'CAP (0-70) (3-Y.O+) (Class G)

4-50 (4-54) **1m 1f 209y** £2,070.00 (£570.00: £270.00) Stalls: High GOING minus 0.59 sec per fur (F)

| | | | | SP | RR | SF |
|---|---|---|---|---|---|---|
| $3575^{2}$ | **Don't Drop Bombs (USA) (39)** (DTThom) **7-9-6v** MissJFeilden(5) (lw: mde virtually all: clr over 3f out: r.o wl) | — | **1** | 2/1$^{1}$ | 49 | 31 |
| $3340^{6}$ | **Royal Thimble (IRE) (57)** (NoelChance) **5-10-10v** MrEJames(4) (hld up: hrd rdn over 2f out: chsd wnr ins fnl f: no imp) | 6 | **2** | 11/2$^{2}$ | 57 | 39 |
| $3860^{2}$ | **Roman Reel (USA) (68)** (GLMoore) **5-11-2$^{(5)}$** MrJGoldstein(7) (lw: a.p: chsd wnr over 3f out tl ins fnl f: one pce) | 1 | **3** | 11/2$^{2}$ | 67 | 49 |
| $745^{5}$ | **Zuno Flyer (USA) (33)** (AMoore) **4-9-0** MrsJMoore(2) (bit bkwd: a.p: one pce fnl 3f) | 2½ | **4** | 25/1 | 28 | 10 |
| $2284^{7}$ | **Kevasingo (54)** (BWHills) **4-10-2$^{(5)}$** MrCBHills(1) (lw: hdwy over 1f out: nvr nrr) | ½ | **5** | 12/1 | 48 | 30 |
| $3802^{8}$ | **Super Serenade (52)** (GBBalding) **7-10-5** MrJThatcher(9) (lw: nvr nr to chal) | 3 | **6** | 11/1 | 41 | 23 |
| $3702^{7}$ | **Bellas Gate Boy (52)** (JPearce) **4-10-5** MrsLPearce(6) (lw: bhd fnl 4f) | 7 | **7** | 6/1$^{3}$ | 30 | 12 |
| $3611^{6}$ | **Fabulous Mtoto (54)** (MSSaunders) **6-10-7** MrKGoble(8) (b: lw: s.s: a bhd) | 10 | **8** | 8/1 | 16 | — |
| 3808* | **Sharp Gazelle (43)** (BSmart) **6-9-10** MissVMarshall(3) (lw: prom over 6f) | ¾ | **9** | 7/1 | 4 | — |

(SP 121.9%) **9 Rn**

**2m 1.1** (2.80) CSF £13.71 CT £50.29 TOTE £2.50: £1.10 £3.20 £1.10 (£9.30) Trio £12.20 OWNER Miss J. Feilden (NEWMARKET) BRED Hurstland Farm Incorporated
LONG HANDICAP Zuno Flyer (USA) 8-13

**3575 Don't Drop Bombs (USA)** followed up last year's success in this race. Making virtually all the running, he forged clear entering the straight to win in decisive style. (2/1: op 3/1)
**3340 Royal Thimble (IRE)**, who won over hurdles at Hereford eleven days earlier, chased the leaders. Under pressure over a quarter of a mile from home, she eventually won the battle for second prize inside the final furlong. (11/2: 7/2-6/1)
**3860 Roman Reel (USA)**, always handy, moved into second place over three furlongs from home, but he failed to reel in the winner and was collared for the runner-up spot inside the final furlong. (11/2)
**485 Zuno Flyer (USA)**, carrying condition for this first run in four months, was never far away, but he received little assistance from the saddle and could only plod on in his own time in the straight. He is still a maiden after nineteen attempts. (25/1)
**1685 Kevasingo**, racing at the back of the field, passed beaten horses to be nearest at the line. (12/1: op 7/1)

T/Plpt: £36.50 (309.28 Tckts). T/Qdpt: £10.40 (74.25 Tckts). AK

## 3706-YORK (L-H) (Good, Good to firm patches)
## Wednesday September 4th
WEATHER: overcast WIND: slt against

### 3981 LEVY BOARD STRAVINSKY VODKA CLAIMING STKS (3-Y.O+) (Class D)
2-10 (2-16) **1m 205y** £5,481.00 (£1,638.00: £784.00: £357.00) Stalls: Low GOING minus 0.35 sec per fur (F)

| | | | | SP | RR | SF |
|---|---|---|---|---|---|---|
| 3509[2] | **Darling Clover (74)** (DMorley) **4-9-0** RCochrane(1) (trckd ldrs: led 1f out: r.o u.p) | — | 1 | 4/1[1] | 78 | 38 |
| 3854[2] | **Mellottie (85)** (MrsMReveley) **11-9-7** KDarley(13) (lw: hld up: hdwy over 3f out: chsd wnr fnl f: r.o towards fin) | s.h | 2 | 9/2[2] | 85 | 45 |
| 3833[9] | **Equerry (83)** (MJohnston) **5-9-1** MHills(3) (led to 1f out: no ex) | 1½ | 3 | 11/2[3] | 76 | 36 |
| 3831* | **Ballpoint (68)** (RHannon) **3-8-11** RPerham(12) (trckd ldrs: ev ch 3f out: nt qckn fnl f) | 1¼ | 4 | 9/1 | 76 | 30 |
| 3785[7] | **Myfontaine (62)** (KTIvory) **9-9-1** JCarroll(7) (b: bhd: hdwy over 2f out: r.o towards fin) | 1 | 5 | 20/1 | 72 | 32 |
| 3480[3] | **North Ardar (62)** (DNicholls) **6-8-12** AlexGreaves(4) (bhd: hdwy on ins 4f out: one pce fnl 2f) | hd | 6 | 20/1 | 69 | 29 |
| 3806[5] | **Toujours Riviera (76)** (JPearce) **6-9-5** GBardwell(2) (plld hrd: a.p: chal over 3f out: wknd over 1f out) | 1 | 7 | 8/1 | 74 | 34 |
| 3854* | **Tame Deer (57)** (MCChapman) **4-8-8**(3) PMcCabe(5) (bhd tl sme late hdwy) | 11 | 8 | 14/1 | 47 | 7 |
| | **Count of Flanders (IRE) (82)** (KAMorgan) **6-9-1v[1]** RMcGhin(6) (dwlt: a bhd) | 3½ | 9 | 33/1 | 44 | 4 |
| 545[9] | **Eastleigh (40)** (RHollinshead) **7-8-9**(3) FLynch(8) (bit bkwd: cl up tl wknd over 3f out) | 8 | 10 | 50/1 | 27 | — |
| 3854[6] | **Rainbow Top (95)** (WJHaggas) **4-9-7** KFallon(10) (chsd ldrs: sn pushed along: wknd fnl 3f) | 16 | 11 | 4/1[1] | 7 | — |
| 3118[5] | **Sandblaster (50)** (DNicholls) **3-8-2** NKennedy(9) (s.i.s: hdwy & in tch ent st: rdn & wknd 3f out) | 3 | 12 | 20/1 | — | — |
| | | | | (SP 120.5%) | **12 Rn** | |

**1m 52.64** (3.44) CSF £21.49 TOTE £4.00: £1.10 £1.60 £2.70 (£8.30) Trio £9.90 OWNER Mr K. Craddock (NEWMARKET) BRED Astalon Ltd
WEIGHT FOR AGE 3yo-6lb
Darling Clover clmd RBastiman £14,000

**3509 Darling Clover**, a real tough and consistent sort, travels well, but found the line coming only just in time. (4/1)
**3854 Mellottie** takes time to get going these days and, although he kept responding to pressure, the line came that stride too soon. Once he wins, he will be retired. (9/2)
**3430 Equerry**, back to his front-running tactics, put up a useful performance, but was never good enough in the final furlong. (11/2: op 7/2)
**3831* Ballpoint** had his chances and looked a big danger early in the straight, but he was always short of a turn of foot to take it over this shorter trip. (9/1)
**3457 Myfontaine** showed definite signs of coming back to form here and, over further, should certainly be kept in mind. (20/1)
**3480 North Ardar** had plenty on at these weights and ran pretty well in the circumstances. (20/1)
**3806 Toujours Riviera** raced too freely for his own good early on. (8/1)
**3854* Tame Deer** (14/1: 10/1-16/1)
**3854 Rainbow Top** was obviously feeling his testing run in the mud last week and ran no sort of race this time. (4/1)

### 3982 BEST BUY PRODUCTS MAIDEN AUCTION STKS (2-Y.O) (Class F)
2-40 (2-49) **7f 202y** £6,836.00 (£2,048.00: £984.00: £452.00) Stalls: Low GOING minus 0.35 sec per fur (F)

| | | | | SP | RR | SF |
|---|---|---|---|---|---|---|
| 3762[2] | **Lady Godiva (70)** (MJPolglase) **2-8-4**ow1 KDarley(18) (in tch: hdwy 4f out: led over 1f out: r.o) | — | 1 | 6/1[2] | 72 | 18 |
| 3080[7] | **Double Espresso (IRE)** (MJohnston) **2-7-9**(3) MHenry(11) (in tch: hdwy 2f out: r.o wl towards fin) | ½ | 2 | 10/1 | 65 | 12 |
| 3227[2] | **Sandbaggedagain (70)** (MWEasterby) **2-8-3** DaleGibson(20) (in tch: c wd st: hdwy u.p 3f out: hung lft: r.o) | ¾ | 3 | 11/1 | 69 | 16 |
| *3417[4]* | **Gresatre (62)** (CADwyer) **2-8-8** RCochrane(21) (bhd: hdwy over 2f out: r.o: nrst fin) | 1¼ | 4 | 16/1 | 71 | 18 |
| 3159[11] | **Sound Appeal** (AGFoster) **2-7-7**(5) CAdamson(3) (chsd ldrs: led 3f out tl over 1f out: no ex) | s.h | 5 | 14/1 | 61 | 8 |
| 3685[4] | **Smugurs (IRE) (69)** (RJRWilliams) **2-8-0** GCarter(15) (mid div: effrt ½-wy: hdwy over 2f out: nt qckn fnl f) | nk | 6 | 12/1 | 62 | 9 |
| 3837[6] | **Blooming Amazing** (JLEyre) **2-8-8** KFallon(12) (b.hind: chsd ldrs: n.m.r ent st: hrd rdn over 2f out: btn over 1f out) | 1 | 7 | 6/1[2] | 68 | 15 |
| 3796[7] | **Righty Ho** (PTWalwyn) **2-8-5** TQuinn(23) (c wd & hdwy over 4f out: sn rdn: nvr able to chal) | 3 | 8 | 12/1 | 59 | 6 |
| 2396[10] | **Jack Says (68)** (TDEasterby) **2-8-3** BDoyle(5) (w ldrs tl wknd fnl 2½f) | nk | 9 | 11/1 | 57 | 4 |
| 2923[4] | **Warrlin (77)** (CWFairhurst) **2-8-8** DeanMcKeown(17) (lw: mid div: effrt ½-wy: nvr able to chal) | s.h | 10 | 33/1 | 62 | 9 |
| | **Smart Spirit (IRE)** (MrsMReveley) **2-8-3** LCharnock(6) (rangy: bit bkwd: nvr nr to chal) | ½ | 11 | 25/1 | 55 | 2 |
| | **Tartan Party** (PFICole) **2-7-12**(5) MartinDwyer(7) (cmpt: unf: bit bkwd: bhd tl sme hdwy fnl 3f) | 4 | 12 | 10/1 | 47 | — |
| 3423[4] | **Leviticus (IRE) (80)** (TPTate) **2-8-8** ACulhane(24) (lw: racd wd: hdwy u.p 4f out: btn & eased fnl 2f) | ¾ | 13 | 4/1[1] | 51 | — |
| | **Pertemps Mission** (JPearce) **2-8-3** GBardwell(14) (rangy: unf: c wd & effrt over 3f out: no imp) | 3 | 14 | 20/1 | 40 | — |
| 3848[7] | **Jukebox Jive** (CMurray) **2-7-12** JQuinn(10) (chsd ldrs tl wknd fnl 3½f) | 3 | 15 | 14/1 | 29 | — |
| | **Gymcrak Gorjos** (GHolmes) **2-8-3** TWilliams(19) (w'like: bit bkwd: mid div: hdwy over 4f out: wknd over 2f out) | 1½ | 16 | 25/1 | 31 | — |
| 3821[3] | **Select Star (IRE)** (APJarvis) **2-8-0**(3) DWright(8) (led tl hdd & wknd 3f out) | nk | 17 | 8/1[3] | 30 | — |
| | **Good Judge (IRE)** (MDHammond) **2-8-5** WRyan(9) (lengthy: bkwd: chsd ldr to ½-wy: wknd) | ¾ | 18 | 25/1 | 31 | — |
| 3462[6] | **Flower Hill Lad (IRE) (76)** (DJSCosgrove) **2-8-3** JStack(22) (s.i.s: c wd st: n.d) | 1¼ | 19 | 12/1 | 26 | — |
| 3848[13] | **Bella Daniella** (TTClement) **2-7-5**(7) RMullen(25) (racd wd: a outpcd & bhd) | 2½ | 20 | 33/1 | 16 | — |
| 3807[11] | **Distinctive Dream (IRE)** (KTIvory) **2-8-3** CScally(4) (s.i.s: n.d) | 2 | 21 | 14/1 | 17 | — |
| 3769[8] | **Oddfellows Girl (44)** (NBycroft) **2-7-12** JLowe(16) (a bhd) | nk | 22 | 33/1 | 11 | — |
| 3082[4] | **Sandmoor Zoe** (TDEasterby) **2-8-4**ow1 MBirch(13) (w ldrs tl wknd fnl 3f) | 2 | 23 | 14/1 | 13 | — |
| *3779[5]* | ***Plutarch Angel*** (WTKemp) **2-8-4b[1]**ow1 JCarroll(1) (Withdrawn not under Starter's orders: Veterinary advice) | | W | 50/1 | — | — |
| | | | | (SP 177.2%) | **23 Rn** | |

**1m 40.98** (4.18) CSF £81.90 TOTE £5.90: £2.00 £6.90 £2.80 (£205.90) Trio £342.70 OWNER Keen Racing (NEWMARKET) BRED Major-Gen Sir George Burns

**3762 Lady Godiva** did well from her draw. Getting first run on the second, she made full use of it. (6/1)
**3080 Double Espresso (IRE)** is improving fast and, judging by the way she finished, the longer the trip, the better it will suit. (10/1)
**3227 Sandbaggedagain** appreciated this trip and ran well from an impossible draw. Responding to pressure in the last three furlongs, he finished well, despite continually hanging left. (11/1)
**3417 Gresatre**, who had a lot of running to do from his draw, was putting in all his best work at the end. (16/1)
**Sound Appeal**, a free-runner, had every chance, but had given her best when collared approaching the last furlong. (14/1)
**3685 Smugurs (IRE)** always kept the leaders within sight, but had to work hard to do so from her draw, and she finally gave up approaching the last furlong. (12/1)

**3837 Blooming Amazing** raced a bit too freely and got messed about at various stages. There is better to come once he gets his act together. (6/1)
**3796 Righty Ho** was always being forced wide from his draw and this was not a bad effort in the circumstances. (12/1)
**Tartan Party** (10/1: op 6/1)
**3423 Leviticus (IRE)** had an impossible task from his draw. Always having to race wide, he finally gave up approaching the last quarter-mile. (4/1: op 6/1)

## 3983 BATLEYS CASH & CARRY H'CAP (0-90) (3-Y.O+) (Class C)

3-10 (3-20) **1m 5f 194y** £8,545.00 (£2,560.00: £1,230.00: £565.00) Stalls: Low GOING minus 0.35 sec per fur (F)

| | | | | SP | RR | SF |
|---|---|---|---|---|---|---|
| 3504[2] | **Jiyush (88)** (HThomsonJones) **3-9-9** RHills(15) (swtg: cl up: led 7f out: rdn 2f out: hung lft: kpt on wl) | — | **1** | 9/1[2] | 100 | 71 |
| 2912[6] | **Midyan Blue (IRE) (72)** (JMPEustace) **6-9-4** RCochrane(16) (a.p: effrt 3f out: hdwy 2f out: chsd wnr fnl f: kpt on wl) | ½ | **2** | 10/1[3] | 83 | 65 |
| 2046[5] | **Beaumont (IRE) (59)** (JEBanks) **6-8-5** JQuinn(5) (swtg: outpcd & bhd 6f out: hdwy 3f out: r.o towards fin) | 2½ | **3** | 20/1 | 68 | 50 |
| *3610*[2] | **Mighty Phantom (USA) (73)** (JWHills) **3-8-8** MHills(7) (lw: hdwy appr st: chsng ldrs & nt clr run over 2f out: rdn & one pce appr fnl f) | s.h | **4** | 14/1 | 82 | 53 |
| 2912[7] | **Secret Service (IRE) (74)** (CWThornton) **4-9-6** DeanMcKeown(17) (mid div: effrt appr st: no imp) | 3 | **5** | 16/1 | 79 | 61 |
| 3689[19] | **Foundry Lane (78)** (MrsMReveley) **5-9-10** ACulhane(13) (lw: rr div: effrt on outside ent st: edgd lft 3f out: styd on: nrst fin) | 1½ | **6** | 10/1[3] | 81 | 63 |
| 3621[4] | **Exactly (IRE) (72)** (JLEyre) **3-8-7** TWilliams(18) (cl up: chal 6f out tl wknd fnl 2½f) | nk | **7** | 16/1 | 75 | 46 |
| 3441[4] | **Belmarita (IRE) (74)** (MHTompkins) **3-8-6**(3) MHenry(2) (swtg: hmpd after 2f: hdwy over 3f out: sn rdn: nvr able to chal) | hd | **8** | 16/1 | 77 | 48 |
| 3504[7] | **Arctic Fancy (USA) (83)** (PWHarris) **3-9-4** GHind(12) (lw: chsd ldrs: effrt over 4f out: wknd over 2f out) | 3 | **9** | 16/1 | 82 | 53 |
| 1005[6] | **Trainglot (77)** (JGFitzGerald) **9-9-9** JCarroll(11) (b: bhd: hdwy over 1f out: r.o) | 4 | **10** | 12/1 | 72 | 54 |
| 3813[2] | **Children's Choice (IRE) (56)** (CNAllen) **5-7-11**(5) MartinDwyer(8) (chsd ldrs: drvn along over 5f out: one pce after) | s.h | **11** | 20/1 | 51 | 33 |
| 3617[3] | **Nuzu (IRE) (78)** (BWHills) **3-8-13** WRyan(14) (in tch tl lost pl over 6f out: styd on u.p fnl 3f) | 1 | **12** | 12/1 | 72 | 43 |
| 3683* | **Welcome Parade (88)** (HRACecil) **3-9-9** PatEddery(19) (racd wd: a.p: outpcd over 3f out: wknd & eased fnl 2f) | 2 | **13** | 11/4[1] | 79 | 50 |
| 3855[8] | **Non Vintage (IRE) (53)** (MCChapman) **5-7-13** NKennedy(4) (bhd: drvn along appr st: n.d) | 1 | **14** | 25/1 | 43 | 25 |
| 3598* | **En Vacances (IRE) (77)** (AGFoster) **4-9-9** KDarley(6) (bhd: pushed along 5f out: nvr nr to chal) | 5 | **15** | 12/1 | 61 | 43 |
| 3816[2] | **Villeggiatura (73)** (MrsJRRamsden) **3-8-8** KFallon(10) (lw: bhd: hdwy 4f out: sn rdn: eased whn btn fnl 2f) | 2 | **16** | 12/1 | 55 | 26 |
| 3689[13] | **Benfleet (74)** (RWArmstrong) **5-9-6** RPrice(1) (hmpd after 2f: mid div: outpcd over 6f out: sn btn) | 25 | **17** | 20/1 | 27 | 9 |
| 3689[18] | **Dreams End (75)** (PBowen) **8-9-2**(5) PPMurphy(9) (in tch: drvn along 7f out: sn wknd) | 6 | **18** | 20/1 | 21 | 3 |
| 3594[12] | **Ambassadori (USA) (70)** (CEBrittain) **3-8-5** BDoyle(3) (led to 7f out: wknd 5f out) | ¾ | **19** | 33/1 | 15 | — |
| | | | | (SP 141.6%) | **19 Rn** | |

**2m 57.64** (1.44) CSF £99.69 CT £1,672.09 TOTE £9.00: £2.10 £2.00 £8.90 £3.30 (£32.50) Trio £554.00 OWNER Mr Hamdan Al Maktoum (NEWMARKET) BRED Shadwell Estate Company Limited
WEIGHT FOR AGE 3yo-11lb

**3504 Jiyush** sweated up as he often does. He looks useful when on the bridle but, when pressure was applied, he tended to hang into the rail and only just found enough. (9/1)
**2912 Midyan Blue (IRE)** at last showed signs of coming back to form and, with a little further to go, would probably have made it. He is now off a useful mark. (10/1)
**2046 Beaumont (IRE)** has done most of his winning on easier ground over shorter distances but, judging by the way he finished, he either needs further or much softer ground these days. (20/1)
**3610 Mighty Phantom (USA)** is in good form. She would have been in the shake up had she got a run when she first wanted it but, in the end, she was always short of speed. (14/1)
**2912 Secret Service (IRE)**, after over six weeks off, ran much better, but was still never able to offer a live threat, despite staying on. (16/1)
**2330 Foundry Lane**, given plenty to do, finished quite well, but was inclined to edge left and could never get in a blow. (10/1)
**3441 Belmarita (IRE)** did not have the best of runs and can be forgiven this. (16/1)
**1005 Trainglot** never showed in the race until finishing particularly well. He is worth keeping in mind under both codes. (12/1: op 8/1)

## 3984 LAWRENCE BATLEY RATED STKS H'CAP (0-105) (3-Y.O+) (Class B)

3-40 (3-51) **6f** £17,063.00 (£6,317.00: £3,033.50: £1,242.50: £496.25: £197.75) Stalls: Low GOING: 0.35 sec per fur (G)

| | | | | SP | RR | SF |
|---|---|---|---|---|---|---|
| 3672* | **Options Open (96)** (MrsJRRamsden) **4-8-12** KFallon(7) (lw: in tch: hdwy ½-wy: led ins fnl f: r.o) | — | **1** | 4/1[2] | 105 | 63 |
| 3672[4] | **Cyrano's Lad (IRE) (97)** (CADwyer) **7-8-13** WRSwinburn(13) (lw: led tl ins fnl f: kpt on) | ½ | **2** | 10/1 | 105 | 63 |
| 3672[2] | **Double Splendour (IRE) (95)** (PSFelgate) **6-8-11** KDarley(14) (lw: in tch: hdwy over 2f out: sn rdn: chal over 1f out: nt qckn) | nk | **3** | 100/30[1] | 102 | 60 |
| 3946[4] | **Lago Di Varano (91)** (RMWhitaker) **4-8-7v** DeanMcKeown(10) (lw: cl up: effrt over 2f out: nt qckn) | 2½ | **4** | 16/1 | 91 | 49 |
| | **Kassbaan (USA) (105)** (SbinSuroor) **6-9-7** JReid(8) (chsd ldrs: rdn 2f out: nt qckn) | 2 | **5** | 7/1[3] | 100 | 58 |
| 3783[4] | **Red Nymph (91)** (WJarvis) **3-8-2**(3) FLynch(1) (lw: in tch: rdn ½-wy: kpt on) | 1¼ | **6** | 10/1 | 83 | 39 |
| 3782[5] | **Hard to Figure (100)** (RJHodges) **10-9-2** RCochrane(12) (bhd: hdwy 2f out: nrst fin) | nk | **7** | 33/1 | 91 | 49 |
| 3693[4] | **Rushcutter Bay (91)** (TTClement) **3-8-5** JStack(9) (s.i.s: sme late hdwy) | 1 | **8** | 16/1 | 79 | 35 |
| 3759[11] | **Sea Dane (105)** (PWHarris) **3-9-5** GHind(6) (b: lw: chsd ldrs tl wknd fnl 2f) | s.h | **9** | 25/1 | 93 | 49 |
| 3296[15] | **Stylish Ways (IRE) (91)** (MissSEHall) **4-8-2**(5) MartinDwyer(5) (outpcd ½-wy: n.d after) | ½ | **10** | 16/1 | 78 | 36 |
| 3222[2] | **Tropical Dance (USA) (93)** (MrsJCecil) **3-8-7** BDoyle(15) (s.i.s: nvr trbld ldrs) | 2½ | **11** | 16/1 | 73 | 29 |
| 3672[15] | **April The Eighth (94)** (BWHills) **3-8-8b**[1] MHills(3) (cl up tl wknd fnl 2f) | 3 | **12** | 14/1 | 66 | 22 |
| 3875[2] | **Bowden Rose (91)** (MBlanshard) **4-8-7b** JQuinn(2) (prom: sn drvn along: wknd fr ½-wy) | ½ | **13** | 10/1 | 62 | 20 |
| 3622[16] | **Double Blue (99)** (MJohnston) **7-9-1b** RHills(4) (a bhd: eased whn btn fnl 2f) | 1¾ | **14** | 20/1 | 65 | 23 |
| 2328[9] | **Dovebrace (100)** (ABailey) **3-9-0** PatEddery(11) (spd to ½-wy: sn wknd) | 2½ | **15** | 14/1 | 59 | 15 |
| | | | | (SP 131.3%) | **15 Rn** | |

**1m 11.24** (0.24) CSF £44.17 CT £145.91 TOTE £5.40: £2.30 £2.70 £1.80 (£18.60) Trio £15.90 OWNER Mr Jonathan Ramsden (THIRSK) BRED D. H. Jones
LONG HANDICAP Lago Di Varano 8-3 Stylish Ways (IRE) 8-6 Bowden Rose 8-6 Rushcutter Bay 8-2
WEIGHT FOR AGE 3yo-2lb

**3672* Options Open** is thriving and, after producing a storming run to settle it inside the final furlong, he was idling in the closing stages. (4/1)

**3672 Cyrano's Lad (IRE)**, who has bags of speed, tried to pinch this by quickening from halfway and, when collared, kept fighting back. Should he try his luck at Doncaster next week in the Portland Handicap, the distance should be ideal. (10/1)
**3672 Double Splendour (IRE)** kept tabs on the winner throughout but he could never summon the same turn of foot when it mattered. (100/30)
**3946 Lago Di Varano** has plenty of speed but, when the pace was really on over this longer distance, he was just found wanting. (16/1)
**Kassbaan (USA)** has really come to form whilst racing on Sand in Dubai and showed plenty of speed here after a lengthy absence, but he got left behind when the tap was really turned on in the last two furlongs. (7/1)
**3783 Red Nymph** did well from her draw, but was struggling some way out and never able to offer a threat. (10/1)
**3782 Hard to Figure** is dropping down the weights and, judging by the way he finished, he still has ability. (33/1)
**2436 April The Eighth** (14/1: 10/1-16/1)

## 3985 MCIVOR SCOTCH WHISKY H'CAP (0-80) (3-Y.O+) (Class D)

4-10 (4-23) **7f 202y** £7,096.00 (£2,128.00: £1,024.00: £236.00: £236.00) Stalls: Low GOING minus 0.35 sec per fur (F)

| | | | | SP | RR | SF |
|---|---|---|---|---|---|---|
| $3799^{5}$ | **Seventeens Lucky (75)** (BobJones) **4-9-12** MWigham(14) (hdwy ½-wy: led ins fnl f: r.o) | — | **1** | 16/1 | 84 | 58 |
| $3770^{3}$ | **Royal Ceilidh (IRE) (76)** (DenysSmith) **3-9-8** JReid(2) (lw: a.p: led over 1f out tl ins fnl f: kpt on) | ½ | **2** | 16/1 | 84 | 53 |
| $3815^{4}$ | **Quilling (66)** (MDods) **4-9-0**$^{(3)}$ FLynch(12) (lw: in tch: qcknd to ld over 3f out: hdd over 1f out: no ex) | 1¼ | **3** | 16/1 | 72 | 46 |
| $2885^{6}$ | **Duello (64)** (MBlanshard) **5-9-1** RCochrane(4) (hdwy u.p 3f out: nvr trbld ldrs) | hd | **4** | 16/1 | 69 | 43 |
| $3295^{7}$ | **Raed (70)** (PTWalwyn) **3-9-2** RHills(5) (hdwy 4f out: swtchd lft & ch over 2f out: rdn & nt qckn appr fnl f) | d.h | **4** | 33/1 | 75 | 44 |
| $3958^{8}$ | **Nobby Barnes (45)** (DonEnricoIncisa) **7-7-10** KimTinkler(10) (hdwy ½-wy: chsng ldrs 2f out: kpt on one pce) | 3 | **6** | 66/1 | 44 | 18 |
| $3805^{7}$ | **Mountgate (77)** (MPBielby) **4-10-0** TQuinn(3) (lw: prom: effrt & ch 3f out: one pce fnl 2f) | 2 | **7** | 16/1 | 72 | 46 |
| $3279^{6}$ | **Pride of Pendle (65)** (DNicholls) **7-9-2** AlexGreaves(9) (in tch: effrt 3f out: sn chsng ldrs & rdn: no imp) | 1 | **8** | $11/1^{3}$ | 58 | 32 |
| 3655* | **Eurobox Boy (56)** (APJarvis) **3-7-13**$^{(3)}$ DWright(20) (chsd ldrs: effrt over 3f out: btn over 1f out) | ½ | **9** | $11/1^{3}$ | 48 | 17 |
| $3513^{6}$ | **Stackattack (IRE) (68)** (PRWebber) **3-9-0** KFallon(19) (hdwy on ins 4f out: hmpd over 2f out: nt rcvr) | 1 | **10** | 12/1 | 58 | 27 |
| $3805^{6}$ | **Master Beveled (71)** (PDEvans) **6-9-8** JFEgan(22) (mid div: hdwy u.p over 2f out: btn over 1f out) | ¾ | **11** | $11/1^{3}$ | 60 | 34 |
| 3501* | **Tatika (74)** (GWragg) **6-9-4**$^{(7)}$ GMilligan(18) (lw: bhd: effrt 3f out: sme late hdwy) | ½ | **12** | $10/1^{2}$ | 62 | 36 |
| *$3603^{7}$* | **Young Annabel (USA) (65)** (CADwyer) **3-8-11** StephenDavies(23) (dwlt: rdn 3f out: n.d) | 1¾ | **13** | 25/1 | 49 | 18 |
| $3830^{8}$ | **Polar Prospect (74)** (BHanbury) **3-9-6** WRyan(7) (led tl over 3f out: grad wknd) | s.h | **14** | 14/1 | 58 | 27 |
| $3471^{14}$ | **Manabar (50)** (MJPolglase) **4-8-1** WHollick(1) (chsd ldrs: wkng whn hmpd over 2f out) | nk | **15** | 50/1 | 33 | 7 |
| $3777^{3}$ | **My Godson (57)** (JLEyre) **6-8-5b**$^{(3)}$ CTeague(8) (dwlt: sn pushed along: n.d) | ¾ | **16** | 16/1 | 39 | 13 |
| $2577^{16}$ | **Bellacardia (60)** (GLewis) **3-8-6** GHind(15) (a bhd) | 9 | **17** | 16/1 | 24 | — |
| 3592* | **Celebration Cake (IRE) (70)** (MissLAPerratt) **4-9-7** PatEddery(16) (lw: cl up tl wknd fnl 3f) | 1½ | **18** | $11/4^{1}$ | 31 | 5 |
| $1323^{6}$ | **He's My Love (IRE) (72)** (JEBanks) **3-9-4** BDoyle(6) (in tch tl wknd fnl 3½f) | 1¾ | **19** | 33/1 | 29 | — |
| $3817^{7}$ | **Mahool (USA) (74)** (JLEyre) **7-9-8**$^{(3)}$ OPears(11) (a bhd) | hd | **20** | 25/1 | 31 | 5 |
| | **Robsera (IRE) (66)** (JJQuinn) **5-9-3** JQuinn(17) (a bhd) | ½ | **21** | 33/1 | 22 | — |
| $3254^{7}$ | **Axeman (IRE) (65)** (DNicholls) **4-9-2** KDarley(21) (a bhd) | ¾ | **22** | 33/1 | 19 | — |
| $2693^{4}$ | **Mbulwa (63)** (RAFahey) **10-9-0** GCarter(24) (cl up tl wknd fnl 3f) | ½ | **23** | 14/1 | 16 | — |

(SP 145.9%) **23 Rn**

**1m 39.98** (3.18) CSF £254.05 CT £3,885.90 TOTE £18.60: £4.40 £4.10 £3.80 R£3.90 D£2.70 (£318.70) Trio £540.80 OWNER Mr D. M. Cameron (NEWMARKET) BRED D. E. Weeden
LONG HANDICAP Nobby Barnes 7-5
WEIGHT FOR AGE 3yo-5lb

**3799 Seventeens Lucky** likes this track and stays further. Once he struck the front inside the final furlong, he was not going to stop. (16/1)
**3770 Royal Ceilidh (IRE)** ran a game race and kept fighting back when headed, which makes this a really good performance off a mark 7lb above anything she has previously won off. (16/1)
**3815 Quilling**, who almost parted company with his jockey leaving the stalls, had to make ground on the outside and ran a cracker, only to run out of steam in the final furlong. (16/1)
**2885 Duello**, after six and a half weeks off, took some driving to get going, but he certainly finished well. On easier ground, he should do even better. (16/1)
**1687 Raed** travelled well when tracking the leaders, but failed to quicken when it mattered. (33/1)
**3333 Nobby Barnes** ran a decent race, but it is anybody's guess as to whether he will ever win again. (66/1)
**3279 Pride of Pendle** showed signs of coming back to form here after a most unsuccessful season. (11/1)
**3513 Stackattack (IRE)** was just beginning to make useful progress when he got virtually knocked over approaching the last two furlongs. That was his chance gone. (12/1)
**3805 Master Beveled** could never overcome his draw. (11/1)
**3592* Celebration Cake (IRE)** looked superb. He must have shot his bolt by going too fast to take a good position early on, as he dropped out tamely once into the straight. (11/4)

## 3986 MAYFIELD BITTER & LAGER MAIDEN STKS (3-Y.O) (Class D)

4-40 (4-52) **1m 2f 85y** £6,368.00 (£1,904.00: £912.00: £416.00) Stalls: Low GOING minus 0.35 sec per fur (F)

| | | | | SP | RR | SF |
|---|---|---|---|---|---|---|
| $707^{4}$ | **Mohawk River (IRE)** (MRStoute) **3-9-0** WRSwinburn(2) (hld up: swtchd & qcknd to ld ins fnl f: comf) | — | **1** | $4/1^{3}$ | 92 | 48 |
| | **Filmore West** (PFICole) **3-9-0** TQuinn(10) (bhd: hdwy on ins 4f out: nt clr run over 2f out to 1f out: r.o wl) | 1¼ | **2** | 11/1 | 90 | 46 |
| | **Torremolinos (USA)** (HRACecil) **3-9-0** WRyan(7) (lengthy: unf: trckd ldrs: chal over 2f out: hrd rdn appr fnl f: r.o one pce) | 3 | **3** | 6/1 | 86 | 42 |
| $3505^{3}$ | **Gulliver (78)** (BWHills) **3-9-0** PatEddery(3) (lw: led tl hdd & no ex ins fnl f) | 2 | **4** | $3/1^{2}$ | 82 | 38 |
| $3472^{4}$ | **Melt The Clouds (CAN) (77)** (PWHarris) **3-9-0** GHind(6) (cl up: chal ent st: wknd appr fnl f) | 2½ | **5** | 11/1 | 79 | 35 |
| $2610^{3}$ | **Radiant Star (82)** (GWragg) **3-9-0** MHills(1) (lw: chsd ldrs: chal over 2f out: btn 1f out) | ½ | **6** | $11/4^{1}$ | 78 | 34 |
| $3656^{9}$ | **Galaka** (LMCumani) **3-8-9** OUrbina(4) (outpcd 5f out: kpt on u.p: no imp) | 2 | **7** | 25/1 | 70 | 26 |
| $3505^{5}$ | **Reticent** (JHMGosden) **3-9-0** JCarroll(9) (b.hind: outpcd ent st: no imp after) | 15 | **8** | 10/1 | 52 | 8 |
| | **Flaming June (USA)** (HRACecil) **3-8-9** AMcGlone(5) (lw: in tch tl rdn & btn over 3f out) | 7 | **9** | 11/1 | 36 | — |
| $3642^{8}$ | **Grand Popo** (SEKettlewell) **3-9-0** NRodgers(12) (a outpcd & wl bhd) | 5 | **10** | 50/1 | 33 | — |
| $3653^{4}$ | **Formidable Partner (67)** (RWArmstrong) **3-9-0** GCarter(8) (hdwy to chse ldrs 7f out: sn pushed along: wknd over 3f out) | ½ | **11** | 14/1 | 32 | — |
| $2996^{9}$ | **Jeopardize** (CEBrittain) **3-8-9** BDoyle(11) (prom: rdn 6f out: wknd over 3f out) | 30 | **12** | 33/1 | — | — |

(SP 135.5%) **12 Rn**

**2m 12.58** (2.88) CSF £49.80 TOTE £3.70: £1.30 £5.30 £2.80 (£32.20) Trio £119.80 OWNER Sheikh Mohammed (NEWMARKET) BRED Sheikh Mohammed bin Rashid al Maktoum

**707 Mohawk River (IRE)** won in useful style and looks the sort to go on improving. (4/1)
**Filmore West** would probably have made a race of it had he got a run sooner but, judging from the way he travelled and by the way he finished, better will be seen over further. (11/1)
**Torremolinos (USA)** travelled on the bridle but, when the pressure was on, he had only the one speed. He has previously run in America, but this was his first outing on grass and he may need a bit further. (6/1)
**3505 Gulliver**, made plenty of use of this time, looked short of speed when tackled. (3/1: op 2/1)
**3472 Melt The Clouds (CAN)**, stepping up in distance, again had his chances but was found wanting in the last two furlongs. (11/1)
**2610 Radiant Star** had his chances but failed to come up with the goods when the pressure was on in the last quarter-mile. (11/4)
**Galaka** ran as though longer trips should see improvement. (25/1)

## 3987 KNIGHTSBRIDGE GIN MAIDEN STKS (2-Y.O) (Class D)

5-10 (5-20) **6f 214y** £6,316.00 (£1,888.00: £904.00: £412.00) Stalls: High GOING minus 0.35 sec per fur (F)

| | | | | SP | RR | SF |
|---|---|---|---|---|---|---|
| | **Fantastic Fellow (USA)** (CEBrittain) **2-9-0** BDoyle(11) (w'like: str: bit bkwd: hld up: stdy hdwy 2f out: led over 1f out: r.o) | — | **1** | 7/1 | 89+ | 30 |
| | **Haltarra (USA)** (SbinSuroor) **2-9-0** JReid(9) (unf: bhd: hdwy ½-wy: sn rdn: chsd wnr fnl f: styd on wl) | ½ | **2** | 5/2[1] | 88+ | 29 |
| | **Mengaab (USA)** (JHMGosden) **2-9-0** GHind(6) (b.hind: w'like: lengthy: bhd: hdwy 3f out: r.o fnl f) | ½ | **3** | 12/1 | 87+ | 28 |
| 3588[2] | **China Red (USA)** (JWHills) **2-9-0** MHills(3) (lw: trckd ldrs: nt qckn fnl 2f) | 3 | **4** | 8/1 | 80 | 21 |
| 3706[3] | **Wasp Ranger (USA)** (PFICole) **2-9-0** TQuinn(2) (lw: cl up: led over 2f out tl over 1f out: sn btn) | hd | **5** | 11/4[2] | 80 | 21 |
| 3407[3] | **Stanton Harcourt (USA)** (JLDunlop) **2-9-0** PatEddery(10) (chsd ldrs tl outpcd fnl 2f) | 2½ | **6** | 7/2[3] | 74 | 15 |
| 1197[3] | **Rainbow Rain (USA)** (MJohnston) **2-9-0** JCarroll(4) (led tl over 2f out: sn btn) | 1½ | **7** | 14/1 | 70 | 11 |
| | **Solo Mio (IRE)** (BWHills) **2-9-0** RHills(5) (gd sort: bit bkwd: s.s & swvd lft: bhd tl sme late hdwy) | 1½ | **8** | 12/1 | 67 | 8 |
| | **Sioux** (CWThornton) **2-8-9** DeanMcKeown(1) (leggy: unf: sn outpcd & bhd) | ¾ | **9** | 50/1 | 60 | 1 |
| | **Kalinini (USA)** (LMCumani) **2-9-0** OUrbina(7) (lengthy: bit bkwd: outpcd after 3f: n.d after) | 2½ | **10** | 20/1 | 60 | 1 |
| | **Zalotto (IRE)** (TJEtherington) **2-9-0** KDarley(8) (rangy: unf: a outpcd & bhd) | 10 | **11** | 25/1 | 37 | — |
| | | | | (SP 133.7%) | **11 Rn** | |

**1m 26.27** (3.27) CSF £26.95 TOTE £15.30: £3.00 £1.80 £5.20 (£26.50) Trio £114.50 OWNER The Thoroughbred Corporation (NEWMARKET) BRED Mrs J. G. Jones

**Fantastic Fellow (USA)** looked likely to be all the better for this, but he still won well and there would seem to be a fair bit of improvement in him. (7/1)
**Haltarra (USA)** took time to realise what was required but, judging by the way he picked up in the last two furlongs, plenty more will be heard of him as he tries longer trips. (5/2)
**Mengaab (USA)**, given plenty to do, finished in useful style and should know much more about it next time. (12/1)
**3588 China Red (USA)** went pretty well here and should find a race or two in due course. (8/1)
**3706 Wasp Ranger (USA)** has plenty of speed, but failed to last it out on this occasion. (11/4: 2/1-3/1)
**3407 Stanton Harcourt (USA)** is still learning and, after chasing the leaders, found this company too hot in the final two furlongs. (7/2)
**1197 Rainbow Rain (USA)**, after three and a half months off, ran fast until blowing up in the last quarter-mile. (14/1)
**Solo Mio (IRE)** is a useful type, but he has a lot to learn about racing, although he did show fair signs of ability. (12/1: op 8/1)

T/Jkpt: Not won; £10,275.40 to York 5/9/96. T/Plpt: £276.20 (134.58 Tckts). T/Qdpt: £108.60 (18.45 Tckts). AA

# 3694-**SALISBURY (R-H) (Firm)**
## Thursday September 5th

Race 5: flip start
WEATHER: fine WIND: almost nil

## 3988 E.B.F. QUIDHAMPTON MAIDEN STKS (2-Y.O F) (Class D)

2-20 (2-21) **6f 212y** £4,406.00 (£1,328.00: £644.00: £302.00) Stalls: High GOING minus 0.56 sec per fur (F)

| | | | | SP | RR | SF |
|---|---|---|---|---|---|---|
| | **Sarayir (USA)** (MajorWRHern) **2-8-11** RHills(10) (leggy: unf: mde virtually all: qcknd clr 2f out: easily) | — | **1** | 10/11[1] | 99++ | 37 |
| | **Calypso Grant (IRE)** (PWHarris) **2-8-11** GHind(5) (w'like: hld up: hdwy over 2f out: chsd wnr fnl f: no imp) | 5 | **2** | 7/1[2] | 88+ | 26 |
| | **Lady of The Lake** (JLDunlop) **2-8-11** PatEddery(14) (w'like: scope: bit bkwd: hld up & bhd: hdwy fnl 2f: r.o) | 2½ | **3** | 9/1 | 82+ | 20 |
| 3593[18] | **Wing And A Prayer (IRE)** (RHannon) **2-8-11** JReid(6) (w wnr: outpcd 2f out: wknd fnl f) | 2 | **4** | 33/1 | 77 | 15 |
| | **Georgina (IRE)** (MajorWRHern) **2-8-11** TSprake(2) (lengthy: scope: hld up & bhd: rdn & hdwy wl over 1f out: r.o) | 1½ | **5** | 16/1 | 74+ | 12 |
| | **Off The Rails** (HCandy) **2-8-11** CRutter(11) (str: scope: hld up: hdwy 2f out: nt rch ldrs) | 1 | **6** | 33/1 | 71 | 9 |
| | **Brave Kris (IRE)** (LMCumani) **2-8-11** OUrbina(4) (scope: prom over 4f) | 1¼ | **7** | 8/1[3] | 69 | 7 |
| 3593[16] | **Racing Heart** (PJMakin) **2-8-11** RHughes(9) (bit bkwd: prom tl rdn & wknd over 2f out) | ¾ | **8** | 33/1 | 67 | 5 |
| | **Ceanothus (IRE)** (JHMGosden) **2-8-11** RCochrane(7) (leggy: unf: bkwd: nvr trbld ldrs) | s.h | **9** | 10/1 | 67 | 5 |
| 3660[7] | **Attribute** (RCharlton) **2-8-11** SSanders(1) (n.d) | ¾ | **10** | 16/1 | 65 | 3 |
| 3820[4] | **Permission** (RHannon) **2-8-11** DaneO'Neill(3) (lw: prom over 4f) | ¾ | **11** | 7/1[2] | 63 | 1 |
| | **Pointe Fine (FR)** (JWHills) **2-8-8(3)** MHenry(15) (str: cmpt: bit bkwd: prom over 4f) | ½ | **12** | 33/1 | 62 | — |
| 3245[9] | **Classic Line** (JLDunlop) **2-8-11** SWhitworth(12) (prom 4f) | 1¾ | **13** | 33/1 | 58 | — |
| | **Tyrolean Dancer (IRE)** (SPCWoods) **2-8-11** DBiggs(8) (w'like: scope: prom tl hrd rdn & wknd over 2f out) | 2 | **14** | 33/1 | 54 | — |
| | **La Belle Affair (USA)** (PMitchell) **2-8-11** AClark(13) (w'like: s.s: bhd whn rdn over 4f out: t.o) | 12 | **15** | 33/1 | 26 | — |
| | | | | (SP 139.9%) | **15 Rn** | |

**1m 27.13** (1.13) CSF £9.12 TOTE £2.20: £1.20 £2.10 £2.90 (£6.20) Trio £84.60 OWNER Mr Hamdan Al Maktoum (LAMBOURN) BRED Shadwell Farm Inc. and Shadwell Estate Co. Ltd.

**Sarayir (USA)** is a sister to Bashayer and Wijdan and a half-sister to Nashwan and Unfuwain. Living up to her home reputation, she made an impressive start to her career and seems perfectly capable of carrying on the family name. (10/11: Evens-5/4)
**Calypso Grant (IRE)**, a sister to Poppy Carew, found she had caught a tartar, but will not always meet one so smart. (7/1)
**Lady of The Lake**, a half-sister to seven-furlong juvenile winner Llia, shaped promisingly in the latter stages and seems sure to come on for the outing. (9/1: 6/1-10/1)
**Wing And A Prayer (IRE)**, a half-sister to Sky Dome, fared a lot better than on her Newbury debut, but may be better off reverting to six for the time being. (33/1)
**Georgina (IRE)**, a half-sister to stayer Hal Hoo Yaroom, is bred to need further and this stable-companion of the winner will do better in due course. (16/1)

**Off The Rails**, another who will do better over longer trips, possesses the right sort of physique to go on from here. (33/1)
**Brave Kris (IRE)**, a half-sister to Divina Luna, ran well until the winner was set alight. (8/1: op 4/1)
**Racing Heart**, a half-sister to Northern Goddess amongst others, was still in need of this. (33/1)
**Ceanothus (IRE)** (10/1: op 6/1)
**1346 Permission** (7/1: 5/1-8/1)

## 3989 'WESSEX STALLIONS' H'CAP (0-85) (3-Y.O+ F & M) (Class D)

2-50 (2-50) **6f 212y** £4,464.50 (£1,346.00: £653.00: £306.50) Stalls: High GOING minus 0.56 sec per fur (F)

| | Horse | Dist | Pos | SP | RR | SF |
|---|---|---|---|---|---|---|
| 3210[13] | **High Summer (USA) (80)** (RCharlton) **3-9-7** PatEddery(11) (lw: mde all: clr 3f out: easily) | — | 1 | 5/1[2] | 98+ | 71 |
| 3599[2] | **Faraway Lass (75)** (LordHuntingdon) **3-8-11**(5) AimeeCook(9) (lw: hld up & plld hrd: hdwy over 2f out: r.o ins fnl f: no ch w wnr) | 6 | 2 | 8/1 | 79 | 52 |
| 3933[3] | **Rebel County (IRE) (74)** (ABailey) **3-9-1** 5x DBiggs(10) (lw: a.p: chsd wnr over 1f out: no imp) | nk | 3 | 11/4[1] | 78 | 51 |
| 3516[11] | **Catch The Lights (85)** (RHannon) **3-9-12** DaneO'Neill(8) (lw: hld up & bhd: hdwy over 1f out: r.o) | 3 | 4 | 20/1 | 82 | 55 |
| 3810[10] | **Prima Silk (67)** (MJRyan) **5-8-12** AClark(13) (no hdwy fnl 2f) | 2 | 5 | 20/1 | 59 | 36 |
| 3812[2] | **Charlton Imp (USA) (56)** (RJHodges) **3-7-8**(3) MHenry(2) (lw: prom tl rdn & wknd 3f out) | 3 | 6 | 12/1 | 41 | 14 |
| 2920[3] | **Tawaaded (IRE) (85)** (PTWalwyn) **3-9-12** RHills(6) (prom: chsd wnr over 2f out tl edgd lft over 1f out: eased whn btn fnl f) | 1¾ | 7 | 20/1 | 66 | 39 |
| 3790[7] | **With Care (78)** (WJarvis) **3-9-5** MTebbutt(5) (lw: mid div: rdn 3f out: bhd fnl 2f) | ¾ | 8 | 7/1[3] | 57 | 30 |
| | **Legendary Leap (70)** (LordHuntingdon) **6-9-1** SSanders(14) (b: bkwd: nvr trbld ldrs) | s.h | 9 | 16/1 | 49 | 26 |
| 3702[6] | **Always Grace (61)** (MissGayKelleway) **4-8-6** TSprake(12) (lw: s.s: a bhd) | 1½ | 10 | 16/1 | 37 | 14 |
| 2134[14] | **Sand Star (65)** (DHaydnJones) **4-8-10** AMackay(1) (s.i.s: hdwy 3f out: hung rt over 2f out: eased whn btn over 1f out) | 3 | 11 | 33/1 | 34 | 11 |
| 3599[4] | **Highland Rhapsody (IRE) (74)** (IABalding) **3-9-1** JReid(7) (lw: chsd wnr over 3f: wknd over 2f out) | 2½ | 12 | 8/1 | 37 | 10 |
| 1493[4] | **Fly Tip (IRE) (84)** (BJMeehan) **3-9-11** BDoyle(3) (lw: bhd fnl 3f: t.o) | 14 | 13 | 20/1 | 15 | — |
| *3672[W]* | ***Silent Expression (82)*** (BJMeehan) **6-9-13** RHughes(4) (Withdrawn not under Starter's orders: lame at s: dead) | | W | 12/1 | — | — |

(SP 127.2%) **13 Rn**

**1m 24.98** (0.65 under best) (-1.02) CSF £39.64 CT £107.37 TOTE £5.30: £1.80 £1.90 £1.70 (£14.80) Trio £7.40 OWNER Mr K. Abdulla (BECKHAMPTON) BRED Juddmonte Farms
WEIGHT FOR AGE 3yo-4lb

**2718* High Summer (USA)** suffers from a deteriorating breathing problem and ran with her tongue tied down for the first time. Dropped 6lb following her disappointing run at Goodwood, she broke the course-record here, but had things very much her own way, and should still be treated with a shade of caution. (5/1)
**3599 Faraway Lass** seemed to get the extra furlong well enough, but was never going to bother the winner. (8/1)
**3933 Rebel County (IRE)**, again running under a penalty, was due to go up a further 6lb at the weekend. (11/4: 2/1-100/30)
**2974* Catch The Lights** seems in the Handicapper's grip, having been raised 16lb for a hat-trick in July. (20/1)
**3601 Prima Silk** is still 4lb higher than when successful at Lingfield in May. (20/1)
**3812 Charlton Imp (USA)**, up 2lb, was dropping back from a mile and probably found the ground too lively. (12/1: op 8/1)

## 3990 DICK POOLE CONDITIONS STKS (2-Y.O F) (Class B)

3-20 (3-23) **6f** £6,725.50 (£2,504.50: £1,214.75: £511.25: £218.13: £100.87) Stalls: High GOING minus 0.56 sec per fur (F)

| | Horse | Dist | Pos | SP | RR | SF |
|---|---|---|---|---|---|---|
| 3444[3] | **Dancing Drop (95)** (RHannon) **2-8-12** RHughes(6) (chsd wnr: led 1f out: r.o wl) | — | 1 | 13/8[1] | 87 | 44 |
| 3105* | **Carati** (RBoss) **2-8-9** SSanders(4) (led: rdn 2f out: hdd 1f out: unable qckn) | 1¼ | 2 | 10/1 | 81 | 38 |
| 3282* | **Alumisiyah (USA)** (HThomsonJones) **2-8-12** RHills(7) (lw: hld up: rdn & hdwy over 2f out: wknd wl over 1f out) | 5 | 3 | 4/1[2] | 70 | 27 |
| 2770[3] | **Arruhan (IRE)** (PTWalwyn) **2-8-12** RCochrane(2) (lw: stdd s: hdwy over 2f out: wknd wl over 1f out) | hd | 4 | 9/1 | 70 | 27 |
| 2051[W] | **Cowrie** (RFJohnsonHoughton) **2-8-12** TSprake(8) (lw: hld up: rdn & hdwy 3f out: wknd over 1f out) | s.h | 5 | 11/2[3] | 70 | 27 |
| 3613[5] | **Bride's Reprisal (90)** (MRChannon) **2-8-9** BDoyle(5) (swtg: nvr nr to chal) | ½ | 6 | 11/2[3] | 66 | 23 |
| 3707[6] | **Eye Shadow (93)** (BJMeehan) **2-8-9** MTebbutt(3) (lw: prom over 3f) | hd | 7 | 12/1 | 65 | 22 |

(SP 115.6%) **7 Rn**

**1m 13.48** (0.48) CSF £16.61 TOTE £2.80: £1.70 £3.30 (£15.70) OWNER Mr Mohamed Suhail (MARLBOROUGH) BRED Gainsborough Stud Management Ltd

**3444 Dancing Drop**, reverting back to six, took a while to gain the upper hand and gave the impression the stiff finish helped. (13/8)
**3105* Carati** made a brave bid from the front and should stay further. (10/1: 6/1-12/1)
**3282* Alumisiyah (USA)**, a half-sister to three-year-old Mutamanni, should have appreciated this longer trip but this was a fair bit hotter than her Brighton maiden. (4/1: op 6/1)
**2770 Arruhan (IRE)** at least settled better than at Doncaster after her rider took a pull leaving the stalls. (9/1)
**1643* Cowrie** was equipped with a Monty Roberts blanket after refusing to go into the stalls in the Queen Mary. (11/2)
**3613 Bride's Reprisal** seemed to find the minimum too sharp in listed company last time and was again quite highly tried here. (11/2: op 11/4)

## 3991 WINTERBOURNE H'CAP (0-65) (3-Y.O+) (Class F)

3-50 (3-51) **1m** £3,456.00 (£966.00: £468.00) Stalls: High GOING minus 0.56 sec per fur (F)

| | Horse | Dist | Pos | SP | RR | SF |
|---|---|---|---|---|---|---|
| 3333[11] | **Master M-E-N (IRE) (52)** (NMBabbage) **4-9-1v** BDoyle(1) (hdwy 2f out: hrd rdn to ld wl ins fnl f: r.o wl) | — | 1 | 20/1 | 64 | 39 |
| 3686[10] | **Honorable Estate (IRE) (63)** (RHannon) **3-9-7** DaneO'Neill(7) (a.p: led on bit 3f out: rdn over 1f out: hdd wl ins fnl f) | 2 | 2 | 14/1 | 71 | 41 |
| 3812[12] | **Mr Cube (IRE) (50)** (JMBradley) **6-8-6b**(7) CLowther(9) (plld hrd mid div: swtchd lft & hdwy fnl f: fin wl) | nk | 3 | 16/1 | 57 | 32 |
| 3694[2] | **Jaazim (51)** (MMadgwick) **6-9-0** JReid(11) (plld hrd: a.p: r.o one pce fnl f) | 1 | 4 | 11/4[1] | 56 | 31 |
| 3443[8] | **Audrey Grace (46)** (MissGayKelleway) **5-8-9** OUrbina(6) (hdwy 3f out: one pce fnl 2f) | nk | 5 | 16/1 | 51 | 26 |
| 3518[16] | **Dawalib (USA) (59)** (DHaydnJones) **6-9-8** RCochrane(8) (a.p: rdn over 1f out: wknd ins fnl f) | ¾ | 6 | 16/1 | 62 | 37 |
| 3501[8] | **Artful Dane (IRE) (65)** (MJHeaton-Ellis) **4-10-0** AClark(4) (no hdwy fnl 2f) | 1¼ | 7 | 20/1 | 66 | 41 |
| *3877[8]* | **Superior Force (60)** (MissBSanders) **3-9-4** SSanders(17) (prom: rdn over 2f out: eased whn btn wl ins fnl f) | hd | 8 | 12/1 | 61 | 31 |
| 3067[8] | **Squared Away (49)** (JWPayne) **4-8-12** MTebbutt(13) (hld up & bhd: hdwy over 1f out: r.o) | s.h | 9 | 13/2[2] | 50 | 25 |
| 1841[13] | **Easy Choice (USA) (55)** (PMitchell) **4-9-4** RHughes(15) (bhd fnl 2f) | 1 | 10 | 20/1 | 54 | 29 |
| 3765[2] | **Milos (60)** (TJNaughton) **5-9-9** TSprake(16) (prom 5f) | nk | 11 | 10/1[3] | 58 | 33 |
| 3694[13] | **Roi de la Mer (IRE) (59)** (JAkehurst) **5-9-8** SWhitworth(12) (hld up & bhd: hdwy on ins 3f out: nt clr run & swtchd lft: nvr nr to chal) | ½ | 12 | 12/1 | 56 | 31 |

3496[12] **Racing Hawk (USA) (50)** (MSSaunders) **4-8-8**(5) PPMurphy(5) (prom: hrd rdn & ev ch 2f out: wknd fnl f)........1 **13** 25/1 45 20
2994[11] **Careful (IRE) (60)** (BWHills) **3-8-13**(5) JDSmith(10) (hdwy 3f out: wknd 2f out)........6 **14** 20/1 43 13
3220[6] **Fairelaine (48)** (KCBailey) **4-8-11** PatEddery(3) (a bhd)........3 **15** 16/1 25 —
3341[6] **Severn Mill (58)** (JMBradley) **5-9-7** NAdams(14) (led 5f: sn wknd)........2 **16** 33/1 31 6
3812[6] **Set the Fashion (60)** (DLWilliams) **7-9-9v** GBardwell(18) (rdn 5f out: a bhd)........3½ **17** 10/1[3] 26 1
2342[7] **Cats Bottom (53)** (AGNewcombe) **4-9-2** DRMcCabe(2) (a bhd: t.o)........18 **18** 20/1 — —
(SP 134.4%) **18 Rn**

**1m 41.93** (1.53) CSF £265.53 CT £4,302.31 TOTE £23.10: £4.30 £2.80 £2.90 £1.20 (£197.10) Trio £183.40 OWNER Mr Alan Craddock (CHELTENHAM) BRED Mrs Mary Gilmore
WEIGHT FOR AGE 3yo-5lb
**1894 Master M-E-N (IRE)** sprang a surprise on this drop back to a mile. (20/1)
**3458* Honorable Estate (IRE)**, raised 3lb, seemed to find this trip just beyond her best. (14/1)
**3606 Mr Cube (IRE)** likes fast ground and had dropped to a mark 5lb lower than the last of his three wins last summer. (16/1)
**3694 Jaazim** was 2lb lower than when running over course and distance a fortnight ago. (11/4: op 7/1)
**3167 Audrey Grace** is still trying to lose her maiden tag. (16/1)
**3151 Dawalib (USA)** did not appear to see out this stiff mile. (16/1)
**2440 Squared Away** (13/2: 9/2-7/1)
**2898* Roi de la Mer (IRE)**, whose two wins have come in selling company, did not get the run of the race. (12/1: op 8/1)

## 3992 SALISBURY FESTIVAL CONDITIONS STKS (3-Y.O+) (Class C)
4-20 (4-21) **1m 6f** £5,220.00 (£1,820.00: £885.00: £375.00) GOING minus 0.56 sec per fur (F)

SP RR SF
3614[4] **Samraan (USA) (107)** (JLDunlop) **3-9-1** PatEddery(3) (hld up & plld hrd: wnt 2nd over 6f out: led over 2f out: drvn out)........— **1** 2/1[2] 116 54
2223* **Haleakala (IRE)** (MJohnston) **3-8-4** BDoyle(1) (hld up: hrd rdn over 2f out: chsd wnr over 1f out: r.o)........½ **2** 5/2[3] 104 42
3797[2] **Double Leaf (110)** (MRStoute) **3-8-7** JReid(4) (led: rdn & hdd over 2f out: wknd fnl f)........8 **3** 11/10[1] 98 36
3673[7] **Latahaab (USA) (96)** (RAkehurst) **5-9-4** TIves(2) (chsd ldr over 7f: bhd fnl 4f: t.o)........dist **4** 20/1 — —
(SP 114.3%) **4 Rn**

**2m 58.91** (0.21) CSF £7.08 TOTE £3.50: (£3.40) OWNER Mr K. M. Al-Mudhaf (ARUNDEL) BRED Mrs Afaf A. Al Essa
WEIGHT FOR AGE 3yo-11lb
**3614 Samraan (USA)** held on well under pressure and will now take his chance as an outsider in the St Leger. (2/1: Evens-5/2)
**2223* Haleakala (IRE)** stays well and lost no caste in defeat. (5/2)
**3797 Double Leaf**, stepping up in trip, found this ground totally different to that he encountered at Windsor. (11/10: Evens-10/11)

## 3993 BLANDFORD H'CAP (0-80) (3-Y.O+) (Class D)
4-50 (4-57) **5f** £4,029.00 (£1,212.00: £586.00: £273.00) Stalls: High GOING minus 0.56 sec per fur (F)

SP RR SF
3930* **Squire Corrie (63)** (GHarwood) **4-8-4b**(7) 6x GayeHarwood(14) (a.p: led 3f out: all out)........— **1** 15/2[3] 69 51
3793[5] **Mousehole (70)** (RGuest) **4-9-4b** JReid(15) (lw: a.p: nt clr run on ins over 2f out: swtchd lft over 1f out: r.o wl ins fnl f)........s.h **2** 7/1[2] 76 58
3868[5] **Ned's Bonanza (59)** (MDods) **7-8-7** AClark(16) (lw: a.p: ev ch fnl f: r.o)........s.h **3** 10/1 65 47
3360* **Pharaoh's Joy (61)** (JWPayne) **3-8-8** RCochrane(11) (a.p: ev ch over 1f out: unable qckn)........1 **4** 13/2[1] 64 45
3167[5] **Supreme Thought (61)** (LGCottrell) **4-8-9** SSanders(2) (swtg: hld up: hdwy over 2f out: r.o one pce fnl f)........½ **5** 16/1 62 44
3793* **Moon Strike (FR) (80)** (HAkbary) **6-10-0** DBiggs(10) (b: lw: gd hdwy fnl f: nvr nrr)........1½ **6** 10/1 76 58
3862[5] **Red Time (55)** (MSSaunders) **3-8-2** FNorton(17) (lw: prom: wknd fnl f)........nk **7** 33/1 50 31
3864[2] **Imposing Time (63)** (MissGayKelleway) **5-8-11b** DaneO'Neill(3) (dwlt: hdwy over 1f out: nt rch ldrs)........½ **8** 7/1[2] 57 39
3827[4] **Tart and a Half (72)** (BJMeehan) **4-9-6** MTebbutt(12) (hdwy 2f out: wknd ins fnl f)........½ **9** 12/1 64 46
3097[4] **Tachycardia (48)** (RJO'Sullivan) **4-7-7**(3) NVarley(1) (led 2f: wknd over 1f out)........1½ **10** 20/1 35 17
3851* **Windrush Boy (60)** (JRBosley) **6-8-3**(5) 6x AimeeCook(8) (swtg: hdwy over 2f out: wknd over 1f out)........½ **11** 12/1 46 28
3810[5] **Nellie North (59)** (GMMcCourt) **3-8-6v** PatEddery(13) (hld up mid div: nvr trbld ldrs)........nk **12** 10/1 44 25
3862[6] **Mac Oates (51)** (DWPArbuthnot) **3-7-12** CRutter(9) (lw: s.s: a bhd)........nk **13** 33/1 35 16
3661* **Ashkernazy (IRE) (48)** (NEBerry) **5-7-5**(5) CAdamson(5) (prom 3f)........hd **14** 14/1 31 13
3477[5] **Millesime (IRE) (60)** (BHanbury) **4-8-8** JStack(4) (b: bhd fnl 2f)........½ **15** 33/1 42 24
3338[3] **Spender (76)** (PWHarris) **7-9-10** GHind(6) (s.s: a bhd)........1 **16** 10/1 55 37
3698[4] **Superlao (BEL) (48)** (JJBridger) **4-7-7**(3) DarrenMoffatt(7) (b.nr hind: prom over 2f)........1 **17** 33/1 23 5
(SP 130.9%) **17 Rn**

**59.83 secs** (-0.17) CSF £57.72 CT £355.43 TOTE £9.20: £2.00 £1.80 £2.10 £1.90 (£25.60) Trio £41.90 OWNER Mr G. Harwood (PULBOROUGH) BRED Whitsbury Manor Stud
LONG HANDICAP Ashkernazy (IRE) 7-5 Tachycardia 7-6 Superlao (BEL) 7-1
WEIGHT FOR AGE 3yo-1lb
**3930* Squire Corrie** just managed to defy a penalty and forced the pace over this stiff five. (15/2)
**3793 Mousehole**, with the blinkers refitted, was supported in the Ring, but could not quite peg back the winner. (7/1: 8/1-12/1)
**3868 Ned's Bonanza** was due to go down 1lb in future handicaps and that might just have made the difference. (10/1: 8/1-12/1)
**3360* Pharaoh's Joy** could not overcome a 3lb hike in the Ratings. (13/2)
**3167 Supreme Thought**, reverting to sprinting, should now be approaching her peak. (16/1)
**3793* Moon Strike (FR)**, raised 6lb, found this trip inadequate on this occasion. (10/1: 8/1-12/1)

T/Plpt: £74.60 (147.22 Tckts). T/Qdpt: £17.40 (35.09 Tckts). KH

# 3981-YORK (L-H) (Good, Good to firm patches)
## Thursday September 5th
WEATHER: fine WIND: slt half against

## 3994 WEATHERBYS/HISCOX HOUSEHOLD INSURANCE MAIDEN STKS (2-Y.O) (Class D)
2-10 (2-12) **6f** £6,680.00 (£2,000.00: £960.00: £440.00) Stalls: Low GOING minus 0.42 sec per fur (F)

SP RR SF
**Tycoon Todd (USA)** (DRLoder) **2-9-0** OPeslier(13) (leggy: unf: lw: trckd ldrs: shkn up to ld over 1f out: r.o strly)........— **1** 15/8[1] 84++ 49

| | | | | | | |
|---|---|---|---|---|---|---|
| | **Harry Wolton** (HRACecil) **2-9-0** WRyan(9) (leggy: scope: lw: mid div: shkn up ½-wy: styd on appr fnl f: r.o wl towards fin) | 2½ | **2** | 7/1[3] | 77+ | 42 |
| | **Speedball (IRE)** (IABalding) **2-9-0** JFEgan(7) (w'like: dwlt: sn chsng ldrs: outpcd ½-wy: hdwy over 1f out: styd on wl towards fin) | nk | **3** | 14/1 | 77 | 42 |
| 3637[4] | **Daring Flight (USA)** (LordHuntingdon) **2-9-0** DHarrison(14) (w ldr: nt qckn appr fnl f) | hd | **4** | 12/1 | 76 | 41 |
| 1480[3] | **Queen's Pageant** (JLSpearing) **2-8-9** KFallon(1) (a chsng ldrs: kpt on same pce fnl 2f) | hd | **5** | 10/1 | 71 | 36 |
| 3668[5] | **Out of Sight (IRE)** (BAMcMahon) **2-9-0** GCarter(3) (a chsng ldrs: nt qckn fnl 2f) | 1½ | **6** | 14/1 | 76 | 37 |
| | **Wind Cheetah (USA)** (MRStoute) **2-9-0** WRSwinburn(6) (wl grwn: bit bkwd: led tl over 1f out: wknd ins fnl f) | d.h | **6** | 9/4[2] | 72+ | 37 |
| 1315[5] | **John Emms (IRE)** (MBell) **2-9-0** MFenton(5) (chsd ldrs: outpcd fnl 2f) | 3½ | **8** | 33/1 | 63 | 28 |
| | **Thornton (USA)** (JHMGosden) **2-9-0** JCarroll(11) (cmpt: scope: hld up: outpcd ½-wy: n.d after) | 3 | **9** | 10/1 | 55 | 20 |
| | **Muliere** (MJohnston) **2-8-9** MHills(12) (unf: scope: w ldrs over 3f: sn wknd) | hd | **10** | 14/1 | 49 | 14 |
| 3464[7] | **Style Dancer (IRE)** (RMWhitaker) **2-9-0** JFanning(8) (cl up over 3f: sn wknd) | hd | **11** | 50/1 | 54 | 19 |
| | **Yorkie George** (LMCumani) **2-9-0** KDarley(2) (w'like: str: s.i.s: a outpcd & bhd) | nk | **12** | 14/1 | 53 | 18 |
| | **Broad River (USA)** (EALDunlop) **2-9-0** TQuinn(16) (w'like: unf: a outpcd & bhd) | 1½ | **13** | 16/1 | 49 | 14 |
| | **Amico** (CWThornton) **2-9-0** DeanMcKeown(10) (leggy: unf: dwlt: a outpcd & bhd) | ¾ | **14** | 33/1 | 47 | 12 |
| | **Yam-Sing** (TDEasterby) **2-9-0** MBirch(4) (w'like: s.s: a bhd) | 3 | **15** | 33/1 | 39 | 4 |
| | **Night Chorus** (BSRothwell) **2-9-0** LCharnock(15) (cmpt: bit bkwd: s.i.s: a bhd) | 2 | **16** | 50/1 | 34 | — |

(SP 149.2%) **16 Rn**

**1m 11.95** (0.95) CSF £19.19 TOTE £2.90: £1.40 £3.70 £6.20 (£13.40) Trio £347.00 OWNER Lucayan Stud (NEWMARKET) BRED Patricia S. Purdy

**Tycoon Todd (USA)** may not be much to look at, but he certainly has a good engine. Ridden with tremendous confidence, seven furlongs will be no problem. (15/8)

**Harry Wolton**, who is very much on the leg at present, took time to get going. Staying on in most determined fashion at the finish, he is crying out for seven. (7/1)

**Speedball (IRE)**, badly tapped for foot at halfway, like the runner-up was putting in all his best work at the finish. He too needs a step up in distance. (14/1)

**3637 Daring Flight (USA)**, who showed plenty of knee-action going down, displayed the benefit of his initial outing. (12/1: op 8/1)

**1480 Queen's Pageant**, absent for over three months, was possibly worst drawn and, in the circumstances, was far from disgraced. (10/1)

**3668 Out of Sight (IRE)** tries hard, but seems to lack anything in the way of gears. (14/1)

**Wind Cheetah (USA)**, a quality colt, looked as if the outing would do him good and the way he ran confirmed it. After travelling strongly for much of the way, he was leg-weary in the closing stages. He will be a different proposition next time. (9/4: op 4/1)

## 3995 QUINTIN GILBEY SILVER TROPHY H'CAP (0-75) (3-Y.O+) (Class D)

2-40 (2-42) **6f 214y** £9,325.00 (£2,800.00: £1,350.00: £625.00) GOING minus 0.42 sec per fur (F)

| | | | | SP | RR | SF |
|---|---|---|---|---|---|---|
| 3623[15] | **Ochos Rios (IRE) (56)** (BSRothwell) **5-8-7**(3) FLynch(8) (b.off hind: chsd ldrs: led over 2f out: hung bdly rt over 1f out: kpt on) | — | **1** | 16/1 | 65 | 28 |
| *3603*[5] | **Wild Palm (72)** (WAO'Gorman) **4-9-12v** EmmaO'Gorman(27) (lw: hdwy on outside ½-wy: hmpd over 1f out: styd on same pce) | 1 | **2** | 33/1 | 79 | 42 |
| 2154[5] | **Foist (44)** (MWEasterby) **4-7-12** DaleGibson(15) (mid div: effrt & n.m.r ½-wy: hdwy over 2f out: styd on wl appr fnl f) | s.h | **3** | 12/1 | 51 | 14 |
| 3702[4] | **Safey Ana (USA) (60)** (BHanbury) **5-9-0** WRyan(26) (b: b.hind: swtg: bhd: hdwy on outside over 2f out: styd on same pce fnl f) | nk | **4** | 16/1 | 66 | 29 |
| *3877*[11] | **Our Shadee (USA) (49)** (KTIvory) **6-8-3v** CScally(21) (swtg: bhd: hdwy on outside over 2f out: styd on wl fnl f) | ½ | **5** | 33/1 | 54 | 17 |
| 3703* | **Sylvan Princess (67)** (CNAllen) **3-8-12**(5) MartinDwyer(1) (lw: bhd: hdwy ½-wy: sn chsng ldrs: nt qckn appr fnl f) | ½ | **6** | 9/1[1] | 71 | 30 |
| 3623[10] | **Lunch Party (56)** (DNicholls) **4-8-10** JCarroll(19) (swtg: hdwy to trck ldrs ½-wy: hung rt over 1f out: eased ins fnl f) | 2½ | **7** | 11/1[3] | 54 | 17 |
| 3686[6] | **Pointer (58)** (MrsPNDutfield) **4-8-12** TQuinn(25) (trckd ldrs on outside: effrt 2f out: kpt on one pce) | ½ | **8** | 20/1 | 55 | 18 |
| 3518[3] | **White Settler (70)** (RJHodges) **3-9-6** SDrowne(18) (a chsng ldrs: rdn 2f out: no imp) | ¾ | **9** | 10/1[2] | 65 | 24 |
| 3867* | **Naissant (71)** (RMMcKellar) **3-9-0**(7) [6x] KSked(2) (chsd ldrs: rdn ½-wy: wknd over 1f out) | ½ | **10** | 10/1[2] | 65 | 24 |
| 3458[8] | **Morning Surprise (58)** (APJarvis) **3-8-1**(7) CCarver(6) (lw: in tch: no ch whn n.m.r over 1f out) | nk | **11** | 33/1 | 51 | 10 |
| 3881* | **Scathebury (60)** (KRBurke) **3-8-10b** [6x] GCarter(20) (b.nr fore: sn bhd & pushed along: sme hdwy 2f out: n.d) | 1¼ | **12** | 25/1 | 50 | 9 |
| *3601*[10] | **Dancing Sioux (65)** (DNicholls) **4-9-5** AlexGreaves(14) (s.i.s: bhd tl sme late hdwy) | hd | **13** | 25/1 | 55 | 18 |
| 3151[3] | **Zain Dancer (55)** (DNicholls) **4-8-2**(7) JBramhill(24) (a bhd) | ½ | **14** | 20/1 | 44 | 7 |
| 3833[5] | **Tael of Silver (66)** (ABailey) **4-9-6** GDuffield(13) (lw: hdwy ½-wy: sn chsng ldrs: wknd 2f out) | nk | **15** | 11/1[3] | 54 | 17 |
| 3815[3] | **Pine Ridge Lad (IRE) (65)** (JLEyre) **6-9-2**(3) OPears(10) (lw: chsd ldrs tl lost pl over 2f out) | ½ | **16** | 14/1 | 52 | 15 |
| 2490* | **Stand Tall (60)** (CWThornton) **4-9-0** DeanMcKeown(11) (swtg: mid div: stdy hdwy ½-wy: eased whn n.m.r over 1f out) | ¾ | **17** | 20/1 | 45 | 8 |
| 3844[8] | **Mister Joel (59)** (MWEasterby) **3-8-4b**(5) GParkin(23) (lw: led tl hdd & wknd over 2f out) | s.h | **18** | 33/1 | 44 | 3 |
| 3702[3] | **Samsolom (59)** (PHowling) **8-8-13** KFallon(5) (b.hind: lw: no ch whn hmpd over 1f out) | 1¼ | **19** | 14/1 | 41 | 4 |
| 3937[16] | **Playmaker (66)** (DNicholls) **3-9-2b[1]** JFEgan(12) (trckd ldrs: wknd & eased 2f out) | 1¼ | **20** | 25/1 | 46 | 5 |
| *3089*[6] | **Lady Silk (48)** (MissJFCraze) **5-8-2** AMcGlone(7) (in tch tl rdn & lost pl ½-wy) | hd | **21** | 33/1 | 27 | — |
| 2630[8] | **Legal Issue (IRE) (68)** (WWHaigh) **4-9-8** RLappin(4) (prom tl lost pl over 2f out) | 1 | **22** | 20/1 | 45 | 8 |
| 3777* | **Euro Sceptic (IRE) (61)** (TDEasterby) **4-8-12b**(3) RHavlin(16) (chsd ldrs: n.m.r over 1f: hrd rdn: lost pl over 2f out) | 4 | **23** | 14/1 | 29 | — |
| | **Ben Gunn (74)** (PTWalwyn) **4-10-0** KDarley(22) (hld up: a bhd) | 1½ | **24** | 33/1 | 38 | 1 |
| 3777[4] | **Gool Lee Shay (USA) (51)** (RMWhitaker) **3-8-1v[1]** JFanning(9) (lw: chsd ldrs to ½-wy: sn wknd) | 6 | **25** | 25/1 | 2 | — |
| 3703[2] | **Spanish Stripper (USA) (56)** (MCChapman) **5-8-7**(3) PMcCabe(3) (a bhd) | nk | **26** | 20/1 | 6 | — |
| 3881[6] | **Magic Lake (49)** (EJAlston) **3-7-13** StephenDavies(17) (lw: a bhd & sn drvn along) | ½ | **27** | 33/1 | — | — |

(SP 144.1%) **27 Rn**

**1m 25.57** (2.57) CSF £453.20 CT £5,892.88 TOTE £14.50: £2.80 £10.10 £4.00 £4.10 (£187.40) Trio £2,392.80; £2,696.14 to Haydock 6/9/96
OWNER Mrs H. A. Burn (MALTON) BRED Capt P. W. Kennedy
WEIGHT FOR AGE 3yo-4lb

**OFFICIAL EXPLANATION Ochos Rios (IRE): explaining the improvement in form, connections reported that the gelding does not like to be crowded, which he had been in his previous race, and that he needs the run of the race to produce his best form.**

**3151 Ochos Rios (IRE)**, well backed at long odds, ended a losing sequence of twenty-five, but he showed what an unreliable character he is, hanging badly right into the whip. (16/1)
**3603 Wild Palm**, who wore a tongue-strap, was drawn on the wide outside. 8lb higher in the weights compared with when he won a handicap at Yarmouth four runs ago, he ran really well, but the interference he suffered from the winner was only slight and made no difference whatsoever. (33/1)
**2154 Foist**, absent for over two months, does not do anything in a hurry. After having to wait for an opening, he was staying on in most determined fashion at the line. A proven All-Weather performer, he is better on turf with some give underfoot. (12/1)
**3702 Safey Ana (USA)**, a confirmed seven-furlong fast-ground specialist, is weighted up to the hilt. (16/1)
**3606 Our Shadee (USA)** is much better suited by All-Weather surfaces and Lingfield in particular. (33/1)
**3703* Sylvan Princess** has been running well in condition events, but here she was a stone higher than when she last won a handicap a month earlier. (9/1)
**3623 Lunch Party** has ability but also has problems and, after hanging, his rider sensibly eased him off with his chance gone. (11/1)
**3833 Tael of Silver** (11/1: 16/1-10/1)

## 3996 STRENSALL STKS (Listed) (3-Y.O+) (Class A)

3-10 (3-16) **1m 205y** £13,402.50 (£4,020.00: £1,935.00: £892.50) Stalls: Low GOING minus 0.42 sec per fur (F)

| | | | | SP | RR | SF |
|---|---|---|---|---|---|---|
| 3671[5] | **Even Top (IRE) (123)** (MHTompkins) **3-8-10** TQuinn(1) (lw: trckd ldr: rdn to ld wl over 1f out: styd on wl) | — | **1** | 10/11[1] | 112 | 49 |
| 3503[3] | **Tamhid (USA) (104)** (HThomsonJones) **3-8-10** GCarter(8) (a chsng ldrs: kpt on u.p fnl 2f: no ch w wnr) | 3 | **2** | 10/1 | 107 | 44 |
| 3158[2] | **Missile (101)** (WJHaggas) **3-8-10** MHills(4) (hld up & plld hrd: effrt over 3f out: n.m.r over 1f out: styd on) | ½ | **3** | 7/2[2] | 106 | 43 |
| 3658* | **Maralinga (IRE) (100)** (LadyHerries) **4-9-2** DeclanO'Shea(6) (lw: led: qcknd over 4f out: hdd wl over 1f out: one pce) | 1 | **4** | 16/1 | 104 | 47 |
| | **Celestial Key (USA) (105)** (MJohnston) **6-9-2** DeanMcKeown(7) (hld up: n.m.r over 3f out: nt clr run over 1f out: kpt on wl) | ¾ | **5** | 20/1 | 103 | 46 |
| 3710[11] | **Kala Sunrise (81)** (CSmith) **3-8-10** KDarley(2) (prom: drvn along & outpcd over 4f out: kpt on fnl 2f) | 1 | **6** | 100/1 | 101? | 38 |
| 3670[6] | **Punishment (115)** (CEBrittain) **5-9-2** OPeslier(9) (in tch: effrt over 4f out: sn rdn & no imp) | 2½ | **7** | 13/2[3] | 96 | 39 |
| 1509[8] | **Star Selection (103)** (JMackie) **5-9-2** JQuinn(3) (bhd: sme hdwy over 3f out: sn lost pl) | 5 | **8** | 66/1 | 87 | 30 |
| 3691* | **Amrak Ajeeb (IRE) (99)** (BHanbury) **4-9-2** MRimmer(5) (lw: chsd ldrs: drvn along over 3f out: lost pl 2f out) | 1¼ | **9** | 10/1 | 85 | 28 |
| | | | | (SP 119.2%) | **9 Rn** | |

**1m 50.33** (1.13) CSF £10.90 TOTE £1.90: £1.40 £2.40 £1.20 (£10.00) Trio £9.40 OWNER Mr B. Schmidt-Bodner (NEWMARKET) BRED M. Dwan

WEIGHT FOR AGE 3yo-6lb

**3671 Even Top (IRE)** had a simple task on paper, but his rider had to earn his fee. A galloper rather than a horse who can do anything in a hurry, he had to be really rousted along to hit the front. Hanging slightly left and looking unhappy on the ground, he was kept right up to his work. He will have to find plenty if he is to have any impact in the Champion Stakes. (10/11: Evens-5/4)
**3503 Tamhid (USA)** seemed to run his best race so far. (10/1: 7/1-11/1)
**3158 Missile**, who was slightly lame behind after Goodwood, was fresh and took a keen grip. Not enjoying the best of runs, he was staying on nicely inside the last and this was a highly satisfactory Cambridgeshire trial. (7/2)
**3658* Maralinga (IRE)**, who had his tongue tied down, tried to pinch it from the front. (16/1)
**Celestial Key (USA)**, ridden to conserve his stamina, shaped promisingly and should soon be adding to his record. (20/1)
**2621 Kala Sunrise** was probably flattered, being kept right up to his work all the way to the line. (100/1)
**3670 Punishment**, warm beforehand, did not run up to his International effort. (13/2)

## 3997 SUN LIFE OF CANADA GARROWBY RATED STKS H'CAP (0-105) (3-Y.O) (Class B)

3-40 (3-45) **1m 3f 195y** £13,140.00 (£4,860.00: £2,330.00: £950.00: £375.00: £145.00) Stalls: Low GOING minus 0.42 sec per fur (F)

| | | | | SP | RR | SF |
|---|---|---|---|---|---|---|
| 3828* | **Arabian Story (88)** (LordHuntingdon) **3-8-4** 3x DHarrison(6) (b: lw: trckd ldrs gng wl: led on bit over 2f out: pushed out) | — | **1** | 10/11[1] | 101+ | 42 |
| 3124[5] | **Quakers Field (105)** (GLMoore) **3-9-7** KFallon(4) (lw: hld up: effrt over 4f out: rdn to ld 3f out: sn hdd: no ch w wnr) | 2½ | **2** | 10/1[3] | 115 | 56 |
| 3683[7] | **Dear Life (USA) (88)** (MrsJCecil) **3-7-13**(5) MartinDwyer(10) (lw: sn chsng ldrs: one pce fnl 2f) | 2 | **3** | 20/1 | 95 | 36 |
| 3710[3] | **General Macarthur (92)** (JLDunlop) **3-8-8** GDuffield(11) (in tch: drvn along 6f out: rdn & one pce fnl 3f) | 1¼ | **4** | 5/1[2] | 97 | 38 |
| 3594[2] | **Brandon Magic (96)** (IABalding) **3-8-12** WRSwinburn(3) (hld up: effrt on outside over 2f out: sn rdn: styd on fnl f) | ¾ | **5** | 10/1[3] | 100 | 41 |
| 3669[6] | **Warbrook (88)** (IABalding) **3-8-4** KDarley(1) (lw: hld up: effrt over 4f out: sn rdn & hung lft: styd on fnl 2f) | s.h | **6** | 25/1 | 92 | 33 |
| 3766* | **Traceability (88)** (SCWilliams) **3-8-4** GCarter(2) (lw: bhd & pushed along 7f out: kpt on fnl 2f: n.d) | s.h | **7** | 14/1 | 92 | 33 |
| | **Gentilhomme (105)** (PFICole) **3-9-7** TQuinn(8) (swtg: chsd ldr: led over 3f out: sn hdd & wknd) | 8 | **8** | 14/1 | 98 | 39 |
| 2502[17] | **Pleasant Surprise (94)** (MJohnston) **3-8-10** MHills(5) (hld up: effrt over 3f out: lost pl over 2f out) | 8 | **9** | 11/1 | 77 | 18 |
| 3617[4] | **Eagle Canyon (IRE) (88)** (BHanbury) **3-7-11**(7) GMilligan(9) (reard s: sn trckng ldrs: lost pl over 3f out: eased) | 15 | **10** | 25/1 | 50 | — |
| 3691[11] | **Qasida (IRE) (89)** (CEBrittain) **3-8-5**ow1 OPeslier(7) (led tl over 3f out: sn lost pl: virtually p.u) | 28 | **11** | 20/1 | 14 | — |
| | | | | (SP 126.1%) | **11 Rn** | |

**2m 29.69** (1.89) CSF £11.84 CT £114.02 TOTE £1.90: £1.30 £2.30 £6.30 (£7.90) Trio £124.40 OWNER The Queen (WEST ILSLEY) BRED The Queen

LONG HANDICAP Arabian Story 7-13 Traceability 7-12 Dear Life (USA) 7-12 Warbrook 8-0 Eagle Canyon (IRE) 7-10 Qasida (IRE) 8-2

**3828* Arabian Story**, who had 5lb in hand at these weights on his revised mark, travelled comfortably and, quickening through on the inside, scored in good style. He looks the type to make an even better four-year-old. (10/11: Evens-11/10)
**3124 Quakers Field**, who looked an absolute picture, showed his fine Goodwood effort was no fluke. (10/1)
**3290* Dear Life (USA)** ran well from 6lb out of the handicap. (20/1)
**3710 General Macarthur** was the first in trouble. (5/1)
**3594 Brandon Magic**, up in distance, travelled strongly off the pace. Picking up ground late in the day, he should do better now he has proved his stamina to connections. (10/1)
**1175 Warbrook**, back in distance, wanted to do nothing but hang left. When he did reach the running rail, he consented to stay on. (25/1)
**3766* Traceability**, 6lb out of the handicap, struggled to go the pace. Putting in some good work at the finish, he might be worth a try over further. (14/1)

## 3998 HUNTINGTON NURSERY H'CAP (2-Y.O) (Class C)

4-10 (4-11) **7f 202y** £7,895.00 (£2,360.00: £1,130.00: £515.00) Stalls: Low GOING minus 0.42 sec per fur (F)

| | | | SP | RR | SF |
|---|---|---|---|---|---|
| 3678* | **General's Star (75)** (MRStoute) **2-8-10** KDarley(2) (mde all: drvn along over 2f out: styd on strly) .................— | **1** | 4/1 3 | 80 | 29 |
| 2972 3 | **Party Romance (USA) (86)** (BHanbury) **2-9-0**(7) GMilligan(1) (lw: hld up: hdwy on ins & nt clr run fr over 2f out tl over 1f out: styd on: no ch w wnr) ........3½ | **2** | 7/2 2 | 84+ | 33 |
| 3485 3 | **Maradi (IRE) (77)** (DMorley) **2-8-12** MHills(10) (lw: hld up & bhd: effrt on outside 2f out: styd on wl fnl f) .........¾ | **3** | 9/1 | 73+ | 22 |
| 3936 7 | **Grate Times (78)** (EWeymes) **2-8-13** KFallon(4) (chsd ldrs: drvn along over 4f out: edgd rt & kpt on fnl f)........1 | **4** | 16/1 | 72 | 21 |
| 3577 6 | **Dee Pee Tee Cee (IRE) (65)** (MWEasterby) **2-8-0** JFEgan(3) (lw: hld up: effrt & nt clr run 3f out: styd on fnl f) ........s.h | **5** | 25/1 | 59 | 8 |
| 3659 7 | **Blue Movie (73)** (MBell) **2-8-8** MFenton(5) (chsd ldrs: rdn & hung rt over 1f out: sn wknd) ........5 | **6** | 20/1 | 57 | 6 |
| 3467 5 | **Irtifa (77)** (PTWalwyn) **2-8-12** TQuinn(6) (plld hrd: trckd ldrs: wkng whn hmpd over 1f out)........hd | **7** | 10/1 | 61 | 10 |
| 3880 3 | **Zorba (64)** (CWThornton) **2-7-13** JQuinn(8) (plld hrd: trckd ldrs: effrt over 2f out: btn whn hmpd over 1f out) ........1¼ | **8** | 8/1 | 46 | — |
| 3512* | **Sparky (65)** (MWEasterby) **2-8-0b** DaleGibson(9) (lw: bhd & pushed along: no ch whn hmpd 2f out) ..............4 | **9** | 10/1 | 38 | — |
| 3835 5 | **Mudflap (84)** (SirMarkPrescott) **2-9-5** GDuffield(11) (prom tl wknd over 2f out)........1¾ | **10** | 11/4 1 | 54 | 3 |
| 3616 7 | **Soden (IRE) (72)** (TGMills) **2-8-7** JCarroll(7) (swtg: trckd ldrs: effrt over 4f out: lost pl 2f out: eased) ............1¼ | **11** | 10/1 | 39 | — |

(SP 131.8%) **11 Rn**

**1m 39.88** (3.08) CSF £19.81 CT £119.36 TOTE £5.70: £2.10 £1.70 £3.20 (£13.10) Trio £45.10 OWNER Mr Saeed Suhail (NEWMARKET) BRED Meon Valley Stud

STEWARDS' ENQUIRY Fenton susp. 14, 16-17/9/96 (careless riding).

**3678* General's Star**, who again wore a tongue-strap, was allowed to dominate. Setting his own pace, he went for home halfway up the straight and, with the majority of his rivals getting in each other's way, he was in no danger in the final furlong. (4/1)

**2972 Party Romance (USA)**, drawn one, found himself trapped on the inner. His young rider had no option but to sit and suffer until a gap came entering the final furlong. He was asked to do just enough to secure second spot, but would not have beaten the winner under any circumstances. (7/2)

**3485 Maradi (IRE)**, a keen-going sort, was settled too far off the pace in what was basically a three-furlong sprint. Making up a lot of ground in the final furlong, he is well capable of finding a similar event. (9/1)

**3512 Grate Times**, tapped for foot at halfway, kept going all the way to the line. He is definitely best with give underfoot. (16/1)

**3251 Dee Pee Tee Cee (IRE)**, stepping up to a mile, was given a patient ride. Meeting trouble, he was staying on in good style at the finish and should find another opening in lesser company. (25/1)

**1437 Blue Movie** hung right under pressure, causing trouble, and his rider was handed a suspension. (20/1)

**3835 Mudflap**, drawn eleven of eleven, was never able to dominate. (11/4)

## 3999 PRINCE OF WALES'S OWN REGIMENT OF YORKSHIRE MAIDEN STKS (3-Y.O) (Class D)

4-40 (4-41) **7f 202y** £6,108.00 (£1,824.00: £872.00: £396.00) Stalls: Low GOING minus 0.42 sec per fur (F)

| | | | SP | RR | SF |
|---|---|---|---|---|---|
| 3788 2 | **Van Gurp (90)** (BAMcMahon) **3-9-0** GDuffield(3) (hld up & plld hrd: hmpd over 5f out: swtchd outside & led over 1f out: hung lft: drvn out) ........— | **1** | 5/2 1 | 93 | 30 |
| 3841 3 | **Mount Pleasant (IRE)** (PFICole) **3-9-0** TQuinn(1) (sn outpcd & pushed along: hdwy over 1f out: r.o wl towards fin)........2 | **2** | 9/2 3 | 89 | 26 |
| 3839 2 | **Zurs (IRE) (80)** (MissGayKelleway) **3-9-0** WRSwinburn(2) (chsd ldrs: rdn & outpcd over 2f out: styd on fnl f)........2½ | **3** | 4/1 2 | 84 | 21 |
| 2572 4 | **Stellar Line (USA) (76)** (BWHills) **3-9-0** KFallon(5) (chsd ldrs: drvn along 4f out: wknd fnl f) ........3 | **4** | 9/1 | 78 | 15 |
| | **Winnebago** (CWThornton) **3-8-9** DeanMcKeown(6) (sn outpcd: sme hdwy 3f out: styd on fnl f)........1½ | **5** | 14/1 | 70 | 7 |
| | **Amington Lass** (PDEvans) **3-8-9** JFEgan(4) (led tl hdd & wknd over 1f out) ........¾ | **6** | 33/1 | 68 | 5 |
| 3767 2 | **Meznh (IRE)** (HThomsonJones) **3-8-9** GCarter(7) (chsd ldr: rdn over 2f out: wknd over 1f out: eased)........2 | **7** | 5/2 1 | 64 | 1 |

(SP 114.9%) **7 Rn**

**1m 40.13** (3.33) CSF £13.51 TOTE £3.20: £2.00 £2.30 (£6.00) OWNER Barouche Stud Ltd (TAMWORTH) BRED Barouche Stud Ltd

**3788 Van Gurp** has plenty of ability but is a tricky customer. Taking a keen grip, he was hampered between horses on the turn. When switched to get a run, he looked like winning on the bridle but, after being sent to the front, all he wanted to do was hang left. (5/2)

**3841 Mount Pleasant (IRE)**, dropped in distance, struggled to go the pace. Really finding his stride inside the last, he is capable of better when stepped back up again. (9/2)

**3839 Zurs (IRE)**, badly tapped for foot at one stage, was staying on at the finish. His future lies in handicaps over further. (4/1)

**2572 Stellar Line (USA)** again produced little under pressure. (9/1)

**Winnebago** looks as though she still needs more time yet, but she did show some ability, staying on nicely in the closing stages. (14/1)

**Amington Lass**, who had two runs at two, set a good clip and held a useful lead at halfway. Once collared, she quickly dropped away, but she would be an interesting proposition in handicap company over seven. (33/1)

**3767 Meznh (IRE)** ran poorly, dropping away over a furlong out and being eased. Perhaps her stamina gave out, but this was still not a good effort. (5/2)

## 4000 RACING SCHOOLS APPRENTICE H'CAP (0-70) (3-Y.O+) (Class E)

5-10 (5-12) **1m 2f 85y** £4,532.50 (£1,360.00: £655.00: £302.50) Stalls: Low GOING minus 0.42 sec per fur (F)

| | | | SP | RR | SF |
|---|---|---|---|---|---|
| 3412 3 | **Gold Desire (44)** (MBrittain) **6-8-5** RMullen(11) (trckd ldrs: chal over 3f out: styd on to ld ins fnl f) ................— | **1** | 12/1 | 55 | 37 |
| 3918* | **Minster Glory (47)** (MWEasterby) **5-8-8b** 5x FLynch(9) (swtg: chsd ldr: led over 4f out tl over 1f out: styd on ins fnl f)........½ | **2** | 7/1 2 | 57 | 39 |
| 2066 6 | **Calder King (63)** (JLEyre) **5-9-10b** CTeague(3) (s.i.s: gd hdwy 3f out: led over 1f out: hung lft & hdd ins fnl f) ........1¼ | **3** | 14/1 | 71 | 53 |
| 3800 5 | **Cuban Reef (45)** (WJMusson) **4-8-6** GMilligan(19) (hld up & bhd: hdwy on outside over 3f out: kpt on same pce fnl f) ........1 | **4** | 12/1 | 52 | 34 |
| 3414 3 | **Mels Baby (IRE) (56)** (JLEyre) **3-8-10** DSweeney(12) (hld up: hdwy over 3f out: kpt on same pce fnl 2f).........½ | **5** | 14/1 | 62 | 37 |
| 3845 2 | **Cumbrian Maestro (57)** (TDEasterby) **3-8-11** RHavlin(2) (lw: sn chsng ldrs: one pce fnl 3f) ........1 | **6** | 11/2 1 | 62 | 37 |
| 3918 5 | **Rasayel (USA) (63)** (PDEvans) **6-9-10** JWilkinson(4) (s.i.s: hdwy over 3f out: rdn & one pce fnl 2f) ..............1¼ | **7** | 9/1 3 | 66 | 48 |
| *3630 9* | **Taniyar (FR) (35)** (RHollinshead) **4-7-10** KSked(8) (a in tch: no hdwy fnl 3f) ........5 | **8** | 25/1 | 30 | 12 |
| 3812 4 | **Alfayza (44)** (JDBethell) **3-7-6**(6) NicolaStokes(20) (hld up & bhd: hdwy 2f out: nvr nr ldrs)........3½ | **9** | 16/1 | 33 | 8 |
| 3220 2 | **Ring of Vision (IRE) (57)** (MrsMReveley) **4-9-4** SCopp(5) (lw: s.i.s: sme hdwy 3f out: n.d) ........½ | **10** | 10/1 | 46 | 28 |
| 3461 4 | **Road Racer (IRE) (57)** (MrsJRRamsden) **3-8-11** AEddery(13) (mid div: drvn along 3f out: no imp)........4 | **11** | 7/1 2 | 40 | 15 |

2567$^{10}$ **Bowcliffe (47)** (MrsAMNaughton) **5-8-5**$^{(3)}$ JMcAuley(10) (lw: trckd ldrs: hung lft & lost pl over 2f out) ...½ **12** 16/1 29 11
3280$^{2}$ **Troubadour Song (52)** (WWHaigh) **4-8-13** DGriffiths(17) (hld up & bhd: sme hdwy over 2f out: n.d) ...¾ **13** 10/1 33 15
3452$^{2}$ **Double Up (66)** (LadyHerries) **3-9-6** PDoe(16) (lw: chsd ldrs tl lost pl over 2f out) ...3½ **14** 12/1 41 16
3653$^{5}$ **Slapy Dam (50)** (JMackie) **4-8-11v** MBaird(7) (lw: s.i.s: sme hdwy 2f out: n.d) ...nk **15** 11/1 25 7
3785$^{12}$ **Open Affair (62)** (APJarvis) **3-8-13**$^{(3)}$ CCarver(1) (a in rr) ...8 **16** 25/1 24 —
3586$^{9}$ **Jean Pierre (56)** (JPearce) **3-8-10** SDrowne(14) (nvr bttr than mid div) ...4 **17** 16/1 12 —
3698$^{10}$ **Summerhill Special (IRE) (57)** (MrsPNDutfield) **5-9-1b**$^{(3)}$ RSmith(15) (plld hrd: led & racd wd: hdd over 4f out: sn wknd) ...1¾ **18** 25/1 11 —
1836$^{4}$ **Most Wanted (IRE) (50)** (JJO'Neill) **3-8-1**$^{(3)}$ AMcCarthy(6) (a rr div) ...1½ **19** 25/1 1 —
(SP 146.3%) **19 Rn**

**2m 12.2** (2.50) CSF £99.10 CT £1,130.45 TOTE £19.30: £4.00 £1.70 £4.40 £5.40 (£52.00) Trio £890.90; £878.37 to Haydock 6/9/96 OWNER Northgate Lodge Racing Club (WARTHILL) BRED Northgate Lodge Stud Ltd
WEIGHT FOR AGE 3yo-7lb

**3412 Gold Desire** made it six wins from fifty starts under a most confident ride. Rated only 44, he might struggle for opportunities from now on. (12/1)
**3918* Minster Glory**, under a 5lb penalty and with a top apprentice in the saddle, fought all the way to the line. (7/1)
**2066 Calder King**, an exasperating character, tried to come from last to first. After hitting the front possibly too soon, all he did was hang left and he threw it away. (14/1)
**3800 Cuban Reef**, given a patient ride, seemed to stay the trip alright. (12/1)
**3414 Mels Baby (IRE)**, ridden to get the trip but off the bit as usual, could do no more than plug on at the one pace. (14/1)
**3845 Cumbrian Maestro** was under pressure and getting nowhere halfway up the straight. (11/2)
**3918 Rasayel (USA)**, bidding to repeat last year's victory, was struggling after a sluggish break and could make no ground at all in the final quarter-mile. (9/1)
**3812 Alfayza**, who received no assistance at all from the saddle, ran creditably in the circumstances. (16/1)

T/Jkpt: £3,873.10 (3.31 Tckts). T/Plpt: £114.10 (287.31 Tckts). T/Qdpt: £4.30 (510.3 Tckts). WG

## 4001a-4022a (Irish Racing) - See Computer Raceform

## 3727a-CURRAGH (Newbridge, Ireland) (R-H) (Good to yielding)
### Saturday August 31st

### 4023a FUTURITY STKS (Gp 3) (2-Y.O)
3-30 (3-32) **1m** £16,250.00 (£4,750.00: £2,250.00: £750.00)

SP RR SF
3143$^{3}$ **Equal Rights (IRE)** (PWChapple-Hyam) **2-8-10** JReid (hld up in rr: hdwy 2f out: led ins fnl f: r.o) ...— **1** 100/30$^{2}$ 106 41
2619* **Recondite (IRE)** (MRChannon) **2-8-10** KDarley (trckd ldrs: 4th st: ev ch 1f out: nt qckn ins fnl f) ...1½ **2** 8/1 103 38
**Beautiful Fire (IRE)** (DKWeld,Ireland) **2-8-10** MJKinane (hld up in rr: 5th st: nt clr run on ins 2f out: swtchd lft 1f out: r.o wl) ...1½ **3** 4/1$^{3}$ 100 35
2503* **Groom's Gordon (FR)** (JLDunlop) **2-8-10** JPMurtagh (prom: disp ld after 3f: led & rdn over 2f out: hdd u.p ins fnl f: no ex) ...hd **4** 5/1 100 35
3243$^{3}$ **Quest Express** (MBell) **2-8-10** MFenton (led tl over 2f out: no imp fnl f) ...2½ **5** 14/1 95 30
**Menja (USA)** (APO'Brien,Ireland) **2-8-8**$^{ow1}$ CRoche (hld up: 6th st: hdwy & effrt over 1f out: wknd u.p ins fnl f) ...hd **6** 6/1 93 27
**Swift Gulliver (IRE)** (JSBolger,Ireland) **2-8-10** KJManning (prom: disp ld bef st: wknd 2f out: eased: lame) ..10 **7** 3/1$^{1}$ 75 10
(SP 116.8%) **7 Rn**

**1m 39.9** (4.90) OWNER R. E. Sangster (MARLBOROUGH) BRED Swettenham Stud
**3143 Equal Rights (IRE)** was given a restrained ride this time and the tactics worked with tremendous effect. He showed a nice turn of foot and this is obviously the correct way to ride him. He will be an interesting Royal Lodge Stakes contender. (100/30)
**2619* Recondite (IRE)** had every chance in second place with a furlong to run, but just could not quicken. (8/1)
**Beautiful Fire (IRE)** had a luckless run, finding his way blocked on the inside two furlong out. Switched to the outside with a furlong left to run, he ran on well to snatch third close home. The horse was hardly to blame. (4/1: op 5/2)
**2503* Groom's Gordon (FR)**, in front and being driven along with over two furlongs to race, could only battle on at the same pace under pressure inside the last. (5/1)
**3243 Quest Express** was soon beaten once headed. (14/1: op 8/1)
**Swift Gulliver (IRE)**, equipped with a tongue-strap, improved to dispute the lead before the straight, but weakened quickly two furlongs out and soon dropped away. He was found to be lame after. (3/1)

### 4024a TATTERSALLS BREEDERS STKS (2-Y.O)
4-00 (4-06) **6f** £73,500.00 (£28,500.00: £18,500.00: £8,500.00)

SP RR SF
3247* **Miss Stamper (IRE)** (RHannon) **2-8-7** DHarrison (mid div: hdwy over 2f out: led wl over 1f out: qcknd clr) ...— **1** 3/1$^{1}$ 103 45
3502* **Paddy Lad (IRE)** (RGuest) **2-8-10** PBloomfield (sn prom stands' side: led 2f out: hdd wl over 1f out: kpt on)...3 **2** 16/1 98 40
3321$^{2}$ **Pelham (IRE)** (RHannon) **2-8-10** WJO'Connor (mid div & rdn ½-wy: r.o fnl 2f: nrst fin) ...2½ **3** 10/1$^{3}$ 91 33
**Fairy Song (IRE)** (CO'Brien,Ireland) **2-8-7b**$^{1}$ NGMcCullagh (mid div ½-wy: hmpd 2f out: swtchd rt: edgd lft u.p early fnl f: r.o) ...nk **4** 12/1 88 30
**Melleray (IRE)** (APO'Brien,Ireland) **2-8-8**$^{ow1}$ CRoche (prom: led far side over 2f out: rdn & kpt on) ...nk **5** 3/1$^{1}$ 88 29
3620$^{2}$ **Mujova (IRE)** (RHollinshead) **2-8-10** SCraine (cl up far side: kpt on u.p last 2f) ...1½ **6** 14/1 86 28
**Keeping The Faith (IRE)** (TCarmody,Ireland) **2-8-7b**$^{1}$ RMBurke (mid div & rdn ½-wy: kpt on fnl 2f: nvr nrr) ....1 **7** 14/1 80 22
**Distinctly West (IRE)** (APO'Brien,Ireland) **2-8-10** JAHeffernan (chsd ldrs stands' side: hmpd 2f out: sltly hmpd jst ins fnl f: r.o) ...nk **8** 20/1 82 24
**Treasure Hill (IRE)** (KPrendergast,Ireland) **2-8-10** GMMoylan (towards rr appr ½-wy: kpt on fnl 2f: nvr nrr) ..nk **9** 33/1 82 24
**Thats Logic (IRE)** (DHassett,Ireland) **2-8-10** DPMcDonogh (sn rdn: mid div ½-wy: kpt on fnl f) ...hd **10** 33/1 81 23
**Gunfire (IRE)** (DGillespie,Ireland) **2-8-10** MJKinane (led far side tl over 2f out) ...hd **11** 6/1$^{2}$ 81 23
**Blue Jazz (IRE)** (MJGrassick,Ireland) **2-8-7** JJBehan (bhd: hdwy u.p after ½-wy: nvr nr to chal) ...s.h **12** 50/1 78 20
**Sherabi (IRE)** (APO'Brien,Ireland) **2-8-7** RTFitzpatrick (racd centre: nvr trbld ldrs) ...s.h **13** 20/1 78 20
**West Side Story** (CO'Brien,Ireland) **2-8-10** WJSupple (led stands' side after 2f to 2f out: sn btn) ...1½ **14** 16/1 77 19

| | Horse (Trainer) Age-Wt Jockey (comment) | Dist | Pos | SP | RR | SF |
|---|---|---|---|---|---|---|
| 3160[3] | **Top of The Form (IRE)** (MJohnston) **2-8-7** JReid (racd centre tl jnd stands' side ½-wy: in tch 2f out: wknd over 1f out) | s.h | **15** | 12/1 | 74 | 16 |
| | **Sandomierz (IRE)** (JSBolger,Ireland) **2-8-7** KJManning (towards rr stands' side ½-wy: nt clr run & swtchd rt wl over 1f out: n.d) | 1 | **16** | 14/1 | 71 | 13 |
| 3659* | **Kaiser Kache (IRE)** (KMcAuliffe) **2-8-10** PJSmullen (chsd ldrs stands' side: n.d fr ½-wy) | ½ | **17** | 20/1 | 73 | 15 |
| 3230[2] | **Falls O'Moness (IRE)** (KRBurke) **2-8-7b[1]** AWhelan (sn jnd stands' side: prom to ½-wy: sn wknd: n.d whn hmpd ins fnl f) | 1 | **18** | 25/1 | 67 | 9 |
| 3411[2] | **Jack Flush (IRE)** (BSRothwell) **2-8-10** MFenton (chsd ldrs stands' side: n.d fr ½-wy) | hd | **19** | 25/1 | 70 | 12 |
| | **Binneas (IRE)** (MKauntze,Ireland) **2-8-7** WJSmith (mid div: u.p ½-wy: n.d) | ½ | **20** | 33/1 | 65 | 7 |
| 3224[5] | **Ballymote** (JBerry) **2-8-10** KDarley (led stands' side 2f: in tch tl wknd fr 2f out) | nk | **21** | 25/1 | 68 | 10 |
| | **Tropical Lass (IRE)** (MJGrassick,Ireland) **2-8-7** EAhern (in tch far side: c centre bef ½-wy: n.d) | s.h | **22** | 50/1 | 64 | 6 |
| | **Amocachi (IRE)** (MissITOakes,Ireland) **2-8-10** JPMurtagh (sn rdn & in tch: c centre: u.p ½-wy: sn n.d) | 1 | **23** | 50/1 | 65 | 7 |
| 3454[2] | **Ciro's Pearl (IRE)** (MHTompkins) **2-8-7** RPrice (mid div: rdn appr ½-wy: n.d) | ¾ | **24** | 16/1 | 60 | 2 |
| 3687[9] | **Imperial Or Metric (IRE)** (JBerry) **2-8-10** GCoogan (s.s: a bhd) | s.h | **25** | 50/1 | 63 | 5 |
| | **Kenaftor (IRE)** (BTevels,Belgium) **2-8-10b[1]** RVindevogel (sn in tch stands' side: wkng whn drifted lft 2f out) | ¾ | **26** | 20/1 | 61 | 3 |
| 3620[4] | **Bollero (IRE)** (JBerry) **2-8-7** JoannaMorgan (in tch far side tl wknd over 2f out) | 1 | **27** | 33/1 | 55 | — |
| | **Broken Innate (IRE)** (BTevels,Belgium) **2-8-9**ow2 CDehens (n.d fr ½-wy) | 5 | **28** | 20/1 | 44 | — |
| | **Forlorn Point (IRE)** (APO'Brien,Ireland) **2-8-7** FrancesCrowley (sn wl bhd) | hd | **29** | 40/1 | 41 | — |
| | **Elinor Dashwood (IRE)** (PJFlynn,Ireland) **2-8-7** DJO'Donohoe (n.d: eased fnl f) | ½ | **30** | 33/1 | 40 | — |
| | | | | (SP 186.7%) | **30 Rn** | |

**1m 13.7** (3.20) OWNER J B R Leisure Ltd (MARLBOROUGH) BRED Eamon O'Mahony

**3247* Miss Stamper (IRE)** did not have all that clear a passage early on, but she worked her way to the front just under a furlong and a half out and soon quickened up nicely to go well clear inside the last. She can certainly step up with some confidence into either listed or Group company, and she gets this trip well. (3/1: op 2/1)

**3502* Paddy Lad (IRE)** hit the front on the stands' side two furlongs out, but was readily outpaced by the winner, although keeping on to be a very creditable runner-up. (16/1)

**3321 Pelham (IRE)** ran on to some purpose over the last furlong and a half to be nearest at the finish. (10/1)

**Fairy Song (IRE)**, from her number-one draw, encountered traffic problems two furlongs out. Switched, she edged left again under pressure inside the last, but still ran on to some purpose. (12/1)

**Melleray (IRE)**, well supported, had no chance from her draw on the far side, although racing prominently until over a furlong out. (3/1: op 6/1)

**3620 Mujova (IRE)** kept on nicely over the last two furlongs without ever looking likely to win. He finished second on the far side, only beaten over there by the well-backed joint-favourite, so this has to go down as a very good effort, and he is one to follow. (14/1)

**3160 Top of The Form (IRE)** elected to come up the middle of the track and made her way over to join the stands'-side group at halfway. (12/1: op 8/1)

**3659* Kaiser Kache (IRE)** was close up behind the leaders on the stands' side until weakening before halfway. (20/1)

**3230 Falls O'Moness (IRE)** came over to the stands' side and was prominent to halfway. She was out of contention when hampered inside the last. (25/1)

**3411 Jack Flush (IRE)** chased the leaders on the stands' side until getting outpaced from halfway. (25/1)

**3224 Ballymote** disputed it up the stands' side early on, but was a spent force from two furlongs out. (25/1)

**3454 Ciro's Pearl (IRE)** was not a threat from halfway. (16/1)

**3462 Imperial Or Metric (IRE)** came out slowly from the stalls and was always behind. (50/1)

**3620 Bollero (IRE)** stayed in touch with the leaders on the far side until weakening over two furlongs out. (33/1)

## 4026a CURRAGH H'CAP (0-110) (3-Y.O+)

5-00 (5-02) **1m 2f** £13,000.00 (£3,800.00: £1,800.00: £600.00)

| | Horse (Trainer) Age-Wt Jockey (comment) | Dist | Pos | SP | RR | SF |
|---|---|---|---|---|---|---|
| | **Hill Society (IRE)** (NMeade,Ireland) **4-7-1**(8) DPMcDonogh (led: 6l clr ½-wy: edgd lft over 1f out: r.o wl) | — | 1 | 9/1 | 82 | 41 |
| | **Escrito (USA)** (DKWeld,Ireland) **3-8-8b** MJKinane (chsd wnr: 3rd st: sn rdn: kpt on: no imp) | 5 | 2 | 6/1[3] | 95 | 46 |
| 3125[9] | **Special Dawn (IRE)** (JLDunlop) **6-8-9** JReid (towards rr: hdwy 2f out: r.o fnl f: nrst fin) | ½ | 3 | 8/1 | 87 | 46 |
| | **Graduated (IRE)** (JSBolger,Ireland) **4-8-8** KJManning (cl up: 3rd ½-wy: 2nd st: rdn over 1f out: kpt on same pce) | 1 | 4 | 5/1[2] | 85 | 44 |
| 2825a[3] | **Sheraka (IRE)** (JOxx,Ireland) **3-9-1** JPMurtagh (in tch: 4th ½-wy: 5th st: rdn & sme hdwy 2f out: no imp fr over 1f out) | s.h | 5 | 5/2[1] | 100 | 51 |
| | **Grief (IRE)** (JOxx,Ireland) **3-7-11** WJSmith (in tch: 5th ½-wy: 4th st: effrt 2f out: one pce) | s.h | 6 | 7/1 | 81 | 32 |
| | **Wood Leopard (USA)** (CO'Brien,Ireland) **4-8-2** 5x NGMcCullagh (hld up in rr: rdn & kpt on fnl 2f: nvr able to chal) | ¾ | 7 | 7/1 | 77 | 36 |
| | **Inchacooley (IRE)** (MBrassil,Ireland) **4-8-8** SCraine (hld up: 6th st: no imp fnl 2f) | 4½ | 8 | 8/1 | 76 | 35 |
| 1249a[6] | **Rescue Time (IRE)** (KPrendergast,Ireland) **3-7-12b[1]** WJSupple (bhd: n.d) | ¾ | 9 | 12/1 | 73 | 24 |
| 2459a[5] | **Nayil** (KPrendergast,Ireland) **4-8-4**(6) GMMoylan (hld up: 6th ½-wy: lost pl appr st: n.d fnl 2f) | 1½ | 10 | 14/1 | 74 | 33 |
| | | | | (SP 131.1%) | **10 Rn** | |

**2m 8.7** (4.70) OWNER P. Garvey (NAVAN)

**Hill Society (IRE)**, bounced out in front, was clear at halfway and, despite edging left with over a furlong to race, was always in complete control. (9/1)

**Escrito (USA)**, always aware of the winner's front-running ability, chased that one, but could not get on terms. (6/1: op 4/1)

**2742 Special Dawn (IRE)**, well behind until making headway from two furlongs out, ran on inside the last to be nearest at the finish. There might be a race for him this season. (8/1)

## 4027a ANGLESEY STKS (Gp 3) (2-Y.O)

5-30 (5-30) **6f** £16,250.00 (£4,750.00: £2,250.00: £750.00)

| | Horse (Trainer) Age-Wt Jockey (comment) | Dist | Pos | SP | RR | SF |
|---|---|---|---|---|---|---|
| | **Air Of Distinction (IRE)** (APO'Brien,Ireland) **2-8-7** JAHeffernan (a.p: led 1f out: r.o u.p) | — | 1 | 9/2[3] | 79 | — |
| 3018a[5] | **Sharemono (USA)** (APO'Brien,Ireland) **2-8-10** CRoche (hld up: swtchd rt 2f out: effrt to disp ld briefly over 1f out: sn rdn: no ex) | 1½ | 2 | 9/2[3] | 78 | — |
| 2470a[3] | **Quws** (KPrendergast,Ireland) **2-8-10** WJSupple (led tl over 1f out: kpt on same pce) | 1½ | 3 | 7/4[2] | 74 | — |
| 3561a[6] | **Azra (IRE)** (JSBolger,Ireland) **2-8-7** KJManning (disp ld: 2nd ½-wy: sn u.p: no imp over 1f out: kpt on nr fin) | ½ | 4 | 6/4[1] | 70 | — |
| | | | | (SP 112.7%) | **4 Rn** | |

**1m 18.0** (7.50) OWNER Mrs John Magnier (PILTOWN)

**IN-FOCUS: This looked a very below par Group Three with little confidence in any of the four runners. In the absence of any serious pace, the form should not be taken at face value.**

**Air Of Distinction (IRE)** came through between horses to lead a furlong out, and ran on willingly enough under pressure. (9/2)
**Sharemono (USA)** made his bid on the outer to dispute it briefly a furlong out, but found little. (9/2: op 3/1)
**2470a Quws** led and disputed the lead until over a furlong out before finding only one pace. (7/4)
**3018a* Azra (IRE)**, desperately weak in the market, was in second place and under pressure at halfway. She looked like dropping right out, but was going on again towards the end. A pair of blinkers might change her attitude. (6/4)
NR

## 3913a-BADEN-BADEN (Germany) (L-H) (Good)
### Tuesday August 27th

### 4028a OETTIGEN-RENNEN (Gp 3) (3-Y.O+)
3-25 (3-30) **1m** £33,784.00 (£13,514.00: £6,757.00: £3,604.00)

| | | | | SP | RR | SF |
|---|---|---|---|---|---|---|
| 3395a3 | **La Blue (GER)** (BSchutz,Germany) **3-8-6** AStarke | — | 1 | | 118 | — |
| 2843a7 | **Sinyar** (BSchutz,Germany) **4-9-2** THellier | ½ | 2 | | 121 | — |
| 2843a3 | **Mill King (GER)** (HBlume,Germany) **3-8-6** ASuborics | 2½ | 3 | | 112 | — |
| 3905a9 | **Silca Blanka (IRE)** (MRChannon) **4-8-9** WNewnes (btn over 5½l) | | 6 | | — | — |
| 3072* | **Yeast** (WJHaggas) **4-9-0** RCochrane (btn over 8l) | | 8 | | — | — |

**9 Rn**

**1m 36.78** TOTE 38DM: 18DM 28DM 20DM OWNER Gestut Wittekindshof BRED Gestut Wittekindshof
**3395a La Blue (GER)**, who ran so well against Timarida and Germany in Munich, franked the form. Although she stays further, she seems best at this trip.
**3905a Silca Blanka (IRE)** raced at the rear of the field. Asked for an effort three furlongs out, he could not quicken.
**3072* Yeast** was prominent early on in the race, but was ridden and beaten over two furlongs out.

## 3914a-DEAUVILLE (France) (R-H) (Good to soft)
### Tuesday August 27th

### 4029a PRIX DU HARAS DE LA HUDERIE (Listed) (2-Y.O C & G)
2-25 (2-23) **7f** £18,445.00 (£6,324.00: £3,953.00: £2,055.00)

| | | | | SP | RR | SF |
|---|---|---|---|---|---|---|
| 3032a2 | **Alpha Plus (USA)** (AFabre,France) **2-9-2** TJarnet | — | 1 | | 95 | — |
| 3150* | **Papua** (IABalding) **2-9-2** LDettori | ¾ | 2 | | 93 | — |
| | **Speedfriend (GER)** (RCollet,France) **2-9-2** SGuillot | 2½ | 3 | | 88 | — |

**7 Rn**

**1m 27.1** (3.10) P-M 1.90F: 1.10F 1.60F OWNER Mr K. Abdullah (CHANTILLY)
**3150* Papua** put up a decent performance. Making the early running and then settling just off the pace, he challenged from two furlongs out, but hung left in the closing stages. A tough sort whose two wins have been on much faster ground, he was beaten by a decent horse, and looks up to winning a listed race.

### 4030a PRIX QUINCEY (Gp 3) (3-Y.O+)
3-30 (3-30) **1m** £28,986.00 (£10,540.00: £5,270.00: £2,635.00)

| | | | | SP | RR | SF |
|---|---|---|---|---|---|---|
| | **Rising Colours** (PDemercastel,France) **3-8-8** AJunk | — | 1 | | 112 | — |
| | **Trojan Sea (USA)** (DSmaga,France) **5-9-0** DBoeuf | nk | 2 | | 111 | — |
| 1141a6 | **Barricade (USA)** (AFabre,France) **3-8-10** TJarnet | 1 | 3 | | 111 | — |
| 3033a3 | **Royal Philosopher** (JWHills) **4-9-2** OPeslier | 1½ | 4 | | 108 | — |

**7 Rn**

**1m 38.9** (2.90) P-M 6.20F: 3.60F 3.60F OWNER N. Pharaon BRED Naji Pharaon
**Rising Colours**, held up until bursting through to lead a furlong from home, held on well in the closing stages, and is clearly on the upgrade. He is likely to be seen next in the Prix du Rond-Point during Arc weekend.
**Trojan Sea (USA)** put in a determined challenge from the furlong marker, but could not peg back the winner.
**Barricade (USA)** was putting in his best work at the finish. He is still trying to find his feet in Group class, but a listed race should come his way.
**3033a Royal Philosopher** appreciated the underfoot conditions. Up with the pace throughout, he got serious two furlongs from home and, when headed a furlong out, could only keep on at one pace. He may prefer a turning track.

### 4031a PRIX MICHEL HOUYVET (Listed) (3-Y.O)
4-00 (3-58) **1m 5f 110y** £18,445.00 (£6,324.00: £3,953.00: £2,055.00)

| | | | | SP | RR | SF |
|---|---|---|---|---|---|---|
| | **Baddamix (FR)** (JEHammond,France) **3-9-2** CAsmussen | — | 1 | | 108 | — |
| | **Alexandre Farnese (FR)** (JdeRoualle,France) **3-9-2** GMosse | s.h | 2 | | 108 | — |
| | **Porto Novo (FR)** (PBary,France) **3-9-2b1** OPeslier | 5 | 3 | | 102 | — |
| 28864 | **Alzabella (IRE)** (JWHills) **3-8-13** LDettori | ½ | 4 | | 98 | — |

**5 Rn**

**3m 4.3** (12.30) P-M 2.40F: 1.70F 1.60F OWNER D. Thompson (CHANTILLY) BRED SNC Lagardere Elevage
**2886 Alzabella (IRE)**, stepping up in trip, led in the early stages. She was one-paced in the last two and a half furlongs, but is consistent and genuine at this level.

## 4028a-BADEN-BADEN (Germany) (L-H) (Good)
### Wednesday August 28th

### 4032a BADENER STEHER CUP (Listed) (3-Y.O+)
2-10 (2-12) **2m** £22,522.00 (£9,009.00: £5,405.00: £3,604.00)

| | | | | SP | RR | SF |
|---|---|---|---|---|---|---|
| 1752a* | **Camp David (GER)** (AWohler,Germany) **6-9-7** ABoschert | — | 1 | | 116 | — |

| | | | SP | RR | SF |
|---|---|---|---|---|---|
| 3531a* | **Lord Jim (IRE)** (LordHuntingdon) **4-9-3b** DHarrison ....4 | **2** | | 108 | — |
| 1054a[2] | **Flamingo Paradise** (HBlume,Germany) **5-9-7** ASuborics ....nk | **3** | | 112 | — |
| 2117[3] | **Old Rouvel (USA)** (DJGMurraySmith) **5-9-1b** RHughes (btn approx 23½l) .... | **6** | | — | — |

**7 Rn**

**3m 26.97** TOTE 18DM: 13DM 19DM 18DM OWNER D. Gabel BRED Frau & I. Brunotte
**1752a* Camp David (GER)** continued in good form with another easy win, and currently looks to be Germany's best stayer.
**3531a* Lord Jim (IRE)** made the early running, but was under strong pressure when headed approaching the final furlong, and could not respond to the winner's challenge.
**2117 Old Rouvel (USA)** raced in third until three furlongs out before weakening quickly.

## 4033a JACOBS GOLDENE PEITSCHE (Gp 2) (3-Y.O+)
3-25 (3-28) **6f** £56,306.00 (£22,523.00: £11,261.00: £7,207.00)

| | | | SP | RR | SF |
|---|---|---|---|---|---|
| 3562a* | **Daring Destiny** (KRBurke) **5-8-12b** RHughes (s.s: bhd to ½-wy: str run fnl f to ld cl home) ....— | **1** | | 118 | — |
| 3708[3] | **Hever Golf Rose** (TJNaughton) **5-8-12** PatEddery (led: clr ½-wy: ct cl home)....s.h | **2** | | 118 | — |
| 3573a[6] | **A Magicman (FR)** (HSteguweit,Germany) **4-9-2** AHelfenbein (hld up: r.o wl fnl 2f: nvr nrr)....1¼ | **3** | | 119 | — |
| | **Glenlivet (SWE)** (LKelp,Sweden) **8-9-2** KWoodburn (in rr: kpt on fnl 2f: nrst fin)....1¾ | **4** | | 114 | — |
| 3572a[2] | **Waky Nao** (HBlume,Germany) **3-8-12** ASuborics (trckd ldrs tl wknd 1f out)....3½ | **5** | | 104 | — |
| 1945a[3] | **Munaaji (USA)** (AWohler,Germany) **5-9-2** ABoschert (prom: ev ch 2f out: wknd)....1½ | **6** | | 101 | — |
| | **Senador (IRE)** (Germany) **4-9-2** SusanneBerneklint (chsd ldr: btn 2f out) ....2 | **7** | | 95 | — |
| | **Never Come Back (GER)** (Germany) **3-8-12** ABest (chsd ldrs to ½-wy: sn btn)....2½ | **8** | | 88 | — |
| 3394a[2] | **Sharp Prod (USA)** (Germany) **6-9-2** PSchiergen (spd 3f)....6 | **9** | | 73 | — |

**9 Rn**

**1m 10.21** TOTE 163DM: 31DM 13DM 19DM OWNER Mrs A. E. M. Wright (WANTAGE) BRED Mrs Ann E. M. Wright
**3562a* Daring Destiny** was slowly away and raced towards the rear until halfway. Hughes persuaded the mare to produce a strong run inside the final furlong to take the lead close home. She is likely to run next in the Diadem Stakes, but her long-term target is the International Bowl at Sha Tin in December.
**3708 Hever Golf Rose** made the early running and was clear at halfway. Unfortunately, this tough mare was caught in the final strides to record her fourth second place of the year. She may run in the Haydock Park Sprint Cup, but has an alternative in the Taby Open Sprint in Stockholm, which she won last year.
**2843a A Magicman (FR)** came back in trip for this race and, although he ran on well in the closing stages, he found the principals too quick.

# BORDEAUX (France) (R-H) (Good)
## Wednesday August 28th

## 4034a CRITERIUM DU BEQUET (Listed) (2-Y.O)
3-50 (3-51) **6f** £15,810.00 (£5,270.00: £2,635.00: £1,318.00)

| | | | SP | RR | SF |
|---|---|---|---|---|---|
| | **Griega (IRE)** (CLaffon-Parias,France) **2-8-6** FSanchez ....— | **1** | | — | — |
| | **Little Kris (FR)** (DSoubagne,France) **2-8-12b[1]** CNora ....1½ | **2** | | — | — |
| 3590[4] | **Sous Le Nez** (RGuest) **2-8-6** PBloomfield ....3 | **3** | | — | — |
| 3164[2] | **Dalmeny Dancer** (BJMeehan) **2-8-9** BDoyle (btn over 6l).... | **5** | | — | — |

**8 Rn**

**No Time Taken** P-M 1.90F: 1.50F 1.70F 3.80F (12.80F) OWNER Mr F. Hinojosa (CHANTILLY) BRED Leo Collins
**3590 Sous Le Nez** came here to get black type against her name, and completed the task successfully.
**3164 Dalmeny Dancer** would have appreciated the ground, but his only win was over five furlongs, and he may have struggled at this trip.

# 4032a-BADEN-BADEN (Germany) (L-H) (Good)
## Friday August 30th

## 4035a MOET & CHANDON-RENNEN (Gp 2) (2-Y.O)
3-25 (3-26) **6f** £45,045.00 (£18,018.00: £9,009.00: £4,505.00)

| | | | SP | RR | SF |
|---|---|---|---|---|---|
| 3561a[2] | **Muchea** (MRChannon) **2-9-2** RHughes (hld up: n.m.r 2f out: qcknd wl to ld ins fnl f: comf) ....— | **1** | | 102 | — |
| 3843[2] | **Omaha City (IRE)** (BGubby) **2-9-2** WNewnes (a.p: led ½-wy tl ins fnl f: no ex) ....1½ | **2** | | 98 | — |
| 3390a[2] | **Dyhim Diamond (IRE)** (CLaffon-Parias,France) **2-9-2** FSanchez (a.p: ev ch 2f out: nt qckn) ....1 | **3** | | 95 | — |
| 3396a* | **Shy Lady (FR)** (BSchutz,Germany) **2-8-12** AStarke (hld up: no ex fr 2f out)....6 | **4** | | 75 | — |
| | **Alte Kunst (IRE)** (Germany) **2-8-12** ABest (prom to ½-wy: sn btn) ....nk | **5** | | 75 | — |
| | **Kasamir (GER)** (Germany) **2-9-2** THellier (led to ½-wy)....8 | **6** | | 57 | — |

**6 Rn**

**1m 10.58** TOTE 19DM: 16DM 32DM OWNER Albion Investments Ltd (UPPER LAMBOURN) BRED Lady Richard Wellesley
**3561a Muchea** was held up and found little room two furlongs out, but was able to quicken into the lead inside the final furlong to score a comfortable victory. He has picked up place money in some good races recently, and thoroughly deserved to win this Group Two.
**3843 Omaha City (IRE)** was always prominent and took the lead at the halfway mark until headed inside the final furlong, from which point he could find no extra.

## 4036a PREIS DER STADT BADEN-BADEN (Listed) (3-Y.O+)
4-35 (4-35) **1m 2f** £18,018.00 (£7,207.00: £4,505.00: £2,703.00)

| | | | SP | RR | SF |
|---|---|---|---|---|---|
| | **Metaxas** (HRemmert,Germany) **3-8-4** ABrockhausen ....— | **1** | | 95 | — |
| | **Silver Blade (FR)** (AWohler,Germany) **3-8-2** EDubravka ....1¼ | **2** | | 91 | — |
| 3691[8] | **Hoh Express** (IABalding) **4-9-6** RHughes ....nk | **3** | | 101 | — |
| 4028a[6] | **Silca Blanka (IRE)** (MRChannon) **4-9-2** KWoodburn (btn approx 8l) .... | **8** | | — | — |

**9 Rn**

**2m 4.81** TOTE 82DM: 24DM 31DM 22DM OWNER J. Erhadt BRED Whitsbury Manor Stud
**3691 Hoh Express**, waited with, made good headway from three furlongs out. He had every chance a furlong out, but began to hang left and could find no more in the closing stages.

**4028a Silca Blanka (IRE)**, having his second race in four days, raced in mid-division. He lost his place four furlongs out and was unable to recover.

## 3029a-**EVRY (France)** (R-H) (Good)
### Friday August 30th

### 4037a PRIX DE MEREVILLE CLAIMING (2-Y.O F)
2-20 (2-23) **7f** £7,905.00

| | Horse | Dist | Pos | SP | RR | SF |
|---|---|---|---|---|---|---|
| | **Blue Danish** (CBoutin,France) **2-8-7** MBoutin | — | 1 | | 75 | — |
| | **Helette** (France) **2-8-10** TGillet | 2 | 2 | | 73 | — |
| | **Sister Chouchou (FR)** (France) **2-8-7** BMarchand | s.nk | 3 | | 70 | — |
| 3343* | **Jay-Gee-Em** (JParkes) **2-9-0** SHamel (btn over 10¼l) | | 11 | | — | — |

**17 Rn**

**1m 27.62** (3.32) P-M 6.80F: 2.20F 2.40F 3.20F (17.30F)
OWNER C. Boutin BRED W. L. Caley
**3343* Jay-Gee-Em**, who raced in mid-division, was at the rear of the field turning into the straight and, from then on, she was struggling.

## 3917a-**SAN SIRO (Milan, Italy)** (R-H) (Soft)
### Saturday August 31st

### 4038a PREMIO VERGOBBIO (2-Y.O C & G)
4-15 **7f 110y** £12,180.00

| | Horse | Dist | Pos | SP | RR | SF |
|---|---|---|---|---|---|---|
| | **Sopran Glasik** (GVerricelli,Italy) **2-9-0** SDettori | — | 1 | | — | — |
| | **Bacchereto (IRE)** (Italy) **2-9-0** MEsposito | ¾ | 2 | | — | — |
| | **Sunny Sample (IRE)** (Italy) **2-9-0** GForte | 6¾ | 3 | | — | — |
| | **Yavlensky (IRE)** (JLDunlop) **2-9-0** FJovine (btn approx 13¼l) | | 9 | | — | — |

**11 Rn**

**1m 35.5** (11.00) TOTE 102L: 34L 39L 58L (582L) OWNER Qualin Stable BRED Az. Agr. San Uberto
**Yavlensky (IRE)** produced a very disappointing performance. This son of Caerleon soon dropped to the rear and was behind for the final four furlongs.

### 4039a PREMIO MENAGGIO (2-Y.O F)
4-40 **7f 110y** £10,150.00 (£4,466.00)

| | Horse | Dist | Pos | SP | RR | SF |
|---|---|---|---|---|---|---|
| | **Ronken (IRE)** (GMaggi,Italy) **2-8-11** EBotti | — | 1 | | — | — |
| 2666a* | **Folgore (USA)** (JLDunlop) **2-8-9** GForte | 1½ | 2 | | — | — |
| | **Scorribanda (ITY)** (Italy) **2-9-0** MEsposito | 2¾ | 3 | | — | — |

**6 Rn**

**1m 35.4** (10.90) TOTE 44L: 19L 17L (60L) OWNER Scuderia Gabriella BRED Az. Agr. San Jore
**2666a* Folgore (USA)** dwelt at the start, and was in the rear as the field turned into the home straight. Hard ridden from over two furlongs out, she kept on well but was never able to get on terms with the winner.

## 4035a-**BADEN-BADEN (Germany)** (L-H) (Good)
### Sunday September 1st

### 4040a MERCEDES-BENZ GROSSER PREIS VON BADEN (Gp 1) (3-Y.O+)
3-45 (3-51) **1m 4f** £146,396.00 (£58,559.00: £29,279.00: £13,513.00)

| | Horse | Dist | Pos | SP | RR | SF |
|---|---|---|---|---|---|---|
| 3728a* | **Pilsudski (IRE)** (MRStoute) **4-9-6** WRSwinburn (trckd ldrs: cl 5th st: hrd rdn over 1f out: led wl ins fnl f) | — | 1 | | 126 | — |
| 3395a2 | **Germany (USA)** (BSchutz,Germany) **5-9-6** LDettori (led: hrd rdn over 1f out: ct wl ins fnl f) | ¾ | 2 | | 125 | — |
| 3567a2 | **Sunshack** (AFabre,France) **5-9-6** SGuillot (hld up mid div: 4th st: chal 2f out: ev ch ins fnl f: no ex) | 1¾ | 3 | | 123 | — |
| 25465 | **Definite Article** (DKWeld,Ireland) **4-9-6** MJKinane (hld up: 6th st: hrd rdn & hung lft over 1f out: styd on one pce) | 1¼ | 4 | | 121 | — |
| 3574a4 | **Agnelli** (HJentzsch,Germany) **3-8-9** PSchiergen (hld up: last st: effrt whn sltly hmpd over 1f out: no ex) | 2½ | 5 | | 116 | — |
| 3203a3 | **Protektor (GER)** (ALowe,Germany) **7-9-6** THellier (hdwy on ins 4f out: 3rd st: ev ch 2f out: sn btn) | 1½ | 6 | | 116 | — |
| 2480a3 | **Poliglote** (MmeCHead,France) **4-9-6** FHead (trckd ldr pllng hrd: 2nd st: sn hrd rdn: wknd appr fnl f) | 1 | 7 | | 114 | — |

**7 Rn**

**2m 26.74** TOTE 120DM: 21DM 13DM 14DM OWNER Lord Weinstock/Exors of late S Weinstock (NEWMARKET) BRED Ballymacoll Stud Co
**3728a* Pilsudski (IRE)** gave Swinburn his biggest success since his return from injury. He was hard ridden over a furlong out and took the lead well inside the final furlong, running on well towards the finish. His main target would seem to be the Arc and, given the improvement he has shown this year, he could be a live outsider.
**3395a Germany (USA)**, soon in front, was hard ridden over a furlong out. He ran on gamely, but could not withstand the winner's late challenge. He would have preferred a little cut in the ground, and will probably renew rivalry with the winner at Longchamp.
**3567a Sunshack**, held up in mid-division, was in fourth place turning into the straight and made his challenge two furlongs from home. With every chance inside the last, he had little in reserve to get to the leaders.
**2546 Definite Article**, held up, was in sixth place turning into the straight. Hard ridden, he began to hang left over a furlong out and could only stay on at the one pace.
**Agnelli** was in last place as the field entered the straight. Making an effort, he was slightly hampered over a furlong out and found little from then on.
**2479a* Protektor (GER)** made headway up the inside rail from four furlongs out. After having every chance two furlongs out, he was soon beaten.
**2480a Poliglote** tracked the early leader and, pulling hard, was in second place turning into the straight. However, his jockey was soon hard at work and he dropped away. He is better served by settling in front.

# 3587-HAYDOCK (L-H) (Good)
## Friday September 6th
WEATHER: fine WIND: nil

## 4041 R.N.L.I. 'SARAH EMILY HARROP' MEDIAN AUCTION MAIDEN STKS (2-Y.O) (Class E)
2-15 (2-16) **1m 30y** £3,257.50 (£985.00: £480.00: £227.50) Stalls: High GOING minus 0.59 sec per fur (F)

| Form | Horse | Dist | Pos | SP | RR | SF |
|---|---|---|---|---|---|---|
| 3423[3] | **Palio Sky** (JLDunlop) **2-9-0** TQuinn(8) (lw: chsd ldrs: led over 1f out: rdn out) | — | 1 | 11/10[1] | 80 | 18 |
| 3682[10] | **Supreme Sound** (PWHarris) **2-9-0** GHind(3) (plld hrd: led tl over 1f out: r.o) | 2 | 2 | 16/1 | 76 | 14 |
| 3485[5] | **Tirage** (CEBrittain) **2-9-0** BDoyle(4) (plld hrd: a.p: ev ch 2f out: rdn & wknd over 1f out) | 2 | 3 | 14/1[3] | 72 | 10 |
| 3595[2] | **In Question** (BWHills) **2-9-0** KFallon(2) (lw: prom: rdn 3f out: wknd 2f out) | 2 | 4 | 5/4[2] | 68 | 6 |
| 3620[5] | **Bollin Terry** (TDEasterby) **2-9-0** MBirch(9) (plld hrd: prom tl wknd 2f out) | 4 | 5 | 25/1 | 60 | — |
| | **Heart of Gold (IRE)** (MissSEHall) **2-9-0** AMcGlone(6) (w'like: leggy: unf: scope: bit bkwd: s.s: nvr nr to chal) | 3½ | 6 | 25/1 | 54+ | — |
| 3821[W] | **Presentiment** (JBerry) **2-9-0** KDarley(11) (hld up: hdwy over 3f out: wknd over 2f out) | 5 | 7 | 20/1 | 44 | — |
| 2211[8] | **Megan Carew** (DMoffatt) **2-8-6**(3) DarrenMoffatt(5) (mid div: rdn & wknd 3f out) | 1 | 8 | 50/1 | 37 | — |
| | **Welcome Home** (PTDalton) **2-8-9** LCharnock(1) (leggy: unf: bkwd: prom tl wknd 3f out) | hd | 9 | 50/1 | 37 | — |
| *2746*[8] | **Real Fire (IRE)** (MGMeagher) **2-9-0** JCarroll(12) (bhd fnl 3f) | 3½ | 10 | 33/1 | 35 | — |
| 3807[8] | **Motcombs Club** (NACallaghan) **2-9-0** SDrowne(7) (sn bhd) | nk | 11 | 20/1 | 34 | — |
| 3448[6] | **Dance Melody** (GROldroyd) **2-8-9** DaleGibson(10) (bhd fnl 4f) | s.h | 12 | 50/1 | 29 | — |
| | **Bonne Ville** (BPalling) **2-8-9** TSprake(13) (bkwd: a bhd) | ¾ | 13 | 50/1 | 27 | — |
| | **Cool Grey** (JJO'Neill) **2-8-9** JFEgan(14) (leggy: scope: bkwd: s.s: rn green: a bhd) | 2½ | 14 | 33/1 | 23 | — |

(SP 135.6%) **14 Rn**

**1m 43.94** (3.34) CSF £22.17 TOTE £2.20: £1.10 £5.00 £2.70 (£59.70) Trio £186.10 OWNER Mr J. E. Nash (ARUNDEL) BRED Montealto Stud Establishment

**3423 Palio Sky**, well backed, was more experienced this time and appreciated the extra furlong. (11/10: 6/4-Evens)

**Supreme Sound**, a half-brother to Top Cees, improved considerably on his debut. Well suited to this step up to a mile, he should soon go one better. (16/1)

**Tirage**, travelling best entering the final quarter-mile, looks to be on the upgrade. (14/1: op 8/1)

**3595 In Question** should have been suited to this longer trip and we will probably not see the best of him until next year. (5/4: op 4/5)

**3620 Bollin Terry** did not help his chances of staying a mile by taking a strong hold. (25/1)

**Heart of Gold (IRE)**, a brother to Yorkshire Cup winner Key to My Heart, should come on for this, but probably needs more time. (25/1)

## 4042 BOLLINGER CHAMPAGNE CHALLENGE SERIES GENTLEMENS' H'CAP (0-70) (3-Y.O) (Class E)
2-45 (2-46) **1m 3f 200y** £3,078.75 (£930.00: £452.50: £213.75) Stalls: Low GOING minus 0.59 sec per fur (F)

| Form | Horse | Dist | Pos | SP | RR | SF |
|---|---|---|---|---|---|---|
| 3584[2] | **Dauphin (IRE) (36)** (WJMusson) **3-9-9**ow2 MrTMcCarthy(8) (a.p: led 2f out: rdn clr 1f out: eased nr fin) | — | 1 | 7/1[3] | 49 | 29 |
| *3422*[3] | **Induna Mkubwa (47)** (CFWall) **3-10-2**(4) MrRWakley(12) (chsd ldr: led over 3f out to 2f out: one pce fnl f) | 5 | 2 | 16/1 | 53 | 35 |
| 3819* | **Ceilidh Star (IRE) (69)** (BWHills) **3-11-10b**(4) MrCBHills(7) (lw: hld up: hdwy 2f out: n.m.r 1f out: styd on) | 4 | 3 | 9/2[2] | 70 | 52 |
| 3705[2] | **Soldier Mak (60)** (AHide) **3-11-1**(4) MrVLukaniuk(5) (prom: rdn & outpcd over 3f out: btn whn edgd lft 1f out) | 1¼ | 4 | 7/1[3] | 59 | 41 |
| 3882[5] | **Arc of The Diver (IRE) (55)** (JBerry) **3-11-0b** MrRHale(10) (led over 8f: sn wknd) | 2 | 5 | 14/1 | 52 | 34 |
| 954[3] | **Siege Perilous (IRE) (66)** (SCWilliams) **3-11-11** MrPPritchard-Gordon(2) (hld up & bhd: styd on fnl 3f: n.d) | 9 | 6 | 4/1[1] | 51 | 33 |
| 3657[2] | **Atlantic Mist (60)** (BRMillman) **3-11-1**(4) MrLJefford(3) (bhd tl sme late hdwy) | 1½ | 7 | 4/1[1] | 42 | 24 |
| 3325[2] | **What Jim Wants (IRE) (39)** (JJO'Neill) **3-9-12** MrRThornton(15) (prom tl rdn & wknd over 3f out) | nk | 8 | 14/1 | 21 | 3 |
| 3918[9] | **Kingfisher Brave (64)** (MGMeagher) **3-11-5**(4) MrPMurray(4) (hdwy 8f out: rdn & wknd over 3f out) | 5 | 9 | 20/1 | 39 | 21 |
| 1498[12] | **Quiet Moments (IRE) (39)** (PGMurphy) **3-9-8**(4) MrMatthewWells(1) (a bhd) | 4 | 10 | 33/1 | 9 | — |
| 3575[4] | **Fairy Highlands (IRE) (53)** (JSHaldane) **3-10-8**(4) MrJAStack(6) (bhd fnl 3f) | 17 | 11 | 16/1 | — | — |
| 3780[15] | **Fergal (USA) (34)** (MissJFCraze) **3-9-3**(4) MrWWenyon(14) (chsd ldrs over 8f) | ¾ | 12 | 50/1 | — | — |
| | **Young Saffy (40)** (MrsMReveley) **3-9-13** MrKGoble(11) (bit bkwd: bhd fnl 3f) | 1¼ | 13 | 20/1 | — | — |
| 2591[4] | **Aren't We Lucky (IRE) (55)** (JJO'Neill) **3-10-10**(4) MrLCorcoran(13) (s.s: racd wd: p.u & dismntd 6f out: fin lame) | | P | 33/1 | — | — |

(SP 125.6%) **14 Rn**

**2m 34.12** (4.72) CSF £105.35 CT £521.95 TOTE £8.30: £2.50 £5.10 £2.10 (£138.90) Trio £165.80 OWNER Mrs Rita Brown (NEWMARKET) BRED Patrick H. Dillon

LONG HANDICAP Fergal (USA) 9-5

STEWARDS' ENQUIRY Wells susp. 16-17/9/96 (excessive use of whip).

**OFFICIAL EXPLANATION Aren't We Lucky (IRE): the jockey reported that the colt had lost his action on the bend and he had felt it prudent to pull him up.**

**3584 Dauphin (IRE)** had given notice he was finding his form last time and, including overweight, defied a 4lb higher mark. (7/1)

**3422 Induna Mkubwa** ran his best race to date, but could not cope with the winner. (16/1)

**3819* Ceilidh Star (IRE)**, 2lb higher than when last in a handicap, never threatened the two principals in the home straight. (9/2)

**3705 Soldier Mak** needs more give underfoot. (7/1)

**3882 Arc of The Diver (IRE)** will need more patient tactics to get this sort of distance. (14/1)

**954 Siege Perilous (IRE)** should be sharper for this first outing for four months. (4/1)

**3657 Atlantic Mist** never seemed likely to take a hand. (4/1)

## 4043 E.B.F. VOLVO S40 MAIDEN STKS (2-Y.O) (Class D)
3-15 (3-19) **5f** £3,785.50 (£1,144.00: £557.00: £263.50) Stalls: Low GOING minus 0.59 sec per fur (F)

| Form | Horse | Dist | Pos | SP | RR | SF |
|---|---|---|---|---|---|---|
| 3494[4] | **Hattab (IRE)** (PTWalwyn) **2-9-0** TSprake(12) (chsd ldr: led 1f out: r.o wl) | — | 1 | 13/2 | 84 | 32 |
| 3429[3] | **Fruitana (IRE) (81)** (JBerry) **2-9-0** JCarroll(14) (led 4f: wknd nr fin) | 3½ | 2 | 13/2 | 73 | 21 |
| 3853[2] | **Caution** (MrsJRRamsden) **2-8-9** KFallon(6) (rdn & hdwy 2f out: r.o ins fnl f) | ¾ | 3 | 7/2[2] | 65 | 13 |
| | **Danetime (IRE)** (NACallaghan) **2-8-11**(3) FLynch(8) (w'like: a.p: one pce fnl 2f) | ½ | 4 | 2/1[1] | 69 | 17 |
| | **Alvilde** (JRFanshawe) **2-8-9** DHarrison(5) (neat: unf: s.s: hdwy fnl 2f: r.o) | 1¾ | 5 | 8/1 | 58 | 6 |
| | **Trailblazer** (CWThornton) **2-9-0** DeanMcKeown(4) (bkwd: outpcd: staying on whn n.m.r over 1f out) | 1½ | 6 | 33/1 | 58+ | 6 |
| 3581[2] | **Batsman** (WJMusson) **2-9-0** AMcGlone(11) (b: nvr nr to chal) | 2½ | 7 | 10/1 | 50 | — |
| 3128[5] | **Effervescence (80)** (RHannon) **2-9-0** DaneO'Neill(9) (lw: outpcd fr ½-wy) | 1¼ | 8 | 9/2[3] | 46 | — |

| | Horse | Dist | Pos | SP | RR | SF |
|---|---|---|---|---|---|---|
| | **La Dolce Vita** (TDBarron) **2-8-9** JFanning(13) (lengthy: bit bkwd: s.s: sme hdwy over 2f out: wknd over 1f out) | hd | **9** | 25/1 | 41 | — |
| 2879$^{14}$ | **Expectation (IRE)** (PRWebber) **2-8-9** KDarley(3) (outpcd fr ½-wy) | 1½ | **10** | 14/1 | 36 | — |
| 3853$^{7}$ | **Sparkling Harry** (MissLCSiddall) **2-9-0** GHind(10) (racd wd: outpcd fr ½-wy) | 2½ | **11** | 33/1 | 33 | — |
| 3879$^{6}$ | **Miss Fugit Penance** (PDEvans) **2-8-9** JFEgan(2) (spd over 2f) | ¾ | **12** | 33/1 | 26 | — |
| 3502$^{9}$ | **Tukapa** (MrsALMKing) **2-9-0** SDrowne(7) (swtg: unruly s: a bhd) | 1 | **13** | 33/1 | 28 | — |
| 3792$^{6}$ | **Anokato (69)** (KTIvory) **2-9-0** CScally(1) (chsd ldrs over 2f) | ½ | **14** | 16/1 | 26 | — |

(SP 148.8%) **14 Rn**

**60.16 secs** (0.96) CSF £55.04 TOTE £8.50: £2.40 £1.80 £2.00 (£11.90) Trio £24.20 OWNER Mr Hamdan Al Maktoum (LAMBOURN) BRED Shadwell Estate Company Limited

**3494 Hattab (IRE)**, a half-brother to Marjaana and Intiaash, showed plenty of speed, and looked a different animal over the minimum trip. (13/2)
**3429 Fruitana (IRE)** soon had all bar the winner in trouble, but barely gets even this trip. (13/2)
**3853 Caution**, a half-sister to Fairywings, can get off the mark over an extra furlong. (7/2)
**Danetime (IRE)**, a half-brother to a juvenile winner in Ireland, was strongly supported in the Ring. Not seeming to stride out on this ground, which was probably on the fast side, he deserves another chance. (2/1)
**Alvilde** will know more next time and shaped as though she will do better when tackling further. (8/1: 6/1-10/1)
**Trailblazer**, a 30,000 guinea half-brother to several winners, did not look fit enough to do himself justice and was taken off his legs for much of the trip. Improvement can be expected, but he will need further. (33/1)

## 4044 ROYAL BANK OF SCOTLAND LIMITED STKS (0-80) (3-Y.O) (Class D)

3-50 (3-50) **6f** £3,597.00 (£1,086.00: £528.00: £249.00) Stalls: Low GOING minus 0.59 sec per fur (F)

| | Horse | Dist | Pos | SP | RR | SF |
|---|---|---|---|---|---|---|
| *3953$^{4}$* | **No Monkey Nuts (78)** (JBerry) **3-9-0** JCarroll(4) (mde all: rdn over 1f out: drvn out) | — | **1** | 6/1 | 87 | 35 |
| 3518$^{12}$ | **Cross of Valour (76)** (JARToller) **3-9-0** TQuinn(5) (lw: a.p: chsd wnr over 2f out: sn rdn: no imp) | 1¾ | **2** | 16/1 | 82 | 30 |
| 2548$^{9}$ | **Forentia (80)** (JRFanshawe) **3-8-8** DHarrison(8) (hld up: hdwy 2f out: hung lft over 1f out: r.o one pce) | 1½ | **3** | 16/1 | 72 | 20 |
| 3844$^{5}$ | **First Maite (75)** (SRBowring) **3-8-11b** KFallon(1) (a.p: rdn over 2f out: one pce) | s.h | **4** | 9/2$^{2}$ | 75 | 23 |
| 3519$^{2}$ | **Alpine Hideaway (IRE) (78)** (BHanbury) **3-8-11** JStack(9) (lw: prom tl wknd over 1f out) | 2½ | **5** | 11/2$^{3}$ | 69 | 17 |
| *2171$^{13}$* | **Little Noggins (IRE) (73)** (CADwyer) **3-8-4**$^{(7)}$ JoHunnam(6) (swtg: chsd wnr over 3f: sn wknd) | 1 | **6** | 25/1 | 66 | 14 |
| 2861* | **Navigate (USA) (80)** (RHannon) **3-9-0** DaneO'Neill(2) (sn outpcd: hdwy 2f out: wknd over 1f out) | 4 | **7** | 5/2$^{1}$ | 58 | 6 |
| 2238$^{5}$ | **Precious Girl (78)** (DMoffatt) **3-8-8v**$^{(3)}$ DarrenMoffatt(3) (outpcd) | 4 | **8** | 8/1 | 45 | — |
| 3844$^{4}$ | **Croeso Cynnes (71)** (BPalling) **3-9-0** TSprake(7) (prom over 3f) | nk | **9** | 6/1 | 47 | — |

(SP 117.4%) **9 Rn**

**1m 12.72** (1.02) CSF £81.38 TOTE £7.00: £1.50 £4.40 £3.30 (£27.90) Trio £298.80 OWNER The Monkey Partnership (COCKERHAM) BRED Miss C. Tagart

OFFICIAL EXPLANATION **Navigate (USA): lost his action.**

**3953 No Monkey Nuts** travelled strongly at the head of affairs and produced what was required when let down. (6/1)
**2950 Cross of Valour** did nothing wrong, but simply met one too good. (16/1)
**Forentia**, without the visor this time, looked a difficult ride. (16/1)
**3844 First Maite** may find a return to the Southwell Sand paying dividends. (9/2)
**3519 Alpine Hideaway (IRE)** continues to prove expensive to follow. (11/2)

## 4045 R.N.L.I. VOLUNTEER (S) H'CAP (0-60) (3-Y.O+) (Class G)

4-20 (4-26) **6f** £1,771.00 (£1,771.00: £378.00) Stalls: Low GOING minus 0.59 sec per fur (F)

| | Horse | Dist | Pos | SP | RR | SF |
|---|---|---|---|---|---|---|
| 3851$^{5}$ | **Petraco (IRE) (56)** (NASmith) **8-9-3**$^{(7)}$ JBramhill(24) (w ldr stands' side: r.o wl ins fnl f) | — | **1** | 14/1 | 66 | 36 |
| 3851$^{3}$ | **Superbit (49)** (BAMcMahon) **4-9-3** TQuinn(23) (lw: mde all stands' side: r.o wl) | — | **1** | 8/1 | 59 | 29 |
| 3525$^{7}$ | **Polar Refrain (50)** (CADwyer) **3-9-2** JFEgan(14) (prom stands' side: hrd rdn over 1f out: r.o ins fnl f) | nk | **3** | 11/4$^{1}$ | 59+ | 27 |
| 3868$^{4}$ | **Dominelle (52)** (TDEasterby) **4-9-6** MBirch(4) (lw: a.p: led far side over 1f out: r.o) | 2½ | **4** | 7/1$^{3}$ | 55 | 25 |
| 3937$^{18}$ | **John's Law (IRE) (50)** (MJHeaton-Ellis) **3-9-2v**$^{1}$ SDrowne(20) (hdwy stands' side over 1f out: r.o ins fnl f) | hd | **5** | 33/1 | 52 | 20 |
| 3817$^{4}$ | **Densben (48)** (DenysSmith) **12-9-2** KFallon(5) (hdwy far side over 1f out: r.o ins fnl f) | ½ | **6** | 13/2$^{2}$ | 49 | 19 |
| 3442$^{7}$ | **Judgement Call (49)** (PHowling) **9-9-3** FNorton(7) (b: w ldr far side: wknd over 1f out) | 1 | **7** | 16/1 | 47 | 17 |
| | **Havana Miss (45)** (BPalling) **4-8-13** DHarrison(1) (led far side over 4f: wknd fnl f) | ½ | **8** | 33/1 | 42 | 12 |
| 3700$^{7}$ | **Brookhead Lady (43)** (PDEvans) **5-8-4**$^{(7)}$ AMcCarthy(3) (no hdwy fnl 2f) | ½ | **9** | 16/1 | 39 | 9 |
| 3652$^{6}$ | **Scored Again (46)** (MJHeaton-Ellis) **6-8-9**$^{(5)}$ AmandaSanders(10) (b: w ldrs far side over 4f) | 1 | **10** | 20/1 | 39 | 9 |
| 3761* | **Speedy Snaps Pride (49)** (PDCundell) **4-9-0b**$^{(3)}$ FLynch(12) (s.i.s: nvr nrr) | 1¾ | **11** | 9/1 | 37 | 7 |
| 3698$^{7}$ | **Needle Match (55)** (CFWall) **3-9-7** JCarroll(13) (chsd ldrs: eased whn btn fnl f) | s.h | **12** | 16/1 | 43 | 11 |
| 3644$^{7}$ | **Members Welcome (IRE) (52)** (JMBradley) **3-9-4v** LCharnock(22) (nvr nr ldrs) | hd | **13** | 20/1 | 40 | 8 |
| 3650$^{7}$ | **Quinntessa (53)** (BPalling) **3-9-5** TSprake(8) (prom far side 4f) | 1¼ | **14** | 33/1 | 38 | 6 |
| *3953$^{9}$* | **Boffy (IRE) (50)** (BPJBaugh) **3-8-9**$^{(7)}$ IonaWands(19) (prom stands' side 4f) | hd | **15** | 20/1 | 34 | 2 |
| 3453$^{5}$ | **Naughty Pistol (USA) (47)** (PDEvans) **4-8-8v**$^{1(7)}$ AnthonyBond(16) (s.s: a bhd) | nk | **16** | 16/1 | 31 | 1 |
| 3680$^{3}$ | **Miss Pigalle (43)** (MissLAPerratt) **5-8-11b** DaleGibson(6) (a bhd) | 1 | **17** | 20/1 | 24 | — |
| 3789$^{5}$ | **Ginas Girl (45)** (MissJBower) **3-8-11** TWilliams(15) (w ldrs stands' side over 3f) | 1½ | **18** | 33/1 | 22 | — |
| 1780$^{11}$ | **Flood's Fancy (55)** (LJBarratt) **3-9-7b** NAdams(9) (bhd fnl 3f) | 1¾ | **19** | 33/1 | 27 | — |
| 661$^{12}$ | **Larrylukeathugh (45)** (JJO'Neill) **3-8-11** JFanning(2) (a bhd) | 4 | **20** | 25/1 | 7 | — |
| 3851$^{14}$ | **Fiery Footsteps (46)** (SWCampion) **4-9-0** SDWilliams(11) (s.s: a wl bhd t.o) | 10 | **21** | 33/1 | — | — |
| 3677$^{9}$ | **Duo Master (58)** (MrsMReveley) **3-9-10b**$^{1}$ KDarley(18) (rel to r: a t.o) | ½ | **22** | 20/1 | — | — |
| *3957$^{12}$* | ***Penny Parkes (52)*** (JBerry) **3-8-13v**$^{1(5)}$ PRoberts(21) (withdrawn not under Starter's orders: uns rdr & bolted) | | **W** | 14/1 | — | — |

(SP 155.8%) **22 Rn**

**1m 13.34** (1.64) CSF P & S £63.15 S & P £59.16 CT P, S & PR £192.15 S, P & PR £185.47 TOTE P £7.70 S £3.80: P £3.90 S £1.90 PR £1.50 D £2.00 (£41.20) Trio £260.00 OWNER Mr Bernard Gover (UPTON SNODSBURY)/Mr Neville Smith (TAMWORTH) BRED Mrs M. Beaumont/A. D. Bottomley

WEIGHT FOR AGE 3yo-2lb

No bids; Needle Match clmd Clayton Bigley Partnership £6,000

**3851 Petraco (IRE)**, dropped in class, appreciated the return to six and, to the surprise of most, got up on the nod to share the spoils. (14/1)
**3851 Superbit**, dropped into a seller for this step up in trip, held on well, but had to settle for a share of the prize. (8/1)
**473 Polar Refrain** really needs softer ground over this trip. (11/4)
**3868 Dominelle**, reverting to selling company, was the first home on the far side. (7/1)
**2970 John's Law (IRE)**, lowered in grade, showed improvement in the first-time visor. (33/1)
**3817 Densben** was running off the same mark as when winning this race last year. (13/2)

## 4046 VOLVO V40 CLAIMING STKS (2-Y.O) (Class F)

4-50 (5-00) **6f** £2,955.00 (£830.00: £405.00) Stalls: High GOING minus 0.59 sec per fur (F)

| Form | Horse | Dist | Pos | SP | RR | SF |
|---|---|---|---|---|---|---|
| $2772^{4}$ | **Commander Jones (IRE) (76)** (BJMeehan) **2-8-7** MTebbutt(20) (mde all stands' side: hung bdly lft ins fnl f: r.o) | — | 1 | $5/1^{3}$ | 78 | 15 |
| $3879^{5}$ | **Contravene (IRE) (58)** (JBerry) **2-7-11** NCarlisle(2) (led far side: r.o fnl f) | 1½ | 2 | 10/1 | 64 | 1 |
| $1632^{5}$ | **Bonnie Lassie** (CWThornton) **2-8-10** DeanMcKeown(3) (prom far side: ev ch 1f out: r.o) | hd | 3 | 14/1 | 77 | 14 |
| $3969^{5}$ | **Abstone Queen (58)** (PDEvans) **2-7-13v**$^{ow1}$ JFEgan(12) (prom stands' side: r.o ins fnl f) | s.h | 4 | 8/1 | 66 | 2 |
| $3871^{*}$ | **Dowry (77)** (RHannon) **2-8-5** DaneO'Neill(13) (lw: chsd wnr stands' side: rdn 3f out: one pce fnl 2f) | 1¼ | 5 | $3/1^{1}$ | 68 | 5 |
| $3871^{3}$ | **Russian Sable (60)** (MRChannon) **2-7-12** AMackay(5) (prom far side: one pce fnl 2f) | 2 | 6 | $9/2^{2}$ | 56 | — |
| $3838^{2}$ | **Tinker's Surprise (IRE) (59)** (BJMeehan) **2-8-1b** BDoyle(17) (no hdwy fnl 2f) | 2 | 7 | 10/1 | 54 | — |
| $3969^{9}$ | **Preskidul (IRE) (56)** (DWPArbuthnot) **2-7-11**(3) DarrenMoffatt(18) (nvr nrr) | hd | 8 | 20/1 | 52 | — |
| $2625^{4}$ | **Donna's Dancer (IRE)** (TDBarron) **2-8-5** JFanning(15) (no hdwy fnl 2f) | 1¾ | 9 | 12/1 | 53 | — |
| $3763^{3}$ | **Will To Win (61)** (PGMurphy) **2-8-1** SDrowne(7) (chsd ldrs far side 4f) | 1¼ | 10 | 14/1 | 45 | — |
| $3869^{4}$ | **My Saltarello (IRE)** (ABMulholland) **2-8-12** MBirch(16) (sme late hdwy) | ½ | 11 | 33/1 | 55 | — |
| $2044^{10}$ | **Chateauherault (IRE)** (PCHaslam) **2-8-4**(7) FBoyle(19) (nvr bttr than mid div) | 3½ | 12 | 33/1 | 45 | — |
| $3838^{W}$ | **Shotley Princess (48)** (NBycroft) **2-8-0** TWilliams(10) (w ldr stands' side: wknd 2f out) | 2½ | 13 | 33/1 | 27 | — |
| $3941^{12}$ | **Globetrotter (IRE)** (MJohnston) **2-8-12** KDarley(9) (sn outpcd) | 1¼ | 14 | 10/1 | 36 | — |
| $3941^{15}$ | **Crosby Nod** (EWeymes) **2-8-5** GHind(8) (bit bkwd: bhd fnl 2f) | 3½ | 15 | 33/1 | 19 | — |
| *$3629^{5}$* | **Read Your Contract (IRE)** (JBerry) **2-8-5v** JCarroll(11) (lw: s.s: a bhd) | 1 | 16 | 20/1 | 17 | — |
| $3871^{8}$ | **Koordinaite** (WJMusson) **2-7-11** FNorton(4) (b: sn wl bhd) | nk | 17 | 33/1 | 8 | — |
| | **Propellant** (CWThornton) **2-9-3** LCharnock(6) (leggy: bkwd: a bhd) | hd | 18 | 25/1 | 28 | — |
| | **See You Soon** (CWThornton) **2-8-7** DaleGibson(1) (unf: bkwd: s.v.s: a bhd) | 7 | 19 | 25/1 | — | — |
| | ***Patrita Park*** (WWHaigh) **2-7-7**(7) JBramhill(21) (withdrawn not under Starter's orders: faulty tack) | | W | 33/1 | — | — |

(SP 154.1%) **19 Rn**

**1m 13.73** (2.03) CSF £59.99 TOTE £7.70: £2.60 £3.80 £3.50 (£106.90) Trio Not won; £729.13 to Haydock 7/9/96 OWNER E H Jones (Paints) Ltd (UPPER LAMBOURN) BRED Cesare Turri

**2772 Commander Jones (IRE)**, without the blinkers this time, proved too good for these, despite doing his best to throw it away in the closing stages. (5/1)

**3879 Contravene (IRE)** seemed more at home back over six. (10/1: 7/1-11/1)

**1632 Bonnie Lassie**, a half-sister to Keep Your Distance, seems to have benefited from being given time. (14/1)

**3969 Abstone Queen** holds her form remarkably well. (8/1)

**3871* Dowry** may need seven unless there is give underfoot. (3/1)

**3871 Russian Sable** could not turn the tables on the favourite, despite being 5lb better off than when beaten two necks at Lingfield. (9/2: 5/2-5/1)

**3838 Tinker's Surprise (IRE)** (10/1: 8/1-12/1)

**Globetrotter (IRE)** (10/1: 7/1-12/1)

## 4047 R.N.L.I. 'MEXICO' MEMORIAL H'CAP (0-80) (3-Y.O) (Class D)

5-20 (5-26) **1m 2f 120y** £3,909.00 (£1,182.00: £576.00: £273.00) Stalls: Low GOING minus 0.59 sec per fur (F)

| Form | Horse | Dist | Pos | SP | RR | SF |
|---|---|---|---|---|---|---|
| $3586^{*}$ | **Sawa-Id (71)** (JHMGosden) **3-9-2** JCarroll(10) (lw: a.p: shkn up to ld over 1f out: hung lft: drvn out) | — | 1 | $2/1^{1}$ | 83 | 38 |
| $3825^{*}$ | **Shalateeno (60)** (BRMillman) **3-8-5** $^{4x}$ TSprake(9) (led: rdn & hdd over 1f out: r.o) | hd | 2 | $11/4^{2}$ | 72 | 27 |
| $3589^{*}$ | **General Glow (63)** (PDEvans) **3-8-8** JFEgan(2) (hld up: hdwy 3f out: styd on ins fnl f) | 5 | 3 | 7/1 | 67 | 22 |
| *$2201^{6}$* | **Shady Girl (IRE) (68)** (BWHills) **3-8-13** KFallon(5) (bhd & pushed along: styd on fnl 3f: nt rch ldrs) | s.h | 4 | 20/1 | 72 | 27 |
| $3785^{11}$ | **Premier Generation (IRE) (60)** (DWPArbuthnot) **3-8-5** TQuinn(6) (b: nvr nr to chal) | hd | 5 | 20/1 | 64 | 19 |
| $3788^{6}$ | **Poetic Dance (USA) (73)** (JLDunlop) **3-9-4** KDarley(11) (lw: sn pushed along: nvr nr ldrs) | 5 | 6 | $6/1^{3}$ | 69 | 24 |
| *$1993^{4}$* | **Sharp Command (58)** (PEccles) **3-8-3** LCharnock(7) (prom tl wknd over 3f out) | 9 | 7 | 25/1 | 41 | — |
| $2486^{3}$ | **Sing And Dance (51)** (EWeymes) **3-7-10** JLowe(3) (prom tl wknd over 3f out) | nk | 8 | 16/1 | 33 | — |
| $3592^{2}$ | **Falcon's Flame (USA) (58)** (MrsJRRamsden) **3-8-3** SDrowne(4) (lw: plld hrd: prom tl wknd over 3f out) | 6 | 9 | 8/1 | 31 | — |
| $3788^{9}$ | **Fourdaned (IRE) (70)** (PWHarris) **3-9-1** GHind(1) (lw: hld up: edgd rt over 3f out: sn bhd) | 1 | 10 | 16/1 | 42 | — |

(SP 123.0%) **10 Rn**

**2m 13.49** (1.99) CSF £8.21 CT £30.59 TOTE £3.10: £1.30 £1.80 £2.10 (£4.10) Trio £9.30 OWNER Mr Hamdan Al Maktoum (NEWMARKET) BRED Mrs W. H. Gibson Fleming

LONG HANDICAP Sing And Dance 7-6

**3586* Sawa-Id**, up 4lb, again showed a tendency to go left and did not win anything like as easily as had seemed likely. (2/1: op 3/1)

**3825* Shalateeno**, under a penalty, was due to go up a further 5lb and battled on bravely to give favourite-backers a few anxious moments. (11/4)

**3589* General Glow** was a stone higher in the Ratings than when winning over course and distance last month. (7/1)

**1776 Shady Girl (IRE)**, stepping up in trip after a break, shaped as though she may need even further. (20/1)

**1119 Premier Generation (IRE)** was never going to take advantage of a 2lb lower mark. (20/1)

T/Plpt: £490.40 (33.6 Tckts). T/Qdpt: £139.60 (8.56 Tckts). KH

# 3681-KEMPTON (R-H) (Good)

## Friday September 6th

WEATHER: warm WIND: almost nil

## 4048 WATFORD H'CAP (0-70) (3-Y.O+) (Class E)

2-05 (2-06) **1m 6f 92y** £3,176.25 (£960.00: £467.50: £221.25) Stalls: High GOING minus 0.35 sec per fur (F)

| Form | Horse | Dist | Pos | SP | RR | SF |
|---|---|---|---|---|---|---|
| $3480^{2}$ | **Durham (54)** (HSHowe) **5-9-2b** SWhitworth(8) (lw: a.p: led 2f out: r.o wl) | — | 1 | 10/1 | 67 | 33 |
| $3968^{*}$ | **Ayunli (64)** (SCWilliams) **5-9-12** GCarter(14) (lw: a.p: led over 3f out to 2f out: unable qckn) | 4 | 2 | $6/1^{2}$ | 73 | 39 |
| $3802^{4}$ | **Euphonic (61)** (IABalding) **6-9-9** PatEddery(3) (a.p: hrd rdn over 2f out: one pce) | 2½ | 3 | $6/1^{2}$ | 67 | 33 |
| $3801^{8}$ | **Nordansk (54)** (MMadgwick) **7-8-13**(3) NVarley(13) (lw: stdy hdwy over 3f out: hung rt over 1f out: one pce) | nk | 4 | $7/1^{3}$ | 60 | 26 |
| *$3600^{3}$* | **Tirolette (IRE) (57)** (RJRWilliams) **4-9-0b**(5) AimeeCook(10) (lw: hld up: rdn over 2f out: one pce) | 1 | 5 | 20/1 | 61 | 27 |
| $3514^{6}$ | **Supreme Star (USA) (61)** (PRHedger) **5-9-9** RHughes(1) (hld up: rdn over 2f out: wknd fnl f) | 1 | 6 | $5/1^{1}$ | 64 | 30 |
| $3355^{4}$ | **Sarasota Storm (51)** (MBell) **4-8-13** MFenton(6) (hdwy over 3f out: one pce fnl 2f) | ½ | 7 | 14/1 | 54 | 20 |
| $3520^{3}$ | **El Volador (51)** (CNAllen) **9-8-8**(5) MartinDwyer(4) (nvr nrr) | s.h | 8 | 14/1 | 54 | 20 |

| Form | Horse | Dist | Pos | SP | RR | SF |
|---|---|---|---|---|---|---|
| 1803[12] | **Stalled (IRE) (51)** (PTWalwyn) **6-8-13** RCochrane(12) (lw: nvr nrr) | 3½ | **9** | 14/1 | 50 | 16 |
| 3813[4] | **Requested (51)** (PBurgoyne) **9-8-13** DRMcCabe(2) (a bhd) | 2 | **10** | 14/1 | 48 | 14 |
| 3297[14] | **Outstayed Welcome (54)** (MJHaynes) **4-8-13**(3) DWright(11) (b.off hind: led 11f) | 1¾ | **11** | 12/1 | 49 | 15 |
| 3664[2] | **Greenwich Again (60)** (TGMills) **4-9-8** JReid(5) (bhd fnl 5f) | 1½ | **12** | 12/1 | 53 | 19 |
| *3437*[6] | **The Lad (51)** (LMontagueHall) **7-8-13** MHills(9) (a bhd) | 1 | **13** | 16/1 | 43 | 9 |
| 3948[11] | **Norsong (55)** (RAkehurst) **4-9-3** SSanders(7) (lw: prom 12f) | 13 | **14** | 10/1 | 32 | — |
| | | | | (SP 128.6%) | **14 Rn** | |

**3m 10.28** (7.28) CSF £68.24 CT £372.28 TOTE £9.00: £3.50 £2.80 £2.40 (£37.30) Trio £112.10 OWNER The Secret Partnership (TIVERTON) BRED Highclere Stud Ltd

**3480 Durham,** formerly with Rod Simpson, made a winning debut for his new stable. Once sent to the front two furlongs out, he soon put his mark on the race. (10/1)

**3968* Ayunli,** successful at Pontefract on Tuesday, did not seem to have a problem with this longer trip. (6/1)

**3802 Euphonic** was made to look very pedestrian in the straight. Acceleration is most definitely not his forte. (6/1)

**3801 Nordansk,** back over a more suitable trip, cruised into contention turning for home, but he gave his rider steering problems below the distance and could only struggle on at the one pace. (7/1)

**3600 Tirolette (IRE)** failed to find the necessary turn of foot in the straight. (20/1)

**3514 Supreme Star (USA),** asked for his effort in the straight, failed to quicken and tired inside the final furlong. (5/1)

## 4049 STANMORE NURSERY H'CAP (2-Y.O) (Class D)

2-35 (2-37) **6f** £3,777.50 (£1,145.00: £560.00: £267.50) Stalls: Low GOING minus 0.35 sec per fur (F)

| Form | Horse | Dist | Pos | SP | RR | SF |
|---|---|---|---|---|---|---|
| 3577[3] | **Jeffrey Anotherred (78)** (KMcAuliffe) **2-8-13** RHughes(14) (hld up: rdn over 2f out: led wl ins fnl f: r.o wl) | — | **1** | 12/1 | 74 | 31 |
| 3697[2] | **Dancethenightaway (82)** (BJMeehan) **2-8-12**(5) MartinDwyer(5) (lw: a.p: led over 2f out tl wl ins fnl f: r.o) | ½ | **2** | 8/1[3] | 77 | 34 |
| 3408[8] | **Lucky Oakwood (USA) (76)** (MBell) **2-8-4**(7) GFaulkner(11) (lw: rdn & hdwy 2f out: r.o wl ins fnl f) | 1½ | **3** | 14/1 | 67 | 24 |
| 3502[10] | **Tailwind (68)** (WRMuir) **2-8-3** GDuffield(8) (prom over 4f) | 5 | **4** | 12/1 | 45 | 2 |
| 3803[5] | **Bapsford (73)** (GLMoore) **2-8-8** RPerham(4) (hdwy over 1f out: nvr nrr) | 3 | **5** | 20/1 | 42 | — |
| 3423[7] | **Hurgill Times (72)** (JWWatts) **2-8-7b[1]** MHills(6) (a.p: led over 3f out tl over 2f out: wknd over 1f out) | nk | **6** | 8/1[3] | 41 | — |
| 3259[3] | **Shuwaikh (72)** (RHannon) **2-8-7** PatEddery(1) (lw: prom over 4f) | s.h | **7** | 11/4[1] | 40 | — |
| 3467[12] | **Bluebell Miss (75)** (MJRyan) **2-8-10** AClark(3) (nvr nr to chal) | s.h | **8** | 16/1 | 43 | — |
| 2199* | **Kilcullen Lad (IRE) (61)** (PMooney) **2-7-3**(7) RMullen(7) (lw: led over 2f: rdn 3f out: wknd over 1f out) | hd | **9** | 16/1 | 29 | — |
| 3502[3] | **Regal Equity (75)** (BJMeehan) **2-8-10** JReid(2) (lw: hdwy & nt clr run over 3f out: wknd over 2f out) | ½ | **10** | 8/1[3] | 42 | — |
| 3408[7] | **Rock Fantasy (68)** (CMurray) **2-8-3b[1]** DRMcCabe(13) (outpcd) | 1 | **11** | 25/1 | 32 | — |
| 3631* | **Love Has No Pride (USA) (76)** (RHannon) **2-8-11** SSanders(10) (sme hdwy 2f out: sn wknd) | 3½ | **12** | 5/1[2] | 31 | — |
| 2916* | **Zugudi (85)** (BHanbury) **2-9-6** MRimmer(9) (lw: a bhd) | 1¾ | **13** | 10/1 | 35 | — |
| 3803[4] | **Miss Barcelona (IRE) (65)** (MJPolglase) **2-8-0** JQuinn(15) (outpcd) | 12 | **14** | 20/1 | — | — |
| | | | | (SP 132.9%) | **14 Rn** | |

**1m 13.97** (2.67) CSF £105.50 CT £1,310.84 TOTE £14.90: £3.10 £3.00 £6.00 (£30.50) Trio £133.70 OWNER Highgrove Developments Ltd (LAMBOURN) BRED John Rose

LONG HANDICAP Kilcullen Lad (IRE) 7-5

**3577 Jeffrey Anotherred** began to get serious in the final quarter-mile and, after a protracted duel with the leader, eventually got on top in the closing stages. (12/1)

**3697 Dancethenightaway** had no problem with this slightly longer trip and went on over a quarter of a mile from home. With only the winner to worry about from below the distance, she was worried out of it in the closing stages. She should be able to win a nursery. (8/1)

**3307 Lucky Oakwood (USA)** found this shorter trip too sharp and was, not surprisingly, doing all her best work in the final quarter-mile. A return to seven furlongs would be in her favour. (14/1)

**Tailwind** came to the end of his tether over a furlong out. (12/1)

**3803 Bapsford** struggled on past beaten horses in the last furlong and a half. (20/1)

**2865 Hurgill Times,** fitted with blinkers for the first time, went on just before halfway. Collared over a quarter of a mile from home, he grimly tried to hold on but had shot his bolt below the distance. (8/1)

## 4050 MILCARS CHERTSEY LOCK CONDITIONS STKS (2-Y.O C & G) (Class C)

3-05 (3-08) **7f (Jubilee)** £4,623.20 (£1,728.80: £844.40: £362.00: £161.00: £80.60) Stalls: High GOING minus 0.35 sec per fur (F)

| Form | Horse | Dist | Pos | SP | RR | SF |
|---|---|---|---|---|---|---|
| 3682[2] | **Falak (USA)** (MajorWRHern) **2-8-10** RHills(7) (lw: mde all: drvn out) | — | **1** | 5/1[2] | 83 | 43 |
| | **Captain Collins (IRE)** (PWChapple-Hyam) **2-8-10** JReid(9) (unf: scope: a.p: swtchd lft & rdn over 2f out: r.o wl: bttr for r) | hd | **2** | 4/6[1] | 83+ | 43 |
| 3494* | **Mukaddar (USA)** (CJBenstead) **2-9-1** RCochrane(4) (lw: chsd wnr: ev ch fnl 2f: r.o) | nk | **3** | 10/1[3] | 87 | 47 |
| | **King Sound** (JHMGosden) **2-8-10** WRyan(10) (w'like: scope: s.s: stdy hdwy over 1f out: r.o: bttr for r) | 3½ | **4** | 5/1[2] | 74+ | 34 |
| | **Catienus (USA)** (MRStoute) **2-8-10** RHughes(2) (w'like: hld up: rdn over 2f out: one pce) | ½ | **5** | 33/1 | 73 | 33 |
| 3682[8] | **Padauk** (MJHaynes) **2-8-10** GCarter(11) (outpcd: nvr nrr) | 8 | **6** | 50/1 | 55 | 15 |
| | **Freedom Chance (IRE)** (JWHills) **2-8-10** MHills(6) (leggy: scope: lw: a bhd) | nk | **7** | 33/1 | 54 | 14 |
| | **Triple Hay** (RHannon) **2-8-10** RPerham(5) (w'like: scope: prom over 5f) | 2 | **8** | 50/1 | 49 | 9 |
| 3615[11] | **Tango King** (JLDunlop) **2-8-10** PatEddery(3) (s.s: hdwy over 3f out: wknd over 2f out) | 1¼ | **9** | 20/1 | 47 | 7 |
| | **Zimiri** (JARToller) **2-8-10** SSanders(8) (w'like: scope: bit bkwd: prom 5f) | 2 | **10** | 33/1 | 42 | 2 |
| | ***Fatal Baraari*** (MRStoute) **2-8-10** WRSwinburn(1) (Withdrawn not under Starter's orders: ref to ent stalls) | | **W** | 14/1 | — | — |
| | | | | (SP 126.6%) | **10 Rn** | |

**1m 26.38** (1.88) CSF £8.33 TOTE £5.00: £1.50 £1.10 £1.80 (£2.80) Trio £5.00 OWNER Mr Hamdan Al Maktoum (LAMBOURN) BRED Shadwell Farm Inc

**OFFICIAL EXPLANATION King Sound: the rider reported that the colt is fractious and lacks confidence at home, and became unsettled in the stalls when another horse played up. He missed the break as a result and did not get a clear run in the early stages. He was then unable to go with the leaders as they quickened.**

**3682 Falak (USA),** who showed promise here on his debut two weeks ago, made that experience count with a pillar-to-post victory, but found the line only just saving him. (5/1: 3/1-11/2)

**Captain Collins (IRE),** a rangy colt who needs time to develop, is well regarded at home and is a brother to Colonel Collins, who was placed in the 2000 Guineas and the Epsom and Irish Derbies. Mounting his challenge in the final quarter-mile, he ran on in good style and would probably have succeeded with a little further to go. He is sure to benefit a great deal from this and looks a ready-made winner. (4/6)

**3494* Mukaddar (USA),** small in comparison with some of his rivals, threw down his challenge to the winner in the final quarter-mile. Battling his heart out, he did little wrong and was only just worried out of it. This run proved his Salisbury victory to be no fluke, and he should soon regain the winning thread. (10/1: 8/1-12/1)

**King Sound**, a deep-girthed individual who is a half-brother to winners in the USA and Japan, caught the eye in no uncertain terms. Given extremely tender handling which did not go unnoticed by the Stewards, he crept closer in the final quarter-mile to finish a highly-encouraging fourth. This experience will stand him in good stead, and he looks a sure-fire future winner. (5/1)
**Catienus (USA)**, a plain colt, did not catch the eye nearly as much as some of the others. (33/1)

## 4051 MILCARS TEMPLE FORTUNE STKS (Listed) (3-Y.O+) (Class A)

3-40 (3-41) **1m (Jubilee)** £12,125.25 (£3,672.00: £1,793.50: £854.25) Stalls: High GOING minus 0.35 sec per fur (F)

| | | | | SP | RR | SF |
|---|---|---|---|---|---|---|
| 3503* | **Centre Stalls (IRE) (103)** (RFJohnsonHoughton) **3-8-9** JReid(2) (hdwy to chse ldr over 2f out: led 1f out: rdn out) | — | **1** | 8/1 | 121 | 65 |
| 3822* | **Wizard King (114)** (SirMarkPrescott) **5-9-0** GDuffield(8) (led to 1f out: unable qckn) | 1¾ | **2** | 2/1[1] | 118 | 67 |
| 3445[10] | **Verzen (IRE) (100)** (DRLoder) **4-9-0** DRMcCabe(7) (chsd ldr over 5f: one pce) | 3½ | **3** | 20/1 | 111 | 60 |
| 3596[5] | **Hammerstein (110)** (MRStoute) **3-8-9** PatEddery(6) (lw: a.p: rdn over 2f out: one pce) | nk | **4** | 3/1[2] | 110 | 54 |
| 3125[11] | **Chief Burundi (USA) (100)** (LMCumani) **4-9-0** OUrbina(5) (swtg: bmpd over 2f out: nvr nr to chal) | 3½ | **5** | 16/1 | 103 | 52 |
| 2337[5] | **Ramooz (USA) (106)** (BHanbury) **3-8-9** WRyan(1) (lw: swtchd rt over 2f out: sme hdwy wl over 1f out: sn wknd) | ½ | **6** | 6/1 | 102 | 46 |
| 3712[5] | **Sergeyev (IRE) (112)** (RHannon) **4-9-0** RHughes(4) (lw: plld hrd: bhd fnl 4f) | 2½ | **7** | 5/1[3] | 97 | 46 |
| 3811[3] | **Mawjud** (HThomsonJones) **3-8-9** RHills(3) (prom over 5f) | 15 | **8** | 33/1 | 67 | 11 |

(SP 114.0%) **8 Rn**

**1m 37.18** (-0.02) CSF £23.30 TOTE £9.90: £2.40 £1.10 £3.50 (£10.10) OWNER Mr Anthony Pye-Jeary (DIDCOT) BRED Limestone Stud
WEIGHT FOR AGE 3yo-5lb

**3503* Centre Stalls (IRE)**, a fast-improving three-year-old, put up a polished display to land his first listed race. In second place approaching the final quarter-mile, he struck the front entering the final furlong and was ridden along to stamp his authority. (8/1)
**3822* Wizard King** continues in tremendous form and, although his winning run came to an end, he lost nothing in defeat. His very astute trainer has placed him to such great effect during his career to win eleven races, including three conditions races and two listed races, and a similar event should soon get him back to the winner's enclosure. (2/1: 5/4-9/4)
**2920* Verzen (IRE)**, collared for second approaching the final quarter-mile, could only plod on at one insufficient pace. (20/1)
**3596 Hammerstein**, back in a more suitable class, was never far away, but disappointingly failed to quicken in the last two furlongs. (3/1)
**1484 Chief Burundi (USA)** continues to disappoint following his third in the Whitsun Cup at Sandown back in May, and could never get into it. (16/1)
**2337 Ramooz (USA)** again disappointed and ran a lifeless race. (6/1)
**3712 Sergeyev (IRE)** pulled far too hard for his own good and, as a result, ran no race at all. He needs a fast pace to allow him to settle and, in that respect, would be better suited by a drop in distance. (5/1)

## 4052 MILCARS CONDITIONS STKS (2-Y.O F) (Class C)

4-10 (4-10) **7f (Jubilee)** £4,576.80 (£1,711.20: £835.60: £358.00: £159.00: £79.40) Stalls: High GOING minus 0.35 sec per fur (F)

| | | | | SP | RR | SF |
|---|---|---|---|---|---|---|
| | **One So Wonderful** (LMCumani) **2-8-8** OUrbina(4) (w'like: scope: a.p: shkn up over 2f out: led over 1f out: comf) | — | **1** | 5/1[3] | 86+ | 45 |
| | **Alphabet** (MRStoute) **2-8-8** RCochrane(7) (b.hind: unf: scope: a.p: ev ch over 1f out: unable qckn) | 3½ | **2** | 5/1[3] | 78 | 37 |
| | **Noble Dane (IRE)** (PWHarris) **2-8-8** PatEddery(5) (w'like: scope: bit bkwd: hdwy 4f out: rdn over 2f out: one pce: bttr for r) | 1½ | **3** | 4/1[1] | 75 | 34 |
| 3499[7] | **Kafaf (USA)** (JHMGosden) **2-8-8** RHills(1) (a.p: rdn over 2f out: one pce) | hd | **4** | 8/1 | 74 | 33 |
| | **Dust Dancer** (JLDunlop) **2-8-8** MHills(3) (leggy: unf: scope: s.s: stdy hdwy over 1f out: r.o: bttr for r) | ¾ | **5** | 14/1 | 73 | 32 |
| | **Western Hour (USA)** (PWChapple-Hyam) **2-8-8** JReid(8) (leggy: unf: scope: rdn over 2f out: hdwy over 1f out: nvr nrr) | hd | **6** | 9/2[2] | 72 | 31 |
| 3647* | **All Is Fair (85)** (SirMarkPrescott) **2-8-13** GDuffield(11) (plld hrd: a.p: led over 2f out tl over 1f out: wknd fnl f) | ¾ | **7** | 9/2[2] | 76 | 35 |
| | **Desert Beauty (IRE)** (MRStoute) **2-8-9**ow1 WRSwinburn(6) (w'like: scope: bit bkwd: stdy hdwy over 2f out: wknd over 1f out: bttr for r) | 2 | **8** | 7/1 | 67 | 25 |
| | **Top Shelf** (CEBrittain) **2-8-5**(3) MHenry(10) (w'like: bit bkwd: rdn over 4f out: hdwy on ins over 2f out: wknd over 1f out) | 1¾ | **9** | 20/1 | 62 | 21 |
| 3449[4] | **Laguna Bay (IRE)** (APJarvis) **2-8-8** SWhitworth(2) (prom over 4f) | 9 | **10** | 33/1 | 42 | 1 |
| 3873[3] | **Northern Pass (USA)** (RAkehurst) **2-8-8** SSanders(9) (led over 4f) | 4 | **11** | 16/1 | 32 | — |

(SP 133.6%) **11 Rn**

**1m 26.04** (1.54) CSF £32.39 TOTE £8.40: £1.70 £2.80 £1.50 (£25.60) Trio £132.10 OWNER Helena Springfield Ltd (NEWMARKET) BRED Meon Valley Stud

**One So Wonderful**, a good-bodied filly who is a half-sister to Craven and Dante winner Alnasr Alwasheek, and to Rockfel winner Relatively Special, was the paddock pick and put up a very decent display as she swept into the lead approaching the final furlong and stormed clear to win with plenty in hand. She could turn out to be very useful and further success awaits her. Indeed, it would be no surprise if she took her place in the Fillies' Mile at Ascot. (5/1: op 3/1)
**Alphabet**, whose dam won the Nell Gwyn, showed a great deal of promise and had every chance below the distance, before the winner's turn of foot put her in her place. A plain filly who needs time to develop but has the scope to do so, she should have no problems finding a race. (5/1: 4/1-7/1)
**Noble Dane (IRE)**, a good-looking filly with plenty of scope, is well thought of at home and showed plenty of promise on this debut before failing to quicken in the last two furlongs. A sister to the useful handicapper Amrak Ajeeb, she should not be difficult to win with. (4/1)
**Kafaf (USA)**, a plain filly, was never far away but failed to quicken in the last two furlongs. (8/1)
**Dust Dancer**, a tall half-sister to numerous winners including the very useful Bulaxie, was not given a hard time, but was noted staying on steadily in the last furlong and a half to be nearest at the finish. The experience will not be lost on her, and improvement can be expected. (14/1: 10/1-16/1)
**Western Hour (USA)** . a plain filly who needs time to develop, was bustled along early in the straight and, although she stayed on in the last furlong and a half, she never seriously threatened the principals. (9/2: op 2/1)
**3647* All Is Fair** (9/2: 3/1-6/1)
**Desert Beauty (IRE)** (7/1: 9/2-8/1)

## 4053 RADLETT MAIDEN H'CAP (0-70) (3-Y.O+) (Class E)

4-40 (4-42) **7f (round)** £3,355.00 (£1,015.00: £495.00: £235.00) Stalls: High GOING minus 0.35 sec per fur (F)

| | | | | SP | RR | SF |
|---|---|---|---|---|---|---|
| 3655[7] | **Sharp Shuffle (IRE) (68)** (RHannon) **3-9-10** RHughes(9) (lw: hld up: nt clr run over 2f out: led ins fnl f: r.o wl) | — | **1** | 8/1[3] | 80 | 58 |

3800[3] **Time of Night (USA) (66)** (RGuest) **3-9-3**(5) DGriffiths(5) (nt clr run 2f out: swtchd lft: hdwy over 1f out: r.o wl ins fnl f)....1¼ **2** 7/1[1] 75 53
2966[2] **Night of Glass (55)** (DMorris) **3-8-11v** NDay(15) (a.p: led over 2f out tl ins fnl f: unable qckn)....hd **3** 7/1[1] 64 42
3215[8] **Paojiunic (IRE) (70)** (LMCumani) **3-9-12** OUrbina(1) (b.hind: lw: rdn over 2f out: hdwy over 1f out: r.o)....1½ **4** 7/1[1] 76 54
3930[12] **Sea Danzig (64)** (JJBridger) **3-9-6** RCochrane(12) (a.p: rdn over 2f out: one pce)....1¾ **5** 20/1 66 44
**Godmersham Park (68)** (MJHeaton-Ellis) **4-10-0** JReid(4) (lw: hld up: nt clr run over 2f out & over 1f out: r.o one pce)....hd **6** 25/1 69 51
3767[3] **Out Line (68)** (MMadgwick) **4-9-11**(3) NVarley(6) (a.p: rdn over 2f out: wknd fnl f)....1½ **7** 9/1 66 48
3586[8] **Yeath (IRE) (52)** (RAkehurst) **4-8-12** SSanders(14) (lw: prom 5f)....½ **8** 16/1 49 31
3519[4] **Alrayyih (USA) (68)** (JHMGosden) **3-9-10** RHills(10) (swtg: rdn over 3f out: hdwy on ins over 2f out: n.m.r on ins over 1f out: eased whn btn ins fnl f)....2 **9** 7/1[1] 60 38
3650[8] **Inaminit (60)** (HJCollingridge) **3-9-2** JQuinn(7) (a mid div)....3½ **10** 25/1 44 22
2345[4] **Multan (52)** (GLMoore) **4-8-12** SWhitworth(16) (w ldr: led over 5f out tl over 4f out: wknd wl over 1f out)....hd **11** 14/1 36 18
**Reem Fever (IRE) (70)** (DWPArbuthnot) **3-9-12** RPrice(8) (lw: rdn over 2f out: hdwy over 1f out: sn wknd)....¾ **12** 25/1 52 30
3513[5] **Sovereigns Court (69)** (MajorDNChappell) **3-9-11** MHills(13) (lw: led over 1f: led over 4f out tl over 2f out: sn wknd)....2 **13** 10/1 47 25
3513[9] **Redskin Lady (56)** (DRCElsworth) **3-8-12** GBardwell(2) (lw: a bhd)....nk **14** 14/1 33 11
3513[10] **Country Thatch (65)** (CAHorgan) **3-9-7** PatEddery(17) (a bhd)....1½ **15** 15/2[2] 39 17
3681[9] **Scimitar (60)** (PJMakin) **3-9-2** AClark(11) (a bhd)....2½ **16** 20/1 28 6
3765[9] **Mansab (USA) (70)** (PGMurphy) **3-9-12** JTate(3) (lw: prom over 4f)....3½ **17** 25/1 30 8
(SP 136.1%) **17 Rn**

**1m 26.23** (1.73) CSF £63.40 CT £397.53 TOTE £7.30: £2.00 £2.70 £1.90 £2.50 (£38.40) Trio £62.90 OWNER Mrs H. F. Prendergast (MARLBOROUGH) BRED W. Tierney
WEIGHT FOR AGE 3yo-4lb

**3655 Sharp Shuffle (IRE)**, momentarily stuck for room early in the straight, moved up entering the final quarter-mile and, sweeping into the lead just inside the final furlong, soon had the race wrapped up. (8/1)
**3800 Time of Night (USA)** found traffic problems at a vital stage, but soon managed to extricate herself. Running on really strongly from that point, she swept through for second place, but found the damage had already been done. (7/1)
**2966 Night of Glass** probably found this seven furlongs more to his liking, as he tired in the closing stages over a mile last time out. Sent on early in the straight, he was collared just inside the final furlong and failed to quicken. (7/1)
**2861 Paojiunic (IRE)** was suited by the step up in distance, and was doing all his best work in the last furlong and a half. (7/1)
**3519 Sea Danzig** was made to look rather pedestrian in the straight. (20/1)
**Godmersham Park**, lumbered with topweight for this belated reappearance, looked pretty straight, but he met with traffic problems in the straight and, when he did find daylight, he could only stay on at the one pace. (25/1)
**2345 Multan** (14/1: 8/1-16/1)
**3513 Sovereigns Court** (10/1: op 6/1)

T/Jkpt: Not won; £4,293.71 to Haydock 7/9/96. T/Plpt: £155.50 (159.23 Tckts). T/Qdpt: £11.50 (141.47 Tckts). AK

# 4041-HAYDOCK (L-H) (Good to firm)
## Saturday September 7th
WEATHER: sunny periods WIND: almost nil

## 4054 STANLEY LEISURE GROUP H'CAP (0-90) (3-Y.O+) (Class C)
2-00 (2-02) **7f 30y** £6,125.00 (£1,850.00: £900.00: £425.00) Stalls: Low GOING minus 0.45 sec per fur (F)

SP RR SF
2725[14] **Primo Lara (82)** (PWHarris) **4-9-6** PatEddery(9) (mde all: drvn clr over 1f out: hld on cl home)....— **1** 12/1 93 51
3650* **Dummer Golf Time (66)** (LordHuntingdon) **3-7-11v**(3) MHenry(2) (lw: in tch: effrt 2f out: r.o wl ins fnl f)....¾ **2** 8/1[3] 75 29
3295[4] **Herodian (USA) (87)** (JHMGosden) **3-9-7b[1]** LDettori(10) (chsd wnr: rdn 2f out: kpt on ins fnl f)....hd **3** 10/1 96 50
3833* **Persian Fayre (75)** (JBerry) **4-8-13** JCarroll(16) (lw: rdn to chal over 2f out: one pce ins fnl f: fin 5th, 1½l: plcd 4th).... **4** 10/1 81 39
3790[2] **Trafalgar Lady (USA) (79)** (RCharlton) **3-8-13** JReid(5) (hld up: hdwy over 2f out: sn rdn: nt rch ldrs: fin 6th, ½l: plcd 5th).... **5** 7/1[2] 84 38
3811[5] **Sharp Prospect (80)** (VSoane) **6-9-4** RCochrane(4) (trckd ldrs on ins: rdn over 2f out: one pce)....¾ **7** 33/1 83 41
3974* **Maple Bay (IRE) (81)** (ABailey) **7-9-2**(3) 5x DWright(8) (lw: in tch: effrt & hrd drvn over 3f out: wknd over 1f out)....¾ **8** 8/1[3] 82 40
3920[10] **Highborn (IRE) (89)** (PSFelgate) **7-9-13** WRyan(13) (trckd ldrs: wkng whn hmpd ins fnl f)....hd **9** 16/1 90 48
3933[8] **Knobbleeneeze (78)** (MRChannon) **6-9-2v** RHughes(1) (effrt over 3f out: edgd lft 1f out: btn whn hmpd ins fnl f)....hd **10** 16/1 79 37
3210[18] **Ood Dancer (USA) (86)** (LMCumani) **3-9-6** KFallon(15) (lw: hld up: hdwy over 2f out: sn rdn: styng on whn n.m.r ins fnl f)....s.h **11** 9/1 87 41
917[3] **Warming Trends (85)** (SirMarkPrescott) **3-9-5** GDuffield(3) (bit bkwd: hmpd after 1f: effrt on ins over 2f out: sn rdn & no imp)....1¾ **12** 7/1[2] 82 36
3102[8] **Nkapen Rocks (SPA) (67)** (CaptJWilson) **3-7-12**(3)ow5 FLynch(11) (lw: hld up & plld hrd: nvr trbld ldrs)....2½ **13** 33/1 58 7
3833[12] **Fame Again (76)** (MrsJRRamsden) **4-9-0** MFenton(12) (lw: dwlt: hdwy 4f out: rdn & wknd over 2f out: t.o)....9 **14** 14/1 47 5
2858* **Young Duke (IRE) (70)** (MrsSDWilliams) **8-8-5**(3) PMcCabe(14) (s.i.s: bhd: hdwy on ins over 2f out: nt clr run & swtchd rt ins fnl f: fin wl: fin 3rd, d.h: disq: plcd last).... **D** 5/1[1] 79 37
(SP 124.1%) **14 Rn**

**1m 28.88** (1.38) CSF £98.91 CT £944.10 TOTE £13.40: £3.80 £2.30 £2.90 (£65.40) Trio £291.90 OWNER Thanet Leasing Ltd (BERKHAMSTED) BRED Pendley Farm
WEIGHT FOR AGE 3yo-4lb
STEWARDS' ENQUIRY McCabe susp. 16-21 & 23-25/9/96 & 1 day (irresponsible riding). Henry susp. 16/9/96 & 1 day (careless riding).

**2328 Primo Lara** returned to form after a two-month break with a game all-the-way success, and won far more easily than the margin suggests. (12/1)
**3650* Dummer Golf Time** had much more to do this time, but he gave of his best and, on this evidence, should stay at least another furlong. (8/1)
**3295 Herodian (USA)** lacked the experience of some of these seasoned handicappers, but he responded well to his first-time blinkers and ran without doubt the best race of his short career. (10/1)

**3833* Persian Fayre** was unable to get to the front, but he pushed the pace hard and was only tapped for toe inside the distance. (10/1)
**3790 Trafalgar Lady (USA)** began to thread her way through inside the last quarter-mile, but could not quite summon the pace to deliver a challenge. She is very lightly-raced and should have more improvement in her at this late stage of the season. (7/1)
**2858* Young Duke (IRE)** was unable to maintain his winning sequence, possibly due to the fact that he had trouble obtaining a clear passage, but he did cause mayhem when weaving his way through and, though he did finish best of all, his disqualification was a formality. Despite his advanced age, he has not stopped winning yet. (5/1)

## 4055 CECIL FRAIL RATED STKS H'CAP (0-100) (3-Y.O+) (Class B)

2-30 (2-32) **1m 3f 200y** £8,263.60 (£3,072.40: £1,486.20: £621.00: £260.50: £116.30) Stalls: High GOING minus 0.45 sec per fur (F)

| | | | | SP | RR | SF |
|---|---|---|---|---|---|---|
| 3710[4] | **Dacha (IRE) (91)** (HRACecil) **4-8-12** PatEddery(9) (lw: chsd ldr: led over 2f out: rdn & edgd rt ins fnl f: r.o) | — | **1** | 11/2[2] | 101 | 75 |
| 3683[6] | **Romios (IRE) (86)** (PFICole) **4-8-7** RCochrane(1) (led tl over 2f out: rdn & swtchd rt ins fnl f: r.o) | ½ | **2** | 16/1 | 95 | 69 |
| 2620[5] | **Mattawan (90)** (MJohnston) **3-8-2b[1]** JFanning(5) (chsd ldrs: outpcd over 2f out: n.d after) | 6 | **3** | 12/1 | 91 | 56 |
| 3710[7] | **Lombardic (USA) (90)** (MrsJCecil) **5-8-11** JReid(12) (chsd ldng pair: sn drvn along: outpcd over 2f out) | hd | **4** | 11/1 | 91 | 65 |
| 3689[5] | **Remaadi Sun (86)** (MDIUsher) **4-8-7** RStreet(6) (hld up & bhd: styd on fnl 2f: nvr nrr) | 5 | **5** | 11/1 | 80 | 54 |
| 3760[7] | **Mystic Hill (90)** (GHarwood) **5-8-11** AClark(2) (hld up in tch: pushed along & outpcd 3f out: sn btn) | 3½ | **6** | 12/1 | 80 | 54 |
| 3791[9] | **Ionio (USA) (92)** (CEBrittain) **5-8-13** BDoyle(4) (sn bhd & pushed along: n.d) | 1¼ | **7** | 25/1 | 80 | 54 |
| 3614[6] | **Whitechapel (USA) (88)** (LordHuntingdon) **8-8-9** RHughes(10) (lw: lost pl ½-wy: n.d after) | 1¾ | **8** | 9/1[3] | 74 | 48 |
| 3691[6] | **Grand Selection (IRE) (88)** (MBell) **4-8-9** MFenton(7) (hld up & a bhd) | s.h | **9** | 12/1 | 74 | 48 |
| 3934[2] | **Leonato (FR) (100)** (PDEvans) **4-9-7** JFEgan(8) (trckd ldrs over 8f) | hd | **10** | 12/1 | 86 | 60 |
| 3594* | **Greenstead (USA) (99)** (JHMGosden) **3-8-11** LDettori(3) (hld up & bhd: effrt over 3f out: sn rdn & outpcd) | hd | **11** | 7/4[1] | 84 | 49 |
| 3689[15] | **Time for Action (IRE) (86)** (MHTompkins) **4-8-4(3)** MHenry(11) (trckd ldrs: saddle slipped early: eased fnl 3f: t.o) | dist | **12** | 12/1 | — | — |
| | | | | (SP 126.6%) | **12 Rn** | |

**2m 27.18** (-2.22) CSF £84.18 CT £950.59 TOTE £5.20: £1.90 £5.10 £4.90 (£78.00) Trio £212.10 OWNER Cliveden Stud (NEWMARKET) BRED Cliveden Stud
LONG HANDICAP Romios (IRE) 8-5 Remaadi Sun 8-4 Time for Action (IRE) 8-6
WEIGHT FOR AGE 3yo-9lb
STEWARDS' ENQUIRY Obj. to Dacha (IRE) by Cochrane overruled.
**OFFICIAL EXPLANATION Greenstead (USA): did not act on the ground.**
**Time For Action (IRE): slipped.**
**3710 Dacha (IRE)**, who along with the runner-up drew clear halfway up the straight, had to work much harder than was expected after gaining command. He is a very progressive youngster and is now finding his way. (11/2)
**2862 Romios (IRE)** looked ill-at-ease cantering to post, but he still produced a sparkling display in defeat and a belated success for this term is long overdue. (16/1)
**2620 Mattawan**, taking on handicappers and fitted with blinkers for the first time, was sitting pretty in behind the principals three furlongs out but, once they stepped on the gas, he was left in their wake. (12/1)
**3710 Lombardic (USA)** has been finding it difficult to recover his true form since the spring, but there was nothing to question his commitment here, and it is possible any easing of the ground will be in his favour. (11/1)
**3594* Greenstead (USA)** was one of many caught out when the tempo picked up early in the straight, and he was soon hard at work and going nowhere. (7/4)

## 4056 ST ANNES CONDITIONS STKS (2-Y.O) (Class B)

3-00 (3-01) **1m 30y** £6,276.62 (£2,273.50: £1,099.25: £458.75: £191.88) Stalls: Low GOING minus 0.45 sec per fur (F)

| | | | | SP | RR | SF |
|---|---|---|---|---|---|---|
| 3779* | **Besiege** (HRACecil) **2-8-12** PatEddery(2) (lw: hld up: hdwy over 2f out: led over 1f out: rdn & styd on gamely) | — | **1** | 6/4[1] | 93 | 59 |
| 3684[5] | **Sandstone (IRE)** (JLDunlop) **2-8-12** LDettori(1) (hld up & bhd: hdwy u.p over 1f out: jnd wnr ins fnl f: unable qckn nr fin) | hd | **2** | 7/1 | 93 | 59 |
| 3485* | **Further Outlook (USA)** (MRStoute) **2-8-12** KFallon(4) (b.off hind: led 1f: led over 3f out tl over 1f out: sn rdn: one pce) | 6 | **3** | 15/8[2] | 81 | 47 |
| 3208* | **Union Town (IRE) (98)** (SirMarkPrescott) **2-8-12** GDuffield(3) (hld up & bhd: sn pushed along: hdwy over 3f out: nvr able to chal) | s.h | **4** | 4/1[3] | 81 | 47 |
| 3684[7] | **Bareeq (85)** (HThomsonJones) **2-8-12b[1]** GCarter(5) (led after 1f tl over 3f out: eased whn btn fnl 2f) | 12 | **5** | 16/1 | 57 | 23 |
| | | | | (SP 113.2%) | **5 Rn** | |

**1m 40.69** (0.73 under 2y best) (0.09) CSF £10.83 TOTE £2.40: £1.40 £1.90 (£4.80) OWNER Mr K. Abdulla (NEWMARKET) BRED Juddmonte Farms
**3779* Besiege** looks to be a lazy type and, as in his previous outing, took time to find top gear, but he did respond to forceful handling and broke the track record in the process. (6/4)
**3684 Sandstone (IRE)**, facing his biggest test, lost nothing in defeat, and the way he battled on under pressure would suggest this longer trip is what he really needs. (7/1)
**3485* Further Outlook (USA)** set sail for home soon after entering the straight, but rivals were queueing up to challenge, and he was made to look very one-paced in the dash to the post. (15/8)
**3208* Union Town (IRE)** struggled with the pace and for most of the way looked out of his depth but, with stamina coming into play, did stay on, if unable to trouble the leaders. (4/1)
**3684 Bareeq** ran much too freely in his first-time blinkers, and was allowed to complete in his own time. (16/1)

## 4057 HAYDOCK PARK SPRINT CUP STKS (Gp 1) (3-Y.O+) (Class A)

3-30 (3-32) **6f** £77,249.50 (£28,370.50: £13,435.25: £5,288.75: £1,894.38: £536.62) Stalls: High GOING minus 0.45 sec per fur (F)

| | | | | SP | RR | SF |
|---|---|---|---|---|---|---|
| 3573a[4] | **Iktamal (USA) (118)** (EALDunlop) **4-9-0** WRyan(9) (lw: hld up: hdwy over 2f out: r.o strly to ld wl ins fnl f) | — | **1** | 10/1 | 126 | 86 |
| 3573a[5] | **Blue Duster (USA) (119)** (DRLoder) **3-8-9** JReid(11) (w ldrs: led over 1f out tl wl ins fnl f) | 1 | **2** | 9/1 | 120 | 78 |
| 3708[5] | **Catch The Blues (IRE)** (APO'Brien,Ireland) **4-8-11v** CRoche(4) (a in tch: drvn along ½-wy: hrd rdn appr fnl f: kpt on) | 1¼ | **3** | 20/1 | 117 | 77 |
| 4033a[2] | **Hever Golf Rose (114)** (TJNaughton) **5-8-11** JFortune(10) (w ldrs: led over 2f out tl over 1f out: unable qckn) | ½ | **4** | 7/1[3] | 116 | 76 |
| 2622[2] | **Lucayan Prince (USA) (119)** (DRLoder) **3-8-12b** LDettori(1) (lw: hld up & bhd: swtchd lft wl over 1f out: nrst fin) | ½ | **5** | 3/1[2] | 117 | 75 |

| Form | Horse | Dist | Pos | SP | RR | SF |
|---|---|---|---|---|---|---|
| 3708$^{4}$ | **Mind Games (118)** (JBerry) **4-9-0** RHughes(6) (w ldrs: rdn & hung rt over 1f out: sn btn) | 1½ | **6** | 14/1 | 113 | 73 |
| 3573a$^{2}$ | **Miesque's Son (USA)** (JEHammond,France) **4-9-0** CAsmussen(3) (lw: hld up: effrt over 2f out: no imp) | hd | **7** | 5/2$^{1}$ | 113 | 73 |
| 3759$^{3}$ | **Rambling Bear (113)** (MBlanshard) **3-8-12** RCochrane(8) (sn bhd: pushed along & a outpcd) | ½ | **8** | 20/1 | 112 | 70 |
| 3132* | **Royal Applause (111)** (BWHills) **3-8-12** KFallon(2) (led tl hdd & wknd over 2f out) | 1½ | **9** | 16/1 | 108 | 66 |
| 3708$^{7}$ | **Cool Jazz (113)** (CEBrittain) **5-9-0** BDoyle(7) (lw: trckd ldrs: drvn along ½-wy: sn outpcd) | 1¼ | **10** | 33/1 | 104 | 64 |
| 3573a$^{3}$ | **Danehill Dancer (IRE) (115)** (NACallaghan) **3-8-12** PatEddery(5) (chsd ldrs: pushed along ½-wy: sn outpcd) | 6 | **11** | 7/1$^{3}$ | 88 | 46 |

(SP 122.7%) **11 Rn**

**1m 9.92** (0.80 under best) (-1.78) CSF £90.87 TOTE £11.80: £2.80 £2.50 £4.20 (£42.60) Trio £198.90 OWNER Maktoum Al Maktoum (NEWMARKET) BRED Green Ireland Properties Ltd

WEIGHT FOR AGE 3yo-2lb

OFFICIAL EXPLANATION **Miesque's Son (USA): did not act on the ground, causing him to hang right.**

**3573a Iktamal (USA)** gained his most important success yet with a convincing win in record time and, on his day, is out of the top drawer. (10/1)

**3573a Blue Duster (USA)** would have been a comfortable winner with Iktamal out of the way and, now that her stable has struck form, she should not be long in making amends. (9/1)

**3708 Catch The Blues (IRE)**, who may well benefit from more yielding ground, ran a fine race back over her ideal trip, and there will be plenty more opportunities for her to get black type by her name. (20/1)

**4033a Hever Golf Rose** turned in another genuine performance on ground plenty fast enough and, though she has not collected this season, it can only be a matter of time before she does. (7/1)

**2622 Lucayan Prince (USA)**, drawn out in the centre of the track, was really clawing the leaders back inside the final furlong but, on this fast ground, he always had a shade too much to do. He is really coming to himself this year. (3/1)

**3708 Mind Games** failed to end his racing career on a winning note, but he did give it his best shot which, in this sort of class, was just not good enough. (14/1)

**3573a Miesque's Son (USA)**, very keen to post, had trouble holding his pitch on ground as fast as this and, though he did try to mount a challenge, he was unable to muster the speed to do so. There is no doubting he is better than this. (5/2)

**3132* Royal Applause**, a very speedy colt, had the foot to set the pace from his low stall, but he is nowhere near as effective when he can not get his toe in, and he folded up quickly once collared. (16/1)

## 4058 LADBROKE H'CAP (0-80) (3-Y.O+) (Class D)

4-00 (4-02) **6f** £4,084.50 (£1,236.00: £603.00: £286.50) Stalls: High GOING minus 0.45 sec per fur (F)

| Form | Horse | Dist | Pos | SP | RR | SF |
|---|---|---|---|---|---|---|
| 2005$^{20}$ | **Oggi (59)** (PJMakin) **5-8-7** PatEddery(22) (a trckng ldrs: hrd rdn over 1f out: r.o to ld ins fnl f: sn clr) | — | **1** | 12/1 | 71 | 53 |
| 3937* | **Another Nightmare (IRE) (52)** (RMMcKellar) **4-7-7**(7) JMcAuley(14) (lw: led tl hdd & no ex ins fnl f) | 1½ | **2** | 10/1$^{3}$ | 60 | 42 |
| 3793$^{6}$ | **French Grit (IRE) (69)** (MDods) **4-9-3** AClark(21) (lw: w ldrs: rdn & no ex wl ins fnl f) | 1 | **3** | 12/1 | 74 | 56 |
| 3639$^{11}$ | **Castlerea Lad (75)** (RHollinshead) **7-9-6**(3) FLynch(16) (hdwy 2f out: kpt on wl ins fnl f) | 1¾ | **4** | 14/1 | 76 | 58 |
| 3932$^{10}$ | **Cretan Gift (68)** (NPLittmoden) **5-9-2b** LDettori(19) (hdwy over 1f out: nrst fin) | 1¼ | **5** | 8/1$^{2}$ | 65 | 47 |
| 3844$^{11}$ | **Bollin Dorothy (58)** (TDEasterby) **3-8-4** BDoyle(24) (mid div: rdn over 2f out: kpt on wl ins fnl f) | nk | **6** | 10/1$^{3}$ | 55 | 35 |
| 3868$^{3}$ | **The Happy Fox (IRE) (75)** (BAMcMahon) **4-9-9** GCarter(5) (a chsng ldrs far side: unable qckn ins fnl f) | nk | **7** | 10/1$^{3}$ | 71 | 53 |
| 3868$^{14}$ | **Garnock Valley (76)** (JBerry) **6-9-10** JCarroll(13) (hdwy to chse ldrs ½-wy: wknd over 1f out) | 1 | **8** | 16/1 | 69 | 51 |
| 3817$^{5}$ | **Halmanerror (70)** (MrsJRRamsden) **6-9-4** KFallon(17) (hdwy 2f out: nvr nr to chal) | s.h | **9** | 15/2$^{1}$ | 63 | 45 |
| 1786$^{5}$ | **Miss Aragon (48)** (MissLCSiddall) **8-7-10** NCarlisle(11) (lw: s.i.s. sme hdwy wl over 1f out: nvr nrr) | 3½ | **10** | 25/1 | 32 | 14 |
| 3868$^{6}$ | **Rich Glow (62)** (NBycroft) **5-8-10** RCochrane(8) (nvr trbld ldrs) | ¾ | **11** | 16/1 | 44 | 26 |
| 3863$^{3}$ | **Polly Golightly (65)** (MBlanshard) **3-8-11v$^{1}$** JQuinn(1) (racd alone far side: gd spd over 4f) | s.h | **12** | 16/1 | 47 | 27 |
| 2713$^{10}$ | **Denbrae (IRE) (70)** (DJGMurraySmith) **4-9-4** GDuffield(10) (trckd ldrs 4f) | 1¼ | **13** | 14/1 | 48 | 30 |
| 3489$^{6}$ | **Mister Westsound (65)** (MissLAPerratt) **4-8-13b** MTebbutt(15) (s.i.s: a in rr) | nk | **14** | 20/1 | 42 | 24 |
| 571$^{4}$ | **Erupt (76)** (GBBalding) **3-9-8** JReid(9) (chsd ldrs over 3f) | 5 | **15** | 16/1 | 40 | 20 |
| 2725$^{17}$ | **High Domain (IRE) (71)** (JLSpearing) **5-9-5** WRyan(23) (in tch: rdn over 2f out: sn wknd) | 2 | **16** | 12/1 | 30 | 12 |
| 3844$^{2}$ | **Never Think Twice (66)** (KTIvory) **3-8-12b** CScally(3) (b: s.s: a bhd) | 1¾ | **17** | 10/1$^{3}$ | 20 | — |
| 3932$^{5}$ | **Fantasy Racing (IRE) (72)** (MRChannon) **4-9-6** RHughes(6) (lw: n.d) | 1¼ | **18** | 14/1 | 23 | 5 |
| *3064*$^{10}$ | **Willie Miles (72)** (JWWatts) **3-9-4** NConnorton(12) (a outpcd) | s.h | **19** | 20/1 | 23 | 3 |
| 2794$^{12}$ | **Sotonian (HOL) (58)** (PSFelgate) **3-8-1**(3)ow8 PMcCabe(4) (a bhd & outpcd) | 7 | **20** | 33/1 | — | — |
| 3643$^{D}$ | **Sonderise (52)** (NTinkler) **7-7-11b**(3) MHenry(2) (prom over 3f) | ¾ | **21** | 16/1 | — | — |
| 3973$^{8}$ | **Aquado (56)** (SRBowring) **7-8-4b** JFEgan(20) (ref to r: t.n.p) | | **R** | 14/1 | — | — |

(SP 154.7%) **22 Rn**

**1m 11.72** (0.02) CSF £139.63 CT £1,436.31 TOTE £14.90: £3.20 £2.70 £3.40 £4.10 (£84.50) Trio £395.90 OWNER Skyline Racing Ltd (MARLBOROUGH) BRED H. D. and M. J. Gee

LONG HANDICAP Miss Aragon 7-9

WEIGHT FOR AGE 3yo-2lb

**Oggi** has been out of sorts in previous outings this term, but was produced fresh and well without the headgear. He brushed these rivals aside without much trouble and, if he can be relied upon to give a repeat performance, a follow-up is on the cards. (12/1)

**3937* Another Nightmare (IRE)** would seem to be ahead of the Handicapper if this good effort is anything to go by. Her game attempt to make all only just failed to materialise, and she is on a high at present. (10/1)

**3793 French Grit (IRE)**, in the firing-line from the break, failed to find anything extra when a final effort was called for, but he ran up to his mark and is knocking at the door. (12/1)

**1829 Castlerea Lad** has given his supporters little to shout about this season, but this was a bit more like his old self, and he still has the ability when he cares to use it. (14/1)

**3810 Cretan Gift** has shown nothing to suggest that he could open his account on turf in such a competitive event, but punters banked on the Dettori magic, although even that was not good enough to enable him to trouble the Judge. (8/1)

**3844 Bollin Dorothy**, hard at work up the stands'-side rail at halfway, kept battling away, but found the race over before she could get to terms. (10/1)

**3868 The Happy Fox (IRE)**, pushing the pace out in the centre of the track, was there with every chance until the sixth furlong again proved just too much. (10/1)

**3817 Halmanerror** may have had trouble finding a way through, but he was only getting into top gear when the race was as good as over. (15/2)

## 4059 SPEKE LIMITED STKS (0-70) (3-Y.O+) (Class E)

4-30 (4-30) **1m 30y** £3,129.00 (£942.00: £456.00: £213.00) Stalls: Low GOING minus 0.45 sec per fur (F)

| Form | Horse | Dist | Pos | SP | RR | SF |
|---|---|---|---|---|---|---|
| 3786$^{3}$ | **Embankment (IRE) (70)** (RHannon) **6-9-0** PatEddery(2) (chsd ldrs: swtchd rt 2f out: rdn to ld wl ins fnl f) | — | **1** | 3/1$^{1}$ | 78 | 57 |
| 3655$^{4}$ | **Budby (68)** (ACStewart) **3-8-8** LDettori(4) (trckd ldrs: hdwy to ld ins fnl f: hdd & no ex towards fin) | ½ | **2** | 7/2$^{2}$ | 76 | 50 |

| | | | | SP | RR | SF |
|---|---|---|---|---|---|---|
| $2917^{3}$ | **Bubble Wings (FR) (66)** (SPCWoods) **4-9-1** WRyan(8) (lw: hld up: effrt over 2f out: styd on u.p fnl f) | 1¾ | **3** | $4/1^{3}$ | 75 | 54 |
| $2701^{3}$ | **Mr Teigh (67)** (BSmart) **4-9-4** MTebbutt(7) (chsd ldr: led over 4f out tl hdd & wknd ins fnl f) | 3½ | **4** | 13/2 | 71 | 50 |
| $3985^{10}$ | **Stackattack (IRE) (68)** (PRWebber) **3-8-9** KFallon(1) (sn pushed along: styd on appr fnl f) | hd | **5** | 11/2 | 67 | 41 |
| $3634^{6}$ | **Quinze (70)** (SirMarkPrescott) **3-8-11** GDuffield(6) (stdd s: effrt over 3f out: no imp) | hd | **6** | 5/1 | 68 | 42 |
| $3280^{5}$ | **Ladykirk (67)** (JWWatts) **3-8-6** JCarroll(5) (led over 3f: wknd qckly) | 4 | **7** | 12/1 | 55 | 29 |
| $3770^{6}$ | **Mubariz (IRE) (70)** (CSmith) **4-9-0** MFenton(3) (b: sn pushed along: a bhd: t.o fnl 2f) | dist | **8** | 33/1 | — | — |

(SP 123.2%) **8 Rn**

**1m 41.05** (0.45) CSF £14.44 TOTE £4.30: £1.50 £1.40 £1.50 (£3.60) OWNER Lady Tennant (MARLBOROUGH) BRED Rathasker Stud
WEIGHT FOR AGE 3yo-5lb

**3786 Embankment (IRE)** completed a nap-hand for Eddery with a readily-gained success, which was his first since the spring of 1994. (3/1)
**3655 Budby** looked to hold all the aces when poking his head in front 200 yards out, but the winner answered his jockey's every call and took his measure nearing the line. (7/2)
**2917 Bubble Wings (FR)** stuck on really well in the closing stages and stamina would seem to be her strong suit. (4/1)
**2701 Mr Teigh** lacks pace at the business end of races and, over a trip possibly on the short side, was left for dead inside the distance. (13/2)
**3985 Stackattack (IRE)**, soon nudged along in the rear, made up quite a lot of ground in the latter stages, and he looks to need a trip at least as far as this. (11/2)
**3634 Quinze**, steadied at the start in an attempt to get him to settle, did eventually stop pulling but, when he did, the leaders had got away and he was never a factor. (5/1: 3/1-11/2)

## 4060 E.B.F. ALTRINCHAM MAIDEN STKS (2-Y.O) (Class D)

5-00 (5-00) **7f 30y** £3,805.00 (£1,150.00: £560.00: £265.00) Stalls: Low GOING minus 0.45 sec per fur (F)

| | | | | SP | RR | SF |
|---|---|---|---|---|---|---|
| | **Apprehension** (DRLoder) **2-9-0** LDettori(5) (gd sort: trckd ldrs: shkn up over 2f out: led over 1f out: pushed clr) | — | **1** | $8/15^{1}$ | 84+ | 40 |
| $3221^{6}$ | **Social Pillar (USA)** (JHMGosden) **2-9-0** JReid(10) (hld up in tch: effrt & ev ch over 2f out: one pce appr fnl f) | 5 | **2** | $4/1^{2}$ | 73 | 29 |
| $3499^{8}$ | **Beryllium** (RHannon) **2-9-0** RHughes(4) (chsd ldr: led over 2f out tl over 1f out: sn rdn & outpcd) | nk | **3** | 11/1 | 72 | 28 |
| | **Highway** (BWHills) **2-9-0** KFallon(2) (lt-f: unf: s.i.s: shkn up & hdwy 3f out: kpt on u.p fnl f) | 2½ | **4** | $13/2^{3}$ | 67 | 23 |
| | **Court Express** (TJEtherington) **2-9-0** MTebbutt(1) (leggy: bit bkwd: s.i.s: a in rr) | 5 | **5** | 20/1 | 55 | 11 |
| $3837^{11}$ | **Beau Roberto** (MJohnston) **2-9-0** BDoyle(8) (trckd ldrs 4f) | 1¼ | **6** | 20/1 | 53 | 9 |
| $1003^{9}$ | **Rake Hey** (RFJohnsonHoughton) **2-9-0** GDuffield(9) (led tl over 2f out: sn rdn & wknd) | s.h | **7** | 16/1 | 52 | 8 |

(SP 122.3%) **7 Rn**

**1m 29.4** (1.17 under 2y best) (1.90) CSF £3.74 TOTE £1.60: £1.20 £1.90 (£2.00) Trio £13.00 OWNER Sheikh Mohammed (NEWMARKET) BRED Sheikh Mohammed Bin Rashid Al Maktoum

**Apprehension** came here with a glowing reputation and, though he did not impress to post, he showed what he is made of with a runaway success in record time. It will come as a big disappointment if he does not go on from here. (8/15)
**3221 Social Pillar (USA)** looked to be the one to beat entering the last quarter-mile but, when the winner was let loose, it was then a race for the places. (4/1)
**Beryllium** is gaining experience and ran his best race yet, but it will not do his confidence much good if he comes up against many as useful as the winner. (11/1)
**Highway**, an unfurnished debutant who could need time, did not fare badly after missing the break. He is sure to be much wiser next time. (13/2)

T/Jkpt: Not won; £11,374.49 to Southwell 9/9/96. T/Plpt: £1,249.00 (25.73 Tckts). T/Qdpt: £113.10 (11.18 Tckts). IM

# 4048-KEMPTON (R-H) (Good)
## Saturday September 7th
WEATHER: fine WIND: almost nil

## 4061 GROSVENOR CASINO RAMSGATE E. B. F. MAIDEN STKS (I) (2-Y.O F) (Class D)

1-45 (1-48) **6f** £3,111.25 (£940.00: £457.50: £216.25) Stalls: Low GOING minus 0.37 sec per fur (F)

| | | | | SP | RR | SF |
|---|---|---|---|---|---|---|
| | **Blane Water (USA)** (JRFanshawe) **2-8-11** DHarrison(4) (unf: hld up: led over 1f out: rdn: r.o wl) | — | **1** | 12/1 | 91 | 41 |
| | **Lochangel** (IABalding) **2-8-6**(5) MartinDwyer(3) (w'like: scope: lw: s.s: wl bhd 3f: swtchd rt: rapid hdwy 2f out: r.o wl ins fnl f) | 4 | **2** | 14/1 | 80+ | 30 |
| | **Silver Kristal** (RAkehurst) **2-8-11** TQuinn(5) (str: scope: bkwd: led over 4f: unable qckn) | 1 | **3** | $7/2^{2}$ | 78 | 28 |
| | **Villarica (IRE)** (PWChapple-Hyam) **2-8-8**(3) RHavlin(11) (leggy: a.p: rdn over 2f out: one pce) | ¾ | **4** | 10/1 | 76 | 26 |
| $3475^{3}$ | **Bold Tina (IRE) (78)** (RHannon) **2-8-11** DaneO'Neill(12) (a.p: rdn over 2f out: wknd over 1f out) | 3 | **5** | $6/1^{3}$ | 68 | 18 |
| | **Native Princess (IRE)** (BWHills) **2-8-6**(5) JDSmith(1) (w'like: scope: bit bkwd: outpcd: nvr nrr) | 1½ | **6** | 16/1 | 64 | 14 |
| $3494^{9}$ | **Ar Hyd Y Knos** (RCharlton) **2-8-11** TSprake(14) (a mid div) | ¾ | **7** | 50/1 | 62 | 12 |
| | **Cugina** (GBBalding) **2-8-11** SDrowne(7) (w'like: scope: bkwd: outpcd: nvr nrr) | 1 | **8** | 50/1 | 59 | 9 |
| $3773^{6}$ | **Marytavy** (SirMarkPrescott) **2-8-11** CNutter(6) (outpcd) | hd | **9** | 33/1 | 59 | 9 |
| $3685^{10}$ | **Wrn Princess** (BJMeehan) **2-8-11** SSanders(13) (prom over 3f) | ½ | **10** | 16/1 | 57 | 7 |
| | **Beveled Crystal** (CJames) **2-8-11** CRutter(2) (small: bhd fnl 4f) | 1½ | **11** | 50/1 | 53 | 3 |
| $3593^{6}$ | **Injazaat (USA)** (MajorWRHern) **2-8-11** WCarson(10) (prom over 3f) | 4 | **12** | $6/4^{1}$ | 43 | — |
| $3660^{5}$ | **Good News (IRE)** (MMadgwick) **2-8-11** RPerham(8) (prom over 3f) | 2 | **13** | 33/1 | 37 | — |
| | **Teutonic Lass (IRE)** (PTWalwyn) **2-8-11** RHills(9) (w'like: scope: bit bkwd: a bhd) | 5 | **14** | 14/1 | 24 | — |

(SP 130.2%) **14 Rn**

**1m 12.96** (1.66) CSF £161.60 TOTE £15.80: £3.30 £3.50 £2.20 (£50.90) Trio £148.70 OWNER C I T Racing Ltd (NEWMARKET) BRED Fittocks Stud

**Blane Water (USA)**, with a lot less to like about her than many in the field, went on a furlong and a half from home and soon asserted her authority. (12/1: 8/1-14/1)
**Lochangel**, an attractive half-sister to Lochsong, has plenty of substance and scope, but showed her inexperience, losing far more ground at the start than she was beaten by. Well adrift of the field until past halfway, she made tremendous headway a quarter of a mile out and really ate up the ground to swoop into second place in the closing stages. She will be a lot wiser for this and should soon pick up a race. (14/1: 8/1-16/1)
**Silver Kristal**, a strongly-made filly, looked extremely fat in the paddock and, in the circumstances, ran surprisingly well, taking the field along until collared a furlong and a half out. Sure to strip a lot fitter for this, she should soon find a race. (7/2)

**Villarica (IRE)** is a quite tall half-sister to several winners. (10/1: 4/1-11/1)
**3475 Bold Tina (IRE)** had experience on her side and raced up with the pace until tiring below the distance. (6/1: op 4/1)
**Native Princess (IRE)**, a round-bodied filly who is a half-sister to several winners in the USA and Italy, did not look fully wound up. After being taken off her feet, she did make a little late headway. (16/1)
**3593 Injazaat (USA)** was very disappointing and tamely dropped out of the action after showing up until approaching the final quarter-mile. (6/4)
**Teutonic Lass (IRE)** (14/1: 8/1-16/1)

## 4062 GROSVENOR CASINO RAMSGATE E.B.F. MAIDEN STKS (II) (2-Y.O F) (Class D)

2-15 (2-19) **6f** £3,095.00 (£935.00: £455.00: £215.00) Stalls: Low GOING minus 0.37 sec per fur (F)

| | | | | SP | RR | SF |
|---|---|---|---|---|---|---|
| | **Calypso Lady (IRE)** (RHannon) **2-8-11** RPerham(9) (leggy: scope: lw: s.s: outpcd: hdwy over 1f out: led ins fnl f: r.o wl) | — | **1** | 50/1 | 77 | 37 |
| 3593[11] | **Flourishing Way** (RCharlton) **2-8-11** TSprake(3) (a.p: rdn over 1f out: r.o wl ins fnl f) | ¾ | **2** | 12/1 | 75 | 35 |
| 3807[3] | **Hopesay** (JHMGosden) **2-8-11** AMcGlone(12) (a.p: led over 1f out tl ins fnl f: unable qckn) | 1 | **3** | 5/1[2] | 72 | 32 |
| | **Always On My Mind** (PJMakin) **2-8-8**(3) RHavlin(7) (unf: scope: a.p: ev ch over 1f out: one pce) | 1¼ | **4** | 50/1 | 69 | 29 |
| | **Spanish Knot (USA)** (LordHuntingdon) **2-8-11** WRSwinburn(13) (leggy: lt-f: hdwy & nt clr run over 1f out: nvr nrr) | 1¼ | **5** | 16/1 | 66 | 26 |
| | **Rosy Outlook (USA)** (IABalding) **2-8-11** TQuinn(1) (unf: scope: hld up: rdn over 2f out: n.m.r over 1f out: wknd fnl f) | 2 | **6** | 11/2[3] | 60 | 20 |
| | **Junie (IRE)** (TGMills) **2-8-11** OUrbina(4) (leggy: lw: hld up: rdn over 1f out: wknd fnl f) | hd | **7** | 50/1 | 60 | 20 |
| 3464[3] | **Sylvan Dancer (IRE)** (CFWall) **2-8-11** SSanders(11) (a.p: ev ch over 1f out: n.m.r 1f out: sn wknd) | s.h | **8** | 16/1 | 60 | 20 |
| | **Silent Miracle (IRE)** (MBell) **2-8-11** JTate(6) (w'like: s.s: bhd fnl 3f) | 1 | **9** | 25/1 | 57 | 17 |
| 3234[5] | **Miss Riviera Rose** (GWragg) **2-8-11** MHills(10) (lw: hld up: rdn over 2f out: wknd fnl f) | 1½ | **10** | 8/1 | 53 | 13 |
| 3433[2] | **Alikhlas** (HThomsonJones) **2-8-11** RHills(8) (led over 4f) | ½ | **11** | 15/8[1] | 52 | 12 |
| 1678[7] | **First Page** (WJarvis) **2-8-11** DaneO'Neill(5) (lw: s.s: a bhd) | 7 | **12** | 33/1 | 33 | — |
| | **Jade's Gem** (GBBalding) **2-8-11** SDrowne(2) (unf: scope: bit bkwd: s.s: a bhd) | ½ | **13** | 50/1 | 32 | — |
| 1954[9] | **Mystery (76)** (SDow) **2-8-11** DHarrison(14) (lw: bhd fnl 4f) | ¾ | **14** | 16/1 | 30 | — |
| | | | | (SP 117.9%) | **14 Rn** | |

**1m 13.3** (2.00) CSF £487.71 TOTE £15.20: £2.70 £5.00 £2.10 (£165.80) Trio £369.10; £389.98 to 9/9/96 OWNER Mrs D. M. Wight (MARLBOROUGH) BRED Scuderia Milano

**Calypso Lady (IRE)**, an angular filly, looked extremely well and was the paddock pick, making her starting price a complete joke. Losing ground at the start and totally taken off her feet, her prospects did not look very good at halfway but she really found her stride from below the distance and swept into the lead inside the final furlong. She will be better served by further. (50/1)
**Flourishing Way**, all the better for her initial run, kept on really well inside the final furlong for second prize. A well-bred filly, she should soon find a race. (12/1: op 6/1)
**3807 Hopesay**, although one of the stable's lesser lights, should be able to find a race round one of the smaller tracks. (5/1)
**Always On My Mind**, with the frame to develop, had every chance below the distance before tapped for toe. A half-sister to two winning hurdlers as well as middle-distance performer Addicted to Love, she should be able to find a race when stepped up in distance. (50/1)
**Spanish Knot (USA)**, a sparely-made filly, met with traffic problems below the distance as she picked up ground, but did stay on to finish fifth. (16/1)
**Rosy Outlook (USA)**, a plain, narrow filly out of a half-sister to European champion two-year-old filly of 1985 Baiser Vole, chased the leaders until eventually tiring in the final furlong. (11/2)
**3433 Alikhlas** did not take the eye in the paddock, but still took the field along until tamely folding up when collared below the distance. (15/8: Evens-2/1)

## 4063 GROSVENOR CONNOISSEUR CASINO CONDITIONS STKS (3-Y.O+ F & M) (Class C)

2-45 (2-45) **1m 4f** £4,629.00 (£1,731.00: £845.50: £362.50: £161.25: £80.75) Stalls: High GOING minus 0.37 sec per fur (F)

| | | | | SP | RR | SF |
|---|---|---|---|---|---|---|
| 3711[6] | **Poppy Carew (IRE) (106)** (PWHarris) **4-9-2** WRSwinburn(6) (lw: hld up: led over 2f out: rdn: r.o wl) | — | **1** | 100/30[1] | 107 | 62 |
| 3836[7] | **Ellie Ardensky (96)** (JRFanshawe) **4-9-2** TQuinn(1) (hdwy over 4f out: chsd wnr over 2f out: unable qckn) | 1¼ | **2** | 13/2[3] | 105 | 60 |
| 3658[2] | **Kinlochewe (97)** (HRACecil) **3-8-11** AMcGlone(7) (lw: a.p: rdn over 2f out: one pce) | 3½ | **3** | 11/2[2] | 105 | 51 |
| 3711[4] | **Bathilde (IRE) (98)** (MRStoute) **3-8-13** RHills(2) (chsd ldr: led over 3f out tl over 2f out: one pce) | hd | **4** | 11/2[2] | 107 | 53 |
| 2869* | **Berenice (80)** (GWragg) **3-8-11** MHills(3) (rdn over 2f out: nvr nr to chal) | 2½ | **5** | 16/1 | 101 | 47 |
| | **Subterfuge** (HRACecil) **3-8-7** DHarrison(5) (a bhd) | 7 | **6** | 8/1 | 88 | 34 |
| 3497[3] | **Ta Awun (USA) (96)** (ACStewart) **3-8-11** WCarson(4) (lw: led over 8f: wknd over 2f out) | nk | **7** | 100/30[1] | 92 | 38 |
| | | | | (SP 107.2%) | **7 Rn** | |

**2m 31.96** (1.26) CSF £21.36 TOTE £2.60: £1.70 £3.60 (£9.50) OWNER Mrs P. W. Harris (BERKHAMSTED) BRED Pendley Farm
WEIGHT FOR AGE 3yo-9lb

**3711 Poppy Carew (IRE)** put up a tremendous performance to register her first victory over this trip. Sent on over a quarter of a mile from home, she lengthened her stride in good style and proved too strong for the runner-up. (100/30)
**2145 Ellie Ardensky** bounced back to form to put to rest fears that this trip was beyond her. Almost on terms with the winner over a quarter of a mile from home, she pulled well clear of the remainder. (13/2)
**3658 Kinlochewe** was firmly put in her place in the last two furlongs. (11/2: 7/2-6/1)
**3711 Bathilde (IRE)** was 13lb worse off with the winner for beating that rival just over four lengths at York last month. (11/2: 7/2-6/1)

## 4064 GEOFFREY HAMLYN H'CAP (0-80) (3-Y.O) (Class D)

3-15 (3-17) **1m (Jubilee)** £3,956.25 (£1,200.00: £587.50: £281.25) Stalls: High GOING minus 0.37 sec per fur (F)

| | | | | SP | RR | SF |
|---|---|---|---|---|---|---|
| 3852* | **Veni Vidi Vici (IRE) (62)** (MJHeaton-Ellis) **3-8-3**ow2 DaneO'Neill(12) (hdwy & nt clr run over 1f out: hrd rdn: led wl ins fnl f: r.o wl) | — | **1** | 9/1[3] | 76 | 43 |
| 3799[4] | **Forest Robin (80)** (RFJohnsonHoughton) **3-9-7** TQuinn(10) (b: lw: hld up: rdn over 2f out: r.o) | ¾ | **2** | 14/1 | 93 | 62 |
| 3679* | **Roushan (77)** (SCWilliams) **3-9-4** JTate(8) (w ldr: led over 3f out: hrd rdn over 1f out: hdd wl ins fnl f: unable qckn) | nk | **3** | 12/1 | 89 | 58 |
| 3634[7] | **Mystic Dawn (61)** (SDow) **3-7-11**(5)ow4 ADaly(17) (lw: hdwy 2f out: rdn over 1f out: one pce) | 2½ | **4** | 25/1 | 68 | 33 |
| 2585[7] | **Hippy (75)** (CEBrittain) **3-9-2** MHills(6) (a.p: rdn over 2f out: one pce) | ¾ | **5** | 10/1 | 80 | 49 |
| 3818[4] | **Midday Cowboy (USA) (73)** (GHarwood) **3-9-0** RHills(18) (rdn over 2f out: hdwy & nt clr run over 1f out: one pce fnl f) | nk | **6** | 16/1 | 78 | 47 |
| 3995[6] | **Sylvan Princess (67)** (CNAllen) **3-8-3**(5) MartinDwyer(14) (rdn over 2f out: hdwy over 1f out: nvr nrr) | s.h | **7** | 6/1[1] | 72 | 41 |

| | | | | SP | RR | SF |
|---|---|---|---|---|---|---|
| *3421*[4] | **Biscay (70)** (RCharlton) **3-8-11** TSprake(19) (hld up: nt clr run 2f out tl over 1f out: one pce) | 1½ | **8** | 16/1 | 72 | 41 |
| 3790[6] | **Press On Nicky (72)** (WRMuir) **3-8-13** OUrbina(13) (lw: a mid div) | 1 | **9** | 12/1 | 72 | 41 |
| 2885[5] | **Willisa (65)** (JDBethell) **3-8-6** WCarson(5) (prom over 5f) | hd | **10** | 16/1 | 65 | 34 |
| 3696* | **Blue Flyer (IRE) (74)** (RIngram) **3-9-1** DRMcCabe(9) (led over 4f: wknd over 1f out) | ¾ | **11** | 8/1[2] | 72 | 41 |
| 3806[3] | **Proud Monk (77)** (GLMoore) **3-9-4** SWhitworth(16) (lw: prom over 6f) | ½ | **12** | 14/1 | 74 | 43 |
| 3967[4] | **Quality (IRE) (78)** (WAO'Gorman) **3-9-5** EmmaO'Gorman(1) (a bhd) | hd | **13** | 14/1 | 75 | 44 |
| 3496[5] | **Mimosa (57)** (SDow) **3-7-5**(7)ow2 DSalt(3) (lw: s.s: a bhd) | 2½ | **14** | 33/1 | 49 | 16 |
| 3287[3] | **Generous Present (59)** (JWPayne) **3-8-0** DeclanO'Shea(15) (lw: prom 6f) | ¾ | **15** | 14/1 | 49 | 18 |
| 3609* | **Designer Lines (75)** (CJames) **3-9-2v** CRutter(7) (lw: bhd fnl 2f) | 1¾ | **16** | 16/1 | 62 | 31 |
| | **Squire's Occasion (CAN) (68)** (RAkehurst) **3-8-9** SSanders(11) (a bhd) | 2½ | **17** | 11/1 | 50 | 19 |
| 1438[7] | **Warren Knight (67)** (CAHorgan) **3-8-8** DHarrison(2) (a bhd) | ½ | **18** | 33/1 | 48 | 17 |
| 3516[4] | **Phonetic (77)** (GBBalding) **3-9-4** SDrowne(4) (bhd fnl 3f) | ½ | **19** | 20/1 | 57 | 26 |

(SP 132.9%) **19 Rn**

**1m 38.63** (1.43) CSF £124.45 CT £1,416.14 TOTE £9.60: £2.20 £3.40 £2.60 £9.90 (£62.70) Trio £319.20 OWNER Mr R. A. Bicker (WROUGHTON) BRED Michael Moran
LONG HANDICAP Mimosa 7-6

**3852* Veni Vidi Vici (IRE)**, who did not get a clear run as he picked up ground below the distance, responded well to pressure in the final furlong to get up in the last 50 yards. (9/1)

**3799 Forest Robin** is still a maiden and is having a tough time of it in handicap company off his current mark. (14/1)

**3679* Roushan**, who went down to the start fifteen minutes before post time, ran a sound race and was only worried out of it in the closing stages. (12/1)

**2605 Mystic Dawn** failed to find another gear from below the distance. She is still a maiden after twelve attempts. (25/1)

**2437 Hippy** failed to quicken in the last two furlongs. (10/1)

**3818 Midday Cowboy (USA)** was one of several who did not get a clear run below the distance but, when a gap did appear, he could only plod on at one pace. (16/1)

**3995 Sylvan Princess**, making a quick reappearance, stayed on from below the distance, but now appears to be in the Handicapper's grip. (6/1)

**Squire's Occasion (CAN)** (11/1: 8/1-12/1)

## 4065 GROSVENOR CASINOS SIRENIA STKS (Listed) (2-Y.O) (Class A)

3-45 (3-46) **6f** £9,576.00 (£2,898.00: £1,414.00: £672.00) Stalls: Low GOING minus 0.37 sec per fur (F)

| | | | | SP | RR | SF |
|---|---|---|---|---|---|---|
| 3707[2] | **Arethusa (100)** (RHannon) **2-8-6** DaneO'Neill(5) (b.off fore: hld up: rdn over 1f out: led ins fnl f: r.o wl) | — | **1** | 11/4[2] | 96 | 43 |
| 3792[8] | **Maserati Monk (95)** (BJMeehan) **2-8-11** SSanders(1) (led: rdn over 1f out: hdd ins fnl f: r.o) | nk | **2** | 20/1 | 100 | 47 |
| 3773* | **Starborough** (DRLoder) **2-8-11** TQuinn(7) (lw: racd centre: a.p: rdn over 2f out: unable qckn) | nk | **3** | 11/10[1] | 99 | 46 |
| 3796* | **Johnny Staccato** (JMPEustace) **2-8-11** JTate(2) (dwlt: hdwy & nt clr run over 1f out: r.o ins fnl f) | ¾ | **4** | 8/1 | 97 | 44 |
| 3707[5] | **Moonshine Girl (USA) (100)** (MRStoute) **2-8-6** WCarson(4) (lw: a.p: ev ch over 1f out: one pce) | 1 | **5** | 9/2[3] | 90 | 37 |
| 3483[2] | **Double-J (IRE) (87)** (KMcAuliffe) **2-8-11** TSprake(3) (bhd fnl 2f) | 2 | **6** | 40/1 | 89? | 36 |
| 3444[9] | **Papita (IRE) (85)** (SDow) **2-8-6** MHills(6) (spd over 4f) | 5 | **7** | 25/1 | 71 | 18 |

(SP 114.6%) **7 Rn**

**1m 12.46** (1.16) CSF £41.59 TOTE £3.40: £1.80 £5.80 (£33.80) OWNER Lord Carnarvon (MARLBOROUGH) BRED P. and Mrs Venner
STEWARDS' ENQUIRY Urbina susp. 16-18/9/96 (excessive use of whip)

**3707 Arethusa**, held up travelling really well, was woken up below the distance and came through to lead inside the last 100 yards. (11/4)

**3792 Maserati Monk**, with plenty of experience on his side, took the field along and, although collared in the last 100 yards, stuck to his task well. (20/1)

**3773* Starborough** elected to race in the centre of the track and was always handy. However, his jockey was niggling him along soon after halfway and, although he was only beaten two necks, he never looked like finding the required turn of foot. He should soon return to the winner's enclosure. (11/10)

**3796* Johnny Staccato** is not that big, but acquitted himself well in this company, staying on nicely inside the final furlong, having not had a clear run below the distance. (8/1)

**3707 Moonshine Girl (USA)**, led round by two handlers in the paddock, was on level terms with the leader below the distance before quicker rivals had her measure. (9/2: 3/1-5/1)

## 4066 GROSVENOR CASINOS SEPTEMBER STKS (Gp 3) (3-Y.O+) (Class A)

4-15 (4-16) **1m 3f 30y** £19,470.00 (£7,371.00: £3,610.50: £1,648.50) Stalls: High GOING minus 0.37 sec per fur (F)

| | | | | SP | RR | SF |
|---|---|---|---|---|---|---|
| 1390a* | **Sacrament (110)** (MRStoute) **5-9-5** WRSwinburn(5) (chsd ldr: led over 1f out: drvn out) | — | **1** | 11/2[3] | 124 | 68 |
| 3798[2] | **Salmon Ladder (USA) (113)** (PFICole) **4-9-0** TQuinn(7) (swtg: led over 9f: hrd rdn & ev ch fnl f: r.o) | nk | **2** | 7/4[1] | 119 | 63 |
| 3431[2] | **Ela-Aristokrati (IRE) (116)** (LMCumani) **4-9-0** OUrbina(6) (b.off hind: hdwy over 2f out: hrd rdn over 1f out: r.o wl ins fnl f) | nk | **3** | 2/1[2] | 118 | 62 |
| 2038[5] | **Cezanne (110)** (SbinSuroor) **7-9-0** RHills(4) (lw: hld up: hrd rdn over 1f out: r.o ins fnl f) | hd | **4** | 11/2[3] | 118 | 62 |
| 3710[2] | **Sheer Danzig (IRE) (96)** (RWArmstrong) **4-9-0** MHills(1) (lw: prom over 6f) | 5 | **5** | 14/1 | 111 | 55 |
| 3791* | **Ball Gown (95)** (DTThom) **6-8-11** DRMcCabe(2) (b.hind: hdwy over 2f out: sn wknd) | 1 | **6** | 25/1 | 106 | 50 |
| 3658[5] | **Lomberto (92)** (RHannon) **3-8-6b**[1] DaneO'Neill(3) (lw: bhd fnl 5f) | 7 | **7** | 40/1 | 99 | 35 |

(SP 113.4%) **7 Rn**

**2m 19.58** (0.78) CSF £15.03 TOTE £7.00: £3.40 £1.80 (£6.30) OWNER Cheveley Park Stud (NEWMARKET) BRED Cheveley Park Stud Ltd
WEIGHT FOR AGE 3yo-8lb
STEWARDS' ENQUIRY Urbina susp. 16-18/9/96 (excessive use of whip).

**1390a* Sacrament**, given a four-month break, put up a fine performance and, showing narrowly ahead below the distance, held on well in a tremendous finish. (11/2)

**3798 Salmon Ladder (USA)** sweated up badly in the paddock and, by the time he went into the stalls, he was in a dreadful state, but that did not stop him running his usual gutsy race. Bowling along in front, he was collared over a furlong out, but he showed a tremendous never-say-die attitude and battled his heart out to the very last stride. A Group Three race is waiting for him. (7/4)

**3431 Ela-Aristokrati (IRE)** would have won this had his jockey not given him such a bad ride. Firstly, Urbina was too far off the two principals turning into the straight, and then he lost his reins for a brief time at a critical stage over a quarter of a mile from home, costing him precious time he could ill-afford to waste. Coming under pressure below the distance, his rider went for his stick and the colt really began to pick up. Closing fast, desperation set in as the line approached and Urbina hit his mount twelve times in the last furlong and a half, but the combination just failed. The Stewards handed him a three-day suspension for his use of the whip. Consolation is richly deserved and it may well come in listed or Group Three company. (2/1)

**2038 Cezanne** looked in fine fettle for this first run in nearly two months. In third place entering the straight, he stuck to his task in commendable style inside the final furlong. (11/2: 4/1-6/1)
**3710 Sheer Danzig (IRE)** was out of his depth. (14/1)
**3791* Ball Gown** was outclassed. (25/1)

## 4067 GROSVENOR VICTORIA CASINO H'CAP (0-90) (3-Y.O+) (Class C)

4-45 (4-51) **1m 4f** £6,174.00 (£1,872.00: £916.00: £438.00) Stalls: High GOING minus 0.37 sec per fur (F)

| Form | Horse | Dist | Pos | SP | RR | SF |
|---|---|---|---|---|---|---|
| 3683[3] | **Leading Spirit (IRE) (83)** (CFWall) **4-9-12** RHills(8) (a.p: chsd ldr over 8f out: led 3f out: rdn out) | — | **1** | 12/1 | 93 | 66 |
| 3260* | **Wild Rita (74)** (WRMuir) **4-9-3** OUrbina(11) (rdn over 3f out: hdwy over 1f out: r.o wl ins fnl f) | ½ | **2** | 12/1 | 83 | 56 |
| 3683[5] | **Artic Courier (82)** (DJSCosgrove) **5-9-6**(5) LNewton(6) (hdwy & nt clr run over 1f out: swtchd rt: r.o wl ins fnl f) | ½ | **3** | 14/1 | 91 | 64 |
| 2882[5] | **Fitzwilliam (USA) (85)** (IABalding) **3-9-0**(5) MartinDwyer(13) (chsd ldr over 3f: chsd wnr over 2f out tl ins fnl f: one pce) | nk | **4** | 7/1[2] | 93 | 57 |
| 3479* | **Pistol (IRE) (77)** (CAHorgan) **6-9-6** WRSwinburn(2) (b.nr hind: hdwy over 1f out: r.o wl ins fnl f) | ¾ | **5** | 15/2[3] | 84 | 57 |
| 3689[10] | **My Learned Friend (83)** (AHide) **5-9-12** AMcGlone(5) (hld up: rdn 3f out: one pce) | nk | **6** | 16/1 | 90 | 63 |
| 3828[2] | **Fairy Knight (64)** (RHannon) **4-8-7** DaneO'Neill(1) (lw: hdwy over 1f out: nvr nrr) | 1½ | **7** | 11/2[1] | 69 | 42 |
| 3155[10] | **Nereus (83)** (BWHills) **3-8-12**(5) JDSmith(18) (lw: hld up: rdn 4f out: wknd fnl f) | ½ | **8** | 25/1 | 87 | 51 |
| 3828[9] | **Roisin Clover (66)** (SDow) **5-8-9** SSanders(7) (nvr nr to chal) | ¾ | **9** | 16/1 | 69 | 42 |
| 3683[2] | **Haya Ya Kefaah (63)** (NMBabbage) **4-8-6** TSprake(14) (prom 10f) | s.h | **10** | 8/1 | 66 | 39 |
| 3710[15] | **Mattimeo (IRE) (72)** (APJarvis) **3-8-6** SDrowne(15) (hdwy & n.m.r over 2f out: nt clr run over 1f out: nt rcvr) | ½ | **11** | 16/1 | 75 | 39 |
| 3479[3] | **Tappeto (70)** (HCandy) **4-8-13** CRutter(9) (hdwy 2f out: nt clr run over 1f out: sn wknd) | ½ | **12** | 14/1 | 72 | 45 |
| 3575* | **Gold Blade (71)** (JPearce) **7-9-0** MWigham(3) (lw: a bhd) | hd | **13** | 14/1 | 73 | 46 |
| 3522* | **Stately Dancer (75)** (GWragg) **3-8-9** MHills(10) (lw: prom over 10f) | 3 | **14** | 14/1 | 73 | 37 |
| 3876[7] | **Mr Browning (USA) (71)** (RAkehurst) **5-9-0b** TQuinn(16) (led 9f) | 9 | **15** | 8/1 | 57 | 30 |
| 968[8] | **No Pattern (72)** (GLMoore) **4-9-1** SWhitworth(12) (lw: hdwy & nt clr run on ins over 2f out: nt clr run on ins over 1f out: sn wknd) | ½ | **16** | 33/1 | 57 | 30 |
| 3760[6] | **Swan Hunter (75)** (DJSCosgrove) **3-8-9** DRMcCabe(17) (a bhd) | 16 | **17** | 25/1 | 39 | 3 |
| 3710[10] | **Alaflak (IRE) (79)** (MajorWRHern) **5-9-8** WCarson(4) (lw: a bhd: p.u 2f out: dismntd) | | **P** | 16/1 | — | — |

(SP 138.1%) **18 Rn**

**2m 32.8** (2.10) CSF £149.24 CT £1,912.05 TOTE £15.80: £2.80 £1.30 £5.00 £2.40 (£76.90) Trio £738.20 OWNER Induna Racing Partners Two (NEWMARKET) BRED Sir Peter Nugent and Ascot Stables
WEIGHT FOR AGE 3yo-9lb

**3683 Leading Spirit (IRE)**, 10lb higher than when winning here in June, goes well on this track. Sent on three furlongs from home, he was rousted along to keep his rivals at bay. (12/1)
**3260* Wild Rita**, racing in midfield, picked up ground from below the distance but, despite running on strongly, was never going to get there in time. (12/1)
**3683 Artic Courier** met with interference below the distance but, to his credit, ran on strongly inside the final furlong. He is not easy to win with. (14/1)
**2882 Fitzwilliam (USA)** regained second place early in the straight, but he failed to master the winner and was collared for the runner-up berth inside the final furlong. (7/1)
**3479* Pistol (IRE)** is in tremendous form at present and was putting in some sound work in the last furlong and a half. (15/2)
**2690 My Learned Friend** never looked like quickening up in the straight. (16/1)
**3333* Mattimeo (IRE)** had no luck in running and his jockey unwisely tried for a run through the middle of the pack in the straight. Not surprisingly, he met with traffic problems which sealed his fate. There were also excuses for his last run but, prior to that, he had won a Nottingham handicap. With a bit of luck, he could well bounce back, and he is certainly one to bear in mind. (16/1)
**771 No Pattern**, who reportedly had a wind operation, hence his four-month absence, continually met with interference as he tried for a run up the inside in the straight. All three of his wins to date have come at Lingfield, two on the Equitrack and, with this run sure to have brought him on and now racing off a 1lb lower mark than his last win, he looks one to bear in mind, especially if returning to his favourite track. (33/1)

## 4068 GROSVENOR CASINO READING APPRENTICE H'CAP (0-70) (3-Y.O+) (Class E)

5-15 (5-21) **1m 2f (Jubilee)** £3,225.00 (£975.00: £475.00: £225.00) Stalls: High GOING minus 0.37 sec per fur (F)

| Form | Horse | Dist | Pos | SP | RR | SF |
|---|---|---|---|---|---|---|
| 3785[8] | **Harvey White (IRE) (56)** (JPearce) **4-8-13**(3) PDoe(17) (hdwy over 3f out: led over 2f out: hrd rdn over 1f out: r.o wl) | — | **1** | 12/1 | 68 | 58 |
| 3802[7] | **Fern's Governor (46)** (WJMusson) **4-8-3**(3) JWilkinson(3) (hld up: ev ch fnl 2f: r.o wl) | s.h | **2** | 7/1[1] | 58 | 48 |
| 3414[2] | **Urgent Swift (67)** (APJarvis) **3-9-1**(5) CCarver(1) (lw: led over 6f: unable qckn fnl 2f) | 6 | **3** | 10/1[3] | 69 | 52 |
| 3318[8] | **In The Band (51)** (LordHuntingdon) **3-8-4** AimeeCook(9) (rdn over 2f out: gd hdwy over 1f out: r.o) | 4 | **4** | 16/1 | 47 | 30 |
| 3111[5] | **Premier League (IRE) (58)** (JELong) **6-8-13**(5) TField(13) (no hdwy fnl 2f) | 1¼ | **5** | 14/1 | 52 | 42 |
| 1996[5] | **Golden Touch (USA) (63)** (DJSCosgrove) **4-9-4**(5) MNutter(7) (lw: lost pl 4f out: one pce fnl 2f) | 2½ | **6** | 16/1 | 53 | 43 |
| 3095[5] | **Wet Patch (IRE) (60)** (RHannon) **4-8-13**(7) GGallagher(11) (lw: stdy hdwy wl over 1f out: nvr nrr) | 2 | **7** | 16/1 | 47 | 37 |
| 3681[3] | **Laughing Buccaneer (45)** (MJHeaton-Ellis) **3-7-7**(5) JFowle(8) (prom over 6f out) | hd | **8** | 14/1 | 32 | 15 |
| *3437*[11] | **Burning Flame (46)** (RMFlower) **3-7-10b**[1](3) KSked(5) (hld up: rdn over 2f out: sn wknd) | ¾ | **9** | 33/1 | 31 | 14 |
| *3608*[9] | **Early Warning (47)** (CREgerton) **3-8-0** AEddery(4) (nvr nrr) | 2 | **10** | 33/1 | 29 | 12 |
| 3800[9] | **Press Again (48)** (PHayward) **4-8-3**(5) AMcCarthy(18) (lw: prom over 7f) | 2½ | **11** | 33/1 | 26 | 16 |
| 759[6] | **Warm Spell (62)** (GLMoore) **6-9-5**(3) JDennis(12) (lw: nvr nrr) | 1¼ | **12** | 20/1 | 38 | 28 |
| 3681[2] | **Absolutelystunning (56)** (MrsBarbaraWaring) **3-8-9** IonaWands(6) (b: a.p: led over 3f out tl over 2f out: sn wknd) | ¾ | **13** | 7/1[1] | 31 | 14 |
| 3785[2] | **Pat's Splendour (43)** (HJCollingridge) **5-8-3** JoHunnam(20) (b.hind: bhd fnl 4f) | hd | **14** | 9/1[2] | 18 | 8 |
| 3484[2] | **Isitoff (69)** (SCWilliams) **3-9-8** GMilligan(14) (b.off hind: prom over 8f) | 2½ | **15** | 7/1[1] | 40 | 23 |
| 3592[7] | **Flag Fen (USA) (59)** (MartynMeade) **5-9-0**(5) ClaireAngell(2) (prom over 7f) | ¾ | **16** | 16/1 | 29 | 19 |
| 3262[7] | **Koraloona (IRE) (55)** (GBBalding) **3-8-5**(3) GayeHarwood(16) (bhd fnl 3f) | ½ | **17** | 10/1[3] | 24 | 7 |
| 3635[3] | **Ma Petite Anglaise (68)** (WJarvis) **4-9-7**(7) TThomas(19) (bhd fnl 3f) | 1¼ | **18** | 10/1[3] | 35 | 25 |

(SP 132.9%) **18 Rn**

**2m 5.8** (2.30) CSF £92.52 CT £818.92 TOTE £15.00: £2.20 £2.10 £3.20 £4.30 (£87.20) Trio £655.70; £101.59 to 9/9/96 OWNER The Harvey White Partnership (NEWMARKET) BRED Mrs C. L. Weld
WEIGHT FOR AGE 3yo-7lb

**3785 Harvey White (IRE)** went on over a quarter of a mile from home, but was given no peace by the runner-up. Engaged in a tremendous duel with that rival, he prevailed by the skin of his teeth. (12/1)

**3471* Fern's Governor** threw down a determined challenge in the final quarter-mile but, despite giving her all, failed by a whisker. She is a winner without a penalty. (7/1)
**3414 Urgent Swift** set the pace, but was left for dead by the front two in the final quarter-mile. (10/1)
**248 In The Band**, in a different parish for much of the race, really found her stride below the distance and ran on past beaten horses to finish a moderate fourth. (16/1)
**3111 Premier League (IRE)** was made to look very pedestrian in the straight. (14/1)
**1996 Golden Touch (USA)**, who has changed stables since his last run, was made to look very one-paced in the straight. (16/1)

T/Plpt: £1,369.80 (14.33 Tckts). T/Qdpt: £66.50 (23.03 Tckts). AK

# 3769-**THIRSK (L-H) (Good to firm)**
## Saturday September 7th
WEATHER: overcast WIND: almost nil

## 4069 E.B.F. UNDERWOOD MAIDEN STKS (2-Y.O) (Class D)
2-15 (2-17) **1m** £3,834.00 (£1,152.00: £556.00: £258.00) Stalls: Low GOING minus 0.46 sec per fur (F)

| Form | Horse | Dist | Pos | SP | RR | SF |
|---|---|---|---|---|---|---|
| 3779[2] | **Ivan Luis (FR) (88)** (MBell) **2-8-9**(5) GFaulkner(4) (lw: trckd ldrs: led 2f out: rdn & r.o) | — | 1 | 11/10[1] | 87 | 40 |
| 2580[10] | **Generous Gift** (EALDunlop) **2-9-0** JStack(5) (in tch: hdwy over 2f out: ev ch ins fnl f: r.o) | ½ | 2 | 16/1 | 86 | 39 |
| 3159[12] | **Ink Pot (USA)** (MRStoute) **2-8-9v[1]** MBirch(2) (led tl hdd 2f out: kpt on) | 1¾ | 3 | 16/1 | 78 | 31 |
| | **River Foyle (USA)** (JHMGosden) **2-9-0** AGarth(3) (neat: scope: b.hind: s.i.s: hdwy appr st: styd on wl fnl 2f: nrst fin) | ¾ | 4 | 14/1[3] | 81+ | 34 |
| 3615[8] | **Invermark** (JRFanshawe) **2-9-0** NDay(12) (prom: effrt ent st: edgd lft & no imp) | 6 | 5 | 3/1[2] | 69 | 22 |
| 3588[8] | **Don't Worry Mike** (FHLee) **2-9-0** KDarley(6) (chsd ldrs: effrt 3f out: wknd fnl 2f) | 5 | 6 | 50/1 | 59 | 12 |
| 3695[6] | **Bold Saint (IRE)** (PWHarris) **2-9-0** GHind(1) (lw: in tch: effrt 2f out: sn btn) | ½ | 7 | 16/1 | 58 | 11 |
| 3874[4] | **Greenwich Fore** (TGMills) **2-8-11**(3) AWhelan(15) (in tch: rdn 3f out: no imp) | ¾ | 8 | 14/1[3] | 57 | 10 |
| 3675[3] | **Gilding The Lily (IRE)** (MJohnston) **2-8-9** TWilliams(10) (lw: prom to st: sn rdn & btn) | 1¼ | 9 | 16/1 | 49 | 2 |
| | **Domino Style** (MJCamacho) **2-8-9** LCharnock(11) (unf: bkwd: sn drvn along & a bhd) | 2 | 10 | 50/1 | 45 | — |
| | **Lawn Lothario** (MJohnston) **2-9-0** DeanMcKeown(14) (w'like: scope: bkwd: a outpcd & bhd) | nk | 11 | 25/1 | 49 | 2 |
| 3423[6] | **Burlesque** (JDBethell) **2-9-0** GBardwell(9) (sn drvn along & bhd) | 1 | 12 | 20/1 | 47 | — |
| *3625*[4] | **Count Tony** (SPCWoods) **2-9-0** DBiggs(8) (a bhd) | 1¼ | 13 | 50/1 | 45 | — |
| 3773[7] | **William's Well** (MWEasterby) **2-8-9**(5) GParkin(7) (chsd ldrs tl wknd fnl 3f) | 2 | 14 | 50/1 | 41 | — |
| | **Ibn Masirah** (MrsMReveley) **2-8-9**(5) SCopp(13) (rangy: scope: bkwd: s.s: a bhd) | 9 | 15 | 50/1 | 23 | — |

(SP 127.9%) **15 Rn**

**1m 38.5** (0.60 under 2y best) (2.00) CSF £20.01 TOTE £2.00: £1.30 £5.00 £3.00 (£29.70) Trio £103.40 OWNER Mr Luciano Gaucci (NEWMARKET) BRED Rodrigo Investments
**3779 Ivan Luis (FR)** spent much of the race on the bridle but, once in front, he seemed to idle and needed driving out. There would seem to be more to come. (11/10: 6/4-Evens)
**Generous Gift**, returning after two months off, went really well and a similar event should not be long in being found. (16/1)
**Ink Pot (USA)** had the visor on for the first time and it really sharpened her up, but she was never quite good enough in the last two furlongs, despite trying hard. (16/1)
**River Foyle (USA)** showed enough to suggest that there is a race or two in him, and he should improve a fair deal for this experience. (14/1)
**Invermark** did not seem entirely suited by this sharp track and, running slightly wide on the turn, was then always inclined to hang when the pressure was on. (3/1)
**Don't Worry Mike** is learning and, as he strengthens, he looks the type to do better. (50/1)
**Bold Saint (IRE)** took the eye in the paddock, but never made any impression in the race. He is still learning. (16/1)

## 4070 YORKSHIRE-TYNE TEES TELEVISION (S) STKS (3-Y.O+) (Class G)
2-50 (2-51) **1m** £2,670.00 (£745.00: £360.00) Stalls: Low GOING minus 0.46 sec per fur (F)

| Form | Horse | Dist | Pos | SP | RR | SF |
|---|---|---|---|---|---|---|
| *3951*[11] | **Power Game (61)** (JBerry) **3-9-1b** KDarley(2) (lw: rr div: hdwy over 2f out: r.o to ld cl home) | — | 1 | 5/2[2] | 65 | 28 |
| 3758[6] | **Lucky Revenge (63)** (MartynMeade) **3-8-4** DeanMcKeown(14) (lw: trckd ldrs gng wl: led 2f out: nt qckn u.p & hdd towards fin) | hd | 2 | 9/4[1] | 54 | 17 |
| 3958[6] | **Roseate Lodge (44)** (SEKettlewell) **10-8-13**(7) JennyBenson(4) (in tch: hdwy 2f out: sn chsng ldrs: nt qckn ins fnl f) | 1¾ | 3 | 14/1 | 61 | 29 |
| 3854[9] | **Anonym (IRE) (60)** (DNicholls) **4-9-6b[1]** AlexGreaves(6) (s.i.s: gd hdwy over 2f out: rdn & nt qckn appr fnl f) | ¾ | 4 | 9/1 | 60 | 28 |
| 3862[2] | **Tonic Chord (55)** (JRFanshawe) **3-8-4** NDay(3) (b: lw: bhd: hdwy over 2f out: hmpd over 1f out: swtchd & styd on one pce) | 1½ | 5 | 5/1[3] | 46 | 9 |
| 1803[11] | **Mcgillycuddy Reeks (IRE) (39)** (NTinkler) **5-8-9** LCharnock(8) (hdwy & swtchd wl over 1f out: nvr able to chal) | 1¾ | 6 | 33/1 | 42 | 10 |
| 3354[11] | **Dispol Duchess (35)** (JLEyre) **3-8-4** RLappin(13) (n.m.r appr st: hdwy 2f out: styd on towards fin) | 2½ | 7 | 20/1 | 37 | — |
| *3420*[4] | **Dark Shot (IRE) (62)** (NTinkler) **4-9-0v** KimTinkler(11) (led tl hdd 2f out: grad wknd) | 1½ | 8 | 11/1 | 39 | 7 |
| 3410[9] | **Noble Colours (40)** (JJQuinn) **3-8-9** ACulhane(12) (bhd: effrt over 2f out: nvr rchd ldrs) | 1¾ | 9 | 33/1 | 36 | — |
| 3645[11] | **Mill Dancer (IRE) (31)** (EJAlston) **4-8-9** StephenDavies(1) (cl up: wkng whn hmpd over 1f out) | nk | 10 | 25/1 | 30 | — |
| 3780[14] | **Baraqueta (53)** (JLEyre) **4-9-0** TWilliams(7) (shkn up after s: chsd ldrs: wknd fnl 2f) | 2½ | 11 | 20/1 | 30 | — |
| 3654[5] | **Sweet Amoret (49)** (PHowling) **3-8-10** FNorton(10) (lw: mid div: btn whn hmpd over 1f out) | 2½ | 12 | 16/1 | 26 | — |
| 3325[6] | **Cameron Edge (33)** (ABMulholland) **3-8-4**(5)ow5 GFaulkner(9) (b: swtg: mid div & rn wd st: n.d) | nk | 13 | 33/1 | 25 | — |
| 3578[11] | **Euro Express (40)** (TDEasterby) **3-8-9b** MBirch(5) (lost tch after 2f: n.d afterwards) | 1½ | 14 | 20/1 | 22 | — |
| 3958[9] | **Top Skipper (IRE) (50)** (MartynWane) **4-8-11**(3) AWhelan(15) (chsd ldrs tl wknd fnl 3f) | 1¼ | 15 | 33/1 | 19 | — |
| 3642[5] | **Nexsis Star (58)** (MrsSJSmith) **3-8-4**(5) PRoberts(17) (chsd ldrs to st: sn lost pl) | nk | 16 | 16/1 | 19 | — |
| | **Lady Swift** (KWHogg) **5-8-9** SDWilliams(18) (a bhd) | 6 | 17 | 33/1 | 2 | — |
| 3654[8] | **Nanny-B** (PHowling) **3-8-4** JStack(16) (b.hind: lost tch fr ½-wy) | 4 | 18 | 33/1 | — | — |

(SP 148.6%) **18 Rn**

**1m 39.8** (3.30) CSF £9.70 TOTE £4.50: £1.60 £1.70 £3.50 (£6.00) Trio £21.90 OWNER Countrywide Racing (COCKERHAM) BRED Bearstone Stud
WEIGHT FOR AGE 3yo-5lb
No bid
STEWARDS' ENQUIRY Benson susp.16-17/9/96 (careless riding)

**3789 Power Game** was always going nicely and, when the pressure was on, he did just enough to take it late on. (5/2: op 5/1)
**3758 Lucky Revenge** travelled really well but, after leading two furlongs out, she just failed to see it out. She can win at this trip, but seven furlongs looks ideal. (9/4)
**3958 Roseate Lodge** ran well in a race where he looked to have plenty on at the weights, and is obviously in really good form. (14/1)
**3060 Anonym (IRE)**, in blinkers for the first time, gave ground away at the start and then showed enough to suggest that he is coming back to form. (9/1)
**3862 Tonic Chord** got a shade warm in the preliminaries and would have been a good bit closer had she not run into trouble approaching the last furlong. (5/1)
**Mcgillycuddy Reeks (IRE)**, taking a drop in distance, ran better but, judging by the way she was staying on, she does need further. It is probably her recent hurdling that has sharpened her up. (33/1)
**3102 Dispol Duchess**, having her first run for her new stable, ran reasonably without offering a threat. (20/1)

## 4071 BRENTWOOD GROUP ANNIVERSARY H'CAP (0-75) (3-Y.O+ F & M) (Class D)

3-20 (3-21) **1m** £4,612.25 (£1,388.00: £671.50: £313.25) Stalls: Low GOING minus 0.46 sec per fur (F)

| | | | | SP | RR | SF |
|---|---|---|---|---|---|---|
| 3866$^{2}$ | **Society Girl (58)** (CWThornton) **3-8-12** DeanMcKeown(12) (lw: cl up: led 1f out: all out) | — | **1** | 13/2$^{3}$ | 67 | 32 |
| 3985$^{8}$ | **Pride of Pendle (65)** (DNicholls) **7-9-10** AlexGreaves(11) (hld up: hdwy over 2f out: rdn over 1f out: r.o: jst falied) | s.h | **2** | 2/1$^{1}$ | 74 | 44 |
| 3152$^{6}$ | **Desert Lynx (IRE) (70)** (TRWatson) **3-9-7**(3) OPears(4) (hld up: nt clr run & swtchd over 2f out: r.o wl towards fin) | ½ | **3** | 25/1 | 78 | 43 |
| 3133$^{8}$ | **Kazimiera (IRE) (65)** (CWCElsey) **3-9-0**(5) GFaulkner(5) (led tl hdd 1f out: kpt on same pce) | nk | **4** | 11/1 | 72 | 37 |
| 3866$^{4}$ | **Lapu-Lapu (52)** (MJCamacho) **3-8-6** LCharnock(6) (lw: a chsng ldrs: n.m.r 1f out: r.o one pce) | ¾ | **5** | 9/1 | 58 | 23 |
| 3681$^{5}$ | **Princess Pamgaddy (47)** (PFICole) **3-8-1** FNorton(14) (b.hind: in tch: hdwy over 1f out: nt qckn ins fnl f) | nk | **6** | 10/1 | 52 | 17 |
| 3650$^{6}$ | **Encore M'Lady (IRE) (60)** (FHLee) **5-9-5** ACulhane(1) (hld up & bhd: effrt over 2f out: sme late hdwy) | 3 | **7** | 20/1 | 59 | 29 |
| 2801$^{16}$ | **Broughton's Pride (IRE) (50)** (JLEyre) **5-8-9** TWilliams(3) (bhd: sme hdwy 2f out: nvr rchd ldrs) | hd | **8** | 25/1 | 49 | 19 |
| 3867$^{2}$ | **Special-K (55)** (EWeymes) **4-9-0** GHind(9) (cl up tl wknd fnl 2f) | nk | **9** | 11/2$^{2}$ | 53 | 23 |
| 3845$^{9}$ | **Perpetual Light (59)** (JJQuinn) **3-8-13** DaleGibson(10) (lw: in tch tl wknd fnl 2f) | ½ | **10** | 14/1 | 56 | 21 |
| 3639* | **Formidable Liz (61)** (MDHammond) **6-9-6** KDarley(7) (lw: hdwy on ins 3f out: nt clr run over 1f out: eased whn btn) | 2½ | **11** | 9/1 | 53 | 23 |
| 3866$^{6}$ | **Rainbows Rhapsody (38)** (DWChapman) **5-7-8**(3)ow1 NVarley(13) (in tch: effrt ent st: wknd fnl 2½f) | 1¼ | **12** | 33/1 | 28 | — |
| 3844$^{10}$ | **Comic Fantasy (AUS) (67)** (MartynWane) **3-9-7** RLappin(8) (lw: a bhd) | 2 | **13** | 25/1 | 53 | 18 |
| 3854$^{4}$ | **Dispol Diamond (63)** (GROldroyd) **3-9-3** MBirch(15) (chsd ldrs to st: sn wknd) | 3½ | **14** | 20/1 | 42 | 7 |
| | | | | (SP 130.1%) | **14 Rn** | |

**1m 39.1** (2.60) CSF £20.33 CT £313.28 TOTE £6.00: £2.00 £1.60 £10.30 (£11.20) Trio £114.90 OWNER Mr Guy Reed (MIDDLEHAM) BRED G. Reed

LONG HANDICAP Rainbows Rhapsody 7-6

WEIGHT FOR AGE 3yo-5lb

**3866 Society Girl** is a game and consistent sort and that won her the day here as she refused to be passed. (13/2)
**3985 Pride of Pendle** is really coming to form but, despite a gallant effort, just failed to make it. (2/1)
**3152 Desert Lynx (IRE)** looked very unlucky here and would have won had she got a clear run earlier. (25/1)
**2754 Kazimiera (IRE)** keeps running well, but has yet to win a race. (11/1)
**3866 Lapu-Lapu** ran pretty well, despite being a bit short of room at various stages, and is worth keeping in mind. (9/1)
**3681 Princess Pamgaddy** was never doing things quickly enough to get into it, but was staying on and, over this trip, a more galloping track could be the answer. (10/1)
**3101 Encore M'Lady (IRE)**, held up to get the trip, failed to get into it but, judging by the way she finished, she remains in good heart. (20/1)

## 4072 LLOYDS PRIVATE BANKING MAIDEN AUCTION STKS (2-Y.O) (Class F)

3-50 (3-53) **7f** £3,002.50 (£840.00: £407.50) Stalls: Low GOING minus 0.46 sec per fur (F)

| | | | | SP | RR | SF |
|---|---|---|---|---|---|---|
| 3593$^{7}$ | **Rose Carnival** (DRLoder) **2-8-4** KDarley(3) (lw: trckd ldrs: led 1½f out: rdn & r.o) | — | **1** | 10/11$^{1}$ | 78 | 23 |
| 3826$^{2}$ | **River of Fortune (IRE) (78)** (MHTompkins) **2-8-4** NDay(6) (lw: a chsng ldrs: ev ch 2f out: nt qckn fnl f) | 2 | **2** | 100/30$^{2}$ | 73 | 18 |
| 2588$^{6}$ | **Gipsy Princess (60)** (MWEasterby) **2-7-12b$^{1}$** DaleGibson(7) (a chsng ldrs: ev ch 2f out: nt qckn) | 3 | **3** | 33/1 | 61 | 6 |
| 3796$^{4}$ | **Jack The Lad (IRE) (73)** (CMurray) **2-8-9** GBardwell(11) (styd on u.p fnl 3f: nrst fin) | 1½ | **4** | 14/1 | 68 | 13 |
| 3687$^{4}$ | **Head Girl (IRE) (72)** (CWThornton) **2-8-0** AMackay(5) (lw: plld hrd: effrt 3f out: hung lft & no imp) | 1½ | **5** | 11/2$^{3}$ | 56 | 1 |
| 3227$^{10}$ | **Classic Partygoer** (MWEasterby) **2-8-2b$^{1}$**(5) GParkin(8) (a abt same pl) | 3½ | **6** | 50/1 | 55 | — |
| 3429$^{2}$ | **Loch-Hurn Lady (73)** (KWHogg) **2-7-12** LCharnock(9) (led tl hdd & wknd 1½f out) | 1 | **7** | 11/1 | 43 | — |
| 3080$^{10}$ | **Lady Salome** (JGFitzGerald) **2-8-4** GHind(10) (in tch tl outpcd fnl 3f) | ½ | **8** | 50/1 | 48 | — |
| | **Hello There** (NTinkler) **2-8-5** KimTinkler(1) (leggy: scope: bkwd: s.i.s: n.d) | 10 | **9** | 33/1 | 26 | — |
| 910$^{6}$ | **Hiltons Executive (IRE)** (EJAlston) **2-8-0** StephenDavies(4) (stdd s: hdwy & c wd st: hung lft 2f out: wknd qckly) | 2 | **10** | 66/1 | 17 | — |
| 3332$^{4}$ | **Mint Condition** (MrsLStubbs) **2-8-7** ACulhane(2) (a bhd: eased fnl 2f: t.o) | 27 | **11** | 50/1 | — | — |
| | | | | (SP 119.1%) | **11 Rn** | |

**1m 26.6** (2.40) CSF £4.45 TOTE £1.80: £1.30 £1.20 £3.50 (£2.80) Trio £62.20 OWNER Mr P. D. Player (NEWMARKET) BRED P. D. and Mrs Player

**3593 Rose Carnival** was always going nicely and won well, despite carrying her head quite high. (10/11: 4/5-Evens)
**3826 River of Fortune (IRE)** keeps finishing second, but her attitude seems alright, and she should go one better in due course. (100/30)
**2588 Gipsy Princess**, trying a longer trip and blinkered for the first time, ran better, particularly after two months off. (33/1)
**3796 Jack The Lad (IRE)**, trying a longer trip, had to really work to improve, but did keep on well all the way to the line. (14/1)
**3687 Head Girl (IRE)** has plenty of ability, but also has a mind of her own and things were never going her way here. (11/2)
**568 Classic Partygoer** had blinkers on for the first time, but they had little effect. (50/1)
**3429 Loch-Hurn Lady** is doing well physically and, after a month off, should be all the better for this. (11/1)

## 4073 TOTE HAMBLETON CUP H'CAP (0-80) (3-Y.O+) (Class D)

4-20 (4-23) **1m 4f** £5,959.00 (£1,792.00: £866.00: £403.00) Stalls: High GOING minus 0.46 sec per fur (F)

| | | | | SP | RR | SF |
|---|---|---|---|---|---|---|
| 3587$^{3}$ | **Far Ahead (79)** (JLEyre) **4-9-13** RLappin(9) (hdwy on ins 6f out: led over 1f out: r.o wl) | — | **1** | 12/1 | 89 | 49 |
| 3710$^{17}$ | **Tessajoe (68)** (MJCamacho) **4-9-2** LCharnock(13) (a.p: chal over 1f out: kpt on wl) | hd | **2** | 8/1$^{3}$ | 78 | 38 |
| | **Kalou (66)** (CWCElsey) **5-9-0** GHind(4) (bit bkwd: swtg: led tl hdd over 1f out: no ex) | 2 | **3** | 20/1 | 73 | 33 |

| Form | Horse | Dist | Pos | SP | RR | SF |
|---|---|---|---|---|---|---|
| 3043[3] | **Once More for Luck (IRE) (66)** (MrsMReveley) **5-9-0** ACulhane(10) (lw: hld up: effrt u.p 5f out: styd on fnl 2f: nrst fin) | hd | **4** | 6/1[1] | 73 | 33 |
| 3621[7] | **Master Hyde (USA) (57)** (WStorey) **7-8-2**(3) NVarley(1) (chsd ldrs: effrt 3f out: r.o one pce) | 3 | **5** | 16/1 | 60 | 20 |
| 3856* | **Wafir (IRE) (82)** (PCalver) **4-10-2** MBirch(5) (lw: chsd ldrs: effrt over 3f out: one pce appr fnl f) | ½ | **6** | 10/1 | 84 | 44 |
| *3955*[2] | **Shahik (USA) (63)** (DHaydnJones) **6-8-11** FNorton(14) (in tch: effrt over 3f out: no imp) | 1½ | **7** | 16/1 | 63 | 23 |
| 3587[2] | **Canton Venture (76)** (SPCWoods) **4-9-10** DBiggs(7) (lw: chsd ldrs: hmpd bnd after 2f: rdn over 1f out: kpt on same pce) | 3 | **8** | 7/1[2] | 72 | 32 |
| 3828[6] | **Loki (IRE) (72)** (GLewis) **8-9-3**(3) AWhelan(19) (bhd: effrt on outside 3f out: hung lft: styd on) | ½ | **9** | 10/1 | 68 | 28 |
| 3968[3] | **Snow Falcon (64)** (MBell) **3-7-10**(7) RMullen(6) (lw: sddle slipped: nvr trbld ldrs) | s.h | **10** | 12/1 | 60 | 11 |
| 3856[4] | **Break the Rules (72)** (MrsMReveley) **4-9-6** KDarley(11) (hld up: stdy hdwy 2f out: nvr plcd to chal) | ½ | **11** | 14/1 | 67 | 27 |
| 3947[15] | **Exemption (65)** (HCandy) **5-8-13** DeanMcKeown(8) (in tch tl outpcd fnl 3f) | 1½ | **12** | 14/1 | 58 | 18 |
| 482[8] | **Desert Fighter (75)** (MrsMReveley) **5-9-4**(5) GLee(18) (hld up: swtchd ins over 2f out: n.d) | ¾ | **13** | 33/1 | 67 | 27 |
| 3968[5] | **Ashover (57)** (TDBarron) **6-8-5** StephenDavies(2) (n.d) | 1 | **14** | 25/1 | 48 | 8 |
| 3939[2] | **Nigel's Lad (IRE) (75)** (PCHaslam) **4-9-4**(5) MBaird(16) (in tch: effrt appr st: sn btn) | 3½ | **15** | 6/1[1] | 61 | 21 |
| 620[9] | **Keen To The Last (FR) (57)** (MDHammond) **4-8-5** DaleGibson(3) (a bhd) | 2½ | **16** | 33/1 | 40 | — |
| 3813[6] | **Double Echo (IRE) (51)** (JDBethell) **8-7-13** GBardwell(17) (in tch tl wknd fnl 4f) | 1 | **17** | 14/1 | 32 | — |
| *18*[10] | **Colorful Ambition (70)** (MrsASwinbank) **6-9-4** JSupple(15) (hld up & a bhd) | 1 | **18** | 50/1 | 50 | 10 |
| 3640[7] | **Access Adventurer (IRE) (70)** (RBoss) **5-8-13**(5) GFaulkner(12) (trckd ldrs: rdn appr st: sn wknd) | 10 | **19** | 25/1 | 37 | — |

(SP 137.8%) **19 Rn**

**2m 33.7** (3.70) CSF £106.13 CT £1,802.40 TOTE £16.30: £2.70 £1.80 £6.20 £1.90 (£29.40) Trio £334.70 OWNER Sunpak Potatoes (HAMBLETON) BRED Sir John Astor

WEIGHT FOR AGE 3yo-9lb

**3587 Far Ahead** was winning her second race over this course and distance this season and always gave the impression that, had he needed it, there was a bit more to come. (12/1)

**3276 Tessajoe** won over this course and distance in April and, off a decent mark now, looks to be coming back to form. (8/1)

**Kalou** trotted up in this last year, but this was her first run of the season and she was also 10lb higher. In the circumstances, she ran really well. (20/1)

**3043 Once More for Luck (IRE)**, after a quiet run over too short a trip last time, was well fancied, but he took time to get into his stride and, when he did, it was all too late. When things go his way, he is quite useful, but he is not one to trust entirely. (6/1)

**3290 Master Hyde (USA)** ran reasonably, always being in contention, but he failed to pick up when ridden in the home straight. (16/1)

**3856* Wafir (IRE)** ran a sound race, but the extra distance coupled with his testing victory last week probably just found him out. (10/1)

**3828 Loki (IRE)** never got into this, but was making some late headway and, given easier ground, can do better. (10/1)

**3856 Break the Rules** failed to get into this, but showed enough under tender handling to suggest that he is not done with yet. (14/1)

## 4074 CHARTERHOUSE ADVERTISING AND MARKETING MAIDEN STKS (3-Y.O+) (Class D)

4-50 (5-01) **6f** £4,367.00 (£1,316.00: £638.00: £299.00) Stalls: High GOING minus 0.46 sec per fur (F)

| Form | Horse | Dist | Pos | SP | RR | SF |
|---|---|---|---|---|---|---|
| 3624[3] | **River Tern (62)** (JBerry) **3-8-12v** KDarley(3) (b: chsd ldrs far side: rdn to ld over 1f out: styd on) | — | **1** | 15/2[3] | 65 | 9 |
| | **Minoletti** (EALDunlop) **3-8-12** JStack(2) (b.nr hind: chsd ldrs far side: disp ld 2f out: nt qckn fnl f) | 2 | **2** | 10/1 | 60 | 4 |
| | **Dewhurst House** (WWHaigh) **3-8-7** RLappin(22) (unf: scope: bit bkwd: racd stands' side: led 2f out: kpt on) | hd | **3** | 66/1 | 54 | — |
| | **Daisy Bates (IRE)** (PWHarris) **3-8-7** GHind(17) (lt-f: scope: cl up stands' side: nt qckn fnl f) | ½ | **4** | 14/1 | 53 | — |
| 3624[4] | **Foreign Relation (IRE)** (PRWebber) **3-8-7** DaleGibson(1) (b.hind: led far side tl hdd & wknd over 1f out) | 1 | **5** | 16/1 | 50 | — |
| 3665[2] | **Shavinsky (72)** (PHowling) **3-8-12** NDay(20) (prom stands' side: kpt on one pce fnl 2f) | 3 | **6** | 100/30[2] | 47 | — |
| 2298[6] | **Wollstonecraft (IRE)** (JHMGosden) **3-8-7** AGarth(8) (racd far side: prom: rdn ½-wy: sn btn) | 1½ | **7** | 6/4[1] | 38 | — |
| 3513[11] | **Saving Power** (PWHarris) **3-8-12** NKennedy(4) (lw: racd far side tl hung bdly rt ½-wy: styd on: n.d) | d.h | **7** | 33/1 | 43 | — |
| 3642[3] | **White Hare** (MrsMReveley) **3-8-7** LCharnock(12) (lw: racd stands' side: nvr trbld ldrs) | s.h | **9** | 16/1 | 38 | — |
| 3624[13] | **Honeyhall** (NBycroft) **3-8-4**(3) NVarley(18) (racd stands' side: n.d) | s.h | **10** | 100/1 | 38 | — |
| 3335[17] | **Masai Man (USA) (35)** (MissJBower) **5-9-0** SDWilliams(14) (racd stands' side: outpcd fr ½-wy) | 1 | **11** | 100/1 | 41 | — |
| 3256[6] | **Dona Filipa (30)** (MissLCSiddall) **3-8-4**(3) DarrenMoffatt(19) (outpcd stands' side fr ½-wy) | 1¾ | **12** | 50/1 | 31 | — |
| 2777[7] | **Hotcake** (MissSEHall) **3-8-7**(5) GLee(15) (b: hdwy stands' side 2f out: nvr nr to chal) | 1¾ | **13** | 50/1 | 31 | — |
| 3862[4] | **Frutina** (CMurray) **3-8-7** GBardwell(11) (racd stands' side: sn bhd) | ¾ | **14** | 25/1 | 24 | — |
| 3847[6] | **Soul Sister** (DHaydnJones) **3-8-7** FNorton(21) (bit bkwd: racd stands' side: bhd fr ½-wy) | 5 | **15** | 50/1 | 11 | — |
| 3609[9] | **Imperial Red (IRE)** (HJCollingridge) **3-8-9**(3) AWhelan(16) (sn bhd stands' side) | 3 | **16** | 100/1 | 8 | — |
| | **Born On The Wild** (SEKettlewell) **3-8-7** NRodgers(6) (unf: bit bkwd: racd far side: a bhd) | 1 | **17** | 50/1 | — | — |
| 3642[9] | **Rupert Manners** (EJAlston) **3-8-12** JLowe(10) (racd stands' side: hung lft most of wy: n.d) | 5 | **18** | 50/1 | — | — |
| | **Hill House Teacher** (MPBielby) **4-8-9** DeanMcKeown(9) (wl grwn: unf: bit bkwd: racd far side: sn bhd) | 9 | **19** | 66/1 | — | — |
| | ***Gemini Dream*** (RFJohnsonHoughton) **3-8-12** MBirch(13) (Withdrawn not under Starter's orders: unruly in paddock) | | **W** | 16/1 | — | — |
| *3353*[11] | ***Beano Script*** (MissSEHall) **3-8-7**(5) GFaulkner(7) (Withdrawn not under Starter's orders: unruly in stalls) | | **W** | 33/1 | — | — |

(SP 133.7%) **19 Rn**

**1m 13.2** (3.50) CSF £74.20 TOTE £7.40: £2.50 £3.60 £23.20 (£22.90) Trio Not won; £382.98 to 9/9/96 OWNER Mr T G & Mrs M E Holdcroft (COCKERHAM) BRED Bearstone Stud

WEIGHT FOR AGE 3yo-2lb

**3624 River Tern** raced up the far rail and did it well, but this was a poor event. (15/2)

**Minoletti** was with the winner up the far side but, on this first run of the season, just failed to last out. (10/1)

**Dewhurst House** came out best of those on the stands' rail and looked likely to be all the better for this. (66/1)

**Daisy Bates (IRE)**, having her first run, showed up well throughout on the stands' side, but was run out of it in the last furlong and a half. (14/1)

**3624 Foreign Relation (IRE)**, stepping up a furlong, was made too much use of here and cried enough entering the last furlong. (16/1)

**3665 Shavinsky** had his chances, but looked slow when the pressure was on. (100/30: 5/1-3/1)

**2298 Wollstonecraft (IRE)** (6/4: Evens-13/8)

**Saving Power**, wandering about, tried all sides of the track. If he can be straightened out, there is obviously better to come. (33/1)

## 4075 YORKSHIRE CANCER RESEARCH MAIDEN H'CAP (0-60) (3-Y.O+) (Class F)

5-20 (5-35) **5f** £3,142.50 (£880.00: £427.50) Stalls: High GOING minus 0.46 sec per fur (F)

| Form | Horse | Dist | Pos | SP | RR | SF |
|---|---|---|---|---|---|---|
| *2940*[16] | **Present 'n Correct (45)** (CBBBooth) **3-8-13** LCharnock(19) (hdwy stands' side ½-wy: r.o fnl f to ld nr fin) | — | **1** | 14/1 | 51 | 32 |
| 3883[11] | **Manolo (FR) (53)** (JBerry) **3-9-7** KDarley(22) (lw; chsd ldrs stands' side: led over 1f out: hdd & nt qckn towards fin) | nk | **2** | 12/1 | 58 | 39 |

| | | Dist | Pos | SP | RR | SF |
|---|---|---|---|---|---|---|
| 3342[7] | **Young Ben (IRE) (36)** (JSWainwright) **4-7-12b**[1](7) JBramhill(23) (b: b.hind: hdwy stands' side over 1f out: edgd lft & kpt on wl) | 2 | **3** | 11/1[3] | 35 | 17 |
| 2029[3] | **Gymcrak Gem (IRE) (60)** (GHolmes) **3-10-0b** DeanMcKeown(8) (b.hind: led far side: nt qckn ins fnl f) | 1 | **4** | 8/1[2] | 55 | 36 |
| 3643[12] | **China Hand (IRE) (36)** (MartynWane) **4-8-2**(3)ow2 AWhelan(21) (led stands' side tl hdd over 1f out: no ex) | 1¼ | **5** | 14/1 | 27 | 7 |
| 3288[3] | **La Finale (50)** (DNicholls) **3-9-4b** AlexGreaves(7) (lw: chsd ldrs far side: edgd lft & nt qckn fnl f) | ½ | **6** | 12/1 | 40 | 21 |
| 3774[4] | **Good To Talk (43)** (TDEasterby) **3-8-11v** MBirch(3) (lw: w ldr far side: rdn over 1f out: nt qckn) | ½ | **7** | 9/2[1] | 31 | 12 |
| 3700[8] | **Desert Skimmer (USA) (48)** (MBell) **3-8-11**(5) GFaulkner(12) (racd far side: nvr trbld ldrs) | nk | **8** | 20/1 | 35 | 16 |
| 3937[15] | **Samsung Lovelylady (IRE) (31)** (EWeymes) **4-8-0v** JFanning(6) (chsd ldrs far side over 3f) | nk | **9** | 25/1 | 17 | — |
| 3453[8] | **Swifty Nifty (IRE) (44)** (WWHaigh) **3-8-12** RLappin(11) (lw: racd far side: prom tl rdn & btn appr fnl f) | ½ | **10** | 20/1 | 29 | 10 |
| 3624[9] | **Petarina (43)** (MissJFCraze) **3-8-11v**[1] JLowe(1) (chsd ldrs far side: no imp fnl 1½f) | nk | **11** | 33/1 | 27 | 8 |
| 3780[7] | **In A Tizzy (31)** (PCHaslam) **3-7-13** TWilliams(2) (racd far side: chsd ldrs tl wknd 1f out) | ½ | **12** | 25/1 | 13 | — |
| 3863[4] | **Pendley Rose (46)** (PWHarris) **3-9-0** GHind(4) (racd far side: prom: rdn 2f out: sn btn) | ½ | **13** | 8/1[2] | 27 | 8 |
| 3863[8] | **Allstars Dancer (31)** (TJNaughton) **3-7-13** AGarth(15) (racd stands' side :n.d) | s.h | **14** | 16/1 | 11 | — |
| 3100[8] | **Chelwood (42)** (LRLloyd-James) **4-8-4b**[1](7) CLowther(10) (racd far side: nvr trbld ldrs) | nk | **15** | 33/1 | 21 | 3 |
| 3774[8] | **Harriet's Beau (31)** (MWEasterby) **3-7-13v**[1] DaleGibson(13) (lw: racd stands' side: spd 3f) | nk | **16** | 20/1 | 10 | — |
| 3453[10] | **Sallyoreally (IRE) (35)** (WStorey) **5-8-4** NKennedy(5) (lw: chsd ldrs far side over 3f) | nk | **17** | 25/1 | 13 | — |
| 3135[8] | **Fancy Clancy (38)** (MissLCSiddall) **3-8-3b**[1](3) DarrenMoffatt(17) (racd stands' side: n.d) | 1 | **18** | 20/1 | 12 | — |
| 3294[16] | **Time Ticks On (40)** (MWEllerby) **3-8-8** VHalliday(24) (racd stands' side: dwlt: a bhd) | hd | **19** | 25/1 | 14 | — |
| 3525[12] | **Sizzling Romp (50)** (DTThom) **4-9-5** JStack(20) (b.hind: racd stands' side: a bhd) | ½ | **20** | 16/1 | 22 | 4 |
| 3624[5] | **Superfrills (53)** (MissLCSiddall) **3-9-4**(3) OPears(18) (lw: racd stands' side: a bhd) | 1¼ | **21** | 20/1 | 21 | 2 |
| *3602*[12] | **Belinda Blue (46)** (RAFahey) **4-9-1v**[1] SDWilliams(14) (lw: dwlt: racd stands' side: a bhd) | 1 | **22** | 20/1 | 11 | — |
| 3851[10] | **Mister Sean (IRE) (40)** (JWPayne) **3-8-8** GBardwell(16) (b.hind: cl up stands' side tl wknd wl over 1f out) | 1¾ | **23** | 16/1 | — | — |
| 2791[4] | **Deardaw (37)** (MissLCSiddall) **4-8-6** FNorton(9) (chsd ldrs far side over 3f) | 1¾ | **24** | 20/1 | — | — |

(SP 149.7%) **24 Rn**

**59.5 secs** (1.50) CSF £180.43 CT £1,094.91 TOTE £24.00: £5.40 £3.20 £2.00 £2.00 (£135.90) Trio £96.20 OWNER Mr A. Lyons (FLAXTON) BRED A. Lyons

WEIGHT FOR AGE 3yo-1lb

**2316 Present 'n Correct** failed to act on the All-Weather last time and was back to form in style here, making up a fair amount of ground to score nicely. (14/1: 10/1-16/1)

**2849 Manolo (FR)** made full use of his draw up the stands' side but, despite trying hard, was just touched off. (12/1)

**3294 Young Ben (IRE)** had the blinkers on for the first time and ran a decent race, keeping on well in the closing stages. The ability is certainly there. (11/1)

**2029 Gymcrak Gem (IRE)** ran well up the far side and, considering she had not run for almost three months, this was a decent effort. (8/1)

**3310 China Hand (IRE)** has bags of speed and ability, but his attitude does seem to be the problem. (14/1)

**3288 La Finale** looks in good trim, but she seems to be her own worst enemy. (12/1)

**3774 Good To Talk** had his chances throughout, racing up the far side, but failed to respond when pressure was applied in the last couple of furlongs. (9/2)

T/Plpt: £179.60 (64.14 Tckts). T/Qdpt: £75.70 (7.91 Tckts). AA

# 3950-WOLVERHAMPTON (L-H) (Standard)

## Saturday September 7th

WEATHER: fine WIND: nil

## 4076 DEAUVILLE MAIDEN H'CAP (0-65) (3-Y.O+) (Class F)

7-00 (7-00) **1m 100y (Fibresand)** £2,070.00 (£570.00: £270.00) Stalls: Low GOING minus 0.12 sec per fur (FST)

| | | Dist | Pos | SP | RR | SF |
|---|---|---|---|---|---|---|
| *3421*[6] | **Nicola's Princess (50)** (BAMcMahon) **3-8-12** GCarter(1) (lw: a.p: led ins fnl f: rdn out) | — | **1** | 6/1[3] | 63 | 40 |
| 3354[8] | **Angus McCoatup (IRE) (55)** (BAMcMahon) **3-9-0**(3) PMcCabe(2) (lw: led tl ins fnl f: r.o) | nk | **2** | 7/1 | 67 | 44 |
| 3165[7] | **Tea Party (USA) (61)** (KOCunningham-Brown) **3-9-9** BDoyle(4) (lw: plld hrd: a.p: nt clr run ins fnl f: swtchd lft: r.o) | hd | **3** | 5/1[2] | 73 | 50 |
| 3134[7] | **Amusing Aside (IRE) (62)** (JWWatts) **3-9-10** GDuffield(3) (a.p: ev ch wl over 1f out: wknd fnl f) | 5 | **4** | 8/1 | 65 | 42 |
| 3138[3] | **Silver Harrow (57)** (AGNewcombe) **3-9-0**(5) DGriffiths(5) (hmpd & lost pl after 1f: hdwy on ins over 2f out: one pce) | ¾ | **5** | 4/1[1] | 58 | 35 |
| 1539[7] | **Old Hush Wing (IRE) (54)** (PCHaslam) **3-9-2** SDrowne(10) (prom 6f) | s.h | **6** | 16/1 | 55 | 32 |
| 3703[7] | **Basood (USA) (60)** (SPCWoods) **3-9-8v** DBiggs(11) (lw: chsd ldrs tl wknd over 2f out) | nk | **7** | 9/1 | 61 | 38 |
| *1719*[15] | **Juba (50)** (DrJDScargill) **4-9-3** MFenton(13) (nvr nr ldrs) | 3 | **8** | 20/1 | 45 | 27 |
| 3456[14] | **Nakhal (53)** (DJGMurraySmith) **3-8-12b**(3) FLynch(6) (a bhd) | 5 | **9** | 7/1 | 39 | 16 |
| 3947[20] | **Melomania (USA) (50)** (TJNaughton) **4-9-3** NAdams(12) (s.i.s: hdwy over 6f out: rdn 4f out: wknd 3f out) | 5 | **10** | 11/1 | 26 | 8 |
| 3474[9] | **Bath Knight (55)** (DJSffrenchDavis) **3-9-0**(3) MHenry(8) (prom 4f) | 3 | **11** | 20/1 | 25 | 2 |
| 3314[9] | **Blossomville (50)** (MAJarvis) **3-8-12** PBloomfield(7) (bhd fnl 4f) | 2½ | **12** | 25/1 | 16 | — |
| *3626*[8] | **Kass Alhawa (60)** (DWChapman) **3-9-8** ACulhane(9) (bhd most of wy) | 1½ | **13** | 16/1 | 23 | — |

(SP 130.5%) **13 Rn**

**1m 49.9** (4.90) CSF £48.39 CT £181.85 TOTE £4.80: £1.20 £3.20 £1.90 (£11.80) Trio £81.60; £23.01 to 9/9/96 OWNER Mr J. D. Graham (TAMWORTH) BRED J. D. Graham

WEIGHT FOR AGE 3yo-5lb

**3062 Nicola's Princess** had a change of luck following her saddle slipping on two of her last three runs. (6/1)

**3089 Angus McCoatup (IRE)** certainly got the trip well enough. (7/1)

**3165 Tea Party (USA)**, fourth in a small race at Deauville last time, seemed held when forced to switch in the closing stages on this first outing on the Sand. (5/1)

**3134 Amusing Aside (IRE)** was making his debut on this surface. (8/1)

**3138 Silver Harrow** was yet another having his first run on Sand, and had a lot to do after being forced to snatch up on the paddock bend. (4/1)

## 4077 SANTA ANITA CLAIMING STKS (3-Y.O+) (Class F)

7-30 (7-30) **7f (Fibresand)** £2,070.00 (£570.00: £270.00) Stalls: High GOING minus 0.12 sec per fur (FST)

| | | Dist | Pos | SP | RR | SF |
|---|---|---|---|---|---|---|
| 3866[8] | **Sis Garden (50)** (TDEasterby) **3-7-13b** JQuinn(5) (a.p: led over 2f out: rdn out) | — | **1** | 7/1 | 64 | 40 |

| | | | | SP | RR | SF |
|---|---|---|---|---|---|---|
| *3601*$^{5}$ | **I'm Your Lady (68)** (BAMcMahon) **5-9-4** GCarter(6) (led over 4f: r.o one pce fnl 2f) | 3½ | **2** | 3/1$^{2}$ | 71 | 51 |
| *3951** | **People Direct (62)** (KMcAuliffe) **3-9-0** JFEgan(1) (b.hind: w ldrs: one pce fnl 2f) | ½ | **3** | 9/2$^{3}$ | 70 | 46 |
| 3995$^{13}$ | **Dancing Sioux (73)** (DNicholls) **4-9-9** MWigham(7) (a.p: no hdwy fnl 2f) | 3 | **4** | 6/1 | 68 | 48 |
| 2928$^{4}$ | **The Great Flood (45)** (CADwyer) **3-9-5** CDwyer(8) (chsd ldrs: no hdwy fnl 3f) | 2½ | **5** | 14/1 | 62 | 38 |
| 3700$^{10}$ | **Fiaba (40)** (MrsNMacauley) **8-8-3v**$^{(3)}$ CTeague(11) (b: wl bhd tl gd late hdwy: nrst fin) | 2 | **6** | 25/1 | 41 | 21 |
| *3953*$^{10}$ | **Jigsaw Boy (67)** (PGMurphy) **7-9-6** SDrowne(10) (hdwy 5f out: rdn & wknd over 3f out) | 2 | **7** | 11/4$^{1}$ | 50 | 30 |
| 3995$^{21}$ | **Lady Silk (50)** (MissJFCraze) **5-9-1** NConnorton(3) (bhd fnl 4f) | nk | **8** | 16/1 | 45 | 25 |
| *3951*$^{6}$ | **Dragonjoy (58)** (NPLittmoden) **3-8-13b** BDoyle(2) (bhd fnl 4f) | 9 | **9** | 16/1 | 26 | 2 |
| 3694$^{11}$ | **Great Hall (40)** (PDCundell) **7-8-6b**$^{(5)}$ DGriffiths(12) (b.hind: s.s: a t.o) | 7 | **10** | 25/1 | 4 | — |
| *3951*$^{13}$ | **Flowing Ocean (76)** (DWChapman) **6-8-11** ACulhane(9) (sn outpcd: t.o) | 6 | **11** | 25/1 | — | — |
| 3977$^{11}$ | **February (42)** (AJChamberlain) **3-8-7**ow2 TGMcLaughlin(4) (prom: rdn 5f out: sn wknd: t.o) | 1½ | **12** | 50/1 | — | — |
| | | | | (SP 128.6%) | **12 Rn** | |

**1m 27.6** (2.90) CSF £29.07 TOTE £8.70: £2.40 £2.00 £1.80 (£24.00) Trio £19.60 OWNER Mr Lin Cheng Lee (MALTON) BRED Mrs J. Mackie and Major W. R. Paton Smith
WEIGHT FOR AGE 3yo-4lb
Sis Garden clmd A Spargo £3,000

**3427* Sis Garden**, upped in class when disappointing last time, had been put in on a useful mark here. (7/1)
**3601 I'm Your Lady** was trying to concede a lot of weight to the winner. (3/1)
**3951* People Direct** has only registered one of her six wins at short of a mile. (9/2)
**1609 Dancing Sioux** had not been disgraced following a sluggish start at York two days earlier. (6/1: op 4/1)
**2928 The Great Flood** is struggling to find a trip. (14/1: op 8/1)
**2940* Fiaba** is not the most consistent of animals. (25/1)
**1460* Jigsaw Boy** never really seemed likely to justify the support in the market. (11/4: op 5/1)

## 4078 WEATHERBYS DATA SERVICES H'CAP (0-85) (3-Y.O+) (Class D)

8-00 (8-01) **1m 1f 79y (Fibresand)** £4,125.90 (£1,234.20: £591.60: £270.30) Stalls: Low GOING minus 0.12 sec per fur (FST)

| | | | | SP | RR | SF |
|---|---|---|---|---|---|---|
| *3627*$^{4}$ | **South Eastern Fred (75)** (HJCollingridge) **5-9-6** MRimmer(11) (lw: plld hrd: a.p: hrd rdn to ld ins fnl f: r.o wl) | — | **1** | 20/1 | 79 | 55 |
| *3627*$^{3}$ | **Super High (81)** (PHowling) **4-9-12b** KFallon(7) (lw: a.p: led over 6f out: rdn over 3f out: hdd ins fnl f) | 1½ | **2** | 10/1 | 82 | 58 |
| 3703$^{5}$ | **Bentico (75)** (MrsNMacauley) **7-9-3**$^{(3)}$ CTeague(10) (hld up & bhd: hdwy 3f out: r.o ins fnl f) | 1¼ | **3** | 20/1 | 74 | 50 |
| *3955*$^{3}$ | **Heathyards Lady (USA) (69)** (RHollinshead) **5-8-11**$^{(3)}$ FLynch(2) (hld up: hdwy over 2f out: one pce fnl f) | ½ | **4** | 12/1 | 67 | 43 |
| *3627*$^{7}$ | **Cool Fire (75)** (SPCWoods) **3-9-0** DBiggs(4) (a.p: one pce fnl 2f) | hd | **5** | 16/1 | 73 | 43 |
| 1071$^{2}$ | **Classic Flyer (IRE) (80)** (RHarris) **3-9-5** AMackay(8) (lw: plld hrd early: no hdwy fnl 2f) | nk | **6** | 6/1$^{2}$ | 78 | 48 |
| 3211$^{11}$ | **Exalted (IRE) (82)** (SirMarkPrescott) **3-9-7** GDuffield(3) (lw: prom over 6f) | 5 | **7** | 9/1$^{3}$ | 71 | 41 |
| 3933* | **My Gallery (IRE) (83)** (ABailey) **5-9-11**$^{(3)}$ DWright(12) (hld up & bhd: hdwy 3f out: eased whn btn fnl f) | s.h | **8** | Evens$^{1}$ | 72 | 48 |
| *3627*$^{10}$ | **Le Sport (74)** (ABailey) **3-8-13** BDoyle(6) (lw: a bhd) | s.h | **9** | 33/1 | 63 | 33 |
| 3694$^{10}$ | **Just Harry (80)** (MJRyan) **5-9-6**$^{(5)}$ MBaird(5) (hld up & bhd: hdwy 3f out: wknd wl over 1f out) | 2½ | **10** | 20/1 | 65 | 41 |
| 3649$^{3}$ | **China Castle (72)** (PCHaslam) **3-8-11** GCarter(9) (lw: a bhd) | nk | **11** | 6/1$^{2}$ | 56 | 26 |
| *3419*$^{5}$ | **Johnnie the Joker (75)** (JPLeigh) **5-9-6b** DeanMcKeown(13) (led over 3f: wknd over 3f out) | 4 | **12** | 20/1 | 52 | 28 |
| 3765$^{3}$ | **Nordinex (IRE) (69)** (RWArmstrong) **4-9-0** RPrice(1) (b.nr fore: rdn over 6f out: bhd fnl 4f: sn t.o) | 13 | **13** | 9/1$^{3}$ | 24 | — |
| | | | | (SP 143.2%) | **13 Rn** | |

**2m 0.6** (4.60) CSF £217.28 CT £3,755.75 TOTE £23.60: £7.70 £2.60 £4.50 (£41.30) Trio £130.10 OWNER South Eastern Electrical Plc (NEWMARKET) BRED L. Audus
WEIGHT FOR AGE 3yo-6lb
STEWARDS' ENQUIRY McKeown susp. 16-20/9/96 (careless riding).

**3627 South Eastern Fred**, dropped 2lb, may have been well beaten over course and distance last time, but that was a hot contest by Wolverhampton's standards. (20/1)
**3627 Super High** had finished a length and a half in front of the winner on 2lb better terms in a very competitive handicap here last month. (10/1)
**3703 Bentico**, without the visor this time, was 7lb higher than when successful over course and distance in June. (20/1)
**3955 Heathyards Lady (USA)** was racing off the same mark as the previous week. (12/1)
**819 Cool Fire** seems to be coming to hand and a drop back to a mile may help. (16/1)
**1071 Classic Flyer (IRE)** may just have needed this first run on the Sand. (6/1)
**3933* My Gallery (IRE)** probably started at a false price because of the hype surrounding her bid to equal the record of nine handicap wins in a season. (Evens)
**3765 Nordinex (IRE)** (9/1: op 6/1)

## 4079 TATTERSALLS MAIDEN AUCTION STKS (2-Y.O) (Class E)

8-30 (8-31) **6f (Fibresand)** £3,028.00 (£904.00: £432.00: £196.00) Stalls: Low GOING minus 0.12 sec per fur (FST)

| | | | | SP | RR | SF |
|---|---|---|---|---|---|---|
| 3848$^{2}$ | **Pericles (78)** (MJohnston) **2-8-5** BDoyle(6) (lw: mde virtually all: clr over 1f out: easily) | — | **1** | 4/5$^{1}$ | 77+ | 33 |
| | **Venture Connect** (CPEBrooks) **2-8-3** CRutter(13) (lt-f: hdwy 3f out: sn rdn: chsd wnr fnl f: no imp) | 4 | **2** | 6/1$^{3}$ | 64 | 20 |
| *3950*$^{2}$ | **The Wyandotte Inn (65)** (RHollinshead) **2-8-1**$^{(3)}$ FLynch(1) (outpcd: gd hdwy over 1f out: r.o) | 2½ | **3** | 11/2$^{2}$ | 59 | 15 |
| 3795$^{3}$ | **Senate Swings (50)** (WRMuir) **2-8-9** KFallon(3) (a.p: chsd wnr on ins over 2f out: wknd over 1f out) | hd | **4** | 8/1 | 63 | 19 |
| 3826$^{6}$ | **Red Garter (IRE) (63)** (KMcAuliffe) **2-7-13**$^{(5)}$ow1 LNewton(12) (w ldrs 4f) | 5 | **5** | 16/1 | 45 | — |
| | **Lochlass (IRE)** (SPCWoods) **2-8-5** DBiggs(9) (neat: prom over 3f) | s.h | **6** | 16/1 | 46 | 2 |
| 3582$^{10}$ | **Flo's Choice (IRE)** (JAHarris) **2-8-4** JO'Reilly(2) (nvr trbld ldrs) | 5 | **7** | 33/1 | 32 | — |
| | **Verinder's Gift** (DrJDScargill) **2-8-3** MFenton(8) (w'like: s.i.s: nvr nr ldrs) | nk | **8** | 16/1 | 30 | — |
| 3848$^{8}$ | **No Class** (RHarris) **2-7-13** AMackay(10) (w ldrs over 3f: eased whn btn fnl f) | hd | **9** | 20/1 | 26 | — |
| 3515$^{9}$ | **Dom Ruinart (IRE)** (JWHills) **2-8-2**$^{(3)}$ MHenry(7) (sn bhd) | 2 | **10** | 8/1 | 26 | — |
| 3682$^{15}$ | **Always Alight** (KRBurke) **2-8-5** SDrowne(4) (outpcd) | 1 | **11** | 33/1 | 24 | — |
| 3919$^{6}$ | **Nesbet** (BRCambidge) **2-8-4**ow1 ACulhane(11) (a bhd) | ¾ | **12** | 50/1 | 21 | — |
| 3941$^{14}$ | **Rising Glory** (MissJFCraze) **2-8-9** SDWilliams(5) (prom 3f) | 1½ | **13** | 50/1 | 22 | — |
| | | | | (SP 139.7%) | **13 Rn** | |

**1m 14.8** (0.50 under 2y best) (3.40) CSF £8.12 TOTE £2.10: £1.50 £1.90 £1.60 (£7.50) Trio £6.50 OWNER Mr David Abell (MIDDLEHAM) BRED Elsdon Farms

**3848 Pericles** made mincemeat of this opposition. (4/5)
**Venture Connect** only cost 3,000 guineas, but has apparently shown plenty at home and had been supported in the Offices in Ireland. He came up against a useful sort in the winner for this type of event. (6/1: tchd 4/1)

**3950 The Wyandotte Inn** had pulled too hard when tried over seven at Leicester, but does seem to need that trip on this evidence. (11/2)
**3795 Senate Swings** does seem to like to get his toe in. (8/1: op 12/1)
**3826 Red Garter (IRE)** was trying her luck on the Sand. (16/1)
**Lochlass (IRE)** is a half-sister to Level Xing and X My Heart. (16/1)
**Dom Ruinart (IRE)** (8/1: op 7/2)

## 4080 VULCAN KIRKLAND (S) H'CAP (0-60) (3, 4 & 5-Y.O) (Class G)

9-00 (9-00) **1m 4f (Fibresand)** £2,070.00 (£570.00: £270.00) Stalls: Low GOING minus 0.12 sec per fur (FST)

| | | | | SP | RR | SF |
|---|---|---|---|---|---|---|
| *3066[6]* | **Heighth of Fame (55)** (DBurchell) **5-9-5**(7) KSked(2) (lw: mde all: clr over 2f out: rdn & r.o wl) | — | **1** | 14/1 | 79 | 56 |
| *3872[3]* | **Pearl Anniversary (IRE) (49)** (MJohnston) **3-8-11** BDoyle(9) (lw: s.i.s: hdwy 7f out: chsd wnr over 2f out: no imp) | 6 | **2** | 7/2[2] | 65 | 33 |
| 3705[7] | **Sylvella (50)** (MAJarvis) **3-8-12** PBloomfield(7) (lw: prom: rdn 6f out: no hdwy fnl 3f) | 8 | **3** | 12/1 | 55 | 23 |
| 3705[4] | **Sahhar (56)** (RWArmstrong) **3-9-4** RPrice(3) (chsd wnr tl wknd over 2f out) | 2½ | **4** | 12/1 | 58 | 26 |
| 3761[15] | **David James' Girl (52)** (ABailey) **4-9-6**(3) DWright(1) (lw: lost pl 7f out: sn hrd rdn: rallied over 3f out: wknd over 1f out) | 1¼ | **5** | 10/1 | 52 | 29 |
| 2537[5] | **Fijon (IRE) (53)** (JPearce) **3-9-1** GBardwell(5) (sn rdn along: a bhd) | 5 | **6** | 16/1 | 47 | 15 |
| *3955[6]* | **Zatopek (53)** (JCullinan) **4-9-7v1**(3) FLynch(10) (hld up: hrd rdn & wknd over 4f out) | 8 | **7** | 6/1[3] | 36 | 13 |
| 3824* | **Indira (58)** (PGMurphy) **3-9-6** SDrowne(11) (prom 6f) | 4 | **8** | 13/2 | 36 | 4 |
| 3849[2] | **Dannistar (49)** (PDEvans) **4-9-6** JFEgan(8) (lw: wl bhd fnl 6f) | 4 | **9** | 9/4[1] | 21 | — |
| 3849[5] | **Yuppy Girl (IRE) (55)** (CaptJWilson) **3-9-3** GCarter(12) (hdwy 8f out: wknd over 3f out: t.o) | 15 | **10** | 16/1 | 7 | — |
| 3507[7] | **Ever Friends (40)** (RHarris) **4-8-11** AMackay(6) (rdn 8f out: sn wl bhd: t.o) | 5 | **11** | 33/1 | — | — |
| | | | | (SP 126.5%) | **11 Rn** | |

**2m 39.3** (6.80) CSF £63.14 CT £581.95 TOTE £13.90: £2.60 £1.40 £4.10 (£29.90) Trio £53.90 OWNER Mr Simon Lewis (EBBW VALE) BRED Paul Mellon
WEIGHT FOR AGE 3yo-9lb
No bid; Pearl Anniversary (IRE) clmd MissSWilton £6,000
OFFICIAL EXPLANATION **Dannistar: pulled hard early on and would not face the kickback.**
**2631 Heighth of Fame** found forcing tactics over this shorter trip enabling him to run this field of platers ragged. (14/1)
**3872 Pearl Anniversary (IRE)** was claimed by Sue Wilton presumably to go jumping. (7/2)
**3357 Sylvella** was dropped into a seller for this debut on the Sand. (12/1: op 8/1)
**3705 Sahhar** paid the penalty for trying to go the pace set by the winner. (12/1: op 7/1)
**3603 David James' Girl** was stepping up considerably in distance. (10/1)
**3849 Dannistar** was most disappointing. (9/4)

## 4081 CHANTILLY H'CAP (0-70) (3-Y.O+) (Class E)

9-30 (9-31) **6f (Fibresand)** £3,003.00 (£833.00: £399.00) Stalls: Low GOING minus 0.12 sec per fur (FST)

| | | | | SP | RR | SF |
|---|---|---|---|---|---|---|
| 3973[7] | **Pageboy (67)** (PCHaslam) **7-9-13** SDrowne(5) (lw: a.p: rdn to ld ins fnl f: r.o wl) | — | **1** | 4/1[1] | 71 | 54 |
| *3602[4]* | **Napier Star (61)** (MrsNMacauley) **3-9-2v**(3) CTeague(6) (led 5f out tl ins fnl f) | 1¾ | **2** | 10/1 | 60 | 41 |
| *3602[3]* | **Itsinthepost (64)** (VSoane) **3-9-8** AMcGlone(11) (led 1f: outpcd over 2f out: rallied over 1f out: r.o ins fnl f) | ¾ | **3** | 5/1[2] | 61 | 42 |
| 3957* | **Marjorie Rose (IRE) (67)** (ABailey) **3-9-4**(7) 7x AngelaGallimore(8) (b: hdwy over 5f out: r.o) | ¾ | **4** | 6/1[3] | 62 | 43 |
| 3342[5] | **Ramsey Hope (60)** (CWFairhurst) **3-9-4v** KFallon(4) (lw: prom: ev ch 2f out: wknd fnl f) | 1 | **5** | 20/1 | 53 | 34 |
| 3313[6] | **Red Admiral (63)** (CMurray) **6-9-9** DeanMcKeown(7) (nvr nr to chal) | 3½ | **6** | 14/1 | 46 | 29 |
| *1971[5]* | **Kung Frode (63)** (BAMcMahon) **4-9-9** GDuffield(2) (lw: s.i.s: sn hmpd: nvr nr to chal) | hd | **7** | 8/1 | 46 | 29 |
| *3420[2]* | **Efficacy (58)** (APJarvis) **5-8-11**(7) CCarver(10) (prom over 3f) | ½ | **8** | 12/1 | 40 | 23 |
| 3583[10] | **Niteowl Raider (IRE) (60)** (JAHarris) **3-9-4** JO'Reilly(13) (lw: chsd ldrs 3f) | 3 | **9** | 25/1 | 34 | 15 |
| 1521[4] | **Leigh Crofter (65)** (PDCundell) **7-9-4**(7) NLovelock(12) (outpcd) | 2 | **10** | 14/1 | 33 | 16 |
| 3639[12] | **Cheeky Chappy (62)** (DWChapman) **5-9-5b**(3) OPears(1) (bhd: hdwy on ins over 2f out: wknd wl over 1f out) | 4 | **11** | 8/1 | 20 | 3 |
| 3700[5] | **Times of Times (IRE) (66)** (MJRyan) **3-9-10** MTebbutt(9) (lw: prom 3f) | s.h | **12** | 7/1 | 24 | 5 |
| 3864[3] | **Another Batchworth (58)** (EAWheeler) **4-9-4** TSprake(3) (chsd ldrs: sltly hmpd over 3f out: wknd over 2f out) | 2½ | **13** | 8/1 | 9 | — |
| | | | | (SP 135.5%) | **13 Rn** | |

**1m 14.7** (3.30) CSF £46.06 CT £206.41 TOTE £7.80: £2.50 £2.90 £1.90 (£53.60) Trio £86.10 OWNER Lord Scarsdale (MIDDLEHAM) BRED K. T. Ivory and Partners
WEIGHT FOR AGE 3yo-2lb
**3758 Pageboy** continues in fine form, and had no intention of being a bridesmaid here. (4/1)
**3602 Napier Star** ran a sound race off a mark 10lb higher than when winning over the minimum distance here in July. (10/1)
**3602 Itsinthepost**, supported in the Ring, again seemed to find six inadequate. (5/1)
**3957* Marjorie Rose (IRE)**, as a result of a penalty, was running off a mark a stone higher than when successful over five here in July. (6/1)
**3342 Ramsey Hope** gave the impression that he may find five far enough on the Sand. (20/1)
**3168 Red Admiral** could not get to his favourite front-running position. (14/1)
**1971 Kung Frode**, held up to get the trip, can do better than this. (8/1)
**1521 Leigh Crofter** (14/1: 10/1-16/1)

T/Plpt: £199.50 (55.6 Tckts). T/Qdpt: £34.50 (13.31 Tckts). KH

# 3473-BATH (L-H) (Good to firm)

## Monday September 9th

WEATHER: unsettled WIND: mod across

## 4082 AUTUMN (S) H'CAP (0-60) (3 & 4-Y.O) (Class G)

1-45 (1-48) **1m 5y** £2,598.00 (£728.00: £354.00) Stalls: Low GOING minus 0.56 sec per fur (F)

| | | | | SP | RR | SF |
|---|---|---|---|---|---|---|
| 3619[6] | **Richard House Lad (41)** (RHollinshead) **3-8-8** LDettori(6) (lw: led 1f: led over 3f out: clr over 1f out: rdn out) | — | **1** | 9/1 | 45 | 22 |

| | | | | SP | RR | SF |
|---|---|---|---|---|---|---|
| 3285$^{5}$ | **Samara Song (55)** (WGMTurner) **3-9-8** TSprake(2) (lw: a.p: chsd wnr over 1f out: r.o) | 1 | **2** | 16/1 | 57 | 34 |
| 3165$^{13}$ | **Shouldbegrey (44)** (WRMuir) **3-8-11** JReid(15) (hdwy 3f out: r.o one pce fnl f) | 1½ | **3** | 16/1 | 43 | 20 |
| 3761$^{5}$ | **Jilly Beveled (39)** (PRWebber) **4-8-11** RPerham(11) (b.hind: hld up: hdwy on ins 4f out: one pce fnl 2f) | 1¼ | **4** | 7/1$^{2}$ | 36 | 18 |
| 3469$^{2}$ | **Tomal (44)** (RIngram) **4-9-2** SWhitworth(4) (hdwy over 3f out: r.o ins fnl f) | s.h | **5** | 100/30$^{1}$ | 40 | 22 |
| 3496$^{13}$ | **Wilfull Lad (IRE) (55)** (MartynMeade) **3-9-1**$^{(7)}$ DSweeney(7) (led after 1f: hdd over 3f out: wknd over 1f out) | nk | **6** | 14/1 | 51 | 28 |
| 3257$^{15}$ | **Acquittal (IRE) (45)** (AStreeter) **4-9-0v**$^{(3)}$ RHavlin(10) (nvr nr to chal) | 1¼ | **7** | 14/1 | 38 | 20 |
| 3861$^{9}$ | **Park Ridge (39)** (TGMills) **4-8-11hb** NAdams(9) (s.i.s: nvr nrr) | ½ | **8** | 33/1 | 31 | 13 |
| 3500$^{9}$ | **Hawanafa (45)** (RHannon) **3-8-12** PatEddery(12) (lw: prom over 5f) | 1¼ | **9** | 7/1$^{2}$ | 35 | 12 |
| 3681$^{6}$ | **Spiral Flyer (IRE) (40)** (MDIUsher) **3-8-7** JCarroll(5) (lw: hld up & plld hrd: n.d) | ½ | **10** | 25/1 | 29 | 6 |
| 3761$^{3}$ | **Shermood (39)** (KTIvory) **3-8-1**$^{(5)}$ MartinDwyer(17) (b.off fore: b.hind: nvr nr ldrs) | ¾ | **11** | 15/2$^{3}$ | 26 | 3 |
| 3473$^{2}$ | **Cedar Dancer (35)** (RJHodges) **4-8-2**$^{(5)}$ AmandaSanders(13) (a bhd) | nk | **12** | 10/1 | 22 | 4 |
| 2130$^{16}$ | **Northern Grey (49)** (DrJDScargill) **4-9-7b** MFenton(3) (s.i.s: sn rcvrd: wknd over 2f out) | 1 | **13** | 16/1 | 34 | 16 |
| 3978$^{9}$ | **Lady Magnum (IRE) (37)** (JNeville) **3-8-4** AClark(1) (dwlt: a bhd) | 3 | **14** | 25/1 | 16 | — |
| 3456$^{13}$ | **Zdenka (42)** (MBlanshard) **3-8-9** TQuinn(16) (prom 4f) | 1¼ | **15** | 16/1 | 18 | — |
| 3525$^{8}$ | **Infantry Dancer (53)** (GCBravery) **3-9-1**$^{(5)}$ LNewton(8) (prom 4f) | 2 | **16** | 16/1 | 25 | 2 |
| 2192$^{21}$ | **Adilov (54)** (KOCunningham-Brown) **4-9-12** BDoyle(18) (lw: a bhd) | 2½ | **17** | 33/1 | 21 | 3 |
| | **Okay Baby (IRE) (44)** (JMBradley) **4-9-2** DaneO'Neill(14) (chsd ldrs 4f: rn wd bnd over 3f out: sn bhd) | ½ | **18** | 33/1 | 10 | — |
| | | | | (SP 138.2%) | **18 Rn** | |

**1m 41.1** (2.60) CSF £144.66 CT £2,166.00 TOTE £10.60: £2.30 £3.70 £4.30 £2.20 (£75.60) Trio £278.90; £294.67 to Lingfield 10/9/96
OWNER Mr D. Morrall (UPPER LONGDON) BRED Mrs E. M. Gauvain
WEIGHT FOR AGE 3yo-5lb
No bid
**3619 Richard House Lad**, dropped 3lb, seemed to benefit from more forceful tactics. (9/1)
**2966 Samara Song**, without the visor, was reverting to a mile. (16/1)
**3000 Shouldbegrey** was dropped into selling company. (16/1)
**3761 Jilly Beveled** was again a shade disappointing. (7/1)
**3469 Tomal** could not take advantage of a return to selling company. (100/30)
**1119 Wilfull Lad (IRE)**, back at a mile, was dropped in class. (14/1)

## 4083 BRISTOL ROVERS MAIDEN STKS (3-Y.O+) (Class D)
2-15 (2-16) **1m 3f 144y** £3,848.75 (£1,160.00: £562.50: £263.75) GOING minus 0.56 sec per fur (F)

| | | | | SP | RR | SF |
|---|---|---|---|---|---|---|
| 3470$^{7}$ | **Far Dawn (USA) (72)** (GHarwood) **3-8-12** AClark(8) (lw: a.p: led wl over 1f out: drvn out) | — | **1** | 7/2$^{2}$ | 70 | 31 |
| 2223$^{4}$ | **Madame Steinlen (75)** (BWHills) **3-8-7** PatEddery(1) (led tl wl over 1f out: hrd rdn: r.o one pce) | 1½ | **2** | 2/1$^{1}$ | 63 | 24 |
| 3505$^{7}$ | **Namoodaj** (ACStewart) **3-8-12** DHarrison(4) (a.p: ev ch 2f out: sn rdn: unable qckn) | hd | **3** | 2/1$^{1}$ | 68 | 29 |
| 3505$^{13}$ | **Wybara** (JHMGosden) **3-8-7** LDettori(3) (hld up: hdwy over 3f out: ev ch over 2f out: wknd fnl f) | 5 | **4** | 6/1$^{3}$ | 56 | 17 |
| | **Mu-Tadil** (RJBaker) **4-9-7** NAdams(9) (nvr gng wl: rdn over 4f out: sn wl bhd: t.o) | 18 | **5** | 50/1 | 36 | 6 |
| 3472$^{17}$ | **Monte Felice (IRE)** (GHarwood) **3-8-12** TQuinn(2) (prom: rdn 4f out: wknd 3f out: t.o) | s.h | **6** | 16/1 | 36 | — |
| 3505$^{11}$ | **Soldier Blue** (PJHobbs) **3-8-12** JReid(5) (hld up & plld hrd: wl bhd fnl 4f: t.o) | 7 | **7** | 25/1 | 27 | — |
| | **Haddit** (AGNewcombe) **3-8-12** MFenton(6) (leggy: lt-f: unf: bit bkwd: s.s: a bhd: t.o fnl 5f) | 5 | **8** | 40/1 | 20 | — |
| | **Minneola** (ABarrow) **4-8-11**$^{(5)}$ SophieMitchell(7) (a bhd: t.o fnl 4f) | 30 | **9** | 100/1 | — | — |
| | | | | (SP 118.3%) | **9 Rn** | |

**2m 29.8** (3.10) CSF £10.78 TOTE £4.90: £1.30 £1.30 £1.60 (£7.90) Trio £5.10 OWNER Mr Peter Wiegand (PULBOROUGH) BRED Galbreath/Phillips Racing Partnership
WEIGHT FOR AGE 3yo-9lb
**2744 Far Dawn (USA)**, back in a maiden, has taken time to come to hand. (7/2)
**2223 Madame Steinlen**, coming back after a break, is proving expensive to follow. (2/1)
**3505 Namoodaj**, trying a longer trip, failed to deliver the goods after looking to be going best. (2/1)
**Wybara** appeared not to stay. (6/1)

## 4084 DESMOND BARTON NURSERY H'CAP (2-Y.O) (Class C)
2-45 (2-48) **1m 5y** £5,307.75 (£1,602.00: £778.50: £366.75) GOING minus 0.56 sec per fur (F)

| | | | | SP | RR | SF |
|---|---|---|---|---|---|---|
| 3616$^{2}$ | **Sheer Face (86)** (WRMuir) **2-9-5** JReid(1) (lw: a.p: led over 1f out: drvn out) | — | **1** | 9/2$^{2}$ | 90 | 26 |
| 3792$^{12}$ | **Fletcher (88)** (PFICole) **2-9-7** TQuinn(7) (hld up: hdwy over 3f out: edgd lft fnl f: r.o) | 1 | **2** | 9/1 | 90 | 26 |
| 3764$^{3}$ | **Elrayahin (80)** (MajorWRHern) **2-8-13b$^{1}$** WCarson(5) (rdn along & sn led: rdn & hdd over 1f out: nt qckn) | hd | **3** | 6/1$^{3}$ | 82 | 18 |
| 3662* | **Princess of Hearts (68)** (BJMeehan) **2-8-1**$^{ow2}$ BDoyle(4) (bhd tl hdwy fnl 2f: r.o) | 2 | **4** | 14/1 | 66 | — |
| 3408$^{3}$ | **Hen Harrier (85)** (JLDunlop) **2-9-4** PatEddery(11) (hdwy over 3f out: hrd rdn over 2f out: one pce) | hd | **5** | 5/2$^{1}$ | 83 | 19 |
| 3826$^{5}$ | **Misty Cay (IRE) (70)** (SDow) **2-7-12**$^{(5)}$ ADaly(2) (swtg: hld up: hdwy 3f out: hrd rdn 2f out: no imp) | 2 | **6** | 11/1 | 64 | — |
| 3493$^{3}$ | **Salabatni (70)** (EALDunlop) **2-8-3** DHarrison(3) (bhd fnl 3f) | 2½ | **7** | 7/1 | 59 | — |
| 3498$^{4}$ | **Running Free (IRE) (63)** (MJFetherston-Godley) **2-7-7b**$^{(3)}$ MHenry(10) (a bhd) | 3 | **8** | 11/1 | 46 | — |
| 3467$^{8}$ | **Hil Rhapsody (80)** (BPalling) **2-8-13** TSprake(8) (prom 5f) | 1 | **9** | 33/1 | 61 | — |
| 3493$^{9}$ | **River King (70)** (RHannon) **2-8-3**$^{ow4}$ DaneO'Neill(6) (lw: a bhd) | 1 | **10** | 16/1 | 49 | — |
| 3230$^{6}$ | **Midatlantic (72)** (PTWalwyn) **2-8-5** JCarroll(9) (lw: prom over 5f) | 5 | **11** | 33/1 | 41 | — |
| | | | | (SP 118.6%) | **11 Rn** | |

**1m 41.7** (3.20) CSF £41.25 CT £226.86 TOTE £5.80: £1.60 £3.00 £2.10 (£20.40) Trio £40.40 OWNER Mr A J de V Patrick (LAMBOURN) BRED Mrs C. R. Philipson
LONG HANDICAP Running Free (IRE) 7-8
**3616 Sheer Face** was well suited by the step up in distance. (9/2)
**2878 Fletcher** has gone left-handed before and does not seem one to trust implicitly. (9/1)
**3764 Elrayahin**, whose rider was intent on making the running, did not find the blinkers doing the trick. (6/1)
**3662* Princess of Hearts**, given a lot to do over this longer trip, was not disgraced in this stronger company. (14/1)
**3408 Hen Harrier** was trying her luck at a mile. (5/2)
**3826 Misty Cay (IRE)** had been dropped 4lb for this first attempt at a mile. (11/1: op 7/1)

## 4085 SHERSTON CONDITIONS STKS (2-Y.O F) (Class C)
3-15 (3-16) **1m 5y** £5,922.00 (£1,638.00) GOING minus 0.56 sec per fur (F)

| | | | | SP | RR | SF |
|---|---|---|---|---|---|---|
| 2582$^{6}$ | **Khassah** (JHMGosden) **2-8-12** WCarson(2) (trckd ldr: led on bit ins fnl f: cleverly) | — | **1** | 11/8$^{2}$ | 95+ | 33 |

| | | | | SP | RR | SF |
|---|---|---|---|---|---|---|
| 2863* | **Ovation** (PFICole) **2-8-12** TQuinn(1) (led: rdn over 1f out: hdd ins fnl f) | 1¼ | **2** | 4/7[1] | 93? | 31 |
| | | | | (SP 105.7%) | **2 Rn** | |

**1m 40.3** (0.40 under 2y best) (1.80) TOTE £2.30 OWNER Mr Hamdan Al Maktoum (NEWMARKET) BRED Shadwell Estate Company Limited

**2582 Khassah** had finished lame on her off-hind when disappointing in the Cherry Hinton. (11/8)

**2863* Ovation** found the winner galloping all over her in the final quarter-mile. (4/7)

## 4086 KEITH PONTER MAIDEN H'CAP (0-70) (3-Y.O+) (Class E)

3-45 (3-49) **1m 5f 22y** £3,304.50 (£996.00: £483.00: £226.50) Stalls: High GOING minus 0.56 sec per fur (F)

| | | | | SP | RR | SF |
|---|---|---|---|---|---|---|
| 3855[11] | **Arcady (58)** (PTWalwyn) **3-8-8** JCarroll(13) (mde virtually all: rdn over 2f out: r.o wl) | — | **1** | 12/1 | 70 | 19 |
| *3872*[2] | **Miss Prism (51)** (JLDunlop) **3-8-1** TSprake(5) (hld up: chsd wnr fnl 3f: one pce) | 2½ | **2** | 10/1 | 60 | 9 |
| 3398[8] | **Lepikha (USA) (62)** (BWHills) **3-8-7**(5) JDSmith(9) (hld up & bhd: hdwy 6f out: rdn over 2f out: styd on fnl f) | ½ | **3** | 10/1 | 70 | 19 |
| 3667[8] | **Go With The Wind (62)** (MBell) **3-8-12** MFenton(8) (a.p: rdn 3f out: one pce fnl 2f) | ½ | **4** | 20/1 | 70 | 19 |
| 3802[6] | **Spread The Word (51)** (LGCottrell) **4-8-11v** JReid(1) (hld up & bhd: hdwy 7f out: one pce fnl 2f) | 1¼ | **5** | 7/1[3] | 57 | 16 |
| 1104[10] | **Hoofprints (IRE) (68)** (GHarwood) **3-9-4** AClark(12) (bit bkwd: prom: hrd rdn over 2f out: wknd over 1f out) | 1¾ | **6** | 12/1 | 72 | 21 |
| 3514[8] | **Crested Knight (IRE) (51)** (CAHorgan) **4-8-11** DHarrison(7) (hld up & bhd: hdwy over 3f out: wknd 2f out) | 2½ | **7** | 8/1 | 52 | 11 |
| 3831[4] | **Chocolate Ice (64)** (CACyzer) **3-8-11b**[1](3) MHenry(11) (prom tl wknd over 2f out) | 5 | **8** | 12/1 | 59 | 8 |
| 3667[3] | **Perfect Gift (56)** (PFICole) **3-8-6** TQuinn(15) (prom: rdn 4f out: wknd over 2f out) | 3½ | **9** | 3/1[1] | 47 | — |
| 3141[8] | **Seven Crowns (USA) (57)** (RHannon) **3-8-7** DaneO'Neill(6) (gd hdwy on ins 8f out: wknd 4f out) | nk | **10** | 20/1 | 47 | — |
| 2613[7] | **Dtoto (55)** (RJBaker) **4-9-1** NAdams(3) (a bhd) | 1½ | **11** | 66/1 | 43 | 2 |
| *2086*[5] | **Brentability (IRE) (54)** (GLewis) **3-8-1**(3) AWhelan(4) (bkwd: a bhd) | 1¾ | **12** | 20/1 | 40 | — |
| | **Faustino (47)** (PJHobbs) **4-8-7** PatEddery(2) (lw: a bhd) | ¾ | **13** | 4/1[2] | 32 | — |
| 1079[11] | **Liberatrice (FR) (53)** (EALDunlop) **3-8-3** WCarson(14) (sn bhd) | hd | **14** | 25/1 | 38 | — |
| *296*[7] | **Verde Luna (64)** (DWPArbuthnot) **4-9-10** SWhitworth(10) (prom 8f) | 3 | **15** | 33/1 | 46 | 5 |
| | | | | (SP 132.4%) | **15 Rn** | |

**2m 50.7** (5.00) CSF £125.27 CT £1,169.36 TOTE £12.60: £3.50 £2.00 £2.70 (£72.60) Trio £388.00; £65.58 to Lingfield 10/9/96 OWNER Windsor House Racing (LAMBOURN) BRED A. D. G. Oldrey

WEIGHT FOR AGE 3yo-10lb

**3283 Arcady**, probably unsuited by the soft last time, has gradually been slipping down the Ratings. (12/1)

**3872 Miss Prism** was 6lb higher than when demoted from second place at Nottingham. (10/1)

**3398 Lepikha (USA)** needs even further on this evidence. (10/1)

**3218 Go With The Wind** is not overblessed with finishing speed. (20/1)

**3802 Spread The Word** could not sustain her effort, despite a 2lb lower mark. (7/1)

**Hoofprints (IRE)** did not look fully wound up for this comeback. (12/1)

**3667 Perfect Gift** failed to justify her market support. (3/1: tchd 5/1)

## 4087 TWERTON MAIDEN AUCTION STKS (2-Y.O F) (Class E)

4-15 (4-18) **5f 11y** £3,051.00 (£918.00: £444.00: £207.00) Stalls: High GOING minus 0.56 sec per fur (F)

| | | | | SP | RR | SF |
|---|---|---|---|---|---|---|
| | **Loving And Giving** (HCandy) **2-8-2** CRutter(7) (w'like: hdwy 2f out: rdn to ld wl ins fnl f: r.o) | — | **1** | 100/30[1] | 75 | 9 |
| 3796[16] | **Hype Energy** (GLewis) **2-8-4**(3) AWhelan(12) (hld up: hdwy 2f out: r.o wl ins fnl f) | ½ | **2** | 33/1 | 78 | 12 |
| 3796[3] | **Northern Girl (IRE) (75)** (BJMeehan) **2-8-1** BDoyle(13) (w ldr: led over 2f out: hdd wl ins fnl f) | ¾ | **3** | 5/1[3] | 70 | 4 |
| 2995[3] | **Keen Waters** (JRArnold) **2-7-12**(3) MHenry(5) (chsd ldrs: one pce fnl 2f) | 2 | **4** | 7/1 | 64 | — |
| | **Ma Vielle Pouque (IRE)** (WGMTurner) **2-8-3**[ow1] DHarrison(10) (leggy: unf: a.p: rdn over 2f out: one pce) | ¾ | **5** | 16/1 | 63 | — |
| 3853[5] | **Gold Edge** (MRChannon) **2-8-3**[ow2] CandyMorris(4) (no hdwy fnl 2f) | 1¼ | **6** | 14/1 | 59 | — |
| | **Shalstayholy (IRE)** (GLMoore) **2-8-6** SWhitworth(1) (str: bkwd: nvr nrr) | s.h | **7** | 8/1 | 62 | — |
| 3796[2] | **Parijazz (IRE)** (MartynMeade) **2-7-13** NAdams(3) (led over 2f: wknd over 1f out) | 1¾ | **8** | 9/2[2] | 50 | — |
| | **Tayovullin (IRE)** (RCharlton) **2-8-7** TSprake(8) (w'like: bhd fnl 2f) | 2 | **9** | 9/2[2] | 51 | — |
| 3796[9] | **Java Bay** (MBlanshard) **2-8-7** TQuinn(9) (prom: rdn over 2f out: sn wknd) | nk | **10** | 20/1 | 50 | — |
| 3475[5] | **Sarabi** (JPearce) **2-8-5** GBardwell(6) (a bhd) | 3 | **11** | 16/1 | 39 | — |
| 3454[12] | **Christmas Rose** (HThomsonJones) **2-8-7**[ow1] PatEddery(11) (outpcd: t.o fnl 2f) | 7 | **12** | 12/1 | 19 | — |
| | | | | (SP 133.5%) | **12 Rn** | |

**62.5 secs** (2.00) CSF £97.33 TOTE £4.10: £1.70 £8.10 £2.70 (£48.80) Trio £182.60 OWNER Mrs J. E. L. Wright (WANTAGE) BRED Wheelersland Stud

**Loving And Giving**, a sister to Speed On, had apparently been showing ability at home. (100/30)

**Hype Energy**, a half-sister to Runs in the Family, showed nothing on her debut, but is going the right way. (33/1)

**3796 Northern Girl (IRE)** was dropping back to the minimum trip. (5/1)

**2995 Keen Waters** is out of a half-sister to good sprinter Sizzling Melody. (7/1)

**Ma Vielle Pouque (IRE)** is the first foal of an Irish ten furlong winner. (16/1)

**3853 Gold Edge** is a half-sister to Chemcast. (14/1: 7/1-16/1)

**Shalstayholy (IRE)**, a half-sister to Arch Angel and Benzoe, seems capable of improvement. (8/1: op 4/1)

**Tayovullin (IRE)** (9/2: op 3/1)

**Christmas Rose** (12/1: 8/1-14/1)

## 4088 LEVY BOARD SEVENTH RACE H'CAP (0-80) (3-Y.O+) (Class D)

4-45 (4-47) **5f 161y** £4,030.75 (£1,216.00: £590.50: £277.75) Stalls: High GOING minus 0.56 sec per fur (F)

| | | | | SP | RR | SF |
|---|---|---|---|---|---|---|
| 3930[4] | **Longwick Lad (67)** (WRMuir) **3-9-0** JReid(6) (hdwy over 2f out: led over 1f out: drvn out) | — | **1** | 9/2[2] | 74 | 34 |
| 3993[3] | **Ned's Bonanza (58)** (MDods) **7-8-7** AClark(11) (lw: a.p: nt clr run & swtchd rt over 1f out: sn rdn: ev ch ins fnl f: unable qckn) | ¾ | **2** | 9/1 | 63 | 25 |
| 3930[6] | **John O'Dreams (49)** (MrsALMKing) **11-7-12** NAdams(2) (chsd ldrs on ins: r.o one pce fnl f) | 1¼ | **3** | 14/1 | 50 | 12 |
| 3930[3] | **Jucea (72)** (JLSpearing) **7-9-7** PatEddery(8) (gd hdwy over 1f out: r.o ins fnl f) | 1¼ | **4** | 7/2[1] | 70 | 32 |
| 3696[3] | **Winsome Wooster (63)** (PGMurphy) **5-8-12** TSprake(7) (lw: s.s: gd hdwy over 1f out: r.o) | ½ | **5** | 16/1 | 60 | 22 |
| 3973[4] | **Robellion (69)** (DWPArbuthnot) **5-9-4v** TQuinn(9) (b.hind: gd hdwy fnl f: fin wl) | hd | **6** | 10/1 | 65 | 27 |
| 1677[3] | **Stoppes Brow (77)** (GLMoore) **4-9-12** SWhitworth(5) (s.s: gd late hdwy: nrst fin) | ¾ | **7** | 20/1 | 71 | 33 |
| 3844[16] | **Princely Sound (64)** (MBell) **3-8-11** MFenton(1) (led 3f: wknd over 1f out) | hd | **8** | 16/1 | 58 | 18 |
| 3810[12] | **Rockcracker (IRE) (63)** (GGMargarson) **4-8-12b** DBiggs(14) (hdwy over 2f out: wknd over 1f out) | ½ | **9** | 25/1 | 56 | 18 |
| 3758[2] | **Don Pepe (62)** (RBoss) **5-8-11** BDoyle(3) (prom over 3f) | ¾ | **10** | 7/1[3] | 52 | 14 |
| 3477[7] | **Walk the Beat (65)** (MartynMeade) **6-8-7**(7) DSweeney(4) (prom tl n.m.r & wknd over 1f out) | ¾ | **11** | 16/1 | 53 | 15 |

| Form | Horse / details | Dist | Pos | SP | RR | SF |
|---|---|---|---|---|---|---|
| 3661[14] | **Paley Prince (USA) (54)** (MDIUsher) **10-7-10**(7) RBrisland(12) (a.p: led over 2f out tl wknd over 1f out) | 2½ | **12** | 33/1 | 35 | — |
| 3700[4] | **Rambold (64)** (NEBerry) **5-8-13** RPerham(10) (prom 3f) | 2 | **13** | 16/1 | 40 | 2 |
| 3465[5] | **Miss Bigwig (68)** (JBerry) **3-9-1** JCarroll(15) (spd over 3f) | 2½ | **14** | 16/1 | 37 | — |
| 2858[7] | **Xenophon of Cunaxa (IRE) (80)** (MJFetherston-Godley) **3-9-13** DHarrison(16) (outpcd) | 7 | **15** | 25/1 | 29 | — |
| 3518[8] | **Master Millfield (IRE) (67)** (CJHill) **4-9-2** DaneO'Neill(13) (bhd fnl 2f) | s.h | **16** | 12/1 | 16 | — |
| | | | | (SP 131.2%) | **16 Rn** | |

**1m 10.8** (1.30) CSF £44.81 CT £526.49 TOTE £5.40: £1.30 £1.90 £3.60 £1.80 (£24.30) Trio £57.00 OWNER Mrs Marion Wickham (LAMBOURN) BRED Mrs Wickham

WEIGHT FOR AGE 3yo-2lb

**3930 Longwick Lad** had run well from a poor draw at Sandown last time. (9/2)

**3993 Ned's Bonanza** continues in good form and was travelling on the bridle until forced to switch to find daylight. (9/1)

**3930 John O'Dreams** was only 1lb higher than when successful at Newbury in June. (14/1)

**3930 Jucea** is 2lb higher than the highest mark off which she has won. (7/2)

**3696 Winsome Wooster**, reverting to sprinting, did not help her chance with a poor start. (16/1)

**3973 Robellion** only found top gear when the race was virtually over. (10/1)

**1677 Stoppes Brow** really needs further than this and looks set for a profitable autumn campaign. (20/1)

T/Plpt: £370.40 (37.01 Tckts). T/Qdpt: £38.00 (26.14 Tckts). KH

# 3600-SOUTHWELL (L-H) (Standard)

## Monday September 9th

WEATHER: overcast WIND: fresh across

## 4089 AMSTERDAM AMATEUR H'CAP (0-70) (3-Y.O+) (Class G)

2-00 (2-01) **1m (Fibresand)** £2,070.00 (£570.00: £270.00) Stalls: Low GOING minus 0.16 sec per fur (FST)

| Form | Horse / details | Dist | Pos | SP | RR | SF |
|---|---|---|---|---|---|---|
| 3981[6] | **North Ardar (52)** (DNicholls) **6-10-7**(3) MrRThornton(9) (hld up: hdwy over 2f out: led ins fnl f: r.o) | — | **1** | 11/2[2] | 63 | 41 |
| 3861[6] | **Twin Creeks (59)** (VSoane) **5-10-10**(7) MrFQuinlan(13) (lw: led: clr ½-wy: hdd & no ex ins fnl f) | 1½ | **2** | 12/1 | 67 | 45 |
| 3606[7] | **Sporting Risk (43)** (PWHarris) **4-10-1** MissAElsey(5) (lw: a chsng ldrs: kpt on fnl 3f: nvr able to chal) | 3½ | **3** | 8/1 | 44 | 22 |
| 3786[6] | **Montone (IRE) (58)** (JRJenkins) **6-10-11v**(5) DrMMannish(3) (bhd: hdwy over 2f out: styd on: nrst fin) | nk | **4** | 7/1 | 58 | 36 |
| *3877*[5] | **Hawaii Storm (FR) (55)** (DJSffrenchDavis) **8-10-6**(7) MissEFolkes(6) (dwlt: hdwy fnl 2f: nrst fin) | 1¾ | **5** | 20/1 | 52 | 30 |
| 3958[10] | **Pc's Cruiser (IRE) (48)** (JLEyre) **4-10-6b** MissDianaJones(8) (a.p: one pce fnl 3f) | nk | **6** | 13/2[3] | 44 | 22 |
| *2935*[6] | **Sandmoor Denim (58)** (SRBowring) **9-10-11**(5) MrsMMorris(1) (trckd ldrs: effrt & swtchd 2f out: r.o one pce) | 3 | **7** | 10/1 | 48 | 26 |
| 3862* | **Mogin (55)** (TJNaughton) **3-10-3**(5) MrsJNaughton(16) (prom tl outpcd fnl 2½f) | s.h | **8** | 9/2[1] | 45 | 18 |
| *3603*[10] | **No Submission (USA) (55)** (DWChapman) **10-10-10v**(3) MissRClark(10) (lw: bhd: c v.wd st: r.o towards fin) | ½ | **9** | 20/1 | 44 | 22 |
| 3461[8] | **Lucky Bea (58)** (MWEasterby) **3-10-11** MrNWilson(7) (s.i.s: hdwy after 3f: rdn & wknd fnl 2f) | nk | **10** | 12/1 | 47 | 20 |
| 2284[11] | **Sarum (47)** (JELong) **10-9-12**(7) MrTWaters(15) (b: cl up tl wknd fnl 3f) | nk | **11** | 33/1 | 35 | 13 |
| *3955*[7] | **Bold Habit (45)** (JPearce) **11-10-3** MrsLPearce(12) (b.nr hind: nvr trbld ldrs) | 6 | **12** | 14/1 | 21 | — |
| | **Shared Risk (47)** (JNorton) **4-10-2**(3) MrPScott(4) (sn bhd) | 8 | **13** | 20/1 | 7 | — |
| 3866[13] | **Prudent Pet (57)** (CWFairhurst) **4-10-12**(3) MrsSBosley(14) (outpcd ½-wy: sn lost tch) | 20 | **14** | 16/1 | — | — |
| 3819[4] | **Classic Colours (USA) (65)** (RHarris) **3-10-11b**[1](7) MrRBarrett(11) (spd 3f: wknd qckly) | 11 | **15** | 16/1 | — | — |
| | | | | (SP 130.6%) | **15 Rn** | |

**1m 46.8** (6.80) CSF £68.86 CT £511.53 TOTE £4.40: £2.10 £5.40 £3.90 (£57.10) Trio £119.20 OWNER Mr M. Rodgers (THIRSK) BRED Mrs H.Seddington

WEIGHT FOR AGE 3yo-5lb

**OFFICIAL EXPLANATION Prudent Pet: had made a noise.**

**3981 North Ardar** last won on this surface over three years ago, but he showed here he handles it as well as turf. Despite this trip being short of his best, he won really well. (11/2)

**3861 Twin Creeks** looked to have stolen this when going several lengths clear just after halfway, but it turned out he had done too much too soon and he was picked off inside the last furlong. In this mood his luck will surely change. (12/1)

**3052 Sporting Risk** has yet to win on this surface, but he showed enough here to suggest that he is capable of rectifying that. (8/1)

**3786 Montone (IRE)**, normally up with the pace, got left behind on this occasion, but he did finish to some purpose to show he retains his ability. (7/1)

**3078 Hawaii Storm (FR)** missed the break, but then finished really well, albeit too late. (20/1)

**3603* Pc's Cruiser (IRE)**, after a poor run on turf last time, ran better here, but was well held in the last couple of furlongs. (13/2)

**2935 Sandmoor Denim**, after seven weeks off, ran well enough to suggest that, despite his years, he is not done with yet. (10/1)

## 4090 COPENHAGEN CLAIMING STKS (I) (3-Y.O+) (Class F)

2-30 (2-31) **5f (Fibresand)** £2,031.00 (£556.00: £261.00) GOING minus 0.16 sec per fur (FST)

| Form | Horse / details | Dist | Pos | SP | RR | SF |
|---|---|---|---|---|---|---|
| 3146[13] | **Palacegate Jack (IRE) (78)** (JBerry) **5-9-0**(5) PRoberts(4) (mde all: clr appr fnl f) | — | **1** | 6/4[1] | 81 | 49 |
| *514*[3] | **Primula Bairn (61)** (DNicholls) **6-8-7**ow1 MRichardson(7) (a cl up: rdn 2f out: kpt on same pce) | 5 | **2** | 11/2[3] | 53 | 20 |
| 3959[D] | **Hoh Majestic (IRE) (61)** (MartynWane) **3-8-6v** JFEgan(3) (a chsng ldrs: kpt on fnl f) | hd | **3** | 8/1 | 53 | 20 |
| *896*[8] | **Bold Aristocrat (IRE) (52)** (RHollinshead) **5-8-4**(3) FLynch(5) (in tch: hdwy over 1f out: nvr able to chal) | nk | **4** | 12/1 | 52 | 20 |
| 3453[11] | **Souperficial (59)** (JAGlover) **5-8-9v** JFortune(12) (lw: chsd ldrs: rdn & no imp fnl 2f) | 1¼ | **5** | 7/2[2] | 50 | 18 |
| *3953*[7] | **Featherstone Lane (69)** (MissLCSiddall) **5-8-13v** GHind(10) (chsd ldrs: effrt 2f out: no imp) | 2 | **6** | 7/1 | 47 | 15 |
| 3851[13] | **Brin-Lodge (IRE) (40)** (KSBridgwater) **3-8-1** AMackay(6) (prom: rdn ½-wy: sn outpcd) | 4 | **7** | 33/1 | 24 | — |
| 3937[7] | **Mill End Lady (42)** (MWEasterby) **3-8-4b**(5) GParkin(9) (sn outpcd & wl bhd: sme late hdwy) | 1½ | **8** | 20/1 | 27 | — |
| | **She's a Madam (46)** (LRLloyd-James) **5-8-0**(7) CLowther(1) (prom tl wknd wl over 1f out) | 7 | **9** | 50/1 | 1 | — |
| | **Silent System (IRE)** (DWChapman) **3-7-9**(7) JBramhill(2) (sn wl bhd) | 1¾ | **10** | 50/1 | — | — |
| *3064*[12] | **Foreverfree** (RFMarvin) **3-7-13** FNorton(8) (s.i.s: effrt ½-wy: sn btn) | 14 | **11** | 33/1 | — | — |
| 3883[W] | **Just Lady (57)** (WGMTurner) **3-7-10**(3) NVarley(11) (unruly leaving paddock: spd over 1f: sn rdn & wknd qckly) | 7 | **12** | 7/1 | — | — |
| | | | | (SP 136.0%) | **12 Rn** | |

**59.3 secs** (2.30) CSF £12.03 TOTE £2.50: £1.20 £2.20 £2.80 (£9.00) Trio £9.90 OWNER Mr N. Warburton (COCKERHAM) BRED Brendan and Sheila Powell

WEIGHT FOR AGE 3yo-1lb

Palacegate Jack (IRE) clmd IPrice £10,000

**2508 Palacegate Jack (IRE)**, at his first attempt on this surface, handled it really well and was different class to this lot. (6/4)
**514 Primula Bairn**, from a yard that is just coming to form, ran a sound race, particularly after five and a half months off. (11/2)
**3959 Hoh Majestic (IRE)** ran reasonably at his first attempt on this surface and, should he really take to it, he certainly has more ability than he has been showing on turf. (8/1)
**342* Bold Aristocrat (IRE)** was always finding this trip a bit sharp after a lengthy lay-off, but he was staying on well at the end. (12/1)
**3331* Souperficial** had his chances until finding things too much approaching the final furlong. (7/2)
**3652 Featherstone Lane** has more ability than he cares to show sometimes, but he only seems to win once every Sheffield flood. (7/1: 5/1-8/1)
**3256* Mill End Lady** found this trip too sharp, but she was picking up well at the end. (20/1)

## 4091 E.B.F. COLOGNE MAIDEN STKS (2-Y.O) (Class D)

3-00 (3-03) **7f (Fibresand)** £4,012.50 (£1,200.00: £575.00: £262.50) Stalls: Low GOING minus 0.16 sec per fur (FST)

| | | | | SP | RR | SF |
|---|---|---|---|---|---|---|
| | **Waiting Game (IRE)** (DRLoder) **2-9-0** WRSwinburn(7) (w'like: w ldr: led over 2f out: rdn & styd on wl fnl f) | — | **1** | 1/2[1] | 82+ | 32 |
| 3869[2] | **Davis Rock** (SirMarkPrescott) **2-8-9** GDuffield(4) (led tl over 2f out: kpt on same pce) | 3½ | **2** | 100/30[2] | 69 | 19 |
| 3245[7] | **Return of Amin** (JDBethell) **2-9-0** SDrowne(8) (lw: a chsng ldrs: kpt on fnl 2f: no imp) | 5 | **3** | 14/1 | 63 | 13 |
| 3293[7] | **Good Day** (CWThornton) **2-9-0** DeanMcKeown(9) (in tch: styd on wl fnl 2f: nvr nr to chal) | 3 | **4** | 12/1[3] | 56 | 6 |
| 3837[12] | **Shaded (IRE)** (JWWatts) **2-9-0** LCharnock(6) (s.i.s: styd on fnl 3f: nvr nr to chal) | 2½ | **5** | 25/1 | 50 | — |
| 3662[2] | **Heavenly Dancer** (MrsNMacauley) **2-8-9** KDarley(14) (in tch: hdwy over 2f out: no imp) | 5 | **6** | 12/1[3] | 34 | — |
| 3637[8] | **King Uno** (MrsJRRamsden) **2-9-0** KFallon(1) (bhd: shkn up & hdwy 2f out: n.d) | 5 | **7** | 14/1 | 27 | — |
| 3848[16] | **Smart Prospect** (BJMeehan) **2-9-0** MTebbutt(10) (chsd ldrs tl wknd fnl 3f) | nk | **8** | 33/1 | 27 | — |
| 3687[16] | **Mellwood (IRE)** (MHTompkins) **2-9-0** NDay(11) (a outpcd & bhd) | 8 | **9** | 33/1 | 8 | — |
| 3840[7] | **Merryhill Mariner** (JLHarris) **2-8-11**(3) CTeague(3) (sn bhd) | 3 | **10** | 33/1 | 1 | — |
| | **Hurgill King (IRE)** (JWWatts) **2-9-0** NConnorton(13) (leggy: scope: bit bkwd: in tch 4f: sn wknd & eased) | 1¾ | **11** | 20/1 | — | — |
| 3807[12] | **Duston Boy** (JWhite) **2-9-0** DaleGibson(2) (hld up: n.d) | 10 | **12** | 33/1 | — | — |
| 3840[10] | **What's That Amy** (NBycroft) **2-8-9** JQuinn(12) (b.off hind: spd to ½-wy: wknd qckly) | 20 | **13** | 50/1 | — | — |
| | | | | (SP 140.8%) | | **13 Rn** |

**1m 31.5** (4.70) CSF £3.76 TOTE £1.60: £1.10 £1.10 £3.80 (£1.80) Trio £13.30 OWNER Sheikh Mohammed (NEWMARKET) BRED Sheikh Mohammed Bin Rashid Al Maktoum

**Waiting Game (IRE)** had to work to win this, but the further they went, the stronger he got. (1/2)
**3869 Davis Rock** keeps running well, but also keeps finding a useful opponent. That will surely change before long. (100/30)
**1344 Return of Amin** is coming to himself looks-wise and, although well beaten, this was not a bad effort. (14/1)
**Good Day**, on the upgrade, was not knocked about here and looks one to keep an eye on, especially in nurseries. (12/1)
**Shaded (IRE)**, slowly out, got better as the race progressed and should have learnt something. (25/1)
**3662 Heavenly Dancer** found this company too hot and failed to make the slightest impression. (12/1)
**King Uno** (14/1: 10/1-20/1)

## 4092 MILAN H'CAP (0-65) (3-Y.O+) (Class F)

3-30 (3-34) **1m 6f (Fibresand)** £2,381.00 (£656.00: £311.00) GOING minus 0.16 sec per fur (FST)

| | | | | SP | RR | SF |
|---|---|---|---|---|---|---|
| 3249[8] | **Batoutoftheblue (58)** (WWHaigh) **3-8-10** DRMcCabe(17) (lw: bhd: hdwy 5f out: r.o u.p to ld wl ins fnl f) | — | **1** | 16/1 | 68 | 12 |
| 3870* | **Star Performer (IRE) (46)** (MrsMReveley) **5-8-9** KDarley(3) (lw: chsd ldrs: pushed along 7f out: led 2f out: hrd drvn, hdd & nt qckn wl ins fnl f) | 1¼ | **2** | 5/1[1] | 55 | 10 |
| *3872[8]* | **Harbet House (FR) (57)** (CACyzer) **3-8-6**(3) FLynch(15) (chsd ldrs: effrt 4f out: one pce fnl 2f) | 3½ | **3** | 14/1 | 62 | 6 |
| 3878[7] | **Bayrak (USA) (59)** (MJRyan) **6-9-8** MTebbutt(13) (lw: trckd ldrs: led 3f out to 2f out: one pce) | 1¾ | **4** | 14/1 | 62 | 17 |
| 3850[4] | **Classic Affair (USA) (53)** (RHarris) **3-8-5** AMackay(16) (b.hind: hld up: hdwy 5f out: sn chsng ldrs: rdn & one pce fnl 2f) | 1¾ | **5** | 6/1[2] | 54 | — |
| *3952[2]* | **Drama King (44)** (SRBowring) **4-8-7b** JQuinn(6) (hdwy 4f out: rdn & no imp) | 10 | **6** | 10/1 | 33 | — |
| 3297[8] | **Hasta la Vista (42)** (MWEasterby) **6-8-0b**(5) GParkin(12) (mde most tl hdd 3f out: grad wknd) | 2 | **7** | 10/1 | 29 | — |
| 3882[4] | **Tabriz (58)** (JDBethell) **3-8-10** SDrowne(4) (lw: w ldr tl wknd fnl 3½f) | 6 | **8** | 16/1 | 38 | — |
| *3952[7]* | **Teen Jay (51)** (BJLlewellyn) **6-9-0v** VSlattery(8) (in tch: effrt 5f out: sn outpcd) | 8 | **9** | 11/1 | 22 | — |
| *3952[3]* | **Well Arranged (IRE) (63)** (MJPolglase) **5-9-12b** SSanders(5) (nvr trbld ldrs) | ¾ | **10** | 10/1 | 33 | — |
| 3813[3] | **Inn At the Top (56)** (JNorton) **4-9-5** DaleGibson(2) (effrt ½-wy: sn rdn: wknd fnl 3f) | ¾ | **11** | 12/1 | 25 | — |
| 3922[9] | **Hill Farm Dancer (62)** (WMBrisbourne) **5-9-11** AGarth(9) (hld up & bhd: n.d) | 7 | **12** | 20/1 | 23 | — |
| *3952[8]* | **Claque (65)** (DWChapman) **4-10-0b** ACulhane(7) (n.d) | 10 | **13** | 16/1 | 15 | — |
| 3813[10] | **Rose of Glenn (44)** (BPalling) **5-8-2**(5)ow2 GFaulkner(10) (bhd fr ½-wy) | 10 | **14** | 33/1 | — | — |
| | **Swings'N'Things (USA) (60)** (BPalling) **4-9-9** JFEgan(14) (in tch tl wknd fnl 5f) | nk | **15** | 25/1 | — | — |
| 3318[3] | **Supermick (47)** (WRMuir) **5-8-10** KFallon(1) (drvn along ½-wy: sn bhd) | 18 | **16** | 15/2[3] | — | — |
| *256[10]* | **Modest Hope (USA) (50)** (BRichmond) **9-8-10**(3) CTeague(11) (b: a bhd: t.o) | dist | **17** | 20/1 | — | — |
| | | | | (SP 133.3%) | | **17 Rn** |

**3m 11.9** (12.90) CSF £94.34 CT £1,098.80 TOTE £25.50: £3.40 £1.60 £4.60 £5.90 (£74.80) Trio £616.90 OWNER Dr C. I. Emmerson (MALTON) BRED Side Hill Stud
WEIGHT FOR AGE 3yo-11lb

**2067 Batoutoftheblue**, whose style of running has suggested that this surface coupled with a longer trip would suit him well, found all the stamina and courage to make it. Now he has broken his duck, he should go on. (16/1)
**3870* Star Performer (IRE)** stays well and responded to pressure in good style, but was just worried out of it. He is certainly going the right way. (5/1)
**2372 Harbet House (FR)** seems to save his best for this track but, despite trying hard, was never good enough in the last two furlongs. (14/1)
**2798 Bayrak (USA)** has never won on this surface, but he showed plenty here, only to find this trip just beyond him. (14/1)
**3850 Classic Affair (USA)** was happy to sit on the bridle but, when a real effort was required in the home straight, there was little more to come. (6/1)
**3952 Drama King** has risen 8lb since winning at Wolverhampton and was always fighting a lost cause. (10/1)
**2423 Hasta la Vista** is off a decent mark on this surface and might well just have needed the run after five weeks off. (10/1)
**3335 Teen Jay** (11/1: op 20/1)

## 4093 ROME NURSERY (S) H'CAP (0-65) (2-Y.O) (Class G)

4-00 (4-01) **5f (Fibresand)** £2,070.00 (£570.00: £270.00) Stalls: High GOING minus 0.16 sec per fur (FST)

| | | | | SP | RR | SF |
|---|---|---|---|---|---|---|
| *3604[3]* | **Make Ready (60)** (JNeville) **2-9-4** KFallon(6) (mde all: kpt on wl fnl f) | — | **1** | 9/2[1] | 57 | 18 |

| | | | | SP | RR | SF |
|---|---|---|---|---|---|---|
| 4046[7] | **Tinker's Surprise (IRE) (63)** (BJMeehan) **2-9-7** MTebbutt(5) (a cl up: nt qckn fnl f) | 2 | **2** | 7/1[2] | 54 | 15 |
| 3853[6] | **Strelitza (IRE) (55)** (MWEasterby) **2-8-8b**[1](5) GParkin(17) (lw: sn outpcd & bhd: r.o wl fnl f) | 2 | **3** | 11/1 | 39 | — |
| 3846[7] | **Singforyoursupper (55)** (GGMargarson) **2-8-13** PBloomfield(13) (a.p: effrt ½-wy: nt pce to chal) | hd | **4** | 10/1 | 39 | — |
| 3879[4] | **Wedding Music (56)** (PCHaslam) **2-9-0v**[1] JFortune(1) (a chsng ldrs: rdn ½-wy: no imp) | 2½ | **5** | 12/1 | 32 | — |
| 3607[3] | **Hever Golf Stormer (IRE) (59)** (TJNaughton) **2-9-3** SSanders(11) (chsd ldrs: hrd drvn ½-wy: sn btn) | ¾ | **6** | 10/1 | 33 | — |
| *1491*[3] | **Fit For The Job (IRE) (54)** (WGMTurner) **2-8-9**(3) NVarley(16) (cl up tl wknd appr fnl f) | ½ | **7** | 9/1 | 26 | — |
| 2161[6] | **Rahona (IRE) (52)** (BSRothwell) **2-8-10** JStack(15) (outpcd fr ½-wy) | 2 | **8** | 20/1 | 18 | — |
| *3950*[3] | **My Girl (53)** (JBerry) **2-8-11b** KDarley(10) (b.nr hind: s.i.s: nvr nr ldrs) | 1½ | **9** | 9/1 | 14 | — |
| 2207[3] | **Run For Us (IRE) (45)** (CADwyer) **2-7-10**(7) JoHunnam(4) (s.i.s: n.d) | 1¼ | **10** | 20/1 | 2 | — |
| 2781[8] | **Risky Flight (42)** (ASmith) **2-8-0** LCharnock(3) (in tch: sn drvn along: wknd fnl 2f) | hd | **11** | 25/1 | — | — |
| 3871[4] | **Summer Risotto (54)** (DJSffrenchDavis) **2-8-12** NCarlisle(14) (a outpcd & bhd) | ½ | **12** | 8/1[3] | 9 | — |
| 3840[5] | **Petrine Gray (53)** (TDEasterby) **2-8-11** JQuinn(7) (a outpcd & bhd) | ¾ | **13** | 9/1 | 5 | — |
| 3511[7] | **Thewrightone (IRE) (47)** (GROldroyd) **2-8-5b** JLowe(9) (a outpcd & wl bhd) | hd | **14** | 16/1 | — | — |
| 4046[13] | **Shotley Princess (48)** (NBycroft) **2-8-6** TWilliams(2) (prom 3f: wknd) | 2½ | **15** | 20/1 | — | — |
| | | | | (SP 130.0%) | **15 Rn** | |

**61.1 secs** (4.10) CSF £36.26 CT £322.01 TOTE £4.50: £1.90 £3.90 £5.10 (£10.10) Trio £175.40 OWNER Mr J. Neville (NEWPORT, GWENT) BRED J. Neville

No bid

**3604 Make Ready** has only ever run on this track over this distance and again showed her liking for the place, winning convincingly. (9/2)

**3838 Tinker's Surprise (IRE)**, without the blinkers, ran a sound race, but just found the winner too determined. (7/1)

**3853 Strelitza (IRE)** had blinkers on for the first time, but she found this trip too sharp and, despite finishing like an express train, never had a hope of making it. (11/1)

**3763* Singforyoursupper** ran quite well at her first attempt on this surface. She ought to be able to pick up a race and should stay a bit further. (10/1)

**3879 Wedding Music**, wearing a visor for the first time, had her chances but was never doing enough under pressure. (12/1)

**3607 Hever Golf Stormer (IRE)**, at his first attempt on the Sand, showed up but was under pressure and treading water from halfway. (10/1)

## 4094 COPENHAGEN CLAIMING STKS (II) (3-Y.O+) (Class F)

4-30 (4-33) **5f (Fibresand)** £2,031.00 (£556.00: £261.00) Stalls: High GOING minus 0.16 sec per fur (FST)

| | | | | SP | RR | SF |
|---|---|---|---|---|---|---|
| *3601*[6] | **Elton Ledger (IRE) (70)** (MrsNMacauley) **7-8-11v** EmmaO'Gorman(12) (b: a.p: kpt on u.p to ld cl home) | — | **1** | 7/2[2] | 77 | 35 |
| 3661[10] | **Step On Degas (62)** (MJFetherston-Godley) **3-8-4**(3) FLynch(8) (cl up: led ins fnl f: hdd & no ex cl home) | hd | **2** | 12/1 | 74 | 31 |
| 3851[2] | **Palacegate Touch (72)** (JBerry) **6-9-5b** GCarter(10) (lw: disp ld tl hdd ins fnl f: no ex towards fin) | ½ | **3** | 11/8[1] | 83 | 41 |
| | **One for Jeannie (70)** (ABailey) **4-8-1v**(3) DWright(4) (b: disp ld tl ins fnl f: one pce) | 1¼ | **4** | 6/1 | 64 | 22 |
| 2518[9] | **Klipspinger (67)** (BSRothwell) **3-8-7b**[1] JStack(5) (chsd ldrs: rdn 2f out: btn 1f out) | 5 | **5** | 4/1[3] | 52 | 9 |
| | **Lawsimina** (MissJFCraze) **3-8-11** NConnorton(9) (neat: unruly gng to s: chsd ldrs tl grad wknd appr fnl f) | 2½ | **6** | 25/1 | 48 | 5 |
| 3957[11] | **Arasong (56)** (EWeymes) **4-8-0** JQuinn(7) (outpcd after 2f: nvr trbld ldrs) | s.h | **7** | 12/1 | 36 | — |
| 4075[24] | **Deardaw (37)** (MissLCSiddall) **4-8-0** FNorton(1) (spd 3f: sn btn) | 5 | **8** | 20/1 | 20 | — |
| 3525[11] | **Christian Flight (IRE) (34)** (SGollings) **7-8-8** VHalliday(11) (lw: a outpcd & bhd) | nk | **9** | 25/1 | 27 | — |
| *2632*[8] | **New Technique (FR) (25)** (KMcAuliffe) **3-8-5** JFEgan(3) (s.i.s: a bhd) | s.h | **10** | 33/1 | 25 | — |
| 2987[5] | **Mr Blue (30)** (GPKelly) **4-8-2**(3) DarrenMoffatt(6) (b.off fore: swtg: a outpcd & wl bhd) | 5 | **11** | 50/1 | 8 | — |
| 3883[14] | **Super Sonata (45)** (TWall) **4-7-12b** DaleGibson(2) (b: spd 3f: sn lost pl) | 7 | **12** | 16/1 | — | — |
| | | | | (SP 137.2%) | **12 Rn** | |

**59.7 secs** (2.70) CSF £47.96 TOTE £4.40: £1.20 £2.50 £1.20 (£26.00) Trio £10.40 OWNER The Posse (MELTON MOWBRAY) BRED Thomas Doherty

WEIGHT FOR AGE 3yo-1lb

**3089 Elton Ledger (IRE)** loves this track and can win over various trips. Ridden to perfection, he hit the front where it mattered. (7/2)

**2244 Step On Degas** put in a sound first effort on this surface and will no doubt find a race in due course. (12/1)

**3851 Palacegate Touch** has been in fine form on turf, but never really fired on this surface, and was worried out of it inside the final furlong. (11/8: 11/10-7/4)

**One for Jeannie**, after over a year off, showed bags of speed and will obviously be all the better for it. (6/1: 4/1-7/1)

**2084 Klipspinger** had blinkers on for the first time, but they failed to have the desired effect. (4/1)

**Lawsimina** gave problems aplenty going to the start, but showed a fair amount of ability in the race. If she settles down, there is better to come. (25/1)

## 4095 MUNICH MAIDEN H'CAP (0-65) (3-Y.O+) (Class F)

5-00 (5-01) **1m 3f (Fibresand)** £2,381.00 (£656.00: £311.00) Stalls: Low GOING minus 0.16 sec per fur (FST)

| | | | | SP | RR | SF |
|---|---|---|---|---|---|---|
| 3703[10] | **Mansur (IRE) (63)** (DRLoder) **4-10-0** DRMcCabe(6) (lw: cl up: led 7f out: styd on wl fnl 2f) | — | **1** | 8/1 | 72 | 25 |
| *3630*[3] | **Chevalier (USA) (63)** (ICampbell) **4-10-0** MWigham(1) (lw: led 4f: cl up: drvn along 3f out: kpt on wl) | 2 | **2** | 10/1 | 69 | 22 |
| 1841[12] | **Yaverland (IRE) (57)** (CADwyer) **4-9-8** MTebbutt(11) (bhd: hdwy 5f out: chsng ldrs over 2f out: no imp) | 5 | **3** | 10/1 | 56 | 9 |
| 3496[8] | **Warspite (41)** (RJO'Sullivan) **6-8-6** JQuinn(8) (hdwy ½-wy: chsng ldrs 3f out: rdn & one pce) | s.h | **4** | 12/1 | 40 | — |
| *1969*[4] | **Magic Heights (50)** (JEBanks) **3-8-2**(5) GFaulkner(12) (chsd ldrs tl outpcd fnl 3½f) | ¾ | **5** | 3/1[1] | 48 | — |
| 3584[4] | **The Boozing Brief (USA) (57)** (MAJarvis) **3-9-0** KDarley(10) (hld up: hdwy 5f out: chsng ldrs over 2f out: sn btn) | 15 | **6** | 5/1[2] | 33 | — |
| *3877*[6] | **Classic Royale (USA) (50)** (RHarris) **3-8-7** AMackay(14) (hld up: hdwy 5f out: chsng ldrs over 2f out: sn btn) | 2 | **7** | 12/1 | 23 | — |
| 3780[4] | **El Bardador (IRE) (53)** (WJarvis) **3-8-10** AMcGlone(7) (prom tl lost pl 6f out: n.d after) | 18 | **8** | 7/1[3] | — | — |
| 3496[11] | **Indian Nectar (58)** (GBBalding) **3-9-1** SDrowne(15) (hld up: effrt 5f out: sn rdn & btn) | 2 | **9** | 12/1 | 2 | — |
| 3854[8] | **Hill Farm Blues (49)** (JLEyre) **3-8-6** RLappin(3) (s.i.s: sn drvn along: n.d) | nk | **10** | 16/1 | — | — |
| *3952*[6] | **Precedency (62)** (KMcAuliffe) **4-9-13** JFortune(4) (b.hind: chsd ldrs tl wknd fnl 3f) | 16 | **11** | 10/1 | — | — |
| 1833[4] | **Jelali (IRE) (61)** (DJGMurraySmith) **3-9-4v**[1] SSanders(2) (chsd ldrs tl rdn & wknd 4f out) | 2½ | **12** | 14/1 | — | — |
| *3630*[8] | **Nordic Hero (IRE) (49)** (APJarvis) **3-8-6** JFEgan(16) (prom tl wknd 5f out) | ½ | **13** | 20/1 | — | — |
| | **Upper Club (IRE) (45)** (PRWebber) **4-8-10** KFallon(13) (outpcd & lost tch 5f out) | nk | **14** | 20/1 | — | — |
| 3500[13] | **Dalwhinnie (65)** (JWHills) **3-9-8** OUrbina(9) (lw: outpcd & wl bhd fnl 7f) | 3 | **15** | 10/1 | — | — |
| *3630*[4] | **Miss Pravda (50)** (BJLlewellyn) **3-8-7** TWilliams(5) (sn drvn along: t.o fnl 6f) | 4 | **16** | 9/1 | — | — |
| | | | | (SP 156.8%) | **16 Rn** | |

**2m 30.5** (10.50) CSF £99.76 CT £792.25 TOTE £11.10: £3.00 £3.00 £3.80 £2.70 (£24.00) Trio £100.20 OWNER Mr Michael Worth (NEWMARKET) BRED M. J. Worth

WEIGHT FOR AGE 3yo-8lb

**2372 Mansur (IRE)**, who likes this surface, stays well and saw it out in determined fashion. (8/1: 5/1-10/1)
**3630 Chevalier (USA)** keeps running well, albeit without winning, but his luck should change before long. (10/1)
**871 Yaverland (IRE)**, after three months off, ran well on this first outing on the All-Weather, and he should be all the better for it. (10/1: op 5/1)
**Warspite** showed his first real signs of form for a long time and may well be worth keeping in mind for a modest event. (12/1: op 8/1)
**1969 Magic Heights**, taking a big step up in trip, had his chances, but was under pressure turning for home and making no further impression. (3/1)
**3584 The Boozing Brief (USA)** tried to come from way off the pace, but ran out of steam when pressure was applied early in the straight. (5/1)

T/Jkpt: Not won; £15,243.78 to Lingfield 10/9/96. T/Plpt: £21.30 (711.21 Tckts). T/Qdpt: £5.50 (199.23 Tckts). AA

# 3650-**LEICESTER** (R-H) (Firm)
## Tuesday September 10th
WEATHER: overcast WIND: almost nil

## 4096 E.B.F. FILBERT MAIDEN STKS (2-Y.O F) (Class D)
2-15 (2-16) **1m 8y** £3,993.30 (£1,193.40: £571.20: £260.10) Stalls: High GOING minus 0.52 sec per fur (F)

| | | | | SP | RR | SF |
|---|---|---|---|---|---|---|
| | **Idrica** (JHMGosden) **2-8-11** LDettori(5) (leggy: scope: dwlt: swtchd lft & hdwy ½-wy: led over 2f out: pushed out) | — | **1** | 10/11[1] | 64+ | 3 |
| 3663[2] | **Mutribah (USA)** (HThomsonJones) **2-8-11** RHills(2) (led over 5f: ev ch & rdn 1f out: rallied cl home) | nk | **2** | Evens[2] | 63 | 2 |
| 3820[8] | **Clear The Air** (PFICole) **2-8-11** MHills(3) (chsd ldrs: rdn over 2f out: sn outpcd) | 10 | **3** | 20/1[3] | 44 | — |
| | **Tracks of My Tears** (WGMTurner) **2-8-4**(7) DMcGaffin(1) (w'like: bit bkwd: prom: rdn along 3f out: sn outpcd: t.o) | 7 | **4** | 33/1 | 30 | — |
| 3848[14] | **Ela Patricia (IRE)** (DJGMurraySmith) **2-8-8**(3) DWright(4) (a bhd: t.o fnl 3f) | 4 | **5** | 33/1 | 22 | — |

(SP 113.0%) **5 Rn**

**1m 39.9** (4.90) CSF £2.18 TOTE £1.80: £1.10 £1.10 (£1.10) OWNER Sheikh Mohammed (NEWMARKET) BRED Sheikh Mohammed Bin Rashid Al Maktoum

**Idrica**, quite an attractive filly with plenty of scope, was given an ideal introduction to racing and won this without resort to the stick. She will much more effective when she can get her toe in and her future looks bright. (10/11: 4/6-Evens)
**3663 Mutribah (USA)** tried to put her previous experience to full use and ran a race full of promise but had to admit the winner too good. (Evens)

## 4097 RANCLIFFE NURSERY (S) H'CAP (0-65) (2-Y.O) (Class G)
2-45 (2-46) **1m 8y** £2,637.00 (£732.00: £351.00) Stalls: High GOING minus 0.52 sec per fur (F)

| | | | | SP | RR | SF |
|---|---|---|---|---|---|---|
| 3663[7] | **Chairmans Daughter (58)** (PFICole) **2-9-3b[1]** RHills(5) (hld up: hdwy 2f out: led wl ins fnl f: sn clr) | — | **1** | 10/1 | 66+ | 15 |
| 3648[5] | **Jingoist (IRE) (53)** (JLHarris) **2-8-12b** BDoyle(7) (hld up: hdwy to ld over 1f out: hdd & nt qckn ins fnl f) | 2 | **2** | 16/1 | 57 | 6 |
| 3943[4] | **Spondulicks (IRE) (60)** (RHannon) **2-9-5** MHills(4) (hld up mid div: hdwy over 1f out: r.o ins fnl f) | 1½ | **3** | 8/1[3] | 61 | 10 |
| 3678[3] | **Cajun Sunset (IRE) (56)** (TDEasterby) **2-9-1** KDarley(3) (chsd ldrs: pushed along ½-wy: kpt on ins fnl f) | 2½ | **4** | 3/1[1] | 52 | 1 |
| *3950*[5] | **Sheraton Girl (51)** (MJohnston) **2-8-10** LDettori(15) (hld up: hdwy over 2f out: kpt on u.p: nvr able to chal) | ½ | **5** | 12/1 | 46 | — |
| 3769[4] | **Time Can Tell (62)** (CMurray) **2-9-7v[1]** DeanMcKeown(9) (b: hld up in tch: rdn wl over 1f out: styd on fnl f) | 1¼ | **6** | 9/2[2] | 55 | 4 |
| 3943[7] | **Poly Moon (58)** (MRChannon) **2-9-3** JFortune(2) (hld up: effrt & drvn along 3f out: nt rch ldrs) | ½ | **7** | 8/1[3] | 50 | — |
| *3954*[5] | **Shandana (48)** (PCHaslam) **2-8-2v**(5) MartinDwyer(13) (mde most tl hdd & wknd over 1f out) | 2½ | **8** | 20/1 | 35 | — |
| 3871[5] | **Hopperetta (57)** (BPalling) **2-9-2** TSprake(14) (lw: plld hrd: prom tl outpcd fnl 2f) | ½ | **9** | 14/1 | 43 | — |
| 3924[8] | **Chopin (IRE) (60)** (RFJohnsonHoughton) **2-9-5b** AMcGlone(1) (prom: ev ch over 2f out: sn wknd) | 1¼ | **10** | 20/1 | 43 | — |
| 3498[9] | **Top Titfer (42)** (AGFoster) **2-7-10v[1]**(5) CAdamson(10) (b.hind: trckd ldrs over 5f) | ½ | **11** | 33/1 | 24 | — |
| 2959[7] | **Foolish Flutter (IRE) (45)** (GROldroyd) **2-8-4v** DaleGibson(6) (a bhd) | hd | **12** | 33/1 | 27 | — |
| 3976[4] | **Ginny Wossername (58)** (WGMTurner) **2-9-0b**(3) RHavlin(8) (prom over 5f) | nk | **13** | 10/1 | 39 | — |
| 3512[7] | **Clonavon Girl (IRE) (52)** (MJCamacho) **2-8-11** LCharnock(12) (lw: prom 5f: sn rdn & wknd: t.o) | 9 | **14** | 14/1 | 15 | — |
| 1904[4] | **Riva La Belle (51)** (JWharton) **2-8-10** KFallon(11) (in rr: rdn 3f out: no imp: t.o) | 15 | **15** | 20/1 | — | — |

(SP 130.7%) **15 Rn**

**1m 39.2** (4.20) CSF £152.27 CT £1,247.01 TOTE £13.50: £4.60 £4.60 £2.10 (£72.90) Trio £176.20 OWNER Mr Yahya Nasib (WHATCOMBE) BRED Hamilton Bloodstock (UK) Ltd
Sold JPearce 7000gns

**Chairmans Daughter** did not look happy striding to post but proved a different class to these rivals and won with any amount in hand. (10/1: op 6/1)
**3648 Jingoist (IRE)** travelled strongly in behind the leaders and gained command below the distance but, once the winner was let loose, she quite simply had no answer. (16/1)
**3943 Spondulicks (IRE)** stayed on really well inside the distance but the leading pair had taken first run and he was unable to deliver his challenge. (8/1)
**3678 Cajun Sunset (IRE)** showed plenty of knee action and, on ground as fast as this, could not muster the pace to prove troublesome. He will win when conditions favour him. (3/1)
**3950 Sheraton Girl**, running over a more suitable trip, was unable to mount a challenge but she did stay on and will find her way. (12/1: op 8/1)
**3769 Time Can Tell** appeared to get outpaced when the tempo lifted two furlongs out but he responded to pressure and was staying on well again nearing the finish. (9/2)

## 4098 WEATHERBYS STALLION BOOK H'CAP (0-70) (3-Y.O+) (Class E)
3-15 (3-16) **7f 9y** £3,916.50 (£1,176.00: £567.00: £262.50) Stalls: High GOING minus 0.52 sec per fur (F)

| | | | | SP | RR | SF |
|---|---|---|---|---|---|---|
| 3812[3] | **Don't Get Caught (IRE) (46)** (JLHarris) **4-8-6** DeanMcKeown(10) (lw: trckd ldrs: led over 1f out: drvn clr) | — | **1** | 16/1 | 57+ | 27 |
| 3844[15] | **Sharp Monty (60)** (RHollinshead) **3-8-13**(3) FLynch(12) (hld up: hdwy to ld over 2f out: hdd over 1f out: one pce) | 2½ | **2** | 14/1 | 65 | 31 |
| 3852[2] | **Windswept (IRE) (56)** (DJSffrenchDavis) **3-8-9**(3) PMcCabe(4) (hld up: hdwy over 2f out: rdn & r.o wl ins fnl f) | hd | **3** | 13/2[1] | 61 | 27 |

| | | | | SP | RR | SF |
|---|---|---|---|---|---|---|
| 2179[3] | **Ivor's Deed (54)** (CFWall) **3-8-10** GDuffield(17) (hld up & bhd: hdwy over 2f out: fin wl) | ½ | **4** | 7/1[2] | 58 | 24 |
| 3867[3] | **Perilous Plight (64)** (MrsLStubbs) **5-9-10** KFallon(13) (hld up: hdwy & nt clr run over 1f out: swtchd rt: fin wl) | ¾ | **5** | 9/1 | 66 | 36 |
| 3456[3] | **Mister Woodstick (IRE) (57)** (MAJarvis) **3-8-13** KDarley(3) (hdwy over 2f out: kpt on u.p ins fnl f) | ½ | **6** | 7/1[2] | 58 | 24 |
| 3995[5] | **Our Shadee (USA) (49)** (KTIvory) **6-8-9v** CScally(9) (hld up: hdwy 2f out: sn ev ch: rdn & one pce fnl f) | ¾ | **7** | 8/1[3] | 48 | 18 |
| 3702[5] | **Awesome Venture (51)** (MCChapman) **6-8-11** DRMcCabe(7) (trckd ldrs: effrt 2f out: no imp) | nk | **8** | 16/1 | 50 | 20 |
| 3867[5] | **Morocco (IRE) (54)** (MRChannon) **7-8-7**(7) AEddery(2) (hld up: hdwy & nt clr run 2f out: wknd appr fnl f) | ¾ | **9** | 14/1 | 51 | 21 |
| 3702[8] | **Bright Diamond (52)** (JRArnold) **3-8-3**(5) MartinDwyer(5) (chsd ldrs over 5f) | 1 | **10** | 20/1 | 47 | 13 |
| 3761[13] | **Euphyllia (57)** (BobJones) **4-9-3v** MWigham(18) (hld up mid div: effrt & rdn 2f out: no imp) | hd | **11** | 20/1 | 52 | 22 |
| 3165[9] | **Dungeon Princess (IRE) (62)** (CMurray) **3-9-4** JFortune(14) (trckd ldrs over 4f) | 2 | **12** | 25/1 | 52 | 18 |
| *3602*[8] | **Anita's Contessa (IRE) (56)** (BPalling) **4-9-2** TSprake(11) (led over 4f: rdn & wknd appr fnl f) | ¾ | **13** | 16/1 | 44 | 14 |
| 748[15] | **Rothley Imp (IRE) (45)** (JWharton) **3-8-1** LCharnock(16) (prom tl wknd over 2f out) | 5 | **14** | 33/1 | 22 | — |
| *419*[6] | **Tirra-Lirra (IRE) (59)** (CEBrittain) **4-9-5** BDoyle(19) (bit bkwd: a bhd) | 1¼ | **15** | 25/1 | 33 | 3 |
| 3456[12] | **Oriole (46)** (NTinkler) **3-8-2** KimTinkler(15) (trckd ldrs 4f) | 1 | **16** | 33/1 | 18 | — |
| *84*[9] | **Chalky Dancer (42)** (HJCollingridge) **4-8-2** DaleGibson(8) (bit bkwd: prom to ½-wy) | hd | **17** | 33/1 | 14 | — |
| 3777[11] | **Welcome Lu (45)** (JLHarris) **3-8-1** FNorton(20) (prom: rdn ½-wy: sn wknd) | ½ | **18** | 10/1 | 15 | — |
| 971[13] | **Media Express (55)** (PSFelgate) **4-8-12**(3) DWright(1) (t.o) | 11 | **19** | 25/1 | — | — |
| 3244[8] | **Mystical Maid (55)** (HThomsonJones) **3-8-11** GCarter(6) (t.o) | ½ | **20** | 25/1 | — | — |

(SP 133.2%) **20 Rn**

**1m 24.7** (1.70) CSF £213.12 CT £1,511.54 TOTE £29.00: £6.00 £2.90 £1.50 £1.80 (£184.50) Trio £442.40; £373.89 to Doncaster 11/9/96
OWNER Mrs P. W. McGrath (MELTON MOWBRAY) BRED Brownstown Stud Farm
WEIGHT FOR AGE 3yo-4lb

**3812 Don't Get Caught (IRE),** turned out in tip top condition, was always running away just off the pace and, given the office below the distance, stormed clear to win readily. (16/1)

**3655 Sharp Monty,** waiting on the leaders, nosed ahead entering the last quarter-mile but could never get away and the winner brushed him aside with ease. (14/1)

**3852 Windswept (IRE)** came very late on the scene and it would seem the waiting tactics were overdone. (13/2)

**2179 Ivor's Deed,** produced fresh and well after a ten week break, had to sidestep several rivals to obtain any sort of run at all when delivering his challenge and, meeting plenty of trouble, found the race over when he did get room. (7/1)

**3867 Perilous Plight** had his full quota of weight to contend with and, unable to get a trouble-free run when making progress, was never any closer than at the finish. (9/1)

**3456 Mister Woodstick (IRE)** obtained a clear run on the outside and was close enough to pose a threat entering the final furlong but he does lack a turn of pace and was never able to put in his bid. (7/1)

**3995 Our Shadee (USA)** looked a serious threat on the approach to the final furlong but he may have got there too soon for he had nothing more to give in the sprint to the line. (8/1)

## 4099 LEICESTERSHIRE MAIDEN STKS (3-Y.O+) (Class D)

3-45 (3-46) **1m 1f 218y** £4,391.10 (£1,315.80: £632.40: £290.70) Stalls: High GOING minus 0.52 sec per fur (F)

| | | | | SP | RR | SF |
|---|---|---|---|---|---|---|
| 3704[2] | **Polar Champ (77)** (SPCWoods) **3-9-0v** LDettori(1) (led after 4f: hrd drvn fnl 2f: hld on gamely) | — | **1** | 4/5[1] | 72 | 48 |
| 3704[6] | **Mutanassib (IRE)** (ACStewart) **3-9-0** WCarson(9) (bit bkwd: led after 1f to 6f out: ev ch & rdn fnl 2f: no ex nr fin) | 1 | **2** | 7/2[2] | 70 | 46 |
| | **King Kato** (GHarwood) **3-9-0** KDarley(11) (w'like: leggy: bit bkwd: s.i.s: sn prom: ev ch & rn v.green over 1f out: kpt on towards fin) | s.h | **3** | 10/1 | 70+ | 46 |
| 1668[5] | **Flamanda** (CEBrittain) **3-8-9** BDoyle(3) (hld up: hdwy over 3f out: nt rch ldrs) | 4 | **4** | 4/1[3] | 59+ | 35 |
| 2869[3] | **Snowy Mantle** (JDBethell) **3-8-9** GCarter(8) (plld hrd: prom tl rdn & wknd fnl 2f) | 11 | **5** | 33/1 | 41 | 17 |
| | **Magic Role** (MAJarvis) **3-9-0** PBloomfield(5) (w'like: leggy: bit bkwd: a in rr) | 8 | **6** | 20/1 | 34 | 10 |
| | **Good (IRE) (35)** (DTThom) **4-9-7** DRMcCabe(4) (led 1f: lost pl ent st: t.o fnl 3f) | 13 | **7** | 66/1 | 13 | — |
| 3776[6] | **Kaye's Secret** (CSmith) **3-8-9** FNorton(2) (a in rr: t.o fnl 3f) | 5 | **8** | 66/1 | — | — |

(SP 117.6%) **8 Rn**

**2m 4.8** (1.10) CSF £4.24 TOTE £1.60: £1.10 £1.70 £2.40 (£2.60) Trio £8.30 OWNER Mr P. K. L. Chu (NEWMARKET) BRED High Point Bloodstock Ltd and Victor Sujanani
WEIGHT FOR AGE 3yo-7lb

**3704 Polar Champ** was certainly not winning out of turn but he had a fight on his hands for the last couple of furlongs before the prize was his. (4/5: 8/13-Evens)

**3704 Mutanassib (IRE),** much straighter in condition than he was at Yarmouth, gave the winner a hard time, and it is on the cards, if they clash again, that the boot would be on the other foot. (7/2)

**King Kato,** a tall individual who has obviously needed time, would have won this had he not wandered about when sent about his business, and with his stable now recovering from a period in the doldrums he looks nailed on to add to their score. (10/1: op 6/1)

**1668 Flamanda** was unable to get herself into it but she did stay on promisingly in the latter stages and is not without hope. (4/1: 3/1-9/2)

## 4100 REMPSTONE MAIDEN STKS (2-Y.O) (Class D)

4-15 (4-17) **7f 9y** £4,689.45 (£1,407.60: £678.30: £313.65) Stalls: High GOING minus 0.52 sec per fur (F)

| | | | | SP | RR | SF |
|---|---|---|---|---|---|---|
| 2132[W] | **Sunbeam Dance (USA)** (SbinSuroor) **2-9-0** GCarter(2) (gd sort: s.i.s: hdwy ½-wy: drvn to chal ent fnl f: led post) | — | **1** | 2/1[1] | 87+ | 39 |
| | **Kahal** (EALDunlop) **2-9-0** WCarson(1) (wl grwn: bit bkwd: a.p: led over 1f out: hrd drvn & hdd fnl stride) | s.h | **2** | 6/1[3] | 87+ | 39 |
| 3407[6] | **Cosmic Prince (IRE)** (MAJarvis) **2-9-0** KDarley(11) (led after 2f tl over 1f out: one pce) | 4 | **3** | 14/1 | 78 | 30 |
| 3214[2] | **Zaretski (79)** (CEBrittain) **2-9-0** BDoyle(8) (plld hrd: led 2f: prom tl rdn & wknd appr fnl f) | 3 | **4** | 8/1 | 71 | 23 |
| | **Desert Track** (JHMGosden) **2-9-0** LDettori(13) (b.hind: unf: bit bkwd: trckd ldrs tl outpcd & eased appr fnl f) | nk | **5** | 5/1[2] | 70 | 22 |
| | **Vanishing Trick (USA)** (HRACecil) **2-8-9** AMcGlone(9) (w'like: str: bkwd: dwlt: bhd tl sme hdwy fnl 2f: nvr nrr) | 2½ | **6** | 11/1 | 60 | 12 |
| | **Atlantic Desire (IRE)** (MJohnston) **2-8-9** MHills(5) (scope: bit bkwd: prom over 4f) | 1½ | **7** | 25/1 | 56 | 8 |
| 3794[5] | **Jalb (IRE)** (ACStewart) **2-9-0** RHills(7) (dwlt: nvr nr ldrs) | 1 | **8** | 14/1 | 59 | 11 |
| 2596[9] | **Mendoza** (DJGMurraySmith) **2-8-11**(3) FLynch(3) (trckd ldrs tl rdn & outpcd fnl 2f) | s.h | **9** | 50/1 | 59 | 11 |
| 3493[6] | **Swan Island** (BPalling) **2-8-9** TSprake(14) (b: a in rr) | hd | **10** | 33/1 | 54 | 6 |
| 3349[8] | **Spaniard's Mount** (MHTompkins) **2-8-11**(3) MHenry(10) (chsd ldrs over 4f) | ¾ | **11** | 25/1 | 57 | 9 |
| | **Hartshorn** (JLDunlop) **2-9-0** GDuffield(4) (lt-f: unf: a bhd & outpcd) | 2½ | **12** | 14/1 | 51 | 3 |

| | | | | SP | RR | SF |
|---|---|---|---|---|---|---|
| | **Crystal Gold** (MRStoute) **2-9-0** KFallon(12) (w'like: scope: chsd ldrs over 4f) | 1¾ | **13** | 13/2 | 47 | — |
| | | | | (SP 129.7%) | | **13 Rn** |

**1m 24.3** (1.30) CSF £15.41 TOTE £3.10: £1.10 £3.10 £6.60 (£13.60) Trio £98.90 OWNER Godolphin (NEWMARKET) BRED Gainsborough Farm Inc

**Sunbeam Dance (USA)**, withdrawn after being kicked at the start on his intended debut at Headquarters in June, is a highly thought-of youngster with engagements in many of the top-class Autumn two-year-old races. An imposing-looking colt, he handled this lively ground extremely well and he does look set to go places. (2/1: 6/4-3/1)

**Kahal**, half asleep walking round the paddock, woke up once in action and made the winner pull out all the stops to collar him on the line. Sure to be much sharper for the run, he does look to have a future. (6/1)

**3407 Cosmic Prince (IRE)** again ran very freely and made most of the running until worn down on the approach to the final furlong. Experience should teach him to settle. (14/1)

**3214 Zaretski**, another free-running sort, had a running battle with Cosmic Prince which in the end only contributed to their defeat. (8/1)

**Desert Track**, an unfurnished half-brother to two winners, may well have been concerned in the finish had his jockey not eased him and looked down at both forelegs inside the distance, obviously thinking something was wrong. He looked to be sound enough on pulling up but there may well be problems in the morning. (5/1: op 5/2)

**Vanishing Trick (USA)**, a strongly-made filly looking far from fully wound up, impressed to post but lost ground at the start and was wisely given an educational debut. (11/1: op 5/1)

## 4101 PRESTWOLD CONDITIONS STKS (3-Y.O+) (Class C)

4-45 (4-46) **5f 2y** £5,711.46 (£1,824.36: £874.18) Stalls: High GOING minus 0.52 sec per fur (F)

| | | | | SP | RR | SF |
|---|---|---|---|---|---|---|
| 3524$^{7}$ | **Croft Pool (104)** (JAGlover) **5-8-10** SDWilliams(2) (lw: mde virtually all: clr appr fnl f: comf) | — | **1** | 5/4$^{1}$ | 96+ | 35 |
| 3932$^{4}$ | **Ziggy's Dancer (USA) (84)** (EJAlston) **5-8-10** KFallon(1) (lw: sn bhd & outpcd: rdn over 1f out: r.o ins fnl f) | 2½ | **2** | 7/2$^{3}$ | 88 | 27 |
| 3232$^{18}$ | **Espartero (IRE) (104)** (SirMarkPrescott) **4-8-10** GDuffield(3) (lw: w wnr 3f: rdn & outpcd appr fnl f) | 1½ | **3** | 13/8$^{2}$ | 83 | 22 |
| | | | | (SP 104.8%) | | **3 Rn** |

**59.4 secs** (0.90) CSF £4.55 TOTE £2.20: (£3.50) OWNER Countrywide Classics Ltd (WORKSOP) BRED J. S. Bell

**3524 Croft Pool** had no option but to make the running and, gradually forging clear, could hardly have found an easier opening for such a rewarding prize. (5/4: op Evens)

**3932 Ziggy's Dancer (USA)**, taken off his legs in the early stages, picked up in fine style inside the distance but the winner had gone beyond recall. (7/2)

**2880 Espartero (IRE)** does the majority of his racing at six furlongs and he was unable to match strides when the winner quickened things up and it must be admitted he ran a bit flat. (13/8)

## 4102 STAG APPRENTICE H'CAP (0-75) (3-Y.O+) (Class E)

5-15 (5-16) **1m 1f 218y** £3,118.50 (£945.00: £462.00: £220.50) Stalls: High GOING minus 0.52 sec per fur (F)

| | | | | SP | RR | SF |
|---|---|---|---|---|---|---|
| 3947$^{7}$ | **White Plains (IRE) (71)** (MBell) **3-9-1**$^{(5)}$ RMullen(11) (lw: trckd ldrs: led wl over 1f out: sn clr: easily) | — | **1** | 7/2$^{2}$ | 81+ | 35 |
| 3297$^{5}$ | **Hawkish (USA) (50)** (DMorley) **7-8-6** FLynch(4) (lw: hld up: stdy hdwy 3f out: r.o wl ins fnl f: no ch w wnr) | 2 | **2** | 100/30$^{1}$ | 57 | 18 |
| 3812$^{8}$ | **Rival Bid (USA) (64)** (MrsNMacauley) **8-9-6** CTeague(9) (lw: s.s: hdwy on ins 3f out: nt clr run & swtchd 2f out: fin wl) | ½ | **3** | 12/1 | 70 | 31 |
| 2348$^{3}$ | **Sea God (44)** (MCChapman) **5-8-0** DRMcCabe(12) (led tl wl over 1f out: sn rdn: one pce) | 2½ | **4** | 10/1 | 46 | 7 |
| 3289$^{3}$ | **Diamond Crown (IRE) (47)** (MartynWane) **5-8-3**$^{ow2}$ RHavlin(7) (hld up: hdwy 4f out: rdn & one pce fnl f) | ¾ | **5** | 14/1 | 48 | 7 |
| 3348* | **Essayeffsee (60)** (MrsMReveley) **7-9-2** GLee(5) (lw: mid div: rdn over 3f out: nt rch ldrs) | 2 | **6** | 6/1$^{3}$ | 58 | 19 |
| *486*$^{4}$ | **Tuigamala (42)** (RIngram) **5-7-9**$^{(3)ow1}$ AmandaSanders(1) (bit bkwd: prom early: effrt over 3f out: no imp) | 1¾ | **7** | 20/1 | 37 | — |
| 2906$^{4}$ | **Spice and Sugar (40)** (BRCambidge) **6-7-7**$^{(3)}$ IonaWands(10) (trckd ldrs: rdn over 2f out: sn btn) | s.h | **8** | 50/1 | 35 | — |
| 3878$^{4}$ | **Ambidextrous (IRE) (51)** (EJAlston) **4-8-7** DWright(6) (a in rr: rdn 3f out: no rspnse) | 1¾ | **9** | 11/1 | 43 | 4 |
| 3808$^{7}$ | **Milltown Classic (IRE) (40)** (JParkes) **4-7-10** PFessey(2) (mid div tl wknd u.p 3f out) | ¾ | **10** | 11/1 | 31 | — |
| 3509$^{4}$ | **Aeroking (USA) (72)** (GHarwood) **5-10-0** MHenry(3) (lw: chsd ldr: led over 2f out tl wl over 1f out: wkng whn hit in face ins fnl f) | ½ | **11** | 7/1 | 62 | 23 |
| 3780$^{16}$ | **Prince Zizim (47)** (RCSpicer) **3-7-10** MartinDwyer(8) (sddle slipped: bhd fr ½-wy: t.o) | 22 | **12** | 50/1 | 2 | — |
| | | | | (SP 120.9%) | | **12 Rn** |

**2m 7.1** (3.40) CSF £15.13 CT £116.08 TOTE £5.90: £2.80 £1.20 £2.30 (£10.50) Trio £42.80 OWNER Deln Ltd (NEWMARKET) BRED Howard Kaskel

LONG HANDICAP Milltown Classic (IRE) 7-3 Spice and Sugar 6-12 Prince Zizim 7-5

WEIGHT FOR AGE 3yo-7lb

**3327* White Plains (IRE)** would have won no supporters with his action to post but he showed no ill effects on the way back and had the prize in safe-keeping before he had reached the final furlong. (7/2)

**3297 Hawkish (USA)**, attempting to follow up his success in this event last year, was doing all his best work inside the distance but the winner had long gone and was not for catching. (100/30)

**3457 Rival Bid (USA)** did look a very unlucky loser after losing so much ground at the start but this is regular for him, and his attempt to make progress up the inside rail may not have been a wise decision. (12/1)

**2348 Sea God** decided to blaze a trail and, in doing so, ran one of his better races. There could be more success to follow. (10/1)

**3289 Diamond Crown (IRE)** stayed on relentlessly up the inside rail from the turn in, but could not quicken sufficiently to get to terms. (14/1)

**3348* Essayeffsee** has done all his winning at this trip but he does appear to need a stiffer track than this and he was never in a position to give his supporters much hope. (6/1)

**3509 Aeroking (USA)** looked to be a man's ride and, though he helped force the pace, was just feeling the strain when he was given a crack across the face by the rider of Rival Bid inside the distance. (7/1)

T/Plpt: £33.40 (390.12 Tckts). T/Qdpt: £9.70 (75.22 Tckts). IM

# 3871-LINGFIELD (L-H) (Turf Good to firm, AWT Standard)

## Tuesday September 10th

WEATHER: fine WIND: almost nil

## 4103 GODSTONE RATING RELATED MAIDEN STKS (0-70) (2-Y.O) (Class E)

2-00 (2-00) **6f** £2,988.30 (£890.40: £424.20: £191.10) Stalls: High GOING minus 0.40 sec per fur (F)

| | | | | SP | RR | SF |
|---|---|---|---|---|---|---|
| 3962$^{2}$ | **Saint Who (USA) (65)** (WAO'Gorman) **2-9-0** EmmaO'Gorman(1) (a.p: led over 2f out: clr over 1f out: r.o wl) | — | **1** | 6/4$^{1}$ | 76? | 10 |

| | | | | | | |
|---|---|---|---|---|---|---|
| 3846[4] | **Manikato (USA) (70)** (DJSCosgrove) **2-9-0** MRimmer(6) (lw: a.p: ev ch over 2f out: unable qckn)....6 | **2** | 4/1[3] | 60 | — |
| 3809[3] | **Hallmark (IRE) (70)** (RHannon) **2-9-0** SSanders(2) (lw: led over 3f: one pce)....½ | **3** | 2/1[2] | 59 | — |
| 3823[6] | **Nervous Rex (64)** (WRMuir) **2-9-0** JReid(4) (a.p: ev ch over 2f out: wknd over 1f out)....1¾ | **4** | 10/1 | 54 | — |
| 3795[4] | **Zanabay (62)** (MartynMeade) **2-8-4**(7) DSweeney(3) (a.p: ev ch over 2f out: wknd over 1f out)....nk | **5** | 16/1 | 50 | — |

(SP 108.3%) **5 Rn**

**1m 12.82** (3.82) CSF £7.13 TOTE £2.60: £1.30 £1.50 (£6.80) OWNER Times of Wigan (NEWMARKET) BRED Rafter T Horses
**3962 Saint Who (USA)** scooted up after easing his way into the lead over a quarter of a mile from home. (6/4)
**3846 Manikato (USA)**, looking in good shape in the paddock, was in the firing-line throughout and had every chance over two furlongs from home before the winner was let loose. (4/1)
**3809 Hallmark (IRE)** looked very well beforehand and held a slender lead until collared over two furlongs from home. An extra furlong may well help offset his lack of acceleration. (2/1)
**2595 Nervous Rex**, up with the pace from the start, had every chance over a quarter of a mile from home, but had come to the end of his tether below the distance. A return to five furlongs is required. (10/1: 6/1-11/1)
**3795 Zanabay** was in the firing-line until tiring over a furlong out. (16/1)

## 4104 E.B.F. NUTFIELD MAIDEN STKS (I) (2-Y.O F) (Class D)
2-30 (2-31) **7f** £3,448.70 (£1,028.60: £490.80: £221.90) Stalls: High GOING minus 0.40 sec per fur (F)

| | | | SP | RR | SF |
|---|---|---|---|---|---|
| 3756[5] | **Indihash (USA)** (RWArmstrong) **2-8-11** RPrice(6) (mde all: pushed out)....— | **1** | 7/1 | 81+ | 31 |
| 3756[3] | **Woodsia** (DRLoder) **2-8-11** WRSwinburn(2) (lw: a.p: ev ch over 1f out: unable qckn)....1¾ | **2** | 11/4[1] | 77+ | 27 |
| 2611[9] | **Etoile (FR)** (PWChapple-Hyam) **2-8-11** JReid(8) (plld hrd: a.p: ev ch over 1f out: one pce)....hd | **3** | 8/1 | 77 | 27 |
| | **Tempting Prospect** (LordHuntingdon) **2-8-11** DHarrison(11) (leggy: unf: a.p: rdn over 2f out: r.o one pce)..1¾ | **4** | 9/2[2] | 73 | 23 |
| | **Flyaway Hill (FR)** (PWHarris) **2-8-11** GHind(9) (leggy: hld up: rdn 3f out: one pce)....1 | **5** | 5/1[3] | 71 | 21 |
| | **Regal Academy (IRE)** (CAHorgan) **2-8-11** MFenton(4) (unf: nvr nr to chal)....1½ | **6** | 50/1 | 67 | 17 |
| | **Daintree (IRE)** (HJCollingridge) **2-8-11** MRimmer(14) (b.hind: leggy: prom over 5f)....s.h | **7** | 50/1 | 67 | 17 |
| | **Bout** (JHMGosden) **2-8-11** JCarroll(10) (w'like: bit bkwd: hld up: rdn over 2f out: wknd over 1f out)....¾ | **8** | 16/1 | 65 | 15 |
| | **Mary Culi** (HCandy) **2-8-11** CRutter(5) (w'like: bit bkwd: a bhd)....5 | **9** | 25/1 | 54 | 4 |
| | **Perfect Angel (IRE)** (MHTompkins) **2-8-11** NDay(12) (leggy: bhd fnl 3f)....5 | **10** | 50/1 | 42 | — |
| 3593[8] | **Curzon Street** (MRStoute) **2-8-11** RCochrane(13) (b.hind: bhd fnl 2f)....2 | **11** | 11/2 | 38 | — |
| 3137[3] | **Coal To Diamonds** (GFJohnsonHoughton) **2-8-11** MTebbutt(3) (bhd fnl 4f)....19 | **12** | 50/1 | — | — |

(SP 118.1%) **12 Rn**

**1m 24.15** (2.55) CSF £24.94 TOTE £10.40: £2.60 £1.70 £2.80 (£9.70) Trio £34.00 OWNER Mr Hamdan Al Maktoum (NEWMARKET) BRED Shadwell Farm Inc. and Shadwell Estate Co. Ltd.
**3756 Indihash (USA)**, who ran disappointingly on easy ground last time, was much happier on this sounder surface. (7/1: 9/2-8/1)
**3756 Woodsia** stood out in the paddock. Launching her challenge in the final quarter-mike, she stuck on well, but found the winner too strong. Her turn is not far away. (11/4: 6/4-3/1)
**2611 Etoile (FR)** took a very keen hold but, despite that, still had every chance below the distance before tapped for toe. She can find a race when she learns to settle better. (8/1: 6/1-10/1)
**Tempting Prospect**, a half-sister to recent Group Two Geoffrey Freer winner Phantom Gold, does not have much substance at present. Rather tapped for toe over a quarter of a mile from home, she did stay on again in the final furlong. (9/2)
**Flyaway Hill (FR)**, a tall newcomer, chased the leaders, but never looked like quickening in the second half of the race. (5/1)
**3593 Curzon Street** (11/2: 4/1-6/1)

## 4105 E.B.F. NUTFIELD MAIDEN STKS (II) (2-Y.O F) (Class D)
3-00 (3-01) **7f** £3,448.70 (£1,028.60: £490.80: £221.90) Stalls: High GOING minus 0.40 sec per fur (F)

| | | | SP | RR | SF |
|---|---|---|---|---|---|
| | **Corsini** (HRACecil) **2-8-11** WRyan(5) (leggy: unf: lw: a.p: led over 4f out: rdn out)....— | **1** | 5/4[1] | 81+ | 31 |
| 3593[5] | **Chorus Song (USA)** (PWChapple-Hyam) **2-8-11** JReid(13) (a.p: rdn over 2f out: unable qckn)....1½ | **2** | 9/4[2] | 78 | 28 |
| | **Hope Chest** (DRLoder) **2-8-11** WRSwinburn(4) (neat: lw: led over 2f: rdn over 2f out: one pce)....hd | **3** | 7/1[3] | 77 | 27 |
| | **Viva Verdi (IRE)** (JLDunlop) **2-8-11** SWhitworth(8) (w'like: scope: lw: nt clr run over 4f out: swtchd lft 2f out: gd hdwy over 1f out: r.o: bttr for r)....hd | **4** | 12/1 | 77+ | 27 |
| 3159[15] | **Silver Sands** (TPMcGovern) **2-8-11** JFEgan(9) (a.p: rdn over 3f out: one pce)....5 | **5** | 100/1 | 66 | 16 |
| | **Babe (IRE)** (MHTompkins) **2-8-11** NDay(7) (neat: no hdwy fnl 3f)....5 | **6** | 33/1 | 54 | 4 |
| | **Little Miss Rocker** (IABalding) **2-8-11** RCochrane(2) (neat: a mid div)....hd | **7** | 25/1 | 54 | 4 |
| | **Fauna (IRE)** (NAGraham) **2-8-11** DHarrison(12) (w'like: s.s: nvr nrr)....1¼ | **8** | 16/1 | 51 | 1 |
| | **Fable** (JARToller) **2-8-11** SSanders(14) (unf: prom over 4f)....1¾ | **9** | 50/1 | 47 | — |
| | **Well Done** (MBell) **2-8-11** MFenton(6) (neat: bkwd: bhd fnl 5f)....4 | **10** | 25/1 | 38 | — |
| | **Persian Blue** (RHannon) **2-8-11** DaneO'Neill(11) (neat: bhd fnl 2f)....2 | **11** | 20/1 | 34 | — |
| | **Mish Mish** (WJarvis) **2-8-11** StephenDavies(3) (neat: bit bkwd: a bhd)....1½ | **12** | 25/1 | 30 | — |
| | **Pirongia** (PHowling) **2-8-11** JQuinn(1) (neat: a bhd)....2 | **13** | 100/1 | 26 | — |
| 3494[12] | **Topps Trio** (KOCunningham-Brown) **2-8-11** CMunday(10) (s.s: bhd fnl 4f)....2½ | **14** | 100/1 | 20 | — |

(SP 125.5%) **14 Rn**

**1m 24.08** (2.48) CSF £4.60 TOTE £2.30: £1.20 £1.10 £1.70 (£2.00) Trio £2.50 OWNER Mr K. Abdulla (NEWMARKET) BRED Juddmonte Farms
**Corsini**, a tall filly, may not have much substance but she looked extremely well and was the subject of encouraging home reports. These proved well founded as she moved to the front over half a mile from home and, ridden along, kept on really well. (5/4: 7/4-11/10)
**3593 Chorus Song (USA)** was never far away, but did not look like finding that vital turn of foot in the last two furlongs. (9/4)
**Hope Chest** may not be that big but she looked in good shape for this debut. The early leader, she remained well in contention until tapped for toe in the last two furlongs. (7/1: op 3/1)
**Viva Verdi (IRE)**, a good-bodied filly, is a half-sister to German Group Three winner Vialli and Spanish Champion filly La Strada. Looking in good shape in the preliminaries, she was really getting her act together in the last two furlongs and would surely have taken second prize with a little further to go. She is sure to have learnt a great deal from this and should have no problems finding a race. (12/1)
**Silver Sands** failed to quicken in the last three furlongs. (100/1)
**Babe (IRE)**, a plain filly, was making little impression on the principals in the second half of the race. (33/1)

## 4106 ORIGIN NURSERY H'CAP (0-75) (2-Y.O) (Class E)
3-30 (3-32) **7f 140y** £3,643.50 (£1,092.00: £525.00: £241.50) Stalls: High GOING minus 0.40 sec per fur (F)

| | | | SP | RR | SF |
|---|---|---|---|---|---|
| 3880[4] | **Stride (74)** (MartynMeade) **2-9-0**(7) DSweeney(13) (lw: hld up: led over 1f out: rdn out)....— | **1** | 10/1[3] | 75 | 26 |
| 3493[8] | **Julietta Mia (USA) (61)** (BWHills) **2-8-3**(5) JDSmith(11) (lw: s.s: hdwy over 1f out: r.o ins fnl f)....1¼ | **2** | 20/1 | 59 | 10 |

3493[7] **Palaemon (70)** (GBBalding) **2-9-3** SDrowne(5) (rdn over 3f out: hdwy over 1f out: unable qckn ins fnl f).......1½ **3** 12/1 65 16
3821[7] **Castles Burning (USA) (60)** (CACyzer) **2-8-7** MHamblett(1) (hdwy over 3f out: ev ch ins fnl f: one pce).......s.h **4** 33/1 55 6
3962[5] **Silca's My Key (IRE) (69)** (MRChannon) **2-9-2** RPerham(7) (a.p: rdn over 2f out: one pce)..........................hd **5** 12/1 64 15
3982[4] **Gresatre (62)** (CADwyer) **2-8-9** RCochrane(2) (dwlt: hdwy over 1f out: r.o)..........................½ **6** 11/2[2] 56 7
3837[13] **Philosophic (55)** (SirMarkPrescott) **2-8-2** SSanders(17) (hld up: rdn over 2f out: r.o one pce fnl f)................hd **7** 14/1 49 —
3962* **Rumbustious (72)** (RHannon) **2-9-5** 5x DaneO'Neill(15) (a.p: rdn over 2f out: ev ch over 1f out: one pce).......½ **8** 11/4[1] 65 16
3230[7] **Trading Aces (66)** (MBell) **2-8-13** MFenton(16) (led over 1f: ev ch 2f out: wknd over 1f out)..........................3 **9** 25/1 52 3
3408[4] **Strat's Quest (68)** (DWPArbuthnot) **2-9-1** DHarrison(14) (b: lw: nvr nrr)..........................¾ **10** 14/1 53 4
1531[6] **Dive Master (IRE) (55)** (CMurray) **2-8-2** JFEgan(9) (lw: rdn over 3f out: sme hdwy over 1f out: sn wknd).......nk **11** 20/1 39 —
3846[6] **Sharp Return (52)** (MJRyan) **2-7-13** GBardwell(10) (sme hdwy over 1f out: sn wknd)..........................nk **12** 33/1 36 —
3943[11] **Rons Revenge (49)** (MJRyan) **2-7-3b**[1](7) AMcCarthy(6) (bmpd s: led 6f out tl over 1f out: sn wknd)..............nk **13** 33/1 32 —
3848[4] **Mystic Quest (IRE) (74)** (KMcAuliffe) **2-9-7** PatEddery(4) (prom 6f)..........................¾ **14** 10/1[3] 55 6
3632[3] **Janglynyve (55)** (SPCWoods) **2-8-2** DBiggs(12) (prom 6f)..........................1¼ **15** 10/1[3] 34 —
3943[3] **Summerville Wood (68)** (PMooney) **2-9-1b** StephenDavies(8) (prom 5f)..........................3½ **16** 10/1[3] 39 —

(SP 129.3%) **16 Rn**

**1m 32.88** (4.08) CSF £180.43 CT £2,296.23 TOTE £9.20: £2.10 £6.90 £3.60 £22.20 (£177.50) Trio £372.10 OWNER Ladyswood Racing Club (MALMESBURY) BRED Side Hill Stud

LONG HANDICAP Rons Revenge 7-9

OFFICIAL EXPLANATION **Medland (IRE): the trainer felt that this race may have come too quickly.**

**3880 Stride**, tucked in behind the front rank travelling really well, got a split and, coming through to lead below the distance, was ridden along to assert. (10/1: op 6/1)

**2985 Julietta Mia (USA)** ran her best race to date on this nursery debut, putting in some good work in the last furlong and a half from the back of the field to take second prize. (20/1)

**1437 Palaemon** made his effort on the outside of the field below the distance but, having almost got on terms, failed to quicken in the last 150 yards. (12/1: 8/1-14/1)

**1531 Castles Burning (USA)** moved up at halfway and threw down his challenge from below the distance, but his rider looked absolutely dreadful in the final furlong, indeed he looked as if he might fall off, and the combination failed to quicken. (33/1)

**3962 Silca's My Key (IRE)** failed to find another gear in the last two furlongs. (12/1)

**3982 Gresatre** stayed on from the back of the field from below the distance. (11/2)

**Philosophic** (14/1: 10/1-16/1)

**3962* Rumbustious**, who has risen 10lb since her Brighton victory last week, had every chance below the distance before her rise in the weights took its toll. (11/4)

## 4107 GRAHAM POTTER ASSOCIATES (S) H'CAP (0-60) (3-Y.O+) (Class G)

4-00 (4-02) **1m 2f (Equitrack)** £2,532.00 (£702.00: £336.00) Stalls: Low GOING minus 0.55 sec per fur (FST)

SP RR SF

2056[2] **Comedy River (42)** (NEBerry) **9-8-10** GHind(5) (hld up: led 1f out: r.o wl)..........................— **1** 9/1 56 39
*3435*[3] **Awesome Power (51)** (JWHills) **10-9-5** AClark(4) (a.p: led 3f out to 1f out: unable qckn)..........................3 **2** 6/1[2] 60 43
3831[3] **Cherry Garden (IRE) (51)** (TJNaughton) **3-8-12b**[1] DHarrison(11) (hld up: rdn 3f out: wknd wl over 1f out).....10 **3** 11/1 44 20
3611[8] **Yellow Dragon (IRE) (49)** (BAPearce) **3-8-10** NCarlisle(1) (b: s.i.s: rdn over 3f out: hdwy over 1f out: nvr nrr)..........................2 **4** 10/1 39 15
3860[6] **One In The Eye (50)** (JRPoulton) **3-8-11** LeesaLong(2) (a.p: rdn over 3f out: wknd 2f out)..........................½ **5** 33/1 39 15
3944[13] **Zamalek (USA) (60)** (GLMoore) **4-10-0** SWhitworth(3) (led 7f: wknd over 2f out)..........................1¾ **6** 8/1 46 29
*3435*[5] **Silver Tzar (51)** (RTPhillips) **4-9-5** RPerham(6) (chsd ldr over 6f)..........................nk **7** 20/1 37 20
**Court Jester (40)** (MJRyan) **5-8-1b**(7) AMcCarthy(10) (nvr nrr)..........................¾ **8** 33/1 25 8
3978[7] **Multi Franchise (58)** (BGubby) **3-9-5** JQuinn(7) (prom over 6f)..........................2 **9** 7/1[3] 40 16
3333[13] **Classic Delight (USA) (48)** (RHarris) **3-8-9** AMackay(12) (a bhd)..........................¾ **10** 33/1 28 4
3824[4] **Ultimate Warrior (58)** (CACyzer) **6-9-12** JCarroll(13) (a bhd)..........................3 **11** 6/1[2] 34 17
*3951*[2] **Medland (IRE) (45)** (BJMcMath) **6-8-13** RCochrane(9) (b: lw: hld up: rdn over 4f out: wknd over 3f out).........nk **12** 5/2[1] 20 3
3786[7] **Camden's Ransom (USA) (55)** (HGRowsell) **9-9-2**(7) DSweeney(8) (a bhd)..........................s.h **13** 14/1 30 13
746[7] **Kellaire Girl (IRE) (44)** (AMoore) **4-8-9**(3) AWhelan(14) (b.hind: bhd fnl 6f)..........................28 **14** 20/1 — —

(SP 133.2%) **14 Rn**

**2m 5.76** (1.46) CSF £63.82 CT £568.31 TOTE £13.40: £2.80 £1.50 £3.10 (£27.20) Trio £63.90 OWNER The Group 1 Racing Club (UPPER LAMBOURN) BRED Dr S. M. Foster

WEIGHT FOR AGE 3yo-7lb

No bid

OFFICIAL EXPLANATION **Take Notice: the jockey reported that the colt stumbled on the crossing and he thought he had gone wrong behind.**

**2056 Comedy River**, whose only previous victory came in Jersey three years ago, bounced back from a three-month absence. Coming through to lead a furlong from home, he soon put the issue beyond doubt. (9/1: 5/1-10/1)

**3435 Awesome Power** went on three furlongs from home but, collared inside the distance, was firmly put in his place. A mile and a quarter on the Equitrack in sellers or claimers is definitely his grade. (6/1: 4/1-13/2)

**3831 Cherry Garden (IRE)**, fitted with blinkers for the first time, was left for dead by the front two in the short home straight. (11/1: 8/1-12/1)

**1970* Yellow Dragon (IRE)** was well supported in the market, despite having shown nothing since winning a seller at Southwell in June. Moving into midfield in the second half of the race, he stayed on in the straight to finish a moderate fourth. (10/1)

**1050 One In The Eye** was close up until tiring turning for home. (33/1)

**Zamalek (USA)** has shown nothing this season, but that did not stop him being well supported in the market for this All-Weather debut. Bowling along in front, he was collared three furlongs from home and was soon in trouble. (8/1: op 20/1)

## 4108 CHAMPAGNE JACQUART MAIDEN STKS (3-Y.O+) (Class D)

4-30 (4-31) **7f** £4,490.55 (£1,346.40: £647.70: £298.35) Stalls: High GOING minus 0.40 sec per fur (F)

SP RR SF

2529[3] **Jumairah Sunset** (ACStewart) **3-8-9** SWhitworth(1) (lw: racd far side: led over 4f out: drvn out)..........................— **1** 12/1 71 29
3788[10] **Regal Splendour (CAN)** (PFICole) **3-9-0** CRutter(7) (lw: racd far side: led over 2f: hrd rdn 2f out: r.o wl)......nk **2** 20/1 75 33
3472[3] **Don Bosio (USA) (84)** (MRStoute) **3-9-0v**[1] WRSwinburn(4) (lw: a.p: rdn over 1f out: unable qckn)..............2½ **3** 5/2[1] 70 28
**Lacandona (USA)** (PWChapple-Hyam) **3-8-9** JReid(9) (leggy: unf: scope: s.s: hdwy over 2f out: rdn over 1f out: one pce)..........................1½ **4** 12/1 61 19
**Hazel** (MissGayKelleway) **4-8-8**(5) DGriffiths(10) (bit bkwd: nvr nr to chal)..........................hd **5** 50/1 61 23
3832[2] **Hannalou (FR) (70)** (SPCWoods) **3-8-9** DBiggs(13) (a.p: rdn over 2f out: one pce)..........................1 **6** 12/1 59 17

3832[8] **Girl of My Dreams (IRE)** (MJHeaton-Ellis) **3-8-9** SDrowne(8) (prom over 5f) ....1½ **7** 50/1 55 13
3686[9] **Sharp Move (37)** (MrsJCecil) **4-8-13** AClark(14) (lw: prom over 4f) ....1¾ **8** 50/1 51 13
**Fencer's Quest (IRE)** (RCharlton) **3-8-7**(7) RBrisland(2) (w'like: scope: lw: nvr nrr) ....nk **9** 25/1 56 14
**Corporal Nym (USA) (97)** (PFICole) **3-9-0** TQuinn(5) (bkwd: hdwy over 4f out: wknd over 1f out) ....2½ **10** 6/1[3] 50 8
3788[3] **Take Notice (80)** (GHarwood) **3-9-0** PatEddery(18) (prom over 3f) ....½ **11** 11/4[2] 49 7
**Rainy Day Song** (LordHuntingdon) **3-8-9** DHarrison(12) (bit bkwd: a bhd) ....hd **12** 20/1 44 2
**Perpetual Hope** (PMitchell) **3-8-9** JQuinn(16) (w'like: bit bkwd: s.s: a bhd) ....hd **13** 50/1 43 1
3656[14] **Sterin** (MarkCampion) **3-8-9** RPerham(6) (a bhd) ....½ **14** 50/1 42 —
3832[11] **Classic Warrior** (RHarris) **3-9-0** AMackay(15) (a bhd) ....1¼ **15** 50/1 44 2
(SP 117.7%) **15 Rn**

**1m 24.16** (2.56) CSF £187.32 TOTE £11.30: £2.50 £5.20 £1.60 (£562.00) Trio £265.70 OWNER Sheikh Ahmed Al Maktoum (NEWMARKET)
BRED Mount Coote Stud
WEIGHT FOR AGE 3yo-4lb
OFFICIAL EXPLANATION **Take Notice: stumbled on the crossing and his jockey felt the horse had gone wrong behind.**
IN-FOCUS: **The first two elected to tack over to the far side which proved a highly successful move, as the ground was undoubtedly faster there.**

**2529 Jumairah Sunset** was given a very enterprising ride and was one of only two to tack over to the far rail. In front over half a mile from home, she had a ding-dong battle with the runner-up but, responding well to pressure, just succeeded. (12/1: 8/1-14/1)
**Regal Splendour (CAN)** left his debut run well behind. The early leader, he then gave chase to the winner on the far rail but, despite giving his all, just failed to get his head back in front. (20/1)
**3472 Don Bosio (USA)** moved into the lead on the stands' side half a mile from home, but was still many lengths off the two racing on the far side. Despite all Swinburn's efforts, he was unable to peg back his two rivals. That first victory is still eluding him. (5/2)
**Lacandona (USA)**, a tall filly who needs time to develop, moved up over a quarter of a mile from home, but then could only plod on at one insufficient pace. (12/1: op 8/1)
**Hazel**, not looking fully wound up for her first run in sixteen months, could never get in a blow. (50/1)
**3832 Hannalou (FR)** was close up on the stands' side until made to look very pedestrian in the last two furlongs. (12/1: op 8/1)

## 4109 H.B.L.B. BLINDLEY HEATH H'CAP (0-80) (3-Y.O+) (Class D)

5-00 (5-03) **7f** £4,291.65 (£1,285.20: £617.10: £283.05) Stalls: High GOING minus 0.40 sec per fur (F)

SP RR SF

2976[9] **Chewit (77)** (AMoore) **4-9-13** CandyMorris(10) (s.s: hdwy on ins 2f out: led ins fnl f: r.o wl) ....— **1** 16/1 81 59
3777[7] **Utmost Zeal (USA) (61)** (PWHarris) **3-8-7** GHind(1) (led: rdn 2f out: hdd ins fnl f: r.o) ....½ **2** 13/2[2] 64 38
3833[8] **Rakis (IRE) (75)** (MrsLStubbs) **6-9-11** JFEgan(4) (a.p: rdn over 1f out: unable qckn) ....1½ **3** 11/1 74 52
3926[5] **Caricature (IRE) (80)** (GLewis) **3-9-9b**(3) AWhelan(2) (a.p: rdn over 2f out: one pce) ....hd **4** 7/1[3] 79 53
3518[10] **Nunsharpa (74)** (JRFanshawe) **3-9-3**(3) NVarley(13) (racd stands' side: a.p: rdn over 2f out: r.o) ....1¼ **5** 12/1 70 44
3767[4] **Really A Dream (IRE) (70)** (MRStoute) **3-9-2v[1]** WRSwinburn(3) (nvr nr to chal) ....1½ **6** 8/1 63 37
1680[6] **Sharp 'n Smart (61)** (BSmart) **4-8-11** RCochrane(11) (prom over 5f) ....1 **7** 16/1 52 30
3967[3] **Sharp Imp (58)** (RMFlower) **6-8-8b** DaneO'Neill(14) (racd stands' side: nvr nrr) ....s.h **8** 12/1 49 27
3989[5] **Prima Silk (67)** (MJRyan) **5-9-3** GBardwell(12) (nvr nrr) ....1¼ **9** 12/1 55 33
*4081*[12] **Times of Times (IRE) (67)** (MJRyan) **3-8-6**(7) AMcCarthy(8) (nvr nrr) ....2½ **10** 16/1 49 23
1680[7] **Quintus Decimus (68)** (BJMeehan) **4-9-4** MTebbutt(16) (racd stands' side: outpcd) ....1¼ **11** 20/1 47 25
3830[10] **Sweet Wilhelmina (70)** (LordHuntingdon) **3-8-11**(5) AimeeCook(5) (b.nr hind: prom over 4f) ....½ **12** 20/1 48 22
4064[6] **Midday Cowboy (USA) (73)** (GHarwood) **3-9-5** AClark(18) (lw: racd stands' side: a bhd) ....s.h **13** 12/1 51 25
3995[19] **Samsolom (59)** (PHowling) **8-8-9** JQuinn(9) (lw: a bhd) ....½ **14** 16/1 36 14
3799[10] **Sejaal (IRE) (73)** (RAkehurst) **4-9-9** SSanders(6) (lw: bhd fnl 2f) ....s.h **15** 16/1 50 28
2974[4] **Shadow Casting (72)** (BWHills) **3-9-4** PatEddery(7) (hdwy 5f out: wknd over 1f out) ....1¾ **16** 9/2[1] 45 19
646[15] **Fran Godfrey (65)** (PTWalwyn) **3-8-11** JCarroll(15) (lw: racd stands' side: bhd fnl 4f) ....1¾ **17** 33/1 34 8
3937[17] **Beldray Park (IRE) (62)** (MrsALMKing) **3-8-8** JReid(17) (racd stands' side: bhd fnl 3f) ....nk **18** 33/1 30 4
(SP 139.0%) **18 Rn**

**1m 22.64** (1.04) CSF £119.93 CT £1,165.70 TOTE £38.70: £7.30 £3.70 £3.30 £2.60 (£447.10) Trio £592.40; £333.79 to Doncaster 11/9/96
OWNER Ballard (1834) Ltd (BRIGHTON) BRED B. Minty
WEIGHT FOR AGE 3yo-4lb
STEWARDS' ENQUIRY Really A Dream(IRE), drawn 3, started from stall 4, and Rakis(IRE) vice versa. Swinburn fined £125 under instruction G1.

**2548 Chewit** slipped through on the inside a quarter of a mile from home and, after moving to the front inside the final furlong, kept on well to gain his first victory on turf. (16/1)
**3777 Utmost Zeal (USA)** was very well supported and bowled along in front. Collared inside the final furlong, he stuck on commendably to the line. (13/2)
**2400 Rakis (IRE)** failed to quicken from below the distance. (11/1)
**3926 Caricature (IRE)** was almost on terms with the leader below the distance before tapped for toe. (7/1)
**3167 Nunsharpa** led the stands'-side group, but they were well adrift of the runners racing on the opposite side of the track. She stuck to her task well in the last two furlongs, but could never close the deficit. (12/1)
**3767 Really A Dream (IRE)**, tried in a visor, made some late headway without posing a threat. (8/1)

## 4110 MARSH GREEN MAIDEN STKS (3-Y.O+) (Class D)

5-30 (5-31) **1m 3f 106y** £4,125.90 (£1,234.20: £591.60: £270.30) Stalls: High GOING minus 0.40 sec per fur (F)

SP RR SF

3522[3] **Possessive Artiste (71)** (MRStoute) **3-8-7** JReid(4) (b.hind: a.p: led over 1f out: rdn out) ....— **1** 9/2[2] 74 30
3505[4] **Ballet High (IRE)** (IABalding) **3-8-12** RCochrane(9) (chsd ldr 2f: chsd ldr over 7f out: ev ch over 1f out: unable qckn) ....1¼ **2** 5/1[3] 77 33
3818[3] **Classic Dame (FR)** (RHarris) **3-8-7** AMackay(5) (hld up: rdn over 2f out: r.o) ....1½ **3** 5/1[3] 70 26
2990[2] **Macmorris (USA) (75)** (PFICole) **3-8-12** TQuinn(2) (led: rn wd st: rdn over 2f out: hdd over 1f out: one pce) ....¾ **4** 4/1[1] 74 30
3942[5] **Calendula** (DMorley) **3-8-7** MFenton(6) (rdn over 2f out: hdwy over 1f out: nvr nrr) ....1¼ **5** 16/1 67 23
**Laazim Afooz** (RTPhillips) **3-8-12** RPerham(10) (no hdwy fnl 3f) ....2 **6** 33/1 70 26
3356[2] **Lucky Hoof** (CEBrittain) **3-8-7** SSanders(8) (nvr nr to chal) ....8 **7** 6/1 53 9
3776[2] **Safa (USA)** (ACStewart) **3-8-7** SWhitworth(3) (bhd fnl 8f) ....¾ **8** 11/2 52 8
*3626*[5] **Theme Arena** (SMellor) **3-8-7** WRyan(7) (s.s: a bhd) ....1½ **9** 33/1 50 6
**Chili-Wah-Wah** (CASmith) **5-9-7** DHarrison(1) (s.s: a bhd) ....6 **10** 50/1 48 12
**Toby Brown** (MrsALMKing) **3-8-12** JQuinn(12) (w'like: bit bkwd: s.s: a bhd) ....7 **11** 50/1 37 —

1507[9] **Veronica Franco (62)** (BAPearce) **3-8-7** GBardwell(11) (hdwy 10f out: chsd ldr over 9f out tl over 7f out: wknd over 3f out)........1¾ **12** 50/1 30 —
(SP 118.8%) **12 Rn**

**2m 28.58** (4.38) CSF £25.69 TOTE £4.90: £1.10 £2.30 £2.50 (£11.40) Trio £35.10 OWNER Mrs Doreen Swinburn (NEWMARKET) BRED Rockwell Bloodstock
WEIGHT FOR AGE 3yo-8lb
**3522 Possessive Artiste** at last came good. Appreciating the longer trip, she struck the front below the distance and was rousted along to score. (9/2: 5/2-5/1)
**3505 Ballet High (IRE)**, in second place for much of the contest, had every chance below the distance but, once again, his lack of acceleration was exposed. (5/1)
**3818 Classic Dame (FR)** chased the leaders but, despite keeping on in the final quarter-mile, failed to get on terms with the front two. (5/1: 6/1-4/1)
**2990 Macmorris (USA)** set the pace, but did not handle the home turn very well. Headed below the distance, he could only plod on in his own time. (4/1)
**3942 Calendula** stayed on in the final quarter-mile without ever posing a threat. (16/1)

T/Jkpt: Not won; £21,334.74 to Doncaster 11/9/96. T/Plpt: £69.40 (205.93 Tckts). T/Qdpt: £20.50 (40.59 Tckts). AK

# 3149-DONCASTER (L-H) (Good, Rnd crse Good to firm patches)
## Wednesday September 11th
WEATHER: overcast WIND: mod half against

## 4111 QUEEN'S OWN YORKSHIRE DRAGOONS CONDITIONS STKS (2-Y.O) (Class C)
1-30 (1-30) **7f** £4,838.75 (£1,745.00: £837.50: £342.50: £136.25) Stalls: High GOING minus 0.22 sec per fur (GF)

SP RR SF

2335* **Benny The Dip (USA)** (JHMGosden) **2-9-1** LDettori(3) (chsd ldrs: shkn up over 2f out: led over 1f out: r.o wl)........— **1** 7/4[2] 99+ 46
3794* **Desert Story (IRE)** (MRStoute) **2-9-1** KFallon(1) (lw: trckd ldrs: chal over 1f out: nt qckn ins fnl f)........1½ **2** 4/1[3] 96 43
**Furnish** (BWHills) **2-8-3** KDarley(4) (w'like: scope: trckd ldrs: plld hrd: led & stumbled over 2f out: hdd over 1f out: sn outpcd)........1½ **3** 11/2 80+ 27
3778* **Out West (USA)** (HRACecil) **2-8-10** PatEddery(5) (lw: chsd ldr: led ½-wy tl over 2f out: sn wl outpcd: styd on ins fnl f)........1¾ **4** 13/8[1] 83 30
3251[4] **Isle of Corregidor (USA)** (MrsJCecil) **2-8-13** AClark(2) (lw: led to ½-wy: lost pl over 2f out)........11 **5** 20/1 61 8
(SP 114.6%) **5 Rn**

**1m 26.52** (2.92) CSF £8.75 TOTE £2.70: £1.40 £2.00 (£5.50) OWNER Mr Landon Knight (NEWMARKET) BRED Landon Knight
**2335* Benny The Dip (USA)**, not the best of walkers, had to be shaken up to get into full stride. Once in front, he scored in good style. A mile will be no problem. (7/4)
**3794* Desert Story (IRE)**, who carried plenty of condition, showed a fair bit of knee-action going down. Moving up looking to be going better than the winner at one stage, he had to settle for second best in the end. (4/1: 3/1-9/2)
**Furnish** proved very keen. Stumbling as she hit the front, she was outpaced by the first two in the final furlong. Once she learns to settle, she will make her mark. (11/2)
**3778* Out West (USA)**, badly outpaced when the race began in earnest, was switched towards the centre and was staying on at the line. Still inexperienced, she definitely needs a mile. (13/8)
**3251 Isle of Corregidor (USA)**, who wore a Monty Roberts-type rope-headcollar, dropped away tamely when headed. (20/1)

## 4112 SITWELL ARMS MALLARD H'CAP (0-105) (3-Y.O+) (Class B)
2-00 (2-02) **1m 6f 132y** £10,290.00 (£3,810.00: £1,830.00: £750.00: £300.00: £120.00) Stalls: Low GOING minus 0.22 sec per fur (GF)

SP RR SF

3689[3] **Corradini (99)** (HRACecil) **4-9-10** KFallon(3) (sn pushed along: hdwy & swtchd outside 3f out: led over 1f out: hung lft: drvn out)........— **1** Evens[1] 113 81
3266[4] **Candle Smile (USA) (88)** (MRStoute) **4-8-13** JReid(7) (trckd ldrs: led over 3f out: hung lft: hdd over 1f out: nt qckn fnl f)........1 **2** 15/2[3] 101 69
3760[2] **Tudor Island (80)** (CEBrittain) **7-8-5** BDoyle(8) (lw: sn chsng ldrs: one pce fnl 3f)........5 **3** 10/1 87 55
3486* **Rushen Raider (72)** (KWHogg) **4-7-11** LCharnock(5) (chsd ldrs: rdn along 6f out: hung lft & one pce fnl 3f)....6 **4** 15/2[3] 73 41
3816* **Highflying (82)** (GMMoore) **10-8-7** JTate(1) (lw: w ldr: led over 4f out tl over 3f out: wknd over 1f out)........8 **5** 14/1 74 42
3834[7] **Deano's Beeno (76)** (MJohnston) **4-8-1** TWilliams(4) (lw: led tl over 4f out: wknd over 3f out)........nk **6** 16/1 68 36
3834[2] **Embryonic (IRE) (78)** (RFFisher) **4-8-3** KDarley(6) (hld up: effrt over 3f out: sn wknd)........13 **7** 8/1 56 24
3699* **Generosa (89)** (HCandy) **3-8-2** CRutter(9) (swtg: hld up: effrt 4f out: sn rdn & lost pl)........1½ **8** 7/1[2] 65 21
(SP 118.8%) **8 Rn**

**3m 4.47** (0.87) CSF £9.30 CT £47.29 TOTE £1.90: £1.30 £2.20 £2.00 (£5.30) Trio £10.80 OWNER Mr K. Abdulla (NEWMARKET) BRED Juddmonte Farms
WEIGHT FOR AGE 3yo-12lb
**3689 Corradini**, running off the same mark as in the Ebor, made his rider earn his fee. After hitting the front, he hung left and swished his tail, but did sufficient. (Evens)
**3266 Candle Smile (USA)** travelled strongly. After hitting the front, he hung left, onto the rail and, in the final furlong, the winner proved too good. He does not find as much as expected off the bridle and, a real stayer, is probably better suited by extreme distances. (15/2)
**3760 Tudor Island** ran another sound race, but looks in the grip of the Handicapper. (10/1)
**3486* Rushen Raider**, up in class and from a 4lb higher mark, hung left under pressure and was left behind in the final three furlongs. (15/2)
**3816* Highflying**, a grand old stager, made the best of his way home on the home turn, but was very tired over a furlong out. (14/1: 10/1-16/1)

## 4113 E.B.F. CARRIE RED NURSERY H'CAP (2-Y.O F) (Class C)
2-35 (2-39) **6f 110y** £17,730.00 (£6,570.00: £3,160.00: £1,300.00: £525.00: £215.00) Stalls: High GOING minus 0.22 sec per fur (GF)

SP RR SF

1143[4] **Nightbird (IRE) (84)** (BWHills) **2-8-13** MHills(19) (lw: bhd: hdwy & swtchd lft over 2f out: r.o wl to ld post)........— **1** 12/1 83 —

| | | | | | | |
|---|---|---|---|---|---|---|
| 2338[6] | **Naked Poser (IRE) (83)** (RHannon) **2-8-12** DBiggs(1) (chsd ldr far side: led over 1f out tl ct last stride)........s.h | **2** | 16/1 | 82 | — |
| 3475[4] | **Oneknight With You (74)** (MJFetherston-Godley) **2-8-3** ACulhane(2) (racd far side: chsd ldrs: kpt on wl fnl f).......nk | **3** | 25/1 | 72 | — |
| 3707[9] | **Halowing (USA) (92)** (PAKelleway) **2-9-7** DRMcCabe(18) (carried lft & hdwy over 2f out: styd on wl fnl f)........2 | **4** | 33/1 | 85 | — |
| 3475[2] | **Blues Queen (79)** (MRChannon) **2-8-8** PatEddery(3) (racd far side: led tl over 1f out: eased nr fin)................hd | **5** | 11/1 3 | 72 | — |
| 3846[5] | **Song Mist (IRE) (80)** (PFICole) **2-8-2**(7) DavidO'Neill(15) (s.i.s: bhd: hdwy to chse ldrs ½-wy: kpt on same pce).......hd | **6** | 16/1 | 73 | — |
| 3593* | **Catechism (USA) (87)** (JHMGosden) **2-9-2** LDettori(13) (unruly s: trckd ldrs: effrt over 2f out: kpt on same pce).......hd | **7** | 4/1 1 | 80 | — |
| 3128[7] | **Can Can Lady (72)** (MJohnston) **2-8-1** JFanning(11) (lw: chsd ldrs: rdn & outpcd ½-wy: kpt on fnl f) .............nk | **8** | 16/1 | 64 | — |
| 3483[5] | **Skyers Flyer (IRE) (85)** (RonaldThompson) **2-9-0** NConnorton(22) (sme hdwy over 2f out: nvr nr to chal) .......2 | **9** | 33/1 | 72 | — |
| 3685* | **Hoh Flyer (USA) (76)** (MBell) **2-8-5** MFenton(6) (s.i.s: racd far side: bhd tl styd on fnl 2f: n.d)...............¾ | **10** | 11/1 3 | 61 | — |
| 3171* | **Undercover Agent (IRE) (85)** (JLDunlop) **2-9-0** GCarter(8) (lw: swtchd lft & racd far side: sme hdwy over 2f out: sn wknd).......½ | **11** | 12/1 | 69 | — |
| 3971[5] | **Perfect Bliss (77)** (PDEvans) **2-7-13**(7) RFfrench(10) (w ldr tl wknd over 1f out).............hd | **12** | 16/1 | 61 | — |
| 3921[5] | **Stone Flower (USA) (88)** (PWChapple-Hyam) **2-9-3** JReid(14) (lw: trckd ldrs: effrt over 2f out: sn wknd)......s.h | **13** | 16/1 | 71 | — |
| 3803* | **Farewell My Love (IRE) (84)** (PFICole) **2-8-8**(5) PPMurphy(21) (b.hind: lw: led stands' side tl wknd over 1f out).......hd | **14** | 11/1 3 | 67 | — |
| 3807[2] | **Gee Bee Dream (78)** (APJarvis) **2-8-7** JFortune(9) (lw: chsd ldrs tl wknd over 2f out)..............1¼ | **15** | 12/1 | 58 | — |
| 3835[9] | **Top of The Wind (IRE) (78)** (JJO'Neill) **2-8-7** RCochrane(20) (bolted gng to s: w ldrs tl rdn & wknd over 2f out).......1¼ | **16** | 16/1 | 55 | — |
| 3814[3] | **Mystic Circle (IRE) (75)** (JWWatts) **2-8-4** JCarroll(7) (racd far side: outpcd fr ½-wy)..............¾ | **17** | 25/1 | 50 | — |
| 3581* | **Stygian (USA) (73)** (BWHills) **2-8-2** WCarson(12) (lw: chsd ldrs: drvn along over 2f out: sn wknd) ..........½ | **18** | 9/1 2 | 47 | — |
| 3843[3] | **Just Visiting (90)** (CaptJWilson) **2-9-5** KFallon(16) (w ldrs tl wknd over 2f out) ..............4 | **19** | 14/1 | 54 | — |
| 2728[5] | **Express Girl (80)** (DMoffatt) **2-8-6**(3) DarrenMoffatt(5) (racd far side: bhd fnl 2f)..............1¼ | **20** | 33/1 | 41 | — |
| 3835[15] | **Double Gold (81)** (BJMeehan) **2-8-10** BDoyle(17) (prom to ½-wy: sn lost pl)..............6 | **21** | 16/1 | 27 | — |
| 3843[7] | **Daylight Dreams (85)** (CACyzer) **2-9-0** KDarley(4) (in tch far side to ½-wy: eased & sn bhd) ..............5 | **22** | 25/1 | 19 | — |
| | | | (SP 146.3%) | **22 Rn** | | |

**1m 21.12** CSF £196.06 CT £4,395.92 TOTE £16.90: £4.10 £4.90 £6.40 £14.10 (£99.20) Trio Not won; £1,648.48 to Doncaster 12/9/96
OWNER Mr S. P. Tindall (LAMBOURN) BRED S. Tindall and Stowell Hill Ltd

**1143 Nightbird (IRE)**, absent since disappointing in much hotter company at Newbury over three months ago, looked bright and well. Switched towards the centre, she had a lot of running to do, but showed real grit and determination to get up in the last stride. The full seven will suit her even better. (12/1: op 8/1)
**2338 Naked Poser (IRE)**, suited by this better ground, had the prize whipped from under her nose right on the line. (16/1)
**3475 Oneknight With You**, a narrow type, proved suited by the step up in distance. (25/1)
**2703* Halowing (USA)**, out of her depth at York last time, was carried towards the centre when the winner switched. Staying on in fine style at the finish, she will be suited by seven furlongs. (33/1)
**3475 Blues Queen** showed plenty of pace on the far side but, with her stamina giving out, she was not ridden right out, otherwise she would have finished fourth. (11/1)
**3846 Song Mist (IRE)**, dropped 5lb, missed the break slightly but, in the firing-line at halfway, had no excuse. (16/1)
**3593* Catechism (USA)**, taken to post early, proved mulish at the start. She does not lack ability, but has more than her fair share of temperament. (4/1)
**3685* Hoh Flyer (USA)**, taken quietly to post, finished in good style after a slow break and will do better soon. (11/1)
**3807 Gee Bee Dream** (12/1: 20/1-33/1)
**3581* Stygian (USA)** (9/1: 6/1-10/1)

## 4114 STONES BITTER PARK HILL STKS (Gp 3) (3-Y.O+ F & M) (Class A)

3-10 (3-11) **1m 6f 132y** £21,044.00 (£7,796.00: £3,748.00: £1,540.00: £620.00: £252.00) Stalls: Low GOING minus 0.22 sec per fur (GF)

| | | | SP | RR | SF |
|---|---|---|---|---|---|
| 3711* | **Eva Luna (USA)** (HRACecil) **4-9-3** PatEddery(5) (lw: mde all: styd on strly fnl 3f) ..............— | **1** | 2/1 1 | 111+ | 80 |
| 3711[2] | **Time Allowed (91)** (MRStoute) **3-8-6**ow1 JReid(4) (trckd ldrs: wnt 2nd 2f out: kpt on u.p: no imp) ..........1¾ | **2** | 7/2 3 | 110 | 66 |
| 3689[2] | **Beauchamp Jade (95)** (HCandy) **4-9-3** GCarter(1) (lw: trckd ldrs: effrt over 4f out: kpt on same pce fnl 2f)......5 | **3** | 7/2 3 | 104 | 73 |
| 3688[6] | **Russian Snows (IRE)** (SbinSuroor) **4-9-8** LDettori(2) (chsd wnr: effrt over 3f out: wknd over 1f out)..........5 | **4** | 11/4 2 | 103 | 72 |
| 3073[2] | **Beyond Doubt (82)** (LordHuntingdon) **4-9-3** WRSwinburn(3) (lw: hld up: effrt 4f out: sn wknd)..........25 | **5** | 20/1 | 71 | 40 |
| 4031a[4] | **Alzabella (IRE) (98)** (JWHills) **3-8-5** MHills(6) (lw: chsd ldrs: rdn 7f out: bhd fnl 4f) ..............20 | **6** | 33/1 | 49 | 6 |
| | | | (SP 112.1%) | **6 Rn** | |

**3m 3.93** (0.33) CSF £8.94 TOTE £2.40: £1.60 £2.20 (£4.20) OWNER Mr K. Abdulla (NEWMARKET) BRED Juddmonte Farms
WEIGHT FOR AGE 3yo-12lb

**3711* Eva Luna (USA)** set a sensible pace. Still a shade green, she kept up the gallop in tremendous style. A winner of a maiden, a listed and now a Group Three on her only three outings, there is plenty more improvement in her and she could well be a Cup horse next year. (2/1: 5/4-9/4)
**3711 Time Allowed**, who was very warm beforehand, went to post keenly. When sent in pursuit of the winner, she tried hard, but could make no impression. (7/2)
**3689 Beauchamp Jade** travelled strongly but, with the winner stepping up the gallop in front, she had to be pushed along once in line for home. It was clear two furlongs out that she was no match. (7/2)
**3688 Russian Snows (IRE)**, who looked very lean beforehand, was flat out early in the straight and dropped away over a furlong out. (11/4)

## 4115 DONCASTER BLOODSTOCK SALES SCARBROUGH STKS (Listed) (Class A)

3-40 (3-41) **5f** £11,267.60 (£4,168.40: £1,999.20: £816.00: £323.00: £125.80) Stalls: High GOING minus 0.22 sec per fur (GF)

| | | | SP | RR | SF |
|---|---|---|---|---|---|
| 2114[17] | **Anzio (IRE) (108)** (MissGayKelleway) **5-9-12b** RCochrane(6) (lw: sn pushed along: hdwy & swtchd lft 1f out: fin fast to ld post)..........— | **1** | 14/1 | 109 | 67 |
| 3875[7] | **Amazing Bay (97)** (IABalding) **3-9-1** LDettori(3) (trckd ldrs: effrt over 1f out: rdn to ld wl ins fnl f: jst ct) ..........hd | **2** | 14/1 | 99 | 56 |
| 3875[4] | **Brave Edge (103)** (RHannon) **5-9-10** KFallon(8) (lw: sn outpcd & pushed along: hdwy over 1f out: r.o wl towards fin)..........s.h | **3** | 8/1 | 107 | 65 |
| 3693* | **Blue Iris (103)** (MAJarvis) **3-9-1** PatEddery(7) (w ldrs: chal over 1f out: rdn & nt qckn ins fnl f) ..........½ | **4** | 13/8 1 | 97 | 54 |
| 4101* | **Croft Pool (104)** (JAGlover) **5-9-7** SDWilliams(2) (lw: sn pushed along: hdwy to ld over 1f out: hdd wl ins fnl f) ..........hd | **5** | 13/2 3 | 102 | 60 |

3132[3] **Speed On (103)** (HCandy) **3-9-6** CRutter(5) (lw: hld up: effrt over 1f out: kpt on: nvr rchd ldrs)........................¾ **6** 13/2[3] 99 56
3875* **Lucky Parkes (100)** (JBerry) **6-9-2** JCarroll(1) (lw: sn led: hdd over 1f out: kpt on same pce) ..........................½ **7** 6/1[2] 93 51
3759[5] **Westcourt Magic (108)** (MWEasterby) **3-9-9** JReid(9) (lw: led early: w ldrs tl wknd over 1f out)..............2½ **8** 12/1 93 50
3875[3] **Fond Embrace (95)** (HCandy) **3-9-1** GCarter(4) (chsd ldrs tl wknd over 1f out) ..........................................2½ **9** 8/1 77 34
(SP 122.3%) **9 Rn**

**59.8 secs** (1.40) CSF £168.12 TOTE £13.20: £2.50 £4.30 £2.60 (£67.70) Trio £337.80 OWNER Mr Tommy Staunton (WHITCOMBE) BRED Rathduff Stud

WEIGHT FOR AGE 3yo-1lb

**IN-FOCUS: The suspicion was that the leaders went too fast for their own good here.**

**2114 Anzio (IRE)**, absent since running below expectations in the Wokingham, looked to have it all on under topweight. Forced to wait for an opening, he came flying through to get up on the line. (14/1)

**3495 Amazing Bay**, happy to get a lead, responded to pressure to lead inside the last 50 yards, only to have the prize whipped from under her nose. This was probably her best ever effort. (14/1)

**3875 Brave Edge**, who likes to come from off a strong pace, put in some sterling work in the final furlong and, in the end, just failed to get there. (8/1)

**3693* Blue Iris** travelled strongly up with the pace, but was treading water in the last 100 yards. Considering the pace the leaders went, this was probably a good effort. (13/8)

**4101* Croft Pool**, having his second outing in two days, struggled slightly to go the pace. After taking it up on the wide outside, he was going up and down in the same place in the final 75 yards. (13/2)

**3132 Speed On** tracked the leaders, looking to be travelling comfortably but, when called on for his effort, he could only stay on at the same pace. Some give underfoot will not come amiss. (13/2)

**3875* Lucky Parkes**, put in last as usual, seemed to set a tremendous pace and had no more to give in the final furlong. (6/1)

**3759 Westcourt Magic**, edgy beforehand, flew out of the traps, but dropped away over a furlong out. He does not seem to be progressing at all. (12/1)

## 4116 TOTE-PORTLAND H'CAP (0-110) (3-Y.O+) (Class B)

4-10 (4-14) **5f 140y** £17,316.00 (£6,444.00: £3,122.00: £1,310.00: £555.00: £253.00) Stalls: High GOING minus 0.22 sec per fur (GF)

SP RR SF

1975[5] **Musical Season (84)** (TDBarron) **4-8-5** KDarley(16) (lw: mde all stands' side: rdn 2f out: r.o wl)....................— **1** 33/1 94 57
3232[15] **Sylva Paradise (IRE) (91)** (CEBrittain) **3-8-10** BDoyle(14) (chsd ldrs far side: effrt over 1f out: r.o)................1¼ **2** 16/1 98 59
3984[4] **Lago Di Varano (85)** (RMWhitaker) **4-8-6v** DeanMcKeown(19) (dwlt: bhd tl hdwy 2f out: r.o ins fnl f) ............s.h **3** 10/1[3] 91 54
3946[7] **Tedburrow (90)** (MrsAMNaughton) **4-8-11** JCarroll(17) (a chsng ldrs: drvn along 2f out: styd on) ....................½ **4** 14/1 95 58
3622[4] **Bolshoi (IRE) (89)** (JBerry) **4-8-10b** EmmaO'Gorman(22) (s.i.s: hdwy & swtchd centre ½-wy: nt qckn appr fnl f) ...................................................................................................nk **5** 14/1 93 56
3810[3] **For the Present (84)** (TDBarron) **6-8-2**(3) FLynch(11) (hdwy far side ½-wy: r.o u.p fnl f).............................hd **6** 14/1 88 51
3910a[3] **Bold Effort (FR) (83)** (KOCunningham-Brown) **4-8-4v** RCochrane(4) (chsd ldrs far side: led over 1f out: r.o).nk **7** 12/1 86 49
3783[11] **Ansellman (83)** (JBerry) **6-8-4v** GCarter(15) (swtchd rt s: sn chsng ldrs: kpt on same pce fnl 2f)....................hd **8** 25/1 86 49
3783[5] **Sir Joey (USA) (88)** (PGMurphy) **7-8-9** SDrowne(2) (hdwy far side ½-wy: styd on fnl f)...................................¾ **9** 12/1 89 52
3693[15] **Midnight Escape (94)** (CFWall) **3-8-13** NCarlisle(3) (led far side tl over 1f out: kpt on)..................................hd **10** 20/1 94 55
3672[11] **Saint Express (83)** (MrsMReveley) **6-8-4** ACulhane(20) (lw: s.i.s: bhd tl styd on appr fnl f) .........................hd **11** 10/1[3] 83 46
*3953** **Sea-Deer (88)** (CADwyer) **7-8-9** LDettori(18) (lw: bhd: sme hdwy over 1f out: n.d) ...........................................nk **12** 8/1[2] 87 50
3984[9] **Sea Dane (105)** (PWHarris) **3-9-10** KFallon(8) (b: lw: s.s: hdwy far side whn nt clr run over 1f out: styd on towards fin).................................................................................................s.h **13** 33/1 104 65
3622[7] **Perryston View (83)** (PCalver) **4-8-4** MBirch(6) (chsd ldrs far side tl rdn & wknd 2f out).............................1¼ **14** 16/1 78 41
3875[6] **That Man Again (94)** (GLewis) **4-9-1b** PatEddery(7) (lw: w ldrs far side tl wknd fnl f)........................................s.h **15** 10/1[3] 89 52
3672[18] **Tiler (IRE) (84)** (MJohnston) **4-8-5** MHills(21) (chsd ldrs tl wknd 2f out)................................................................1¾ **16** 25/1 74 37
3946[12] **Double Quick (IRE) (95)** (MJohnston) **4-9-2** JReid(13) (racd far side: nvr nr ldrs).............................................1¼ **17** 33/1 82 45
3984[8] **Rushcutter Bay (88)** (TTClement) **3-8-2**(5) GFaulkner(12) (sn in tch far side: rdn ½-wy: sn btn) ......................1½ **18** 25/1 71 32
3984[2] **Cyrano's Lad (IRE) (97)** (CADwyer) **7-9-4** WRSwinburn(10) (lw: w ldrs far side tl lost pl 2f out: eased).........2½ **19** 4/1[1] 72 35
*3953*[11] **Lady Sheriff (83)** (RHollinshead) **5-7-11b**(7) KSked(9) (mid div far side: effrt ½-wy: sn wknd) ..........................nk **20** 25/1 58 21
3875[9] **High Priority (IRE) (90)** (MRChannon) **3-8-9** RPerham(1) (lw: racd far side: eased fnl 2f)................................14 **21** 33/1 25 —
(SP 137.4%) **21 Rn**

**1m 7.94** (0.94) CSF £463.82 CT £5,102.22 TOTE £36.10: £8.60 £5.20 £2.30 £4.00 (£751.80) Trio £2,829.80 OWNER Mr P. D. Savill (THIRSK) BRED G. R. and B. Davies

WEIGHT FOR AGE 3yo-2lb

**1975 Musical Season**, who has taken time to get his confidence back after injury, looked in good trim, despite an absence of three months. Forcing the pace on the stands' side, he scored in decisive fashion in the end. (33/1)

**3038 Sylva Paradise (IRE)**, absent since disappointing in the Stewards' Cup, probably ran right up to his best. (16/1)

**3984 Lago Di Varano** lost more ground at the start than he was eventually beaten by. (10/1)

**3038 Tedburrow** ran a genuine race over his best trip. (14/1)

**3622 Bolshoi (IRE)** tried to come from last to first as usual. Drawn on the stands' rail, he had to switch up the centre to find room to make his effort. (14/1)

**3810 For the Present**, who gave a problem or two in the stalls, did best of those racing on the far side. (14/1)

**3910a Bold Effort (FR)**, back on home soil, has slipped down the weights. (12/1)

**3672 Saint Express** again hinted at a return to form, putting in his best work at the finish after missing the break slightly. (10/1)

**2332* Sea Dane**, who benefited from Iktamal's disqualification at Newcastle in June, has run poorly on his three subsequent starts. Giving away ground at the start, he was making real inroads when running out of room over a furlong out. Sticking on again at the finish, he is one to keep an eye on. (33/1)

## 4117 LEGER RADIO LIMITED STKS (0-80) (3-Y.O) (Class D)

4-40 (4-44) **1m 2f 60y** £4,425.00 (£1,320.00: £630.00: £285.00) Stalls: Low GOING minus 0.22 sec per fur (GF)

SP RR SF

3248[5] **Oops Pettie (78)** (MrsJCecil) **3-8-10** WRSwinburn(1) (lw: hld up: stdy hdwy over 3f out: led over 1f out: r.o strly).......................................................................................................— **1** 11/2[3] 85 69
2033[3] **Trojan Risk (78)** (GLewis) **3-8-13** PatEddery(5) (b: s.i.s: hld up: effrt & swtchd rt 2f out: styd on ins fnl f: no ch w wnr)...............................................................................................3½ **2** 4/1[1] 83 67
3791[11] **Infamous (USA) (79)** (PFICole) **3-8-13** WCarson(10) (hld up: effrt over 3f out: rdn & one pce fnl f)................1¾ **3** 16/1 80 64
3923[8] **Bowled Over (79)** (CACyzer) **3-8-13** KFallon(4) (in tch: sn pushed along: styd on fnl 2f).................................1 **4** 20/1 78 62

| | | | | SP | RR | SF |
|---|---|---|---|---|---|---|
| 3806$^{2}$ | **Maid For Baileys (IRE) (78)** (MJohnston) **3-8-8** JReid(7) (trckd ldr: led over 3f out: hdd over 1f out: one pce) | ½ | **5** | 5/1$^{2}$ | 73 | 57 |
| *4078$^{6}$* | **Classic Flyer (IRE) (80)** (RHarris) **3-8-8** AMackay(2) (chsd ldrs: effrt & rdn 2f out: sn wknd) | 5 | **6** | 8/1 | 65 | 49 |
| 3633* | **King of Sparta (78)** (LMCumani) **3-8-13** OUrbina(3) (trckd ldrs: effrt over 3f out: wknd 2f out) | 6 | **7** | 6/1 | 60 | 44 |
| | **Dance Star (79)** (MAJarvis) **3-8-8** EmmaO'Gorman(9) (s.i.s: hld up: effrt on outside 3f out: no imp whn sltly hmpd 2f out) | 6 | **8** | 20/1 | 46 | 30 |
| 3806$^{7}$ | **Iberian Dancer (CAN) (80)** (JWHills) **3-8-10** MHills(6) (in tch: effrt over 2f out: wkng whn hmpd over 1f out) | 2 | **9** | 7/1 | 45 | 29 |
| 2943$^{5}$ | **Ailesbury Hill (USA) (66)** (PWChapple-Hyam) **3-8-8** LDettori(11) (led tl over 3f out: wknd & eased over 1f out) | 1¼ | **10** | 16/1 | 41 | 25 |
| 3926$^{10}$ | **Deadline Time (IRE) (80)** (MrsMReveley) **3-9-1** KDarley(8) (lw: hld up: effrt over 2f out: sn sltly hmpd & wknd: eased: fin lame) | 12 | **11** | 8/1 | 29 | 13 |
| | | | | (SP 122.3%) | **11 Rn** | |

**2m 8.02** (1.02) CSF £27.30 TOTE £6.50: £2.00 £1.80 £3.90 (£9.70) Trio £58.30 OWNER Mrs D. MacRae (NEWMARKET) BRED D. Macrae

**3248 Oops Pettie** really took the eye in the paddock. Ridden for speed, she showed plenty of it. A late developer, she is almost certainly a step ahead of her handicap mark. (11/2)

**2033 Trojan Risk**, absent for three months and from a stable showing real signs of a revival, fell out of the traps. Forced to switch to get a run, he stuck on to finish second best and should soon do better. (4/1)

**2905 Infamous (USA)**, with the blinkers left off, proved woefully one-paced at the business end over this trip. (16/1)

**2665a Bowled Over**, a keen-going type, ran easily his best race for some time. (20/1)

**3806 Maid For Baileys (IRE)**, runner-up eight times, looked sure to be closely involved in the finish when going on, but proved completely lacking in anything resembling finishing speed yet again when off the bridle. (5/1)

**4078 Classic Flyer (IRE)** (8/1: 6/1-9/1)

**3633* King of Sparta** (6/1: op 4/1)

**3063* Deadline Time (IRE)** looked to suffer a serious leg injury. (8/1)

T/Jkpt: Not won; £30,726.17 to Doncaster 12/9/96. T/Plpt: £2,722.00 (9.85 Tckts). T/Qdpt: £716.50 (2.69 Tckts). WG

# 3826-EPSOM (L-H) (Good to firm)
## Wednesday September 11th

WEATHER: sunny WIND: almost nil

## 4118 LANGLEY VALE MEDIAN AUCTION MAIDEN STKS (2-Y.O) (Class E)

2-10 (2-10) **7f** £3,127.50 (£945.00: £460.00: £217.50) Stalls: Low GOING minus 0.29 sec per fur (GF)

| | | | | SP | RR | SF |
|---|---|---|---|---|---|---|
| 3615$^{2}$ | **Shii-Take** (RAkehurst) **2-9-0** SSanders(1) (lw: jinked s: mde all: pushed out) | — | **1** | 4/6$^{1}$ | 92+ | 32 |
| | **Supply And Demand** (GLMoore) **2-9-0** SWhitworth(4) (w'like: s.s: hdwy on ins over 3f out: chsd wnr over 2f out: r.o: bttr for r) | 3 | **2** | 12/1 | 85+ | 25 |
| 3695$^{2}$ | **Another Night (IRE)** (RHannon) **2-9-0** DaneO'Neill(7) (lw: rdn & hdwy 2f out: r.o one pce) | 4 | **3** | 11/2$^{2}$ | 76 | 16 |
| 3964$^{3}$ | **Heart of Armor** (PFICole) **2-9-0** TQuinn(6) (lw: a.p: chsd wnr over 3f out tl over 2f out: wandered: one pce) | ½ | **4** | 9/1 | 75 | 15 |
| 3494$^{6}$ | **Sudest (IRE)** (IABalding) **2-8-9**(5) MartinDwyer(5) (s.s: hdwy over 2f out: one pce) | nk | **5** | 25/1 | 74 | 14 |
| 3494$^{5}$ | **Amyas (IRE)** (BWHills) **2-8-9**(5) JDSmith(3) (bhd fnl 3f) | 2½ | **6** | 13/2$^{3}$ | 69 | 9 |
| 3475$^{10}$ | **Sea Mist (IRE)** (PWChapple-Hyam) **2-8-6**(3) RHavlin(2) (lw: chsd wnr over 1f: wknd 3f out) | nk | **7** | 33/1 | 63 | 3 |
| 3407$^{12}$ | **Swift** (MJPolglase) **2-9-0** GDuffield(9) (lw: chsd wnr over 5f out tl over 3f out: wknd over 2f out) | 7 | **8** | 50/1 | 52 | — |
| 2600$^{5}$ | **Palisander (IRE) (77)** (SDow) **2-9-0** WRyan(8) (prom over 3f) | 8 | **9** | 25/1 | 34 | — |
| | | | | (SP 119.0%) | **9 Rn** | |

**1m 23.63** (3.33) CSF £9.88 TOTE £1.60: £1.10 £1.10 £1.30 (£6.40) Trio £10.70 OWNER Mr Clive Batt (EPSOM) BRED Alan Coogan

**3615 Shii-Take** confirmed the promise of his first two runs with a pillar-to-post victory. (4/6)

**Supply And Demand**, a plain-looking gelding, made a promising debut. Taking second place over two furlongs from home, he was given one or two gentle reminders and kept on in very pleasing style. Sure to have learnt a lot from this, he can find an ordinary maiden. (12/1)

**3695 Another Night (IRE)** struggled on in the final quarter-mile to snatch third prize, but never threatened the front two. He needs a mile. (11/2: op 3/1)

**3964 Heart of Armor** failed to handle the switch-back track last week at Brighton, so it was rather surprising to see him brought here. He again looked ill-at-ease, but nevertheless showed in second place for a brief time early in the straight, before wandering around and failing to quicken. He needs a more conventional course. (9/1: 6/1-10/1)

**3494 Sudest (IRE)** made an effort over a quarter of a mile from home, but could then only tread water. (25/1)

**3494 Amyas (IRE)** (13/2: 5/1-8/1)

## 4119 GERALD EVE H'CAP (0-90) (3-Y.O+) (Class C)

2-45 (2-45) **5f** £5,394.00 (£1,632.00: £796.00: £378.00) Stalls: High GOING minus 0.29 sec per fur (GF)

| | | | | SP | RR | SF |
|---|---|---|---|---|---|---|
| 3932$^{11}$ | **Tuscan Dawn (74)** (JBerry) **6-8-7**(5) PRoberts(6) (swtg: chsd ldr: rdn over 1f out: led wl ins fnl f: r.o wl) | — | **1** | 12/1 | 81 | 54 |
| 3993$^{9}$ | **Tart and a Half (71)** (BJMeehan) **4-8-9b** MTebbutt(8) (hrd rdn over 1f out: hdwy fnl f: r.o wl) | ½ | **2** | 7/1 | 76 | 49 |
| 3827* | **Portelet (83)** (RGuest) **4-9-7** PBloomfield(4) (led: rdn over 1f out: hdd wl ins fnl f: r.o) | hd | **3** | 9/4$^{1}$ | 88 | 61 |
| 3827$^{3}$ | **Midnight Spell (68)** (JWHills) **4-8-3**(3) MHenry(5) (hld up: swtchd lft over 2f out: one pce) | 1¾ | **4** | 6/1$^{3}$ | 68 | 41 |
| 3827$^{7}$ | **Twice as Sharp (90)** (PWHarris) **4-10-0** GHind(7) (lw: hld up: rdn over 2f out: one pce) | s.h | **5** | 12/1 | 89 | 62 |
| 3864* | **La Belle Dominique (58)** (SGKnight) **4-7-10** FNorton(2) (b.off hind: a.p: rdn over 2f out: ev ch over 1f out: wknd ins fnl f) | 1¼ | **6** | 12/1 | 53 | 26 |
| 2143$^{12}$ | **Tarf (USA) (85)** (PTWalwyn) **3-9-8** RHills(9) (lw: swtchd lft & hdwy over 1f out: wknd ins fnl f) | 2 | **7** | 10/1 | 74 | 46 |
| 3827$^{2}$ | **Youdontsay (83)** (TJNaughton) **4-9-7** DaneO'Neill(3) (dwlt: a bhd) | 4 | **8** | 5/1$^{2}$ | 59 | 32 |
| | | | | (SP 106.4%) | **8 Rn** | |

**55.37 secs** (0.87) CSF £77.38 CT £199.55 TOTE £14.10: £2.80 £1.40 £1.60 (£22.10) Trio £25.30 OWNER Mrs Chris Deuters (COCKERHAM) BRED F. Hines

LONG HANDICAP La Belle Dominique 7-8

WEIGHT FOR AGE 3yo-1lb

STEWARDS' ENQUIRY Norton susp: 20-21/9/96 (excessive use of whip)

**3827 Tuscan Dawn** bounced back to form. Racing in second place, he was shaken up below the distance and managed to get on top in the last 50 yards. (12/1)

**3827 Tart and a Half** had the blinkers back on here, but still looks a difficult ride. Nevertheless, she picked up ground well in the final furlong to snatch second prize in the dying strides. She has a very poor wins-to-runs ratio and should be left alone. (7/1)

**3827* Portelet**, who beat the winner nearly seven lengths here recently, failed to confirm the form on 4lb worse terms. (9/4)
**3827 Midnight Spell**, switched to the outside at halfway, failed to find the necessary turn of foot. (6/1)
**2694 Twice as Sharp** is high in the handicap at present as he was rated 90 here, but is yet to win off more than 84. (12/1: op 8/1)
**3864* La Belle Dominique** regained the losing thread and, after having every chance below the distance, tired in the last 100 yards. (12/1: 7/1-14/1)

## 4120 CHALK LANE RATED STKS H'CAP (0-105) (3-Y.O+) (Class B)

3-20 (3-21) **1m 2f 18y** £7,543.80 (£2,824.20: £1,382.10: £595.50: £267.75: £136.65) Stalls: Low GOING minus 0.29 sec per fur (GF)

| | | | | SP | RR | SF |
|---|---|---|---|---|---|---|
| 3947* | **Ninia (USA) (85)** (MJohnston) **4-8-10** RHills(7) (lw: chsd ldr: led over 3f out: clr 2f out: comf) | — | **1** | 5/1$^{1}$ | 102+ | 63 |
| 3691$^{5}$ | **Clan Ben (IRE) (96)** (HRACecil) **4-9-7** WRyan(8) (lw: rdn & hdwy on ins over 3f out: nt clr run on ins over 1f out: r.o one pce) | 6 | **2** | 11/2$^{2}$ | 104 | 65 |
| 3791$^{3}$ | **Double Bluff (IRE) (90)** (IABalding) **3-8-3**(5) MartinDwyer(1) (lw: led over 6f: rdn: one pce) | hd | **3** | 7/1$^{3}$ | 97 | 51 |
| 3923$^{3}$ | **Champagne Prince (88)** (PWHarris) **3-8-6** GHind(2) (a.p: rdn over 3f out: one pce) | 2 | **4** | 15/2 | 92 | 46 |
| 3766$^{3}$ | **Diminutive (USA) (85)** (JWHills) **3-8-0**(3) MHenry(5) (lw: hdwy over 3f out: rdn over 2f out: one pce) | hd | **5** | 12/1 | 89 | 43 |
| 3791$^{12}$ | **Major Change (90)** (RHannon) **4-9-1** DaneO'Neill(3) (a.p: rdn over 3f out: one pce) | ¾ | **6** | 16/1 | 93 | 54 |
| 3709$^{6}$ | **Star Manager (USA) (86)** (PFICole) **6-8-11** TQuinn(4) (nvr nrr) | 3½ | **7** | 10/1 | 83 | 44 |
| 1520$^{8}$ | **Tremplin (USA) (90)** (NACallaghan) **4-9-1** GDuffield(11) (s.s: a bhd) | 1¾ | **8** | 33/1 | 85 | 46 |
| 3791$^{4}$ | **Bardon Hill Boy (IRE) (92)** (BHanbury) **4-9-3** JStack(9) (bhd fnl 3f) | 1 | **9** | 8/1 | 85 | 46 |
| 3947$^{10}$ | **Hardy Dancer (87)** (GLMoore) **4-8-12** SWhitworth(10) (lw: bhd fnl 4f) | 21 | **10** | 11/2$^{2}$ | 47 | 8 |
| 3594$^{10}$ | **Wot No Fax (89)** (SDow) **3-8-7** SSanders(6) (lw: hdwy 8f out: wknd 5f out: t.o) | 20 | **11** | 16/1 | 17 | — |
| | | | | (SP 114.3%) | **11 Rn** | |

**2m 5.37** (0.97) CSF £29.60 CT £174.40 TOTE £4.20: £2.00 £2.10 £2.60 (£10.30) Trio £34.80 OWNER Mrs D. R. Schreiber (MIDDLEHAM) BRED Newgate Stud Farm Inc
WEIGHT FOR AGE 3yo-7lb
**OFFICIAL EXPLANATION Hardy Dancer: finished distressed.**
**Wot No Fax: travelled badly down the hill, and the rider, fearing something was amiss, allowed him to come home in his own time.**
**3947* Ninia (USA)** completed the hat-trick in emphatic style, despite another rise in the weights. Going on entering the straight, she forged clear a quarter of a mile from home to win with a ton in hand. The Handicapper will not be pleased with this. (5/1: op 3/1)
**3691 Clan Ben (IRE)** picked up ground along the inside rail turning into the straight. He did not have a clear run below the distance, but this made little difference to his chances, although he did stay on to snatch second prize in the last couple of strides. (11/2)
**3791 Double Bluff (IRE)**, collared over three furlongs from home, could then only go up and down in the same place. (7/1)
**3923 Champagne Prince** was made to look very one-paced in the straight. (15/2)
**3766 Diminutive (USA)**, who failed to handle the easy ground last time, took closer order entering the straight, but could then only tread water. (12/1)
**1961* Major Change** was made to look very pedestrian in the straight. (16/1)

## 4121 SOUTHERN MOBILE H'CAP (0-85) (3-Y.O+) (Class D)

3-50 (3-55) **1m 4f 10y** £4,357.50 (£1,320.00: £645.00: £307.50) Stalls: Low GOING minus 0.29 sec per fur (GF)

| | | | | SP | RR | SF |
|---|---|---|---|---|---|---|
| 3997$^{3}$ | **Dear Life (USA) (82)** (MrsJCecil) **3-9-6**(5) MartinDwyer(7) (lw: hdwy 9f out: led 3f out: clr 2 out: r.o wl) | — | **1** | 9/2$^{2}$ | 95+ | 68 |
| 3876$^{3}$ | **Shining Dancer (60)** (SDow) **4-8-12** WRyan(3) (hld up: hrd rdn over 2f out: chsd wnr ins fnl f: r.o one pce) | 3½ | **2** | 13/2$^{3}$ | 68 | 50 |
| 3802$^{2}$ | **Strat's Legacy (44)** (DWPArbuthnot) **9-7-7**(3) MHenry(5) (hdwy over 3f out: chsd wnr over 2f out tl ins fnl f: one pce) | 1¼ | **3** | 20/1 | 51 | 33 |
| 4073$^{9}$ | **Loki (IRE) (72)** (GLewis) **8-9-7**(3) AWhelan(10) (lw: stdy hdwy over 3f out: rdn over 2f out: one pce) | 3 | **4** | 10/1 | 75 | 57 |
| 3828$^{4}$ | **Artic Bay (64)** (MrsPNDutfield) **4-9-2** TSprake(13) (hdwy over 5f out: wknd over 1f out) | hd | **5** | 12/1 | 67 | 49 |
| 3272$^{5}$ | **Apollono (74)** (JRFanshawe) **4-9-12** NDay(12) (rdn over 3f out: hdwy over 1f out: nvr nrr) | 1¾ | **6** | 8/1 | 74 | 56 |
| 3944$^{4}$ | **Rising Dough (IRE) (70)** (GLMoore) **4-9-8** SSanders(11) (lw: hdwy over 4f out: wknd 2f out) | 5 | **7** | 10/1 | 64 | 46 |
| 3947$^{19}$ | **Early Peace (IRE) (65)** (MJPolglase) **4-9-3** MRimmer(8) (b.off hind: lw: rdn over 3f out: nvr nrr) | 1¼ | **8** | 33/1 | 57 | 39 |
| 3991$^{10}$ | **Easy Choice (USA) (55)** (PMitchell) **4-8-7** JQuinn(6) (a bhd) | 1 | **9** | 33/1 | 46 | 28 |
| 3947$^{12}$ | **Filial (IRE) (82)** (GHarwood) **3-9-11** RHills(1) (lw: prom over 8f) | 1½ | **10** | 10/1 | 71 | 44 |
| 3828$^{10}$ | **Proton (69)** (RAkehurst) **6-9-7** TQuinn(4) (lw: a.p: ev ch 3f out: wkng whn hmpd on ins over 2f out) | 7 | **11** | 4/1$^{1}$ | 48 | 30 |
| 3235$^{4}$ | **Shaha (70)** (RHannon) **3-8-13b** DaneO'Neill(2) (lw: led 9f) | 4 | **12** | 10/1 | 44 | 17 |
| 3923$^{6}$ | **Ski Academy (IRE) (84)** (PWChapple-Hyam) **3-9-10**(3) RHavlin(9) (lw: prom over 6f) | 1½ | **13** | 25/1 | 56 | 29 |
| | | | | (SP 121.2%) | **13 Rn** | |

**2m 37.77** (2.77) CSF £32.11 CT £488.18 TOTE £4.40: £2.60 £1.90 £4.40 (£13.20) Trio £62.30 OWNER Lady Howard de Walden (NEWMARKET) BRED Lord Howard de Walden
LONG HANDICAP Strat's Legacy 7-7
WEIGHT FOR AGE 3yo-9lb
**3997 Dear Life (USA)**, who ran well in a Class B Handicap last week, appreciated the drop in class and scooted up. (9/2)
**3876 Shining Dancer**, struggling on in the straight, eventually managed to take second place inside the final furlong. (13/2)
**3802 Strat's Legacy** began a forward move from the back of the field entering the straight and was soon in second place. However, he never looked like reeling in the winner and was caught for the runner-up berth inside the final furlong. (20/1)
**4073 Loki (IRE)**, making a quick reappearance, steadily weaved his way through the field running down Tattenham Hill, but failed to find another gear in the last two furlongs. (10/1: 8/1-12/1)
**3828 Artic Bay** had come to the end of his tether below the distance. (12/1: 10/1-16/1)
**3272 Apollono**, who did not handle Tattenham Corner very well, stayed on in the last furlong and a half without posing a threat. (8/1: 6/1-9/1)
**3505* Filial (IRE)** (10/1: 8/1-12/1)
**3235 Shaha** (10/1: 8/1-12/1)

## 4122 RUBBING HOUSE CONDITIONS STKS (3-Y.O+) (Class C)

4-20 (4-23) **6f** £4,645.60 (£1,740.40: £852.70: £368.50: £166.75: £86.05) Stalls: High GOING minus 0.29 sec per fur (GF)

| | | | | SP | RR | SF |
|---|---|---|---|---|---|---|
| 3618$^{5}$ | **Selhurstpark Flyer (IRE) (88)** (JBerry) **5-8-7**(5) PRoberts(8) (b: mde all: rdn out) | — | **1** | 11/1 | 100+ | 55 |
| 3672$^{3}$ | **Marl (89)** (RAkehurst) **3-8-5** SSanders(5) (rdn over 3f out: hdwy over 1f out: r.o one pce) | 2½ | **2** | 7/2$^{1}$ | 88 | 41 |
| 3596$^{8}$ | **Green Perfume (USA) (106)** (PFICole) **4-9-12** TQuinn(7) (lw: chsd wnr over 4f out: rdn over 2f out: one pce) | nk | **3** | 7/2$^{1}$ | 107 | 62 |
| 3445$^{12}$ | **Defined Feature (IRE) (94)** (MRStoute) **3-8-5** WRyan(2) (lw: lost pl over 3f out: rallied fnl f: r.o) | nk | **4** | 10/1$^{3}$ | 87 | 40 |

| | | | | SP | RR | SF |
|---|---|---|---|---|---|---|
| 3517[3] | **Loch Patrick (105)** (MMadgwick) **6-9-4** DHarrison(3) (lw: rdn over 3f out: hdwy fnl f: nvr nrr) | nk | **5** | 4/1[2] | 97 | 52 |
| 3920[6] | **Prends Ca (IRE) (86)** (RHannon) **3-8-2b[1]**(3) AWhelan(10) (hld up: rdn over 2f out: one pce) | ½ | **6** | 12/1 | 85 | 38 |
| 3984[11] | **Tropical Dance (USA) (93)** (MrsJCecil) **3-8-0**(5) MartinDwyer(9) (lw: rdn over 3f out: hdwy over 1f out: one pce) | hd | **7** | 14/1 | 84 | 37 |
| 3612[6] | **Shamanic (86)** (RHannon) **4-8-12** DaneO'Neill(4) (lw: s.s: a bhd) | 2½ | **8** | 12/1 | 83 | 38 |
| 3524[8] | **Amaniy (USA) (94)** (HThomsonJones) **3-8-5** RHills(1) (chsd wnr over 1f: wknd over 3f out) | 7 | **9** | 25/1 | 59 | 12 |

(SP 107.8%) **9 Rn**

**1m 9.06** (1.06) CSF £43.38 TOTE £7.90: £1.70 £1.10 £1.70 (£13.60) Trio £13.10 OWNER Mr Chris Deuters (COCKERHAM) BRED Gay O'Callaghan

WEIGHT FOR AGE 3yo-2lb

**3618 Selhurstpark Flyer (IRE)** made every post a winning one and, ridden along, kept on too strongly for his rivals. (11/1)

**3672 Marl**, struggling to go with the pace, stayed on in the last furlong and a half to snatch second prize. (7/2)

**3596 Green Perfume (USA)** was unable to dominate on this occasion and did not look entirely happy about it. Ridden along over a quarter of a mile from home, he failed to get the better of the winner and was run out of second place in the last few strides. (7/2)

**2919 Defined Feature (IRE)** got outpaced rounding Tattenham Corner, but did stay on again in the final furlong. (10/1)

**3517 Loch Patrick**, unable to go the pace, was doing all his best work in the final furlong. (4/1)

**3920 Prends Ca (IRE)**, fitted with blinkers for the first time, chased the leaders, but never looked like quickening up in the last two furlongs. (12/1)

**3612 Shamanic** (12/1: 8/1-14/1)

## 4123 E.B.F. MAIDEN STKS (2-Y.O) (Class D)

4-50 (4-51) **6f** £3,550.00 (£1,075.00: £525.00: £250.00) Stalls: High GOING minus 0.29 sec per fur (GF)

| | | | | SP | RR | SF |
|---|---|---|---|---|---|---|
| 3114[3] | **Cryhavoc (82)** (JRArnold) **2-9-0** DHarrison(3) (a.p: hrd rdn over 1f out: led ins fnl f: r.o wl) | — | **1** | 10/1 | 76 | 35 |
| 3685[2] | **Test The Water (IRE) (80)** (RHannon) **2-9-0** DaneO'Neill(4) (b.nr hind: lw: a.p: rdn over 3f out: r.o ins fnl f) | 1 | **2** | 9/2[2] | 73 | 32 |
| 3593[2] | **Nopalea** (CEBrittain) **2-8-6**(3) MHenry(5) (lw: led: rdn 2f out: hdd ins fnl f: unable qckn) | ½ | **3** | 3/1[1] | 67 | 26 |
| 3206[4] | **Zaima (IRE)** (JLDunlop) **2-8-9** TSprake(10) (lw: rdn over 2f out: hdwy & edgd lft over 1f out: 4th whn nt clr run ins fnl f) | 1¼ | **4** | 10/1 | 64 | 23 |
| 3695[5] | **Around Fore Alliss** (TGMills) **2-9-0** GHind(6) (lw: hdwy 3f out: hdwy over 1f out: nvr nrr) | 3 | **5** | 20/1 | 61 | 20 |
| 3919[3] | **Count Roberto (USA)** (PWChapple-Hyam) **2-8-11**(3) RHavlin(16) (lw: hld up: rdn over 3f out: one pce) | 2 | **6** | 10/1 | 55 | 14 |
| 3807[9] | **Contentment (IRE)** (JWHills) **2-9-0** RHills(14) (bmpd s: no hdwy fnl 3f) | 3 | **7** | 8/1 | 47 | 6 |
| | **Swinging The Blues (IRE)** (RAkehurst) **2-9-0** TQuinn(13) (str: scope: dwlt & bmpd s: outpcd: nvr nrr) | ½ | **8** | 7/1[3] | 46 | 5 |
| 3581[4] | **Hever Golf Mover** (TJNaughton) **2-8-9** AMcGlone(9) (outpcd: nvr nrr) | nk | **9** | 25/1 | 40 | — |
| 3259[9] | **V I P Charlie** (JRJenkins) **2-9-0** SSanders(8) (lw: outpcd: nvr nrr) | 1¼ | **10** | 50/1 | 42 | 1 |
| 3963[8] | **M R Poly (55)** (MRChannon) **2-8-7**(7) AEddery(7) (lw: prom 2f) | nk | **11** | 50/1 | 41 | — |
| 3485[6] | **Secret Pass (USA)** (EALDunlop) **2-9-0** WRyan(2) (lw: a bhd) | ½ | **12** | 25/1 | 40 | — |
| 3502[6] | **Stock Hill Dancer** (KRBurke) **2-8-9** JQuinn(1) (prom over 1f) | ¾ | **13** | 25/1 | 33 | — |
| 3829[5] | **Right Man** (GLewis) **2-9-0** SWhitworth(11) (s.s & hmpd s: a bhd) | ½ | **14** | 25/1 | 36 | — |
| 3685[17] | **Marengo** (JAkehurst) **2-9-0v** GDuffield(15) (swvd lft s: chsd wnr 3f: rdn over 2f out: rel to r fnl 2f) | 3½ | **15** | 20/1 | 27 | — |

(SP 122.9%) **15 Rn**

**1m 10.59** (2.59) CSF £51.64 TOTE £20.30: £4.20 £1.40 £1.80 (£40.90) Trio £14.40 OWNER Mr A. H. Robinson (UPPER LAMBOURN) BRED Al Dahlawi Stud Co Ltd

**3114 Cryhavoc** came under pressure below the distance and managed to get on top inside the final furlong. (10/1: 8/1-12/1)

**3685 Test The Water (IRE)** had to settle for being the bridesmaid for the third successive time. An extra furlong may help him break his duck. (9/2)

**3593 Nopalea** was overhauled inside the final furlong. She can find a small maiden. (3/1)

**3206 Zaima (IRE)** did not look entirely happy on this tricky course and drifted over to the rail when picking up ground below the distance. She was staying on nicely when failing to get a clear run in the closing stages, and looks one to note. (10/1: 8/1-12/1)

**3919 Count Roberto (USA)** (10/1: 8/1-12/1)

**3685 Marengo** had the headgear back on but, once again, looked thoroughly ungenuine. He should be avoided at all costs. (20/1)

## 4124 DOWNS MAIDEN STKS (3-Y.O) (Class D)

5-20 (5-20) **1m 114y** £3,566.25 (£1,080.00: £527.50: £251.25) Stalls: Low GOING minus 0.29 sec per fur (GF)

| | | | | SP | RR | SF |
|---|---|---|---|---|---|---|
| 3935[3] | **Supamova (USA) (80)** (PFICole) **3-8-9** TQuinn(3) (lw: w ldrs: led 4f out: hrd rdn over 1f out: r.o wl) | — | **1** | 9/2[2] | 84 | 36 |
| 3790[5] | **Lucky Archer (79)** (CEBrittain) **3-9-0** WRyan(7) (lw: hdwy 4f out: rdn over 2f out: n.m.r over 1f out: swtchd rt: r.o) | ¾ | **2** | 7/1[3] | 88 | 40 |
| 3709[18] | **Axford (USA) (87)** (PWChapple-Hyam) **3-8-11**(3) RHavlin(6) (lw: led over 4f: rdn over 2f out: unable qckn fnl f) | 1¼ | **3** | 2/1[1] | 85 | 37 |
| 3123[8] | **Golden Thunderbolt (FR) (78)** (JHMGosden) **3-9-0** GHind(10) (lw: a.p: rdn over 3f out: one pce) | 1¾ | **4** | 8/1 | 82 | 34 |
| 2687[4] | **Philosopher (IRE) (78)** (RHannon) **3-9-0** DaneO'Neill(8) (lost pl 6f out: rallied fnl f: r.o one pce) | 1¾ | **5** | 10/1 | 79 | 31 |
| 3949[2] | **Yukon Hope (USA) (75)** (RCharlton) **3-8-9** TSprake(5) (lw: a.p: rdn over 2f out: eased whn btn ins fnl f) | 6 | **6** | 9/2[2] | 62 | 14 |
| 2383[8] | **El Presidente** (GPEnright) **3-8-9**(5) ADaly(4) (lw: bhd fnl 4f) | ¾ | **7** | 25/1 | 66 | 18 |
| 863[14] | **Petros Pride (55)** (MJBolton) **3-8-9** JQuinn(9) (a bhd) | 6 | **8** | 66/1 | 50 | 2 |
| 3832[9] | **Prove The Point (IRE)** (MrsPNDutfield) **3-8-9** MTebbutt(1) (lw: s.s: a bhd) | 1½ | **9** | 50/1 | 47 | — |

(SP 109.7%) **9 Rn**

**1m 45.4** (3.40) CSF £31.17 TOTE £4.00: £1.80 £2.60 £1.40 (£11.70) Trio £17.20 OWNER Mr M. Arbib (WHATCOMBE) BRED Janus Bloodstock

**3935 Supamova (USA)** appreciated the drop in distance and, after disputing the lead, was sent on rounding Tattenham Corner. Responding well to pressure, she kept on too well for her rivals. (9/2)

**3790 Lucky Archer** moved up from the rear rounding Tattenham Corner. Running on inside the final furlong, he came through to snatch second prize. (7/1)

**970 Axford (USA)** is becoming expensive to follow and the excuses are beginning to run out. (2/1)

**2572 Golden Thunderbolt (FR)** never looked like quickening up in the straight. (8/1: op 9/2)

**2687 Philosopher (IRE)** got outpaced after only a couple of furlongs, but did stay on again in the last 200 yards. (10/1: 8/1-12/1)

**3949 Yukon Hope (USA)** was never far away, but the distress signals were being sent out in the final quarter-mile and she was eased down when all chance had gone inside the last 150 yards. (9/2)

T/Plpt: £8.20 (1,751.66 Tckts). T/Qdpt: £5.50 (139.72 Tckts). AK

## 3820-CHEPSTOW (L-H) (Good to firm)
### Thursday September 12th
WEATHER: fine but cloudy WIND: mod bhd

**4125** SCANIA 4-SERIES TROPHY H'CAP (0-80) (3-Y.O+) (Class D)
2-10 (2-16) **1m 2f 36y** £4,099.00 (£1,237.00: £601.00: £283.00) GOING minus 0.54 sec per fur (F)

SP RR SF

3635[4] **Soviet Bride (IRE) (68)** (SDow) **4-8-11**(5) ADaly(8) (hld up: rdn & hdwy over 2f out: r.o wl to ld fnl stride) ......— **1** 14/1 79 45
3947[11] **Game Ploy (POL) (78)** (DHaydnJones) **4-9-12** RCochrane(2) (hld up: hdwy 2f out: nt clr run over 1f out: hrd rdn: r.o wl) ......s.h **2** 13/2[2] 89 55
3856[7] **Another Time (73)** (SPCWoods) **4-9-7** DBiggs(10) (hdwy over 4f out: led ins fnl f: hdd last stride)......s.h **3** 12/1 84 50
3944* **Roufontaine (80)** (WRMuir) **5-9-11**(3) RHavlin(11) (hld up: hdwy on ins 4f out: led wl over 1f out tl ins fnl f)......2 **4** 7/1[3] 88 54
3786[2] **Pay Homage (73)** (IABalding) **8-9-2**(5) MartinDwyer(9) (lw: rdn & hdwy over 2f out: btn whn hmpd wl ins fnl f)......1½ **5** 8/1 78 44
3496[14] **Monument (68)** (JSKing) **4-9-2** BDoyle(4) (chsd ldr: rdn over 1f out: wknd fnl f)......1¾ **6** 20/1 71 37
3785[6] **Maradata (IRE) (60)** (RHollinshead) **4-8-8** GCarter(16) (dwlt: hdwy on ins over 3f out: nt clr run over 2f out: sn wknd)......1¼ **7** 16/1 61 27
3929[2] **Apache Len (USA) (72)** (RHannon) **3-8-13b** DaneO'Neill(7) (led over 8f: hmpd over 1f out: wknd fnl f)......hd **8** 9/1 73 32
2883[10] **Danegold (IRE) (78)** (MRChannon) **4-9-5v**(7) AEddery(6) (s.s: nvr nrr)......½ **9** 20/1 78 44
650[13] **Blaze of Oak (USA) (60)** (JMBradley) **5-8-8** TSprake(12) (bkwd: plld hrd: prom over 7f)......3 **10** 33/1 55 21
3635[2] **Mister O'Grady (IRE) (54)** (RAkehurst) **5-8-2** SSanders(3) (lw: prom over 7f)......2 **11** 6/1[1] 46 12
*3627*[12] **Ethbaat (USA) (70)** (MJHeaton-Ellis) **5-9-4** SDrowne(13) (lw: a bhd)......s.h **12** 20/1 62 28
**Alltime Dancer (IRE) (59)** (OSherwood) **4-8-4**(3) MHenry(14) (bkwd: bhd fnl 2f)......1½ **13** 11/1 48 14
3825[8] **Hand of Straw (IRE) (55)** (PGMurphy) **4-8-3v** NAdams(15) (a bhd)......7 **14** 25/1 33 —
3947[5] **Bakers Daughter (54)** (JRArnold) **4-8-2** AClark(5) (prom 6f: t.o)......16 **15** 8/1 7 —

(SP 122.0%) **15 Rn**

**2m 6.7** (1.40) CSF £95.07 CT £1,046.17 TOTE £18.60: £3.50 £2.30 £4.90 (£102.10) Trio £156.20 OWNER Mr Terry Shepherd (EPSOM) BRED Gainsborough Stud Management Ltd
WEIGHT FOR AGE 3yo-7lb

**3635 Soviet Bride (IRE)** seems at her best on undulating tracks. (14/1)
**2883 Game Ploy (POL)**, 7lb higher than when completing a hat-trick in July, was only beaten by inches and may have been a shade unlucky. (13/2)
**3272* Another Time**, 3lb higher than when winning at Lingfield, was a flop in the mud last time. (12/1)
**3944* Roufontaine** had been raised another 9lb following her easy win at Sandown. (7/1)
**3786 Pay Homage** would have finished closer but for running out of room on the inside in the last 150 yards. (8/1)
**3260 Monument** was 3lb higher than when scoring by the minimum margin at Windsor in July. (20/1)
**3635 Mister O'Grady (IRE)** could not confirm the Brighton form with the winner on 2lb worse terms. (6/1)
**Alltime Dancer (IRE)** (11/1: 7/1-12/1)

**4126** SILURIAN SCANIA CONDITIONS STKS (3-Y.O F) (Class C)
2-45 (2-47) **1m 2f 36y** £4,941.00 (£1,721.00: £835.50: £352.50) GOING minus 0.54 sec per fur (F)

SP RR SF

3497[2] **Min Alhawa (USA) (101)** (MajorWRHern) **3-8-10** RHills(4) (chsd ldr: led over 3f out: qcknd clr wl over 1f out: r.o wl)......— **1** 9/4[2] 111 32
3945[2] **Miss Universal (IRE) (106)** (CEBrittain) **3-8-10** BDoyle(1) (lw: led over 6f: rdn & outpcd 2f out: rallied ins fnl f)......3½ **2** 5/6[1] 106 27
3945[8] **Obsessive (USA) (97)** (MRStoute) **3-8-10** RCochrane(2) (swtg: hld up: hdwy to chse wnr fnl 2f: no imp) ......s.h **3** 7/1[3] 105 26
3836[6] **El Opera (IRE) (96)** (PFICole) **3-8-13** SSanders(3) (lw: hld up: hdwy 4f out: rdn over 2f out: wknd over 1f out)......4 **4** 9/1 102 23

(SP 107.8%) **4 Rn**

**2m 7.7** (2.40) CSF £4.35 TOTE £3.00 (£1.90) OWNER Mr Hamdan Al Maktoum (LAMBOURN) BRED Shadwell Farm Inc
**3497 Min Alhawa (USA)** benefited from the introduction of forcing tactics. (9/4)
**3945 Miss Universal (IRE)** did not find a return to a mile and a quarter doing the trick. (5/6)
**2465a Obsessive (USA)** has not been able to reproduce her Musidora form. (7/1)
**3836 El Opera (IRE)** was the first beaten. (9/1: 9/2-10/1)

**4127** SCANIA 4-SERIES 'HORSEPOWER' MAIDEN STKS (2-Y.O) (Class D)
3-20 (3-22) **7f 16y** £3,837.50 (£1,160.00: £565.00: £267.50) GOING minus 0.54 sec per fur (F)

SP RR SF

2972[4] **Royal Amaretto (IRE)** (BJMeehan) **2-9-0** MTebbutt(6) (lw: a.p: led wl over 1f out: rdn out)......— **1** 100/30[2] 86 41
3757[3] **Blue Goblin (USA)** (LMCumani) **2-9-0** OUrbina(9) (hld up: hdwy over 2f out: ev ch fnl f: unable qckn)......½ **2** 15/8[1] 85 40
**Waterspout (USA)** (GHarwood) **2-9-0** AClark(19) (w'like: scope: s.s: swtchd lft: hdwy over 3f out: one pce fnl f)......4 **3** 10/1 76 31
3848[5] **Saffron Rose** (MBlanshard) **2-8-9** NAdams(14) (led over 5f: one pce)......1¾ **4** 20/1 67 22
3259[W] **Mara River** (IABalding) **2-8-4**(5) MartinDwyer(7) (lw: a.p: no hdwy fnl 2f)......1¼ **5** 11/1 64 19
3499[3] **American Whisper** (PWHarris) **2-9-0** GHind(13) (hdwy over 2f out: wknd over 1f out)......3½ **6** 6/1[3] 61 16
**Sellette (IRE)** (DHaydnJones) **2-8-9** RCochrane(5) (unf: scope: bkwd: s.i.s: hld up & bhd: nvr plcd to chal)...nk **7** 12/1 55 10
**Nemisto** (CEBrittain) **2-8-11**(3) MHenry(1) (unf: scope: bkwd: nvr nr to chal)......3 **8** 33/1 54 9
**Village Pub (FR)** (KOCunningham-Brown) **2-9-0** TSprake(17) (lt-f: unf: bit bkwd: prom tl n.m.r over 2f out: bttr for r)......s.h **9** 33/1 54 9
2243[5] **Soda Pop (IRE)** (CEBrittain) **2-9-0** BDoyle(18) (prom over 4f)......s.h **10** 20/1 53 8
**Avanti Blue** (KMcAuliffe) **2-9-0** JCarroll(12) (w'like: bit bkwd: prom over 4f)......1¼ **11** 33/1 51 6
3682[14] **Warring** (MRChannon) **2-9-0** RPerham(3) (prom over 4f)......3½ **12** 50/1 43 —
3988[8] **Racing Heart** (PJMakin) **2-8-9** SSanders(16) (n.d)......½ **13** 33/1 37 —
**Sadler's Blaze (IRE)** (PWHarris) **2-9-0** FNorton(8) (cmpt: bkwd: a bhd)......1¾ **14** 20/1 38 —
3787[5] **Golden Melody** (RHannon) **2-8-9** RHills(10) (a bhd)......1¾ **15** 25/1 29 —
**Rock And Reign** (PGMurphy) **2-8-9** SDrowne(20) (lt-f: unf: a bhd)......½ **16** 33/1 28 —
**Alpine Music (IRE)** (JMBradley) **2-9-0** NCarlisle(2) (w'like: leggy: bit bkwd: s.s: bhd fnl 2f)......6 **17** 50/1 19 —

| | | | | SP | RR | SF |
|---|---|---|---|---|---|---|
| | **Chief Predator (USA)** (RHannon) **2-9-0** DBiggs(15) (lt-f: bit bkwd: a bhd) | 3 | **18** | 33/1 | 12 | — |

(SP 137.0%) **18 Rn**

**1m 20.8** (0.60 under 2y best) (0.80) CSF £10.48 TOTE £4.20: £1.90 £1.60 £2.90 (£4.30) Trio £106.30 OWNER The Harlequin Partnership (UPPER LAMBOURN) BRED Patrick Doyle

**2972 Royal Amaretto (IRE)**, who has taken a little time to come to hand, held on well in the closing stages. (100/30: 6/4-7/2)
**3757 Blue Goblin (USA)** ran a sound race in defeat and is knocking on the door. (15/8)
**Waterspout (USA)**, a half-brother to mile juvenile winner Waterland, gave the impression that something may have gone amiss with his tack which makes this an even more promising debut. (10/1: 4/1-12/1)
**3848 Saffron Rose**, a half-sister to Scots Law, was stepping up from an Auction race. (20/1)
**2600 Mara River**, a half-sister to fourteen-furlong winner Arrastra, gives the impression that whatever she does this year will be a bonus. (11/1: 7/1-12/1)
**3499 American Whisper** has not progressed from his debut on this evidence but is another who is bred not to come into his own until next season. (6/1: op 4/1)
**Sellette (IRE)**, a half-sister to Irish listed winner Dashing Colours, was given a nice introduction and this kindness will be repaid. (12/1: 7/1-14/1)
**Village Pub (FR)** ran much better than his finishing position suggests and is really bred to be a sprinter. (33/1)

## 4128 SCANIA 1996 TRUCK OF THE YEAR TROPHY H'CAP (0-60) (3-Y.O+) (Class F)

3-50 (3-53) **7f 16y** £3,212.50 (£900.00: £437.50) GOING minus 0.54 sec per fur (F)

| | | | | SP | RR | SF |
|---|---|---|---|---|---|---|
| *3877** | **Speedy Classic (USA) (54)** (MJHeaton-Ellis) **7-9-8** AClark(15) (b.nr hind: mde all: clr over 1f out: r.o wl) | — | **1** | 6/1[3] | 63 | 46 |
| 3991[6] | **Dawalib (USA) (59)** (DHaydnJones) **6-9-13** SWhitworth(6) (chsd wnr: hrd rdn over 1f out: no imp) | 3 | **2** | 15/2 | 61 | 44 |
| 3789[12] | **Ivory's Grab Hire (60)** (KTIvory) **3-9-10b** DBiggs(13) (a.p: r.o one pce fnl f) | s.h | **3** | 20/1 | 62 | 41 |
| 3973[14] | **Thai Morning (60)** (PWHarris) **3-9-10** GHind(7) (lw: hdwy over 2f out: rdn over 1f out: one pce) | 1¼ | **4** | 20/1 | 59 | 38 |
| 2710[8] | **Classic Look (IRE) (55)** (MajorDNChappell) **3-9-5** GCarter(8) (b.nr fore: s.s: hdwy over 1f out: nvr nrr) | 1 | **5** | 16/1 | 52 | 31 |
| 3977[2] | **Secret Pleasure (IRE) (60)** (RHannon) **3-9-10** DaneO'Neill(2) (b.nr hind: s.s: sn rcvrd: no hdwy fnl 2f) | nk | **6** | 9/1 | 56 | 35 |
| 3973[13] | **Deerly (53)** (CASmith) **3-9-3** CRutter(10) (no hdwy fnl 2f) | nk | **7** | 20/1 | 49 | 28 |
| 3686[2] | **Paddy's Rice (56)** (MBlanshard) **5-9-10** RCochrane(11) (hld up: hdwy over 2f out: edgd lft: eased whn btn over 1f out) | ¾ | **8** | 9/2[1] | 50 | 33 |
| 3991[11] | **Milos (60)** (TJNaughton) **5-10-0** TSprake(18) (hld up: hdwy over 1f out: nvr nrr) | ¾ | **9** | 6/1[3] | 52 | 35 |
| 4000[18] | **Summerhill Special (IRE) (57)** (MrsPNDutfield) **5-9-4b**(7) RSmith(4) (lw: plld hrd: prom over 4f) | 2 | **10** | 33/1 | 45 | 28 |
| 3703[6] | **Galapino (52)** (CEBrittain) **3-9-2b**[1] BDoyle(5) (lw: bhd fnl 2f) | nk | **11** | 16/1 | 39 | 18 |
| 3694[7] | **Astral Invader (IRE) (50)** (MSSaunders) **4-9-4** OUrbina(12) (b: a bhd) | 1½ | **12** | 16/1 | 34 | 17 |
| 3694[5] | **Desert Calm (IRE) (46)** (MrsPNDutfield) **7-8-11b**(3) RHavlin(16) (s.s & wnt lft: a bhd) | nk | **13** | 16/1 | 29 | 12 |
| 3686[14] | **Blushing Grenadier (IRE) (55)** (MJFetherston-Godley) **4-9-9** JStack(9) (a bhd) | 1¼ | **14** | 20/1 | 35 | 18 |
| 3151[8] | **Soaking (52)** (PBurgoyne) **6-9-6** DRMcCabe(3) (s.s: a bhd) | ½ | **15** | 11/2[2] | 31 | 14 |
| 3650[9] | **Duke Valentino (58)** (RHollinshead) **4-9-7**(5) DGriffiths(20) (prom tl rdn & wknd over 2f out) | ½ | **16** | 11/1 | 36 | 19 |

(SP 137.8%) **16 Rn**

**1m 21.0** (1.00) CSF £53.05 CT £851.63 TOTE £6.70: £2.20 £2.70 £4.50 £5.00 (£27.80) Trio £403.20; £227.17 to Doncaster 13/9/96 OWNER Mr Mel Davies (WROUGHTON) BRED Lagrange Chance Partnership & Overbrook Farm
WEIGHT FOR AGE 3yo-4lb

**3877* Speedy Classic (USA)**, 9lb lower than when scoring on the Equitrack last time, was rated 2lb below the mark off which he last won on turf, here over two years ago. (6/1)
**3991 Dawalib (USA)**, back to his best trip, was due to go down 4lb and probably came up against a well-handicapped horse in the winner. (15/2: 4/1-8/1)
**3301 Ivory's Grab Hire** is still 7lb higher than when winning at Lingfield in June. (20/1)
**3863 Thai Morning** may have found this trip beyond his best. (20/1)
**1333 Classic Look (IRE)**, a half-sister to Brief Glimpse, may need more cut in the ground. (16/1)
**3977 Secret Pleasure (IRE)** was already due to drop 3lb in future handicaps. (9/1)
**3686 Paddy's Rice**, having his first run for his new stable, was not given a hard time when his chance was deemed to have gone. (9/2: op 3/1)
**2602* Soaking** (11/2: 12/1-5/1)
**3592 Duke Valentino** (11/1: 8/1-12/1)

## 4129 SILURIAN SCANIA KNOW HOW (S) STKS (3-Y.O+) (Class G)

4-20 (4-27) **1m 14y** £2,668.00 (£748.00: £364.00) GOING minus 0.54 sec per fur (F)

| | | | | SP | RR | SF |
|---|---|---|---|---|---|---|
| 3852[3] | **Cointosser (IRE) (63)** (MCPipe) **3-8-7**(5) MartinDwyer(3) (hdwy over 2f out: led ins fnl f: r.o) | — | **1** | 13/8[1] | 71 | 49 |
| *3062*[6] | **Mustn't Grumble (IRE) (55)** (MissSJWilton) **6-9-3v** SWhitworth(15) (a.p: led 2f out: hrd rdn & hdd ins fnl f) | 1¼ | **2** | 33/1 | 69 | 52 |
| 3786[4] | **Cape Pigeon (USA) (65)** (LGCottrell) **11-9-8v** MFenton(7) (led: swtchd stands' side: hdd 2f out: r.o one pce) | 1½ | **3** | 6/1[3] | 71 | 54 |
| *4076*[5] | **Silver Harrow (57)** (AGNewcombe) **3-8-7**(5) DGriffiths(4) (a.p: ev ch 2f out: one pce) | nk | **4** | 8/1 | 65 | 43 |
| 3161[12] | **Captain's Day (55)** (TGMills) **4-9-3** JCarroll(13) (lw: hdwy over 1f out: r.o) | 3½ | **5** | 14/1 | 58 | 41 |
| 3978[3] | **Helios (64)** (NJHWalker) **8-9-1**(7) MatthewWilliams(20) (a.p: no hdwy fnl 2f) | ½ | **6** | 5/1[2] | 62 | 45 |
| | **Baba Au Rhum (IRE)** (IPWilliams) **4-9-3** RCochrane(5) (lw: plld hrd: prom over 5f) | 4 | **7** | 20/1 | 49 | 32 |
| 3785[13] | **Miss Laughter (50)** (JWHills) **4-9-3** OUrbina(2) (w ldrs over 5f) | 1½ | **8** | 14/1 | 46 | 29 |
| 3978[5] | **Ketabi (USA) (60)** (RAkehurst) **5-9-8** SSanders(12) (lw: nvr trbld ldrs) | 1¼ | **9** | 14/1 | 49 | 32 |
| 3985[15] | **Manabar (50)** (MJPolglase) **4-9-3** WHollick(17) (prom 5f) | ¾ | **10** | 33/1 | 42 | 25 |
| 661[2] | **Everset (FR) (60)** (ABailey) **8-9-0**(3) DWright(8) (b: bkwd: s.s: nvr nr ldrs) | ¾ | **11** | 14/1 | 41 | 24 |
| 3473[6] | **Shanghai Lil (28)** (MJFetherston-Godley) **4-8-12** CRutter(16) (a bhd) | 3 | **12** | 25/1 | 30 | 13 |
| *4077*[12] | **February (42)** (AJChamberlain) **3-8-7** TGMcLaughlin(11) (b: a bhd) | 3½ | **13** | 66/1 | 23 | 1 |
| 3970[13] | **Safa Dancer (32)** (BAMcMahon) **3-8-2**(5) LNewton(14) (a bhd) | 1¼ | **14** | 40/1 | 20 | — |
| | **Blakenmor** (JNeville) **3-8-12** SDrowne(18) (b: a bhd) | 2½ | **15** | 25/1 | 20 | — |
| 3472[16] | **Bunty Bagshaw** (JLSpearing) **3-8-7** NAdams(19) (bit bkwd: dwlt: a bhd) | 7 | **16** | 66/1 | 1 | — |
| 3849[12] | **Hangoninthere (40)** (NMBabbage) **5-9-3** MTebbutt(1) (a bhd) | ¾ | **17** | 50/1 | 5 | — |
| | **Faro Flyer** (KTIvory) **3-8-12** StephenDavies(6) (b: b.hind: w'like: bkwd: a bhd: t.o) | 20 | **18** | 33/1 | — | — |
| 3609[6] | **Desert Scout (34)** (KMcAuliffe) **3-8-12v** BDoyle(9) (lw: v.rel to r: a t.o) | dist | **19** | 50/1 | — | — |

(SP 137.4%) **19 Rn**

**1m 32.5** (0.00) CSF £57.86 TOTE £2.50: £1.50 £4.90 £2.50 (£50.60) Trio £74.00 OWNER Mr Jim Ennis (WELLINGTON) BRED Mellon Stud
WEIGHT FOR AGE 3yo-5lb
Bt in 6,800 gns

**3852 Cointosser (IRE)** appreciated this return to a lower grade. (13/8)
**3062 Mustn't Grumble (IRE)**, reverting to turf, came up against a useful sort for this type of event. (33/1)
**3786 Cape Pigeon (USA)**, back in the right sort of grade, did not throw in the towel when headed. (6/1: op 3/1)
**4076 Silver Harrow** could not take advantage of a drop into a seller. (8/1: 6/1-9/1)
**Captain's Day** ran his best race for some time. (14/1: op 8/1)
**3978 Helios** is presumably thought to now be too high in the Ratings for handicaps. (5/1)
**3978 Ketabi (USA)** (14/1: 10/1-16/1)

## 4130 SCANIA 4-SERIES 'KING OF THE ROAD' TROPHY H'CAP (0-70) (3-Y.O+) (Class E)

4-50 (4-58) **5f 16y** £3,246.00 (£978.00: £474.00: £222.00) Stalls: High GOING minus 0.54 sec per fur (F)

| | | | | SP | RR | SF |
|---|---|---|---|---|---|---|
| 3930[W] | **Malibu Man (63)** (EAWheeler) **4-9-9** TSprake(7) (lw: mde all: sn clr: rdn out) | — | **1** | 9/2[1] | 71 | 45 |
| 3993[14] | **Ashkernazy (IRE) (45)** (NEBerry) **5-8-5**ow2 RPerham(12) (a.p: r.o ins fnl f) | 2 | **2** | 7/1 | 47 | 19 |
| 3993[8] | **Imposing Time (63)** (MissGayKelleway) **5-9-9b** RCochrane(10) (a.p: chsd wnr over 1f out: hrd rdn: r.o one pce) | ¾ | **3** | 11/2[2] | 62 | 36 |
| 3686[8] | **Al Shaati (FR) (36)** (RJO'Sullivan) **6-7-10** NAdams(15) (a.p: one pce fnl 2f) | hd | **4** | 9/1 | 35 | 9 |
| 4088[12] | **Paley Prince (USA) (54)** (MDIUsher) **10-9-0** SWhitworth(11) (lw: hdwy fnl f: nrst fin) | 1¼ | **5** | 25/1 | 49 | 23 |
| 3789[11] | **Maraschino (37)** (BJMeehan) **3-7-10** DeclanO'Shea(6) (lw: a.p: no hdwy fnl 2f) | nk | **6** | 40/1 | 31 | 4 |
| 3883[4] | **Songsheet (66)** (MartynMeade) **3-9-4**(7) DSweeney(4) (lw: nvr nr to chal) | ¾ | **7** | 8/1 | 58 | 31 |
| 2286[13] | **Rowlandsons Stud (IRE) (55)** (PBurgoyne) **3-8-7**(7) JBosley(13) (nvr trbld ldrs) | ¾ | **8** | 40/1 | 44 | 17 |
| 2791[7] | **Colston-C (61)** (PDEvans) **4-9-7** ACulhane(9) (stdd s: nvr nrr) | 2½ | **9** | 10/1 | 43 | 17 |
| 3864[7] | **Logie Pert Lad (42)** (JJBridger) **4-7-11**(5)ow6 ADaly(16) (bhd fnl 2f) | 1¼ | **10** | 50/1 | 20 | — |
| 3863[2] | **Tymeera (57)** (BPalling) **3-8-13v**1(3) MHenry(1) (prom over 3f) | ½ | **11** | 6/1[3] | 33 | 6 |
| 773[10] | **Amy Leigh (IRE) (61)** (CaptJWilson) **3-9-6** CRutter(14) (bkwd: prom 3f) | 1¾ | **12** | 25/1 | 32 | 5 |
| 2244[8] | **Halbert (56)** (PBurgoyne) **7-9-2v** DRMcCabe(2) (bkwd: a bhd) | ¾ | **13** | 20/1 | 24 | — |
| 3652[4] | **Marino Street (56)** (PDEvans) **3-9-1v** OUrbina(3) (lw: outpcd) | hd | **14** | 10/1 | 24 | — |
| *4094*[12] | **Super Sonata (46)** (TWall) **4-8-3v**(3) DWright(8) (b: bhd fnl 2f) | 4 | **15** | 33/1 | 1 | — |
| 3851[7] | **Nineacres (51)** (NMBabbage) **5-8-11v** AClark(5) (s.s: sn t.o) | 14 | **16** | 12/1 | — | — |
| | | | | (SP 129.6%) | **16 Rn** | |

**57.8 secs** (0.80) CSF £35.85 CT £170.63 TOTE £5.40: £1.30 £1.80 £1.30 £2.40 (£19.00) Trio £15.60 OWNER Church Racing Partnership (PANGBOURNE) BRED Mrs M. Chubb
LONG HANDICAP Logie Pert Lad 7-0 Maraschino 7-7 Al Shaati (FR) 7-6
WEIGHT FOR AGE 3yo-1lb
**2992 Malibu Man**, withdrawn on his last two intended starts, showed far too much speed for these rivals. (9/2)
**3661* Ashkernazy (IRE)**, excluding the overweight, was back to the mark off which she won at Windsor. (7/1)
**3864 Imposing Time** was meeting the runner-up on the same terms as when beaten a neck at Windsor. (11/2)
**41 Al Shaati (FR)**, 4lb out of the handicap, was supported in the Offices and repaid any each-way money. (9/1)
**Paley Prince (USA)**, making a quick reappearance, could not go the furious pace set by the winner. (25/1)
**3061 Maraschino**, carrying 3lb more than her long-handicap mark, was reverting to the minimum trip. (40/1)
**Colston-C** (10/1: op 6/1)

T/Plpt: £164.20 (62.44 Tckts). T/Qdpt: £10.40 (92.58 Tckts). KH

# 4111-DONCASTER (L-H) (Good to firm)
## Thursday September 12th

WEATHER: overcast WIND: fresh bhd

## 4131 RALPH RAPER MEMORIAL PRINCE OF WALES CUP NURSERY H'CAP (2-Y.O) (Class C)

2-00 (2-02) **1m (straight)** £18,310.00 (£6,790.00: £3,270.00: £1,350.00: £550.00: £230.00) Stalls: High GOING minus 0.49 sec per fur (F)

| | | | | SP | RR | SF |
|---|---|---|---|---|---|---|
| 3821* | **Al Azhar (85)** (IABalding) **2-8-10** PatEddery(5) (led 2f: led wl over 2f out: rdn & r.o) | — | **1** | 7/2[2] | 85+ | 43 |
| 3982[3] | **Sandbaggedagain (71)** (MWEasterby) **2-7-3**(7) RMullen(12) (prom stands' side: hdwy & hung lft 2f out: r.o wl towards fin) | 1 | **2** | 20/1 | 69 | 27 |
| 3807[10] | **Princess Topaz (71)** (CACyzer) **2-7-10** JQuinn(1) (trckd ldrs: effrt 3f out: nt qckn fnl f) | 2 | **3** | 16/1 | 65 | 23 |
| 3835* | **The Fly (93)** (BWHills) **2-9-4** MHills(2) (hld up: effrt over 3f out: hung lft: sn chsng ldrs: nt qckn fnl 2f) | ½ | **4** | 9/4[1] | 86 | 44 |
| 2865* | **Southerly Wind (75)** (MrsJRRamsden) **2-8-0** JFanning(16) (hld up: hdwy 2f out: rdn & styd on wl) | 3½ | **5** | 11/1 | 61 | 19 |
| 3307* | **Peartree House (IRE) (89)** (BWHills) **2-9-0** WCarson(8) (in tch: outpcd 3f out: kpt on fnl 2f) | 1 | **6** | 16/1 | 73 | 31 |
| 3616[3] | **Mister Pink (90)** (RFJohnsonHoughton) **2-9-1** JReid(9) (sn outpcd & bhd: styd on fnl 2f) | ¾ | **7** | 14/1 | 73 | 31 |
| 3998* | **General's Star (82)** (MRStoute) **2-8-4**(3) 8x FLynch(13) (chsd ldrs: effrt 3f out: wknd fnl 2f) | ¾ | **8** | 15/2[3] | 63 | 21 |
| 3837[8] | **Puzzlement (73)** (CEBrittain) **2-7-7**(5)ow2 MBaird(3) (cl up: led after 2f tl wl over 2f out: wknd) | nk | **9** | 33/1 | 53 | 9 |
| 3936[4] | **Exit To Rio (CAN) (94)** (MrsJRRamsden) **2-9-5** KFallon(4) (in tch tl outpcd fnl 3f) | 1¾ | **10** | 16/1 | 71 | 29 |
| 3835[19] | **The Deejay (IRE) (71)** (MBrittain) **2-7-10v**1 JLowe(7) (led stands' side tl wknd fnl 2½f) | 4 | **11** | 33/1 | 40 | — |
| 3685[3] | **Champagne Toast (78)** (RHannon) **2-8-3**ow1 DHarrison(17) (lw: a rr div) | 3 | **12** | 20/1 | 41 | — |
| 3843[4] | **For Your Eyes Only (96)** (TDEasterby) **2-9-7** MBirch(6) (b: lw: cl up over 5f) | 1¼ | **13** | 20/1 | 56 | 14 |
| 4024a[17] | **Kaiser Kache (IRE) (82)** (KMcAuliffe) **2-8-7** JFortune(15) (chsd ldrs 5f) | hd | **14** | 25/1 | 42 | — |
| 3874* | **Sad Mad Bad (USA) (80)** (MJohnston) **2-8-5** KDarley(11) (swtg: cl up over 5f) | s.h | **15** | 14/1 | 40 | — |
| 4034a[5] | **Dalmeny Dancer (88)** (BJMeehan) **2-8-13** TQuinn(10) (chsd ldrs over 5f) | 3 | **16** | 25/1 | 42 | — |
| 3706[6] | **Millroy (USA) (87)** (PAKelleway) **2-8-12** OPeslier(14) (wl bhd fr ½-wy) | 13 | **17** | 33/1 | 15 | — |
| | | | | (SP 134.9%) | **17 Rn** | |

**1m 38.05** (1.03 under 2y best) (1.05) CSF £71.81 CT £978.34 TOTE £4.20: £1.40 £6.80 £3.20 £1.20 (£43.60) Trio £513.90 OWNER Al Muallim Partnership (KINGSCLERE) BRED P. D. and Mrs Player
LONG HANDICAP Puzzlement 7-8 Sandbaggedagain 7-9 Princess Topaz 7-9
**3821* Al Azhar**, a good-looking colt, was off a useful mark here. Leaving nothing to chance and kicking a long way out, he won most convincingly. (7/2)
**3982 Sandbaggedagain**, despite hanging left yet again, ran a cracking race, staying on determinedly throughout the last three furlongs to be nearest at the finish. He really does deserve a change of luck. (20/1)

**3054 Princess Topaz**, an excitable filly who needed two lads in the preliminaries, got the trip and the track she needed here. After looking dangerous, she failed to prolong the effort in the final furlong. She is off a useful mark at present. (16/1)
**3835* The Fly** raced closer to the pace this time but, when asked for an effort, he was always inclined to hang left, and failed to get in a blow. This was certainly not his true form. (9/4)
**2865* Southerly Wind** had been off the track for eight weeks and ran as though this was just needed. He should be well worth keeping in mind. (11/1: 8/1-12/1)
**3307* Peartree House (IRE)** was off the bit some way out, but did keep battling on to suggest that he is still in good heart. (16/1)
**3616 Mister Pink** failed to go the pace until picking up well when it was all over. (14/1)

## 4132 BRITAIN'S FASTEST RAILWAY PARK STKS (Gp 3) (3-Y.O+) (Class A)

2-35 (2-36) **1m (round)** £21,392.00 (£7,928.00: £3,814.00: £1,570.00: £635.00: £261.00) GOING minus 0.49 sec per fur (F)

| | | | | SP | RR | SF |
|---|---|---|---|---|---|---|
| 3784[2] | **Bishop of Cashel (111)** (JRFanshawe) **4-9-4** WRSwinburn(5) (lw: hld up: hdwy on bit 2f out: led 1f out: rdn & r.o) | — | **1** | 4/1[2] | 122 | 58 |
| 3596* | **Bin Rosie (113)** (DRLoder) **4-9-4b** LDettori(4) (hld up & bhd: hdwy 2f out: r.o towards fin) | ¾ | **2** | 4/1[2] | 121 | 57 |
| 3784[4] | **Restructure (IRE) (116)** (MrsJCecil) **4-9-4** JReid(8) (lw: cl up: led over 2f out to 1f out: kpt on) | 1¼ | **3** | 7/2[1] | 118 | 54 |
| 3784[5] | **Distant Oasis (USA)** (HRACecil) **3-8-6** PatEddery(2) (trckd ldrs gng wl: effrt & swtchd rt over 2f out: styd on towards fin) | ½ | **4** | 7/2[1] | 110 | 41 |
| 3784[6] | **Gothenberg (IRE) (118)** (MJohnston) **3-9-1** OPeslier(6) (trckd ldrs: effrt over 3f out: outpcd fnl 2f) | 8 | **5** | 20/1 | 103 | 34 |
| 3712* | **Ruznama (USA) (100)** (BWHills) **3-8-6** WCarson(3) (in tch: effrt over 3f out: rdn & btn 2f out) | nk | **6** | 6/1[3] | 93 | 24 |
| 810[10] | **Nijo (109)** (DRLoder) **5-9-0** KDarley(7) (hld up: effrt 3f out: sn rdn & no imp) | nk | **7** | 12/1 | 96 | 32 |
| 4030a[4] | **Royal Philosopher (105)** (JWHills) **4-9-0** MHills(1) (led tl hdd & wknd over 2f out) | 5 | **8** | 16/1 | 86 | 22 |
| | | | | (SP 117.1%) | **8 Rn** | |

**1m 36.85** (0.35) CSF £19.64 TOTE £4.40: £1.50 £1.40 £2.00 (£5.80) OWNER Cheveley Park Stud (NEWMARKET) BRED Carroll Bloodstock Ltd
WEIGHT FOR AGE 3yo-5lb

**3784 Bishop of Cashel** again travelled on the bridle and this time kicked with a furlong to go. Although he does not find as much as looks likely when let down, he was always doing just enough. (4/1)
**3596* Bin Rosie**, who has to come from behind, took time to get going. Although really flying at the death, he had given the winner too much start. (4/1)
**3784 Restructure (IRE)** is an honest sort who keeps trying hard, but he was again tapped for foot at the business end. (7/2)
**3784 Distant Oasis (USA)** looked to be going quite well here but, when short of room, proved short of the necessary speed to make up for it. Judging by the way she finished though, she should have no difficulty in staying further, and she should also improve when doing so. (7/2)
**3784 Gothenberg (IRE)** tried different tactics here and was held up. This certainly did not work and he ran poorly. (20/1)
**3712* Ruznama (USA)** found this more competitive and, when short of room halfway up the straight, she came under pressure and soon gave up altogether. (6/1)
**Nijo**, returning after a lengthy absence, never gave any hopes of getting into it. (12/1)
**4030a Royal Philosopher**, very warm beforehand, was well outclassed in the race. (16/1)

## 4133 MAY HILL STKS (Gp 3) (2-Y.O F) (Class A)

3-10 (3-13) **1m (round)** £16,280.00 (£6,020.00: £2,885.00: £1,175.00: £462.50: £177.50) Stalls: Low GOING minus 0.49 sec per fur (F)

| | | | | SP | RR | SF |
|---|---|---|---|---|---|---|
| 3756* | **Reams of Verse (USA)** (HRACecil) **2-8-9** PatEddery(11) (trckd ldrs: disp ld over 2f out: led over 1f out: rdn & r.o) | — | **1** | 2/1[1] | 95 | 29 |
| 2582[8] | **Dame Laura (IRE) (100)** (PFICole) **2-8-9** TQuinn(2) (tckd ldrs: disp ld over 2f out tl over 1f out: nt pce of wnr) | 2 | **2** | 16/1 | 91 | 25 |
| 2997[6] | **Gretel** (MRStoute) **2-8-9** WRSwinburn(10) (lw: plld hrd: bhd: hdwy whn nt clr run over 2f out: swtchd over 1f out: r.o wl towards fin) | hd | **3** | 14/1 | 91+ | 25 |
| 3756[2] | **Bint Baladee** (SbinSuroor) **2-8-9** LDettori(12) (hld up: hdwy 3f out: hung lft 2f out: nt qckn) | 3½ | **4** | 5/2[2] | 84 | 18 |
| 3068[3] | **Raindancing (IRE) (100)** (RHannon) **2-8-9** JReid(1) (chsd ldrs: effrt 3f out: outpcd whn hmpd over 1f out) | nk | **5** | 14/1 | 83 | 17 |
| 3835[3] | **Vagabond Chanteuse (79)** (TJEtherington) **2-8-9** LCharnock(3) (trckd ldrs: effrt over 2f out: r.o one pce) | 4 | **6** | 50/1 | 75 | 9 |
| 3159* | **Quintellina** (LMCumani) **2-8-9** KDarley(6) (lw: in tch: effrt over 3f out: no imp) | 1¼ | **7** | 9/2[3] | 73 | 7 |
| 3663* | **The In-Laws (IRE)** (SirMarkPrescott) **2-8-9** GDuffield(5) (cl up: led after 3f tl over 2f out: btn whn hmpd over 1f out) | ¾ | **8** | 16/1 | 71 | 5 |
| 3444* | **Catwalk** (WJHaggas) **2-8-12** MHills(9) (led 3f: wknd fnl 3f) | 6 | **9** | 20/1 | 62 | — |
| 3454[W] | **Attitre (FR)** (CEBrittain) **2-8-9** KFallon(4) (w'like: leggy: bkwd: hld up: hmpd appr st: a bhd) | hd | **10** | 33/1 | 59 | — |
| 3131[3] | **Mrs Miniver (USA)** (PAKelleway) **2-8-9** OPeslier(7) (hld up & bhd: outpcd fr ½-wy) | 9 | **11** | 25/1 | 41 | — |
| *3804[2]* | ***Fernanda (100)*** (JLDunlop) **2-8-9b** WCarson(8) (Withdrawn not under Starter's orders: ref to ent stalls) | | **W** | 16/1 | — | — |
| | | | | (SP 124.6%) | **11 Rn** | |

**1m 38.87** (2.37) CSF £31.25 TOTE £3.00: £1.40 £3.40 £3.10 (£30.80) Trio £214.80 OWNER Mr K. Abdulla (NEWMARKET) BRED Juddmonte Farms

**3756* Reams of Verse (USA)**, from a yard that farms this event, made no mistake. Despite edging slightly left under pressure when in front, she was always in command. (2/1)
**2582 Dame Laura (IRE)**, taking a step up in trip, got it well. This tough filly made a real fight of it, but had to admit defeat inside the last furlong. (16/1)
**2997 Gretel** again took a fierce hold and, after being dropped out the back, met with all sorts of trouble. She left the impression that, should she ever learn to settle, she will be extremely useful. (14/1)
**3756 Bint Baladee** was yet another runner from this yard that looked ultra-fit and very hard trained. She had her chances but again spoilt them by hanging left, giving her rider all sorts of problems. (5/2)
**3068 Raindancing (IRE)** had her chances, but was already struggling and going nowhere when Bint Baladee hung into her over a furlong out. (14/1)
**3835 Vagabond Chanteuse** travelled quite well, but found this company too hot in the last two and a half furlongs. (50/1)
**3159* Quintellina** looked a picture, but ran moderately, never firing at any stage. Something would seem to be wrong with her. (9/2)
**3663* The In-Laws (IRE)**, from a yard that is masterful at taking big steps up in class, proved disappointing, dropping away tamely in the last couple of furlongs. (16/1)

## 4134 EAST COAST DONCASTER CUP STKS (Gp 3) (3-Y.O+) (Class A)

3-40 (3-42) **2m 2f** £19,072.00 (£7,048.00: £3,374.00: £1,370.00: £535.00: £201.00) Stalls: High GOING minus 0.49 sec per fur (F)

| | | | | SP | RR | SF |
|---|---|---|---|---|---|---|
| 2071[2] | **Double Trigger (IRE) (119)** (MJohnston) **5-9-7** LDettori(5) (lw: mde most: qcknd over 4f out: r.o wl) | — | **1** | Evens[1] | 128+ | 63 |

3673* **Celeric (107)** (DMorley) **4-9-0** WCarson(2) (lw: hld up: effrt 3f out: chsng wnr appr fnl f: styd on wl: nvr able to chal) ....2 **2** 13/8[2] 119 54
3753a[3] **Lear White (USA) (112)** (PAKelleway) **5-9-0** OPeslier(3) (trckd ldrs: wnt 2nd over 3f out: sn hrd drvn & no imp) ....2 **3** 13/2[3] 117 52
3157[7] **Admiral's Well (IRE) (103)** (RAkehurst) **6-9-0** TQuinn(1) (trckd wnr: effrt 4f out: one pce) ....2 **4** 25/1 116 51
4032a[6] **Old Rouvel (USA) (100)** (DJGMurraySmith) **5-9-0** KDarley(6) (prom: rdn over 4f out: no imp after) ....4 **5** 50/1 112 47
3751a[5] **Assessor (IRE) (107)** (RHannon) **7-9-3** JReid(4) (hld up: effrt 4f out: n.d) ....7 **6** 25/1 109 44
(SP 111.1%) **6 Rn**

**3m 53.0** (2.60 under best) (1.00) CSF £2.90 TOTE £1.80: £1.40 £1.30 (£1.60) OWNER Mr R. W. Huggins (MIDDLEHAM) BRED Dene Investments N V

**2071 Double Trigger (IRE)** has had his training problems this year, but was back to something like his best here. Dominating throughout, he really stepped on the gas in the last half-mile and was never in any danger. (Evens)
**3673* Celeric**, held up as usual, got the trip well and kept staying on, but the winner was always too good for him. (13/8)
**3753a Lear White (USA)**, taking another step up in distance, looked a big danger early in the straight but, when serious stamina came into it, he was found wanting in this company. (13/2)
**2117* Admiral's Well (IRE)** ran his usual game race, but was well outpointed in the last half-mile. On the same terms here, he was beaten half a length further than the previous year. (25/1)
**4032a Old Rouvel (USA)** showed up well but, once an effort was required in the home straight, soon cried enough. (50/1)
**3751a Assessor (IRE)** won this three years ago and is certainly not the force he was. (25/1)

## 4135 KYOTO SCEPTRE STKS (Listed) (3-Y.O+ F & M) (Class A)

4-10 (4-11) **7f** £10,971.80 (£4,056.20: £1,943.10: £790.50: £310.25: £118.15) Stalls: High GOING minus 0.49 sec per fur (F)

SP RR SF
3127[13] **My Branch (112)** (BWHills) **3-8-6** MHills(2) (lw: hld up: a gng wl: led ins fnl f: r.o) ....— **1** 7/2[2] 106 45
3989* **High Summer (USA) (80)** (RCharlton) **3-8-6** PatEddery(7) (led tl ins fnl f: kpt on) ....1¼ **2** 100/30[1] 103 42
3524[2] **Dance Sequence (USA) (108)** (MRStoute) **3-8-6** OPeslier(3) (prom: rdn over 2f out: sn outpcd: kpt on fnl f) .1¼ **3** 100/30[1] 100 39
3517[5] **Polska (USA)** (DRLoder) **3-8-6** LDettori(1) (chsd ldrs: rdn over 2f out: ch over 1f out: nt qckn) ....nk **4** 12/1 100 39
3712[3] **Forest Cat (IRE) (101)** (MrsJCecil) **4-8-10** JReid(5) (cl up: effrt over 2f out: wknd appr fnl f) ....½ **5** 4/1[3] 99 42
3127[3] **Tamnia (102)** (JLDunlop) **3-8-6b[1]** TQuinn(6) (chsd ldrs: rdn 3f out: one pce) ....2 **6** 8/1 94 33
3945[9] **Thea (USA) (93)** (JRFanshawe) **3-8-6** DHarrison(4) (outpcd & bnd 3f) ....11 **7** 9/1 69 8
(SP 117.2%) **7 Rn**

**1m 24.01** (0.41) CSF £15.28 TOTE £3.70: £2.10 £1.80 (£8.90) OWNER Mr Wafic Said (LAMBOURN) BRED Addison Racing Ltd Inc
WEIGHT FOR AGE 3yo-4lb

OFFICIAL EXPLANATION **My Branch: accounting for the filly's apparent improvement since her last run, her trainer said she had run disappointingly from a bad draw at Goodwood, following some hard races, and had been turned out and freshened up since.**

**1567a My Branch**, back to her brilliant best here, was on the bridle throughout and won really well. (7/2)
**3989* High Summer (USA)** had her tongue tied down for the second time and ran a useful race, attempting to make all again, but was well outpointed in the final furlong. (100/30)
**3524 Dance Sequence (USA)**, an edgy filly, is proving difficult to win with this season but, judging from the way she finished here, she should get further. (100/30)
**3517 Polska (USA)** had plenty on in this company and, after having her chances, was done with entering the final furlong. This was still not a bad effort. (12/1)
**3712 Forest Cat (IRE)** has had some stiffish tasks this season and was always finding things too tough on this occasion. (4/1)
**3127 Tamnia** had blinkers on for the first time and they failed to have the desired effect. Off the bit from halfway, she was going nowhere thereafter. (8/1)

## 4136 DONCASTER FREE PRESS LADIES DAY H'CAP (0-90) (3-Y.O+) (Class C)

4-40 (4-44) **7f** £6,945.00 (£2,085.00: £1,005.00: £465.00) Stalls: High GOING minus 0.49 sec per fur (F)

SP RR SF
3985[3] **Quilling (66)** (MDods) **4-8-1**(3) FLynch(7) (lw: disp ld to ½-wy: sn rdn: styd on wl to ld post) ....— **1** 15/2[3] 74 27
3937[2] **Wardara (71)** (CADwyer) **4-8-2v**(7) JoHunnam(3) (w ldrs: led ½-wy tl ct nr fin) ....hd **2** 14/1 79 32
3810* **Lough Erne (78)** (CFWall) **4-9-2** WCarson(20) (lw: effrt 3f out: hdwy over 1f out: styd on wl towards fin) ....½ **3** 11/2[1] 85 38
3833[2] **Keston Pond (IRE) (76)** (MrsVAAconley) **6-9-0** MDeering(13) (prom: effrt 3f out: ev ch over 1f out: kpt on one pce) ....½ **4** 11/1 82 35
3926[3] **Consort (86)** (GHarwood) **3-9-6** PatEddery(11) (hld up: effrt & n.m.r 3f out to 2f out: styd on u.p) ....nk **5** 7/1[2] 91 40
2053[21] **Wild Rice (90)** (GWragg) **4-10-0** MHills(6) (b: hld up: effrt over 2f out: sn chsng ldrs: nt qckn fnl f) ....nk **6** 20/1 94 47
3920[8] **Champagne Grandy (77)** (MRChannon) **6-8-10**(5) PPMurphy(9) (bhd: styd on fnl 2f: nrst fin) ....1¾ **7** 20/1 77 30
3933[18] **Air Commodore (IRE) (88)** (DWPArbuthnot) **5-9-12** MBirch(4) (b: bhd: hdwy over 2f out: styd on) ....s.h **8** 33/1 88 41
3981[3] **Equerry (82)** (MJohnston) **5-9-6** JReid(8) (chsd ldrs: rdn ½-wy: wknd over 1f out) ....nk **9** 20/1 81 34
3973[11] **Cavers Yangous (65)** (MJohnston) **5-8-3v** TWilliams(18) (disp ld to ½-wy: grad wknd) ....2½ **10** 20/1 59 12
3920[5] **Chickawicka (IRE) (87)** (BPalling) **5-9-6**(5) SCopp(15) (lw: cl up tl wknd 2f out) ....1¼ **11** 20/1 78 31
4109[14] **Samsolom (59)** (PHowling) **8-7-11** JQuinn(16) (hld up: effrt 3f out: n.d) ....1 **12** 33/1 48 1
3995* **Ochos Rios (IRE) (60)** (BSRothwell) **5-7-12** 4x LCharnock(12) (b.off hind: chsd ldrs: edgd rt 3f out: wknd over 1f out) ....hd **13** 10/1 48 1
3933[17] **King Rat (IRE) (79)** (TJEtherington) **5-9-3b** GDuffield(19) (outpcd whn n.m.r 3f out: n.d after) ....4 **14** 20/1 58 11
3232[30] **Statoyork (82)** (BWHills) **3-9-2** KFallon(2) (a bhd) ....1¼ **15** 16/1 58 7
1186[19] **Barrel of Hope (80)** (JLEyre) **4-9-4b** JFortune(1) (chsd ldrs: sn drvn along: wknd fnl 3f) ....2 **16** 25/1 52 5
3790[9] **Wisam (87)** (RHannon) **3-9-7** LDettori(10) (b.off fore: trckd ldrs tl wknd fnl 3f) ....nk **17** 12/1 58 7
*1601** **Northern Fan (IRE) (77)** (NTinkler) **4-9-1** KDarley(17) (a rr div) ....9 **18** 20/1 27 —
3322[3] **Arterxerxes (81)** (MJHeaton-Ellis) **3-9-1** TQuinn(14) (disp ld to ½-wy: wknd qckly & eased) ....5 **19** 14/1 20 —
*3920[14]* ***Royal Mark (IRE) (88)*** (JWWatts) **3-9-8** WRSwinburn(5) (Withdrawn not under Starter's orders: lame at s) .... **W** 14/1 — —
(SP 133.7%) **19 Rn**

**1m 25.4** (1.80) CSF £95.86 CT £517.74 TOTE £8.30: £2.10 £6.10 £1.80 £2.20 (£66.60) Trio £275.80 OWNER Mr A. G. Watson (DARLINGTON) BRED Hesmonds Stud Ltd
WEIGHT FOR AGE 3yo-4lb

**3985 Quilling** came up with the goods at last, but it was a desperate thing. He was well handled to get his head in front at the right time, and does look exceptionally well at the moment. (15/2)
**3937 Wardara**, given a fine ride, was in the thick of things throughout, but she has never won over this trip and was just worried out of it. (14/1)

**3810* Lough Erne** ran a fine race, staying on strongly at the end. Her stands'-side draw probably made all the difference. (11/2)
**3833 Keston Pond (IRE)** does not seem to know how to run a bad race and, after a busy season, is as well as ever. (11/1)
**3926 Consort** was a shade unlucky. He was short of room at vital stages, but did finish in determined style. (7/1: op 9/2)
**1703 Wild Rice** looked to be going quite well in behind the leaders, but then failed to find as much as looked likely when ridden. After three months off, this was still not a bad effort. (20/1)
**3265 Champagne Grandy** was noted staying on at the end. Once the ground eases, she can do even better. (20/1)
**Air Commodore (IRE)** ran as though he is steadily coming to hand. (33/1)

T/Jkpt: £7,682.90 (4.63 Tckts). T/Plpt: £18.20 (2,001.64 Tckts). T/Qdpt: £9.30 (158.84 Tckts). AA

## 4137a-4155a (Irish Racing) - See Computer Raceform

# 4021a-CURRAGH (Newbridge, Ireland) (R-H) (Good)
## Sunday September 8th

### 4156a GO AND GO ROUND TOWER STKS (Listed) (2-Y.O)
2-45 (2-45) **6f** £9,675.00 (£2,775.00: £1,275.00: £375.00)

| | | | | SP | RR | SF |
|---|---|---|---|---|---|---|
| | **Desert Ease (IRE)** (DKWeld,Ireland) **2-8-7** MJKinane (a cl up: effrt 2f out: led over 1f out: hdd briefly ins fnl f: r.o) | — | 1 | 9/4 [1] | 81+ | 40 |
| 2834a[4] | **Classic Park** (APO'Brien,Ireland) **2-8-8**ow1 JReid (hld up trckng ldrs: chal & led briefly ins fnl f: kpt on u.p) | hd | 2 | 5/1 | 82 | 40 |
| 3561a[8] | **Check The Band (USA)** (APO'Brien,Ireland) **2-9-0** CRoche (w ldrs: led over 2f out tl over 1f out: kpt on) | 1 | 3 | 100/30 [3] | 85 | 44 |
| 2470a[4] | **Mosconi (IRE)** (JSBolger,Ireland) **2-8-10** KJManning (hld up: rdn over 1f out: kpt on: n.d) | 4½ | 4 | 8/1 | 69 | 28 |
| | **Stonehaven (IRE)** (TStack,Ireland) **2-8-10** PJSmullen (led & disp ld: hdd over 2f out: rdn over 1f out: sn btn) | 1½ | 5 | 11/4 [2] | 65 | 24 |
| | **Maratana (IRE)** (EJKearnsJnr,Ireland) **2-8-7** WJSmith (prom: rdn wl over 1f out: sn wknd) | 1 | 6 | 10/1 | 59 | 18 |

(SP 117.4%) **6 Rn**

**1m 13.7** (3.20) OWNER Moyglare Stud Farm (CURRAGH)
**Desert Ease (IRE)**, well regarded, made this look quite easy, despite only getting home by a head. She raced on the outside throughout and, with Kinane only waving the whip at her, she put in a sustained challenge over the last furlong and was always in command. The Group Three C.L. Weld Park Stakes here will be her late-season target. (9/4)
**2834a Classic Park**, who has had plenty of experience, came through between horses to flatter a furlong out, but she was always held by the winner. (5/1)
**3018a Check The Band (USA)**, with his penalty, was always vulnerable and found nothing under pressure. (100/30)
**2470a Mosconi (IRE)** adopted waiting tactics, but they might have been overdone here and he was never able to get in a blow. (8/1)

### 4159a MOYGLARE STUD STKS (Gp 1) (2-Y.O F)
4-15 (4-16) **7f** £84,300.00 (£28,800.00: £13,800.00: £4,800.00)

| | | | | SP | RR | SF |
|---|---|---|---|---|---|---|
| 3707* | **Bianca Nera** (DRLoder) **2-8-11** KDarley (hld up trckng ldrs: nt clr run over 1f out: swtchd lft jst ins fnl f: led wl ins fnl f: r.o) | — | 1 | 3/1 [2] | 106+ | 49 |
| 2315* | **Ryafan (USA)** (JHMGosden) **2-8-11** PatEddery (cl up: chsd ldr 3f out: led over 2f out: hdd over 1f out: r.o u.p) | ½ | 2 | 9/2 | 105 | 48 |
| 4027a[4] | **Azra (IRE)** (JSBolger,Ireland) **2-8-11b[1]** KJManning (hld up: hdwy to jn ldrs ½-wy: rdn to ld over 1f out: edgd rt jst ins fnl f: sn hdd: kpt on) | nk | 3 | 14/1 | 104 | 47 |
| | **Velvet Appeal (IRE)** (MHalford,Ireland) **2-8-11** WJSupple (hld up towards rr: hdwy fr 2f out: 5th 1f out: r.o wl u.p) | hd | 4 | 40/1 | 104 | 47 |
| 3561a[5] | **Star Profile (IRE)** (DKWeld,Ireland) **2-8-11** MJKinane (hld up in rr: swtchd lft & pushed along ½-wy: 4th u.p early fnl f: no ex) | ½ | 5 | 4/1 [3] | 103 | 46 |
| 2877* | **Crystal Crossing (IRE)** (PWChapple-Hyam) **2-8-11** JReid (hld up: nt clr run fr 2f out: r.o towards fin) | 1 | 6 | 5/2 [1] | 101+ | 44 |
| 4027a* | **Air Of Distinction (IRE)** (APO'Brien,Ireland) **2-8-11** JAHeffernan (prom tl wknd qckly 1f out) | 4 | 7 | 14/1 | 91 | 34 |
| | **Family Tradition (IRE)** (APO'Brien,Ireland) **2-8-11** CRoche (n.d fr ½-wy: bhd & rdn 2f out: sme late hdwy) | hd | 8 | 6/1 | 91 | 34 |
| | **Fastnet View (IRE)** (APO'Brien,Ireland) **2-8-11** KFallon (sn disp ld: 2nd & pushed along 4f out: wknd over 2f out) | 4½ | 9 | 33/1 | 81 | 24 |
| | **Peace Melody (IRE)** (APO'Brien,Ireland) **2-8-11** JPMurtagh (led after 2f tl over 2f out: sn wknd) | d.h | 9 | 33/1 | 81 | 24 |

(SP 127.7%) **10 Rn**

**1m 26.3** (3.30) OWNER S. Frisby (NEWMARKET) BRED Miss S. McCreery and Stowell Hill Ltd
**3707* Bianca Nera** should have won by a wider margin, although this might not have been the greatest Group One two-year-old contest. She got no sort of run at all from well over a furlong out and had to be switched to deliver. Once she saw daylight, she quickened up well and it would be wrong to say she had a hard race in the process. She has a definite turn of foot and, if she does run again this season, it will be in the Prix Marcel Boussac. (3/1)
**2315* Ryafan (USA)**, always in the front rank, took a definite advantage two furlongs out and, after being headed, came back again at the finish. She certainly does not have anything like the speed of the winner, but was not disgraced. (9/2)
**4027a Azra (IRE)**, blinkered for the first time, put up a different performance and, after leading briefly a furlong and a half out, bustled on unhesitatingly to the end. (14/1)
**Velvet Appeal (IRE)** is still a maiden but ran on with serious purpose from the rear of the field to take fourth place close home. (40/1)
**3561a Star Profile (IRE)** could not go the pace early on and then encountered difficulty when making her run on the outside from two furlongs out. If she had been able to maintain her position inside the last, the winner would not have got out in time. (4/1)
**2877* Crystal Crossing (IRE)**, held up, found herself faced with traffic problems throughout the last furlong and a half, and this run can be disregarded. (5/2)
**4027a* Air Of Distinction (IRE)** was unable to reproduce her Anglesey Stakes form here and was outpaced over the last three furlongs. (14/1: op 8/1)

### 4160a TRUSTED PARTNER MATRON STKS (Gp 3) (3-Y.O+ F & M)
4-45 (4-47) **1m (New)** £16,250.00 (£4,750.00: £2,250.00: £750.00)

| | | | | SP | RR | SF |
|---|---|---|---|---|---|---|
| 2609[3] | **Donna Viola** (CFWall) **4-9-0** JReid (hld up: wnt 3rd bef st: rdn 2f out: r.o u.p to ld fnl 50y) | — | 1 | 5/2 [2] | 108 | 40 |

| | Horse | Details | Dist | Pos | SP | RR | SF |
|---|---|---|---|---|---|---|---|
| 3836* | **Hagwah (USA)** | (BHanbury) **4-9-0** WRyan (led: rdn 2f out: kpt on wl: hdd fnl 50y) | ½ | 2 | 9/4 1 | 107 | 39 |
| 3530a3 | **Charlock (IRE)** | (JOxx,Ireland) **3-8-9** JPMurtagh (hld up: edgd rt 5f out: 4th st: swtchd lft wl over 1f out: 3rd over 1f out: r.o u.p) | hd | 3 | 8/1 | 107 | 34 |
| 39454 | **Arabride** | (LordHuntingdon) **4-9-0** PatEddery (chsd ldr: rdn over 2f out: 3rd & one pce over 1f out) | 6 | 4 | 3/1 3 | 95 | 27 |
| 3530a2 | **Proud Titania (IRE)** | (APO'Brien,Ireland) **3-8-9** JAHeffernan (bhd: hung lft ½-wy: last & rdn st: n.d) | 1 | 5 | 10/1 | 93 | 20 |
| | **Sheffield (USA)** | (JSBolger,Ireland) **3-8-9b** KJManning (in tch whn chckd & lost pl 5f out: 5th & pushed along appr st: no imp last 2f) | 1 | 6 | 9/1 | 91 | 18 |
| | | | | | (SP 114.5%) | | **6 Rn** |

**1m 39.9** (4.90) OWNER Kieran Scott (NEWMARKET) BRED Lady Juliet de Chair
**2609 Donna Viola** put in a sustained run over the last furlong and a half to wear down Hagwah virtually on the line. She needs a bit further than this and the Prix de l'Opera at Longchamp was the suggestion after the race. (5/2)
**3836* Hagwah (USA)** tried to make all the running, and the tactics looked likely to succeed until she began to tie up in the last 150 yards. (9/4: op 6/4)
**3530a Charlock (IRE)**, fifth into the straight, ran on strongly over the last furlong to be nearest at the finish. (8/1: op 9/2)
**3945 Arabride** ran in second place until crying enough two furlongs out. (3/1)
NR

## 4037a-EVRY (France) (R-H) (Good to firm)
## Tuesday September 3rd

### 4162a PRIX RIDGWAY (Listed) (3-Y.O C & G)
2-25 (2-23) **1m 1f** £18,445.00 (£6,324.00: £3,953.00)

| | Horse | Details | Dist | Pos | SP | RR | SF |
|---|---|---|---|---|---|---|---|
| 1756a6 | **Rupert (FR)** | (JdeRoualle,France) **3-9-2** GMosse | — | 1 | | 111 | — |
| | **Nero Zilzal (USA)** | (ELellouche,France) **3-9-2** TThulliez | nk | 2 | | 111 | — |
| 27246 | **Winter Romance** | (EALDunlop) **3-9-2** MHills | ½ | 3 | | 110 | — |
| 36914 | **Wood Magic** | (DRLoder) **3-9-2** RHughes (btn approx 4l) | | 7 | | — | — |
| | | | | | | | **10 Rn** |

**1m 40.29** P-M 6.40F: 2.70F 3.40F 6.90F (47.60F) OWNER Mr Z. Hakam BRED Haras du Bois Roussel
**2724 Winter Romance**, last early on, came with a run up the centre of the track but, after taking the lead a furlong out, could not go through with his effort. Still a good effort as he is much better when there is cut in the ground, he could now go for the Cambridgeshire.
**3691 Wood Magic**, prominent, was in trouble halfway down the straight and gradually faded out of contention. The plan had been for him to make all, but he got into a pocket on the rail and was unable to get out and force the pace. This can be ignored.
DS

## 4038a-SAN SIRO (Milan, Italy) (R-H) (Good)
## Saturday September 7th

### 4163a PREMIO GOFFS (2-Y.O)
5-00 (5-10) **6f** £10,150.00

| | Horse | Details | Dist | Pos | SP | RR | SF |
|---|---|---|---|---|---|---|---|
| | **Milliardaire (IRE)** | (GColleo,Italy) **2-9-3** MLatorre | — | 1 | | — | — |
| | **Jaunty Jack** | (LMCumani) **2-8-12** MCangiano | 1 | 2 | | — | — |
| | **Sun Sweet (ITY)** | (VPanici,Italy) **2-8-12** LPanici | ¾ | 3 | | — | — |
| | **Al Blu (IRE)** | (LMCumani) **2-8-12** FJovine (btn approx 6 3/4l) | | 6 | | — | — |
| | | | | | | | **7 Rn** |

**1m 13.1** (5.10) TOTE 19L: 13L 18L (47L) OWNER Scuderia Andy Capp BRED Scuderia Andy Capp Spa
**Jaunty Jack** showed good early speed and kept on well inside the final furlong, but could not quite get on terms with the winner. He is sure to pick up a small race.
**Al Blu (IRE)**, who fell out of the stalls, was slowly into his stride and never able to get on terms. He will come on for the run and better can be expected next time.

## 0497a-HANOVER (Germany) (L-H) (Good)
## Sunday September 8th

### 4164a PREIS DER HANNOVERSCHEN SPARKASSEN (Gp 3) (3-Y.O+ F & M)
3-25 (3-30) **1m 4f** £32,658.00 (£13,063.00: £6,532.00)

| | Horse | Details | Dist | Pos | SP | RR | SF |
|---|---|---|---|---|---|---|---|
| 2478a2 | **Anno Luce** | (UOstmann,Germany) **3-8-9b** GBocskai | — | 1 | | 112 | — |
| | **The Blade (GER)** | (HRemmert,Germany) **3-8-9** ABrockhausen | 2½ | 2 | | 109 | — |
| 3203a6 | **Night Petticoat (GER)** | (BSchutz,Germany) **3-8-9** AStarke | 1½ | 3 | | 107 | — |
| | | | | | | | **13 Rn** |

**2m 28.6** TOTE 21DM: 12DM 29DM 17DM OWNER Sheikh Mohammed BRED Sheikh Mohammed
**Anno Luce** gained her first Pattern success. This was a well-deserved win and she can go on from here.
**1750a* Night Petticoat (GER)**, who would have appreciated a little more cut in the ground, seems to be coming back to form.

## 2664a-LONGCHAMP (Paris, France) (R-H) (Good to firm)
## Sunday September 8th

### 4165a EMIRATES PRIX DU MOULIN DE LONGCHAMP (Gp 1) (3-Y.O+ C & F)
2-25 (2-28) **1m** £118,577.00 (£47,431.00: £23,715.00: £11,858.00)

| | Horse | Details | Dist | Pos | SP | RR | SF |
|---|---|---|---|---|---|---|---|
| 20392 | **Ashkalani (IRE)** | (AdeRoyerDupre,France) **3-8-11** GMosse (trckd ldrs: hdwy to ld over 1f out: qcknd clr ins fnl f: easily) | — | 1 | 4/5 1 | 132+ | 39 |
| 3745a* | **Spinning World (USA)** | (JEPease,France) **3-8-11** CAsmussen (a.p: rdn 2f out: ev ch over 1f out: kpt on) | 1½ | 2 | 7/2 2 | 129 | 36 |

| | | | | SP | RR | SF |
|---|---|---|---|---|---|---|
| 2052* | **Shake the Yoke** (ELellouche,France) **3-8-8** SGuillot (bhd early: plld out 2f out: rdn & r.o fr 1f out: nrst fin) | s.h | 3 | 7/2 2 | 126 | 33 |
| 3745a2 | **Vetheuil (USA)** (AFabre,France) **4-9-2** OPeslier (racd in 5th early: u.p st: styd on fnl f) | 2 | 4 | 15/2 3 | 125 | 37 |
| 3749a* | **Carling (FR)** (MmePBarbe,France) **4-8-12** TThulliez (chsd ldr to st: rdn to ld over 2f out: hdd over 1f out: no ex) | s.nk | 5 | 11/1 | 121 | 33 |
| 3745a3 | **Shaanxi (USA)** (ELellouche,France) **4-8-12** MEbina (racd in 6th early: rdn over 2f out: nt qckn) | 2½ | 6 | 11/1 | 116 | 28 |
| 3745a5 | **Grey Risk (FR)** (PDemercastel,France) **3-8-11** TJarnet (hld up: nvr rchd ldrs) | ¾ | 7 | 21/1 | 118 | 25 |
| 3745a8 | **Le Triton (USA)** (MmeCHead,France) **3-8-11** FHead (a in rr) | 1½ | 8 | 26/1 | 115 | 22 |
| | **Metaphor (USA)** (JEPease,France) **3-8-8** FSanchez (set str pce to st: hdd over 2f out: wknd) | 20 | 9 | 7/2 2 | 72 | — |
| | | | | (SP 158.9%) | | **9 Rn** |

**1m 37.2** (2.20) P-M 1.80F: 1.10F 1.10F 1.10F (2.90F) OWNER Aga Khan (CHANTILLY) BRED Aga Khan's Studs S.C.
**IN-FOCUS: For betting purposes Spinning World (USA) and Metaphor (USA) were cpld, as were Shaanxi (USA) and Carling (FR).**
**2039 Ashkalani (IRE)**, reappearing after nearly three months, looked splendid in the paddock and put up the most impressive performance seen at Longchamp this year. Coasting throughout, he showed tremendous acceleration just over a furlong out to have it sewn up in a matter of strides. He will now go for the Queen Elizabeth II Stakes, back at Ascot where he was produced too early when run out of the St. James's Palace Stakes in the final furlong. It will take a very special horse to beat him this time. (4/5)
**3745a* Spinning World (USA)**, who did nothing wrong, lost nothing in defeat but must be sick of the sight of Ashkalani as this was the fourth time he has finished behind him. It is possible that softer ground would have turned things more in his favour. He will avoid meeting the winner for a fifth time at Ascot and will instead be aimed at the Breeders' Cup Mile. (7/2)
**2052* Shake the Yoke** was given an awful lot to do. Held up for a late run, she had to be extricated in the straight to make her challenge and, making up a lot of late ground, would have taken second place in another couple of strides. She will take on the winner again at Ascot, where she is already a course and distance winner, and she may have the assistance of Olivier Peslier, which should be to her advantage. (7/2)
**3745a Vetheuil (USA)**, racing on the rail for much of the race, made his challenge from two furlongs out, but did not have the necessary speed on this ground. He looks best on a straight track, but was taking on the best milers in Europe here. (15/2)

## 4166a PRIX DES CHENES (Gp 3) (2-Y.O C & G)
3-30 (3-37) **1m** £28,986.00 (£10,540.00: £5,270.00)

| | | | | SP | RR | SF |
|---|---|---|---|---|---|---|
| 3201a2 | **Nombre Premier** (AdeRoyerDupre,France) **2-9-2** PSogorb | — | 1 | | 92 | — |
| | **Majorien** (MmeCHead,France) **2-9-2** FHead | ¾ | 2 | | 91 | — |
| | **Peintre Celebre (USA)** (AFabre,France) **2-9-2** OPeslier | ½ | 3 | | 90 | — |
| | | | | | | **7 Rn** |

**1m 44.8** (9.80) P-M 4.30F: 1.90F 2.20F OWNER Marquesa de Moratalla (CHANTILLY) BRED Marquesa de Moratalla
**3201a Nombre Premier**, given a very confident ride by his young jockey who was winning his first Group race, produced a good turn of foot and strode out really well in the final furlong. He certainly appreciated this extra distance and will now take his chance in the Gran Criterium.
**Majorien**, held up on this occasion, made his challenge up the middle of the track, but appeared to hesitate halfway up the straight before running on again at the finish. He would have been better suited to a much stronger pace.
**Peintre Celebre (USA)** was slightly hemmed in halfway up the straight but, when in the clear, could only run on at one pace. He was a disappointing favourite, but should be given another chance.

## 4167a PRIX GLADIATEUR (Gp 3) (3-Y.O+)
4-00 (4-09) **1m 7f 110y** £28,986.00 (£10,540.00: £5,270.00)

| | | | | SP | RR | SF |
|---|---|---|---|---|---|---|
| 36732 | **Always Aloof (USA)** (MRStoute) **5-9-4** OPeslier | — | 1 | | 125 | 55 |
| 3751a* | **Kassani (IRE)** (AdeRoyerDupre,France) **4-9-8** GMosse | ¾ | 2 | | 128 | 58 |
| 3751a4 | **Ming Dynasty (IRE)** (DSmaga,France) **5-9-2b** CAsmussen | 5 | 3 | | 117 | 47 |
| | | | | | | **6 Rn** |

**3m 19.1** (3.10) P-M 5.80F: 2.30F 1.50F OWNER Mr S. Hanson (NEWMARKET) BRED Northern and Pacific Investments
**3673 Always Aloof (USA)** was given a fine ride and ran a most courageous race. Always in the first two, he stole several lengths early in the straight and then held on gamely in the final furlong. He will be back at Longchamp in early October to contest the Group One Prix du Cadran.
**3751a* Kassani (IRE)**, giving 5lb to the winner, was held up for a late run, but his jockey may have been taken by surprise when the winner accelerated in the straight. He arrived late on the scene and was cutting down the leeway with every stride in the final furlong. He will give Double Trigger plenty to think about in the Cadran providing the ground does not become soft.
**3751a Ming Dynasty (IRE)** raced behind the leaders and ran on gamely to take third place. He is really not up to this class.

## 4168a PRIX DE LIANCOURT (Listed) (3-Y.O F)
4-30 (4-32) **1m 2f** £18,445.00 (£6,324.00: £3,953.00)

| | | | | SP | RR | SF |
|---|---|---|---|---|---|---|
| | **Otaiti (IRE)** (AFabre,France) **3-9-0** OPeslier | — | 1 | | 108 | 23 |
| | **Vicomtesse Mag (FR)** (JEHammond,France) **3-9-0** SGuillot | ½ | 2 | | 107 | 22 |
| 3916a4 | **Honest Guest (IRE)** (MHTompkins) **3-9-0** TQuinn | nk | 3 | | 107 | 22 |
| | | | | | | **10 Rn** |

**2m 5.2** (5.20) P-M 4.50F: 2.00F 2.60F 1.80F (22.70F) OWNER D. Wildenstein (CHANTILLY) BRED Dayton Ltd
**Otaiti (IRE)** looked very useful here.
**3916a Honest Guest (IRE)**, always prominent, took the lead entering the straight. Hard ridden, she stuck to her guns right to the line, but finally had to be satisfied with third place. She is thoroughly game and her trainer will now be looking for another listed race.

# 3394a-MUNICH (Germany) (L-H) (Soft)
## Sunday September 8th

## 4169a BAYERISCHER FLIEGERPREIS DER BMW (Listed) (3-Y.O+)
3-15 (3-19) **6f 110y** £10,811.00 (£4,324.00: £2,207.00)

| | | | | SP | RR | SF |
|---|---|---|---|---|---|---|
| 3572a3 | **Takin (GER)** (FrauEMader,Germany) **5-8-10** LMader | — | 1 | | 98 | — |
| 3524* | **Monaassib** (EALDunlop) **5-9-5** WCarson | nk | 2 | | 106 | — |
| | **Ace High (USA)** (HJentzsch,Germany) **3-8-13** RHughes | ½ | 3 | | 101 | — |
| | | | | | | **10 Rn** |

**1m 20.8** TOTE 34DM: 12DM 11DM 14DM OWNER Stall Reckendorf BRED Gotz Meyer zu Reckendorf

**3524* Monaassib** put up a gutsy display under topweight. He raced in third and quickened well to take up the running two furlongs out. Although he ran on well, he just failed to hold off the late run of the winner, but would probably have won had the going been firmer.

## 4163a-SAN SIRO (Milan, Italy) (R-H) (Good)
### Sunday September 8th

### 4170a PREMIO METANOPOLI (3-Y.O F)
2-30 (2-37) **1m 3f** £10,150.00

| | | | | SP | RR | SF |
|---|---|---|---|---|---|---|
| 1393a[5] | **Grey Way (USA)** (GBotti,Italy) **3-8-9** EBotti | — | 1 | | 76 | — |
| | **Croa (IRE)** (GMaggi,Italy) **3-8-11** NMulas | 7 | 2 | | 68 | — |
| 3441[7] | **Candrika** (LMCumani) **3-8-7** LSorrentino | ½ | 3 | | 63 | — |
| | | | | | | **6 Rn** |

**2m 17.5** (9.50) TOTE 12L: 11L 13L (18L) OWNER C. Vittadini (ITALY) BRED C. Vittadini
**Candrika** was never able to get on terms with the easy winner. Racing in third, she made headway over three furlongs out and went third a furlong and a half out, but then failed to quicken further.

### 4171a PREMIO GUDO (2-Y.O)
4-30 (4-40) **1m** £8,120.00

| | | | | SP | RR | SF |
|---|---|---|---|---|---|---|
| | **Kaffir (IRE)** (GVerricelli,Italy) **2-9-0** SDettori | — | 1 | | — | — |
| | **Columella (ITY)** (PCaravati,Italy) **2-9-0** GForte | 2½ | 2 | | — | — |
| | **Sopran Big Bir (ITY)** (TManili,Italy) **2-8-10** MPlanard | s.h | 3 | | — | — |
| | **Lajatta** (LMCumani) **2-9-0** LSorrentino (btn approx 6l) | | 6 | | — | — |
| | | | | | | **10 Rn** |

**No Time Taken** TOTE 35L: 18L 31L 46L (196L) OWNER Scuderia Fert BRED Azienda Agricola le Tiglio
**Lajatta** put up a fair performance on this debut. He raced in fourth in the middle of the track but, when asked for an effort two furlongs out, found very little and was soon outpaced. He will come on for the run.

### 4172a PREMIO FEDERICO TESIO (Gp 3) (4-Y.O+)
5-00 (5-15) **1m 3f** £25,554.00 (£11,614.00: £6,443.00)

| | | | | SP | RR | SF |
|---|---|---|---|---|---|---|
| 1135a[7] | **Slicious** (VCaruso,Italy) **4-8-11** MEsposito | — | 1 | | 116 | — |
| 3754a[3] | **Concepcion (GER)** (HJentzsch,Germany) **6-8-11** SEccles | 2¾ | 2 | | 112 | — |
| 327a* | **Galtee (IRE)** (UweStoltefuss,Germany) **4-8-11** JQuinn | 1½ | 3 | | 110 | — |
| | | | | | | **6 Rn** |

**2m 15.3** (7.30) TOTE 20L: 13L 15L (25L) OWNER Laghi Stable BRED F. C. T. Wilson
**623a* Slicious**, returning to winning form, had to be hard ridden to put it beyond doubt.

## 1943a-TABY (Stockholm, Sweden) (L-H) (Good)
### Sunday September 8th

### 4173a TABY OPEN SPRINT CHAMPIONSHIP (Listed) (3-Y.O+)
2-00 **6f** £34,985.00 (£9,718.00: £7,775.00)

| | | | | SP | RR | SF |
|---|---|---|---|---|---|---|
| 3759[4] | **Jayannpee** (IABalding) **5-9-4** LDettori (fin 3rd, hd, hd: awrdd r) | — | 1 | | 101 | — |
| | **Humbert's Landing (IRE)** (ALund,Norway) **5-9-4** JTandari (fin 1st: disq: plcd 2nd) | | 2 | | 103 | — |
| | **Subzero** (WUppstrom,Sweden) **4-9-4** CCordrey (fin 4th, nse: plcd 3rd) | | 3 | | 101 | — |
| 1943a[3] | **Hakiki (IRE)** (WNeuroth,Norway) **4-9-4** FJohansson (fin 2nd, hd: disq: plcd 4th) | | 4 | | 102 | — |
| | | | | | | **12 Rn** |

**1m 9.0** TOTE 36.50KR: 19.40KR 92.90KR 95.20KR (1,088.60KR) OWNER Mr J. Paniccia (KINGSCLERE) BRED C. H. Bothway
**3759 Jayannpee**, in third place entering the straight, was carried over by Humbert's Landing and ran on well to the line. The first two were disqualified for two separate incidents, so Jayannpee was promoted to first.

### 4174a STOCKHOLM CUP (Gp 3) (3-Y.O+)
2-30 **1m 4f** £58,309.00 (£19,436.00: £9,718.00)

| | | | | SP | RR | SF |
|---|---|---|---|---|---|---|
| 2843a[6] | **Kill the Crab (IRE)** (WNeuroth,Norway) **4-9-2** FJohansson | — | 1 | | 112 | — |
| 3754a[2] | **Dulford Lad** (JFretheim,Norway) **5-9-6** MSantos | 1 | 2 | | 115 | — |
| | **Inchrory** (AHyldmo,Norway) **3-8-12** GNordling | 2 | 3 | | 113 | — |
| 3386a[7] | **Overbury (IRE)** (SbinSuroor) **5-9-6** LDettori (btn approx 9¼l) | 6 | 4 | | 104 | — |
| 3754a[6] | **Glide Path (USA)** (JWHills) **7-9-6** JWeaver (btn approx 20 3/4l) | | 9 | | — | — |
| | | | | | | **14 Rn** |

**2m 27.0** TOTE 66.30KR: 20.70KR 49.50KR 18.90KR (927.60KR) OWNER Stall Tricolor BRED Deerpark Stud in Ireland
**3386a Overbury (IRE)** made some headway to go fourth entering the straight, but was never able to get in an effective challenge.
**3754a Glide Path (USA)**, the winner of this event last year, never looked like repeating that performance.

## 4131-DONCASTER (L-H) (Good to firm, Rnd crse Good patches)
### Friday September 13th
WEATHER: fine but cloudy WIND: fresh hlf bhd

### 4175 AMCO MAIDEN STKS (2-Y.O) (Class D)
1-30 (1-31) **1m (straight)** £3,840.00 (£1,140.00: £540.00: £240.00) Stalls: High GOING minus 0.44 sec per fur (F)

| | | | | SP | RR | SF |
|---|---|---|---|---|---|---|
| 3757[4] | **Cape Cross (IRE)** (JHMGosden) **2-9-0** LDettori(7) (b.hind: hld up: shkn up over 2f out: r.o wl to ld jst ins fnl f: pushed out) | — | 1 | 3/1[2] | 91+ | 36 |

| | | | Pos | SP | RR | SF |
|---|---|---|---|---|---|---|
| | **Shaya** (MajorWRHern) **2-9-0** WCarson(4) (w'like: lengthy: chsd ldrs: pushed along over 2f out: led over 1f out: sn hdd: nt pce of wnr) | 1¼ | **2** | 11/4$^{1}$ | 89+ | 34 |
| | **Voyagers Quest (USA)** (PWChapple-Hyam) **2-9-0** GDuffield(2) (w'like: hld up & plld hrd: effrt ½-wy: sn rdn & outpcd: styd on fnl 2f) | 3 | **3** | 12/1 | 83 | 28 |
| | **Recourse (USA)** (HRACecil) **2-9-0** MJKinane(8) (w'like: leggy: trckd ldr: hung lft thrght: led ½-wy: put hd in air & hdd over 1f out: sn wknd) | 1 | **4** | 6/1 | 81 | 26 |
| | **Lookout** (BWHills) **2-8-9** MHills(9) (w'like: scope: bit bkwd: hld up: effrt over 2f out: kpt on: nvr nr to chal) | 1¾ | **5** | 6/1 | 72+ | 17 |
| 3982$^{14}$ | **Pertemps Mission** (JPearce) **2-9-0** GBardwell(6) (led to ½-wy: wknd over 1f out) | 3 | **6** | 50/1 | 71 | 16 |
| 3757$^{2}$ | **Flirting Around (USA)** (MRStoute) **2-9-0** JReid(5) (lw: chsd ldrs: effrt over 2f out: sn wl outpcd) | nk | **7** | 100/30$^{3}$ | 70 | 15 |
| | **Fruitie O'Flarety** (CEBrittain) **2-9-0** BDoyle(3) (unf: bit bkwd: s.i.s: sn pushed along: wl outpcd fr ½-wy) | 3 | **8** | 20/1 | 64 | 9 |
| 3485$^{4}$ | **Ibin St James** (JDBethell) **2-9-0** JFortune(10) (pushed along & outpcd fr ½-wy) | s.h | **9** | 33/1 | 64 | 9 |
| | **Wellcome Inn** (JAHarris) **2-9-0** KFallon(1) (wl grwn: bkwd: s.s: sn chsng ldrs & pushed along: lost pl 3f out: sn bhd) | 23 | **10** | 33/1 | 18 | — |

(SP 123.6%) **10 Rn**

**1m 39.52** (2.52) CSF £11.98 TOTE £4.50: £1.30 £1.50 £3.80 (£6.80) Trio £46.00 OWNER Sheikh Mohammed (NEWMARKET) BRED Sheikh Mohammed Bin Rashid Al Maktoum

**3757 Cape Cross (IRE)**, a lazy walker, had to be put about his task. Showing a nice turn of foot, he won in good style in the end. He will be even better next year when he fills to his frame. (3/1)

**Shaya**, an athletic, much-touted newcomer, was a shade green going to post. After being driven through to take the lead, he was soon headed and could not match the winner for foot. This was a sprint from halfway and he should be a different proposition next time. (11/4: 11/10-3/1)

**Voyagers Quest (USA)** would not settle and, after being caught flat-footed, was staying on at the finish. (12/1: op 8/1)

**Recourse (USA)**, a tall newcomer, was very green going to post. Hanging left and carrying his head high, he never really took hold of his bit. Hopefully this will have opened his eyes. (6/1: op 4/1)

**Lookout**, an attractive filly, was green going to post. Not knocked about at any stage, the outing should bring her on a good deal. (6/1)

**Pertemps Mission**, a good walker, made the running, but was well and truly outpaced once the race began in earnest. (50/1)

**3757 Flirting Around (USA)** showed a very poor action going down and was probably suited by the give underfoot on his debut. (100/30)

## 4176 JOY U.K. H'CAP (0-100) (3-Y.O+) (Class C)

2-00 (2-02) **1m 4f** £5,120.00 (£1,520.00: £720.00: £320.00) Stalls: Low GOING minus 0.19 sec per fur (GF)

| | | | Pos | SP | RR | SF |
|---|---|---|---|---|---|---|
| 3710$^{9}$ | **Spillo (88)** (LMCumani) **3-8-11** KDarley(8) (lw: bhd: effrt 4f out: styd on wl u.p to ld towards fin) | — | **1** | 5/1$^{2}$ | 100 | 73 |
| 3710$^{5}$ | **Daunt (92)** (JHMGosden) **4-9-10** LDettori(5) (lw: hld up: stdy hdwy over 2f out: rdn to ld over 1f out: hdd & nt qckn wl ins fnl f) | ¾ | **2** | 4/1$^{1}$ | 103 | 85 |
| 4055$^{12}$ | **Time for Action (IRE) (85)** (MHTompkins) **4-9-0**(3) MHenry(2) (lw: led tl over 1f out: styd on same pce) | 2 | **3** | 7/1$^{3}$ | 93 | 75 |
| 3711$^{9}$ | **Pike Creek (USA) (85)** (IABalding) **3-8-8** KFallon(1) (a chsng ldrs: drvn 7f out: styd on same pce fnl 2f) | 1¾ | **4** | 10/1 | 91 | 64 |
| 3710$^{22}$ | **Three Hills (85)** (BWHills) **3-8-8b$^{1}$** MHills(13) (trckd ldrs: chal 3f out: sn rdn: one pce appr fnl f) | 1¼ | **5** | 10/1 | 89 | 62 |
| 4073$^{8}$ | **Canton Venture (76)** (SPCWoods) **4-8-8** WCarson(12) (chsd ldrs: wknd 2f out: eased) | 8 | **6** | 12/1 | 70 | 52 |
| *184*$^{10}$ | **Endowment (74)** (MrsMReveley) **4-8-6** ACulhane(10) (hld up & bhd: sme hdwy fnl 2f: nvr nr to chal) | 5 | **7** | 20/1 | 61 | 43 |
| 3939$^{7}$ | **Manful (67)** (CWCElsey) **4-7-13b** NKennedy(14) (sn pushed along: nvr nr ldrs) | 2 | **8** | 20/1 | 51 | 33 |
| 3497$^{6}$ | **Wight (85)** (RHannon) **3-8-8** MJKinane(3) (a in rr) | 8 | **9** | 14/1 | 59 | 32 |
| 3710$^{13}$ | **Askern (75)** (DHaydnJones) **5-8-7** AMackay(7) (lw: hdwy on outside to chse ldrs over 5f out: lost pl 3f out) | 1¼ | **10** | 12/1 | 47 | 29 |
| 3791$^{5}$ | **Jagellon (USA) (84)** (WRMuir) **5-9-2** JReid(9) (lw: chsd ldrs tl lost pl over 4f out) | 3 | **11** | 12/1 | 52 | 34 |
| 3997$^{9}$ | **Pleasant Surprise (94)** (MJohnston) **3-9-3** BDoyle(6) (sn pushed along: chsd ldr tl lost pl over 4f out) | hd | **12** | 14/1 | 62 | 35 |
| 3704$^{4}$ | **Royal Action (77)** (JEBanks) **3-7-9b$^{1(5)}$** MBaird(11) (sn pushed along: a in rr: lost tch 4f out) | 27 | **13** | 10/1 | 9 | — |

(SP 122.4%) **13 Rn**

**2m 31.02** (1.02) CSF £24.45 CT £128.95 TOTE £5.30: £1.70 £1.80 £3.20 (£7.00) Trio £23.10 OWNER Mrs Luca Cumani (NEWMARKET) BRED Limestone Stud

WEIGHT FOR AGE 3yo-9lb

**3145 Spillo**, who looked particularly well in the paddock, moved with more freedom than he had at York. Responding to pressure, he stuck on willingly to get up near the line. All he does is stay. (5/1)

**3710 Daunt**, who made all the running when successful at Newbury in July, was ridden with plenty of confidence, but it turned out misplaced in the end. After cruising through onto the heels of the leaders, he was shaken up to hit the front but, once there, he did not find as much as was expected and was worn down near the line. (4/1: 3/1-9/2)

**3351* Time for Action (IRE)**, who likes to dominate, made the running and stuck on willingly if at the same pace. (7/1)

**3315* Pike Creek (USA)**, struggling to keep up some way from home, stuck on under pressure and will be suited by a stiffer test. (10/1)

**2690 Three Hills**, tried in blinkers, moved up looking as if he could take the leader at any time but, when the chips were down, he did not find a lot and could only stay on at the same pace. (10/1: 7/1-12/1)

**3587 Canton Venture** was eased up when beaten and has probably had enough for the time being. (12/1)

**Endowment**, dropped in at the start, came through nicely in the closing stages. His new connections are obviously still learning and he is one to bear in mind. (20/1)

## 4177 RJB MINING CONDITIONS STKS (3, 4 & 5-Y.O) (Class B)

2-35 (2-35) **1m 2f 60y** £7,130.00 (£2,630.00: £1,255.00: £505.00: £192.50: £67.50) Stalls: Low GOING minus 0.19 sec per fur (GF)

| | | | Pos | SP | RR | SF |
|---|---|---|---|---|---|---|
| | **Forest Buck (USA)** (HRACecil) **3-8-9** AMcGlone(2) (trckd ldr: led over 2f out: rdn & r.o wl ins fnl f) | — | **1** | 10/1 | 114+ | 62 |
| 3798$^{3}$ | **Storm Trooper (USA) (112)** (HRACecil) **3-9-1** MJKinane(5) (trckd ldrs: effrt 2f out: sn rdn & no imp) | 2½ | **2** | 8/15$^{1}$ | 116 | 64 |
| 3798$^{4}$ | **Prince of My Heart (103)** (BWHills) **3-8-13** MHills(4) (led tl over 2f out: one pce) | 3½ | **3** | 11/1 | 109 | 57 |
| 1520$^{4}$ | **Wijara (IRE) (103)** (RHannon) **4-9-2** JReid(6) (lw: hld up: effrt over 3f out: sn rdn: nvr nr to chal) | 2 | **4** | 6/1$^{2}$ | 102 | 57 |
| 725$^{5}$ | **Maiden Castle** (JHMGosden) **3-8-11** LDettori(1) (b: lw: hld up: effrt over 4f out: sn chsng ldrs: wknd over 2f out) | 1½ | **5** | 8/1$^{3}$ | 101 | 49 |
| 3503$^{8}$ | **Tarte Aux Pommes (USA) (80)** (CEBrittain) **4-8-11** BDoyle(3) (trckd ldrs: effrt 3f out: sn wknd) | 2½ | **6** | 33/1 | 90? | 45 |

(SP 111.0%) **6 Rn**

**2m 9.07** (2.07) CSF £15.56 TOTE £9.90: £2.90 £1.10 (£3.40) OWNER Buckram Oak Holdings (NEWMARKET) BRED Buckram Oak Farm

WEIGHT FOR AGE 3yo-7lb

**Forest Buck (USA)**, winner of a maiden at Leicester in October, has been operated on for chips in his knee. Taking a keen grip, he took time to get into full stride once he hit the front, but he scored in decisive fashion in the end. This was clearly a surprise to connections, but there is no doubt he is a talented colt. (10/1)

**3798 Storm Trooper (USA)** travelled strongly as usual but, after looking to be going easily best at one stage, he did not find as much as expected once under pressure. A brilliant winner at Newmarket first time out, he has flattered to deceive since. (8/15)

**986 Prince of My Heart** set a strong pace, but was easily swept aside. (11/1: 8/1-12/1)
**1520 Wijara (IRE)**, a confirmed autumn performer, did not impress with his action going down. The first under pressure, he stayed on in his own time. This, his first outing in over three months, will no doubt bring him on. (6/1: op 4/1)
**725 Maiden Castle**, absent since flopping at Newbury in April, made a brief effort halfway up the straight, but was soon in trouble. (8/1)
**Tarte Aux Pommes (USA)** has now finished last in all her four starts here this year. (33/1)

## 4178 O & K TROY STKS (Listed) (3-Y.O+) (Class A)

3-05 (3-11) **1m 4f** £11,563.40 (£4,280.60: £2,055.30: £841.50: £335.75: £133.45) Stalls: Low GOING minus 0.19 sec per fur (GF)

| | | | | SP | RR | SF |
|---|---|---|---|---|---|---|
| 3841* | **Busy Flight (105)** (BWHills) **3-8-6** MHills(7) (lw: mde all: styd on strly fnl 2f) | — | 1 | 5/1[3] | 119 | 78 |
| 3157[6] | **Kalabo (USA) (113)** (SbinSuroor) **4-9-1** LDettori(2) (swtg: hld up: effrt over 3f out: swtchd outside over 2f out: styd on wl ins fnl f: nt rch wnr) | 1¼ | 2 | 9/2[2] | 117 | 85 |
| 3597[2] | **Minds Music (USA) (113)** (HRACecil) **4-9-1** KFallon(9) (lw: drvn along 9f out: hdwy over 4f out: nt qckn fnl 2f) | 1½ | 3 | 100/30[1] | 115 | 83 |
| 3409[3] | **Desert Shot (113)** (MRStoute) **6-9-1** JReid(6) (stdd s: hld up: hdwy on ins over 3f out: nt qckn fnl 2f) | 1¼ | 4 | 13/2 | 114 | 82 |
| 3749a[2] | **Bal Harbour (110)** (HRACecil) **5-9-6** MJKinane(4) (lw: chsd ldrs: rdn over 2f out: wknd over 1f out) | 6 | 5 | 9/2[2] | 111 | 79 |
| 1427[4] | **Smart Play (USA) (95)** (MrsJCecil) **3-8-6** KDarley(1) (hld up: hdwy on ins over 4f out: sn chsng ldrs: wknd over 1f out) | hd | 6 | 20/1 | 106 | 65 |
| 3992[2] | **Haleakala (IRE)** (MJohnston) **3-8-1** WCarson(8) (b.nr fore: swtg: drvn along 7f out: bhd fnl 3f) | 1 | 7 | 15/2 | 99 | 58 |
| 3781[7] | **Weet-A-Minute (IRE) (105)** (RHollinshead) **3-8-6** FLynch(5) (chsd ldrs tl wknd over 2f out) | s.h | 8 | 33/1 | 104 | 63 |
| 3972[3] | **Anchor Clever (109)** (PAKelleway) **4-9-1** DRMcCabe(3) (lw: trckd wnr tl wknd over 3f out: sn bhd & eased) | 19 | 9 | 33/1 | 79 | 47 |

(SP 111.8%) **9 Rn**

**2m 29.72** (0.23 under best) (-0.28) CSF £25.12 TOTE £5.90: £1.90 £1.90 £1.30 (£23.60) Trio £19.20 OWNER Mr S. WingfieldDigby (LAMBOURN) BRED S. Wingfield Digby
WEIGHT FOR AGE 3yo-9lb

**3841* Busy Flight** is obviously a progressive young stayer. Setting a strong gallop, he kept it up in tremendous style to score in record time. He looks a smart prospect, especially for next year. (5/1)
**3157 Kalabo (USA)**, who presumably failed to stay two miles last time, stuck on strongly after being switched but, after giving the winner plenty of rope, he was never going to close the gap in time. A mile and six might prove his ideal trip. (9/2)
**3597 Minds Music (USA)** was soon hard at work. Only keeping on at the same pace in the last two furlongs, he needs a longer trip. (100/30)
**3409 Desert Shot**, steadied at the start, was ridden to conserve his stamina. Creeping up on the inner halfway up the straight, he could do little more than stay on at the same pace when pressure was applied. A mile and three might prove his optimum trip. (13/2)
**3749a Bal Harbour**, who did not impress with his action going down, would appreciate easier ground. (9/2)
**1427 Smart Play (USA)**, absent since well beaten here in May, made a rapid move on the inner once in line for home, but his stamina seemed to give way over a furlong out. (20/1)

## 4179 LAURENT-PERRIER CHAMPAGNE STKS (Gp 2) (2-Y.O C & G) (Class A)

3-35 (3-39) **7f** £45,939.70 (£16,015.70: £7,662.85: £3,106.75) Stalls: High GOING minus 0.44 sec per fur (F)

| | | | | SP | RR | SF |
|---|---|---|---|---|---|---|
| 3243* | **Bahhare (USA)** (JLDunlop) **2-8-10** WCarson(3) (lw: hld up: shkn up over 2f out: rdn to ld over 1f out: qcknd clr) | — | 1 | 4/6[1] | 106+ | 62 |
| 3668[3] | **In Command (IRE)** (BWHills) **2-8-10** MHills(1) (lw: trckd ldr: led over 2f out tl over 1f out: unable qckn) | 3½ | 2 | 9/1 | 98 | 54 |
| 3040* | **Musheer (USA)** (MissGayKelleway) **2-8-10** KFallon(5) (lw: led: sn pushed along: hdd over 2f out: kpt on same pce) | 1¾ | 3 | 9/2[3] | 94 | 50 |
| 3588* | **Reliquary (USA)** (DRLoder) **2-8-10** LDettori(4) (lw: hld up: effrt & swtchd lft over 2f out: rdn & no imp over 1f out: eased) | 4 | 4 | 4/1[2] | 85 | 41 |

(SP 108.2%) **4 Rn**

**1m 23.21** (1.19 under 2y best) (-0.39) CSF £5.73 TOTE £1.60: (£3.90) OWNER Mr Hamdan Al Maktoum (ARUNDEL) BRED Shadwell Farm Inc

**3243* Bahhare (USA)**, awkward to load, had to be pushed along to get into full stride. After hitting the front, he carried his head slightly high and thrashed his tail, but he quickened clear in the style of a top-class colt. He scored in record time and has set the standard for next year's 2000 Guineas. (4/6)
**3668 In Command (IRE)**, who would not settle when held up at York, made the best of his way home, but had no answer when the winner swept by. (9/1)
**3040* Musheer (USA)** made the running and was pushed along to set a record pace but, when the chips were down, he found nothing in the way of finishing speed. He had two handlers in the paddock. (9/2: 5/2-5/1)
**3588* Reliquary (USA)**, on edge in the parade ring, needed two handlers. Dropped in last of the four, he looked to be travelling strongly but, when switched off the rail to make his effort, he found disappointingly little and, with all chance gone inside the last, was eased. It remains to be seen whether he goes on and confirms the high promise he showed on his debut. (4/1)

## 4180 H. LEVERTON H'CAP (0-80) (3-Y.O+) (Class D)

4-10 (4-11) **5f** £3,840.00 (£1,140.00: £540.00: £240.00) Stalls: High GOING minus 0.44 sec per fur (F)

| | | | | SP | RR | SF |
|---|---|---|---|---|---|---|
| 3085[8] | **Surprise Mission (70)** (MrsJRRamsden) **4-9-5** ACulhane(15) (lw: stdd s: hld up: stdy hdwy 2f out: r.o to ld ins fnl f) | — | 1 | 14/1 | 81 | 64 |
| 3930[2] | **Gone Savage (65)** (WJMusson) **8-9-0** LDettori(11) (sn chsng ldrs: ev ch fnl f: n.m.r: r.o) | ½ | 2 | 9/2[1] | 74 | 57 |
| 3622[12] | **Daawe (USA) (66)** (MrsVAAconley) **5-9-1v** MDeering(21) (led: edgd lft & hdd ins fnl f) | ½ | 3 | 16/1 | 74 | 57 |
| 3973[2] | **Kira (70)** (JLEyre) **6-9-5** WCarson(20) (lw: a chsng ldrs: sn drvn along: kpt on same pce fnl 2f) | 2½ | 4 | 15/2[3] | 70 | 53 |
| 3932[3] | **Insider Trader (77)** (MrsJRRamsden) **5-9-7**(5) GFaulkner(2) (led far side: edgd rt & nt qckn fnl f) | ½ | 5 | 14/1 | 75 | 58 |
| 3932* | **Panther (IRE) (72)** (PDEvans) **6-9-7v** MJKinane(12) (styd on u.p fnl 2f: nt rch ldrs) | nk | 6 | 12/1 | 69 | 52 |
| 3774* | **Oatey (65)** (MrsJRRamsden) **3-8-13** KFallon(3) (chsd ldrs far side: sn drvn along: styd on fnl f) | nk | 7 | 7/1[2] | 61 | 43 |
| 3693[9] | **Literary Society (USA) (69)** (JARToller) **3-9-3** GDuffield(18) (sn outpcd & drvn along: styd on fnl 2f) | ¾ | 8 | 14/1 | 63 | 45 |
| 3995[20] | **Playmaker (64)** (DNicholls) **3-8-12b** AlexGreaves(19) (lw: chsd ldrs tl wknd over 1f out) | ½ | 9 | 25/1 | 56 | 38 |
| 3793[2] | **Tropical Beach (66)** (JBerry) **3-9-0** EmmaO'Gorman(6) (reard, s.s & swtchd rt: bhd tl sme hdwy over 1f out) | 1¼ | 10 | 16/1 | 54 | 36 |
| 3296[16] | **Blessingindisguise (76)** (MWEasterby) **3-9-5**(5) GParkin(17) (lw: sn bhd) | nk | 11 | 33/1 | 63 | 45 |
| 2119[7] | **Saddlehome (USA) (71)** (TDBarron) **7-9-6** JFortune(14) (hld up: sme hdwy 2f out: sn wknd) | ½ | 12 | 14/1 | 57 | 40 |
| 3868* | **Just Dissident (IRE) (62)** (RMWhitaker) **4-8-11** DeanMcKeown(22) (lw: chsd ldrs: drvn along ½-wy: wknd over 1f out) | s.h | 13 | 12/1 | 48 | 31 |
| 3232[21] | **Master of Passion (75)** (JMPEustace) **7-9-10** MTebbutt(7) (racd far side: hld up: effrt over 2f out: sn wknd) | 1½ | 14 | 20/1 | 56 | 39 |

| | | | | | |
|---|---|---|---|---|---|
| 2363[12] **Miss Waterline (72)** (PDEvans) **3-8-13**(7) AnthonyBond(10) (racd centre: outpcd fr ½-wy) ..........s.h | **15** | 33/1 | 53 | 35 |
| 3932[7] **Chadwell Hall (67)** (SRBowring) **5-9-2b** SDWilliams(16) (chsd ldrs 3f: sn wknd) ..........nk | **16** | 20/1 | 47 | 30 |
| 3932[12] **Beau Venture (USA) (68)** (BPalling) **8-9-3** KDarley(5) (chsd ldrs far side 3f: sn wknd) ..........1½ | **17** | 33/1 | 43 | 26 |
| 3868[9] **Royal Dome (IRE) (75)** (MartynWane) **4-9-5**(5) PRoberts(8) (chsd ldrs far side 3f: sn wknd) ..........¾ | **18** | 20/1 | 47 | 30 |
| *4081*[11] **Cheeky Chappy (75)** (DWChapman) **5-9-7b**(3) OPears(9) (racd far side: a in rr) ..........nk | **19** | 33/1 | 47 | 30 |
| 3793[4] **Barranak (IRE) (67)** (GMMcCourt) **4-9-2** AMcGlone(13) (lw: chsd ldrs: sn drvn along: lost pl ½-wy) ..........s.h | **20** | 25/1 | 38 | 21 |
| *3953*[2] **Sing With the Band (70)** (BAMcMahon) **5-9-5** JReid(4) (w ldrs far side tl wknd 2f out) ..........hd | **21** | 16/1 | 41 | 24 |
| | | (SP 135.9%) **21 Rn** | | |

**58.47 secs** (0.07) CSF £74.69 CT £983.21 TOTE £18.70: £4.10 £1.50 £3.60 £1.70 (£62.10) Trio £783.70 OWNER Mr D. R. Brotherton (THIRSK) BRED D. R. Brotherton

WEIGHT FOR AGE 3yo-1lb

STEWARDS' ENQUIRY Deering susp. 23-24/9/96 (careless riding).

**3085 Surprise Mission**, who really took the eye in the paddock, had the draw in his favour for once. A keen-going sort who has more speed than stamina, he came from off the pace to get up near the line. (14/1)

**3930 Gone Savage** continues to run well and is overdue a change of luck. (9/2)

**3424 Daawe (USA)**, back to five, certainly does not lack speed. Edging off a true line inside the last, he slightly hampered the runner-up. (16/1)

**3973 Kira** was never able to dominate and her rider was soon hard at work. (15/2)

**3932 Insider Trader**, with the visor again left off, came out best of the far-side group. (14/1)

**3932* Panther (IRE)** struggled from a 4lb higher mark. (12/1)

**3774* Oatey**, raised 5lb, finished second best on the far side. (7/1)

## 4181 SUN PRINCESS CONDITIONS STKS (3-Y.O) (Class C)

4-40 (4-42) **1m (round)** £4,560.00 (£1,680.00: £800.00: £320.00: £120.00: £40.00) Stalls: High GOING minus 0.19 sec per fur (GF)

| | | SP | RR | SF |
|---|---|---|---|---|
| 3229[3] **Kammtarra (USA) (101)** (SbinSuroor) **3-9-0** LDettori(7) (trckd ldrs: led over 2f out: r.o wl) ..........— | **1** | 7/2[2] | 111 | 71 |
| 3712[2] **Ali-Royal (IRE) (111)** (HRACecil) **3-9-4** MJKinane(4) (trckd ldrs: effrt 2f out: sn rdn: no imp fnl f) ..........1½ | **2** | 7/4[1] | 112 | 72 |
| 3691[7] **Tawkil (USA) (97)** (BWHills) **3-8-11** WCarson(2) (trckd ldrs: effrt & n.m.r 2f out: kpt on same pce) ..........2½ | **3** | 11/2[3] | 100 | 60 |
| 3996[6] **Kala Sunrise (81)** (CSmith) **3-8-11** JFortune(6) (bhd: styd on u.p fnl 3f: nvr nr to chal) ..........3½ | **4** | 33/1 | 93 | 53 |
| 2337[4] **World Premier (105)** (CEBrittain) **3-8-11** BDoyle(1) (lw: led tl over 2f out: wknd over 1f out) ..........2½ | **5** | 8/1 | 88 | 48 |
| 695[4] **Pommard (IRE)** (JHMGosden) **3-8-11** KDarley(8) (sn bhd: rdn over 3f out: nvr nr ldrs) ..........3 | **6** | 9/1 | 82 | 42 |
| 3811[2] **Bonarelli (IRE) (94)** (MRStoute) **3-8-11** KFallon(5) (sn outpcd & pushed along: n.d) ..........6 | **7** | 10/1 | 70 | 30 |
| 3822[5] **Dublin River (USA) (97)** (HThomsonJones) **3-8-11** NCarlisle(3) (lw: chsd ldrs: pushed along 5f out: lost pl over 2f out) ..........1 | **8** | 25/1 | 68 | 28 |
| 3999* **Van Gurp (90)** (BAMcMahon) **3-9-0** GDuffield(9) (lw: hld up: effrt over 3f out: hung lft: n.d) ..........3½ | **9** | 14/1 | 64 | 24 |
| | | (SP 117.6%) **9 Rn** | | |

**1m 37.62** (1.12) CSF £9.85 TOTE £3.50: £1.10 £1.40 £2.10 (£3.80) Trio £8.40 OWNER Mr Saeed Maktoum Al Maktoum (NEWMARKET) BRED Gainsborough Farm Inc.

**3229 Kammtarra (USA)** seems more settled these days and won this in good style. He should make an even better four-year-old. (7/2: 3/1-9/2)

**3712 Ali-Royal (IRE)** did not pull out as much as expected after travelling strongly for much of the way. Seven furlongs possibly suits him fractionally better. (7/4)

**1817 Tawkil (USA)**, back at a mile, did not have a lot of room on the inside, but it was his lack of pace that was his downfall. (11/2)

**3996 Kala Sunrise** appeared to run another good race, keeping on under strong pressure. After York and here, he will shoot up in the weights and will find it tough going. (33/1)

**2337 World Premier**, reappearing after a break, tired coming to the final furlong. (8/1)

**695 Pommard (IRE)**, keen in the early stages, went flat at halfway and never looked like picking up. It is hard to know what to make of this one. (9/1: 6/1-10/1)

T/Jkpt: £7,100.00 (0.1 Tckts); £5,366.00 to Doncaster 14/9/96. T/Plpt: £14.60 (1,722.59 Tckts). T/Qdpt: £3.90 (410.94 Tckts). WG

# 3801-GOODWOOD (R-H) (St crse Good, Rnd crse Good to firm)
## Friday September 13th

WEATHER: fine WIND: almost nil

## 4182 EYDON HALL FARM MACMILLAN NURSES NURSERY H'CAP (2-Y.O) (Class D)

2-10 (2-11) **7f** £4,854.00 (£1,452.00: £696.00: £318.00) Stalls: High GOING minus 0.20 sec per fur (GF)

| | | SP | RR | SF |
|---|---|---|---|---|
| 3809* **Brandon Jack (78)** (IABalding) **2-9-3** RCochrane(3) (lw: rdn over 2f out: hdwy over 1f out: led wl ins fnl f: r.o wl) ..........— | **1** | 7/1[3] | 78 | 40 |
| 3762[4] **Right Tune (81)** (BHanbury) **2-9-6** WRyan(7) (lw: led: rdn over 2f out: hdd ins fnl f: r.o) ..........1¼ | **2** | 5/2[1] | 78 | 40 |
| 3515* **Salty Jack (IRE) (81)** (SDow) **2-9-1**(5) ADaly(11) (a.p: rdn over 2f out: led ins fnl f: sn hdd: unable qckn) ..........hd | **3** | 16/1 | 78 | 40 |
| 3969* **Burlington House (USA) (83)** (PFICole) **2-9-8** 7x TQuinn(1) (hld up: rdn over 2f out: one pce fnl f) ..........1¾ | **4** | 11/4[2] | 76 | 38 |
| 3873[5] **Petrel (67)** (LordHuntingdon) **2-8-6v**[1] DHarrison(10) (rdn over 3f out: hdwy over 1f out: nvr nrr) ..........2 | **5** | 7/1[3] | 55 | 17 |
| 3674[6] **Dickie Bird (IRE) (82)** (RHannon) **2-9-7** DaneO'Neill(8) (lw: dwlt: rdn over 3f out: nvr nr to chal) ..........½ | **6** | 7/1[3] | 69 | 31 |
| 3962[4] **Supercharmer (75)** (CEBrittain) **2-9-0** RHills(5) (lw: prom over 5f) ..........13 | **7** | 16/1 | 33 | — |
| 4046[6] **Russian Sable (66)** (MRChannon) **2-8-5** CRutter(4) (dwlt: a bhd) ..........1¾ | **8** | 25/1 | 20 | — |
| 3620[7] **Caspian Morn (76)** (APJarvis) **2-9-1** JTate(6) (prom over 4f) ..........1¼ | **9** | 20/1 | 27 | — |
| 1871[12] **Eaton Park (IRE) (77)** (RAkehurst) **2-9-2** SSanders(2) (bhd fnl 2f) ..........2½ | **10** | 20/1 | 22 | — |
| | | (SP 117.9%) **10 Rn** | | |

**1m 28.6** (3.80) CSF £23.91 CT £256.54 TOTE £7.10: £1.90 £1.70 £2.40 (£17.70) Trio £63.80 OWNER Mr R. P. B. Michaelson (KINGSCLERE) BRED Highclere Stud Ltd

**3809* Brandon Jack**, still only sixth a quarter of a mile from home, produced a sustained effort from below the distance to sweep into the lead in the closing stages. (7/1)

**3762 Right Tune** looked extremely well in the paddock and was far happier on this faster surface, having been below form on softish ground last time out. A return to the winner's enclosure looks imminent. (5/2)

**3515* Salty Jack (IRE)** had been done no favours by the Handicapper on this nursery debut. (16/1)

**3969* Burlington House (USA)** is small and not built to carry such big weights. He looked a real danger entering the final quarter mile, but the seventh furlong caught him out. He needs to drop back to six. (11/4: 2/1-3/1)

**3873 Petrel**, tried in a visor for the first time, stayed on from below the distance without threatening. (7/1: 5/1-8/1)

## 4183 BELLWAY HOMES STARDOM STKS (Listed) (2-Y.O) (Class A)

2-40 (2-41) **1m** £12,678.75 (£3,780.00: £1,802.50: £813.75) Stalls: High GOING minus 0.20 sec per fur (GF)

| | | | | SP | RR | SF |
|---|---|---|---|---|---|---|
| 3927[2] | **Falkenham (100)** (PFICole) **2-8-11** TQuinn(5) (hld up: led 2f out: hrd rdn ins fnl f: r.o wl) | — | **1** | 8/11[1] | 104 | 52 |
| 3927[4] | **Hello (IRE) (100)** (JLDunlop) **2-8-11** WRyan(3) (lw: hdwy over 1f out: ev ch ins fnl f: r.o) | 1 | **2** | 5/1[2] | 102 | 50 |
| 3908a[8] | **Double Park (FR) (97)** (MJohnston) **2-8-6** TWilliams(4) (lw: led 6f: ev ch 1f out: unable qckn) | 3 | **3** | 8/1 | 91 | 39 |
| 3444[4] | **Lady Mail (IRE) (94)** (JMPEustace) **2-8-6** RCochrane(1) (hdwy over 2f out: ev ch over 1f out: wknd fnl f) | 1¼ | **4** | 8/1 | 89 | 37 |
| 3762* | **Blue River (IRE) (90)** (TGMills) **2-8-11** JCarroll(2) (lw: chsd ldr 5f) | 15 | **5** | 11/2[3] | 64 | 12 |

(SP 112.2%) **5 Rn**

**1m 39.83** (2.63) CSF £4.73 TOTE £1.60: £1.10 £1.80 (£2.90) OWNER Mr T. M. Hely-Hutchinson (WHATCOMBE) BRED Kirtlington Stud Ltd

**3927 Falkenham** carried his head rather high and awkwardly, just as he had done at Sandown two weeks ago but, having said that, he did nothing wrong, and found another gear when given a few reminders inside the final furlong. (8/11: op Evens)

**3927 Hello (IRE)**, just over three lengths behind the winner at Sandown two weeks ago, ran a lot better here and looked the likely winner entering the final furlong, before the winner found another gear. (5/1)

**3908a Double Park (FR)** did a good job of pacemaking. (8/1)

**3444 Lady Mail (IRE)** found lack of stamina her undoing in the final furlong. A return to seven furlongs would probably be in her favour. (8/1)

**3762* Blue River (IRE)** looked extremely well in the paddock, which made this performance even more disappointing. (11/2: 4/1-6/1)

## 4184 SCHRODER INVESTMENT MANAGEMENT H'CAP (0-100) (3-Y.O+) (Class C)

3-10 (3-11) **1m 1f** £14,726.25 (£4,410.00: £2,117.50: £971.25) Stalls: High GOING minus 0.20 sec per fur (GF)

| | | | | SP | RR | SF |
|---|---|---|---|---|---|---|
| 3805[13] | **Autumn Cover (70)** (PRHedger) **4-8-0** DBiggs(1) (lw: led over 7f out: hrd rdn & edgd rt wl ins fnl f: r.o wl) | — | **1** | 25/1 | 80 | 33 |
| 3786* | **Night Wink (USA) (78)** (GLMoore) **4-8-8** SWhitworth(13) (lw: a.p: rdn over 1f out: r.o) | nk | **2** | 16/1 | 88 | 41 |
| 3709[2] | **North Song (94)** (JHMGosden) **3-9-4** GHind(17) (a.p: nt clr run on ins over 2f out: rdn over 1f out: unable qckn) | 1¼ | **3** | 4/1[1] | 101 | 48 |
| 3148* | **Panata (IRE) (84)** (LMCumani) **3-8-8** OUrbina(12) (nt clr run over 3f out tl over 2f out: swtchd lft & hdwy over 1f out: r.o) | 1¼ | **4** | 5/1[2] | 89 | 36 |
| 3623[4] | **Ron's Secret (73)** (JWPayne) **4-8-3b**[1]ow2 SSanders(11) (a.p: rdn over 2f out: one pce) | 1 | **5** | 10/1 | 76 | 27 |
| 3799[3] | **Orsay (78)** (WRMuir) **4-8-8** TQuinn(8) (hld up: rdn over 2f out: one pce) | ¾ | **6** | 10/1 | 80 | 33 |
| 3805[14] | **Menas Gold (78)** (SDow) **4-8-3**(5) ADaly(3) (rdn over 1f out: gd hdwy fnl f: r.o) | nk | **7** | 40/1 | 79 | 32 |
| 3806* | **Conspicuous (IRE) (84)** (LGCottrell) **6-9-0** JQuinn(14) (lw: hdwy & nt clr run over 1f out: nvr nrr) | 1 | **8** | 7/1[3] | 84 | 37 |
| 4036a[3] | **Hoh Express (98)** (IABalding) **4-10-0** RCochrane(2) (lw: rdn & hdwy on ins over 3f out: nt clr run on ins over 1f out: one pce) | nk | **9** | 20/1 | 97 | 50 |
| 3799[2] | **Hilaala (USA) (85)** (PTWalwyn) **3-8-9** RHills(7) (lw: prom over 7f) | ¾ | **10** | 14/1 | 83 | 30 |
| 3811* | **Kayvee (95)** (GHarwood) **7-9-11** AClark(5) (rdn & hdwy 2f out: wknd fnl f) | hd | **11** | 16/1 | 93 | 46 |
| 3226* | **Royal Result (USA) (84)** (MRStoute) **3-8-8** MFenton(15) (hld up: rdn over 2f out: wknd over 1f out) | ½ | **12** | 12/1 | 81 | 28 |
| 2677[7] | **Sayeh (IRE) (95)** (MajorWRHern) **4-9-11** WRyan(9) (led over 1f: wknd over 5f out) | 1¼ | **13** | 33/1 | 89 | 42 |
| 3765[5] | **Fionn de Cool (IRE) (69)** (RAkehurst) **5-7-13** DeclanO'Shea(10) (lw: bhd fnl 4f) | ½ | **14** | 20/1 | 63 | 16 |
| 3521[4] | **Czarna (IRE) (76)** (CEBrittain) **5-8-6** JCarroll(4) (lw: prom over 7f) | 6 | **15** | 25/1 | 59 | 12 |
| 731[10] | **Roman Gold (IRE) (83)** (RHannon) **3-8-7** DaneO'Neill(16) (a bhd) | 1½ | **16** | 33/1 | 63 | 10 |
| 3856[10] | **Ki Chi Saga (USA) (82)** (JLDunlop) **4-8-12** GCarter(6) (lw: s.s: a bhd) | 2½ | **17** | 33/1 | 58 | 11 |

(SP 122.0%) **17 Rn**

**1m 55.4** (4.00) CSF £334.06 CT £1,832.37 TOTE £28.80: £4.60 £4.10 £1.40 £2.20 (£421.90) Trio £379.40 OWNER Mr G. A. Alexander (CHICHESTER) BRED P. and Mrs Venner

WEIGHT FOR AGE 3yo-6lb

STEWARDS' ENQUIRY Biggs susp. 23-24/9/96 (careless riding).

**3805 Autumn Cover** battled on well to gain his fifth victory of the season. Unfortunately, his rider was very harshly handed a two-day suspension for careless riding. (25/1)

**3786* Night Wink (USA)** made the winner work really hard in the final furlong and only just failed to succeed. (16/1)

**3709 North Song** has been a model of consistency this season and has yet to be out of the first three, winning twice. (4/1)

**3148* Panata (IRE)** has been in cracking form this season, but she met with serious traffic problems on this occasion and can be considered very unlucky. Compensation can soon be found. (5/1)

**3623 Ron's Secret,** fitted with blinkers for the first time, was always to the fore and does seem to be gradually coming to form. (10/1)

**3799 Orsay,** back on a sounder surface, failed to find the necessary turn of foot in the last two furlongs. (10/1)

**1440 Menas Gold** was given a strange ride, for her jockey did not seem very bothered and only really started to get at her below the distance. With only two behind her a furlong from home, she then sprouted wings to come through at the finish. She has been slipping down the handicap after some poor efforts and is now 6lb lower than when she last won back in September 1994. (40/1)

**3806* Conspicuous (IRE),** winner of this race last year off a 15lb lower mark, encountered all sorts of traffic problems. This run is best forgotten, although his steep rise in the handicap last year has made life tough for him this season. (7/1)

**3226* Royal Result (USA)** (12/1: op 8/1)

## 4185 BMW 3 SERIES TROPHY CONDITIONS STKS (3-Y.O) (Class C)

3-40 (3-40) **7f** £6,396.00 (£2,364.00: £1,132.00: £460.00: £180.00: £68.00) Stalls: High GOING minus 0.20 sec per fur (GF)

| | | | | SP | RR | SF |
|---|---|---|---|---|---|---|
| 3712[6] | **Polar Prince (IRE) (103)** (MAJarvis) **3-9-5** RCochrane(7) (hdwy over 2f out: nt clr run wl over 1f out: led ins fnl f: r.o wl) | — | **1** | 5/2[2] | 111 | 56 |
| 3822[2] | **Russian Music (103)** (MissGayKelleway) **3-9-1** TQuinn(8) (lw: w ldr: led wl over 1f out: hrd rdn: hdd ins fnl f: unable qckn) | 1¼ | **2** | 9/4[1] | 104 | 49 |
| | **Silver Prey (USA)** (EALDunlop) **3-8-12** GCarter(1) (hdwy over 2f out: rdn over 1f out: r.o one pce) | hd | **3** | 6/1[3] | 101 | 46 |
| 3517[4] | **Lonely Leader (IRE) (100)** (RHannon) **3-9-1** DaneO'Neill(2) (lw: a.p: ev ch wl over 1f out: one pce) | s.h | **4** | 6/1[3] | 104 | 49 |
| 3524[9] | **King of Peru (103)** (APJarvis) **3-8-12** SDrowne(6) (hdwy over 2f out: rdn over 1f out: wknd fnl f) | 5 | **5** | 11/1 | 89 | 34 |
| 3516[14] | **Lilli Claire (88)** (AGFoster) **3-8-9**(5) CAdamson(5) (a bhd) | nk | **6** | 16/1 | 91 | 36 |
| 3658[4] | **Civil Liberty (90)** (GLewis) **3-9-1b**[1] WRyan(3) (lw: led over 5f) | 4 | **7** | 12/1 | 83 | 28 |
| 3984[15] | **Dovebrace (100)** (ABailey) **3-8-12b**[1] SSanders(4) (a bhd) | 4 | **8** | 33/1 | 70 | 15 |

(SP 112.8%) **8 Rn**

**1m 27.34** (2.54) CSF £8.10 TOTE £3.50: £1.50 £1.10 £1.70 (£3.80) OWNER Mrs Christine Stevenson (NEWMARKET) BRED Michael Morrin

**3712 Polar Prince (IRE)** was the one true seven-furlong specialist in this field and he made that tell as he quickened nicely to settle it. (5/2)

**3822 Russian Music**, finishing second for the third time in a row and the fifth this season, is probably better off at a mile. (9/4)
**Silver Prey (USA)** looked in good shape considering this was his first run in thirteen months and stayed on well in the final furlong, only just failing to take second prize. He will probably be seen to better effect over further. (6/1)
**3517 Lonely Leader (IRE)**, almost two lengths behind Russian Music at Salisbury last time, finished a lot closer here. (6/1)
**1327* King of Peru** had come to the end of his tether in the final furlong. (11/1)

## 4186 WEATHERBYS H'CAP (0-70) (3-Y.O+) (Class E)

4-15 (4-17) **1m** £4,792.50 (£1,440.00: £695.00: £322.50) Stalls: High GOING minus 0.20 sec per fur (GF)

| Form | Horse | Dist | Pos | SP | RR | SF |
|---|---|---|---|---|---|---|
| 3947$^{6}$ | **Ashby Hill (IRE) (59)** (RRowe) **5-9-7** GCarter(15) (lw: s.s: stdy hdwy over 2f out: hmpd over 1f out: swtchd lft: r.o wl ins fnl f: fin 2nd, s.h: awrdd r) | — | 1 | 7/1$^{1}$ | 69 | 51 |
| 4064$^{4}$ | **Mystic Dawn (57)** (SDow) **3-8-9**(5) ADaly(10) (lw: hdwy over 2f out: edgd rt & led over 1f out: rdn out: fin 1st: disq: plcd 2nd) | | 2 | 10/1$^{3}$ | 67 | 44 |
| 3785* | **Thatchmaster (IRE) (58)** (CAHorgan) **5-9-6** DHarrison(1) (lw: led 1f: rdn 3f out: led 2f out tl over 1f out: unable qckn) | 1¾ | 3 | 7/1$^{1}$ | 64 | 46 |
| 3985$^{4}$ | **Duello (64)** (MBlanshard) **5-9-12** RCochrane(8) (lw: rdn over 3f out: hdwy over 2f out: r.o wl) | ½ | 4 | 8/1$^{2}$ | 69 | 51 |
| 3686$^{3}$ | **Racing Telegraph (40)** (CNAllen) **6-7-11**(5) MartinDwyer(14) (lw: hld up: rdn over 2f out: one pce) | 3½ | 5 | 14/1 | 38 | 20 |
| 3703$^{3}$ | **Mr Rough (55)** (DMorris) **5-9-3** StephenDavies(18) (lw: a.p: rdn over 2f out: ev ch over 1f out: wknd fnl f) | ¾ | 6 | 12/1 | 52 | 34 |
| 3852$^{6}$ | **Ca'd'oro (60)** (GBBalding) **3-9-3** SDrowne(12) (lw: nvr nr to chal) | nk | 7 | 16/1 | 56 | 33 |
| 2705$^{5}$ | **Ameer Alfayaafi (IRE) (58)** (RAkehurst) **3-9-1** TQuinn(4) (rdn over 3f out: nvr nrr) | ½ | 8 | 8/1$^{2}$ | 53 | 30 |
| 3845$^{6}$ | **Pride of Kashmir (52)** (PWHarris) **3-8-9** GHind(11) (a mid div) | ½ | 9 | 20/1 | 45 | 22 |
| *3877$^{3}$* | **Rocky Waters (USA) (52)** (PBurgoyne) **7-8-11v**(3) PMcCabe(17) (b.hind: led 7f out: clr 5f out: hdd 2f out: sn wknd) | 7 | 10 | 16/1 | 31 | 13 |
| 3991$^{7}$ | **Artful Dane (IRE) (65)** (MJHeaton-Ellis) **4-9-13** AClark(7) (lw: nvr nrr) | 1 | 11 | 20/1 | 42 | 24 |
| *4089$^{8}$* | **Mogin (55)** (TJNaughton) **3-8-7**(5) JDSmith(20) (swtg: s.s: hdwy on ins over 4f out: wknd over 2f out) | ½ | 12 | 14/1 | 31 | 8 |
| 3258$^{9}$ | **Persian Dawn (46)** (MajorDNChappell) **3-8-3** CRutter(19) (lw: prom over 5f) | s.h | 13 | 33/1 | 22 | — |
| 3876$^{10}$ | **Classy Chief (70)** (RBoss) **3-9-13** JCarroll(9) (a mid div) | ¾ | 14 | 33/1 | 45 | 22 |
| *4089$^{5}$* | **Hawaii Storm (FR) (38)** (DJSffrenchDavis) **8-8-0** DeclanO'Shea(21) (lw: s.s: a bhd) | nk | 15 | 16/1 | 12 | — |
| *3630$^{7}$* | **Mazirah (47)** (PJMakin) **5-8-9** SSanders(2) (lw: a bhd) | 2½ | 16 | 33/1 | 16 | — |
| 3525$^{4}$ | **Yezza (IRE) (55)** (APJarvis) **3-8-12** WRyan(6) (lw: a bhd) | nk | 17 | 33/1 | 24 | 1 |
| 3825$^{7}$ | **Persian Butterfly (56)** (RMStronge) **4-9-4** VSlattery(3) (lw: bhd fnl 5f) | 1½ | 18 | 33/1 | 22 | 4 |
| 2581$^{17}$ | **Yoxall Lodge (62)** (HJCollingridge) **6-9-10** VSmith(5) (a bhd) | ½ | 19 | 25/1 | 27 | 9 |
| 3800$^{11}$ | **Narbonne (55)** (BJMcMath) **5-9-3** DBiggs(16) (prom over 4f: t.o) | dist | 20 | 20/1 | — | — |

(SP 127.8%) **20 Rn**

**1m 40.83** (3.63) CSF £68.67 CT £473.51 TOTE £7.80: £2.10 £3.80 £1.60 £2.00 (£71.60) Trio £83.10 OWNER Miss Meriel Tufnell (PULBOROUGH) BRED Patrick Aspell
WEIGHT FOR AGE 3yo-5lb

**3947 Ashby Hill (IRE)**, who likes to hear her feet rattle, was hampered by Mystic Dawn below the distance. She ran on strongly inside the final furlong and, after failing by only a whisker, it was a foregone conclusion that she would be awarded the race in the Stewards' Room. (7/1)
**4064 Mystic Dawn** moved to the front below the distance, but she drifted right in the process, hampering Ashby Hill and, although she held on by a whisker, it looked a formality she would lose the race in the Stewards' Room. (10/1)
**3785* Thatchmaster (IRE)**, beaten a neck by the winner at Salisbury, was meeting that rival on 5lb worse terms. He is holding his form really well this season. (7/1)
**3985 Duello** may be a consistent sort, but his record now stands at just two wins from forty-one starts, and both of those came on soft ground. (8/1)
**3686 Racing Telegraph** has now won just once from thirty-four starts. (14/1: 10/1-16/1)
**3703 Mr Rough** has gained all three of his wins to date over a mile on fast ground. (12/1)

## 4187 EQUITY FINANCIAL COLLECTIONS LIMITED STKS (0-80) (3-Y.O+) (Class D)

4-50 (4-50) **1m 4f** £4,308.00 (£1,284.00: £612.00: £276.00) Stalls: Low GOING minus 0.20 sec per fur (GF)

| Form | Horse | Dist | Pos | SP | RR | SF |
|---|---|---|---|---|---|---|
| 3617* | **Willie Conquer (80)** (RAkehurst) **4-9-7** TQuinn(3) (lw: hld up: rdn over 1f out: led nr fin) | — | 1 | 9/4$^{1}$ | 88 | 62 |
| 4067$^{2}$ | **Wild Rita (74)** (WRMuir) **4-9-4** OUrbina(1) (chsd ldr: led 3f out: rdn over 2f out: hdd nr fin) | nk | 2 | 9/4$^{1}$ | 85 | 59 |
| 3504$^{6}$ | **Steamroller Stanly (80)** (CACyzer) **3-8-12** GCarter(4) (lw: lost pl 6f out: rallied over 1f out: r.o) | 1 | 3 | 6/1$^{3}$ | 86 | 51 |
| 3355$^{2}$ | **Farringdon Hill (77)** (MajorWRHern) **5-9-7b** WRyan(2) (led & sn clr: hdd 3f out: sn wknd) | 4 | 4 | 7/2$^{2}$ | 81 | 55 |
| 3521$^{3}$ | **Alambar (IRE) (78)** (PTWalwyn) **3-8-12** RHills(5) (lw: rdn 3f out: wknd over 1f out) | 1½ | 5 | 9/1 | 79 | 44 |

(SP 108.0%) **5 Rn**

**2m 37.29** (4.09) CSF £7.15 TOTE £2.40: £1.70 £1.20 (£2.10) OWNER Mr Raymond Tooth (EPSOM) BRED W. and R. Barnett Ltd
WEIGHT FOR AGE 3yo-9lb

**3617* Willie Conquer** was given a fine ride by Quinn who sat the gelding behind the leader in the straight, and then pounced in the final furlong. (9/4)
**4067 Wild Rita** can always be relied upon to give a good account of herself and only just lost out here. (9/4)
**3504 Steamroller Stanly** lost his pitch running to the top of the hill and looked certain to finish tailed off, but got a second wind in the final quarter-mile. (6/1)
**3355 Farringdon Hill** did a good job of pacemaking, but was soon beaten when headed. (7/2)
**3521 Alambar (IRE)** failed to see out this longer trip. (9/1)

## 4188 E.B.F. CUCUMBER MAIDEN STKS (2-Y.O) (Class D)

5-20 (5-24) **6f** £5,427.50 (£1,625.00: £780.00: £357.50) Stalls: Low GOING minus 0.20 sec per fur (GF)

| Form | Horse | Dist | Pos | SP | RR | SF |
|---|---|---|---|---|---|---|
| 3837$^{2}$ | **Hurricane State (USA)** (PWChapple-Hyam) **2-8-11**(3) RHavlin(3) (lw: mde all: rdn over 1f out: r.o wl) | — | 1 | 6/4$^{1}$ | 99 | 64 |
| 3757$^{6}$ | **Kumait (USA) (99)** (SbinSuroor) **2-9-0** WRyan(7) (a.p: chsd wnr over 2f out: rdn over 1f out: unable qckn) | 5 | 2 | 2/1$^{2}$ | 86 | 51 |
| 3690$^{8}$ | **Select Choice (IRE)** (APJarvis) **2-9-0** SDrowne(8) (hld up: rdn over 2f out: one pce) | 6 | 3 | 20/1 | 70 | 35 |
| 3773$^{2}$ | **Indian Blaze** (PWHarris) **2-9-0** GHind(1) (hld up: rdn over 2f out: one pce) | ¾ | 4 | 8/1$^{3}$ | 68 | 33 |
| 3807$^{6}$ | **Mon Bruce** (WRMuir) **2-9-0** SSanders(5) (chsd wnr over 3f: wknd over 1f out) | 1¾ | 5 | 25/1 | 63 | 28 |
| 3147$^{5}$ | **Linden's Lad (IRE)** (JRJenkins) **2-9-0** SWhitworth(4) (nvr nr to chal) | s.h | 6 | 50/1 | 63 | 28 |
| 3809$^{4}$ | **With A Will** (HCandy) **2-8-8**(7)ow1 LJames(6) (b.hind: prom over 2f out) | hd | 7 | 25/1 | 64 | 28 |
| | **Waterville Boy (IRE)** (RHannon) **2-9-0** DaneO'Neill(9) (leggy: lt-f: nvr nrr) | 2 | 8 | 12/1 | 57 | 22 |
| 3807$^{18}$ | **Rosenkavalier (IRE)** (LGCottrell) **2-9-0** JQuinn(11) (nvr nrr) | hd | 9 | 50/1 | 57 | 22 |

**Cheval Roc** (RHannon) **2-9-0** RPerham(14) (w'like: lw: dwlt: sme hdwy over 2f out: wknd wl over 1f out).....s.h **10** 25/1 57 22
**Bicton Park** (DMorley) **2-9-0** RCochrane(2) (w'like: scope: a bhd) ....................1¼ **11** 16/1 54 19
1118[8] **Heart Full of Soul** (PFICole) **2-9-0** TQuinn(13) (bit bkwd: a bhd)....................nk **12** 25/1 53 18
**Dandy Regent** (CACyzer) **2-9-0** MFenton(10) (leggy: unf: scope: a bhd) ....................2½ **13** 25/1 46 11
3637[6] **Chaluz** (MJohnston) **2-9-0** TWilliams(12) (bhd fnl 2f) ....................9 **14** 16/1 22 —
*3837[7]* ***Hachiyah (IRE)*** (HThomsonJones) **2-8-9** RHills(15) (Withdrawn not under Starter's orders: ref to ent stalls).................... **W** 16/1 — —
(SP 137.7%) **14 Rn**

**1m 11.15** (1.15) CSF £5.34 TOTE £2.60: £1.30 £1.40 £7.00 (£2.50) Trio £14.80 OWNER Mrs B. V. Sangster (MARLBOROUGH) BRED Clovelly Farms, Division of Gnl Agri Services

**3837 Hurricane State (USA)** confirmed the promise shown on his Newcastle debut with this pillar-to-post victory, pulling right away in the final furlong for a thoroughly convincing success. (6/4)
**3757 Kumait (USA)** appreciated the drop back in distance and the sounder surface, but failed to match the winner from below the distance, although he finished well clear of the remainder. There is a race waiting for him. (2/1)
**1871 Select Choice (IRE)**, out of his depth in a Group Two last time, was much happier back in this class and reached the frame for the first time, if looking one-paced in the last two furlongs. (20/1)
**3773 Indian Blaze** was made to look pedestrian in the final quarter-mile. (8/1: tchd 12/1)
**Mon Bruce** had come to the end of his tether below the distance. (25/1)

T/Plpt: £7.30 (2,763.62 Tckts). T/Qdpt: £2.70 (450.18 Tckts). AK

## 4175-DONCASTER (L-H) (Good to firm)
## Saturday September 14th
WEATHER: fine WIND: slt against

## 4189 EAST COAST CONDITIONS STKS (2-Y.O) (Class C)
2-00 (2-00) **6f** £4,918.00 (£1,822.00: £876.00: £360.00: £145.00: £59.00) Stalls: High GOING minus 0.08 sec per fur (G)

SP RR SF
3792* **Magical Times (100)** (RBoss) **2-9-1** KFallon(4) (chsd ldrs: rdn to ld ent fnl f: styd on strly u.p) ....................— **1** 7/2[2] 101 54
3829* **Tomba (81)** (BJMeehan) **2-9-1** MTebbutt(7) (swtg: chsd ldrs: nt clr run appr fnl f: r.o ins fnl f: no ch w wnr)...2½ **2** 11/1 94 47
3843[5] **Young Bigwig (IRE) (100)** (JBerry) **2-8-11** JCarroll(2) (trckd ldrs: effrt 2f out: disp ld over 1f out: rdn & nt qckn) ....................¾ **3** 3/1[1] 88 41
3971[2] **Nigrasine (100)** (JLEyre) **2-9-7** DeanMcKeown(1) (lw: a cl up: disp ld wl over 1f out: edgd lft, sn rdn & btn)...hd **4** 6/1 98 51
**Farhan (USA)** (PTWalwyn) **2-8-8** RHills(8) (rangy: unf: hld up: effrt over 2f out: rn green: styd on: no imp)......2 **5** 11/1 80+ 33
3931[4] **Osomental (97)** (DHaydnJones) **2-8-11b** AMackay(6) (led over 4f: wknd) ....................1¼ **6** 11/1 79 32
3206* **Caerfilly Dancer** (RAkehurst) **2-8-10** TQuinn(5) (s.i.s: effrt ½-wy: no imp) ....................4 **7** 4/1[3] 68 21
3620[3] **Mumkin (85)** (TThomsonJones) **2-8-13** WCarson(9) (hld up: outpcd after 2f: n.d after) ....................½ **8** 11/1 69 22
(SP 114.8%) **8 Rn**

**1m 13.7** (2.70) CSF £35.98 TOTE £4.20: £1.50 £3.90 £1.30 (£28.40) Trio £50.80 OWNER Ms Lynn Bell (NEWMARKET) BRED White Lodge Farm Stud

**3792* Magical Times**, who has been running well all season, showed what an improved performer he is by really stamping his authority on this entering the last furlong. (7/2)
**3829* Tomba** was a shade unlucky here as he was stopped approaching the final furlong when trying to get up the rail. Judging from the way he finished, he should get further. (11/1)
**3843 Young Bigwig (IRE)** had his chances but, strongly ridden in the last two furlongs, lacked that final dash to make an impression. (3/1)
**3971 Nigrasine** had plenty on here in trying to give weight all round. Going to his right under pressure, he cried enough approaching the final furlong. (6/1)
**Farhan (USA)**, a big sort, certainly needed the experience, but showed enough to suggest that, over further, plenty will be seen of him. (11/1: 8/1-12/1)
**3931 Osomental** had the blinkers back on and tried to run his field into the ground, but he gave up some way out when the pressure was applied. (11/1)

## 4190 ROTHMANS ROYALS NORTH SOUTH CHALLENGE SERIES SEMI-FINAL H'CAP (0-100) (3-Y.O+) (Class C)
2-30 (2-34) **1m (round)** £19,950.00 (£6,000.00: £2,900.00: £1,350.00) Stalls: High GOING minus 0.08 sec per fur (G)

SP RR SF
3866* **Gladys Althorpe (IRE) (67)** (JLEyre) **3-8-0** AMackay(14) (bhd: hdwy on outside over 2f out: hrd rdn to ld cl home) ....................— **1** 12/1 78 46
3646[3] **Impulsive Air (IRE) (63)** (EWeymes) **4-8-1** JQuinn(23) (a chsng ldrs: rdn over 2f out: kpt on wl towards fin)..nk **2** 25/1 73 46
4071[2] **Pride of Pendle (67)** (DNicholls) **7-8-5**ow1 AlexGreaves(3) (trckd ldrs: smooth hdwy to ld over 1f out: rdn, hdd & nt qckn towards fin)....................hd **3** 15/2[2] 77 49
4070[4] **Anonym (IRE) (58)** (DNicholls) **4-7-3b**(7) JBramhill(4) (s.i.s: wnt prom ½-wy: styng on whn n.m.r towards fin)..1 **4** 33/1 66 39
3933[10] **High Premium (68)** (RAFahey) **8-8-6** ACulhane(12) (chsd ldrs: rdn ½-wy: kpt on: nvr able to chal) ..............s.h **5** 25/1 76 49
3640[2] **Hawksley Hill (IRE) (80)** (MrsJRRamsden) **3-8-13** KFallon(8) (lw: mid div & pushed along 3f out: swtchd outside over 1f out: r.o towards fin)....................hd **6** 5/1[1] 88 56
3856[5] **Sandmoor Chambray (82)** (TDEasterby) **5-9-6** MBirch(15) (chsd ldrs: led 2f out tl over 1f out: btn whn hmpd towards fin)....................½ **7** 16/1 89 62
3709[8] **Tertium (IRE) (87)** (MartynWane) **4-9-11** JCarroll(6) (trckd ldrs: n.m.r 2f out: effrt over 1f out: styng on whn nt clr run ent fnl f)....................hd **8** 20/1 94 67
3640[5] **Master Charter (83)** (MrsJRRamsden) **4-9-7** JFortune(5) (swtg: hdwy on ins over 3f out: styd on u.p fnl f: nvr able to chal)....................1 **9** 10/1 88 61
3279[4] **Scaraben (73)** (SEKettlewell) **8-8-11** JStack(18) (s.i.s: bhd tl styd on fnl 2f)....................1 **10** 16/1 76 49
3985[2] **Royal Ceilidh (IRE) (78)** (DenysSmith) **3-8-11** JReid(7) (a chsng ldrs: effrt 3f out: r.o one pce) ....................hd **11** 9/1[3] 81 49
3842[2] **Bollin Frank (71)** (TDEasterby) **4-8-9** LCharnock(2) (led to 2f out: grad wknd) ....................½ **12** 11/1 73 46
3974[8] **Flying North (IRE) (75)** (MrsMReveley) **3-8-8** KDarley(24) (bhd: effrt on outside ½-wy: nvr able to chal)........hd **13** 20/1 76 44
3989[3] **Rebel County (IRE) (80)** (ABailey) **3-8-13** DBiggs(13) (bhd tl sme late hdwy)....................½ **14** 16/1 80 48
3985[23] **Mbulwa (63)** (RAFahey) **10-8-1** DaleGibson(20) (effrt ½-wy: no imp) ....................1 **15** 25/1 61 34
3974[10] **Rambo Waltzer (64)** (DNicholls) **4-7-9**(7) JoHunnam(25) (chsd ldrs tl wknd fnl 3f)....................nk **16** 25/1 62 35
3933[12] **Gymcrak Premiere (86)** (GHolmes) **8-9-10v** DeanMcKeown(19) (b.hind: bhd: hdwy on outside 2f out: n.d)..s.h **17** 25/1 84 57

| | | | | SP | RR | SF |
|---|---|---|---|---|---|---|
| 3623[11] | **Hawwam (58)** (EJAlston) **10-7-10** JLowe(9) (n.d) | ¾ | **18** | 50/1 | 54 | 27 |
| 3985[7] | **Mountgate (75)** (MPBielby) **4-8-13** MTebbutt(17) (bhd: nt clr run & swtchd over 2f out: n.d) | 2½ | **19** | 25/1 | 66 | 39 |
| 3933[13] | **Band on the Run (90)** (BAMcMahon) **9-10-0** TQuinn(11) (in tch: hung lft & lost pl over 2f out) | ¾ | **20** | 20/1 | 80 | 53 |
| 3279[9] | **Winston (72)** (JDBethell) **3-8-5** SDrowne(10) (n.d) | ¾ | **21** | 20/1 | 60 | 28 |
| 4054[8] | **Maple Bay (IRE) (81)** (ABailey) **7-9-0**(5) GFaulkner(16) (lw: chsd ldrs over 4f: sn lost pl) | 3½ | **22** | 16/1 | 62 | 35 |
| 3937[20] | **Elpidos (61)** (MDHammond) **4-7-13**ow1 WCarson(21) (wl bhd fr ½-wy) | 1¼ | **23** | 50/1 | 40 | 12 |
| 3920[7] | **Queens Consul (IRE) (83)** (BSRothwell) **6-9-7** DHarrison(22) (effrt & n.m.r 3f out: sn lost tch) | hd | **24** | 20/1 | 61 | 34 |
| 3933[6] | **Somerton Boy (IRE) (70)** (PCalver) **6-8-8** WRyan(1) (a bhd) | nk | **25** | 16/1 | 48 | 21 |
| | | | | (SP 146.7%) | **25 Rn** | |

**1m 39.58** (3.08) CSF £280.54 CT £2,264.82 TOTE £10.50: £2.40 £5.00 £1.90 £10.90 (£225.20) Trio £1,801.40; £279.10 to 16/9/96 OWNER Mr T. S. Ely (HAMBLETON) BRED Mrs R. Kitchin
LONG HANDICAP Anonym (IRE) 7-6 Hawwam 7-1
WEIGHT FOR AGE 3yo-5lb
STEWARDS' ENQUIRY Mackay susp. 23-24/9/96 (careless riding).

**3866* Gladys Althorpe (IRE)** produced a run from behind as she has to and, responding to some strong driving, got up late on. She will certainly know she has been in a race here. (12/1)
**3646 Impulsive Air (IRE)** ran his heart out, being in the thick of things throughout, and was staying on well at the end. (25/1)
**4071 Pride of Pendle** travelled particularly well, but just saw too much daylight too soon and was worried out of it near the finish. She is in top form at the moment. (15/2)
**4070 Anonym (IRE)** has bags of ability and is running well just now, but was a shade unlucky as he was short of room late on. (33/1)
**1810* High Premium** had his chances, but was off the bit some way out. To his credit, he did keep staying on and is really well at present. (25/1)
**3640 Hawksley Hill (IRE)** had all sorts of trouble in getting a run and, when extricated, it was just too late. (5/1)
**3709 Tertium (IRE)** ran well. He appeared unlucky and seems to coming back to form. (20/1)
**3640 Master Charter** had problems in trying to get a run up the inner and should not be written off yet. (10/1)
**3279 Scaraben**, given plenty to do, was never any nearer than at the end. (16/1)
**3842 Bollin Frank** (11/1: 10/1-1/2)

## 4191 POLYPIPE PLC FLYING CHILDERS STKS (Gp 2) (2-Y.O) (Class A)

3-05 (3-06) **5f** £26,000.40 (£9,573.60: £4,554.30: £1,816.50: £675.75: £219.45) Stalls: High GOING minus 0.08 sec per fur (G)

| | | | | SP | RR | SF |
|---|---|---|---|---|---|---|
| 3690[4] | **Easycall (100)** (BJMeehan) **2-9-3** MTebbutt(1) (lw: trckd ldrs: rdn to ld ins fnl f: r.o) | — | **1** | 5/1[3] | 112 | 53 |
| 3690[2] | **Compton Place (100)** (JARToller) **2-8-12** SSanders(7) (lw: led tl ins fnl f: r.o) | 1½ | **2** | 9/4[1] | 102 | 43 |
| 3213[3] | **Deep Finesse (100)** (MAJarvis) **2-9-3** PatEddery(3) (hmpd after 1½f: sn drvn along: hdwy 2f out: styd on: nvr able to chal) | 1¼ | **3** | 5/1[3] | 103 | 44 |
| 3903a[2] | **Head Over Heels (IRE) (100)** (JHMGosden) **2-8-7** LDettori(5) (b.hind: lw: prom: effrt ½-wy: sn hrd drvn: nt pce to chal) | nk | **4** | 7/2[2] | 92 | 33 |
| 3692* | **Janib (USA) (100)** (HThomsonJones) **2-8-12** RHills(4) (cl up over 3f: grad wknd) | 2 | **5** | 5/1[3] | 91 | 32 |
| 3018a[3] | **Nevada (IRE)** (APO'Brien,Ireland) **2-8-12v1** KFallon(6) (trckd ldrs: effrt 2f out: hrd rdn & no ex) | 1¼ | **6** | 10/1 | 87 | 28 |
| 3692[5] | **Fredrik The Fierce (IRE) (100)** (JBerry) **2-8-12v1** KDarley(2) (drvn along after 2f: n.d after) | ½ | **7** | 25/1 | 85 | 26 |
| | | | | (SP 115.9%) | **7 Rn** | |

**60.08 secs** (1.68) CSF £16.35 TOTE £9.40: £3.40 £1.90 (£10.40) OWNER Easycall Partnership (UPPER LAMBOURN) BRED Mrs Susan Feddern

**3690 Easycall**, back over what appeared his best trip, won well. (5/1)
**3690 Compton Place** ran a game race, but was just tapped for foot in the final furlong and seems better over a shade further. (9/4)
**3213 Deep Finesse** had to be switched after being short of room early on and then did quite well without offering a live threat. (5/1)
**3903a Head Over Heels (IRE)**, getting all the allowances, had her chances, but lacked the necessary turn of foot to take them. (7/2)
**3692* Janib (USA)** showed plenty of speed, but disappointingly was the first to crack once the pressure was applied. (5/1)
**3018a Nevada (IRE)** had the visor on for the first time and looked to be back over his ideal trip but, once off the bit, he proved very disappointing. (10/1)
**3160* Fredrik The Fierce (IRE)**, who had the visor on for the first time, found it failing to have any effect. (25/1)

## 4192 PERTEMPS ST LEGER STKS (Gp 1) (3-Y.O C & F) (Class A)

3-40 (3-41) **1m 6f 132y** £174,688.40 (£64,355.60: £30,642.80: £12,254.00: £4,592.00: £1,527.20) Stalls: Low GOING minus 0.08 sec per fur (G)

| | | | | SP | RR | SF |
|---|---|---|---|---|---|---|
| 3797* | **Shantou (USA) (115)** (JHMGosden) **3-9-0** LDettori(10) (lw: a in tch: effrt & swtchd over 2f out: chal 1f out: hrd rdn to ld cl home) | — | **1** | 8/1 | 125 | 84 |
| 3671* | **Dushyantor (USA) (120)** (HRACecil) **3-9-0** PatEddery(9) (lw: hld up: smooth hdwy 4f out: led 2f out: rdn ins fnl f: hdd & nt qckn towards fin) | nk | **2** | 2/1[1] | 125 | 84 |
| 3992* | **Samraan (USA) (107)** (JLDunlop) **3-9-0** JCarroll(3) (hld up: hdwy whn n.m.r over 2f out: squeezed thro: styd on wl: nt pce to chal) | 4 | **3** | 28/1 | 120 | 79 |
| 3671[2] | **Mons (119)** (LMCumani) **3-9-0** OUrbina(5) (swtg: led to 4f out: kpt on u.p: n.m.r 2f out: styd on) | 3½ | **4** | 5/1[2] | 117 | 76 |
| 3124* | **St Mawes (FR) (110)** (JLDunlop) **3-9-0b** KDarley(8) (hld up: effrt over 4f out: sn rdn: styd on: nvr rchd ldrs) | 1¼ | **5** | 8/1 | 115 | 74 |
| 3669[2] | **Wilawander (99)** (BWHills) **3-9-0** RHills(1) (chsd ldrs: rdn 4f out: outpcd fnl 2f) | 2½ | **6** | 16/1 | 112 | 71 |
| 3781* | **Sharaf Kabeer (107)** (SbinSuroor) **3-9-0** TQuinn(6) (cl up: led 4f out to 2f out: btn whn hmpd wl over 1f out) | 2 | **7** | 11/1 | 110 | 69 |
| 3597* | **Heron Island (IRE) (113)** (PWChapple-Hyam) **3-9-0** JReid(12) (lw: hld up & bhd: effrt over 4f out: no imp) | 1¾ | **8** | 10/1 | 108 | 67 |
| 3760* | **Flying Legend (USA) (94)** (HRACecil) **3-9-0** WRyan(7) (chsd ldrs tl rdn & wknd wl over 2f out) | 8 | **9** | 18/1 | 100 | 59 |
| 2054* | **Gordi (USA)** (DKWeld,Ireland) **3-9-0** KFallon(11) (hld up: effrt & pushed along 6f out: sn prom: outpcd fnl 4f) | hd | **10** | 7/1[3] | 99 | 58 |
| 3124[7] | **Desert Boy (IRE) (112)** (PWChapple-Hyam) **3-9-0** WCarson(4) (bhd: lost tch fnl 4f) | dist | **11** | 50/1 | — | — |
| | | | | (SP 118.7%) | **11 Rn** | |

**3m 5.1** (1.50) CSF £23.41 TOTE £7.10: £2.10 £1.50 £6.10 (£8.10) Trio £122.70 OWNER Sheikh Mohammed (NEWMARKET) BRED Darley Stud Management Inc
STEWARDS' ENQUIRY Dettori susp. 23-26/9/96 & Eddery susp. 23-24/9/96 (excessive use of whip).
**IN-FOCUS: This was the second time this season that whip-related suspensions have been handed out after the finish of a Classic. The BHB are now understood to be taking a serious look at the Rules as they stand. It can only be hoped they reach a sensible conclusion.**
**3797* Shantou (USA)** needed every yard of the trip and, given some very strong assistance, proved to be game, despite carrying his head quite high. He looks a real stayer. (8/1)

**3671* Dushyantor (USA)** looked to have done everything right and was on the bridle in the straight but, when the chips were down in the closing stages, was comprehensively outstayed. (2/1)
**3992* Samraan (USA)** stays well and was a shade unlucky here. He got hit over the head by a whip in the last two furlongs, and was also a bit short of room at the same time. He would never have seriously troubled the front two. (28/1)
**3671 Mons**, over his longest trip to date, needed every yard of it and, after looking likely to drop away halfway up the straight, he kept on well to the end. He gives the impression that, with some cut in the ground, he could really come into his own. (5/1)
**3124* St Mawes (FR)** made his effort early in the straight, but took an age to get going and failed to offer any sort of threat, despite staying on. (8/1)
**3669 Wilawander** was always close enough if good enough, but his limitations were well exposed in the last three furlongs. (16/1)
**3781* Sharaf Kabeer** has won over this trip previously, but did not appear to get it in this company. (11/1)
**3597* Heron Island (IRE)** could never make any impression and would seem to have found this ground too fast. (10/1)
**3760* Flying Legend (USA)**, taking a big step up in class, was found wanting in the last three furlongs. (18/1)
**2054* Gordi (USA)** looked lean and was getting very warm before the start. Off the bit some way out, he did not run any sort of race. He is an excitable sort and may have been over the top here. (7/1: 5/1-15/2)
**2844a Desert Boy (IRE)** was completely outclassed. (50/1)

## 4193 LADBROKE H'CAP (0-95) (3-Y.O+) (Class C)

4-15 (4-16) **1m 2f 60y** £15,692.00 (£5,828.00: £2,814.00: £1,170.00: £485.00: £211.00) Stalls: Low GOING minus 0.08 sec per fur (G)

| | | | | SP | RR | SF |
|---|---|---|---|---|---|---|
| 3947$^{3}$ | **Clifton Fox (82)** (JAGlover) **4-9-1** DHarrison(11) (rr div: hdwy 2f out: swtchd lft ins 1f out: r.o to ld nr fin) | — | **1** | 10/1 | 93 | 76 |
| 3947$^{2}$ | **Angus-G (79)** (MrsMReveley) **4-8-12** KDarley(15) (lw: bhd: hdwy 4f out: led over 1f out: r.o: jst ct) | nk | **2** | 5/1$^{2}$ | 90 | 73 |
| 3691$^{12}$ | **Billy Bushwacker (88)** (MrsMReveley) **5-9-7** ACulhane(17) (hld up & bhd: hdwy 3f out: disp ld 1f out: nt qckn towards fin) | ½ | **3** | 10/1 | 98 | 81 |
| 3649* | **Mentalasanythin (70)** (DHaydnJones) **7-8-3** AMackay(5) (bhd: hdwy 3f out: styd on wl: nrst fin) | 3 | **4** | 16/1 | 75 | 58 |
| 3805$^{9}$ | **Serendipity (FR) (84)** (JLDunlop) **3-8-10** TQuinn(1) (a.p: effrt & ev ch over 1f out: sltly hmpd ins fnl f: no ex) | ¾ | **5** | 14/1 | 88 | 64 |
| 3947$^{9}$ | **Fahs (USA) (68)** (RAkehurst) **4-8-1** DRMcCabe(3) (hld up: effrt whn nt clr run 2f out: nvr able to chal) | ½ | **6** | 16/1 | 71 | 54 |
| 871$^{4}$ | **Obelos (USA) (69)** (MrsJCecil) **5-8-2** GBardwell(13) (cl up: led over 2f out tl over 1f out: sn outpcd) | nk | **7** | 20/1 | 72 | 55 |
| 3704* | **Trick (IRE) (73)** (LMCumani) **3-7-13** JQuinn(8) (prom: effrt 3f out: one pce fnl 2f) | nk | **8** | 8/1$^{3}$ | 75 | 51 |
| 3985$^{11}$ | **Master Beveled (69)** (PDEvans) **6-7-9**(7) RFfrench(12) (chsd ldrs: effrt & ev ch over 2f out: nt qckn ins fnl f) | s.h | **9** | 20/1 | 71 | 54 |
| 3923* | **Gold Disc (USA) (91)** (BWHills) **3-9-3** PatEddery(9) (swtg: hld up & bhd: hdwy on ins 3f out: nt clr run: no imp) | 2½ | **10** | 10/1 | 89 | 65 |
| 3710$^{19}$ | **Skillington (USA) (89)** (IABalding) **3-9-1** LDettori(2) (lw: led tl over 2f out: wknd 1f out) | nk | **11** | 9/1 | 87 | 63 |
| 4120* | **Ninia (USA) (90)** (MJohnston) **4-9-9** 5x RHills(7) (lw: in tch: lost pl ent st: nt clr run after) | 1½ | **12** | 7/2$^{1}$ | 85 | 68 |
| 4073$^{13}$ | **Desert Fighter (70)** (MrsMReveley) **5-8-3** LCharnock(10) (nvr nr ldrs) | ¾ | **13** | 50/1 | 64 | 47 |
| 3710* | **Celestial Choir (91)** (JLEyre) **6-9-7**(3) OPears(18) (lw: hld up: effrt on outside 3f out: n.d) | ½ | **14** | 10/1 | 85 | 68 |
| 3791$^{10}$ | **Kings Assembly (79)** (PWHarris) **4-8-12** GHind(14) (chsd ldrs tl wknd fnl 3f) | ¾ | **15** | 20/1 | 71 | 54 |
| 4073$^{15}$ | **Nigel's Lad (IRE) (74)** (PCHaslam) **4-8-7** JFortune(16) (nvr trbld ldrs) | ¾ | **16** | 16/1 | 65 | 48 |
| 1200$^{4}$ | **Samim (USA) (75)** (SGollings) **3-8-1b** SSanders(4) (chsd ldrs: hrd drvn over 3f out: sn wknd) | 20 | **17** | 33/1 | 35 | 11 |
| | | | | (SP 139.9%) | **17 Rn** | |

**2m 9.18** (2.18) CSF £62.69 CT £502.50 TOTE £13.00: £2.70 £1.60 £2.30 £3.20 (£22.40) Trio £95.80 OWNER P and S Partnership (WORKSOP) BRED Crest Stud Ltd
WEIGHT FOR AGE 3yo-7lb
**3947 Clifton Fox** needed a lot of luck in running and got it. Producing a tremendous burst to settle it in the closing stages, he should have a real chance in the Cambridgeshire given easier ground. (10/1)
**3947 Angus-G** is improving and ran his heart out here, only to be caught near the line. (5/1)
**3071 Billy Bushwacker** is a real character who has the ability to win races at any time, but he needs things to go just right. He is the type to consider in big handicaps. (10/1)
**3649* Mentalasanythin** ran a cracking race, making up heaps of ground in the last three furlongs, and is obviously in top form. (16/1)
**3123 Serendipity (FR)** had his chances, but was going nowhere when the winner slightly hampered him entering the last furlong. (14/1)
**3205 Fahs (USA)** is a difficult customer to win with, but he had no luck in running here. (16/1)
**871 Obelos (USA)** ran well after four and a half months off and should be all the better for it. (20/1)
**3985 Master Beveled** is running well at present and should be kept in mind if the ground eases. (20/1)
**3923* Gold Disc (USA)** tried the impossible when attempting a run up the rail and never saw daylight. (10/1)
**4120* Ninia (USA)**, normally up with the pace, was dropped in on this occasion and Hills got what he deserved for those tactics, never getting a run at any stage. Tactics are the most important part of race riding and this was an unbelievable performance. (7/2)

## 4194 PORCELANOSA RATED STKS H'CAP (0-105) (3-Y.O+) (Class B)

4-45 (4-46) **1m (straight)** £13,557.60 (£5,018.40: £2,409.20: £986.00: £393.00: £155.80) Stalls: High GOING minus 0.08 sec per fur (G)

| | | | | SP | RR | SF |
|---|---|---|---|---|---|---|
| 810$^{12}$ | **Decorated Hero (100)** (JHMGosden) **4-9-4** LDettori(1) (hld up: stdy hdwy over 2f out: r.o wl fnl f to ld nr fin) | — | **1** | 9/1 | 110 | 79 |
| 3709$^{9}$ | **Hi Nod (100)** (MJCamacho) **6-9-4** LCharnock(7) (lw: a.p: rdn to ld wl ins fnl f: hdd & no ex towards fin) | ½ | **2** | 14/1 | 109 | 78 |
| 3071$^{9}$ | **Jarah (USA) (98)** (SbinSuroor) **3-8-11** RHills(6) (lw: prom: led 2f out: hrd rdn 1f out: r.o: hdd wl ins fnl f: no ex towards fin) | nk | **3** | 14/1 | 106 | 70 |
| 3984$^{12}$ | **April The Eighth (91)** (BWHills) **3-8-4** JCarroll(4) (hld up: hdwy over 2f out: rdn & btn appr fnl f) | 1½ | **4** | 16/1 | 96 | 60 |
| *4078*$^{8}$ | **My Gallery (IRE) (89)** (ABailey) **5-8-4**(3) DWright(2) (hld up: hdwy over 2f out: sn chsng ldrs: rdn & btn 1f out) | 1½ | **5** | 9/1 | 91 | 60 |
| *3627** | **Hal's Pal (92)** (DRLoder) **3-8-5b**ow3 PatEddery(5) (hld up & bhd: nt clr run 2f out: nt rcvr) | hd | **6** | 4/1$^{1}$ | 94+ | 55 |
| 3731a$^{4}$ | **Blomberg (IRE) (103)** (JRFanshawe) **4-9-7** DHarrison(8) (lw: trckd ldrs: effrt 3f out: wknd 2f out) | 3½ | **7** | 15/2$^{3}$ | 98 | 67 |
| 3842$^{4}$ | **Saleemah (USA) (95)** (JLDunlop) **3-8-8** WCarson(11) (cl up: rdn over 2f out: wknd wl over 1f out) | 5 | **8** | 5/1$^{2}$ | 80 | 44 |
| 3996$^{4}$ | **Maralinga (IRE) (100)** (LadyHerries) **4-9-4** DeclanO'Shea(9) (led to 2f out: sn rdn & btn) | 1 | **9** | 9/1 | 83 | 52 |
| 3709$^{7}$ | **Beauchamp Jazz (92)** (JLDunlop) **4-8-10v**$^{1}$ JReid(3) (cl up tl rdn & wknd wl over 1f out) | 2½ | **10** | 9/1 | 70 | 39 |
| 3709$^{5}$ | **Nagnagnag (IRE) (94)** (SDow) **4-8-12** TQuinn(10) (in tch: effrt 3f out: wknd fnl 2f) | 6 | **11** | 5/1$^{2}$ | 60 | 29 |
| | | | | (SP 124.3%) | **11 Rn** | |

**1m 38.58** (2.08) CSF £117.03 CT £1,641.62 TOTE £10.30: £2.70 £5.00 £4.70 (£57.90) Trio £274.90 OWNER Mr Herbert Allen (NEWMARKET) BRED Reg Griffin and Jim McGrath
WEIGHT FOR AGE 3yo-5lb

**600 Decorated Hero**, patiently ridden, swooped to conquer once a gap appeared in the closing stages to score a shade cleverly. He looks worth following this back-end. (9/1)
**3083 Hi Nod** ran his usual game race but, despite trying hard, had no answer to the winner's late burst. (14/1)
**2354* Jarah (USA)** ran well and kept responding to pressure. He looks to be in really good heart. (14/1)
**2436 April The Eighth**, without the blinkers this time and stepping up in trip, ran particularly well, but failed to see out the last furlong. (16/1)
**4078 My Gallery (IRE)** has not surprisingly shot up the weights and that seemed to anchor her here. (9/1)
**3627* Hal's Pal**, held up, never got a run until too late. This is best ignored. (4/1)

## 4195 BATTLE OF BRITAIN NURSERY H'CAP (0-85) (2-Y.O) (Class D)

5-15 (5-19) **6f** £5,010.00 (£1,500.00: £720.00: £330.00) Stalls: High GOING minus 0.08 sec per fur (G)

| | | | | SP | RR | SF |
|---|---|---|---|---|---|---|
| 3846* | **Sharp Hat (78)** (RHannon) **2-9-4** LDettori(2) (hld up: stdy hdwy to ld over 1f out: r.o) | — | **1** | 6/1$^{2}$ | 83 | 60 |
| 3687$^{3}$ | **Petite Danseuse (75)** (SDow) **2-8-10**$^{(5)}$ ADaly(9) (trckd ldrs: effrt over 1f out: r.o wl: jst failed) | hd | **2** | 9/1 | 80 | 57 |
| 3969$^{4}$ | **In Good Nick (63)** (MWEasterby) **2-8-3b$^{1}$** DaleGibson(3) (chsd ldrs: ev ch over 1f out: kpt on) | 1¾ | **3** | 14/1 | 63 | 40 |
| 3792$^{5}$ | **Plan For Profit (IRE) (74)** (MJohnston) **2-9-0** JReid(10) (bhd: shkn up ½-wy: hung lft & styd on: nrst fin) | 1½ | **4** | 9/1 | 70 | 47 |
| 3448* | **Little Blue (IRE) (61)** (TDEasterby) **2-8-1** JLowe(6) (led tl over 1f out: kpt on same pce) | 1½ | **5** | 20/1 | 53 | 30 |
| 1774$^{5}$ | **Mantles Prince (81)** (GLewis) **2-9-7** PatEddery(4) (lw: hld up: effrt over 2f out: styd on: n.d) | 2 | **6** | 6/1$^{2}$ | 68 | 45 |
| 3647$^{5}$ | **The Four Isles (62)** (DHaydnJones) **2-8-2** AMackay(8) (s.i.s: hld up & bhd: hdwy over 2f out: rdn & btn over 1f out) | d.h | **6** | 14/1 | 49 | 26 |
| 3879* | **Lunar Music (74)** (MartynMeade) **2-8-7**$^{(7)}$ DSweeney(7) (chsd ldrs: hung lft wl over 1f out: sn btn) | 1¼ | **8** | 14/1 | 57 | 34 |
| 3936* | **I Can't Remember (78)** (PDEvans) **2-9-1**$^{(3)}$ DWright(12) (outpcd & bhd ½-wy: sme late hdwy) | 1¾ | **9** | 9/1 | 57 | 34 |
| 4024a$^{27}$ | **Bollero (IRE) (75)** (JBerry) **2-8-10**$^{(5)}$ PFessey(1) (chsd ldr tl wknd fnl 2f) | 1 | **10** | 20/1 | 51 | 28 |
| 3464$^{10}$ | **Cairn Dhu (65)** (MrsJRRamsden) **2-8-5** SSanders(5) (s.i.s: sme hdwy whn hmpd wl over 1f out: n.d) | ½ | **11** | 16/1 | 40+ | 17 |
| *3950** | **Imperial Garden (IRE) (65)** (PCHaslam) **2-8-5** SDrowne(11) (prom 4f) | 1½ | **12** | 20/1 | 36 | 13 |
| 3674$^{8}$ | **Cherokee Flight (74)** (MrsJRRamsden) **2-9-0** KFallon(13) (lw: s.i.s: effrt ½-wy: no imp) | nk | **13** | 13/2$^{3}$ | 44 | 21 |
| 3838* | **Keen To Please (63)** (DenysSmith) **2-8-3** WCarson(16) (gd spd 4f: wknd) | 5 | **14** | 11/2$^{1}$ | 20 | — |
| 3659$^{W}$ | **Masterstroke (74)** (BJMeehan) **2-9-0** MTebbutt(14) (outpcd & bhd fr ½-wy) | 1 | **15** | 12/1 | 28 | 5 |
| 3840$^{2}$ | **Unknown Territory (IRE) (69)** (RonaldThompson) **2-8-9** JQuinn(15) (bhd fr ½-wy) | 9 | **16** | 20/1 | — | — |
| | | | | (SP 139.9%) | **16 Rn** | |

**1m 13.46** (2.46) CSF £60.99 CT £704.47 TOTE £5.10: £1.60 £2.90 £4.10 £2.00 (£27.50) Trio £808.20 OWNER Mr J. C. Smith (MARLBOROUGH) BRED Littleton Stud
**3846* Sharp Hat** went very freely to post, but this made little difference and getting first run on the runner-up won him the day. (6/1)
**3687 Petite Danseuse** gave the impression that she should have won this but, by the time she found her stride, the winner had stolen it. (9/1)
**3969 In Good Nick** ran well in the first-time blinkers and kept staying on under pressure. (14/1)
**3792 Plan For Profit (IRE)** was never going that well and was always tending to hang, but he did keep staying on. (9/1)
**3448* Little Blue (IRE)** showed her customary speed, but she had given her best approaching the last furlong. (20/1)
**1774 Mantles Prince** ran well after over three months off. (6/1)
**3647 The Four Isles** has plenty more ability but, as yet, has never put his heart into it. (14/1: op 25/1)
**3291 Cairn Dhu** gave the impression that he is learning and, just when he was beginning to run here, he was virtually knocked over. (16/1)

T/Jkpt: Not won; £13,671.92 to Nottingham 16/9/96. T/Plpt: £863.80 (50.04 Tckts). T/Qdpt: £132.20 (15.19 Tckts). AA

# 4182-GOODWOOD (R-H) (St crse Good, Rnd crse Good to firm)
## Saturday September 14th

WEATHER: fine WIND: almost nil

## 4196 FOOD BROKERS RATED STKS H'CAP (0-105) (3-Y.O+) (Class B)

2-15 (2-24) **7f** £9,924.60 (£3,671.40: £1,760.70: £718.50: £284.25: £110.55) Stalls: High GOING minus 0.11 sec per fur (G)

| | | | | SP | RR | SF |
|---|---|---|---|---|---|---|
| 3691$^{13}$ | **Star of Zilzal (USA) (93)** (MRStoute) **4-8-9** AClark(6) (mde all: clr over 2f out: pushed out) | — | **1** | 10/1 | 105 | 54 |
| 3832* | **Grand Musica (91)** (IABalding) **3-7-12**$^{(5)}$ MartinDwyer(7) (chsd wnr: rdn over 2f out: no imp) | 2½ | **2** | 5/1$^{3}$ | 97 | 42 |
| 3271$^{6}$ | **Please Suzanne (98)** (RHannon) **3-8-10** DaneO'Neill(8) (rdn & hdwy over 2f out: one pce) | 3 | **3** | 12/1 | 97 | 42 |
| 3996$^{5}$ | **Celestial Key (USA) (105)** (MJohnston) **6-9-7** BDoyle(2) (hld up: rdn over 2f out: one pce) | ¾ | **4** | 4/1$^{1}$ | 103 | 52 |
| 3920$^{2}$ | **My Best Valentine (94)** (JWhite) **6-8-7**$^{(3)}$ AWhelan(5) (lw: a.p: rdn over 2f out: one pce) | s.h | **5** | 13/2 | 92 | 41 |
| 3445$^{11}$ | **Almuhimm (USA) (91)** (EALDunlop) **4-8-7** GDuffield(3) (lw: sme hdwy over 2f out: wknd over 1f out) | ¾ | **6** | 5/1$^{3}$ | 87 | 36 |
| 3822$^{4}$ | **Resounder (USA) (96)** (JHMGosden) **3-8-8** AMcGlone(4) (lw: hld up: rdn over 2f out: wknd over 1f out) | nk | **7** | 5/1$^{3}$ | 91 | 36 |
| 2471a$^{6}$ | **Tarawa (IRE) (104)** (NACallaghan) **4-9-6** CAsmussen(1) (a bhd) | ¾ | **8** | 5/1$^{3}$ | 98 | 47 |
| *3782$^{2}$* | ***Law Commission (95)*** (DRCElsworth) **6-8-11** RCochrane(9) (Withdrawn not under Starter's orders: broke out of stalls & bolted) | | **W** | 9/2$^{2}$ | — | — |
| | | | | (SP 135.0%) | **8 Rn** | |

**1m 27.31** (2.51) CSF £55.33 CT £431.33 TOTE £10.90: £2.60 £1.40 £3.00 (£23.10) Trio £74.80 OWNER Mr Mana Al Maktoum (NEWMARKET) BRED Gainsborough Farm Inc
LONG HANDICAP Almuhimm (USA) 8-5 Grand Musica 8-0
WEIGHT FOR AGE 3yo-4lb
**3263 Star of Zilzal (USA)** did not take the eye in the paddock, but connections decided to use different tactics this time and, instead of holding him up, allowed the gelding to make his own running. The move paid handsome dividends as he forged clear over two furlongs from home to win his first handicap. (10/1)
**3832* Grand Musica** ran well on this handicap debut, despite carrying his head rather high. (5/1: 9/2-7/1)
**3271 Please Suzanne** has been mainly disappointing since her Kempton victory back in May. (12/1)
**3996 Celestial Key (USA)**, winner of a listed race last year, has now climbed to 105 in the Ratings, 9lb above his last handicap success, and found the weight anchoring him. (4/1)
**3920 My Best Valentine** has been raised 6lb for his 'moral victory' at Chester and is now 9lb higher than his last handicap success. (13/2)
**3445 Almuhimm (USA)** again disappointed and appears to have gone off the boil having had a sparkling mid-summer. (5/1)

## 4197 WESTMINSTER TAXI INSURANCE SELECT STKS (Gp 3) (3-Y.O+) (Class A)

2-45 (2-51) **1m 2f** £23,590.00 (£8,827.00: £4,238.50: £1,844.50) Stalls: High GOING minus 0.11 sec per fur (G)

| | | | | SP | RR | SF |
|---|---|---|---|---|---|---|
| 2583$^{2}$ | **Singspiel (IRE) (122)** (MRStoute) **4-9-3** CAsmussen(2) (mde all: qcknd over 1f out: pushed out) | — | **1** | 11/10$^{1}$ | 126 | 77 |

3746a[4] **Wall Street (USA) (110)** (SbinSuroor) **3-8-7** RCochrane(3) (lw: chsd wnr over 4f: n.m.r on ins over 2f out: chsd wnr over 1f out: r.o) ....1 **2** 9/4[2] 121 65
3671[4] **Farasan (IRE) (115)** (HRACecil) **3-8-7** GDuffield(1) (hld up: rdn over 2f out: sn wknd) ....8 **3** 9/2[3] 109 53
2844a[4] **Prize Giving (112)** (GWragg) **3-8-7** AClark(4) (lw: hld up: chsd wnr over 5f out tl over 1f out: sn wknd) ....2½ **4** 9/1 105 49
(SP 106.6%) **4 Rn**

**2m 7.38** (1.88) CSF £3.64 TOTE £1.80: (£1.70) OWNER Sheikh Mohammed (NEWMARKET) BRED Sheikh Mohammed bin Rashid al Maktoum
WEIGHT FOR AGE 3yo-7lb

**2583 Singspiel (IRE)** has suffered badly from seconditis over the last couple of seasons but, back over his ideal trip, found this was his day, quickening nicely approaching the final furlong to keep the runner-up at bay. (11/10)
**3746a Wall Street (USA)** got the split between horses and looked a real threat to the winner over a furlong out before his rival changed gear, but did finish well clear of the remainder. He is a very decent three-year-old and should be able to find another listed race, or even a Group Three event, before the season is out. (9/4: 3/1-2/1)
**3671 Farasan (IRE)** is not really up to this class. (9/2: op 2/1)
**2844a Prize Giving** looked extremely well in the paddock after a nine-week break. (9/1: 6/1-10/1)

## 4198 WILLIAM HILL SPRINT CUP H'CAP (0-95) (3-Y.O+) (Class C)

3-20 (3-23) **6f** £14,915.00 (£4,520.00: £2,210.00: £1,055.00) Stalls: Low GOING minus 0.11 sec per fur (G)

SP RR SF
3693[2] **Clan Chief (79)** (JRArnold) **3-9-1** AClark(2) (b.hind: swtg: mde virtually all: all out) ....— **1** 8/1[2] 87 60
3758[5] **Indian Relative (76)** (RGuest) **3-8-7**(5) DGriffiths(10) (swtg: hld up: rdn over 1f out: ev ch fnl f: r.o wl) ....nk **2** 25/1 83 56
4058* **Oggi (65)** (PJMakin) **5-8-3** GDuffield(18) (hld up: rdn over 2f out: ev ch fnl f: r.o wl) ....hd **3** 13/2[1] 72 47
3666[2] **Scissor Ridge (58)** (JJBridger) **4-7-3**(7) RMullen(13) (swtg: a.p: rdn over 2f out: ev ch fnl f: r.o) ....½ **4** 33/1 64 39
3993[6] **Moon Strike (FR) (80)** (HAkbary) **6-9-1**(3) RHavlin(15) (b: hld up: ev ch over 1f out: r.o) ....½ **5** 14/1 84 59
3296[9] **So Intrepid (IRE) (80)** (JMBradley) **6-9-4** TWilliams(4) (lw: rdn over 2f out: hdwy over 1f out: r.o) ....nk **6** 20/1 84 59
3696[2] **Ortolan (80)** (RHannon) **3-9-2** DaneO'Neill(1) (rdn over 2f out: hdwy over 1f out: r.o) ....s.h **7** 11/1 83 56
3338[8] **Go Hever Golf (79)** (TJNaughton) **4-9-3** AMcGlone(21) (swtg: a.p: rdn over 2f out: ev ch 1f out: unable qckn) ....1¼ **8** 33/1 79 54
3993* **Squire Corrie (66)** (GHarwood) **4-7-11b**(7) GayeHarwood(22) (lw: a.p: rdn over 2f out: ev ch over 1f out: one pce) ....s.h **9** 14/1 66 41
4058[4] **Castlerea Lad (73)** (RHollinshead) **7-8-8**(3) FLynch(20) (hdwy over 1f out: one pce) ....s.h **10** 11/1 73 48
3973* **Grand Chapeau (IRE) (61)** (DNicholls) **4-7-10**(3) MHenry(17) (a.p: rdn over 2f out: ev ch over 1f out: wknd fnl f) ....½ **11** 9/1[3] 59 34
3758[3] **Almasi (IRE) (69)** (CFWall) **4-8-0**(7) PClarke(16) (hdwy over 1f out: nt clr run ins fnl f: one pce) ....¾ **12** 20/1 65 40
3783[12] **No Extras (IRE) (81)** (GLMoore) **6-9-5** SWhitworth(12) (b.off hind: swtg: rdn over 2f out: nvr nrr) ....nk **13** 14/1 77 52
2298[4] **Montserrat (77)** (LGCottrell) **4-9-1v** CAsmussen(8) (no hdwy fnl 2f) ....½ **14** 20/1 71 46
3810[7] **Bayin (USA) (74)** (MDIUsher) **7-8-12** RStreet(19) (b: sme hdwy over 1f out: sn wknd) ....nk **15** 25/1 68 43
3810[2] **Kildee Lad (81)** (APJones) **6-9-5** BDoyle(3) (lw: a bhd) ....½ **16** 16/1 73 48
3933[7] **Portend (90)** (SRBowring) **4-10-0b** SDWilliams(6) (spd over 4f) ....1¼ **17** 20/1 79 54
3758* **Bee Health Boy (70)** (MWEasterby) **3-8-1**(5) GParkin(7) (spd over 3f) ....1 **18** 14/1 56 29
3783[8] **Lennox Lewis (76)** (APJarvis) **4-9-0** JTate(9) (lw: spd over 4f) ....1½ **19** 20/1 58 33
3967[6] **Pride of Hayling (IRE) (62)** (PRHedger) **5-8-0** JFanning(5) (swtg: spd over 3f) ....5 **20** 33/1 31 6
4119[8] **Youdontsay (83)** (TJNaughton) **4-9-2**(5) JDSmith(14) (lw: a bhd) ....4 **21** 20/1 41 16
(SP 128.7%) **21 Rn**

**1m 12.06** (2.06) CSF £174.97 CT £1,286.83 TOTE £7.10: £1.90 £9.00 £2.40 £4.40 (£282.90) Trio £838.00 OWNER Mr P. G. Lowe (UPPER LAMBOURN) BRED D. Gill
LONG HANDICAP Scissor Ridge 7-8
WEIGHT FOR AGE 3yo-2lb

**3693 Clan Chief** continues in the form of his life, despite a rise of 21lb since his first victory of the season, and gained the biggest win of his career on his first venture over six furlongs. The Handicapper will not be very amused. (8/1)
**3758 Indian Relative** ran surely her best race to date and battled hard for the lead in the final furlong, going down by only a neck. (25/1)
**4058* Oggi**, beaten under a length in this race last year, went even closer on this occasion and only just lost out. (13/2)
**3666 Scissor Ridge** has been a model of consistency this season in lower-grade races than this but, despite the step up in class, gave a thoroughly good account of himself and showed real battling qualities. (33/1)
**3993 Moon Strike (FR)** is probably best at seven furlongs but, having said that, he had every chance below the distance and stuck on well to the line. (14/1)
**2228* So Intrepid (IRE)** was doing all his best work in the last furlong and a half, but just failed to get there in time. (20/1)
**3696 Ortolan** has won four claimers this year, including once over this course and distance, but that was on soft ground where stamina came into play. On a faster surface, he found it all happening too quickly on this downhill track, but he is certainly better than claiming company and should soon pick up his first handicap. (11/1)
**Go Hever Golf** ran his best race for a very long time and, at the line, was beaten only about two and a half lengths. (33/1)
**3993* Squire Corrie** is best at five furlongs and that was borne out here for, after having every chance below the distance, he failed to find another gear in the last 200 yards. He remains in good form nevertheless. (14/1)
**4058 Castlerea Lad** (11/1: 16/1-10/1)

## 4199 HIGHLAND SPRING/ROA H'CAP (0-90) (3-Y.O+) (Class C)

3-55 (3-56) **2m** £7,765.00 (£2,320.00: £1,110.00: £505.00) Stalls: High GOING minus 0.11 sec per fur (G)

SP RR SF
3834[10] **Great Easeby (IRE) (60)** (WStorey) **6-8-3** JFanning(5) (hld up: rdn over 3f out: led over 2f out: r.o wl) ....— **1** 10/1 69 55
3801* **French Ivy (USA) (67)** (FMurphy) **9-8-10** RCochrane(3) (b: lw: stdy hdwy over 2f out: rdn over 1f out: r.o) ....nk **2** 4/1[1] 76 62
3948* **Ivor's Flutter (82)** (DRCElsworth) **7-9-6**(5) DGriffiths(12) (nt clr run & swtchd lft 2f out: hdwy over 1f out: r.o ins fnl f) ....nk **3** 9/1 90 76
3928[2] **Candle Smoke (USA) (72)** (GHarwood) **3-7-9**(7) GayeHarwood(7) (a.p: ev ch over 2f out: unable qckn fnl f) .1½ **4** 7/1[3] 79 52
3948[4] **Blaze Away (USA) (76)** (IABalding) **5-9-0**(5) MartinDwyer(1) (lw: rdn over 3f out: hdwy over 2f out: one pce) 1¼ **5** 7/1[3] 82 68
3922[7] **Shirley Sue (70)** (MJohnston) **3-7-11**(3) MHenry(13) (lw: nvr nr to chal) ....nk **6** 12/1 75 48
3834[3] **Harbour Island (81)** (MRStoute) **4-9-10b** CAsmussen(10) (led 14f out to 9f out: wknd wl over 1f out) ....1¾ **7** 6/1[2] 85 71
79* **Miroswaki (USA) (65)** (RAkehurst) **6-8-8** StephenDavies(4) (lw: a.p: rdn over 3f out: wknd over 1f out) ....½ **8** 8/1 68 54
3598[3] **Salaman (FR) (82)** (JLDunlop) **4-9-11b** BDoyle(9) (lw: hdwy 3f out: wkng whn n.m.r on ins wl over 1f out) ....½ **9** 10/1 85 71
449[19] **Meant to Be (79)** (LadyHerries) **6-9-1**(7) PDoe(2) (led 2f: led 9f out tl over 2f out: sn wknd) ....11 **10** 25/1 71 57
3948[12] **Polo Kit (IRE) (68)** (RJO'Sullivan) **5-8-11** GDuffield(6) (b: lw: a bhd) ....5 **11** 20/1 55 41

| | | | | SP | RR | SF |
|---|---|---|---|---|---|---|
| | **Inchcailloch (IRE) (62)** (JSKing) **7-8-5** AClark(8) (a bhd: t.o) | | **12** | 33/1 | — | — |
| 2511[2] | **Labeed (USA) (70)** (RAkehurst) **3-8-0** AMcGlone(11) (6th whn broke leg over 4f out: dead) | | **P** | 11/1 | — | — |

(SP 126.2%) **13 Rn**

**3m 28.8** (4.80) CSF £49.27 CT £356.73 TOTE £14.00: £3.40 £1.60 £3.90 (£33.20) Trio £418.80 OWNER Mr D. C. Batey (CONSETT) BRED Swettenham Stud

WEIGHT FOR AGE 3yo-13lb

OFFICIAL EXPLANATION **Great Easeby (IRE): accounting for the gelding's apparent improvement on his last run, his owner said that Great Easeby is a lazy horse and needs strong handling to get him going, but on the previous outing had been ridden by N. Kennedy who was not familiar with the horse.**

**2857 Great Easeby (IRE)** at last gained his first victory on the Flat, having finished second four times this year. (10/1)

**3801* French Ivy (USA)** continues in fine form but, despite staying on really well in the straight, was never going to overhaul the winner in time. (4/1)

**3948* Ivor's Flutter** is no easy ride, but at last picked up ground below the distance, if never going to get there in time. (9/1)

**3928 Candle Smoke (USA)** has risen 6lb for being beaten a whisker at Sandown last time. (7/1)

**3948 Blaze Away (USA)**, reportedly being aimed at the Cesarewitch and The Sport of Kings Hurdle Series, is coming along nicely. (7/1)

**3922 Shirley Sue**, winner of four races this year, looks in the Handicapper's grip at present. (12/1)

**79* Miroswaki (USA)**, who did well over hurdles last winter and finished second to Blaze Away over them at Ascot in April on his last outing, played an active role until tiring early in the final quarter-mile. This run will have put him straight and he should soon be winning, whether it be on the Flat or over jumps. (8/1)

**3598 Salaman (FR)** (10/1: 7/1-11/1)

**2511 Labeed (USA)** (11/1: 8/1-12/1)

## 4200 ROYAL NAVY MAIDEN STKS (2-Y.O) (Class D)

4-30 (4-35) **1m** £4,620.00 (£1,380.00: £660.00: £300.00) Stalls: High GOING minus 0.11 sec per fur (G)

| | | | | SP | RR | SF |
|---|---|---|---|---|---|---|
| 3245[11] | **Home Alone** (JHMGosden) **2-8-11**(3) RHavlin(3) (mde all: pushed out) | — | **1** | 16/1 | 83 | 40 |
| 3615[5] | **Mardi Gras (IRE)** (JLDunlop) **2-9-0** CAsmussen(9) (hld up: rdn & edgd rt over 1f out: r.o wl ins fnl f) | ¾ | **2** | 4/6[1] | 82 | 39 |
| | **Hibernate (IRE)** (RCharlton) **2-9-0** AMcGlone(2) (w'like: scope: bit bkwd: a.p: chsd wnr over 3f out tl wl ins fnl f: unable qckn) | ¾ | **3** | 6/1[2] | 80 | 37 |
| | **Cadbury Castle** (MBlanshard) **2-8-9** AClark(6) (w'like: bit bkwd: a.p: rdn over 2f out: sn wknd) | 8 | **4** | 50/1 | 59 | 16 |
| | **Zingaro (IRE)** (CEBrittain) **2-9-0** BDoyle(7) (w'like: rdn over 3f out: edgd rt over 2f out: nvr nr to chal) | nk | **5** | 16/1 | 63 | 20 |
| | **Allied Academy** (SCWilliams) **2-9-0** JTate(8) (leggy: scope: lw: s.s: hdwy over 2f out: sn wknd) | 6 | **6** | 33/1 | 51 | 8 |
| | **Sand Cay (USA)** (RHannon) **2-9-0** DaneO'Neill(4) (w'like: bit bkwd: a bhd) | ½ | **7** | 9/1[3] | 50 | 7 |
| | **Grandpa Lex (IRE)** (IABalding) **2-9-0** RCochrane(1) (leggy: unf: scope: s.s: a bhd) | ½ | **8** | 6/1[2] | 49 | 6 |
| 3682[7] | **Frost King** (MissBSanders) **2-8-11**(3) AWhelan(5) (swtg: prom over 4f) | 4 | **9** | 50/1 | 41 | — |

(SP 117.2%) **9 Rn**

**1m 42.02** (4.82) CSF £26.76 TOTE £17.70: £2.60 £1.10 £2.00 (£11.60) Trio £28.00 OWNER Mr D. H. Armitage (NEWMARKET) BRED Highclere Stud Ltd

IN-FOCUS: **This was a very ordinary maiden event.**

**Home Alone**, who finished last on his Newmarket debut, was a totally different kettle of fish on this occasion, but it is worth noting that he was taken down very quietly to the start some time after the others, and he may be just a little bit of an awkward customer. (16/1)

**3615 Mardi Gras (IRE)**, who met with all sorts of problems on his debut, had no such excuses here and took an age to find top gear. He did run on strongly inside the final furlong and managed to snatch second place close home. (4/6: 4/7-10/11)

**Hibernate (IRE)**, a flashy, good-bodied colt with plenty of scope, did not look fully fit but still showed plenty of promise. He should have no problems winning a race. (6/1)

**Cadbury Castle**, a plain filly, looked as though the run was needed and so that proved as she tired a quarter of a mile from home. (50/1)

**Zingaro (IRE)** proved rather green on this debut. (16/1)

**Sand Cay (USA)** (9/1: 5/1-10/1)

**Grandpa Lex (IRE)** (6/1: op 4/1)

## 4201 CITY OF PORTSMOUTH MAIDEN STKS (3-Y.O) (Class D)

5-00 (5-03) **1m 2f** £4,620.00 (£1,380.00: £660.00: £300.00) Stalls: High GOING minus 0.11 sec per fur (G)

| | | | | SP | RR | SF |
|---|---|---|---|---|---|---|
| 3505[8] | **Raheefa (USA)** (JHMGosden) **3-8-9** AMcGlone(5) (a.p: rdn over 1f out: led last strides) | — | **1** | 10/1 | 78 | 41 |
| 3656[4] | **Opalette** (LadyHerries) **3-8-9** RCochrane(3) (led: rdn over 1f out: hdd last strides) | hd | **2** | 9/2[2] | 78 | 41 |
| 3161[8] | **Pasternak (75)** (SirMarkPrescott) **3-9-0** GDuffield(2) (lw: plld hrd: stdy hdwy over 3f out: rdn over 1f out: r.o wl) | hd | **3** | 3/1[1] | 83 | 46 |
| 2996[6] | **Infatuation** (LadyHerries) **3-8-11**(3) FLynch(8) (lw: rdn over 2f out: hdwy over 1f out: r.o wl ins fnl f) | s.h | **4** | 9/2[2] | 83 | 46 |
| 3505[6] | **Prospero** (GHarwood) **3-9-0** CAsmussen(11) (a.p: rdn over 1f out: unable qckn fnl f) | 3½ | **5** | 15/2[3] | 77 | 40 |
| 3788[8] | **Latin Quarter (USA)** (RCharlton) **3-9-0** BDoyle(7) (chsd ldr 8f) | 3½ | **6** | 9/1 | 71 | 34 |
| 3847[4] | **Itkan (IRE)** (CJBenstead) **3-8-9** TWilliams(1) (rdn over 3f out: hdwy over 2f out: wknd over 1f out) | 8 | **7** | 20/1 | 54 | 17 |
| 3788[7] | **Silvretta (IRE)** (ACStewart) **3-8-9** SWhitworth(6) (bhd fnl 5f) | 2½ | **8** | 8/1 | 50 | 13 |
| | **Sacred Loch (USA)** (GHarwood) **3-9-0** AClark(4) (leggy: scope: swtg: bhd fnl 3f) | 2½ | **9** | 16/1 | 51 | 14 |
| 3505[9] | **Porlock Castle** (KRBurke) **3-9-0** JTate(12) (bhd fnl 3f) | 17 | **10** | 33/1 | 23 | — |
| 3656[15] | **Locket** (JABennett) **3-8-6**(3) MHenry(9) (a bhd: t.o) | dist | **11** | 66/1 | — | — |
| 3472[8] | **Sovereign Crest (IRE)** (CAHorgan) **3-9-0** NAdams(10) (bhd whn stmbld & fell over 7f out) | | **F** | 33/1 | — | — |

(SP 121.3%) **12 Rn**

**2m 11.02** (5.52) CSF £52.27 TOTE £14.30: £3.10 £1.40 £1.90 (£22.10) Trio £27.70 OWNER Mr Hamdan Al Maktoum (NEWMARKET) BRED David Garvin

IN-FOCUS: **This looked another very ordinary maiden.**

**Raheefa (USA)** stepped up on her Sandown debut and came through in the final furlong to get up in a desperate finish. (10/1)

**3656 Opalette** attempted to make all the running but, in a desperate finish, was worried out if it in the last few strides. (9/2: op 5/2)

**2894 Pasternak**, a big, imposing individual, looked outstanding in the paddock, but took a very keen hold in the early stages. Nevertheless, he appeared to be travelling well as he eased his way into the action in the straight and, in a tight finish, only just lost out. In a faster-run race, he should finally lose his maiden tag. (3/1)

**2996 Infatuation** stepped up on his gentle introduction, but was noted flashing his tail each time he was hit. Nevertheless, he ran on strongly and only just failed in a blanket finish. (9/2)

**3505 Prospero** carried his head rather high and failed to quicken in the last 200 yards. (15/2)

**3788 Silvretta (IRE)** (8/1: 5/1-9/1)

## 4202 BATTLE OF BRITAIN WESTHAMPNETT AMATEUR LIMITED STKS (0-70) (3-Y.O+) (Class E)

5-30 (5-34) **7f** £4,045.00 (£1,210.00: £580.00: £265.00) Stalls: High GOING minus 0.11 sec per fur (G)

| | | | | SP | RR | SF |
|---|---|---|---|---|---|---|
| 3510* | **Polly Peculiar (60)** (BSmart) **5-10-3**(5) MissVMarshall(15) (stdy hdwy over 2f out: led over 1f out: sn clr: r.o wl) | — | **1** | 10/1 | 79 | 41 |
| 4059* | **Embankment (IRE) (70)** (RHannon) **6-10-11** MrCVigors(6) (a.p: led 2f out tl over 1f out: unable qckn) | 5 | **2** | 11/4 $^{2}$ | 71 | 33 |
| 3770$^{5}$ | **Serious Sensation (70)** (SirMarkPrescott) **3-10-7** MrPScott(7) (lw: hdwy to ld over 3f out: hdd 2f out: one pce) | 1¼ | **3** | 2/1 $^{1}$ | 68 | 26 |
| 3926$^{12}$ | **Carmarthen Bay (70)** (GLMoore) **3-10-5** MrKGoble(1) (lw: hdwy over 1f out: r.o) | 1¼ | **4** | 12/1 | 63 | 21 |
| 3257$^{6}$ | **Tauten (IRE) (38)** (PBurgoyne) **6-10-1v**(5) MissMO'Sullivan(14) (hdwy 2f out: r.o one pce) | s.h | **5** | 66/1 | 60 | 22 |
| 3465$^{8}$ | **Sabaah Elfull (70)** (ACStewart) **3-9-13**(5) MrVLukaniuk(10) (lw: a.p: ev ch 2f out: wknd fnl f) | nk | **6** | 7/1 $^{3}$ | 61 | 19 |
| | **Jato (68)** (SCWilliams) **7-10-4**(5) MrsSEddery(4) (b: hdwy over 3f out: ev ch 2f out: wknd fnl f) | 3½ | **7** | 9/1 | 54 | 16 |
| 1685$^{5}$ | **Kingchip Boy (63)** (MJRyan) **7-10-6v**(5) MrSLavallin(9) (bit bkwd: hld up: rdn over 2f out: wknd over 1f out) | ½ | **8** | 9/1 | 55 | 17 |
| 3944$^{7}$ | **Delight of Dawn (64)** (RMStronge) **4-10-3**(5) MrJDewhurst(11) (b: nvr nr to chal) | 2 | **9** | 16/1 | 47 | 9 |
| 4053$^{12}$ | **Reem Fever (IRE) (65)** (DWPArbuthnot) **3-10-2b** MrsDArbuthnot(3) (lw: hdwy over 4f out: wknd over 1f out) | 2½ | **10** | 25/1 | 40 | — |
| 3817$^{11}$ | **Winter Scout (USA) (58)** (CPEBrooks) **8-10-6**(5) MissJRussell(5) (lw: bhd fnl 3f) | 1½ | **11** | 25/1 | 41 | 3 |
| *3877*$^{10}$ | **Justinianus (IRE) (38)** (JJBridger) **4-10-4**(5) MrDBridger(12) (lw: led over 3f) | 4 | **12** | 100/1 | 30 | — |
| *402*$^{11}$ | **Cultural Icon (USA) (37)** (PMitchell) **4-10-7**(5)ow3 MrMJeffries(2) (a bhd) | 1¾ | **13** | 100/1 | 29 | — |
| *4089*$^{11}$ | **Sarum (35)** (JELong) **10-10-6**(5) MrTWaters(16) (b: prom over 3f) | hd | **14** | 100/1 | 28 | — |
| 3849$^{15}$ | **Colebrook Willie (32)** (JRBosley) **3-10-5v** MrsSBosley(17) (prom over 2f) | 2 | **15** | 100/1 | 21 | — |
| | **Masbro Bird (42)** (TMJones) **3-10-2**(5)ow5 MrPMiddleton(13) (w ldr over 3f) | 1¾ | **16** | 100/1 | 19 | — |
| 3474$^{12}$ | **Indian Wolf (30)** (BJLlewellyn) **3-10-5** MrJLLlewellyn(8) (lw: prom over 4f) | 1½ | **17** | 100/1 | 14 | — |
| | | | | (SP 130.3%) | **17 Rn** | |

**1m 30.07** (5.27) CSF £37.44 TOTE £12.30: £2.10 £1.60 £1.50 (£16.10) Trio £9.60 OWNER Miss Victoria Marshall (LAMBOURN) BRED Aston Park Stud

WEIGHT FOR AGE 3yo-4lb

**3510* Polly Peculiar** followed up her Beverley victory in emphatic style, storming to the front over a furlong out and soon putting the issue beyond doubt. (10/1)

**4059* Embankment (IRE)** has done all his winning at a mile and was unable to cope with the winner over this shorter trip. (11/4)

**3770 Serious Sensation** ran his best race on turf to date but, when headed a quarter of a mile from home, failed to find another gear. (2/1)

**2974 Carmarthen Bay** seems best on Sand but put in some good work in the last furlong and a half. (12/1)

**3257 Tauten (IRE)** was well adrift until staying on through the pack in the straight. She is still a maiden after twenty-six attempts. (66/1)

**3100* Sabaah Elfull**, whose only victory to date came over five furlongs, had come to the end of her tether inside the distance. (7/1)

T/Plpt: £76.90 (295.76 Tckts). T/Qdpt: £9.00 (137.8 Tckts). AK

# 3808-NOTTINGHAM (L-H) (St crse Good to firm, Firm patches, Rnd crse Firm)

## Monday September 16th

WEATHER: fine WIND: almost nil

## 4203 CARLTON H'CAP (0-65) (3-Y.O+) (Class F)

2-00 (2-01) **2m 9y** £2,381.00 (£656.00: £311.00) Stalls: High GOING minus 0.47 sec per fur (F)

| | | | | SP | RR | SF |
|---|---|---|---|---|---|---|
| 3928$^{8}$ | **Broughtons Formula (34)** (WJMusson) **6-8-0b** JQuinn(8) (hld up: hdwy 3f out: led wl over 1f out: sn qcknd clr: r.o wl) | — | **1** | 16/1 | 44 | 25 |
| 4048$^{10}$ | **Requested (48)** (PBurgoyne) **9-9-0** DRMcCabe(17) (s.s: gd hdwy 2f out: r.o wl ins fnl f) | 1½ | **2** | 10/1 | 57 | 38 |
| *3066*$^{5}$ | **Iota (55)** (JLHarris) **7-9-7** BDoyle(9) (hld up: hdwy over 3f out: ev ch 2f out: r.o one pce) | ½ | **3** | 14/1 | 63 | 44 |
| 3979$^{12}$ | **Zeliba (37)** (MrsNMacauley) **4-7-10**(7) JoHunnam(20) (hld up & bhd: gd hdwy over 2f out: r.o one pce fnl f) | nk | **4** | 14/1 | 45 | 26 |
| *3605*$^{6}$ | **Atienza (USA) (49)** (SCWilliams) **3-8-3**ow1 JTate(1) (a.p: outpcd wl over 1f out: styd on fnl f) | hd | **5** | 25/1 | 57 | 25 |
| 3850$^{6}$ | **Mizyan (IRE) (56)** (JEBanks) **8-9-3**(5) GFaulkner(14) (hld up: hdwy 5f out: wknd over 1f out) | 4 | **6** | 10/1 | 60 | 41 |
| *4092*$^{5}$ | **Classic Affair (USA) (64)** (RHarris) **3-9-4** AMackay(7) (lw: bhd tl gd late hdwy: nvr nrr) | nk | **7** | 6/1 $^{3}$ | 67 | 36 |
| 3979$^{4}$ | **Lucky Coin (54)** (PHowling) **4-9-6** FNorton(13) (prom: rdn 4f out: wknd 2f out) | ½ | **8** | 14/1 | 57 | 38 |
| 3801$^{5}$ | **Prague Spring (60)** (LadyHerries) **4-9-12b**$^{1}$ RCochrane(3) (b: plld hrd: led 4f: rdn 8f out: wknd over 2f out) | hd | **9** | 10/1 | 63 | 44 |
| 2182$^{14}$ | **Bobby's Dream (33)** (MHTompkins) **4-7-13** GBardwell(11) (bit bkwd: nvr nr to chal) | ½ | **10** | 25/1 | 35 | 16 |
| 3225$^{3}$ | **Alisura (62)** (JRFanshawe) **3-9-2** DHarrison(10) (mid div: bhd fnl 2f) | 1¼ | **11** | 11/2 $^{2}$ | 63 | 32 |
| 3775* | **Jalcanto (55)** (MrsMReveley) **6-9-7** ACulhane(5) (s.s: rdn & hdwy over 3f out: wknd 2f out) | s.h | **12** | 8/1 | 56 | 37 |
| 3775$^{2}$ | **Kesanta (35)** (WGMTurner) **6-7-10**(5) CAdamson(4) (b: hld up & plld hrd: hdwy over 3f out: wknd over 2f out) | s.h | **13** | 12/1 | 36 | 17 |
| | **Sea Buck (49)** (HCandy) **10-8-8**(7)ow8 LJames(15) (bkwd: a bhd) | 6 | **14** | 40/1 | 44 | 17 |
| 4048$^{3}$ | **Euphonic (60)** (IABalding) **6-9-12** LDettori(19) (led after 4f tl wl over 1f out: wknd qckly) | 1¾ | **15** | 3/1 $^{1}$ | 53 | 34 |
| | **Arc Bright (IRE) (49)** (RHollinshead) **6-8-12**(3) FLynch(18) (bkwd: a bhd) | 2½ | **16** | 20/1 | 40 | 21 |
| 3991$^{17}$ | **Set the Fashion (58)** (DLWilliams) **7-9-5**(5) DGriffiths(2) (prom tl wknd over 3f out) | 1 | **17** | 25/1 | 48 | 29 |
| 2756$^{8}$ | **Atherton Green (IRE) (51)** (JAGlover) **6-9-3** MBirch(12) (prom tl wknd 3f out) | 1¾ | **18** | 16/1 | 39 | 20 |
| *4092*$^{9}$ | **Teen Jay (56)** (BJLlewellyn) **6-9-8** VSlattery(16) (lw: prom 11f) | s.h | **19** | 16/1 | 44 | 25 |
| *4107*$^{8}$ | **Court Jester (40)** (MJRyan) **5-8-6b** AClark(6) (prom tl wknd over 3f out) | 1 | **20** | 33/1 | 27 | 8 |
| | | | | (SP 160.1%) | **20 Rn** | |

**3m 27.6** (4.60) CSF £190.55 CT £2,191.61 TOTE £19.30: £3.60 £3.80 £3.30 £4.80 (£308.40) Trio Not won; £536.44 to Sandown 17/9/96 OWNER Crawford Gray & Aylett (NEWMARKET) BRED The Lavington Stud

WEIGHT FOR AGE 3yo-12lb

**69 Broughtons Formula** bounced back to form having slipped to a mark a stone lower than when he last won on turf over a year ago. (16/1)

**3813 Requested** was back to the mark off which he ran when second at Ascot in June. (10/1)

**2423* Iota** was 5lb higher than when successful at Catterick in July. (14/1)

**3664 Zeliba**, back to the mark of the second of her two selling victories, was stepping up in distance. (14/1: 10/1-16/1)

**2928 Atienza (USA)**, trying her luck at two miles, was 5lb lower than when a well-beaten second in a weakly-contested event at Musselburgh in July. (25/1)

**3335 Mizyan (IRE)**, 4lb lower than when he last won, has never been successful beyond a mile and three-quarters. (10/1)

**3775* Jalcanto** (8/1: op 5/1)
**3775 Kesanta** (12/1: op 8/1)
**4048 Euphonic** should have been suited by this longer trip, but went out like a light. (3/1)

## 4204 E.B.F. NOTTINGHAM MAIDEN STKS (2-Y.O) (Class D)

2-30 (2-31) **1m 54y** £3,957.00 (£1,185.00: £569.00: £261.00) Stalls: High GOING minus 0.47 sec per fur (F)

| | | | | SP | RR | SF |
|---|---|---|---|---|---|---|
| 2909[2] | **Happy Minstral (USA)** (MJohnston) **2-9-0** RHills(2) (led after 1f: qcknd clr over 1f out: rdn out) | — | **1** | 8/1 | 75 | 28 |
| 3873[4] | **Sword Arm** (RCharlton) **2-9-0** TSprake(6) (hld up: hdwy over 3f out: chsd wnr over 1f out: no imp) | 1½ | **2** | 3/1[2] | 72 | 25 |
| | **Over To You (USA)** (EALDunlop) **2-9-0** KFallon(5) (lt-f: unf: s.s: hdwy over 2f out: rdn over 1f out: one pce) | 1¾ | **3** | 8/1 | 69 | 22 |
| 3682[11] | **Silver Patriarch (IRE)** (JLDunlop) **2-9-0** KDarley(9) (bit bkwd: hld up: hdwy over 2f out: sn edgd lft: one pce) | 2 | **4** | 6/1[3] | 65 | 18 |
| 3821[4] | **Rasmussen (IRE)** (JHMGosden) **2-9-0** LDettori(3) (b.hind: s.i.s: sn prom: rdn over 2f out: wknd over 1f out) | nk | **5** | 11/8[1] | 64 | 17 |
| 3757[8] | **Dixie Jamboree (USA)** (LMCumani) **2-9-0** SSanders(1) (no hdwy fnl 2f) | 1¼ | **6** | 10/1 | 62 | 15 |
| | **Polar Flight** (MJohnston) **2-9-0** BDoyle(4) (unf: scope: bkwd: prom tl wknd 2f out) | 2 | **7** | 25/1 | 58 | 11 |
| 3615[16] | **Beauchamp Lion** (JLDunlop) **2-9-0** GCarter(8) (bit bkwd: hld up: a bhd) | s.h | **8** | 16/1 | 58 | 11 |
| | **Canton Ron** (CADwyer) **2-9-0** TGMcLaughlin(7) (wl grwn: bkwd: plld hrd: led 1f: wknd 2f out) | 13 | **9** | 25/1 | 33 | — |

(SP 126.3%) **9 Rn**

**1m 44.6** (3.30) CSF £33.41 TOTE £9.00: £1.60 £1.30 £2.80 (£13.20) Trio £53.00 OWNER Atlantic Racing Ltd (MIDDLEHAM) BRED Hartland Farm

**2909 Happy Minstral (USA)**, a half-brother to Double Bass and good Irish winner Punctilio, quickened from the front in a race run at a muddling pace. He returned with a nasty cut having been struck into behind. (8/1)
**3873 Sword Arm** confirmed the form of his Salisbury debut with Rasmussen. (3/1)
**Over To You (USA)** should be better for the experience, but does lack substance. (8/1: op 4/1)
**Silver Patriarch (IRE)**, a half-brother to Silver Singing and My Patriarch, gave the impression he may have been feeling the ground. (6/1: op 3/1)
**3821 Rasmussen (IRE)** could prefer better ground. (11/8)
**Dixie Jamboree (USA)** was stepping up to a mile. (10/1: op 6/1)

## 4205 NOTTINGHAM 'GOOSE FAIR' H'CAP (0-70) (3-Y.O+) (Class E)

3-00 (3-01) **5f 13y** £3,698.10 (£1,108.80: £533.40: £245.70) Stalls: High GOING minus 0.47 sec per fur (F)

| | | | | SP | RR | SF |
|---|---|---|---|---|---|---|
| 4058[5] | **Cretan Gift (66)** (NPLittmoden) **5-9-10b** LDettori(15) (hdwy wl over 1f out: str run to ld wl ins fnl f) | — | **1** | 7/2[1] | 75 | 53 |
| *4081*[13] | **Another Batchworth (53)** (EAWheeler) **4-8-11b**[1] SWhitworth(18) (led over 3f out: clr over 1f out: hdd wl ins fnl f) | 1¾ | **2** | 10/1 | 57 | 35 |
| 4045* | **Superbit (53)** (BAMcMahon) **4-8-11** SSanders(3) (lw: led centre: r.o one pce fnl f) | nk | **3** | 7/1[3] | 56 | 34 |
| 3937[9] | **Camionneur (IRE) (49)** (TDEasterby) **3-8-6b** JLowe(1) (hdwy over 1f out: r.o) | nk | **4** | 12/1 | 51 | 28 |
| 3777[10] | **Coolowen Flash (IRE) (41)** (JLEyre) **5-7-13** TWilliams(16) (led over 1f: btn whn edgd rt wl ins fnl f) | 1 | **5** | 12/1 | 39 | 17 |
| *4090*[5] | **Souperficial (50)** (JAGlover) **5-8-8v** JFortune(11) (lw: a.p: no hdwy fnl 2f) | s.h | **6** | 13/2[2] | 48 | 26 |
| 931[7] | **Stephensons Rocket (56)** (DNicholls) **5-9-0** AlexGreaves(19) (hdwy wl over 1f out: btn whn bdly hmpd wl ins fnl f) | 1 | **7** | 10/1 | 51 | 29 |
| 3793[10] | **Lloc (54)** (CADwyer) **4-8-5**(7) JoHunnam(4) (swtg: prom far side over 3f) | ½ | **8** | 11/1 | 48 | 26 |
| 4058[12] | **Polly Golightly (65)** (MBlanshard) **3-9-8v** JQuinn(17) (nvr nr to chal) | ½ | **9** | 9/1 | 57 | 34 |
| 3868[8] | **Serious Hurry (39)** (RMMcKellar) **8-7-4b**(7) JMcAuley(10) (prom over 3f) | 2 | **10** | 16/1 | 25 | 3 |
| 3643[11] | **Tutu Sixtysix (38)** (DonEnricoIncisa) **5-7-10b** KimTinkler(14) (swtg: prom over 3f) | 1¼ | **11** | 50/1 | 20 | — |
| *4094*[8] | **Deardaw (38)** (MissLCSiddall) **4-7-10** FNorton(8) (n.d) | ¾ | **12** | 33/1 | 17 | — |
| 3993[11] | **Windrush Boy (58)** (JRBosley) **6-8-11**(5) AimeeCook(12) (n.d) | ¾ | **13** | 12/1 | 35 | 13 |
| 4058[20] | **Sotonian (HOL) (50)** (PSFelgate) **3-8-7** DHarrison(5) (outpcd) | 2½ | **14** | 25/1 | 19 | — |
| 1985[7] | **Welsh Mountain (68)** (MJHeaton-Ellis) **3-9-11** SDrowne(13) (bit bkwd: outpcd) | ½ | **15** | 16/1 | 35 | 12 |
| 3310[3] | **Hamilton Gold (50)** (MGMeagher) **3-8-7**[ow2] KFallon(7) (s.s: a bhd) | 3½ | **16** | 12/1 | 6 | — |
| 3932[14] | **Silk Cottage (62)** (RMWhitaker) **4-9-6v** ACulhane(6) (lw: outpcd) | 2½ | **17** | 20/1 | 10 | — |
| | **Dazzle Me (38)** (AGNewcombe) **4-7-7b**[1](3) NVarley(2) (swtg: spd far side over 2f) | 1 | **18** | 50/1 | — | — |

(SP 142.6%) **18 Rn**

**59.4 secs** (0.80) CSF £41.94 CT £241.26 TOTE £4.80: £1.40 £4.00 £2.30 £4.40 (£34.40) Trio £42.00 OWNER R A M Racecourses Ltd (WOLVERHAMPTON) BRED Hesmonds Stud Ltd
LONG HANDICAP Tutu Sixtysix 6-10 Deardaw 7-9 Dazzle Me 6-13
WEIGHT FOR AGE 3yo-1lb

**4058 Cretan Gift**, dropped 2lb, was gaining his first success on grass and will now go for the Silver Cup at Ayr on Saturday. (7/2)
**3864 Another Batchworth** was blinkered after disappointing on the Sand last time. (10/1)
**4045* Superbit**, raised 4lb, continues in top form at the moment. (7/1)
**3465 Camionneur (IRE)** was probably unsuited by the soft ground last time. (12/1)
**1865 Coolowen Flash (IRE)**, dropped 9lb this season, was a springer in the Offices and showed considerable improvement. (12/1)
**4090 Souperficial** was 4lb higher than when winning over course and distance last month. (13/2)
**931 Stephensons Rocket**, without the blinkers for this comeback, would have finished a bit closer had his rider not been forced to snatch up. (10/1)

## 4206 WEATHERBYS INSURANCE SERVICES H'CAP (0-70) (3-Y.O+ F & M) (Class E)

3-30 (3-34) **6f 15y** £3,889.20 (£1,167.60: £562.80: £260.40) Stalls: High GOING minus 0.47 sec per fur (F)

| | | | | SP | RR | SF |
|---|---|---|---|---|---|---|
| 3930[7] | **Merrie le Bow (49)** (PatMitchell) **4-8-4**(5) AmandaSanders(15) (gd hdwy over 1f out: led nr fin) | — | **1** | 12/1 | 60 | 25 |
| 4045[4] | **Dominelle (51)** (TDEasterby) **4-8-11** MBirch(22) (gd hdwy over 1f out: fin wl) | s.h | **2** | 13/2[2] | 62 | 27 |
| 4071[11] | **Formidable Liz (60)** (MDHammond) **6-9-6** JFortune(7) (lw: a.p: led far side over 1f out: hdd nr fin) | ¾ | **3** | 8/1[3] | 69 | 34 |
| 4058[2] | **Another Nightmare (IRE) (54)** (RMMcKellar) **4-8-7**(7) JMcAuley(9) (prom centre: ev ch over 1f out: unable qckn) | nk | **4** | 5/1[1] | 62 | 27 |
| 4130[14] | **Marino Street (56)** (PDEvans) **3-9-0v** JFEgan(16) (led stands' side: one pce fnl f) | nk | **5** | 20/1 | 63 | 26 |
| 3650[4] | **Whispered Melody (60)** (PWHarris) **3-9-4** GHind(4) (led far side over 3f: one pce) | 1¾ | **6** | 10/1 | 63 | 26 |
| 4088[5] | **Winsome Wooster (63)** (PGMurphy) **5-9-9** SDrowne(5) (lw: hdwy over 1f out: r.o) | nk | **7** | 16/1 | 65 | 30 |
| *4077*[8] | **Lady Silk (46)** (MissJFCraze) **5-8-6** NConnorton(1) (hdwy over 1f out: nt rch ldrs) | 1¼ | **8** | 25/1 | 45 | 10 |
| 4128[7] | **Deerly (48)** (CASmith) **3-8-6** CRutter(21) (nvr nr to chal) | 1 | **9** | 20/1 | 44 | 7 |
| 4088[13] | **Rambold (64)** (NEBerry) **5-9-10** RPerham(14) (w ldrs stands' side over 3f) | nk | **10** | 16/1 | 59 | 24 |

| | Horse | Dist | Pos | SP | RR | SF |
|---|---|---|---|---|---|---|
| 3977[7] | **Time Clash (55)** (BPalling) **3-8-13** TSprake(2) (no hdwy fnl 2f) | ½ | **11** | 33/1 | 49 | 12 |
| 3680[5] | **Ballard Lady (IRE) (45)** (JSWainwright) **4-7-12**(7) JBramhill(6) (nvr trbld ldrs) | ¾ | **12** | 14/1 | 37 | 2 |
| | **Galacia (IRE) (55)** (WGMTurner) **4-8-8**(7) DMcGaffin(24) (spd over 3f) | nk | **13** | 33/1 | 46 | 11 |
| 3698[5] | **Calandrella (46)** (GBBalding) **3-8-4** AMcGlone(18) (bhd fnl 2f) | nk | **14** | 20/1 | 36 | — |
| 3122[5] | **Shashi (IRE) (63)** (WWHaigh) **4-9-9** RLappin(19) (bhd fnl 2f) | nk | **15** | 12/1 | 53 | 18 |
| 4058[10] | **Miss Aragon (45)** (MissLCSiddall) **8-8-5** NCarlisle(12) (lw: bhd fnl 2f) | nk | **16** | 12/1 | 34 | — |
| *3601*[11] | **Flirty Gertie (60)** (RBoss) **4-9-6** DHarrison(13) (lw: bhd fnl 2f) | 1¼ | **17** | 20/1 | 45 | 10 |
| 3700[6] | **Lillibella (61)** (IABalding) **3-9-0b**[1](5) MartinDwyer(20) (lw: a bhd) | 1¼ | **18** | 10/1 | 43 | 6 |
| 4075[6] | **La Finale (48)** (DNicholls) **3-8-6** AClark(10) (lw: bhd fnl 2f) | 1¼ | **19** | 14/1 | 27 | — |
| 2869[4] | **Smiling Bess (48)** (RHollinshead) **3-8-3**(3) FLynch(23) (swtg: a bhd) | 1¾ | **20** | 20/1 | 22 | — |
| 3959[8] | **Branston Danni (65)** (MrsJRRamsden) **3-9-9** KFallon(3) (b.nr hind: stumbled s: bhd fnl 3f) | 1 | **21** | 12/1 | 37 | — |
| 4109[10] | **Times of Times (IRE) (66)** (MJRyan) **3-9-3b**[1](7) AMcCarthy(8) (bhd fnl 2f) | nk | **22** | 20/1 | 37 | — |
| 3700[2] | **L A Touch (55)** (JJQuinn) **3-8-13** JStack(11) (prom 3f) | 4 | **23** | 8/1[3] | 15 | — |
| 3255[8] | **Angel Face (USA) (50)** (BPreece) **3-8-8** VSlattery(17) (t.o) | dist | **24** | 33/1 | — | — |
| | | | | (SP 167.5%) | **24 Rn** | |

**1m 12.5** (2.00) CSF £104.15 CT £664.98 TOTE £18.80: £4.50 £2.70 £2.90 £1.60 (£56.50) Trio £465.90 OWNER Mrs Anna Sanders (NEWMARKET) BRED Mrs J. R. Hine and Miss J. Bunting

WEIGHT FOR AGE 3yo-2lb

**3700 Merrie le Bow** appreciated this return to six. (12/1)

**4045 Dominelle** continues in top form and another stride would probably have sufficed. (13/2)

**3639* Formidable Liz**, who tried a mile last time, ran a fine race for one who has only ever won on turning courses. (8/1)

**4058 Another Nightmare (IRE)**, 7lb higher than when winning at Ripon, seems to handle all sorts of ground and did not have much to race with up the centre of the course. (5/1)

**3652 Marino Street** bounced back to form after her recent disappointing run over the minimum trip at Chepstow. (20/1)

**3650 Whispered Melody**, trying her luck at sprinting, had been supported in the morning with one of the Independents. (10/1)

## 4207 COLWICK NURSERY H'CAP (0-75) (2-Y.O F) (Class E)

4-00 (4-04) **6f 15y** £3,752.70 (£1,125.60: £541.80: £249.90) Stalls: High GOING minus 0.47 sec per fur (F)

| | Horse | Dist | Pos | SP | RR | SF |
|---|---|---|---|---|---|---|
| 3846[8] | **Heavenly Miss (IRE) (64)** (DBurchell) **2-9-1** KFallon(14) (a.p: led over 1f out: drvn out) | — | **1** | 8/1[3] | 77 | 25 |
| 3975[6] | **Aybeegirl (66)** (MrsJCecil) **2-8-12v**(5) MartinDwyer(8) (prom: led 4f out tl over 1f out: one pce) | 3½ | **2** | 4/1[1] | 70 | 18 |
| 3687[18] | **Hit Or Miss (63)** (PCHaslam) **2-9-0** JFortune(7) (lw: a.p: rdn 2f out: one pce) | 1¾ | **3** | 12/1 | 62 | 10 |
| *3954** | **Impy Fox (IRE) (60)** (CADwyer) **2-8-4**(7) JoHunnam(2) (led 2f: r.o ins fnl f) | nk | **4** | 5/1[2] | 58 | 6 |
| 3462[5] | **Danehill Princess (IRE) (70)** (RHollinshead) **2-9-4v**(3) FLynch(5) (s.s: hdwy 3f out: r.o one pce fnl 2f) | s.h | **5** | 8/1[3] | 68 | 16 |
| 3982[22] | **Oddfellows Girl (45)** (NBycroft) **2-7-10** JQuinn(10) (prom 4f) | 1½ | **6** | 33/1 | 39 | — |
| *3604*[4] | **Breffni (IRE) (56)** (RDickin) **2-8-7** DaleGibson(11) (lw: hrd rdn & hung lft over 1f out: no hdwy) | 1¼ | **7** | 12/1 | 47 | — |
| 3796[8] | **Circle of Magic (65)** (PJMakin) **2-9-2** SSanders(9) (nvr nr to chal) | nk | **8** | 8/1[3] | 55 | 3 |
| *3088*[6] | **Mirror Four Sport (57)** (MJohnston) **2-8-8** RHills(1) (lw: hdwy over 1f out: wknd qckly ins fnl f) | ½ | **9** | 10/1 | 46 | — |
| 3976[5] | **Dozen Roses (54)** (TMJones) **2-8-5b** NCarlisle(13) (b.off hind: bhd fnl 3f) | 1¼ | **10** | 12/1 | 40 | — |
| 3976[2] | **Silent Valley (55)** (BJMeehan) **2-8-6** BDoyle(12) (a bhd) | nk | **11** | 4/1[1] | 40 | — |
| 3975[10] | **Statuette (66)** (BPalling) **2-9-3** TSprake(4) (led 2f: wknd over 1f out) | 3½ | **12** | 10/1 | 42 | — |
| 3763[6] | **Dancing Star (IRE) (51)** (PDEvans) **2-8-2v** JFEgan(6) (t.o) | 25 | **13** | 12/1 | — | — |
| *3962*[3] | ***Life On The Street (68)*** (RHannon) **2-9-5** KDarley(3) (Withdrawn not under Starter's orders: Veterinary advice) | | **W** | 5/1[2] | — | — |
| | | | | (SP 158.6%) | **13 Rn** | |

**1m 12.9** (2.40) CSF £44.69 CT £393.14 TOTE £10.20: £2.40 £1.80 £3.60 (£31.00) Trio £89.60 OWNER Mr T. R. Pearson (EBBW VALE) BRED Edward and Mrs S. Hannigan

LONG HANDICAP Oddfellows Girl 7-9

**3651* Heavenly Miss (IRE)** found her last run coming too soon and also failed to handle the sharp course at Warwick. (8/1)

**3975 Aybeegirl** was stepping up from the minimum trip. (4/1)

**3488* Hit Or Miss** was 7lb lower than when last seen in a nursery. (12/1)

**3954* Impy Fox (IRE)** may need seven on ground as fast as this. (5/1)

**3462 Danehill Princess (IRE)**, although under topweight, was running off a 6lb lower mark than her other run in a nursery. (8/1)

**3576 Oddfellows Girl** was 1lb out of the handicap. (33/1)

**3976 Silent Valley**, narrowly beaten in a seller last time, ran no race at all on this drop back to six. (4/1)

## 4208 LEVY BOARD MAIDEN STKS (2-Y.O) (Class D)

4-30 (4-32) **6f 15y** £4,598.55 (£1,382.40: £667.70: £310.35) Stalls: High GOING minus 0.47 sec per fur (F)

| | Horse | Dist | Pos | SP | RR | SF |
|---|---|---|---|---|---|---|
| 2892[4] | **Telemania (IRE)** (WJHaggas) **2-8-9** DaneO'Neill(7) (swtg: hdwy 2f out: rdn & r.o wl to ld nr fin) | — | **1** | 15/2 | 75 | 20 |
| 3940[4] | **The Gay Fox (93)** (BAMcMahon) **2-9-0** RCochrane(9) (a.p: led over 2f out: clr over 1f out: hdd nr fin) | ½ | **2** | 6/4[1] | 79 | 24 |
| 3807[5] | **Mayflower** (IABalding) **2-8-9** KDarley(2) (lw: chsd ldrs: rdn over 2f out: r.o ins fnl f) | ¾ | **3** | 6/1[2] | 72 | 17 |
| | **Restless Spirit (USA)** (MJohnston) **2-9-0** RHills(15) (w'like: bkwd: trckd ldrs: swtchd lft over 2f out: r.o ins fnl f) | 1 | **4** | 10/1 | 74+ | 19 |
| 3615[10] | **Al Masroor (USA)** (JWPayne) **2-9-0** AMcGlone(5) (hdwy over 1f out: nt rch ldrs) | 3 | **5** | 20/1 | 66 | 11 |
| | **Forgotten Times (USA)** (EALDunlop) **2-8-9** WRyan(3) (w'like: s.s: effrt over 2f out: eased whn btn ins fnl f) | 3½ | **6** | 14/1 | 52 | — |
| | **Cimmerian** (MrsJRRamsden) **2-8-9** KFallon(12) (leggy: lt-f: prom: rdn over 2f out: sn wknd) | hd | **7** | 14/1 | 52 | — |
| | **Mungo Park** (MrsJRRamsden) **2-9-0** JFortune(4) (wl grwn: bkwd: nvr nrr) | ½ | **8** | 33/1 | 55 | — |
| 1678[3] | **Seva (IRE)** (DRLoder) **2-8-9** DRMcCabe(10) (lw: prom: ev ch whn hung rt wl over 1f out: sn wknd) | nk | **9** | 7/1[3] | 50 | — |
| | **Bally Souza (IRE)** (MJohnston) **2-8-9** BDoyle(8) (lt-f: a bhd) | ¾ | **10** | 20/1 | 48 | — |
| | **In Your Dreams (IRE)** (HCandy) **2-8-9** GCarter(1) (unf: scope: s.i.s: a bhd) | 1¾ | **11** | 12/1 | 43 | — |
| 3809[6] | **Two Bills** (AStreeter) **2-8-11**(3) RHavlin(13) (prom over 3f) | 1¾ | **12** | 20/1 | 43 | — |
| 4062[13] | **Jade's Gem** (GBBalding) **2-8-9** SDrowne(11) (bit bkwd: s.i.s: a bhd) | ¾ | **13** | 33/1 | 36 | — |
| 3853[9] | **Five-O-Fifty** (JLEyre) **2-9-0** TWilliams(14) (b.hind: swtg: led over 3f: hmpd wl over 1f out: sn wknd) | nk | **14** | 10/1 | 41 | — |
| | **Kanawa** (APJones) **2-8-9** AClark(16) (lt-f: unf: swtg: s.s: a bhd) | nk | **15** | 33/1 | 35 | — |
| | | | | (SP 140.9%) | **15 Rn** | |

**1m 12.9** (2.40) CSF £20.99 TOTE £14.90: £3.40 £1.10 £2.60 (£15.40) Trio £23.00 OWNER Mr J. D. Ashenheim (NEWMARKET) BRED Jack Ashenheim

**2892 Telemania (IRE)** is the type who gets worked up, but does seem to be going the right way. (15/2)

**3940 The Gay Fox** may have preferred softer ground, but looked to have it in the bag below the distance. (6/4)
**3807 Mayflower** will do better when she tackles further. (6/1)
**Restless Spirit (USA)**, a half-brother to the stayer Syrtos, will come on a lot for this debut. (10/1)
**Al Masroor (USA)**, a $100,000 colt, did not seem suited by this drop back to six, but could be on the upgrade. (20/1)
**Forgotten Times (USA)**, a half-sister to Hadaad, will be better for the experience. (14/1)
**1678 Seva (IRE)** (7/1: 5/1-8/1)

## 4209 TRENT LIMITED STKS (0-65) (3-Y.O+) (Class F)

5-00 (5-00) **1m 1f 213y** £2,381.00 (£656.00: £311.00) Stalls: High GOING minus 0.47 sec per fur (F)

| | | | | SP | RR | SF |
|---|---|---|---|---|---|---|
| 3819$^{5}$ | **Lady of Leisure (USA) (65)** (MrsJCecil) **4-9-0** KDarley(2) (a.p: swtchd rt wl over 1f out: qcknd to ld 1f out: drvn out) | — | **1** | 11/4$^{1}$ | 73 | 40 |
| 1414$^{4}$ | **George Bull (62)** (MajorWRHern) **4-9-3** TSprake(6) (lw: hld up: led over 1f out: sn hdd: hrd rdn: unable qckn) | 1½ | **2** | 3/1$^{2}$ | 74 | 41 |
| 3966* | **Afon Alwen (63)** (SCWilliams) **3-8-10** JTate(1) (b.nr hind: led tl over 1f out: wknd ins fnl f) | 4 | **3** | 11/2 | 66 | 27 |
| 4102$^{3}$ | **Rival Bid (USA) (64)** (MrsNMacauley) **8-9-2**(3) CTeague(3) (dwlt: hdwy over 2f out: sn rdn: r.o ins fnl f) | 1½ | **4** | 5/1$^{3}$ | 67 | 34 |
| 3500$^{10}$ | **Lady Bankes (IRE) (64)** (WGMTurner) **3-8-3**(7) DSweeney(7) (lw: hld up: rdn over 2f out: wknd over 1f out) | 2½ | **5** | 11/4$^{1}$ | 60 | 21 |
| 3845$^{3}$ | **Lila Pedigo (IRE) (60)** (MissJFCraze) **3-8-10** NConnorton(5) (plld hrd: chsd ldr: rdn 3f out: wknd wl over 1f out) | 4 | **6** | 8/1 | 53 | 14 |
| 3866$^{7}$ | **Lomond Lassie (USA) (32)** (MissJFCraze) **3-8-8** JLowe(4) (hld up: rdn over 3f out: bhd fnl 2f) | 10 | **7** | 40/1 | 35 | — |
| 3703$^{9}$ | **Saltando (IRE) (40)** (PatMitchell) **5-9-3** KFallon(8) (lw: nvr gng wl: a bhd) | 2½ | **8** | 25/1 | 34 | 1 |

(SP 127.8%) **8 Rn**

**2m 4.9** (2.40) CSF £12.47 TOTE £3.50: £1.70 £2.40 £1.10 (£6.00) OWNER Mrs Anna Sanders (NEWMARKET) BRED Arthur B. Hancock III
WEIGHT FOR AGE 3yo-6lb
**3819 Lady of Leisure (USA)** was a different animal without the tongue-strap. (11/4)
**1414 George Bull**, coming back after a summer break, could not cope with the winner when the chips were down, but would have been better off in a handicap. (3/1: 2/1-7/2)
**3966* Afon Alwen** found this more competitive than Brighton. (11/2: 4/1-6/1)
**4102 Rival Bid (USA)** had no excuses this time. (5/1: 4/1-6/1)
**2924 Lady Bankes (IRE)** had run too freely when tried over a mile and a half last time. (11/4)
**3845 Lila Pedigo (IRE)** proved a handful to settle. (8/1)

T/Jkpt: Not won; £17,797.08 to Sandown 17/9/96. T/Plpt: £652.60 (29.24 Tckts). T/Qdpt: £6.60 (343.37 Tckts). KH

# 3943-SANDOWN (R-H) (Good to firm)
## Tuesday September 17th

WEATHER: sunny WIND: str half bhd

## 4210 SEPTEMBER MAIDEN AUCTION STKS (2-Y.O) (Class D)

2-15 (2-16) **5f 6y** £3,403.75 (£1,030.00: £502.50: £238.75) Stalls: Low GOING minus 0.58 sec per fur (F)

| | | | | SP | RR | SF |
|---|---|---|---|---|---|---|
| 3853$^{4}$ | **Gaelic Storm** (MJohnston) **2-8-3** BDoyle(2) (lw: a.p: led over 1f out: rdn & r.o wl) | — | **1** | 15/2$^{3}$ | 84 | 38 |
| | **Heart Throb** (WJHaggas) **2-8-1**(3) FLynch(9) (neat: lw: s.s: stdy hdwy over 2f out: edgd lft ins fnl f: r.o wl: bttr for r) | 1¾ | **2** | 9/4$^{2}$ | 79+ | 33 |
| 2595$^{2}$ | **Rise 'n Shine (78)** (CACyzer) **2-8-7**ow3 PatEddery(13) (lw: led over 3f: unable qckn) | 3½ | **3** | 8/1 | 71 | 22 |
| 4087$^{3}$ | **Northern Girl (IRE) (75)** (BJMeehan) **2-7-12** CRutter(12) (a.p: hrd rdn over 1f out: one pce) | hd | **4** | 8/1 | 62 | 16 |
| 4087$^{2}$ | **Hype Energy** (GLewis) **2-8-1**(3) AWhelan(5) (lw: chsd ldrs: rdn over 3f out: wknd over 1f out) | 3 | **5** | 15/8$^{1}$ | 58 | 12 |
| 2712$^{8}$ | **Wee Dram** (RHannon) **2-7-12** JQuinn(8) (nvr nr to chal) | s.h | **6** | 20/1 | 52 | 6 |
| 4118$^{8}$ | **Swift** (MJPolglase) **2-8-6** KDarley(11) (lw: a.p: rdn over 2f out: wknd over 1f out) | ¾ | **7** | 50/1 | 58 | 12 |
| 2309$^{9}$ | **Geordie Lad** (JABennett) **2-8-3** AClark(10) (a.p: rdn over 2f out: wknd over 1f out) | s.h | **8** | 33/1 | 55 | 9 |
| | **Hever Golf Lover (IRE)** (TJNaughton) **2-8-1**ow3 SSanders(3) (w'like: s.s: nvr nrr) | ½ | **9** | 16/1 | 51 | 2 |
| | **Come Together** (DWPArbuthnot) **2-8-1** GCarter(14) (unf: bit bkwd: s.s: a bhd) | s.h | **10** | 20/1 | 51 | 5 |
| *4079*$^{10}$ | **Dom Ruinart (IRE)** (JWHills) **2-8-0**(3) MHenry(1) (hld up: rdn over 2f out: sn wknd) | 1¼ | **11** | 25/1 | 49 | 3 |
| 3963$^{6}$ | **Kingsdown Trix (IRE)** (AMoore) **2-8-3** DaneO'Neill(4) (a bhd) | 1½ | **12** | 20/1 | 44 | — |
| 4123$^{11}$ | **M R Poly (55)** (MRChannon) **2-8-6** AMackay(7) (lw: bhd fnl 2f) | 4 | **13** | 50/1 | 35 | — |
| | **Flahive's First** (JSMoore) **2-7-12**(5) PPMurphy(6) (neat: a bhd) | 1¾ | **14** | 33/1 | 26 | — |

(SP 133.4%) **14 Rn**

**59.85 secs** (0.05) CSF £25.88 TOTE £7.60: £2.00 £1.70 £1.80 (£22.40) Trio £42.70 OWNER H C Racing Club (MIDDLEHAM) BRED A. D. G. Oldrey
**3853 Gaelic Storm** was much happier back on this fast ground and, leading over a furlong out, quickly sprinted clear. (15/2)
**Heart Throb**, a narrow filly, was very well supported in the morning but lack of experience found her out as she lost several lengths at the start. Given considerate handling, she caught the eye as she moved through the field but, despite running on really strongly to finish a clear second best, she had no hope of catching the winner. Sure to have learnt a great deal from this, she can pick up a similar event before long. (9/4)
**2595 Rise 'n Shine** was having her first run in ten weeks, but lack of acceleration is beginning to become a bit of a problem. (8/1)
**4087 Northern Girl (IRE)** ran another solid race, but probably needs to return to six furlongs, the distance over which she nearly won her first race at Salisbury last month. (8/1: op 9/2)
**4087 Hype Energy** failed to confirm the promise shown at Bath last week. (15/8)

## 4211 E.B.F. MAIDEN STKS (2-Y.O F) (Class D)

2-50 (2-52) **1m 14y** £3,468.75 (£1,050.00: £512.50: £243.75) Stalls: High GOING minus 0.58 sec per fur (F)

| | | | | SP | RR | SF |
|---|---|---|---|---|---|---|
| | **Fiji** (HRACecil) **2-8-11** PatEddery(2) (gd sort: mde virtually all: pushed out) | — | **1** | 4/7$^{1}$ | 80+ | 28 |
| 4052$^{2}$ | **Alphabet** (MRStoute) **2-8-11** WRSwinburn(1) (b.hind: chsd wnr: ev ch 1f out: unable qckn) | 1¾ | **2** | 5/2$^{2}$ | 77 | 25 |
| | **Listed Account (USA)** (LMCumani) **2-8-11** KDarley(5) (b.nr hind: leggy: scope: bit bkwd: s.s: hdwy over 1f out: r.o: bttr for r) | 1½ | **3** | 10/1$^{3}$ | 74+ | 22 |
| 3873$^{6}$ | **Logica (IRE) (73)** (PAKelleway) **2-8-11** JReid(3) (hld up: rdn over 2f out: r.o one pce) | s.h | **4** | 40/1 | 74 | 22 |
| 3764$^{6}$ | **French Mist** (CEBrittain) **2-8-11** BDoyle(6) (a.p: rdn over 2f out: wknd fnl f) | 5 | **5** | 33/1 | 64 | 12 |

| Form | Horse / details | Dist | Pos | SP | RR | SF |
|---|---|---|---|---|---|---|
| 3820[6] | **Indian Rapture** (RHannon) **2-8-11** DaneO'Neill(4) (a bhd) | s.h | **6** | 33/1 | 63 | 11 |
| 3593[17] | **Push A Venture** (SPCWoods) **2-8-11** DBiggs(7) (plld hrd: bhd fnl 2f) | 7 | **7** | 66/1 | 50 | — |
| | | | | (SP 111.1%) | **7 Rn** | |

**1m 43.38** (2.18) CSF £2.30 TOTE £1.60: £1.10 £1.50 (£1.50) OWNER H R H Prince Fahd Salman (NEWMARKET) BRED Newgate Stud Co

**Fiji**, a well-made, imposing filly with bags of substance and scope, is well thought of at home and, although the runner-up looked a very serious threat to her in the straight, she was able to brush her aside in the last 150 yards. Connections are already thinking about next year's Oaks but, while her trainer wants to run her again this year, he does not want her to have a hard time and will look for a suitable opportunity. She looks very useful. (4/7)

**4052 Alphabet**, who came up against a potentially useful filly in One So Wonderful on her debut at Kempton recently, had the misfortune to come up against another one here. Nevertheless, she matched strides with the winner in the straight and appeared to be going the better below the distance before she was put in her place in the last 150 yards. She looks nailed on next time out. (5/2: 7/4-11/4)

**Listed Account (USA)**, quite a tall, plain filly, looked as though this debut was just needed. She showed her inexperience by losing several lengths at the start, but put in eyecatching work in the last furlong and a half to snatch third prize on the line. Sure to be a lot wiser for this, she looks a ready-made winner. (10/1: op 4/1)

**3873 Logica (IRE)** ran her best race since her Lingfield second in July but she was not in the same league as the first two and has had plenty of chances. (40/1)

## 4212 WEATHERBYS SPONSORSHIP IN RACING H'CAP (0-80) (3-Y.O+) (Class D)

3-25 (3-26) **7f 16y** £4,053.75 (£1,230.00: £602.50: £288.75) Stalls: High GOING minus 0.58 sec per fur (F)

| Form | Horse / details | Dist | Pos | SP | RR | SF |
|---|---|---|---|---|---|---|
| 4109[3] | **Rakis (IRE) (75)** (MrsLStubbs) **6-9-11** PatEddery(4) (lw: a.p: rdn over 2f out: led 1f out: drvn out) | — | **1** | 11/4[1] | 83 | 48 |
| 4098* | **Don't Get Caught (IRE) (51)** (JLHarris) **4-8-1** 5x BDoyle(7) (lw: hld up: nt clr run over 1f out: swtchd lft: r.o wl ins fnl f) | ½ | **2** | 3/1[2] | 58+ | 23 |
| 3052[7] | **Glowing Jade (68)** (JAGlover) **6-9-4** GCarter(6) (nt clr run over 2f out: hdwy & nt clr run over 1f out: r.o ins fnl f) | 1 | **3** | 12/1 | 73 | 38 |
| 2602[15] | **Dancing Heart (67)** (BJMeehan) **4-9-3** MTebbutt(5) (chsd ldr: led over 2f out to 1f out: unable qckn) | nk | **4** | 14/1 | 71 | 36 |
| 4064[11] | **Blue Flyer (IRE) (74)** (RIngram) **3-9-7** SWhitworth(3) (hld up: rdn over 2f out: one pce) | 2 | **5** | 7/1 | 73 | 35 |
| 3881[2] | **Miletrian City (57)** (JBerry) **3-8-4b** KDarley(2) (lw: hld up: rdn over 2f out: one pce) | nk | **6** | 15/2 | 56 | 18 |
| 3929[5] | **Hadadabble (49)** (PatMitchell) **3-7-10** NCarlisle(8) (lw: led over 4f: wknd wl over 1f out) | 1½ | **7** | 50/1 | 44 | 6 |
| 3817* | **Daryabad (IRE) (77)** (TJNaughton) **4-9-8**(5) JDSmith(1) (a bhd) | ¾ | **8** | 9/2[3] | 71 | 36 |
| 3812[14] | **Barbrallen (55)** (MrsLCJewell) **4-8-0**(5)ow9 SophieMitchell(9) (a bhd) | 4 | **9** | 50/1 | 40? | — |
| | | | | (SP 112.4%) | **9 Rn** | |

**1m 29.82** (1.22) CSF £10.60 CT £72.82 TOTE £3.00: £1.80 £1.30 £2.60 (£3.90) Trio £23.50 OWNER Mr P. G. Shorrock (WARTHILL) BRED The Mount Coote Partnership

LONG HANDICAP Hadadabble 7-0 Barbrallen 7-0

WEIGHT FOR AGE 3yo-3lb

**4109 Rakis (IRE)** was only 3lb higher than when winning here in June and has now won nine races, all of which were over this trip. (11/4)

**4098* Don't Get Caught (IRE)**, reportedly in foal to Pursuit of Love, failed to get a clear run at a critical stage below the distance and, although she ran on really strongly inside the final furlong, was never going to get to the winner in time. However, it should be noted that Eddery reported afterwards he would have won more easily on Rakis had there been a faster pace. (3/1: op 2/1)

**739* Glowing Jade** met with traffic problems as she tried for a run through the pack and, when a gap did appear, she ran on inside the final furlong to snatch third prize. (12/1)

**2193 Dancing Heart** ran his best race for some time but, headed a furlong from home, failed to find another gear. (14/1: 10/1-16/1)

**3696* Blue Flyer (IRE)** could only struggle on at one pace in the final quarter-mile. (7/1)

**3881 Miletrian City** has been running well in claimers and sellers this year and, although he finished second in a 0-70 Handicap at Musselburgh last time out, this was a much tougher test. (15/2)

**3817* Daryabad (IRE)** (9/2: op 3/1)

## 4213 SANDOWN FUTURITY CONDITIONS STKS (2-Y.O) (Class C)

4-00 (4-00) **1m 14y** £4,954.80 (£1,606.80: £788.40) Stalls: High GOING minus 0.58 sec per fur (F)

| Form | Horse / details | Dist | Pos | SP | RR | SF |
|---|---|---|---|---|---|---|
| 3873* | **Barnum Sands** (JLDunlop) **2-9-1** PatEddery(3) (lw: chsd ldr: led wl over 1f out: shkn up & r.o wl) | — | **1** | 5/6[1] | 95+ | 23 |
| 2852* | **Cinema Paradiso** (PFICole) **2-9-1** TQuinn(2) (hld up: rdn over 3f out: chsd wnr ins fnl f: r.o one pce) | 3 | **2** | 11/10[2] | 89 | 17 |
| 4084[4] | **Princess of Hearts (66)** (BJMeehan) **2-8-6** BDoyle(1) (led over 6f: wknd fnl f) | 2½ | **3** | 20/1[3] | 75? | 3 |
| | | | | (SP 106.9%) | **3 Rn** | |

**1m 44.26** (3.06) CSF £1.98 TOTE £1.90: (£1.10) OWNER Aylesfield Farms Stud (ARUNDEL) BRED Aylesfield Farms Stud

**3873* Barnum Sands** was certainly the pick of the three runners, with far more scope than his two rivals. In a falsely-run race, he went on early inside the final quarter-mile and, shaken up, soon asserted, although the form should not be taken too literally. He may have one more run this year over a mile on softish ground. (5/6)

**2852* Cinema Paradiso** is very short on substance and it took a long time for him to get going, eventually taking second place early inside the final furlong. (11/10)

**4084 Princess of Hearts**, whose only victory came in a seller, set a very moderate pace. Collared well over a furlong from home, she held on until put in her place inside the last 200 yards. (20/1)

## 4214 SURBITON H'CAP (0-95) (3-Y.O F) (Class C)

4-30 (4-31) **1m 14y** £5,504.50 (£1,666.00: £813.00: £386.50) Stalls: High GOING minus 0.58 sec per fur (F)

| Form | Horse / details | Dist | Pos | SP | RR | SF |
|---|---|---|---|---|---|---|
| 3133[2] | **Fatefully (USA) (88)** (SbinSuroor) **3-9-5** JReid(1) (chsd ldr: led over 3f out: rdn out) | — | **1** | 7/4[1] | 103 | 57 |
| 3830[4] | **Sandhill (IRE) (89)** (JHMGosden) **3-9-6** PatEddery(4) (led over 4f: hrd rdn over 1f out: unable qckn) | 2½ | **2** | 8/1 | 99 | 53 |
| 4064[5] | **Hippy (75)** (CEBrittain) **3-8-6** BDoyle(8) (lw: a.p: rdn over 2f out: one pce) | ¾ | **3** | 8/1 | 84 | 38 |
| 3926[4] | **Tsarnista (79)** (JLDunlop) **3-8-10** GCarter(2) (hdwy 6f out: rdn over 2f out: one pce) | 1¼ | **4** | 11/2[3] | 85 | 39 |
| 3926[2] | **Blessed Spirit (79)** (CFWall) **3-8-10** SSanders(5) (lw: rdn & hdwy 2f out: 4th & no ch whn nt clr run ins fnl f) | ½ | **5** | 5/1[2] | 84 | 38 |
| 3806[4] | **Tarneem (USA) (79)** (MRStoute) **3-8-10** WRSwinburn(9) (hld up: rdn over 2f out: one pce) | 1½ | **6** | 8/1 | 81 | 35 |
| 3926[6] | **Kirov Lady (IRE) (75)** (RHannon) **3-8-6** DaneO'Neill(6) (hung rt 2f out: a bhd) | 1¼ | **7** | 14/1 | 75 | 29 |
| 3167[8] | **Marjaana (IRE) (69)** (PTWalwyn) **3-8-0** JQuinn(7) (lw: bhd fnl 2f) | 1 | **8** | 16/1 | 67 | 21 |
| 3945[11] | **Agnella (IRE) (90)** (GLMoore) **3-9-2**(5) DGriffiths(3) (bhd fnl 3f) | 6 | **9** | 33/1 | 76 | 30 |
| | | | | (SP 117.2%) | **9 Rn** | |

**1m 41.13** (-0.07) CSF £15.55 CT £83.60 TOTE £2.50: £1.20 £3.20 £1.90 (£12.00) Trio £38.80 OWNER Godolphin (NEWMARKET) BRED Darley Stud Management Co Ltd

**3133 Fatefully (USA)** again raced with her tongue tied down and, poking a nostril in front early in the straight, stormed clear from below the distance to win in a time over two seconds faster than either of the two juvenile races over this trip. She is certainly going the right way. (7/4)
**3830 Sandhill (IRE)** adopted her usual front-running role and, although collared early in the straight, was not put in her place until inside the distance. (8/1)
**4064 Hippy** was once again tapped for toe and may need to be dropped a few more pounds in the handicap. (8/1)
**3926 Tsarnista** never looked like finding another gear in the last two furlongs. (11/2)
**3926 Blessed Spirit**, 3lb worse off with the winner for beating that rival a head at Doncaster in July, could never get in a telling blow on this occasion. (5/1)
**3806 Tarneem (USA)**, who probably did not stay nine furlongs last time out, once again had her lack of pace well exposed. (8/1)

## 4215 WILLOW CLAIMING STKS (3-Y.O+) (Class E)

5-00 (5-01) **5f 6y** £3,111.25 (£940.00: £457.50: £216.25) Stalls: Low GOING minus 0.58 sec per fur (F)

| | | | | SP | RR | SF |
|---|---|---|---|---|---|---|
| *4094*[3] | **Palacegate Touch (73)** (JBerry) **6-8-9b** GCarter(4) (a.p: hrd rdn over 1f out: led nr fin) | — | 1 | 6/1[3] | 81 | 61 |
| 3618[7] | **Lord High Admiral (CAN) (85)** (MJHeaton-Ellis) **8-8-9** JReid(12) (racd far side: led: clr 3f out: rdn over 1f out: hdd nr fin) | 1¼ | 2 | 7/4[1] | 77 | 57 |
| *4090** | **Palacegate Jack (IRE) (78)** (CADwyer) **5-9-5** CDwyer(2) (hdwy 2f out: rdn over 1f out: r.o) | 1¼ | 3 | 8/1 | 83 | 63 |
| 4198[19] | **Lennox Lewis (76)** (APJarvis) **4-9-1v[1]** JTate(8) (hdwy 2f out: hrd rdn over 1f out: r.o one pce) | hd | 4 | 8/1 | 79 | 59 |
| 3930[5] | **Purple Fling (70)** (LGCottrell) **5-9-0** JQuinn(14) (b: racd centre: a.p: rdn over 2f out: one pce) | ½ | 5 | 10/1 | 76 | 56 |
| 525[3] | **Night Harmony (IRE) (56)** (RHannon) **3-8-6** DaneO'Neill(10) (b: a.p: rdn over 2f out: one pce) | 1 | 6 | 16/1 | 66 | 45 |
| 3827[10] | **Tafahhus (70)** (MJPolglase) **4-8-4b** GDuffield(13) (racd far side: chsd ldrs: rdn over 2f out: wknd fnl f) | 1 | 7 | 14/1 | 60 | 40 |
| 4045* | **Petraco (IRE) (60)** (NASmith) **8-7-11**(7) JBramhill(7) (bhd fnl 3f) | 3 | 8 | 16/1 | 50 | 30 |
| 3864[4] | **Lift Boy (USA) (50)** (AMoore) **7-8-5** CandyMorris(9) (lw: bhd fnl 2f) | hd | 9 | 33/1 | 51 | 31 |
| 2013[11] | **Blue Suede Hoofs (64)** (BJMeehan) **3-8-4** BDoyle(11) (prom 3f) | 2 | 10 | 33/1 | 45 | 24 |
| 3693[16] | **Zalotti (IRE) (79)** (MHTompkins) **3-8-13** KDarley(3) (lw: prom 2f) | ¾ | 11 | 5/1[2] | 51 | 30 |
| 3506[5] | **Oscilights Gift (26)** (PBurgoyne) **4-8-2** JStack(6) (a bhd) | 1½ | 12 | 50/1 | 34 | 14 |
| 2286[21] | **Coalisland (15)** (RIngram) **6-8-5b** SWhitworth(1) (bit bkwd: s.s: a wl bhd) | 17 | 13 | 66/1 | — | — |
| | | | | (SP 126.4%) | **13 Rn** | |

**58.82 secs** (0.42 under best) (-0.98) CSF £16.96 TOTE £7.40: £1.60 £1.70 £3.30 (£8.30) Trio £20.90 OWNER Laurel (Leisure) Ltd (COCKERHAM) BRED The Woodhaven Stud
WEIGHT FOR AGE 3yo-1lb
**4094 Palacegate Touch** took the field along on the stands' side and clawed back the tiring leader inside the final furlong to get on top near the line and smash the course record which had stood for six years by the best part of half a second. He has now won fourteen times, including seven claimers and one seller. (6/1)
**3432 Lord High Admiral (CAN)** elected to tack over to the far rail, where the ground is often faster, but he went off very fast and the uphill finish took its toll as he was caught near the line. Winner of four races here, including two claimers, he should soon make amends on his favourite track. (7/4)
**4090* Palacegate Jack (IRE)**, claimed for £10,000 out of Jack Berry's stable after winning at Southwell last week, had no easy task at these weights but ran on up the hill to take third prize. (8/1)
**1334 Lennox Lewis** was tried in a visor but yet again disappointed, considering this was only a claimer. (8/1)
**3930 Purple Fling** was one of three who elected to break away from the stands'-side group but, instead of tacking right over to the far rail, he elected to race in the centre, which was a poor move as the ground is often slower there. (10/1)
**525 Night Harmony (IRE)** looked straight for this first run in nearly six months, but failed to quicken in the final quarter-mile. (16/1)

## 4216 SURREY RACING H'CAP (0-70) (3-Y.O) (Class E)

5-35 (5-35) **1m 3f 91y** £3,501.25 (£1,060.00: £517.50: £246.25) Stalls: High GOING minus 0.58 sec per fur (F)

| | | | | SP | RR | SF |
|---|---|---|---|---|---|---|
| 1641[4] | **Tart (66)** (RFJohnsonHoughton) **3-9-5** JReid(9) (a.p: led over 2f out: clr over 1f out: r.o wl) | — | 1 | 11/2[2] | 78 | 43 |
| 3825[5] | **Domettes (IRE) (57)** (RHannon) **3-8-10** DaneO'Neill(14) (lw: a.p: rdn over 3f out: r.o one pce) | 5 | 2 | 12/1 | 62 | 27 |
| 3944[3] | **Royal Diversion (IRE) (66)** (JLDunlop) **3-9-5** WRSwinburn(5) (rdn & hdwy over 2f out: r.o one pce) | s.h | 3 | 10/1 | 71 | 36 |
| 3283[5] | **Nikita's Star (IRE) (65)** (DJGMurraySmith) **3-9-1**(3) FLynch(6) (gd hdwy over 4f out: led over 3f out tl over 2f out: one pce) | 1¼ | 4 | 11/1 | 68 | 33 |
| 2876[3] | **Amadour (IRE) (63)** (PMitchell) **3-9-2** GCarter(8) (lw: hld up: rdn over 2f out: one pce) | ¾ | 5 | 14/1 | 65 | 30 |
| 4068[13] | **Absolutelystunning (56)** (MrsBarbaraWaring) **3-8-9** AClark(11) (b: hdwy over 1f out: nvr nrr) | nk | 6 | 14/1 | 58 | 23 |
| 3611[4] | **Get Tough (60)** (SDow) **3-8-13** TQuinn(3) (hdwy over 2f out: one pce) | ¾ | 7 | 13/2[3] | 61 | 26 |
| 4042[7] | **Atlantic Mist (59)** (BRMillman) **3-8-12** SDrowne(10) (lw: hld up: rdn over 2f out: wknd fnl f) | 1¾ | 8 | 8/1 | 57 | 22 |
| 3459[9] | **Agdistis (61)** (HThomsonJones) **3-9-0** KDarley(1) (hdwy over 2f out: wknd over 1f out) | 3½ | 9 | 14/1 | 54 | 19 |
| 3983[19] | **Ambassadori (USA) (65)** (CEBrittain) **3-9-4** BDoyle(12) (bhd fnl 2f) | 7 | 10 | 25/1 | 49 | 14 |
| 3522[6] | **Temptress (64)** (PTWalwyn) **3-9-3** GDuffield(15) (led 8f) | 1 | 11 | 11/1 | 46 | 11 |
| *2934*[6] | **Red Rusty (USA) (57)** (DMorris) **3-8-10** CRutter(7) (lw: a bhd) | 4 | 12 | 33/1 | 34 | — |
| 3876[6] | **Claire's Dancer (IRE) (64)** (AndrewTurnell) **3-8-10**(7) CScudder(13) (lw: prom 9f) | 1¼ | 13 | 20/1 | 39 | 4 |
| | **Chalcuchima (67)** (RCharlton) **3-9-6** SSanders(4) (a bhd) | 3 | 14 | 20/1 | 38 | 3 |
| 4042[3] | **Ceilidh Star (IRE) (68)** (BWHills) **3-9-7b** PatEddery(2) (prom over 7f) | 5 | 15 | 3/1[1] | 32 | — |
| | | | | (SP 134.6%) | **15 Rn** | |

**2m 25.38** (1.98) CSF £70.92 CT £618.55 TOTE £5.90: £1.60 £3.70 £2.70 (£54.70) Trio £185.90 OWNER Lady Rothschild (DIDCOT) BRED Exors of the late Mrs D. M. de Rothschild
OFFICIAL EXPLANATION **Ceilidh Star (IRE): ran very free early on down the hill and was never going.**
**1641 Tart**, who injured a joint at Leicester in June that subsequently became poisoned, hence her absence, bounced back in emphatic style. (11/2)
**3825 Domettes (IRE)** is only small but stuck on well to win the battle for second prize. (12/1)
**3944 Royal Diversion (IRE)** saw out this longer trip, but she never looked like finding the required turn of foot. She is still a maiden. (10/1)
**3283 Nikita's Star (IRE)** made up rapid ground to sweep into the lead early in the straight, but it may have been a case of too much too soon. (11/1)
**2876 Amadour (IRE)** looked in good shape for this first run in nine weeks, but never looked like quickening up in the straight. (14/1)
**3681 Absolutelystunning** stayed on from the back of the field in the straight without posing a threat. (14/1)
**3522 Temptress** (11/1: 8/1-12/1)
**4042 Ceilidh Star (IRE)** (3/1: op 5/1)

**T/Jkpt: £3,182.80 (7.65 Tckts). T/Plpt: £17.30 (1,052.11 Tckts). T/Qdpt: £4.10 (212.34 Tckts). AK**

# 3700-YARMOUTH (L-H) (Good)

## Tuesday September 17th

WEATHER: sunny periods WIND: str across

### 4217 BROOKE CLAIMING STKS (3-Y.O) (Class E)

2-35 (2-36) **1m 3f 101y** £3,206.70 (£957.60: £457.80: £207.90) Stalls: High GOING minus 0.32 sec per fur (GF)

| Form | Horse | Dist | Pos | SP | RR | SF |
|---|---|---|---|---|---|---|
| 3938$^{3}$ | **Tart (FR) (73)** (JRFanshawe) **3-8-13** DHarrison(8) (lw: a.p: led 2f out: hrd rdn fnl f: hld on) | — | 1 | 15/8$^{1}$ | 74 | 43 |
| 3981$^{4}$ | **Ballpoint (75)** (RHannon) **3-9-7** RPerham(7) (hld up in tch: hdwy over 2f out: hrd rdn & ev ch fnl f: unable qckn) | nk | 2 | 9/2$^{2}$ | 82 | 51 |
| 3808$^{6}$ | **Clued Up (47)** (PDEvans) **3-8-4v$^{1}$** JFEgan(1) (hld up: hdwy on ins over 2f out: kpt on u.p towards fin) | 1½ | 3 | 25/1 | 63 | 32 |
| 4086$^{8}$ | **Chocolate Ice (64)** (CACyzer) **3-8-9** JFortune(9) (led after 2f to 2f out: rdn & one pce fnl f) | nk | 4 | 20/1 | 67 | 36 |
| 3623$^{17}$ | **Irish Sea (USA) (67)** (DNicholls) **3-8-7** WRyan(5) (hld up: hdwy centre over 2f out: rdn & no ex ins fnl f) | ½ | 5 | 16/1 | 64 | 33 |
| 3768$^{5}$ | **State Approval (63)** (APJarvis) **3-8-6**$^{(7)}$ CCarver(6) (plld hrd: led 2f: prom tl outpcd wl over 2f out: rallied ins fnl f) | ½ | 6 | 7/1$^{3}$ | 70 | 39 |
| *4080$^{8}$* | **Indira (58)** (PGMurphy) **3-7-8**$^{(7)}$ RFfrench(2) (hld up: effrt & rdn wl over 2f out: no imp) | 2½ | 7 | 8/1 | 54 | 23 |
| 3918$^{3}$ | **Time For Tea (IRE) (62)** (CACyzer) **3-9-2** LDettori(11) (hld up in rr: effrt 3f out: no imp) | nk | 8 | 8/1 | 69 | 38 |
|  | **Far Atlantic** (CADwyer) **3-8-7**$^{ow3}$ KFallon(10) (lt-f: unf: bit bkwd: trckd ldrs: pushed along ent st: wknd 3f out: t.o) | 23 | 9 | 20/1 | 28 | — |
| 3354$^{10}$ | **Seeking Destiny (IRE) (44)** (MCChapman) **3-8-7** DRMcCabe(4) (dwlt: a bhd: t.o fnl 3f) | dist | 10 | 50/1 | — | — |

(SP 108.9%) **10 Rn**

**2m 27.1** (4.10) CSF £9.46 TOTE £2.30: £1.10 £2.10 £5.80 (£6.50) Trio £65.50 OWNER Lord Vestey (NEWMARKET) BRED Lord Samuel Vestey
Ballpoint clmd GMoore £12,000; Tart (FR) clmd JPearce £10,500

**3938 Tart (FR)** was the first of the Tarts to win today. She appreciated the faster ground and the drop in class, but had to work hard to break her duck. (15/8)

**3981 Ballpoint** did not look entirely happy on this ever-drying ground, but he put in a determined late challenge that only just failed. (9/2: 3/1-5/1)

**3808 Clued Up**, visored for the first time, did not really find top gear until far too late and was never nearer than at the finish. (25/1)

**3831 Chocolate Ice** did not wear the blinkers that he carried on his previous outing and finished much closer to the runner-up than he did on much worse terms at Epsom. (20/1)

**3481 Irish Sea (USA)**, pulled wide to deliver his challenge, kept staying on, but lacked the speed to get to terms. (16/1)

**3422* State Approval** raced freely for almost a mile before losing his pitch. Driven along, he was back into his stride again inside the distance and there is still time for him to get back to winning ways. (7/1)

**3824* Indira** (8/1: 6/1-9/1)

### 4218 JOHN MUSKER STKS (Listed) (3-Y.O+ F & M) (Class A)

3-10 (3-10) **1m 2f 21y** £12,869.00 (£2,839.00: £2,839.00: £833.00) Stalls: High GOING minus 0.32 sec per fur (GF)

| Form | Horse | Dist | Pos | SP | RR | SF |
|---|---|---|---|---|---|---|
| 3836$^{2}$ | **Flame Valley (USA) (94)** (MRStoute) **3-8-7** KFallon(1) (hld up: hdwy over 2f out: sn rdn: led ent fnl f: drvn clr) | — | 1 | 5/1$^{3}$ | 111 | 63 |
| 4063$^{5}$ | **Berenice (90)** (GWragg) **3-8-7** MHills(3) (lw: hld up: hdwy 3f out: rdn & r.o wl ins fnl f) | 3½ | 2 | 25/1 | 106 | 58 |
| 3711$^{7}$ | **Balalaika (105)** (LMCumani) **3-8-7** JFortune(7) (a.p: rdn to ld over 2f out: hdd 1f out: one pce) | d.h | 2 | 11/1 | 106 | 58 |
| 3847* | **Inchyre (82)** (RCharlton) **3-8-7** TSprake(4) (hld up: hdwy on ins over 3f out: kpt on: nt pce to chal) | 1¼ | 4 | 20/1 | 104 | 56 |
| 3711$^{5}$ | **Annaba (IRE) (106)** (JHMGosden) **3-8-7** LDettori(6) (b: led tl over 3f out: rdn & hmpd over 1f out: nt rcvr) | s.h | 5 | 4/1$^{2}$ | 103+ | 55 |
| 3916a$^{3}$ | **Bint Shadayid (USA) (115)** (SbinSuroor) **3-8-7** RHills(8) (prom: led over 3f out tl over 2f out: rdn & edgd lft over 1f out: sn btn) | 1¾ | 6 | 9/4$^{1}$ | 101 | 53 |
| 708$^{5}$ | **Paloma Bay (IRE) (98)** (MBell) **3-8-7** RCochrane(9) (bit bkwd: a in rr: t.o) | 8 | 7 | 20/1 | 88 | 40 |
| 3497$^{7}$ | **Sardonic (102)** (HRACecil) **3-8-11** AMcGlone(2) (lw: prom tl rdn & wknd wl over 2f out: t.o) | hd | 8 | 16/1 | 92 | 44 |
| 3945$^{3}$ | **Yamuna (USA) (102)** (HRACecil) **3-8-7** WRyan(5) (s.v.s: a wl bhd: t.o) | 20 | 9 | 11/2 | 56 | 8 |

(SP 110.4%) **9 Rn**

**2m 4.7** (0.30) CSF F V & Bal £24.58; F V & Ber £44.55 TOTE £6.20: £1.40 Bal £3.10 Ber £4.10 (F V & Bal £16.40; F V & Ber £21.00) Trio £134.80 OWNER Cheveley Park Stud (NEWMARKET) BRED Flaxman Holdings Ltd

**3836 Flame Valley (USA)** looked to be in trouble entering the last quarter-mile but she responded to pressure to nose ahead passing the furlong marker, and the rest was easy. This strongly-run race suited her a treat. (5/1)

**2869* Berenice**, hard at work from some way out, kept on willingly towards the finish without ever threatening to get close enough to cause concern. (25/1)

**3711 Balalaika** shows some knee-action and will probably come into her own when she can get her toe in. Running well all the way, she proved very one-paced in the race to the line. (11/1: 8/1-12/1)

**3847* Inchyre**, facing by far her biggest test yet, could not muster the pace to mount a serious challenge. (20/1)

**3711 Annaba (IRE)**, hard driven and looking held when stopped in her tracks below the distance, had little hope of getting back into it, but she did rally and would definitely have finished in the prizes. (4/1)

**3916a Bint Shadayid (USA)** drifted left into the path of Annaba when hard ridden over a furlong out and the way her stride shortened inside the final furlong must cast doubts about her ability to stay the trip. (9/4: op 6/4)

**3945 Yamuna (USA)** (11/2: 7/2-6/1)

### 4219 WILLIAM BULWER LONG MEMORIAL MAIDEN STKS (3-Y.O+) (Class D)

3-45 (3-46) **5f 43y** £4,152.00 (£1,236.00: £588.00: £264.00) Stalls: Low GOING minus 0.32 sec per fur (GF)

| Form | Horse | Dist | Pos | SP | RR | SF |
|---|---|---|---|---|---|---|
| 943$^{2}$ | **Saheeel (USA)** (SbinSuroor) **3-8-13** LDettori(4) (bit bkwd: led after 1f: pushed clr appr fnl f: easily) | — | 1 | 4/5$^{1}$ | 90+ | 37 |
| 4074$^{7}$ | **Wollstonecraft (IRE) (70)** (JHMGosden) **3-8-8** GHind(5) (hld up: hdwy whn nt clr run over 1f out: swtchd lft & r.o wl towards fin) | 3 | 2 | 4/1$^{2}$ | 76+ | 23 |
| 2615$^{8}$ | **Smithereens (69)** (PTWalwyn) **3-8-8** RCochrane(6) (a.p: hrd drvn & one pce appr fnl f) | 1¾ | 3 | 7/1 | 70 | 17 |
| 3999$^{6}$ | **Amington Lass (65)** (PDEvans) **3-8-8** JFEgan(1) (a.p: rdn wl over 1f out: sn outpcd) | 2 | 4 | 14/1 | 64 | 11 |
| 4074$^{6}$ | **Shavinsky (70)** (PHowling) **3-8-13** KFallon(2) (lw: led 1f: rdn whn bmpd over 1f out: sn btn) | 2½ | 5 | 6/1$^{3}$ | 62 | 9 |
|  | **Timely Times** (CADwyer) **3-8-1**$^{(7)}$ JoHunnam(3) (dwlt: a outpcd: t.o) | 9 | 6 | 40/1 | 29 | — |

(SP 111.4%) **6 Rn**

**62.5 secs** (2.00) CSF £4.35 TOTE £1.50: £1.10 £2.00 (£2.20) OWNER Godolphin (NEWMARKET) BRED Darley Stud Management

**943 Saheeel (USA)**, whose only previous run was in the early part of May, did not look fully wound up here, but he was a class apart from this opposition and, in the end, won with any amount in hand. (4/5)

**2298 Wollstonecraft (IRE)** found trouble when trying to come between horses approaching the final furlong and, though he did run on strongly once free, the damage had already been done. (4/1: op 5/2)
**1652 Smithereens**, stepping back down to the minimum trip, did not possess the speed to go with the winner when that rival stepped on the gas. (7/1: 8/1-12/1)
**3999 Amington Lass** ran over a mile on her previous outing this term, but she was back to sprinting here and found demands too great after showing up for three furlongs. (14/1)
**4074 Shavinsky** showed up with the pace, but he was at full stretch and struggling when the runner-up barged her way through just over a furlong out. (6/1: op 4/1)

## 4220 BRIAN TAYLOR MEMORIAL H'CAP (0-90) (3-Y.O+) (Class C)

4-15 (4-16) **5f 43y** £5,439.90 (£1,621.20: £772.60: £348.30) Stalls: Low GOING minus 0.32 sec per fur (GF)

| Form | Horse | | Pos | SP | RR | SF |
|---|---|---|---|---|---|---|
| 3827[6] | **Canovas Heart (72)** (BobJones) **7-9-0** NDay(7) (chsd ldr: led over 1f out: drvn out) | — | **1** | 6/1[3] | 79 | 44 |
| 4088* | **Longwick Lad (74)** (WRMuir) **3-9-1** [7x] LDettori(2) (hdwy 2f out: kpt on u.p ins fnl f) | 1 | **2** | 4/1[2] | 78 | 42 |
| 4119[3] | **Portelet (83)** (RGuest) **4-9-11** PBloomfield(8) (led tl over 1f out: rdn & no ex fnl f) | ¾ | **3** | 2/1[1] | 85 | 50 |
| 3482[4] | **Premium Gift (60)** (CBBBooth) **4-8-2** LCharnock(4) (lw: a chsng ldrs: kpt on fnl f: nt pce to chal) | ½ | **4** | 15/2 | 60 | 25 |
| 3930[14] | **Sally Slade (74)** (CACyzer) **4-9-2** JFortune(6) (bhd: effrt & swtchd lft over 1f out: nvr nrr) | ¾ | **5** | 16/1 | 72 | 37 |
| 3993[16] | **Spender (76)** (PWHarris) **7-9-4** GHind(5) (lw: outpcd: a bhd) | 2½ | **6** | 8/1 | 66 | 31 |
| 2292[12] | **Sweet Magic (82)** (PHowling) **5-9-10** FNorton(1) (b.off hind: lw: nvr gng pce) | 1½ | **7** | 16/1 | 67 | 32 |
| *4090[2]* | **Primula Bairn (56)** (DNicholls) **6-7-12b** DaleGibson(3) (lw: a bhd & outpcd) | 2½ | **8** | 8/1 | 34 | — |

(SP 113.4%) **8 Rn**

**62.1 secs** (1.60) CSF £27.97 CT £58.62 TOTE £7.80: £2.00 £1.60 £1.10 (£21.30) OWNER Mr M J Osborne and Mrs J Woods (NEWMARKET) BRED M. J. Hall
WEIGHT FOR AGE 3yo-1lb
**3827 Canovas Heart** helped set a furious pace for the first three furlongs and proved the stronger to sustain the tempo and gain his revenge over the favourite. (6/1)
**4088* Longwick Lad** had a 7lb penalty to overcome and, though he tried his heart out, the winner was always holding him. (4/1)
**4119 Portelet** has only got one way of running and, although she carried the weight remarkably well, this bumper bundle would have been enough to stop a train. (2/1)
**3482 Premium Gift** ran her usual game race, but she was at full stretch all the way and lacked the pace to mount a challenge. (15/2)
**2232 Sally Slade**, switched towards the centre of the track in an attempt to deliver her bid, could not summon up the pace to land a blow, despite staying on. (16/1)
**3338 Spender** (8/1: 6/1-9/1)

## 4221 CAISTER (S) STKS (3-Y.O+) (Class G)

4-45 (4-49) **7f 3y** £2,868.00 (£798.00: £384.00) Stalls: Low GOING minus 0.32 sec per fur (GF)

| Form | Horse | | Pos | SP | RR | SF |
|---|---|---|---|---|---|---|
| 3973[10] | **How's Yer Father (63)** (RJHodges) **10-8-9**(5) AmandaSanders(3) (hld up: hdwy 2f out: r.o to ld wl ins fnl f) | — | **1** | 9/1 | 65 | 43 |
| 3304[6] | **Best Kept Secret (50)** (PDEvans) **5-8-7v**(7) AnthonyBond(13) (prom tl lost pl ½-wy: sn rdn: r.o wl appr fnl f) | 1½ | **2** | 25/1 | 62 | 40 |
| 4070[2] | **Lucky Revenge (62)** (MartynMeade) **3-8-3**(3) RHavlin(2) (a w ldrs: drifted rt ½-wy: led over 2f out tl wl ins fnl f) | ½ | **3** | 9/2[1] | 55 | 30 |
| 3644[9] | **Oriel Lad (62)** (PDEvans) **3-8-11b** JFEgan(17) (hdwy 2f out: hrd rdn & r.o ins fnl f) | 1 | **4** | 12/1 | 58 | 33 |
| 3995[11] | **Morning Surprise (56)** (APJarvis) **3-7-13**(7) CCarver(18) (s.i.s: sn chsng ldrs: rdn & r.o wl ins fnl f) | ½ | **5** | 6/1[2] | 52 | 27 |
| 3881[10] | **Uncle George (59)** (MHTompkins) **3-8-11v** NDay(6) (hld up: hdwy over 3f out: one pce fnl 2f) | 3 | **6** | 15/2 | 50 | 25 |
| 4045[22] | **Duo Master (58)** (MrsMReveley) **3-8-11** JFortune(1) (dwlt: sn chsng ldrs: nvr nr to chal) | hd | **7** | 16/1 | 50 | 25 |
| 3839[4] | **Miss Walsh** (CBBBooth) **3-8-6** LCharnock(10) (trckd ldrs over 5f) | ½ | **8** | 12/1 | 44 | 19 |
| 4070[8] | **Dark Shot (IRE) (62)** (NTinkler) **4-9-0b[1]** KimTinkler(7) (chsd ldrs over 5f) | s.h | **9** | 25/1 | 49 | 27 |
| 3995[26] | **Spanish Stripper (USA) (56)** (MCChapman) **5-9-0** DRMcCabe(15) (s.s: nvr nrr) | nk | **10** | 9/1 | 48 | 26 |
| 4045[18] | **Ginas Girl (41)** (MissJBower) **3-8-6** AMcGlone(19) (a in rr) | 3 | **11** | 40/1 | 36 | 11 |
| 3761[6] | **Square Mile Miss (IRE) (45)** (PHowling) **3-8-6** GHind(8) (prom over 4f) | ¾ | **12** | 20/1 | 34 | 9 |
| 3217[4] | **Mediate (IRE) (39)** (AHide) **4-9-0b** WRyan(5) (lw: hld up: effrt 3f out: eased whn no ch wl over 1f out) | 3½ | **13** | 12/1 | 32 | 10 |
| 4074[14] | **Frutina** (CMurray) **3-8-6** PBloomfield(9) (nvr trbld ldrs) | 1¼ | **14** | 40/1 | 24 | — |
| 3761[14] | **Farfeste (33)** (DMorris) **3-8-6v** DHarrison(4) (rdn ½-wy: sn lost tch) | 5 | **15** | 33/1 | 12 | — |
| 4070[18] | **Nanny-B (28)** (PHowling) **3-8-6** FNorton(14) (b.hind: a in rr) | 2½ | **16** | 40/1 | 7 | — |
| 3510[W] | **Khattat (USA) (66)** (JAHarris) **6-9-0** KFallon(12) (bkwd: led over 4f: sn rdn & wknd) | 1 | **17** | 7/1[3] | 9 | — |
| 3252[R] | **Venus Victorious (IRE) (40)** (RBastiman) **5-8-9b** RPerham(16) (s.v.s: a wl bhd) | 1 | **18** | 40/1 | 2 | — |
| | **Wahab** (RFMarvin) **3-8-11** TGMcLaughlin(20) (b.off hind: wl grwn: bkwd: a in rr) | 1¾ | **19** | 50/1 | 3 | — |
| 4074[11] | **Masai Man (USA) (35)** (MissJBower) **5-9-0** SDWilliams(11) (lost pl ½-wy: sn bhd) | 2 | **20** | 33/1 | — | — |

(SP 135.7%) **20 Rn**

**1m 26.6** (2.40) CSF £204.42 TOTE £8.40: £3.60 £8.20 £2.10 (£69.60) Trio £98.20 OWNER Mrs Anna Sanders (SOMERTON) BRED Lord Edwin McAlpine
WEIGHT FOR AGE 3yo-3lb
No bid
**3339 How's Yer Father** needed to drop to selling company to win at this trip, but he did it comfortably enough and he is a grand old campaigner. He must have given his connections plenty of fun. (9/1: 6/1-10/1)
**2392 Best Kept Secret** again ran his race in snatches, but he was galloping on strongly at the finish and is capable of winning at this trip. (25/1)
**4070 Lucky Revenge** gave away more ground than she was beaten by in her manoeuvre to get to the stands' rail and she had used up all her speed by the time the winner was let loose. (9/2)
**3301 Oriel Lad** responded to strong pressure in the closing stages without being able to quicken sufficiently to cause concern. (12/1: 8/1-14/1)
**3458 Morning Surprise**, slowly into her stride, stuck on well in the latter stages, but the principals had the legs of her and she was always fighting a lost cause. (6/1)
**3789 Uncle George** was close enough if good enough two furlongs out but, once push came to shove, decided that was sufficient. (15/2)

## 4222 JACK LEADER MEMORIAL CHALLENGE TROPHY NURSERY H'CAP (2-Y.O F) (Class D)

5-20 (5-20) **7f 3y** £3,947.50 (£1,180.00: £565.00: £257.50) Stalls: Low GOING minus 0.32 sec per fur (GF)

| Form | Horse | | Pos | SP | RR | SF |
|---|---|---|---|---|---|---|
| 2187[2] | **Madame Chinnery (72)** (JMPEustace) **2-9-2** RCochrane(2) (lw: hld up: hdwy ½-wy: led 2f out: rdn clr) | — | **1** | 5/1[3] | 77 | 41 |

| | | | | SP | RR | SF |
|---|---|---|---|---|---|---|
| 3988[10] | **Attribute (72)** (RCharlton) **2-9-2** TSprake(5) (hld up: hdwy wl over 1f out: rdn & kpt on ins fnl f) | 2 | **2** | 15/2 | 72 | 36 |
| 4049[3] | **Lucky Oakwood (USA) (77)** (MBell) **2-9-2**(5) GFaulkner(3) (trckd ldrs: effrt & ev ch 2f out: sn rdn & one pce) | ¾ | **3** | 7/2[2] | 76 | 40 |
| 4046[4] | **Abstone Queen (63)** (PDEvans) **2-8-7v** JFEgan(1) (a.p: slt ld over 2f out: sn rdn & hdd: one pce) | 1½ | **4** | 9/1 | 58 | 22 |
| 4084[6] | **Misty Cay (IRE) (70)** (SDow) **2-8-9**(5) ADaly(4) (trckd ldrs: hrd rdn 2f out: styd on towards fin) | ½ | **5** | 12/1 | 64 | 28 |
| *4093*[4] | **Singforyoursupper (55)** (GGMargarson) **2-7-13** GBardwell(8) (led over 4f: sn drvn along: grad wknd) | 3½ | **6** | 20/1 | 41 | 5 |
| 3848* | **Scarlet Crescent (75)** (PTWalwyn) **2-9-5** RHills(7) (lw: chsd ldrs over 4f: sn hrd drvn & outpcd) | ¾ | **7** | 100/30[1] | 60 | 24 |
| 3859* | **Chain Reaction (IRE) (70)** (MAJarvis) **2-9-0** PBloomfield(6) (prom over 4f) | nk | **8** | 11/2 | 54 | 18 |
| | | | | (SP 111.6%) | | **8 Rn** |

**1m 26.9** (2.70) CSF £36.74 CT £130.80 TOTE £6.20: £1.50 £2.20 £2.00 (£18.60) OWNER The Chinnery Partnership (NEWMARKET) BRED Aston Park Stud

**2187 Madame Chinnery**, fresh and well after a mid-summer break, showed her rivals a clean pair of heels inside the distance and she should have little trouble in following up. (5/1)

**3660 Attribute** will come into her own when the emphasis is on stamina and that first success can not be far away. (15/2)

**4049 Lucky Oakwood (USA)** pushed the pace, but seemed reluctant to let herself down. She will return to form once the rains arrive. (7/2)

**4046 Abstone Queen** ran up to her mark, but the principals proved too strong for her in the sprint to the line. (9/1)

**4084 Misty Cay (IRE)** travelled well in behind the leaders but, with the pressure being maintained, could not step up a gear when it was called for. (12/1)

**3848* Scarlet Crescent** found this step up in class to much for her and she was feeling the strain and going backwards entering the final quarter-mile. (100/30)

**3859* Chain Reaction (IRE)** (11/2: op 7/2)

T/Plpt: £72.40 (243.63 Tckts). T/Qdpt: £7.00 (188.92 Tckts). IM

## 3775-**BEVERLEY** (R-H) (Good to firm, Firm patches)
## Wednesday September 18th

WEATHER: fine & cloudy WIND: fresh half against

## 4223 HUMBER ESTUARY NURSERY (S) H'CAP (0-65) (2-Y.O) (Class G)

2-10 (2-12) **7f 100y** £2,565.00 (£715.00: £345.00) Stalls: High GOING minus 0.67 sec per fur (HD)

| | | | | SP | RR | SF |
|---|---|---|---|---|---|---|
| 3498[6] | **Scarrots (59)** (SCWilliams) **2-9-4** KDarley(15) (chsd ldr: led over 3f out: hld on wl towards fin) | — | **1** | 11/1 | 64 | 35 |
| 4097[2] | **Jingoist (IRE) (53)** (JLHarris) **2-8-9b**(3) FLynch(16) (lw: trckd ldrs: effrt 2f out: styd on same pce ins fnl f) | nk | **2** | 9/4[1] | 57 | 28 |
| 3769* | **Soviet Lady (IRE) (62)** (JLEyre) **2-9-7** TWilliams(7) (hdwy to chse ldrs ½-wy: rdn & hung rt over 1f out: one pce) | 3½ | **3** | 13/2[3] | 59 | 30 |
| 4097[5] | **Sheraton Girl (51)** (MJohnston) **2-8-10** JCarroll(8) (lw: a chsng ldrs: hung rt & one pce fnl 2f) | hd | **4** | 11/1 | 48 | 19 |
| 3943[10] | **Lycius Touch (57)** (MJohnston) **2-9-2** GDuffield(12) (lw: a chsng ldrs: one pce fnl 2f) | 3 | **5** | 12/1 | 47 | 18 |
| 3943[5] | **Marsh Marigold (56)** (MartynMeade) **2-8-8**(7) DSweeney(4) (bhd tl styd on fnl 2f) | 2½ | **6** | 11/1 | 41 | 12 |
| 4041[7] | **Presentiment (60)** (JBerry) **2-9-5** JFortune(3) (mid div: effrt over 2f out: n.d) | nk | **7** | 12/1 | 44 | 15 |
| 3448[11] | **Superboots (46)** (WWHaigh) **2-7-12**(7) JBramhill(10) (hmpd after 1f: mid div & sn drvn along: nvr nr to chal) | 2 | **8** | 16/1 | 26 | — |
| *4093*[8] | **Rahona (IRE) (52)** (BSRothwell) **2-8-11** LCharnock(6) (in tch: rdn over 2f out: sn wknd) | nk | **9** | 20/1 | 31 | 2 |
| 3678[6] | **Apiculate (IRE) (46)** (WTKemp) **2-7-12**(7) KSked(5) (s.i.s: bhd whn hmpd over 3f out: swtchd outside: styd on appr fnl f) | nk | **10** | 25/1 | 25 | — |
| 3976[8] | **Fly Down To Rio (IRE) (49)** (DWPArbuthnot) **2-8-8** MBirch(9) (mid div: drvn along ½-wy: sn wknd) | 4 | **11** | 16/1 | 19 | — |
| 1869[9] | **Midyans Song (55)** (JJO'Neill) **2-9-0** TSprake(14) (hmpd after 1f: in tch tl lost pl over 2f out) | 1¾ | **12** | 16/1 | 21 | — |
| 4072[6] | **Classic Partygoer (54)** (MWEasterby) **2-8-8**(5) GParkin(2) (sn bhd) | 3½ | **13** | 16/1 | 13 | — |
| 3769[9] | **Silver Raj (54)** (WTKemp) **2-8-13** ACulhane(13) (s.s: a bhd: eased fnl 2f) | 18 | **14** | 33/1 | — | — |
| 3803[6] | **Muscatana (58)** (BWHills) **2-9-3** KFallon(1) (lw: bhd whn hmpd ½-wy: eased) | 4 | **15** | 4/1[2] | — | — |
| 3809[7] | **Miss Alice (50)** (JNorton) **2-8-9** JLowe(17) (led: hdd & fell over 3f out) | | **F** | 25/1 | — | — |
| 3838[4] | **Not A Lot (60)** (MWEasterby) **2-9-5** DaleGibson(11) (lw: plld hrd: hmpd after 1f: mid div whn bdly hmpd & uns rdr over 3f out) | | **U** | 16/1 | — | — |
| | | | | (SP 149.3%) | | **17 Rn** |

**1m 33.2** (1.20) CSF £40.78 CT £190.37 TOTE £14.90: £3.10 £1.30 £1.70 £2.60 (£28.90) Trio £47.00 OWNER Mr Bruce Wyatt (NEWMARKET) BRED R. G. Percival

No bid

**2733 Scarrots** . who took it up at halfway, outbattled the runner-up where it mattered most. (11/1)

**4097 Jingoist (IRE)** looked to be travelling best for much of the way but, when the chips were down, the winner proved just the more determined. (9/4: op 7/2)

**3769* Soviet Lady (IRE)** tended to hang under pressure, possibly feeling the firmish ground. (13/2)

**4097 Sheraton Girl**, with the blinkers again left off, tended to hang under pressure. (11/1)

**3943 Marsh Marigold** (11/1: 8/1-12/1)

## 4224 TATTERSALLS MAIDEN AUCTION STKS (2-Y.O) (Class E)

2-40 (2-42) **7f 100y** £3,964.00 (£1,192.00: £576.00: £268.00) Stalls: High GOING minus 0.67 sec per fur (HD)

| | | | | SP | RR | SF |
|---|---|---|---|---|---|---|
| 2624[12] | **White Hot** (EALDunlop) **2-8-10** KDarley(6) (chsd ldrs: rdn over 2f out: hung rt over 1f out: styd on to ld wl ins fnl f) | — | **1** | 7/1 | 85 | 39 |
| 4072[2] | **River of Fortune (IRE) (74)** (MHTompkins) **2-7-12**(3) MHenry(11) (lw: a chsng ldrs: rdn 2f out: styd on to ld ins fnl f: sn hdd & no ex) | 1¼ | **2** | 11/10[1] | 73 | 27 |
| 4046[14] | **Globetrotter (IRE)** (MJohnston) **2-8-7** GDuffield(10) (lw: led tl ins fnl f) | 1½ | **3** | 20/1 | 76 | 30 |
| 3982[8] | **Righty Ho** (PTWalwyn) **2-8-4** TSprake(3) (in tch: rdn & lost pl ½-wy: hung rt & styd on wl appr fnl f) | nk | **4** | 6/1 | 73 | 27 |
| 3982[18] | **Good Judge (IRE)** (MDHammond) **2-8-4** JFanning(7) (bhd: kpt on fnl 2f: nvr nr to chal) | 5 | **5** | 25/1 | 62 | 16 |
| 3982[W] | **Plutarch Angel** (WTKemp) **2-7-10**(7) KSked(2) (in tch: rdn & outpcd ½-wy: n.d) | s.h | **6** | 50/1 | 61 | 15 |
| 3963[2] | **Swiss Coast (IRE) (81)** (NTinkler) **2-8-8v** LCharnock(8) (lw: chsd ldrs: rdn 2f out: sn wknd) | 1½ | **7** | 5/1[3] | 62 | 16 |
| | **Moorbird (IRE)** (MJohnston) **2-8-6** TWilliams(9) (wl grwn: scope: bit bkwd: s.s: bhd & rdn along: styd on appr fnl f) | 1½ | **8** | 16/1 | 57 | 11 |
| 3869[5] | **Willskip (USA)** (JBerry) **2-8-9** JCarroll(12) (in tch tl outpcd ½-wy) | 2 | **9** | 33/1 | 56 | 10 |
| 4024a[18] | **Falls O'Moness (IRE) (73)** (KRBurke) **2-7-11**(3) NVarley(4) (chsd ldrs: chal & edgd lft 2f out: wknd over 1f out) | ¾ | **10** | 7/2[2] | 45 | — |

| | | | | SP | RR | SF |
|---|---|---|---|---|---|---|
| | **Murray Grey** (EWeymes) **2-8-1**(3) FLynch(1) (b: w'like: scope: bkwd: sn bhd & pushed along) | 1¾ | **11** | 20/1 | 46 | — |
| 3941[13] | **Sam Peeb** (RAFahey) **2-8-4** ACulhane(5) (hld up & plld hrd: a bhd) | 10 | **12** | 33/1 | 24 | — |
| | | | | (SP 140.4%) | **12 Rn** | |

**1m 32.1** (0.10) CSF £17.14 TOTE £7.80: £2.00 £1.10 £5.40 (£7.10) Trio £82.30 OWNER The Serendipity Partnership (NEWMARKET) BRED Broughton Bloodstock

**2353 White Hot** proved suited by the step up in distance. Tending to hang under pressure, he was skilfully handled. (7/1)

**4072 River of Fortune (IRE)** again found one just too good. (11/10)

**Globetrotter (IRE),** who looks as though he can be made fitter, made the running and ran easily his best race so far. (20/1)

**3982 Righty Ho** seemed to have trouble handling the bend and dropped right out. Staying on strongly at the finish, despite his tendency to hang he might be suited by a left-handed track. (6/1)

**Good Judge (IRE),** who looks as though he still needs more time, shaped by no means badly and should improve further in time. (25/1)

**3963 Swiss Coast (IRE),** whose stamina is uncertain, seemed to give in tamely. (5/1)

## 4225 E.B.F. GARROWBY MAIDEN STKS (2-Y.O F) (Class D)

3-10 (3-12) **7f 100y** £3,756.00 (£1,128.00: £544.00: £252.00) Stalls: High GOING minus 0.67 sec per fur (HD)

| | | | | SP | RR | SF |
|---|---|---|---|---|---|---|
| | **Lyrical Bid (USA)** (DRLoder) **2-8-11** KDarley(1) (unf: scope: lw: trckd ldrs: shkn up over 2f out: carried lft fnl f: styd on to ld post) | — | **1** | 3/1[2] | 75 | 29 |
| 4062[2] | **Flourishing Way** (RCharlton) **2-8-11** TSprake(4) (lw: led: rdn & edgd lft over 1f out: jst ct) | s.h | **2** | 4/5[1] | 75 | 29 |
| | **Perfect Poppy** (JRFanshawe) **2-8-8**(3) NVarley(5) (lt-f: bit bkwd: uns rdr gng to s: s.i.s: sn trckng ldrs: effrt over 2f out: nt qckn appr fnl f) | 1½ | **3** | 10/1 | 72 | 26 |
| | **Fellwah (IRE)** (EALDunlop) **2-8-11** KFallon(2) (leggy: scope: dwlt: effrt over 3f out: styd on fnl 2f: nvr nr to chal) | 3 | **4** | 7/1[3] | 65 | 19 |
| 4061[6] | **Native Princess (IRE)** (BWHills) **2-8-11** GDuffield(3) (trckd ldr tl lost pl over 2f out) | 1¼ | **5** | 8/1 | 63 | 17 |
| | | | | (SP 113.3%) | **5 Rn** | |

**1m 33.1** (1.10) CSF £5.86 TOTE £3.10: £1.60 £1.10 (£2.20) OWNER Cheveley Park Stud (NEWMARKET) BRED Cheveley Park Stud

**Lyrical Bid (USA),** who is not very big, answered her rider's calls, despite being carried out towards the centre, and she put her head in front right on the line. She lacks any scope. (3/1: op 7/4)

**4062 Flourishing Way** set her own pace. Edging left, out towards the centre, and taking the winner with her, the winning partnership proved just the stronger near the line. (4/5: op 6/4)

**Perfect Poppy,** who lacks substance, unseated her rider going to the start. She raced keenly on the heels of the leaders and was left with the door open by the winner, but could find no more coming to the final furlong. The outing should bring her on a little. (10/1)

**Fellwah (IRE)** did not seem to have any idea, but was picking up ground late in the day. (7/1)

## 4226 JOHN MANGLES MEMORIAL H'CAP (0-65) (3-Y.O+) (Class F)

3-45 (3-49) **1m 100y** £3,210.00 (£960.00: £460.00: £210.00) Stalls: High GOING minus 0.67 sec per fur (HD)

| | | | | SP | RR | SF |
|---|---|---|---|---|---|---|
| 3974[4] | **Thatched (IRE) (47)** (REBarr) **6-8-4**(7) KSked(17) (trckd ldrs: styd on appr fnl f: led wl ins fnl f: jst hld on) | — | **1** | 9/1 | 49 | 32 |
| 4125[7] | **Maradata (IRE) (60)** (RHollinshead) **4-9-7**(3) FLynch(7) (lw: hld up: stdy hdwy over 2f out: led over 1f out tl wl ins fnl f) | hd | **2** | 16/1 | 62 | 45 |
| 3995[3] | **Foist (46)** (MWEasterby) **4-8-5**(5) GParkin(1) (lw: gd hdwy on outside 3f out: sn ev ch: styd on wl ins fnl f) | s.h | **3** | 8/1 | 48 | 31 |
| 3120[8] | **Murphy's Gold (IRE) (51)** (RAFahey) **5-9-1** ACulhane(5) (bhd: gd hdwy 2f out: styd on ins fnl f) | hd | **4** | 11/1 | 53 | 36 |
| 3452[3] | **Mazilla (56)** (AStreeter) **4-9-3**(3) RHavlin(12) (trckd ldrs: n.m.r 2f out: styd on same pce) | 6 | **5** | 10/1 | 46 | 29 |
| *4078[3]* | **Bentico (55)** (MrsNMacauley) **7-9-2**(3) CTeague(16) (bhd tl styd on fnl 2f) | 1¼ | **6** | 16/1 | 43 | 26 |
| *4078** | **South Eastern Fred (46)** (HJCollingridge) **5-8-10** MRimmer(14) (chsd ldrs tl wknd over 1f out) | 1½ | **7** | 7/1[2] | 31 | 14 |
| 3978[6] | **Soldier Cove (USA) (55)** (MartynMeade) **6-8-12**(7) DSweeney(9) (hdwy on outside ½-wy: sn chsng ldrs: n.m.r 2f out: outpcd appr fnl f) | hd | **8** | 33/1 | 40 | 23 |
| 4071[9] | **Special-K (54)** (EWeymes) **4-9-4** GDuffield(18) (lw: led 2f: w ldr tl led over 2f out: hdd over 1f out: sn wknd) | ½ | **9** | 15/2[3] | 38 | 21 |
| | **Kilnamartyra Girl (49)** (JParkes) **6-8-13** LChamock(10) (bit bkwd: mid div: sn drvn along: n.d) | 1¼ | **10** | 33/1 | 31 | 14 |
| 4071* | **Society Girl (60)** (CWThornton) **3-9-6** JFortune(11) (lw: chsd ldrs: wkng whn hmpd wl over 1f out) | ½ | **11** | 4/1[1] | 41 | 20 |
| 3867[4] | **Cee-Jay-Ay (53)** (JBerry) **9-8-12**(5) PRoberts(6) (s.s: sme hdwy whn nt clr run over 1f out: n.d) | hd | **12** | 16/1 | 33 | 16 |
| 3808[17] | **Born A Lady (52)** (SRBowring) **3-8-12b** SDWilliams(19) (led after 2f tl over 2f out: sn wknd) | 2½ | **13** | 25/1 | 28 | 7 |
| 4071[7] | **Encore M'Lady (IRE) (58)** (FHLee) **5-9-8** JCarroll(8) (hdwy over 3f out: sn prom: n.m.r & lost pl 2f out) | ½ | **14** | 20/1 | 33 | 16 |
| 3490[3] | **Gulf of Siam (60)** (MissSEHall) **3-9-6** KDarley(15) (sn drvn along: hung rt over 1f out: n.d) | s.h | **15** | 10/1 | 35 | 14 |
| 3958[7] | **Flyaway Blues (47)** (MrsMReveley) **4-8-6v**(5) GLee(2) (bhd: sme hdwy over 3f out: sn wknd) | 1 | **16** | 20/1 | 20 | 3 |
| 4047[9] | **Falcon's Flame (USA) (56)** (MrsJRRamsden) **3-9-2** KFallon(3) (lw: bhd: drvn along ½-wy: n.d) | nk | **17** | 9/1 | 28 | 7 |
| 3985[16] | **My Godson (57)** (JLEyre) **6-9-7b** RLappin(4) (unruly in stalls: s.s: a bhd) | nk | **18** | 14/1 | 29 | 12 |
| 3974[15] | **Firle Phantasy (65)** (PCalver) **3-9-11** MBirch(13) (chsd ldrs tl lost pl over 2f out: sn bhd) | 14 | **19** | 33/1 | 10 | — |
| | | | | (SP 148.4%) | **19 Rn** | |

**1m 44.9** (0.90) CSF £153.87 CT £1,164.49 TOTE £13.40: £2.50 £5.50 £1.80 £3.90 (£182.70) Trio Not won; £1,126.72 to Ayr 19/9/96 OWNER Mr C. W. Marwood (MIDDLESBROUGH) BRED D. P. O'Brien

WEIGHT FOR AGE 3yo-4lb

**3974 Thatched (IRE),** ideally suited by coming from off the pace, lay closer than usual. Well handled, he scraped home in a tight finish. (9/1)

**3785 Maradata (IRE),** who looked a picture, possibly hit the front too soon and was worried out of it near the line. (16/1)

**3995 Foist,** worst drawn, had to make his effort on the outside. Staying on really well at the line, he definitely stayed the trip. (8/1)

**3120 Murphy's Gold (IRE)** reserves his best for here and ran one of his better races this year. (11/1)

**3452 Mazilla,** dropped in distance, found herself trapped on the inner, but it was lack of pace that proved her downfall. (10/1)

**3867 Special-K** (15/2: op 12/1)

**4071* Society Girl,** stepping up in distance, was already beaten when short of room over a furlong out. (4/1)

## 4227 FREDA AND JAMES HETHERINGTON H'CAP (0-75) (3-Y.O+) (Class D)

4-15 (4-18) **1m 3f 216y** £4,081.00 (£1,228.00: £594.00: £277.00) Stalls: High GOING minus 0.67 sec per fur (HD)

| | | | | SP | RR | SF |
|---|---|---|---|---|---|---|
| 3878[3] | **Campaspe (44)** (JGFitzGerald) **4-7-13**(3)ow2 FLynch(11) (hld up: smooth hdwy to ld over 3f out: sn rdn clr) | — | **1** | 10/1 | 59 | 41 |
| 4086[3] | **Lepikha (USA) (62)** (BWHills) **3-8-12** JFortune(15) (hld up: smooth hdwy over 4f out: rdn over 2f out: styd on: no ch w wnr) | 9 | **2** | 8/1 | 65 | 41 |
| 4000[11] | **Road Racer (IRE) (53)** (MrsJRRamsden) **3-8-3** JCarroll(4) (lw: hld up: effrt & swtchd rt over 2f out: n.m.r: kpt on one pce) | 1¼ | **3** | 12/1 | 54 | 30 |

| | Horse | Btn | Pos | SP | RR | SF |
|---|---|---|---|---|---|---|
| 3961[2] | **Totem Dancer (68)** (JLEyre) **3-9-4** RLappin(1) (lw: a chsng ldrs: styd on one pce fnl 2f) | s.h | **4** | 6/1[2] | 69 | 45 |
| 3621[3] | **South Sea Bubble (IRE) (66)** (LMCumani) **4-9-10** KDarley(12) (lw: chsd ldrs: ev ch & rdn over 2f out: wknd over 1f out) | 5 | **5** | 7/4[1] | 61 | 45 |
| 3818[6] | **Indiana Princess (60)** (MrsMReveley) **3-8-10** ACulhane(10) (unruly in stalls: bhd tl styd on fnl 3f) | 1½ | **6** | 14/1 | 53 | 29 |
| 3939[6] | **Taufan Boy (73)** (PWHarris) **3-9-6**(3) MHenry(7) (lw: w ldr: rdn 4f out: wknd 2f out) | 1¼ | **7** | 10/1 | 64 | 40 |
| 4073[3] | **Kalou (66)** (CWCElsey) **5-9-10** LCharnock(9) (swtg: hdwy to chse ldrs over 4f out: rdn & wknd over 2f out) | 3½ | **8** | 7/1[3] | 52 | 36 |
| 3878[12] | **Noir Esprit (47)** (JMCarr) **3-7-11v[1]** NKennedy(6) (bhd: sme hdwy & hung lft over 2f out: n.d) | 2 | **9** | 33/1 | 31 | 7 |
| 4070[16] | **Nexsis Star (48)** (MrsSJSmith) **3-7-12** JLowe(14) (sn bhd & pushed along) | 1½ | **10** | 25/1 | 30 | 6 |
| 3816[4] | **Mister Aspecto (IRE) (72)** (MJohnston) **3-9-8v** TWilliams(13) (lw: mde most tl over 3f out: wandered & sn wknd) | 1 | **11** | 7/1[3] | 52 | 28 |
| 4073[12] | **Exemption (60)** (HCandy) **5-9-4b[1]** GDuffield(5) (mid div & drvn along ½-wy: sn bhd) | 2½ | **12** | 10/1 | 37 | 21 |
| | **Devilry (58)** (RCraggs) **6-8-13**(3) RHavlin(3) (bit bkwd: chsd ldrs: rdn along ½-wy: sn wknd) | 14 | **13** | 33/1 | 16 | — |
| 3398[6] | **Shenango (IRE) (69)** (GWragg) **3-8-12**(7) GMilligan(8) (hld up: effrt on outside over 4f out: nt run on) | nk | **14** | 12/1 | 27 | 3 |

(SP 145.8%) **14 Rn**

**2m 31.3** (-1.10) CSF £96.73 CT £936.02 TOTE £8.90: £1.80 £3.40 £6.40 (£48.40) Trio £684.30; £674.70 to Ayr 19/9/96 OWNER Mr J. G. FitzGerald (MALTON) BRED J. G. FitzGerald
WEIGHT FOR AGE 3yo-8lb

**3878 Campaspe,** suited by the strong pace, scored by a wide margin. She seems hard to catch right. (10/1)
**4086 Lepikha (USA)** ran easily her best race so far, travelling strongly most of the way in what was a fast-run race. (8/1)
**3461 Road Racer (IRE)** met trouble when making his effort, but it was his lack of pace that got him into trouble in the first place. He might be worth a try over a mile and six. (12/1)
**3961 Totem Dancer,** raised 2lb, raced up with the pace in a strongly-run race. Significantly, the two leaders finished well beaten. (6/1)
**3621 South Sea Bubble (IRE),** again heavily backed, had every chance this time. She is proving expensive to follow. (7/4)
**3818 Indiana Princess,** on her handicap debut, played up in the stalls and was behind until staying on from the home turn (14/1)
**3479 Taufan Boy** sat on the heals of the leader in what was a strongly-run race, but he called enough two furlongs from home. (10/1)
**4073 Kalou** did not impress in the paddock. (7/1)
**Exemption** (10/1: op 16/1)

## 4228 ARAGON MAIDEN STKS (2-Y.O) (Class D)

4-50 (4-51) **5f** £3,735.00 (£1,125.00: £545.00: £255.00) Stalls: High GOING minus 0.67 sec per fur (HD)

| | Horse | Btn | Pos | SP | RR | SF |
|---|---|---|---|---|---|---|
| | **Jhazi** (DRLoder) **2-9-0** KDarley(3) (w'like: lw: trckd ldrs: led on bit ½-wy: pushed clr 1f out: easily) | — | **1** | 1/3[1] | 85++ | 47 |
| | **Archello (IRE)** (GROldroyd) **2-8-5**(5)ow1 GParkin(6) (leggy: bit bkwd: in tch: styd on appr fnl f: no ch w wnr) | 4 | **2** | 33/1 | 68 | 29 |
| | **Bishops Court** (MrsJRRamsden) **2-9-0** KFallon(2) (w'like: str: bit bkwd: swvd lft s: hld up: stdy hdwy ½-wy: r.o wl fnl f: improve) | ½ | **3** | 14/1 | 71+ | 33 |
| 3994[11] | **Style Dancer (IRE) (70)** (RMWhitaker) **2-8-11**(3) RHavlin(11) (a chsng ldrs: one pce fnl 2f) | 2 | **4** | 33/1 | 64 | 26 |
| 3994[10] | **Muliere** (MJohnston) **2-8-9** JFanning(13) (bit bkwd: w ldrs tl wknd over 1f out) | 2 | **5** | 13/2[2] | 53 | 15 |
| | **Dominant Air** (SirMarkPrescott) **2-9-0** GDuffield(12) (neat: scope: mid div: styd on appr fnl f: n.d) | 1¼ | **6** | 8/1[3] | 54 | 16 |
| 4046[W] | **Patrita Park** (WWHaigh) **2-8-9** RLappin(15) (unf: mid div & sn rdn along: styd on appr fnl f) | s.h | **7** | 33/1 | 49 | 11 |
| 3956[5] | **Bold Gayle** (MrsJRRamsden) **2-8-9** JFortune(4) (bit bkwd: hld up & bhd: sme hdwy 2f out: nvr nr ldrs) | ¾ | **8** | 14/1 | 46+ | 8 |
| 3330[5] | **One Lady** (JLEyre) **2-8-9** TWilliams(16) (led to ½-wy: wknd over 1f out) | ¾ | **9** | 33/1 | 44 | 6 |
| 3994[16] | **Night Chorus** (BSRothwell) **2-9-0** LCharnock(14) (sn outpcd & bhd) | 5 | **10** | 33/1 | 33 | — |
| 3773[10] | **Onemoretime** (BWMurray) **2-8-9** TSprake(9) (b.hind: sn bhd) | 2 | **11** | 33/1 | 21 | — |
| *4093[11]* | **Risky Flight (42)** (ASmith) **2-9-0b[1]** MBirch(8) (chsd ldrs: sn rdn: lost pl ½-wy) | 2½ | **12** | 33/1 | 18 | — |
| | **Il Principe (IRE)** (JohnBerry) **2-9-0** MRimmer(10) (unf: bit bkwd: s.i.s: a wl bhd) | 8 | **13** | 20/1 | — | — |
| | **Aspecto Lad (IRE)** (MJohnston) **2-8-11**(3) MHenry(5) (w'like: bkwd: s.s: a wl bhd & sn rdn along) | 5 | **14** | 20/1 | — | — |
| | **Jonny's Joker** (FHLee) **2-9-0** ACulhane(7) (leggy: scope: bit bkwd: s.s: rn green & a wl bhd) | 15 | **15** | 25/1 | — | — |

(SP 146.7%) **15 Rn**

**61.3 secs** (0.20 under 2y best) (-0.20) CSF £27.32 TOTE £1.50: £1.20 £20.60 £3.00 (£93.80) Trio £283.60 OWNER Abdullah Saeed Bul Hab (NEWMARKET) BRED Bottisham Heath Stud

**Jhazi,** who looked particularly fit and well on his debut, is a son of Arazi and he cost 88,000 guineas as a yearling. He proved different class to this lot and won very easily. He will be an interesting proposition if he goes for the Two Year Old Trophy at Redcar. (1/3: op 4/6)
**Archello (IRE),** cheaply bought, is a poor walker. Sticking on inside the last, she had no chance with the winner. (33/1)
**Bishops Court,** a sturdily-made brother to Surprise Mission, ran an eye-catcher on this debut. After ducking left at the start, he made ground on the bridle at halfway and, with any assistance at all from the saddle, would have finished second. He looked as though the outing would do him good and should make a useful sprint handicapper in time. (14/1: op 7/1)
**Style Dancer (IRE)** was well beaten on his three previous outings and his position casts doubt over the overall value of the form. (33/1)
**Muliere** still looked in need of the outing and was leg-weary coming to the final furlong. (13/2)
**Dominant Air,** a close-coupled newcomer, ran a shade green and the outing will bring him on. (8/1)
**3956 Bold Gayle,** dropped in at the start, showed some ability, staying on nicely under a quiet ride. Her long-term future lies in handicaps. (14/1: op 8/1)

## 4229 END OF SEASON MAIDEN STKS (3-Y.O+) (Class D)

5-20 (5-33) **5f** £3,925.00 (£1,180.00: £570.00: £265.00) Stalls: High GOING minus 0.67 sec per fur (HD)

| | Horse | Btn | Pos | SP | RR | SF |
|---|---|---|---|---|---|---|
| 4075[2] | **Manolo (FR) (58)** (JBerry) **3-8-13b[1]** JCarroll(4) (lw: mde virtually all: clr over 1f out: drvn out) | — | **1** | 5/2[2] | 68 | 41 |
| 4074[5] | **Foreign Relation (IRE)** (PRWebber) **3-8-8** KFallon(11) (b.hind: hdwy ½-wy: styd on wl fnl f: nt rch wnr) | 2 | **2** | 5/1[3] | 57 | 30 |
| | **Gad Yakoun** (MGMeagher) **3-8-13** JFortune(1) (unf: bit bkwd: s.i.s: sn chsng ldrs: kpt on wl fnl f) | 1¼ | **3** | 25/1 | 58 | 31 |
| 3446[9] | **Present Imperfect** (IABalding) **3-8-8** TSprake(14) (chsd ldrs: outpcd ½-wy: kpt on fnl f) | 1¼ | **4** | 11/8[1] | 49 | 22 |
| 4075[3] | **Young Ben (IRE) (36)** (JSWainwright) **4-8-7b**(7) JBramhill(7) (sn bhd & rdn: sme hdwy 2f out: nvr nr ldrs) | 1½ | **5** | 25/1 | 49 | 23 |
| 4074[3] | **Dewhurst House** (WWHaigh) **3-8-8** RLappin(8) (lw: w ldrs tl wknd appr fnl f) | 1¾ | **6** | 6/1 | 38 | 11 |
| 4075[7] | **Good To Talk (43)** (TDEasterby) **3-8-13** MBirch(5) (hld up: stdy hdwy ½-wy: rdn over 1f out: no imp) | 1 | **7** | 14/1 | 40 | 13 |
| 4075[10] | **Swifty Nifty (IRE) (40)** (WWHaigh) **3-8-5**(3) RHavlin(9) (chsd ldrs to ½-wy: sn wknd) | 1¼ | **8** | 20/1 | 31 | 4 |
| 2208[9] | **Bent Raiwand (USA) (70)** (DonEnricoIncisa) **3-8-8** KimTinkler(3) (bit bkwd: sn outpcd & rdn along) | 1½ | **9** | 25/1 | 26 | — |
| 3592[11] | **Paper Maze (29)** (EHOwenjun) **3-8-1**(7) RCody-Boutcher(12) (sn bhd) | s.h | **10** | 25/1 | 26 | — |
| *2684[9]* | **Avant Huit (45)** (MrsNMacauley) **4-8-6v**(3) CTeague(13) (w ldrs: rdn 2f out: sn wknd) | 5 | **11** | 25/1 | 10 | — |
| | **Gay Breeze** (PSFelgate) **3-8-13** GDuffield(6) (str: cmpt: bkwd: s.s: a wl bhd) | 9 | **12** | 20/1 | — | — |
| *4090[7]* | **Brin-Lodge (IRE) (35)** (KSBridgwater) **3-8-5**(3) NVarley(2) (chsd ldrs to ½-wy: sn wknd) | 1 | **13** | 25/1 | — | — |
| | **Macs Clan** (MissJBower) **3-8-8** SDWilliams(10) (v.unruly gng to s: s.s: a wl bhd) | 25 | **14** | 25/1 | — | — |

*4074[4]* ***Daisy Bates (IRE)*** (PWHarris) **3-8-8** KDarley(15) (Withdrawn not under Starter's orders: bolted bef s).............. **W** 5/2[2] — —
(SP 173.3%) **14 Rn**

**61.6 secs** (0.10) CSF £16.78 TOTE £3.60: £1.40 £2.00 £11.30 (£25.00) Trio £441.70; £348.43 to Ayr 19/9/96 OWNER Lucayan Stud (COCKERHAM) BRED Baron Guy De Rothschild
WEIGHT FOR AGE 3yo-1lb

**4075 Manolo (FR)** was in blinkers for the first time and they clearly had the desired effect. To be honest though, this race was no better than a seller. (5/2)

**4074 Foreign Relation (IRE)**, badly drawn at Thirsk last time, stuck on strongly late in the day. An easy six would suit. (5/1: tchd 8/1)

**Gad Yakoun**, who was cheaply bought last year, is nothing to look at, but clearly possesses some ability. Worst drawn, the outing should have taught him something. (25/1)

**Present Imperfect**, a gangly filly, struggled badly to keep up at halfway and might be suited by a flatter and more galloping track. (11/8: Evens-9/4)

**4074 Dewhurst House** (6/1: op 4/1)

T/Plpt: £85.80 (138.16 Tckts). T/Qdpt: £70.00 (8.75 Tckts). WG

# 4210-SANDOWN (R-H) (Good to firm, Firm patches)
## Wednesday September 18th
WEATHER: fine WIND: str half bhd

## 4230 'DISMISSAL' CLAIMING STKS (2-Y.O) (Class D)
2-15 (2-16) **5f 6y** £3,338.75 (£1,010.00: £492.50: £233.75) Stalls: Low GOING minus 0.46 sec per fur (F)

| | | | | SP | RR | SF |
|---|---|---|---|---|---|---|
| 3975[3] | **Clara Bliss (IRE) (72)** (BJMeehan) **2-8-6** MTebbutt(8) (a.p: led over 1f out: drvn out) | — | 1 | 3/1[2] | 68 | 41 |
| 3976[3] | **Danehill Prince** (GLMoore) **2-8-7** SWhitworth(1) (dwlt: rdn & hdwy over 1f out: r.o wl ins fnl f) | nk | 2 | 12/1 | 68 | 41 |
| 3615[12] | **Ellens Lad (IRE)** (RHannon) **2-8-7** DaneO'Neill(4) (lw: a.p: rdn over 1f out: r.o) | hd | 3 | 7/1[3] | 68 | 41 |
| 3803[7] | **Suite Factors (73)** (KRBurke) **2-8-9** TQuinn(7) (w ldr: led over 2f out tl over 1f out: unable qckn) | 2½ | 4 | 10/1 | 62 | 35 |
| 3803[2] | **Last Chance (81)** (CNAllen) **2-9-0** PatEddery(6) (led over 2f: rdn & one pce) | s.h | 5 | 7/4[1] | 67 | 40 |
| 3823[5] | **Just Loui (62)** (WGMTurner) **2-7-13**(5) CAdamson(5) (lw: no hdwy fnl 2f) | 2 | 6 | 16/1 | 50 | 23 |
| 2429[5] | **Jilly Woo (59)** (DRCElsworth) **2-8-1**ow1 SDrowne(10) (bhd 3f) | 3½ | 7 | 14/1 | 36 | 8 |
| 3803[11] | **Rusty (IRE) (63)** (JBerry) **2-8-2** GCarter(2) (lw: bhd fnl 3f) | 3 | 8 | 7/1[3] | 28 | 1 |
| 3129[13] | **Swift Refusal (70)** (MJHaynes) **2-8-6b[1]** CRutter(9) (lw: bhd fnl 3f) | 1 | 9 | 16/1 | 28 | 1 |
| *4079[5]* | **Red Garter (IRE) (63)** (KMcAuliffe) **2-7-13v[1]**(5) LNewton(3) (prom over 2f) | 2½ | 10 | 20/1 | 18 | — |

(SP 126.3%) **10 Rn**

**60.44 secs** (0.64) CSF £37.95 TOTE £5.00: £1.70 £3.00 £1.80 (£25.70) Trio £109.10 OWNER Mr Gary Catchpole (UPPER LAMBOURN) BRED Martyn J. McEnery

**3975 Clara Bliss (IRE)** has some solid form to her name and, sent on below the distance, responded well to pressure and held on gamely. (3/1: tchd 9/2)

**3976 Danehill Prince**, formerly with Mick Channon, is a huge horse who carries plenty of condition and was putting in some sterling work in the last furlong and a half. The drop in distance was against him and, back over seven furlongs - this gelding would have no problems carrying big weights - he should be able to find a small race. (12/1)

**3114 Ellens Lad (IRE)** looked extremely well beforehand and, appreciating the drop in class, made sure the winner fought hard to the line. (7/1)

**3332* Suite Factors**, with plenty of experience on his side, was happier on this faster ground but, after leading at halfway, was collared below the distance and tapped for toe. (10/1)

**3803 Last Chance** was having his first run for his new stable but, after leading to halfway, could then only keep on at one pace. (7/4)

## 4231 C. GORDON MEDLEN AND SONIA P. COE MEMORIAL LIMITED STKS (0-80) (3-Y.O) (Class D)
2-50 (2-50) **7f 16y** £3,745.00 (£1,135.00: £555.00: £265.00) Stalls: High GOING minus 0.46 sec per fur (F)

| | | | | SP | RR | SF |
|---|---|---|---|---|---|---|
| 4064[3] | **Roushan (80)** (SCWilliams) **3-9-1** JTate(8) (mde all: hrd rdn over 1f out: r.o wl) | — | 1 | 15/8[1] | 95 | 61 |
| 3833[4] | **Divine Quest (76)** (HRACecil) **3-8-12** PatEddery(3) (lw: chsd wnr: ev ch over 1f out: unable qckn) | ¾ | 2 | 5/2[2] | 90 | 56 |
| 4124[2] | **Lucky Archer (79)** (CEBrittain) **3-8-12** BDoyle(2) (lw: hld up: rdn over 2f out: one pce) | 3 | 3 | 11/4[3] | 84 | 50 |
| 3609[2] | **Diamond Beach (80)** (BWHills) **3-8-12** TQuinn(6) (hld up: rdn over 2f out: one pce) | 3½ | 4 | 9/1 | 76 | 42 |
| 4064[12] | **Proud Monk (76)** (GLMoore) **3-8-12** SWhitworth(7) (hmpd on ins 6f out: a bhd) | 3½ | 5 | 16/1 | 68 | 34 |
| 3599[6] | **Elite Force (IRE) (76)** (PWChapple-Hyam) **3-8-12** JReid(5) (dwlt: a bhd) | nk | 6 | 14/1 | 67 | 33 |
| *423[5]* | **Miss Pickpocket (IRE) (64)** (MissGayKelleway) **3-8-9** DaneO'Neill(1) (b: swtg: plld hrd: hdwy 4f out: wknd 3f out) | 4 | 7 | 33/1 | 55 | 21 |

(SP 115.5%) **7 Rn**

**1m 28.66** (0.06) CSF £6.94 TOTE £3.50: £1.90 £2.10 (£3.40) OWNER Mr R. J. Cummings (NEWMARKET) BRED Mascalls Stud Farm

**4064 Roushan**, who was taken down very early to post, put up a game performance from the front and, responding well to pressure, kept the runner-up at bay. (15/8)

**3833 Divine Quest** looked extremely well in the paddock and loomed up looking a serious threat to the winner in the straight. However, she gave the impression that she did not want to go past and had to accept defeat inside the final furlong. (5/2: 7/4-11/4)

**4124 Lucky Archer** was not suited by the drop back in distance, and failed to quicken in the last two furlongs. A return to a mile is needed. (11/4)

**3609 Diamond Beach** chased the leaders, but never threatened to quicken in the last three furlongs. (9/1: 6/1-10/1)

**3599 Elite Force (IRE)** (14/1: 7/1-16/1)

## 4232 SCOTTISH EQUITABLE/JOCKEYS ASSOCIATION H'CAP (0-80) (3-Y.O) (Class D)
3-20 (3-22) **1m 14y** £6,343.00 (£1,924.00: £942.00: £451.00) Stalls: High GOING minus 0.46 sec per fur (F)

| | | | | SP | RR | SF |
|---|---|---|---|---|---|---|
| 3991[8] | **Superior Force (58)** (MissBSanders) **3-8-7** SSanders(1) (lw: chsd ldr: rdn over 2f out: led last strides) | — | 1 | 12/1 | 66 | 47 |
| 2294[6] | **No Cliches (70)** (GLewis) **3-9-5b** PatEddery(7) (lw: led: hrd rdn over 1f out: hdd last strides) | hd | 2 | 7/1[2] | 78 | 59 |
| 3852[9] | **Witherkay (61)** (RHannon) **3-8-10** DaneO'Neill(10) (a.p: rdn over 2f out: one pce) | 3½ | 3 | 11/1 | 62 | 43 |
| 3866[9] | **Sistar Act (66)** (MRChannon) **3-9-1** TQuinn(9) (lw: rdn over 3f out: hdwy over 1f out: r.o one pce) | nk | 4 | 12/1 | 66 | 47 |
| 4054[2] | **Dummer Golf Time (69)** (LordHuntingdon) **3-9-4v** JReid(3) (a.p: rdn over 3f out: one pce) | hd | 5 | 3/1[1] | 69 | 50 |
| 3522[4] | **Seeking Fortune (USA) (72)** (JRFanshawe) **3-9-7** WRSwinburn(5) (lw: hld up: drvn over 1f out: no rspnse) | 2½ | 6 | 3/1[1] | 67 | 48 |
| 3800[8] | **Disallowed (IRE) (69)** (MBell) **3-9-4** MFenton(2) (nvr nr to chal) | 2 | 7 | 12/1 | 60 | 41 |

4128[5] **Classic Look (IRE) (55)** (MajorDNChappell) **3-8-4** GCarter(8) (a bhd) ....4 **8** 9/1[3] 38 19
4064[15] **Generous Present (58)** (JWPayne) **3-8-4**(3) DWright(6) (lw: a bhd) ....¾ **9** 12/1 40 21
4053[15] **Country Thatch (60)** (CAHorgan) **3-8-9** BDoyle(4) (a bhd) ....5 **10** 33/1 32 13
3995[12] **Scathebury (59)** (KRBurke) **3-8-8b** SDrowne(11) (plld hrd: hld up: rdn over 2f out: sn wknd) ....7 **11** 12/1 17 —
(SP 122.2%) **11 Rn**

**1m 41.94** (0.74) CSF £88.70 CT £901.38 TOTE £15.10: £3.60 £2.80 £2.80 (£36.40) Trio £133.20 OWNER Copyforce Ltd (EPSOM) BRED Ahmed M. Foustok

**3501 Superior Force** has gradually come down in the handicap and bounced back to form. Engaged in a tremendous battle with the leader in the straight, he managed to get up in the last couple of strides. (12/1)
**2294 No Cliches**, in tremendous shape for this first run in nearly twelve weeks and following a drop of 10lb since the beginning of the season, bounced back with a gutsy effort. Bowling along in front, he had a tremendous set-to with the winner in the straight and only lost out in the last couple of strides. He is a winner without a penalty. (7/1: 5/1-8/1)
**2234 Witherkay** ran better here, but failed to find another gear in the final quarter mile. (11/1)
**3845 Sistar Act** comes from a stable that is out of form at present and, although staying on in the last furlong and a half, she never threatened to get in a serious blow. (12/1)
**4054 Dummer Golf Time** raced in a handy position, but was tapped for toe in the straight. (3/1)
**3522 Seeking Fortune (USA)** did not look an easy ride and, when shown the persuader in the final quarter mile, failed to respond at all. (3/1)
**3881* Scathebury** (12/1: 8/1-14/1)

## 4233 E.B.F. 'GRASS WIDOWS' MAIDEN STKS (2-Y.O) (Class D)

3-55 (3-57) **7f 16y** £3,810.00 (£1,155.00: £565.00: £270.00) Stalls: High GOING minus 0.46 sec per fur (F)

SP RR SF

**Sleepytime (IRE)** (HRACecil) **2-8-9** PatEddery(3) (wl grwn: a.p: led over 2f out: qcknd over 1f out: hrd hld: v.impressive) ....— **1** 30/100[1] 79++ 46
841[5] **Tough Act** (GHarwood) **2-9-0** AClark(16) (a.p: rdn over 2f out: unable qckn) ....5 **2** 33/1 73 40
4050[W] **Fatal Baraari** (MRStoute) **2-9-0** JReid(5) (w'like: scope: led over 1f: led over 3f out tl over 2f out: one pce)....¾ **3** 8/1[3] 71 38
**Crystal Hearted** (HCandy) **2-9-0** AMcGlone(8) (w'like: scope: bit bkwd: hdwy over 1f out: nvr nrr) ....1¼ **4** 50/1 68 35
3682[6] **Shalaal (USA)** (EALDunlop) **2-9-0** SWhitworth(9) (hld up: rdn over 2f out: one pce) ....hd **5** 25/1 68 35
3668[7] **Drive Assured** (CEBrittain) **2-9-0** BDoyle(6) (a.p: rdn over 2f out: one pce) ....s.h **6** 25/1 68 35
3615[4] **Haydn James (USA)** (PWHarris) **2-9-0** GHind(11) (lw: w ldr: led over 5f out tl over 3f out: wknd over 1f out) ....1¼ **7** 7/1[2] 65 32
**Attitude** (HCandy) **2-9-0** CRutter(12) (w'like: scope: nvr nrr) ....¾ **8** 33/1 63 30
**Bobbitt** (WJarvis) **2-8-9** TQuinn(7) (w'like: bit bkwd: nvr nrr) ....3 **9** 25/1 52 19
2245[6] **Bathe In Light (USA)** (LordHuntingdon) **2-8-9** WRSwinburn(1) (lw: a mid div) ....hd **10** 33/1 51 18
**Ortelius** (RHannon) **2-9-0** DaneO'Neill(4) (w'like: scope: a bhd) ....6 **11** 25/1 43 10
**Peter Perfect** (GLewis) **2-8-11**(3) AWhelan(2) (str: scope: bit bkwd: prom 3f) ....nk **12** 50/1 42 9
**Double-E-I-B-A** (CNAllen) **2-8-9**(5) MartinDwyer(14) (w'like: bit bkwd: a bhd) ....2½ **13** 100/1 36 3
**Serenade (IRE)** (MJHaynes) **2-9-0** GCarter(10) (w'like: bkwd: a bhd) ....5 **14** 100/1 25 —
**Oaken Wood (IRE)** (NACallaghan) **2-9-0** DRMcCabe(13) (str: bit bkwd: a bhd) ....8 **15** 66/1 7 —
(SP 132.1%) **15 Rn**

**1m 29.56** (0.96) CSF £17.15 TOTE £1.40: £1.10 £5.50 £2.00 (£12.10) Trio £43.30 OWNER Greenbay Stables Ltd (NEWMARKET) BRED C. H. Wacker III

**Sleepytime (IRE)** is highly regarded at home, following sparkling work on the gallops, which has seen her trounce work-companions who have already won this season. Anticipation was high, but the performance she put up had to be seen to be believed. Cruising into the lead over a quarter of a mile from home, she showed a tremendous turn of foot to sweep clear in a matter of strides and, with Eddery having a strangle-hold on the filly inside the final furlong, the winning distance is certainly no true reflection of her superiority. Indeed, she was value for a good fifteen lengths. A very imposing filly who already looks like a three-year-old, she looks extremely high-class and it is going to take something exceptional to beat her this year. (30/100)
**Tough Act**, given a five-month break and stepped up in trip, left his debut run behind and, although having absolutely no chance with the winner, eventually managed to win the battle for second prize. (33/1)
**Fatal Baraari**, a good-bodied colt, went on entering the straight but was firmly put in his place by the winner over two furlongs from home. A half-brother to four winners including Irish and Italian Oaks winner Possessive Dancer, he should soon pick up a race. (8/1: 4/1-9/1)
**Crystal Hearted**, a scopey newcomer, looked as though the run would do him good, but caught the eye, staying on in the last furlong and a half. He is sure to come on a lot for this. (50/1)
**3682 Shalaal (USA)** chased the leaders, but never looked like quickening up in the straight. (25/1)
**2132 Drive Assured** raced in a handy position, but was made to look very pedestrian in the straight. (25/1)
**3615 Haydn James (USA)** (7/1: 5/1-8/1)

## 4234 DAVID WARD BENEFIT NURSERY H'CAP (2-Y.O) (Class D)

4-25 (4-29) **5f 6y** £3,940.00 (£1,195.00: £585.00: £280.00) Stalls: Low GOING minus 0.46 sec per fur (F)

SP RR SF

3829[3] **Polish Warrior (IRE) (78)** (PWChapple-Hyam) **2-9-5** JReid(6) (lw: a.p: qcknd & led 1f out: all out) ....— **1** 7/2[1] 83 62
3429[5] **Hangover Square (IRE) (78)** (RHannon) **2-9-5** DaneO'Neill(4) (lw: rdn & hdwy over 1f out: r.o wl ins fnl f).....hd **2** 10/1 83 62
4043[14] **Anokato (65)** (KTIvory) **2-8-1b**(5) MartinDwyer(2) (a.p: led 2f out to 1f out: unable qckn) ....3 **3** 9/1 60 39
4103[2] **Manikato (USA) (70)** (DJSCosgrove) **2-8-6**(5) LNewton(12) (lw: hdwy over 1f out: hrd rdn: one pce) ....2 **4** 12/1 59 38
3809[2] **Cambridge Ball (IRE) (71)** (MJohnston) **2-8-12** PatEddery(10) (rdn over 2f out: hdwy over 1f out: nvr nrr)......¾ **5** 4/1[2] 57 36
3924[5] **Tear White (IRE) (75)** (TGMills) **2-9-2b** TQuinn(9) (led 3f) ....½ **6** 10/1 60 39
3871[6] **Sparkling Edge (57)** (CADwyer) **2-7-5**(7) RMullen(8) (nvr nrr) ....½ **7** 10/1 40 19
3823[7] **Northern Sal (72)** (JBerry) **2-8-13** GCarter(11) (b.nr hind: a.p: ev ch wl over 1f out: sn wknd) ....1¾ **8** 20/1 50 29
3523[6] **Battle Ground (IRE) (55)** (NACallaghan) **2-7-10** DeclanO'Shea(7) (a bhd) ....hd **9** 20/1 32 11
4034a[3] **Sous Le Nez (80)** (RGuest) **2-9-7** PBloomfield(1) (prom over 2f) ....¾ **10** 13/2[3] 55 34
3796[17] **Mike's Double (IRE) (55)** (GLewis) **2-7-10** RStreet(5) (s.s: a bhd) ....1¼ **11** 20/1 26 5
4049[10] **Regal Equity (75)** (BJMeehan) **2-9-2b[1]** BDoyle(3) (a.p: ev ch 2f out: wknd over 1f out) ....1¼ **12** 9/1 42 21
(SP 124.8%) **12 Rn**

**59.89 secs** (0.09) CSF £37.44 CT £264.57 TOTE £3.20: £1.40 £3.70 £4.20 (£18.00) Trio £57.90 OWNER Mrs D. Weatherby (MARLBOROUGH) BRED J. Ford

LONG HANDICAP Battle Ground (IRE) 7-9

**3829 Polish Warrior (IRE)**, unsuited by Epsom's tricky course previously, showed a fine turn of foot to sweep into the lead a furlong out. However, this was probably too soon for him and, with the runner-up finishing in good style, he had little to spare at the line. (7/2)

**3429 Hangover Square (IRE)** ran his best race to date and, eating up the ground in the last furlong and a half, may well have overhauled the winner in a few more strides. (10/1)
**3792 Anokato** put some disappointing runs behind him and, after leading a quarter of a mile out, was collared by the winner a furlong out. (9/1)
**4103 Manikato (USA)** made an effort from the rear below the distance, but could then make no further impression. (12/1)
**3809 Cambridge Ball (IRE)** was not helped by the drop in distance and, after being unable to go the early pace, was doing all her best work from below the distance. (4/1)
**3924 Tear White (IRE)** is not an easy ride and, having set the pace, was collared two furlongs from home. (10/1)

## 4235 KENNINGTON OVAL MAIDEN STKS (3-Y.O) (Class D)

5-00 (5-04) **1m 2f 7y** £3,745.00 (£1,135.00: £555.00: £265.00) Stalls: High GOING minus 0.46 sec per fur (F)

| | | | | SP | RR | SF |
|---|---|---|---|---|---|---|
| 3042[5] | **Congo Man** (MRStoute) **3-9-0** JReid(4) (hld up: rdn over 2f out: led ins fnl f: r.o wl) | — | **1** | 11/4[2] | 80 | 46 |
| 3986[3] | **Torremolinos (USA)** (HRACecil) **3-9-0** PatEddery(3) (lw: led: rdn over 2f out: hdd ins fnl f: unable qckn) | 1½ | **2** | 6/5[1] | 78 | 44 |
| 707[7] | **Enriched (IRE)** (JHMGosden) **3-8-9** GHind(1) (b.hind: bit bkwd: hld up: chsd ldr over 6f out: rdn over 2f out: ev ch ins fnl f: one pce) | hd | **3** | 11/4[2] | 72 | 38 |
| | **Mr Wild (USA)** (BHanbury) **3-9-0** JStack(2) (w'like: scope: chsd ldr over 3f: wknd 2f out) | 8 | **4** | 20/1 | 65 | 31 |
| | **Unassailable** (CEBrittain) **3-8-9** BDoyle(5) (w'like: scope: s.s: a in rr: t.o) | 20 | **5** | 16/1[3] | 28 | — |
| | | | | (SP 109.4%) | **5 Rn** | |

**2m 8.67** (1.97) CSF £6.22 TOTE £3.90: £1.60 £1.40 (£2.30) OWNER Mr J. D. Ashenheim (NEWMARKET) BRED Jack Ashenheim
**3042 Congo Man**, given a break since his debut nearly eight weeks ago, chased the leaders. Produced from below the distance, he gradually whittled down the front two to get on top inside the final furlong. (11/4)
**3986 Torremolinos (USA)** looked in good shape in the paddock and attempted to make all the running. Engaged in a real battle with the third, they were both passed by the winner inside the final furlong. He should soon make amends. (6/5: 4/6-5/4)
**Enriched (IRE)** was carrying plenty of condition for this first run in five months, and had a tremendous ding-dong battle with the runner-up in the straight, only for them both to be passed by the winner inside the final furlong. There is a race waiting for her. (11/4)
**Mr Wild (USA)**, a good-bodied gelding, had shot his bolt two furlongs from home. (20/1)

## 4236 END OF SEASON APPRENTICE H'CAP (0-70) (3-Y.O+) (Class E)

5-30 (5-36) **1m 2f 7y** £2,855.00 (£875.00: £435.00: £215.00) Stalls: High GOING minus 0.46 sec per fur (F)

| | | | | SP | RR | SF |
|---|---|---|---|---|---|---|
| 4000[4] | **Cuban Reef (45)** (WJMusson) **4-8-8** JDennis(9) (gd hdwy over 1f out: str run fnl f: led last stride) | — | **1** | 6/1[2] | 56 | 20 |
| 2226[7] | **Rock The Barney (IRE) (48)** (PBurgoyne) **7-8-4**(7) JBosley(6) (lw: stdy hdwy 3f out: led 2f out: rdn fnl f: hdd last stride) | s.h | **2** | 12/1 | 59 | 23 |
| 4068[7] | **Wet Patch (IRE) (60)** (RHannon) **4-8-13**(10) KSalt(13) (lw: a.p: led over 2f out: sn hdd: ev ch fnl f: r.o) | ½ | **3** | 16/1 | 70 | 34 |
| | **Lucy Tufty (39)** (JPearce) **5-7-6**(10)ow6 LisaMoncrieff(1) (hdwy over 2f out: r.o) | 2½ | **4** | 33/1 | 45 | 3 |
| 4000* | **Gold Desire (48)** (MBrittain) **6-8-6**(5) JFowle(7) (b.nr fore: hdwy over 2f out: one pce fnl f) | 1 | **5** | 11/2[1] | 53 | 17 |
| 3785[4] | **Lady Sabina (35)** (WJMusson) **6-7-7**(5)ow1 KerryBaker(4) (lw: hdwy over 1f out: nvr nrr) | hd | **6** | 10/1[3] | 39 | 2 |
| *152*[8] | **Father Dan (IRE) (56)** (MissGayKelleway) **7-8-9**(10) BFord(5) (b: lw: led over 1f: one pce fnl 2f) | s.h | **7** | 20/1 | 60 | 24 |
| 3970[4] | **Guesstimation (USA) (60)** (JPearce) **7-9-4**(5) MatthewWilliams(16) (a.p: nt clr run on ins over 2f out: wknd over 1f out) | 2 | **8** | 6/1[2] | 61 | 25 |
| 3965[4] | **Eskimo Kiss (IRE) (44)** (MJFetherston-Godley) **3-7-10v**(5)ow5 DavidO'Neill(2) (lw: a mid div) | s.h | **9** | 12/1 | 45 | — |
| 2440[6] | **Princely Affair (51)** (MBell) **3-8-5**(3) RMullen(14) (lw: nvr nrr) | 2 | **10** | 11/2[1] | 49 | 7 |
| 3944[11] | **Bronze Runner (38)** (EAWheeler) **12-7-10b**(5)ow5 EmilyJoyce(11) (hld up: rdn over 2f out: sn wknd) | 1¾ | **11** | 25/1 | 33 | — |
| *604*[5] | **Nautical Jewel (48)** (MDIUsher) **4-8-6**(5) RBrisland(12) (bit bkwd: hdwy over 1f out: sn wknd) | 1¾ | **12** | 25/1 | 40 | 4 |
| 4068[4] | **In The Band (49)** (LordHuntingdon) **3-7-12v[1]**(8) CCogan(15) (bhd fnl 2f) | 1½ | **13** | 10/1[3] | 39 | — |
| *3435*[10] | **Elly Fleetfoot (IRE) (53)** (MJRyan) **4-8-8b**(8) AMcCarthy(10) (lw: a.p: led 4f out tl over 2f out: wknd wl over 1f out) | nk | **14** | 12/1 | 42 | 6 |
| | **Special Risk (IRE) (47)** (RAkehurst) **6-8-7**(3) DDenby(8) (bit bkwd: a bhd) | 2½ | **15** | 16/1 | 32 | — |
| 3471[12] | **Misty View (42)** (JWhite) **7-8-0**(5)ow5 AnthonyBond(3) (hld up: rdn 3f out: sn wknd) | 6 | **16** | 33/1 | 18 | — |
| 3974[6] | **Wickins (65)** (HJCollingridge) **6-10-0** CWebb(17) (s.s: plld hrd: gd hdwy to ld over 8f out: hdd 4f out: wknd qckly 2f out) | s.h | **17** | 10/1[3] | 41 | 5 |
| | | | | (SP 139.8%) | **17 Rn** | |

**2m 11.33** (4.63) CSF £79.21 CT £1,051.66 TOTE £7.90: £1.80 £2.60 £2.40 £10.40 (£78.20) Trio £237.00 OWNER Mr K. L. West (NEWMARKET) BRED Angley Stud Ltd
LONG HANDICAP Lucy Tufty 7-7 Bronze Runner 7-2 Eskimo Kiss (IRE) 7-8
WEIGHT FOR AGE 3yo-6lb
**4000 Cuban Reef**, still out with the washing entering the straight, showed a tremendous turn of foot to sweep through and snatch the spoils right on the line. (6/1)
**1655 Rock The Barney (IRE)** bounced back to form here and, travelling really well, struck the front a quarter of a mile from home. However, this was probably too early for him and he was caught right on the line. (12/1)
**3095 Wet Patch (IRE)** was in one of his better moods and, vying for the lead in the last three furlongs, was only just worried out of it. (16/1)
**Lucy Tufty**, without a run since finishing second in a selling handicap hurdle at Fakenham last December, stayed on in the straight to take fourth prize. (33/1)
**4000* Gold Desire**, racing in midfield, closed up in the straight, but failed to quicken inside the distance. (11/2)
**3785 Lady Sabina**, out with the washing until well into the straight, stayed on through beaten rivals to be nearest at the line. One win from thirty-six starts says it all. (10/1)

T/Jkpt: Not won; £3,910.01 to Ayr 19/9/96. T/Plpt: £152.70 (104.73 Tckts). T/Qdpt: £23.00 (43.15 Tckts). AK

# 4217-YARMOUTH (L-H) (Good to firm)

## Wednesday September 18th

WEATHER: Fine, strong sea breeze, cool WIND: gale force across

## 4237 NEWTON (S) STKS (3-Y.O+) (Class G)

2-00 (2-04) **1m 2f 21y** £2,763.00 (£768.00: £369.00) Stalls: High GOING minus 0.44 sec per fur (F)

| | | | | SP | RR | SF |
|---|---|---|---|---|---|---|
| *4095*[8] | **El Bardador (IRE) (53)** (WJarvis) **3-8-11b[1]** MHills(5) (lw: hld up: gd hdwy 2f out: led ins fnl f: drvn clr) | — | **1** | 12/1 | 61 | 39 |

3991[12] **Roi de la Mer (IRE) (59)** (JAkehurst) **5-9-8** RHughes(11) (lw: hld up in rr: hdwy over 2f out: ev ch fnl f: unable qckn)........2½ **2** 9/2[2] 62 46
4125[10] **Blaze of Oak (USA) (60)** (JMBradley) **5-8-10**(7) RFfrench(9) (b: hdwy ½-wy: led 2f out tl hdd & no ex ins fnl f)........½ **3** 14/1 56 40
4070[6] **Mcgillycuddy Reeks (IRE) (36)** (NTinkler) **5-8-12** WRyan(17) (hld up: hdwy 3f out: kpt on u.p fnl f)........1 **4** 25/1 50 34
4217[5] **Irish Sea (USA) (67)** (DNicholls) **3-8-11** MWigham(18) (hld up: hdwy 3f out: kpt on u.p appr fnl f)........hd **5** 10/1[3] 55 33
3970[2] **Shabanaz (64)** (WRMuir) **11-9-8** LDettori(3) (lw: hld up in tch: effrt 3f out: sn drvn along: nt pce to chal)........1 **6** 13/8[1] 58 42
3974[9] **Desert Zone (USA) (46)** (JLHarris) **7-9-3** RCochrane(7) (b: hdwy 3f out: sn rdn: nvr able to chal)........1 **7** 25/1 51 35
*3626*[4] **Mrs Drummond (IRE)** (APJarvis) **3-7-13**(7) CCarver(2) (in tch: effrt & rdn over 2f out: no imp)........2 **8** 33/1 43 21
690[16] **Quillwork (USA) (60)** (JPearce) **4-8-12** GBardwell(6) (b.nr hind: bit bkwd: in tch: effrt & rdn 3f out: no imp)........¾ **9** 12/1 42 26
3584[10] **Junior Ben (IRE) (41)** (PHowling) **4-9-3b** FNorton(4) (led after 2f tl over 3f out: sn rdn: grad wknd)........1 **10** 25/1 45 29
**Arak (USA) (70)** (GCBravery) **8-9-3** NDay(10) (b: bkwd: prom: led over 3f out to 2f out: wknd qckly)........½ **11** 14/1 45 29
4070[12] **Sweet Amoret (47)** (PHowling) **3-8-11** JQuinn(1) (b.off hind: led 2f: rdn & wknd 3f out)........2½ **12** 25/1 41 19
**Superensis** (JohnBerry) **6-9-8** RMcGhin(14) (trckd ldrs 7f: sn wknd)........3½ **13** 25/1 40 24
**Anaxagoras** (SGollings) **6-9-3** VHalliday(12) (bkwd: tckd ldrs tl wknd wl over 2f out)........nk **14** 33/1 35 19
3878[5] **Jabaroot (IRE) (24)** (RMMcKellar) **5-8-10**(7) JMcAuley(13) (a in rr: t.o)........8 **15** 25/1 22 6
2895[7] **Tom Swift (IRE) (56)** (RCSpicer) **3-8-11** RPerham(16) (a in rr: t.o)........2 **16** 33/1 19 —
3944[15] **Griffin's Girl (30)** (PMooney) **4-8-12** CScally(15) (plld hrd: prom tl wknd over 3f out: t.o)........2½ **17** 50/1 10 —
4110[10] **Chili-Wah-Wah** (CASmith) **5-9-3** DHarrison(8) (bit bkwd: a bhd: t.o)........2½ **18** 50/1 11 —
(SP 129.9%) **18 Rn**

**2m 6.9** (2.50) CSF £63.57 TOTE £13.70: £2.70 £2.70 £4.00 (£38.10) Trio £197.50 OWNER The Spotted Hats (NEWMARKET) BRED Grangemore Stud
WEIGHT FOR AGE 3yo-6lb
Bt in 5,250 gns
**3780 El Bardador (IRE)** stepped down in grade to open his account with a comfortable win, and the first-time blinkers worked the oracle. (12/1)
**3991 Roi de la Mer (IRE)**, skilfully settled off the pace, came to win his race entering the final furlong, but the winner easily had the legs of him when the chips were down. (9/2)
**Blaze of Oak (USA)**, still to win a race, performed much better in this lower grade, and his turn will come. (14/1)
**4070 Mcgillycuddy Reeks (IRE)** has not won for over two years, but she did have last year off, and she is only just getting back to complete fitness. (25/1)
**4217 Irish Sea (USA)** filled the same position in a better-class event less than twenty-four hours earlier and, though he gave of his best, could never land a blow. (10/1: op 4/1)
**3970 Shabanaz** was making hard work of it from a long way out and, though he did stay on, was never a serious factor. (13/8)
**Arak (USA)**, returning after a long absence, was walked to the start. Once in action, he helped share the pace until blowing up and being eased from below the distance. (14/1: op 8/1)

## 4238 GOLDEN JUBILEE CHALLENGE TROPHY H'CAP (0-90) (3-Y.O+) (Class C)

2-30 (2-32) **1m 2f 21y** £6,378.50 (£1,910.00: £917.00: £420.50) Stalls: High GOING minus 0.44 sec per fur (F)

SP RR SF

3447[11] **Secret Aly (CAN) (80)** (CEBrittain) **6-9-9** MRoberts(9) (lw: hld up & bhd: hdwy & swtchd rt over 2f out: r.o strly to ld nr fin)........— **1** 14/1 90 63
3134[3] **Rory (74)** (MrsJCecil) **5-8-12**(5) AmandaSanders(3) (hld up: hdwy over 3f out: led ins fnl f: hdd cl home)........½ **2** 8/1[2] 83 56
**Opulent (72)** (CADwyer) **5-8-8**(7) JoHunnam(5) (trckd ldrs: outpcd 3f out: swtchd ins: fin wl)........nk **3** 33/1 81 54
2621[17] **Al Shadeedah (USA) (82)** (LMCumani) **3-9-5** LDettori(2) (chsd ldrs: led wl over 1f out tl ins fnl f: btn whn hmpd nr fin)........¾ **4** 9/1[3] 90 57
3447[9] **Sadler's Walk (73)** (GWragg) **5-9-2b** MHills(16) (hld up: hdwy to jn ldrs 2f out: rdn & unable qckn ins fnl f)........½ **5** 12/1 80 53
3981* **Darling Clover (78)** (RBastiman) **4-9-2**(5) HBastiman(1) (trckd ldrs: ev ch 2f out: sn rdn: one pce)........1½ **6** 11/1 82 55
3623[13] **Chabrol (CAN) (67)** (TTClement) **3-7-13**(5) ADaly(4) (led 2f: rdn over 1f out: one pce)........hd **7** 20/1 71 38
3770[2] **Dilazar (USA) (79)** (JRFanshawe) **3-9-2** DHarrison(14) (b.hind: led after 2f tl wl over 1f out: one pce)........1¼ **8** 12/1 81 48
3942[8] **Roi du Nord (FR) (70)** (SWCampion) **4-8-13** RCochrane(6) (prom: hrd rdn over 1f out: grad wknd)........s.h **9** 33/1 72 45
4067[13] **Gold Blade (71)** (JPearce) **7-9-0** MWigham(11) (s.s: a bhd)........1¾ **10** 16/1 70 43
3938[2] **Princess Danielle (61)** (WRMuir) **4-8-4** JQuinn(10) (a in rr)........½ **11** 11/1 60 33
3970* **Action Jackson (56)** (BJMcMath) **4-7-6**(7) RFfrench(8) (prom: ev ch 3f out: sn rdn & wknd)........2½ **12** 12/1 51 24
3148[W] **Jezyah (USA) (80)** (RWArmstrong) **3-9-3** RPrice(15) (bit bkwd: prom tl wknd wl over 1f out)........3½ **13** 20/1 69 36
3981[5] **Myfontaine (65)** (KTIvory) **9-8-8** GBardwell(13) (b: hld up in rr: effrt & rdn over 3f out: no imp)........1 **14** 11/1 53 26
3815* **King's Academy (IRE) (86)** (HRACecil) **3-9-9** WRyan(12) (lw: hld up: pushed along 4f out: no imp)........2½ **15** 100/30[1] 70 37
3947[18] **Vindaloo (82)** (JLHarris) **4-9-11** RHughes(7) (hld up in rr: effrt 3f out: sn rdn & no imp: eased: t.o)........dist **16** 33/1 — —
(SP 123.2%) **16 Rn**

**2m 5.4** (1.00) CSF £112.72 CT £3,284.07 TOTE £15.70: £3.00 £3.20 £12.70 £3.00 (£51.40) Trio Not won; £765.26 to Ayr 19/9/96 OWNER Mr B. H. Voak (NEWMARKET) BRED Northern Equine Thoroughbred Productions
WEIGHT FOR AGE 3yo-6lb
STEWARDS' ENQUIRY Sanders susp. 27/9/96 (careless riding)
**2299 Secret Aly (CAN)** responded to a magical ride from Michael Roberts on his return from injury to grab the lead in the shadow of the post for a well deserved success. (14/1)
**3134 Rory** did everything right and looked to have timed his effort to perfection when leading inside the final furlong, but the sustained late swoop of the winner just proved too much. He deserves another chance after such a good effort. (8/1)
**Opulent**, an ex-Irish gelding having his first run in this country, ran exceptionally well considering he did not look fully wound up. When he gets the ground conditions in his favour, he can soon make amends. (33/1)
**2188* Al Shadeedah (USA)**, always in the action, did look to be labouring to hold her pitch when squeezed for room inside the last 50 yards. (9/1)
**766 Sadler's Walk**, very lightly-raced this term, produced a determined challenge entering the last quarter-mile and only missed out in the battle to the finish. He is ready to return to form. (12/1)
**3981* Darling Clover**, having her first outing for her new connections, did not fail for the want of trying, and will find easier races than this. (11/1)
**3357* Chabrol (CAN)** ran well all the way and there would seem to be more success in the pipe-line. (20/1)
**3981 Myfontaine** (11/1: 8/1-12/1)
**3815* King's Academy (IRE)** ran very moderately, and was being bustled along to no effect from the turn into the straight. (100/30)

## 4239 DANNY WRIGHT MEMORIAL CONDITIONS STKS (3-Y.O+) (Class C)

3-00 (3-01) **6f 3y** £6,780.20 (£1,857.80) Stalls: Low GOING minus 0.44 sec per fur (F)

| | | | | SP | RR | SF |
|---|---|---|---|---|---|---|
| 3759[8] | **Russian Revival (USA) (109)** (SbinSuroor) **3-8-11** LDettori(1) (mde all: qckmd appr fnl f: sn clr) | — | 1 | 7/4[2] | 116? | 14 |
| 4051[7] | **Sergeyev (IRE) (112)** (RHannon) **4-8-13** RHughes(2) (lw: plld hrd: hld up: rdn over 1f out: sn outpcd) | 5 | 2 | 1/2[1] | 103 | 3 |
| | | | | (SP 103.0%) | **2 Rn** | |

**1m 14.1** (3.20) TOTE £2.00 OWNER Godolphin (NEWMARKET) BRED Swettenham Stud
WEIGHT FOR AGE 3yo-2lb

**3132 Russian Revival (USA)** had no option but to make the running, but he is a six-furlong specialist and the speed he showed to forge clear approaching the final furlong left no doubt who was boss. (7/4)

**4051 Sergeyev (IRE)** runs more often over longer trips now and, though he did take a bit of settling, quite simply had no answer to the finishing speed of the winner. (1/2)

## 4240 SHADWELL STUD SERIES APPRENTICE H'CAP (0-70) (3-Y.O+) (Class E)

3-30 (3-32) **7f 3y** £3,113.00 (£944.00: £462.00: £221.00) Stalls: Low GOING minus 0.44 sec per fur (F)

| | | | | SP | RR | SF |
|---|---|---|---|---|---|---|
| 4088[10] | **Don Pepe (62)** (RBoss) **5-9-6** ADaly(11) (hld up gng wl: hdwy over 1f out: ev ch ins fnl f: unable qckn: fin 2nd, 1½l: awrdd r) | — | 1 | 8/1[2] | 71 | 49 |
| 3985[9] | **Eurobox Boy (56)** (APJarvis) **3-8-6**(5) CCarver(16) (lw: led tl hdd & no ex ins fnl f: fin 3rd, hd: plcd 2nd) | | 2 | 8/1[2] | 64 | 39 |
| *4078*[12] | **Johnnie the Joker (50)** (JPLeigh) **5-8-8b** PFessey(10) (a.p: rdn over 1f out: kpt on fnl f: fin 4th, 1¼l: plcd 3rd) | | 3 | 16/1 | 56 | 34 |
| 3274[7] | **Irrepressible (IRE) (45)** (RJHodges) **5-8-3** PPMurphy(12) (trckd ldrs: rdn over 1f out: sltly hmpd jst ins fnl f: nt rcvr: fin 5th, 1l: plcd 4th) | | 4 | 14/1 | 48 | 26 |
| 688[12] | **East Barns (IRE) (38)** (SGollings) **8-7-7b**(3) RFfrench(9) (bkwd: a.p: rdn over 1f out: one pce: fin 6th, s.h: plcd 5th) | | 5 | 33/1 | 41 | 19 |
| 3991[3] | **Mr Cube (IRE) (50)** (JMBradley) **6-8-3b**(5) CLowther(6) (hdwy over 1f out: nvr nrr) | hd | 7 | 8/1[2] | 53 | 31 |
| 4098[8] | **Awesome Venture (51)** (MCChapman) **6-8-9** DGriffiths(4) (trckd ldrs: rdn over 1f out: one pce) | ¾ | 8 | 12/1[3] | 52 | 30 |
| *3877*[7] | **Four of Spades (52)** (RJHodges) **5-8-10v** AmandaSanders(1) (hld up: hdwy 3f out: sn ev ch: rdn & wknd over 1f out) | nk | 9 | 16/1 | 53 | 31 |
| 4098[4] | **Ivor's Deed (54)** (CFWall) **3-8-4**(5) PClarke(14) (lw: hld up: effrt & n.m.r appr fnl f: n.d) | ¾ | 10 | 9/2[1] | 53 | 28 |
| 4186[5] | **Racing Telegraph (40)** (CNAllen) **6-7-12** IonaWands(3) (mid div tl wknd 2f out) | 1½ | 11 | 16/1 | 35 | 13 |
| 2412[8] | **Ahjay (46)** (GLMoore) **6-8-4**ow5 JDSmith(13) (a in rr) | 3½ | 12 | 25/1 | 33 | 6 |
| 3977* | **Just Millie (USA) (58)** (JEBanks) **3-8-13v** GFaulkner(5) (a in rr) | ½ | 13 | 8/1[2] | 44 | 19 |
| 3852[5] | **Fairly Sure (IRE) (47)** (NEBerry) **3-8-2** JoHunnam(2) (a bhd) | ¾ | 14 | 16/1 | 32 | 7 |
| 3967[8] | **Super Park (57)** (JPearce) **4-9-1** HBastiman(7) (prom: rdn 2f out: btn whn hmpd wl over 1f out) | 2 | 15 | 20/1 | 37 | 15 |
| 4082[11] | **Shermood (41)** (KTIvory) **3-7-10** MBaird(8) (b: a bhd) | 4 | 16 | 20/1 | 12 | — |
| 3833[10] | **Ertlon (70)** (CEBrittain) **6-9-9**(5) JGotobed(15) (hld up & bhd: rapid hdwy & barged thro to ld ins fnl f: sn clr: fin 1st: disq: plcd last) | | D | 12/1[3] | 82 | 60 |
| | | | | (SP 124.5%) | **16 Rn** | |

**1m 25.4** (1.20) CSF £66.49 CT £932.95 TOTE £9.20: £2.60 £3.00 £2.90 £4.30 (£31.60) Trio £368.60 OWNER Mrs Elaine Aird (NEWMARKET) BRED Patrick Eddery Ltd
LONG HANDICAP Shermood 7-8
WEIGHT FOR AGE 3yo-3lb
STEWARDS' ENQUIRY Gotobed susp. 27-30/9/96 (irresponsible riding)

**3758 Don Pepe**, put back over possibly his ideal trip, was most fortunate to be awarded the race in the Stewards' Room, for Ertlon beat him for toe in no uncertain terms. (8/1)

**3655* Eurobox Boy** did his best to make it all but, over a trip short of his best, was tapped for speed in the last 200 yards. (8/1)

**3419 Johnnie the Joker** does most of his racing on the All-Weather nowadays, but he was far from disgraced here and he can act on livelier ground. (16/1)

**2994 Irrepressible (IRE)**, looking very wintry in his coat, did his best to hold the strong-finishing Ertlon in on the rail from below the distance, but he was knocked out of his stride when that rival surged past, and at least gained reward for doing so. (14/1)

**East Barns (IRE)** looked as fat as a bull after four months out of action, but he performed with credit and can only improve on this. (33/1)

**3991 Mr Cube (IRE)** was unable to get himself into contention, but he was into his stride nearing the finish and is no back-number yet. (8/1)

**4098 Ivor's Deed** usually comes from behind, but he was never really travelling on this occasion and the fact he was denied a clear run could not have had much bearing on such a poor display. (9/2)

**3265 Ertlon**, patiently waiting for an opening on the stands' rail, was forced to barge his way through to take command inside the final furlong and, in winning going away, was the unfortunate one to lose out in the end. Compensation awaits. (12/1)

## 4241 E.B.F. HALVERGATE MAIDEN STKS (2-Y.O F) (Class D)

4-05 (4-05) **6f 3y** £3,987.55 (£1,194.40: £573.70: £263.35) Stalls: Low GOING minus 0.44 sec per fur (F)

| | | | | SP | RR | SF |
|---|---|---|---|---|---|---|
| | **The Faraway Tree** (GWragg) **2-8-11** MHills(4) (w'like: leggy: hld up in tch: hdwy 2f out: led ins fnl f: qcknd clr) | — | 1 | 100/30[1] | 80+ | 27 |
| 3706[7] | **Our Way** (CEBrittain) **2-8-11** MRoberts(5) (mde most tl ins fnl f) | 2 | 2 | 12/1 | 75 | 22 |
| 3675[4] | **Thahabyah (USA)** (HThomsonJones) **2-8-11** RHills(3) (hld up in tch: hdwy ½-wy: ev ch 1f out: unable qckn) | 1¼ | 3 | 7/2[2] | 71 | 18 |
| 3859[3] | **City Gambler** (GCBravery) **2-8-11** NDay(9) (lw: trckd ldrs: rdn over 1f out: one pce) | 1¾ | 4 | 16/1 | 67 | 14 |
| | **Star Entry** (WJarvis) **2-8-11** WRyan(10) (neat: scope: bit bkwd: s.i.s: bhd tl sme hdwy appr fnl f) | 3½ | 5 | 12/1 | 57+ | 4 |
| | **Rochea** (WJHaggas) **2-8-11** RMcGhin(8) (cmpt: bkwd: prom tl wknd over 1f out) | hd | 6 | 33/1 | 57 | 4 |
| | **Missfortuna** (SirMarkPrescott) **2-8-11** CNutter(7) (w'like: str: bkwd: s.s: a bhd) | 2½ | 7 | 14/1 | 51 | — |
| 3259[21] | **Biba (IRE)** (RBoss) **2-8-6**(5) GFaulkner(6) (prom tl wknd wl over 1f out) | ¾ | 8 | 33/1 | 49 | — |
| | **Mythical** (SirMarkPrescott) **2-8-11** RPerham(2) (w'like: scope: bkwd: a bhd & outpcd) | ½ | 9 | 14/1 | 47 | — |
| 3988[4] | **Wing And A Prayer (IRE)** (RHannon) **2-8-11** RHughes(12) (w ldrs 4f: wknd qckly) | s.h | 10 | 9/2[3] | 47 | — |
| | **Eurolink Profile** (LMCumani) **2-8-11** LDettori(1) (leggy: unf: hld up: hdwy 3f out: wknd over 1f out: eased) | 1 | 11 | 7/2[2] | 44 | — |
| 3963[7] | **Fontcaudette (IRE)** (JEBanks) **2-8-11** JQuinn(11) (sn bhd & outpcd) | 1½ | 12 | 33/1 | 40 | — |
| | | | | (SP 129.1%) | **12 Rn** | |

**1m 13.1** (2.20) CSF £43.08 TOTE £4.90: £1.70 £1.90 £1.60 (£23.40) Trio £38.00 OWNER Mr A. E. Oppenheimer (NEWMARKET) BRED Hascombe and Valiant Studs

**The Faraway Tree**, a May filly from a useful winning family, turned in an impressive racecourse debut and she may well be even more effective over a longer trip. (100/30: op 2/1)
**3438 Our Way** showed how much she is progressing with a brave attempt to make all, and she will not be long in getting off the mark. (12/1)
**3675 Thahabyah (USA)** still looked as though she had a little bit left to work on, and the way she ran only serves to prove that point. (7/2)
**3859 City Gambler**, a free-running filly, pushed the pace all the way, but could not produce anything extra when the final battle really got under way. (16/1)
**Star Entry**, sluggish leaving the stalls and soon well outpaced, caught the eye, picking up steadily in the latter stages. She will be all the wiser next time. (12/1: 7/1-14/1)
**Rochea**, a late filly very much in need of the run and the experience, was struggling approaching the final furlong, but she would have learnt plenty here. (33/1)
**Missfortuna** (14/1: 8/1-16/1)
**Eurolink Profile** (7/2: op 2/1)

## 4242 E.B.F. FLEGGBOROUGH MAIDEN STKS (2-Y.O) (Class D)

4-35 (4-38) **7f 3y** £4,201.40 (£1,260.20: £606.60: £279.80) Stalls: Low GOING minus 0.44 sec per fur (F)

| | | | | SP | RR | SF |
|---|---|---|---|---|---|---|
| 3994[2] | **Harry Wolton** (HRACecil) **2-9-0** WRyan(2) (hld up: hdwy 3f out: led 1f out: r.o wl) | — | **1** | 5/4[1] | 82+ | 45 |
| | **Chivalric (IRE)** (DRLoder) **2-9-0** LDettori(16) (lt-f: unf: a.p: led over 2f out to 1f out: one pce) | 1¼ | **2** | 4/1[2] | 79 | 42 |
| | **Superbelle** (MAJarvis) **2-8-9** EmmaO'Gorman(14) (leggy: lt-f: trckd ldrs: kpt on one pce fnl f) | 3½ | **3** | 40/1 | 66 | 29 |
| 3764[5] | **Pretty Sharp** (APJarvis) **2-8-9** FNorton(10) (hld up: hdwy 2f out: styd on wl ins fnl f) | 1¾ | **4** | 50/1 | 62 | 25 |
| 3837[4] | **Noble Investment** (JMPEustace) **2-9-0** RCochrane(17) (trckd ldrs: outpcd 2f out: styd on u.p appr fnl f) | s.h | **5** | 10/1[3] | 67 | 30 |
| 2195[10] | **Harmony Hall** (JRFanshawe) **2-9-0** DBiggs(7) (b.hind: bkwd: prom: drvn along 3f out: one pce) | nk | **6** | 40/1 | 66 | 29 |
| 3682[9] | **Bold Words (CAN)** (EALDunlop) **2-9-0** RHughes(11) (bit bkwd: s.s: hdwy ½-wy: wknd over 1f out) | 1¾ | **7** | 40/1 | 62 | 25 |
| | **Travelmate** (JRFanshawe) **2-9-0** DHarrison(3) (leggy: unf: bit bkwd: nvr trbld ldrs) | ¾ | **8** | 33/1 | 61 | 24 |
| 3919[4] | **Gentleman's Word (USA)** (MRStoute) **2-9-0** KBradshaw(9) (mid div: no hdwy fnl 2f) | ½ | **9** | 14/1 | 60 | 23 |
| 4041[3] | **Tirage (76)** (CEBrittain) **2-9-0** MRoberts(1) (hdwy over 3f out: sn hrd drvn: wknd wl over 1f out) | 1¼ | **10** | 20/1 | 57 | 20 |
| 3407[5] | **Silk St John** (MJRyan) **2-9-0** RPrice(6) (a bhd) | 2 | **11** | 20/1 | 52 | 15 |
| | **Hadidi** (DMorley) **2-9-0** RHills(4) (w'like: scope: bkwd: s.i.s: a bhd) | nk | **12** | 16/1 | 51 | 14 |
| | **Red Guard** (GWragg) **2-9-0** MHills(8) (w'like: leggy: a in rr) | 1½ | **13** | 10/1[3] | 48 | 11 |
| 4171a[6] | **Lajatta** (LMCumani) **2-8-7**(7) RFfrench(13) (bit bkwd: prom 4f) | 2 | **14** | 33/1 | 43 | 6 |
| 4104[10] | **Perfect Angel (IRE)** (MHTompkins) **2-8-9** NDay(5) (a bhd) | nk | **15** | 40/1 | 38 | 1 |
| 3701[6] | **Mujazi (IRE)** (RWArmstrong) **2-9-0b1** RPerham(12) (plld hrd: w ldr over 4f: sn wknd) | ¾ | **16** | 40/1 | 41 | 4 |
| 3809[8] | **Priory Gardens (IRE)** (JMBradley) **2-9-0** JQuinn(15) (led tl hdd & wknd over 2f out: t.o) | 23 | **17** | 50/1 | — | — |
| | | | | (SP 126.7%) | **17 Rn** | |

**1m 25.6** (1.40) CSF £6.88 TOTE £1.80: £1.10 £1.70 £13.40 (£4.00) Trio £284.80; £52.16 to Ayr 19/9/96 OWNER Old Road Securities Plc (NEWMARKET) BRED T. D. Holland-Martin

**3994 Harry Wolton** confirmed the promise he showed on his debut at York with a very comfortably-gained success, and this could just be the start. (5/4)
**Chivalric (IRE)**, a half-brother to four winners, is not much to look at, but he knew what was needed and, if he had not come up against one as useful as the winner, there would be no doubting his ability. (4/1)
**Superbelle** could not match strides with the colts in the run to the line, but she did nothing wrong and the experience will not be lost. (40/1)
**3764 Pretty Sharp** is getting to realise what the game is all about, and she should not be long in improving on this good effort. (50/1)
**3837 Noble Investment** failed to hold his pitch when the pace lifted two furlongs out, but he was getting down to serious work towards the finish and will find his way. (10/1: 12/1-8/1)
**Harmony Hall** looked decidedly burly after three months on the sidelines, but he did not fare badly and looks to have ability. (40/1)
**Red Guard** (10/1: 7/1-12/1)

## 4243 NORTH SEA H'CAP (0-80) (3-Y.O+) (Class D)

5-10 (5-10) **1m 3y** £4,159.05 (£1,244.40: £596.70: £272.85) Stalls: Low GOING minus 0.44 sec per fur (F)

| | | | | SP | RR | SF |
|---|---|---|---|---|---|---|
| 3805[3] | **Sue's Return (76)** (APJarvis) **4-10-0** RHughes(12) (lw: hld up: hdwy 2f out: hrd rdn to ld cl home) | — | **1** | 9/2[1] | 87 | 45 |
| 3852[4] | **Missile Toe (IRE) (58)** (JEBanks) **3-8-6** NDay(13) (lw: hld up: hdwy 3f out: led over 1f out tl ct post) | hd | **2** | 7/1[2] | 69 | 23 |
| 3861[3] | **Talathath (FR) (71)** (CADwyer) **4-9-2v**(7) JoHunnam(9) (a.p: jnd ldrs 3f out: hrd drvn & no ex fnl f) | 1¼ | **3** | 14/1 | 79 | 37 |
| 2001[5] | **Lituus (USA) (77)** (JHMGosden) **3-9-11** LDettori(10) (trckd ldrs: rdn 2f out: kpt on same pce) | 1¼ | **4** | 8/1[3] | 83 | 37 |
| 4071[4] | **Kazimiera (IRE) (65)** (CWCElsey) **3-8-8**(5) PFessey(8) (prom: led over 2f out tl over 1f out: one pce) | 1¼ | **5** | 11/1 | 68 | 22 |
| 4184[5] | **Ron's Secret (71)** (JWPayne) **4-9-9b** RCochrane(2) (lw: in tch: rdn 3f out: kpt on one pce) | hd | **6** | 8/1[3] | 74 | 32 |
| 3805[8] | **Confronter (71)** (SDow) **7-9-9** MRoberts(3) (racd centre: prom: rdn over 2f out: sn wknd) | 2 | **7** | 10/1 | 70 | 28 |
| 4053[4] | **Paojiunic (IRE) (68)** (LMCumani) **3-8-9**(7) RFfrench(1) (nvr trbld ldrs) | nk | **8** | 7/1[2] | 67 | 21 |
| 3981[7] | **Toujours Riviera (75)** (JPearce) **6-9-13** GBardwell(6) (trckd ldrs: rdn over 2f out: sn btn) | 1¼ | **9** | 16/1 | 71 | 29 |
| 3861[2] | **Sooty Tern (69)** (JMBradley) **9-9-0**(7) CLowther(7) (led 2f: wknd over 2f out) | 4 | **10** | 14/1 | 57 | 15 |
| 4073[19] | **Access Adventurer (IRE) (66)** (RBoss) **5-8-13b1**(5) GFaulkner(5) (led after 2f tl over 2f out: sn rdn & wknd) | nk | **11** | 25/1 | 53 | 11 |
| 4071[3] | **Desert Lynx (IRE) (70)** (TRWatson) **3-9-4** DHarrison(4) (a in rr: t.o) | 5 | **12** | 10/1 | 48 | 2 |
| 3403* | **Gloriana (68)** (LadyHerries) **4-9-6** JQuinn(11) (hld up: effrt wl over 2f out: no imp: t.o) | nk | **13** | 8/1[3] | 45 | 3 |
| | | | | (SP 126.1%) | **13 Rn** | |

**1m 38.1** (2.80) CSF £35.59 CT £303.78 TOTE £6.20: £2.40 £2.60 £3.30 (£31.30) Trio £315.80 OWNER Mr A. L. R. Morton (ASTON UPTHORPE) BRED J. R. C. and Mrs Wren
WEIGHT FOR AGE 3yo-4lb

**3805 Sue's Return**, winning her first race in two years, produced a brave display under topweight, answering her rider's every call to get up on the line. (9/2)
**3852 Missile Toe (IRE)** set sail for home inside the distance and soon had the measure of his nearest pursuers but, hard as he tried, the post arrived a stride too late. (7/1: op 14/1)
**3861 Talathath (FR)**, engaged in a fierce battle for the last two furlongs, had to admit his measure had been taken inside the distance. (14/1)
**2001 Lituus (USA)** is slowly coming to hand and that initial success can not be far away. (8/1)
**4071 Kazimiera (IRE)** tries her heart out, but she remains a maiden, and luck must favour her one of these days. (11/1)
**4184 Ron's Secret** was going nowhere three furlongs out and looked likely to finish in the ruck, but she did decide to stay on in the latter stages, and she could be worth keeping in mind when the ground eases. (8/1)

T/Plpt: £463.90 (23.09 Tckts). T/Qdpt: £23.40 (27.15 Tckts). IM

# 3675-AYR (L-H) (Good to firm)
## Thursday September 19th

WEATHER: fine WIND: fresh half bhd

## 4244 MOTHERWELL BRIDGE SUPPORT MACMILLAN NURSES (S) STKS (2-Y.O) (Class E)

2-10 (2-12) **5f** £3,947.50 (£1,180.00: £565.00: £257.50) Stalls: High GOING minus 0.33 sec per fur (GF)

| | Horse / details | Dist | Pos | SP | RR | SF |
|---|---|---|---|---|---|---|
| 4195[5] | **Little Blue (IRE) (61)** (TDEasterby) **2-8-11** MBirch(12) (lw: mde all: rdn & hung lft over 1f out: styd on) | — | **1** | 15/2 | 70 | 30 |
| 4087[6] | **Gold Edge** (MRChannon) **2-8-6** KDarley(15) (lw: chsd ldrs: hmpd & swtchd ½-wy: ev ch over 1f out: nt qckn) | 1 | **2** | 5/1[1] | 62 | 22 |
| 3659[3] | **Nightingale Song (76)** (MartynMeade) **2-8-4**(7) DSweeney(7) (a in tch: hdwy & ev ch over 1f out: nt qckn) | 2 | **3** | 5/1[1] | 60 | 20 |
| 3838[3] | **Robec Girl (IRE) (66)** (JBerry) **2-8-11** JCarroll(9) (mid div: styd on wl appr fnl f: nvr nr to chal) | 1¼ | **4** | 12/1 | 56 | 16 |
| 3512[8] | **Rivonia (USA) (65)** (MrsJRRamsden) **2-8-6** KFallon(13) (lw: mid div: sn drvn along: styd on appr fnl f: nt rch ldrs) | 1½ | **5** | 5/1[1] | 47 | 7 |
| | **Waltz Time** (MissLAPerratt) **2-8-6** GCarter(16) (bit bkwd: unruly s: s.s: wl bhd tl styd on appr fnl f) | nk | **6** | 20/1 | 46 | 6 |
| 4043[9] | **La Dolce Vita** (TDBarron) **2-8-6** JFortune(1) (chsd ldrs to ½-wy: grad wknd) | 1½ | **7** | 7/1[3] | 41 | 1 |
| 3869[3] | **Mr Fortywinks (IRE) (67)** (JLEyre) **2-8-8**(3) FLynch(4) (outpcd ½-wy: n.d after) | nk | **8** | 12/1 | 45 | 5 |
| | **Pupil Master (IRE)** (DenysSmith) **2-8-11** LCharnock(8) (leggy: sn outpcd: sme hdwy fnl f: n.d) | nk | **9** | 25/1 | 44 | 4 |
| 3336[6] | **Impulsion (IRE) (67)** (RHannon) **2-8-11** JReid(14) (w wnr tl wknd 2f out) | nk | **10** | 6/1[2] | 43 | 3 |
| 3879[2] | **Melbourne Princess (64)** (RMWhitaker) **2-8-6** ACulhane(2) (chsd ldrs: outpcd ½-wy: sn lost pl) | ½ | **11** | 14/1 | 36 | — |
| | **Stakis Casinos Lad (IRE)** (MJohnston) **2-8-11** JWeaver(11) (leggy: unf: s.i.s: a bhd) | 2½ | **12** | 20/1 | 33 | — |
| *4093*[15] | **Shotley Princess (48)** (NBycroft) **2-8-6** TWilliams(5) (chsd ldr 3f: wknd qckly) | 2 | **13** | 100/1 | 22 | — |
| 4043[12] | **Miss Fugit Penance** (PDEvans) **2-8-6** JFEgan(3) (mid div: drvn along ½-wy: sn bhd) | ½ | **14** | 33/1 | 20 | — |
| 3840[12] | **Cantsaynowt (40)** (RMMcKellar) **2-7-13**(7) KSked(6) (mid div: rdn ½-wy: sn bhd) | nk | **15** | 50/1 | 19 | — |
| | **Jive Boogie** (NBycroft) **2-8-4b**[1](7) JBramhill(10) (bkwd: s.s: a wl bhd: t.o) | 30 | **16** | 100/1 | — | — |

(SP 130.9%) **16 Rn**

**59.09 secs** (2.09) CSF £44.83 TOTE £9.90: £3.10 £1.80 £2.00 (£33.20) Trio £43.00 OWNER Ryedale Associates (MALTON) BRED A. T. Robinson

No bid

**4195 Little Blue (IRE)** is certainly going the right way and does not lack speed. Despite hanging out towards the centre, she never looked in any danger in the final furlong. (15/2)

**4087 Gold Edge** showed a moderate action going down. Short of room and forced to switch at halfway, she was almost upsides coming to the final furlong but could then do no more. Easier ground would help her cause. (5/1)

**3659 Nightingale Song**, racing towards the centre, drew almost upsides over a furlong out but could then do no more. Five furlongs seems to suit her best. (5/1)

**3838 Robec Girl (IRE)** did not get going until too late and needs further. (12/1)

**3512 Rivonia (USA)**, dropping back more than two furlongs, was run off her feet. Staying on at the finish, she is not a five-furlong filly. (5/1)

**Waltz Time**, who gave a lot of trouble at the stalls, missed the break and came from a long way back. Provided temperament does not get the better of her, she should improve. (20/1)

**La Dolce Vita** was struggling from halfway from a poor draw. (7/1)

**3869 Mr Fortywinks (IRE)** (12/1: tchd 141/)

## 4245 HOLIDAY IN AYRSHIRE & ARRAN E.B.F. MAIDEN STKS (2-Y.O) (Class D)

2-40 (2-42) **7f** £4,581.00 (£1,368.00: £654.00: £297.00) Stalls: High GOING minus 0.33 sec per fur (GF)

| | Horse / details | Dist | Pos | SP | RR | SF |
|---|---|---|---|---|---|---|
| 2416[3] | **Brave Montgomerie** (MissLAPerratt) **2-9-0** JCarroll(4) (sn trckng ldrs: nt clr run over 1f out: r.o wl u.p to ld nr fin) | — | **1** | 5/1[3] | 77 | 6 |
| 3237[4] | **Canadian Fantasy (83)** (MJohnston) **2-9-0** JWeaver(6) (led 2f: led over 1f out: hrd rdn & wandered: hdd cl home) | 1¼ | **2** | 2/1[2] | 74 | 3 |
| | **Mystique Air (IRE)** (EWeymes) **2-8-9** LCharnock(5) (neat: sn trckng ldrs: drvn along & outpcd over 3f out: hdwy & ev ch over 1f out: nt qckn) | 1 | **3** | 8/1 | 67 | — |
| 2720[2] | **Jackson Falls** (TDEasterby) **2-9-0** MBirch(2) (lw: trckd ldrs: led over 2f out tl over 1f out: wknd ins fnl f) | 3 | **4** | 11/8[1] | 65 | — |
| | **As-Is** (MJohnston) **2-9-0** KDarley(3) (neat: outpcd & drvn along 4f out: n.d) | 5 | **5** | 12/1 | 54 | — |
| | **Swiftway** (KWHogg) **2-9-0** SDWilliams(1) (w'like: bit bkwd: s.s: sme hdwy ½-wy: sn wl outpcd) | 3 | **6** | 50/1 | 47 | — |
| 3880[9] | **Chanson d'Amour (IRE) (54)** (MissLAPerratt) **2-8-6**(3) DWright(7) (trckd ldrs: led after 2f tl over 2f out: wknd qckly over 1f out) | 4 | **7** | 50/1 | 33 | — |

(SP 114.8%) **7 Rn**

**1m 29.58** (5.58) CSF £15.05 TOTE £6.90: £2.20 £1.70 (£8.80) OWNER Mr C. J. C. McLaren (AYR) BRED P. and Mrs Venner

**2416 Brave Montgomerie**, absent for eleven weeks, overcame difficulty in running to get up near the line. Open to further improvement, he looks a likely type for a mile nursery. (5/1)

**3237 Canadian Fantasy**, who ran unaccountably badly on his previous outing almost seven weeks ago, carried his head high, hung both ways and swished his tail under pressure, and was worried out of it near the line. He is clearly one to have reservations about. (2/1: 6/4-9/4)

**Mystique Air (IRE)**, who looked as if the outing would do her good, moved up on the outside on the turn for home. Running green and tapped for toe, she recovered to have every chance but could then find no more. The outing and experience will bring her on a good deal and she should not be hard to place. (8/1)

**2720 Jackson Falls**, absent for over two months, went to post very keenly and, after hitting the front, his stamina gave out in the final 150 yards. The way he runs, six might suit him better. (11/8)

**As-Is** needs more time yet. (12/1)

## 4246 LADBROKE SPRINT H'CAP (0-80) (3-Y.O+) (Class D)

3-10 (3-13) **5f** £7,096.00 (£2,128.00: £1,024.00: £472.00) Stalls: High GOING minus 0.33 sec per fur (GF)

| | Horse / details | Dist | Pos | SP | RR | SF |
|---|---|---|---|---|---|---|
| 3932[13] | **Able Sheriff (56)** (MWEasterby) **4-8-5b** ACulhane(15) (chsd ldrs: styd on wl u.p fnl f: led nr fin) | — | **1** | 16/1 | 64 | 43 |
| *4081** | **Pageboy (65)** (PCHaslam) **7-9-0** JFortune(17) (lw: chsd ldrs: led over 1f out tl nr fin) | ½ | **2** | 12/1[3] | 71 | 50 |
| 3937[5] | **Amron (55)** (JBerry) **9-8-4** GCarter(16) (sn outpcd & bhd: hdwy 2f out: styd on wl ins fnl f) | ¾ | **3** | 16/1 | 59 | 38 |
| 4088[14] | **Miss Bigwig (68)** (JBerry) **3-8-11**(5) PFessey(20) (led tl over 1f out: kpt on same pce) | ½ | **4** | 20/1 | 70 | 48 |
| 3959* | **Natural Key (66)** (DHaydnJones) **3-9-0** AMackay(18) (lw: sn bhd & drvn along: hdwy 2f out: styd on wl ins fnl f) | hd | **5** | 12/1[3] | 68 | 46 |

| | | | | SP | RR | SF |
|---|---|---|---|---|---|---|
| 4058[11] | **Rich Glow (61)** (NBycroft) **5-8-10** JWeaver(11) (sn outpcd & bhd: hdwy over 1f out: r.o wl nr fin) | ¾ | **6** | 14/1 | 61 | 40 |
| 4198[11] | **Grand Chapeau (IRE) (61)** (DNicholls) **4-8-10** AlexGreaves(14) (w ldrs: nt qckn appr fnl f) | nk | **7** | 10/1[1] | 60 | 39 |
| 4205[4] | **Camionneur (IRE) (49)** (TDEasterby) **3-7-11b** JLowe(21) (s.s: bhd: hdwy over 1f out: styng on whn nt clr run ins fnl f) | s.h | **8** | 10/1[1] | 48 | 26 |
| 4205[7] | **Stephensons Rocket (56)** (DNicholls) **5-8-5b** MBirch(22) (lw: w ldr: wkng whn n.m.r 1f out) | s.h | **9** | 10/1[1] | 54 | 33 |
| 4180[5] | **Insider Trader (77)** (MrsJRRamsden) **5-9-12** KFallon(12) (trckd ldrs: effrt 2f out: kpt on same pce) | hd | **10** | 10/1[1] | 75 | 54 |
| 3957[4] | **Sunday Mail Too (IRE) (47)** (MissLAPerratt) **4-7-10** NKennedy(19) (in tch: styd on same pce fnl 2f) | hd | **11** | 25/1 | 45 | 24 |
| 3883[9] | **Six for Luck (58)** (DANolan) **4-8-7** GDuffield(3) (racd far side: chsd ldrs over 3f) | 1¼ | **12** | 40/1 | 52 | 31 |
| 3579[7] | **Pallium (IRE) (48)** (MrsAMNaughton) **8-7-11**ow1 TWilliams(4) (racd far side: sn bhd: hdwy over 1f out: styd on towards fin) | ¾ | **13** | 33/1 | 39 | 17 |
| 4180[6] | **Panther (IRE) (72)** (PDEvans) **6-9-7v** JFEgan(7) (lw: racd centre: sn drvn along & outpcd: sme hdwy 2f out: n.d) | s.h | **14** | 14/1 | 63 | 42 |
| 3883[3] | **Kalar (56)** (DWChapman) **7-8-5b** JCarroll(6) (led far side tl wknd ins fnl f) | hd | **15** | 14/1 | 47 | 26 |
| 3993[4] | **Pharaoh's Joy (61)** (JWPayne) **3-8-9** JReid(9) (racd centre: sn outpcd) | s.h | **16** | 11/1[2] | 52 | 30 |
| 3883[2] | **Johayro (61)** (JSGoldie) **3-8-4b**(5) GLee(5) (lw: w ldr far side tl wknd over 1f out) | 2 | **17** | 12/1[3] | 45 | 23 |
| 4180[13] | **Just Dissident (IRE) (62)** (RMWhitaker) **4-8-8**(3) FLynch(8) (racd centre: w ldrs tl wknd 2f out) | ½ | **18** | 20/1 | 45 | 24 |
| *4081*[5] | **Ramsey Hope (60)** (CWFairhurst) **3-8-8** LCharnock(1) (racd far side: sn wl outpcd) | 1¾ | **19** | 40/1 | 37 | 15 |
| 3932[8] | **Myttons Mistake (68)** (ABailey) **3-8-13**(3) DWright(10) (sn outpcd & bhd) | nk | **20** | 25/1 | 44 | 22 |
| 3883[6] | **Leading Princess (IRE) (52)** (MissLAPerratt) **5-7-8b**(7) JBramhill(13) (lw: chsd ldr 3f: sn wknd) | hd | **21** | 25/1 | 28 | 7 |
| 3844[12] | **Goretski (IRE) (70)** (NTinkler) **3-9-4** KDarley(2) (racd far side: bhd fnl 2f) | 5 | **22** | 25/1 | 30 | 8 |

(SP 132.3%) **22 Rn**

**58.02 secs** (1.02) CSF £185.03 CT £2,871.79 TOTE £27.30: £5.70 £2.50 £3.10 £10.30 (£168.50) Trio £711.00 OWNER Early Morning Breakfast Syndicate (SHERIFF HUTTON) BRED Theakston Stud

LONG HANDICAP Sunday Mail Too (IRE) 7-9

WEIGHT FOR AGE 3yo-1lb

**3482 Able Sheriff** proved most persistent under pressure and forced his head in front near the line. Nobody could say he did not deserve this success. (16/1)

**4081* Pageboy**, generally regarded as a six-furlong horse, was just edged out near the line. (12/1)

**3937 Amron**, on a losing run of twenty-eight, struggled to go the pace. When the ground eases, there is still time for him to find a race this back-end. (16/1)

**3465 Miss Bigwig**, who has slipped down the weights, proved very keen going to post and showed all her old speed. (20/1)

**3959* Natural Key** struggled badly to go the pace. Putting in all her best work at the finish, she is better suited by six. (12/1)

**3868 Rich Glow** invariably runs well here. (14/1)

**3973* Grand Chapeau (IRE)**, 6lb higher than at Pontefract, seemed to run up to his best. (10/1)

**4205 Camionneur (IRE)** missed the break and met trouble. He is by no means a reliable performer. (10/1)

**4205 Stephensons Rocket**, with the blinkers back on, was getting the worst of the argument with Miss Bigwig when tightened up entering the final furlong. (10/1)

**4180 Insider Trader**, with the visor again left off, was struggling from his midfield draw. (10/1)

## 4247 TIMEFORM HARRY ROSEBERY TROPHY STKS (Listed) (2-Y.O) (Class A)

3-40 (3-42) **5f** £9,681.00 (£3,579.00: £1,714.50: £697.50: £273.75: £104.25) Stalls: High GOING minus 0.33 sec per fur (GF)

| | | | | SP | RR | SF |
|---|---|---|---|---|---|---|
| 3823[2] | **Conspiracy (92)** (JLDunlop) **2-8-6** KDarley(2) (lw: trckd ldrs: led over 1f out: pushed clr) | — | **1** | 3/1[2] | 91+ | 50 |
| 2726[6] | **Superior Premium (88)** (RAFahey) **2-8-11** ACulhane(3) (outpcd & pushed along ½-wy: styd on wl fnl f: no ch w wnr) | 3 | **2** | 20/1 | 86 | 45 |
| 3613[4] | **Snap Crackle Pop (IRE) (94)** (RFJohnsonHoughton) **2-8-6** JReid(5) (swvd rt s: trckd ldrs: outpcd over 1f out: styd on wl ins fnl f) | ½ | **3** | 15/2 | 80 | 39 |
| 3660* | **Joza** (HCandy) **2-8-6** CRutter(7) (lw: sltly hmpd s: plld hrd: led over 3f tl over 1f out: wknd ins fnl f) | ½ | **4** | 15/8[1] | 78 | 37 |
| 3940* | **For Old Times Sake (100)** (JBerry) **2-9-2** GCarter(9) (sn outpcd: hung lft & hdwy over 1f out: kpt on) | 1 | **5** | 5/1[3] | 85 | 44 |
| 3975* | **Perpetual (74)** (SirMarkPrescott) **2-8-6** GDuffield(4) (led over 1f: chsd ldrs tl wknd jst ins fnl f) | 1½ | **6** | 12/1 | 70 | 29 |
| 4189[6] | **Osomental (97)** (DHaydnJones) **2-8-11b** AMackay(6) (sltly hmpd s: outpcd & bhd: sme hdwy over 1f out: n.d) | ¾ | **7** | 16/1 | 73 | 32 |
| 3975[4] | **Bold African (85)** (PDEvans) **2-8-11b** JFEgan(8) (swvd lft s: chsd ldrs tl lost pl 2f out) | 1¾ | **8** | 20/1 | 67 | 26 |
| 3843[6] | **The Lambton Worm (86)** (DenysSmith) **2-8-11** KFallon(1) (sn outpcd & drvn along: eased fnl f) | ¾ | **9** | 50/1 | 65 | 24 |

(SP 113.3%) **9 Rn**

**57.62 secs** (0.18 under 2y best) (0.62) CSF £49.09 TOTE £3.50: £1.20 £3.60 £1.60 (£34.80) Trio £47.30 OWNER Lord Chelsea (ARUNDEL) BRED Somerhall Bloodstock Ltd and Lord Chelsea

**3823 Conspiracy**, who did not impress going to post, was meeting Perpetual on no less than 23lb better terms. She was pushed clear to score in tremendous style by what looked far more than the official margin, breaking a 52-year-old track juvenile record in the process. (3/1)

**2726 Superior Premium** stuck on strongly inside the last and is worth a try over six now. (20/1)

**3613 Snap Crackle Pop (IRE)** was another putting in her best work at the finish. She will be suited by six furlongs now. (15/2)

**3660* Joza**, who went to post keenly, would not settle. She looks the type who lives on her nerves and it remains to be seen how far she progresses. (15/8)

**3940* For Old Times Sake**, under a 5lb penalty, was soon being run off his legs. (5/1)

**3975* Perpetual**, who had no chance with the winner on Chepstow form, showed bags of toe, but was very leg-weary just inside the last. (12/1)

## 4248 TEXSTYLE WORLD BOGSIDE CUP H'CAP (0-85) (3-Y.O) (Class D)

4-10 (4-11) **1m 7f** £8,220.00 (£2,460.00: £1,180.00: £540.00) GOING minus 0.33 sec per fur (GF)

| | | | | SP | RR | SF |
|---|---|---|---|---|---|---|
| 3939[3] | **Etterby Park (USA) (69)** (MJohnston) **3-8-13** JWeaver(4) (lw: led 4f: led over 2f out: drvn clr over 1f out: eased nr fin) | — | **1** | 6/1[3] | 84+ | 45 |
| 3928[3] | **Roseberry Avenue (IRE) (75)** (LadyHerries) **3-9-5** KDarley(3) (chsd ldrs: sn pushed along: outpcd over 3f out: styd on appr fnl f: no ch w wnr) | 7 | **2** | 9/4[1] | 83 | 44 |
| 4047[3] | **General Glow (62)** (PDEvans) **3-8-6** JFEgan(1) (trckd ldrs: drvn along over 4f out: one pce fnl 2f) | 3½ | **3** | 9/1 | 66 | 27 |
| 3816[3] | **Aztec Flyer (USA) (56)** (MrsMReveley) **3-8-0** LCharnock(7) (hld up: effrt over 3f out: styd on fnl f: nvr nr to chal) | 1¼ | **4** | 16/1 | 59 | 20 |
| 3968[2] | **Mock Trial (IRE) (65)** (MrsJRRamsden) **3-8-9** KFallon(2) (trckd ldrs: effrt over 3f out: wl outpcd fnl 2f) | 5 | **5** | 7/1 | 62 | 23 |
| 3398[5] | **Silverdale Knight (57)** (KWHogg) **3-8-1** NKennedy(6) (chsd ldrs: led over 4f out tl over 2f out: wknd over 1f out) | 3½ | **6** | 10/1 | 50 | 11 |

| Form | Horse / details | Dist | Pos | SP | RR | SF |
|---|---|---|---|---|---|---|
| 3772* | **Dirab (77)** (TDBarron) **3-9-7** JFortune(5) (lw: trckd ldr: led 11f out tl over 4f out: lost pl over 3f out: eased) | 21 | **7** | 11/4[2] | 48 | 9 |
| | | | | (SP 109.2%) | **7 Rn** | |

**3m 15.67** (4.97) CSF £18.32 TOTE £7.30: £2.60 £1.60 (£8.60) OWNER Mr G. Middlebrook (MIDDLEHAM) BRED Jayeff "B" Stables

**3939 Etterby Park (USA)**, suited by this longer trip, took the race by the horns once in line for home and was soon in no danger. (6/1)

**3928 Roseberry Avenue (IRE)** was soon pushed along. Badly tapped for toe turning in, he was staying on in the final furlong and would be suited by less firm ground. (9/4)

**4047 General Glow**, stepped up in distance, seemed to stay alright but only in his own time. (9/1: op 6/1)

**3816 Aztec Flyer (USA)**, humoured along in the rear, decided to stay on late in the day. The ability is there if ever he gets his act together. (16/1)

**3968 Mock Trial (IRE)** was left behind in the final two furlongs. Whether it was lack of stamina or of pace, only time will tell. (7/1)

**3398 Silverdale Knight**, who won over hurdles five days earlier, seemed to run out of stamina. (10/1)

**3772* Dirab** had much more use made of him. Dropping out once in line for home, he was allowed to come home in his own time. (11/4)

## 4249 SOTHEBY'S AMATEUR H'CAP (0-70) (3-Y.O+) (Class E)

4-40 (4-41) **1m 2f 192y** £3,626.00 (£1,088.00: £524.00: £242.00) Stalls: High GOING minus 0.33 sec per fur (GF)

| Form | Horse / details | Dist | Pos | SP | RR | SF |
|---|---|---|---|---|---|---|
| 3580[4] | **Rex Mundi (56)** (PDEvans) **4-10-9**(5) MrWMcLaughlin(6) (s.i.s: sn trckng ldrs: led & edgd rt over 1f out: styd on towards fin) | — | **1** | 12/1 | 66 | 48 |
| 4000[3] | **Calder King (64)** (JLEyre) **5-11-8v** MissDianaJones(14) (hld up: stdy hdwy 3f out: styd on ins fnl f: nt rch wnr) | ½ | **2** | 13/2 | 73 | 55 |
| 3677* | **Stormless (53)** (PMonteith) **5-10-8**(3) MrRThornton(5) (hdwy 4f out: led over 2f out tl over 1f out: kpt on same pce) | 1¾ | **3** | 9/2[2] | 60 | 42 |
| 3980[7] | **Bellas Gate Boy (50)** (JPearce) **4-10-8** MrsLPearce(1) (dwlt s: bhd: gd hdwy over 2f out: edgd lft & styd on ins fnl f) | nk | **4** | 16/1 | 56 | 38 |
| 3325* | **He's Got Wings (IRE) (53)** (MrsJRRamsden) **3-9-13**(5) MissERamsden(2) (lw: hdwy to chse ldrs 6f out: no imp fnl 2f) | 1¼ | **5** | 10/1 | 57 | 32 |
| 4000[10] | **Ring of Vision (IRE) (57)** (MrsMReveley) **4-10-10**(5) MissHDudgeon(3) (lw: mid div: hdwy over 2f out: nt clr run ins fnl f: kpt on) | ½ | **6** | 12/1 | 61 | 43 |
| 4193[4] | **Mentalasanythin (70)** (DHaydnJones) **7-11-9**(5) MrACharles-Jones(7) (hld up: sme hdwy over 3f out: nvr nr ldrs) | 2½ | **7** | 4/1[1] | 70 | 52 |
| | **Supertop (53)** (LLungo) **8-10-11** MrMHNaughton(13) (hld up: hdwy on ins over 2f out: swtchd rt ins fnl f: kpt on wl) | s.h | **8** | 25/1 | 53 | 35 |
| 3426[8] | **Manoy (52)** (JHetherton) **3-10-3b** MrTMcCarthy(11) (chsd ldrs: chal 3f out: wknd over 1f out: hmpd nr fin) | nk | **9** | 20/1 | 52 | 27 |
| 4000[6] | **Cumbrian Maestro (59)** (TDEasterby) **3-10-10** MrCBonner(8) (chsd ldrs: led 4f out tl over 2f out: sn wknd) | s.h | **10** | 7/1 | 58 | 33 |
| 4073[14] | **Ashover (52)** (TDBarron) **6-10-5**(5) MissMKeuthen(4) (mid div: edgd rt & kpt on appr fnl f: n.d) | 2½ | **11** | 25/1 | 48 | 30 |
| 3348[9] | **Commander Glen (IRE) (55)** (MDHammond) **4-10-8**(5) MissMCarson(16) (lw: s.i.s: bhd: sme hdwy 2f out: n.d) | 3½ | **12** | 25/1 | 46 | 28 |
| 3677[5] | **Swandale Flyer (39)** (NBycroft) **4-9-11** MrsDKettlewell(12) (chsd ldrs to 4f out: sn wknd) | 2 | **13** | 40/1 | 27 | 9 |
| 4042[2] | **Induna Mkubwa (49)** (CFWall) **3-9-9**(5)ow2 MrRWakley(18) (gd hdwy 5f out: sn chsng ldrs: edgd lft & wknd over 1f out) | hd | **14** | 6/1[3] | 37 | 10 |
| 3426[10] | **Hutchies Lady (38)** (RMMcKellar) **4-9-5**(5) MrsCWilliams(19) (a bhd) | 3 | **15** | 40/1 | 21 | 3 |
| | **Pipers Glen (36)** (CParker) **4-9-8** MissPRobson(15) (a bhd) | ½ | **16** | 66/1 | 18 | — |
| 3882[6] | **Philgem (42)** (CWFairhurst) **3-9-4**(3) MrsSBosley(17) (a in rr) | ½ | **17** | 100/1 | 24 | — |
| *3951[8]* | **Tolepa (IRE) (45)** (JJO'Neill) **3-9-3**(7) MissSKerswell(9) (chsd ldrs: rdn along 4f out: sn lost pl) | nk | **18** | 50/1 | 26 | 1 |
| 3490[2] | **Black and Blues (35)** (JSGoldie) **10-9-7** MrsAFarrell(10) (led to 4f out: wknd qckly 2f out: t.o) | 12 | **19** | 66/1 | — | — |
| | | | | (SP 135.8%) | **19 Rn** | |

**2m 22.79** (6.89) CSF £88.30 CT £388.25 TOTE £18.30: £3.00 £1.50 £1.40 £4.70 (£67.90) Trio £128.30 OWNER Mr J. W. Littler (WELSHPOOL) BRED J. W. Littler

LONG HANDICAP Philgem 8-2 Black and Blues 8-8

WEIGHT FOR AGE 3yo-7lb

**3580 Rex Mundi**, dropped in distance, gave away ground at the start. Edging right under pressure, he was persuaded to do just enough. (12/1)

**4000 Calder King**, who hit the front far too soon at York, possibly overdid the waiting tactics here. Sticking on inside the last, he could not quite get upsides the winner. (13/2)

**3677* Stormless**, 5lb higher in the weights, ran as well as could be expected. (9/2)

**469 Bellas Gate Boy** lost ground at the start and was set an impossible task, so did well to finish so close. (16/1)

**3325* He's Got Wings (IRE)**, having his first outing for his new connections, was not knocked about by his inexperienced rider. (10/1: 8/1-12/1)

**4193 Mentalasanythin** (4/1: op 6/1)

**Supertop** seemed to shape well in what was almost certainly a warm-up for hurdles. (25/1)

## 4250 TATTERSALLS MAIDEN AUCTION STKS (2-Y.O) (Class E)

5-10 (5-18) **6f** £4,240.00 (£1,270.00: £610.00: £280.00) Stalls: High GOING minus 0.33 sec per fur (GF)

| Form | Horse / details | Dist | Pos | SP | RR | SF |
|---|---|---|---|---|---|---|
| 4043[3] | **Caution** (MrsJRRamsden) **2-8-1** GCarter(4) (hdwy & swtchd rt ½-wy: styd on to ld jst ins fnl f: edgd lft: styd on wl) | — | **1** | 100/30[2] | 79 | 41 |
| 4087[8] | **Parijazz (IRE)** (MartynMeade) **2-7-9**(3) DWright(10) (led: hung bdly lft over 1f out: hdd jst ins fnl f) | 2½ | **2** | 16/1 | 69 | 31 |
| 4123[2] | **Test The Water (IRE) (80)** (RHannon) **2-8-7** JReid(5) (sn outpcd: rdn ½-wy: styd on fnl 2f) | 3½ | **3** | 6/4[1] | 69 | 31 |
| | **Shantarskie (IRE)** (CFWall) **2-8-5** GDuffield(11) (cmpt: lw: chsd ldrs tl outpcd fnl 2f) | nk | **4** | 4/1[3] | 66 | 28 |
| 3956[6] | **Murron Wallace** (RMWhitaker) **2-8-1** AMackay(3) (swvd lft s: bhd tl styd on fnl 2f) | 3 | **5** | 50/1 | 54 | 16 |
| 3941[2] | **Hurgill Lady** (JWWatts) **2-8-1** JFanning(6) (lw: trckd ldrs: plld hrd: effrt over 2f out: wknd over 1f out) | 1¼ | **6** | 7/1 | 51 | 13 |
| | **Morning Star** (MJohnston) **2-7-12** TWilliams(7) (neat: w ldrs: rdn over 2f out: wknd over 1f out) | 3 | **7** | 33/1 | 40 | 2 |
| 3941[3] | **Treasure Touch (IRE)** (GMMoore) **2-8-5** JTate(1) (chsd ldrs: edgd rt & wknd 2f out) | hd | **8** | 8/1 | 47 | 9 |
| | **Zigse** (TDBarron) **2-8-6** JFortune(8) (neat: leggy: s.i.s: a in rr) | 2½ | **9** | 20/1 | 41 | 3 |
| | **Fairy Ring (IRE)** (RMWhitaker) **2-7-13**(3)ow1 FLynch(2) (neat: leggy: unruly s: s.s: a bhd) | ¾ | **10** | 16/1 | 35 | — |
| *3291[2]* | ***Red Romance (68)*** (DenysSmith) **2-8-3** LCharnock(9) (Withdrawn not under Starter's orders: burst out of stalls) | | **W** | 20/1 | — | — |
| | | | | (SP 132.9%) | **10 Rn** | |

**1m 10.91** (1.11) CSF £52.75 TOTE £4.10: £1.60 £4.20 £1.10 (£47.00) Trio £18.60 OWNER L C and A E Sigsworth (THIRSK) BRED L. C. and Mrs A. E. Sigsworth

**4043 Caution** needed every yard of this six but, in the end, scored in decisive fashion. (100/30)
**3796 Parijazz (IRE)** helped throw it away by hanging badly left but, judging by the way the winner finished, she would have only come second anyway. (16/1)
**4123 Test The Water (IRE)** showed a very poor action going down. Never able to go the pace, he was staying on in the final furlong, and probably needs further and softer. (6/4)
**Shantarskie (IRE)**, a sharp sort, was badly outpaced in the final two furlongs. Hopefully the outing will bring him on. (4/1)
**3956 Murron Wallace**, difficult at the stalls, lost a lot of ground at the start and, in the circumstances, shaped creditably. (50/1)
**3941 Hurgill Lady** proved too keen for her own good. (7/1)

T/Jkpt: Not won; £8,149.78 to Ayr 20/9/96. T/Plpt: £203.60 (117.65 Tckts). T/Qdpt: £38.60 (39.81 Tckts). WG

# 4103-LINGFIELD (L-H) (Turf Firm, AWT Standard)
## Thursday September 19th
WEATHER: raining WIND: slt half against

## 4251 HORSE RACING ENTERPRISES (S) STKS (2-Y.O) (Class G)
2-20 (2-21) **6f (Equitrack)** £2,448.00 (£678.00: £324.00) Stalls: High GOING minus 0.45 sec per fur (FST)

| Form | Horse | Dist | Pos | SP | RR | SF |
|---|---|---|---|---|---|---|
| 3455[6] | **Eager To Please (64)** (JBerry) **2-9-2** TQuinn(6) (chsd ldr: led 2f out: r.o wl) | — | **1** | 7/1 | 70 | 8 |
| *3954*[2] | **Windborn (57)** (KMcAuliffe) **2-8-6** SSanders(4) (a.p: rdn over 2f out: chsd wnr fnl f: one pce) | 3 | **2** | 4/1[1] | 52 | — |
| *4093*[2] | **Tinker's Surprise (IRE) (63)** (BJMeehan) **2-8-9**(7) GHannon(5) (sn led: hdd 2f out: one pce) | 3 | **3** | 9/2[2] | 54 | — |
| 3975[8] | **Whizz Kid (62)** (JJBridger) **2-8-4**(7) RMullen(12) (hdwy 3f out: rdn 2f out: one pce) | 3½ | **4** | 6/1 | 40 | — |
| *4093*[6] | **Hever Golf Stormer (IRE) (59)** (TJNaughton) **2-8-11** DaneO'Neill(3) (sn rdn along in mid div: sme hdwy fnl f: nvr nrr) | 3½ | **5** | 10/1 | 30 | — |
| 4097[7] | **Poly Moon (58)** (MRChannon) **2-8-11** LDettori(1) (chsd ldrs: rdn over 2f out: wknd over 1f out) | 1¼ | **6** | 5/1[3] | 27 | — |
| *4079*[8] | **Verinder's Gift** (DrJDScargill) **2-8-11** MFenton(9) (mid div: rdn 3f out: grad wknd) | 5 | **7** | 20/1 | 14 | — |
| | **Parquet** (JJSheehan) **2-8-6** AMorris(8) (lt-f: a bhd) | 1¼ | **8** | 33/1 | 5 | — |
| 3336[5] | **Lake Spring (IRE)** (RJHodges) **2-8-11** SDrowne(2) (sn rdn along: bhd fnl 4f) | 1¾ | **9** | 33/1 | 6 | — |
| 1471[7] | **Life's A Roar (IRE)** (CADwyer) **2-8-11v**[1] JStack(11) (s.i.s: a bhd) | hd | **10** | 14/1 | 5 | — |
| 3846[9] | **Face It (45)** (WGMTurner) **2-8-6b**[1] AClark(10) (chsd ldr 4f) | 2½ | **11** | 16/1 | — | — |
| *4093*[10] | **Run For Us (IRE) (45)** (CADwyer) **2-8-6** DHarrison(7) (a bhd) | ¾ | **12** | 25/1 | — | — |

(SP 117.8%) **12 Rn**

**1m 14.58** (3.98) CSF £32.80 TOTE £5.30: £1.40 £1.90 £2.00 (£11.30) Trio £12.80 OWNER The Totally Original Partnership (COCKERHAM) BRED Mrs Sara Hood
Sold CSparrowhawk 6,600gns; Windborn clmd AMoore £6,000
**3455 Eager To Please** clearly appreciated this Equitrack surface and won this uncompetitive seller in emphatic style. (7/1)
**3954 Windborn** was always struggling to go the pace. (4/1: 3/1-9/2)
**4093 Tinker's Surprise (IRE)** appears best at five furlongs. (9/2)
**2944 Whizz Kid** (6/1: 4/1-7/1)

## 4252 JARDINE INSURANCE SERVICES H'CAP (0-70) (3-Y.O+) (Class E)
2-50 (2-53) **1m 6f** £3,916.50 (£1,176.00: £567.00: £262.50) Stalls: High GOING minus 0.36 sec per fur (F)

| Form | Horse | Dist | Pos | SP | RR | SF |
|---|---|---|---|---|---|---|
| *3872** | **Mischief Star (59)** (DRCElsworth) **3-8-4**(5) DGriffiths(6) (hld up in tch: chsd ldr over 1f out: hrd rdn ins fnl f: led nr fin) | — | **1** | 11/2[2] | 69 | 23 |
| 3434[3] | **Diego (66)** (CEBrittain) **3-9-2** MRoberts(4) (chsd ldrs: led 2f out: hrd rdn ins fnl f: hdd nr fin) | hd | **2** | 9/2[1] | 76 | 30 |
| 4067[9] | **Roisin Clover (64)** (SDow) **5-9-5**(5) ADaly(9) (hld up in mid div: hdwy 2f out: rdn over 1f out: styd on one pce ins fnl f) | 3½ | **3** | 7/1 | 70 | 34 |
| *2631*[4] | **Great Tern (43)** (NMBabbage) **4-7-12**(5)ow2 PPMurphy(17) (mid div: rdn over 2f out: styd on one pce ins fnl f) | 1¾ | **4** | 50/1 | 47 | 9 |
| 4086[6] | **Hoofprints (IRE) (68)** (GHarwood) **3-9-4** AClark(13) (chsd ldr: led over 3f out: hdd 2f out: wknd ins fnl f) | 2 | **5** | 14/1 | 70 | 24 |
| 3979[8] | **Rocquaine Bay (37)** (MJBolton) **9-7-6**(5) CAdamson(11) (nvr nrr) | 1¾ | **6** | 14/1 | 37 | 1 |
| 4128[10] | **Summerhill Special (IRE) (55)** (MrsPNDutfield) **5-9-1** MTebbutt(15) (hld up in rr: sme hdwy fnl 2f: nvr nrr) | 2½ | **7** | 33/1 | 52 | 16 |
| 4048[12] | **Greenwich Again (58)** (TGMills) **4-9-4** DaneO'Neill(10) (hld up in rr: hdwy 5f out: rdn 3f out: one pce) | hd | **8** | 16/1 | 55 | 19 |
| 1660[4] | **Guest Alliance (IRE) (47)** (AMoore) **4-8-7** CandyMorris(3) (a mid div) | 4 | **9** | 14/1 | 39 | 3 |
| 3876[5] | **Arktikos (IRE) (68)** (JHMGosden) **3-9-4v** LDettori(12) (b.hind: chsd ldrs: rdn over 2f out: grad wknd) | 1 | **10** | 6/1[3] | 59 | 13 |
| 4048[14] | **Norsong (54)** (RAkehurst) **4-9-0** TQuinn(2) (led: hdd over 3f out: wknd over 1f out) | 5 | **11** | 10/1 | 39 | 3 |
| 2594[6] | **Allez Pablo (36)** (RRowe) **6-7-3**(7) PDoe(8) (chsd ldrs tl wknd over 2f out) | 3½ | **12** | 50/1 | 17 | — |
| 3316[10] | **Trapper Norman (37)** (RIngram) **4-7-11** DeclanO'Shea(14) (bhd fnl 4f: t.o) | 13 | **13** | 33/1 | 3 | — |
| | **Extremely Friendly (50)** (BobJones) **3-8-0** SDrowne(18) (a bhd: t.o) | s.h | **14** | 33/1 | 16 | — |
| 2407[5] | **Ben Bowden (50)** (MBlanshard) **3-8-0** JQuinn(16) (bhd fnl 4f: t.o) | 5 | **15** | 33/1 | 11 | — |
| 3849[3] | **Flight Master (58)** (PJMakin) **4-9-4** SSanders(7) (t: a bhd: t.o) | 9 | **16** | 9/1 | 8 | — |
| 3694[14] | **Little Wobbly (39)** (PCClarke) **6-7-6**(7)ow3 CherylBone(5) (prom early: bhd fnl 5f: t.o) | dist | **17** | 100/1 | — | — |
| 2155[10] | **Quest Again (62)** (DWPArbuthnot) **5-9-8** SWhitworth(19) (hld up in rr: hdwy 5f out: mid div whn p.u & dismntd wl over 1f out) | | **P** | 14/1 | — | — |

(SP 128.7%) **18 Rn**

**3m 5.85** (7.55) CSF £29.58 CT £169.23 TOTE £7.40: £1.90 £1.50 £1.70 £4.20 (£15.60) Trio £38.30 OWNER Mrs P. J. Sheen (WHITCOMBE) BRED Mrs John Trotter
LONG HANDICAP Little Wobbly 7-4 Allez Pablo 6-12
WEIGHT FOR AGE 3yo-10lb
**3872* Mischief Star** showed improved form to win on the All-Weather last time and proved herself here just as effective on the turf. A return to two miles will suit. (11/2)
**3434 Diego** was one of the few here certain to get the trip and his rider made full use of his stamina, only just losing out in a driving finish. (9/2)
**3235 Roisin Clover** was ridden to get the trip and saw it out well enough. (7/1)
**866 Great Tern** ran her best race so far and is obviously a stayer. (50/1)
**4086 Hoofprints (IRE)** put up an improved performance and can find a small handicap, especially if dropped in distance. (14/1)

## 4253 HUNGERFORD MAIDEN STKS (2-Y.O) (Class D)

3-20 (3-22) **7f 140y** £4,201.40 (£1,260.20: £606.60: £279.80) Stalls: High GOING minus 0.36 sec per fur (F)

| | | | | SP | RR | SF |
|---|---|---|---|---|---|---|
| 1960[5] | **Bandore (IRE)** (DRLoder) **2-9-0** WRSwinburn(7) (mde all: rdn ins fnl f: r.o) | — | 1 | 2/1[1] | 72 | 28 |
| 3129[7] | **Logic** (CEBrittain) **2-8-9** MRoberts(9) (chsd ldrs: rdn over 1f out: styd on strly ins fnl f) | hd | 2 | 11/4[2] | 67 | 23 |
| 3773[3] | **All In Leather** (WJHaggas) **2-8-9** TQuinn(8) (hld up in tch: chsd wnr over 1f out tl ins fnl f: one pce) | 1¾ | 3 | 6/1[3] | 63 | 19 |
| 3963[3] | **Here's To Howie (USA)** (RHannon) **2-9-0** DaneO'Neill(3) (a.p: rdn over 1f out: one pce) | hd | 4 | 15/2 | 68 | 24 |
| 4038a[9] | **Yavlensky (IRE)** (JLDunlop) **2-9-0** DHarrison(10) (rr: rdn over 2f out: styd on one pce ins fnl f) | 1 | 5 | 12/1 | 66 | 22 |
| | **Pietro Bembo (IRE)** (SirMarkPrescott) **2-9-0** SSanders(4) (leggy: rr: rdn over 3f out: kpt on one pce ins fnl f) | ¾ | 6 | 20/1 | 64 | 20 |
| | **Indium** (JHMGosden) **2-9-0** LDettori(11) (unf: scope: hld up: hdwy over 1f out: sn rdn: one pce) | ½ | 7 | 6/1[3] | 63 | 19 |
| 3682[12] | **State of Gold (IRE)** (WJHaggas) **2-9-0** MFenton(6) (chsd ldrs: rdn 2f out: wknd fnl f) | 1½ | 8 | 20/1 | 60 | 16 |
| 4069[8] | **Greenwich Fore** (TGMills) **2-9-0** JQuinn(2) (mid div: rdn over 2f out: wknd over 1f out) | nk | 9 | 20/1 | 59 | 15 |
| 3493[11] | **Fantasy Girl (IRE)** (JLDunlop) **2-8-9** JStack(5) (mid div: rdn over 2f out: sn wknd) | 2½ | 10 | 25/1 | 49 | 5 |
| 3259[5] | **Penlop** (BJMeehan) **2-9-0** MTebbutt(12) (a bhd) | 2½ | 11 | 25/1 | 49 | 5 |
| | | | | (SP 130.0%) | | **11 Rn** |

**1m 32.33** (3.53) CSF £8.70 TOTE £2.90: £1.90 £1.10 £1.20 (£4.00) Trio £12.00 OWNER Lady Harrison (NEWMARKET) BRED Denis McDonnell

OFFICIAL EXPLANATION **Penlop: the rider reported that the colt travelled well until attempting to jump a path and losing his action. The trainer added that the colt had been injured as a yearling and had been hard to keep sound this summer.**

**1960 Bandore (IRE)** was beaten in a good race last time. (2/1: 6/4-9/4)

**3129 Logic** had run poorly last time after a promising debut but bounced back to form here, putting in a determined challenge in the final furlong. She can find a race soon, especially over further. (11/4)

**3773 All In Leather** was never far away, but found quickening beyond her. (6/1: 5/1-8/1)

**3963 Here's To Howie (USA)**, as on his debut, was just found wanting for a turn of foot. (15/2: 8/1-12/1)

**4038a Yavlensky (IRE)** took a while to get going when asked to improve, but was staying on strongly at the finish. He will come into his own over further and will probably be seen at his best as a three-year-old. (12/1: 8/1-14/1)

**Pietro Bembo (IRE)** was very green early on, but showed signs late in the race that he was learning the game. (20/1)

**Indium** (6/1: 3/1-7/1)

## 4254 HBLB LIMITED STKS (0-80) (3-Y.O+) (Class D)

3-50 (3-53) **7f 140y** £3,827.55 (£1,142.40: £545.70: £247.35) Stalls: High GOING minus 0.36 sec per fur (F)

| | | | | SP | RR | SF |
|---|---|---|---|---|---|---|
| 4109* | **Chewit (77)** (AMoore) **4-9-3** CandyMorris(3) (hld up gng wl: led over 2f out: sn clr: easily) | — | 1 | 6/4[1] | 85+ | 45 |
| | **High Hope Henry (USA) (80)** (RAkehurst) **3-8-13** TQuinn(2) (keen hold: led over 4f out: hdd over 2f out: one pce) | 3½ | 2 | 3/1[3] | 78 | 34 |
| 4212[5] | **Blue Flyer (IRE) (74)** (RIngram) **3-8-13b** SWhitworth(1) (led 3f: rdn over 2f out: one pce) | 2 | 3 | 13/2 | 74 | 30 |
| 3999[3] | **Zurs (IRE) (80)** (MissGayKelleway) **3-8-10** WRSwinburn(4) (prom: rdn 3f out: nt run on: eased ins fnl f) | 13 | 4 | 11/4[2] | 43 | — |
| | | | | (SP 105.0%) | | **4 Rn** |

**1m 30.97** (2.17) CSF £5.52 TOTE £2.50 (£2.40) OWNER Ballard (1834) Ltd (BRIGHTON) BRED B. Minty

WEIGHT FOR AGE 3yo-4lb

**4109* Chewit** hacked up and is in really good heart at present. (6/4: op 5/2)

**High Hope Henry (USA)** did not help himself by pulling hard in the early stages. (3/1: op 6/4)

**4212 Blue Flyer (IRE)** was simply not good enough. (13/2)

**3999 Zurs (IRE)** looked far from keen. (11/4)

## 4255 DIBB LUPTON & BROOMHEAD H'CAP (0-95) (3-Y.O+) (Class C)

4-20 (4-23) **6f** £5,884.50 (£1,758.00: £841.00: £382.50) Stalls: High GOING minus 0.36 sec per fur (F)

| | | | | SP | RR | SF |
|---|---|---|---|---|---|---|
| 3946[6] | **Seigneurial (86)** (GHarwood) **4-9-10** AClark(4) (lw: stdd s: hld up: hdwy over 3f out: edgd rt over 1f out: led ent fnl f: r.o) | — | 1 | 3/1[1] | 94 | 49 |
| 3790[8] | **White Emir (87)** (BJMeehan) **3-9-9b** WRSwinburn(3) (a.p: led 4f out: hdd & edgd rt ent fnl f: one pce) | 1½ | 2 | 6/1 | 91 | 44 |
| 3672[5] | **Lord Olivier (IRE) (78)** (WJarvis) **6-9-2** MTebbutt(5) (a.p: rdn & sltly outpcd over 2f out: styng on whn n.m.r ent fnl f: swtchd lft: r.o) | hd | 3 | 4/1[2] | 82 | 37 |
| 3810[14] | **Kind of Light (79)** (RGuest) **3-9-1** DaneO'Neill(7) (chsd ldrs: outpcd ½-wy: hrd rdn 2f out: styd on ins fnl f) | hd | 4 | 6/1 | 83 | 36 |
| 4088[6] | **Robellion (68)** (DWPArbuthnot) **5-8-6v** TQuinn(2) (b.hind: chsd ldrs: rdn over 2f out: one pce) | ¾ | 5 | 9/2[3] | 70 | 25 |
| 3216[10] | **Scharnhorst (77)** (SDow) **4-8-10(5)** ADaly(6) (chsd ldrs: outpcd ½-wy: hrd rdn & swtchd lft over 1f out: one pce) | 1½ | 6 | 10/1 | 75 | 30 |
| 4044* | **No Monkey Nuts (83)** (JBerry) **3-9-0(5)** PRoberts(1) (lw: b: b.nr hind: led 2f: rdn over 2f out: grad wknd) | 2 | 7 | 7/1 | 75 | 28 |
| | | | | (SP 113.3%) | | **7 Rn** |

**1m 10.9** (1.90) CSF £19.38 TOTE £3.40: £2.00 £4.30 (£17.90) OWNER The PBT Group (PULBOROUGH) BRED Richard M. Whitaker

WEIGHT FOR AGE 3yo-2lb

**3946 Seigneurial** looked like winning comfortably when moving up to challenge below the distance, but he made life difficult for himself by edging right, towards his rivals. Straightened out, he saw it out well. (3/1)

**3215 White Emir** made most of the running, but does not find much off the bridle. (6/1)

**3672 Lord Olivier (IRE)** has incredibly never won a handicap, but would have gone close here with a clear run. (4/1: 3/1-9/2)

**3270 Kind of Light** gave the strong impression that a return to seven furlongs would suit. (6/1)

**4088 Robellion** was struggling from some way out. (9/2)

**1442* Scharnhorst** could not go the pace from halfway. (10/1)

## 4256 JARDINES H'CAP (0-70) (3-Y.O+) (Class E)

4-50 (4-56) **7f** £3,889.20 (£1,167.60: £562.80: £260.40) Stalls: High GOING minus 0.36 sec per fur (F)

| | | | | SP | RR | SF |
|---|---|---|---|---|---|---|
| 4098[9] | **Morocco (IRE) (54)** (MRChannon) **7-8-7(7)** AEddery(6) (racd far side: hld up mid div: hdwy 2f out: led 1f out: r.o) | — | 1 | 20/1 | 62 | 44 |
| 2621[13] | **Amber Fort (67)** (DRCElsworth) **3-9-5v[1](5)** DGriffiths(7) (chsd ldrs far side: rdn & ev ch 1f out: one pce) | 1½ | 2 | 16/1 | 72 | 51 |
| 4053[6] | **Godmersham Park (68)** (MJHeaton-Ellis) **4-10-0** AClark(1) (racd far side: chsd ldrs: rdn & ev ch 1f out: one pce) | nk | 3 | 9/1[3] | 72 | 54 |
| 4053[5] | **Sea Danzig (62)** (JJBridger) **3-9-5** SSanders(16) (led stands' side group: rdn over 1f out: one pce) | ½ | 4 | 20/1 | 65 | 44 |

4098[7] **Our Shadee (USA) (49)** (KTIvory) **6-8-9v** CScally(14) (racd stands' side: bhd: hdwy over 1f out: r.o ins fnl f) .nk **5** 16/1 51 33
3832[3] **Onefortheditch (USA) (65)** (JHMGosden) **3-9-8** LDettori(2) (racd far side: led: hdd 1f out: no ex) ....................½ **6** 4/1[1] 66 45
3698[8] **Dark Menace (47)** (EAWheeler) **4-8-2**(5) ADaly(4) (racd far side: chsd ldrs tl wknd over 1f out) .......................2½ **7** 20/1 42 24
4109[8] **Sharp Imp (58)** (RMFlower) **6-9-4b** TQuinn(17) (racd stands' side: chsd ldrs: rdn over 1f out: wknd ins fnl f)..nk **8** 14/1 53 35
3991[2] **Honorable Estate (IRE) (63)** (RHannon) **3-9-6** DaneO'Neill(15) (racd stands' side: prom over 5f) ..................hd **9** 10/1 57 36
4128[2] **Dawalib (USA) (55)** (DHaydnJones) **6-9-1** SWhitworth(11) (racd far side: hld up: hdwy over 2f out: rdn over 1f out: grad wknd) ....................½ **10** 15/2[2] 48 30
3991[18] **Cats Bottom (49)** (AGNewcombe) **4-8-9** SDrowne(12) (racd stands' side: chsd ldrs 5f) ..................hd **11** 16/1 42 24
4098[11] **Euphyllia (57)** (BobJones) **4-9-3v** MWigham(5) (racd far side: a bhd)..................1 **12** 20/1 48 30
4098[3] **Windswept (IRE) (56)** (DJSffrenchDavis) **3-8-13** DHarrison(13) (racd stands' side: bhd fnl 2f)..................1 **13** 10/1 44 23
3686[4] **Whatever's Right (IRE) (65)** (MDIUsher) **7-9-11** WRSwinburn(3) (racd far side: w ldrs tl wknd over 1f out) ....¾ **14** 10/1 52 34
4064[18] **Warren Knight (64)** (CAHorgan) **3-9-7** MFenton(8) (racd far side: a bhd)..................1¼ **15** 25/1 48 27
*4089*[2] **Twin Creeks (50)** (VSoane) **5-8-10** JStack(10) (racd stands' side: bhd fnl 2f)..................1¾ **16** 12/1 30 12
4128[8] **Paddy's Rice (56)** (MBlanshard) **5-9-2** JQuinn(18) (racd stands' side: bhd fnl 2f)..................½ **17** 12/1 35 17
4128[3] **Ivory's Grab Hire (60)** (KTIvory) **3-9-3b** MTebbutt(9) (racd far side: chsd ldrs over 4f)..................1½ **18** 14/1 35 14
(SP 138.3%) **18 Rn**

**1m 23.46** (1.86) CSF £301.84 CT £2,842.21 TOTE £26.40: £3.10 £4.00 £3.00 £5.50 (£1,749.60) Trio Not won; £795.26 to Ayr 20/9/96
OWNER Mr Martin Myers (UPPER LAMBOURN) BRED Nikita Investments
WEIGHT FOR AGE 3yo-3lb

**3867 Morocco (IRE)** got a dream of a run up the far rail and won nicely. (20/1)
**2621 Amber Fort** ran a good race, but is an enigmatic character as his record of one win in fourteen starts shows. (16/1)
**4053 Godmersham Park** ran a really good race under his big weight. (9/1)
**4053 Sea Danzig** made all the running on the unfavoured stands' side. (20/1)
**4098 Our Shadee (USA)** finished strongly as usual and, along with Sea Danzig, finished clear of his stands'-side rivals. (16/1)
**3832 Onefortheditch (USA)** ran a sound enough race on her handicap debut. (4/1)

## 4257 C & H (HAULIERS) H'CAP (0-75) (3-Y.O+) (Class D)

5-20 (5-24) **1m 2f** £4,556.85 (£1,366.80: £657.90: £303.45) Stalls: High GOING minus 0.36 sec per fur (F)

SP RR SF

4102* **White Plains (IRE) (70)** (MBell) **3-8-12**(7) RMullen(7) (a.p: led over 1f out: hrd rdn ins fnl f: r.o)..................— **1** 4/1[1] 80 46
3220[4] **Elashath (USA) (65)** (JHMGosden) **3-9-0** LDettori(4) (chsd ldrs: rdn 2f out: styd on ins fnl f)..................nk **2** 4/1[1] 75 41
3825[9] **Printers Quill (50)** (MajorDNChappell) **4-8-0**(5)ow5 SophieMitchell(3) (hld up mid div: rdn 2f out: styd on wl ins fnl f)..................hd **3** 20/1 59 26
4000[14] **Double Up (66)** (LadyHerries) **3-8-8**(7) PDoe(2) (a.p: rdn 2f out: n.m.r ins fnl f: r.o) ..................s.h **4** 14/1 75 41
3986[5] **Melt The Clouds (CAN) (75)** (PWHarris) **3-9-10** GHind(6) (lw: led: hdd over 1f out: one pce) ..................1½ **5** 16/1 82 48
4067[7] **Fairy Knight (63)** (RHannon) **4-9-4** DaneO'Neill(16) (hld up: hdwy over 2f out: nt clr run on ins fnl 2f: nt rcvr)..................s.h **6** 11/2[2] 70 42
3856[9] **Law Dancer (IRE) (68)** (TGMills) **3-9-3** JQuinn(14) (chsd ldrs: rdn over 1f out: one pce) ..................¾ **7** 16/1 74 40
4082[5] **Tomal (44)** (RIngram) **4-7-13** DeclanO'Shea(9) (nvr nrr)..................2½ **8** 16/1 46 18
2945[3] **Rubbiyati (52)** (CEBrittain) **4-8-7** MRoberts(12) (mid div: rdn 2f out: no hdwy)..................2 **9** 10/1 50 22
3253[4] **Russian Request (IRE) (71)** (MRStoute) **3-9-6** WRSwinburn(1) (prom: rdn 2f out: sn wknd)..................2½ **10** 8/1[3] 65 31
1515[12] **Dutosky (60)** (JohnBerry) **6-9-1** RMcGhin(8) (bhd fnl 6f) ..................2 **11** 25/1 51 23
4068[6] **Golden Touch (USA) (63)** (DJSCosgrove) **4-9-4** JStack(15) (nvr nrr) ..................nk **12** 14/1 54 26
3985[4] **Raed (70)** (PTWalwyn) **3-9-5** AClark(5) (in tch: rdn over 2f out: sn wknd) ..................3 **13** 10/1 56 22
3977[8] **To The Whire (51)** (GLMoore) **3-8-0**ow1 SDrowne(10) (mid div: rdn over 2f out: sn wknd) ..................1½ **14** 25/1 35 —
1092[7] **Lovely Prospect (67)** (RGuest) **3-9-2** DHarrison(11) (a bhd: t.o fnl 4f) ..................dist **15** 20/1 — —
(SP 132.9%) **15 Rn**

**2m 8.17** (3.47) CSF £21.24 CT £278.19 TOTE £2.90: £1.50 £2.30 £18.90 (£8.80) Trio £333.10; £117.31 to Ayr 20/9/96 OWNER Deln Ltd (NEWMARKET) BRED Howard Kaskel
WEIGHT FOR AGE 3yo-6lb

**4102* White Plains (IRE)** was unpenalised for his win in an Apprentice race last time and was officially 6lb well in here. He will find life more difficult in future. (4/1)
**3220 Elashath (USA)** kept on really well and can win again off his present mark. (4/1)
**3341* Printers Quill** took a while to pick up when asked to challenge, but was staying on strongly at the finish. (20/1)
**3452 Double Up** was a bit short of room in the closing stages, but for which she would have gone close. (14/1)
**3986 Melt The Clouds (CAN)** tried different tactics here and this aggressive style of running could well succeed if dropped back in trip. (16/1)
**3828 Fairy Knight** was very unlucky. Continually denied a run in the final two furlongs, he gave the very strong impression that he would have won with a clear passage. Compensation awaits. (11/2)

T/Plpt: £386.60 (21.79 Tckts). T/Qdpt: £318.20 (1.37 Tckts). SM

# 4237-YARMOUTH (L-H) (Good to firm)

## Thursday September 19th

WEATHER: overcast, cool WIND: gale across

## 4258 TED PILLAR CONDITIONS STKS (2-Y.O) (Class C)

2-30 (2-31) **6f 3y** £4,854.60 (£1,749.60: £838.80: £342.00: £135.00) Stalls: High GOING minus 0.40 sec per fur (F)

SP RR SF

3927[3] **Air Express (IRE) (100)** (CEBrittain) **2-8-11** BDoyle(1) (lw: mde all: drvn out fnl f)..................— **1** 5/4[1] 104 42
2070[5] **Grand Lad (IRE) (100)** (RWArmstrong) **2-9-1** RHills(5) (bit bkwd: plld hrd: hld up: hdwy over 1f out: chal ins fnl f: unable qckn)..................1¾ **2** 9/4[2] 103 41
4024a[2] **Paddy Lad (IRE) (96)** (RGuest) **2-8-11** PBloomfield(2) (chsd ldrs: rdn 2f out: kpt on fnl f)..................1¼ **3** 100/30[3] 96 34
3990[5] **Cowrie (85)** (RFJohnsonHoughton) **2-8-10** TSprake(3) (dwlt: a bhd: rdn over 2f out: no real imp)..................½ **4** 33/1 94? 32
3931[3] **Braveheart (IRE) (98)** (MRChannon) **2-8-11** RHughes(4) (lw: prom tl wknd wl over 1f out: eased whn btn)...2½ **5** 16/1 88 26
(SP 107.1%) **5 Rn**

**1m 12.3** (1.40) CSF £4.12 TOTE £1.80: £1.20 £1.80 (£3.00) OWNER Mr Mohamed Obaida (NEWMARKET) BRED Gainsborough Stud Management Ltd

**3927 Air Express (IRE)** has been very highly tried and he found this much easier, despite being brought back to six furlongs. (5/4: Evens-7/4)

**2070 Grand Lad (IRE)**, sure to strip fitter for this first run in three months, was attempting the impossible in trying to concede weight to the useful winner. (9/4: 3/1-2/1)
**4024a Paddy Lad (IRE)**, runner-up in a valuable race in Ireland last month, could not get in a blow against the leading pair, but he did stay on and could well need a stiffer test. (100/30: 9/4-7/2)
**3990 Cowrie** lost all chance with a slow break. (33/1)
**3931 Braveheart (IRE)** was in trouble below the distance and was not persevered with when beaten. (16/1)

## 4259 WILLIAM YOUNGER EAST ANGLIA H'CAP (0-60) (3-Y.O+) (Class F)

3-00 (3-01) **6f 3y** £3,548.00 (£1,064.00: £512.00: £236.00) Stalls: High GOING minus 0.40 sec per fur (F)

| | | | | SP | RR | SF |
|---|---|---|---|---|---|---|
| 3977[4] | **Corniche Quest (IRE) (52)** (MRChannon) **3-9-4** RHughes(18) (lw: hld up: hdwy over 1f out: rdn to ld last stride) | — | **1** | 10/1[3] | 60 | 40 |
| 4206* | **Merrie le Bow (56)** (PatMitchell) **4-9-5**[(5) 7x] AmandaSanders(1) (lw: a.p: led ins fnl f: ct cl home) | hd | **2** | 8/1[2] | 64 | 46 |
| 4045[3] | **Polar Refrain (53)** (CADwyer) **3-8-12**[(7)] JoHunnam(11) (a.p: rdn over 1f out: rallied nr fin) | s.h | **3** | 4/1[1] | 61 | 41 |
| 3932[15] | **Allwight Then (IRE) (60)** (DJSCosgrove) **5-10-0** RHills(20) (plld hrd: hld up: effrt & n.m.r appr fnl f: r.o towards fin) | ½ | **4** | 12/1 | 66 | 48 |
| *3602*[16] | **Dissentor (IRE) (43)** (JAGlover) **4-8-11v** NCarlisle(16) (a.p: rdn over 1f out: kpt on nr fin) | 1½ | **5** | 20/1 | 45 | 27 |
| 4206[4] | **Another Nightmare (IRE) (54)** (RMMcKellar) **4-9-8** PatEddery(2) (led tl hdd & wknd ins fnl f) | s.h | **6** | 4/1[1] | 56 | 38 |
| 4240[8] | **Awesome Venture (51)** (MCChapman) **6-9-0**[(5)] MBaird(17) (chsd ldrs: effrt u.p over 1f out: eased nr fin) | s.h | **7** | 14/1 | 53 | 35 |
| 4075[13] | **Pendley Rose (45)** (PWHarris) **3-8-11** NDay(14) (hdwy 2f out: kpt on u.p ins fnl f) | ¾ | **8** | 20/1 | 45 | 25 |
| 4221[10] | **Spanish Stripper (USA) (56)** (MCChapman) **5-9-10** DRMcCabe(10) (hdwy over 2f out: rdn & nt pce to chal) | hd | **9** | 16/1 | 56 | 38 |
| 3967[5] | **Waders Dream (IRE) (55)** (PatMitchell) **7-9-6v**[(3)] NVarley(3) (trckd ldrs over 4f) | 1 | **10** | 12/1 | 52 | 34 |
| 4045[7] | **Judgement Call (47)** (PHowling) **9-9-1** FNorton(15) (b: prom over 4f) | s.h | **11** | 16/1 | 44 | 26 |
| 4045[13] | **Members Welcome (IRE) (48)** (JMBradley) **3-9-0v** GBardwell(4) (s.i.s: swtchd rt: nvr nr to chal) | s.h | **12** | 20/1 | 45 | 25 |
| | **Saint Amigo (40)** (RMWhitaker) **4-8-8** MHills(8) (nvr gng pce of ldrs) | ½ | **13** | 33/1 | 36 | 18 |
| 3930[8] | **Face the Future (52)** (VSoane) **7-9-6** AMcGlone(13) (nvr trbld ldrs) | nk | **14** | 12/1 | 47 | 29 |
| 4136[12] | **Samsolom (59)** (PHowling) **8-9-13** BDoyle(12) (lw: b: outpcd) | hd | **15** | 14/1 | 53 | 35 |
| 4098[14] | **Rothley Imp (IRE) (45)** (JWharton) **3-8-11** TSprake(7) (lw: outpcd) | 2½ | **16** | 25/1 | 33 | 13 |
| | **Rapier Point (IRE) (50)** (CMurray) **5-9-4** PBloomfield(9) (b: bkwd: led stands' side over 4f) | hd | **17** | 16/1 | 38 | 20 |
| 3518[15] | **Masruf (IRE) (59)** (TThomsonJones) **4-9-13b**[1] WRyan(6) (spd far side 4f: wknd qckly: t.o) | 12 | **18** | 20/1 | 15 | — |
| | | | | (SP 140.1%) | | **18 Rn** |

**1m 12.9** (2.00) CSF £91.13 CT £368.99 TOTE £7.90: £1.80 £2.10 £1.50 £3.90 (£65.00) Trio £46.40 OWNER Mr M. Bishop (UPPER LAMBOURN) BRED K. Molloy
WEIGHT FOR AGE 3yo-2lb
STEWARDS' ENQUIRY Hughes susp. 30/9 & 2/10/96 (careless riding).
**3977 Corniche Quest (IRE)**, stepping back to sprinting, needed to work hard to get up on the line. (10/1)
**4206* Merrie le Bow**, making a quick reappearance, tried hard to defy a 7lb penalty and was unlucky to be shaded on the post. (8/1: op 5/1)
**4045 Polar Refrain** showed much-improved form to fail narrowly and will not remain a maiden for much longer. She is one to keep in mind. (4/1)
**1049 Allwight Then (IRE)**, restrained at this first attempt at the trip, would have taken all the beating but for being impeded entering the final furlong. (12/1)
**592 Dissentor (IRE)** has only won on the All-Weather, but he performed with credit here and he is ready to pick up another prize. (20/1)
**4206 Another Nightmare (IRE)**, having her second outing of the week, attempted to blaze a trail again, but she was feeling the strain inside the final furlong. (4/1)
**3702 Awesome Venture** does nearly all his racing over a longer trip nowadays, but he ran really well here until eased when slightly impeded nearing the finish. (14/1: 10/1-16/1)

## 4260 THOMAS PRIOR MEMORIAL STAYERS H'CAP (0-95) (3-Y.O+) (Class C)

3-30 (3-30) **2m 2f 51y** £5,637.50 (£1,682.00: £803.00: £363.50) Stalls: High GOING minus 0.19 sec per fur (GF)

| | | | | SP | RR | SF |
|---|---|---|---|---|---|---|
| 3983* | **Jiyush (93)** (HThomsonJones) **3-9-7** RHills(3) (lw: a gng wl: trckd ldng pair: led over 1f out: sn clr) | — | **1** | 3/1[1] | 111+ | 62 |
| 1783[2] | **Flocheck (USA) (85)** (JLDunlop) **3-8-13** PatEddery(4) (led tl over 1f out: sn outpcd) | 5 | **2** | 7/2[2] | 99 | 50 |
| 3598[8] | **Toy Princess (USA) (73)** (CEBrittain) **4-9-0** BDoyle(1) (chsd ldr: disp ld 2f out: rdn & one pce appr fnl f) | 3½ | **3** | 12/1 | 84 | 48 |
| 3504[5] | **Pearl Venture (78)** (SPCWoods) **4-9-5** WRyan(9) (hld up & bhd: styd on fnl 2f: nvr nrr) | 4 | **4** | 9/1[3] | 85 | 49 |
| 4187[3] | **Steamroller Stanly (80)** (CACyzer) **3-8-8** TSprake(8) (lw: trckd ldrs: rdn 3f out: no imp) | 2 | **5** | 14/1 | 85 | 36 |
| 3850* | **Golden Arrow (IRE) (85)** (MCPipe) **5-9-12** RHughes(5) (hld up: effrt u.p over 2f out: eased whn btn appr fnl f) | 3½ | **6** | 7/2[2] | 87 | 51 |
| 3801[6] | **Paradise Navy (68)** (CREgerton) **7-8-9b** MHills(7) (lw: hld up: a in rr) | 2½ | **7** | 12/1 | 68 | 32 |
| 3983[14] | **Non Vintage (IRE) (59)** (MCChapman) **5-7-7**[(7)ow4] JoHunnam(6) (a in rr) | 1¾ | **8** | 25/1 | 58 | 18 |
| | | | | (SP 105.3%) | | **8 Rn** |

**4m 1.1** (5.90 under best) (6.50) CSF £12.02 CT £74.54 TOTE £3.10: £1.50 £1.50 £1.60 (£4.40) Trio £22.20 OWNER Mr Hamdan Al Maktoum (NEWMARKET) BRED Shadwell Estate Company Limited
LONG HANDICAP Non Vintage (IRE) 7-5
WEIGHT FOR AGE 3yo-13lb
**3983* Jiyush** has really found his form since trying extended trips and, after this effortless success, will carry a 4lb penalty in the Cesarewitch. (3/1)
**1783 Flocheck (USA)**, reappearing after a mid-summer holiday, failed in his attempt to make all, but he did very little wrong and should be much sharper with this run under his belt. (7/2)
**2319 Toy Princess (USA)** looked the only danger to the winner two furlongs out, but she could not wear him down. (12/1)
**3504 Pearl Venture** looked ill-at-ease on the fast ground and was never able to get himself into the action. (9/1)
**4187 Steamroller Stanly** had finished way behind the winner last month and was never going well enough to put the record straight. (14/1)
**3850* Golden Arrow (IRE)** had had a six-hour cross-country trip to the races and this could have been the reason for his very lack-lustre performance. (7/2)

## 4261 E.B.F. FREETHORPE MAIDEN STKS (2-Y.O) (Class D)

4-00 (4-02) **1m 3y** £3,712.60 (£1,109.80: £531.40: £242.20) Stalls: High GOING minus 0.19 sec per fur (GF)

| | | | | SP | RR | SF |
|---|---|---|---|---|---|---|
| | **High Roller (IRE)** (HRACecil) **2-9-0** WRyan(12) (leggy: scope: hld up in tch: hdwy to ld 1f out: sn clr: impressive) | — | **1** | 10/11[1] | 94++ | 45 |

| | | | | SP | RR | SF |
|---|---|---|---|---|---|---|
| | **Teofilio (IRE)** (DRLoder) **2-9-0** RHughes(5) (w'like: str: bkwd: a.p: styd on ins fnl f: no ch w wnr) | 5 | **2** | 8/1 | 84+ | 35 |
| 3925$^{5}$ | **Indifferent Guy** (CEBrittain) **2-9-0** BDoyle(7) (w ldr: led 3f to 1f out: sn rdn & outpcd) | ¾ | **3** | 50/1 | 83 | 34 |
| | **Malik (IRE)** (SbinSuroor) **2-9-0** PatEddery(15) (w'like: str: bkwd: led 5f: wknd wl over 1f out) | 5 | **4** | 7/2$^{2}$ | 73 | 24 |
| | **Talib (USA)** (DMorley) **2-9-0** RHills(2) (leggy: lt-f: sn chsng ldrs: hrd drvn over 2f out: sn outpcd) | 1 | **5** | 20/1 | 71 | 22 |
| | **Include Me Out** (JRFanshawe) **2-9-0** NDay(11) (gd sort: bkwd: bhd tl sme hdwy fnl 2f: nvr nrr) | 3 | **6** | 33/1 | 65 | 16 |
| 4069$^{13}$ | **Count Tony** (SPCWoods) **2-9-0** DBiggs(1) (nvr nrr) | ¾ | **7** | 50/1 | 63 | 14 |
| | **Perfect Paradigm (IRE)** (JHMGosden) **2-9-0** AMcGlone(3) (w'like: leggy: nvr nrr) | ¾ | **8** | 16/1 | 62 | 13 |
| | **Joli's Prince** (CMurray) **2-9-0** PBloomfield(4) (w'like: leggy: bkwd: trckd ldrs over 5f) | ¾ | **9** | 33/1 | 60 | 11 |
| | **Ramadour (IRE)** (JRFanshawe) **2-8-11**(3) NVarley(13) (wl grwn: bkwd: nvr trbld ldrs) | hd | **10** | 50/1 | 60 | 11 |
| 3757$^{5}$ | **Baaheth (USA)** (RWArmstrong) **2-9-0** WCarson(9) (s.i.s: hrd drvn 3f out: no imp) | hd | **11** | 4/1$^{3}$ | 60 | 11 |
| | **Marsul (USA)** (JHMGosden) **2-9-0** MHills(14) (gd sort: bkwd: s.s: effrt ½-wy: wknd 2f out) | 2 | **12** | 16/1 | 56 | 7 |
| | **Aquavita** (CACyzer) **2-8-9** TSprake(8) (leggy: unf: bit bkwd: s.s: a bhd) | 2 | **13** | 50/1 | 47 | — |
| | **Sipowitz** (CACyzer) **2-9-0** MRimmer(6) (leggy: unf: bkwd: sn pushed along in rr) | 6 | **14** | 50/1 | 40 | — |
| | **She's A Cracker** (CADwyer) **2-8-2**(7) JoHunnam(10) (cmpt: bkwd: a bhd & outpcd) | ½ | **15** | 50/1 | 34 | — |
| | | | | (SP 139.9%) | **15 Rn** | |

**1m 38.8** (3.50) CSF £10.82 TOTE £1.80: £1.70 £2.60 £4.00 (£12.20) Trio £70.70 OWNER Baron G Von Ullmann (NEWMARKET) BRED S. Niarchos

**High Roller (IRE)** confirmed all the promise of his homework with a very impressive display and was immediately quoted at 16/1 for the 1997 Derby. (10/11: 4/6-11/10)

**Teofilio (IRE)**, nowhere near as forward in condition as the winner, nevertheless showed plenty of promise and could go places. (8/1: op 4/1)

**3925 Indifferent Guy**, the most experienced member of the field, shared the running until being made to look pedestrian when the winner showed his paces. (50/1)

**Malik (IRE)**, a very moderate mover on such lively ground, helped put pace to the race until blowing up below the distance. (7/2)

**Talib (USA)**, a leggy colt who showed plenty of knee-action, turned in a very encouraging first run and looks to have ability. (20/1)

**Include Me Out** is bred to need extreme trips and was only finding his stride when it was all over. (33/1)

## 4262 LOTTIE AND ALBERT BOTTON MEMORIAL NURSERY H'CAP (0-85) (2-Y.O) (Class D)

4-30 (4-33) **1m 3y** £3,529.30 (£1,053.40: £503.20: £228.10) Stalls: High GOING minus 0.19 sec per fur (GF)

| | | | | SP | RR | SF |
|---|---|---|---|---|---|---|
| 4113$^{8}$ | **Can Can Lady (72)** (MJohnston) **2-8-9** MHills(6) (lw: a.p: led over 1f out: rdn & edgd rt: r.o wl) | — | **1** | 7/1 | 71 | 35 |
| 3982$^{17}$ | **Select Star (IRE) (68)** (APJarvis) **2-8-5** WRyan(8) (lw: chsd ldrs: rdn over 1f out: styd on wl towards fin) | 1¼ | **2** | 12/1 | 65 | 29 |
| 3998$^{3}$ | **Maradi (IRE) (77)** (DMorley) **2-9-0** WCarson(13) (lw: trckd ldrs: effrt over 1f out: kpt on ins fnl f) | nk | **3** | 9/2$^{2}$ | 73 | 37 |
| 3936$^{3}$ | **Sinecure (USA) (84)** (JHMGosden) **2-9-7** AMcGlone(10) (a.p: led over 3f out tl over 1f out: no ex fnl f) | ¾ | **4** | 6/1$^{3}$ | 78 | 42 |
| 4131$^{9}$ | **Puzzlement (69)** (CEBrittain) **2-8-6** BDoyle(9) (mde most over 4f: rdn & nt clr run ins fnl f: swtchd lft: r.o) | 1¼ | **5** | 11/1 | 61 | 25 |
| 4106$^{6}$ | **Gresatre (68)** (CADwyer) **2-7-12**(7) JoHunnam(12) (hld up: effrt 2f out: nt pce to chal) | hd | **6** | 8/1 | 60 | 24 |
| 3975$^{2}$ | **Bold Oriental (IRE) (72)** (NACallaghan) **2-8-9** PatEddery(2) (lw: trckd ldrs: swtchd rt 3f out: sn rdn: no imp) | hd | **7** | 11/4$^{1}$ | 64 | 28 |
| 3998$^{11}$ | **Soden (IRE) (76)** (TGMills) **2-8-13** RHughes(5) (hld up & bhd: hdwy u.p over 1f out: no imp) | hd | **8** | 20/1 | 67 | 31 |
| 3046$^{8}$ | **Fan of Vent-Axia (61)** (CNAllen) **2-7-7**(5) MartinDwyer(4) (in tch tl wknd u.p 2f out) | 3 | **9** | 20/1 | 46 | 10 |
| 4106$^{4}$ | **Castles Burning (USA) (60)** (CACyzer) **2-7-8**(3) NVarley(7) (hld up: effrt 3f out: sn rdn & wknd) | 1¾ | **10** | 8/1 | 42 | 6 |
| 4106$^{5}$ | **Silca's My Key (IRE) (68)** (MRChannon) **2-8-5** TSprake(3) (hld up: rdn wl over 2f out: no imp) | 2 | **11** | 14/1 | 46 | 10 |
| 4049$^{11}$ | **Rock Fantasy (63)** (CMurray) **2-8-0b** DRMcCabe(11) (lost pl ½-wy: t.o) | 19 | **12** | 33/1 | 3 | — |
| | | | | (SP 129.0%) | **12 Rn** | |

**1m 39.4** (4.10) CSF £85.43 CT £400.42 TOTE £9.90: £2.60 £5.90 £1.90 (£81.20) Trio £107.40 OWNER Mr A. W. Robinson (MIDDLEHAM) BRED Godolphin Management Co Ltd

**2797 Can Can Lady** appreciated this step up in trip and won with a bit more in hand than the margin suggests. (7/1)

**3821 Select Star (IRE)** would seem to be coming to himself fast now and should be able to find an opening before the season ends. (12/1)

**3998 Maradi (IRE)** needs all of this trip and will make his mark when faced with a stiffer test of stamina. (9/2)

**3936 Sinecure (USA)** only got shaken off inside the distance and there was no disgrace in this defeat. (6/1)

**Puzzlement**, still holding every chance but being nudged along when forced to switch 200 yards out, lost his momentum and whatever chance remained. (11/1: 8/1-12/1)

**4106 Gresatre** failed to deliver his bid, despite staying on, and there would seem to be more improvement to come. (8/1)

## 4263 WILLIAM YOUNGER EAST ANGLIA MAIDEN H'CAP (0-60) (3-Y.O+) (Class F)

5-00 (5-03) **1m 3y** £3,548.00 (£1,064.00: £512.00: £236.00) GOING minus 0.19 sec per fur (GF)

| | | | | SP | RR | SF |
|---|---|---|---|---|---|---|
| 4053$^{3}$ | **Night of Glass (55)** (DMorris) **3-9-9v** NDay(18) (hld up: drvn along 3f out: hdwy to ld over 1f out: sn clr) | — | **1** | 7/2$^{1}$ | 64 | 48 |
| 2745$^{9}$ | **Diebiedale (45)** (RBoss) **4-8-12**(5) GFaulkner(19) (lw: trckd ldrs: led 2f out tl over 1f out: one pce) | 2 | **2** | 25/1 | 50 | 38 |
| 4082$^{13}$ | **Northern Grey (49)** (DrJDScargill) **4-9-7** NCarlisle(12) (hld up & bhd: gd hdwy 2f out: rdn & r.o wl ins fnl f) | 1 | **3** | 14/1 | 52 | 40 |
| 979$^{9}$ | **Framed (IRE) (49)** (SCWilliams) **6-9-2**(5) MartinDwyer(10) (in tch: hdwy 3f out: ev ch whn veered rt ent fnl f) | 2 | **4** | 14/1 | 48 | 36 |
| 4098$^{17}$ | **Chalky Dancer (42)** (HJCollingridge) **4-9-0** MRimmer(1) (trckd ldrs: ev ch 2f out: rdn & no ex fnl f) | 1½ | **5** | 25/1 | 38 | 26 |
| 3958$^{3}$ | **Riccarton (50)** (PCalver) **3-9-4** WRyan(17) (hld up: hdwy & swtchd lft 3f out: sn rdn: nt rch ldrs) | 5 | **6** | 6/1$^{2}$ | 36 | 20 |
| 2437$^{5}$ | **College Night (IRE) (46)** (CADwyer) **4-9-4** WCarson(16) (effrt u.p over 2f out: wnt lame & eased ins fnl f) | ¾ | **7** | 6/1$^{2}$ | 31 | 19 |
| 3881$^{4}$ | **Creeking (52)** (SirMarkPrescott) **3-9-6** CNutter(14) (prom: disp ld 3f out: sn rdn & wknd) | 1½ | **8** | 8/1$^{3}$ | 34 | 18 |
| 3978$^{4}$ | **Office Hours (52)** (CACyzer) **4-9-10** PBloomfield(6) (rdn & effrt 2f out: n.d) | 1¾ | **9** | 12/1 | 30 | 18 |
| 3991$^{16}$ | **Severn Mill (44)** (JMBradley) **5-9-2** TSprake(15) (chsd ldrs over 5f) | s.h | **10** | 33/1 | 22 | 10 |
| 4070$^{5}$ | **Tonic Chord (48)** (JRFanshawe) **3-9-2** AMcGlone(4) (sn pushed along: nvr bttr than mid div) | d.h | **10** | 16/1 | 26 | 10 |
| 4186$^{17}$ | **Yezza (IRE) (55)** (APJarvis) **3-9-9v** PatEddery(13) (hld up: a bhd) | 1¾ | **12** | 10/1 | 30 | 14 |
| 3995$^{25}$ | **Gool Lee Shay (USA) (50)** (RMWhitaker) **3-9-4** MHills(5) (w ldr: led ½-wy to 2f out: wknd qckly) | 1¾ | **13** | 14/1 | 21 | 5 |
| *4095*$^{7}$ | **Classic Royale (USA) (55)** (RHarris) **3-9-9** RPrice(20) (a in rr) | 1½ | **14** | 25/1 | 23 | 7 |
| 3966$^{4}$ | **Charisse Dancer (53)** (CFWall) **3-9-7** RHills(3) (a bhd) | 1 | **15** | 10/1 | 19 | 3 |
| 3986$^{12}$ | **Jeopardize (50)** (CEBrittain) **3-9-4** BDoyle(9) (a bhd) | 1½ | **16** | 20/1 | 13 | — |
| 3852$^{15}$ | **Flying Harold (46)** (MRChannon) **3-9-0** RHughes(8) (led 4f: rdn & wknd 3f out) | 1½ | **17** | 16/1 | 6 | — |
| 3051$^{3}$ | **Topup (55)** (JWHills) **3-9-9** OUrbina(2) (prom to ½-wy: sn lost tch: t.o) | 25 | **18** | 10/1 | — | — |
| | | | | (SP 147.9%) | **18 Rn** | |

**1m 39.4** (4.10) CSF £94.91 CT £1,136.01 TOTE £4.40: £2.20 £7.80 £4.40 £5.10 (£101.10) Trio £343.50; £387.11 to Ayr 20/09/96 OWNER Mr K Silvester and Mr B Silvester (NEWMARKET) BRED Brian Silvester and Kenneth Paul Silvester

WEIGHT FOR AGE 3yo-4lb

**4053 Night of Glass** opened his account with a fairly straightforward success, but his jockey left nothing to chance and drove him out firmly to the finish. (7/2)

**2305 Diebiedale**, fresh and well after a two-month holiday, ran extremely well at this first attempt at a mile. She will soon be paying her way. (25/1)
**1691 Northern Grey** wore blinkers in his previous race, but they were done away with this time and he produced probably his best effort yet. (14/1)
**688 Framed (IRE)** would have taken all the beating had he not drifted over to the far rail inside the final furlong, giving away more ground than he was beaten by. (14/1: 10/1-20/1)
**Chalky Dancer** joined issue two furlongs out and looked to be going as well as any, but a turn of speed was missing when he was put to the test. (25/1)
**2437 College Night (IRE)** was staying on really well when she appeared to go lame, and was eased right up inside the last furlong. (6/1)
**3881 Creeking** (8/1: op 5/1)
**3777 Gool Lee Shay (USA)** (14/1: op 7/1)
**3051 Topup** (10/1: op 6/1)

T/Plpt: £71.80 (162.39 Tckts). T/Qdpt: £21.10 (29.39 Tckts). IM

## 4264a-4267a (Irish Racing) - See Computer Raceform

## 0660a-GALWAY (Ireland) (R-H) (Good to firm)
## Tuesday September 10th

### 4268a ARDILAUN HOUSE HOTEL OYSTER STKS (Listed) (3-Y.O+)
5-00 (5-04) **1m 4f** £9,675.00 (£2,775.00: £1,275.00: £375.00)

| | | Dist | Pos | SP | RR | SF |
|---|---|---|---|---|---|---|
| 3728a[3] | **Predappio** (JOxx,Ireland) **3-8-13** JPMurtagh (chsd ldrs: swtchd to chal over 1f out: rdn & styd on to ld ins fnl f) | — | 1 | 2/1[2] | 115+ | — |
| 3728a[2] | **I'm Supposin (IRE)** (KPrendergast,Ireland) **4-9-5** WJSupple (hld up: chsd ldr over 2f out: led over 1f out tl ins fnl fnl f: kpt on) | ½ | 2 | 15/8[1] | 111 | — |
| 3728a[5] | **Fill the Bill (IRE)** (APO'Brien,Ireland) **4-9-5** CRoche (hld up towards rr: hdwy 3f out: chsng ldrs over 1f out: no ex u.p fnl f) | 4½ | 3 | 5/1 | 105 | — |
| 3531a[6] | **Ceirseach (IRE)** (JSBolger,Ireland) **3-8-10b** KJManning (led tl over 5f out: outpcd over 2f out: styd on ins fnl f) | s.h | 4 | 9/1 | 105 | — |
| | **Munif (IRE)** (DKWeld,Ireland) **4-9-5b** MJKinane (chsd ldr tl led over 5f out: rdn over 2f out: hdd over 1f out: sn wknd) | 5 | 5 | 100/30[3] | 99 | — |
| | | | | (SP 117.9%) | | **5 Rn** |

**2m 39.1** OWNER Sheikh Mohammed (CURRABEG)
**3728a Predappio**, with blinkers left off, hacked up and the winning margin is in no way a true reflection. He will almost certainly go to Dubai this winter and has a solid future. (2/1)
**3728a I'm Supposin (IRE)** led approaching the last furlong, but was totally outpaced close home. (15/8)
**3531a Fill the Bill (IRE)** could only stay on at the one pace. (5/1)
**3531a Ceirseach (IRE)** ran along in front to halfway and kept on again from the rear inside the last. (9/1: op 6/1)
**Munif (IRE)**, in front from halfway to early in the straight, was outclassed. (100/30)
NR

## 4269a-4279a (Irish Racing) - See Computer Raceform

## 3892a-LEOPARDSTOWN (Dublin, Ireland) (L-H) (Good)
## Saturday September 14th

### 4280a FLYING FIVE (Gp 3) (2-Y.O)
3-25 (3-29) **5f** £16,250.00 (£4,750.00: £2,250.00: £750.00)

| | | Dist | Pos | SP | RR | SF |
|---|---|---|---|---|---|---|
| 3708[2] | **Eveningperformance** (HCandy) **5-9-6** CRutter (mde all: rdn ins fnl f: r.o) | — | 1 | 9/10[1] | 117+ | 77 |
| 2816a* | **Ailleacht (USA)** (JSBolger,Ireland) **4-9-6** KJManning (cl up: 2nd & pushed along 2f out: u.p 1f out: kpt on wl) | ½ | 2 | 6/1[3] | 115? | 75 |
| 4057[3] | **Catch The Blues (IRE)** (APO'Brien,Ireland) **4-9-6b** MJKinane (bhd & sn outpcd: rdn ½-wy: hdwy to go 3rd early fnl f: r.o wl u.p) | nk | 3 | 3/1[2] | 114 | 74 |
| | **Symboli Kildare (IRE)** (JOxx,Ireland) **3-9-8b[1]** JPMurtagh (chsd ldrs: 3rd briefly over 1f out: no imp ins fnl f) | 3 | 4 | 9/1 | 107 | 67 |
| 3562a[6] | **Sunset Reigns (IRE)** (APO'Brien,Ireland) **3-9-5** SCraine (prom: rdn wl over 1f out: sn btn) | 4 | 5 | 9/1 | 91 | 51 |
| | **Really Chuffed** (WPMullins,Ireland) **2-8-0** WJSmith (chsd ldrs: dropped bhd & n.d fr 2f out) | 5 | 6 | 25/1 | 78 | 16 |
| | | | | (SP 115.8%) | | **6 Rn** |

**57.8 secs** (0.30) OWNER Mrs David Blackburn (WANTAGE) BRED Mrs R. D. Peacock
**3708 Eveningperformance** got a bit warm in the preliminaries and had to be hooded to go into the stalls. She made all and, shaken up inside the last, never looked like being seriously challenged. Third in the Prix de l'Abbaye last year, she goes for the same race again, and looks the biggest danger to Anabaa. (9/10)
**2816a* Ailleacht (USA)** chased the winner unavailingly throughout to be nearest at the finish, but is almost certainly flattered by her proximity at the line. (6/1: op 4/1)
**4057 Catch The Blues (IRE)** either could not or would not go the early pace and had plenty to do from halfway. She ran on under pressure inside the last and this again demonstrated the necessity of a sixth furlong for her. (3/1: op 2/1)
**Symboli Kildare (IRE)** had no chance at these weights, but ran on well enough to suggest his turn will come again this season over a longer trip, possibly in a handicap. (9/1: op 6/1)

### 4281a IRISH CHAMPION STKS (Gp 1) (3-Y.O+ C & F)
4-00 (4-00) **1m 2f** £90,300.00 (£28,800.00: £13,800.00: £4,800.00)

| | | Dist | Pos | SP | RR | SF |
|---|---|---|---|---|---|---|
| 3907a* | **Timarida (IRE)** (JOxx,Ireland) **4-9-1** JPMurtagh (hld up: last st: swtchd rt & gd hdwy wl over 1f out: qcknd & edgd lft ins fnl f: sn led: r.o wl) | — | 1 | 3/1[2] | 121+ | 70 |

2837a* **Dance Design (IRE)** (DKWeld,Ireland) **3-8-8** MJKinane (set slow pce: rdn & qckned 2f out: u.p 1f out: hdd & outpcd ins fnl f)....1½ **2** 9/2[3] 119 61
3912a[4] **Glory of Dancer** (PAKelleway) **3-8-11** OPeslier (hld up in tch: 4th st: trckng ldrs whn sltly hmpd ins fnl f: rdn & r.o)....nk **3** 10/1 121 63
3070[3] **Shaamit (IRE)** (WJHaggas) **3-8-11** MHills (hld up: 3rd on ins st: no imp over 1f out: shkn up & nt qckn ins fnl f)....1½ **4** 5/4[1] 119 61
3731a* **Idris (IRE)** (JSBolger,Ireland) **6-9-4** KJManning (hld up: 5th on ins st: nt clr run 2f out: swtchd rt 1f out: rdn & kpt on)....nk **5** 14/1 118 67
3431* **Tamayaz (CAN)** (SbinSuroor) **4-9-4** GCarter (chsd ldr: rdn 2f out: lost pl 1f out: kpt on same pce)....nk **6** 6/1 118 67
(SP 117.7%) **6 Rn**

**2m 6.2** (2.20) OWNER H H Aga Khan (CURRABEG) BRED H.H. Aga Khan's Studs S.C.
**3907a* Timarida (IRE)** had no difficulty at all in adapting to a slow pace. Last into the straight, she began getting her head down with less than two furlongs to race and, despite edging left when quickening up early inside the last, she was in total command over the last half-furlong and only had to be hand ridden. She boasts a turn of foot and seems adaptable to any tactics. (3/1)
**2837a* Dance Design (IRE)** set only a moderate pace and, when Kinane asked her to quicken early in the straight, the response was immediate. It was no disgrace for her to find herself outpaced by Timarida inside the last. (9/2)
**3912a Glory of Dancer** was right in contention when slightly inconvenienced by the winner early inside the last. He ran on with some purpose but was held near the finish. (10/1)
**3070 Shaamit (IRE)**, well placed throughout and apparently going well on the inside turning for home in third place, found himself with no space on the inner from two furlongs out. He had his chance early inside the last, but just could not quicken when asked. (5/4)
**3731a* Idris (IRE)** was another who found traffic problems on this, one of his favourite tracks. Switched out with a furlong to run, he was nearest at the end. (14/1)
**3431* Tamayaz (CAN)** ran second until finding himself flat-footed from a furlong out. He would have appreciated a stronger gallop. (6/1)

## 4282a-4284a (Irish Racing) - See Computer Raceform

## 4162a-EVRY (France) (R-H) (Good)
### Tuesday September 10th

### 4285a PRIX D'ARENBERG (Gp 3) (2-Y.O)
2-30 (2-25) **5f 110y** £28,986.00 (£10,540.00: £5,270.00: £2,635.00)

| | | | | SP | RR | SF |
|---|---|---|---|---|---|---|
| 3750a[3] | **Pas De Reponse (USA)** (MmeCHead,France) **2-8-8** FHead | — | **1** | | 101+ | — |
| | **Heaven's Command** (NClement,France) **2-8-8** GMosse | 1½ | **2** | | 97 | — |
| 3748a* | **Ballade Viennoise (FR)** (J-PGauvin,France) **2-8-8** EAntoniat | 1 | **3** | | 94 | — |
| 3903a[3] | **Jennelle** (CADwyer) **2-8-8** JoHunnam | 1½ | **4** | | 89 | — |

**5 Rn**

**65.06 secs** (0.66) P-M 1.50F: 1.10F 1.10F OWNER Wertheimer Brothers (CHANTILLY) BRED Wertheimer & Frere
**3750a Pas De Reponse (USA)** won like an odds-on favourite, totally outclassing her field and leading from pillar-to-post. She is definitely going the right way and is now likely to head for the Cheveley Park Stakes, which her trainer has won twice before with fillies that have gone on to win the 1000 Guineas. She has already won over six furlongs and should give a good account of herself at Newmarket.
**Heaven's Command** tried in vain to tackle the winner in the closing stages. She is probably only of listed standard, but is a game performer.
**Ballade Viennoise (FR)**, held up, was putting in her best work at the finish.
**3903a Jennelle** tracked the winner from the start, but was beaten with a furlong left to run.

## 1580a-CAPANNELLE (Rome, Italy) (R-H) (Good)
### Wednesday September 11th

### 4286a PREMIO OLA (Unraced 2-Y.O F)
4-00 (4-07) **7f 110y** £12,180.00

| | | | SP | RR | SF |
|---|---|---|---|---|---|
| **Regal Dynasty (IRE)** (LCamici,Italy) **2-9-0** MCangiano | — | **1** | | — | — |
| **Fabiana Sciumbata** (Italy) **2-9-0** GBietolini | 1½ | **2** | | — | — |
| **Valentina Crown (USA)** (Italy) **2-9-0** VMezzatesta | 4 | **3** | | — | — |
| **Shareef Allah** (KMcAuliffe) **2-9-0** FJovine | 1½ | **4** | | — | — |

**11 Rn**

**1m 31.7** TOTE 52L: 16L 18L 13L (183L) OWNER Allevamento Gialloblu BRED Massimo Marchetti
**Shareef Allah**, racing in mid-division, was switched to the outside for a run in the straight and kept on well inside the final furlong for fourth place.

### 4287a PREMIO STRATFORD (Unraced 2-Y.O C & G)
4-30 (4-40) **7f 110y** £12,180.00

| | | | SP | RR | SF |
|---|---|---|---|---|---|
| **General Song (IRE)** (KMcAuliffe) **2-9-0** FJovine | — | **1** | | — | — |
| **Rio Napo (IRE)** (Italy) **2-9-0** MPasquale | 4½ | **2** | | — | — |
| **Mont Royal** (Italy) **2-9-0** DZarroli | 2 | **3** | | — | — |

**14 Rn**

**1m 31.0** TOTE 48L: 20L 22L 29L (168L) OWNER Scuderia Gen Horse (LAMBOURN) BRED T. J. Hurley
**General Song (IRE)**, who tracked the leader, took over two furlongs out. From there he quickened clear and came home in impressive style.

## 1946a-BELMONT PARK (New York, USA) (L-H)
### Saturday September 14th

### 4288a MAN O'WAR STKS (Gp 1) (3-Y.O+)
9-10 **1m 3f (Turf)** £154,839.00 (£51,613.00: £28,387.00: £15,484.00)

| | | | SP | RR | SF |
|---|---|---|---|---|---|
| **Diplomatic Jet (USA)** (JPicou,USA) **4-9-0** JChavez | — | **1** | | 129 | — |

| | | | SP | RR | SF |
|---|---|---|---|---|---|
| 3912a* | **Mecke (USA)** (ETortora,USA) **4-9-0** RobbieDavis | 2 **2** | | 126 | — |
| 3911a* | **Marlin (USA)** (DWLukas,USA) **3-8-8** SSellers | ¾ **3** | | 127 | — |
| 3395a⁴ | **Montjoy (USA)** (PFICole) **4-9-0** GStevens | ¾ **4** | | 124 | — |

**8 Rn**

**2m 14.37** P-M 25.20: (1-2) 11.60 7.00 (1-2-3) 8.10 4.60 5.40 OWNER F. Hooper BRED F. Hooper
**3395a Montjoy (USA)** was backed down to second favourite, but could not justify the support.

# VELIEFENDI (Istanbul, Turkey) (R-H) (Good to firm)
## Saturday September 14th

## 4289a TOPKAPI KOSUSU (Listed) (3-Y.O+)
3-00 (3-02) **1m** £38,710.00 (£15,484.00: £7,742.00)

| | | | SP | RR | SF |
|---|---|---|---|---|---|
| 3153⁴ | **Cadeaux Tryst** (EALDunlop) **4-9-6** TSprake | — **1** | | 112 | — |
| | **Airman (TUR)** (Turkey) **4-9-6** HKaratas | hd **2** | | 112 | — |
| 3945⁵ | **Lap of Luxury** (WJarvis) **7-9-3** NDay | nk **3** | | 108 | — |
| | **I Nanu (TUR)** (Turkey) **4-9-3** AAtci | s.h **4** | | 108 | — |
| | **Gelinim (TUR)** (Turkey) **5-9-3** AOzdeniz | **5** | | — | — |
| | **Blow Up (TUR)** (Turkey) **3-8-8** SAkdi | **6** | | — | — |
| | **Mr Black (TUR)** (Turkey) **6-9-6** YTunc | **7** | | — | — |
| | **Binba Star (TUR)** (Turkey) **6-9-6b¹** MCilgin | **8** | | — | — |
| | **Moon Shine (TUR)** (Turkey) **6-9-6** MAkbulut | **9** | | — | — |
| | **Shank (RUS)** (Turkey) **3-8-11** SPshukov | **10** | | — | — |
| | **Lydhurst (USA)** (Turkey) **3-8-11b¹** Jean-PierreLopez | **11** | | — | — |

**11 Rn**

**1m 36.87** TOTE 1.60L: 2.50L 2.20L 3.55L (14.75L) OWNER Maktoum Al Maktoum (NEWMARKET) BRED Gainsborough Stud Management Ltd
**3153 Cadeaux Tryst**, held up well off the pace, began his challenge down the outside. He only managed to get on top near the line, but would have preferred more of an early pace.
**Airman (TUR)** went on two furlongs out, but was caught close home.
**3945 Lap of Luxury**, with the winner, was held up off the pace and made her effort on the outside. She is very game and ran well, but could give no more in the closing stages.

# 3034a-FRANKFURT (Germany) (L-H) (Good)
## Sunday September 15th

## 4290a MADE IN EUROPE-TROPHY (Gp 2) (3-Y.O+)
3-05 (3-14) **1m 2f** £54,054.00 (£21,622.00: £9,910.00: £4,505.00)

| | | | SP | RR | SF |
|---|---|---|---|---|---|
| 3905a* | **Artan (IRE)** (MRolke,Germany) **4-9-2** RCochrane (chsd ldrs: 2nd st: qcknd to ld over 2f out: sn clr: eased) | — **1** | | 117+ | — |
| 3034a² | **Sir Warren (IRE)** (HBlume,Germany) **3-8-5** ABrockhausen (hld up in rr: r.o fnl 2f: no ch w wnr) | 1 **2** | | 111 | — |
| 3746a³ | **Zero Problemo (IRE)** (BSchutz,Germany) **3-8-5** AStarke (a.p: 3rd st: rdn & one pce fnl 2f) | 3 **3** | | 107 | — |
| 3753a⁵ | **Wind Of Chance (GER)** (BSchutz,Germany) **3-8-5** LHammer-Hansen (mid div: 5th st: kpt on same pce) | 1¼ **4** | | 105 | — |
| 3842* | **Almond Rock** (JRFanshawe) **4-9-0** DHarrison (mid div: 7th st: sn rdn & one pce) | 2 **5** | | 103 | — |
| 3034a³ | **Silent Lake (GER)** (Germany) **5-9-0** RHughes (in tch tl no ex fr 2f out) | 1¾ **6** | | 101 | — |
| 4063* | **Poppy Carew (IRE)** (PWHarris) **4-8-9** GHind (mid div: one pce fr over 2f out) | 1¼ **7** | | 94 | — |
| 904a* | **Ardilan (IRE)** (Germany) **3-8-9ow2** ATylicki (chsd ldr: wknd 4f out) | 3 **8** | | 96 | — |
| | **No Dancer (GER)** (Germany) **5-9-0b** NGrant (mid div: btn 3f out) | 2½ **9** | | 90 | — |
| 2668a¹⁰ | **My Happy Guest (IRE)** (Germany) **3-8-5** AHelfenbein (a in rr) | nk **10** | | 87 | — |
| | **Favourite Prince (IRE)** (Germany) **5-9-0** RLudtke (led tl over 2f out: wknd qckly) | nk **11** | | 89 | — |

**11 Rn**

**2m 10.48** TOTE 34DM: 14DM 22DM 13DM OWNER Stall Brandenburg BRED J. Brennen
**3905a* Artan (IRE)**, a son of Be My Native, kicked clear two furlongs out and Cochrane had the confidence to ease him right down before the line.
**3842* Almond Rock** is a decent handicapper at best and was taking a huge step up in class here. He could never threaten the leaders and seemed slightly one-paced.
**4063* Poppy Carew (IRE)**, stepping up in class, never threatened to take a hand in proceedings.

# 4165a-LONGCHAMP (Paris, France) (R-H) (Good)
## Sunday September 15th

## 4291a PRIX D'AUMALE (Gp 3) (2-Y.O F)
1-30 (1-29) **1m** £28,986.00 (£10,540.00: £5,270.00)

| | | | SP | RR | SF |
|---|---|---|---|---|---|
| 2269a² | **Joyeuse Entree** (AdeRoyerDupre,France) **2-8-9** GMosse | — **1** | | 104 | 46 |
| | **Dissertation (FR)** (MmeCHead,France) **2-8-9** FHead | 2 **2** | | 100 | 42 |
| | **Nawal (FR)** (JdeRoualle,France) **2-8-9** CAsmussen | nk **3** | | 99 | 41 |

**11 Rn**

**1m 39.1** (4.10) P-M 2.60F: 1.40F 3.40F 3.20F (24.80F) OWNER Marquesa de Moratalla (CHANTILLY) BRED Marquesa de Moratalla
**Joyeuse Entree** is a very classy filly in the making. Slowly away and pulling hard, she found a gap halfway up the straight and showed top-class acceleration to win in fine style. She is an experienced but still-improving filly and she will be difficult to beat in the Prix Marcel Boussac.
**Dissertation (FR)** was soon in the lead, but had no answer when passed by the winner in the closing stages. However, she did battle on gamely to hold second place.
**Nawal (FR)** was hampered in the straight, but then put in a decent effort in the final furlong. She was probably unlucky not to have taken second place.

## 4292a PRIX VERMEILLE (Gp 1) (3-Y.O F)

2-40 (2-40) **1m 4f** £105,402.00 (£42,161.00: £21,080.00: £10,540.00)

| | | | | SP | RR | SF |
|---|---|---|---|---|---|---|
| 3570a[3] | **My Emma** (RGuest) **3-9-0** CAsmussen (mid div: 4th st: gd hdwy on ins over 1f out: rdn to ld ins fnl f: r.o wl) | — | **1** | 291/10 | 117 | 57 |
| 3688[2] | **Papering (IRE)** (LMCumani) **3-9-0** LDettori (led: qcknd 4f out: hdd ins fnl f: kpt on: fin 3rd, s.nk: plcd 2nd) | | **2** | 26/10[2] | 117 | 57 |
| 1949a[2] | **Miss Tahiti (IRE)** (AFabre,France) **3-9-0** OPeslier (chsd ldr pllng hrd: rdn 2f out: r.o one pce cl home: fin 4th, nk: plcd 3rd) | | **3** | 24/10[1] | 116 | 56 |
| 3392a[5] | **Leonila (IRE)** (RCollet,France) **3-9-0** DBoeuf (hld up in rr: swtchd lft 2f out: hmpd over 1f out: kpt on: fin 5th, s.nk: plcd 4th) | | **4** | 245/10 | 116 | 56 |
| 3021a* | **Zafzala (IRE)** (JOxx,Ireland) **3-9-0** JPMurtagh (mid div: rdn 2f out: r.o & hung lft u.p over 1f out: fin 2nd, hd: disq: plcd 5th) | | **5** | 7/2[3] | 117 | 57 |
| 3916a* | **Luna Wells (IRE)** (AFabre,France) **3-9-0** TJamet (hld up in rr: n.m.r 2f out: sn swtchd rt: r.o) | ½ | **6** | 26/10[2] | 115 | 55 |
| 3688[4] | **Shamadara (IRE)** (AdeRoyerDupre,France) **3-9-0** GMosse (racd in 4th: rdn 2f out: no hdwy) | 3 | **7** | 7/2[3] | 111 | 51 |
| 2069* | **Tulipa (USA)** (AFabre,France) **3-9-0** SGuillot (racd in 7th: rdn 2f out: one pce) | 3 | **8** | 26/10[2] | 107 | 47 |
| 3916a[2] | **Bint Salsabil (USA)** (JLDunlop) **3-9-0** WCarson (prom tl rdn & outpcd over 2f out) | ½ | **9** | 102/10 | 107 | 47 |
| 1388a[3] | **Camille (FR)** (PDemercastel,France) **3-9-0** AJunk (plld hrd: a in rr) | 8 | **10** | 18/1 | 96 | 36 |

(SP 178.6%) **10 Rn**

**2m 31.3** (5.30) P-M 30.10F: 4.80F 2.40F 1.50F (145.40F) OWNER Matthews Breeding and Racing (NEWMARKET) BRED Lord Matthews

**IN-FOCUS: For betting purposes Shamadara (IRE) and Zafzala (IRE) were cpld, as were Tulipa (USA) and Papering (IRE).**

**3570a My Emma** was given an outstanding ride by Asmussen to snaeak up the rail inside the final furlong and hold on bravely to the line. At Deauville she was totally unsuited by the lack of pace but, on this occasion, the race was run to suit her. Great credit must be given to her trainer who was winning his first Group One race. This beautifuuly-bred filly will now be retired for the season, and will be aimed at the Arc de Triomphe next year. (291/10)

**3688 Papering (IRE)** was promoted to second place on the disqualification of Zafzala. She put in a really game effort, leading from the start until well inside the final furlong. She stays really well, but is probably just a little one-paced. She has several options now and will either go for the Princess Royal, Prix de Royallieu or the Sun Chariot Stakes. (26/10)

**1949a Miss Tahiti (IRE)** was moved up a place in the Stewards' Room. She was perfectly placed to challenge for the lead in the straight, but did not have the necessary stamina in the final furlong. She is now back to her best after a difficult spring, and could go on to the Prix de l'Opera, rather than the Arc. (24/10)

**3916a Bint Salsabil (USA)** was given every possible chance, but faded in the straight after receiving some interference with a furlong and a half left to run. It is probably safe to state now that she does not stay a mile and a half in top-class company. (102/10)

## 4293a PRIX NIEL (Gp 2) (3-Y.O C & F)

3-10 (3-12) **1m 4f** £52,701.00 (£21,080.00: £10,540.00: £5,270.00)

| | | | | SP | RR | SF |
|---|---|---|---|---|---|---|
| 2480a* | **Helissio (FR)** (ELellouche,France) **3-9-2** OPeslier (mde all: r.o strly) | — | **1** | 4/5[1] | 123+ | 65 |
| 3035a* | **Darazari (IRE)** (AdeRoyerDupre,France) **3-9-2** GMosse (6th st: rdn & hdwy over 1f out: r.o: nt rch wnr) | 1 | **2** | 41/10[2] | 122 | 64 |
| 2844a* | **Radevore** (AFabre,France) **3-9-2** TJarnet (a cl up: wnt 2nd st: no ex fnl f) | 1½ | **3** | 20/1 | 120 | 62 |
| 3670[4] | **Grape Tree Road** (AFabre,France) **3-9-2** SGuillot (5th st: effrt on ins 2f out: no ex fnl f) | 1 | **4** | 181/10 | 118 | 60 |
| 3746a[7] | **Arbatax (IRE)** (PBary,France) **3-9-2** CAsmussen (hld up: 6th st: effrt 2f out: nvr nr to chal) | 3 | **5** | 16/1 | 114 | 56 |
| 3915a[2] | **Tarator (USA)** (ELellouche,France) **3-9-2** TQuinn (prom: 4th st: one pce fnl 2f) | s.nk | **6** | 11/1 | 114 | 56 |
| 3915a[7] | **Water Poet (IRE)** (AFabre,France) **3-9-2** LDettori (hld up: 8th st: nvr able to chal) | nk | **7** | 21/1 | 114 | 56 |
| 3746a[5] | **Le Destin (FR)** (PDemercastel,France) **3-9-2** AJunk (hld up in rr: hdwy 4f out: 7th st: sn btn) | 3 | **8** | 25/1 | 110 | 52 |
| 2473a[2] | **Polaris Flight (USA)** (PWChapple-Hyam) **3-9-2** JReid (trckd wnr tl wl over 2f out: 3rd st: sn wknd) | 1½ | **9** | 52/10[3] | 108 | 50 |
| | **Palatal (USA)** (FPoulsen,Denmark) **3-9-2** FJohansson (a towards rr: last & btn st) | 2½ | **10** | 27/1 | 104 | 46 |

(SP 127.5%) **10 Rn**

**2m 30.4** (4.40) P-M 1.80F: 1.10F 1.40F 2.30F (3.30F) OWNER Enrique Sarasola BRED Ecurie Skymarc Farm

**2480a* Helissio (FR)** was given a superb ride, and made every yard of the running to win without being put under severe pressure. Quickening in the straight to build up a lead of several lengths, he was just encouraged with hands and heels in the final furlong to hold his advantage. He has done extremely well during the summer and was reported to only be 80% fit on this occasion. He stays well and has a terrific turn of foot, so looks a good favourite for the Arc, and he is adaptable, and can either be held up or settled in front. (4/5)

**3035a* Darazari (IRE)**, racing just behind the leaders, did not have the best of luck when his jockey wanted to challenge in the straight. Once in the clear, he strode out well and was running on throughout the final furlong. This impressive colt is improving with every race. He takes up the challenge again in the Arc and may be better suited if there is more cut in the ground then there was here. (41/10)

**2844a* Radevore** was always well up and battled on gamely throughout the final furlong and a half. He was not quite up to this task, so he will miss the Arc and go instead for the Prix de Conseil de Paris. (20/1)

**3670 Grape Tree Road** looked extremely dangerous on the rail a furlong and a half out, but he could not go through with his effort. It appears that ten furlongs is the best distance for this colt who won the Grand Prix de Paris in June. (181/10)

**2473a Polaris Flight (USA)** ran very freely and was in second place until early in the straight, before going out like a light. This performance is probably best forgotten. (52/10)

## 4294a PRIX DE LA SALAMANDRE (Gp 1) (2-Y.O C & F)

3-40 (3-41) **7f** £52,701.00 (£21,080.00: £10,540.00: £5,270.00)

| | | | | SP | RR | SF |
|---|---|---|---|---|---|---|
| 3668* | **Revoque (IRE)** (PWChapple-Hyam) **2-9-0** JReid (hld up: 3rd st: rdn 2f out: qcknd to ld ins fnl f: r.o wl) | — | **1** | 21/10[2] | 114 | 69 |
| 3690[3] | **The West (USA)** (PFICole) **2-9-0** TQuinn (rdn & slt ld over 2f out: no ex fnl f) | 3 | **2** | 53/10[3] | 107 | 62 |
| 3750a[2] | **Zamindar (USA)** (AFabre,France) **2-9-0** TJarnet (led tl over 2f out: kpt on u.p: hdd & no ex ins fnl f) | s.h | **3** | 1/2[1] | 107 | 62 |
| 3908a[2] | **Dame D'Harvard (USA)** (RCollet,France) **2-8-11** OPeslier (hld up in rr: 4th st: kpt on fnl 2f) | nk | **4** | 69/10 | 103 | 58 |
| | **Sacristan** (AFabre,France) **2-9-0b[1]** SGuillot (s.i.s: 3rd st: sn eased: t.o) | dist | **5** | 1/2[1] | — | — |

(SP 194.1%) **5 Rn**

**1m 20.9** (1.90) P-M 3.10F: 3.70F 7.10F OWNER Mr R. E. Sangster (MARLBOROUGH) BRED Minch Bloodstock

**IN-FOCUS: For betting purposes Sacristan and Zamindar (USA) were cpld.**

**3668* Revoque (IRE)** was being niggled at early in the straight when three lengths adrift of the leaders. He was kept up to his task though and gradually wore down his rivals to take the lead half a furlong out, before striding out to an impressive victory. He is a big colt with plenty of scope, and he might now be left alone until next season, when his principal target will be the 2000 Guineas. (21/10)

**3690 The West (USA)** was one of the leaders from the start. He hit the front early in the straight and looked the likely winner two out but, come the furlong marker, he had shot his bolt. He might be better than this, particularly if his energies are not used up early. He will probably be rested until next year, although the Grand Criterium will be considered. (53/10)

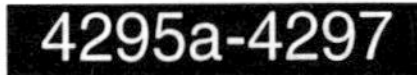



**3750a Zamindar (USA)** had another wretched race. His pacemaker missed the break and was then totally useless, never making it to the front, so he soon found himself sharing the lead at a fast pace. He looked beaten early in the straight but fought back gamely, and battled all the way to the line. Connections wanted to drop him out in his last two races but have been frustrated. He should be given another chance. (1/2)
**3908a Dame D'Harvard (USA)** was outpaced early on before putting in her best work at the finish. She is not quite up to this class and may have been flattered as the runner-up and third were at the end of their tether. (69/10)

## 4295a PRIX FOY (Gp 3) (4-Y.O+ C & F)

4-15 (4-11) **1m 4f** £28,986.00 (£10,540.00: £5,270.00)

| | | | Pos | SP | RR | SF |
|---|---|---|---|---|---|---|
| 2480a$^{2}$ | **Swain (IRE)** (AFabre,France) **4-9-2** TJarnet (hld up: wnt 2nd over 4f out: rdn 2f out: led appr fnl f: rdn out) | — | 1 | Evens$^{2}$ | 121+ | 41 |
| 3070* | **Pentire** (GWragg) **4-9-2** MHills (hld up in rr: led after 3f: rdn & hdd appr fnl f: kpt on one pce) | ½ | 2 | 4/5$^{1}$ | 120+ | 40 |
| 3915a$^{5}$ | **Leeds (IRE)** (HVandePoele,France) **4-9-2** SGuillot (4th st: styd on one pce) | 3 | 3 | 136/10$^{3}$ | 116 | 36 |
| | | | | (SP 112.4%) | | **5 Rn** |

**2m 33.9** (7.90) P-M 2.00F: 1.10F 1.10F OWNER Sheikh Mohammed (CHANTILLY) BRED Sheikh Mohammed
**2480a Swain (IRE)** had everything in his favour on this occasion, as Pentire took up the running after three furlongs and set a decent pace. He took the lead one and a half furlongs out and then held on well in the final furlong without being given a particularly hard race. This outing will have put him spot on for the Arc de Triomphe, a race in which he finished third a year ago, and he again represents excellent each-way value. (Evens)
**3070* Pentire** played into the hands of Swain. Considering he has a turn of foot, it was strange that he was taken into the lead when he could have turned out best of all in a sprint finish. He stayed on one-paced after being passed by the winner halfway up the straight, but things will be different in the Arc and he should not be written off. The Prix Foy is often a strangely-run race, so can produce a false result, and it was also the slowest of all the Arc trials. (4/5)
**3035a Leeds (IRE)**, racing in fourth place, ran on to finish third without ever looking likely to trouble the winner and runner-up. He is not up to this class, but is a game and consistent performer. (136/10)

# 4244-AYR (L-H) (Good to firm, Firm patches)
## Friday September 20th
WEATHER: fine WIND: fresh half bhd

## 4296 WILLIAMS DE BROE CLAIMING STKS (3-Y.O+) (Class E)

2-00 (2-02) **1m** £4,402.50 (£1,320.00: £635.00: £292.50) Stalls: High GOING minus 0.26 sec per fur (GF)

| | | | Pos | SP | RR | SF |
|---|---|---|---|---|---|---|
| 4136$^{9}$ | **Equerry (81)** (MJohnston) **5-8-13** JWeaver(8) (lw: trckd ldr: rdn to ld 2f out: clr fnl f) | — | 1 | 13/8$^{1}$ | 76 | 64 |
| 4190$^{5}$ | **High Premium (68)** (RAFahey) **8-9-3** KDarley(14) (sn pushed along: hmpd & lost pl 4f out: gd hdwy over 2f out: r.o wl fnl f) | 3 | 2 | 7/2$^{2}$ | 74 | 62 |
| 3815$^{5}$ | **Broctune Gold (67)** (MrsMReveley) **5-9-1** ACulhane(2) (lw: led to 2f out: kpt on same pce) | nk | 3 | 8/1$^{3}$ | 71 | 59 |
| *4089** | **North Ardar (62)** (DNicholls) **6-8-6**(7) JBramhill(1) (trckd ldrs: effrt over 2f out: wknd over 1f out) | 6 | 4 | 14/1 | 57 | 45 |
| 3866$^{3}$ | **Scenicris (IRE) (55)** (RHollinshead) **3-7-13**(3)ow4 FLynch(11) (bhd: effrt over 2f out: nvr nr to chal) | 1 | 5 | 9/1 | 48 | 28 |
| 3442$^{13}$ | **Indian Rhapsody (47)** (ABailey) **4-7-11**(3) DWright(9) (bhd: sme hdwy over 2f out: nvr nr ldrs) | 3 | 6 | 12/1 | 36 | 24 |
| 4070* | **Power Game (58)** (JBerry) **3-8-9b** JCarroll(6) (chsd ldrs: rdn over 2f out: sn wknd) | 2½ | 7 | 20/1 | 44 | 28 |
| 3878$^{8}$ | **Seconds Away (28)** (JSGoldie) **5-8-5** TWilliams(7) (sn bhd: sme hdwy 2f out: n.d) | ½ | 8 | 66/1 | 35 | 23 |
| 3929* | **Prima Volta (67)** (RHannon) **3-9-2** DHarrison(5) (sn bhd) | s.h | 9 | 10/1 | 50 | 34 |
| 4070$^{3}$ | **Roseate Lodge (48)** (SEKettlewell) **10-7-12**(7) JennyBenson(10) (a bhd) | 1 | 10 | 25/1 | 33 | 21 |
| 3426$^{11}$ | **Giddy (45)** (JHetherton) **3-8-0** NKennedy(3) (chsd ldrs tl lost pl 3f out) | 8 | 11 | 66/1 | 16 | — |
| 2080$^{8}$ | **Arabian Design** (GMMoore) **4-9-3** JTate(13) (chsd ldrs tl lost pl 3f out: sn bhd) | 15 | 12 | 66/1 | — | — |
| | | | | (SP 118.0%) | | **12 Rn** |

**1m 38.49** (1.09) CSF £7.47 TOTE £2.50: £1.40 £1.60 £3.40 (£4.10) Trio £9.80 OWNER Mr J. R. Good (MIDDLEHAM) BRED J. R. and Mrs P. Good
WEIGHT FOR AGE 3yo-4lb
Equerry clmd AGWatson £8,000
**3981 Equerry**, in a foul mood beforehand, did nothing wrong in the race and his rider left nothing to chance, driving him well clear a furlong out. (13/8)
**4190 High Premium**, attempting to repeat last year's success in this event, dropped right back when hampered on the home turn. Last of all two furlong from home, he made inroads in the final furlong but far too late to trouble the winner. (7/2)
**3815 Broctune Gold** set a strong pace but it was obvious two furlongs out that he was no match for the winner. (8/1)
**3866 Scenicris (IRE)** (9/1: 6/1-10/1)
**3929* Prima Volta** (10/1: op 6/1)

## 4297 FAUCETS FOR MEYNELL SAFEMIX THERMOSTATIC VALVES AND SHOWERS H'CAP (0-90) (3-Y.O+ F & M) (Class C)

2-35 (2-36) **1m 2f** £5,952.00 (£1,776.00: £848.00: £384.00) Stalls: High GOING minus 0.26 sec per fur (GF)

| | | | Pos | SP | RR | SF |
|---|---|---|---|---|---|---|
| 4190$^{14}$ | **Rebel County (IRE) (80)** (ABailey) **3-9-5** DBiggs(5) (lw: hld up: hdwy over 2f out: led over 1f out: jst hld on) | — | 1 | 15/2 | 86 | 50 |
| 3923$^{2}$ | **Daira (65)** (JDBethell) **3-8-4** SDrowne(4) (hld up: stdy hdwy 4f out: r.o wl fnl f: jst failed) | hd | 2 | 6/1$^{3}$ | 71 | 35 |
| 3815$^{2}$ | **Fairywings (82)** (MrsJRRamsden) **3-9-7** KFallon(1) (lw: sn bhd & pushed along: styd on wl u.p fnl 2f: nrst fin) | 2 | 3 | 5/1$^{2}$ | 85 | 49 |
| 3938* | **Ground Game (82)** (DRLoder) **3-9-7** KDarley(3) (lw: trckd ldr: led over 3f out tl over 2f out: kpt on same pce appr fnl f) | hd | 4 | 6/4$^{1}$ | 85 | 49 |
| 1775$^{8}$ | **Dee-Lady (75)** (WGMTurner) **4-8-13**(7) DSweeney(6) (trckd ldrs: led over 2f out tl over 1f out: one pce) | ½ | 5 | 33/1 | 77 | 47 |
| 3947$^{17}$ | **Frezeliere (85)** (JLDunlop) **3-9-10** JFortune(7) (trckd ldrs: rdn 2f out: wknd appr fnl f) | 6 | 6 | 8/1 | 77 | 41 |
| 1854$^{5}$ | **Circled (USA) (75)** (BWHills) **3-9-0** JCarroll(8) (led: rdn & hdd over 3f out: wknd over 1f out) | 2 | 7 | 10/1 | 64 | 28 |
| 4047$^{8}$ | **Sing And Dance (57)** (EWeymes) **3-7-10** NKennedy(2) (sn pushed along: bhd fnl 3f) | ½ | 8 | 25/1 | 45 | 9 |
| | | | | (SP 109.7%) | | **8 Rn** |

**2m 8.56** (3.96) CSF £45.15 CT £207.69 TOTE £9.60: £2.10 £1.60 £1.80 (£50.30) OWNER Showtime Ice Cream Concessionaire (TARPORLEY) BRED C. J. Foy
LONG HANDICAP Sing And Dance 7-0
WEIGHT FOR AGE 3yo-6lb
**3989 Rebel County (IRE)**, stepping back up in distance, travelled strongly for much of the way but, in the end, the post came just in time. (15/2)

**3923 Daira**, whose jockey seemed if anything guilty of over-confidence, waited until inside the last to make his effort. She was eating up ground all the way to the line, but the post came just too soon. Her luck must change before long. (6/1)
**3815 Fairywings** took a walk in the market. Her rider really earned his fee and only his persistence got her into third spot near the line. (5/1: op 11/4)
**3938* Ground Game** raced a trifle too keenly. After being headed, she rallied gamely, but could do no more in the final furlong. (6/4)
**1520 Dee-Lady**, who wore a restraining bridle and bit, took it up travelling strongly but, once challenged, did not find a lot. (33/1)
**3039 Frezeliere** was too keen for her own good. (8/1: 6/1-9/1)

## 4298 LADBROKE RACING MILE NURSERY H'CAP (2-Y.O) (Class C)

3-05 (3-06) **1m** £7,895.00 (£2,360.00: £1,130.00: £515.00) Stalls: High GOING minus 0.26 sec per fur (GF)

| | | | | SP | RR | SF |
|---|---|---|---|---|---|---|
| 3835[10] | **Foxes Tail (72)** (MissSEHall) **2-8-5**(3) FLynch(3) (chsd ldr: chal over 2f out: styd on wl u.p to ld ins fnl f) | — | **1** | 14/1 | 77 | 13 |
| 4131[5] | **Southerly Wind (75)** (MrsJRRamsden) **2-8-11** KFallon(5) (lw: bhd: hdwy over 2f out: n.m.r & swtchd: styd on wl appr fnl f: nt rch wnr) | 1 | **2** | 9/2[2] | 78 | 14 |
| 4131[2] | **Sandbaggedagain (66)** (MWEasterby) **2-7-9**(7) RMullen(6) (trckd ldrs: led over 2f out: sn rdn & hung lft: hdd ins fnl f) | s.h | **3** | 5/4[1] | 69 | 5 |
| 4195[9] | **I Can't Remember (78)** (PDEvans) **2-9-0** JFEgan(4) (hld up: effrt over 2f out: nt clr run & swtchd over 1f out: kpt on) | 3 | **4** | 12/1 | 75 | 11 |
| 3998[5] | **Dee Pee Tee Cee (IRE) (65)** (MWEasterby) **2-8-1** LCharnock(7) (chsd ldrs: hung lft over 1f out: one pce) | nk | **5** | 11/1 | 61 | — |
| 2909[3] | **Hurgill Dancer (73)** (JWWatts) **2-8-9** GDuffield(1) (trckd ldrs: effrt over 3f out: hmpd over 1f out: kpt on) | ½ | **6** | 33/1 | 68 | 4 |
| 4060[6] | **Beau Roberto (65)** (MJohnston) **2-8-1** TWilliams(2) (led tl over 2f out: wknd over 1f out) | 2 | **7** | 20/1 | 56 | — |
| 3982[9] | **Jack Says (61)** (TDEasterby) **2-7-11**ow1 AMackay(9) (hld up & bhd: effrt over 3f out: sn wknd) | 9 | **8** | 20/1 | 34 | — |
| 4106* | **Stride (79)** (MartynMeade) **2-8-8**(7) 5x DSweeney(8) (lw: gd hdwy on outside over 4f out: chsd ldrs tl rdn & wknd over 2f out) | 1 | **9** | 6/1[3] | 50 | — |
| 3846[3] | **Nant Y Gamer (FR) (85)** (JBerry) **2-9-7** JCarroll(10) (bhd & pushed along over 3f out: sn lost tch) | 11 | **10** | 9/1 | 34 | — |

(SP 122.1%) **10 Rn**

**1m 43.24** (5.84) CSF £73.81 CT £127.14 TOTE £18.20: £4.30 £1.90 £1.30 (£26.10) Trio £32.20 OWNER Mrs Joan Hodgson (MIDDLEHAM) BRED Miss S. E. Hall
**3512 Foxes Tail** proved most persistent under pressure and finally gained his reward. (14/1)
**4131 Southerly Wind**, who had plenty to do with the favourite on Doncaster running, again took time to warm to his task. Making up several lengths in the final furlong, he needs either a stiffer track or less firm ground. (9/2)
**4131 Sandbaggedagain** looked to have a golden chance at the weights on his Doncaster running. Racing towards the centre, he hung left when he took it up and his young rider persisted in using his whip in his right hand. Inside the last, they were well worried out of it. (5/4)
**3936* I Can't Remember**, who found six furlongs too short at Doncaster, was staying on when messed about coming to the final furlong. (12/1)
**3998 Dee Pee Tee Cee (IRE)** hung left under pressure coming to the final furlong, causing problems on his inside. (11/1)
**2909 Hurgill Dancer**, flat out early in the straight, was only sticking on at the same pace when hampered over a furlong out. He looks to have plenty of weight for what he has actually achieved. (33/1)

## 4299 SHADWELL STUD FIRTH OF CLYDE STKS (Listed) (2-Y.O F) (Class A)

3-35 (3-37) **6f** £18,233.60 (£6,742.40: £3,231.20: £1,316.00: £518.00: £198.80) Stalls: High GOING minus 0.34 sec per fur (GF)

| | | | | SP | RR | SF |
|---|---|---|---|---|---|---|
| 3804[4] | **Queen Sceptre (IRE) (98)** (BWHills) **2-8-11** KFallon(1) (trckd ldrs: led over 1f out: edgd lft & rdn clr) | — | **1** | 8/1 | 95 | 67 |
| 4191[4] | **Head Over Heels (IRE) (100)** (JHMGosden) **2-8-13** GHind(2) (b.hind: bmpd & swtchd rt s: w ldr: nt qckn appr fnl f) | 2 | **2** | 9/2[2] | 92 | 64 |
| 4024a* | **Miss Stamper (IRE) (100)** (RHannon) **2-8-13** DHarrison(5) (sn pushed along: nt clr run over 2f out: swtchd lft over 1f out: kpt on same pce) | hd | **3** | 8/13[1] | 91 | 63 |
| 3921[2] | **Olympic Spirit (100)** (JBerry) **2-8-11** JCarroll(6) (led tl over 1f out: kpt on one pce) | 1½ | **4** | 15/2[3] | 85 | 57 |
| 3170[2] | **Song of Skye (83)** (TJNaughton) **2-8-8** JWeaver(4) (sltly hmpd s: effrt ½-wy: sn chsng ldrs: hrd rdn & wknd over 1f out) | 3 | **5** | 12/1 | 74 | 46 |
| 3956* | **Solfegietto (80)** (MBell) **2-8-8** MFenton(3) (lw: hmpd s: effrt ½-wy: sn rdn & wknd) | 2 | **6** | 33/1 | 69 | 41 |

(SP 113.6%) **6 Rn**

**1m 9.74** (-0.06) CSF £39.37 TOTE £11.40: £3.20 £2.30 (£27.70) OWNER Sceptre Racing (LAMBOURN) BRED Mrs E. McMahon
**3804 Queen Sceptre (IRE)**, held by Head Over Heels and Olympic Spirit on their running together at five furlongs at Newbury, turned the tables in decisive fashion, scoring in good style in the end. (8/1)
**4191 Head Over Heels (IRE)**, bumped slightly by Queen Sceptre on her outer at the start, was then switched right to try and get close to the rail, causing serious interference to Solfegietto and, to a lesser extent, Song of Skye. Her rider seemed very lucky to escape censure. (9/2)
**4024a* Miss Stamper (IRE)** showed a fluent action going to post but, in the race, was never travelling at all. Short of room soon after halfway, when she was switched outside over a furlong out she did not find enough to even overtake Head Over Heels let alone trouble the winner. It turned out that she was in season, which helped to explain this below-par effort. (8/13)
**3921 Olympic Spirit** made the running but her stamina seemed to give out in the closing stages. She is probably better over the minimum. (15/2)
**3170 Song of Skye** was slightly squeezed out at the start but had recovered to chase the leaders by halfway. (12/1: op 20/1)
**3956* Solfegietto** was never travelling after being badly bumped by Head Over Heels coming out of the stalls. (33/1)

## 4300 LADBROKES AYRSHIRE H'CAP (0-90) (3-Y.O+) (Class C)

4-10 (4-11) **1m** £22,012.50 (£6,600.00: £3,175.00: £1,462.50) Stalls: High GOING minus 0.26 sec per fur (GF)

| | | | | SP | RR | SF |
|---|---|---|---|---|---|---|
| 4190[3] | **Pride of Pendle (66)** (DNicholls) **7-8-5** AlexGreaves(3) (hld up: stdy hdwy over 2f out: qcknd to ld ins fnl f: r.o wl) | — | **1** | 6/1[2] | 80 | 56 |
| 4190[6] | **Hawksley Hill (IRE) (80)** (MrsJRRamsden) **3-9-1** KFallon(16) (sn bhd & drvn along: hdwy over 2f out: swtchd outside: hung lft & styd on fnl f) | ¾ | **2** | 7/1[3] | 93 | 65 |
| 3295* | **Give Me A Ring (IRE) (84)** (CWThornton) **3-9-5** JFortune(2) (w ldr: led after 2f tl ins fnl f: no ex) | nk | **3** | 10/1 | 96 | 68 |
| 4193[12] | **Ninia (USA) (90)** (MJohnston) **4-9-8**(7) 5x KSked(7) (lw: hmpd after s: bhd: hdwy on outside 2f out: edgd lft & styd on wl fnl f) | 1¼ | **4** | 9/2[1] | 99 | 75 |
| 3985[18] | **Celebration Cake (IRE) (70)** (MissLAPerratt) **4-8-9** JWeaver(6) (hld up: hdwy over 2f out: nt clr run: styd on fnl f) | s.h | **5** | 10/1 | 79 | 55 |
| 4190[8] | **Tertium (IRE) (87)** (MartynWane) **4-9-12** JCarroll(12) (hld up: hdwy on outside over 2f out: sn chsng ldrs: wknd fnl f) | 2½ | **6** | 12/1 | 91 | 67 |
| 4190[24] | **Queens Consul (IRE) (83)** (BSRothwell) **6-9-8** MFenton(8) (wl bhd tl styd on wl fnl 2f) | s.h | **7** | 33/1 | 87 | 63 |

| Form | Horse | Dist | Pos | SP | RR | SF |
|---|---|---|---|---|---|---|
| 4136* | **Quilling (71)** (MDods) **4-8-7**$^{(3)}$ $^{5x}$ FLynch(15) (in tch: effrt over 2f out: kpt on: no imp) | 2 | **8** | 12/1 | 71 | 47 |
| $3974^{11}$ | **Spanish Verdict (64)** (DenysSmith) **9-8-3** GDuffield(5) (chsd ldrs: one pce whn n.m.r 1f out) | 1¾ | **9** | 33/1 | 61 | 37 |
| $4181^{4}$ | **Kala Sunrise (83)** (CSmith) **3-9-4** KDarley(1) (lw: hdwy on ins over 3f out: sn rdn: wkng whn hmpd over 1f out) | ½ | **10** | 14/1 | 79 | 51 |
| 3958* | **King Curan (USA) (68)** (DHaydnJones) **5-8-7b** AMackay(13) (lw: led 2f: chsd ldrs tl edgd lft & wknd over 1f out) | 2 | **11** | 14/1 | 60 | 36 |
| $4190^{10}$ | **Scaraben (73)** (SEKettlewell) **8-8-12** JStack(9) (hld up: effrt over 2f out: sn wknd) | 1¼ | **12** | 8/1 | 62 | 38 |
| $4136^{14}$ | **King Rat (IRE) (79)** (TJEtherington) **5-9-4** JTate(14) (lw: prom tl lost pl over 1f out) | 4 | **13** | 33/1 | 60 | 36 |
| 2773* | **Ret Frem (IRE) (68)** (CParker) **3-8-3** GHind(4) (chsd ldrs tl wknd over 2f out) | 1¾ | **14** | 33/1 | 46 | 18 |
| $1672^{3}$ | **Coureur (70)** (MDHammond) **7-8-9** DHarrison(18) (sn bhd & drvn along) | 2 | **15** | 20/1 | 44 | 20 |
| $4054^{7}$ | **Sharp Prospect (77)** (VSoane) **6-9-2** RCochrane(17) (lw: chsd ldrs tl lost pl over 1f out) | nk | **16** | 16/1 | 50 | 26 |
| $3995^{23}$ | **Euro Sceptic (IRE) (60)** (TDEasterby) **4-7-10b**$^{(3)}$ DWright(11) (lw: sn bhd & drvn along) | s.h | **17** | 33/1 | 33 | 9 |
| $2883^{11}$ | **Some Horse (IRE) (80)** (MGMeagher) **3-9-1** ACulhane(10) (sn bhd & pushed along) | 5 | **18** | 33/1 | 43 | 15 |
| | | | | (SP 131.3%) | | **18 Rn** |

**1m 38.55** (1.15) CSF £45.15 CT £388.26 TOTE £6.20: £1.70 £2.90 £2.90 £2.10 (£20.20) Trio £116.30 OWNER Mrs Linda Miller (THIRSK) BRED James Simpson

WEIGHT FOR AGE 3yo-4lb

**4190 Pride of Pendle** was ridden to perfection. Biding her time, she was never going to be beaten once she hit the front. This is her ground and this is the way to ride her, as at Doncaster last week she saw too much daylight on the inside. (6/1)

**4190 Hawksley Hill (IRE)**, poorly drawn, was soon flat out. Yet again hanging left under pressure, he stuck on strongly, but was never going to overhaul the winner. (7/1)

**3295* Give Me A Ring (IRE)** made light of an absence of over six weeks. Showing the right sort of spirit, he was only collared inside the last and deserves to win another race. (10/1)

**4193 Ninia (USA)** again did not have luck on her side. Squeezed out soon after the start, she was outpaced and behind until staying on strongly at the death. Unfortunately, she will have more to do in future handicaps after her runaway Epsom success. (9/2)

**3985 Celebration Cake (IRE)** had too much use made of him when running poorly at York so did well to finish so close after a poor run. (10/1)

**4190 Tertium (IRE)**, awkward at the start, had to make his effort on the wide outside and, as a result, saw too much daylight. (12/1: 8/1-14/1)

**3770* Queens Consul (IRE)**, who ran poorly last time, was well behind until making considerable late ground. (33/1)

## 4301 CLARENDON CARPETS GROUP CONDITIONS STKS (2-Y.O) (Class D)

4-40 (4-42) **7f** £4,581.00 (£1,368.00: £654.00: £297.00) Stalls: High GOING minus 0.26 sec per fur (GF)

| Form | Horse | Dist | Pos | SP | RR | SF |
|---|---|---|---|---|---|---|
| $3478^{4}$ | **What Happened Was (71)** (MartynMeade) **2-8-4**$^{(7)}$ DSweeney(2) (mde virtually all: hung rt over 3f out: styd on wl ins fnl f) | — | **1** | 25/1 | 84? | 29 |
| $4113^{4}$ | **Halowing (USA) (92)** (PAKelleway) **2-8-13** JWeaver(6) (w wnr: chal 3f out: nt qckn ins fnl f) | ½ | **2** | 2/1 $^{2}$ | 85 | 30 |
| $4050^{5}$ | **Catienus (USA)** (MRStoute) **2-8-12** KDarley(4) (lw: trckd ldrs: effrt over 3f out: sn outpcd & hung lft: styd on fnl f) | 1 | **3** | 11/8 $^{1}$ | 82 | 27 |
| $3349^{7}$ | **Coral Strand** (JWWatts) **2-8-7** JCarroll(1) (hld up: effrt over 3f out: rdn & one pce over 1f out) | 2 | **4** | 25/1 | 72 | 17 |
| $4024a^{6}$ | **Mujova (IRE) (87)** (RHollinshead) **2-9-1**$^{(3)}$ FLynch(3) (trckd ldrs: effrt over 2f out: wknd over 1f out) | 2 | **5** | 6/1 $^{3}$ | 78 | 23 |
| $4060^{4}$ | **Highway** (BWHills) **2-8-12** KFallon(5) (lw: s.s: a bhd: lost tch 3f out) | 10 | **6** | 7/1 | 50 | — |
| | | | | (SP 109.9%) | | **6 Rn** |

**1m 27.75** (3.75) CSF £69.67 TOTE £14.00: £2.50 £2.10 (£29.20) OWNER Beyts Livestock Ltd (MALMESBURY) BRED Grange Thoroughbreds

**3478 What Happened Was**, a winner over five furlongs at Beverley, pulled off a shock, but it seemed no fluke. After having trouble making the turn, she stuck on really strongly to get right on top in the final 75 yards. (25/1)

**4113 Halowing (USA)** threw down a strong challenge but had to give best near the line. (2/1)

**4050 Catienus (USA)** came unstuck in what turned out to be a three-and-a-half-furlong sprint. Caught out by his lack of experience, he stuck on inside the last and will do better over a mile in a more truly-run event. (11/8)

**Coral Strand**, rousted along once in line for home, looks to need more time yet. (25/1)

**4024a Mujova (IRE)** dropped out over a furlong from home, as if running out of stamina. (6/1)

**4060 Highway**, who showed a very poor action going down, started slowly and ran badly. (7/1: op 4/1)

## 4302 ROBERT WYPER MOTORS H'CAP (0-75) (3-Y.O+) (Class D)

5-10 (5-12) **2m 1f 105y** £5,010.00 (£1,500.00: £720.00: £330.00) Stalls: Low GOING minus 0.26 sec per fur (GF)

| Form | Horse | Dist | Pos | SP | RR | SF |
|---|---|---|---|---|---|---|
| $3428^{4}$ | **Good Hand (USA) (64)** (SEKettlewell) **10-9-5** JFortune(6) (lw: prom: pushed along 9f out: sn outpcd & bhd: hdwy & hrd rdn 3f out: led over 1f out: hld on wl towards fin) | — | **1** | 7/1 | 75 | 52 |
| $4199^{6}$ | **Shirley Sue (70)** (MJohnston) **3-8-13** JWeaver(12) (led after 2f to 8f out: one pce fnl 2f: fin 3rd, 3l: plcd 2nd) | | **2** | 7/1 | 78 | 43 |
| $3486^{3}$ | **Great Oration (IRE) (54)** (FWatson) **7-8-9** KFallon(1) (lw: bhd: hdwy on outside whn sltly hmpd over 1f out: one pce: fin 4th, 3l: plcd 3rd) | | **3** | 9/2 $^{2}$ | 59 | 36 |
| $4112^{4}$ | **Rushen Raider (72)** (KWHogg) **4-9-13** LCharnock(5) (lw: led 2f: trckd ldrs: led over 2f out tl over 1f out: one pce: fin 5rd, 1¼l: plcd 4th) | | **4** | 3/1 $^{1}$ | 76 | 53 |
| $1022^{4}$ | **Palace of Gold (43)** (LLungo) **6-7-12**$^{ow2}$ TWilliams(8) (s.s: bhd tl sme hdwy fnl 2f: nvr nr ldrs: fin 6th, 5l: plcd 5th) | | **5** | 20/1 | 43 | 18 |
| $4073^{16}$ | **Keen To The Last (FR) (52)** (MDHammond) **4-8-7** JCarroll(4) (trckd ldrs tl wknd 2f out) | 1 | **7** | 50/1 | 51 | 28 |
| *$3600^{6}$* | **Alwarqa (60)** (DNicholls) **3-8-3** AMackay(7) (trckd ldrs: led 8f out tl over 2f out: wknd over 1f out) | 2 | **8** | 8/1 | 57 | 22 |
| *$4092^{2}$* | **Star Performer (IRE) (51)** (MrsMReveley) **5-8-6** KDarley(2) (chsd ldrs: drvn along 6f out: wknd 2f out) | s.h | **9** | 6/1 $^{3}$ | 48 | 25 |
| $3855^{12}$ | **Zamhareer (USA) (53)** (WStorey) **5-8-1**$^{(7)}$ IonaWands(9) (sn pushed along: lost pl after 5f: sn wl bhd) | 8 | **10** | 16/1 | 42 | 19 |
| $2871^{4}$ | **Philmist (48)** (CWCElsey) **4-8-3b** NKennedy(10) (hdwy ½-wy: sn prom: wkng whn hmpd over 2f out) | 4 | **11** | 16/1 | 34 | 11 |
| 3855* | **Uncle Doug (61)** (MrsMReveley) **5-9-2** ACulhane(3) (hld up: effrt & swtchd rt over 2f out: gd hdwy & ev ch ins fnl f: no ex nr fin: fin 2nd, nk: disq: plcd last) | | **D** | 7/1 | 72 | 49 |
| | | | | (SP 124.6%) | | **11 Rn** |

**3m 49.26** (6.76) CSF £53.93 CT £230.10 TOTE £7.90: £2.40 £1.90 £2.00 (£28.80) Trio £50.80 OWNER Uncle Jacks Pub (MIDDLEHAM) BRED Tauner Dunlap, Jr. and Brereton C. Jones

LONG HANDICAP Palace of Gold 7-7

WEIGHT FOR AGE 3yo-12lb

STEWARDS' ENQUIRY Culhane susp. 29-30/9 & 1-3/10/96 (irresponsible riding).

**3428 Good Hand (USA)**, whose confidence has been boosted by two recent facile hurdle successes, has dropped down the weights steadily on the Flat this year. Picking up the bit once in line for home, he showed tremendous resolution in a tight finish. His new trainer has certainly done well with him. (7/1)

**4199 Shirley Sue** is as tough as old boots and very willing. (7/1)
**3486 Great Oration (IRE)**, put into the stalls last as usual, was only staying on at the same pace when sllightly hampered by Uncle Doug over two furlongs out. (9/2)
**4112 Rushen Raider**, back in his right class, made the best of his way home early in the straight but, once collared, could find no more. (3/1)
**3855* Uncle Doug**, travelling strongly just off the pace, was short of room two furlongs out. Barging his way through, he was almost level halfway through the final furlong but was making no impression near the line. Inevitably he was disqualified and his rider was handed a five-day ban for irresponsible riding. (7/1)

T/Jkpt: Not won; £15,586.75 to Ayr 21/9/96. T/Plpt: £100.80 (241.31 Tckts). T/Qdpt: £39.00 (29 Tckts). WG

## 3612-NEWBURY (L-H) (Good to firm)
## Friday September 20th

Race 3: hand-timed
WEATHER: overcast WIND: mod bhd

### 4303 HOME STUD NURSERY H'CAP (2-Y.O) (Class C)
2-10 (2-11) **7f 64y (round)** £5,712.00 (£1,716.00: £828.00: £384.00) Stalls: Low GOING minus 0.39 sec per fur (F)

| | | | | SP | RR | SF |
|---|---|---|---|---|---|---|
| 3684$^{6}$ | **Bali Paradise (USA) (89)** (PFICole) **2-9-6** TQuinn(1) (lw: mde all: rdn & qcknd clr wl over 1f out: r.o wl) | — | 1 | 6/1$^{2}$ | 91 | 57 |
| 4049* | **Jeffrey Anotherred (83)** (KMcAuliffe) **2-9-0** RHughes(10) (hld up: swtchd rt & hdwy 2f out: edgd rt over 1f out: r.o one pce fnl f) | 1½ | 2 | 11/2$^{1}$ | 82 | 48 |
| 4182$^{3}$ | **Salty Jack (IRE) (81)** (SDow) **2-8-7**(5) ADaly(4) (a.p: chsd wnr wl over 1f out: btn whn edgd rt fnl f) | 1¼ | 3 | 6/1$^{2}$ | 77 | 43 |
| 3807$^{4}$ | **Eurolink Spartacus (81)** (JLDunlop) **2-8-12** LDettori(11) (a.p: rdn over 3f out: one pce fnl 2f) | 2½ | 4 | 8/1 | 72 | 38 |
| 3962$^{9}$ | **Merciless Cop (65)** (BJMeehan) **2-7-5b$^{1}$**(5) MartinDwyer(8) (plld hrd early: hdwy over 3f out: edgd rt over 1f out: one pce) | 1¼ | 5 | 16/1 | 53 | 19 |
| 3941* | **Certain Magic (75)** (WRMuir) **2-8-6** JReid(5) (nvr nr to chal) | 4 | 6 | 7/1$^{3}$ | 54 | 20 |
| 3821$^{5}$ | **Homestead (70)** (RHannon) **2-8-1** SSanders(13) (sn rdn along: nvr trbld ldrs) | nk | 7 | 8/1 | 48 | 14 |
| 4106$^{10}$ | **Strat's Quest (68)** (DWPArbuthnot) **2-7-10**(3) DarrenMoffatt(3) (prom over 4f) | hd | 8 | 20/1 | 46 | 12 |
| 4182$^{6}$ | **Dickie Bird (IRE) (82)** (RHannon) **2-8-13** PatEddery(9) (lw: prom: rdn & ev ch 2f out: sn wknd) | 3½ | 9 | 10/1 | 52 | 18 |
| 2398$^{5}$ | **Talisman (IRE) (70)** (SDow) **2-8-1** JQuinn(6) (dwlt: a bhd) | 2 | 10 | 40/1 | 36 | 2 |
| 3963* | **Interdream (79)** (RHannon) **2-8-10** DaneO'Neill(2) (bhd fnl 2f) | 5 | 11 | 10/1 | 34 | — |
| 3483$^{4}$ | **Largesse (90)** (JohnBerry) **2-9-7** MRimmer(7) (a bhd) | 2½ | 12 | 14/1 | 40 | 6 |

(SP 116.6%) **12 Rn**

**1m 29.32** (1.22) CSF £35.78 CT £191.73 TOTE £7.10: £2.50 £2.30 £1.70 (£17.20) Trio £31.10 OWNER Al Muallim Partnership (WHATCOMBE) BRED Galbreath/Phillips Racing Partnership
LONG HANDICAP Merciless Cop 7-9

**3684 Bali Paradise (USA)** may just have needed his comeback run at Kempton a month ago. (6/1)
**4049* Jeffrey Anotherred**, raised 5lb, did not seem bothered by this longer trip, but the winner had got first run. (11/2: 4/1-6/1)
**4182 Salty Jack (IRE)** gave his rider plenty of problems in trying to keep him straight in the closing stages. (6/1)
**3807 Eurolink Spartacus** did get the step up in distance, but the Handicapper had not taken any chances with him. (8/1: 6/1-9/1)
**3494 Merciless Cop**, tried in blinkers, was 5lb lower after disappointing when well backed last time. (16/1)
**3941* Certain Magic**, moving up in distance, found this ground much faster than at Ripon. (7/1)
**3674 Dickie Bird (IRE)** (10/1: 8/1-12/1)

### 4304 TONY STRATTON SMITH MEMORIAL CONDITIONS STKS (3-Y.O+) (Class B)
2-40 (2-41) **5f 34y** £7,663.00 (£2,857.00: £1,388.50: £587.50: £253.75: £120.25) Stalls: High GOING minus 0.39 sec per fur (F)

| | | | | SP | RR | SF |
|---|---|---|---|---|---|---|
| 3708$^{6}$ | **Struggler (110)** (DRLoder) **4-9-4** LDettori(2) (lw: a gng wl: led ins fnl f: r.o wl) | — | 1 | 11/2$^{2}$ | 109 | 76 |
| 4057$^{4}$ | **Hever Golf Rose (114)** (TJNaughton) **5-8-9** PatEddery(5) (lw: w ldr: led 2f out: rdn & hdd ins fnl f: unable qckn) | 1 | 2 | 4/6$^{1}$ | 97 | 64 |
| 4115$^{2}$ | **Amazing Bay (97)** (IABalding) **3-8-8** TQuinn(9) (hld up: hdwy over 1f out: r.o ins fnl f) | ¾ | 3 | 9/1$^{3}$ | 95 | 61 |
| 3932$^{9}$ | **Crofters Ceilidh (75)** (BAMcMahon) **4-8-9b$^{1}$** SSanders(3) (trckd ldrs: rdn over 1f out: one pce) | ¾ | 4 | 66/1 | 92 | 59 |
| 3946$^{11}$ | **Kunucu (IRE) (90)** (TDBarron) **3-8-8** MHills(4) (led 3f: wknd fnl f) | 1½ | 5 | 33/1 | 88 | 54 |
| 2880$^{7}$ | **Averti (IRE) (107)** (WRMuir) **5-9-4** JReid(7) (chsd ldrs over 3f) | nk | 6 | 14/1 | 96 | 63 |
| 3047$^{5}$ | **Ya Malak (105)** (IABalding) **5-9-0** AMcGlone(8) (lw: hld up & bhd: swtchd lft & hdwy over 1f out: nvr plcd to chal) | s.h | 7 | 14/1 | 92 | 59 |
| 3946$^{3}$ | **Top Banana (95)** (HCandy) **5-9-0b$^{1}$** CRutter(6) (hdwy over 2f out: hrd rdn & wknd over 1f out) | 1 | 8 | 9/1$^{3}$ | 88 | 55 |
| 3984$^{13}$ | **Bowden Rose (95)** (MBlanshard) **4-8-13b** JQuinn(1) (prom: rdn over 2f out: sn wknd) | 1¼ | 9 | 33/1 | 84 | 51 |

(SP 116.1%) **9 Rn**

**59.77 secs** (0.03 under best) (-0.43) CSF £9.26 TOTE £5.80: £1.60 £1.10 £1.40 (£3.50) Trio £4.50 OWNER Sir Andrew Lloyd Webber (NEWMARKET) BRED Hesmonds stud Ltd
WEIGHT FOR AGE 3yo-1lb

**3708 Struggler** decisively turned around the Nunthorpe form with Hever Golf Rose on 6lb worse terms. (11/2)
**4057 Hever Golf Rose**, well suited by race conditions because she had failed to win this year, had finished two and three-quarter lengths in front of the winner in the Nunthorpe when receiving only 3lb. It now seems essential that she gets some cut in the ground to be seen at her best. (4/6)
**4115 Amazing Bay** ran another fine race and is certainly doing her handicap mark no favours. (9/1)
**2694 Crofters Ceilidh** had a tough task here, but showed improved form in the blinkers. (66/1)
**1188* Kunucu (IRE)** was another showing signs of a return to form, despite being highly tried. (33/1)
**2498* Averti (IRE)** has never won over the minimum trip. (14/1)
**3047 Ya Malak**, who has changed stables, gave the impression he can do better than this form suggests. (14/1)

### 4305 POLYGRAM MONSTER COLLECTION CONDITIONS STKS (2-Y.O F) (Class B)
3-10 (3-29) **7f (straight)** £6,416.00 (£2,384.00: £1,152.00: £480.00: £200.00: £88.00) Stalls: High GOING minus 0.39 sec per fur (F)

| | | | | SP | RR | SF |
|---|---|---|---|---|---|---|
| 4104$^{3}$ | **Etoile (FR)** (PWChapple-Hyam) **2-8-8** JReid(4) (mde all: drvn out) | — | 1 | 7/1 | 91 | 62 |
| | **My Valentina** (BWHills) **2-8-8** MHills(1) (str: scope: a.p: ev ch 2f out: no imp) | 2½ | 2 | 8/1 | 85 | 56 |

| | | | Pos | SP | RR | SF |
|---|---|---|---|---|---|---|
| 4062* | **Calypso Lady (IRE)** (RHannon) **2-8-13** RPerham(2) (lw: chsd ldrs: rdn 3f out: r.o one pce fnl f) | ½ | **3** | 15/2 | 89 | 60 |
| 3508[3] | **Sleepless** (NAGraham) **2-8-8** TQuinn(6) (a.p: rdn over 2f out: one pce) | 1½ | **4** | 7/2[2] | 81 | 52 |
| 3787[3] | **Siyadah (USA)** (SbinSuroor) **2-8-8** RHills(3) (chsd wnr: rdn & ev ch over 2f out: wknd wl over 1f out) | 1 | **5** | 100/30[1] | 78 | 49 |
| | **Will You Dance** (JLDunlop) **2-8-8** WRyan(10) (str: scope: bkwd: hld up mid div: no hdwy fnl 2f) | ¾ | **6** | 16/1 | 77 | 48 |
| | **Entice (FR)** (BWHills) **2-8-8** BDoyle(8) (gd sort: hld up & bhd: nvr nr to chal) | ½ | **7** | 5/1[3] | 76 | 47 |
| | **Dulcinea** (IABalding) **2-8-8** PatEddery(7) (lw: dwlt: a bhd) | 12 | **8** | 6/1 | 48 | 19 |
| | **Nick of Time** (JLDunlop) **2-8-8** TSprake(9) (unf: scope: a bhd) | 1¼ | **9** | 20/1 | 45 | 16 |
| | ***Messhed (USA)*** (BHanbury) **2-8-8** WCarson (Withdrawn not under Starter's orders: kicked & inj jockey in paddock) | | **W** | | — | — |

(SP 122.3%) **9 Rn**

**1m 24.3** (-0.20) CSF £58.46 TOTE £8.00: £2.20 £2.00 £2.00 (£57.30) Trio £32.20 OWNER I M S Racing (MARLBOROUGH) BRED STE Aland

**4104 Etoile (FR)** settled much better in front and looked the likely winner some way out. (7/1)

**My Valentina**, a sister to Hawaash and half-sister to Averti (IRE), possesses the physique to progress from this promising debut. (8/1: op 5/1)

**4062* Calypso Lady (IRE)**, a half-sister to Strutting and Slip Jig, kept plugging away under her penalty and should not be inconvenienced by a mile. (15/2)

**3508 Sleepless** caught a tartar in Bianca Nera when dropped back from six to five at Beverley last time. (7/2: 6/4-3/1)

**3787 Siyadah (USA)** proved a disappointment and was one of the first beaten. (100/30)

**Will You Dance**, a half-sister to Polar Boy, will undoubtedly come on for the outing. (16/1)

**Entice (FR)**, out of a half-sister to Blushing Groom, will be better for the experience. (5/1: 8/1-16/1)

## 4306 HAYNES, HANSON AND CLARK CONDITIONS STKS (2-Y.O C & G) (Class B)

3-40 (3-59) **1m** £9,223.20 (£3,448.80: £1,684.40: £722.00: £321.00: £160.60) Stalls: High GOING minus 0.39 sec per fur (F)

| | | | Pos | SP | RR | SF |
|---|---|---|---|---|---|---|
| 4050[4] | **King Sound** (JHMGosden) **2-8-10** WRyan(8) (lw: hld up & bhd: swtchd lft 2f out: gd hdwy over 1f out: led ins fnl f: rdn out) | — | **1** | 13/8[1] | 90 | 42 |
| 3987[8] | **Solo Mio (IRE)** (BWHills) **2-8-10** MHills(6) (lw: hld up: hdwy over 3f out: ev ch 1f out: unable qckn) | ½ | **2** | 33/1 | 89 | 41 |
| 3987[2] | **Haltarra (USA)** (SbinSuroor) **2-8-10** LDettori(5) (w ldr: led over 2f out tl ins fnl f: unable qckn) | s.h | **3** | 5/2[2] | 89 | 41 |
| | **Slip The Net (IRE)** (PFICole) **2-8-10** TQuinn(1) (w'like: scope: prom: rdn over 2f out: wknd over 1f out) | 3½ | **4** | 15/2[3] | 82+ | 34 |
| | **Rainwatch** (JLDunlop) **2-8-10** TSprake(9) (w'like: hld up & bhd: pushed along over 3f out: nvr nr to chal) | nk | **5** | 33/1 | 81 | 33 |
| | **Hint** (PFICole) **2-8-10** PatEddery(7) (w'like: chsd ldrs: rdn 5f out: wknd over 1f out) | 2½ | **6** | 20/1 | 76 | 28 |
| 3615[7] | **Fallah** (MajorWRHern) **2-8-10** RHills(3) (prom over 5f) | ½ | **7** | 12/1 | 75 | 27 |
| | **Burundi (IRE)** (PWChapple-Hyam) **2-8-10** JReid(4) (w'like: scope: lw: s.i.s: sn rcvrd: rdn over 2f out: sn wknd) | hd | **8** | 14/1 | 75 | 27 |
| | **Baubigny (USA)** (MRChannon) **2-8-10** RHughes(2) (lengthy: led over 5f: wknd qckly over 1f out) | 9 | **9** | 8/1 | 57 | 9 |

(SP 114.5%) **9 Rn**

**1m 38.96** (0.69 under 2y best) (1.96) CSF £41.49 TOTE £2.80: £1.30 £3.00 £1.40 (£37.10) Trio £28.80 OWNER Sheikh Mohammed (NEWMARKET) BRED Newgate Stud Co

**4050 King Sound** looks a smart prospect and lowered the juvenile course record, despite idling towards the finish. He seems likely to go for the Racing Post Trophy. (13/8)

**3987 Solo Mio (IRE)**, a 160,000 guinea half-brother to a couple of useful performers in France, had finished nearly ten lengths behind the third at York. Coming up against a potentially smart sort in the winner, he is certainly going the right way. (33/1)

**3987 Haltarra (USA)**, a brother to Kammtarra and a half-brother to Lammtarra, is obviously well regarded and Dettori may have had the option of riding the winner. Time may show this to be a pretty good effort. (5/2: 6/4-3/1)

**Slip The Net (IRE)**, a brother to Ellie Ardensky and a half-brother to Lady Shipley, was the subject of good reports and will soon step up on this. (15/2: 3/1-8/1)

**Rainwatch**, a half-brother to Tria Kemata, is out of a mare who won the Ribblesdale. Taking a long time to get the message, staying will be his game next season. (33/1)

**Hint**, a half-brother to juvenile scorer Wavey, did not seem to know what was required and should have learnt a lot. (20/1)

**3615 Fallah** may have found this ground too lively. (12/1: 10/1-16/1)

## 4307 KPMG SILVER CLEF LADIES' H'CAP (0-70) (3-Y.O+) (Class E)

4-15 (4-29) **1m 4f 5y** £5,117.50 (£1,540.00: £745.00: £347.50) Stalls: Low GOING minus 0.39 sec per fur (F)

| | | | Pos | SP | RR | SF |
|---|---|---|---|---|---|---|
| 4073[17] | **Double Echo (IRE) (46)** (JDBethell) **8-9-12** MissEJohnsonHoughton(5) (lw: a.p: led 3f out: sn clr: jst hld on) | — | **1** | 20/1 | 57 | 38 |
| 3825[2] | **Rising Spray (57)** (CAHorgan) **5-10-9** MrsAPerrett(6) (lw: hld up & bhd: gd hdwy over 3f out: r.o wl ins fnl f: jst failed) | hd | **2** | 11/2[1] | 68 | 49 |
| 4048[9] | **Stalled (IRE) (49)** (PTWalwyn) **6-10-1** MarchionessBlandford(17) (lw: s.s: gd hdwy over 2f out: str run fnl f: fin wl) | nk | **3** | 14/1 | 60 | 41 |
| 3983[11] | **Children's Choice (IRE) (55)** (CNAllen) **5-10-7b1** MrsDKettlewell(4) (hdwy over 3f out: r.o one pce fnl 2f) | 3 | **4** | 11/1 | 62 | 43 |
| *4092*[16] | **Supermick (38)** (WRMuir) **5-9-4** MissJAllison(12) (bhd tl gd hdwy fnl 2f: r.o) | 1 | **5** | 12/1 | 43 | 24 |
| 4048[11] | **Outstayed Welcome (51)** (MJHaynes) **4-10-3** MissYHaynes(18) (led 9f: wknd over 1f out) | 1¾ | **6** | 14/1 | 54 | 35 |
| 2574[10] | **Typhoon Eight (IRE) (66)** (BWHills) **4-11-4** MissPJones(1) (lw: prom: outpcd 5f out: styd on fnl 2f) | nk | **7** | 25/1 | 68 | 49 |
| 3510[3] | **Breezed Well (38)** (BRCambidge) **10-9-4** MrsHNoonan(13) (plld hrd: prom tl wknd wl over 1f out) | ¾ | **8** | 25/1 | 39 | 20 |
| 4067[12] | **Tappeto (69)** (HCandy) **4-11-2(5)** MrsCDunwoody(2) (nvr nrr) | ¾ | **9** | 14/1 | 69 | 50 |
| 3979[2] | **Voices in the Sky (48)** (AGNewcombe) **5-10-0** MissMCarson(19) (lw: n.d) | ½ | **10** | 11/1 | 48 | 29 |
| | **Red Raja (65)** (PMitchell) **3-10-9** MrsJNaughton(8) (nvr nr ldrs) | 3 | **11** | 33/1 | 61 | 34 |
| 4121[3] | **Strat's Legacy (41)** (DWPArbuthnot) **9-9-7** MrsDArbuthnot(16) (hdwy over 2f out: wknd over 1f out) | s.h | **12** | 10/1 | 37 | 18 |
| 4042* | **Dauphin (IRE) (45)** (WJMusson) **3-9-3** MrsJMoore(21) (prom 8f) | nk | **13** | 15/2[3] | 40 | 13 |
| 4202[5] | **Tauten (IRE) (50)** (PBurgoyne) **6-9-11v(5)ow12** MissMO'Sullivan(9) (s.s: last whn hmpd 8f out) | 3 | **14** | 25/1 | 31 | 10 |
| *319** | **Your Most Welcome (54)** (DJSffrenchDavis) **5-10-1(5)** MissEFolkes(14) (a bhd) | 6 | **15** | 20/1 | 37 | 18 |
| 4202[11] | **Winter Scout (USA) (58)** (CPEBrooks) **8-10-5(5)** MissJRussell(7) (a bhd) | hd | **16** | 33/1 | 41 | 22 |
| 3965* | **Colour Counsellor (46)** (RMFlower) **3-9-4b** MrsAFarrell(22) (prom: hrd rdn over 2f out: wknd qckly) | 3½ | **17** | 16/1 | 25 | — |
| 3849[7] | **Arcatura (51)** (CJames) **4-9-12(5)** MissCCorbett(10) (prom tl wknd qckly over 2f out) | 4 | **18** | 33/1 | 24 | 5 |
| 2989[9] | **Paper Cloud (54)** (RTPhillips) **4-10-6** MissKEllis(15) (prom 7f) | 3 | **19** | 33/1 | 23 | 4 |
| 2133[11] | **Straight Thinking (USA) (55)** (JLSpearing) **3-9-8(5)** MissAShirley-Priest(20) (plld hrd: prom over 8f) | 6 | **20** | 50/1 | 16 | — |
| | **Great Simplicity (42)** (RCurtis) **9-9-8b** MrsSEddery(3) (b: a bhd) | 4 | **21** | 50/1 | — | — |

| | | | | SP | RR | SF |
|---|---|---|---|---|---|---|
| 3520$^{4}$ | **Nosey Native (51)** (JPearce) **3-9-9** MrsLPearce(11) (bhd whn hmpd & fell 8f out) | | F | 13/2$^{2}$ | — | — |
| | | | | (SP 136.6%) | | **22 Rn** |

**2m 36.0** (6.00) CSF £124.90 CT £1,514.59 TOTE £22.60: £4.10 £1.80 £2.50 £2.50 (£124.00) Trio £921.00 OWNER Mrs John Lee (MIDDLE-HAM) BRED A. Tarry
WEIGHT FOR AGE 3yo-8lb
STEWARDS' ENQUIRY Blandford susp. 30/9 & 1/10/96 (careless riding).
**3813 Double Echo (IRE)**, dropped 5lb, stays well and the tactics of throwing down the gauntlet just paid off. (20/1)
**3825 Rising Spray**, up a further 2lb, again came up against a rival who slipped the field at a crucial stage. (11/2)
**961 Stalled (IRE)**, down 2lb, made up a tremendous amount of ground, but the enterprising ride given to the winner caught him out. (14/1)
**3813 Children's Choice (IRE)**, tried in blinkers, really needs softer ground over this trip. (11/1: 8/1-12/1)
**3318 Supermick**, disappointing on the Sand last time, again gave the impression he really needs further. (12/1: op 8/1)
**2989 Outstayed Welcome**, having disappointed, was racing off a 6lb lower mark than when third at Chepstow in July. (14/1)

## 4308 VICTOR CHANDLER H'CAP (0-95) (3-Y.O+) (Class C)

4-45 (5-00) **7f 64y (round)** £6,193.00 (£1,864.00: £902.00: £421.00) Stalls: Low GOING minus 0.39 sec per fur (F)

| | | | | SP | RR | SF |
|---|---|---|---|---|---|---|
| 4186$^{4}$ | **Duello (64)** (MBlanshard) **5-7-11** JQuinn(4) (hld up: rdn over 2f out: gd hdwy over 1f out: led ins fnl f: r.o wl) | — | **1** | 15/2$^{3}$ | 72 | 43 |
| 4064$^{9}$ | **Press On Nicky (70)** (WRMuir) **3-7-11**(3) MHenry(8) (lw: plld hrd: led tl ins fnl f) | 1½ | **2** | 20/1 | 75 | 43 |
| 4054$^{D}$ | **Young Duke (IRE) (77)** (MrsSDWilliams) **8-8-10** JReid(6) (hdwy over 1f out: r.o ins fnl f) | ¾ | **3** | 9/4$^{1}$ | 80 | 51 |
| 4054$^{10}$ | **Knobbleeneeze (78)** (MRChannon) **6-8-11v** RHughes(2) (prom: rdn 2f out: r.o one pce fnl f) | nk | **4** | 10/1 | 80 | 51 |
| 3782$^{6}$ | **Jawaal (85)** (LadyHerries) **6-9-4** TSprake(9) (hld up & plld hrd: gd hdwy fnl f: fin wl) | ½ | **5** | 12/1 | 86 | 57 |
| *379*$^{5}$ | **Secret Spring (FR) (83)** (PRHedger) **4-9-2** AMcGlone(11) (hld up & bhd: hdwy on ins over 3f out: r.o fnl f) | ¾ | **6** | 20/1 | 83 | 54 |
| 1296a$^{7}$ | **Anastina (79)** (NAGraham) **4-8-12** LDettori(7) (a.p: rdn 2f out: wknd ins fnl f) | s.h | **7** | 14/1 | 79 | 50 |
| 3709$^{3}$ | **Moments of Fortune (USA) (95)** (BHanbury) **4-10-0** WRyan(3) (chsd ldr: wknd fnl f) | hd | **8** | 8/1 | 94 | 65 |
| 3995$^{2}$ | **Wild Palm (74)** (WAO'Gorman) **4-8-7v** EmmaO'Gorman(5) (hld up & plld hrd: nvr nrr) | ½ | **9** | 7/1$^{2}$ | 72 | 43 |
| 3995$^{4}$ | **Safey Ana (USA) (63)** (BHanbury) **5-7-5**(5) MartinDwyer(1) (rdn & hdwy on ins over 3f out: wknd fnl f) | ½ | **10** | 10/1 | 60 | 31 |
| 3989$^{2}$ | **Faraway Lass (75)** (LordHuntingdon) **3-8-0**(5) AimeeCook(12) (hld up & bhd: nvr trbld ldrs) | hd | **11** | 15/2$^{3}$ | 72 | 40 |
| 4044$^{2}$ | **Cross of Valour (79)** (JARToller) **3-8-9** SSanders(10) (hld up: rdn & n.m.r wl over 1f out: sn bhd) | 9 | **12** | 20/1 | 56 | 24 |
| | | | | (SP 124.7%) | | **12 Rn** |

**1m 28.7** (0.60) CSF £131.27 CT £405.40 TOTE £9.10: £2.60 £10.30 £1.50 (£205.40) Trio £451.60 OWNER H C Promotions Ltd (UPPER LAM-BOURN) BRED P. D. and Mrs Player
LONG HANDICAP Safey Ana (USA) 7-8
WEIGHT FOR AGE 3yo-3lb
**4186 Duello** was hardly winning out of turn. (15/2)
**3790 Press On Nicky** was 5lb lower then when making her debut in handicap company following her win in a maiden at Salisbury. (20/1)
**4054 Young Duke (IRE)**, up 7lb on the assumption that he would have won convincingly at Haydock, was 12lb higher than the first of his two wins this season. (9/4: 2/1-3/1)
**3612 Knobbleeneeze** is still 11lb higher than when successful at Chester in June and was 5lb worse off than when beaten a neck by the winner over the same course in May. (10/1)
**3782 Jawaal** could not take advantage of a 6lb lower mark, but at least showed signs of a return to form. (12/1)
**243* Secret Spring (FR)** shaped well after a long lay-off and is one to keep an eye on. (20/1)

## 4309 KINTBURY MAIDEN STKS (3-Y.O) (Class D)

5-15 (5-30) **1m** £4,175.00 (£1,250.00: £600.00: £275.00) Stalls: High GOING minus 0.39 sec per fur (F)

| | | | | SP | RR | SF |
|---|---|---|---|---|---|---|
| 526$^{7}$ | **Threadneedle (USA)** (LordHuntingdon) **3-9-0** LDettori(10) (a.p: rdn over 3f out: led ins fnl f: r.o) | — | **1** | 7/1 | 81 | 27 |
| 3949$^{10}$ | **Scarpetta (USA)** (JWHills) **3-8-9** RHills(1) (led: rdn over 1f out: hdd ins fnl f: r.o) | ½ | **2** | 5/1$^{3}$ | 75 | 21 |
| 550$^{12}$ | **Zilclare (IRE)** (EALDunlop) **3-8-9** WRyan(12) (hld up mid div: hdwy over 1f out: r.o ins fnl f) | 1½ | **3** | 7/1 | 72 | 18 |
| | **Medfee** (RCharlton) **3-8-9** PatEddery(8) (scope: lw: hld up & bhd: gd hdwy fnl f: fin wl) | hd | **4** | 3/1$^{1}$ | 72 | 18 |
| 4231$^{4}$ | **Diamond Beach (80)** (BWHills) **3-9-0** MHills(3) (hld up mid div: hdwy & swtchd lft over 1f out: one pce fnl f) | 1½ | **5** | 11/2 | 74 | 20 |
| 4108$^{10}$ | **Corporal Nym (USA) (97)** (PFICole) **3-9-0** TQuinn(4) (lw: prom: ev ch 2f out: wknd ins fnl f) | 2½ | **6** | 100/30$^{2}$ | 69 | 15 |
| | **The Fugative** (PMitchell) **3-8-9** SSanders(6) (str: scope: bkwd: plld hrd: w ldr: ev ch 2f out: wknd qckly fnl f) | 3 | **7** | 33/1 | 58 | 4 |
| 3788$^{11}$ | **Bello Carattere** (LordHuntingdon) **3-9-0** OUrbina(7) (bhd: rdn over 3f out: n.d) | 1¼ | **8** | 25/1 | 60 | 6 |
| 3949$^{14}$ | **Stolen Music (IRE)** (MajorDNChappell) **3-8-9** AClark(5) (hld up & bhd: nvr nr ldrs) | ¾ | **9** | 50/1 | 54 | — |
| 2919$^{5}$ | **With The Tempo (IRE)** (DrJDScargill) **3-8-9** JQuinn(11) (a bhd) | ½ | **10** | 16/1 | 53 | — |
| 1667$^{12}$ | **Blue Jumbo (IRE)** (WJMusson) **3-8-9** DRMcCabe(9) (bhd fnl 3f) | 6 | **11** | 50/1 | 41 | — |
| | **Hotstepper** (RJPrice) **3-8-6**(3) AWhelan(2) (str: scope: bkwd: bhd: rdn over 3f out: t.o fnl 2f) | 16 | **12** | 33/1 | 9 | — |
| | | | | (SP 124.7%) | | **12 Rn** |

**1m 40.83** (3.83) CSF £41.26 TOTE £6.80: £1.90 £1.90 £2.40 (£32.40) Trio £66.00 OWNER The Queen (WEST ILSLEY) BRED The Queen
**Threadneedle (USA)**, a brother to Magic Junction and a half-brother to Twilight Sleep, prevailed, despite being rather caught out when the slow pace quickened past halfway. (7/1: tchd 12/1)
**921 Scarpetta (USA)** set a slow pace until after halfway and is bred to need a stiffer test of stamina. (5/1: 3/1-11/2)
**Zilclare (IRE)** had not shown much on her debut back in the spring but is clearly on the upgrade now. (7/1: 8/1-12/1)
**Medfee**, a half-sister to stayer Cross Talk, seemed to get undone by the slowly-run race, but looks a ready-made future winner. (3/1: 9/4-7/2)
**4231 Diamond Beach** has had plenty of chances. (11/2: 3/1-6/1)
**Corporal Nym (USA)** may still have just needed this. (100/30: 2/1-7/2)
**The Fugative** ran well until blowing up in the closing stages. (33/1)

T/Plpt: £23.20 (808.97 Tckts). T/Qdpt: £19.10 (51.08 Tckts). KH

# 4296-AYR (L-H) (Good to firm, Firm patches)

## Saturday September 21st

WEATHER: overcast WIND: mod half bhd

## 4310 E.B.F. TOP FLIGHT LEISURE MAIDEN STKS (2-Y.O) (Class D)

1-55 (1-56) **1m** £4,347.00 (£1,296.00: £618.00: £279.00) Stalls: High GOING minus 0.32 sec per fur (GF)

| | | | | SP | RR | SF |
|---|---|---|---|---|---|---|
| 3756$^{8}$ | **Double Flight** (MJohnston) **2-8-9** JWeaver(3) (trckd ldrs: shkn up to ld over 1f out: drvn out) | — | **1** | 2/5$^{1}$ | 66 | 39 |

| | | | | SP | RR | SF |
|---|---|---|---|---|---|---|
| $4069^{11}$ | **Lawn Lothario** (MJohnston) **2-9-0** TWilliams(1) (bit bkwd: led tl over 1f out: hung lft & kpt on same pce) | 2 | **2** | 16/1 | 67? | 40 |
| $4245^{4}$ | **Jackson Falls** (TDEasterby) **2-9-0** MBirch(4) (trckd ldr: effrt over 3f out: sn rdn: wknd 2f out) | 13 | **3** | $3/1^{2}$ | 41 | 14 |
| | **Manileno** (JHetherton) **2-9-0** KFallon(2) (unf: s.i.s: sn wl bhd: t.o fr ½-wy) | dist | **4** | $14/1^{3}$ | — | — |
| | | | | (SP 109.0%) | | **4 Rn** |

**1m 40.11** (2.71) CSF £5.72 TOTE £1.50: (£4.30) OWNER The 3rd Middleham Partnership (MIDDLEHAM) BRED Shadwell Estate Company Limited

**3277 Double Flight**, who was presumably wrong last time, took this soft race in decisive fashion. There is not a lot of her. (2/5)

**Lawn Lothario**, well beaten first time, still looked in need of an outing. Showing plenty of knee-action going down, he hung as if feeling the ground. (16/1)

**4245 Jackson Falls**, who struggled to stay seven furlongs here two days earlier, fell in a heap two furlongs from home. (3/1: 2/1-7/2)

**Manileno**, a narrow, unattractive type, showed plenty of knee-action going down and was soon left trailing. Even so, he picked up £289 prizemoney, likely to be his biggest ever pay day. (14/1: 16/1-25/1)

## 4311 SAM HALL AND DICK PEACOCK NURSERY H'CAP (2-Y.O) (Class D)

2-25 (2-27) **6f** £4,698.00 (£1,404.00: £672.00: £306.00) Stalls: Low GOING minus 0.32 sec per fur (GF)

| | | | | SP | RR | SF |
|---|---|---|---|---|---|---|
| $4113^{5}$ | **Blues Queen (78)** (MRChannon) **2-8-4** JCarroll(2) (lw: w ldrs: led 2f out: r.o wl u.p fnl f) | — | **1** | $5/1^{2}$ | 78 | 48 |
| $3835^{16}$ | **Bolero Boy (95)** (MWEasterby) **2-9-2**(5) GParkin(9) (racd centre: chsd ldrs: edgd lft & kpt on wl ins fnl f) | 1¼ | **2** | 16/1 | 92 | 62 |
| $3969^{2}$ | **Burkes Manor (83)** (TDBarron) **2-8-9** JFortune(4) (a chsng ldrs: styd on same pce appr fnl f) | 4 | **3** | $6/1^{3}$ | 69 | 39 |
| $3674^{9}$ | **Hawait (IRE) (87)** (BWHills) **2-8-13** KFallon(6) (trckd ldrs: n.m.r 2f out: sn rdn: kpt on same pce) | 1 | **4** | $3/1^{1}$ | 70 | 40 |
| $3987^{7}$ | **Rainbow Rain (USA) (80)** (MJohnston) **2-8-6** JWeaver(1) (lw: led to 2f out: one pce) | 1½ | **5** | 13/2 | 59 | 29 |
| $4084^{9}$ | **Hil Rhapsody (76)** (BPalling) **2-7-13**(3)ow2 FLynch(10) (swvd rt s: racd centre: bhd tl sme hdwy fnl f: n.d) | 2½ | **6** | 16/1 | 49 | 17 |
| $3956^{2}$ | **Night Flight (75)** (JJO'Neill) **2-8-1** JFEgan(8) (w ldrs: drvn along over 2f out: hung rt & wknd over 1f out) | 1¼ | **7** | 8/1 | 44 | 14 |
| $4113^{9}$ | **Skyers Flyer (IRE) (84)** (RonaldThompson) **2-8-5**(5) ADaly(11) (s.i.s: a in rr) | 1¼ | **8** | 16/1 | 50 | 20 |
| $3468^{4}$ | **Secret Combe (IRE) (86)** (PJMakin) **2-8-9**(3) RHavlin(5) (chsd ldrs: drvn along ½-wy: sn wknd) | ½ | **9** | 10/1 | 51 | 21 |
| 3840* | **Naivasha (70)** (JBerry) **2-7-5**(5) PFessey(7) (chsd ldrs: sn pushed along: lost pl over 2f out) | nk | **10** | 12/1 | 34 | 4 |
| $3921^{4}$ | **Martine (80)** (ABailey) **2-8-3**(3) DWright(3) (sn wl outpcd & pushed along) | ½ | **11** | 16/1 | 43 | 13 |
| | | | | (SP 120.7%) | | **11 Rn** |

**1m 10.73** (0.93) CSF £73.09 CT £463.00 TOTE £4.90: £1.60 £3.20 £2.10 (£27.30) Trio £44.90 OWNER Maygain Ltd (UPPER LAMBOURN) BRED Major C. R. Philipson

LONG HANDICAP Naivasha 7-8

**4113 Blues Queen**, well drawn with the stalls on the far side, scored in decisive fashion. This was a less-competitive nursery than the one at Doncaster she ran in on her previous outing. (5/1: 7/2-6/1)

**3674 Bolero Boy**, dropping back from a mile, raced up the centre with just one to keep him company. Edging left, towards the far side under pressure, he faltered for a stride or two inside the last but, to his credit, kept on all the way to the line. (16/1)

**3969 Burkes Manor**, put in last, did not have time to misbehave in the stalls this time. (6/1)

**3269* Hawait (IRE)**, heavily backed, was short of room soon after halfway, but that is no excuse. (3/1: 7/1-11/4)

**3987 Rainbow Rain (USA)** proved very one-paced when headed. (13/2)

## 4312 LADBROKE (AYR) SILVER CUP H'CAP (3-Y.O+) (Class B)

3-05 (3-05) **6f** £12,427.50 (£3,720.00: £1,785.00: £817.50) Stalls: Low GOING minus 0.32 sec per fur (GF)

| | | | | SP | RR | SF |
|---|---|---|---|---|---|---|
| 4205* | **Cretan Gift (68)** (NPLittmoden) **5-8-12b** TGMcLaughlin(27) (lw: hdwy ½-wy: led over 1f out: hrd rdn & edgd lft: jst hld on) | — | **1** | $10/1^{2}$ | 76 | 59 |
| $3639^{13}$ | **Thwaab (65)** (FWatson) **4-8-9b**[1] GHind(25) (s.s: hdwy ½-wy: str run fnl f: jst failed) | s.h | **2** | 14/1 | 73 | 56 |
| $3783^{15}$ | **La Petite Fusee (79)** (RJO'Sullivan) **5-9-6**(3) RHavlin(22) (led stands' side: hdd over 1f out: kpt on wl) | 1 | **3** | 20/1 | 84 | 67 |
| $4136^{2}$ | **Wardara (69)** (CADwyer) **4-8-13v** SDrowne(5) (lw: chsd ldr far side: led over 1f out: r.o) | hd | **4** | $12/1^{3}$ | 74 | 57 |
| $4058^{13}$ | **Denbrae (IRE) (70)** (DJGMurraySmith) **4-9-0** JWeaver(18) (sn bhd: gd hdwy over 1f out: styd on wl nr fin) | s.h | **5** | 25/1 | 75 | 58 |
| $4180^{15}$ | **Miss Waterline (72)** (PDEvans) **3-9-0** JFEgan(26) (hdwy ½-wy: styd on wl fnl f) | s.h | **6** | 33/1 | 77 | 58 |
| $4198^{2}$ | **Indian Relative (76)** (RGuest) **3-8-13**(5) DGriffiths(20) (in tch: hdwy & ev ch over 1f out: nt qckn) | 1 | **7** | $15/2^{1}$ | 78 | 59 |
| $4136^{4}$ | **Keston Pond (IRE) (75)** (MrsVAAconley) **6-9-5** MDeering(24) (s.i.s: sn chsng ldrs: wkng whn sltly hmpd ins fnl f) | s.h | **8** | $10/1^{2}$ | 77 | 60 |
| $4198^{18}$ | **Bee Health Boy (70)** (MWEasterby) **3-8-5b**(7) RMullen(28) (chsd ldrs: kpt on same pce fnl 2f) | hd | **9** | 20/1 | 72 | 53 |
| $3672^{10}$ | **Stuffed (71)** (MWEasterby) **4-8-10b**[1](5) GParkin(12) (swtchd rt s: hdwy ½-wy: sn prom: wknd over 1f out) | hd | **10** | 14/1 | 72 | 55 |
| $4058^{8}$ | **Garnock Valley (76)** (JBerry) **6-9-6** JCarroll(29) (wl bhd tl styd on appr fnl f) | s.h | **11** | 20/1 | 77 | 60 |
| $3672^{14}$ | **Bollin Harry (79)** (TDEasterby) **4-9-9** MBirch(1) (lw: led far side tl hdd & wknd over 1f out) | nk | **12** | 40/1 | 79 | 62 |
| $3973^{9}$ | **Dictation (USA) (62)** (JJO'Neill) **4-8-6** DaneO'Neill(23) (chsd ldrs tl wknd 2f out) | s.h | **13** | 50/1 | 62 | 45 |
| $4198^{6}$ | **So Intrepid (IRE) (80)** (JMBradley) **6-9-10** TWilliams(9) (racd far side: sn outpcd: sme hdwy over 1f out: n.d) | 1¾ | **14** | 25/1 | 76 | 59 |
| $2725^{15}$ | **Palo Blanco (79)** (TDBarron) **5-9-9** JFortune(6) (racd far side: bhd tl sme hdwy over 1f out: n.d) | 1¼ | **15** | 28/1 | 71 | 54 |
| $4088^{7}$ | **Stoppes Brow (77)** (GLMoore) **4-9-7v** SWhitworth(7) (racd far side: s.s: a in rr) | hd | **16** | 50/1 | 69 | 52 |
| $3868^{2}$ | **Brecongill Lad (69)** (MissSEHall) **4-8-13** EmmaO'Gorman(8) (lw: racd far side: chsd ldrs tl wknd 2f out) | ½ | **17** | 22/1 | 60 | 43 |
| $4246^{3}$ | **Amron (58)** (JBerry) **9-8-2** AMcGlone(14) (lw: bhd: sme hdwy over 1f out: n.d) | s.h | **18** | 16/1 | 49 | 32 |
| $3154^{7}$ | **Pharmacy (75)** (JWWatts) **3-9-3** TSprake(19) (chsd ldrs tl lost pl over 2f out) | 1½ | **19** | 40/1 | 62 | 43 |
| $3995^{10}$ | **Naissant (65)** (RMMcKellar) **3-8-0**(7) KSked(4) (racd far side: bhd fr ½-wy) | s.h | **20** | 22/1 | 51 | 32 |
| $4180^{7}$ | **Oatey (65)** (MrsJRRamsden) **3-8-7** KFallon(3) (lw: racd far side: a in rr) | 1¾ | **21** | 20/1 | 47 | 28 |
| $4180^{14}$ | **Master of Passion (75)** (JMPEustace) **7-9-5** DRMcCabe(10) (racd far side: a bhd) | 1¼ | **22** | 33/1 | 53 | 36 |
| $3446^{2}$ | **Nilgiri Hills (IRE) (82)** (JLDunlop) **3-9-10** JStack(16) (lw: prom tl lost pl over 2f out) | hd | **23** | 20/1 | 60 | 41 |
| $3868^{11}$ | **King of Show (IRE) (60)** (RAllan) **5-7-13v**(5) ADaly(15) (sn outpcd) | s.h | **24** | 50/1 | 38 | 21 |
| $3622^{6}$ | **The Scythian (73)** (BobJones) **4-9-3** NDay(17) (edgd lft & bhd fr ½-wy) | s.h | **25** | 22/1 | 51 | 34 |
| $4119^{2}$ | **Tart and a Half (72)** (BJMeehan) **4-9-2b** DeanMcKeown(11) (racd far side: chsd ldrs over 3f: sn wknd) | 1 | **26** | 25/1 | 47 | 30 |
| $3844^{3}$ | **Middle East (73)** (TDBarron) **3-8-12**(3) FLynch(13) (in tch tl lost pl ½-wy) | 7 | **27** | 20/1 | 30 | 11 |
| $4058^{14}$ | **Mister Westsound (65)** (MissLAPerratt) **4-8-2b**(7) PClarke(21) (sddle slipped: bhd whn uns rdr ins fnl f) | | **U** | 33/1 | — | — |
| | | | | (SP 133.0%) | | **28 Rn** |

**1m 10.48** (0.68) CSF £131.98 CT £2,534.51 TOTE £10.50: £3.20 £3.20 £3.20 £5.20 (£36.60) Trio £158.50 OWNER R A M Racecourses Ltd (WOLVERHAMPTON) BRED Hesmonds Stud Ltd

WEIGHT FOR AGE 3yo-2lb

OFFICIAL EXPLANATION **Mister Westsound: saddle slipped.**

IN-FOCUS: **Those drawn high enjoyed an advantage and filled the first three places.**

**4205* Cretan Gift**, who broke his duck on turf earlier in the week, ran without a penalty. With his rider using his whip in vigorous fashion, he edged left towards the centre and, in the end, the post came just in time. (10/1)
**3639 Thwaab**, in blinkers rather than the usual visor, was taken to post early. Last away, he would have made it in one more stride. (14/1)
**3518* La Petite Fusee** put a poor effort last time behind her, leading the stands'-side group. (20/1)
**4136 Wardara** came out best of those drawn on the far side and, at the line, was only just over a length down. (12/1)
**2347* Denbrae (IRE)**, after two moderate efforts, finished best of all. (25/1)
**1101 Miss Waterline**, kept off the track all summer, came through strongly in the closing stages and is relatively fresh. (33/1)
**4198 Indian Relative** had every chance but, in truth, never looked like justifying the market support. (15/2: op 12/1)
**4136 Keston Pond (IRE)** was weakening when hampered slightly by the winner inside the last. (10/1)
**2329 Stuffed**, with the blinkers on, ran well from a middle draw. (14/1)
**2911 Garnock Valley**, soon trailing, came tearing through at the death. (20/1)

## 4313 STAKIS CASINOS DOONSIDE CUP STKS (Listed) (3-Y.O+) (Class A)

3-35 (3-36) **1m 2f 192y** £12,243.60 (£4,532.40: £2,176.20: £891.00: £355.50: £141.30) Stalls: High GOING minus 0.32 sec per fur (GF)

| | | | | SP | RR | SF |
|---|---|---|---|---|---|---|
| 3614[5] | **Key to My Heart (IRE) (113)** (MissSEHall) **6-8-11** JWeaver(3) (b: trckd ldrs: shkn up to ld over 2f out: r.o strly) | — | **1** | 6/4[1] | 116 | 73 |
| 4178[4] | **Desert Shot (113)** (MRStoute) **6-8-11** KFallon(6) (hld up: effrt over 3f out: styd on u.p fnl f: no imp) | 3 | **2** | 2/1[2] | 112 | 69 |
| 3798[5] | **Behaviour (107)** (MrsJCecil) **4-8-11** JCarroll(2) (lw: hld up: effrt over 2f out: styd on same pce appr fnl f) | 1¾ | **3** | 6/1[3] | 109 | 66 |
| 4162a[7] | **Wood Magic (104)** (DRLoder) **3-8-4** DRMcCabe(1) (led tl over 2f out: wknd over 1f out) | 6 | **4** | 6/1[3] | 100 | 50 |
| 2620[6] | **Flyfisher (IRE) (100)** (GLewis) **3-8-4** AMcGlone(4) (lw: trckd ldr: effrt over 3f out: wknd 2f out) | 6 | **5** | 9/1 | 91 | 41 |
| | **Done Well (USA) (83)** (PMonteith) **4-8-11** AMackay(7) (lw: hld up: effrt over 3f out: sn bhd & eased) | 18 | **6** | 66/1 | 65 | 22 |
| 3882* | **Ragtime Cowgirl (42)** (DANolan) **3-7-13** PFessey(5) (lw: trckd ldrs tl lost pl 3f out: sn bhd) | 1½ | **7** | 150/1 | 33 t | 8 |
| | | | | (SP 114.1%) | | **7 Rn** |

**2m 15.43** (-0.47) CSF £4.83 TOTE £2.50: £1.60 £1.90 (£1.90) OWNER Mrs Maureen Pickering (MIDDLEHAM) BRED Miss Fiona Meehan
WEIGHT FOR AGE 3yo-7lb
**3614 Key to My Heart (IRE)**, given a more patient ride than on some occasions in the past, made it third time lucky in this race. Once he was sent to the front, there was only one winner but, in truth, this was not the strongest listed race ever. (6/4)
**4178 Desert Shot** could have done with a stronger pace. Sticking on under pressure, he finished clear second but was never going to bother the winner. (2/1)
**3071* Behaviour**, who ran poorly on soft ground at Windsor last time, seemed to run up to his very best. (6/1: op 7/2)
**4162a Wood Magic**, below-par in France last time, led on sufferance. (6/1)
**2620 Flyfisher (IRE)** was quickly put in his place once the race began in earnest. (9/1)

## 4314 LADBROKE (AYR) GOLD CUP H'CAP (3-Y.O+) (Class B)

4-15 (4-17) **6f** £51,630.00 (£15,540.00: £7,520.00: £3,510.00) Stalls: Low GOING minus 0.32 sec per fur (GF)

| | | | | SP | RR | SF |
|---|---|---|---|---|---|---|
| 3232* | **Coastal Bluff (104)** (TDBarron) **4-9-10** JFortune(28) (b.hind: w ldrs: shkn up to ld stands' side over 2f out: drvn along: r.o wl) | — | **1** | 3/1[1] | 118+ | 84 |
| 3406[2] | **Mr Bergerac (IRE) (83)** (BPalling) **5-8-3** TSprake(29) (hld up: hdwy 2f out: r.o wl ins fnl f) | 1½ | **2** | 20/1 | 93 | 59 |
| 3445[2] | **Prince Babar (95)** (JEBanks) **5-8-10(5)** DGriffiths(27) (w ldrs: styd on u.p fnl f) | nk | **3** | 10/1[3] | 104 | 70 |
| 3984[3] | **Double Splendour (IRE) (95)** (PSFelgate) **6-9-1** GHind(25) (sn chsng ldrs: kpt on same pce fnl 2f) | 1½ | **4** | 7/1[2] | 100 | 66 |
| 3783* | **Wildwood Flower (98)** (RHannon) **3-9-2** DaneO'Neill(2) (s.i.s: racd far side: hdwy 2f out: r.o wl ins fnl f) | nk | **5** | 16/1 | 102 | 66 |
| 3232[16] | **Emerging Market (100)** (JLDunlop) **4-9-6** AMcGlone(20) (lw: hdwy to chse ldrs ½-wy: sn rdn: kpt on one pce) | nk | **6** | 16/1 | 104 | 70 |
| 4116* | **Musical Season (91)** (TDBarron) **4-8-11** 7x JFEgan(13) (led far side tl over 2f out: kpt on same pce) | s.h | **7** | 20/1 | 95 | 61 |
| 4116[5] | **Bolshoi (IRE) (89)** (JBerry) **4-8-9b** EmmaO'Gorman(8) (racd far side: hdwy over 2f out: styd on fnl f) | nk | **8** | 33/1 | 92 | 58 |
| 3622[5] | **Bollin Joanne (88)** (TDEasterby) **3-8-6** MBirch(5) (b: chsd ldr far side: led over 2f out tl hdd & wknd ins fnl f) | nk | **9** | 28/1 | 90 | 54 |
| 3672[13] | **Benzoe (IRE) (84)** (MrsJRRamsden) **6-8-4**ow1 KFallon(15) (hdwy ½-wy: sn drvn along: no imp fnl 2f) | 1 | **10** | 28/1 | 83 | 48 |
| 4116[3] | **Lago Di Varano (87)** (RMWhitaker) **4-8-7v** DeanMcKeown(9) (racd far side: in tch: rdn over 2f out: no imp) | s.h | **11** | 28/1 | 86 | 52 |
| 3946[8] | **Bajan Rose (84)** (MBlanshard) **4-7-13(5)** ADaly(3) (chsd ldrs far side tl wknd over 1f out) | hd | **12** | 50/1 | 83 | 49 |
| 4101[2] | **Ziggy's Dancer (USA) (85)** (EJAlston) **5-8-5**ow1 RLappin(1) (chsd ldrs far side: rdn 2f out: grad wknd) | ¾ | **13** | 50/1 | 82 | 47 |
| 4116[6] | **For the Present (84)** (TDBarron) **6-8-1(3)** FLynch(22) (chsd ldrs over 3f: sn wknd) | 1½ | **14** | 14/1 | 77 | 43 |
| 3984[7] | **Hard to Figure (100)** (RJHodges) **10-9-1(5)** GLee(6) (lw: racd far side: sn bhd: sme hdwy 2f out: n.d) | hd | **15** | 50/1 | 93 | 59 |
| 2532* | **Babsy Babe (94)** (JJQuinn) **3-8-12** AMackay(19) (lw: in tch tl lost pl over 2f out) | ½ | **16** | 40/1 | 85 | 49 |
| 3672[6] | **Double Bounce (91)** (PJMakin) **6-8-8(3)** RHavlin(16) (b: hld up: sme hdwy over 2f out: sn wknd) | nk | **17** | 12/1 | 81 | 47 |
| 3672[9] | **Golden Pound (USA) (84)** (MissGayKelleway) **4-8-4** DRMcCabe(23) (lw: w ldrs tl wknd over 2f out) | s.h | **18** | 28/1 | 74 | 40 |
| 3599* | **Patsy Grimes (92)** (JSMoore) **6-8-7(5)** PPMurphy(4) (racd far side: n.d) | s.h | **19** | 50/1 | 82 | 48 |
| 4116[4] | **Tedburrow (91)** (MrsAMNaughton) **4-8-11** JCarroll(14) (swtchd rt s: prom over 3f) | ¾ | **20** | 22/1 | 79 | 45 |
| 4116[12] | **Sea-Deer (88)** (CADwyer) **7-8-8** JStack(21) (lw: nvr nr ldrs) | 1½ | **21** | 28/1 | 72 | 38 |
| 4122* | **Selhurstpark Flyer (IRE) (91)** (JBerry) **5-8-6(5)** 3x PRoberts(18) (b: led stands' side tl over 2f out: sn wknd) | s.h | **22** | 16/1 | 75 | 41 |
| | **Don't Care (IRE) (90)** (MissLAPerratt) **5-8-10b** JWeaver(24) (chsd ldrs tl lost pl over 2f out) | ½ | **23** | 18/1 | 73 | 39 |
| 4116[9] | **Sir Joey (USA) (88)** (PGMurphy) **7-8-8** SDrowne(10) (lw: s.s: racd far side: a bhd) | ½ | **24** | 28/1 | 69 | 35 |
| 4116[16] | **Tiler (IRE) (84)** (MJohnston) **4-8-4** TWilliams(17) (bhd fr ½-wy) | 2½ | **25** | 33/1 | 59 | 25 |
| 3440[3] | **Hawa Al Nasamaat (USA) (85)** (EALDunlop) **4-8-5** SWhitworth(7) (racd far side: bhd fr ½-wy) | 1¼ | **26** | 50/1 | 56 | 22 |
| 4122[8] | **Shamanic (86)** (RHannon) **4-8-6** RPerham(11) (lw: racd far side: a rr div) | 2½ | **27** | 50/1 | 51 | 17 |
| 4116[2] | **Sylva Paradise (IRE) (91)** (CEBrittain) **3-8-6(3)** DWright(12) (lw: racd far side: virtually p.u after 2f: fin lame) | dist | **28** | 25/1 | — | — |
| | | | | (SP 142.4%) | | **28 Rn** |

**1m 9.54** (-0.26) CSF £62.02 CT £409.35 TOTE £4.10: £2.20 £3.30 £2.70 £1.80 (£31.30) Trio £70.70 OWNER Mrs D. E. Sharp (THIRSK) BRED R. M. West
WEIGHT FOR AGE 3yo-2lb
**OFFICIAL EXPLANATION Sylva Paradise: was lame on pulling up.**
**IN-FOCUS: As in the Silver Cup, those drawn towards the stands' rail enjoyed a big headstart. Indeed, the first three home were drawn 28, 29 and 27, prompting the Tricast dividend to be chopped to an unbelievably tight figure.**
**3232* Coastal Bluff**, 13lb higher than Goodwood, showed a scratchy action going down on the firm ground. Gaining the plum stands'-side rail, he had to be pushed along to take charge but, in the end, scored with considerable authority. He should be a major contender for top sprint honours next year, as he is still unfurnished and can only improve over another winter. (3/1: op 9/2)

**3406 Mr Bergerac (IRE)**, absent for six weeks, had no option but to bide his time after the winner beat him to the stands'-side rail. Picking up ground inside the last, he secured second spot near the line. (20/1)
**3445 Prince Babar**, 9lb higher compared with the Wokingham, ran another blinder and has now been placed in four valuable handicaps this year. (10/1)
**3984 Double Splendour (IRE)** ran his usual sound race. (7/1)
**3783* Wildwood Flower**, who had the worst of the draw in the Stewards' Cup, came out best of the far-side group. Surely she deserves to find a good prize. (16/1)
**2623 Emerging Market** had plenty of use made of him. He seems best coming from off a strong pace. (16/1)
**4116* Musical Season**, under a 7lb penalty, finished second best on the far side. (20/1)
**4116 Bolshoi (IRE)** stayed on on the far side when it was all over, finishing third of that group. (33/1)

## 4315 JOHNNIE WALKER WHISKY H'CAP (0-90) (3-Y.O+) (Class C)

4-45 (4-47) **1m 5f 13y** £6,264.00 (£1,872.00: £896.00: £408.00) Stalls: Low GOING minus 0.32 sec per fur (GF)

| | | | | SP | RR | SF |
|---|---|---|---|---|---|---|
| 4048* | **Durham (60)** (HSHowe) **5-8-3b** SWhitworth(3) (lw: bhd: pushed along 4f out: hdwy to ld over 1f out: hung lft: drvn clr) | — | 1 | 3/1 [1] | 74 | 46 |
| 3922[2] | **Floating Line (68)** (EJAlston) **8-8-11** KFallon(4) (led early: chsd ldrs: led over 2f out tl over 1f out: kpt on same pce) | 5 | 2 | 5/1 [3] | 76 | 48 |
| 4073* | **Far Ahead (83)** (JLEyre) **4-9-12** RLappin(10) (lw: bhd: hdwy 2f out: sn rdn & styd on one pce) | 3 | 3 | 4/1 [2] | 87 | 59 |
| 4249[7] | **Mentalasanythin (70)** (DHaydnJones) **7-8-13** AMackay(2) (hld up: effrt over 2f out: styd on fnl f) | 1 | 4 | 7/1 | 73 | 45 |
| 4125[14] | **Hand of Straw (IRE) (54)** (PGMurphy) **4-7-11v**ow1 TWilliams(5) (trckd ldrs: ev ch tl wknd over 1f out) | ¾ | 5 | 50/1 | 56 | 27 |
| 3928[5] | **Ela Man Howa (54)** (ABailey) **5-7-8b[1]**(3)ow1 DWright(7) (bhd: stdy hdwy on outside 3f out: rdn & wknd 2f out) | 6 | 6 | 12/1 | 49 | 20 |
| 3958[12] | **Lord Advocate (58)** (DANolan) **8-7-8b**(7)ow5 KSked(1) (w ldrs: stumbled & lost pl 4f out: sme hdwy on outside 2f out) | 6 | 7 | 50/1 | 45 | 12 |
| 4112[6] | **Deano's Beeno (72)** (MJohnston) **4-9-1** JWeaver(8) (sn led: hdd over 2f out: sn wknd) | ¾ | 8 | 5/1 [3] | 58 | 30 |
| | **Cois Na Farraige (IRE) (75)** (MissLAPerratt) **3-8-9** JCarroll(6) (hld up: jnd ldrs 4f out: wknd 2f out) | 2½ | 9 | 20/1 | 58 | 21 |
| 3939[11] | **Marchant Ming (IRE) (58)** (MDHammond) **4-7-10**(5) PFessey(9) (chsd ldrs tl lost pl 2f out) | 1½ | 10 | 14/1 | 40 | 12 |
| | **Shonara's Way (85)** (PMonteith) **5-9-7**(7) JBramhill(11) (sn bhd: hdwy on outside 10f out: sn lost pl: bhd fnl 5f: t.o) | 22 | 11 | 25/1 | 40 | 12 |
| | | | | (SP 117.7%) | **11 Rn** | |

**2m 47.51** (2.71) CSF £17.46 CT £54.79 TOTE £4.30: £1.60 £2.40 £1.70 (£12.50) Trio £12.30 OWNER The Secret Partnership (TIVERTON) BRED Highclere Stud Ltd
LONG HANDICAP Lord Advocate 7-3 Hand of Straw (IRE) 7-9 Ela Man Howa 7-4
WEIGHT FOR AGE 3yo-9lb
**4048* Durham**, who usually has plenty of use made of him, came from off the pace this time. Despite hanging when he hit the front, he came right away and seems a reformed character. (3/1)
**3922 Floating Line**, dropping back in distance, turned in another commendable effort. Surely it can only be a question of time before his luck changes. (5/1)
**4073* Far Ahead**, 4lb higher, was making hard work of it throughout. (4/1)
**4193 Mentalasanythin** ran better on his second outing in three days. (7/1)
**1838 Hand of Straw (IRE)**, who has slipped down the weights, travelled strongly but found very little under pressure. (50/1)

## 4316 SPH PROPERTY SEARCH H'CAP (0-90) (3-Y.O+) (Class C)

5-15 (5-17) **7f** £6,420.00 (£1,920.00: £920.00: £420.00) Stalls: High GOING minus 0.32 sec per fur (GF)

| | | | | SP | RR | SF |
|---|---|---|---|---|---|---|
| 4300[5] | **Celebration Cake (IRE) (70)** (MissLAPerratt) **4-8-9** JWeaver(10) (hld up: hdwy over 3f out: swtchd over 1f out: r.o wl to ld towards fin) | — | 1 | 9/2 [2] | 82 | 52 |
| 3817[6] | **Superpride (62)** (MrsMReveley) **4-8-1** TWilliams(9) (lw: reminders after s: led tl jst ins fnl f: kpt on) | 1½ | 2 | 16/1 | 71 | 41 |
| 4136[7] | **Champagne Grandy (74)** (MRChannon) **6-8-8**(5) PPMurphy(2) (lw: hld up: hdwy on ins over 2f out: led jst ins fnl f: hdd & no ex fnl 50y) | ½ | 3 | 13/2 [3] | 81 | 51 |
| 4300[11] | **King Curan (USA) (68)** (DHaydnJones) **5-8-7v** GHind(5) (chsd ldrs: sn drvn along: one pce appr fnl f) | 1¼ | 4 | 14/1 | 73 | 43 |
| 3770[4] | **Cashmere Lady (74)** (JLEyre) **4-8-13** RLappin(8) (s.i.s: pushed along over 3f out: styd on fnl 2f) | hd | 5 | 13/2 [3] | 78 | 48 |
| 4194[5] | **My Gallery (IRE) (89)** (ABailey) **5-9-11**(3) DWright(6) (hld up: effrt over 2f out: swtchd & sltly hmpd over 1f out: nvr nr to chal) | 2 | 6 | 100/30 [1] | 89 | 59 |
| 4054[4] | **Persian Fayre (75)** (JBerry) **4-9-0** JCarroll(11) (chsd ldrs: ev ch tl wknd over 1f out) | nk | 7 | 9/2 [2] | 74 | 44 |
| 4246[5] | **Natural Key (66)** (DHaydnJones) **3-8-2** AMackay(3) (lw: bhd: effrt over 3f out: sltly hmpd over 1f out: n.d) | 1 | 8 | 7/1 | 63 | 30 |
| 4045[17] | **Miss Pigalle (58)** (MissLAPerratt) **5-7-6b**(5)ow1 PFessey(12) (chsd ldrs: wkng whn sltly hmpd over 1f out) | 1 | 9 | 100/1 | 53 | 22 |
| 2725[12] | **Murray's Mazda (IRE) (57)** (JLEyre) **7-7-3**(7) AMcCarthy(7) (in tch: drvn along over 3f out: lost pl over 2f out) | 3½ | 10 | 14/1 | 44 | 14 |
| 4054[14] | **Fame Again (73)** (MrsJRRamsden) **4-8-12** KFallon(4) (hld up: effrt over 2f out: sn lost pl) | 2 | 11 | 12/1 | 55 | 25 |
| | | | | (SP 126.5%) | **11 Rn** | |

**1m 25.23** (1.23) CSF £69.33 CT £449.36 TOTE £5.50: £2.20 £4.50 £2.60 (£53.10) Trio £264.00 OWNER Lightbody of Hamilton Ltd (AYR) BRED John Davison
LONG HANDICAP Miss Pigalle 6-8 Murray's Mazda (IRE) 7-5
WEIGHT FOR AGE 3yo-3lb
**4300 Celebration Cake (IRE)**, having his second outing in two days, did well to get there considering this trip is on the sharp side for him. Having to switch to get an opening, he caused a domino effect involving three other horses. The Stewards kept the locals happy by deeming that no interference took place, but it did not look that way at all. (9/2)
**3817 Superpride**, rousted along after the start, kept on surprisingly well to fight off all but the winner. (16/1)
**4136 Champagne Grandy** again shaped as if on the way back and should find another opening once the ground eases. (13/2)
**3958* King Curan (USA)**, having his second race in two days, ran much better, sticking on under pressure. (14/1)
**3770 Cashmere Lady**, better known as an All-Weather performer, found this trip on the short side. When stepped up to a mile or beyond, she will surely break her duck on turf. (13/2)
**4194 My Gallery (IRE)** found the ground on the fast side for her and did not have the run of the race. She must not be written off yet. (100/30)

T/Jkpt: £12,448.20 (1.29 Tckts). T/Plpt: £30.20 (1,002.72 Tckts). T/Qdpt: £8.30 (251.77 Tckts). WG

# 3575-CATTERICK (L-H) (Good to firm, Good patches)

## Saturday September 21st

WEATHER: sunny periods WIND: str across

## 4317 HAPPY BIRTHDAY JFS 55 TODAY (S) STKS (3-Y.O) (Class G)

2-20 (2-20) **1m 5f 175y** £2,406.00 (£666.00: £318.00) Stalls: Low GOING minus 0.24 sec per fur (GF)

| | | | | SP | RR | SF |
|---|---|---|---|---|---|---|
| $3775^{4}$ | **Havana Heights (IRE) (37)** (JLEyre) **3-8-5** JQuinn(4) (hld up in tch: reminder over 3f out: hdwy ent st: led ins fnl f: r.o) | — | **1** | $11/2^{3}$ | 45 | 10 |
| $4042^{5}$ | **Arc of The Diver (IRE) (52)** (JBerry) **3-8-10b** GCarter(7) (lw: trckd ldrs: led over 2f out tl ins fnl f: rallied u.p cl home) | ¾ | **2** | $3/1^{2}$ | 49 | 14 |
| $2215^{9}$ | **The Butterwick Kid (45)** (RAFahey) **3-8-10** ACulhane(9) (bit bkwd: hld up & bhd: hdwy u.p ent st: styd on fnl f) | 3½ | **3** | 14/1 | 45 | 10 |
| $2683^{5}$ | **Champagne Warrior (IRE) (46)** (MJCamacho) **3-8-5b$^{1}$** LCharnock(3) (lw: chsd ldr: rdn & outpcd over 2f out: styd on same pce) | 2½ | **4** | $4/6^{1}$ | 37 | 2 |
| | **Chancancook** (JLEyre) **3-8-0**$^{(7)ow2}$ SBuckley(6) (lt-f: unf: dwlt: hld up on ins: outpcd over 2f out: styd on ins fnl f) | 1¾ | **5** | 10/1 | 37 | — |
| $4249^{17}$ | **Philgem (23)** (CWFairhurst) **3-8-5** NKennedy(5) (prom tl rdn & one pce fnl 2f) | nk | **6** | 20/1 | 35 | — |
| | **Aydigo** (JPearce) **3-8-10** GBardwell(2) (lt-f: unf: bkwd: bhd: drvn along & outpcd ½-wy: sme late hdwy) | ½ | **7** | 12/1 | 39 | 4 |
| $3961^{8}$ | **Ship's Dancer (40)** (DonEnricoIncisa) **3-8-5v** KimTinkler(10) (nvr nr to chal) | 2½ | **8** | 16/1 | 31 | — |
| $1523^{8}$ | **Storm Wind (IRE) (40)** (KRBurke) **3-8-10** MFenton(1) (bit bkwd: led & sn clr: hdd over 2f out: wknd qckly) | 2 | **9** | 25/1 | 34 | — |
| $2175^{9}$ | **Brogans Brush (37)** (JSHaldane) **3-8-10** JFanning(8) (chsd ldrs over 9f: sn lost tch: t.o) | dist | **10** | 25/1 | — | — |

(SP 142.2%) **10 Rn**

**3m 6.4** (10.90) CSF £26.15 TOTE £6.30: £1.50 £1.40 £3.20 (£11.00) Trio £30.70 OWNER Mr Anthony Cross (HAMBLETON) BRED Golden Vale Stud

No bid

**3775 Havana Heights (IRE)** timed her effort to perfection, but needed to see out the trip to ward off a determined rival. (11/2)

**4042 Arc of The Diver (IRE)** got the better of the long-time leader to take over on straightening up but, after looking to be in control, failed to last home. (3/1)

**2215 The Butterwick Kid**, a youngster with plenty of size about him to go jumping, stayed on relentlessly inside the distance and it would seem he lacks nothing as regards stamina. (14/1)

**2683 Champagne Warrior (IRE)**, tried in blinkers this time, was off the bit soon after reaching the straight and, failing to respond to pressure, proved a big disappointment. (4/6: op 5/4)

**Chancancook**, a very unfurnished newcomer, did not fare badly after losing ground at the start and could prove better than a selling plater when she strengthens up. (10/1)

**3882 Philgem** failed to see out the trip after travelling well and looking a danger to all turning in. (20/1)

**Aydigo** (12/1: 8/1-14/1)

## 4318 E.B.F. MAIDEN STKS (2-Y.O) (Class D)

2-50 (2-50) **5f 212y** £4,012.50 (£1,200.00: £575.00: £262.50) Stalls: High GOING minus 0.24 sec per fur (GF)

| | | | | SP | RR | SF |
|---|---|---|---|---|---|---|
| $4118^{6}$ | **Amyas (IRE)** (BWHills) **2-8-9**$^{(5)}$ JDSmith(8) (lw: hld up in tch: hdwy 2f out: led ins fnl f: drvn clr) | — | **1** | $7/2^{2}$ | 69 | 26 |
| $4123^{7}$ | **Contentment (IRE)** (JWHills) **2-9-0** MFenton(6) (lw: chsd ldr: led over 2f out tl hdd & no ex ins fnl f) | 2 | **2** | 6/1 | 64 | 21 |
| $3773^{5}$ | **Erosion (IRE)** (MJohnston) **2-9-0** GBardwell(4) (bit bkwd: led: hrd drvn & hdd over 2f out: one pce fnl f) | 1¾ | **3** | $5/1^{3}$ | 59 | 16 |
| $2720^{6}$ | **Barresbo** (CWFairhurst) **2-9-0** LCharnock(7) (plld hrd: hld up: hdwy wl over 1f out: nt rch ldrs) | 1¾ | **4** | 10/1 | 54 | 11 |
| *$4091^{7}$* | **King Uno** (MrsJRRamsden) **2-9-0** JQuinn(3) (hld up: hdwy ent st: sn rdn: nt pce to chal) | ½ | **5** | 20/1 | 53 | 10 |
| | **Come Dancing** (MJohnston) **2-8-9** JFanning(9) (leggy: lt-f: bit bkwd: s.s: hdwy ½-wy: wknd over 1f out: improve) | 1½ | **6** | 9/1 | 44+ | 1 |
| $3464^{5}$ | **Toronto (76)** (JBerry) **2-9-0** GCarter(5) (lw: chsd ldng pair 4f: sn rdn & btn) | 4 | **7** | $9/4^{1}$ | 38 | — |
| *$4091^{5}$* | **Shaded (IRE)** (JWWatts) **2-9-0** NConnorton(2) (lw: hld up in rr: smooth hdwy on ins whn bdly hmpd wl over 1f out: nt rcvr) | ½ | **8** | 14/1 | 37+ | — |
| $1479^{3}$ | **Bailieborough Boy (IRE)** (TDBarron) **2-9-0** ACulhane(1) (a bhd & outpcd) | 1¼ | **9** | 7/1 | 34 | — |

(SP 127.0%) **9 Rn**

**1m 14.6** (3.70) CSF £25.52 TOTE £3.80: £1.90 £1.60 £1.90 (£10.30) Trio £30.20 OWNER Mrs J. M. Corbett (LAMBOURN) BRED Mrs Helen Smith

**3494 Amyas (IRE)** showed a good turn of speed to take over 100 yards out and win with quite a bit in hand. (7/2)

**Contentment (IRE)**, a half-brother to St Leger winner Bob's Return, will surely need further in time, but this was his best effort yet and he is getting the hang of the game. (6/1)

**3773 Erosion (IRE)** still looks to have something left to work on, but he showed he is progressing in the right direction with a pleasing display. More will be heard of him. (5/1)

**2720 Barresbo** has a long way to go to be in the same class as his smart half-sister Blue Iris, but he was not disgraced here after ten weeks out of action and can soon put matters straight. (10/1)

**King Uno**, showing his first glimpse of form, could not really get himself into the action, but the promise is there and he has got time on his side. (20/1)

**Come Dancing**, very green in the preliminaries and the race, probably gave away more ground at the start than she was beaten by, and it is to be hoped the experience will not be lost. (9/1: 5/1-10/1)

**4091 Shaded (IRE)**, trying for an ambitious run up the inside from the turn into the straight, was almost put over the rail below the distance and, forced to take avoiding action, was unable to recover. (14/1)

## 4319 RED ONION NURSERY H'CAP (0-75) (2-Y.O) (Class E)

3-20 (3-23) **7f** £3,444.00 (£1,032.00: £496.00: £228.00) Stalls: Low GOING minus 0.24 sec per fur (GF)

| | | | | SP | RR | SF |
|---|---|---|---|---|---|---|
| $4072^{3}$ | **Gipsy Princess (62)** (MWEasterby) **2-8-9** LCharnock(5) (lw: mde all: hrd drvn 1f out: hld on gamely) | — | **1** | $4/1^{1}$ | 61 | 9 |
| $3840^{3}$ | **Juicy Ting (64)** (PCHaslam) **2-8-11** GCarter(2) (lw: a.p: effrt on ins 2f out: kpt on wl towards fin) | nk | **2** | $4/1^{1}$ | 62 | 10 |
| $3462^{8}$ | **Lord Discord (65)** (TDEasterby) **2-8-12** NConnorton(4) (hld up: hdwy & swtchd ins 2f out: r.o wl ins fnl f) | ½ | **3** | 16/1 | 62 | 10 |
| $3771^{3}$ | **Super Saint (65)** (TDBarron) **2-8-12** ACulhane(7) (plld hrd: chsd wnr most of wy: rdn & unable qckn fnl f) | ½ | **4** | $11/2^{3}$ | 61 | 9 |
| $3577^{5}$ | **Madison Welcome (IRE) (65)** (MrsJRRamsden) **2-8-12** JFanning(3) (lw: hld up in rr: hdwy over 1f out: styng on whn nt clr run nr fin) | 1 | **5** | $9/2^{2}$ | 59 | 7 |

| | | | SP | RR | SF |
|---|---|---|---|---|---|
| 3880$^{6}$ | **Italian Symphony (IRE) (74)** (MJohnston) **2-9-7** JQuinn(9) (chsd ldrs: rdn over 1f out: wknd fnl f)......................1 | **6** | 6/1 | 66 | 14 |
| 3969$^{6}$ | **Epic Stand (60)** (MrsJRRamsden) **2-8-0**$^{(7)}$ TFinn(8) (lw: effrt on outside 3f out: one pce appr fnl f)..................½ | **7** | 16/1 | 50 | — |
| 3814$^{2}$ | **Tom Mi Dah (65)** (MDHammond) **2-8-12** NKennedy(6) (hld up in rr: outpcd fnl 2f)..............................................3 | **8** | 11/2$^{3}$ | 49 | — |
| 3848$^{15}$ | **Ballydinero (IRE) (53)** (CaptJWilson) **2-8-0** GBardwell(1) (lw: s.i.s: a bhd: outpcd) ............................................2 | **9** | 25/1 | 32 | — |
| | | | (SP 118.8%) | | **9 Rn** |

**1m 29.1** (5.50) CSF £19.86 CT £213.22 TOTE £4.20: £1.70 £1.90 £4.40 (£21.10) Trio £117.50; £117.51 to Musselburgh 23/9/96 OWNER Lady Manton (SHERIFF HUTTON) BRED Mrs A. Scott

**4072 Gipsy Princess**, allowed to stride on from the off, showed the right attitude in a nail-biting finish and deservedly emerged as the winner. (4/1)
**3840 Juicy Ting**, stepping up from selling company, ran by far his best race in defeat and it should not be long before he goes one better. (4/1)
**2517 Lord Discord**, short of room when staying on in the latter part of the race, was not knocked about afterwards. He could be one to keep an eye on. (16/1)
**3771 Super Saint** handled the track much better over this longer trip, but he took such a fearsome hold that he only succeeded in beating himself. (11/2)
**3577 Madison Welcome (IRE)**, set alight approaching the final furlong, had no luck at all when attempting to deliver his challenge between horses, but whether he would have made it with a clear passage is open to debate. (9/2: op 3/1)
**3880 Italian Symphony (IRE)**, conceding weight all round, left the impression that he is not yet seeing this trip out. (6/1)

## 4320 CONSTANT SECURITY SERVICES H'CAP (0-85) (3-Y.O+) (Class D)

3-50 (3-50) **1m 3f 214y** £4,012.50 (£1,200.00: £575.00: £262.50) Stalls: Low GOING minus 0.24 sec per fur (GF)

| | | | SP | RR | SF |
|---|---|---|---|---|---|
| 4073$^{2}$ | **Tessajoe (71)** (MJCamacho) **4-9-2** LCharnock(7) (b.hind: lw: hld up in tch: hdwy to ld over 1f out: rdn & r.o wl)..........— | **1** | 11/4$^{1}$ | 79 | 39 |
| 4067$^{3}$ | **Artic Courier (83)** (DJSCosgrove) **5-9-9**$^{(5)}$ LNewton(3) (hld up & bhd: gd hdwy 2f out: rdn & r.o wl nr fin) .......½ | **2** | 4/1$^{2}$ | 90 | 50 |
| 3942$^{2}$ | **Classic Parisian (IRE) (74)** (RHarris) **3-8-11** RPrice(9) (lw: chsd ldr: led over 3f out tl over 1f out: one pce) .1½ | **3** | 7/1 | 79 | 31 |
| | **Mad Militant (IRE) (55)** (AStreeter) **7-8-0** JQuinn(4) (bit bkwd: hld up: hdwy 5f out: drvn along ent st: styd on)..........1¼ | **4** | 20/1 | 59 | 19 |
| 4067$^{8}$ | **Nereus (81)** (BWHills) **3-8-13**$^{(5)}$ JDSmith(1) (b.hind: a.p: hrd drvn over 1f out: one pce) ..........................s.h | **5** | 7/1 | 85 | 37 |
| 4073$^{4}$ | **Once More for Luck (IRE) (66)** (MrsMReveley) **5-8-11** ACulhane(2) (hld up: hdwy 3f out: hrd drvn wl over 1f out: nt pce to chal)..........¾ | **6** | 4/1$^{2}$ | 69 | 29 |
| 4073$^{5}$ | **Master Hyde (USA) (56)** (WStorey) **7-8-1** JFanning(8) (lw: hld up: hdwy ½-wy: one pce fnl 2f)..........................3 | **7** | 9/2$^{3}$ | 55 | 15 |
| 3828$^{11}$ | **Persian Elite (IRE) (82)** (CREgerton) **5-9-13** GCarter(5) (led over 8f: wknd 2f out: t.o)....................................16 | **8** | 20/1 | 59 | 19 |
| 4073$^{18}$ | **Colorful Ambition (67)** (MrsASwinbank) **6-8-12** NConnorton(6) (s.s: a bhd: t.o) ...............................................6 | **9** | 25/1 | 36 | — |
| | | | (SP 123.2%) | | **9 Rn** |

**2m 37.8** (6.40) CSF £12.94 CT £57.90 TOTE £3.10: £1.90 £1.30 £2.60 (£6.10) Trio £9.00 OWNER Riley Partnership (MALTON) BRED A. and Mrs Rhodes

WEIGHT FOR AGE 3yo-8lb

**4073 Tessajoe**, like most of his stablemates, was turned out to perfection and, though he does carry a lot of condition, he had the race run to suit and won with more ease than the margin might suggest. (11/4: 2/1-3/1)
**4067 Artic Courier** was given plenty to do after the winner had first run on him and he was never going to reel him in. His luck will change one of these days. (4/1)
**3942 Classic Parisian (IRE)**, taking on handicappers for the first time, ran well and it will come as a big surprise if she can not find an opening in the coming weeks. (7/1)
**Mad Militant (IRE)** does perform well when fresh, but he did look a bit ring-rusty after an absence of almost a year and could be as good as ever. (20/1)
**2876* Nereus** did not look at all happy on such a tight track and was hard at work to no avail inside the last quarter-mile. (7/1)
**4073 Master Hyde (USA)**, subject of quite a gamble, was galloping on the spot for the last couple of furlongs. An easing of the ground may well be what he requires. (9/2: op 10/1)

## 4321 SKYRAM H'CAP (0-65) (3-Y.O+) (Class F)

4-25 (4-28) **1m 7f 177y** £3,078.00 (£858.00: £414.00) Stalls: Low GOING minus 0.24 sec per fur (GF)

| | | | SP | RR | SF |
|---|---|---|---|---|---|
| 3870$^{4}$ | **Onefourseven (42)** (JLEyre) **3-7-5**$^{(5)}$ CAdamson(2) (hld up mid div: hdwy 4f out: led on bit ent st: pushed clr fnl f)..........— | **1** | 16/1 | 53 | 25 |
| 2756* | **Hullbank (60)** (WWHaigh) **6-9-12** GCarter(15) (b: lw: a.p: hrd rdn over 1f out: r.o one pce)............................2½ | **2** | 9/1 | 69 | 53 |
| 4203* | **Broughtons Formula (39)** (WJMusson) **6-8-5b** $^{5x}$ JQuinn(8) (lw: chsd ldrs: rdn & outpcd ent st: styd on ins fnl f) ..........nk | **3** | 7/4$^{1}$ | 47 | 31 |
| 3580* | **Marsayas (IRE) (57)** (MJCamacho) **3-8-11** LCharnock(6) (lw: a.p: led 5f out tl over 2f out: sn rdn & btn).......3½ | **4** | 8/1$^{3}$ | 62 | 34 |
| 3520$^{2}$ | **Spinning Mouse (60)** (DMorley) **3-9-0** MFenton(1) (hld up: hdwy 7f out: hmpd & lost pl 4f out: nt rcvr) ............6 | **5** | 11/4$^{2}$ | 59 | 31 |
| 3878$^{10}$ | **Monaco Gold (IRE) (41)** (MrsMReveley) **4-8-7** ACulhane(3) (styd on fnl 3f: nvr nrr)..........................................2½ | **6** | 9/1 | 37 | 21 |
| 2423$^{7}$ | **Superhoo (30)** (RCraggs) **5-7-10** GBardwell(11) (swtg: led 2f: rdn along ½-wy: no imp fnl 4f)..........................2½ | **7** | 25/1 | 24 | 8 |
| 3855$^{5}$ | **Jundi (IRE) (44)** (JDBethell) **5-8-5b**$^{(5)ow1}$ JDSmith(5) (hld up in rr: sme hdwy fnl 3f: fin lame) ........................12 | **8** | 25/1 | 25 | 8 |
| 4042$^{P}$ | **Aren't We Lucky (IRE) (57)** (JJO'Neill) **3-8-4**$^{(7)ow2}$ SOlley(12) (trckd ldrs 12f: sn lost tch: t.o) ..........................3½ | **9** | 33/1 | 35 | 5 |
| 2627$^{10}$ | **Alzotic (IRE) (46)** (JNorton) **3-7-7v**$^{(7)ow4}$ JoHunnam(13) (bit bkwd: led after 2f to 5f out: sn wknd: t.o)..............4 | **10** | 20/1 | 20 | — |
| 3970$^{6}$ | **Highfield Fizz (41)** (CWFairhurst) **4-8-7** NConnorton(9) (a bhd: t.o) ........................................................2½ | **11** | 25/1 | 12 | — |
| 2756$^{4}$ | **Longcroft (40)** (SEKettlewell) **4-8-6** NKennedy(4) (a bhd: t.o fnl 6f) ......................................................1¾ | **12** | 16/1 | 9 | — |
| 3870$^{6}$ | **Clash of Swords (54)** (PCalver) **3-8-8b** JFanning(7) (lw: chsd ldrs tl wknd over 4f out: t.o)...............................2½ | **13** | 14/1 | 21 | — |
| 3865$^{6}$ | **Penny Peppermint (34)** (REBarr) **4-7-7**$^{(7)}$ JMcAuley(14) (t.o fnl 6f)...................................................................9 | **14** | 50/1 | — | — |
| 542$^{12}$ | **Doctor's Remedy (30)** (MrsJJordan) **10-7-3b**$^{(7)}$ JennyBenson(10) (bkwd: lost pl ½-wy: t.o)............................1½ | **15** | 50/1 | — | — |
| | | | (SP 135.7%) | | **15 Rn** |

**3m 30.0** (8.50) CSF £154.58 CT £357.86 TOTE £17.00: £2.50 £4.40 £1.60 (£137.30) Trio £212.60 OWNER Mr J. Roundtree (HAMBLETON) BRED Peter Storey

LONG HANDICAP Onefourseven 7-4 Superhoo 7-8 Doctor's Remedy 7-3

WEIGHT FOR AGE 3yo-12lb

**3870 Onefourseven** won this with so much in hand that one wondered why he has not produced some real sign of ability before. He is only a three-year-old and, with a featherweight to carry, may have thought he was loose. (16/1)
**2756* Hullbank** found the task of conceding two and a half stone to a younger rival beyond him, but he never gave up trying and his heart is in the right place. (9/1)
**4203* Broughtons Formula** found the 5lb penalty just that bit too much of a handicap but, at these weights, there was no way he was going to beat the winner. (7/4)

**3580* Marsayas (IRE)** broke his duck over course and distance last month, but he was flat to the boards soon after joining in, and had to admit the principals much too good for him on the day. (8/1)
**3520 Spinning Mouse**, creeping through on the inside rail when stopped in her stride at the end of the back straight, lost far too much ground to have any hope of recovery. She must be given the chance to make amends. (11/4)
**3878 Monaco Gold (IRE)** was threading his way through in the latter stages, but always had far too much to do. (9/1)

## 4322 'GO RACING IN YORKSHIRE' MAIDEN STKS (3-Y.O) (Class D)

5-00 (5-01) **7f** £4,142.50 (£1,240.00: £595.00: £272.50) Stalls: Low GOING minus 0.24 sec per fur (GF)

| | | | | SP | RR | SF |
|---|---|---|---|---|---|---|
| 4108[3] | **Don Bosio (USA) (84)** (MRStoute) **3-9-0v** NConnorton(6) (a.p: led wl over 1f out: drew clr: v.easily) | — | **1** | 4/5[1] | 87+ | 39 |
| 3767[9] | **Danlora** (WJarvis) **3-8-9** JQuinn(9) (lw: trckd ldrs: rdn 2f out: styd on: no ch w wnr) | 6 | **2** | 8/1 | 68 | 20 |
| 4074[2] | **Minoletti** (EALDunlop) **3-9-0** MFenton(7) (b.nr hind: lw: led: rdn & hdd over 2f out: one pce appr fnl f) | nk | **3** | 8/1 | 73 | 25 |
| 3999[4] | **Stellar Line (USA) (74)** (BWHills) **3-8-9**(5) JDSmith(13) (a.p: rdn to ld over 2f out: sn hdd & outpcd) | ¾ | **4** | 6/1[3] | 71 | 23 |
| | **Classic Ribbon (IRE)** (RHarris) **3-8-9** RPrice(11) (leggy: unf: in tch: effrt & rdn wl over 1f out: kpt on) | hd | **5** | 33/1 | 66 | 18 |
| 3425[W] | **Jungle Fresh** (JDBethell) **3-9-0** GBardwell(1) (dwlt: nvr nrr) | 8 | **6** | 33/1 | 52 | 4 |
| 1901[17] | **Proud Look (69)** (BWHills) **3-9-0** LCharnock(12) (lw: in tch tl wknd 2f out) | hd | **7** | 8/1 | 52 | 4 |
| *4076*[13] | **Kass Alhawa (75)** (DWChapman) **3-9-0** ACulhane(3) (a in rr) | nk | **8** | 25/1 | 52 | 4 |
| 4074[17] | **Born On The Wild** (SEKettlewell) **3-8-9** NKennedy(4) (a bhd & outpcd) | nk | **9** | 50/1 | 46 | — |
| 3457[8] | **John-T (75)** (JBerry) **3-9-0** GCarter(8) (a bhd & outpcd) | hd | **10** | 20/1 | 51 | 3 |
| | **Man On A Mission** (AStreeter) **3-8-9**(5) LNewton(2) (w'like: bkwd: s.s: a wl bhd: t.o) | 6 | **11** | 50/1 | 37 | — |
| 3492[9] | **Ballykissangel (28)** (NBycroft) **3-8-9**(5) CAdamson(10) (mid div tl wknd over 2f out: t.o) | 5 | **12** | 100/1 | 25 | — |
| 3642[2] | **Mighty Keen** (MJohnston) **3-9-0** JFanning(5) (plld hrd: prom 4f: sn wknd: t.o) | 5 | **13** | 5/1[2] | 14 | — |

(SP 139.2%) **13 Rn**

**1m 26.6** (3.00) CSF £10.26 TOTE £1.80: £1.10 £3.40 £1.70 (£8.50) Trio £14.40 OWNER Sultan Al Kabeer (NEWMARKET) BRED Poole Investments

**4108 Don Bosio (USA)** was faced with a simple task to open his account and hardly needed to break sweat, but he left the impression that this ground was plenty fast enough for him. (4/5: op Evens)
**3446 Danlora** worked hard in the closing stages to gain the runner-up prize and she looks the type who will come into her own over a longer trip. (8/1: 6/1-9/1)
**4074 Minoletti**, tackling a slightly longer trip, gave his best, but was made to look very one-paced when the winner lengthened up. (8/1: op 5/1)
**3999 Stellar Line (USA)**, taking a step down in distance, kicked for home early in the straight, but lacked the pace to get away and he was brushed aside with ease when the battle to the line really developed. (6/1)
**Classic Ribbon (IRE)** showed signs of ability on this racecourse debut and, if there is any improvement to come, ought to be able to pay her way. (33/1)

## 4323 BROUGH PARK H'CAP (0-60) (3-Y.O+ F & M) (Class F)

5-30 (5-33) **7f** £3,288.00 (£918.00: £444.00) Stalls: Low GOING minus 0.24 sec per fur (GF)

| | | | | SP | RR | SF |
|---|---|---|---|---|---|---|
| 3761[2] | **Komlucky (48)** (ABMulholland) **4-8-11v**(5) LNewton(3) (a.p: led over 1f out: hld on wl cl home) | — | **1** | 6/1[3] | 57 | 35 |
| 3578[4] | **Regal Fanfare (IRE) (53)** (MrsLStubbs) **4-9-0b**(7) JoHunnam(10) (hld up: hdwy over 2f out: jnd wnr ent fnl f: r.o) | hd | **2** | 12/1 | 62 | 40 |
| *4077** | **Sis Garden (48)** (JCullinan) **3-8-8b**(5) AimeeCook(12) (hld up: hdwy 2f out: rdn & r.o wl ins fnl f) | 1¼ | **3** | 3/1[1] | 54 | 29 |
| 4206[19] | **La Finale (48)** (DNicholls) **3-8-6b**(7) JennyBenson(5) (led tl over 1f out: no ex fnl f) | hd | **4** | 25/1 | 54 | 29 |
| 4206[8] | **Lady Silk (46)** (MissJFCraze) **5-9-0** NConnorton(4) (hld up: hdwy on outside over 2f out: nrst fin) | nk | **5** | 16/1 | 51 | 29 |
| 2253[8] | **Bold Enough (53)** (BWHills) **3-8-13**(5) JDSmith(8) (hdwy 2f out: kpt on: nt pce to chal) | 1 | **6** | 14/1 | 56 | 31 |
| 4226[9] | **Special-K (54)** (EWeymes) **4-9-1v**[1](7) CLowther(2) (lw: dwlt: hdwy on ins & nt clr run ent st: swtchd rt & kpt on appr fnl f) | s.h | **7** | 5/1[2] | 57 | 35 |
| 4206[3] | **Formidable Liz (60)** (MDHammond) **6-9-11**(3) OPears(16) (lw: hld up: hdwy 2f out: nt clr run: nvr able to chal) | ¾ | **8** | 5/1[2] | 61 | 39 |
| *4089*[14] | **Prudent Pet (49)** (CWFairhurst) **4-9-3** LCharnock(13) (hld up: hdwy on outside 3f out: hrd rdn over 1f out: no imp) | 1 | **9** | 20/1 | 48 | 26 |
| 3973[15] | **Cruz Santa (54)** (TDBarron) **3-9-5** ACulhane(18) (nvr trbld ldrs) | hd | **10** | 25/1 | 52 | 27 |
| 3461[6] | **Funky (50)** (DNicholls) **3-9-1** AlexGreaves(6) (prom tl wknd wl over 1f out) | 1½ | **11** | 10/1 | 45 | 20 |
| 3166[7] | **My Millie (46)** (DWBarker) **3-8-11** JFanning(17) (nvr nr to chal) | nk | **12** | 25/1 | 40 | 15 |
| 3844[6] | **Madam Zando (46)** (JBalding) **3-8-4**(7) JEdmunds(14) (lw: a in rr) | 3 | **13** | 20/1 | 33 | 8 |
| 3959[3] | **Charming Bride (55)** (SCWilliams) **3-9-6** GCarter(7) (b.nr hind: prom tl wknd over 2f out) | ½ | **14** | 8/1 | 41 | 16 |
| 4000[19] | **Most Wanted (IRE) (45)** (JJO'Neill) **3-8-10** RPrice(11) (a in rr) | 1¼ | **15** | 16/1 | 28 | 3 |
| | **Emei Shan (45)** (WGMTurner) **3-8-3**(7) DMcGaffin(1) (chsd ldrs over 4f) | 1 | **16** | 50/1 | 26 | 1 |
| 3578[8] | **Belbay Star (48)** (JLEyre) **3-8-13** JQuinn(9) (mid div to ½-wy: sn lost tch: t.o) | 6 | **17** | 14/1 | 15 | — |
| 3100[7] | **Lady Seren (IRE) (42)** (SEKettlewell) **4-8-10** NKennedy(15) (dwlt: a bhd: t.o) | 2½ | **18** | 25/1 | 4 | — |

(SP 152.5%) **18 Rn**

**1m 27.6** (4.00) CSF £85.82 CT £263.20 TOTE £6.80: £1.80 £4.20 £1.40 £15.30 (£56.90) Trio £81.40 OWNER Hambleton Lodge Equine Premix Ltd (HAMBLETON) BRED T. Barratt
WEIGHT FOR AGE 3yo-3lb

**3761 Komlucky** travelled well throughout and deservedly held on after losing out in a photo-finish last time. She supplied her trainer with his first success. (6/1)
**3578 Regal Fanfare (IRE)** has not won beyond six furlongs, but she stuck on grimly here in an all-out battle to the finish and there could be another race to be won. (12/1)
**4077* Sis Garden**, ridden with more restraint, stayed on well inside the last furlong, but could not get in a blow against the leading pair. (3/1: op 6/1)
**4075 La Finale** set out to make it all, but she was forced to give best below the distance and had nothing more to offer inside the final furlong. (25/1)
**2940 Lady Silk** struggles a bit on such lively ground, but was pegging back the leaders in the closing stages and is due another win. (16/1)
**2016 Bold Enough** could not get in a blow on this step back to seven furlongs, but she was far from disgraced and will be fresher than most for an autumn campaign. (14/1)
**3867 Special-K** did not have the run of the race in her first-time visor, but she ran on to finish a close-up seventh and there is still time for her to score before the season ends. (5/1)

T/Plpt: £145.30 (61.12 Tckts). T/Qdpt: £7.00 (59.18 Tckts). IM

## 4303-NEWBURY (L-H) (Good to firm)
## Saturday September 21st
WEATHER: fine WIND: slt half bhd

### 4324 WEST BYFLEET SOCIAL CLUB NURSERY H'CAP (2-Y.O) (Class C)
1-40 (1-40) **5f 34y** £5,186.00 (£1,568.00: £764.00: £362.00) Stalls: High GOING minus 0.42 sec per fur (F)

| Form | Horse | Dist | Pos | SP | RR | SF |
|---|---|---|---|---|---|---|
| 3940[5] | **Meliksah (IRE) (87)** (MBell) **2-8-7**(5) GFaulkner(3) (b.nr fore: lw: mde all: rdn out) | — | 1 | 11/2[3] | 83 | 44 |
| 4049[4] | **Tailwind (71)** (WRMuir) **2-7-3**(7) PDoe(5) (lost pl over 3f out: rallied over 1f out: r.o wl) | ½ | 2 | 16/1 | 65 | 26 |
| 3936[5] | **Lamorna (81)** (MRChannon) **2-7-13**(7) AEddery(2) (outpcd: hdwy fnl f: r.o wl) | ¾ | 3 | 11/2[3] | 73 | 34 |
| 4049[2] | **Dancethenightaway (86)** (BJMeehan) **2-8-6**(5) MartinDwyer(6) (a.p: rdn 2f out: unable qckn) | ½ | 4 | 2/1[2] | 77 | 38 |
| 3675* | **Silca Key Silca (77)** (MRChannon) **2-8-2** CRutter(7) (a.p: rdn 2f out: one pce) | s.h | 5 | 15/8[1] | 67 | 28 |
| | | | | (SP 104.8%) | | **5 Rn** |

**61.19 secs** (0.99) CSF £50.47 TOTE £7.70: £2.90 £3.30 (£37.30) OWNER Mr Yucel Birol (NEWMARKET) BRED Ron Con Ltd
LONG HANDICAP Tailwind 7-3

**3940 Meliksah (IRE)** was certainly the paddock pick. Having failed to handle the soft ground last time out, he was much happier back on a faster surface. (11/2: 4/1-6/1)

**4049 Tailwind** ran his best race do date and, after getting outpaced over three furlongs from home, came with a wet sail from below the distance to snatch second prize. (16/1)

**3936 Lamorna** failed to stay seven furlongs last time, but found the drop back to the minimum trip too sharp. A return to six furlongs would be ideal. (11/2: 4/1-6/1)

**4049 Dancethenightaway** was 4lb higher for her narrow Kempton defeat. (2/1: 6/4-9/4)

**3675* Silca Key Silca** was tapped for toe in the final quarter-mile. (15/8)

### 4325 KPMG CONDITIONS STKS (3-Y.O+) (Class C)
2-10 (2-10) **1m 1f** £4,967.00 (£1,853.00: £901.50: £382.50: £166.25: £79.75) Stalls: Low GOING minus 0.22 sec per fur (GF)

| Form | Horse | Dist | Pos | SP | RR | SF |
|---|---|---|---|---|---|---|
| 3503[2] | **Phantom Quest (105)** (HRACecil) **3-8-11** PatEddery(7) (lw: chsd ldr: led wl over 1f out: rdn out) | — | 1 | 9/4[1] | 109 | 38 |
| 3996[2] | **Tamhid (USA) (104)** (HThomsonJones) **3-8-9** RHills(1) (hld up: rdn & ev ch fnl 2f: r.o wl) | s.h | 2 | 11/4[2] | 107 | 36 |
| 4196[4] | **Celestial Key (USA) (105)** (MJohnston) **6-8-11**(3) MHenry(4) (hdwy on ins over 3f out: rdn 2f out: unable qckn fnl f) | 2½ | 3 | 7/1 | 103 | 37 |
| | **Red Carnival (USA) (109)** (MRStoute) **4-8-9** LDettori(6) (b.hind: hld up: nt clr run over 2f out: rdn & swtchd rt wl over 1f out: no rspnse) | 1½ | 4 | 3/1[3] | 95 | 29 |
| | **Proper Blue (USA) (90)** (TGMills) **3-8-9** WRyan(3) (bit bkwd: nvr nr to chal) | nk | 5 | 33/1 | 99 | 28 |
| 4185[4] | **Lonely Leader (IRE) (100)** (RHannon) **3-8-11** RHughes(5) (lw: led over 7f) | hd | 6 | 10/1 | 101 | 30 |
| 2248[4] | **Night City (102)** (LadyHerries) **5-9-6** DeclanO'Shea(8) (s.s: a bhd) | 5 | 7 | 16/1 | 96 | 30 |
| | | | | (SP 112.9%) | | **7 Rn** |

**1m 54.59** (4.29) CSF £8.49 TOTE £2.90: £1.70 £1.90 (£4.10) OWNER Mr K. Abdulla (NEWMARKET) BRED Juddmonte Farms
WEIGHT FOR AGE 3yo-5lb

**3503 Phantom Quest** at last came good but only after a tremendous fight with the runner-up in the final quarter-mile. Interestingly, Eddery never went for his whip. (9/4)

**3996 Tamhid (USA)** would surely have prevailed in another stride. He is yet to get his head in front this year, but richly deserves a change of luck. (11/4)

**4196 Celestial Key (USA)** has yet to win beyond a mile but gave a good account of himself. (7/1)

**Red Carnival (USA)**, a classy individual, had been off the course for eleven months. When asked for her effort in the final quarter-mile, she did not look overkeen and found nothing. (3/1: op 2/1)

**Proper Blue (USA)** did not look fully fit and could never get in a blow. (33/1)

### 4326 COURAGE H'CAP (0-105) (3-Y.O+) (Class B)
2-40 (2-40) **1m 2f 6y** £16,042.50 (£6,007.50: £2,941.25: £1,268.75: £571.88: £293.12) Stalls: Low GOING minus 0.22 sec per fur (GF)

| Form | Horse | Dist | Pos | SP | RR | SF |
|---|---|---|---|---|---|---|
| 4125[2] | **Game Ploy (POL) (81)** (DHaydnJones) **4-8-5** RCochrane(12) (hdwy over 1f out: led ins fnl f: pushed out) | — | 1 | 5/1[2] | 94 | 66 |
| 3658[3] | **Inquisitor (USA) (104)** (JHMGosden) **4-10-0** LDettori(7) (b: b.hind: lw: stdy hdwy over 3f out: led over 2f out tl ins fnl f: unable qckn) | 3 | 2 | 15/2 | 112 | 84 |
| 4193[6] | **Fahs (USA) (72)** (RAkehurst) **4-7-5**(5) MartinDwyer(2) (led over 7f: one pce) | 1¼ | 3 | 11/1 | 78 | 50 |
| 3947[13] | **Edan Heights (74)** (SDow) **4-7-12** NCarlisle(1) (lw: hdwy on ins over 3f out: hrd rdn over 1f out: one pce) | 1½ | 4 | 20/1 | 78 | 50 |
| 3710[8] | **At Liberty (IRE) (84)** (RHannon) **4-8-8** DBiggs(14) (lw: rdn & hdwy 2f out: one pce fnl f) | ½ | 5 | 20/1 | 87 | 59 |
| 4176[10] | **Askern (72)** (DHaydnJones) **5-7-10** DeclanO'Shea(8) (rdn over 2f out: hdwy over 1f out: nvr nrr) | 5 | 6 | 33/1 | 67 | 39 |
| 4120[5] | **Diminutive (USA) (84)** (JWHills) **3-7-13**(3) MHenry(11) (rdn over 2f out: hdwy over 1f out: nvr nrr) | 1¾ | 7 | 20/1 | 76 | 42 |
| 4120[2] | **Clan Ben (IRE) (96)** (HRACecil) **4-9-6** PatEddery(13) (lw: nvr nrr) | nk | 8 | 4/1[1] | 88 | 60 |
| 4117[2] | **Trojan Risk (81)** (GLewis) **3-7-13** CRutter(4) (lw: stdy hdwy over 3f out: wknd over 1f out) | ½ | 9 | 6/1[3] | 72 | 38 |
| 4120[10] | **Hardy Dancer (87)** (GLMoore) **4-8-8**(3) AWhelan(3) (lw: prom 6f) | ¾ | 10 | 25/1 | 77 | 49 |
| 3640[10] | **Milford Sound (80)** (JRFanshawe) **3-7-9**(3) NVarley(5) (lw: prom over 7f) | 8 | 11 | 33/1 | 57 | 23 |
| 4176[5] | **Three Hills (83)** (BWHills) **3-8-1b** RHills(15) (lw: prom over 7f) | 1 | 12 | 12/1 | 58 | 24 |
| 3997[5] | **Brandon Magic (96)** (IABalding) **3-9-0b[1]** RHughes(10) (lw: bhd fnl 4f) | ¾ | 13 | 16/1 | 70 | 36 |
| 3791[7] | **King Athelstan (USA) (81)** (BAMcMahon) **8-8-5** SSanders(9) (lw: prom over 8f) | 3 | 14 | 40/1 | 50 | 22 |
| | **Gone for a Burton (IRE) (85)** (PJMakin) **6-8-9** GDuffield(16) (bhd fnl 3f) | 3½ | 15 | 14/1 | 49 | 21 |
| 4120[9] | **Bardon Hill Boy (IRE) (92)** (BHanbury) **4-9-2** WRyan(6) (prom over 6f) | 11 | 16 | 16/1 | 38 | 10 |
| 4026a[3] | **Special Dawn (IRE) (88)** (JLDunlop) **6-8-12** JTate(17) (lw: a bhd) | 15 | 17 | 10/1 | 10 | — |
| | | | | (SP 132.7%) | | **17 Rn** |

**2m 4.57** (0.77) CSF £42.69 CT £381.89 TOTE £5.10: £1.50 £1.90 £2.40 £8.10 (£21.60) Trio £81.60 OWNER Mr Kevan Kynaston (PONTYPRIDD) BRED C. Olsen Ltd
LONG HANDICAP Fahs (USA) 7-6
WEIGHT FOR AGE 3yo-6lb

**4125 Game Ploy (POL)** has risen 16lb since his first handicap success this season, but that did not stop him registering his fourth victory of the year. (5/1)

**3658 Inquisitor (USA)** ran his best race so far in a light campaign this season but, after grabbing the initiative over a quarter of a mile from home, failed to cope with the winner. (15/2)
**4193 Fahs (USA)** is at his best when allowed to force the pace but, although running well here, is yet to win in this country. (11/1)
**3447 Edan Heights** was racing off a mark 9lb higher than his last victory and would have been happier with some give in the ground. (20/1)
**3710 At Liberty (IRE)** took closer order a quarter of a mile from home but, despite grimly trying to get on terms, failed to quicken inside the distance. (20/1)
**3346* Askern** was doing all his best work in the last furlong and a half. (33/1)

## 4327 TOTE BOOKMAKERS AUTUMN CUP H'CAP (0-100) (3-Y.O+) (Class C)

3-10 (3-11) **1m 5f 61y** £9,590.00 (£9,590.00: £2,180.00: £1,040.00) Stalls: Low GOING minus 0.22 sec per fur (GF)

| | | | | SP | RR | SF |
|---|---|---|---|---|---|---|
| 2724$^{13}$ | **Kutta (97)** (RWArmstrong) **4-10-0** RHills(12) (hdwy over 3f out: ev ch fnl 2f: led post) | — | **1** | 9/1 | 109 | 83 |
| 3504* | **Ballynakelly (77)** (RAkehurst) **4-8-8** SSanders(6) (lw: a.p: chsd ldr over 8f out: led over 4f out: all out) | — | **1** | 13/8$^{1}$ | 89 | 63 |
| 4055$^{8}$ | **Whitechapel (USA) (88)** (LordHuntingdon) **8-9-5** LDettori(2) (hdwy over 3f out: hrd rdn over 1f out: unable qckn) | 6 | **3** | 6/1$^{3}$ | 93 | 67 |
| 4055$^{5}$ | **Remaadi Sun (83)** (MDIUsher) **4-9-0** RStreet(4) (hdwy over 2f out: hrd rdn over 1f out: one pce) | 3 | **4** | 10/1 | 84 | 58 |
| 3997$^{4}$ | **General Macarthur (92)** (JLDunlop) **3-9-0** PatEddery(3) (lw: rdn over 2f out: hdwy over 1f out: one pce) | 3½ | **5** | 13/2 | 89 | 54 |
| 3983$^{2}$ | **Midyan Blue (IRE) (74)** (JMPEustace) **6-8-5** RCochrane(9) (nvr nr to chal) | 9 | **6** | 9/2$^{2}$ | 60 | 34 |
| 3398$^{4}$ | **Sharaf (IRE) (82)** (WRMuir) **3-8-4b** OUrbina(11) (lw: led 9f) | 12 | **7** | 20/1 | 54 | 19 |
| 2882$^{14}$ | **Lalindi (IRE) (75)** (DRCElsworth) **5-8-6b** NCarlisle(10) (lw: hdwy over 3f out: wknd over 2f out) | 8 | **8** | 25/1 | 37 | 11 |
| 4067$^{16}$ | **No Pattern (70)** (GLMoore) **4-7-10**$^{(5)}$ MartinDwyer(1) (lw: a bhd) | 2 | **9** | 25/1 | 30 | 4 |
| | **High Summer (70)** (TThomsonJones) **6-8-1**$^{ow1}$ DBiggs(7) (b: bit bkwd: chsd ldr 5f: wknd over 4f out) | 1 | **10** | 66/1 | 28 | 1 |
| 4117$^{4}$ | **Bowled Over (78)** (CACyzer) **3-8-0**$^{ow1}$ JTate(13) (prom 10f) | 1½ | **11** | 25/1 | 35 | — |
| 2339$^{5}$ | **Truancy (80)** (CJMann) **3-7-13**$^{(3)}$ MHenry(8) (a bhd: t.o) | dist | **12** | 50/1 | — | — |

(SP 122.7%) **12 Rn**

**2m 48.28** (1.78) CSF K & B £11.81 B & K £8.42 CT K, B & W £46.69 B, K & W £35.06 TOTE K £6.10 B £1.40: K £3.00 B £1.60 £1.60 (£17.60) Trio £25.60 OWNER Mr Hamdan Al Maktoum (NEWMARKET)/Y Y Partnership (EPSOM) BRED Shadwell Estate Company Limited/Crest Stud

WEIGHT FOR AGE 3yo-9lb

**Kutta** appeared to be travelling better than the winner as he threw down his challenge in the final quarter-mile but he had met a real tartar in the winner. Nevertheless, he gave his all and managed to force a dead-heat on the line. (9/1)
**3504* Ballynakelly** is in the form of his life and extended his quite remarkable sequence to eight, despite a rise of 26lb since his first turf victory. He is as tough and genuine as they come and is a real credit to his trainer. (13/8)
**3614 Whitechapel (USA)**, winner of this event last year off a mark of 80, is now rated 88 but has never won off more than 84. (6/1)
**3689 Remaadi Sun**, whose rider gave him several reminders below the distance when using it above shoulder height, looked very ungainly in the process. Street can consider himself lucky that the Stewards did not notice. (10/1)
**3997 General Macarthur** ran disappointingly and could never get in a blow. (13/2)
**3983 Midyan Blue (IRE)** ran well last time, but he failed to live up to that here and has now not won in over a year. (9/2)

## 4328 BONUSPRINT MILL REEF STKS (Gp 2) (2-Y.O) (Class A)

3-40 (3-42) **6f 8y** £33,085.00 (£12,411.25: £5,985.63: £2,633.12) Stalls: High GOING minus 0.42 sec per fur (F)

| | | | | SP | RR | SF |
|---|---|---|---|---|---|---|
| 3843* | **Indian Rocket (100)** (JLDunlop) **2-8-12** RHills(1) (a.p: led 2f out: rdn out) | — | **1** | 100/30$^{3}$ | 108 | 65 |
| 3690$^{9}$ | **Proud Native (IRE) (100)** (APJarvis) **2-8-12** RCochrane(7) (lw: hld up: rdn over 2f out: unable qckn) | 2½ | **2** | 25/1 | 101? | 58 |
| 3707$^{3}$ | **Seebe (USA) (100)** (IABalding) **2-8-10** LDettori(10) (lw: hdwy over 1f out: hrd rdn: one pce) | nk | **3** | 11/4$^{1}$ | 99 | 56 |
| 3931* | **Andreyev (IRE) (100)** (RHannon) **2-8-12** RHughes(9) (lw: hdwy over 1f out: hrd rdn: one pce) | 1½ | **4** | 4/1 | 97 | 54 |
| 3921* | **Sambac (USA) (100)** (HRACecil) **2-8-7** WRyan(5) (lw: hld up: hrd rdn over 1f out: one pce) | hd | **5** | 3/1$^{2}$ | 91 | 48 |
| 4035a$^{2}$ | **Omaha City (IRE) (100)** (BGubby) **2-8-12** PatEddery(6) (chsd ldr 4f) | 4 | **6** | 10/1 | 86 | 43 |
| 4287a* | **General Song (IRE)** (KMcAuliffe) **2-8-12** GDuffield(2) (scope: bhd fnl 2f) | ½ | **7** | 14/1 | 84 | 41 |
| 4065$^{2}$ | **Maserati Monk (95)** (BJMeehan) **2-8-12** SSanders(3) (led 4f) | nk | **8** | 16/1 | 84 | 41 |
| 4131$^{17}$ | **Millroy (USA) (87)** (PAKelleway) **2-8-12b** CRutter(4) (lw: a bhd) | 3½ | **9** | 50/1 | 74 | 31 |
| 1003* | **Vasari (IRE)** (MRChannon) **2-8-12** OUrbina(8) (bhd fnl 3f: t.o) | dist | **10** | 14/1 | — | — |

(SP 128.9%) **10 Rn**

**1m 11.52** (-0.28) CSF £73.34 TOTE £3.80: £1.40 £5.90 £1.50 (£57.50) Trio £92.80 OWNER Mr Khalil Alsayegh (ARUNDEL) BRED Red House Stud

**3843* Indian Rocket** continues to go from strength to strength and, let loose into the lead a quarter of a mile from home, readily asserted. (100/30)
**3156 Proud Native (IRE)** showed his York run to be all wrong and, although no match for the winner, still finished a good second. (25/1)
**3707 Seebe (USA)** had no excuses this time and appeared to be travelling well at the back of the field. However, after picking up ground below the distance, she could make no further impression. Another furlong would be a great advantage. (11/4)
**3931* Andreyev (IRE)** was unable to cope with the step up in class and, after taking closer order below the distance, failed to find another gear. (4/1)
**3921* Sambac (USA)** found her winning run coming to an end and, when pressure was applied below the distance, she failed to find what was required. (3/1)

## 4329 ROTHMANS ROYALS NORTH SOUTH CHALLENGE SERIES SEMI-FINAL H'CAP (0-100) (3-Y.O+) (Class C)

4-10 (4-12) **1m 7y (round)** £17,750.00 (£5,375.00: £2,625.00: £1,250.00) Stalls: Low GOING minus 0.42 sec per fur (F)

| | | | | SP | RR | SF |
|---|---|---|---|---|---|---|
| 4186$^{11}$ | **Artful Dane (IRE) (65)** (MJHeaton-Ellis) **4-7-10v**$^{1}$ NCarlisle(9) (lw: stdy hdwy over 2f out: led over 1f out: rdn out) | — | **1** | 33/1 | 78 | 37 |
| 3640$^{8}$ | **Mo-Addab (IRE) (73)** (ACStewart) **6-8-4** WRyan(1) (lw: rdn over 3f out: hdwy over 1f out: r.o ins fnl f) | 1¼ | **2** | 8/1$^{3}$ | 84 | 43 |
| 4136$^{8}$ | **Air Commodore (IRE) (85)** (DWPArbuthnot) **5-9-2** PatEddery(3) (b: hrd rdn over 2f out: hdwy over 1f out: r.o) | 1¾ | **3** | 5/1$^{2}$ | 92 | 51 |
| 3765$^{4}$ | **Bon Luck (IRE) (70)** (JRFanshawe) **4-7-12**$^{(3)}$ NVarley(14) (lw: hld up: rdn over 2f out: unable qckn) | nk | **4** | 12/1 | 76 | 35 |
| 4125$^{9}$ | **Danegold (IRE) (76)** (MRChannon) **4-8-0v**$^{(7)}$ AEddery(8) (lw: rdn over 2f out: hdwy over 1f out: r.o) | s.h | **5** | 16/1 | 82 | 41 |
| 3815$^{7}$ | **Saifan (85)** (DMorris) **7-9-2v** LDettori(7) (lw: s.s: hdwy over 1f out: nvr nrr) | nk | **6** | 9/1 | 91 | 50 |
| 3765$^{6}$ | **Blaze of Song (72)** (RHannon) **4-8-3v**$^{1}$ DBiggs(15) (b: lw: chsd ldr over 5f: hrd rdn: one pce) | nk | **7** | 25/1 | 77 | 36 |
| 3989$^{4}$ | **Catch The Lights (82)** (RHannon) **3-8-9** RCochrane(12) (rdn over 2f out: hdwy over 1f out: r.o) | s.h | **8** | 12/1 | 87 | 42 |
| 3920* | **Concer Un (97)** (SCWilliams) **4-10-0** JTate(6) (b.nr fore: lw: led over 6f: wknd ins fnl f) | ½ | **9** | 9/2$^{1}$ | 101 | 60 |
| 4064$^{7}$ | **Sylvan Princess (69)** (CNAllen) **3-7-5**$^{(5)}$ MartinDwyer(4) (lw: nvr nr to chal) | 4 | **10** | 14/1 | 65 | 20 |

| | | | | SP | RR | SF |
|---|---|---|---|---|---|---|
| 3933[5] | **Absolute Magic (74)** (WJHaggas) **6-8-5** RHills(10) (lw: a bhd) | ¾ | **11** | 12/1 | 69 | 28 |
| 2858[3] | **Easy Jet (POL) (74)** (LordHuntingdon) **4-8-5** OUrbina(16) (prom over 5f) | nk | **12** | 9/1 | 68 | 27 |
| 3933[11] | **Shamrock Fair (IRE) (70)** (LordHuntingdon) **4-7-12**(3) MHenry(11) (lw: a bhd) | 7 | **13** | 16/1 | 50 | 9 |
| 3830[3] | **Slip Jig (IRE) (81)** (RHannon) **3-8-8** CRutter(13) (b.hind: bhd fnl 3f) | 3½ | **14** | 16/1 | 54 | 9 |
| 3830[2] | **Mazcobar (80)** (PJMakin) **3-8-7** SSanders(2) (prom over 4f) | ¾ | **15** | 8/1[3] | 52 | 7 |
| *4078[5]* | **Cool Fire (70)** (SPCWoods) **3-7-11** DeclanO'Shea(5) (lw: prom over 3f) | 15 | **16** | 25/1 | 12 | — |
| | | | | (SP 135.1%) | **16 Rn** | |

**1m 38.42** (2.42) CSF £276.34 CT £1,502.10 TOTE £93.20: £11.10 £2.00 £1.50 £3.40 (£358.70) Trio £811.40; £914.36 to Musselburgh 23/9/96 OWNER S P Lansdown Racing (WROUGHTON) BRED R. A. Keogh

LONG HANDICAP Sylvan Princess 7-8 Artful Dane (IRE) 7-9

WEIGHT FOR AGE 3yo-4lb

**3340* Artful Dane (IRE)** bounced back to form and was ridden along to assert. (33/1)

**3640 Mo-Addab (IRE)** has been steadily coming down the handicap after some poor efforts and, as a result, ran his best race of the season. (8/1)

**4136 Air Commodore (IRE)** is steadily coming to hand and was doing all his best work in the last furlong and a half. All four of his victories to date have come over a mile. (5/1)

**3765 Bon Luck (IRE)** never looked like quickening up in the last two furlongs. He remains a maiden. (12/1)

**2603 Danegold (IRE)** stayed on from the back of the field without ever posing a threat. (16/1)

**3450 Saifan** was rated 85 here, but has never won off a mark higher than 78 and appears to be in the Handicapper's grip at present. (9/1)

## 4330 E.B.F. HARWELL MAIDEN STKS (2-Y.O) (Class D)

4-40 (4-44) **6f 8y** £4,198.00 (£1,264.00: £612.00: £286.00) Stalls: High GOING minus 0.42 sec per fur (F)

| | | | | SP | RR | SF |
|---|---|---|---|---|---|---|
| 3994[3] | **Speedball (IRE)** (IABalding) **2-9-0** PatEddery(22) (a.p: rdn over 2f out: led nr fin) | — | **1** | 11/10[1] | 82 | 55 |
| 4062[3] | **Hopesay** (JHMGosden) **2-8-9** LDettori(5) (a.p: rdn over 1f out: led ins fnl f: hdd nr fin) | nk | **2** | 4/1[2] | 76 | 49 |
| | **Sabina** (IABalding) **2-8-4**(5) MartinDwyer(6) (neat: a.p: led over 2f out tl ins fnl f: one pce) | 1½ | **3** | 33/1 | 72 | 45 |
| | **Begorrat (IRE)** (BJMeehan) **2-9-0** DBiggs(20) (leggy: scope: hld up: rdn over 2f out: one pce) | 3 | **4** | 50/1 | 69 | 42 |
| | **Refuse To Lose** (JMPEustace) **2-9-0** RCochrane(16) (str: scope: hdwy over 1f out: nvr nrr) | 2½ | **5** | 20/1 | 63 | 36 |
| 3874[2] | **Inclination** (MBlanshard) **2-8-4**(5) MBaird(15) (led over 3f: wknd over 1f out) | ½ | **6** | 12/1[3] | 56 | 29 |
| | **Lonely Heart** (MajorDNChappell) **2-8-6**(3) NVarley(11) (w'like: scope: rdn over 4f out: hdwy over 1f out: nvr nrr) | nk | **7** | 50/1 | 56 | 29 |
| 3319[9] | **Klondike Charger (USA)** (BWHills) **2-9-0** RHughes(9) (hdwy over 1f out: nvr nrr) | hd | **8** | 16/1 | 60 | 33 |
| | **Gee Bee Boy** (APJarvis) **2-9-0** JTate(19) (leggy: scope: nvr nrr) | 1½ | **9** | 50/1 | 56 | 29 |
| 3234[4] | **Shifting Time** (IABalding) **2-8-9** WRyan(4) (prom 4f) | ½ | **10** | 14/1 | 50 | 23 |
| | **Misty Rain** (BWHills) **2-8-9** RStreet(12) (leggy: lt-f: nvr nrr) | s.h | **11** | 50/1 | 50 | 23 |
| | **Mutasawwar** (EALDunlop) **2-9-0** RHills(2) (b: w'like: scope: hdwy 3f out: wknd over 1f out) | hd | **12** | 14/1 | 55 | 28 |
| | **Rhapsody In White (IRE)** (MAJarvis) **2-9-0** PBloomfield(1) (w'like: a mid div) | 1 | **13** | 50/1 | 52 | 25 |
| | **Rotor Man (IRE)** (JDBethell) **2-9-0** OUrbina(8) (w'like: scope: hld up: rdn over 2f out: sn wknd) | nk | **14** | 50/1 | 51 | 24 |
| | **Mr Majica** (BJMeehan) **2-9-0** MTebbutt(13) (w'like: nvr nrr) | 1 | **15** | 12/1[3] | 49 | 22 |
| 3620[6] | **Bewitching Lady** (DWPArbuthnot) **2-8-6**(3) DarrenMoffatt(7) (prom over 3f) | 2 | **16** | 33/1 | 38 | 11 |
| 3695[4] | **Tom Tailor (GER)** (DRCElsworth) **2-9-0** NCarlisle(21) (bhd fnl 2f) | 2½ | **17** | 33/1 | 37 | 10 |
| | **Mr Paradise (IRE)** (TJNaughton) **2-9-0** SSanders(3) (leggy: scope: s.s: a bhd) | hd | **18** | 50/1 | 36 | 9 |
| | **Despina** (HCandy) **2-8-9** CRutter(17) (leggy: scope: a bhd) | 1¼ | **19** | 20/1 | 28 | 1 |
| | **Island Prince** (NACallaghan) **2-8-7**(7) AEddery(24) (leggy: a bhd) | ½ | **20** | 50/1 | 32 | 5 |
| | **Welcome Heights** (MJFetherston-Godley) **2-9-0** DeclanO'Shea(10) (str: bkwd: s.s: a bhd) | 4 | **21** | 50/1 | 21 | — |
| | **Sharpest** (JLDunlop) **2-8-11**(7)ow4 CScudder(18) (leggy: lt-f: a bhd) | 4 | **22** | 33/1 | 14 | — |
| | **Isca Maiden** (PHayward) **2-8-9** VSlattery(23) (neat: a bhd) | 2 | **23** | 50/1 | — | — |
| 1626[6] | **Carlton (IRE)** (GLewis) **2-8-11**(3) AWhelan(14) (bit bkwd: bhd fnl 3f) | 1 | **24** | 50/1 | 3 | — |
| | | | | (SP 145.1%) | **24 Rn** | |

**1m 12.32** (0.52) CSF £6.62 TOTE £2.10: £1.30 £1.90 £7.80 (£3.10) Trio £66.00 OWNER Mr J. C. Smith (KINGSCLERE) BRED Frank Barry

**3994 Speedball (IRE)**, in the firing-line throughout, was being bustled along in the second half of the race and only managed to get in front near the line. An extra furlong would not go amiss. (11/10)

**4062 Hopesay** put her experience to good use but, after getting to the front inside the final furlong, was worried out of it near the line. There is a race waiting for her round one of the smaller tracks. (4/1)

**Sabina** is not very big but that did not stop her moving to the front over a quarter of a mile from home before collared inside the final furlong. A race should be found for her. (33/1)

**Begorrat (IRE)**, a tall gelding with substance, chased the leaders but never looking like quickening up in the second half of the race. (50/1)

**Refuse To Lose**, a half-brother to numerous winners, stayed on in the last furlong and a half. (20/1)

**3874 Inclination** was taking a drop in distance and, after taking the field along until after halfway, was soon in trouble. (12/1)

**Lonely Heart**, an attractive filly, found this trip far too sharp and was doing all her best work in the closing stages. She will do better over further. (50/1)

**3234 Shifting Time** (14/1: op 7/1)

T/Plpt: £2,183.00 (11.98 Tckts). T/Qdpt: £34.50 (55.92 Tckts). AK

# 4076-WOLVERHAMPTON (L-H) (Standard)

## Saturday September 21st

WEATHER: overcast WIND: slt against

## 4331 E.B.F. MALI MAIDEN STKS (2-Y.O) (Class D)

7-00 (7-00) **1m 100y (Fibresand)** £3,633.60 (£1,084.80: £518.40: £235.20) Stalls: Low GOING minus 0.12 sec per fur (FST)

| | | | | SP | RR | SF |
|---|---|---|---|---|---|---|
| 4106[14] | **Mystic Quest (IRE) (74)** (KMcAuliffe) **2-9-0v[1]** MTebbutt(8) (a.p: led over 3f out: rdn over 2f out: hdd over 1f out: led ins fnl f: edgd lft: r.o) | — | **1** | 14/1 | 83 | 31 |
| 3701[4] | **Ferny Hill (IRE)** (SirMarkPrescott) **2-9-0** GDuffield(2) (lw: a.p: rdn over 4f out: ev ch 1f out: one pce) | 1¾ | **2** | 10/11[1] | 80 | 28 |
| 3319[10] | **As Friendly** (MRStoute) **2-9-0** KBradshaw(4) (led 5f: hrd rdn to ld over 1f out: hdd ins fnl f) | ¾ | **3** | 7/1[3] | 78 | 26 |
| 3982[2] | **Double Espresso (IRE)** (MJohnston) **2-8-6**(3) MHenry(9) (hdwy over 3f out: one pce fnl 2f) | 4 | **4** | 9/4[2] | 66 | 14 |
| 3685[14] | **Royal Roulette** (SPCWoods) **2-8-9** DBiggs(7) (prom tl wknd over 2f out) | 3 | **5** | 33/1 | 60 | 8 |

| | | | | SP | RR | SF |
|---|---|---|---|---|---|---|
| 3796[12] | **Jack Brown** (TTClement) **2-8-9**(5) GFaulkner(3) (bhd fnl 3f) | 1¼ | **6** | 50/1 | 63 | 11 |
| 3963[4] | **Carlys Quest** (JNeville) **2-8-7**(7) JFowle(11) (s.i.s: a wl bhd) | 3 | **7** | 16/1 | 57 | 5 |
| | **Digital Option (IRE)** (PRWebber) **2-8-7**(7) RStudholme(5) (w'like: s.i.s: a bhd) | 10 | **8** | 20/1 | 38 | — |
| 3349[6] | **Terry's Rose** (RHollinshead) **2-8-2**(7) SCrawford(12) (prom 5f) | 2½ | **9** | 25/1 | 28 | — |
| | **Don't Fool Me (IRE)** (PMooney) **2-8-11**(3) AWhelan(6) (lengthy: dwlt: a bhd) | 3½ | **10** | 50/1 | 27 | — |
| | **Southern Chief** (WGMTurner) **2-8-11**(3) CTeague(10) (leggy: bkwd: sn t.o) | 14 | **11** | 33/1 | — | — |
| 3511[11] | **Ohio Royale** (PCHaslam) **2-8-7**(7) DSweeney(1) (bhd fnl 3f: t.o) | 3 | **12** | 50/1 | — | — |

(SP 128.6%) **12 Rn**

**1m 51.1** (6.10) CSF £28.09 TOTE £12.30: £2.10 £1.70 £2.30 (£10.30) Trio £15.30 OWNER Delamere Cottage Racing Partners (1996) (LAMBOURN) BRED John O'Connor and Jeremiah Aherne

**3848 Mystic Quest (IRE)**, disappointing last time, found the first-time visor doing the trick. (14/1: 10/1-16/1)

**3701 Ferny Hill (IRE)**, stepping up from six, came under pressure at halfway but stuck to his guns. His promising debut suggests he is capable of better than this on grass. (10/11)

**As Friendly**, out of a half-sister to Golden Fleece, had shown nothing when backed on his Kempton debut and one could only assume that he had been working well on the All-Weather at home, hence the switch. (7/1)

**3982 Double Espresso (IRE)**, who only cost 1,500 guineas, could not sustain her effort over this longer trip. (9/4)

**Royal Roulette** is a sister to seven-furlong juvenile scorer Personal Hazard, who went on to win twice over hurdles. (33/1)

## 4332 MOZAMBIQUE LIMITED STKS (0-60) (3-Y.O+) (Class F)

7-30 (7-31) **1m 6f 166y (Fibresand)** £2,070.00 (£570.00: £270.00) Stalls: High GOING minus 0.12 sec per fur (FST)

| | | | | SP | RR | SF |
|---|---|---|---|---|---|---|
| *4092** | **Batoutoftheblue (63)** (WWHaigh) **3-8-9** DRMcCabe(4) (hld up: pushed along 6f out: gd hdwy 2f out: led ins fnl f: styd on wl) | — | **1** | 5/2[1] | 73 | 18 |
| 4086* | **Arcady (60)** (PTWalwyn) **3-8-6** TSprake(10) (a.p: led 6f out: rdn clr over 3f out: hdd ins fnl f) | 5 | **2** | 9/2[3] | 65 | 10 |
| 3356[4] | **Supermodel (55)** (MrsNMacauley) **4-8-12**(3) CTeague(8) (b: hdwy over 5f out: ev ch over 1f out: one pce) | 1 | **3** | 11/1 | 62 | 18 |
| 3802[5] | **Duty Sergeant (IRE) (37)** (PMitchell) **7-9-1**(3) MHenry(7) (wl bhd tl hdwy over 5f out: one pce fnl 2f) | 4 | **4** | 14/1 | 60 | 16 |
| *4080[2]* | **Pearl Anniversary (IRE) (48)** (MissSJWilton) **3-8-11** SWhitworth(2) (led after 1f: hdd 6f out: wknd over 2f out) | 13 | **5** | 6/1 | 50 | — |
| *4095[16]* | **Miss Pravda (50)** (BJLlewellyn) **3-7-11**(7) JBramhill(9) (prom tl wknd 3f out) | d.h | **5** | 33/1 | 43 | — |
| 4203[3] | **Iota (60)** (JLHarris) **7-9-5** GDuffield(6) (prom 9f) | 5 | **7** | 7/2[2] | 42 | — |
| *4092[3]* | **Harbet House (FR) (56)** (CACyzer) **3-8-6**(3) FLynch(3) (hld up: bhd fnl 7f: t.o) | 12 | **8** | 9/1 | 30 | — |
| 2988[8] | **Cross Talk (IRE) (55)** (NTinkler) **4-9-6** KimTinkler(11) (s.i.s: sn rcvrd: lost pl after 4f: bhd fnl 6f: t.o) | 9 | **9** | 25/1 | 20 | — |
| *4092[4]* | **Bayrak (USA) (56)** (MJRyan) **6-9-6** MTebbutt(5) (led 1f: wknd over 5f out: t.o) | 4 | **10** | 8/1 | 16 | — |

(SP 126.2%) **10 Rn**

**3m 19.9** (12.50) CSF £14.89 TOTE £3.70: £1.40 £2.00 £2.00 (£9.10) Trio £25.90 OWNER Dr C. I. Emmerson (MALTON) BRED Side Hill Stud

WEIGHT FOR AGE 3yo-11lb

**4092* Batoutoftheblue** continued from where he left off last time and gives the impression he will stay all day. (5/2)

**4086* Arcady** threw down the gauntlet leaving the back straight but had no answer to the winner in the closing stages. (9/2)

**3356 Supermodel** had shown she could handle the Fibresand when second over two miles at Southwell back in January. (11/1: 8/1-12/1)

**3802 Duty Sergeant (IRE)** had not been seen out on the Sand since running over an inadequate trip some eighteen months ago. (14/1: op 33/1)

## 4333 BEACON RADIO DISC JOCKEY DERBY H'CAP (0-70) (3-Y.O+) (Class E)

8-00 (8-00) **6f (Fibresand)** £2,929.50 (£812.00: £388.50) Stalls: Low GOING minus 0.12 sec per fur (FST)

| | | | | SP | RR | SF |
|---|---|---|---|---|---|---|
| *4081[6]* | **Red Admiral (60)** (CMurray) **6-9-8** DeanMcKeown(13) (w ldrs: led over 1f out: rdn out) | — | **1** | 12/1 | 72 | 29 |
| 4130[3] | **Imposing Time (63)** (MissGayKelleway) **5-9-6b**(5) DGriffiths(11) (chsd ldrs: r.o ins fnl f) | nk | **2** | 4/1[1] | 74 | 31 |
| 3578[5] | **Shontaine (61)** (MJohnston) **3-9-4**(3) MHenry(9) (reminders & outpcd over 4f out: gd hdwy fnl f: fin wl) | 2½ | **3** | 10/1 | 66 | 21 |
| 4130[8] | **Rowlandsons Stud (IRE) (62)** (PBurgoyne) **3-9-1**(7) JBosley(12) (prom: nt clr run over 3f out: r.o fnl f) | 1½ | **4** | 25/1 | 63 | 18 |
| *3603[2]* | **Theatre Magic (65)** (SRBowring) **3-9-6**(5) MartinDwyer(10) (chsd ldrs: one pce appr fnl f) | s.h | **5** | 8/1 | 65 | 20 |
| 4098[13] | **Anita's Contessa (IRE) (57)** (BPalling) **4-9-5** TSprake(8) (no hdwy fnl 2f) | 1¼ | **6** | 16/1 | 54 | 11 |
| *4081[7]* | **Kung Frode (61)** (BAMcMahon) **4-9-9** GDuffield(2) (lw: w ldrs: ev ch over 1f out: wknd ins fnl f) | hd | **7** | 10/1 | 58 | 15 |
| *4081[2]* | **Napier Star (62)** (MrsNMacauley) **3-9-5v**(3) CTeague(6) (lw: a.p: led 2f out: hdd over 1f out: wknd fnl f) | ½ | **8** | 5/1[2] | 58 | 13 |
| *3953[6]* | **Bold Street (IRE) (65)** (ABailey) **6-9-13b** DBiggs(7) (b: hdwy on ins over 2f out: wknd over 1f out) | 2 | **9** | 7/1[3] | 55 | 12 |
| *4081[3]* | **Itsinthepost (64)** (VSoane) **3-9-10** MFenton(1) (led 4f: wknd over 1f out) | 1½ | **10** | 7/1[3] | 50 | 5 |
| *4094[5]* | **Klipspinger (67)** (BSRothwell) **3-9-10**(3) FLynch(5) (prom tl wknd fnl f) | nk | **11** | 16/1 | 52 | 7 |
| 3930[9] | **Queens Check (63)** (MissJFCraze) **3-9-9** DRMcCabe(3) (stdd s: a bhd) | ¾ | **12** | 14/1 | 46 | 1 |
| *4081[10]* | **Leigh Crofter (62)** (PDCundell) **7-9-3**(7) NLovelock(4) (a bhd) | 3 | **13** | 20/1 | 37 | — |

(SP 125.7%) **13 Rn**

**1m 16.2** (4.80) CSF £58.62 CT £369.25 TOTE £14.00: £3.20 £2.00 £4.70 (£46.20) Trio £87.40 OWNER Sackville House Racing (NEWMARKET) BRED Hesmonds Stud Ltd

WEIGHT FOR AGE 3yo-2lb

**4081 Red Admiral**, always up with the pace this time, took advantage of a 3lb lower mark. (12/1)

**4130 Imposing Time**, making his All-Weather debut, could not peg back the winner in time and might be worth a try at seven. (4/1)

**3151 Shontaine** ran his best race on the artificial surface, but got taken off his legs and found the trip inadequate. (10/1)

**743 Rowlandsons Stud (IRE)** was 7lb higher than when scoring over this trip on the Equitrack at Lingfield in March. (25/1)

**3603 Theatre Magic**, up 3lb, just lacked the necessary finishing kick over this shorter distance. (8/1)

**4081 Napier Star** (5/1: 4/1-6/1)

## 4334 PLYVINE CATERING H'CAP (0-60) (3-Y.O+) (Class F)

8-30 (8-32) **1m 4f (Fibresand)** £2,070.00 (£570.00: £270.00) Stalls: Low GOING minus 0.12 sec per fur (FST)

| | | | | SP | RR | SF |
|---|---|---|---|---|---|---|
| 3876[2] | **Glow Forum (56)** (LMontagueHall) **5-9-5**(5) MartinDwyer(4) (a.p: led over 3f out: rdn clr over 1f out: eased ins fnl f) | — | **1** | 6/4[1] | 68 | 31 |
| 2756[5] | **All On (43)** (JHetherton) **5-8-11** SWhitworth(5) (bhd tl gd hdwy over 1f out: nt trble wnr) | 6 | **2** | 14/1 | 47 | 10 |
| *3955[4]* | **Sommersby (IRE) (51)** (MrsNMacauley) **5-9-2**(3) CTeague(1) (b: a.p: rdn over 2f out: one pce) | 2½ | **3** | 11/2[2] | 52 | 15 |
| 3948[7] | **Todd (USA) (54)** (PMitchell) **5-9-8** GCarter(3) (lw: w ldr: led 5f out tl over 3f out: wknd over 1f out) | s.h | **4** | 20/1 | 55 | 18 |
| *3952[9]* | **Platinum Plus (55)** (CADwyer) **4-9-9** CDwyer(12) (b: nvr trbld ldrs) | 12 | **5** | 10/1 | 40 | 3 |
| | **Blue And Royal (IRE) (52)** (VSoane) **4-9-6** MFenton(6) (nvr nr ldrs) | hd | **6** | 33/1 | 37 | — |

| | | | SP | RR | SF |
|---|---|---|---|---|---|
| *6541*0 | **Last Roundup (53)** (CWThornton) **4-9-7** DeanMcKeown(11) (hld up: bhd fnl 4f) ....10 | **7** | 20/1 | 24 | — |
| 38653 | **In the Money (IRE) (60)** (RHollinshead) **7-9-11**(3) FLynch(10) (lw: bhd fnl 5f) ....5 | **8** | 7/1 3 | 25 | — |
| 40688 | **Laughing Buccaneer (53)** (MJHeaton-Ellis) **3-8-13v1** SDrowne(9) (prom tl rdn & wknd over 5f out) ....10 | **9** | 16/1 | 4 | — |
| 38243 | **Siesta Time (USA) (48)** (DBurchell) **6-9-2** RPrice(8) (wnt lft s: hdwy 8f out: wknd over 6f out) ....1¾ | **10** | 10/1 | — | — |
| *34224* | **Newbridge Boy (59)** (MGMeagher) **3-9-5** DRMcCabe(2) (led 7f: rdn & wknd 4f out) ....¾ | **11** | 9/1 | 7 | — |
| 39688 | **De-Veers Currie (IRE) (53)** (MartinTodhunter) **4-9-7** TSprake(7) (hmpd & stumbled s: a bhd: t.o fnl 6f) ....dist | **12** | 25/1 | — | — |

(SP 124.9%) **12 Rn**

**2m 42.9** (10.40) CSF £23.29 CT £94.43 TOTE £2.50: £1.10 £3.50 £2.10 (£22.90) Trio £101.00; £113.82 to Musselburgh 23/9/96 OWNER Mr Andy Smith (EPSOM) BRED Forum Bloodstock Ltd

WEIGHT FOR AGE 3yo-8lb

**3876 Glow Forum** had been raised no less than 17lb following two wins at Southwell, but still had no problems with this opposition. (6/4)
**2756 All On** made up a lot of ground in the home straight and needs a stiffer test of stamina. (14/1)
**3955 Sommersby (IRE)** has slipped to a mark 7lb lower than when winning over the course and distance a year ago. (11/2)
**3785 Todd (USA)** has yet to prove he really stays a mile and a half. (20/1)

## 4335 DUNSTALL PARK SERIES NURSERY (S) H'CAP (Final) (2-Y.O) (Class E)

9-00 (9-02) **7f (Fibresand)** £4,191.00 (£1,248.00: £594.00: £267.00) Stalls: High GOING minus 0.12 sec per fur (FST)

| | | | SP | RR | SF |
|---|---|---|---|---|---|
| 40462 | **Contravene (IRE) (56)** (JBerry) **2-8-13** GCarter(2) (mde all: clr over 1f out: pushed out) ....— | **1** | 7/2 3 | 65 | 1 |
| 38462 | **Tinkerbell (64)** (MissSJWilton) **2-9-7v** SWhitworth(1) (a.p: r.o ins fnl f: no ch w wnr) ....5 | **2** | 9/4 2 | 62 | — |
| *39543* | **Mujadil Express (IRE) (55)** (JSMoore) **2-8-9**(3) MHenry(7) (w wnr: one pce fnl 2f) ....1¼ | **3** | 12/1 | 50 | — |
| 42224 | **Abstone Queen (56)** (PDEvans) **2-8-10v**(3) FLynch(3) (hld up: hdwy 4f out: chsd wnr: hung rt & c wd st: eased whn btn ins fnl f) ....3 | **4** | 5/1 | 44 | — |
| *4251*12 | **Run For Us (IRE) (43)** (CADwyer) **2-7-7**(7)ow3 JoHunnam(6) (nvr nr ldrs) ....4 | **5** | 40/1 | 22 | — |
| 3943* | **Run Lucy Run (63)** (MissGayKelleway) **2-9-6** GDuffield(5) (chsd ldrs: rdn over 3f out: sn wknd) ....2 | **6** | 15/8 1 | 37 | — |
| 40979 | **Hopperetta (57)** (BPalling) **2-9-0b1** TSprake(4) (s.i.s: sn rcvd: wknd over 3f out) ....7 | **7** | 14/1 | 15 | — |

(SP 121.2%) **7 Rn**

**1m 32.2** (7.50) CSF £12.24 TOTE £3.50: £1.80 £2.40 (£4.50) OWNER Mr William Burns (COCKERHAM) BRED E. O'Leary
Bt in 8,000 gns. Tinkerbell clmd JJannaway £7,000

OFFICIAL EXPLANATION **Run Lucy Run: the trainer felt that the filly ran very flat and may have been coming into season.**
**4046 Contravene (IRE)** is useful in this sort of grade and found no problem with the extra furlong. (7/2)
**3846 Tinkerbell** was 4lb lower than when second over an inadequate trip on grass last time at Warwick. (9/4)
**3954 Mujadil Express (IRE)** was stepping up in distance. (12/1: op 8/1)
**4222 Abstone Queen**, despite use of the whip, did not handle the home turn at all well and was soon under the stands' rail. (5/1)
**3943* Run Lucy Run** disappointed on her first run for her new stable. (15/8)

## 4336 KEY JOINERY MAIDEN H'CAP (0-70) (3-Y.O+) (Class E)

9-30 (9-31) **1m 100y (Fibresand)** £2,490.00 (£690.00: £330.00) Stalls: Low GOING minus 0.12 sec per fur (FST)

| | | | SP | RR | SF |
|---|---|---|---|---|---|
| *40763* | **Tea Party (USA) (61)** (KOCunningham-Brown) **3-9-5** TSprake(8) (a.p: led over 1f out: rdn out) ....— | **1** | 9/2 2 | 81 | 38 |
| 37038 | **What A Fuss (65)** (BHanbury) **3-9-9** JStack(6) (led 2f: led 4f out: rdn 2f out: hdd over 1f out: one pce) ....3½ | **2** | 11/2 3 | 78 | 35 |
| *40762* | **Angus McCoatup (IRE) (55)** (BAMcMahon) **3-8-8**(5) LNewton(11) (lw: a.p: rdn over 3f out: r.o one pce fnl 2f) .2 | **3** | 11/2 3 | 65 | 22 |
| *40775* | **The Great Flood (55)** (CADwyer) **3-8-6**(7) JoHunnam(10) (lw: hdwy wl over 1f out: r.o) ....5 | **4** | 11/2 3 | 55 | 12 |
| 40477 | **Sharp Command (54)** (PEccles) **3-8-12** GCarter(12) (nvr nr to chal) ....5 | **5** | 25/1 | 45 | 2 |
| | **Mustang (60)** (CWThornton) **3-9-4** DeanMcKeown(2) (prom over 4f) ....4 | **6** | 12/1 | 43 | — |
| 398517 | **Bellacardia (55)** (GLewis) **3-8-10**(3) AWhelan(4) (led over 6f out to 4f out: wknd over 2f out) ....1¼ | **7** | 16/1 | 36 | — |
| 39773 | **Rawi (59)** (MissGayKelleway) **3-9-3** GDuffield(9) (sme hdwy on ins over 2f out: wknd wl over 1f out) ....1¾ | **8** | 7/2 1 | 36 | — |
| 39188 | **Crabbie's Pride (66)** (MGMeagher) **3-9-10** DRMcCabe(1) (a bhd: t.o) ....12 | **9** | 16/1 | 21 | — |
| 31404 | **Dashing Dancer (IRE) (55)** (BPJBaugh) **5-9-3** WLord(7) (chsd ldrs 4f: t.o) ....5 | **10** | 14/1 | — | — |
| 31127 | **Kowtow (52)** (MDIUsher) **3-8-10** RStreet(3) (a bhd: t.o) ....5 | **11** | 25/1 | — | — |
| | **Alaska (66)** (MGMeagher) **3-9-3**(7) RStudholme(13) (bhd fnl 5f: t.o) ....6 | **12** | 25/1 | — | — |

(SP 124.2%) **12 Rn**

**1m 50.8** (5.80) CSF £29.06 CT £129.09 TOTE £4.70: £1.90 £2.70 £1.50 (£6.70) Trio £5.40 OWNER Mr A. J. Richards (STOCKBRIDGE) BRED W. S. Farish and Bayard Sharp

WEIGHT FOR AGE 3yo-4lb

**4076 Tea Party (USA)** gives the impression he will get a mile and a quarter. (9/2)
**3418 What A Fuss** does seem better suited to Sand than the turf. (11/2: 7/2-6/1)
**4076 Angus McCoatup (IRE)** was off the same mark as when runner-up in a similar event here two weeks ago. (11/2)
**4077 The Great Flood**, supported in the Ring, seems to need a return to even further. (11/2: 8/1-5/1)
**3977 Rawi** was the third beaten favourite of the evening for his stable. (7/2)

T/Plpt: £92.00 (111.83 Tckts). T/Qdpt: £47.70 (7.58 Tckts). KH

# 4096-LEICESTER (R-H) (Firm)

## Monday September 23rd

WEATHER: overcast WIND: almost nil

## 4337 HIGHFIELDS LIMITED STKS (0-60) (3-Y.O+) (Class F)

2-15 (2-17) **1m 8y** £3,380.60 (£941.60: £453.80) Stalls: High GOING minus 0.47 sec per fur (F)

| | | | SP | RR | SF |
|---|---|---|---|---|---|
| 41292 | **Mustn't Grumble (IRE) (55)** (MissSJWilton) **6-9-0v** SWhitworth(4) (hld up: hdwy over 2f out: hrd rdn to ld wl ins fnl f) ....— | **1** | 12/1 | 70 | 35 |
| 42432 | **Missile Toe (IRE) (58)** (JEBanks) **3-8-10** NDay(2) (lw: a.p: led over 1f out tl wl ins fnl f: kpt on u.p) ....nk | **2** | 7/2 2 | 69 | 30 |
| 42266 | **Bentico (55)** (MrsNMacauley) **7-9-0v**(3) CTeague(6) (lw: w ldrs: ev ch over 1f out: unable qckn fnl f) ....2 | **3** | 14/1 | 68 | 33 |
| 41862 | **Mystic Dawn (62)** (SDow) **3-8-2**(5) ADaly(9) (lw: a.p: rdn wl over 1f out: nt pce to chal) ....¾ | **4** | 11/4 1 | 61 | 22 |
| *4078*10 | **Just Harry (60)** (MJRyan) **5-8-7**(7) AMcCarthy(5) (prom tl rdn & one pce appr fnl f) ....3 | **5** | 16/1 | 58 | 23 |
| 3991* | **Master M-E-N (IRE) (56)** (NMBabbage) **4-9-3v** BDoyle(15) (lw: trckd ldrs: shkn up wl over 1f out: one pce) ...nk | **6** | 10/1 | 60 | 25 |
| *40779* | **Dragonjoy (49)** (NPLittmoden) **3-9-2** AMcGlone(1) (chsd ldrs: rdn over 2f out: no imp) ....1¼ | **7** | 33/1 | 61 | 22 |

$4237^{3}$ **Blaze of Oak (USA) (58)** (JMBradley) **5-9-0** KFallon(10) (hld up: hdwy 3f out: nt rch ldrs) ....nk **8** 16/1 54 19

$4226^{2}$ **Maradata (IRE) (58)** (RHollinshead) **4-9-0**(3) FLynch(17) (lw: hld up: swtchd lft & hdwy over 2f out: nt rch ldrs) ....1¼ **9** 11/2 $^{3}$ 55 20

$4098^{10}$ **Bright Diamond (50)** (JRArnold) **3-8-7b$^{1}$** CRutter(7) (trckd ldrs over 5f) ....1¼ **10** 16/1 46 7

$4221^{2}$ **Best Kept Secret (50)** (PDEvans) **5-8-7v**(7) AnthonyBond(16) (racd alone far side: led tl hdd & wknd over 1f out) ....1¼ **11** 12/1 47 12

$3766^{4}$ **Zacaroon (58)** (JFfitch-Heyes) **5-8-11** SSanders(12) (chsd ldrs over 5f: wknd qckly) ....6 **12** 25/1 32 —

$3458^{9}$ **Royal Intrusion (44)** (RJHodges) **3-8-10** SDrowne(8) (lw: a in rr: t.o) ....13 **13** 50/1 9 —

$4098^{19}$ **Media Express (50)** (PSFelgate) **4-8-11**(3) DWright(13) (a bhd: t.o) ....4 **14** 33/1 1 —

**Native Lass (IRE) (25)** (JBalding) **7-8-4**(7) JEdmunds(3) (bkwd: led stands' side 4f: sn wknd: t.o) ....dist **15** 66/1 — —

$4129^{13}$ **February (33)** (AJChamberlain) **3-8-7** TSprake(11) (stumbled & uns rdr leaving stalls) .... **U** 66/1 — —

(SP 127.7%) **16 Rn**

**1m 37.2** (2.20) CSF £52.50 TOTE £15.30: £5.20 £1.50 £2.40 (£23.90) Trio £154.70 OWNER Mr John Pointon (STOKE-ON-TRENT) BRED Rathduff Stud

WEIGHT FOR AGE 3yo-4lb

**4129 Mustn't Grumble (IRE)**, running his first race at a mile, was stepping up in class. He does seem to perform better at this time of year. (12/1: op 8/1)

**4243 Missile Toe (IRE)**, making a quick reappearance in an attempt to gain compensation for his narrow defeat at Yarmouth, suffered the same fate again and luck is not favouring him at present. (7/2)

**4078 Bentico**, twice a winner over course and distance in the autumn, tried his best to add to the score, but a turn of finishing speed was missing when it was most needed. (14/1)

**4186 Mystic Dawn** had a bit more use made of her than she did at Goodwood and could never muster the pace to land a blow. (11/4)

**3606 Just Harry** finished closest of those drawn on the far side, but his measure had been taken before reaching the final furlong. (16/1)

**3991* Master M-E-N (IRE)** was able to keep tabs on the leaders but, when an extra effort was called for, there was little more to come. (10/1)

**4221 Best Kept Secret** (12/1: tchd 8/1)

## 4338 KEGWORTH CONDITIONS STKS (2-Y.O) (Class C)

2-45 (2-45) **7f 9y** £5,915.14 (£1,891.24: £907.62) Stalls: High GOING minus 0.47 sec per fur (F)

SP RR SF

$3068^{5}$ **Imroz (USA)** (HRACecil) **2-8-11** WRyan(3) (mde all: shkn up ins fnl f: hld on wl) ....— **1** 1/4 $^{1}$ 90 23

$3971^{6}$ **Musical Dancer (USA) (100)** (EALDunlop) **2-9-2** KFallon(1) (lw: hld up: wnt 2nd ½-wy: rdn to chal ent fnl f: r.o) ....hd **2** 6/1 $^{3}$ 95 28

1499* **Reunion (IRE)** (JWHills) **2-8-9** RHills(2) (chsd wnr over 3f: swtchd lft & rdn appr fnl f: nt pce to chal) ....2 **3** 11/2 $^{2}$ 83 16

(SP 109.7%) **3 Rn**

**1m 25.8** (2.80) CSF £2.14 TOTE £1.20 (£1.30) OWNER Mr K. Abdulla (NEWMARKET) BRED Juddmonte Farms

**3068 Imroz (USA)**, back in her own class here, did not win like an odds-on shot should, but she showed the right commitment. (1/4)

**3971 Musical Dancer (USA)**, a likeable youngster who should improve with time, gave supporters of the hotpot a worrying time here, and he is certainly progressing in the right direction. (6/1: op 3/1)

**1499* Reunion (IRE)** had an absence of four months to overcome and was struggling with the pace two furlongs out, but she renewed her effort inside the distance. But for being eased when held, she could have finished at least a length closer. (11/2)

## 4339 RIVER NURSERY H'CAP (0-75) (2-Y.O) (Class E)

3-15 (3-17) **5f 218y** £3,588.90 (£1,075.20: £516.60: £237.30) Stalls: High GOING minus 0.47 sec per fur (F)

SP RR SF

$4113^{18}$ **Stygian (USA) (73)** (BWHills) **2-9-2**(5) JDSmith(7) (a.p: led over 2f out: rdn & edgd lft over 1f out: drvn clr) ....— **1** 4/1 $^{2}$ 77 11

$4049^{9}$ **Kilcullen Lad (IRE) (56)** (PMooney) **2-8-4** JQuinn(2) (a.p: rdn & hung rt over 1f out: slightly hmpd ent fnl f: r.o one pce) ....2½ **2** 5/1 53 —

$1779^{5}$ **Rockaroundtheclock (65)** (PDEvans) **2-8-13** JFEgan(6) (swtg: hld up: hdwy u.p 2f out: kpt on ins fnl f) ....½ **3** 9/1 61 —

$4207^{5}$ **Danehill Princess (IRE) (70)** (RHollinshead) **2-9-1**(3) FLynch(8) (dwlt: hdwy ½-wy: rdn over 1f out: sn btn) ....nk **4** 11/4 $^{1}$ 65 —

$4207^{7}$ **Breffni (IRE) (56)** (RDickin) **2-8-4** DaneO'Neill(4) (bolted bef s: hld up in rr: a bhd) ....4 **5** 12/1 41 —

$4087^{4}$ **Keen Waters (63)** (JRArnold) **2-8-11** CRutter(1) (hld up pllng hrd: effrt & rdn wl over 1f out: no imp) ....1¼ **6** 9/2 $^{3}$ 44 —

$4207^{13}$ **Dancing Star (IRE) (51)** (PDEvans) **2-7-6**(7) RMullen(3) (s.i.s: a in rr) ....1 **7** 10/1 30 —

*$2554^{2}$* **Grovefair Dancer (IRE) (73)** (MissSJWilton) **2-9-7v$^{1}$** SWhitworth(5) (led tl over 2f out: grad wknd) ....½ **8** 14/1 50 —

(SP 115.0%) **8 Rn**

**1m 13.9** (3.90) CSF £22.67 CT £154.14 TOTE £4.70: £1.70 £2.00 £4.00 (£15.60) OWNER Mr K. Abdulla (LAMBOURN) BRED Juddmonte Farms

**3581* Stygian (USA)** returned to form with a clear-cut success but she did cause some interference inside the last quarter-mile by drifting off a true course. (4/1: 3/1-9/2)

**2199* Kilcullen Lad (IRE)**, turning in a most-improved performance, caused some of his own trouble by hanging right and then had the winner cross in front of him, but that rival proved far superior, and there were no hard-luck stories. (5/1)

**1779 Rockaroundtheclock**, out of action since the first week in June, stayed on strongly in the closing stages. He should come into his own when tackling a slightly longer trip. (9/1)

**4207 Danehill Princess (IRE)** once again found that she can not forfeit ground at the start and then come and beat her rivals like Damon Hill occasionally does. But then again, she probably has not got a Williams-Renault engine. (11/4)

**3604 Breffni (IRE)** carted her jockey to the mile start and may well have gone further but for the high fence at the end of the straight. Never able to get amongst the leaders, she is probably better than this. (12/1: op 7/1)

**4087 Keen Waters**, who still looks to be carrying condition, took quite a keen tug but was restrained behind the leaders. When asked for her effort, she was unable to respond, but left the impression she could be a different proposition next year. (9/2)

**2554 Grovefair Dancer (IRE)** (14/1: 10/1-16/1)

## 4340 GOLDEN HAND (S) STKS (3-Y.O) (Class G)

3-45 (3-46) **1m 1f 218y** £2,658.00 (£738.00: £354.00) Stalls: High GOING minus 0.47 sec per fur (F)

SP RR SF

$3965^{8}$ **In Cahoots (30)** (AGNewcombe) **3-8-11** JQuinn(12) (a.p: led over 3f out: clr appr fnl f: drvn out) ....— **1** 10/1 55 30

$1888^{W}$ **Haute Cuisine (50)** (RJRWilliams) **3-8-11** DaneO'Neill(9) (hld up: rdn 3f out: gd hdwy appr fnl f: fin wl) ....1 **2** 6/1 $^{2}$ 53 28

$2251^{5}$ **Totally Yours (IRE) (36)** (MRChannon) **3-7-13**(7) AEddery(4) (hld up in rr: hdwy on ins 3f out: hrd rdn appr fnl f: one pce) ....3½ **3** 7/2 $^{1}$ 43 18

$4226^{13}$ **Born A Lady (52)** (SRBowring) **3-8-11b** KFallon(3) (hld up in tch: effrt & rdn 2f out: nvr able to chal) ....1¾ **4** 7/2 $^{1}$ 45 20

$2740^{6}$ **Areish (IRE) (39)** (JFfitch-Heyes) **3-8-6** SSanders(5) (bit bkwd: trckd ldrs: rdn & one pce fnl 2f) ....3½ **5** 20/1 34 9

| Prev | Horse | Dist | Pos | SP | RR | SF |
|---|---|---|---|---|---|---|
| | **Candy's Delight (40)** (MrsSJSmith) **3-8-6** NCarlisle(13) (led tl over 3f out: rdn & wknd wl over 1f out) | 11 | **6** | 9/1 | 17 | — |
| 3619$^{10}$ | **Needwood Fantasy (32)** (BCMorgan) **3-8-6** GCarter(6) (b.nr hind: a in rr) | 3½ | **7** | 16/1 | 11 | — |
| 3619$^{18}$ | **Brownie's Promise (27)** (MBrittain) **3-8-4**$^{(7)}$ RMullen(2) (bit bkwd: trckd ldrs over 6f: sn rdn & wknd) | 3 | **8** | 33/1 | 11 | — |
| | **Lunar Gris (45)** (RMStronge) **3-8-6** VSlattery(1) (bkwd: in tch to ½-wy: grad wknd: t.o) | 3 | **9** | 33/1 | 2 | — |
| *3628$^{10}$* | **Miss Impulse (55)** (MissJBower) **3-8-6** DRMcCabe(7) (a bhd: t.o) | 2 | **10** | 7/1$^{3}$ | — | — |
| 4129$^{19}$ | **Desert Scout (30)** (KMcAuliffe) **3-8-11** MTebbutt(10) (lw: rel to r: a t.o) | dist | **11** | 33/1 | — | — |
| 4129$^{18}$ | **Faro Flyer** (KTIvory) **3-8-6**$^{(5)}$ MartinDwyer(11) (b: b.hind: bkwd: plld hrd: prom 6f: wknd qckly: t.o) | nk | **12** | 33/1 | — | — |

(SP 112.7%) **12 Rn**

**2m 7.1** (3.40) CSF £59.77 TOTE £10.70: £3.20 £2.20 £1.40 (£34.80) Trio £45.00 OWNER Duckhaven Stud (BARNSTAPLE) BRED Duckhaven Stud

No bid

**In Cahoots**, allowed to go with the pace, kicked on soon after straightening up and, though he was being reeled in at the finish, he already had the race won. (10/1: op 5/1)

**Haute Cuisine**, rather surprisingly for a son of Petong, appears to have plenty of stamina and, though he did not put it to use until too late here, it is possible more forceful tactics will be employed in the future. (6/1)

**2251 Totally Yours (IRE)** has enjoyed a three-month rest and was fully expected to open her account, but she lacked the pace to get herself in with a chance. (7/2)

**3602 Born A Lady** would only get this trip in a horsebox and it came as no great surprise that she was galloping on the spot for the final quarter-mile. (7/2)

## 4341 CHARNWOOD CLAIMING STKS (3 & 4-Y.O) (Class F)

4-15 (4-17) **5f 218y** £3,333.00 (£928.00: £447.00) Stalls: High GOING minus 0.47 sec per fur (F)

| Prev | Horse | Dist | Pos | SP | RR | SF |
|---|---|---|---|---|---|---|
| 4045$^{16}$ | **Naughty Pistol (USA) (46)** (PDEvans) **4-8-2v** JFEgan(8) (stumbled s: hld up: hdwy 2f out: str run to ld wl ins fnl f) | — | **1** | 10/1 | 59 | 24 |
| *4090$^{3}$* | **Hoh Majestic (IRE) (58)** (MartynWane) **3-7-12v**$^{(3)}$ FLynch(3) (a.p: rdn to ld ins fnl f: sn hdd & no ex) | 1½ | **2** | 7/1$^{3}$ | 56 | 19 |
| 4215$^{7}$ | **Tafahhus (70)** (MJPolglase) **4-8-7b** MRoberts(5) (led 4f: ev ch ins fnl f: unable qckn) | 2 | **3** | 3/1$^{1}$ | 55 | 20 |
| *3953$^{12}$* | **Vax New Way (60)** (JLSpearing) **3-8-9b** SDrowne(9) (a.p centre: led 2f out tl ins fnl f: one pce) | ½ | **4** | 8/1 | 57 | 20 |
| | **Needwood Limelight** (BCMorgan) **3-8-1** CRutter(11) (bit bkwd: hdwy over 1f out: fin wl: broke leg after line: dead) | 2½ | **5** | 50/1 | 43 | 6 |
| 3780$^{10}$ | **Rocky Stream (40)** (RMWhitaker) **3-7-10** FNorton(1) (trckd ldrs: rdn & no hdwy fnl 2f) | nk | **6** | 33/1 | 37 | — |
| 4045$^{8}$ | **Havana Miss (42)** (BPalling) **4-7-9**$^{(3)}$ MHenry(4) (chsd ldrs: rdn & one pce appr fnl f) | ½ | **7** | 16/1 | 36 | 1 |
| 3661$^{3}$ | **Mister Raider (47)** (EAWheeler) **4-8-6b**$^{(5)}$ ADaly(15) (lw: led far side: rdn & one pce appr fnl f) | ¾ | **8** | 12/1 | 47 | 12 |
| 3139$^{14}$ | **Meranti (54)** (JMBradley) **3-7-8**$^{(7)}$ RFfrench(7) (nvr trbld ldrs) | 1¾ | **9** | 20/1 | 34 | — |
| 4045$^{14}$ | **Quinntessa (50)** (BPalling) **3-8-0** TSprake(18) (sme late hdwy: nvr nrr) | ¾ | **10** | 20/1 | 31 | — |
| 4186$^{13}$ | **Persian Dawn (36)** (MajorDNChappell) **3-7-13**$^{(5)}$ SophieMitchell(12) (outpcd) | nk | **11** | 16/1 | 34 | — |
| 4074* | **River Tern (73)** (JBerry) **3-9-3b$^{1}$** GCarter(19) (b: lw: s.s: hdwy ½-wy: sn rdn: no imp) | 4 | **12** | 9/2$^{2}$ | 36 | — |
| 4221$^{4}$ | **Oriel Lad (62)** (PDEvans) **3-8-6b**$^{ow1}$ KFallon(10) (outpcd) | ½ | **13** | 10/1 | 24 | — |
| | **Viennese Dancer** (RJRWilliams) **3-8-4** DRMcCabe(6) (b.hind: lt-f: unf: s.s: a outpcd) | 2½ | **14** | 33/1 | 15 | — |
| 3789$^{7}$ | **Siberian Rose** (JWharton) **3-7-10** JQuinn(14) (outpcd) | ¾ | **15** | 33/1 | 5 | — |
| 3339$^{7}$ | **Time Goes On (35)** (RJHodges) **4-7-12**$^{(5)ow1}$ PPMurphy(2) (outpcd) | 1¾ | **16** | 50/1 | 6 | — |
| *4094$^{11}$* | **Mr Blue (30)** (GPKelly) **4-8-5**$^{(3)ow5}$ CTeague(16) (outpcd: t.o) | 16 | **17** | 100/1 | — | — |

(SP 127.7%) **17 Rn**

**1m 11.6** (1.60) CSF £75.18 TOTE £14.60: £3.50 £2.10 £1.10 (£43.70) Trio £60.10 OWNER Mr Colin Booth (WELSHPOOL) BRED Brereton C. Jones

WEIGHT FOR AGE 3yo-2lb

**3453 Naughty Pistol (USA)**, in her glory on this galloping track, produced a telling burst of speed to nose ahead 100 yards out and win going away. She should be able to carry on from here. (10/1)

**4090 Hoh Majestic (IRE)** looked to have timed his run to perfection, but was swamped for speed when the winner came on the scene. He has not yet won beyond the minimum trip, but his turn will come. (7/1: op 9/2)

**3285* Tafahhus** held the overall lead in the centre of the track without company all the way and had nothing in reserve for a final flourish. (3/1)

**3049 Vax New Way** will probably have to return to the All-Weather to get back to winning ways, but he ran well and further success will come as no surprise. (8/1)

**3427 Rocky Stream** did not shape badly on this return to sprinting, and it would seem there is a race in her. (33/1)

**Havana Miss** has not won since her two-year-old days, but he has got speed to burn and will put it to good use one of these days. (16/1)

**4074* River Tern** (9/2: 3/1-5/1)

## 4342 LIGHTNING H'CAP (0-80) (3-Y.O+) (Class D)

4-45 (4-45) **5f 2y** £3,827.55 (£1,142.40: £545.70: £247.35) Stalls: High GOING minus 0.47 sec per fur (F)

| Prev | Horse | Dist | Pos | SP | RR | SF |
|---|---|---|---|---|---|---|
| 4205$^{6}$ | **Souperficial (50)** (JAGlover) **5-8-0v** SSanders(2) (hld up in tch: hdwy to ld wl ins fnl f: sn clr) | — | **1** | 7/2$^{2}$ | 58 | 18 |
| 4215$^{3}$ | **Palacegate Jack (IRE) (78)** (CADwyer) **5-10-0** KFallon(1) (led: clr 2f out: rdn & hdd wl ins fnl f) | 1½ | **2** | 7/4$^{1}$ | 81 | 41 |
| 4198$^{15}$ | **Bayin (USA) (73)** (MDIUsher) **7-9-9** RStreet(5) (s.i.s: hdwy 2f out: str run fnl f: r.o) | s.h | **3** | 13/2 | 76 | 36 |
| 3864$^{5}$ | **Sharp Pearl (74)** (JWhite) **3-9-9** RHughes(6) (a.p: hrd drvn appr fnl f: kpt on) | 1½ | **4** | 10/1 | 72 | 31 |
| 4198$^{10}$ | **Castlerea Lad (71)** (RHollinshead) **7-9-4**$^{(3)}$ FLynch(4) (s.s: hdwy ½-wy: rdn over 1f out: nt rch ldrs) | s.h | **5** | 4/1$^{3}$ | 69 | 29 |
| 4180$^{20}$ | **Barranak (IRE) (65)** (GMMcCourt) **4-9-1** CRutter(7) (prom over 3f: sn outpcd) | 6 | **6** | 12/1 | 44 | 4 |
| 4130$^{13}$ | **Halbert (52)** (PBurgoyne) **7-8-2v** DRMcCabe(3) (w ldr to ½-wy: rdn & outpcd over 1f out) | 5 | **7** | 20/1 | 15 | — |

(SP 113.5%) **7 Rn**

**60.1 secs** (1.60) CSF £9.73 CT £32.85 TOTE £5.40: £2.70 £1.20 (£6.30) OWNER Mr J. A. Glover (WORKSOP) BRED C. L. Loyd

WEIGHT FOR AGE 3yo-1lb

**4205 Souperficial** only wins in his turn, but he is smart on his day and this was one of those days. (7/2)

**4215 Palacegate Jack (IRE)** did his very best to concede 28lb to the winner, but he found it beyond him in the sprint to the line. (7/4)

**3219 Bayin (USA)** is hardly up to winning at this trip nowadays and was only finding top gear when the race was over. (13/2)

**3864 Sharp Pearl** ran without blinkers and turned in a good display, if just lacking the speed to get to terms. (10/1)

**4058 Castlerea Lad**, having a rare outing at the minimum trip, lost all chance with a tardy start and was unable to get himself into it. (4/1: 3/1-9/2)

T/Jkpt: Not won; £3,529.50 to Nottingham 24/9/96. T/Plpt: £56.10 (272.28 Tckts). T/Qdpt: £23.60 (45.7 Tckts). IM

# 3878-MUSSELBURGH (R-H) (Good to firm)

## Monday September 23rd

WEATHER: overcast WIND: almost nil

### 4343 E.B.F. RATING RELATED MAIDEN STKS (0-60) (2-Y.O F) (Class F)

2-00 (2-03) **5f** £2,697.00 (£816.00: £398.00: £189.00) Stalls: High GOING minus 0.34 sec per fur (GF)

| Runner | Btn | Pl | SP | RR | SF |
|---|---|---|---|---|---|
| 3840[6] **Skyers Tryer (55)** (RonaldThompson) **2-8-11** NConnorton(4) (lw: led 1f: cl up: led ins fnl f: styd on wl) | — | **1** | 9/1 | 70 | 26 |
| 3467[6] **Molly Music (60)** (GGMargarson) **2-8-11v[1]** KDarley(1) (lw: cl up: led ½-wy tl ins fnl f: kpt on) | 1¾ | **2** | 6/1[3] | 64 | 20 |
| 3941[5] **Compact Disc (IRE) (60)** (MJohnston) **2-8-11** JWeaver(6) (chsd ldrs: rdn ½-wy: r.o one pce) | 2 | **3** | 4/5[1] | 58 | 14 |
| 4072[10] **Hiltons Executive (IRE) (55)** (EJAlston) **2-8-11** JFortune(5) (led after 1f to ½-wy: sn rdn & btn) | 3 | **4** | 14/1 | 48 | 4 |
| *4093*[14] **Thewrightone (IRE) (47)** (GROldroyd) **2-8-6b(5)** GParkin(2) (prom: rdn ½-wy: no imp after) | nk | **5** | 50/1 | 47 | 3 |
| 3956[7] **Trulyfan (IRE) (50)** (RAFahey) **2-8-11v[1]** ACulhane(3) (dwlt: gd hdwy ½-wy: sn ev ch: wknd appr fnl f) | s.h | **6** | 25/1 | 47 | 3 |
| 3807[17] **Florentine Diamond (IRE) (60)** (SirMarkPrescott) **2-8-8(3)** RHavlin(8) (lw: s.i.s: drvn along thrght: no imp) | s.h | **7** | 4/1[2] | 47 | 3 |
| *4244*[15] ***Cantsaynowt (40)*** (RMMcKellar) **2-8-4b[1](7)** JMcAuley(7) (Withdrawn not under Starter's orders: Veterinary advice) | | **W** | 66/1 | — | — |
| | | | (SP 113.8%) | | **7 Rn** |

**60.0 secs** (2.30) CSF £54.31 TOTE £11.70: £2.60 £3.60 (£21.60) OWNER Mrs J. Carney (DONCASTER) BRED Miss H. K. Monteith

**3840 Skyers Tryer** probably needs a bit further, but found a poor race here and won it convincingly. (9/1)

**3467 Molly Music**, in a visor for the first time, showed she has the speed to win a modest race at the minimum trip. (6/1)

**3941 Compact Disc (IRE)** failed to impress on looks and was always struggling with the pace. (4/5: 10/11-Evens)

**Hiltons Executive (IRE)**, beaten out of sight previously, did show something here, but there is still plenty more needed. (14/1)

**3291 Thewrightone (IRE)** has yet to show anything really positive. (50/1)

**2059 Trulyfan (IRE)**, in a visor for the first time, threw away all chances at the start. (25/1)

**Florentine Diamond (IRE)**, in a poor event, failed to show anything. (4/1: op 9/4)

### 4344 ROYAL CALEDONIAN HUNT CUP H'CAP (0-70) (3-Y.O+) (Class E)

2-30 (2-30) **1m 7f 16y** £3,061.00 (£928.00: £454.00: £217.00) Stalls: High GOING minus 0.34 sec per fur (GF)

| Runner | Btn | Pl | SP | RR | SF |
|---|---|---|---|---|---|
| 4048[7] **Sarasota Storm (50)** (MBell) **4-8-12** MFenton(3) (lw: hld up: hdwy ent st: racd alone stands' side: led 2f out: r.o wl) | — | **1** | 7/2[2] | 64 | 15 |
| 4248* **Etterby Park (USA) (73)** (MJohnston) **3-9-10** 4x JWeaver(7) (lw: led: qcknd ent st: hdd 2f out: kpt on wl) | 3½ | **2** | 1/2[1] | 83 | 23 |
| 2756[6] **Vain Prince (44)** (NTinkler) **9-8-6b** LCharnock(2) (lw: trckd ldrs: effrt 3f out: r.o one pce) | 3½ | **3** | 8/1[3] | 51 | 2 |
| *339*[10] **Peep O Day (41)** (JLEyre) **5-8-3** TWilliams(1) (b.off hind: chsd ldrs: wnt 2nd appr st: outpcd fnl 2f) | ¾ | **4** | 25/1 | 47 | — |
| 4237[15] **Jabaroot (IRE) (34)** (RMMcKellar) **5-7-3(7)** JMcAuley(8) (dwlt: hdwy ent st: rdn & no imp) | 1¼ | **5** | 50/1 | 38 | — |
| 3427[13] **Boundary Bird (IRE) (45)** (MJohnston) **3-7-5(5)** PFessey(6) (prom tl outpcd fnl 3½f) | 3½ | **6** | 100/1 | 46 | — |
| 3961[5] **Hallikeld (46)** (TJEtherington) **3-7-8(3)ow1** DarrenMoffatt(4) (lost pl 8f out: n.d after) | hd | **7** | 20/1 | 47 | — |
| 3865* **Latvian (62)** (RAllan) **9-9-10v** JFortune(5) (chsd ldrs tl wknd fnl 3½f) | 1½ | **8** | 10/1 | 61 | 12 |
| | | | (SP 120.6%) | | **8 Rn** |

**3m 21.1** (10.60) CSF £5.77 CT £11.87 TOTE £4.20: £1.30 £1.00 £2.50 (£2.30) OWNER Mr B. J. Warren (NEWMARKET) BRED B. J. Warren

LONG HANDICAP Boundary Bird (IRE) 7-8 Hallikeld 7-2 Jabaroot (IRE) 7-0

WEIGHT FOR AGE 3yo-11lb

**3355 Sarasota Storm** gained his fourth win from as many outings on this track and has yet to show anything really positive elsewhere. (7/2)

**4248* Etterby Park (USA)** tried to quicken it up from the home turn, but was easily picked off by the winner. Despite running on, he was always well second best. (1/2)

**2756 Vain Prince** is certainly off a decent mark just now and ran better here. He looks likely to pick up a race before long, especially over timber. (8/1)

**Peep O Day**, having her first run in six months, put up a decent effort and should be kept in mind, especially if returning to hurdles. (25/1)

**3878 Jabaroot (IRE)** ran reasonably from 10lb out of the handicap. (50/1)

### 4345 WEATHERBYS GROUP H'CAP (0-70) (3-Y.O+) (Class E)

3-00 (3-01) **1m 4f 31y** £3,139.00 (£952.00: £466.00: £223.00) Stalls: High GOING minus 0.34 sec per fur (GF)

| Runner | Btn | Pl | SP | RR | SF |
|---|---|---|---|---|---|
| 4048[2] **Ayunli (64)** (SCWilliams) **5-9-8** JWeaver(7) (lw: trckd ldrs: led over 3f out: r.o: comf) | — | **1** | 1/2[1] | 73+ | 36 |
| 3621[8] **Soba Up (70)** (TJEtherington) **6-10-0** ACulhane(2) (hld up: hdwy to chse wnr over 2f out: r.o u.p) | 2½ | **2** | 7/1[2] | 76 | 39 |
| 3974[13] **Royal Legend (58)** (JPearce) **4-9-2** GBardwell(3) (lw: plld hrd: effrt over 3f out: styd on: no imp) | 4 | **3** | 10/1[3] | 58 | 21 |
| 3638[3] **Crambella (IRE) (38)** (GPKelly) **4-7-10** LCharnock(5) (chsd ldrs tl outpcd 3f out: no imp after) | 4 | **4** | 33/1 | 33 | — |
| 3297[13] **Eden Dancer (52)** (MrsMReveley) **4-8-10** KDarley(6) (led tl over 3f out: sn btn) | 5 | **5** | 7/1[2] | 41 | 4 |
| 3592[12] **Meadow Blue (47)** (MissLCSiddall) **3-7-11ow1** TWilliams(1) (bhd: hdwy ent st: sn rdn & n.d) | 10 | **6** | 100/1 | 22 | — |
| 3645[3] **Moofaji (48)** (FWatson) **5-8-3(3)ow9** RHavlin(4) (sddle slipped after s: prom tl lost pl appr st) | 13 | **7** | 10/1[3] | 6 | — |
| | | | (SP 113.8%) | | **7 Rn** |

**2m 39.6** (6.60) CSF £4.72 TOTE £1.50: £1.10 £2.60 (£3.00) OWNER Mr I. A. Southcott (NEWMARKET) BRED I. A. Southcott

LONG HANDICAP Meadow Blue 7-7 Crambella (IRE) 7-5

WEIGHT FOR AGE 3yo-8lb

**4048 Ayunli** looked a good thing and, once striking the front early in the straight, was always in command. (1/2)

**3098 Soba Up** has been disappointing most of the season, but she did keep battling away after all had appeared lost. She may at last be coming right. (7/1: op 9/2)

**79 Royal Legend** showed his first real signs of form since joining his new stable. He is now dropping down the handicap. (10/1)

**3638 Crambella (IRE)** ran reasonably from 5lb out of the handicap, but she was going nowhere in the last three furlongs. (33/1)

**Eden Dancer** probably still needed this, and should now begin to show signs of improvement. (7/1)

**3645 Moofaji** was hampered by a slipping saddle from early on. This should be completely ignored. (10/1)

### 4346 PINKIE NURSERY H'CAP (0-75) (2-Y.O) (Class E)

3-30 (3-33) **5f** £2,905.00 (£880.00: £430.00: £205.00) Stalls: High GOING minus 0.34 sec per fur (GF)

| Runner | Btn | Pl | SP | RR | SF |
|---|---|---|---|---|---|
| 4024a[21] **Ballymote (73)** (JBerry) **2-9-7** KDarley(3) (mde all: rdn & styd on wl fnl f) | — | **1** | 7/4[1] | 73 | 42 |
| 4046[9] **Donna's Dancer (IRE) (65)** (TDBarron) **2-8-13b[1]** JFortune(2) (s.i.s: outpcd & bhd tl hdwy 2f out: styd on u.p) | 1½ | **2** | 7/1[3] | 60 | 29 |

| | | | | SP | RR | SF |
|---|---|---|---|---|---|---|
| 4228[4] | **Style Dancer (IRE) (70)** (RMWhitaker) **2-9-1**(3) RHavlin(1) (lw: hdwy to chse wnr ½-wy: sn rdn: no imp fnl f) .. | ½ | **3** | 5/2[2] | 64 | 33 |
| 4207[3] | **Hit Or Miss (63)** (PCHaslam) **2-8-11** JWeaver(4) (lw: chsd wnr to ½-wy: sn btn) .... | 12 | **4** | 5/2[2] | 18 | — |
| | | | | (SP 106.0%) | **4 Rn** | |

**59.6 secs** (1.90) CSF £10.35 TOTE £2.50 (£6.30) OWNER Manny Bernstein (Racing) Ltd (COCKERHAM) BRED J. A. and Mrs Duffy

**4024a Ballymote** had the early pace to burn the opposition off and, shaken up entering the final furlong, was never going to stop. (7/4)

**2625 Donna's Dancer (IRE)**, in blinkers for the first time, needed plenty of driving to get him going after a poor start, and it was always too late when he decided to run on seriously. (7/1)

**4228 Style Dancer (IRE)** has the looks of something better and ran reasonably but, once the pressure was on from halfway, was never good enough. (5/2)

**4207 Hit Or Miss**, who seems to be going backwards these days, quickly lost ground when the pressure was on at halfway. (5/2)

## 4347 CARBERRY TOWER CLAIMING STKS (2-Y.O) (Class F)

4-00 (4-01) **1m 16y** £2,827.00 (£856.00: £418.00: £199.00) Stalls: High GOING minus 0.34 sec per fur (GF)

| | | | | SP | RR | SF |
|---|---|---|---|---|---|---|
| 4024a[25] | **Imperial Or Metric (IRE) (73)** (JBerry) **2-9-2** JCarroll(7) (lw: trckd ldrs: led over 2f out: r.o) .... | — | **1** | 9/4[1] | 71 | 19 |
| 4097[6] | **Time Can Tell (60)** (CMurray) **2-8-8** DeanMcKeown(12) (b: bhd: hdwy over 2f out: r.o wl towards fin) .... | ¾ | **2** | 7/2[2] | 62 | 10 |
| 4069[15] | **Ibn Masirah** (MrsMReveley) **2-8-5**(5) SCopp(2) (bit bkwd: s.i.s: hdwy & hung lft 2f out: styd on: nrst fin) .... | 3 | **3** | 50/1 | 58 | 6 |
| 3962[8] | **Fancy A Fortune (IRE) (69)** (JPearce) **2-9-4** GBardwell(1) (lw: outpcd & bhd: hdwy whn bmpd ent st: styd on: no imp) .... | 2½ | **4** | 11/2[3] | 61 | 9 |
| 4223[5] | **Lycius Touch (57)** (MJohnston) **2-8-5** TWilliams(5) (cl up: led 3f out: sn hdd & wknd) .... | 3 | **5** | 8/1 | 42 | — |
| *4079*[13] | **Rising Glory** (MissJFCraze) **2-8-10** NConnorton(8) (lw: s.s: bhd tl sme late hdwy) .... | 5 | **6** | 33/1 | 37 | — |
| 4245[7] | **Chanson d'Amour (IRE) (54)** (MissLAPerratt) **2-8-13** JWeaver(10) (rdn ½-wy: nvr bttr than mid div) .... | 6 | **7** | 16/1 | 28 | — |
| 4224[6] | **Plutarch Angel** (WTKemp) **2-7-9**(7) KSked(11) (rdn ½-wy: nvr trbld ldrs) .... | ½ | **8** | 14/1 | 16 | — |
| 4223[14] | **Silver Raj (54)** (WTKemp) **2-8-2b** LCharnock(9) (n.d) .... | 1 | **9** | 50/1 | 14 | — |
| *4091*[11] | **Hurgill King (IRE)** (JWWatts) **2-9-4b**[1] GDuffield(4) (lw: prom: rdn & hung lft appr st: sn btn) .... | 1 | **10** | 25/1 | 28 | — |
| 4223[4] | **Sheraton Girl (48)** (MJohnston) **2-8-5** KDarley(6) (cl up: led appr st: hdd 3f out: sn lost pl) .... | 1¾ | **11** | 8/1 | 11 | — |
| 3082[5] | **Samspet (46)** (RAFahey) **2-8-6v**[1] ACulhane(3) (led tl rn wd appr st: sn bhd) .... | 4 | **12** | 33/1 | 5 | — |
| | | | | (SP 116.8%) | **12 Rn** | |

**1m 44.0** (5.40) CSF £9.94 TOTE £3.00: £1.10 £1.80 £16.70 (£9.30) Trio £324.50; £137.13 to Epsom 24/9/96 OWNER Clayton Bigley Partnership Ltd (COCKERHAM) BRED Patrick J. Duffy

**4024a Imperial Or Metric (IRE)** travelled well, which won him the race as, by the time the second got going, he was home and dried. (9/4)

**4097 Time Can Tell**, well drawn, lost his pitch altogether before the turn and then flew at the death, but had been set too much to do. He failed to run up to his form last time with the blinkers on and will obviously win a race or two without them. (7/2)

**Ibn Masirah** is still learning and still needed this, but showed enough to suggest that, in time, there is better to come. (50/1)

**3632 Fancy A Fortune (IRE)**, poorly drawn, also lacked pace on this sharp track and could never get into it. Better should be seen on a more galloping track. (11/2)

**3648 Lycius Touch** had her chances, but was well outpaced in the last two furlongs and probably needs easier ground. (8/1)

**Rising Glory** looks a bit of a handful but, after a bad start, did finish quite well to show the ability is there. (33/1)

**3779 Plutarch Angel** (14/1: op 8/1)

**4223 Sheraton Girl** (8/1: 7/1-12/1)

## 4348 HONEST TOUN MAIDEN H'CAP (0-60) (3-Y.O+) (Class F)

4-30 (4-34) **7f 15y** £2,996.00 (£908.00: £444.00: £212.00) Stalls: High GOING minus 0.34 sec per fur (GF)

| | | | | SP | RR | SF |
|---|---|---|---|---|---|---|
| 1689[10] | **Society Magic (USA) (54)** (IABalding) **3-9-8** KDarley(6) (in tch: hdwy 3f out: led 1½f out: r.o) .... | — | **1** | 9/2[1] | 65 | 35 |
| 3592[8] | **Red March Hare (30)** (DMoffatt) **5-7-12**(3) DarrenMoffatt(13) (rr div: hdwy 3f out: chsng wnr over 1f out: r.o) .... | 1¼ | **2** | 10/1 | 38 | 11 |
| 3289[5] | **The Barnsley Belle (IRE) (42)** (JLEyre) **3-8-10** RLappin(14) (led to 1½f out: one pce) .... | 1½ | **3** | 6/1[2] | 47 | 17 |
| 4071[12] | **Rainbows Rhapsody (33)** (DWChapman) **5-8-4** LCharnock(10) (a chsng ldrs: effrt 3f out: styd on one pce) .... | 1¾ | **4** | 14/1 | 34 | 7 |
| 3624[6] | **Glen Garnock (IRE) (56)** (DNicholls) **4-9-13** DeanMcKeown(5) (lw: racd wd: in tch: rdn over 3f out: styd on: no imp) .... | nk | **5** | 6/1[2] | 56 | 29 |
| 4108[7] | **Girl of My Dreams (IRE) (55)** (MJHeaton-Ellis) **3-9-9** GDuffield(4) (s.i.s: hdwy 2f out: nrst fin) .... | hd | **6** | 10/1 | 55 | 25 |
| 3492[6] | **Shaa Spin (41)** (JBerry) **4-8-12** JCarroll(12) (chsd ldrs tl outpcd fnl 3f) .... | 4 | **7** | 33/1 | 32 | 5 |
| 3256[12] | **Nutcracker Suite (IRE) (35)** (JLEyre) **4-8-3**(3)ow1 RHavlin(2) (sme hdwy over 2f out: nvr trbld ldrs) .... | 1¼ | **8** | 20/1 | 23 | — |
| 3817[10] | **Polish Lady (IRE) (38)** (CMurray) **3-8-6** TWilliams(1) (bhd: effrt ½-wy: n.d) .... | ¾ | **9** | 9/1 | 24 | — |
| 3403[3] | **Katie Komaite (43)** (CaptJWilson) **3-8-11** JWeaver(8) (lw: cl up tl wknd fnl 2½f) .... | 1¼ | **10** | 10/1 | 27 | — |
| 4075[15] | **Chelwood (38)** (LRLloyd-James) **4-8-2**(7) CLowther(11) (b.nr hind: lost tch fr ½-wy) .... | ¾ | **11** | 33/1 | 20 | — |
| 3591[7] | **Gold Lining (IRE) (35)** (EJAlston) **3-8-3v** MFenton(9) (cl up: rn wd st: sn wknd) .... | s.h | **12** | 33/1 | 17 | — |
| 2432[10] | **Truly Bay (50)** (TDBarron) **3-9-4** JFortune(7) (s.i.s & drvn along: a bhd) .... | 1½ | **13** | 6/1[2] | 28 | — |
| 3881[3] | **Fisiostar (37)** (MDods) **3-8-5b** ACulhane(3) (b.hind: in tch tl wknd fnl 3f) .... | 6 | **14** | 7/1[3] | 2 | — |
| | | | | (SP 131.1%) | **14 Rn** | |

**1m 29.2** (3.70) CSF £49.43 CT £263.84 TOTE £3.90: £3.20 £3.10 £2.80 (£62.70) Trio £222.40 OWNER Miss A. V. Hill (KINGSCLERE) BRED Brereton C. Jones

WEIGHT FOR AGE 3yo-3lb

OFFICIAL EXPLANATION **Truly Bay: the trainer reported that the gelding was unable to handle the track.**

**Society Magic (USA)** got a shade warm beforehand, but there were never any doubts in the race and he scored nicely, although he did need to be kept up to his work. (9/2)

**Red March Hare** ran well, staying on determinedly in the last three furlongs, and could well appreciate a bit further nowadays. (10/1)

**3289 The Barnsley Belle (IRE)** has been disappointing this season, but did run one of her better races this time, although she was outbattled in the final furlong. (6/1)

**3866 Rainbows Rhapsody** keeps running reasonably, but is basically short of a turn of foot at the business end. (14/1: op 8/1)

**3624 Glen Garnock (IRE)**, a big sort, was not really suited to this track and was struggling from the home turn. (6/1)

**Girl of My Dreams (IRE)**, after a poor start, ran as though further should suit. (10/1)

**3578 Polish Lady (IRE)** (9/1: op 5/1)

**2150 Truly Bay**, well backed, got his hind leg stuck over the rail when kicking out leaving the paddock, and may well have injured himself as he ran no sort of race. (6/1: 7/1-12/1)

T/Plpt: £258.80 (44.65 Tckts). T/Qdpt: £10.60 (74.77 Tckts). AA

# 4118-EPSOM (L-H) (Good to firm, Good patches)
## Tuesday September 24th
WEATHER: fine WIND: slt across

### 4349 WALTER NIGHTINGALL MAIDEN STKS (2-Y.O) (Class D)
2-15 (2-16) **1m 114y** £3,241.25 (£980.00: £477.50: £226.25) Stalls: Low GOING minus 0.13 sec per fur (G)

| | | | | SP | RR | SF |
|---|---|---|---|---|---|---|
| 4100$^{7}$ | **Atlantic Desire (IRE)** (MJohnston) **2-8-9** JWeaver(1) (mde all: clr over 2f out: r.o wl) | — | 1 | 4/1$^{2}$ | 77+ | 31 |
| | **Tommy Tortoise** (PFICole) **2-9-0** TQuinn(3) (str: scope: bit bkwd: rdn over 3f out: hdwy over 1f out: chsd wnr ins fnl: r.o one pce) | 6 | 2 | 6/1$^{3}$ | 71 | 25 |
| 3499$^{4}$ | **High Extreme (IRE)** (PWChapple-Hyam) **2-9-0** JReid(4) (chsd wnr 2f: chsd wnr over 3f out tl ins fnl f: one pce) | 2½ | 3 | 13/8$^{1}$ | 66 | 20 |
| 4188$^{8}$ | **Waterville Boy (IRE)** (RHannon) **2-9-0** RPerham(5) (chsd wnr over 6f out tl over 3f out: wknd over 1f out) | 4 | 4 | 10/1 | 59 | 13 |
| 4100$^{9}$ | **Mendoza** (DJGMurraySmith) **2-9-0** RHughes(2) (dwlt: sme hdwy over 2f out: wknd over 1f out) | 4 | 5 | 33/1 | 51 | 5 |
| | **Slightly Oliver (IRE)** (GLewis) **2-9-0** SWhitworth(6) (w'like: dwlt: hdwy 6f out: wknd over 3f out) | 8 | 6 | 12/1 | 36 | — |
| *4175$^{8}$* | ***Fruitie O'Flarety*** (CEBrittain) **2-9-0** BDoyle(7) (Withdrawn not under Starter's orders: unruly in stalls) | | W | 7/1 | — | — |
| | | | | (SP 104.6%) | | **6 Rn** |

**1m 47.25** (5.25) CSF £18.32 TOTE £3.20: £1.40 £1.90 (£7.20) OWNER Atlantic Racing Ltd (MIDDLEHAM) BRED Hamwood Stud

**Atlantic Desire (IRE)**, all the fitter for her recent run, forged clear in the straight to win this weak race. (4/1)

**Tommy Tortoise**, an attractive, round-bodied colt with plenty of strength and substance, looked as though this run would do him good. Staying is obviously his game and improvement can be expected on a more galloping track. (6/1: 4/1-7/1)

**3499 High Extreme (IRE)** was taking another step up in distance, but that still could not stop him looking one-paced. (13/8)

**Waterville Boy (IRE)**, collared for second early in the straight, held on grimly until tiring below the distance. (10/1: op 6/1)

**Slightly Oliver (IRE)** (12/1: 6/1-14/1)

### 4350 STAFF INGHAM NURSERY H'CAP (2-Y.O) (Class D)
2-45 (2-45) **6f** £3,355.00 (£1,015.00: £495.00: £235.00) Stalls: High GOING minus 0.13 sec per fur (G)

| | | | | SP | RR | SF |
|---|---|---|---|---|---|---|
| 3464* | **Balladoole Bajan (75)** (MJohnston) **2-8-10** JWeaver(6) (rdn over 2f out: hdwy over 1f out: led ins fnl f: drvn out) | — | 1 | 11/4$^{1}$ | 82 | 41 |
| 4195$^{6}$ | **Mantles Prince (80)** (GLewis) **2-9-1** RHughes(2) (chsd ldrs: rdn over 4f out: nt clr run over 2f out: swtchd rt: r.o ins fnl f) | ½ | 2 | 6/1$^{3}$ | 86 | 45 |
| 4195$^{2}$ | **Petite Danseuse (78)** (SDow) **2-8-8**(5) ADaly(3) (hld up: led over 1f out tl ins fnl f: unable qckn) | 1½ | 3 | 11/4$^{1}$ | 80 | 39 |
| 4230* | **Clara Bliss (IRE) (78)** (BJMeehan) **2-8-13** 6x TQuinn(4) (chsd ldr: led over 2f out tl over 1f out: one pce) | 1 | 4 | 11/2$^{2}$ | 77 | 36 |
| 3975$^{5}$ | **Chingachgook (64)** (PWHarris) **2-7-13** FNorton(5) (bhd whn stumbled over 4f out) | 6 | 5 | 11/2$^{2}$ | 47 | 6 |
| 4182$^{10}$ | **Eaton Park (IRE) (67)** (RAkehurst) **2-8-2** SSanders(1) (lw: led over 3f: wknd over 1f out) | 2½ | 6 | 25/1 | 43 | 2 |
| 2879$^{8}$ | **Class Distinction (IRE) (86)** (RHannon) **2-9-7** RPerham(7) (lw: spd over 2f) | 4 | 7 | 9/1 | 52 | 11 |
| | | | | (SP 112.2%) | | **7 Rn** |

**1m 10.83** (2.83) CSF £17.69 TOTE £3.00: £2.00 £2.40 (£16.60) OWNER Mr R. H. A. Smith (MIDDLEHAM) BRED Normanby Stud Ltd

**3464* Balladoole Bajan** appreciated the extra furlong and came with a good run to lead inside the final furlong. (11/4)

**4195 Mantles Prince** found it all happening too fast on this tricky course, but did run on inside the final furlong. (6/1)

**4195 Petite Danseuse** failed to confirm Doncaster form with the runner-up on 4lb worse terms. (11/4)

**4230* Clara Bliss (IRE)**, successful in a Sandown claimer last week, had a tougher task here. (11/2)

**1046 Eaton Park (IRE)** continues to go the wrong way since finishing second at Lingfield on his debut back in May. (25/1)

### 4351 STANLEY WOOTTON CONDITIONS STKS (3-Y.O+) (Class C)
3-20 (3-20) **1m 2f 18y** £4,881.60 (£1,709.60: £837.30: £361.50) Stalls: Low GOING minus 0.13 sec per fur (G)

| | | | | SP | RR | SF |
|---|---|---|---|---|---|---|
| 3596$^{3}$ | **Magellan (USA) (111)** (CEBrittain) **3-8-8** TQuinn(3) (mde all: clr over 3f out: rdn over 2f out: r.o wl) | — | 1 | 8/11$^{1}$ | 117 | 52 |
| 3992$^{3}$ | **Double Leaf (110)** (MRStoute) **3-8-8** RCochrane(4) (lw: hld up: chsd wnr over 2f out: rdn over 1f out: nt r.o) | 2 | 2 | 6/4$^{2}$ | 114 | 49 |
| 3788* | **Province** (GLewis) **3-8-12** RHughes(1) (lw: chsd wnr over 7f) | 19 | 3 | 7/1$^{3}$ | 88 | 23 |
| 4121$^{9}$ | **Easy Choice (USA) (50)** (PMitchell) **4-9-0** AClark(2) (lw: hdwy over 5f out: wknd over 3f out: t.o) | dist | 4 | 100/1 | — | — |
| | | | | (SP 111.4%) | | **4 Rn** |

**2m 8.05** (3.65) CSF £2.21 TOTE £1.90 (£1.40) OWNER Mr Mohamed Obaida (NEWMARKET) BRED Gainsborough Farm Inc

WEIGHT FOR AGE 3yo-6lb

**3596 Magellan (USA)**, hugging the rail rounding Tattenham Corner, soon forged clear and proved far more willing than the runner-up to register his first victory in this country. (8/11)

**3992 Double Leaf**, held up, came down the centre of the track in the straight. His jockey was very keen not to let him down until the last possible minute and, when he did below the distance, the colt put his head up and failed to put his best foot forward. (6/4: op Evens)

**3788* Province** was taking a step up in class. (7/1)

### 4352 RON SMYTH RATED STKS H'CAP (0-100) (3-Y.O+) (Class B)
3-50 (3-51) **1m 114y** £7,592.96 (£2,836.64: £1,383.32: £590.60: £260.30: £128.18) Stalls: Low GOING minus 0.13 sec per fur (G)

| | | | | SP | RR | SF |
|---|---|---|---|---|---|---|
| 4196* | **Star of Zilzal (USA) (100)** (MRStoute) **4-9-7** AClark(1) (mde virtually all: hung rt fnl 3f: rdn out) | — | 1 | 100/30$^{1}$ | 109 | 63 |
| 4194$^{11}$ | **Nagnagnag (IRE) (94)** (SDow) **4-9-1** RHughes(4) (rdn over 3f out: hdwy over 1f out: r.o wl) | 1 | 2 | 4/1$^{2}$ | 101 | 55 |
| 4194$^{4}$ | **April The Eighth (90)** (BWHills) **3-8-6** RCochrane(2) (a.p: nt clr run over 2f out: r.o) | nk | 3 | 6/1$^{3}$ | 97 | 46 |
| 4185$^{7}$ | **Civil Liberty (88)** (GLewis) **3-8-4** TQuinn(6) (hrd rdn & hdwy over 2f out: unable qckn ins fnl f) | hd | 4 | 8/1 | 94 | 43 |
| 4184$^{2}$ | **Night Wink (USA) (86)** (GLMoore) **4-8-0**(7) JDennis(11) (lw: rdn over 2f out: hdwy over 1f out: one pce ins fnl f) | ½ | 5 | 12/1 | 91 | 45 |
| 3923$^{9}$ | **Kamari (USA) (88)** (ACStewart) **3-8-4** RHills(5) (lw: chsd wnr: rdn over 2f out: one pce) | s.h | 6 | 11/1 | 93 | 42 |
| 4196$^{5}$ | **My Best Valentine (93)** (JWhite) **6-9-0** SSanders(10) (lw: hdwy over 2f out: hrd rdn over 1f out: wknd ins fnl f) | 1¾ | 7 | 12/1 | 95 | 49 |
| 4231$^{3}$ | **Lucky Archer (88)** (CEBrittain) **3-7-13**(5)ow2 ADaly(8) (lw: prom 7f) | 1¼ | 8 | 14/1 | 88 | 35 |
| 3148$^{3}$ | **Blue Zulu (IRE) (86)** (JRFanshawe) **4-8-7** NDay(9) (prom 5f) | 5 | 9 | 10/1 | 76 | 30 |

4054[3] **Herodian (USA) (90)** (JHMGosden) **3-8-6b** GHind(3) (bhd fnl 2f) ....15 **10** 9/1 52 1
(SP 117.9%) **10 Rn**

**1m 45.09** (3.09) CSF £16.43 CT £68.78 TOTE £3.60: £2.00 £1.80 £2.80 (£5.80) Trio £10.60 OWNER Mr Mana Al Maktoum (NEWMARKET) BRED Gainsborough Farm Inc
LONG HANDICAP Night Wink (USA) 8-2 Blue Zulu (IRE) 8-5 Lucky Archer 8-0
WEIGHT FOR AGE 3yo-5lb

**4196* Star of Zilzal (USA)** again adopted the front-running tactics that were so successful at Goodwood last time out and, despite hanging right into the centre of the track in the straight, just managed to hold off his challengers. (100/30)
**3709 Nagnagnag (IRE)**, who ran no race at all last time, goes well around here and bounced back to form, running on nicely in the last furlong and a half. (4/1)
**4194 April The Eighth**, although slightly interfered with over a quarter of a mile from home, stuck on nicely in the last furlong and a half. (6/1: 9/2-7/1)
**3658 Civil Liberty** was without the blinkers this time. (8/1)
**4184 Night Wink (USA)** was 8lb higher for his recent narrow defeat at Goodwood. (12/1)
**3923 Kamari (USA)**, tailed off last time, has been done no favours by the Handicapper. (11/1: 8/1-12/1)
**4196 My Best Valentine** found this trip too far. (12/1)

## 4353 EPSOM AND WALTON DOWNS MAIDEN STKS (3-Y.O) (Class D)

4-20 (4-27) **1m 4f 10y** £3,647.50 (£1,105.00: £540.00: £257.50) Stalls: Low GOING minus 0.13 sec per fur (G)

| | | | | SP | RR | SF |
|---|---|---|---|---|---|---|
| 3999[2] | **Mount Pleasant (IRE) (86)** (PFICole) **3-9-0** TQuinn(2) (lw: a.p: led 5f out: rdn over 2f out: clr over 1f out: r.o wl) | — | **1** | 10/11[1] | 88 | 65 |
| 1773[11] | **Matthias Mystique (50)** (MissBSanders) **3-8-9** SSanders(6) (rdn over 3f out: hdwy over 1f out: r.o) | 6 | **2** | 66/1 | 75 | 52 |
| 4110[6] | **Laazim Afooz** (RTPhillips) **3-9-0** RHughes(9) (hld up: rdn over 4f out: unable qckn) | ½ | **3** | 14/1 | 79 | 56 |
| 3041[2] | **Serenus (USA) (80)** (LordHuntingdon) **3-9-0** JWeaver(8) (lw: led over 1f: rdn over 3f out: wknd over 1f out) | 1 | **4** | 15/8[2] | 78 | 55 |
| 4124[8] | **Petros Pride (55)** (MJBolton) **3-8-9** RCochrane(4) (bhd fnl 5f) | 19 | **5** | 66/1 | 48 | 25 |
| 3155[6] | **Gumair (USA) (72)** (RHannon) **3-9-0** RPerham(3) (lw: led over 10f out to 5f out: sn wknd) | ½ | **6** | 6/1[3] | 52 | 29 |
| 3505[14] | **Sliparis (40)** (KOCunningham-Brown) **3-8-9** SWhitworth(7) (a bhd: t.o fnl 8f) | dist | **7** | 66/1 | — | — |
| *4235[5]* | ***Unassailable*** (CEBrittain) **3-8-9** AClark(1) (Withdrawn not under Starter's orders: ref to ent stalls) | | **W** | 20/1 | — | — |

(SP 117.4%) **7 Rn**

**2m 38.48** (3.48) CSF £33.06 TOTE £1.80: £1.30 £8.60 (£25.20) Trio £19.80 OWNER H R H Prince Fahd Salman (WHATCOMBE) BRED Newgate Stud Co

**3999 Mount Pleasant (IRE)**, back over a more suitable trip, violently flashed his tail every time he was hit in the straight, although he still forged clear in the final quarter-mile for a clear-cut success. (10/11)
**Matthias Mystique**, looking fit for this first run in nearly four months, had shown nothing previously. Not too much should be read into this as it was a very poor contest. (66/1)
**Laazim Afooz** looks extremely one-paced and one should certainly not get excited about this performance. (14/1: 10/1-16/1)
**3041 Serenus (USA)** lacks pace, and this trip appeared to be stretching his stamina to the limit. (15/8)

## 4354 LADBROKE H'CAP (0-75) (3-Y.O+) (Class D)

4-50 (4-54) **1m 114y** £4,474.50 (£1,356.00: £663.00: £316.50) Stalls: Low GOING minus 0.13 sec per fur (G)

| | | | | SP | RR | SF |
|---|---|---|---|---|---|---|
| 4117[5] | **Maid For Baileys (IRE) (75)** (MJohnston) **3-9-10** JWeaver(12) (a.p: led over 2f out: hrd rdn: r.o wl) | — | **1** | 13/2[3] | 86 | 64 |
| 4212[2] | **Don't Get Caught (IRE) (52)** (JLHarris) **4-8-6** RCochrane(9) (lw: rdn & hdwy over 2f out: r.o wl ins fnl f) | ¾ | **2** | 5/2[1] | 62 | 45 |
| 3978* | **Mr Nevermind (IRE) (62)** (GLMoore) **6-9-2** SWhitworth(1) (hld up: rdn over 2f out: ev ch ins fnl f: unable qckn) | ½ | **3** | 10/1 | 71 | 54 |
| 3944[5] | **Absolute Utopia (USA) (66)** (NEBerry) **3-9-1** RPerham(5) (lw: rdn over 2f out: hdwy over 1f out: r.o) | 1 | **4** | 25/1 | 73 | 51 |
| 3856[11] | **North Reef (IRE) (71)** (SirMarkPrescott) **5-9-11** GDuffield(4) (w ldr 5f: hrd rdn over 2f out: one pce) | ¾ | **5** | 10/1 | 76 | 59 |
| 3967[2] | **Balance of Power (72)** (RAkehurst) **4-9-12** TQuinn(10) (rdn & hdwy over 2f out: wknd 1f out) | 3 | **6** | 7/2[2] | 72 | 55 |
| 4129[6] | **Helios (64)** (NJHWalker) **8-9-4** RHughes(8) (lw: a.p: hrd rdn over 2f out: wknd over 1f out) | 1 | **7** | 14/1 | 62 | 45 |
| 4109[15] | **Sejaal (IRE) (68)** (RAkehurst) **4-9-8** SSanders(7) (hdwy over 4f out: wknd 3f out) | 2½ | **8** | 20/1 | 61 | 44 |
| 4232* | **Superior Force (63)** (MissBSanders) **3-8-9**(3) 5x AWhelan(3) (lw: prom 3f) | ¾ | **9** | 7/1 | 55 | 33 |
| 3765[7] | **Bernard Seven (IRE) (74)** (CEBrittain) **4-10-0b** AClark(2) (led: styd far side st: rdn 3f out: hdd over 2f out: wknd fnl f) | 2½ | **10** | 25/1 | 61 | 44 |
| *3953[13]* | **Dancing Lawyer (66)** (BJMeehan) **5-9-6** JReid(6) (bhd fnl 3f) | 2 | **11** | 16/1 | 49 | 32 |
| 3315[4] | **Typhoon Lad (72)** (SDow) **3-9-2**(5) ADaly(11) (lw: styd far side st: a bhd) | 3 | **12** | 20/1 | 50 | 28 |

(SP 124.6%) **12 Rn**

**1m 45.36** (3.36) CSF £23.05 CT £154.00 TOTE £6.60: £1.80 £1.10 £2.60 (£8.80) Trio £29.60 OWNER G R Bailey Ltd (Baileys Horse Feeds) (MIDDLEHAM) BRED Mrs C. Van C. Anthony
WEIGHT FOR AGE 3yo-5lb

**4117 Maid For Baileys (IRE)** at last managed to lose her maiden tag, and grimly responded to pressure to hold on. (13/2)
**4212 Don't Get Caught (IRE)** had no excuses this time and was never going to overhaul the winner in time. (5/2)
**3978* Mr Nevermind (IRE)**, more at home in claimers, had more on his plate here but acquitted himself really well. (10/1)
**3944 Absolute Utopia (USA)** ran his best race to date as he stayed on in the last furlong and a half. (25/1)
**3856 North Reef (IRE)** failed to cope with the extremely testing conditions last time. (10/1)
**3967 Balance of Power** is now 9lb higher than when last successful and that surely proved to be his undoing. (7/2)

T/Plpt: £95.30 (165.58 Tckts). T/Qdpt: £10.50 (111.31 Tckts). AK

# 4203-NOTTINGHAM (L-H) (Good to firm, Firm patches)
## Tuesday September 24th

WEATHER: overcast WIND: almost nil

## 4355 BOLLINGER CHAMPAGNE SERIES GENTLEMENS' H'CAP (0-70) (3-Y.O+) (Class F)

2-00 (2-02) **1m 1f 213y** £3,150.00 (£875.00: £420.00) Stalls: Low GOING minus 0.32 sec per fur (GF)

| | | | | SP | RR | SF |
|---|---|---|---|---|---|---|
| 4068[2] | **Fern's Governor (51)** (WJMusson) **4-10-12** MrTMcCarthy(4) (b: hld up: gd hdwy 3f out: led on bit over 2f out: sn clr: v.easily) | — | **1** | 100/30[1] | 62+ | 51 |

4236[7] **Father Dan (IRE) (56)** (MissGayKelleway) **7-10-13**(4) MrNMoran(2) (b: hld up: hdwy over 2f out: hrd rdn: r.o: no ch w wnr)....1¼ **2** 8/1 65 54
4102[5] **Diamond Crown (IRE) (45)** (MartynWane) **5-10-2**(4) MrRDGreen(9) (swtg: hld up & bhd: rdn & hdwy fnl 2f: r.o)....2½ **3** 20/1 50 39
3980[5] **Kevasingo (52)** (BWHills) **4-10-9**(4) MrCBHills(14) (a.p: one pce fnl 2f)....½ **4** 14/1 56 45
3970[3] **Bold Top (42)** (BSRothwell) **4-10-3b** MrMHNaughton(8) (a.p: rdn & ev ch over 2f out: one pce)....hd **5** 13/2[3] 46 35
3584[11] **Red Tie Affair (USA) (53)** (MBell) **3-10-8** MrRWakley(6) (b.nr fore: lw: a.p: no hdwy fnl 2f)....1¼ **6** 20/1 55 38
3970[5] **Hi Rock (42)** (JNorton) **4-10-3** MrPScott(1) (nvr nrr)....4 **7** 16/1 38 27
*4089*[4] **Montone (IRE) (63)** (JRJenkins) **6-11-6v**(4) DrMMannish(15) (led over 7f: wknd over 1f out)....nk **8** 12/1 58 47
4202[9] **Delight of Dawn (64)** (RMStronge) **4-11-7**(4) MrJDewhurst(12) (b: prom 8f)....1 **9** 20/1 58 47
4125[12] **Ethbaat (USA) (67)** (MJHeaton-Ellis) **5-11-10**(4) MrFBrennan(3) (lw: hdwy over 3f out: wknd 2f out)....½ **10** 16/1 60 49
3575[3] **Never Time (IRE) (42)** (MrsVAAconley) **4-9-13**(4) MrGMarkham(16) (nvr bttr than mid div)....½ **11** 20/1 34 23
4209[6] **Lila Pedigo (IRE) (60)** (MissJFCraze) **3-10-11**(4) MrWWenyon(11) (s.i.s: a bhd)....hd **12** 14/1 52 35
3970[9] **Hunza Story (45)** (NPLittmoden) **4-10-2**(4)ow13 MrDVerco(7) (b.hind: prom 7f)....2½ **13** 33/1 33 9
3786[10] **Mezzoramio (50)** (KAMorgan) **4-10-11v** MrRThornton(10) (prom: hrd rdn & wknd over 3f out)....nk **14** 12/1 37 26
*3951*[10] **Peutetre (55)** (FJordan) **4-11-2** MrGShenkin(5) (prom tl rdn & wknd over 3f out: t.o)....10 **15** 33/1 26 15
4226[5] **Mazilla (56)** (AStreeter) **4-10-13**(4) MrPClinton(13) (hld up: a bhd: t.o)....1½ **16** 4/1[2] 25 14
(SP 132.9%) **16 Rn**

**2m 8.1** (5.60) CSF £31.18 CT £450.75 TOTE £4.20: £1.60 £2.40 £2.00 £2.90 (£14.40) Trio £94.90 OWNER Fern Components Ltd (NEWMARKET) BRED E. A. Badger
WEIGHT FOR AGE 3yo-6lb
**OFFICIAL EXPLANATION Mazilla: the trainer reported that the filly did not take as strong a hold as usual and found nothing when asked to quicken.**
**4068 Fern's Governor**, up 5lb, did not like the rain-softened ground when disappointing at Goodwood two outings ago, and the winning margin gave no reflection of her superiority. (100/30)
**152 Father Dan (IRE)**, with the winner easing right down, is greatly flattered by the margin of defeat. (8/1: op 5/1)
**4102 Diamond Crown (IRE)**, dropped 2lb, is another greatly flattered by his proximity to the easy winner. (20/1)
**3980 Kevasingo**, down 2lb, has never won beyond a mile but, although unable to go with the winner, seemed to stay well enough. (14/1)
**3970 Bold Top** was 5lb higher than when runner-up in a similar event at Pontefract last month. (13/2)
**3000 Red Tie Affair (USA)** was 4lb lower than when third over this trip at Sandown in July. (20/1)
**3443* Mezzoramio** (12/1: op 7/1)

## 4356 ASHTON CORRUGATED MIDLANDS LIMITED STKS (0-60) (3-Y.O+) (Class F)
2-30 (2-36) **6f 15y** £3,594.80 (£1,002.80: £484.40) Stalls: High GOING minus 0.03 sec per fur (G)

SP RR SF
3767[7] **Shining Cloud (60)** (MBell) **3-8-8** MFenton(24) (mde all stands' side: clr over 1f out: r.o wl)....— **1** 7/1[2] 71 51
4130[6] **Maraschino (34)** (BJMeehan) **3-8-8** MTebbutt(4) (prom far side: r.o one pce fnl f)....6 **2** 33/1 55 35
4256[18] **Ivory's Grab Hire (58)** (KTIvory) **3-8-9b**(5) MartinDwyer(20) (b: swtg: hdwy stands' side over 1f out: nt trble wnr)....s.h **3** 14/1 61 41
4128* **Speedy Classic (USA) (59)** (MJHeaton-Ellis) **7-9-5** SDrowne(7) (hld up far side: hdwy 2f out: one pce fnl f)....1 **4** 7/1[2] 61 43
4053[17] **Mansab (USA) (60)** (PGMurphy) **3-8-11** JFEgan(23) (prom stands' side: no hdwy fnl 2f)....nk **5** 16/1 55 35
4130[16] **Nineacres (48)** (NMBabbage) **5-8-13v** JQuinn(5) (lw: hdwy over 1f out: nvr nrr)....½ **6** 25/1 53 35
4259[10] **Waders Dream (IRE) (55)** (PatMitchell) **7-9-2v** KDarley(22) (hdwy over 1f out: r.o)....1 **7** 16/1 54 36
4075[4] **Gymcrak Gem (IRE) (60)** (GHolmes) **3-8-8b** KFallon(6) (b.hind: lw: a.p: led far side over 3f out tl wknd over 1f out)....½ **8** 13/2[1] 46 26
4215[6] **Night Harmony (IRE) (56)** (RHannon) **3-8-11** DaneO'Neill(1) (b: led far side over 2f: wknd over 1f out)....½ **9** 9/1[3] 48 28
4215[8] **Petraco (IRE) (60)** (NASmith) **8-8-9**(7) JBramhill(8) (nvr nr to chal)....hd **10** 16/1 51 33
4259[2] **Merrie le Bow (49)** (PatMitchell) **4-8-11**(5) AmandaSanders(11) (lw: spd centre over 4f)....nk **11** 9/1[3] 50 32
3812[7] **Oh Susannah (35)** (JAHarris) **5-8-10** TSprake(2) (n.d)....2 **12** 33/1 39 21
4246[19] **Ramsey Hope (60)** (CWFairhurst) **3-8-11** DeanMcKeown(18) (lw: n.d)....¾ **13** 25/1 40 20
2518[7] **Plum First (59)** (DWChapman) **6-8-13** ACulhane(21) (a bhd)....hd **14** 10/1 40 22
4205[3] **Superbit (53)** (BAMcMahon) **4-9-2** JFortune(10) (lw: prom far side 4f)....nk **15** 10/1 42 24
4088[9] **Rockcracker (IRE) (60)** (GGMargarson) **4-9-5b** GCarter(3) (outpcd)....½ **16** 20/1 43 25
3460[7] **Flashy's Son (58)** (FMurphy) **8-8-13** JTate(19) (b: a bhd)....hd **17** 12/1 37 19
3993[12] **Nellie North (58)** (GMMcCourt) **3-8-8v** CRutter(12) (s.i.s: sn rcvrd: wknd over 2f out)....1¼ **18** 10/1 31 11
2964[8] **Hickleton Miss (47)** (MrsVAAconley) **3-8-8** NCarlisle(9) (a bhd)....½ **19** 33/1 30 10
3977[13] **Heights of Love (37)** (JWHills) **3-8-5**(3) MHenry(15) (spd stands' side over 3f)....1¾ **20** 50/1 25 5
4323[13] **Madam Zando (46)** (JBalding) **3-8-1**(7) JEdmunds(16) (a bhd)....s.h **21** 33/1 25 5
3937[8] **Mullagh Hill Lad (IRE) (44)** (BAMcMahon) **3-8-6**(5) LNewton(14) (s.i.s: a bhd)....½ **22** 33/1 26 6
4202[10] **Reem Fever (IRE) (60)** (DWPArbuthnot) **3-8-8** RPrice(13) (a bhd)....hd **23** 20/1 23 3
*3832*[W] ***Animation (37)*** (KMcAuliffe) **3-8-8** JCarroll(17) (Withdrawn not under Starter's orders: bolted bef s).... **W** 50/1 — —
(SP 153.5%) **23 Rn**

**1m 13.2** (2.70) CSF £223.98 TOTE £7.50: £2.00 £30.10 £4.00 (£338.20) Trio Not won; £847.60 to Goodwood 25/9/96 OWNER Mrs Anne Yearley (NEWMARKET) BRED Mrs A. Yearley
WEIGHT FOR AGE 3yo-2lb
**Shining Cloud** has needed time to recover from a bad case of the virus in the spring. Well in at the weights, she landed a touch in fine style on her first run for her new stable. (7/1)
**4130 Maraschino** would have been much better off with the winner in a handicap and it was a case of finishing best of the rest. (33/1)
**4128 Ivory's Grab Hire** seems to find this trip on the short side. (14/1)
**4128* Speedy Classic (USA)** is probably better suited to seven these days. (7/1)
**755 Mansab (USA)**, a $400,000 yearling, was bought for 13,500 guineas out of John Dunlop's yard at Newmarket July Sales, and gave the first indication his gelding operation may have worked. (16/1)
**Nineacres** ran much better than when slowly away at Chepstow last time, having seemed to get a reasonable start for a change. (25/1)
**4215 Night Harmony (IRE)** (9/1: op 6/1)

## 4357 DHL INTERNATIONAL MAIDEN STKS (2-Y.O F) (Class D)
3-05 (3-05) **6f 15y** £3,987.55 (£1,194.40: £573.70: £263.35) Stalls: High GOING minus 0.03 sec per fur (G)

SP RR SF
**Much Commended** (GWragg) **2-8-11** MHills(2) (w'like: leggy: hld up: hdwy 2f out: led ins fnl f: pushed out) — **1** 9/4[2] 83+ 29

| | | | SP | RR | SF |
|---|---|---|---|---|---|
| | **Dragonada (USA)** (HRACecil) **2-8-11** WRyan(8) (unf: scope: led tl ins fnl f) ....¾ | **2** | 10/11[1] | 81+ | 27 |
| | **Made Bold** (HCandy) **2-8-11** CRutter(9) (w'like: scope: bit bkwd: a.p: r.o ins fnl f) ....2½ | **3** | 14/1 | 74 | 20 |
| 4123[3] | **Nopalea (80)** (CEBrittain) **2-8-11** MRoberts(4) (plld hrd: a.p: one pce fnl 2f) ....3 | **4** | 4/1[3] | 67 | 13 |
| | **Tycoon Girl (IRE)** (BJMeehan) **2-8-11** MTebbutt(3) (lt-f: unf: dwlt: nvr nrr) ....1¼ | **5** | 25/1 | 63 | 9 |
| 4043[5] | **Alvilde** (JRFanshawe) **2-8-11** DHarrison(6) (prom: swtchd lft 2f out: wknd over 1f out) ....s.h | **6** | 10/1 | 63 | 9 |
| 4241[7] | **Missfortuna** (SirMarkPrescott) **2-8-11** CNutter(7) (bit bkwd: s.s: rdn over 3f out: a bhd) ....1 | **7** | 20/1 | 61 | 7 |
| 2245[8] | **Dayrella** (WRMuir) **2-8-11** KFallon(5) (w ldr tl rdn & wknd wl over 1f out) ....9 | **8** | 50/1 | 37 | — |
| 4105[10] | **Well Done** (MBell) **2-8-11** MFenton(1) (a bhd: t.o) ....6 | **9** | 50/1 | 21 | — |

(SP 131.4%) **9 Rn**

**1m 15.0** (4.50) CSF £5.27 TOTE £3.30: £1.20 £1.20 £3.90 (£2.30) Trio £9.30 OWNER Mr A. E. Oppenheimer (NEWMARKET) BRED Hascombe and Valiant Studs

**Much Commended**, a sister to Prize Giving, was subsequently described as a nice filly who will improve, and may go for the valuable Redcar Trophy. (9/4)

**Dragonada (USA)**, a sister to three winners including Galtres Stakes winner Professional Girl, is bred to require further and will not have to improve much to win a race. (10/11: Evens-4/5)

**Made Bold**, a half-sister to Abso and Simply Sooty, only cost 6,200 guineas as a yearling, but shaped well without being unduly knocked about. (14/1: 10/1-25/1)

**4123 Nopalea** did not help her chances by refusing to settle. (4/1: 3/1-5/1)

**Tycoon Girl (IRE)**, a 17,000 guinea yearling, should be better for the experience. (25/1)

**4043 Alvilde** should have done better over this extra furlong and may have found the ground too lively. (10/1: op 5/1)

## 4358 MANN EGERTON LEVY BOARD H'CAP (0-70) (3-Y.O) (Class E)

3-35 (3-35) **2m 9y** £3,343.20 (£999.60: £478.80: £218.40) Stalls: High GOING minus 0.32 sec per fur (GF)

| | | | SP | RR | SF |
|---|---|---|---|---|---|
| 4086[4] | **Go With The Wind (60)** (MBell) **3-9-0** MFenton(3) (hld up: stdy hdwy on ins over 3f out: led on bit 1f out: shkn up: sn clr) ....— | **1** | 5/1 | 73 | 23 |
| 3667[4] | **Influence Pedler (62)** (CEBrittain) **3-9-2** MRoberts(2) (led: rdn over 2f out: hdd 1f out: no ch w wnr) ....6 | **2** | 6/4[1] | 69 | 19 |
| 3965[3] | **Duncombe Hall (42)** (CACyzer) **3-7-10** JQuinn(1) (a.p: wnt 2nd over 4f out: hrd rdn & one pce fnl 2f) ....1¼ | **3** | 9/2[3] | 48 | — |
| 3459[3] | **Dancing Cavalier (62)** (RHollinshead) **3-8-13**(3) FLynch(4) (hld up: rdn 5f out: hdwy over 3f out: wknd over 2f out) ....6 | **4** | 9/4[2] | 62 | 12 |
| | **Topaglow (IRE) (45)** (PTDalton) **3-7-13** LCharnock(6) (bit bkwd: hld up & plld hrd: hdwy over 3f out: wknd over 2f out) ....1½ | **5** | 50/1 | 43 | — |
| 3028a[8] | **Ewar Bold (67)** (KOCunningham-Brown) **3-9-7** KDarley(5) (chsd ldr tl rdn over 4f out: wknd over 3f out: t.o) .21 | **6** | 11/1 | 44 | — |

(SP 115.9%) **6 Rn**

**3m 33.2** (10.20) CSF £13.00 TOTE £5.80: £3.30 £1.40 (£4.20) OWNER Mrs B. Long (NEWMARKET) BRED B. Long

LONG HANDICAP Duncombe Hall 7-7

**4086 Go With The Wind**, although not one to rely on, does stay well and was suited by being covered up in a small field. (5/1)

**3667 Influence Pedler**, dropped 5lb, found the winner galloping all over him in the final quarter-mile. (6/4: Evens-7/4)

**3965 Duncombe Hall**, 3lb wrong at the weights, had finished third in a seller last time. (9/2)

**3459 Dancing Cavalier**, with both his wins having come at Southwell, probably found this ground too fast. (9/4)

**Topaglow (IRE)** ran too freely, but should at least come on for the outing. (50/1)

## 4359 MSAS CARGO INTERNATIONAL MAIDEN STKS (2-Y.O F) (Class D)

4-05 (4-07) **1m 54y** £3,804.25 (£1,138.00: £545.50: £249.25) Stalls: Low GOING minus 0.32 sec per fur (GF)

| | | | SP | RR | SF |
|---|---|---|---|---|---|
| 4133[10] | **Attitre (FR)** (CEBrittain) **2-8-11** MRoberts(1) (mde all: qcknd 2f out: sn clr: r.o wl) ....— | **1** | 6/1[3] | 74 | 31 |
| | **Nightlark (IRE)** (DRLoder) **2-8-11** WRSwinburn(2) (lt-f: unf: a.p: chsd wnr 3f out: sn rdn: unable qckn) ....1½ | **2** | 7/2[2] | 71 | 28 |
| 4127[7] | **Sellette (IRE)** (DHaydnJones) **2-8-11** KFallon(4) (bhd: rdn & hdwy over 1f out: r.o) ....3 | **3** | 10/1 | 65 | 22 |
| 3988[3] | **Lady of The Lake** (JLDunlop) **2-8-11** KDarley(7) (hld up: rdn & n.m.r 2f out: one pce) ....1¼ | **4** | 4/6[1] | 63 | 20 |
| | **Seattle Swing** (JHMGosden) **2-8-11** JCarroll(10) (b.hind: unf: scope: s.i.s: hld up: rdn & no hdwy fnl 2f) ....s.h | **5** | 10/1 | 63 | 20 |
| 4211[6] | **Indian Rapture** (RHannon) **2-8-11** DaneO'Neill(3) (s.i.s: sn rcvrd: rdn & wknd over 2f out) ....hd | **6** | 14/1 | 63 | 20 |
| 3663[8] | **Control Freak** (AGFoster) **2-8-8**(3) MHenry(6) (chsd wnr over 5f: wknd qckly) ....8 | **7** | 100/1 | 47 | 4 |
| | **Miss Kalaglow** (CFWall) **2-8-11** AMcGlone(8) (leggy: unf: plld hrd early: bhd fnl 3f) ....5 | **8** | 25/1 | 37 | — |
| | **Rose Sharp** (CSmith) **2-8-11** JFortune(9) (w'like: bit bkwd: s.s: a bhd: t.o) ....16 | **9** | 66/1 | 6 | — |

(SP 127.7%) **9 Rn**

**1m 45.2** (3.90) CSF £28.57 TOTE £8.50: £1.70 £1.50 £2.60 (£13.30) Trio £126.70 OWNER Mr R. A. Pledger (NEWMARKET) BRED Gainsborough Stud Management Ltd

**Attitre (FR)**, a half-sister to Please Suzanne, had twice been a 14/1 chance when withdrawn prior to being highly tried on her debut in the May Hill at Doncaster. (6/1)

**Nightlark (IRE)**, a half-sister to Overbury and Overruled, not surprisingly seemed to get the mile well enough. (7/2: 2/1-4/1)

**4127 Sellette (IRE)** only got going late in the day but seems to be progressing along the right lines. (10/1: op 6/1)

**3988 Lady of The Lake** may not be seen at her best until next year. (4/6: op Evens)

**Seattle Swing** is a half-sister to a couple of winners in the States. (10/1: op 7/2)

**3820 Indian Rapture** has now managed to finish sixth on all three of her starts. (14/1: 10/1-16/1)

## 4360 DYNASTY INTERNATIONAL MAIDEN STKS (3-Y.O+) (Class D)

4-35 (4-37) **1m 54y** £4,391.10 (£1,315.80: £632.40: £290.70) Stalls: Low GOING minus 0.32 sec per fur (GF)

| | | | SP | RR | SF |
|---|---|---|---|---|---|
| 550[8] | **Dawawin (USA)** (EALDunlop) **3-8-9** MHills(8) (hld up: edgd lft & hdwy 3f out: edgd lft wl over 1f out: sn led: r.o wl) ....— | **1** | 11/2[3] | 78 | 43 |
| 732[13] | **Kutman (USA)** (MRStoute) **3-9-0** WRSwinburn(7) (bit bkwd: hld up: hdwy over 1f out: r.o ins fnl f) ....1¾ | **2** | 12/1 | 80 | 45 |
| 613[2] | **Lost Lagoon (USA)** (HRACecil) **4-9-4** WRyan(5) (bit bkwd: plld hrd: a.p: led wl over 1f out: sn hdd: one pce) 1 | **3** | 4/6[1] | 78 | 47 |
| 544[6] | **Family Man** (JRFanshawe) **3-9-0** DHarrison(6) (bit bkwd: a.p: one pce fnl 2f) ....1¼ | **4** | 9/1 | 75 | 40 |
| 3591[6] | **Holloway Melody (42)** (BAMcMahon) **3-8-9** JFortune(4) (a.p: rdn & no hdwy fnl 2f) ....¾ | **5** | 50/1 | 69 | 34 |
| | **Sufuf** (DMorley) **3-8-9** GCarter(1) (lt-f: unf: s.s: sn rcvrd: hdwy 3f out: one pce fnl 2f) ....nk | **6** | 25/1 | 68 | 33 |
| 2437[7] | **Fresh Fruit Daily (70)** (PAKelleway) **4-8-10**(3) DWright(10) (bit bkwd: led: hrd rdn & hdd wl over 1f out: wknd fnl f) ....1½ | **7** | 33/1 | 65 | 34 |
| 3832[5] | **Intimation** (JARToller) **3-8-9** KFallon(16) (rdn over 3f out: no hdwy) ....2 | **8** | 16/1 | 61 | 26 |
| | **Saxon Bay** (KOCunningham-Brown) **4-9-4** KDarley(13) (bkwd: s.s: a bhd) ....9 | **9** | 50/1 | 49 | 18 |

| | | | | SP | RR | SF |
|---|---|---|---|---|---|---|
| 4108[2] | **Regal Splendour (CAN)** (PFICole) **3-9-0** CRutter(15) (wl bhd fnl 3f) | ½ | **10** | 4/1[2] | 48 | 13 |
| | **La Thuile (24)** (TJEtherington) **4-8-13** LCharnock(11) (plld hrd: prom: edgd lft over 3f out: wknd 2f out) | 1¾ | **11** | 100/1 | 40 | 9 |
| 3776[5] | **Euphoric Illusion** (MrsSJSmith) **5-9-3**(3)ow2 OPears(14) (bit bkwd: s.s: wl bhd fnl 4f) | 2½ | **12** | 100/1 | 42 | 9 |
| 4098[15] | **Tirra-Lirra (IRE) (55)** (CEBrittain) **4-8-13** MRoberts(2) (w ldr tl wknd over 3f out) | 1¾ | **13** | 25/1 | 31 | — |
| | **Romantic Warrior** (KSBridgwater) **3-9-0** VSlattery(9) (tall: bkwd: wl bhd fnl 4f) | 5 | **14** | 100/1 | 27 | — |
| | **Western Country** (EAWheeler) **4-9-4** TSprake(12) (bkwd: plld hrd: t.o whn rn wd ent st) | dist | **15** | 100/1 | — | — |

(SP 137.5%) **15 Rn**

**1m 43.8** (2.50) CSF £72.00 TOTE £7.10: £3.60 £2.90 £1.20 (£20.00) Trio £14.50 OWNER Mr Hamdan Al Maktoum (NEWMARKET) BRED John C. Oxley

WEIGHT FOR AGE 3yo-4lb

**550 Dawawin (USA)** showed plenty of promise on her debut last back-end, but did not come to herself when being prepared as a pacemaker in the 1000 Guineas. With the patience now paying off, she is one to keep on the right side. (11/2)

**Kutman (USA)**, a half-brother to several winners in France, had not been out since making his debut at Newbury in April. He should be suited by further. (12/1: op 8/1)

**613 Lost Lagoon (USA)**, having only his third run, again did not help his cause by proving difficult to settle. (4/6: 4/5-Evens)

**544 Family Man**, yet another on the sidelines since the spring, is out of a mare who was placed at up to two miles. (9/1)

**3591 Holloway Melody** probably ran her best race to date. (50/1)

**Sufuf**, a half-sister to Karayb, was not given a hard time and improvement can be expected. (25/1)

**4108 Regal Splendour (CAN)** (4/1: op 5/2)

## 4361 HAMBLIN GRAND CASINO NURSERY H'CAP (0-75) (2-Y.O) (Class E)

5-05 (5-06) **1m 1f 213y** £3,261.30 (£974.40: £466.20: £212.10) Stalls: Low GOING minus 0.32 sec per fur (GF)

| | | | | SP | RR | SF |
|---|---|---|---|---|---|---|
| 3762[3] | **Swallow Breeze (64)** (DrJDScargill) **2-8-10** MRoberts(4) (bhd & pushed along: carried wd ent st: hdwy over 3f out: led over 1f out: edgd lft: r.o wl) | — | **1** | 7/2[2] | 65 | 12 |
| 4097* | **Chairmans Daughter (65)** (JPearce) **2-8-11** GBardwell(5) (hld up & plld hrd: hrd rdn over 3f out: hdwy over 2f out: ev ch ins fnl f: unable qckn) | 1½ | **2** | 6/1 | 64 | 11 |
| 3982[10] | **Warrlin (65)** (CWFairhurst) **2-8-11** DeanMcKeown(9) (lw: led over 3f: led over 3f out tl over 1f out: one pce) | ¾ | **3** | 14/1 | 62 | 9 |
| 4046[12] | **Chateauherault (IRE) (60)** (PCHaslam) **2-8-6** JFortune(8) (a.p: ev ch over 2f out: one pce) | 1¾ | **4** | 25/1 | 55 | 2 |
| 3581[5] | **Auction Hall (66)** (MBell) **2-8-7**(5) GFaulkner(12) (lw: hld up: bmpd ent st: hdwy 3f out: one pce fnl 2f) | 2 | **5** | 13/2 | 57 | 4 |
| 4084[10] | **River King (66)** (RHannon) **2-8-12** DaneO'Neill(3) (lw: prom: ev ch over 2f out: wknd over 1f out) | ¾ | **6** | 14/1 | 56 | 3 |
| 4097[3] | **Spondulicks (IRE) (60)** (RHannon) **2-8-6** JCarroll(2) (s.i.s: sn rcvrd: no hdwy fnl 3f) | 1¼ | **7** | 8/1 | 48 | — |
| 3964[4] | **Triple Term (75)** (JLDunlop) **2-9-7** KDarley(7) (hld up & plld hrd: hdwy over 3f out: ev ch over 2f out: wknd over 1f out) | nk | **8** | 11/4[1] | 63 | 10 |
| 4097[12] | **Foolish Flutter (IRE) (50)** (GROldroyd) **2-7-10b[1]** NCarlisle(1) (lw: s.i.s: n.d) | 3½ | **9** | 50/1 | 32 | — |
| 3931[6] | **Prairie Minstrel (USA) (70)** (RDickin) **2-9-2** MHills(10) (hld up: hdwy over 3f out: ev ch over 2f out: wknd over 1f out) | 2½ | **10** | 10/1 | 48 | — |
| 4213[3] | **Princess of Hearts (66)** (BJMeehan) **2-8-12** MTebbutt(11) (unruly stalls: hdwy over 3f out: ev ch over 2f out: wknd over 1f out) | 4 | **11** | 11/2[3] | 38 | — |
| 4097[15] | **Riva La Belle (50)** (JWharton) **2-7-10b[1]** JQuinn(6) (lw: plld hrd: sn prom: led over 6f out tl over 3f out: sn wknd: t.o) | 17 | **12** | 33/1 | — | — |
| 3779[4] | **Wildmoor (65)** (JDBethell) **2-8-11** KFallon(13) (hld up & bhd: bmpd ent st: hdwy over 3f out: sn nt clr run & eased) | 8 | **13** | 12/1 | — | — |

(SP 141.9%) **13 Rn**

**2m 9.6** (7.10) CSF £28.27 CT £268.91 TOTE £4.20: £3.10 £3.10 £6.70 (£15.50) Trio £218.50 OWNER Foreneish Racing (NEWMARKET) BRED Godolphin Management Co Ltd

LONG HANDICAP Foolish Flutter (IRE) 7-0 Riva La Belle 7-6

OFFICIAL EXPLANATION **Wildmoor: suffered interference shortly after turning into the home straight.**

**3762 Swallow Breeze**, with plenty of stamina in her pedigree on the dam's side, was only 1lb higher than when third at Newmarket. (7/2)

**4097* Chairmans Daughter**, with her new trainer deciding to leave the blinkers off, had to contend with a 7lb higher mark but her attitude could not be faulted. (6/1)

**2122 Warrlin** was certainly ridden as if the trip would not be a problem. (14/1)

**Chateauherault (IRE)**, a half-brother to Muchtarak, showed his first sign of ability over this stamina test. (25/1)

**2315 Auction Hall** was amazingly taking a big step up in distance having been dropped back to the bare minimum last time. (13/2)

**River King** may be better back at a mile for the time being. (14/1)

**3964 Triple Term** proved too headstrong to get this sort of distance. (11/4)

T/Jkpt: Not won; £6,973.92 to Goodwood 25/9/96. T/Plpt: £183.90 (85.63 Tckts). T/Qdpt: £9.30 (117.1 Tckts). KH

# 3931-CHESTER (L-H) (Good)
## Wednesday September 25th

WEATHER: fine & sunny WIND: almost nil

## 4362 CARDEN MAIDEN STKS (3-Y.O+) (Class D)

2-20 (2-21) **1m 5f 89y** £4,107.00 (£1,236.00: £598.00: £279.00) Stalls: Low GOING: 0.30 sec per fur (G)

| | | | | SP | RR | SF |
|---|---|---|---|---|---|---|
| 3042[3] | **Ginger Fox (USA) (84)** (HRACecil) **3-8-12** WRyan(5) (lw: mde virtually all: hrd drvn fnl f: hld on gamely) | — | **1** | 5/2[2] | 92 | 65 |
| 3935[2] | **Heart (82)** (MRStoute) **3-8-7** KFallon(9) (chsd wnr thrght: rdn over 2f out: disp ld ent fnl f: unable qckn) | ¾ | **2** | 6/4[1] | 86 | 59 |
| 4110[2] | **Ballet High (IRE) (75)** (IABalding) **3-8-12** RCochrane(7) (lw: sn chsng ldng pair: hrd drvn 5f out: sn lost tch) | 14 | **3** | 11/2 | 74 | 47 |
| 4083[4] | **Wybara** (JHMGosden) **3-8-7** GHind(8) (hld up: outpcd 4f out: sn btn) | 8 | **4** | 16/1 | 60 | 33 |
| | **St Honorine (IRE)** (CMurray) **4-9-2** JFortune(6) (b: s.s: hdwy 6f out: outpcd over 3f out) | 3½ | **5** | 50/1 | 56 | 38 |
| 3986[4] | **Gulliver (79)** (BWHills) **3-8-12** MHills(1) (lw: hld up: pushed along & outpcd 4f out: t.o) | 16 | **6** | 5/1[3] | 42 | 15 |
| 4237[18] | **Chili-Wah-Wah** (CASmith) **5-9-7** DeanMcKeown(4) (swtg: bit bkwd: a bhd: lost tch 7f out: t.o) | dist | **7** | 100/1 | — | — |
| 1638[14] | **Pats Folly (17)** (FJYardley) **5-9-2** MTebbutt(2) (prom 4f: sn lost pl: t.o fr ½-wy) | hd | **8** | 100/1 | — | — |

(SP 110.4%) **8 Rn**

**2m 59.3** (9.30) CSF £6.15 TOTE £3.30: £1.50 £1.20 £1.10 (£2.40) Trio £3.90 OWNER H R H Prince Fahd Salman (NEWMARKET) BRED Newgate Stud Farm Inc.

WEIGHT FOR AGE 3yo-9lb

**3042 Ginger Fox (USA)**, waiting in front, set a sedate pace and won the battle of what turned out to be a two-horse race for the final half-mile, and could just be about to find his way. (5/2)
**3935 Heart** is not having much luck at this venue, and had to settle for the runner-up prize for the second time running. She stuck to her task willingly and she is due a win. (6/4)
**4110 Ballet High (IRE)** failed to get in a blow against the principals, and was going in reverse a long way from home. (11/2)

## 4363 MARFORD MAIDEN STKS (2-Y.O) (Class D)

2-50 (2-51) **7f 2y** £3,626.00 (£1,088.00: £524.00: £242.00) Stalls: Low GOING: 0.30 sec per fur (G)

| | | | | SP | RR | SF |
|---|---|---|---|---|---|---|
| 4060[3] | **Beryllium (78)** (RHannon) **2-9-0** DaneO'Neill(2) (mde all: hrd drvn appr fnl f: r.o wl) | — | 1 | 7/1 | 88 | 50 |
| 3988[2] | **Calypso Grant (IRE)** (PWHarris) **2-8-9** GHind(1) (a.p: chal ent st: hrd drvn & unable qckn appr fnl f) | 1 | 2 | 3/1[2] | 81 | 43 |
| 4208[10] | **Bally Souza (IRE)** (MJohnston) **2-8-9** JWeaver(5) (hld up: hdwy over 2f out: sn hrd rdn: nt pce to chal) | 2 | 3 | 12/1 | 76 | 38 |
| 3221[5] | **Maftool** (JHMGosden) **2-9-0** WRyan(4) (outpcd ½-wy: effrt wl over 1f out: one pce fnl f) | 1½ | 4 | 5/2[1] | 78 | 40 |
| | **Showcase** (MRStoute) **2-8-9** WRSwinburn(3) (lengthy: unf: bit bkwd: s.s: bhd tl styd on fnl 2f) | 2 | 5 | 5/1[3] | 68+ | 30 |
| | **Dead Aim (IRE)** (IABalding) **2-9-0** KDarley(8) (trckd ldrs to ½-wy: sn pushed along & outpcd) | 3 | 6 | 10/1 | 66 | 28 |
| 4060[5] | **Court Express** (TJEtherington) **2-9-0** MTebbutt(6) (hld up in tch: wknd over 2f out) | nk | 7 | 33/1 | 66 | 28 |
| 4062[6] | **Rosy Outlook (USA)** (IABalding) **2-8-9** RCochrane(7) (lw: hld up: hdwy 3f out: wknd qckly wl over 1f out) | 5 | 8 | 5/1[3] | 49 | 11 |
| 1525[12] | **Honourable Felix** (EJAlston) **2-9-0** KFallon(10) (bkwd: a bhd: t.o) | 10 | 9 | 50/1 | 31 | — |
| | **Glimmering Hope (IRE)** (MissJFCraze) **2-9-0** NConnorton(9) (w'like: bkwd: s.s: a bhd: t.o) | dist | 10 | 50/1 | — | — |
| | | | | (SP 123.1%) | **10 Rn** | |

**1m 31.4** (6.20) CSF £28.36 TOTE £9.90: £2.20 £1.50 £5.40 (£12.30) Trio £65.00 OWNER Lostford Manor Stud (MARLBOROUGH) BRED Halevale Ltd

**4060 Beryllium**, a locally-owned winner in the colours carried by Mind Games, will never be as good as him, but turned in a brave display from the front and deservedly held on. (7/1)
**3988 Calypso Grant (IRE)** almost got to terms on straightening up, but the winner, with the help of the inside rail, kept pulling out more and she had to admit she had met her match. (3/1)
**Bally Souza (IRE)** performed much better than she did on her debut, but she had a punishing race and may not forget it in a hurry. (12/1)
**3221 Maftool**, looking as though he would benefit from the run after six weeks off, was having his first race on a turning track, and was never going well enough to offer his supporters much encouragement. (5/2)
**Showcase**, not over-big, is choicely bred and was given a quiet introduction after losing ground at the start, but she will be all the wiser next time. (5/1)
**Dead Aim (IRE)** has already been gelded. Looking far from fully wound up, he was hard at work before reaching the straight, and it is to be hoped he will improve for the experience. (10/1)
**4062 Rosy Outlook (USA)** closed up out in the country, and was soon within striking range, but she stopped as if shot on entering the straight, and proved most disappointing. (5/1)

## 4364 TATTERSALLS AUCTION NURSERY H'CAP (2-Y.O) (Class C)

3-20 (3-22) **7f 2y** £5,865.00 (£1,770.00: £860.00: £405.00) Stalls: Low GOING: 0.30 sec per fur (G)

| | | | | SP | RR | SF |
|---|---|---|---|---|---|---|
| 3982[6] | **Smugurs (IRE) (60)** (RJRWilliams) **2-7-8**(3) DWright(3) (a.p: led over 1f out: rdn out) | — | 1 | 7/1 | 62 | 37 |
| 3998[4] | **Grate Times (76)** (EWeymes) **2-8-13** KDarley(4) (trckd ldrs: rdn along 4f out: swtchd ins over 1f out: fin fast) | hd | 2 | 10/1 | 78 | 53 |
| 4182* | **Brandon Jack (84)** (IABalding) **2-9-7** RCochrane(2) (lw: hld up in rr: hdwy 3f out: str run fnl f: nrst fin) | 1 | 3 | 3/1[1] | 84 | 59 |
| 4207[2] | **Aybeegirl (66)** (MrsJCecil) **2-7-12**(5) MartinDwyer(6) (lw: hld up: hdwy on outside over 2f out: wknd ins fnl f) | 2½ | 4 | 13/2[3] | 60 | 35 |
| 4046* | **Commander Jones (IRE) (75)** (BJMeehan) **2-8-12** MTebbutt(5) (a.p: rdn & edgd lft over 1f out: one pce) | 2½ | 5 | 10/1 | 63 | 38 |
| *4079** | **Pericles (80)** (MJohnston) **2-9-3** JWeaver(1) (lw: set str pce: rdn & hdd over 1f out: sn btn) | 1 | 6 | 9/2[2] | 66 | 41 |
| 4224[2] | **River of Fortune (IRE) (74)** (MHTompkins) **2-8-8**(3) MHenry(12) (hdwy 3f out: sn rdn: no imp) | s.h | 7 | 8/1 | 60 | 35 |
| 4127[4] | **Saffron Rose (74)** (MBlanshard) **2-8-11** JQuinn(11) (a in rr) | 1½ | 8 | 14/1 | 56 | 31 |
| 3826* | **Shall We Go (IRE) (70)** (RHannon) **2-8-7** DaneO'Neill(7) (chsd ldrs over 4f: sn rdn & outpcd) | 4 | 9 | 8/1 | 43 | 18 |
| 3687[13] | **Al Ava Consonant (68)** (JDBethell) **2-8-0**(5) PFessey(8) (a bhd: t.o) | 14 | 10 | 20/1 | 9 | — |
| 3588[6] | **Heathyards Pearl (USA) (74)** (RHollinshead) **2-8-8**(3) FLynch(9) (swtg: a bhd: eased whn btn 2f out: t.o) | 10 | 11 | 20/1 | — | — |
| 3590[6] | **Nomore Mr Niceguy (82)** (EJAlston) **2-9-5** KFallon(10) (a bhd: t.o) | 10 | 12 | 16/1 | — | — |
| | | | | (SP 131.5%) | **12 Rn** | |

**1m 31.13** (5.93) CSF £75.26 CT £209.12 TOTE £9.20: £2.20 £2.90 £2.00 (£47.50) Trio £37.30 OWNER Mugs Us (NEWMARKET) BRED Joseph O'Brien

**3982 Smugurs (IRE)**, falling out of the bottom of the handicap but not winning out of turn, kicked on below the distance and held on grimly to the line. (7/1)
**3998 Grate Times** looked to be in serious trouble at halfway but, with stamina coming into play, put in a sustained last-furlong challenge and only just failed. (10/1)
**4182* Brandon Jack** usually comes from off the pace but, on such a tight track, was almost trying the impossible. Had he not hung left though inside the final furlong, he would have gone very close. (3/1)
**4207 Aybeegirl**, a winner over the minimum trip here, tried hard to make her presence felt, but stamina seemed to desert her inside the last furlong. (13/2)
**4046* Commander Jones (IRE)** again drifted left when asked for his effort inside then final furlong and, losing his momentum, easily got brushed aside. (10/1)
**4079* Pericles** was not afraid to force a strong pace, but several rivals kept tabs on him and beat him for toe when the chips were down. (9/2)

## 4365 BOOKER CASH & CARRY H'CAP (0-80) (3-Y.O+) (Class D)

3-50 (3-53) **1m 7f 195y** £5,962.50 (£1,800.00: £875.00: £412.50) Stalls: Low GOING: 0.30 sec per fur (G)

| | | | | SP | RR | SF |
|---|---|---|---|---|---|---|
| 3983[3] | **Beaumont (IRE) (59)** (JEBanks) **6-8-11** JQuinn(1) (hld up: stdy hdwy 5f out: hrd drvn 3f out: led over 1f out: sn clr: hld on) | — | 1 | 6/1[3] | 72 | 47 |
| 3928[7] | **Amiarge (44)** (MBrittain) **6-7-10** GBardwell(12) (lost pl 9f out: gd hdwy ent st: styd on strly fnl f) | 1¾ | 2 | 20/1 | 55 | 30 |
| 3922* | **Izza (57)** (WStorey) **5-8-9** NKennedy(4) (hld up & bhd: stdy hdwy over 5f out: n.m.r ent st: kpt on ins fnl f) | 1 | 3 | 4/1[2] | 67 | 42 |
| 3855[6] | **Bowcliffe Court (IRE) (62)** (BWHills) **4-9-0** MHills(8) (trckd ldrs: effrt & hrd drvn 3f out: styd on fnl f) | 2½ | 4 | 12/1 | 70 | 45 |
| 3922[3] | **The Swan (80)** (JLDunlop) **3-9-6** TSprake(10) (b: chsd ldrs: led 5f out tl over 1f out: one pce) | 2 | 5 | 7/2[1] | 86 | 49 |
| 3948[3] | **Bob's Ploy (74)** (MHTompkins) **4-9-9**(3) MHenry(13) (lw: hld up: hdwy 5f out: nt clr run ent st: wknd appr fnl f) | 2½ | 6 | 10/1 | 77 | 52 |
| 642[2] | **Love The Blues (65)** (DNicholson) **4-9-3** KDarley(7) (bkwd: prom: ev ch 2f out: wknd appr fnl f) | hd | 7 | 14/1 | 68 | 43 |

**Needwood Muppet (50)** (AJWilson) **9-7-9**$^{(7)ow4}$ KSked(3) (bkwd: in tch to ½-wy: sn lost pl: n.d after)......8 **8** 33/1 45 16
$4048^{5}$ **Tirolette (IRE) (55)** (RJRWilliams) **4-8-7b** RCochrane(5) (lw: trckd ldrs: hrd drvn 3f out: sn btn)......1 **9** 20/1 49 24
$4000^{7}$ **Rasayel (USA) (62)** (PDEvans) **6-9-0** JFEgan(6) (hdwy ½-wy: wknd 4f out: t.o)......20 **10** 16/1 36 11
$3928^{9}$ **Rivercare (IRE) (61)** (MJPolglase) **3-7-10**$^{(5)ow5}$ AmandaSanders(11) (chsd clr ldr tl rdn & wknd 6f out: t.o)......5 **11** 33/1 30 —
$3983^{10}$ **Trainglot (76)** (JGFitzGerald) **9-10-0** KFallon(14) (b: a in rr: t.o fnl 5f)......5 **12** 10/1 40 15
$4315^{6}$ **Ela Man Howa (47)** (ABailey) **5-7-10b**$^{(3)}$ DWright(2) (b: led & sn clr: wknd & hdd 5f out: t.o)......13 **13** 16/1 — —
$3834^{4}$ **Noufari (FR) (75)** (RHollinshead) **5-9-10**$^{(3)}$ FLynch(15) (a bhd: rdn 5f out: no rspnse: t.o)......1 **14** 12/1 25 —
$3037^{14}$ **Argyle Cavalier (IRE) (56)** (BJMeehan) **6-8-8** MTebbutt(9) (bhd fr ½-wy: t.o)......27 **15** 16/1 — —
(SP 129.8%) **15 Rn**

**3m 37.43** (14.53) CSF £112.94 CT £503.18 TOTE £6.00: £1.90 £11.10 £2.20 (£133.80) Trio £346.10 OWNER Mr P. Cunningham (NEWMARKET) BRED Mount Coote Stud in Ireland
LONG HANDICAP Rivercare (IRE) 7-7 Amiarge 7-7
WEIGHT FOR AGE 3yo-12lb

**3983 Beaumont (IRE)** gave notice in his previous race that he is not short on stamina and, after taking command below the distance, quickly put the issue beyond doubt. (6/1)
**3463 Amiarge**, a very in-and-out performer, made up a lot of ground in the latter stages and the ability is there when he cares to use it. (20/1)
**3922* Izza**, denied any kind of run turning in, did get space approaching the final furlong but, by then, the winner had the prize in sake-keeping. It could prove costly to consider her an unlucky loser. (4/1)
**3855 Bowcliffe Court (IRE)** looks to be a very hard ride, but he does stay, and more testing ground should give him the chance to get back to winning ways. (12/1)
**3922 The Swan**, forced to accept a lead for eleven furlongs, could not get away from the pursuing pack and she was fighting a lost cause inside the distance. (7/2)
**3948 Bob's Ploy**, hard at work when he ran into trouble entering the straight, lacked the speed to get out of it, and he called enough on the approach to the final furlong. There is nothing to say he will not be suited to this trip. (10/1)
**642 Love The Blues** has not been out since the spring and it was obvious this run was needed, but she ran extremely well and, if her attention is switched to hurdles, she could prove useful in staying events. (14/1)

## 4366 HESWALL CONDITIONS STKS (2-Y.O) (Class C)
4-20 (4-20) **7f 122y** £5,292.00 (£1,852.00: £906.00: £390.00) Stalls: Low GOING: 0.30 sec per fur (G)

SP RR SF
3682* **Entrepreneur** (MRStoute) **2-9-0** WRSwinburn(3) (lw: hld up in rr: hdwy to chse ldr ent st: qcknd to ld 100y out: impressive)......— **1** 1/6$^{1}$ 95+ 44
$3971^{3}$ **Kharir (IRE)** (HThomsonJones) **2-9-0** GCarter(4) (lw: led: qcknd 4f out: hdd & outpcd wl ins fnl f)......2½ **2** 11/1$^{3}$ 90 39
3964* **Rapier** (RHannon) **2-9-0** DaneO'Neill(2) (lw: chsd ldr to ½-wy: rdn wl over 2f out: sn outpcd)......6 **3** 10/1$^{2}$ 77 26
$4301^{5}$ **Mujova (IRE) (87)** (RHollinshead) **2-8-11** JFortune(1) (s.i.s: hdwy & 2nd ½-wy: rdn & outpcd wl over 1f out)....3 **4** 14/1 68 17
(SP 109.8%) **4 Rn**

**1m 39.25** (7.25) CSF £2.80 TOTE £1.20 (£2.00) OWNER Mr M Tabor & Mrs John Magnier (NEWMARKET) BRED Cheveley Park Stud Ltd

**3682* Entrepreneur** adopted totally different tactics in this small field and was the backmarker until approaching the straight, but he lengthened impressively when given the office and left his rivals for dead. His next intended outing is in the Dewhurst at Newmarket and, at this stage of his career, he looks one of our leading juveniles. (1/6)
**3971 Kharir (IRE)** attempted to get to the bottom of the winner by setting a testing gallop but, hard as he tried, he only looked second rate when the race began in earnest. (11/1)
**3964* Rapier** did nothing wrong, but he was out of his depth here and could not do much about it. (10/1)
**4301 Mujova (IRE)** has shown plenty of promise in the past, but he is some way below top-class and it showed here. (14/1)

## 4367 TARPORLEY H'CAP (0-85) (3-Y.O+) (Class D)
4-50 (4-51) **5f 16y** £4,467.50 (£1,340.00: £645.00: £297.50) Stalls: Low GOING: 0.30 sec per fur (G)

SP RR SF
$4304^{4}$ **Crofters Ceilidh (75)** (BAMcMahon) **4-9-5b** JFortune(7) (a.p: led ins fnl f: rdn out)......— **1** 5/1$^{1}$ 86 48
$4198^{8}$ **Go Hever Golf (76)** (TJNaughton) **4-9-6** JWeaver(5) (lw: hld up in rr: effrt & nt clr run ent st: gd hdwy fnl f: unlucky)......1¼ **2** 7/1$^{2}$ 83 45
$3352^{9}$ **Gondo (52)** (EJAlston) **9-7-3v**$^{(7)}$ RFfrench(1) (hld up: hdwy on ins ent st: fin wl)......s.h **3** 33/1 59 21
4119* **Tuscan Dawn (77)** (JBerry) **6-9-2**$^{(5)}$ PRoberts(6) (led tl hdd & no ex ins fnl f)......¾ **4** 7/1$^{2}$ 82 44
3338* **Friendly Brave (USA) (74)** (MissGayKelleway) **6-9-4** WRSwinburn(11) (b.hind: lw: hld up in tch: effrt wl over 1f out: nvr able to chal)......1 **5** 8/1 75 37
$4246^{17}$ **Johayro (61)** (JSGoldie) **3-8-4** JQuinn(12) (prom: hrd drvn over 1f out: one pce)......1 **6** 20/1 59 20
$4246^{6}$ **Rich Glow (61)** (NBycroft) **5-8-5** KDarley(4) (lw: hdwy u.p appr fnl f: nrst fin)......½ **7** 15/2$^{3}$ 58 20
$3946^{10}$ **Pride of Brixton (85)** (GLewis) **3-10-0** WRyan(9) (swtg: hld up mid div: effrt ent st: nvr plcd to chal)......1¼ **8** 10/1 78 39
$4246^{14}$ **Panther (IRE) (71)** (PDEvans) **6-9-1v** JFEgan(10) (mid div on outside: hrd rdn 2f out: no imp)......¾ **9** 10/1 61 23
$3932^{6}$ **Glorious Aragon (82)** (RFJohnsonHoughton) **4-9-12** ACulhane(8) (hld up: rdn & outpcd 2f out: sn btn)......½ **10** 12/1 71 33
$4058^{7}$ **The Happy Fox (IRE) (75)** (BAMcMahon) **4-9-5** GCarter(13) (lw: in tch: effrt & rdn over 2f out: sn outpcd)....1¼ **11** 12/1 60 22
*4094*$^{4}$ **One for Jeannie (64)** (ABailey) **4-8-5b**$^{1(3)}$ DWright(3) (s.i.s: sn drvn along: a bhd)......nk **12** 15/2$^{3}$ 48 10
$4130^{12}$ **Amy Leigh (IRE) (60)** (CaptJWilson) **3-8-0**$^{(3)ow3}$ FLynch(2) (spd 3f)......¾ **13** 16/1 42 —
(SP 123.5%) **13 Rn**

**64.79 secs** (4.79) CSF £38.44 CT £1,008.87 TOTE £5.30: £2.60 £3.60 £2.10 (£20.10) Trio £117.10 OWNER Mrs Mary Meddings (TAMWORTH) BRED Rowcliffe Stud
LONG HANDICAP Gondo 6-7
WEIGHT FOR AGE 3yo-1lb

**4304 Crofters Ceilidh** ran the best race of her career at Newbury last weekend and she is sure to be penalised for it, so this quick return to action was a shrewd move and she landed the spoils readily. (5/1)
**4198 Go Hever Golf**, unable to go the early pace, was repeatedly denied a clear run when poised to challenge entering the straight and, though he finished like a train, the winner had gone beyond recall. He should not be long in making amends. (7/1)
**2910 Gondo** stuck to the inside rail and delivered a determined challenge once in line for home, but the winner had got away and he had to make do with small pickings. (33/1)
**4119* Tuscan Dawn** is probably more effective these days when not so much use is made of him, for he does seem to run himself into the ground. (7/1)
**3338* Friendly Brave (USA)** did not appear entirely happy on such a sharp track, but he ran up to his mark and it would seem there is more to come. (8/1)
**3883 Johayro** was taking on the big boys this time and he lost no caste in defeat. He would seem a very progressive youngster. (20/1)

**4246 Rich Glow** did not get going until far too late, and he does need a stiffer test on such an easy track. (15/2)

T/Plpt: £31.20 (519.95 Tckts). T/Qdpt: £18.60 (42.11 Tckts). IM

# 4196-GOODWOOD (R-H) (Good to firm)
## Wednesday September 25th

WEATHER: warm WIND: almost nil

## 4368 DEEKS & STEERE BUILDING CONTRACTORS GOLDEN ANNIVERSARY (S) STKS (2-Y.O) (Class E)

2-30 (2-31) **7f** £3,622.50 (£1,080.00: £515.00: £232.50) Stalls: High GOING minus 0.22 sec per fur (GF)

| Form | Horse | Dist | Pos | SP | RR | SF |
|---|---|---|---|---|---|---|
| 4262[11] | **Silca's My Key (IRE) (68)** (MRChannon) **2-8-6v1**(5) PPMurphy(9) (hrd rdn over 3f out: hdwy over 2f out: led over 1f out tl ins fnl f: led last strides) | — | **1** | 3/1 [1] | 64 | 19 |
| 4223[6] | **Marsh Marigold (56)** (MartynMeade) **2-8-6** JReid(5) (hdwy & nt clr run 2f out: swtchd rt over 1f out: led ins fnl f: hrd rdn: hdd last strides) | hd | **2** | 10/1 | 59 | 14 |
| 4106[16] | **Summerville Wood (64)** (PMooney) **2-8-4**(7) PDoe(4) (hdwy over 3f out: hrd rdn & hung lft 3f out: hung rt 2f out: one pce fnl f) | 5 | **3** | 5/1 [3] | 52 | 7 |
| *4251*[4] | **Whizz Kid (62)** (JJBridger) **2-7-13**(7) RMullen(10) (chsd ldr: led over 2f out tl over 1f out: one pce) | 2 | **4** | 6/1 | 43 | — |
| | **Seretse's Nephew** (SCWilliams) **2-8-11** JTate(7) (nvr nr to chal) | 1¾ | **5** | 11/1 | 44 | — |
| 4046[8] | **Preskidul (IRE) (53)** (DWPArbuthnot) **2-8-6** TQuinn(2) (b: b.hind: a.p: rdn over 2f out: wknd over 1f out) | 2 | **6** | 8/1 | 34 | — |
| 4049[5] | **Bapsford (69)** (GLMoore) **2-8-11** SSanders(6) (swtg: hdwy over 3f out: rdn over 2f out: wknd over 1f out) | 3½ | **7** | 7/2 [2] | 31 | — |
| 4208[13] | **Jade's Gem** (GBBalding) **2-8-6** SDrowne(1) (a bhd) | 1½ | **8** | 25/1 | 23 | — |
| | **Foxford Lad** (TMJones) **2-8-11** RPerham(8) (w'like: bit bkwd: bhd fnl 5f) | s.h | **9** | 40/1 | 28 | — |
| 3840[4] | **Municipal Girl (IRE) (54)** (BPalling) **2-8-6** DHarrison(3) (led over 4f) | ¾ | **10** | 16/1 | 21 | — |
| | | | | (SP 118.9%) | **10 Rn** | |

**1m 29.77** (4.97) CSF £30.79 TOTE £3.50: £1.50 £1.70 £2.20 (£9.10) Trio £27.00 OWNER Aldridge Racing Ltd (UPPER LAMBOURN) BRED Sheikh Mohammed Bin Rashid Al Maktoum

No bid

**4106 Silca's My Key (IRE)** is more at home in this grade where his only previous victory came, and had the added help of the first-time visor. (3/1: 7/4-100/30)

**3943 Marsh Marigold** looked like losing her maiden tag as she came through to lead inside the final furlong, only to be caught by the persistent winner in the last couple of strides. (10/1)

**3943 Summerville Wood** was out of his depth in a nursery last time out, and was much happier in this grade, where his only previous victory came. (5/1)

**2944 Whizz Kid** was once again running in her correct grade. (6/1)

**Seretse's Nephew** was rather surprisingly making his debut over seven furlongs, considering his breeding. Nevertheless, he stayed on from the rear in the final furlong and a half, despite not looking fully wound up. (11/1: 7/1-12/1)

**807 Preskidul (IRE)** failed to last home over this longer trip. (8/1)

**4049 Bapsford** did not stay this longer trip. (7/2)

## 4369 HOSHIZAKI ICEMAKERS AUCTION STKS (2-Y.O) (Class C)

3-00 (3-03) **7f** £5,536.50 (£2,053.50: £989.25: £408.75: £166.88: £70.12) Stalls: High GOING minus 0.22 sec per fur (GF)

| Form | Horse | Dist | Pos | SP | RR | SF |
|---|---|---|---|---|---|---|
| 4224* | **White Hot** (EALDunlop) **2-8-9** RHills(14) (lw: w ldr: led over 1f out: drvn out) | — | **1** | 14/1 | 99 | 43 |
| 2714* | **Kalinka (IRE)** (PFICole) **2-7-10** FNorton(12) (a.p: rdn over 1f out: r.o) | s.h | **2** | 7/4 [1] | 86 | 30 |
| 4024a[3] | **Pelham (IRE) (96)** (RHannon) **2-9-0** PatEddery(13) (led over 5f: unable qckn fnl f) | 3½ | **3** | 5/1 [2] | 96 | 40 |
| 4084* | **Sheer Face (90)** (WRMuir) **2-8-9** JReid(6) (lw: hdwy over 2f out: rdn: one pce) | ½ | **4** | 15/2 [3] | 90 | 34 |
| 4118[2] | **Supply And Demand** (GLMoore) **2-8-10** SWhitworth(5) (rdn & hdwy over 2f out: one pce) | hd | **5** | 5/1 [2] | 91 | 35 |
| 4065[7] | **Papita (IRE) (84)** (SDow) **2-7-12**(5) ADaly(9) (rdn over 2f out: hdwy over 1f out: nvr nrr) | 2 | **6** | 12/1 | 79 | 23 |
| 3848[3] | **Gift Token** (MajorDNChappell) **2-7-10** NCarlisle(2) (lw: nvr nr to chal) | nk | **7** | 12/1 | 71 | 15 |
| 4241[4] | **City Gambler** (GCBravery) **2-7-13** DRMcCabe(4) (nvr nrr) | 3 | **8** | 33/1 | 67 | 11 |
| 3982[12] | **Tartan Party** (PFICole) **2-8-1** CRutter(7) (s.s: nvr nrr) | 5 | **9** | 33/1 | 58 | 2 |
| 3964[7] | **Streamline (IRE)** (GLewis) **2-8-1**(3) AWhelan(8) (hld up: rdn over 3f out: wknd 2f out) | nk | **10** | 50/1 | 60 | 4 |
| 2629[2] | **Iechyd-Da (IRE) (91)** (MBell) **2-8-8** MFenton(3) (a bhd) | 4 | **11** | 10/1 | 55 | — |
| 4105[9] | **Fable** (JARToller) **2-7-10** DeclanO'Shea(15) (lw: bhd whn hmpd on ins over 2f out) | ¾ | **12** | 50/1 | 41 | — |
| 2224[13] | **Tulsa (IRE)** (BGubby) **2-8-4v1** SSanders(1) (prom over 4f) | 2½ | **13** | 50/1 | 44 | — |
| | **Sylvan Jubilacion** (PMitchell) **2-8-3**ow2 AClark(10) (s.s: a bhd) | 5 | **14** | 50/1 | 31 | — |
| 3796[10] | **The Commodore (IRE)** (WJarvis) **2-8-7** StephenDavies(11) (prom over 3f) | 9 | **15** | 50/1 | 15 | — |
| | | | | (SP 128.3%) | **15 Rn** | |

**1m 27.5** (2.70) CSF £38.52 TOTE £14.90: £2.70 £1.30 £2.00 (£11.40) Trio £19.50 OWNER The Serendipity Partnership (NEWMARKET) BRED Broughton Bloodstock

**4224* White Hot**, forging ahead below the distance, proved more willing than the runner-up. (14/1)

**2714* Kalinka (IRE)**, when asked to go and challenge the winner, looked far from happy and, carrying her head very high, was not putting it all in, despite failing by a whisker. Had she been more resolute, she would certainly have carried the day. (7/4)

**4024a Pelham (IRE)** has been running really well this season but, on this occasion, he had no easy task conceding weight all round. (5/1: 7/2-11/2)

**4084* Sheer Face** was not helped by the drop back in distance and a return back to a mile is required. (15/2: op 5/1)

**4118 Supply And Demand**, bustled along to close over a quarter of a mile from home, was then only treading water. Another furlong will help him find a small race. (5/1)

**3444 Papita (IRE)** (12/1: 8/1-14/1)

**2629 Iechyd-Da (IRE)** (10/1: 6/1-11/1)

## 4370 ST. IVEL 'GOLD CUP' MAIDEN STKS (2-Y.O) (Class D)

3-30 (3-34) **1m** £4,270.75 (£1,276.00: £610.50: £277.75) Stalls: High GOING minus 0.22 sec per fur (GF)

| Form | Horse | Dist | Pos | SP | RR | SF |
|---|---|---|---|---|---|---|
| 4175[3] | **Voyagers Quest (USA)** (PWChapple-Hyam) **2-9-0** JReid(2) (a.p: chsd ldr 5f out: rdn over 2f out: led nr fin) | — | **1** | 11/8 [1] | 93 | 43 |
| 3987[6] | **Stanton Harcourt (USA)** (JLDunlop) **2-9-0** PatEddery(9) (hld up: rdn over 2f out: led ins fnl f: hdd nr fin) | nk | **2** | 4/1 [3] | 92 | 42 |
| 3682[4] | **Pennys From Heaven** (HCandy) **2-9-0** CRutter(6) (led: rdn 2f out: hdd ins fnl f: one pce) | 3½ | **3** | 11/1 | 85 | 35 |

| | | | | SP | RR | SF |
|---|---|---|---|---|---|---|
| | **Heritage** (JHMGosden) **2-9-0** JCarroll(1) (a.p: rdn over 2f out: wknd over 1f out) | 4 | **4** | 11/1 | 77 | 27 |
| 4050[6] | **Padauk** (MJHaynes) **2-9-0** AMcGlone(8) (chsd ldr 3f: rdn over 2f out: wknd wl over 1f out) | ½ | **5** | 50/1 | 76 | 26 |
| 4127[3] | **Waterspout (USA)** (GHarwood) **2-9-0** AClark(5) (hld up: rdn over 2f out: sn wknd) | hd | **6** | 7/2[2] | 76 | 26 |
| 2708[9] | **Elhafid (USA)** (MajorWRHern) **2-9-0** RHills(3) (a bhd) | 5 | **7** | 25/1 | 66 | 16 |
| 2712[4] | **Noble Hero** (JJSheehan) **2-9-0** SDrowne(4) (bhd fnl 2f) | nk | **8** | 50/1 | 66 | 16 |
| | **Utah (IRE)** (LMontagueHall) **2-9-0** SSanders(10) (bhd fnl 2f) | 3½ | **9** | 33/1 | 59 | 9 |
| | **Bentnose** (LadyHerries) **2-9-0** DeclanO'Shea(7) (a bhd) | ¾ | **10** | 20/1 | 57 | 7 |
| | **Sheffield Shark (IRE)** (DWPArbuthnot) **2-9-0** TQuinn(12) (s.s: a bhd) | hd | **11** | 25/1 | 57 | 7 |
| *4100[10]* | ***Swan Island*** (BPalling) **2-8-9** DHarrison(11) (Withdrawn not under Starter's orders: Veterinary advice) | | **W** | 33/1 | — | — |

(SP 123.3%) **11 Rn**

**1m 40.78** (3.58) CSF £7.42 TOTE £2.30: £1.30 £1.40 £2.10 (£4.10) Trio £11.40 OWNER Mr Richard Kaster (MARLBOROUGH) BRED Gulf States Racing Stables II

**4175 Voyagers Quest (USA)** looks a bit on the lazy side and needed every yard of this trip, Reid really having to get at him to get him up near the line. (11/8)

**3987 Stanton Harcourt (USA)** ran his best race to date over this longer trip and looked booked for the winner's enclosure when striking the front early inside the final furlong, only to be collared near the line. He should now be ready to open his account. (4/1: op 5/2)

**3682 Pennys From Heaven** is extremely tall and towered over his rivals in the paddock. Bowling along in front, he gamely tried to hold on, but was eventually collared inside the final furlong. He is going the right way and should soon find a race. (11/1: 8/1-12/1)

**Heritage** was close up until lack of a run took its toll over a furlong out. (11/1: 7/1-12/1)

**Padauk** was in the thick of the action until tiring early in the final quarter-mile. (50/1)

**4127 Waterspout (USA)** was very disappointing following his encouraging Chepstow debut. (7/2: 5/2-4/1)

## 4371 R.O.A. FOUNDATION STKS (Listed) (3-Y.O+) (Class A)

4-00 (4-01) **1m 2f** £17,787.50 (£5,300.00: £2,525.00: £1,137.50) Stalls: High GOING minus 0.22 sec per fur (GF)

| | | | | SP | RR | SF |
|---|---|---|---|---|---|---|
| 4160a[2] | **Hagwah (USA) (103)** (BHanbury) **4-8-9** MRoberts(3) (mde all: sn clr: qcknd 4f out: rdn 2f out: r.o wl) | — | **1** | 5/2[2] | 115 | 48 |
| 4174a[4] | **Overbury (IRE)** (SbinSuroor) **5-9-7** TQuinn(1) (hld up: chsd wnr over 3f out: rdn 2f out: unable qckn fnl f) | 2½ | **2** | 9/1 | 123 | 56 |
| 3691[2] | **Fahim (108)** (ACStewart) **3-8-8** RHills(5) (dwlt: rdn over 3f out: hdwy over 2f out: eased whn btn ins fnl f) | 2½ | **3** | 2/1[1] | 112 | 39 |
| 1575a[4] | **Sanoosea (USA) (110)** (MRStoute) **4-9-0** JReid(2) (bhd fnl 3f) | ½ | **4** | 6/1 | 111 | 44 |
| 4178[5] | **Bal Harbour (110)** (HRACecil) **5-9-0** PatEddery(4) (chsd wnr over 6f) | s.h | **5** | 7/2[3] | 111 | 44 |

(SP 108.4%) **5 Rn**

**2m 8.93** (3.43) CSF £18.79 TOTE £3.60: £2.10 £2.00 (£19.30) OWNER Mr Abdullah Ali (NEWMARKET) BRED Gainsborough Farm Inc

WEIGHT FOR AGE 3yo-6lb

**4160a Hagwah (USA)** was given a superb ride by Roberts who out-manoeuvred his rivals. She may now go for the Prix de l'Opera. (5/2)

**4174a Overbury (IRE)**, winner of a Group One in Hong Kong back in April, was making his first appearance in this country this season. (9/1)

**3691 Fahim** is a very progressive three-year-old and richly deserved this step up in class. Although he failed to gain the day, tactics played a very large part in this race and he is well worth another chance in this company. (2/1)

**1575a Sanoosea (USA)** did not look fully fit for this first run in four months and was in trouble in the last three furlongs. (6/1)

**4178 Bal Harbour** runs his best races when allowed to dominate, but he was unable to do that here. (7/2)

## 4372 FRIALATOR INTERNATIONAL H'CAP (0-70) (3-Y.O+) (Class E)

4-30 (4-33) **5f** £4,012.50 (£1,200.00: £575.00: £262.50) Stalls: Low GOING minus 0.22 sec per fur (GF)

| | | | | SP | RR | SF |
|---|---|---|---|---|---|---|
| 4198[4] | **Scissor Ridge (58)** (JJBridger) **4-8-10**(7) RMullen(19) (racd far side: a.p: led over 1f out: rdn out) | — | **1** | 8/1[3] | 66 | 40 |
| 4198[20] | **Pride of Hayling (IRE) (62)** (PRHedger) **5-9-7** SDrowne(4) (rdn over 2f out: hdwy over 1f out: r.o wl ins fnl f) | nk | **2** | 20/1 | 69 | 43 |
| 4088[3] | **John O'Dreams (49)** (MrsALMKing) **11-8-8** MRoberts(1) (rdn over 2f out: hdwy over 1f out: r.o wl ins fnl f) | hd | **3** | 13/2[2] | 56 | 30 |
| 4198[9] | **Squire Corrie (66)** (GHarwood) **4-9-4b**(7) GayeHarwood(8) (a.p: ev ch over 1f out: r.o) | s.h | **4** | 9/1 | 73 | 47 |
| 4088[11] | **Walk the Beat (63)** (MartynMeade) **6-9-1**(7) DSweeney(16) (stdy hdwy over 1f out: r.o ins fnl f) | s.h | **5** | 16/1 | 69 | 43 |
| 4053[7] | **Out Line (68)** (MMadgwick) **4-9-10**(3) NVarley(6) (rdn 3f out: hdwy over 1f out: r.o wl ins fnl f) | 2½ | **6** | 25/1 | 66 | 40 |
| 4130* | **Malibu Man (69)** (EAWheeler) **4-10-0** JReid(9) (led over 3f: wknd ins fnl f) | ¾ | **7** | 5/1[1] | 65 | 39 |
| 3693[17] | **Mindrace (68)** (KTIvory) **3-9-12** TQuinn(12) (a.p: ev ch over 1f out: wknd ins fnl f) | hd | **8** | 14/1 | 64 | 37 |
| 3993[10] | **Tachycardia (43)** (RJO'Sullivan) **4-8-2**ow1 SSanders(18) (racd far side: a.p: ev ch over 1f out: wknd fnl f) | 1 | **9** | 14/1 | 36 | 9 |
| 4045[10] | **Scored Again (44)** (MJHeaton-Ellis) **6-8-3** AClark(13) (a.p: ev ch over 1f out: eased whn btn ins fnl f) | ¾ | **10** | 16/1 | 34 | 8 |
| 3993[7] | **Red Time (52)** (MSSaunders) **3-8-10** DHarrison(5) (nvr nrr) | ¾ | **11** | 25/1 | 40 | 13 |
| 3937[6] | **Runs in the Family (51)** (GMMcCourt) **4-8-10** PatEddery(15) (a mid div) | ½ | **12** | 8/1[3] | 37 | 11 |
| 4205[12] | **Deardaw (37)** (MissLCSiddall) **4-7-10** FNorton(11) (sme hdwy over 2f out: wknd over 1f out) | ½ | **13** | 40/1 | 22 | — |
| 4130[2] | **Ashkernazy (IRE) (46)** (NEBerry) **5-8-5** RPerham(14) (prom 2f) | ¾ | **14** | 10/1 | 28 | 2 |
| 4119[6] | **La Belle Dominique (56)** (SGKnight) **4-9-1** VSlattery(10) (hld up: rdn 2f out: sn wknd) | hd | **15** | 16/1 | 38 | 12 |
| 4130[5] | **Paley Prince (USA) (51)** (MDIUsher) **10-8-10** SWhitworth(17) (a bhd) | 1 | **16** | 20/1 | 30 | 4 |
| 3977[12] | **Kealbra Lady (38)** (MSSaunders) **3-7-3**(7) PDoe(3) (bhd fnl 2f) | 1 | **17** | 66/1 | 13 | — |
| 3166[12] | **Double Or Bust (38)** (AGNewcombe) **3-7-10** NCarlisle(20) (racd far side: outpcd) | 1½ | **18** | 50/1 | 9 | — |
| 3863[11] | **Into Debt (38)** (JRPoulton) **3-7-10** DeclanO'Shea(7) (s.s: a bhd) | hd | **19** | 50/1 | 8 | — |
| *4090[12]* | **Just Lady (57)** (WGMTurner) **3-8-10**(5) ADaly(2) (bhd fnl 2f) | 9 | **20** | 33/1 | — | — |

(SP 130.3%) **20 Rn**

**59.05 secs** (2.35) CSF £147.17 CT £1,050.46 TOTE £8.80: £1.80 £4.10 £1.70 £2.00 (£71.00) Trio £272.80 OWNER Mr Donald Smith (LIPHOOK) BRED J. K. Keegan

LONG HANDICAP Double Or Bust 7-3 Into Debt 7-8 Kealbra Lady 6-6

WEIGHT FOR AGE 3yo-1lb

**4198 Scissor Ridge**, a tough and consistent gelding who was having his seventeenth race of the season, was coming back to this trip for the first time in over two years and was winning for the first time over it. (8/1)

**3967 Pride of Hayling (IRE)** is better at six, but ran on really strongly in the last furlong and a half, only just failing to get there. (20/1)

**4088 John O'Dreams** has won just once in over two years, but this OAP really ate up the ground from below the distance and only just failed to get there. (13/2)

**4198 Squire Corrie** is running very well at present and was back at the trip where all four of his victories to date have come. (9/1)

**3323 Walk the Beat** returned to form here. He appeared to be cruising as he steadily picked up ground below the distance but, despite running on inside the final furlong, he just failed to get there. (16/1)

**3767 Out Line** found this fast five furlongs far too sharp for her and a return to six or seven is required for this maiden. (25/1)

**4130* Malibu Man** had a stiff task under topweight, but was only done with inside the final furlong. (5/1)

**3652 Scored Again** has slipped down the handicap following a string of disappointing efforts, and ran much better here. (16/1)

## 4373 TETLEY FOODSERVICE CLAIMING H'CAP (0-60) (3-Y.O+) (Class E)
5-00 (5-03) **1m** £4,467.50 (£1,340.00: £645.00: £297.50) Stalls: High GOING minus 0.22 sec per fur (GF)

| | | | | SP | RR | SF |
|---|---|---|---|---|---|---|
| 4086[7] | **Crested Knight (IRE) (47)** (CAHorgan) **4-9-2** DHarrison(17) (chsd ldr: led over 2f out: drvn 1f out: r.o wl) | — | **1** | 9/1 | 59 | 45 |
| 4256[11] | **Cats Bottom (49)** (AGNewcombe) **4-8-13**(5) DGriffiths(18) (hld up: hrd rdn & edgd lft over 2f out: chsd wnr over 1f out: r.o) | ½ | **2** | 20/1 | 60 | 46 |
| 3977[6] | **Velvet Jones (52)** (GFHCharles-Jones) **3-9-3** SWhitworth(13) (hdwy over 1f out: r.o wl ins fnl f) | ¾ | **3** | 33/1 | 62 | 44 |
| 2994* | **King Parrot (IRE) (55)** (LordHuntingdon) **8-9-5**(5) AimeeCook(15) (rdn over 2f out: hdwy over 1f out: r.o) | 2 | **4** | 11/2[1] | 61 | 47 |
| *3630*[11] | **Baron Hrabovsky (52)** (PFICole) **3-9-3** TQuinn(16) (rdn over 2f out: hdwy over 1f out: r.o one pce) | s.h | **5** | 20/1 | 57 | 39 |
| 4128[15] | **Soaking (52)** (PBurgoyne) **6-9-7** DRMcCabe(21) (rdn over 2f out: hdwy over 1f out: nvr nrr) | 1½ | **6** | 12/1 | 54 | 40 |
| 3694[3] | **Queen of Shannon (IRE) (50)** (AWCarroll) **8-8-12v**(7) RStudholme(11) (s.s: hdwy 2f out: one pce) | ½ | **7** | 11/1 | 51 | 37 |
| 3989[6] | **Charlton Imp (USA) (56)** (RJHodges) **3-9-7** SDrowne(19) (a.p: rdn over 3f out: wknd over 1f out) | hd | **8** | 12/1 | 57 | 39 |
| 3991[4] | **Jaazim (49)** (MMadgwick) **6-9-4** JReid(9) (a.p: rdn 2f out: wknd fnl f) | s.h | **9** | 6/1[2] | 50 | 36 |
| 4186[10] | **Rocky Waters (USA) (49)** (PBurgoyne) **7-9-4v** JStack(22) (led over 5f) | 2 | **10** | 14/1 | 46 | 32 |
| 4256[5] | **Our Shadee (USA) (49)** (KTIvory) **6-9-4v** CScally(12) (nvr nrr) | 1¼ | **11** | 16/1 | 44 | 30 |
| 2945[11] | **Mam'selle Bergerac (IRE) (54)** (PMitchell) **3-9-5** AClark(20) (hdwy on ins over 1f out: sn wknd) | hd | **12** | 33/1 | 48 | 30 |
| 4068[5] | **Premier League (IRE) (56)** (JELong) **6-9-11** RPrice(7) (nvr nrr) | 3½ | **13** | 16/1 | 43 | 29 |
| *4107*[6] | **Zamalek (USA) (56)** (GLMoore) **4-9-11** CandyMorris(10) (nvr nrr) | 1½ | **14** | 33/1 | 40 | 26 |
| 4237[2] | **Roi de la Mer (IRE) (59)** (JAkehurst) **5-10-0** RHughes(8) (hld up: rdn over 2f out: sn wknd) | 1¾ | **15** | 8/1[3] | 40 | 26 |
| 4129[5] | **Captain's Day (50)** (TGMills) **4-9-5** JCarroll(6) (a bhd) | nk | **16** | 14/1 | 30 | 16 |
| 3469[4] | **Proud Brigadier (IRE) (51)** (PBurgoyne) **8-9-3**(3) AWhelan(2) (bhd fnl 2f) | 1¾ | **17** | 16/1 | 28 | 14 |
| 4000[16] | **Open Affair (57)** (APJarvis) **3-9-8** PatEddery(5) (bhd fnl 2f) | 2½ | **18** | 16/1 | 29 | 11 |
| 4263[9] | **Office Hours (52)** (CACyzer) **4-9-7** MRoberts(3) (prom over 5f) | 2½ | **19** | 20/1 | 19 | 5 |
| 3698[11] | **Real Gem (51)** (PJMakin) **3-9-2** SSanders(1) (a bhd) | 1¾ | **20** | 33/1 | 14 | — |
| *4089*[3] | **Sporting Risk (47)** (PWHarris) **4-9-2** AMcGlone(14) (prom over 4f) | 2½ | **21** | 14/1 | 5 | — |

(SP 144.1%) **21 Rn**

**1m 40.79** (3.59) CSF £176.86 CT £5,180.94 TOTE £15.00: £3.90 £6.30 £12.00 £1.10 (£486.00) Trio £2,070.60; £2,041.52 to Goodwood 26/9/96 OWNER Mrs B. Sumner (PULBOROUGH) BRED The Casual Partnership

WEIGHT FOR AGE 3yo-4lb

**1618 Crested Knight (IRE)** has been failing to stay over much further than this and, back over a more suitable distance, was able to lose his maiden tag. (9/1: 12/1-8/1)

**1613 Cats Bottom** ran her best race for some time, but she has basically deteriorated badly, and her only victory to date came on her two-year-old debut. (20/1)

**3977 Velvet Jones** ran on past beaten horses in the last furlong and a half to take third place, but this exposed maiden is extremely moderate, and one should not get too excited about this performance. (33/1)

**2994* King Parrot (IRE)** has gained three of his four victories this year for this pilot but, despite the combination running on in the last furlong and a half, they never looked like getting there in time. (11/2)

**2859 Baron Hrabovsky** looks extremely moderate, but did struggle on to be nearest at the line. (20/1)

**2602* Soaking** has never won over this far, but stayed on in the last furlong to be nearest at the line. (12/1)

## 4374 MERBURY CATERING CONSULTANTS H'CAP (0-80) (3-Y.O) (Class D)
5-30 (5-32) **1m 4f** £4,628.25 (£1,386.00: £665.50: £305.25) Stalls: Low GOING minus 0.22 sec per fur (GF)

| | | | | SP | RR | SF |
|---|---|---|---|---|---|---|
| 3594[11] | **Fasil (IRE) (80)** (CJBenstead) **3-9-7** RHills(3) (hdwy over 2f out: led over 1f out: edgd rt: r.o wl) | — | **1** | 14/1 | 92 | 62 |
| 4073[10] | **Snow Falcon (62)** (MBell) **3-8-3** MFenton(6) (s.s: hdwy 2f out: led wl over 1f out: sn hdd: unable qckn fnl f) | 2 | **2** | 8/1[3] | 71 | 41 |
| 3768[3] | **Major Dundee (IRE) (74)** (RHannon) **3-9-1** JReid(9) (hld up: rdn over 2f out: r.o ins fnl f) | 1¾ | **3** | 11/1 | 81 | 51 |
| 4067[11] | **Mattimeo (IRE) (72)** (APJarvis) **3-8-13** PatEddery(2) (hdwy over 2f out: ev ch over 1f out: wknd fnl f) | 1¼ | **4** | 11/4[1] | 77 | 47 |
| 3929[4] | **Quiet Arch (IRE) (60)** (CACyzer) **3-8-1** SDrowne(1) (a.p: hrd rdn over 2f out: ev ch over 1f out: sn wknd) | 3½ | **5** | 33/1 | 61 | 31 |
| 4083* | **Far Dawn (USA) (75)** (GHarwood) **3-9-2** AClark(4) (hld up: hrd rdn over 2f out: ev ch over 1f out: sn wknd) | ½ | **6** | 12/1 | 75 | 45 |
| 3657[5] | **Kitty Kitty Cancan (70)** (LadyHerries) **3-8-4**(7) PDoe(7) (hdwy 7f out: wknd over 3f out) | 3 | **7** | 14/1 | 66 | 36 |
| *3608*[2] | **Dhulikhel (56)** (DMarks) **3-7-4**(7) RMullen(5) (bhd fnl 2f) | nk | **8** | 25/1 | 52 | 22 |
| 3960* | **Divine (67)** (ACStewart) **3-8-8** MRoberts(8) (chsd ldr: led over 4f out tl wl over 1f out: sn wknd) | 2 | **9** | 11/4[1] | 60 | 30 |
| 4047[2] | **Shalateeno (65)** (BRMillman) **3-8-6** SSanders(10) (led over 7f) | 10 | **10** | 4/1[2] | 45 | 15 |

(SP 120.6%) **10 Rn**

**2m 37.14** (3.94) CSF £112.33 CT £1,180.11 TOTE £15.90: £2.80 £2.20 £2.30 (£48.00) Trio £138.30 OWNER Mr Hamdan Al Maktoum (EPSOM) BRED Ballyvolane Stud

**2128* Fasil (IRE)** bounced back to form and, striking the front below the distance, proved just too strong for the runner-up. (14/1: op 8/1)

**3968 Snow Falcon** poked his head in front early in the final quarter-mile, only to be collared by the winner soon afterwards. Grimly trying to hold on to that rival, he was tapped for toe in the last 100 yards. (8/1)

**3768 Major Dundee (IRE)** does not have a great turn of foot, but did stay on in the final furlong to take third prize. (11/1: 8/1-12/1)

**4067 Mattimeo (IRE)** had no excuses this time and had every chance below the distance before tiring. (11/4)

**3929 Quiet Arch (IRE)** may have found this just too far and, after having every chance over a furlong out, was soon in trouble. (33/1)

**4083* Far Dawn (USA)** was easily beaten in handicaps off slightly higher marks than this prior to his Bath maiden win and, once again, was in trouble in the final furlong having had every chance below the distance. (12/1: 8/1-14/1)

T/Jkpt: Not won; £11,305.98 to Goodwood 26/9/96. T/Plpt: £71.40 (258.55 Tckts). T/Qdpt: £33.00 (24.08 Tckts). AK

# 4368-GOODWOOD (R-H) (Good to firm)
## Thursday September 26th

Visibility: poor race 7

WEATHER: drizzle WIND: str half against

## 4375 VULCANA GAS APPLIANCES NURSERY H'CAP (0-85) (2-Y.O) (Class D)
2-30 (2-31) **1m** £4,127.75 (£1,232.00: £588.50: £266.75) Stalls: High GOING: 0.00 sec per fur (G)

| | | | | SP | RR | SF |
|---|---|---|---|---|---|---|
| 4262[7] | **Bold Oriental (IRE) (72)** (NACallaghan) **2-8-9** PatEddery(2) (stdy hdwy on ins over 2f out: n.m.r on ins over 1f out: led ins fnl f: rdn out) | — | **1** | 5/1[2] | 76 | 40 |

| Horse / details | Dist | Pos | SP | RR | SF |
|---|---|---|---|---|---|
| 4049[12] **Love Has No Pride (USA) (72)** (RHannon) **2-8-9** DaneO'Neill(5) (a.p: rdn over 2f out: led over 1f out tl ins fnl f: r.o) | nk | **2** | 8/1 | 75 | 39 |
| 3936[6] **Northern Sun (84)** (TGMills) **2-9-7** TQuinn(10) (hld up: rdn over 3f out: r.o one pce) | 3½ | **3** | 9/1 | 80 | 44 |
| 4303[5] **Merciless Cop (64)** (BJMeehan) **2-8-1b** CRutter(7) (led over 6f out tl over 1f out: wknd fnl f) | 3 | **4** | 10/1 | 54 | 18 |
| 4106[3] **Palaemon (70)** (GBBalding) **2-8-7** SDrowne(8) (lw: no hdwy fnl 2f) | 1 | **5** | 7/2[1] | 58 | 22 |
| 3964[5] **Mutahadeth (66)** (NAGraham) **2-8-3**ow1 DHarrison(6) (nvr nr to chal) | 4 | **6** | 16/1 | 46 | 9 |
| 4262[2] **Select Star (IRE) (68)** (APJarvis) **2-8-5** TSprake(3) (hdwy 4f out: wknd over 3f out) | 6 | **7** | 5/1[2] | 36 | — |
| 4303[10] **Talisman (IRE) (70)** (SDow) **2-8-7** MRoberts(4) (lw: led over 1f: wknd 3f out) | 7 | **8** | 33/1 | 24 | — |
| 3616[8] **Goodwood Lass (IRE) (76)** (JLDunlop) **2-8-13** KDarley(9) (lw: prom 4f) | nk | **9** | 6/1[3] | 30 | — |
| 3762[8] **Sun O'Tirol (IRE) (67)** (MRChannon) **2-8-4** JCarroll(1) (hdwy 4f out: wknd over 3f out) | 2 | **10** | 25/1 | 17 | — |

(SP 112.7%) **10 Rn**

**1m 42.35** (5.15) CSF £39.38 CT £321.97 TOTE £5.50: £2.20 £2.10 £3.30 (£22.00) Trio £50.80 OWNER Mr M. Tabor (NEWMARKET) BRED Leo Collins

OFFICIAL EXPLANATION **Select Star (IRE): lost a front plate during the race.**

**3975 Bold Oriental (IRE)** has been tried over a variety of trips, but it was over this longer distance that he finally opened his account. (5/1)
**3631* Love Has No Pride (USA)** had no problems with this longer trip and, although collared inside the final furlong, kept on well to the line. (8/1: 6/1-9/1)
**3936 Northern Sun** is a real stayer and had no trouble with this longer trip - the problem on this occasion was lack of acceleration. (9/1)
**4303 Merciless Cop** found this trip too far and, having set the pace, had little more to offer when collared below the distance. (10/1)
**4106 Palaemon** ran his best race to date at Lingfield last time, but was only treading water in the final quarter-mile here. (7/2)
**4262 Select Star (IRE)** ran no race at all, but his pilot later said the colt had lost a front plate during the contest. (5/1)

## 4376 J. S. HUMIDIFIERS H'CAP (0-85) (3-Y.O) (Class D)

3-00 (3-04) **7f** £4,592.50 (£1,375.00: £660.00: £302.50) Stalls: High GOING: 0.00 sec per fur (G)

| Horse / details | Dist | Pos | SP | RR | SF |
|---|---|---|---|---|---|
| 4322* **Don Bosio (USA) (86)** (MRStoute) **3-9-12v** 6x TQuinn(9) (swtg: hld up: qcknd to ld over 1f out: comf) | — | **1** | 6/1[3] | 102+ | 65 |
| 4202[4] **Carmarthen Bay (65)** (GLMoore) **3-8-5** GDuffield(15) (lw: nt clr run on ins over 3f out: nt clr run on ins over 2f out tl over 1f out: hdwy 1f out: r.o wl) | 2½ | **2** | 25/1 | 75 | 38 |
| 4064[13] **Quality (IRE) (78)** (WAO'Gorman) **3-9-4b** EmmaO'Gorman(10) (lw: rdn over 2f out: hdwy over 1f out: r.o) | 2½ | **3** | 16/1 | 83 | 46 |
| 4186[7] **Ca'd'oro (59)** (GBBalding) **3-7-10**(3) NVarley(1) (rdn over 3f out: hdwy over 1f out: r.o) | nk | **4** | 14/1 | 63 | 26 |
| 4109[4] **Caricature (IRE) (78)** (GLewis) **3-9-1b**(3) AWhelan(11) (a.p: rdn over 2f out: wknd fnl f) | 1 | **5** | 8/1 | 80 | 43 |
| 3767* **Kerry Ring (81)** (JHMGosden) **3-9-7** PatEddery(14) (lw: a.p: rdn 2f out: wknd fnl f) | ½ | **6** | 9/2[1] | 82 | 45 |
| 4058[17] **Never Think Twice (66)** (KTIvory) **3-8-6b** DBiggs(5) (b: hdwy 4f out: rdn over 2f out: wknd fnl f) | ¾ | **7** | 25/1 | 65 | 28 |
| 4308[2] **Press On Nicky (70)** (WRMuir) **3-8-10** JReid(8) (lw: led over 5f) | 2½ | **8** | 7/1 | 63 | 26 |
| 4198[7] **Ortolan (79)** (RHannon) **3-9-5** DaneO'Neill(2) (rdn over 2f out: hdwy over 1f out: wknd fnl f) | 1¾ | **9** | 11/2[2] | 68 | 31 |
| 4256[4] **Sea Danzig (63)** (JJBridger) **3-8-3**ow1 DHarrison(4) (lw: prom over 4f) | ¾ | **10** | 16/1 | 50 | 12 |
| 4136[15] **Statoyork (79)** (BWHills) **3-9-0**(5) JDSmith(7) (lw: prom over 4f) | 2 | **11** | 14/1 | 62 | 25 |
| 676[4] **Waypoint (73)** (RCharlton) **3-8-13** TSprake(6) (lw: hld up: rdn 2f out: sn wknd) | ½ | **12** | 14/1 | 55 | 18 |
| 3949* **Ruwy (77)** (CJBenstead) **3-9-3** RCochrane(12) (bhd fnl 2f) | hd | **13** | 14/1 | 58 | 21 |
| 4221[3] **Lucky Revenge (64)** (MartynMeade) **3-8-4**ow2 MRoberts(3) (a bhd) | 1¼ | **14** | 20/1 | 43 | 4 |

(SP 122.3%) **14 Rn**

**1m 28.52** (3.72) CSF £127.21 CT £2,074.67 TOTE £7.00: £2.50 £8.00 £6.80 (£106.70) Trio £547.50 OWNER Sultan Al Kabeer (NEWMARKET) BRED Poole Investments

**4322* Don Bosio (USA)** has had problems breaking his duck, but he did so without breaking sweat in a very small race at Catterick last week, which appears to have given him confidence. Despite topweight, he showed a fine turn of foot to sweep into the lead approaching the final furlong, and settled the issue in a matter of strides. (6/1)
**4202 Carmarthen Bay** had a nightmare run in the straight, and did extremely well to burst through and take second place. After an encouraging run here twelve days ago, he does seem to be returning to form and, as both his victories to date have come on the Equitrack, he looks one to note when returning to the Sand. (25/1)
**3967 Quality (IRE)** was doing all his best work in the last furlong and a half, but was never going to get there in time. Although he has won twice over this trip, his other three wins have come over further and a step up in distance may be in his favour. (16/1)
**3852 Ca'd'oro** found this trip rather sharp and was only running on at the death. A return to a mile would help. (14/1)
**4109 Caricature (IRE)** has been gradually slipping down the handicap but, after racing prominently, had come to the end of his tether entering the final furlong. (8/1)
**3767* Kerry Ring** scrambled home in an ordinary maiden at Sandown last month, and has been done no favours by the Handicapper. (9/2)
**4308 Press On Nicky** (7/1: 5/1-8/1)

## 4377 ROOF UNITS RATED STKS H'CAP (0-100) (3-Y.O+) (Class B)

3-30 (3-31) **2m** £7,967.96 (£2,941.64: £1,405.82: £568.10: £219.05: £79.43) Stalls: High GOING: 0.00 sec per fur (G)

| Horse / details | Dist | Pos | SP | RR | SF |
|---|---|---|---|---|---|
| 4112[2] **Candle Smile (USA) (90)** (MRStoute) **4-8-13** JReid(3) (mde all: pushed out) | — | **1** | 7/4[1] | 103 | 69 |
| 2533[9] **Asterita (98)** (DRLoder) **4-9-7** PatEddery(1) (lw: stdy hdwy over 3f out: chsd wnr over 2f out: rdn over 1f out: unable qckn) | 6 | **2** | 9/1 | 105 | 71 |
| 4178[7] **Haleakala (IRE) (95)** (MJohnston) **3-8-6** MRoberts(5) (b.nr fore: swtg: hld up: rdn over 3f out: wknd over 1f out) | 3½ | **3** | 9/4[2] | 99 | 53 |
| 3142* **Southern Power (IRE) (91)** (RAkehurst) **5-9-0** TQuinn(7) (b.nr hind: a.p: rdn over 4f out: wknd over 3f out: lame) | 13 | **4** | 3/1[3] | 82 | 48 |
| 3797[6] **Captain's Guest (IRE) (95)** (GHarwood) **6-9-4** AClark(2) (lw: a.p: rdn over 3f out: sn wknd) | 5 | **5** | 16/1 | 81 | 47 |
| **Blaaziing Joe (IRE) (95)** (DLWilliams) **5-9-4** DHarrison(4) (bit bkwd: a bhd: t.o fnl 4f) | dist | **6** | 66/1 | — | — |

(SP 109.5%) **6 Rn**

**3m 29.8** (5.80) CSF £14.89 TOTE £2.30: £1.20 £3.70 (£9.10) OWNER Maktoum Al Maktoum (NEWMARKET) BRED Maple Leaf Farm
WEIGHT FOR AGE 3yo-12lb

OFFICIAL EXPLANATION **Southern Power: finshed lame on his near-hind leg.**

**4112 Candle Smile (USA)** put up a fine display from the front and, nudged along, disposed of his only serious rival from below the distance. He will now head for the Cesarewitch, for which he just misses a penalty. (7/4)
**1128 Asterita**, who has changed stables since her last run nearly twelve weeks ago, looked in good shape and ran her best race of the year, looking a real threat to the winner below the distance before tapped for toe. She should soon make up for lost time. (9/1: 6/1-10/1)
**3992 Haleakala (IRE)** is short on experience, but still showed up well until tiring below the distance. (9/4)
**3142* Southern Power (IRE)** was extremely disappointing, but it later transpired that he had finished lame behind. This run is best ignored. (3/1)

**Captain's Guest (IRE)** was having only his second run on the Flat since winning the '94 Cesarewitch and ran a lot better until tiring three furlongs out. His trainer later reported he would have needed the run, and he is keen to get another race into him before he returns for the '96 Newmarket marathon. (16/1)

## 4378 CHARLTON HUNT SUPREME STKS (Gp 3) (3-Y.O+) (Class A)

4-00 (4-02) **7f** £23,430.00 (£8,778.00: £4,224.00: £1,848.00) Stalls: High GOING: 0.00 sec per fur (G)

| | | | | SP | RR | SF |
|---|---|---|---|---|---|---|
| 1574a[5] | **Tagula (IRE) (117)** (IABalding) **3-8-9** KDarley(7) (a.p: chsd ldr over 1f out: rdn fnl f: led last strides) | — | **1** | 4/1[3] | 119 | 65 |
| 4051[2] | **Wizard King (115)** (SirMarkPrescott) **5-8-12** GDuffield(6) (led: rdn over 1f out: hdd last strides) | hd | **2** | 5/2[2] | 119 | 68 |
| 3596[7] | **Thrilling Day (112)** (NAGraham) **3-8-10** DHarrison(9) (hmpd over 5f out: rdn over 3f out: hdwy & nt clr run on ins over 1f out: r.o one pce) | 6 | **3** | 12/1 | 106 | 52 |
| 4135* | **My Branch (112)** (BWHills) **3-8-6** MHills(4) (lw: hld up: nt clr run over 2f out: rdn over 1f out: wknd fnl f) | ½ | **4** | 2/1[1] | 101 | 47 |
| 3752a* | **Personal Love (USA)** (HSteinmetz,Germany) **3-8-6** ABest(5) (unf: chsd ldr over 5f) | 4 | **5** | 33/1 | 92 | 38 |
| 4239[2] | **Sergeyev (IRE) (112)** (RHannon) **4-9-2** RHughes(2) (stdd s: hdwy 2f out: wknd over 1f out) | 1 | **6** | 20/1 | 97 | 46 |
| 4254* | **Chewit (78)** (AMoore) **4-8-12** CandyMorris(3) (hld up: rdn over 2f out: wknd over 1f out) | 1¼ | **7** | 33/1 | 90 | 39 |
| 3517[8] | **Brief Glimpse (IRE) (100)** (MajorDNChappell) **4-8-9** PatEddery(1) (sme hdwy 2f out: wknd over 1f out) | 4 | **8** | 33/1 | 78 | 27 |
| 4185* | **Polar Prince (IRE) (110)** (MAJarvis) **3-8-9** RCochrane(8) (bhd whn hmpd over 5f out: nt rcvr) | 15 | **9** | 11/2 | 46 | — |
| | | | | (SP 118.6%) | **9 Rn** | |

**1m 27.17** (2.37) CSF £14.20 TOTE £5.60: £1.90 £1.70 £2.60 (£9.50) Trio £33.30 OWNER Robert & Elizabeth Hitchins (KINGSCLERE) BRED Sean and Patrick Twomey

WEIGHT FOR AGE 3yo-3lb

**1574a Tagula (IRE)** has had a series of problems including back trouble and, as a result, was having his first run in four months. Well suited by the drop to seven, he put up a useful display and gradually reeled in the leader to get up in the last couple of strides. The Prix de la Foret is his next target. (4/1: 3/1-9/2)

**4051 Wizard King** is a gutsy as they come and once again ran his heart out. Doing it the hard way as usual, he grimly held on until overhauled in the last couple of strides. He will now go for the Group Three Coolmore Home of Champions Concorde Stakes at Tipperary, where he was beaten a short-head last year. He richly deserves his first Group success. (5/2)

**3596 Thrilling Day**, who got involved in scrimmaging over five furlongs out, stayed on for third without ever looking a serious threat. Her trainer later reported that the filly was struck into by Polar Prince, and sustained an injury in the process. (12/1: op 8/1)

**4135* My Branch** is very much in and out and, after a brilliant display last time, disappointed here, never really getting into the action. (2/1)

**3752a* Personal Love (USA)**, winner of a listed race in her native Germany this year, raced in second place until calling it a day over a furlong out. (33/1)

**4239 Sergeyev (IRE)** seems to be a shadow of his former self, and yet again proved very disappointing. (20/1)

**4185* Polar Prince (IRE)** was at the back of the field when badly hampered over five out, causing him to lose a lot of ground. He could never recover and this run is best forgotten. (11/2)

## 4379 CRANE FLUID SYSTEMS ABV MAIDEN STKS (3-Y.O) (Class D)

4-30 (4-32) **1m 2f** £4,342.25 (£1,298.00: £621.50: £283.25) Stalls: High GOING: 0.00 sec per fur (G)

| | | | | SP | RR | SF |
|---|---|---|---|---|---|---|
| 3986[2] | **Filmore West** (PFICole) **3-9-0** TQuinn(2) (mde all: rdn over 2f out: clr over 1f out: r.o wl) | — | **1** | 5/4[1] | 85 | 34 |
| 2601[3] | **Renzo (IRE) (82)** (GHarwood) **3-9-0** AClark(1) (a.p: rdn over 2f out: r.o one pce) | 3 | **2** | 2/1[2] | 80 | 29 |
| 4125[8] | **Apache Len (USA) (70)** (RHannon) **3-9-0v[1]** RHughes(4) (hld up: rdn over 3f out: nt clr run over 1f out: one pce) | ¾ | **3** | 33/1 | 79 | 28 |
| 4243[4] | **Lituus (USA) (77)** (JHMGosden) **3-9-0** JCarroll(8) (chsd wnr: ev ch over 2f out: edgd lft over 1f out: one pce) | 1 | **4** | 13/2[3] | 77 | 26 |
| | **Brother Roy** (TGMills) **3-9-0** JReid(3) (hld up: rdn over 3f out: wknd over 2f out) | 10 | **5** | 33/1 | 61 | 10 |
| | **Harlestone Heath** (JLDunlop) **3-8-9** GDuffield(7) (lt-f: a bhd: t.o fnl 6f) | 6 | **6** | 25/1 | 47 | — |
| 4201[F] | **Sovereign Crest (IRE)** (CAHorgan) **3-9-0** SWhitworth(9) (s.s: a bhd: t.o fnl 6f) | 3 | **7** | 50/1 | 47 | — |
| | **Questing Star** (GWragg) **3-8-9** MHills(6) (w'like: hld up: rdn over 3f out: wknd over 2f out: t.o) | 1½ | **8** | 10/1 | 40 | — |
| | **Thatcham Island** (DLWilliams) **3-8-9** DHarrison(5) (w'like: s.s: a bhd: t.o fnl 5f) | dist | **9** | 66/1 | — | — |
| | | | | (SP 113.4%) | **9 Rn** | |

**2m 13.58** (8.08) CSF £3.92 TOTE £1.90: £1.30 £1.20 £3.40 (£2.50) Trio £23.50 OWNER Mr Christopher Wright (WHATCOMBE) BRED Meon Valley Stud

**3986 Filmore West** dictated matters from the front and forged clear in the final quarter-mile to win a poor race. (5/4)

**2601 Renzo (IRE)**, not helped by the drop back in distance, got rather outpaced early in the straight and, although carrying his head rather high, did struggle on to take second inside the final furlong. A return to a mile and a half is required. (2/1)

**3929 Apache Len (USA)** chased the leaders and, although done no favours by the fourth below the distance, was looking one-paced at the time. He ran well in claiming company last month and a return to that class might help. (33/1)

**4243 Lituus (USA)** is certainly one of the stable's lesser lights and once again had his lack of pace well exposed. (13/2)

**Brother Roy**, without a run since May last year, found lack of a recent run taking its toll over two furlongs out. (33/1)

**Questing Star** (10/1: op 5/1)

## 4380 E.B.F. IMI AIR CONDITIONING MAIDEN STKS (2-Y.O) (Class D)

5-00 (5-04) **6f** £4,413.75 (£1,320.00: £632.50: £288.75) Stalls: Low GOING: 0.00 sec per fur (G)

| | | | | SP | RR | SF |
|---|---|---|---|---|---|---|
| 3245[2] | **Bachelors Pad** (WJarvis) **2-9-0** PatEddery(11) (a.p: led over 1f out: r.o wl) | — | **1** | 5/6[1] | 96+ | 56 |
| 3245[10] | **Moonshiner (USA)** (GWragg) **2-9-0** MHills(8) (a.p: led 2f out tl over 1f out: unable qckn) | 3½ | **2** | 11/2[2] | 87 | 47 |
| 4188[3] | **Select Choice (IRE) (82)** (APJarvis) **2-9-0** KDarley(6) (led 4f: one pce) | 2½ | **3** | 14/1 | 80 | 40 |
| | **Royal Born** (WJarvis) **2-9-0** StephenDavies(10) (rdn over 2f out: gd hdwy fnl f: r.o wl: bttr for r) | nk | **4** | 33/1 | 79+ | 39 |
| 3277[4] | **Dawam Allail (78)** (MAJarvis) **2-9-0** RCochrane(9) (lw: hld up: rdn over 2f out: one pce) | s.h | **5** | 9/1 | 79 | 39 |
| 4062[7] | **Junie (IRE)** (TGMills) **2-8-9** TQuinn(17) (hdwy over 2f out: rdn over 1f out: one pce) | s.h | **6** | 16/1 | 74 | 34 |
| 4127[9] | **Village Pub (FR)** (KOCunningham-Brown) **2-9-0** TSprake(7) (lw: prom 3f) | 1½ | **7** | 25/1 | 75 | 35 |
| 4188[10] | **Cheval Roc** (RHannon) **2-9-0** DaneO'Neill(2) (lw: prom 3f) | hd | **8** | 20/1 | 75 | 35 |
| | **Rock To The Top (IRE)** (JJSheehan) **2-9-0** SDrowne(4) (leggy: scope: lw: prom over 2f) | 1¼ | **9** | 50/1 | 71 | 31 |
| 3502[11] | **Bon Guest (IRE)** (TJNaughton) **2-8-9(5)** JDSmith(14) (hld up: rdn over 2f out: wknd over 1f out) | s.h | **10** | 33/1 | 71 | 31 |
| 1959[6] | **Smokebush** (LordHuntingdon) **2-9-0** DHarrison(3) (bhd fnl 3f) | 1¼ | **11** | 14/1 | 68 | 28 |
| 924[5] | **Janie's Boy** (JohnBerry) **2-9-0** RHughes(13) (hld up: rdn over 2f out: wknd over 1f out) | 1¼ | **12** | 33/1 | 65 | 25 |
| | **Buzzby Babe** (AGFoster) **2-8-4(5)** CAdamson(1) (neat: bhd fnl 3f) | 1 | **13** | 50/1 | 57 | 17 |
| 4123[14] | **Right Man** (GLewis) **2-9-0** SWhitworth(12) (s.s: a bhd) | s.h | **14** | 33/1 | 62 | 22 |
| 3807[19] | **Little Progress** (TMJones) **2-9-0** RPerham(16) (hdwy over 2f out: wknd over 1f out) | s.h | **15** | 66/1 | 62 | 22 |

| | | | | SP | RR | SF |
|---|---|---|---|---|---|---|
| 2252$^{4}$ | **Debonair** (GLewis) **2-8-6**(3) AWhelan(5) (b.nr hind: bit bkwd: dwlt: a bhd) | 2½ | **16** | 33/1 | 50 | 10 |
| | **Desert Warrior (IRE)** (MissGayKelleway) **2-9-0** JReid(18) (b.hind: str: scope: s.s: a bhd) | 1 | **17** | 8/1$^{3}$ | 52 | 12 |

(SP 139.0%) **17 Rn**

**1m 12.91** (2.91) CSF £7.42 TOTE £1.90: £1.20 £2.50 £3.50 (£7.40) Trio £32.00 OWNER Mrs Doris Allen (NEWMARKET) BRED Mrs F. G. Allen

**3245 Bachelors Pad** confirmed the promise shown on his Newmarket debut and, sent on approaching the final furlong, quickly asserted. His trainer thinks a lot of him. (5/6)

**3245 Moonshiner (USA)** left his debut run well behind and should soon pick up a race. (11/2)

**4188 Select Choice (IRE)**, once again, was made to look very one-paced in the last two furlongs. (14/1: 8/1-16/1)

**Royal Born** caught the eye on this debut. With only four behind him at the distance, he made up a tremendous amount of ground in the final furlong, only just missing out on third prize. Sure to be a lot wiser for this, he should pick up a race in due course. (33/1)

**3277 Dawam Allail** was once again caught short of acceleration when the real race began in the final quarter-mile. (9/1: 6/1-10/1)

**Junie (IRE)** was tapped for toe below the distance. (16/1)

**Desert Warrior (IRE)** (8/1: 4/1-10/1)

## 4381 FANS DIRECT 100% CASH BACK APPRENTICE H'CAP (0-80) (3-Y.O+) (Class E)

5-35 (5-38) **1m 1f** £3,980.00 (£1,190.00: £570.00: £260.00) Stalls: High GOING: 0.00 sec per fur (G)

| | | | | SP | RR | SF |
|---|---|---|---|---|---|---|
| 3765* | **Koathary (USA) (70)** (LGCottrell) **5-9-7** DGriffiths(9) (lw: hdwy 3f out: led 2f out: clr over 1f out: r.o wl) | — | **1** | 5/2$^{2}$ | 86 | 35 |
| 4047* | **Sawa-Id (77)** (JHMGosden) **3-9-6**(3) AEddery(3) (hld up: ev ch 2f out: unable qckn) | 5 | **2** | 7/2$^{3}$ | 84 | 28 |
| 4125$^{5}$ | **Pay Homage (72)** (IABalding) **8-9-2**(7) RFowley(8) (lw: chsd ldr: led 3f out to 2f out: one pce) | 1 | **3** | 13/2 | 77 | 26 |
| *337$^{4}$* | **By The Bay (52)** (SDow) **4-8-3** ADaly(6) (hdwy over 1f out: r.o) | 1 | **4** | 33/1 | 56 | 5 |
| 4238$^{2}$ | **Rory (74)** (MrsJCecil) **5-9-8**(3) AmandaSanders(2) (hdwy over 3f out: wknd over 2f out) | 2½ | **5** | 9/4$^{1}$ | 73 | 22 |
| *553$^{7}$* | **Hatta Sunshine (USA) (45)** (AMoore) **6-7-10** CAdamson(5) (hdwy over 3f out: wknd over 2f out) | 3½ | **6** | 33/1 | 38 | — |
| 3496$^{10}$ | **Runic Symbol (45)** (MBlanshard) **5-7-5**(5) KerryBaker(1) (bhd fnl 5f) | nk | **7** | 25/1 | 37 | — |
| 1825$^{6}$ | **Queen of All Birds (IRE) (71)** (RBoss) **5-9-5**(3) GFaulkner(4) (hdwy over 3f out: wknd over 2f out) | 4 | **8** | 9/1 | 56 | 5 |
| 4047$^{4}$ | **Shady Girl (IRE) (67)** (BWHills) **3-8-13b$^{1}$** JDSmith(7) (led & sn clr: c wd st: hdd 3f out: sn wknd) | 18 | **9** | 14/1 | 20 | — |

(SP 121.3%) **9 Rn**

**1m 59.19** (7.79) CSF £11.88 CT £46.63 TOTE £4.00: £1.90 £1.60 £1.80 (£5.00) Trio £17.80 OWNER Mr E. J. S. Gadsden (CULLOMPTON) BRED Calumet Farm

LONG HANDICAP Runic Symbol 7-6 Hatta Sunshine (USA) 7-5

WEIGHT FOR AGE 3yo-5lb

**3765* Koathary (USA)** annihilated the opposition to complete the hat-trick, despite a rise of 7lb in the handicap. (5/2)

**4047* Sawa-Id** has risen another 6lb in the weights for his last win and, after having every chance a quarter of a mile out, was left standing by the winner. (7/2: op 9/4)

**4125 Pay Homage**, without a win since May '95, had his hopes of victory dashed when he was left standing in the final quarter-mile. (13/2)

**337 By The Bay**, off the track since February, is still a maiden. (33/1)

**4238 Rory** was 2lb well-in at the weights, making this performance even more disappointing. (9/4)

T/Jkpt: £3,416.80 (4.15 Tckts). T/Plpt: £72.60 (287.79 Tckts). T/Qdpt: £3.40 (313.75 Tckts). AK

# 3968-PONTEFRACT (L-H) (Good to firm, Firm patches)

## Thursday September 26th

WEATHER: changeable WIND: mod across

## 4382 AMEC DEVELOPMENTS H'CAP (0-70) (3-Y.O+) (Class E)

2-45 (2-46) **5f** £3,314.00 (£992.00: £476.00: £218.00) Stalls: Low GOING minus 0.01 sec per fur (G)

| | | | | SP | RR | SF |
|---|---|---|---|---|---|---|
| 3959$^{2}$ | **Bowlers Boy (68)** (JJQuinn) **3-9-9**(5) GParkin(18) (lw: racd wd: hld up: gd hdwy over 1f out: r.o wl to ld towards fin: cleverly) | — | **1** | 14/1 | 75 | 56 |
| 3973$^{6}$ | **Captain Carat (61)** (MrsJRRamsden) **5-9-8** KFallon(4) (stumbled s: bhd: gd hdwy ½-wy: hmpd & swtchd rt ins fnl f: r.o) | ¾ | **2** | 4/1$^{1}$ | 66 | 48 |
| 4088$^{2}$ | **Ned's Bonanza (61)** (MDods) **7-9-5**(3) FLynch(9) (lw: trckd ldrs: led ins fnl f: hdd & no ex towards fin) | ½ | **3** | 5/1$^{2}$ | 64 | 46 |
| 4180$^{10}$ | **Tropical Beach (66)** (JBerry) **3-9-5**(7) CLowther(6) (s.i.s: bhd tl styd on fnl 2f: nt rch ldrs) | 1½ | **4** | 14/1 | 64 | 45 |
| 4246$^{18}$ | **Just Dissident (IRE) (62)** (RMWhitaker) **4-9-9** DeanMcKeown(3) (lw: w ldr: led ½-wy tl ins fnl f) | s.h | **5** | 11/1 | 60 | 42 |
| 4180$^{16}$ | **Chadwell Hall (65)** (SRBowring) **5-9-9b**(3) CTeague(7) (led to ½-wy: edgd lft & wknd ins fnl f) | nk | **6** | 14/1 | 62 | 44 |
| 4071$^{13}$ | **Comic Fantasy (AUS) (64)** (JLEyre) **3-9-7b**(3) OPears(12) (bhd: hdwy on outside over 1f out: nvr nr ldrs) | 2 | **7** | 20/1 | 55 | 36 |
| 4205$^{8}$ | **Lloc (54)** (CADwyer) **4-9-1** MTebbutt(17) (racd wd: hdwy over 1f out: nvr nr to chal) | s.h | **8** | 16/1 | 45 | 27 |
| 4206$^{6}$ | **Whispered Melody (60)** (PWHarris) **3-8-13**(7) JoHunnam(10) (chsd ldrs: rdn ½-wy: wknd over 1f out) | hd | **9** | 14/1 | 50 | 31 |
| 3465$^{10}$ | **Chalice (65)** (JBalding) **3-9-4**(7) JEdmunds(5) (hld up & bhd: stdy hdwy on ins over 1f out: nvr plcd to chal) | ½ | **10** | 33/1 | 54 | 35 |
| 4088$^{8}$ | **Princely Sound (62)** (MBell) **3-9-8** MFenton(14) (lw: in tch: rdn ½-wy: sn lost pl) | nk | **11** | 10/1 | 50 | 31 |
| 4130$^{9}$ | **Colston-C (56)** (PDEvans) **4-9-3** JFEgan(16) (racd wd: outpcd ½-wy: sltly hmpd over 1f out: eased) | 1¾ | **12** | 12/1 | 38 | 20 |
| 4246$^{2}$ | **Pageboy (65)** (PCHaslam) **7-9-12** JFortune(15) (lw: chsd ldrs: effrt over 1f out: sn wknd & eased) | ¾ | **13** | 6/1$^{3}$ | 45 | 27 |
| 2481$^{11}$ | **Thick as Thieves (48)** (RonaldThompson) **4-8-9** NConnorton(2) (trckd ldrs to ½-wy: sn bhd) | hd | **14** | 33/1 | 27 | 9 |
| 3793$^{8}$ | **Shadow Jury (66)** (DWChapman) **6-9-13b** LCharnock(8) (chsd ldrs tl wknd 2f out: eased) | 1 | **15** | 16/1 | 42 | 24 |
| 4108$^{8}$ | **Sharp Move (44)** (MrsJCecil) **4-8-0**(5) MartinDwyer(1) (sn outpcd: n.d) | s.h | **16** | 14/1 | 20 | 2 |
| 3995$^{18}$ | **Mister Joel (58)** (MWEasterby) **3-9-4b** ACulhane(11) (trckd ldrs: hmpd ½-wy: n.d after) | s.h | **17** | 20/1 | 34 | 15 |
| 4180$^{9}$ | **Playmaker (61)** (DNicholls) **3-9-7b** AlexGreaves(13) (lw: sltly hmpd ½-wy: n.d) | 1¼ | **18** | 14/1 | 33 | 14 |

(SP 143.2%) **18 Rn**

**64.1 secs** (3.30) CSF £74.16 CT £323.09 TOTE £20.40: £3.80 £1.60 £1.20 £3.40 (£63.20) Trio £47.20 OWNER Bowlers Racing (MALTON) BRED Roldvale Ltd

WEIGHT FOR AGE 3yo-1lb

STEWARDS' ENQUIRY Egan susp. 5-7/10/96 (failure to obtain best possible placing). Evans fined £300.

**3959 Bowlers Boy,** dropped back to five and from a 4lb higher mark than at Hamilton, raced wide, possibly on the better-watered ground. Almost last once in line for home, he showed a tremendous turn of foot and won cheekily in the end. He was a revelation here. (14/1)

**3352 Captain Carat,** not for the first time, gave trouble in the stalls and lost ground. Staying on when trying for an ambitious run between horses inside the last, he had to be switched but would not have beaten the winner. (4/1: op 6/1)

**4088 Ned's Bonanza** seems to be at the top of his form at present. (5/1)

**3793 Tropical Beach,** an ideal ride for an inexperienced pilot, finished strongly after missing the break yet again. (14/1)

**3868* Just Dissident (IRE)**, ideally drawn, showed all his old speed. (11/1)
**3618 Chadwell Hall** came of a true line under pressure, leaving Captain Carat with no room. (14/1)
**3135 Chalice** has slipped down the weights 7lb after three unplaced runs and ran an eye-opener here. (33/1)

## 4383 E.B.F. HIGH BAY WAREHOUSE MAIDEN STKS (2-Y.O) (Class D)

3-20 (3-21) **6f** £4,435.50 (£1,344.00: £657.00: £313.50) Stalls: Low GOING minus 0.01 sec per fur (G)

| | | | | SP | RR | SF |
|---|---|---|---|---|---|---|
| $3293^{2}$ | **Intikhab (USA)** (DMorley) **2-9-0** RHills(7) (lw: trckd ldrs gng wl: smooth hdwy to ld over 1f out: readily) | — | **1** | 1/2 [1] | 83+ | 38 |
| $4204^{7}$ | **Polar Flight** (MJohnston) **2-9-0** JWeaver(4) (sn rdn along & hung lft: hdwy & swtchd outside over 1f out: styd on: no ch w wnr) | 2½ | **2** | 12/1 [3] | 76 | 31 |
| | **Tayseer (USA)** (EALDunlop) **2-9-0** KFallon(2) (leggy: scope: s.s: hdwy ½-wy: nt clr run over 1f out: kpt on same pace) | 1½ | **3** | 10/1 [2] | 72 | 27 |
| $4241^{6}$ | **Rochea** (WJHaggas) **2-8-9** MFenton(10) (w ldrs: led over 2f out tl over 1f out: kpt on same pce) | 1¼ | **4** | 16/1 | 64 | 19 |
| $4253^{6}$ | **Pietro Bembo (IRE)** (SirMarkPrescott) **2-9-0** SSanders(1) (hld up & bhd: hdwy 2f out: styd on ins fnl f) | 6 | **5** | 10/1 [2] | 53 | 8 |
| $2413^{5}$ | **Wobble** (WJHaggas) **2-9-0** NDay(6) (bhd: hdwy over 1f out: nvr nr ldrs) | 1½ | **6** | 20/1 | 49 | 4 |
| $2219^{6}$ | **Baileys Imp (IRE)** (MJohnston) **2-9-0** DeanMcKeown(3) (led tl over 2f out: wknd over 1f out) | ½ | **7** | 20/1 | 48 | 3 |
| $4123^{5}$ | **Around Fore Alliss** (TGMills) **2-9-0** JFortune(9) (lw: chsd ldrs tl wknd over 2f out) | hd | **8** | 14/1 | 47 | 2 |
| $3757^{12}$ | **Dawn Summit** (BHanbury) **2-9-0** JStack(5) (bit bkwd: in tch: effrt over 2f out: sn wl outpcd) | 2½ | **9** | 25/1 | 41 | — |
| | **Freedom of Troy** (JLEyre) **2-9-0** RLappin(8) (leggy: unf: pushed along ½-wy: sn wl outpcd) | 1¾ | **10** | 25/1 | 36 | — |
| $4072^{9}$ | **Hello There** (NTinkler) **2-9-0** KimTinkler(11) (a outpcd & bhd) | s.h | **11** | 50/1 | 36 | — |
| $3879^{8}$ | **True Perspective** (JDBethell) **2-9-0** GBardwell(12) (swtg: w ldrs over 3f: sn wknd) | 3½ | **12** | 50/1 | 27 | — |
| | | | | (SP 126.2%) | **12 Rn** | |

**1m 18.7** (4.40) CSF £8.86 TOTE £1.50: £1.10 £2.20 £2.10 (£6.30) Trio £7.30 OWNER Mr Hamdan Al Maktoum (NEWMARKET) BRED J. I. Racing Inc. and Marvin Little Jr

**3293 Intikhab (USA)** showed bags of promise first time and stood out in the paddock here. He showed a fluent action going down and, travelling best throughout, had only to be nudged along to score in good style. (1/2)
**Polar Flight** is still learning. Struggling to go the pace and tending to hang towards the rail, he stuck on when switched to the outside, but the winner was in a different league. (12/1: op 8/1)
**Tayseer (USA)**, who is on the leg, missed the break. Pushed along to improve at halfway, he ran into trouble over a furlong out but, when he saw daylight, he could only stick on at the same pace. The outing is sure to bring him on. (10/1: op 5/1)
**4241 Rochea** is a keen-going type. (16/1)
**4253 Pietro Bembo (IRE)**, dropped in at the start, is definitely not without ability and needs one more run to qualify for handicaps. (10/1)
**2413 Wobble**, taken to post slowly, took a while to get the hang of things, but the way he was staying on at the finish, suggests there is better to come in time. (20/1)

## 4384 WAKEFIELD EUROPORT FAST TRACK TO EUROPE NURSERY H'CAP (0-85) (2-Y.O) (Class D)

3-50 (3-52) **1m 4y** £4,110.00 (£1,230.00: £590.00: £270.00) Stalls: Low GOING minus 0.01 sec per fur (G)

| | | | | SP | RR | SF |
|---|---|---|---|---|---|---|
| $4298^{2}$ | **Southerly Wind (75)** (MrsJRRamsden) **2-9-1** KFallon(3) (lw: hdwy to chse ldrs ½-wy: led over 1f out: styd on strly) | — | **1** | 5/4 [1] | 74 | 41 |
| $4298^{4}$ | **I Can't Remember (78)** (PDEvans) **2-9-4** JFEgan(7) (a chsng ldrs: kpt on u.p fnl f: no ch w wnr) | 1¼ | **2** | 12/1 | 75 | 42 |
| $3319^{6}$ | **Ikatania (78)** (JLDunlop) **2-9-4** GCarter(11) (lw: sn bhd & pushed along: hdwy 2f out: styd on ins fnl f) | ¾ | **3** | 8/1 [3] | 73 | 40 |
| $3685^{11}$ | **Ellway Lady (IRE) (65)** (IABalding) **2-8-0**(5) MartinDwyer(10) (bhd: hdwy on outside 2f out: styd on fnl f) | ¾ | **4** | 14/1 | 59 | 26 |
| 4262* | **Can Can Lady (76)** (MJohnston) **2-9-2** 6x JWeaver(1) (led tl over 1f out: wknd towards fin) | ¾ | **5** | 11/2 [2] | 68 | 35 |
| $4223^{U}$ | **Not A Lot (60)** (MWEasterby) **2-8-0** LCharnock(6) (hld up: hdwy 2f out: kpt on: nvr nr to chal) | 1¼ | **6** | 25/1 | 50 | 17 |
| $4262^{6}$ | **Gresatre (64)** (CADwyer) **2-8-4** JQuinn(2) (chsd ldrs tl outpcd over 1f out) | ½ | **7** | 12/1 | 53 | 20 |
| $3998^{9}$ | **Sparky (63)** (MWEasterby) **2-8-3b** JFanning(9) (lw: racd wd: chsd ldrs: rdn & wandered 3f out: wknd over 1f out) | 7 | **8** | 16/1 | 38 | 5 |
| $3835^{12}$ | **Ninth Symphony (78)** (PCHaslam) **2-9-4** JFortune(12) (hld up & bhd: hung bdly rt & rn wd ent st) | 9 | **9** | 9/1 | 35 | 2 |
| $3936^{8}$ | **Skelton Sovereign (IRE) (68)** (RHollinshead) **2-8-5**(3) FLynch(8) (lw: s.i.s: effrt over 3f out: sn wknd) | nk | **10** | 20/1 | 24 | — |
| $4084^{3}$ | **Elrayahin (81)** (MajorWRHern) **2-9-7b** RHills(4) (chsd ldrs tl wknd 2f out) | nk | **11** | 17/2 | 36 | 3 |
| $4041^{10}$ | **Real Fire (IRE) (57)** (MGMeagher) **2-7-8b1**(3)ow1 DWright(5) (a bhd: lost tch over 2f out) | 7 | **12** | 40/1 | — | — |
| | | | | (SP 130.4%) | **12 Rn** | |

**1m 47.3** (5.80) CSF £18.63 CT £95.66 TOTE £2.30: £1.20 £2.00 £2.80 (£13.10) Trio £51.80 OWNER Mr M. J. Simmonds (THIRSK) BRED M. J. Simmonds

LONG HANDICAP Real Fire (IRE) 7-9

**4298 Southerly Wind**, who will be put up 3lb in future after his unlucky Ayr effort, made no mistakes, but his rider earned his fee. He took plenty of rousting along and, once in front, tended to wander. He scored decisively in the end though and is a promising young stayer. (5/4)
**4298 I Can't Remember** is as tough as they come and stayed this stiff mile really well. (12/1)
**3319 Ikatania**, very lethargic, was staying on when it was all over. It seems all he does is stay. (8/1)
**3438 Ellway Lady (IRE)**, who looked to have been given plenty to do at the weights, appreciated the step up in distance and will improve for an even stiffer test. (14/1)
**4262* Can Can Lady**, from a 4lb higher mark, tried hard to make all but she was leg-weary inside the last. (11/2)

## 4385 WAKEFIELD EUROPORT DALBY SCREW-DRIVER RATED STKS H'CAP (0-95) (3-Y.O+) (Class C)

4-20 (4-21) **1m 2f 6y** £6,720.80 (£2,487.20: £1,193.60: £488.00: £194.00: £76.40) Stalls: Low GOING minus 0.01 sec per fur (G)

| | | | | SP | RR | SF |
|---|---|---|---|---|---|---|
| $3981^{2}$ | **Mellottie (84)** (MrsMReveley) **11-8-10** ACulhane(3) (lw: hld up: nt clr run over 3f out: swtchd outside & gd hdwy over 1f out: r.o wl to ld nr fin) | — | **1** | 12/1 | 101 | 71 |
| $4193^{11}$ | **Skillington (USA) (88)** (IABalding) **3-8-3v1**(5) MartinDwyer(4) (lw: led: clr over 1f out: edgd rt: hdd & no ex nr fin) | nk | **2** | 7/1 | 105 | 69 |
| $4193^{14}$ | **Celestial Choir (91)** (JLEyre) **6-9-3** JFortune(5) (hld up: effrt over 3f out: gd hdwy over 1f out: r.o) | 3 | **3** | 9/2 [1] | 103 | 73 |
| $3791^{2}$ | **Henry Island (IRE) (89)** (GWragg) **3-8-9** RHills(9) (chsd ldrs: effrt over 2f out: wknd fnl f) | 3½ | **4** | 5/1 [2] | 95 | 59 |
| $4125^{4}$ | **Roufontaine (81)** (WRMuir) **5-8-4**(3) RHavlin(7) (chsd ldrs: chal over 4f out: wknd appr fnl f) | 2½ | **5** | 14/1 | 83 | 53 |
| $3229^{7}$ | **Polar Eclipse (91)** (MJohnston) **3-8-11** JWeaver(2) (a in tch: drvn along & no imp fnl 3f) | 1½ | **6** | 16/1 | 91 | 55 |
| $3145^{11}$ | **Frog (81)** (SirMarkPrescott) **3-8-1** SSanders(1) (lw: chsd ldrs: rdn 3f out: wknd over 1f out) | 2½ | **7** | 9/1 | 77 | 41 |
| $4308^{8}$ | **Moments of Fortune (USA) (95)** (BHanbury) **4-9-7** WRyan(10) (drvn over 5f out: lost pl over 3f out: eased fnl f) | 12 | **8** | 9/1 | 72 | 42 |
| $3669^{7}$ | **Private Song (USA) (92)** (RCharlton) **3-8-12** AMcGlone(6) (chsd ldr: drvn 5f out: lost pl over 3f out: eased) | 1½ | **9** | 13/2 [3] | 66 | 30 |

3691[14] **Al Shafa (95)** (JLDunlop) **3-9-1** GCarter(8) (a bhd: drvn along 5f out: eased fnl 2f)........................................21 **10** 8/1 36 —
1841[5] **Hand Craft (IRE) (81)** (WJHaggas) **4-8-7** KFallon(11) (hld up & bhd: sme hdwy over 2f out: sn wknd: eased).¾ **11** 14/1 21 —
(SP 118.7%) **11 Rn**

**2m 11.2** (2.90) CSF £86.32 CT £403.26 TOTE £8.90: £2.00 £2.50 £1.90 (£33.80) Trio £44.80 OWNER Mrs J. G. Fulton (SALTBURN) BRED Mrs G. R. Reveley and Partners
LONG HANDICAP Roufontaine 8-6 Hand Craft (IRE) 8-5 Frog 8-0
WEIGHT FOR AGE 3yo-6lb

**3981 Mellottie** signed off what has been a brilliant career, winning his sixteenth Flat race from sixty-three starts, after starting out winning bumpers and then over hurdles. (12/1)
**3145 Skillington (USA)**, tried in a visor, set a strong pace and had all but the winner in trouble at halfway. Showing several lengths clear over a furlong out, he came off the rail as he tired and was just caught. (7/1)
**3710* Celestial Choir** put a poor effort last time behind her, and stayed on in most determined fashion. (9/2)
**3791 Henry Island (IRE)**, with a senior jockey aboard this time, tired entering the final furlong after being hard at work some way out. (5/1)
**4125 Roufontaine** tried to match strides with the winner from halfway, but was very leg-weary entering the last. (14/1)
**3145 Frog**, absent for almost two months, should come on for the outing. (9/1)

## 4386 WAKEFIELD EUROPORT MAIDEN STKS (2-Y.O) (Class D)
4-50 (4-50) **1m 4y** £3,468.75 (£1,050.00: £512.50: £243.75) Stalls: Low GOING minus 0.01 sec per fur (G)

SP RR SF
3821[2] **Panama City (USA)** (PWChapple-Hyam) **2-8-11**(3) RHavlin(4) (trckd ldr: led over 2f out: r.o wl)....................— **1** 6/4[1] 81 28
3964[2] **St Lawrence (CAN)** (CEBrittain) **2-9-0** BDoyle(8) (trckd ldrs: effrt over 2f out: kpt on fnl f: no ch w wnr) .......2½ **2** 9/2[2] 76 23
3987[10] **Kalinini (USA)** (LMCumani) **2-9-0** OUrbina(9) (bit bkwd: in tch: hdwy to chse ldrs ½-wy: effrt & hung lft over 1f out: styd on one pce)........................................1¾ **3** 9/2[2] 73 20
2967[3] **Love Me Do (USA)** (MJohnston) **2-9-0** JWeaver(2) (lw: led tl over 2f out: wknd towards fin) ..........................¾ **4** 6/1[3] 71 18
4105[7] **Little Miss Rocker** (IABalding) **2-8-4**(5) MartinDwyer(5) (chsd ldrs: rdn & outpcd over 2f out: styd on fnl f) ......2 **5** 20/1 62 9
**Moonlight Invader (IRE)** (EALDunlop) **2-9-0** WRyan(1) (wl grwn: scope: bit bkwd: dwlt: bhd: effrt over 2f out: rn green: styd on ins fnl f)........................................nk **6** 10/1 66 13
4050[9] **Tango King** (JLDunlop) **2-9-0** AMcGlone(7) (s.i.s: hld up: effrt & outpcd over 2f out: kpt on appr fnl f)............3 **7** 14/1 60 7
**Whirlawhile (USA)** (EALDunlop) **2-9-0** KFallon(3) (b.hind: rangy: scope: bit bkwd: chsd ldrs: drvn along over 3f out: lost pl over 1f out)........................................1 **8** 12/1 31 6
3809[10] **Bert** (PTWalwyn) **2-9-0** GCarter(10) (swvd bdly rt s: a in rr)........................................hd **9** 33/1 58 5
**The Tig** (LRLloyd-James) **2-9-0** TWilliams(6) (b.nr hind: w'like: bkwd: s.s: a bhd)........................................7 **10** 50/1 44 —
(SP 123.8%) **10 Rn**

**1m 48.6** (7.10) CSF £9.22 TOTE £2.20: £1.40 £1.90 £1.50 (£3.50) Trio £13.10 OWNER Mr R. E. Sangster (MARLBOROUGH) BRED Swettenham Stud

**3821 Panama City (USA)**, beaten by a subsequent smart nursery winner first time up, had a straightforward task and carried it out with the minimum of fuss. (6/4)
**3964 St Lawrence (CAN)**, much better suited by this stiffer track, finished clear second best but was never going to trouble the winner. (9/2)
**Kalinini (USA)**, who could only beat one on his debut three weeks earlier, tended to hang slightly under pressure and still lacks experience. (9/2)
**2967 Love Me Do (USA)**, absent for two months, showed bags of toe, but tired as if in need of the outing towards the finish. (6/1)
**Little Miss Rocker**, badly tapped for toe turning in, will be suited by further. (20/1)
**Moonlight Invader (IRE)** has plenty of size and scope, but looked to be in need of the outing. Missing the break, he ran very green but stuck on at the finish. (10/1: op 6/1)

## 4387 HERMES ASSET MANAGEMENT LIMITED STKS (0-70) (3-Y.O+) (Class E)
5-20 (5-20) **1m 2f 6y** £3,035.00 (£920.00: £450.00: £215.00) Stalls: Low GOING minus 0.01 sec per fur (G)

SP RR SF
4209* **Lady of Leisure (USA) (65)** (MrsJCecil) **4-9-1** GBardwell(8) (lw: trckd ldrs pllng hrd: styd on to ld wl ins fnl f: all out)........................................— **1** 5/2[2] 77 57
4232[2] **No Cliches (70)** (GLewis) **3-8-10b** JWeaver(4) (sn led: pushed along 5f out: hdd & no ex wl ins fnl f).............½ **2** 13/8[1] 77 51
3704[8] **Sinking Sun (66)** (BWHills) **3-8-7v** KFallon(2) (hld up: stdy hdwy over 4f out: sn chsng ldrs: rdn & wnt bdly rt ins fnl f: styd on towards fin) ........................................½ **3** 12/1 73 47
3918[2] **Hareb (USA) (67)** (JWHills) **3-8-7**(3) MHenry(1) (lw: led early: chsd ldrs tl wknd over 2f out)............................9 **4** 7/2[3] 62 36
4257[15] **Lovely Prospect (67)** (RGuest) **3-8-7** PBloomfield(6) (lw: sn bhd & pushed along: n.d) ..............................13 **5** 16/1 38 12
4238[9] **Roi du Nord (FR) (70)** (SWCampion) **4-9-2** GCarter(3) (sn bhd: hdwy to chse ldrs 4f out: lost pl over 2f out) .12 **6** 14/1 22 2
3845[11] **Naseem Alsahar (65)** (MajorWRHern) **3-8-7b** RHills(7) (swtg: sn trckng ldrs: ev ch tl wknd over 2f out).........10 **7** 9/1 3 —
4340[6] **Candy's Delight (40)** (MrsSJSmith) **3-8-4**(3) FLynch(5) (chsd ldrs: drvn along & hung rt over 3f out: sn bhd) .10 **8** 100/1 — —
(SP 120.1%) **8 Rn**

**2m 13.6** (5.30) CSF £7.16 TOTE £3.60: £1.40 £1.40 £2.00 (£2.70) OWNER Mrs Anna Sanders (NEWMARKET) BRED Arthur B. Hancock III
WEIGHT FOR AGE 3yo-6lb

**4209* Lady of Leisure (USA)**, who took a keen grip, stuck on under pressure to get up near the line. (5/2)
**4232 No Cliches**, soon setting a strong pace, was only worn down near the line. (13/8: 11/10-7/4)
**3425 Sinking Sun**, who had run poorly on her two previous starts, would have won this had she kept straight. Weaving badly right under pressure inside the last, she finished almost under the stands' rail, but was still closing the gap at the line. (12/1: op 8/1)
**3918 Hareb (USA)**, carrying his head high, found nothing under pressure, and looks one to have reservations about. (7/2)

T/Plpt: £9.70 (1,513.66 Tckts). T/Qdpt: £4.50 (182.45 Tckts). WG

## 4388a-4395a (Irish Racing) - See Computer Raceform

# 4155a-CURRAGH (Newbridge, Ireland) (R-H) (St crse Good, Rnd Good to firm)
## Saturday September 21st

## 4396a MACDONAGH & BOLAND STKS (Listed) (3-Y.O+)
3-15 (3-16) **7f** £9,675.00 (£2,775.00: £1,275.00: £375.00)

SP RR SF
**Wandering Thoughts (IRE)** (PJFlynn,Ireland) **7-9-0** NGMcCullagh (sn trckng ldrs: wnt 2nd over 1f out: led early fnl f: qckd & r.o wl)........................................— **1** 14/1 106 45

| | | | | SP | RR | SF |
|---|---|---|---|---|---|---|
| 4051[6] | **Ramooz (USA)** (BHanbury) **3-9-1** JReid (hld up in rr: nt clr run fr 2f out: wnt 4th & swtchd lft 1f out: rdn & wnt 2nd 100y out: r.o wl) | ¾ | **2** | 6/1[3] | 108 | 44 |
| 2471a[5] | **Burden Of Proof (IRE)** (CO'Brien,Ireland) **4-9-0** WRSwinburn (hld up: nt clr run fr 2f out: swtchd rt over 1f out: swtchd lft ins fnl f: r.o wl) | 1 | **3** | 4/1[2] | 102 | 41 |
| 2839a[4] | **Al Mohaajir (USA)** (JSBolger,Ireland) **5-9-4** KJManning (hld up in tch: hdwy 2f out: rdn & wnt 2nd briefly early fnl f: kpt on) | nk | **4** | 7/1 | 105 | 44 |
| 3731a[3] | **Peace Prize (IRE)** (DKWeld,Ireland) **3-8-11b[1]** MJKinane (led: rdn & qcknd 2f out: hdd ins fnl f: no ex) | 1½ | **5** | 6/1[3] | 98 | 34 |
| 3731a[2] | **Raiyoun (IRE)** (JOxx,Ireland) **3-8-11** JPMurtagh (hld up in rr: rdn & styd on fnl 2f: nvr able to chal) | 1½ | **6** | 6/4[1] | 95 | 31 |
| 1247a[5] | **No Animosity (IRE)** (DHassett,Ireland) **3-8-11** WJSupple (prom: pushed along over 3f out: wknd qckly u.p over 1f out) | 4½ | **7** | 16/1 | 84 | 20 |
| 2472a[13] | **Sir Silver Sox (USA)** (TStack,Ireland) **4-9-0b** PJSmullen (prom: rdn 2f out: wknd qckly u.p over 1f out) | hd | **8** | 25/1 | 84 | 23 |
| 1246a[5] | **Highly Motivated** (APO'Brien,Ireland) **3-8-8** JAHeffernan (bhd: rdn 3f out: n.d) | s.h | **9** | 25/1 | 81 | 17 |
| | | | | (SP 121.3%) | **9 Rn** | |

**1m 26.5** (3.50) OWNER William Mythen (CARRICK-ON-SUIR) BRED Mrs Anne Grace

**Wandering Thoughts (IRE)** is certainly approaching the veteran stage now, but still possesses a turn of foot. His opportunities are limited as he is a bit too good for handicaps, even at this stage of his career. (14/1)

**4051 Ramooz (USA)** grabbed second place inside the last 100 yards. He ran on well, but looked desperately unlucky. (6/1)

**2471a Burden Of Proof (IRE)** ran on well but needs softer ground to demonstrate his full ability. (4/1)

**2839a Al Mohaajir (USA)** had every chance when going second briefly inside the last. He needs softer ground and a bit further. (7/1)

**3731a Peace Prize (IRE)** took them along until headed inside the last. (6/1: op 4/1)

## 4397a JEFFERSON SMURFIT MEMORIAL IRISH ST. LEGER (Gp 1) (3-Y.O+)

3-50 (3-53) **1m 6f** £85,800.00 (£28,800.00: £13,800.00: £4,800.00)

| | | | | SP | RR | SF |
|---|---|---|---|---|---|---|
| 3070[4] | **Oscar Schindler (IRE)** (KPrendergast,Ireland) **4-9-8** SCraine (hld up in tch: 4th st: wnt 2nd on bit over 2f out: led over 1f out: rdn & qcknd early fnl f: r.o wl) | — | **1** | 4/1[2] | 125+ | 59 |
| 3688* | **Key Change (IRE)** (JOxx,Ireland) **3-8-9** JPMurtagh (prom: wnt 2nd over 10f out: led ent st: pushed along over 2f out: hdd over 1f out: unable qckn) | 3½ | **2** | 11/4[1] | 118 | 42 |
| 4066* | **Sacrament** (MRStoute) **5-9-8** WRSwinburn (hld up in tch: disp 3rd whn hmpd ent st: lost pl, 5th & n.m.r over 1f out: rdn & styd on ins fnl f) | 2 | **3** | 9/2[3] | 119 | 53 |
| 3614[2] | **Posidonas** (PFICole) **4-9-8** TQuinn (chsd ldr tl over 10f out: disp 3rd pl whn hmpd ent st: 3rd & no ex over 1f out: kpt on) | s.h | **4** | 9/2[3] | 119 | 53 |
| 4268a[2] | **I'm Supposin (IRE)** (KPrendergast,Ireland) **4-9-8** WJSupple (hld up in rr: hdwy after 5f: hdwy 2f out: 4th over 1f out: no imp ins fnl f) | 2 | **5** | 14/1 | 116 | 50 |
| 4192[10] | **Gordi (USA)** (DKWeld,Ireland) **3-8-12** MJKinane (hld up: hdwy over 2f out: sn rdn & btn) | 5 | **6** | 8/1 | 111 | 35 |
| 2474a* | **Blushing Flame (USA)** (MRStoute) **5-9-8** JReid (led tl ent st: sn wknd) | 4½ | **7** | 10/1 | 106 | 40 |
| 1912a[5] | **Viaticum (IRE)** (NMeade,Ireland) **4-9-5b** JoannaMorgan (a bhd) | 9 | **8** | 50/1 | 92 | 26 |
| 4268a[3] | **Fill the Bill (IRE)** (APO'Brien,Ireland) **4-9-8** JAHeffernan (a bhd) | s.h | **9** | 25/1 | 95 | 29 |
| | | | | (SP 115.7%) | **9 Rn** | |

**2m 59.1** (6.10) OWNER Oliver Lehane (CURRAGH) BRED Oliver Lehane

**3070 Oscar Schindler (IRE)**, going supremely well in fourth place turning into the straight, was upsides the leader with two furlongs to race and, leading well over a furlong out, quickened clear inside the last for an easy win. This was a good performance in a fast time and, if the ground is good or good to firm in Paris, he has an outsider's chance, but the Melbourne, and possibly the Japan Cup are other attractive targets. (4/1)

**3688* Key Change (IRE)** was no match for the winner once he took over, but she still beat the rest of these comfortably enough and her end of season targets could include the Gran Premio Del Jockey Club Italiano or the Royal-Oak, but she needs cut in the ground. (11/4)

**4066* Sacrament**, in third place when hampered entering the straight, lost his place but stayed on again inside the last. (9/2)

**3614 Posidonas** was involved in a bit of scrimmaging turning into the straight and, after recovering, appeared to edge left over the last two furlongs (9/2)

**4268a I'm Supposin (IRE)** made headway two furlongs out to go fourth over a furlong out, but could not find anything extra inside the last. In this company and at level weights, he appeared to find the trip beyond him. (14/1)

**4192 Gordi (USA)** again disappointed. He made a bit of headway over a furlong out, but was soon ridden and beaten. (8/1: op 5/1)

**2474a* Blushing Flame (USA)** was headed in the straight and then dropped right away. (10/1)

## 4398a AGA KHAN'S STUDS NATIONAL STKS (Gp 1) (2-Y.O C & F)

4-30 (4-30) **7f** £112,600.00 (£38,600.00: £18,600.00: £6,600.00)

| | | | | SP | RR | SF |
|---|---|---|---|---|---|---|
| | **Desert King (IRE)** (APO'Brien,Ireland) **2-9-0** WRSwinburn (hld up in rr: stdy hdwy fr 2f out: 4th over 1f out: r.o wl to ld fnl 50y) | — | **1** | 11/1 | 96 | 54 |
| 3807* | **Referendum (IRE)** (GLewis) **2-9-0** JReid (waited w in ld: qcknd 2f out: rdn ent fnl f: r.o: hdd fnl 50y) | nk | **2** | 10/1 | 95 | 53 |
| 4159a[3] | **Azra (IRE)** (JSBolger,Ireland) **2-8-11b** KJManning (a cl up: wnt 3rd over 1f out: sn rdn: kpt on ins fnl f) | 1 | **3** | 10/1 | 90 | 48 |
| 3987* | **Fantastic Fellow (USA)** (CEBrittain) **2-9-0** MRoberts (prom: wnt 2nd 2f out: ev ch: no ex ins fnl f) | s.h | **4** | 7/1 | 93 | 51 |
| | **Johan Cruyff** (APO'Brien,Ireland) **2-9-0** JPMurtagh (hld up: pushed along over 2f out: 6th over 1f out: r.o) | nk | **5** | 11/1 | 92 | 50 |
| 3561a[3] | **Verglas (IRE)** (KPrendergast,Ireland) **2-9-0** WJSupple (hld up: hdwy on outside & rdn 2f out: r.o ins fnl f) | s.h | **6** | 4/1[2] | 92 | 50 |
| 3143[D] | **Sahm (USA)** (JLDunlop) **2-9-0** TQuinn (hld up in tch: rdn under 2f out: 5th over 1f out: no ex ins fnl f) | hd | **7** | 6/4[1] | 92 | 50 |
| 2470a* | **Daylight In Dubai (USA)** (PWChapple-Hyam) **2-9-0** KDarley (sn chsng ldr: rdn & lost pl 2f out: sn btn) | 1½ | **8** | 8/1 | 89 | 47 |
| 4023a[3] | **Beautiful Fire (IRE)** (DKWeld,Ireland) **2-9-0** MJKinane (cl up: rdn wl over 2f out: btn over 1f out) | 3½ | **9** | 11/2[3] | 81 | 39 |
| 4156a[5] | **Stonehaven (IRE)** (TStack,Ireland) **2-9-0** PJSmullen (bhd: n.d fnl 2f) | hd | **10** | 25/1 | 80 | 38 |
| | | | | (SP 137.7%) | **10 Rn** | |

**1m 25.7** (2.70) OWNER Michael Tabor (PILTOWN)

**Desert King (IRE)** had only two behind him at the two-furlong marker and wove his way through the field in quite spectacular fashion to lead close home. He has some decent maiden form, but only broke his duck at the third attempt in very sticky ground at Tralee. The Dewhurst was being optimistically mentioned as a possible future target. (11/1: op 7/1)

**3807* Referendum (IRE)** soon led and was waited with in front. Ridden and quickening the pace over a furlong and a half out, he looked the winner until headed close home. (10/1)

**4159a Azra (IRE)** did her bit to uphold the Moyglare form, going third a furlong and a half out and keeping on under pressure inside the last. (10/1)

**3987* Fantastic Fellow (USA)**, always close up, found himself outpaced inside the last. He is still a bit green, but would have derived benefit from this run. (7/1)

**Johan Cruyff**, settled in the rear, hung badly left over the last furlong and a half, but still stayed on to be nearest at the finish. (11/1: op 7/1)
**3561a Verglas (IRE)** again disappointed, making headway on the outer two furlongs out, but finding absolutely nothing in the way of a tum of foot. (4/1)
**3143 Sahm (USA)**, tucked away in mid-division, was fifth over a furlong out, but never had the pace to challenge seriously. (6/4)
**2470a* Daylight In Dubai (USA)**, close up two furlongs out, was beaten soon after. (8/1)

## 4399a-4404a (Irish Racing) - See Computer Raceform

## 2844a-SAINT-CLOUD (France) (L-H) (Good)
### Monday September 16th

### 4405a PRIX DE LA COCHERE (Listed) (3-Y.O F)
2-45 (2-52) **1m** £18,445.00 (£6,324.00: £3,953.00: £2,055.00)

| | | | | SP | RR | SF |
|---|---|---|---|---|---|---|
| 3158[9] | **Golden Pond (IRE)** (CFWall) **3-8-12** JReid | — | 1 | | 102 | — |
| 3568a[2] | **Folle Tempete (FR)** (JEHammond,France) **3-8-12** MBoutin | s.h | 2 | | 102 | — |
| 3909a[3] | **Miss Riviera** (GWragg) **3-8-12** MHills | nk | 3 | | 101 | — |
| | **Sherema (USA)** (AdeRoyerDupre,France) **3-8-12** GMosse | d.h | 3 | | 101 | — |
| | | | | | | **12 Rn** |

**1m 39.6** (1.10) P-M 22.60F: 5.70F 5.10F MR 2.70F SH 2.20F (205.50F) OWNER Tullamaine Castle Stud & Partners (NEWMARKET) BRED Tullamaine Castle Stud and Partners
**2544 Golden Pond (IRE)**, who held the lead almost throughout, was passed in the straight but rallied to win in game style. The plan for her was to go to the States, but with this run to her name, her future is uncertain.
**3909a Miss Riviera** had every chance but could give no more inside the final furlong.
DS

## 3387a-MAISONS-LAFFITTE (France) (Good to soft)
### Tuesday September 17th

### 4406a PRIX DE SEINE-ET-OISE (Gp 3) (3-Y.O+)
2-55 (2-56) **6f** £28,986.00 (£10,540.00: £5,270.00: £2,635.00)

| | | | | SP | RR | SF |
|---|---|---|---|---|---|---|
| 3914a* | **Kistena (FR)** (MmeCHead,France) **3-8-11** ODoleuze | — | 1 | | 110+ | — |
| 2841a[3] | **Don't Worry Me (IRE)** (GHenrot,France) **4-8-10** AJunk | 2½ | 2 | | 100 | — |
| 3909a* | **Moon Is Up (USA)** (JEHammond,France) **3-8-9** CAsmussen | 2 | 3 | | 96 | — |
| 3759[2] | **Atraf** (DMorley) **3-9-1** WCarson (btn approx 9 3/4l) | | 8 | | — | — |
| | | | | | | **10 Rn** |

**1m 11.3** (1.60) P-M 2.30F: 1.20F 2.60F 1.70F (16.10L) OWNER Wertheimer Brothers (CHANTILLY) BRED J.Wertheimer & Frere
**3914a* Kistena (FR)** is a pretty useful second string to her crack stablemate Anabaa, and was winning her second Group race in excellent style here. Racing on the rail, she hit the front a furlong out and drew clear to win emphatically. She appears to be getting better with every race and, as the sprint season is drawing to a close, she will probably take on Anabaa in the Prix de l'Abbaye, and will not let him have it all his own way.
**2841a Don't Worry Me (IRE)**, fast away, led a furlong out, but had no answer to the winner. She is a thoroughly game filly.
**Moon Is Up (USA)** ran a decent race as she was coming back to six furlongs after winning a listed race over a mile. Putting in her best work at the end, this distance is obviously a little sharp for her, and she looks sure to become Miesque's fourth Group race-winning progeny soon.
**3759 Atraf** fell when being pulled up before the start, which might have effected his chance. He led for much of the race, but was a spent force when collared a furlong out. He usually battles on to the line and his connections feel sure he did not run up to his best.
DS

## 4170a-SAN SIRO (Milan, Italy) (R-H) (Good)
### Tuesday September 17th

### 4407a PREMIO GALBIATE MAIDEN (2-Y.O)
3-50 **6f** £8,120.00

| | | | | SP | RR | SF |
|---|---|---|---|---|---|---|
| | **Poseidon** (MRChannon) **2-8-13** RHughes | — | 1 | | — | — |
| | **Ipponatte (ITY)** (Italy) **2-9-0** GForte | 1 | 2 | | — | — |
| | **Evensong (ITY)** (Italy) **2-9-0** LPanici | s.nk | 3 | | — | — |
| | | | | | | **8 Rn** |

**1m 12.9** (4.90) TOTE 15L: 13L 23L 34L (134L) OWNER Allevamento La Nuovo Sbarra (UPPER LAMBOURN) BRED Mrs W. H. Gibson Fleming
**Poseidon**, a debutante, scored an impressive victory by making all and quickening up well approaching the final furlong.

## 4407a-SAN SIRO (Milan, Italy) (R-H) (Holding)
### Friday September 20th

### 4408a PREMIO MELZO (2-Y.O)
1-45 **6f** £8,120.00

| | | | | SP | RR | SF |
|---|---|---|---|---|---|---|
| | **Lonely Man (USA)** (GBotti,Italy) **2-9-5** EBotti | — | 1 | | — | — |
| | **Tetris (IRE)** (CFWall) **2-8-7** FJovine | 2¼ | 2 | | — | — |
| | **Sweeping Stakes (ITY)** (Italy) **2-8-7** GForte | 2½ | 3 | | — | — |
| | | | | | | **5 Rn** |

**1m 15.7** (7.70) TOTE 25L: 13L 13L (25L) OWNER Scuderia Siba (ITALY) BRED Scuderia Siba
**Tetris (IRE)** produced a fair display on her first racecourse appearance and was close up throughout. Disputing the lead until just inside the final furlong, she could only run on at the one pace in the closing stages.

## 3396a-COLOGNE (Germany) (R-H) (Good)
### Saturday September 21st

### 4409a GROSSER KAUFHOF-PREIS (Gp 2) (3-Y.O+)
3-45 (3-47) **1m** £32,685.00 (£13,063.00: £6,532.00: £4,054.00)

| | Horse | Details | Dist | Pos | SP | RR | SF |
|---|---|---|---|---|---|---|---|
| 2274a[2] | **Accento** | (RSuerland,Germany) **3-8-9** AHelfenbein (led 4f: 2nd st: rdn to ld 1f out: r.o wl) | — | 1 | | 117 | — |
| 4033a[3] | **A Magicman (FR)** | (HSteguweit,Germany) **4-9-3** ASuborics (bhd early: hdwy to ld 4f out: hdd 1f out: kpt on wl) | nk | 2 | | 120 | — |
| 3905a[2] | **Devil River Peek (USA)** | (BSchutz,Germany) **4-9-3** AStarke (hld up: 7th st: r.o strly fnl f) | 1¾ | 3 | | 117 | — |
| 1052a[4] | **Chato (USA)** | (HSteinmetz,Germany) **4-9-1** ABest (a.p: wnt 3rd 2f out: no ex cl home) | nk | 4 | | 114 | — |
| 3397a* | **Orfijar (FR)** | (PLautner,Germany) **6-9-3** WNewnes (a.p: 3rd st: ev ch 1½f out: no ex ins fnl f) | hd | 5 | | 116 | — |
| | **Ladoni** | (Germany) **4-9-1** KWoodburn (hld up: kpt on fnl 2f: nvr plcd to chal) | ½ | 6 | | 113 | — |
| 3397a[3] | **Kalatos (GER)** | (AWohler,Germany) **4-9-1** ABoschert (a in tch: no ex fr 2f out) | 1¾ | 7 | | 110 | — |
| 2843a[10] | **Tres Heureux (GER)** | (FrauEMader,Germany) **6-9-1** PSchiergen (bhd to ½-wy: nvr nrr) | hd | 8 | | 109 | — |
| 4169a* | **Takin (GER)** | (FrauEMader,Germany) **5-9-1** LMader (a in rr) | 1¼ | 9 | | 107 | — |
| 4028a[2] | **Sinyar** | (BSchutz,Germany) **4-9-3** THellier (mid div tl wknd 2f out) | ¾ | 10 | | 107 | — |
| 4194[7] | **Blomberg (IRE)** | (JRFanshawe) **4-9-3** DHarrison (in tch: 4th st: btn 2f out) | 3 | 11 | | 101 | — |
| 4132[3] | **Restructure (IRE)** | (MrsJCecil) **4-9-3** AClark (lost pl over 4f out: btn 3f out) | 1¾ | 12 | | 98 | — |

**12 Rn**

**1m 38.39** (8.39) TOTE 156DM: 38DM 22DM 22DM OWNER Stall Avantage BRED Daleside Nurseries Ltd
**3731a Blomberg (IRE)** raced in touch during the early stages and was well up in fourth as the field turned into the straight. He was slightly hampered on the turn and was beaten two furlongs out.
**4132 Restructure (IRE)** raced with the pace until losing his place over four furlongs out, and was beaten from three furlongs out.

## 4406a-MAISONS-LAFFITTE (France) (Very Soft)
### Saturday September 21st

### 4410a LA COUPE DE MAISONS-LAFFITTE (Gp 3) (4-Y.O+)
2-25 (2-26) **1m 2f** £28,986.00 (£10,540.00: £5,270.00: £2,635.00)

| | Horse | Details | Dist | Pos | SP | RR | SF |
|---|---|---|---|---|---|---|---|
| 3567a[3] | **Running Flame (FR)** | (JEHammond,France) **4-8-11** OPeslier | — | 1 | | 119 | — |
| 4165a[5] | **Carling (FR)** | (MmePBarbe,France) **4-9-0** TThulliez | 1½ | 2 | | 120 | — |
| | **Edessa (IRE)** | (DSepulchre,France) **4-8-8** CAsmussen | ½ | 3 | | 113 | — |
| 3905a[3] | **Musetta (IRE)** | (CEBrittain) **4-8-10** BDoyle | 5 | 4 | | 107 | — |
| | **Beneficial** | (GWragg) **6-8-11** MHills | 2 | 5 | | 105 | — |

**8 Rn**

**2m 6.3** (4.30) P-M 6.60F: 1.10F 1.10F 1.10F (3.80F) OWNER Mr Gary Biszantz (CHANTILLY) BRED Caraibes Farm
**3905a Musetta (IRE)** finished a remote fourth after fading badly inside the final furlong.
**Beneficial**, making his seasonal debut, faded inside the final furlong to finish a well beaten fifth.

### 4411a PRIX R. T. L. H'CAP (3-Y.O+)
2-55 (3-00) **6f** £22,388.00

| | Horse | Details | Dist | Pos | SP | RR | SF |
|---|---|---|---|---|---|---|---|
| 4116[7] | **Bold Effort (FR)** | (KOCunningham-Brown) **4-9-1b** FSanchez | — | 1 | | 86 | — |
| | **Strimmer** | (France) **8-8-1** CHanotel | ½ | 2 | | 71 | — |
| | **Capitaine Achab (FR)** | (France) **4-8-6** ASanglard | s.nk | 3 | | 75 | — |

**18 Rn**

**1m 13.9** (4.20) P-M 7.90F: 3.10F 2.70F 4.80F (23.80) OWNER Mr A. J. Richards (STOCKBRIDGE) BRED Ewar Stud Farm
**4116 Bold Effort (FR)**, who finished seventh in the Portland at Doncaster earlier in the month, put up another good display. It appears that he is getting used to this going, and he was back to his preferred distance here.
DS

## 4409a-COLOGNE (Germany) (R-H) (Good)
### Sunday September 22nd

### 4412a IDUNA/NOVA-FLEIGER-PREIS (Listed)
1-35 (1-43) **5f** £9,009.00 (£3,604.00: £1,802.00)

| | Horse | Details | Dist | Pos | SP | RR | SF |
|---|---|---|---|---|---|---|---|
| | **Matula (USA)** | (RSuerland,Germany) **4-9-12** AHelfenbein | — | 1 | | 109 | — |
| 4033a[6] | **Munaaji (USA)** | (AWohler,Germany) **5-9-12b** ABoschert | ½ | 2 | | 107 | — |
| 4115[7] | **Lucky Parkes** | (JBerry) **6-9-8** JCarroll | hd | 3 | | 103 | — |

**12 Rn**

**56.93 secs** (2.43) TOTE 78DM: 23DM 19DM 19DM OWNER Stall Primavera BRED Meadow Grove Farm
**4115 Lucky Parkes** disputed it until taking the lead at halfway, but was caught 50 yards out. She may stay in Germany to contest a listed race at Dortmund.

### 4413a EMS KURLEPOST EUROPA-PREIS (Gp 1) (3-Y.O+)
3-25 (3-28) **1m 4f** £135,135.00 (£54,054.00: £27,027.00: £13,514.00)

| | Horse | Details | Dist | Pos | SP | RR | SF |
|---|---|---|---|---|---|---|---|
| 3574a[2] | **Lavirco (GER)** | (PRau,Germany) **3-8-10** TMundry (chsd ldrs: cl up 4f out: led over 2f out: sn clr: impressive) | — | 1 | | 126+ | — |
| 4040a[6] | **Protektor (GER)** | (ALowe,Germany) **7-9-6** THellier (hld up in rr: hdwy fr 3f out: r.o strly 1f out: kpt on) | 3½ | 2 | | 123 | — |
| 3753a[2] | **Hollywood Dream (GER)** | (UOstmann,Germany) **5-9-2** JReid (hld up in rr: hdwy 4f out: r.o fr 2f out) | ¾ | 3 | | 118 | — |
| 3753a* | **Luso** | (CEBrittain) **4-9-6** MJKinane (racd in 3rd: chsd wnr over 2f out: no ex fnl f) | nk | 4 | | 122 | — |
| 4134[3] | **Lear White (USA)** | (PAKelleway) **5-9-6** JWeaver (chsd ldr tl wknd 2f out) | 7 | 5 | | 113 | — |
| 2110a* | **Mongol Warrior (USA)** | (LordHuntingdon) **3-8-10** DHarrison (racd in 5th: rdn & btn 2f out) | 2½ | 6 | | 107 | — |

| | | | | SP | RR | SF |
|---|---|---|---|---|---|---|
| 3753a$^{8}$ | **Caballo (GER)** (HJentzsch,Germany) **5-9-6** PSchiergen (set gd pce tl hdd over 2f out: wknd qckly) | 10 | **7** | | 96 | — |

**7 Rn**

**2m 28.63** (1.63) TOTE 22DM: 14DM 19DM 20DM OWNER Gestut Fahrhof BRED Gestut Fahrhof Stiftung
**3574a Lavirco (GER)** bounced back to form with this very impressive victory.
**3753a* Luso** was close up in third during the early stages and chased the winner over the final two furlongs, but could find no extra inside the final furlong.
**4134 Lear White (USA)** raced in second until weakening over two furlongs out.
**2110a* Mongol Warrior (USA)** raced in fifth, but was ridden and beaten over two furlongs out.

## 1059a-DIELSDORF (Zurich, Switzerland) (L-H) (Good)
## Sunday September 22nd

### 4414a GRAND PRIX JOCKEY CLUB (3-Y.O+)
2-45 (2-56) **1m 4f 68y** £26,816.00 (£10,726.00: £8,045.00: £5,363.00)

| | | | | SP | RR | SF |
|---|---|---|---|---|---|---|
| 4055$^{3}$ | **Mattawan** (MJohnston) **3-8-4b** MRoberts | — | **1** | | 85 | — |
| | **Coro (SWI)** (RStadelmann,Switzerland) **4-9-4** J-MBreux | ¾ | **2** | | 90 | — |
| 2110a$^{2}$ | **Shturm (RUS)** (MWeiss,Switzerland) **3-9-1** NJeanpierre | 2 | **3** | | 92 | — |

**10 Rn**

**2m 39.4** TOTE 2.10SF: 1.30SF 1.40SF 1.30SF OWNER Sheikh Mohammed (MIDDLEHAM) BRED Sheikh Mohammed Bin Rashid Al Maktoum
**4055 Mattawan** made all the running and, when challenged early in the straight, Roberts managed to get more out of the colt.

## 4291a-LONGCHAMP (Paris, France) (R-H) (Very Soft)
## Sunday September 22nd

### 4415a PRIX DE LA ROCHETTE (Gp 3) (2-Y.O C & G)
2-20 (2-19) **1m** £28,986.00 (£10,540.00: £5,270.00)

| | | | | SP | RR | SF |
|---|---|---|---|---|---|---|
| 3748a$^{2}$ | **Fine Fellow (IRE)** (MmeCHead,France) **2-8-11** FHead | — | **1** | | 96 | 13 |
| 4029a* | **Alpha Plus (USA)** (AFabre,France) **2-8-11** TJarnet | nk | **2** | | 95 | 12 |
| 4029a$^{3}$ | **Speedfriend (GER)** (RCollet,France) **2-8-11** SGuillot | 1½ | **3** | | 92 | 9 |

**6 Rn**

**1m 48.8** (13.80) P-M 4.30F: 1.40F 1.10F OWNER Maktoum Al Maktoum (CHANTILLY) BRED Mrs Elizabeth Hayes
**Fine Fellow (IRE)** made all and fended off the challenge of the odds-on favourite.

### 4416a PRIX DU PRINCE D'ORANGE (Gp 3) (3-Y.O)
3-25 (3-24) **1m 2f** £28,986.00 (£10,540.00: £5,270.00)

| | | | | SP | RR | SF |
|---|---|---|---|---|---|---|
| | **Baroud d'Honneur (FR)** (JBernard,France) **3-8-11** FBlondel | — | **1** | | 119 | 12 |
| 3746a$^{2}$ | **Android (USA)** (AFabre,France) **3-9-0** OPeslier | 1½ | **2** | | 120 | 13 |
| 3431$^{8}$ | **Acharne** (CEBrittain) **3-8-11** BDoyle | 2 | **3** | | 113 | 6 |

**5 Rn**

**2m 17.5** (17.50) P-M 9.50F: 2.00F 1.10F OWNER Mlle A. Negre BRED Haras d'Etreham
**Baroud d'Honneur (FR)** beat the odds-on favourite a shade comfortably.
**2844a Acharne** led, and looked to be going well when kicking early in the straight, but he was done for foot when the principals made their effort.

### 4417a PRIX DU PIN (Listed) (3-Y.O+)
3-55 (3-56) **7f** £18,445.00 (£6,324.00: £3,953.00: £2,055.00)

| | | | | SP | RR | SF |
|---|---|---|---|---|---|---|
| 3745a$^{6}$ | **Zarannda (IRE)** (AdeRoyerDupre,France) **3-8-8** GMosse | — | **1** | | 111 | 72 |
| | **Winning Smile (FR)** (TClout,France) **6-8-11b$^{1}$** SGuillot | 1½ | **2** | | 108 | 72 |
| | **Naninja (USA)** (AFabre,France) **3-8-8** OPeslier | ¾ | **3** | | 106 | 67 |
| 3144$^{4}$ | **Sorbie Tower (IRE)** (MissGayKelleway) **3-8-8** TQuinn (btn approx 4l) | | **7** | | — | — |

**10 Rn**

**1m 25.7** (6.70) P-M 3.70F: 1.90F 2.70F 3.00F (37.90) OWNER Aga Khan (CHANTILLY) BRED H. H. Aga Khan's Studs S. C.
**3144 Sorbie Tower (IRE)** ran his first disappointing race of the campaign. He took control soon after entering the straight, but had nothing more to give inside the final furlong. He has had a long year and may now be put away.

## 4408a-SAN SIRO (Milan, Italy) (R-H) (Heavy)
## Sunday September 22nd

### 4418a PREMIO MOLVEDO (3-Y.O+)
1-45 (1-50) **7f 110y** £25,169.00

| | | | | SP | RR | SF |
|---|---|---|---|---|---|---|
| 903a$^{6}$ | **Alabastro (IRE)** (LCamici,Italy) **3-8-12** MCangiano | — | **1** | | 106 | — |
| 3712$^{7}$ | **How Long** (LMCumani) **3-8-12** LDettori | 1¼ | **2** | | 103 | — |
| 1137a$^{3}$ | **Sharp Reproach** (Ld'Auria,Italy) **3-8-12** MDemuro | ¾ | **3** | | 102 | — |

**8 Rn**

**1m 35.5** (11.00) TOTE 54L: 22L 26L 22L (263L) OWNER Scuderia Blueberry BRED Scuderia Blueberry SRL
**2888 How Long** raced in fifth during the early stages before making progress to be second at halfway. Ridden over two furlongs out, he kept on in the closing stages.

### 4419a PREMIO FERIA (3-Y.O+ F & M)
2-15 (2-20) **1m** £25,619.00

| | | | | SP | RR | SF |
|---|---|---|---|---|---|---|
| | **Rapiddima (IRE)** (VOriani,Italy) **5-9-0** MEsposito | — | **1** | | 89 | — |

| | Horse | | Pos | SP | RR | SF |
|---|---|---|---|---|---|---|
| | **Bemont Park (ITY)** (Italy) **5-9-9** GBietolini | s.nk | **2** | | 98 | — |
| 1758a[5] | **Sagar Pride (IRE)** (JGBurns,Ireland) **3-8-10** GForte | ¾ | **3** | | 87 | — |
| | | | | | | **11 Rn** |

**1m 44.4** (14.40) TOTE 109L: 18L 12L 13L (129L) OWNER The RHT
**1758a Sagar Pride (IRE)** was held up at the back of the field, and made a strong challenge two and a half furlongs out, but the exertions may have taken their toll and she had little more to give inside the final furlong.

## 4420a PREMIO SIGNORINETTA (2-Y.O F)
3-15 (3-25) **7f 110y** £32,805.00

| | Horse | | Pos | SP | RR | SF |
|---|---|---|---|---|---|---|
| 4039a[2] | **Folgore (USA)** (JLDunlop) **2-8-11** FJovine | — | **1** | | — | — |
| | **Lady Bi (IRE)** (RBrogi,Italy) **2-8-11** GBietolini | 1¼ | **2** | | — | — |
| | **Cristin (ITY)** (VSarti,Italy) **2-8-11** GForte | 2½ | **3** | | — | — |
| | | | | | | **16 Rn** |

**1m 39.3** (14.80) TOTE 30L: 17L 35L 62L (231L) OWNER Allevamento Annarosa (ARUNDEL) BRED Allevamento Annarosa
**4039a Folgore (USA)** raced in mid-division on the inside and made headway from two furlongs out to take the lead well inside the final furlong. From there, she ran on well to win comfortably.

## 4421a GRAN PREMIO D'ITALIA (3-Y.O)
4-15 (4-28) **1m 4f** £101,500.00 (£44,660.00: £24,360.00: £12,180.00)

| | Horse | | Pos | SP | RR | SF |
|---|---|---|---|---|---|---|
| | **Toto le Moko (IRE)** (AVerdesi,Italy) **3-9-2** MMonteriso | — | **1** | | 118 | — |
| 1580a[3] | **Coral Reef (ITY)** (GColleo,Italy) **3-9-2** MPlanard | nk | **2** | | 118 | — |
| 2670a* | **Snake Snap** (VCaruso,Italy) **3-9-2** MEsposito | 3¼ | **3** | | 113 | — |
| 3781[4] | **Freequent** (LMCumani) **3-9-2** LDettori | 3½ | **4** | | 109 | — |
| | | | | | | **15 Rn** |

**2m 38.3** (18.30) TOTE 663L: 121L 23L 29L (3076L) OWNER Gerecon Italia BRED Leo Collins
**3781 Freequent** was prominent during the early stages and was third as they turned into the straight. Dettori had the colt in a challenging position three furlongs out, but he could only run on at the one pace inside the final two furlongs. He was never that happy on the heavy going.

# 3662-FOLKESTONE (R-H) (Good to firm, Good patches)
## Friday September 27th
WEATHER: fine WIND: almost nil

## 4422 EUROTUNNEL DEVELOPMENTS PREMIER SITE MAIDEN STKS (3-Y.O+ F & M) (Class D)
1-50 (1-52) **1m 1f 149y** £3,960.15 (£1,183.20: £566.10: £257.55) Stalls: High GOING minus 0.28 sec per fur (GF)

| | Horse | | Pos | SP | RR | SF |
|---|---|---|---|---|---|---|
| 3938[5] | **Omara (USA) (75)** (HRACecil) **3-8-10** WRyan(1) (hld up: led on bit 1f out: shkn up: comf) | — | **1** | 7/2[2] | 71++ | 17 |
| 3949[4] | **Kentucky Fall (FR)** (LadyHerries) **3-8-10** AClark(3) (a.p: chsd ldr over 5f out: led over 2f out to 1f out: unable qckn) | 4 | **2** | 9/1[3] | 64 | 10 |
| 1656[11] | **Seirenes (78)** (PTWalwyn) **3-8-10** TQuinn(6) (lw: chsd ldr 4f: rdn over 4f out: lost pl over 3f out: r.o one pce fnl f) | 4 | **3** | 10/1 | 58 | 4 |
| 3505[2] | **Unalloyed (USA)** (DRLoder) **3-8-10** WRSwinburn(10) (led 7f: wknd over 1f out: b.b.v) | 3½ | **4** | 1/2[1] | 52 | — |
| 1119[15] | **Smile Forever (USA) (60)** (MissGayKelleway) **3-8-5(5)** DGriffiths(8) (lw: plld hrd: hld up: rdn over 3f out: one pce) | nk | **5** | 50/1 | 52 | — |
| 4212[7] | **Hadadabble (39)** (PatMitchell) **3-8-10** MFenton(11) (nvr nr to chal) | 1 | **6** | 50/1 | 50 | — |
| 3852[12] | **Bianca Cappello (IRE) (25)** (PSFelgate) **3-8-10** GDuffield(2) (lw: a bhd) | 10 | **7** | 66/1 | 33 | — |
| 3785[14] | **Queens Fancy (35)** (SDow) **3-8-10** SSanders(5) (a bhd) | s.h | **8** | 66/1 | 33 | — |
| 4108[13] | **Perpetual Hope** (PMitchell) **3-8-10** JQuinn(4) (a bhd) | 1¾ | **9** | 40/1 | 30 | — |
| 3861[8] | **Sweet Allegiance (23)** (JRPoulton) **6-9-2** AMorris(7) (bhd fnl 8f) | 21 | **10** | 100/1 | — | — |
| *3058[2]* | ***Classic Form (IRE)*** (RHarris) **3-8-10** RPrice(9) (Withdrawn not under Starter's orders; Veterinary advice) | | **W** | 12/1 | — | — |
| | | | | | (SP 126.0%) | **10 Rn** |

**2m 4.2** (6.50) CSF £30.69 TOTE £4.60: £1.10 £1.40 £1.80 (£14.10) Trio £12.40 OWNER Mr F. Hinojosa (NEWMARKET) BRED Indian Creek, H. Lascelles, A. Stroud and W. B. Is
WEIGHT FOR AGE 3yo-6lb
**3938 Omara (USA)** needs to do it all on the bridle and that was exactly what she was able to do in this small race, eventually losing her maiden tag at the eleventh attempt. She is no easy ride and is certainly not one to stake your life on. (7/2: 9/4-4/1)
**3949 Kentucky Fall (FR)** is going the right way and should find a small maiden before long. (9/1: 5/1-10/1)
**1123 Seirenes** has been off the course since flopping at Windsor back in June, but returned looking in good shape. She will probably do better on a slightly easier surface. (10/1)
**3505 Unalloyed (USA)** broke a blood-vessel, which would account for this poor performance. (1/2)
**Smile Forever (USA)** has changed stables since her last run nearly five months ago, but looked in good heart. (50/1)

## 4423 WIGGINS GROUP CLAIMING STKS (2-Y.O) (Class F)
2-20 (2-21) **6f** £2,857.00 (£792.00: £379.00) Stalls: Low GOING minus 0.28 sec per fur (GF)

| | Horse | | Pos | SP | RR | SF |
|---|---|---|---|---|---|---|
| *4251** | **Eager To Please (51)** (MissGayKelleway) **2-9-2** TQuinn(6) (b: lw: a.p: rdn over 1f out: led ins fnl f: r.o wl) | — | **1** | 9/2[3] | 65 | 23 |
| 3963[5] | **Hever Golf Charger (IRE) (75)** (TJNaughton) **2-9-2** SSanders(1) (led tl ins fnl f: r.o) | hd | **2** | 5/1 | 65 | 23 |
| 4182[8] | **Russian Sable (59)** (MRChannon) **2-8-5** CRutter(7) (swtchd rt & hdwy over 1f out: ev ch ins fnl f: r.o) | nk | **3** | 8/1 | 53 | 11 |
| *4093[12]* | **Summer Risotto (54)** (DJSffrenchDavis) **2-7-8(5)** MartinDwyer(2) (lw: a.p: rdn 2f out: unable qckn) | 1¾ | **4** | 14/1 | 42 | — |
| 4046[5] | **Dowry (66)** (RHannon) **2-8-11** DaneO'Neill(8) (lw: hdwy over 1f out: nvr nrr) | nk | **5** | 11/4[1] | 54 | 12 |
| 3962[6] | **Hoh Surprise (IRE) (56)** (MBell) **2-8-5** MFenton(5) (lw: a.p: ev ch over 1f out: wknd ins fnl f) | 1 | **6** | 7/2[2] | 45 | 3 |
| 3796[18] | **Major Twist (IRE)** (RHannon) **2-8-12** RPerham(10) (bhd fnl 2f) | 5 | **7** | 16/1 | 39 | — |
| | **Sam's Yer Man** (SCWilliams) **2-8-11(3)** MHenry(3) (w'like: bit bkwd: a bhd) | 4 | **8** | 25/1 | 30 | — |
| 2714[6] | **Gibb's Beach (IRE)** (CADwyer) **2-8-5** JQuinn(11) (spd over 4f) | 6 | **9** | 33/1 | 5 | — |
| 4062[12] | **First Page** (WJarvis) **2-8-8** AMcGlone(9) (spd over 4f) | 2 | **10** | 10/1 | 3 | — |
| | | | | | (SP 123.3%) | **10 Rn** |

**1m 14.0** (3.80) CSF £27.13 TOTE £4.10: £1.30 £1.90 £3.10 (£9.00) Trio £22.50 OWNER Miss Jo Crowley (WHITCOMBE) BRED Mrs Sara Hood

**4251* Eager To Please**, sold out of Jack Berry's stable for 6,600 guineas after winning a seller on the Equitrack a week earlier, stood out in the paddock. (9/2)
**3963 Hever Golf Charger (IRE)** was headed inside the final furlong but, to his credit, kept on well to the bitter end. (5/1)
**4046 Russian Sable** ran a solid race and was one of three in line inside the final furlong before just being worried out of it. (8/1: op 5/1)
**3871 Summer Risotto** was once again made to look pedestrian in the last two furlongs. (14/1)
**4046 Dowry** found this six furlongs on a fast surface too sharp and may now need seven furlongs if there is no cut in the ground. (11/4)
**3962 Hoh Surprise (IRE)**, who went down early, has been running well in these type of races but probably needs some give to be seen to best effect - her only win came in the mud at Windsor last month. (7/2: 5/2-4/1)

## 4424 E. B. F. BLUE CIRCLE RATING RELATED MAIDEN STKS (0-65) (2-Y.O) (Class F)

2-50 (2-51) **5f** £2,571.40 (£710.40: £338.20) Stalls: Low GOING minus 0.28 sec per fur (GF)

| | | | | SP | RR | SF |
|---|---|---|---|---|---|---|
| 4234$^{3}$ | **Anokato (65)** (KTIvory) **2-8-9b**$^{(5)}$ MartinDwyer(1) (mde all: rdn out) | — | **1** | 5/2$^{2}$ | 71 | 39 |
| 4339$^{6}$ | **Keen Waters (63)** (JRArnold) **2-8-11** SSanders(5) (chsd wnr: rdn over 1f out: ev ch ins fnl f: unable qckn) | 1¼ | **2** | 10/1 | 64 | 32 |
| 4324$^{2}$ | **Tailwind (64)** (WRMuir) **2-9-0** TQuinn(3) (hld up: rdn 2f out: one pce) | 5 | **3** | 4/5$^{1}$ | 51 | 19 |
| 4049$^{14}$ | **Miss Barcelona (IRE) (61)** (MJPolglase) **2-8-11** WRyan(4) (swtg: bhd fnl 2f) | 2½ | **4** | 10/1 | 40 | 8 |
| 3660$^{13}$ | **Show Off (60)** (WJarvis) **2-8-11** AMcGlone(2) (hdwy over 2f out: sn wknd) | 2 | **5** | 8/1$^{3}$ | 34 | 2 |
| | | | | (SP 113.4%) | **5 Rn** | |

**59.6 secs** (2.00) CSF £20.78 TOTE £3.90: £1.20 £4.30 (£37.50) OWNER Mr K. T. Ivory (RADLETT) BRED Mrs P. A. Brown
**4234 Anokato**, who seems at his best when fitted with blinkers, made every yard to win a dreadful race. (5/2)
**4339 Keen Waters**, in pursuit of the winner throughout, found him too strong inside the last 100 yards. (10/1: 6/1-12/1)
**4324 Tailwind** found this trip too sharp and, if he is to win a race, it will have to be over further. (4/5: op Evens)
**3803 Miss Barcelona (IRE)** is very moderate and has had plenty of chances. (10/1)
**3054 Show Off** (8/1: 4/1-9/1)

## 4425 EUROTUNNEL DEVELOPMENTS FAST TRACK NURSERY H'CAP (0-85) (2-Y.O) (Class D)

3-20 (3-21) **5f** £3,468.20 (£1,034.60: £493.80: £223.40) Stalls: Low GOING minus 0.28 sec per fur (GF)

| | | | | SP | RR | SF |
|---|---|---|---|---|---|---|
| 4230$^{3}$ | **Ellens Lad (IRE) (72)** (RHannon) **2-8-12** DaneO'Neill(3) (lw: racd stands' side: hld up: led over 1f out: hrd rdn: r.o wl) | — | **1** | 5/1$^{2}$ | 68 | 41 |
| 4324$^{5}$ | **Silca Key Silca (77)** (MRChannon) **2-9-3** CRutter(1) (racd stands' side: rdn over 2f out: hdwy over 1f out: r.o wl) | ¾ | **2** | 7/1 | 71 | 44 |
| 4247$^{6}$ | **Perpetual (74)** (SirMarkPrescott) **2-9-0** GDuffield(5) (lw: a.p: rdn over 2f out: ev ch ins fnl f: unable qckn) | 1 | **3** | 6/5$^{1}$ | 64 | 37 |
| 1959$^{2}$ | **Cadeaux Cher (81)** (BWHills) **2-9-2**$^{(5)}$ JDSmith(8) (b.hind: lw: outpcd: hung lft & hdwy over 1f out: r.o) | 1½ | **4** | 8/1 | 67 | 40 |
| 4234$^{6}$ | **Tear White (IRE) (75)** (TGMills) **2-8-12b**$^{(3)}$ AWhelan(2) (lw: racd stands' side: led over 3f) | hd | **5** | 10/1 | 60 | 33 |
| 4230$^{4}$ | **Suite Factors (73)** (KRBurke) **2-8-13** DRMcCabe(7) (hdwy over 1f out: eased whn btn ins fnl f) | 2½ | **6** | 12/1 | 50 | 23 |
| 4210$^{3}$ | **Rise 'n Shine (78)** (CACyzer) **2-9-4** TQuinn(4) (lw: hld up: rdn over 2f out: wknd over 1f out) | 6 | **7** | 6/1$^{3}$ | 36 | 9 |
| 4207$^{12}$ | **Statuette (66)** (BPalling) **2-8-3**$^{(3)}$ MHenry(6) (gd spd 3f) | 8 | **8** | 20/1 | — | — |
| | | | | (SP 121.6%) | **8 Rn** | |

**59.4 secs** (1.80) CSF £37.95 CT £63.80 TOTE £6.00: £2.00 £1.60 £1.50 (£24.30) OWNER Mrs Chris Harrington (MARLBOROUGH) BRED Mrs Chris Harrington
OFFICIAL EXPLANATION **Unalloyed (USA): finished distressed.**
**4230 Ellens Lad (IRE)**, one of three who elected to race on the favoured stands' side, responded to pressure to keep his head in front. (5/1)
**4324 Silca Key Silca**, who would probably be better served by a return to six furlongs, was doing all her best work in the last furlong and a half. (7/1)
**4247 Perpetual** elected to tack over to the far side but, although having control on that side in the final quarter-mile, was unable to match her two rivals on the opposite rail. She has been a model of consistency this season and can find another race before long. (6/5)
**1959 Cadeaux Cher** was unable to go the pace and, when he did start to pick up ground below the distance, he drifted badly into the centre of the track. (8/1: 6/1-9/1)
**4234 Tear White (IRE)** is a very tricky customer but led the field on the stands' side until collared below the distance. (10/1)

## 4426 LOCATE IN KENT H'CAP (0-70) (3-Y.O+) (Class E)

3-50 (3-54) **1m 7f 92y** £3,670.80 (£1,100.40: £529.20: £243.60) Stalls: Low GOING minus 0.28 sec per fur (GF)

| | | | | SP | RR | SF |
|---|---|---|---|---|---|---|
| 4345* | **Ayunli (69)** (SCWilliams) **5-9-12**$^{(3)}$ $^{5x}$ MHenry(1) (a.p: led 3f out: clr 2f out: r.o wl) | — | **1** | 5/1$^{3}$ | 82 | 51 |
| 4086$^{2}$ | **Miss Prism (51)** (JLDunlop) **3-8-0** JQuinn(15) (hld up: rdn over 3f out: chsd wnr fnl f: no imp) | 6 | **2** | 15/2 | 58 | 16 |
| 4260$^{7}$ | **Paradise Navy (68)** (CREgerton) **7-9-9b**$^{(5)}$ AimeeCook(5) (s.s: stdy hdwy 3f out: r.o one pce) | ¾ | **3** | 11/1 | 74 | 43 |
| 3163$^{4}$ | **Mr Copyforce (45)** (MissBSanders) **6-8-5** GDuffield(9) (a.p: rdn 3f out: chsd wnr wl over 1f out to 1f out: one pce) | nk | **4** | 7/1 | 51 | 20 |
| 4252$^{5}$ | **Hoofprints (IRE) (66)** (GHarwood) **3-9-1** AClark(12) (hdwy on ins 6f out: rdn 4f out: one pce) | 2½ | **5** | 14/1 | 69 | 27 |
| 4121$^{8}$ | **Early Peace (IRE) (60)** (MJPolglase) **4-9-6** MRimmer(7) (b.off hind: rdn over 3f out: hdwy over 1f out: nvr nrr) | 2 | **6** | 33/1 | 61 | 30 |
| *4092*$^{14}$ | **Rose of Glenn (40)** (BPalling) **5-8-0** CRutter(8) (a.p: led 4f out to 3f out: wknd over 1f out) | ¾ | **7** | 33/1 | 40 | 9 |
| 4203$^{4}$ | **Zeliba (40)** (MrsNMacauley) **4-7-7**$^{(7)ow3}$ JoHunnam(2) (nvr nrr) | 2 | **8** | 9/1 | 38 | 4 |
| 1618$^{11}$ | **White Claret (56)** (RAkehurst) **4-9-2** TQuinn(13) (bit bkwd: led over 2f: ev ch 3f out: wknd over 1f out) | 1½ | **9** | 4/1$^{2}$ | 53 | 22 |
| 3476$^{4}$ | **Aude la Belle (FR) (40)** (SGKnight) **8-8-0** FNorton(10) (nvr nrr) | 7 | **10** | 16/1 | 29 | — |
| 3813$^{5}$ | **Sterling Fellow (56)** (RHannon) **3-8-5b** DaneO'Neill(11) (bhd fnl 7f) | nk | **11** | 5/2$^{1}$ | 45 | 3 |
| 1614$^{18}$ | **Dance Model (59)** (JJSheehan) **3-8-5**$^{(3)ow9}$ AWhelan(3) (s.s: a bhd) | hd | **12** | 33/1 | 48 | — |
| 3970$^{10}$ | **Brown Eyed Girl (37)** (BJMcMath) **4-7-6**$^{(5)ow1}$ MartinDwyer(4) (hdwy over 7f out: wknd over 4f out) | 9 | **13** | 33/1 | 17 | — |
| 1679$^{5}$ | **Chez Catalan (47)** (RAkehurst) **5-8-7b** SSanders(14) (bit bkwd: bhd fnl 8f) | 5 | **14** | 16/1 | 21 | — |
| | **Emnala (IRE) (43)** (EAWheeler) **4-7-12**$^{(5)}$ ADaly(16) (bit bkwd: a bhd) | nk | **15** | 33/1 | 17 | — |
| 4110$^{12}$ | **Veronica Franco (56)** (BAPearce) **3-8-5** DRMcCabe(6) (led 13f out to 4f out: sn wknd: t.o) | dist | **16** | 20/1 | — | — |
| | | | | (SP 145.7%) | **16 Rn** | |

**3m 25.9** (7.90) CSF £46.27 CT £383.36 TOTE £5.70: £2.00 £1.20 £2.70 £1.60 (£16.70) Trio £74.70 OWNER Mr I. A. Southcott (NEWMARKET) BRED I. A. Southcott
LONG HANDICAP Brown Eyed Girl 7-9
WEIGHT FOR AGE 3yo-11lb

**4345* Ayunli**, making a quick reappearance, drifted in the market, but she had no problems with this longer trip. (5/1: op 5/2)
**4086 Miss Prism** once again had to settle for being the bridesmaid and never looked like reeling in the winner. (15/2)
**3801 Paradise Navy** needs to be given the kid-glove treatment and that is exactly what his rider did as the combination steadily crept closer in the last half-mile. (11/1: 6/1-12/1)
**3163 Mr Copyforce** never looked like finding the necessary turn of foot. (7/1)
**4252 Hoofprints (IRE)** was only treading water in the last three furlongs. (14/1: 12/1-20/1)
**1506* Early Peace (IRE)** has gained his only victory over a mile, but did seem to stay this longer trip adequately. (33/1)
**4203 Zeliba** (9/1: 5/1-10/1)
**3813 Sterling Fellow** was heavily backed, but never gave his supporters anything to cheer about. (5/2)

## 4427 KINGS HILL LIMITED STKS (0-70) (3-Y.O+) (Class E)

4-20 (4-21) **1m 4f** £3,425.10 (£1,024.80: £491.40: £224.70) Stalls: High GOING minus 0.28 sec per fur (GF)

| | | | | SP | RR | SF |
|---|---|---|---|---|---|---|
| 3947[14] | **Ocean Park (68)** (LadyHerries) **5-9-5** AClark(7) (b: lw: hdwy 6f out: rdn to ld wl ins fnl f: r.o wl) | — | **1** | 9/2[1] | 72 | 30 |
| 4201[5] | **Prospero (70)** (GHarwood) **3-8-9** TQuinn(10) (a.p: rdn over 2f out: r.o ins fnl f) | 1¾ | **2** | 5/1[2] | 68 | 18 |
| 4327[9] | **No Pattern (70)** (GLMoore) **4-9-3v** SWhitworth(11) (lw: hdwy over 4f out: led 2f out: hrd rdn over 1f out: hdd wl ins fnl f: unable qckn) | hd | **3** | 10/1 | 68 | 26 |
| 4067[15] | **Mr Browning (USA) (69)** (RAkehurst) **5-9-3b** SSanders(5) (a.p: led 7f out to 2f out: wknd fnl f: fin 5th, 3/4l: plcd 4th) | | **4** | 9/2[1] | 64 | 22 |
| 4209[4] | **Rival Bid (USA) (64)** (MrsNMacauley) **8-9-2**(3) CTeague(6) (swtg: s.s: hdwy over 1f out: one pce: fin 6th, 2l: plcd 5th) | | **5** | 10/1 | 64 | 22 |
| 3800[7] | **Classic Romance (68)** (RHarris) **3-8-6** RPrice(8) (hdwy 6f out: rdn & ev ch 2f out: sn wknd) | 3½ | **7** | 8/1 | 54 | 4 |
| 754[9] | **Not Quite Grey (68)** (KMcAuliffe) **3-8-9** MTebbutt(9) (a bhd) | 9 | **8** | 20/1 | 45 | — |
| 4083[2] | **Madame Steinlen (70)** (BWHills) **3-8-6** WRyan(1) (prom 9f) | 3½ | **9** | 9/2[1] | 37 | — |
| 4217[4] | **Chocolate Ice (60)** (CACyzer) **3-8-9** DRMcCabe(2) (led 5f: wknd over 4f out) | 19 | **10** | 20/1 | 15 | — |
| 2284[13] | **Begger's Opera (22)** (PatMitchell) **4-9-3** MFenton(4) (bhd fnl 5f: t.o) | dist | **11** | 50/1 | — | — |
| 3819[3] | **Almuhtaram (67)** (MissGayKelleway) **4-9-5b** DaneO'Neill(3) (hld up: hrd rdn over 1f out: r.o one pce: fin 4th, btn 1¾l: disq: plcd last) | | **D** | 7/1[3] | 67 | 25 |

(SP 124.5%) **11 Rn**

**2m 39.0** (7.80) CSF £27.24 TOTE £5.80: £1.90 £2.10 £4.70 (£27.50) Trio £140.40 OWNER Mr E. Reitel (LITTLEHAMPTON) BRED Mrs H. Khan
WEIGHT FOR AGE 3yo-8lb
STEWARDS' ENQUIRY O'Neill susp. 6-7/10/96 (failing to weigh-in). Obj. by Clerk of Scales to Almuhtaram sustained (failure to weigh in).
**547* Ocean Park**, all the better for his recent run at Sandown, regained the winning thread to register his fifth victory of the year. (9/2: op 7/1)
**4201 Prospero** appreciated the longer trip but, although running on inside the final furlong to snatch second, was not going to trouble the winner. (5/1)
**4067 No Pattern** ran his best race for some time. His jockey gave him the full treatment, but the combination were unable to hold on in the closing stages. (10/1: 7/1-12/1)
**3876 Mr Browning (USA)** took a while to get to the head of affairs and, once collared a quarter of a mile out, was soon in trouble. (9/2)
**4209 Rival Bid (USA)** (10/1: 8/1-12/1)
**2384 Classic Romance** (8/1: 6/1-9/1)
**3819 Almuhtaram**, tackling a slightly longer trip, did stay on from below the distance. Unfortunately, his jockey failed to weigh-in and he was subsequently disqualified. (7/1)

## 4428 LEVY BOARD APPRENTICE H'CAP (0-70) (3-Y.O+) (Class E)

4-50 (4-51) **6f 189y** £3,670.80 (£1,100.40: £529.20: £243.60) Stalls: High GOING minus 0.28 sec per fur (GF)

| | | | | SP | RR | SF |
|---|---|---|---|---|---|---|
| 4240[7] | **Mr Cube (IRE) (50)** (JMBradley) **6-8-5b**(5) CLowther(6) (lw: a.p: led 1f out: rdn out) | — | **1** | 15/2 | 60 | 20 |
| 3989[11] | **Sand Star (55)** (DHaydnJones) **4-9-1** DRMcCabe(1) (s.s: hdwy & swvd lft 1f out: fin wl) | 1½ | **2** | 20/1 | 62 | 22 |
| 4256* | **Morocco (IRE) (57)** (MRChannon) **7-9-0**(3) 5x AEddery(4) (hdwy over 1f out: r.o ins fnl f) | nk | **3** | 11/2[3] | 63 | 23 |
| 3761[11] | **Sapphire Son (IRE) (49)** (PCClarke) **4-8-9** DaneO'Neill(8) (lw: a.p: hrd rdn over 1f out: unable qckn) | 1¼ | **4** | 14/1 | 52 | 12 |
| 3316[7] | **Mystery Matthias (49)** (MissBSanders) **3-8-6v** AWhelan(5) (w ldr: led over 3f out to 1f out: wknd ins fnl f) | 1¾ | **5** | 20/1 | 48 | 5 |
| *4089*[12] | **Bold Habit (45)** (JPearce) **11-8-0**(5) PDoe(10) (b.off fore: b.nr hind: lw: hdwy over 1f out: nvr nrr) | hd | **6** | 33/1 | 44 | 4 |
| 3285[4] | **Pearl Dawn (IRE) (62)** (GLMoore) **6-9-3**(5) JDennis(13) (nvr nr to chal) | 2 | **7** | 12/1 | 56 | 16 |
| 4109[2] | **Utmost Zeal (USA) (61)** (PWHarris) **3-9-4** MHenry(7) (prom over 4f) | s.h | **8** | 2/1[1] | 55 | 12 |
| 4202[7] | **Jato (68)** (SCWilliams) **7-10-0** ADaly(11) (b.nr hind: lw: a.p: rdn over 1f out: sn wknd) | hd | **9** | 6/1 | 62 | 22 |
| 4217[8] | **Time For Tea (IRE) (62)** (CACyzer) **3-8-12**(7) RSawyer(12) (lw: nvr nrr) | 1 | **10** | 16/1 | 53 | 10 |
| 4232[11] | **Scathebury (59)** (KRBurke) **3-9-2v** RHavlin(9) (lw: led over 3f: wknd over 1f out) | 1¾ | **11** | 12/1 | 46 | 3 |
| 4108[5] | **Hazel (61)** (MissGayKelleway) **4-9-7** DGriffiths(14) (b.hind: bhd fnl 2f) | nk | **12** | 9/2[2] | 47 | 7 |
| *1601*[10] | **Moi Canard (59)** (BAPearce) **3-8-9**(7) DSalt(16) (lw: mid div over 5f) | nk | **13** | 25/1 | 45 | 2 |
| 1156[5] | **Southern Dominion (50)** (CNAllen) **4-8-10** MartinDwyer(2) (lw: bhd fnl 2f) | hd | **14** | 9/1 | 36 | — |
| | **Arzani (USA) (63)** (DJSCosgrove) **5-9-4**(5) MNutter(3) (a bhd) | 2 | **15** | 33/1 | 44 | 4 |
| *1993*[11] | **Little Millie (60)** (JWMullins) **3-8-12**(5) DDenby(15) (lw: bhd fnl 2f) | nk | **16** | 33/1 | 40 | — |

(SP 153.1%) **16 Rn**

**1m 25.8** (4.20) CSF £160.73 CT £611.95 TOTE £8.20: £2.00 £2.30 £2.10 £3.00 (£125.00) Trio £106.00 OWNER Mr R. Miles (CHEPSTOW) BRED Lyonstown Stud
WEIGHT FOR AGE 3yo-3lb
**4240 Mr Cube (IRE)** gained his first victory in over a year. (15/2)
**1121 Sand Star** ran her best race for a long time but, having said that, she swerved violently left under pressure as she picked up ground below the distance. To her credit though she was flying at the death. (20/1)
**4256* Morocco (IRE)** is not very consistent but did run on in the last furlong and a half, only just losing the runner-up spot. (11/2)
**3585 Sapphire Son (IRE)**, who would be more at home in a seller or a claimer, failed to quicken in the last two furlongs. (14/1)
**3316 Mystery Matthias** is still a maiden after nineteen attempts. (20/1)
**Bold Habit**, with just one win since the beginning of 1992, is well past his sell-by date, although he did stay on from below the distance. (33/1)
**3285 Pearl Dawn (IRE)** (12/1: 8/1-14/1)
**1156 Southern Dominion** (9/1: 9/2-10/1)

T/Plpt: £291.10 (35.87 Tckts). T/Qdpt: £46.10 (16.86 Tckts). AK

# 4054-HAYDOCK (L-H) (Good)
## Friday September 27th
WEATHER: fine & sunny WIND: slt against

## 4429 STANLEY GOLDEN NUMBERS MAIDEN STKS (3-Y.O) (Class D)
2-00 (2-03) **1m 2f 120y** £3,985.25 (£1,202.00: £583.50: £274.25) Stalls: High GOING: 0.08 sec per fur (G)

| Form | Horse | Dist | Pos | SP | RR | SF |
|---|---|---|---|---|---|---|
| | **Naazeq** (ACStewart) **3-8-9** RHills(5) (w'like: scope: hld up: brought stands' side: hdwy to ld over 2f out: sn clr: easily) | — | **1** | 9/1 | 83 | 56 |
| $3656^{5}$ | **Grand Splendour** (LadyHerries) **3-8-9** KFallon(7) (lw: hld up: hdwy 4f out: led far side over 2f out: kpt on: no ch w wnr) | 3½ | **2** | $7/1^{3}$ | 78 | 51 |
| $4201^{4}$ | **Infatuation** (LadyHerries) **3-9-0** DeclanO'Shea(2) (lw: hld up: hdwy over 2f out: one pce fnl f) | ½ | **3** | $4/1^{2}$ | 82 | 55 |
| $3923^{5}$ | **Raise A Prince (FR) (74)** (JWHills) **3-9-0** RHughes(10) (lw: hld up: hdwy far side 3f out: disp ld 2f out: wknd ins fnl f) | ¾ | **4** | 9/1 | 81 | 54 |
| $3949^{6}$ | **Diamond Dance (IRE)** (JHMGosden) **3-8-9** LDettori(16) (b: bit bkwd: led after 2f tl over 2f out: wknd over 1f out) | 7 | **5** | $7/4^{1}$ | 65 | 38 |
| | **Tiutchev** (RCharlton) **3-9-0** TSprake(8) (leggy: scope: bit bkwd: hld up in tch: wknd wl over 1f out) | nk | **6** | 10/1 | 70 | 43 |
| $3999^{5}$ | **Winnebago** (CWThornton) **3-8-9** DeanMcKeown(3) (chsd ldrs tl wknd wl over 1f out) | 2 | **7** | 12/1 | 62 | 35 |
| | **Roberto Riva** (JLDunlop) **3-9-0** DHarrison(12) (prom: c stands' side st: wknd over 2f out) | 6 | **8** | 14/1 | 58 | 31 |
| $4099^{6}$ | **Magic Role** (MAJarvis) **3-9-0** RCochrane(9) (prom: c stands' side st: wknd over 2f out) | 2½ | **9** | 25/1 | 54 | 27 |
| $4083^{7}$ | **Soldier Blue** (PJHobbs) **3-9-0** MRoberts(15) (wl grwn: bkwd: led 2f: c stands' side: hdd & wknd over 2f out: t.o) | 27 | **10** | 33/1 | 13 | — |
| $4322^{6}$ | **Jungle Fresh** (JDBethell) **3-9-0** GBardwell(14) (a in rr: t.o) | 24 | **11** | 33/1 | — | — |
| | **Evening In Paris** (JWHills) **3-8-9** OUrbina(11) (small: str: bkwd: s.s: a t.o) | 11 | **12** | 25/1 | — | — |
| | **I Say Dancer (IRE)** (LJBarratt) **3-8-6**(3) DWright(4) (w'like: bkwd: s.s: a t.o) | ¾ | **13** | 33/1 | — | — |
| | **Shirlaty** (CWThornton) **3-8-9** SDrowne(6) (prom tl sddle slipped & wknd qckly 3f out: t.o) | 5 | **14** | 33/1 | — | — |
| | **Dunston Queen** (PJBevan) **3-8-9** NCarlisle(1) (lengthy: bkwd: a bhd: t.o) | 18 | **15** | 33/1 | — | — |

(SP 134.7%) **15 Rn**

**2m 17.29** (5.79) CSF £70.72 TOTE £13.90: £2.90 £2.10 £1.50 (£78.00) Trio £83.70 OWNER Mr Hamdan Al Maktoum (NEWMARKET) BRED Shadwell Estate Company Limited

OFFICIAL EXPLANATION **Shirlaty: his saddle slipped during the race.**

**Naazeq** produced an impressive winning debut with a clear-cut success, and this is only the start. (9/1)

**3656 Grand Splendour** won the race on the far side, but the winner proved just too smart for her. She is going the right way and her turn will come. (7/1)

**4201 Infatuation** seems to have inherited the stamina of his dam, and may well come into his own over a slightly longer trip. (4/1)

**3923 Raise A Prince (FR),** who wore a tongue-strap and was ridden with more restraint, joined the leader on the far side two furlongs out, but could not force his head in front. (9/1)

**3949 Diamond Dance (IRE)**, bandaged all round and still looking just short of peak-fitness, did her share of the pacemaking until weakening after being collared entering the final quarter-mile. (7/4)

**Tiutchev**, a leggy gelding with plenty of stamina in his breeding, was very much on his toes. Settled behind the leaders, he cried enough below the distance and gradually dropped away. He should be able to win races. (10/1)

## 4430 STANLEY CREDIT CLAIMING H'CAP (0-70) (3-Y.O+) (Class E)
2-30 (2-33) **6f** £3,582.50 (£1,085.00: £530.00: £252.50) Stalls: High GOING: 0.08 sec per fur (G)

| Form | Horse | Dist | Pos | SP | RR | SF |
|---|---|---|---|---|---|---|
| $4045^{6}$ | **Densben (47)** (DenysSmith) **12-8-6** ACulhane(13) (lw: hld up: swtchd lft & gd hdwy over 1f out: str run to ld post) | — | **1** | 12/1 | 55 | 35 |
| $4109^{9}$ | **Prima Silk (63)** (MJRyan) **5-9-8** RHughes(18) (b.nr hind: a.p: led appr fnl f: hdd last stride) | hd | **2** | 16/1 | 71 | 51 |
| $3973^{3}$ | **Barato (61)** (MrsJRRamsden) **5-9-6** KFallon(22) (hld up: hdwy & ev ch 1f out: rdn & no ex fnl f) | 1¼ | **3** | $6/1^{2}$ | 65 | 45 |
| $4180^{12}$ | **Saddlehome (USA) (69)** (TDBarron) **7-10-0** LDettori(14) (hld up: hdwy 2f out: nrst fin) | 1¾ | **4** | 10/1 | 69 | 49 |
| $4259^{4}$ | **Allwight Then (IRE) (60)** (DJSCosgrove) **5-9-5** RCochrane(11) (stdd s: hdwy over 1f out: unable qckn fnl f) | 1¼ | **5** | 10/1 | 56 | 36 |
| $3278^{4}$ | **Double Oscar (IRE) (58)** (DNicholls) **3-9-1** AlexGreaves(7) (hdwy over 2f out: ev ch over 1f out: wknd fnl f) | 1¼ | **6** | 20/1 | 51 | 29 |
| $4128^{14}$ | **Blushing Grenadier (IRE) (49)** (MJFetherston-Godley) **4-8-8v** PatEddery(16) (hdwy 2f out: r.o wl ins fnl f) | s.h | **7** | 12/1 | 42 | 22 |
| $4128^{9}$ | **Milos (60)** (TJNaughton) **5-9-5** TSprake(8) (nvr nrr) | 1½ | **8** | 16/1 | 49 | 29 |
| $4356^{9}$ | **Night Harmony (IRE) (56)** (RHannon) **3-8-13** DeanMcKeown(10) (prom: ev ch tl wknd fnl f) | 1½ | **9** | 14/1 | 41 | 19 |
| 4341* | **Naughty Pistol (USA) (52)** (PDEvans) **4-8-11v** 6x JFEgan(24) (prom stands' side: drvn over 1f out: sn btn) | hd | **10** | $7/1^{3}$ | 37 | 17 |
| $3844^{9}$ | **Standown (69)** (JBerry) **3-9-7**(5) PRoberts(2) (spd over 3f) | 4 | **11** | 25/1 | 43 | 21 |
| $2426^{8}$ | **Bargash (60)** (PDEvans) **4-9-5b** OUrbina(20) (prom: ev ch over 1f out: sn hrd rdn & wknd) | 4 | **12** | 16/1 | 23 | 3 |
| $4045^{5}$ | **John's Law (IRE) (48)** (MJHeaton-Ellis) **3-8-5b**[1] SDrowne(9) (lw: nvr trbld ldrs) | s.h | **13** | 20/1 | 11 | — |
| *$2084^{7}$* | **Maybank (IRE) (46)** (AStreeter) **4-8-5** BDoyle(5) (prom far side 3f) | 1½ | **14** | 33/1 | 5 | — |
| $3930^{13}$ | **Nakami (66)** (PJMakin) **4-9-11** DHarrison(6) (b: prom far side 3f) | 1½ | **15** | 20/1 | 21 | 1 |
| $4206^{2}$ | **Dominelle (51)** (TDEasterby) **4-8-10** MBirch(23) (hld up: effrt & nt clr run 2f out: nt rcvr) | 1 | **16** | $5/1^{1}$ | 4 | — |
| $3579^{10}$ | **Bashful Brave (67)** (BPJBaugh) **5-9-12** WLord(12) (led over 3f out tl appr fnl f: wknd qckly) | ½ | **17** | 33/1 | 18 | — |
| $4246^{20}$ | **Myttons Mistake (68)** (ABailey) **3-9-8**(3) DWright(15) (a in rr) | hd | **18** | 16/1 | 19 | — |
| | **Comeonup (60)** (JMBradley) **5-8-12**(7) RFfrench(17) (b: bkwd: outpcd) | ¾ | **19** | 25/1 | 9 | — |
| $2222^{6}$ | **Purple Memories (64)** (MJohnston) **3-9-7** MRoberts(3) (outpcd) | 1¼ | **20** | 20/1 | 10 | — |
| $4259^{6}$ | **Another Nightmare (IRE) (54)** (RMMcKellar) **4-8-6**(7) JMcAuley(4) (spd far side over 3f) | ½ | **21** | 16/1 | — | — |
| *$2367^{11}$* | **Gormire (60)** (JHetherton) **3-9-3** NCarlisle(1) (s.s: a bhd) | ½ | **22** | 33/1 | 3 | — |
| $3959^{4}$ | **Craignairn (61)** (JBerry) **3-9-4b** GCarter(19) (led over 2f: sn rdn & outpcd: wknd wl over 1f out: t.o) | 4 | **23** | 20/1 | — | — |

(SP 153.4%) **23 Rn**

**1m 16.13** (4.43) CSF £203.64 CT £1,215.22 TOTE £13.80: £2.50 £4.40 £2.10 £3.00 (£174.50) Trio £284.80 OWNER Mrs Janet Pike (BISHOP AUCKLAND) BRED D. W. Pike

WEIGHT FOR AGE 3yo-2lb

**4045 Densben,** the winner of this event twelve months ago, has been unable to trouble the Judge since, but he knows where the winning post is here and timed his run to perfection. (12/1)

**3989 Prima Silk**, brought back to sprinting, looked to have the edge when leading into the final furlong, but the determined late challenge of the winner proved just too strong. (16/1)

**3973 Barato**, usually produced at the last minute, rather surprisingly joined issue entering the final furlong and he did not appear to go through with his effort. (6/1)
**1113 Saddlehome (USA)**, possibly better at the minimum trip, ran his best race for quite some time on this step down in class and, if he is going to get back on the winning trail, this could be the grade where it will happen. (10/1)
**4259 Allwight Then (IRE)** loomed up as a live threat passing the furlong marker but, once there, lacked the speed to wrap things up. His turn could be near at hand. (10/1)
**3278 Double Oscar (IRE)**, having his first outing since changing stables and running without his usual headgear, showed plenty of promise, holding every chance at the distance before getting done for toe in the sprint to the line. (20/1)
**2376* Blushing Grenadier (IRE)** came late on the scene on this return to sprinting and, with a bit more cut in the ground, he showed he is still capable of picking up another prize. (12/1)
**4206 Dominelle** had little chance of getting through this tightly-packed field and this mediocre effort can safely be ignored. (5/1)

## 4431 STANLEY RACING H'CAP (0-90) (3-Y.O+) (Class C)

3-00 (3-05) **1m 3f 200y** £6,157.50 (£1,860.00: £905.00: £427.50) Stalls: High GOING: 0.08 sec per fur (G)

| | | | | SP | RR | SF |
|---|---|---|---|---|---|---|
| 4067$^{10}$ | **Haya Ya Kefaah (63)** (NMBabbage) **4-8-9** TSprake(4) (a.p: led over 3f out: hrd rdn: hld on gamely)............— | **1** | | 16/1 | 72 | 54 |
| 3939* | **Sugar Mill (71)** (MrsMReveley) **6-9-3** ACulhane(2) (hld up: hrd rdn 3f out: hdwy 2f out: ev ch ins fnl f: r.o).....nk | **2** | | 13/2$^{2}$ | 80 | 62 |
| 3939$^{4}$ | **Rusk (73)** (JPearce) **3-8-11** MWigham(13) (hld up: hdwy & nt clr run over 1f out: swtchd rt ins fnl f: fin wl)......½ | **3** | | 12/1 | 81 | 55 |
| 4249* | **Rex Mundi (60)** (PDEvans) **4-8-6** $^{4x}$ JFEgan(3) (a.p: hrd rdn over 2f out: ev ch fnl f: r.o).........................s.h | **4** | | 14/1 | 68 | 50 |
| 3791$^{6}$ | **House of Riches (84)** (LMCumani) **3-9-8** LDettori(10) (hld up: effrt & n.m.r fnl 2f: nvr able to chal)..................1 | **5** | | 8/1$^{3}$ | 91 | 65 |
| 3828$^{7}$ | **Lord Hastie (USA) (65)** (CWThornton) **8-8-11** RCochrane(15) (hld up: hdwy & nt clr run over 2f out: swtchd lft appr fnl f: kpt on wl)....................nk | **6** | | 9/1 | 71 | 53 |
| 3983$^{5}$ | **Secret Service (IRE) (73)** (CWThornton) **4-9-5** DeanMcKeown(12) (hld up: rdn & no hdwy fnl 2f) ................1¼ | **7** | | 10/1 | 77 | 59 |
| 4249$^{2}$ | **Calder King (64)** (JLEyre) **5-8-10b** KFallon(8) (dwlt: nvr trbld ldrs)....................¾ | **8** | | 5/1$^{1}$ | 67 | 49 |
| 2882$^{8}$ | **Shadow Leader (78)** (CREgerton) **5-9-10** RHughes(6) (lw: plld hrd: prom: led over 4f out tl over 3f out: hrd rdn & wknd appr fnl f)....................1 | **9** | | 14/1 | 80 | 62 |
| 2895* | **Circus Star (73)** (DNicholson) **3-8-11** JReid(5) (plld hrd: hld up in tch: wknd over 2f out) ....................½ | **10** | | 8/1$^{3}$ | 74 | 48 |
| 3997$^{10}$ | **Eagle Canyon (IRE) (80)** (BHanbury) **3-9-4** PatEddery(1) (led over 7f: rdn & wknd 2f out)....................½ | **11** | | 9/1 | 81 | 55 |
| 3754a$^{7}$ | **Otto E Mezzo (75)** (MJPolglase) **4-9-7** WHollick(11) (hld up & bhd: effrt 3f out: wknd 2f out)....................1¼ | **12** | | 33/1 | 74 | 56 |
| 3997$^{7}$ | **Traceability (83)** (SCWilliams) **3-9-7** GCarter(14) (prom tl wknd over 2f out: t.o) ....................5 | **13** | | 10/1 | 75 | 49 |
| 4174a$^{9}$ | **Glide Path (USA) (82)** (JWHills) **7-10-0** JOsborne(7) (hld up: hdwy centre & ev ch over 2f out: sn rdn & wknd: t.o)....................10 | **14** | | 20/1 | 61 | 43 |
| 4176$^{7}$ | **Endowment (72)** (MrsMReveley) **4-8-13**$^{(5)}$ SCopp(9) (s.s: a bhd: t.o) ....................¾ | **15** | | 20/1 | 50 | 32 |
| | | | | (SP 129.8%) | | **15 Rn** |

**2m 36.26** (6.86) CSF £114.61 CT £1,218.30 TOTE £18.10: £5.60 £2.30 £5.00 (£53.50) Trio £303.60 OWNER Mr Alan Craddock (CHELTENHAM) BRED Sheikh Ahmed bin Rashid al Maktoum
WEIGHT FOR AGE 3yo-8lb

IN-FOCUS: **In the majority of races on the Round Course at this meeting, the whole field came across to the stands' side once straightened up for home. With so many runners, general bunching was inevitable and there were bound to be many hard luck stories.**
**3683 Haya Ya Kefaah** retains his form remarkably well, and he thoroughly deserved this success after such a gutsy display. (16/1)
**3939* Sugar Mill** failed in his bid to complete the hat-trick, but he stuck to his guns in this slightly better-class event, and could still have more improvement in him than most, even at this late stage of the season. (13/2: 9/2-7/1)
**3939 Rusk**, still to get off the mark, may have been a shade unlucky here, for with a clear run he would probably have won with a bit to spare. (12/1)
**4249* Rex Mundi**, in the firing-line from the start, put in a determined bid inside the final furlong and only lost out close home. (14/1)
**3791 House of Riches** was one of the unlucky ones and never got a sight of the front until it was all too late. (8/1)
**3710 Lord Hastie (USA)**, poised to challenge from the turn into the straight, was searching for room for the final quarter-mile and, though he ran on strongly after being switched, the post was always going to beat him. (9/1)
**4249 Calder King** should have finished ahead of Rex Mundi on these terms but he failed to fire after a sluggish start, and finished a never-nearer eighth. (5/1: op 8/1)

## 4432 STANLEY LEISURE PLC DREAM MILE H'CAP (0-85) (3-Y.O+) (Class D)

3-30 (3-34) **1m 30y** £4,822.00 (£1,456.00: £708.00: £334.00) Stalls: Low GOING: 0.08 sec per fur (G)

| | | | | SP | RR | SF |
|---|---|---|---|---|---|---|
| 4296$^{2}$ | **High Premium (68)** (RAFahey) **8-9-2** ACulhane(12) (hld up: hdwy 3f out: led over 1f out: drvn out)..............— | **1** | | 11/2$^{1}$ | 80 | 46 |
| 4190* | **Gladys Althorpe (IRE) (70)** (JLEyre) **3-9-0** KFallon(1) (hld up: hdwy & swtchd rt over 1f out: r.o wl towards fin)....................1¾ | **2** | | 6/1$^{2}$ | 79 | 41 |
| 3800$^{2}$ | **Pomona (78)** (PJMakin) **3-9-8** PatEddery(10) (prom: ev ch over 1f out: no ex fnl f)....................nk | **3** | | 7/1 | 86 | 48 |
| 4128$^{16}$ | **Duke Valentino (58)** (RHollinshead) **4-8-3**$^{(3)}$ FLynch(15) (lw: hld up: hdwy over 3f out: kpt on ins fnl f) .........1½ | **4** | | 16/1 | 63 | 29 |
| 4212* | **Rakis (IRE) (78)** (MrsLStubbs) **6-9-12** $^{5x}$ JFEgan(6) (hld up: nt clr run over 2f out: swtchd lft ins fnl f: r.o wl)....................nk | **5** | | 12/1 | 82 | 48 |
| 4190$^{22}$ | **Maple Bay (IRE) (80)** (ABailey) **7-9-9**$^{(5)}$ GFaulkner(16) (lw: hld up & bhd: rdn & hdwy over 1f out: eased whn btn fnl f)....................1¾ | **6** | | 14/1 | 81 | 47 |
| 3974$^{2}$ | **Courageous Dancer (IRE) (76)** (BHanbury) **4-9-10** LDettori(18) (b: lw: led tl hdd & wknd over 1f out)............nk | **7** | | 13/2$^{3}$ | 76 | 42 |
| 4329$^{7}$ | **Blaze of Song (72)** (RHannon) **4-9-6v** RHughes(9) (hld up: no hdwy fnl 2f)....................1½ | **8** | | 14/1 | 69 | 35 |
| 4190$^{16}$ | **Rambo Waltzer (62)** (DNicholls) **4-8-10** AlexGreaves(2) (hld up: hdwy 3f out: ev ch over 1f out: wknd appr fnl f) ....................1¼ | **9** | | 20/1 | 57 | 23 |
| 4098$^{6}$ | **Mister Woodstick (IRE) (58)** (MAJarvis) **3-8-2**$^{ow1}$ BDoyle(14) (nvr nr ldrs) ....................nk | **10** | | 20/1 | 52 | 13 |
| 2183$^{11}$ | **Dragon's Back (IRE) (69)** (MrsJCecil) **3-8-13** JReid(5) (prom tl hrd rdn & wknd over 2f out)....................6 | **11** | | 16/1 | 52 | 14 |
| 4243$^{10}$ | **Sooty Tern (69)** (JMBradley) **9-8-10**$^{(7)}$ RFfrench(7) (trckd ldrs over 5f)....................s.h | **12** | | 16/1 | 52 | 18 |
| 4068$^{16}$ | **Flag Fen (USA) (59)** (MartynMeade) **5-8-7** TSprake(11) (lw: nvr trbld ldrs) ....................1¼ | **13** | | 20/1 | 39 | 5 |
| 4297$^{5}$ | **Dee-Lady (75)** (WGMTurner) **4-9-2**$^{(7)}$ DSweeney(8) (prom tl wknd over 2f out)....................nk | **14** | | 25/1 | 55 | 21 |
| 4108* | **Jumairah Sunset (70)** (ACStewart) **3-9-0** MRoberts(17) (s.i.s: a bhd)....................2 | **15** | | 6/1$^{2}$ | 46 | 8 |
| 3800$^{6}$ | **Elite Hope (USA) (68)** (CREgerton) **4-9-2b$^{1}$** OUrbina(13) (nt clr run over 2f out: sn bhd) ....................3½ | **16** | | 25/1 | 37 | 3 |
| 4054$^{13}$ | **Nkapen Rocks (SPA) (58)** (CaptJWilson) **3-8-2** GCarter(4) (s.i.s: a bhd: t.o)....................8 | **17** | | 33/1 | 11 | — |
| | | | | (SP 133.4%) | | **17 Rn** |

**1m 46.68** (6.08) CSF £39.05 CT £234.75 TOTE £7.90: £1.80 £1.40 £2.00 £3.80 (£18.80) Trio £36.20 OWNER Mr J. C. Parsons (MALTON) BRED M.E Wates
WEIGHT FOR AGE 3yo-4lb

**4296 High Premium** made amends for a luckless run last week with a fairly clear-cut success, but fortune favoured him this time. (11/2)
**4190* Gladys Althorpe (IRE)** had a nightmare run through inside the distance and only saw daylight when it was all too late. With a clear run, she would have kept up her winning sequence. (6/1)
**3800 Pomona**, still searching for that first success, performed with credit, trying to give weight to the principals, and she is ready to strike when conditions are in her favour. (7/1)
**3592 Duke Valentino** runs better when produced from off the pace and, though he was unable to trouble the principals on this occasion, was far from disgraced in defeat. (16/1)

## 4433 STANLEY SNOOKER NURSERY H'CAP (0-85) (2-Y.O) (Class D)

4-00 (4-01) **6f** £3,623.00 (£1,094.00: £532.00: £251.00) Stalls: High GOING: 0.08 sec per fur (G)

| Form | Horse | Dist | Pos | SP | RR | SF |
|---|---|---|---|---|---|---|
| 4106[9] | **Trading Aces (62)** (MBell) **2-7-8**(7) RMullen(9) (hld up: hdwy & swtchd lft 2f out: led fnl 100y: r.o wl) | — | **1** | 12/1 | 74 | 18 |
| *2746** | **Dayville (USA) (75)** (RCharlton) **2-9-0** TSprake(7) (chsd ldr: led over 1f out: hdd & unable qckn wl ins fnl f) | 1¾ | **2** | 3/1[1] | 82 | 26 |
| *4335*[4] | **Abstone Queen (63)** (PDEvans) **2-8-2v** JFEgan(3) (hdwy over 1f out: r.o wl ins fnl f) | 1½ | **3** | 11/1 | 66 | 10 |
| 4195[11] | **Cairn Dhu (61)** (MrsJRRamsden) **2-8-0** GCarter(8) (dwlt: hdwy fnl f: nvr nrr) | 4 | **4** | 8/1 | 54 | — |
| 4195[13] | **Cherokee Flight (72)** (MrsJRRamsden) **2-8-11v**[1] KFallon(6) (racd keenly: led tl over 1f out: sn rdn & btn) | ¾ | **5** | 7/1 | 63 | 7 |
| *4091*[4] | **Good Day (70)** (CWThornton) **2-8-9** DeanMcKeown(1) (nvr rchd ldrs) | ¾ | **6** | 13/2[3] | 59 | 3 |
| 3941[6] | **Why O Six (68)** (RAFahey) **2-8-7** ACulhane(4) (chsd ldrs: rdn ½-wy: wknd over 1f out) | 1 | **7** | 4/1[2] | 54 | — |
| 2588[2] | **Rum Lad (73)** (JJQuinn) **2-8-7**(5) GParkin(5) (outpcd) | 2 | **8** | 10/1 | 54 | — |
| 3687[12] | **Veerapong (IRE) (61)** (MWEasterby) **2-8-0b**[ow1] JFanning(10) (chsd ldng pair: edgd rt over 2f out: sn btn) | 4 | **9** | 10/1 | 31 | — |
| 3988[11] | **Permission (82)** (RHannon) **2-9-7** LDettori(2) (a bhd & outpcd) | 5 | **10** | 8/1 | 39 | — |

(SP 127.3%) **10 Rn**

**1m 17.06** (5.36) CSF £49.44 CT £402.98 TOTE £14.10: £2.70 £1.70 £3.40 (£28.50) Trio £72.60 OWNER Mr R. P. B. Michaelson (NEWMARKET) BRED Limestone Stud
**2323 Trading Aces**, from a yard in top form, had enough in hand to switch from the rail and then drift further left, but still win going away. (12/1: op 8/1)
**2746* Dayville (USA)**, a winner on the All-Weather on her previous outing ten weeks earlier, looked set to follow up until the winner beat her for toe in the dash to the line. (3/1: op 2/1)
**4335 Abstone Queen** struggled with the pace and only found top gear when the race was all but over. (11/1)
**4195 Cairn Dhu**, flat-footed as the stalls opened, was unable to recover, and his finishing position was as close as he got. (8/1: 5/1-10/1)
**3050* Cherokee Flight** raced far too freely in his first-time visor and was legless when collared approaching the final furlong. (7/1: op 4/1)
**4091 Good Day** showed his first glimpse of form over a slightly longer trip last time, but the pace was always too hot for him here. (13/2: 4/1-7/1)
**3941 Why O Six** (4/1: op 10/1)

## 4434 STANLEY CASINO CONDITIONS STKS (3-Y.O+) (Class C)

4-30 (4-32) **1m 6f** £5,282.00 (£1,842.00: £896.00: £380.00) Stalls: Centre GOING: 0.08 sec per fur (G)

| Form | Horse | Dist | Pos | SP | RR | SF |
|---|---|---|---|---|---|---|
| 726[3] | **Moonax (IRE) (119)** (BWHills) **5-9-1** PatEddery(5) (a.p: led over 2f out: rdn & r.o wl) | — | **1** | 11/10[1] | 106 | 49 |
| 1482[3] | **Court of Honour (IRE) (117)** (PWChapple-Hyam) **4-9-1** JReid(2) (bit bkwd: led tl over 2f out: rdn & kpt on fnl f) | 1 | **2** | 11/10[1] | 105 | 48 |
| 3934[7] | **Poltarf (USA) (103)** (JHMGosden) **5-9-1** LDettori(3) (lw: dropped rr 8f out: effrt 3f out: ev ch appr fnl f: one pce) | 1¼ | **3** | 9/1[2] | 103 | 46 |
| 2250[2] | **Edipo Re** (PJHobbs) **4-9-1** RHughes(4) (b: plld hrd: wnt 2nd 6f out: drvn along over 3f out: sn outpcd) | 20 | **4** | 25/1[3] | 81 | 24 |

(SP 109.1%) **4 Rn**

**3m 8.13** (9.93) CSF £2.60 TOTE £1.90 (£1.20) OWNER Sheikh Mohammed (LAMBOURN) BRED Liscannor Stud Ltd in Ireland
**726 Moonax (IRE)** had to be led down to the start for this first outing since the spring. Settled going well, he did not need to get serious to succeed here, and is a class act on his day. (11/10)
**1482 Court of Honour (IRE)** looked to be carrying more condition than the winner after a four-month break, but he ran extremely well and should gain more success in the coming weeks. (11/10)
**3934 Poltarf (USA)**, by far the fittest member of the field, looked a live threat when challenging for the lead at the distance, but the leading pair proved too strong for him. (9/1)
**2250 Edipo Re** needs more cut in the ground than he had here, but he was far from fully wound up after a lengthy holiday, and he was left behind early in the straight. (25/1)

T/Jkpt: Not won; £3,337.56 to Ascot 28/9/96. T/Plpt: £164.20 (114.4 Tckts). T/Qdpt: £11.10 (104.42 Tckts). IM

# 3814-REDCAR (L-H) (Firm, Good to firm patches)
## Friday September 27th

WEATHER: sunny periods WIND: mod half bhd

## 4435 NEWBY MEDIAN AUCTION MAIDEN STKS (2-Y.O F) (Class E)

2-10 (2-11) **7f** £3,377.50 (£1,015.00: £490.00: £227.50) Stalls: Centre GOING minus 0.56 sec per fur (F)

| Form | Horse | Dist | Pos | SP | RR | SF |
|---|---|---|---|---|---|---|
| | **Priena (IRE)** (DRLoder) **2-8-11** KDarley(7) (lengthy: unf: lw: disp ld tl led 2f out: easily) | — | **1** | 4/7[1] | 78+ | 25 |
| 4242[4] | **Pretty Sharp** (APJarvis) **2-8-11** JFortune(3) (disp ld 5f: rdn & no ch w wnr) | 7 | **2** | 7/4[2] | 62 | 9 |
| 3809[9] | **Go For Green** (DrJDScargill) **2-8-11** JStack(5) (hld up: hdwy 3f out: sn rdn & no imp) | 1¾ | **3** | 16/1 | 58 | 5 |
| 3988[14] | **Tyrolean Dancer (IRE)** (SPCWoods) **2-8-11** DBiggs(4) (prom: effrt 3f out: r.o one pce) | 2½ | **4** | 10/1[3] | 52 | — |
| | **Diamond Eyre** (JLEyre) **2-8-11** RLappin(2) (unf: bkwd: prom: rdn ½-wy: sn btn) | 1½ | **5** | 33/1 | 49 | — |
| 4041[12] | **Dance Melody (48)** (GROldroyd) **2-8-8**(3) NVarley(8) (chsd ldrs tl outpcd fnl 3f) | 2 | **6** | 50/1 | 44 | — |
| 4041[8] | **Megan Carew** (DMoffatt) **2-8-8**(3) DarrenMoffatt(6) (prom: effrt ½-wy: sn btn) | 3½ | **7** | 50/1 | 36 | — |
| | **Daunting Times** (BWMurray) **2-8-11** VHalliday(1) (unf: bkwd: b.hind: chsd ldrs: hung bdly lft fr ½-wy: sn wknd) | 6 | **8** | 50/1 | 23 | — |

(SP 123.8%) **8 Rn**

**1m 25.0** (2.00) CSF £2.24 TOTE £2.00: £1.20 £1.10 £1.90 (£1.30) OWNER Cuadra Africa (NEWMARKET) BRED Almagro de Actividades Comerciales S A
**Priena (IRE)** has plenty of scope about her but is as yet only lightly-made. She did look fit though, and had the perfect introduction here, winning as she liked from moderate opposition. (4/7)
**4242 Pretty Sharp** is going the right way but, despite a valiant effort, was completely outclassed. (7/4)

**Go For Green** never really got into this, but showed enough to suggest that she has the ability to win a small race. (16/1)
**Tyrolean Dancer (IRE)** showed some ability and seemed to stay well enough. (10/1)
**Diamond Eyre** is not much to look at and certainly needed this, so in the circumstances did not run too badly. (33/1)

## 4436 MISSISSIPPI AMATEUR H'CAP (0-70) (3-Y.O+) (Class E)

2-40 (2-43) **1m** £3,787.00 (£1,141.00: £553.00: £259.00) Stalls: Centre GOING minus 0.56 sec per fur (F)

| | | | | SP | RR | SF |
|---|---|---|---|---|---|---|
| 4000$^{5}$ | **Mels Baby (IRE) (56)** (JLEyre) **3-10-10** MissDianaJones(11) (in tch: hdwy over 2f out: r.o to ld cl home) | — | **1** | 10/1$^{3}$ | 69 | 47 |
| 4259$^{7}$ | **Awesome Venture (50)** (MCChapman) **6-10-8** MrRThornton(19) (w ldrs centre: kpt on wl fnl f) | 1 | **2** | 14/1 | 61 | 43 |
| 4226$^{12}$ | **Cee-Jay-Ay (53)** (JBerry) **9-10-11** MrRHale(13) (s.i.s: hdwy ½-wy: led 2f out tl ct cl home) | hd | **3** | 14/1 | 64 | 46 |
| 4307$^{8}$ | **Breezed Well (38)** (BRCambidge) **10-9-5**(5) MrsHNoonan(8) (chsd ldrs centre: ev ch 2f out: r.o one pce) | 1¼ | **4** | 25/1 | 46 | 28 |
| 3991$^{9}$ | **Squared Away (49)** (JWPayne) **4-10-2b**(5) MissCLake(28) (lw: bhd: hdwy over 2f out: styd on wl nr fin) | nk | **5** | 11/1 | 57 | 39 |
| 4202* | **Polly Peculiar (60)** (BSmart) **5-10-13**(5) MissVMarshall(10) (s.i.s: wnt prom centre ½-wy: ev ch over 2f out: btn over 1f out) | nk | **6** | 7/2$^{1}$ | 67 | 49 |
| 3958$^{13}$ | **Habeta (USA) (45)** (JWWatts) **10-9-12**(5) MissERamsden(21) (styd on fnl 3f: nvr nrr) | 1½ | **7** | 33/1 | 49 | 31 |
| 3845$^{7}$ | **Dispol Gem (67)** (GROldroyd) **3-11-7** MrTMcCarthy(9) (chsd ldrs centre: wknd fnl 2f) | 1½ | **8** | 20/1 | 68 | 46 |
| 4348$^{4}$ | **Rainbows Rhapsody (35)** (DWChapman) **5-9-2**(5) MrMKneafsey(16) (in tch: hdwy over 2f out: nvr able to chal) | 1¾ | **9** | 20/1 | 33 | 15 |
| 4226* | **Thatched (IRE) (53)** (REBarr) **6-10-11** 6x MrSSwiers(7) (lw: effrt ½-wy: nvr trbld ldrs) | 1¼ | **10** | 8/1$^{2}$ | 48 | 30 |
| 2929$^{8}$ | **Peacefull Reply (USA) (35)** (FHLee) **6-9-2**(5) MrCWatson(17) (in tch: rdn & no imp fnl 3f) | 1½ | **11** | 33/1 | 27 | 9 |
| 4323$^{5}$ | **Lady Silk (46)** (MissJFCraze) **5-9-13**(5) MrWWenyon(22) (bhd stands' side tl styd on fnl 2f) | s.h | **12** | 14/1 | 38 | 20 |
| 4263$^{3}$ | **Northern Grey (44)** (DrJDScargill) **4-9-11**(5) MrEBabington(25) (in tch stands' side: no imp fnl 3f) | s.h | **13** | 12/1 | 36 | 18 |
| 4226$^{8}$ | **Soldier Cove (USA) (55)** (MartynMeade) **6-10-8**(5) MrsDMcHale(24) (n.d) | ½ | **14** | 25/1 | 46 | 28 |
| *4089*$^{10}$ | **Lucky Bea (58)** (MWEasterby) **3-10-12** MrNWilson(18) (nvr trbld ldrs) | 3 | **15** | 33/1 | 43 | 21 |
| 3453$^{3}$ | **Upex le Gold Too (35)** (DWChapman) **4-9-2**(5) MrsCWilliams(12) (in tch 5f) | 1¼ | **16** | 33/1 | 17 | — |
| | **Bill Moon (35)** (DTThom) **10-9-7** MissJFeilden(2) (chsd ldr far side: chal 3f out: wknd fnl 2f) | 1½ | **17** | 25/1 | 14 | — |
| 2776$^{11}$ | **Islay Brown (IRE) (45)** (CWCElsey) **3-9-13b** MissAElsey(6) (lw: led far side tl hdd & wknd 2f out) | s.h | **18** | 66/1 | 24 | 2 |
| 3443$^{W}$ | **Love Legend (41)** (DWPArbuthnot) **11-9-13** MrsDArbuthnot(27) (n.d fr ½-wy) | hd | **19** | 25/1 | 20 | 2 |
| 3973$^{W}$ | **Statistician (57)** (JohnBerry) **4-11-1** MrsJLeBrocq(20) (in tch over 5f) | hd | **20** | 33/1 | 36 | 18 |
| 4102$^{11}$ | **Aeroking (USA) (70)** (GHarwood) **5-12-0** MrsAPerrett(29) (lw: in tch stands' side over 5f) | s.h | **21** | 12/1 | 49 | 31 |
| 4307$^{20}$ | **Straight Thinking (USA) (55)** (JLSpearing) **3-10-4**(5) MissAShirley-Priest(14) (cl up centre over 5f: wknd) | nk | **22** | 50/1 | 33 | 11 |
| 4323$^{9}$ | **Prudent Pet (49)** (CWFairhurst) **4-10-7** MrsSBosley(15) (n.d) | ½ | **23** | 25/1 | 26 | 8 |
| 4226$^{10}$ | **Kilnamartyra Girl (49)** (JParkes) **6-10-7** MrsDKettlewell(4) (n.d) | nk | **24** | 25/1 | 26 | 8 |
| 3958$^{14}$ | **Great Bear (45)** (DWChapman) **4-10-3** MissRClark(26) (bhd fr ½-wy) | 2½ | **25** | 16/1 | 17 | — |
| 4356$^{12}$ | **Oh Susannah (41)** (JAHarris) **5-9-8**(5)ow6 MrGWoodward(1) (n.d) | 1¾ | **26** | 16/1 | 9 | — |
| *255*$^{9}$ | **Natural Path (43)** (MrsVAAconley) **5-9-10**(5)ow3 MrGMarkham(23) (swtg: spd centre 5f) | 3½ | **27** | 100/1 | 4 | — |
| | **Marsh's Law (43)** (GPKelly) **9-9-10**(5)ow8 MrSLavallin(5) (bhd fr ½-wy) | 11 | **28** | 100/1 | — | — |
| | | | | (SP 150.6%) | **28 Rn** | |

**1m 38.3** (2.60) CSF £147.83 CT £1,879.86 TOTE £8.40: £2.00 £4.40 £3.40 £4.70 (£84.60) Trio £175.60 OWNER Mr John Roberts (Wakefield) (HAMBLETON) BRED A. F. O'Callaghan
LONG HANDICAP Bill Moon 9-2 Upex le Gold Too 9-0 Peacefull Reply (USA) 9-2 Rainbows Rhapsody 9-5 Marsh's Law 9-6
WEIGHT FOR AGE 3yo-4lb
**4000 Mels Baby (IRE)** at last got it right and, in doing so, was given a fine ride. This should have boosted his confidence. (10/1)
**4259 Awesome Venture** has not won Turf for three years, but this was a sound effort and there could be a race to be found, especially when there is some give underfoot. (14/1)
**3867 Cee-Jay-Ay** came sailing through from halfway and probably hit the front too soon, only to be worried out of it late on. (14/1)
**3510 Breezed Well**, despite his years, is running well at present, but just lacks that final dash. (25/1)
**2440 Squared Away** made up an incredible amount of ground in the last three furlongs and would seem to be better suited by further. (11/1)
**4202* Polly Peculiar** gave away a fair few lengths at the start and that probably made all the difference. (7/2)
**3344 Habeta (USA)** showed he is still in good heart by running on well when it was all over. (33/1)

## 4437 SCARBOROUGH MAIDEN (S) STKS (3-Y.O) (Class G)

3-10 (3-11) **1m 3f** £2,637.00 (£732.00: £351.00) Stalls: Low GOING minus 0.56 sec per fur (F)

| | | | | SP | RR | SF |
|---|---|---|---|---|---|---|
| 3960$^{3}$ | **Dunrowan** (MrsMReveley) **3-8-9** KDarley(9) (hld up: hdwy 4f out: chsng ldrs 2f out: hrd rdn to ld wl ins fnl f) | — | **1** | 3/1$^{2}$ | 58 | 30 |
| 4323$^{12}$ | **My Millie (46)** (DWBarker) **3-8-9** LCharnock(8) (a.p: led 3f out tl ct wl ins fnl f) | 1 | **2** | 12/1 | 57 | 29 |
| *4080*$^{3}$ | **Sylvella (50)** (MAJarvis) **3-8-9** PBloomfield(13) (lw: cl up: led wl over 3f out: hdd 3f out: sn outpcd: styd on ins fnl f) | 1¼ | **3** | 9/4$^{1}$ | 55 | 27 |
| 2931$^{6}$ | **Dino's Mistral (30)** (FHLee) **3-9-0** RLappin(6) (hdwy over 4f out: sn in tch: one pce fnl 2f) | 5 | **4** | 33/1 | 53 | 25 |
| 2180$^{9}$ | **Cocoon (IRE) (40)** (CWThornton) **3-8-9** TWilliams(7) (prom: chal 4f out: edgd rt: one pce fnl 2f) | 6 | **5** | 25/1 | 39 | 11 |
| 3780$^{13}$ | **Reinhardt (IRE) (52)** (JSWainwright) **3-8-7b**$^{1}$(7) JBramhill(14) (hdwy to chse ldrs ent st: c wd: one pce fnl 3f) | 1 | **6** | 6/1$^{3}$ | 42 | 14 |
| 3831$^{6}$ | **Whothehellisharry (53)** (JBerry) **3-9-0** JCarroll(15) (chsd ldrs tl wknd fnl 2½f) | s.h | **7** | 8/1 | 42 | 14 |
| 4237$^{8}$ | **Mrs Drummond (IRE)** (APJarvis) **3-8-9** JFortune(1) (effrt 4f out: sme late hdwy: n.d) | 1¼ | **8** | 7/1 | 35 | 7 |
| 3619$^{17}$ | **Swynford Supreme (50)** (JFBottomley) **3-9-0** NKennedy(11) (nvr trbld ldrs) | 3 | **9** | 20/1 | 36 | 8 |
| 3960$^{4}$ | **Magical Midnight (30)** (DonEnricoIncisa) **3-8-9b** KimTinkler(10) (bhd: sme hdwy 2f out: n.d) | ¾ | **10** | 33/1 | 30 | 2 |
| 3970$^{11}$ | **Irish Oasis (IRE) (43)** (BSRothwell) **3-9-0** JStack(2) (cl up tl wknd fnl 4f) | 1¾ | **11** | 16/1 | 32 | 4 |
| 4209$^{7}$ | **Lomond Lassie (USA) (32)** (MissJFCraze) **3-8-9** NConnorton(3) (in tch tl wknd fnl 3½f) | 3 | **12** | 12/1 | 23 | — |
| | **Shoja** (MrsVAAconley) **3-8-7**(7) GMilligan(16) (bkwd: a bhd) | 7 | **13** | 20/1 | 18 | — |
| 4259$^{16}$ | **Rothley Imp (IRE) (42)** (JWharton) **3-8-9** JWeaver(5) (swtg: a bhd) | s.h | **14** | 14/1 | 13 | — |
| | **Colway Bridge** (MrsMReveley) **3-8-9**(5) GLee(4) (bit bkwd: led tl hdd wl over 3f out: sn btn) | s.h | **15** | 25/1 | 18 | — |
| 4070$^{9}$ | **Noble Colours (30)** (JJQuinn) **3-9-0** DBiggs(12) (ref to r: t.n.p) | | **R** | 33/1 | — | — |
| | | | | (SP 147.6%) | **16 Rn** | |

**2m 20.7** (2.70) CSF £44.81 TOTE £3.60: £1.70 £5.80 £1.60 (£156.90) Trio £50.90 OWNER Mr R. R. J. Scott (SALTBURN) BRED R. R. J. Scott
Bt in 3,600 gns
**3960 Dunrowan**, taking a big drop in class, did the business but really had to work to do so. She gave the impression that she should improve over further. (3/1)
**My Millie**, taking a big step up in trip, ran much better, only to be just touched off. (12/1)
**4080 Sylvella** has the ability and, judging by the way she kept on towards the finish, should appreciate further. (9/4)

**Dino's Mistral** has shown next to nothing previously, but did give a little encouragement here. (33/1)
**171 Cocoon (IRE)**, trying her longest trip to date, threw her chances away by hanging right. (25/1)
**3056 Reinhardt (IRE)**, in blinkers for the first time, failed to produce the goods when ridden in the straight. (6/1)

## 4438 HORNSEA H'CAP (0-80) (3-Y.O+) (Class D)

3-40 (3-41) **1m 2f** £4,159.00 (£1,252.00: £606.00: £283.00) Stalls: Low GOING minus 0.56 sec per fur (F)

| Form | Horse | Dist | Pos | SP | RR | SF |
|---|---|---|---|---|---|---|
| 4068$^{3}$ | **Urgent Swift (67)** (APJarvis) **3-8-13** JFortune(3) (a.p: chal over 2f out: disp ld over 1f out: led ins fnl f: hrd rdn & r.o) | — | **1** | 8/1 | 77 | 27 |
| 4257$^{2}$ | **Elashath (USA) (65)** (JHMGosden) **3-8-11** JWeaver(5) (lw: cl up: disp ld 3f out: kpt on u.p) | hd | **2** | 11/10$^{1}$ | 75 | 25 |
| 4193$^{13}$ | **Desert Fighter (66)** (MrsMReveley) **5-8-13**(5) GLee(2) (led tl hdd ins fnl f: kpt on wl) | hd | **3** | 10/1 | 76 | 32 |
| 4102$^{6}$ | **Essayeffsee (60)** (MrsMReveley) **7-8-12** KDarley(8) (lw: hld up & bhd: hdwy 4f out: styd on wl towards fin) | 1 | **4** | 8/1 | 68 | 24 |
| 4121$^{6}$ | **Apollono (72)** (JRFanshawe) **4-9-7**(3) NVarley(4) (lw: in tch: effrt over 3f out: nvr able to chal) | 1 | **5** | 13/2$^{3}$ | 79 | 35 |
| 4300$^{9}$ | **Spanish Verdict (64)** (DenysSmith) **9-9-2** TWilliams(10) (lw: chsd ldrs tl outpcd fnl 3f) | 1¾ | **6** | 25/1 | 68 | 24 |
| 3961$^{7}$ | **Ordained (58)** (EJAlston) **3-8-4** GHind(9) (trckd ldrs: effrt over 3f out: btn 2f out) | ½ | **7** | 8/1 | 61 | 11 |
| 3938$^{4}$ | **Forest Fantasy (56)** (JWharton) **3-8-2** JStack(7) (trckd ldrs: chal over 3f out: wknd over 2f out) | 4 | **8** | 11/2$^{2}$ | 53 | 3 |
| 4109$^{17}$ | **Fran Godfrey (62)** (PTWalwyn) **3-8-8** JCarroll(6) (a bhd) | 11 | **9** | 14/1 | 41 | — |
| 4320$^{9}$ | **Colorful Ambition (67)** (MrsASwinbank) **6-9-5** JSupple(1) (ref to r: t.n.p) | | **R** | 40/1 | — | — |

(SP 131.7%) **10 Rn**

**2m 6.8** (3.20) CSF £18.77 CT £95.95 TOTE £10.30: £2.80 £1.50 £2.20 (£8.00) Trio £80.70 OWNER Mrs Ann Jarvis (ASTON UPTHORPE) BRED Home Stud Ltd
WEIGHT FOR AGE 3yo-6lb

**4068 Urgent Swift** is a bit of a character and took some keeping straight here, but he was given an absolutely tremendous ride and that won the day. (8/1: 6/1-9/1)
**4257 Elashath (USA)** has shown previously that he does not possess a change of gear and much more use should have been made of him here. (11/10)
**Desert Fighter**, from a yard that is really coming to form, ran his best race, and is worth keeping in mind, especially over hurdles. (10/1)
**4102 Essayeffsee** would have appreciated a stronger gallop and, despite finishing well, it was always too late. He is in fine form. (8/1)
**4121 Apollono** ran reasonably, but lacked a turn of foot to ever take the opportunity. (13/2: 5/2-7/1)
**3842 Spanish Verdict** looks well enough, but is not showing his sparkle at the moment. (25/1)

## 4439 CONSTANT SECURITY H'CAP (0-85) (3-Y.O+) (Class D)

4-10 (4-11) **7f** £4,107.00 (£1,236.00: £598.00: £279.00) Stalls: Centre GOING minus 0.56 sec per fur (F)

| Form | Horse | Dist | Pos | SP | RR | SF |
|---|---|---|---|---|---|---|
| 4300$^{8}$ | **Quilling (69)** (MDods) **4-9-1** JFortune(1) (lw: cl up: disp ld over 2f out: edgd rt: led over 1f out: hrd drvn: r.o) | — | **1** | 7/2$^{1}$ | 78 | 58 |
| 4212$^{3}$ | **Glowing Jade (68)** (JAGlover) **6-9-0** KDarley(6) (hld up: hdwy 2f out: ev ch ins fnl f: kpt on) | nk | **2** | 7/2$^{1}$ | 76 | 56 |
| 4190$^{4}$ | **Anonym (IRE) (58)** (DNicholls) **4-7-11b**(7) JBramhill(9) (lw: trckd ldrs: disp ld over 2f out tl over 1f out: nt r.o) | ¾ | **3** | 7/2$^{1}$ | 65 | 45 |
| 4316$^{10}$ | **Murray's Mazda (IRE) (52)** (JLEyre) **7-7-12** TWilliams(4) (hld up: effrt over 2f out: styd on: nvr able to chal) | 3 | **4** | 12/1$^{3}$ | 52 | 32 |
| 4255$^{5}$ | **Robellion (68)** (DWPArbuthnot) **5-9-0v** JWeaver(8) (b: hld up: hdwy 3f out: one pce appr fnl f) | 2 | **5** | 8/1$^{2}$ | 63 | 43 |
| 3817$^{8}$ | **Kid Ory (55)** (PCalver) **5-7-12**(3) NVarley(3) (w ldrs: n.m.r wl over 1f out: one pce after) | s.h | **6** | 8/1$^{2}$ | 50 | 30 |
| 3833$^{11}$ | **Tinklers Folly (65)** (DenysSmith) **4-8-11** LCharnock(10) (led tl hdd over 2f out: sn btn) | 2 | **7** | 16/1 | 56 | 36 |
| 4300$^{13}$ | **King Rat (IRE) (79)** (TJEtherington) **5-9-11b** JTate(5) (trckd ldrs: n.m.r 2f out: sn btn) | hd | **8** | 8/1$^{2}$ | 69 | 49 |
| 4259$^{9}$ | **Spanish Stripper (USA) (56)** (MCChapman) **5-7-11**(5) PFessey(2) (effrt ½-wy: no imp) | 2½ | **9** | 14/1 | 41 | 21 |
| 4206$^{15}$ | **Shashi (IRE) (63)** (WWHaigh) **4-8-9b** RLappin(7) (sddle slipped & lost tch fnl 3f) | 8 | **10** | 20/1 | 29 | 9 |

(SP 125.0%) **10 Rn**

**1m 22.5** (-0.50) CSF £16.65 CT £44.95 TOTE £4.40: £2.00 £2.30 £1.50 (£7.60) Trio £8.00 OWNER Mr A. G. Watson (DARLINGTON) BRED Hesmonds Stud Ltd

**4136* Quilling** was given the strongest assistance going and gave his all to hold on. (7/2)
**4212 Glowing Jade** produced a run from the back of the field, but was never quite doing enough, despite staying on. He looks on good terms with himself. (7/2)
**4190 Anonym (IRE)** is a real character and probably saw too much daylight too soon on this occasion. (7/2)
**2590 Murray's Mazda (IRE)** ran reasonably and looks to be coming back to form. (12/1)
**4255 Robellion** has never won over further than six furlongs on Turf, and his run here came to an end approaching the last furlong. (8/1)
**3328 Kid Ory** has had a disappointing year. Should he ever regain his form, he is certainly well handicapped at present. (8/1)

## 4440 MICHAELMAS NURSERY H'CAP (0-85) (2-Y.O) (Class D)

4-40 (4-40) **7f** £3,853.50 (£1,158.00: £559.00: £259.50) Stalls: Centre GOING minus 0.56 sec per fur (F)

| Form | Horse | Dist | Pos | SP | RR | SF |
|---|---|---|---|---|---|---|
| 4123$^{4}$ | **Zaima (IRE) (79)** (JLDunlop) **2-9-7** KDarley(1) (hld up: hdwy ½-wy: led appr fnl f: r.o) | — | **1** | 11/4$^{2}$ | 78 | 47 |
| 4195$^{4}$ | **Plan For Profit (IRE) (74)** (MJohnston) **2-9-2** JWeaver(3) (cl up: led wl over 1f out: sn hdd: kpt on) | ½ | **2** | 7/4$^{1}$ | 72 | 41 |
| *4093*$^{3}$ | **Strelitza (IRE) (55)** (MWEasterby) **2-7-11b** NKennedy(8) (chsd ldrs: effrt & hung lft 2f out: kpt on nr fin) | ½ | **3** | 7/1 | 52 | 21 |
| 3873$^{7}$ | **Danka (70)** (PTWalwyn) **2-8-12v$^{1}$** JCarroll(7) (led over 5f: one pce) | 4 | **4** | 16/1 | 58 | 27 |
| 4024a$^{19}$ | **Jack Flush (IRE) (73)** (BSRothwell) **2-9-1** JStack(9) (in tch: effrt over 2f out: nt pce to chal) | ¾ | **5** | 11/1 | 59 | 28 |
| 4131$^{11}$ | **The Deejay (IRE) (68)** (MBrittain) **2-8-10** RLappin(6) (lw: outpcd & lost tch 3f out: sme late hdwy) | 1½ | **6** | 8/1 | 50 | 19 |
| 4319$^{4}$ | **Super Saint (65)** (TDBarron) **2-8-7** JFortune(4) (lw: plld hrd: trckd ldrs tl rdn & btn 2f out) | ½ | **7** | 6/1$^{3}$ | 46 | 15 |
| 3423$^{10}$ | **Broctune Line (57)** (MrsMReveley) **2-7-13** LCharnock(5) (lw: hld up: outpcd ½-wy: n.d after) | ½ | **8** | 7/1 | 37 | 6 |
| 4182$^{9}$ | **Caspian Morn (70)** (APJarvis) **2-8-12** JTate(2) (prom tl wknd 2½f) | 1¾ | **9** | 16/1 | 46 | 15 |

(SP 133.5%) **9 Rn**

**1m 23.9** (0.90) CSF £9.14 CT £31.86 TOTE £3.00: £2.70 £1.10 £2.60 (£3.20) Trio £14.40 OWNER Prince A A Faisal (ARUNDEL) BRED Nawara Stud Co Ltd

**4123 Zaima (IRE)**, patiently ridden, appreciated the longer trip and did it nicely. (11/4)
**4195 Plan For Profit (IRE)** gives the impression that, as he strengthens, he will improve. He certainly stays well enough and better is likely. (7/4)
**4093 Strelitza (IRE)** is certainly a hard ride as she hangs quite badly, but she was keeping on well at the end, and obviously appreciated this longer trip. (7/1)
**3499 Danka**, in a visor for the first time, tried to make all but found little when the pressure was on. (16/1)
**4024a Jack Flush (IRE)** keeps running well without success. (11/1)
**3208 The Deejay (IRE)**, normally up with the pace, was dropped out here and that proved to be the wrong tactics. (8/1)

T/Plpt: £14.70 (726.55 Tckts). T/Qdpt: £2.40 (261.34 Tckts). AA

## 3204-ASCOT (R-H) (Good to firm, Good patches)
## Saturday September 28th
WEATHER: fine WIND: almost nil

### 4441 CUMBERLAND LODGE STKS (Gp 3) (3-Y.O+) (Class A)
2-00 (2-00) **1m 4f** £31,400.00 (£11,882.50: £5,816.25: £2,651.25) Stalls: High GOING minus 0.12 sec per fur (G)

| Form | Horse | Dist | Pos | SP | RR | SF |
|---|---|---|---|---|---|---|
| 4197$^{2}$ | **Wall Street (USA) (114)** (SbinSuroor) **3-8-6** LDettori(7) (mde all: rdn out) | — | 1 | 2/1$^{1}$ | 121 | 74 |
| 4066$^{2}$ | **Salmon Ladder (USA) (113)** (PFICole) **4-9-0** TQuinn(4) (swtg: chsd wnr: hrd drvn & ev ch fnl 2f: unable qckn nr fin) | ½ | 2 | 4/1$^{3}$ | 120 | 81 |
| 3711$^{3}$ | **Priolina (IRE)** (JCHayden,Ireland) **3-8-3b** JQuinn(1) (lw: rdn & hdwy over 2f out: one pce) | 4 | 3 | 25/1 | 112 | 65 |
| 3671$^{3}$ | **Royal Court (IRE) (116)** (PWChapple-Hyam) **3-8-6** JReid(5) (b.nr fore: hld up: rdn over 3f out: r.o one pce fnl 2f) | 1½ | 4 | 11/4$^{2}$ | 113 | 66 |
| 4178$^{2}$ | **Kalabo (USA) (113)** (SbinSuroor) **4-9-0** MJKinane(8) (swtg: a.p: hrd rdn over 2f out: wknd over 1f out) | hd | 5 | 8/1 | 113 | 74 |
| 4192$^{5}$ | **St Mawes (FR) (111)** (JLDunlop) **3-8-9** KDarley(6) (bhd whn nt clr run on ins over 7f out: bhd whn hmpd on ins over 3f out: nvr nr to chal) | ¾ | 6 | 9/1 | 115 | 68 |
| 3997$^{2}$ | **Quakers Field (107)** (GLMoore) **3-8-6** GDuffield(2) (prom 9f) | 3½ | 7 | 25/1 | 107 | 60 |

(SP 108.8%) **7 Rn**

**2m 31.09** (1.09) CSF £9.44 TOTE £2.70: £1.70 £1.80 (£4.30) OWNER Godolphin (NEWMARKET) BRED Darley Stud Management Inc
WEIGHT FOR AGE 3yo-8lb

IN-FOCUS: **Inconsistency among Stewards was once again glaringly obvious here after they failed to have Quinn in for use of the whip after he had hit Salmon Ladder nine times, several times above shoulder height and very severely. Surely it is about time the BHB sorted out the whole whip problem once and for all before British racing becomes the laughing stock of the world.**

**4197 Wall Street (USA)** had no problems staying this longer trip and put up a fine performance under a lovely ride to make all the running, winning his first Group race in the process. He is a very decent three-year-old and will stay in training next year. (2/1)

**4066 Salmon Ladder (USA)** once again ran his heart out. Sweating up badly by the time the runners left the paddock, although not quite as badly as at Kempton, he had a tremendous battle with the winner in the final quarter-mile and lost absolutely nothing in defeat. He is a real credit to his trainer, and this tough campaigner richly deserves to get back into the winner's enclosure. (4/1)

**3711 Priolina (IRE)** certainly knows how to get into the money, but has only one win to her name and that came in a maiden. This class is probably a bit beyond her. (25/1)

**3671 Royal Court (IRE)** was already being slightly niggled at coming out of Swinley Bottom and was really tapped for toe when the race began in earnest in the last three furlongs. He will surely do a lot better when stepped up in distance. (11/4)

**4178 Kalabo (USA)** is not really up to this class. (8/1: 6/1-9/1)

**4192 St Mawes (FR)** did not have the blinkers on this time but, even though he met several problems in running, the simple fact was that he was not good enough. (9/1)

### 4442 RACAL DIADEM STKS (Gp 2) (3-Y.O+) (Class A)
2-35 (2-36) **6f** £58,350.00 (£21,905.00: £10,577.50: £4,667.50) Stalls: Low GOING minus 0.12 sec per fur (G)

| Form | Horse | Dist | Pos | SP | RR | SF |
|---|---|---|---|---|---|---|
| 2337$^{9}$ | **Diffident (FR) (113)** (SbinSuroor) **4-9-0** LDettori(10) (a.p: n.m.r & swtchd rt 1f out: led wl ins fnl f: drvn out) | — | 1 | 12/1 | 114 | 70 |
| 4057$^{5}$ | **Lucayan Prince (USA) (119)** (DRLoder) **3-8-12b** WRSwinburn(1) (nt clr run over 2f out to 1f out: gd hdwy & n.m.r fnl f: fin wl) | s.h | 2 | 15/8$^{1}$ | 114++ | 68 |
| 3914a$^{4}$ | **Leap for Joy (105)** (JHMGosden) **4-8-11** RHills(13) (lw: hld up: rdn over 1f out: led ins fnl f: sn hdd: r.o) | s.h | 3 | 14/1 | 111 | 67 |
| 4314$^{28}$ | **Sylva Paradise (IRE) (91)** (CEBrittain) **3-8-12** BDoyle(11) (a.p: led over 1f out tl ins fnl f: unable qckn) | ¾ | 4 | 66/1 | 112 | 66 |
| 3596$^{6}$ | **Lucky Lionel (USA) (112)** (RHannon) **3-8-12** OPeslier(3) (lw: hld up: nt clr run over 2f out tl over 1f out: n.m.r ins fnl f: r.o) | nk | 5 | 20/1 | 111 | 65 |
| 3222* | **Royale Figurine (IRE) (107)** (MJFetherston-Godley) **5-8-11** JReid(4) (hld up: nt clr run over 2f out & over 1f out: r.o) | nk | 6 | 7/1$^{2}$ | 107 | 63 |
| 3712$^{8}$ | **Branston Abby (IRE) (108)** (MJohnston) **7-8-11** JWeaver(2) (rdn & hdwy over 1f out: nvr nrr) | 1½ | 7 | 14/1 | 103 | 59 |
| 4173a* | **Jayannpee (107)** (IABalding) **5-9-0** RCochrane(6) (lw: a.p: n.m.r over 1f out: sn wknd) | 2 | 8 | 10/1 | 101 | 57 |
| 4033a* | **Daring Destiny (111)** (KRBurke) **5-9-1b** RHughes(12) (stdd s: hdwy over 1f out: wknd fnl f) | nk | 9 | 8/1$^{3}$ | 101 | 57 |
| 4304$^{6}$ | **Averti (IRE) (107)** (WRMuir) **5-9-0** PatEddery(9) (led over 4f) | ½ | 10 | 25/1 | 99 | 55 |
| 3759* | **Carranita (IRE) (108)** (BPalling) **6-8-11** TSprake(8) (prom over 4f) | 2½ | 11 | 7/1$^{2}$ | 89 | 45 |
| 4057$^{10}$ | **Cool Jazz (110)** (CEBrittain) **5-9-0** MJKinane(5) (s.s: a bhd) | 6 | 12 | 12/1 | 76 | 32 |

(SP 118.8%) **12 Rn**

**1m 15.36** (1.36) CSF £33.09 TOTE £12.00: £3.00 £1.40 £4.30 (£20.20) Trio £126.10 OWNER Godolphin (NEWMARKET) BRED Haras d'Etreham & R Ades in France
WEIGHT FOR AGE 3yo-2lb

**1129 Diffident (FR)**, winner of the President's Cup in Abu Dhabi over the Winter, has been a bitter disappointment since his return to this country, but bounced back here to land his first Group Two victory. Managing to get on top well inside the final furlong, the unlucky runner-up was absolutely flying and he found the line coming not a stride too soon. There can be absolutely no doubting that, had Lucayan Prince had more luck in running, Diffident would definitely have been second best. (12/1)

**4057 Lucayan Prince (USA)** was without a shadow of doubt the hard luck story of the day. Unfortunately, he has to be brought with a late run from the back, which means he is always likely to encounter traffic problems. Absolutely flying in the final furlong, he would undoubtedly have got up in a couple more strides. He was the moral victor of this race, and the Breeders' Cup sprint is now a possibility. (15/8)

**3914a Leap for Joy** ran a fine race on ground faster than she would have liked. Nevertheless, she managed to get to the front inside the final furlong and was only just worried out of it. She wants it on the soft side and will now head for the Group Three Premio Omenoni in Milan, a race she won last year. (14/1)

**4116 Sylva Paradise (IRE)** looked completely out of his depth here, but ran very well and showed in front below the distance before collared inside the final furlong. He will not run again this season according to his trainer. (66/1)

**3596 Lucky Lionel (USA)**, the paddock pick, put some disappointing efforts behind him here and, although encountering traffic problems, ran on to finish on the heels of the principals. He now looks ready to win his first race of the season, possibly in Group Three company. (20/1)

**3222* Royale Figurine (IRE)** has had a throat infection since winning a small race at Newmarket last month and has had a rushed preparation according to her trainer. Nevertheless, she ran well and, after meeting interference on a couple of occasions, kept on nicely inside the final furlong. (7/1)

**3708 Cool Jazz**, the winner of this race last year, ran no race at all, and his jockey later reported the horse finished distressed. (12/1)

## 4443 QUEEN ELIZABETH II STKS (Gp 1) (3-Y.O+) (Class A)

3-20 (3-23) **1m (round)** £199,020.00 (£73,978.50: £35,114.25: £14,837.25) Stalls: High GOING minus 0.12 sec per fur (G)

| Form | Horse | Dist | Pos | SP | RR | SF |
|---|---|---|---|---|---|---|
| 3784* | **Mark of Esteem (IRE) (129)** (SbinSuroor) **3-8-11** LDettori(5) (hld up: rdn 1f out: led ins fnl f: r.o wl) | — | **1** | 100/30[2] | 138 | 85 |
| 939* | **Bosra Sham (USA) (118)** (HRACecil) **3-8-8** PatEddery(7) (lw: chsd ldr: led over 1f out tl ins fnl f: unable qckn) | 1¼ | **2** | 100/30[2] | 133 | 80 |
| 3670[2] | **First Island (IRE) (124)** (GWragg) **4-9-1** MHills(4) (lw: hld up: rdn over 2f out: one pce) | 4 | **3** | 11/2[3] | 128 | 79 |
| 3745a[4] | **Charnwood Forest (IRE) (122)** (SbinSuroor) **4-9-1** MJKinane(3) (lw: a.p: rdn over 2f out: one pce) | ½ | **4** | 14/1 | 127 | 78 |
| 4165a* | **Ashkalani (IRE)** (AdeRoyerDupre,France) **3-8-11** GMosse(2) (lw: rdn 2f out: nvr nr to chal) | ¾ | **5** | 9/4[1] | 125 | 72 |
| 3670[3] | **Bijou d'Inde (127)** (MJohnston) **3-8-11** JWeaver(1) (led over 6f) | 1¼ | **6** | 10/1 | 123 | 70 |
| 2037[5] | **Soviet Line (IRE) (120)** (MRStoute) **6-9-1** TQuinn(6) (stdd s: a bhd) | 1 | **7** | 25/1 | 121 | 72 |

(SP 111.9%) **7 Rn**

**1m 40.95** (0.15) CSF £13.87 TOTE £3.70: £2.10 £2.50 (£8.10) OWNER Godolphin (NEWMARKET) BRED Sheikh Mohammed Bin Rashid Al Maktoum

WEIGHT FOR AGE 3yo-4lb

IN-FOCUS: **This was undoubtedly the mile Championship race of Europe.**

**3784* Mark of Esteem (IRE)**, who looked well in the paddock but had sweated up by the time they were paraded, put up a brilliant display to firmly stamp himself as the number one miler in Europe. Traveling supremely well, he was woken up by Dettori at the distance and swept into the lead inside the final furlong for a thoroughly convincing performance. He will now go for the Breeders' Cup Mile and, in this sort of form, will give a real fright to the best in the World. (100/30)

**939* Bosra Sham (USA)** returned with a badly bruised and bleeding foot after winning the 1000 Guineas and it had been an uphill struggle to get her ready for this. It was asking a lot of her after a near five-month absence, and her trainer reported that she would come on for the run, but she ran an absolute blinder. Although finishing well clear of the remainder, she was unable to cope with the race-fit winner inside the final furlong. Connections must have been absolutely delighted with this performance and, as long as all is well, she will now head for the Dubai Champion Stakes and a possible mouthwatering clash with Halling. (100/30)

**3670 First Island (IRE)** is certainly one of the most improved horses in training this year, but worries that his victory in a Group One win came in a sub-standard Sussex Stakes were borne out here. Nevertheless, he ran a sound race, if left for dead by the front two in the final quarter-mile. Connections are now contemplating a crack at the Breeders' Cup Mile and a return clash with the winner. (11/2)

**3745a Charnwood Forest (IRE)**, racing with his tongue tied down, was the only non-Group One winner in the field, but acquitted himself as well as could be expected, running up to his Sussex Stakes form. (14/1)

**4165a* Ashkalani (IRE)**, regarded by his trainer as the best horse he has ever trained, suffered his only previous career defeat here in the St James's Palace Stakes. Looking absolutely magnificent in the paddock, he took a very keen hold on the way to post and was a major disappointment. Put to sleep at the back of the field, he was a long way off the principals entering the straight, considering there had not been much pace early. His jockey reported afterwards that he ran flat and there can be no doubting this was not his true running. (9/4)

**3670 Bijou d'Inde** has the heart of a lion, and has run some tremendous races this season, including when beating Ashkalani in the St James's Palace Stakes, but those hard contests appear to have taken their toll, and his trainer was not confident that he was as well as in June, as his recent gallops have not been as good. (10/1)

**2037 Soviet Line (IRE)**, third in this race last year, ran no race at all. (25/1)

## 4444 TOTE FESTIVAL H'CAP (3-Y.O+) (Class B)

3-55 (3-59) **7f** £50,102.50 (£15,070.00: £7,285.00: £3,392.50) Stalls: Low GOING minus 0.12 sec per fur (G)

| Form | Horse | Dist | Pos | SP | RR | SF |
|---|---|---|---|---|---|---|
| 4194* | **Decorated Hero (108)** (JHMGosden) **4-9-13** 5x LDettori(22) (stdy hdwy 2f out: led 1f out: rdn out) | — | **1** | 7/1[2] | 120 | 96 |
| 4184[11] | **Kayvee (95)** (GHarwood) **7-9-0** AClark(26) (a.p: ev ch 1f out: unable qckn) | 3½ | **2** | 20/1 | 99 | 75 |
| 4185[2] | **Russian Music (103)** (MissGayKelleway) **3-9-5** MJKinane(2) (lw: a.p: led over 1f out: sn hdd: one pce) | ½ | **3** | 16/1 | 106 | 79 |
| 4396a[2] | **Ramooz (USA) (106)** (BHanbury) **3-9-8** WRSwinburn(13) (lw: rdn & hdwy over 1f out: one pce ins fnl f) | ½ | **4** | 12/1 | 108 | 81 |
| 4352[7] | **My Best Valentine (94)** (JWhite) **6-8-13** RHughes(1) (lw: nt clr run over 2f out: hdwy over 1f out: r.o) | hd | **5** | 40/1 | 96 | 72 |
| 3445[8] | **Green Barries (96)** (MJohnston) **3-8-12** MHills(12) (lw: rdn & hdwy over 1f out: one pce fnl f) | 1¼ | **6** | 33/1 | 95 | 68 |
| 4136[5] | **Consort (86)** (GHarwood) **3-8-2** CRutter(14) (lw: rdn & hdwy over 1f out: nvr nrr) | 1¼ | **7** | 20/1 | 82 | 55 |
| 4196[6] | **Almuhimm (USA) (89)** (EALDunlop) **4-8-8** RHills(15) (hdwy over 1f out: nvr nrr) | 1¾ | **8** | 33/1 | 81 | 57 |
| 4314[3] | **Prince Babar (95)** (JEBanks) **5-9-0** PatEddery(23) (rdn & hdwy over 1f out: wknd ins fnl f) | 1 | **9** | 8/1[3] | 85 | 61 |
| 4184[6] | **Orsay (78)** (WRMuir) **4-7-8**(3) MHenry(9) (a.p: ev ch over 1f out: sn wknd) | hd | **10** | 33/1 | 67 | 43 |
| 4316[6] | **My Gallery (IRE) (89)** (ABailey) **5-8-5**(3) DWright(4) (nvr nrr) | 1½ | **11** | 40/1 | 75 | 51 |
| 3709[10] | **Gold Spats (USA) (86)** (MRStoute) **3-8-2** JQuinn(18) (a mid div) | nk | **12** | 16/1 | 71 | 44 |
| 4314[17] | **Double Bounce (91)** (PJMakin) **6-8-10** KDarley(17) (nvr nrr) | 1¼ | **13** | 25/1 | 73 | 49 |
| 4314[19] | **Patsy Grimes (92)** (JSMoore) **6-8-6**(5) PPMurphy(21) (nvr nrr) | 3 | **14** | 50/1 | 67 | 43 |
| 2704[6] | **Queenfisher (88)** (GLMoore) **4-8-2**(5) MartinDwyer(6) (lw: a mid div) | ¾ | **15** | 50/1 | 62 | 38 |
| 4312[11] | **Garnock Valley (77)** (JBerry) **6-7-10** DeclanO'Shea(20) (a mid div) | s.h | **16** | 100/1 | 51 | 27 |
| 3263[4] | **Sabot (94)** (BWHills) **3-8-10** JReid(10) (b.nr hind: lw: prom over 4f) | nk | **17** | 50/1 | 67 | 40 |
| 3612[13] | **Mullitover (87)** (MJHeaton-Ellis) **6-8-6** GDuffield(25) (prom 4f) | s.h | **18** | 25/1 | 60 | 36 |
| 4308[5] | **Jawaal (85)** (LadyHerries) **6-8-4** SSanders(19) (lw: stumbled s: prom over 4f) | ½ | **19** | 16/1 | 57 | 33 |
| 4135[2] | **High Summer (USA) (85)** (RCharlton) **3-8-1** 5x TSprake(3) (w ldr over 4f) | ¾ | **20** | 5/2[1] | 55 | 28 |
| 4054* | **Primo Lara (87)** (PWHarris) **4-8-6** 5x TQuinn(7) (lw: led over 5f) | ¾ | **21** | 20/1 | 55 | 31 |
| 4181[5] | **World Premier (105)** (CEBrittain) **3-9-7** BDoyle(24) (lw: bhd fnl 3f) | s.h | **22** | 50/1 | 73 | 46 |
| 4190[19] | **Mountgate (77)** (MPBielby) **4-7-10** NCarlisle(5) (a bhd) | 1½ | **23** | 50/1 | 42 | 18 |
| 3210[4] | **Unconditional Love (IRE) (98)** (MJohnston) **3-9-0** JWeaver(8) (swtg: prom 3f) | 1 | **24** | 33/1 | 60 | 33 |
| 4194[2] | **Hi Nod (100)** (MJCamacho) **6-9-5** LCharnock(11) (bhd fnl 3f) | 2½ | **25** | 12/1 | 57 | 33 |
| 4325[3] | **Celestial Key (USA) (105)** (MJohnston) **6-9-10** OPeslier(16) (lw: prom 4f) | 1 | **26** | 25/1 | 59 | 35 |

(SP 138.5%) **26 Rn**

**1m 27.67** (0.47) CSF £134.61 CT £2,058.08 TOTE £9.30: £3.00 £4.10 £2.50 £3.00 (£130.70) Trio £817.30 OWNER Mr Herbert Allen (NEWMARKET) BRED Reg Griffin and Jim McGrath

LONG HANDICAP Garnock Valley 7-9

WEIGHT FOR AGE 3yo-3lb

OFFICIAL EXPLANATION **High Summer (USA): choked a furlong and a half out.**

**4194* Decorated Hero** put up a thoroughly-impressive display under topweight. Steadily creeping into the action in the final quarter-mile and drifting over towards the stands' side, he struck the front a furlong out and soon asserted. After this performance, he will now surely have to be campaigned in listed or Group Three company. (7/1: 12/1-6/1)

**3811* Kayvee**, third in this event in 1993 and 1994, goes really well in these big competitive handicaps without actually winning. (20/1)

**4185 Russian Music** is a model of consistency, and has never been out of the first three, but he does have a problem in winning - he has just one victory to his name. (16/1)
**4396a Ramooz (USA)** failed to find another gear inside the final furlong. Connections will probably now be looking at another conditions race or a listed event. (12/1)
**4352 My Best Valentine**, making a quick reappearance, was racing off 94 here, but has never won off more than 85. Nevertheless, he acquitted himself really well and put in some good work in the last furlong and a half. (40/1)
**3445 Green Barries** is finding it tough off a 10lb higher mark than when completing an impressive hat-trick at Goodwood last month and, after picking up ground below the distance, was making no further impression inside the final furlong. (33/1)
**4135 High Summer (USA)**, racing with her tongue tied down, appeared to be a handicap snip as she was due to rise 20lb in future handicaps. Unfortunately, she suffered a recurrence of her breathing problems, and her jockey reported that while she was fine bowling along, as soon as the pressure was applied she started to gurgle and stopped quickly. (5/2)

## 4445 ROSEMARY RATED STKS H'CAP (0-105) (Listed) (3-Y.O+ F & M) (Class A)

4-30 (4-32) **1m (straight)** £19,129.20 (£7,162.80: £3,506.40: £1,512.00: £681.00: £348.60) Stalls: Low GOING minus 0.12 sec per fur (G)

| | Horse / details | Dist | Pos | SP | RR | SF |
|---|---|---|---|---|---|---|
| 4214* | **Fatefully (USA) (95)** (SbinSuroor) **3-9-0** LDettori(6) (lw: hld up: squeezed thro to ld over 1f out: edgd lft ins fnl f: drvn out) | — | 1 | 7/4[1] | 106 | 84 |
| 3782[4] | **Abeyr (100)** (MAJarvis) **3-9-5** RCochrane(8) (nt clr run over 2f out: hdwy over 1f out: r.o wl ins fnl f) | nk | 2 | 25/1 | 110 | 88 |
| 3127[5] | **Prancing (95)** (DRLoder) **3-9-0** OPeslier(14) (hld up: rdn & ev ch 1f out: unable qckn) | 1¾ | 3 | 33/1 | 102 | 80 |
| 3791[8] | **Questonia (89)** (HRACecil) **3-8-8** PatEddery(17) (lw: s.s: hdwy over 6f out: led over 2f out tl over 1f out: 4th & btn whn nt clr run ins fnl f) | 1¼ | 4 | 8/1[3] | 93 | 71 |
| 3920[4] | **Divina Luna (88)** (JWHills) **3-8-7** MHills(15) (lw: hdwy over 2f out: rdn over 1f out: one pce) | 1½ | 5 | 20/1 | 89 | 67 |
| 4122[2] | **Marl (90)** (RAkehurst) **3-8-9** TQuinn(11) (hdwy over 1f out: nvr nrr) | 1¼ | 6 | 14/1 | 89 | 67 |
| 1441[8] | **Darling Flame (USA) (102)** (JHMGosden) **3-9-7** RHughes(9) (nt clr run over 2f out: hdwy over 1f out: nvr nrr) | nk | 7 | 25/1 | 100 | 78 |
| 4184[4] | **Panata (IRE) (85)** (LMCumani) **3-8-4**[ow1] OUrbina(3) (hld up: rdn over 2f out: one pce) | ½ | 8 | 7/1[2] | 82 | 59 |
| 3836[5] | **Cabaret (IRE) (95)** (PWChapple-Hyam) **3-9-0** JReid(5) (lw: nvr nrr) | 1¼ | 9 | 16/1 | 90 | 68 |
| 1481* | **Aerleon Jane (92)** (JHMGosden) **3-8-11** BDoyle(12) (hld up: nt clr run over 2f out & over 1f out: sn wknd) | s.h | 10 | 33/1 | 87 | 65 |
| 4300[4] | **Ninia (USA) (95)** (MJohnston) **4-9-4** JWeaver(13) (led over 5f: wknd over 1f out) | ½ | 11 | 10/1 | 89 | 71 |
| 4135[4] | **Polska (USA) (102)** (DRLoder) **3-9-7** WRSwinburn(19) (bhd fnl 2f) | 4 | 12 | 11/1 | 88 | 66 |
| 3945[10] | **Najiya (102)** (JLDunlop) **3-9-7** KDarley(7) (a bhd) | 2 | 13 | 33/1 | 84 | 62 |
| 4124* | **Supamova (USA) (84)** (PFICole) **3-8-3** CRutter(10) (prom over 5f) | 7 | 14 | 33/1 | 52 | 30 |
| 3909a[5] | **Satin Bell (95)** (JLDunlop) **3-9-0** MJKinane(18) (mid div over 6f) | 3½ | 15 | 25/1 | 56 | 34 |
| 4308[7] | **Anastina (84)** (NAGraham) **4-8-7** SSanders(1) (prom 5f) | 10 | 16 | 40/1 | 25 | 7 |
| 4126* | **Min Alhawa (USA) (102)** (MajorWRHern) **3-9-7** RHills(16) (prom over 5f) | 2 | 17 | 9/1 | 39 | 17 |
| 4218[7] | **Paloma Bay (IRE) (96)** (MBell) **3-9-1** MFenton(2) (virtually ref to r: a t.o) | dist | 18 | 33/1 | — | — |
| | | | | (SP 133.4%) | **18 Rn** | |

**1m 41.76** (0.56) CSF £46.80 CT £1,144.01 TOTE £3.00: £1.40 £6.40 £9.70 £2.00 (£98.60) Trio £2,100.00; £1,478.90 to Ascot 29/9/96
OWNER Godolphin (NEWMARKET) BRED Darley Stud Management Co Ltd
LONG HANDICAP Anastina 8-2 Supamova (USA) 7-13
WEIGHT FOR AGE 3yo-4lb

**4214* Fatefully (USA)** has been raised 7lb for her recent Sandown victory, but that was not enough to stop her, as she squeezed through a small gap to strike the front below the distance and hold on in a driving finish. According to connections, this is as good as she is. (7/4)
**3782 Abeyr** bounced back to form and, running on really strongly in the last furlong and a half, made the winner pull out all the stops. A fast-run race over a mile is just what she wants, and she might return here in a fortnight for a listed event. (25/1)
**3127 Prancing** was taking a step up in trip and, after having every chance a furlong out, failed to find another gear. (33/1)
**3791 Questonia** was probably unsuited by the rain-softened ground when flopping last time and ran much better here. (8/1: op 12/1)
**3920 Divina Luna** ran another solid race. (20/1)
**4122 Marl** appeared to see out this longer trip, and was doing all her best work in the final furlong and a half. (14/1)
**4300 Ninia (USA)** (10/1: 8/1-12/1)
**4135 Polska (USA)** (11/1: 8/1-12/1)

## 4446 BLUE SEAL CONDITIONS STKS (2-Y.O F) (Class B)

5-00 (5-00) **6f** £12,335.50 (£4,498.00: £2,199.00: £945.00: £422.50) Stalls: Low GOING minus 0.12 sec per fur (G)

| | Horse / details | Dist | Pos | SP | RR | SF |
|---|---|---|---|---|---|---|
| 4061[2] | **Lochangel** (IABalding) **2-8-8** LDettori(5) (lw: mde all: shkn up over 1f out: r.o wl) | — | 1 | 5/4[1] | 88 | 37 |
| 4105* | **Corsini** (HRACecil) **2-8-11** PatEddery(1) (chsd wnr: rdn over 2f out: r.o) | ¾ | 2 | 5/4[1] | 89 | 38 |
| 4052[5] | **Dust Dancer** (JLDunlop) **2-8-8** TQuinn(3) (a.p: rdn over 2f out: wknd over 1f out) | 5 | 3 | 11/1[3] | 73 | 22 |
| | **Plaisir d'Amour (IRE)** (NACallaghan) **2-8-8** OPeslier(4) (scope: bit bkwd: hld up: rdn over 2f out: wknd over 1f out) | 2½ | 4 | 15/2[2] | 66 | 15 |
| | **Chili Bouchier (USA)** (DMarks) **2-8-8** GDuffield(2) (w'like: bkwd: a bhd) | 6 | 5 | 66/1 | 50 | — |
| | | | | (SP 110.5%) | **5 Rn** | |

**1m 17.38** (3.38) CSF £3.10 TOTE £2.70: £1.50 £1.20 (£1.60) OWNER Mr J. C. Smith (KINGSCLERE) BRED Littleton Stud

**4061 Lochangel**, looking in good shape in the paddock, was a lot wiser for her Kempton introduction and put up a polished display. (5/4)
**4105* Corsini**, a narrow filly, may lack substance but certainly has ability. After giving chase to the winner, she threw down a determined challenge but, despite keeping on, was unable to get on top. (5/4: 4/5-11/8)
**4052 Dust Dancer** was not helped by the drop in distance, and was left standing by the front two in the final quarter-mile. She caught the eye on her debut and, when stepping back up in trip, looks one to note. (11/1: 6/1-12/1)
**Plaisir d'Amour (IRE)**, a sister to Danehill Dancer, was not expected to win by connections and they were not disappointed. She should come on a lot for this. (15/2)

## 4447 GORDON CARTER H'CAP (0-95) (3-Y.O+) (Class C)

5-35 (5-36) **2m 45y** £14,655.00 (£4,440.00: £2,170.00: £1,035.00) Stalls: High GOING minus 0.12 sec per fur (G)

| | Horse / details | Dist | Pos | SP | RR | SF |
|---|---|---|---|---|---|---|
| 2330[12] | **Fujiyama Crest (IRE) (86)** (MRStoute) **4-9-10v** LDettori(1) (b.hind: mde virtually all: all out) | — | 1 | 2/1[1] | 98 | 80 |
| 3776* | **Northern Fleet (80)** (GHarwood) **3-8-6** PatEddery(17) (a.p: rdn over 4f out: chsd wnr over 2f out: r.o) | nk | 2 | 9/1[3] | 92 | 62 |
| 4199[8] | **Miroswaki (USA) (65)** (RAkehurst) **6-8-3** SSanders(12) (rdn & gd hdwy over 1f out: r.o wl) | 2 | 3 | 12/1 | 75 | 57 |
| 4199[3] | **Ivor's Flutter (84)** (DRCElsworth) **7-9-3**(5) DGriffiths(2) (rapid hdwy over 1f out: r.o wl ins fnl f) | hd | 4 | 10/1 | 94 | 76 |

| | | | | | | |
|---|---|---|---|---|---|---|
| 4121[2] | **Shining Dancer (61)** (SDow) **4-7-13** JQuinn(6) (lw: rdn & hdwy over 1f out: r.o wl ins fnl f) | ½ | **5** | 25/1 | 70 | 52 |
| 4112[7] | **Embryonic (IRE) (76)** (RFFisher) **4-9-0** WRSwinburn(18) (hdwy over 2f out: rdn over 1f out: one pce) | ½ | **6** | 14/1 | 85 | 67 |
| 4260[4] | **Pearl Venture (75)** (SPCWoods) **4-8-13** RHughes(15) (lw: a.p: rdn over 2f out: wknd over 1f out) | 6 | **7** | 20/1 | 78 | 60 |
| 4344[2] | **Etterby Park (USA) (76)** (MJohnston) **3-7-13**(3) MHenry(5) (hdwy over 1f out: nvr nrr) | nk | **8** | 16/1 | 78 | 48 |
| 3850[2] | **Upper Gallery (IRE) (80)** (PWChapple-Hyam) **3-8-6** JReid(13) (lw: a.p: rdn over 3f out: wknd 2f out) | ½ | **9** | 10/1 | 82 | 52 |
| 4176[4] | **Pike Creek (USA) (83)** (IABalding) **3-8-9** RCochrane(9) (swtg: a mid div) | ½ | **10** | 16/1 | 84 | 54 |
| 4315* | **Durham (68)** (HSHowe) **5-8-6b** SWhitworth(14) (hld up: rdn over 3f out: eased whn btn fnl f) | 2½ | **11** | 9/2 2 | 67 | 49 |
| 3828[8] | **Silently (78)** (IABalding) **4-9-2** KDarley(11) (dwlt: nvr nrr) | 2 | **12** | 25/1 | 75 | 57 |
| 4199[10] | **Meant to Be (76)** (LadyHerries) **6-8-7**(7) PDoe(16) (prom over 13f) | 3 | **13** | 25/1 | 70 | 52 |
| 4112[3] | **Tudor Island (78)** (CEBrittain) **7-9-2** BDoyle(7) (lw: prom 13f) | 8 | **14** | 12/1 | 64 | 46 |
| 4260[2] | **Flocheck (USA) (88)** (JLDunlop) **3-9-0** JWeaver(10) (lw: a bhd) | 1½ | **15** | 10/1 | 73 | 43 |
| 2882[10] | **Reimei (70)** (RAkehurst) **7-8-8** TQuinn(4) (bhd fnl 2f) | hd | **16** | 20/1 | 55 | 37 |
| 3948[9] | **Shooting Light (IRE) (75)** (PGMurphy) **3-8-1** TSprake(8) (a bhd) | 2½ | **17** | 33/1 | 57 | 27 |
| 3834[9] | **Sea Victor (79)** (JLHarris) **4-9-3** MJKinane(3) (bhd fnl 3f) | 13 | **18** | 25/1 | 48 | 30 |

(SP 150.5%) **18 Rn**

**3m 31.04** (3.84) CSF £24.92 CT £196.49 TOTE £3.60: £1.90 £1.80 £3.50 £2.90 (£23.00) Trio £517.50 OWNER Mr Seisuke Hata (NEWMARKET) BRED B. Kennedy

WEIGHT FOR AGE 3yo-12lb

IN-FOCUS: **This was a quite remarkable feat by Frankie Dettori to go through a fiercely-competitive card and complete a 25,095-1 seven-timer, becoming the first ever jockey to achieve this. The scenes after the final leg will live long in the memories of those present.**

**2042 Fujiyama Crest (IRE)** followed up last year's victory in this race, despite racing off a 7lb higher mark. Making virtually all the running, he was given no peace by the runner-up but, to the enormous delight of the crowd, held on. (2/1: 3/1-6/4)

**3776* Northern Fleet** was thrown in at the deep-end, but ran a tremendous race. In second place early in the straight, he made the winner fight really hard and only just failed. He should soon find a similar event. (9/1)

**4199 Miroswaki (USA)** put in giant strides through the field below the distance and, running on strongly, finished a highly-commendable third. He certainly looks one to note. (12/1: op 8/1)

**4199 Ivor's Flutter** stormed through the pack to finish fourth, although having no chance of getting near the principals. (10/1)

**4121 Shining Dancer** was another who was doing all her best work in the last furlong and a half. (25/1)

**3834 Embryonic (IRE)** made good headway early in the straight, but failed to find another gear below the distance. (14/1)

**3850 Upper Gallery (IRE)** (10/1: 7/1-11/1)

T/Jkpt: £279.00 (42.4 Tckts). T/Plpt: £51.70 (1,090.47 Tckts). T/Qdpt: £18.50 (222.06 Tckts). AK

## 4429-HAYDOCK (L-H) (Good)

## Saturday September 28th

Race 6: hand-timed

WEATHER: overcast WIND: mod half against

## 4448 SEPTEMBER MAIDEN H'CAP (0-70) (3-Y.O+) (Class E)

2-05 (2-07) **1m 6f** £3,241.25 (£980.00: £477.50: £226.25) Stalls: Centre GOING minus 0.20 sec per fur (GF)

| | | | | SP | RR | SF |
|---|---|---|---|---|---|---|
| 4252[4] | **Great Tern (41)** (NMBabbage) **4-7-12**(7) RFfrench(5) (a cl up: led over 3f out: clr over 1f out: comf) | — | **1** | 10/1 | 53 | 34 |
| 3398[9] | **Taharqa (IRE) (70)** (JHMGosden) **3-9-10** GHind(11) (trckd ldrs: c stands' side st: rdn to ld group over 2f out: no imp) | 4 | **2** | 10/1 | 77 | 48 |
| 2736[5] | **Forever Noble (IRE) (60)** (MRChannon) **3-9-0** RPerham(8) (in tch: lost pl ½-wy: c stands' side st: rallied over 2f out: nvr nrr) | 3 | **3** | 16/1 | 64 | 35 |
| 4227[2] | **Lepikha (USA) (62)** (BWHills) **3-9-2** DeanMcKeown(20) (hld up in tch: rdn over 2f out: one pce) | 1¼ | **4** | 5/1 1 | 65 | 36 |
| 4227[6] | **Indiana Princess (58)** (MrsMReveley) **3-8-12** ACulhane(16) (lw: mid div: rdn over 2f out: styd on) | 2½ | **5** | 12/1 | 58 | 29 |
| *2936*[14] | **Sicarian (55)** (MJHeaton-Ellis) **4-9-5** DaneO'Neill(9) (lw: led tl rdn & hdd over 3f out: sn btn) | 2½ | **6** | 25/1 | 52 | 33 |
| 3948[2] | **Compass Pointer (62)** (JMPEustace) **3-9-2** MTebbutt(7) (hld up: hdwy 5f out: c stands' side: rdn & hdd over 2f out: sn btn) | 8 | **7** | 6/1 2 | 50 | 21 |
| | **Sedvicta (46)** (MrsMReveley) **4-8-5**(5) GLee(12) (bkwd: sme late hdwy: nvr nrr) | 1½ | **8** | 16/1 | 32 | 13 |
| *4095*[15] | **Dalwhinnie (65)** (JWHills) **3-8-12**(7) AMcCarthy(6) (prom: rdn over 2f out: sn btn) | 2½ | **9** | 25/1 | 48 | 19 |
| *3872*[5] | **Pleasureland (IRE) (60)** (PJMakin) **3-8-11b1**(3) RHavlin(18) (hdwy ½-wy: rdn & carried wd ent st: sn wknd) | ½ | **10** | 20/1 | 43 | 14 |
| 4237[10] | **Junior Ben (IRE) (41)** (PHowling) **4-8-5** FNorton(17) (a in rr) | 2½ | **11** | 25/1 | 21 | 2 |
| 2247[8] | **Veiled Dancer (IRE) (70)** (JLDunlop) **3-9-10** KFallon(19) (bit bkwd: hld up: effrt & rdn ent st: wknd 2f out: eased whn btn over 1f out) | 3½ | **12** | 8/1 3 | 46 | 17 |
| 3870[12] | **So Keen (55)** (ABailey) **3-8-9** GCarter(15) (s.i.s: a bhd) | 3½ | **13** | 25/1 | 27 | — |
| 4110[7] | **Lucky Hoof (65)** (CEBrittain) **3-9-5** MRoberts(1) (a bhd: rdn 6f out: sn no rspnse) | 3½ | **14** | 10/1 | 33 | 4 |
| *4336*[9] | **Crabbie's Pride (63)** (MGMeagher) **3-8-10**(7) RStudholme(14) (a bhd) | 3½ | **15** | 33/1 | 27 | — |
| 4203[11] | **Alisura (62)** (JRFanshawe) **3-8-13**(3) NVarley(10) (chsd ldrs: drvn along & lost tch 5f out) | 2½ | **16** | 14/1 | 23 | — |
| 3986[7] | **Galaka (67)** (LMCumani) **3-9-7** JStack(3) (bit bkwd: bhd fr ½-wy: t.o) | 2½ | **17** | 9/1 | 25 | — |
| 4216[14] | **Chalcuchima (65)** (RCharlton) **3-9-5** WRyan(13) (bit bkwd: chsd ldr 7f: sn lost tch: t.o) | 1½ | **18** | 20/1 | 21 | — |
| | **Menoo Who (IRE) (60)** (SGollings) **4-9-7**(3) FLynch(4) (bkwd: a bhd: t.o) | 21 | **19** | 33/1 | — | — |

(SP 136.3%) **19 Rn**

**3m 5.28** (7.08) CSF £106.17 CT £1,492.83 TOTE £10.60: £2.10 £3.10 £4.30 £1.80 (£138.60) Trio £338.40; £238.34 to Ascot 29/9/96 OWNER Mr John Cantrill (CHELTENHAM) BRED Theakston Stud

WEIGHT FOR AGE 3yo-10lb

**4252 Great Tern** appreciated having more use made of her and, with stamina no real problem, had the prize sewn up from some way out. (10/1)

**3042 Taharqa (IRE)**, tackling this extended trip for the first time, won the race on his side, but the winner had got away, and he had little chance of reeling her in. He is bred to stay, and should be able to find an opening. (10/1)

**2251 Forever Noble (IRE)** ran well after a lengthy break and the way he stayed on in the latter stages suggested that staying is his game. (16/1)

**4227 Lepikha (USA)** promises so much, yet up to date has achieved little, and her slow, relentless gallop may well be better suited to testing conditions. (5/1)

**4227 Indiana Princess**, with stamina coming to play, stayed on steadily inside the distance. It is possible she needs all of two miles. (12/1: 8/1-14/1)

**2572 Sicarian**, a grand-looking individual who looks made for the winter game, forced the pace as he had in his previous race, but he was a spent force after being headed. A little more restraint could solve the problem. (25/1)
**3948 Compass Pointer** would have taken all the beating had he been able to reproduce the improved performance over this trip on his most recent outing, but he elected to race on the slower stands' side, and was struggling to hold on in the last quarter-mile. (6/1)
**3986 Galaka** (9/1: 6/1-10/1)

## 4449 SALE MAIDEN STKS (2-Y.O F) (Class D)

2-40 (2-41) **1m 30y** £3,452.50 (£1,045.00: £510.00: £242.50) Stalls: Low GOING minus 0.20 sec per fur (GF)

| | | | | SP | RR | SF |
|---|---|---|---|---|---|---|
| | **Myrtlebank** (HRACecil) **2-8-11** WRyan(8) (lengthy: unf: led after 1f: hrd rdn over 1f out: styd on strly) | — | 1 | 8/15[1] | 91+ | 29 |
| | **Valencia** (RCharlton) **2-8-11** KFallon(5) (lt-f: unf: chsd ldrs: jnd wnr 2f out: rdn & no ex fnl f) | 1¼ | 2 | 8/1[3] | 89+ | 27 |
| 3919[5] | **Eponine** (MRChannon) **2-8-11** RPerham(7) (led 1f: prom: rdn & outpcd 2f out: sn btn) | 7 | 3 | 33/1 | 75 | 13 |
| 3820[2] | **Nile Valley (IRE)** (PWChapple-Hyam) **2-8-8**(3) RHavlin(6) (prom: drvn 3f out: one pce fnl 2f) | ½ | 4 | 9/2[2] | 74 | 12 |
| | **Old Colony** (PFICole) **2-8-11** DaneO'Neill(10) (lt-f: unf: trckd ldrs tl outpcd ½-wy: n.d afterwards) | 4 | 5 | 14/1 | 66 | 4 |
| 4104[8] | **Bout** (JHMGosden) **2-8-11** GHind(4) (bit bkwd: sn trckng ldrs: effrt over 2f out: no imp) | 1½ | 6 | 12/1 | 63 | 1 |
| | **Noisette** (JHMGosden) **2-8-11** AGarth(2) (w'like: scope: bit bkwd: hld up: hdwy over 2f out: eased whn btn fnl f) | 4 | 7 | 12/1 | 55 | — |
| 3982[11] | **Smart Spirit (IRE)** (MrsMReveley) **2-8-11** ACulhane(9) (a bhd) | 1¾ | 8 | 33/1 | 52 | — |
| 4041[9] | **Welcome Home** (PTDalton) **2-8-11** DeanMcKeown(3) (hld up & plld hrd: a bhd: t.o) | 7 | 9 | 50/1 | 38 | — |
| | **Mazara (IRE)** (AGFoster) **2-8-11** GCarter(1) (lt-f: a wl bhd: t.o) | 14 | 10 | 66/1 | 10 | — |

(SP 125.9%) **10 Rn**

**1m 45.7** (5.10) CSF £6.64 TOTE £1.70: £1.10 £1.80 £4.70 (£5.70) Trio £42.40 OWNER Sir David Wills (NEWMARKET) BRED Sir David Wills
**Myrtlebank** came here with a glowing reputation and landed some substantial wagers, but she was made to work hard before gaining complete control inside the final 100 yards. (8/15)
**Valencia**, a still unfurnished filly from a good family, did momentarily look to be travelling best when joining issue two furlongs out but, when it developed into a slog, she was the first to crack. Given time to strengthen, she could prove to be just as good as her half-brother Source of Light. (8/1: 6/1-9/1)
**3919 Eponine**, by far the most experienced member of the field, is still waiting for more suitable underfoot conditions, and it was apparent inside the last quarter-mile that this lively ground is not for her. (33/1)
**3820 Nile Valley (IRE)** was having trouble holding her pitch from halfway and, though she did keep staying on, it was very much at her one inadequate pace. (9/2: op 5/2)
**Old Colony**, a lightly-made debutante, travelled comfortably behind the leaders until losing touch early in the straight. Bustled along, she did attempt to rally, but it came to little, and she could well need more time. (14/1: op 8/1)
**Bout** was unable to improve on her debut, but she was tenderly handled when held, and is still very much in the process of learning. (12/1: op 6/1)
**Noisette** (12/1: op 8/1)

## 4450 AKZO NOBEL PREMIER H'CAP (0-90) (3-Y.O+) (Class C)

3-10 (3-11) **1m 2f 120y** £6,125.00 (£1,850.00: £900.00: £425.00) Stalls: High GOING minus 0.20 sec per fur (GF)

| | | | | SP | RR | SF |
|---|---|---|---|---|---|---|
| 4083[3] | **Namoodaj (71)** (ACStewart) **3-8-3** DHarrison(9) (lw: chsd ldrs: led over 2f out: rdn out) | — | 1 | 13/2 | 82 | 34 |
| 4193[7] | **Obelos (USA) (69)** (MrsJCecil) **5-8-8** GBardwell(5) (led after 1f tl over 2f out: hrd dvm & r.o one pce u.p) | 1¾ | 2 | 9/2[2] | 77 | 36 |
| 4329[5] | **Danegold (IRE) (76)** (MRChannon) **4-9-1v** RPerham(4) (prom: rdn & outpcd over 2f out: kpt on ins fnl f) | 2½ | 3 | 13/2 | 81 | 40 |
| 4117[8] | **Dance Star (74)** (MAJarvis) **3-8-6** EmmaO'Gorman(3) (lw: s.i.s: hld up: hdwy ent st: kpt on one pce fnl 2f) | 3 | 4 | 11/1 | 74 | 26 |
| 4193[17] | **Samim (USA) (72)** (SGollings) **3-8-1b**(3) FLynch(2) (lw: hld up: drvn over 3f out: nvr nrr) | 2½ | 5 | 20/1 | 68 | 20 |
| 4238* | **Secret Aly (CAN) (83)** (CEBrittain) **6-9-8** MRoberts(8) (lw: hld up & bhd: pushed along ½-wy: nvr nr to chal) | 7 | 6 | 4/1[1] | 69 | 28 |
| 3710[20] | **Quango (89)** (JGFitzGerald) **4-10-0b**[1] KFallon(1) (lw: hld up: hrd drvn over 2f out: sn no imp: t.o) | 7 | 7 | 12/1 | 64 | 23 |
| 3947[8] | **A-Aasem (74)** (HThomsonJones) **3-8-6** GCarter(6) (lw: plld hrd: led 1f: wknd over 3f out: t.o) | 9 | 8 | 6/1 | 35 | — |
| 4073[6] | **Wafir (IRE) (82)** (PCalver) **4-9-7** MBirch(7) (lw: bhd: rdn 4f out: eased whn btn over 1f out: t.o) | 5 | 9 | 11/2[3] | 36 | — |

(SP 115.3%) **9 Rn**

**2m 16.47** (4.97) CSF £33.38 CT £180.80 TOTE £8.20: £2.40 £1.60 £1.80 (£30.00) Trio £50.20 OWNER Sheikh Ahmed Al Maktoum (NEWMARKET) BRED Sheikh Ahmed Bin Rashid Al Maktoum
WEIGHT FOR AGE 3yo-7lb
OFFICIAL EXPLANATION **Stolen Kiss (IRE): choked throughout the race.**
**4083 Namoodaj**, quite an attractive individual, came good at the first time of asking against handicappers, staying on much too strongly for his pursuers after forging ahead over two furlongs out. (13/2)
**4193 Obelos (USA)** was always going to be the one to beat here, but he lacks anything in the way of finishing speed and, once off the bridle, his chances of getting back were slim. (9/2)
**4329 Danegold (IRE)** is taking time to recover his useful form of last season and, though he did rally after getting outpaced, the progress was slow, and he was always fighting a lost cause. (13/2)
**Dance Star** could not muster the pace to trouble the principals, and it is possible that she may not have come to herself yet this season. (11/1: 8/1-12/1)
**4238* Secret Aly (CAN)** did not stride out with any freedom on the way to post, and was reluctant to let himself down on the way back, running very flat indeed. (4/1)
**3457 A-Aasem** (6/1: op 4/1)
**4073 Wafir (IRE)** (11/2: op 7/2)

## 4451 E. B. F. KNUTSFORD MAIDEN STKS (2-Y.O) (Class D)

3-45 (3-48) **7f 30y** £3,943.00 (£1,189.00: £577.00: £271.00) Stalls: Low GOING minus 0.20 sec per fur (GF)

| | | | | SP | RR | SF |
|---|---|---|---|---|---|---|
| | **River Usk** (HRACecil) **2-9-0** WRyan(11) (neat: scope: bit bkwd: hld up gng wl: hdwy over 2f out: led over 1f out: drifted lft ins fnl f: r.o) | — | 1 | 8/11[1] | 81+ | 21 |
| 4189[5] | **Farhan (USA)** (PTWalwyn) **2-9-0** GCarter(7) (lw: chsd ldrs: outpcd over 1f out: styd on strly ins fnl f) | nk | 2 | 15/2[3] | 80 | 20 |
| | **Delilah (IRE)** (MRStoute) **2-8-9** KFallon(5) (leggy: scope: bit bkwd: hld up in tch: rdn & ev ch fr 2f out: unable qckn ins fnl f) | 1¼ | 3 | 15/2[3] | 73+ | 13 |
| | **Agony Aunt** (MrsJCecil) **2-8-9** GBardwell(10) (w'like: str: bit bkwd: s.s: bhd: pushed along ½-wy: styd on appr fnl f) | hd | 4 | 20/1 | 72 | 12 |
| | **Maylane** (ACStewart) **2-9-0** MRoberts(3) (lt-f: lw: hld up in tch: slt ld over 2f out: hdd over 1f out: sn btn) | 2½ | 5 | 12/1 | 72 | 12 |
| | **Noirie** (MBrittain) **2-9-0** MWigham(6) (w'like: scope: bit bkwd: wl bhd tl styd on fnl 2f) | 4 | 6 | 66/1 | 63 | 3 |
| 4245[5] | **As-Is** (MJohnston) **2-9-0** DeanMcKeown(2) (led tl over 2f out: sn rdn & wknd) | 1 | 7 | 33/1 | 61 | 1 |

| | | | | SP | RR | SF |
|---|---|---|---|---|---|---|
| 4105[2] | **Chorus Song (USA)** (PWChapple-Hyam) **2-8-6**(3) RHavlin(12) (in tch: shkn up over 3f out: wknd over 1f out) | hd | **8** | 9/2[2] | 55 | — |
| 3994[15] | **Yam-Sing** (TDEasterby) **2-9-0** MBirch(8) (trckd ldrs: rdn over 2f out: sn wknd) | 1½ | **9** | 66/1 | 57 | — |
| | **Russian Aspect** (MWEasterby) **2-9-0** ACulhane(13) (leggy: unf: bkwd: in tch 4f: sn wknd) | 1¾ | **10** | 50/1 | 53 | — |
| 4188[11] | **Bicton Park** (DMorley) **2-9-0** JStack(9) (bkwd: a in rr: t.o fnl 3f) | 5 | **11** | 66/1 | 42 | — |
| | **Ocean Light** (ABailey) **2-8-9** GHind(4) (lt-f: s.i.s: racd alone far side st: hdwy ½-wy: wknd over 2f out: t.o) | hd | **12** | 66/1 | 37 | — |

(SP 122.9%) **12 Rn**

**1m 32.89** (5.39) CSF £7.36 TOTE £1.80: £1.20 £2.00 £1.10 (£5.00) Trio £9.70 OWNER Mr K. Abdulla (NEWMARKET) BRED Juddmonte Farms

**River Usk**, who, like his brother Tenby, is not over-big, did not win as cosily as it seemed he would, but he was inclined to run green after striking the front. He will be all the wiser and so much sharper when he next appears. (8/11)

**4189 Farhan (USA)** may have an opportunity to cross swords with the winner in The Racing Post Trophy, and one would have to respect his chance for he was eating up ground at the finish after getting outpaced at a crucial time. (15/2: 13/2-8/12)

**Delilah (IRE)**, a filly with plenty of scope, is very much on the leg at present. Turning in a very encouraging first appearance, she should come into her own as a three-year-old. (15/2)

**Agony Aunt**, a strongly-made filly, did well to finish so close after losing ground at the start, and it would seem she has ability. (20/1)

**Maylane** looked well forward in condition, and made the winner put his best foot forward, but he tied up rather quickly inside the last furlong and may have needed the outing more than was apparent. (12/1)

**Noirie**, sure to strip fitter with this run under his belt, trailed the field by quite a long way until staying on to reach his final placing. (66/1)

**4105 Chorus Song (USA)**, hard at work and trying to hold her pitch soon after halfway, responded willingly but had the misfortune to run into a wall of horses below the distance, and the position had to be accepted. She is worth keeping in mind. (9/2)

## 4452 AKZO NOBEL HOLDINGS H'CAP (0-90) (3-Y.O+) (Class C)

4-20 (4-21) **5f** £5,865.00 (£1,770.00: £860.00: £405.00) Stalls: High GOING minus 0.20 sec per fur (GF)

| | | | | SP | RR | SF |
|---|---|---|---|---|---|---|
| 4215[2] | **Lord High Admiral (CAN) (82)** (MJHeaton-Ellis) **8-9-8v** MRoberts(18) (mde all: sn wl clr: rdn over 1f out: r.o wl) | — | **1** | 5/2[1] | 93 | 54 |
| 4180[2] | **Gone Savage (67)** (WJMusson) **8-8-7** JStack(5) (hld up: hdwy over 2f out: r.o ins fnl f: no ch w wnr) | 1¼ | **2** | 11/2[2] | 74 | 35 |
| 4180[18] | **Royal Dome (IRE) (73)** (MartynWane) **4-8-10**(3) RHavlin(6) (cl up centre: rdn over 1f out: r.o) | 1¼ | **3** | 16/1 | 76 | 37 |
| 4180* | **Surprise Mission (75)** (MrsJRRamsden) **4-9-1** KFallon(9) (hld up: hdwy 2f out: rdn over 1f out: kpt on: nvr nrr) | nk | **4** | 13/2[3] | 77 | 38 |
| 4116[8] | **Ansellman (81)** (JBerry) **6-9-7v** GCarter(13) (hdwy over 1f out: fin wl) | s.h | **5** | 14/1 | 83 | 44 |
| 3810[11] | **Sailormaite (82)** (SRBowring) **5-9-8b** DHarrison(14) (dwlt: hdwy wl over 1f out: nrst fin) | ¾ | **6** | 16/1 | 82 | 43 |
| 3432[21] | **Tadeo (87)** (MJohnston) **3-9-9**(3) FLynch(7) (chsd ldrs: rdn over 2f out: one pce) | ½ | **7** | 20/1 | 85 | 45 |
| 4180[4] | **Kira (72)** (JLEyre) **6-8-9**(3) NVarley(15) (b.off hind: prom: rdn 2f out: sn btn) | 1 | **8** | 11/1 | 67 | 28 |
| 4180[21] | **Sing With the Band (68)** (BAMcMahon) **5-8-1**(7) AMcCarthy(1) (hdwy ½-wy: sn rdn: nvr able to chal) | nk | **9** | 20/1 | 62 | 23 |
| 4180[3] | **Daawe (USA) (68)** (MrsVAAconley) **5-8-8v** MDeering(8) (outpcd fr ½-wy) | 1½ | **10** | 16/1 | 57 | 18 |
| 4088[4] | **Jucea (72)** (JLSpearing) **7-8-12** WRyan(12) (outpcd) | 1½ | **11** | 12/1 | 56 | 17 |
| 4119[5] | **Twice as Sharp (88)** (PWHarris) **4-10-0** GHind(17) (lw: spd 3f) | nk | **12** | 10/1 | 71 | 32 |
| 4246[4] | **Miss Bigwig (67)** (JBerry) **3-8-1**(5) PFessey(16) (lw: spd over 2f) | nk | **13** | 16/1 | 49 | 9 |
| 2694[20] | **Stolen Kiss (IRE) (74)** (MWEasterby) **4-9-0b** ACulhane(10) (bit bkwd: a in rr: t.o) | 8 | **14** | 14/1 | 31 | — |
| 3672[21] | **Snipe Hall (85)** (TRWatson) **5-9-8**(3) OPears(4) (b.hind: bhd fr ½-wy: t.o) | 7 | **15** | 33/1 | 19 | — |

(SP 131.7%) **15 Rn**

**61.24 secs** (2.04) CSF £17.55 CT £186.96 TOTE £3.10: £1.60 £1.80 £6.10 (£7.00) Trio £86.10 OWNER Elite Racing Club (WROUGHTON) BRED Windfields Farm

WEIGHT FOR AGE 3yo-1lb

OFFICIAL EXPLANATION **Stolen Kiss (IRE): choked throughout the race.**

**4215 Lord High Admiral (CAN)** just loves this track and often seems fortunate enough to end up with a plum high draw and, with his favourite jockey, simply galloped the opposition into the ground. (5/2)

**4180 Gone Savage** put in a sustained challenge under strong pressure up the centre of the course inside the last furlong, but had little hope of pegging back the runaway winner. (11/2)

**3432* Royal Dome (IRE)** did his best to keep tabs on the winner from his low draw, but he was always at full stretch to do so and it is to his credit that he was able to get so close at the finish. (16/1)

**4180* Surprise Mission** tried hard to get himself into the action in the latter stages, but he had given himself just too much to do and was never going to finish any closer. (13/2)

**3216 Ansellman** produced a determined late challenge, but found the race over before he could land a blow. (14/1)

**3432 Sailormaite** lost his chance with a sluggish start and, in such a fiercely-contested sprint, did extremely well in the circumstances to finish as close as he did. (16/1)

**2676 Tadeo** showed a bit of his old fire here and could be on the way back. (20/1)

**1501 Stolen Kiss (IRE)** (14/1: 12/1-6/1)

## 4453 CASTLE IRWELL H'CAP (0-80) (3-Y.O) (Class D)

4-55 (4-56) **7f 30y** £4,258.25 (£1,286.00: £625.50: £295.25) Stalls: Low GOING minus 0.20 sec per fur (GF)

| | | | | SP | RR | SF |
|---|---|---|---|---|---|---|
| 4109[5] | **Nunsharpa (74)** (JRFanshawe) **3-8-12**(3) NVarley(5) (mde all: drvn clr over 1f out: easily) | — | **1** | 14/1 | 87 | 35 |
| *3953*[3] | **Oberon's Dart (IRE) (70)** (PJMakin) **3-8-11** MRoberts(12) (trckd ldrs: effrt 2f out: edgd lft & kpt on wl fnl f) | 3 | **2** | 14/1 | 76 | 24 |
| 4243[12] | **Desert Lynx (IRE) (70)** (TRWatson) **3-8-11** WRyan(13) (hld up: hdwy u.p over 2f out: kpt on wl fnl f) | 1½ | **3** | 20/1 | 73 | 21 |
| 3679[2] | **Mezzanotte (IRE) (76)** (LMCumani) **3-9-3** KFallon(9) (hld up: hdwy 3f out: rdn & r.o wl ins fnl f) | hd | **4** | 5/2[1] | 79 | 27 |
| 2918* | **Muhandis (80)** (JHMGosden) **3-9-7** GHind(10) (hld up: hdwy u.p wl over 1f out: nrst fin) | 1¼ | **5** | 11/2[3] | 80 | 28 |
| 4064[8] | **Biscay (69)** (RCharlton) **3-8-10** DHarrison(4) (lw: prom: chsd wnr over 4f out: rdn over 1f out: wknd fnl f) | nk | **6** | 14/1 | 68 | 16 |
| 4243[5] | **Kazimiera (IRE) (64)** (CWCElsey) **3-8-0**(5) PFessey(14) (prom: c wd ent st: rdn 2f out: grad wknd) | 3 | **7** | 14/1 | 57 | 5 |
| 4064* | **Veni Vidi Vici (IRE) (68)** (MJHeaton-Ellis) **3-8-9** DaneO'Neill(6) (lw: trckd ldrs: drvn along 3f out: no imp) | nk | **8** | 3/1[2] | 60 | 8 |
| 3920[13] | **Ocean Grove (IRE) (77)** (PWChapple-Hyam) **3-9-1**(3) RHavlin(16) (stdd s: hld up: effrt & nt clr run 2f out: nt rcvr) | s.h | **9** | 14/1 | 69 | 17 |
| 4312[20] | **Naissant (70)** (RMMcKellar) **3-8-4**(7) JMcAuley(1) (b.hind: nvr trbld ldrs) | 4 | **10** | 16/1 | 53 | 1 |
| 2754[6] | **Mybotye (78)** (GROldroyd) **3-9-2**(3) OPears(15) (a in rr) | 2½ | **11** | 14/1 | 55 | 3 |
| 4180[11] | **Blessingindisguise (73)** (MWEasterby) **3-9-0** ACulhane(3) (lw: hld up: effrt u.p 3f out: eased whn btn fnl f) | 1¼ | **12** | 16/1 | 47 | — |
| 3999[7] | **Meznh (IRE) (74)** (HThomsonJones) **3-9-1** GCarter(11) (lw: s.s: effrt on ins 3f out: wknd 2f out) | hd | **13** | 14/1 | 48 | — |
| 4044[4] | **First Maite (74)** (SRBowring) **3-9-1b** DeanMcKeown(2) (lw: trckd ldrs 4f: sn wknd: t.o) | 5 | **14** | 16/1 | 37 | — |

| | | | | SP | RR | SF |
|---|---|---|---|---|---|---|
| 3799[11] | **Oh Whataknight (78)** (JWHills) **3-9-2**(3) FLynch(7) (prom: drifted rt & wknd over 3f out: t.o) | 14 | **15** | 25/1 | 10 | — |
| | | | | (SP 141.9%) | **15 Rn** | |

**1m 31.7** (4.20) CSF £200.94 CT £3,707.83 TOTE £25.30: £5.30 £3.80 £6.80 (£149.50) Trio Not won; £674.72 to Ascot 29/9/96 OWNER Mr T. D. Holland-Martin (NEWMARKET) BRED The Overbury Stud

**4109 Nunsharpa** has taken time to get off the mark, but she has always promised to do so and this runaway success could be the start of something good. (14/1)

**3953 Oberon's Dart (IRE)** is not quite so fleet-footed on such lively ground and he took time to find top gear, but he went down fighting, and another success is near at hand. (14/1)

**4071 Desert Lynx (IRE)**, brought to the centre of the track, stayed on from off the pace to reach her finishing position and, ridden this way, would seem to need at least a mile. (20/1)

**3679 Mezzanotte (IRE)**, pitted against handicappers for the first time, never promised to take a hand in proceedings until staying on when it was all too late. (5/2)

**2918* Muhandis**, doing all his best work late on, was never a serious factor and he could have needed this blow out after over two months out of action. (11/2)

**3421 Biscay** moved into second place early in the straight, and for a few strides looked set to take over, but the winner put her head down and galloped on, and she had to accept the inevitable. (14/1)

**4064* Veni Vidi Vici (IRE)** struggled with the pace over this shorter trip and was in trouble before reaching the quarter-mile pole. (3/1)

T/Plpt: £248.90 (71.84 Tckts). T/Qdpt: £134.80 (5.74 Tckts). IM

## 4435-REDCAR (L-H) (Firm, Good to firm patches)
## Saturday September 28th

WEATHER: overcast WIND: fresh half bhd

### 4454 PARTRIDGE MAIDEN STKS (2-Y.O F) (Class D)
2-25 (2-25) **6f** £2,369.75 (£2,369.75: £527.00: £243.50) Stalls: Centre GOING minus 0.62 sec per fur (F)

| | | | | SP | RR | SF |
|---|---|---|---|---|---|---|
| 4241[3] | **Thahabyah (USA)** (HThomsonJones) **2-8-11** RPrice(6) (lw: trckd ldrs: led & hung rt over 2f out: hdd ins fnl f: rallied nr fin) | — | **1** | 5/4[1] | 75 | 40 |
| | **St Lucinda (CAN)** (DRLoder) **2-8-11** DRMcCabe(2) (unf: w ldrs: drvn along over 2f out: styd on to ld ins fnl f: jst lasted) | — | **1** | 9/4[2] | 75 | 40 |
| 4228[2] | **Archello (IRE)** (GROldroyd) **2-8-6**(5) GParkin(1) (hld up tl led over 2f out: styd on same pce fnl f) | 1¼ | **3** | 7/2[3] | 72 | 37 |
| 4228[5] | **Muliere** (MJohnston) **2-8-11** TWilliams(3) (w ldrs: drvn along over 3f out: sn outpcd & hung lft) | 5 | **4** | 6/1 | 58 | 23 |
| 4208[7] | **Cimmerian** (MrsJRRamsden) **2-8-11** JFortune(4) (hld up: effrt & swtchd rt over 3f out: n.d) | 1¾ | **5** | 16/1 | 54 | 19 |
| | **Gollaccia** (GMMoore) **2-8-11** JTate(5) (w'like: bkwd: s.i.s: sn drvn along & t.o: sme hdwy fnl f) | 13 | **6** | 100/1 | 19 | — |
| | | | | (SP 118.6%) | **6 Rn** | |

**1m 10.4** (0.20) CSF SL & T £2.86; T & SL £2.37 TOTE SL £1.10; T £1.20: SL £1.10; T £1.60 (£2.10) OWNER Mr Hamdan Al Maktoum (NEWMARKET)/Mr Dean Grimm (NEWMARKET) BRED Scuderia Italia SRL/Dean Grimm

**4241 Thahabyah (USA)** wanted to do nothing but hang right and ended up under the stands' rail. Coming again under pressure, she dead-heated right on the line. (5/4: Evens-11/8)

**St Lucinda (CAN)**, who did not impress at all in the paddock, is a poor walker, but moved better on the way to post. After taking a narrow advantage inside the last, she had to share the spoils in the end. This looked anything but a vintage contest. (9/4)

**4228 Archello (IRE)**, a poor walker, showed a fair bit of knee-action. She might do better on easier ground. (7/2)

**4228 Muliere**, who did not impress going to post, ran about badly under pressure, possibly feeling the firm ground. (6/1)

**Cimmerian**, who wore a tongue-strap, was settled off the pace. (16/1)

### 4455 QUAIL (S) H'CAP (0-60) (3-Y.O+) (Class G)
2-55 (2-56) **1m 2f** £2,847.00 (£792.00: £381.00) Stalls: Low GOING minus 0.62 sec per fur (F)

| | | | | SP | RR | SF |
|---|---|---|---|---|---|---|
| 3645[5] | **Brambles Way (41)** (MrsMReveley) **7-8-10v**(5) SCopp(4) (w ldr: led 6f out: styd on u.p fnl 2f) | — | **1** | 12/1 | 55 | 37 |
| 4082[7] | **Acquittal (IRE) (39)** (AStreeter) **4-8-8v**(5) LNewton(11) (lw: a chsng ldrs: styd on same pce fnl 2f) | 6 | **2** | 9/2[1] | 43 | 25 |
| 4355[4] | **Kevasingo (52)** (BWHills) **4-9-12** AMcGlone(2) (lw: b.hind: a in tch: effrt 4f out: styd on same pce fnl 2f) | 1 | **3** | 15/2 | 55 | 37 |
| 4355[3] | **Diamond Crown (IRE) (45)** (MartynWane) **5-9-5** MRimmer(3) (bhd: hdwy 4f out: kpt on one pce fnl 2f) | s.h | **4** | 7/1 | 48 | 30 |
| 4355[7] | **Hi Rock (42)** (JNorton) **4-8-11v**[1](5) GParkin(17) (chsd ldrs: rdn 4f out: wknd ins fnl f) | 1½ | **5** | 20/1 | 42 | 24 |
| 4237[4] | **Mcgillycuddy Reeks (IRE) (42)** (NTinkler) **5-9-2** KimTinkler(7) (lw: lost pl over 4f out: styd on fnl 2f) | hd | **6** | 14/1 | 42 | 24 |
| 3589[4] | **Raindeer Quest (45)** (JLEyre) **4-9-5** RLappin(16) (in tch: drvn along 4f out: wknd over 1f out) | hd | **7** | 5/1[2] | 45 | 27 |
| 4190[18] | **Hawwam (49)** (EJAlston) **10-9-9** SDrowne(6) (in tch: drvn along over 3f out: no imp) | s.h | **8** | 8/1 | 49 | 31 |
| 4000[15] | **Slapy Dam (50)** (JMackie) **4-9-5v**(5) GFaulkner(10) (lw: hld up: effrt on outside over 4f out: nvr nr ldrs) | 6 | **9** | 12/1 | 40 | 22 |
| 3305[3] | **Risky Rose (42)** (RHollinshead) **4-9-2** JFortune(5) (hld up & bhd: hdwy u.p 4f out: nvr nr ldrs) | ¾ | **10** | 14/1 | 31 | 13 |
| 1001[15] | **Tee Tee Too (IRE) (45)** (MissMKMilligan) **4-9-5** JFanning(9) (bit bkwd: hld up & bhd: swtchd rt over 1f out: n.d) | 1¾ | **11** | 100/1 | 31 | 13 |
| *4080[9]* | **Dannistar (54)** (PDEvans) **4-10-0** JFEgan(15) (hld up: a in rr) | 3 | **12** | 14/1 | 36 | 18 |
| 3414[10] | **Pinkerton Polka (41)** (JParkes) **4-9-1** KRutter(12) (bhd: hrd rdn & hung lft over 2f out) | 2½ | **13** | 33/1 | 19 | 1 |
| 4348[7] | **Shaa Spin (41)** (JBerry) **4-8-10**(5) PRoberts(8) (swtg: led to 6f out: lost pl over 2f out) | hd | **14** | 33/1 | 18 | — |
| *4080[10]* | **Yuppy Girl (IRE) (49)** (CaptJWilson) **3-8-10**(7) DSweeney(14) (hld up: racd wd: effrt on over 4f out: sn wknd) | 3 | **15** | 16/1 | 22 | — |
| *4257[8]* | ***Tomal (42)*** (RIngram) **4-9-2** DRMcCabe(1) (Withdrawn not under Starter's orders: lame at s) | | **W** | 6/1[3] | — | — |
| | | | | (SP 137.4%) | **15 Rn** | |

**2m 5.1** (1.50) CSF £56.39 CT £311.00 TOTE £18.60: £4.10 £2.60 £3.10 (£77.30) Trio £238.50; £124.34 to Ascot 29/9/96 OWNER Mr Nigel Jones (SALTBURN) BRED W. P. S. Johnson

WEIGHT FOR AGE 3yo-6lb

No bid

**IN-FOCUS: This was, even by selling-race standards, a poor race.**

**3645 Brambles Way**, a winner over hurdles a month earlier, made it twenty-ninth time lucky on the Flat. Given an enterprising ride, he was in no danger in the final furlong. (12/1)

**3257 Acquittal (IRE)** bounced back after three disappointing efforts to finish second best. (9/2)

**4355 Kevasingo**, dropped slightly in class, probably ran up to the best he is capable of these days. (15/2)

**4355 Diamond Crown (IRE)** was closely matched with Kevasingo on Nottingham running four days earlier. (7/1)

**4237 Mcgillycuddy Reeks (IRE)** does not seem to have a trip. (14/1)

## 4456 SNIPE MAIDEN STKS (3-Y.O+) (Class D)
3-25 (3-25) **7f** £4,081.00 (£1,228.00: £594.00: £277.00) Stalls: Centre GOING minus 0.62 sec per fur (F)

| | | | | SP | RR | SF |
|---|---|---|---|---|---|---|
| 2208$^{10}$ | **Royal Jade (79)** (BWHills) **3-8-9** RPrice(1) (b.hind: trckd ldrs: effrt over 2f out: led over 1f out: r.o u.p) | — | **1** | 11/4$^{2}$ | 76 | 39 |
| 4108$^{6}$ | **Hannalou (FR) (68)** (SPCWoods) **3-8-9** DBiggs(7) (led tl over 1f out: kpt on same pce) | 1¼ | **2** | 7/2$^{3}$ | 73 | 36 |
| 4074$^{W}$ | **Beano Script** (MissSEHall) **3-9-0** JFEgan(9) (b.hind: hdwy & pushed along ½-wy: edgd rt & ev ch over 2f out: kpt on same pce) | 1 | **3** | 14/1 | 76 | 39 |
| 3446$^{6}$ | **La Mafarr (USA)** (JHMGosden) **3-9-0** AMcGlone(10) (lw: trckd ldrs: effrt over 2f out: sn rdn & outpcd: no imp) | 3½ | **4** | 10/11$^{1}$ | 68 | 31 |
| 4322$^{8}$ | **Kass Alhawa (75)** (DWChapman) **3-8-11**$^{(3)}$ PMcCabe(5) (swtg: sn drvn along & outpcd: styd on fnl 2f: n.d) | 3½ | **5** | 66/1 | 60 | 23 |
| 4074$^{12}$ | **Dona Filipa (30)** (MissLCSiddall) **3-8-9** RLappin(3) (trckd ldrs: rdn 3f out: sn wknd) | 2 | **6** | 50/1 | 50 | 13 |
| 4074$^{10}$ | **Honeyhall** (NBycroft) **3-8-9** JFanning(8) (trckd ldrs: drvn along ½-wy: wknd over 2f out) | 2½ | **7** | 100/1 | 45 | 8 |
| 3774$^{9}$ | **Time To Fly (42)** (BWMurray) **3-9-0** VHalliday(6) (trckd ldrs: rdn over 2f out: wandered & sn wknd) | nk | **8** | 50/1 | 49 | 12 |
| | **Keen Sally** (JohnBerry) **3-8-9** TWilliams(2) (w'like: bkwd: s.s: sn wl bhd: t.o fr ½-wy) | dist | **9** | 25/1 | — | — |

(SP 118.2%) **9 Rn**

**1m 23.2** (0.20) CSF £12.58 TOTE £4.20: £1.30 £1.10 £2.50 (£8.70) Trio £48.20 OWNER Mr D. J. Deer (LAMBOURN) BRED D. J. and Mrs Deer

**2208 Royal Jade**, who ran too badly to be true last time, answered her rider's calls in willing fashion to take a run-of-the-mill Maiden. (11/4)

**4108 Hannalou (FR)** has now finished second four times. (7/2)

**Beano Script**, who has a pronounced knee-action, was tailed off first time and then, on his second intended outing, was unruly at the start and had to be withdrawn. The way he ran here showed he is not without ability, and he might do better on easier ground. (14/1: op 50/1)

**3446 La Mafarr (USA)**, who cost $525,000 as a yearling, showed a scratchy action going down. Looking to be travelling nicely to past halfway, he was badly tapped for toe when the race began in earnest. Perhaps he might do better when the ground eases. (10/11: 4/6-Evens)

**932 Kass Alhawa**, with the blinkers again left off, struggled to go the pace. He is not a sprinter. (66/1)

## 4457 TOTE BOOKMAKERS RATED STKS H'CAP (0-95) (3-Y.O+) (Class C)
3-55 (3-55) **1m 6f 19y** £5,356.40 (£1,868.40: £909.20: £386.00) Stalls: Low GOING minus 0.62 sec per fur (F)

| | | | | SP | RR | SF |
|---|---|---|---|---|---|---|
| 4302* | **Good Hand (USA) (69)** (SEKettlewell) **10-8-10** JFortune(4) (hld up: pushed along over 5f out: rdn over 3f out: led over 2f out: sn drew clr: eased towards fin) | — | **1** | 7/2$^{3}$ | 81+ | 31 |
| 3983$^{4}$ | **Mighty Phantom (USA) (73)** (JWHills) **3-8-4** AMcGlone(1) (lw: trckd ldr: chal 7f out: led over 4f out tl over 2f out: styd on same pce) | 5 | **2** | 4/5$^{1}$ | 79 | 19 |
| 4112$^{5}$ | **Highflying (81)** (GMMoore) **10-9-8** JTate(2) (lw: trckd ldrs: effrt & chal 4f out: kpt on one pce fnl 2f) | nk | **3** | 100/30$^{2}$ | 87 | 37 |
| 3822$^{6}$ | **Classic Eagle (92)** (RHarris) **3-9-9** RPrice(3) (led tl over 4f out: sn lost pl & eased) | dist | **4** | 8/1 | — | — |

(SP 112.0%) **4 Rn**

**3m 2.0** (2.70) CSF £6.75 TOTE £3.50 (£2.90) OWNER Uncle Jacks Pub (MIDDLEHAM) BRED Tauner Dunlap, Jr. and Brereton C. Jones
WEIGHT FOR AGE 3yo-10lb

**4302* Good Hand (USA)**, from a 5lb higher mark, was suited by the flat-out gallop. After taking time to get into full stride, he drew well clear and was able to ease right up. He carries a 4lb penalty in the Cesarewitch and must not be underestimated, even at his advanced age. (7/2)

**3983 Mighty Phantom (USA)** made the best of his way home, but the winner proved much too strong. (4/5)

**4112 Highflying**, happy to get a lead, kept on gamely in the final two furlongs but, like the runner-up, had no chance with the winner. (100/30)

**986 Classic Eagle**, who has a pronounced round action, finished eleventh in the Derby. Racing with his tongue tied down, he set a strong pace but, once overtaken, dropped out in two strides, and was allowed to come home in his own time. He looked in poor shape beforehand, and seems to have lost his way altogether. His shareholders will not be best pleased. (8/1: 6/1-9/1)

## 4458 E. B. F. GROUSE MAIDEN STKS (2-Y.O) (Class D)
4-25 (4-25) **1m 1f** £3,652.00 (£1,096.00: £528.00: £244.00) Stalls: Low GOING minus 0.62 sec per fur (F)

| | | | | SP | RR | SF |
|---|---|---|---|---|---|---|
| | **Windsor Castle** (PFICole) **2-9-0** MRimmer(2) (w'like: dwlt s: sn pushed along & in tch: outpcd over 4f out: styd on to ld over 1f out: drvn out) | — | **1** | 1/2$^{1}$ | 63+ | — |
| 4250$^{9}$ | **Zigse** (TDBarron) **2-9-0** JFortune(6) (led tl over 1f out: kpt on same pce) | 1¾ | **2** | 25/1 | 60 | — |
| 4245$^{6}$ | **Swiftway** (KWHogg) **2-8-7**$^{(7)}$ DSweeney(4) (trckd ldr: effrt over 3f out: kpt on same pce appr fnl f) | 1 | **3** | 16/1$^{3}$ | 58 | — |
| 3687$^{19}$ | **Ocean Breeze** (JSWainwright) **2-8-7**$^{(7)}$ JBramhill(3) (s.i.s: sn in tch & pushed along: outpcd 4f out: rdn & hung lft over 2f out: wknd & eased over 1f out) | 13 | **4** | 66/1 | 35 | — |
| | **Kosevo (IRE)** (MRStoute) **2-9-0v$^{1}$** JTate(1) (w'like: lengthy: dwlt s: reluctant to r: rdn 4f out: nt run on: virtually p.u) | dist | **5** | 2/1$^{2}$ | — | — |

(SP 111.2%) **5 Rn**

**1m 55.8** (6.00) CSF £10.18 TOTE £1.70: £1.10 £2.10 (£4.40) OWNER H R H Prince Fahd Salman (WHATCOMBE) BRED Newgate Stud Co

**Windsor Castle**, who showed plenty of knee-action going down, missed the break and was soon pushed along. Running green, he stayed on up the wide outside and scored decisively in the end. He is obviously a real stayer. (1/2)

**Zigse** was stepping up considerably in distance. Making the running at a sensible pace, the winner proved simply too strong in the end. (25/1)

**Swiftway**, who possesses plenty of size and scope, still looked as if the outing would do him good. Travelling strongly for much of the way, he tired slightly in the final furlong, but can be expected to improve given slightly more time. (16/1)

**Ocean Breeze**, tailed off in a seller over a much shorter trip first time, is not without some ability. (66/1)

**Kosevo (IRE)**, in a visor on his debut, proved most reluctant and, failing to respond to pressure, his rider eventually gave up. (2/1)

## 4459 PHEASANT NURSERY H'CAP (0-75) (2-Y.O) (Class E)
4-55 (4-56) **5f** £3,172.75 (£952.00: £335.13: £335.13) Stalls: Centre GOING minus 0.62 sec per fur (F)

| | | | | SP | RR | SF |
|---|---|---|---|---|---|---|
| 4339$^{2}$ | **Kilcullen Lad (IRE) (56)** (PMooney) **2-8-3** DRMcCabe(8) (hmpd s: bhd: hdwy ½-wy: hung rt & swtchd rt ins fnl f: r.o wl to ld post) | — | **1** | 9/2$^{2}$ | 53 | 29 |
| 4346$^{2}$ | **Donna's Dancer (IRE) (65)** (TDBarron) **2-8-12b** JFortune(10) (lw: reminders after s: chsd ldrs: led over 1f out tl last stride) | s.h | **2** | 5/1$^{3}$ | 62 | 38 |
| 4195$^{14}$ | **Keen To Please (63)** (DenysSmith) **2-8-10** JFanning(1) (hdwy to ld over 3f out: hdd over 1f out: kpt on wl u.p) | ½ | **3** | 11/2 | 58 | 34 |
| 4069$^{14}$ | **William's Well (56)** (MWEasterby) **2-8-3b$^{1}$** JFEgan(4) (w ldrs: nt qckn appr fnl f) | d.h | **3** | 33/1 | 51 | 27 |
| 4244* | **Little Blue (IRE) (69)** (TDEasterby) **2-8-11**$^{(5)}$ GFaulkner(9) (lw: sn outpcd: hdwy over 1f out: nvr nr ldrs) | 2½ | **5** | 9/4$^{1}$ | 56 | 32 |
| 4195$^{12}$ | **Imperial Garden (IRE) (60)** (PCHaslam) **2-8-7** SDrowne(2) (b.off hind: chsd ldrs 3f: grad wknd) | hd | **6** | 16/1 | 47 | 23 |
| 4195$^{8}$ | **Lunar Music (74)** (MartynMeade) **2-9-0**$^{(7)}$ DSweeney(6) (lw: sn outpcd: styd on appr fnl f: nvr nr to chal) | 1½ | **7** | 9/1 | 56 | 32 |

| Form | Horse | Dist | Pos | SP | RR | SF |
|---|---|---|---|---|---|---|
| 4234[8] | **Northern Sal (65)** (JBerry) **2-8-7**(5) PRoberts(5) (b.nr hind: led over 1f: wknd 2f out) | 2 | **8** | 12/1 | 41 | 17 |
| 2728[7] | **Molly Drummond (68)** (CWCElsey) **2-9-1** NConnorton(11) (w ldrs tl lost pl ½-wy) | ½ | **9** | 10/1 | 42 | 18 |
| 3660[9] | **Poker Princess (57)** (MBell) **2-8-4** JTate(3) (sn wl outpcd & bhd) | 5 | **10** | 7/1 | 15 | — |
| 4244[13] | **Shotley Princess (49)** (NBycroft) **2-7-10** NKennedy(7) (swvd s: outpcd & bhd fr ½-wy) | s.h | **11** | 150/1 | 7 | — |
| | | | | (SP 129.8%) | **11 Rn** | |

**57.8 secs** (0.30) CSF £28.47 CT KL DD & KTP £62.07; KL DD & WW £323.81 TOTE £6.10: £3.00 £1.50 KTP £1.40 WW £4.10 (£8.80) Trio KL DD & KTP £9.30; KL DD & WW £77.50; £65.57 to Ascot 29/09/96 OWNER Mr George Tobitt (RADLETT) BRED S. W. D. McIlveen

LONG HANDICAP Shotley Princess 7-3

**4339 Kilcullen Lad (IRE)** would have been an unlucky loser after being knocked sideways at the start. Again hanging badly, he was switched violently right inside the last and stayed on strongly to get up on the line. (9/2)

**4346 Donna's Dancer (IRE)**, given some sharp reminders soon after the start, was caught right on the line. (5/1)

**3838* Keen To Please**, dropped back to five and with her tongue tied down, showed a return to form. (11/2)

**William's Well**, in blinkers for the first time, ran much better. (33/1)

**4244* Little Blue (IRE)**, as usual, did not impress going to post. Not getting her usual quick start, she was out of contention until staying on late in the day. She is better than she showed here. (9/4)

**3879* Lunar Music** (9/1: op 6/1)

**Poker Princess** (7/1: op 4/1)

## 4460 DUCK APPRENTICE H'CAP (0-80) (3-Y.O+) (Class E)

5-25 (5-26) **6f** £3,285.00 (£990.00: £480.00: £225.00) Stalls: Centre GOING minus 0.62 sec per fur (F)

| Form | Horse | Dist | Pos | SP | RR | SF |
|---|---|---|---|---|---|---|
| 4430[3] | **Barato (61)** (MrsJRRamsden) **5-8-10**(5) TFinn(11) (sn prom: led over 1f out: kpt on) | — | **1** | 7/1[3] | 72 | 53 |
| 4058[3] | **French Grit (IRE) (69)** (MDods) **4-9-9** CTeague(6) (chsd ldrs: led over 2f out tl over 1f out: r.o same pce) | ¾ | **2** | 4/1[1] | 78 | 59 |
| 4136[10] | **Cavers Yangous (62)** (MJohnston) **5-8-13v**(3) KSked(16) (a in tch: edgd lft & kpt on appr fnl f) | 2½ | **3** | 16/1 | 64 | 45 |
| 4259[5] | **Dissentor (IRE) (42)** (JAGlover) **4-7-10v** MBaird(15) (lw: bhd: hdwy u.p 2f out: edgd lft: kpt on wl: nt rch ldrs) | s.h | **4** | 10/1 | 44 | 25 |
| 4342[5] | **Castlerea Lad (71)** (RHollinshead) **7-9-11** GParkin(14) (s.i.s: bhd tl hdwy 2f out: hung lft: nt rch ldrs) | ¾ | **5** | 4/1[1] | 71 | 52 |
| 4246[8] | **Camionneur (IRE) (54)** (TDEasterby) **3-8-3b**(3)ow4 GFaulkner(10) (s.i.s: hdwy to chse ldrs ½-wy: nt qckn appr fnl f) | nk | **6** | 11/2[2] | 53 | 28 |
| 4180[19] | **Cheeky Chappy (72)** (DWChapman) **5-9-12b** PMcCabe(12) (led tl over 2f out: kpt on one pce) | nk | **7** | 33/1 | 71 | 52 |
| 4246[13] | **Pallium (IRE) (49)** (MrsAMNaughton) **8-8-0**(3)ow3 DSweeney(2) (sn outpcd: hrd rdn & sme hdwy over 1f out: n.d) | ¾ | **8** | 10/1 | 46 | 24 |
| 4312[U] | **Mister Westsound (64)** (MissLAPerratt) **4-8-13b**(5) PClarke(7) (lw: s.s: wl bhd: hdwy on stands' side 2f out: hmpd over 1f out: styd on towards fin) | 1¼ | **9** | 14/1 | 57 | 38 |
| 4206[16] | **Miss Aragon (43)** (MissLCSiddall) **8-7-11** ADaly(13) (s.i.s: bhd tl some hdwy 2f out: n.d) | ½ | **10** | 16/1 | 35 | 16 |
| 3957[3] | **Ragazzo (IRE) (42)** (JSWainwright) **6-7-5b**(5) JBramhill(9) (b.nr hind: chsd ldrs: sn drvn along: wl outpcd fnl 2f) | ½ | **11** | 33/1 | 33 | 14 |
| 4205[15] | **Welsh Mountain (66)** (MJHeaton-Ellis) **3-9-4v** SDrowne(3) (lw: prom: rdn ½-wy: sn wknd) | ½ | **12** | 20/1 | 55 | 34 |
| 4058[9] | **Halmanerror (69)** (MrsJRRamsden) **6-9-9** DRMcCabe(5) (hld up: nvr plcd to chal) | 1 | **13** | 10/1 | 56 | 37 |
| 4356[17] | **Flashy's Son (58)** (FMurphy) **8-8-5b**1(7) DHayden(4) (b: trckd ldrs: drvn along ½-wy: sn lost pl) | hd | **14** | 25/1 | 44 | 25 |
| 4229[8] | **Swifty Nifty (IRE) (44)** (WWHaigh) **3-7-10** DarrenMoffatt(18) (chsd ldrs tl lost pl ½-wy) | 3 | **15** | 25/1 | 22 | 1 |
| 1405[12] | **Montrestar (66)** (PDEvans) **3-8-13b**(5) AnthonyBond(17) (chsd ldrs: wandered 2f out: sn wknd) | 1¼ | **16** | 16/1 | 41 | 20 |
| 3252[6] | **Invigilate (48)** (MartynWane) **7-8-2** PRoberts(8) (sn drvn along & outpcd: bhd fr ½-wy) | 6 | **17** | 14/1 | 7 | — |
| | | | | (SP 144.5%) | **17 Rn** | |

**1m 9.7** (-0.50) CSF £38.66 CT £445.92 TOTE £5.90: £1.40 £2.30 £2.70 £3.00 (£16.10) Trio £56.50 OWNER Mr David Young (THIRSK) BRED J. Carr and Miss L. Charlton

LONG HANDICAP Dissentor (IRE) 7-8 Swifty Nifty (IRE) 7-2 Ragazzo (IRE) 6-8

WEIGHT FOR AGE 3yo-2lb

STEWARDS' ENQUIRY Sweeney susp. 7-9/10/96 (excessive use of whip)

**4430 Barato**, having his second race in two days, saw a lot of daylight for him, as he normally likes to come late, but he always looked to be holding the runner-up's challenge. (7/1)

**4058 French Grit (IRE)** ran another sound race and is knocking on the door. (4/1)

**3817 Cavers Yangous**, never far away, stayed on late in the day and is better over seven. (16/1)

**4259 Dissentor (IRE)**, soon detatched on the stands' side, was putting in her best work at the finish. Well handicapped on his All-Weather form, he might be suited by a step up to seven. (10/1)

**4342 Castlerea Lad** missed the break. Hanging left, he was putting his best work in at the finish. He is a top-of-the-ground performer and will need luck with the weather from now on. (4/1: op 7/1)

**4246 Camionneur (IRE)** again lost ground at the start. (11/2)

**3489 Mister Westsound**, out of luck at Ayr, ambled out of the stalls and was soon over ten lengths behind. Making his way over to the stands' side, he was squeezed out coming to the final furlong, but was still flying at the death. There is no doubt he is capable of winning off this sort of mark when everything goes right. (14/1)

T/Plpt: £80.40 (105.41 Tckts). T/Qdpt: £21.60 (12.78 Tckts). WG

# 4441-ASCOT (R-H) (Good)

## Sunday September 29th

WEATHER: overcast WIND: mod half against

## 4461 SUNDAY CONDITIONS STKS (2-Y.O) (Class B)

2-00 (2-00) **7f** £12,544.00 (£4,696.00: £2,298.00: £990.00: £445.00: £227.00) Stalls: Low GOING minus 0.08 sec per fur (G)

| Form | Horse | Dist | Pos | SP | RR | SF |
|---|---|---|---|---|---|---|
| 4100[2] | **Kahal** (EALDunlop) **2-8-11** RHills(4) (lw: chsd ldr: led on bit 2f out: pushed out) | — | **1** | 9/2 | 98+ | 67 |
| | **Ricky Ticky Tavie (USA)** (DRLoder) **2-8-11** WRSwinburn(9) (scope: a.p: hrd rdn & ev ch over 1f out: unable qckn) | 3½ | **2** | 11/4[1] | 90+ | 59 |
| 4111[3] | **Furnish** (BWHills) **2-8-6** PatEddery(3) (plld hrd: rdn over 2f out: hdwy over 1f out: r.o one pce) | 2 | **3** | 4/1[3] | 80 | 49 |
| 4100* | **Sunbeam Dance (USA)** (SbinSuroor) **2-9-0** LDettori(2) (lw: led 5f: wknd over 1f out) | 1¾ | **4** | 7/2[2] | 84 | 53 |
| | **Ursa Major** (PAKelleway) **2-8-11** MRoberts(7) (cmpt: bit bkwd: swtg: hld up: rdn over 2f out: wknd over 1f out) | 2½ | **5** | 50/1 | 76 | 45 |

| | Horse | Dist | Pos | SP | RR | SF |
|---|---|---|---|---|---|---|
| | **Truly Parched (USA)** (PWChapple-Hyam) **2-8-11** JReid(6) (unf: scope: bit bkwd: s.s: nvr nr to chal) | 2½ | **6** | 25/1 | 70 | 39 |
| | **Cybertechnology** (BWHills) **2-8-11** MHills(8) (unf: scope: bit bkwd: nvr nrr) | 5 | **7** | 50/1 | 59 | 28 |
| | **E-Mail (IRE)** (JMPEustace) **2-8-11** RCochrane(11) (neat: bit bkwd: a bhd) | nk | **8** | 66/1 | 58 | 27 |
| | **Shahboor (USA)** (MRStoute) **2-8-11** KDarley(10) (scope: bit bkwd: a bhd) | 3½ | **9** | 20/1 | 50 | 19 |
| | **Mandilak (USA)** (LMCumani) **2-8-11** OUrbina(5) (w'like: scope: bit bkwd: hld up: rdn over 3f out: sn wknd) | 1¾ | **10** | 20/1 | 46 | 15 |
| | **Purchasing Power (IRE)** (NACallaghan) **2-8-11** MJKinane(1) (scope: bhd fnl 3f) | ¾ | **11** | 20/1 | 44 | 13 |
| | | | | (SP 110.6%) | **11 Rn** | |

**1m 29.11** (1.91) CSF £15.33 TOTE £5.30: £2.00 £1.60 £1.40 (£12.10) Trio £12.30 OWNER Mr Hamdan Al Maktoum (NEWMARKET) BRED Shadwell Estate Company Limited

**4100 Kahal**, 3lb better off with Sunbeam Dance for a short-head beating on his debut, made no mistake this time with a very polished display, cruising into the lead on the bridle a quarter of a mile from home and needing only to be pushed out. An attractive colt who is sixteen hands plus, he has no neck or hind-quarters to speak of according to his trainer, but has always worked nicely. He will not run again this year and looks the sort who could make up into a useful three-year-old. (9/2: op 3/1)

**Ricky Ticky Tavie (USA)**, an athletic colt with room for development, made a very pleasing debut and was the only threat to the winner over a furlong out before put in his place. He looks a ready-made winner. (11/4)

**4111 Furnish** once again took a keen hold and, although staying on in the last furlong and a half to take third, never seriously threatened the front two. Once she learns to settle, success will come her way. (4/1)

**4100* Sunbeam Dance (USA)** is well thought of at home which made this performance rather disappointing. A mile on fast ground would suit him better than seven furlongs on a rain-softened surface such as this. (7/2: 5/2-4/1)

**Ursa Major**, a close-coupled colt, looked as though the run would do him good. (50/1)

## 4462 GTECH ROYAL LODGE STKS (Gp 2) (2-Y.O C & G) (Class A)

2-35 (2-35) **1m (round)** £69,330.00 (£26,114.00: £12,682.00: £5,674.00) Stalls: High GOING minus 0.08 sec per fur (G)

| Form | Horse | Dist | Pos | SP | RR | SF |
|---|---|---|---|---|---|---|
| 4111* | **Benny The Dip (USA)** (JHMGosden) **2-8-11** WRSwinburn(3) (chsd ldr: led over 1f out: hrd rdn: r.o wl) | — | **1** | 9/4$^{1}$ | 109 | 60 |
| 4111$^{2}$ | **Desert Story (IRE)** (MRStoute) **2-8-11** MJKinane(7) (hld up: swtchd lft wl over 1f out: rdn & ev ch ins fnl f: unable qckn) | ¾ | **2** | 10/1 | 108 | 59 |
| 4056* | **Besiege** (HRACecil) **2-8-11** PatEddery(4) (lw: led: rdn over 2f out: hdd over 1f out: unable qckn) | 1¼ | **3** | 3/1$^{2}$ | 105 | 56 |
| 4023a* | **Equal Rights (IRE) (100)** (PWChapple-Hyam) **2-9-0** JReid(6) (rdn over 2f out: hdwy over 1f out: r.o one pce) | nk | **4** | 9/1$^{3}$ | 107 | 58 |
| 3925* | **Medaaly (100)** (SbinSuroor) **2-8-11** LDettori(1) (hld up: rdn over 2f out: one pce) | 1½ | **5** | 3/1$^{2}$ | 101 | 52 |
| 4258* | **Air Express (IRE) (100)** (CEBrittain) **2-8-11** BDoyle(8) (hdwy on ins over 1f out: one pce) | nk | **6** | 20/1 | 101 | 52 |
| 3595* | **State Fair (100)** (BWHills) **2-8-11** MHills(5) (bhd fnl 2f) | 5 | **7** | 25/1 | 91 | 42 |
| 4023a$^{2}$ | **Recondite (IRE) (100)** (MRChannon) **2-8-11** KDarley(2) (a.p: rdn over 2f out: wkng whn n.m.r wl over 1f out) | 13 | **8** | 25/1 | 65 | 16 |
| | | | | (SP 112.3%) | **8 Rn** | |

**1m 43.67** (2.87) CSF £21.86 TOTE £3.10: £1.10 £2.00 £1.50 (£14.40) OWNER Mr Landon Knight (NEWMARKET) BRED Landon Knight

IN-FOCUS: **This did not look a vintage Royal Lodge and the field did finish a bit too close for comfort. Nevertheless, there were some nice sorts.**

**4111* Benny The Dip (USA)** seemed well suited by the slightly longer trip and the slight easing in the ground. Rated one of the besttwo-year-olds he has trained, John Gosden does not believe he will stay the Derby trip next year and thinks a mile and a quarter will be his limit. (9/4)

**4111 Desert Story (IRE)** renewed rivalry with the winner and managed to get closer to him this time. He will now be put away for the season. (10/1)

**4056* Besiege** does not do things quickly and, collared below the distance, failed to find another gear. (3/1)

**4023a* Equal Rights (IRE)** was lumbered with a 3lb penalty for his recent Group Three success at the Curragh. He will not run again this season and looks a good middle-distance prospect for next year. (9/1)

**3925* Medaaly** was rather disappointing, for when Dettori woke him up early in the straight, he could only go up and down in the same place. (3/1: op 6/4)

**4258* Air Express (IRE)**, taking a step up in distance, has been placed in several Group races this season, but he was not up to this class. (20/1)

## 4463 MAIL ON SUNDAY MILE H'CAP (Final) (3-Y.O+) (Class B)

3-10 (3-11) **1m (straight)** £29,700.00 (£9,000.00: £4,400.00: £2,100.00) Stalls: Low GOING minus 0.08 sec per fur (G)

| Form | Horse | Dist | Pos | SP | RR | SF |
|---|---|---|---|---|---|---|
| 3996$^{9}$ | **Amrak Ajeeb (IRE) (99)** (BHanbury) **4-10-0** MRimmer(2) (lw: hdwy & nt clr run over 1f out: led wl ins fnl f: r.o wl) | — | **1** | 33/1 | 111 | 98 |
| 4194$^{6}$ | **Hal's Pal (89)** (DRLoder) **3-9-0b** LDettori(8) (swtg: hld up: rdn over 1f out: led ins fnl f: sn hdd: unable qckn) | 1¼ | **2** | 6/1$^{1}$ | 99 | 82 |
| 3805$^{10}$ | **Zajko (USA) (74)** (LadyHerries) **6-8-0**$^{(3)ow2}$ FLynch(13) (hdwy 2f out: rdn over 1f out: r.o) | 3 | **3** | 20/1 | 78 | 63 |
| 4184* | **Autumn Cover (74)** (PRHedger) **4-8-3** DBiggs(6) (led: hrd rdn over 1f out: hdd ins fnl f: sn wknd) | s.h | **4** | 20/1 | 77 | 64 |
| 4297* | **Rebel County (IRE) (84)** (ABailey) **3-8-9** KDarley(10) (rdn over 2f out: hdwy over 1f out: nvr nrr) | 2 | **5** | 25/1 | 83 | 66 |
| 4243$^{3}$ | **Talathath (FR) (71)** (CADwyer) **4-8-0v** JQuinn(9) (a.p: rdn over 2f out: one pce) | ¾ | **6** | 25/1 | 69 | 56 |
| 4202$^{2}$ | **Embankment (IRE) (72)** (RHannon) **6-8-1**$^{ow2}$ SSanders(5) (rdn 3f out: lost pl over 2f out: r.o one pce fnl f) | 1¾ | **7** | 33/1 | 66 | 51 |
| 4193$^{9}$ | **Master Beveled (71)** (PDEvans) **6-8-0**$^{ow3}$ JFEgan(25) (lw: rdn over 3f out: nvr nr to chal) | ¾ | **8** | 20/1 | 64 | 48 |
| 3861$^{10}$ | **Broughtons Turmoil (73)** (WJMusson) **7-8-2** GHind(4) (b: swtg: nt clr run on ins & lost pl over 2f out: hmpd over 1f out: nt rcvr) | ½ | **9** | 33/1 | 65 | 52 |
| 3985* | **Seventeens Lucky (78)** (BobJones) **4-8-7** NDay(17) (prom over 6f) | nk | **10** | 25/1 | 69 | 56 |
| 4240$^{D}$ | **Ertlon (73)** (CEBrittain) **6-8-2** BDoyle(23) (hld up: rdn 3f out: wknd over 1f out) | nk | **11** | 25/1 | 64 | 51 |
| 4329$^{2}$ | **Mo-Addab (IRE) (76)** (ACStewart) **6-8-5** MRoberts(15) (swtg: nt clr run over 2f out: hdwy & nt clr run over 1f out: nvr plcd to chal) | ½ | **12** | 8/1$^{2}$ | 66 | 53 |
| 3805$^{12}$ | **Mihriz (IRE) (68)** (RAkehurst) **4-7-6**$^{(5)ow1}$ MartinDwyer(20) (hld up: rdn over 2f out: wknd over 1f out) | ¾ | **13** | 20/1 | 56 | 42 |
| 4300* | **Pride of Pendle (71)** (DNicholls) **7-8-0** AMcGlone(12) (a mid div) | hd | **14** | 10/1$^{3}$ | 59 | 46 |
| 3450$^{10}$ | **Moscow Mist (IRE) (80)** (LadyHerries) **5-8-9** DeclanO'Shea(19) (swtg: a mid div) | nk | **15** | 25/1 | 67 | 54 |
| 3805$^{2}$ | **Present Situation (67)** (LordHuntingdon) **5-7-3**$^{(7)}$ IonaWands(7) (prom over 5f) | 1 | **16** | 25/1 | 52 | 39 |
| 3805* | **Sky Dome (IRE) (88)** (MHTompkins) **3-8-10**$^{(3)}$ MHenry(26) (prom over 6f) | nk | **17** | 12/1 | 73 | 56 |
| 4212$^{8}$ | **Daryabad (IRE) (75)** (TJNaughton) **4-8-4b** GCarter(3) (prom over 5f) | 1¾ | **18** | 25/1 | 56 | 43 |
| 4243$^{7}$ | **Confronter (69)** (SDow) **7-7-12** CRutter(22) (hdwy over 1f out: wknd fnl f) | ½ | **19** | 33/1 | 49 | 36 |
| 4243* | **Sue's Return (79)** (APJarvis) **4-8-8** MJKinane(16) (a bhd) | 1¾ | **20** | 14/1 | 56 | 43 |
| 3799* | **Admirals Flame (IRE) (79)** (CFWall) **5-8-8** GDuffield(14) (bhd fnl 2f) | 1¼ | **21** | 16/1 | 53 | 40 |
| 3790$^{3}$ | **Jerry Cutrona (IRE) (82)** (NACallaghan) **3-8-7** PatEddery(18) (s.s: a bhd) | 1½ | **22** | 14/1 | 53 | 36 |

| Form | Horse | Dist | Pos | SP | RR | SF |
|---|---|---|---|---|---|---|
| 4193[5] | **Serendipity (FR) (84)** (JLDunlop) **3-8-9b[1]** TQuinn(11) (prom 6f) | 3 | **23** | 16/1 | 49 | 32 |
| 4316[3] | **Champagne Grandy (75)** (MRChannon) **6-7-13**(5)ow1 PPMurphy(1) (a bhd) | 3 | **24** | 25/1 | 34 | 20 |
| 4190[7] | **Sandmoor Chambray (82)** (TDEasterby) **5-8-11** MBirch(24) (bhd fnl 2f) | 3½ | **25** | 33/1 | 34 | 21 |
| | | | | (SP 131.8%) | **25 Rn** | |

**1m 42.08** (0.88) CSF £203.69 CT £3,761.72 TOTE £34.20: £8.50 £2.00 £6.60 £6.40 (£84.60) Trio £1,335.10 OWNER Mr A. Merza (NEWMARKET) BRED Ovidstown Investments Ltd

LONG HANDICAP Mihriz (IRE) 7-9 Present Situation 7-3

WEIGHT FOR AGE 3yo-4lb

**3691* Amrak Ajeeb (IRE)** is anything but consistent but, despite a 7lb rise since his last victory, was back on song here and managed to get up in the closing stages. He must have rain according to his trainer, who hopes he will be able to win a Group Three with him in Germany or Italy. (33/1)

**4194 Hal's Pal** travelled sweetly but, when he got to the front inside the final furlong, he did not look over-enthusiastic and carried his head rather high. Soon collared by the winner, he failed to find another gear. (6/1)

**2526 Zajko (USA)** has slipped down the handicap after some poor efforts this year and, as a result, ran his best race of the season. (20/1)

**4184* Autumn Cover** has given connections plenty to cheer about this season and ran another fine race, despite carrying a staggering 30lb more than when first successful back at Brighton in April. (20/1)

**4297* Rebel County (IRE)** put in some good work in the last furlong and a half without ever posing a threat. (25/1)

**4243 Talathath (FR)** acquitted himself well in this better-class race, if failing to find another gear in the final two furlongs. (25/1)

**3686* Broughtons Turmoil** may not be the easiest of rides, but he had absolutely no luck in running on this occasion. Although 7lb higher than when last successful, he could pick up another handicap when dropped in class - his five wins to date have come in Class E or F events. (33/1)

**4329 Mo-Addab (IRE)**, winner of this race last year off a 3lb lower mark, bounced back to form at Newbury the previous weekend, but was given a very curious ride. Failing to get any sort of run in the critical part of the race, his pilot was as quiet as a mouse on him and eased him down in the final furlong. Described as an autumn horse by his trainer, it would be no surprise to see him lift a decent handicap, possibly the Rothmans North South Final at Newmarket next month. (8/1)

## 4464 FILLIES' MILE STKS (Gp 1) (2-Y.O F) (Class A)

3-50 (3-51) **1m (round)** £91,840.00 (£34,434.50: £16,592.25: £7,283.25) Stalls: High GOING minus 0.08 sec per fur (G)

| Form | Horse | Dist | Pos | SP | RR | SF |
|---|---|---|---|---|---|---|
| 4133* | **Reams of Verse (USA)** (HRACecil) **2-8-10** MJKinane(2) (lw: hld up: rdn over 2f out: led 1f out: edgd rt ins fnl f: r.o wl) | — | **1** | 5/1[3] | 110 | 53 |
| 4085* | **Khassah** (JHMGosden) **2-8-10** RHills(5) (lw: rdn & hdwy over 1f out: r.o) | 1¼ | **2** | 10/1 | 108 | 51 |
| 4233* | **Sleepytime (IRE)** (HRACecil) **2-8-10** PatEddery(8) (a.p: nt clr run wl over 1f out tl hmpd ins fnl f: nt rcvr) | nk | **3** | 6/4[1] | 107+ | 50 |
| 3804* | **Red Camellia (100)** (SirMarkPrescott) **2-8-10** GDuffield(7) (lw: led to 1f out: edgd lft ins fnl f: unable qckn) | s.h | **4** | 2/1[2] | 107 | 50 |
| 4253[2] | **Logic** (CEBrittain) **2-8-10** LDettori(6) (lw: nvr nr to chal) | 3½ | **5** | 50/1 | 100? | 43 |
| 4133[11] | **Mrs Miniver (USA)** (PAKelleway) **2-8-10** MRoberts(3) (sme hdwy 3f out: wknd over 2f out) | 1¼ | **6** | 100/1 | 97? | 40 |
| 4085[2] | **Ovation** (PFICole) **2-8-10** TQuinn(1) (chsd ldr over 5f) | 2 | **7** | 25/1 | 93 | 36 |
| 4133[3] | **Gretel** (MRStoute) **2-8-10** WRSwinburn(4) (plld hrd: a bhd) | 1 | **8** | 20/1 | 91 | 34 |
| | | | | (SP 110.6%) | **8 Rn** | |

**1m 44.32** (3.52) CSF £45.12 TOTE £6.80: £1.70 £1.90 £1.20 (£11.80) OWNER Mr K. Abdulla (NEWMARKET) BRED Juddmonte Farms

**IN-FOCUS: a very unsatisfactory ending to what looked an informative race on paper.**

**4133* Reams of Verse (USA)** continues to progress but must be considered a fortunate winner of this Group One event. Gaining control a furlong out, she gave her stablemate Sleepytime no room to get out and kept on well to the line. Described by her trainer as a lazy filly, although she does travel well in her races, she will now be put away for the winter. She looks an exciting prospect for next year and a live Guineas prospect. (5/1: 9/2-7/1)

**4085* Khassah** went down well to post and began to pick up ground below the distance. Running on inside the final furlong, she just managed to win the battle for second prize. (10/1)

**4233* Sleepytime (IRE)** came into this race with expectations running high, but had a nightmare run and a fair amount of criticism has to be levelled at Eddery. Racing in third place, there was a gap for her to go through, but Eddery was oozing confidence and decided not to let the filly go, but the opening then closed and she had nowhere to go. Desperation began to set in inside the final furlong, and she was hampered, lost ground and dropped back to fourth. Nevertheless, she managed to squeeze through and snatch third on the line. With a clear run, there can be no doubt she would have won this, and her reputation would have soared further. Cecil rates her in the same league as Bosra Sham. (6/4: Evens-13/8)

**3804* Red Camellia,** so impressive at Goodwood last month, was not fluent going to post and found this mile just a bit too far at this stage of her career. Bowling along in front, she was collared a furlong out and, edging slightly to her left, not helping Sleepytime at all, failed to find another gear. She too looks an exciting prospect for next year. (2/1)

**4253 Logic** was not in the same class as her rivals. (50/1)

**3131 Mrs Miniver (USA)** was blatantly out of her depth. (100/1)

## 4465 TOTE SUNDAY SPECIAL H'CAP (3-Y.O+) (Class B)

4-25 (4-27) **1m 4f** £44,740.00 (£13,420.00: £6,460.00: £2,980.00) Stalls: High GOING minus 0.08 sec per fur (G)

| Form | Horse | Dist | Pos | SP | RR | SF |
|---|---|---|---|---|---|---|
| 3689[7] | **Better Offer (IRE) (98)** (GHarwood) **4-9-6** MJKinane(14) (rdn & swtchd rt 2f out: gd hdwy over 1f out: led ins fnl f: r.o wl) | — | **1** | 9/1[3] | 111 | 75 |
| 4066[5] | **Sheer Danzig (IRE) (96)** (RWArmstrong) **4-9-4** MHills(11) (lw: lost pl 8f out: rdn over 2f out: gd hdwy over 1f out: fin wl) | 1¼ | **2** | 16/1 | 107 | 71 |
| 4055* | **Dacha (IRE) (95)** (HRACecil) **4-9-3** 4x PatEddery(17) (lw: a.p: led over 4f out tl ins fnl f: unable qckn) | 1 | **3** | 7/1[2] | 105 | 69 |
| 3691[3] | **Dance So Suite (88)** (PFICole) **4-8-10** TQuinn(9) (hdwy over 5f out: ev ch over 1f out: one pce) | ½ | **4** | 20/1 | 97 | 61 |
| 4187* | **Willie Conquer (84)** (RAkehurst) **4-8-6** 4x SSanders(13) (a.p: rdn over 1f out: one pce) | ¾ | **5** | 25/1 | 92 | 56 |
| 4114[3] | **Beauchamp Jade (94)** (HCandy) **4-9-2** GCarter(4) (rdn over 2f out: gd hdwy over 1f out: r.o wl ins fnl f) | 1 | **6** | 9/1[3] | 101 | 65 |
| 3689[16] | **Lakeline Legend (IRE) (91)** (MAJarvis) **3-8-5** EmmaO'Gorman(20) (swtg: a.p: rdn over 2f out: one pce) | 1¼ | **7** | 20/1 | 96 | 52 |
| 4055[2] | **Romios (IRE) (84)** (PFICole) **4-8-6** CRutter(16) (a.p: ev ch 2f out: wknd over 1f out) | 1¼ | **8** | 14/1 | 88 | 52 |
| 4326[5] | **At Liberty (IRE) (84)** (RHannon) **4-8-6** DaneO'Neill(18) (lw: nvr nr to chal) | nk | **9** | 33/1 | 87 | 51 |
| 4176[2] | **Daunt (92)** (JHMGosden) **4-9-0** LDettori(12) (lw: hdwy over 2f out: wknd over 1f out) | 3½ | **10** | 9/1[3] | 91 | 55 |
| 4055[10] | **Leonato (FR) (100)** (PDEvans) **4-9-8** JFEgan(3) (nvr nrr) | 3 | **11** | 50/1 | 95 | 59 |
| 4327[3] | **Whitechapel (USA) (88)** (LordHuntingdon) **8-8-10** WRSwinburn(10) (lw: nvr nrr) | ½ | **12** | 12/1 | 82 | 46 |
| 4067[6] | **My Learned Friend (83)** (AHide) **5-8-5** AMcGlone(2) (lw: a mid div) | 1 | **13** | 40/1 | 76 | 40 |

| | | | | SP | RR | SF |
|---|---|---|---|---|---|---|
| 3997* | **Arabian Story (97)** (LordHuntingdon) **3-8-11** 4x DHarrison(6) (b: a mid div) | nk | **14** | 5/1[1] | 89 | 45 |
| 3754a[9] | **Son of Sharp Shot (IRE) (102)** (JLDunlop) **6-9-10** KDarley(15) (lw: a bhd) | 1 | **15** | 33/1 | 93 | 57 |
| 1109[2] | **Polydamas (86)** (MRStoute) **4-8-8** JReid(5) (prom over 9f) | 1 | **16** | 20/1 | 76 | 40 |
| | **Zaralaska (92)** (LMCumani) **5-9-0** OUrbina(7) (prom over 9f) | hd | **17** | 12/1 | 81 | 45 |
| 4327[4] | **Remaadi Sun (83)** (MDIUsher) **4-8-5** RStreet(1) (lw: a bhd) | 3 | **18** | 33/1 | 68 | 32 |
| 4176[3] | **Time for Action (IRE) (85)** (MHTompkins) **4-8-4**(3) MHenry(19) (led over 7f: wknd over 2f out) | 13 | **19** | 25/1 | 53 | 17 |
| 1767[3] | **Korambi (92)** (CEBrittain) **4-9-0** BDoyle(8) (lw: prom over 7f: t.o) | dist | **20** | 40/1 | — | — |
| | | | | (SP 124.7%) | | **20 Rn** |

**2m 33.31** (3.31) CSF £130.77 CT £988.25 TOTE £8.10: £1.80 £4.40 £2.20 £5.40 (£73.80) Trio £327.00 OWNER Mrs Wendy Sainer (PULBOROUGH) BRED John McLoughlin

WEIGHT FOR AGE 3yo-8lb

**3689 Better Offer (IRE)**, runner-up in this race last year, has been running well of late and a drop of 2lb was enough to get him back into the winner's enclosure. (9/1)

**4066 Sheer Danzig (IRE)**, 11lb higher than when winning the Hong Kong Trophy at Sandown in July, did not have much luck on his side, but flew through the field in the last furlong and a half, only to find the line coming too soon. (16/1)

**4055* Dacha (IRE)** is progressing nicely and made his bid for glory over half a mile out. Collared inside the final furlong, he failed to find another gear. (7/1)

**3691 Dance So Suite** was back over his best trip. (20/1)

**4187* Willie Conquer** was facing a far more competitive field after two wins in small handicaps. (25/1)

**4114 Beauchamp Jade**, set to rise 6lb in future handicaps, put in some fine work form the rear in the last furlong and a half, but was never going to get there in time. (9/1)

**Zaralaska** (12/1: 8/1-14/1)

## 4466 ASCOT RATED STKS H'CAP (0-105) (3-Y.O+) (Class B)

5-00 (5-01) **5f** £15,854.00 (£5,936.00: £2,905.50: £1,252.50: £563.75: £288.25) Stalls: Low GOING minus 0.08 sec per fur (G)

| | | | | SP | RR | SF |
|---|---|---|---|---|---|---|
| 4314[8] | **Bolshoi (IRE) (90)** (JBerry) **4-8-7b** EmmaO'Gorman(6) (s.s: stdy hdwy 2f out: led over 1f out: r.o wl) | — | **1** | 11/1 | 100 | 66 |
| 3783[2] | **Samwar (90)** (MissGayKelleway) **4-8-7** RCochrane(5) (b: hdwy over 1f out: r.o wl ins fnl f) | 1½ | **2** | 11/4[1] | 95 | 61 |
| 4115[5] | **Croft Pool (104)** (JAGlover) **5-9-7** GCarter(12) (rdn & hdwy over 1f out: r.o wl ins fnl f) | 2 | **3** | 12/1 | 103 | 69 |
| 3946[13] | **Duel At Dawn (90)** (JHMGosden) **3-8-6** LDettori(8) (b: b.hind: lw: led over 3f: one pce) | ¾ | **4** | 20/1 | 86 | 51 |
| 4116[13] | **Sea Dane (102)** (PWHarris) **3-9-4** WRSwinburn(15) (rdn over 1f out: gd hdwy fnl f: r.o wl) | s.h | **5** | 25/1 | 98 | 63 |
| 3232[19] | **Astrac (IRE) (90)** (MissGayKelleway) **5-8-7** MHills(4) (a.p: rdn over 1f out: one pce) | 1½ | **6** | 20/1 | 81 | 47 |
| 3946* | **Crowded Avenue (101)** (PJMakin) **4-9-4** PatEddery(9) (a.p: rdn over 1f out: wknd fnl f) | ¾ | **7** | 6/1[2] | 90 | 56 |
| 4122[5] | **Loch Patrick (104)** (MMadgwick) **6-9-7** JReid(16) (nvr nrr) | ½ | **8** | 20/1 | 91 | 57 |
| 4116[15] | **That Man Again (92)** (GLewis) **4-8-9b** KDarley(1) (hld up: rdn over 1f out: wknd fnl f) | ¾ | **9** | 12/1 | 77 | 43 |
| 4116[17] | **Double Quick (IRE) (92)** (MJohnston) **4-8-9** MRoberts(10) (a.p: rdn over 2f out: wknd over 1f out) | s.h | **10** | 20/1 | 77 | 43 |
| 4116[10] | **Midnight Escape (93)** (CFWall) **3-8-9** NCarlisle(13) (a.p: rdn over 2f out: wknd over 1f out) | s.h | **11** | 25/1 | 78 | 43 |
| 3232[10] | **To the Roof (IRE) (98)** (PWHarris) **4-9-1** GHind(2) (hld up: nt clr run over 2f out tl over 1f out: eased whn btn fnl f) | 1½ | **12** | 14/1 | 78 | 44 |
| 4411a* | **Bold Effort (FR) (90)** (KOCunningham-Brown) **4-8-7v** BDoyle(11) (mid div over 3f) | 2½ | **13** | 14/1 | 62 | 28 |
| 4115[6] | **Speed On (102)** (HCandy) **3-9-4** CRutter(14) (a bhd) | 6 | **14** | 14/1 | 55 | 20 |
| 4304[3] | **Amazing Bay (98)** (IABalding) **3-9-0** TQuinn(7) (hld up: shkn up over 2f out: wknd wl over 1f out) | 2 | **15** | 17/2[3] | 44 | 9 |
| 3946[9] | **Takadou (IRE) (90)** (MissLCSiddall) **5-8-7** MJKinane(3) (a bhd) | 2 | **16** | 20/1 | 30 | — |
| 4304[9] | **Bowden Rose (95)** (MBlanshard) **4-8-12b** JQuinn(17) (racd centre: bhd fnl 2f) | nk | **17** | 33/1 | 34 | — |
| | | | | (SP 129.6%) | | **17 Rn** |

**61.1 secs** (1.10) CSF £40.69 CT £374.56 TOTE £14.00: £2.80 £1.70 £3.00 £2.80 (£23.00) Trio £142.10 OWNER Mrs David Brown (COCKERHAM) BRED David John Brown

LONG HANDICAP Bolshoi (IRE) 8-5 Takadou (IRE) 8-6 Samwar 8-6 Bold Effort (FR) 8-4 Duel At Dawn 8-1

WEIGHT FOR AGE 3yo-1lb

**4314 Bolshoi (IRE)**, 2lb out of the handicap, was a thoroughly convincing winner having struck the front at the distance, readily asserting. (11/1: 8/1-12/1)

**3783 Samwar** found this five furlongs a bit on the sharp side, but ran on strongly from below the distance to take second place. Some rain would be in his favour. (11/4: op 9/2)

**4115 Croft Pool** has been running well this year, despite just one win, and ran on nicely in the last furlong and a half to take third prize. (12/1: op 8/1)

**2584 Duel At Dawn**, 5lb out of the handicap, took the field along but, headed at the distance, was soon beaten. (20/1)

**4116 Sea Dane** seems to be coming back to form after a spell in the doldrums, and put in some eyecatching work in the final furlong to finish in tremendous style. This trip was too sharp for him and, back over six where all three of his victories have come, he looks one to note. (25/1)

**2497 Astrac (IRE)**, having his first run for his new stable, probably found this trip too sharp and failed to quicken in the last furlong and a half. He has done all his winning over six and seven. (20/1)

**4115 Speed On** (14/1: 10/1-16/1)

## 4467 HARVEST STKS (Listed) (3-Y.O+ F & M) (Class A)

5-35 (5-35) **1m 4f** £24,622.50 (£7,455.00: £3,640.00: £1,732.50) Stalls: High GOING minus 0.08 sec per fur (G)

| | | | | SP | RR | SF |
|---|---|---|---|---|---|---|
| 3836[4] | **Altamura (USA) (103)** (JHMGosden) **3-8-9** LDettori(3) (lw: hdwy over 2f out: led over 1f out: rdn out) | — | **1** | 13/2[3] | 115 | 68 |
| 4114[2] | **Time Allowed (106)** (MRStoute) **3-8-6** JReid(6) (b: hdwy to ld 2f out: hdd over 1f out: unable qckn) | 2 | **2** | 6/4[1] | 109 | 62 |
| 4114[4] | **Russian Snows (IRE)** (SbinSuroor) **4-9-0** MJKinane(5) (nt clr run & lost pl 2f out: rallied fnl f: r.o) | 2½ | **3** | 4/1[2] | 106 | 67 |
| 4218[4] | **Inchyre (82)** (RCharlton) **3-8-6** DHarrison(8) (hdwy 3f out: ev ch 2f out: one pce) | hd | **4** | 20/1 | 106 | 59 |
| 4218[2] | **Balalaika (105)** (LMCumani) **3-8-6** OPeslier(7) (lw: rdn over 2f out: hdwy over 1f out: r.o ins fnl f) | nk | **5** | 10/1 | 106 | 59 |
| 3571a[4] | **Alessandra (95)** (BWHills) **3-8-6** MHills(4) (prom over 8f) | 8 | **6** | 25/1 | 95 | 48 |
| 4063[2] | **Ellie Ardensky (98)** (JRFanshawe) **4-9-0** WRSwinburn(1) (prom over 10f) | 5 | **7** | 20/1 | 88 | 49 |
| 4168a[3] | **Honest Guest (IRE) (110)** (MHTompkins) **3-8-6** TQuinn(2) (chsd ldr 9f out to 2f out: sn wknd) | 6 | **8** | 11/1 | 80 | 33 |
| 2886[3] | **Place de L'Opera (98)** (HRACecil) **3-8-6** PatEddery(10) (lw: a bhd) | ¾ | **9** | 9/1 | 79 | 32 |
| 4063[7] | **Ta Awun (USA) (96)** (ACStewart) **3-8-6b[1]** RHills(9) (led 10f) | 1¾ | **10** | 33/1 | 77 | 30 |
| | | | | (SP 117.1%) | | **10 Rn** |

**2m 32.9** (2.90) CSF £16.02 TOTE £6.70: £2.10 £1.40 £1.70 (£6.50) Trio £7.10 OWNER Sheikh Mohammed (NEWMARKET) BRED Darley Stud Management Inc

WEIGHT FOR AGE 3yo-8lb

**3836 Altamura (USA)** has no problems with this longer trip and, moving through to take the lead below the distance, was ridden along to pull away. The Princess Royal Stakes at the next meeting here is probably her next target. (13/2: op 4/1)
**4114 Time Allowed** was finishing bridesmaid for the fifth time in six outings. A return clash with the winner in the Princess Royal Stakes looks likely. (6/4)
**4114 Russian Snows (IRE)**, who failed to stay a mile and three-quarters last time, was the hard-luck story of the race. Travelling really well, she was shuffled back to the rear of the field a quarter of a mile out and appeared in a hopeless position, but she ran on strongly inside the distance to take third in the last couple of strides. She is yet to win in this country but that should soon be rectified. (4/1)
**4218 Inchyre**, taking a step up in trip, acquitted herself well. (20/1)
**4218 Balalaika** took a while to get going, but ran on nicely from below the distance. A drop of rain may be in her favour. (10/1: 6/1-11/1)
**4168a Honest Guest (IRE)** (11/1: 8/1-12/1)

T/Jkpt: Not won; £5,586.87 to Bath 30/9/96. T/Plpt: £144.50 (285.27 Tckts). T/Qdpt: £53.10 (60.18 Tckts). AK

# 3956-**HAMILTON** (R-H) (Good, Good to soft patches)
## Sunday September 29th
WEATHER: sunny periods WIND: mod half against

### 4468 E. B. F. MEDIAN AUCTION MAIDEN STKS (2-Y.O) (Class E)
2-15 (2-15) **5f 4y** £3,376.80 (£1,022.40: £499.20: £237.60) Stalls: Low GOING minus 0.10 sec per fur (G)

| | | | | SP | RR | SF |
|---|---|---|---|---|---|---|
| 4228[3] | **Bishops Court** (MrsJRRamsden) **2-9-0** KFallon(1) (trckd ldrs: smooth hdwy to ld appr fnl f: easily) | — | **1** | 10/11[1] | 78+ | 35 |
| 4250[6] | **Hurgill Lady** (JWWatts) **2-8-9** NConnorton(2) (lw: cl up: led 1½f out: sn hdd & no ch w wnr) | 1½ | **2** | 5/1[2] | 68 | 25 |
| 3956[3] | **Changed To Baileys (IRE) (68)** (JBerry) **2-9-0** JFortune(6) (chsd ldrs: effrt 2f out: r.o one pce) | 2½ | **3** | 13/2[3] | 65 | 22 |
| | **Forcing Bid** (SirMarkPrescott) **2-9-0** MFenton(7) (w'like: scope: sn outpcd & bhd: hdwy over 1f out: styd on wl) | 1¼ | **4** | 5/1[2] | 61+ | 18 |
| | **Lightning Bolt (IRE)** (MJohnston) **2-8-9** JWeaver(5) (led tl hdd 1½f out: grad wknd) | hd | **5** | 10/1 | 56 | 13 |
| | **Tipperary Sunset (IRE)** (JJQuinn) **2-9-0** DRMcCabe(4) (cmpt: scope: bit bkwd: s.s: a wl bhd) | 16 | **6** | 33/1 | 10 | — |

(SP 111.1%) **6 Rn**

**61.5 secs** (3.20) CSF £5.66 TOTE £1.60: £1.30 £1.60 (£3.90) OWNER Mr D. R. Brotherton (THIRSK) BRED D. R. Brotherton
**4228 Bishops Court** confirmed the promise shown at Beverley and won in useful style. He looks one to keep following. (10/11)
**4250 Hurgill Lady** was completely outclassed by the winner, but did stay on well when all was lost. She should be able to pick up a race. (5/1)
**3956 Changed To Baileys (IRE)** ran another sound race but failed to pick up in the closing stages. (13/2)
**Forcing Bid**, a useful-looking newcomer, found this trip too sharp. Judging by the way he finished, better should now be seen especially over further. (5/1)
**Lightning Bolt (IRE)**, an Irish import, had shown next to nothing previously but, after failing to impress on looks, did give some signs of hope. (10/1)

### 4469 E. B. F. MAIDEN STKS (2-Y.O) (Class D)
2-50 (2-51) **6f 5y** £3,631.25 (£1,100.00: £537.50: £256.25) Stalls: Low GOING minus 0.10 sec per fur (G)

| | | | | SP | RR | SF |
|---|---|---|---|---|---|---|
| 3994[12] | **Yorkie George** (LMCumani) **2-9-0** JFortune(8) (s.i.s: sn in tch: led wl over 1f out: edgd lft: r.o) | — | **1** | 9/2[2] | 71 | 40 |
| 4250[10] | **Fairy Ring (IRE)** (RMWhitaker) **2-8-6**(3) RHavlin(2) (lw: hld up: hdwy 2f out: r.o) | 1¾ | **2** | 33/1 | 61 | 30 |
| 4043[6] | **Trailblazer** (CWThornton) **2-9-0** DeanMcKeown(4) (lw: chsd ldrs: effrt over 2f out: kpt on: nvr able to chal) | 1¼ | **3** | 7/4[1] | 63 | 32 |
| | **Sang d'Antibes (FR)** (DJSCosgrove) **2-8-4**(5) LNewton(3) (w'like: lw: hung rt thrght: cl up: led 2½f out tl wl over 1f out: nt qckn) | 2½ | **4** | 8/1 | 51 | 20 |
| 4104[11] | **Curzon Street (74)** (MRStoute) **2-8-9** KFallon(7) (trckd ldrs: effrt 2f out: nt qckn) | 1¼ | **5** | 6/1 | 48 | 17 |
| 4244[6] | **Waltz Time** (MissLAPerratt) **2-8-9** TSprake(5) (cl up tl hung rt & wknd wl over 1f out) | ¾ | **6** | 14/1 | 46 | 15 |
| 3631[2] | **Allegro** (DRLoder) **2-9-0** DRMcCabe(6) (lw: led over 3f: wknd) | 2½ | **7** | 11/2[3] | 44 | 13 |
| | **Cee-N-K (IRE)** (MJohnston) **2-9-0** JWeaver(1) (str: bit bkwd: s.i.s: a outpcd & bhd) | 20 | **8** | 14/1 | — | — |

(SP 111.6%) **8 Rn**

**1m 13.5** (3.50) CSF £91.40 TOTE £5.10: £1.70 £5.20 £1.70 (£72.00) Trio £147.40; £20.77 to Hamilton 30/9/96 OWNER Mr M. J. Dawson (NEWMARKET) BRED Robert Charles Key
**Yorkie George**, an excitable sort, needs to brush up on his starting, but he is obviously improving fast and won this in decent style. (9/2)
**Fairy Ring (IRE)** looked pretty fit and ran well, staying on strongly at the finish. He should improve over further. (33/1)
**4043 Trailblazer**, a laid-back individual, was inclined to hang in a rather messy race, but did keep on at the end to suggest that there is better to come, especially over further. (7/4)
**Sang d'Antibes (FR)** took the eye in the paddock, but all she wanted to do was hang right, giving her rider all sorts of problems. There is plenty more ability there if she can be persuaded. (8/1)
**3593 Curzon Street**, very much on her toes, was taken to post early and, after racing freely, failed to pick up when ridden. She seems her own worst enemy. (6/1: op 4/1)
**4244 Waltz Time** behaved better this time and ran reasonably, but was still in need of this. She has the ability if she can fully get it together. (14/1: 16/1-25/1)
**3631 Allegro** looked fit enough, but again failed to see out the trip. (11/2: op 7/2)
**Cee-N-K (IRE)** (14/1: 8/1-16/1)

### 4470 LIZARS BINOCULARS H'CAP (0-90) (3-Y.O+) (Class C)
3-25 (3-25) **1m 1f 36y** £6,152.80 (£1,863.40: £910.20: £433.60) Stalls: High GOING minus 0.10 sec per fur (G)

| | | | | SP | RR | SF |
|---|---|---|---|---|---|---|
| 2142[7] | **Consordino (80)** (LMCumani) **3-9-8** JFortune(7) (mde all: styd on wl fnl 2f) | — | **1** | 9/2[2] | 93 | 63 |
| 4190[13] | **Flying North (IRE) (73)** (MrsMReveley) **3-8-10**(5) GLee(4) (hld up: hdwy on ins 4f out: swtchd 2f out: styd on wl towards fin) | 1½ | **2** | 10/1 | 83 | 53 |
| 4316[4] | **King Curan (USA) (68)** (DHaydnJones) **5-9-1v** LCharnock(8) (chsd ldrs: hdwy to chal wl over 1f out: wknd ins fnl f) | 2 | **3** | 5/1[3] | 75 | 50 |
| 4184[12] | **Royal Result (USA) (82)** (MRStoute) **3-9-10** KFallon(1) (bhd: hdwy 3f out: styd on u.p: nvr able to chal) | 6 | **4** | 4/1[1] | 78 | 48 |
| 3623[8] | **Bulsara (61)** (CWFairhurst) **4-8-8** DeanMcKeown(5) (prom: effrt over 3f out: r.o one pce) | 11 | **5** | 14/1 | 38 | 13 |
| 4238[6] | **Darling Clover (76)** (RBastiman) **4-9-4**(5) HBastiman(2) (lw: prom tl outpcd fnl 3f) | 1¾ | **6** | 6/1 | 50 | 25 |
| 4316* | **Celebration Cake (IRE) (75)** (MissLAPerratt) **4-9-8** JWeaver(6) (lw: hld up: effrt 4f out: no imp) | 2½ | **7** | 4/1[1] | 45 | 20 |

| | Horse | Details | Dist | Pos | SP | RR | SF |
|---|---|---|---|---|---|---|---|
| 4184[17] | **Ki Chi Saga (USA) (77)** | (JLDunlop) **4-9-10b[1]** TSprake(3) (cl up tl rdn & wknd wl over 2f out) | 13 | **8** | 16/1 | 24 | — |

(SP 110.8%) **8 Rn**

**1m 58.2** (3.90) CSF £40.91 CT £201.22 TOTE £5.80: £1.50 £2.60 £2.10 (£12.40) OWNER Sheikh Mohammed (NEWMARKET) BRED Lord Rotherwick

WEIGHT FOR AGE 3yo-5lb

**1481 Consordino,** having her first run for over three months, has obviously had problems, but does stay well. Given a fine ride, she won in useful style and should improve for the run. (9/2)

**3640 Flying North (IRE)** got the best ground up the far rail when making his run and, judging by the way he finished, he is at last coming to hand. (10/1: op 6/1)

**4316 King Curan (USA)** normally has to make it, but that was never on here. He still ran well though, only finding it too tough in the last furlong. (5/1)

**3226* Royal Result (USA)** tried to come from behind and did the right thing by sticking to the rail but, when a real effort was required, he was never doing anything like enough. (4/1)

**3280 Bulsara,** from a yard that is well out of form, ran reasonably, but failed to offer a live threat. (14/1: 8/1-16/1)

**4238 Darling Clover** has been set stiffish tasks by the Handicapper of late and was back-pedalling fully three furlongs out. (6/1)

**4316* Celebration Cake (IRE),** trying a longer trip, was dropped out and, refusing to settle, had run himself out halfway up the straight. (4/1: 3/1-9/2)

## 4471 TELEWEST COMMUNICATIONS CONDITIONS STKS (2-Y.O) (Class C)

4-00 (4-02) **1m 65y** £4,664.64 (£1,745.76: £853.88: £367.40: £164.70: £83.62) Stalls: High GOING minus 0.10 sec per fur (G)

| | Horse | Details | Dist | Pos | SP | RR | SF |
|---|---|---|---|---|---|---|---|
| 4056[3] | **Further Outlook (USA)** | (MRStoute) **2-9-2** KFallon(5) (b.hind: cl up: disp ld 3f out: hrd drvn fnl f: kpt on wl) | — | **1** | 100/30[1] | 96 | 49 |
| *4091** | **Waiting Game (IRE)** | (DRLoder) **2-9-2** DRMcCabe(7) (lw: led tl disp ld 3f out: edgd lft u.p fnl f: no ex towards fin) | hd | **2** | 6/1 | 96 | 49 |
| 4069* | **Ivan Luis (FR) (85)** | (MBell) **2-8-11**(5) GFaulkner(3) (hld up: hdwy ½-wy: chsng ldrs fnl 2f: nt pce to chal) | 2½ | **3** | 7/2[2] | 91 | 44 |
| 3880* | **Ben's Ridge (82)** | (PCHaslam) **2-8-11** JFortune(6) (lw: a chsng ldrs: rdn & one pce fnl 3f) | 3½ | **4** | 33/1 | 79 | 32 |
| 4133[7] | **Quintellina (93)** | (LMCumani) **2-8-11** JWeaver(1) (hld up: swtchd lft & effrt over 3f out: sn btn) | ½ | **5** | 4/1[3] | 78 | 31 |
| 3837* | **Redwing** | (JLDunlop) **2-9-2** TSprake(4) (in tch: effrt over 3f out: edgd rt & r.o one pce) | ½ | **6** | 7/2[2] | 82 | 35 |
| 4133[8] | **The In-Laws (IRE)** | (SirMarkPrescott) **2-8-11** MFenton(2) (lw: in tch tl outpcd fnl 3f) | 1¾ | **7** | 14/1 | 74 | 27 |

(SP 111.4%) **7 Rn**

**1m 48.6** (4.50) CSF £20.98 TOTE £3.40: £1.60 £2.70 (£8.80) OWNER Mr Mana Al Maktoum (NEWMARKET) BRED Gainsborough Farm Inc.

**4056 Further Outlook (USA)** certainly stays and is particularly game. Given a very forceful ride, he needed both those qualities to hold on. (100/30)

**4091* Waiting Game (IRE),** made plenty of use of, kept fighting back, but edging left in the closing stages probably just made the difference. He stays really well and should find plenty of success on Turf in due course. (6/1)

**4069* Ivan Luis (FR)** ran a sound race, but was never good enough to seriously trouble the front two. This may turn out to have been a decent event. (7/2)

**3880* Ben's Ridge** is running consistently well at present and was not disgraced here. (33/1)

**4133 Quintellina,** edgy beforehand, has lost her way of late. She was racing on the slower ground though and did make some late headway. (4/1)

**3837* Redwing** did not appear suited by this undulating track. (7/2)

**4133 The In-Laws (IRE)** (14/1: 8/1-16/1)

## 4472 CHIMS CLAIMING STKS (3-Y.O) (Class E)

4-35 (4-36) **1m 65y** £3,050.25 (£924.00: £451.50: £215.25) Stalls: High GOING minus 0.10 sec per fur (G)

| | Horse | Details | Dist | Pos | SP | RR | SF |
|---|---|---|---|---|---|---|---|
| 4296[7] | **Power Game (58)** | (JBerry) **3-9-1b** JFortune(2) (s.i.s: hdwy on ins 4f out: rdn to ld ins fnl f: r.o) | — | **1** | 7/2[2] | 70 | 48 |
| 3978[2] | **Western Venture (IRE) (50)** | (JWPayne) **3-8-11** MFenton(10) (led tl hdd ins fnl f: kpt on same pce) | 1¾ | **2** | 7/2[2] | 63 | 41 |
| 3881[8] | **Termon (52)** | (MissLAPerratt) **3-8-10** JWeaver(8) (a chsng ldrs: rdn & one pce fnl 3f) | 10 | **3** | 14/1 | 42 | 20 |
| 4249[18] | **Tolepa (IRE) (40)** | (JJO'Neill) **3-8-12** KFallon(1) (dwlt: hdwy on ins 4f out: nrst fin) | 2½ | **4** | 40/1 | 40 | 18 |
| 4323[4] | **La Finale (45)** | (DNicholls) **3-8-1b**(7) JBramhill(4) (cl up tl wknd fnl 3f) | ½ | **5** | 7/1[3] | 35 | 13 |
| 1714[5] | **Cd Super Targeting (IRE) (64)** | (MRChannon) **3-9-2** TSprake(9) (trckd ldrs: effrt over 2f out: wknd wl over 1f out) | ½ | **6** | 3/1[1] | 42 | 20 |
| 3102[13] | **Cerise (IRE) (44)** | (CWCElsey) **3-7-13b**(5) PFessey(3) (nvr trbld ldrs) | 5 | **7** | 20/1 | 20 | — |
| 3961[4] | **Mystic Times (39)** | (BMactaggart) **3-8-6** DeanMcKeown(6) (prom: outpcd ½-wy: grad wknd) | 1½ | **8** | 10/1 | 19 | — |
| *3951[12]* | **Harsh Times (43)** | (TDEasterby) **3-8-4b** LCharnock(5) (in tch tl outpcd ½-wy) | 7 | **9** | 9/1 | 4 | — |
| *1719[16]* | **Bashtheboards (61)** | (JJQuinn) **3-8-12**(5) GParkin(11) (in tch tl wknd over 3f out) | nk | **10** | 25/1 | 16 | — |
| 3965[10] | **Royal Rigger (32)** | (CSmith) **3-7-13**(3) NVarley(7) (in tch tl wknd fnl 4f) | 6 | **11** | 66/1 | — | — |
| | **Inchella** | (MissLAPerratt) **3-8-8** NKennedy(12) (cmpt: bkwd: s.s: a t.o) | 15 | **12** | 33/1 | — | — |

(SP 123.2%) **12 Rn**

**1m 48.6** (4.50) CSF £16.04 TOTE £3.40: £1.20 £2.20 £3.50 (£4.20) Trio £48.20 OWNER Countrywide Racing (COCKERHAM) BRED Bearstone Stud

**4070* Power Game** had plenty to do after a poor start, but his rider was one of the few aware that the better ground was up the far rail. Improving early in the straight, he won really well. (7/2)

**3978 Western Venture (IRE)** did the right thing and made it, getting the best ground throughout but, despite leaving the remainder well behind, he had found one just too good. (7/2)

**3491 Termon** ran her best race for a while, but was well outpointed in the last three furlongs. (14/1: 12/1-20/1)

**3058 Tolepa (IRE)** ran a useful race here after a bad start and is now beginning to get the hang of things. (40/1)

**4323 La Finale,** stepping up in trip again, was found wanting when the pressure was on in the last half-mile. (7/1)

**1714 Cd Super Targeting (IRE)** looked to be travelling well but, once off the bit with three furlongs to go, the response was disappointing. (3/1)

## 4473 RACING CHANNEL SATURDAY SERVICE H'CAP (0-75) (3-Y.O+) (Class D)

5-10 (5-11) **5f 4y** £4,038.40 (£1,223.20: £597.60: £284.80) Stalls: Low GOING minus 0.10 sec per fur (G)

| | Horse | Details | Dist | Pos | SP | RR | SF |
|---|---|---|---|---|---|---|---|
| 4316[8] | **Natural Key (65)** | (DHaydnJones) **3-9-7** LCharnock(14) (lw: racd far side: cl up: led over 1f out: r.o wl) | — | **1** | 7/2[1] | 74 | 48 |
| 4246[9] | **Stephensons Rocket (56)** | (DNicholls) **5-8-13** AlexGreaves(15) (lw: outpcd far side: hdwy 2f out: styd on wl towards fin) | 1¼ | **2** | 5/1[2] | 61 | 36 |

| | | | | SP | RR | SF |
|---|---|---|---|---|---|---|
| *1716[9]* | **My Cherrywell (54)** (LRLloyd-James) **6-8-4v(7)** CLowther(2) (b.hind: chsd ldrs stands' side: kpt on wl fnl f) | 1 | **3** | 50/1 | 56 | 31 |
| 4246[15] | **Kalar (55)** (DWChapman) **7-8-12b** JWeaver(4) (led stands' side: nt qckn fnl f) | ¾ | **4** | 10/1 | 54 | 29 |
| 3937[11] | **Craigie Boy (50)** (NBycroft) **6-8-7v[1]** KFallon(1) (hdwy stands' side over 1f out: styd on wl towards fin) | s.h | **5** | 9/1 | 49 | 24 |
| 4382[13] | **Pageboy (67)** (PCHaslam) **7-9-10** JFortune(7) (lw: racd stands' side: in tch: kpt on one pce fnl 2f) | hd | **6** | 7/1[3] | 66 | 41 |
| 4205[17] | **Silk Cottage (57)** (RMWhitaker) **4-9-0v** DeanMcKeown(12) (lw: racd far side: trckd ldrs: effrt 2f out: hung bdly lft: nvr able to chal) | hd | **7** | 14/1 | 56 | 31 |
| 4246[12] | **Six for Luck (57)** (DANolan) **4-9-0** TSprake(8) (led far side 1½f: cl up tl wknd fnl 2f) | ½ | **8** | 14/1 | 54 | 29 |
| 3957[5] | **Kabcast (42)** (DWChapman) **11-7-8b(5)** PFessey(11) (led far side after 1½f tl hdd & wknd over 1f out) | hd | **9** | 20/1 | 39 | 14 |
| 4341[2] | **Hoh Majestic (IRE) (58)** (MartynWane) **3-9-0v** MFenton(6) (racd stands' side: outpcd fr ½-wy) | 2 | **10** | 10/1 | 48 | 22 |
| 4205[5] | **Coolowen Flash (IRE) (40)** (JLEyre) **5-7-11** TWilliams(5) (cl up stands' side tl wknd appr fnl f) | nk | **11** | 10/1 | 29 | 4 |
| 4246[11] | **Sunday Mail Too (IRE) (45)** (MissLAPerratt) **4-8-2** NKennedy(10) (racd far side: sn drvn along: bhd fr ½-wy) | ½ | **12** | 10/1 | 33 | 8 |
| 3310[8] | **Never Say so (42)** (CSmith) **4-7-10(3)** NVarley(9) (racd far side: outpcd & bhd fr ½-wy) | 6 | **13** | 50/1 | 11 | — |

(SP 119.8%) **13 Rn**

**61.1 secs** (2.80) CSF £20.23 CT £699.36 TOTE £4.70: £1.80 £2.50 £9.60 (£23.90) Trio £140.40 OWNER Mr Hugh O'Donnell (PONTYPRIDD) BRED Cheveley Park Stud Ltd

WEIGHT FOR AGE 3yo-1lb

**4246 Natural Key** had a good draw and made full use of it to gain his fourth course win of the season. (7/2)

**4246 Stephensons Rocket**, without the blinkers this time but well drawn, got left behind. Judging by the way he stayed on, he is in good heart. (5/1)

**1492 My Cherrywell** ran a super race up the stands' side and was finishing in most determined style. (50/1)

**3883 Kalar** ran his heart out towards the stands' side, but just found it all too much in the final furlong. This was a decent effort from a yard that is out of form at present. (10/1)

**3424 Craigie Boy**, in a visor for the first time, only stayed on when it was too late and is probably better over a bit further. (9/1)

**4246 Pageboy** could never dominate over this shorter trip, but he still looks well enough and this was not a bad effort from his draw. (7/1)

## 4474 PETER GRANT TESTIMONIAL H'CAP (0-70) (3-Y.O) (Class E)

5-40 (5-41) **1m 4f 17y** £3,317.70 (£1,005.60: £491.80: £234.90) Stalls: High GOING minus 0.10 sec per fur (G)

| | | | | SP | RR | SF |
|---|---|---|---|---|---|---|
| 4317[3] | **The Butterwick Kid (45)** (RAFahey) **3-7-10** LCharnock(10) (chsd ldrs: led over 2f out: all out) | — | **1** | 12/1 | 51 | 15 |
| *4095[6]* | **The Boozing Brief (USA) (57)** (MAJarvis) **3-8-8b[1]** PBloomfield(6) (w ldr: led 4f out tl over 2f out: hrd rdn & styd on fnl f: jst failed) | s.h | **2** | 6/1 | 63 | 27 |
| 4201[8] | **Silvretta (IRE) (60)** (ACStewart) **3-8-11** SWhitworth(12) (bhd: hdwy on ins 3f out: hmpd over 2f out: styd on strly towards fins) | 2½ | **3** | 4/1[2] | 63 | 27 |
| 4227[3] | **Road Racer (IRE) (54)** (MrsJRRamsden) **3-8-5[ow1]** KFallon(7) (lw: mid div: effrt over 3f out: wandered u.p: one pce appr fnl f) | hd | **4** | 3/1[1] | 57 | 20 |
| 3845* | **Contract Bridge (IRE) (50)** (CWThornton) **3-7-8(7)** AMcCarthy(9) (s.i.s: hdwy 5f out: nt clr run & swtchd 3f out: styd on) | nk | **5** | 5/1[3] | 52 | 16 |
| 4355[6] | **Red Tie Affair (USA) (53)** (MBell) **3-8-4** MFenton(11) (lw: b.nr fore: hld up & bhd: c wd st: nrst fin) | 5 | **6** | 8/1 | 49 | 13 |
| 4317[6] | **Philgem (45)** (CWFairhurst) **3-7-10** NKennedy(3) (in tch tl outpcd fnl 4f) | 13 | **7** | 50/1 | 23 | — |
| 4047[6] | **Poetic Dance (USA) (70)** (JLDunlop) **3-9-7** TSprake(4) (lw: led tl hdd 4f out: sn rdn & btn) | ¾ | **8** | 7/1 | 47 | 11 |
| 4313[7] | **Ragtime Cowgirl (45)** (DANolan) **3-7-5(5)** PFessey(5) (a bhd) | 5 | **9** | 12/1 | 16 | — |
| 4322[12] | **Ballykissangel (46)** (NBycroft) **3-7-8(3)[ow1]** NVarley(2) (prom tl wknd fnl 4f) | 9 | **10** | 100/1 | 5 | — |
| 4323[15] | **Most Wanted (IRE) (46)** (JJO'Neill) **3-7-11[ow1]** TWilliams(1) (prom tl wknd fnl 4f) | 5 | **11** | 16/1 | — | — |

(SP 123.8%) **11 Rn**

**2m 40.9** (8.90) CSF £79.70 CT £318.91 TOTE £24.10: £3.50 £1.50 £2.30 (£32.30) Trio £25.50 OWNER The Butterwick Race Co (MALTON) BRED Scorrier Stud

LONG HANDICAP The Butterwick Kid 7-9 Philgem 5-13 Ragtime Cowgirl 7-7 Ballykissangel 6-7 Most Wanted (IRE) 7-7

**4317 The Butterwick Kid** has improved tremendously since trying further, and he showed fine determination to hold on here. (12/1)

**4095 The Boozing Brief (USA)**, in blinkers for the first time, was inclined to hang when ridden but, to his credit, he did fight back and would probably have won in another stride. (6/1)

**3788 Silvretta (IRE)** did the right thing by sticking to the far rail when improving up the straight but, in so doing, also found a little trouble, and only got going when it was too late. She seems to be coming right. (4/1: 3/1-9/2)

**4227 Road Racer (IRE)** had his chances, but was never producing the goods when required. (3/1)

**3845* Contract Bridge (IRE)** never really had things going her way here, but she did stay on well at the end to suggest that she remains in good heart. (5/1)

**4355 Red Tie Affair (USA)**, pulled wide in to the straight and onto the slower ground, ran quite well but, despite staying on, could never get into it. (8/1: op 5/1)

T/Plpt: £74.70 (125.96 Tckts). T/Qdpt: £46.00 (8.19 Tckts). AA

# 4082-BATH (L-H) (Good becoming Good to soft)
## Monday September 30th

WEATHER: raining WIND: nil

## 4475 E.B.F. TORMARTON MAIDEN STKS (2-Y.O) (Class D)

2-00 (2-03) **5f 161y** £3,738.25 (£1,126.00: £545.50: £255.25) Stalls: High GOING minus 0.10 sec per fur (G)

| | | | | SP | RR | SF |
|---|---|---|---|---|---|---|
| 4330[3] | **Sabina** (IABalding) **2-8-9** LDettori(12) (mde all: clr whn shkn up 1f out: rdn & wknd nr fin) | — | **1** | 7/4[1] | 81 | 35 |
| 1959[5] | **Tigrello** (GLewis) **2-9-0** PatEddery(8) (a.p: rdn over 3f out: chsd wnr fnl f: r.o one pce) | 1¾ | **2** | 4/1[3] | 81 | 35 |
| 1822[4] | **Just Nick** (WRMuir) **2-9-0** JReid(13) (chsd ldrs: r.o one pce fnl f) | 1¼ | **3** | 15/2 | 78 | 32 |
| 4210[6] | **Wee Dram** (RHannon) **2-8-9** RPerham(1) (chsd wnr: one pce fnl f) | nk | **4** | 33/1 | 72 | 26 |
| | **Za-Im** (BWHills) **2-9-0** RHills(11) (w'like: scope: prom: rdn & no hdwy fnl 2f) | 1¾ | **5** | 12/1 | 72 | 26 |
| 4087[9] | **Tayovullin (IRE)** (RCharlton) **2-8-9** TSprake(9) (no hdwy fnl 3f) | ¾ | **6** | 33/1 | 65 | 19 |
| 3593[15] | **Perchance To Dream (IRE)** (BRMillman) **2-8-9** BDoyle(14) (nvr trbld ldrs) | 2½ | **7** | 100/1 | 58 | 12 |
| 4228[6] | **Dominant Air** (SirMarkPrescott) **2-9-0** SSanders(7) (dwlt: a bhd) | 1¾ | **8** | 20/1 | 58 | 12 |
| | **Sweet Bettsie** (AGFoster) **2-8-4(5)** CAdamson(10) (w'like: dwlt: a bhd) | 1¼ | **9** | 50/1 | 50 | 4 |
| 3994[4] | **Daring Flight (USA)** (LordHuntingdon) **2-9-0** DHarrison(3) (prom: rdn over 3f out: wknd over 2f out) | nk | **10** | 2/1[2] | 54 | 8 |

4127$^{17}$ **Alpine Music (IRE)** (JMBradley) **2-9-0** CRutter(4) (a bhd) ....................5 **11** 100/1 40 —
**Keepsake (IRE)** (MDIUsher) **2-8-9** RStreet(2) (w'like: bkwd: s.s: a t.o) ....................16 **12** 100/1 — —
(SP 124.7%) **12 Rn**

**1m 13.0** (3.50) CSF £9.54 TOTE £2.90: £1.30 £1.60 £1.90 (£8.50) Trio £17.10 OWNER The Queen (KINGSCLERE) BRED Mrs Mary Taylor
IN-FOCUS: **the ground looked on the soft side of good.**
**4330 Sabina** seemed to get tired in the rain-softened ground, and may be more effective at the minimum trip for the time being. (7/4)
**1959 Tigrello** has presumably been waiting for some decent ground. Perhaps a shade flattered by his proximity to the leg-weary winner, a longer trip should help. (4/1)
**1822 Just Nick**, who has changed stables, was a springer in the market and kept on to reward any each-way money. (15/2)
**Wee Dram** ran her best race to date. (33/1)
**Za-Im** was the only one to travel as well as the winner for the first half of the race, and may do better over further. (12/1: op 6/1)
**Tayovullin (IRE)** will need much further than this in time on her breeding. (33/1)

## 4476 WEATHERBYS DATA SERVICES CHUCKLESTONE H'CAP (0-80) (3-Y.O+) (Class D)

2-30 (2-31) **2m 1f 34y** £3,757.75 (£1,132.00: £548.50: £256.75) Stalls: High GOING minus 0.10 sec per fur (G)

SP RR SF
3983$^{12}$ **Nuzu (IRE) (78)** (BWHills) **3-9-3b$^{1}$** MHills(6) (hld up: stdy hdwy 6f out: rdn to ld over 2f out: r.o wl) ....................— **1** 7/1$^{3}$ 93 44
4199$^{12}$ **Inchcailloch (IRE) (62)** (JSKing) **7-8-13** AClark(11) (hld up: hdwy over 5f out: rdn & chsd wnr fnl 2f: no imp)...4 **2** 7/1$^{3}$ 73 36
*4095*$^{12}$ **Jelali (IRE) (62)** (DJGMurraySmith) **3-8-1**$^{ow1}$ TSprake(3) (hld up & bhd: gd hdwy 3f out: hrd rdn & one pce fnl 2f) ....................7 **3** 50/1 67 17
3928$^{6}$ **Sea Freedom (60)** (GBBalding) **5-8-11v** JReid(12) (lw: chsd ldr: wknd 2f out) ....................1½ **4** 10/1 63 26
4203$^{19}$ **Teen Jay (50)** (BJLlewellyn) **6-8-1** DeclanO'Shea(4) (tk keen hold: sn prom: rdn over 4f out: led over 3f out tl over 2f out: sn wknd) ....................23 **5** 20/1 32 —
3850$^{8}$ **Bold Classic (IRE) (79)** (JLDunlop) **3-9-4v$^{1}$** TQuinn(7) (lw: prom: rdn over 2f out: eased whn btn over 1f out) .1 **6** 10/1 60 11
4252$^{6}$ **Rocquaine Bay (45)** (MJBolton) **9-7-10** JQuinn(9) (nvr nr ldrs) ....................¾ **7** 25/1 25 —
3850$^{5}$ **Bellara (60)** (NMBabbage) **4-8-11** LDettori(8) (hld up: hdwy on ins 7f out: wknd 4f out) ....................1 **8** 100/30$^{2}$ 39 2
4199$^{5}$ **Blaze Away (USA) (75)** (IABalding) **5-9-12** PatEddery(10) (hld up: rdn 6f out: wknd 4f out) ....................7 **9** 2/1$^{1}$ 48 11
4083$^{5}$ **Mu-Tadil (45)** (RJBaker) **4-7-10** FNorton(1) (a bhd) ....................3 **10** 50/1 15 —
4187$^{4}$ **Farringdon Hill (77)** (MajorWRHern) **5-10-0b** RHills(5) (led over 13f: eased whn btn fnl 2f) ....................13 **11** 10/1 35 —
4307$^{21}$ **Great Simplicity (45)** (RCurtis) **9-7-10b** GBardwell(2) (b: a bhd: t.o fnl 3f) ....................10 **12** 100/1 — —
(SP 122.2%) **12 Rn**

**3m 51.8** (10.80) CSF £52.72 CT £2,097.64 TOTE £9.60: £2.60 £1.70 £10.30 (£31.20) Trio £356.50; £150.66 to Newmarket 1/10/96 OWNER Sheikh Mohammed (LAMBOURN) BRED Darley Stud Management Co Ltd
LONG HANDICAP Rocquaine Bay 6-12 Great Simplicity 7-7
WEIGHT FOR AGE 3yo-12lb
**3617 Nuzu (IRE)**, aided by the blinkers, was also helped by an extended trip with cut in the ground. (7/1)
**Inchcailloch (IRE)**, 1lb lower than when fourth in last year's Cesarewitch, was supported in the ring and stepped up considerably on his reappearance at Goodwood earlier in the month. (7/1: op 14/1)
**Jelali (IRE)** was given an awful lot to do on his first attempt at this sort of trip. (50/1)
**3801 Sea Freedom** was 2lb lower than when runner-up at Goodwood two outings ago. (10/1)
**3850 Bellara**, dropped 5lb, was only 2lb higher than the second of her two wins in the spring. (100/30: 2/1-7/2)

## 4477 E.B.F. DODINGTON MAIDEN STKS (2-Y.O) (Class D)

3-00 (3-01) **1m 2f 46y** £3,397.00 (£1,021.00: £493.00: £229.00) Stalls: Low GOING minus 0.10 sec per fur (G)

SP RR SF
**Eldorado (IRE)** (MJohnston) **2-9-0** JReid(1) (wl grwn: hld up: pushed along over 5f out: rdn & hdwy 2f out: led ins fnl f: r.o wl) ....................— **1** 11/2$^{2}$ 86+ 42
4306$^{4}$ **Slip The Net (IRE)** (PFICole) **2-9-0** TQuinn(3) (w ldr: led 8f out: rdn over 3f out: hdd ins fnl f) ....................2½ **2** 2/7$^{1}$ 82 38
4233$^{6}$ **Drive Assured (82)** (CEBrittain) **2-9-0** BDoyle(4) (plld hrd: a.p: chsd ldr 4f out: rdn over 2f out: eased whn btn ins fnl f) ....................13 **3** 13/2$^{3}$ 62 18
**Wesley's Lad (IRE)** (JNeville) **2-9-0** AClark(5) (cmpt: bkwd: hld up: hdwy 3f out: rdn & wknd 2f out) ....................nk **4** 50/1 61 17
4041$^{13}$ **Bonne Ville** (BPalling) **2-8-9** TSprake(2) (hld up: wknd over 2f out) ....................s.h **5** 40/1 56 12
*4331*$^{11}$ **Southern Chief** (WGMTurner) **2-9-0** RPerham(6) (bit bkwd: led over 2f: wknd over 2f out: t.o) ....................23 **6** 66/1 25 —
(SP 112.4%) **6 Rn**

**2m 13.6** (6.10) CSF £7.43 TOTE £5.80: £2.80 £1.10 (£1.90) OWNER Mr R. W. Huggins (MIDDLEHAM) BRED Joseph Kruger II
**Eldorado (IRE)**, a 10,000 guinea half-brother to a middle-distance winner in Ireland, is out of a half-sister to Snurge. It was a case of the further he went the better he got, and he looks a ready-made candidate for the Zetland Stakes at Newmarket. (11/2: op 5/2)
**4306 Slip The Net (IRE)** seemed to have a simple enough task on paper, but one had not reckoned on a fine staying performance by the newcomer. (2/7)
**4233 Drive Assured** kept on the fairway, but did not see out this monster par five as well as the first two. (13/2)
**Wesley's Lad (IRE)** only cost 2,000 Irish guineas, but showed signs of ability and will strip fitter for the run. (50/1)

## 4478 EUROPEAN FRICTION INDUSTRIES ANNIVERSARY MAIDEN STKS (3-Y.O+) (Class D)

3-30 (3-32) **1m 2f 46y** £3,757.75 (£1,132.00: £548.50: £256.75) Stalls: Low GOING minus 0.10 sec per fur (G)

SP RR SF
4201$^{3}$ **Pasternak (75)** (SirMarkPrescott) **3-8-12** SSanders(7) (lw: hld up: hdwy 3f out: led over 1f out: hdd ins fnl f: led post) ....................— **1** 9/2 85 61
4099$^{3}$ **King Kato** (GHarwood) **3-8-12** JReid(8) (a.p: led over 2f out tl over 1f out: led ins fnl f: hdd post) ....................s.h **2** 4/1$^{3}$ 85 61
4309$^{4}$ **Medfee** (RCharlton) **3-8-7** PatEddery(5) (lw: a.p: rdn & one pce fnl 2f) ....................10 **3** 9/4$^{1}$ 64 40
4360$^{2}$ **Kutman (USA)** (MRStoute) **3-8-12** WRyan(10) (hld up & bhd: hdwy 3f out: one pce fnl 2f) ....................2½ **4** 5/2$^{2}$ 65 41
**War Shanty** (LadyHerries) **3-8-7** AClark(1) (bkwd: nvr nr to chal) ....................nk **5** 50/1 60 36
4099$^{2}$ **Mutanassib (IRE)** (ACStewart) **3-8-12** RHills(9) (lw: led over 7f: sn wknd) ....................1¼ **6** 13/2 63 39
3986$^{8}$ **Reticent (73)** (JHMGosden) **3-8-12** LDettori(11) (swtg: prom over 7f) ....................6 **7** 20/1 54 30
4099$^{4}$ **Flamanda** (CEBrittain) **3-8-7** BDoyle(3) (prom over 6f) ....................12 **8** 25/1 30 6
*4336*$^{11}$ **Kowtow (49)** (MDIUsher) **3-8-7** RStreet(4) (prom tl wknd over 2f out) ....................5 **9** 100/1 22 —
4083$^{8}$ **Haddit** (AGNewcombe) **3-8-12** SDrowne(2) (s.i.s: a bhd: t.o) ....................9 **10** 100/1 13 —
(SP 123.4%) **10 Rn**

**2m 10.9** (3.40) CSF £22.95 TOTE £6.90: £1.90 £1.90 £1.30 (£17.40) Trio £24.90 OWNER Mr Graham Rock (NEWMARKET) BRED Hesmonds Stud Ltd

**4201 Pasternak** again took the eye in the paddock. Settling much better this time, he got back up to snatch the verdict on the nod. (9/2)
**4099 King Kato** was very easy to back in the Ring but ran a great race and only got touched off on the line. (4/1: 2/1-9/2)
**4309 Medfee**, stepping up in distance, was a little disappointing and could not go with the two principals in the final quarter-mile. (9/4)
**4360 Kutman (USA)** should have been suited by this extra quarter-mile, but could not sustain his run. (5/2)
**War Shanty**, a half-sister to the sprinter Brave Edge, will derive considerable benefit from this belated seasonal debut. (50/1)
**4099 Mutanassib (IRE)** did nothing more than cut out the donkey-work and may be better suited to a longer trip. (13/2)

## 4479 MORRIS DANCER CONDITIONS STKS (3-Y.O+) (Class C)

4-00 (4-01) **1m 5y** £4,851.00 (£1,809.00: £879.50: £372.50: £161.25: £76.75) Stalls: Low GOING minus 0.10 sec per fur (G)

| | | | Pos | SP | RR | SF |
|---|---|---|---|---|---|---|
| 4181² | **Ali-Royal (IRE) (111)** (HRACecil) **3-9-4** PatEddery(6) (hld up: hdwy to ld over 2f out: sn clr) | — | 1 | 11/10¹ | 119 | 75 |
| 4132⁷ | **Nijo (109)** (DRLoder) **5-9-0v¹** LDettori(5) (led over 5f: no ch w wnr) | 12 | 2 | 7/2² | 87 | 47 |
| 1393a⁷ | **Story Line** (BWHills) **3-8-5** TQuinn(4) (hld up & bhd: hdwy over 2f out: r.o one pce) | 3½ | 3 | 13/2 | 75 | 31 |
| 4194⁹ | **Maralinga (IRE) (100)** (LadyHerries) **4-9-4** DeclanO'Shea(1) (chsd ldr tl wknd over 2f out) | 3½ | 4 | 10/1 | 77 | 37 |
| 4194³ | **Jarah (USA) (99)** (SbinSuroor) **3-9-0** RHills(3) (hld up & bhd: effrt over 2f out: sn wknd) | hd | 5 | 5/1³ | 77 | 33 |
| 3211¹² | **Iamus (83)** (PTWalwyn) **3-8-12** JReid(2) (prom over 4f) | hd | 6 | 50/1 | 75 | 31 |

(SP 110.9%) **6 Rn**

**1m 40.4** (1.90) CSF £5.15 TOTE £1.90: £1.40 £2.00 (£3.00) OWNER Greenbay Stables Ltd (NEWMARKET) BRED C. H. WACKER III
WEIGHT FOR AGE 3yo-4lb
IN-FOCUS: **This was a strongly-run race.**
**4181 Ali-Royal (IRE)** has been taking on some useful types and, ridden more aggressively than at Doncaster, quickly put the issue beyond doubt. (11/10)
**4132 Nijo** set a strong pace in the first-time visor until swept aside by the winner. (7/2)
**1393a Story Line** did not have enough time to read the script over this shorter distance. (13/2)
**3996 Maralinga (IRE)** is another who seems to need further. (10/1)
**4194 Jarah (USA)** could not make the transition from handicap company. (5/1)
**2181* Iamus** would have been much better off in a handicap. (50/1)

## 4480 ALDIE MAIDEN APPRENTICE H'CAP (0-60) (3-Y.O+) (Class F)

4-30 (4-32) **1m 5y** £3,125.00 (£875.00: £425.00) Stalls: Low GOING minus 0.10 sec per fur (G)

| | | | Pos | SP | RR | SF |
|---|---|---|---|---|---|---|
| 4082³ | **Shouldbegrey (42)** (WRMuir) **3-8-10** AmandaSanders(9) (plld hrd: a.p: led ins fnl f: r.o) | — | 1 | 13/2³ | 51 | 28 |
| 4082⁴ | **Jilly Beveled (39)** (PRWebber) **4-8-6**(5) DavidO'Neill(12) (swtg: led: edgd rt wl over 1f out: hdd ins fnl f) | 1¼ | 2 | 9/1 | 46 | 27 |
| 4053¹⁶ | **Scimitar (53)** (PJMakin) **3-9-7** DSweeney(15) (gd hdwy over 1f out: r.o wl ins fnl f) | 1 | 3 | 20/1 | 58 | 35 |
| *4107*⁵ | **One In The Eye (47)** (JRPoulton) **3-9-1** RMullen(18) (a.p: rdn & ev ch 2f out: one pce) | hd | 4 | 33/1 | 51 | 28 |
| 4263⁷ | **College Night (IRE) (46)** (CADwyer) **4-9-4** JoHunnam(16) (hdwy over 1f out: nvr nrr) | hd | 5 | 9/1 | 50 | 31 |
| 4263² | **Diebiedale (45)** (RBoss) **4-9-3** GFaulkner(13) (a.p: no hdwy fnl 2f) | 2½ | 6 | 9/2¹ | 44 | 25 |
| 3949¹² | **Rose Tint (IRE) (55)** (LordHuntingdon) **3-9-9** AimeeCook(14) (hdwy 2f out: nt rch ldrs) | 1¾ | 7 | 16/1 | 51 | 28 |
| 4128⁶ | **Secret Pleasure (IRE) (55)** (RHannon) **3-9-9** KSked(2) (s.i.s: nvr nrr) | 3½ | 8 | 11/2² | 44 | 21 |
| 3681⁷ | **Northern Saga (IRE) (41)** (CJDrewe) **3-8-6**(3) RFfrench(6) (no hdwy fnl 3f) | s.h | 9 | 12/1 | 30 | 7 |
| *2934*¹⁵ | **Covered Girl (IRE) (55)** (BWHills) **3-9-9** GMilligan(11) (hld up: lost pl 4f out: n.d after) | nk | 10 | 25/1 | 43 | 20 |
| 3808¹⁰ | **Fastini Gold (35)** (MDIUsher) **4-8-2**(5) RBrisland(4) (a bhd) | 1¼ | 11 | 11/1 | 21 | 2 |
| 4082² | **Samara Song (55)** (WGMTurner) **3-9-2**(7) DMcGaffin(17) (lw: prom over 5f) | 1¾ | 12 | 15/2 | 37 | 14 |
| | **River Wye (IRE) (40)** (GHYardley) **4-8-9**(3) DDenby(3) (bhd whn hung rt & c wd over 2f out) | 1¼ | 13 | 33/1 | 20 | 1 |
| 2994¹⁰ | **Impetuous Lady (USA) (48)** (NEBerry) **3-9-2** AEddery(7) (lw: a bhd) | 2 | 14 | 20/1 | 24 | 1 |
| 4206¹⁴ | **Calandrella (43)** (GBBalding) **3-8-11** IonaWands(8) (lw: chsd ldr tl wknd over 2f out) | ¾ | 15 | 20/1 | 17 | — |
| *1809*⁹ | **Duralock Fencer (50)** (PGMurphy) **3-9-1**(3) JDennis(1) (s.s: a bhd) | ¾ | 16 | 33/1 | 23 | — |
| 3966⁶ | **Lovely Morning (60)** (DJGMurraySmith) **3-9-11**(3) PDoe(10) (a bhd: t.o) | dist | 17 | 33/1 | — | — |

(SP 130.5%) **17 Rn**

**1m 44.3** (5.80) CSF £61.77 CT £1,025.93 TOTE £10.30: £1.30 £1.90 £5.80 £6.20 (£38.80) Trio £416.10 OWNER Mr Brian Levy (LAMBOURN) BRED B. A. Levy
WEIGHT FOR AGE 3yo-4lb
**4082 Shouldbegrey** was dropped 2lb after his third last time over course and distance in a seller. (13/2)
**4082 Jilly Beveled** finished a length and a quarter behind the winner last time but, excluding her rider's allowance, was 2lb worse off. (9/1)
**Scimitar**, 17lb lower than when first seen in a handicap, seems to be finding his form. (20/1)
**4107 One In The Eye** was dropping back to a mile. (33/1)
**4263 College Night (IRE)**, tried in a visor two outings ago, only got going late in the day. (9/1)
**4263 Diebiedale** was running off the same mark as when runner-up at Yarmouth. (9/2)
**4082 Samara Song** (15/2: 5/1-8/1)

T/Jkpt: £7,333.50 (0.09 Tckts); £9,399.38 to Newmarket 1/10/96. T/Plpt: £180.50 (88.47 Tckts). T/Qdpt: £8.60 (125.2 Tckts). KH

# 4468-HAMILTON (R-H) (Good to soft, Good patches)
## Monday September 30th

WEATHER: sunny spells WIND: fresh across

## 4481 E.B.F BOTHWELL BRIDGE MEDIAN AUCTION MAIDEN STKS (2-Y.O) (Class F)

2-15 (2-17) **1m 65y** £2,836.00 (£796.00: £388.00) Stalls: High GOING minus 0.01 sec per fur (G)

| | | | Pos | SP | RR | SF |
|---|---|---|---|---|---|---|
| 3264² | **Hindsight (IRE)** (WJHaggas) **2-9-0** KFallon(4) (lw: hld up: hdwy ½-wy: disp ld over 2f out: styd on wl fnl f) | — | 1 | 2/5¹ | 72 | 30 |
| 3809⁵ | **Lightning Rebel** (CWThornton) **2-9-0** DeanMcKeown(1) (hld up & bhd: hdwy 5f out: disp ld over 2f out: nt qckn towards fin) | ¾ | 2 | 16/1 | 71? | 29 |
| 4224⁸ | **Moorbird (IRE)** (MJohnston) **2-9-0** JWeaver(5) (bit bkwd: w ldr: led over 4f out tl over 2f out: one pce) | 7 | 3 | 14/1 | 57 | 15 |
| 3941⁷ | **Coral Island** (JGFitzGerald) **2-9-0** KDarley(3) (cl up tl grad wknd fnl 3f) | 11 | 4 | 7/1² | 36 | — |
| 4310⁴ | **Manileno** (JHetherton) **2-9-0b¹** NKennedy(6) (led tl over 4f out: ev ch tl wknd fnl 2f) | ¾ | 5 | 100/1 | 34 | — |
| 3685⁸ | **Blown-Over** (ACStewart) **2-8-9** SWhitworth(2) (lw: cl up tl wknd fnl 3f) | s.h | 6 | 8/1³ | 29 | — |

(SP 108.6%) **6 Rn**

**1m 51.1** (7.00) CSF £6.77 TOTE £1.40: £1.10 £4.70 (£5.50) OWNER Mr M. Tabor (NEWMARKET) BRED M. Ervine

**3264 Hindsight (IRE)**, who wore a net-muzzle for the first time, was taken to post last and very steadily. He looked particularly fit, but this was never easy and he had to really work to gain the upper hand. (2/5)
**3809 Lightning Rebel** got the best ground in the straight and ran a cracking race. He seems to be improving. (16/1)
**Moorbird (IRE)** still needed this and ran well until blowing up in the last couple of furlongs. (14/1: op 8/1)
**3941 Coral Island** is a decent type, but does not yet look fully wound up and gives the impression time is needed. (7/1: 10/1-6/1)
**4310 Manileno** had blinkers on this time and ran better, but there is still some way to go. (100/1)
**3438 Blown-Over** ran on the worst ground in the straight and dropped tamely away in the last three furlongs. (8/1: op 4/1)

## 4482 LORD HAMILTON OF DALZELL NURSERY H'CAP (0-75) (2-Y.O) (Class E)

2-45 (2-46) **1m 65y** £3,376.80 (£1,022.40: £499.20: £237.60) Stalls: High GOING minus 0.01 sec per fur (G)

| | | | | SP | RR | SF |
|---|---|---|---|---|---|---|
| 4097[4] | **Cajun Sunset (IRE) (56)** (TDEasterby) **2-8-3** KDarley(7) (trckd ldrs: styd on to ld ins fnl f) | — | **1** | 11/2 | 61 | 15 |
| 4223[7] | **Presentiment (56)** (JBerry) **2-8-3** JTate(6) (trckd ldrs: led over 4f out tl ins fnl f: kpt on) | 1¼ | **2** | 10/1 | 59 | 13 |
| 3982[13] | **Leviticus (IRE) (74)** (TPTate) **2-9-7** DeanMcKeown(4) (cl up: rdn over 3f out: sn outpcd: styd on nr fin) | 1¾ | **3** | 5/2[1] | 73 | 27 |
| 4319[3] | **Lord Discord (66)** (TDEasterby) **2-8-13** MBirch(2) (hld up & bhd: hdwy ½-wy: chsd ldrs over 1f out: nt qckn) | 1½ | **4** | 7/2[2] | 62 | 16 |
| 4049[6] | **Hurgill Times (68)** (JWWatts) **2-9-1** GDuffield(3) (lw: prom tl outpcd over 3f out: n.d after) | 9 | **5** | 9/1 | 47 | 1 |
| 4319[2] | **Juicy Ting (66)** (PCHaslam) **2-8-13** JFortune(1) (lw: hld up: effrt & hung lft 4f out: sn btn) | 10 | **6** | 4/1[3] | 26 | — |
| 4347[7] | **Chanson d'Amour (IRE) (54)** (MissLAPerratt) **2-7-10v**[1](5) PFessey(5) (led tl over 4f out: wandered u.p & sn wknd) | 5 | **7** | 40/1 | 4 | — |
| | | | | (SP 107.7%) | | **7 Rn** |

**1m 51.7** (7.60) CSF £46.82 TOTE £4.90: £3.00 £3.00 (£13.30) OWNER Mr P. D. Savill (MALTON) BRED Rathasker Stud
**4097 Cajun Sunset (IRE)** does not do anything quickly, but he does stay and that was all that was needed here. (11/2: 4/1-6/1)
**Presentiment** got the run of the race and the best ground, but just found the winner too determined. (10/1)
**3982 Leviticus (IRE)** is basically short of toe but he certainly stays and, had he been able top make it here, would have done a deal better. (5/2)
**4319 Lord Discord** tried to come from behind which is hard on this track, and ran out of fuel approaching the final furlong. He is still learning. (7/2)
**4049 Hurgill Times** had the blinkers taken off this time and ran poorly. (9/1)
**4319 Juicy Ting** looked particularly well, but spoilt his chances by continually hanging left in the straight, giving his rider no help at all. (4/1)

## 4483 BILL MCHARG MEMORIAL H'CAP (0-70) (4-Y.O+) (Class E)

3-15 (3-16) **1m 4f 17y** £3,486.00 (£1,056.00: £516.00: £246.00) Stalls: High GOING minus 0.01 sec per fur (G)

| | | | | SP | RR | SF |
|---|---|---|---|---|---|---|
| 4426* | **Ayunli (69)** (SCWilliams) **5-9-13** 5x JTate(12) (lw: mde all: styd on strly fnl 3f) | — | **1** | 7/2[1] | 82 | 60 |
| 4345[2] | **Soba Up (70)** (TJEtherington) **6-10-0** MBirch(10) (lw: chsd ldrs: effrt 3f out: styd on: no imp) | 5 | **2** | 16/1 | 76 | 54 |
| 3939[5] | **Eau de Cologne (65)** (CWThornton) **4-9-9** DeanMcKeown(2) (a.p: effrt & c wd 3f out: styd on: no imp) | 3 | **3** | 7/1[2] | 67 | 45 |
| 4073[11] | **Break the Rules (70)** (MrsMReveley) **4-10-0** KDarley(6) (bhd: hdwy on outside fnl 3f: nrst fin) | hd | **4** | 12/1 | 72 | 50 |
| 4315[7] | **Lord Advocate (46)** (DANolan) **8-8-1b**(3) NVarley(3) (bhd: effrt 4f out: swtchd outside: styd on strly nr fin) | 1 | **5** | 33/1 | 47 | 25 |
| 4249[13] | **Swandale Flyer (38)** (NBycroft) **4-7-3**(7) JBramhill(4) (hdwy 5f out: sn in tch: one pce fnl 2f) | 1½ | **6** | 50/1 | 37 | 15 |
| 4249[11] | **Ashover (49)** (TDBarron) **6-8-7** JFortune(9) (chsd ldrs tl wknd fnl 2f) | 1 | **7** | 10/1 | 47 | 25 |
| *3603*[4] | **Giftbox (USA) (57)** (SirMarkPrescott) **4-9-1** GDuffield(1) (cl up tl wknd fnl 3f) | hd | **8** | 16/1 | 55 | 33 |
| 3309[3] | **Pharly Dancer (61)** (WWHaigh) **7-9-0**(5) LNewton(7) (rr div: effrt 4f out: n.d) | s.h | **9** | 9/1 | 58 | 36 |
| 4190[23] | **Elpidos (56)** (MDHammond) **4-8-11**(3) FLynch(14) (lw: nvr trbld ldrs) | 4 | **10** | 15/2[3] | 48 | 26 |
| 4315[4] | **Mentalasanythin (68)** (DHaydnJones) **7-9-12** JWeaver(5) (prom: effrt 3f out: sn wknd) | 2½ | **11** | 7/2[1] | 57 | 35 |
| 4125[6] | **Monument (67)** (JSKing) **4-9-6**(5) DGriffiths(13) (lost tch fnl 4f) | 10 | **12** | 20/1 | 43 | 21 |
| 3346[9] | **Victor Laszlo (40)** (RAllan) **4-7-7**(5)ow2 PFessey(8) (a bhd) | 3 | **13** | 25/1 | 12 | — |
| 972[7] | **Astral Weeks (IRE) (60)** (LLungo) **5-9-4** KFallon(11) (a bhd: t.o) | 25 | **14** | 33/1 | — | — |
| | | | | (SP 123.7%) | | **14 Rn** |

**2m 39.5** (7.50) CSF £54.59 CT £352.51 TOTE £4.70: £2.70 £4.50 £3.50 (£15.50) Trio £76.50 OWNER Mr I. A. Southcott (NEWMARKET) BRED I. A. Southcott
LONG HANDICAP Swandale Flyer 7-8 Victor Laszlo 7-8
**4426* Ayunli**, on a track well suited to front-running, made all in tremendous style and seems to be getting better all the time. (7/2: 9/4-4/1)
**4345 Soba Up** is running well and always kept tabs on the winner, but was never good enough when the pressure was on. (16/1)
**3939 Eau de Cologne** was short of toe at a vital stage and had to race wide in the slower ground, but did well in the end. (7/1)
**4073 Break the Rules** produced his run on the outside of the field in the slower ground, so this was not a bad effort. (12/1)
**3649 Lord Advocate**, normally up with the pace, had to come from behind and really finished well, but it was always too late. He is slipping back down to a useful mark. (33/1)
**3677 Swandale Flyer** has run reasonable races at various distances, but has yet to seriously trouble the Judge. (50/1)
**3968 Ashover** (10/1: op 16/1)

## 4484 SHAWFIELD CLAIMING STKS (3-Y.O+) (Class E)

3-45 (3-48) **1m 3f 16y** £2,954.70 (£894.60: £436.80: £207.90) Stalls: High GOING minus 0.01 sec per fur (G)

| | | | | SP | RR | SF |
|---|---|---|---|---|---|---|
| 4176[8] | **Manful (64)** (CWCElsey) **4-9-8b** NKennedy(4) (mde all: styd on wl fnl 3f) | — | **1** | 7/2[2] | 75 | 54 |
| 4326[6] | **Askern (70)** (DHaydnJones) **5-9-8** JWeaver(8) (trckd wnr: chal 5f out: rdn 3f out: one pce) | 5 | **2** | 13/8[1] | 68 | 47 |
| 4317[2] | **Arc of The Diver (IRE) (49)** (JBerry) **3-8-9** KDarley(1) (lw: a.p: effrt 4f out: nt pce to chal) | 1¾ | **3** | 8/1 | 59 | 31 |
| 4296[4] | **North Ardar (60)** (DNicholls) **6-9-2** AlexGreaves(2) (hld up: effrt 4f out: sn rdn: nvr rchd ldrs) | 1½ | **4** | 9/2[3] | 57 | 36 |
| 4344[8] | **Latvian (62)** (RAllan) **9-8-12v** KFallon(5) (bhd: brought wd & effrt over 4f out: n.d) | 12 | **5** | 7/1 | 36 | 15 |
| 4345[7] | **Moofaji (39)** (FWatson) **5-8-12** JFortune(3) (lw: chsd ldrs: outpcd 4f out: sn wknd) | 2 | **6** | 20/1 | 33 | 12 |
| *281*[7] | **Bridlington Bay (35)** (JLEyre) **3-7-13**(7)ow1 SBuckley(10) (b.nr fore: plld hrd: prom tl wknd over 4f out) | 10 | **7** | 66/1 | 19 | — |
| *4334*[12] | **De-Veers Currie (IRE) (53)** (MartinTodhunter) **4-8-11** DMcKeown(7) (effrt 5f out: sn btn) | 15 | **8** | 20/1 | — | — |
| *1488*[8] | **Walk In The Wild** (DANolan) **4-8-8**(3) NVarley(6) (a bhd: t.o) | 26 | **9** | 200/1 | — | — |
| 2731[11] | **Midas Man** (DANolan) **5-8-7**(5) PFessey(9) (a bhd: t.o) | 21 | **10** | 400/1 | — | — |
| | | | | (SP 113.9%) | | **10 Rn** |

**2m 26.5** (7.10) CSF £8.93 TOTE £5.70: £1.30 £1.80 £1.50 (£7.70) Trio £18.60 OWNER Mr C. D. Barber-Lomax (MALTON) BRED John Rose
WEIGHT FOR AGE 3yo-7lb
North Ardar clmd TWall £7,000
**2296 Manful** went off in front, giving him the best ground, and he was always too strong for the runner-up. (7/2)
**4326 Askern** sat on the winner's heels but, when it came down to a fight in the last three furlongs, he was found wanting on this occasion. (13/8)

**4317 Arc of The Diver (IRE)** looked particularly fit and ran reasonably, but was well short of speed when the pressure was on in the last half-mile. (8/1)
**4089* North Ardar** failed to impress on looks and ran moderately. He was later claimed for the third time this season. (9/2)
**3865* Latvian** was pulled wide for an effort early in the straight, but wanted nothing to do with it. (7/1)
**4345 Moofaji** had plenty to do at the weights and was left behind in the last half-mile. (20/1)

## 4485 TENNENT'S LAGER CONDITIONS STKS (3-Y.O+) (Class C)

4-15 (4-16) **6f 5y** £5,087.20 (£1,904.80: £932.40: £402.00: £181.00: £92.60) Stalls: Low GOING minus 0.01 sec per fur (G)

| | | | | SP | RR | SF |
|---|---|---|---|---|---|---|
| | **Midnight Blue** (WJarvis) **3-8-7** JWeaver(8) (racd centre: cl up: led over 2f out: styd on wl) | — | 1 | 15/2 | 89+ | 50 |
| 4185[5] | **King of Peru (101)** (APJarvis) **3-8-12** RCochrane(6) (racd stands' side: trckd ldrs: effrt over 2f out: hung rt & styd on one pce) | 1½ | 2 | 7/1[3] | 90 | 51 |
| 3875[5] | **King of The East (IRE) (98)** (MRStoute) **3-9-4** KFallon(9) (lw: racd centre: a chsng ldrs: kpt on one pce fnl f) | hd | 3 | 4/1[2] | 96 | 57 |
| 4304[5] | **Kunucu (IRE) (90)** (TDBarron) **3-8-7** KDarley(10) (racd towards far side: cl up: rdn 2f out: nt qckn) | 1½ | 4 | 14/1 | 81 | 42 |
| 4453[10] | **Naissant (70)** (RMMcKellar) **3-8-0**(7) JMcAuley(4) (bhd stands' side tl styd on strly fnl f) | nk | 5 | 100/1 | 80 | 41 |
| 4101[3] | **Espartero (IRE) (102)** (SirMarkPrescott) **4-9-0b**[1] GDuffield(7) (lw: hld up centre: effrt over 2f out: no imp) | 5 | 6 | 7/2[1] | 72 | 35 |
| 4314[22] | **Selhurstpark Flyer (IRE) (93)** (JBerry) **5-9-1**(5) PRoberts(2) (b: led stands' side: hung rt: hdd over 2f out: sn wknd) | s.h | 7 | 10/1 | 78 | 41 |
| 3822[3] | **Montendre (103)** (RJHodges) **9-9-0** MBirch(5) (lw: in tch stands' side: rdn ½-wy: sn btn) | 1¼ | 8 | 4/1[2] | 68 | 31 |
| 4185[8] | **Dovebrace (92)** (ABailey) **3-8-12v**[1] JFortune(1) (racd stands' side: prom 4f) | 4 | 9 | 20/1 | 58 | 19 |
| 3875[8] | **Princely Hush (IRE) (100)** (MBell) **4-9-0** MFenton(11) (racd towards far side: prom tl wknd appr fnl f) | 1½ | 10 | 7/1[3] | 54 | 17 |

(SP 120.5%) **10 Rn**

**1m 12.8** (2.80) CSF £55.83 TOTE £5.30: £1.60 £2.80 £1.60 (£19.60) Trio £41.40 OWNER Sussex-Essex Racing (NEWMARKET) BRED P. V. And Mrs J. P. Jackson
WEIGHT FOR AGE 3yo-2lb
**Midnight Blue**, having only her second ever race and her first race of the season, has had problems with a chipped knee, but obviously relishes easier ground. Scoring really well, she looks likely to benefit from it. (15/2: 5/1-8/1)
**4185 King of Peru** seems to like a bit of cut in the ground and ran a better race, but was inclined to hang under pressure and was never quite good enough. (7/1)
**3875 King of The East (IRE)** appreciates this easier ground and ran particularly well. He should pick up a race this back-end. (4/1)
**4304 Kunucu (IRE)** had a good draw, but did not make full use of it. This trip may have been stretching things a bit. (14/1: 12/1-20/1)
**3867* Naissant** ran a cracker, coming from off the pace to finish best of all. She should not be written off yet. (100/1)
**4101 Espartero (IRE)**, in blinkers for the first time, pulled pretty hard early on and then failed to come up with the goods when asked the question. (7/2)
**4122* Selhurstpark Flyer (IRE)** was always tending to hang right and did not give his true running. (10/1: op 6/1)
**3822 Montendre** was never going at any stage. (4/1)

## 4486 TENNENT'S 80/- APPRENTICE H'CAP (0-60) (3-Y.O+) (Class F)

4-45 (4-48) **6f 5y** £2,725.00 (£835.00: £415.00: £205.00) Stalls: High GOING minus 0.01 sec per fur (G)

| | | | | SP | RR | SF |
|---|---|---|---|---|---|---|
| 3624[12] | **Bataleur (55)** (MissJBower) **3-9-8** CScudder(16) (lw: chsd ldrs far side: led 2f out: hung lft: jst hld on) | — | 1 | 20/1 | 62 | 42 |
| *3953*[5] | **Desert Invader (IRE) (49)** (DWChapman) **5-9-4** LJames(10) (cl up centre: chal & hung lft over 1f out: styd on wl towards fin) | s.h | 2 | 16/1 | 56 | 38 |
| 3995[27] | **Magic Lake (44)** (EJAlston) **3-8-11v**[1] JFowle(6) (hld up centre: hdwy whn hmpd over 1f out: styd on nr fin) | 2 | 3 | 10/1[3] | 46 | 26 |
| 3937[4] | **Disco Boy (42)** (PDEvans) **6-8-8**(3) ABond(2) (chsd ldrs stands' side: nt qckn fnl f) | 1 | 4 | 14/1 | 41 | 23 |
| 4246[21] | **Leading Princess (IRE) (50)** (MissLAPerratt) **5-9-5b** PClarke(9) (led 4f: hmpd over 1f out: styd on one pce) | 1½ | 5 | 20/1 | 45 | 27 |
| 4460[10] | **Miss Aragon (43)** (MissLCSiddall) **8-8-9**(3) TSiddall(5) (hdwy centre over 2f out: hmpd over 1f out: styd on wl towards fin) | ½ | 6 | 20/1 | 37 | 19 |
| 3306[14] | **Blow Dry (IRE) (43)** (MartynWane) **6-8-12** SBuckley(7) (racd centre: outpcd & bhd ½-wy: swtchd stands' side & styd on towards fin) | s.h | 7 | 16/1 | 37 | 19 |
| 4430[21] | **Another Nightmare (IRE) (55)** (RMMcKellar) **4-9-7**(3) JMcAuley(4) (chsd ldrs centre tl wknd fnl 2f) | 4 | 8 | 14/1 | 38 | 20 |
| 3995[7] | **Lunch Party (56)** (DNicholls) **4-9-11** TFinn(13) (lw: dwlt & hmpd s: hdwy ½-wy: nvr able to chal) | ½ | 9 | 7/1[2] | 38 | 20 |
| 3957[2] | **Henry the Hawk (50)** (MDods) **5-9-5** PFredericks(1) (b: swtg: racd stands' side: a outpcd) | hd | 10 | 10/1[3] | 31 | 13 |
| 4473[5] | **Craigie Boy (50)** (NBycroft) **6-9-5v** AMcCarthy(8) (lw: in tch: hdwy far side 2f out: sn rdn & btn) | 1¼ | 11 | 5/1[1] | 28 | 10 |
| 4473[10] | **Hoh Majestic (IRE) (58)** (MartynWane) **3-9-11v** CLowther(17) (spd far side: outpcd ½-wy: no imp after) | ½ | 12 | 10/1[3] | 35 | 15 |
| 3694[6] | **Dil Dil (43)** (MrsJRRamsden) **3-8-7**(3) ClaireWest(3) (lw: racd stands' side: a outpcd) | 1 | 13 | 20/1 | 17 | — |
| 4460[17] | **Invigilate (48)** (MartynWane) **7-8-9**(8) GWright(11) (chsd ldrs far side tl wknd fnl 2f) | ½ | 14 | 33/1 | 21 | 3 |
| 4473[12] | **Sunday Mail Too (IRE) (45)** (MissLAPerratt) **4-8-9**(5) NPollard(14) (lw: sn drvn along far side: n.d) | hd | 15 | 16/1 | 17 | — |
| 4045[9] | **Brookhead Lady (41)** (TWall) **5-8-5**(5) SCrawford(18) (b: spd far side 4f: sn btn) | 3 | 16 | 7/1[2] | 5 | — |
| 3959[7] | **Butterwick Belle (IRE) (57)** (RAFahey) **3-9-5**(5)ow1 KPrendergast(15) (lw: bhd far side: hdwy ½-wy: wknd over 1f out) | 3½ | 17 | 20/1 | 12 | — |
| 4205[16] | **Hamilton Gold (47)** (MGMeagher) **3-8-11**(3) RStudholme(12) (dwlt: effrt far side ½-wy: sn btn) | 2 | 18 | 10/1[3] | — | — |

(SP 135.8%) **18 Rn**

**1m 14.4** (4.40) CSF £297.30 CT £3,194.88 TOTE £38.30: £4.40 £4.40 £5.10 £4.30 (£237.80) Trio £921.40; £1,038.26 to Newmarket 1/10/96 OWNER Mr Michael Worth (SOUTHWELL) BRED M. J. Worth
WEIGHT FOR AGE 3yo-2lb
**3624 Bataleur** did his best to throw this away by hanging badly left when in front, and the line came just in time. (20/1)
**3953 Desert Invader (IRE)** ran a super race and, despite hanging left when ridden, stayed on to only just to fail. (16/1)
**3881 Magic Lake**, an in-and-out performer, ran well over this shorter trip and would seem to be in good heart just now. (10/1: op 20/1)
**3937 Disco Boy** would probably have taken some beating with a favourable draw. (14/1: 10/1-16/1)
**3883 Leading Princess (IRE)** showed plenty of speed and, after being hampered over a furlong out, did struggle on. (20/1)
**1786 Miss Aragon** showed her first signs of form for a while and looks one to keep an eye on. (20/1)
**2391 Blow Dry (IRE)** is certainly well handicapped and this was not a bad effort. (16/1)
**3995 Lunch Party** got messed about at the start and, in the circumstances, ran well. (7/1)
**3345 Brookhead Lady** (7/1: op 14/1)
**3310 Hamilton Gold** (10/1: 7/1-12/1)

T/Plpt: £443.30 (30.98 Tckts). T/Qdpt: £116.30 (11.49 Tckts). AA

# 3788-NEWMARKET (R-H) (Good)
## Tuesday October 1st
WEATHER: sunny periods WIND: slt half bhd

## 4487 NGK SPARK PLUGS RATED STKS H'CAP (0-100) (3-Y.O+) (Class B)
1-30 (1-32) **1m 4f (Rowley)** £8,067.50 (£2,982.50: £1,428.75: £581.25: £228.13: £86.87) Stalls: High GOING minus 0.49 sec (F)

| | | | | SP | RR | SF |
|---|---|---|---|---|---|---|
| 4121* | **Dear Life (USA) (90)** (MrsJCecil) **3-8-9**(5) MartinDwyer(6) (lw: a.p: led over 2f out: r.o wl) | — | **1** | 5/1[2] | 101 | 61 |
| 4067[4] | **Fitzwilliam (USA) (85)** (IABalding) **3-8-9** TQuinn(9) (lw: trckd ldrs: rdn over 4f out: r.o wl ins fnl f) | 1¼ | **2** | 13/2 | 94 | 54 |
| 4055[7] | **Ionio (USA) (90)** (CEBrittain) **5-9-7** MRoberts(4) (led tl over 2f out: sn rdn: one pce fnl f) | 3½ | **3** | 16/1 | 95 | 62 |
| 4114[5] | **Beyond Doubt (82)** (LordHuntingdon) **4-8-13** DHarrison(7) (hld up: hdwy 3f out: outpcd over 1f out: styd on fnl f) | hd | **4** | 11/2[3] | 87 | 54 |
| 4177[5] | **Maiden Castle (94)** (JHMGosden) **3-9-4** LDettori(2) (b: lw: stdd s: hdwy 4f out: no imp fnl 2f) | 9 | **5** | 7/1 | 87 | 47 |
| 4176* | **Spillo (93)** (LMCumani) **3-9-3** KDarley(1) (lw: hld up: pushed along 5f out: nvr nr to chal) | 3 | **6** | 4/1[1] | 82 | 42 |
| 844[10] | **Vaugrenier (IRE) (76)** (RHannon) **4-8-7** DaneO'Neill(8) (bit bkwd: nvr plcd to chal) | 3½ | **7** | 25/1 | 60 | 27 |
| 4099* | **Polar Champ (77)** (SPCWoods) **3-8-1v** DBiggs(5) (chsd ldr: ev ch tl wknd over 3f out) | 1½ | **8** | 12/1 | 59 | 19 |
| 4178[6] | **Smart Play (USA) (95)** (MrsJCecil) **3-9-5** JReid(3) (hld up: effrt over 4f out: no imp: t.o) | 13 | **9** | 5/1[2] | 60 | 20 |

(SP 112.0%) **9 Rn**

**2m 30.14** (-0.36) CSF £33.26 CT £432.67 TOTE £6.00: £1.80 £1.50 £2.10 (£15.60) Trio £57.80 OWNER Lady Howard de Walden (NEWMARKET) BRED Lord Howard de Walden

WEIGHT FOR AGE 3yo-7lb

**4121* Dear Life (USA)** has really found her true form now and succeeded in this high-class event almost as easily as she did at Epsom. (5/1)

**4067 Fitzwilliam (USA)**, struggling with the pace some way out, got better the further they went, but the winner had got away and he was unable to reel her in. (13/2)

**2534 Ionio (USA)** adopted new tactics this time and it was only the concession of so much weight that was holding him inside the distance. (16/1)

**3073 Beyond Doubt** looked to be getting on terms until she failed to handle the run into the Dip. She stayed on again up the final climb, but the damage had been done. (11/2: 4/1-6/1)

**4177 Maiden Castle**, a very attractive colt taking on handicappers for the first time, again failed to go through with the effort and he could be taking after his dam, who proved most disappointing as a three-year-old. (7/1)

**4176* Spillo**, bustled along soon after halfway, failed to pick up at all and he is probably best playing away from home. (4/1)

## 4488 TATTERSALLS HOUGHTON SALES CONDITIONS STKS (2-Y.O) (Class B)
2-05 (2-12) **7f (Rowley)** £23,909.90 (£8,914.10: £4,332.05: £1,832.75: £791.38: £374.82) Stalls: High GOING minus 0.49 sec per fur (F)

| | | | | SP | RR | SF |
|---|---|---|---|---|---|---|
| 4029a[2] | **Papua (100)** (IABalding) **2-9-0** JReid(8) (lw: hld up in tch: effrt over 1f out: hrd rdn to ld cl home) | — | **1** | 10/1 | 96 | 53 |
| 4050[3] | **Mukaddar (USA)** (CJBenstead) **2-9-0** RHills(14) (a.p: led over 2f out: hrd rdn & hdd fnl strides) | hd | **2** | 14/1 | 96 | 53 |
| 2504[4] | **Granny's Pet (100)** (PFICole) **2-9-0** TQuinn(7) (bit bkwd: hld up pllng hrd: hdwy over 1f out: fin strly) | nk | **3** | 25/1 | 95 | 52 |
| 3690* | **Abou Zouz (USA) (100)** (DRLoder) **2-9-0** LDettori(21) (h.d.w: hld up in tch: sltly outpcd & n.m.r wl over 1f out: styd on u.p) | nk | **4** | 7/4[1] | 94 | 51 |
| 4056[2] | **Sandstone (IRE)** (JLDunlop) **2-9-0** MJKinane(18) (a.p: rdn & n.m.r appr fnl f: kpt on u.p) | ¾ | **5** | 7/1[3] | 93 | 50 |
| 4061* | **Blane Water (USA)** (JRFanshawe) **2-8-9** DHarrison(10) (chsd ldrs: rdn 2f out: kpt on ins fnl f) | s.h | **6** | 10/1 | 88 | 45 |
| 4200* | **Home Alone** (JHMGosden) **2-9-0** RHavlin(13) (b.hind: led over 4f: rdn & edgd rt ent fnl f: one pce) | 1¾ | **7** | 33/1 | 89 | 46 |
| 3566a[4] | **Boojum** (BWHills) **2-8-9** MHills(6) (lw: s.i.s: gd hdwy appr fnl f: fin wl) | ½ | **8** | 33/1 | 82 | 39 |
| 2878[3] | **Wolf Mountain** (RHannon) **2-9-0** RHughes(4) (plld hrd: hld up: effrt over 2f out: one pce fnl f) | nk | **9** | 10/1 | 87 | 44 |
| 3706[2] | **Swiss Law** (JGFitzGerald) **2-9-0** KFallon(22) (lw: in tch: hdwy 3f out: no imp appr fnl f) | 1¾ | **10** | 6/1[2] | 83 | 40 |
| 4023a[4] | **Groom's Gordon (FR) (100)** (JLDunlop) **2-9-0** PatEddery(17) (chsd ldrs: rdn 3f out: sn lost tch) | ½ | **11** | 12/1 | 82 | 39 |
| 4234[4] | **Manikato (USA) (70)** (DJSCosgrove) **2-9-0** MRimmer(23) (hdwy 4f out: one pce fnl 2f) | 1 | **12** | 100/1 | 79 | 36 |
| 3668[6] | **Get The Point** (RHollinshead) **2-9-0** WRyan(11) (a bhd & outpcd) | ¾ | **13** | 100/1 | 78 | 35 |
| 4242[5] | **Noble Investment** (JMPEustace) **2-9-0** RCochrane(2) (hdwy ½-wy: ev ch over 2f out: sn rdn & btn) | 1½ | **14** | 66/1 | 74 | 31 |
| 4049[13] | **Zugudi (80)** (BHanbury) **2-9-0** JStack(19) (prom: rdn & ev ch 3f out: sn wknd) | nk | **15** | 100/1 | 74 | 31 |
| 4253* | **Bandore (IRE)** (DRLoder) **2-9-0** WRSwinburn(12) (prom centre: eased whn btn appr fnl f) | nk | **16** | 20/1 | 73 | 30 |
| 4233[5] | **Shalaal (USA)** (EALDunlop) **2-9-0** SWhitworth(9) (rdn 3f out: a bhd) | hd | **17** | 50/1 | 73 | 30 |
| 4133[5] | **Raindancing (IRE) (100)** (RHannon) **2-8-9** DaneO'Neill(3) (b: in tch to ½-wy) | 1¼ | **18** | 20/1 | 65 | 22 |
| 3835[4] | **Rich In Love (IRE) (99)** (CACyzer) **2-8-9** MRoberts(20) (sn in rr & drvn along: no imp) | nk | **19** | 25/1 | 64 | 21 |
| 3835[20] | **Lycility (IRE) (90)** (CEBrittain) **2-8-9** BDoyle(5) (chsd ldrs over 4f) | nk | **20** | 40/1 | 63 | 20 |
| | **Telloff** (MAJarvis) **2-8-9** GDuffield(1) (lt-f: neat: a bhd & outpcd) | 1 | **21** | 66/1 | 61 | 18 |
| 4211[5] | **French Mist** (CEBrittain) **2-8-9** KDarley(16) (prom over 4f) | ½ | **22** | 100/1 | 60 | 17 |
| | **Midnight Shift (IRE)** (RGuest) **2-8-9** PBloomfield(15) (cmpt: bit bkwd: dwlt: a bhd: t.o) | 4 | **23** | 66/1 | 51 | 8 |

(SP 140.7%) **23 Rn**

**1m 24.87** (0.37) CSF £142.09 TOTE £10.70: £2.60 £5.80 £5.60 (£90.00) Trio £1,536.00 OWNER Robert & Elizabeth Hitchins (KINGSCLERE) BRED Exors of the late D. Macrae

**4029a Papua**, narrowly beaten in France on his previous outing, was awash with sweat in the preliminaries. Travelling well just behind the leaders, he stuck his neck out and just prevailed in an all-out duel to the line. (10/1)

**4050 Mukaddar (USA)** moved through smoothly to show in front and always looked to be holding on, but the hill proved just too much and he was forced to give best right on the line. (14/1)

**2504 Granny's Pet**, fresh and well after almost three months on the sidelines, got this extended trip extremely well. With this outing under his belt, he can only go on to better things. (25/1)

**3690* Abou Zouz (USA)**, tightened up on the far rail and tapped for toe running into the Dip, rallied gamely on the hill. Losses will soon be recovered. (7/4)

**4056 Sandstone (IRE)**, always waiting to pounce, did not get a lot of room in which to manoeuvre in the Dip and, though he battled on once free, he lacked the pace to deliver a challenge. (7/1)

**4061* Blane Water (USA)** ran well for one lacking experience and she certainly has the right commitment. (10/1)

**4200* Home Alone**, walked to the start, soon pulled his way into the lead and, though he had been collared, would have finished closer had he not drifted towards the far rail up the hill. (33/1)

**3566a Boojum** never fully recovered from a sluggish start, but she was eating up ground at the finish and is a filly to keep in mind. (33/1)

## 4489 SHADWELL STUD SERIES APPRENTICE H'CAP (Final) (0-85) (3-Y.O+) (Class E)

2-35 (2-42) **1m 2f (Rowley)** £7,295.00 (£2,210.00: £1,080.00: £515.00) Stalls: High GOING minus 0.49 sec per fur (F)

| | | Dist | Pos | SP | RR | SF |
|---|---|---|---|---|---|---|
| 3766[2] | **Step Aloft (76)** (LordHuntingdon) **4-9-6** AimeeCook(6) (a.p: led over 3f out: clr over 1f out: r.o) | — | **1** | 12/1 | 87 | 69 |
| 4059[3] | **Bubble Wings (FR) (66)** (SPCWoods) **4-8-10** MHenry(4) (hld up & bhd: hdwy 2f out: r.o wl fnl f) | 2½ | **2** | 8/1[3] | 73 | 55 |
| 4068* | **Harvey White (IRE) (62)** (JPearce) **4-8-3**(3) PDoe(11) (swtg: a.p: chsd wnr 3f out tl hrd rdn & one pce ins fnl f) | 1 | **3** | 7/1[2] | 67 | 49 |
| 4193[8] | **Trick (IRE) (73)** (LMCumani) **3-8-9**(3) RFfrench(10) (hld up: hdwy wl over 1f out: fin wl) | 2 | **4** | 7/1[2] | 75 | 52 |
| 4307* | **Double Echo (IRE) (52)** (JDBethell) **8-7-10** PFessey(5) (hdwy 4f out: one pce fnl 2f) | 1¼ | **5** | 20/1 | 52 | 34 |
| 3470[2] | **Vola Via (USA) (82)** (IABalding) **3-9-7** MartinDwyer(7) (hld up: hdwy 3f out: sn rdn: wknd over 1f out) | hd | **6** | 10/1 | 82 | 59 |
| 3856[3] | **Cheerful Aspect (IRE) (75)** (EALDunlop) **3-9-0** PRoberts(2) (chsd ldrs: effrt 3f out: sn rdn & outpcd) | 1¼ | **7** | 12/1 | 73 | 50 |
| 4257[3] | **Printers Quill (52)** (MajorDNChappell) **4-7-10** IonaWands(12) (nvr nr ldrs) | 1¾ | **8** | 12/1 | 47 | 29 |
| 4184[7] | **Menas Gold (77)** (SDow) **4-9-7** ADaly(14) (bhd: effrt over 2f out: no real imp) | 3½ | **9** | 9/1 | 67 | 49 |
| *4078*[2] | **Super High (55)** (PHowling) **4-7-13b** MBaird(8) (disp ld 7f: sn wknd) | s.h | **10** | 12/1 | 45 | 27 |
| 4238[3] | **Opulent (73)** (CADwyer) **5-9-3** JoHunnam(13) (rdn along 4f out: no imp) | ½ | **11** | 6/1[1] | 62 | 44 |
| 4257* | **White Plains (IRE) (75)** (MBell) **3-9-0** GFaulkner(3) (trckd ldrs tl wknd qckly over 2f out: t.o) | 11 | **12** | 6/1[1] | 46 | 23 |
| 4177[6] | **Tarte Aux Pommes (USA) (80)** (CEBrittain) **4-9-5**(5) JGotobed(9) (dwlt: a in rr: t.o) | 8 | **13** | 33/1 | 38 | 20 |
| 1047* | **Zidac (75)** (PJMakin) **4-9-5** RHavlin(1) (mde most tl hdd & wknd 3f out: t.o) | 1 | **14** | 12/1 | 32 | 14 |
| | | | | (SP 129.9%) | **14 Rn** | |

**2m 3.01** (-0.59) CSF £103.27 CT £682.84 TOTE £10.90: £3.10 £2.40 £2.90 (£41.00) Trio £230.70 OWNER The Queen (WEST ILSLEY) BRED The Queen

LONG HANDICAP Double Echo (IRE) 7-9 Printers Quill 7-9

WEIGHT FOR AGE 3yo-5lb

**3766 Step Aloft** put her best foot forward for her female apprentice and won with a ton in hand. (12/1)

**4059 Bubble Wings (FR)** performed with credit on this first attempt at the trip, but she had been given plenty to do and is capable of better. (8/1)

**4068* Harvey White (IRE)** tried hard to keep tabs on the winner, but she was always galloping all over him, and he called enough on reaching the hill. (7/1)

**3704* Trick (IRE)**, covered up in the pack, only got going late on and, by then, the race was over. (7/1)

**4307* Double Echo (IRE)** finds this trip inadequate even on this track, and he was never within striking range of the winner. (20/1)

**3470 Vola Via (USA)** made progress in the centre of the track three furlongs out, but he was fighting a lost cause when swishing his tail under pressure below the distance, and appears to have a mind of his own. (10/1)

**4184 Menas Gold** (9/1: op 6/1)

**4238 Opulent** failed to fire on this second outing in this country, and he showed at Yarmouth that he is better than this. (6/1)

**4257* White Plains (IRE)** has enjoyed a successful season, but he was a spent force passing the Bushes and weakened to finish tailed off. He may well have had enough for now. (6/1)

## 4490 E.B.F. JERSEY LILY NURSERY H'CAP (2-Y.O F) (Class C)

3-10 (3-13) **7f (Rowley)** £19,087.50 (£5,700.00: £2,725.00: £1,237.50) Stalls: High GOING minus 0.49 sec per fur (F)

| | | Dist | Pos | SP | RR | SF |
|---|---|---|---|---|---|---|
| 4113* | **Nightbird (IRE) (89)** (BWHills) **2-9-7** MHills(9) (racd centre: hld up in tch: hdwy to ld appr fnl f: r.o wl) | — | **1** | 5/1[1] | 95 | 56 |
| *4335*[2] | **Tinkerbell (74)** (WRMuir) **2-8-6v** JReid(5) (lw: led over 2f: led over 2f out tl appr fnl f: rallied cl home) | ½ | **2** | 33/1 | 79 | 40 |
| 4208* | **Telemania (IRE) (83)** (WJHaggas) **2-9-1** KFallon(6) (hld up: hdwy over 2f out: sn rdn: r.o wl ins fnl f) | 1¾ | **3** | 5/1[1] | 84 | 45 |
| 3982* | **Lady Godiva (70)** (MJPolglase) **2-8-2** NCarlisle(2) (a.p stands' side: ev ch over 2f out: one pce fnl f) | hd | **4** | 14/1 | 71 | 32 |
| 4222* | **Madame Chinnery (77)** (JMPEustace) **2-8-9** RCochrane(8) (hld up: rdn ½-wy: r o wl fnl f) | nk | **5** | 10/1[3] | 77 | 38 |
| 4113[6] | **Song Mist (IRE) (78)** (PFICole) **2-8-10** TQuinn(12) (lw: prom far side: ev ch 2f out: wknd fnl f) | 1¼ | **6** | 12/1 | 75 | 36 |
| 4113[15] | **Gee Bee Dream (76)** (APJarvis) **2-8-8** MJKinane(4) (in tch: rdn over 2f out: kpt on ins fnl f) | ¾ | **7** | 12/1 | 71 | 32 |
| 4113[2] | **Naked Poser (IRE) (87)** (RHannon) **2-9-5** PatEddery(3) (lw: w ldrs centre: ev ch over 2f out: sn rdn: btn over 1f out) | hd | **8** | 15/2[2] | 82 | 43 |
| 4072* | **Rose Carnival (79)** (DRLoder) **2-8-11** LDettori(1) (chsd ldrs centre: bhd fnl 2f) | nk | **9** | 5/1[1] | 74 | 35 |
| 4113[7] | **Catechism (USA) (85)** (JHMGosden) **2-9-3** GHind(10) (stdd s: plld hrd: led over 4f tl over 2f out: sn wknd) | 1¼ | **10** | 11/1 | 77 | 38 |
| 3208[6] | **Briska (IRE) (79)** (RHannon) **2-8-11** DaneO'Neill(13) (pushed along ½-wy: a bhd) | nk | **11** | 25/1 | 70 | 31 |
| 4084[5] | **Hen Harrier (84)** (JLDunlop) **2-9-2** KDarley(14) (chsd ldrs far side: rdn & btn over 2f out) | s.h | **12** | 14/1 | 75 | 36 |
| 4311* | **Blues Queen (85)** (MRChannon) **2-9-3** JCarroll(7) (s.s: a in rr) | hd | **13** | 12/1 | 76 | 37 |
| 4241[2] | **Our Way (73)** (CEBrittain) **2-8-5** BDoyle(11) (racd far side: lost tch ½-wy: t.o) | 8 | **14** | 16/1 | 45 | 6 |
| | | | | (SP 128.3%) | **14 Rn** | |

**1m 25.15** (0.65) CSF £139.05 CT £817.58 TOTE £6.20: £2.60 £5.50 £2.70 (£111.40) Trio £363.90 OWNER Mr S. P. Tindall (LAMBOURN) BRED S. Tindall and Stowell Hill Ltd

**4113* Nightbird (IRE)**, a useful filly conceding weight all round, kicked for home in the Dip and, from then on, there was only going to be one winner. (5/1)

**4335 Tinkerbell** is obviously far superior to selling company, and courage alone will always win her her share of prizes. (33/1)

**4208* Telemania (IRE)** continued to progress with another pleasing performance. She will soon get back to winning ways. (5/1)

**3982* Lady Godiva**, in the action all the way, was really into her stride on meeting the rising ground, but she could not peg back the principals. She does stay well and there will be some back-end nurseries made to measure. (14/1)

**4222* Madame Chinnery**, shaken up to take hold of her bit over three furlongs out, did keep staying on, but the leaders were not stopping and she was unable to land a blow. (10/1)

**4113 Song Mist (IRE)**, driven along to hold every chance passing the Bushes, found her stride shortening up the hill. It would seem this trip is just beyond her. (12/1)

**4113 Naked Poser (IRE)** had her chance to gain revenge on the winner, but she was labouring running into the Dip and her chance had gone. (15/2)

**4072* Rose Carnival** found this step up in class too much for her and she was beating a retreat inside the last quarter-mile. (5/1)

## 4491 SHADWELL STUD CHEVELEY PARK STKS (Gp 1) (2-Y.O F) (Class A)

3-45 (3-46) **6f (Rowley)** £69,178.50 (£25,681.50: £12,390.75: £5,141.25: £2,120.63: £912.37) Stalls: High GOING minus 0.49 sec per fur (F)

| | | Dist | Pos | SP | RR | SF |
|---|---|---|---|---|---|---|
| 4285a* | **Pas De Reponse (USA)** (MmeCHead,France) **2-8-11** FHead(3) (w'like: unf: a.p: led over 1f out: shkn up & r.o strly) | — | **1** | 7/1[3] | 105 | 63 |

| | | | | SP | RR | SF |
|---|---|---|---|---|---|---|
| 3068[2] | **Moonlight Paradise (USA) (100)** (SbinSuroor) **2-8-11** LDettori(6) (lt-f: hld up in tch: effrt over 1f out: rdn & r.o wl fnl f) | 1 | **2** | 11/2[2] | 102 | 60 |
| 3561a[4] | **Ocean Ridge (USA)** (PWChapple-Hyam) **2-8-11** JReid(9) (lw: led tl over 1f out: rdn & kpt on fnl f) | 1 | **3** | 12/1 | 100 | 58 |
| 2582* | **Dazzle** (MRStoute) **2-8-11** KFallon(4) (h.d.w: hld up & bhd: plld out over 2f out: rdn & no ex ins fnl f) | ½ | **4** | 4/9[1] | 98 | 56 |
| 4065* | **Arethusa (100)** (RHannon) **2-8-11** DaneO'Neill(2) (b: hld up in rr: hdwy over 1f out: nvr nrr) | 2½ | **5** | 16/1 | 92 | 50 |
| 4299* | **Queen Sceptre (IRE) (98)** (BWHills) **2-8-11** PatEddery(7) (lw: w ldrs tl outpcd over 1f out: sn btn) | 2½ | **6** | 16/1 | 85 | 43 |
| 4247[3] | **Snap Crackle Pop (IRE) (94)** (RFJohnsonHoughton) **2-8-11** AMcGlone(5) (prom 4f: sn rdn & outpcd) | 2 | **7** | 50/1 | 80 | 38 |
| 3990[2] | **Carati (89)** (RBoss) **2-8-11** GDuffield(8) (chsd ldrs: rdn over 2f out: sn outpcd) | hd | **8** | 50/1 | 79 | 37 |

(SP 120.5%) **8 Rn**

**1m 11.16** (-0.64) CSF £43.36 TOTE £6.50: £1.20 £1.30 £2.20 (£9.60) Trio £29.30 OWNER Wertheimer et Frere (CHANTILLY) BRED Wertheimer & Frere

**4285a* Pas De Reponse (USA)** is not a lot to look at, but looks are only skin-deep and she reproduced her top-class French form to hold off the field readily. Her price for the 1000 Guineas has been cut drastically, but there must be a doubt about her staying a mile. (7/1: 9/2-15/2)

**3068 Moonlight Paradise (USA)** ran her best race yet and the way she battled on nearing the finish would suggest she must be one of our top contenders when the prizes for the fillies' Classics are distributed next year. (11/2)

**3561a Ocean Ridge (USA)**, very free to post, tried hard to make all and rallied bravely up the hill to go down fighting. (12/1)

**2582* Dazzle**, in the opinion of many paddock watchers, is still in the process of growing and, though she did look fit after almost three months off the track, she could not quicken in the same fashion as she had done in the past. She had plenty to do and was not beaten far, but may be best put away until next year. (4/9)

**4065* Arethusa**, doing all her best work on meeting the rising ground, was not disgraced in this company and there are plenty more good prizes to be won with her. (16/1)

**4299* Queen Sceptre (IRE)** ran fast up with the pace, but she was out of her class when the contest really developed in the Dip. (16/1)

## 4492 E.B.F. EQUITY FINANCIAL COLLECTIONS MAIDEN STKS (2-Y.O C & G) (Class D)

4-20 (4-20) **1m (Rowley)** £5,526.50 (£1,652.00: £791.00: £360.50) Stalls: High GOING minus 0.49 sec per fur (F)

| | | | | SP | RR | SF |
|---|---|---|---|---|---|---|
| | **Asas** (SbinSuroor) **2-8-11** RHills(10) (gd sort: led 2f: led wl over 1f out: clr fnl f) | — | **1** | 14/1 | 93++ | 42 |
| 4163a[2] | **Jaunty Jack** (LMCumani) **2-8-11** OUrbina(1) (lw: s.i.s: hdwy over 2f out: kpt on ins fnl f: no ch w wnr) | 2½ | **2** | 20/1 | 88+ | 37 |
| 2543[3] | **Dark Green (USA)** (PFICole) **2-8-11** TQuinn(6) (bit bkwd: in tch: hdwy & rn green over 2f out: one pce fnl f) | nk | **3** | 9/2[3] | 87 | 36 |
| | **Desert Horizon** (JHMGosden) **2-8-11** LDettori(2) (gd sort: bkwd: hld up & bhd: hdwy 2f out: drifted rt fnl f: nvr nrr) | 3 | **4** | 20/1 | 81+ | 30 |
| 4242[2] | **Chivalric (IRE)** (DRLoder) **2-8-11** WRSwinburn(5) (led after 2f tl wl over 1f out: wknd fnl f) | s.h | **5** | 7/4[1] | 81 | 30 |
| | **Catchable** (HRACecil) **2-8-11** PatEddery(8) (gd sort: scope: bit bkwd: chsd ldrs tl wknd over 1f out) | ¾ | **6** | 3/1[2] | 80 | 29 |
| | **Percy Isle (IRE)** (MRStoute) **2-8-11** MJKinane(12) (neat: bkwd: bhd: sme hdwy fnl 2f: nvr nrr) | 1¾ | **7** | 20/1 | 76+ | 25 |
| | **Royal Crown (IRE)** (PWChapple-Hyam) **2-8-11** JReid(7) (gd sort: leggy: bkwd: prom tl rdn & lost pl after 3f: sn btn) | 5 | **8** | 12/1 | 66 | 15 |
| 4261[6] | **Include Me Out** (JRFanshawe) **2-8-11** NDay(4) (nvr trbld ldrs) | ¾ | **9** | 50/1 | 65 | 14 |
| | **Harik** (BHanbury) **2-8-11** JStack(11) (leggy: scope: chsd ldrs: rdn 3f out: grad wknd) | hd | **10** | 33/1 | 65 | 14 |
| | **Michael Venture** (SPCWoods) **2-8-11** WRyan(3) (w'like: scope: s.s: a bhd: t.o) | 5 | **11** | 50/1 | 55 | 4 |
| 4233[13] | **Double-E-I-B-A** (CNAllen) **2-8-6**(5) MartinDwyer(9) (a in rr: t.o) | hd | **12** | 100/1 | 54 | 3 |

(SP 116.0%) **12 Rn**

**1m 38.59** (1.29) CSF £219.62 TOTE £11.40: £3.00 £2.90 £1.40 (£116.40) Trio £123.20 OWNER Mr Hamdan Al Maktoum (NEWMARKET) BRED Shadwell Estate Company Limited

**Asas**, a tall colt, made a very impressive winning debut and, as he is bred to stay, he could go a long way up the ladder next season. (14/1)

**4163a Jaunty Jack**, who made his racecourse debut in Italy, missed a beat at the start, but stayed on pleasingly in the latter stages. More will be heard of him. (20/1)

**2543 Dark Green (USA)**, given three months to recover his form after his initial outing, is sure to strip fitter for the run, but he ran well and should be able to go on from here. (9/2)

**Desert Horizon** began to stay on inside the final quarter-mile, but did show signs of greenness, and will know more next time. (20/1)

**4242 Chivalric (IRE)** helped force the pace but he had kept nothing in reserve, and the final climb caught him out. (7/4)

**Catchable** strode out well to post and then sat in behind the leaders travelling strongly until blowing up approaching the final furlong. He looks sure to be a leading light next year. (3/1)

**Royal Crown (IRE)** (12/1: 6/1-14/1)

T/Jkpt: Not won; £14,877.77 to Brighton 2/10/96. T/Plpt: £1,472.80 (18.05 Tckts). T/Qdpt: £196.20 (13.3 Tckts). IM

# 3975-BRIGHTON (L-H) (Good)

## Wednesday October 2nd

WEATHER: warm WIND: almost nil

## 4493 FINAL (S) STKS (2-Y.O) (Class G)

2-20 (2-23) **5f 59y** £2,070.00 (£570.00: £270.00) Stalls: Low GOING minus 0.36 sec per fur (F)

| | | | | SP | RR | SF |
|---|---|---|---|---|---|---|
| 2195[11] | **Royal Blackbird** (JEBanks) **2-7-13**(7) RMullen(1) (hdwy 3f out: led 2f out: rdn over 1f out: r.o wl) | — | **1** | 16/1 | 67 | 22 |
| 3879[3] | **Le Shuttle (59)** (MHTompkins) **2-8-6** LDettori(2) (swtg: led over 2f: ev ch ins fnl f: unable qckn) | 2 | **2** | 7/1 | 61 | 16 |
| 4244[2] | **Gold Edge (62)** (MRChannon) **2-8-6** RPerham(4) (lw: a.p: led over 2f out: sn hdd: one pce fnl f) | ½ | **3** | 9/4[2] | 59 | 14 |
| 4210[4] | **Northern Girl (IRE) (66)** (BJMeehan) **2-8-6b[1]** BDoyle(6) (hld up: c stands' side st: hrd rdn over 1f out: r.o) | ½ | **4** | 2/1[1] | 58 | 13 |
| 3975[9] | **Castle House (57)** (JAkehurst) **2-9-2** GDuffield(5) (lw: a.p: c stands' side st: hrd rdn over 1f out: one pce) | 1 | **5** | 12/1 | 65 | 20 |
| 4368[5] | **Seretse's Nephew** (SCWilliams) **2-8-11** JTate(3) (b: a.p: rdn over 2f out: wknd over 1f out) | 5 | **6** | 5/1[3] | 45 | — |
| 4207[10] | **Dozen Roses (51)** (TMJones) **2-8-6b** NCarlisle(7) (b.off hind: lw: s.s: a bhd) | ½ | **7** | 14/1 | 38 | — |
| *4251*[8] | **Parquet** (JJSheehan) **2-8-6** AMorris(8) (lw: a bhd) | 10 | **8** | 50/1 | 8 | — |

(SP 115.5%) **8 Rn**

**62.3 secs** (2.30) CSF £109.51 TOTE £16.40: £4.70 £1.70 £1.30 (£53.30) OWNER Mr E. Carter (NEWMARKET) BRED Red House Stud
Bt in 6,000 gns

**Royal Blackbird** proved very troublesome and had to be led all the way to the start, but it was to be a different story on the way back. (16/1)

**3879 Le Shuttle** has had plenty of chances in this company, and was still battling for the advantage inside the final furlong when tapped for toe. (7/1: 6/1-9/1)

**4244 Gold Edge** has found her class and was only tapped for toe in the final furlong. (9/4)
**4210 Northern Girl (IRE)**, fitted with blinkers for the first time and dropped into selling company, was one of two who elected to come over to the stands' side in search of better ground. Carrying her head slightly awkwardly in the final quarter-mile, she stuck on well inside the final furlong but has had plenty of chances. (2/1)
**1713 Castle House** was taking a step down in class but failed to quicken in the last two furlongs. (12/1: op 8/1)
**4368 Seretse's Nephew** played an active role until coming to the end of his tether below the distance. (5/1)
**3976 Dozen Roses** (14/1: 6/1-16/1)

## 4494 E.B.F. SOMPTING MAIDEN STKS (2-Y.O) (Class D)

2-50 (2-52) **6f 209y** £4,059.60 (£1,213.80: £581.40: £265.20) Stalls: Low GOING minus 0.36 sec per fur (F)

| | | | | SP | RR | SF |
|---|---|---|---|---|---|---|
| 4100$^{3}$ | **Cosmic Prince (IRE)** (MAJarvis) **2-9-0** PBloomfield(15) (mde virtually all: clr over 1f out: r.o wl) | — | **1** | 6/1 | 86 | 41 |
| 4062$^{5}$ | **Spanish Knot (USA)** (LordHuntingdon) **2-8-9** LDettori(2) (nt clr run over 2f out: swtchd rt: hdwy over 1f out: r.o one pce) | 1¼ | **2** | 11/2$^{3}$ | 78 | 33 |
| | **Speedboat (USA)** (LMCumani) **2-9-0** OUrbina(8) (w'like: hdwy 2f out: rdn over 1f out: r.o one pce) | s.h | **3** | 8/1 | 83 | 38 |
| *4331*$^{2}$ | **Ferny Hill (IRE)** (SirMarkPrescott) **2-9-0** GDuffield(4) (a.p: hrd rdn over 1f out: one pce) | 1½ | **4** | 11/2$^{3}$ | 80 | 35 |
| 4369$^{5}$ | **Supply And Demand** (GLMoore) **2-9-0** SWhitworth(3) (s.s: hdwy over 2f out: r.o one pce) | 1½ | **5** | 5/1$^{2}$ | 76 | 31 |
| 4233$^{14}$ | **Serenade (IRE)** (MJHaynes) **2-9-0** JTate(1) (bit bkwd: hdwy over 1f out: nvr nrr) | 5 | **6** | 50/1 | 65 | 20 |
| 4200$^{5}$ | **Zingaro (IRE)** (CEBrittain) **2-9-0** BDoyle(10) (prom over 5f) | ¾ | **7** | 20/1 | 63 | 18 |
| 4210$^{13}$ | **M R Poly (55)** (MRChannon) **2-9-0** RPerham(7) (prom over 5f) | 1½ | **8** | 50/1 | 59 | 14 |
| 4363$^{5}$ | **Showcase** (MRStoute) **2-8-4**(5) MartinDwyer(14) (rdn & hdwy over 1f out: wknd fnl f) | 1 | **9** | 6/1 | 52 | 7 |
| 4253$^{8}$ | **State of Gold (IRE)** (WJHaggas) **2-9-0** MRoberts(6) (nvr nrr) | 2½ | **10** | 20/1 | 51 | 6 |
| 4330$^{4}$ | **Begorrat (IRE)** (BJMeehan) **2-9-0** DBiggs(12) (bhd fnl 3f) | s.h | **11** | 9/2$^{1}$ | 51 | 6 |
| 4210$^{12}$ | **Kingsdown Trix (IRE) (67)** (AMoore) **2-9-0** CRutter(5) (swtg: bhd fnl 3f) | 1¾ | **12** | 50/1 | 47 | 2 |
| 4233$^{12}$ | **Peter Perfect** (GLewis) **2-8-11**(3) AWhelan(16) (bit bkwd: prom 5f) | 2½ | **13** | 50/1 | 42 | — |
| 4380$^{9}$ | **Rock To The Top (IRE)** (JJSheehan) **2-9-0** MRimmer(9) (lw: prom over 5f) | 2 | **14** | 50/1 | 37 | — |
| 4105$^{6}$ | **Babe (IRE)** (MHTompkins) **2-8-9** NDay(11) (a bhd) | 5 | **15** | 50/1 | 20 | — |
| | | | | (SP 126.6%) | **15 Rn** | |

**1m 22.1** (2.10) CSF £37.49 TOTE £7.30: £2.60 £1.80 £2.90 (£16.30) Trio £148.20; £81.44 to Newmarket 3/10/96 OWNER Cosmic Greyhound Racing Partnership (NEWMARKET) BRED R. V. Young
**4100 Cosmic Prince (IRE)** strode off in front and forged clear in the final quarter-mile, to win in decisive style. (6/1: op 4/1)
**4062 Spanish Knot (USA)** did not have the best of runs but stayed on in the last furlong and a half, and never looked like getting to the winner in time. (11/2)
**Speedboat (USA)** comes from a stable that has a 36% strike rate here, but even though he stayed on, he never threatened to improve on the stable's record. (8/1: 5/1-9/1)
**4331 Ferny Hill (IRE)** was tackling his third new distance in the last three runs, but failed to quicken in the last furlong and a half. (11/2)
**Serenade (IRE)** still did not look fit, but he did stay on from the rear of the field in the last furlong and a half. (50/1)

## 4495 A.R. DENNIS BOOKMAKERS OCTOBER NURSERY H'CAP (0-75) (2-Y.O) (Class E)

3-20 (3-21) **6f 209y** £3,479.70 (£1,041.60: £499.80: £228.90) Stalls: Low GOING minus 0.36 sec per fur (F)

| | | | | SP | RR | SF |
|---|---|---|---|---|---|---|
| 2559$^{5}$ | **Impulsif (USA) (74)** (DJSffrenchDavis) **2-9-3**(3) PMcCabe(1) (a.p: led over 1f out: rdn out) | — | **1** | 11/1 | 80 | 32 |
| 4188$^{12}$ | **Heart Full of Soul (70)** (PFICole) **2-9-2b**$^{1}$ CRutter(4) (lw: hld up: swtchd rt over 1f out: rdn: r.o wl ins fnl f) | hd | **2** | 20/1 | 76 | 28 |
| 3976* | **Irish Fiction (IRE) (66)** (DJSCosgrove) **2-8-12** MRimmer(6) (hld up: rdn over 2f out: r.o one pce) | 4 | **3** | 10/1$^{3}$ | 63 | 15 |
| 2429$^{3}$ | **Suave Star (58)** (CADwyer) **2-8-4** JTate(3) (lw: s.s: hdwy & nt clr run on ins over 1f out: r.o one pce) | hd | **4** | 14/1 | 54 | 6 |
| 4182$^{7}$ | **Supercharmer (72)** (CEBrittain) **2-9-4** BDoyle(2) (led over 5f: wknd fnl f) | ½ | **5** | 16/1 | 67 | 19 |
| 4118$^{7}$ | **Sea Mist (IRE) (66)** (PWChapple-Hyam) **2-8-9**(3) RHavlin(9) (lw: a.p: rdn over 2f out: wknd over 1f out) | 1 | **6** | 20/1 | 59 | 11 |
| 4207$^{11}$ | **Silent Valley (55)** (BJMeehan) **2-8-1b**$^{1}$ DeclanO'Shea(14) (nvr nrr) | 2 | **7** | 25/1 | 43 | — |
| *4335*$^{6}$ | **Run Lucy Run (67)** (MissGayKelleway) **2-8-13** GDuffield(5) (lost pl 3f out: one pce fnl 2f) | 1½ | **8** | 12/1 | 52 | 4 |
| *4251*$^{6}$ | **Poly Moon (57)** (MRChannon) **2-7-12**(5)ow5 PPMurphy(10) (prom 5f) | 1¼ | **9** | 20/1 | 39 | — |
| 3685$^{16}$ | **Chilli Boom (50)** (TJNaughton) **2-7-10** GBardwell(15) (b.hind: nvr nrr) | nk | **10** | 33/1 | 31 | — |
| *4331** | **Mystic Quest (IRE) (75)** (KMcAuliffe) **2-9-7v** JFEgan(7) (hld up: rdn over 2f out: sn wknd) | ¾ | **11** | 16/1 | 55 | 7 |
| 4049$^{7}$ | **Shuwaikh (72)** (RHannon) **2-9-4** DBiggs(11) (rdn & sme hdwy over 1f out: sn wknd) | 2½ | **12** | 6/1$^{2}$ | 46 | — |
| 4207$^{4}$ | **Impy Fox (IRE) (57)** (CADwyer) **2-7-10**(7) JoHunnam(12) (bhd fnl 3f) | nk | **13** | 12/1 | 30 | — |
| 4222$^{2}$ | **Attribute (73)** (RCharlton) **2-9-0**(5) MartinDwyer(13) (bhd fnl 5f) | 1 | **14** | 100/30$^{1}$ | 44 | — |
| 4222$^{5}$ | **Misty Cay (IRE) (67)** (SDow) **2-8-13** MRoberts(16) (a bhd) | nk | **15** | 12/1 | 37 | — |
| 4123$^{12}$ | **Secret Pass (USA) (70)** (EALDunlop) **2-9-2** SWhitworth(17) (prom over 4f) | | **16** | 20/1 | — | — |
| | | | | (SP 122.1%) | **16 Rn** | |

**1m 23.3** (3.30) CSF £187.48 CT £1,274.35 TOTE £16.00: £3.00 £5.80 £2.00 £6.30 (£198.20) Trio £225.60 OWNER Mrs Mary Moloney (UPPER LAMBOURN) BRED Major Michael G. Wyatt
LONG HANDICAP Chilli Boom 7-3
**OFFICIAL EXPLANATION Attribute: was unsuited by the track and was never travelling well.**
**2559 Impulsif (USA)** appreciated the step up in distance and, striking the front below the distance, just managed to hold on. (11/1)
**Heart Full of Soul** was fitted with blinkers for the first time on this handicap debut, and left previous form well behind. Really motoring in the final furlong, he would surely have prevailed in a few more strides. (20/1)
**3976* Irish Fiction (IRE)**, whose two wins to date have both come in sellers, acquitted himself well in this better class race. (10/1)
**2429 Suave Star**, chopped for room as she picked up ground along the inside rail below the distance, stayed on and only just lost out on third prize. (14/1)
**3962 Supercharmer** cut out the running but was collared below the distance and soon had nothing more to offer. (16/1)
**Sea Mist (IRE)** raced up with the pace but was hung out to dry below the distance. (20/1)

## 4496 LEVY BOARD MAIDEN H'CAP (0-70) (3-Y.O+) (Class E)

3-50 (3-51) **1m 3f 196y** £3,343.20 (£999.60: £478.80: £218.40) Stalls: High GOING minus 0.36 sec per fur (F)

| | | | | SP | RR | SF |
|---|---|---|---|---|---|---|
| 4216$^{5}$ | **Amadour (IRE) (63)** (PMitchell) **3-9-10** OUrbina(7) (lw: hdwy over 2f out: hrd rdn & squeezed thro on ins ins fnl f: led last strides) | — | **1** | 20/1 | 72 | 46 |
| 4042$^{4}$ | **Soldier Mak (58)** (AHide) **3-9-5** GBardwell(6) (a.p: led 6f out: hrd rdn over 1f out: hdd last strides) | hd | **2** | 12/1 | 67 | 41 |
| 4216$^{3}$ | **Royal Diversion (IRE) (67)** (JLDunlop) **3-10-0** GDuffield(4) (hrd rdn & hdwy over 1f out: r.o wl ins fnl f) | 1¼ | **3** | 4/1$^{1}$ | 74 | 48 |

| Form | Horse | Dist | Pos | SP | RR | SF |
|---|---|---|---|---|---|---|
| 4076[7] | **Basood (USA) (55)** (SPCWoods) **3-8-9v**(7) CWebb(8) (hdwy 4f out: rdn over 2f out: one pce) | ¾ | **4** | 20/1 | 61 | 35 |
| 3841[5] | **Give And Take (57)** (LordHuntingdon) **3-9-4** LDettori(11) (lw: hdwy over 1f out: r.o one pce) | ¾ | **5** | 7/1[3] | 62 | 36 |
| 4353[2] | **Matthias Mystique (50)** (MissBSanders) **3-8-6**(5) ADaly(3) (swtg: hrd rdn & hdwy over 1f out: nvr nrr) | hd | **6** | 5/1[2] | 55 | 29 |
| 3258[7] | **Coh Sho No (60)** (SDow) **3-9-7** MRoberts(9) (led 6f: rdn over 2f out: eased whn btn over 1f out) | 4 | **7** | 7/1[3] | 60 | 34 |
| 4068[9] | **Burning Flame (43)** (RMFlower) **3-8-4b** DBiggs(12) (hdwy 5f out: wknd 2f out) | 1¾ | **8** | 33/1 | 40 | 14 |
| 4422[5] | **Smile Forever (USA) (60)** (MissGayKelleway) **3-9-2**(5) DGriffiths(14) (lw: nvr nr to chal) | 1¾ | **9** | 25/1 | 55 | 29 |
| 1462[10] | **Fro (52)** (TJNaughton) **3-8-13** SWhitworth(2) (hld up: rdn over 3f out: wknd over 2f out) | 2½ | **10** | 33/1 | 44 | 18 |
| 3249[16] | **Future's Trader (60)** (RHannon) **3-9-7** JFEgan(5) (lw: bhd fnl 2f) | 2½ | **11** | 25/1 | 48 | 22 |
| 4236[4] | **Lucy Tufty (35)** (JPearce) **5-7-10**(7) LisaMoncrieff(1) (s.s: hdwy over 5f out: mid div whn hmpd on ins over 4f out: sn wknd) | 5 | **12** | 16/1 | 17 | — |
| 3966[2] | **Golden Fawn (58)** (LadyHerries) **3-8-12**(7) PDoe(10) (bhd fnl 4f) | 1½ | **13** | 5/1[2] | 38 | 12 |
| 3274[13] | **Rockusa (40)** (PRHedger) **4-8-8** RPerham(15) (a bhd) | hd | **14** | 33/1 | 19 | — |
| 4203[5] | **Atienza (USA) (53)** (SCWilliams) **3-9-0** JTate(13) (b.hind: prom 6f) | 5 | **15** | 12/1 | 26 | — |
| 4086[9] | **Perfect Gift (54)** (PFICole) **3-9-1b**[1] CRutter(16) (lw: prom 7f) | 1½ | **16** | 15/2 | 25 | — |

(SP 137.4%) **16 Rn**

**2m 32.5** (4.90) CSF £240.83 CT £1,077.46 TOTE £23.60: £3.80 £2.90 £1.40 £14.00 (£90.00) Trio £161.50; £54.61 to Newmarket 3/10/96
OWNER Mr Derek Crowson BRED Pierce Molony
WEIGHT FOR AGE 3yo-7lb

**4216 Amadour (IRE)** bravely squeezed through a narrow gap along the inside rail, to force his head in front in the last couple of strides and to give his trainer his first winner in over four months. (20/1)
**4042 Soldier Mak** at last looked like losing his maiden tag at the twelfth attempt of asking as he went on at halfway, but with the winner squeezing up his inner, he was caught a couple of strides from the line. (12/1)
**4216 Royal Diversion (IRE)** took an age to get going but she did run on from below the distance, although she was never going to get there in time. She has had plenty of chances but is lacking on the acceleration front. (4/1)
**1589 Basood (USA)** appeared to see out this longer trip but failed to quicken in the final quarter-mile. (20/1)
**3841 Give And Take** was taking a big drop in class for this handicap debut, but despite staying on, never threatened. (7/1)
**4353 Matthias Mystique** was flattered by her run at Epsom last week and this performance is a better assesment of her ability. (5/1: op 5/2)
**1614 Coh Sho No** (7/1: op 16/1)
**4086 Perfect Gift** (15/2: 12/1-7/1)

## 4497 STEYNING H'CAP (0-60) (3-Y.O+) (Class F)

4-20 (4-24) **1m 1f 209y** £2,381.00 (£656.00: £311.00) Stalls: High GOING minus 0.36 sec per fur (F)

| Form | Horse | Dist | Pos | SP | RR | SF |
|---|---|---|---|---|---|---|
| 3500* | **Kristal Breeze (49)** (WRMuir) **4-9-3** LDettori(14) (hdwy over 2f out: led over 1f out: r.o wl) | — | **1** | 7/2[1] | 64 | 43 |
| 3966[3] | **Tallulah Belle (44)** (NPLittmoden) **3-8-7** NCarlisle(17) (swtchd lft over 2f out: hdwy to chse wnr over 1f out: no imp) | 3½ | **2** | 14/1 | 53 | 27 |
| 4240[11] | **Racing Telegraph (40)** (CNAllen) **6-8-3**(5) MartinDwyer(6) (lw: a.p: led over 4f out tl over 1f out: sn wknd) | 5 | **3** | 11/1 | 41 | 20 |
| 4128[11] | **Galapino (50)** (CEBrittain) **3-8-13** BDoyle(3) (hdwy over 1f out: nvr nrr) | 1¼ | **4** | 16/1 | 49 | 23 |
| 664[11] | **Barbason (54)** (AMoore) **4-9-8** CandyMorris(15) (hdwy over 1f out: nvr nrr) | nk | **5** | 25/1 | 53 | 32 |
| 4186[9] | **Pride of Kashmir (50)** (PWHarris) **3-8-13** GDuffield(12) (hdwy over 1f out: nvr nrr) | ¾ | **6** | 12/1 | 48 | 22 |
| 4323[6] | **Bold Enough (50)** (BWHills) **3-8-13** CRutter(11) (lw: nvr nr to chal) | 1¼ | **7** | 7/1[2] | 46 | 20 |
| 4102[7] | **Tuigamala (41)** (RIngram) **5-8-9** SWhitworth(18) (lw: nvr nrr) | s.h | **8** | 7/1[2] | 37 | 16 |
| 4053[11] | **Multan (50)** (GLMoore) **4-9-4** RPerham(13) (b: prom over 7f) | nk | **9** | 16/1 | 45 | 24 |
| | **Shoofk (52)** (SDow) **5-9-1**(5) ADaly(1) (lw: lost pl 5f out: one pce fnl 3f) | 1¾ | **10** | 16/1 | 44 | 23 |
| 2127[11] | **Ottavio Farnese (59)** (AHide) **4-9-13** GBardwell(19) (lw: nvr nrr) | hd | **11** | 20/1 | 51 | 30 |
| 1956[8] | **Hever Golf Eagle (49)** (TJNaughton) **3-8-12** MRoberts(7) (prom 8f) | 1¼ | **12** | 16/1 | 39 | 13 |
| 4217[3] | **Clued Up (54)** (PDEvans) **3-9-3v** JFEgan(16) (prom over 7f) | ½ | **13** | 12/1 | 43 | 17 |
| 4236[3] | **Wet Patch (IRE) (60)** (RHannon) **4-9-7**(7) GGallagher(9) (a bhd) | 4 | **14** | 15/2[3] | 43 | 22 |
| 4082[8] | **Park Ridge (35)** (TGMills) **4-8-0**(3) AWhelan(5) (led over 5f: wknd over 2f out) | 1½ | **15** | 33/1 | 15 | — |
| 4236[10] | **Princely Affair (51)** (MBell) **3-8-7**(7) RMullen(2) (lw: hdwy 4f out: wknd over 2f out) | ¾ | **16** | 12/1 | 30 | 4 |
| *87*[3] | **Tonka (57)** (PJMakin) **4-9-8**(3) RHavlin(8) (prom 6f) | 9 | **17** | 25/1 | 22 | 1 |
| 2577[15] | **Bellateena (43)** (HJCollingridge) **4-8-11** MRimmer(10) (prom over 5f) | 2½ | **18** | 33/1 | 4 | — |
| 3303[10] | **Moving Up (IRE) (46)** (TEPowell) **3-8-6**(3) PMcCabe(4) (lw: a bhd) | 21 | **19** | 16/1 | — | — |

(SP 144.8%) **19 Rn**

**2m 1.6** (3.30) CSF £56.60 CT £493.65 TOTE £4.00: £1.20 £4.90 £3.30 £4.40 (£73.00) Trio £295.50; £249.72 to Newmarket 3/10/96 OWNER Mr S. Lamb (LAMBOURN) BRED R. and Mrs Heathcote
WEIGHT FOR AGE 3yo-5lb

**3500* Kristal Breeze** notched up her fourth win of the year and gave Frankie his 100th winner of the season, as she struck the front below the distance and soon asserted for a clear-cut success. (7/2)
**3966 Tallulah Belle** picked up ground to go in pursuit of the winner below the distance, but had no hope of reeling in that rival. She remains a maiden after 21 attempts. (14/1: 10/1-16/1)
**4186 Racing Telegraph** failed to see out this longer trip and after showing in front over half a mile from home, was collared below the distance and soon done with. One win from 36 starts says it all. (11/1)
**3703 Galapino** put in some good work in the last furlong and a half without ever posing a threat. (16/1)
**320* Barbason** was having his first run in nearly six months, but did make a little late headway. (25/1)
**3845 Pride of Kashmir** struggled on to be nearest at the line but remains a very exposed maiden after eighteen attempts. (12/1)
**366* Tuigamala** (7/1: op 14/1)

## 4498 EASTBOURNE LIMITED STKS (0-65) (3-Y.O) (Class F)

4-50 (4-53) **7f 214y** £2,381.00 (£656.00: £311.00) Stalls: Low GOING minus 0.36 sec per fur (F)

| Form | Horse | Dist | Pos | SP | RR | SF |
|---|---|---|---|---|---|---|
| 3525[5] | **Misrule (USA) (65)** (JHMGosden) **3-8-11** LDettori(3) (chsd ldr: led over 2f out: clr over 1f out: r.o wl) | — | **1** | 7/2[3] | 67 | 45 |
| 4109[12] | **Sweet Wilhelmina (65)** (LordHuntingdon) **3-8-6**(5) AimeeCook(6) (hdwy over 1f out: chsd wnr ins fnl f: no imp) | 4 | **2** | 12/1 | 59 | 37 |
| 4240[13] | **Just Millie (USA) (58)** (JEBanks) **3-8-9**(5) GFaulkner(4) (hld up: chsd wnr over 1f out tl ins fnl f: sn wknd) | 2½ | **3** | 20/1 | 57 | 35 |
| 3863[7] | **Memphis Beau (IRE) (62)** (JARToller) **3-9-3b** MRoberts(2) (lw: hld up: rdn over 2f out: wknd over 1f out) | 1¼ | **4** | 20/1 | 57 | 35 |
| 3664[6] | **Classic Beauty (IRE) (65)** (RHarris) **3-9-0** RPrice(1) (b.hind: lw: led over 5f: wknd wl over 1f out) | 8 | **5** | 16/1 | 38 | 16 |
| 4296[9] | **Prima Volta (65)** (RHannon) **3-9-0** JFEgan(8) (nvr nr to chal) | 1 | **6** | 5/2[2] | 36 | 14 |
| 4376[2] | **Carmarthen Bay (65)** (GLMoore) **3-9-0** GDuffield(5) (lw: nvr gng wl: bhd fnl 4f) | 4 | **7** | 13/8[1] | 28 | 6 |

3609[8] **The Grey Weaver (28)** (RMFlower) **3-9-0b[1]** DBiggs(7) (a bhd: t.o) ....dist **8** 50/1 — —
(SP 113.9%) **8 Rn**

**1m 34.0** (1.80) CSF £38.06 TOTE £4.20: £1.70 £1.20 £2.00 (£10.60) OWNER Mr K. Abdulla (NEWMARKET) BRED Juddmonte Farms
**OFFICIAL EXPLANATION Carmarthen Bay: finished distressed.**
**3525 Misrule (USA)** moved to the front over a quarter of a mile out and forged clear to lose her maiden tag. (7/2)
**Sweet Wilhelmina** ran her best race so far this season but, although snatching second place inside the final furlong, had no hope with the winner. (12/1)
**3977* Just Millie (USA)**, who flopped after winning here at the beginning of last month, ran better on this return, but after showing in second place, had nothing more to offer when collared for that position inside the final furlong. (20/1)
**3317* Memphis Beau (IRE)**, not at all keen to go down, failed to see out the trip and had been hung out to dry below the distance. (20/1)
**3490* Classic Beauty (IRE)** took the field along, but she was collared over a quarter of a mile from home and had soon shot her bolt. (16/1)
**3929* Prima Volta** (5/2: op 4/1)
**4376 Carmarthen Bay** looked ill at ease on this tricky switchback track and, never travelling well, her supporters knew their fate soon after the start. (13/8)

## 4499 HANNINGTONS MACMILLAN CHAPEL APPEAL MAIDEN STKS (3-Y.O+) (Class D)
5-20 (5-21) **7f 214y** £3,761.25 (£1,122.00: £535.50: £242.25) Stalls: Low GOING minus 0.36 sec per fur (F)

| | | | | SP | RR | SF |
|---|---|---|---|---|---|---|
| 4309[3] | **Zilclare (IRE)** (EALDunlop) **3-8-9** SWhitworth(9) (lw: hdwy over 3f out: led ins fnl f: r.o wl) | — | **1** | 9/4[2] | 82 | 35 |
| 4124[4] | **Golden Thunderbolt (FR) (78)** (JHMGosden) **3-9-0** LDettori(4) (lw: hld up: rdn 2f out: ev ch 1f out: unable qckn) | 1¾ | **2** | 2/1[1] | 84 | 37 |
| 4109[6] | **Really A Dream (IRE) (67)** (MRStoute) **3-8-9** MRoberts(7) (hdwy 3f out: led 1f out tl ins fnl f: one pce) | ½ | **3** | 13/2 | 78 | 31 |
| 3933[9] | **Blatant Outburst (73)** (GCBravery) **6-9-3** NDay(6) (hld up: rdn over 2f out: n.m.r over 1f out: one pce) | hd | **4** | 16/1 | 82 | 38 |
| 4201[6] | **Latin Quarter (USA)** (RCharlton) **3-9-0** BDoyle(1) (a.p: rdn over 2f out: wknd over 1f out) | 6 | **5** | 6/1[3] | 70 | 23 |
| 4129[7] | **Baba Au Rhum (IRE)** (IPWilliams) **4-9-3** NCarlisle(8) (s.s: stdy hdwy over 2f out: one pce) | ¾ | **6** | 40/1 | 69 | 25 |
| 3123[9] | **Smooth Asset (IRE) (70)** (PWChapple-Hyam) **3-8-6**(3) RHavlin(2) (led 5f out to 1f out: sn wknd) | 2½ | **7** | 20/1 | 59 | 12 |
| 4108[12] | **Rainy Day Song** (LordHuntingdon) **3-8-4**(5) AimeeCook(3) (nvr nrr) | ¾ | **8** | 33/1 | 57 | 10 |
| 4109[13] | **Midday Cowboy (USA) (70)** (GHarwood) **3-9-0b[1]** CRutter(11) (bhd fnl 3f) | 1¼ | **9** | 9/1 | 60 | 13 |
| *2749*[12] | **Express Routing (51)** (VSoane) **4-9-3** GDuffield(5) (bit bkwd: a bhd) | 12 | **10** | 33/1 | 36 | — |
| 3977[10] | **Embroidered (27)** (RMFlower) **3-8-9b** DBiggs(12) (led 3f: wknd over 2f out) | 15 | **11** | 66/1 | 1 | — |
| 4074[W] | **Gemini Dream** (RFJohnsonHoughton) **3-9-0** RPrice(10) (w'like: scope: bit bkwd: bhd fnl 4f) | 1 | **12** | 25/1 | 4 | — |

(SP 126.0%) **12 Rn**

**1m 34.8** (2.60) CSF £7.39 TOTE £3.50: £1.40 £1.40 £2.30 (£4.40) Trio £7.70 OWNER Maktoum Al Maktoum (NEWMARKET) BRED GAINSBOROUGH STUD MANAGEMENT LTD
WEIGHT FOR AGE 3yo-3lb
**4309 Zilclare (IRE)** looked in good shape in the paddock and confirmed the promise shown at Newbury, managing to get on top inside the final furlong. (9/4)
**4124 Golden Thunderbolt (FR)** has had his chances and is now looking pretty exposed. His main chance would be over further. (2/1)
**4109 Really A Dream (IRE)** has disappointed on several occasions this year, and although showing in front for a brief time around the furlong pole, he has had plenty of chances. (13/2: 5/1-8/1)
**3933 Blatant Outburst** has not been running badly in maidens this season, but was tapped for toe in the last furlong and a half. (16/1)
**Latin Quarter (USA)** raced up with the pace but was sending out distress signals below the distance. (6/1)

T/Jkpt: Not won; £19,002.74 to Newmarket 3/10/96. T/Plpt: £684.00 (19.2 Tckts). T/Qdpt: £563.20 (1.29 Tckts) AK

# 3833-NEWCASTLE (L-H) (Good to firm)
## Wednesday October 2nd
Races 1 & 4 - hand-timed
WEATHER: fine WIND: slt half against

## 4500 E.B.F. HEBBURN MAIDEN STKS (2-Y.O) (Class D)
2-00 (2-01) **1m 3y (straight)** £3,485.00 (£1,055.00: £515.00: £245.00) Stalls: High GOING minus 0.65 sec per fur (HD)

| | | | | SP | RR | SF |
|---|---|---|---|---|---|---|
| | **Stowaway** (MAJarvis) **2-9-0** RCochrane(7) (wl grwn: hld up: effrt & nt clr run over 2f out: led over 1f out: r.o strly) | — | **1** | 2/1[2] | 93+ | — |
| 4052[4] | **Kafaf (USA)** (JHMGosden) **2-8-9** KDarley(2) (w ldrs: led over 2f out tl over 1f out: no ch w wnr) | 4 | **2** | 8/1 | 80 | — |
| | **Our People** (MJohnston) **2-9-0** JWeaver(5) (rangy: unf: bit bkwd: sn trckng ldrs: drvn along & outpcd over 2f out: styd on appr fnl f) | nk | **3** | 12/1 | 84+ | — |
| 4069[3] | **Ink Pot (USA)** (MRStoute) **2-8-9v** KFallon(3) (led tl over 2f out: r.o one pce) | ½ | **4** | 5/1[3] | 78 | — |
| 4175[4] | **Recourse (USA)** (HRACecil) **2-9-0** WRyan(1) (trckd ldrs: hung lft ½-wy: wknd ins fnl f) | 1 | **5** | 4/5[1] | 81 | — |
| 4261[5] | **Talib (USA)** (DMorley) **2-9-0** GCarter(6) (outpcd & drvn along ½-wy: sn bhd) | 11 | **6** | 10/1 | 60 | — |

(SP 133.4%) **6 Rn**

**1m 39.1** CSF £18.96 TOTE £2.30: £1.60 £3.00 (£26.50) OWNER Mr Mohammed Bin Hendi (NEWMARKET) BRED Hesmonds Stud Ltd
**Stowaway**, who has plenty of size and scope, showed a fair amount of knee-action going down and took a keen grip. Settled on the heels of the leaders, after having to wait for an opening he eventually won this in fine style. He looks potentially a very useful stayer. (2/1: 7/4-Evens)
**4052 Kafaf (USA)** wore a tongue strap and showed a pronounced round action going down, and was outclassed by the winner. (8/1: op 5/1)
**Our People**, out of a winning stayer, needs to furnish and looked on the backward side. Showing a pronounced knee-action going down, he was staying on nicely at the finish and can only improve. (12/1)
**4069 Ink Pot (USA)** did not impress with her action going down, and after making the running, was easily swept aside. (5/1)
**4175 Recourse (USA)**, a good walker, went to post in exemplary fashion, but on the way back wanted to do nothing but hang left and he found little under pressure. He is one to have reservations about, especially after his temperamental display on his debut at Doncaster. (4/5: Evens-7/4)

## 4501 BRUNTON LANE RATING RELATED MAIDEN STKS (0-65) (2-Y.O) (Class F)
2-30 (2-32) **7f** £2,557.50 (£720.00: £352.50) Stalls: High GOING minus 0.65 sec per fur (HD)

| | | | | SP | RR | SF |
|---|---|---|---|---|---|---|
| 4106[2] | **Julietta Mia (USA) (63)** (BWHills) **2-8-6**(5) JDSmith(2) (hld up: stdy hdwy ½-wy: led over 1f out: drvn out) | — | **1** | 11/4[2] | 61 | 21 |

$3762^{5}$ **Going For Broke (65)** (PCHaslam) **2-9-0** JFortune(3) (lw: chsd ldrs: rdn over 2f out: ev ch over 1f out: nt qckn) .......... 1¼ **2** 9/4$^{1}$ 61 21
$3998^{8}$ **Zorba (65)** (CWThornton) **2-9-0** DeanMcKeown(1) (trckd ldrs: effrt over 2f out: kpt on same pce) .......... 1¾ **3** 13/2$^{3}$ 57 17
$4069^{6}$ **Don't Worry Mike (65)** (FHLee) **2-9-0** JWeaver(6) (mde most tl over 1f out: sn wknd) .......... 4 **4** 14/1 48 8
$4195^{3}$ **In Good Nick (63)** (MWEasterby) **2-8-6b**(5) GParkin(5) (chsd ldrs: rdn ½-wy: lost pl over 2f out) .......... 8 **5** 11/4$^{2}$ 27 —
$3454^{7}$ **Maremma (64)** (DonEnricoIncisa) **2-8-11** KimTinkler(9) (s.i.s: a in rr) .......... 1¾ **6** 25/1 23 —
$4361^{13}$ **Wildmoor (65)** (JDBethell) **2-9-0b$^{1}$** GCarter(7) (w ldrs tl rdn & wknd 2f out) .......... 3 **7** 12/1 19 —
$3576^{W}$ **Kitty Galore (IRE) (56)** (MDods) **2-8-8**(3) CTeague(4) (hld up & plld hrd: drvn along ½-wy: nt run on) .......... 3 **8** 33/1 9 —
$4223^{10}$ **Apiculate (IRE) (46)** (WTKemp) **2-9-0** KFallon(8) (chsd ldrs: rdn over 4f out: lost pl over 2f out) .......... 1 **9** 50/1 10 —
(SP 120.5%) **9 Rn**

**1m 26.39** (1.89) CSF £9.48 TOTE £3.40: £1.60 £1.10 £1.90 (£4.60) Trio £19.80 OWNER Mr D. J. Deer (LAMBOURN) BRED Newbiggin Ltd

**4106 Julietta Mia (USA)**, an excitable type, who carries her head high, was skillfully handled and, in the end, scored in decisive fashion. (11/4)

**3762 Going For Broke**, who showed a fluent action going down, was almost upsides over a furlong out but could never find sufficient to worry the winner out of it. (9/4)

**3880 Zorba** settled better this time, but in truth did not find an awful lot under pressure. (13/2)

**4069 Don't Worry Mike**, a handful at the start, seemed to run out of gas and might be suited by a drop back to six. (14/1)

**4195 In Good Nick** showed a very poor action going to post. Hard at work at halfway, she soon dropped out of contention. (11/4: 2/1-3/1)

## 4502 E.B.F. POLWARTH MAIDEN STKS (2-Y.O) (Class D)

3-00 (3-00) **6f** £3,403.75 (£1,030.00: £502.50: £238.75) Stalls: High GOING minus 0.65 sec per fur (HD)

SP RR SF

$4043^{4}$ **Danetime (IRE)** (NACallaghan) **2-9-0** RCochrane(3) (lw: w ldr: led over 2f out: drvn out) .......... — **1** 6/4$^{2}$ 93 25
**Indian Brave** (MJohnston) **2-9-0** JWeaver(1) (leggy: unf: scope: reminders after s: led tl over 2f out: hung lft & nt qckn fnl f) .......... 1½ **2** 7/2$^{3}$ 89+ 21
$4188^{2}$ **Kumait (USA) (92)** (SbinSuroor) **2-9-0** WRyan(4) (lw: trckd ldrs: effrt over 2f out: edgd rt & no imp) .......... 1¼ **3** 10/11$^{1}$ 86 18
**Kalousion** (CWCElsey) **2-9-0** KFallon(5) (unf: bit bkwd: dwlt s: sn wl bhd) .......... 23 **4** 25/1 24 —
$4383^{11}$ **Hello There** (NTinkler) **2-9-0** KimTinkler(2) (s.i.s: a wl outpcd & bhd) .......... hd **5** 100/1 24 —
(SP 119.4%) **5 Rn**

**1m 12.9** (1.40) CSF £7.39 TOTE £2.30: £1.10 £1.20 (£4.50) OWNER Mr M. Tabor (NEWMARKET) BRED Holborn Trust Co

**4043 Danetime (IRE)**, heavily backed on his debut, recovered the losses but he had to battle all the way to the line. (6/4)

**Indian Brave**, coltish in the paddock, settled down once he had a man on his back. Given some reminders soon after the start, he hung left and showed inexperience under pressure. The outing should help settle him down and bring him on. (7/2)

**4188 Kumait (USA)** wore a tongue strap and looked unhappy with it going down to the start. When called on for an effort, all he wanted to do was duck in behind the first two. (10/11)

## 4503 BOLLINGER CHAMPAGNE CHALLENGE SERIES GENTLEMENS' H'CAP (0-70) (3-Y.O+) (Class E)

3-30 (3-31) **1m (round)** £2,931.00 (£888.00: £434.00: £207.00) Stalls: Low GOING minus 0.65 sec per fur (HD)

SP RR SF

$4355^{8}$ **Montone (IRE) (63)** (JRJenkins) **6-11-10v**(4) DrMMannish(9) (w ldr: led ½-wy: hrd rdn over 1f out: styd on wl) .......... — **1** 10/1 74 42
$4263^{5}$ **Chalky Dancer (34)** (HJCollingridge) **4-9-9**(4) MrPClose(5) (trckd ldrs: chal over 1f out: nt qckn ins fnl f) .......... 1¼ **2** 11/2 43 11
3060* **Sir Arthur Hobbs (56)** (JLEyre) **9-11-3**(4) MrVLukaniuk(1) (chsd ldrs: hrd rdn & kpt on one pce appr fnl f) .......... 4 **3** 5/1$^{3}$ 57 25
$3958^{11}$ **Nizaal (USA) (35)** (RAllan) **5-10-0** MrKGoble(6) (in tch: effrt & hung lft over 2f out: kpt on one pce) .......... ½ **4** 6/1 35 3
$3808^{13}$ **Langtonian (31)** (JLEyre) **7-9-10b** MrMHNaughton(4) (s.s: bhd: hdwy on ins over 2f out: hung lft over 1f out: hrd rdn: nt rchd ldrs) .......... ¾ **5** 20/1 29 —
$4296^{8}$ **Seconds Away (28)** (JSGoldie) **5-9-3**(4) MrOMcPhail(2) (effrt over 2f out: kpt on appr fnl f: nvr nr ldrs) .......... hd **6** 16/1 26 —
$4226^{4}$ **Murphy's Gold (IRE) (51)** (RAFahey) **5-11-2** MrSSwiers(8) (hld up: hdwy over 1f out: rdn 2f out: no imp) .......... nk **7** 5/2$^{1}$ 48 16
$4436^{10}$ **Thatched (IRE) (48)** (REBarr) **6-10-13** MrRHale(10) (mid div: drvn along & lost pl over 2f out: styd on ins fnl f) .......... 1¼ **8** 9/2$^{2}$ 43 11
$4436^{11}$ **Peacefull Reply (USA) (30)** (FHLee) **6-9-5**(4) MrCWatson(7) (effrt over 3f out: rdn & hung lft over 2f out: sn wknd) .......... 2½ **9** 33/1 20 —
$4436^{25}$ **Great Bear (45)** (DWChapman) **4-10-10** MrTMcCarthy(3) (a bhd) .......... 4 **10** 20/1 27 —
$4237^{11}$ **Arak (USA) (60)** (GCBravery) **8-11-7**(4) MrDCrossland(11) (b: racd wd: led to ½-wy: wknd qckly over 2f out) ... 7 **11** 10/1 28 —
(SP 129.6%) **11 Rn**

**1m 43.4** (4.40) CSF £65.37 CT £298.34 TOTE £12.40: £2.60 £3.40 £2.70 (£58.60) Trio £234.70 OWNER Mr B. Shirazi (ROYSTON) BRED Sean Gorman

STEWARDS' ENQUIRY Naughton. susp 11-12/10/96 (improper use of whip)

**4089 Montone (IRE)** and his rider, who is certainly no stylist, have certainly struck up a fine understanding. (10/1)

**4263 Chalky Dancer** does not run that often but threw down a strong challenge, although in the closing stages he was definitely second best. (11/2)

**3060* Sir Arthur Hobbs**, from a 4lb higher mark, had an absence of 68 days to overcome. He certainly did not lack encouragement from his rider's whip. (5/1: op 3/1)

**3677 Nizaal (USA)**, gambled on to stage a recovery, did not look to be giving his all under pressure. (6/1: 10/1-11/2)

**3452 Langtonian** has more ability than he cares to show. (20/1)

**4226 Murphy's Gold (IRE)**, an exasperating type, saw more daylight than is good for him and, under pressure, pulled out very little. (5/2)

## 4504 GATESHEAD LIMITED STKS (0-80) (3-Y.O+) (Class D)

4-00 (4-00) **7f** £3,550.00 (£1,075.00: £525.00: £250.00) Stalls: High GOING minus 0.65 sec per fur (HD)

SP RR SF

$4231^{2}$ **Divine Quest (76)** (HRACecil) **3-8-11** WRyan(3) (lw: effrt ½-wy: hrd rdn & styd on to ld ins fnl f: all out) .......... — **1** 11/10$^{1}$ 85 37
$4312^{8}$ **Keston Pond (IRE) (75)** (MrsVAAconley) **6-9-2** JWeaver(4) (led tl ins fnl f: nt qckn nr fin) .......... nk **2** 6/4$^{2}$ 87 41
$3842^{7}$ **Knotty Hill (74)** (RCraggs) **4-9-0** JFortune(2) (trckd ldr: effrt over 2f out: ev ch over 1f out: kpt on one pce) .. 1¾ **3** 14/1 81 35
$3799^{9}$ **Green Bopper (USA) (77)** (MBell) **3-9-0** MFenton(1) (lw: green: racd wd: hld up: effrt ½-wy: rdn over 2f out: no rspnse) .......... 6 **4** 5/1$^{3}$ 70 22
(SP 111.0%) **4 Rn**

**1m 24.94** (0.44) CSF £3.10 TOTE £1.80 (£1.20) OWNER Lady Howard de Walden (NEWMARKET) BRED Lord Howard de Walden

WEIGHT FOR AGE 3yo-2lb

**4231 Divine Quest** does nothing in a hurry but, answering her rider's every call, took this with nothing at all to spare. (11/10)

**4312 Keston Pond (IRE)** set out to make all and battled on all the way to the line. (6/4)

**3101 Knotty Hill** put two poor efforts behind him to have every chance. (14/1: 10/1-16/1)
**584* Green Bopper (USA)**, absent for 39 days, looked fresh and well but found nothing at all when put under pressure. (5/1)

## 4505 JARROW SPRINT H'CAP (0-85) (3-Y.O+) (Class D)

4-30 (4-31) **5f** £3,728.75 (£1,130.00: £552.50: £263.75) Stalls: High GOING minus 0.65 sec per fur (HD)

| | | | | SP | RR | SF |
|---|---|---|---|---|---|---|
| 4220[3] | **Portelet (83)** (RGuest) **4-9-7**(5) JDSmith(12) (mde all: hld on wl) | — | **1** | 8/1[3] | 93 | 43 |
| 4246[10] | **Insider Trader (76)** (MrsJRRamsden) **5-9-5** JFortune(1) (b.off fore: chsd ldrs: edgd rt: ev ch fnl f: r.o) | ½ | **2** | 10/1 | 84 | 34 |
| 4116[11] | **Saint Express (81)** (MrsMReveley) **6-9-5b[1]**(5) GLee(10) (lw: a chsng ldrs: effrt 2f out: kpt on same pce) | 1½ | **3** | 4/1[2] | 85 | 35 |
| 4382[7] | **Comic Fantasy (AUS) (64)** (JLEyre) **3-8-7b** TWilliams(14) (chsd ldrs: sn rdn along: kpt on one pce fnl 2f) | 1¼ | **4** | 16/1 | 64 | 14 |
| 4382[3] | **Ned's Bonanza (63)** (MDods) **7-8-3**(3) FLynch(8) (lw: mid div: styd on fnl 2f: nvr nr to chal) | ½ | **5** | 9/1 | 61 | 11 |
| 4246* | **Able Sheriff (61)** (MWEasterby) **4-8-4b**[ow1] WRyan(6) (hdwy ½-wy: sn rdn: nvr rchd ldrs) | s.h | **6** | 9/1 | 59 | 8 |
| 4382[2] | **Captain Carat (63)** (MrsJRRamsden) **5-8-6**[ow2] KFallon(3) (b.nr fore: bmpd & swtchd rt s: bhd: sme hdwy ½-wy: nvr nr ldrs) | 3 | **7** | 11/4[1] | 51 | — |
| 2143[14] | **Eastern Prophets (84)** (TJNaughton) **3-9-13** JWeaver(13) (effrt & sltly hmpd 2f out: nvr nr ldrs) | s.h | **8** | 20/1 | 72 | 22 |
| 4215* | **Palacegate Touch (77)** (JBerry) **6-9-6b** GCarter(5) (racd wd: chsd ldrs tl wandered & wknd over 1f out) | nk | **9** | 10/1 | 64 | 14 |
| 4367[7] | **Rich Glow (61)** (NBycroft) **5-8-4** LCharnock(9) (sn outpcd: swtchd lft 2f out: n.d) | 1 | **10** | 12/1 | 45 | — |
| 4116[14] | **Perryston View (81)** (PCalver) **4-9-10** MBirch(7) (in tch: rdn & hung lft ½-wy: sn wknd) | 1¼ | **11** | 12/1 | 61 | 11 |
| 4246[22] | **Goretski (IRE) (67)** (NTinkler) **3-8-10** KDarley(2) (swvd rt s: a bhd) | 2 | **12** | 20/1 | 41 | — |
| 4460[7] | **Cheeky Chappy (72)** (DWChapman) **5-9-1b** RCochrane(4) (sn bhd) | 2½ | **13** | 16/1 | 38 | — |
| | | | | (SP 132.6%) | **13 Rn** | |

**59.05 secs** (0.65) CSF £85.97 CT £355.41 TOTE £9.50: £2.60 £4.20 £2.10 (£38.50) Trio £138.60 OWNER Matthews Breeding and Racing (NEWMARKET) BRED Lord Victor Matthews

**4220 Portelet**, very keen going to post, likes to dominate and showed the right sort of spirit when hotly challenged. (8/1)
**4246 Insider Trader**, with the visor left off again, had the worst of the draw. Edging right towards the stands' side, he threw down a strong challenge in the final furlong, but could not force his head in front of a most determined opponent. (10/1)
**4116 Saint Express**, who has slipped right down the weights, was tried in blinkers. Most reluctant to leave the paddock, he never seemed to be putting his best foot forward. (4/1)
**3465 Comic Fantasy (AUS)** ran a much better race for her new trainer. (16/1)
**4382 Ned's Bonanza** (9/1: op 6/1)
**4382 Captain Carat**, drawn on the outside, took a bump at the start. Switched towards the stands' side, he tried to improve at halfway, but was never a factor. (11/4)

## 4506 HOLYSTONE H'CAP (0-75) (3-Y.O) (Class D)

5-00 (5-01) **2m 19y** £3,663.75 (£1,110.00: £542.50: £258.75) Stalls: High GOING minus 0.65 sec per fur (HD)

| | | | | SP | RR | SF |
|---|---|---|---|---|---|---|
| 4249[5] | **He's Got Wings (IRE) (53)** (MrsJRRamsden) **3-8-0** GCarter(7) (hld up: gd hdwy over 2f out: styd on wl u.p to ld ins fnl f) | — | **1** | 7/1 | 63+ | 20 |
| 3641[2] | **Forgie (IRE) (63)** (PCalver) **3-8-10** MBirch(5) (chsd ldrs: led over 2f out tl ins fnl f: unable qckn) | 2½ | **2** | 7/1 | 71 | 28 |
| 4227[11] | **Mister Aspecto (IRE) (70)** (MJohnston) **3-9-3v** JWeaver(9) (chsd ldr: led after 5f tl over 2f out: styd on one pce) | nk | **3** | 10/1 | 77 | 34 |
| 4358* | **Go With The Wind (64)** (MBell) **3-8-11** [4x] MFenton(11) (hld up: gd hdwy over 3f out: hung lft & kpt on fnl f) | hd | **4** | 3/1[2] | 71 | 28 |
| 4321* | **Onefourseven (50)** (JLEyre) **3-7-6**(5)[ow1] CAdamson(10) (hld up: hdwy 6f out: styd on u.p fnl 2f: nvr nr to chal) | s.h | **5** | 5/2[1] | 57 | 13 |
| 4317[8] | **Ship's Dancer (49)** (DonEnricoIncisa) **3-7-10v** KimTinkler(6) (sn bhd: sme hdwy over 2f out: n.d) | 8 | **6** | 100/1 | 48 | 5 |
| 3948[5] | **Desert Dunes (74)** (NAGraham) **3-9-7** RCochrane(8) (trckd ldrs: effrt & hung lft 3f out: wknd over 1f out) | 2½ | **7** | 13/2[3] | 71 | 28 |
| 4248[4] | **Aztec Flyer (USA) (53)** (MrsMReveley) **3-8-0** LCharnock(2) (hld up: sme hdwy over 3f out: n.d) | 8 | **8** | 7/1 | 42 | — |
| 3242[8] | **Northern Motto (51)** (WStorey) **3-7-9**(3) NVarley(4) (chsd ldrs: sn drvn along: edgd rt over 2f out: sn lost pl) | ¾ | **9** | 9/1 | 39 | — |
| 4344[7] | **Hallikeld (49)** (TJEtherington) **3-7-3**(7) JBramhill(1) (led 5f: drvn along 6f out: lost pl over 4f out) | 12 | **10** | 50/1 | 25 | — |
| 3991[14] | **Careful (IRE) (55)** (BWHills) **3-8-2** JStack(3) (wl bhd fnl 5f: t.o) | 30 | **11** | 20/1 | 1 | — |
| | | | | (SP 131.2%) | **11 Rn** | |

**3m 28.66** (3.16) CSF £56.73 CT £468.00 TOTE £10.30: £2.70 £2.30 £2.90 (£37.30) Trio £92.70 OWNER Mr Bernard Hathaway (THIRSK) BRED Citadel Stud

LONG HANDICAP Hallikeld 6-12 Ship's Dancer 6-13

**4249 He's Got Wings (IRE)** appreciated this stamina test. Responding to his rider's calls, he stayed on in good style to get on top inside the last. (7/1)
**3641 Forgie (IRE)**, off the same mark as at Pontefract, made the best of his way home, but the winner proved too strong where it mattered most. (7/1)
**3816 Mister Aspecto (IRE)** put two poor efforts behind him and stuck on in grim fashion. (10/1)
**4358* Go With The Wind**, patiently ridden as usual, swished his tail and looked anything but happy under pressure. (3/1: op 5/1)
**4321* Onefourseven** sat off the pace in a strongly-run race. Sticking on under pressure in the final two furlongs, he never looked like landing a blow off a 7lb higher mark than Catterick. (5/2)

T/Plpt: £679.20 (12.55 Tckts). T/Qdpt: £17.10 (30.4 Tckts). WG

# 3988-SALISBURY (R-H) (Good to soft)

## Wednesday October 2nd

Race 3: flip start
WEATHER: fine WIND: nil

## 4507 E. B. F. MARLBOROUGH MAIDEN STKS (I) (2-Y.O) (Class D)

1-40 (1-44) **1m** £3,353.00 (£1,004.00: £482.00: £221.00) GOING minus 0.20 sec per fur (GF)

| | | | | SP | RR | SF |
|---|---|---|---|---|---|---|
| 4242[7] | **Bold Words (CAN)** (EALDunlop) **2-9-0** MHills(4) (lw: a.p: led over 1f out: rdn out) | — | **1** | 25/1 | 74 | 30 |
| | **Flagship** (MajorWRHern) **2-8-9** TSprake(2) (unf: led: rdn & hdd over 1f out: r.o wl) | hd | **2** | 14/1 | 69 | 25 |
| 4359[3] | **Sellette (IRE)** (DHaydnJones) **2-8-9** DHarrison(1) (trckd ldrs: rdn over 1f out: swtchd rt & r.o wl ins fnl f) | 1¾ | **3** | 15/2 | 65 | 21 |

| | | | | SP | RR | SF |
|---|---|---|---|---|---|---|
| | **Corinthian (IRE)** (RHannon) **2-9-0** PatEddery(3) (w'like: scope: dwlt: sn w ldr: rdn over 2f out: one pce fnl f) | 2½ | **4** | 8/1 | 65 | 21 |
| | **Sausalito Bay** (IABalding) **2-9-0** AMcGlone(8) (w'like: scope: prom tl wknd over 1f out) | 4 | **5** | 5/2$^{1}$ | 57 | 13 |
| | **Other Club** (JARToller) **2-9-0** SSanders(13) (w'like: scope: a.p: hrd rdn over 2f out: wknd over 1f out) | ½ | **6** | 13/2$^{2}$ | 56 | 12 |
| $4100^{12}$ | **Hartshorn** (JLDunlop) **2-9-0** RHills(6) (nvr trbld ldrs) | 5 | **7** | 33/1 | 46 | 2 |
| | **Trooper** (PFICole) **2-9-0** TQuinn(11) (unf: scope: nvr gng wl: a bhd) | ¾ | **8** | 7/1$^{3}$ | 45 | 1 |
| | **Crystal Hills (IRE)** (JHMGosden) **2-9-0** GHind(12) (wl grwn: a bhd) | 1¼ | **9** | 9/1 | 42 | — |
| $4306^{9}$ | **Baubigny (USA)** (MRChannon) **2-9-0** JCarroll(7) (prom 6f) | s.h | **10** | 7/1$^{3}$ | 42 | — |
| $4370^{11}$ | **Sheffield Shark (IRE)** (DWPArbuthnot) **2-9-0** MTebbutt(9) (uns rdr bef s: bhd fnl 2f) | 3½ | **11** | 40/1 | 35 | — |
| $2878^{5}$ | **Kinship (IRE)** (PWChapple-Hyam) **2-9-0** JReid(5) (prom 3f) | 5 | **12** | 12/1 | 25 | — |
| $3498^{8}$ | **Fistral Flame** (JSMoore) **2-8-9** JQuinn(10) (a bhd: t.o) | 10 | **13** | 40/1 | — | — |

(SP 125.8%) **13 Rn**

**1m 45.71** (5.31) CSF £308.24 TOTE £20.90: £4.40 £5.30 £2.20 (£510.40) Trio £170.50; £144.15 to Newmarket 3/10/96 OWNER Maktoum Al Maktoum (NEWMARKET) BRED Crow's Nest & Hermitage Farm

**IN-FOCUS: The runners raced stands' side.**

**Bold Words (CAN)** broke better than on his previous two starts and seemed well suited by this longer trip. (25/1)

**Flagship**, by the Arc winner Rainbow Quest out of an Oaks winner, should stay much further and is an interesting prospect for next season following this promising debut. (14/1)

**4359 Sellette (IRE)** again suggested she is well up to winning a race or two. (15/2)

**Corinthian (IRE)** did not impress going to post but he came back well enough, and has a physique which bodes well for the future. (8/1: 5/1-9/1)

**Sausalito Bay** showed plenty of pace on this debut. (5/2)

**Other Club**, a good-looking sort, is from a winning family and showed enough to suggest he can follow in their footsteps in due course. (13/2)

**Trooper**, off the bridle throughout, never gave his supporters any hope. (7/1: op 4/1)

**Crystal Hills (IRE)** (9/1: 6/1-10/1)

## 4508 E.B.F. MARLBOROUGH MAIDEN STKS (II) (2-Y.O) (Class D)

2-10 (2-13) **1m** £3,327.00 (£996.00: £478.00: £219.00) GOING minus 0.20 sec per fur (GF)

| | | | | SP | RR | SF |
|---|---|---|---|---|---|---|
| | **Yorkshire (IRE)** (PFICole) **2-9-0** TQuinn(7) (unf: a.p: led on bit 3f out: rdn clr fnl f) | — | **1** | 2/1$^{2}$ | 97+ | 41 |
| | **Nordic Crest (IRE)** (PWHarris) **2-9-0** GHind(2) (str; scope: hdwy 2f out: swtchd rt & r.o ins fnl f: no ch w wnr) | 7 | **2** | 33/1 | 83+ | 27 |
| $4253^{7}$ | **Indium** (JHMGosden) **2-9-0** AMcGlone(9) (a.p: ev ch over 2f out: one pce) | hd | **3** | 10/1 | 83 | 27 |
| $3499^{10}$ | **Norman Conquest (USA)** (IABalding) **2-9-0** MHills(1) (led over 2f: one pce fnl 3f) | 2½ | **4** | 25/1 | 78 | 22 |
| $4200^{2}$ | **Mardi Gras (IRE)** (JLDunlop) **2-9-0** PatEddery(3) (chsd ldr: led over 5f out tl over 3f out: eased whn btn ins fnl f) | 4 | **5** | Evens$^{1}$ | 70 | 14 |
| | **Brynkir** (DJGMurraySmith) **2-9-0** DHarrison(6) (str: scope: rdn & hdwy 3f out: nvr nr to chal) | 1¾ | **6** | 33/1 | 66 | 10 |
| | **Walk On By** (RHannon) **2-9-0** DaneO'Neill(4) (w'like: scope: prom over 5f) | 2 | **7** | 16/1 | 62 | 6 |
| $3820^{3}$ | **Moonspell** (RCharlton) **2-8-9** SSanders(11) (bhd most of wy) | 2½ | **8** | 8/1 | 52 | — |
| $3874^{6}$ | **Mister Jay** (PTWalwyn) **2-9-0** JCarroll(10) (bhd whn hmpd over 1f out: eased) | 10 | **9** | 33/1 | 37 | — |
| $3319^{4}$ | **My Hero (IRE)** (TGMills) **2-8-9** RHills(8) (bhd fnl 4f) | 1½ | **10** | 12/1 | 29 | — |
| | **Saxonbury** (MRStoute) **2-9-0** WRSwinburn(5) (str: bit bkwd: nvr gng wl: a bhd) | 2½ | **11** | 7/1$^{3}$ | 29 | — |
| $4200^{4}$ | **Cadbury Castle** (MBlanshard) **2-8-9** AClark(12) (sn bhd: t.o) | 9 | **12** | 25/1 | 6 | — |
| *$4306^{8}$* | ***Burundi (IRE)*** (PWChapple-Hyam) **2-9-0** JReid(13) (Withdrawn not under Starter's orders: lame) | | **W** | 9/1 | — | — |

(SP 156.1%) **12 Rn**

**1m 44.61** (4.21) CSF £69.06 TOTE £3.50: £1.50 £3.10 £6.10 (£58.50) Trio £185.20; £130.49 to Newmarket 3/10/96 OWNER H R H Prince Fahd Salman (WHATCOMBE) BRED Newgate Stud Co

**IN-FOCUS: The runners raced stands' side.**

**Yorkshire (IRE)**, a son of Generous, is nothing special to look at but was fit and knew his job. His prospects depend on how much he strengthens during the winter but this was an excellent start to his career. (2/1)

**Nordic Crest (IRE)** took the eye both in the paddock and in the manner in which he picked up at the end of the race. (33/1)

**Indium** was ridden with more enterprise than on his debut, and it was not his fault that the winner proved to be in a different league. (10/1: 6/1-12/1)

**3040 Norman Conquest (USA)** has looked moderate to date but showed early pace, only to be left standing by the impressive winner. (25/1)

**4200 Mardi Gras (IRE)** is proving expensive to follow. (Evens)

**Brynkir** has plenty to commend him on looks, but his prospects probably lie in the long term. (33/1)

**3820 Moonspell** (8/1: 6/1-10/1)

**Saxonbury**, carrying plenty of condition for this debut, showed no signs of ability. There are winning hurdlers in his family and he may end up in that sphere, unless considerable improvement is forthcoming. (7/1)

## 4509 HURDLERS CLAIMING H'CAP (0-60) (3-Y.O+) (Class F)

2-40 (2-40) **1m 6f** £3,036.00 (£846.00: £408.00) Stalls: Low GOING minus 0.20 sec per fur (GF)

| | | | | SP | RR | SF |
|---|---|---|---|---|---|---|
| $3649^{5}$ | **Nothing Doing (IRE) (34)** (WJMusson) **7-8-7** PatEddery(7) (mde all: r.o wl) | — | **1** | 11/2$^{1}$ | 48 | 26 |
| $4426^{7}$ | **Rose of Glenn (40)** (BPalling) **5-8-13** TSprake(20) (plld hrd: a.p: jnd wnr 3f out: one pce fnl f) | 1¾ | **2** | 33/1 | 52 | 30 |
| $3801^{3}$ | **Ginka (35)** (JWMullins) **5-8-8** VSlattery(4) (rdn 6f out: hdwy fnl 3f: nvr nrr) | 8 | **3** | 12/1 | 38 | 16 |
| $3965^{11}$ | **Sam Rockett (49)** (CAHorgan) **3-8-13** DHarrison(19) (bhd tl hdwy 3f out: one pce fnl 2f) | 1 | **4** | 33/1 | 51 | 20 |
| $4086^{5}$ | **Spread The Word (48)** (LGCottrell) **4-9-7v** JQuinn(5) (b: prom tl wknd over 2f out) | 3 | **5** | 8/1$^{3}$ | 46 | 24 |
| $3507^{6}$ | **Dots Dee (30)** (JMBradley) **7-8-3** SDrowne(10) (b.nr fore: rdn & hdwy 4f out: wknd 2f out) | 2 | **6** | 14/1 | 26 | 4 |
| $4365^{11}$ | **Rivercare (IRE) (53)** (MJPolglase) **3-8-12**(5) AmandaSanders(17) (lw: prom tl wknd 3f out) | 2½ | **7** | 16/1 | 46 | 15 |
| | **Spring to Glory (32)** (PHayward) **9-8-5** DaneO'Neill(12) (prom tl wknd over 2f out) | nk | **8** | 33/1 | 25 | 3 |
| $3520^{7}$ | **Bresil (USA) (32)** (KRBurke) **7-7-12**(7) EmilyJoyce(16) (lw: plld hrd: prom tl wknd over 3f out) | nk | **9** | 25/1 | 25 | 3 |
| $4252^{7}$ | **Summerhill Special (IRE) (50)** (MrsPNDutfield) **5-9-9** MTebbutt(3) (bhd whn swtchd stands' side over 3f out: n.d) | ½ | **10** | 9/1 | 42 | 20 |
| $4448^{3}$ | **Forever Noble (IRE) (60)** (MRChannon) **3-9-10** JCarroll(9) (hdwy 6f out: wknd over 2f out) | ¾ | **11** | 10/1 | 51 | 20 |
| $4252^{12}$ | **Allez Pablo (30)** (RRowe) **6-8-3** GHind(8) (a bhd) | 4 | **12** | 33/1 | 17 | — |
| $2599^{8}$ | **Native Song (39)** (MJHaynes) **3-8-3** AMcGlone(18) (chsd ldr: wknd over 3f out) | 2 | **13** | 16/1 | 23 | — |
| *$4095^{14}$* | **Upper Club (IRE) (38)** (PRWebber) **4-8-11b**$^{1}$ MWigham(14) (plld hrd: a bhd) | 1¾ | **14** | 33/1 | 20 | — |
| $4236^{2}$ | **Rock The Barney (IRE) (49)** (PBurgoyne) **7-9-8** DRMcCabe(15) (a bhd) | 6 | **15** | 11/2$^{1}$ | 24 | 2 |
| $3825^{13}$ | **Studio Thirty (36)** (CASmith) **4-8-9**ow1 JReid(2) (bhd fnl 2f) | s.h | **16** | 25/1 | 11 | — |

3785[3] **War Requiem (IRE) (36)** (RJO'Sullivan) **6-8-9** TQuinn(1) (hdwy 5f out: swtchd stands' side over 3f out: eased whn btn over 1f out)....20 **17** 6/1[2] — —
*4095*[4] **Warspite (41)** (RJO'Sullivan) **6-9-0** SSanders(11) (prom 10f: t.o)....1¼ **18** 14/1 — —
4353[7] **Sliparis (40)** (KOCunningham-Brown) **3-8-4** CMunday(13) (a bhd: t.o fnl 4f)....¾ **19** 14/1 — —
**Jolis Absent (41)** (MJRyan) **6-9-0** AClark(6) (a bhd: t.o fnl 4f)....3½ **20** 20/1 — —
(SP 141.9%) **20 Rn**

**3m 7.77** (9.07) CSF £175.96 CT £1,958.41 TOTE £5.90: £1.40 £3.80 £2.70 £6.20 (£105.80) Trio £180.10 OWNER Broughton Bloodstock (NEWMARKET) BRED Cleaboy Stud
WEIGHT FOR AGE 3yo-9lb
**3649 Nothing Doing (IRE)**, gamely rallying when joined by the runner-up, seemed well-suited by the longer trip. (11/2)
**9 Rose of Glenn**, who has been running unplaced in conventional handicaps, has done all her winning in sellers and claimers. (33/1)
**3801 Ginka** has finished well in recent races and a test of stamina should be in her favour. (12/1)
**Sam Rockett** showed belated signs of ability and is worth persevering with over this sort of trip. (33/1)
**4086 Spread The Word** has yet to prove she stays this far. (8/1)
**4448 Forever Noble (IRE)** made a promising move early in the straight but found the weight concession beyond him. (10/1)
**4236 Rock The Barney (IRE)** has only ever won on good or fast ground. (11/2)

## 4510 CRANBORNE CONDITIONS STKS (2-Y.O) (Class C)
3-10 (3-10) **6f** £4,553.60 (£1,702.40: £831.20: £356.00: £158.00: £78.80) Stalls: Low GOING minus 0.20 sec per fur (GF)

SP RR SF
4189[2] **Tomba (99)** (BJMeehan) **2-9-1** MTebbutt(3) (hld up: swtchd rt & hdwy to ld over 1f out: drvn out)....— **1** 9/2[3] 94 40
4330* **Speedball (IRE)** (IABalding) **2-9-1** MHills(1) (led after 1f tl over 3f out: swtchd rt over 1f out: hrd rdn & unable qckn ins fnl f)....2½ **2** 6/4[1] 87 33
4189* **Magical Times (100)** (RBoss) **2-9-6** PatEddery(2) (lw: w ldrs: led over 3f out tl over 1f out: one pce)....2½ **3** 7/4[2] 86 32
4207* **Heavenly Miss (IRE) (72)** (DBurchell) **2-8-7** TSprake(6) (led 1f: wknd fnl f)....3½ **4** 20/1 63 9
3940[3] **Big Ben (95)** (RHannon) **2-9-1** DaneO'Neill(5) (w ldrs tl wknd over 1f out)....½ **5** 11/1 70 16
4111[5] **Isle of Corregidor (USA) (85)** (MrsJCecil) **2-8-12** TQuinn(4) (lw: hld up: rdn 2f out: btn whn n.m.r ins fnl f: eased)....5 **6** 16/1 54 —
(SP 113.5%) **6 Rn**

**1m 16.16** (3.16) CSF £11.49 TOTE £6.20: £2.30 £1.50 (£8.10) OWNER Mr J. R. Good (UPPER LAMBOURN) BRED Mrs P. Good
**IN-FOCUS: The runners raced stands' side.**
**4189 Tomba**, 5lb better off with the third on Doncaster running, turned the tables in no uncertain fashion. He holds his form well. (9/2)
**4330* Speedball (IRE)** lost his position on the stands' rail approaching halfway, and from then on, little went right for him. He is capable of winning more races when things go his way. (6/4)
**4189* Magical Times**, a winner on soft ground in August, failed to confirm Doncaster form with the winner. (7/4)
**4207* Heavenly Miss (IRE)** ran well for a long way but was ultimately outclassed by some useful rivals. (20/1)
**3940 Big Ben** has been running over five and the extra furlong was his downfall on this occasion. (11/1: 8/1-12/1)
**4111 Isle of Corregidor (USA)**, still in contention below the distance, was allowed to coast in once beaten. (16/1)

## 4511 GOLDING CHALKE H'CAP (0-70) (3-Y.O+) (Class E)
3-40 (3-42) **1m** £3,600.00 (£1,080.00: £520.00: £240.00) Stalls: Low GOING minus 0.20 sec per fur (GF)

SP RR SF
4186* **Ashby Hill (IRE) (65)** (RRowe) **5-9-9** AClark(10) (a.p: led ins fnl f: rdn out)....— **1** 4/1[1] 75 45
4184[14] **Fionn de Cool (IRE) (67)** (RAkehurst) **5-9-11** TQuinn(11) (lw: hdwy to ld over 2f out tl over 1f out: one pce)....2 **2** 10/1 73 43
4053[13] **Sovereigns Court (65)** (MajorDNChappell) **3-9-6** RHills(15) (stdd s: sn prom: led over 1f out tl ins fnl f)....½ **3** 20/1 70 37
4354[7] **Helios (64)** (NJHWalker) **8-9-1**(7) MatthewWilliams(18) (lw: a.p: r.o one pce fnl 2f)....1¼ **4** 25/1 67 37
4047[5] **Premier Generation (IRE) (59)** (DWPArbuthnot) **3-9-0** TSprake(7) (gd hdwy stands' side 2f out: r.o ins fnl f) .½ **5** 20/1 61 28
*3603*[12] **Northern Celadon (IRE) (62)** (MJHeaton-Ellis) **5-9-6** DaneO'Neill(17) (w ldr: led over 3f out tl over 2f out: one pce)....½ **6** 14/1 63 33
4128[4] **Thai Morning (57)** (PWHarris) **3-8-12** GHind(4) (led stands' side: one pce fnl 2f)....2 **7** 16/1 54 21
4373[17] **Proud Brigadier (IRE) (51)** (PBurgoyne) **8-8-9** DRMcCabe(6) (hdwy stands' side 3f out: wknd over 1f out)...11 **8** 20/1 26 —
4256[3] **Godmersham Park (68)** (MJHeaton-Ellis) **4-9-12** JReid(8) (prom stands' side over 5f)....2½ **9** 9/1[3] 38 8
943[4] **Flint And Steel (65)** (BobJones) **3-9-1**(5) LNewton(1) (b: n.d)....3 **10** 14/1 29 —
3469[11] **Deevee (60)** (CJBenstead) **7-9-4** MWigham(14) (s.s: eased whn no ch ins fnl f)....s.h **11** 12/1 23 —
4232[3] **Witherkay (61)** (RHannon) **3-9-2** PatEddery(12) (bhd fnl 2f)....½ **12** 9/1[3] 23 —
701[8] **Whispering Dawn (63)** (MRChannon) **3-9-4** JCarroll(3) (swtg: prom stands' side over 5f)....3 **13** 12/1 19 —
4256[10] **Dawalib (USA) (57)** (DHaydnJones) **6-9-1** MHills(13) (lw: mid div: hrd rdn over 2f out: eased whn no ch fnl f).½ **14** 14/1 12 —
4428* **Mr Cube (IRE) (50)** (JMBradley) **6-8-1b**(7) CLowther(16) (led over 4f: wknd qckly)....½ **15** 7/1[2] 4 —
4109[11] **Quintus Decimus (65)** (BJMeehan) **4-9-9** DHarrison(2) (lw: w ldr stands' side over 5f)....8 **16** 25/1 3 —
**Kirov Royale (60)** (MarkCampion) **5-9-4** AMcGlone(5) (swtg: a bhd)....3½ **17** 50/1 — —
**Renata's Prince (IRE) (70)** (KRBurke) **3-9-11** JQuinn(9) (wl bhd fnl 3f)....¾ **18** 25/1 — —
(SP 130.6%) **18 Rn**

**1m 45.07** (4.67) CSF £43.16 CT £689.40 TOTE £5.50: £2.00 £3.00 £12.10 £6.80 (£25.10) Trio £586.10; £181.64 to Newmarket 3/10/96
OWNER Miss Meriel Tufnell (PULBOROUGH) BRED Patrick Aspell
WEIGHT FOR AGE 3yo-3lb
**IN-FOCUS: The far side group had an advantage.**
**4186* Ashby Hill (IRE)**, a consistent mare, did not mind the cut in the ground and defied a 6lb rise in the weights. (4/1)
**3765 Fionn de Cool (IRE)** has slipped to a mark 3lb lower than when scoring over course and distance in August last year. (10/1)
**3513 Sovereigns Court**, 4lb lower than when making his handicap debut last time, appeared to stay the mile well enough and perhaps some give in the ground is the key to him. (20/1)
**4129 Helios**, back to the mark off which he was awarded a race here in August, won on this ground two years ago. (25/1)
**4047 Premier Generation (IRE)** dropped a further 1lb, seemed to relish the easier ground and was the first home on the stands' side. (20/1)
**2551 Northern Celadon (IRE)** ran well and has obviously been waiting for the ground to ease. (14/1)
**4128 Thai Morning**, rather surprisingly stepping up to a mile, did most of the donkey work on the unfavoured stands' side. (16/1)

## 4512 AUTUMN MAIDEN STKS (I) (2-Y.O) (Class D)
4-10 (4-13) **6f 212y** £3,476.50 (£1,042.00: £501.00: £230.50) Stalls: Low GOING minus 0.20 sec per fur (GF)

SP RR SF
4305[7] **Entice (FR)** (BWHills) **2-8-9** PatEddery(14) (a.p: led ins fnl f: pushed out)....— **1** 5/1[2] 88+ 33

3987[5] **Wasp Ranger (USA)** (PFICole) **2-9-0** TQuinn(12) (lw: a.p: led over 1f out: hdd ins fnl f: r.o)....½ **2** 7/2[1] 92 37
**Eshtiaal (USA)** (JLDunlop) **2-9-0** RHills(15) (leggy: scope: s.s: hld up & bhd: shkn up to over 3f out: gd hdwy over 1f out: fin wl)....3 **3** 7/1 85+ 30
**Sir Talbot** (RHannon) **2-9-0** DaneO'Neill(18) (unf: scope: a.p: one pce fnl 2f)....1 **4** 25/1 83 28
**Great Child** (MRStoute) **2-9-0** WRSwinburn(2) (str: scope: bit bkwd: mid div: hdwy fnl 2f: r.o)....hd **5** 11/2[3] 82 27
4061[8] **Cugina** (GBBalding) **2-8-9** SDrowne(7) (mid div: hdwy 2f out: r.o one pce fnl f)....hd **6** 33/1 77 22
**Academy Star** (JRFanshawe) **2-8-9** DHarrison(11) (leggy: unf: hdwy over 2f out: nvr nr to chal)....1¼ **7** 14/1 74 19
4043[8] **Effervescence (77)** (RHannon) **2-9-0** MWigham(9) (nvr nr to chal)....1½ **8** 33/1 76 21
3829[2] **Bold Spring (IRE) (77)** (RHannon) **2-9-0v[1]** JReid(13) (led: sn clr: hdd over 1f out: wknd qckly)....½ **9** 8/1 75 20
**Burning Truth (USA)** (RCharlton) **2-9-0** TSprake(5) (unf: scope: bit bkwd: dwlt: pushed along: hdwy over 2f out: wknd over 1f out)....3½ **10** 12/1 67 12
4127[12] **Warring** (MRChannon) **2-9-0** JCarroll(8) (a bhd)....4 **11** 33/1 58 3
**Woodland Nymph** (DJGMurraySmith) **2-8-9** DRMcCabe(1) (w'like: scope: bkwd: s.s: a bhd)....2 **12** 33/1 48 —
4052[11] **Northern Pass (USA)** (RAkehurst) **2-8-9** SSanders(4) (prom over 4f)....hd **13** 33/1 48 —
**Blue Imperial (FR)** (JWHills) **2-9-0** MHills(19) (scope: bkwd: mid div: rdn 3f out: sn bhd)....1¼ **14** 25/1 50 —
4380[7] **Village Pub (FR)** (KOCunningham-Brown) **2-9-0** JQuinn(3) (lw: chsd ldr over 3f: sn wknd)....2½ **15** 33/1 44 —
4104[5] **Flyaway Hill (FR)** (PWHarris) **2-8-9** GHind(17) (prom over 3f: eased whn btn fnl 2f)....1¾ **16** 6/1 35 —
**Chickamauga (USA)** (IABalding) **2-8-9** MTebbutt(16) (unf: a bhd)....6 **17** 16/1 21 —
**Nitwitty** (PDCundell) **2-9-0** AMcGlone(10) (w'like: bit bkwd: a bhd: t.o fnl 4f)....¾ **18** 33/1 25 —
**Top of The Green (IRE)** (PJMakin) **2-9-0** AClark(6) (leggy: a bhd)....1½ **19** 33/1 21 —
(SP 143.6%) **19 Rn**

**1m 29.82** (3.82) CSF £23.50 TOTE £7.10: £2.30 £2.00 £3.10 (£12.80) Trio £33.40 OWNER Sheikh Mohammed (LAMBOURN) BRED Darley Stud Management Co. Ltd.

IN-FOCUS: **The runners raced far side.**

**4305 Entice (FR)** has obviously learnt from her Newbury debut and was by no means flat out to hold the runner-up. Further improvement can be expected. (5/1)
**3987 Wasp Ranger (USA)** lost nothing in defeat and simply met one too good in the winner. (7/2: 3/1-9/2)
**Eshtiaal (USA)** finished in eye-catching style and is one to note. (7/1)
**Sir Talbot** made a promising-enough debut but may need more time. (25/1)
**Great Child**, a well-made 25,000 guineas newcomer, shaped promisingly and will be sharper for the run. (11/2: 3/1-6/1)
**Cugina** benefited from this extra furlong. (33/1)
**Academy Star** is a half-sister to Stoney Valley. (14/1)
**3829 Bold Spring (IRE)**, trying a longer trip, went off far too quickly in the first-time visor. (8/1)

## 4513 FONTHILL H'CAP (0-70) (3-Y.O+) (Class E)

4-40 (4-42) **1m 1f 209y** £3,834.00 (£1,152.00: £556.00: £258.00) GOING minus 0.20 sec per fur (GF)

SP RR SF

4073[7] **Shahik (USA) (61)** (DHaydnJones) **6-9-6** RHills(9) (gd hdwy over 2f out: led over 1f out: drvn out)....— **1** 14/1 74 47
4216[11] **Temptress (59)** (PTWalwyn) **3-8-13v** TSprake(6) (led tl over 1f out: r.o wl)....nk **2** 14/1 72 40
4238[11] **Princess Danielle (59)** (WRMuir) **4-9-4** JReid(12) (lw: hld up: hdwy 3f out: nt clr run over 1f out: r.o ins fnl f)....2½ **3** 3/1[1] 68 41
3314[6] **It'sthebusiness (55)** (SDow) **4-9-0** TQuinn(16) (a.p: ev ch over 1f out: one pce)....½ **4** 12/1 63 36
4125[15] **Bakers Daughter (54)** (JRArnold) **4-8-13** AClark(11) (swtg: a.p: rdn over 2f out: no hdwy)....3½ **5** 12/1 56 29
3459[5] **Parsa (USA) (63)** (JLDunlop) **3-9-3** PatEddery(17) (hld up & bhd: gd hdwy 3f out: wknd over 1f out)....7 **6** 13/2[2] 54 22
**Peppers (IRE) (66)** (KRBurke) **3-9-6** DHarrison(15) (prom tl wknd over 2f out)....s.h **7** 33/1 57 25
2251[15] **Ember (58)** (RTPhillips) **3-8-12** JQuinn(18) (s.s: hdwy 3f out: swtchd lft over 1f out: sn wknd)....2 **8** 33/1 46 14
4059[6] **Quinze (67)** (SirMarkPrescott) **3-9-7** SSanders(3) (nvr nr ldrs)....5 **9** 12/1 47 15
4124[7] **El Presidente (60)** (GPEnright) **3-9-0** AMcGlone(13) (lw: rdn over 5f out: a mid div)....hd **10** 20/1 39 7
3949[8] **Dark Truffle (66)** (MrsJCecil) **3-9-6** MHills(14) (hld up: hdwy on ins 3f out: nt clr run 2f out: sn wknd)....2 **11** 7/1[3] 42 10
4355[16] **Mazilla (56)** (AStreeter) **4-8-10v(5)** LNewton(5) (n.d)....2½ **12** 14/1 28 1
4059[5] **Stackattack (IRE) (63)** (PRWebber) **3-9-3** DaneO'Neill(1) (chsd ldr tl wknd 3f out)....4 **13** 10/1 29 —
4232[4] **Sistar Act (66)** (MRChannon) **3-9-6** JCarroll(7) (lw: a bhd)....1½ **14** 9/1 29 —
*4095*[9] **Indian Nectar (58)** (GBBalding) **3-8-12** SDrowne(10) (prom 6f)....¾ **15** 25/1 20 —
*3952*[11] **Mapengo (65)** (JCullinan) **5-9-10** VSlattery(2) (prom: hrd rdn & wkng whn n.m.r over 2f out)....hd **16** 33/1 27 —
3611[7] **Two Socks (63)** (PBurgoyne) **3-9-3** DRMcCabe(8) (a bhd: eased whn no ch over 1f out)....5 **17** 14/1 17 —
4358[6] **Ewar Bold (67)** (KOCunningham-Brown) **3-9-7b** MTebbutt(4) (bhd: hrd rdn 4f out: eased whn no ch fnl 2f)..dist **18** 33/1 — —
(SP 140.0%) **18 Rn**

**2m 10.51** (5.21) CSF £195.37 CT £695.92 TOTE £20.30: £4.40 £3.70 £1.20 £3.40 (£447.90) Trio £138.70 OWNER Mr S. Hunter (PONTYPRIDD)

WEIGHT FOR AGE 3yo-5lb

**3955 Shahik (USA)**, down 2lb and dropped in distance, seemed to relish the yielding going. (14/1)
**3522 Temptress**, back to 1lb lower mark than when winning at Newbury in June, had not shown improvement when tried in a visor last year, and it may well be that the softer ground was an even bigger help. (14/1)
**3938 Princess Danielle** acts on this ground but had to overcome some traffic problems and found the front two had got the first run. (3/1)
**3314 It'sthebusiness**, still 4lb higher than when winning at Lingfield in May, appeared freshened up by a two-month break. (12/1)
**3947 Bakers Daughter**, 7lb higher than when successful at Windsor in July, may have found the ground too fast when disappointing last time out. (12/1: 8/1-14/1)
**3459 Parsa (USA)**, back to a more suitable trip, did not seem to get home in this easier going. (13/2)
**4059 Quinze** (12/1: op 8/1)

## 4514 AUTUMN MAIDEN STKS (II) (2-Y.O) (Class D)

5-10 (5-17) **6f 212y** £3,476.50 (£1,042.00: £501.00: £230.50) Stalls: Low GOING minus 0.20 sec per fur (GF)

SP RR SF

**Dacoit (USA)** (MRStoute) **2-9-0** WRSwinburn(15) (w'like: scope: a.p: led 1f out: pushed out)....— **1** 7/1[3] 90+ 24
**Crimson Tide (IRE)** (JWHills) **2-9-0** MHills(17) (leggy: scope: s.s: hld up: hdwy & nt clr run 2f out: r.o wl ins fnl f)....½ **2** 8/1 89+ 23
**Titta Ruffo** (BJMeehan) **2-9-0** MTebbutt(14) (w'like: bhd: gd hdwy on ins over 1f out: rdn & r.o wl ins fnl f) ..3½ **3** 25/1 81+ 15
**River's Source (USA)** (BWHills) **2-9-0** PatEddery(4) (w'like: scope: gd hdwy to ld over 1f out: sn hdd: one pce)....hd **4** 4/1[2] 81 15

| | | | | SP | RR | SF |
|---|---|---|---|---|---|---|
| | **Arapi** (SirMarkPrescott) **2-8-9** SSanders(5) (unf: bit bkwd: a.p: led wl over 1f out: sn hdd: one pce) | nk | **5** | 11/1 | 75 | 9 |
| 3859[4] | **Phylida** (PJMakin) **2-8-9** DHarrison(8) (w ldr: led 3f out tl wl over 1f out: wknd fnl f) | 1¾ | **6** | 50/1 | 71 | 5 |
| 4163a[6] | **Al Blu (IRE)** (LMCumani) **2-9-0** DRMcCabe(10) (no hdwy fnl 2f) | ½ | **7** | 25/1 | 75 | 9 |
| 4233[2] | **Tough Act** (GHarwood) **2-9-0** AClark(13) (prom: j.path over 2f out: wknd over 1f out) | ¾ | **8** | 9/4[1] | 73 | 7 |
| 4062[14] | **Mystery (65)** (SDow) **2-8-9** GHind(1) (hdwy 3f out: ev ch 2f out: sn wknd) | 4 | **9** | 33/1 | 59 | — |
| 4330[22] | **Sharpest** (JLDunlop) **2-9-0** TSprake(12) (bhd: rdn 3f out: nvr nrr) | ¾ | **10** | 33/1 | 62 | — |
| | **Star Precision** (GBBalding) **2-8-9** SDrowne(3) (unf: s.s: bhd: rdn over 3f out: n.d) | 1½ | **11** | 50/1 | 54 | — |
| | **Prince of Denial** (DWPArbuthnot) **2-9-0** TQuinn(7) (leggy: bit bkwd: s.i.s: mid div whn rdn 3f out: n.d) | nk | **12** | 33/1 | 58 | — |
| | **Kafil (USA)** (HThomsonJones) **2-9-0** RHills(2) (w'like: scope: prom: ev ch 2f out: sn rdn & wknd) | 1½ | **13** | 7/1[3] | 55 | — |
| | **Brave Envoy** (MJHeaton-Ellis) **2-9-0** JReid(9) (leggy: scope: bhd fnl 2f) | 2 | **14** | 25/1 | 50 | — |
| | **Petsong** (RHannon) **2-9-0** DaneO'Neill(18) (w'like: scope: led 4f: sn wknd) | 2½ | **15** | 12/1 | 44 | — |
| | **Gore Hill** (MBlanshard) **2-8-9** JQuinn(16) (neat: bkwd: dwlt: a bhd) | 6 | **16** | 50/1 | 25 | — |
| | **Agent Mulder** (PDCundell) **2-9-0** AMcGlone(11) (unf: scope: a bhd) | ¾ | **17** | 50/1 | 29 | — |
| 4127[18] | **Chief Predator (USA)** (RHannon) **2-9-0** JCarroll(6) (prom tl wknd qckly over 3f out: t.o) | 11 | **18** | 50/1 | 3 | — |
| | | | | (SP 133.1%) | **18 Rn** | |

**1m 31.08** (5.08) CSF £61.14 TOTE £7.80: £2.90 £3.40 £13.60 (£56.40) Trio £290.80; £163.86 to Newmarket 3/10/96 OWNER Sheikh Mohammed (NEWMARKET) BRED Double "D" Ranch
IN-FOCUS: **The runners raced far side.**
**Dacoit (USA)** has the physique to show better things next year. (7/1: op 4/1)
**Crimson Tide (IRE)** certainly did not get the run of the race and looks a ready-made future winner. (8/1)
**Titta Ruffo** stayed on to secure the minor berth and seems to require a mile. (25/1)
**River's Source (USA)** is bred to need further. (4/1: 2/1-9/2)
**Arapi** will come on for this debut. (11/1: 7/2-12/1)
**Phylida** stepped up on her two previous outings, and may be an interesting proposition in a nursery over six on this sort of going. (50/1)
**Kafil (USA)** (7/1: op 3/1)

T/Plpt: £1,063.60 (9.64 Tckts). T/Qdpt: £41.90 (14.65 Tckts) KH

## 4487-NEWMARKET (R-H) (Good to firm)
## Thursday October 3rd
WEATHER: overcast WIND: fresh to strong across

## 4515 PORT OF FELIXSTOWE CLAIMING STKS (3-Y.O+) (Class E)
1-30 (1-38) **1m 4f (Rowley)** £4,110.00 (£1,230.00: £590.00: £270.00) Stalls: High GOING minus 0.53 sec per fur (F)

| | | | | SP | RR | SF |
|---|---|---|---|---|---|---|
| 3500[11] | **Evidence In Chief (62)** (DRCElsworth) **3-8-5v** DHarrison(9) (lw: hld up & bhd: stdy hdwy 5f out: chal wl over 1f out: led wl ins fnl f: hld on wl) | — | **1** | 7/1 | 64 | 39 |
| 4320[6] | **Once More for Luck (IRE) (65)** (MrsMReveley) **5-9-2**(5) GLee(15) (lw: hld up & bhd: hdwy 4f out: chal & hung rt ins fnl f: no ex towards fin) | s.h | **2** | 4/1[2] | 73 | 55 |
| 4374[5] | **Quiet Arch (IRE) (60)** (CACyzer) **3-8-10** JWeaver(1) (hdwy ½-wy: led wl over 1f out tl wl ins fnl f: nt qckn) | ¾ | **3** | 12/1 | 68 | 43 |
| 4121[4] | **Loki (IRE) (70)** (GLewis) **8-8-9**(3) AWhelan(17) (b.hind: in tch: effrt 3f out: styd on: nt pce to chal) | 3 | **4** | 5/2[1] | 59 | 41 |
| 2921[4] | **Petoskin (50)** (JPearce) **4-8-12**(7) PDoe(18) (mde most tl hdd, hung lft & wknd wl over 1f out) | 3 | **5** | 25/1 | 62 | 44 |
| 4217[6] | **State Approval (63)** (APJarvis) **3-8-1**(7) CCarver(4) (cl up: disp ld 7f out to 3f out: grad wknd fnl 2f) | 1¾ | **6** | 7/1 | 56 | 31 |
| 4237[9] | **Quillwork (USA) (55)** (JPearce) **4-8-8** GBardwell(2) (hld up: hdwy to chal 3f out: wknd wl over 1f out) | ½ | **7** | 14/1 | 48 | 30 |
| 4203[10] | **Bobby's Dream (33)** (MHTompkins) **4-8-4**(3) MHenry(3) (effrt 5f out: nvr trbld ldrs) | 2½ | **8** | 25/1 | 44 | 26 |
| 4237[6] | **Shabanaz (62)** (WRMuir) **11-8-12** JReid(16) (lw: prom tl wknd fnl 3½f) | 2 | **9** | 4/1[2] | 46 | 28 |
| 4362[5] | **St Honorine (IRE)** (CMurray) **4-9-0** JFortune(11) (b: chsd ldrs tl wknd fnl 3f) | 7 | **10** | 20/1 | 39 | 21 |
| 4216[2] | **Domettes (IRE) (58)** (RHannon) **3-8-3** DaneO'Neill(7) (prom tl wknd fnl 4f) | 2 | **11** | 5/1 | 32 | 7 |
| *4095[11]* | **Precedency (50)** (KMcAuliffe) **4-8-12** JFEgan(5) (b.hind: chsd ldrs tl wknd over 3f out) | 17 | **12** | 20/1 | 11 | — |
| | **Needwood Native** (AJWilson) **8-8-12** VSlattery(13) (rdn & lost pl 6f out: t.o) | dist | **13** | 20/1 | — | — |
| *3944[2]* | ***Kaafih Homm (IRE) (72)*** (NACallaghan) **5-9-13** LDettori(8) (Withdrawn not under Starter's orders: veterinary advice) | | **W** | 9/2[3] | — | — |
| | ***Squandamania*** (PFICole) **3-9-6** MHills(10) (Withdrawn not under Starter's orders: veterinary advice) | | **W** | 8/1 | — | — |
| | ***Broughtons Champ*** (WJMusson) **4-9-3** DRMcCabe(12) (Withdrawn not under Starter's orders: uns rdr & bolted) | | **W** | 33/1 | — | — |
| | | | | (SP 178.8%) | **13 Rn** | |

**2m 31.73** (1.23) CSF £40.66 TOTE £17.30: £3.70 £1.40 £4.80 (£35.60) Trio £63.60 OWNER Mr Raymond Tooth (WHITCOMBE) BRED N. Abbott
WEIGHT FOR AGE 3yo-7lb
**OFFICIAL EXPLANATION Needwood Native: finished distressed.**
**2975* Evidence In Chief** returned here looking particularly well after almost two months off and, after travelling on the bridle, proved too determined for the runner-up. (7/1: 8/1-12/1)
**4073 Once More for Luck (IRE)** should have won this, but he is his own worst enemy and failed to go through with it. He will win a race but is likely to throw plenty away. (4/1)
**4374 Quiet Arch (IRE)**, in a messy race, came there going well, but just failed to see it out. By the looks of things, he can pick up a race on turf in due course. (12/1: 12/1-20/1)
**4121 Loki (IRE)** ran quite well, but just failed to pick up sufficiently when ridden. (5/2)
**2921 Petoskin** obviously had a problem last time and this was something like his true form. (25/1)
**4217 State Approval** is not very big and went freely to post. After running in the same manner, he stopped in the last two furlongs. (7/1: 6/1-9/1)
**Quillwork (USA)**, having her second run for her new stable, shaped reasonably well until finding this trip too far in the last furlong and a half. (14/1: 14/1-25/1)

## 4516 E.B.F. EQUITY FINANCIAL COLLECTIONS WESTLEY MAIDEN STKS (2-Y.O) (Class D)
2-00 (2-09) **7f (Rowley)** £7,515.00 (£2,250.00: £1,080.00: £495.00) Stalls: Low GOING minus 0.32 sec per fur (GF)

| | | | | SP | RR | SF |
|---|---|---|---|---|---|---|
| | **Mashhaer (USA)** (SbinSuroor) **2-9-0** RHills(7) (lt-f: unf: chsd ldrs: hdwy to ld ins fnl f: r.o) | — | **1** | 6/1[3] | 83+ | 53 |
| | **Courtship** (HRACecil) **2-9-0** PatEddery(10) (gd srt: scope: w ldrs: outpcd 2f out: styd on to chal ins fnl f: kpt on) | 1¼ | **2** | 11/4[1] | 80+ | 50 |

4242[13] **Red Guard** (GWragg) **2-9-0** MHills(3) (lw: led tl ins fnl f: kpt on same pce)........1 **3** 4/1[2] 78 48
4060[2] **Social Pillar (USA)** (JHMGosden) **2-9-0** LDettori(4) (chsd ldrs: outpcd over 2f out: kpt on fnl f)........2 **4** 6/1[3] 73 43
**Regal Thunder (USA)** (MRStoute) **2-9-0** KDarley(16) (w'like: scope: mid div: styd on wl fnl 2f)........1½ **5** 7/1 70 40
**Spy Knoll** (MRStoute) **2-9-0** JReid(14) (w'like: leggy: bkwd: mid div: styd on wl fnl f)........s.h **6** 20/1 70 40
**Green Card (USA)** (SPCWoods) **2-9-0** RHughes(17) (w'like: in tch: rdn over 2f out: no imp)........¾ **7** 33/1 68 38
**Unshaken** (JRFanshawe) **2-9-0** DHarrison(12) (cmpt: scope: chsd ldrs tl wknd fnl 2f)........¾ **8** 33/1 66 36
**Aerleon Pete (IRE)** (MRStoute) **2-9-0** WRSwinburn(15) (neat: mid div: shkn up over 2f out: sme late hdwy)..½ **9** 12/1 65 35
**Kamin (USA)** (RWArmstrong) **2-9-0** JWeaver(13) (cmpt: scope: dwlt: n.d)........4 **10** 16/1 56 26
**Craven Hill (IRE)** (NAGraham) **2-9-0** GDuffield(2) (w'like: outpcd & bhd: sme late hdwy)........¾ **11** 33/1 54 24
4330[20] **Island Prince** (NACallaghan) **2-9-0** DaneO'Neill(9) (nvr nr ldrs)........1½ **12** 33/1 51 21
**Fantail** (MHTompkins) **2-9-0** RCochrane(6) (gd sort: s.i.s: nvr trbld ldrs)........¾ **13** 33/1 49 19
**Wonderboy (IRE)** (RAkehurst) **2-9-0** SSanders(8) (leggy: lt-f: chsd ldrs: sn rdn along: wknd over 2f out)........¾ **14** 33/1 48 18
**Oliver (IRE)** (RWArmstrong) **2-9-0** RPrice(1) (w'like: scope: s.s: drvn along & nt rcvr)........nk **15** 25/1 47 17
**Salsee Lad** (JRFanshawe) **2-9-0** NDay(5) (wl grwn: bkwd: dwlt: sn wl bhd: t.o)........dist **16** 33/1 — —
(SP 130.5%) **16 Rn**

**1m 26.07** (1.57) CSF £21.93 TOTE £6.40: £2.00 £1.80 £1.60 (£6.10) Trio £25.80 OWNER Mr Hamdan Al Maktoum (NEWMARKET) BRED Shadwell Estate Co., Ltd. and Shadwell Farm Inc.

**Mashhaer (USA)** is nothing special to look at and won an ordinary race, but had to really knuckle down to the job in hand and, in the end, won really well. (6/1)
**Courtship** looked the part, but was found out on the downhill section approaching the final furlong and, despite battling on, was always second best. He will stay further and should have learnt from this. (11/4)
**Red Guard** had obviously learnt plenty from his debut run and put in a much-improved effort this time, but was tapped for toe late on. He lacks a change of gear, but should pick up a race in due course., (4/1: op 5/2)
**4060 Social Pillar (USA)** looked and moved really well, but was short of toe at a vital stage and, after getting well outpaced, stayed on to suggest that longer trips might see improvement. (6/1)
**Regal Thunder (USA)** needed this and showed some promise, picking up in pleasing style at the end. Better now looks likely. (7/1: 4/1-8/1)
**Spy Knoll**, very much in need of this, gave the impression that, with experience, there is a fair bit of improvement in him. (20/1)
**Green Card (USA)**, a shade fractious in the stalls, ran reasonably until blowing up in the last couple of furlongs. (33/1)
**Unshaken**, looking likely to be all the better for the run, showed useful speed until stopping approaching the final furlong. (33/1)

## 4517 BAILEYS HORSE FEEDS NURSERY H'CAP (2-Y.O) (Class C)

2-35 (2-36) **5f (Rowley)** £7,570.00 (£2,260.00: £1,080.00: £490.00) Stalls: Low GOING minus 0.32 sec per fur (GF)

SP RR SF
4324* **Meliksah (IRE) (89)** (MBell) **2-9-2**(5) GFaulkner(2) (mde all: rdn & r.o wl fnl f)........— **1** 9/2[2] 98 63
4043* **Hattab (IRE) (88)** (PTWalwyn) **2-9-6** RHills(3) (s.i.s: sn in tch: hdwy to chse wnr over 1f out: nt qckn towards fin)........1½ **2** 6/4[1] 92 57
4424* **Anokato (70)** (KTIvory) **2-7-13b**(3) 7x MHenry(5) (a chsng ldrs: rdn 2f out: r.o one pce)........3 **3** 15/2 65 30
4024a[15] **Top of The Form (IRE) (87)** (MJohnston) **2-9-5** JWeaver(1) (cl up: rdn 2f out: r.o one pce)........nk **4** 7/1 81 46
4468[3] **Changed To Baileys (IRE) (68)** (JBerry) **2-7-9b**[1](5) PFessey(4) (dwlt: hdwy ½-wy: rdn & no imp)........1¼ **5** 14/1 58 23
4210[7] **Swift (64)** (MJPolglase) **2-7-3**(7) RFfrench(7) (prom: effrt 2f out: no imp after)........4 **6** 33/1 41 6
3924[7] **Bramble Bear (72)** (MBlanshard) **2-8-4** JQuinn(6) (cl up tl wknd wl over 1f out)........d.h **6** 25/1 62 27
4230[5] **Last Chance (78)** (CNAllen) **2-8-5**(5) MartinDwyer(8) (lw: hld up: outpcd ½-wy: n.d)........2½ **8** 14/1 47 12
4350[4] **Clara Bliss (IRE) (72)** (BJMeehan) **2-8-1**(3) FLynch(9) (outpcd & bhd fr ½-wy)........2 **9** 6/1[3] 34 —
(SP 116.9%) **9 Rn**

**59.52 secs** (0.82) CSF £11.36 CT £45.09 TOTE £6.00: £2.00 £1.30 £2.80 (£2.80) Trio £18.60 OWNER Mr Yucel Birol (NEWMARKET) BRED Ron Con Ltd

**4324* Meliksah (IRE)** is a bad-actioned colt, but he has certainly come right of late and won this with plenty of authority. (9/2)
**4043* Hattab (IRE)** ran well after a poor start and this may turn out to be a decent race. (6/4)
**4424* Anokato** put in a determined effort, but the struggle proved too much approaching the final furlong. (15/2)
**4024a Top of The Form (IRE)** could never dominate this time and it all proved too much in the last two furlongs but, after a month off, this was still not a bad effort. (7/1)
**4468 Changed To Baileys (IRE)**, in blinkers for the first time, threw away all chances with a slow start. (14/1)

## 4518 JRA NAKAYAMA ROUS STKS (Listed) (3-Y.O+) (Class A)

3-05 (3-05) **5f (Rowley)** £10,971.80 (£4,056.20: £1,943.10: £790.50: £310.25: £118.15) Stalls: Low GOING minus 0.32 sec per fur (GF)

SP RR SF
4466[3] **Croft Pool (104)** (JAGlover) **5-8-12** GCarter(5) (trckd ldrs: rdn to ld ins fnl f: r.o)........— **1** 4/1[2] 111 72
4115[4] **Blue Iris (103)** (MAJarvis) **3-8-7** LDettori(6) (led tl ins fnl f: kpt on)........¾ **2** 11/4[1] 104 65
4115* **Anzio (IRE) (109)** (MissGayKelleway) **5-9-4b** RCochrane(2) (lw: cl up: rdn 2f out: r.o one pce)........1 **3** 11/4[1] 111 72
4115[3] **Brave Edge (106)** (RHannon) **5-9-1** PatEddery(4) (outpcd & bhd 2f out: styd on towards fin)........3½ **4** 4/1[2] 97 58
1316[4] **Music Gold (IRE) (92)** (WAO'Gorman) **3-8-12b** EmmaO'Gorman(3) (dwlt: sn in tch: rdn & no imp fnl 2f)........nk **5** 33/1 93 54
4304[7] **Ya Malak (102)** (IABalding) **5-8-12** AMcGlone(7) (trckd ldrs: effrt 2f out: sn rdn & btn)........2½ **6** 11/1[3] 85 46
(SP 104.6%) **6 Rn**

**58.5 secs** (-0.20) CSF £13.50 TOTE £5.40: £2.60 £1.40 (£7.00) OWNER Countrywide Classics Ltd (WORKSOP) BRED J. S. Bell

**4466 Croft Pool**, patiently ridden, produced a run to settle it emphatically inside the final furlong. He is game and consistent. (4/1)
**4115 Blue Iris** was allowed to dictate things and, quickening it up from halfway, shook off all but the winner. (11/4)
**4115* Anzio (IRE)** likes to come from behind and was always seeing too much daylight too soon on this occasion. (11/4)
**4115 Brave Edge** would have preferred a faster pace early on, as he got caught flat-footed when things hotted up at halfway, and his chance had then gone. (4/1)
**1316 Music Gold (IRE)**, after over four months off, missed the break and was always fighting a lost cause thereafter. (33/1)
**4304 Ya Malak** travelled well but, once off the bit, the response was disappointing. (11/1: 7/1-12/1)

## 4519 MIDDLE PARK STKS (Gp 1) (2-Y.O C) (Class A)

3-40 (3-41) **6f (Rowley)** £81,532.50 (£30,367.50: £14,733.75: £6,206.25: £2,653.13: £1,231.87) Stalls: Low GOING minus 0.32 sec per fur (GF)

SP RR SF
3750a* **Bahamian Bounty** (DRLoder) **2-8-11** LDettori(2) (hld up: nt clr run 2f out: hdwy over 1f out: r.o wl to ld wl ins fnl f)........— **1** 7/4[1] 109 66

4035a* **Muchea (100)** (MRChannon) **2-8-11** RHughes(1) (bhd: swtchd & hdwy over 1f out: led ins fnl f: r.o: jst ct) .....hd **2** 16/1 109 66
4179[2] **In Command (IRE)** (BWHills) **2-8-11** MHills(8) (a.p: effrt 2f out: r.o) ......1 **3** 8/1 106 63
4398a[4] **Fantastic Fellow (USA)** (CEBrittain) **2-8-11** OPeslier(9) (a.p: led appr fnl f: hdd ins fnl f: kpt on) ......s.h **4** 10/1 106 63
4191[3] **Deep Finesse (100)** (MAJarvis) **2-8-11** PatEddery(3) (w ldrs: led 2f out tl appr fnl f: no ex) ......1¼ **5** 16/1 103 60
4191* **Easycall (100)** (BJMeehan) **2-8-11** MTebbutt(10) (lw: trckd ldrs: effrt 2f out: sn hrd rdn & r.o one pce) ......1 **6** 7/1 100 57
4188* **Hurricane State (USA)** (PWChapple-Hyam) **2-8-11** JReid(7) (lw: cl up: effrt 2f out: sn drvn: wknd 1f out) .....nk **7** 13/2[3] 99 56
4328[4] **Andreyev (IRE) (100)** (RHannon) **2-8-11** DaneO'Neill(4) (in tch: effrt over 2f out: no imp) ......1½ **8** 33/1 95 52
3750a[4] **Rich Ground (100)** (JDBethell) **2-8-11** JWeaver(5) (led 4f: wknd) ......3½ **9** 33/1 86 43
4328* **Indian Rocket (100)** (JLDunlop) **2-8-11** RHills(11) (lw: wnt rt s: sn prom: ev ch 2f out: wknd over 1f out: eased) ......½ **10** 9/2[2] 85 42
4100[4] **Zaretski (79)** (CEBrittain) **2-8-11** MRoberts(6) (effrt ½-wy: sn btn) ......6 **11** 100/1 69 26

(SP 119.2%) **11 Rn**

**1m 11.95** (0.15) CSF £27.94 TOTE £2.80: £1.50 £2.90 £2.80 (£30.70) Trio £37.70 OWNER Maktoum Al Maktoum (NEWMARKET) BRED Clarents Racing Ltd

**3750a* Bahamian Bounty** went to post like an old sheep, but he certainly livened up in the race and, after looking in serious trouble when having nowhere to go, he got a gap approaching the final furlong and produced the sparkle that was required. Whether he will stay further is open to debate, but he certainly has the right attitude. (7/4)

**4035a* Muchea**, like the winner short of room at the back of the field, if anything got first run, but was then beaten fair and square. (16/1)

**4179 In Command (IRE)**, in a field full of good-looking colts, was without doubt one of the best and ran a fine race. He looks the type to improve no end next year as he tries further. (8/1: 6/1-10/1)

**4398a Fantastic Fellow (USA)**, a super-looking individual, was always finding this trip a bit on the sharp side, but he did keep plugging on. (10/1)

**4191 Deep Finesse**, stepping up to six for the first time, was always up with the pace, but just failed to see it out in this company. (16/1)

**4191* Easycall** ran a sound race, but he left the impression that, at present, he is at his best over the minimum trip. (7/1)

**4188* Hurricane State (USA)**, taking a big step up in class, ran well but was found wanting in the last furlong and a half. (13/2: 4/1-7/1)

**4328* Indian Rocket** was very much on edge beforehand and never really fired. He was sympathetically handled when beaten and this is best completely ignored. (9/2)

## 4520 JOEL STKS (Listed) (3-Y.O+) (Class A)

4-15 (4-15) **1m (Rowley)** £11,464.80 (£4,243.20: £2,036.60: £833.00: £331.50: £130.90) Stalls: Low GOING minus 0.32 sec per fur (GF)

SP RR SF

4028a[8] **Yeast (107)** (WJHaggas) **4-9-0** RCochrane(8) (lw: racd centre: mde most: r.o wl fnl 2f) ......— **1** 11/2[3] 114 70
4409a[12] **Restructure (IRE) (114)** (MrsJCecil) **4-9-7** MRoberts(1) (chsd ldrs stands' side: effrt over 2f out: styd on: nt pce to chal) ......1¼ **2** 7/2[1] 119 75
4135[6] **Tamnia (100)** (JLDunlop) **3-8-6** KDarley(3) (swtg: in tch stands' side: effrt over 2f out: styd on wl towards fin) ......hd **3** 20/1 106 59
4325* **Phantom Quest (107)** (HRACecil) **3-8-11** PatEddery(6) (lw: hld up stands' side: hdwy u.p 2f out: nvr able to chal) ......½ **4** 9/2[2] 110 63
4051[4] **Hammerstein (110)** (MRStoute) **3-8-11** RHughes(7) (led stands' side tl rdn & btn over 1f out) ......½ **5** 7/1 109 62
4185[3] **Silver Prey (USA) (100)** (EALDunlop) **3-8-11** WRyan(4) (chsd ldrs stands' side tl rdn & btn 2f out: lame) ......6 **6** 11/2[3] 97 50
4122[3] **Green Perfume (USA) (106)** (PFICole) **4-9-0** MHills(5) (hld up & bhd stands' side: effrt over 2f out: no imp) ...¾ **7** 10/1 96 52
4439[2] **Glowing Jade (68)** (JAGlover) **6-8-9** GCarter(9) (chsd wnr centre: rdn 3f out: sn wknd) ......13 **8** 66/1 65 21
982* **El Penitente (IRE)** (DRLoder) **3-8-11** LDettori(2) (trckd ldrs stands' side: wknd fnl 2f) ......2½ **9** 13/2 65 18

(SP 112.4%) **9 Rn**

**1m 37.43** (0.13) CSF £23.00 TOTE £6.60: £2.00 £1.70 £5.50 (£11.50) Trio £199.60 OWNER Mr B. Haggas (NEWMARKET) BRED R. T. and Mrs Watson

WEIGHT FOR AGE 3yo-3lb

**OFFICIAL EXPLANATION Silver Prey (USA): returned home lame.**

**4028a Yeast** was able to have things his own way by racing up the centre of the course. In front virtually throughout, he was always too strong for the main body on the stands' rail. (11/2)

**4409a Restructure (IRE)** does not do anything quickly, but he does respond to pressure, and stayed on well to beat the stands'-side group, if never looking likely to trouble the winner in the centre of the track. (7/2)

**4135 Tamnia**, happier without the blinkers, ran much better and was keeping on really well at the end. (20/1)

**4325* Phantom Quest** failed to impress with his action going to post. Asked for an effort some way out, he was never giving it his best shot. (9/2)

**4051 Hammerstein** moved moderately to post and, after making the running up the stands' side, folded up when the pressure was applied over a furlong out. (7/1: 5/1-15/2)

**4185 Silver Prey (USA)**, stepping up in distance, was a big disappointment and was beaten too far out to say he did not stay. (11/2)

**4122 Green Perfume (USA)** was held up this time, which did not suit him. (10/1)

**982* El Penitente (IRE)** (13/2: 4/1-7/1)

## 4521 FITZWILLIAM H'CAP (0-80) (3-Y.O) (Class D)

4-50 (4-51) **5f (Rowley)** £4,620.00 (£1,380.00: £660.00: £300.00) Stalls: Low GOING minus 0.32 sec per fur (GF)

SP RR SF

3932[2] **Swynford Dream (79)** (JFBottomley) **3-9-6** LDettori(3) (mde all: rdn & r.o strly fnl f) ......— **1** 7/2[2] 88 70
4180[8] **Literary Society (USA) (68)** (JARToller) **3-8-9** SSanders(1) (chsd ldrs: hdwy u.p 2f out: no ex ins fnl f) ......1¼ **2** 10/1 73 55
4356* **Shining Cloud (67)** (MBell) **3-8-8** 7x MFenton(12) (a cl up: effrt 2f out: kpt on same pce) ......nk **3** 3/1[1] 71 53
4372[8] **Mindrace (68)** (KTIvory) **3-8-4**(5) MartinDwyer(13) (a chsng ldrs: rdn 2f out: r.o one pce) ......1 **4** 12/1 69 51
3693[14] **U-No-Harry (IRE) (72)** (RHollinshead) **3-8-10**(3) FLynch(7) (mid div: rdn over 2f out: styd on wl fnl f) ......1¾ **5** 20/1 67 49
4220[2] **Longwick Lad (77)** (WRMuir) **3-9-4** JReid(10) (in tch: hrd rdn over 1f out: nvr able to chal) ......s.h **6** 6/1[3] 72 54
*4094*[2] **Step On Degas (62)** (MJFetherston-Godley) **3-7-10**(7) RFfrench(9) (lw: in tch: effrt ½-wy: no imp) ......1¼ **7** 11/1 53 35
4342[4] **Sharp Pearl (74)** (JWhite) **3-9-1** RHughes(2) (bhd: hdwy ½-wy: sn rdn & n.d) ......1¼ **8** 25/1 61 43
1628[10] **Air Wing (75)** (MHTompkins) **3-9-2** RCochrane(15) (racd alone centre: hung lft ½-wy: in tch tl wknd over 1f out) ......¾ **9** 16/1 60 42
4382[4] **Tropical Beach (66)** (JBerry) **3-8-7** KDarley(16) (sn outpcd) ......¾ **10** 10/1 48 30
4202[6] **Sabaah Elfull (66)** (ACStewart) **3-8-7** MRoberts(11) (dwlt: n.d) ......½ **11** 14/1 47 29
4382[10] **Chalice (66)** (JBalding) **3-8-0**(7)ow1 JEdmunds(4) (lw: sn outpcd) ......hd **12** 33/1 46 27
3665[3] **Il Doria (IRE) (60)** (AHide) **3-8-1** AMcGlone(5) (b.hind: s.i.s: a rr div) ......3 **13** 20/1 31 13
4219[3] **Smithereens (68)** (PTWalwyn) **3-8-9** PatEddery(8) (nvr wnt pce) ......¾ **14** 16/1 36 18

| | | | | SP | RR | SF |
|---|---|---|---|---|---|---|
| 3406[5] | **Mijas (71)** (LMontagueHall) **3-8-12** DaneO'Neill(14) (outpcd & lost tch fr ½-wy) | ¾ | **15** | 33/1 | 37 | 19 |
| | | | | (SP 133.4%) | | **15 Rn** |

**59.07 secs** (0.37) CSF £39.75 CT £115.66 TOTE £5.30: £1.90 £3.70 £2.00 (£40.40) Trio £59.10 OWNER Qualitair Holdings Ltd (MALTON) BRED Qualitair Stud Ltd

**3932 Swynford Dream** seems to be an autumn horse and was back to something like his best here. (7/2)
**3465* Literary Society (USA)**, a real trier, was always in pursuit of the winner but, despite a valiant effort, was never good enough.(10/1: 8/1-12/1)
**4356* Shining Cloud**, taking a drop in distance, ran well, always being in the front rank, but was just sort of a turn of foot at the business end. (3/1)
**3477 Mindrace** was up with the pace throughout, but just lacked a turn of foot.. (12/1)
**3465 U-No-Harry (IRE)** ran a decent race after six weeks off and was finishing in determined fashion. (20/1)
**4220 Longwick Lad** seems to have plenty on at present and, although always in sight of the leaders, was struggling some way out and never able to make a serious impression. (6/1)

T/Jkpt: Not won; £32,006.61 to Newmarket 4/10/96. T/Plpt: £186.10 (167.26 Tckts). T/Qdpt: £16.20 (153.91 Tckts). AA

## 4522a-4536a (Irish Racing) - See Computer Raceform

## 0772a-LISTOWEL (Ireland) (L-H) (Good, Chases Good to firm)
### Saturday September 28th

### 4537b LISTOWEL RACES SUPPORTERS' CLUB SLAN ABHAILE Q.R. RACE STKS (4-Y.O+) (Class E)
5-05 **2m**

| | | | SP | RR | SF |
|---|---|---|---|---|---|
| **Theatreworld (IRE)** (APO'Brien,Ireland) **4-11-1**(3) MrBMCash (hld up; led 5f out: r.o: easily) | — | **1** | 7/4[2] | 85+ | — |
| **Mystical City (IRE)** (WPMullins,Ireland) **6-10-8**(5) MrRWalsh (ran 2nd over 3f out: no imp cl home) | 12 | **2** | 11/10[1] | 68 | — |
| **Nazmi (IRE)** (PO'Leary,Ireland) **4-10-7**(7) MrAKWyse (bhd: rdn over 2fout: nvr nrr) | 7 | **3** | 9/1 | 62 | — |
| **Sheregori (IRE)** (APO'Brien,Ireland) **6-10-8**(3) MrDValentine (hld up: chsd ldrs over 4f out: styd on nr fin) | hd | **4** | 14/1 | 59 | — |
| **Adaramann (IRE)** (TMWalsh,Ireland) **4-10-0**(7) MrAFleming (led: rdn st: nt qckn fnl f) | 15 | **5** | 25/1 | 40 | — |
| **Blue Drifter (IRE)** (MBrassil,Ireland) **7-10-0**(7) MrKRO'Ryan (chsd ldrs: hdwy over 4fout: rdn & one pce) | 3 | **6** | 33/1 | 37 | — |
| **Reeves (IRE)** (WPMullins,Ireland) **4-10-7**(7) MrJSaville (bhd: effrt ½-wy: rdn & no hdwy fr 2f out) | 10 | **7** | 6/1[3] | 34 | — |
| **Cara Alanna (IRE)** (TGWalsh,Ireland) **9-9-11**(7) MrJCKelly (chsd ldrs: rdn over 2f out: nt qckn) | 14 | **8** | 50/1 | 10 | — |
| **No Spoken Word (IRE)** (LComer,Ireland) **5-9-13**(7)ow1 MrGElliott (n.d) | dist | **9** | 66/1 | — | — |
| | | | (SP 125.2%) | | **9 Rn** |

**No Time Taken** (PILTOWN) BRED I. Allen, K. C. Choo and Calogo Bloodstock Ag

## 4418a-SAN SIRO (Milan, Italy) (R-H) (Heavy)
### Tuesday September 24th

### 4538a PREMIO SERIO (2-Y.O)
4-20 (4-25) **1m** £8,120.00

| | | | | SP | RR | SF |
|---|---|---|---|---|---|---|
| 3695[3] | **Passi d'Orlando (IRE)** (JLDunlop) **2-9-0** GForte | — | **1** | | — | — |
| | **Mr Tamburino (USA)** (Italy) **2-9-0** EBotti | 4½ | **2** | | — | — |
| | **Setmatt** (Italy) **2-9-0** FJovine | 3¾ | **3** | | — | — |
| | | | | | | **9 Rn** |

**1m 43.9** (13.90) TOTE 25L: 13L 16L 13L (92L) OWNER I. Tudini (ARUNDEL) BRED Scuderia Aterno
**3695 Passi d'Orlando (IRE)**, stepping up to a mile, outclassed his rivals here for an easy success.

## 4405a-SAINT-CLOUD (France) (L-H) (Soft)
### Friday September 27th

### 4539a PRIX JOUBERT (Listed) (3-Y.O F)
3-25 (3-27) **1m 4f** £18,445.00 (£6,324.00: £3,953.00)

| | | | | SP | RR | SF |
|---|---|---|---|---|---|---|
| 3571a[2] | **Met Mech Nich (FR)** (J-PPelat,France) **3-8-11** OPeslier | — | **1** | | 105 | — |
| | **Loophole (FR)** (PBary,France) **3-8-11** GMosse | ½ | **2** | | 104 | — |
| | **Truly Generous (IRE)** (RCollet,France) **3-8-11** GGuignard | s.nk | **3** | | 104 | — |
| 3839* | **Lothlorien (USA)** (PWChapple-Hyam) **3-8-11** ODoleuze (btn over 7 3/4l) | | **7** | | — | — |
| | | | | | | **7 Rn** |

**2m 40.7** (11.40) P-M 2.10F: 1.50F 3.00F OWNER Mr G. Samama BRED G. Samama
**3839* Lothlorien (USA)** ran well to the straight, but then failed to get home. This trip may have been a little too far for her.

## 2274a-DORTMUND (Germany) (R-H) (Good)
### Saturday September 28th

### 4540a RESTAURANT LA TABLE-RENNEN DORTMUNDER FLIEGERPREIS (Listed) (3-Y.O+)
2-43 **5f** £22,522.00 (£9,009.00: £6,757.00)

| | | | | SP | RR | SF |
|---|---|---|---|---|---|---|
| | **Nautiker (GER)** (PRemmert,Germany) **5-8-9** ASuborics | — | **1** | | 105 | — |
| 4412a[2] | **Munaaji (USA)** (AWohler,Germany) **5-8-9b** ABoschert | nk | **2** | | 104 | — |
| 4412a* | **Matula (USA)** (RSuerland,Germany) **4-9-1** AHelfenbein | ½ | **3** | | 108 | — |
| 4412a[3] | **Lucky Parkes** (JBerry) **6-8-9** JCarroll (btn over 6½l) | | **11** | | — | — |
| | | | | | | **12 Rn** |

**57.7 secs** TOTE 191DM: 33DM 16DM 18DM OWNER Stall Hufe
**4412a Lucky Parkes**, who has remained in Germany since her previous run, never showed any of her customary early zip. Something was clearly amiss and this run can be ignored.

# 4286a-CAPANNELLE (Rome, Italy) (R-H) (Soft)
## Sunday September 29th

### 4541a PREMIO LYDIA TESIO (Gp 2) (3-Y.O+ F & M)
3-10 (3-41) **1m 2f** £39,135.00 (£18,023.00: £10,067.00: £5,033.00)

| | | | | SP | RR | SF |
|---|---|---|---|---|---|---|
| 4170a* | **Grey Way (USA)** (GBotti,Italy) **3-8-7** EBotti (hld up in rr: 7th st: gd hdwy on ins to ld 2f out: r.o wl: eased cl home) | — | 1 | | 111 | — |
| | **Karpacka (IRE)** (GVerricelli,Italy) **5-8-11** SDettori (hld up in rr: 10th st: hdwy on outside 2f out: wnt 2nd ins fnl f: no ch w wnr) | 2 | 2 | | 106 | — |
| 1393a[3] | **Bog Wild (USA)** (EBorromeo,Italy) **3-8-6** FJovine (racd in 8th: hdwy to go 4th 3f out: ev ch over 1f out: wknd ins fnl f) | 2¼ | 3 | | 103 | — |
| | **Germignaga (ITY)** (LCamici,Italy) **3-8-6** MCangiano (mid div st: styd on one pce fnl 2f) | 3 | 4 | | 98 | — |
| | **Blu Tascheta (ITY)** (Italy) **3-8-6** MMonteriso (cl up: 4th st: wknd fr over 1f out) | ½ | 5 | | 98 | — |
| | **Nenna (IRE)** (Italy) **4-8-11** LFicuciello (in rr st: n.d) | 1 | 6 | | 95 | — |
| 1393a[8] | **Bellflower (FR)** (Italy) **3-8-6** VMezzatesta (prom: 3rd st: led over 2f out to 2f out: wknd) | 1 | 7 | | 94 | — |
| 1396a[4] | **Beauty To Petriolo (IRE)** (Italy) **3-8-6** MPasquale (mid div st: rdn & btn over 2f out) | 8 | 8 | | 82 | — |
| | **Robreva (IRE)** (Italy) **3-8-6** JacquelineFreda (a bhd) | 4 | 9 | | 75 | — |
| 4419a[2] | **Bemont Park (ITY)** (Italy) **3-8-11** GBietolini (set str pce tl over 2f out: wknd qckly) | ¾ | 10 | | 79 | — |
| | **Blu Meltimi (ITY)** (Italy) **3-8-6** DZarroli (fin lame) | 15 | 11 | | 50 | — |
| | | | | | | **11 Rn** |

**2m 2.1** TOTE 32L: 14L 36L 15L (330L) OWNER Dr Carlo Vittadini (ITALY) BRED C. Vittadini
**Grey Way (USA)** put in a good performance to take this easily. She may now go for a race at Santa Anita.
**Karpacka (IRE)** is flattered by her proximity to the winner. Finding her feet inside the final furlong, she was never going to get there.

# 4540a-DORTMUND (Germany) (R-H) (Soft)
## Sunday September 29th

### 4542a BMW ST LEGER (Gp 2) (3-Y.O)
3-25 (3-31) **1m 6f** £54,054.00 (£21,622.00: £10,810.00: £5,405.00)

| | | | | SP | RR | SF |
|---|---|---|---|---|---|---|
| 3913a* | **Wurftaube (GER)** (HRemmert,Germany) **3-8-12** KWoodburn (hld up: 5th st: swtchd outside & led 2f out: sn clr: v.easily) | — | 1 | | 122+ | — |
| 4164a[3] | **Night Petticoat (GER)** (BSchutz,Germany) **3-8-12** AStarke (a.p: wnt 2nd bef ½-wy: led over 2f out to 2f out: one pce) | 11 | 2 | | 109 | — |
| 4040a[5] | **Agnelli** (HJentzsch,Germany) **3-9-2** PSchiergen (mid div: 4th st: sn rdn & one pce) | 5 | 3 | | 108 | — |
| 3913a[2] | **Narrabeth (IRE)** (Germany) **3-9-2** CAsmussen (hld up: 6th st: one pce) | 1¾ | 4 | | 106 | — |
| 4192[3] | **Samraan (USA)** (JLDunlop) **3-9-2** JCarroll (set v.slow pce: rn wd bnd: dropped bk to 3rd: rdn 3f out: sn btn) | 6 | 5 | | 99 | — |
| 2668a[3] | **Albaran (GER)** (Germany) **3-9-2** ATylicki (a bhd) | 4 | 6 | | 94 | — |
| 4164a* | **Anno Luce** (Germany) **3-8-12b** GBocskai (chsd ldr pllng hrd: carried wd bnd: led sn after: hdd over 2f out: wknd) | 3 | 7 | | 87 | — |
| | **Eduardo (ITY)** (Germany) **3-9-2b[1]** THellier (a bhd) | 7 | 8 | | 83 | — |
| | | | | | | **8 Rn** |

**3m 2.3** TOTE 32DM: 15DM 25DM 29DM OWNER Gestut Ravensberg BRED Gestut Ravensberg
**3913a* Wurftaube (GER)**, who is unbeaten in her last six races, won this impressively. Storming clear after taking the lead two furlongs out, she became the first filly to win the Deutsches St Leger since 1988. She will stay in training, but will not race again this year.
**4164a Night Petticoat (GER)** had no reply as the winner took the lead and could only stay on to finish best of the rest.
**4192 Samraan (USA)** was a reluctant early leader at a very slow pace. Attempting to duck out passing the racecourse stables, he was shuffled back to third, a position he maintained until weakening quickly early in the straight. He needs a truly-run race.

# WOODBINE (Toronto, Canada) (L-H) (Soft)
## Sunday September 29th

### 4543a CANADIAN INTERNATIONAL (Gp 1) (3-Y.O+)
9-40 (9-41) **1m 4f** £283,019.00 (£94,340.00: £51,887.00)

| | | | | SP | RR | SF |
|---|---|---|---|---|---|---|
| 4197* | **Singspiel (IRE)** (MRStoute) **4-9-0** GStevens | — | 1 | | 131 | — |
| | **Chief Bearhart (USA)** (MFrostad,Canada) **3-8-6** SHawley | 2 | 2 | | 128 | — |
| 4288a[2] | **Mecke (USA)** (ETortora,USA) **4-9-0** RobbieDavis | 3½ | 3 | | 124 | — |
| | | | | | | **7 Rn** |

**2m 33.2** P-M 5.80: (1-2) 3.80 5.70 (1-2-3) 2.80 3.10 2.60 (45.30) OWNER Sheikh Mohammed (NEWMARKET) BRED Sheikh Mohammed bin Rashid al Maktoum
**4197* Singspiel (IRE)** was racing on Lasix for the first time in an attempt to alleviate a minor bleeding problem. Settled well in third as Windsharp set a gentle pace, he moved to the front two and a half furlongs out and quickened clear at the top of the straight when challenged by the runner-up. He won with plenty in hand and will return for the Breeders' Cup Turf on October 26th.

# 4251-LINGFIELD (L-H) (Good, Good to firm patches)
## Friday October 4th
WEATHER: showers WIND: almost nil

### 4544 E. B. F. SLEEPING PARTNER MAIDEN STKS (I) (2-Y.O) (Class D)
1-20 (1-21) **6f** £3,570.90 (£1,066.20: £509.60: £231.30) Stalls: High GOING minus 0.06 sec per fur (G)

| | | | | SP | RR | SF |
|---|---|---|---|---|---|---|
| 3994[6] | **Wind Cheetah (USA)** (MRStoute) **2-9-0** BDoyle(12) (a.p: chsd ldr 3f out: led over 1f out: edgd rt: pushed out) | — | 1 | 4/9[1] | 88+ | 52 |

| Form | Horse and details | Dist | Pos | SP | RR | SF |
|---|---|---|---|---|---|---|
| 4061[12] | **Injazaat (USA)** (MajorWRHern) **2-8-9b[1]** TSprake(10) (led over 4f: n.m.r 1f out: unable qckn) | 2½ | **2** | 5/1[2] | 76 | 40 |
| 3807[13] | **Saltimbanco** (IABalding) **2-8-9**(5) MartinDwyer(6) (lw: a.p: rdn over 2f out: one pce) | 2½ | **3** | 20/1 | 75 | 39 |
| 4349[4] | **Waterville Boy (IRE)** (RHannon) **2-9-0** RPerham(7) (lost pl over 3f out: no hdwy fnl 2f) | 11 | **4** | 20/1 | 45 | 9 |
| 4188[7] | **With A Will** (HCandy) **2-8-8**(7)ow1 LJames(3) (b.hind: no hdwy fnl 3f) | 1½ | **5** | 16/1 | 42 | 5 |
| | **Wild Hadeer** (WJHaggas) **2-8-11**(3) FLynch(9) (w'like: outpcd: nvr nrr) | ½ | **6** | 25/1 | 40 | 4 |
| | **Happy** (PTWalwyn) **2-9-0** JCarroll(8) (w'like: bit bkwd: prom over 2f) | 2½ | **7** | 10/1[3] | 33 | — |
| 4383[5] | **Pietro Bembo (IRE)** (SirMarkPrescott) **2-9-0** GDuffield(5) (s.s: a bhd) | 1¾ | **8** | 16/1 | 29 | — |
| 4242[14] | **Lajatta** (LMCumani) **2-9-0** OUrbina(1) (a bhd) | nk | **9** | 20/1 | 28 | — |
| 4105[5] | **Silver Sands** (TPMcGovern) **2-8-9** JFEgan(11) (b.hind: chsd ldr 3f) | 3½ | **10** | 25/1 | 14 | — |
| 4357[9] | **Well Done** (MBell) **2-8-9** MFenton(2) (a bhd) | 3 | **11** | 33/1 | 6 | — |
| | **Forward Miss** (MrsLCJewell) **2-8-4**(5) SophieMitchell(4) (neat: bit bkwd: s.s: a wl bhd) | 11 | **12** | 100/1 | — | — |

(SP 132.7%) **12 Rn**

**1m 11.81** (2.81) CSF £4.33 TOTE £1.30: £1.10 £1.30 £2.80 (£2.40) Trio £12.10 OWNER Cheveley Park Stud (NEWMARKET) BRED Fawn Leap Farm Inc.

STEWARDS' ENQUIRY Obj. to Wind Cheetah (USA) by Sprake overruled. Sprake fined £60 (failure to have reasonable grounds for an objection).

**3994 Wind Cheetah (USA)** confirmed the promise shown at York and needed only to be nudged along for a cosy success. (4/9)

**4061 Injazaat (USA)** was fitted with blinkers here after flopping badly at Kempton last month and ran a lot better. Her jockey decided to object for the interference, but was fined for failing to have grounds for an objection. (5/1)

**3069 Saltimbanco** looked in very good shape in the paddock. (20/1)

**4349 Waterville Boy (IRE)**, who failed to stay an extended mile last time, returned to six furlongs, only to lack the necessary pace in the second half of the race. Maybe seven furlongs would help. (20/1)

**3809 With A Will** was making little impression in the second half of the race. (16/1)

**Wild Hadeer**, a medium-sized colt, failed to go the pace but did pass beaten horses in the closing stages. (25/1)

**Happy** (10/1: 6/1-12/1)

## 4545 DITCHLING MAIDEN STKS (2-Y.O) (Class D)

1-50 (1-50) **5f** £3,712.60 (£1,109.80: £531.40: £242.20) Stalls: High GOING minus 0.06 sec per fur (G)

| Form | Horse and details | Dist | Pos | SP | RR | SF |
|---|---|---|---|---|---|---|
| 4210[2] | **Heart Throb** (WJHaggas) **2-8-6**(3) FLynch(3) (lw: hld up: led 1f out: rdn out) | — | **1** | 11/8[1] | 79 | 57 |
| 4234[2] | **Hangover Square (IRE) (82)** (RHannon) **2-9-0** DaneO'Neill(8) (lw: a.p: ev ch fnl 2f: r.o) | nk | **2** | 7/2[2] | 83 | 61 |
| 4357[4] | **Nopalea (80)** (CEBrittain) **2-8-9** BDoyle(7) (led 4f out to 1f out: wknd ins fnl f) | 3 | **3** | 9/1 | 68 | 46 |
| | **Hajat** (HThomsonJones) **2-8-9** GCarter(6) (neat: s.s: rdn & hdwy over 1f out: one pce) | 1¼ | **4** | 6/1[3] | 64 | 42 |
| 1683[4] | **Don Sebastian** (WJHaggas) **2-9-0** MTebbutt(10) (s.s: shkn up over 1f out: hdwy fnl f: nvr nrr) | hd | **5** | 25/1 | 69+ | 47 |
| 1179[6] | **Copperbeech (IRE)** (PWChapple-Hyam) **2-8-6**(3) RHavlin(9) (lw: a.p: rdn 2f out: wknd over 1f out) | ½ | **6** | 14/1 | 63 | 41 |
| 4357[8] | **Dayrella** (WRMuir) **2-8-9** JFortune(5) (lw: a bhd) | 2 | **7** | 50/1 | 56 | 34 |
| 3924[4] | **Myrmidon (84)** (JLDunlop) **2-9-0** TSprake(4) (lw: rdn & sme hdwy over 1f out: wknd fnl f) | 1¾ | **8** | 7/1 | 56 | 34 |
| 4230[9] | **Swift Refusal (64)** (MJHaynes) **2-8-9** CRutter(2) (lw: led 1f: wknd over 2f out) | hd | **9** | 50/1 | 50 | 28 |
| *2633*[11] | **Littlestone Rocket** (WRMuir) **2-9-0** DHarrison(1) (b: bit bkwd: prom over 3f) | 9 | **10** | 100/1 | 26 | 4 |

(SP 116.5%) **10 Rn**

**58.74 secs** (1.74) CSF £6.48 TOTE £2.30: £1.10 £1.30 £2.10 (£4.20) Trio £7.60 OWNER Mr B. Haggas (NEWMARKET) BRED The Wickfield Stud Ltd

**4210 Heart Throb** put her Sandown experience to good use. (11/8)

**4234 Hangover Square (IRE)** appears to have got the hang of things now and may now be ready to strike in a small race. (7/2)

**4357 Nopalea** was dropping to the minimum trip for the first time. (9/1)

**Hajat**, a January foal, is not as big and strong as many of the Thomson Jones inmates. (6/1: op 3/1)

**1683 Don Sebastian**, given a four-month rest, was rather surprisingly brought back to five furlongs. Given the kid-glove treatment, he was out the back until staying on in the final furlong to be nearest at the finish, just as in his two other races. With three runs under his belt, he is now qualified for nurseries and looks one to bear in mind, especially if tackling further. (25/1)

**1179 Copperbeech (IRE)** looked in good order considering this was her first run since May. (14/1: op 5/1)

**3924 Myrmidon** (7/1: 3/1-8/1)

## 4546 BLETCHINGLY CLAIMING STKS (2-Y.O) (Class F)

2-20 (2-23) **6f** £2,381.00 (£656.00: £311.00) Stalls: High GOING minus 0.06 sec per fur (G)

| Form | Horse and details | Dist | Pos | SP | RR | SF |
|---|---|---|---|---|---|---|
| 4364[5] | **Commander Jones (IRE) (75)** (BJMeehan) **2-9-1** MTebbutt(18) (a.p: swtchd lft over 2f out: led over 1f out: r.o wl) | — | **1** | 13/2[3] | 78 | 59 |
| 4350[3] | **Petite Danseuse (78)** (SDow) **2-8-7**(5) ADaly(10) (rdn over 2f out: hdwy to chse wnr over 1f out: r.o) | 2 | **2** | 3/1[1] | 70 | 51 |
| 4423[5] | **Dowry (66)** (RHannon) **2-8-10** DaneO'Neill(9) (lw: racd far side: a.p: swtchd lft over 3f out: rdn over 1f out: one pce) | 4 | **3** | 6/1[2] | 57 | 38 |
| 4440[9] | **Caspian Morn (70)** (APJarvis) **2-8-8v[1]** JFortune(12) (led over 4f: sn wknd) | 1 | **4** | 14/1 | 52 | 33 |
| 4195[15] | **Masterstroke (72)** (BJMeehan) **2-9-3** RHughes(2) (racd far side: a.p: hrd rdn over 2f out: eased whn btn ins fnl f) | 2½ | **5** | 12/1 | 55 | 36 |
| 3128[8] | **Aficionado (IRE) (76)** (RFJohnsonHoughton) **2-9-3b** GDuffield(11) (outpcd: rdn & hdwy over 1f out: nvr nrr) | s.h | **6** | 6/1[2] | 55 | 36 |
| 2031[11] | **Lochinvar** (JSMoore) **2-8-7** JFEgan(13) (w ldr over 3f) | nk | **7** | 50/1 | 44 | 25 |
| 4423[3] | **Russian Sable (59)** (MRChannon) **2-8-2** CRutter(7) (racd far side: outpcd: hdwy fnl f: nvr nrr) | hd | **8** | 10/1 | 39 | 20 |
| 4369[13] | **Tulsa (IRE)** (BGubby) **2-8-13v** AClark(6) (racd far side: outpcd: hdwy over 1f out: one pce) | ½ | **9** | 50/1 | 48 | 29 |
| 3763[7] | **Silver Lining (73)** (APJones) **2-8-11** TSprake(5) (racd far side: hdwy over 1f out: one pce) | s.h | **10** | 25/1 | 46 | 27 |
| 4423[2] | **Hever Golf Charger (IRE) (73)** (TJNaughton) **2-9-3** SSanders(4) (racd far side: prom 4f) | 1½ | **11** | 11/1 | 48 | 29 |
| 4423[4] | **Summer Risotto (54)** (DJSffrenchDavis) **2-7-7**(5) MartinDwyer(19) (outpcd) | s.h | **12** | 16/1 | 29 | 10 |
| 4369[15] | **The Commodore (IRE)** (WJarvis) **2-8-13** JCarroll(8) (racd far side: outpcd) | 2½ | **13** | 25/1 | 37 | 18 |
| | **Witney-La-Roche** (JSMoore) **2-8-5** NAdams(3) (w'like: bit bkwd: racd far side: bhd fnl 4f) | ¾ | **14** | 25/1 | 27 | 8 |
| 4230[7] | **Jilly Woo (55)** (DRCElsworth) **2-8-4** BDoyle(14) (a bhd) | 1½ | **15** | 14/1 | 22 | 3 |
| 3982[21] | **Distinctive Dream (IRE)** (KTIvory) **2-9-7** DBiggs(15) (b: b.hind: bhd fnl 3f) | 1½ | **16** | 16/1 | 35 | 16 |
| | **Jo Coleman** (DMorris) **2-8-8** NDay(17) (leggy: a bhd) | ¾ | **17** | 20/1 | 20 | 1 |
| *4251*[10] | **Life's A Roar (IRE)** (CADwyer) **2-8-5v** GHind(16) (b: swtg: prom 3f) | 1¼ | **18** | 50/1 | 14 | — |

(SP 139.3%) **18 Rn**

**1m 11.41** (2.41) CSF £27.71 TOTE £8.70: £3.10 £1.60 £2.90 (£11.60) Trio £20.90 OWNER E H Jones (Paints) Ltd (UPPER LAMBOURN) BRED Cesare Turri

Petite Danseuse clmd IMoss £10,000

**4364 Commander Jones (IRE)**, not the easiest of rides, appreciated the return to claiming company. This is his class, his trainer later reported. (13/2)
**4350 Petite Danseuse** has not been allowed to eat the bread of idleness this season, this being her twelfth outing, and she once again ran a sound race. (3/1)
**4423 Dowry** found this trip too sharp at Folkestone last week and, although she raced up with the pace on the far side, she was found wanting at the business end. Seven furlongs is needed. (6/1)
**3620 Caspian Morn**, collared below the distance, was soon in trouble. (14/1)
**3208 Masterstroke** was bang in the firing-line on the far side until eased when all chance had gone. (12/1)
**2734 Aficionado (IRE)** continues to disappoint, despite the drop in class. (6/1)
**2429 Jilly Woo** (14/1: 10/1-16/1)

## 4547 E. B. F. SLEEPING PARTNER MAIDEN STKS (II) (2-Y.O) (Class D)
2-55 (2-56) **6f** £3,570.90 (£1,066.20: £509.60: £231.30) Stalls: High GOING minus 0.06 sec per fur (G)

| | | | | SP | RR | SF |
|---|---|---|---|---|---|---|
| | **Bint Albaadiya (USA)** (MRStoute) **2-8-9** DHarrison(3) (unf: a.p: rdn over 2f out: led over 1f out: r.o wl) | — | **1** | 11/2$^{3}$ | 67+ | 34 |
| 4330$^{10}$ | **Shifting Time** (IABalding) **2-8-4**(5) MartinDwyer(9) (w ldr: rdn over 1f out: ev ch ins fnl f: r.o wl) | hd | **2** | 4/1$^{1}$ | 67 | 34 |
| 3697$^{4}$ | **Aim Seven (77)** (RHannon) **2-9-0** DaneO'Neill(7) (lw: led over 4f: rdn: r.o) | ½ | **3** | 13/2 | 70 | 37 |
| | **Al Muallim (USA)** (JWPayne) **2-9-0** AMcGlone(2) (w'like: dwlt: rdn & hdwy over 1f out: unable qckn ins fnl f) | ¾ | **4** | 16/1 | 68 | 35 |
| 4104$^{7}$ | **Daintree (IRE)** (HJCollingridge) **2-8-9** MRimmer(8) (b.hind: a.p: ev ch over 1f out: one pce) | 1¼ | **5** | 8/1 | 60 | 27 |
| 4200$^{6}$ | **Allied Academy** (SCWilliams) **2-9-0** GCarter(6) (lw: hld up: rdn over 2f out: one pce) | ½ | **6** | 33/1 | 64 | 31 |
| 1954$^{6}$ | **Catria (IRE)** (JHMGosden) **2-8-9** GHind(4) (hld up: shkn up over 2f out: one pce) | 1¼ | **7** | 5/1$^{2}$ | 55 | 22 |
| | **Atnab (USA)** (PTWalwyn) **2-8-9** JCarroll(5) (w'like: bkwd: outpcd: nvr nrr) | s.h | **8** | 11/1 | 55 | 22 |
| | **Dorado Beach** (BWHills) **2-8-4**(5) JDSmith(11) (w'like: bit bkwd: a bhd) | 5 | **9** | 12/1 | 42 | 9 |
| | **Lulu** (SirMarkPrescott) **2-8-9** GDuffield(10) (leggy; unf: prom 4f) | 1 | **10** | 15/2 | 39 | 6 |
| | **Mighty Flyer (IRE)** (DRLoder) **2-8-9** DRMcCabe(12) (w'like: lw: bhd fnl 2f) | 1¾ | **11** | 4/1$^{1}$ | 35 | 2 |
| | **Ewar Arrangement** (CEBrittain) **2-9-0** RHughes(1) (leggy: bhd fnl 2f) | 18 | **12** | 20/1 | — | — |

(SP 137.9%) **12 Rn**

**1m 12.73** (3.73) CSF £30.67 TOTE £8.50: £3.60 £1.30 £1.90 (£25.50) Trio £96.20 OWNER Sheikh Ahmed Al Maktoum (NEWMARKET) BRED Swettenham Stud
IN-FOCUS: **This was by far the slowest of the three two-year-old races run over this trip.**
**Bint Albaadiya (USA)**, quite a weak-looking filly, hung on well. (11/2: 5/2-6/1)
**3234 Shifting Time** had less on her plate here and, as a result, only just failed to get off the mark. In similar company, she can find a race. (4/1: op 7/1)
**3697 Aim Seven** returned to form and stuck to his guns well to the bitter end. (13/2)
**Al Muallim (USA)** proved troublesome in the paddock when mounted, but ran a lot better. This was a pleasing debut and he will do better over further. (16/1)
**Daintree (IRE)** stepped up on her initial run here. (8/1: op 14/1)
**Allied Academy** found the drop in distance too sharp. (33/1)
**1954 Catria (IRE)** was having her first run in nearly four months and was certainly looked after. Buried in midfield, her jockey did wiggle his arms around a bit, but the filly never looked like quickening. She looks one to keep an eye on, especially when she is qualified for nurseries. (5/1)
**Lulu** (15/2: 5/1-8/1)
**Mighty Flyer (IRE)** (4/1: op 5/2)

## 4548 AUTUMN MAIDEN STKS (3-Y.O+) (Class D)
3-25 (3-26) **1m 6f** £4,092.75 (£1,224.00: £586.50: £267.75) Stalls: High GOING minus 0.06 sec per fur (G)

| | | | | SP | RR | SF |
|---|---|---|---|---|---|---|
| 3781$^{5}$ | **Zaforum (100)** (LMontagueHall) **3-8-12b**[1] RHughes(3) (mde virtually all: rdn over 2f out: r.o wl) | — | **1** | 7/2$^{2}$ | 85 | 43 |
| 3983$^{8}$ | **Belmarita (IRE) (72)** (MHTompkins) **3-8-7** GDuffield(1) (a.p: ev ch 2f out: unable qckn) | 3½ | **2** | 8/1$^{3}$ | 76 | 34 |
| 4379$^{2}$ | **Renzo (IRE) (82)** (GHarwood) **3-8-12** AClark(9) (hdwy 7f out: ev ch 2f out: nt r.o) | ½ | **3** | 7/2$^{2}$ | 80 | 38 |
| 4362$^{2}$ | **Heart (82)** (MRStoute) **3-8-7** BDoyle(5) (lw: chsd wnr: ev ch 2f out: sn wknd) | 7 | **4** | 5/4$^{1}$ | 67 | 25 |
| 3776$^{3}$ | **Shirley Venture (72)** (SPCWoods) **3-8-7** DBiggs(11) (a.p: rdn 4f out: sn wknd) | 4 | **5** | 10/1 | 63 | 21 |
| 3980$^{4}$ | **Zuno Flyer (USA) (32)** (AMoore) **4-9-7** CandyMorris(10) (prom over 9f) | 1¼ | **6** | 66/1 | 66 | 33 |
| | **Hayling-Billy** (PRHedger) **3-8-12** SDrowne(6) (unf: nvr nr to chal) | 6 | **7** | 50/1 | 60 | 18 |
| 2556$^{11}$ | **Brick Court (IRE) (32)** (RFJohnsonHoughton) **4-8-9**(7) BarrySmith(13) (bhd fnl 6f) | 1½ | **8** | 100/1 | 53 | 20 |
| 4426$^{16}$ | **Veronica Franco (56)** (BAPearce) **3-8-7** StephenDavies(4) (s.s: a bhd) | nk | **9** | 100/1 | 53 | 11 |
| 2786$^{5}$ | **Private Percival** (JRPoulton) **3-8-12** AMorris(2) (bhd fnl 7f) | 9 | **10** | 100/1 | 47 | 5 |
| 847$^{11}$ | **Executive Officer** (RMFlower) **3-8-12** GHind(8) (a bhd) | ¾ | **11** | 100/1 | 46 | 4 |
| 4110$^{9}$ | **Theme Arena** (SMellor) **3-8-7** AMcGlone(12) (a bhd) | 1 | **12** | 50/1 | 40 | — |
| 4110$^{11}$ | **Toby Brown** (MrsALMKing) **3-8-9**(3) FLynch(7) (a bhd) | 5 | **13** | 100/1 | 40 | — |

(SP 119.5%) **13 Rn**

**3m 6.92** (8.62) CSF £29.32 TOTE £4.30: £1.20 £1.90 £1.50 (£12.20) Trio £49.30 OWNER Mr Andy Smith (EPSOM) BRED Forum Bloodstock Ltd
WEIGHT FOR AGE 3yo-9lb
**3781 Zaforum** has been given some very unrealistic targets this year, but was fitted with blinkers for the first time and taking a well deserved drop in class. That was enough for him to open his account with a pillar-to-post victory. (7/2)
**3983 Belmarita (IRE)** managed to get into the prizemoney, but lack of acceleration is becoming a real problem, even over this trip. (8/1: 6/1-10/1)
**4379 Renzo (IRE)** was better suited by this longer trip, but he carried his head very high when the crunch came and threw in the towel. (7/2)
**4362 Heart** quite simply failed to stay this longer trip. She appeared to be going far better than her rivals entering the straight but, when let down approaching the final quarter-mile, completely fell in a heap. (5/4)
**3776 Shirley Venture** had given up the ghost turning into the straight. (10/1: 7/1-12/1)
**3980 Zuno Flyer (USA)** is extremely exposed and this poor performer is now a maiden after twenty attempts. (66/1)

## 4549 UPHAM NURSERY H'CAP (0-75) (2-Y.O) (Class E)
4-00 (4-01) **7f** £3,943.80 (£1,184.40: £571.20: £264.60) Stalls: High GOING minus 0.06 sec per fur (G)

| | | | | SP | RR | SF |
|---|---|---|---|---|---|---|
| 4375$^{4}$ | **Merciless Cop (61)** (BJMeehan) **2-8-8b** MTebbutt(13) (a.p: led over 1f out: r.o wl) | — | **1** | 8/1 | 71 | 54 |

4242[11] **Silk St John (73)** (MJRyan) **2-9-6** AClark(5) (racd far side: hld up: led over 3f out tl over 1f out: unable qckn) ....4 **2** 6/1[3] 74 57
4262[10] **Castles Burning (USA) (58)** (CACyzer) **2-8-5** GCarter(7) (racd far side: outpcd: hdwy over 1f out: r.o) ....2 **3** 20/1 54 37
4253[9] **Greenwich Fore (74)** (TGMills) **2-9-7** JFortune(10) (a.p: rdn over 2f out: one pce) ....s.h **4** 20/1 70 53
4106[8] **Rumbustious (69)** (RHannon) **2-9-2** DaneO'Neill(4) (racd far side: a.p: rdn over 2f out: one pce) ....nk **5** 9/1 65 48
4364[9] **Shall We Go (IRE) (70)** (RHannon) **2-9-3** RPerham(1) (racd far side: a.p: rdn over 2f out: one pce) ....1 **6** 12/1 63 46
4423* **Eager To Please (62)** (MissGayKelleway) **2-8-9** 7x GDuffield(17) (lw: rdn over 3f out: swtchd lft over 2f out: hdwy over 1f out: nvr nrr) ....1½ **7** 9/2[1] 52 35
4084[11] **Midatlantic (65)** (PTWalwyn) **2-8-12v[1]** JCarroll(2) (lw: racd far side: led over 3f) ....1 **8** 20/1 53 36
4242[10] **Tirage (74)** (CEBrittain) **2-9-7** BDoyle(15) (prom over 4f) ....1 **9** 10/1 59 42
4364[8] **Saffron Rose (74)** (MBlanshard) **2-9-7** NAdams(14) (prom over 4f) ....½ **10** 20/1 58 41
4127[13] **Racing Heart (65)** (PJMakin) **2-8-12** AMcGlone(3) (racd far side: bhd fnl 4f) ....1 **11** 10/1 47 30
4424[4] **Miss Barcelona (IRE) (61)** (MJPolglase) **2-8-8** DHarrison(16) (prom over 3f) ....1½ **12** 20/1 39 22
4123[10] **V I P Charlie (63)** (JRJenkins) **2-8-10** SSanders(18) (lw: s.s: a bhd) ....s.h **13** 5/1[2] 41 24
3829[7] **No Comment (66)** (MBell) **2-8-13** MFenton(6) (lw: racd far side: s.s: a bhd) ....s.h **14** 9/1 44 27
3687[17] **Schisandra (59)** (MJFetherston-Godley) **2-8-6** StephenDavies(11) (hdwy over 2f out: wknd over 1f out) ....s.h **15** 33/1 37 20
4084[8] **Running Free (IRE) (61)** (MJFetherston-Godley) **2-8-5v[1](3)** FLynch(9) (bhd fnl 4f) ....¾ **16** 16/1 37 20
4204[6] **Dixie Jamboree (USA) (72)** (LMCumani) **2-9-5** OUrbina(8) (lw: bhd fnl 4f) ....2 **17** 12/1 44 27
(SP 146.4%) **17 Rn**

**1m 24.29** (2.69) CSF £61.27 CT £937.24 TOTE £13.50: £2.00 £2.60 £4.10 £9.00 (£99.30) Trio £437.90; £123.38 to Newmarket 5/10/96
OWNER Mr Mario Lanfranchi (UPPER LAMBOURN) BRED G. S. Shropshire

**4375 Merciless Cop** has been dropped 9lb since his handicap debut. (8/1)
**3407 Silk St John** ran well on this handicap debut. Collared by the stands'-side winner below the distance, he failed to match that rival. (6/1)
**4106 Castles Burning (USA)**, unable to go the pace on the far side, was doing all his best work in the last furlong and a half. A return to a mile would help. (20/1)
**3874 Greenwich Fore**, given a lot of weight on this handicap debut, failed to quicken in the last two furlongs. (20/1)
**4106 Rumbustious** has been running well this season. (9/1)
**3826* Shall We Go (IRE)** failed to find another gear in the final quarter-mile. (12/1: op 8/1)
**4423* Eager To Please** has done all his winning in selling or claiming company and, even though he was well in here - he was set to rise 10lb in future handicaps - that was not enough to get him into the action. (9/2)
**3988 Racing Heart** (10/1: 8/1-16/1)
**4204 Dixie Jamboree (USA)** (12/1: op 6/1)

## 4550 LEVY BOARD H'CAP (0-70) (3-Y.O) (Class E)

4-35 (4-38) **7f** £3,616.20 (£1,083.60: £520.80: £239.40) Stalls: High GOING minus 0.06 sec per fur (G)

SP RR SF

4376[10] **Sea Danzig (62)** (JJBridger) **3-8-13** DHarrison(18) (mde all: hrd rdn over 1f out: r.o wl) ....— **1** 14/1 72 47
4256[2] **Amber Fort (68)** (DRCElsworth) **3-9-0v(5)** DGriffiths(13) (hld up: rdn over 2f out: ev ch ins fnl f: unable qckn) ....¾ **2** 9/2[3] 76 51
4202[3] **Serious Sensation (67)** (SirMarkPrescott) **3-9-4** GDuffield(4) (lw: racd far side: a.p: rdn over 2f out: ev ch ins fnl f: unable qckn) ....2½ **3** 4/1[2] 70 45
4376[4] **Ca'd'oro (59)** (GBBalding) **3-8-10** SDrowne(1) (lw: racd far side: hld up: rdn over 2f out: r.o) ....nk **4** 12/1 61 36
2715[4] **Maristax (70)** (PJMakin) **3-9-7** SSanders(8) (a.p: rdn over 2f out: one pce) ....hd **5** 20/1 72 47
2428[9] **Wire Act (USA) (60)** (MartynMeade) **3-8-4(7)** DSweeney(11) (nvr nr to chal) ....5 **6** 20/1 50 25
4216[10] **Ambassadori (USA) (60)** (CEBrittain) **3-8-11** BDoyle(7) (racd far side: a.p: rdn over 2f out: wknd fnl f) ....hd **7** 7/1 50 25
4256[9] **Honorable Estate (IRE) (63)** (RHannon) **3-9-0** DaneO'Neill(17) (a mid div) ....1 **8** 14/1 51 26
3832[6] **Octavia Hill (62)** (PWHarris) **3-8-13** GHind(15) (lw: nvr nrr) ....2½ **9** 16/1 44 19
4229[2] **Foreign Relation (IRE) (59)** (PRWebber) **3-8-10** JFEgan(14) (a mid div) ....2 **10** 10/1 36 11
4098[12] **Dungeon Princess (IRE) (58)** (CMurray) **3-8-9** JFortune(2) (lw: racd far side: hld up: rdn over 2f out: wknd over 1f out) ....s.h **11** 33/1 35 10
4348* **Society Magic (USA) (60)** (IABalding) **3-8-6(5)** 6x MartinDwyer(12) (bhd fnl 5f) ....¾ **12** 3/1[1] 36 11
3317[3] **School Boy (69)** (TJNaughton) **3-9-6** RHughes(16) (prom over 5f) ....¾ **13** 12/1 43 18
3949[5] **Polish Rhythm (IRE) (69)** (MHTompkins) **3-9-6** NDay(5) (lw: racd far side: bhd fnl 4f) ....½ **14** 14/1 42 17
4243[8] **Paojiunic (IRE) (67)** (LMCumani) **3-9-4** OUrbina(6) (racd far side: prom over 5f) ....½ **15** 7/1 39 14
3832[4] **Ashanti Dancer (IRE) (65)** (MJHaynes) **3-9-2** GCarter(3) (racd far side: a bhd) ....s.h **16** 14/1 37 12
*3064*[6] **Mrs McBadger (59)** (BSmart) **3-8-10** MTebbutt(9) (lw: racd far side: bhd fnl 3f) ....¾ **17** 33/1 29 4
4428[13] **Moi Canard (59)** (BAPearce) **3-8-10** DRMcCabe(10) (a bhd) ....18 **18** 20/1 — —
(SP 165.4%) **18 Rn**

**1m 25.23** (3.63) CSF £93.04 CT £311.08 TOTE £18.70: £4.30 £1.40 £1.90 £3.60 (£64.10) Trio £101.70 OWNER Mr P. Cook (LIPHOOK) BRED Theobalds Stud

**4256 Sea Danzig** at last lost his maiden tag at the eighteenth attempt with a pillar-to-post victory. (14/1)
**4256 Amber Fort** proved a thorn in the side of the winner and had every chance inside the final furlong before that rival found a bit extra. (9/2)
**4202 Serious Sensation** ran another sound race. Rated 84 when second on the All-Weather at Wolverhampton in August, he was racing off just 67 here on Turf Ratings and may be ready to strike on either surface. (4/1)
**4376 Ca'd'oro** ran on nicely inside the final furlong and only just failed to snatch third prize. He will be better served by a return to a mile. (12/1)
**2715 Maristax**, off the track for nearly three months, has been dropped 5lb in the handicap, but still failed to quicken in the last two furlongs. (20/1)
**1888* Wire Act (USA)**, given a three-month break, never threatened to get into the action. (20/1)
**4053 Paojiunic (IRE)** (7/1: 5/1-15/2)

## 4551 LEWES AMATEUR LIMITED STKS (0-65) (3-Y.O+) (Class F)

5-05 (5-05) **1m 3f 106y** £2,381.00 (£656.00: £311.00) Stalls: High GOING minus 0.06 sec per fur (G)

SP RR SF

4121[5] **Artic Bay (63)** (MrsPNDutfield) **4-10-8(6)** MrLJefford(8) (lw: a.p: led over 2f out: r.o wl) ....— **1** 20/1 78 60
4252[3] **Roisin Clover (63)** (SDow) **5-10-11** MrTMcCarthy(7) (lw: a.p: hrd rdn over 1f out: r.o) ....2½ **2** 5/1[2] 72 54
4483* **Ayunli (64)** (SCWilliams) **5-11-1** 2x MrsAPerrett(4) (led over 1f: led 4f out tl over 2f out: one pce) ....2 **3** 4/5[1] 73 55

| | | | | SP | RR | SF |
|---|---|---|---|---|---|---|
| 3830$^{6}$ | **Allstars Express (64)** (TJNaughton) **3-10-4**$^{(6)}$ MrsJNaughton(10) (hdwy over 2f out: one pce) | 3½ | **4** | 16/1 | 69 | 45 |
| 4427$^{3}$ | **No Pattern (65)** (GLMoore) **4-10-8v**$^{(4)}$ MrKGoble(13) (lw: hdwy over 2f out: one pce) | 1½ | **5** | 5/1$^{2}$ | 63 | 45 |
| 4307$^{6}$ | **Outstayed Welcome (51)** (MJHaynes) **4-10-12** MissYHaynes(9) (led 10f out to 4f out: wknd over 2f out) | 2 | **6** | 25/1 | 60 | 42 |
| 4436$^{4}$ | **Breezed Well (38)** (BRCambidge) **10-10-6**$^{(6)}$ MrsHNoonan(5) (prom 10f) | 1¼ | **7** | 50/1 | 58 | 40 |
| 4355$^{2}$ | **Father Dan (IRE) (56)** (MissGayKelleway) **7-10-8**$^{(4)}$ MrRWakley(14) (b: lw: nvr nr to chal) | hd | **8** | 12/1$^{3}$ | 58 | 40 |
| 4321$^{5}$ | **Spinning Mouse (59)** (DMorley) **3-10-5** MissDianaJones(11) (prom 8f) | 1½ | **9** | 5/1$^{2}$ | 55 | 31 |
| 4082$^{17}$ | **Adilov (48)** (JJBridger) **4-10-6**$^{(6)}$ MrDBridger(1) (lw: bhd fnl 6f) | 2½ | **10** | 50/1 | 53 | 35 |
| 3965$^{2}$ | **Ela Agapi Mou (USA) (52)** (AMoore) **3-10-0**$^{(6)}$ MrsJMoore(3) (s.s: a bhd) | 1¼ | **11** | 20/1 | 51 | 27 |
| 4216$^{4}$ | **Nikita's Star (IRE) (65)** (DJGMurraySmith) **3-10-6**$^{(4)}$ MrRThornton(12) (bhd fnl 6f) | 4 | **12** | 16/1 | 49 | 25 |
| *3418*$^{5}$ | **Tathmin (55)** (JRBosley) **3-10-2**$^{(4)}$ MrsSBosley(15) (a bhd) | 5 | **13** | 50/1 | 38 | 14 |
| 4436$^{22}$ | **Straight Thinking (USA) (55)** (JLSpearing) **3-10-0**$^{(6)}$ MissAShirley-Priest(6) (a bhd) | s.h | **14** | 50/1 | 38 | 14 |
| | | | | (SP 146.2%) | | **14 Rn** |

**2m 32.83** (8.63) CSF £129.71 TOTE £27.40: £3.90 £2.00 £1.40 (£76.20) Trio £67.40 OWNER Mrs Nerys Dutfield (SEATON) BRED Mrs Nerys Dutfield

WEIGHT FOR AGE 3yo-6lb

**4121 Artic Bay** proved too strong for these. The plan is for him to run in an amateur riders' race at Ascot and then give him a break before schooling him over hurdles. (20/1)

**4252 Roisin Clover** stayed on to win the battle for second prize but failed to get on terms with the winner. (5/1)

**4483* Ayunli** is in cracking form at present and won four races last month. However, this race was her fourth in twelve days - she won at Hamilton on Monday - and she is now probably beginning to feel the effects. (4/5)

**3830 Allstars Express** made his effort on the outside of the field over a quarter of a mile from home, but could then only tread water. (16/1)

**4427 No Pattern** took closer order two furlongs from home, but could then make no further impression. (5/1: op 3/1)

**4307 Outstayed Welcome** did a lot of the donkey work, but was hung out to dry over two furlongs from home. Two wins in thirty-one starts says it all. (25/1)

**4355 Father Dan (IRE)** (12/1: 9/1-14/1)

T/Plpt: £75.20 (140.51 Tckts). T/Qdpt: £75.00 (8.22 Tckts). AK

## 4515-NEWMARKET (R-H) (Good to firm)
## Friday October 4th

WEATHER: fine & sunny WIND: fresh half bhd

### 4552 NGK SPARK PLUGS RATED STKS H'CAP (0-105) (3-Y.O+ F & M) (Class B)

2-00 (2-02) **6f (Rowley)** £8,053.00 (£2,977.00: £1,426.00: £580.00: £227.50: £86.50) Stalls: High GOING minus 0.44 sec per fur (F)

| | | | | SP | RR | SF |
|---|---|---|---|---|---|---|
| 4122$^{6}$ | **Prends Ca (IRE) (86)** (RHannon) **3-9-0** PatEddery(8) (a.p: chal 1f out: rdn to ld wl ins fnl f) | — | **1** | 13/2 | 99 | 70 |
| 4314$^{12}$ | **Bajan Rose (82)** (MBlanshard) **4-8-11** RCochrane(3) (a.p: led wl over 1f out tl wl ins fnl f) | nk | **2** | 6/1$^{3}$ | 94 | 66 |
| 4122$^{4}$ | **Defined Feature (IRE) (91)** (MRStoute) **3-9-5** WRSwinburn(6) (b.hind: led tl wl over 1f out: rdn & kpt on one pce fnl f) | 3 | **3** | 5/1$^{2}$ | 95 | 66 |
| 4122$^{7}$ | **Tropical Dance (USA) (89)** (MrsJCecil) **3-9-3** KDarley(1) (lw: hld up: effrt over 1f out: kpt on towards fin) | 2 | **4** | 12/1 | 88 | 59 |
| 3693$^{11}$ | **Galine (87)** (WAO'Gorman) **3-9-1** EmmaO'Gorman(4) (hld up: pushed along ½-wy: effrt & rdn wl over 1f out: nvr nrr) | ½ | **5** | 9/2$^{1}$ | 85 | 56 |
| 3790$^{10}$ | **Shanghai Girl (84)** (DRLoder) **3-8-12v** LDettori(2) (trckd ldrs: brought wd & ev ch over 1f out: wknd fnl f) | s.h | **6** | 15/2 | 81 | 52 |
| 4314$^{16}$ | **Babsy Babe (93)** (JJQuinn) **3-9-7** JQuinn(7) (hld up: effrt over 2f out: sn outpcd) | 1½ | **7** | 12/1 | 86 | 57 |
| 4255$^{4}$ | **Kind of Light (79)** (RGuest) **3-8-7** MRoberts(5) (chsd ldrs: hrd drvn over 1f out: sn btn) | 1½ | **8** | 5/1$^{2}$ | 68 | 39 |
| 4044$^{3}$ | **Forentia (78)** (JRFanshawe) **3-8-6** KFallon(9) (lw: drvn along ½-wy: sn outpcd) | 6 | **9** | 25/1 | 51 | 22 |
| | | | | (SP 110.1%) | | **9 Rn** |

**1m 11.2** (-0.60) CSF £39.58 CT £180.84 TOTE £8.30: £2.40 £1.70 £1.90 (£21.70) Trio £90.80 OWNER Mr P. B. Adams (MARLBOROUGH) BRED Sheikh Mohammed Bin Rashid Al Maktoum

LONG HANDICAP Forentia 8-3

WEIGHT FOR AGE 3yo-1lb

**4122 Prends Ca (IRE)**, much happier without the blinkers, needed all of this trip, particularly the hill, to get on top nearing the line. (13/2)

**3618 Bajan Rose**, much more of a sprinter than the winner, did look to have the measure of that rival 200 yards out, but the final climb proved just too much. This was a very good effort on such lively ground and she can soon make amends if the rains arrive in time. (6/1)

**4122 Defined Feature (IRE)**, surprisingly weak in the market after such a promising run last time, got outpaced running into the Dip but, to her credit, was coming back for more at the finish. (5/1)

**3222 Tropical Dance (USA)** has not produced her true form this term and one would question whether she has trained on, but she probably has as she has shown plenty of promise on more than the one occasion. (12/1)

**3047 Galine**, just beginning to get her winter coat, was never going the pace of the leaders, but she did run on up the hill to be nearest at the finish. (9/2)

**2950 Shanghai Girl** joined issue running into the Dip, but failed to sustain the run when the pressure was on and was well outpaced on meeting the rising ground. (15/2: 5/1-8/1)

### 4553 RACING POST GODOLPHIN STKS (Listed) (3-Y.O+) (Class A)

2-35 (2-35) **1m 4f (Rowley)** £12,161.80 (£4,205.80: £2,017.90: £824.50) Stalls: High GOING minus 0.44 sec per fur (F)

| | | | | SP | RR | SF |
|---|---|---|---|---|---|---|
| 4178* | **Busy Flight (113)** (BWHills) **3-8-11** MHills(5) (lw: mde all: drvn clr appr fnl f) | — | **1** | 11/8$^{1}$ | 121 | 76 |
| 4313* | **Key to My Heart (IRE) (114)** (MissSEHall) **6-9-4** JWeaver(3) (b: lw: chsd wnr: effrt & shkn up 2f out: no imp) | 4 | **2** | 3/1$^{2}$ | 116 | 78 |
| 4192$^{7}$ | **Sharaf Kabeer (107)** (SbinSuroor) **3-8-11** LDettori(2) (hld up: plld wd & hdwy over 3f out: outpcd appr fnl f) | 1½ | **3** | 3/1$^{2}$ | 114 | 69 |
| 4192$^{8}$ | **Heron Island (IRE) (113)** (PWChapple-Hyam) **3-8-7** RCochrane(4) (lw: unruly stalls: s.i.s: hld up in rr: effrt 3f out: one pce fnl 2f) | nk | **4** | 6/1$^{3}$ | 109 | 64 |
| | | | | (SP 106.4%) | | **4 Rn** |

**2m 28.19** (-2.31) CSF £5.20 TOTE £2.20: (£2.90) OWNER Mr S. WingfieldDigby (LAMBOURN) BRED S. Wingfield Digby

WEIGHT FOR AGE 3yo-7lb

**4178* Busy Flight** completed his hat-trick with another gutsy all-the-way success and, though he gives the impression that he does need to get his toe in, he showed no signs of stopping. He looks set to go a long way. (11/8)

**4313* Key to My Heart (IRE)**, a very handsome colt, could not quite concede weight to an improving three-year-old, but he never once stopped trying and at least his heart is in the right place. (3/1)
**4192 Sharaf Kabeer** may well need a stiffer test of stamina, for he lacked the speed to deliver a challenge after looking to be travelling strongly for most of the way. (3/1)
**4192 Heron Island (IRE)** again ran somewhat flat and, as he has been on the go since the spring, he gives the impression that he has had enough for the time being. (6/1: 7/2-13/2)

## 4554 CHARLES WELLS BOMBARDIER BITTER RATED STKS H'CAP (0-100) (3-Y.O+) (Class B)

3-05 (3-07) **7f (Rowley)** £8,676.50 (£3,213.50: £1,544.25: £633.75: £254.38: £102.62) Stalls: High GOING minus 0.44 sec (F)

| | | | | SP | RR | SF |
|---|---|---|---|---|---|---|
| $4054^{9}$ | **Highborn (IRE) (89)** (PSFelgate) **7-8-10** WRyan(11) (chsd ldrs: rdn 3f out: rallied appr fnl f: led last 100y) | — | **1** | 25/1 | 98 | 67 |
| $2880^{10}$ | **Madly Sharp (100)** (JWWatts) **5-9-7** MHills(10) (lw: a.p: slt ld 4f out: hrd drvn & hdd wl ins fnl f) | 1 | **2** | 11/1 | 107 | 76 |
| $3782^{7}$ | **Saseedo (USA) (90)** (WAO'Gorman) **6-8-11** EmmaO'Gorman(12) (mid div: sn pushed along: outpcd 3f out: r.o strly fnl f) | ½ | **3** | 14/1 | 96 | 65 |
| $4314^{13}$ | **Ziggy's Dancer (USA) (86)** (EJAlston) **5-8-7** KFallon(6) (trckd ldrs: effrt over 1f out: nt pce to chal) | 2 | **4** | 14/1 | 87 | 56 |
| $4196^{W}$ | **Law Commission (95)** (DRCElsworth) **6-9-2** JWeaver(7) (hld up in rr: gd hdwy 2f out: sn rdn: nt rch ldrs) | ¾ | **5** | 6/1 [3] | 94 | 63 |
| 4255* | **Seigneurial (91)** (GHarwood) **4-8-12** MRoberts(2) (lw: plld hrd: bhd: effrt over 2f out: nvr rchd ldrs) | nk | **6** | 14/1 | 90 | 59 |
| 4376* | **Don Bosio (USA) (95)** (MRStoute) **3-9-0v** 3x WRSwinburn(3) (lw: trckd ldrs: drvn 2f out: outpcd appr fnl f) | ¾ | **7** | 100/30 [1] | 92 | 59 |
| 4231* | **Roushan (86)** (SCWilliams) **3-8-5** JTate(1) (led 3f: prom tl wknd appr fnl f) | ½ | **8** | 12/1 | 82 | 49 |
| $4314^{6}$ | **Emerging Market (99)** (JLDunlop) **4-9-6** KDarley(5) (hld up in rr: hdwy over 1f out: no ex ins fnl f) | s.h | **9** | 11/2 [2] | 95 | 64 |
| $2853^{2}$ | **Everglades (IRE) (98)** (RCharlton) **8-9-5** PatEddery(4) (plld hrd: prom tl outpcd appr fnl f: eased whn btn) | 1¾ | **10** | 13/2 | 90 | 59 |
| $3445^{9}$ | **Maid For The Hills (91)** (DRLoder) **3-8-10** RCochrane(8) (plld hrd: hld up & bhd: hdwy over 2f out: wknd fnl f) | s.h | **11** | 25/1 | 83 | 50 |
| $4196^{7}$ | **Resounder (USA) (94)** (JHMGosden) **3-8-13v[1]** LDettori(9) (trckd ldrs far side: rdn & wknd over 1f out) | nk | **12** | 10/1 | 85 | 52 |

(SP 118.9%) **12 Rn**

**1m 23.74** (-0.76) CSF £245.41 CT £2,213.72 TOTE £36.90: £6.30 £2.80 £3.60 (£259.10) Trio £521.50 OWNER Yorkshire Racing Club Owners Group 1990 (MELTON MOWBRAY) BRED Mrs P. F. McQuillan
LONG HANDICAP Ziggy's Dancer (USA) 8-6 Roushan 8-0
WEIGHT FOR AGE 3yo-2lb

**2722 Highborn (IRE)** caused quite an upset after looking to be one of the first beaten, but he won fairly and squarely in the end. There was no fluke about this success. (25/1)
**1107 Madly Sharp** has shown a liking for this track in the past, but his successes have come in the spring and this performance under topweight gives every indication that he is still as good as ever. (11/1)
**3445 Saseedo (USA)** was never travelling and did look destined to finish in the pack, but he found his stride on meeting the hill and finished best of all. (14/1)
**4101 Ziggy's Dancer (USA)** is usually at his best produced late, but he was never far away here, though he was short of a turn of finishing speed in the dash to the line. (14/1)
**3782 Law Commission** needs to deliver his challenge as late as possible, but he is always best coming from off a strong pace and, with this race not being run to suit, he once again made a fool of his jockey. (6/1)
**4255* Seigneurial** did not give his jockey much help by pulling too hard on this first attempt at the trip and his final placing was as close as he got. (14/1)
**4376* Don Bosio (USA)** was thrown in at the deep-end against these experienced older handicappers and, though he held his pitch in the chasing group, he quite simply got left behind when the race really developed. (100/30: 9/4-7/2)

## 4555 SOMERVILLE TATTERSALL STKS (Listed) (2-Y.O C & G) (Class A)

3-40 (3-40) **7f (Rowley)** £9,116.80 (£3,371.20: £1,615.60: £658.00: £259.00: £99.40) Stalls: High GOING minus 0.44 sec per fur (F)

| | | | | SP | RR | SF |
|---|---|---|---|---|---|---|
| $3143^{2}$ | **Grapeshot (USA) (100)** (LMCumani) **2-8-9** LDettori(5) (lw: led 1f: led 3f out: drew clr fnl f) | — | **1** | 5/4 [1] | 99 | 69 |
| $4338^{2}$ | **Musical Dancer (USA) (100)** (EALDunlop) **2-8-9** KFallon(2) (hld up: hdwy 2f out: edgd rt & ev ch 1f out: no ex fnl f) | 1¾ | **2** | 20/1 | 95 | 65 |
| 4050* | **Falak (USA)** (MajorWRHern) **2-8-9** RHills(7) (led after 1f to 3f out: ev ch tl unable qckn fnl f) | ¾ | **3** | 5/1 [2] | 93 | 63 |
| $2040^{6}$ | **Shock Value (IRE)** (MRStoute) **2-8-9** WRSwinburn(6) (chsd ldrs: rdn 2f out: styd on fnl f) | 1 | **4** | 7/1 | 91 | 61 |
| 4380* | **Bachelors Pad** (WJarvis) **2-8-9** MHills(4) (lw: hld up in rr: outpcd 2f out: styd on ins fnl f) | 1¼ | **5** | 6/1 [3] | 88 | 58 |
| $4065^{4}$ | **Johnny Staccato** (JMPEustace) **2-8-9** RCochrane(8) (s.s: hld up: effrt over 2f out: btn appr fnl f) | 1½ | **6** | 10/1 | 85 | 55 |
| $3925^{2}$ | **Imperial President (100)** (HRACecil) **2-8-9** PatEddery(3) (prom: pushed along 3f out: wknd appr fnl f) | 2½ | **7** | 8/1 | 79 | 49 |
| $1766^{4}$ | **Rude Awakening (89)** (GLewis) **2-8-9** KDarley(1) (bkwd: s.s: a bhd: lost tch 2f out: t.o) | 29 | **8** | 33/1 | 13 | — |

(SP 115.8%) **8 Rn**

**1m 23.47** (-1.03) CSF £22.86 TOTE £2.30: £1.40 £2.10 £1.90 (£15.60) OWNER Mrs Timothy von Halle (NEWMARKET) BRED Jody Huckabay and Dr Stuart Brown

**3143 Grapeshot (USA)** won this in workmanlike rather than impressive fashion, but he always looked to be in charge, and proved his point nearing the finish. (5/4)
**4338 Musical Dancer (USA)** showed that stamina is his strong suit for, after struggling from some way out, he stayed on really well up the hill. He should come into his own next term. (20/1)
**4050* Falak (USA)**, who ran with his tongue tied down, raced freely and probably did too much too soon, but he was still only outpointed inside the last furlong. (5/1)
**2040 Shock Value (IRE)**, out of action since Royal Ascot and trying his luck over a slightly longer trip, was hard at work and going nowhere at halfway, but he got better the further he went, and should not be long in improving on this. (7/1)
**4380* Bachelors Pad** got outpaced just when he was trying to take closer order running into the Dip and, though he found his feet again up the hill, he had allowed the principals to get away. This was not a bad performance and he looks to have what it takes. (6/1)
**4065 Johnny Staccato** has not mastered the art of trapping but he needs to be held up to get the trip and, on such a testing track, he had to admit he lacked the stamina to see it out. (10/1)
**3925 Imperial President**, whose trainer stated beforehand that he was beginning to go in his coat, ran a bit of a lack-lustre race and was not persevered with when all chance had gone. (8/1)

## 4556 JAMES LEVETT H'CAP (0-100) (3-Y.O) (Class C)

4-15 (4-15) **1m 2f (Rowley)** £7,830.00 (£2,340.00: £1,120.00: £510.00) Stalls: High GOING minus 0.44 sec per fur (F)

| | | | | SP | RR | SF |
|---|---|---|---|---|---|---|
| | **Najm Mubeen (IRE) (85)** (ACStewart) **3-8-12** MRoberts(2) (plld hrd: a.p: led over 1f out: drvn out nr fin) | — | **1** | 16/1 | 102 | 68 |

| | | | | SP | RR | SF |
|---|---|---|---|---|---|---|
| 4117* | **Oops Pettie (83)** (MrsJCecil) **3-8-10** WRSwinburn(9) (lw: hld up: hdwy to chal over 1f out: rdn & unable qckn ins fnl f) | 1¼ | **2** | 9/4[1] | 98 | 64 |
| 4463[22] | **Jerry Cutrona (IRE) (82)** (NACallaghan) **3-8-9** RCochrane(1) (hld up & bhd: effrt 2f out: r.o strly towards fin) | hd | **3** | 12/1 | 97 | 63 |
| 3997[6] | **Warbrook (84)** (IABalding) **3-8-11** KDarley(11) (prom: outpcd & lost pl 3f out: styd on fnl f) | 5 | **4** | 25/1 | 91 | 57 |
| 4297[2] | **Daira (69)** (JDBethell) **3-7-5**(5) PFessey(5) (trckd ldrs tl n.m.r & outpcd wl over 1f out: kpt on one pce) | 3 | **5** | 13/2 | 71 | 37 |
| 3211[5] | **Mawingo (IRE) (83)** (GWragg) **3-8-3**(7) GMilligan(8) (hld up: effrt over 3f out: nt trble ldrs) | s.h | **6** | 9/2[3] | 85 | 51 |
| 4326[13] | **Brandon Magic (94)** (IABalding) **3-9-7** MHills(4) (w ldrs: slt ld 3f out tl over 1f out: wknd fnl f) | ¾ | **7** | 14/1 | 95 | 61 |
| 2514[7] | **Albaha (USA) (77)** (JEBanks) **3-8-4** JStack(3) (lw: s.s: a in rr) | 1¾ | **8** | 25/1 | 75 | 41 |
| 3926* | **Select Few (86)** (LMCumani) **3-8-13** LDettori(7) (led to 3f out: wknd over 1f out) | hd | **9** | 7/2[2] | 84 | 50 |
| 4193[10] | **Gold Disc (USA) (91)** (BWHills) **3-9-4** PatEddery(10) (prom tl wknd 2f out: eased whn btn) | ¾ | **10** | 11/1 | 88 | 54 |
| | | | | (SP 120.8%) | | **10 Rn** |

**2m 2.64** (-0.96) CSF £51.30 CT £425.43 TOTE £19.70: £3.90 £1.30 £3.30 (£55.80) Trio £92.60 OWNER Sheikh Ahmed Al Maktoum (NEWMARKET) BRED Kilfrush Stud Ltd

LONG HANDICAP Daira 7-9

**Najm Mubeen (IRE)**, whose last appearance on a racecourse was at this meeting twelve months ago, found the task of taking on handicappers no problem at all, and a lot of the credit must go to his trainer for producing him fit after such a long break. (16/1)

**4117* Oops Pettie** delivered her challenge at the same time as the winner but, after a brief struggle, had to admit he was too strong for her. Time may show this to be a better than average performance. (9/4)

**3790 Jerry Cutrona (IRE)** did not get the trip when tried as a two-year-old but, restrained in the rear, he stayed on stoutly up the hill, and there could be more success to come in the near future. (12/1)

**3997 Warbrook** has been tackling longer trips and he was tapped for toe before reaching the bushes, and then stayed on again towards the finish. (25/1)

**4297 Daira**, restrained just behind the leaders, did not enjoy the smoothest of runs into the Dip and, losing her momentum, was unable to recover. (13/2)

**3211 Mawingo (IRE)**, unable to get himself into the race, gave the impression that this trip was just too far for him on such a stiff track. (9/2)

**3926* Select Few** (7/2: op 2/1)

**4193 Gold Disc (USA)** (11/1: 8/1-12/1)

## 4557 FURTHER FLIGHT H'CAP (0-90) (3-Y.O+) (Class C)

4-50 (4-50) **1m 6f (Rowley)** £6,628.00 (£1,984.00: £952.00: £436.00) Stalls: High GOING minus 0.44 sec per fur (F)

| | | | | SP | RR | SF |
|---|---|---|---|---|---|---|
| 4315[2] | **Floating Line (69)** (EJAlston) **8-9-7** KFallon(6) (lw: hld up: hdwy ½-wy: sn chsng ldr: led over 3f out: sn clr: unchal) | — | **1** | 5/2[2] | 83 | 65 |
| 4327[8] | **Lalindi (IRE) (72)** (DRCElsworth) **5-9-10b** LDettori(4) (lw: led after 2f: qcknd clr 8f out: hdd over 3f out: sn outpcd) | 5 | **2** | 9/2[3] | 80 | 62 |
| 3961* | **Full Throttle (70)** (MHTompkins) **3-8-10**(3) MHenry(5) (hld up: effrt & rdn 3f out: no real imp) | 8 | **3** | 6/4[1] | 69 | 42 |
| 4327[7] | **Sharaf (IRE) (79)** (WRMuir) **3-9-8** PatEddery(2) (led 2f: rdn over 3f out: sn lost tch) | 1 | **4** | 10/1 | 77 | 50 |
| 4216[15] | **Ceilidh Star (IRE) (68)** (BWHills) **3-8-11b** MHills(1) (chsd ldr 8f: dropped rr 5f out: sn rdn & no imp) | ¾ | **5** | 5/1 | 65 | 38 |
| | | | | (SP 112.5%) | | **5 Rn** |

**2m 56.83** (0.83) CSF £12.67 TOTE £3.10: £1.30 £2.10 (£6.80) OWNER Mr G. Lowe (PRESTON) BRED R. Kalman

WEIGHT FOR AGE 3yo-9lb

**4315 Floating Line**, winner of this event last year, set sail for home some way out and, gradually forging clear, found this a simple task. (5/2)

**2430* Lalindi (IRE)** tried hard to slip her rivals a mile out, but she could never gain enough leeway and, once the winner had taken her measure, she just had to settle for second best. (9/2)

**3961* Full Throttle** did not produce his true running on this step up in class and it may have been asking a lot against such an experienced handicapper as the winner but, then again, he was unable to get in a blow against the runner-up. (6/4)

**3398 Sharaf (IRE)** was throwing out distress signals over three furlongs out and it would appear the Handicapper has his measure. (10/1: op 6/1)

**4042 Ceilidh Star (IRE)** travelled well for the first mile, but then lost her pitch and, from then on, was fighting a lost cause. (5/1)

T/Jkpt: Not won; £58,846.54 to Newmarket 5/10/96. T/Plpt: £422.20 (81.6 Tckts). T/Qdpt: £62.10 (34.36 Tckts). IM

# 4448-HAYDOCK (L-H) (Soft)

## Saturday October 5th

WEATHER: fine & sunny WIND: mod half against

## 4558 WALNUT MAIDEN STKS (2-Y.O) (Class D)

1-40 (1-41) **5f** £3,485.00 (£1,055.00: £515.00: £245.00) Stalls: Centre GOING: 0.50 sec per fur (GS)

| | | | | SP | RR | SF |
|---|---|---|---|---|---|---|
| 3994[5] | **Queen's Pageant** (JLSpearing) **2-8-9** SDrowne(11) (lw: w ldrs: led over 2f out: hung lft: hld on wl nr fin) | — | **1** | 2/1[1] | 68 | 40 |
| 3224[7] | **Fine Times (56)** (CWFairhurst) **2-9-0** DeanMcKeown(5) (mid div: effrt & swtchd lft over 1f out: nt qckn ins fnl f) | ¾ | **2** | 33/1 | 71 | 43 |
| 2699[3] | **Midyan Queen** (RHollinshead) **2-8-4**(5) DGriffiths(1) (w ldrs: nt qckn fnl f) | 1¼ | **3** | 14/1 | 62 | 34 |
| | **Savona (IRE)** (PJMakin) **2-8-9** KDarley(12) (w'like: scope: dwlt: hdwy to chse ldrs ½-wy: kpt on same pce) | 1¾ | **4** | 10/1 | 56 | 28 |
| | **Hyde Park (IRE)** (SirMarkPrescott) **2-9-0** SSanders(7) (wl grwn: scope: bkwd: chsd ldrs: effrt over 2f out: wknd fnl f) | s.h | **5** | 5/2[2] | 61+ | 33 |
| 4043[11] | **Sparkling Harry (65)** (MissLCSiddall) **2-8-11**(3) PMcCabe(2) (in tch: drvn along & outpcd ½-wy: kpt on fnl f) | s.h | **6** | 50/1 | 61 | 33 |
| 3921[3] | **Ruby Tuesday (80)** (BAMcMahon) **2-8-9** JFortune(9) (lw: led tl over 2f out: wknd over 1f out) | 6 | **7** | 9/2[3] | 37 | 9 |
| 3508[7] | **Something Blue** (TRWatson) **2-8-9** JCarroll(4) (b.hind: sn outpcd) | 1 | **8** | 50/1 | 33 | 5 |
| 4318[7] | **Toronto (71)** (JBerry) **2-8-9**(5) PRoberts(6) (w ldrs: hung lft ½-wy: sn lost pl) | 1 | **9** | 16/1 | 35 | 7 |
| 4208[8] | **Mungo Park** (MrsJRRamsden) **2-9-0** MWigham(10) (bit bkwd: s.s: a in rr) | nk | **10** | 20/1 | 34 | 6 |
| 4043[2] | **Fruitana (IRE) (81)** (JBerry) **2-9-0** GCarter(8) (lw: trckd ldrs: shkn up over 1f out: wknd qckly ins fnl f) | 1½ | **11** | 13/2 | 29 | 1 |
| 4228[7] | **Patrita Park** (WWHaigh) **2-8-9** RLappin(3) (sn pushed along & outpcd) | 1½ | **12** | 33/1 | 20 | — |
| | | | | (SP 129.6%) | | **12 Rn** |

**64.88 secs** (5.68) CSF £61.45 TOTE £3.00: £1.40 £6.90 £5.50 (£116.30) Trio £179.00 OWNER Mrs Robert Heathcote (ALCESTER) BRED R. and Mrs Heathcote

**3994 Queen's Pageant**, bred to be suited by soft ground, struggled home in what was almost certainly a very moderate race. (2/1)
**1537 Fine Times** bounced back after running poorly on his three previous outings. (33/1)
**2699 Midyan Queen**, on her toes beforehand, ran well from the worst of the draw. (14/1)
**Savona (IRE)**, a bad walker, showed plenty of knee-action going down and showed ability after a slow start, almost certainly appreciating the soft ground. (10/1: op 6/1)
**Hyde Park (IRE)**, a medium-sized, attractive colt, looked badly in need of the outing. He showed promise and can be expected to do considerably better in due course. (5/2: 5/4-11/4)
**Sparkling Harry** seemed to run his best race so far and will be suited by six or even seven. (50/1)

## 4559 RALLI BROTHERS AND CONEY H'CAP (0-80) (3-Y.O) (Class D)

2-10 (2-12) **1m 2f 120y** £4,212.75 (£1,272.00: £618.50: £291.75) Stalls: High GOING: 0.50 sec per fur (GS)

| | | | | SP | RR | SF |
|---|---|---|---|---|---|---|
| $4307^{F}$ | **Nosey Native (57)** (JPearce) **3-7-7**$^{(5)ow2}$ MBaird(2) (s.s: sn bhd & pushed along: effrt & nt clr run over 3f out: styd on strly to ld over 1f out: sn clr: eased towards fin) | — | **1** | 16/1 | 77 | 30 |
| $4257^{5}$ | **Melt The Clouds (CAN) (74)** (PWHarris) **3-9-1** FNorton(4) (led: clr over 3f out: hdd over 1f out: no ch w wnr) | 8 | **2** | 12/1 | 82 | 37 |
| $4326^{11}$ | **Milford Sound (77)** (JRFanshawe) **3-9-1**$^{(3)}$ NVarley(17) (a chsng ldrs: drvn along 6f out: one pce fnl 3f) | 7 | **3** | 14/1 | 74 | 29 |
| $3979^{9}$ | **Love Bateta (IRE) (66)** (JEBanks) **3-8-7** JStack(13) (a.p: one pce fnl 3f) | hd | **4** | 20/1 | 63 | 18 |
| *$4334^{11}$* | **Newbridge Boy (55)** (MGMeagher) **3-7-10** NKennedy(1) (lw: hdwy u.p 3f out: kpt on: nvr nr to chal) | 1¼ | **5** | 25/1 | 50 | 5 |
| $4450^{5}$ | **Samim (USA) (67)** (SGollings) **3-8-8b** VHalliday(15) (mid div: sn drvn along: no imp fnl 4f) | 2½ | **6** | 16/1 | 58 | 13 |
| $1783^{4}$ | **Ledgendry Line (68)** (MrsMReveley) **3-8-9** KDarley(14) (s.i.s: bhd tl styd on fnl 2f) | 1¼ | **7** | 12/1 | 58 | 13 |
| $1508^{14}$ | **Formidable Flame (60)** (WJMusson) **3-8-1** CRutter(5) (hld up & bhd: pushed along & styd on fnl 2f: nvr nr ldrs) | s.h | **8** | 14/1 | 49 | 4 |
| $3960^{2}$ | **Vanadium Ore (60)** (JLEyre) **3-8-1v**$^{1}$ TWilliams(19) (chsd ldrs: bmpd after 3f: rdn & edgd lft 3f out: sn wknd) | 1¼ | **9** | 8/1$^{3}$ | 48 | 3 |
| $4438^{7}$ | **Ordained (56)** (EJAlston) **3-7-4**$^{(7)}$ JFowle(11) (hld up & bhd: sme hdwy over 3f out: n.d) | 6 | **10** | 16/1 | 34 | — |
| $4201^{2}$ | **Opalette (70)** (LadyHerries) **3-8-11** DeclanO'Shea(6) (lw: hld up: sme hdwy 3f out: sn wknd) | 1 | **11** | 13/2$^{2}$ | 47 | 2 |
| $4110^{5}$ | **Calendula (66)** (DMorley) **3-8-7** MFenton(18) (lw: chsd ldrs tl wknd over 3f out) | 4 | **12** | 16/1 | 37 | — |
| 4470* | **Consordino (85)** (LMCumani) **3-9-12** JFortune(9) (lw: chsd ldrs: rdn over 4f out: lost pl 3f out) | 3½ | **13** | 6/1$^{1}$ | 51 | 6 |
| $4187^{5}$ | **Alambar (IRE) (76)** (PTWalwyn) **3-9-3** JCarroll(8) (mid div: effrt 4f out: sn wknd & eased) | ½ | **14** | 14/1 | 41 | — |
| $4322^{10}$ | **John-T (65)** (JBerry) **3-8-6** GCarter(12) (a in rr) | nk | **15** | 25/1 | 29 | — |
| $3947^{16}$ | **Kriscliffe (80)** (MissGayKelleway) **3-9-7** MRimmer(7) (b: a bhd: hmpd after 1f) | 5 | **16** | 20/1 | 37 | — |
| 3665* | **Failed To Hit (72)** (SirMarkPrescott) **3-8-13** SSanders(10) (prom: drvn along 5f out: sn wknd) | 1¾ | **17** | 8/1$^{3}$ | 26 | — |
| $873^{18}$ | **Sizzling Symphony (55)** (RAFahey) **3-7-5**$^{(5)}$ PFessey(3) (wl bhd fnl 3f) | 11 | **18** | 33/1 | — | — |
| $4117^{6}$ | **Classic Flyer (IRE) (75)** (RHarris) **3-9-2** RPrice(16) (chsd ldrs: bmpd after 3f: sn rdn: lost pl 4f out: virtually p.u) | dist | **19** | 16/1 | — | — |

(SP 134.8%) **19 Rn**

**2m 23.72** (12.22) CSF £190.61 CT £2,552.78 TOTE £20.60: £3.80 £4.00 £3.20 £9.00 (£143.40) Trio £413.70; £466.25 to Haydock 6/10/96
OWNER Mr Jeff Pearce (NEWMARKET) BRED Lady Jennifer Green
LONG HANDICAP Newbridge Boy 7-7 Nosey Native 7-6

**3520 Nosey Native** came from last to first in what was a strongly-run race. (16/1)
**4257 Melt The Clouds (CAN)** set a very strong gallop and showed with a clear advantage just under half a mile from home but, in the end, proved no match for the winner. (12/1)
**3051* Milford Sound**, who has a pronounced knee-action, was hard at work some way from home. He has plenty of weight for what he has actually achieved. (14/1)
**3657 Love Bateta (IRE)** put a poor effort last time behind her. (20/1)
**3422 Newbridge Boy** was 3lb higher in the weights than when winning at Wolverhampton three runs ago. (25/1)
**1200 Samim (USA)**, who is slipping down the weights, almost certainly has as much temperament as ability. (16/1)
**1783 Ledgendry Line**, who showed plenty of knee-action going down, shaped nicely after an absence of 120 days. Staying on at the death, he will be suited by further. (12/1)
**4470* Consordino**, a very poor mover, was 5lb higher in the weights than when winning at Hamilton six days earlier. She ran too badly to be true here. (6/1)

## 4560 IMACO H'CAP (0-80) (3-Y.O+ F & M) (Class D)

2-45 (2-46) **7f 30y** £4,053.50 (£1,223.00: £594.00: £279.50) Stalls: Low GOING: 0.50 sec per fur (GS)

| | | | | SP | RR | SF |
|---|---|---|---|---|---|---|
| 3800* | **Q Factor (75)** (DHaydnJones) **4-9-10** SDrowne(1) (lw: chsd ldrs: led 2f out: hld on towards fin) | — | **1** | 6/1$^{1}$ | 85 | 35 |
| *$3419^{9}$* | **Princess Efisio (57)** (BAMcMahon) **3-8-4** SSanders(12) (bhd: gd hdwy over 2f out: styd on wl fnl f: jst failed) | s.h | **2** | 12/1 | 67 | 15 |
| $4453^{3}$ | **Desert Lynx (IRE) (70)** (TRWatson) **3-9-3** TWilliams(10) (lw: in tch: effrt over 3f out: carried lft: hrd rdn, hung rt & styd on one pce fnl 2f) | 3 | **3** | 11/1 | 73 | 21 |
| $3995^{15}$ | **Tael of Silver (63)** (ABailey) **4-8-12** KDarley(5) (in tch: kpt on one pce fnl 3f) | 5 | **4** | 12/1 | 55 | 5 |
| $4058^{6}$ | **Bollin Dorothy (56)** (TDEasterby) **3-8-3** MFenton(8) (lw: trckd ldrs: led over 3f out to 2f out: sn wknd) | 2½ | **5** | 15/2$^{2}$ | 42 | — |
| $3926^{8}$ | **Salmis (77)** (JRFanshawe) **3-9-7**$^{(3)}$ NVarley(13) (effrt over 3f out: kpt on: nvr nr ldrs) | 1¼ | **6** | 10/1 | 61 | 9 |
| $3426^{12}$ | **Best of All (IRE) (65)** (JBerry) **4-9-0** JFortune(3) (led tl over 3f out: lost pl over 1f out) | 1¼ | **7** | 20/1 | 46 | — |
| $4312^{6}$ | **Miss Waterline (72)** (PDEvans) **3-8-12**$^{(7)}$ AnthonyBond(6) (hld up: effrt over 2f out: nvr nr to chal) | hd | **8** | 14/1 | 53 | 1 |
| $4439^{10}$ | **Shashi (IRE) (62)** (WWHaigh) **4-8-11** RLappin(15) (chsd ldrs: rdn & edgd lft 3f out: grad wknd) | ¾ | **9** | 20/1 | 41 | — |
| $4381^{8}$ | **Queen of All Birds (IRE) (69)** (RBoss) **5-9-4v**$^{1}$ MRimmer(4) (b: s.i.s: hdwy u.p 3f out: sn chsng ldrs: wandered: wknd over 1f out) | 1¾ | **10** | 12/1 | 44 | — |
| $4316^{11}$ | **Fame Again (70)** (MrsJRRamsden) **4-9-5** MWigham(16) (lw: hld up: effrt over 3f out: sn wknd) | 3½ | **11** | 12/1 | 37 | — |
| $2146^{4}$ | **Kiss Me Again (IRE) (77)** (RHannon) **3-9-10** RPerham(9) (rr div: effrt over 3f out: n.d) | 1¾ | **12** | 14/1 | 40 | — |
| $3817^{9}$ | **Gymcrak Flyer (67)** (GHolmes) **5-9-2** DeanMcKeown(7) (b.hind: s.i.s: a bhd) | 2½ | **13** | 12/1 | 25 | — |
| $3949^{7}$ | **Summer Beauty (67)** (JHMGosden) **3-9-0** JCarroll(11) (a bhd: rdn over 3f out: no rspnse) | 24 | **14** | 8/1$^{3}$ | — | — |
| $4074^{9}$ | **White Hare (57)** (MrsMReveley) **3-8-4** JFanning(14) (racd wd: a bhd) | 3½ | **15** | 14/1 | — | — |

(SP 122.6%) **15 Rn**

**1m 37.5** (10.00) CSF £70.12 CT £723.04 TOTE £4.70: £2.20 £4.20 £3.10 (£38.80) Trio £138.70 OWNER Mr H. G. Collis (PONTYPRIDD) BRED A. Sofroniou and H. Collis
WEIGHT FOR AGE 3yo-2lb

**3800* Q Factor**, in good form all season, held on by the skin of her teeth. (6/1)

**2937 Princess Efisio**, a very poor mover, proved well suited by the give underfoot and, in the end, was only just denied. She stayed the trip alright. (12/1)
**4453 Desert Lynx (IRE)**, taken to post quietly, again showed her appreciation of give underfoot. (11/1)
**3833 Tael of Silver**, who showed a very poor action going down, appears to be in the grip of the handicapper. (12/1)
**4058 Bollin Dorothy**, who has slipped down the weights, travelled strongly but, when collared, soon faded. (15/2)
**3107* Salmis** again wore a tongue-strap. (10/1)

## 4561 RALLI BROTHERS AND CONEY CONDITIONS STKS (3-Y.O+) (Class C)

3-20 (3-20) **5f** £4,727.60 (£1,768.40: £864.20: £371.00: £165.50: £83.30) Stalls: Centre GOING: 0.50 sec per fur (GS)

| | | | | SP | RR | SF |
|---|---|---|---|---|---|---|
| 4452[7] | **Tadeo (87)** (MJohnston) **3-8-12** DeanMcKeown(7) (lw: mde all: hung lft fr ½-wy: styd on wl) | — | **1** | 9/1 | 99 | 57 |
| 4452[5] | **Ansellman (81)** (JBerry) **6-8-12b** GCarter(5) (a chsng ldrs: rdn over 1f out: no imp) | 2½ | **2** | 10/1 | 91 | 49 |
| 4367* | **Crofters Ceilidh (83)** (BAMcMahon) **4-8-7b** JFortune(4) (hdwy to trck ldrs ½-wy: rdn over 1f out: kpt on same pce) | 4 | **3** | 7/2[2] | 73 | 31 |
| 4219* | **Saheeel (USA)** (SbinSuroor) **3-9-0** JCarroll(2) (lw: trckd ldrs: edgd lft & wknd over 1f out) | 1¼ | **4** | 7/4[1] | 76 | 34 |
| 4466[16] | **Takadou (IRE) (89)** (MissLCSiddall) **5-8-12** RLappin(3) (lw: sn outpcd & pushed along: kpt on fnl f: n.d) | s.h | **5** | 12/1 | 74 | 32 |
| 4485[4] | **Kunucu (IRE) (90)** (TDBarron) **3-8-7** KDarley(6) (chsd wnr tl lost pl ½-wy: n.d) | 1½ | **6** | 4/1[3] | 64 | 22 |
| 4119[7] | **Tarf (USA) (81)** (PTWalwyn) **3-8-7** SSanders(1) (trckd ldrs: drvn along & edgd lft ½-wy: sn wknd & eased) | 13 | **7** | 14/1 | 23 | — |
| | | | | (SP 112.0%) | | **7 Rn** |

**64.03 secs** (4.83) CSF £77.03 TOTE £15.40: £3.40 £3.00 (£38.20) OWNER Mr J. R. Good (MIDDLEHAM) BRED J. R. and Mrs P. Good
**4452 Tadeo**, relatively fresh, showed these rivals a clear pair of heels throughout. (9/1)
**4452 Ansellman** ran well and would have been meeting the winner on 3lb better terms if it had been a handicap. (10/1)
**4367* Crofters Ceilidh**, with the blinkers on again, travelled strongly but did not seem to get home in the ground. (7/2)
**4219* Saheeel (USA)** edged out towards the centre. His rider reported that he was never travelling in the soft ground. (7/4)
**1321 Takadou (IRE)** ran his usual race, being outpaced and staying on late in the day. (12/1)
**4485 Kunucu (IRE)**, having her second outing in five days, was in trouble before halfway. (4/1)

## 4562 MAPLE NURSERY (S) H'CAP (0-65) (2-Y.O) (Class G)

3-55 (3-57) **6f** £2,473.50 (£696.00: £340.50) Stalls: Centre GOING: 0.50 sec per fur (GS)

| | | | | SP | RR | SF |
|---|---|---|---|---|---|---|
| 4368[2] | **Marsh Marigold (60)** (MartynMeade) **2-8-9**(7) DSweeney(15) (lw: trckd ldrs: led over 1f out: hung lft & sn clr) | — | **1** | 15/2[1] | 61 | 27 |
| 4433[9] | **Veerapong (IRE) (56)** (MWEasterby) **2-8-12b** JFanning(16) (sn bhd & pushed along: hdwy over 1f out: edgd lft: kpt on) | 3½ | **2** | 16/1 | 48 | 14 |
| 4106[12] | **Sharp Return (47)** (MJRyan) **2-7-12**(5) MBaird(24) (led: edgd lft ½-wy: hdd over 1f out: kpt on same pce) | s.h | **3** | 14/1 | 39 | 5 |
| 3840[8] | **Fearless Cavalier (54)** (RHollinshead) **2-8-5**(5) DGriffiths(4) (a chsng ldrs: one pce fnl 2f) | 6 | **4** | 16/1 | 30 | — |
| 4423[6] | **Hoh Surprise (IRE) (56)** (MBell) **2-8-12** MFenton(11) (lw: hdwy ½-wy: styd on u.p: nvr nr to chal) | 1½ | **5** | 15/2[1] | 28 | — |
| 4440[8] | **Broctune Line (53)** (MrsMReveley) **2-8-9** KDarley(14) (hdwy u.p ½-wy: kpt on: nvr nr ldrs) | nk | **6** | 12/1[3] | 24 | — |
| 4495[9] | **Poly Moon (52)** (MRChannon) **2-8-8** CRutter(20) (lw: chsd ldrs tl outpcd fnl 2f) | s.h | **7** | 8/1[2] | 23 | — |
| 4347[12] | **Samspet (46)** (RAFahey) **2-8-2v** FNorton(5) (a in tch: drvn along ½-wy: no imp) | 1¾ | **8** | 25/1 | 12 | — |
| 3969[11] | **Mazil (65)** (TDEasterby) **2-9-4b**(3) RHavlin(13) (chsd ldrs tl wknd over 1f out) | ½ | **9** | 20/1 | 30 | — |
| *4093*[9] | **My Girl (45)** (JBerry) **2-7-10b**(5) PFessey(18) (s.s: wl bhd & rdn along: hdwy & wandered over 1f out: n.d) | ½ | **10** | 16/1 | 8 | — |
| 3976[7] | **Champagne On Ice (54)** (PDEvans) **2-8-10** RPerham(8) (a mid div & sn drvn along) | hd | **11** | 16/1 | 17 | — |
| 4223[11] | **Fly Down To Rio (IRE) (45)** (DWPArbuthnot) **2-7-12b**[1](3) DarrenMoffatt(10) (nvr wnt pce) | ¾ | **12** | 20/1 | 6 | — |
| *4093*[13] | **Petrine Gray (53)** (TDEasterby) **2-8-9** MBirch(7) (chsd ldrs over 3f: sn wknd) | nk | **13** | 12/1[3] | 13 | — |
| 4223[F] | **Miss Alice (50)** (JNorton) **2-8-6** TWilliams(21) (bhd: sme hdwy whn hmpd over 1f out: n.d) | ¾ | **14** | 25/1 | 8 | — |
| 4223[8] | **Superboots (43)** (WWHaigh) **2-7-6b**[1](7) JBramhill(12) (swtg: chsd ldrs: rdn ½-wy: sn wknd) | nk | **15** | 20/1 | — | — |
| *4079*[4] | **Senate Swings (56)** (WRMuir) **2-8-12** SWhitworth(17) (a rr div) | 1½ | **16** | 12/1[3] | 9 | — |
| 4384[12] | **Real Fire (IRE) (52)** (MGMeagher) **2-8-1**(7)ow4 RStudholme(19) (lw: bhd fr ½-wy) | 1½ | **17** | 16/1 | 1 | — |
| 4223[2] | **Jingoist (IRE) (56)** (JLHarris) **2-8-12b** DeanMcKeown(6) (lw: sn bhd & drvn along) | ½ | **18** | 8/1[2] | 4 | — |
| 3429[9] | **Impish (IRE) (57)** (TJEtherington) **2-8-13b**[1] JCarroll(22) (chsd ldrs tl rdn & wknd 2f out) | 2½ | **19** | 14/1 | — | — |
| 2429[8] | **Full Traceability (IRE) (60)** (JBerry) **2-9-2v** JFortune(9) (prom tl lost pl ½-wy) | 1¼ | **20** | 16/1 | — | — |
| 3840[11] | **Lucybod (40)** (NTinkler) **2-7-10** NKennedy(23) (bhd: sme hdwy ½-wy: sn lost pl) | ½ | **21** | 20/1 | — | — |
| *3954*[6] | **Silver Moon (47)** (BAMcMahon) **2-8-3** SSanders(1) (racd far side: bhd fnl 2f) | 3 | **22** | 25/1 | — | — |
| 4223[13] | **Classic Partygoer (53)** (MWEasterby) **2-8-4b**(5)ow2 GParkin(2) (racd far side: eased & bhd fnl 2f) | ½ | **23** | 25/1 | — | — |
| | | | | (SP 151.9%) | | **23 Rn** |

**1m 19.98** (8.28) CSF £128.61 CT £1,582.39 TOTE £6.90: £2.10 £5.80 £3.60 £6.80 (£60.80) Trio £391.80 OWNER Ladyswood Racing Club (MALMESBURY) BRED R. M. West
Bt in 7,200 gns
**4368 Marsh Marigold**, well suited by the give underfoot, found the drop back in distance no problem. (15/2)
**3082 Veerapong (IRE)** bounced back after three poor efforts. (16/1)
**1169 Sharp Return**, bred to go in the soft, was drawn on the stands' side but his apprentice let him drift away from the rail. He would not have beaten the winner under any circumstances. (14/1)
**3651 Fearless Cavalier** ran better. (16/1)
**4423 Hoh Surprise (IRE)**, who wore a tongue-strap, was out with the washing until staying on late in the day. (15/2)

## 4563 RACING SCHOOLS' APPRENTICE H'CAP (0-70) (3-Y.O+) (Class E)

4-30 (4-31) **1m 6f** £3,241.25 (£980.00: £477.50: £226.25) Stalls: Centre GOING: 0.50 sec per fur (GS)

| | | | | SP | RR | SF |
|---|---|---|---|---|---|---|
| 3459* | **Sweetness Herself (62)** (MJRyan) **3-9-7** MBaird(2) (bhd: hdwy 3f out: styd on to ld ins fnl f) | — | **1** | 11/1[3] | 72 | 44 |
| | **Bang in Trouble (IRE) (52)** (JJO'Neill) **5-9-6** CTeague(18) (bit bkwd: sn trckng ldrs: led & c wd 4f out: sn clr: edgd lft & hdd ins fnl f) | nk | **2** | 25/1 | 62 | 43 |
| 4307[4] | **Children's Choice (IRE) (55)** (CNAllen) **5-9-9** DDenby(4) (lw: mid div: pushed along 5f out: styd on fnl 2f) | 2½ | **3** | 11/1[3] | 62 | 43 |
| 4474* | **The Butterwick Kid (48)** (RAFahey) **3-8-7** PFessey(1) (a in tch: hrd rdn 3f out: kpt on: no imp) | 3½ | **4** | 11/1[3] | 51 | 23 |
| 4307[3] | **Stalled (IRE) (53)** (PTWalwyn) **6-9-7** RHavlin(14) (lw: hld up: hdwy 7f out: sn prom: edgd rt: hrd rdn & kpt on fnl 2f) | ¾ | **5** | 5/1[1] | 55 | 36 |
| *3952*[4] | **Charlie Bigtime (41)** (RHarris) **6-8-3**(6)ow1 WendyRose(19) (b.hind: hdwy on outside 7f out: edgd lft & kpt on fnl 2f) | nk | **6** | 16/1 | 43 | 23 |
| 3845[5] | **Gunner B Special (40)** (SRBowring) **3-7-13b** KSked(10) (b: b.hind: chsd ldrs: c wd over 3f out: one pce) | 1¼ | **7** | 20/1 | 40 | 12 |

| | | | | SP | RR | SF |
|---|---|---|---|---|---|---|
| | **La Brief (57)** (MJRyan) **4-9-8**$^{(3)}$ AMcCarthy(8) (bit bkwd: sn wl bhd: styd on fnl 2f: nt rch ldrs) | ¾ | **8** | 12/1 | 56 | 37 |
| *3955*$^{9}$ | **Forzair (52)** (JJO'Neill) **4-9-0**$^{(6)}$ SOlley(16) (chsd ldrs: outpcd 4f out: kpt on fnl 2f) | nk | **9** | 25/1 | 51 | 32 |
| *4332*$^{4}$ | **Duty Sergeant (IRE) (35)** (PMitchell) **7-8-3** IonaWands(20) (chsd ldrs tl wknd 3f out) | 3½ | **10** | 16/1 | 30 | 11 |
| *3952** | **Backwoods (57)** (WMBrisbourne) **3-9-2** DSweeney(15) (sme hdwy 2f out: n.d) | ½ | **11** | 11/1$^{3}$ | 51 | 23 |
| 4436$^{14}$ | **Soldier Cove (USA) (43)** (MartynMeade) **6-8-8**$^{(3)}$ TField(6) (prom: effrt over 3f out: wknd over 2f out) | ½ | **12** | 25/1 | 37 | 18 |
| 3780$^{3}$ | **Monte Cavo (31)** (MBrittain) **5-7-10**$^{(3)}$ JFowle(11) (chsd ldrs tl wknd over 3f out) | 13 | **13** | 14/1 | 10 | — |
| 4448$^{8}$ | **Sedvicta (46)** (MrsMReveley) **4-9-0** SCopp(12) (rr div: rdn 4f out: sn bhd) | 2½ | **14** | 10/1$^{2}$ | 22 | 3 |
| 4317* | **Havana Heights (IRE) (48)** (JLEyre) **3-8-1**$^{(6)ow3}$ RWinks(3) (a bhd) | 2½ | **15** | 11/1$^{3}$ | 21 | — |
| 4307$^{5}$ | **Supermick (38)** (WRMuir) **5-8-6** JWilkinson(9) (mid div: c wd over 4f out: n.d) | s.h | **16** | 12/1 | 11 | — |
| *4080*$^{6}$ | **Fijon (IRE) (53)** (JPearce) **3-8-12** PDoe(7) (a bhd) | 1½ | **17** | 20/1 | 25 | — |
| 3825$^{4}$ | **Course Fishing (44)** (BAMcMahon) **5-8-12** GMilligan(5) (lw: chsd ldrs tl lost pl over 3f out) | 3½ | **18** | 12/1 | 12 | — |
| 4448$^{6}$ | **Sicarian (52)** (MJHeaton-Ellis) **4-9-6** SDrowne(13) (led to 4f out: wknd qckly over 2f out) | 4 | **19** | 14/1 | 15 | — |
| 3922$^{4}$ | **Shakiyr (FR) (49)** (RHollinshead) **5-9-3** DGriffiths(17) (a bhd: c wd & rdn over 4f out) | ¾ | **20** | 10/1$^{2}$ | 11 | — |

(SP 145.8%) **20 Rn**

**3m 15.94** (17.74) CSF £260.10 CT £2,864.96 TOTE £13.40: £3.20 £6.90 £2.80 £2.70 (£777.00) Trio £496.00; £565.97 to Haydock 6/10/96
OWNER Mrs M. J. Lavell (NEWMARKET) BRED Stud-On-The-Chart
WEIGHT FOR AGE 3yo-9lb
STEWARDS' ENQUIRY Havlin susp. 14-15/10/96 (excessive use of whip).

**3459* Sweetness Herself** proved suited by the step up distance and the give underfoot. This was her first outing for 54 days and should bring her on again. (11/1)
**Bang in Trouble (IRE)** looked burly on his first outing since running over hurdles in January. After coming wide and getting the best ground on the stands' side, his rider made the mistake of letting him drift towards the middle and they were pipped in the closing stages. (25/1)
**4307 Children's Choice (IRE)**, with no blinkers fitted this time, struggled to go the pace but put in some solid late work. (11/1)
**4474* The Butterwick Kid**, who did not lack assistance from the saddle, was racing from a 3lb higher mark. (11/1)
**4307 Stalled (IRE)**, raised 4lb in the weights, did not keep straight despite his rider's use of the stick. (5/1)
**La Brief**, absent since winning three of her last four outings in November, came from a different parish turning in to be staying on in pleasing fashion at the line. (12/1)

## 4564 WHITEBEAM MAIDEN STKS (2-Y.O F) (Class D)

5-00 (5-02) **1m 30y** £3,485.00 (£1,055.00: £515.00: £245.00) Stalls: Low GOING: 0.50 sec per fur (GS)

| | | | | SP | RR | SF |
|---|---|---|---|---|---|---|
| 4052$^{3}$ | **Noble Dane (IRE)** (PWHarris) **2-8-11** FNorton(1) (trckd ldrs gng wl: led on bit over 1f out: shkn up & hung lft: styd on) | — | **1** | 11/4$^{2}$ | 75 | 11 |
| | **Almi Ad (USA)** (DMorley) **2-8-11** MFenton(7) (lengthy: unf: trckd ldrs: swtchd lft over 1f out: ev ch ins fnl f: r.o) | ½ | **2** | 11/1 | 74+ | 10 |
| 4449$^{8}$ | **Smart Spirit (IRE)** (MrsMReveley) **2-8-6**$^{(5)}$ GLee(8) (hld up: stdy hdwy 2f out: kpt on wl fnl f) | 6 | **3** | 33/1 | 62+ | — |
| 4433$^{10}$ | **Permission (78)** (RHannon) **2-8-11** RPerham(2) (trckd ldrs: effrt over 2f out: wknd over 1f out) | 5 | **4** | 14/1 | 52 | — |
| | **Misellina (FR)** (DRLoder) **2-8-8**$^{(3)}$ PMcCabe(6) (lengthy: unf: trckd ldrs: drvn along & outpcd over 3f out: wknd over 1f out) | hd | **5** | 5/1$^{3}$ | 52 | — |
| 4370$^{W}$ | **Swan Island** (BPalling) **2-8-11** CRutter(4) (b: led tl over 2f out: wknd over 1f out) | 1¾ | **6** | 33/1 | 49 | — |
| 4211$^{3}$ | **Listed Account (USA)** (LMCumani) **2-8-11** KDarley(9) (lw: trckd ldrs: led over 2f out tl over 1f out: sn wknd) | ½ | **7** | 10/11$^{1}$ | 48 | — |
| *2172*$^{5}$ | **Tycoon Tina** (WMBrisbourne) **2-8-11** SDrowne(5) (dwlt: outpcd & pushed along over 3f out: sn bhd) | 8 | **8** | 50/1 | 32 | — |

(SP 118.6%) **8 Rn**

**1m 53.29** (12.69) CSF £29.84 TOTE £3.90: £1.20 £2.80 £4.10 (£6.70) Trio £69.10 OWNER The Bestbee Partnership (BERKHAMSTED) BRED Ovidstown Investments Ltd

**4052 Noble Dane (IRE)**, a sister to Amrak Ajeeb, looked to be in second gear much of the way but, once she hit the front, she hung left and made hard work of it. She might appreciate being waited with longer. (11/4)
**Almi Ad (USA)**, who showed plenty of knee-action going down, travelled almost as strongly as the winner. Having to wait for an opening, in the end he was just held at bay. The first two finished well clear. (11/1)
**Smart Spirit (IRE)**, on her toes beforehand and having her third outing, was by no means knocked about and should definitely win races in handicap company at three. (33/1)
**1346 Permission**, who shows plenty of knee-action, was last of ten in a Nursery on her previous start. (14/1)
**Misellina (FR)**, a poor mover, ought to have been suited by the give underfoot. Badly tapped for toe halfway up the straight, she tired over a furlong out as if needing the outing. (5/1)
**4211 Listed Account (USA)** presumably failed to handle the ground. Taking it up travelling nicely, she fell in a heap over a furlong out. (10/11: Evens-11/10)

T/Plpt: £7,045.90 (1.84 Tckts). T/Qdpt: £362.10 (2.2 Tckts). WG

# 4552-NEWMARKET (R-H) (Good to firm)
## Saturday October 5th

WEATHER: sunny periods WIND: fresh half bhd

## 4565 OH SO SHARP STKS (Listed) (2-Y.O F) (Class A)

1-50 (1-51) **7f (Rowley)** £9,279.20 (£3,432.80: £1,646.40: £672.00: £266.00: £103.60) Stalls: Low GOING minus 0.37 sec per fur (F)

| | | | | SP | RR | SF |
|---|---|---|---|---|---|---|
| 3988* | **Sarayir (USA)** (MajorWRHern) **2-8-9** RHills(5) (s.i.s: sn cl up: led wl over 1f out: rdn & r.o ins fnl f) | — | **1** | 4/7$^{1}$ | 96 | 68 |
| 4133$^{W}$ | **Fernanda (100)** (JLDunlop) **2-8-9b** TSprake(8) (lw: in tch: effrt wl over 1f out: hdwy to chse wnr ins fnl f: nt qckn) | 1¼ | **2** | 8/1$^{3}$ | 93 | 65 |
| 3990* | **Dancing Drop (95)** (RHannon) **2-8-9** DaneO'Neill(6) (w ldrs: rdn 2f out: r.o one pce) | 2½ | **3** | 9/1 | 87 | 59 |
| 4189$^{7}$ | **Caerfilly Dancer** (RAkehurst) **2-8-9** TQuinn(7) (a chsng ldrs: rdn 2f out: nt qckn) | 1¾ | **4** | 25/1 | 83 | 55 |
| 4359* | **Attitre (FR)** (CEBrittain) **2-8-9** MRoberts(4) (lw: led tl hdd & wknd wl over 1f out) | 1¾ | **5** | 14/1 | 79 | 51 |
| 4301$^{2}$ | **Halowing (USA) (90)** (PAKelleway) **2-8-9** DRMcCabe(2) (lw: in tch: rdn 3f out: sn btn) | 2½ | **6** | 25/1 | 74 | 46 |
| 4096* | **Idrica** (JHMGosden) **2-8-9** PatEddery(3) (s.s: drvn along thrght: no rspnse) | 21 | **7** | 6/1$^{2}$ | 26 | — |

(SP 113.4%) **7 Rn**

**1m 24.05** (-0.45) CSF £5.77 TOTE £1.60: £1.30 £3.30 (£4.60) OWNER Mr Hamdan Al Maktoum (LAMBOURN) BRED Shadwell Farm Inc. and Shadwell Estate Co. Ltd.

**3988* Sarayir (USA)**, stepped up in class here, passed the test with flying colours and, having to work to put it beyond doubt, she will have learnt plenty. She is a very tall filly who should improve a good deal with another year behind her as she does need to strengthen. (4/7)
**3804 Fernanda**, in a better mood this time, looked particularly well and ran her usual sound race but the winner was always holding her in the final furlong. (8/1)
**3990* Dancing Drop** almost ran her form with the runner-up to the pound and this would seem to be as good as she is. (9/1)
**3206* Caerfilly Dancer** jumped off on terms this time but had her limitations exposed when the pressure was on in the last couple of furlongs. (25/1)
**4359* Attitre (FR)**, a sturdy filly, was very much on her toes and, after going freely to post, came back in similar fashion and had shot her bolt over a furlong out. (14/1: 10/1-16/1)
**4301 Halowing (USA)** needed two attendants in the paddock and, taken to post early, never really threatened in the race. (25/1)
**4096* Idrica** needed the Monty Roberts treatment at the start and was in a mulish mood throughout the race. She would have nothing to do with it and, although tailed off, finished with her ears pricked. (6/1)

## 4566 NGK SPARK PLUGS PERFORMANCE NURSERY H'CAP (2-Y.O) (Class C)

2-20 (2-21) **6f (Rowley)** £6,576.00 (£1,968.00: £944.00: £432.00) Stalls: Low GOING minus 0.37 sec per fur (F)

| | | | | SP | RR | SF |
|---|---|---|---|---|---|---|
| 3293* | **Serenity (83)** (JRFanshawe) **2-8-11** DHarrison(5) (hld up & bhd: n.m.r over 2f out: hdwy over 1f out: r.o wl to ld wl ins fnl f) | — | 1 | 8/1 2 | 93 | 59 |
| 4195* | **Sharp Hat (82)** (RHannon) **2-8-10** PatEddery(11) (cl up: led wl over 1f out tl wl ins fnl f: kpt on) | 1¼ | 2 | 4/1 1 | 89 | 55 |
| 4182[4] | **Burlington House (USA) (85)** (PFICole) **2-8-8**(5) GFaulkner(6) (lw: prom: effrt & nt clr run over 1f out: styd on wl fnl f) | 1 | 3 | 8/1 2 | 89 | 55 |
| 3792[11] | **Ricasso (73)** (DRLoder) **2-8-1** DRMcCabe(2) (lw: w ldrs: rdn over 2f out: kpt on one pce fnl f) | nk | 4 | 12/1 | 76 | 42 |
| 4208[2] | **The Gay Fox (88)** (BAMcMahon) **2-9-2** RCochrane(12) (bhd: hdwy over 2f out: chsng ldrs over 1f out: kpt on) | 1 | 5 | 14/1 | 89 | 55 |
| 3637* | **A Breeze (80)** (DMorris) **2-8-8** NDay(3) (lw: bhd: styd on fnl 2f: nrst fin) | ½ | 6 | 12/1 | 79 | 45 |
| 4222[3] | **Lucky Oakwood (USA) (77)** (MBell) **2-7-12**(7) RMullen(13) (lw: prom: effrt over 2f out: kpt on one pce) | s.h | 7 | 14/1 | 76 | 42 |
| 4303[7] | **Homestead (70)** (RHannon) **2-7-12** JQuinn(16) (outpcd ½-wy: styd on fnl f: no imp) | 1½ | 8 | 25/1 | 65 | 31 |
| 4339* | **Stygian (USA) (80)** (BWHills) **2-8-5**(3) JDSmith(4) (mid div: hdwy u.p 2f out: sn btn) | s.h | 9 | 12/1 | 75 | 41 |
| 3829[4] | **Marsad (IRE) (75)** (CJBenstead) **2-8-3** RHills(7) (lw: led over 4f: sn struck into & eased) | nk | 10 | 8/1 2 | 69 | 35 |
| 4258[4] | **Cowrie (93)** (RFJohnsonHoughton) **2-9-7** TSprake(8) (chsd ldrs: btn whn hmpd wl over 1f out) | 2 | 11 | 25/1 | 82 | 48 |
| 4113[17] | **Mystic Circle (IRE) (75)** (JWWatts) **2-8-3b1** LCharnock(1) (outpcd & bhd tl sme late hdwy) | 1 | 12 | 25/1 | 61 | 27 |
| 4103* | **Saint Who (USA) (78)** (WAO'Gorman) **2-8-6** EmmaO'Gorman(9) (prom tl outpcd & lost pl ½-wy: n.d after) | s.h | 13 | 9/1 3 | 64 | 30 |
| 4131[14] | **Kaiser Kache (IRE) (80)** (KMcAuliffe) **2-8-8v1** BDoyle(14) (outpcd fr ½-wy) | s.h | 14 | 25/1 | 66 | 32 |
| 4131[16] | **Dalmeny Dancer (85)** (BJMeehan) **2-8-13b1** MTebbutt(10) (lw: spd over 3f: wknd qckly) | 2½ | 15 | 25/1 | 64 | 30 |
| 4324[3] | **Lamorna (81)** (MRChannon) **2-8-2**(7) AEddery(15) (prom 4f) | 3 | 16 | 14/1 | 52 | 18 |
| | | | | (SP 125.6%) | **16 Rn** | |

**1m 12.18** (0.38) CSF £36.92 CT £239.55 TOTE £6.50: £1.60 £1.30 £2.30 £3.20 (£8.30) Trio £40.60 OWNER Dr Catherine Wills (NEWMARKET) BRED Hyde Stud

**3293* Serenity**, after two months off, looked fairly useful here and, coming from almost last to first and meeting trouble in running, still won in tremendous style. (8/1)
**4195* Sharp Hat** again pulled extremely hard going to post but still ran a cracking race and kept battling on when looking well beaten. (4/1)
**4182 Burlington House (USA)** might well have had a serious chance here had he not met with interference and looks worth following. (8/1)
**3792 Ricasso** has been very disappointing previously but, off a decent mark here, showed he has the ability to win a modest race. (12/1)
**4208 The Gay Fox** keeps running well but seems to have his fair share of weight at present. (14/1)
**3637* A Breeze** ran a sound race after almost seven weeks off and, by the way he finished, he is likely to pick up a similar event before the season ends. (12/1)
**3829 Marsad (IRE)** had just been headed when he hung slightly left and was badly struck into over a furlong out. He was then wisely eased a good deal. (8/1)

## 4567 SUN CHARIOT STKS (Gp 2) (3-Y.O+ F & M) (Class A)

2-55 (2-56) **1m 2f (Rowley)** £34,561.00 (£12,799.00: £6,149.50: £2,522.50: £1,011.25: £406.75) Stalls: Low GOING minus 0.37 sec per fur (F)

| | | | | SP | RR | SF |
|---|---|---|---|---|---|---|
| 3231* | **Last Second (IRE) (114)** (SirMarkPrescott) **3-8-11** GDuffield(8) (trckd ldrs: smooth hdwy to ld 1f out: shkn up & r.o strly) | — | 1 | 9/4 1 | 121 | 72 |
| 3392a[3] | **Spout (109)** (RCharlton) **4-8-13** PatEddery(2) (hld up: hdwy 2f out: chsd wnr fnl f: nt pce to chal) | 2 | 2 | 7/1 | 115 | 71 |
| 4218* | **Flame Valley (USA) (94)** (MRStoute) **3-8-8** KFallon(5) (cl up: effrt 2f out: r.o one pce) | 2½ | 3 | 13/2 3 | 111 | 62 |
| 4292a[9] | **Bint Salsabil (USA) (113)** (JLDunlop) **3-8-8** RHills(3) (led: rdn 2f out: hdd 1f out: sn btn) | ½ | 4 | 10/1 | 110 | 61 |
| 3945* | **Wandering Star (USA) (108)** (JRFanshawe) **3-8-8** NDay(4) (prom: effrt 3f out: r.o one pce) | s.h | 5 | 9/1 | 110 | 61 |
| 4126[2] | **Miss Universal (IRE) (105)** (CEBrittain) **3-8-8** BDoyle(7) (chsd ldrs tl outpcd fnl 2f) | 5 | 6 | 40/1 | 102 | 53 |
| 4292a[3] | **Miss Tahiti (IRE)** (AFabre,France) **3-8-8** SGuillot(9) (leggy: lt-f: hld up & bhd: rdn over 2f out: n.d) | 5 | 7 | 7/2 2 | 94 | 45 |
| 4218[2] | **Berenice (90)** (GWragg) **3-8-8** MHills(6) (rr div: effrt 3f out: n.d) | nk | 8 | 33/1 | 93 | 44 |
| 4132[4] | **Distant Oasis (USA) (109)** (HRACecil) **3-8-8** WRyan(1) (chsd ldrs: rdn 3f out: sn btn) | 14 | 9 | 8/1 | 71 | 22 |
| | | | | (SP 114.4%) | **9 Rn** | |

**2m 2.84** (-0.76) CSF £17.03 TOTE £3.00: £1.50 £2.20 £2.20 (£11.80) Trio £24.30 OWNER Mr Faisal Salman (NEWMARKET) BRED Miss K. Rausing and Mrs S. M. Rogers
WEIGHT FOR AGE 3yo-5lb

**3231* Last Second (IRE)** looked really good here, travelling well throughout. When sent about her business in the final furlong, she quickly shook off all opposition and was not given a hard time. (9/4)
**3392a Spout** likes things to go her way and, up to a point, they did here, but in the end she was no match for the useful winner. (7/1)
**4218* Flame Valley (USA)** had her chances throughout and kept trying hard but she was firmly put in her place in the last furlong and a half. (13/2)
**4292a Bint Salsabil (USA)** sailed along on the bridle but, when it came to a real effort approaching the final furlong, she failed to pick up. (10/1)
**3945* Wandering Star (USA)**, stepped up in class and distance, ran reasonably but was found out when the pace was seriously on in the last three furlongs. (9/1)
**4126 Miss Universal (IRE)** has yet to win a race and this company proved far too hot. (40/1)
**4292a Miss Tahiti (IRE)** never fired at all and this was obviously not her true running. (7/2)
**4132 Distant Oasis (USA)** (8/1: 6/1-9/1)

## 4568 TOTE CAMBRIDGESHIRE H'CAP (3-Y.O+) (Class B)

3-35 (3-37) **1m 1f (Rowley)** £55,252.50 (£20,647.50: £10,073.75: £4,306.25: £1,903.13: £941.87) Stalls: Low GOING minus 0.37 sec per fur (F)

| | | | | SP | RR | SF |
|---|---|---|---|---|---|---|
| 4193* | **Clifton Fox (85)** (JAGlover) **4-8-2** 5x NDay(17) (chsd ldrs stands' side: led wl over 1f out: r.o wl) | — | **1** | 14/1 | 103 | 79 |
| 3996[3] | **Missile (101)** (WJHaggas) **3-8-11**(3) FLynch(21) (hdwy centre over 2f out: r.o: nt pce of wnr) | 2½ | **2** | 15/2[2] | 115 | 87 |
| 4193[2] | **Angus-G (79)** (MrsMReveley) **4-7-10** JQuinn(16) (lw: chsd ldrs stands' side: led over 2f out tl wl over 1f out: r.o one pce) | 2½ | **3** | 12/1 | 88 | 64 |
| 4125[3] | **Another Time (79)** (SPCWoods) **4-7-10** GBardwell(15) (mid div stands' side: hdwy 2f out: kpt on one pce fnl f) | ½ | **4** | 66/1 | 87 | 63 |
| 4300[2] | **Hawksley Hill (IRE) (83)** (MrsJRRamsden) **3-7-10** LCharnock(37) (bhd far side tl hdwy over 2f out: prom & hung rt appr fnl f: nt qckn) | 1½ | **5** | 28/1 | 89 | 61 |
| 4297[3] | **Fairywings (83)** (MrsJRRamsden) **3-7-10** NAdams(13) (hdwy stands' side 2f out: r.o: nrst fin) | nk | **6** | 66/1 | 88 | 60 |
| 4196[8] | **Tarawa (IRE) (104)** (NACallaghan) **4-9-7** MRoberts(34) (racd far side: hdwy & prom 2f out: nt qckn) | nk | **7** | 40/1 | 109 | 85 |
| 4120[3] | **Double Bluff (IRE) (90)** (IABalding) **3-7-12**(5) MartinDwyer(22) (led centre: rdn 3f out: r.o one pce) | s.h | **8** | 40/1 | 94 | 66 |
| 4177[3] | **Prince of My Heart (103)** (BWHills) **3-8-13**(3) JDSmith(7) (racd stands' side: styd on fnl 2f: n.d) | hd | **9** | 66/1 | 107 | 79 |
| 4120[7] | **Star Manager (USA) (87)** (PFICole) **6-8-4**ow1 TQuinn(28) (racd centre: hdwy 2f out: styd on wl towards fin) | ¾ | **10** | 66/1 | 90 | 65 |
| 4300[3] | **Give Me A Ring (IRE) (84)** (CWThornton) **3-7-11** NCarlisle(25) (lw: chsd ldrs centre: effrt over 3f out: no imp) | nk | **11** | 50/1 | 86 | 58 |
| 4463[17] | **Sky Dome (IRE) (88)** (MHTompkins) **3-7-12**(3) MHenry(3) (lw: in tch stands' side: outpcd 2f out: no imp after) | ¾ | **12** | 50/1 | 89 | 61 |
| 4184[3] | **North Song (94)** (JHMGosden) **3-8-7** BDoyle(30) (lw: chsd ldrs far side: hdwy 3f out: btn wl over 1f out) | 1 | **13** | 14/1 | 93 | 65 |
| 4385[8] | **Moments of Fortune (USA) (95)** (BHanbury) **4-8-12** MTebbutt(18) (swtg: racd stands' side: nvr trbld ldrs) | hd | **14** | 66/1 | 94 | 70 |
| 4181* | **Kammtarra (USA) (101)** (SbinSuroor) **3-9-0** RHills(12) (chsd ldrs stands' side: rdn & btn appr fnl f) | hd | **15** | 11/2[1] | 100 | 72 |
| 3947[4] | **Sharpical (83)** (SirMarkPrescott) **4-8-0**ow3 GDuffield(14) (lw: racd stands' side: prom tl outpcd fnl 2f) | s.h | **16** | 16/1 | 82 | 55 |
| 4193[16] | **Nigel's Lad (IRE) (79)** (PCHaslam) **4-7-3**(7) RMullen(20) (chsd ldrs stands' side tl wknd fnl 2f) | s.h | **17** | 66/1 | 78 | 54 |
| 4308[6] | **Secret Spring (FR) (83)** (PRHedger) **4-8-0** AMcGlone(10) (lw: in tch stands' side tl wknd fnl 2f) | 1¼ | **18** | 33/1 | 80 | 56 |
| 4326* | **Game Ploy (POL) (86)** (DHaydnJones) **4-8-3**ow3 5x RCochrane(35) (hdwy far side 3f out: wknd over 1f out) | 1¼ | **19** | 11/1[3] | 80 | 53 |
| 3211[3] | **Crown Court (USA) (91)** (LMCumani) **3-8-4**ow2 PatEddery(2) (racd stands' side: chsd ldrs: ev ch over 2f out: wknd over 1f out) | s.h | **20** | 11/1[3] | 85 | 55 |
| 3646[9] | **Bold Amusement (85)** (WSCunningham) **6-7-11b**(5)ow6 ADaly(19) (w ldrs centre tl wknd fnl 2½f) | s.h | **21** | 150/1 | 79 | 49 |
| 4190[9] | **Master Charter (83)** (MrsJRRamsden) **4-8-0** JTate(5) (lw: outpcd stands' side fr ½-wy: n.d) | 1½ | **22** | 16/1 | 74 | 50 |
| 4326[8] | **Clan Ben (IRE) (96)** (HRACecil) **4-8-13b1** WRyan(40) (lw: led & clr far side tl hdd & wknd over 2f out) | hd | **23** | 33/1 | 87 | 63 |
| 4193[3] | **Billy Bushwacker (88)** (MrsMReveley) **5-8-5b** ACulhane(23) (racd centre: rdn 3f out: sn btn) | 2½ | **24** | 20/1 | 75 | 51 |
| 2053[15] | **Stone Ridge (IRE) (92)** (RHannon) **4-8-9** DaneO'Neill(39) (bkwd: racd far side: n.d) | 1 | **25** | 50/1 | 77 | 53 |
| 4120[4] | **Champagne Prince (89)** (PWHarris) **3-8-2**ow1 GHind(29) (chsd ldrs far side tl wknd fnl 2½f) | 1 | **26** | 66/1 | 72 | 43 |
| 4184[8] | **Conspicuous (IRE) (84)** (LGCottrell) **6-8-1** TSprake(38) (racd far side: n.d) | nk | **27** | 33/1 | 67 | 43 |
| 4444[2] | **Kayvee (95)** (GHarwood) **7-8-12** AClark(33) (in tch far side: no imp fnl 3f) | ½ | **28** | 33/1 | 77 | 53 |
| 4300[6] | **Tertium (IRE) (87)** (MartynWane) **4-8-1**(3) AWhelan(9) (lw: racd stands' side: bhd fnl 2f) | nk | **29** | 66/1 | 68 | 44 |
| 4463[4] | **Autumn Cover (79)** (PRHedger) **4-7-5**(5) 5x CAdamson(11) (lw: chsd ldrs stands' side 6f: wknd) | ¾ | **30** | 66/1 | 59 | 35 |
| 4432[8] | **Blaze of Song (79)** (RHannon) **4-7-3v**(7) RFfrench(31) (racd far side: n.d) | 1 | **31** | 150/1 | 57 | 33 |
| 765[12] | **Show Faith (IRE) (82)** (RHannon) **6-7-13** DBiggs(32) (bit bkwd: racd far side: n.d) | d.h | **31** | 66/1 | 62 | 38 |
| 4352[2] | **Nagnagnag (IRE) (94)** (SDow) **4-8-11** RHughes(6) (lw: a bhd stands' side) | 1¼ | **33** | 33/1 | 70 | 46 |
| 4520* | **Yeast (112)** (WJHaggas) **4-10-1** 5x KFallon(4) (lw: led stands' side tl hdd over 2f out: wknd) | nk | **34** | 14/1 | 87 | 63 |
| 4463[20] | **Sue's Return (79)** (APJarvis) **4-7-7**(3) DWright(27) (lw: n.d) | 1 | **35** | 50/1 | 53 | 29 |
| 4290a[5] | **Almond Rock (94)** (JRFanshawe) **4-8-11** DHarrison(36) (racd far side: n.d) | 2½ | **36** | 33/1 | 63 | 39 |
| 3791[13] | **Silver Groom (IRE) (81)** (RAkehurst) **6-7-12**ow1 DRMcCabe(24) (lw: racd centre: bhd fr ½-wy) | ¾ | **37** | 50/1 | 49 | 24 |
| *4078*[13] | **Nordinex (IRE) (88)** (RWArmstrong) **4-7-12**(7)ow9 AEddery(1) (a bhd stands' side) | ¾ | **38** | 100/1 | 55 | 22 |

(SP 141.1%) **38 Rn**

**1m 48.54** (-2.46) CSF £107.89 CT £1,238.38 TOTE £18.80: £4.00 £3.60 £2.60 £17.50 (£109.40) Trio £260.50 OWNER P and S Partnership (WORKSOP) BRED Crest Stud Ltd

LONG HANDICAP Bold Amusement 7-3 Autumn Cover 7-1 Blaze of Song 7-3 Angus-G 7-7 Hawksley Hill (IRE) 7-7 Fairywings 7-9 Sue's Return 7-7 Nigel's Lad (IRE) 7-3 Another Time 7-4 Nordinex (IRE) 7-6

WEIGHT FOR AGE 3yo-4lb

**OFFICIAL EXPLANATION Kammtarra (USA): was found to have a bruised foot on returning home.**

**4193* Clifton Fox** likes a strongly-run event and this was just up his street. Once he saw the front, he fairly sprinted away. (14/1)

**3996 Missile** has not stopped improving all year. He ran another cracking race here and next season should see him really come into his own. (15/2)

**4193 Angus-G** is a real game and consistent sort who just keeps plugging away, but he is possibly short of a change of gear and longer trips could be the answer. (12/1)

**4125 Another Time** ran really well from 6lb out of the handicap but he was being held in the last one hundred yards and this would seem to be his absolute best. (66/1)

**4300 Hawksley Hill (IRE)** ran a super race on what turned out to be the unfavoured far side and, with a better draw, would have made them all go. (28/1)

**4297 Fairywings** has been on the go all season and has never stopped improving and this was yet another fine effort. Despite finishing well, the run was always too late. (66/1)

**2471a Tarawa (IRE)** ran a useful race on the unfavoured far side and was just second best of that group. (40/1)

**4120 Double Bluff (IRE)** just gallops but has not got a change of pace and he was tapped for toe here in the last couple of furlongs. (40/1)

**4177 Prince of My Heart**, highly tried this year, ran as though longer trips will see improvement from now on. (66/1)

**3709 Star Manager (USA)** ran well from a moderate draw and was putting in some good late work. (66/1)

**4181* Kammtarra (USA)** had his chances but was found out when this really got competitive in the last two furlongs. (11/2)

## 4569 JOCKEY CLUB CUP STKS (Gp 3) (3-Y.O+) (Class A)

4-10 (4-14) **2m (Rowley)** £20,580.00 (£7,620.00: £3,660.00: £1,500.00: £600.00: £240.00) Stalls: High GOING minus 0.37 sec per fur (F)

| | | | | SP | RR | SF |
|---|---|---|---|---|---|---|
| 4134[2] | **Celeric (111)** (DMorley) **4-9-0** RHills(4) (lw: trckd ldrs gng wl: chal on bit 2f out: rdn to ld ins fnl f: all out) | — | **1** | 11/4[2] | 118 | 76 |
| 3673[3] | **Sanmartino (IRE) (105)** (BWHills) **4-9-0** KFallon(1) (lw: hld up & bhd: hdwy 4f out: rdn to ld 2f out: hdd ins fnl f: rallied) | hd | **2** | 8/1[3] | 118 | 76 |

| | | | | SP | RR | SF |
|---|---|---|---|---|---|---|
| 3157[3] | **Persian Punch (IRE) (105)** (DRCElsworth) **3-8-3** RCochrane(2) (lw: in tch: hdwy 3f out: chal wl over 1f out: r.o one pce) | 2½ | **3** | 8/1[3] | 115 | 62 |
| 4114* | **Eva Luna (USA) (108)** (HRACecil) **4-9-0** PatEddery(7) (lw: led: edgd lft most of wy: hdd 2f out: sn btn) | 5 | **4** | 11/8[1] | 110 | 68 |
| 4134[5] | **Old Rouvel (USA) (103)** (DJGMurraySmith) **5-9-0** GDuffield(8) (hld up & bhd: hdwy on ins 5f out: sn rdn & no imp) | ½ | **5** | 50/1 | 110 | 68 |
| 4434[3] | **Poltarf (USA) (103)** (JHMGosden) **5-9-0** GHind(6) (lw: chsd ldr: chal 10f out: wknd fnl 3f) | dist | **6** | 16/1 | — | — |
| 2352[3] | **Further Flight (110)** (BWHills) **10-9-3** MHills(3) (b.hind: hld up: effrt 4f out: sn rdn & btn) | 5 | **7** | 9/1 | — | — |
| 4134[4] | **Admiral's Well (IRE) (107)** (RAkehurst) **6-9-0** TQuinn(5) (lw: chsd ldrs tl wknd over 3f out: t.o) | dist | **8** | 33/1 | — | — |
| | | | | (SP 111.8%) | **8 Rn** | |

**3m 21.91** (1.21 under best) (-1.39) CSF £22.05 TOTE £2.60: £1.20 £1.90 £1.70 (£17.00) OWNER Mr Christopher Spence (NEWMARKET) BRED Chieveley Manor Enterprises

WEIGHT FOR AGE 3yo-11lb

**4134 Celeric** looked likely to romp in for much of the trip but, in the end, it was a desperate thing and he needed plenty of persuading to do the business. He perhaps saw too much daylight too soon. (11/4)

**3673 Sanmartino (IRE)** was given some ride here and that almost won the day when all looked lost. Obviously these longer trips bring out the best in him. (8/1: op 20/1)

**3157 Persian Punch (IRE)** ran a tremendous race after over two months off and is obviously coming back to his very best. (8/1: 6/1-9/1)

**4114* Eva Luna (USA)**, edgy beforehand, was then inclined to hang left in the race and put up little fight at the business end. This was not her true running. (11/8)

**4134 Old Rouvel (USA)** is a funny customer and was always finding the effort required beyond him. (50/1)

**4434 Poltarf (USA)** stopped as though something was wrong in the last three furlongs. (16/1)

**2352 Further Flight**, going for his sixth consecutive win in this event, has had his problems this year and they took their toll here for a most disappointing effort. (9/1: op 11/2)

**4134 Admiral's Well (IRE)** ran as though something was amiss and virtually pulled up in the last two furlongs. (33/1)

## 4570 ALINGTON MAIDEN STKS (2-Y.O F) (Class D)

4-45 (4-50) **6f (Rowley)** £5,572.00 (£1,666.00: £798.00: £364.00) Stalls: Low GOING minus 0.37 sec per fur (F)

| | | | | SP | RR | SF |
|---|---|---|---|---|---|---|
| 3593[3] | **Elegant Warning (IRE)** (BWHills) **2-8-11** MHills(3) (hld up: hdwy gng wl 2f out: led jst ins fnl f: r.o wl) | — | **1** | 3/1[2] | 83 | 60 |
| | **Meshhed (USA)** (BHanbury) **2-8-11** RHills(5) (unf: scope: trckd ldrs gng wl: led over 1f out: sn rdn & hdd: kpt on) | 1½ | **2** | 3/1[2] | 79 | 56 |
| 3206[5] | **Etna** (LMCumani) **2-8-11** OUrbina(10) (bit bkwd: prom: effrt over 2f out: chal 1f out: nt qckn) | nk | **3** | 12/1 | 78 | 55 |
| | **Polish Romance (USA)** (MRStoute) **2-8-11** KFallon(1) (lt-f: unf: s.i.s: gd hdwy 2f out: ev ch over 1f out: no ex) | 1¼ | **4** | 11/4[1] | 75+ | 52 |
| | **Jamrat Samya (IRE)** (LMCumani) **2-8-4**(7) RFfrench(7) (w'like: scope: bit bkwd: led tl hdd & hrd rdn over 1f out: sn outpcd) | 1½ | **5** | 33/1 | 71 | 48 |
| | **Lady Diesis (USA)** (BWHills) **2-8-8**(3) JDSmith(4) (lt-f: unf: hld up & bhd: r.o stdly fnl f) | 1¼ | **6** | 50/1 | 68 | 45 |
| | **Raaha** (RWArmstrong) **2-8-11** MRoberts(6) (lt-f: unf: w ldrs tl wknd appr fnl f) | hd | **7** | 14/1 | 67 | 44 |
| | **Blueygreen** (PWChapple-Hyam) **2-8-11** NDay(14) (w'like: scope: bkwd: s.i.s: hdwy ½-wy: btn appr fnl f) | 3½ | **8** | 16/1 | 58 | 35 |
| | **Tajrebah (USA)** (PTWalwyn) **2-8-11** PatEddery(11) (w'like: cmpt: bkwd: nvr nr to chal) | 3 | **9** | 9/1[3] | 50 | 27 |
| *4079[6]* | **Lochlass (IRE)** (SPCWoods) **2-8-11** DBiggs(13) (bit bkwd: w ldr over 3f: wknd) | ¾ | **10** | 50/1 | 48 | 25 |
| | **Jovian** (RGuest) **2-8-11** GDuffield(2) (w'like: scope: bkwd: prom tl outpcd fnl 2f) | ¾ | **11** | 25/1 | 46 | 23 |
| | **Kilshanny** (LMCumani) **2-8-11** DRMcCabe(9) (b.nr hind: w'like: bkwd: s.s: a wl bhd) | s.h | **12** | 14/1 | 46 | 23 |
| 4242[15] | **Perfect Angel (IRE)** (MHTompkins) **2-8-8**(3) MHenry(12) (dwlt: a wl bhd) | 2 | **13** | 33/1 | 41 | 18 |
| *3660[4]* | ***Noble Story*** (RAkehurst) **2-8-11** TQuinn(8) (Withdrawn not under Starter's orders: veterinary advice) | | **W** | 16/1 | — | — |
| | | | | (SP 133.1%) | **13 Rn** | |

**1m 12.13** (0.33) CSF £12.73 TOTE £3.60: £1.30 £1.80 £3.50 (£7.10) Trio £31.20 OWNER Mr Pip Elson (LAMBOURN) BRED Charlton Down Stud

**3593 Elegant Warning (IRE)** won this in good style, showing a fine turn of foot in the last furlong, and this should have boosted her confidence no end. (3/1: 5/1-11/4)

**Meshhed (USA)**, who injured Willie Carson on her intended debut at Newbury, was treated with a deal of caution here and was mounted in the saddling boxes. She ran promisingly, travelling on the bridle, but lack of experience told late on. (3/1: 2/1-7/2)

**3206 Etna**, still just needing this, ran well and further improvement looks likely. (12/1: op 8/1)

**Polish Romance (USA)** missed the kick and then did well to get into it and should be all the better for the experience. (11/4)

**Jamrat Samya (IRE)**, who is likely to need further, ran a decent race until getting tapped for foot in the closing stages. (33/1)

**Lady Diesis (USA)**, given a kind introduction, showed that there is better to come in due course. (50/1)

**Blueygreen** needed this and showed enough to suggest that, given time, much better will be seen. (16/1)

**Kilshanny** (14/1: 33/1-50/1)

## 4571 LINKS H'CAP (0-90) (3-Y.O+) (Class C)

5-20 (5-21) **7f (Rowley)** £6,872.50 (£2,062.00: £993.00: £458.50) Stalls: Low GOING minus 0.37 sec per fur (F)

| | | | | SP | RR | SF |
|---|---|---|---|---|---|---|
| 4354[2] | **Don't Get Caught (IRE) (56)** (JLHarris) **4-7-10** LCharnock(1) (lw: in tch: hdwy over 2f out: chal 1f out: r.o to ld wl ins fnl f) | — | **1** | 7/1[3] | 66 | 42 |
| 4463[9] | **Broughtons Turmoil (73)** (WJMusson) **7-8-13** PatEddery(3) (trckd ldrs gng wl: led 1f out: hrd rdn & r.o: hdd & no ex wl ins fnl f) | ½ | **2** | 3/1[1] | 82 | 58 |
| 4308* | **Duello (69)** (MBlanshard) **5-8-9** JQuinn(8) (in tch: effrt 2f out: styd on wl fnl f) | 1¾ | **3** | 10/1 | 74 | 50 |
| 4312[2] | **Thwaab (70)** (FWatson) **4-8-10b** KFallon(10) (hld up & bhd: hdwy whn nt clr run & swtchd over 2f out: hdwy over 1f out: nt qckn ins fnl f) | nk | **4** | 11/2[2] | 74 | 50 |
| 4444[11] | **My Gallery (IRE) (87)** (ABailey) **5-9-10**(3) DWright(14) (hld up: effrt over 2f out: edgd lft & styd on: no imp) | 1½ | **5** | 14/1 | 88 | 64 |
| 4356[4] | **Speedy Classic (USA) (59)** (MJHeaton-Ellis) **7-7-13** NCarlisle(4) (w ldrs: led 3f out to 1f out: sn btn) | hd | **6** | 16/1 | 60 | 36 |
| 4240* | **Don Pepe (62)** (RBoss) **5-8-2** BDoyle(12) (bhd: effrt over 2f out: styd on: nvr able to chal) | ½ | **7** | 14/1 | 61 | 37 |
| 4308[9] | **Wild Palm (72)** (WAO'Gorman) **4-8-12v** EmmaO'Gorman(13) (chsd ldrs tl outpcd over 2f out: n.d) | ¾ | **8** | 20/1 | 70 | 46 |
| 4198[3] | **Oggi (66)** (PJMakin) **5-8-6** DHarrison(6) (nvr trbld ldrs) | nk | **9** | 9/1 | 63 | 39 |
| 4254[2] | **High Hope Henry (USA) (78)** (RAkehurst) **3-9-2** TQuinn(5) (lw: nvr wnt pce) | 1½ | **10** | 20/1 | 72 | 46 |
| 4352[8] | **Lucky Archer (84)** (CEBrittain) **3-9-8** MRoberts(15) (lw: w ldrs tl wknd appr fnl f) | ½ | **11** | 12/1 | 76 | 50 |
| 4308[4] | **Knobbleeneeze (78)** (MRChannon) **6-8-13v**(5) PPMurphy(16) (chsd ldrs: n.m.r 2f out: r.o one pce) | nk | **12** | 20/1 | 70 | 46 |
| 4198[12] | **Almasi (IRE) (69)** (CFWall) **4-8-2**(7) PClarke(7) (lw: dwlt: hld up & bhd: effrt over 2f out: n.d) | hd | **13** | 33/1 | 61 | 37 |

| Form | Horse / details | Btn | Pos | SP | RR | SF |
|---|---|---|---|---|---|---|
| 4376[6] | **Kerry Ring (79)** (JHMGosden) **3-9-3** GHind(11) (cl up: outpcd whn hmpd wl over 1f out: nt rcvr) | 4 | **14** | 12/1 | 61 | 35 |
| 4376[11] | **Statoyork (74)** (BWHills) **3-8-9**(3) JDSmith(9) (led to 3f out: wandered u.p: sn lost pl) | 1½ | **15** | 33/1 | 53 | 27 |
| 3789* | **Northern Judge (59)** (BHanbury) **3-7-6**(5)ow1 MartinDwyer(2) (drvn along 3f out: n.d) | hd | **16** | 10/1 | 38 | 11 |

(SP 135.8%) **16 Rn**

**1m 25.23** (0.73) CSF £29.54 CT £215.42 TOTE £7.10: £1.50 £1.70 £3.60 £1.70 (£22.20) Trio £110.30 OWNER Mrs P. W. McGrath (MELTON MOWBRAY) BRED Brownstown Stud Farm

LONG HANDICAP Don't Get Caught (IRE) 7-8 Northern Judge 7-7

WEIGHT FOR AGE 3yo-2lb

**4354 Don't Get Caught (IRE)** has been unlucky of late and put that right here with a determined run in the last two furlongs to settle it where it mattered. (7/1)

**4463 Broughtons Turmoil** travelled particularly well and was given a superb ride but was always second best in the last half-furlong. In this form he should find another race before long. (3/1: op 9/2)

**4308* Duello** is in really good heart and, judging from the way he finished, he should pick up another race before the season ends. (10/1: 8/1-12/1)

**4312 Thwaab** ran well but had traffic problems and, in the end, probably found this trip just too far. (11/2: 10/1-5/1)

**4316 My Gallery (IRE)** keeps trying hard but her rise in the weights has put an end to her finishing dash and she failed to get in a serious blow. (14/1)

**4356 Speedy Classic (USA)** had his chances but was well outpointed in the final furlong. (16/1)

**4240* Don Pepe** could never get his run going soon enough and was never any nearer than at the finish. (14/1)

**4376 Kerry Ring** (12/1: op 8/1)

T/Jkpt: £17,556.80 (3.4 Tckts). T/Plpt: £34.30 (1,318.44 Tckts). T/Qdpt: £14.20 (131.54 Tckts). AA

## 4331-WOLVERHAMPTON (L-H) (Standard)

## Saturday October 5th

WEATHER: cloudy WIND: almost nil

### 4572 PINK ICE MEDIAN AUCTION MAIDEN STKS (2-Y.O) (Class F)

7-00 (7-03) **6f (Fibresand)** £2,519.00 (£694.00: £329.00) Stalls: Low GOING minus 0.04 sec per fur (STD)

| Form | Horse / details | Btn | Pos | SP | RR | SF |
|---|---|---|---|---|---|---|
| *4091*[2] | **Davis Rock (69)** (SirMarkPrescott) **2-8-9** SSanders(11) (w ldrs: led 2f out: rdn out) | — | **1** | Evens [1] | 69 | 33 |
| 4188[5] | **Mon Bruce** (WRMuir) **2-9-0** JFortune(6) (w ldrs: ev ch & rdn over 1f out: sn edgd lft & unable qckn) | 1¾ | **2** | 13/2 [3] | 69 | 33 |
| 3859[2] | **Brazilia (69)** (PTWalwyn) **2-8-9** JCarroll(8) (led after 1f to 2f out: wknd fnl f) | 3 | **3** | 8/1 | 56 | 20 |
| 4383[4] | **Rochea** (WJHaggas) **2-8-9** MFenton(4) (lw: chsd ldrs: no imp fnl 2f) | 2½ | **4** | 7/2 [2] | 50 | 14 |
| 4204[9] | **Canton Ron** (CADwyer) **2-9-0** TGMcLaughlin(5) (in tch over 3f) | s.h | **5** | 50/1 | 55 | 19 |
| | **Morning Line (IRE)** (RJRWilliams) **2-8-9** TSprake(7) (lt-f: unf: effrt over 2f out: nvr nr ldrs) | 2 | **6** | 33/1 | 44 | 8 |
| 4228[14] | **Aspecto Lad (IRE)** (MJohnston) **2-9-0** DeanMcKeown(9) (wl bhd tl sme hdwy fnl 2f) | 2 | **7** | 20/1 | 44 | 8 |
| 4339[3] | **Rockaroundtheclock (65)** (PDEvans) **2-9-0** GCarter(2) (s.v.s: nt rcvr) | 3½ | **8** | 12/1 | 35 | — |
| 1453[8] | **Master Foley** (NPLittmoden) **2-8-11**(3) FLynch(10) (lw: led 1f: wknd over 2f out) | 4 | **9** | 50/1 | 24 | — |
| *3950*[6] | **Jay Tee Ef (IRE)** (BAMcMahon) **2-8-9**(5) LNewton(1) (sn bhd) | 11 | **10** | 50/1 | — | — |
| | **Diamonds Are** (DTThom) **2-8-9b**[1] MWigham(3) (cmpt: bkwd: a bhd) | 9 | **11** | 50/1 | — | — |

(SP 119.9%) **11 Rn**

**1m 15.5** (4.10) CSF £8.14 TOTE £1.90: £1.40 £1.90 £1.70 (£12.70) Trio £6.30 OWNER Hesmonds Stud (NEWMARKET) BRED Hesmonds Stud Ltd

**4091 Davis Rock** moved down well on this occasion and finally broke her duck with some authority. (Evens)

**4188 Mon Bruce**, for whom this was a drop in class, kept plugging away after the winner in the straight, but was never doing enough. (13/2)

**3859 Brazilia** got very stirred up before the race being mounted on the course. Ridden without irons and having to be led some of the way to the start, she may prove better at the minimum trip, but is becoming expensive to follow. (8/1)

**4383 Rochea**, making her debut on this surface, could never quite get into a challenging position and was a beaten horse on straightening up. (7/2)

**Canton Ron** ran better than on his debut, but never looked like taking a hand. (50/1)

**Morning Line (IRE)**, a lightly-made filly, soon got behind, but did some running in the second half of the race. (33/1)

**4339 Rockaroundtheclock** lost all chance at the start and this is best ignored. (12/1: op 7/1)

### 4573 AMETHYST CLAIMING STKS (3-Y.O+) (Class F)

7-30 (7-32) **7f (Fibresand)** £2,415.00 (£665.00: £315.00) Stalls: High GOING minus 0.04 sec per fur (STD)

| Form | Horse / details | Btn | Pos | SP | RR | SF |
|---|---|---|---|---|---|---|
| 4439[8] | **King Rat (IRE) (77)** (TJEtherington) **5-9-2b** JCarroll(11) (lw: trckd ldrs: led 2f out: sn rdn clr) | — | **1** | 7/4 [1] | 77 | 56 |
| 4337[3] | **Bentico (75)** (MrsNMacauley) **7-9-5v**(3) CTeague(5) (b: hld up: rdn & hdwy 3f out: no imp appr fnl f) | 3 | **2** | 4/1 [2] | 76 | 55 |
| 4337[7] | **Dragonjoy (52)** (NPLittmoden) **3-8-9v**[1] AMcGlone(8) (lw: in tch: rdn 3f out: r.o fnl 2f) | 1¼ | **3** | 25/1 | 62 | 39 |
| 3981[10] | **Eastleigh (45)** (RHollinshead) **7-8-3**(5) DGriffiths(10) (sn pushed along & outpcd: r.o fnl 2f) | 6 | **4** | 33/1 | 46 | 25 |
| 4342[7] | **Halbert (43)** (PBurgoyne) **7-8-10** DRMcCabe(7) (led 1f: led 3f out to 2f out: sn btn) | 2 | **5** | 50/1 | 43 | 22 |
| 4430[12] | **Bargash (48)** (PDEvans) **4-8-4** GCarter(1) (prom: rdn 3f out: one pce) | 1¼ | **6** | 20/1 | 34 | 13 |
| *3877*[13] | **Jolto (50)** (KMcAuliffe) **7-8-13**(5) AimeeCook(4) (nvr trbld ldrs) | nk | **7** | 25/1 | 48 | 27 |
| *4077*[4] | **Dancing Sioux (70)** (DNicholls) **4-8-10** MWigham(3) (lw: prom: rdn 3f out: sn wknd) | ¾ | **8** | 5/1 [3] | 38 | 17 |
| 4354[11] | **Dancing Lawyer (76)** (BJMeehan) **5-9-4** MTebbutt(6) (a bhd) | 1½ | **9** | 9/1 | 42 | 21 |
| 4430[17] | **Bashful Brave (67)** (BPJBaugh) **5-9-4** WLord(12) (stdd s: effrt over 2f out: sn btn) | 5 | **10** | 25/1 | 31 | 10 |
| *2306*[8] | **Young Benson (61)** (TWall) **4-8-10b** SSanders(9) (b: led after 1f: hdd & wknd 3f out) | 4 | **11** | 10/1 | 14 | — |
| *114*[7] | **Mixed Mood (52)** (BJLlewellyn) **4-7-6**(7) JBramhill(2) (sn wl bhd) | 13 | **12** | 50/1 | — | — |

(SP 115.3%) **12 Rn**

**1m 28.2** (3.50) CSF £8.57 TOTE £3.00: £1.40 £1.60 £2.30 (£7.20) Trio £32.40 OWNER Mr Paul Daniels (MALTON) BRED Airlie Stud

WEIGHT FOR AGE 3yo-2lb

King Rat (IRE) clmd JGMO'Shea £9,000

**3817 King Rat (IRE)** has inexplicably run only once on the All-Weather, over a suitably long trip, since winning this race two years ago. Always travelling best, he looks as good as ever. (7/4)

**4337 Bentico** ran a fine race over a trip short of his best. (4/1)

**3951 Dragonjoy**, with the combination of the jockey who has ridden him to all his five victories and a first-time visor, returned to form. (25/1)

**501 Eastleigh**, having his second run back after a five month break, is, not for the first time, in the middle of a long losing run, but did run one of his best races in a long time. (33/1)
**1716 Halbert** has had precious little racing in his career at beyond six furlongs and did not appear to stay. (50/1)
**1609 Bargash** has yet to prove as effective on the All-Weather as he is on Turf. (20/1)

## 4574 PETER LAST MEMORIAL H'CAP (0-60) (3-Y.O+) (Class F)

8-00 (8-02) **1m 4f (Fibresand)** £2,519.00 (£694.00: £329.00) Stalls: Low GOING minus 0.04 sec per fur (STD)

| | | | | SP | RR | SF |
|---|---|---|---|---|---|---|
| *4334*[2] | **All On (43)** (JHetherton) **5-8-11** SWhitworth(9) (trckd ldrs: led over 2f out: sn qcknd clr: easily) | — | **1** | 6/1[3] | 61++ | 40 |
| *4332*[2] | **Arcady (57)** (PTWalwyn) **3-9-4** JCarroll(7) (led 2f: led 5f out tl over 2f out: no ch w wnr) | 10 | **2** | 100/30[2] | 62 | 34 |
| *4076*[6] | **Old Hush Wing (IRE) (50)** (PCHaslam) **3-8-11** JFortune(4) (lw: in tch: rdn 4f out: r.o wl fnl 2f) | ½ | **3** | 6/1[3] | 54 | 26 |
| | **Expansive Runner (USA) (50)** (PWHarris) **4-9-4** MFenton(10) (a.p: one pce fnl 3f) | ¾ | **4** | 20/1 | 53 | 32 |
| | **Weeheby (USA) (57)** (MFBarraclough) **7-9-11** SSanders(8) (hdwy 5f out: nvr able to chal) | ¾ | **5** | 20/1 | 59 | 38 |
| | **Al Helal (47)** (JRJenkins) **4-9-1** AMcGlone(2) (lw: dwlt: sn in tch: effrt 4f out: no imp) | 2½ | **6** | 25/1 | 46 | 25 |
| 2506[10] | **Needwood Epic (57)** (BCMorgan) **3-9-4** GCarter(3) (prom tl rdn & wknd 5f out) | ¾ | **7** | 33/1 | 55 | 27 |
| *2935** | **Ihtimaam (FR) (57)** (MrsASwinbank) **4-9-11** JSupple(1) (in tch: lost pl 9f out: rdn 4f out: no imp) | 5 | **8** | 20/1 | 48 | 27 |
| 3340[3] | **Orchard Gold (48)** (JPearce) **5-9-2** NDay(12) (b.nr fore: stdd s: led after 2f: hdd 5f out: sn wknd) | 10 | **9** | 7/1 | 26 | 5 |
| | **Rousitto (55)** (RHollinshead) **8-9-6**(3) FLynch(6) (rdn 5f out: a bhd) | 6 | **10** | 7/1 | 25 | 4 |
| 4315[5] | **Hand of Straw (IRE) (60)** (PGMurphy) **4-10-0v** SDrowne(11) (lw: chsd ldrs 6f) | ¾ | **11** | 10/1 | 29 | 8 |
| 1454[3] | **Bella Sedona (55)** (LadyHerries) **4-9-9** AClark(5) (rdn & lost pl 8f out: sn wl bhd) | 15 | **12** | 5/2[1] | 4 | — |

(SP 135.4%) **12 Rn**

**2m 40.5** (8.00) CSF £28.55 CT £125.06 TOTE £7.10: £2.50 £1.60 £3.10 (£4.30) Trio £23.30 OWNER Mr N. Hetherton (MALTON) BRED N. Hetherton
WEIGHT FOR AGE 3yo-7lb
**4334 All On**, on her toes beforehand, returned to her very best, winning in impressive style. She could have won by much further and should be followed. (6/1: op 4/1)
**4332 Arcady** caught a real tartar and still looks weighted to win on this surface. (100/30: 9/4-7/2)
**885 Old Hush Wing (IRE)**, taking a big step up in trip, stayed on well to the line and will come into his own when tackling further still. (6/1)
**Expansive Runner (USA)** is very lightly-raced and moved down well, although racing with his tongue down. He looked fit enough, but proved short of gears in the last half-mile. (20/1)
**Weeheby (USA)** ran a sound race and looks set for a return to hurdling. (20/1)
**Al Helal**, having his first run in this country since his two-year-old debut for Major Hern, had lost his form in Ireland in recent months and never looked like taking a hand. (25/1)
**4315 Hand of Straw (IRE)** (10/1: 12/1-8/1)
**1454 Bella Sedona** (5/2: 4/1-9/4)

## 4575 S. J. DIXON & SONS H'CAP (0-70) (3-Y.O+) (Class E)

8-30 (8-31) **1m 1f 79y (Fibresand)** £3,502.40 (£1,047.20: £501.60: £228.80) Stalls: Low GOING minus 0.04 sec per fur (STD)

| | | | | SP | RR | SF |
|---|---|---|---|---|---|---|
| *4095** | **Mansur (IRE) (67)** (DRLoder) **4-9-11** DRMcCabe(3) (prom: outpcd 6f out: rallied 3f out: r.o wl to ld nr fin) | — | **1** | 4/1[2] | 82 | 64 |
| *4336** | **Tea Party (USA) (68)** (KOCunningham-Brown) **3-9-8** TSprake(7) (lw: plld hrd: led 6f out: clr 2f out: sn rdn: ct nr fin) | nk | **2** | 7/2[1] | 83 | 61 |
| *4333*[5] | **Theatre Magic (63)** (SRBowring) **3-9-3** DeanMcKeown(6) (a.p: rdn over 2f out: one pce) | 5 | **3** | 12/1 | 69 | 47 |
| *4078*[4] | **Heathyards Lady (USA) (69)** (RHollinshead) **5-9-10**(3) FLynch(10) (lw: hld up: hdwy 4f out: one pce appr fnl f) | 1¾ | **4** | 4/1[2] | 72 | 54 |
| *3603*[9] | **Penmar (56)** (TJEtherington) **4-9-0b** JCarroll(12) (chsd ldrs tl rdn & wknd 2f out) | ½ | **5** | 20/1 | 58 | 40 |
| *3955*[8] | **Sweet Supposin (IRE) (69)** (JohnBerry) **5-9-6v**(7) JoHunnam(5) (in tch: rdn 5f out: nt pce to chal) | hd | **6** | 12/1 | 71 | 53 |
| *4078*[11] | **China Castle (70)** (PCHaslam) **3-9-10** GCarter(8) (wl bhd: gd hdwy 3f out: hmpd over 1f out: nvr plcd to chal) | nk | **7** | 10/1 | 71 | 49 |
| 2541[6] | **Lady Dignity (IRE) (67)** (PJMakin) **3-9-7** SSanders(4) (in tch: sn pushed along: no imp fnl f) | 2 | **8** | 14/1 | 65 | 43 |
| *2934*[4] | **Domino Flyer (60)** (MrsASwinbank) **3-9-0** JFortune(1) (lw: led over 3f: wknd 4f out) | 7 | **9** | 16/1 | 46 | 24 |
| *4095*[2] | **Chevalier (USA) (63)** (ICampbell) **4-9-7** MWigham(13) (lw: prom tl wknd 4f out: eased whn btn) | 22 | **10** | 5/1[3] | 11 | — |
| *4077*[11] | **Flowing Ocean (60)** (DWChapman) **6-9-4** ACulhane(2) (a bhd) | nk | **11** | 33/1 | 8 | — |
| 2058[10] | **Our Tom (64)** (JWharton) **4-9-8** NCarlisle(9) (bhd fnl 6f) | nk | **12** | 20/1 | 11 | — |

(SP 128.4%) **12 Rn**

**2m 0.8** (4.80) CSF £19.05 CT £150.71 TOTE £3.80: £2.00 £2.40 £4.10 (£4.50) Trio £31.10 OWNER Mr Michael Worth (NEWMARKET) BRED M. J. Worth
WEIGHT FOR AGE 3yo-4lb
**4095* Mansur (IRE)**, with his tongue tied down, has got his act together at long last, but only just got going in time and really needs further than this. (4/1)
**4336* Tea Party (USA)**, keen in the early stages, kicked for home a long way out and the tactics all but worked, the rest being well beaten. (7/2)
**4333 Theatre Magic**, stepping up in trip, raced with the leaders, but was clearly in trouble turning for home. (12/1)
**4078 Heathyards Lady (USA)** continues to run to form, but gets no respite from the Handicapper. (4/1)
**2372 Penmar**, back on his winning mark over this course and distance, raced wide throughout and faded in the straight. (20/1)
**3955 Sweet Supposin (IRE)**, off since running badly here five weeks ago, was among the first off the bit, but kept plugging away. (12/1)
**3649 China Castle** surely needs further than this, but was making eyecatching progress when, having been brought to the stands' rail, he was stopped in this tracks approaching the final furlong. He is very much one to note. (10/1)

## 4576 JACK KIRKLAND MEMORIAL NURSERY (S) H'CAP (0-65) (2-Y.O) (Class G)

9-00 (9-03) **5f (Fibresand)** £2,070.00 (£570.00: £270.00) Stalls: Low GOING minus 0.04 sec per fur (STD)

| | | | | SP | RR | SF |
|---|---|---|---|---|---|---|
| 4244[4] | **Robec Girl (IRE) (62)** (JBerry) **2-9-1**(5) PRoberts(11) (lw: prom: led wl over 1f out: sn rdn clr: edgd lft & kpt on) | — | **1** | 5/1[3] | 66 | 26 |
| 4046[10] | **Will To Win (61)** (PGMurphy) **2-9-5** SDrowne(6) (lw: w ldrs: ev ch 2f out: sn rdn: r.o fnl f) | 1¾ | **2** | 10/1 | 59 | 19 |
| 3853[8] | **Magyar Titok (IRE) (51)** (BobJones) **2-8-9** NDay(10) (lw: rdn 2f out: hdwy over 1f out: r.o wl ins fnl f) | ¾ | **3** | 7/2[1] | 47 | 7 |
| 4493[5] | **Castle House (57)** (JAkehurst) **2-9-1v**[1] SSanders(4) (w ldrs: one pce fnl 2f) | 3 | **4** | 7/1 | 43 | 3 |
| 4343[4] | **Hiltons Executive (IRE) (50)** (EJAlston) **2-8-8** DeanMcKeown(7) (lw: led over 3f) | nk | **5** | 20/1 | 35 | — |
| *4093*[7] | **Fit For The Job (IRE) (54)** (WGMTurner) **2-8-5b**[1](7) DSweeney(1) (hdwy 2f out: nt rch ldrs) | nk | **6** | 12/1 | 39 | — |

| | | | | | | |
|---|---|---|---|---|---|---|
| *4335*[5] | **Run For Us (IRE) (43)** (CADwyer) **2-7-8**(7)ow5 JoHunnam(8) (dwlt: nvr nr ldrs) | 1¾ | **7** | 33/1 | 22 | — |
| 4343* | **Skyers Tryer (63)** (RonaldThompson) **2-9-7** NConnorton(5) (chsd ldrs: rdn over 2f out: sn btn) | ¾ | **8** | 9/2[2] | 40 | — |
| 4339[7] | **Dancing Star (IRE) (52)** (PDEvans) **2-8-10** ACulhane(2) (s.i.s: a bhd) | 1¾ | **9** | 16/1 | 23 | — |
| 2406[3] | **Emma's Risk (53)** (RHarris) **2-8-11** MTebbutt(9) (sn bhd) | 1 | **10** | 14/1 | 21 | — |
| 4230[8] | **Rusty (IRE) (60)** (JBerry) **2-9-4v**[1] GCarter(3) (lw: chsd ldrs 3f) | 4 | **11** | 5/1[3] | 15 | — |

(SP 123.3%) **11 Rn**

**63.1 secs** (4.40) CSF £51.51 CT £187.70 TOTE £4.80: £2.10 £2.50 £2.00 (£21.10) Trio £72.50; £91.91 to Haydock 6/10/96 OWNER Highgrove Developments Ltd (COCKERHAM) BRED Michael Fleming
LONG HANDICAP Run For Us (IRE) 7-9
No bid
**4244 Robec Girl (IRE)** took to this surface in good style and could easily follow up. (5/1)
**3763 Will To Win** looked in fine condition and kept the winner at full stretch in the last furlong. (10/1: op 5/1)
**Magyar Titok (IRE)**, an edgy individual who moved keenly to post, does not give the impression he needs six furlongs, at least on this surface. (7/2: 4/1-5/2)
**4493 Castle House** ended up going the reverse way to the start, but did nothing wrong in the race. (7/1)
**4343 Hiltons Executive (IRE)**, taken down quietly, broke well, but proved one-paced once headed. (20/1)
**1491 Fit For The Job (IRE)** raced at the rear of the main group until making a little progress late in the day. He takes a good hold, but will probably stay another furlong. (12/1: op 7/1)
**4343* Skyers Tryer** (9/2: 3/1-5/1)
**3511* Rusty (IRE)** (5/1: op 8/1)

## 4577 RUBY H'CAP (0-65) (3-Y.O+) (Class F)

9-30 (9-33) **6f (Fibresand)** £2,070.00 (£570.00: £270.00) Stalls: Low GOING minus 0.04 sec per fur (STD)

| | | | | SP | RR | SF |
|---|---|---|---|---|---|---|
| 4372[5] | **Walk the Beat (60)** (MartynMeade) **6-9-2**(7) DSweeney(8) (lw: a.p: led over 1f out: rdn out) | — | **1** | 100/30[1] | 69 | 51 |
| *4090*[4] | **Bold Aristocrat (IRE) (55)** (RHollinshead) **5-9-1**(3) FLynch(13) (lw: hdwy over 2f out: r.o wl fnl f: nt rch wnr) | ¾ | **2** | 10/1 | 62 | 44 |
| 4505[13] | **Cheeky Chappy (60)** (DWChapman) **5-9-9b** ACulhane(3) (w ldrs: kpt on fnl f) | 2½ | **3** | 20/1 | 60 | 42 |
| *4333*[8] | **Napier Star (61)** (MrsNMacauley) **3-9-6v**(3) CTeague(4) (lw: led over 4f: wknd ins fnl f) | s.h | **4** | 10/1 | 61 | 42 |
| 3937[10] | **Prudent Princess (54)** (AHide) **4-8-10b**(7) JoHunnam(12) (dwlt: hdwy over 2f out: one pce fnl f) | 2 | **5** | 33/1 | 49 | 31 |
| 2617[10] | **Prime Partner (57)** (WRMuir) **3-9-5** SWhitworth(1) (chsd ldrs 3f) | 3 | **6** | 20/1 | 44 | 25 |
| *4081*[4] | **Marjorie Rose (IRE) (65)** (ABailey) **3-9-6**(7) AngelaGallimore(10) (b: prom tl rdn & btn over 2f out) | 1 | **7** | 8/1 | 49 | 30 |
| 4255[7] | **No Monkey Nuts (63)** (JBerry) **3-9-11** GCarter(6) (b.hind: bhd: rdn 3f out: nvr nr ldrs) | s.h | **8** | 9/2[2] | 47 | 28 |
| *4333** | **Red Admiral (65)** (CMurray) **6-10-0** DeanMcKeown(5) (sn rdn along: bhd fnl 2f) | 3½ | **9** | 6/1[3] | 40 | 22 |
| 4486[17] | **Butterwick Belle (IRE) (56)** (RAFahey) **3-8-13**(5) PFessey(2) (sn pushed along: chsd ldrs 3f) | 1½ | **10** | 33/1 | 27 | 8 |
| *270*[10] | **Gulf Shaadi (65)** (EJAlston) **4-9-11**(3) DWright(7) (s.s: a wl bhd) | ¾ | **11** | 33/1 | 34 | 16 |
| 4430[22] | **Gormire (56)** (JHetherton) **3-9-4** NCarlisle(9) (hmpd after 1f: no ch after) | nk | **12** | 33/1 | 24 | 5 |
| *3602** | **Delrob (55)** (DHaydnJones) **5-9-4b** SDrowne(11) (a bhd) | 3 | **13** | 9/2[2] | 15 | — |

(SP 124.3%) **13 Rn**

**1m 15.1** (3.70) CSF £34.82 CT £543.15 TOTE £7.60: £2.10 £2.70 £3.00 (£43.20) Trio £72.60 OWNER The Country Life Partnership (MALMESBURY) BRED R. B. Warren
WEIGHT FOR AGE 3yo-1lb
**4372 Walk the Beat** showed he is back to his best, but had to struggle late in the day after looking like winning decisively. (100/30)
**4090 Bold Aristocrat (IRE)**, taken off his feet after the first couple of furlongs, ran on strongly in the home straight. To date, his wins have all been at Southwell. (10/1)
**3223 Cheeky Chappy** has been on the go since the turn of the year and ran a fine race off a much higher mark than he has ever scored off on this surface, coming back for more at the end. (20/1)
**4081 Napier Star** does not appear to quite stay a sixth furlong when ridden in such an aggressive fashion. (10/1)
**2937 Prudent Princess** has flattered to deceive in the past, but did appear to shape with some promise. (33/1)
**2325 Prime Partner** performed reasonably on his first run on this surface as he ideally needs another furlong. (20/1)

T/Plpt: £30.50 (367.12 Tckts). T/Qdpt: £26.20 (12.89 Tckts). Dk

# 4558-HAYDOCK (L-H) (Soft, Heavy patches)
## Sunday October 6th

WEATHER: overcast & showery WIND: slt against

## 4578 DEAUVILLE MAIDEN STKS (I) (2-Y.O) (Class D)

1-30 (1-31) **7f 30y** £3,062.50 (£925.00: £450.00: £212.50) Stalls: High GOING: 0.56 sec per fur (GS)

| | | | | SP | RR | SF |
|---|---|---|---|---|---|---|
| | **Poteen (USA)** (LMCumani) **2-9-0** OUrbina(3) (leggy: scope: hld up & bhd: hdwy 2f out: led wl ins fnl f: comf) | — | **1** | 3/1[2] | 87+ | 33 |
| | **Ghataas** (JLDunlop) **2-9-0** GCarter(11) (lt-f: unf: a.p: led on bit over 2f out: rdn & hdd wl ins fnl f) | nk | **2** | 8/1 | 86+ | 32 |
| 3588[4] | **Bea's Ruby (IRE)** (ABailey) **2-8-9** DHarrison(4) (trckd ldrs: ev ch 2f out: sn rdn & one pce) | 6 | **3** | 16/1 | 68 | 14 |
| 3998[2] | **Party Romance (USA) (88)** (BHanbury) **2-9-0** MRimmer(8) (led: rdn & hdd over 2f out: wknd over 1f out) | 1¼ | **4** | 2/1[1] | 70 | 16 |
| 4188[4] | **Indian Blaze (81)** (PWHarris) **2-9-0** GHind(5) (lw: trckd ldrs: effrt over 2f out: sn rdn & no imp) | ¾ | **5** | 7/1 | 68 | 14 |
| 3787[2] | **Caribbean Star (90)** (MRStoute) **2-8-9** KFallon(2) (hld up: effrt over 2f out: wknd appr fnl f) | hd | **6** | 11/2[3] | 63 | 9 |
| 3779[7] | **Captain Carparts** (JLEyre) **2-9-0** TWilliams(10) (b.nr fore: lw: chsd ldr: shkn up ½-wy: sn ev ch: wknd wl over 1f out) | 5 | **7** | 33/1 | 57 | 3 |
| *3950*[4] | **Sandweld** (CADwyer) **2-9-0** CDwyer(6) (plld hrd: sn chsng ldrs: wknd over 2f out) | s.h | **8** | 25/1 | 57 | 3 |
| 3994[14] | **Amico** (CWThornton) **2-9-0** DeanMcKeown(9) (a bhd) | 2½ | **9** | 33/1 | 51 | — |
| | **Fullopep** (MrsMReveley) **2-9-0** ACulhane(7) (w'like: leggy: bkwd: s.s: a bhd) | 1¼ | **10** | 20/1 | 48 | — |
| 4451[9] | **Yam-Sing** (TDEasterby) **2-9-0** MBirch(1) (lw: a bhd: t.o) | 25 | **11** | 33/1 | — | — |

(SP 120.6%) **11 Rn**

**1m 37.18** (9.68) CSF £26.15 TOTE £4.00: £1.50 £2.80 £2.70 (£27.10) Trio £54.00 OWNER Lord Vestey (NEWMARKET) BRED Dr and Mrs E. A. Neuman
**Poteen (USA)**, a very late foal who is a brother to mud-lover Bog Trotter, won this with the minimum of fuss and is set to go places. (3/1: op 2/1)
**Ghataas**, an unfurnished colt closely related to two winners, did not look the type to handle this bottomless ground, but he gave a good account of himself and, on a sounder surface, should have little trouble finding an opening. (8/1: op 5/1)

**3588 Bea's Ruby (IRE)** improved on her initial outing over this slightly longer trip, but she found the colts too strong for her in the battle to the line. (16/1)
**3998 Party Romance (USA)** has proved a bit of a disappointment since performing so well on his debut at Royal Ascot, but he has had far more use made of him in recent races and, on this showing, it would seem to be the wrong way to ride him. (2/1: op 5/4)
**4188 Indian Blaze** coped well enough with this more testing ground, but he was never able to land a blow and, as yet, is not lasting the trip. (7/1: 10/1-13/2)
**3787 Caribbean Star** could never make her presence felt and began to fade before reaching the final furlong. (11/2)

## 4579 AUTEUIL CONDITIONS STKS (2-Y.O) (Class C)
2-00 (2-00) **5f** £4,484.00 (£1,676.00: £818.00: £350.00: £155.00: £77.00) Stalls: Low GOING: 0.56 sec per fur (GS)

| | Horse / details | Dist | Pos | SP | RR | SF |
|---|---|---|---|---|---|---|
| 4247[2] | **Superior Premium (96)** (RAFahey) **2-8-11** ACulhane(1) (lw: swvd rt s: hdwy ½-wy: led appr fnl f: rdn out) | — | 1 | 7/2[2] | 90 | 41 |
| 4285a[4] | **Jennelle (100)** (CADwyer) **2-8-4**(7) JoHunnam(2) (hmpd s: sn bhd & outpcd: hdwy u.p over 2f out: r.o wl towards fin) | nk | 2 | 3/1[1] | 89 | 40 |
| 4328[10] | **Vasari (IRE) (90)** (MRChannon) **2-9-0** JFortune(6) (led tl over 1f out: kpt on u.p fnl f) | ¾ | 3 | 7/1 | 90 | 41 |
| 4087* | **Loving And Giving** (HCandy) **2-8-6** GCarter(3) (prom: led over 1f out: sn hdd: wknd fnl f) | 4 | 4 | 5/1 | 69 | 20 |
| 4510[5] | **Big Ben (95)** (RHannon) **2-9-0** RPerham(5) (lw: prom tl lost pl wl over 1f out) | 4 | 5 | 7/1 | 64 | 15 |
| 4299[4] | **Olympic Spirit (100)** (JBerry) **2-9-0** JCarroll(4) (b.hind: lw: gd spd to ½-wy: sn drvn & wknd: t.o) | 10 | 6 | 4/1[3] | 32 | — |
| | | | | (SP 108.9%) | | **6 Rn** |

**65.18 secs** (5.98) CSF £13.14 TOTE £4.30: £2.10 £2.30 (£6.10) OWNER Mr J. C. Parsons (MALTON) BRED Giles W. Pritchard-Gordon
STEWARDS' ENQUIRY Obj. to Superior Premium by Hunnam overruled.
**4247 Superior Premium**, content to bide his time, lengthened up when given the office approaching the final furlong and won with more in hand than the margin might suggest. (7/2)
**4285a Jennelle**, slightly impeded by the winner leaving the stalls, never got going until far too late, and her jockey's objection was bordering on the lines of frivolous. (3/1)
**1003* Vasari (IRE)** got the best of the start from his stands'-side stall and battled on willingly after being collared, but the winner had taken his measure inside the distance. (7/1)
**4087* Loving And Giving**, a daughter of Sharpo, should have been in her element in these testing conditions, but her stride shortened rather quickly passing the furlong marker and she was soon brushed aside. (5/1)

## 4580 LONGCHAMP H'CAP (0-85) (3-Y.O+) (Class D)
2-35 (2-36) **1m 3f 200y** £3,988.75 (£1,210.00: £592.50: £283.75) Stalls: Low GOING: 0.56 sec per fur (GS)

| | Horse / details | Dist | Pos | SP | RR | SF |
|---|---|---|---|---|---|---|
| 4431[2] | **Sugar Mill (73)** (MrsMReveley) **6-9-6** ACulhane(17) (lw: racd wd: lost pl ent st: rallied u.p over 1f out: styd on to ld wl ins fnl f) | — | 1 | 13/2[3] | 83 | 56 |
| 3447[3] | **Voila Premiere (IRE) (66)** (MHTompkins) **4-8-10**(3) MHenry(5) (lw: chsd ldrs: led over 2f out: hrd rdn & hdd wl ins fnl f) | 1 | 2 | 9/2[1] | 75 | 48 |
| 1783[6] | **Bellator (74)** (GBBalding) **3-9-0** SDrowne(10) (bit bkwd: hld up & bhd: gd hdwy over 2f out: ev ch ins fnl f: no ex cl home) | ½ | 3 | 16/1 | 82 | 48 |
| 3398[7] | **Bechstein (77)** (JLDunlop) **3-9-3b[1]** GCarter(15) (hld up: hdwy over 2f out: one pce ins fnl f) | ¾ | 4 | 11/1 | 84 | 50 |
| 4431[3] | **Rusk (74)** (JPearce) **3-9-0** MWigham(6) (hld up: hdwy u.p fnl 2f: nvr nrr) | 1½ | 5 | 6/1[2] | 79 | 45 |
| 2793[4] | **Debutante Days (68)** (CREgerton) **4-8-10**(5) SophieMitchell(19) (prom: rdn over 2f out: styd on same pce) | 1¾ | 6 | 14/1 | 71 | 44 |
| 4187[2] | **Wild Rita (76)** (WRMuir) **4-9-9** KFallon(16) (lw: rdn ent st: styd on fnl 2f: nvr nrr) | 1 | 7 | 9/1 | 77 | 50 |
| 4320[3] | **Classic Parisian (IRE) (74)** (RHarris) **3-9-0** RPrice(1) (hld up in tch: styd centre: wknd over 2f out) | 1½ | 8 | 10/1 | 73 | 39 |
| 4483[2] | **Soba Up (70)** (TJEtherington) **6-9-3** MBirch(9) (trckd ldrs: rdn 3f out: wknd over 1f out) | ½ | 9 | 10/1 | 69 | 42 |
| 3979* | **Naval Gazer (IRE) (73)** (DRLoder) **3-8-13** DRMcCabe(18) (s.i.s: hdwy centre over 2f out: eased whn btn ins fnl f) | nk | 10 | 10/1 | 71 | 37 |
| 4374[6] | **Far Dawn (USA) (72)** (GHarwood) **3-8-12** AClark(3) (in tch: rdn over 3f out: sn wknd) | 3½ | 11 | 16/1 | 66 | 32 |
| 4483[11] | **Mentalasanythin (68)** (DHaydnJones) **7-9-1** LCharnock(14) (led tl hdd & wknd wl over 2f out) | 3½ | 12 | 14/1 | 57 | 30 |
| 1524[8] | **Johns Act (USA) (66)** (DHaydnJones) **6-8-13** DHarrison(2) (bit bkwd: prom: styd centre st: wknd over 2f out) | 1½ | 13 | 25/1 | 53 | 26 |
| 1005[18] | **Evezio Rufo (70)** (NPLittmoden) **4-9-3v** TGMcLaughlin(7) (w ldrs tl wknd wl over 2f out: t.o) | 8 | 14 | 33/1 | 46 | 19 |
| 4431[5] | **House of Riches (84)** (LMCumani) **3-9-10** OUrbina(11) (lw: hld up mid div: wknd over 2f out: eased whn btn: t.o) | 1¼ | 15 | 10/1 | 58 | 24 |
| 4315[9] | **Cois Na Farraige (IRE) (75)** (MissLAPerratt) **3-9-1** JCarroll(12) (racd wd back st: lost tch over 3f out: t.o) | ½ | 16 | 25/1 | 49 | 15 |
| *4078[7]* | **Exalted (IRE) (82)** (SirMarkPrescott) **3-9-8** SSanders(13) (lw: prom: led wl over 2f out: sn hdd & wknd: t.o) | s.h | 17 | 14/1 | 56 | 22 |
| 1426[6] | **Blackpatch Hill (73)** (NTinkler) **7-9-6** KimTinkler(4) (bkwd: a bhd: t.o) | 1 | 18 | 25/1 | 45 | 18 |
| | | | | (SP 146.7%) | | **18 Rn** |

**2m 43.14** (13.74) CSF £39.76 CT £454.31 TOTE £5.80: £1.90 £2.70 £4.80 £3.70 (£34.40) Trio £601.40 OWNER Mr C. C. Buckley (SALTBURN) BRED Snailwell Stud Co Ltd
WEIGHT FOR AGE 3yo-7lb
**4431 Sugar Mill** won this courtesy of his superior stamina, for he was only third best 200 yards out, before the leading pair cracked. (13/2)
**3447 Voila Premiere (IRE)**, tackling this extended trip for the first time, would have succeeded had the going not been so stamina-sapping. He should go one better once he recovers from these exertions. (9/2: op 12/1)
**1783 Bellator** acts on the ground and stays extremely well, but lack of peak-fitness after a four-month break took its toll after he looked all over the winner into the final furlong. (16/1)
**1180 Bechstein** began to stay on inside the last quarter-mile, but he always had too much to do and was never going to make it. (11/1)
**4431 Rusk** finished much closer to the winner on identical terms on his most recent outing, but he struggled in this ground and was never a serious factor. (6/1)
**2793 Debutante Days** failed to make any impression when asked for a final effort and her three-month holiday was probably having its effect in the closing stages. (14/1)
**4187 Wild Rita** has done all her winning on a sound surface and was never travelling until staying on to finish seventh. (9/1: op 6/1)

## 4581 D. H. WELTON & CO H'CAP (0-90) (3-Y.O+) (Class C)
3-10 (3-11) **6f** £6,031.00 (£1,828.00: £894.00: £427.00) Stalls: Low GOING: 0.56 sec per fur (GS)

| | Horse / details | Dist | Pos | SP | RR | SF |
|---|---|---|---|---|---|---|
| 4444[16] | **Garnock Valley (74)** (JBerry) **6-8-13b[1]** GCarter(4) (hld up: hdwy 2f out: qcknd to ld ins fnl f: sn clr) | — | 1 | 25/1 | 94 | 83 |
| 4198[14] | **Montserrat (75)** (LGCottrell) **4-9-0v** MFenton(5) (lw: a.p: led wl over 1f out: hdd ins fnl f: kpt on: no ch w wnr) | 5 | 2 | 14/1 | 82 | 71 |

| | | | | SP | RR | SF |
|---|---|---|---|---|---|---|
| 4136[3] | **Lough Erne (78)** (CFWall) **4-9-3** SSanders(9) (lw: hdwy ½-wy: disp ld ent fnl f: one pce) | hd | **3** | 7/1[2] | 84 | 73 |
| 4136[16] | **Barrel of Hope (78)** (JLEyre) **4-9-3b** RLappin(13) (hdwy fnl 2f: nrst fin) | 1¾ | **4** | 25/1 | 80 | 69 |
| 4367[5] | **Friendly Brave (USA) (74)** (MissGayKelleway) **6-8-13** MRimmer(1) (b.hind: lw: hld up: hdwy over 2f out: one pce fnl f) | 1¼ | **5** | 14/1 | 72 | 61 |
| 4452[6] | **Sailormaite (80)** (SRBowring) **5-9-5b** DeanMcKeown(18) (hld up: hdwy & nt clr run over 2f out: swtchd rt & lft: nt rch ldrs) | ¾ | **6** | 11/1 | 76 | 65 |
| 4314[21] | **Sea-Deer (86)** (CADwyer) **7-9-11** CDwyer(19) (hld up & bhd: sme hdwy over 1f out: nvr nrr) | 1½ | **7** | 12/1 | 78 | 67 |
| 1898[6] | **Charlie Sillett (82)** (BWHills) **4-9-4**(3) JDSmith(8) (bit bkwd: s.s: effrt over 1f out: nt rch ldrs) | 1¼ | **8** | 14/1 | 71 | 60 |
| 4058[16] | **High Domain (IRE) (70)** (JLSpearing) **5-8-9** SDrowne(11) (mde most tl hdd & wknd over 1f out) | ¾ | **9** | 25/1 | 57 | 46 |
| 3693[8] | **Norwegian Blue (IRE) (84)** (APJarvis) **3-9-8v** JFortune(10) (trckd ldrs: nt clr run over 2f out: sn btn) | 1¼ | **10** | 20/1 | 68 | 56 |
| 4314[23] | **Don't Care (IRE) (88)** (MissLAPerratt) **5-9-13b** JCarroll(2) (nvr trbld ldrs) | hd | **11** | 20/1 | 72 | 61 |
| 4314[25] | **Tiler (IRE) (81)** (MJohnston) **4-9-6** BDoyle(23) (lw: racd stands' side: bhd fnl 2f) | 7 | **12** | 16/1 | 46 | 35 |
| 4312[12] | **Bollin Harry (78)** (TDEasterby) **4-9-3** MBirch(3) (lw: w ldrs 4f: sn rdn & wknd) | hd | **13** | 16/1 | 43 | 32 |
| 4215[5] | **Purple Fling (71)** (LGCottrell) **5-8-5**(5) DGriffiths(20) (prom 4f) | ¾ | **14** | 12/1 | 34 | 23 |
| 2078[8] | **Antonias Melody (81)** (SRBowring) **3-9-2**(3) CTeague(14) (bit bkwd: nvr plcd to chal) | s.h | **15** | 25/1 | 43 | 31 |
| 4309[6] | **Corporal Nym (USA) (73)** (PFICole) **3-8-11** ACulhane(17) (s.s: a in rr) | ¾ | **16** | 20/1 | 33 | 21 |
| 4314[10] | **Benzoe (IRE) (82)** (MrsJRRamsden) **6-9-7** KFallon(12) (hrd drvn ½-wy: no imp) | 1¼ | **17** | 13/2[1] | 39 | 28 |
| 3984[6] | **Red Nymph (90)** (WJarvis) **3-9-11**(3) FLynch(7) (prom over 3f) | 2½ | **18** | 16/1 | 40 | 28 |
| 3693[19] | **Splicing (80)** (WJHaggas) **3-9-4** DHarrison(16) (chsd ldrs over 3f) | ½ | **19** | 20/1 | 29 | 17 |
| 4342[2] | **Palacegate Jack (IRE) (78)** (CADwyer) **5-8-12**(5) PRoberts(15) (prom over 3f) | 1 | **20** | 9/1[3] | 24 | 13 |
| 3085[12] | **Cross The Border (89)** (DNicholls) **3-9-13** AlexGreaves(24) (a bhd) | 1¼ | **21** | 33/1 | 32 | 20 |
| 4058[15] | **Erupt (74)** (GBBalding) **3-8-12v** AClark(22) (outpcd) | ½ | **22** | 16/1 | 16 | 4 |

(SP 140.5%) **22 Rn**

**1m 16.09** (4.39) CSF £334.09 CT £2,513.33 TOTE £37.90: £13.30 £4.90 £2.00 £4.70 (£412.40) Trio £2,365.70; £1,166.22 to Pontefract 7/10/96 OWNER Mr Robert Aird (COCKERHAM) BRED Sunley Stud

WEIGHT FOR AGE 3yo-1lb

**4312 Garnock Valley**, with a combination of first-time blinkers and soft ground, improved vastly, and the ease of the success had to be seen to be believed. (25/1)

**2298 Montserrat**, a totally different animal on soft ground, ran up to her best and there could still be more success to follow if it does remain wet. (14/1)

**4136 Lough Erne**, produced to win her race approaching the final furlong, had no answer when the winner came on the scene, but she ran her race out to the finish and will be still be fresher than most for the remaining weeks. (7/1)

**935 Barrel of Hope** needs a stiffer test than this on such an easy track and only found top gear when it was all but over. (25/1)

**4367 Friendly Brave (USA)**, a very versatile animal who wins from five furlongs to seven furlongs on all types of ground, could not quite summon up the speed to get serious. (14/1)

**4452 Sailormaite** can expect, from to time, to encounter trouble when trying to weave his way through such a big field, but nothing seemed to go right for him here and, if there was a hard-luck story, then his was a case to consider. (11/1)

**3953* Sea-Deer** was never in a position to pose a threat, but he was motoring on at the finish, and there is still time for him to strike again. (12/1)

**1334 Charlie Sillett**, the winner of this event twelve months ago, was race-fit then, but he did look a bit rusty here after almost four months out of action, and a sluggish start did nothing to help his cause. In such a large field, it says a lot that he was able to finish on the heels of the leaders. (14/1)

**3223* Benzoe (IRE)** once again forfeited ground at the start and, failing to pick up when ridden, ran no race at all. (13/2)

## 4582 SAINT-CLOUD LIMITED STKS (0-70) (3-Y.O+) (Class E)

3-40 (3-41) **1m 2f 120y** £3,139.00 (£952.00: £466.00: £223.00) Stalls: Low GOING: 0.56 sec per fur (GS)

| | | | | SP | RR | SF |
|---|---|---|---|---|---|---|
| 4463[8] | **Master Beveled (68)** (PDEvans) **6-9-2** KFallon(1) (stdd s: stdy hdwy 3f out: led over 1f out: edgd lft: sn clr) | — | **1** | 7/2[1] | 80 | 54 |
| 4483[4] | **Break the Rules (70)** (MrsMReveley) **4-9-4** DHarrison(9) (hld up: hdwy 2f out: rdn & styd on wl fnl f) | 2½ | **2** | 10/1 | 78 | 52 |
| 4227[5] | **South Sea Bubble (IRE) (65)** (LMCumani) **4-8-13** OUrbina(3) (led after 2f tl over 2f out: kpt on one pce fnl f) | nk | **3** | 8/1[3] | 73 | 47 |
| 4243[6] | **Ron's Secret (69)** (JWPayne) **4-8-13** JCarroll(16) (hrd rdn & hdwy over 3f out: styd on wl fnl f) | hd | **4** | 6/1[2] | 73 | 47 |
| 4513[14] | **Sistar Act (66)** (MRChannon) **3-8-6**(7) AEddery(5) (dwlt: hdwy on ins 5f out: led over 2f out tl over 1f out: sn wknd) | 1¾ | **5** | 14/1 | 76 | 44 |
| 4243[13] | **Gloriana (68)** (LadyHerries) **4-9-1** JQuinn(13) (prom tl rdn & wknd over 2f out) | s.h | **6** | 12/1 | 72 | 46 |
| 2027[4] | **Alsahib (USA) (70)** (WRMuir) **3-8-10** SSanders(10) (stdd s: a in rr) | 11 | **7** | 16/1 | 56 | 24 |
| 646[4] | **Doctor Bravious (IRE) (70)** (MBell) **3-8-10v** MFenton(6) (trckd ldrs tl wknd over 2f out) | 2 | **8** | 10/1 | 53 | 21 |
| 4438* | **Urgent Swift (70)** (APJarvis) **3-8-12** JFortune(4) (hld up: hdwy over 3f out: wknd over 2f out) | 8 | **9** | 11/1 | 43 | 11 |
| 2998[4] | **Shu Gaa (IRE) (70)** (WJHaggas) **3-8-10** GHind(11) (nvr bttr than mid div) | hd | **10** | 10/1 | 41 | 9 |
| 4249[3] | **Stormless (53)** (PMonteith) **5-8-13**(7) JBramhill(2) (mid div: effrt & rdn over 2f out: no imp) | 1¼ | **11** | 16/1 | 43 | 17 |
| 3426[7] | **Tissue of Lies (USA) (68)** (MJohnston) **3-8-10** BDoyle(15) (led 2f: prom tl wknd over 3f out) | 1½ | **12** | 12/1 | 37 | 5 |
| 1023[5] | **Kathryn's Pet (67)** (MrsMReveley) **3-8-7** ACulhane(8) (a bhd) | 4 | **13** | 20/1 | 28 | — |
| | **Surrey Dancer (63)** (MrsMReveley) **8-8-11**(5) SCopp(12) (s.s: a bhd: t.o) | 11 | **14** | 20/1 | 14 | — |
| 4110[3] | **Classic Dame (FR) (68)** (RHarris) **3-8-7** RPrice(14) (trckd ldrs 7f) | s.h | **15** | 12/1 | 11 | — |

(SP 134.3%) **15 Rn**

**2m 23.42** (11.92) CSF £40.02 TOTE £3.90: £1.70 £3.80 £3.70 (£23.70) Trio £45.20 OWNER Mrs E. J. Williams (WELSHPOOL) BRED C. R. Black

WEIGHT FOR AGE 3yo-6lb

**4193 Master Beveled**, winning his first race in two years, gave away considerable ground by veering over to the far rail after taking control, but he proved superior to these rivals to record his first success at the trip. (7/2: 9/2-3/1)

**4483 Break the Rules** has been performing over longer trips of late and it took him quite some time to find his stride, but he finished best of all and gave his supporters hope for the future. (10/1)

**4227 South Sea Bubble (IRE)** is still struggling to find an opening, but she ran another promising race and her turn is long overdue. (8/1)

**4243 Ron's Secret**, running without blinkers and held up to get the trip, only decided to put her best foot forward inside the distance and, by then, the winner had shot clear. (6/1)

**4232 Sistar Act** reserves her best for a much sounder surface, but she was far from disgraced here and is running well enough to find another small race. (14/1)

**3403* Gloriana** ran a bit too free to last home over this trip and was throwing out distress signals below the distance. (12/1)

**646 Doctor Bravious (IRE)** (10/1: op 6/1)

## 4583 MAISONS-LAFFITTE H'CAP (0-90) (3-Y.O) (Class C)

4-10 (4-11) **1m 30y** £5,823.00 (£1,764.00: £862.00: £411.00) Stalls: High GOING: 0.56 sec per fur (GS)

| Form | Horse | Dist | Pos | SP | RR | SF |
|---|---|---|---|---|---|---|
| $4463^{5}$ | **Rebel County (IRE) (84)** (ABailey) **3-9-1** DBiggs(9) (s.i.s: hld up: hdwy over 2f out: rdn to ld wl ins fnl f) | — | 1 | $4/1^{1}$ | 94 | 55 |
| $4054^{12}$ | **Warming Trends (85)** (SirMarkPrescott) **3-9-2** SSanders(2) (a.p: led wl over 2f out tl wl ins fnl f) | 1¼ | 2 | $5/1^{2}$ | 93 | 54 |
| $3456^{7}$ | **Le Teteu (FR) (65)** (BobJones) **3-7-10** JQuinn(1) (lw: hld up: hdwy over 2f out: hrd rdn: one pce fnl f) | 3½ | 3 | 8/1 | 66 | 27 |
| $3933^{2}$ | **Jo Mell (84)** (TDEasterby) **3-9-1** MBirch(11) (lw: hld up: stdy hdwy 3f out: ev ch 2f out: rdn & wknd fnl f) | hd | 4 | $5/1^{2}$ | 85 | 46 |
| $4054^{5}$ | **Trafalgar Lady (USA) (79)** (RCharlton) **3-8-10** TSprake(3) (lw: hld up: hdwy over 2f out: sn rdn & wknd) | 10 | 5 | $7/1^{3}$ | 60 | 21 |
| $3985^{14}$ | **Polar Prospect (72)** (BHanbury) **3-8-3** JStack(7) (mde most tl hdd wl over 2f out: sn wknd) | 3½ | 6 | 12/1 | 46 | 7 |
| $2041^{31}$ | **Manaloj (USA) (86)** (PTWalwyn) **3-9-3** JFortune(10) (bkwd: prom: ev ch tl rdn & wknd over 2f out) | 2½ | 7 | 20/1 | 55 | 16 |
| $2041^{25}$ | **Therhea (IRE) (83)** (BRMillman) **3-9-0** BDoyle(4) (bkwd: in tch: rdn & wknd over 3f out) | ½ | 8 | $7/1^{3}$ | 51 | 12 |
| $4352^{10}$ | **Herodian (USA) (90)** (JHMGosden) **3-9-7b** JCarroll(6) (b: lw: chsd ldrs over 4f: sn rdn & wknd: t.o) | 5 | 9 | 10/1 | 48 | 9 |
| $4184^{16}$ | **Roman Gold (IRE) (81)** (RHannon) **3-8-12** RPerham(8) (lw: a bhd: t.o) | ¾ | 10 | 12/1 | 38 | — |
| $3920^{9}$ | **Sualtach (IRE) (83)** (RHollinshead) **3-9-0v¹** DHarrison(5) (prom over 6f: sn wknd: t.o) | 1¾ | 11 | 14/1 | 36 | — |
| $3430^{4}$ | **Nasrudin (USA) (80)** (DRLoder) **3-8-11** DRMcCabe(12) (bhd: hrd rdn over 3f out: no rspnse: t.o) | dist | 12 | 9/1 | — | — |

(SP 135.3%) **12 Rn**

**1m 49.57** (8.97) CSF £26.49 CT £153.98 TOTE £5.40: £1.90 £2.20 £3.50 (£14.00) Trio £156.30 OWNER Showtime Ice Cream Concessionaire (TARPORLEY) BRED C. J. Foy

LONG HANDICAP Le Teteu (FR) 7-8

**OFFICIAL EXPLANATION Nasrudin (USA): was choking throughout the race.**

**4463 Rebel County (IRE)** is enjoying one hell of a season and, though she has continued to scale the heights, she holds her form well and is a credit to her connections. (4/1)

**917 Warming Trends** usually comes good at this time of year but, as yet, his successes have come at shorter trips. If an excuse were needed here, it could be said that he failed to last home. (5/1)

**3456 Le Teteu (FR)** kept staying on in the latter stages, but he lacked the speed of the principals and was never going to make it. (8/1)

**3933 Jo Mell** should have had the beating of the winner on these terms, but once again failed to put his best foot forward when the pressure was on. He may well need a pair of blinkers. (5/1)

**4054 Trafalgar Lady (USA)** acts on this ground, but she looks to be something of a short-runner and this trip proved beyond her. (7/1)

**3594 Polar Prospect** bowled along in the lead for over five furlongs, but had kept very little in reserve and was back-pedalling passing the quarter-mile marker. (12/1)

## 4584 DEAUVILLE MAIDEN STKS (II) (2-Y.O) (Class D)

4-40 (4-43) **7f 30y** £3,046.25 (£920.00: £447.50: £211.25) Stalls: High GOING: 0.56 sec per fur (GS)

| Form | Horse | Dist | Pos | SP | RR | SF |
|---|---|---|---|---|---|---|
| | **Future Perfect** (MWEasterby) **2-8-9**(5) GParkin(10) (leggy: unf: bhd: hrd rdn over 2f out: gd hdwy to ld ent fnl f: r.o strly) | — | 1 | 16/1 | 77 | 15 |
| | **Daniel Deronda** (PWHarris) **2-9-0** GHind(7) (w'like: scope: bit bkwd: hld up & bhd: hdwy 2f out: kpt on wl ins fnl f) | 1¼ | 2 | 9/1 | 74 | 12 |
| $2057^{5}$ | **Mutabari (USA)** (DMorley) **2-9-0** MFenton(9) (b.nr hind: bit bkwd: a.p: led wl over 1f out tl hdd ent fnl f: one pce) | hd | 3 | $15/8^{1}$ | 74 | 12 |
| | **Itatinga (USA)** (MRStoute) **2-8-9** KFallon(2) (unf: bkwd: s.s: hdwy ent st: jnd ldr over 2f out: wknd over 1f out) | 4 | 4 | $5/2^{2}$ | 60 | — |
| | **Drumgor Prince** (APJarvis) **2-9-0** JFortune(4) (leggy: scope: chsd ldrs: rdn 4f out: wknd over 1f out) | 2½ | 5 | 14/1 | 59 | — |
| $3874^{5}$ | **Kennemara Star (IRE)** (JLDunlop) **2-9-0** GCarter(3) (plld hrd: ev ch wl over 1f out: wknd appr fnl f) | 1½ | 6 | $11/2^{3}$ | 56 | — |
| $4200^{7}$ | **Sand Cay (USA)** (RHannon) **2-9-0** RPerham(8) (led tl hdd & wknd wl over 1f out) | 2½ | 7 | 10/1 | 50 | — |
| $4046^{18}$ | **Propellant** (CWThornton) **2-9-0** DeanMcKeown(11) (bkwd: bhd: effrt over 3f out: sn rdn & lost tch) | 1¼ | 8 | 33/1 | 48 | — |
| $4224^{11}$ | **Murray Grey** (EWeymes) **2-8-9** JQuinn(6) (b: bkwd: chsd ldrs over 4f: sn lost tch) | 4 | 9 | 33/1 | 34 | — |
| $4502^{4}$ | **Kalousion** (CWCElsey) **2-9-0** JCarroll(5) (a bhd) | 4 | 10 | 33/1 | 30 | — |
| | **Dunston Gold** (PJBevan) **2-9-0** NCarlisle(1) (lt-f: unf: bkwd: s.s: hdwy on ins over 5f out: wknd over 3f out) | 3½ | 11 | 33/1 | 22 | — |

(SP 122.1%) **11 Rn**

**1m 38.91** (11.41) CSF £138.43 TOTE £13.60: £2.90 £2.50 £1.30 (£206.60) Trio £210.20 OWNER R O M Racing (SHERIFF HUTTON) BRED Mrs E. C. York

**Future Perfect** looked sure to finish out with the washing halfway up the straight, but suddenly started to pick up and, coming back on the bridle, led inside the final furlong and won very cosily indeed. (16/1)

**Daniel Deronda**, a scopey individual who comes from a winning family, looked far from fully wound up, but he was starting to realise what was required in the closing stages and looks a ready-made winner. (9/1)

**2057 Mutabari (USA)**, carrying a summer bloom on his coat, looked just in need of the run after a break since June, and that was the deciding factor in the run to the line. (15/8)

**Itatinga (USA)** has got a bit of filling out to do and she can also be made much fitter, but she showed promise after a slow start and will be all the wiser with this experience under her belt. (5/2: op 6/4)

**Drumgor Prince** did not shape badly and will be so much wiser the next time he appears. (14/1)

**3874 Kennemara Star (IRE)** had the edge in experience and loomed up to look a serious threat below the distance, but he was unable to sustain the run and was going in reverse entering the final furlong. (11/2)

**Sand Cay (USA)** would have learnt much more this time, striding along in the lead until feeling the strain and calling enough below the distance. (10/1)

T/Jkpt: Not won; £2,140.55 to Pontefract 7/10/96. T/Plpt: £497.50 (34.42 Tckts). T/Qdpt: £46.20 (34.97 Tckts). IM

# 4382-PONTEFRACT (L-H) (Good, Good to firm patches)

## Monday October 7th

WEATHER: overcast WIND: slt half bhd

## 4585 E.B.F. CLAXTON BAY MAIDEN STKS (2-Y.O) (Class D)

2-15 (2-20) **1m 2f 6y** £4,201.50 (£1,272.00: £621.00: £295.50) Stalls: Low GOING minus 0.22 sec per fur (GF)

| Form | Horse | Dist | Pos | SP | RR | SF |
|---|---|---|---|---|---|---|
| $4204^{4}$ | **Silver Patriarch (IRE)** (JLDunlop) **2-9-0** PatEddery(10) (hld up: hdwy 6f out: led over 1f out: drvn clr: eased nr fin) | — | 1 | $7/2^{2}$ | 82+ | 37 |

| | | | | SP | RR | SF |
|---|---|---|---|---|---|---|
| 4261$^{8}$ | **Perfect Paradigm (IRE)** (JHMGosden) **2-9-0** LDettori(1) (led tl over 1f out: kpt on: no ch w wnr) | 3 | **2** | 3/1$^{1}$ | 77 | 32 |
| 4245$^{2}$ | **Canadian Fantasy (82)** (MJohnston) **2-9-0b$^{1}$** JWeaver(4) (lw: hld up: effrt over 2f out: styd on same pce: nvr nr to chal) | 1¾ | **3** | 13/2 | 74 | 29 |
| | **Vicki Romara** (MJohnston) **2-8-9** RHills(9) (lt-f: s.i.s: bhd: hdwy over 3f out: styd on same pce) | ¾ | **4** | 33/1 | 68 | 23 |
| | **Premier** (MJohnston) **2-9-0** BDoyle(3) (unf: a chsng ldrs: one pce fnl 2f) | nk | **5** | 11/2$^{3}$ | 73 | 28 |
| 4349$^{2}$ | **Tommy Tortoise** (PFICole) **2-9-0** TQuinn(5) (b.nr hind: lw: a chsng ldrs: drvn along over 3f out: one pce) | 2 | **6** | 7/2$^{2}$ | 70 | 25 |
| 4175$^{6}$ | **Pertemps Mission** (JPearce) **2-9-0** GBardwell(2) (chsd ldrs: drvn along ½-wy: lost pl over 2f out) | 1 | **7** | 10/1 | 68 | 23 |
| *4331$^{6}$* | **Jack Brown** (TTClement) **2-9-0** KFallon(8) (s.i.s: a in rr) | 1¼ | **8** | 50/1 | 66 | 21 |
| 4096$^{4}$ | **Tracks of My Tears** (WGMTurner) **2-8-2**(7) DMcGaffin(7) (sn bhd) | 5 | **9** | 50/1 | 53 | 8 |
| 4361$^{3}$ | **Warrlin (66)** (CWFairhurst) **2-9-0** DeanMcKeown(6) (chsd ldr tl wknd over 2f out) | 7 | **10** | 14/1 | 47 | 2 |

(SP 120.8%) **10 Rn**

**2m 13.9** (1.60 under 2y best) (5.60) CSF £14.33 TOTE £4.50: £1.30 £1.70 £2.20 (£7.30) Trio £14.50 OWNER Mr Peter Winfield (ARUNDEL) BRED Peter Winfield

**4204 Silver Patriarch (IRE)**, who has plenty of furnishing to do, took this in good style and it took his jockey all his time to pull him up. He should make a useful staying handicapper at three. (7/2)

**Perfect Paradigm (IRE)** showed a good strong action going down. Allowed to stride along in front, he had no answer when the winner swept by. (3/1)

**4245 Canadian Fantasy**, tried in blinkers, was set a fair bit to do. Sticking on from the turn, he was never going to get near either of the first two. (13/2)

**Vicki Romara** is nothing to look at, lacking both size and substance, but she obviously has some ability and can be expected to do better next year. (33/1)

**Premier**, very green to post, showed ability and can only improve. (11/2)

**4349 Tommy Tortoise** certainly took the eye in the paddock, but is a poor walker. Hard at work before the home turn, he proved painfully one-paced. (7/2)

## 4586 LEVY BOARD NURSERY H'CAP (0-75) (2-Y.O) (Class E)

2-45 (2-49) **6f** £3,548.00 (£1,064.00: £512.00: £236.00) Stalls: Low GOING minus 0.22 sec per fur (GF)

| | | | | SP | RR | SF |
|---|---|---|---|---|---|---|
| 4123$^{6}$ | **Count Roberto (USA) (75)** (PWChapple-Hyam) **2-9-4**(3) RHavlin(8) (w ldrs: led 1f out: r.o wl) | — | **1** | 12/1 | 88 | 45 |
| 4546$^{3}$ | **Dowry (64)** (RHannon) **2-8-10** PatEddery(17) (lw: racd v.wd: led: swtchd lft over 2f out: hdd 1f out: nt qckn) | 3½ | **2** | 8/1 | 68 | 25 |
| 4384$^{8}$ | **Sparky (61)** (MWEasterby) **2-8-7b** JFanning(2) (lw: bhd: hdwy & swtchd over 1f out: styd on wl towards fin) | 3½ | **3** | 25/1 | 55 | 12 |
| 4546$^{5}$ | **Masterstroke (72)** (BJMeehan) **2-9-4** MTebbutt(14) (lw: in tch: rdn over 2f out: kpt on same pce) | s.h | **4** | 16/1 | 66 | 23 |
| 4459$^{2}$ | **Donna's Dancer (IRE) (67)** (TDBarron) **2-8-13b** JFortune(4) (lw: a chsng ldrs: rdn 2f out: one pce) | 1¾ | **5** | 7/1$^{3}$ | 57 | 14 |
| 4433$^{8}$ | **Rum Lad (70)** (JJQuinn) **2-8-9**(7) GMilligan(1) (bhd tl styd on fnl 2f) | nk | **6** | 16/1 | 59 | 16 |
| 3969$^{3}$ | **Brutal Fantasy (IRE) (70)** (JLEyre) **2-9-2** RLappin(12) (b.off hind: w ldrs tl wknd over 1f out) | 1¼ | **7** | 6/1$^{2}$ | 55 | 12 |
| 4318$^{4}$ | **Barresbo (69)** (CWFairhurst) **2-9-1** DeanMcKeown(3) (lw: drvn along & outpcd: sme hdwy over 1f out: n.d) | 1½ | **8** | 12/1 | 50 | 7 |
| 4318$^{5}$ | **King Uno (67)** (MrsJRRamsden) **2-8-13** JCarroll(9) (bhd: sme hdwy over 1f out: nvr nr ldrs) | 1½ | **9** | 16/1 | 44 | 1 |
| 3771$^{4}$ | **Mill End Boy (67)** (MWEasterby) **2-8-8**(5) GParkin(15) (bhd: sme hdwy over 1f out: n.d) | ½ | **10** | 20/1 | 43 | — |
| 3523$^{3}$ | **Our Kevin (68)** (KMcAuliffe) **2-9-0** SSanders(6) (swtg: a in rr) | 1 | **11** | 20/1 | 41 | — |
| 4433$^{3}$ | **Abstone Queen (63)** (PDEvans) **2-8-9v** ACulhane(7) (prom: rdn 2f out: sn lost pl) | ½ | **12** | 14/1 | 35 | — |
| 4087$^{11}$ | **Sarabi (65)** (JPearce) **2-8-11** KFallon(18) (racd wd: chsd ldrs: swtchd lft over 2f out: rdn & wknd over 1f out) | 2½ | **13** | 20/1 | 30 | — |
| 4224$^{3}$ | **Globetrotter (IRE) (74)** (MJohnston) **2-9-6** JWeaver(5) (nvr wnt pce) | nk | **14** | 12/1 | 39 | — |
| 4339$^{4}$ | **Danehill Princess (IRE) (69)** (RHollinshead) **2-9-1v** LDettori(13) (swtg: reminders after s: a in rr) | 1¼ | **15** | 11/2$^{1}$ | 30 | — |
| 4311$^{6}$ | **Hil Rhapsody (70)** (BPalling) **2-9-2** TSprake(16) (swtg: a outpcd & bhd) | nk | **16** | 25/1 | 31 | — |
| *3050$^{6}$* | ***Colonel's Pride (69)*** (RMWhitaker) **2-9-1** KDarley(11) (Withdrawn not under Starter's orders: veterinary advice) | | **W** | 33/1 | — | — |
| *4350$^{5}$* | ***Chingachgook (60)*** (PWHarris) **2-8-6** GHind(10) (Withdrawn not under Starter's orders: tried to break out & damaged stall) | | **W** | 12/1 | — | — |

(SP 133.3%) **16 Rn**

**1m 17.4** (3.10) CSF £92.34 CT £1,943.37 TOTE £12.10: £2.60 £2.00 £3.80 £8.70 (£72.30) Trio £408.60; £518.04 to Redcar 8/10/96 OWNER Manton House Syndicate (MARLBOROUGH) BRED Viking Group V and Ashford Stud

**3919 Count Roberto (USA)** looked to have plenty on here at the weights but, in the end, scored in decisive fashion in a race in which very few took a serious hand. (12/1)

**4546 Dowry**, having her second race in three days, was kept very wide from stall seventeen on the unwatered ground. Switched the width of the track soon after halfway, the winner proved much too strong in the end. (8/1)

**3512* Sparky** struggled to go the pace. Staying on at the finish, he needs seven or even a mile. (25/1)

**4546 Masterstroke** was having his second run in three days. (16/1)

**4459 Donna's Dancer (IRE)** takes plenty of stoking up. (7/1)

**2588 Rum Lad** could not go the pace early on. (16/1)

**4339 Danehill Princess (IRE)**, given some sharp reminders leaving the stalls, never picked up her bit at any stage. (11/2)

## 4587 PONTEFRACT SERIES FINAL APPRENTICE H'CAP (0-60) (3-Y.O+) (Class F)

3-15 (3-19) **1m 4f 8y** £2,856.50 (£872.00: £431.00: £210.50) Stalls: Low GOING minus 0.22 sec per fur (GF)

| | | | | SP | RR | SF |
|---|---|---|---|---|---|---|
| 2060$^{5}$ | **Howqua River (43)** (PWChapple-Hyam) **4-8-6**(7) RCody-Boutcher(10) (chsd ldrs: led 2f out: hld on towards fin) | — | **1** | 12/1 | 54 | 39 |
| 4484$^{3}$ | **Arc of The Diver (IRE) (49)** (JBerry) **3-8-9b**(3) CLowther(14) (a chsng ldrs: ev ch fnl 2f: nt qckn towards fin) | hd | **2** | 7/1$^{3}$ | 60 | 38 |
| 4483$^{7}$ | **Ashover (49)** (TDBarron) **6-9-0**(5) PFredericks(1) (lw: bhd: hmpd after 1f: gd hdwy over 1f out: styd on towards fin) | 4 | **3** | 6/1$^{2}$ | 55 | 40 |
| 4307$^{12}$ | **Strat's Legacy (43)** (DWPArbuthnot) **9-8-13** AEddery(7) (swtg: bhd: hdwy on outside over 2f out: kpt on: nvr nr to chal) | 1¼ | **4** | 7/1$^{3}$ | 47 | 32 |
| 620$^{14}$ | **Colosse (49)** (JLEyre) **4-9-0**(5) SBuckley(4) (lw: s.i.s: bhd: gd hdwy over 2f out: sn chsng ldrs: wknd over 1f out) | 2 | **5** | 12/1 | 50 | 35 |
| 3845$^{8}$ | **May King Mayhem (48)** (MrsALMKing) **3-8-11** DDenby(17) (trckd ldrs: drvn along & lost pl 5f out: styd on fnl 2f) | 3½ | **6** | 20/1 | 45 | 23 |
| 3705$^{5}$ | **Parrot's Hill (IRE) (50)** (MHTompkins) **3-8-13** GMilligan(12) (hdwy on outside 4f out: sn prom: wknd over 1f out) | 1¼ | **7** | 8/1 | 45 | 23 |

| | | | | SP | RR | SF |
|---|---|---|---|---|---|---|
| 4474[4] | **Road Racer (IRE) (53)** (MrsJRRamsden) **3-8-11**(5) ClaireWest(8) (lw: bhd: hmpd after 4f: sme hdwy over 2f out: nvr nr ldrs) | 2½ | **8** | 9/2 [1] | 45 | 23 |
| 4355[5] | **Bold Top (40)** (BSRothwell) **4-8-10b** KSked(18) (led to 2f out: sn wknd) | 7 | **9** | 9/1 | 22 | 7 |
| 4355[11] | **Never Time (IRE) (42)** (MrsVAAconley) **4-8-7**(5) TFinn(11) (s.i.s: bhd: gd hdwy 5f out: sn prom: wknd over 2f out) | 1¾ | **10** | 33/1 | 22 | 7 |
| 4455[11] | **Tee Tee Too (IRE) (40)** (MissMKMilligan) **4-8-5**(5) JennyBenson(3) (nvr nr ldrs) | 1¾ | **11** | 50/1 | 18 | 3 |
| 3852[10] | **Irish Kinsman (56)** (GHYardley) **3-9-0**(5) JFowle(2) (mid div: drvn along ½-wy: sme hdwy over 2f out: sn wknd) | ½ | **12** | 33/1 | 33 | 11 |
| 4257[11] | **Dutosky (58)** (JohnBerry) **6-10-0** GFaulkner(5) (hdwy ½-wy: sn trckng ldrs: wknd 2f out) | 3½ | **13** | 25/1 | 30 | 15 |
| *4334*[8] | **In the Money (IRE) (52)** (RHollinshead) **7-9-8** RMullen(16) (racd wd: sn pushed along: sn in tch: lost pl over 2f out) | 1¼ | **14** | 12/1 | 23 | 8 |
| 4237[5] | **Irish Sea (USA) (57)** (DNicholls) **3-9-6b[1]** JBramhill(13) (trckd ldrs tl wknd qckly 2f out: sn t.o) | 18 | **15** | 9/1 | 4 | — |
| 4437[2] | **My Millie (52)** (DWBarker) **3-9-1** JEdmunds(15) (plld hrd: sddle slipped: w ldr tl wknd qckly 4f out: t.o 2f out) | 1 | **16** | 14/1 | — | — |
| | | | | (SP 134.8%) | | **16 Rn** |

**2m 40.7** (6.40) CSF £94.97 CT £529.53 TOTE £18.10: £3.60 £1.70 £2.30 £1.70 (£65.10) Trio £224.60 OWNER Mrs Jane Chapple-Hyam (MARLBOROUGH)

WEIGHT FOR AGE 3yo-7lb

IN-FOCUS: **This was 18-year-old Cody-Boutcher's first success.**

**1472 Howqua River**, who has never really fulfilled his potential, showed more battling qualities than the runner-up. (12/1: op 7/1)

**4484 Arc of The Diver (IRE)**, almost upsides once in line for home, did not seem as keen to be giving his all in a close-run thing. (7/1)

**3968 Ashover**, who has slipped down the weights, tried to do this the hard way. Almost last three furlongs from home, he was staying on really strongly for his inexperienced rider at the line. (6/1)

**4121 Strat's Legacy** can be relied upon to run well for an inexperienced rider. (7/1)

**4474 Road Racer (IRE)**, knocked back when short of room on the bend a mile from home, stuck on in half-hearted fashion from the turn. He lacks pace and does not look 100%. (9/2)

**3865 In the Money (IRE)** (12/1: op 8/1)

## 4588 TRINIDAD & TOBAGO H'CAP (0-70) (3-Y.O+) (Class E)

3-45 (3-48) **2m 1f 22y** £3,786.75 (£1,134.00: £544.50: £249.75) Stalls: Centre GOING minus 0.22 sec per fur (GF)

| | | | | SP | RR | SF |
|---|---|---|---|---|---|---|
| 4302[8] | **Alwarqa (57)** (MDHammond) **3-8-7** JFortune(12) (lw: chsd ldrs: led over 1f out: styd on strly) | — | **1** | 20/1 | 71 | 39 |
| 2530[3] | **Lostris (IRE) (35)** (MDods) **5-7-10** NKennedy(10) (led after 3f tl over 1f out: kpt on same pce) | 3 | **2** | 25/1 | 46 | 25 |
| 4302[3] | **Great Oration (IRE) (54)** (FWatson) **7-9-1** LDettori(6) (hld up: stdy hdwy 3f out: styd on same pce appr fnl f) | ½ | **3** | 7/2 [2] | 65 | 44 |
| 4302[2] | **Shirley Sue (70)** (MJohnston) **3-9-6** JWeaver(2) (prom: hmpd & lost pl 9f out: sn drvn along: swtchd 3f out: styd on) | 2½ | **4** | 6/1 [3] | 78 | 46 |
| 4302[9] | **Star Performer (IRE) (49)** (MrsMReveley) **5-8-10** KDarley(14) (bhd: hdwy u.p 3f out: nvr rchd ldrs) | 4 | **5** | 16/1 | 54 | 33 |
| 4426[6] | **Early Peace (IRE) (55)** (MJPolglase) **4-9-2** MRimmer(8) (b.off hind: chsd ldrs: drvn along 6f out: one pce fnl 3f) | 2½ | **6** | 33/1 | 57 | 36 |
| 4506* | **He's Got Wings (IRE) (57)** (MrsJRRamsden) **3-8-7** 4x KFallon(7) (b.nr hind: bhd: hdwy u.p 4f out: nvr nr ldrs) | 2½ | **7** | 7/4 [1] | 57 | 25 |
| 4203[6] | **Mizyan (IRE) (56)** (JEBanks) **8-8-12**(5) GFaulkner(3) (lw: bhd: gd hdwy on outside 10f out: lost pl 3f out) | 8 | **8** | 14/1 | 49 | 28 |
| 4302[7] | **Keen To The Last (FR) (50)** (MDHammond) **4-8-11** JCarroll(4) (led 3f: chsd ldrs tl wknd over 2f out) | 5 | **9** | 33/1 | 38 | 17 |
| 4321[2] | **Hullbank (63)** (WWHaigh) **6-9-7**(3) PMcCabe(1) (b: lw: gd hdwy 9f out: sn trckng ldrs: wknd 2f out) | 1 | **10** | 8/1 | 50 | 29 |
| 4203[16] | **Arc Bright (IRE) (49)** (RHollinshead) **6-8-10** DeanMcKeown(5) (s.i.s: sn chsng ldrs: lost pl 3f out) | 1¾ | **11** | 25/1 | 34 | 13 |
| | **Rainelle (57)** (JWWatts) **4-9-4b[1]** NConnorton(13) (gd hdwy 10f out: sn trckng ldrs: wkng whn hmpd 3f out) | ½ | **12** | 100/1 | 42 | 21 |
| 4110[8] | **Safa (USA) (70)** (ACStewart) **3-9-6** RHills(11) (swtg: dropped rr ½-wy: n.d) | 18 | **13** | 12/1 | 38 | 6 |
| 3775[3] | **Top Prize (35)** (MBrittain) **8-7-10v** GBardwell(9) (a bhd: t.o 3f out) | 23 | **14** | 25/1 | — | — |
| | | | | (SP 127.4%) | | **14 Rn** |

**3m 47.3** (7.80) CSF £388.63 CT £1,985.72 TOTE £27.30: £7.40 £5.90 £1.70 (£358.50) Trio £255.30 OWNER Mr John Barton (MIDDLEHAM)
BRED Shadwell Estate Company Limited

LONG HANDICAP Lostris (IRE) 7-8 Top Prize 7-7

WEIGHT FOR AGE 3yo-11lb

STEWARDS' ENQUIRY Weaver susp. 16-19/10/96 (irresponsible riding). 5 days outstanding also added to current susp. 21-25/10/96

**3056 Alwarqa** proved well suited by this stout test of stamina. Showing a powerful action, she won decisively in the end and will be even better on easier ground or possibly an All-Weather surface. (20/1)

**2530 Lostris (IRE)**, having her first run for three months and 2lb wrong at the weights, was soon bowling along in front. She stuck on strongly, but the winner had her measure entering the last. (25/1)

**4302 Great Oration (IRE)** was patiently ridden as usual and stuck to the inner on the run round the home turn. When picked up, he could do no more than stick on at the same pace. (7/2)

**4302 Shirley Sue**, who is certainly being kept busy with four wins already under her belt this year, was possibly a shade unlucky not to be more closely involved in the finish. Chopped off at the halfway mark, she was soon flat out and had to switch to get an opening. Staying on at the finish, she is not finished yet. (6/1)

**4506* He's Got Wings (IRE)**, under a 4lb penalty, was possibly flattered by his Newcastle success as the leaders almost certainly went too fast. Hard at work and trying to pick up ground half a mile from home, he kept on, but was never a factor. (7/4)

## 4589 BUCCOO REEF CLAIMING STKS (3-Y.O) (Class F)

4-15 (4-17) **6f** £3,174.50 (£882.00: £423.50) Stalls: Low GOING minus 0.22 sec per fur (GF)

| | | | | SP | RR | SF |
|---|---|---|---|---|---|---|
| 4376[9] | **Ortolan (79)** (RHannon) **3-8-13** PatEddery(4) (w ldrs: rdn to ld 2f out: drvn clr fnl f) | — | **1** | 8/11 [1] | 89 | 51 |
| 4430[11] | **Standown (65)** (JBerry) **3-8-7** KDarley(1) (lw: a chsng ldrs: styd on u.p ins fnl f: no ch w wnr) | 3 | **2** | 15/2 [3] | 75 | 37 |
| 4312[27] | **Middle East (72)** (TDBarron) **3-8-12** JFortune(12) (mde most to 2f out: kpt on same pce) | 1 | **3** | 7/1 [2] | 77 | 39 |
| 4044[6] | **Little Noggins (IRE) (70)** (CADwyer) **3-7-11**(7) JoHunnam(14) (racd wd: w ldrs tl wknd over 1f out) | 2½ | **4** | 16/1 | 63 | 25 |
| 4341[13] | **Oriel Lad (58)** (DonEnricoIncisa) **3-8-3** KimTinkler(16) (mid div: styd on appr fnl f) | 2½ | **5** | 100/1 | 55 | 17 |
| 4356[22] | **Mullagh Hill Lad (IRE) (40)** (BAMcMahon) **3-8-7** SSanders(15) (lw: racd wd: trckd ldrs tl rdn & wknd 2f out) | s.h | **6** | 50/1 | 59 | 21 |
| 4486[12] | **Hoh Majestic (IRE) (56)** (MartynWane) **3-8-0v**(3) FLynch(7) (sme hdwy 2f out: nvr nr to chal) | 1¾ | **7** | 16/1 | 50 | 12 |
| 4341[12] | **River Tern (73)** (JBerry) **3-8-2v**(5) PRoberts(10) (b: trckd ldrs: effrt 2f out: nt r.o) | 1½ | **8** | 14/1 | 50 | 12 |
| | **Bairn Atholl** (RJHodges) **3-8-1**ow1 SDrowne(2) (neat: s.i.s: bhd tl sme hdwy appr fnl f) | ½ | **9** | 50/1 | 43 | 4 |
| 4428[11] | **Scathebury (57)** (KRBurke) **3-8-7b** KFallon(17) (swtchd lft s: nvr nr ldrs) | hd | **10** | 20/1 | 49 | 11 |

| | | | Pos | SP | RR | SF |
|---|---|---|---|---|---|---|
| | **Sarasota Ryde** (JEBanks) **3-7-11**$^{(7)}$ RMullen(9) (unf: n.d) | 1¼ | **11** | 33/1 | 42 | 4 |
| $4206^{21}$ | **Branston Danni (61)** (MrsJRRamsden) **3-7-13** JQuinn(6) (b.nr hind: nvr nr ldrs) | ½ | **12** | 14/1 | 36 | — |
| $2392^{5}$ | **The Frisky Farmer (67)** (WGMTurner) **3-8-0**$^{(7)}$ DMcGaffin(5) (lw: w ldrs tl wknd 2f out) | ½ | **13** | 20/1 | 43 | 5 |
| $4221^{8}$ | **Miss Walsh** (CBBBooth) **3-7-12** LCharnock(13) (a outpcd) | 2½ | **14** | 33/1 | 27 | — |
| $3970^{17}$ | **Forecast (45)** (JWharton) **3-8-4** DeanMcKeown(18) (a bhd) | ½ | **15** | 100/1 | 32 | — |
| $3937^{3}$ | **Doug's Folly (42)** (MWEasterby) **3-8-2b** JFanning(3) (s.s: bhd: nt clr run on ins 2f out: n.d) | hd | **16** | 25/1 | 29 | — |
| $3957^{7}$ | **Orange And Blue (33)** (MissJFCraze) **3-8-6** AMcGlone(8) (a rr div) | 2½ | **17** | 100/1 | 27 | — |
| $4453^{15}$ | **Oh Whataknight (70)** (JWHills) **3-8-4** RHills(11) (a outpcd & bhd) | 11 | **18** | 20/1 | — | — |

(SP 138.2%) **18 Rn**

**1m 16.4** (2.10) CSF £8.55 TOTE £1.70: £1.30 £2.40 £2.20 (£10.50) Trio £11.20 OWNER J. Lazzari (MARLBOROUGH) BRED Filletts Farm Stud
Ortolan clmd Diamond Racing Ltd. £14,000

**4198 Ortolan** won his fifth race of this type this season. He had to be really rousted along to take charge, but is equally effective over six and seven. (8/11: op Evens)

**3140 Standown** bounced back, sticking on under pressure to finish second best. (15/2)

**3844 Middle East**, who was badly drawn in the Silver Cup at Ayr, showed plenty of toe to lead them for four furlongs. (7/1: op 4/1)

**443* Little Noggins (IRE)**, poorly drawn, showed plenty of speed, but ran out of gas coming to the final furlong. She is probably better suited by five. (16/1)

## 4590 MARAVAL H'CAP (0-80) (3-Y.O) (Class D)

4-45 (4-48) **1m 4y** £5,526.50 (£1,652.00: £791.00: £360.50) Stalls: Low GOING minus 0.22 sec per fur (GF)

| | | | Pos | SP | RR | SF |
|---|---|---|---|---|---|---|
| 4436* | **Mels Baby (IRE) (58)** (JLEyre) **3-8-0** TWilliams(3) (lw: trckd ldrs: nt clr run on ins over 1f out: squeezed thro & r.o wl to ld towards fin) | — | **1** | 8/1 | 68 | 30 |
| $4387^{2}$ | **No Cliches (73)** (GLewis) **3-9-1b** PatEddery(2) (led over 6f out: hrd rdn & edgd rt fnl f: jst ct) | nk | **2** | 7/2 $^{1}$ | 82 | 44 |
| $4296^{5}$ | **Scenicris (IRE) (60)** (RHollinshead) **3-7-13**$^{(3)ow5}$ FLynch(5) (hdwy over 2f out: styd on strly ins fnl f) | hd | **3** | 25/1 | 69 | 26 |
| $4214^{5}$ | **Blessed Spirit (78)** (CFWall) **3-9-6** SSanders(7) (swtg: hld up: hdwy & nt clr run over 1f out: styd on wl ins fnl f) | nk | **4** | 7/1 | 87 | 49 |
| 4053* | **Sharp Shuffle (IRE) (72)** (RHannon) **3-9-0** RHughes(8) (trckd ldrs: ev ch 2f out: styd on same pce fnl f) | hd | **5** | 8/1 | 80 | 42 |
| 4354* | **Maid For Baileys (IRE) (79)** (MJohnston) **3-9-7** JWeaver(10) (led over 1f: ev ch 2f out: wknd jst ins fnl f) | 2 | **6** | 6/1 $^{3}$ | 83 | 45 |
| $4214^{8}$ | **Marjaana (IRE) (67)** (PTWalwyn) **3-8-9v**$^{1}$ RHills(12) (hdwy & nt clr run over 1f out: kpt on: nvr rchd ldrs) | ½ | **7** | 14/1 | 70 | 32 |
| $4240^{10}$ | **Ivor's Deed (54)** (CFWall) **3-7-10** NCarlisle(9) (lw: bhd: sme hdwy over 2f out: nvr nr to chal) | 2½ | **8** | 11/1 | 52 | 14 |
| $4337^{2}$ | **Missile Toe (IRE) (60)** (JEBanks) **3-8-2** NDay(4) (lw: hdwy ½-wy: effrt over 2f out: sn wknd) | 1½ | **9** | 5/1 $^{2}$ | 55 | 17 |
| $4226^{17}$ | **Falcon's Flame (USA) (54)** (MrsJRRamsden) **3-7-10** JQuinn(6) (trckd ldrs tl grad wknd fnl 2f) | ½ | **10** | 20/1 | 48 | 10 |
| $3986^{9}$ | **Flaming June (USA) (67)** (HRACecil) **3-8-9** WRyan(11) (in tch: effrt over 2f out: sn wknd) | 8 | **11** | 10/1 | 46 | 8 |
| *$4336^{12}$* | **Alaska (62)** (MGMeagher) **3-8-4b** JFanning(1) (hld up & plld hrd: a bhd) | ¾ | **12** | 100/1 | 39 | 1 |

(SP 121.6%) **12 Rn**

**1m 45.3** (3.80) CSF £34.93 CT £630.12 TOTE £9.80: £2.50 £1.80 £5.00 (£18.90) Trio £178.10 OWNER Mr John Roberts (Wakefield) (HAMBLETON) BRED A. F. O'Callaghan
LONG HANDICAP Falcon's Flame (USA) 7-9

**4436* Mels Baby (IRE)**, from just a 2lb higher mark, had to sit and suffer on the inside until an opening appeared with the leader coming off the fence. He showed the right sort of spirit to squeeze through and get up near the line. He would have been a very unlucky loser. (8/1)

**4387 No Cliches** came off the rail under strong pressure, leaving the door open for the winner to come through. (7/2)

**3866 Scenicris (IRE)** seemed to run easily his best race, making great strides inside the last. (25/1)

**4214 Blessed Spirit** seems to find plenty of trouble. Having to wait for an opening, she was staying on in good style at the line. (7/1)

**4053* Sharp Shuffle (IRE)**, raised 5lb, could find no more under pressure in the final furlong. (8/1)

**4354* Maid For Baileys (IRE)**, 4lb higher, could not dominate on this occasion and faded just inside the last. (6/1)

**2729 Marjaana (IRE)**, in a visor for the first time, was another to have no luck in running. (14/1)

## 4591 CARONI MAIDEN STKS (3-Y.O) (Class D)

5-15 (5-16) **1m 4y** £3,988.75 (£1,210.00: £592.50: £283.75) Stalls: Low GOING minus 0.22 sec per fur (GF)

| | | | Pos | SP | RR | SF |
|---|---|---|---|---|---|---|
| | **Canyon Creek (IRE)** (JHMGosden) **3-9-0** LDettori(10) (unf: lw: trckd ldrs: shkn up over 2f out: led 1f out: sn qcknd clr: eased towards fin) | — | **1** | 11/8 $^{1}$ | 86+ | 49 |
| $4124^{6}$ | **Yukon Hope (USA) (73)** (RCharlton) **3-8-9** TSprake(14) (trckd ldrs: led over 1f out: sn hdd: no ch w wnr) | 2 | **2** | 16/1 | 77 | 40 |
| $4124^{3}$ | **Axford (USA) (82)** (PWChapple-Hyam) **3-8-11**$^{(3)}$ RHavlin(13) (w ldr: led over 3f out tl over 1f out: kpt on same pce) | 1 | **3** | 6/1 $^{3}$ | 80 | 43 |
| $4360^{4}$ | **Family Man** (JRFanshawe) **3-9-0** DHarrison(2) (trckd ldrs: effrt over 2f out: kpt on same pce) | 2½ | **4** | 9/2 $^{2}$ | 75 | 38 |
| $4379^{5}$ | **Brother Roy** (TGMills) **3-9-0** JFortune(5) (s.s: hdwy to chse ldrs ½-wy: drvn along 3f out: no imp) | 2½ | **5** | 20/1 | 70 | 33 |
| $4044^{5}$ | **Alpine Hideaway (IRE) (76)** (BHanbury) **3-9-0** JStack(3) (a chsng ldrs: drvn along over 3f out: one pce) | 1¼ | **6** | 11/1 | 68 | 31 |
| $4429^{7}$ | **Winnebago** (CWThornton) **3-8-9** DeanMcKeown(8) (effrt over 3f out: kpt on fnl 2f: n.d) | 6 | **7** | 33/1 | 51 | 14 |
| $3839^{3}$ | **State of Caution (85)** (JLDunlop) **3-9-0b**$^{1}$ PatEddery(11) (b: hld up: hdwy 3f out: shkn up over 1f out: nt r.o) | 2½ | **8** | 6/1 $^{3}$ | 51 | 14 |
| $4456^{3}$ | **Beano Script** (MissSEHall) **3-9-0** MBirch(1) (bhd: effrt over 2f out: nvr nr ldrs) | 1½ | **9** | 25/1 | 48 | 11 |
| $2181^{7}$ | **Great Chief** (HRACecil) **3-9-0** WRyan(12) (rr div: effrt 3f out: wknd over 1f out) | 1 | **10** | 9/1 | 46 | 9 |
| | **Ostia** (MrsJCecil) **3-8-9** KDarley(9) (plld hrd: led tl over 3f out: wkng whn n.m.r 2f out) | ¾ | **11** | 33/1 | 39 | 2 |
| $3973^{16}$ | **Surf City (60)** (WWHaigh) **3-8-11**$^{(3)}$ PMcCabe(4) (hld up & plld hrd: a bhd) | 3½ | **12** | 100/1 | 37 | — |
| $4297^{8}$ | **Sing And Dance (47)** (EWeymes) **3-8-9** KFallon(6) (sn outpcd & pushed along: a in rr) | nk | **13** | 100/1 | 32 | — |
| | **Dunston Star (IRE)** (PJBevan) **3-9-0** NCarlisle(7) (cmpt: bkwd: sn bhd & drvn along: t.o fnl 3f) | 24 | **14** | 66/1 | — | — |

(SP 131.0%) **14 Rn**

**1m 44.7** (3.20) CSF £25.72 TOTE £2.30: £1.60 £3.30 £1.50 (£20.40) Trio £27.80 OWNER Sheikh Mohammed (NEWMARKET) BRED Sheikh Mohammed bin Rashid al Maktoum

**Canyon Creek (IRE)** lacks size and substance and has noticeably small feet. Showing a sharp action, he had to be shaken up, but quickened clear to score in impressive fashion in the end. (11/8)

**4124 Yukon Hope (USA)** left her poor effort at Epsom behind her, but had met a tartar in the winner. (16/1)

**4124 Axford (USA)** is certainly proving hard to win with. (6/1)

**4360 Family Man**, tucked away on the inner, was by no means knocked about. Now he is qualified for a handicap mark, he can be expected to do better. (9/2)

T/Jkpt: Not won; £5,991.22 to Redcar 8/10/96. T/Plpt: £271.20 (79.68 Tckts). T/Qdpt: £42.20 (38.2 Tckts). WG

## 4454-**REDCAR** (L-H) (Good to firm, Firm patches)
## Tuesday October 8th

WEATHER: sunny WIND: almost nil

### 4592 GUISBOROUGH MAIDEN STKS (3-Y.O) (Class D)

2-15 (2-16) **6f** £4,003.00 (£1,204.00: £582.00: £271.00) Stalls: Centre GOING minus 0.24 sec per fur (GF)

| Form | Horse | Dist | Pos | SP | RR | SF |
|---|---|---|---|---|---|---|
| | **Volley (IRE)** (JBerry) **3-8-9** GCarter(3) (unf: hdwy ½-wy: hmpd over 2f out: led ins fnl f: r.o) | — | **1** | 10/1 | 87 | 50 |
| 4219[2] | **Wollstonecraft (IRE) (73)** (JHMGosden) **3-8-9** LDettori(14) (cl up: led ½-wy tl ins fnl f: nt qckn) | 2½ | **2** | 9/2[2] | 80 | 43 |
| 4312[23] | **Nilgiri Hills (IRE) (81)** (JLDunlop) **3-9-0** KDarley(1) (lw: sn chsng ldrs: edgd rt 3f out: ev ch 2f out: rdn & no ex) | 1 | **3** | 11/8[1] | 83 | 46 |
| 4322[3] | **Minoletti (74)** (EALDunlop) **3-9-0** KFallon(5) (b.nr hind: swtg: hld up: hdwy ½-wy: nt clr run over 2f out: styd on one pce after) | 2½ | **4** | 7/1[3] | 76 | 39 |
| | **Carreamia** (JLEyre) **3-8-9** RLappin(8) (leggy: unf: bhd: hdwy 3f out: styd on: nvr able to chal) | ½ | **5** | 33/1 | 70 | 33 |
| 4229[3] | **Gad Yakoun** (MGMeagher) **3-9-0** JFortune(12) (lw: chsd ldrs: rdn over 2f out: r.o one pce) | ¾ | **6** | 10/1 | 73 | 36 |
| 4229[W] | **Daisy Bates (IRE)** (PWHarris) **3-8-9** GHind(10) (chsd ldrs: sddle slipped: eased fnl 3f) | 1 | **7** | 8/1 | 65 | 28 |
| 4229[9] | **Bent Raiwand (USA) (62)** (DonEnricoIncisa) **3-8-9** KimTinkler(13) (b.hind: spd 3f: sn outpcd) | 5 | **8** | 100/1 | 52 | 15 |
| 3844[14] | **Merrily (63)** (MissSEHall) **3-8-4**(5) GFaulkner(11) (sn outpcd) | 5 | **9** | 12/1 | 38 | 1 |
| 4229[6] | **Dewhurst House** (WWHaigh) **3-8-9** DRMcCabe(6) (led 3f: wknd 2f out) | 1¼ | **10** | 25/1 | 35 | — |
| *4094*[6] | **Lawsimina** (MissJFCraze) **3-8-9** NConnorton(7) (swtg: bit bkwd: outpcd fr ½-wy) | nk | **11** | 33/1 | 34 | — |
| 4108[11] | **Take Notice (80)** (GHarwood) **3-9-0** AClark(9) (bhd & drvn along: n.d) | 2½ | **12** | 9/1 | 33 | — |
| 4456[7] | **Honeyhall (38)** (NBycroft) **3-8-9** ACulhane(4) (chsd ldrs: hmpd over 2f out: sn wknd) | 3½ | **13** | 100/1 | 18 | — |
| 4340[12] | **Faro Flyer** (KTIvory) **3-9-0** DBiggs(2) (b: b.hind: p.u lame ½-wy: uns rdr: dead) | | **P** | 100/1 | — | — |

(SP 132.5%) **14 Rn**

**1m 11.8** (1.60) CSF £56.09 TOTE £19.80: £3.90 £2.00 £1.10 (£44.20) Trio £41.00 OWNER Three Shires Racing (COCKERHAM) BRED Rathduff Stud

STEWARDS' ENQUIRY Darley susp. 17 & 21/10/96 (careless riding)

**OFFICIAL EXPLANATION Daisy Bates IIRE): the saddle slipped forward in the early stages, as a result her jockey was unable to ride her out as vigorously as he would have liked.**

**Volley (IRE)**, making her debut, won a poor race, but did it well, and should improve further. (10/1)

**4219 Wollstonecraft (IRE)**, taken to post early as usual, had her chances but was short of a change of gear. (9/2)

**3446 Nilgiri Hills (IRE)** has plenty of ability but, tending to hang right, failed to come up with the goods yet again. (11/8)

**4322 Minoletti**, a very sweaty individual, takes a strong hold and obviously has more ability should he ever settle down. (7/1)

**Carreamia** has not got a lot to recommend her on looks, but she obviously has ability, and she made useful progress in the second half of the race. (33/1)

**4229 Gad Yakoun** showed useful speed, but his limitations were well exposed approaching the final furlong. (10/1: 12/1-8/1)

**4074 Daisy Bates (IRE)**, taken to post early, looked to be having trouble with her saddle on the way down and it certainly slipped on the way back. She was eased considerably from halfway. (8/1)

### 4593 E.B.F. PICKERING MAIDEN STKS (2-Y.O F) (Class D)

2-45 (2-50) **6f** £3,834.00 (£1,152.00: £556.00: £258.00) Stalls: Centre GOING minus 0.24 sec per fur (GF)

| Form | Horse | Dist | Pos | SP | RR | SF |
|---|---|---|---|---|---|---|
| 4357[5] | **Tycoon Girl (IRE)** (BJMeehan) **2-8-11** BDoyle(3) (lw: s.i.s: sn rcvrd & cl up: led 2f out: r.o) | — | **1** | 5/1[3] | 73 | 38 |
| 4446[4] | **Plaisir d'Amour (IRE)** (NACallaghan) **2-8-11** LDettori(7) (a.p: effrt over 2f out: wandered u.p: nt pce of wnr) | 2½ | **2** | 15/8[2] | 66 | 31 |
| 3773[4] | **Splashed** (TDBarron) **2-8-11** JFortune(1) (chsd ldrs: rdn & nt qckn fnl 2f) | 1 | **3** | 20/1 | 64 | 29 |
| 3756[4] | **Santa Rosa (IRE)** (JLDunlop) **2-8-11** KDarley(5) (prom: rdn 2f out: sn btn) | 3½ | **4** | 5/4[1] | 54 | 19 |
| 4318[6] | **Come Dancing** (MJohnston) **2-8-11** MRoberts(8) (lw: led: edgd lft: hdd 2f out: sn btn) | 2 | **5** | 16/1 | 49 | 14 |
| 3593[19] | **Flood's Hot Stuff** (MRChannon) **2-8-11** AClark(6) (chsd ldrs over 3f: sn outpcd) | 4 | **6** | 25/1 | 38 | 3 |
| 4454[6] | **Gollaccia** (GMMoore) **2-8-11** JTate(4) (sn outpcd & wl bhd: sme late hdwy) | 1¾ | **7** | 100/1 | 34 | — |

(SP 111.4%) **7 Rn**

**1m 12.8** (2.60) CSF £14.00 TOTE £6.80: £1.10 £2.20 (£4.80) OWNER Mr F. C. T. Wilson (UPPER LAMBOURN) BRED Ballinacurra Stud

**4357 Tycoon Girl (IRE)** took the eye in the paddock and won nicely, continuing her stable's brilliant run with juveniles. (5/1)

**4446 Plaisir d'Amour (IRE)** looked well enough but, when it came down to a struggle, she was inclined to hang off a true line and did not possess a turn of foot. (15/8: Evens-2/1)

**3773 Splashed** ran a fine race, but just failed to pick up in the last two furlongs, and is still learning. (20/1)

**3756 Santa Rosa (IRE)** looks weak as yet and proved disappointing when asked for an effort. (5/4)

**4318 Come Dancing** is only small and lightly-made and obviously has problems as she was taken to post early. Always inclined to hang, she soon packed it in when passed two furlongs out. (16/1)

**Gollaccia** could not go early on yet again and obviously needs further. (100/1)

### 4594 MALTON CLAIMING STKS (2-Y.O) (Class F)

3-15 (3-17) **7f** £3,120.00 (£870.00: £420.00) Stalls: Centre GOING minus 0.24 sec per fur (GF)

| Form | Horse | Dist | Pos | SP | RR | SF |
|---|---|---|---|---|---|---|
| 4303[4] | **Eurolink Spartacus (79)** (JLDunlop) **2-9-2** LDettori(11) (lw: a.p: led over 1f out: pushed along & rdn out) | — | **1** | 11/8[1] | 81 | 42 |
| 4364[7] | **River of Fortune (IRE) (73)** (MHTompkins) **2-8-6**(5) GFaulkner(5) (cl up: led over 2f out tl over 1f out: kpt on) | 1½ | **2** | 100/30[2] | 73 | 34 |
| 4319[6] | **Italian Symphony (IRE) (72)** (MJohnston) **2-9-2b[1]** KDarley(7) (lw: trckd ldrs: disp ld & hung lft over 1f out: nt qckn) | ¾ | **3** | 14/1 | 76 | 37 |
| 4244[5] | **Rivonia (USA) (62)** (MrsJRRamsden) **2-8-1** SSanders(8) (in tch: effrt & n.m.r over 1f out: styd on one pce) | 1 | **4** | 6/1[3] | 59 | 20 |
| 4250[5] | **Murron Wallace** (RMWhitaker) **2-8-3** FNorton(1) (in tch: nt clr run & swtchd over 1f out: nvr able to chal) | 3½ | **5** | 12/1 | 53 | 14 |
| 4495[7] | **Silent Valley (55)** (BJMeehan) **2-8-3b** BDoyle(2) (led tl over 2f out: grad wknd) | 1¼ | **6** | 16/1 | 50 | 11 |
| 4562[13] | **Petrine Gray (53)** (TDEasterby) **2-8-1** DRMcCabe(19) (styd on fnl 2f: nrst fin) | ¾ | **7** | 25/1 | 46 | 7 |
| 4501[6] | **Maremma (64)** (DonEnricoIncisa) **2-7-13** KimTinkler(16) (s.i.s: styd on wl fnl 2f) | 1¼ | **8** | 100/1 | 41 | 2 |
| 4298[8] | **Jack Says (56)** (TDEasterby) **2-8-8b[1]** MBirch(17) (effrt ½-wy: nvr rchd ldrs) | ¾ | **9** | 16/1 | 48 | 9 |
| 4347[3] | **Ibn Masirah** (MrsMReveley) **2-8-7**(5) SCopp(15) (bhd tl stdy late hdwy) | s.h | **10** | 20/1 | 52 | 13 |
| 4244[9] | **Pupil Master (IRE)** (DenysSmith) **2-8-8** LCharnock(10) (bit bkwd: bhd: sme hdwy 2f out: n.d) | nk | **11** | 25/1 | 48 | 9 |
| *4331*[8] | **Digital Option (IRE)** (PRWebber) **2-9-2** KFallon(18) (bit bkwd: nvr nr to chal) | nk | **12** | 25/1 | 55 | 16 |

| | | | | | | |
|---|---|---|---|---|---|---|
| 2422[5] | **Captain Flint** (ASmith) **2-8-4** DeanMcKeown(12) (s.i.s: n.d) | ¾ | **13** | 200/1 | 41 | 2 |
| 4207[6] | **Oddfellows Girl (40)** (NBycroft) **2-8-1** JFanning(9) (sn drvn along: outpcd fr ½-wy) | 1¾ | **14** | 100/1 | 34 | — |
| 4347[10] | **Hurgill King (IRE)** (JWWatts) **2-8-10** GHind(14) (s.i.s: a bhd) | 1½ | **15** | 100/1 | 40 | 1 |
| 4501[8] | **Kitty Galore (IRE) (56)** (MDods) **2-8-5** RLappin(6) (prom 4f) | 9 | **16** | 50/1 | 14 | — |
| | **Bold Engagement** (MDods) **2-8-7** NKennedy(3) (dipped backed: outpcd & bhd fr ½-wy) | 3 | **17** | 50/1 | 9 | — |
| 3769[5] | **Norbreck House (53)** (JBerry) **2-9-0b[1]** GCarter(13) (sn w ldrs: wknd 2½f out) | 4 | **18** | 33/1 | 7 | — |
| | **Eurolink Rascal (IRE)** (RAkehurst) **2-9-2** RCochrane(20) (leggy: unf: shkn up ½-wy: sn bhd) | 5 | **19** | 16/1 | — | — |
| 4343[W] | **Cantsaynowt (40)** (RMMcKellar) **2-7-10**(7) JMcAuley(4) (chsd ldrs to ½-wy: wknd qckly) | 16 | **20** | 200/1 | — | — |

(SP 138.6%) **20 Rn**

**1m 26.1** (3.10) CSF £7.15 TOTE £2.40: £1.40 £1.50 £4.30 (£4.60) Trio £8.10 OWNER Eurolink Group Plc (ARUNDEL) BRED A. G. Antoniades
Eurolink Spartacus clmd KBjorning £10,000

**4303 Eurolink Spartacus** won this nicely, but was not doing a lot in front and had his ears pricked all the way to the line. There is plenty more to come if he can be persuaded. (11/8)

**4224 River of Fortune (IRE)** helped force the pace and plugged on when headed, but was always well held. Surely her luck will change. (100/30)

**4319 Italian Symphony (IRE)** had the blinkers on for the first time and it made a difference, but he still refused to go through with it. (14/1)

**4244 Rivonia (USA)** had her chances, but was short of both pace and room at a vital stage. (6/1)

**4250 Murron Wallace** ran as though he is gradually getting the hang of things. (12/1)

**4207 Silent Valley**, having her second run in the blinkers, went to post keenly and raced in similar fashion, but found little when tackled. (16/1)

**1845 Maremma** ran reasonably, but this combination has been without success for some considerable time. (100/1)

## 4595 CASTLETON CONDITIONS STKS (3-Y.O+) (Class C)

3-45 (3-45) **7f** £4,829.40 (£1,794.60: £867.30: £361.50: £150.75: £66.45) Stalls: Centre GOING minus 0.24 sec per fur (GF)

| | | | | SP | RR | SF |
|---|---|---|---|---|---|---|
| 4445[7] | **Darling Flame (USA) (101)** (JHMGosden) **3-8-7** LDettori(4) (lw: trckd ldrs gng wl: hdwy on bit to ld wl ins fnl f: v.cleverly) | — | **1** | 3/1[2] | 100+ | 54 |
| 4169a[2] | **Monaassib (107)** (EALDunlop) **5-9-6** KFallon(3) (b.hind: led tl wl ins fnl f: no ch w wnr) | ½ | **2** | 15/8[1] | 110 | 66 |
| 2844a[7] | **General Academy (IRE)** (PAKelleway) **3-8-12** MRoberts(2) (in tch: swtchd & effrt 2f out: hung lft: styd on wl towards fin) | 1¼ | **3** | 7/1 | 101 | 55 |
| 4444[25] | **Hi Nod (102)** (MJCamacho) **6-9-0** LCharnock(6) (lw: chsd ldrs: pushed along 3f out: r.o one pce) | hd | **4** | 3/1[2] | 101 | 57 |
| 4485[2] | **King of Peru (101)** (APJarvis) **3-8-12** RCochrane(5) (hld up: effrt over 2f out: rdn & nt qckn) | 1 | **5** | 6/1[3] | 99 | 53 |
| 4444[23] | **Mountgate (75)** (MPBielby) **4-9-0** DRMcCabe(1) (w ldr tl outpcd fnl 2f) | 11 | **6** | 100/1 | 73 | 29 |

(SP 112.6%) **6 Rn**

**1m 24.4** (1.40) CSF £8.78 TOTE £3.60: £1.60 £1.10 (£4.90) OWNER Sheikh Mohammed (NEWMARKET) BRED Darley Stud Management Inc
WEIGHT FOR AGE 3yo-2lb

OFFICIAL EXPLANATION **Highland Fizz: accounting for the apparent improvement in form, the rider stated that his instructions were to ride the filly in a handy position, and that the more trouble she found the better she appeared to go. Her trainer added that the filly had shown a tendency to be ingenuine in her earlier races.**

**674 Darling Flame (USA)** was short of room for much of the trip, but Dettori refused to panic. When a gap finally appeared, she cruised through on the bridle and could have won by a street. She has really come good and should be followed. (3/1)

**4169a Monaassib** tried hard to make all but the winner was laughing at him throughout the final furlong. (15/8)

**2844a General Academy (IRE)** takes some riding as he is a big colt who tends to hang left, but he was making useful progress at the end. There is obviously plenty of ability there. (7/1)

**4194 Hi Nod** was off the bit some way out, but he did keep battling on, albeit in vain. (3/1)

**4485 King of Peru** tried to come from off the pace but, when put into the race, was never doing enough. (6/1)

**3445 Mountgate** had too much on in this company. (100/1)

## 4596 BEVERLEY H'CAP (0-80) (3-Y.O+) (Class D)

4-15 (4-16) **1m 6f 19y** £3,951.00 (£1,188.00: £574.00: £267.00) Stalls: Low GOING minus 0.24 sec per fur (GF)

| | | | | SP | RR | SF |
|---|---|---|---|---|---|---|
| 4321[11] | **Highfield Fizz (43)** (CWFairhurst) **4-7-10** LCharnock(7) (hld up & bhd: hdwy whn bmpd over 2f out: styd on wl to ld wl ins fnl f) | — | **1** | 100/1 | 50 | 32 |
| 4227[4] | **Totem Dancer (68)** (JLEyre) **3-8-12** RLappin(5) (hld up: nt clr run over 2f out: swtchd appr fnl f: fin fast) | nk | **2** | 9/2[3] | 75 | 48 |
| 4374[2] | **Snow Falcon (65)** (MBell) **3-8-4**(5) GFaulkner(3) (trckd ldrs: led on bit appr fnl f: sn rdn: hdd & nt qckn wl ins fnl f) | nk | **3** | 11/4[1] | 71 | 44 |
| 4447[18] | **Sea Victor (75)** (JLHarris) **4-10-0** BDoyle(4) (hld up: effrt over 3f out: styd on strly towards fin) | hd | **4** | 8/1 | 81 | 63 |
| 4483[9] | **Pharly Dancer (61)** (WWHaigh) **7-9-0** DRMcCabe(1) (mde most tl hdd & wknd appr fnl f) | 2½ | **5** | 12/1 | 64 | 46 |
| 3486[4] | **Double Agent (73)** (MJohnston) **3-9-3** MRoberts(8) (lw: cl up: chal 4f out: wknd fnl 2f) | 2 | **6** | 4/1[2] | 74 | 47 |
| 4426[5] | **Hoofprints (IRE) (62)** (GHarwood) **3-8-6** AClark(2) (lw: prom: effrt whn hmpd over 2f out: one pce) | 2 | **7** | 11/1 | 61 | 34 |
| 4506[2] | **Forgie (IRE) (63)** (PCalver) **3-8-7** MBirch(9) (chsd ldrs tl wknd over 2f out) | 6 | **8** | 4/1[2] | 55 | 28 |
| | **Ralitsa (IRE) (62)** (MDHammond) **4-9-1** JFortune(6) (bhd: hdwy appr st: wknd fnl 3f) | 5 | **9** | 16/1 | 48 | 30 |

(SP 118.9%) **9 Rn**

**3m 4.7** (5.40) CSF £462.35 CT £1,566.72 TOTE £94.00: £11.80 £1.80 £1.80 (£110.60) Trio £290.50 OWNER Mrs P. J. Taylor-Garthwaite (MIDDLEHAM) BRED K. and P. J. Garthwaite
LONG HANDICAP Highfield Fizz 7-3
WEIGHT FOR AGE 3yo-9lb

**3402 Highfield Fizz**, in a messy race, produced a run to settle it late on. This did though look the sort of event in which there would have been a different result were it run every day of the week. (100/1)

**4227 Totem Dancer** should have won this, but got into all sorts of trouble and only got out when it was too late. (9/2)

**4374 Snow Falcon** looked to be hacking up for much of the trip but, when sent on, proved disappointing under pressure. (11/4)

**3266* Sea Victor**, showing his first signs of form for a while, finished in useful style and looks worth keeping in mind. (8/1)

**3309 Pharly Dancer** gets very warm before his races these days, but he still ran quite well here. (12/1)

**3486 Double Agent** raced with every chance, but was tapped for toe, and may need further. (4/1: 3/1-9/2)

**4426 Hoofprints (IRE)** had a barging match with the winner over two furlongs out and lacked the pace to get out of trouble. (11/1)

## 4597 SCARBOROUGH H'CAP (0-70) (3-Y.O+) (Class E)

4-45 (4-48) **1m 1f** £3,377.50 (£1,015.00: £490.00: £227.50) Stalls: Centre GOING minus 0.24 sec per fur (GF)

| | | | | SP | RR | SF |
|---|---|---|---|---|---|---|
| 4307[15] | **Your Most Welcome (54)** (DJSffrenchDavis) **5-8-11**(5) GParkin(8) (bhd & pushed along 5f out: hdwy over 2f out: r.o to ld ins fnl f) | — | **1** | 20/1 | 65 | 44 |

4438[6] **Spanish Verdict (62)** (DenysSmith) **9-9-10** KFallon(5) (lw: chsd ldrs: led 1½f out tl ins fnl f: kpt on) ..............1¼ **2** 12/1[3] 71 50
4436[3] **Cee-Jay-Ay (53)** (JBerry) **9-8-10**(5) PRoberts(7) (s.i.s: hdwy 3f out: r.o towards fin) ..........................................hd **3** 8/1[2] 62 41
4256[6] **Onefortheditch (USA) (65)** (JHMGosden) **3-9-9** LDettori(10) (trckd ldrs: ev ch ins fnl f: r.o one pce) .............hd **4** 2/1[1] 73 48
4438[4] **Essayeffsee (60)** (MrsMReveley) **7-9-8** KDarley(4) (hdwy 4f out: n.m.r 2f out: styd on u.p) ............................2½ **5** 8/1[2] 64 43
3974[3] **Advance East (56)** (MDods) **4-9-4** JFortune(9) (bhd: hdwy u.p 3f out: nrst fin) ...............................................1¾ **6** 16/1 57 36
4240[2] **Eurobox Boy (56)** (APJarvis) **3-9-0** RCochrane(3) (lw: prom: nt clr run over 2f out: r.o one pce) .....................hd **7** 8/1[2] 57 32
4439[9] **Spanish Stripper (USA) (54)** (MCChapman) **5-8-13**(3) PMcCabe(2) (hld up & bhd: hdwy 3f out: nvr rchd ldrs) ..........nk **8** 33/1 54 33
4470[5] **Bulsara (60)** (CWFairhurst) **4-9-8** DeanMcKeown(11) (in tch: hdwy & ev ch 2f out: wknd appr fnl f)...............1¼ **9** 14/1 58 37
4559[9] **Vanadium Ore (60)** (JLEyre) **3-9-4v** TWilliams(13) (mid div: hrd drvn over 3f out: no imp) .............................½ **10** 25/1 57 32
4436[8] **Dispol Gem (64)** (GROldroyd) **3-9-3**(5) GFaulkner(14) (cl up: led wl over 2f out tl over 1f out: wknd)..............nk **11** 14/1 61 36
4436[2] **Awesome Venture (50)** (MCChapman) **6-8-12** DRMcCabe(12) (plld hrd: cl up tl wknd fnl 2½f) ..................1½ **12** 12/1[3] 44 23
4354[4] **Absolute Utopia (USA) (65)** (NEBerry) **3-9-6**(3) DarrenMoffatt(6) (swtg: unruly leaving paddock: prom tl wknd appr fnl 3f)..........3 **13** 14/1 54 29
4436[5] **Squared Away (49)** (JWPayne) **4-8-11b** AClark(16) (lw: bhd & bmpd ent st: hrd drvn & n.d) ........................1¼ **14** 8/1[2] 35 14
4472[2] **Western Venture (IRE) (54)** (RMMcKellar) **3-8-12** SSanders(1) (led tl hdd & wknd wl over 2f out).................3½ **15** 14/1 34 9
3961[9] **Khabar (61)** (RBastiman) **3-9-0**(5) HBastiman(15) (a bhd)...........................................................8 **16** 14/1 27 2
(SP 143.9%) **16 Rn**

**1m 53.8** (4.00) CSF £250.42 CT £1,949.36 TOTE £86.70: £19.30 £3.90 £4.00 £1.70 (£1,396.60) Trio £562.50; £633.90 to York 9/10/96
OWNER Mrs J. E. Lambert (UPPER LAMBOURN) BRED Collin Stud
WEIGHT FOR AGE 3yo-4lb
**319* Your Most Welcome** had a lot of running to do from early in the straight, but he answered his rider's calls and, keeping out of trouble, did it well. (20/1)
**4438 Spanish Verdict** is coming back to form, but was just tapped for foot late on. (12/1)
**4436 Cee-Jay-Ay** did his usual, finishing well after a poor start, but the effort was always too late. (8/1)
**4256 Onefortheditch (USA)** had her chances, but this lightly-made sort failed to pick up when asked. (2/1)
**4438 Essayeffsee** met with trouble in running and lacked the pace to do anything about it. (8/1)
**3974 Advance East**, a disappointing sort, was having his first run for his new stable here and, yet again, showed hints of ability. (16/1)
**4240 Eurobox Boy** was short of room at a vital stage. This effort is best ignored. (8/1)

## 4598 SETTRINGTON H'CAP (0-70) (3-Y.O) (Class E)

5-15 (5-17) **7f** £3,718.75 (£1,120.00: £542.50: £253.75) Stalls: Centre GOING minus 0.24 sec per fur (GF)

SP RR SF
2617[5] **Chirico (USA) (66)** (JHMGosden) **3-9-7** LDettori(14) (lw: hld up: hdwy 3f out: led 1f out: r.o) .........................— **1** 2/1[1] 82 63
4348[3] **The Barnsley Belle (IRE) (41)** (JLEyre) **3-7-10** TWilliams(4) (lw: cl up: led over 3f out to 1f out: kpt on)........1½ **2** 12/1 54 35
4472* **Power Game (61)** (JBerry) **3-9-2b** KDarley(8) (hdwy over 2f out: chsng ldrs over 1f out: nt qckn) .................3½ **3** 9/1 66 47
3306[7] **Too Hasty (52)** (TDEasterby) **3-8-7** MRoberts(15) (bhd tl styd on wl stands' side fnl 2f) ..............................2½ **4** 14/1 51 32
4356[3] **Ivory's Grab Hire (58)** (KTIvory) **3-8-13b** DBiggs(17) (b: chsd ldrs: wandered u.p 2f out: kpt on)...................s.h **5** 8/1[3] 57 38
4456[6] **Dona Filipa (45)** (MissLCSiddall) **3-8-0**ow4 DRMcCabe(16) (styd on fnl 2f: nrst fin).........................................nk **6** 50/1 43 20
4259* **Corniche Quest (IRE) (55)** (MRChannon) **3-8-3**(7) AEddery(18) (lw: styd on fnl 3f: nrst fin)...........................1¼ **7** 10/1 50 31
4430[6] **Double Oscar (IRE) (55)** (DNicholls) **3-8-10** AlexGreaves(7) (bmpd after 1f: nvr nr to chal) ............................3 **8** 20/1 43 24
3810[6] **Agent (60)** (JLEyre) **3-9-1** DeanMcKeown(20) (in tch stands' side: no imp fnl 3f)..............................................1¼ **9** 25/1 46 27
4259[3] **Polar Refrain (54)** (CADwyer) **3-8-9** KFallon(21) (effrt stands' side 3f out: n.d)..................................................½ **10** 4/1[2] 38 19
*4333*[4] **Rowlandsons Stud (IRE) (52)** (PBurgoyne) **3-8-0**(7) JBosley(3) (chsd ldrs over 4f)..........................................1 **11** 25/1 34 15
4550[7] **Ambassadori (USA) (60)** (CEBrittain) **3-9-1** BDoyle(13) (led to ½-wy: sn outpcd) ..............................................nk **12** 14/1 41 22
4221[5] **Morning Surprise (52)** (APJarvis) **3-8-7** RCochrane(19) (w ldrs: sn btn) ...........................................................2½ **13** 14/1 28 9
4098[16] **Oriole (43)** (NTinkler) **3-7-12** KimTinkler(12) (a outpcd) ..........................................................................nk **14** 50/1 18 —
4240[14] **Fairly Sure (IRE) (47)** (NEBerry) **3-7-13**(3) DarrenMoffatt(9) (a rr div)............................................................s.h **15** 12/1 22 3
4589[16] **Doug's Folly (42)** (MWEasterby) **3-7-11b** LCharnock(6) (in tch: chal ½-wy: wknd over 2f out)..........................2½ **16** 33/1 11 —
3333[15] **Our Albert (IRE) (55)** (JAGlover) **3-8-10** SSanders(11) (w ldrs over 4f: wknd) .................................................½ **17** 50/1 23 4
*4090*[10] **Silent System (IRE) (41)** (DWChapman) **3-7-10** NKennedy(2) (a bhd) ..............................................................¾ **18** 50/1 7 —
4240[16] **Shermood (47)** (KTIvory) **3-7-9**(7)ow6 KSked(1) (b.hind: w ldrs 4f: wknd qckly).................................................1¼ **19** 25/1 10 —
4226[19] **Firle Phantasy (55)** (PCalver) **3-8-10b**[1] MBirch(10) (prom 5f: wknd qckly).......................................................9 **20** 20/1 — —
(SP 150.8%) **20 Rn**

**1m 24.8** (1.80) CSF £31.41 CT £199.38 TOTE £3.50: £2.10 £2.20 £3.00 £2.90 (£33.70) Trio £117.40 OWNER Sheikh Mohammed (NEWMARKET) BRED Darley Stud Management Inc
LONG HANDICAP The Barnsley Belle (IRE) 7-9 Silent System (IRE) 6-13 Shermood 7-8 Dona Filipa 6-13
**2617 Chirico (USA)**, despite tending to hang left, always had the edge for speed when it mattered. (2/1)
**4348 The Barnsley Belle (IRE)** is running really well at present, but just found the winner too good in the last furlong. (12/1)
**4472* Power Game** looked a big danger two furlongs out but, when the pressure was applied, he failed to come up with the goods. (9/1)
**3102 Too Hasty**, poorly drawn, made up heaps of ground to show he still has ability if caught in the mood. (14/1)
**4356 Ivory's Grab Hire** had his chances but rather spoilt them by hanging left. (8/1: op 14/1)
**3256 Dona Filipa**, with little to recommend her previously, caught the eye here, finishing quite well. (50/1)

T/Jkpt: Not won; £10,114.32 to York 9/10/96. T/Plpt: £17.90 (948.55 Tckts). T/Qdpt: £10.80 (97.21 Tckts). AA

# 3846-WARWICK (L-H) (Firm, Good to firm fnl 8f)

## Tuesday October 8th

WEATHER: overcast with rain WIND: almost nil

## 4599 E.B.F BRINKLOW MAIDEN STKS (I) (2-Y.O C & G) (Class D)

1-30 (1-32) **7f** £3,427.50 (£752.50: £752.50: £217.50) Stalls: Low GOING minus 0.47 sec per fur (F)

SP RR SF
2702[10] **Ihtiyati (USA)** (JLDunlop) **2-8-11** TSprake(2) (hld up: smooth hdwy on ins to ld ins fnl f: r.o wl).....................— **1** 25/1 84+ 28
4451[2] **Farhan (USA)** (PTWalwyn) **2-8-11** RHills(6) (chsd ldr: led 2f out: hrd rdn & hdd ins fnl f) ..................................1½ **2** 8/13[1] 81 25
4330[13] **Rhapsody In White (IRE)** (MAJarvis) **2-8-11** PBloomfield(4) (led to 2f out: rdn & ev ch ins fnl f: nt qckn) .....d.h **2** 16/1 81 25
4383[2] **Polar Flight** (MJohnston) **2-8-11** JWeaver(10) (trckd ldrs: drvn & outpcd ent st: edgd lft over 1f out: kpt on towards fin)..........1¼ **4** 7/2[2] 78 22

| | | | | SP | RR | SF |
|---|---|---|---|---|---|---|
| 3994[9] | **Thornton (USA)** (JHMGosden) **2-8-11** JCarroll(5) (b: bit bkwd: chsd ldrs: rdn & outpcd 2f out: sltly hmpd over 1f out: styd on towards fin) | nk | 5 | 7/1[3] | 77 | 21 |
| 3615[15] | **Myosotis** (PJMakin) **2-8-11b[1]** GDuffield(1) (hld up in rr: rdn wl over 1f out: no imp) | 2½ | 6 | 66/1 | 71 | 15 |
| | **Regal Reprimand** (GLewis) **2-8-11** SWhitworth(3) (b.hind: unf: scope: bkwd: a bhd: hrd rdn over 2f out: no imp) | ¾ | 7 | 25/1 | 70 | 14 |
| | **Cold Lazarus** (RTPhillips) **2-8-11** RPerham(9) (w'like: scope: bkwd: dwlt: sn chsng ldrs: shkn up over 1f out: one pce) | nk | 8 | 50/1 | 69 | 13 |
| 4369[9] | **Tartan Party** (PFICole) **2-8-11** CRutter(8) (b.hind: a in rr: t.o) | 5 | 9 | 25/1 | 58 | 2 |
| | **Prince Jordan** (ICampbell) **2-8-11** NAdams(7) (leggy: bkwd: a bhd: t.o) | 5 | 10 | 66/1 | 46 | — |
| | **Such Presence** (KSBridgwater) **2-8-11** VSlattery(11) (leggy: lt-f: a bhd & outpcd: t.o) | 7 | 11 | 100/1 | 30 | — |
| | | | | (SP 120.0%) | **11 Rn** | |

**1m 27.0** (2.40) CSF I & F £20.10; I & R I W £160.72 TOTE £50.00: £7.20 F £1.10 R I W £3.40 (I & F £11.40; I & R I W £147.30) Trio £118.20 OWNER Mr Hamdan Al Maktoum (ARUNDEL) BRED John F. and Kirsten B. Swift

**Ihtiyati (USA)**, given plenty of time to strengthen up, came back fresh and well after almost three months off the track, and won with plenty in hand. (25/1)

**4451 Farhan (USA)**, in the same ownership as the winner but from a different stable, looked to have found a suitable opportunity to open his account but, when the race was on inside the distance, he lacked that bit of extra finishing pace to retain his lead. (8/13)

**Rhapsody In White (IRE)** performed much better than he did on his debut and showed he is heading in the right direction with a very pleasing display. He should not remain a maiden for long. (16/1)

**4383 Polar Flight**, caught a bit flat-footed turning in, was finding his stride again nearing the finish. A return to a mile could be the answer. (7/2)

**Thornton (USA)**, still not quite the finished article, stuck on really well inside the distance and should now be ready to show what he is made of. (7/1: op 3/1)

**Myosotis**, a half-brother to winning sprinter Thatcherella and fitted with blinkers for the first time, never got a look in at the leaders. He is taking time to realise what the game is all about. (66/1)

**Cold Lazarus**, a late foal who is a half-brother to a middle-distance winner, showed plenty of promise on this debut and he can only improve on this. (50/1)

## 4600 TATTERSALLS MAIDEN AUCTION STKS (2-Y.O) (Class E)

2-00 (2-04) **6f** £4,170.85 (£1,250.80: £601.90: £277.45) Stalls: Low GOING minus 0.47 sec per fur (F)

| | | | | SP | RR | SF |
|---|---|---|---|---|---|---|
| 2195[4] | **Craigievar** (JRFanshawe) **2-8-7** DHarrison(7) (lw: chsd ldrs: led over 1f out: sn clr: r.o wl) | — | 1 | 9/4[1] | 73 | 40 |
| 4050[8] | **Triple Hay** (RHannon) **2-8-9** DaneO'Neill(2) (trckd ldrs: swtchd rt & effrt over 1f out: kpt on u.p) | 2 | 2 | 8/1 | 70 | 37 |
| 4468[4] | **Forcing Bid** (SirMarkPrescott) **2-8-8** GDuffield(5) (led tl hrd rdn & hdd over 1f out: outpcd fnl f) | 3 | 3 | 6/1[3] | 61 | 28 |
| | **Risky Missile** (JEBanks) **2-8-0**ow2 NDay(14) (prom tl rdn & wknd 1f out) | 1¾ | 4 | 12/1 | 48 | 13 |
| 3796[15] | **Star Turn (IRE)** (MBell) **2-8-6** MFenton(3) (hmpd sn after s: chsd ldrs over 4f: one pce) | ½ | 5 | 20/1 | 53 | 20 |
| | **Lady Shirl (IRE)** (PMitchell) **2-8-0** JQuinn(4) (lengthy: nvr nr to chal) | 1½ | 6 | 16/1 | 43 | 10 |
| 2993[2] | **Gablesea** (BPJBaugh) **2-8-4** WLord(9) (s.i.s: sn rdn to chse ldrs: no hdwy fnl 2f) | ¾ | 7 | 4/1[2] | 45 | 12 |
| | **Wing of A Prayer** (WJarvis) **2-8-9** JReid(11) (leggy: unf: hmpd s: nvr nrr) | 1¼ | 8 | 12/1 | 46 | 13 |
| 4210[9] | **Hever Golf Lover (IRE)** (TJNaughton) **2-7-10**(3) MHenry(8) (b.hind: prom tl wknd over 1f out) | 1 | 9 | 11/1 | 34 | 1 |
| | **Ballerina's Dream** (MartynMeade) **2-7-13** NAdams(6) (leggy: lt-f: unf: s.s: a bhd) | nk | 10 | 33/1 | 33 | — |
| | **Spicetress** (JLSpearing) **2-7-9**(3) NVarley(12) (leggy: unf: bkwd: sn drvn along: a bhd & outpcd) | ½ | 11 | 33/1 | 31 | — |
| | **Inkwell** (AHide) **2-8-3** AMcGlone(10) (w'like: s.s: a bhd) | nk | 12 | 33/1 | 35 | 2 |
| | **Fleuve d'Or (IRE)** (DHaydnJones) **2-8-1** SDrowne(15) (leggy: unf: bkwd: a bhd: t.o) | 3½ | 13 | 20/1 | 23 | — |
| 4330[23] | **Isca Maiden** (PHayward) **2-7-12** CRutter(13) (a bhd & outpcd: t.o) | s.h | 14 | 66/1 | 20 | — |
| | **College Princess** (CADwyer) **2-7-8**(7)ow3 JoHunnam(1) (l-f: unf: prom to ½-wy: sn lost tch: t.o) | 4 | 15 | 25/1 | 13 | — |
| | | | | (SP 129.5%) | **15 Rn** | |

**1m 12.9** (0.90) CSF £21.32 TOTE £3.40: £1.60 £3.10 £3.00 (£16.90) Trio £17.90 OWNER Mr D. I. Russell (NEWMARKET) BRED C. R. and V. M. Withers

**2195 Craigievar**, closely-related to three winners abroad, was supported to the exclusion of the rest and the confidence was rewarded with a clear-cut success that should be the first of many. (9/4)

**Triple Hay**, lowered in class, turned in a most-improved performance and, on the strength of this, should have no trouble in winning races. (8/1)

**4468 Forcing Bid** adopted more forceful tactics over this slightly longer trip, but the winner cruised past without much trouble and his stride shortened quickly inside the final furlong. (6/1: op 4/1)

**Risky Missile** had the speed to push the pace on this debut and only called enough approaching the final furlong. (12/1: 6/1-14/1)

**Star Turn (IRE)**, short of room soon after leaving the start, recovered to track the leaders until getting left behind once in line for home. (20/1)

**Lady Shirl (IRE)**, a daughter of a middle-distance winner, found this trip too short and was only getting into her stride at the finish. (16/1)

**Wing of A Prayer**, knocked out of his stride when a rival swerved on leaving the stalls, had little hope of recovering the lost ground and this effort can be ignored. (12/1: op 6/1)

**Hever Golf Lover (IRE)** (11/1: op 5/1)

## 4601 E.B.F. BRINKLOW MAIDEN STKS (II) (2-Y.O C & G) (Class D)

2-30 (2-33) **7f** £3,427.50 (£1,020.00: £485.00: £217.50) Stalls: Low GOING minus 0.47 sec per fur (F)

| | | | | SP | RR | SF |
|---|---|---|---|---|---|---|
| 4233[4] | **Crystal Hearted** (HCandy) **2-8-11** AMcGlone(6) (lw: mde all: qcknd clr 2f out: eased towards fin) | — | 1 | 5/2[2] | 92+ | 42 |
| 4508[W] | **Burundi (IRE)** (PWChapple-Hyam) **2-8-11** JReid(8) (lw: chsd ldrs: drvn ent st: chsd wnr fnl 3f: no imp) | 1¾ | 2 | 4/1[3] | 88 | 38 |
| 4380[4] | **Royal Born** (WJarvis) **2-8-11** StephenDavies(1) (plld hrd: hld up in tch: one pce fnl 2f) | 4 | 3 | 9/4[1] | 79 | 29 |
| | **Present Chance** (BAMcMahon) **2-8-6**(5) LNewton(9) (str: scope: bkwd: in tch: kpt on appr fnl f: nt pce to chal) | 1½ | 4 | 33/1 | 75 | 25 |
| | **Ginzbourg** (JLDunlop) **2-8-11** TSprake(5) (b: scope: bkwd: s.i.s: bhd tl hdwy over 1f out: nvr nrr) | s.h | 5 | 14/1 | 75 | 25 |
| 4363[6] | **Dead Aim (IRE)** (IABalding) **2-8-11** WRyan(10) (hld up: effrt 2f out: nvr nr to chal) | ½ | 6 | 8/1 | 74 | 24 |
| | **Sharp Deed (IRE)** (PJMakin) **2-8-11** GDuffield(7) (w'like: leggy: bkwd: nvr trbld ldrs) | s.h | 7 | 12/1 | 74 | 24 |
| 4383[6] | **Wobble** (WJHaggas) **2-8-11** RMcGhin(4) (s.s: plld hrd: sddle slipped: a bhd) | ½ | 8 | 16/1 | 73 | 23 |
| | **Prix de Clermont (IRE)** (GLewis) **2-8-8**(3) AWhelan(3) (leggy: unf: chsd ldrs tl outpcd wl over 1f out) | s.h | 9 | 33/1 | 73 | 23 |
| 3701[5] | **Manwal (IRE)** (BHanbury) **2-8-11** RHills(2) (chsd wnr 4f: sn rdn & wknd: t.o) | 13 | 10 | 9/1 | 43 | — |
| | | | | (SP 126.6%) | **10 Rn** | |

**1m 25.8** (1.20) CSF £13.68 TOTE £3.50: £1.40 £1.80 £1.70 (£5.40) Trio £5.70 OWNER Mrs C. M. Poland (WANTAGE) BRED Newgate Stud Co

**4233 Crystal Hearted**, subject of some inspired support in the Ring, won this with a ton in hand. This good-looking colt looks set to go a long way. (5/2)
**Burundi (IRE)** ran over a mile on his initial outing and looked very much in need of the experience, but he knew much more this time and finished clear of the rest. (4/1: op 7/4)
**4380 Royal Born** should have found this step up in trip ideal, but he pulled too hard for his own good and could only stay on at the one pace in the dash to the line. (9/4)
**Present Chance**, carrying plenty of surplus condition for this racecourse debut, ran extremely well in what looked a hot heat. He looks sure to make the grade. (33/1)
**Ginzbourg**, a June foal from a very good family, lost his chance with a slow start, but he did show a glimpse of promise and the experience will not be lost. (14/1: 8/1-16/1)
**4363 Dead Aim (IRE)** stayed on in the closing stages, but could not get himself into the action. (8/1: tchd 12/1)
**3701 Manwal (IRE)** (9/1: 6/1-10/1)

## 4602 CHEF'S LARDER NURSERY H'CAP (0-85) (2-Y.O) (Class D)

3-00 (3-04) **1m** £4,354.15 (£1,307.20: £630.10: £291.55) Stalls: Low GOING minus 0.47 sec per fur (F)

| Form | Horse | Dist | Pos | SP | RR | SF |
|---|---|---|---|---|---|---|
| 4495[2] | **Heart Full of Soul (70)** (PFICole) **2-8-8b** PatEddery(20) (racd wd: mde all: drvn clr 2f out: unchal) | — | **1** | 4/1[1] | 76 | 37 |
| 4369[8] | **City Gambler (72)** (GCBravery) **2-8-10** MHills(8) (lw: prom: hrd rdn ent st: kpt on ins fnl f) | 1½ | **2** | 8/1[2] | 75 | 36 |
| 3880[2] | **Hello Dolly (IRE) (63)** (KRBurke) **2-8-1** StephenDavies(10) (trckd ldrs: rdn over 1f out: kpt on towards fin) | ½ | **3** | 14/1 | 65 | 26 |
| 4223* | **Scarrots (63)** (SCWilliams) **2-7-12**(3) MHenry(6) (prom: hmpd & lost pl over 3f out: rallied u.p appr fnl f) | 2½ | **4** | 14/1 | 60 | 21 |
| 4384[2] | **I Can't Remember (79)** (PDEvans) **2-9-3** JFEgan(16) (trckd ldrs: r.o one pce fnl 2f) | ½ | **5** | 10/1[3] | 75 | 36 |
| 4262[4] | **Sinecure (USA) (83)** (JHMGosden) **2-9-7** JCarroll(18) (hld up in tch: effrt over 2f out: swtchd rt wl over 1f out: kpt on) | hd | **6** | 8/1[2] | 79 | 40 |
| 4361[11] | **Princess of Hearts (70)** (BJMeehan) **2-8-8** MTebbutt(19) (prom: hrd drvn over 1f out: wknd fnl f) | ½ | **7** | 25/1 | 65 | 26 |
| 4224[4] | **Righty Ho (70)** (PTWalwyn) **2-8-8** TSprake(12) (prom tl rdn & outpcd wl over 1f out) | nk | **8** | 10/1[3] | 64 | 25 |
| 4370[8] | **Noble Hero (68)** (JJSheehan) **2-8-6** CRutter(15) (hld up: hdwy & nt clr run over 3f out: nt rcvr) | s.h | **9** | 25/1 | 62 | 23 |
| *3417*[11] | **Flotilla (79)** (SirMarkPrescott) **2-9-3** GDuffield(13) (prom over 4f: sn rdn: grad lost tch) | ½ | **10** | 12/1 | 72 | 33 |
| 4384[10] | **Skelton Sovereign (IRE) (64)** (RHollinshead) **2-7-13**(3) FLynch(14) (nvr nr to chal) | s.h | **11** | 20/1 | 57 | 18 |
| 4361[2] | **Chairmans Daughter (67)** (JPearce) **2-8-5** RHills(5) (nvr nr ldrs) | ¾ | **12** | 11/1 | 59 | 20 |
| 4349[3] | **High Extreme (IRE) (75)** (PWChapple-Hyam) **2-8-13** JReid(17) (chsd wnr tl wknd over 2f out) | s.h | **13** | 10/1[3] | 66 | 27 |
| 3943[2] | **Maraud (71)** (JLSpearing) **2-8-9** SDrowne(7) (chsd ldrs over 4f: wknd qckly) | ¾ | **14** | 20/1 | 61 | 22 |
| 4349[5] | **Mendoza (63)** (DJGMurraySmith) **2-8-1** NAdams(1) (s.s: a bhd) | s.h | **15** | 33/1 | 53 | 14 |
| 4303[11] | **Interdream (77)** (RHannon) **2-9-1** DaneO'Neill(9) (a in rr) | 1 | **16** | 20/1 | 65 | 26 |
| 4298[5] | **Dee Pee Tee Cee (IRE) (64)** (MWEasterby) **2-8-2**ow1 AMcGlone(2) (bhd fnl 3f) | ½ | **17** | 11/1 | 51 | 11 |
| 4118[5] | **Sudest (IRE) (78)** (IABalding) **2-8-11**(5) MartinDwyer(11) (lw: a bhd) | ¾ | **18** | 14/1 | 63 | 24 |
| 4188[9] | **Rosenkavalier (IRE) (67)** (LGCottrell) **2-8-5** JQuinn(4) (a bhd) | 1¼ | **19** | 20/1 | 50 | 11 |
| *4331*[7] | **Carlys Quest (73)** (JNeville) **2-8-11** RHughes(3) (b.hind: t.o whn p.u ins fnl f) | | **P** | 25/1 | — | — |
| | | | | (SP 147.4%) | | **20 Rn** |

**1m 38.0** (1.60) CSF £40.03 CT £424.98 TOTE £5.10: £1.50 £2.80 £3.30 £4.20 (£46.80) Trio £341.60 OWNER Mr Terence Shand (WHATCOMBE) BRED Stratford Place Stud
**4495 Heart Full of Soul** seemed well suited by this step up to a mile and, making doubly sure it would be a true test of stamina, had the prize sewn up from the turn into the straight. (4/1)
**4241 City Gambler** produced her best effort yet in this first handicap, staying on strongly right to the end, but she is somewhat flattered to have got so close to the winner. (8/1: op 5/1)
**3880 Hello Dolly (IRE)**, a consistent filly tackling a mile for the first time, was knuckling down to some serious work at the finish and this could prove to be her trip. (14/1)
**4223* Scarrots**, forced to take avoiding action when poised to challenge on the home turn, renewed his effort willingly and would certainly have made the frame but for that incident. (14/1)
**4384 I Can't Remember**, never far away, did not pick up when the pressure was applied entering the final quarter-mile, but he did keep staying on and, at the weights, there was no disgrace in this. (10/1: 8/1-12/1)
**4262 Sinecure (USA)** did not enjoy a trouble-free run below the distance, but he was hard at work at the time and it is doubtful if it denied him the opportunity of making the prizes. (8/1: 6/1-9/1)
**4213 Princess of Hearts** once again failed to see the trip out after being in the thick of the action from the start. (25/1)
**4224 Righty Ho** had much more use made of him this time, but he was struggling to hold on soon after entering the final quarter-mile. He will get the trip when ridden with more restraint. (10/1)
**4361 Chairmans Daughter** (11/1: 8/1-12/1)

## 4603 WROXHALL CLAIMING H'CAP (0-60) (3-Y.O+) (Class F)

3-30 (3-31) **1m 2f 169y** £3,428.20 (£955.20: £460.60) Stalls: Low GOING minus 0.47 sec per fur (F)

| Form | Horse | Dist | Pos | SP | RR | SF |
|---|---|---|---|---|---|---|
| *4107** | **Comedy River (44)** (NEBerry) **9-8-12** DaneO'Neill(6) (hld up & bhd: gd hdwy over 1f out: led wl ins fnl f: r.o wl) | — | **1** | 7/1[2] | 56 | 37 |
| *3951*[4] | **Proud Image (60)** (GMMcCourt) **4-10-0** JReid(15) (hld up: gd hdwy over 1f out: ev ch ins fnl f: r.o) | 1 | **2** | 12/1 | 71 | 52 |
| 4068[14] | **Pat's Splendour (43)** (HJCollingridge) **5-8-11** MRimmer(14) (gd hdwy over 1f out: led ins fnl f: sn hdd: unable qckn) | nk | **3** | 11/1 | 53 | 34 |
| 4455[3] | **Kevasingo (51)** (BWHills) **4-9-5b**[1] MHills(11) (a.p: led over 4f out: qcknd clr 2f out: wknd & hdd ins fnl f) | 3 | **4** | 5/1[1] | 57 | 38 |
| 4513[4] | **It'sthebusiness (55)** (SDow) **4-9-4v**(5) ADaly(3) (swtg: led over 1f: rdn 4f out: one pce fnl 2f) | ¾ | **5** | 7/1[2] | 60 | 41 |
| 3785[16] | **Back By Dawn (52)** (DRCElsworth) **3-9-0** DHarrison(9) (b.hind: prom: rdn over 3f out: wknd wl over 1f out) | 8 | **6** | 33/1 | 45 | 20 |
| 4513[18] | **Ewar Bold (60)** (KOCunningham-Brown) **3-9-8b** TSprake(4) (nvr nr to chal) | hd | **7** | 33/1 | 53 | 28 |
| 4353[5] | **Petros Pride (52)** (MJBolton) **3-9-0** PBloomfield(17) (nvr nrr) | ¾ | **8** | 33/1 | 43 | 18 |
| *4092*[12] | **Hill Farm Dancer (46)** (WMBrisbourne) **5-8-9**(5) DGriffiths(13) (dwlt: sn rcvrd: no hdwy fnl 3f) | ¾ | **9** | 16/1 | 36 | 17 |
| 4129[9] | **Ketabi (USA) (57)** (RAkehurst) **5-9-4**(7) DDenby(5) (b: swtg: nvr trbld ldrs) | nk | **10** | 12/1 | 47 | 28 |
| 3966[5] | **Chesteine (48)** (PJMakin) **3-8-10** WRyan(18) (nvr nr ldrs) | 1 | **11** | 16/1 | 36 | 11 |
| 4337[8] | **Blaze of Oak (USA) (50)** (JMBradley) **5-8-11**(7) RFfrench(1) (plld hrd mid div: hdwy 3f out: wknd over 1f out) | 2½ | **12** | 11/1 | 35 | 16 |
| 2056[11] | **Araboybill (54)** (JNeville) **5-9-8b** RHughes(12) (n.d) | nk | **13** | 20/1 | 38 | 19 |
| 4480[12] | **Samara Song (55)** (WGMTurner) **3-8-10**(7) DMcGaffin(10) (a bhd) | 1½ | **14** | 16/1 | 37 | 12 |
| 4340* | **In Cahoots (49)** (AGNewcombe) **3-8-11** JCarroll(7) (led 9f out: hdd & hrd rdn over 4f out: wknd qckly wl over 1f out) | 3½ | **15** | 8/1[3] | 26 | 1 |

| | | | Pos | SP | RR | SF |
|---|---|---|---|---|---|---|
| 3958[2] | **Racing Brenda (45)** (BCMorgan) **5-8-13** SWhitworth(19) (a bhd) | 2 | **16** | 5/1[1] | 19 | — |
| 4053[10] | **Inaminit (53)** (HJCollingridge) **3-9-1b[1]** JQuinn(20) (s.s: a bhd) | 4 | **17** | 16/1 | 21 | — |
| 4497[13] | **Clued Up (54)** (PDEvans) **3-9-2b** JFEgan(8) (prom: rdn over 4f out: wknd 2f out) | 5 | **18** | 10/1 | 14 | — |
| 4083[6] | **Monte Felice (IRE) (49)** (GHarwood) **3-8-11** GDuffield(2) (plld hrd: prom tl wknd over 3f out) | 3½ | **19** | 16/1 | 4 | — |
| | | | | (SP 153.6%) | **19 Rn** | |

**2m 16.3** (2.80) CSF £99.15 CT £892.20 TOTE £7.70: £1.70 £6.40 £3.10 £1.30 (£219.90) Trio Not won; £433.94 to York 9/10/96 OWNER Group 1 Racing (1994) Ltd (UPPER LAMBOURN) BRED Dr S. M. Foster

WEIGHT FOR AGE 3yo-6lb

**4107* Comedy River** showed his well-being on the Fibresand last time and was 2lb higher then when runner-up in a seller at Nottingham on his previous outing. (7/1)

**3951 Proud Image**, who has never won beyond a mile, was ridden to get the trip. (12/1)

**3785 Pat's Splendour** does not seem the most consistent of animals. (11/1)

**4455 Kevasingo**, sharpened up by the blinkers, threw down the gauntlet once in the home straight, but his stamina limitations were exposed. (5/1)

**4513 It'sthebusiness** was running off the same mark as at Salisbury last week. (7/1)

**4340* In Cahoots** (8/1: 6/1-9/1)

**3958 Racing Brenda**, raised 2lb, ran so badly that one could not put it down to simply the longer trip. (5/1)

## 4604 RACING SCHOOLS' APPRENTICE H'CAP (0-70) (3-Y.O+) (Class F)

4-00 (4-01) **2m 20y** £3,118.80 (£866.80: £416.40) Stalls: Low GOING minus 0.47 sec per fur (F)

| | | | Pos | SP | RR | SF |
|---|---|---|---|---|---|---|
| 4476[2] | **Inchcailloch (IRE) (62)** (JSKing) **7-9-9** RHavlin(3) (lw: hld up: hdwy 4f out: led over 1f out: drvn out) | — | **1** | 100/30[1] | 74 | 47 |
| *604*[9] | **Parklife (IRE) (39)** (PCHaslam) **4-8-0** RMullen(5) (bit bkwd: s.s: hdwy over 3f out: chsd wnr & edgd lft fnl f: no imp) | 2 | **2** | 25/1 | 49 | 22 |
| 4321[3] | **Broughtons Formula (41)** (WJMusson) **6-8-2b** MBaird(1) (lw: hld up & bhd: hdwy 3f out: r.o ins fnl f) | 1¼ | **3** | 6/1[3] | 50 | 23 |
| 4426[3] | **Paradise Navy (67)** (CREgerton) **7-10-0b** FLynch(9) (hld up & bhd: hdwy 4f out: one pce fnl 2f) | ¾ | **4** | 7/1 | 75 | 48 |
| 4563[3] | **Children's Choice (IRE) (55)** (CNAllen) **5-9-2** GMilligan(2) (no hdwy fnl 2f) | nk | **5** | 7/1 | 63 | 36 |
| 4307[11] | **Red Raja (65)** (PMitchell) **3-9-1** SDrowne(6) (bit bkwd: prom tl wknd wl over 1f out) | 5 | **6** | 50/1 | 68 | 30 |
| 4252* | **Mischief Star (64)** (DRCElsworth) **3-9-0** DGriffiths(11) (lw: prom: led 3f out tl over 1f out: wknd fnl f) | ½ | **7** | 4/1[2] | 66 | 28 |
| 3142[8] | **Coleridge (53)** (JJSheehan) **8-9-0b** CWebb(7) (bit bkwd: s.s: hdwy 5f out: wknd 3f out) | ¾ | **8** | 11/1 | 55 | 28 |
| *4332*[7] | **Iota (59)** (JLHarris) **7-9-6** CTeague(4) (prom: led over 4f out to 3f out: wknd 2f out) | 2 | **9** | 12/1 | 59 | 32 |
| *3437*[9] | **Acrow Line (38)** (DBurchell) **11-7-13** PFessey(8) (bit bkwd: a bhd) | 11 | **10** | 9/1 | 27 | — |
| 4236[15] | **Special Risk (IRE) (47)** (RAkehurst) **6-8-8** DDenby(12) (prom 12f: t.o) | 23 | **11** | 12/1 | 13 | — |
| | **Saafi (IRE) (43)** (RJBaker) **5-8-0**(4) AMcCarthy(10) (swtg: bit bkwd: plld hrd: led: clr after 4f: wknd & hdd over 4f out: t.o) | dist | **12** | 50/1 | — | — |
| | | | | (SP 123.8%) | **12 Rn** | |

**3m 30.7** (4.70) CSF £74.01 CT £452.39 TOTE £3.60: £1.40 £5.30 £2.20 (£81.10) Trio £65.00 OWNER Mr F. J. Carter (SWINDON) BRED Hascombe and Valiant Studs

WEIGHT FOR AGE 3yo-11lb

**4476 Inchcailloch (IRE)** travelled well through the race and will now have another crack at the Cesarewitch. (100/30)

**604 Parklife (IRE)**, stepping up in distance after a six-month lay-off, was inclined to duck in behind the winner in the closing stages. (25/1)

**4321 Broughtons Formula** was 7lb higher than when winning at Nottingham. (6/1: op 4/1)

**4426 Paradise Navy**, 1lb lower than when third at Folkestone, is the type who needs things to go all his own way. (7/1: 6/1-9/1)

**4563 Children's Choice (IRE)**, third at Haydock the previous weekend, had to contend with both a longer trip and much faster ground. (7/1)

**Red Raja** had his stamina limitations exposed in the home straight. (50/1)

**4252* Mischief Star** could not defy a 5lb hike in the Ratings. (4/1)

## 4605 E.B.F. MAIDEN STKS (2-Y.O F) (Class D)

4-30 (4-31) **7f** £4,565.00 (£1,370.00: £660.00: £305.00) Stalls: Low GOING minus 0.47 sec per fur (F)

| | | | Pos | SP | RR | SF |
|---|---|---|---|---|---|---|
| 4357[2] | **Dragonada (USA)** (HRACecil) **2-8-11** PatEddery(14) (mde all: qcknd clr wl over 1f out: easily) | — | **1** | Evens[1] | 90+ | 49 |
| 4242[3] | **Superbelle** (MAJarvis) **2-8-11** EmmaO'Gorman(4) (a.p: r.o ins fnl f: no ch w wnr) | 5 | **2** | 4/1[2] | 79 | 38 |
| | **Sweeten Up** (HRACecil) **2-8-11** WRyan(13) (w'like: bit bkwd: hld up: hdwy 2f out: m green & edgd lft over 1f out: r.o) | ½ | **3** | 12/1 | 77 | 36 |
| 3433[5] | **Royal Orchid (IRE) (78)** (RHannon) **2-8-11** DaneO'Neill(6) (b.nr hind: bit bkwd: a.p: one pce fnl 2f) | ¾ | **4** | 14/1 | 76 | 35 |
| 4208[3] | **Mayflower (79)** (IABalding) **2-8-11** DHarrison(2) (lw: hld up: rdn 2f out: no hdwy) | 3½ | **5** | 6/1[3] | 68 | 27 |
| 4330[7] | **Lonely Heart** (MajorDNChappell) **2-8-11** RHills(1) (swtg: rdn & no hdwy fnl 2f) | nk | **6** | 14/1 | 67 | 26 |
| 4233[9] | **Bobbitt** (WJarvis) **2-8-11** JWeaver(5) (dwlt: nvr nrr) | 1¾ | **7** | 16/1 | 63 | 22 |
| 4449[4] | **Nile Valley (IRE)** (PWChapple-Hyam) **2-8-11** JReid(3) (prom: hmpd & lost pl on ins over 3f out: n.d after) | hd | **8** | 8/1 | 63 | 22 |
| | **She's Dawan (IRE)** (PMitchell) **2-8-11** JQuinn(9) (w'like: bit bkwd: hdwy over 3f out: wknd 2f out) | hd | **9** | 20/1 | 63 | 22 |
| 4061[14] | **Teutonic Lass (IRE)** (PTWalwyn) **2-8-11** JCarroll(7) (bkwd: prom 5f) | ¾ | **10** | 50/1 | 61 | 20 |
| 3454[11] | **Fair Relation** (PFICole) **2-8-11** TSprake(11) (a bhd) | 2½ | **11** | 25/1 | 55 | 14 |
| 4105[13] | **Pirongia** (PHowling) **2-8-11** GDuffield(10) (bhd fnl 3f: t.o) | 18 | **12** | 100/1 | 14 | — |
| | **Aquatic Queen** (RJWeaver) **2-8-6**(5) ADaly(8) (unf: scope: bit bkwd: t.o) | 10 | **13** | 50/1 | — | — |
| | | | | (SP 135.8%) | **13 Rn** | |

**1m 25.2** (0.60) CSF £6.66 TOTE £1.60: £1.10 £1.50 £3.40 (£6.50) Trio £28.00 OWNER Niarchos Family (NEWMARKET) BRED Flaxman Holdings Ltd

**4357 Dragonada (USA)**, appreciating this extra furlong, made short work of these rivals and should go on from here. (Evens)

**4242 Superbelle**, a sister to a winner in Norway and a half-sister to Super High, got the better of the separate race for the runner-up spot. (4/1)

**Sweeten Up**, a sister to Honey Mount and a half-sister to Orthorhombus, will need further in time and will come on considerably for the experience. (12/1: op 8/1)

**3129 Royal Orchid (IRE)**, out of a half-sister to the sprinter Mistertopogigo, was trying her luck at seven. (14/1)

**4208 Mayflower** should have been suited by this longer trip. (6/1)

**4330 Lonely Heart** should have benefited from the step up in distance. (14/1: op 8/1)

## 4606 MOP FAIR LIMITED STKS (0-70) (3-Y.O+) (Class E)

5-00 (5-02) **1m** £3,807.30 (£1,142.40: £550.20: £254.10) Stalls: Low GOING minus 0.47 sec per fur (F)

| | | | Pos | SP | RR | SF |
|---|---|---|---|---|---|---|
| 4582* | **Master Beveled (68)** (PDEvans) **6-9-4** 3x JFEgan(7) (a.p: led ins fnl f: drvn out) | — | **1** | 9/2[2] | 73 | 50 |

| | | | | SP | RR | SF |
|---|---|---|---|---|---|---|
| 4257[13] | **Raed (70)** (PTWalwyn) **3-8-12** RHills(16) (hld up: hdwy over 1f out: r.o wl ins fnl f) | nk | **2** | 7/1 | 69 | 43 |
| 4232[7] | **Disallowed (IRE) (67)** (MBell) **3-8-12v[1]** MFenton(3) (hdwy 4f out: r.o wl ins fnl f) | ¾ | **3** | 12/1 | 68 | 42 |
| 3424[14] | **Detachment (USA) (70)** (PWChapple-Hyam) **3-8-12** JReid(4) (bit bkwd: led after 1f: clr wl over 1f out: sn rdn & edgd rt: hdd ins fnl f) | s.h | **4** | 14/1 | 68 | 42 |
| 4322[2] | **Danlora (70)** (WJarvis) **3-8-9** JWeaver(14) (hdwy over 2f out: r.o ins fnl f) | 1¼ | **5** | 9/2[2] | 62 | 36 |
| 4354[5] | **North Reef (IRE) (70)** (SirMarkPrescott) **5-9-1** GDuffield(11) (lw: swtg: a.p: rdn & one pce fnl 2f) | ¾ | **6** | 4/1[1] | 64 | 41 |
| 4422[6] | **Hadadabble (39)** (PatMitchell) **3-8-9** DaneO'Neill(1) (nvr nr to chal) | 2½ | **7** | 50/1 | 56 | 30 |
| *294*[7] | **Tormount (USA) (69)** (LordHuntingdon) **3-8-12** DHarrison(15) (bit bkwd: nvr nrr) | nk | **8** | 20/1 | 58 | 32 |
| *1448*[3] | **Distinct Beauty (IRE) (66)** (WAO'Gorman) **3-8-12** EmmaO'Gorman(8) (bkwd: n.d) | nk | **9** | 12/1 | 58 | 32 |
| 3974[7] | **Singapore Sting (USA) (67)** (HRACecil) **3-8-12** PatEddery(6) (led 1f: hrd rdn & wknd wl over 1f out) | ¾ | **10** | 13/2[3] | 56 | 30 |
| 4212[4] | **Dancing Heart (67)** (BJMeehan) **4-9-1** MTebbutt(12) (lw: prom: hrd rdn over 2f out: wknd wl over 1f out) | 1 | **11** | 12/1 | 54 | 31 |
| 4205[9] | **Polly Golightly (64)** (MBlanshard) **3-8-9** JQuinn(10) (hld up: a bhd) | 1 | **12** | 20/1 | 49 | 23 |
| 4356[6] | **Nineacres (48)** (NMBabbage) **5-9-1v** RHughes(2) (a bhd) | 6 | **13** | 20/1 | 40 | 17 |
| 3918[6] | **Shalta Chief (43)** (EHOwenjun) **4-8-8**(7) RCody-Boutcher(5) (a bhd: t.o) | 5 | **14** | 66/1 | 30 | 7 |
| | | | | (SP 129.7%) | **14 Rn** | |

**1m 37.6** (1.20) CSF £36.42 TOTE £5.40: £2.00 £2.00 £3.90 (£31.90) Trio £141.10 OWNER Mrs E. J. Williams (WELSHPOOL) BRED C. R. Black

WEIGHT FOR AGE 3yo-3lb

**4582* Master Beveled** was easy to back on ground much quicker that at Haydock two days earlier, but it had been raining all afternoon. (9/2: 9/4-5/1)

**3985 Raed** may have found the ground too firm when disappointing last time, having run well on his previous outing at York. (7/1)

**3470 Disallowed (IRE)** showed improvement in the first-time visor. (12/1: op 7/1)

**2687 Detachment (USA)** is bred to stay a mile, but appeared to find it beyond him, having seemingly had the race in the bag. (14/1: op 8/1)

**4322 Danlora** was stepping up to a mile. (9/2: 3/1-5/1)

**4354 North Reef (IRE)** possibly finds this trip short of his best these days. (4/1)

**1448 Distinct Beauty (IRE)** (12/1: 8/1-14/1)

**4212 Dancing Heart** (12/1: op 7/1)

T/Plpt: £19.50 (676.95 Tckts). T/Qdpt: £11.10 (78.85 Tckts). IM/KH

## 4355-NOTTINGHAM (L-H) (Good, Good to firm patches)
## Wednesday October 9th

WEATHER: cloudy WIND: fresh across

### 4607 JOHN MOUNTENEY (S) STKS (2-Y.O) (Class G)

2-10 (2-15) **1m 54y** £2,070.00 (£570.00: £270.00) Stalls: Low GOING minus 0.25 sec per fur (GF)

| | | | | SP | RR | SF |
|---|---|---|---|---|---|---|
| 4347[2] | **Time Can Tell (66)** (CMurray) **2-8-11** DeanMcKeown(17) (b: chsd ldrs: led 2f out: clr fnl f) | — | **1** | 5/2[1] | 62 | 25 |
| *4251*[7] | **Verinder's Gift** (DrJDScargill) **2-8-11** KDarley(13) (b.hind: hld up: hdwy over 3f out: chsd wnr fnl f: no imp) | 5 | **2** | 33/1 | 52 | 15 |
| *3954*[4] | **Corncrake (IRE) (58)** (BJMeehan) **2-8-6** BDoyle(3) (lw: led & sn wl clr: wknd & hdd 2f out: rallied nr fin) | s.h | **3** | 11/2[3] | 47 | 10 |
| 4349[6] | **Slightly Oliver (IRE)** (GLewis) **2-8-11b[1]** SWhitworth(8) (trckd ldrs: rdn 2f out: one pce) | 1¼ | **4** | 14/1 | 50 | 13 |
| 4359[7] | **Control Freak** (AGFoster) **2-8-6** TSprake(4) (chsd clr ldr 5f: wknd wl over 1f out) | 5 | **5** | 10/1 | 35 | — |
| | **Riverside Girl (IRE)** (JSMoore) **2-8-6** JFEgan(15) (leggy: lt-f: unf: hld up: hdwy u.p 2f out: nt rch ldrs) | 1 | **6** | 33/1 | 33 | — |
| 4368[3] | **Summerville Wood (61)** (PMooney) **2-9-2** DRMcCabe(14) (nvr nrr) | 3½ | **7** | 10/1 | 36 | — |
| | **Chipet** (APJones) **2-8-6** RCochrane(18) (lt-f: unf: bit bkwd: hdwy 5f out: rdn & wknd 3f out) | ¾ | **8** | 4/1[2] | 25 | — |
| | **Mustang Scally** (JMackie) **2-8-6** JFanning(12) (lengthy: bkwd: hld up: hdwy 3f out: wknd 2f out) | ¾ | **9** | 20/1 | 23 | — |
| 3687[14] | **The Dubious Goose** (JGFitzGerald) **2-8-11** WRyan(2) (nvr trbld ldrs) | ¾ | **10** | 14/1 | 27 | — |
| | **Macari** (BPJBaugh) **2-8-11** WLord(7) (w'like: bkwd: a in rr) | 2½ | **11** | 33/1 | 22 | — |
| 4210[14] | **Flahive's First** (JSMoore) **2-8-6**(5) PPMurphy(5) (a in rr) | s.h | **12** | 33/1 | 22 | — |
| 4347[6] | **Rising Glory (50)** (MissJFCraze) **2-8-11** NConnorton(10) (plld hrd: prom tl over 3f out: sn wknd: t.o) | 9 | **13** | 14/1 | 5 | — |
| 4104[12] | **Coal To Diamonds** (GFJohnsonHoughton) **2-8-6b[1]** StephenDavies(1) (s.s: a bhd: t.o) | 7 | **14** | 33/1 | — | — |
| | ***Cathies Flower*** (JAHarris) **2-8-6** JO'Reilly(16) (Withdrawn not under Starter's orders: ref to ent stalls) | | **W** | 20/1 | — | — |
| 4331[10] | **Don't Fool Me (IRE)** (PMooney) **2-8-8**(3) PMcCabe(6) (Withdrawn not under Starter's orders: bolted bef s) | | **W** | 33/1 | — | — |
| | | | | (SP 129.3%) | **14 Rn** | |

**1m 46.4** (5.10) CSF £78.41 TOTE £3.00: £1.60 £4.60 £2.10 (£31.80) Trio £159.30; £26.93 to York 10/10/96 OWNER Mr Darren Croft (NEWMARKET) BRED J. G. and Mrs J. M. Brearley

Bt in 5,200 gns

**4347 Time Can Tell** sat much closer to the pace this time and had little trouble striding clear for a very easy success. (5/2)

**Verinder's Gift**, having his first outing on Turf and tackling a longer trip, failed to make any impression on the winner inside the distance, but this was his first glimpse of form, and there is a race to be won at this level. (33/1)

**3954 Corncrake (IRE)**, who set off at a rate of knots, looked done for when collared entering the final quarter-mile, but she ran on again after getting her second wind, and there is definitely a race in her. (11/2: 4/1-6/1)

**Slightly Oliver (IRE)** ran much better in the first-time blinkers, but he was being made to work inside the final quarter-mile and lacked the pace to mount a challenge. (14/1: op 8/1)

**Control Freak** did her best to keep tabs on the clear leader, but she only succeeded in beating herself and was a spent force below the distance. (10/1: 6/1-12/1)

**Riverside Girl (IRE)** was beginning to realise what was needed in the latter stages, and will be all the wiser for the experience. (33/1)

**Chipet** (4/1: 6/1-10/1)

### 4608 E.B.F. MAIDEN STKS (2-Y.O F) (Class D)

2-40 (2-43) **1m 54y** £3,926.45 (£1,175.60: £564.30: £258.65) Stalls: Low GOING minus 0.25 sec per fur (GF)

| | | | | SP | RR | SF |
|---|---|---|---|---|---|---|
| | **Fascinating Rhythm** (HRACecil) **2-8-11** PatEddery(9) (w'like: scope: a.p: pushed along 3f out: led over 1f out: drvn out) | — | **1** | 10/11[1] | 84+ | 30 |
| 3988[7] | **Brave Kris (IRE)** (LMCumani) **2-8-11** WRyan(4) (hld up in tch: effrt & hrd drvn 2f out: styd on fnl f) | 1½ | **2** | 20/1 | 81 | 27 |
| 3764[2] | **Elbaaha** (MAJarvis) **2-8-11** RCochrane(7) (swtg: chsd ldrs: effrt & hung lft 2f out: one pce) | 3 | **3** | 12/1 | 75 | 21 |
| | **Liffre (IRE)** (JHMGosden) **2-8-11** LDettori(13) (b.hind: w'like: scope: s.s: hdwy on ins over 3f out: one pce fnl 2f) | 1 | **4** | 13/2 | 73 | 19 |

| Form | Horse | Dist | Pos | SP | RR | SF |
|---|---|---|---|---|---|---|
| | **Graceful Lass** (DRLoder) **2-8-11** DRMcCabe(8) (w'like: plld hrd: hld up: sme late hdwy: nvr nrr) | ½ | **5** | 20/1 | 72 | 18 |
| | **Grapevine (IRE)** (PWChapple-Hyam) **2-8-11** JReid(5) (lengthy: scope: hld up: stdy hdwy fnl 2f: nvr nrr) | ½ | **6** | 6/1[3] | 71 | 17 |
| 4211[2] | **Alphabet** (MRStoute) **2-8-11** MRimmer(11) (b.hind: led: rdn & hdd over 1f out: sn btn) | nk | **7** | 4/1[2] | 71 | 17 |
| | **Thornby Park** (JLDunlop) **2-8-11** TSprake(12) (w'like: nvr nr ldrs) | 3 | **8** | 25/1 | 65 | 11 |
| | **Irish Pet** (JMPEustace) **2-8-11** BDoyle(2) (w'like: scope: a bhd) | hd | **9** | 40/1 | 65 | 11 |
| 4104[2] | **Woodsia** (DRLoder) **2-8-11** KDarley(10) (prom: rdn & ev ch over 2f out: wknd qckly) | nk | **10** | 9/1 | 64 | 10 |
| 4451[4] | **Agony Aunt** (MrsJCecil) **2-8-11** GBardwell(3) (hld up: a in rr) | 1½ | **11** | 12/1 | 61 | 7 |
| *4331[5]* | **Royal Roulette** (SPCWoods) **2-8-11** DBiggs(1) (plld hrd: hld up: a bhd: t.o) | 5 | **12** | 66/1 | 52 | — |
| 4449[5] | **Old Colony** (PFICole) **2-8-11** CRutter(6) (mid div tl wknd 3f out: t.o) | 1 | **13** | 33/1 | 50 | — |
| | | | | (SP 145.6%) | **13 Rn** | |

**1m 45.9** (4.60) CSF £26.01 TOTE £1.80: £1.20 £4.20 £3.80 (£99.40) Trio £182.20; £102.68 to York 10/10/96 OWNER Helena Springfield Ltd (NEWMARKET) BRED Meon Valley Stud

**Fascinating Rhythm** kept up her stable's impressive recorded with late-developing two-year-olds on this track, but made hard work of it. It will be interesting to see if the race brings her on. (10/11: Evens-11/10)

**3988 Brave Kris (IRE)** put her previous experience to good use and made the winner know she had been in a race. She would seem to be a very progressive youngster. (20/1)

**3764 Elbaaha** continues to knock at the door, but she was inclined to edge in behind the runner-up in the closing stages, and gave the impression she was not enjoying pressure being applied. (12/1: op 8/1)

**Liffre (IRE)** gave away quite a lot of ground at the start and, in the circumstances, must be considered to have put up a pleasing display, upon which she can only improve. (13/2: op 4/1)

**Graceful Lass,** very keen in the early stages, stayed on well inside the distance and should soon improve on this. (20/1)

**Grapevine (IRE)** benefited from a quiet introduction and stayed on to show promise for the future. (6/1: op 3/1)

**4211 Alphabet** appeared to have a bit too much use made of her, and her front-running tactics had come to an end once the winner was sent about her business. (4/1)

**4104 Woodsia** (9/1: op 5/1)

**4451 Agony Aunt** (12/1: op 7/1)

## 4609 TOMMY LAWTON H'CAP (0-70) (3-Y.O+) (Class E)

3-10 (3-10) **1m 54y** £3,889.20 (£1,167.60: £562.80: £260.40) Stalls: Low GOING minus 0.25 sec per fur (GF)

| Form | Horse | Dist | Pos | SP | RR | SF |
|---|---|---|---|---|---|---|
| 2925[3] | **Castan (IRE) (69)** (JLDunlop) **3-9-10** PatEddery(2) (hld up: hdwy 3f out: led over 1f out: all out) | — | **1** | 6/1[2] | 81 | 47 |
| 4186[14] | **Classy Chief (65)** (RBoss) **3-9-1**(5) GFaulkner(18) (lw: a.p: led over 2f out tl over 1f out: rallied u.p nr fin) | nk | **2** | 33/1 | 76 | 42 |
| 982[11] | **Waft (USA) (60)** (BWHills) **3-9-1** RCochrane(1) (hld up: hdwy over 3f out: r.o u.p ins fnl f) | s.h | **3** | 10/1 | 71 | 37 |
| 4428[3] | **Morocco (IRE) (58)** (MRChannon) **7-8-9**(7) AEddery(7) (hld up in tch: hdwy 2f out: nrst fin) | 1¾ | **4** | 13/2[3] | 66 | 35 |
| 4439[3] | **Anonym (IRE) (58)** (DNicholls) **4-8-9b**(7) JBramhill(12) (trckd ldrs: rdn 2f out: nt pce to chal) | ¾ | **5** | 8/1 | 65 | 34 |
| 817[17] | **Explosive Power (55)** (GCBravery) **5-8-13** DRMcCabe(15) (hld up: hdwy 3f out: one pce fnl 2f) | 2 | **6** | 33/1 | 58 | 27 |
| 4453[8] | **Veni Vidi Vici (IRE) (68)** (MJHeaton-Ellis) **3-9-9** SDrowne(9) (lw: in tch: effrt 3f out: one pce fnl 2f) | 1¾ | **7** | 7/1 | 67 | 33 |
| 4300[17] | **Euro Sceptic (IRE) (59)** (TDEasterby) **4-9-0b**(3) RHavlin(3) (chsd ldrs: wkng whn nt clr run 2f out) | ½ | **8** | 16/1 | 57 | 26 |
| 4308[10] | **Safey Ana (USA) (61)** (BHanbury) **5-9-5** WRyan(13) (b: swtg: bhd: rdn over 2f out: nvr nr to chal) | 2½ | **9** | 13/2[3] | 54 | 23 |
| 4463[19] | **Confronter (67)** (SDow) **7-9-11** LDettori(5) (hld up in rr: effrt & rdn over 2f out: no imp) | hd | **10** | 10/1 | 60 | 29 |
| 3640[11] | **Parliament Piece (60)** (CaptJWilson) **10-9-4** KDarley(6) (hld up: hdwy on ins 3f out: nt clr run 2f out: no imp) | 3 | **11** | 20/1 | 47 | 16 |
| 4430[19] | **Comeonup (56)** (JMBradley) **5-9-0** TSprake(11) (nvr bttr than mid div) | 1¼ | **12** | 20/1 | 41 | 10 |
| 4337* | **Mustn't Grumble (IRE) (55)** (MissSJWilton) **6-8-13v** SWhitworth(10) (dwlt: a in rr) | ½ | **13** | 11/2[1] | 39 | 8 |
| 4428[15] | **Arzani (USA) (60)** (DJSCosgrove) **5-9-4** MRimmer(14) (s.s: a bhd) | hd | **14** | 33/1 | 44 | 13 |
| | **Daytona Beach (IRE) (57)** (DJSffrenchDavis) **6-8-10**(5) PPMurphy(4) (bit bkwd: led tl hdd & wknd over 2f out) | 2½ | **15** | 12/1 | 36 | 5 |
| 4428[2] | **Sand Star (60)** (DHaydnJones) **4-9-4** JReid(8) (prom: ev ch over 2f out: sn wknd) | nk | **16** | 6/1[2] | 38 | 7 |
| 3830[7] | **Classic Ballet (FR) (64)** (RHarris) **3-9-5** RPrice(17) (swtg: hld up: c wd st: a bhd) | 3½ | **17** | 33/1 | 36 | 2 |
| | | | | (SP 147.3%) | **17 Rn** | |

**1m 45.4** (4.10) CSF £189.88 CT £1,908.86 TOTE £6.30: £2.20 £10.90 £4.40 £2.70 (£171.10) Trio £228.00; £256.95 to York 10/10/96 OWNER Mr James Hartnett (ARUNDEL) BRED Taupo Ltd

WEIGHT FOR AGE 3yo-3lb

**2925 Castan (IRE)**, very much on his toes in the preliminaries, had to put his best foot forward in the closing stages, but he always looked up to it and ran out a worthy winner. (6/1)

**3656 Classy Chief** was in no mood to give best and fought back strongly inside the final furlong. A repeat of this effort could be good enough to see him get off the mark. (33/1)

**Waft (USA)**, very lightly-raced and returning to action after a lengthy absence, ran by far her best race yet and, if she can step up on this, she will not be long in getting winning brackets by her name. (10/1)

**4428 Morocco (IRE)** only does as much as he needs to and, though he did not enjoy the smoothest of passages when making his run, it is doubtful when he would have troubled the principals. (13/2)

**4439 Anonym (IRE)** is quite consistent but he only wins in his turn, and this was never going to be one of those days. (8/1)

**424* Explosive Power** has not yet won on Turf, but shaped promisingly here after almost six months off the track. If he returns to the Sand over a slightly longer trip, the hint should be taken. (33/1)

**4337* Mustn't Grumble (IRE)**, sluggish leaving the stalls, ran a very lack-lustre race and there seemed no viable excuse. (11/2)

**Daytona Beach (IRE)** was quietly fancied to make a winning seasonal debut, but he had been collared early in the straight as lack of peak-fitness caught him out. (12/1)

## 4610 PAVIS CHALLENGE H'CAP (0-70) (3-Y.O+) (Class E)

3-40 (3-41) **5f 13y** £3,643.50 (£1,092.00: £525.00: £241.50) Stalls: High GOING minus 0.25 sec per fur (GF)

| Form | Horse | Dist | Pos | SP | RR | SF |
|---|---|---|---|---|---|---|
| 4205[2] | **Another Batchworth (55)** (EAWheeler) **4-9-0b** SWhitworth(19) (mde all stands' side: rdn & hld on wl) | — | **1** | 7/1[3] | 66 | 21 |
| 4430[16] | **Dominelle (53)** (TDEasterby) **4-8-12** MBirch(11) (lw: prom centre: rdn & r.o wl ins fnl f) | ¾ | **2** | 12/1 | 62 | 17 |
| 4382[6] | **Chadwell Hall (64)** (SRBowring) **5-9-6b**(3) CTeague(16) (chsd wnr stands' side: kpt on u.p fnl f) | hd | **3** | 6/1[2] | 72 | 27 |
| 4430[9] | **Night Harmony (IRE) (55)** (RHannon) **3-9-0** PatEddery(10) (swtg: a.p centre: rdn wl over 1f out: unable qckn fnl f) | 1¾ | **4** | 16/1 | 58 | 13 |
| 4356[15] | **Superbit (54)** (BAMcMahon) **4-8-13** WRyan(15) (lw: chsd ldrs: rdn over 1f out: one pce) | nk | **5** | 14/1 | 56 | 11 |
| 4382[8] | **Lloc (52)** (CADwyer) **4-8-4**(7) JoHunnam(7) (swtg: hdwy over 1f out: fin wl) | 1 | **6** | 20/1 | 51 | 6 |
| 4372[2] | **Pride of Hayling (IRE) (63)** (PRHedger) **5-9-8** SDrowne(17) (swtg: hdwy appr fnl f: nrst fin) | nk | **7** | 9/1 | 61 | 16 |
| 4180[17] | **Beau Venture (USA) (65)** (BPalling) **8-9-10** TSprake(12) (chsd ldrs centre: no hdwy fnl 2f) | hd | **8** | 33/1 | 62 | 17 |

| | | | | SP | RR | SF |
|---|---|---|---|---|---|---|
| 4367[12] | **One for Jeannie (61)** (ABailey) **4-8-13**(7) AngelaGallimore(5) (b: nvr nrr) | 1 | **9** | 33/1 | 55 | 10 |
| 4486[14] | **Invigilate (43)** (MartynWane) **7-7-9**(7) RFfrench(22) (nvr gng pce of ldrs) | hd | **10** | 33/1 | 37 | — |
| 4342* | **Souperficial (55)** (JAGlover) **5-9-0v** LDettori(21) (outpcd: effrt u.p 2f out: no imp) | nk | **11** | 2/1[1] | 48 | 3 |
| 4246[16] | **Pharaoh's Joy (61)** (JWPayne) **3-9-6** RCochrane(18) (nvr nr ldrs) | hd | **12** | 9/1 | 54 | 9 |
| 4075[21] | **Superfrills (50)** (MissLCSiddall) **3-8-9** DeanMcKeown(2) (spd far side 4f) | hd | **13** | 50/1 | 42 | — |
| 4356[5] | **Mansab (USA) (56)** (PGMurphy) **3-9-1** JFEgan(6) (a in rr) | hd | **14** | 25/1 | 48 | 3 |
| *1455*[13] | **Margaretrose Anna (43)** (BPJBaugh) **4-8-2** WLord(8) (outpcd) | 1 | **15** | 50/1 | 32 | — |
| 4473[4] | **Kalar (53)** (DWChapman) **7-8-7**(5) MBaird(3) (prom far side 4f) | 1¼ | **16** | 12/1 | 38 | — |
| 4367[13] | **Amy Leigh (IRE) (55)** (CaptJWilson) **3-9-0** CRutter(13) (swtg: outpcd) | 1¼ | **17** | 33/1 | 36 | — |
| 3352[W] | **Swan At Whalley (69)** (MartynWane) **4-9-9**(5) PRoberts(4) (lw: prom far side 3f) | 1¼ | **18** | 20/1 | 46 | 1 |
| 4205[14] | **Sotonian (HOL) (45)** (PSFelgate) **3-8-1**(3) PMcCabe(20) (outpcd: t.o) | 7 | **19** | 50/1 | — | — |
| | | | | (SP 139.1%) | **19 Rn** | |

**61.9 secs** (3.30) CSF £90.13 CT £520.21 TOTE £12.30: £1.60 £3.20 £1.90 £6.50 (£103.70) Trio £144.80 OWNER Mrs Mr Mr Price Wakefield O'Toole (PANGBOURNE) BRED Mrs D. Price

**4205 Another Batchworth** had finished in front of most of these rivals here last month when just failing to hang on, but she was always calling the tune on this occasion, and deservedly got back to winning ways. (7/1)

**4430 Dominelle** once again found one too good for her, but did not fail for the want of trying and another success will not come out of turn. (12/1)

**4382 Chadwell Hall** probably needs a bit more cut in the ground than he found here, but he gave it his best shot and is certainly a trier. (6/1)

**4215 Night Harmony (IRE)** showed with the pace all the way and was only shaken off well inside the final furlong. It seems strange that he is still a maiden. (16/1)

**4205 Superbit** ran up to his mark, and was only found wanting in the closing stages after being in contention from the start. (14/1)

**3360 Lloc** possibly needs more yielding ground to recapture her form, but she showed her well-being by running on best of all when it was all too late. (20/1)

**4372 Pride of Hayling (IRE)** did not find top gear until far too late, and she does appear to need a slightly stiffer test of stamina. (9/1: 6/1-10/1)

**4342* Souperficial**, backed as if defeat was out of the question, quite simply failed to fire and was always in the ruck. (2/1: op 4/1)

## 4611 NOTTS COUNTY MAIDEN STKS (I) (3-Y.O) (Class D)

4-10 (4-10) **1m 1f 213y** £3,604.60 (£1,073.80: £511.40: £230.20) Stalls: Low GOING minus 0.25 sec per fur (GF)

| | | | | SP | RR | SF |
|---|---|---|---|---|---|---|
| 1656[5] | **Smilin N Wishin (USA) (80)** (PWChapple-Hyam) **3-8-9** JReid(8) (bit bkwd: a.p: led over 2f out: drvn clr) | — | **1** | 11/4[3] | 77 | 7 |
| 4309[2] | **Scarpetta (USA) (76)** (JWHills) **3-8-9** KDarley(1) (led tl over 2f out: rdn & btn appr fnl f) | 4 | **2** | 5/2[2] | 71 | 1 |
| | **Sea Wedding** (HRACecil) **3-8-9** WRyan(9) (gd sort: s.s: hdwy 3f out: shkn up 2f out: styd on) | 1 | **3** | 6/4[1] | 69 | — |
| 4422[W] | **Classic Form (IRE)** (RHarris) **3-8-9** RPrice(7) (hdwy ½-wy: one pce fnl 2f) | 6 | **4** | 8/1 | 59 | — |
| 4429[9] | **Magic Role** (MAJarvis) **3-9-0** PBloomfield(3) (chsd ldrs: rdn over 2f out: sn btn) | hd | **5** | 25/1 | 64 | — |
| 4360[14] | **Romantic Warrior** (KSBridgwater) **3-9-0** VSlattery(2) (hld up: chsd ldrs: wknd over 2f out) | 3½ | **6** | 100/1 | 59 | — |
| | **Needwood Legend** (BCMorgan) **3-9-0** SWhitworth(10) (w'like: bkwd: trckd ldrs tl wknd over 2f out) | nk | **7** | 100/1 | 58 | — |
| | **Ajkuit (IRE)** (JJSheehan) **3-8-9**(5) PPMurphy(5) (hld up in tch: drvn along & outpcd 3f out: sn bhd) | s.h | **8** | 50/1 | 58 | — |
| 4548[7] | **Hayling-Billy** (PRHedger) **3-9-0** SDrowne(4) (bit bkwd: stumbled s: a in rr) | nk | **9** | 100/1 | 58 | — |
| 2949[5] | **Partita** (CEBrittain) **3-8-9** BDoyle(6) (swtg: w ldr to ½-wy: wknd qckly: t.o) | 28 | **10** | 25/1 | 8 | — |
| | | | | (SP 119.0%) | **10 Rn** | |

**2m 10.8** (8.30) CSF £9.88 TOTE £3.10: £1.10 £1.40 £1.30 (£6.20) Trio £2.30 OWNER Mr R. E. Sangster (MARLBOROUGH) BRED Marion G. Montanari

**1656 Smilin N Wishin (USA)** came back fresh and well after her summer holidays and opened her account with a runaway success. She does likes to get her toe in and should be able to go from here. (11/4)

**4309 Scarpetta (USA)** seemed to not last out over this slightly longer trip, but she did have plenty of use made of her, and it may be worth riding her with more restraint again over this trip. (5/2)

**Sea Wedding** missed a beat at the start. Picking up ground once in line for home, she was treading water passing the two-furlong marker, but did stay on, and the experience will not be wasted. (6/4: 4/5-13/8)

**3058 Classic Form (IRE)**, given a long break since making her debut in May, was struggling to hold on from below the distance, and it could be that this step up in distance was more than she could cope with at this stage of her career. (8/1: tchd 12/1)

**Magic Role** played an active role until the contest began in earnest. (25/1)

## 4612 'MAGPIES' H'CAP (0-60) (3-Y.O+) (Class F)

4-40 (4-40) **2m 1f 188y** £2,381.00 (£656.00: £311.00) Stalls: High GOING minus 0.25 sec per fur (GF)

| | | | | SP | RR | SF |
|---|---|---|---|---|---|---|
| 4365[2] | **Amiarge (44)** (MBrittain) **6-9-2** GBardwell(16) (hld up: hdwy 6f out: led over 2f out: rdn out) | — | **1** | 5/1[2] | 55 | 40 |
| 4426[8] | **Zeliba (35)** (MrsNMacauley) **4-8-0**(7) JoHunnam(1) (hld up mid div: hdwy 5f out: ev ch ent fnl f: unable qckn) | 1½ | **2** | 7/1 | 45 | 30 |
| 4426[11] | **Sterling Fellow (56)** (RHannon) **3-9-2b** PatEddery(18) (lw: sn prom: rdn over 2f out: styd on strly) | nk | **3** | 7/1 | 65 | 38 |
| 4509[3] | **Ginka (35)** (JWMullins) **5-8-7** VSlattery(10) (rdn 10f out: styd on fnl 3f: nvr nrr: fin 5th, 3l: plcd 4th) | | **4** | 10/1 | 36 | 21 |
| 542[8] | **Bark'n'bite (50)** (MrsMReveley) **4-9-8** KDarley(9) (bit bkwd: hld up & bhd: styd on fnl 2f: nvr nrr: fin 6th, 4l: plcd 5th) | | **5** | 6/1[3] | 48 | 33 |
| 4509[7] | **Rivercare (IRE) (53)** (MJPolglase) **3-8-13** MRimmer(6) (prom: led 7f out tl over 2f out: sn wknd) | hd | **7** | 33/1 | 51 | 24 |
| 2530* | **Fortunes Course (IRE) (50)** (JSKing) **7-9-8** SDrowne(14) (bit bkwd: led 11f: wknd wl over 2f out) | 3 | **8** | 12/1 | 45 | 30 |
| 4426[12] | **Dance Model (50)** (JJSheehan) **3-8-10** AMorris(12) (nvr nrr) | ½ | **9** | 33/1 | 45 | 18 |
| 4426[2] | **Miss Prism (51)** (JLDunlop) **3-8-11** LDettori(2) (mid div: rdn 4f out: gd hdwy 3f out: wknd fnl 2f: eased) | ¾ | **10** | 2/1[1] | 45 | 18 |
| 3801[7] | **King William (36)** (NEBerry) **11-8-5**(3) PMcCabe(4) (bit bkwd: a in rr) | 2 | **11** | 20/1 | 28 | 13 |
| 4365[8] | **Needwood Muppet (46)** (AJWilson) **9-9-4** JReid(17) (a in rr) | ½ | **12** | 20/1 | 38 | 23 |
| 1454[5] | **Royrace (37)** (WMBrisbourne) **4-8-9** RCochrane(7) (bit bkwd: a bhd) | 2½ | **13** | 33/1 | 27 | 12 |
| 4563[7] | **Gunner B Special (40)** (SRBowring) **3-8-0b** NAdams(5) (b: b.hind: plld hrd: hdwy 10f out: wknd 3f out) | ¾ | **14** | 14/1 | 29 | 2 |
| 3870[9] | **Victoria Day (27)** (BAMcMahon) **4-7-6**(7) RFfrench(3) (trckd ldrs 12f: sn lost pl) | 1¾ | **15** | 33/1 | 14 | — |
| 4496[15] | **Atienza (USA) (53)** (SCWilliams) **3-8-13** BDoyle(8) (b.hind: hld up: hdwy over 5f out: bdly hmpd over 3f out: nt rcvr: t.o) | 7 | **16** | 14/1 | 34 | 7 |
| 4358[3] | **Duncombe Hall (39)** (CACyzer) **3-7-13** DRMcCabe(11) (w ldrs 13f: grad wknd: t.o) | 5 | **17** | 16/1 | 16 | — |
| *4334*[6] | **Blue And Royal (IRE) (52)** (VSoane) **4-9-10** TSprake(15) (chsd ldrs 12f: sn lost tch: t.o) | 29 | **18** | 33/1 | 3 | — |

4496[10] **Fro (52)** (TJNaughton) **3-8-9**(3) JDSmith(13) (hdwy 9f out: edgd lft over 3f out: one pce fnl 2f: fin 4th, 6l: disq: plcd last) ... **D** 33/1 56 29

(SP 152.5%) **18 Rn**

**4m 0.8** CSF £44.79 CT £241.81 TOTE £7.30: £1.40 £2.10 £2.30 £2.20 (£31.80) Trio £165.80 OWNER Miss D. J. Woods (WARTHILL) BRED Follies Partnership

WEIGHT FOR AGE 3yo-12lb

STEWARDS' ENQUIRY Smith susp. 18-19 & 21-23/10/96 (irresponsible riding).

**4365 Amiarge**, winner of his only previous race here some fourteen months ago, found this extended trip made to measure and, though he did have to do battle, he never looked in danger of losing out. (5/1)

**4203 Zeliba** delivered a serious-looking challenge approaching the final furlong, and kept her head down right to the line, but then had to admit the winner just too strong for her. She does stay extremely well and there is more to come. (7/1)

**4426 Sterling Fellow**, under stronger handling, showed he is not short of stamina but, on these terms, he had it all to do for a three-year-old. (7/1)

**4509 Ginka** is certainly running well enough to win a race, though she does seem to need a lot of stoking up, and stamina does not appear to be a problem. (10/1)

**542 Bark'n'bite**, sure to strip fitter for this first run in six months, made up quite a lot of ground in the last half-mile, and he could pay his way before being returned to hurdles. (6/1)

**4426 Miss Prism** has had some punishing races without success in the past couple of months, and this very much below-par performance could be an indication that she has had enough for the time being. (2/1)

**4203 Atienza (USA)**, taking closer order and travelling well when stopped in her tracks early in the straight, was unable to recover, and this performance can safely be ignored. (14/1)

**Fro** caused interference when wandering about over three furlongs out and, though she stayed on to be a well-beaten fourth, was disqualified and placed last. (33/1)

## 4613 NOTTS COUNTY MAIDEN STKS (II) (3-Y.O) (Class D)

5-10 (5-12) **1m 1f 213y** £3,604.60 (£1,073.80: £511.40: £230.20) Stalls: Low GOING minus 0.25 sec per fur (GF)

| | Horse / details | Dist | Pos | SP | RR | SF |
|---|---|---|---|---|---|---|
| 4235[2] | **Torremolinos (USA)** (HRACecil) **3-9-0** PatEddery(8) (mde all: sn clr: r.o wl) | — | 1 | 5/4[1] | 87 | 26 |
| 4429[4] | **Raise A Prince (FR) (74)** (JWHills) **3-9-0** KDarley(6) (lw: hld up in rr: hdwy over 3f out: nt clr run over 1f out: swtchd rt: r.o wl fnl f) | 4 | 2 | 3/1[2] | 81 | 20 |
| | **Benning (USA)** (JHMGosden) **3-8-9** LDettori(10) (w'like: b.hind: dwlt: sn in tch: chsd wnr fnl 2f: rdn & edgd lft over 1f out: one pce) | 1 | 3 | 3/1[2] | 74 | 13 |
| 4235[4] | **Mr Wild (USA)** (BHanbury) **3-9-0** MRimmer(4) (a.p: rdn over 2f out: one pce) | s.h | 4 | 12/1 | 79 | 18 |
| 4322[4] | **Stellar Line (USA) (74)** (BWHills) **3-9-0** RCochrane(3) (lw: hld up: stdy hdwy over 3f out: wknd 2f out) | 6 | 5 | 8/1[3] | 69 | 8 |
| | **On The Green** (AHide) **3-8-9** PBloomfield(1) (w'like: plld hrd: chsd ldrs over 7f) | 7 | 6 | 50/1 | 53 | — |
| | **Alarico (FR)** (IPWilliams) **3-9-0** BDoyle(5) (scope: bkwd: s.s: a in rr) | 1 | 7 | 33/1 | 56 | — |
| | **Needwood Nutkin** (BCMorgan) **3-8-9** TSprake(9) (w'like: bkwd: plld hrd: trckd ldrs tl wknd over 2f out) | 1 | 8 | 50/1 | 50 | — |
| 4317[7] | **Aydigo** (JPearce) **3-9-0** GBardwell(7) (sn pushed along: a bhd: t.o) | 15 | 9 | 100/1 | 31 | — |
| | **Starlight Waltzer** (KSBridgwater) **3-9-0** VSlattery(2) (unf: bkwd: wl bhd fnl 3f: t.o) | nk | 10 | 100/1 | 30 | — |

(SP 122.1%) **10 Rn**

**2m 8.9** (6.40) CSF £5.70 TOTE £1.80: £1.30 £1.10 £2.30 (£5.10) Trio £3.30 OWNER The Thoroughbred Corporation (NEWMARKET) BRED Mr & Mrs John C. Mabee

**4235 Torremolinos (USA)** put the emphasis on stamina and galloped his rivals into the ground. This success was not coming out of turn. (5/4: 4/5-11/8)

**4429 Raise A Prince (FR)** looked as though he would have given the winner a race had he not been forced to switch approaching the final furlong, for he finished strongly. An early success will come as no surprise. (3/1: op 5/1)

**Benning (USA)** turned in a promising display on this debut and, as she still has a bit left to work on, she should not be long in opening her account. (3/1: op 2/1)

**4235 Mr Wild (USA)** finished much closer to the winner than he did on his debut, and would seem to be going the right way. (12/1: op 8/1)

**4322 Stellar Line (USA)**, ridden with restraint over this longer trip, dropped in a heap two furlongs out and is proving something of a problem. (8/1)

T/Plpt: £103.20 (111.75 Tckts). T/Qdpt: £32.50 (19.99 Tckts). IM

# 3994-YORK (L-H) (Good)
## Wednesday October 9th

WEATHER: overcast WIND: mod half against

## 4614 EQUITY FINANCIAL COLLECTIONS NURSERY H'CAP (2-Y.O) (Class C)

2-00 (2-01) **6f** £6,212.00 (£1,856.00: £888.00: £404.00) Stalls: High GOING minus 0.12 sec per fur (G)

| | Horse / details | Dist | Pos | SP | RR | SF |
|---|---|---|---|---|---|---|
| 4318* | **Amyas (IRE) (78)** (BWHills) **2-9-3** MHills(11) (bhd: swtchd & hdwy 2f out: led ins fnl f: easily) | — | 1 | 7/2[1] | 84+ | 42 |
| 4346[3] | **Style Dancer (IRE) (70)** (RMWhitaker) **2-8-4**(5) MartinDwyer(2) (chsd ldrs: led over 1f out tl ins fnl f: nt qckn) | 2 | 2 | 14/1 | 71 | 29 |
| 4311[3] | **Burkes Manor (82)** (TDBarron) **2-9-7** DHarrison(3) (hdwy ½-wy: sn in tch: kpt on fnl f) | ¾ | 3 | 7/1 | 81 | 39 |
| 3969[15] | **Nostalgic Air (USA) (70)** (EWeymes) **2-8-9** JQuinn(6) (s.i.s: sn in tch: chal 2f out: no ex fnl f) | nk | 4 | 25/1 | 68 | 26 |
| 4424[3] | **Tailwind (70)** (WRMuir) **2-8-9** JWeaver(12) (in tch: effrt 2f out: styd on: nt pce to chal) | s.h | 5 | 11/1 | 68 | 26 |
| 4210* | **Gaelic Storm (82)** (MJohnston) **2-9-7** MRoberts(5) (s.i.s: sn rcvrd & chsd ldrs: ev ch & edgd lft 2f out: nt qckn) | nk | 6 | 4/1[2] | 79 | 37 |
| 3982[7] | **Blooming Amazing (75)** (JLEyre) **2-9-0** TWilliams(1) (cl up: led over 2f out tl over 1f out: sn btn) | hd | 7 | 12/1 | 72 | 30 |
| 4488[15] | **Zugudi (77)** (BHanbury) **2-9-2** JStack(9) (hld up & bhd: effrt 2f out: n.d) | 1 | 8 | 16/1 | 71 | 29 |
| 4350[7] | **Class Distinction (IRE) (80)** (RHannon) **2-9-5** DaneO'Neill(4) (nvr trbld ldrs) | ½ | 9 | 12/1 | 73 | 31 |
| 3250[6] | **Step N Go (IRE) (71)** (MrsJRRamsden) **2-8-10** KFallon(8) (lw: hld up & bhd: n.d) | 8 | 10 | 10/1 | 42 | — |
| 4210[11] | **Dom Ruinart (IRE) (58)** (JWHills) **2-7-8**(3)ow1 MHenry(10) (chsd ldrs tl wknd wl over 1f out) | 8 | 11 | 25/1 | 8 | — |
| 3869* | **Levelled (78)** (MRChannon) **2-9-3** RHughes(7) (led tl hdd & wknd over 2f out) | 9 | 12 | 13/2[3] | 4 | — |

(SP 121.1%) **12 Rn**

**1m 14.45** (3.45) CSF £47.74 CT £304.06 TOTE £3.70: £1.60 £3.90 £2.50 (£37.50) Trio £187.90 OWNER Mrs J. M. Corbett (LAMBOURN) BRED Mrs Helen Smith

**4318* Amyas (IRE)** has come good in a big way and made up a tremendous amount of ground to win on the bridle. (7/2)

**4346 Style Dancer (IRE)** is improving with experience but, despite a gallant effort, the winner was different class. (14/1)
**4311 Burkes Manor** keeps running well, but was never doing enough, despite staying on. (7/1)
**3275 Nostalgic Air (USA)** showed her first signs of form for a while, and might be worth keeping an eye on. (25/1)
**4424 Tailwind** has the ability to do better but, as yet, seems to be his own worst enemy. (11/1)
**4210* Gaelic Storm** just missed the kick. He never seemed on good terms with himself, despite getting into the argument, and this is best ignored. (4/1)

## 4615 BODDINGTONS LIMITED STKS (0-80) (3-Y.O+) (Class D)

2-30 (2-31) **1m 3f 195y** £6,056.00 (£1,808.00: £864.00: £392.00) Stalls: Low GOING minus 0.12 sec per fur (G)

| | | | | SP | RR | SF |
|---|---|---|---|---|---|---|
| 3235[3] | **Puce (80)** (LMCumani) **3-8-8** OUrbina(8) (lw: hld up & bhd: stdy hdwy on outside to ld 1f out: r.o) | — | 1 | 9/2[2] | 89 | 49 |
| 4489* | **Step Aloft (76)** (LordHuntingdon) **4-8-8**(5) AimeeCook(3) (swtg: trckd ldrs: squeezed out over 4f out: hdwy over 2f out: nt pce of wnr) | 2 | 2 | 13/8[1] | 84 | 51 |
| 4447[12] | **Silently (75)** (IABalding) **4-9-2** TQuinn(5) (led 1f: led over 4f out to 1f out: no ex u.p) | nk | 3 | 10/1 | 87 | 54 |
| 4227[7] | **Taufan Boy (70)** (PWHarris) **3-8-9** GHind(9) (trckd ldrs: chal 4f out: rdn over 2f out: btn over 1f out) | 1¼ | 4 | 20/1 | 85 | 45 |
| 3521[5] | **Annecy (USA) (74)** (HRACecil) **3-8-6** KFallon(4) (swtg: hld up: effrt 4f out: sn hrd drvn & no imp) | 7 | 5 | 7/1 | 73 | 33 |
| 3441[3] | **Lady Joshua (IRE) (78)** (JLDunlop) **3-8-6** JFortune(11) (swtg: rr div: hdwy 4f out: rdn & nvr trbld ldrs) | 1¾ | 6 | 5/1[3] | 70 | 30 |
| 4487[7] | **Vaugrenier (IRE) (76)** (RHannon) **4-9-2** RHughes(6) (hld up: hdwy on ins 4f out: sn rdn: btn 2f out) | 2 | 7 | 12/1 | 71 | 38 |
| 4432[14] | **Dee-Lady (73)** (WGMTurner) **4-8-13** AClark(2) (b: swtg: hld up & bhd: effrt 4f out: n.d) | nk | 8 | 20/1 | 67 | 34 |
| 4260[5] | **Steamroller Stanly (77)** (CACyzer) **3-8-11** JWeaver(10) (in tch tl wknd 4f out) | 1¾ | 9 | 11/1 | 70 | 30 |
| 4176[13] | **Royal Action (77)** (JEBanks) **3-8-2**(7) RMullen(7) (sn trckd ldrs: effrt 4f out: sn wknd) | 1 | 10 | 20/1 | 67 | 27 |
| 4580[18] | **Blackpatch Hill (73)** (NTinkler) **7-9-2b[1]** KimTinkler(1) (led after 1f tl over 4f out: wknd qckly: t.o) | dist | 11 | 50/1 | — | — |

(SP 126.8%) **11 Rn**

**2m 32.69** (4.89) CSF £12.67 TOTE £5.10: £1.80 £1.10 £2.30 (£4.90) Trio £19.60 OWNER Fittocks Stud (NEWMARKET) BRED Fittocks Stud
WEIGHT FOR AGE 3yo-7lb
**3235 Puce** returned here in style and, confidently ridden, won authoritatively. (9/2)
**4489* Step Aloft**, although getting messed about early in the straight, still had her chances, but it was the lack of a change of speed that was the difference in the end. (13/8)
**3617 Silently** looked tremendous, but yet again, when the chips were down, he swished his tail under pressure and refused to struggle. (10/1)
**4227 Taufan Boy**, with plenty to do at the weights, ran well in the circumstances. (20/1)
**3521 Annecy (USA)** needed some strong persuading to improve early in the straight, but she was never up to the task. (7/1)
**3441 Lady Joshua (IRE)**, after two months off, never gave any signs of getting into the battle. (5/1)

## 4616 NEWINGTON HOTEL YORK RACEGOERS H'CAP (0-80) (3-Y.O+) (Class D)

3-00 (3-02) **5f** £6,576.00 (£1,968.00: £944.00: £432.00) Stalls: High GOING minus 0.12 sec per fur (G)

| | | | | SP | RR | SF |
|---|---|---|---|---|---|---|
| 4452[2] | **Gone Savage (69)** (WJMusson) **8-9-5** JStack(5) (in tch: hdwy to ld ins fnl f: r.o wl) | — | 1 | 15/2[2] | 81 | 64 |
| 4312[10] | **Stuffed (70)** (MWEasterby) **4-9-1b**(5) GParkin(7) (trckd ldrs gng wl: effrt over 1f out: kpt on) | 1¼ | 2 | 12/1 | 78 | 61 |
| 4372[4] | **Squire Corrie (67)** (GHarwood) **4-8-10b**(7) GayeHarwood(9) (led tl ins fnl f: kpt on same pce) | 1½ | 3 | 14/1 | 70 | 53 |
| 4521[2] | **Literary Society (USA) (68)** (JARToller) **3-9-4** SSanders(6) (in tch: hdwy over 1f out: nt qckn ins fnl f) | nk | 4 | 14/1 | 70 | 53 |
| 4452[11] | **Jucea (70)** (JLSpearing) **7-9-3**(3) FLynch(8) (lw: styd on fnl 2f: nrst fin) | 1½ | 5 | 20/1 | 67 | 50 |
| 4312[17] | **Brecongill Lad (70)** (MissSEHall) **4-9-1**(5) MartinDwyer(18) (cl up stands' side: nt qckn appr fnl f) | nk | 6 | 16/1 | 67 | 50 |
| 4220[5] | **Sally Slade (72)** (CACyzer) **4-9-8** JWeaver(10) (hdwy u.p 2f out: styd on: nvr able to chal) | hd | 7 | 25/1 | 68 | 51 |
| 4382[15] | **Shadow Jury (63)** (DWChapman) **6-8-13b** JCarroll(11) (w ldrs tl rdn & btn over 1f out) | 1¼ | 8 | 33/1 | 55 | 38 |
| 4505[2] | **Insider Trader (76)** (MrsJRRamsden) **5-9-12** JFortune(14) (b.off fore: chsd ldrs: rdn 2f out: grad wknd) | ½ | 9 | 9/1[3] | 67 | 50 |
| 4452[4] | **Surprise Mission (75)** (MrsJRRamsden) **4-9-11** KFallon(21) (hdwy stands' side ½-wy: rdn & nvr able to chal) | ½ | 10 | 15/2[2] | 64 | 47 |
| 4430[4] | **Saddlehome (USA) (68)** (TDBarron) **7-9-4** TQuinn(19) (bhd: effrt ½-wy: no imp) | hd | 11 | 7/1[1] | 57 | 40 |
| 4452[3] | **Royal Dome (IRE) (73)** (MartynWane) **4-9-9** MRoberts(13) (lw: prom tl outpcd fnl 2f) | 1¼ | 12 | 10/1 | 58 | 41 |
| 4246[7] | **Grand Chapeau (IRE) (60)** (DNicholls) **4-8-10** AlexGreaves(16) (prom over 3f) | nk | 13 | 16/1 | 44 | 27 |
| 4367[6] | **Johayro (59)** (JSGoldie) **3-8-4b**(5) GLee(4) (cl up 3f: sn wknd) | ¾ | 14 | 25/1 | 40 | 23 |
| 4452[8] | **Kira (70)** (JLEyre) **6-9-3**(3) OPears(17) (racd stands' side: nvr wnt pce) | 1½ | 15 | 20/1 | 47 | 30 |
| 4367[11] | **The Happy Fox (IRE) (72)** (BAMcMahon) **4-9-8b** GDuffield(1) (lw: racd far side: sn drvn along: no imp) | s.h | 16 | 33/1 | 48 | 31 |
| 3868[13] | **Here Comes a Star (69)** (JMCarr) **8-9-5** ACulhane(20) (a bhd stands' side) | nk | 17 | 25/1 | 44 | 27 |
| 4372[7] | **Malibu Man (68)** (EAWheeler) **4-8-13**(5) ADaly(23) (led stands' side 3f: sn wknd) | 1¼ | 18 | 20/1 | 39 | 22 |
| 4452[10] | **Daawe (USA) (67)** (MrsVAAconley) **5-9-3b[1]** MDeering(2) (led far side: rdn & no imp fnl 2f) | hd | 19 | 16/1 | 38 | 21 |
| 4521[9] | **Air Wing (75)** (MHTompkins) **3-9-11** RHills(15) (bhd fr ½-wy) | s.h | 20 | 25/1 | 46 | 29 |
| 4473[2] | **Stephensons Rocket (58)** (DNicholls) **5-8-8** AClark(3) (racd far side: no ch fnl 2f) | 1½ | 21 | 16/1 | 24 | 7 |
| 4452[14] | **Stolen Kiss (IRE) (74)** (MWEasterby) **4-9-10b** RHughes(22) (racd stands' side: outpcd fr ½-wy) | hd | 22 | 25/1 | 40 | 23 |
| 3215[6] | **Gwespyr (67)** (JBerry) **3-9-3** GCarter(12) (reard s: a bhd) | nk | 23 | 25/1 | 32 | 15 |

(SP 142.9%) **23 Rn**

**59.35 secs** (1.65) CSF £96.60 CT £1,180.73 TOTE £6.80: £1.60 £2.70 £4.80 £3.80 (£43.80) Trio £555.20 OWNER The Square Table (NEWMARKET) BRED Mrs C. F. Van Straubenzee and R. Mead
**4452 Gone Savage** has been very unlucky this season and gained just reward here, winning in good style on this easier ground. (15/2)
**4312 Stuffed** travelled well, but just did not pick up as well as the winner when asked. Judging by this, he is on good terms with himself at present. (12/1)
**4372 Squire Corrie** is still in good form and tried really hard but, headed inside the final furlong, had run himself out. (14/1)
**4521 Literary Society (USA)** was a bit short of room at one stage, but did stay on well to show he is still in good heart. (14/1)
**4088 Jucea** was picking up in pleasing style at the end and is now slipping back to a decent mark. (20/1)
**3868 Brecongill Lad** ran best of those towards the stands' side and has plenty more ability if caught in the mood. (16/1)
**4430 Saddlehome (USA)** was never doing enough to get into this with any chance. (7/1)

## 4617 BOOKER CHEF'S LARDER H'CAP (0-85) (3-Y.O+) (Class D)

3-30 (3-34) **1m 2f 85y** £6,888.00 (£2,064.00: £992.00: £456.00) Stalls: Low GOING minus 0.12 sec per fur (G)

| | | | | SP | RR | SF |
|---|---|---|---|---|---|---|
| 4478* | **Pasternak (80)** (SirMarkPrescott) **3-9-4** 5x GDuffield(7) (lw: hld up & bhd: nt clr run several times in st: swtchd over 1f out: r.o wl to ld cl home) | — | 1 | 5/1[2] | 91 | 65 |
| 4450[2] | **Obelos (USA) (69)** (MrsJCecil) **5-8-7**(5) MartinDwyer(5) (chsd ldr: disp ld 3f out: led wl ins fnl f: hdd & no ex towards fin) | ¾ | 2 | 8/1[3] | 79 | 58 |

4465[19] **Time for Action (IRE) (84)** (MHTompkins) **4-9-13** RHills(19) (lw: mde most tl hdd wl ins fnl f)........................nk **3** 20/1 93 72
4484* **Manful (69)** (CWCElsey) **4-8-12b** 5x NKennedy(20) (mid div: styd on fnl 3f: nrst fin) ........................................1¾ **4** 20/1 76 55
4438[5] **Apollono (70)** (JRFanshawe) **4-8-13** SSanders(11) (trckd ldrs: effrt 4f out: ch 2f out: one pce)..............................1 **5** 14/1 75 54
4355* **Fern's Governor (60)** (WJMusson) **4-8-3** GCarter(4) (bhd: pushed along 8f out: styd on fnl 2f: nrst fin)..........nk **6** 3/1[1] 65 44
4326[15] **Gone for a Burton (IRE) (83)** (PJMakin) **6-9-12** JFortune(9) (bhd: hdwy 3f out: styd on: nt qckn ins fnl f).....................................................................................................................................1¾ **7** 16/1 85 64
4067[14] **Stately Dancer (75)** (GWragg) **3-8-13** MHills(3) (lw: in tch tl grad wknd fnl 3f) ..........................................2½ **8** 14/1 73 47
4431[8] **Calder King (65)** (JLEyre) **5-8-8b** TWilliams(8) (drvn along over 4f out: n.d)..............................................5 **9** 14/1 55 34
4427* **Ocean Park (75)** (LadyHerries) **5-9-4** AClark(18) (b: lw: in tch: effrt 4f out: no imp)........................................½ **10** 10/1 65 44
4556[5] **Daira (68)** (JDBethell) **3-8-6** DHarrison(13) (hmpd 8f out: effrt whn n.m.r over 2f out: no imp) ........................1½ **11** 14/1 55 29
4385[11] **Hand Craft (IRE) (78)** (WJHaggas) **4-9-7** RMcGhin(17) (dwlt: a bhd)..........................................................1½ **12** 20/1 63 42
4300[7] **Queens Consul (IRE) (82)** (BSRothwell) **6-9-11** MFenton(15) (s.i.s: gd hdwy on outside over 4f out: btn 2f out)......................................................................................................................................nk **13** 20/1 67 46
4315[3] **Far Ahead (83)** (JLEyre) **4-9-12** RLappin(16) (chsd ldrs: effrt 4f out: grad wknd) ..........................................2 **14** 14/1 65 44
4337[9] **Maradata (IRE) (60)** (RHollinshead) **4-8-0**(3) FLynch(1) (effrt over 3f out: n.d)...........................................4 **15** 16/1 35 14
4297[6] **Frezeliere (82)** (JLDunlop) **3-9-6b** MRoberts(2) (lw: plld hrd: in tch tl wknd over 3f out).....................................8 **16** 14/1 45 19
4193[15] **Kings Assembly (77)** (PWHarris) **4-9-6** GHind(12) (chsd ldrs tl lost pl over 3f out)........................................¾ **17** 20/1 39 18
4327[11] **Bowled Over (75)** (CACyzer) **3-8-13** KFallon(6) (chsd ldrs tl wknd over 4f out).............................................5 **18** 20/1 29 3
4064[2] **Forest Robin (84)** (RFJohnsonHoughton) **3-9-8** TQuinn(10) (b: lw: a bhd) ...............................................7 **19** 14/1 27 1
3401[4] **Drummer Hicks (53)** (EWeymes) **7-7-10** JQuinn(14) (a in rr)..................................................................2½ **20** 20/1 — —
(SP 153.6%) **20 Rn**

**2m 13.27** (3.57) CSF £46.38 CT £693.30 TOTE £8.30: £1.90 £2.50 £9.50 £8.10 (£29.90) Trio £695.80 OWNER Mr Graham Rock (NEWMARKET) BRED Hesmonds Stud Ltd
LONG HANDICAP Drummer Hicks 7-5
WEIGHT FOR AGE 3yo-5lb

**4478* Pasternak** put up an incredible performance, coming from a long way behind in the straight after finding all sorts of trouble. He is obviously a progressive individual and another year should see plenty of improvement. (5/1)
**4450 Obelos (USA)** had a real tussle for the lead throughout but, just when he got his head in front, he was swamped by the winner. (8/1)
**4176 Time for Action (IRE)** made this a real test by setting a strong pace, but he finally had to cry enough in the last 100 yards. (20/1)
**4484* Manful** is in really good form at present and kept staying on. Either a bit further or easier ground would have suited. (20/1)
**4438 Apollono** was close enough if good enough halfway up the straight but, despite being given some strong assistance, never came up with the goods. (14/1)
**4355* Fern's Governor** trotted up over this trip last time, but ran here as though a mile and a half is a must. (3/1)
**Gone for a Burton (IRE)**, having his second run of the season, showed signs of something better. (16/1)

## 4618 CONSTANT SECURITY MEDIAN AUCTION MAIDEN STKS (2-Y.O) (Class E)

4-00 (4-02) **7f 202y** £6,628.00 (£1,984.00: £952.00: £436.00) Stalls: Low GOING minus 0.12 sec per fur (G)

SP RR SF

4461[7] **Cybertechnology** (BWHills) **2-9-0** MHills(14) (chsd ldrs: led 2f out: r.o u.p fnl f) ..............................................— **1** 7/1[3] 84 30
4305[6] **Will You Dance** (JLDunlop) **2-8-9** KFallon(1) (bhd: pushed along appr st: gd hdwy to disp ld over 1f out: styd on wl).......................................................................................................................................½ **2** 7/1[3] 78 24
3040[2] **Snow Partridge (USA)** (PFICole) **2-9-0** TQuinn(8) (cl up: chal 3f out: sn rdn: one pce fnl 2f) ...........................3½ **3** 5/4[1] 76 22
4386[3] **Kalinini (USA)** (LMCumani) **2-9-0** OUrbina(5) (in tch: effrt 3f out: styd on: nt pce to chal)..............................1¼ **4** 4/1[2] 73 19
4512[4] **Sir Talbot** (RHannon) **2-9-0** DaneO'Neill(3) (trckd ldrs: outpcd over 3f out: styd on appr fnl f) ............................½ **5** 7/1[3] 72 18
4507[8] **Trooper** (PFICole) **2-9-0** RHills(2) (bhd: hdwy ½-wy: nt pce to chal)...........................................................2½ **6** 20/1 67 13
4041[6] **Heart of Gold (IRE)** (MissSEHall) **2-9-0** RHughes(6) (swtg: s.i.s: hld up & bhd: shkn up 2f out: stdy late hdwy)......................................................................................................................................¾ **7** 16/1 66+ 12
3873[9] **Absolute Liberty (USA)** (SPCWoods) **2-9-0** AClark(12) (led tl hdd & wknd 2f out)..........................................¾ **8** 50/1 64 10
4359[8] **Miss Kalaglow** (CFWall) **2-8-9** GDuffield(7) (b.hind: swtg: a rr div) ..........................................................5 **9** 50/1 49 —
2211[3] **Ile Distinct (IRE)** (MrsASwinbank) **2-9-0** JFortune(13) (s.i.s: sn in tch: ch over 2f out: sn rdn & wknd) ..........s.h **10** 50/1 54 —
4386[4] **Love Me Do (USA)** (MJohnston) **2-9-0** JWeaver(4) (lw: chsd ldrs tl wknd fnl 2f)...........................................s.h **11** 10/1 54 —
4481[4] **Coral Island** (JGFitzGerald) **2-9-0** JCarroll(10) (outpcd fr ½-wy) ...............................................................¾ **12** 50/1 53 —
**Ziggy's Viola (IRE)** (MrsMReveley) **2-8-9** ACulhane(9) (rangy: unf: a rr div).................................................2½ **13** 33/1 42 —
2802[7] **Mon Performer** (MJCamacho) **2-9-0** LCharnock(11) (bit bkwd: a bhd)...........................................................11 **14** 50/1 25 —
(SP 134.4%) **14 Rn**

**1m 42.48** (5.68) CSF £56.66 TOTE £12.30: £2.90 £1.80 £1.10 (£28.40) Trio £21.80 OWNER Mr W. J. Gredley (LAMBOURN) BRED Stetchworth Park Stud Ltd

**Cybertechnology** has obviously learnt plenty from his Ascot run and showed fine courage here when pressure was applied. (7/1)
**4305 Will You Dance** produced a good turn of foot to challenge approaching the final furlong but, despite responding to pressure, was just being held. Her turn should soon come. (7/1)
**3040 Snow Partridge (USA)** had plenty of chances here, but was short of a turn of speed to do anything about it. (5/4: Evens-11/8)
**4386 Kalinini (USA)** is learning all the time and, judging by the way he was keeping on, it will not be long before he finds a race. (4/1)
**4512 Sir Talbot** had his chances, but he is basically one-paced. Over further and in time, he will come into his own. (7/1)
**4507 Trooper** was clueless a week earlier on his debut, but showed here he is improving, although it is a steady progression. (20/1)
**4041 Heart of Gold (IRE)** had an educational and will no doubt do better in due course. (16/1)

## 4619 E.B.F. SANCTON MAIDEN STKS (2-Y.O) (Class D)

4-30 (4-32) **6f** £5,900.00 (£1,760.00: £840.00: £380.00) Stalls: High GOING minus 0.12 sec per fur (G)

SP RR SF

4488[9] **Wolf Mountain** (RHannon) **2-9-0** RHughes(6) (hld up: hdwy to chal over 2f out: led over 1f out: rdn & r.o wl ins fnl f) ..........................................................................................................................— **1** 7/4[1] 94 57
4380[2] **Moonshiner (USA)** (GWragg) **2-9-0** MHills(3) (cl up: led over 2f out tl over 1f out: kpt on)...............................2½ **2** 2/1[2] 87 50
4502[2] **Indian Brave** (MJohnston) **2-9-0** JWeaver(4) (hld up: hdwy ½-wy: edgd lft u.p: nvr able to chal)...................1½ **3** 4/1[3] 83 46
**Selberry** (PCHaslam) **2-9-0** JFortune(2) (rangy: unf: bit bkwd: a.p: effrt 2f out: r.o one pce)..............................1 **4** 25/1 81 44
**Tal-Y-Llyn (IRE)** (BWHills) **2-9-0** TQuinn(1) (w'like: cmpt: bit bkwd: prom: effrt over 2f out: btn appr fnl f) ..................................................................................................................................hd **5** 9/1 80 43
3838[5] **Figlia** (CBBBooth) **2-8-9b**[1] LCharnock(8) (led tl over 2f out: grad wknd).................................................4 **6** 100/1 65 28
**Ijtinab** (PTWalwyn) **2-9-0** RHills(7) (cmpt: bit bkwd: outpcd & bhd fr ½-wy) ...............................................8 **7** 9/1 48 11

**Frederick James** (MJHeaton-Ellis) **2-9-0** JCarroll(5) (b.hind: lengthy: unf: bkwd: bhd: hdwy ½-wy: wknd 2f out) ....1 **8** 16/1 46 9
(SP 120.4%) **8 Rn**

**1m 13.17** (2.17) CSF £5.89 TOTE £2.70: £1.10 £1.20 £1.40 (£2.50) OWNER Lord Carnarvon (MARLBOROUGH) BRED Highclere Stud Ltd
**2878 Wolf Mountain** at last got it right and, responding to pressure, did it well in the end. This should have taught him plenty. (7/4)
**4380 Moonshiner (USA)** put up another decent show and made the winner really fight, but he was firmly put in his place at the finish. (2/1)
**4502 Indian Brave**, held up this time, did not seem entirely suited to these tactics and never really got in a blow. There is better to come. (4/1)
**Selberry**, who needed this, showed a good action and ran well. He will improve in time. (25/1)
**Tal-Y-Llyn (IRE)** looked likely to benefit from this and did show some ability. (9/1)
**Figlia**, in blinkers for the first time, blasted off, but had run herself out with two furlongs left. (100/1)

## 4620 MICKLEGATE RATED STKS H'CAP (0-100) (3-Y.O+) (Class B)
5-00 (5-01) **7f 202y** £8,531.50 (£3,158.50: £1,516.75: £621.25: £248.13: £98.87) Stalls: Low GOING minus 0.12 sec per fur (G)

| | Horse / details | | Pos | SP | RR | SF |
|---|---|---|---|---|---|---|
| 4300[10] | **Kala Sunrise (84)** (CSmith) **3-8-6**ow1 JFortune(6) (lw: a.p: pushed along 3f out: led ins fnl f: r.o u.p) | — | 1 | 14/1 | 92 | 42 |
| 4463[2] | **Hal's Pal (96)** (DRLoder) **3-9-4b** RHughes(7) (hld up & bhd: smooth hdwy to chal 1f out: rdn & no ex) | ¾ | 2 | 2/1 [1] | 103 | 54 |
| 4352[3] | **April The Eighth (90)** (BWHills) **3-8-12** MHills(1) (w ldr: led over 3f out tl ins fnl f: kpt on) | hd | 3 | 7/1 [3] | 96 | 47 |
| 4196[2] | **Grand Musica (93)** (IABalding) **3-9-1** TQuinn(3) (a chsng ldrs: rdn 3f out: styd on towards fin) | ¾ | 4 | 11/2 [2] | 98 | 49 |
| 4190[17] | **Gymcrak Premiere (83)** (GHolmes) **8-8-8v** KFallon(9) (b.hind: drvn along & bhd ½-wy: sme late hdwy) | 4 | 5 | 10/1 | 80 | 34 |
| 4479[5] | **Jarah (USA) (99)** (SbinSuroor) **3-9-7** RHills(10) (hld up: effrt 4f out: wknd over 2f out) | 3 | 6 | 8/1 | 90 | 41 |
| 4444[19] | **Jawaal (84)** (LadyHerries) **6-8-6**(3) FLynch(8) (hld up: hdwy on ins over 3f out: sn rdn & btn) | nk | 7 | 8/1 | 74 | 28 |
| 4568[29] | **Tertium (IRE) (86)** (MartynWane) **4-8-11** LCharnock(4) (in tch: effrt 4f out: no imp) | nk | 8 | 9/1 | 75 | 29 |
| 4184[10] | **Hilaala (USA) (84)** (PTWalwyn) **3-8-6v1** JCarroll(5) (chsd ldrs tl wknd wl over 2f out) | ½ | 9 | 12/1 | 72 | 23 |
| 4385[6] | **Polar Eclipse (86)** (MJohnston) **3-8-8v1** JWeaver(2) (led tl over 3f out: wknd 2f out) | nk | 10 | 14/1 | 74 | 25 |

(SP 123.6%) **10 Rn**

**1m 40.51** (3.71) CSF £42.68 CT £213.01 TOTE £21.40: £2.90 £1.90 £2.10 (£23.00) Trio £119.90 OWNER Mr A. E. Needham (WELLINGORE) BRED Green Park Investments Ltd
WEIGHT FOR AGE 3yo-3lb
**4181 Kala Sunrise** has been promising to win a race for some time and, given some strong assistance, proved very determined in the closing stages. (14/1)
**4463 Hal's Pal** as usual spent most of the race on the bridle but, when put into it seriously, he failed to produce the necessary goods. He is a most frustrating character. (2/1)
**4352 April The Eighth** is running well at present and gave a good account of himself, fighting back when headed. (7/1)
**4196 Grand Musica**, up there all the way, kept staying on to suggest that he should get further. (11/2)
**3709 Gymcrak Premiere** has been disappointing this year and is slipping down the handicap. (10/1)
**4479 Jarah (USA)** has two ways of running these days. (8/1)

T/Jkpt: Not won; £15,884.32 to York 10/10/96. T/Plpt: £43.60 (502.91 Tckts). T/Qdpt: £14.40 (85.31 Tckts). AA

# 4614-YORK (L-H) (Good)
## Thursday October 10th
WEATHER: fine WIND: almost nil

## 4621 EQUITY FINANCIAL COLLECTIONS CONDITIONS STKS (2-Y.O) (Class C)
2-00 (2-00) **6f 214y** £5,070.40 (£1,873.60: £896.80: £364.00: £142.00: £53.20) Stalls: High GOING minus 0.14 sec per fur (G)

| | Horse / details | | Pos | SP | RR | SF |
|---|---|---|---|---|---|---|
| 3927[6] | **Great Ovation (IRE) (100)** (LMCumani) **2-9-5** LDettori(3) (lw: trckd ldrs: pushed along ½-wy: sn outpcd: rallied to ld wl ins fnl f) | — | 1 | 2/1 [2] | 97 | 48 |
| 4311[2] | **Bolero Boy (99)** (MWEasterby) **2-9-0** PatEddery(1) (lw: trckd ldrs: effrt over 2f out: rdn to ld 1f out: hdd & nt qckn wl ins fnl f) | 1¼ | 2 | 13/8 [1] | 89 | 40 |
| 4363* | **Beryllium (84)** (RHannon) **2-9-0** RHughes(5) (led: rdn over 2f out: hdd 1f out: kpt on wl) | nk | 3 | 6/1 | 88 | 39 |
| 3804[5] | **Mayfair** (PFICole) **2-8-9** TQuinn(2) (trckd ldrs: effrt ½-wy: wknd 2f out) | 5 | 4 | 11/2 [3] | 72 | 23 |
| 3268[2] | **Foot Battalion (IRE) (95)** (RHollinshead) **2-8-8**(3) FLynch(6) (trckd ldrs tl lost pl over 2f out) | 1½ | 5 | 9/1 | 71 | 22 |
| | **Sodelk** (JHetherton) **2-8-6**ow3 MBirch(4) (leggy: bit bkwd: dwlt: hld up & plld hrd: lost pl over 2f out: sn bhd) | 10 | 6 | 50/1 | 43 | — |

(SP 113.1%) **6 Rn**

**1m 26.54** (3.54) CSF £5.57 TOTE £2.50: £1.50 £1.60 (£1.80) OWNER Mrs E. H. Vestey (NEWMARKET) BRED Swettenham Stud
**3927 Great Ovation (IRE)**, whose Sandown outing apparently came too soon, was warm in the paddock but still on good terms with himself. Outpaced in what was a three and a half furlong sprint, he rallied in tremendous style to lead well inside the last, and will be better suited by a mile. (2/1)
**4311 Bolero Boy** looked in tip-top trim. Taking time to warm to his task, he showed ahead a furlong out but had no answer to the winner's late burst. (13/8)
**4363* Beryllium** lacks substance but is tough. Stepping up the gallop soon after halfway, he rallied under pressure towards the finish. (6/1)
**3804 Mayfair**, who has been clipped out, raced keenly but, when the race began in earnest, in truth she did not find much. (11/2)
**3268 Foot Battalion (IRE)** looked as though the outing was needed after an absence of 67 days. (9/1)

## 4622 BODDINGTONS MAIDEN STKS (3-Y.O) (Class D)
2-30 (2-32) **1m 2f 85y** £6,316.00 (£1,888.00: £904.00: £412.00) Stalls: Low GOING minus 0.14 sec per fur (G)

| | Horse / details | | Pos | SP | RR | SF |
|---|---|---|---|---|---|---|
| 3841[2] | **Multicoloured (IRE)** (MRStoute) **3-9-0** JReid(1) (led: shkn up over 2f out: clr over 1f out: eased towards fin) | — | 1 | Evens [1] | 88+ | 65 |
| 4429[2] | **Grand Splendour (71)** (LadyHerries) **3-8-9** KFallon(6) (hld up: effrt over 5f out: styd on u.p fnl 2f: no ch w wnr) | 2½ | 2 | 10/1 | 79 | 56 |
| 4235[3] | **Enriched (IRE)** (JHMGosden) **3-8-9** LDettori(3) (lw: trckd ldrs: effrt over 2f out: styd on same pce) | nk | 3 | 3/1 [2] | 79 | 56 |
| 3942[3] | **Pep Talk (USA) (76)** (HRACecil) **3-9-0** PatEddery(8) (chsd wnr: pushed along over 4f out: outpcd fnl 3f) | 6 | 4 | 15/2 [3] | 74 | 51 |
| 4429[6] | **Tiutchev** (RCharlton) **3-9-0** RHughes(7) (trckd ldrs: kpt on one pce fnl 3f) | 1 | 5 | 16/1 | 73 | 50 |
| | **Bonanza Peak (USA)** (MrsJCecil) **3-9-0** KDarley(5) (w'like: scope: s.i.s: bhd tl styd on u.p fnl 2f: nvr nr ldrs) | 1½ | 6 | 25/1 | 71 | 48 |

**Tumi (USA)** (JHMGosden) **3-8-9** JCarroll(10) (leggy: scope: bit bkwd: sn trckng ldrs: pushed along over 3f out: lost pl over 2f out)........s.h **7** 20/1 66 43
4379$^{8}$ **Questing Star** (GWragg) **3-8-9** MHills(9) (trckd ldrs tl lost pl over 2f out)........7 **8** 20/1 55 32
4201$^{9}$ **Sacred Loch (USA)** (GHarwood) **3-9-0** AClark(2) (swtg: trckd ldrs: effrt over 4f out: sn lost pl)........½ **9** 33/1 59 36
4360$^{6}$ **Sufuf** (DMorley) **3-8-9** RHills(4) (hld up: effrt 4f out: sn lost pl)........3½ **10** 10/1 49 26
(SP 127.1%) **10 Rn**

**2m 12.49** (2.79) CSF £12.97 TOTE £2.00: £1.30 £1.90 £1.40 (£6.00) Trio £6.40 OWNER Lord Weinstock/Exors of late S Weinstock (NEWMARKET) BRED Ballymacoll Stud Farm Ltd

**3841 Multicoloured (IRE)** impressed with his action going to post. Dropping back in distance, he ensured there was no hanging about and, but for being eased, would have won by double the official margin. He looks sure to improve more than most from three to four. (Evens)
**4429 Grand Splendour** clearly has some temperament but also does not lack ability. She stuck on grimly under pressure but to no further avail. (10/1)
**4235 Enriched (IRE)**, who has plenty of size, travelled smoothly but, off the bridle, could only stay on at the same pace. There is still time for her to find a race. (3/1)
**3942 Pep Talk (USA)** seems to lack anything in the way of finishing speed. (15/2)
**4429 Tiutchev**, a keen-going type, needs to learn to settle. (16/1)
**Bonanza Peak (USA)** is not without some hope. (25/1)
**Tumi (USA)** fly-leaped repeatedly on the way to the start. She showed some ability until tiring halfway up the straight. (20/1)

## 4623 ALLIED DUNBAR RATED STKS H'CAP (0-105) (3-Y.O+) (Class B)

3-00 (3-00) **6f 214y** £8,053.00 (£2,977.00: £1,426.00: £580.00: £227.50: £86.50) Stalls: High GOING minus 0.14 sec per fur (G)

SP RR SF

4051$^{3}$ **Verzen (IRE) (102)** (DRLoder) **4-9-5** DRMcCabe(7) (racd stands' side: prom: pushed along ½-wy: hdwy to ld over 1f out: styd on wl)........— **1** 4/1$^{2}$ 110 76
4444$^{26}$ **Celestial Key (USA) (102)** (MJohnston) **6-9-5** JWeaver(5) (lw: hld up: effrt ½-wy: ev ch ins fnl f: nt qckn nr fin)........½ **2** 9/1 109 75
4444$^{21}$ **Primo Lara (90)** (PWHarris) **4-8-7** GHind(2) (mde most tl over 1f out: kpt on same pce)........3 **3** 14/1 90 56
4445$^{10}$ **Aerleon Jane (90)** (JHMGosden) **3-8-5** LDettori(6) (lw: hld up: effrt over 2f out: kpt on one pce)........1 **4** 9/4$^{1}$ 88 52
4554* **Highborn (IRE) (92)** (PSFelgate) **7-8-9** 3x WRyan(4) (sn pushed along: prom: outpcd ½-wy: kpt on u.p fnl 2f)........1½ **5** 9/2$^{3}$ 86 52
1623$^{5}$ **Welton Arsenal (94)** (MRChannon) **4-8-11** RHughes(3) (lw: hld up: smooth hdwy to trck ldrs ½-wy: effrt over 1f out: fnd nil)........4 **6** 8/1 79 45
4352* **Star of Zilzal (USA) (104)** (MRStoute) **4-9-7** AClark(1) (sn trckng ldr: chal over 4f out: rdn over 2f out: sn wknd & eased)........7 **7** 9/2$^{3}$ 73 39
(SP 114.9%) **7 Rn**

**1m 24.25** (1.25) CSF £34.27 TOTE £5.40: £3.00 £3.50 (£26.80) OWNER Mr Saeed Manana (NEWMARKET) BRED Sheikh Mohammed bin Rashid al Maktoum
LONG HANDICAP Primo Lara 8-5
WEIGHT FOR AGE 3yo-2lb

**4051 Verzen (IRE)** raced alone up the stands' side. It is just possible he was on the best ground. (4/1)
**4325 Celestial Key (USA)** looked exceptionally well and ran out of his skin, in the end only just being denied. (9/1)
**4054* Primo Lara**, happy to be back on a turning track, stuck on when headed. (14/1)
**1481* Aerleon Jane**, who presumably needed the outing at Ascot, showed a good action going down but, called on for an effort, could do no more than stay on at the same pace. (9/4)
**4554* Highborn (IRE)**, under a 3lb penalty, was the first to come under pressure. (9/2)
**1623 Welton Arsenal**, a frustrating character, as usual travelled strongly, but pulled out absolutely nothing when asked for an effort. (8/1)
**4352* Star of Zilzal (USA)**, 4lb higher in the weights, was unable to dominate and, calling it a day with over two furlongs left, was sensibly allowed to come home in his own time. (9/2)

## 4624 SASHA LYONS BIRTHDAY CLAIMING STKS (3-Y.O+) (Class D)

3-30 (3-32) **1m 2f 85y** £6,316.00 (£1,888.00: £904.00: £412.00) Stalls: Low GOING minus 0.14 sec per fur (G)

SP RR SF

3691$^{9}$ **Hazard a Guess (IRE) (84)** (DNicholls) **6-9-4** AlexGreaves(3) (hld up: effrt over 3f out: hung lft: swtchd rt & styd on ins fnl f: led post)........— **1** 3/1$^{1}$ 76 58
4515$^{3}$ **Quiet Arch (IRE) (57)** (CACyzer) **3-8-6** GCarter(5) (lw: prom: led over 1f out tl last stride)........s.h **2** 6/1 69 46
3939$^{8}$ **Leif the Lucky (USA) (64)** (MissSEHall) **7-8-3**(5) MartinDwyer(7) (b: trckd ldrs: led 3f out tl over 1f out: kpt on same pce ins fnl f)........1 **3** 5/1$^{3}$ 64 46
4511$^{12}$ **Witherkay (61)** (RHannon) **3-8-6** DaneO'Neill(4) (trckd ldrs: pushed along over 4f out: hung rt & one pce fnl 2f)........3 **4** 12/1 63 40
4559$^{6}$ **Samim (USA) (67)** (SGollings) **3-8-6b** KFallon(1) (sn bhd & drvn along: hdwy 3f out: kpt on: nvr rchd ldrs)......1 **5** 14/1 61 38
3985$^{6}$ **Nobby Barnes (37)** (DonEnricoIncisa) **7-8-6** KimTinkler(11) (bhd: styd on u.p fnl 3f: nvr nr to chal)........3½ **6** 33/1 51 33
2331$^{6}$ **Ten Past Six (88)** (MartynWane) **4-8-11** MHills(9) (hld up: hdwy u.p 4f out: sn wknd)........9 **7** 4/1$^{2}$ 42 24
4136$^{18}$ **Northern Fan (IRE) (74)** (NTinkler) **4-9-2** KDarley(8) (led & sn clr: hdd 3f out: hung lft & sn wknd)........2½ **8** 12/1 43 25
4184$^{15}$ **Czarna (IRE) (74)** (CEBrittain) **5-8-11** BDoyle(6) (hld up: stdy hdwy 4f out: sn rdn: wknd over 2f out)........10 **9** 5/1$^{3}$ 23 5
2913$^{7}$ **Realms of Glory (IRE) (40)** (PMitchell) **3-8-1** JQuinn(10) (mid div: effrt over 4f out: sn bhd)........10 **10** 33/1 2 —
4340$^{8}$ **Brownie's Promise (27)** (MBrittain) **3-8-1v$^{1}$** GBardwell(2) (s.i.s: bhd & drvn along ½-wy: sn lost tch: t.o)........27 **11** 50/1 — —
(SP 122.5%) **11 Rn**

**2m 13.94** (4.24) CSF £21.13 TOTE £3.80: £1.60 £2.00 £1.80 (£9.50) Trio £24.10 OWNER Consultco Ltd (THIRSK) BRED A. F. O'Callaghan in Ireland
WEIGHT FOR AGE 3yo-5lb

**3691 Hazard a Guess (IRE)**, absent for 50 days, made little appeal in the paddock. Hanging left and giving his rider problems, he was persuaded to stay on and lead right on the post. (3/1)
**4515 Quiet Arch (IRE)**, dropped back in trip, was collared in the very last stride. (6/1)
**3939 Leif the Lucky (USA)** as usual travelled strongly. After hitting the front on the bridle, he kept on better than on some occasions in the past when headed. (5/1)
**4232 Witherkay**, who looked to have plenty on at the weights, hung right under pressure and could only keep on at the same pace. (12/1)
**4559 Samim (USA)**, soon flat out, took it into his head to stay on halfway up the straight. (14/1)
**3985 Nobby Barnes** is on a losing run of 44, stretching back over two years. (33/1)

## 4625 GREEN HOWARDS CUP NURSERY H'CAP (2-Y.O) (Class C)

4-00 (4-02) **7f 202y** £6,992.00 (£2,096.00: £1,008.00: £464.00) Stalls: Low GOING minus 0.14 sec per fur (G)

| Ref | Horse and running details | Dist | Pos | SP | RR | SF |
|---|---|---|---|---|---|---|
| 4375[2] | **Love Has No Pride (USA) (76)** (RHannon) **2-8-7** DaneO'Neill(1) (bhd: hdwy ½-wy: led over 2f out: r.o strly) | — | 1 | 7/1[2] | 83 | 44 |
| 4319* | **Gipsy Princess (65)** (MWEasterby) **2-7-10b** LCharnock(4) (hdwy to chse ldrs ½-wy: ev ch over 2f out: kpt on u.p: no ch w wnr) | 4 | 2 | 14/1 | 64 | 25 |
| 4298[3] | **Sandbaggedagain (74)** (MWEasterby) **2-8-5** JCarroll(16) (lw: chsd ldrs: led over 3f out tl over 2f out: kpt on same pce) | nk | 3 | 13/2[1] | 72 | 33 |
| 4131[3] | **Princess Topaz (72)** (CACyzer) **2-8-3** JQuinn(7) (effrt ½-wy: styd on: nvr able to chal) | 1¼ | 4 | 7/1[2] | 68 | 29 |
| 3243[4] | **Mr Bombastique (IRE) (85)** (BWHills) **2-9-2** MHills(2) (a chsng ldrs: one pce fnl 2f: hmpd ins fnl f) | 2½ | 5 | 15/2[3] | 76 | 37 |
| 4361[5] | **Auction Hall (65)** (MBell) **2-7-3**(7) RMullen(12) (bhd & pushed along: sme hdwy over 2f out: kpt on: nvr nr ldrs) | 1¼ | 6 | 14/1 | 53 | 14 |
| 4298[6] | **Hurgill Dancer (70)** (JWWatts) **2-8-1** JFEgan(13) (chsd ldrs: no imp fnl 3f) | nk | 7 | 25/1 | 58 | 19 |
| 4375[3] | **Northern Sun (83)** (TGMills) **2-9-0** JReid(6) (hld up: effrt & n.m.r 4f out: kpt on: nvr nr ldrs) | nk | 8 | 12/1 | 70 | 31 |
| 3512[6] | **Floating Devon (65)** (TDEasterby) **2-7-10** GBardwell(10) (hld up & bhd: sme hdwy over 3f out: n.d) | hd | 9 | 25/1 | 52 | 13 |
| 4347* | **Imperial Or Metric (IRE) (76)** (JBerry) **2-8-7** GCarter(15) (in tch: sn rdn along: one pce fnl 3f) | 1 | 10 | 20/1 | 61 | 22 |
| 4084[2] | **Fletcher (90)** (PFICole) **2-9-7** TQuinn(3) (chsd ldrs: drvn along ½-wy: wknd over 2f out) | s.h | 11 | 12/1 | 75 | 36 |
| 4364* | **Smugurs (IRE) (66)** (RJRWilliams) **2-7-8**(3) DWright(8) (mid div: effrt u.p 3f out: sn wknd) | 3 | 12 | 12/1 | 45 | 6 |
| 4131[8] | **General's Star (82)** (MRStoute) **2-8-13v[1]** KDarley(5) (lw: mde most tl over 3f out: sn lost pl) | 1 | 13 | 9/1 | 59 | 20 |
| *3625[5]* | **Highway Robber (IRE) (70)** (JMPEustace) **2-7-10**(5) MartinDwyer(17) (s.i.s: hdwy on outside over 4f out: hung lft: n.d) | 1½ | 14 | 33/1 | 44 | 5 |
| 2619[4] | **Shimazu (IRE) (86)** (JHMGosden) **2-9-3** LDettori(11) (sn bhd & pushed along: eased appr fnl f) | 1¾ | 15 | 7/1[2] | 56 | 17 |
| 4261[3] | **Indifferent Guy (84)** (CEBrittain) **2-9-1** BDoyle(9) (a bhd) | 2½ | 16 | 14/1 | 49 | 10 |
| 4262[3] | **Maradi (IRE) (77)** (DMorley) **2-8-8** RHills(14) (w ldr: wknd qckly over 2f out) | 10 | 17 | 10/1 | 22 | — |
| | | | | (SP 140.2%) | **17 Rn** | |

**1m 40.25** (3.45) CSF £104.23 CT £660.79 TOTE £7.90: £2.00 £5.10 £1.40 £2.20 (£137.40) Trio £135.70 OWNER Miss L. Regis (MARLBOROUGH) BRED Ralph C. Wilson Jnr

LONG HANDICAP Floating Devon 7-1

**4375 Love Has No Pride (USA)**, from a 4lb higher mark, raced with tremendous enthusiasm and scored decisively and in good style. (7/1)

**4319* Gipsy Princess**, with the blinkers back on, stuck on to finish second best but had no chance whatsoever with the winner. (14/1)

**4298 Sandbaggedagain**, 3lb higher at the weights than compared with Doncaster, made the best of his way home but he seemed to hang fire in front. All legs at present, he should be more the finished article next year. (13/2)

**4131 Princess Topaz** stuck on but lacked the pace to take a hand. She needs more use making of her. (7/1)

**3243 Mr Bombastique (IRE)** looked to have plenty on at the weights. (15/2)

**4361 Auction Hall** only got going late in the day and will be happier reverting to ten furlongs. (14/1)

## 4626 BADGER HILL APPRENTICE H'CAP (0-70) (3-Y.O+) (Class E)

4-30 (4-32) **1m 3f 195y** £7,096.00 (£2,128.00: £1,024.00: £472.00) Stalls: Low GOING minus 0.14 sec per fur (G)

| Ref | Horse and running details | Dist | Pos | SP | RR | SF |
|---|---|---|---|---|---|---|
| 4580[2] | **Voila Premiere (IRE) (66)** (MHTompkins) **4-9-7**(3) RMullen(9) (lw: chsd ldrs: led & hung lft over 1f out: styd on) | — | 1 | 11/2[1] | 82 | 63 |
| 3983[18] | **Dreams End (70)** (PBowen) **8-9-7**(7) RCody-Boutcher(3) (chsd ldrs: led 4f out tl over 1f out: nt qckn ins fnl f) | ¾ | 2 | 20/1 | 85 | 66 |
| 2570[4] | **Karisma (IRE) (65)** (DenysSmith) **3-9-2** ADaly(20) (mid div: pushed along 5f out: styd on u.p fnl 2f) | 6 | 3 | 20/1 | 72 | 46 |
| 4320[4] | **Mad Militant (IRE) (55)** (AStreeter) **7-8-8**(5) DDenby(12) (hld up: hdwy over 4f out: sn chsng ldrs: one pce fnl 2f) | 2½ | 4 | 20/1 | 59 | 40 |
| *4334** | **Glow Forum (52)** (LMontagueHall) **5-8-10** MartinDwyer(8) (a chsng ldrs: styd on one pce fnl 3f) | hd | 5 | 11/2[1] | 55 | 36 |
| 4587[3] | **Ashover (49)** (TDBarron) **6-8-2**(5) JDennis(11) (lw: bhd: styd on fnl 3f: nvr nr ldrs) | nk | 6 | 8/1[3] | 52 | 33 |
| *3610[4]* | **Trilby (69)** (PFICole) **3-8-13**(7) DavidO'Neill(2) (bhd & pushed along: hdwy over 4f out: styd on one pce) | 2 | 7 | 14/1 | 69 | 43 |
| 4236[5] | **Gold Desire (48)** (MBrittain) **6-7-13**(7) JFowle(10) (bhd: hdwy over 4f out: sn prom: no imp fnl 2f) | ½ | 8 | 14/1 | 48 | 29 |
| 3587[6] | **Home Counties (IRE) (60)** (DMoffatt) **7-9-4** CAdamson(21) (bhd: sme hdwy 2f out: n.d) | 4 | 9 | 25/1 | 54 | 35 |
| 4227[8] | **Kalou (65)** (CWCElsey) **5-9-9** PFessey(16) (led 2f: chal over 4f out: wknd over 2f out) | 2½ | 10 | 20/1 | 56 | 37 |
| 4489[5] | **Double Echo (IRE) (51)** (JDBethell) **8-8-6**(3) GFaulkner(13) (mid div: effrt 4f out: sn wknd) | nk | 11 | 12/1 | 42 | 23 |
| *4092[7]* | **Hasta la Vista (51)** (MWEasterby) **6-8-9b** GParkin(18) (chsd ldrs tl wknd over 2f out) | hd | 12 | 20/1 | 41 | 22 |
| 4307[13] | **Dauphin (IRE) (45)** (WJMusson) **3-7-10** MBaird(1) (s.i.s: bhd: sme hdwy over 2f out: n.d) | nk | 13 | 14/1 | 35 | 9 |
| 4497* | **Kristal Breeze (54)** (WRMuir) **4-8-7**(5) 5x JWilkinson(15) (lw: nvr bttr than mid div) | 5 | 14 | 7/1[2] | 37 | 18 |
| 4249[6] | **Ring of Vision (IRE) (57)** (MrsMReveley) **4-9-1** GLee(6) (s.i.s: bhd: sme hdwy 3f out: sn wknd) | s.h | 15 | 16/1 | 40 | 21 |
| 4509[15] | **Rock The Barney (IRE) (49)** (PBurgoyne) **7-8-0**(7) JBosley(7) (s.i.s: a bhd) | nk | 16 | 16/1 | 32 | 13 |
| 4307[10] | **Voices in the Sky (48)** (AGNewcombe) **5-8-1**(5) RFfrench(5) (b.hind: chsd ldrs: wknd & edgd rt over 2f out) | 3 | 17 | 16/1 | 27 | 8 |
| 4216[13] | **Claire's Dancer (IRE) (59)** (AndrewTurnell) **3-8-5**(5) CWebb(17) (in tch tl lost pl over 4f out) | 2½ | 18 | 33/1 | 34 | 8 |
| 4496* | **Amadour (IRE) (68)** (PMitchell) **3-9-5** 5x DGriffiths(19) (chsd ldrs: drvn along 5f out: sn wknd) | s.h | 19 | 16/1 | 43 | 17 |
| 4237* | **El Bardador (IRE) (57)** (WJarvis) **3-8-8b** PRoberts(14) (bhd: sme hdwy on outside 5f out: sn wknd) | 2½ | 20 | 12/1 | 29 | 3 |
| 4320[7] | **Master Hyde (USA) (54)** (WStorey) **7-8-9v**(3) DSweeney(4) (led after 2f to 4f out: sn wknd: bhd whn b.d over 2f out) | | B | 20/1 | — | — |
| | **Claireswan (IRE) (58)** (MHTompkins) **4-8-13**(3) GMilligan(22) (bhd whn hmpd & fell over 2f out) | | F | 20/1 | — | — |
| | | | | (SP 153.4%) | **22 Rn** | |

**2m 32.66** (4.86) CSF £120.80 CT £2,009.80 TOTE £6.40: £1.90 £4.10 £6.90 £4.90 (£41.40) Trio £532.50 OWNER Mr B. W. Gaule (NEWMARKET) BRED Mrs W. Hanson

WEIGHT FOR AGE 3yo-7lb

STEWARDS' ENQUIRY Ffrench susp. 21 & 22/10/96 (careless riding).

**4580 Voila Premiere (IRE)**, who looked in tremendous nick, is on top of his form at present and gained a well-deserved victory. (11/2)

**2008 Dreams End** put two poor runs behind him and was the only one to seriously trouble the winner. (20/1)

**2570 Karisma (IRE)** ran quite well after an absence of ninety-four days. (20/1)

**4320 Mad Militant (IRE)**, having his second run after eleven months off, should be cherry-ripe next time. (20/1)

**4334* Glow Forum** is better suited by the All-Weather surfaces. (11/2)

**4587 Ashover**, having his second outing in three days and his forty-ninth in all, is about a stone better on the All-Weather. (8/1)

T/Jkpt: £7,176.90 (2.47 Tckts). T/Plpt: £61.40 (433.8 Tckts). T/Qdpt: £27.60 (36.16 Tckts). WG

**4627a-4638a** (Irish Racing) - See Computer Raceform

## 4394a-CURRAGH (Newbridge, Ireland) (R-H) (Good to yielding)
## Saturday October 5th

### 4639a BLENHEIM STKS (Listed) (2-Y.O)
3-00 (3-00) **6f** £9,675.00 (£2,775.00: £1,275.00: £375.00) GOING minus 0.17 sec per fur (GF)

| | | | | SP | RR | SF |
|---|---|---|---|---|---|---|
| 4156a[3] | **Check The Band (USA)** (APO'Brien,Ireland) **2-9-1**[ow1] CRoche (a.p: led ½-wy: rdn & r.o fnl f) | — | **1** | 7/2[3] | 102+ | 26 |
| 4024a[4] | **Fairy Song (IRE)** (CO'Brien,Ireland) **2-8-7b** NGMcCullagh (chsd ldrs: 5th & effrt over 1f out: 2nd & kpt on u.p ins last: nt rch wnr) | 1½ | **2** | 9/1 | 90 | 15 |
| | **Gan Ainm (IRE)** (PMullins,Ireland) **2-8-12**[ow1] JPMurtagh (hld up: hdwy ½-wy: chal 2f out: 3rd & no ex ins last) | 1 | **3** | 8/1 | 92 | 16 |
| | **Klinsman (IRE)** (APO'Brien,Ireland) **2-8-10** SCraine (dwlt: plld hrd towards rr: hdwy 2f out: r.o ins fnl f: nrst fin) | ½ | **4** | 12/1 | 89 | 14 |
| 4156a* | **Desert Ease (IRE)** (DKWeld,Ireland) **2-8-12** MJKinane (cl up: effrt 2f out: 4th & no ex 1f out) | 2 | **5** | 5/2[1] | 86 | 11 |
| 1565a[7] | **Daffodil Dale (IRE)** (KPrendergast,Ireland) **2-8-7** WJSupple (chsd ldrs: rdn & nt rch ldrs over 1f out: kpt on ins fnl f) | ½ | **6** | 14/1 | 79 | 4 |
| 4156a[2] | **Classic Park** (APO'Brien,Ireland) **2-8-7** JAHeffernan (in tch: 4th & chal over 1f out: no ex ins fnl f) | hd | **7** | 3/1[2] | 79 | 4 |
| | **Burnt Toast (IRE)** (TStack,Ireland) **2-8-7** PJSmullen (chsd ldrs: effrt 2f out: rdn & no ex fr over 1f out) | 1 | **8** | 25/1 | 76 | 1 |
| | **Better Be Sure (USA)** (TARegan,Ireland) **2-8-7** JoannaMorgan (in tch to ½-wy: rdn & no imp 2f out) | 3½ | **9** | 33/1 | 67 | — |
| 2834a[3] | **Petite Princess (USA)** (JSBolger,Ireland) **2-8-11** KJManning (led & disp ld: hdd ½-wy: ev ch 2f out: sn btn) | 1 | **10** | 7/1 | 68 | — |
| | **Too Easy (IRE)** (KPCotter,Ireland) **2-8-10** RMBurke (disp ld to ½-wy: wknd fr 2f out) | 3½ | **11** | 40/1 | 58 | — |

(SP 133.0%) **11 Rn**

**1m 14.7** (4.20) OWNER John Jones jr (PILTOWN)

**4156a Check The Band (USA)**, turning out for the second time in a week following an easy Navan success, showed himself to be in tremendous form. He took over at halfway and was in complete command throughout the final furlong. (7/2)
**4024a Fairy Song (IRE)** put up an improved performance, going second under pressure inside the last without ever getting on terms with the winner. (9/1)
**Gan Ainm (IRE)**, third and finding no extra inside the last, kept on well. (8/1)
**Klinsman (IRE)** showed plenty of promise, despite dwelling at the start and then running freely early on. He made progress from the rear two furlongs out and kept on nicely inside the last to be nearest at the finish. (12/1)
**4156a* Desert Ease (IRE)** was a bit disappointing, finding nothing in fourth place from the furlong marker. (5/2)
**Daffodil Dale (IRE)** put up an improved performance but in doing so, destroyed a tempting nursery mark. (14/1)
**4156a Classic Park**, the shortest priced of the three O'Brien runners, challenged a furlong and a half out but found little extra inside the last. (3/1)

### 4642a C. L. WELD PARK STKS (Gp 3) (2-Y.O F)
4-30 (4-32) **7f** £17,875.00 (£5,225.00: £2,475.00: £825.00) GOING minus 0.17 sec per fur (GF)

| | | | | SP | RR | SF |
|---|---|---|---|---|---|---|
| | **Token Gesture (IRE)** (DKWeld,Ireland) **2-8-9** PJSmullen (mde all: rdn over 1f out: kpt on u.p: hld on wl) | — | **1** | 10/1 | 81 | 41 |
| 4024a[5] | **Melleray (IRE)** (APO'Brien,Ireland) **2-8-11**[ow2] CRoche (hld up: 6th ½-wy: 3rd & trckd ldrs over 1f out: swtchd rt ins fnl f: r.o u.p) | hd | **2** | 7/2[3] | 83 | 41 |
| | **Absolute Glee (USA)** (DKWeld,Ireland) **2-8-9** MJKinane (chsd ldr: rdn to chal over 1f out: ev ch ins fnl f: r.o u.p) | s.h | **3** | 3/1[2] | 81 | 41 |
| 4398a[3] | **Azra (IRE)** (JSBolger,Ireland) **2-8-9b** KJManning (hld up in tch: hdwy over 2f out: 4th & chal over 1f out: kpt on u.p ins fnl f: no ex) | ¾ | **4** | 5/2[1] | 79 | 39 |
| | **Moon Flower (IRE)** (APO'Brien,Ireland) **2-8-9** JAHeffernan (cl up: 3rd ½-wy: sn rdn: 5th u.p & no ex 1½f out: kpt on same pce) | 3½ | **5** | 9/1 | 71 | 31 |
| | **Charita (IRE)** (JGBurns,Ireland) **2-8-9b**[1] NGMcCullagh (hld up towards rr: rdn & chsd ldrs over 2f out: nt trble ldrs 1f out) | 2½ | **6** | 14/1 | 65 | 25 |
| 4159a[4] | **Velvet Appeal (IRE)** (MHalford,Ireland) **2-8-9** WJSupple (hld up towards rr: rdn & chsd ldrs 2f out: no imp over 1f out: kpt on) | s.h | **7** | 9/2 | 65 | 25 |
| | **Trapped (IRE)** (PJFlynn,Ireland) **2-8-9** SCraine (hld up: 5th & hdwy ½-wy: rdn & no ex over 1f out) | s.h | **8** | 12/1 | 65 | 25 |

(SP 127.4%) **8 Rn**

**1m 26.2** (3.20) OWNER Moyglare Stud Farm (CURRAGH)

**Token Gesture (IRE)**, who won her maiden at Galway, made all the running here, keeping on strongly under pressure and just holding on. (10/1)
**4024a Melleray (IRE)**, in third place and tracking the leaders over a furlong out, she switched right inside the last and ran on well under pressure in the straight. (7/2)
**Absolute Glee (USA)**, the better fancied stable companion of the winner, raced in second placed and made her challenge a furlong and a half out. She had every chance but just could not quicken under pressure close home. (3/1)
**4398a Azra (IRE)** shows commendable consistency in her ability to gain placings, but this effort, fourth and under pressure from over a furlong out, hardly rates with her two recent Group One placings here. (5/2)
**Moon Flower (IRE)**, under pressure over a furlong out, was outpaced inside the last. (9/1: op 6/1)
**Charita (IRE)** found herself getting left behind over the last furlong. (14/1)
**4159a Velvet Appeal (IRE)**, still a maiden, was making no impression over a furlong and a half out. (9/2: op 3/1)

### 4643a IRISH CESAREWITCH H'CAP (0-110) (3-Y.O+)
5-00 (5-02) **2m** £13,000.00 (£3,800.00: £1,800.00: £600.00) GOING minus 0.17 sec per fur (GF)

| | | | | SP | RR | SF |
|---|---|---|---|---|---|---|
| | **Miltonfield** (JEMulhern,Ireland) **7-8-6**(4)[ow1] TEDurcan (hld up towards rr: hdwy over 6f out: led 1½f out: rdn & r.o) | — | **1** | 12/1 | 83 | 39 |
| | **Notcomplainingbut (IRE)** (PMullins,Ireland) **5-7-13**(8) JPSpencer (hld up: hmpd ½-wy: hdwy 6f out: chal over 2f out: ev ch 1½f out: rdn & styd on) | 1 | **2** | 9/1[3] | 79 | 36 |
| | **Antapoura (IRE)** (APO'Brien,Ireland) **4-8-2** JAHeffernan (towards rr: hdwy ½-wy: mid div & n.m.r on ins bef st: rdn & hdwy 3f out: styd on wl fnl 1½f) | 3½ | **3** | 25/1 | 71 | 28 |

| | | | | SP | RR | SF |
|---|---|---|---|---|---|---|
| | **Academy House (IRE)** (APO'Brien,Ireland) **3-7-6**(8) RJCondon (cl up: 5th 6f out: chal & ev ch over 2f out: no ex u.p over 1f out) | nk | **4** | 12/1 | 79 | 25 |
| | **Afarka (IRE)** (JOxx,Ireland) **3-8-5**(2) PJSmullen (towards rr: hmpd & hdwy 6f out: rdn & chsd ldrs st: 5th & nt rch ldrs 1½f out: kpt on) | ½ | **5** | 10/1 | 86 | 32 |
| 4026a[10] | **Nayil** (KPrendergast,Ireland) **4-9-3**(6) GMMoylan (hld up: hdwy 6f out: 4th, rdn & chsd ldrs st: no imp 1½f out) | 2 | **6** | 25/1 | 89 | 46 |
| | **Magic Combination (IRE)** (KPrendergast,Ireland) **3-8-11** WJSupple (hld up towards rr: hmpd & stumbled under 7f out: chsd ldrs 3f out: kpt on) | 2 | **7** | 20/1 | 86 | 32 |
| 4537b* | **Theatreworld (IRE)** (APO'Brien,Ireland) **4-9-2** 5x CRoche (sn in tch: 3rd ½-wy: sn led & disp ld: rdn clr & c wd st: hdd u.p over 1f out: one pce) | 1 | **8** | 5/1[1] | 79 | 36 |
| | **Gan Saru** (PJFlynn,Ireland) **3-9-4** NGMcCullagh (hld up: chsd ldrs 4f out: rdn & chal 3f out: no ex 2f out) | 3½ | **9** | 5/1[1] | 88 | 34 |
| | **Real Guest (IRE)** (CCollins,Ireland) **3-8-0** RMBurke (hld up in tch: 9th ½-wy: wnt 2nd 4f out: rdn & chsd ldrs: wknd fr 2f out) | 5½ | **10** | 25/1 | 65 | 11 |
| | **Private Encore (IRE)** (JMuldoon,Ireland) **5-8-0b**(6) RTFitzpatrick (chsd ldrs: hmpd under 7f out: rdn st: nt trble ldrs 2f out: one pce) | 3½ | **11** | 20/1 | 56 | 13 |
| | **Star Defector (IRE)** (JMuldoon,Ireland) **5-8-11**ow1 JPMurtagh (mid div: hdwy to chse ldrs 5f out: 6th & rdn 3f out: no imp fr 2f out) | ¾ | **12** | 20/1 | 60 | 16 |
| | **All the Vowels (IRE)** (JEMulhern,Ireland) **5-7-12b**(4) 7x EAhern (in tch: 9th & chsd ldrs bef st: no imp fr 2f out) | 1 | **13** | 14/1 | 50 | 7 |
| | **Celtic Lore** (DKWeld,Ireland) **4-9-10b** MJKinane (towards rr: rdn & no imp 3f out: kpt on) | s.h | **14** | 14/1 | 72 | 29 |
| | **Metastasio (IRE)** (DGMcArdle,Ireland) **4-7-13** AJNolan (disp ld to 5f out: wknd: no imp early st: kpt on) | 7 | **15** | 20/1 | 40 | — |
| | **Tarthooth (IRE)** (ALTMoore,Ireland) **5-7-13** JoannaMorgan (led & disp ld early: 4th ½-wy: hmpd under 7f out: sn lost pl: n.d 3f out: kpt on) | 1 | **16** | 14/1 | 39 | — |
| | **Mazamet (USA)** (JOxx,Ireland) **3-8-7** DHogan (in tch: 6th ½-wy: 5th, rdn & chsd ledrs st: no imp over 2f out) | ¾ | **17** | 16/1 | 58 | 4 |
| | **No Dunce (IRE)** (PMullins,Ireland) **6-7-10**(8)ow7 JJMullins (towards rr: hdwy bef ½-wy: chsd ldrs 6f out: wknd bef st: no imp 3f out) | ¾ | **18** | 20/1 | 43 | — |
| | **Temerity (IRE)** (WPMullins,Ireland) **3-7-11** AO'Rourke (mid div: rdn & wknd 5f out: n.d early st) | 1 | **19** | 40/1 | 46 | — |
| | **Radanpour (IRE)** (WPMullins,Ireland) **4-8-12** SCraine (hld up: 8th, rdn & chsd ldrs 6f out: btn early st) | 1 | **20** | 11/2[2] | 49 | 6 |
| | **Betterbebob (IRE)** (WPMullins,Ireland) **5-8-0**(6) GCoogan (cl up: 5th ½-wy: wknd 6f out: n.d last 4f) | 2 | **21** | 33/1 | 41 | — |
| | **Magical Lady (IRE)** (APO'Brien,Ireland) **4-7-10**(2)ow3 FrancesCrowley (mid div: hdwy 6f out: chsd ldrs: wknd bef st: n.d) | ½ | **22** | 20/1 | 32 | — |
| 4537b[2] | **Mystical City (IRE)** (WPMullins,Ireland) **6-8-12** KJManning (towards rr: sme hdwy ½-wy: n.d last 4f) | s.h | **23** | 14/1 | 46 | 3 |
| | **Three Rivers** (WPMullins,Ireland) **3-7-4**(6) DPMcDonogh (sn led & disp ld to 7f out: sn wknd qckly: dropped bhd bef st) | | **24** | 33/1 | — | — |
| | **Fishin Cabin (IRE)** (PMatthews,Ireland) **4-7-7** LO'Shea (n.d: dropped bhd appr st) | | **25** | 100/1 | — | — |
| | **Tidjani (IRE)** (FBerry,Ireland) **4-8-13**(8) FMBerry (mid div: rdn & lost pl ½-wy: dropped bhd: wl t.o 4f out) | | **26** | 20/1 | — | — |
| | | | | (SP 169.9%) | **26 Rn** | |

**3m 32.7** (8.70) OWNER J. C. Savage (CURRAGH)
NR

## 4644a-4648a (Irish Racing) - See Computer Raceform

## 0515a-TIPPERARY (Ireland) (L-H) (Good to yielding, Chases Good)
## Sunday October 6th

### 4649a COOLMORE STUD HOME OF CHAMPIONS CONCORDE STKS (Gp 3) (3-Y.O+)
3-30 (3-31) **7f** £16,250.00 (£4,750.00: £2,250.00: £750.00)

| | | | | SP | RR | SF |
|---|---|---|---|---|---|---|
| 4378[2] | **Wizard King** (SirMarkPrescott) **5-8-11** GDuffield (mde all: qcknd 2f out: rdn & r.o) | — | **1** | 7/4[1] | 113+ | — |
| 3782[3] | **Cool Edge (IRE)** (MHTompkins) **5-8-11** NDay (chsd wnr after 2f: rdn to chal wl over 1f out: kpt on) | 1½ | **2** | 12/1 | 110 | — |
| 4281a[5] | **Idris (IRE)** (JSBolger,Ireland) **6-9-4** KJManning (hld up: 4th & hdwy st: sn rdn & effrt: 3rd 1f out: kpt on u.p: nt trble wnr) | ½ | **3** | 2/1[2] | 115 | — |
| 4396a[3] | **Burden Of Proof (IRE)** (CO'Brien,Ireland) **4-8-11** CRoche (hld up towards rr: 5th & rdn over 1f out: r.o u.p ins last: nt rch wnr) | hd | **4** | 5/2[3] | 108 | — |
| | **Wandering Thoughts (IRE)** (PJFlynn,Ireland) **7-8-11** NGMcCullagh (chsd wnr early: rdn & chsd ldrs st: 4th & btn 1f out) | 2½ | **5** | 6/1 | 103 | — |
| | | | | (SP 120.2%) | **5 Rn** | |

**1m 32.8** OWNER Sh Ahmed Bin Saeed Al Maktoum (NEWMARKET) BRED Sheikh Mohammed bin Rashid al Maktoum

**4378 Wizard King**, just touched off in this race last year, had the edge on him on ratings now and made all the running. Asked to quicken up two furlongs out, he did all that was required. A return visit to Ireland for next months Listed Knockaire Stakes at Leopardstown is a possibility. (7/4)

**3782 Cool Edge (IRE)** ran well, and, soon in second place, challenged persistently from under two furlongs out but could make no impression inside the last. (12/1: op 6/1)

**4281a Idris (IRE)**, with his penalty and over a trip short of his best, was always a bit uneasy. He went third a furlong out and kept on under pressure without ever seriously challenging the winner. (2/1)

**4396a Burden Of Proof (IRE)**, waited with in the rear, ran on from last place a furlongs and a half out, but had no prospect of getting to the winner. (5/2: op 4/1)

**4396a* Wandering Thoughts (IRE)** (6/1: op 4/1)

## 3574a-HOPPEGARTEN (Berlin, Germany) (R-H) (Good)
## Thursday October 3rd

### 4650a PRIX ZINO DAVIDOFF-PREIS DER DEUTSCHEN EINHEIT (Gp 3) (3-Y.O+)
3-20 (3-43) **1m 2f** £38,739.00 (£16,216.00: £8,108.00)

| | | | | SP | RR | SF |
|---|---|---|---|---|---|---|
| 2479a[5] | **Oxalagu (GER)** (BSchutz,Germany) **4-9-6** AStarke | — | **1** | | 116 | — |

4172a[3] **Galtee (IRE)** (UweStoltefuss,Germany) **4-9-6** CAsmussen ....hd **2** 116 —
4290a[2] **Sir Warren (IRE)** (HBlume,Germany) **3-8-13** ABrockhausen ....½ **3** 113 —
3912a[7] **Needle Gun (IRE)** (CEBrittain) **4-9-6** BDoyle (btn over 6½l).... **7** — —
**14 Rn**

**2m 7.5** TOTE 96DM: 28DM 37DM 44DM OWNER Gestut Rietberg
**3912a Needle Gun (IRE)** headed the chasing group as Ledok set a very strong pace. Moving to the front half a mile from home, he was collared at the two-furlong pole and had nothing more to give. He has visited both Dubai and America during a globe-trotting season, and may be beginning to lose his edge.

## 4539a-SAINT-CLOUD (France) (L-H) (Soft)
### Friday October 4th

### 4651a PRIX L'EXPRESS (Claimer) (4-Y.O+)
1-50 (1-55) **4f** £7,905.00

| | | | | SP | RR | SF |
|---|---|---|---|---|---|---|
| | **Baba Thong (USA)** (MmeCHead,France) **4-8-5**(5) NGuesdon | — | **1** | | 83 | — |
| 4367[2] | **Go Hever Golf** (TJNaughton) **4-9-2** CAsmussen | ½ | **2** | | 87 | — |
| | **Stitched Up (IRE)** (France) **7-8-7** GGuignard | 1½ | **3** | | 72 | — |

**16 Rn**

**47.5 secs** P-M 4.00F: 1.60F 2.10F 2.80F (8.20F) OWNER Wertheimer Brothers (CHANTILLY) BRED Bloodstock Trading
**4367 Go Hever Golf**, who has been running well in decent handicaps of late, was dropped in class here for this extraordinary event.
DS

## 4288a-BELMONT PARK (New York, USA) (L-H) (Firm)
### Saturday October 5th

### 4652a TURF CLASSIC INVITATIONAL (Gp 1) (3-Y.O+)
9-42 **1m 4f** £193,548.00 (£64,516.00: £35,484.00)

| | | | | SP | RR | SF |
|---|---|---|---|---|---|---|
| 4288a* | **Diplomatic Jet (USA)** (JPicou,USA) **4-9-0** JChavez | — | **1** | | 126 | — |
| 3912a[2] | **Awad (USA)** (DDonk,USA) **6-9-0** PDay | ¾ | **2** | | 125 | — |
| 4288a[3] | **Marlin (USA)** (DWLukas,USA) **3-8-9** SSellers | 3¼ | **3** | | 123 | — |
| 4040a[4] | **Definite Article** (DKWeld,Ireland) **4-9-0** GStevens (btn approx 6½l) | | **6** | | — | — |
| 4397a[4] | **Posidonas** (PFICole) **4-9-0** JSantos (btn approx 17½l) | | **10** | | — | — |

**10 Rn**

**2m 27.51** P-M 13.40: (1-2) 6.10 4.30 (1-2-3) 4.00 3.10 5.40 OWNER F. Hooper BRED F. Hooper
**4040a Definite Article** raced in fifth place before coming under pressure and finding little at the top of the stretch.
**4397a Posidonas** was prominent until he began to weaken soon after halfway.

## 4415a-LONGCHAMP (Paris, France) (R-H) (Soft)
### Saturday October 5th

### 4653a PRIX DE CONDE (Gp 3) (2-Y.O C & G)
1-30 (1-29) **1m 1f** £28,986.00 (£10,540.00: £5,270.00: £2,635.00)

| | | | | SP | RR | SF |
|---|---|---|---|---|---|---|
| | **New Frontier (IRE)** (AFabre,France) **2-9-2** TJarnet (fin 2nd, s.h: awrdd r) | — | **1** | | 90 | 21 |
| 3615* | **Monza (USA)** (PWChapple-Hyam) **2-9-2** JReid (fin 1st: disq: plcd 2nd) | | **2** | | 90 | 21 |
| | **Kaldou Star** (ELellouche,France) **2-9-2** OPeslier | ½ | **3** | | 89 | 20 |

**7 Rn**

**2m 1.3** (13.30) P-M 6.00F: 2.80F 2.40F (32.10F) OWNER Mr M. Tabor (CHANTILLY) BRED Irelandia Holdings Ltd
STEWARDS' ENQUIRY Reid susp. 14-17/10/96 (careless riding)
**New Frontier (IRE)**, who was supplemented into this race, may have been a somewhat fortunate winner. After going under by a short-head after challenging for the lead throughout the final furlong, he was awarded the prize in the Stewards' Room. Nevertheless, it was a game performance and he now heads for the Criterium de Saint-Cloud.
**3615* Monza (USA)**, held up for a late run, came to the fore with a furlong left to run, but had edged to the right a little earlier and interfered with the fading Keroub. He was disqualified and his jockey given a four-day suspension, which may have been a rather harsh decision. He can take his revenge in the Criterium de Saint-Cloud.
**Kaldou Star**, held up for a late run, looked fairly dangerous at the furlong marker. From then on though, he only stayed on at one pace, and this distance is possibly just a little too far.

### 4654a PRIX DE ROYALLIEU (Gp 2) (3-Y.O+ F & M)
2-00 (2-02) **1m 4f 110y** £39,526.00 (£15,810.00: £7,905.00: £3,953.00) GOING: 0.51 sec per fur (GS)

| | | | | SP | RR | SF |
|---|---|---|---|---|---|---|
| 4218[5] | **Annaba (IRE)** (JHMGosden) **3-8-7** LDettori (chsd ldr to st: led over 1f out: sn clr: r.o wl) | — | **1** | | 119 | 77 |
| 3688[5] | **Whitewater Affair** (MRStoute) **3-8-7** JWeaver (a cl up: chsd wnr fr over 1f out: rallied wl cl home) | 4 | **2** | | 114 | 72 |
| 4292a[5] | **Zafzala (IRE)** (JOxx,Ireland) **3-8-7** GMosse (hld up in rr: rdn 2f out: gd hdwy fnl f: fin wl) | s.h | **3** | | 114 | 72 |
| 2273a* | **Dance Treat (USA)** (DSepulchre,France) **4-9-1** ODoleuze (mid div: smooth hdwy fr 2f out: rdn over 1f out: kpt on one pce) | 1½ | **4** | | 113 | 78 |
| 4168a* | **Otaiti (IRE)** (AFabre,France) **3-8-7** OPeslier (in rr early: sme late hdwy) | 2½ | **5** | | 109 | 67 |
| 3392a[2] | **Camporese (IRE)** (PWChapple-Hyam) **3-8-7** JReid (prom: rdn over 2f out: outpcd fnl 2f) | hd | **6** | | 109 | 67 |
| | **Truly Generous (FR)** (RCollet,France) **3-8-7** GGuignard (in rr early: styd on fnl f: nvr plcd to chal) | s.nk | **7** | | 108 | 66 |
| | **Blue Water (FR)** (JEHammond,France) **4-9-1** MBoutin (chsd ldrs: rdn 2f out: one pce) | nk | **8** | | 109 | 74 |
| 2277a[3] | **Spanish Falls** (MmeCHead,France) **3-8-7** FHead (a in rr) | 5 | **9** | | 102 | 60 |
| 3570a[2] | **Binary** (AFabre,France) **3-8-7** TJarnet (prom early: outpcd st) | 4 | **10** | | 96 | 54 |
| 3688[3] | **Mezzogiorno** (GWragg) **3-8-7** CAsmussen (n.d) | | **11** | | — | — |
| 3571a* | **Vadsa Honor (FR)** (AFabre,France) **3-8-7** AJunk (n.d) | | **12** | | — | — |

| | | | | | | |
|---|---|---|---|---|---|---|
| | **Haramayda (FR)** (AdeRoyerDupre,France) **3-8-7** PCoppin (led tl over 1f out: wknd qckly) | | **13** | | — | — |
| | | | | | | **13 Rn** |

**2m 43.2** (8.70) P-M 10.20F: 5.30F 5.30F 1.50F (181.20F) OWNER Sheikh Mohammed (NEWMARKET) BRED Sheikh Mohammed Bin Rashid Al Maktoum

**4218 Annaba (IRE)**, close up until bursting into the lead halfway up the straight, seemed to benefit from the increased distance and soft ground. She will hopefully stay in training next year.

**3688 Whitewater Affair**, always well up, had absolutely no reply when the winner surged into the lead. She battled on gamely to hold second place by the narrowest of margins, but this distance might just have been beyond her.

**3021a* Zafzala (IRE)**, held up, came with a promising-looking effort halfway up the straight. However, in the final furlong, she just stayed on, and did not quite show the sparkle she did in the Vermeille.

**2273a* Dance Treat (USA)** ran the race of her career. Her jockey looked to have a double handful halfway up the straight, but she found nothing when asked a serious question, and appeared not to stay the final furlong.

**3392a Camporese (IRE)** was never far away and chased the winner through early in the straight, but her effort petered out and she dropped out of contention.

**3688 Mezzogiorno** was never really at the races and made no show on this occasion.

## 4655a PRIX DU CADRAN (Gp 1) (4-Y.O+)

3-10 (3-14) **2m 4f** £65,876.00 (£26,350.00: £13,175.00: £6,588.00) GOING: 0.51 sec per fur (GS)

| | | | | SP | RR | SF |
|---|---|---|---|---|---|---|
| 3751a[2] | **Nononito (FR)** (JLesbordes,France) **5-9-2** TJarnet (mid div: led gng wl 2f out: kpt on wl cl home) | — | **1** | 187/10 | 127 | 76 |
| 4434* | **Moonax (IRE)** (BWHills) **5-9-2** LDettori (mid div: rdn & swrvd lft over 1f out: r.o wl fnl f: nt rch wnr) | 1 | **2** | 26/10[2] | 126 | 75 |
| 1397a[5] | **Always Earnest (USA)** (MmeMBollack-Badel,France) **8-9-2** ABadel (rr early: u.p 5f out: r.o st: nvr rchd ldrs) | 2½ | **3** | 17/1 | 124 | 73 |
| 4032a* | **Camp David (GER)** (AWohler,Germany) **6-9-2** ABoschert (trckd ldrs: kpt on u.p st) | 1½ | **4** | 11/1 | 123 | 72 |
| 4134* | **Double Trigger (IRE)** (MJohnston) **5-9-2** JWeaver (chsd ldrs: u.p ent st: one pce) | 3 | **5** | 19/10[1] | 121 | 70 |
| 4167a* | **Always Aloof (USA)** (MRStoute) **5-9-2** OPeslier (chsd ldr to st: unable qckn) | 5 | **6** | 94/10[3] | 117 | 66 |
| | **Separate Lives (SWE)** (ASpanu,France) **5-9-2** FSanchez (led to 2f out: wknd) | 10 | **7** | 18/1 | 109 | 58 |
| 4167a[2] | **Kassani (IRE)** (AdeRoyerDupre,France) **4-9-2** GMosse (in rr early: outpcd st) | 2½ | **8** | 26/10[2] | 107 | 56 |
| 4032a[3] | **Flamingo Paradise** (HBlume,Germany) **5-9-2** THellier (n.d) | 8 | **9** | 72/1 | 100 | 49 |
| | **Juste Ciel (FR)** (DCharbonnier,France) **4-8-13** J-FJacquet (bhd fnl 5f: t.o) | dist | **10** | 74/1 | — | — |
| | | | | (SP 126.6%) | | **10 Rn** |

**4m 31.5** (16.50) P-M 19.70F: 3.70F 1.90F 3.30F (29.30F) OWNER Mr Patrick Sebagh

**3751a Nononito (FR)**, who cruised into the lead two furlongs out, was put under pressure inside the final furlong and was beginning to run out of steam by the post. It was a game effort and a well-deserved victory for his small stable, and he thoroughly appreciated the cut in the ground on this occasion. He will now be allowed to take his chance in the Prix Royal-Oak at the end of the month. (187/10)

**4434* Moonax (IRE)** is a very dodgy character. He was just being manouevred for a run when he decided he fancied going back to the paddock and, diving to the left, he lost many lengths and possibly the race. Straightened up by Dettori as quickly as possible, he flew in the later stages, probably in a bid to have a bite at Nononito. He may also line up for the Royal-Oak, but there is a hurdles campaign planned. (26/10)

**Always Earnest (USA)**, trying to win this race for the second consecutive year, was brought with his usual late run and was still making progress at the finish. Age is probably taking its toll now, but he is still good for a couple of staying races a year. (17/1)

**4032a* Camp David (GER)** put up a decent performance in this company without ever promising to reach the lead. The distance might have been a little far for him, but it was a good effort for a German stayer. (11/1)

**4134* Double Trigger (IRE)** failed to draw the string out of his rivals, which was rather the case a year ago in the same race. It was surprising he did not take the lead much further out and set a really decent pace, which would have been to his advantage. Instead he raced in third place, and was under pressure and going nowhere soon after entering the straight. He has now been beaten in his last three runs in Group One company, but this was still a disappointing run, although the softish ground was against him. (19/10)

**4167a* Always Aloof (USA)**, well up as usual, was still well there at the entrance to the straight but proved one-paced thereafter. He had had a hard race in the Prix Gladiateur and the ground had changed considerably in the interim. (94/10)

## 4656a PRIX DOLLAR (Gp 2) (3-Y.O+)

3-45 (3-52) **1m 1f 165y** £39,526.00 (£15,810.00: £7,605.00: £3,953.00) GOING: 0.51 sec per fur (GS)

| | | | | SP | RR | SF |
|---|---|---|---|---|---|---|
| | **Flemensfirth (USA)** (JHMGosden) **4-9-0** LDettori (smooth hdwy to ld over 1f out: rdn & qcknd wl: r.o) | — | **1** | | 127 | 63 |
| 3915a[3] | **Percutant** (DSmaga,France) **5-9-0** DBoeuf (in rr early: trckd wnr ent st: rdn 2f out: no imp) | 2 | **2** | | 124 | 60 |
| | **El Angelo (USA)** (PBary,France) **4-9-0** TJarnet (in rr early tl st: hdwy over 1f out: wnt 3rd cl home) | 2½ | **3** | | 120 | 56 |
| 4290a[3] | **Zero Problemo (IRE)** (BSchutz,Germany) **3-8-9** AStarke (in rr early: hdwy to ld 2f out tl over 1f out: one pce) | 3 | **4** | | 115 | 46 |
| 2843a* | **Manzoni (GER)** (JEHammond,France) **4-9-4** CAsmussen (mid div: unable qckn st) | ½ | **5** | | 118 | 54 |
| 2276a[10] | **Martiniquais (IRE)** (AFabre,France) **3-8-9** OPeslier (mid div: unable qckn st) | s.h | **6** | | 114 | 45 |
| 3747a[3] | **Madrileno (IRE)** (RMartin-Sanchez,Spain) **4-9-0** JReid (n.d) | 5 | **7** | | 106 | 42 |
| 1052a[3] | **Silvering (FR)** (MmeCHead,France) **4-9-0** FHead (chsd ldr: rdn & btn over 1f out) | 4 | **8** | | 99 | 35 |
| 3754a* | **Federico (USA)** (SJensen,Denmark) **4-9-0** JWeaver (led to 2f out: wknd) | nk | **9** | | 99 | 35 |
| | **Solid Illusion (USA)** (PDemercastel,France) **5-9-0** GMosse (racd in 3rd early: outpcd st) | 2½ | **10** | | 94 | 30 |
| 3996[7] | **Punishment** (CEBrittain) **5-9-0** FSanchez (n.d) | | **11** | | — | — |
| | | | | | | **11 Rn** |

**2m 7.7** (9.20) P-M 2.90F: 1.50F 1.60F 5.00F (6.50F) OWNER Sheikh Mohammed (NEWMARKET) BRED Mill Ridge Farm Ltd in USA

**Flemensfirth (USA)** had absolutely no problem in landing this race for the second year, and it must go down as a great training achievement, as he had not been out since that win. Always travelling well within himself, he cruised into the lead halfway up the straight and soon had it sewn up. He is a fresh horse, so should continue to have a successful autumn, with his targets the Premio Roma and then the Dubai World Cup.

**3915a Percutant** raced in last place for much of the race and then put in a decent late run, but never looked likely to trouble the winner. He has had a good season and goes particularly well when it is soft. He has been put forward for races in Japan and Hong Kong.

**El Angelo (USA)** was putting in his best work at the finish. He is now off to America as he was sold at the Goffs soon after the race.

**3746a Zero Problemo (IRE)** hit the front just over a furlong out, having been in mid-division early on, but could not maintain the effort and stayed on at the one pace. This colt appears to need better ground to show his best.

**3996 Punishment** was always well behind.

## 4657a PRIX DE LUTECE (Gp 3) (3-Y.O)

4-15 (4-23) **1m 7f** £28,986.00 (£10,540.00: £5,270.00: £2,635.00) GOING: 0.51 sec per fur (GS)

| | | | | SP | RR | SF |
|---|---|---|---|---|---|---|
| 4293a[6] | **Tarator (USA)** (ELellouche,France) **3-9-2** TJarnet | — | **1** | | 121 | 74 |

| | | | | SP | RR | SF |
|---|---|---|---|---|---|---|
| 3202a[2] | **Kharizmi (FR)** (AdeRoyerDupre,France) **3-8-11** GMosse | nk | 2 | | 116 | 69 |
| 3751a[3] | **Chief Contender (IRE)** (PWChapple-Hyam) **3-8-11** JReid | ¾ | 3 | | 115 | 68 |
| 3689* | **Clerkenwell (USA)** (MRStoute) **3-8-9** LDettori (btn over 15½l) | | 7 | | 96 | 49 |
| | | | | | | **8 Rn** |

**3m 18.6** (12.60) P-M 2.80F: 1.40F 1.90F 1.60F (11.30F) OWNER Mr Wafic Said BRED Clovelly Farms
**3915a Tarator (USA)** put in a really gutsy performance having taken the advantage over a furlong out, and battled on well in the final stages to win his second Group race of the season. He was giving 5lb and upwards to his rivals, and this tough and consistent performer will make a fine four-year-old. He made an early start this year, so may now be rested, but he has been nominated for races later in the year in Japan and Hong Kong.
**3202a Kharizmi (FR)** was always there and battled on throughout the final stages. He was later fetched for top price at Goffs, and he will now be sent to Saudi Arabia.
**3751a Chief Contender (IRE)** made a gallant effort to make all. He never gave in and could return to France for the Prix Royal-Oak.
**3689* Clerkenwell (USA)** raced in mid-division, but went out like a light early in the straight. This certainly was not his true form, and maybe this came a little late in the season. This was very different ground to that which he encountered when winning the Ebor Handicap.
DS

## 4538a-SAN SIRO (Milan, Italy) (R-H) (Good to soft)
### Saturday October 5th

### 4658a PREMIO BRESSO MAIDEN (2-Y.O)
1-45 (1-46) **7f 110y** £8,120.00 (£3,573.00: £1,949.00)

| | | | | SP | RR | SF |
|---|---|---|---|---|---|---|
| | **Vicoumtess Brave (IRE)** (LordHuntingdon) **2-8-10** EBotti | — | 1 | | — | — |
| | **Risiat (IRE)** (EBorromeo,Italy) **2-8-13** FJovine | 3¾ | 2 | | — | — |
| | **Ozark (IRE)** (DCrisanti,Italy) **2-8-13** MEsposito | 4¾ | 3 | | — | — |
| | | | | | | **9 Rn** |

**1m 36.9** (12.40) TOTE 42L: 13L 11L 15L (291L) OWNER Scuderia San Pancrazio (WEST ILSLEY)
**Vicoumtess Brave (IRE)** raced in mid-division. Taking the lead a furlong out, she only needed to be pushed out with hands and heels to give her trainer his first juvenile winner of the season outside selling company.

## 3203a-DUSSELDORF (Germany) (R-H) (Soft)
### Sunday October 6th

### 4659a GROSSER PREIS VON DUSSELDORF (Gp 2) (3-Y.O+)
3-40 (3-53) **1m 110y** £36,036.00 (£14,414.00: £7,207.00: £3,604.00)

| | | | | SP | RR | SF |
|---|---|---|---|---|---|---|
| | **Village Storm (FR)** (SJensen,Denmark) **6-9-0** THellier (mde all: clr ent st: unchal) | — | 1 | | 116 | — |
| 4409a[8] | **Tres Heureux (GER)** (FrauEMader,Germany) **6-9-0** LMader (hld up: r.o fr 2f out: nvr nrr) | 5 | 2 | | 107 | — |
| 4028a[3] | **Mill King (GER)** (HBlume,Germany) **3-8-8** ASuborics (racd in 4th: one pce fnl 2f) | 1¾ | 3 | | 100 | — |
| 4409a[4] | **Chato (USA)** (HSteinmetz,Germany) **4-9-0** ABest (hld up: 5th st: sn rdn & one pce) | 6 | 4 | | 92 | — |
| 4409a[5] | **Orfijar (FR)** (Germany) **6-9-2** WNewnes (prom: wknd 3f out) | 3 | 5 | | 88 | — |
| 1395a[4] | **Peppito (GER)** (Germany) **3-8-8** LHammer-Hansen (mid div: wknd over 3f out: t.o fnl f) | 16 | 6 | | 53 | — |
| | | | | | | **6 Rn** |

**1m 47.8** TOTE 82DM: 34DM 28DM OWNER S. Thynell
**Village Storm (FR)** took a very weak Group Two. Making all the running, he comfortably beat last year's winner.
**1759a Tres Heureux (GER)** won this last year, but never looked like catching the winner.

## 4653a-LONGCHAMP (Paris, France) (R-H) (Good to soft)
### Sunday October 6th

### 4660a PRIX DE L'ABBAYE DE LONGCHAMP (Gp 1) (C & F)
1-30 (1-32) **5f** £65,876.00 (£26,350.00: £13,175.00: £6,588.00) GOING: 0.51 sec per fur (GS)

| | | | | SP | RR | SF |
|---|---|---|---|---|---|---|
| 4406a* | **Kistena (FR)** (MmeCHead,France) **3-9-8** ODoleuze (in rr: hdwy over 1f out: rdn to ld cl home) | — | 1 | 146/10 | 125 | 65 |
| 3573a* | **Anabaa (USA)** (MmeCHead,France) **4-9-11** FHead (s.i.s: rdn ½-wy: led 1f out tl hdd & no ex cl home) | nk | 2 | 30/100[1] | 127 | 67 |
| 4304[2] | **Hever Golf Rose** (TJNaughton) **5-9-8** PatEddery (prom: rdn 2f out: chal 1f out: one pce fnl f) | 2 | 3 | 89/10[3] | 118 | 58 |
| 1581a[2] | **Easy Option (IRE)** (SbinSuroor) **4-9-8** LDettori (in rr: hdwy whn hmpd over 1f out: nrst fin) | ½ | 4 | 74/10[2] | 116 | 56 |
| 3707[4] | **Carmine Lake (IRE)** (PWChapple-Hyam) **2-8-4** TQuinn (last early: hdwy 2f out: n.m.r cl home) | 1 | 5 | 271/10 | 114 | 35 |
| 4280a* | **Eveningperformance** (HCandy) **5-9-8** CRutter (led early tl hdd 1f out: sn wknd) | nse | 6 | 126/10 | 113 | 53 |
| 4304* | **Struggler** (DRLoder) **4-9-11** OPeslier (sme hdwy ½-wy: no imp) | hd | 7 | 161/10 | 115 | 55 |
| 4406a[2] | **Don't Worry Me (IRE)** (GHenrot,France) **4-9-8** AJunk (prom 3f) | 1 | 8 | 476/10 | 109 | 49 |
| 4057[8] | **Rambling Bear** (MBlanshard) **3-9-11** RCochrane (gd spd 3f) | 3 | 9 | 57/1 | 103 | 43 |
| 4280a[2] | **Ailleacht (USA)** (JSBolger,Ireland) **4-9-8** MJKinane (prom 3f: wknd) | nk | 10 | 577/10 | 99 | 39 |
| | | | | (SP 127.6%) | | **10 Rn** |

**59.3 secs** (4.80) P-M 15.60F: 1.10F 1.10F 1.10F (4.20F) OWNER Wertheimer Brothers (CHANTILLY) BRED J.Wertheimer & Frere
**4406a* Kistena (FR)** was one of the slowest away, but came with a sweeping late run which gave her victory over her better fancied stable-companion in the final 50 yards. She has improved with every race this season and has always been held in high esteem by her trainer, who may now prepare her for the Breeders' Cup Sprint on the dirt at Woodbine. She will remain in training as a four-year-old. (146/10)
**3573a* Anabaa (USA)** started slowly from his outside draw. He was being niggled at from halfway, but took the lead a furlong out, only to be outpaced by the winner in the final stages. Five furlongs is not his ideal distance and he was beaten by a specialist at this trip, but neither the ground or the draw was blamed for this defeat, and he could now go for the Breeders' Cup Mile or a valuable sprint in Japan. (30/100)
**4304 Hever Golf Rose**, never far from the lead, battled on gamely to the bitter end. She appears to have lost a little of her old sparkle this season, but may well be sent to Milan for the Premio Omenoni next Sunday. She will stay in training next year. (89/10)
**1581a Easy Option (IRE)**, none too quickly into her stride, did not have the best of runs when challenging a furlong out, but ran almost pound to pound with Anabaa as when they met in the Prix du Gros Chene at Deauville. (74/10)

**3707 Carmine Lake (IRE)**, outpaced early on, was putting in her best work at the finish. It was a good effort by the only two-year-old in the race. (271/10)
**4280a* Eveningperformance**, fast away, led until after halfway, but her stride began to shorten in the final furlong and she finished a rather disappointing sixth. She stays in training next year. (126/10)
**4304* Struggler** was in the same position throughout and could not quicken in the final stages. He is a much better prospect on firmer ground. (161/10)
**3759 Rambling Bear** forced the starting stalls open and delayed the start. He was never really seen with a chance and was well beaten by the end. (57/1)
**4280a Ailleacht (USA)**, smartly into her stride, was still second at the halfway stage, but then ran out of puff. (577/10)

## 4661a PRIX MARCEL BOUSSAC (Gp 1) (2-Y.O F)

2-05 (2-06) **1m** £105,402.00 (£42,161.00: £21,080.00: £10,540.00) GOING: 0.01 sec per fur (G)

| | | | | SP | RR | SF |
|---|---|---|---|---|---|---|
| 4159a[2] | **Ryafan (USA)** (JHMGosden) **2-8-11** LDettori (a.p: rdn st: hdwy to chal ins fnl f: led cl home) | — | **1** | 2/1[1] | 107 | 46 |
| 2997[2] | **Yashmak (USA)** (HRACecil) **2-8-11** PatEddery (chsd ldr: led 2f out: qcknd wl: hdd cl home: rallied) | hd | **2** | 2/1[1] | 107 | 46 |
| 4159a[8] | **Family Tradition (IRE)** (APO'Brien,Ireland) **2-8-11** WRSwinburn (prom: outpcd ent st: r.o fnl f) | 2½ | **3** | 26/1 | 102 | 41 |
| 4159a* | **Bianca Nera** (DRLoder) **2-8-11** KDarley (mid div early: rdn 2f out: sme late hdwy) | 1½ | **4** | 24/10[2] | 99 | 38 |
| | **Veiled Threat (IRE)** (RCollet,France) **2-8-11** SGuillot (in rr early: r.o fr 1f out: nrst fin) | nk | **5** | 457/10 | 98 | 37 |
| 4291a[2] | **Dissertation (FR)** (MmeCHead,France) **2-8-11** FHead (led early: hdd 2f out: wknd) | hd | **6** | 97/10 | 98 | 37 |
| 3908a[3] | **Green Lady (IRE)** (AFabre,France) **2-8-11** TJarnet (mid div early: rdn 2f out: unable qckn) | hd | **7** | 88/10 | 98 | 37 |
| | **Spring Dance (FR)** (PBary,France) **2-8-11** GMosse (in rr early: hdwy 2f out: no imp fnl f) | 2 | **8** | 92/10 | 94 | 33 |
| 4291a[3] | **Nawal (FR)** (JdeRoualle,France) **2-8-11** CAsmussen (n.d) | 1 | **9** | 20/1 | 92 | 31 |
| 3908a* | **Shigeru Summit** (CBoutin,France) **2-8-11** MBoutin (hld up early: bhd st) | 1½ | **10** | 72/10[3] | 89 | 28 |
| 2051* | **Dance Parade (USA)** (PFICole) **2-8-11** TQuinn (racd in 5th: wknd st) | | **11** | 97/10 | — | — |
| 4294a[4] | **Dame D'Harvard (USA)** (RCollet,France) **2-8-11** OPeslier (n.d) | | **12** | 92/10 | — | — |
| | **Dancing Fire (FR)** (PBogoev,Bulgaria) **2-8-11** BYasmianov (s.i.s: hdwy ½-wy: wknd st) | | **13** | 624/10 | — | — |
| | | | | (SP 169.0%) | | **13 Rn** |

**1m 39.8** (4.80) P-M 3.00F: 2.80F 2.70F 6.40F (10.70F) OWNER No Owner (NEWMARKET) BRED Juddmonte Farms
IN-FOCUS: **For betting purposes Ryafan (USA) and Yashmak (USA) were cpld, as were Dame D'Harvard (USA) and Spring Dance (FR).**
**4159a Ryafan (USA)**, always prominent, challenged from the furlong marker and just managed to pull out a little extra near the line. She pulled a little in the early stages, but looks capable of staying further and is very much a classic prospect. (2/1)
**2997 Yashmak (USA)**, in second place before taking the lead halfway up the straight, was involved in a ding-dong battle and only gave up the lead in the final few strides. A top-class filly in the making, she will do better when raced over a longer distance. There are no plans for her at present, but she looks out of the top drawer. (2/1)
**Family Tradition (IRE)**, always in the leading group, had no answer when the winner and runner-up drew clear in the final stages. She will be suited by a longer distance. (26/1)
**4159a* Bianca Nera**, racing in mid-division, made her effort from a furlong and a half furlong out. She did not have the best of runs before putting in her best work at the finish, but probably did not show her best on this occasion. (24/10)
**2051* Dance Parade (USA)**, prominent until halfway up the straight, went into reverse gear rather quickly. She had not been out for nearly four months and was racing over a mile for the first time. (97/10)

## 4662a FORTE MERIDIEN PRIX DE L'ARC DE TRIOMPHE (Gp 1) (3-Y.O+ C & F)

2-50 (2-50) **1m 4f** £527,009.00 (£210,804.00: £105,402.00: £52,701.00) GOING: 0.01 sec per fur (G)

| | | | | SP | RR | SF |
|---|---|---|---|---|---|---|
| 4293a* | **Helissio (FR)** (ELellouche,France) **3-8-11** OPeslier (led early: qcknd & wnt clr fr 2f out: easily) | — | **1** | 18/10[1] | 136+ | 70 |
| 4040a* | **Pilsudski (IRE)** (MRStoute) **4-9-5** WRSwinburn (racd in 2nd: rdn over 2f out: kpt on one pce) | 5 | **2** | 221/10 | 130 | 71 |
| 4397a* | **Oscar Schindler (IRE)** (KPrendergast,Ireland) **4-9-5** CAsmussen (in rr early: gd hdwy over 1f out: r.o wl) | s.nk | **3** | 148/10 | 130 | 71 |
| 4295a* | **Swain (IRE)** (AFabre,France) **4-9-5** TJarnet (mid div: rdn over 2f out: styd on towards fin) | 1 | **4** | 5/2[2] | 129 | 70 |
| 4292a[6] | **Luna Wells (IRE)** (AFabre,France) **3-8-8** TThulliez (mid div: r.o cl home) | 1½ | **5** | 61/1 | 123 | 57 |
| 4293a[8] | **Le Destin (FR)** (PDemercastel,France) **3-8-11** DBoeuf (in rr early: sme late hdwy: nrst fin) | ¾ | **6** | 47/1 | 125 | 59 |
| 4281a[4] | **Shaamit (IRE)** (WJHaggas) **3-8-11** PatEddery (a mid div) | ½ | **7** | 22/1 | 124 | 58 |
| 4295a[3] | **Leeds (IRE)** (HVandePoele,France) **4-9-5** ODoleuze (nrst fin) | 1½ | **8** | 52/1 | 123 | 64 |
| 4292a[4] | **Leonila (IRE)** (RCollet,France) **3-8-8** GGuignard (a cl up: chal over 1f out: wknd fnl f) | s.h | **9** | 59/1 | 119 | 53 |
| 4295a[2] | **Pentire** (GWragg) **4-9-5** MHills (s.s: a mid div) | 1 | **10** | 73/10 | 122 | 63 |
| 4293a[2] | **Darazari (IRE)** (AdeRoyerDupre,France) **3-8-11** GMosse (mid div: btn st) | s.nk | **11** | 8/1 | 120 | 54 |
| 4293a[3] | **Radevore** (AFabre,France) **3-8-11** SGuillot (in tch to st: sn outpcd) | 3 | **12** | 60/1 | 116 | 50 |
| 2473a* | **Zagreb (USA)** (DKWeld,Ireland) **3-8-11** MJKinane (plld hrd: racd in 3rd tl over 1f out: wknd qckly) | nk | **13** | 66/10[3] | 116 | 50 |
| | **Tamure (IRE)** (JHMGosden) **4-9-5** FHead (a bhd) | 1½ | **14** | 5/2[2] | 115 | 56 |
| 3070[2] | **Classic Cliche (IRE)** (SbinSuroor) **4-9-5** LDettori (racd in 5th: wknd st: eased fnl f) | 15 | **15** | 5/2[2] | 95 | 36 |
| 4293a[9] | **Polaris Flight (USA)** (PWChapple-Hyam) **3-8-11** JReid (in rr whn broke leg & fell 2f out: dead) | | **F** | 47/1 | — | — |
| | | | | (SP 183.7%) | | **16 Rn** |

**2m 29.9** (3.90) OWNER E. Sarasola BRED Ecurie Skymarc Farm
IN-FOCUS: **For betting purposes Swain (IRE), Tamure (IRE) and Classic Cliche (IRE) were cpld.**
**4293a* Helissio (FR)** put up a superb performance under one of the greatest rides ever seen in the Arc by Peslier, who had the nerve to take command of the race soon after the start and dictate from then on. Covering each furlong in roughly twelve seconds, he turned in his quickest one at the entrance to the straight, where he drew clear and made his rivals look rather ordinary. Great credit must go to his trainer who produced him in the finest condition, and his next target is said to be the Japan Cup. There is a good chance he will stay in training next year. (18/10)
**4040a* Pilsudski (IRE)** ran a thoroughly honest race, but was beaten by a superior horse. Tracking the winner, he had no answer when that one accelerated early in the straight, and just stayed on at one pace. He will now be aimed at the Breeders' Cup Turf race, and will stay in training next year. (221/10)
**4397a* Oscar Schindler (IRE)**, who looked extremely well, was last early on and had a rotten run in the straight. Finishing like a train, he would have taken second in a few more strides, and connections later stated they were unhappy with the way he was ridden, considering him to have been given too much to do. He now goes for the Melbourne Cup. (148/10)
**4295a* Swain (IRE)**, not helped by his outside draw, was a long way out of his ground for a horse who needs to be up with the pace. In tenth place and on the outside, he came up the middle of the track and stayed on steadily through the final two furlongs. He was thought to be lame after the race, but this proved not to be the case, and connections will be looking to the Breeders' and Japan Cups. (5/2)
**4281a Shaamit (IRE)** raced in third place early on and was fifth into the straight, but then lacked the necessary speed to take a hand in the finish. (22/1)

**4295a Pentire**, slowly away, raced on the rail but made very little progress in the final two furlongs. This was a lack-lustre performance, but he would have preferred better ground. (73/10)
**2473a* Zagreb (USA)**, racing a little freely early on but soon settled into third, still looked dangerous in the straight, but dropped out quickly with a furlong and a half left to run. He was probably in need of the run and may turn out for the Champion Stakes at Newmarket. (66/10)
**Tamure (IRE)** was always at the tail-end of the field. (5/2)
**3070 Classic Cliche (IRE)** moved up just behind the leaders on the descent to the straight, but was beaten soon after and dropped out of contention. (5/2)
**4293a Polaris Flight (USA)**, in the rear when he broke his off-fore early in the straight, tragically had to be put down. (47/1)

## 4663a SUNSET & VINE PRIX DE L'OPERA (Gp 2) (3-Y.O+ F & M)
3-40 (3-41) **1m 1f 55y** £52,701.00 (£21,080.00: £10,540.00: £5,270.00) GOING: 0.01 sec per fur (G)

| | | | SP | | RR | SF |
|---|---|---|---|---|---|---|
| 4160a* | **Donna Viola** (CFWall) **4-8-13** JReid (in rr early: n.m.r 2f out: hdwy over 1f out: led nr fin) | — | | **1** | 117 | 67 |
| 4028a* | **La Blue (GER)** (BSchutz,Germany) **3-8-12** CAsmussen (in rr early tl st: hdwy fr over 1f out to ld 1f out: r.o wl: hdd nr fin) | ½ | | **2** | 119 | 65 |
| 3570a* | **Sangria (USA)** (AFabre,France) **3-8-10** TJarnet (mid div: rdn 2f out: one pce fr over 1f out: nrst fin) | ½ | | **3** | 116 | 63 |
| 3907a[4] | **Khalisa (IRE)** (AdeRoyerDupre,France) **3-8-12** GMosse (hld up early: hdwy 2f out: ev ch 1f out: one pce cl home) | ½ | | **4** | 117 | 64 |
| 3568a* | **Hill Silver (USA)** (PBary,France) **3-8-10** SGuillot (in rr early: r.o fnl f) | ¾ | | **5** | 114 | 61 |
| 4371* | **Hagwah (USA)** (BHanbury) **4-8-13** WRyan (led early tl hdd 1f out: wknd) | 2½ | | **6** | 109 | 60 |
| 4419a[3] | **Sagar Pride (IRE)** (JGBurns,Ireland) **3-8-10** LDettori (mid div: nvr plcd to chal) | 2½ | | **7** | 106 | 53 |
| | **Ski Iberia (ARG)** (AFabre,France) **4-8-13** OPeslier (4th st: chal over 1f out: wknd cl home) | 2 | | **8** | 101 | 53 |
| 4292a[10] | **Camille (FR)** (PDemercastel,France) **3-8-10** DBoeuf (cl up early: wknd st) | ¾ | | **9** | 101 | 49 |
| 3144[10] | **Matiya (IRE)** (BHanbury) **3-9-0** RHills (trckd ldr early: btn st) | 10 | | **10** | 87 | 37 |

**10 Rn**

**1m 55.5** (3.50) P-M 14.70F: 3.40F 2.00F 2.80F (28.90F) OWNER K. Scott (NEWMARKET) BRED Lady Juliet de Chair
**4160a* Donna Viola** came with a beautifully-timed run to lead in the last 200 yards and was going away from some pretty useful rivals at the end. She has had a highly-successful year and may now be heading for even greater things, races such as the E. P. Taylor Stakes and Breeders' Cup are now being considered. She is a thoroughly game and consistent filly.
**4028a* La Blue (GER)**, well backed, looked all over the winner as they hit the furlong marker, but she had no reply to the winner's burst in the closing stages. A top-class performer, she should make her mark in similar company in the future and is certainly one of the best fillies trained in Germany.
**3570a* Sangria (USA)** ran on bravely in the final stages. She fought on well to the post, but lacked a little acceleration at the end.
**3907a Khalisa (IRE)**, dropped out last and given a lot to do in the straight, made up a lot of ground in the centre of the track, but her run petered out with 100 yards left. She is better than she showed on this occasion.
**4371* Hagwah (USA)** led until halfway up the straight, but then dropped out of contention. She is not really up to this level.
**4419a Sagar Pride (IRE)**, always in mid-division, failed to make any impression on the leaders in the straight.
**1949a Matiya (IRE)** was none too quickly into her stride, but soon moved up into second place. She was still thereabouts halfway up the straight, but then dropped out completely. She has had a long, hard season.

## 4664a PRIX DU ROND-POINT (Gp 2) (3-Y.O+)
4-20 (4-19) **1m** £52,701.00 (£21,080.00: £10,540.00: £5,270.00) GOING: 0.01 sec per fur (G)

| | | | SP | | RR | SF |
|---|---|---|---|---|---|---|
| 3784[3] | **Alhaarth (IRE)** (MajorWRHern) **3-8-12** RHills (set str pce: rdn & r.o wl fr over 1f out) | — | | **1** | 128 | 59 |
| 4165a[6] | **Shaanxi (USA)** (ELellouche,France) **4-9-0** OPeslier (3rd st: rdn & hdwy 2f out: no imp fnl f) | 1½ | | **2** | 124 | 58 |
| 4132[2] | **Bin Rosie** (DRLoder) **4-9-1** LDettori (in rr tl st: hdwy fr over 1f out: wnt 3rd cl home) | 2½ | | **3** | 120 | 54 |
| 4132* | **Bishop of Cashel** (JRFanshawe) **4-9-1** WRSwinburn (mid div to st: unable qckn whn rdn 2f out: sme late hdwy) | 2 | | **4** | 116 | 50 |
| | **River Bay (USA)** (France) **3-8-12** SGuillot (in rr: r.o fnl f) | s.h | | **5** | 116 | 47 |
| 4030a[3] | **Barricade (USA)** (AFabre,France) **3-8-12** TJarnet (nvr plcd to chal) | 1½ | | **6** | 113 | 44 |
| 2276a[5] | **Blackwater (USA)** (MZilber,France) **3-8-12** DBoeuf (6th st: rdn & ev ch over 1f out: wknd fnl f) | 1½ | | **7** | 110 | 41 |
| 4051* | **Centre Stalls (IRE)** (RFJohnsonHoughton) **3-8-12** JReid (mid div: unable qckn) | 1½ | | **8** | 107 | 38 |
| 4443[7] | **Soviet Line (IRE)** (MRStoute) **6-9-5** TQuinn (trckd ldr early: dropped back fr 2f out) | 3 | | **9** | 105 | 39 |
| 4406a[3] | **Moon Is Up (USA)** (JEHammond,France) **3-8-8** CAsmussen (4th st: qckly wknd) | 15 | | **10** | 67 | — |

**10 Rn**

**1m 38.6** (3.60) P-M 9.10F: 2.10F 1.30F 1.80F (14.50) OWNER Mr Hamdan Al Maktoum (LAMBOURN) BRED Shadwell Estate Company Limited
**3784 Alhaarth (IRE)** won his first race of the season in good style, making every yard of the running and holding off the concerted effort of the runner-up with some ease. He appeared to like the cut in the ground and the track, and there look to be some more good races in him. He could come back for the Prix de la Foret, and stays in training next season.
**3745a Shaanxi (USA)** did her very best to win this race for the second consecutive year. Following the winner throughout, she did not have the necessary speed to go with him in the final furlong, but may now turn out for a potential rematch in the Prix de la Foret.
**4132 Bin Rosie** arrived late on the scene and was putting in his best work at the finish. He never looked like catching the first two though, who had the final stages to themselves.
**4132* Bishop of Cashel**, held up early, gradually made up ground in the straight, but never had a chance of finishing in the first two. There was a good pace from the start here and the leaders never came back to the rest of the field.
**4051* Centre Stalls (IRE)**, racing in mid-division, just stayed on at one pace in the straight.
**4443 Soviet Line (IRE)** was well up early on, but dropped out rapidly in the straight.
DS

# 4658a-SAN SIRO (Milan, Italy) (R-H) (Good to soft)
## Sunday October 6th

## 4665a PREMIO DUCA D'AOSTA (Listed) (3-Y.O+)
2-15 (2-18) **1m 7f** £20,300.00 (£8,932.00: £4,872.00)

| | | | SP | | RR | SF |
|---|---|---|---|---|---|---|
| 3934[3] | **Snow Princess (IRE)** (LordHuntingdon) **4-8-12** JWeaver | — | | **1** | 109 | — |
| 3972[2] | **Kristal's Paradise (IRE)** (JLDunlop) **4-8-12** GForte | 5¾ | | **2** | 103 | — |

| | | | | SP | RR | SF |
|---|---|---|---|---|---|---|
| | **Saeta Rubia (USA)** (VSarti,Italy) **5-8-12** MPlanard | 3¾ | **3** | | 99 | — |
| | | | | | | **6 Rn** |

**3m 16.6** (18.60) TOTE 24L: 13L 12L (17L) OWNER Lord Weinstock (WEST ILSLEY) BRED Ballymacoll Stud Co
**3934 Snow Princess (IRE)**, never far away, took the lead a furlong and a half from home and pulled clear for an easy victory. The winner of last year's November Handicap, she is an autumn filly and her trainer may now look for a similar opening on the continent.
**3972 Kristal's Paradise (IRE)** went to the front half a mile from home, but had no answer to the winner's finishing burst.

## 4666a PREMIO DEL DADO (Listed) (2-Y.O)
3-15 (3-23) **1m** £20,300.00 (£8,932.00: £4,872.00)

| | | | | SP | RR | SF |
|---|---|---|---|---|---|---|
| 4183[2] | **Hello (IRE)** (JLDunlop) **2-8-11** FJovine | — | **1** | | 101+ | — |
| | **White Gulch** (GBotti,Italy) **2-8-11** EBotti | 9¼ | **2** | | 83 | — |
| 2671a* | **Kingsinger (IRE)** (PCeriotti,Italy) **2-9-5** AParravani | 5 | **3** | | 81 | — |
| | | | | | | **7 Rn** |

**1m 40.7** (10.70) TOTE 15L: 12L 16L (21L) OWNER Mr P. Wroughton (ARUNDEL) BRED H Volz
**4183 Hello (IRE)** has been running creditably in good company and found this much easier, tracking the leaders until quickening clear passing the two-furlong marker.

## 4667a PREMIO VITTORIO DI CAPUA (Gp 1) (3-Y.O+)
3-45 (3-54) **1m** £54,084.00 (£29,929.00: £14,456.00)

| | | | | SP | RR | SF |
|---|---|---|---|---|---|---|
| 3596[2] | **Mistle Cat (USA)** (SPCWoods) **5-8-13** RHughes (mde all: rdn over 3f out: r.o wl) | — | **1** | | 122 | — |
| 4132[5] | **Gothenberg (IRE)** (MJohnston) **3-8-9** JWeaver (plld hrd 3f: a.p: no imp fnl f) | 2 | **2** | | 117 | — |
| 1759a* | **Morigi** (ITellini,Italy) **5-8-13** MTellini (mid div: outpcd 3f out: rallied ins fnl f) | 3¼ | **3** | | 112 | — |
| 1759a[2] | **Ravier (ITY)** (EBorromeo,Italy) **5-8-13** FJovine (4th st: hdwy 3f out: wknd fnl f) | nk | **4** | | 111 | — |
| | **Les Boyer** (Italy) **5-8-13** EBotti (in rr st: nvr able to chal) | 2½ | **5** | | 106 | — |
| | **Thomire** (Italy) **4-8-13** GForte (a in rr) | 7½ | **6** | | 91 | — |
| | | | | | | **6 Rn** |

**1m 40.3** (10.30) TOTE 46L: 24L 24L (81L) OWNER Mr P. K. L. Chu (NEWMARKET) BRED Henry H. Fitzgibbon & Overbrook Farm
**3596 Mistle Cat (USA)** made all and never looked like being caught. This was a very weak Group One - the time was only 0.4 seconds quicker than the preceding juvenile event - and he will find life much tougher in his next race, which could be either the Prix de la Foret or the Breeders' Cup Mile. Nevertheless, this was a deserved reward for his consistency.
**4132 Gothenberg (IRE)** pulled hard in the early stages. Tracking the winner throughout, he was always well held, but kept the others at bay easily enough. He has been on the go all season and deservedly earned a nice pay cheque here.

# 1952a-FUCHU (Tokyo, Japan) (L-H) (Firm)
## Sunday October 6th

## 4668a MAINICHI OKAN (Gp 2) (3-Y.O+)
6-40 **1m 1f** £405,308.00

| | | | | SP | RR | SF |
|---|---|---|---|---|---|---|
| 3798* | **Annus Mirabilis (FR)** (SbinSuroor) **4-9-0** DHolland | — | **1** | | 120 | — |
| | **Toyo Lyphard (JPN)** (YMatsunaga,Japan) **6-9-2** MMatsunaga | 1½ | **2** | | 119 | — |
| | **Bubble Gum Fellow (JPN)** (KFujisawa,Japan) **3-8-12** YOkabe | nk | **3** | | 119 | — |
| | | | | | | **12 Rn** |

**1m 45.8** TOTE 1020Y: 350Y 660Y250Y (16870Y) OWNER Godolphin (NEWMARKET) BRED Darley Stud Management Co Ltd
**3798* Annus Mirabilis (FR)** was turned out in peak condition. Tucked in behind the leaders, he went for home almost two furlongs out and stayed on really well to give a relieved Holland the first victory of his three month stay. He could return for the Japan Cup.

# 4461-ASCOT (R-H) (Good, Good to soft patches)
## Friday October 11th
WEATHER: overcast WIND: almost nil

## 4669 BOLLINGER CHAMPAGNE CHALLENGE SERIES GENTLEMEN'S H'CAP (Final) (0-80) (3-Y.O+) (Class E)
2-00 (2-01) **1m 4f** £4,396.50 (£1,332.00: £651.00: £310.50) Stalls: High GOING: 0.06 sec per fur (G)

| | | | | SP | RR | SF |
|---|---|---|---|---|---|---|
| 4257[6] | **Fairy Knight (63)** (RHannon) **4-10-12** MrCBonner(2) (lw: hdwy over 2f out: led over 1f out: r.o wl) | — | **1** | 4/1[1] | 74 | 42 |
| 3470[5] | **Country Lover (67)** (LordHuntingdon) **5-11-2v** MrABalding(7) (lw: hld up: rdn over 2f out: chsd wnr fnl f: r.o) | 1¾ | **2** | 12/1 | 76 | 44 |
| 4450* | **Namoodaj (74)** (ACStewart) **3-10-12**(4) MrVLukaniuk(16) (plld hrd: a.p: led 5f out: hung lft over 2f out: hrd rdn: swvd bdly lft & hdd over 1f out: one pce) | 7 | **3** | 9/2[2] | 73 | 34 |
| 4068[12] | **Warm Spell (60)** (GLMoore) **6-10-9** MrKGoble(11) (b: hld up: rdn over 2f out: one pce) | 2½ | **4** | 14/1 | 56 | 24 |
| 4431[4] | **Rex Mundi (61)** (PDEvans) **4-10-10** MrMRimell(10) (a.p: hrd rdn over 2f out: sn wknd) | 3 | **5** | 7/1 | 53 | 21 |
| 4509[4] | **Sam Rockett (51)** (CAHorgan) **3-9-3**(4) MrJCrowley(3) (hdwy over 1f out: nvr nrr) | hd | **6** | 33/1 | 43 | 4 |
| 3471[11] | **Golden Hadeer (44)** (MJRyan) **5-9-3**(4) MrSLavallin(5) (nvr nrr) | 1¾ | **7** | 50/1 | 34 | 2 |
| | **Harding (58)** (SMellor) **5-10-7** MrJRees(6) (a mid div) | 5 | **8** | 33/1 | 41 | 9 |
| 4551* | **Artic Bay (68)** (MrsPNDutfield) **4-10-13**(4) 5x MrLJefford(8) (a.p: hrd rdn over 2f out: wknd over 1f out) | 3 | **9** | 8/1 | 47 | 15 |
| 3479[2] | **Newport Knight (73)** (RAkehurst) **5-11-8** MrRThornton(1) (b.off hind: lw: prom over 8f) | 7 | **10** | 6/1[3] | 43 | 11 |
| | **Desert Challenger (IRE) (46)** (JRJenkins) **6-9-9**ow2 MrRWakley(14) (bhd fnl 6f) | 6 | **11** | 50/1 | 8 | — |
| 4385[5] | **Roufontaine (79)** (WRMuir) **5-12-0** MrTMcCarthy(4) (hdwy 6f out: wknd over 2f out) | ½ | **12** | 9/1 | 40 | 8 |
| *2304*[5] | **Red Phantom (IRE) (64)** (SMellor) **4-10-13** MrPScott(12) (lw: bhd fnl 7f) | ½ | **13** | 33/1 | 24 | — |
| 3944[12] | **Bajan (IRE) (63)** (LadyHerries) **5-10-12** MrPPritchard-Gordon(9) (a bhd) | 3 | **14** | 14/1 | 19 | — |
| 3785[19] | **Persian Conquest (IRE) (50)** (RIngram) **4-9-9b**(4) MrKSantana(15) (led 7f: wknd over 2f out) | 1¾ | **15** | 50/1 | 4 | — |
| 4503* | **Montone (IRE) (66)** (JRJenkins) **6-11-1v** 5x DrMMannish(13) (s.s: a bhd) | ¾ | **16** | 14/1 | 19 | — |
| | | | | (SP 128.5%) | | **16 Rn** |

**2m 42.88** (12.88) CSF £50.12 CT £212.18 TOTE £4.70: £1.50 £2.40 £1.80 £3.00 (£30.20) Trio £66.40 OWNER P & S Lever Partners (MARLBOROUGH) BRED Peter McCalmont
LONG HANDICAP Sam Rockett 9-5 Golden Hadeer 8-13

WEIGHT FOR AGE 3yo-7lb

**4257 Fairy Knight** gained compensation for his unlucky run at Lingfield with a thoroughly-convincing victory, moving to the front below the distance and quickly asserting. (4/1)

**3470 Country Lover** saw out this trip well enough and, although unable to peg back the winner, finished well clear of the rest. (12/1)

**4450* Namoodaj** was given a far from sensible ride by his pilot in the straight for, as the gelding began to drift into the centre of the course, his rider whacked him with his whip in his right hand, causing him to swerve and end up on the stands' rail. (9/2: 3/1-5/1)

**Warm Spell** has been out of form this season, but this was not a bad run, and he is at his best this time of the year with some cut in the ground. (14/1)

**4431 Rex Mundi** was at the end of his tether early in the straight. (7/1)

**4509 Sam Rockett** is probably flattered to have finished so close, as he was only passing beaten horses. (33/1)

**4551* Artic Bay** (8/1: 6/1-9/1)

**4503* Montone (IRE)** (14/1: 10/1-16/1)

## 4670 TRIPLEPRINT MAIDEN STKS (2-Y.O) (Class D)

2-30 (2-30) **6f** £6,937.50 (£2,100.00: £1,025.00: £487.50) Stalls: Low GOING: 0.06 sec per fur (G)

| Horse | Dist | Pos | SP | RR | SF |
|---|---|---|---|---|---|
| **Dances With Dreams** (PWChapple-Hyam) **2-8-9** JReid(3) (unf: scope: lw: nt clr run over 1f out: hdwy 1f out: qcknd to ld wl ins fnl f: r.o wl) | — | **1** | 12/1 | 76 t | 44 |
| **Bintang Timor (USA)** (PFICole) **2-9-0** TQuinn(4) (w'like: scope: lw: hld up: rdn & n.m.r over 2f out: swtchd rt over 1f out: hrd rdn & ev ch wl ins fnl f: unable qckn) | ¾ | **2** | 1/2 [1] | 79 t | 47 |
| **Nariskin (IRE)** (JLDunlop) **2-9-0** LDettori(6) (scope: lw: a.p: led over 1f out tl wl ins fnl f: one pce) | ½ | **3** | 13/2 [2] | 78 t | 46 |
| **Musharak** (JLDunlop) **2-9-0** RHills(5) (unf: scope: led over 4f out tl over 1f out: one pce) | 2½ | **4** | 10/1 [3] | 71 t | 39 |
| **Blushing Desert** (RHannon) **2-8-9** DaneO'Neill(7) (unf: scope: hdwy 2f out: ev ch over 1f out: wknd fnl f) | 1¼ | **5** | 20/1 | 63 t | 31 |
| **Praeditus** (RHannon) **2-9-0** PatEddery(2) (w'like: scope: bit bkwd: s.s: hdwy over 3f out: wknd fnl f) | 1½ | **6** | 12/1 | 64 t | 32 |
| **Labeq (IRE)** (PTWalwyn) **2-9-0** MJKinane(1) (str: scope: bkwd: led over 1f: rdn over 2f out: wkng whn n.m.r on ins 1f out) | ¾ | **7** | 16/1 | 62 t | 30 |

(SP 115.1%) **7 Rn**

**1m 17.97** (3.97) CSF £18.54 TOTE £6.20: £2.00 £1.30 (£3.80) OWNER Dr Anne J F Gillespie & Mr John Wilson (MARLBOROUGH) BRED Dr A. Gillespie

STEWARDS' ENQUIRY Reid susp. 21-23/10/96 (careless riding)

**IN-FOCUS: This did not look a particularly strong event.**

**Dances With Dreams** looked in good shape for this debut and, after looking in a bit of trouble as she failed to get a clear run, she was switched and produced a lovely run to get up in the closing stages. (12/1: op 8/1)

**Bintang Timor (USA)** cost $180,000 as a yearling and was the subject of encouraging reports, so he was all the rage in the market. Given a very hard race on this debut, connections must have been disappointed, but he should recoup losses soon, possibly over a bit further. (1/2)

**Nariskin (IRE)**, not as big as the others, was only worried out of it in the closing stages. A race should soon be found. (13/2: 7/2-7/1)

**Musharak**, who has the scope to develop, did a lot of the pacemaking. (10/1: op 6/1)

**Blushing Desert**, rather weak at present, had every chance until tiring in the final furlong. (20/1)

**Praeditus** looked as though the run would do him good. (12/1: op 6/1)

## 4671 BONUSPRINT OCTOBER STKS (Listed) (3-Y.O+ F & M) (Class A)

3-05 (3-10) **1m (round)** £17,750.00 (£5,375.00: £2,625.00: £1,250.00) Stalls: High GOING: 0.06 sec per fur (G)

| Prev | Horse | Dist | Pos | SP | RR | SF |
|---|---|---|---|---|---|---|
| 4445* | **Fatefully (USA) (102)** (SbinSuroor) **3-8-11** LDettori(2) (hld up: led over 1f out: hrd rdn & edgd rt ins fnl f: r.o wl) | — | **1** | 6/1 [3] | 110 | 71 |
| 3836[9] | **Scarlet Plume (96)** (JLDunlop) **3-8-8** MRoberts(3) (led over 1f: led over 2f out tl over 1f out: unable qckn) | 1½ | **2** | 20/1 | 104 | 65 |
| 3497[5] | **Parrot Jungle (IRE) (97)** (JLDunlop) **3-8-8** TSprake(4) (lw: hdwy over 2f out: hrd rdn over 1f out: r.o wl ins fnl f) | nk | **3** | 50/1 | 103 | 64 |
| 3945[7] | **Awaamir (90)** (JHMGosden) **3-8-8** MHills(6) (swtg: led over 6f out tl over 2f out: ev ch over 1f out: one pce) | 2 | **4** | 20/1 | 99 | 60 |
| 4445[2] | **Abeyr (106)** (MAJarvis) **3-8-8** RCochrane(5) (swtg: rdn over 2f out: hdwy over 1f out: nvr nrr) | 1¼ | **5** | 3/1 [2] | 97 | 58 |
| 4568[33] | **Nagnagnag (IRE) (95)** (SDow) **4-8-11** RHughes(7) (rdn over 2f out: hdwy over 1f out: nvr nrr) | hd | **6** | 20/1 | 97 | 61 |
| 3656* | **Turning Wheel (USA)** (HRACecil) **3-8-8** PatEddery(10) (a.p: rdn 2f out: wknd over 1f out) | 1¼ | **7** | 2/1 [1] | 94 | 55 |
| 4325[4] | **Red Carnival (USA) (109)** (MRStoute) **4-8-11** TQuinn(1) (b.hind: swtg: prom over 6f) | 3½ | **8** | 7/1 | 87 | 51 |
| 4445[3] | **Prancing (98)** (DRLoder) **3-8-8** KDarley(12) (bhd fnl 3f) | 5 | **9** | 14/1 | 77 | 38 |
| 4445[15] | **Satin Bell (93)** (JLDunlop) **3-8-8** JReid(8) (lw: prom 5f) | 1½ | **10** | 25/1 | 74 | 35 |
| 2337[8] | **Tereshkova (USA)** (SbinSuroor) **4-9-0** MJKinane(9) (lw: bhd fnl 3f) | 7 | **11** | 16/1 | 63 | 27 |
| 4360* | **Dawawin (USA) (78)** (EALDunlop) **3-8-8** RHills(11) (a bhd) | 3 | **12** | 25/1 | 54 | 15 |

(SP 121.6%) **12 Rn**

**1m 43.76** (2.96) CSF £104.56 TOTE £6.00: £1.80 £6.00 £5.00 (£183.40) Trio £901.10 OWNER Godolphin (NEWMARKET) BRED Darley Stud Management Co Ltd

WEIGHT FOR AGE 3yo-3lb

**4445* Fatefully (USA)** continues to improve and, although meeting Abeyr on 8lb worse terms for beating her a neck here two weeks ago, finished five lengths to the good. (6/1: op 7/2)

**2991 Scarlet Plume** may have gone in her coat, but she found the easier ground and drop in distance ideal and, as a result, ran her best race of the season. (20/1)

**3497 Parrot Jungle (IRE)**, given a two-month break, bounced back to form and, running on nicely in the straight, only just failed to take second prize. (50/1)

**3640* Awaamir** disappointed in similar company last time, but ran better here. Although collared early in the straight, she still had every chance below the distance before tapped for toe. (20/1)

**4445 Abeyr** was very disappointing as she was weighted to reverse form with the winner. (3/1)

**4352 Nagnagnag (IRE)** is not up to this class. (20/1)

**3656* Turning Wheel (USA)** was disappointing and failed to cope with the step up in class. (2/1)

**4445 Prancing** (14/1: 10/1-16/1)

## 4672 BUCKHOUND NURSERY H'CAP (2-Y.O) (Class C)

3-40 (3-42) **7f** £8,754.00 (£2,652.00: £1,296.00: £618.00) Stalls: Low GOING: 0.06 sec per fur (G)

| Prev | Horse | Dist | Pos | SP | RR | SF |
|---|---|---|---|---|---|---|
| 4250[3] | **Test The Water (IRE) (85)** (RHannon) **2-9-2** PatEddery(13) (lw: rdn over 3f out: hdwy over 2f out: led 1f out: r.o wl) | — | **1** | 12/1 | 90 | 55 |

4488[12] **Manikato (USA) (68)** (DJSCosgrove) **2-7-13v[1]** CRutter(3) (swtg: hld up: rdn & ev ch 1f out: unable qckn) ....1¾ **2** 10/1 69 34
4549* **Merciless Cop (65)** (BJMeehan) **2-7-10b** [5x] JQuinn(5) (led over 5f out to 1f out: one pce) ....nk **3** 4/1[2] 65 30
4127[2] **Blue Goblin (USA) (90)** (LMCumani) **2-9-7** LDettori(2) (hld up: nt clr run over 2f out: rdn over 1f out: one pce) ....2½ **4** 100/30[1] 85 50
4433* **Trading Aces (69)** (MBell) **2-7-7**(7) RMullen(8) (hrd rdn over 2f out: hdwy over 1f out: nvr nrr) ....5 **5** 12/1 52 17
4113[14] **Farewell My Love (IRE) (82)** (PFICole) **2-8-13** TQuinn(1) (b.off hind: led over 1f: ev ch over 1f out: wknd fnl f) ....nk **6** 20/1 65 30
4368* **Silca's My Key (IRE) (72)** (MRChannon) **2-7-12v**(5)ow5 PPMurphy(4) (nvr nrr) ....½ **7** 16/1 53 13
4602[5] **I Can't Remember (79)** (PDEvans) **2-8-10** JFEgan(6) (prom over 5f) ....nk **8** 14/1 60 25
3925[6] **Orontes (USA) (85)** (RHannon) **2-9-2** DaneO'Neill(7) (prom over 3f) ....6 **9** 20/1 52 17
4369[6] **Papita (IRE) (81)** (SDow) **2-8-12** MRoberts(12) (bhd fnl 2f) ....3 **10** 20/1 41 6
4113[3] **Oneknight With You (77)** (MJFetherston-Godley) **2-8-5b[1]**(3) FLynch(9) (bhd fnl 2f) ....hd **11** 11/2[3] 37 2
4234[7] **Sparkling Edge (69)** (CADwyer) **2-7-7**(7)ow4 JoHunnam(11) (a bhd) ....8 **12** 50/1 11 —
4364[2] **Grate Times (81)** (EWeymes) **2-8-12** KDarley(10) (bhd fnl 2f) ....5 **13** 14/1 11 —
(SP 118.4%) **13 Rn**

**1m 31.57** (4.37) CSF £113.65 CT £536.34 TOTE £11.30: £2.60 £4.10 £2.10 (£181.20) Trio £549.40 OWNER Mr J. S. Threadwell (MARLBOROUGH) BRED Kilnamoragh Stud
LONG HANDICAP Sparkling Edge 7-0 Merciless Cop 7-4
**4250 Test The Water (IRE)** has been crying out for further and the slight easing in the ground gave him the chance to break his duck. (12/1: 8/1-14/1)
**4234 Manikato (USA)**, set to rise 12lb, had every chance a furlong from home before the winner asserted. (10/1: 8/1-12/1)
**4549* Merciless Cop** did much of the donkey-work but, when passed by the winner a furlong out, failed to find another gear. (4/1)
**4127 Blue Goblin (USA)** met with traffic problems but, when an opening did appear below the distance, failed to find that vital turn of foot. (100/30)
**4433* Trading Aces** has been raised 7lb for her recent win and, after struggling at the back of the field, passed beaten horses to finish a moderate fifth. (12/1: 8/1-14/1)
**3803* Farewell My Love (IRE)** did not run badly, but the extra furlong found her out. (20/1)

## 4673 WYNDHAM H'CAP (0-90) (3-Y.O+) (Class C)

4-15 (4-15) **2m 45y** £9,525.75 (£2,886.00: £1,410.50: £672.75) Stalls: High GOING: 0.06 sec per fur (G)

SP RR SF

4447[15] **Flocheck (USA) (85)** (JLDunlop) **3-9-6** MJKinane(3) (lw: chsd ldr over 14f out: led 9f out: clr over 2f out: r.o wl) ....— **1** 9/1 100 60
4476[4] **Sea Freedom (60)** (GBBalding) **5-8-6v** GHind(1) (hdwy over 6f out: rdn over 2f out: r.o one pce) ....3½ **2** 14/1 72 43
3983[17] **Benfleet (71)** (RWArmstrong) **5-9-3** RPrice(7) (lw: hdwy over 2f out: hrd rdn over 1f out: one pce) ....nk **3** 20/1 82 53
4199[7] **Harbour Island (80)** (MRStoute) **4-9-12b** LDettori(15) (hld up: n.m.r & swtchd rt over 2f out: n.m.r on ins over 1f out: r.o one pce) ....3 **4** 7/1[3] 88 59
4447[2] **Northern Fleet (82)** (GHarwood) **3-9-3** PatEddery(4) (lw: a.p: chsd wnr 7f out tl wl over 1f out: sn wknd) ....2½ **5** 5/2[1] 88 48
4365[6] **Bob's Ploy (74)** (MHTompkins) **4-9-6** RCochrane(5) (rdn & hdwy over 2f out: one pce) ....¾ **6** 20/1 79 50
4427[4] **Mr Browning (USA) (69)** (RAkehurst) **5-9-1** TQuinn(10) (hld up: nt clr run over 4f out: wknd fnl f) ....1¾ **7** 20/1 72 43
4365[3] **Izza (57)** (WStorey) **5-8-3** NKennedy(16) (nvr nrr) ....2½ **8** 9/2[2] 58 29
2499[3] **Raffles Rooster (59)** (AGNewcombe) **4-8-5** SDrowne(8) (a mid div) ....1½ **9** 16/1 58 29
4447[10] **Pike Creek (USA) (80)** (IABalding) **3-9-1** KDarley(11) (swtg: hld up: rdn over 5f out: wknd 4f out) ....7 **10** 20/1 73 33
4557[4] **Sharaf (IRE) (79)** (WRMuir) **3-9-0** JReid(13) (lw: bhd whn nt clr run over 5f out) ....1½ **11** 33/1 70 30
3163[8] **Mull House (55)** (GPEnright) **9-8-1** NAdams(6) (b: bit bkwd: a bhd) ....20 **12** 100/1 26 —
4327[10] **High Summer (69)** (TThomsonJones) **6-9-1** DBiggs(14) (b: prom over 12f) ....d.h **12** 50/1 40 11
3801[4] **Durshan (USA) (50)** (JRJenkins) **7-7-10** DeclanO'Shea(2) (bhd fnl 4f) ....¾ **14** 100/1 21 —
1194[11] **Muse (82)** (DRCElsworth) **9-9-9**(5) DGriffiths(9) (swtg: bit bkwd: a bhd) ....18 **15** 25/1 35 6
4431[11] **Eagle Canyon (IRE) (79)** (BHanbury) **3-9-0** WRyan(12) (led 7f: wknd over 5f out) ....1¾ **16** 25/1 30 —
(SP 115.4%) **16 Rn**

**3m 37.21** (10.01) CSF £110.23 CT £2,209.76 TOTE £11.00: £2.30 £2.20 £4.00 £1.80 (£64.80) Trio £242.10 OWNER Stonethorn Stud Farms Ltd (ARUNDEL) BRED G. W. Jennings
LONG HANDICAP Durshan (USA) 6-12
WEIGHT FOR AGE 3yo-11lb
OFFICIAL EXPLANATION **Flocheck (USA): was unable to dominate proceedings the time before, but was able to do so here.**
**4260 Flocheck (USA)** flopped last time, but bounced back here. Going on running into Swinley Bottom, he forged clear early in the straight to win in fine style. (9/1)
**4476 Sea Freedom** is extremely frustrating and is still a maiden after twenty-eight attempts. (14/1)
**2973 Benfleet** looked in good shape beforehand and ran his best race so far this season. (20/1)
**3834 Harbour Island** is a real stayer and, although not having the best of runs in the straight, struggled on for fourth. (7/1)
**4447 Northern Fleet** was rather disappointing. Eddery was bustling him along half a mile from home, and the writing was on the wall in the straight. (5/2)
**4365 Bob's Ploy** has won just once from nineteen starts. (20/1)

## 4674 MAYFLOWER CONDITIONS APPRENTICE STKS (3-Y.O+) (Class E)

4-45 (4-48) **1m (straight)** £4,187.25 (£1,278.00: £631.50: £308.25) Stalls: Low GOING: 0.06 sec per fur (G)

SP RR SF

4444[9] **Prince Babar (98)** (JEBanks) **5-8-9**(3) RMullen(11) (a.p: led 5f out: r.o wl) ....— **1** 3/1[2] 89 68
4444[3] **Russian Music (104)** (MissGayKelleway) **3-9-1** DGriffiths(10) (a.p: rdn over 1f out: ev ch ins fnl f: unable qckn) ....¾ **2** 2/1[1] 94 70
2881[6] **Kings Witness (USA) (100)** (WJHaggas) **3-8-6**(3) GFaulkner(6) (b.off fore: hdwy 4f out: hrd rdn over 1f out: one pce) ....1¾ **3** 5/1[3] 84 60
4064[14] **Mimosa (51)** (SDow) **3-8-4** ADaly(12) (swtg: hdwy over 1f out: nvr nrr) ....4 **4** 50/1 71 47
4181[9] **Van Gurp (90)** (BAMcMahon) **3-9-1** LNewton(13) (lw: hdwy 4f out: wknd over 1f out) ....5 **5** 12/1 72 48
4445[6] **Marl (89)** (RAkehurst) **3-8-4** MartinDwyer(3) (hdwy over 2f out: wknd over 1f out) ....½ **6** 11/2 60 36
4341[11] **Persian Dawn (36)** (MajorDNChappell) **3-8-1**(3) IonaWands(5) (prom 4f) ....1 **7** 100/1 58 34
2432* **Rivers Magic (78)** (MajorDNChappell) **3-8-12**(3) AimeeCook(14) (led 3f: wknd 2f out) ....½ **8** 10/1 68 44
4499[6] **Baba Au Rhum (IRE)** (IPWilliams) **4-8-7**(5) RFfrench(8) (a bhd) ....2½ **9** 100/1 57 36
4209[8] **Saltando (IRE) (40)** (PatMitchell) **5-8-12** AmandaSanders(7) (a bhd) ....5 **10** 100/1 47 26

| | | | | SP | RR | SF |
|---|---|---|---|---|---|---|
| 4568[31] | **Show Faith (IRE) (82)** (RHannon) **6-8-12** MBaird(9) (lw: sme hdwy over 3f out: wknd over 2f out) | 1½ | **11** | 16/1 | 44 | 23 |
| 4360[15] | **Western Country (30)** (EAWheeler) **4-8-7**(5) JWilkinson(2) (swtg: bhd fnl 5f: t.o) | dist | **12** | 100/1 | — | — |
| 3472[14] | **Endaxi Sam** (RIngram) **3-8-4**(5) CWebb(4) (bhd fnl 4f: t.o) | ½ | **13** | 100/1 | — | — |
| | **Fruit Town (IRE)** (PButler) **7-8-12** CAdamson(1) (bkwd: s.s: a wl bhd: t.o) | | **14** | 100/1 | — | — |
| | | | | (SP 121.0%) | | **14 Rn** |

**1m 44.53** (3.33) CSF £9.04 TOTE £4.40: £1.60 £1.30 £1.40 (£3.10) Trio £6.70 OWNER Mr Giles Pritchard-Gordon (NEWMARKET)
WEIGHT FOR AGE 3yo-3lb
OFFICIAL EXPLANATION **Baba Au Rhum (IRE): the rider explained that his instructions were to switch the gelding off in mid division, as he tends to pull in his races, and thereafter to do his best. The gelding pulled extremely hard going down expending valuable energy. In the latter stages after pulling hard again in the race, he had nothing left when asked to quicken. Thereafter he was only able to hold his mount together and would not have been any closer with a more vigorous ride.**
IN-FOCUS: **This was an uncompetitive event.**
**4314 Prince Babar** gained his first victory of the season after some good efforts in hot handicaps. (3/1)
**4444 Russian Music** has been a model of consistency this season, but has cost punters dear, and once again settled for second best. (2/1)
**2535 Kings Witness (USA)**, given a three-month break, was left standing from below the distance. (5/1)
**3496 Mimosa** is flattered to have finished so close as she stayed on past beaten horses. (50/1)
**3999* Van Gurp** is not an easy ride and had shot his bolt below the distance. (12/1)
**4445 Marl** (11/2: 4/1-6/1)

## 4675 TANKERVILLE H'CAP (0-90) (3-Y.O+) (Class C)

5-20 (5-23) **1m 4f** £7,652.50 (£2,320.00: £1,135.00: £542.50) Stalls: High GOING: 0.06 sec per fur (G)

| | | | | SP | RR | SF |
|---|---|---|---|---|---|---|
| 4431[9] | **Shadow Leader (76)** (CREgerton) **5-9-0** RHughes(2) (stdy hdwy over 3f out: led 1f out: hrd rdn: r.o wl) | — | **1** | 12/1 | 86 | 63 |
| 4465[16] | **Polydamas (84)** (MRStoute) **4-9-8** JReid(5) (a.p: led over 1f out: sn hdd: unable qckn) | 2 | **2** | 7/1[1] | 91 | 68 |
| 4465[4] | **Dance So Suite (89)** (PFICole) **4-9-13** TQuinn(14) (swtg: a.p: ev ch 1f out: one pce) | nk | **3** | 7/1[1] | 96 | 73 |
| 4063[6] | **Subterfuge (82)** (HRACecil) **3-8-13** WRyan(1) (hdwy over 3f out: rdn over 2f out: r.o one pce) | 1¼ | **4** | 10/1[3] | 87 | 57 |
| 573[16] | **River Keen (IRE) (84)** (RWArmstrong) **4-9-8** MHills(10) (lw: led over 10f) | 7 | **5** | 7/1[1] | 80 | 57 |
| 4431[12] | **Otto E Mezzo (73)** (MJPolglase) **4-8-11** KDarley(3) (a.p: rdn over 2f out: sn wknd) | 1¾ | **6** | 33/1 | 67 | 44 |
| 4487[4] | **Beyond Doubt (82)** (LordHuntingdon) **4-9-6** DHarrison(8) (hld up: rdn over 2f out: sn wknd) | hd | **7** | 10/1[3] | 76 | 53 |
| 4374* | **Fasil (IRE) (86)** (CJBenstead) **3-9-3** RHills(4) (lw: bhd fnl 5f) | 3½ | **8** | 8/1[2] | 75 | 45 |
| 4326[4] | **Edan Heights (73)** (SDow) **4-8-6**(5) ADaly(7) (lw: a mid div) | nk | **9** | 8/1[2] | 61 | 38 |
| 4465[13] | **My Learned Friend (81)** (AHide) **5-9-0**(5) MartinDwyer(15) (bhd fnl 2f) | 3 | **10** | 20/1 | 65 | 42 |
| 1353[7] | **Bit on the Side (IRE) (82)** (NEBerry) **7-9-3**(3) PMcCabe(12) (a bhd) | ¾ | **11** | 16/1 | 65 | 42 |
| 2006[7] | **More Than You Know (IRE) (87)** (RHannon) **3-9-4** DaneO'Neill(9) (lw: a bhd) | 14 | **12** | 33/1 | 52 | 22 |
| 3669[5] | **Liefling (USA) (79)** (JHMGosden) **3-8-10** LDettori(13) (prom 10f) | 2½ | **13** | 8/1[2] | 40 | 10 |
| 4447[16] | **Reimei (70)** (RAkehurst) **7-8-8** SSanders(11) (b.off fore: bhd fnl 3f) | 1¼ | **14** | 16/1 | 30 | 7 |
| 4320[2] | **Artic Courier (85)** (DJSCosgrove) **5-9-9** MRimmer(6) (mid div whn hmpd 10f out: bhd fnl 8f) | 5 | **15** | 14/1 | 38 | 15 |
| | | | | (SP 125.8%) | | **15 Rn** |

**2m 36.03** (6.03) CSF £89.49 CT £591.31 TOTE £17.10: £4.80 £2.90 £3.50 (£44.30) Trio £287.00 OWNER Mr James Blackshaw (CHADDLE-WORTH) BRED A. J. Sexton
WEIGHT FOR AGE 3yo-7lb
**Shadow Leader** bounced back to form with a thoroughly convincing display. Always travelling well, he struck the front a furlong out and, given a few reminders, quickly had the race in hand. (12/1)
**1109 Polydamas** ran better but, after showing briefly in front below the distance, was soon passed by the winner. (7/1)
**4465 Dance So Suite** ran well and still had every chance a furlong out. (7/1)
**Subterfuge** struggled on in the straight without ever looking likely to find that vital turn of foot. (10/1)
**392* River Keen (IRE)** has been off since April, but looked extremely well and did a fine job from the front until lack of run took its toll. He is one to note. (7/1)
**3754a Otto E Mezzo** has yet to win in this country and, after racing in a prominent position, had given his best early in the straight. (33/1)

T/Jkpt: Not won; £5,909.80 to Ascot 12/10/96. T/Plpt: £385.50 (87.58 Tckts). T/Qdpt: £64.90 (31.73 Tckts). AK

# 4669-ASCOT (R-H) (Good, Good to soft patches)
## Saturday October 12th

WEATHER: fine WIND: almost nil

## 4676 AUTUMN STKS (Listed) (2-Y.O) (Class A)

2-00 (2-00) **1m (round)** £12,195.00 (£3,690.00: £1,800.00: £855.00) Stalls: High GOING: 0.09 sec per fur (G)

| | | | | SP | RR | SF |
|---|---|---|---|---|---|---|
| 4261* | **High Roller (IRE)** (HRACecil) **2-8-11** PatEddery(1) (hld up: n.m.r over 2f out: chsd ldr over 1f out: hrd rdn: led last strides) | — | **1** | 2/5[1] | 106 | 61 |
| 4213* | **Barnum Sands (100)** (JLDunlop) **2-8-11** TQuinn(3) (hld up: led over 3f out: rdn over 1f out: hdd last strides) | s.h | **2** | 9/2[2] | 106 | 61 |
| 4369[4] | **Sheer Face (90)** (WRMuir) **2-8-11** JReid(4) (hld up: rdn 2f out: wknd over 1f out) | 8 | **3** | 33/1 | 90 | 45 |
| 4133[9] | **Catwalk (98)** (WJHaggas) **2-8-10** LDettori(5) (led 7f out tl over 3f out: wknd over 1f out) | 2½ | **4** | 8/1[3] | 84 | 39 |
| 4183[5] | **Blue River (IRE) (90)** (TGMills) **2-8-11** BDoyle(2) (swtg: led 1f: rdn over 2f out: sn wknd) | 12 | **5** | 25/1 | 61 | 16 |
| | | | | (SP 107.5%) | | **5 Rn** |

**1m 44.91** (4.11) CSF £2.51 TOTE £1.30: £1.10 £1.30 (£1.70) OWNER Baron G Von Ullmann (NEWMARKET) BRED S. Niarchos
**4261* High Roller (IRE)**, already favourite for next year's Derby, was all the rage in the market, but nearly let his supporters down. Short of room for a few strides early in the straight having given the leader a nice head start, Eddery had to get serious on the colt and gave him twelve smacks to get him up in the last couple of strides. This was a disappointing display and, not surprisingly, his odds lengthened for next year's Blue Riband event. He did look green though. (2/5)
**4213* Barnum Sands** went to the front turning for home and poached a useful lead on the favourite. He appeared to falter a few times in the final quarter-mile, and was caught in the last couple of strides. (9/2)
**4369 Sheer Face** is not up to this class. (33/1)
**3444* Catwalk** was feared by her trainer to have gone over the top. (8/1)
**4183 Blue River (IRE)** was rather edgy in the paddock and got warm. (25/1)

## 4677 WILLMOTT DIXON CORNWALLIS STKS (Gp 3) (2-Y.O) (Class A)

2-30 (2-30) **5f** £22,295.00 (£8,438.50: £4,131.75: £1,884.75) Stalls: Low GOING: 0.09 sec per fur (G)

| | | | | SP | RR | SF |
|---|---|---|---|---|---|---|
| $4519^{6}$ | **Easycall (100)** (BJMeehan) **2-9-4** MTebbutt(12) (a.p: led over 2f out: hrd rdn fnl f: r.o wl) | — | **1** | 11/2$^{2}$ | 112 | 77 |
| 4639a* | **Check The Band (USA)** (APO'Brien,Ireland) **2-8-12** CRoche(1) (a.p: rdn over 1f out: unable qckn) | 1½ | **2** | 9/2$^{1}$ | 101 | 66 |
| $4258^{2}$ | **Grand Lad (IRE) (100)** (RWArmstrong) **2-8-12** RHills(8) (swtg: led over 3f out tl over 2f out: rdn over 1f out: one pce) | ½ | **3** | 11/1 | 100 | 65 |
| $4328^{6}$ | **Omaha City (IRE) (100)** (BGubby) **2-8-12** BDoyle(10) (hld up: rdn over 2f out: one pce) | 2 | **4** | 16/1 | 93 | 58 |
| 4579* | **Superior Premium (96)** (RAFahey) **2-8-12** ACulhane(4) (lw: hld up: hrd rdn over 1f out: one pce) | 1¼ | **5** | 25/1 | 89 | 54 |
| 3924* | **Rudi's Pet (IRE) (96)** (RHannon) **2-8-12** DaneO'Neill(5) (nvr nr to chal) | 2 | **6** | 20/1 | 83 | 48 |
| 3750a$^{5}$ | **Blue Ridge (100)** (RHannon) **2-8-12** MJKinane(3) (bhd fnl 2f) | 5 | **7** | 25/1 | 67 | 32 |
| $4299^{2}$ | **Head Over Heels (IRE) (100)** (JHMGosden) **2-8-7** LDettori(11) (b.hind: lw: sme hdwy over 2f out: sn wknd) | ½ | **8** | 7/1$^{3}$ | 60 | 25 |
| 4475* | **Sabina** (IABalding) **2-8-7** TQuinn(2) (prom over 3f) | hd | **9** | 8/1 | 60 | 25 |
| $4519^{5}$ | **Deep Finesse (100)** (MAJarvis) **2-9-1** PatEddery(7) (s.s: a bhd) | 8 | **10** | 9/2$^{1}$ | 42 | 7 |
| 4517* | **Meliksah (IRE) (89)** (MBell) **2-8-12** MFenton(9) (lw: led over 1f: wknd 2f out) | nk | **11** | 10/1 | 38 | 3 |

(SP 111.1%) **11 Rn**

**61.94 secs** (1.94) CSF £26.95 TOTE £4.70: £2.10 £2.00 £2.80 (£13.20) Trio £97.90 OWNER Easycall Partnership (UPPER LAMBOURN) BRED Mrs Susan Feddern

**4519 Easycall** responded well to pressure and made it five wins from seven starts this year. (11/2: op 7/2)
**4639a* Check The Band (USA)**, winner of two races in Ireland last week, goes well with some cut. (9/2)
**4258 Grand Lad (IRE)** liked this slightly easier surface and ran well in this valuable event. (11/1)
**4035a Omaha City (IRE)** can get into the money in this type of event, but is not up to winning one. (16/1)
**4579* Superior Premium** had gained both his wins with some cut and, after coming under strong pressure below the distance, failed to find another gear. (25/1)
**3924* Rudi's Pet (IRE)** is not up to this company. (20/1)
**4519 Deep Finesse** ran diabolically. (9/2)

## 4678 PRINCESS ROYAL STKS (Gp 3) (3-Y.O+ F & M) (Class A)

3-00 (3-00) **1m 4f** £32,300.00 (£12,227.50: £5,988.75: £2,733.75) Stalls: High GOING: 0.09 sec per fur (G)

| | | | | SP | RR | SF |
|---|---|---|---|---|---|---|
| $4467^{2}$ | **Time Allowed (106)** (MRStoute) **3-8-7** JReid(4) (b: led over 10f: hrd rdn: led last stride) | — | **1** | 15/2 | 112 | 76 |
| $4567^{2}$ | **Spout (109)** (RCharlton) **4-9-3** PatEddery(1) (swtg: hld up: rdn over 2f out: led over 1f out: hrd rdn: hdd last stride) | s.h | **2** | 4/1$^{2}$ | 115 | 86 |
| $3711^{8}$ | **Ninotchka (USA) (101)** (JLDunlop) **3-8-7** TQuinn(5) (b: swtg: hrd rdn & hdwy over 1f out: one pce) | 4 | **3** | 33/1 | 107 | 71 |
| 4292a$^{2}$ | **Papering (IRE) (112)** (LMCumani) **3-8-7** KDarley(2) (a.p: rdn over 2f out: wknd fnl f) | 1¼ | **4** | 9/2$^{3}$ | 105 | 69 |
| 4467* | **Altamura (USA) (112)** (JHMGosden) **3-8-7** LDettori(8) (a.p: rdn over 2f out: wknd over 1f out) | hd | **5** | 5/2$^{1}$ | 105 | 69 |
| $4377^{2}$ | **Asterita (95)** (DRLoder) **4-9-0** WRSwinburn(9) (lw: hdwy over 1f out: nvr nrr) | s.h | **6** | 33/1 | 105 | 76 |
| $3836^{2}$ | **Roses In The Snow (IRE) (88)** (JWHills) **3-8-7** FLynch(11) (nvr nr to chal) | 1¼ | **7** | 40/1 | 103 | 67 |
| $4467^{3}$ | **Russian Snows (IRE) (111)** (SbinSuroor) **4-9-5** MJKinane(3) (a.p: rdn over 2f out: wknd over 1f out) | 6 | **8** | 9/1 | 100 | 71 |
| 4290a$^{7}$ | **Poppy Carew (IRE) (106)** (PWHarris) **4-9-0** GHind(10) (lw: a bhd) | 4 | **9** | 16/1 | 90 | 61 |
| $4441^{3}$ | **Priolina (IRE)** (JCHayden,Ireland) **3-8-7b** OPeslier(7) (lw: nvr gng wl: a bhd) | 7 | **10** | 14/1 | 80 | 44 |
| 4429* | **Naazeq** (ACStewart) **3-8-7** RHills(6) (bhd fnl 2f) | 21 | **11** | 14/1 | 52 | 16 |

(SP 116.1%) **11 Rn**

**2m 33.44** (3.44) CSF £34.86 TOTE £9.40: £2.20 £1.90 £5.90 (£20.10) Trio £128.50 OWNER Mr R. Barnett (NEWMARKET) BRED W. and R. Barnett Ltd

WEIGHT FOR AGE 3yo-7lb

**4467 Time Allowed** gained a richly-deserved victory after a string of near-misses to land her first Group success. After a tremendous set-to, she just had a whisker in front at the line. (15/2)
**4567 Spout** failed by only a whisker to land her third Group race. Engaged in a tremendous tussle with the winner, it looked as if she had prevailed, but she just lost out. (4/1)
**2533 Ninotchka (USA)** acts best on an easier surface and, after picking up ground below the distance, failed to get on terms with the front two. (33/1)
**4292a Papering (IRE)** was never far away, but had come to the end of her tether inside the distance. (9/2: op 3/1)
**4467* Altamura (USA)**, 3lb better off with the winner for her two length beating, was very disappointing and had given her all below the distance. (5/2)
**4377 Asterita** looked extremely well beforehand, but never got into the shake up. She needs further. (33/1)
**4441 Priolina (IRE)** (14/1: 10/1-16/1)

## 4679 WILLMOTT DIXON H'CAP (0-110) (3-Y.O+) (Class B)

3-35 (3-36) **5f** £18,237.50 (£5,525.00: £2,700.00: £1,287.50) Stalls: Low GOING: 0.09 sec per fur (G)

| | | | | SP | RR | SF |
|---|---|---|---|---|---|---|
| 4561* | **Tadeo (91)** (MJohnston) **3-8-12** MRoberts(14) (lw: mde all: rdn out) | — | **1** | 20/1 | 101 | 71 |
| $4466^{12}$ | **To the Roof (IRE) (96)** (PWHarris) **4-9-3** GHind(1) (lw: rdn & hdwy over 1f out: r.o ins fnl f) | 1 | **2** | 15/2$^{3}$ | 103 | 73 |
| $4314^{24}$ | **Sir Joey (USA) (86)** (PGMurphy) **7-8-7** SDrowne(4) (swtg: hrd rdn & hdwy over 1f out: r.o wl ins fnl f) | 1 | **3** | 20/1 | 90 | 60 |
| 4466* | **Bolshoi (IRE) (100)** (JBerry) **4-9-7b** EmmaO'Gorman(3) (nt clr run over 1f out: gd hdwy fnl f: r.o wl) | ½ | **4** | 9/1 | 102 | 72 |
| $4552^{6}$ | **Shanghai Girl (80)** (DRLoder) **3-8-1v** DRMcCabe(12) (lw: hdwy over 1f out: unable qckn fnl f) | nk | **5** | 33/1 | 81 | 51 |
| $4505^{9}$ | **Palacegate Touch (76)** (JBerry) **6-7-11b** NCarlisle(16) (a.p: hrd rdn over 1f out: one pce) | nk | **6** | 33/1 | 76 | 46 |
| $4314^{7}$ | **Musical Season (90)** (TDBarron) **4-8-11** KDarley(10) (lw: a.p: hrd rdn over 1f out: one pce) | hd | **7** | 15/2$^{3}$ | 90 | 60 |
| $4442^{6}$ | **Royale Figurine (IRE) (107)** (MJFetherston-Godley) **5-10-0** JReid(17) (rdn & hdwy over 1f out: one pce fnl f) | nk | **8** | 14/1 | 106 | 76 |
| $4116^{20}$ | **Lady Sheriff (81)** (RHollinshead) **5-7-13**$^{(3)}$ FLynch(7) (hld up: rdn 2f out: one pce) | nk | **9** | 33/1 | 79 | 49 |
| 4372* | **Scissor Ridge (75)** (JJBridger) **4-7-3**$^{(7)}$ RMullen(11) (swtg: nvr nrr) | 1½ | **10** | 50/1 | 68 | 38 |
| 4521* | **Swynford Dream (85)** (JFBottomley) **3-8-6** LDettori(6) (a.p: rdn over 1f out: sn wknd) | ¾ | **11** | 7/1$^{2}$ | 76 | 46 |
| $4314^{11}$ | **Lago Di Varano (86)** (RMWhitaker) **4-8-7v** PatEddery(5) (lw: bhd fnl 2f) | ½ | **12** | 10/1 | 75 | 45 |
| $4616^{12}$ | **Royal Dome (IRE) (75)** (MartynWane) **4-7-3**$^{(7)}$ RFfrench(15) (prom over 3f) | 1¼ | **13** | 33/1 | 60 | 30 |
| 4651a$^{2}$ | **Go Hever Golf (79)** (TJNaughton) **4-8-0**$^{ow2}$ SSanders(13) (prom 2f) | 1¼ | **14** | 12/1 | 60 | 28 |
| $4466^{2}$ | **Samwar (95)** (MissGayKelleway) **4-9-2** MJKinane(9) (b: s.s: hdwy & nt clr run over 1f out: eased whn btn ins fnl f) | 2½ | **15** | 100/30$^{1}$ | 68 | 38 |

4255[2] **White Emir (86)** (BJMeehan) **3-8-7b** OPeslier(8) (prom 3f)....¾ **16** 16/1 57 27
4505* **Portelet (88)** (RGuest) **4-8-6**(3) JDSmith(2) (prom over 2f)....1¼ **17** 14/1 55 25
(SP 128.4%) **17 Rn**

**61.96 secs** (1.96) CSF £155.72 CT £2,907.28 TOTE £27.30: £4.20 £2.80 £4.40 £2.30 (£145.50) Trio £926.80 OWNER Mr J. R. Good (MIDDLEHAM) BRED J. R. and Mrs P. Good

LONG HANDICAP Scissor Ridge 6-10 Royal Dome (IRE) 7-8

**4561* Tadeo** followed up last week's Haydock win with a pillar-to-post success. (20/1)

**2114 To the Roof (IRE)** was a different proposition from his last outing here and ran on well in the last quarter-mile. (15/2)

**3783 Sir Joey (USA)** picked up well below the distance and ran on strongly for third, but he has never won off a mark as high as this. (20/1)

**4466* Bolshoi (IRE)** goes well for Emma O'Gorman, but has been raised 10lb for his last win, and failed to get the run of the race, doing well to come through for fourth. (9/1)

**4552 Shanghai Girl** ran better here but, after making her effort below the distance, failed to find another gear in the last 200 yards. (33/1)

**4215* Palacegate Touch** was up against it here, but still ran well. (33/1)

**4651a Go Hever Golf** (12/1: 8/1-14/1)

**4466 Samwar** was very disappointing. (100/30)

## 4680 MITRE RATED STKS H'CAP (0-105) (3-Y.O+) (Class B)

4-10 (4-15) **1m 2f** £12,242.40 (£4,581.60: £2,240.80: £964.00: £432.00: £219.20) Stalls: High GOING: 0.09 sec per fur (G)

SP RR SF

4325[5] **Proper Blue (USA) (90)** (TGMills) **3-8-2** SSanders(5) (rdn over 2f out: nt clr run over 1f out: hdwy to ld 1f out: r.o wl)....— **1** 12/1 101 68
2724* **Wilcuma (97)** (PJMakin) **5-9-0** PatEddery(6) (bit bkwd: swtchd rt & hdwy over 1f out: ev ch ins fnl f: unable qckn)....1¾ **2** 4/1[1] 105 77
**Alkateb (91)** (MissGayKelleway) **4-8-8** JReid(4) (hdwy over 1f out: ev ch whn edgd rt 1f out: one pce)....2 **3** 11/1 96 68
4184[9] **Hoh Express (96)** (IABalding) **4-8-13** TQuinn(8) (lw: a.p: rdn over 2f out: wkng whn hmpd ins fnl f)....2 **4** 9/2[2] 98 70
4465[10] **Daunt (95)** (JHMGosden) **4-8-12** LDettori(3) (a.p: led over 7f out to 1f out: sn wknd)....1 **5** 4/1[1] 95 67
4445[11] **Ninia (USA) (95)** (MJohnston) **4-8-12** BDoyle(2) (a.p: rdn over 2f out: wknd over 1f out)....1¼ **6** 11/2[3] 93 65
4066[7] **Lomberto (92)** (RHannon) **3-8-4b** DaneO'Neill(7) (led over 2f: wknd over 2f out)....9 **7** 25/1 76 43
1131[2] **Medaille Militaire (104)** (JLDunlop) **4-9-7** MJKinane(1) (hdwy 3f out: wknd wl over 1f out)....¾ **8** 9/2[2] 87 59
(SP 111.6%) **8 Rn**

**2m 10.06** (3.26) CSF £53.96 CT £490.88 TOTE £15.70: £2.30 £1.80 £2.30 (£29.40) OWNER Mr M. J. Legg (EPSOM) BRED Claiborne Farm and The Gamely Corporation

WEIGHT FOR AGE 3yo-5lb

**4325 Proper Blue (USA)**, still last entering the straight, failed to get a clear run below the distance but, when a gap did appear, he showed a tremendous turn of foot to sweep into the lead. (12/1)

**2724* Wilcuma** did not look fully fit for this first run in three months but, having said that, he came to hold every chance early inside the final furlong, before the winner asserted. (4/1)

**Alkateb** had been off the course for eleven months, but ran really well. He should soon make up for lost time. (11/1)

**4036a Hoh Express** was already feeling the pinch when hampered early inside the final furlong. He has been fighting a losing battle with the Handicapper this season. (9/2)

**4176 Daunt** gained control coming out of Swinley Bottom and still appeared to be travelling early in the straight. Collared a furlong out, he was quickly done with. (4/1: op 5/2)

**4300 Ninia (USA)** has gone off the boil. (11/2)

## 4681 HYPERION CONDITIONS STKS (2-Y.O) (Class B)

4-40 (4-45) **7f** £7,178.40 (£2,685.60: £1,312.80: £564.00: £252.00: £127.20) Stalls: Low GOING: 0.09 sec per fur (G)

SP RR SF

4519[8] **Andreyev (IRE) (100)** (RHannon) **2-8-13** MJKinane(4) (lw: a.p: shkn up to ld over 1f out: comf)....— **1** 100/30[2] 102+ 62
4514* **Dacoit (USA)** (MRStoute) **2-8-11** WRSwinburn(3) (a.p: rdn over 2f out: r.o one pce fnl f)....3½ **2** 7/2[3] 92 52
4118* **Shii-Take (94)** (RAkehurst) **2-8-11** LDettori(5) (lw: led over 5f: one pce)....hd **3** 5/2[1] 92 52
4488[3] **Granny's Pet (100)** (PFICole) **2-9-1** TQuinn(2) (lw: hdwy over 2f out: wknd fnl f)....4 **4** 4/1 87 47
4370[5] **Padauk (74)** (MJHaynes) **2-8-11** JReid(6) (a bhd)....2½ **5** 50/1 77? 37
4461[5] **Ursa Major** (PAKelleway) **2-8-11** MRoberts(1) (prom 5f)....½ **6** 13/2 76 36
(SP 109.2%) **6 Rn**

**1m 30.87** (3.67) CSF £13.93 TOTE £4.40: £2.10 £2.10 (£8.30) OWNER Mr J. Palmer-Brown (MARLBOROUGH) BRED T. F. Moorhead

**4328 Andreyev (IRE)** was taking a drop in class and had no problems collecting. (100/30)

**4514* Dacoit (USA)** was not helped by the slow early pace and, when Swinburn really rousted him along over a quarter of a mile from home, the response was not immediate. He did stay on in the final furlong but, by then, it was all over. He should soon be winning again, maybe over a bit further. (7/2: 5/2-4/1)

**4118* Shii-Take** set a very moderate pace until quickening things up over a quarter of a mile from home. Collared below the distance, he looked likely to hold on for second, but was worried out of it in the last couple of strides. (5/2)

**4488 Granny's Pet** looked in good shape, but she could never throw down a challenge, and was done with in the final furlong. (4/1)

**4461 Ursa Major** (13/2: 10/1-6/1)

## 4682 DUKE OF EDINBURGH H'CAP (0-90) (3-Y.O+) (Class C)

5-15 (5-21) **1m (straight)** £9,456.00 (£2,868.00: £1,404.00: £672.00) Stalls: Low GOING: 0.09 sec per fur (G)

SP RR SF

4432* **High Premium (73)** (RAFahey) **8-8-12** ACulhane(7) (a.p: led 3f out: edgd rt ins fnl f: all out)....— **1** 14/1 82 64
4582[7] **Alsahib (USA) (66)** (WRMuir) **3-8-2** MFenton(21) (lw: hdwy 2f out: hrd rdn over 1f out: r.o ins fnl f)....1¼ **2** 40/1 73 52
4511[2] **Fionn de Cool (IRE) (67)** (RAkehurst) **5-8-6** TQuinn(6) (lw: rdn over 2f out: hdwy over 1f out: r.o wl ins fnl f)....½ **3** 9/1[2] 73 55
4444[7] **Consort (85)** (GHarwood) **3-9-7** WRSwinburn(2) (lw: a.p: hrd rdn over 1f out: unable qckn)....s.h **4** 8/1[1] 90 69
4329* **Artful Dane (IRE) (71)** (MJHeaton-Ellis) **4-8-10v** SDrowne(18) (swtg: a.p: rdn over 2f out: one pce fnl f)....¾ **5** 20/1 75 57
4432[6] **Maple Bay (IRE) (79)** (ABailey) **7-8-13**(5) GFaulkner(1) (a.p: rdn over 2f out: one pce)....1 **6** 33/1 81 63
4243[9] **Toujours Riviera (72)** (JPearce) **6-8-11** OPeslier(22) (a.p: ev ch over 1f out: wknd fnl f)....½ **7** 16/1 73 55
4463[21] **Admirals Flame (IRE) (79)** (CFWall) **5-8-11**(7) PClarke(24) (b: hdwy 2f out: wknd fnl f)....1½ **8** 33/1 77 59
2142[3] **Medieval Lady (86)** (IABalding) **3-9-3**(5) MartinDwyer(8) (swtg: nvr nrr)....1¾ **9** 8/1[1] 81 60
4379[3] **Apache Len (USA) (70)** (RHannon) **3-8-6b** DaneO'Neill(17) (lw: a.p: ev ch over 2f out: wknd over 1f out)....½ **10** 25/1 64 43

| | | | | SP | RR | SF |
|---|---|---|---|---|---|---|
| 3799[8] | **Comanche Companion (70)** (TJNaughton) **6-8-9** PatEddery(13) (swtg: nvr nr to chal) | 1 | **11** | 9/1[2] | 62 | 44 |
| 4120[8] | **Tremplin (USA) (87)** (NACallaghan) **4-9-12** MRoberts(11) (nvr nrr) | s.h | **12** | 33/1 | 79 | 61 |
| 3744a[10] | **Wakeel (USA) (83)** (SDow) **4-9-8** JReid(14) (nvr nrr) | 1¼ | **13** | 16/1 | 73 | 55 |
| 3926[7] | **Alhawa (USA) (80)** (CJBenstead) **3-9-2b[1]** RHills(4) (prom over 5f) | hd | **14** | 25/1 | 70 | 49 |
| 4450[3] | **Danegold (IRE) (76)** (MRChannon) **4-9-1v** RPerham(23) (prom over 5f) | nk | **15** | 20/1 | 65 | 47 |
| 4354[6] | **Balance of Power (70)** (RAkehurst) **4-8-9** SSanders(9) (prom over 5f) | nk | **16** | 25/1 | 58 | 40 |
| 4254[3] | **Blue Flyer (IRE) (74)** (RIngram) **3-8-10** DRMcCabe(20) (hdwy over 1f out: eased whn btn ins fnl f) | 1 | **17** | 33/1 | 60 | 39 |
| 2581[16] | **A Chef Too Far (72)** (RRowe) **3-8-5**(3) RHavlin(10) (led 5f) | ¾ | **18** | 12/1[3] | 57 | 36 |
| 4352[5] | **Night Wink (USA) (85)** (GLMoore) **4-9-10** SWhitworth(19) (swtg: hdwy over 2f out: wknd over 1f out) | nk | **19** | 20/1 | 69 | 51 |
| 4463[3] | **Zajko (USA) (75)** (LadyHerries) **6-8-11**(3) FLynch(5) (hld up: rdn over 2f out: sn wknd) | 3 | **20** | 8/1[1] | 53 | 35 |
| 4354[9] | **Superior Force (62)** (MissBSanders) **3-7-12** NAdams(16) (prom over 4f) | 4 | **21** | 40/1 | 32 | 11 |
| 1330[10] | **Night Dance (89)** (GLewis) **4-9-11**(3) AWhelan(3) (bhd fnl 3f) | 11 | **22** | 16/1 | 37 | 19 |
| 4309* | **Threadneedle (USA) (81)** (LordHuntingdon) **3-9-3** LDettori(15) (a bhd) | 1¾ | **23** | 8/1[1] | 26 | 5 |
| | **That Old Feeling (IRE) (86)** (JWhite) **4-9-11** BDoyle(25) (swtg: uns rdr & bolted bef s: bhd fnl 5f: t.o) | 20 | **24** | 66/1 | — | — |
| | | | | (SP 140.4%) | **24 Rn** | |

**1m 45.18** (3.98) CSF £446.53 CT £4,876.28 TOTE £17.30: £3.40 £27.80 £2.30 £2.70 (£1,712.90) Trio Not won; £2,497.36 to 14/10/96
OWNER Mr J. C. Parsons (MALTON) BRED M.E Wates
WEIGHT FOR AGE 3yo-3lb
**OFFICIAL EXPLANATION Threadneedle (USA): lost his action completely in the later stages.**
**4432* High Premium** followed up his recent Haydock victory, but was all out to hold on. (14/1)
**2027 Alsahib (USA)** ran his best race to date and kept on nicely inside the final furlong. (40/1)
**4511 Fionn de Cool (IRE)** ran on really strongly in the final furlong. He is not easy to win with and has won just once in forty starts. (9/1)
**4136 Consort** failed to find the necessary turn of foot below the distance. (8/1)
**4329* Artful Dane (IRE)** is an in-and-out performer these days, but did not run badly here. (20/1)
**3974* Maple Bay (IRE)** has won nine times this year, but is now 17lb higher than in April. (33/1)
**1195* A Chef Too Far** (12/1: op 25/1)

T/Jkpt: Not won; £15,629.81 to 14/10/96. T/Plpt: £370.80 (98.12 Tckts). T/Qdpt: £84.10 (17.01 Tckts). AK

## 4621-YORK (L-H) (Good, Good to firm patches)
## Saturday October 12th

WEATHER: sunny periods WIND: mod across

### 4683 EQUITY FINANCIAL COLLECTIONS H'CAP (0-85) (3-Y.O+) (Class D)

2-15 (2-17) **1m 5f 194y** £8,480.00 (£2,540.00: £1,220.00: £560.00) Stalls: Low GOING minus 0.46 sec per fur (F)

| | | | | SP | RR | SF |
|---|---|---|---|---|---|---|
| 4365* | **Beaumont (IRE) (61)** (JEBanks) **6-8-8** JQuinn(6) (in tch: led over 2f out: sn clr: r.o wl) | — | **1** | 9/1[3] | 75+ | 42 |
| 4327[6] | **Midyan Blue (IRE) (74)** (JMPEustace) **6-9-7** RCochrane(1) (trckd ldrs: outpcd 4f out: styd on wl u.p fnl 2f: nvr able to chal) | 4 | **2** | 5/1[1] | 83 | 50 |
| 4447[11] | **Durham (68)** (HSHowe) **5-9-1b** OUrbina(4) (a.p: effrt over 3f out: hung lft over 2f out: styd on one pce) | 1½ | **3** | 8/1[2] | 76 | 43 |
| | **Broctune Bay (53)** (MrsMReveley) **7-8-0** TWilliams(19) (hld up & bhd: effrt over 4f out: styd on: no imp) | 3½ | **4** | 25/1 | 57 | 26 |
| | **Turnpole (IRE) (70)** (MrsMReveley) **5-8-12**(5) GLee(14) (hld up & bhd: c wd st & stdy hdwy fnl 4f) | s.h | **5** | 14/1 | 74 | 41 |
| 1837[2] | **Domappel (75)** (MrsJCecil) **4-9-8** JWeaver(20) (cl up: rdn to ld wl over 4f out: hung lft: hdd & wknd over 2f out) | 6 | **6** | 11/1 | 72 | 40 |
| 3855[3] | **Ski For Gold (68)** (JLDunlop) **3-8-6** TSprake(12) (rr div & drvn along over 4f out: styd on: n.d) | ½ | **7** | 9/1[3] | 64 | 25 |
| 3878[2] | **Blenheim Terrace (65)** (CBBBooth) **3-8-3** LCharnock(18) (hld up: smooth hdwy 4f out: effrt over 2f out: hung lft & sn btn) | 1½ | **8** | 11/1 | 59 | 21 |
| 4447[13] | **Meant to Be (70)** (LadyHerries) **6-9-3** AClark(2) (cl up: ev ch over 4f out: wknd fnl 3f) | 1½ | **9** | 14/1 | 63 | 32 |
| 4431[6] | **Lord Hastie (USA) (64)** (CWThornton) **8-8-11** JFortune(7) (hdwy 4f out: sn in tch: rdn & btn 2f out) | s.h | **10** | 9/1[3] | 57 | 27 |
| 3111[8] | **Fighting Times (56)** (CASmith) **4-8-3** CRutter(5) (b.off hind: in tch tl wknd fnl 3½f) | 1 | **11** | 25/1 | 47 | 18 |
| 3161[6] | **Lookingforarainbow (IRE) (72)** (BobJones) **8-9-5** MWigham(16) (in tch: effrt ent st: one pce) | ½ | **12** | 14/1 | 63 | 32 |
| 4448[7] | **Compass Pointer (62)** (JMPEustace) **3-8-0** NKennedy(15) (hld up & bhd: hdwy 5f out: wknd 3f out) | ¾ | **13** | 16/1 | 52 | 14 |
| 4556[4] | **Warbrook (82)** (IABalding) **3-9-6** MHills(8) (lw: chsd ldrs: effrt 4f out: wknd over 2½f out) | s.h | **14** | 11/1 | 72 | 33 |
| 4483[3] | **Eau de Cologne (62)** (CWThornton) **4-8-9** DeanMcKeown(11) (in tch tl outpcd fnl 2½f) | 1¼ | **15** | 12/1 | 51 | 21 |
| 4315[10] | **Marchant Ming (IRE) (55)** (MDHammond) **4-8-2** GCarter(9) (outpcd appr st: n.d after) | 5 | **16** | 20/1 | 38 | 10 |
| | **Dawadar (USA) (69)** (JSGoldie) **9-9-2** AMcGlone(10) (a bhd) | 6 | **17** | 66/1 | 45 | 17 |
| 1976[7] | **Kadastrof (FR) (78)** (RDickin) **6-9-11** JCarroll(3) (led tl hdd & wknd wl over 4f out) | s.h | **18** | 25/1 | 54 | 25 |
| 4457[3] | **Highflying (81)** (GMMoore) **10-9-9**(5) DGriffiths(13) (rdn & lost pl 6f out: n.d after) | 26 | **19** | 16/1 | 27 | 2 |
| | | | | (SP 140.0%) | **19 Rn** | |

**2m 58.78** (2.58) CSF £55.82 CT £368.64 TOTE £7.50: £2.00 £1.50 £2.10 £21.20 (£14.60) Trio £41.90 OWNER Mr P. Cunningham (NEWMARKET) BRED Mount Coote Stud in Ireland
WEIGHT FOR AGE 3yo-9lb
**4365* Beaumont (IRE)** is in tremendous form at present and ought to be able to win again. (9/1)
**4327 Midyan Blue (IRE)** got tapped for toe early in the straight but, judging by the way he was picking up at the finish, he should stay further. (5/1)
**4315* Durham** ran another decent race but, when it came to a struggle, he was inclined to hang, and was going nowhere in the last two furlongs. (8/1)
**Broctune Bay** put in a useful effort and looks well worth keeping in mind, especially over timber. (25/1)
**Turnpole (IRE)**, whose rider certainly had the kid-gloves on, put up a most-promising display. Whether or not there is time for him to score on the level this season is questionable, but he should be followed over hurdles. (14/1)
**1837 Domappel**, trying a longer trip, helped force the pace and did not seem to last out. (11/1)
**3855 Ski For Gold**, returning here after six weeks off, ran reasonably in the circumstances, and this should have done him good. (9/1)
**3878 Blenheim Terrace** travelled on the bridle but, once asked for an effort halfway up the straight, the response was disappointing. (11/1)

### 4684 E.B.F. SURFACHEM MAIDEN STKS (2-Y.O) (Class D)

2-45 (2-47) **7f 202y** £6,212.00 (£1,856.00: £888.00: £404.00) Stalls: Low GOING minus 0.46 sec per fur (F)

| | | | | SP | RR | SF |
|---|---|---|---|---|---|---|
| 2708[5] | **Hidden Meadow** (IABalding) **2-9-0** MHills(11) (mde all: racd far side: r.o strly fnl 2f) | — | **1** | 9/4[2] | 86 | 21 |

| | | | | SP | RR | SF |
|---|---|---|---|---|---|---|
| 4261[2] | **Teofilio (IRE)** (DRLoder) **2-9-0** RHughes(1) (lw: trckd ldrs: led stands' side over 4f out: r.o & edgd lft fnl 2f: nt pce of wnr) | 1 | **2** | 5/4[1] | 84 | 19 |
| | **Saafeya (IRE)** (JHMGosden) **2-8-9** JCarroll(10) (w'like: unf: dwlt: stdy hdwy ½-wy: effrt over 2f out: no imp) | 4 | **3** | 6/1[3] | 71 | 7 |
| 4451[6] | **Noirie** (MBrittain) **2-9-0** MWigham(3) (chsd ldrs: rdn & one pce fnl 3f) | 6 | **4** | 20/1 | 64 | 2 |
| 4245[3] | **Mystique Air (IRE)** (EWeymes) **2-8-9** LCharnock(2) (hld up: racd far side & chsd wnr 4f out: rdn & btn 2f out) | ½ | **5** | 9/1 | 58 | — |
| 4242[12] | **Hadidi** (DMorley) **2-9-0** RCochrane(4) (hld up & bhd: effrt ½-wy: no imp) | 1½ | **6** | 10/1 | 60 | — |
| 4475[12] | **Keepsake (IRE)** (MDIUsher) **2-8-9** RStreet(5) (bit bkwd: bhd: effrt over 4f out: n.d) | ¾ | **7** | 50/1 | 53 | — |
| | **Arisaig (IRE)** (PCalver) **2-9-0** MBirch(6) (leggy: scope: hld up & bhd: effrt ½-wy: sn btn) | nk | **8** | 33/1 | 58 | — |
| 4451[10] | **Russian Aspect** (MWEasterby) **2-8-9**(5) GParkin(7) (bhd: effrt ½-wy: sn btn) | 1 | **9** | 33/1 | 56 | — |
| | **Polarize** (TDBarron) **2-9-0** JFortune(9) (unf: prom to ½-wy: sn rdn & btn) | 1 | **10** | 33/1 | 54 | — |
| 4224[5] | **Good Judge (IRE)** (MDHammond) **2-9-0** KFallon(8) (prom tl rdn & wknd over 3f out) | hd | **11** | 33/1 | 53 | — |

(SP 127.1%) **11 Rn**

**1m 40.8** (4.00) CSF £5.73 TOTE £4.20: £1.50 £1.30 £1.60 (£2.60) Trio £4.00 OWNER Mr George Strawbridge (KINGSCLERE) BRED I. A. Balding

**2708 Hidden Meadow** was one of the few to stick to the far rail in the straight at this meeting. That proved a good move as he won really well. He is obviously improving. (9/4)
**4261 Teofilio (IRE)** looked particularly well and, although racing on the opposite side of the track to the winner, he had his chances, but was never quite good enough. His turn will come. (5/4: op 4/5)
**Saafeya (IRE)** put in a decent first effort and should have learnt plenty. (6/1)
**4451 Noirie** showed promise on this debut and put up another fair run, but found this company too hot in the last couple of furlongs. (20/1)
**4245 Mystique Air (IRE)** was the only one to race on the far side with the winner, and was well outclassed in the last couple of furlongs. (9/1)
**Hadidi** looks the type to get better in time. (10/1: 8/1-14/1)

## 4685 COLDSTREAM GUARDS ROCKINGHAM STKS (Listed) (2-Y.O) (Class A)

3-15 (3-18) **6f** £9,846.00 (£3,546.00: £1,698.00: £690.00: £270.00) Stalls: High GOING minus 0.46 sec per fur (F)

| | | | | SP | RR | SF |
|---|---|---|---|---|---|---|
| 4490* | **Nightbird (IRE) (89)** (BWHills) **2-8-6** MHills(3) (lw: led 1f: trckd ldr: led wl over 1f out: shkn up & r.o) | — | **1** | 7/4[2] | 91+ | 52 |
| 3931[5] | **Victory Dancer (95)** (BJMeehan) **2-8-11b** JWeaver(5) (led after 1f tl wl over 1f out: r.o one pce) | 3½ | **2** | 11/1 | 87 | 48 |
| 4179[4] | **Reliquary (USA)** (DRLoder) **2-8-11** RHughes(1) (hld up: stdy hdwy over 2f out: wnt 2nd & rdn 1½f out: sn btn) | ½ | **3** | 6/5[1] | 85 | 47 |
| 4247[5] | **For Old Times Sake (100)** (JBerry) **2-8-11** GCarter(4) (lw: trckd ldrs: effrt over 2f out: no imp) | 2 | **4** | 11/2[3] | 80 | 42 |
| 3150[5] | **Samsung Spirit (79)** (EWeymes) **2-8-6** JQuinn(2) (prom tl rdn & btn over 2f out) | 3½ | **5** | 25/1 | 66? | 29 |

(SP 109.4%) **5 Rn**

**1m 10.99** (-0.01) CSF £15.71 TOTE £2.30: £1.50 £2.80 (£9.00) OWNER Mr S. P. Tindall (LAMBOURN) BRED S. Tindall and Stowell Hill Ltd

**4490* Nightbird (IRE)** is improving and won in useful style. She looks one to watch next year in any company and especially over further. (7/4)
**3931 Victory Dancer** ran a sound race, but was well and truly put in his place in the last couple of furlongs. (11/1)
**4179 Reliquary (USA)** seems to be his own worst enemy and, after giving a few problems at the start, then raced too freely and found little when off the bit. (6/5)
**4247 For Old Times Sake** was always finding this company too hot but, as usual, tried his heart out. (11/2)
**3150 Samsung Spirit** was well outclassed in the last two furlongs. (25/1)

## 4686 CROWTHER HOMES H'CAP (0-80) (3-Y.O+) (Class D)

3-45 (3-47) **1m 205y** £10,800.00 (£3,240.00: £1,560.00: £720.00) Stalls: Low GOING minus 0.46 sec per fur (F)

| | | | | SP | RR | SF |
|---|---|---|---|---|---|---|
| 4626[2] | **Dreams End (70)** (PBowen) **8-9-6** RCochrane(26) (hdwy 4f out: styd on to ld ins fnl f: kpt on wl) | — | **1** | 12/1 | 81 | 47 |
| 4326[9] | **Trojan Risk (80)** (GLewis) **3-9-12** RHughes(17) (b.off fore: s.i.s: hdwy 3f out: styd on wl) | 1½ | **2** | 14/1 | 88 | 51 |
| 4463[6] | **Talathath (FR) (71)** (CADwyer) **4-9-7v** KFallon(21) (in tch: effrt ½-wy: led over 1f out tl ins fnl f: no ex) | ½ | **3** | 14/1 | 78 | 45 |
| 4071[5] | **Lapu-Lapu (52)** (MJCamacho) **3-7-12** LCharnock(27) (bhd: hdwy to chal over 1f out: nt qckn ins fnl f) | hd | **4** | 16/1 | 59 | 24 |
| 4071[8] | **Broughton's Pride (IRE) (48)** (JLEyre) **5-7-12** TWilliams(20) (a.p: effrt 4f out: ev ch over 1f out: sn btn) | 1¾ | **5** | 25/1 | 52 | 21 |
| 2943[6] | **Shining Example (74)** (PJMakin) **4-9-10** JFortune(15) (c v.wd st: styd on wl fnl 3f) | 3 | **6** | 20/1 | 73 | 40 |
| 4463[10] | **Seventeens Lucky (78)** (BobJones) **4-10-0** MWigham(23) (sn pushed along & bhd: styd on fnl 3f) | nk | **7** | 11/1 | 76 | 44 |
| 4489[3] | **Harvey White (IRE) (64)** (JPearce) **4-8-9**(5) MBaird(8) (styd on fnl 3f: nrst fin) | 1 | **8** | 14/1 | 60 | 29 |
| 4236* | **Cuban Reef (47)** (WJMusson) **4-7-8**(3) MHenry(3) (hdwy & in tch ent st: racd far side: no imp fnl 3f) | 1¾ | **9** | 12/1 | 40 | 11 |
| 1502[4] | **Shaffishayes (64)** (MrsMReveley) **4-9-0** DeanMcKeown(12) (racd far side: in tch tl rdn & no imp fnl 3f) | ½ | **10** | 20/1 | 56 | 26 |
| 4226[3] | **Foist (46)** (MWEasterby) **4-7-10b**[1] NKennedy(2) (lw: racd freely: led & sn clr: racd far side: wknd & hdd over 1f out) | 2 | **11** | 7/1[1] | 35 | 6 |
| 4606* | **Master Beveled (77)** (PDEvans) **6-9-13** 4x JFEgan(22) (lw: effrt 4f out: sn hrd drvn & in tch: btn 2f out) | 1¾ | **12** | 8/1[2] | 63 | 32 |
| 4432[9] | **Rambo Waltzer (61)** (DNicholls) **4-8-4**(7) JoHunnam(13) (in tch: racd far side: one pce fnl 4f) | 2½ | **13** | 25/1 | 42 | 13 |
| 4348[5] | **Glen Garnock (IRE) (53)** (DNicholls) **4-8-3** GDuffield(16) (chsd ldrs tl wknd over 2f out) | 2 | **14** | 20/1 | 31 | 3 |
| 4190[2] | **Impulsive Air (IRE) (65)** (EWeymes) **4-9-1** JQuinn(24) (in tch: no imp fnl 4f) | s.h | **15** | 10/1 | 43 | 13 |
| 4387* | **Lady of Leisure (USA) (72)** (MrsJCecil) **4-9-8** GBardwell(18) (lw: chsd ldrs: racd far side: wknd fnl 3f) | 3 | **16** | 10/1 | 44 | 15 |
| 4316[5] | **Cashmere Lady (72)** (JLEyre) **4-9-8** RLappin(19) (bhd: effrt ½-wy: n.d) | hd | **17** | 16/1 | 44 | 15 |
| 4626[8] | **Gold Desire (48)** (MBrittain) **6-7-9**(3) NVarley(10) (nvr bttr than mid div) | 1 | **18** | 20/1 | 18 | — |
| 4463[14] | **Pride of Pendle (71)** (DNicholls) **7-9-7** AlexGreaves(6) (lw: effrt over 4f out: nvr trbld ldrs) | nk | **19** | 9/1[3] | 41 | 12 |
| 4582[6] | **Gloriana (66)** (LadyHerries) **4-9-2** MHills(14) (chsd ldrs: racd far side: outpcd fnl 3f) | nk | **20** | 14/1 | 35 | 7 |
| 4436[7] | **Habeta (USA) (46)** (JWWatts) **10-7-7**(3) DWright(1) (a bhd) | s.h | **21** | 25/1 | 15 | — |
| 4432[16] | **Elite Hope (USA) (65)** (NTinkler) **4-8-10**(5) AimeeCook(5) (n.d) | 5 | **22** | 33/1 | 25 | — |
| 4470[6] | **Darling Clover (74)** (RBastiman) **4-9-5**(5) HBastiman(9) (n.d) | 2½ | **23** | 16/1 | 30 | 2 |
| | **Rafters (53)** (JMBradley) **7-8-3** TSprake(25) (n.d) | s.h | **24** | 50/1 | 9 | — |
| | **Time Leader (65)** (RDickin) **4-9-1** JCarroll(7) (a bhd) | 3 | **25** | 50/1 | 15 | — |
| 690[17] | **Our Main Man (51)** (RMWhitaker) **6-8-1** FNorton(4) (bhd fr ½-wy) | 1 | **26** | 33/1 | — | — |
| 4470[3] | **King Curan (USA) (68)** (DHaydnJones) **5-9-4b** DHarrison(11) (rdn over 4f out: sn bhd) | 30 | **27** | 16/1 | — | — |

(SP 166.1%) **27 Rn**

**1m 51.3** (2.10) CSF £192.05 CT £2,288.19 TOTE £12.10: £3.10 £4.80 £4.90 £5.80 (£207.00) Trio £1,401.00 OWNER Mr T. G. Price (HAVERFORDWEST) BRED Hascombe and Valiant Studs

LONG HANDICAP Habeta (USA) 7-9

WEIGHT FOR AGE 3yo-4lb

**4626 Dreams End** confirmed his promise of only a couple of days previously and won this in useful style. Now he is in form, he should be watched under both Rules. (12/1)
**4117 Trojan Risk** looks in good heart and came from a long way behind but, despite finishing well, could never get in a blow at the winner. (14/1)
**4463 Talathath (FR)** never seems to run a bad race these days but, despite a valiant effort, just failed to last it out this time. (14/1)
**4071 Lapu-Lapu** ran a super race after a five-week break. There could be another prize to be picked up with her before the season ends. (16/1)
**1650 Broughton's Pride (IRE)** is slipping back down to a useful mark, and ran well enough to suggest she is in good form. (25/1)
**2943 Shining Example** put in a useful effort after almost three months off, and is likely to be all the better for it. (20/1)
**3985* Seventeens Lucky** took an age to get going and never got into it. (11/1)
**4489 Harvey White (IRE)** found this trip a bit too sharp and only ran on when it was all too late. (14/1)
**4226 Foist** ran far too freely with the blinkers on over this longer trip, and had run himself into the ground approaching the final furlong. (7/1)

## 4687 CORAL SPRINT TROPHY H'CAP (0-100) (3-Y.O+) (Class C)

4-15 (4-18) **6f** £17,610.00 (£5,280.00: £2,540.00: £1,170.00) Stalls: High GOING minus 0.46 sec per fur (F)

| | | | | SP | RR | SF |
|---|---|---|---|---|---|---|
| 4314[9] | **Bollin Joanne (87)** (TDEasterby) **3-8-9**(5) GParkin(7) (b: trckd ldrs: led over 1f out: r.o wl) | — | **1** | 6/1[1] | 100 | 76 |
| 4314[4] | **Double Splendour (IRE) (96)** (PSFelgate) **6-9-10** WRyan(19) (lw: hld up: effrt ½-wy: r.o: nrst fin) | 2 | **2** | 6/1[1] | 104 | 80 |
| 4552[2] | **Bajan Rose (85)** (MBlanshard) **4-8-13** RCochrane(8) (in tch: kpt on u.p fnl 2f: nrst fin) | hd | **3** | 14/1 | 92 | 70 |
| 4466[6] | **Astrac (IRE) (88)** (MissGayKelleway) **5-9-2** MHills(12) (lw: cl up: rdn over 2f out: kpt on same pce) | ½ | **4** | 10/1[3] | 94 | 71 |
| 4312[15] | **Palo Blanco (78)** (TDBarron) **5-8-6** JFortune(21) (bhd & drvn along tl styd on wl fnl 1½f) | 1 | **5** | 16/1 | 81 | 59 |
| 4116[19] | **Cyrano's Lad (IRE) (100)** (CADwyer) **7-9-7**(7) JoHunnam(10) (cl up: led ½-wy tl over 1f out: wknd) | s.h | **6** | 16/1 | 103 | 80 |
| 4554[6] | **Seigneurial (90)** (GHarwood) **4-9-4** AClark(18) (chsd ldrs: outpcd over 2f out: kpt on towards fin) | hd | **7** | 16/1 | 93 | 70 |
| 4314[2] | **Mr Bergerac (IRE) (86)** (BPalling) **5-9-0** TSprake(11) (lw: mid div: sn drvn along: kpt on: no imp) | ½ | **8** | 7/1[2] | 88 | 65 |
| 4561[5] | **Takadou (IRE) (81)** (MissLCSiddall) **5-8-9** DHarrison(14) (lw: styd on fnl 2f: n.d) | ¾ | **9** | 33/1 | 81 | 59 |
| 4581* | **Garnock Valley (86)** (JBerry) **6-9-0b** GCarter(9) (lw: bhd: rdn ½-wy: sme late hdwy) | s.h | **10** | 12/1 | 86 | 63 |
| 4255[3] | **Lord Olivier (IRE) (77)** (WJarvis) **6-8-5** AMcGlone(5) (in tch: drvn along ½-wy: no imp) | ¾ | **11** | 16/1 | 75 | 53 |
| 3984[14] | **Double Blue (95)** (MJohnston) **7-9-9v[1]** JWeaver(20) (outpcd fr ½-wy) | 1½ | **12** | 33/1 | 89 | 66 |
| 3946[5] | **Pearl d'Azur (USA) (86)** (DRLoder) **3-8-13** RHughes(15) (plld hrd: effrt ½-wy: no imp) | nk | **13** | 10/1[3] | 79 | 56 |
| 4312* | **Cretan Gift (74)** (NPLittmoden) **5-8-2b** GDuffield(13) (sn outpcd & wl bhd: sme late hdwy) | 1¼ | **14** | 11/1 | 63 | 42 |
| 4198[17] | **Portend (88)** (SRBowring) **4-9-2b** SDWilliams(1) (sn outpcd) | ½ | **15** | 25/1 | 76 | 54 |
| 4314[20] | **Tedburrow (90)** (MrsAMNaughton) **4-9-4** JCarroll(22) (trckd ldr stands' side: rdn & n.d fr ½-wy) | nk | **16** | 16/1 | 77 | 56 |
| 4505[3] | **Saint Express (81)** (MrsMReveley) **6-8-4**(5) GLee(23) (spd stands' side 4f: sn btn) | 1½ | **17** | 16/1 | 64 | 43 |
| 4581[11] | **Don't Care (IRE) (85)** (MissLAPerratt) **5-8-13b** MBirch(16) (spd 4f: wknd qckly) | 1½ | **18** | 33/1 | 64 | 43 |
| 3984[10] | **Stylish Ways (IRE) (87)** (MissSEHall) **4-9-1** JFEgan(17) (in tch 4f) | 1½ | **19** | 33/1 | 62 | 41 |
| 4581[17] | **Benzoe (IRE) (80)** (MrsJRRamsden) **6-8-8** KFallon(2) (sn pushed along: n.d) | 2½ | **20** | 16/1 | 49 | 29 |
| 4342[3] | **Bayin (USA) (71)** (MDIUsher) **7-7-13** RStreet(3) (effrt ½-wy: sn rdn & btn) | s.h | **21** | 14/1 | 40 | 20 |
| 4581[15] | **Antonias Melody (80)** (SRBowring) **3-8-4b[1]**(3) CTeague(4) (led to ½-wy: sn wknd) | nk | **22** | 25/1 | 48 | 27 |
| 4376[5] | **Caricature (IRE) (78)** (GLewis) **3-8-2b**(3) MHenry(6) (outpcd & lost tch fr ½-wy) | nk | **23** | 20/1 | 45 | 24 |
| | | | | (SP 154.0%) | | **23 Rn** |

**1m 9.87** (-1.13) CSF £46.49 CT £488.71 TOTE £12.90: £3.20 £2.00 £3.10 £2.80 (£73.40) OWNER Lady Westbrook (MALTON) BRED Sir Neil and Lady Westbrook
WEIGHT FOR AGE 3yo-1lb

**3622 Bollin Joanne** won most authoritatively and would appear to be in tip-top form. (6/1: op 10/1)
**4314 Double Splendour (IRE)** ran yet another cracking race and was not helped by his high draw. (6/1)
**4552 Bajan Rose** is running consistently well at the moment and deserves to find a race. (14/1)
**4466 Astrac (IRE)** keeps running well, but is just short of finishing pace, and may well be better suited by more give in the ground. (10/1)
**2725 Palo Blanco** is coming back to form and this was a particularly good effort from his draw. (16/1)
**3984 Cyrano's Lad (IRE)** ran miserably last time and put up a much better performance here. He seems to like a race where he can dominate. (16/1)

## 4688 ROYAL BRITISH LEGION INSURANCE SERVICES H'CAP (0-85) (3-Y.O+) (Class D)

4-45 (4-49) **6f 214y** £11,034.00 (£3,312.00: £1,596.00: £738.00) Stalls: High GOING minus 0.46 sec per fur (F)

| | | | | SP | RR | SF |
|---|---|---|---|---|---|---|
| 4316[7] | **Persian Fayre (75)** (JBerry) **4-9-4** KFallon(8) (trckd ldrs: led wl over 2f out: r.o u.p) | — | **1** | 20/1 | 84 | 65 |
| 4583[2] | **Warming Trends (88)** (SirMarkPrescott) **3-10-1** GDuffield(22) (lw: racd stands' side: hdwy 3f out: r.o fnl f: nrst fin) | ½ | **2** | 9/1[2] | 96 | 75 |
| 4583[4] | **Jo Mell (84)** (TDEasterby) **3-9-11** MBirch(9) (trckd ldrs: chal 2f out: rdn & nt qckn) | 1¼ | **3** | 12/1 | 89 | 68 |
| 4312[19] | **Pharmacy (71)** (JWWatts) **3-8-12** WRyan(10) (gd hdwy 3f out: sn chsng ldrs: nt qckn fnl f) | 1 | **4** | 33/1 | 74 | 54 |
| 4560[7] | **Best of All (IRE) (60)** (JBerry) **4-8-3b[1]** GCarter(3) (bhd: styd on fnl 3f: nrst fin) | 1¾ | **5** | 33/1 | 59 | 42 |
| 4190[25] | **Somerton Boy (IRE) (68)** (PCalver) **6-8-11** JCarroll(14) (lw: bhd: gd hdwy 3f out: nvr rchd ldrs) | 1¼ | **6** | 25/1 | 64 | 47 |
| 4460[9] | **Mister Westsound (60)** (MissLAPerratt) **4-8-3b** AMcGlone(27) (racd stands' side: effrt ½-wy: nrst fin) | nk | **7** | 25/1 | 55 | 39 |
| 4571[3] | **Duello (69)** (MBlanshard) **5-8-12** JQuinn(21) (bhd tl styd on strly fnl 2f) | hd | **8** | 14/1 | 64 | 47 |
| 4460[13] | **Halmanerror (66)** (MrsJRRamsden) **6-8-9** OUrbina(13) (hdwy over 2f out: nvr nr to chal) | ½ | **9** | 16/1 | 60 | 43 |
| 4439* | **Quilling (72)** (MDods) **4-9-1** JFortune(25) (nvr rchd ldrs) | 1½ | **10** | 12/1 | 62 | 46 |
| 4560[11] | **Fame Again (67)** (MrsJRRamsden) **4-8-10** JFanning(15) (hdwy ½-wy: sn in tch: no imp fnl 1½f) | nk | **11** | 20/1 | 57 | 40 |
| 3989[8] | **With Care (76)** (WJarvis) **3-9-3** JWeaver(19) (bhd tl styd on fnl 2f) | ¾ | **12** | 25/1 | 64 | 45 |
| 4453* | **Nunsharpa (83)** (JRFanshawe) **3-9-7**(3) NVarley(4) (led tl wl over 2f out: sn btn) | ¾ | **13** | 12/1 | 69 | 50 |
| *4078[9]* | **Le Sport (68)** (DNicholls) **3-8-6**(3) DWright(16) (sn drvn along & wl bhd: sme late hdwy) | 2 | **14** | 33/1 | 50 | 32 |
| 4432[5] | **Rakis (IRE) (78)** (MrsLStubbs) **6-9-7** JFEgan(18) (n.d) | hd | **15** | 16/1 | 59 | 43 |
| 3995[16] | **Pine Ridge Lad (IRE) (65)** (JLEyre) **6-8-8** TWilliams(17) (prom: sn drvn along: wknd fnl 3f) | s.h | **16** | 25/1 | 46 | 31 |
| 4136[13] | **Ochos Rios (IRE) (59)** (BSRothwell) **5-7-11**(5) MBaird(11) (chsd ldrs over 4f: sn wknd) | nk | **17** | 20/1 | 40 | 25 |
| 4300[16] | **Sharp Prospect (75)** (VSoane) **6-9-4** RCochrane(24) (n.d) | ½ | **18** | 20/1 | 54 | 38 |
| 4511[3] | **Sovereigns Court (64)** (MajorDNChappell) **3-8-5** TSprake(26) (n.d) | ½ | **19** | 11/1[3] | 42 | 25 |
| 4504[2] | **Keston Pond (IRE) (78)** (MrsVAAconley) **6-9-2**(5) DGriffiths(20) (hdwy u.p ½-wy: sn btn) | s.h | **20** | 14/1 | 56 | 40 |
| 4571[12] | **Knobbleeneeze (77)** (MRChannon) **6-9-6v** RHughes(12) (in tch 4f) | ¾ | **21** | 16/1 | 53 | 38 |
| 4232[5] | **Dummer Golf Time (68)** (LordHuntingdon) **3-8-9v** DHarrison(23) (n.d) | s.h | **22** | 14/1 | 44 | 27 |
| 3995[22] | **Legal Issue (IRE) (68)** (WWHaigh) **4-8-8**(3) PMcCabe(6) (in tch 4f) | 2 | **23** | 33/1 | 40 | 25 |
| 4316[2] | **Superpride (63)** (MrsMReveley) **4-8-6** AClark(5) (chsd ldrs 4f: wknd qckly) | 4 | **24** | 14/1 | 26 | 12 |

| | Horse | Dist | Pos | SP | RR | SF |
|---|---|---|---|---|---|---|
| 4456* | **Royal Jade (75)** (BWHills) **3-9-2** MHills(2) (b.hind: lw: chsd ldrs 4f: wknd) | ¾ | **25** | 5/1[1] | 36 | 20 |
| 4581[4] | **Barrel of Hope (76)** (JLEyre) **4-9-5b** RLappin(7) (spd to ½-wy: wknd qckly) | ¾ | **26** | 11/1[3] | 35 | 21 |
| 4581[6] | **Sailormaite (78)** (SRBowring) **5-9-7b** DeanMcKeown(1) (rel to r: swvd lft & uns rdr leaving stalls) | | **U** | 20/1 | — | — |

(SP 161.7%) **27 Rn**

**1m 22.85** (-0.15) CSF £208.30 CT £2,154.87 TOTE £43.40: £11.10 £3.40 £3.70 £7.60 (£343.90) OWNER Mr Murray Grubb (COCKERHAM) BRED Aramstone Stud Co

WEIGHT FOR AGE 3yo-2lb

**4054 Persian Fayre** put up his best performance to date and saw it out most determinedly. (20/1)

**4583 Warming Trends** made up a lot of ground in the last three furlongs. Easier ground would have suited him better. (9/1)

**4583 Jo Mell** keeps knocking at the door but, despite travelling well, never quite comes up with goods. He deserves a change of luck. (12/1)

**2773 Pharmacy** put up her best effort for a while, but might be better suited by a drop back to six. (33/1)

**2874 Best of All (IRE)** had the blinkers for the first time and they certainly improved her. (33/1)

**3933 Somerton Boy (IRE)** made useful ground halfway through the race to suggest he is in good heart. (25/1)

**4460 Mister Westsound** had a lot of running to do from halfway and, despite finishing well up the stands' rail, could never get anywhere near. If he decides to, he certainly has the ability. (25/1)

**4058 Halmanerror** could have another race in him. (16/1)

**3255* With Care** gave signs of coming back to form here by finishing well, albeit too late. (25/1)

## 4689 SAMPLERITE LIMITED STKS (0-75) (3-Y.O+) (Class D)

5-15 (5-17) **6f** £6,212.00 (£1,856.00: £888.00: £404.00) Stalls: High GOING minus 0.46 sec per fur (F)

| | Horse | Dist | Pos | SP | RR | SF |
|---|---|---|---|---|---|---|
| 4308[11] | **Faraway Lass (75)** (LordHuntingdon) **3-9-1** DHarrison(10) (a cl up: chal 1f out: styd on to ld nr fin) | — | **1** | 11/2[3] | 82 | 64 |
| 4460[2] | **French Grit (IRE) (71)** (MDods) **4-8-13** AClark(3) (lw: mde most tl ct cl home) | nk | **2** | 4/1[2] | 78 | 61 |
| 4616[19] | **Daawe (USA) (67)** (MrsVAAconley) **5-9-8** MDeering(2) (disp ld tl hung lft over 1f out: kpt on towards fin) | ¾ | **3** | 16/1 | 85 | 68 |
| 4312[25] | **The Scythian (72)** (BobJones) **4-8-13** MWigham(8) (in tch: hdwy over 1f out: styd on towards fin) | ¾ | **4** | 12/1 | 74 | 57 |
| 4453[12] | **Blessingindisguise (70)** (MWEasterby) **3-8-12** JQuinn(9) (unruly s: bhd tl styd on appr fnl f) | 1¾ | **5** | 12/1 | 70 | 52 |
| 4460[5] | **Castlerea Lad (68)** (RHollinshead) **7-8-8**(5) DGriffiths(6) (lw: a.p: effrt 2f out: r.o one pce fnl f) | ½ | **6** | 10/1 | 68 | 52 |
| 4382* | **Bowlers Boy (73)** (JJQuinn) **3-8-13**(5) GParkin(7) (lw: bhd: hdwy u.p 2f out: nvr able to chal) | 2½ | **7** | 7/2[1] | 68 | 50 |
| 4581[5] | **Friendly Brave (USA) (72)** (MissGayKelleway) **6-9-11** RHughes(4) (b.hind: bhd: hdwy over 2f out: nvr rchd ldrs) | s.h | **8** | 12/1 | 73 | 57 |
| 4485[5] | **Naissant (79)** (RMMcKellar) **3-8-8**(7) KSked(13) (b.hind: a outpcd & bhd) | 3½ | **9** | 9/1 | 55 | 39 |
| 4560[8] | **Miss Waterline (72)** (PDEvans) **3-8-9** JFEgan(5) (a outpcd & bhd) | 3 | **10** | 6/1 | 41 | 26 |
| 4616[20] | **Air Wing (71)** (MHTompkins) **3-8-12** RCochrane(1) (cl up over 4f) | ½ | **11** | 14/1 | 43 | 27 |
| 3995[24] | **Ben Gunn (74)** (PTWalwyn) **4-8-13** JCarroll(12) (outpcd & bhd fr ½-wy) | 2 | **12** | 14/1 | 37 | 23 |
| 2200[9] | **Faith Alone (67)** (CFWall) **3-8-12** GDuffield(11) (outpcd & bhd fr ½-wy) | 5 | **13** | 12/1 | 24 | 10 |

(SP 141.0%) **13 Rn**

**1m 10.78** (-0.22) CSF £31.11 TOTE £6.70: £2.00 £1.80 £5.40 (£15.60) Trio £174.30 OWNER Mr J. Rose (WEST ILSLEY) BRED John Rose

WEIGHT FOR AGE 3yo-1lb

**3989 Faraway Lass** needed all her courage to win this, and the ability to stay further served her well. (11/2)

**4460 French Grit (IRE)** is in fine form but, despite a gallant effort, was just touched off. (4/1)

**4180 Daawe (USA)** has been on the go all year, but was having his first run with blinkers or a visor, and put up a fine effort. (16/1)

**3622 The Scythian** has been generally disappointing this season, but did show signs of form here, running on well at the end. (12/1)

**2532 Blessingindisguise** gave problems at the start, but then ran well, finishing in good style. He may yet return to form. (12/1)

**4460 Castlerea Lad** has not found his finishing dash this season and it was again missing. (10/1)

T/Plpt: £503.00 (72.88 Tckts). T/Qdpt: £252.50 (6.23 Tckts). AA

# 4337-LEICESTER (R-H) (Good to firm, Firm back st)

## Monday October 14th

WEATHER: overcast WIND: fresh half bhd

## 4690 DORMOUSE MAIDEN APPRENTICE STKS (I) (3-Y.O) (Class G)

1-30 (1-31) **7f 9y** £2,224.00 (£614.00: £292.00) Stalls: High GOING minus 0.51 sec per fur (F)

| | Horse | Dist | Pos | SP | RR | SF |
|---|---|---|---|---|---|---|
| 3413[2] | **Robamaset (IRE) (88)** (LMCumani) **3-8-9**(3) RFfrench(11) (bit bkwd: a.p: rdn to ld appr fnl f: drvn clr) | — | **1** | 5/2[1] | 87 | 48 |
| 4571[11] | **Lucky Archer (80)** (CEBrittain) **3-8-7b**[1](5) JGotobed(5) (plld hrd: a.p: led 2f out tl appr fnl f: one pce) | 5 | **2** | 4/1[2] | 76 | 37 |
| | **Rash Gift** (LordHuntingdon) **3-8-7** AimeeCook(6) (h.d.w: bit bkwd: trckd ldrs: rdn & r.o wl ins fnl f) | nk | **3** | 11/2 | 70 | 31 |
| 4337[10] | **Bright Diamond (47)** (JRArnold) **3-8-2**(5) RCody-Boutcher(4) (trckd ldrs: effrt 2f out: sn rdn: kpt on) | ½ | **4** | 33/1 | 69 | 30 |
| 4499[2] | **Golden Thunderbolt (FR) (75)** (JHMGosden) **3-8-12** AEddery(1) (bhd: hdwy & rdn over 2f out: veered rt appr fnl f: nrst fin) | hd | **5** | 9/2[3] | 74 | 35 |
| 4456[2] | **Hannalou (FR) (65)** (SPCWoods) **3-8-4**(3) CWebb(10) (led to 2f out: sn rdn: one pce) | 1½ | **6** | 8/1 | 65 | 26 |
| 949[3] | **Will Do** (MartynMeade) **3-8-12** DSweeney(8) (bit bkwd: trckd ldrs tl wknd over 2f out) | 1¼ | **7** | 16/1 | 67 | 28 |
| 1709[5] | **All Stand** (MajorDNChappell) **3-8-7** SCopp(2) (in tch: hrd drvn over 2f out: sn btn) | 3 | **8** | 25/1 | 56 | 17 |
| *4094*[10] | **New Technique (FR) (25)** (KMcAuliffe) **3-8-4**(3) PDoe(7) (a in rr: t.o) | 6 | **9** | 66/1 | 42 | 3 |
| *3626*[2] | **Eccentric Dancer (25)** (MPBielby) **3-8-8b**(7)ow8 SRitchie(3) (outpcd: a bhd) | 1¼ | **10** | 66/1 | 47 | — |
| 4422[9] | **Perpetual Hope** (PMitchell) **3-8-4**(3) DDenby(13) (outpcd: a bhd: t.o fr ½-wy) | 4 | **11** | 66/1 | 30 | — |
| 3832[10] | **Martindale (IRE)** (BWHills) **3-8-9**(3) JWilkinson(9) (b.hind: chsd ldrs: rdn 3f out: sn wknd: t.o) | 9 | **12** | 20/1 | 15 | — |
| 4309[12] | **Hotstepper** (RJPrice) **3-8-7** JoHunnam(12) (t.o fnl 3f) | 14 | **13** | 66/1 | — | — |

(SP 116.7%) **13 Rn**

**1m 23.4** (0.40) CSF £11.96 TOTE £2.60: £1.10 £1.90 £2.20 (£6.90) Trio £16.20 OWNER Scuderia Rencati Srl (NEWMARKET) BRED Azienda Agricola Francesca

**3413 Robamaset (IRE)**, who has not been rushed, won this lower-grade event with any amount in hand and could strike again while the iron is hot. (5/2: 11/10-11/4)

**4231 Lucky Archer** has been highly tried and, with the first-time blinkers, was strongly fancied to get off the mark but, if anything, he ran a bit too free and had kept nothing in hand for the final battle. (4/1)

**Rash Gift**, making a belated seasonal debut, ran a race full of promise and, given the easier ground that she looks to need, she should not have too much trouble in finding an opening. (11/2: 3/1-6/1)

**3702 Bright Diamond** has not shown much sign of ability in the past, but she did not fare badly here and could at last be getting it together. (33/1)

**4499 Golden Thunderbolt (FR)**, who ran with his tongue tied down, went from one side of the course to the other when making progress in the latter stages and he was still closing at the line. (9/2)
**4456 Hannalou (FR)** adopted her usual tactics and blazed a trail, but her lack of finishing speed was fully exposed when the contest really hotted up. She is getting her winter coat and may have to wait until next year to gain winning brackets. (8/1: 6/1-9/1)

## 4691 SHELDUCK H'CAP (0-70) (3-Y.O+ F & M) (Class E)

2-00 (2-01) **1m 8y** £3,916.50 (£1,176.00: £567.00: £262.50) Stalls: High GOING minus 0.51 sec per fur (F)

| Form | Horse | Dist | Pos | SP | RR | SF |
|---|---|---|---|---|---|---|
| 4337$^{4}$ | **Mystic Dawn (62)** (SDow) **3-9-3** TQuinn(10) (hld up & bhd: gd hdwy 2f out: led ins fnl f: r.o wl) | — | **1** | 13/2$^{2}$ | 77 | 57 |
| 4373$^{2}$ | **Cats Bottom (53)** (AGNewcombe) **4-8-6**$^{(5)ow4}$ GParkin(9) (led to 2f out: ev ch ins fnl f: unable qckn) | 1½ | **2** | 15/2 | 65 | 44 |
| 4453$^{7}$ | **Kazimiera (IRE) (62)** (CWCElsey) **3-8-12**$^{(5)}$ MartinDwyer(16) (a.p: led 2f out tl ins fnl f: r.o) | nk | **3** | 20/1 | 73 | 53 |
| 4513$^{6}$ | **Parsa (USA) (61)** (JLDunlop) **3-9-2** PatEddery(13) (hld up & bhd: rdn & hdwy over 2f out: swtchd rt & ev ch ins fnl f: no ex) | hd | **4** | 7/1$^{3}$ | 72 | 52 |
| 4597$^{4}$ | **Onefortheditch (USA) (65)** (JHMGosden) **3-9-6** LDettori(5) (hld up: effrt & rdn 2f out: styd on ins fnl f) | 1 | **5** | 5/1$^{1}$ | 74 | 54 |
| 4606$^{3}$ | **Disallowed (IRE) (67)** (MBell) **3-9-8v** MFenton(3) (lw: trckd ldrs: rdn 3f out: one pce fnl 2f) | nk | **6** | 10/1 | 76 | 56 |
| 4360$^{5}$ | **Holloway Melody (52)** (BAMcMahon) **3-8-7** SSanders(8) (trckd ldrs: rdn wl over 1f out: one pce) | 2 | **7** | 16/1 | 57 | 37 |
| 4099$^{5}$ | **Snowy Mantle (52)** (JDBethell) **3-8-7** DHarrison(18) (prom: ev ch 2f out: wknd appr fnl f) | 1½ | **8** | 33/1 | 54 | 34 |
| 4560$^{13}$ | **Gymcrak Flyer (67)** (GHolmes) **5-9-11** KFallon(2) (b.hind: trckd ldrs: hrd drvn 2f out: wknd ins fnl f) | 1 | **9** | 14/1 | 67 | 50 |
| 4376$^{14}$ | **Lucky Revenge (60)** (MartynMeade) **3-8-8**$^{(7)}$ TField(4) (hld up: rdn over 2f out: edgd rt & wknd over 1f out) | ½ | **10** | 33/1 | 59 | 39 |
| 3205$^{11}$ | **La Fille de Cirque (44)** (RJRWilliams) **4-8-2** DBiggs(6) (nvr nr ldrs) | ½ | **11** | 33/1 | 42 | 25 |
| 4582$^{5}$ | **Sistar Act (65)** (MRChannon) **3-9-6** RHughes(20) (a in rr) | ½ | **12** | 14/1 | 62 | 42 |
| 4348$^{6}$ | **Girl of My Dreams (IRE) (50)** (MJHeaton-Ellis) **3-8-5** SDrowne(7) (a bhd) | 4 | **13** | 16/1 | 39 | 19 |
| 4513$^{8}$ | **Ember (55)** (RTPhillips) **3-8-10** JQuinn(19) (chsd ldrs 5f) | 3½ | **14** | 20/1 | 37 | 17 |
| 4550$^{8}$ | **Honorable Estate (IRE) (61)** (RHannon) **3-9-2** DaneO'Neill(12) (prom 5f) | 2 | **15** | 14/1 | 39 | 19 |
| 4560$^{3}$ | **Desert Lynx (IRE) (70)** (TRWatson) **3-9-8**$^{(3)}$ OPears(14) (a in rr) | 1 | **16** | 14/1 | 46 | 26 |
| 3977$^{9}$ | **Honestly (57)** (BSmart) **3-8-12** MTebbutt(11) (plld hrd: prom tl wknd 3f out) | 1¾ | **17** | 33/1 | 29 | 9 |
| 2242$^{4}$ | **Miss Charlie (49)** (ABailey) **6-8-7** RLappin(17) (bit bkwd: plld hrd: bhd fnl 3f: t.o) | 8 | **18** | 12/1 | 5 | — |
| *194*$^{7}$ | **Miss Carottene (50)** (MJRyan) **3-8-0**$^{(5)}$ MBaird(1) (bit bkwd: w ldr 5f: wknd qckly: t.o) | 15 | **19** | 16/1 | — | — |
| | | | | (SP 136.7%) | **19 Rn** | |

**1m 35.1** (0.10) CSF £54.92 CT £872.82 TOTE £7.80: £3.00 £1.90 £4.80 £2.50 (£37.20) Trio £322.40 OWNER Up and Downer Partnership (EPSOM) BRED Mrs M. Upsdell
WEIGHT FOR AGE 3yo-3lb
**4337 Mystic Dawn** benefited from a return to more patient tactics and, ridden to perfection by a more experience jockey, won this turning handsprings. (13/2)
**4373 Cats Bottom** attempted to make it all and fought back bravely after being headed to go down fighting. She is at the top of her form just now and thoroughly deserves to win another race. (15/2)
**4243 Kazimiera (IRE)** came to win her race entering the last quarter-mile and gave her all in battle, but had to admit the winner much too fleet-footed for her in the sprint to the line. (20/1)
**4513 Parsa (USA)** did not relish this step down in distance and was only finding top gear when it was as good as over. She has had a lightish season and there is still time for her to score again. (7/1)
**4597 Onefortheditch (USA)**, driven along to mount a challenge below the distance, kept staying on without having the speed to get to terms. She is beginning to look wintry and may well have had enough for the time being. (5/1: 7/2-11/2)
**4606 Disallowed (IRE)** sat in behind the leaders, travelling strongly, but needed a reminder to concentrate on her work three furlongs out. Staying on without being able to quicken, she did not appear to be giving it her best shot when the whips were cracking. (10/1)
**2869 Snowy Mantle** ran much better than her finishing position suggests in his first handicap, and this lightly-raced filly is worth keeping in mind. (33/1)

## 4692 BADGER LIMITED STKS (0-60) (3-Y.O+) (Class F)

2-30 (2-31) **1m 8y** £3,475.80 (£968.80: £467.40) Stalls: High GOING minus 0.51 sec per fur (F)

| Form | Horse | Dist | Pos | SP | RR | SF |
|---|---|---|---|---|---|---|
| 4463$^{16}$ | **Present Situation (60)** (LordHuntingdon) **5-8-12**$^{(5)}$ AimeeCook(15) (a gng wl: led 2f out: sn clr: easily) | — | **1** | 11/2$^{2}$ | 77+ | 59 |
| *4573*$^{2}$ | **Bentico (53)** (MrsNMacauley) **7-9-0**$^{(5)}$ GFaulkner(6) (hld up: hdwy over 2f out: hrd rdn & chsd wnr appr fnl f: no imp) | 3 | **2** | 6/1$^{3}$ | 73 | 55 |
| 4609$^{13}$ | **Mustn't Grumble (IRE) (55)** (MissSJWilton) **6-9-5v** SWhitworth(2) (hld up: hdwy over 2f out: r.o wl fnl f) | 1¾ | **3** | 12/1 | 70 | 52 |
| 4428$^{7}$ | **Pearl Dawn (IRE) (60)** (GLMoore) **6-9-2** LDettori(4) (hld up: hdwy over 2f out: nt rch ldrs) | 3 | **4** | 11/1 | 61 | 43 |
| 4337$^{5}$ | **Just Harry (58)** (MJRyan) **5-8-10**$^{(7)}$ AMcCarthy(1) (hld up: hdwy fnl 2f: r.o) | 2 | **5** | 20/1 | 58 | 40 |
| 4609$^{3}$ | **Waft (USA) (60)** (BWHills) **3-8-11** MHills(9) (trckd ldrs: effrt 2f out: sn rdn: nt pce to chal) | ½ | **6** | 7/2$^{1}$ | 54 | 33 |
| 4240$^{3}$ | **Johnnie the Joker (49)** (JPLeigh) **5-9-5b** DeanMcKeown(13) (w ldr: led over 2f out: sn hdd: wknd fnl f) | 2 | **7** | 25/1 | 55 | 37 |
| 4373$^{3}$ | **Velvet Jones (50)** (GFHCharles-Jones) **3-9-0** KFallon(19) (nvr nr to chal) | 1¼ | **8** | 16/1 | 50 | 29 |
| 3589$^{7}$ | **Maurangi (39)** (BWMurray) **5-8-12**$^{(5)}$ GParkin(7) (bhd: rdn 3f out: kpt on appr fnl f) | ½ | **9** | 33/1 | 49 | 31 |
| 4503$^{2}$ | **Chalky Dancer (35)** (HJCollingridge) **4-8-10**$^{(7)}$ JoHunnam(5) (lw: prom tl wknd wl over 1f out) | s.h | **10** | 33/1 | 49 | 31 |
| 4550$^{10}$ | **Foreign Relation (IRE) (57)** (PRWebber) **3-8-11** JFEgan(8) (nvr plcd to chal) | 1¾ | **11** | 16/1 | 43 | 22 |
| 4263* | **Night of Glass (59)** (DMorris) **3-9-2v** NDay(20) (hld up: hdwy 2f out: sn rdn: wknd fnl f) | 1 | **12** | 9/1 | 46 | 25 |
| 4480$^{8}$ | **Secret Pleasure (IRE) (53)** (RHannon) **3-8-11** DaneO'Neill(3) (b.nr hind: prom 5f) | ½ | **13** | 16/1 | 40 | 19 |
| 4550$^{6}$ | **Wire Act (USA) (58)** (MartynMeade) **3-9-2b** NAdams(14) (trckd ldrs: rdn over 2f out: wknd wl over 1f out) | ½ | **14** | 20/1 | 44 | 23 |
| *4076** | **Nicola's Princess (53)** (BAMcMahon) **3-8-13** GCarter(17) (bhd fnl 3f) | 5 | **15** | 20/1 | 31 | 10 |
| 4226$^{14}$ | **Encore M'Lady (IRE) (57)** (FHLee) **5-9-4** PatEddery(16) (hld up: a in rr) | ½ | **16** | 14/1 | 32 | 14 |
| 4387$^{5}$ | **Lovely Prospect (60)** (RGuest) **3-8-11b**$^{1}$ RHills(12) (led tl hdd & wknd over 2f out) | ¾ | **17** | 14/1 | 26 | 5 |
| *3626*$^{7}$ | **Lia Fail (IRE) (56)** (RHollinshead) **3-8-10**$^{(3)}$ FLynch(10) (mid div: effrt & rdn over 2f out: sn wknd) | 4 | **18** | 25/1 | 20 | — |
| 4428$^{16}$ | **Little Millie (54)** (JWMullins) **3-8-11** JQuinn(18) (outpcd: t.o) | 12 | **19** | 33/1 | — | — |
| 4430$^{20}$ | **Purple Memories (60)** (MJohnston) **3-9-0** JWeaver(11) (lw: chsd ldrs to ½-wy: wknd qckly: eased whn btn: t.o) | 2½ | **20** | 20/1 | — | — |
| | | | | (SP 144.5%) | **20 Rn** | |

**1m 34.9** (-0.10) CSF £41.43 TOTE £6.50: £2.50 £1.70 £5.50 (£27.70) Trio £34.20 OWNER Mr Chris van Hoorn (WEST ILSLEY) BRED The Queen
WEIGHT FOR AGE 3yo-3lb
OFFICIAL EXPLANATION **Purple Memories: was hanging both ways and his jockey was unable to ride him out.**
**3805 Present Situation** reserves his best for Aimee Cook and, though he does not often win on such lively ground, he won this readily enough. A follow up is on the cards. (11/2)

**4573 Bentico** made a brave attempt to win this race for the third time in succession, but the winner beat him fair and square and there were no viable excuses. (6/1)
**4609 Mustn't Grumble (IRE)** adopted identical tactics to the ones that were successful over course and distance last month, but the principals had taken first run and he was unable to reel them in. (12/1: 7/1-14/1)
**3285 Pearl Dawn (IRE)** tried hard to get into the action in the latter stages, but the principals were not stopping. (11/1)
**4337 Just Harry**, set alight into the final quarter-mile, did well to finish so close but, on ground faster than he cares for, he was never going to reach the leaders. He usually comes good in the late autumn or early winter and performs much better on the All-Weather nowadays. (20/1)
**4609 Waft (USA)** ran extremely well last week after a long break, but she found this race coming far too soon and was always struggling in an attempt to land a blow. (7/2)
**4240 Johnnie the Joker**, in the firing-line until fading inside the final furlong, does not quite last this trip, but he is ready to strike when returning to seven furlongs on the All-Weather. (25/1)

## 4693 DORMOUSE MAIDEN APPRENTICE STKS (II) (3-Y.O) (Class G)

3-00 (3-02) **7f 9y** £2,224.00 (£614.00: £292.00) Stalls: High GOING minus 0.51 sec per fur (F)

| | | | | SP | RR | SF |
|---|---|---|---|---|---|---|
| 4591[6] | **Alpine Hideaway (IRE) (76)** (BHanbury) **3-8-12** GFaulkner(10) (lw: hld up in tch: hdwy to ld 2f out: drvn clr appr fnl f) | — | **1** | 11/8[1] | 77 | 46 |
| 4360[10] | **Regal Splendour (CAN) (70)** (PFICole) **3-8-7**(5) DavidO'Neill(12) (racd alone far side: a.p: rdn & ev ch 2f out: one pce) | 5 | **2** | 15/8[2] | 66 | 35 |
| *4336*[3] | **Angus McCoatup (IRE) (49)** (BAMcMahon) **3-8-7**(5) AMcCarthy(8) (lw: prom: rdn over 1f out: one pce) | 1¾ | **3** | 12/1 | 62 | 31 |
| 3832[7] | **Balinsky (IRE) (59)** (JBerry) **3-8-2**(5) CLowther(11) (outpcd & bhd: hrd rdn 2f out: kpt on fnl f) | nk | **4** | 14/1 | 56 | 25 |
| 4309[7] | **The Fugative** (PMitchell) **3-8-7** RMullen(4) (trckd ldrs: c stands' side 2f out: no hdwy fnl f) | ½ | **5** | 8/1[3] | 55 | 24 |
| 3458[7] | **Lachesis (56)** (RHollinshead) **3-8-0**(7) SCrawford(9) (lw: nvr rchd ldrs) | 2 | **6** | 20/1 | 50 | 19 |
| 4229[12] | **Gay Breeze** (PSFelgate) **3-8-9**(3) JEdmunds(7) (lw: prom: led over 3f out to 2f out: wknd qckly: t.o) | 9 | **7** | 66/1 | 35 | 4 |
| 4341[14] | **Viennese Dancer** (RJRWilliams) **3-8-7** AimeeCook(2) (b.hind: trckd ldrs: rdn 2f out: sn wknd) | 2 | **8** | 50/1 | 25 | — |
| 3657[10] | **Northern Clan (40)** (AJChamberlain) **3-8-9b**(3) JBramhill(5) (led over 3f: sn rdn & wknd: t.o) | 3 | **9** | 66/1 | 24 | — |
| | **Fair Lady (BEL)** (JMPlasschaert,Belgium) **3-8-4**(3) JDennis(3) (w'like: dwlt: a outpcd: t.o) | ¾ | **10** | 25/1 | 17 | — |
| 4229[14] | **Macs Clan** (MissJBower) **3-8-2**(5) RBrisland(6) (a bhd: t.o) | dist | **11** | 50/1 | — | — |
| *4499*[12] | ***Gemini Dream*** (RFJohnsonHoughton) **3-8-5**(7) BarrySmith(1) (Withdrawn not under Starter's orders: uns rdr at s) | | **W** | 66/1 | — | — |
| | | | | (SP 119.4%) | **11 Rn** | |

**1m 23.6** (0.60) CSF £4.21 TOTE £2.30: £1.10 £1.60 £2.20 (£1.40) Trio £3.90 OWNER Ms Mary Breslin (NEWMARKET) BRED Roseberry Ltd
**4044 Alpine Hideaway (IRE)** has taken time to open his account, but he swooped to conquer here and won in the style of a useful colt. (11/8)
**4108 Regal Splendour (CAN)**, ploughing a lone furrow up the far rail, always looked a serious threat but, once the winner quickened up, he quite simply had no answer. (15/8: Evens-2/1)
**4336 Angus McCoatup (IRE)** ran up to his mark against two as useful as the principals, but he had little chance of wearing then down. (12/1)
**3058 Balinsky (IRE)**, taken off her legs for most of the way, stuck on gamely under strong pressure to be nearest at the finish. (14/1)
**4309 The Fugative** does look to have ability, but she probably found this trip too short and, after drifting over towards the stands' rail in the latter stages, was tapped for toe in the race to the line. (8/1)
**3107 Lachesis** could have needed this run after two months out of action and her finishing position was as close as she could get. (20/1)

## 4694 STOAT (S) STKS (2-Y.O) (Class G)

3-30 (3-34) **1m 1f 218y** £2,553.00 (£708.00: £339.00) Stalls: High GOING minus 0.51 sec per fur (F)

| | | | | SP | RR | SF |
|---|---|---|---|---|---|---|
| 4602[11] | **Skelton Sovereign (IRE) (64)** (RHollinshead) **2-8-8**(3) FLynch(3) (hld up: hdwy over 2f out: led over 1f out: r.o wl) | — | **1** | 5/1[1] | 63 | 19 |
| 4585[9] | **Tracks of My Tears** (WGMTurner) **2-7-13**(7) DMcGaffin(9) (hdwy 5f out: ev ch 2f out: one pce) | 3 | **2** | 33/1 | 53 | 9 |
| | **Blush** (MCPipe) **2-8-1**(5) MartinDwyer(4) (unf: hld up: hdwy & nt clr run 3f out: r.o fnl f) | 1 | **3** | 12/1 | 52+ | 8 |
| 3943[9] | **Grovefair Lad (IRE) (57)** (BJMeehan) **2-8-11** MTebbutt(15) (chsd ldr: led 6f out: rdn over 2f out: hdd over 1f out: one pce) | ¾ | **4** | 5/1[1] | 55 | 11 |
| 4319[9] | **Ballydinero (IRE) (48)** (CaptJWilson) **2-8-11** KFallon(11) (lw: nvr nr to chal) | 3½ | **5** | 20/1 | 50 | 6 |
| 4605[11] | **Fair Relation** (PFICole) **2-8-6** TQuinn(13) (plld hrd: a.p: rdn over 3f out: no hdwy) | ¾ | **6** | 5/1[1] | 44 | — |
| 4594[13] | **Captain Flint** (ASmith) **2-8-11** DeanMcKeown(1) (prom: no hdwy fnl 2f) | hd | **7** | 50/1 | 48 | 4 |
| *4335*[7] | **Hopperetta (55)** (BPalling) **2-8-6** TSprake(14) (hld up & plld hrd: hdwy on ins 2f out: sn rdn & edgd lft: nt rch ldrs) | d.h | **7** | 20/1 | 43 | — |
| 3092[5] | **Poly Dancer** (MRChannon) **2-8-1**(5) PPMurphy(7) (swtg: n.d) | 1¼ | **9** | 40/1 | 41 | — |
| *4335*[3] | **Mujadil Express (IRE) (54)** (JSMoore) **2-8-6** JFEgan(16) (plld hrd: prom tl wknd over 2f out) | 1½ | **10** | 16/1 | 39 | — |
| 4347[4] | **Fancy A Fortune (IRE) (68)** (JPearce) **2-8-11v**[1] GBardwell(2) (hld up & plld hrd: wknd over 2f out) | 2 | **11** | 5/1[1] | 41 | — |
| *3417*[9] | **Bali-Pet (61)** (WGMTurner) **2-8-11b**[1] RPerham(10) (nvr nr ldrs) | nk | **12** | 16/1 | 40 | — |
| 4361[12] | **Riva La Belle (42)** (JWharton) **2-8-6b** NAdams(5) (s.s: a bhd) | 5 | **13** | 33/1 | 27 | — |
| *4091*[6] | **Heavenly Dancer (59)** (MrsNMacauley) **2-8-6** DHarrison(6) (a bhd) | ¾ | **14** | 7/1[2] | 26 | — |
| 4195[16] | **Unknown Territory (IRE) (68)** (RonaldThompson) **2-8-11v**[1] NConnorton(8) (prom tl wknd qckly 4f out: t.o) | dist | **15** | 10/1[3] | — | — |
| *3954*[10] | **Bold Motion** (CMurray) **2-8-6** PBloomfield(12) (led 4f: wknd qckly over 3f out: t.o) | | **16** | 25/1 | — | — |
| | | | | (SP 131.4%) | **16 Rn** | |

**2m 8.1** (4.40) CSF £144.70 TOTE £7.50: £2.40 £5.70 £4.40 (£225.70) Trio Not won; £401.82 to Leicester 15/10/96 OWNER Mr G. Bailey (UPPER LONGDON) BRED Patrick Brady
No bid
**3512 Skelton Sovereign (IRE)**, dropped in class, benefited from this longer trip and may now go for a ten-furlong nursery. (5/1)
**Tracks of My Tears**, descending to selling company, showed a marked improvement on her two previous starts. (33/1)
**Blush** shaped promisingly after not getting the best of runs. (12/1: op 8/1)
**3662 Grovefair Lad (IRE)**, a springer in the market, had plenty of use made of him in this stamina test. (5/1: op 10/1)
**2932 Ballydinero (IRE)** was lowered in grade for this longer trip. (20/1)
**Fair Relation**, trying her luck in a seller, was a bit too keen early on for this sort of distance. (5/1: 5/2-11/2)
**4347 Fancy A Fortune (IRE)** proved disappointing to settle in the first-time visor. (5/1)

## 4695 RABBIT H'CAP (0-85) (3-Y.O) (Class D)

4-00 (4-00) **1m 3f 183y** £4,324.80 (£1,295.40: £622.20: £285.60) Stalls: High GOING minus 0.51 sec per fur (F)

| | | | | SP | RR | SF |
|---|---|---|---|---|---|---|
| 3657* | **Present Arms (USA) (81)** (PFICole) **3-9-7** TQuinn(4) (lw: chsd ldr: led over 3f out: clr over 1f out: r.o wl) | — | **1** | 5/2[2] | 89 | 59 |

| | | | | | |
|---|---|---|---|---|---|
| 4489⁴ | **Trick (IRE) (73)** (LMCumani) **3-8-13** LDettori(5) (hld up: hdwy 3f out: rdn 2f out: chsd wnr fnl f: no imp) ...........3 | **2** | 2/1 1 | 77 | 47 |
| 1201³ | **Mawared (IRE) (73)** (JLDunlop) **3-8-13** RHills(7) (hld up: hdwy on ins over 6f out: rdn & hung rt fnl 2f: r.o) ..........½ | **3** | 10/1 | 76 | 46 |
| 4252² | **Diego (70)** (CEBrittain) **3-8-10** MRoberts(6) (lw: led 2f: outpcd 5f out: styd on fnl f) ..........3 | **4** | 4/1 3 | 69 | 39 |
| 4121¹⁰ | **Filial (IRE) (80)** (GHarwood) **3-9-6** PatEddery(1) (lw: hld up: ev ch over 2f out: sn rdn: wknd fnl f) ..........1¾ | **5** | 10/1 | 77 | 47 |
| 4248³ | **General Glow (62)** (PDEvans) **3-8-2** JFEgan(2) (rdn over 4f out: wknd over 2f out) ..........15 | **6** | 10/1 | 39 | 9 |
| 2321* | **Meltemison (70)** (MDHammond) **3-8-10** JWeaver(3) (bkwd: led after 2f tl over 3f out: sn wknd: t.o) ..........12 | **7** | 16/1 | 30 | — |
| | | | (SP 115.1%) | **7 Rn** | |

**2m 29.8** (0.80) CSF £7.81 TOTE £4.20: £1.70 £1.60 (£3.30) OWNER H R H Prince Fahd Salman (WHATCOMBE) BRED Tri-Star Stable
**3657* Present Arms (USA)**, raised 6lb, did not need the blinkers to put up a good performance, and now goes for the November Handicap under a 4lb penalty. (5/2)
**4489 Trick (IRE)**, trying a longer trip, found the winner too much of a handful. (2/1: 6/4-9/4)
**1201 Mawared (IRE)** did not help his rider by persistently hanging into the far rail. (10/1: op 6/1)
**4252 Diego**, raised 4lb, did not seem suited to this shorter distance. (4/1)
**3505* Filial (IRE)** did not seem to see out the mile and a half. (10/1: op 6/1)

## 4696 HEDGEHOG CONDITIONS STKS (2-Y.O) (Class C)
4-30 (4-30) **1m 1f 218y** £4,789.12 (£1,723.50: £824.25: £333.75: £129.38) Stalls: High GOING minus 0.51 sec per fur (F)

| | | | SP | RR | SF |
|---|---|---|---|---|---|
| 4458* | **Windsor Castle** (PFICole) **2-9-1** TQuinn(4) (sn pushed along: chsd ldr: hmpd 2f out: hrd rdn to ld nr fin) .....— | **1** | 3/1 3 | 87 | 45 |
| 4349* | **Atlantic Desire (IRE) (85)** (MJohnston) **2-8-10** JWeaver(3) (lw: led: rdn & edgd lft 2f out: hdd nr fin) ..........hd | **2** | 7/4 1 | 82 | 40 |
| 4131⁷ | **Mister Pink (89)** (RFJohnsonHoughton) **2-8-11b¹** PatEddery(1) (a.p: ev ch over 2f out: unable qckn fnl f) ....1¼ | **3** | 2/1 2 | 81 | 39 |
| 4585⁴ | **Vicki Romara** (MJohnston) **2-8-6** LDettori(5) (bit bkwd: hld up: hdwy on ins over 2f out: hrd rdn & ev ch over 1f out: wknd fnl f) ..........3 | **4** | 10/1 | 71 | 29 |
| 4564⁴ | **Permission (68)** (RHannon) **2-8-6** DaneO'Neill(2) (lw: hld up: eased whn no ch over 1f out) ..........16 | **5** | 20/1 | 45 | 3 |
| | | | (SP 108.5%) | **5 Rn** | |

**2m 5.3** (1.90 under 2y best) (1.60) CSF £8.14 TOTE £4.40: £1.90 £1.90 (£7.80) OWNER H R H Prince Fahd Salman (WHATCOMBE) BRED Newgate Stud Co
**4458* Windsor Castle**, again showing stamina to be the least of his problems, had to overcome being hit over the head by the runner-up's whip. He will now be put away for next year. (3/1: 9/4-7/2)
**4349* Atlantic Desire (IRE)** did the winner no favours at the quarter-mile pole. (7/4)
**4131 Mister Pink**, having previously once worn a visor, was tried in blinkers here. (2/1: 6/4-9/4)
**4585 Vicki Romara** had more on her plate than last week, but again ran well. (10/1)

## 4697 E.B.F. HARE MAIDEN STKS (2-Y.O F) (Class D)
5-00 (5-01) **7f 9y** £4,662.50 (£1,400.00: £675.00: £312.50) Stalls: High GOING minus 0.51 sec per fur (F)

| | | | SP | RR | SF |
|---|---|---|---|---|---|
| 4100⁶ | **Vanishing Trick (USA)** (HRACecil) **2-8-11** PatEddery(12) (bit bkwd: led 5f: hrd rdn to ld ins fnl f: all out) .....— | **1** | 3/1 2 | 82 | 35 |
| | **Apache Star** (GWragg) **2-8-11** MHills(7) (b.nr hind: w'like: leggy: hld up: hdwy 3f out: led 2f out: sn rdn: hdd ins fnl f) ..........½ | **2** | 7/4 1 | 81+ | 34 |
| 4253³ | **All In Leather** (WJHaggas) **2-8-11** KFallon(5) (a.p: hrd rdn & ev ch ins fnl f: unable qckn) ..........nk | **3** | 8/1 | 80 | 33 |
| 4208⁶ | **Forgotten Times (USA)** (EALDunlop) **2-8-11** WRyan(1) (swvd lft s: rdn & hdwy over 2f out: r.o one pce fnl f) ..........2½ | **4** | 16/1 | 75 | 28 |
| | **Tangshan (CAN)** (MRStoute) **2-8-11** WRSwinburn(9) (leggy: lt-f: bit bkwd: hld up & bhd: hdwy over 2f out: wknd over 1f out) ..........3 | **5** | 9/2 3 | 68 | 21 |
| | **Inimitable** (JLDunlop) **2-8-11** TSprake(10) (leggy: unf: bit bkwd: nvr nr to chal) ..........½ | **6** | 33/1 | 67 | 20 |
| 4359⁴ | **Lady of The Lake** (JLDunlop) **2-8-11** KDarley(4) (hld up: rdn & no hdwy fnl 2f) ..........½ | **7** | 9/1 | 65 | 18 |
| 4435³ | **Go For Green** (DrJDScargill) **2-8-11** MFenton(6) (s.s: nvr trbld ldrs) ..........3 | **8** | 33/1 | 59 | 12 |
| 4052⁹ | **Top Shelf** (CEBrittain) **2-8-11** BDoyle(8) (a bhd) ..........2 | **9** | 25/1 | 54 | 7 |
| | **Jucinda** (JPearce) **2-8-11** GBardwell(3) (leggy: lt-f: bit bkwd: a bhd) ..........nk | **10** | 50/1 | 53 | 6 |
| 4547⁹ | **Dorado Beach** (BWHills) **2-8-8(3)** JDSmith(2) (hld up mid div: wknd fnl 2f) ..........3½ | **11** | 33/1 | 45 | — |
| 4061⁵ | **Bold Tina (IRE) (78)** (RHannon) **2-8-11** DaneO'Neill(11) (prom over 4f) ..........8 | **12** | 16/1 | 27 | — |
| | | | (SP 127.1%) | **12 Rn** | |

**1m 24.4** (1.40) CSF £8.94 TOTE £3.70: £1.40 £1.10 £2.80 (£4.60) Trio £13.90 OWNER Cliveden Stud (NEWMARKET) BRED Clivedon Stud Ltd
**4100 Vanishing Trick (USA)** needed Eddery at his strongest to pull this one out of the hat. (3/1: 6/4-100/30)
**Apache Star**, a half-sister to Stately Dancer, looked all set to score when taking it up, but the winner's previous experience told in the final stages. She should have little difficulty making amends. (7/4)
**4253 All In Leather** lived up to her name and responded to the whip. (8/1: 5/1-10/1)
**4208 Forgotten Times (USA)** is learning all the time. (16/1)
**Tangshan (CAN)**, a $30,000 half-sister to six winners in the States, is sparely-made and probably needs more time. (9/2)
**Inimitable** showed encouragement for the future. (33/1)
**4359 Lady of The Lake** (9/1: 5/1-10/1)

T/Jkpt: £8,049.10 (1.77 Tckts). T/Plpt: £60.50 (263.94 Tckts). T/Qdpt: £22.30 (46.96 Tckts). IM/KH

# 4690-LEICESTER (R-H) (Good to firm, Firm back st)
## Tuesday October 15th
WEATHER: sunny intervals, rain at times WIND: mod half bhd

## 4698 E.B.F. MANNY BERNSTEIN CREDIT DIVISION MAIDEN STKS (I) (2-Y.O C & G) (Class D)
1-30 (1-31) **7f 9y** £3,557.50 (£1,060.00: £505.00: £227.50) Stalls: High GOING minus 0.43 sec per fur (F)

| | | | SP | RR | SF |
|---|---|---|---|---|---|
| 4233⁸ | **Attitude** (HCandy) **2-8-11** CRutter(10) (trckd ldrs: led over 1f out: r.o wl) ..........— | **1** | 14/1 | 76 | 43 |
| 4514⁴ | **River's Source (USA)** (BWHills) **2-8-11** PatEddery(6) (chsd ldr: led over 2f out tl over 1f out: hrd rdn & unable qckn fnl f) ..........2 | **2** | 4/9 1 | 72 | 39 |
| 4516⁹ | **Aerleon Pete (IRE)** (MRStoute) **2-8-11** WRSwinburn(9) (bhd & outpcd: gd hdwy 2f out: swtchd lft over 1f out: fin wl) ..........½ | **3** | 8/1 3 | 70 | 37 |
| 4514¹² | **Prince of Denial** (DWPArbuthnot) **2-8-11** TSprake(11) (b: b.hind: hld up: hdwy over 1f out: nrst fin) ..........1½ | **4** | 50/1 | 67 | 34 |

| | | | | | | |
|---|---|---|---|---|---|---|
| | **Cold Steel** (WJarvis) **2-8-11** WRyan(4) (lengthy: scope: prom: rdn over 2f out: rn green: sn btn) | 1¼ | **5** | 20/1 | 64 | 31 |
| | **Fabled Light (IRE)** (GWragg) **2-8-11** MHills(3) (w'like: str: bkwd: hld up: drifted rt 3f out: no hdwy fnl 2f) | 2 | **6** | 9/2[2] | 60 | 27 |
| | **Boater** (DMorley) **2-8-11** RCochrane(1) (w'like: bkwd: hld up: effrt 2f out: wknd over 1f out) | 2 | **7** | 25/1 | 55 | 22 |
| | **Doc Ryan's** (MJRyan) **2-8-11** GCarter(2) (scope: bkwd: s.s: a in rr) | 1½ | **8** | 33/1 | 52 | 19 |
| 4512[14] | **Blue Imperial (FR)** (JWHills) **2-8-11** RHills(5) (bit bkwd: led over 4f: sn wknd) | ½ | **9** | 50/1 | 50 | 17 |
| | **Sixties Melody** (RBoss) **2-8-11** SSanders(8) (wl grwn: scope: dwlt: rn green: a bhd: t.o) | 11 | **10** | 50/1 | 25 | — |
| | | | | (SP 122.6%) | **10 Rn** | |

**1m 24.3** (1.30) CSF £21.02 TOTE £14.20: £2.60 £1.00 £1.60 (£5.40) Trio £7.30 OWNER Girsonfield Ltd (WANTAGE) BRED Girsonfield Ltd

**Attitude**, a strong individual who shows plenty of knee-action, had little trouble pulling clear of the favourite. (14/1: 10/1-16/1)

**4514 River's Source (USA)**, still carrying a bit of surplus condition, is just starting to get his winter coat. He may well have to wait for next season before he can prove his true worth. (4/9: op 8/11)

**Aerleon Pete (IRE)**, who finished strongly, looks to be a colt who will go on improving. (8/1: op 5/1)

**Prince of Denial** finished much closer to the favourite this time. He is sure to be suited by a longer trip, and should not have much trouble in finding an opening. (50/1)

**Cold Steel**, very much on his toes for this racecourse debut, pulled too hard for his own good and showed signs of greenness in the latter stages. He will be all the wiser for the experience. (20/1)

**Fabled Light (IRE)**, a very attractive brother to Old Hickory, was not straight enough to do himself justice this time, but showed promise and could be a different proposition next season. (9/2: 7/4-5/1)

## 4699 MANNY BERNSTEIN RACING CONDITIONS STKS (2-Y.O) (Class C)

2-00 (2-01) **7f 9y** £4,901.50 (£1,839.00: £882.00: £360.00: £142.50) Stalls: High GOING minus 0.43 sec per fur (F)

| | | | | SP | RR | SF |
|---|---|---|---|---|---|---|
| 3919* | **Amid Albadu (USA) (87)** (JLDunlop) **2-9-2** RHills(4) (led 3f: led over 2f out: rdn & edgd lft wl ins fnl f: hld on) | — | **1** | 3/1[2] | 75 | 62 |
| | **Arabian** (MRStoute) **2-8-10** KDarley(3) (leggy: unf: hld up: hdwy 2f out: sn hrd drvn: sustained chal ins fnl f: jst failed) | s.h | **2** | 10/1 | 69 | 56 |
| | **Sporting Fellow** (MRStoute) **2-8-10** WRSwinburn(6) (unf: scope: bit bkwd: a.p: ev ch wl over 1f out: rdn & one pce ins fnl f) | 4 | **3** | 11/2[3] | 60 | 47 |
| 4451* | **River Usk** (HRACecil) **2-9-2** PatEddery(2) (lw: plld hrd: led 4f out tl over 2f out: sn rdn & btn) | 5 | **4** | 4/7[1] | 54 | 41 |
| 4311[8] | **Skyers Flyer (IRE) (81)** (RonaldThompson) **2-8-5** JQuinn(5) (plld hrd: prom over 4f: sn outpcd) | 4 | **5** | 33/1 | 34 | 21 |
| | | | | (SP 116.1%) | **5 Rn** | |

**1m 24.1** (1.10) CSF £24.78 TOTE £6.00: £1.40 £2.70 (£18.70) OWNER Mr Hamdan Al Maktoum (ARUNDEL) BRED Airlie Stud

**3919* Amid Albadu (USA)** stays this trip extremely well and, putting his previous experience to good use, defied his penalty by the skin of his teeth. (3/1)

**Arabian**, a half-brother to Young Buster, only lost out here due to lack of a previous race. He will be the one to beat from now on wherever he runs. (10/1: 8/1-12/1)

**Sporting Fellow**, a stable-companion to the runner-up, did not look fully wound up and only dropped away as lack of peak condition took its toll. He will win races. (11/2: 5/2-6/1)

**4451* River Usk** had different ground to contend with here and he was hard at work entering the last quarter-mile. (4/7)

## 4700 E.B.F. MANNY BERNSTEIN CREDIT DIVISION MAIDEN STKS (II) (2-Y.O C & G) (Class D)

2-30 (2-31) **7f 9y** £3,557.50 (£1,060.00: £505.00: £227.50) Stalls: High GOING minus 0.43 sec per fur (F)

| | | | | SP | RR | SF |
|---|---|---|---|---|---|---|
| | **Showboat** (BWHills) **2-8-11** PatEddery(8) (w'like: scope: s.i.s: hld up: hdwy to ld over 1f out: pushed clr fnl f) | — | **1** | 2/1[2] | 93+ | 46 |
| 4451[5] | **Maylane** (ACStewart) **2-8-11** MRoberts(10) (lw: plld hrd: hld up in tch: led over 2f out tl over 1f out: no ch w wnr) | 5 | **2** | 7/4[1] | 82 | 35 |
| 3494[13] | **Silver Secret** (MJHeaton-Ellis) **2-8-11** JCarroll(4) (dwlt: sn chsng ldrs: kpt on u.p ins fnl f) | ¾ | **3** | 100/1 | 80 | 33 |
| | **Final Trial (IRE)** (GWragg) **2-8-11** MHills(5) (w'like: scope: trckd ldrs: led wl over 2f out: sn hdd: one pce fnl f) | 1¼ | **4** | 11/4[3] | 77 | 30 |
| 4380[11] | **Smokebush** (LordHuntingdon) **2-8-11** DHarrison(7) (bhd: rdn over 2f out: nvr nrr) | 4 | **5** | 16/1 | 68 | 21 |
| | **The Roundsills** (RFJohnsonHoughton) **2-8-11** AMcGlone(2) (cmpt: bkwd: nvr plcd to chal) | nk | **6** | 20/1 | 67 | 20 |
| 4380[10] | **Bon Guest (IRE)** (TJNaughton) **2-8-11** SSanders(3) (prom over 4f) | nk | **7** | 33/1 | 67 | 20 |
| 4127[11] | **Avanti Blue** (KMcAuliffe) **2-8-11** JFEgan(1) (bit bkwd: hld up in rr: effrt & hung bdly lft over 2f out: sn rdn: nvr nr ldrs) | 4 | **8** | 50/1 | 58 | 11 |
| 4547[12] | **Ewar Arrangement** (CEBrittain) **2-8-11** BDoyle(9) (lw: led tl hdd & wknd wl over 2f out: t.o) | 6 | **9** | 33/1 | 44 | — |
| 4584[11] | **Dunston Gold** (PJBevan) **2-8-11** NCarlisle(6) (s.s: a bhd: t.o) | 3½ | **10** | 100/1 | 36 | — |
| | | | | (SP 116.8%) | **10 Rn** | |

**1m 24.8** (1.80) CSF £5.69 TOTE £3.40: £1.30 £1.20 £13.00 (£2.60) Trio £232.20; £98.12 to Haydock 16/10/96 OWNER Mr R. D. Hollingsworth (LAMBOURN) BRED R. D. Hollingsworth

**Showboat**, a highly thought-of newcomer who is engaged in next year's Derby, put up an impressive performance, winning with the minimum of fuss. He looks extremely useful. (2/1: 5/4-9/4)

**4451 Maylane** was ridden with more restraint. Once the winner lengthened, he found himself out of his depth. (7/4)

**Silver Secret** stayed on particularly well inside the distance, and it would seem he gets stamina from his dam's side. (100/1)

**Final Trial (IRE)**, a choppy mover who also holds a Derby entry, did strike the front, but was unable to hold onto pole position for long and his stride shortened inside the final furlong. (11/4: op 6/4)

## 4701 MANNY BERNSTEIN TRADE DIVISION (S) H'CAP (0-60) (3-Y.O+) (Class G)

3-00 (3-02) **7f 9y** £3,015.00 (£840.00: £405.00) Stalls: High GOING minus 0.43 sec per fur (F)

| | | | | SP | RR | SF |
|---|---|---|---|---|---|---|
| 4129[4] | **Silver Harrow (53)** (AGNewcombe) **3-9-0**(5) GParkin(2) (a.p: led wl over 1f out: r.o wl) | — | **1** | 7/1[1] | 65 | 54 |
| 4436[20] | **Statistician (55)** (JohnBerry) **4-9-9b[1]** RCochrane(5) (hld up: hdwy 3f out: rdn & hung lft: r.o strly towards fin) | ¾ | **2** | 14/1 | 65 | 56 |
| 4609[4] | **Morocco (IRE) (58)** (MRChannon) **7-9-5**(7) AEddery(15) (hld up: hdwy to ld 2f out: sn hdd: unable qckn fnl f) | nk | **3** | 7/1[1] | 68 | 59 |
| 4256[12] | **Euphyllia (52)** (BobJones) **4-9-6** MWigham(7) (a.p: ev ch 2f out: rdn & one pce fnl f) | 1½ | **4** | 14/1 | 58 | 49 |
| 4373[15] | **Roi de la Mer (IRE) (57)** (JAkehurst) **5-9-11** RHughes(8) (lw: chsd ldrs: rdn 2f out: kpt on ins fnl f) | 1¼ | **5** | 15/2[2] | 60 | 51 |
| 4356[7] | **Waders Dream (IRE) (49)** (PatMitchell) **7-9-3v** MFenton(12) (trckd ldrs: hdwy & ev ch wl over 1f out: sn rdn: one pce) | 1¼ | **6** | 14/1 | 50 | 41 |

| | | | SP | RR | SF |
|---|---|---|---|---|---|
| 4221* **How's Yer Father (60)** (RJHodges) **10-9-9**(5) AmandaSanders(9) (hld up: effrt over 2f out: sn rdn & no imp) | ½ | **7** | 15/2[2] | 59 | 50 |
| 4240[15] **Super Park (54)** (JPearce) **4-9-3**(5) MBaird(1) (in tch: effrt over 2f out: no ex appr fnl f) | nk | **8** | 14/1 | 53 | 44 |
| 4692[4] **Pearl Dawn (IRE) (60)** (GLMoore) **6-9-9**(5) LNewton(17) (prom: led over 2f out: sn hdd: wknd appr fnl f) | 1 | **9** | 8/1[3] | 56 | 47 |
| 4129[11] **Everset (FR) (57)** (ABailey) **8-9-8b**(3) DWright(19) (b: lw: racd keenly: led tl over 2f out: sn wknd) | 2 | **10** | 8/1[3] | 49 | 40 |
| 4428[14] **Southern Dominion (48)** (CNAllen) **4-8-11**(5) MartinDwyer(16) (b.hind: w ldrs tl rdn & wknd over 2f out) | hd | **11** | 33/1 | 40 | 31 |
| 4373[7] **Queen of Shannon (IRE) (48)** (AWCarroll) **8-8-9v**(7) RStudholme(11) (a in rr) | ¾ | **12** | 10/1 | 38 | 29 |
| 4323[14] **Charming Bride (55)** (SCWilliams) **3-9-7** WRSwinburn(13) (b: a bhd) | 1 | **13** | 14/1 | 43 | 32 |
| 4045[11] **Speedy Snaps Pride (49)** (PDCundell) **4-8-12b**(5) DGriffiths(20) (hld up in tch: rdn & wknd 2f out) | 1¼ | **14** | 12/1 | 34 | 25 |
| 4551[14] **Straight Thinking (USA) (50)** (JLSpearing) **3-9-2b**[1] GBardwell(4) (dwlt: bhd & rdn over 2f out: no imp) | 1 | **15** | 33/1 | 33 | 22 |
| *2369*[11] **First Gold (54)** (JWharton) **7-9-8** KFallon(6) (bkwd: bhd fnl 3f: t.o) | 5 | **16** | 11/1 | 25 | 16 |
| 4221[7] **Duo Master (52)** (MrsMReveley) **3-9-4** KDarley(14) (a bhd: t.o) | 5 | **17** | 10/1 | 12 | 1 |
| 1485[11] **Janies Girl (IRE) (55)** (KRBurke) **3-9-7** JQuinn(18) (a bhd: t.o) | 15 | **18** | 33/1 | — | — |
| | | | (SP 147.1%) | | **18 Rn** |

**1m 24.2** (1.20) CSF £108.74 CT £702.83 TOTE £7.90: £1.40 £3.80 £2.40 £2.40 (£132.90) Trio £214.30 OWNER Mr M. Patel (BARNSTAPLE) BRED G. A. Bosley and H. Clarkin

WEIGHT FOR AGE 3yo-2lb

No bid

**4129 Silver Harrow**, very keen to post, was not winning out of turn. Now that he has succeeded, maybe there will be more of the same to follow. (7/1)

**3406 Statistician** found something like his true form in his first-time blinkers, but he again gave away a winning chance by hanging badly left in the latter stages, otherwise the prize would have been his. (14/1)

**4609 Morocco (IRE)** looked the likely winner when nosing ahead entering the last quarter-mile, but the winner was onto him in double-quick time and had the legs of him in the sprint to the line. (7/1)

**3151 Euphyllia** has not won a race for twelve months, but she performed much better without the visor and was only shaken off inside the distance. She could be worth keeping in mind for any near-at-hand engagements. (14/1)

**4237 Roi de la Mer (IRE)** has hardly got the speed to win at this trip, but he stuck on strongly in the closing stages, and there could be another prize to be won. (15/2)

**3967 Waders Dream (IRE)**, still to succeed beyond six furlongs, found himself in with every chance below the distance but, when the pressure was on, lacked the pace to do anything about it. (14/1)

**4221* How's Yer Father** did not look at all happy cantering to post and, though he did hold his pitch, was found wanting once the battle to the line developed. Once the rains arrive, he will return to form. (15/2)

**3694 Queen of Shannon (IRE)** (10/1: 12/1-8/1)

## 4702 MANNY BERNSTEIN IN RUNNING H'CAP (0-70) (3-Y.O+) (Class E)

3-30 (3-32) **1m 1f 218y** £3,889.20 (£1,167.60: £562.80: £260.40) Stalls: High GOING minus 0.43 sec per fur (F)

| | | | SP | RR | SF |
|---|---|---|---|---|---|
| 4427[5] **Rival Bid (USA) (63)** (MrsNMacauley) **8-9-7**(3) CTeague(12) (swtg: s.s: gd hdwy & hung rt 2f out: hrd rdn & r.o wl to ld nr fin) | — | **1** | 11/1 | 73 | 58 |
| 4483[8] **Giftbox (USA) (52)** (SirMarkPrescott) **4-8-13** GDuffield(6) (a.p: led over 1f out: hrd rdn & hdd nr fin) | 1¼ | **2** | 12/1 | 60 | 45 |
| 3348[7] **Blurred (IRE) (70)** (MHTompkins) **3-9-12** RHills(8) (led 2f: led over 4f out tl over 1f out: hrd rdn & edgd lft wl ins fnl f) | s.h | **3** | 9/1 | 78 | 58 |
| *2689*[4] **General Haven (68)** (TJNaughton) **3-9-10** JWeaver(16) (lw: hld up & bhd: plld out over 2f out: gd hdwy over 1f out: fin wl) | 1½ | **4** | 14/1 | 74 | 54 |
| 4243[11] **Access Adventurer (IRE) (63)** (RBoss) **5-9-10** WRyan(15) (hld up mid div: hdwy 2f out: one pce fnl f) | 1½ | **5** | 16/1 | 66 | 51 |
| 4186[8] **Ameer Alfayaafi (IRE) (56)** (RAkehurst) **3-8-12** TQuinn(9) (a.p: hrd rdn 3f out: no hdwy) | 2½ | **6** | 10/1 | 55 | 35 |
| 3638[5] **Willy Star (BEL) (48)** (MrsSJSmith) **6-8-9** PBloomfield(10) (nvr nrr) | nk | **7** | 33/1 | 47 | 32 |
| 4559* **Nosey Native (68)** (JPearce) **3-9-10** MWigham(4) (nrst fin) | 1¾ | **8** | 15/2[2] | 64 | 44 |
| 4686[8] **Harvey White (IRE) (64)** (JPearce) **4-9-6**(5) MBaird(14) (lw: nvr trbld ldrs) | ½ | **9** | 5/1[1] | 59 | 44 |
| 4513[2] **Temptress (63)** (PTWalwyn) **3-9-5v** SSanders(13) (led after 2f tl over 4f out: sn wknd) | ½ | **10** | 8/1[3] | 57 | 37 |
| *4334*[5] **Platinum Plus (54)** (CADwyer) **4-9-1** MRimmer(3) (b: swtg: prom 4f) | 3 | **11** | 15/2[2] | 43 | 28 |
| 4209[3] **Afon Alwen (61)** (SCWilliams) **3-9-3** KDarley(2) (b.hind: bhd fnl 3f) | 6 | **12** | 14/1 | 41 | 21 |
| 4582[8] **Doctor Bravious (IRE) (66)** (MBell) **3-9-8v** MFenton(11) (lw: prom 7f) | 3½ | **13** | 14/1 | 40 | 20 |
| 4511[18] **Renata's Prince (IRE) (68)** (KRBurke) **3-9-10b**[1] RCochrane(18) (lw: a bhd) | ¾ | **14** | 25/1 | 41 | 21 |
| 4238[12] **Action Jackson (56)** (BJMcMath) **4-9-3** DBiggs(17) (prom 7f) | 1¾ | **15** | 20/1 | 26 | 11 |
| 3980[3] **Roman Reel (USA) (67)** (GLMoore) **5-10-0** SWhitworth(5) (lw: prom 5f: t.o) | 20 | **16** | 12/1 | 5 | — |
| 4513[17] **Two Socks (60)** (PBurgoyne) **3-9-2** RHughes(19) (lw: bhd fnl 3f out: t.o) | 6 | **17** | 20/1 | — | — |
| | | | (SP 136.3%) | | **17 Rn** |

**2m 5.5** (1.80) CSF £136.44 CT £1,167.79 TOTE £8.10: £1.70 £2.70 £3.80 £8.30 (£71.80) Trio £509.90; £215.49 to Haydock 16/10/96 OWNER Twenty Twenty Racing (MELTON MOWBRAY) BRED Marvin L. Warner Jnr.

WEIGHT FOR AGE 3yo-5lb

**4209 Rival Bid (USA)** looked none too co-operative coming to the final furlong, and needed plenty of persuasion to put his best foot forward. He is likely to run over hurdles in the near future. (11/1)

**3603 Giftbox (USA)**, dropped 5lb, would have preferred more give in the ground and ran a fine race in the circumstances. (12/1)

**3134 Blurred (IRE)** was 2lb higher than when narrowly beaten at Doncaster at the end of July. (9/1)

**2689 General Haven**, 5lb higher than when winning at Windsor, was coming back after a three-month break. (14/1)

**1816 Access Adventurer (IRE)**, disappointing when tried in blinkers last time, has been struggling to find some form. (16/1)

**2705 Ameer Alfayaafi (IRE)**, who has been slipping down the Ratings, was trying a longer trip. (10/1)

**4559* Nosey Native** (15/2: 5/1-8/1)

**4686 Harvey White (IRE)** was 8lb higher than when successful at Kempton last month. (5/1)

**3980 Roman Reel (USA)** (12/1: 8/1-14/1)

## 4703 MANNY BERNSTEIN EARLY BIRDS CLAIMING STKS (3-Y.O+) (Class F)

4-00 (4-04) **1m 3f 183y** £3,190.20 (£887.20: £426.60) Stalls: High GOING minus 0.43 sec per fur (F)

| | | | SP | RR | SF |
|---|---|---|---|---|---|
| 3948[6] **Te Amo (IRE) (62)** (RAkehurst) **4-9-5** SSanders(18) (a.p: led on bit 3f out: rdn out) | — | **1** | 7/2[2] | 68 | 52 |
| 4515[4] **Loki (IRE) (65)** (GLewis) **8-8-10**(3) AWhelan(16) (b.hind: s.i.s: stdy hdwy 6f out: chsd wnr over 1f out: unable qckn) | 1¾ | **2** | 5/2[1] | 60 | 44 |
| 4455[6] **Mcgillycuddy Reeks (IRE) (40)** (NTinkler) **5-8-5** WRyan(19) (hld up: hdwy 4f out: ev ch over 2f out: hrd rdn: one pce) | 3 | **3** | 20/1 | 48 | 32 |

| | | | | SP | RR | SF |
|---|---|---|---|---|---|---|
| 4000$^{8}$ | **Taniyar (FR) (32)** (RHollinshead) **4-9-6**$^{(5)}$ DGriffiths(4) (hld up: hdwy over 3f out: one pce fnl 2f) | 2½ | **4** | 20/1 | 64 | 48 |
| 4509$^{2}$ | **Rose of Glenn (40)** (BPalling) **5-9-0** TSprake(8) (a.p: rdn & ev ch over 2f out: wknd over 1f out) | 2 | **5** | 16/1 | 51 | 35 |
| 4515$^{9}$ | **Shabanaz (60)** (WRMuir) **11-9-2** PatEddery(5) (hld up: hdwy fnl 2f: nvr nrr) | 2 | **6** | 8/1 | 50 | 34 |
| 3808$^{2}$ | **Oakbury (IRE) (37)** (MissLCSiddall) **4-9-2** GHind(12) (nvr nr to chal) | 1½ | **7** | 25/1 | 48 | 32 |
| 2380$^{6}$ | **Precious Island** (PTDalton) **3-8-1** NAdams(10) (nvr nrr) | 6 | **8** | 50/1 | 32 | 9 |
| 4340$^{2}$ | **Haute Cuisine (47)** (RJRWilliams) **3-8-12** DaneO'Neill(7) (nvr trbld ldrs) | 3 | **9** | 10/1 | 39 | 16 |
| 4613$^{9}$ | **Aydigo** (JPearce) **3-8-6** GBardwell(15) (nvr nr ldrs) | 1¾ | **10** | 33/1 | 30 | 7 |
| 4373$^{5}$ | **Baron Hrabovsky (48)** (PFICole) **3-9-4** TQuinn(14) (n.d) | s.h | **11** | 7/1$^{3}$ | 42 | 19 |
| 3808$^{15}$ | **Shuttlecock (34)** (MrsNMacauley) **5-9-5**$^{(3)}$ CTeague(2) (led 9f: eased whn btn over 1f out) | nk | **12** | 25/1 | 39 | 23 |
| 4317$^{5}$ | **Chancancook** (JLEyre) **3-8-4** TWilliams(9) (s.s: bhd whn rdn over 3f out: n.d) | nk | **13** | 12/1 | 27 | 4 |
| *4574*$^{11}$ | **Hand of Straw (IRE) (52)** (PGMurphy) **4-9-2v** SDrowne(11) (a bhd) | ½ | **14** | 14/1 | 32 | 16 |
| 4102$^{10}$ | **Milltown Classic (IRE) (33)** (JParkes) **4-8-5** JFanning(3) (prom 6f: t.o) | 17 | **15** | 16/1 | — | — |
| 4480$^{9}$ | **Northern Saga (IRE) (39)** (CJDrewe) **3-8-6** JQuinn(6) (a bhd: t.o) | ¾ | **16** | 33/1 | 5 | — |
| 4478$^{10}$ | **Haddit** (AGNewcombe) **3-9-4** FNorton(13) (a bhd: t.o) | 4 | **17** | 50/1 | 11 | — |
| | **Bianca's Son (BEL)** (JMPlasschaert,Belgium) **6-9-11** MKeogh(20) (bkwd: a bhd: t.o) | 2 | **18** | 50/1 | 9 | — |
| 4496$^{14}$ | **Rockusa (34)** (PRHedger) **4-9-0v**$^{1}$ GCarter(22) (s.i.s: sn prom: wknd 3f out: eased whn btn: t.o) | 5 | **19** | 33/1 | — | — |
| | **Dunston Knight** (PJBevan) **3-8-6** NCarlisle(17) (cmpt: bkwd: t.o fnl 6f) | 26 | **20** | 50/1 | — | — |
| | | | | (SP 143.5%) | **20 Rn** | |

**2m 31.5** (2.50) CSF £13.72 TOTE £5.00: £1.90 £1.90 £2.90 (£4.50) Trio £46.30 OWNER Fernray Ltd (EPSOM) BRED T. E. Fitzsimons
WEIGHT FOR AGE 3yo-7lb
Te Amo (IRE) clmd FFarrant £6,000
**3948 Te Amo (IRE)**, appreciating this return to a claimer, probably failed to stay the extra quarter-mile at Sandown last time. (7/2)
**4515 Loki (IRE)** comes from a stable struggling to get out of the doldrums. (5/2)
**4455 Mcgillycuddy Reeks (IRE)**, trying a longer trip, was certainly not disgraced on this step up from selling company. (20/1)
**2506 Taniyar (FR)** ran his best race for some time and would have been much better off in a handicap. (20/1)
**4509 Rose of Glenn** seems to need further than this nowadays. (16/1)
**4237 Shabanaz**, ridden to get the trip, did his best work in the latter stages. (8/1)
**4340 Haute Cuisine** (10/1: 8/1-12/1)
**4373 Baron Hrabovsky** (7/1: 10/1-16/1)
**4317 Chancancook** (12/1: op 20/1)
**4315 Hand of Straw (IRE)** (14/1: op 8/1)

## 4704 MANNY BERNSTEIN DOUBLE RESULT CONDITIONS STKS (3-Y.O F) (Class C)

4-30 (4-30) **1m 8y** £4,882.73 (£1,757.48: £840.74: £340.70: £132.35) Stalls: High GOING minus 0.43 sec per fur (F)

| | | | | SP | RR | SF |
|---|---|---|---|---|---|---|
| 4445$^{4}$ | **Questonia (90)** (HRACecil) **3-8-13** PatEddery(2) (lw: led over 6f: hrd rdn to ld last strides) | — | **1** | 11/8$^{2}$ | 105 | 56 |
| 4405a$^{3}$ | **Miss Riviera (97)** (GWragg) **3-8-9** MHills(5) (hld up: led wl over 1f out: rdn & hdd last strides) | hd | **2** | 5/4$^{1}$ | 101 | 52 |
| 4194$^{8}$ | **Saleemah (USA) (95)** (JLDunlop) **3-8-13** RHills(3) (chsd ldr tl wknd wl over 1f out) | 6 | **3** | 5/1$^{3}$ | 93 | 44 |
| 4117$^{9}$ | **Iberian Dancer (CAN) (79)** (JWHills) **3-8-13** RHughes(4) (hld up: rdn over 3f out: bhd fnl 2f) | 9 | **4** | 20/1 | 75 | 26 |
| | **Condition Red** (MSSaunders) **3-8-6** JFEgan(1) (w'like: scope: bkwd: swvd lft s: hld up: rdn 3f out: sn bhd) | 25 | **5** | 100/1 | 18 | — |
| | | | | (SP 109.0%) | **5 Rn** | |

**1m 35.4** (0.40) CSF £3.31 TOTE £2.20: £1.40 £1.10 (£1.30) OWNER Mr K. Abdulla (NEWMARKET) BRED Juddmonte Farms
**4445 Questonia** needed a vintage ride from Eddery to prevail. (11/8)
**4405a Miss Riviera** seemed to have the edge until Eddery conjured up an inspired finish. (5/4: Evens-11/8)
**3842 Saleemah (USA)** was worn down in the final quarter-mile. (5/1: 3/1-6/1)
**3148 Iberian Dancer (CAN)** had a very tough task at the weights. (20/1)

## 4705 E.B.F. MANNY BERNSTEIN MAIDEN STKS (2-Y.O) (Class D)

5-00 (5-01) **1m 8y** £4,272.50 (£1,280.00: £615.00: £282.50) Stalls: High GOING minus 0.43 sec per fur (F)

| | | | | SP | RR | SF |
|---|---|---|---|---|---|---|
| 4500$^{3}$ | **Our People** (MJohnston) **2-9-0** JWeaver(3) (mde all: rdn & edgd rt ins fnl f: r.o wl) | — | **1** | 5/1$^{3}$ | 84 | 54 |
| 4492$^{11}$ | **Michael Venture** (SPCWoods) **2-9-0** KDarley(5) (bit bkwd: a.p: rdn over 2f out: ev ch over 1f out: r.o) | ¾ | **2** | 33/1 | 83 | 53 |
| | **Deep Water (USA)** (PFICole) **2-9-0** TQuinn(12) (unf: scope: bkwd: a.p: ev ch over 1f out: btn whn n.m.r & swtchd lft ins fnl f) | 1 | **3** | 9/4$^{1}$ | 81 | 51 |
| 4516$^{6}$ | **Spy Knoll** (MRStoute) **2-9-0** WRSwinburn(10) (lw: hdwy 3f out: r.o fnl f) | 3½ | **4** | 7/2$^{2}$ | 74 | 44 |
| 4494$^{2}$ | **Spanish Knot (USA)** (LordHuntingdon) **2-8-9** DHarrison(4) (a.p: rdn over 2f out: hung rt over 1f out: one pce) | ¾ | **5** | 11/2 | 67 | 37 |
| | **High Intrigue (IRE)** (HRACecil) **2-9-0** WRyan(1) (leggy: lt-f: nvr nr to chal) | 6 | **6** | 5/1$^{3}$ | 60 | 30 |
| | **High On Life** (ACStewart) **2-9-0** MRoberts(13) (unf: scope: hld up & plld hrd: bhd fnl 2f) | 2 | **7** | 20/1 | 56 | 26 |
| | **Wathbat Nashwan** (LMCumani) **2-8-7**$^{(7)}$ RFfrench(8) (s.s: a bhd) | ½ | **8** | 25/1 | 55 | 25 |
| | **Zibeth** (LMCumani) **2-8-9** OUrbina(6) (w'like: leggy: bkwd: prom over 5f) | 2 | **9** | 10/1 | 46 | 16 |
| 4204$^{8}$ | **Beauchamp Lion** (JLDunlop) **2-9-0** GCarter(2) (hld up: rdn over 3f out: sn bhd) | 2 | **10** | 25/1 | 47 | 17 |
| | **Keen Dancer** (MBell) **2-9-0** MFenton(7) (unf: scope: bkwd: hld up: a bhd) | 3 | **11** | 25/1 | 41 | 11 |
| | **Protocol (IRE)** (JWHills) **2-9-0** MHills(11) (leggy: unf: s.s: sn prom: wknd over 2f out) | 6 | **12** | 33/1 | 29 | — |
| | | | | (SP 133.0%) | **12 Rn** | |

**1m 35.7** (0.10 under 2y best) (0.70) CSF £138.03 TOTE £7.00: £2.10 £12.60 £1.10 (£133.30) Trio £273.20; £76.97 to Haydock 16/10/96
OWNER Dr Fuk To Chang (MIDDLEHAM) BRED Wheelersland Stud
**4500 Our People** is a brother to a winner in Denmark. Doing it the hard way from the front, he chalked up the season's century for his stable. (5/1: 4/1-13/2)
**Michael Venture** had shown nothing on his debut at the beginning of the month and still looked in need of this. (33/1)
**Deep Water (USA)** did not impress in his coat in the paddock, and more should be heard of him next season. (9/4: tchd 6/4)
**4516 Spy Knoll**, bred to eventually require further, seems to be going the right way. (7/2: 3/1-9/2)
**4494 Spanish Knot (USA)** possibly found this ground a bit lively. (11/2: 4/1-6/1)
**High Intrigue (IRE)** will hopefully come on over the winter. (5/1: 2/1-11/2)
**Zibeth** (10/1: op 5/1)

T/Jkpt: Not won; £2,383.22 to Haydock 16/10/96. T/Plpt: £182.70 (84.33 Tckts). T/Qdpt: £23.90 (65.03 Tckts). IM/KH

## 4578-HAYDOCK (L-H) (Heavy)
### Wednesday October 16th
Meeting Abandoned after Race 1: jockeys considered course unsafe.
WEATHER: unsettled WIND: str across

**4706** E.B.F. HAWTHORN MAIDEN STKS (I) (2-Y.O) (Class D)
1-30 (1-32) **7f 30y** £3,160.00 (£955.00: £465.00: £220.00) Stalls: Low GOING: 0.37 sec per fur (GS)

| | | | | SP | RR | SF |
|---|---|---|---|---|---|---|
| 4301[3] | **Catienus (USA)** (MRStoute) **2-9-0** KDarley(2) (mde all: clr fnl 2f: unchal) | — | 1 | 2/1[1] | 89 | 20 |
| | **Outflanker (USA)** (PWChapple-Hyam) **2-9-0** WRSwinburn(1) (w'like: scope: trckd ldrs: shkn up over 2f out: chsd wnr appr fnl f: no imp) | 8 | 2 | 5/1[2] | 71 | 2 |
| | **Right Wing (IRE)** (MajorWRHern) **2-9-0** TSprake(6) (unf: scope: s.s: bhd: hdwy 2f out: nvr nrr) | 3½ | 3 | 6/1[3] | 63 | — |
| | **Spartan Girl (IRE)** (LordHuntingdon) **2-8-9** LDettori(3) (lt-f: unf: sn chsng wnr: wknd over 2f out) | hd | 4 | 5/1[2] | 58 | — |
| 4210[10] | **Come Together** (DWPArbuthnot) **2-8-9** GCarter(9) (plld hrd: chsd ldrs tl wknd over 2f out) | 3 | 5 | 20/1 | 51 | — |
| 4514[11] | **Star Precision** (GBBalding) **2-8-9** SDrowne(11) (hld up: rdn & hdwy over 2f out: nvr nrr) | 4 | 6 | 16/1 | 42 | — |
| | **Raivue** (EWeymes) **2-9-0** JQuinn(8) (wl grwn: bkwd: plld hrd: prom 4f) | 2½ | 7 | 16/1 | 42 | — |
| 4570[9] | **Tajrebah (USA)** (PTWalwyn) **2-8-9** RHills(12) (bit bkwd: trckd ldrs tl lost pl ½-wy: swtchd lft over 2f out: no imp) | nk | 8 | 12/1 | 36 | — |
| 4386[6] | **Moonlight Invader (IRE)** (EALDunlop) **2-9-0** WRyan(4) (bkwd: a bhd: t.o) | 19 | 9 | 5/1[2] | — | — |
| | **Hit The Flag (IRE)** (ABMulholland) **2-9-0** DeanMcKeown(10) (cmpt: bit bkwd: plld hrd: bhd fnl 3f: t.o) | 11 | 10 | 25/1 | — | — |

(SP 125.7%) **10 Rn**

**1m 36.59** (9.09) CSF £13.15 TOTE £2.70: £1.20 £1.90 £2.60 (£4.90) Trio £11.90 OWNER Sheikh Mohammed (NEWMARKET) BRED Darley Stud Management Inc

**4301 Catienus (USA)** made sure the emphasis would be on stamina by making all, and he was out on his own from some way out. (2/1)
**Outflanker (USA)**, thought good enough to warrant an entry in the Middle Park, did not look fully wound up for this racecourse debut, but he stayed on in the latter stages, and will win races in time. (5/1: op 3/1)
**Right Wing (IRE)**, an unfurnished brother to three winners, gave away what chance he had with a slow start, but he did stay on to make the frame, and will certainly know more next time. (6/1)
**Spartan Girl (IRE)**, a lightly-made, unfurnished filly from the family of Sun Princess, is hardly built for mud-larking, but she did push the pace until calling enough entering the last quarter-mile. (5/1)
**Come Together**, a good-quartered filly who was taking a step up in distance, raced freely and tracked the leaders until feeling the strain and dropping away halfway up the straight. (20/1)
**Star Precision**, bred for stamina, was never able to get herself into contention, but the experience will no doubt prove beneficial. (16/1)
**4386 Moonlight Invader (IRE)** looks the type who will always carry plenty of condition, but he was all at sea in this testing ground and was always nearer last than first. It is to be hoped he is better than this. (5/1)

**4707** SYCAMORE NURSERY H'CAP (2-Y.O) (Class D)
**Abandoned** - Course unsafe

**4708** GALA CLUB CONDITIONS STKS (2-Y.O) (Class C)
**Abandoned** - Course unsafe

**4709** TOMMY WALLIS H'CAP (0-80) (3-Y.O+) (Class D)
**Abandoned** - Course unsafe

**4710** KING'S REGIMENT CUP CONDITIONS STKS (3-Y.O+) (Class C)
**Abandoned** - Course unsafe

**4711** BOOKER CASH & CARRY H'CAP (0-80) (3-Y.O) (Class D)
**Abandoned** - Course unsafe

**4712** E.B.F. HAWTHORN MAIDEN STKS (II) (2-Y.O) (Class D)
**Abandoned** - Course unsafe

**4713** HOLLY MAIDEN STKS (3-Y.O+) (Class D)
**Abandoned** - Course unsafe

T/Jkpt: £4.40 (1,578.45 Tckts). T/Plpt: £1.10 (20,543.37 Tckts). T/Qdpt: Void IM

## 4565-NEWMARKET (R-H) (Good to firm)
### Thursday October 17th
WEATHER: fine & sunny WIND: almost nil

**4714** NGK SPARK PLUGS CONDITIONS STKS (3-Y.O+) (Class B)
1-30 (1-30) **1m 2f (Rowley)** £8,937.50 (£3,312.50: £1,593.75: £656.25: £265.63: £109.37) GOING minus 0.25 sec per fur (GF)

| | | | | SP | RR | SF |
|---|---|---|---|---|---|---|
| 725[4] | **Bright Water** (HRACecil) **3-8-9** PatEddery(5) (h.d.w: hld up: hdwy 4f out: led wl over 1f out: r.o wl) | — | 1 | 6/1 | 114 | 71 |
| 4313[2] | **Desert Shot (109)** (MRStoute) **6-9-0v** RCochrane(4) (stdd s: hld up: hdwy over 2f out: styd on u.p cl home) | 2½ | 2 | 7/2[1] | 110 | 72 |
| 1988[3] | **Florid (USA) (108)** (HRACecil) **5-9-5** MRoberts(1) (lw: hld up in tch: rdn over 2f out: kpt on ins fnl f) | s.h | 3 | 6/1 | 115 | 77 |
| 4371[2] | **Overbury (IRE) (114)** (SbinSuroor) **5-9-12** LDettori(8) (lw: trckd ldrs: led 3f out tl wl over 1f out: rdn & one pce fnl f) | 2 | 4 | 4/1[2] | 119 | 81 |
| 4568[9] | **Prince of My Heart (103)** (BWHills) **3-9-0** MHills(2) (hld up & bhd: effrt over 2f out: nvr able to chal) | 1 | 5 | 16/1 | 110 | 67 |
| 4351* | **Magellan (USA) (111)** (CEBrittain) **3-9-0** BDoyle(3) (lw: led 7f: sn rdn & outpcd) | 1¾ | 6 | 11/2[3] | 107 | 64 |
| | **Wahiba Sands** (JLDunlop) **3-8-9** TQuinn(9) (hld up & bhd: nvr nr to chal) | ½ | 7 | 25/1 | 102 | 59 |
| 2050[10] | **Musick House (IRE) (98)** (PWChapple-Hyam) **3-8-12** WRSwinburn(7) (hld up: effrt 3f out: sn pushed along & outpcd: t.o) | 17 | 8 | 25/1 | 77 | 34 |

| Form | Horse / details | Dist | Pos | SP | RR | SF |
|---|---|---|---|---|---|---|
| 1999* | **Shehab (IRE) (84)** (PRHedger) **3-8-9** RMcGhin(6) (lw: plld hrd: w ldrs tl wknd qckly 3f out: t.o) | 5 | **9** | 12/1 | 66 | 23 |

(SP 107.4%) **9 Rn**

**2m 3.91** (0.31) CSF £23.88 TOTE £6.50: £2.20 £1.20 £2.50 (£9.40) Trio £22.00 OWNER Mr K. Abdulla (NEWMARKET) BRED Juddmonte Farms

WEIGHT FOR AGE 3yo-5lb

**725 Bright Water** failed to act on the soft ground at Newbury in the spring and this was his first outing since. Taking command running into the Dip, he lengthened impressively on meeting the rising ground and the long wait proved worthwhile. (6/1)

**4313 Desert Shot**, dropped in at the start, was doing all his best work in the closing stages but the winner had gone clear and was not for catching. (7/2)

**1988 Florid (USA)** came back fresh and well after a four-month break and stuck on determinedly up the final climb. If he is seen out again this term, the hint should be taken. (6/1)

**4371 Overbury (IRE)** had it all to do attempting to concede weight all round. He did look in a class of his own when cruising into the lead, but this trip on such a stiff track plus the weight took the sting out of him in the final 200 yards. (4/1)

**4568 Prince of My Heart**, a very poor mover in this slower paces, is not up to this class, although he did stay on, and was not at all disgraced. (16/1)

**4351* Magellan (USA)** is a genuine colt but he does seem to produce his best when ridden with more restraint, and the front-running tactics employed left him legless when the final battle developed. (11/2: 4/1-6/1)

**1999* Shehab (IRE)** (12/1: op 20/1)

## 4715 EQUITY FINANCIAL COLLECTIONS (S) STKS (2-Y.O) (Class E)

2-00 (2-02) **7f** **(Rowley)** £5,517.00 (£1,656.00: £798.00: £369.00) Stalls: High GOING minus 0.25 sec per fur (GF)

| Form | Horse / details | Dist | Pos | SP | RR | SF |
|---|---|---|---|---|---|---|
| 4594[2] | **River of Fortune (IRE) (73)** (MHTompkins) **2-7-13**(7) RMullen(26) (a.p: led ½-wy: clr appr fnl f: jst hld on) | — | **1** | 7/2[1] | 70 | 38 |
| 4602[7] | **Princess of Hearts (70)** (BJMeehan) **2-8-11b[1]** BDoyle(10) (hld up: hdwy over 2f out: styd on strly cl home) | s.h | **2** | 12/1 | 75 | 43 |
| 4234[9] | **Battle Ground (IRE) (50)** (NACallaghan) **2-8-11** LDettori(12) (a.p: rdn over 1f out: one pce) | 2½ | **3** | 14/1 | 69 | 37 |
| 4607[7] | **Summerville Wood (61)** (PMooney) **2-8-13b**(3) PMcCabe(16) (hld up: hdwy 2f out: kpt on u.p ins fnl f) | nk | **4** | 25/1 | 74 | 42 |
| 4546[6] | **Aficionado (IRE) (73)** (RFJohnsonHoughton) **2-8-11** SSanders(17) (mid div: hdwy u.p 2f out: styd on towards fin) | 1¼ | **5** | 12/1 | 66 | 34 |
| 4562* | **Marsh Marigold (68)** (MartynMeade) **2-8-4**(7) DSweeney(15) (hdwy over 1f out: nrst fin) | hd | **6** | 10/1 | 65 | 33 |
| 3659[6] | **Victoria's Dream (IRE) (66)** (MRChannon) **2-8-11** CandyMorris(21) (trckd ldrs: one pce appr fnl f) | nk | **7** | 16/1 | 65 | 33 |
| 4546[15] | **Jilly Woo (49)** (DRCElsworth) **2-8-6b[1]** MRoberts(13) (a.p: rdn over 1f out: one pce) | d.h | **7** | 25/1 | 60 | 28 |
| 4384[7] | **Gresatre (63)** (CADwyer) **2-8-4**(7) JoHunnam(18) (chsd ldrs: outpcd 2f out: sn rdn: no imp) | hd | **9** | 14/1 | 65 | 33 |
| 4131[12] | **Champagne Toast (75)** (RHannon) **2-8-11** MHills(19) (b: b.hind: in tch: drvn along ½-wy: nvr able to chal) | s.h | **10** | 8/1[3] | 64 | 32 |
| 4512[11] | **Warring (58)** (MRChannon) **2-8-11** NDay(20) (drvn along 2f out: nvr nrr) | 2 | **11** | 25/1 | 60 | 28 |
| 4516[12] | **Island Prince** (NACallaghan) **2-8-11** SWhitworth(8) (hld up & bhd: sme late hdwy: nvr nrr) | 2½ | **12** | 33/1 | 54 | 22 |
| 4380[16] | **Debonair (57)** (GLewis) **2-8-6** PatEddery(7) (b.nr hind: chsd ldrs: outpcd whn nt clr run over 2f out) | 1 | **13** | 10/1 | 47 | 15 |
| 4546[14] | **Witney-La-Roche** (JSMoore) **2-8-11** NAdams(27) (chsd ldrs 4f: sn lost tch) | ½ | **14** | 33/1 | 51 | 19 |
| 4493[6] | **Seretse's Nephew** (SCWilliams) **2-8-8**(3) AWhelan(3) (in tch: eased whn btn fnl 2f) | nk | **15** | 33/1 | 50 | 18 |
| | **Zorro** (RMFlower) **2-8-11** SDrowne(22) (w'like: nvr nr ldrs) | s.h | **16** | 33/1 | 50 | 18 |
| 4507[11] | **Sheffield Shark (IRE)** (DWPArbuthnot) **2-8-11v[1]** TQuinn(5) (b: in tch to ½-wy: sn wknd) | nk | **17** | 16/1 | 49 | 17 |
| 4544[4] | **Waterville Boy (IRE) (68)** (RHannon) **2-8-11** RHughes(6) (a in rr) | 1 | **18** | 16/1 | 47 | 15 |
| *4576*[7] | **Run For Us (IRE) (40)** (CADwyer) **2-8-6** OUrbina(23) (led over 3f: outpcd fnl 2f) | ½ | **19** | 33/1 | 41 | 9 |
| 4492[12] | **Double-E-I-B-A** (CNAllen) **2-8-6**(5) MartinDwyer(14) (lw: a bhd) | nk | **20** | 33/1 | 45 | 13 |
| | **Swynford Charmer** (JFBottomley) **2-8-11** JLowe(24) (b.hind: cmpt: chsd ldrs over 4f: eased whn btn) | ½ | **21** | 7/1[2] | 44 | 12 |
| 4599[10] | **Prince Jordan** (ICampbell) **2-8-6**(5) GFaulkner(1) (s.s: a bhd) | ¾ | **22** | 33/1 | 42 | 10 |
| 4423[8] | **Sam's Yer Man** (SCWilliams) **2-8-4**(7) DarrenWilliams(25) (lw: a bhd) | ¾ | **23** | 33/1 | 41 | 9 |
| 3803[12] | **Racing Carr** (TJNaughton) **2-8-6** AClark(9) (dwlt: a bhd) | ½ | **24** | 33/1 | 34 | 2 |
| 4607[6] | **Riverside Girl (IRE)** (JSMoore) **2-8-1**(5) PPMurphy(11) (bhd fnl 3f) | s.h | **25** | 33/1 | 34 | 2 |
| | **Paddy Hurry (66)** (NACallaghan) **2-8-11** RCochrane(2) (lw: rdn along ½-wy: a bhd) | 5 | **26** | 9/1 | 28 | — |
| *4572*[11] | **Diamonds Are** (DTThom) **2-8-6** DBiggs(4) (bhd fnl 3f: t.o) | dist | **27** | 33/1 | — | — |

(SP 164.3%) **27 Rn**

**1m 27.15** (2.65) CSF £49.10 TOTE £4.80: £2.00 £5.90 £5.80 (£45.10) Trio £119.30 OWNER The B B A Fortune In Mind Partnership (NEWMARKET) BRED Corduff Stud

Bt in 10,500 gns

**4594 River of Fortune (IRE)** had this prize safely under wraps from some way out, but the hill began to take its toll and the line arrived only just in time. (7/2)

**4602 Princess of Hearts** did not impress to post, but the blinkers almost worked the oracle, and she would have made it in another stride. (12/1)

**3523 Battle Ground (IRE)**, tackling the trip for the first time, did not quite last home, but he gave it his best and there is a race to be won. (14/1: 10/1-16/1)

**4368 Summerville Wood**, staying on from off the pace, ran by far his best race yet and these more patient tactics will pay dividends. (25/1)

**4546 Aficionado (IRE)** seemed to appreciate this longer trip, for he was really finding his stride up the hill. (12/1)

**4562* Marsh Marigold** would seem to be able to act on any sort of going and is not short on stamina, but her determined late flourish here was slightly mistimed. (10/1)

**3659 Victoria's Dream (IRE)** may have trouble getting the trip on this track, but she could possibly do so on an easier course, and she showed here she has the ability to pick up another prize. (16/1)

**3685 Champagne Toast** (8/1: op 5/1)

**Paddy Hurry** (9/1: 14/1-8/1)

## 4716 HUNTER PRICE PARTNERSHIP RATED STKS H'CAP (0-100) (3-Y.O+) (Class B)

2-35 (2-36) **1m 4f** **(Rowley)** £7,995.00 (£2,955.00: £1,415.00: £575.00: £225.00: £85.00) Stalls: High GOING: minus 0.25 sec per fur (GF)

| Form | Horse / details | Dist | Pos | SP | RR | SF |
|---|---|---|---|---|---|---|
| 4465[5] | **Willie Conquer (85)** (RAkehurst) **4-8-7** SSanders(4) (hld up: hdwy 3f out: led jst ins fnl f: hld on u.p) | — | **1** | 6/1[3] | 98 | 80 |
| 4465[14] | **Arabian Story (98)** (LordHuntingdon) **3-8-13** WRSwinburn(11) (b: trckd ldrs: led over 2f out tl ins fnl f: kpt on u.p) | ¾ | **2** | 9/2[1] | 110 | 85 |
| 4465[8] | **Romios (IRE) (85)** (PFICole) **4-8-7** TQuinn(7) (hld up & bhd: hdwy over 2f out: styd on wl towards fin) | ¾ | **3** | 11/1 | 96 | 78 |
| 4487* | **Dear Life (USA) (96)** (MrsJCecil) **3-8-6**(5) MartinDwyer(8) (lw: hld up in tch: rdn & lost pl 4f out: styd on ins fnl f) | 6 | **4** | 5/1[2] | 99 | 74 |

4465[15] **Son of Sharp Shot (IRE) (99)** (JLDunlop) **6-9-7** PatEddery(10) (lw: hld up: effrt 3f out: nt rch ldrs)................1½ **5** 7/1 100 82
4465[9] **At Liberty (IRE) (85)** (RHannon) **4-8-7** MHills(9) (hld up in rr: nvr plcd to chal) ..............................................1¾ **6** 25/1 84 66
4055[6] **Mystic Hill (88)** (GHarwood) **5-8-10** AClark(3) (hld up: hdwy over 3f out: rdn & btn 2f out) ...............................4 **7** 12/1 81 63
**Shaft of Light (85)** (LordHuntingdon) **4-8-7** MRoberts(6) (led tl hdd & wknd over 2f out: t.o) ..........................10 **8** 20/1 65 47
4326[12] **Three Hills (85)** (BWHills) **3-8-0** DBiggs(2) (trckd ldrs over 8f: sn wknd: t.o) .................................................2 **9** 20/1 62 37
4675[2] **Polydamas (85)** (MRStoute) **4-8-7v[1]** RCochrane(5) (prom tl wknd over 3f out: t.o)..........................................2 **10** 9/2[1] 60 42
(SP 109.2%) **10 Rn**

**2m 29.26** (-1.24) CSF £29.03 CT £237.87 TOTE £6.40: £1.90 £1.80 £3.30 (£21.80) Trio £67.70 OWNER Mr Raymond Tooth (EPSOM) BRED W. and R. Barnett Ltd

LONG HANDICAP Romios (IRE) 8-6 At Liberty (IRE) 8-5 Willie Conquer 8-6 Shaft of Light 8-5 Polydamas 8-6 Three Hills 7-10
WEIGHT FOR AGE 3yo-7lb

**OFFICIAL EXPLANATION Polydamas: was never travelling and his trainer felt the race had come too soon.**

**4465 Willie Conquer** finished ahead of many of these rivals at Ascot at the end of last month and, setting sail for home, always had the measure of a couple of persistent rivals. (6/1: op 4/1)

**3997* Arabian Story** returned to form here and showed his most recent run to be a one-off, but his spirited rally after being headed was never quite going to succeed. (9/2)

**4055 Romios (IRE)** began his effort passing the Bushes and closed all the way to the line, but the post was always going to arrive too soon. Another success is long overdue. (11/1: 8/1-12/1)

**4487* Dear Life (USA)**, never travelling at any stage, did eventually stay on up the hill, but this was a way below-par performance. (5/1)

**3754a Son of Sharp Shot (IRE)** did not get going until far too late and was never a factor. (7/1)

**4326 At Liberty (IRE)** has still to prove he really stays this trip. (25/1)

**4675 Polydamas** raced very keenly in his first-time visor and had run himself out before the race began in earnest. (9/2)

## 4717 BIRDCAGE NURSERY H'CAP (2-Y.O) (Class C)

3-10 (3-10) **6f (Rowley)** £6,992.00 (£2,096.00: £1,008.00: £464.00) Stalls: High GOING minus 0.25 sec per fur (GF)

SP RR SF

4123* **Cryhavoc (86)** (JRArnold) **2-9-7** SSanders(1) (lw: a.p: led 2f out: hrd rdn & edgd rt fnl f: r.o wl) ......................— **1** 16/1 96 66
4311[5] **Rainbow Rain (USA) (78)** (MJohnston) **2-8-13** MRoberts(3) (in tch: effrt over 1f out: styd on wl towards fin).1½ **2** 25/1 84 54
4113[13] **Stone Flower (USA) (85)** (PWChapple-Hyam) **2-9-6** WRSwinburn(9) (chsd ldrs: hrd rdn over 1f out: r.o wl cl home) ......................................................................................................½ **3** 33/1 90 60
4546[2] **Petite Danseuse (76)** (CADwyer) **2-8-4**(7) JoHunnam(4) (bhd: stdy hdwy over 1f out: fin wl)...........................s.h **4** 16/1 81 51
4566[3] **Burlington House (USA) (85)** (PFICole) **2-9-1**(5) GFaulkner(12) (lw: led 4f: rdn & wknd ins fnl f)....................hd **5** 7/1[2] 89 59
4545* **Heart Throb (81)** (WJHaggas) **2-9-2** RHughes(16) (dwlt: hdwy ½-wy: nt clr run & swtchd lft wl over 1f out: fin wl).......................................................................................................s.h **6** 8/1[3] 85 55
4566[2] **Sharp Hat (84)** (RHannon) **2-9-5** PatEddery(6) (bhd: hdwy ½-wy: unable qckn fnl f)......................................2 **7** 10/1 83 53
4614* **Amyas (IRE) (85)** (BWHills) **2-9-6** 7x MHills(7) (b.nr hind: outpcd & drvn along ½-wy: sme late hdwy).............nk **8** 7/4[1] 83 53
4614[2] **Style Dancer (IRE) (70)** (RMWhitaker) **2-8-5** AClark(17) (trckd ldrs tl outpcd wl over 1f out) ...........................½ **9** 20/1 67 37
*4091*[3] **Return of Amin (66)** (JDBethell) **2-8-1** SDrowne(10) (effrt 2f out: no imp).................................................1½ **10** 33/1 59 29
3796[13] **Broughtons Error (70)** (WJMusson) **2-8-0**(5) MBaird(2) (lw: s.i.s: a in rr) ..............................................nk **11** 25/1 62 32
4364[4] **Aybeegirl (67)** (MrsJCecil) **2-7-11**(5) MartinDwyer(5) (chsd ldrs over 4f).............................................1¼ **12** 25/1 56 26
4544[3] **Saltimbanco (76)** (IABalding) **2-8-11** RCochrane(14) (a bhd & outpcd)..................................................nk **13** 25/1 64 34
4262[5] **Puzzlement (66)** (CEBrittain) **2-8-1** DeclanO'Shea(18) (a bhd & outpcd).............................................s.h **14** 25/1 54 24
4475[10] **Daring Flight (USA) (83)** (LordHuntingdon) **2-9-4** LDettori(15) (trckd ldrs over 3f)........................................1 **15** 10/1 68 38
3924[3] **Feel A Line (78)** (BJMeehan) **2-8-13** BDoyle(8) (prom 4f)....................................................................1¾ **16** 33/1 58 28
4566[16] **Lamorna (80)** (MRChannon) **2-9-1** TQuinn(11) (chsd ldrs 4f) ..................................................................4 **17** 33/1 50 20
4545[7] **Dayrella (64)** (WRMuir) **2-7-6**(7) PDoe(13) (lw: chsd ldrs to ½-wy: sn lost tch: t.o)......................................5 **18** 50/1 20 —
(SP 127.6%) **18 Rn**

**1m 13.08** (1.28) CSF £326.12 CT £11,531.80 TOTE £25.40: £2.60 £3.10 £9.10 £2.60 (£242.40) Trio £348.40 OWNER Mr A. H. Robinson (UPPER LAMBOURN) BRED Al Dahlawi Stud Co Ltd

**OFFICIAL EXPLANATION Daring Flight (USA): the jockey reported that he had not ridden the colt out as he had begun to weaken, and he felt something was amiss.**
**Amyas (IRE): the trainer felt the race had come too soon.**

**4123* Cryhavoc** has really come to himself of late and, in defying topweight with a readily-gained success, looks to be a youngster with a promising future. (16/1)

**4311 Rainbow Rain (USA)** consented to being restrained and produced his best effort to date. A repeat could soon get him off the mark. (25/1)

**3921 Stone Flower (USA)**, with the pace from the start, did not fail for the want of trying in the latter stages and success at this trip is well within her grasp. (33/1)

**4546 Petite Danseuse** does not know how to run a bad race and, though she may have mistimed her run here, she finished best of all. She has not stopped winning yet. (16/1)

**4566 Burlington House (USA)** can win from the front but, in such a hotly-contested handicap, he probably did too much too soon, and was found wanting up the hill. (7/1)

**4545* Heart Throb**, held up to get the trip, did not enjoy the best of runs when making progress, but finished in fine style and, with any luck at all, would have made the prizes. Compensation awaits. (8/1: 6/1-9/1)

**4566 Sharp Hat**, poised to challenge running into the Dip, did not find the expected response when let down and was easily shaken off in the dash to the line. (10/1)

**4614* Amyas (IRE)** was the only one anybody wanted to be on in the Ring, but he was in trouble at halfway and failed to make any impression until staying on past beaten rivals up the hill. (7/4)

## 4718 CHALLENGE STKS (Gp 2) (3-Y.O+) (Class A)

3-40 (3-40) **7f (Rowley)** £35,431.00 (£13,129.00: £6,314.50: £2,597.50: £1,048.75: £429.25) Stalls: High GOING minus 0.25 sec per fur (GF)

SP RR SF

4443[4] **Charnwood Forest (IRE) (122)** (SbinSuroor) **4-9-4** LDettori(8) (lw: trckd ldr: led & qcknd 2f out: r.o wl).........— **1** 15/8[1] 125+ 74
4664a[4] **Bishop of Cashel (118)** (JRFanshawe) **4-9-0** WRSwinburn(3) (lw: sn chsng ldrs: rdn & r.o ins fnl f)..................2 **2** 4/1[3] 116 65
4378[4] **My Branch (112)** (BWHills) **3-8-9** MHills(7) (trckd ldrs: swtchd rt 2f out: kpt on one pce) ..................................2 **3** 15/2 109 56
4378[3] **Thrilling Day (112)** (NAGraham) **3-8-9** TQuinn(2) (hld up in rr: hdwy 2f out: nvr nr to chal)...............................1¼ **4** 12/1 106 53
4442[2] **Lucayan Prince (USA) (119)** (DRLoder) **3-8-12b** RHughes(1) (hld up: swtchd rt sn after s: effrt & nt clr run 2f out: no imp) ..............................................................................................................¾ **5** 9/4[2] 107 54
4378[9] **Polar Prince (IRE) (110)** (MAJarvis) **3-8-12** RCochrane(6) (hld up: effrt & rdn over 2f out: sn btn) ..................nk **6** 20/1 107 54

Troon (RHaugen,Norway) **6-9-0** MSantos(4) (led 5f: sn outpcd)....1½ **7** 100/1 103 52
4442[9] **Daring Destiny (111)** (KRBurke) **5-9-1** OUrbina(5) (hld up: effrt over 2f out: sn rdn & outpcd)....s.h **8** 25/1 104 53
(SP 114.6%) **8 Rn**

**1m 25.12** (0.62) CSF £9.46 TOTE £2.30: £1.10 £1.60 £1.60 (£3.10) OWNER Godolphin (NEWMARKET) BRED Sheikh Mohammed bin Rashid al Maktoum
WEIGHT FOR AGE 3yo-2lb
**4443 Charnwood Forest (IRE)**, always travelling strongly, quickened to pull away from his rivals running into the Dip and did not need to get serious to win very easily indeed. If he comes out of this race alright, he will join his stablemate Mark of Esteem in pursuit of more glory in the Breeders' Cup Mile. (15/8)
**4664a Bishop of Cashel** could never get in a blow against the useful winner but, over a trip short of his best and on ground plenty lively enough, this was a decent effort. (4/1: 3/1-9/2)
**4378 My Branch** gained her revenge over Thrilling Day, but does seem to struggle to stay this trip in such hot company. (15/2)
**4378 Thrilling Day** made up quite a lot of ground to reach her final placing, but was unable to get close enough to cause concern. (12/1)
**4442 Lucayan Prince (USA)** needs to be held up and was travelling strongly for most of the way but, once the winner kicked, he could do little to prevent him getting away. (9/4)

## 4719 MILCARS LEASING H'CAP (0-85) (3-Y.O+) (Class D)

4-15 (4-15) **1m (Rowley)** £3,840.00 (£1,140.00: £540.00: £240.00) GOING minus 0.25 sec per fur (GF)

SP RR SF
4674[10] **Saltando (IRE) (54)** (PatMitchell) **5-7-6**(5)ow1 MartinDwyer(10) (w ldr: led over 2f out: rdn & r.o wl fnl f)....— **1** 50/1 65 42
4682[7] **Toujours Riviera (72)** (JPearce) **6-9-1** NDay(3) (led tl over 2f out: hrd rdn fnl f: kpt on)....1¼ **2** 6/1[3] 81 59
4463[23] **Serendipity (FR) (82)** (JLDunlop) **3-9-8** TQuinn(8) (lw: swtchd centre after 1f: hld up & bhd: effrt over 2f out: nrst fin)....1¼ **3** 11/2[2] 88 63
4499[4] **Blatant Outburst (72)** (GCBravery) **6-9-1** LDettori(2) (led centre: outpcd & rdn 2f out: styd on again fnl f)....1¾ **4** 13/2 75 53
4463[11] **Ertlon (73)** (CEBrittain) **6-9-2** BDoyle(6) (hld up: hdwy 3f out: one pce fnl 2f)....s.h **5** 6/1[3] 75 53
4326[10] **Hardy Dancer (85)** (GLMoore) **4-10-0** SWhitworth(7) (chsd ldrs far side: rdn 3f out: sn btn)....6 **6** 12/1 75 53
3402[4] **Charlie Chang (IRE) (72)** (RHannon) **3-8-12** RHughes(1) (lw: racd centre: effrt 3f out: sn rdn & no imp)....1 **7** 12/1 60 35
4257[12] **Golden Touch (USA) (61)** (DJSCosgrove) **4-8-4** SSanders(9) (trckd ldrs far over 5f)....1½ **8** 14/1 46 24
4590[2] **No Cliches (73)** (GLewis) **3-8-13b** PatEddery(5) (racd centre: prom tl rdn & wknd over 2f out)....3 **9** 4/1[1] 52 27
4511[11] **Deevee (53)** (CJBenstead) **7-7-10** JLowe(4) (racd centre: dropped ½-wy: sn t.o)....5 **10** 8/1 22 —
(SP 112.4%) **10 Rn**

**1m 39.2** (1.90) CSF £285.79 CT £1,809.75 TOTE £64.00: £8.70 £1.90 £2.10 (£273.70) Trio £737.40; £249.26 to Newmarket 18/10/96 OWNER Mrs Sandy Herridge (NEWMARKET) BRED Thoroughbred Trust
LONG HANDICAP Saltando (IRE) 6-11
WEIGHT FOR AGE 3yo-3lb
**1640 Saltando (IRE)** caused a real upset from 13lb out of the handicap, but he kept finding more when challenged and there was certainly no fluke about this success. (50/1)
**3981 Toujours Riviera** looked to have found a suitable race to open his account for the year, but the winner just would not be denied and he was forced to settle for second best. (6/1)
**4193 Serendipity (FR)** won his maiden in the spring, but he has struggled in handicaps since then and, over a trip short of his ideal, was never going to get to terms. (11/2)
**4499 Blatant Outburst**, still to get off the mark, got tapped for toe running into the Dip, but he was finding his stride again up the hill and is worth trying again at ten furlongs. (13/2: 7/2-7/1)
**4240 Ertlon**, poised to challenge passing the Bushes, did not find a lot when popped the question and could do little more than stay on at the one pace. (6/1)
**4068 Golden Touch (USA)** (14/1: 10/1-16/1)
**4590 No Cliches** won at this trip in his first season and would seem to be need much further now. He did run a bit flat here though and is obviously proving difficult to place. (4/1)

## 4720 E.B.F. CHESTERTON MAIDEN STKS (2-Y.O) (Class D)

4-50 (4-53) **1m (Rowley)** £7,281.00 (£2,178.00: £1,044.00: £477.00) GOING minus 0.25 sec per fur (GF)

SP RR SF
**Royal Crusade (USA)** (WJHaggas) **2-9-0** BDoyle(14) (w'like: scope: chsd ldr: led wl over 1f out: rdn out)....— **1** 11/2[3] 86+ 49
4492[6] **Catchable** (HRACecil) **2-9-0** PatEddery(11) (lw: led tl wl over 1f out: kpt on u.p)....3 **2** 13/8[1] 80 43
**Natural Eight (IRE)** (BWHills) **2-9-0** AClark(16) (neat: hld up: stdy hdwy 2f out: styd on wl nr fin)....1 **3** 50/1 78 41
**Valagalore** (BWHills) **2-8-9** RStreet(12) (tall: scope: trckd ldrs far side: one pce ins fnl f)....1 **4** 50/1 71 34
**Galibis (FR)** (PAKelleway) **2-9-0** TQuinn(6) (lt-f: unf: prom: outpcd over 1f out: styd on towards fin)....1½ **5** 25/1 73 36
3595[3] **Davoski** (BWHills) **2-9-0** MHills(2) (hmpd s: pushed along & hdwy ½-wy: one pce fnl 2f)....½ **6** 9/2[2] 72 35
2302[6] **Real Estate** (CFWall) **2-9-0** SSanders(4) (bkwd: mid div tl sme late hdwy)....2½ **7** 33/1 67 30
**Alifandango (IRE)** (ACStewart) **2-8-9** MRoberts(10) (w'like: unf: mid div: outpcd over 3f out: kpt on appr fnl f: no imp)....s.h **8** 20/1 62 25
**Highly Prized** (IABalding) **2-9-0** LDettori(1) (cmpt: unf: hmpd s: trckd ldrs fr ½-wy: wknd fnl 2f)....4 **9** 12/1 59 22
**City Hall (IRE)** (PWChapple-Hyam) **2-9-0** WRSwinburn(17) (leggy: scope: s.s: hdwy 5f out: outpcd 3f out)....½ **10** 10/1 58 21
**Regait** (MAJarvis) **2-9-0** RCochrane(8) (gd sort: bkwd: mid div tl pushed along & wknd over 2f out)....6 **11** 16/1 46 9
4516[13] **Fantail** (MHTompkins) **2-8-7**(7) RMullen(15) (nvr nr ldrs)....nk **12** 66/1 45 8
4233[15] **Oaken Wood (IRE)** (NACallaghan) **2-9-0** SWhitworth(9) (lw: bhd fnl 3f)....½ **13** 100/1 44 7
**Timothy George (IRE)** (GBBalding) **2-9-0** SDrowne(3) (w'like: wnt lft s: a bhd)....1¾ **14** 100/1 41 4
**Gadroon** (PCHaslam) **2-9-0** RHughes(13) (w'like: prom tl wknd over 2f out)....s.h **15** 16/1 41 4
**Rinca** (JPearce) **2-8-9** NDay(5) (w'like: leggy: scope: s.s: a bhd)....¾ **16** 50/1 34 —
4261[9] **Joli's Prince** (CMurray) **2-9-0** PBloomfield(7) (lw: chsd ldrs to ½-wy: grad lost pl)....1½ **17** 100/1 36 —
(SP 122.1%) **17 Rn**

**1m 40.09** (2.79) CSF £13.71 TOTE £7.80: £2.10 £1.40 £5.40 (£8.60) Trio £413.50 OWNER Highclere Thoroughbred Racing Ltd (NEWMARKET) BRED Leo J. Hamel
**Royal Crusade (USA)**, one of the few who took the eye in the paddock, won this with a fair bit in hand and could go on to better things next season. (11/2: 3/1-6/1)
**4492 Catchable** settled down in the lead this time, but he could never shake off the winner and, once that rival had taken command, was always destined for second spot. (13/8)
**Natural Eight (IRE)**, a half-brother to the very sharp Watch Me, did not stride out freely to post but he was beginning to realise what was needed in the latter stages. This was a very promising start. (50/1)

**Valagalore** has plenty of filling out to do, but she ran well here and could prove a useful filly next term. (50/1)
**Galibis (FR)**, an unfurnished colt who needs time, would have been in the shake-up had he been able to come down the hill but, to his credit, he was renewing his challenge towards the finish. He does to look to have ability. (25/1)
**3595 Davoski**, impeded by a swerving rival leaving the start, had to work to recover the lost ground, and was galloping on the spot inside the last quarter-mile. (9/2: 3/1-5/1)
**Highly Prized** looked wintry in his coat and none too happy on this lively ground, but he did reach a challenging position passing the Bushes and only faded running into the Dip. He could be a different proposition next year. (12/1: 6/1-14/1)
**City Hall (IRE)** (10/1: 6/1-12/1)

T/Jkpt: Not won; £3,726.23 to Newmarket 18/10/96. T/Plpt: £559.60 (38.39 Tckts). T/Qdpt: £204.40 (6.97 Tckts). IM

## 4592-REDCAR (L-H) (Good to firm, Firm patches)
## Thursday October 17th

WEATHER: fine & sunny WIND: slt half against

### 4721 CUB HUNTERS RATING RELATED MAIDEN STKS (0-70) (2-Y.O) (Class E)

1-40 (1-40) **1m** £3,195.50 (£959.00: £462.00: £213.50) Stalls: Centre GOING minus 0.49 sec per fur (F)

| | | | | SP | RR | SF |
|---|---|---|---|---|---|---|
| 4544[8] | **Pietro Bembo (IRE) (70)** (SirMarkPrescott) **2-9-0** GDuffield(7) (in tch: drvn along ½-wy: styd on wl to ld wl ins fnl f) | — | **1** | Evens[1] | 67 | 28 |
| 4060[7] | **Rake Hey (65)** (RFJohnsonHoughton) **2-9-0b[1]** AMcGlone(3) (trckd ldr: led over 1f out tl nr fin) | ¾ | **2** | 9/1 | 66 | 27 |
| 4375[7] | **Select Star (IRE) (69)** (APJarvis) **2-9-0** WRyan(8) (lw: hld up: effrt over 2f out: styd on u.p fnl f) | hd | **3** | 100/30[2] | 65 | 26 |
| 4482[5] | **Hurgill Times (65)** (JWWatts) **2-9-0v[1]** JCarroll(4) (led: hdd wl over 1f out: hrd rdn & wknd ins fnl f) | 2½ | **4** | 12/1 | 60 | 21 |
| 4208[9] | **Seva (IRE) (70)** (DRLoder) **2-8-11** DRMcCabe(2) (lw: chsd ldrs: led wl over 1f out: sn hdd & hung bdly lft) | ½ | **5** | 4/1[3] | 56 | 17 |
| 3462[7] | **Shaken Up (69)** (MrsDHaine) **2-9-0** JFortune(6) (unruly in stalls: s.i.s: drvn along & hdwy ½-wy: wknd over 1f out) | 1¾ | **6** | 10/1 | 56 | 17 |
| 4594[8] | **Maremma (58)** (DonEnricoIncisa) **2-8-11** KimTinkler(9) (sn pushed along: bhd fnl 2f) | 5 | **7** | 33/1 | 43 | 4 |
| 4607[13] | **Rising Glory (50)** (MissJFCraze) **2-9-0** NConnorton(5) (s.i.s: sn chsng ldrs: lost pl over 2f out) | 8 | **8** | 100/1 | 30 | — |

(SP 123.8%) **8 Rn**

**1m 38.5** (2.80) CSF £11.41 TOTE £2.00: £1.40 £2.30 £1.10 (£16.20) Trio £22.30 OWNER Mr Cyril Humphris (NEWMARKET) BRED Mrs C. F. Van Straubenzee and Partners
STEWARDS' ENQUIRY Fortune susp. 26 & 28-30/10/96 (improper riding).
**4383 Pietro Bembo (IRE)**, a grand type with size and scope, showed a good action going down. Stepping up to a mile, he needed every yard of it and, with his rider hard at work from halfway, only forced his head in front near the line. He will improve more than most from two to three and should pay his way in handicap company next year. (Evens)
**829 Rake Hey**, stepped up in distance and with the blinkers on, was only collared near the line. (9/1)
**4375 Select Star (IRE)**, who is hardly a model of consistency, never looked to be giving his rider full co-operation. (100/30)
**4482 Hurgill Times**, tried in a visor this time, tended to wander under pressure. (12/1: op 8/1)
**1678 Seva (IRE)**, who looked very fit, threw it away by hanging badly left once she hit the front. (4/1)

### 4722 LESLIE PETCH MEMORIAL H'CAP (0-85) (3-Y.O+) (Class D)

2-10 (2-10) **1m 6f 19y** £4,133.00 (£1,244.00: £602.00: £281.00) Stalls: Low GOING minus 0.49 sec per fur (F)

| | | | | SP | RR | SF |
|---|---|---|---|---|---|---|
| 4476[5] | **Teen Jay (45)** (BJLlewellyn) **6-7-13** TWilliams(4) (trckd ldrs: chal over 2f out: styd on u.p to ld wl ins fnl f) | — | **1** | 20/1 | 57 | 9 |
| 4596[2] | **Totem Dancer (68)** (JLEyre) **3-8-13** RLappin(5) (trckd ldr: led over 2f out: hdd & nt qckn ins fnl f) | ½ | **2** | 11/8[1] | 79 | 22 |
| 4315[8] | **Deano's Beeno (70)** (MJohnston) **4-9-10** DeanMcKeown(1) (led tl over 2f out: styd on same pce) | 3 | **3** | 5/1[3] | 78 | 30 |
| 4302[D] | **Uncle Doug (65)** (MrsMReveley) **5-9-5** ACulhane(2) (trckd ldrs: effrt over 3f out: kpt on same pce fnl 2f) | 2 | **4** | 3/1[2] | 71 | 23 |
| *4332** | **Batoutoftheblue (60)** (WWHaigh) **3-8-5** DRMcCabe(3) (lw: nvr gng wl: bhd: drvn along 6f out: virtually p.u 2f out) | dist | **5** | 3/1[2] | — | — |

(SP 113.5%) **5 Rn**

**3m 6.0** (6.70) CSF £46.98 TOTE £23.70: £3.40 £1.70 (£10.00) OWNER Gemini Associates (BARGOED) BRED Sheikh Mohammed bin Rashid al Maktoum
WEIGHT FOR AGE 3yo-9lb
**3335 Teen Jay**, a keen-going sort, bounced right back to his best and, under a forceful ride, got the better of a prolonged battle to lead near the line. He will now revert to hurdles. (20/1)
**4596 Totem Dancer**, who showed a very poor action going down, had much more use made of her this time, but there was certainly no excuse on this occasion. (11/8)
**3434 Deano's Beeno**, who is by no means a consistent sort, was left behind after making the running once the race began in earnest. (5/1)
**4302 Uncle Doug**, raised 4lb, scratched his way to the start. (3/1)
**4332* Batoutoftheblue** looked in tip-top trim but, opposed in the market on this return to turf, was never going a yard. Driven along and getting nowhere turning out of the back stretch, his rider wisely called it a day. There was something drastically wrong here. (3/1: op 2/1)

### 4723 REDCAR TWO-YEAR-OLD TROPHY STKS (2-Y.O) (Class B)

2-55 (2-56) **6f** £57,417.60 (£21,158.40: £10,079.20: £4,036.00: £1,518.00: £510.80) Stalls: Centre GOING: minus 0.49 sec per fur (F)

| | | | | SP | RR | SF |
|---|---|---|---|---|---|---|
| 4328[2] | **Proud Native (IRE) (100)** (APJarvis) **2-8-7** WRyan(5) (lw: chsd ldrs: led over 1f out: jst hld on) | — | **1** | 13/2[3] | 101 | 58 |
| 4189[4] | **Nigrasine (100)** (JLEyre) **2-8-4** DeanMcKeown(12) (w ldrs: rdn 2f out: edgd lft & styd on wl fnl f) | hd | **2** | 9/1 | 98 | 55 |
| 4357* | **Much Commended** (GWragg) **2-7-10** JQuinn(10) (dwlt: sn in tch: rdn & outpcd over 2f out: styd on strly fnl f) | 1 | **3** | 5/1[1] | 87+ | 44 |
| 4488[6] | **Blane Water (USA)** (JRFanshawe) **2-8-1ow2** DHarrison(17) (swtg: hld up: effrt ½-wy: styd on wl fnl f) | nk | **4** | 8/1 | 91 | 46 |
| 4579[3] | **Vasari (IRE) (90)** (MRChannon) **2-8-1** CRutter(16) (swtg: w ldrs: rdn & outpcd over 2f out: styd on ins fnl f) | s.h | **5** | 16/1 | 91 | 48 |
| 4510* | **Tomba (99)** (BJMeehan) **2-8-7** MTebbutt(1) (chsd ldrs: kpt on same pce fnl 2f) | hd | **6** | 12/1 | 97 | 54 |
| 4490[13] | **Blues Queen (85)** (MRChannon) **2-8-5** JCarroll(8) (hld up & bhd: hdwy & swtchd rt over 2f out: styd on fnl f) | 1¾ | **7** | 66/1 | 90 | 47 |
| 4369[3] | **Pelham (IRE) (96)** (RHannon) **2-8-4** DaneO'Neill(3) (lw: hmpd s: bhd tl styd on wl appr fnl f) | nk | **8** | 16/1 | 88 | 45 |
| 4491[7] | **Snap Crackle Pop (IRE) (91)** (RFJohnsonHoughton) **2-7-13** AMcGlone(14) (trckd ldrs: effrt 2f out: one pce) | nk | **9** | 20/1 | 83 | 40 |

4228* **Jhazi** (DRLoder) **2-9-0** DRMcCabe(22) (lw: chsd ldrs stands' side: kpt on same pce fnl 2f) ..........hd **10** 6/1[2] 97 54
3068[6] **Marathon Maid (91)** (RAFahey) **2-7-13** FNorton(25) (racd stands' side: sn outpcd & pushed along: sme hdwy 2f out: nvr nr ldrs)..........¾ **11** 50/1 80 37
4299[5] **Song of Skye (86)** (TJNaughton) **2-8-5** MFenton(6) (hmpd s: bhd tl sme hdwy fnl 2f)..........nk **12** 50/1 86 43
4639a[7] **Classic Park** (APO'Brien,Ireland) **2-8-2** JFEgan(7) (disp ld: hmpd after s: led over 2f out: hung rt: hdd over 1f out: sn wknd)..........½ **13** 20/1 81 38
4366[4] **Mujova (IRE) (87)** (RHollinshead) **2-8-6**ow[2] KFallon(13) (lw: drvn along ½-wy: nvr nr ldrs) ..........1 **14** 50/1 83 38
4510[2] **Speedball (IRE)** (IABalding) **2-8-7** JFortune(15) (in tch: drvn along & outpcd ½-wy: sn wknd)..........½ **15** 16/1 82 39
4510[3] **Magical Times (100)** (RBoss) **2-8-4** GDuffield(20) (sn bhd: sme hdwy u.p ½-wy: n.d) ..........1 **16** 11/1 77 34
4558* **Queen's Pageant** (JLSpearing) **2-7-10** GBardwell(26) (lw: s.i.s: racd stands' side: outpcd & drvn along ½-wy) ..........hd **17** 33/1 68 25
3919[2] **Nominator Lad** (BAMcMahon) **2-8-1** TSprake(18) (lw: mid div: drvn along ½-wy: n.d) ..........1¼ **18** 50/1 70 27
4461[6] **Truly Parched (USA)** (PWChapple-Hyam) **2-8-10** RHavlin(24) (racd stands' side: outpcd & bhd fr ½-wy).....nk **19** 20/1 78 35
3994[6] **Out of Sight (IRE)** (BAMcMahon) **2-8-12** NConnorton(21) (prom stands' side: rdn 3f out: sn wknd)..........¾ **20** 66/1 78 35
4566[5] **The Gay Fox (88)** (BAMcMahon) **2-8-5**ow[1] ACulhane(11) (chsd ldrs tl wknd 2f out) ..........1 **21** 50/1 69 25
3771[5] **Bayford Thrust (90)** (JBerry) **2-8-4** GCarter(9) (b: b.hind: disp ld over 3f: sn wknd) ..........2 **22** 50/1 62 19
4247[7] **Osomental (95)** (DHaydnJones) **2-8-7b** LCharnock(2) (wnt rt after s: prom to ½-wy: sn lost pl) ..........s.h **23** 50/1 65 22
4065[6] **Double-J (IRE) (89)** (KMcAuliffe) **2-8-4v**[1] JStack(23) (prom stands' side: rdn & lost pl ½-wy)..........1¼ **24** 66/1 59 16
4621[5] **Foot Battalion (IRE) (95)** (RHollinshead) **2-8-7** FLynch(4) (lw: hmpd s: a bhd)..........9 **25** 66/1 38 —
(SP 136.0%) **25 Rn**

**1m 9.6** (0.20 under 2y best) (-0.60) CSF £61.99 TOTE £7.70: £3.30 £3.50 £2.90 (£39.10) Trio £177.20 OWNER Mr L. Fust (ASTON UPTHORPE) BRED Mrs B. A. Headon
STEWARDS' ENQUIRY Charnock susp. 26 & 28-29/10/96 (careless riding).

**4328 Proud Native (IRE)** travelled strongly on the far side for much of the way but, after looking likely to win decisively at one stage, in the end he just hung on. He has been a model of consistency. (13/2)
**4189 Nigrasine** ran his heart out and, in the end, was only just denied. (9/1)
**4357* Much Commended** missed the break and lacked experience. Staying on really well at the finish, he would have won with a bit further to go and clearly needs the seven. (5/1)
**4488 Blane Water (USA)**, a keen-going type, got warm down at the start. Tapped for toe at halfway, he was putting in some solid work at the finish and will be much better back over seven. (8/1)
**4579 Vasari (IRE)**, taken to post early, ran well from a modest draw. Left behind soon after halfway, he was making inroads again at the finish. (16/1)
**4510* Tomba** seemed to run up to his best. (12/1)
**4311* Blues Queen** had plenty on at the weights and made a mockery of her long odds. Happy to sit off the pace, she was switched towards the centre soon after halfway and was staying on in good style at the end. There is still time for her to take another nursery. (66/1)
**4369 Pelham (IRE)** came through late after being involved in some scrimmaging soon after the start. (16/1)
**4228* Jhazi**, winner of his only previous outing, ran creditably from a poor draw, as the middle to far side was the place to be. After showing plenty of toe, he was rather isolated and left behind in the second half of the contest. (6/1)

## 4724 STANLEY RACING H'CAP (0-85) (3-Y.O+) (Class D)
3-25 (3-29) **1m** £4,796.00 (£1,448.00: £704.00: £332.00) Stalls: Centre GOING minus 0.49 sec per fur (F)

SP RR SF
4238[8] **Dilazar (USA) (77)** (JRFanshawe) **3-9-7** DHarrison(6) (trckd ldrs gng wl: led over 2f out: shkn up & wnt clr over 1f out)..........— **1** 8/1 95 74
4059[4] **Mr Teigh (67)** (BSmart) **4-9-0** MTebbutt(12) (lw: hld up: smooth hdwy over 2f out: styd on fnl f: no ch w wnr)...6 **2** 7/1[3] 73 55
4470[4] **Royal Result (USA) (80)** (MRStoute) **3-9-10** WRyan(8) (trckd ldrs: chal 3f out: kpt on same pce appr fnl f)...s.h **3** 8/1 86 65
4597[3] **Cee-Jay-Ay (53)** (JBerry) **9-7-9**(5) PFessey(10) (lw: dwlt: bhd tl hdwy over 2f out: kpt on wl fnl f)..........nk **4** 8/1 58 40
4606[2] **Raed (70)** (PTWalwyn) **3-9-0** RHills(2) (trckd ldr: chal over 2f out: sn rdn: kpt on one pce) ..........3 **5** 5/1[1] 69 48
4597[2] **Spanish Verdict (62)** (DenysSmith) **9-8-9** KFallon(7) (lw: sn outpcd & drvn along: styd on fnl 2f) ..........½ **6** 6/1[2] 60 42
4430* **Densben (53)** (DenysSmith) **12-8-0** JQuinn(3) (sn outpcd & bhd: hdwy over 2f out: kpt on: nvr nr ldrs)..........s.h **7** 14/1 51 33
4439[4] **Murray's Mazda (IRE) (50)** (JLEyre) **7-7-8**(3) DWright(13) (sn bhd & drvn along: n.d)..........9 **8** 12/1 30 12
4559[17] **Failed To Hit (72)** (SirMarkPrescott) **3-9-2** GDuffield(11) (lw: sn bhd & drvn along) ..........4 **9** 14/1 44 23
2032* **Antarctic Storm (63)** (RAFahey) **3-8-7** GCarter(1) (swvd lft s: led: hung rt: hdd over 2f out: sn wknd)..........¾ **10** 16/1 34 13
4231[6] **Elite Force (IRE) (72)** (PWChapple-Hyam) **3-8-13**(3) RHavlin(5) (chsd ldrs: drvn along ½-wy: lost pl 3f out)..2½ **11** 25/1 38 17
4360[11] **La Thuile (49)** (TJEtherington) **4-7-10** LCharnock(4) (in tch tl lost pl ½-wy: sn bhd)..........13 **12** 200/1 — —
4688[10] **Quilling (72)** (MDods) **4-9-5** JFortune(9) (unruly stalls & uns rdr s) .......... **U** 6/1[2] — —
(SP 122.3%) **13 Rn**

**1m 34.7** (0.10 under best) (-1.00) CSF £59.67 CT £446.22 TOTE £10.80: £2.60 £3.90 £3.50 (£48.80) Trio £115.20 OWNER Mr Mana Al Maktoum (NEWMARKET) BRED Anthony Rizzo and Marie Rizzo
LONG HANDICAP La Thuile 5-13
WEIGHT FOR AGE 3yo-3lb

**3770 Dilazar (USA)**, who looked a useful prospect when showing plenty of promise on his first outing this year, came back from a spell in the wilderness. Appreciating the drop back in trip, he shot clear to score by a wide margin. (8/1)
**4059 Mr Teigh**, who travelled strongly on the bridle, was, like the winner, left for dead by the winner. He is about 7lb better on the All-Weather. (7/1)
**4470 Royal Result (USA)**, dropped in distance and slipping down the weights, ran well but his is as good as he is. (8/1)
**4597 Cee-Jay-Ay** ran his usual race, forfeiting ground at the start and deciding to stay on when it was all over. (8/1)
**4606 Raed** is proving hard to win with. (5/1)
**4597 Spanish Verdict** was struggling from start to finish. (6/1)

## 4725 E.B.F. MAIDEN STKS (2-Y.O F) (Class D)
3-55 (3-56) **7f** £3,834.00 (£1,152.00: £556.00: £258.00) Stalls: Centre GOING minus 0.49 sec per fur (F)

SP RR SF
4570[2] **Meshhed (USA)** (BHanbury) **2-8-11** RHills(2) (lw: w ldr gng wl: led over 2f out: pushed out) ..........— **1** 1/2[1] 85+ 55
3787[6] **Nawasib (IRE)** (JLDunlop) **2-8-11** TSprake(4) (trckd ldrs: effrt over 2f out: styd on: no ch w wnr)..........3½ **2** 25/1 77 47
4052[6] **Western Hour (USA)** (PWChapple-Hyam) **2-8-8**(3) RHavlin(5) (trckd ldrs: rdn over 2f out: kpt on same pce)...2 **3** 5/1[2] 72 42
**Amaryllis (IRE)** (JHMGosden) **2-8-11** GHind(7) (unf: s.s: hdwy to chse ldrs ½-wy: rn green & wknd 2f out) .2½ **4** 10/1 67 37
4363[3] **Bally Souza (IRE)** (MJohnston) **2-8-11** TWilliams(3) (led tl over 2f out: sn wknd)..........2½ **5** 8/1[3] 61 31
**Ikhtisar (USA)** (PTWalwyn) **2-8-11** JCarroll(6) (lt-f: leggy: sn drvn along & wl outpcd) ..........6 **6** 14/1 47 17

| | | | | SP | RR | SF |
|---|---|---|---|---|---|---|
| | **Midnight Romance** (APJarvis) **2-8-11** WRyan(1) (unf: scope: s.i.s: sme hdwy ½-wy: sn wknd) | 3 | **7** | 14/1 | 40 | 10 |

(SP 120.7%) **7 Rn**

**1m 22.9** (-0.10) CSF £13.91 TOTE £1.40: £1.10 £4.90 (£10.60) OWNER Mr Hamdan Al Maktoum (NEWMARKET) BRED Shadwell Farm Inc
**4570 Meshhed (USA)** took plenty of persuading to enter the stalls. Never off the bridle, this easy win should have given her plenty of confidence, and there is no doubting that she does not lack ability. (1/2)
**3129 Nawasib (IRE)** ran her best race yet, but the winner was in a different league. (25/1)
**4052 Western Hour (USA)**, a keen-going sort, was put in her place in two strides after travelling almost as well as the winner. (5/1: op 3/1)
**Amaryllis (IRE)** looks as though she needs plenty of time, but she showed some ability after a slow break and then running green. (10/1: op 6/1)
**4363 Bally Souza (IRE)** led on sufferance. (8/1)
**Midnight Romance** (14/1: 5/1-16/1)

## 4726 LEVY BOARD H'CAP (0-65) (3-Y.O+) (Class F)

4-25 (4-25) **1m 5f 135y** £3,605.00 (£1,085.00: £525.00: £245.00) Stalls: Low GOING minus 0.49 sec per fur (F)

| | | | | SP | RR | SF |
|---|---|---|---|---|---|---|
| 4604[3] | **Broughtons Formula (41)** (WJMusson) **6-8-5b** DRMcCabe(3) (hld up: gd hdwy over 1f out: r.o wl to ld wl ins fnl f) | — | **1** | 8/1 | 52 | 28 |
| 4448[5] | **Indiana Princess (55)** (MrsMReveley) **3-8-10** ACulhane(5) (led 3f: trckd ldrs: led ins fnl f: sn hdd & no ex) | 1 | **2** | 14/1 | 65 | 32 |
| 4515* | **Evidence In Chief (57)** (DRCElsworth) **3-8-12v** DHarrison(1) (lw: hld up & bhd: hdwy & wnt rt 2f out: styd on fnl f) | 1 | **3** | 7/1[3] | 66 | 33 |
| 4596[7] | **Hoofprints (IRE) (62)** (GHarwood) **3-9-3** JQuinn(8) (lw: led after 3f: drvn clr 4f out: hdd ins fnl f: one pce) | ½ | **4** | 12/1 | 70 | 37 |
| 4596[3] | **Snow Falcon (65)** (MBell) **3-9-6** MFenton(2) (lw: hld up & bhd: hdwy on outside & sltly hmpd 2f out: nvr rchd ldrs) | 2½ | **5** | 3/1[1] | 70 | 37 |
| 4227* | **Campaspe (54)** (JGFitzGerald) **4-9-1**(3) FLynch(12) (hld up in tch: effrt over 2f out: kpt on same pce) | 2½ | **6** | 6/1[2] | 56 | 32 |
| *4574*[7] | **Needwood Epic (57)** (BCMorgan) **3-8-12v**[1] LCharnock(4) (chsd ldrs: drvn along 4f out: wknd 2f out) | 2½ | **7** | 40/1 | 56 | 23 |
| 4489[8] | **Printers Quill (51)** (MajorDNChappell) **4-8-10**(5) SophieMitchell(13) (chsd ldr: rdn 3f out: one pce) | hd | **8** | 16/1 | 50 | 26 |
| 4587[2] | **Arc of The Diver (IRE) (52)** (JBerry) **3-8-7b** GCarter(10) (lw: bhd & drvn along over 3f out: nvr nr ldrs) | ½ | **9** | 7/1[3] | 51 | 18 |
| 4563[18] | **Course Fishing (43)** (BAMcMahon) **5-8-0**(7) AMcCarthy(14) (s.i.s: bhd: sme hdwy on outside 3f out: sn wknd) | 2 | **10** | 8/1 | 39 | 15 |
| 3939[9] | **Maftun (USA) (53)** (GMMoore) **4-9-3** JFEgan(7) (mid div: effrt & hung rt over 2f out: sn wknd) | ½ | **11** | 12/1 | 49 | 25 |
| 4448[12] | **Veiled Dancer (IRE) (65)** (JLDunlop) **3-9-6** KFallon(9) (a in rr) | 2 | **12** | 20/1 | 58 | 25 |
| | **Joe Jagger (IRE) (44)** (MDHammond) **5-8-8** GDuffield(15) (bkwd: bhd & drvn along 4f out: n.d) | 3 | **13** | 40/1 | 34 | 10 |
| 625[14] | **Dont Forget Curtis (IRE) (62)** (GMMoore) **4-9-12** JFortune(11) (mid div: drvn along over 4f out: sn bhd) | 13 | **14** | 33/1 | 36 | 12 |
| 4588[12] | **Rainelle (57)** (JWWatts) **4-9-7b** NConnorton(6) (b: chsd ldrs tl lost pl over 3f out) | ¾ | **15** | 66/1 | 31 | 7 |

(SP 128.5%) **15 Rn**

**2m 57.2** (4.00) CSF £109.33 CT £770.41 TOTE £9.80: £2.00 £4.70 £2.10 (£48.60) Trio £115.70 OWNER Crawford Gray & Aylett (NEWMARKET) BRED The Lavington Stud
WEIGHT FOR AGE 3yo-9lb
**4604 Broughtons Formula** is useful on his day. Given a confident ride, he only made his move a furlong and a half out and, showing a bright turn of foot, shot to the front nearing the line. (8/1)
**4448 Indiana Princess**, dropped 3lb, raced keenly. Persuaded to put her head in front inside the last, she had the prize whipped from under her almost on the line. (14/1: 10/1-16/1)
**4515* Evidence In Chief** stayed the trip well enough, but his winning efforts seem to be confined to claiming races. (7/1)
**4596 Hoofprints (IRE)**, who has slipped down the weights, was given an enterprising ride. Making the best of his way home once in line for home, he soon showed in a clear lead. When it mattered though, he could do no more than stay on at the same pace. (12/1)
**4596 Snow Falcon** was given plenty to do. Messed about by the third horse two furlongs out, she was never going to get close enough to take a hand from that point on. (3/1)
**4227* Campaspe**, raised 8lb, travelled nicely on the heels of the leaders but, when asked to join issue, she did not find a lot. Perhaps this trip was just beyond her. (6/1)
**4587 Arc of The Diver (IRE)** (7/1: 5/1-15/2)

## 4727 EGTON LIMITED STKS (0-70) (3-Y.O+) (Class E)

5-00 (5-01) **5f** £3,172.75 (£952.00: £458.50: £211.75) Stalls: Centre GOING minus 0.49 sec per fur (F)

| | | | | SP | RR | SF |
|---|---|---|---|---|---|---|
| 4610* | **Another Batchworth (55)** (EAWheeler) **4-8-12b** TSprake(1) (mde all: clr ½-wy: unchal) | — | **1** | 5/1[2] | 71 | 50 |
| 4119[4] | **Midnight Spell (66)** (JWHills) **4-8-12**(3) MHenry(2) (a chsng ldrs: kpt on wl ins fnl f: nt rch wnr) | 1 | **2** | 3/1[1] | 71 | 50 |
| 4616[17] | **Here Comes a Star (69)** (JMCarr) **8-8-12** ACulhane(5) (lw: sltly hmpd s: bhd tl styd on wl appr fnl f) | 1½ | **3** | 13/2[3] | 63 | 42 |
| 4229* | **Manolo (FR) (65)** (JBerry) **3-9-1b** GCarter(12) (effrt ½-wy: sn chsng wnr: rdn & hung lft 2f out: kpt on same pce) | 1 | **4** | 8/1 | 63 | 42 |
| 4452[9] | **Sing With the Band (66)** (BAMcMahon) **5-8-12** JFortune(11) (chsd ldrs: rdn & hung lft 2f out: no imp) | 1¼ | **5** | 5/1[2] | 56 | 35 |
| 4452[13] | **Miss Bigwig (66)** (JBerry) **3-8-4**(5) PFessey(10) (chsd ldrs: rdn ½-wy: no imp) | 1¼ | **6** | 9/1 | 49 | 28 |
| 4610[5] | **Superbit (54)** (BAMcMahon) **4-9-1** GDuffield(8) (lw: in tch: rdn over 3f out: wknd over 1f out) | 1 | **7** | 16/1 | 52 | 31 |
| 4610[18] | **Swan At Whalley (69)** (MartynWane) **4-8-10**(5) PRoberts(3) (chsd wnr to ½-wy: sn wknd) | 2½ | **8** | 7/1 | 44 | 23 |
| 4259[13] | **Saint Amigo (37)** (RMWhitaker) **4-8-9**(3) RHavlin(4) (swvd rt s: sn drvn along & a bhd) | hd | **9** | 50/1 | 40 | 19 |
| 4075[18] | **Fancy Clancy (34)** (MissLCSiddall) **3-8-9b** DHarrison(7) (a bhd) | 2 | **10** | 100/1 | 31 | 10 |
| 4460[15] | **Swifty Nifty (IRE) (36)** (WWHaigh) **3-8-9** DRMcCabe(6) (s.i.s: a bhd) | 2½ | **11** | 50/1 | 23 | 2 |
| *4090*[9] | **She's a Madam (40)** (LRLloyd-James) **5-8-2**(7) CLowther(9) (lw: chsd ldrs tl lost pl ½-wy) | 1½ | **12** | 100/1 | 18 | — |

(SP 117.1%) **12 Rn**

**57.7 secs** (0.20) CSF £19.01 TOTE £5.00: £2.50 £2.00 £1.80 (£8.00) Trio £28.10 OWNER Mrs Mr Mr Price Wakefield O'Toole (PANGBOURNE) BRED Mrs D. Price
**4610* Another Batchworth** was a revelation. Showing speed to burn, she must have been six or seven lengths clear at halfway. (5/1)
**4119 Midnight Spell**, who had the beating of the winner on their running together at Brighton in July, like the rest was completely taken off her legs. Sticking to her task inside the last, she was reeling in the winner at the line but much too late. (3/1)
**3579 Here Comes a Star** has enjoyed little luck this season and it was highlighted here. Left short of room at the start, he was out with the washing until tearing through in the final furlong. (13/2)
**4229* Manolo (FR)**, raised 12lb after his Beverley win, raced wide. Showing second soon after halfway, he hung left under pressure and was never doing anything like enough. (8/1)
**3953 Sing With the Band** never looked happy and persisted in hanging left under pressure. (5/1)

T/Plpt: £149.30 (88.77 Tckts). T/Qdpt: £38.90 (25.26 Tckts). WG

**4728a-4737a** (Irish Racing) - See Computer Raceform

## 0271a-NAAS (Ireland) (L-H) (Good)
## Sunday October 13th

### 4738a ALI RETZA & MAMADI SOUDAVAR GARNET STKS (Listed) (3-Y.O+)
5-00 (5-00) **1m** £9,675.00 (£2,775.00: £1,275.00: £375.00)

| Form | Horse | Dist | Pos | SP | RR | SF |
|---|---|---|---|---|---|---|
| 2837a[5] | **French Ballerina (IRE)** (PJFlynn,Ireland) **3-8-8** WJSmith (bhd: hdwy 3f out: swtchd rt 2f out: r.o wl & edgd lft ins fnl f: led nr fin) | — | 1 | 13/2 | 103+ | — |
| 4026a[8] | **Inchacooley (IRE)** (MBrassil,Ireland) **4-8-11** PShanahan (hld up: gd hdwy over 2f out: led jst ins fnl f tl nr fin: kpt on) | ¾ | 2 | 16/1 | 102 | — |
| | **Oriane** (JOxx,Ireland) **3-8-9**ow1 JPMurtagh (hld up: hdwy over 2f out: ev ch ins fnl f: r.o: sltly hmpd nr fin) | hd | 3 | 3/1 [1] | 102 | — |
| 4214[4] | **Tsarnista** (JLDunlop) **3-8-8** KFallon (hdwy ½-wy: rdn whn hmpd & snatched up ins fnl f: kpt on) | 1 | 4 | 8/1 | 99 | — |
| 4663a[7] | **Sagar Pride (IRE)** (JGBurns,Ireland) **3-8-8** NGMcCullagh (chsd ldrs: hdwy over 2f out: sn rdn: ev ch over 1f out: one pce ins fnl f) | 3 | 5 | 100/30 [2] | 93 | — |
| | **Fairy Lake (IRE)** (JGMurphy,Ireland) **3-8-8** PJSmullen (bhd: r.o fnl 2f: nrst fin) | 3 | 6 | 33/1 | 87 | — |
| 2197[2] | **Idle Fancy** (CCollins,Ireland) **3-8-8** RMBurke (sn prom: 2nd st: ev ch tl wknd over 1f out) | 1 | 7 | 14/1 | 85 | — |
| 4268a[4] | **Ceirseach (IRE)** (JSBolger,Ireland) **3-8-13b** KJManning (prom: 2nd whn stumbled wl over 3f out: 3rd st: rdn over 2f out: sn btn) | ¾ | 8 | 7/1 | 89 | — |
| | **Park Petard** (JSBolger,Ireland) **3-8-8** WJSupple (bhd: nvr nrr) | 1½ | 9 | 14/1 | 81 | — |
| | **Logstown (IRE)** (CCollins,Ireland) **4-8-11** SCraine (led tl ent fnl f: wknd qckly) | 1 | 10 | 12/1 | 79 | — |
| 4571* | **Don't Get Caught (IRE)** (JLHarris) **4-8-11** JFEgan (n.d) | s.h | 11 | 12/1 | 79 | — |
| | **Polygueza (FR)** (EJO'Grady,Ireland) **3-8-8** JAQuinn (sn cl up: 4th st: sn wknd) | ¾ | 12 | 25/1 | 77 | — |
| 2275a[3] | **Identify (IRE)** (DKWeld,Ireland) **3-8-13b** MJKinane (chsd ldrs: 5th st: rdn over 2f out: sn wknd: eased whn btn) | 1½ | 13 | 5/1 [3] | 79 | — |
| | | | | (SP 143.1%) | | **13 Rn** |

**1m 39.8** OWNER Mrs John Magnier (CARRICK-ON-SUIR)
**2837a French Ballerina (IRE)** would prefer a longer trip but was impressive enough. She switched out from the far rail two furlongs out, but went left again inside the final furlong before leading 50 yards out. She was value for more than the official margin. (13/2: op 4/1)
**Inchacooley (IRE)**, wearing a tongue-strap, was always vulnerable to her younger rival. (16/1)
**Oriane** came through to have every chance inside the last, but was slightly hampered by the winner close home. (3/1)
**4214 Tsarnista**, under pressure in fourth place when hampered and having to be snatched up inside the last, kept on well to the line. (8/1: op 4/1)
**4571* Don't Get Caught (IRE)** was totally outclassed. (12/1: op 5/1)

## 4660a-LONGCHAMP (Paris, France) (R-H) (Soft)
## Thursday October 10th

### 4739a PRIX EUGENE DE SAVOIE (Listed) (3-Y.O+)
3-30 (3-48) **1m** £18,445.00 (£6,324.00: £3,953.00: £2,055.00)

| Form | Horse | Dist | Pos | SP | RR | SF |
|---|---|---|---|---|---|---|
| 4444* | **Decorated Hero** (JHMGosden) **4-9-1** TJarnet | — | 1 | | 121+ | — |
| 3199a[2] | **La Fra Angelico (FR)** (JMartens,Belgium) **5-8-12b**[1] DBoeuf | 6 | 2 | | 106 | — |
| | **Hathor Eria (FR)** (MmePBarbe,France) **3-8-13** TThulliez | 1½ | 3 | | 107 | — |
| 4289a* | **Cadeaux Tryst** (EALDunlop) **4-9-5** TSprake | hd | 4 | | 110 | — |
| 1800[7] | **Master Boots** (DRLoder) **3-8-12** OPeslier (btn over 18l) | | 6 | | — | — |
| | | | | | | **6 Rn** |

**1m 42.58** (7.58) P-M 1.70F: 1.30F 2.30F OWNER Mr H. Allen (NEWMARKET) BRED Reg Griffin and Jim McGrath
**4444* Decorated Hero** put up an impressive performance. Racing in second place early, he burst into the lead with two furlongs to go. He drew right away from his rivals and had the race sewn up with more than a furlong left to run. He appears to have peaked and looks quite capable of making his mark in Group company, so it would be no surprise to see him back in France for the Prix Perth.
**4289a* Cadeaux Tryst** raced behind the leaders, but was very one-paced in the straight. Battling well, he only lost third by the narrowest of margins, but was giving 5lb to the winner and weight to the rest of the field, so it was a creditable performance.
**1800 Master Boots** made no show. He was held up for a late run, but was beaten soon after entering the straight.

## PARDUBICE (Czech Republic) (Good)
## Saturday October 12th

### 4740a PIVOVAR PARDUBICE ST. LEGER (3-Y.O+)
2-10 **1m 6f 110y** £10,870.00

| Form | Horse | Dist | Pos | SP | RR | SF |
|---|---|---|---|---|---|---|
| 4203[17] | **Set the Fashion** (DLWilliams) **7-9-9** JRaja | — | 1 | | 59 | — |
| | **Valesan (CZE)** (CzechRepublic) **4-9-9** DCengar | nse | 2 | | 59 | — |
| | **Sexman (POL)** (CzechRepublic) **3-9-2** DAndres | 5 | 3 | | 55 | — |
| | | | | | | **11 Rn** |

**3m 22.0** OWNER Mr R. J. Matthews (NEWBURY) BRED The Queen
**3812 Set the Fashion**, always in the first three, challenged from over a furlong out and just managed to hold on.

## 4412a-COLOGNE (Germany) (R-H) (Soft)
## Sunday October 13th

### 4741a BUCHMACHER SPRINGER STEHER PREIS (Listed) (3-Y.O+)
4-15 (4-21) **1m 5f 110y** £9,009.00 (£3,604.00: £1,802.00: £901.00)

| Form | Horse | Dist | Pos | SP | RR | SF |
|---|---|---|---|---|---|---|
| | **Domain (GER)** (HBlume,Germany) **3-8-4** NGrant | — | 1 | | 102 | — |

| | | | SP | RR | SF |
|---|---|---|---|---|---|
| 4032a[2] | **Lord Jim (IRE)** (LordHuntingdon) **4-9-4b** DHarrison ....½ | 2 | | 107 | — |
| | **Diktys (GER)** (HBlume,Germany) **4-9-2** THellier ....nk | 3 | | 105 | — |
| | | | | | 9 Rn |

**3m 7.7** TOTE 46DM: 14DM 12DM 14DM (141DM) OWNER Gestut Rottgen BRED Gestut Rottgen
**4032a Lord Jim (IRE)**, in second place throughout, made a challenge for the lead inside the final furlong, but was unable to quicken.

# 4739a-LONGCHAMP (Paris, France) (R-H) (Good)
## Sunday October 13th

### 4742a GRAND CRITERIUM (Gp 1) (2-Y.O C & F)
2-30 (2-29) **1m** £131,752.00 (£52,701.00: £26,350.00: £13,175.00)

| | | | SP | RR | SF |
|---|---|---|---|---|---|
| 4294a* | **Revoque (IRE)** (PWChapple-Hyam) **2-9-0** JReid (prom: rdn over 1f out: r.o strly to ld ins fnl f: r.o wl) ....— | 1 | 4/5[1] | 108+ | — |
| 4166a[2] | **Majorien** (MmeCHead,France) **2-9-0** FHead (trckd ldr: rdn to ld 2f out: hdd ins fnl f: kpt on)....2 | 2 | 109/10 | 104 | — |
| 4306* | **King Sound** (JHMGosden) **2-9-0** TJarnet (4th st: rdn 2f out: outpcd 1f out: rallied cl home) ....4 | 3 | 38/10[2] | 96 | — |
| 4398a[2] | **Referendum (IRE)** (GLewis) **2-9-0** PatEddery (led to 2f out: kpt on one pce u.p) ....nk | 4 | 107/10 | 95 | — |
| | **Aneysar (IRE)** (AdeRoyerDupre,France) **2-9-0** GMosse (mid div: rdn over 1f out: n.m.r ins fnl f: nvr trbld ldrs) ....nk | 5 | 101/10 | 95 | — |
| 4166a* | **Nombre Premier** (AdeRoyerDupre,France) **2-9-0** PSogorb (chsd ldrs to st: rdn 2f out: no imp) ....2 | 6 | 76/10[3] | 91 | — |
| | **Olympic Majesty (FR)** (CO'Brien,Ireland) **2-9-0** OPeslier (in rr: nt qckn fnl 2f) ....8 | 7 | 12/1 | 75 | — |
| | **Le Topolino (USA)** (PBogoev,Bulgaria) **2-9-0** MGalabov (a in rr) ....2½ | 8 | 23/1 | 70 | — |
| | **Wild Thyme (USA)** (PBogoev,Bulgaria) **2-9-0** BYasmianov (bhd fr ½-wy) ....2½ | 9 | 23/1 | 65 | — |
| | | | (SP 130.0%) | | 9 Rn |

**1m 37.7** (2.70) P-M 1.80F: 1.10F 1.60F 1.30F (9.30F) OWNER Mr R. E. Sangster (MARLBOROUGH) BRED Minch Bloodstock
IN-FOCUS: **For betting purposes Le Topolino (USA) and Wild Thyme (USA) were cpld**
**4294a* Revoque (IRE)**, a fine individual, looked top class here. Bustled along early on to find a good position and racing on the rail, he found problems soon after entering the straight but, once in the clear, changed gear and began to stretch in fine style. Sweeping past the runner-up inside the final furlong, he won going away. A colt with plenty of scope for further improvement, he recorded an extremely fast time here and could turn out to be the champion European Juvenile. He will not be seen out again in 1996 and could go directly for next year's 2000 Guineas without a run, but that will apparently depend on the spring weather. A stiff, straight track like Newmarket will suit him even better than the likes of Longchamp, and he currently looks good value in the ante-post market. (4/5)
**4166a Majorien** did absolutely nothing wrong. Following the long-time leader before taking over before the furlong pole, he had nothing left when challenged by the winner, but stayed on well. He has begun to settle down and is improving with every race and, like the winner, is to be put away for the season. Next term's agenda is likely to include the Prix de Fontainebleau and then the Dubai Poule d'Essai des Poulains. (109/10)
**4306* King Sound**, never far from the leading group, was outpaced when the leaders accelerated in the straight, but stuck to his task well and looks like a colt who will be better suited by a longer distance. He has plenty of scope and is already being talked about as a possibility for next year's Derby. (38/10)
**4398a Referendum (IRE)** used up some energy early on getting to the head of affairs, but led until over a furlong out and then just stayed on one-paced. At this stage of his career, a mile might be a bit too far and he may not quite be up to this standard, but this was still a game performance. (107/10)
**Olympic Majesty (FR)** was never at the races. He was beaten early in the straight and it was a lot to ask of such an inexperienced colt. (12/1)
DS

# 4169a-MUNICH (Germany) (L-H) (Soft)
## Sunday October 13th

### 4743a GROSSER BUCHMACHER SPRINGER SPRINT-PREIS (Listed) (3-Y.O+)
3-20 (3-25) **6f 110y** £15,766.00 (£6,306.00: £3,153.00: £1,802.00)

| | | | SP | RR | SF |
|---|---|---|---|---|---|
| 4442[7] | **Branston Abby (IRE)** (MJohnston) **6-9-1** MRoberts ....— | 1 | | 113 | — |
| 3572a* | **Macanal (USA)** (HJentzsch,Germany) **4-9-4** PSchiergen ....hd | 2 | | 116 | — |
| 4409a[9] | **Takin (GER)** (FrauEMader,Germany) **5-9-1** LMader ....1¼ | 3 | | 110 | — |
| 3914a[8] | **Warning Star** (BWHills) **4-8-7** JCarroll ....½ | 4 | | 100 | — |
| | | | | | 8 Rn |

**1m 21.0** TOTE 46DM: 14DM 12DM 14DM OWNER Mr David Abell (MIDDLEHAM) BRED John David Abell
**3712 Branston Abby (IRE)** scored a record twenty-third win, which makes her the winning-most British-trained filly or mare of the post-war era. Held up towards the rear early on, she began to make headway from two furlongs out and took the lead in the final strides.
**3914a Warning Star**, who dwelt slightly, made headway on the outside from four furlongs out. She was third and with every chance from a furlong out, but could find no extra inside the final furlong.

# 4665a-SAN SIRO (Milan, Italy) (R-H) (Heavy)
## Sunday October 13th

### 4744a PREMIO OMENONI (Gp 3) (3-Y.O+)
1-45 (1-48) **5f** £30,324.00 (£13,933.00: £7,773.00)

| | | | SP | RR | SF |
|---|---|---|---|---|---|
| 4442[3] | **Leap for Joy** (JHMGosden) **4-8-4** LDettori ....— | 1 | | 107 | — |
| 4518[4] | **Brave Edge** (RHannon) **8-8-7** DaneO'Neill ....1¼ | 2 | | 106 | — |
| 4660a[3] | **Hever Golf Rose** (TJNaughton) **5-8-4** TQuinn ....s.nk | 3 | | 102 | — |
| | | | | | 7 Rn |

**58.9 secs** (3.70) TOTE 22L: 17L 42L (138L) OWNER S. Hata (NEWMARKET) BRED The Overbury Stud
**4442 Leap for Joy** chased Hever Golf Rose on the outside before taking the lead a furlong out and running on well to win this race for the second successive year. She will now be aimed for the Group Three Prix du Petit Couvert at Longchamp on October 27.
**4518 Brave Edge**, outpaced early, stayed on in the final two furlongs to take second in the last strides.
**4660a Hever Golf Rose** led until a furlong out and then stayed on at one pace, but was deprived of second close home.

## 4745a PREMIO BBA ITALIA (2-Y.O)
2-15 (2-19) **1m 1f** £10,150.00 (£4,466.00: £2,436.00)

| Form | Horse | Dist | Pos | SP | RR | SF |
|---|---|---|---|---|---|---|
| 4420a$^{3}$ | **Cristin (ITY)** (VSarti,Italy) **2-8-8** FJovine | — | 1 | | 73 | — |
| 4538a* | **Passi d'Orlando (IRE)** (JLDunlop) **2-8-11** GForte | ½ | 2 | | 75 | — |
| | **Applausi (IRE)** (MCiciarelli,Italy) **2-8-13** AParravani | 4¾ | 3 | | 69 | — |
| | | | | | | **8 Rn** |

**1m 57.1** (14.90) TOTE 52L: 15L 12L 19L (54L) OWNER A. Sansottera

**4538a* Passi d'Orlando (IRE)**, who tracked the leader until taking the lead two and a half furlongs out, was unlucky to be caught close home.

## 4746a PREMIO DORMELLO (Gp 3) (2-Y.O F)
2-45 (2-50) **1m** £31,347.00 (£14,700.00: £8,284.00)

| Form | Horse | Dist | Pos | SP | RR | SF |
|---|---|---|---|---|---|---|
| | **Happy Dancer (USA)** (RCollet,France) **2-8-11** CAsmussen | — | 1 | | — | — |
| | **Genevra (IRE)** (HRemmert,Germany) **2-8-11** KWoodburn | nk | 2 | | — | — |
| | **Sopran Mariduff** (RRossini,Italy) **2-8-11** AMarcialis | ¾ | 3 | | — | — |
| 4211$^{4}$ | **Logica (IRE)** (PAKelleway) **2-8-11** LDettori (btn approx 5 3/4l) | | 8 | | — | — |
| 4420a* | **Folgore (USA)** (JLDunlop) **2-8-11** FJovine (btn approx 6l) | | 9 | | — | — |
| | | | | | | **12 Rn** |

**1m 43.2** (13.20) TOTE 43L: 21L 61L 35L (604L) OWNER P-M Chevalier (CHANTILLY) BRED Walter Armitage

**4211 Logica (IRE)** raced in seventh until the straight, but made no headway in the final two furlongs.

**4420a* Folgore (USA)**, held up towards the rear, began to make headway over three furlongs out, but was never in a position to challenge.

## 4747a GRAN PREMIO DEL JOCKEY-CLUB (Gp 1) (3-Y.O+ C & F)
3-45 (4-01) **1m 4f** £161,386.00 (£83,281.00: £49,025.00: £24,512.00)

| Form | Horse | Dist | Pos | SP | RR | SF |
|---|---|---|---|---|---|---|
| 4192* | **Shantou (USA)** (JHMGosden) **3-8-12** LDettori (hld up: hdwy st: qcknd to ld wl over 1f out: comf) | — | 1 | | 128 | — |
| 4397a$^{3}$ | **Sacrament** (MRStoute) **5-9-4** WRSwinburn (a in tch: mid div st: ev ch 2f out: one pce) | 3 | 2 | | 123 | — |
| 3915a* | **Strategic Choice (USA)** (PFICole) **5-9-4** TQuinn (prom: cl up st: one pce fnl 2f) | 2½ | 3 | | 120 | — |
| 4413a$^{3}$ | **Hollywood Dream (GER)** (UOstmann,Germany) **5-9-1** CAsmussen (hld up: last st: hdwy over 3f out: styd on: nt rch ldrs) | ½ | 4 | | 116 | — |
| 4172a* | **Slicious** (VCaruso,Italy) **4-9-4** MEsposito (rel to ent stalls: in tch: mid div st: effrt over 2f out: sn one pce) | ¾ | 5 | | 118 | — |
| 4421a$^{2}$ | **Coral Reef (ITY)** (GColleo,Italy) **3-8-12** EBotti (led tl wl over 1f out) | 1¾ | 6 | | 117 | — |
| 3917a* | **Tarhelm (IRE)** (GColleo,Italy) **4-9-4** LSorrentino (a in rr) | 4½ | 7 | | 110 | — |
| 4172a$^{2}$ | **Concepcion (GER)** (HJentzsch,Germany) **6-9-4** SEccles (prom: 2nd st: wknd over 3f out) | 1¾ | 8 | | 107 | — |
| | | | | | | **8 Rn** |

**2m 32.4** (12.40) TOTE 24L: 11L 13L 11L (88L) OWNER Sheikh Mohammed (NEWMARKET) BRED Darley Stud Management Inc

**4192* Shantou (USA)** continued the recent successful run in major European races for the jockey-trainer partnership of Dettori and Gosden. Held up towards the rear before quickening approaching the final quarter mile, he took the lead well over a furlong out and won comfortably.

**4397a Sacrament**, always in touch, was fourth coming into the straight. He had every chance over two furlongs out, but could only stay on at the one pace.

**3915a* Strategic Choice (USA)**, prominent in the early stages, was a close third into the straight, but was no better than one-paced in the closing stages.

# 4317-CATTERICK (L-H) (Good)
## Friday October 18th
WEATHER: dry WIND: fresh half bhd

## 4748 E.B.F. ZETLAND MEDIAN AUCTION MAIDEN STKS (2-Y.O F) (Class E)
2-10 (2-11) **7f** £3,288.00 (£984.00: £472.00: £216.00) Stalls: Low GOING: 0.05 sec per fur (G)

| Form | Horse | Dist | Pos | SP | RR | SF |
|---|---|---|---|---|---|---|
| | **Kadeena** (MJohnston) **2-8-11** TWilliams(2) (unf: bit bkwd: chsd ldrs: styd on u.p to ld ins fnl f: r.o) | — | 1 | 10/1 | 78+ | 33 |
| 3675$^{2}$ | **Kalimat** (WJarvis) **2-8-11** KDarley(6) (trckd ldrs: hmpd over 2f out: led over 1f out: hdd & nt qckn ins nl f) | 1¼ | 2 | 15/8$^{1}$ | 75 | 30 |
| 4046$^{3}$ | **Bonnie Lassie** (CWThornton) **2-8-11** DeanMcKeown(10) (chsd ldrs tl lost pl ½-wy: hdwy & ev ch 1f out: nt qckn) | hd | 3 | 11/2 | 75 | 30 |
| 4105$^{8}$ | **Fauna (IRE)** (NAGraham) **2-8-11** AMcGlone(1) (s.i.s: sn trckng ldrs: ev ch 1f out: sn wknd) | 1¾ | 4 | 10/1 | 71 | 26 |
| *4572*$^{3}$ | **Brazilia (69)** (PTWalwyn) **2-8-11** JFortune(3) (led tl over 1f out: sn wknd) | ¾ | 5 | 20/1 | 69 | 24 |
| 4618$^{13}$ | **Ziggy's Viola (IRE)** (MrsMReveley) **2-8-11** ACulhane(4) (bit bkwd: hld up: bhd tl styd on appr fnl f: nvr nr to chal) | 3½ | 6 | 25/1 | 61 | 16 |
| 4684$^{7}$ | **Keepsake (IRE)** (MDIUsher) **2-8-11** RStreet(8) (rr div: styd on appr fnl f: n.d) | 1¼ | 7 | 25/1 | 58 | 13 |
| 4225$^{5}$ | **Native Princess (IRE)** (BWHills) **2-8-11** JCarroll(7) (in tch: effrt 2f out: sn wknd & eased) | 2½ | 8 | 5/1$^{3}$ | 53 | 8 |
| 4488$^{21}$ | **Telloff** (MAJarvis) **2-8-11** GDuffield(11) (sn drvn along: chsd ldrs: hung lft & lost pl 2f out) | 1 | 9 | 4/1$^{2}$ | 50 | 5 |
| 4594$^{6}$ | **Silent Valley (51)** (BJMeehan) **2-8-11b** MTebbutt(5) (a bhd: eased fnl 2f) | 11 | 10 | 25/1 | 25 | — |
| 1845$^{7}$ | **Ramsey Pride** (JHetherton) **2-8-11** NKennedy(9) (chsd ldrs tl lost pl ½-wy: sn bhd & eased: t.o) | dist | 11 | 100/1 | — | — |
| | | | | (SP 122.3%) | | **11 Rn** |

**1m 29.2** (5.60) CSF £28.83 TOTE £11.30: £2.80 £1.10 £2.60 (£17.60) Trio £34.00 OWNER Devonia Stud (MIDDLEHAM) BRED Devonia Stud

**Kadeena**, who did not look fit and also looked in need of more time, showed plenty of knee-action going down. Scoring decisively in the end, she will be even better suited by a mile and a more galloping track, but this race was, in truth, no better than a seller. (10/1: op 5/1)

**3675 Kalimat** was short of room when Brazilia made a move for the favoured stands'-side rail once in line for home. After taking it up, she eventually found the winner much too strong. (15/8)

**4046 Bonnie Lassie** lost a good pitch on the turn for home. Rallying to have every chance a furlong out, she will be better suited by a mile, and should win a claimer or a seller. (11/2)

**Fauna (IRE)**, who recovered from a sluggish start to be soon tracking the leaders going well, faded inside the last as if still in need of the outing. (10/1)

**4572 Brazilia**, who became stirred up last time, did not parade in front of the Stands and was taken straight to post. Racing keenly, she made the running but, when challenged, she did not find much. (20/1)

**Ziggy's Viola (IRE)** still looks in need of more time and raced keenly. Settled at the back, she was staying on at the finish and can do better next year. (25/1)

## 4749 NORTHGATE NORFLEX NURSERY H'CAP (0-85) (2-Y.O) (Class E)

2-45 (2-46) **5f** £3,444.00 (£1,032.00: £496.00: £228.00) Stalls: Low GOING: 0.05 sec per fur (G)

| Form | Horse | Dist | Pos | SP | RR | SF |
|---|---|---|---|---|---|---|
| 4586[13] | **Sarabi (65)** (JPearce) **2-8-9** JQuinn(3) (mde all: styd on wl fnl f: eased nr fin) | — | 1 | 33/1 | 72 | 39 |
| 4586[5] | **Donna's Dancer (IRE) (67)** (TDBarron) **2-8-11b** DeanMcKeown(12) (lw: s.i.s: sn chsng ldrs: kpt on wl ins fnl f) | hd | 2 | 9/1[2] | 74 | 41 |
| 4113[20] | **Express Girl (77)** (DMoffatt) **2-9-4**(3) DarrenMoffatt(2) (chsd wnr far side: kpt on wl fnl f) | 1 | 3 | 10/1[3] | 81 | 48 |
| 4459[3] | **Keen To Please (64)** (DenysSmith) **2-8-8** JCarroll(15) (a chsng ldrs: rdn & kpt on one pce fnl 2f) | 3 | 4 | 9/1[2] | 58 | 25 |
| 4517[9] | **Clara Bliss (IRE) (73)** (BJMeehan) **2-9-3** MTebbutt(14) (a chsng ldrs: nt qckn fnl 2f) | s.h | 5 | 16/1 | 67 | 34 |
| *2635** | **Come Too Mamma's (62)** (JBerry) **2-8-1**(5) PFessey(16) (led stands' side tl hdd & wknd over 1f out) | hd | 6 | 14/1 | 55 | 22 |
| 4459[3] | **William's Well (57)** (MWEasterby) **2-8-1b** JFEgan(10) (a in tch: no imp fnl 2f) | 1¼ | 7 | 14/1 | 46 | 13 |
| 4459* | **Kilcullen Lad (IRE) (59)** (PMooney) **2-8-3** DRMcCabe(5) (in tch: effrt & hung rt 2f out: kpt on same pce) | hd | 8 | 9/2[1] | 48 | 15 |
| 4468[2] | **Hurgill Lady (66)** (JWWatts) **2-8-10** NConnorton(11) (w ldrs tl wknd over 1f out) | ¾ | 9 | 12/1 | 53 | 20 |
| 4208[14] | **Five-O-Fifty (56)** (JLEyre) **2-7-11**(3) MHenry(17) (sn bhd: sme hdwy over 1f out: n.d) | 1 | 10 | 12/1 | 40 | 7 |
| 3637[2] | **Marylebone (IRE) (75)** (JBerry) **2-9-5** KDarley(13) (sn bhd) | 1¼ | 11 | 9/1[2] | 55 | 22 |
| 4586[7] | **Brutal Fantasy (IRE) (70)** (JLEyre) **2-9-0** RLappin(8) (b.hind: nvr nr ldrs) | 1¼ | 12 | 14/1 | 46 | 13 |
| 4424[2] | **Keen Waters (63)** (JRArnold) **2-8-7** GDuffield(1) (sn chsng ldrs far side: lost pl 2f out) | hd | 13 | 12/1 | 38 | 5 |
| 4562[9] | **Mazil (62)** (TDEasterby) **2-8-6** MBirch(6) (sn outpcd) | 1 | 14 | 33/1 | 34 | 1 |
| 4459[9] | **Molly Drummond (65)** (CWCElsey) **2-8-9b1** LCharnock(4) (racd far side: sn outpcd) | 2½ | 15 | 33/1 | 29 | — |
| 4343[3] | **Compact Disc (IRE) (57)** (MJohnston) **2-8-1** TWilliams(9) (prom early: bhd fr ½-wy) | 5 | 16 | 16/1 | 5 | — |
| 4425[6] | **Suite Factors (68)** (KRBurke) **2-8-12** StephenDavies(7) (bhd fr ½-wy) | nk | 17 | 16/1 | 15 | — |
| | | | | (SP 126.8%) | **17 Rn** | |

**60.9 secs** (3.40) CSF £285.66 CT £3,007.77 TOTE £33.00: £9.20 £1.70 £4.90 £3.60 (£344.80) Trio Not won; £543.85 to Newmarket 19/10/96 OWNER Mr Ziad Galadari (NEWMARKET) BRED M. L. Page

OFFICIAL EXPLANATION **Sarabi: regarding the apparent improvement in form, trainer explained that the filly got upset in the stalss last time, then was hampered and as a result ran too freely and too wide. He added that today she was relaxed, and also benifited from the shorter trip.**

**3475 Sarabi**, who has to go in the stalls with the hood on but then have it almost immediately removed, made all on the far side and won with a fraction more in hand than the margin would suggest. His rider eased up near the finish and seemed unaware that the leader on the other side was as close as he was. (33/1)

**4586 Donna's Dancer (IRE)**, closely matched with Kilcullen Lad on Redcar running, managed to give ground away at the start as usual. Showing ahead on the stands' side over a furlong out, he kept on strongly, but the winner just had the edge on the far side. (9/1)

**2728 Express Girl** ran well on the far side, chasing the leaders throughout, and connections reckon she is even better on easier ground. (10/1)

**4459 Keen To Please** wore a tongue-strap but, as at Redcar, could only keep on at the same pace under pressure. (9/1)

**4459* Kilcullen Lad (IRE)**, who tends to hang right, raced towards the far side, but joined the stands'-side group at halfway. Soon flat out, he never looked like taking a hand. (9/2)

## 4750 DARLINGTON BUILDING SOCIETY H'CAP (0-80) (3-Y.O) (Class D)

3-15 (3-15) **1m 7f 177y** £3,785.00 (£1,130.00: £540.00: £245.00) Stalls: Low GOING: 0.05 sec per fur (G)

| Form | Horse | Dist | Pos | SP | RR | SF |
|---|---|---|---|---|---|---|
| 4563[11] | **Backwoods (57)** (WMBrisbourne) **3-7-12**ow2 AGarth(2) (hld up: hdwy & reminder 5f out: styd on wl fnl 2f: led ins fnl f) | — | 1 | 12/1 | 70 | 37 |
| 4447[9] | **Upper Gallery (IRE) (80)** (PWChapple-Hyam) **3-9-4**(3) RHavlin(3) (trckd ldrs: led over 2f out tl ins fnl f: r.o) | ½ | 2 | 7/2[2] | 93 | 62 |
| *4574[2]* | **Arcady (63)** (PTWalwyn) **3-8-4** JCarroll(1) (a.p: hdwy to chal over 2f out: one pce) | 10 | 3 | 8/1 | 65 | 34 |
| 4042[6] | **Siege Perilous (IRE) (66)** (SCWilliams) **3-8-7** KDarley(5) (lw: hdwy ½-wy: drvn along 5f out: ev ch over 2f out: wknd over 1f out) | 8 | 4 | 9/4[1] | 60 | 29 |
| 4321[4] | **Marsayas (IRE) (55)** (MJCamacho) **3-7-10** LCharnock(4) (chsd ldrs: drvn along 6f out: n.m.r over 2f out: sn wknd) | ¾ | 5 | 7/1 | 49 | 18 |
| 4506[3] | **Mister Aspecto (IRE) (70)** (MJohnston) **3-8-11v** DeanMcKeown(6) (chsd ldrs: led over 5f out tl over 2f out: sn wknd) | ½ | 6 | 5/1[3] | 63 | 32 |
| 4596[6] | **Double Agent (73)** (MJohnston) **3-8-11**(3) MHenry(7) (lw: bhd & drvn along 10f out: hdwy u.p 6f out: lost pl 4f out: t.o) | 23 | 7 | 8/1 | 43 | 12 |
| 3638* | **Another Quarter (IRE) (55)** (MCChapman) **3-7-10** NKennedy(8) (b: lw: led tl over 5f out: sn lost pl: t.o) | 2½ | 8 | 20/1 | 22 | — |
| | | | | (SP 116.8%) | **8 Rn** | |

**3m 31.6** (10.10) CSF £51.31 CT £332.51 TOTE £7.80: £1.80 £1.50 £1.50 (£27.90) OWNER Mr P. R. Kirk (NESSCLIFFE) BRED Sheikh Mohammed bin Rashid al Maktoum

LONG HANDICAP Marsayas (IRE) 7-9 Another Quarter (IRE) 7-5

**3952* Backwoods**, who was unsuited by the testing ground on his comeback effort at Haydock, stuck on in determined fashion against the far rail to show ahead inside the last. An All-Weather performer, he has a good, fluent action and wants nothing worse than good ground on turf. (12/1)

**3850 Upper Gallery (IRE)** looked to have his first success in the bag when sneaking through on the inner to take it up once in line for home. Letting the winner up on his inside and flashing his tail under pressure, he was worried out of it near the line. There is surely still time for him to open his account. (7/2)

**4574 Arcady** was left behind in the final two furlongs. This trip is possibly beyond her. (8/1)

**4042 Siege Perilous (IRE)**, absent for forty-two days, ran as if in need of the outing. (9/4)

**4321 Marsayas (IRE)** was already deep in trouble when left short of room in general bunching on the turn for home. (7/1)

**4596 Double Agent** (8/1: op 5/1)

## 4751 E.B.F. RIPLEY MAIDEN STKS (I) (2-Y.O) (Class D)

3-50 (3-50) **5f 212y** £3,242.50 (£970.00: £465.00: £212.50) Stalls: High GOING: 0.05 sec per fur (G)

| Form | Horse | Dist | Pos | SP | RR | SF |
|---|---|---|---|---|---|---|
| 4547[4] | **Al Muallim (USA)** (JWPayne) **2-9-0** AMcGlone(9) (lw: hld up: effrt over 2f out: styd on wl u.p to ld ins fnl f) | — | 1 | 6/4[1] | 70 | 44 |
| 4318[3] | **Erosion (IRE)** (MJohnston) **2-9-0** TWilliams(1) (lw: w ldr: led over 3f out: hdd, hrd rdn & nt qckn ins fnl f) | ¾ | 2 | 3/1[2] | 68 | 42 |
| 4380[12] | **Janie's Boy** (RGuest) **2-9-0** JQuinn(3) (chsd ldrs: styd far side: kpt on wl fnl f) | 1¼ | 3 | 20/1 | 65 | 39 |
| 4593[2] | **Plaisir d'Amour (IRE)** (NACallaghan) **2-8-9** GDuffield(6) (lw: chsd ldrs: rdn over 2f out: sn wl outpcd) | 6 | 4 | 6/4[1] | 44 | 18 |

**Fearless Sioux** (CWThornton) **2-8-9** DeanMcKeown(4) (unf: bkwd: s.i.s: bhd: stdy hdwy 2f out: nvr nr ldrs) ..½ **5** 100/1 42 16
3880[7] **I'm Still Here (60)** (JBerry) **2-9-0** KDarley(7) (w ldrs: rdn 2f out: sn wl outpcd) ....................2½ **6** 50/1 41 15
4454[5] **Cimmerian** (MrsJRRamsden) **2-8-9** JFortune(2) (hld up: bhd & drvn along ½-wy: kpt on appr fnl f: n.d) ........nk **7** 33/1 35 9
4383[10] **Freedom of Troy** (JLEyre) **2-9-0** RLappin(8) (sn bhd) ....................3½ **8** 100/1 30 4
4469[4] **Sang d'Antibes (FR)** (DJSCosgrove) **2-8-9** JCarroll(5) (led tl over 3f out: wknd qckly 2f out: sn wl bhd)........20 **9** 9/1[3] — —
(SP 126.6%) **9 Rn**

**1m 15.0** (4.10) CSF £7.13 TOTE £2.40: £2.00 £1.00 £3.30 (£6.80) Trio £17.70 OWNER Al Muallim Partnership (NEWMARKET) BRED James T. Gottwald

**4547 Al Muallim (USA)**, a bonny little colt, showed a good, fluent action going down. Sticking on strongly, he landed something of a gamble with a fraction in hand at the line. (6/4: op 7/2)
**4318 Erosion (IRE)**, who is only small, looked very fit. Showing a pronounced knee-action going down, he tended to come off a straight line under strong pressure but, in the end, the winner was simply too good. (3/1)
**Janie's Boy**, having his third outing for his third trainer, is small and looked as if the outing was needed. The only one to stick on the far side, he stuck to his guns and stayed on in the final furlong. On his appearance, there ought to be improvement in him. (20/1)
**4593 Plaisir d'Amour (IRE)** looked fit, but is only moderate if this is the best she can do. (6/4: 4/5-13/8)
**Fearless Sioux**, a narrow, backward newcomer, shaped nicely after missing the break. There ought to be improvement in her. (100/1)

## 4752 BROWNE, SMITH, BAKER & PARTNERS RATING RELATED MAIDEN STKS (0-65) (3-Y.O) (Class F)
4-25 (4-26) **1m 3f 214y** £3,015.00 (£840.00: £405.00) Stalls: Low GOING: 0.05 sec per fur (G)

SP RR SF
4353[3] **Laazim Afooz (65)** (RTPhillips) **3-8-12** RPerham(11) (lw: mde all: drew clr 2f out: readily) ....................— **1** 11/4[1] 64 37
4340[3] **Totally Yours (IRE) (36)** (MRChannon) **3-8-4**(5) PPMurphy(6) (gd hdwy over 5f out: chsd wnr over 1f out: kpt on: no imp) ....................1¾ **2** 25/1 59 32
4496[4] **Basood (USA) (54)** (SPCWoods) **3-8-2b[1](7)** CWebb(4) (bhd: hmpd 8f out: gd hdwy on outside over 4f out: styd on fnl 2f: nvr nr to chal) ....................2½ **3** 12/1 55 28
4496[2] **Soldier Mak (60)** (AHide) **3-8-12** GBardwell(9) (lw: a chsng ldrs: drvn along over 3f out: one pce) ....................3 **4** 11/4[1] 54 27
4227[9] **Noir Esprit (41)** (JMCarr) **3-8-12b[1]** LCharnock(1) (a chsng ldrs: one pce fnl 2f) ....................4 **5** 33/1 49 22
4362[4] **Wybara (65)** (JHMGosden) **3-8-9** GHind(10) (chsd ldrs: drvn along 4f out: one pce whn n.m.r over 1f out: eased) ....................1½ **6** 10/1[3] 44 17
4591[13] **Sing And Dance (47)** (EWeymes) **3-8-9** GDuffield(14) (in tch: drvn along & outpcd 4f out: kpt on fnl 2f)........2½ **7** 10/1[3] 41 14
4496[13] **Golden Fawn (58)** (LadyHerries) **3-8-9** JQuinn(5) (lw: mid div: drvn along & outpcd over 3f out: n.d after) ....2½ **8** 10/1[3] 37 10
4474[7] **Philgem (20)** (CWFairhurst) **3-8-9** NKennedy(3) (chsd ldrs tl lost pl 4f out: n.d after) ....................1¼ **9** 66/1 36 9
4227[10] **Nexsis Star (42)** (MrsSJSmith) **3-8-7**(5) PRoberts(13) (s.i.s: wnt prom 7f out: sn drvn along: lost pl over 3f out) ....................7 **10** 66/1 29 2
4437[4] **Dino's Mistral (40)** (FHLee) **3-8-12** RLappin(7) (bhd: hmpd 8f out: sme hdwy 6f out: sn lost pl) ....................½ **11** 33/1 29 2
4437[3] **Sylvella (50)** (MAJarvis) **3-8-9** PBloomfield(15) (chsd ldrs tl wknd qckly over 4f out: sn bhd) ....................16 **12** 14/1 4 —
3780[11] **Craigmore Magic (USA) (40)** (MissMKMilligan) **3-8-12b[1]** KDarley(2) (bhd whn hmpd 8f out: sme hdwy 5f out: sn wknd) ....................12 **13** 50/1 — —
*2751[4]* **Indiphar (46)** (FHLee) **3-8-9** JCarroll(12) (t.o fnl 3f) ....................hd **14** 16/1 — —
4427[8] **Not Quite Grey (65)** (KMcAuliffe) **3-8-12v[1]** JFEgan(8) (chsd ldrs tl wknd qckly 6f out: t.o 3f out) ....................9 **15** 9/1[2] — —
(SP 125.5%) **15 Rn**

**2m 40.9** (9.50) CSF £64.68 TOTE £4.60: £1.80 £4.30 £3.10 (£80.10) Trio £406.40; £343.51 to Newmarket 19/10/96 OWNER Sheikh Ahmed Al Maktoum (LAMBOURN) BRED Sheikh Ahmed bin Rashid al Maktoum

**4353 Laazim Afooz**, who showed a good action going to post, set out to make this a test of stamina and, in the end, took a poor race in good style. (11/4)
**4340 Totally Yours (IRE)**, third in a seller last time, moved into second place over a furlong out but, tending to hang in behind, was never making any impression. (25/1)
**4496 Basood (USA)**, closely matched with Soldier Mak on Brighton form, was behind when hampered on the paddock bend. Sticking on under pressure in the final two furlongs, this looked an improved effort. (12/1: op 8/1)
**4496 Soldier Mak** has had plenty of chances and had no excuse whatsoever here. (11/4: 2/1-3/1)
**4083 Wybara** looked to meet trouble twice in the home straight, but she was probably coming off a true line and her rider was probably just holding her together. She looks very moderate indeed. (10/1)

## 4753 HORNBY CASTLE H'CAP (0-75) (3-Y.O+) (Class D)
5-00 (5-02) **1m 3f 214y** £4,662.50 (£1,400.00: £675.00: £312.50) Stalls: Low GOING: 0.05 sec per fur (G)

SP RR SF
4307[7] **Typhoon Eight (IRE) (66)** (BWHills) **4-9-6** JCarroll(12) (b.hind: trckd ldrs: led over 3f out: jst hld on) ............— **1** 14/1 77 45
4427[D] **Almuhtaram (65)** (GLewis) **4-9-2b**(3) AWhelan(1) (trckd ldrs: n.m.r 3f out: styd on wl fnl f: jst failed) ...............nk **2** 7/1[2] 76 44
4365[10] **Rasayel (USA) (60)** (PDEvans) **6-9-0** JFEgan(2) (s.i.s: hld up: hdwy & n.m.r over 2f out: nt clr run over 1f out: styd on wl) ....................1¼ **3** 20/1 69 37
4320* **Tessajoe (74)** (MJCamacho) **4-10-0** LCharnock(10) (b.hind: lw: hld up: wnt prom 6f out: effrt over 3f out: wknd fnl f) ....................5 **4** 100/30[1] 76 44
*4574** **All On (42)** (JHetherton) **5-7-10** GBardwell(9) (bhd & drvn along 7f out: rdn over 3f out: styd on fnl 2f: nvr nr to chal) ....................1¼ **5** 100/30[1] 43 11
4626[4] **Mad Militant (IRE) (55)** (AStreeter) **7-8-9** JQuinn(13) (lw: hld up: gd hdwy over 2f out: sn chsng ldrs: wknd over 1f out) ....................2½ **6** 9/1[3] 52 20
4102[4] **Sea God (42)** (MCChapman) **5-7-10** FNorton(4) (chsd ldrs: n.m.r & lost pl over 2f out: kpt on) ....................2½ **7** 20/1 36 4
4484[2] **Askern (60)** (DHaydnJones) **5-9-0** DRMcCabe(7) (lw: bhd: sme hdwy u.p 2f out: n.d) ....................5 **8** 100/30[1] 47 15
4615[11] **Blackpatch Hill (68)** (NTinkler) **7-9-8b** KimTinkler(11) (led tl over 3f out: sn wl outpcd) ....................6 **9** 66/1 47 15
4587[5] **Colosse (49)** (JLEyre) **4-8-3** RLappin(8) (lw: trckd ldrs: effrt over 2f out: sn wknd) ....................1½ **10** 7/1[2] 26 —
3492[5] **Shamokin (43)** (FWatson) **4-7-11** NKennedy(5) (hld up & plld hrd: bhd fnl 6f: t.o) ....................dist **11** 100/1 — —
4042[11] **Fairy Highlands (IRE) (50)** (JSHaldane) **3-7-6**(5) PFessey(6) (chsd ldrs: wkng whn n.m.r over 2f out: sn bhd: t.o) ....................5 **12** 25/1 — —
4456[5] **Kass Alhawa (70)** (DWChapman) **3-9-3** ACulhane(3) (sn bhd: t.o 3f out: fin lame) ....................18 **13** 66/1 — —
(SP 128.2%) **13 Rn**

**2m 40.9** (9.50) CSF £106.83 CT £1,829.68 TOTE £16.20: £3.00 £3.10 £4.80 (£41.80) Trio £97.60 OWNER Mr Michael Siu (LAMBOURN) BRED Barronstown Stud and Ron Con Ltd
LONG HANDICAP All On 7-7
WEIGHT FOR AGE 3yo-7lb

**OFFICIAL EXPLANATION Askern: the trainer reported that the gelding needs to race prominently and lost interest after missing the break. Kass Alhawa: the jockey reported him to be moving badly throughout the race. The trainer added that the colt was lame behind after the race.**

**1450 Typhoon Eight (IRE)**, who needed the run last time, his first outing for over two months, kicked on off the bend and poached just sufficient lead to hang on. (14/1)

**4427 Almuhtaram**, having his first outing for his new trainer, was taken gently to post. Short of room when scrimmaging took place turning in, he stayed on well under pressure in the final furlong, but needed three more strides. He certainly stayed the trip. (7/1)

**4000 Rasayel (USA)**, fresh and well beforehand, was possibly the unlucky one. Short of room twice in the straight, she was putting in some good work in the final furlong, but it was just too late. (20/1)

**4320* Tessajoe**, from a 3lb higher mark, went in pursuit of the winner once in line for home, but had bellows to mend entering the final furlong. (100/30)

**4574* All On** was reportedly short of work after a foot injury. Behind and pushed along before halfway, she stayed on when it was all over. The outing should put her spot on and, though better on the All-Weather, there is still time for her to win on turf. (100/30)

**4626 Mad Militant (IRE)** looked a real danger at one stage, but stopped in a matter of strides coming to the final furlong. (9/1)

## 4754 E.B.F. RIPLEY MAIDEN STKS (II) (2-Y.O) (Class D)

5-30 (5-31) **5f 212y** £3,242.50 (£970.00: £465.00: £212.50) Stalls: High GOING: 0.05 sec per fur (G)

| | | | | SP | RR | SF |
|---|---|---|---|---|---|---|
| 4570[6] | **Lady Diesis (USA)** (BWHills) **2-8-9** JCarroll(5) (lw: trckd ldrs gng wl: led on bit over 3f out: v.easily) | — | 1 | 4/11[1] | 63+ | 34 |
| 4578[10] | **Fullopep** (MrsMReveley) **2-9-0** KDarley(4) (bit bkwd: trckd ldrs: outpcd & drvn along over 3f out: styd on fnl f: no ch w wnr) | 3 | 2 | 12/1[3] | 60 | 31 |
| 4475[8] | **Dominant Air** (SirMarkPrescott) **2-9-0** GDuffield(1) (s.i.s: hdwy to ld over 4f out: hdd over 3f out: one pce) | ¾ | 3 | 25/1 | 58 | 29 |
| 3593[13] | **Karawan** (JHMGosden) **2-8-9** GHind(8) (w ldrs: rdn over 1f out: eased towards fin) | 2 | 4 | 3/1[2] | 48 | 19 |
| 4618[14] | **Mon Performer** (MJCamacho) **2-9-0** LCharnock(6) (outpcd ½-wy: sn bhd) | 11 | 5 | 66/1 | 23 | — |
| | **Euroquest** (DNicholls) **2-9-0** AlexGreaves(7) (wl grwn: scope: bit bkwd: sn outpcd & bhd) | 1¼ | 6 | 50/1 | 20 | — |
| 4228[13] | **Il Principe (IRE)** (JohnBerry) **2-9-0** TWilliams(3) (led over 1f: lost pl over 3f out) | 1¾ | 7 | 33/1 | 15 | — |
| | **Whitegate's Son** (BEllison) **2-9-0** JQuinn(2) (unf: bkwd: s.i.s: a bhd) | 7 | 8 | 150/1 | — | — |
| | | | | (SP 116.9%) | | **8 Rn** |

**1m 15.4** (4.50) CSF £6.17 TOTE £1.30: £1.00 £4.50 £4.90 (£8.60) OWNER Mr Peter Williams (LAMBOURN) BRED Romany Investments

**4570 Lady Diesis (USA)** looked to have been found an easy opening and, never out of third gear, all her rider had to do in the last two furlongs was to look round for non-existent dangers. (4/11)

**Fullopep**, who showed plenty of knee-action going down, is a grand sort, but does not yet look fully fit. Badly tapped for toe turning in, he stayed on inside the last, and he is capable of better over further. (12/1)

**4228 Dominant Air**, who showed a very scratchy action going down. proved very one-paced. (25/1)

**Karawan**, very keen going to post, was never racing on an even keel, but would have finished a length nearer the third but for being eased off near the line. (3/1: op 7/4)

T/Plpt: £1,309.10 (10.08 Tckts). T/Qdpt: £89.60 (10.78 Tckts). WG

# 4714-NEWMARKET (R-H) (Good)

## Friday October 18th

WEATHER: overcast WIND: fresh across

## 4755 NEWMARKET CHALLENGE CUP MAIDEN STKS (2-Y.O) (Class G)

1-30 (1-30) **7f (Rowley)** Stalls: Centre GOING minus 0.07 sec per fur (G)

| | | | | SP | RR | SF |
|---|---|---|---|---|---|---|
| | **Squeak** (JHMGosden) **2-8-9** LDettori(1) (lt-f: scope: led 3f: led over 2f out: pushed out) | — | 1 | 2/5[1] | 73+ | 24 |
| | **Flowing Fortune** (EALDunlop) **2-9-0** KFallon(3) (w'like: scope: cl up: led 4f out tl over 2f out: wknd) | 8 | 2 | 7/2[2] | 60 t | 11 |
| | **Kristopher** (JWHills) **2-9-0** MHills(2) (wl grwn: bkwd: dwlt: outpcd & lost tch fr ½-wy) | 9 | 3 | 7/1[3] | 39 t | — |
| | | | | (SP 106.2%) | | **3 Rn** |

**1m 29.91** (5.41) CSF £1.97 TOTE £1.40 (£1.60) OWNER Lord Hartington (NEWMARKET) BRED Side Hill Stud

**Squeak**, a weak-looking individual, did the job required well, but the opposition was not up to much, and her rider left nothing to chance, keeping her going all the way to the line. (2/5)

**Flowing Fortune** gave the winner a fright halfway through the race, but then tied up badly as though well in need of this. (7/2: 6/4-4/1)

**Kristopher**, a heavily-made, backward sort, was never going at any stage. (7/1: 3/1-15/2)

## 4756 E.B.F. TRAVIS PERKINS MAIDEN STKS (2-Y.O) (Class D)

2-00 (2-01) **6f (Rowley)** £5,890.50 (£1,764.00: £847.00: £388.50) Stalls: Centre GOING: minus 0.07 sec per fur (G)

| | | | | SP | RR | SF |
|---|---|---|---|---|---|---|
| | **Baked Alaska** (ACStewart) **2-8-9** DHarrison(3) (w'like: scope: lw: mid div: hdwy 2f out: led ins fnl f: edgd rt & r.o) | — | 1 | 33/1 | 89+ | 52 |
| | **Miss Sancerre** (GWragg) **2-8-9** RCochrane(4) (lengthy: unf: scope: dwlt: hdwy over 2f out: ev ch ins fnl f: kpt on) | 1 | 2 | 20/1 | 86+ | 49 |
| 4502[3] | **Kumait (USA) (88)** (SbinSuroor) **2-9-0** LDettori(10) (lw: trckd ldrs: effrt 2f out: kpt on one pce fnl f) | 1¾ | 3 | 7/1[2] | 87 | 50 |
| 4383[3] | **Tayseer (USA)** (EALDunlop) **2-9-0** KFallon(15) (chsd ldrs: hdwy over 1f out: kpt on u.p) | ½ | 4 | 15/2[3] | 85 | 48 |
| 4570[4] | **Polish Romance (USA)** (MRStoute) **2-8-9** WRSwinburn(22) (b.nr hind: lw: led tl hdd & no ex ins fnl f) | hd | 5 | 11/4[1] | 80 | 43 |
| 4475[2] | **Tigrello** (GLewis) **2-9-0** PatEddery(6) (lw: cl up: outpcd whn sltly hmpd appr fnl f: no ex) | 1½ | 6 | 8/1 | 81 | 44 |
| | **Miss Golden Sands** (GWragg) **2-8-9** MHills(7) (cmpt: prom: effrt 2f out: nt qckn) | nk | 7 | 7/1[2] | 75 | 38 |
| 4514[13] | **Kafil (USA)** (HThomsonJones) **2-9-0** RHills(8) (b: in tch: styd on fnl 2f: no imp) | nk | 8 | 20/1 | 80 | 43 |
| 4488[23] | **Midnight Shift (IRE)** (RGuest) **2-8-9** JReid(5) (chsd ldrs: effrt 2f out: nt qckn) | ½ | 9 | 50/1 | 73 | 36 |
| 4330[14] | **Rotor Man (IRE)** (JDBethell) **2-9-0** GCarter(18) (chsd ldrs: rdn & no imp fnl 2f) | 2 | 10 | 50/1 | 73 | 36 |
| | **Tithcar** (BHanbury) **2-8-9** WRyan(11) (w'like: chsd ldrs tl wknd appr fnl f) | ½ | 11 | 14/1 | 67 | 30 |
| 2184[6] | **Kweilo** (JWPayne) **2-9-0** MFenton(14) (lw: dwlt: stdy hdwy 2f out: nvr plcd to chal) | 1½ | 12 | 50/1 | 68+ | 31 |
| 4380[6] | **Junie (IRE)** (TGMills) **2-8-9** TQuinn(12) (in tch: sn drvn along: nvr able to chal) | 1 | 13 | 33/1 | 60 | 23 |
| | **Wintered Out** (GLMoore) **2-8-9** SWhitworth(2) (neat: bhd: styd on fnl 2f: n.d) | ½ | 14 | 50/1 | 59 | 22 |
| | **Alyportent** (WJHaggas) **2-9-0** MRoberts(13) (neat: dwlt: hdwy over 2f out: hung rt & n.d) | hd | 15 | 25/1 | 63 | 26 |
| | **Double-O** (WJarvis) **2-9-0** SSanders(1) (leggy: scope: sn pushed along: n.d) | 3 | 16 | 33/1 | 55 | 18 |

| | Horse | Dist | Pos | SP | RR | SF |
|---|---|---|---|---|---|---|
| 2195[8] | **Secret Ballot (IRE)** (RHannon) **2-9-0** RHughes(20) (bkwd: outpcd & bhd fr ½-wy) | ½ | **17** | 33/1 | 54 | 17 |
| | **Flying Thatch (IRE)** (RHannon) **2-9-0** DaneO'Neill(16) (w'like: scope: bkwd: sn outpcd) | ¾ | **18** | 20/1 | 52 | 15 |
| | **Julia's Relative** (RGuest) **2-8-9** JFanning(19) (b: neat: s.i.s: a bhd) | hd | **19** | 50/1 | 47 | 10 |
| | **Nor-Do-I** (JMPEustace) **2-9-0** MRimmer(9) (w'like: prom tl wknd 2f out) | ½ | **20** | 25/1 | 50 | 13 |
| | **First Chance (IRE)** (DRCElsworth) **2-8-9** BDoyle(21) (leggy: scope: a rr div) | 2½ | **21** | 33/1 | 39 | 2 |
| | **Water Garden** (GWragg) **2-9-0** AClark(17) (wl grwn: bkwd: s.s: a bhd) | 2 | **22** | 33/1 | 38 | 1 |

(SP 130.6%) **22 Rn**

**1m 14.3** (2.50) CSF £524.60 TOTE £54.00: £10.20 £8.30 £2.20 (£257.00) Trio £617.20; £791.13 to Newmarket 19/10/96 OWNER Cliveden Stud (NEWMARKET) BRED Cliveden Stud Ltd

STEWARDS' ENQUIRY Fenton susp. 28/10-1/11/96 (failure to obtain best possible placing). Payne fined £400 under Rule 51(ii) (schooling in public)

**Baked Alaska** is a decent type and won this well, despite showing signs of greenness. There would seem to be plenty of improvement in her. (33/1)

**Miss Sancerre**, a long, lean individual, showed plenty here after a poor start and, as she strengthens, there should be better things to come. (20/1)

**4502 Kumait (USA)** again had his chances but, when it came down to a struggle, he was yet again found wanting. (7/1)

**4383 Tayseer (USA)** was really taught his job here, and he kept responding, but was never quick enough to make it. A bit further should help. (15/2)

**4570 Polish Romance (USA)** ran just the opposite to last time, going off in front here, but was picked off in the closing stages for a disappointing effort. (11/4: op 6/4)

**4475 Tigrello**, from a yard out of form, ran well, but was done with when short of room in the closing stages. (8/1: 6/1-9/1)

**Miss Golden Sands** got a bit warm beforehand, but still ran well and looks the type to benefit from the experience. (7/1)

**Kafil (USA)**, a really nice type who is still learning, gave the impression that time will bring plenty of improvement. (20/1)

**Tithcar** (14/1: 12/1-20/1)

**Kweilo**, a big individual, had what can only be described as an educational here. This should stand him in good stead. (50/1)

## 4757 BARING INTERNATIONAL DARLEY STKS (Listed) (3-Y.O+) (Class A)

2-35 (2-35) **1m 1f (Rowley)** £11,366.20 (£4,205.80: £2,017.90: £824.50: £327.25: £128.35) Stalls: Centre GOING minus 0.07 sec per fur (G)

| | Horse | Dist | Pos | SP | RR | SF |
|---|---|---|---|---|---|---|
| 4568[7] | **Tarawa (IRE) (102)** (NACallaghan) **4-9-0** RHughes(5) (lw: hld up: smooth hdwy 3f out: led ins fnl f: shkn up & r.o) | — | **1** | 9/2[2] | 116 | 85 |
| 4479[2] | **Nijo (102)** (DRLoder) **5-9-0** LDettori(4) (led: qcknd 3f out: hdd & no ex ins fnl f) | 2½ | **2** | 20/1 | 112 | 81 |
| 4177* | **Forest Buck (USA)** (HRACecil) **3-8-10** PatEddery(2) (cl up: outpcd over 2f out: kpt on u.p) | 1 | **3** | 2/1[1] | 110 | 75 |
| 4409a[11] | **Blomberg (IRE) (103)** (JRFanshawe) **4-9-7** DHarrison(3) (in tch: pushed along 4f out: kpt on: no imp) | 2 | **4** | 25/1 | 113 | 82 |
| 4162a[3] | **Winter Romance (102)** (EALDunlop) **3-8-10** KFallon(6) (bhd: pushed along 4f out: hdwy 2f out: styd on) | s.h | **5** | 8/1 | 106 | 71 |
| 4663a[6] | **Hagwah (USA) (106)** (BHanbury) **4-8-13** WRyan(8) (chsd ldrs: rdn over 2f out: r.o one pce) | nk | **6** | 15/2[3] | 105 | 74 |
| 4520[3] | **Tamnia (102)** (JLDunlop) **3-8-5** TQuinn(9) (hld up: effrt 3f out: n.d) | 8 | **7** | 9/1 | 86 | 51 |
| 4313[3] | **Behaviour (106)** (MrsJCecil) **4-9-0** RHills(1) (chsd ldrs tl wknd fnl 3f) | ¾ | **8** | 14/1 | 90 | 59 |
| 4410a[5] | **Beneficial** (GWragg) **6-9-0** MHills(7) (lw: prom tl wknd wl over 2f out) | 2½ | **9** | 14/1 | 86 | 55 |
| 696* | **Lionize (USA)** (PWChapple-Hyam) **3-8-10** JReid(10) (bhd: rdn 3f out: n.d) | s.h | **10** | 12/1 | 86 | 51 |

(SP 114.0%) **10 Rn**

**1m 51.91** (0.91) CSF £73.34 TOTE £6.30: £1.80 £2.00 £1.70 (£46.90) Trio £46.40 OWNER Mrs J. Callaghan (NEWMARKET) BRED Patrick Eddery Ltd

WEIGHT FOR AGE 3yo-4lb

**4568 Tarawa (IRE)**, drawn on the wrong side in the Cambridgeshire, landed a touch here in good style, and there were never any doubts about the result from some way out. (9/2)

**4479 Nijo**, without the headgear this time, put up a decent show, but was comfortably picked off inside the last furlong. (20/1)

**4177* Forest Buck (USA)**, dropped back in trip here, got outpaced at a vital stage, but was staying on at the end to show that, over further, he will return to form. (2/1)

**4409a Blomberg (IRE)** is certainly a hard ride and, despite being off the bit a long way out, he kept struggling on, although always in vain. (25/1)

**4162a Winter Romance** had the overnight rain required, but still looked very slow here, and it was only his rider's persistence that kept him going. It would appear that even softer ground is needed. (8/1)

**4663a Hagwah (USA)** ran a bit flat here, but she has had some hard races of late and they may have taken their toll. (15/2)

**4313 Behaviour** (14/1: 10/1-16/1)

**696* Lionize (USA)** (12/1: 8/1-14/1)

## 4758 ROCKFEL STKS (Gp 3) (2-Y.O F) (Class A)

3-05 (3-06) **7f (Rowley)** £15,700.00 (£5,800.00: £2,775.00: £1,125.00: £437.50: £162.50) Stalls: Centre GOING minus 0.07 sec per fur (G)

| | Horse | Dist | Pos | SP | RR | SF |
|---|---|---|---|---|---|---|
| 4491[2] | **Moonlight Paradise (USA) (100)** (SbinSuroor) **2-8-12** LDettori(3) (lw: trckd clr ldr: led on bit 2f out: shkn up & r.o strly) | — | **1** | 11/8[1] | 107+ | 70 |
| 4491[4] | **Dazzle (100)** (MRStoute) **2-9-0** WRSwinburn(5) (lw: hld up: stdy hdwy to chal 2f out: rdn & one pce) | 2½ | **2** | 2/1[2] | 103 | 66 |
| 4566* | **Serenity (90)** (JRFanshawe) **2-8-9** DHarrison(4) (lw: hld up centre: swtchd rt after 2½f: hdwy 3f out: styd on: nvr able to chal) | 1¾ | **3** | 8/1 | 94 | 57 |
| 4328[5] | **Sambac (USA) (100)** (HRACecil) **2-8-9** WRyan(2) (h.d.w: hld up: swtchd rt after 2½f: effrt & prom over 2f out: no imp) | 1½ | **4** | 12/1 | 91 | 54 |
| 2051[7] | **More Silver (USA)** (PFICole) **2-8-9** TQuinn(6) (plld hrd: led & sn clr: hdd 2f out: sn btn) | 3 | **5** | 7/1[3] | 84 | 47 |
| 3990[7] | **Eye Shadow (88)** (BJMeehan) **2-8-9** BDoyle(1) (racd centre: outpcd & lost tch over 2f out: styd on nr fin) | 1 | **6** | 66/1 | 82? | 45 |

(SP 108.2%) **6 Rn**

**1m 26.26** (1.76) CSF £4.20 TOTE £2.40: £1.20 £1.30 (£1.90) OWNER Godolphin (NEWMARKET) BRED Allen E. Paulson

**4491 Moonlight Paradise (USA)** really enjoyed the longer trip and, always going well, won in most emphatic style. She is obviously still improving. (11/8)

**4491 Dazzle**, who needed two attendants in the paddock, sat on the winner's heels throughout and, if anything, saw too much daylight too soon, and was well outclassed in the final furlong. She seems much better suited when coming from behind, and no doubt Fallon will be receiving written apologies from all and sundry. (2/1: 6/4-9/4)

**4566* Serenity** had two handlers in the paddock and looked very much on edge, but ran really well in this company without offering a live threat. She basically lacks substance, but certainly has an engine. (8/1)

**4328 Sambac (USA)**, whose rider seemed unsure about where to race, eventually switched to the rail and, off the bit some way out, had her limitations exposed. (12/1)
**2051 More Silver (USA)**, very fresh after her lay-off, virtually took charge and went clear early on, but not surprisingly had run herself out with two furlongs left. This is best ignored. (7/1)
**3707 Eye Shadow**, outclassed here, ran as though longer trips will bring out the best in her. (66/1)

## 4759 DEWHURST STKS (Gp 1) (2-Y.O C & F) (Class A)

3-40 (3-41) **7f (Rowley)** £83,535.00 (£31,065.00: £15,032.50: £6,287.50: £2,643.75: £1,186.25) Stalls: Centre GOING minus 0.07 sec per fur (G)

| Form | Horse / Trainer / Jockey / Comment | Dist | Pos | SP | RR | SF |
|---|---|---|---|---|---|---|
| 4519[3] | **In Command (IRE) (100)** (BWHills) **2-9-0** MHills(2) (a.p: led over 1f out: all out) | — | **1** | 10/1 | 106 | 76 |
| 3245* | **Musical Pursuit** (MHTompkins) **2-9-0** PatEddery(7) (led tl over 2f out: sn outpcd: styd on gamely fnl f: jst failed) | hd | **2** | 13/2 | 106 | 76 |
| 4462[6] | **Air Express (IRE) (100)** (CEBrittain) **2-9-0** BDoyle(6) (lw: cl up: outpcd wl over 1f out: styd on gamely fnl f) | nk | **3** | 50/1 | 105 | 75 |
| 4519* | **Bahamian Bounty** (DRLoder) **2-9-0** LDettori(3) (hld up: effrt & nt clr run wl over 1f out: swtchd lft & styd on one pce) | 1¼ | **4** | 7/2[1] | 102 | 72 |
| 4461* | **Kahal** (EALDunlop) **2-9-0** RHills(4) (lw: w ldr: led over 2f out tl over 1f out: one pce) | nk | **5** | 7/2[1] | 102 | 72 |
| 4398a* | **Desert King (IRE)** (APO'Brien,Ireland) **2-9-0** CRoche(8) (gd sort: cmpt: lw: in tch: outpcd ½-wy: sn lost pl: styd on u.p fnl f) | nk | **6** | 4/1[2] | 101 | 71 |
| 4294a[2] | **The West (USA)** (PFICole) **2-9-0** TQuinn(1) (lw: plld hrd early: effrt over 2f out: no imp whn hmpd appr fnl f) | ½ | **7** | 9/2[3] | 100 | 70 |
| 4544* | **Wind Cheetah (USA)** (MRStoute) **2-9-0** MJKinane(5) (hld up: outpcd ½-wy: sn lost tch: styd on fnl f) | 1½ | **8** | 33/1 | 96? | 66 |

(SP 110.0%) **8 Rn**

**1m 25.93** (1.43) CSF £63.33 TOTE £10.60: £1.40 £2.30 £4.70 (£71.50) OWNER Maktoum Al Maktoum (LAMBOURN) BRED Gainsborough Stud Management Ltd

**4519 In Command (IRE)** showed what a tough customer he is, but he will need to improve over the winter to take a serious hand in next year's Classics. (10/1)
**3245* Musical Pursuit** is improving physically and, showing fine courage here, should continue on the upgrade as he goes over further. (13/2)
**4462 Air Express (IRE)** ran really well and kept fighting back when all looked lost but, like several in the race, just seemed short of a change of speed. (50/1)
**4519* Bahamian Bounty** looked to be travelling well, but was short of room over a furlong out and, when switched, failed to quicken up. It would seem that he is just a sprinter. (7/2: 2/1-4/1)
**4461* Kahal**, a most imposing individual, was facing his stiffest task to date here, but he basically proved short of a turn of foot. To give him the benefit, he may need time to strengthen to his frame. (7/2: op 9/4)
**4398a* Desert King (IRE)** ran as though longer trips or much easier ground is a must for him. (4/1)
**4294a The West (USA)**, a big, long-striding individual, refused to settle early on and beat himself. (9/2)
**4544* Wind Cheetah (USA)**, who had been sweating when brought into the paddock, went freely to post and never got into the race. (33/1)

## 4760 NGK SPARK PLUGS NURSERY H'CAP (2-Y.O) (Class C)

4-15 (4-16) **1m (Rowley)** £6,576.00 (£1,968.00: £944.00: £432.00) Stalls: Centre GOING minus 0.07 sec per fur (G)

| Form | Horse / Trainer / Jockey / Comment | Dist | Pos | SP | RR | SF |
|---|---|---|---|---|---|---|
| 4507* | **Bold Words (CAN) (85)** (EALDunlop) **2-9-5** MHills(1) (disp ld over 6f: rallied to ld ins fnl f: r.o) | — | **1** | 8/1[2] | 91 | 60 |
| 4501* | **Julietta Mia (USA) (68)** (BWHills) **2-8-2** BDoyle(15) (trckd ldrs: led wl over 1f out: put hd in air & hung lft: hdd ins fnl f: kpt on) | ½ | **2** | 14/1 | 73 | 42 |
| 4330[17] | **Tom Tailor (GER) (72)** (DRCElsworth) **2-8-6** DHarrison(10) (bhd tl styd on strly fnl 2f: nrst fin) | 2 | **3** | 16/1 | 73 | 42 |
| 4490[5] | **Madame Chinnery (77)** (JMPEustace) **2-8-11** RCochrane(2) (disp ld over 6f: kpt on same pce) | nk | **4** | 8/1[2] | 77 | 46 |
| 4514[8] | **Tough Act (82)** (GHarwood) **2-9-2** AClark(9) (lw: chsd ldrs: outpcd over 2f out: kpt on fnl f) | hd | **5** | 12/1 | 82 | 51 |
| 4242[9] | **Gentleman's Word (USA) (73)** (MRStoute) **2-8-7v[1]** MJKinane(8) (in tch: hdwy u.p over 1f out: nt pce to chal) | ½ | **6** | 11/1 | 72 | 41 |
| 4625* | **Love Has No Pride (USA) (81)** (RHannon) **2-9-1** 5x DaneO'Neill(13) (hld up: hdwy ½-wy: ev ch & rdn over 2f out: wknd over 1f out) | 1¼ | **7** | 7/2[1] | 78 | 47 |
| 4204[5] | **Rasmussen (IRE) (72)** (JHMGosden) **2-8-6** LDettori(7) (b.hind: hld up: effrt 3f out: styd on: no imp after) | ½ | **8** | 11/1 | 68 | 37 |
| 4602[3] | **Hello Dolly (IRE) (63)** (KRBurke) **2-7-11** DeclanO'Shea(11) (lw: in tch: rdn over 2f out: no imp) | 1 | **9** | 14/1 | 57 | 26 |
| 4100[11] | **Spaniard's Mount (66)** (MHTompkins) **2-7-7**(7) RMullen(18) (outpcd & bhd tl styd on fnl f) | nk | **10** | 20/1 | 59 | 28 |
| 4494[5] | **Supply And Demand (87)** (GLMoore) **2-9-7** SWhitworth(4) (in tch: effrt 2f out: sn wknd) | nk | **11** | 25/1 | 80 | 49 |
| 4310* | **Double Flight (78)** (MJohnston) **2-8-12** MRoberts(12) (lw: nvr nr ldrs) | ½ | **12** | 12/1 | 70 | 39 |
| 4384[3] | **Ikatania (78)** (JLDunlop) **2-8-12** PatEddery(14) (chsd ldrs 6f: wknd) | s.h | **13** | 10/1[3] | 69 | 38 |
| 4602* | **Heart Full of Soul (80)** (PFICole) **2-9-0** 5x TQuinn(16) (in tch tl outpcd 3f out: n.d after) | 2 | **14** | 12/1 | 67 | 36 |
| 3764* | **Happy Go Lucky (84)** (RJO'Sullivan) **2-9-4** SSanders(17) (cl up tl wknd 2f out) | 1¾ | **15** | 10/1[3] | 68 | 37 |
| 4625[8] | **Northern Sun (83)** (TGMills) **2-9-3** WRyan(5) (chsd ldrs 5f) | 1½ | **16** | 25/1 | 64 | 33 |
| 4175[9] | **Ibin St James (77)** (JDBethell) **2-8-11** GCarter(3) (a outpcd & bhd) | 3 | **17** | 33/1 | 52 | 21 |

(SP 137.0%) **17 Rn**

**1m 40.88** (3.58) CSF £115.50 CT £1,701.17 TOTE £9.40: £2.10 £5.10 £6.30 £2.20 (£182.10) Trio £1,800.60; £1,648.51 to Newmarket 19/10/96 OWNER Maktoum Al Maktoum (NEWMARKET) BRED Crow's Nest & Hermitage Farm

**4507* Bold Words (CAN)** stays particularly well and is tough, and that won him the day. (8/1: 7/1-12/1)
**4501* Julietta Mia (USA)** has plenty of ability, but is a real character and, if all her efforts can be channelled into racing, she will improve a lot. (14/1)
**3695 Tom Tailor (GER)** obviously appreciated this step up in trip, as he was eating up the ground in the closing stages. (16/1)
**4490 Madame Chinnery** is a tough sort who stays really well, but was just tapped for speed in the closing stages. (8/1)
**4233 Tough Act** needs these longer trips, and stayed on after looking in trouble two furlongs out. His turn should come. (12/1: 8/1-14/1)
**3919 Gentleman's Word (USA)**, trying a longer trip and wearing a visor, struggled on, but was never doing things fast enough to have a chance. There is certainly more ability there if he can be persuaded. (11/1: 8/1-12/1)
**4625* Love Has No Pride (USA)** had his chance but, when asked for an effort two furlongs out, his response was very disappointing. (7/2)
**3044 Spaniard's Mount** either needs further of softer ground, as the race was over when he finally picked up. (20/1)

## 4761 EQUITY FINANCIAL COLLECTIONS H'CAP (0-95) (3-Y.O) (Class C)

4-50 (4-50) **1m 6f (Rowley)** £5,900.00 (£1,760.00: £840.00: £380.00) Stalls: High GOING minus 0.07 sec per fur (G)

| Form | Horse / Trainer / Jockey / Comment | Dist | Pos | SP | RR | SF |
|---|---|---|---|---|---|---|
| 3935* | **Flamands (IRE) (83)** (LMCumani) **3-8-9** LDettori(3) (lw: trckd ldrs: stdy hdwy 3f out: led ins fnl f: pushed along & r.o) | — | **1** | 11/4[1] | 96 | 55 |

4353* **Mount Pleasant (IRE) (86)** (PFICole) **3-8-12** TQuinn(7) (lw: cl up tl outpcd & lost pl 5f out: hdwy to ld wl over 1f out: hdd ins fnl f: kpt on) ....nk **2** 7/1 99 58
4447[8] **Etterby Park (USA) (73)** (MJohnston) **3-7-13** JFanning(6) (mde most tl hdd wl over 1f out: kpt on same pce) ....5 **3** 8/1 80 39
4327[5] **General Macarthur (92)** (JLDunlop) **3-9-4** MJKinane(5) (hld up: hdwy 3f out: hung rt 2f out: styd on towards fin) ....2 **4** 10/1 97 56
4548[2] **Belmarita (IRE) (73)** (MHTompkins) **3-7-6**(7) RMullen(1) (trckd ldrs gng wl: chal 6f out tl rdn & btn wl over 1f out) ....2½ **5** 11/2[3] 75 34
2616[3] **Prince Kinsky (77)** (LordHuntingdon) **3-8-3** DHarrison(4) (hld up & bhd: hmpd 10f out: effrt 4f out: wandered u.p: nvr able to chal) ....1¾ **6** 8/1 77 36
4431[13] **Traceability (81)** (SCWilliams) **3-8-7** KFallon(2) (a.p: chal 3f out: sn hrd drvn: wknd over 1f out: eased) ....3 **7** 14/1 77 36
3673[6] **Benatom (USA) (95)** (HRACecil) **3-9-7** PatEddery(8) (hld up: effrt 5f out: sn btn) ....22 **8** 7/2[2] 66 25
(SP 114.8%) **8 Rn**

**3m 1.67** (5.67) CSF £20.52 CT £124.18 TOTE £3.60: £1.70 £2.00 £2.40 (£8.30) OWNER Sultan Al Kabeer (NEWMARKET) BRED Lyonstown Stud, Swettenham Stud and Ron Con Ltd

**3935* Flamands (IRE)**, despite flashing her tail in the preliminaries, did nothing wrong in the race and, if anything, won a shade cheekily. (11/4)
**4353* Mount Pleasant (IRE)** looked a bit of a funny customer here, running in snatches, but he did battle back when looking beaten. (7/1)
**4344 Etterby Park (USA)** showed he is still in fine trim, but was just chopped for speed in the last furlong and a half. (8/1: 6/1-9/1)
**4327 General Macarthur** spoilt his chances by hanging right when asked for an effort and is obviously a bit of a thinker. (10/1: op 6/1)
**4548 Belmarita (IRE)** travelled particularly well for much of the trip but, when it came down to a struggle, she was then found wanting. (11/2)
**2616 Prince Kinsky**, after over three months off, got messed about turning into the straight, and was then inclined to wander about when ridden. He is worth another chance. (8/1: 5/1-9/1)

T/Jkpt: £7,100.00 (0.1 Tckts); £7,985.38 to Newmarket 19/10/96. T/Plpt: £1,214.50 (17 Tckts). T/Qdpt: £93.50 (27.03 Tckts). AA

## 4748-CATTERICK (L-H) (Good)
## Saturday October 19th
WEATHER: overcast WIND: fresh half against

### 4762 E.B.F. PROSPECT HILL MAIDEN STKS (2-Y.O) (Class D)
2-05 (2-08) **5f** £3,697.50 (£1,110.00: £535.00: £247.50) Stalls: Low GOING: 0.05 sec per fur (G)

SP RR SF
4244[7] **La Dolce Vita** (TDBarron) **2-8-9** JFanning(12) (hld up: hdwy ½-wy: led jst ins fnl f: styd on wl) ....— **1** 33/1 70 17
4558[5] **Hyde Park (IRE)** (SirMarkPrescott) **2-9-0** GDuffield(13) (chsd ldr: ev ch jst ins fnl f: nt qckn) ....1¼ **2** 13/8[1] 71 18
4545[4] **Hajat** (HThomsonJones) **2-8-9** JFortune(10) (a chsng ldrs: nt qckn fnl f) ....1 **3** 7/2[2] 63 10
4558[10] **Mungo Park** (MrsJRRamsden) **2-9-0** MDeering(14) (sn wl outpcd & wl bhd: styd on strly appr fnl f: nt rch ldrs) ....1 **4** 25/1 65+ 12
4357[6] **Alvilde** (JRFanshawe) **2-8-4**(5) GFaulkner(1) (led far side: edgd rt ½-wy: grad wknd) ....½ **5** 10/1 58 5
4558[3] **Midyan Queen (65)** (RHollinshead) **2-8-6**(3) FLynch(8) (sn in tch: styd on appr fnl f: nvr rchd ldrs: b.b.v) ....hd **6** 12/1 58 5
4558[11] **Fruitana (IRE) (81)** (JBerry) **2-8-9v**[1](5) PRoberts(11) (led & sn clr: wknd & hdd jst ins fnl f) ....1¼ **7** 9/1[3] 59 6
1453[4] **Turtle Moon** (MHTompkins) **2-9-0** KDarley(2) (racd far side: prom: swtchd rt ½-wy: wknd over 1f out) ....1½ **8** 10/1 54 1
4062[8] **Sylvan Dancer (IRE) (70)** (CFWall) **2-8-9** RMcGhin(4) (racd far side: sn outpcd & bhd) ....hd **9** 12/1 49 —
4468[5] **Lightning Bolt (IRE)** (MJohnston) **2-8-9** TWilliams(9) (chsd ldrs tl wknd over 1f out) ....1½ **10** 20/1 44 —
4123[9] **Hever Golf Mover** (TJNaughton) **2-8-9** MFenton(5) (racd far side: a bhd) ....¾ **11** 20/1 41 —
4469[6] **Waltz Time** (MissLAPerratt) **2-8-9** AMcGlone(3) (racd far side: bhd fr ½-wy) ....3½ **12** 33/1 30 —
4593[6] **Flood's Hot Stuff** (MRChannon) **2-8-9** RPerham(7) (sn wl bhd) ....1½ **13** 33/1 25 —
4558[8] **Something Blue** (TRWatson) **2-8-9** JCarroll(6) (b.hind: racd far side: sn wl bhd) ....7 **14** 50/1 3 —
(SP 128.0%) **14 Rn**

**62.2 secs** (4.70) CSF £86.84 TOTE £102.50: £8.20 £1.10 £2.20 (£81.60) Trio £114.40 OWNER Mr I. Fox (THIRSK) BRED D. R. Botterill
**OFFICIAL EXPLANATION Midyan Queen: bled from the nose.**
**4244 La Dolce Vita**, badly drawn at Ayr, took this in decisive fashion, but it was just a run-of-the-mill maiden. (33/1)
**4558 Hyde Park (IRE)** stepped up on his initial effort and there should be better to come, especially over six. (13/8)
**4545 Hajat** looked wintry in her coat, but this is as good as she is. (7/2)
**Mungo Park** has plenty of size and scope, but was out with the washing until coming tearing through in the closing stages. Now qualified for a handicap mark, he is one to bear in mind, especially over further. (25/1)
**4357 Alvilde**, who led on the far side, edged right to join the main body of the field at halfway. She should be capable of better over further. (10/1)
**4558 Midyan Queen** stayed on well, but it transpired she had broken a blood-vessel. (12/1)
**4043 Fruitana (IRE)**, tried in a visor, showed his rivals a clean pair of heels, but the needle was on empty entering the final furlong. (9/1)
**1453 Turtle Moon** (10/1: op 5/1)

### 4763 PLODMIRE WOOD APPRENTICE CLAIMING STKS (3-Y.O+) (Class G)
2-40 (2-41) **1m 3f 214y** £2,637.00 (£732.00: £351.00) Stalls: Low GOING: 0.05 sec per fur (G)

SP RR SF
999[6] **Dana Point (IRE) (58)** (TDBarron) **4-8-3**(7) VictoriaAppleby(3) (b: mde most: clr 3f out: unchal) ....— **1** 11/1 71 39
*4332[9]* **Cross Talk (IRE) (66)** (NTinkler) **4-8-12** FLynch(1) (in tch: hdwy over 4f out: swtchd stands' side 2f out: styd on: nt rch ldr) ....3½ **2** 20/1 68 36
4582[2] **Break the Rules (70)** (MrsMReveley) **4-9-4**(3) GFaulkner(11) (hld up: stdy hdwy 7f out: wnt 2nd over 2f out: sn rdn & no imp) ....6 **3** 8/11[1] 69 37
3463[7] **Kashana (IRE) (34)** (WStorey) **4-8-1v**[1](3) IonaWands(12) (in tch: drvn along 4f out: styd on fnl 2f) ....1 **4** 66/1 51 19
2141[6] **Salty Girl (IRE) (65)** (BWHills) **3-8-4** DarrenMoffatt(9) (prom: effrt over 3f out: sn wknd) ....4 **5** 9/2[3] 53 14
4596[5] **Pharly Dancer (60)** (WWHaigh) **7-9-0** LNewton(5) (lw: w ldrs: rdn 3f out: swtchd rt & wknd 2f out) ....1¾ **6** 4/1[2] 53 21
4515[10] **St Honorine (IRE)** (CMurray) **4-8-11** RHavlin(4) (in tch: drvn along 6f out: wknd 4f out) ....6 **7** 50/1 42 10
3309[7] **Finestatetobein** (FWatson) **3-7-10**(7)ow2 CLowther(6) (s.i.s: sn w ldrs: wknd over 3f out) ....7 **8** 66/1 32 —
**Lost Dream** (CADwyer) **7-8-13**(3) JoHunnam(2) (b: sn bhd) ....1¼ **9** 20/1 36 4
4455[13] **Pinkerton Polka (36)** (JParkes) **4-8-3** ADaly(13) (b.hind: a bhd) ....½ **10** 50/1 23 —
4515[5] **Petoskin (50)** (JPearce) **4-9-2** MBaird(7) (sn wl bhd) ....3½ **11** 12/1 31 —
4437[13] **Shoja** (MrsVAAconley) **3-7-12**(7) RCody-Boutcher(10) (unruly in stalls: s.i.s: a bhd) ....3½ **12** 50/1 22 —

| | | | | SP | RR | SF |
|---|---|---|---|---|---|---|
| 4099[8] | **Kaye's Secret** (JLHarris) **3-8-1** PFessey(8) (sn bhd & rdn along) | 8 | **13** | 66/1 | 8 | — |

(SP 132.0%) **13 Rn**

**2m 40.4** (9.00) CSF £197.45 TOTE £35.50: £11.60 £1.30 £1.10 (£42.40) Trio £87.50 OWNER Mr J. Baggott (THIRSK) BRED T. N. Leonard
WEIGHT FOR AGE 3yo-7lb
Dana Point (IRE) clmd Harvey Smith £4,000

**999 Dana Point (IRE)** seemed to appreciate the step up in distance. Making light of an absence of two months, he shot clear under an enterprising ride turning in and was never in any danger. On pulling up he made a bee-line for the exit gate, giving the girl a nasty-looking fall. (11/1: 8/1-12/1)
**2394 Cross Talk (IRE)** seems to like it round here. (20/1)
**4582 Break the Rules** gave the winner plenty of rope but, under pressure to close the gap once in line for home, the response was most disappointing. (8/11: op 5/4)
**Kashana (IRE)**, racing with her tongue tied down and in a visor for the first time, looks an out-and-out stayer. (66/1)
**2141 Salty Girl (IRE)** was having her first outing for four months. (9/2: op 3/1)
**4596 Pharly Dancer** ran poorly. (4/1)

## 4764 MD FOODS NURSERY H'CAP (0-85) (2-Y.O) (Class E)
3-15 (3-18) **7f** £3,574.00 (£1,072.00: £516.00: £238.00) Stalls: Low GOING: 0.05 sec per fur (G)

| | | | | SP | RR | SF |
|---|---|---|---|---|---|---|
| 4586[12] | **Abstone Queen (64)** (PDEvans) **2-8-0v**ow3 JFEgan(4) (mid div: hdwy & c wd over 2f out: rdn & hung lft: styd on to ld ins fnl f) | — | **1** | 16/1 | 66 | 32 |
| 4625[2] | **Gipsy Princess (67)** (MWEasterby) **2-8-3b** AMcGlone(3) (led over 5f out tl ins fnl f) | 1½ | **2** | 9/2 [1] | 66 | 35 |
| 4501[3] | **Zorba (65)** (CWThornton) **2-8-1** FNorton(6) (in tch: rdn over 2f out: styd on wl ins fnl f) | 2½ | **3** | 9/1 | 58 | 27 |
| 4471[7] | **The In-Laws (IRE) (85)** (SirMarkPrescott) **2-9-7** GDuffield(7) (s.i.s: hdwy & c wd 3f out: styd on same pce appr fnl f) | 1¼ | **4** | 8/1 | 75 | 44 |
| *4335** | **Contravene (IRE) (60)** (JBerry) **2-7-5**(5) PFessey(13) (chsd ldrs: c wd ent st: wknd over 1f out) | 2½ | **5** | 7/1 [3] | 44 | 13 |
| 3853* | **Tribal Mischief (66)** (DMoffatt) **2-7-13**(3) DarrenMoffatt(2) (prom: rdn & hung lft over 1f out: sn wknd) | 6 | **6** | 14/1 | 37 | 6 |
| 4495* | **Impulsif (USA) (82)** (DJSffrenchDavis) **2-8-13**(5) GParkin(16) (racd wd: stdy hdwy ½-wy: effrt over 2f out: sn wknd) | 1¼ | **7** | 6/1 [2] | 50 | 19 |
| 4586[14] | **Globetrotter (IRE) (71)** (MJohnston) **2-8-7** TWilliams(1) (led over 1f: chsd ldrs tl wknd over 1f out) | s.h | **8** | 12/1 | 39 | 8 |
| 4586[9] | **King Uno (64)** (MrsJRRamsden) **2-8-0** MDeering(11) (sn wl bhd: styd on fnl 2f: n.d) | hd | **9** | 20/1 | 31 | — |
| 3969[7] | **Denton Lad (70)** (JWWatts) **2-8-6** NConnorton(5) (prom: effrt over 2f out: sn wknd) | 2½ | **10** | 9/1 | 32 | 1 |
| 4672[13] | **Grate Times (79)** (EWeymes) **2-9-1** MRimmer(9) (sn bhd) | 2½ | **11** | 11/1 | 35 | 4 |
| 2942[10] | **Jonfy (IRE) (60)** (BWHills) **2-7-10** RStreet(8) (sn wl bhd) | ½ | **12** | 25/1 | 15 | — |
| 4495[6] | **Sea Mist (IRE) (64)** (PWChapple-Hyam) **2-7-7**(7)ow1 RCody-Boutcher(12) (sn bhd) | 1 | **13** | 14/1 | 17 | — |
| 2984* | **Mirror Four Life (IRE) (79)** (MHTompkins) **2-8-10**(5) GFaulkner(14) (lw: prom tl lost pl ½-wy: t.o) | 22 | **14** | 10/1 | — | — |
| 4558[9] | **Toronto (69)** (JBerry) **2-8-5**ow2 KDarley(15) (racd wd: prom tl lost pl over 2f out: sn bhd: t.o) | 1½ | **15** | 20/1 | — | — |

(SP 133.8%) **15 Rn**

**1m 28.4** (4.80) CSF £88.58 CT £664.69 TOTE £23.80: £5.90 £2.30 £2.90 (£65.10) Trio £66.20 OWNER Mr J. E. Abbey (WELSHPOOL) BRED Ridgebarn Farm
LONG HANDICAP Jonfy (IRE) 7-8

**4433 Abstone Queen** is certainly tough, this being her twentieth outing this term. (16/1)
**4625 Gipsy Princess** was 2lb higher in the weights. (9/2)
**4501 Zorba** was reeling in the first two at the line and would appreciate a stiffer track. (9/1)
**4133 The In-Laws (IRE)**, out of her depth on her last two starts, had plenty on under topweight. (8/1)

## 4765 CROW HOLE BANK H'CAP (0-85) (3-Y.O+) (Class D)
3-50 (3-52) **5f** £4,110.00 (£1,230.00: £590.00: £270.00) Stalls: Low GOING: 0.05 sec per fur (G)

| | | | | SP | RR | SF |
|---|---|---|---|---|---|---|
| 4679[6] | **Palacegate Touch (74)** (JBerry) **6-8-12b**(5) PFessey(19) (racd stands' side: led to ½-wy: led ins fnl f: hung lft towards fin) | — | **1** | 8/1 [2] | 84 | 51 |
| 4367[8] | **Pride of Brixton (83)** (GLewis) **3-9-12** SWhitworth(16) (w ldrs stands' side: led over 1f out: hdd & no ex nr fin) | 1¼ | **2** | 7/1 [1] | 89 | 56 |
| 4220[6] | **Spender (74)** (PWHarris) **7-9-3** GDuffield(15) (lw: racd stands' side: in tch: hrd rdn over 1f out: swtchd lft: styd on) | 1¼ | **3** | 14/1 | 76 | 43 |
| 4473[7] | **Silk Cottage (55)** (RMWhitaker) **4-7-12v** FNorton(5) (racd far side: in tch: hdwy to ld over 1f out: r.o) | hd | **4** | 20/1 | 57 | 24 |
| 4505[8] | **Eastern Prophets (82)** (TJNaughton) **3-9-11** OUrbina(18) (lw: chsd ldrs stands' side: kpt on same pce appr fnl f) | 1¾ | **5** | 16/1 | 78 | 45 |
| 4610[3] | **Chadwell Hall (66)** (SRBowring) **5-8-6b**(3) CTeague(3) (lw: racd far side: chsd ldrs over 3f) | 2½ | **6** | 9/1 [3] | 54 | 21 |
| 4589[12] | **Branston Danni (57)** (MrsJRRamsden) **3-8-0**ow2 JFanning(20) (s.i.s: bhd tl styd on wl fnl 2f: nt rch ldrs) | hd | **7** | 20/1 | 45 | 10 |
| 4616[9] | **Insider Trader (78)** (MrsJRRamsden) **5-9-7** JFortune(1) (led far side tl over 1f out: sn wknd) | s.h | **8** | 7/1 [1] | 66 | 33 |
| 4505[12] | **Goretski (IRE) (63)** (NTinkler) **3-8-6** KimTinkler(8) (racd centre: gd spd to ½-wy: grad wknd) | hd | **9** | 25/1 | 50 | 17 |
| 4679[9] | **Lady Sheriff (77)** (RHollinshead) **5-9-3**(3) FLynch(17) (in tch stands' side: effrt ½-wy: no imp) | nk | **10** | 9/1 [3] | 63 | 30 |
| 4687[21] | **Bayin (USA) (69)** (MDIUsher) **7-8-12** RStreet(7) (s.i.s: racd far side: swtchd rt 2f out: nvr nr ldrs) | s.h | **11** | 12/1 | 55 | 22 |
| 4581[13] | **Bollin Harry (74)** (TDEasterby) **4-9-0**(3) RHavlin(4) (lw: racd far side: in tch: effrt 2f out: sn wknd) | ¾ | **12** | 10/1 | 58 | 25 |
| 4382[12] | **Colston-C (57)** (PDEvans) **4-8-0**ow1 JFEgan(9) (racd far side: nvr bttr than mid div) | ¾ | **13** | 20/1 | 38 | 4 |
| 4505[6] | **Able Sheriff (60)** (MWEasterby) **4-8-3b** AMcGlone(6) (racd far side: in tch: effrt 2f out: sn wknd) | 1¼ | **14** | 10/1 | 37 | 4 |
| 4044[8] | **Precious Girl (76)** (DMoffatt) **3-9-2v**(3) DarrenMoffatt(10) (racd far side: sn bhd) | hd | **15** | 16/1 | 53 | 20 |
| 4367[4] | **Tuscan Dawn (77)** (JBerry) **6-9-1**(5) PRoberts(2) (w ldr far side tl wknd 2f out) | 1¼ | **16** | 9/1 [3] | 50 | 17 |
| 4581[21] | **Cross The Border (85)** (DNicholls) **3-10-0** KDarley(14) (led stands' side to ½-wy: sn lost pl) | 4 | **17** | 20/1 | 45 | 12 |
| 4727[8] | **Swan At Whalley (68)** (MartynWane) **4-8-11** RPerham(11) (prom stands' side to ½-wy: sn lost pl) | ¾ | **18** | 16/1 | 26 | — |
| 4581[20] | **Palacegate Jack (IRE) (76)** (CADwyer) **5-9-5** JCarroll(12) (racd stands' side: bhd fr ½-wy) | 1¼ | **19** | 10/1 | 30 | — |
| 3844[18] | **Sihafi (USA) (75)** (JMCarr) **3-9-4** MRimmer(13) (a rr div) | 7 | **20** | 33/1 | 6 | — |

(SP 151.2%) **20 Rn**

**60.6 secs** (3.10) CSF £70.16 CT £523.65 TOTE £13.10: £3.20 £3.70 £3.00 £4.80 (£62.10) Trio £98.80 OWNER Laurel (Leisure) Ltd (COCKERHAM) BRED The Woodhaven Stud

**4679 Palacegate Touch**, who normally hangs left, behaved himself from his high draw, apart from dodging left near the finish. (8/1: op 12/1)
**3693 Pride of Brixton**, taken to post early, still has plenty of speed, but is 5lb higher than when he won at Chester in May. (7/1)
**3338 Spender** stuck on under strong pressure and is marginally better on the All-Weather. (14/1)
**3477 Silk Cottage** did best of those racing on the far side. (20/1)

**790a Eastern Prophets** presumably needed the race at Newcastle last time, but it is hard to know what is his best trip. (16/1)
**3774 Branston Danni** made no appeal in the paddock, but again hinted there may be a small handicap in her before the season's end. (20/1)
**4505 Insider Trader**, drawn one, led on the far side. (7/1)

## 4766 THIEVES GILL LIMITED STKS (0-60) (3-Y.O+) (Class F)

4-25 (4-27) **1m 5f 175y** £2,910.00 (£810.00: £390.00) Stalls: Low GOING: 0.05 sec per fur (G)

| Form | Horse | Dist | Pos | SP | RR | SF |
|---|---|---|---|---|---|---|
| 3855[4] | **Los Alamos (60)** (CWThornton) **3-8-8** DeanMcKeown(3) (mde all: drvn along 4f out: styd on wl) | — | **1** | 7/1 | 70 | 40 |
| 4612[10] | **Miss Prism (51)** (JLDunlop) **3-8-6** KDarley(1) (trckd ldrs: chsd wnr fnl 4f: rdn over 2f out: no imp) | 6 | **2** | 15/2 | 61 | 31 |
| 4474[3] | **Silvretta (IRE) (60)** (ACStewart) **3-8-6** JCarroll(5) (chsd ldrs: drvn along & wl outpcd 4f out: kpt on fnl 2f) | 9 | **3** | 4/1[2] | 51 | 21 |
| 4509[11] | **Forever Noble (IRE) (57)** (MRChannon) **3-8-9** RPerham(2) (bhd: hdwy 3f out: styd on fnl 2f: nvr nr to chal) | 5 | **4** | 12/1 | 48 | 18 |
| 4588[6] | **Early Peace (IRE) (52)** (MJPolglase) **4-9-6** MRimmer(9) (chsd ldrs: rdn & outpcd over 3f out: wknd over 1f out) | 9 | **5** | 25/1 | 39 | 18 |
| 4604[5] | **Children's Choice (IRE) (55)** (CNAllen) **5-8-10**(7) DDenby(4) (sn bhd & pushed along: sme hdwy over 4f out: n.d) | hd | **6** | 3/1[1] | 36 | 15 |
| 3480* | **North Bear (55)** (MrsSJSmith) **4-9-3**(3) OPears(6) (sn pushed along: sme hdwy 5f out: sn wknd) | 11 | **7** | 12/1 | 27 | 6 |
| *2936*[9] | **Dispol Dancer (25)** (MrsVAAconley) **5-9-4** MDeering(11) (a bhd) | ½ | **8** | 50/1 | 24 | 3 |
| 4604[9] | **Iota (54)** (JLHarris) **7-9-3** TWilliams(8) (sn drvn along: chsd ldrs tl wknd over 3f out) | 1¾ | **9** | 7/1 | 21 | — |
| *197*[3] | **Reploy (60)** (LordHuntingdon) **3-8-1**(5) AimeeCook(7) (in tch: dropped back after 5f: n.d) | 2½ | **10** | 13/2[3] | 16 | — |
| 4587[6] | **May King Mayhem (45)** (MrsALMKing) **3-8-6**(3) FLynch(10) (a bhd: t.o 3f out) | 27 | **11** | 25/1 | — | — |
| *4574*[4] | **Expansive Runner (USA) (48)** (PWHarris) **4-9-4** GDuffield(12) (trckd wnr: drvn along 7f out: wknd qckly over 3f out: t.o) | 5 | **12** | 14/1 | — | — |
| | | | | (SP 126.8%) | **12 Rn** | |

**3m 5.45** (9.95) CSF £57.78 TOTE £11.00: £3.20 £2.60 £2.00 (£21.80) Trio £32.60 OWNER Mr Guy Reed (MIDDLEHAM) BRED G. Reed
WEIGHT FOR AGE 3yo-9lb
**3855 Los Alamos**, absent for eight weeks, was given an enterprising ride and, in the final half-mile, there were only two in it, but only one winner. (7/1)
**4612 Miss Prism**, who is finding it hard to win, would have been 7lb better off with the winner in a handicap. (15/2)
**4474 Silvretta (IRE)** was stepping up in distance but, judging by the way she ran, she needs even further. (4/1: op 2/1)
**4604 Children's Choice (IRE)** ran a very flat race. Driven along from start to finish, she was never in the contest. (3/1: op 5/1)

## 4767 SOUR BECK CONDITIONS STKS (2-Y.O) (Class D)

4-55 (4-55) **5f** £3,281.50 (£982.00: £471.00: £215.50) Stalls: Low GOING: 0.05 sec per fur (G)

| Form | Horse | Dist | Pos | SP | RR | SF |
|---|---|---|---|---|---|---|
| 4517[6] | **Swift (59)** (MJPolglase) **2-8-11** MRimmer(2) (lw: sn w ldrs: rdn & outpcd 2f out: styd on to ld ins fnl f) | — | **1** | 5/1[3] | 61 | 11 |
| 4749[4] | **Keen To Please (64)** (DenysSmith) **2-8-10** JCarroll(4) (trckd ldr: rdn 2f out: styd on towards fin) | ¾ | **2** | 7/4[1] | 58 | 8 |
| 2699[4] | **Enchantica (70)** (JBerry) **2-8-6** KDarley(3) (led tl ins fnl f) | hd | **3** | 7/4[1] | 53 | 3 |
| 4228[11] | **Onemoretime** (BWMurray) **2-8-6** VHalliday(6) (b.hind: s.i.s: a outpcd: hmpd over 1f out) | 7 | **4** | 20/1 | 31 | — |
| 2681[5] | **Tazibari (70)** (DMoffatt) **2-8-7**(3) DarrenMoffatt(5) (sn outpcd: rdn & wnt lft over 1f out: n.d) | nk | **5** | 9/2[2] | 34 | — |
| | | | | (SP 112.3%) | **5 Rn** | |

**62.7 secs** (5.20) CSF £13.72 TOTE £8.30: £1.70 £1.20 (£7.70) OWNER Gen Sir Geoffrey Howlett (NEWMARKET) BRED Mrs Amschel Rothschild
**Swift**, twice the size of his opponents, would have been 16lb better off with the third in a nursery. He came back to score decisively, and connections will be hoping to turn him out under a penalty. (5/1)
**4749 Keen To Please**, having her second race in two days, again wore a tongue-strap. She is certainly tough and willing. (7/4)
**2699 Enchantica**, absent for three months, ran out of gas inside the last. At least she kept straight this time. (7/4)

## 4768 'CLOSE OF PLAY' H'CAP (0-70) (3-Y.O+) (Class E)

5-30 (5-37) **7f** £3,860.00 (£1,160.00: £560.00: £260.00) Stalls: Low GOING: 0.05 sec per fur (G)

| Form | Horse | Dist | Pos | SP | RR | SF |
|---|---|---|---|---|---|---|
| 3578[6] | **Allinson's Mate (IRE) (56)** (TDBarron) **8-8-9b**(7) VictoriaAppleby(4) (trckd ldrs: qcknd to ld over 2f out: pushed out) | — | **1** | 16/1 | 67 | 50 |
| 4513[13] | **Stackattack (IRE) (60)** (PRWebber) **3-9-4** RPerham(8) (lw: a in tch: chsd wnr fnl 2f: no imp) | 1½ | **2** | 20/1 | 68 | 49 |
| 4428[8] | **Utmost Zeal (USA) (64)** (PWHarris) **3-9-8** AMcGlone(5) (swtg: prom early: bhd ½-wy: gd hdwy over 2f out: styd on fnl f) | 4 | **3** | 10/1 | 62 | 43 |
| 4430[10] | **Naughty Pistol (USA) (54)** (PDEvans) **4-9-0v** JFEgan(6) (prom: rdn & outpcd over 2f out: styd on fnl f) | 1¼ | **4** | 9/1[3] | 50 | 33 |
| 2868[8] | **Sharp 'n' Shady (55)** (CFWall) **3-8-13** GDuffield(1) (bhd: hdwy 2f out: styd on towards fin) | 2½ | **5** | 14/1 | 45 | 26 |
| 4682[11] | **Comanche Companion (66)** (TJNaughton) **6-9-12** OUrbina(12) (mid div: hdwy & c wd over 2f out: nt rch ldrs) | s.h | **6** | 5/1[2] | 56 | 39 |
| 4688[11] | **Fame Again (64)** (MrsJRRamsden) **4-9-10** MWigham(9) (s.i.s: bhd: c wd & styd on fnl 2f) | ¾ | **7** | 14/1 | 52 | 35 |
| 4609[2] | **Classy Chief (68)** (RBoss) **3-9-7**(5) GFaulkner(15) (mid div: hdwy to chse ldrs over 2f out: wknd over 1f out) | ½ | **8** | 10/1 | 55 | 36 |
| *4573*[8] | **Dancing Sioux (59)** (DNicholls) **4-9-5** AlexGreaves(3) (trckd ldrs tl grad wknd fnl 2f) | 1 | **9** | 20/1 | 44 | 27 |
| 4498* | **Misrule (USA) (69)** (JHMGosden) **3-9-13** JCarroll(10) (hld up & bhd: hdwy 2f out: eased ins fnl f) | 1½ | **10** | 9/2[1] | 50 | 31 |
| 4609[11] | **Parliament Piece (67)** (CaptJWilson) **10-9-13** DeanMcKeown(11) (bhd: sme hdwy 2f out: n.d) | 1¼ | **11** | 20/1 | 45 | 28 |
| 4511[9] | **Godmersham Park (68)** (MJHeaton-Ellis) **4-9-9v1**(5) PPMurphy(17) (w ldrs tl wknd 2f out) | ½ | **12** | 20/1 | 45 | 28 |
| 4701[2] | **Statistician (55)** (JohnBerry) **4-9-1b** MFenton(20) (racd wd: chsd ldrs tl wknd 2f out) | ¾ | **13** | 12/1 | 31 | 14 |
| 4226[18] | **My Godson (56)** (JLEyre) **6-8-9b**(7) SBuckley(16) (b.nr hind: s.i.s: a bhd) | 2½ | **14** | 20/1 | 26 | 9 |
| 4486[2] | **Desert Invader (IRE) (54)** (DWChapman) **5-9-0** JFanning(19) (sn trckng ldrs: lost pl 3f out) | ½ | **15** | 16/1 | 23 | 6 |
| 4692[16] | **Encore M'Lady (IRE) (57)** (FHLee) **5-8-12**(5) LNewton(7) (a bhd) | ½ | **16** | 16/1 | 25 | 8 |
| 4323[2] | **Regal Fanfare (IRE) (53)** (MrsLStubbs) **4-8-6b**(7) JoHunnam(13) (s.i.s: bhd: c wd over 2f out: n.d) | ½ | **17** | 10/1 | 19 | 2 |
| 4688[24] | **Superpride (63)** (MrsMReveley) **4-9-9** TWilliams(18) (chsd ldrs tl wknd over 2f out) | 3½ | **18** | 14/1 | 21 | 4 |
| 473[4] | **Chilibang Bang (55)** (JBerry) **3-8-13** KDarley(2) (led tl over 2f out: wknd qckly: t.o) | 17 | **19** | 20/1 | — | — |
| 4430[23] | **Craignairn (57)** (JLEyre) **3-9-1b** RLappin(14) (chsd ldrs tl wknd qckly 3f out: t.o) | 5 | **20** | 20/1 | — | — |
| | | | | (SP 150.8%) | **20 Rn** | |

**1m 28.1** (4.50) CSF £296.40 CT £3,051.97 TOTE £16.20: £5.00 £4.30 £1.10 £3.50 (£275.90) Trio Not won; £586.24 to Pontefract 21/10/96
OWNER Mr Peter Jones (THIRSK) BRED Gay O'Callaghan
WEIGHT FOR AGE 3yo-2lb
**3578 Allinson's Mate (IRE)**, having his ninety-ninth race, pulled off a long-priced treble for his trainer and also a double for his promising young apprentice. He loves turning tracks and pinched it when nipping through on the inner turning in. (16/1)

**4059 Stackattack (IRE)**, dropping back in distance, stuck on under pressure, but was never going to get in a blow at the winner. He is still a maiden. (20/1)
**4109 Utmost Zeal (USA)**, an in-and-out performer, seemed to drop himself out before finishing in good style. (10/1)
**4341* Naughty Pistol (USA)**, who won three times in America in her youth, was staying on when it was all over, and might be suited by a mile. (9/1)
**775 Sharp 'n' Shady**, absent for three months, is capable of better when the soft ground comes along. (14/1)
**455 Comanche Companion**, well supported, came across to race on the stands' side while the first five remained on the far side. She probably needs much softer ground. (5/1: op 10/1)
**3510 Fame Again** (14/1: op 8/1)
**4077 Dancing Sioux** shaped nicely and is one to watch out for on the All-Weather. (20/1)
**4498* Misrule (USA)** ran no race at all and her rider gave up. Connections were at a loss to explain this inept effort. (9/2)
**4323 Regal Fanfare (IRE)** (10/1: 14/1-9/1)

T/Plpt: £217.50 (51.88 Tckts). T/Qdpt: £58.00 (9.93 Tckts). WG

## 4755-NEWMARKET (R-H) (Good)
## Saturday October 19th

WEATHER: sunny periods WIND: fresh half bhd

## 4769 ROTHMANS ROYALS NORTH SOUTH CHALLENGE SERIES H'CAP (Final) (3-Y.O+) (Class B)

1-45 (1-47) **1m (Rowley)** £29,700.00 (£9,000.00: £4,400.00: £2,100.00) Stalls: Centre GOING minus 0.22 sec per fur (GF)

| | | | | SP | RR | SF |
|---|---|---|---|---|---|---|
| 4568[5] | **Hawksley Hill (IRE) (83)** (MrsJRRamsden) **3-8-11** KFallon(19) (swtchd lft s: sn pushed along: hdwy to ld 2f out: hung lft: r.o wl) | — | **1** | 11/2[1] | 96 | 76 |
| 4682* | **High Premium (78)** (RAFahey) **8-8-9** ACulhane(23) (racd centre: hrd drvn ½-wy: hdwy 2f out: chsng wnr ins fnl f: r.o wl) | 1½ | **2** | 10/1[3] | 88 | 71 |
| 4682[5] | **Artful Dane (IRE) (71)** (MJHeaton-Ellis) **4-8-2v** SDrowne(11) (in tch: hdwy 2f out: styd on wl) | 1 | **3** | 20/1 | 79 | 62 |
| 4686[15] | **Impulsive Air (IRE) (65)** (EWeymes) **4-7-10** JQuinn(6) (lw: a.p: hdwy & n.m.r over 1f out: styd on one pce) | ¾ | **4** | 20/1 | 72 | 55 |
| 4609[5] | **Anonym (IRE) (65)** (DNicholls) **4-7-3b(7)** JBramhill(22) (lw: racd centre: hdwy 3f out: styd on wl) | ½ | **5** | 40/1 | 71 | 54 |
| 4463[25] | **Sandmoor Chambray (81)** (TDEasterby) **5-8-12** MBirch(25) (racd centre: hdwy u.p over 2f out: styd on wl) | 1 | **6** | 25/1 | 85 | 68 |
| 4583* | **Rebel County (IRE) (90)** (ABailey) **3-9-4** DBiggs(15) (in tch: hdwy & ch 2f out: one pce fnl f) | nk | **7** | 14/1 | 93 | 73 |
| 4190[21] | **Winston (70)** (JDBethell) **3-7-7(5)** MartinDwyer(8) (bhd: hmpd over 2f out: r.o towards fin) | nk | **8** | 25/1 | 72 | 52 |
| 4329[6] | **Saifan (84)** (DMorris) **7-9-1v** NDay(2) (lw: effrt & nt clr run over 2f out: styd on: nrst fin) | 1 | **9** | 16/1 | 84 | 67 |
| 4190[11] | **Royal Ceilidh (IRE) (79)** (DenysSmith) **3-8-7**ow1 JReid(17) (trckd ldrs: hmpd 3f out: effrt 2f out: nt qckn) | ½ | **10** | 20/1 | 78 | 57 |
| 4432[2] | **Gladys Althorpe (IRE) (72)** (JLEyre) **3-7-11(3)** NVarley(1) (hdwy 3f out: n.m.r & no imp) | ½ | **11** | 13/2[2] | 70 | 50 |
| 4329[8] | **Catch The Lights (82)** (RHannon) **3-8-10** DaneO'Neill(12) (in tch: n.m.r 2f out: no imp) | nk | **12** | 20/1 | 80 | 60 |
| 4682[15] | **Danegold (IRE) (74)** (MRChannon) **4-8-5v** CRutter(7) (sn outpcd & wl bhd: hdwy & swtchd 2f out: nrst fin) | ½ | **13** | 33/1 | 71 | 54 |
| 4686[13] | **Rambo Waltzer (65)** (DNicholls) **4-7-3(7)** PDoe(21) (w ldr centre tl wknd fnl 2½f) | s.h | **14** | 40/1 | 62 | 45 |
| 4329[9] | **Concer Un (97)** (SCWilliams) **4-10-0** TQuinn(4) (b.nr fore: prom: nt clr run 2f out: sn btn) | 1 | **15** | 14/1 | 92 | 75 |
| 4470[2] | **Flying North (IRE) (75)** (MrsMReveley) **3-8-3** GCarter(10) (effrt & n.m.r 2f out: nvr nr to chal) | ½ | **16** | 20/1 | 69 | 49 |
| 4300[12] | **Scaraben (72)** (SEKettlewell) **8-8-3** JStack(26) (led centre ½-wy: sn rdn: wknd fnl 2f) | ½ | **17** | 16/1 | 65 | 48 |
| 4455[8] | **Hawwam (65)** (EJAlston) **10-7-10** JLowe(18) (n.d) | nk | **18** | 100/1 | 57 | 40 |
| 4568[31] | **Blaze of Song (70)** (RHannon) **4-8-1b1** SSanders(20) (b: swtchd lft s: outpcd fnl 3f) | 1 | **19** | 33/1 | 60 | 43 |
| 4682[6] | **Maple Bay (IRE) (78)** (ABailey) **7-8-6(3)** DWright(24) (lw: racd centre: no imp fr ½-wy) | 1 | **20** | 20/1 | 66 | 49 |
| 4190[20] | **Band on the Run (88)** (BAMcMahon) **9-9-5** LDettori(5) (chsd ldrs 6f: sn wknd & eased) | 3½ | **21** | 20/1 | 69 | 52 |
| 4686[19] | **Pride of Pendle (71)** (DNicholls) **7-8-2** GHind(16) (outpcd & lost tch fr ½-wy) | ¾ | **22** | 20/1 | 51 | 34 |
| 4486[3] | **Magic Lake (68)** (EJAlston) **3-7-3v(7)** RFfrench(3) (plld hrd: led & sn clr: hdd 2f out: sn wknd) | nk | **23** | 100/1 | 47 | 27 |
| 4190[12] | **Bollin Frank (71)** (TDEasterby) **4-8-2** LCharnock(27) (lw: led centre to ½-wy: sn btn) | 1½ | **24** | 20/1 | 47 | 30 |
| 4329[16] | **Cool Fire (68)** (SPCWoods) **3-7-10b1** GBardwell(14) (cl up 6f: wknd) | 3 | **25** | 50/1 | 38 | 18 |
| 4329[12] | **Easy Jet (POL) (72)** (LordHuntingdon) **4-8-3v1** DHarrison(13) (sn bhd) | 2½ | **26** | 20/1 | 37 | 20 |
| 4329[14] | **Slip Jig (IRE) (80)** (RHannon) **3-8-8** PatEddery(9) (b.nr fore: lw: lost tch fr ½-wy: eased) | 6 | **27** | 20/1 | 33 | 13 |

(SP 137.7%) **27 Rn**

**1m 37.45** (0.15) CSF £58.00 CT £996.64 TOTE £5.80: £1.90 £2.20 £5.60 £4.20 (£20.50) Trio £260.90 OWNER Mr Hamish Alexander (THIRSK) BRED The Wickfield Stud Ltd

LONG HANDICAP Hawwam 6-7 Magic Lake 6-0 Cool Fire 7-7 Anonym (IRE) 7-3 Rambo Waltzer 7-2

WEIGHT FOR AGE 3yo-3lb

IN-FOCUS: **Following Tarawa's win yesterday, Hawksley Hill made it a clean sweep for the first two home from a high draw in the Cambridgeshire.**

**4568 Hawksley Hill (IRE)** had to really work to improve from halfway and, if anything, then hit the front too soon. Once there, he was not going to give it away and ran on splendidly to show just how unfortunate he was to have a high draw in the Cambridgeshire. (11/2)
**4682* High Premium** is in tremendous form and ran a super race in the smaller group down the centre of the track, but was well held by the winner in the closing stages. (10/1: 7/1-11/1)
**4682 Artful Dane (IRE)** has been much more consistent since wearing a visor and this was another fine effort. (20/1)
**4190 Impulsive Air (IRE)**, a noted poor mover who is difficult to weigh up, ran another fine race here, despite not having much room in which to manoeuvre. (20/1)
**4609 Anonym (IRE)** has so much ability, but does not always put it to full use, although this was a fine effort. (40/1)
**3856 Sandmoor Chambray** kept responding to pressure in good style and this was a cracking effort after his poor showing at Ascot. (25/1)
**4583* Rebel County (IRE)** has improved no end of late and, despite shooting up the weights, is still running her heart out. (14/1: 10/1-16/1)
**3279 Winston**, in a race where there were several hard-luck stories towards the stands' side, seemed to get the worst of it and did finish to some purpose. (25/1)
**4329 Saifan**, despite getting messed about no end, was running on strongly at the finish. (16/1)
**3985 Royal Ceilidh (IRE)** travelled really well, but he received a hefty bump three furlongs out and then failed to pick up. (20/1)

## 4770 OWEN BROWN HOUGHTON CONDITIONS STKS (2-Y.O) (Class B)

2-20 (2-20) **7f (Rowley)** £6,164.00 (£2,276.00: £1,088.00: £440.00: £170.00: £62.00) Stalls: Centre GOING minus 0.22 sec per fur (GF)

| | | | | SP | RR | SF |
|---|---|---|---|---|---|---|
| 4514[2] | **Crimson Tide (IRE)** (JWHills) **2-8-12** MHills(3) (hld up: hdwy ½-wy: shkn up to ld ins fnl f: r.o wl) | — | **1** | 9/4[1] | 92 | 64 |

4502* **Danetime (IRE)** (NACallaghan) **2-9-1** PatEddery(5) (lw: led: qcknd over 2f out: hdd ins fnl f: r.o) ....................1 **2** 7/2$^{2}$ 93 65
**Generous Libra** (DRLoder) **2-8-12** LDettori(2) (gd sort: scope: trckd ldrs: effrt over 2f out: r.o one pce) .......2½ **3** 13/2$^{3}$ 84 56
4670$^{2}$ **Bintang Timor (USA)** (PFICole) **2-8-12** TQuinn(1) (cl up: effrt over 2f out: wknd wl over 1f out) ...............................5 **4** 9/4$^{1}$ 73 45
**Russian Ruler (IRE)** (APJarvis) **2-8-12** JReid(6) (neat: sn cl up: rdn over 2f out: sn btn)..................................1¾ **5** 20/1 69 41
4507$^{6}$ **Other Club** (JARToller) **2-8-12** SSanders(4) (hld up: effrt 3f out: sn rdn & btn)...........................................1¼ **6** 14/1 66 38
(SP 108.5%) **6 Rn**

**1m 25.65** (1.15) CSF £9.57 TOTE £3.30: £1.80 £2.00 (£5.20) OWNER Mr Christopher Wright (LAMBOURN) BRED Barronstown Stud and Roncon Ltd

**4514 Crimson Tide (IRE)**, who travelled well, picked up when asked and won most convincingly to show he is on the upgrade. (9/4)
**4502* Danetime (IRE)** is an honest sort and he got this trip well enough, but the winner always had the edge in the final furlong. (7/2: op 9/4)
**Generous Libra** put in a decent first effort but was tapped for toe in the last two furlongs. No doubt the experience will bring him on. (13/2: 9/2-7/1)
**4670 Bintang Timor (USA)**, who moved poorly to post, disappointed here but had had a hard race at Ascot, and that was probably the reason for this. Time should see him return to form. (9/4)
**Russian Ruler (IRE)**, a quick-actioned individual, needed this experience and, once off the bit, was soon put in his place. (20/1)
**4507 Other Club** would seem to need plenty of time and, once things really hotted up, was quickly put in his place. (14/1: 12/1-20/1)

## 4771 TOTE CESAREWITCH H'CAP (3-Y.O+) (Class B)

3-00 (3-03) **2m 2f (Rowley)** £48,770.00 (£14,660.00: £7,080.00: £3,290.00) Stalls: High GOING minus 0.22 sec per fur (GF)

SP RR SF

4604* **Inchcailloch (IRE) (70)** (JSKing) **7-7-3**(7) RFfrench(15) (in tch: hdwy 3f out: nt clr run over 1f out: squeezed thro ins fnl f: r.o wl to ld cl home)...........................................— **1** 20/1 84 60
3983$^{15}$ **En Vacances (IRE) (79)** (AGFoster) **4-8-5** TSprake(13) (a chsng ldrs: outpcd 3f out: hdwy over 1f out: ev ch wl ins fnl f: styd on)...........................................nk **2** 50/1 93 69
3972* **Canon Can (USA) (84)** (HRACecil) **3-7-13** JQuinn(26) (lw: a chsng ldrs: rdn 4f out: styd on wl & slt ld over 1f out: no ex towards fin)...........................................nk **3** 9/2$^{1}$ 98 63
4557* **Floating Line (70)** (EJAlston) **8-7-7**(3) MHenry(3) (a w ldr: led 4f out tl over 1f out: kpt on) ..............................2 **4** 20/1 82 58
4596$^{4}$ **Sea Victor (79)** (JLHarris) **4-8-5** BDoyle(24) (led tl hdd 4f out: ev ch tl wknd ins fnl f) .............................1½ **5** 40/1 89 65
4327* **Ballynakelly (81)** (RAkehurst) **4-8-7** 4x SSanders(14) (lw: mid div: drvn along 6f out: hdwy 3f out: nt pce to chal)...........................................2 **6** 12/1 90 66
3834* **Orchestra Stall (89)** (JLDunlop) **4-9-1** TQuinn(18) (b: a.p: hdwy u.p over 3f out: ev ch 2f out: wandered u.p: hmpd & eased whn btn ins fnl f)...........................................¾ **7** 6/1$^{2}$ 97 73
4673$^{4}$ **Harbour Island (81)** (MRStoute) **4-8-7b** LDettori(12) (mid div: hdwy u.p over 3f out: styd on wl: nrst fin) ..........5 **8** 20/1 85 61
4365$^{12}$ **Trainglot (77)** (JGFitzGerald) **9-8-3** LCharnock(11) (b: chsd ldrs: rdn over 6f out: no imp after) .....................2½ **9** 20/1 78 54
4447$^{6}$ **Embryonic (IRE) (78)** (RFFisher) **4-8-4** GCarter(10) (mid div: hdwy 4f out: rdn & no imp) ..............................½ **10** 50/1 79 55
4431$^{7}$ **Secret Service (IRE) (73)** (CWThornton) **4-7-10**(3) NVarley(4) (lw: mid div: hdwy 6f out: sn in tch & hrd drvn: one pce fnl 2f)...........................................1½ **11** 33/1 73 49
4260* **Jiyush (92)** (HThomsonJones) **3-8-7** 4x RHills(7) (in tch: effrt 4f out: rdn & grad wknd fnl 2½f)........................2 **12** 9/2$^{1}$ 90 55
4457* **Good Hand (USA) (70)** (SEKettlewell) **10-7-10** 4x GBardwell(5) (bhd: hrd rdn over 5f out: nvr nrr)......................1 **13** 25/1 67 43
4465* **Better Offer (IRE) (102)** (GHarwood) **4-10-0** 4x WRSwinburn(22) (bhd: hdwy u.p 4f out: nvr rchd ldrs) ...........nk **14** 20/1 99 75
**Sea Plane (70)** (ALBates,France) **7-7-10b** WMessina(23) (bhd: gd hdwy 6f out & sn prom: wknd 3f out).........½ **15** 50/1 66 42
3928* **Chris's Lad (71)** (BJMeehan) **5-7-11b**ow1 CRutter(9) (rdn 6f out: n.d)..............................hd **16** 33/1 67 42
4476$^{9}$ **Blaze Away (USA) (76)** (IABalding) **5-7-11**(5) MartinDwyer(6) (lw: hdwy on outside ½-wy: rdn 5f out: sn btn) .nk **17** 50/1 72 48
1835$^{7}$ **Runaway Pete (USA) (70)** (MCPipe) **6-7-10** NCarlisle(16) (bhd: rdn 6f out: n.d).............................2½ **18** 66/1 64 40
3834$^{8}$ **Danjing (IRE) (88)** (MCPipe) **4-9-0** RHughes(19) (chsd ldrs: pushed along 5f out: wknd fnl 3f) .......................1¼ **19** 40/1 80 56
4626$^{F}$ **Claireswan (IRE) (70)** (MHTompkins) **4-7-7**(3) DWright(21) (drvn along & bhd fnl 7f)..............................½ **20** 100/1 62 38
4447$^{4}$ **Ivor's Flutter (82)** (DRCElsworth) **7-8-8** DHarrison(17) (bhd: drvn along 6f out: n.d)...............................s.h **21** 12/1 74 50
4604$^{4}$ **Paradise Navy (70)** (CREgerton) **7-7-3b**(7) RMullen(8) (racd wd: effrt 7f out: sn rdn & btn) .............................. **22** 66/1 — —
4377* **Candle Smile (USA) (88)** (MRStoute) **4-9-0** JReid(25) (prom tl wknd 6f out)........................................ **23** 10/1$^{3}$ — —
2711$^{5}$ **Witney-de-Bergerac (IRE) (70)** (JSMoore) **4-7-10** NAdams(20) (a bhd) ........................................ **24** 100/1 — —
1710$^{6}$ **Granby Bell (70)** (PHayward) **5-7-3**(7) PDoe(1) (cl up tl wknd 7f out)........................................ **25** 150/1 — —
4377$^{5}$ **Captain's Guest (IRE) (95)** (GHarwood) **6-9-7** AClark(2) (rdn 7f out: sn lost tch)........................................ **26** 50/1 — —
(SP 129.0%) **26 Rn**

**3m 51.17** (0.77) CSF £663.50 CT £4,760.16 TOTE £21.00: £3.00 £7.20 £2.20 £4.30 (£422.80) Trio £1,778.10 OWNER Mr F. J. Carter (SWINDON) BRED Hascombe and Valiant Studs

LONG HANDICAP Sea Plane 7-0 Floating Line 7-8 Runaway Pete (USA) 7-5 Claireswan (IRE) 6-12 Inchcailloch (IRE) 7-2 Paradise Navy 7-8 Chris's Lad 7-8 Witney-de-Bergerac (IRE) 6-12 Granby Bell 6-5 Good Hand (USA) 7-4

WEIGHT FOR AGE 3yo-11lb

**4604* Inchcailloch (IRE)** put up a super performance from 8lb out of the handicap and, had a gap come when he first wanted it, he would have won more convincingly. (20/1)
**3598* En Vacances (IRE)** seems to have been trained with this in mind, but she got outpaced at a vital stage three furlongs out and, despite picking up well at the end, always had too much on. (50/1)
**3972* Canon Can (USA)**, due to go up 15lb in future handicaps, ran a smashing race, always being in the thick of things but, when it came down to a battle, he was just short of speed when it mattered. (9/2)
**4557* Floating Line** helped force the pace and really turned it on in the last half-mile, but was just tapped for toe in the final furlong. (20/1)
**4596 Sea Victor** is coming back to form as the season ends and, should an opportunity arise, he should be kept in mind. (40/1)
**4327* Ballynakelly** tried really hard to get into it in the last three-quarters of a mile, but this thorough stayer was just short of the necessary speed, and a stronger earlier pace would have suited him better. (12/1)
**3834* Orchestra Stall** always had a good enough position, but he was inclined to wander about under pressure and, after causing the winner problems, was then eased when beaten. (6/1)
**4673 Harbour Island** took a long time to find his stride and basically lacked the speed to make any impression. (20/1)
**3983 Trainglot**, taken off his legs halfway up the straight, found his chance had then gone. (20/1)
**4447 Embryonic (IRE)** got pretty warm beforehand and, after racing up with the pace, weakened in the last three furlongs. (50/1)

## 4772 OLIVIER DOUIEB MEMORIAL RATED STKS H'CAP (0-100) (3-Y.O+) (Class B)

3-35 (3-38) **5f (Rowley)** £8,966.50 (£3,323.50: £1,599.25: £658.75: £266.88: £110.12) Stalls: Low GOING minus 0.22 sec per fur (GF)

SP RR SF

4466$^{11}$ **Midnight Escape (91)** (CFWall) **3-8-12** NCarlisle(21) (prom far side: hdwy to ld ins fnl f: r.o) ...........................— **1** 25/1 100 76

4679[12] **Lago Di Varano (86)** (RMWhitaker) **4-8-7v** AClark(8) (chsd ldrs stands' side: ev ch ins fnl f: kpt on)................¾ **2** 16/1 93 69
4679[11] **Swynford Dream (86)** (JFBottomley) **3-8-7** JLowe(14) (w ldr: rdn 2f out: kpt on wl fnl f)..................................hd **3** 20/1 92 68
4679[17] **Portelet (87)** (RGuest) **4-8-3**(5) DGriffiths(22) (racd far side: mde most tl hdd ins fnl f: kpt on)........................hd **4** 25/1 93 69
4687[16] **Tedburrow (88)** (MrsAMNaughton) **4-8-9** ACulhane(4) (hdwy stands' side 2f out: hmpd ins fnl f: fin wl).........hd **5** 16/1 94 70
4561[3] **Crofters Ceilidh (86)** (BAMcMahon) **4-8-7b** SSanders(13) (racd far side: hdwy 2f out: hung bdly lft: kpt on wl fnl f)..........s.h **6** 16/1 92 68
4561[2] **Ansellman (86)** (JBerry) **6-8-7b** GCarter(17) (a chsng ldrs far side: kpt on u.p fnl f)........................................s.h **7** 14/1 91 67
4679[4] **Bolshoi (IRE) (100)** (JBerry) **4-9-7b** EmmaO'Gorman(18) (bhd far side: hdwy u.p 2f out: nrst fin)..................nk **8** 9/2[1] 104 80
4466[17] **Bowden Rose (91)** (MBlanshard) **4-8-12b** JQuinn(11) (led stands' side: ev ch over 1f out: edgd rt: kpt on one pce)..........s.h **9** 33/1 95 71
4554[4] **Ziggy's Dancer (USA) (86)** (EJAlston) **5-8-7** KFallon(16) (hdwy ½-wy: sn in tch: nt qckn fnl f).......................1¼ **10** 14/1 86 62
4687[9] **Takadou (IRE) (86)** (MissLCSiddall) **5-8-7** DHarrison(3) (lw: bhd tl r.o fnl f)..........................................nk **11** 25/1 85 61
4198[21] **Youdontsay (86)** (TJNaughton) **4-8-4**(3) MHenry(6) (nvr trbld ldrs)..........................................nk **12** 40/1 84 60
4687[8] **Mr Bergerac (IRE) (86)** (BPalling) **5-8-7** TSprake(10) (sn drvn along & bhd: n.d)..........................................1¼ **13** 11/1 80 56
4581[7] **Sea-Deer (86)** (CADwyer) **7-8-7** RHills(12) (prom tl wknd over 1f out)..........................................1 **14** 16/1 77 53
4466[10] **Double Quick (IRE) (90)** (MJohnston) **4-8-11** MRoberts(20) (chsd ldrs far side tl wknd appr fnl f)..................s.h **15** 20/1 81 57
4466[9] **That Man Again (90)** (SCWilliams) **4-8-11** TQuinn(9) (cl up over 3f)..........................................hd **16** 14/1 81 57
4561[6] **Kunucu (IRE) (90)** (TDBarron) **3-8-11** MHills(19) (racd far side: n.d)..........................................¾ **17** 20/1 78 54
4561[4] **Saheeel (USA) (91)** (SbinSuroor) **3-8-12** LDettori(5) (outpcd & bhd fr ½-wy)..........................................nk **18** 8/1[2] 78 54
4679[3] **Sir Joey (USA) (86)** (PGMurphy) **7-8-7** SDrowne(1) (a bhd)..........................................½ **19** 10/1[3] 72 48
945[7] **Repertory (96)** (MRChannon) **3-9-3** RHughes(15) (lw: chsd ldrs far side tl wknd fnl 2f)..........................................2 **20** 40/1 75 51
4452[12] **Twice as Sharp (86)** (PWHarris) **4-8-7** GHind(7) (lw: cl up stands' side tl wknd wl over 1f out)......................s.h **21** 16/1 65 41
2143[9] **Willow Dale (IRE) (86)** (DRCElsworth) **3-8-7** PatEddery(2) (bhd fr ½-wy)..........................................3 **22** 25/1 56 32
(SP 133.6%) **22 Rn**

**58.82 secs** (0.12) CSF £356.24 CT £7,335.56 TOTE £60.70: £12.10 £4.70 £5.10 £5.80 (£738.90) Trio £2,018.70; £2,274.66 to Pontefract 21/10/96 OWNER Mr Mervyn Ayers (NEWMARKET) BRED M. L. Ayers

LONG HANDICAP Lago Di Varano 8-6 Swynford Dream 8-5 Sea-Deer 8-4 Youdontsay 8-1 Takadou (IRE) 8-0 Crofters Ceilidh 8-3 Ansellman 8-4 Ziggy's Dancer (USA) 8-3 Willow Dale (IRE) 8-0

STEWARDS' ENQUIRY Sanders susp. 28-30/10/96 (careless riding).

**2143* Midnight Escape** bounced back to form here in tremendous style and was always in command in the last half-furlong. (25/1)
**4116 Lago Di Varano** has not run a bad race for a while and this was back to his very best, but he just failed to quicken enough late on. (16/1)
**4521* Swynford Dream** is in terrific form just now and was in the thick of things throughout here. (20/1)
**4505* Portelet** came back to form here after a poor effort last time, and kept fighting back when headed. (25/1)
**4116 Tedburrow** appeared unlucky as he took a hefty knock inside the final furlong. But for this he would have been second at worst. (16/1)
**4561 Crofters Ceilidh** caused a fair amount of trouble by hanging left in the last two furlongs. (16/1)
**4561 Ansellman** is pretty high in the weights, but he still ran a useful race. (14/1)
**4679 Bolshoi (IRE)** could not get into his stride soon enough on this occasion. (9/2)
**3875 Bowden Rose** is liable to come good at this time of year but, when she decided to run on this occasion, it was always too late. (33/1)
**3875 That Man Again** (14/1: 10/1-16/1)

## 4773 DUBAI CHAMPION STKS (Gp 1) (3-Y.O+) (Class A)

4-15 (4-16) **1m 2f** **(Rowley)** £174,126.00 (£64,434.00: £30,917.00: £12,635.00: £5,017.50: £1,970.50) Stalls: Low GOING minus 0.22 sec per fur (GF)

SP RR SF

4443[2] **Bosra Sham (USA) (128)** (HRACecil) **3-8-8** PatEddery(4) (trckd ldrs: stdy hdwy to ld wl over 1f out: edgd lft: rdn & r.o strly)..........— **1** 9/4[2] 134 74
3670* **Halling (USA) (130)** (SbinSuroor) **5-9-2** LDettori(2) (lw: trckd ldr: led & hung rt 3f out: hdd wl over 1f out: kpt on)..........2½ **2** Evens[1] 133 78
4281a* **Timarida (IRE)** (JOxx,Ireland) **4-8-13** JPMurtagh(1) (trckd ldrs: effrt 3f out: ev ch & n.m.r 1½f out: r.o one pce fnl f)..........1 **3** 15/2[3] 128 73
3996* **Even Top (IRE) (123)** (MHTompkins) **3-8-11** TQuinn(3) (lw: led to 3f out: kpt on wl fnl f)..........................hd **4** 14/1 131 71
4443[3] **First Island (IRE) (124)** (GWragg) **4-9-2** MHills(5) (hld up: effrt 3f out: nt pce to chal)..........................2½ **5** 14/1 127 72
4281a[3] **Glory of Dancer (120)** (PAKelleway) **3-8-11** OPeslier(6) (hld up: rdn 3f out: no imp)..........................hd **6** 40/1 127 67
(SP 108.3%) **6 Rn**

**2m 3.71** (0.11) CSF £4.56 TOTE £3.10: £1.50 £1.50 (£2.30) OWNER Mr Wafic Said (NEWMARKET) BRED Gerald W. Leigh

WEIGHT FOR AGE 3yo-5lb

**4443 Bosra Sham (USA)** has had more than her fair share of problems this year, but at last got everything right, and showed what a tremendous filly she is by winning this most authoritatively. (9/4)
**3670* Halling (USA)** may not have been at his very best as he went to his right when first asked a question and was well beaten on entering the final furlong. (Evens)
**4281a* Timarida (IRE)** came here after a coughing scare early in the week, but still ran a tremendous race, and being short of room made little to no difference. (15/2)
**3996* Even Top (IRE)** showed a moderate action, but still ran well and, if anything, did not go fast enough early on. He ran as though longer trips are what he needs. (14/1: 10/1-16/1)
**4443 First Island (IRE)** has run some tremendous races this season and looked past his best here, as he never really threatened to get into it. (14/1)
**4281a Glory of Dancer** has been fancied to win everything bar the FA Cup this season but, to give him credit, he has put up some fine performances. On this occasion though, he never looked likely to make an impression. (40/1)

## 4774 BEDFORD LODGE HOTEL BENTINCK STKS (Listed) (3-Y.O+) (Class A)

4-45 (4-48) **6f** **(Rowley)** £12,253.60 (£4,542.40: £2,186.20: £901.00: £365.50: £151.30) Stalls: Low GOING minus 0.22 sec per fur (GF)

SP RR SF

4239* **Russian Revival (USA) (110)** (SbinSuroor) **3-8-11** WRSwinburn(3) (led after 1f: r.o wl u.p fnl f)....................— **1** 20/1 120 83
2663a[12] **Passion For Life (114)** (GLewis) **3-9-1** PatEddery(1) (cl up: rdn wl over 1f out: r.o)..........................1½ **2** 12/1 120 83
4660a[4] **Easy Option (IRE) (112)** (SbinSuroor) **4-8-7** LDettori(8) (lw: hld up: smooth hdwy over 2f out: squeezed thro over 1f out: no ex ins fnl f)..........1¼ **3** 5/2[1] 108 72
4442[5] **Lucky Lionel (USA) (112)** (RHannon) **3-8-11** OPeslier(9) (outpcd & bhd tl hdwy over 1f out: r.o towards fin)..¾ **4** 8/1[2] 111 74
4314[5] **Wildwood Flower (98)** (RHannon) **3-8-6** DaneO'Neill(4) (chsd ldrs: hdwy 2f out: rdn & btn ins fnl f)..............nk **5** 8/1[2] 105 68

4679$^{8}$ **Royale Figurine (IRE) (107)** (MJFetherston-Godley) **5-8-7** JReid(7) (in tch: outpcd 2f out: kpt on wl fnl f) ......nk **6** 8/1$^{2}$ 104 68

4442$^{11}$ **Carranita (IRE) (108)** (BPalling) **6-8-7** TSprake(5) (chsd ldrs: outpcd 2f out: no imp after)..............................s.h **7** 10/1$^{3}$ 104 68

4743a* **Branston Abby (IRE) (108)** (MJohnston) **7-8-7** MRoberts(12) (hld up: swtchd & effrt 2f out: no ex fnl f) ..........½ **8** 8/1$^{2}$ 103 67

4466$^{5}$ **Sea Dane (102)** (PWHarris) **3-8-11** GHind(2) (b: trckd ldrs: effrt over 2f out: btn over 1f out) ..............................1 **9** 25/1 105 68

4687$^{6}$ **Cyrano's Lad (IRE) (100)** (CADwyer) **7-8-12** CDwyer(10) (led 1f: cl up tl wknd over 1f out) ..............................¾ **10** 33/1 103 67

3612$^{8}$ **Latching (IRE) (85)** (RFJohnsonHoughton) **4-8-7** KFallon(6) (s.i.s: a outpcd & bhd)........................................2½ **11** 100/1 91 55

4660a$^{7}$ **Struggler (112)** (DRLoder) **4-8-12** RHughes(11) (chsd ldrs tl wknd wl over 1f out) ........................................1½ **12** 11/1 92 56

4406a$^{8}$ **Atraf (113)** (DMorley) **3-9-1** RHills(14) (lw: spd over 4f: wknd)..........................................................½ **13** 12/1 95 58

4442$^{10}$ **Averti (IRE) (102)** (WRMuir) **5-8-12** TQuinn(15) (bhd: effrt ½-wy: n.d)..........................................................½ **14** 40/1 90 54

2072$^{16}$ **Tumbleweed Ridge (110)** (BJMeehan) **3-8-11** MTebbutt(13) (s.i.s: pushed along & sn in tch: wknd 2f out) ..2½ **15** 20/1 83 46

(SP 125.6%) **15 Rn**

**1m 11.38** (-0.42) CSF £223.44 TOTE £15.70: £4.60 £3.40 £1.60 (£88.60) Trio £100.60 OWNER Godolphin (NEWMARKET) BRED Swettenham Stud

WEIGHT FOR AGE 3yo-1lb

**4239* Russian Revival (USA)** has been firing too high for most of the season and, back over his best trip here, won in good style. (20/1)

**2663a Passion For Life** ran a fine race from a yard out of form and could be one to follow next year. (12/1)

**4660a Easy Option (IRE)**, held up to get the trip, came sailing through approaching the final furlong, only then to run out of stamina in the last 150 yards. (5/2)

**4442 Lucky Lionel (USA)** was never on the bridle, but kept responding. Judging by the way he finished, he would have been in the shake-up with a little further to go. (8/1)

**4314 Wildwood Flower** had her chances, but was short of room and speed approaching the final furlong, and that was it. (8/1)

**4442 Royale Figurine (IRE)** ran well, but was always short of a turn of foot to make it. (8/1)

**3759* Carranita (IRE)** (10/1: 6/1-11/1)

**4743a* Branston Abby (IRE)** was always finding things happening too quickly in the last two furlongs, and was wisely not knocked about when beaten. When the rain really comes, she will be one to be reckoned with. (8/1: 6/1-9/1)

**4660a Struggler** (11/1: 7/1-12/1)

## 4775 NGK SPARK PLUGS H'CAP (0-95) (3-Y.O+) (Class C)

5-20 (5-23) **7f (Rowley)** £6,836.00 (£2,048.00: £984.00: £452.00) Stalls: Centre GOING minus 0.22 sec per fur (GF)

SP RR SF

4453$^{4}$ **Mezzanotte (IRE) (76)** (LMCumani) **3-8-7** LDettori(20) (lw: in tch: gd hdwy 2f out: led ins fnl f: r.o wl) ............— **1** 11/1 87 70

4688$^{2}$ **Warming Trends (91)** (SirMarkPrescott) **3-9-8** SSanders(13) (cl up: led wl over 1f out: hdd 1f out: r.o u.p) ....nk **2** 9/2$^{1}$ 101 84

4550$^{2}$ **Amber Fort (69)** (DRCElsworth) **3-7-11v**$^{(3)}$ MHenry(22) (a.p: hdwy to ld 1f out: hdd ins fnl f: kpt on u.p)........s.h **3** 16/1 79 62

4136$^{6}$ **Wild Rice (88)** (GWragg) **4-9-7** MHills(7) (b: trckd ldrs: chal 2f out: hrd drvn fnl f: kpt on)..............................s.h **4** 14/1 98 83

4136$^{11}$ **Chickawicka (IRE) (87)** (BPalling) **5-9-6** TSprake(12) (cl up tl wknd over 1f out) ..........................................2½ **5** 33/1 91 76

4571$^{2}$ **Broughtons Turmoil (77)** (WJMusson) **7-8-10** BDoyle(9) (styd on fnl 2f: nvr able to chal) ..............................1 **6** 11/1 79 64

1425$^{4}$ **Delta Soleil (USA) (88)** (PWHarris) **4-9-7** GHind(16) (chsd ldrs: ev ch 2f out: sn rdn & btn) ..............................1 **7** 14/1 88 73

3790$^{15}$ **She's My Love (72)** (JEBanks) **3-8-3** JQuinn(17) (led tl hdd & wknd wl over 1f out) ........................................hd **8** 16/1 72 55

4687$^{7}$ **Seigneurial (89)** (GHarwood) **4-9-8** AClark(15) (chsd ldrs tl wknd appr fnl f)..........................................................1 **9** 20/1 86 71

4554$^{3}$ **Saseedo (USA) (90)** (WAO'Gorman) **6-9-9** EmmaO'Gorman(21) (bhd: styd on fnl 2f: nrst fin)........................s.h **10** 10/1 87 72

4581$^{8}$ **Charlie Sillett (80)** (BWHills) **4-8-13** CRutter(5) (lw: bhd: hdwy over 1f out: nvr trbld ldrs) ..............................s.h **11** 20/1 77 62

4623$^{6}$ **Welton Arsenal (92)** (MRChannon) **4-9-11** RHughes(11) (mid div: effrt over 2f out: n.d)........................................1 **12** 25/1 87 72

4620$^{5}$ **Gymcrak Premiere (80)** (GHolmes) **8-8-13v** KFallon(8) (b.hind: drvn along & bhd tl sme late hdwy) ..............½ **13** 25/1 74 59

4688$^{21}$ **Knobbleeneeze (74)** (MRChannon) **6-8-0v**$^{(7)}$ AEddery(4) (in tch: effrt over 2f out: grad wknd)........................hd **14** 25/1 67 52

4581$^{3}$ **Lough Erne (78)** (CFWall) **4-8-11** RHills(1) (prom: ev ch 2f out: wknd over 1f out) ........................................½ **15** 8/1$^{3}$ 70 55

4554$^{5}$ **Law Commission (95)** (DRCElsworth) **6-10-0** TQuinn(19) (bhd: sme hdwy 2f out: n.d)........................................¾ **16** 14/1 86 71

4432$^{7}$ **Courageous Dancer (IRE) (74)** (BHanbury) **4-8-7** WRyan(6) (a rr div) ..........................................................1¼ **17** 20/1 62 47

4136$^{W}$ **Royal Mark (IRE) (88)** (JWWatts) **3-9-5b** WRSwinburn(2) (a bhd)..........................................................hd **18** 25/1 76 59

4609* **Castan (IRE) (74)** (JLDunlop) **3-8-5**ow1 PatEddery(18) (nvr wnt pce)..........................................................hd **19** 7/1$^{2}$ 61 43

4444$^{5}$ **My Best Valentine (94)** (JWhite) **6-9-13** SDrowne(3) (lw: prom 4f: wknd) ..........................................................5 **20** 20/1 70 55

2577$^{2}$ **Flying Pennant (IRE) (72)** (RHannon) **3-8-3**ow2 DaneO'Neill(14) (a bhd) ..........................................................nk **21** 20/1 47 28

4571$^{5}$ **My Gallery (IRE) (86)** (ABailey) **5-9-2**$^{(3)}$ DWright(10) (dwlt: a outpcd & wl bhd)..............................................¾ **22** 20/1 59 44

(SP 146.2%) **22 Rn**

**1m 24.77** (0.27) CSF £63.57 CT £794.65 TOTE £12.80: £2.20 £2.00 £4.70 £3.50 (£30.30) Trio £183.60 OWNER Mr P. A. Leonard (NEWMARKET) BRED Biddestone Stud

WEIGHT FOR AGE 3yo-2lb

**4453 Mezzanotte (IRE)** took the eye in the paddock and won his first race, quickening really well to do so. (11/1)

**4688 Warming Trends** kept trying hard and more give in the ground would help. (9/2)

**4550 Amber Fort** keeps running well and deserves a change of luck. (16/1)

**4136 Wild Rice** travelled as though this was his for the taking but, when it came down to it, he just failed to quicken enough. He is in good heart at the moment. (14/1)

**3920 Chickawicka (IRE)** ran a sound race, helping to force the pace, but was always short of speed in the closing stages. (33/1)

**4571 Broughtons Turmoil** has gone up 4lb for finishing second last time and ran well again here, but the effort was always too late. (11/1)

**4581 Charlie Sillett** gave the impression that, with some give in the ground, there is a race to be found. (20/1)

T/Jkpt: Not won; £15,794.97 to Pontefract 21/10/96. T/Plpt: £1,295.20 (35.74 Tckts). T/Qdpt: £155.50 (18.53 Tckts). AA

# 4572-WOLVERHAMPTON (L-H) (Standard)

## Saturday October 19th

WEATHER: raining

## 4776 ATHENA H'CAP (0-65) (3-Y.O) (Class F)

7-00 (7-01) **5f (Fibresand)** £2,415.00 (£665.00: £315.00) Stalls: Low GOING minus 0.01 sec per fur (STD)

SP RR SF

4356$^{13}$ **Ramsey Hope (58)** (CWFairhurst) **3-9-0b** LCharnock(8) (mde virtually all: edgd lft fnl f: r.o wl) ........................— **1** 40/1 66 46

4610$^{4}$ **Night Harmony (IRE) (53)** (RHannon) **3-8-9** DHarrison(7) (b: lw: a.p: ev ch 2f out: one pce fnl f)..................1¾ **2** 9/2$^{2}$ 55 35

*4333*$^{12}$ **Queens Check (62)** (MissJFCraze) **3-9-4b** NConnorton(5) (chsd ldrs: outpcd 2f out: rallied ins fnl f: fin wl).....½ **3** 12/1 63 43

*4577*$^{4}$ **Napier Star (59)** (MrsNMacauley) **3-8-12v**$^{(3)}$ CTeague(13) (b.hind: lw: racd wd: a.p: one pce fnl 2f) ................2 **4** 5/2$^{1}$ 53 33

| | Horse | Dist | Pos | SP | RR | SF |
|---|---|---|---|---|---|---|
| 4382[18] | **Playmaker (57)** (DNicholls) **3-8-13b** JFortune(11) (prom 3f) | 3 | **5** | 11/1 | 42 | 22 |
| 4130[7] | **Songsheet (65)** (MartynMeade) **3-9-0**(7) DSweeney(6) (nvr nr to chal) | 1¼ | **6** | 12/1 | 46 | 26 |
| 1964[7] | **Risking (55)** (GLewis) **3-8-8**(3) AWhelan(12) (b: prom 3f) | nk | **7** | 12/1 | 35 | 15 |
| 4130[11] | **Tymeera (55)** (BPalling) **3-8-6**(5) MartinDwyer(2) (chsd ldrs 3f) | s.h | **8** | 12/1 | 35 | 15 |
| 3937[12] | **Need You Badly (55)** (SPCWoods) **3-8-4**(7) CWebb(3) (s.s: a bhd) | 2 | **9** | 10/1 | 28 | 8 |
| 4521[14] | **Smithereens (64)** (PTWalwyn) **3-9-6v[1]** JStack(9) (s.s: sme hdwy & rn v.wd 3f out: sn bhd) | ½ | **10** | 20/1 | 36 | 16 |
| *32[9]* | **Lady Eclat (59)** (JAGlover) **3-9-1b** NDay(10) (bhd fnl 3f) | 5 | **11** | 14/1 | 15 | — |
| 4521[13] | **Il Doria (IRE) (56)** (AHide) **3-8-12** GBardwell(1) (b.hind: a bhd) | 2 | **12** | 20/1 | 5 | — |
| 478[5] | **Gi La High (54)** (JBerry) **3-8-10** GCarter(4) (lw: s.s: a bhd) | 1¾ | **13** | 8/1[3] | — | — |
| | | | | (SP 124.7%) | **13 Rn** | |

**61.7 secs** (3.00) CSF £203.88 CT £2,157.99 TOTE £60.40: £11.20 £2.30 £3.70 (£127.00) Trio Not won; £57.58 to Pontefract 21/10/96
OWNER Mr C. D. Barber-Lomax (MIDDLEHAM) BRED Norton Grove Stud Ltd
**4081 Ramsey Hope**, dropped 2lb, is considered to barely get six, so the minimum is his optimum trip on this surface. (40/1)
**4610 Night Harmony (IRE)**, down 2lb, despite a decent effort last time, was making his debut on the Sand. (9/2)
**3091* Queens Check** was tried over six last time and one can see why on this evidence. (12/1)
**4577 Napier Star** is still 8lb higher than when scoring over course and distance in July. (5/2)
**3223 Playmaker** was trying his luck on the All-Weather, having been disappointing on Turf. (11/1)
**1684 Risking** (12/1: op 8/1)
**3416 Need You Badly** (10/1: 8/1-12/1)

## 4777 HERA CLAIMING STKS (2-Y.O) (Class F)

7-30 (7-37) **6f (Fibresand)** £2,415.00 (£665.00: £315.00) Stalls: Low GOING minus 0.01 sec per fur (STD)

| | Horse | Dist | Pos | SP | RR | SF |
|---|---|---|---|---|---|---|
| 4614[3] | **Burkes Manor (82)** (TDBarron) **2-9-5** DHarrison(4) (a.p: rdn over 3f out: led ins fnl f: edgd lft: r.o wl) | — | **1** | 3/1[2] | 81 | 54 |
| 4230[6] | **Just Loui (70)** (WGMTurner) **2-8-2**(7)ow2 DSweeney(7) (a.p: ev ch over 1f out: unable qckn) | 1½ | **2** | 16/1 | 67 | 38 |
| *4576** | **Robec Girl (IRE) (67)** (JBerry) **2-8-3**(5) PRoberts(2) (a.p: led 4f out tl ins fnl f) | s.h | **3** | 11/1 | 66 | 39 |
| 4493[4] | **Northern Girl (IRE) (60)** (BJMeehan) **2-7-7b**(5)ow2 MartinDwyer(11) (prom tl hrd rdn & wknd over 2f out) | 11 | **4** | 6/1[3] | 27 | — |
| 4546* | **Commander Jones (IRE) (85)** (BJMeehan) **2-9-5** MTebbutt(6) (led 2f: wknd over 2f out) | 2½ | **5** | 5/4[1] | 41 | 14 |
| 4586[11] | **Our Kevin (68)** (KMcAuliffe) **2-8-10v**(3) PMcCabe(5) (rdn & hdwy over 3f out: wknd 2f out) | 3 | **6** | 9/1 | 27 | — |
| 4699[5] | **Skyers Flyer (IRE) (81)** (RonaldThompson) **2-9-0** NConnorton(8) (bhd fnl 2f) | 1¼ | **7** | 14/1 | 25 | — |
| 4600[9] | **Hever Golf Lover (IRE)** (TJNaughton) **2-9-0** GCarter(10) (bhd fnl 2f) | 1½ | **8** | 25/1 | 21 | — |
| *4576[10]* | **Emma's Risk (46)** (RHarris) **2-7-3**(7) AMcCarthy(12) (a bhd) | ½ | **9** | 33/1 | 1 | — |
| 3336[4] | **Select Lady** (APJarvis) **2-7-10**(7)ow3 CCarver(3) (b.nr hind: a bhd) | 5 | **10** | 33/1 | — | — |
| 4346[4] | **Hit Or Miss (60)** (PCHaslam) **2-7-4**(7) RMullen(1) (s.v.s: a bhd) | 2 | **11** | 14/1 | — | — |
| 4459[6] | **Imperial Garden (IRE) (69)** (PCHaslam) **2-8-13** JFortune(13) (a bhd: t.o) | 9 | **12** | 14/1 | — | — |
| *916[10]* | ***Sandkatoon (IRE)*** (JSMoore) **2-8-1**(5)ow2 AimeeCook(9) (Withdrawn not unders Starter's orders: uns rdr gng to s: rdr inj) | | **W** | 33/1 | — | — |
| | | | | (SP 140.6%) | **12 Rn** | |

**1m 14.8** (0.50 under 2y best) (3.40) CSF £52.82 TOTE £3.80: £1.60 £3.60 £2.90 (£51.20) Trio Not won; £96.67 to Pontefract 21/10/96
OWNER M P Burke Developments Ltd (THIRSK) BRED Messinger Stud Ltd
Burkes Manor clmd CBjorling £12,000; Commander Jones (IRE) clmd CBjorling £12,000
**4614 Burkes Manor** has some good form in nurseries and proved too good for this company on his first run on the Sand. (3/1: 4/1-5/2)
**3823 Just Loui** came up against an above-average sort in the winner for this type of event. (16/1)
**4576* Robec Girl (IRE)** did not seem inconvenienced by the extra furlong, and battled it out for the runner-up spot when headed. (11/1)
**4493 Northern Girl (IRE)** was struggling with the surface soon after halfway. (6/1)
**4546* Commander Jones (IRE)** is another who did not seem to relish the Sand. (5/4)
**3299* Skyers Flyer (IRE)** (14/1: op 7/1)
**4346 Hit Or Miss** (14/1: 8/1-16/1)

## 4778 APOLLO H'CAP (0-70) (3-Y.O+) (Class E)

8-00 (8-04) **6f (Fibresand)** £3,210.00 (£960.00: £460.00: £210.00) Stalls: Low GOING minus 0.01 sec per fur (STD)

| | Horse | Dist | Pos | SP | RR | SF |
|---|---|---|---|---|---|---|
| *4333[2]* | **Imposing Time (67)** (MissGayKelleway) **5-9-13b** SSanders(13) (b: a.p: led over 3f out: all out) | — | **1** | 4/1[2] | 76 | 51 |
| *4333[9]* | **Bold Street (IRE) (61)** (ABailey) **6-9-4b**(3) DWright(12) (b: sn outpcd: gd hdwy 2f out: ev ch 1f out: unable qckn) | 1 | **2** | 10/1 | 67 | 42 |
| *4577** | **Walk the Beat (65)** (MartynMeade) **6-9-4**(7) DSweeney(9) (lw: trckd ldrs: rdn & outpcd over 2f out: rallied over 1f out: r.o) | nk | **3** | 7/2[1] | 71 | 46 |
| 3313[8] | **Yo Kiri-B (58)** (TJNaughton) **5-9-4** BDoyle(11) (chsd ldrs: one pce fnl f) | 1¼ | **4** | 11/1 | 60 | 35 |
| 4688[23] | **Legal Issue (IRE) (62)** (WWHaigh) **4-9-8** SWhitworth(8) (s.i.s: hdwy over 1f out: nvr nrr) | 4 | **5** | 14/1 | 54 | 29 |
| 4499[7] | **Smooth Asset (IRE) (65)** (PWChapple-Hyam) **3-9-7**(3) RHavlin(7) (prom tl wknd wl over 1f out) | s.h | **6** | 11/1 | 56 | 30 |
| | **Dieci Anno (IRE) (67)** (BPalling) **3-9-12** TSprake(4) (led over 2f: eased whn btn fnl f: sddle slipped) | 1 | **7** | 20/1 | 56 | 30 |
| *4577[2]* | **Bold Aristocrat (IRE) (57)** (RHollinshead) **5-9-0**(3) FLynch(2) (outpcd) | 2 | **8** | 11/2[3] | 40 | 15 |
| 4460[3] | **Cavers Yangous (68)** (MJohnston) **5-9-7v**(7) KSked(3) (lw: a bhd) | 1¼ | **9** | 10/1 | 48 | 23 |
| 4430[5] | **Allwight Then (IRE) (58)** (DJSCosgrove) **5-9-4** JFortune(1) (chsd ldrs tl wknd wl over 1f out) | nk | **10** | 8/1 | 37 | 12 |
| *4333[13]* | **Leigh Crofter (58)** (PDCundell) **7-8-13b**(5) DGriffiths(5) (bhd fnl 3f) | 1¾ | **11** | 20/1 | 33 | 8 |
| *4577[3]* | **Cheeky Chappy (58)** (DWChapman) **5-9-4b** ACulhane(10) (prom tl wknd wl over 1f out) | 2 | **12** | 15/2 | 27 | 2 |
| | | | | (SP 131.5%) | **12 Rn** | |

**1m 15.6** (4.20) CSF £44.74 CT £146.07 TOTE £4.70: £2.00 £5.40 £1.90 (£28.10) Trio £93.20; £32.82 to Pontefract 21/10/96 OWNER Mr Michael Watt (WHITCOMBE) BRED James H. Slade
WEIGHT FOR AGE 3yo-1lb
OFFICIAL EXPLANATION **Dieci Anno (IRE): hung right coming into the straight, causing the saddle to slip.**
**4333 Imposing Time**, up 4lb, had to dig deep to hold on in the closing stages. (4/1)
**3953 Bold Street (IRE)** has been slipping down the Ratings, and showed definite signs of a return to form. (10/1)
**4577* Walk the Beat** had been penalised 5lb for his course and distance win a fortnight ago. (7/2)
**3313 Yo Kiri-B** was 1lb higher than when runner-up over course and distance in June. (11/1)
**2630 Legal Issue (IRE)**, not helped by a sluggish start, found this trip inadequate. (14/1)
**2913 Smooth Asset (IRE)** was dropping back to sprinting for this first try on the artificial surface. (11/1)
**4460 Cavers Yangous** (10/1: 8/1-12/1)

## 4779 ZEUS H'CAP (0-70) (3-Y.O+) (Class E)

8-30 (8-33) **1m 4f (Fibresand)** £3,210.00 (£960.00: £460.00: £210.00) Stalls: Low GOING minus 0.01 sec per fur (STD)

| | | | | SP | RR | SF |
|---|---|---|---|---|---|---|
| 4626[5] | **Glow Forum (67)** (LMontagueHall) **5-9-6**(5) MartinDwyer(10) (b: hld up: stdy hdwy 6f out: hrd rdn 2f out: led nr fin: all out) | — | **1** | 11/4[1] | 83 | 56 |
| *4080** | **Heighth of Fame (63)** (DBurchell) **5-9-0**(7) KSked(5) (led: hrd rdn 2f out: hdd nr fin) | nk | **2** | 13/2[3] | 79 | 52 |
| 4000[13] | **Troubadour Song (70)** (WWHaigh) **4-9-11**(3) PMcCabe(8) (bhd tl gd hdwy 4f out: styd on fnl f) | ½ | **3** | 10/1 | 85 | 58 |
| *4575[7]* | **China Castle (70)** (PCHaslam) **3-9-7** GCarter(4) (bhd tl gd hdwy 4f out: eased whn btn ins fnl f) | 7 | **4** | 5/1[2] | 76 | 42 |
| 4551[4] | **Allstars Express (63)** (TJNaughton) **3-9-0** SSanders(3) (hld up: hdwy 6f out: hrd rdn 5f out: wknd 4f out) | 7 | **5** | 14/1 | 59 | 25 |
| 4559[4] | **Love Bateta (IRE) (66)** (JEBanks) **3-9-3** JStack(9) (chsd ldrs: reminders 6f out: wknd over 4f out) | 1½ | **6** | 16/1 | 60 | 26 |
| 4568[17] | **Nigel's Lad (IRE) (68)** (PCHaslam) **4-9-12** JFortune(2) (chsd ldr: wknd over 4f out) | 11 | **7** | 7/1 | 48 | 21 |
| *4092[13]* | **Claque (61)** (DWChapman) **4-9-5b** ACulhane(11) (a bhd) | ½ | **8** | 14/1 | 40 | 13 |
| 4513* | **Shahik (USA) (63)** (DHaydnJones) **6-9-7** LCharnock(7) (bhd fnl 4f: t.o) | 10 | **9** | 5/1[2] | 29 | 2 |
| | **Tovarich (62)** (RonaldThompson) **5-9-6** NConnorton(12) (bhd fnl 5f: t.o) | 7 | **10** | 33/1 | 18 | — |
| 3918[7] | **La Pellegrina (IRE) (63)** (PWChapple-Hyam) **3-8-11**(3) RHavlin(6) (prom 7f: t.o) | s.h | **11** | 14/1 | 19 | — |
| 4563[9] | **Forzair (66)** (JJO'Neill) **4-9-3**(7)ow1 DJewett(1) (prom 6f: t.o) | 5 | **12** | 16/1 | 16 | — |
| | | | | (SP 129.6%) | **12 Rn** | |

**2m 40.4** (7.90) CSF £22.05 CT £154.51 TOTE £3.30: £1.10 £2.90 £3.40 (£17.90) Trio £16.30 OWNER Mr Andy Smith (EPSOM) BRED Forum Bloodstock Ltd

WEIGHT FOR AGE 3yo-7lb

**4626 Glow Forum** had to work hard to defy an 11lb hike in the Ratings for her easy win from All On here last month. (11/4: 7/4-3/1)

**4080* Heighth of Fame** did his best to overcome an 8lb penalty for winning a seller here six weeks ago. (13/2)

**3280 Troubadour Song** appreciated the return to twelve furlongs on the Sand. (10/1)

**4575 China Castle** would have finished much closer had his rider not accepted the inevitable in the final 100 yards. (5/1)

## 4780 PLYVINE CATERING (S) STKS (2-Y.O F) (Class F)

9-00 (9-01) **1m 100y (Fibresand)** £2,415.00 (£665.00: £315.00) Stalls: Low GOING minus 0.01 sec per fur (STD)

| | | | | SP | RR | SF |
|---|---|---|---|---|---|---|
| 4477[5] | **Bonne Ville** (BPalling) **2-8-7** TSprake(8) (a.p: led ins fnl f: drvn out) | — | **1** | 16/1 | 71 | 28 |
| 4715[2] | **Princess of Hearts (70)** (BJMeehan) **2-8-12b** BDoyle(11) (a.p: led 3f out tl ins fnl f: r.o) | nk | **2** | 6/4[1] | 75 | 32 |
| 4608[12] | **Royal Roulette** (SPCWoods) **2-8-7** DBiggs(13) (hdwy 4f out: sn hrd rdn: one pce fnl 2f) | 5 | **3** | 11/2[3] | 61 | 18 |
| 4562[2] | **Veerapong (IRE) (58)** (MWEasterby) **2-8-2b**(5) GParkin(12) (dwlt: sme hdwy fnl 2f: n.d) | 5 | **4** | 4/1[2] | 52 | 9 |
| 4339[8] | **Grovefair Dancer (IRE) (67)** (MissSJWilton) **2-8-12v** SWhitworth(9) (hld up: hdwy 6f out: hrd rdn 5f out: wknd over 3f out) | 8 | **5** | 4/1[2] | 41 | — |
| *4576[8]* | **Skyers Tryer (59)** (RonaldThompson) **2-8-12** NConnorton(7) (led after 1f: hdd 3f out: wknd 2f out) | ¾ | **6** | 20/1 | 40 | — |
| 4562[12] | **Fly Down To Rio (IRE) (42)** (DWPArbuthnot) **2-8-7b** DHarrison(3) (bhd fnl 4f) | 4 | **7** | 33/1 | 27 | — |
| 4694[10] | **Mujadil Express (IRE) (53)** (JSMoore) **2-8-2**(5) PPMurphy(4) (led 1f: wknd over 3f out) | 1¼ | **8** | 20/1 | 25 | — |
| *1084[3]* | **Tazio Nuvolari** (WGMTurner) **2-8-0**(7) DMcGaffin(2) (a bhd) | 3½ | **9** | 16/1 | 18 | — |
| 4564[8] | **Tycoon Tina** (WMBrisbourne) **2-8-0**(7) RMullen(1) (a bhd: t.o) | 8 | **10** | 25/1 | 3 | — |
| 4562[7] | **Poly Moon (48)** (MRChannon) **2-8-12** JFortune(10) (hld up: hdwy 6f out: wknd 4f out: t.o) | 9 | **11** | 20/1 | — | — |
| | **Sheeba** (MissAEEmbiricos) **2-8-0**(7) AMcCarthy(5) (lt-f: unf: a bhd: t.o) | 12 | **13** | 50/1 | — | — |
| | | | | (SP 130.2%) | **12 Rn** | |

**1m 51.6** (6.60) CSF £42.08 TOTE £25.40: £4.60 £1.50 £2.50 (£20.40) Trio Not won; £73.98 to Pontefract 21/10/96 OWNER Millbrook Associates (COWBRIDGE) BRED Scorrier Stud

Bt in 10,400 gns

**Bonne Ville**, a half-sister to The Butterwick Kid, was dropped in class for this switch to the Sand. (16/1)

**4715 Princess of Hearts** seemed set to score when taking it up, but found the winner had the edge in the final 200 yards. (6/4)

**4331 Royal Roulette** could not take advantage of this lower grade. (11/2: op 7/2)

**4562 Veerapong (IRE)** was upped in distance for this first outing on the Sand. (4/1)

## 4781 APHRODITE H'CAP (0-60) (3-Y.O+) (Class F)

9-30 (9-32) **1m 100y (Fibresand)** £2,415.00 (£665.00: £315.00) Stalls: Low GOING minus 0.01 sec per fur (STD)

| | | | | SP | RR | SF |
|---|---|---|---|---|---|---|
| 4511[7] | **Thai Morning (55)** (PWHarris) **3-9-6** GHind(9) (a.p: led over 6f out: clr wl over 1f out: easily) | — | **1** | 10/1 | 84+ | 63 |
| 3977[5] | **Allstars Rocket (55)** (TJNaughton) **3-9-6** TSprake(7) (a.p: chsd wnr 3f out: no imp fnl 2f) | 8 | **2** | 5/1[2] | 69 | 48 |
| 4256[16] | **Twin Creeks (59)** (VSoane) **5-9-13** SSanders(11) (a.p: one pce fnl 2f) | 5 | **3** | 7/1[3] | 63 | 45 |
| *4077[3]* | **People Direct (60)** (KMcAuliffe) **3-9-11** JFEgan(8) (b.hind: hdwy 3f out: nt rch ldrs) | 2 | **4** | 7/2[1] | 61 | 40 |
| 1319[18] | **Slievenamon (52)** (JEBanks) **3-8-10**(7) RMullen(12) (chsd ldrs: no hdwy fnl 2f) | nk | **5** | 25/1 | 52 | 31 |
| 4186[15] | **Hawaii Storm (FR) (55)** (DJSffrenchDavis) **8-9-4**(5) CAdamson(10) (dwlt: nvr nrr) | 5 | **6** | 20/1 | 46 | 28 |
| *4575[9]* | **Domino Flyer (58)** (MrsASwinbank) **3-9-9** JFortune(13) (led 2f: wknd over 2f out) | 1¾ | **7** | 10/1 | 45 | 24 |
| 4693[3] | **Angus McCoatup (IRE) (55)** (BAMcMahon) **3-9-6** GCarter(2) (b: prom over 5f) | 1¼ | **8** | 7/1[3] | 40 | 19 |
| 4216[12] | **Red Rusty (USA) (55)** (DMorris) **3-9-6b**[1] NDay(1) (prom over 5f) | hd | **9** | 16/1 | 40 | 19 |
| 4503[11] | **Arak (USA) (55)** (GCBravery) **8-9-9** SWhitworth(6) (b: a bhd) | 3 | **10** | 20/1 | 34 | 16 |
| *4089[7]* | **Sandmoor Denim (55)** (SRBowring) **9-9-6**(3) CTeague(4) (a bhd) | 2½ | **11** | 10/1 | 29 | 11 |
| | **Tanseeq (60)** (MGMeagher) **5-10-0** ACulhane(5) (a bhd: t.o fnl 5f) | 3½ | **12** | 33/1 | 28 | 10 |
| 4484[4] | **North Ardar (52)** (TWall) **6-9-3**(3) PMcCabe(3) (s.s: a t.o) | 14 | **13** | 5/1[2] | — | — |
| | | | | (SP 130.0%) | **13 Rn** | |

**1m 49.2** (4.20) CSF £60.20 CT £357.71 TOTE £13.80: £3.90 £2.70 £3.20 (£62.40) Trio £99.90; £91.48 to Pontefract 21/10/96 OWNER The Thai Connection (BERKHAMSTED) BRED R. G. Percival

WEIGHT FOR AGE 3yo-3lb

**4511 Thai Morning**, dropped 2lb, has been running well and proved a revelation over both the trip and the surface. (10/1)

**3977 Allstars Rocket** could do nothing more than chase the easy winner home. (5/1)

**4089 Twin Creeks** was running off the same mark as when second at Southwell last month. (7/1)

**4077 People Direct** does not seem so effective in handicaps as in claimers and sellers. (7/2)

**Slievenamon**, switching to the Sand, had not started shorter than 33/1 on his three starts in the spring. (25/1)

T/Plpt: £294.10 (34.65 Tckts). T/Qdpt: £38.40 (11.44 Tckts). KH

# 4422-FOLKESTONE (R-H) (Good to soft)
## Monday October 21st
WEATHER: sunny WIND: almost nil

### 4782 WESTENHANGER MAIDEN AUCTION STKS (I) (2-Y.O) (Class E)
1-30 (1-31) **6f 189y** £2,963.60 (£882.80: £420.40: £189.20) Stalls: High GOING: 0.39 sec per fur (GS)

| | Horse | Dist | Pos | SP | RR | SF |
|---|---|---|---|---|---|---|
| 3941[11] | **Havago** (RHannon) **2-8-5** WRyan(7) (lw: w ldr: led 2f out: swvd bdly lft over 1f out: hrd rdn: r.o wl) | — | 1 | 8/1 | 72 | 10 |
| 4545[5] | **Don Sebastian (77)** (WJHaggas) **2-8-10** MTebbutt(3) (hdwy 5f out: rdn over 1f out: unable qckn) | 1½ | 2 | 13/8[1] | 74 | 12 |
| | **Sidney The Kidney** (MJRyan) **2-7-5**(7) AMcCarthy(4) (neat: stdy hdwy over 1f out: r.o: bttr for r) | 2½ | 3 | 20/1 | 56 | — |
| 4087[7] | **Shalstayholy (IRE)** (GLMoore) **2-8-5** SWhitworth(13) (hld up: rdn over 2f out: r.o one pce) | s.h | 4 | 2/1[2] | 63 | 1 |
| | **Eastern Eagle (IRE)** (JMPEustace) **2-8-10** RCochrane(8) (neat: bit bkwd: stdy hdwy over 1f out: nvr nrr) | 3 | 5 | 14/1 | 61 | — |
| 4494[8] | **M R Poly (55)** (MRChannon) **2-8-10** RPerham(10) (a.p: rdn over 2f out: one pce) | ½ | 6 | 33/1 | 59 | — |
| | **Strictly Hard** (GCBravery) **2-7-12** DeclanO'Shea(12) (leggy: s.s: nvr nrr) | ½ | 7 | 20/1 | 46 | — |
| | **Nichol Fifty** (MHTompkins) **2-8-7** NDay(2) (w'like: bit bkwd: nvr nrr) | nk | 8 | 14/1 | 55 | — |
| 4600[5] | **Star Turn (IRE)** (MBell) **2-8-5** MFenton(11) (led 5f: wknd fnl f) | ½ | 9 | 11/2[3] | 51 | — |
| | **Ella Lamees** (WJMusson) **2-8-0** DRMcCabe(1) (unf: bit bkwd: s.i.s: hmpd over 1f out: a bhd) | 1½ | 10 | 14/1 | 43 | — |
| 4600[12] | **Inkwell** (AHide) **2-8-3** AMcGlone(6) (hld up: rdn over 2f out: sn wknd) | 2½ | 11 | 25/1 | 40 | — |
| 4369[10] | **Streamline (IRE) (62)** (GLewis) **2-8-4**(3) AWhelan(9) (bhd fnl 3f) | 8 | 12 | 20/1 | 25 | — |
| 4494[14] | **Rock To The Top (IRE)** (JJSheehan) **2-8-10** SDrowne(5) (bhd fnl 2f) | 3 | 13 | 25/1 | 21 | — |
| | | | | (SP 142.8%) | | **13 Rn** |

**1m 30.9** (9.30) CSF £24.33 TOTE £10.60: £2.30 £1.10 £6.70 (£10.40) Trio £160.70 OWNER Noodles Racing (MARLBOROUGH) BRED Roldvale Ltd

**2538 Havago** showed with a definite lead early in the straight and, although swerving over to the stands' rail cost him several lengths, he still managed to hold off his rivals. (8/1: op 5/1)
**4545 Don Sebastian** was tackling a much more suitable trip on this occasion but, even though the winner steered a very erratic course in the straight, he was unable to take advantage. (13/8)
**Sidney The Kidney**, who cost a mere 1,100 guineas, was given a sympathetic introduction and caught the eye as she steadily crept closer in the last furlong and a half. She will have learnt a lot from this. (20/1)
**4087 Shalstayholy (IRE)** stepped up on her debut. (2/1)
**Eastern Eagle (IRE)** did not look fully wound up, but stayed on through beaten horses to be nearest at the line. (14/1: 7/1-16/1)
**3515 M R Poly** has shown little to date, so this was an improvement. (33/1)
**Nichol Fifty** (14/1: 8/1-16/1)
**4600 Star Turn (IRE)** (11/2: op 11/4)
**Ella Lamees** (14/1: 7/1-16/1)

### 4783 WESTENHANGER MAIDEN AUCTION STKS (II) (2-Y.O) (Class E)
2-00 (2-01) **6f 189y** £2,936.30 (£874.40: £416.20: £187.10) Stalls: High GOING: 0.39 sec per fur (GS)

| | Horse | Dist | Pos | SP | RR | SF |
|---|---|---|---|---|---|---|
| 4601[5] | **Ginzbourg** (JLDunlop) **2-8-10** TSprake(4) (b: lw: hdwy over 2f out: rdn over 1f out: led ins fnl f: r.o wl) | — | 1 | 4/1 | 81 | 18 |
| 4380[3] | **Select Choice (IRE) (84)** (APJarvis) **2-8-5** WRyan(5) (hdwy over 2f out: led over 1f out tl ins fnl f: r.o) | nk | 2 | 11/4[1] | 75 | 12 |
| | **Rechullin** (DRLoder) **2-8-4**ow2 DRMcCabe(10) (neat: bit bkwd: a.p: led over 2f out tl over 1f out: ev ch ins fnl f: unable qckn) | 1½ | 3 | 3/1[2] | 69 | 6 |
| | **Forget To Remindme** (JSMoore) **2-7-9**(3) NVarley(6) (w'like: bit bkwd: hdwy over 1f out: nvr nrr) | 9 | 4 | 33/1 | 44 | — |
| 4087[10] | **Java Bay** (MBlanshard) **2-8-5** AClark(7) (nvr nr to chal) | nk | 5 | 33/1 | 50 | — |
| 4330[18] | **Mr Paradise (IRE)** (TJNaughton) **2-8-4**ow1 SSanders(2) (nvr nrr) | nk | 6 | 20/1 | 48 | — |
| 3943[8] | **Super Scravels (44)** (DrJDScargill) **2-7-12** DeclanO'Shea(12) (a.p: rdn 2f out: sn wknd) | hd | 7 | 33/1 | 42 | — |
| 4601[3] | **Royal Born** (WJarvis) **2-8-7** StephenDavies(1) (lw: a.p: rdn 2f out: sn wknd) | ½ | 8 | 7/2[3] | 50 | — |
| 3685[13] | **Oakbrook Rose** (BSmart) **2-7-11**(5)ow2 ADaly(3) (hld up: rdn over 2f out: sn wknd) | 1 | 9 | 33/1 | 43 | — |
| 4330[21] | **Welcome Heights** (MJFetherston-Godley) **2-8-3** CRutter(11) (a bhd) | 4 | 10 | 33/1 | 34 | — |
| 4600[13] | **Fleuve d'Or (IRE)** (DHaydnJones) **2-8-0** SDrowne(8) (a bhd) | s.h | 11 | 33/1 | 35 | — |
| *4079*[11] | **Always Alight (45)** (KRBurke) **2-8-5b**[1] JFEgan(9) (lw: led over 4f) | 2 | 12 | 33/1 | 32 | — |
| | | | | (SP 119.2%) | | **12 Rn** |

**1m 30.6** (9.00) CSF £13.87 TOTE £4.90: £1.70 £1.30 £1.60 (£6.70) Trio £12.10 OWNER Mr J. L. Dunlop (ARUNDEL) BRED Exors of the late D. Macrae

**4601 Ginzbourg** was a lot wiser here and forced his way to the front inside the final furlong. (4/1: 3/1-5/1)
**4380 Select Choice (IRE)** appreciated the extra furlong. (11/4)
**Rechullin**, with something left to work on, was only brushed aside in the final furlong. (3/1)
**Forget To Remindme**, who cost a mere 1,400 guineas, did not look fully tuned up. (33/1)
**4601 Royal Born** (7/2: 2/1-4/1)

### 4784 BIDDENDEN (S) STKS (3-Y.O) (Class F)
2-30 (2-32) **6f 189y** £2,381.00 (£656.00: £311.00) Stalls: High GOING: 0.39 sec per fur (GS)

| | Horse | Dist | Pos | SP | RR | SF |
|---|---|---|---|---|---|---|
| 4598[7] | **Corniche Quest (IRE) (54)** (MRChannon) **3-9-0** RPerham(12) (hdwy over 2f out: led over 1f out: hung lft ins fnl f: rdn out) | — | 1 | 3/1[2] | 59 | 14 |
| 4589[10] | **Scathebury (55)** (KRBurke) **3-9-5b** GCarter(16) (a.p: rdn over 1f out: ev ch ins fnl f: unable qckn) | 1¾ | 2 | 14/1 | 60 | 15 |
| *4333*[3] | **Shontaine (61)** (MJohnston) **3-8-7**(7) KSked(9) (hld up: rdn over 2f out: r.o one pce fnl f) | ½ | 3 | 5/2[1] | 54 | 9 |
| 2490[5] | **Opening Chorus (51)** (DNicholls) **3-9-0** DHarrison(4) (hld up: rdn over 2f out: one pce) | ¾ | 4 | 8/1 | 52 | 7 |
| 4598[13] | **Morning Surprise (48)** (APJarvis) **3-8-2**(7) CCarver(15) (a.p: rdn over 2f out: one pce) | 1½ | 5 | 10/1 | 44 | — |
| 3166[9] | **Apartments Abroad (38)** (KMcAuliffe) **3-8-9v** JFEgan(2) (b.hind: hdwy on ins over 1f out: nvr nrr) | ½ | 6 | 25/1 | 42 | — |
| 4589[9] | **Bairn Atholl** (RJHodges) **3-8-9** SDrowne(10) (nvr nr to chal) | 1¼ | 7 | 33/1 | 39 | — |
| 4098[20] | **Mystical Maid (52)** (HThomsonJones) **3-8-9b**[1] WRyan(13) (led over 5f: wknd ins fnl f) | ½ | 8 | 13/2[3] | 38 | — |
| 3458[12] | **Duet (30)** (JSKing) **3-8-9** DaneO'Neill(6) (prom over 5f) | ¾ | 9 | 25/1 | 37 | — |
| 4237[12] | **Sweet Amoret (47)** (PHowling) **3-9-0** RCochrane(8) (b.off hind: chsd ldr 5f: wkng whn n.m.r over 1f out) | 3 | 10 | 14/1 | 35 | — |
| *3951*[9] | **Arch Angel (IRE) (44)** (GFHCharles-Jones) **3-8-9** CRutter(7) (lw: bhd fnl 2f) | 2½ | 11 | 33/1 | 24 | — |
| 4219[6] | **Timely Times** (CADwyer) **3-8-2**(7) JoHunnam(3) (a bhd) | ½ | 12 | 33/1 | 23 | — |
| | **Madison's Touch** (RMFlower) **3-8-9** DBiggs(1) (w'like: bit bkwd: a bhd) | 11 | 13 | 20/1 | — | — |

| | | Dist | Pos | SP | RR | SF |
|---|---|---|---|---|---|---|
| 4693[8] | **Viennese Dancer** (RJRWilliams) **3-8-9** DRMcCabe(5) (b.hind: s.i.s: a bhd) | 19 | **14** | 33/1 | — | — |
| 4691[19] | **Miss Carottene (50)** (MJRyan) **3-9-0** AClark(14) (bhd fnl 2f) | 11 | **15** | 10/1 | — | — |
| | | | | (SP 133.7%) | **15 Rn** | |

**1m 31.3** (9.70) CSF £45.18 TOTE £4.70: £2.10 £5.30 £1.40 (£31.70) Trio £38.60 OWNER Mr M. Bishop (UPPER LAMBOURN) BRED K. Molloy No bid

**4259* Corniche Quest (IRE)**, although drifting left inside the final furlong, proved too strong for the runner-up. (3/1)
**3881* Scathebury** ran his best race for some time. (14/1: op 8/1)
**4333 Shontaine** seems to be returning to form, and stayed on well inside the final furlong to snatch third prize. (5/2: op 4/1)
**2490 Opening Chorus**, given a three and a half month break, never looked like quickening in the straight. (8/1)
**4221 Morning Surprise** has yet to win on Turf. (10/1)
**2345 Apartments Abroad** stayed on along the inside rail in the last furlong and a half to be nearest at the line. (25/1)
**2636 Mystical Maid** (13/2: 4/1-7/1)
**131* Miss Carottene** (10/1: op 5/1)

## 4785 SCHATUNOWSKI BROOKS H'CAP (0-60) (3-Y.O) (Class F)

3-00 (3-02) **1m 1f 149y** £3,343.20 (£999.60: £478.80: £218.40) Stalls: High GOING: 0.39 sec per fur (GS)

| | | Dist | Pos | SP | RR | SF |
|---|---|---|---|---|---|---|
| 3961[6] | **Mono Lady (IRE) (51)** (DHaydnJones) **3-8-12** MFenton(10) (a.p: led over 2f out: clr over 1f out: edgd lft ins fnl f: rdn out) | — | **1** | 20/1 | 63 | 9 |
| 4674[4] | **Mimosa (61)** (SDow) **3-9-3**(5) ADaly(5) (lw: gd hdwy 2f out: r.o wl ins fnl f: too much to do) | 1 | **2** | 3/1[1] | 71 | 17 |
| 4624[2] | **Quiet Arch (IRE) (65)** (CACyzer) **3-9-12** GCarter(11) (hdwy 3f out: chsd wnr over 2f out tl wl ins fnl f: r.o one pce) | 1¼ | **3** | 7/2[2] | 73 | 19 |
| 3845[13] | **Nawaji (USA) (48)** (WRMuir) **3-8-9** DaneO'Neill(6) (swtg: rdn & hdwy over 1f out: r.o) | 4 | **4** | 20/1 | 50 | — |
| 4263[12] | **Yezza (IRE) (51)** (APJarvis) **3-8-12** WRyan(14) (hdwy over 1f out: nvr nrr) | 3 | **5** | 14/1 | 48 | — |
| 4232[9] | **Generous Present (57)** (JWPayne) **3-9-4** RCochrane(12) (a.p: shkn up over 1f out: wknd fnl f) | 3 | **6** | 9/1 | 49 | — |
| 4702[6] | **Ameer Alfayaafi (IRE) (56)** (RAkehurst) **3-9-3b1** SSanders(2) (a.p: ev ch over 2f out: sn wknd) | 12 | **7** | 6/1[3] | 28 | — |
| 4513[10] | **El Presidente (55)** (GPEnright) **3-8-11**(5) GFaulkner(8) (hld up: rdn over 3f out: wknd over 1f out) | 3 | **8** | 20/1 | 22 | — |
| 2377[9] | **Sally's Twins (56)** (JSMoore) **3-9-3** JFEgan(3) (a mid div) | 2½ | **9** | 25/1 | 19 | — |
| 1099[9] | **Rowlandsons Charm (IRE) (50)** (MissBSanders) **3-8-11v** AClark(1) (lw: prom over 6f) | 1¼ | **10** | 6/1[3] | 11 | — |
| 4068[17] | **Koraloona (IRE) (52)** (GBBalding) **3-8-13** SDrowne(13) (swtg: a bhd) | 1¼ | **11** | 20/1 | 11 | — |
| 4356[23] | **Reem Fever (IRE) (54)** (DWPArbuthnot) **3-9-1** RPrice(4) (bhd fnl 4f) | 7 | **12** | 20/1 | 1 | — |
| 4548[9] | **Veronica Franco (50)** (BAPearce) **3-8-11** StephenDavies(9) (led 7f) | ¾ | **13** | 33/1 | — | — |
| 3979[13] | **Note of Caution (USA) (50)** (NAGraham) **3-8-11** DHarrison(7) (prom over 5f) | 12 | **14** | 25/1 | — | — |
| 4201[7] | **Itkan (IRE) (52)** (CJBenstead) **3-8-13** MWigham(15) (bhd fnl 4f) | 3½ | **15** | 16/1 | — | — |
| | | | | (SP 132.8%) | **15 Rn** | |

**2m 11.9** (14.20) CSF £81.09 CT £257.02 TOTE £17.00: £3.80 £1.60 £1.80 (£23.70) Trio £25.40 OWNER Monolithic Refractories Ltd (PONTYPRIDD) BRED Dr. Michael Smurfit

**3961 Mono Lady (IRE)** forged clear below the distance and was not going to be caught by the strong-finishing runner-up. (20/1)
**4674 Mimosa** was given a very poor ride by her young pilot, who was obviously brimming with confidence. Waited with at the back of the field, she still had plenty of ground to make up on the leader running down the hill, but her jockey did not seem at all bothered. Getting into top gear in the final quarter-mile, she ran on strongly, but the line was always going to beat her. (3/1)
**4624 Quiet Arch (IRE)** was collared for the runner-up berth in the closing stages. (7/2)
**Nawaji (USA)** ran her best race to date. (20/1)
**3525 Yezza (IRE)** remains a maiden. (14/1)
**3287 Generous Present** appeared to find this longer trip beyond him and had run out of steam in the final furlong. (9/1: 6/1-10/1)

## 4786 CLIFF MEDIAN AUCTION MAIDEN STKS (2-Y.O) (Class F)

3-30 (3-31) **5f** £2,381.00 (£656.00: £311.00) Stalls: Low GOING: 0.39 sec per fur (GS)

| | | Dist | Pos | SP | RR | SF |
|---|---|---|---|---|---|---|
| 4516[8] | **Unshaken** (JRFanshawe) **2-9-0** DHarrison(2) (a.p: shkn up to ld over 1f out: r.o wl) | — | **1** | 4/1[2] | 86 | 42 |
| 4566[10] | **Marsad (IRE) (75)** (CJBenstead) **2-9-0** RCochrane(3) (led 4f out tl over 1f out: unable qckn) | 3½ | **2** | 4/1[2] | 75 | 31 |
| 4600[4] | **Risky Missile** (JEBanks) **2-8-9** NDay(11) (a.p: hrd rdn over 1f out: one pce) | 1¾ | **3** | 5/1[3] | 64 | 20 |
| 4123[13] | **Stock Hill Dancer** (KRBurke) **2-8-9** TSprake(1) (led 1f: lost pl over 2f out: rallied fnl f: r.o) | 2½ | **4** | 50/1 | 56 | 12 |
| 4545[2] | **Hangover Square (IRE) (85)** (RHannon) **2-9-0** DaneO'Neill(13) (lw: a.p: hrd rdn over 1f out: one pce) | ¾ | **5** | 7/4[1] | 59 | 15 |
| 4600[3] | **Forcing Bid** (SirMarkPrescott) **2-9-0** SSanders(7) (lw: hdwy over 2f out: rdn over 1f out: one pce) | s.h | **6** | 11/2 | 59 | 15 |
| 4494[13] | **Peter Perfect** (GLewis) **2-8-11**(3) AWhelan(6) (swtg: nvr nrr) | 2½ | **7** | 33/1 | 51 | 7 |
| | **Dancing Mystery** (EAWheeler) **2-8-9**(5) ADaly(5) (w'like: bit bkwd: dwlt: hdwy over 2f out: wknd wl over 1f out) | ¾ | **8** | 14/1 | 48 | 4 |
| 4546[7] | **Lochinvar** (JSMoore) **2-9-0** JFEgan(4) (a.p: rdn over 2f out: sn wknd) | ½ | **9** | 50/1 | 47 | 3 |
| 4545[9] | **Swift Refusal (64)** (MJHaynes) **2-8-9** CRutter(8) (bhd fnl 2f) | hd | **10** | 50/1 | 41 | — |
| 4600[15] | **College Princess** (CADwyer) **2-8-2**(7) JoHunnam(12) (bhd fnl 2f) | 2½ | **11** | 40/1 | 33 | — |
| 4380[15] | **Little Progress (60)** (TMJones) **2-9-0** RPerham(9) (b.hind: s.s: a bhd) | 2½ | **12** | 50/1 | 30 | — |
| | **Goodbye Gatemen (IRE)** (MJHeaton-Ellis) **2-9-0** SDrowne(10) (unf: bit bkwd: a bhd) | 5 | **13** | 20/1 | 14 | — |
| | | | | (SP 133.1%) | **13 Rn** | |

**62.8 secs** (5.20) CSF £21.62 TOTE £6.90: £2.10 £2.00 £1.30 (£12.60) Trio £52.40 OWNER Mr W. J. Gredley (NEWMARKET) BRED Stetchworth Park Stud Ltd

**4516 Unshaken** appreciated the drop in distance and scored a cosy success. (4/1: 3/1-9/2)
**4566 Marsad (IRE)**, taking a drop to the minimum distance, showed the way for much of the trip. (4/1: 11/4-9/2)
**4600 Risky Missile** is by a mud-loving sire. (5/1)
**3502 Stock Hill Dancer** was given a rather strange ride, for her jockey did not seem at all bothered as she got rather outpaced at halfway. She did stay on again in the final furlong, but it was all over by then. (50/1)
**4545 Hangover Square (IRE)** once again cost his supporters dear. (7/4)
**4600 Forcing Bid**, a big, strapping individual who looked in good shape, was not helped by the drop in trip. (11/2: op 5/2)
**Dancing Mystery** (14/1: 20/1-10/1)

## 4787 LEVY BOARD RATING RELATED MAIDEN STKS (0-60) (2-Y.O) (Class F)

4-00 (4-02) **6f** £2,785.60 (£771.60: £368.80) Stalls: Low GOING: 0.39 sec per fur (GS)

| | | Dist | Pos | SP | RR | SF |
|---|---|---|---|---|---|---|
| 4562[3] | **Sharp Return (49)** (MJRyan) **2-9-0** AClark(9) (a.p: led over 2f out: hrd rdn over 1f out: r.o wl) | — | **1** | 7/1 | 54 | 25 |

4549[3] **Castles Burning (USA) (57)** (CACyzer) **2-9-0** GCarter(8) (lw: hdwy over 2f out: hrd rdn over 1f out: hung lft & ev ch ins fnl f: r.o wl)....hd **2** 13/2 54 25
4715[7] **Jilly Woo (49)** (DRCElsworth) **2-8-11b** TSprake(1) (hld up: hrd rdn over 1f out: swtchd rt ins fnl f: ev ch wl ins fnl f: r.o wl)....s.h **3** 20/1 51 22
**Suite Addition (IRE) (52)** (CAHorgan) **2-8-11** MFenton(4) (a.p: rdn 2f out: ev ch whn hmpd ins fnl f: unable qckn)....2½ **4** 33/1 44 15
4715[3] **Battle Ground (IRE) (50)** (NACallaghan) **2-8-7**(7) RMullen(11) (lw: a.p: rdn 3f out: one pce fnl 2f)....2½ **5** 100/30[1] 40 11
4493[3] **Gold Edge (58)** (MRChannon) **2-8-11** RPerham(2) (led over 3f: wknd over 1f out)....1¼ **6** 9/1 34 5
4546[16] **Distinctive Dream (IRE) (52)** (KTIvory) **2-9-0** CScally(7) (s.s: nvr nr to chal)....1 **7** 33/1 34 5
4493[2] **Le Shuttle (58)** (MHTompkins) **2-8-6**(5) GFaulkner(3) (hdwy over 2f out: hrd rdn over 1f out: wknd fnl f)....½ **8** 6/1[3] 30 1
4514[9] **Mystery (60)** (SDow) **2-8-11** DaneO'Neill(5) (lw: bhd fnl 2f)....2½ **9** 11/2[2] 23 —
4195[6] **The Four Isles (60)** (DHaydnJones) **2-9-0** RCochrane(10) (lw: s.s: a bhd)....2 **10** 13/2 21 —
2512[5] **Impala (60)** (WGMTurner) **2-8-7**(7) DSweeney(12) (prom over 3f)....4 **11** 16/1 10 —
*2746[6]* **Pretty Sally (IRE) (58)** (DJGMurraySmith) **2-8-11** DHarrison(6) (bit bkwd: a bhd)....2½ **12** 33/1 1 —
(SP 121.4%) **12 Rn**

**1m 17.7** (7.50) CSF £49.36 TOTE £8.60: £2.60 £2.50 £4.80 (£38.10) Trio £293.30; £45.44 to Chepstow 22/10/96 OWNER Mrs Teresa Baron (NEWMARKET) BRED Stud-On-The-Chart

**4562 Sharp Return**, who ran well with some cut last time, gained control over quarter of a mile from home and just managed to prevail. (7/1: op 4/1)
**4549 Castles Burning (USA)** drifted to his left from below the distance and, fighting for the lead inside the final furlong, did the fourth no favours. (13/2: 7/2-7/1)
**2429 Jilly Woo** was making a quick reappearance. (20/1)
**Suite Addition (IRE)** was having her first run in three months and was bang in with every chance when hampered by the second inside the final furlong. Her jockey hardly had to stop riding her though. (33/1)
**4715 Battle Ground (IRE)**, making a quick reappearance, was made to look very pedestrian in the final quarter-mile. (100/30: 2/1-7/2)
**4493 Gold Edge** failed to see out this slightly longer trip. (9/1: 6/1-10/1)
**4493 Le Shuttle** does not stay six. (6/1)
**1678 Mystery** (11/2: 9/2-7/1)

## 4788 LYSANDER INSURANCE BROKERS LIMITED STKS (0-70) (3-Y.O+) (Class E)
4-30 (4-41) **6f** £3,343.20 (£999.60: £478.80: £218.40) Stalls: Low GOING: 0.39 sec per fur (GS)

SP RR SF
4581[14] **Purple Fling (70)** (LGCottrell) **5-8-12** RCochrane(1) (a.p: led ins fnl f: rdn out)....— **1** 4/1[1] 74 34
4109[7] **Sharp 'n Smart (55)** (BSmart) **4-8-12** MTebbutt(4) (a.p: hrd rdn 2f out: ev ch ins fnl f: r.o)....hd **2** 16/1 74 34
4360[7] **Fresh Fruit Daily (67)** (PAKelleway) **4-8-9** DRMcCabe(8) (rdn over 2f out: nt clr run over 1f out: hdwy fnl f: r.o wl)....¾ **3** 25/1 69 29
3844[7] **Azwah (USA) (60)** (PTWalwyn) **3-8-8** TSprake(2) (led tl ins fnl f: unable qckn)....hd **4** 12/1 69 28
4329[11] **Absolute Magic (70)** (WJHaggas) **6-8-12** MFenton(7) (lw: s.s: hdwy over 1f out: r.o)....1¼ **5** 8/1 68 28
4430[2] **Prima Silk (68)** (MJRyan) **5-8-12** AClark(10) (a.p: rdn over 1f out: ev ch ins fnl f: one pce)....hd **6** 6/1[3] 68 28
3442[9] **Be Warned (60)** (NACallaghan) **5-8-12** WRyan(11) (nvr nr to chal)....½ **7** 13/2 67 27
4589[4] **Little Noggins (IRE) (68)** (CADwyer) **3-8-1**(7) JoHunnam(5) (a.p: rdn over 1f out: wknd fnl f)....½ **8** 16/1 62 21
4550[5] **Maristax (70)** (PJMakin) **3-8-8** SSanders(12) (a bhd)....1½ **9** 9/2[2] 58 17
*4333[10]* **Itsinthepost (58)** (VSoane) **3-8-8** AMcGlone(9) (hld up: rdn over 2f out: wknd over 1f out)....1¼ **10** 25/1 55 14
1442[6] **Efra (68)** (RHannon) **7-8-12** DaneO'Neill(13) (bit bkwd: bhd fnl 2f)....10 **11** 9/2[2] 31 —
4610[7] **Pride of Hayling (IRE) (62)** (PRHedger) **5-8-12**(3) NVarley(14) (lw: hdwy 3f out: wknd over 1f out)....1½ **12** 10/1 30 —
4356[11] **Merrie le Bow (58)** (PatMitchell) **4-8-10**(5) AmandaSanders(6) (p.u sn after s: dead).... **P** 10/1 — —
*664** ***Deeply Vale (IRE) (66)*** (GLMoore) **5-8-12** SWhitworth(3) (Withdrawn not under Starter's orders: unruly in stalls & taken out: bolted in false s).... **W** 12/1 — —
*4312[5]* ***Denbrae (IRE) (70)*** (DJGMurraySmith) **4-9-1** DHarrison(16) (Withdrawn not unders Starter's orders: hmpd, uns rdr & bolted in false s).... **W** 8/1 — —
(SP 159.2%) **13 Rn**

**1m 16.9** (6.70) CSF £69.92 TOTE £6.20: £1.90 £7.10 £2.70 (£59.00) Trio £252.30 OWNER Mr Simon Mounsey (CULLOMPTON) BRED Mrs P. Lewis
WEIGHT FOR AGE 3yo-1lb

**4215 Purple Fling** gained control inside the final furlong and, rousted along, just managed to hold on. (4/1)
**244* Sharp 'n Smart** disputed the lead from the start and was still battling for the advantage nearing the line. (16/1)
**2124 Fresh Fruit Daily** did not get the best of runs as she tried to pick up ground below the distance. She put in some good work in the final furlong, but is still a maiden after fifteen attempts. (25/1)
**3518 Azwah (USA)**, collared inside the final furlong, then failed to muster another turn of foot. (12/1)
**3933 Absolute Magic** has not won for over two years and has generally been disappointing. (8/1: 7/1-12/1)
**4430 Prima Silk** takes her races well and this was her nineteenth run of the year. (6/1)
**2860 Be Warned** (13/2: 7/1-11/1)
**4610 Pride of Hayling (IRE)** (10/1: 8/1-12/1)

## 4789 LEEDS AMATEUR H'CAP (0-60) (3-Y.O+) (Class G)
5-00 (5-13) **1m 4f** £2,070.00 (£570.00: £270.00) Stalls: High GOING: 0.39 sec per fur (GS)

SP RR SF
4509[10] **Summerhill Special (IRE) (45)** (MrsPNDutfield) **5-10-6**(3) MrKGoble(7) (hdwy over 5f out: led over 2f out: r.o wl)....— **1** 20/1 61 20
4509[5] **Spread The Word (44)** (LGCottrell) **4-10-3v**(5) MrLJefford(9) (hdwy over 3f out: chsd wnr over 1f out: no imp)....2½ **2** 10/1 57 16
4726[3] **Evidence In Chief (57)** (DRCElsworth) **3-10-7v**(7) MrNMoran(12) (rdn over 2f out: hdwy over 1f out: r.o)....5 **3** 13/2[3] 63 15
4563[5] **Stalled (IRE) (51)** (PTWalwyn) **6-10-10**(5) MarchionessBlandford(3) (lw: hdwy over 1f out: nvr nrr)....4 **4** 8/1 52 11
*4336[5]* **Sharp Command (54)** (PEccles) **3-10-11** MrRThornton(17) (w ldr: led over 5f out tl over 2f out: wknd wl over 1f out)....2 **5** 25/1 52 4
4587* **Howqua River (50)** (PWChapple-Hyam) **4-10-9**(5) MrSRutherford(10) (hdwy over 3f out: edgd lft over 1f out: sn wknd)....2 **6** 11/2[2] 45 4
4381[6] **Hatta Sunshine (USA) (40)** (AMoore) **6-9-13**(5) MrsJMoore(2) (lw: s.s: hdwy over 1f out: nvr nrr)....hd **7** 20/1 35 —
**Smuggler's Point (USA) (54)** (JJBridger) **6-10-11**(7) MrDBridger(13) (nvr nr to chal)....¾ **8** 33/1 48 7

4587[4] **Strat's Legacy (42)** (DWPArbuthnot) **9-10-6** MrsDArbuthnot(5) (nvr nrr)....2½ **9** 12/1 33 —
1450[10] **Ilandra (IRE) (43)** (RAkehurst) **4-10-7** MrTMcCarthy(8) (prom over 10f)....1¼ **10** 12/1 32 —
4626[6] **Ashover (49)** (TDBarron) **6-10-8**(5) MissMKeuthen(6) (prom 8f)....1 **11** 11/2[2] 37 —
*4573*[7] **Jolto (57)** (KMcAuliffe) **7-11-7** MissJAllison(15) (b.hind: a.p: ev ch over 2f out: wknd over 1f out)....4 **12** 33/1 40 —
4548[10] **Private Percival (47)** (JRPoulton) **3-9-11**(7) MrsCPoulton(14) (bhd fnl 2f)....½ **13** 33/1 29 —
4509* **Nothing Doing (IRE) (37)** (WJMusson) **7-9-12**(3) MrRWakley(4) (led over 6f: wknd 2f out)....¾ **14** 3/1[1] 18 —
*1814*[6] **Flash In The Pan (IRE) (55)** (JSMoore) **3-10-7**(5) MrsSMoore(16) (bhd fnl 3f)....1¾ **15** 33/1 34 —
**Kadiri (IRE) (54)** (JRBosley) **5-11-1**(3) MrsSBosley(1) (a bhd)....¾ **16** 25/1 32 —
2124[9] **Prestige Lass (58)** (BSmart) **3-10-10**(5) MissVMarshall(18) (bhd fnl 8f)....3½ **17** 16/1 31 —
4360[13] **Tirra-Lirra (IRE) (48)** (CEBrittain) **4-10-7**(5) MrVLukaniuk(11) (bhd fnl 6f)....3 **18** 33/1 17 —
(SP 142.5%) **18 Rn**

**2m 51.2** (20.00) CSF £209.24 CT £1,347.76 TOTE £11.80: £3.50 £1.80 £2.10 £2.10 (£39.30) Trio £125.70 OWNER Mrs Nerys Dutfield (SEATON) BRED Miss Audrey F. Thompson
WEIGHT FOR AGE 3yo-7lb

**2743 Summerhill Special (IRE)**, out of form for a very long time, found this was to be her day and, striking the front over a quarter of a mile from home, kept up the gallop in fine style. (20/1)
**4509 Spread The Word**, despite drawing clear of the remainder, failed to reel in the winner. She is still a maiden after fourteen attempts. (10/1: 8/1-12/1)
**4726 Evidence In Chief** stayed on nicely in the last furlong and a half, but was never going to get there in time. (13/2)
**4563 Stalled (IRE)** is not an easy ride and, although picking up ground in the last furlong and a half, found it all over bar the shouting. (8/1)
**1993 Sharp Command**, a poor performer, cut out a lot of the running until put in his place in the straight. (25/1)
**4587* Howqua River** had shot his bolt below the distance. (11/2)
**4587 Strat's Legacy** (12/1: 8/1-14/1)
**4509* Nothing Doing (IRE)** (3/1: 4/1-5/2)

T/Plpt: £64.10 (175.06 Tckts). T/Qdpt: £42.80 (21.43 Tckts). AK

# 4585-PONTEFRACT (L-H) (Good)
## Monday October 21st
WEATHER: sunny WIND: almost nil

## 4790 BROCKADALE MAIDEN AUCTION STKS (I) (2-Y.O) (Class F)
2-15 (2-19) **6f** £2,388.00 (£668.00: £324.00) Stalls: Low GOING: 0.05 sec per fur (G)

SP RR SF

**Key Largo (IRE)** (MHTompkins) **2-8-5**(3) MHenry(14) (w'like: lengthy: outpcd & bhd: hdwy over 2f out: r.o to ld cl home)....— **1** 20/1 73 23
4514[6] **Phylida (70)** (PJMakin) **2-8-2** GDuffield(7) (swtg: chsd ldrs: rdn ½-wy: led ins fnl f: hdd & no ex towards fin)....hd **2** 6/1[2] 67 17
4558[6] **Sparkling Harry (65)** (MissLCSiddall) **2-8-4b[1]** GHind(5) (chsd ldrs: c wd & effrt over 1f out: styd on)....3 **3** 16/1 61 11
4072[7] **Loch-Hurn Lady (60)** (KWHogg) **2-7-10**(3) DWright(10) (led tl ins fnl f: wknd)....1½ **4** 10/1 52 2
4234[5] **Cambridge Ball (IRE) (69)** (MJohnston) **2-8-5** MRoberts(4) (cl up tl outpcd over 2f out: hdwy whn nt cl run 1f out: nt rcvr)....2½ **5** 6/4[1] 51 1
2059[10] **Chasetown Flyer (USA)** (RHollinshead) **2-8-6** LDettori(1) (in tch: effrt over 2f out: nvr rchd ldrs)....½ **6** 14/1 51 1
4562[17] **Real Fire (IRE) (45)** (MGMeagher) **2-8-6** JFortune(13) (sn outpcd & bhd: styd on u.p fnl 2f)....½ **7** 50/1 49 —
1645[10] **Morritt Magic (40)** (CWThornton) **2-8-0** NCarlisle(12) (mid div: rdn ½-wy: no imp)....hd **8** 66/1 43 —
4600[7] **Gablesea (72)** (BPJBaugh) **2-8-6** ACulhane(15) (w ldr: chal over 1f out: wknd ins fnl f)....s.h **9** 9/1 49 —
4594[14] **Oddfellows Girl (40)** (NBycroft) **2-7-8**(5) PFessey(3) (outpcd fr ½-wy)....½ **10** 66/1 41 —
*4576*[5] **Hiltons Executive (IRE) (50)** (EJAlston) **2-8-1** JQuinn(8) (plld hrd: chsd ldrs over 4f)....1¼ **11** 20/1 39 —
4544[6] **Wild Hadeer** (WJHaggas) **2-8-8**ow1 KFallon(9) (s.i.s: a outpcd & wl bhd)....2½ **12** 8/1[3] 40 —
**Mechilie** (JWPayne) **2-8-0** GBardwell(2) (str: cmpt: bkwd: s.s: a t.o)....dist **13** 33/1 — —
***Loganlea (IRE)*** (WJMusson) **2-8-5** BDoyle(11) (Withdrawn not under Starter's orders: ref to ent stalls)....**W** 16/1 — —
(SP 120.3%) **13 Rn**

**1m 19.8** (5.50) CSF £120.24 TOTE £18.20: £3.60 £1.60 £4.10 (£39.50) Trio £125.20 OWNER Mr M. H. Tompkins (NEWMARKET) BRED Flying Fox Farm

**Key Largo (IRE)**, in a moderate event, took the eye in the paddock. After showing signs of greenness early on, he produced a great run to settle it event late on. (20/1)
**4514 Phylida** certainly did not impress on looks, but ran well, only just to be touched off. (6/1)
**4558 Sparkling Harry** looked in good trim and ran pretty well, but was never doing enough when it mattered. (16/1)
**4072 Loch-Hurn Lady** ran well after another lengthy lay-off and should be all the better for it. (10/1)
**4234 Cambridge Ball (IRE)** proved short of toe at a vital stage and then ran into trouble. She surely needs a bit further. (6/4)
**Chasetown Flyer (USA)** (14/1: op 8/1)
**1166 Real Fire (IRE)** took a long time to get going, but was making steady progress at the end. (50/1)
**2993 Gablesea** (9/1: 8/1-12/1)

## 4791 CHEP H'CAP (0-80) (3-Y.O+) (Class D)
2-45 (2-47) **5f** £4,815.00 (£1,440.00: £690.00: £315.00) Stalls: Low GOING: 0.05 sec per fur (G)

SP RR SF

4616[2] **Stuffed (72)** (MWEasterby) **4-9-3**(5) GParkin(13) (lw: trckd ldrs: led ins fnl f: rdn & r.o)....— **1** 6/1[1] 80 50
4688[U] **Sailormaite (78)** (SRBowring) **5-10-0** DeanMcKeown(17) (s.i.s: hdwy ½-wy: hung lft & r.o fnl 2f)....1 **2** 25/1 83 53
4689[2] **French Grit (IRE) (74)** (MDods) **4-9-7**(3) CTeague(6) (swtg: a chsng ldrs: kpt on u.p fnl f)....½ **3** 8/1[2] 77 47
4616[6] **Brecongill Lad (68)** (MissSEHall) **4-9-4** ACulhane(14) (led tl ins fnl f: wknd towards fin)....nk **4** 11/1 70 40
4521[10] **Tropical Beach (64)** (JBerry) **3-8-7**(7) CLowther(18) (bhd tl r.o wl fnl 2f)....nk **5** 33/1 65 35
4616[7] **Sally Slade (70)** (CACyzer) **4-9-6** MRoberts(8) (bhd: hdwy wl over 1f out: r.o wl)....½ **6** 16/1 70 40
4687[14] **Cretan Gift (73)** (NPLittmoden) **5-9-9b** TGMcLaughlin(9) (bhd: styd on fnl 2f: nrst fin)....2½ **7** 12/1 65 35
4616[11] **Saddlehome (USA) (66)** (TDBarron) **7-9-2** JCarroll(16) (swtg: in tch: effrt 2f out: r.o one pce)....nk **8** 10/1[3] 57 27
4312[7] **Indian Relative (77)** (RGuest) **3-9-8**(5) DGriffiths(7) (swtg: effrt ½-wy: nvr nr to chal)....hd **9** 12/1 67 37
4616[5] **Jucea (68)** (JLSpearing) **7-9-1b**(3) FLynch(4) (trckd ldrs: effrt 2f out: sn btn)....¾ **10** 10/1[3] 56 26

| | | | | |
|---|---|---|---|---|
| 4616[10] **Surprise Mission (73)** (MrsJRRamsden) **4-9-9** KFallon(2) (s.i.s: hdwy ½-wy: no imp)....................1¼ | **11** | 6/1[1] | 57 | 27 |
| 4382[17] **Mister Joel (55)** (MWEasterby) **3-8-5** LCharnock(3) (lw: w ldr tl wknd wl over 1f out)....................s.h | **12** | 25/1 | 39 | 9 |
| 4610[11] **Souperficial (54)** (JAGlover) **5-8-4v** GDuffield(11) (a rr div)....................1 | **13** | 16/1 | 35 | 5 |
| 4505[7] **Captain Carat (63)** (MrsJRRamsden) **5-8-13** JFortune(10) (b.nr fore: dwlt: drvn along wl over 1f out: n.d)......nk | **14** | 10/1[3] | 43 | 13 |
| 4505[5] **Ned's Bonanza (62)** (MDods) **7-8-12** BDoyle(12) (lw: prom over 3f: wknd)....................1¼ | **15** | 20/1 | 38 | 8 |
| 4367[3] **Gondo (50)** (EJAlston) **9-8-0v** JQuinn(15) (sn outpcd & bhd)....................¾ | **16** | 33/1 | 23 | — |
| 4592[2] **Wollstonecraft (IRE) (77)** (JHMGosden) **3-9-13** LDettori(1) (prom: outpcd over 2f out: sn wknd)....................hd | **17** | 8/1[2] | 50 | 20 |
| | | (SP 131.9%) **17 Rn** | | |

**64.4 secs** (3.60) CSF £137.77 CT £1,165.63 TOTE £7.20: £2.10 £5.80 £2.40 £3.20 (£135.00) Trio £224.50 OWNER Early Morning Breakfast Syndicate (SHERIFF HUTTON) BRED Manor Grange Stud Co Ltd

**4616 Stuffed**, without the blinkers this time, did the job required well and, once in front, was not going to stop. (6/1)

**4581 Sailormaite** has so much ability but also his own ideas and, although running on well here, all he really wanted to do was hang left. (25/1)

**4689 French Grit (IRE)**, very warm beforehand, ran a fine race and kept responding to pressure. (8/1)

**4616 Brecongill Lad** showed bags of speed, but was worried out of it when it really mattered. (11/1)

**4382 Tropical Beach** likes to come from off a strong pace and finished fast, but always too late to have a chance. (33/1)

**4220 Sally Slade** flew in the last two furlongs, but had given the leaders too much start. She is in good form at the moment. (16/1)

**4616 Jucea** (10/1: 8/1-12/1)

**3774 Mister Joel** looked particularly well, but stopped quickly in the home straight. With the blinkers refitted, he should do better. (25/1)

## 4792 TOTE SILVER TANKARD STKS (Listed) (2-Y.O) (Class A)

3-15 (3-15) **1m 4y** £12,929.00 (£4,811.00: £2,330.50: £977.50: £413.75: £188.25) Stalls: Low GOING: 0.05 sec per fur (G)

| | | SP | RR | SF |
|---|---|---|---|---|
| 4512* **Entice (FR)** (BWHills) **2-8-6** MHills(3) (hld up & bhd: hdwy over 2f out: qcknd to ld cl home)....................— | **1** | 5/2[1] | 88 | 40 |
| 3695* **Fahris (IRE)** (HThomsonJones) **2-8-11** RHills(1) (lw: trckd ldrs: hdwy to ld over 2f out: hrd rdn fnl f: nt qckn towards fin)....................nk | **2** | 13/2[3] | 92 | 44 |
| 3668[2] **Symonds Inn** (JGFitzGerald) **2-8-11** KFallon(7) (lw: trckd ldrs: disp ld over 2f out tl over 1f out: hrd rdn & r.o one pce)....................½ | **3** | 5/2[1] | 91 | 43 |
| 4461[4] **Sunbeam Dance (USA)** (SbinSuroor) **2-8-11** LDettori(2) (lw: hld up: hdwy over 2f out: rdn & no imp)..............7 | **4** | 3/1[2] | 77 | 29 |
| 4490[2] **Tinkerbell (78)** (WRMuir) **2-8-6v** MRoberts(4) (led tl over 2f out: sn btn)....................10 | **5** | 20/1 | 53 | 5 |
| 4625[10] **Imperial Or Metric (IRE) (76)** (JBerry) **2-8-11** JFortune(6) (chsd ldrs 5f: sn btn)....................6 | **6** | 100/1 | 46 | — |
| 4621[3] **Beryllium (97)** (RHannon) **2-8-11** RHughes(5) (hld up: effrt 3f out: sn rdn & btn)....................5 | **7** | 12/1 | 36 | — |
| | | (SP 108.9%) **7 Rn** | | |

**1m 47.0** (5.50) CSF £16.60 TOTE £3.70: £2.30 £2.50 (£9.00) OWNER Sheikh Mohammed (LAMBOURN) BRED Darley Stud Management Co. Ltd.

OFFICIAL EXPLANATION **Beryllium: hung right and lost his action, effectively stopping his jockey from riding him out for sixth place.**

**4512* Entice (FR)**, a free-runner who has bags of ability, won this useful event in good style in the end. Should she learn to settle fully, she can improve a great deal. (5/2)

**3695* Fahris (IRE)** was the pick of the bunch on looks and tried hard, but was just done for toe late on. (13/2)

**3668 Symonds Inn** had the form, but had not been out for two months and that was probably the difference. He should come into his own next year. (5/2)

**4461 Sunbeam Dance (USA)** was well enough placed until finding this company far too hot for his liking in the last couple of furlongs. (3/1)

**4490 Tinkerbell** found the company far too good, and was quickly dealt with with two furlongs left. (20/1)

**4347* Imperial Or Metric (IRE)** was well outclassed. (100/1)

**4621 Beryllium** gave problems by hanging halfway through the race. This effort is best forgotten. (12/1)

## 4793 CLAYTON BIGLEY PARTNERSHIP H'CAP (0-70) (3-Y.O+) (Class E)

3-45 (3-49) **1m 2f 6y** £5,361.00 (£1,608.00: £774.00: £357.00) Stalls: Low GOING: 0.05 sec per fur (G)

| | | SP | RR | SF |
|---|---|---|---|---|
| 4617[15] **Maradata (IRE) (59)** (RHollinshead) **4-9-3** LDettori(4) (hld up & bhd: stdy hdwy 3f out: r.o to ld wl ins fnl f)....— | **1** | 10/1[3] | 69 | 33 |
| *4575** **Mansur (IRE) (60)** (DRLoder) **4-9-4** RHughes(17) (lw: trckd ldrs: effrt over 2f out: slt ld ins fnl f: nt qckn towards fin)....................¾ | **2** | 6/1[1] | 69 | 33 |
| 4606[6] **North Reef (IRE) (68)** (SirMarkPrescott) **5-9-12** GDuffield(13) (swtg: cl up: led 3f out tl ins fnl f: kpt on)....................hd | **3** | 11/1 | 77 | 41 |
| 4626[14] **Kristal Breeze (57)** (WRMuir) **4-9-1** KFallon(10) (prom: outpcd over 3f out: kpt on wl fnl f)....................1¼ | **4** | 12/1 | 64 | 28 |
| 4702* **Rival Bid (USA) (69)** (MrsNMacauley) **8-9-10**(3) 6x CTeague(5) (hld up & bhd: c wd st: r.o: nrst fin)....................hd | **5** | 11/1 | 76 | 40 |
| 4686[10] **Shaffishayes (62)** (MrsMReveley) **4-9-6** DeanMcKeown(8) (hld up: effrt over 2f out: styd on u.p nr fin).........s.h | **6** | 8/1[2] | 68 | 32 |
| 4503[8] **Thatched (IRE) (48)** (REBarr) **6-8-1**(5) PFessey(15) (hdwy on outside over 2f out: styd on: no imp)....................½ | **7** | 25/1 | 54 | 18 |
| 3426[14] **In Good Faith (62)** (JJQuinn) **4-9-6** JQuinn(7) (hdwy ½-wy: sn rdn: one pce fnl 2f)....................nk | **8** | 16/1 | 67 | 31 |
| 4702[4] **General Haven (68)** (TJNaughton) **3-9-7** JFortune(19) (drvn along ½-wy: nvr nr to chal)....................s.h | **9** | 11/1 | 73 | 32 |
| 754[11] **Name of Our Father (USA) (70)** (PBowen) **3-9-4**(5) PPMurphy(1) (led to 3f out: grad wknd)....................nk | **10** | 50/1 | 75 | 34 |
| 4597[5] **Essayeffsee (59)** (MrsMReveley) **7-8-12**(5) SCopp(6) (hld up & bhd: nvr nr to chal)....................½ | **11** | 12/1 | 63 | 27 |
| 4597* **Your Most Welcome (57)** (DJSffrenchDavis) **5-8-10**(5) GParkin(3) (bhd: drvn along over 3f out: n.d)............1¾ | **12** | 10/1[3] | 58 | 22 |
| 4606[8] **Tormount (USA) (66)** (LordHuntingdon) **3-9-5** MRoberts(14) (chsd ldrs tl wknd over 2f out)....................2 | **13** | 10/1[3] | 64 | 23 |
| 4617[9] **Calder King (63)** (JLEyre) **5-9-7b** TWilliams(18) (in tch: effrt ½-wy: wknd over 2f out)....................2½ | **14** | 14/1 | 57 | 21 |
| 4688[14] **Le Sport (64)** (DNicholls) **3-9-0**(3) DWright(12) (bhd: rdn 6f out: n.d)....................nk | **15** | 25/1 | 57 | 16 |
| *4575[3]* **Theatre Magic (55)** (SRBowring) **3-8-8** SDWilliams(2) (chsd ldrs tl wknd 3f out)....................3½ | **16** | 20/1 | 43 | 2 |
| 4686[26] **Our Main Man (49)** (RMWhitaker) **6-8-4**(3) RHavlin(9) (lw: bhd: sme hdwy over 2f out: sn wknd)....................1¼ | **17** | 50/1 | 35 | — |
| 4688[16] **Pine Ridge Lad (IRE) (65)** (JLEyre) **6-9-9** RLappin(11) (plld hrd: prom tl wknd 3f out)....................nk | **18** | 33/1 | 50 | 14 |
| 3173[8] **Titchwell Lass (59)** (JEBanks) **3-8-12** JStack(16) (s.i.s: gd hdwy ½-wy: wknd qckly 2f out)....................10 | **19** | 20/1 | 28 | — |
| | | (SP 129.7%) **19 Rn** | | |

**2m 17.6** (9.30) CSF £66.36 CT £635.91 TOTE £10.20: £2.20 £2.40 £2.60 £2.50 (£33.80) Trio £268.30 OWNER Mr R. Hollinshead (UPPER LONGDON) BRED His Highness the Aga Khans Studs S. C.

WEIGHT FOR AGE 3yo-5lb

OFFICIAL EXPLANATION **Maradata (IRE): accounting for the filly's improvement in form, her trainer said that she is a difficult ride and appears to give of her best when ridden by L. Dettori.**

**4226 Maradata (IRE)** is a different horse when Dettori is on board and, given a superb ride, won well. (10/1)

**4575* Mansur (IRE)** is in really good form and ran a sound race, only to find the winner too strong. (6/1: op 4/1)

**4606 North Reef (IRE)** helped force the pace and kept battling away, but was short of a change of speed in the closing stages. (11/1)

**4497* Kristal Breeze** got outpaced approaching the home turn, and left the impression that longer trips suit her better. (12/1)

**4702* Rival Bid (USA)** likes to come from off the pace, but had to race very wide here to find a clear passage, and the effort was always too late. (11/1)
**1502 Shaffishayes** was stepping up in trip but still took time to get going, and failed to offer a threat. (8/1)
**In Good Faith** was off the bit some way out, and was always short of the necessary turn of foot. He may need a bit further or softer ground. (16/1)

## 4794 BLUFF COVE H'CAP (0-70) (3-Y.O+) (Class E)

4-15 (4-19) **2m 1f 216y** £3,548.00 (£1,064.00: £512.00: £236.00) Stalls: Centre GOING: 0.05 sec per fur (G)

| Form | Horse | Dist | Pos | SP | RR | SF |
|---|---|---|---|---|---|---|
| 4448[4] | **Lepikha (USA) (62)** (BWHills) **3-9-1** MHills(8) (hdwy 7f out: styd on strly to ld wl ins fnl f) | — | **1** | 7/1[2] | 76 | 51 |
| 4506[5] | **Onefourseven (50)** (JLEyre) **3-8-3** TWilliams(7) (hld up: hdwy 5f out: led over 2f out tl wl ins fnl f: kpt on) | 1¼ | **2** | 10/1[3] | 63 | 38 |
| 4612[3] | **Sterling Fellow (60)** (RHannon) **3-8-13b** RHughes(18) (bhd: hdwy 6f out: chsng ldrs 2f out: kpt on one pce fnl f) | 2½ | **3** | 12/1 | 71 | 46 |
| 4612[D] | **Fro (46)** (TJNaughton) **3-7-8**(5)ow3 MartinDwyer(15) (a chsng ldrs: outpcd 3f out: styd on again towards fin) | 1 | **4** | 16/1 | 56 | 28 |
| 4515[8] | **Bobby's Dream (33)** (MHTompkins) **4-7-8**(3) MHenry(3) (rr div: hdwy 3f out: styd on wl: nrst fin) | s.h | **5** | 25/1 | 43 | 29 |
| 3772[3] | **Arian Spirit (IRE) (53)** (JLEyre) **5-9-3** RLappin(13) (trckd ldrs: disp ld 3f out: sn hdd & one pce) | s.h | **6** | 14/1 | 63 | 49 |
| 4563[4] | **The Butterwick Kid (47)** (RAFahey) **3-8-0** LCharnock(20) (hdwy 10f out: disp ld 3f out: sn hdd & grad wknd) | 1¼ | **7** | 20/1 | 56 | 31 |
| 4612* | **Amiarge (50)** (MBrittain) **6-9-0** GBardwell(6) (bhd: styd on fnl 3f: n.d) | 13 | **8** | 10/1[3] | 47 | 33 |
| 4588* | **Alwarqa (62)** (MDHammond) **3-9-1** JFortune(12) (lw: bhd: hdwy 3f out: nvr rchd ldrs) | nk | **9** | 3/1[1] | 59 | 34 |
| 4588[8] | **Mizyan (IRE) (53)** (JEBanks) **8-9-3** LDettori(5) (chsd ldrs tl wknd fnl 3½f) | ½ | **10** | 14/1 | 49 | 35 |
| 4612[2] | **Zeliba (35)** (MrsNMacauley) **4-7-13** JQuinn(10) (hdwy to chse ldrs 6f out: wknd wl over 1f out) | hd | **11** | 7/1[2] | 31 | 17 |
| 4042[8] | **What Jim Wants (IRE) (44)** (JJO'Neill) **3-7-6**(5)ow1 PFessey(4) (chsd ldrs tl wknd 4f out) | 17 | **12** | 50/1 | 25 | — |
| 4260[8] | **Non Vintage (IRE) (50)** (MCChapman) **5-8-11**(3) PMcCabe(2) (bhd & drvn along 8f out: hdwy & in tch 3f out: sn wknd) | 3 | **13** | 16/1 | 28 | 14 |
| 4563[14] | **Sedvicta (42)** (MrsMReveley) **4-8-6** ACulhane(17) (a bhd) | 8 | **14** | 25/1 | 13 | — |
| *3955[5]* | **Mr Moriarty (IRE) (32)** (SRBowring) **5-7-10** NAdams(1) (b: led tl hdd & wknd 3f out) | ½ | **15** | 33/1 | 2 | — |
| | **Dockmaster (38)** (MissMKMilligan) **5-7-13**(3)ow2 FLynch(19) (a rr div) | s.h | **16** | 50/1 | 8 | — |
| 4612[13] | **Royrace (34)** (WMBrisbourne) **4-7-12** AGarth(16) (wnt prom 10f out: wknd 4f out) | 5 | **17** | 33/1 | — | — |
| 4588[2] | **Lostris (IRE) (36)** (MDods) **5-8-0** NKennedy(11) (chsd ldrs tl wknd fnl 4f) | 2½ | **18** | 10/1[3] | — | — |
| 4683[17] | **Dawadar (USA) (60)** (JSGoldie) **9-9-5**(5) GLee(9) (hdwy to jn ldrs 10f out: wknd over 3f out) | 1 | **19** | 50/1 | 23 | 9 |
| 4612[5] | **Bark'n'bite (50)** (MrsMReveley) **4-9-0** JCarroll(14) (prom to ½-wy: wknd qckly: p.u 2f out) | | **P** | 14/1 | — | — |

(SP 140.9%) **20 Rn**

**4m 4.1** (12.10) CSF £77.81 CT £793.26 TOTE £9.30: £2.10 £2.80 £3.50 £3.30 (£84.50) Trio £111.10 OWNER Mr R. E. Sangster (LAMBOURN) BRED Swettenham Stud

LONG HANDICAP What Jim Wants (IRE) 7-4 Fro 7-7

WEIGHT FOR AGE 3yo-11lb

**OFFICIAL EXPLANATION Bark'n'Bite: lost his action.**

**4448 Lepikha (USA)** has looked slow in the past and this much longer trip suited her down to the ground, with her stamina winning the day. (7/1)
**4506 Onefourseven** is running well and will be interesting if returning to the All-Weather. (10/1)
**4612 Sterling Fellow** does not do anything quickly but he does stay, and kept on well here when all looked lost. (12/1)
**4612 Fro** looks the type that would need another circuit to really come into her own. (16/1)
**1611 Bobby's Dream** never got going here until too late and is still a maiden after eighteen attempts. (25/1)
**3772 Arian Spirit (IRE)** had her chances, but the weight told in the last couple of furlongs. (14/1)
**4612 Bark'n'bite** (14/1: 12/1-20/1)

## 4795 BROOMFIELD NURSERY H'CAP (0-75) (2-Y.O) (Class E)

4-45 (4-49) **1m 4y** £3,704.00 (£1,112.00: £536.00: £248.00) Stalls: Low GOING: 0.05 sec per fur (G)

| Form | Horse | Dist | Pos | SP | RR | SF |
|---|---|---|---|---|---|---|
| *4331[4]* | **Double Espresso (IRE) (63)** (MJohnston) **2-8-12** MRoberts(13) (lw: a.p: led 2f out & qcknd: r.o wl) | — | **1** | 10/1[2] | 75 | 32 |
| 4760[2] | **Julietta Mia (USA) (68)** (BWHills) **2-9-3** MHills(12) (hld up & bhd: stdy hdwy 4f out: effrt & ch over 1f out: put hd in air & nt qckn) | 3½ | **2** | 7/4[1] | 73 | 30 |
| 4625[7] | **Hurgill Dancer (67)** (JWWatts) **2-9-2** JCarroll(6) (prom: effrt 3f out: styd on: nt pce to chal) | 1¾ | **3** | 25/1 | 69 | 26 |
| 4594[4] | **Rivonia (USA) (59)** (MrsJRRamsden) **2-8-8** KFallon(19) (lw: rr div: styd on fnl 3f: nrst fin) | 3½ | **4** | 10/1[2] | 54 | 11 |
| 4594[5] | **Murron Wallace (60)** (RMWhitaker) **2-8-9** LCharnock(9) (mid div & rdn 3f out: styd on towards fin) | hd | **5** | 16/1 | 54 | 11 |
| 4602[17] | **Dee Pee Tee Cee (IRE) (62)** (MWEasterby) **2-8-6**(5) GParkin(15) (lw: mid div: nt clr run 2½f out: styd on towards fin) | 2½ | **6** | 20/1 | 51 | 8 |
| 4207[8] | **Circle of Magic (60)** (PJMakin) **2-8-9** GDuffield(18) (prom: reminders after 2f: effrt over 2f out: sn btn) | 1¼ | **7** | 16/1 | 47 | 4 |
| 4103[3] | **Hallmark (IRE) (69)** (RHannon) **2-9-4b**[1] RHughes(7) (w ldrs: led 3f out to 2f out: sn wknd) | 5 | **8** | 14/1 | 46 | 3 |
| *2633[12]* | **Heggies (IRE) (62)** (CREgerton) **2-8-8**(3) MHenry(8) (chsd ldrs: n.m.r over 2f out: sn btn) | ½ | **9** | 25/1 | 38 | — |
| 4433[6] | **Good Day (66)** (CWThornton) **2-9-1** DeanMcKeown(2) (rdn ½-wy: nvr bttr than mid div) | 1¼ | **10** | 14/1 | 39 | — |
| 4262[9] | **Fan of Vent-Axia (59)** (CNAllen) **2-8-3v**[1](5) MartinDwyer(4) (chsd ldrs tl grad wknd fnl 2f) | nk | **11** | 25/1 | 32 | — |
| 4440[5] | **Jack Flush (IRE) (72)** (BSRothwell) **2-9-7** JStack(16) (cl up tl wknd over 2f out) | 2½ | **12** | 20/1 | 40 | — |
| 3405[6] | **Rebuke (55)** (RFJohnsonHoughton) **2-8-4** JQuinn(5) (nvr nr ldrs) | ¾ | **13** | 25/1 | 21 | — |
| 4694* | **Skelton Sovereign (IRE) (66)** (RHollinshead) **2-8-12**(3) 6x FLynch(17) (a bhd) | 3½ | **14** | 14/1 | 25 | — |
| 4482[2] | **Presentiment (58)** (JBerry) **2-8-7** JFortune(3) (in tch tl wknd fnl 2f) | ¾ | **15** | 16/1 | 16 | — |
| 4495[4] | **Suave Star (58)** (CADwyer) **2-8-7** GHind(1) (a bhd) | 3 | **16** | 12/1[3] | 10 | — |
| 4384[6] | **Not A Lot (57)** (MWEasterby) **2-8-6** ACulhane(11) (hld up & a bhd) | nk | **17** | 25/1 | 8 | — |
| 4618[11] | **Love Me Do (USA) (72)** (MJohnston) **2-9-7** LDettori(10) (lw: a bhd) | 8 | **18** | 10/1[2] | 7 | — |
| 4501[4] | **Don't Worry Mike (61)** (FHLee) **2-8-10** RHills(14) (led tl hdd & wknd 3f out) | 6 | **19** | 20/1 | — | — |

(SP 142.5%) **19 Rn**

**1m 48.5** (7.00) CSF £28.67 CT £436.43 TOTE £9.70: £2.10 £1.10 £5.00 £1.80 (£8.10) Trio £225.60 OWNER Mr R. W. Huggins (MIDDLEHAM) BRED Godolphin Management Co Ltd

**4331 Double Espresso (IRE)** stays well and showed a turn of foot. She looks a progressive sort. (10/1: 7/1-12/1)
**4760 Julietta Mia (USA)** again showed she has plenty of ability, but did not really produce it when the pressure was on. (7/4: op 11/4)
**4298 Hurgill Dancer** ran well, staying on in the last two furlongs, but never looked likely to offer a live threat. (25/1)
**4594 Rivonia (USA)** is slow but sure, and was keeping on well at the end. (10/1)
**4594 Murron Wallace** was staying on in the closing stages as though stamina is her one real asset. (16/1)
**4298 Dee Pee Tee Cee (IRE)** seems to find trouble in his races and it can not all be down to bad luck. (20/1)

## 4796 BROCKADALE MAIDEN AUCTION STKS (II) (2-Y.O) (Class F)
5-15 (5-19) **6f** £2,374.00 (£664.00: £322.00) Stalls: Low GOING: 0.05 sec per fur (G)

| | | | | SP | RR | SF |
|---|---|---|---|---|---|---|
| 4250[2] | **Parijazz (IRE) (72)** (MartynMeade) **2-7-13** NAdams(8) (swtg: mde all: all out) | — | **1** | 15/8[1] | 69 | — |
| 4228[10] | **Night Chorus** (BSRothwell) **2-8-5** JStack(3) (bhd: hdwy 2f out: hung lft: r.o towards fin) | hd | **2** | 25/1 | 75 | 4 |
| 4600[6] | **Lady Shirl (IRE)** (PMitchell) **2-8-3** JQuinn(1) (trckd ldrs: hdwy to chse wnr over 1f out: sn rdn & no ex) | 3 | **3** | 7/1 | 65 | — |
| 4600[11] | **Spicetress** (JLSpearing) **2-7-13**(3)ow4 FLynch(6) (w ldr: rdn 2f out: one pce) | ½ | **4** | 33/1 | 62 | — |
| 4072[5] | **Head Girl (IRE) (72)** (CWThornton) **2-8-0** LCharnock(7) (swtg: in tch: rdn ½-wy: hung lft over 1f out: styd on towards fin) | nk | **5** | 13/2[3] | 60 | — |
| 3462[10] | **Tom Pladdey (67)** (RBastiman) **2-8-4** DeanMcKeown(12) (s.i.s: sn rcvrd & chsng ldrs: wknd wl over 1f out) | 3 | **6** | 20/1 | 56 | — |
| *4576*[3] | **Magyar Titok (IRE) (51)** (BobJones) **2-8-5** FNorton(9) (swtg: chsd ldrs: ev ch 2f out: sn wknd) | 1¼ | **7** | 11/1 | 53 | — |
| 4601[7] | **Sharp Deed (IRE)** (PJMakin) **2-8-5** GDuffield(11) (wnt lft s: nvr trbld ldrs) | 1¾ | **8** | 5/1[2] | 49 | — |
| | **Anetta** (MissSEHall) **2-8-3** TWilliams(2) (b.hind: unf: scope: bit bkwd: bhd: sme hdwy 2f out: n.d) | ½ | **9** | 9/1 | 45 | — |
| 4594[18] | **Norbreck House (50)** (JBerry) **2-8-7**ow2 SDWilliams(13) (prom tl outpcd fr ½-wy) | 2½ | **10** | 20/1 | 43 | — |
| 4343[5] | **Thewrightone (IRE) (47)** (GROldroyd) **2-7-12b** NCarlisle(14) (cl up over 3f: wknd qckly) | 5 | **11** | 33/1 | 20 | — |
| 1827[16] | **T-N-T Express** (JLEyre) **2-8-7** RLappin(5) (a outpcd & bhd) | 2 | **12** | 33/1 | 24 | — |
| 4562[19] | **Impish (IRE) (53)** (TJEtherington) **2-8-5b**ow1 JCarroll(10) (a bhd) | 2½ | **13** | 20/1 | 15 | — |
| | **Gymcrak Jester** (GHolmes) **2-8-5** JFanning(4) (unf: bkwd: a outpcd & bhd) | 3½ | **14** | 25/1 | 6 | — |

(SP 126.4%) **14 Rn**

**1m 21.1** (6.80) CSF £46.51 TOTE £2.70: £1.40 £5.50 £2.20 (£96.80) Trio £63.90 OWNER Baucher, Beyts & Humphrey Partnership (MALMESBURY) BRED David Barry

**4250 Parijazz (IRE)** gave problems going to the start and got extremely warm beforehand. She did the business in the race though and the line came just in time. (15/8)

**Night Chorus** has plenty of ability if he ever learns to run straight. He was not helping his rider at any stage here. (25/1)

**4600 Lady Shirl (IRE)** looked dangerous entering the last two furlongs, but proved disappointing when ridden. (7/1)

**Spicetress** ran better this time, showing useful speed, but was going nowhere in the home straight. (33/1)

**4072 Head Girl (IRE)** is a frustrating character who gives the impression that she has more ability than she sometimes cares to show. (13/2)

**2596 Tom Pladdey** has ability but is inclined to wander about when the pressure was on, and was going nowhere in the last couple of furlongs. (20/1)

T/Jkpt: Not won; £20,163.66 to Chepstow 22/10/96. T/Plpt: £636.50 (29.78 Tckts). T/Qdpt: £67.00 (25.48 Tckts). AA

# 4125-CHEPSTOW (L-H) (Soft)
## Tuesday October 22nd
WEATHER: overcast WIND: almost nil

## 4797 E.B.F. MEADOW MAIDEN STKS (I) (2-Y.O F) (Class D)
1-30 (1-34) **7f 16y** £3,260.50 (£979.00: £472.00: £218.50) Stalls: High GOING: 0.56 sec per fur (GS)

| | | | | SP | RR | SF |
|---|---|---|---|---|---|---|
| 4305[2] | **My Valentina** (BWHills) **2-8-11** MHills(7) (chsd ldrs: qcknd to ld wl ins fnl f) | — | **1** | 13/8[1] | 85 | 45 |
| 4547[7] | **Catria (IRE)** (JHMGosden) **2-8-11** GHind(8) (led: clr ½-wy: wknd & hdd wl ins fnl f) | 1 | **2** | 14/1 | 83 | 43 |
| 4514[5] | **Arapi** (SirMarkPrescott) **2-8-11** GDuffield(6) (led stands' side 3f out: hrd rdn fnl f: nt rch ldrs) | 3½ | **3** | 5/1[2] | 75 | 35 |
| 4605[6] | **Lonely Heart** (MajorDNChappell) **2-8-11** GCarter(3) (swtg: hdwy fnl 2f: nvr nrr) | nk | **4** | 33/1 | 74 | 34 |
| | **Toi Toi (IRE)** (DWPArbuthnot) **2-8-11** SWhitworth(14) (w'like: bkwd: s.s: hdwy over 1f out: nvr nrr) | nk | **5** | 50/1 | 74 | 34 |
| 2230[7] | **Quibbling** (HCandy) **2-8-11** CRutter(6) (trckd ldrs centre: one pce fnl 2f) | 1¼ | **6** | 25/1 | 71 | 31 |
| 4512[6] | **Cugina** (GBBalding) **2-8-11** SDrowne(10) (lw: hdwy 2f out: nvr nr to chal) | ¾ | **7** | 8/1 | 69 | 29 |
| 4547[8] | **Atnab (USA)** (PTWalwyn) **2-8-11** RHills(9) (bit bkwd: chsd ldr tl wknd 2f out) | 1½ | **8** | 10/1 | 66 | 26 |
| 4305[9] | **Nick of Time** (JLDunlop) **2-8-11** TSprake(15) (led stands' side 4f: sn lost tch) | 1½ | **9** | 33/1 | 62 | 22 |
| | **Aunt Daphne** (BAMcMahon) **2-8-11** SSanders(12) (leggy: unf: bit bkwd: nvr nr ldrs) | 1¼ | **10** | 50/1 | 59 | 19 |
| | **Mashkorah (USA)** (RHannon) **2-8-11** DaneO'Neill(5) (leggy: unf: bhd: effrt over 2f out: no imp) | 2 | **11** | 25/1 | 55 | 15 |
| 1643[3] | **Venetian Scene** (PFICole) **2-8-11** TQuinn(4) (bkwd: chsd ldrs over 4f) | s.h | **12** | 14/1 | 55 | 15 |
| | **Snappy Girl (IRE)** (MRStoute) **2-8-11** KFallon(1) (unf: scope: bkwd: s.s: a in rr) | 5 | **13** | 10/1 | 43 | 3 |
| 3982[5] | **Sound Appeal** (AGFoster) **2-8-6**(5) CAdamson(2) (swtg: in tch centre to ½-wy) | 2 | **14** | 33/1 | 39 | — |
| | **Comic Opera (IRE)** (PWChapple-Hyam) **2-8-11** PatEddery(13) (lt-f: unf: s.s: a bhd: t.o) | 6 | **15** | 6/1[3] | 25 | — |
| 4514[16] | **Gore Hill** (MBlanshard) **2-8-11** JQuinn(11) (bit bkwd: prom stands' side 4f: sn wknd: t.o) | 6 | **16** | 50/1 | 12 | — |

(SP 134.1%) **16 Rn**

**1m 28.0** (8.00) CSF £26.93 TOTE £2.60: £1.50 £3.70 £2.10 (£26.40) Trio £92.50 OWNER Mr D. J. Deer (LAMBOURN) BRED D. J. and Mrs Deer

**4305 My Valentina** handled this testing ground extremely well and took the measure of the runner-up readily inside the final 50 yards. (13/8)

**4547 Catria (IRE)** may have had a bit too much use made of her at this first attempt at the trip and she had no answer when the winner launched her challenge. She could make up into a useful three-year-old. (14/1)

**4514 Arapi** took control on the stands' side three furlongs out, but the principals, racing away from her, had too much pace inside the distance. (5/1: 4/1-13/2)

**4605 Lonely Heart** came out of the pack in the closing stages, but was just too late to make the frame. She is the sort who could on improving. (33/1)

**Toi Toi (IRE)**, a daughter of a winning mare, showed plenty of promise after losing ground at the start on this debut. She should be able to pay her way. (50/1)

**Quibbling**, a sparely-made filly who may have trouble handling such testing conditions, held her pitch in the chasing group until feeling the strain inside the last quarter-mile. (25/1)

**1643 Venetian Scene** needed the run after almost five months out of action and was in trouble and going backwards soon after halfway. (14/1)

**Snappy Girl (IRE)** (10/1: 4/1-12/1)

## 4798 E.B.F. MEADOW MAIDEN STKS (II) (2-Y.O F) (Class D)
2-00 (2-03) **7f 16y** £3,237.75 (£972.00: £468.50: £216.75) Stalls: High GOING: 0.56 sec per fur (GS)

| | | | | SP | RR | SF |
|---|---|---|---|---|---|---|
| | **Technicolour (IRE)** (MRStoute) **2-8-11** WRSwinburn(3) (lt-f: stdd s: gd hdwy 2f out: str run u.p to ld last stride) | — | **1** | 7/2[2] | 81+ | 34 |

3613[6] **Summerosa (USA)** (PWChapple-Hyam) **2-8-11** PatEddery(1) (led tl ins fnl f: hrd rdn to ld nr fin: hdd last stride) ....hd **2** 5/4[1] 81 34
**Kawa-Ib (IRE)** (PTWalwyn) **2-8-11** RHills(10) (hld up: hdwy 3f out: led ins fnl f: hdd nr fin) ....hd **3** 11/1 81 34
4369[7] **Gift Token** (MajorDNChappell) **2-8-11** GCarter(15) (swtg: a.p: ev ch 2f out: one pce fnl f) ....3 **4** 12/1 74 27
**Free As A Bird** (MRChannon) **2-8-11** RHughes(4) (lt-f: s.s: hdwy 4f out: ev ch 2f out: eased whn btn ins fnl f) ....6 **5** 16/1 60 13
4104[9] **Mary Culi** (HCandy) **2-8-11** CRutter(9) (prom: rdn 2f out: one pce appr fnl f) ....2 **6** 33/1 56 9
4512[12] **Woodland Nymph** (DJGMurraySmith) **2-8-11** DRMcCabe(6) (chsd ldrs tl wknd wl over 1f out) ....1¼ **7** 50/1 53 6
**Eliza** (LordHuntingdon) **2-8-11** DHarrison(7) (w'like: scope: bkwd: spd over 5f) ....¾ **8** 16/1 51 4
**Bisquet-de-Bouche** (RDickin) **2-8-11** MRoberts(11) (lt-f: s.s: hdwy 3f out: nt rch ldrs) ....¾ **9** 33/1 49 2
**Ginger Rogers** (DWPArbuthnot) **2-8-11** TQuinn(12) (leggy: bkwd: outpcd) ....1¼ **10** 20/1 47 —
**After Hours** (DJSffrenchDavis) **2-8-11** MTebbutt(5) (w'like: bit bkwd: a in rr) ....1 **11** 50/1 44 —
3593[14] **Golden Goddess** (IABalding) **2-8-6**(5) MartinDwyer(8) (bkwd: spd centre over 4f) ....2 **12** 16/1 40 —
**Kilmeena Lady** (JCFox) **2-8-11** AClark(2) (leggy: unf: gd spd 4f: wknd wl over 1f out) ....2½ **13** 66/1 34 —
2538[8] **Moccasin (IRE)** (PRWebber) **2-8-11** RPerham(16) (bhd fnl 3f) ....2½ **14** 33/1 29 —
4600[14] **Isca Maiden** (PHayward) **2-8-11** NAdams(14) (a bhd) ....2½ **15** 66/1 23 —
4605[4] **Royal Orchid (IRE) (76)** (RHannon) **2-8-11** DaneO'Neill(13) (b.nr hind: in rr most of wy) ....2 **16** 8/1[3] 18 —
(SP 131.9%) **16 Rn**

**1m 28.9** (8.90) CSF £8.43 TOTE £4.50: £1.60 £1.30 £3.30 (£4.00) Trio £12.60 OWNER Lord Weinstock/Exors of late S Weinstock (NEWMARKET) BRED Ballymacoll Stud Farm Ltd

**Technicolour (IRE)** had the ground to suit her and was ridden with plenty of confidence, but she did need to show true grit to get on top nearing the finish. (7/2: 9/4-4/1)

**3613 Summerosa (USA)**, stepping up in distance, tried hard to make every post a winning one but, hard as she tried, she just failed to last home. She will know she has been in a race. (5/4: Evens-11/8)

**Kawa-Ib (IRE)** put in a very bold showing on this racecourse debut and, after forcing her head in front, was touched off in the dying strides. She will definitely win races, but may well have to wait until next year. (11/1: 6/1-12/1)

**3848 Gift Token** is not yet lasting the trip and this bottomless ground did not help. She was not disgraced in defeat though and there will be plenty more opportunities. (12/1: 8/1-14/1)

**Free As A Bird**, a lightly-made filly from a winning family, showed plenty of promise after a tardy start and will not let the family name down. (16/1)

**Mary Culi** ran much better than she did on her debut and there is certainly a race or two in her. (33/1)

**Eliza** did not look fully tuned up for this debut, but she displayed plenty of speed and, on a sounder surface, may well have been thereabouts. (16/1)

## 4799 ANNUAL FLAT V JUMP JOCKEYS CHALLENGE H'CAP (0-70) (3-Y.O+) (Class G)

2-30 (2-32) **7f 16y** £2,379.00 (£669.00: £327.00) Stalls: High GOING: 0.56 sec per fur (GS)

SP RR SF

3384a[3] **Jimmy the Skunk (IRE) (60)** (PDEvans) **5-11-0** RHills(6) (mde all: hrd rdn fnl f: hld on gamely) ....— **1** 12/1 70 51
4463[7] **Embankment (IRE) (70)** (RHannon) **6-11-5**(5) CMaude(7) (lw: hld up: hdwy over 2f out: hrd rdn: r.o wl fnl f) ...¾ **2** 5/1[2] 78 59
4430[8] **Milos (58)** (TJNaughton) **5-10-12** GDuffield(9) (hld up: gd hdwy 2f out: ev ch ins fnl f: unable qckn) ....nk **3** 16/1 66 47
*3951*[5] **Yeoman Oliver (70)** (BAMcMahon) **3-11-3**(5) JAMcCarthy(10) (lw: hld up: effrt 3f out: rdn & one pce fnl f) ....1½ **4** 25/1 74 53
2235[8] **Belzao (60)** (DRCElsworth) **3-10-12** TQuinn(3) (swtg: w wnr: rdn 2f out: no ex fnl f) ....4 **5** 16/1 55 34
3636[2] **Mellors (IRE) (64)** (JARToller) **3-11-2** TSprake(8) (nvr nr to chal) ....1 **6** 7/1[3] 57 36
*4778*[2] **Bold Street (IRE) (64)** (ABailey) **6-10-13b**(5) WMarston(12) (b: hld up: hdwy over 2f out: wknd fnl f) ....2 **7** 8/1 52 33
3926[9] **Brighton Road (IRE) (70)** (GBBalding) **3-11-8** TWilliams(5) (sn drvn along: a in rr) ....1 **8** 8/1 56 35
4701[9] **Pearl Dawn (IRE) (60)** (GLMoore) **6-10-9**(5) JFrost(11) (a in rr) ....1¾ **9** 25/1 42 23
4550[3] **Serious Sensation (65)** (SirMarkPrescott) **3-11-3** MHills(4) (swtg: chsd ldrs: hrd rdn over 2f out: wknd wl over 1f out) ....1 **10** 9/4[1] 45 24
2228[9] **Sue Me (IRE) (59)** (WRMuir) **4-10-8**(5) BClifford(1) (chsd ldrs tl wknd 2f out) ....s.h **11** 9/1 39 20
4498[4] **Memphis Beau (IRE) (62)** (JARToller) **3-10-9b**(5) GUpton(2) (dwlt: sn chsng ldrs: wknd fnl 2f) ....s.h **12** 25/1 42 21
(SP 123.2%) **12 Rn**

**1m 29.9** (9.90) CSF £68.60 CT £884.98 TOTE £11.70: £2.80 £1.90 £5.60 (£27.20) Trio £300.50; £296.37 to Newcastle 23/10/96 OWNER Mr Trevor Gallienne (WELSHPOOL) BRED Martyn J. McEnery

WEIGHT FOR AGE 3yo-2lb

**Jimmy the Skunk (IRE)**, who has been racing in Jersey, has shown a liking for the soft ground. Giving his all inside the final furlong, he did well to hold on nearing the finish. (12/1)

**4202 Embankment (IRE)** delivered a determined challenge inside the final furlong but, over a trip short of his best, could not find the speed to put his stamp on proceedings. (5/1: 7/2-11/2)

**3765 Milos** looked sure to score when joining issue 200 yards out, but the winner, with the help of the far rail, proved the stronger in an all-out battle to the line. (16/1)

**3951 Yeoman Oliver**, still to win on Turf, looked a live threat when making his bid approaching the final furlong, but he could do little more than gallop on the spot when the chips were down. (25/1)

**1984 Belzao** had plenty of use made of him, but appeared not to see the trip out in such stamina-testing ground. (16/1)

**3636 Mellors (IRE)**, held up to get the trip, was never near enough to pose a threat, and it is doubtful if the going suited him. (7/1: 5/1-15/2)

**4550 Serious Sensation** has won on the All-Weather, but he did not relish this ground and he was hard at work and in trouble some way out. (9/4)

## 4800 SPINNEY CONDITIONS STKS (3-Y.O+) (Class C)

3-00 (3-03) **1m 14y** £5,054.00 (£1,886.00: £918.00: £390.00: £170.00: £82.00) Stalls: High GOING: 0.56 sec per fur (GS)

SP RR SF

4568[23] **Clan Ben (IRE) (95)** (HRACecil) **4-9-0b** PatEddery(8) (hld up: hdwy over 2f out: hrd rdn to ld ins fnl f: edgd lft: all out) ....— **1** 5/1[3] 97 54
4775[12] **Welton Arsenal (92)** (MRChannon) **4-9-6** RHughes(6) (hld up: stdy hdwy over 2f out: ev ch ins fnl f: sn rdn: nt r.o) ....1½ **2** 33/1 100 57
4615[8] **Dee-Lady (70)** (WGMTurner) **4-8-2**(7) DSweeney(9) (b: a w ldrs: led over 2f out: sn clr: wknd & hdd ins fnl f) ....1¼ **3** 50/1 87 44
4325[7] **Night City (102)** (LadyHerries) **5-9-8** DeclanO'Shea(1) (stdd s: hdwy 3f out: ev ch & rdn over 1f out: one pce) ....¾ **4** 9/2[2] 98 55

| | | | | | | |
|---|---|---|---|---|---|---|
| 4775[5] | **Chickawicka (IRE) (87)** (BPalling) **5-9-0** TSprake(4) (led over 3f: rdn & one pce fnl f) | hd | **5** | 12/1 | 90 | 47 |
| 4623[2] | **Celestial Key (USA) (105)** (MJohnston) **6-9-0** MRoberts(2) (chsd ldrs: rdn over 2f out: wknd wl over 1f out) | 7 | **6** | 11/8[1] | 76 | 33 |
| 4568[14] | **Moments of Fortune (USA) (93)** (BHanbury) **4-9-0b** JStack(7) (swtg: chsd ldrs: led 4f out tl over 2f out: sn rdn & wknd) | hd | **7** | 9/1 | 76 | 33 |
| | **Chai-Yo** (JABOld) **6-8-10**(7)ow6 EGreehy(10) (bit bkwd: nvr nr to chal) | 4 | **8** | 66/1 | 71 | 22 |
| 4214[9] | **Agnella (IRE) (85)** (GLMoore) **3-8-6** GDuffield(5) (prom tl wknd over 2f out) | 4 | **9** | 33/1 | 55 | 9 |
| 4313[5] | **Flyfisher (IRE) (97)** (GLewis) **3-8-11** WRSwinburn(13) (trckd ldrs over 5f: sn lost tch) | nk | **10** | 10/1 | 59 | 13 |
| 1770[9] | **Alessia (85)** (WRMuir) **4-8-9** KFallon(11) (swtg: w ldrs tl wknd qckly over 2f out) | 2½ | **11** | 50/1 | 49 | 6 |
| 4337[12] | **Zacaroon (50)** (JFfitch-Heyes) **5-8-9** DHarrison(3) (a in rr) | 5 | **12** | 100/1 | 39 | — |
| | **Street Kendra (FR)** (BSmart) **4-8-9** MTebbutt(12) (swtg: w ldrs to ½-wy: wknd over 2f out) | ½ | **13** | 33/1 | 38 | — |

(SP 119.0%) **13 Rn**

**1m 41.1** (8.60) CSF £128.46 TOTE £5.10: £1.90 £4.00 £9.10 (£18.70) Trio £246.00 OWNER Angus Dundee Plc (NEWMARKET) BRED T. Hillman

WEIGHT FOR AGE 3yo-3lb

**4120 Clan Ben (IRE)** came good in the autumn last year and this hard-earned success could be the start of his comeback. (5/1: op 3/1)

**4623 Welton Arsenal** was going to win a minute entering the final furlong but, when it came to doing battle, he swished his tail and said no thanks. (33/1)

**4297 Dee-Lady**, who has been tried at all trips, is not quite up to this class, but she is genuine and thoroughly deserves to win another prize. (50/1)

**2248 Night City** won this event twelve months ago on similar ground and may have been squeezed for room on the inside when making progress. He was close enough if good enough at the furlong pole, but could not quicken sufficiently to take charge. (9/2)

**4775 Chickawicka (IRE)**, making a quick reappearance, had trouble getting the trip in these conditions and called enough inside the distance. (12/1)

**4623 Celestial Key (USA)** could not handle the ground and was getting stuck in the mud for the last quarter-mile. (11/8)

**3709 Moments of Fortune (USA)** (9/1: op 6/1)

## 4801 PAT EDDERY 200-IN-A-SEASON MAIDEN STKS (2-Y.O) (Class D)

3-30 (3-34) **1m 14y** £4,076.25 (£1,230.00: £597.50: £281.25) Stalls: High GOING: 0.56 sec per fur (GS)

| | | | | SP | RR | SF |
|---|---|---|---|---|---|---|
| 4507[5] | **Sausalito Bay** (IABalding) **2-9-0** KFallon(8) (w ldrs: led over 1f out: drvn out) | — | **1** | 11/1 | 79 | 38 |
| 4585[2] | **Perfect Paradigm (IRE)** (JHMGosden) **2-9-0** GHind(3) (lw: led tl over 1f out: r.o one pce) | ¾ | **2** | 15/2 | 78 | 37 |
| 4492[7] | **Percy Isle (IRE)** (MRStoute) **2-9-0** WRSwinburn(12) (hdwy 3f out: hrd rdn over 1f out: r.o ins fnl f) | nk | **3** | 11/2[3] | 77 | 36 |
| | **Wellaki (USA)** (JHMGosden) **2-9-0** AMcGlone(18) (w'like: scope: bit bkwd: hdwy 3f out: r.o one pce fnl 2f) | 1¼ | **4** | 25/1 | 74 | 33 |
| 4507[2] | **Flagship** (MajorWRHern) **2-8-9** TSprake(16) (w ldrs: ev ch over 1f out: wknd ins fnl f) | nk | **5** | 9/4[1] | 69 | 28 |
| 4584[5] | **Drumgor Prince** (APJarvis) **2-9-0** JFortune(19) (hdwy & edgd lft fnl 2f: nvr nrr) | 3½ | **6** | 33/1 | 67 | 26 |
| 4507[4] | **Corinthian (IRE)** (RHannon) **2-9-0** PatEddery(14) (a.p: rdn over 2f out: one pce) | 4 | **7** | 7/1 | 59 | 18 |
| | **Night Mirage (USA)** (MJohnston) **2-8-9** MRoberts(20) (lengthy: lw: prom tl wknd over 2f out) | hd | **8** | 20/1 | 54 | 13 |
| | **Montfort (USA)** (PFICole) **2-9-0** TQuinn(13) (unf: scope: chsd ldrs: rdn over 2f out: sn wknd) | nk | **9** | 9/1 | 58 | 17 |
| 4508[6] | **Brynkir** (DJGMurraySmith) **2-9-0** DHarrison(10) (nvr bttr than mid div) | hd | **10** | 50/1 | 58 | 17 |
| 4599[7] | **Regal Reprimand** (GLewis) **2-9-0** SWhitworth(17) (b.hind: hdwy over 2f out: nvr trbld ldrs) | 1¼ | **11** | 20/1 | 56 | 15 |
| | **Swing West (USA)** (PFICole) **2-9-0** CRutter(2) (w'like: scope: prom tl wknd over 2f out) | 1 | **12** | 25/1 | 54 | 13 |
| | **Ramike (IRE)** (MJohnston) **2-9-0** MHills(6) (w'like: scope: outpcd) | 3½ | **13** | 25/1 | 47 | 6 |
| 3821[6] | **Big Bang** (MBlanshard) **2-9-0** JQuinn(4) (outpcd) | 1¼ | **14** | 66/1 | 44 | 3 |
| 4477[4] | **Wesley's Lad (IRE)** (JNeville) **2-9-0** AClark(7) (prom tl wknd over 2f out) | 2 | **15** | 50/1 | 40 | — |
| 4261[4] | **Malik (IRE)** (SbinSuroor) **2-9-0b**[1] RHills(11) (bhd fnl 4f) | hd | **16** | 5/1[2] | 40 | — |
| 4233[11] | **Ortelius** (RHannon) **2-9-0** DaneO'Neill(1) (prom tl wknd over 2f out) | s.h | **17** | 33/1 | 40 | — |
| 3874[7] | **Euro Superstar (FR)** (SDow) **2-9-0** SSanders(9) (bit bkwd: a bhd) | 2 | **18** | 50/1 | 36 | — |
| | **Miss Mezzanine** (EAWheeler) **2-8-4**(5) ADaly(5) (lt-f: outpcd: t.o) | 13 | **19** | 50/1 | 5 | — |
| *3625*[9] | **Ronquista d'Or** (GAHam) **2-9-0** NAdams(15) (bit bkwd: a t.o) | dist | **20** | 100/1 | — | — |

(SP 142.7%) **20 Rn**

**1m 42.6** (10.10) CSF £95.10 TOTE £12.70: £3.50 £2.50 £2.30 (£37.90) Trio £119.80 OWNER Mr J. C. Smith (KINGSCLERE) BRED Littleton Stud

**4507 Sausalito Bay** has no stamina problems. With the leaders all the way, he gained a definite advantage over a furlong out and, driven along, kept finding it all the way to the line. (11/1: 8/1-12/1)

**4585 Perfect Paradigm (IRE)** made a gallant effort to lead throughout. Headed approaching the final furlong, he kept on well and should have no trouble in losing his maiden tag. (15/2: 5/1-8/1)

**Percy Isle (IRE)** took a long time to find top gear. Driven along three furlongs out, he kept staying on, but it was not until the last 100 yards that he really found his stride. Further improvement can be expected. (11/2: 3/1-6/1)

**Wellaki (USA)** came with a good run from three furlongs out but, though staying on to the end, could not quite find the speed to catch the leaders. (25/1)

**4507 Flagship** ran a shade freely, disputing the lead, but still appeared to be running over her rivals at the two-furlong marker. Put to her best, she tired in the closing stages, but gives the impression she could reverse the placings on future occasions. (9/4)

**4584 Drumgor Prince**, despite drifting across the course, ran on in the last two furlongs but was never on terms with the leaders. (33/1)

## 4802 RICHARD HOLDER H'CAP (0-85) (3-Y.O+) (Class D)

4-00 (4-04) **6f 16y** £4,190.00 (£1,265.00: £615.00: £290.00) Stalls: High GOING: 0.56 sec per fur (GS)

| | | | | SP | RR | SF |
|---|---|---|---|---|---|---|
| 4775[11] | **Charlie Sillett (80)** (BWHills) **4-9-13** MHills(18) (hdwy 2f out: r.o to ld last strides) | — | **1** | 15/2[2] | 88 | 57 |
| 4687[23] | **Caricature (IRE) (76)** (GLewis) **3-9-5b**(3) AWhelan(1) (a.p: led over 2f out tl fnl strides) | hd | **2** | 25/1 | 84 | 52 |
| 4312[16] | **Stoppes Brow (76)** (GLMoore) **4-9-9v** SWhitworth(10) (lw: hdwy over 2f out: ev ch 1f out: nt qckn) | 1¼ | **3** | 16/1 | 80 | 49 |
| 4581[19] | **Splicing (75)** (WJHaggas) **3-9-7** KFallon(13) (a.p: ev ch over 1f out: one pce) | 2 | **4** | 25/1 | 74 | 42 |
| 4312[14] | **So Intrepid (IRE) (79)** (JMBradley) **6-9-12** PatEddery(15) (hrd rdn 2f out: hdwy over 1f out: one pce fnl f) | ¾ | **5** | 15/2[2] | 76 | 45 |
| 4560* | **Q Factor (78)** (DHaydnJones) **4-9-11** SDrowne(2) (chsd ldr over 3f: one pce) | 3 | **6** | 9/1[3] | 67 | 36 |
| 3993[5] | **Supreme Thought (60)** (LGCottrell) **4-8-7** JFEgan(20) (swtg: lw: nrst fin) | nk | **7** | 16/1 | 49 | 18 |
| 4592[3] | **Nilgiri Hills (IRE) (80)** (JLDunlop) **3-9-12b**[1] TQuinn(19) (nvr nr to chal) | s.h | **8** | 11/1 | 68 | 36 |
| 4581[2] | **Montserrat (75)** (LGCottrell) **4-9-8v** MFenton(14) (lw: rdn over 2f out: btn whn hmpd over 1f out) | nk | **9** | 100/30[1] | 63 | 32 |
| 4560[12] | **Kiss Me Again (IRE) (75)** (RHannon) **3-9-7** DHarrison(12) (nvr trbld ldrs) | 1¾ | **10** | 25/1 | 58 | 26 |
| 4689[8] | **Friendly Brave (USA) (72)** (MissGayKelleway) **6-9-5** RHughes(5) (b: hld up: effrt & rdn over 2f out: sn wknd) | hd | **11** | 20/1 | 55 | 24 |

| Horse | Dist | Pos | SP | RR | SF |
|---|---|---|---|---|---|
| 4453[9] **Ocean Grove (IRE) (75)** (PWChapple-Hyam) **3-9-4b1(3)** RHavlin(16) (lw: hrd rdn over 2f out: no hdwy) | ½ | **12** | 14/1 | 56 | 24 |
| 4701[7] **How's Yer Father (60)** (RJHodges) **10-8-2(5)** AmandaSanders(11) (n.d) | s.h | **13** | 33/1 | 41 | 10 |
| 3989[13] **Fly Tip (IRE) (79)** (BJMeehan) **3-9-11** MTebbutt(8) (swtg: outpcd) | s.h | **14** | 33/1 | 60 | 28 |
| 4581[9] **High Domain (IRE) (67)** (JLSpearing) **5-9-0** JQuinn(17) (gd spd tl wknd over 1f out) | hd | **15** | 20/1 | 48 | 17 |
| 4674[8] **Rivers Magic (76)** (MajorDNChappell) **3-9-8** RHills(9) (outpcd) | ¾ | **16** | 14/1 | 55 | 23 |
| 4679[14] **Go Hever Golf (76)** (TJNaughton) **4-9-9** SSanders(7) (prom tl wknd 2f out) | 6 | **17** | 16/1 | 39 | 8 |
| 2532[7] **Spotted Eagle (81)** (RHannon) **3-9-13** DaneO'Neill(4) (a bhd) | 5 | **18** | 33/1 | 31 | — |
| 4312[3] **La Petite Fusee (81)** (RJO'Sullivan) **5-10-0** DBiggs(3) (led over 3f: wknd qckly: b.b.v) | 6 | **19** | 11/1 | 15 | — |
| 4581[10] **Norwegian Blue (IRE) (81)** (APJarvis) **3-9-13** JFortune(6) (swtg: prom tl wknd qckly 2f out) | 1½ | **20** | 33/1 | 11 | — |
| | | | (SP 137.1%) | **20 Rn** | |

**1m 16.3** (7.10) CSF £172.06 CT £2,733.76 TOTE £8.70: £2.50 £4.70 £4.40 £7.30 (£92.90) Trio £813.40 OWNER Mr John Sillett (LAMBOURN) BRED J. Sillett

WEIGHT FOR AGE 3yo-1lb

**4775 Charlie Sillett**, revelling in the soft conditions, came with a smooth run two furlongs out. After hesitating momentarily, he ran on to snatch the race in the final stride. (15/2)

**4376 Caricature (IRE)** nipped through on the rail to take up the running over two furlongs out. Gamely as he ran on, he could not quite hold the winner. (25/1)

**4088 Stoppes Brow** moved up rapidly under pressure two furlongs out but, after having every chance entering the final furlong, could find no extra nearing the finish. (16/1)

**2634 Splicing**, well placed from the start, looked a big danger at the distance, but could find no extra inside the last furlong. (25/1)

**4198 So Intrepid (IRE)** was being driven along in midfield a long way from the finish and, though he eventually stayed on take fifth, he never held out any hope of winning. (15/2)

**4560* Q Factor**, in second place to past halfway, kept on at one pace under pressure. (9/1)

**4581 Montserrat** always struggled to go the pace in the middle of the course, and had lost all chance when short of room approaching the final furlong. (100/30)

**4312 La Petite Fusee** weakened quickly after leading for over three furlongs. It transpired that she had broken a blood-vessel. (11/1: 8/1-12/1)

## 4803 COPSE NURSERY H'CAP (0-75) (2-Y.O) (Class E)

4-30 (4-34) **6f 16y** £3,129.00 (£942.00: £456.00: £213.00) Stalls: High GOING: 0.56 sec per fur (GS)

| Horse | Dist | Pos | SP | RR | SF |
|---|---|---|---|---|---|
| 4303[8] **Strat's Quest (64)** (DWPArbuthnot) **2-8-10** DHarrison(9) (b: hld up: led over 2f out: drvn out) | — | **1** | 16/1 | 64 | 17 |
| 4546[12] **Summer Risotto (50)** (DJSffrenchDavis) **2-7-10** NCarlisle(14) (b.hind: lw: hdwy over 1f out: r.o wl ins fnl f) | ½ | **2** | 25/1 | 49 | 2 |
| 4234[11] **Mike's Double (IRE) (51)** (GLewis) **2-7-11b1** JQuinn(5) (hdwy 2f out: ev ch & hrd rdn fnl f: r.o) | hd | **3** | 5/1 2 | 49 | 2 |
| 3975[11] **Wild Nettle (52)** (JCFox) **2-7-12** DeclanO'Shea(17) (swtg: a.p: ev ch 1f out: nt qckn) | nk | **4** | 33/1 | 50 | 3 |
| 4043[10] **Expectation (IRE) (66)** (PRWebber) **2-8-12** KFallon(2) (lw: a.p: ev ch fnl f: no ex nr fin) | nk | **5** | 14/1 | 63 | 16 |
| 4549[5] **Rumbustious (68)** (RHannon) **2-9-0** DaneO'Neill(12) (styd on fnl 2f: nt trble ldrs) | 2½ | **6** | 8/1 | 58 | 11 |
| 4454[4] **Muliere (64)** (MJohnston) **2-8-10** MRoberts(6) (hrd rdn over 2f out: no rspnse) | nk | **7** | 8/1 | 54 | 7 |
| *4576*[2] **Will To Win (61)** (PGMurphy) **2-8-7** SDrowne(16) (b.hind: led stands' side 3f: wknd over 1f out) | 5 | **8** | 12/1 | 37 | — |
| 4242[17] **Priory Gardens (IRE) (50)** (JMBradley) **2-7-10** NAdams(15) (swtg: led stands' side 3f out: sn hdd: wknd over 1f out) | ¾ | **9** | 50/1 | 24 | — |
| *4079*[3] **The Wyandotte Inn (65)** (RHollinshead) **2-8-8(3)** FLynch(10) (swtg: in tch tl wknd 2f out) | ½ | **10** | 20/1 | 38 | — |
| 4549[7] **Eager To Please (68)** (MissGayKelleway) **2-9-0** TQuinn(4) (lw: prom to 2f out) | 1¾ | **11** | 8/1 | 36 | — |
| *4572*[2] **Mon Bruce (75)** (WRMuir) **2-9-4(3)** MHenry(8) (outpcd) | 2 | **12** | 6/1 3 | 38 | — |
| 4545[6] **Copperbeech (IRE) (70)** (PWChapple-Hyam) **2-8-13(3)** RHavlin(7) (b.hind: swtg: led far side: wknd 2f out) | nk | **13** | 9/1 | 32 | — |
| *4572*[8] **Rockaroundtheclock (65)** (PDEvans) **2-8-11** JFEgan(11) (swtg: outpcd) | ½ | **14** | 20/1 | 26 | — |
| 4586[2] **Dowry (67)** (RHannon) **2-8-13** PatEddery(1) (rdn along: w ldrs far side tl wknd qckly over 1f out) | nk | **15** | 4/1 1 | 27 | — |
| 841[6] **Highland Pass (IRE) (70)** (PBurgoyne) **2-9-2** DRMcCabe(13) (bkwd: a bhd) | 6 | **16** | 33/1 | 14 | — |
| | | | (SP 135.7%) | **16 Rn** | |

**1m 18.1** (8.90) CSF £339.93 CT £2,190.15 TOTE £13.00: £3.60 £5.50 £1.60 £12.50 (£519.50) Trio £480.80; £555.34 to Newcastle 23/10/96 OWNER Mr Jack Blumenow (COMPTON) BRED Miss P. E. Decker

LONG HANDICAP Priory Gardens (IRE) 7-5 Summer Risotto 7-6

**3408 Strat's Quest** made a break for home over two furlongs out and, though fast being overhauled at the finish, held on for long enough. (16/1)

**4423 Summer Risotto** had plenty to do from the two-furlong marker and it was not until the last 100 yards that she really started to fly. It was then just too late. (25/1)

**Mike's Double (IRE)**, blinkered for the first time, came with a strong run in the centre of the course to challenge entering the final furlong. After having every chance, he could find no extra near the finish. (5/1)

**Wild Nettle** looked like causing a surprise when challenging strongly from two furlongs out, but was being held near the finish. (33/1)

**2531 Expectation (IRE)** did best of those racing on the far side, being always well placed. She still had every chance near the finish, but could find no more. (14/1)

**4549 Rumbustious** stayed on in the last two furlongs, but was never on terms with the leaders. (8/1)

**4586 Dowry** ran fast on the far rail, but was being hard ridden some way out, and all chance had gone at the two-furlong marker. (4/1)

## 4804 PASTURE H'CAP (0-80) (3-Y.O) (Class D)

5-00 (5-01) **1m 4f 23y** £4,076.25 (£1,230.00: £597.50: £281.25) Stalls: Low GOING: 0.56 sec per fur (GS)

| Horse | Dist | Pos | SP | RR | SF |
|---|---|---|---|---|---|
| 4563* **Sweetness Herself (66)** (MJRyan) **3-8-4(5)** MBaird(4) (hdwy 3f out: led over 1f out: r.o wl) | — | **1** | 4/1 2 | 79 | 51 |
| 4615[4] **Taufan Boy (73)** (PWHarris) **3-9-2** GHind(11) (hdwy 5f out: led over 2f out tl over 1f out: nt qckn) | 1 | **2** | 12/1 | 85 | 57 |
| 4580[3] **Bellator (75)** (GBBalding) **3-9-4** SDrowne(15) (swtg: hdwy 4f out: ev ch over 1f out: one pce) | 6 | **3** | 6/1 3 | 79 | 51 |
| 4626[7] **Trilby (65)** (PFICole) **3-8-8** TQuinn(1) (w ldrs: ev ch 2f out: one pce) | ½ | **4** | 12/1 | 68 | 40 |
| 3979[10] **Mua-Tab (60)** (PTWalwyn) **3-8-3** TSprake(13) (a.p: one pce fnl 3f) | 3 | **5** | 14/1 | 59 | 31 |
| 4448[9] **Dalwhinnie (62)** (JWHills) **3-8-2(3)** MHenry(3) (swtg: led 6f: remained prom: one pce fnl 2f) | hd | **6** | 20/1 | 61 | 33 |
| 1507[8] **Clemente (73)** (RHannon) **3-9-2** DaneO'Neill(16) (nrst fin) | s.h | **7** | 14/1 | 72 | 44 |
| 2905[4] **Baranov (IRE) (62)** (DJGMurraySmith) **3-8-5** DHarrison(12) (bit bkwd: hld up: led on bit over 3f out: hdd & wknd over 2f out) | 5 | **8** | 20/1 | 54 | 26 |
| 4604[6] **Red Raja (60)** (PMitchell) **3-8-3** JQuinn(10) (nvr nr to chal) | 6 | **9** | 33/1 | 44 | 16 |
| 2706[3] **Premier Night (73)** (SDow) **3-9-2** RHughes(9) (swtg: nvr nr to chal) | ¾ | **10** | 16/1 | 56 | 28 |
| 4695[3] **Mawared (IRE) (73)** (JLDunlop) **3-9-2** RHills(18) (w ldrs: led 6f out tl over 3f out: sn wknd) | 8 | **11** | 8/1 | 46 | 18 |
| 4559[8] **Formidable Flame (60)** (WJMusson) **3-8-3** CRutter(8) (n.d) | 8 | **12** | 20/1 | 22 | — |

| | | | | SP | RR | SF |
|---|---|---|---|---|---|---|
| 1956[4] | **Dramatic Act (55)** (CRBarwell) **3-7-12** NAdams(5) (s.s: a bhd) | 1¾ | **13** | 33/1 | 15 | — |
| 4216* | **Tart (74)** (RFJohnsonHoughton) **3-9-3** PatEddery(7) (in tch tl wknd 4f out) | 1¼ | **14** | 11/4[1] | 32 | 4 |
| 4387[3] | **Sinking Sun (68)** (BWHills) **3-8-11b** KFallon(6) (b.hind: hdwy 5f out: wknd 3f out) | 2½ | **15** | 14/1 | 23 | — |
| 4121[13] | **Ski Academy (IRE) (78)** (PWChapple-Hyam) **3-9-4b[1](3)** RHavlin(14) (swtg: jnd ldrs 6f out: rdn & wknd over 3f out: t.o) | 20 | **16** | 20/1 | 7 | — |

(SP 138.3%) **16 Rn**

**2m 45.7** (13.30) CSF £54.13 CT £280.24 TOTE £4.60: £1.50 £2.70 £1.50 £3.20 (£32.40) Trio £77.20 OWNER Mrs M. J. Lavell (NEWMARKET) BRED Stud-On-The-Chart

**4563* Sweetness Herself**, patiently ridden, cut down her rivals as soon as she was switched to the outside in the long straight. She took up the running approaching the final furlong, and stayed on strongly. (4/1)

**4615 Taufan Boy** had all but the winner in trouble when going for gold two and a half furlongs out, but was held decisively in the closing stages. (12/1)

**4580 Bellator** appeared to be travelling well when moving up to challenge three furlongs out but, put to his best, could stay on only at one pace. (6/1)

**3610 Trilby** disputed the lead on the inside from the start but, after having every chance over two furlongs out, could find no extra under pressure. (12/1)

**2384 Mua-Tab**, always chasing the leading group, stayed on at one pace under pressure in the last three furlongs. (14/1)

**2247 Dalwhinnie** led to halfway and chased up the leaders from that point, without being able to find a turn of foot. (20/1)

**2905 Baranov (IRE)** cruised into the lead, apparently running all over his rivals, approaching the three-furlong marker, but found nothing when let down. He may be worth another chance. (20/1)

**4216* Tart**, well enough placed in the early stages, was already beginning to lose her pitch approaching the long straight and, soon under pressure, dropped away tamely. (11/4)

T/Jkpt: Not won; £26,643.08 to Newcastle 23/10/96. T/Plpt: £731.30 (22.57 Tckts). T/Qdpt: £218.40 (4.55 Tckts). IM

## 4500-NEWCASTLE (L-H) (Good to firm, Good patches)
## Wednesday October 23rd

Races 4, 6 & 8 - hand-timed

WEATHER: fine & sunny WIND: fresh half bhd

### 4805 COOPERS & LYBRAND H'CAP (0-70) (I) (3-Y.O+) (Class E)

1-40 (1-42) **6f** £2,762.00 (£836.00: £408.00: £194.00) Stalls: High GOING minus 0.41 sec per fur (F)

| | | | | SP | RR | SF |
|---|---|---|---|---|---|---|
| 4486[5] | **Leading Princess (IRE) (47)** (MissLAPerratt) **5-8-6b** JFortune(1) (mde all: all out) | — | **1** | 12/1 | 54 | 26 |
| 4312[18] | **Amron (55)** (JBerry) **9-9-0** GCarter(6) (sn outpcd & pushed along: hdwy over 1f out: styd on wl) | nk | **2** | 8/1[2] | 61 | 33 |
| 3868[7] | **Indiahra (44)** (JLEyre) **5-8-3** TWilliams(20) (w ldr: led over 2f out: styd on towards fin) | hd | **3** | 10/1[3] | 50 | 22 |
| 4688[7] | **Mister Westsound (56)** (MissLAPerratt) **4-9-1b** JCarroll(15) (s.i.s: racd stands' side: hdwy 2f out: styd on wl ins fnl f) | nk | **4** | 10/1[3] | 61 | 33 |
| 4460* | **Barato (68)** (MrsJRRamsden) **5-9-6(7)** TFinn(3) (lw: trckd wnr: chal over 1f out: nt qckn) | nk | **5** | 7/1[1] | 72 | 44 |
| 4690[4] | **Bright Diamond (47)** (JRArnold) **3-8-5** SSanders(7) (sn bhd: styd on appr fnl f) | hd | **6** | 14/1 | 51 | 22 |
| 4765[11] | **Bayin (USA) (69)** (MDIUsher) **7-10-0** RStreet(8) (lw: s.i.s: sn bhd: hdwy centre over 1f out: styd on wl towards fin) | 1 | **7** | 7/1[1] | 70 | 42 |
| 4486[8] | **Another Nightmare (IRE) (52)** (RMMcKellar) **4-8-4(7)** JMcAuley(5) (b.hind: chsd ldrs: nt qckn appr fnl f) | ¾ | **8** | 14/1 | 51 | 23 |
| 4460[12] | **Welsh Mountain (63)** (MJHeaton-Ellis) **3-9-7v** GDuffield(12) (lw: chsd ldrs tl wknd over 1f out) | ½ | **9** | 25/1 | 61 | 32 |
| 4486[11] | **Craigie Boy (48)** (NBycroft) **6-8-7b** FNorton(19) (in tch stands' side: rdn ½-wy: wknd over 1f out) | ½ | **10** | 20/1 | 45 | 17 |
| 4616[13] | **Grand Chapeau (IRE) (57)** (DNicholls) **4-9-2** AlexGreaves(13) (led stands' side tl over 2f out: wknd over 1f out) | nk | **11** | 10/1[3] | 53 | 25 |
| 4592[8] | **Bent Raiwand (USA) (55)** (DonEnricoIncisa) **3-8-13** KimTinkler(10) (b.hind: sn outpcd) | 3 | **12** | 50/1 | 43 | 14 |
| 4560[9] | **Shashi (IRE) (60)** (WWHaigh) **4-9-5b** DRMcCabe(16) (chsd ldrs stands' side: hung rt & wknd over 1f out) | ¾ | **13** | 25/1 | 46 | 18 |
| 4382[16] | **Sharp Move (41)** (MrsJCecil) **4-7-11(3)** FLynch(14) (in tch stands' side: lost pl 2f out) | 1½ | **14** | 20/1 | 23 | — |
| *1718[4]* | **Principal Boy (IRE) (45)** (TJEtherington) **3-8-3** JFEgan(9) (nvr wnt pce) | hd | **15** | 25/1 | 27 | — |
| 4075* | **Present 'n Correct (51)** (CBBBooth) **3-8-9** LCharnock(2) (s.s: sn chsng ldrs: rdn ½-wy: lost pl 2f out) | 1 | **16** | 7/1[1] | 30 | 1 |
| 3654[6] | **Magic Melody (58)** (JLSpearing) **3-9-2** SDrowne(4) (a bhd) | 1 | **17** | 20/1 | 34 | 5 |
| 4312[24] | **King of Show (IRE) (58)** (RAllan) **5-9-3v** KFallon(17) (racd stands' side: a outpcd & bhd) | 1¾ | **18** | 20/1 | 30 | 2 |
| 4598[16] | **Doug's Folly (40)** (MWEasterby) **3-7-12b** JQuinn(11) (dwlt: a bhd) | nk | **19** | 14/1 | 11 | — |
| 4229[5] | **Young Ben (IRE) (42)** (JSWainwright) **4-7-8b(7)** JBramhill(18) (b.hind: bhd & edgd lft ½-wy: t.o) | 22 | **20** | 25/1 | — | — |

(SP 140.0%) **20 Rn**

**1m 13.74** (2.24) CSF £107.03 CT £969.07 TOTE £14.90: £2.70 £2.40 £3.20 £1.60 (£34.30) Trio £281.20 OWNER Mrs Ruth Wyllie (AYR) BRED Woodford Stud

WEIGHT FOR AGE 3yo-1lb

**OFFICIAL EXPLANATION Shashi (IRE): hung badly to his right.**

**4486 Leading Princess (IRE)**, only 3lb higher than when she won at Carlisle in June, has never lacked speed and, making all on the far side, just lasted home. (12/1)

**4246 Amron** as usual struggled to go the pace. Picking up ground over a furlong out, he could not quite collar the winner on this ground. (8/1)

**3868 Indiahra**, back over six, took a decisive advantage on the stands' side with over two furlongs to go. Lacking company, she stuck on really well and, in the end, was only just edged out of it. (10/1)

**4688 Mister Westsound** ran his usual race, forfeiting ground at the start, and tearing through at the death. When everything goes right he is sure to win another race. (10/1)

**4460* Barato** shadowed the winner on the far side and looked to be going the better but, when the chips were down, off a 7lb higher mark, he could find no more. (7/1)

**4342 Bayin (USA)** gave away ground at the start. Making his effort up the middle, he lacked company, but stayed on strongly towards the finish. (7/1)

### 4806 ALNWICK MAIDEN STKS (2-Y.O F) (Class D)

2-10 (2-13) **7f** £3,387.50 (£1,025.00: £500.00: £237.50) Stalls: High GOING minus 0.41 sec per fur (F)

| | | | | SP | RR | SF |
|---|---|---|---|---|---|---|
| | **Society Rose** (MRStoute) **2-8-11** KFallon(7) (cmpt: bkwd: sn chsng ldrs: rdn to ld over 1f out: styd on strly: eased nr fin) | — | **1** | 1/2[1] | 73+ | 23 |

| | | | | SP | RR | SF |
|---|---|---|---|---|---|---|
| $3837^{9}$ | **Kippilaw** (MJohnston) **2-8-11** TWilliams(2) (led tl over 1f out: no ch w wnr) | 4 | **2** | 13/2 $^{3}$ | 64 | 14 |
| $4593^{4}$ | **Santa Rosa (IRE)** (JLDunlop) **2-8-11** JFortune(5) (lw: chsd ldrs: drvn along ½-wy: styd on same pce) | hd | **3** | 11/4 $^{2}$ | 64 | 14 |
| $4069^{10}$ | **Domino Style** (MJCamacho) **2-8-11** LCharnock(3) (prom: rdn & hung lft ½-wy: sn wl outpcd) | 4 | **4** | 50/1 | 55 | 5 |
| $4558^{12}$ | **Patrita Park** (WWHaigh) **2-8-11** RLappin(8) (hld up & bhd: styd on fnl 2f: n.d) | 3½ | **5** | 33/1 | 47 | — |
| $4584^{9}$ | **Murray Grey** (EWeymes) **2-8-11** GDuffield(1) (b: chsd ldrs: rdn over 2f out: sn wl outpcd) | s.h | **6** | 50/1 | 46 | — |
| | **Whirl Pool** (MJCamacho) **2-8-11** MBirch(4) (s.i.s: sn chsng ldrs: drvn along & lost pl over 4f out: sn bhd) | 11 | **7** | 50/1 | 21 | — |
| $4593^{7}$ | **Gollaccia** (GMMoore) **2-8-11** JFEgan(6) (s.s: a outpcd & bhd) | 1½ | **8** | 50/1 | 18 | — |
| | ***Melodic Squaw*** (MPBielby) **2-8-11** DRMcCabe(9) (Withdrawn not under Starter's orders: v.unruly & ref to ent stalls) | | **W** | 50/1 | — | — |
| | | | | (SP 119.4%) | **8 Rn** | |

**1m 27.81** (3.31) CSF £4.60 TOTE £1.60: £1.00 £1.80 £1.50 (£3.80) Trio £1.30 OWNER Cheveley Park Stud (NEWMARKET) BRED Cheveley Park Stud Ltd

**Society Rose** was found an easy opening on her debut and, after having to be put about her job, soon showed in a commanding lead. (1/2)
**Kippilaw** certainly knew her job but, once the cards were played, the winner proved in a different league. (13/2)
**4593 Santa Rosa (IRE)** ran much better than she had done at Redcar. Driven along at halfway, she was staying on at the finish and needs at least a mile. (11/4: op 7/4)
**Domino Style** gave her rider problems, hanging left under pressure from halfway. (50/1)

## 4807 E.B.F. AMBLE MAIDEN STKS (2-Y.O) (Class D)

2-40 (2-42) **6f** £3,566.25 (£1,080.00: £527.50: £251.25) Stalls: High GOING minus 0.41 sec per fur (F)

| | | | | SP | RR | SF |
|---|---|---|---|---|---|---|
| $2611^{2}$ | **Rihan (USA)** (SbinSuroor) **2-8-9** JCarroll(13) (mde all: shkn up & hung lft over 2f out: styd on wl ins fnl f) | — | **1** | 5/4 $^{1}$ | 78 | 28 |
| $4619^{5}$ | **Tal-Y-Llyn (IRE)** (BWHills) **2-9-0** KFallon(12) (lw: sn chsng ldrs & drvn along: ev ch over 1f out: hrd rdn & kpt on wl) | 1 | **2** | 11/4 $^{2}$ | 80 | 30 |
| $4670^{3}$ | **Nariskin (IRE)** (JLDunlop) **2-9-0** JFortune(6) (trckd ldrs: ev ch & hung lft over 1f out: styd on same pce) | ¾ | **3** | 3/1 $^{3}$ | 78 | 28 |
| $4469^{8}$ | **Cee-N-K (IRE)** (MJohnston) **2-9-0** JFanning(9) (w ldrs tl outpcd appr fnl f) | 4 | **4** | 33/1 | 68 | 18 |
| $4363^{7}$ | **Court Express** (TJEtherington) **2-9-0** ACulhane(4) (sn bhd: styd on fnl 2f: nvr nr ldrs) | 3½ | **5** | 25/1 | 58 | 8 |
| $4451^{7}$ | **As-Is** (MJohnston) **2-9-0** TWilliams(7) (chsd ldrs tl wknd over 1f out) | 4 | **6** | 25/1 | 48 | — |
| $4584^{8}$ | **Propellant** (CWThornton) **2-9-0** DeanMcKeown(5) (s.i.s: bhd: sme late hdwy: n.d) | 5 | **7** | 50/1 | 34 | — |
| $4754^{8}$ | **Whitegate's Son** (BEllison) **2-9-0** JQuinn(1) (in tch tl wknd over 2f out) | 1¼ | **8** | 66/1 | 31 | — |
| $2923^{7}$ | **Dulas Bay** (MWEasterby) **2-8-9**(5) GParkin(10) (sn wl outpcd & bhd) | 1¼ | **9** | 66/1 | 28 | — |
| | **Quezon City** (MJCamacho) **2-9-0** GDuffield(2) (unf: bit bkwd: sn bhd) | 1½ | **10** | 50/1 | 24 | — |
| | **Toon Flyer** (WStorey) **2-9-0** NKennedy(11) (wl grwn: bkwd: s.i.s: a wl outpcd & bhd: t.o) | 22 | **11** | 50/1 | — | — |
| | **Bright Gold** (ASmith) **2-9-0** MBirch(8) (w'like: bit bkwd: s.i.s: a wl bhd: t.o) | 1½ | **12** | 66/1 | — | — |
| | ***Hio Nod*** (MJCamacho) **2-9-0** LCharnock(3) (Withdrawn not under Starter's orders: unruly & ref to ent stalls) | | **W** | 20/1 | — | — |
| | | | | (SP 121.9%) | **12 Rn** | |

**1m 13.76** (2.26) CSF £4.89 TOTE £2.00: £1.00 £1.60 £1.50 (£3.40) Trio £1.70 OWNER Mr Hamdan Al Maktoum (NEWMARKET) BRED Shadwell Farm Inc

**2611 Rihan (USA)**, a particularly good mover, tended to hang left off the rail when first sent about her business. She stayed on strongly to get right on top inside the last, and will be even better suited by seven. (5/4: 4/5-11/8)
**4619 Tal-Y-Llyn (IRE)** took the eye in the paddock, but did not show the best of actions going down. Soon driven along, he stuck to his task in determined fashion and can improve on easier ground. (11/4)
**4670 Nariskin (IRE)** tracked the winner travelling equally as well. Tending to hang left under pressure, he is still learning the ropes. (3/1)
**Cee-N-K (IRE)**, who showed precious little first time, ran much better. (33/1)
**Court Express** was never put in the race, but significantly this qualifies him for handicaps. (25/1)

## 4808 BEDLINGTON CLAIMING H'CAP (0-60) (3-Y.O+) (Class F)

3-10 (3-13) **1m (round)** £2,983.00 (£838.00: £409.00) Stalls: Low GOING minus 0.41 sec per fur (F)

| | | | | SP | RR | SF |
|---|---|---|---|---|---|---|
| $4455^{4}$ | **Diamond Crown (IRE) (44)** (MartynWane) **5-9-0** KFallon(19) (lw: s.i.s: bhd: gd hdwy 2f out: nt clr run: styd on wl to ld nr fin) | — | **1** | 9/1 $^{3}$ | 50 | 22 |
| $4323^{11}$ | **Funky (43)** (DNicholls) **3-8-10** AlexGreaves(6) (in tch: hdwy to ld over 2f out: hdd nr fin) | hd | **2** | 11/1 | 49 | 18 |
| $3761^{12}$ | **Harvest Reaper (45)** (JLHarris) **4-9-1** SSanders(10) (in tch tl lost pl ½-wy: hdwy 2f out: styd on ins fnl f) | 2½ | **3** | 20/1 | 46 | 18 |
| $4503^{3}$ | **Sir Arthur Hobbs (56)** (JLEyre) **9-9-12** RLappin(20) (hld up: hdwy over 2f out: nt clr run & swtchd over 1f out: styd on: nt rch ldrs) | 2 | **4** | 5/1 $^{2}$ | 53 | 25 |
| $4237^{7}$ | **Desert Zone (USA) (46)** (JLHarris) **7-9-2** DeanMcKeown(12) (a chsng ldrs: one pce fnl 2f) | 1 | **5** | 16/1 | 41 | 13 |
| $4478^{9}$ | **Kowtow (49)** (MDIUsher) **3-9-2** RStreet(9) (lw: s.i.s: bhd tl styd on fnl 2f) | 2 | **6** | 16/1 | 40 | 9 |
| $4221^{12}$ | **Square Mile Miss (IRE) (42)** (PHowling) **3-8-9** JQuinn(13) (a in tch: one pce fnl 2f) | nk | **7** | 20/1 | 32 | 1 |
| $4603^{4}$ | **Kevasingo (51)** (BWHills) **4-9-7b** JCarroll(17) (lw: bhd: drvn along ½-wy: styd on fnl 2f) | hd | **8** | 7/2 $^{1}$ | 41 | 13 |
| $4316^{9}$ | **Miss Pigalle (41)** (MissLAPerratt) **5-8-11b** JFortune(4) (led tl over 2f out: sn wknd) | 3 | **9** | 14/1 | 25 | — |
| *$4577^{10}$* | **Butterwick Belle (IRE) (53)** (RAFahey) **3-8-13**(7) RWinston(11) (in tch: drvn along over 2f out: n.m.r & sn wknd) | 2 | **10** | 33/1 | 33 | 2 |
| $4484^{6}$ | **Moofaji (39)** (FWatson) **5-8-2**(7) CLowther(2) (in tch: rdn along & outpcd over 3f out: styd on ins fnl f) | nk | **11** | 20/1 | 18 | — |
| $4692^{9}$ | **Maurangi (39)** (BWMurray) **5-8-4**(5) LNewton(3) (b: chsd ldrs tl wknd 2f out) | hd | **12** | 12/1 | 18 | — |
| $4240^{5}$ | **East Barns (IRE) (38)** (SGollings) **8-8-8b** FNorton(1) (s.i.s: a in rr) | 3 | **13** | 12/1 | 11 | — |
| | **Priddy Fair (50)** (DWBarker) **3-9-3** LCharnock(5) (in tch tl wknd fnl 2f) | 1 | **14** | 33/1 | 21 | — |
| $4436^{15}$ | **Lucky Bea (55)** (MWEasterby) **3-9-3**(5) GParkin(15) (s.i.s: a bhd) | ½ | **15** | 14/1 | 25 | — |
| $4503^{10}$ | **Great Bear (42)** (DWChapman) **4-8-12** ACulhane(18) (racd wd: a in rr) | 3½ | **16** | 14/1 | 5 | — |
| $4045^{21}$ | **Fiery Footsteps (38)** (SWCampion) **4-8-8** DRMcCabe(14) (a bhd) | 6 | **17** | 33/1 | — | — |
| $2731^{7}$ | **Haido'hart (42)** (BSRothwell) **4-8-7**(5) PRoberts(16) (prom tl wknd 2f out) | ¾ | **18** | 20/1 | — | — |
| $1311^{10}$ | **Barik (IRE) (50)** (BMactaggart) **6-9-1**(5) GLee(7) (chsd ldrs tl wknd over 2f out) | 2½ | **19** | 33/1 | — | — |
| $4082^{18}$ | **Okay Baby (IRE) (38)** (JMBradley) **4-8-8** JFEgan(8) (sn bhd & drvn along) | 10 | **20** | 25/1 | — | — |
| | | | | (SP 139.0%) | **20 Rn** | |

**1m 43.4** (4.40) CSF £104.27 CT £1,828.01 TOTE £7.50: £1.70 £2.90 £16.10 £1.40 (£40.30) Trio Not won; £325.26 to Newbury 24/10/96
OWNER Mr J. M. Pickup (RICHMOND) BRED Dene Investments N V
WEIGHT FOR AGE 3yo-3lb

**4455 Diamond Crown (IRE)** was well suited by the strong gallop and uphill finish. Having to look for an opening, he got there in the last strides. (9/1)

**3461 Funky**, who has slipped down the weights and has been tried over a variety of trips, did her best to pinch this, but was just caught near the line. (11/1)
**Harvest Reaper** ran easily his best race this time, recovering well after being badly outpaced at halfway. (20/1)
**4503 Sir Arthur Hobbs**, who presumably needed it last time after a nine-week break, was set an impossible task. Short of room halfway up the straight, he did well to finish so close. (5/1)
**3849 Desert Zone (USA)** has not won for a long time, but ran creditably here. (16/1)
**1061 Kowtow** was given the usual Street ride. At the back after being steadied at the start, she was staying on at the finish. (16/1)

## 4809 COOPERS & LYBRAND H'CAP (0-70) (II) (3-Y.O+) (Class E)

3-40 (3-44) **6f** £2,762.00 (£836.00: £408.00: £194.00) Stalls: High GOING minus 0.41 sec per fur (F)

| Form | Horse | Dist | Pl | SP | RR | SF |
|---|---|---|---|---|---|---|
| $4791^{8}$ | **Saddlehome (USA) (66)** (TDBarron) **7-9-11** JCarroll(5) (hld up far side: hdwy whn nt clr run over 1f out: squeezed thro to ld wl ins fnl f) | — | **1** | 9/1 | 75 | 37 |
| $4341^{4}$ | **Vax New Way (57)** (JLSpearing) **3-9-1b** SDrowne(17) (led stands' side: rdn over 2f out: r.o: no ex nr fin) | nk | **2** | 16/1 | 65 | 26 |
| $4571^{7}$ | **Don Pepe (62)** (RBoss) **5-9-2**$^{(5)}$ ADaly(20) (hld up stands' side: hdwy 2f out: r.o wl towards fin) | ½ | **3** | 12/1 | 69 | 31 |
| $4460^{6}$ | **Camionneur (IRE) (50)** (TDEasterby) **3-8-8b** JQuinn(18) (trckd ldrs gng wl stands' side: effrt 2f out: nt qckn towards fin) | nk | **4** | 14/1 | 56 | 17 |
| $4206^{12}$ | **Ballard Lady (IRE) (44)** (JSWainwright) **4-7-10**$^{(7)}$ JBramhill(12) (in tch stands' side: hung lft fnl 2f: styd on) | ¾ | **5** | 16/1 | 48 | 10 |
| *$4778^{9}$* | **Cavers Yangous (61)** (MJohnston) **5-9-6v** TWilliams(1) (chsd ldrs far side: led ins fnl f: sn hdd & nt qckn) | nk | **6** | 12/1 | 64 | 26 |
| $4791^{12}$ | **Mister Joel (55)** (MWEasterby) **3-8-8b**$^{(5)}$ GParkin(13) (lw: cl up stands' side: rdn 2f out: nt qckn) | ¾ | **7** | 20/1 | 56 | 17 |
| $4598^{17}$ | **Our Albert (IRE) (42)** (JAGlover) **3-7-9v**$^{1(5)}$ PFessey(3) (chsd ldrs far side: one pce fnl 2f) | 1 | **8** | 25/1 | 41 | 2 |
| $4610^{17}$ | **Amy Leigh (IRE) (49)** (CaptJWilson) **3-8-7b**$^{1}$ DeanMcKeown(6) (disp ld far side tl wknd ins fnl f) | ¾ | **9** | 33/1 | 46 | 7 |
| $4486^{15}$ | **Sunday Mail Too (IRE) (42)** (MissLAPerratt) **4-8-1** NKennedy(7) (chsd ldrs far side: hung rt fr ½-wy: no imp) | nk | **10** | 20/1 | 38 | — |
| $4312^{13}$ | **Dictation (USA) (58)** (JJO'Neill) **4-9-3** JFortune(10) (disp ld far side tl wknd appr fnl f) | 2 | **11** | 6/1$^{1}$ | 49 | 11 |
| $4689^{6}$ | **Castlerea Lad (65)** (RHollinshead) **7-9-5v**$^{1(5)}$ DGriffiths(16) (lw: racd stands' side: effrt ½-wy: no imp) | hd | **12** | 13/2$^{2}$ | 55 | 17 |
| $3489^{7}$ | **Rinus Manor (IRE) (45)** (EJAlston) **5-8-4** FNorton(9) (racd far side: effrt ½-wy: n.d) | hd | **13** | 33/1 | 35 | — |
| $4688^{9}$ | **Halmanerror (65)** (MrsJRRamsden) **6-9-10** KFallon(2) (lw: racd far side: nvr plcd to chal) | 2 | **14** | 8/1$^{3}$ | 50 | 12 |
| $4486^{6}$ | **Miss Aragon (38)** (MissLCSiddall) **8-7-11** NCarlisle(4) (racd far side: outpcd fr ½-wy) | 1¼ | **15** | 12/1 | 19 | — |
| $4727^{3}$ | **Here Comes a Star (65)** (JMCarr) **8-9-10** ACulhane(19) (racd stands' side: effrt ½-wy: sn btn) | 2½ | **16** | 9/1 | 40 | 2 |
| $4259^{12}$ | **Members Welcome (IRE) (45)** (JMBradley) **3-8-3v** LCharnock(14) (s.i.s: racd stands' side: n.d) | 6 | **17** | 25/1 | 4 | — |
| $4074^{7}$ | **Saving Power (55)** (PWHarris) **3-8-13** GDuffield(11) (racd stands' side: a bhd) | ¾ | **18** | 10/1 | 12 | — |
| $4460^{14}$ | **Flashy's Son (52)** (FMurphy) **8-8-8**$^{(3)}$ FLynch(8) (b: racd far side: eased fr ½-wy: lame) | 6 | **19** | 16/1 | — | — |
| | | | | (SP 138.3%) | **19 Rn** | |

**1m 14.18** (2.68) CSF £144.35 CT £1,661.74 TOTE £9.70: £2.40 £3.50 £2.40 £3.50 (£117.10) Trio £262.60 OWNER Mr Kevin Shaw (THIRSK) BRED Saddle Home Farm in USA
WEIGHT FOR AGE 3yo-1lb
STEWARDS' ENQUIRY Bramhill susp. 1-2 & 4/11/96 + 1 day (excessive use of whip)
**OFFICIAL EXPLANATION Shashi (IRE): hung badly right.**
**4616 Saddlehome (USA)** is a funny customer these days, but he was certainly in the right mood here and, had he got a run sooner, he would have trotted up. (9/1)
**4341 Vax New Way** is in top form just now and put up a fine performance on the opposite side of the track to the winner but, despite making all on that side, was never quite good enough. (16/1)
**4571 Don Pepe**, dropped out on the stands' side, was just given a shade too much to do and finished best of all. (12/1)
**4460 Camionneur (IRE)** spent most of the race swinging off the bit but, when asked for an effort, he was never doing enough. (14/1)
**3680 Ballard Lady (IRE)** was always close enough if good enough, but she got unbalanced under pressure in the last couple of furlongs. (16/1)
**4460 Cavers Yangous** ran a fair race if short of toe late on, but did finish second to the winner on the far side. (12/1)
**4791 Mister Joel** had the blinkers back on and lasted longer, but he has never won at this trip. (20/1)
**Dictation (USA)** (6/1: op 12/1)
**4688 Halmanerror** never got into this, but should not be written off yet. (8/1)

## 4810 CALDER PRINT H'CAP (0-60) (I) (3-Y.O+) (Class F)

4-10 (4-16) **1m 2f 32y** £2,563.00 (£718.00: £349.00) Stalls: Low GOING minus 0.41 sec per fur (F)

| Form | Horse | Dist | Pl | SP | RR | SF |
|---|---|---|---|---|---|---|
| $4686^{4}$ | **Lapu-Lapu (52)** (MJCamacho) **3-9-1** LCharnock(8) (hld up: hdwy 3f out: r.o to ld wl ins fnl f) | — | **1** | 4/1$^{2}$ | 62 | 28 |
| $4000^{9}$ | **Alfayza (43)** (JDBethell) **3-8-6** SDrowne(5) (hld up: hdwy 3f out: swtchd outside over 1f out: r.o towards fin) | 1¼ | **2** | 25/1 | 51 | 17 |
| $4497^{7}$ | **Bold Enough (48)** (BWHills) **3-8-11** JCarroll(3) (mid div: hdwy over 3f out: rdn to ld ins fnl f: sn hdd & no ex) | nk | **3** | 10/1$^{3}$ | 56 | 22 |
| $4559^{5}$ | **Newbridge Boy (52)** (MGMeagher) **3-9-1** FNorton(14) (trckd ldrs: hdwy & ev ch over 1f out: nt qckn) | ½ | **4** | 14/1 | 59 | 25 |
| $4597^{6}$ | **Advance East (55)** (MDods) **4-9-9** JFortune(11) (trckd ldrs gng wl: led over 2f out: rdn over 1f out: hdd & no ex ins fnl f) | ¾ | **5** | 10/1$^{3}$ | 61 | 32 |
| $4686^{18}$ | **Gold Desire (47)** (MBrittain) **6-8-8**$^{(7)}$ RMullen(4) (bhd tl styd on wl fnl 3f) | 6 | **6** | 14/1 | 43 | 14 |
| $4769^{18}$ | **Hawwam (48)** (EJAlston) **10-9-2** KFallon(13) (rr div: hdwy 3f out: in tch & hrd drvn over 1f out: sn btn) | nk | **7** | 10/1$^{3}$ | 44 | 15 |
| $4483^{5}$ | **Lord Advocate (43)** (DANolan) **8-8-8b**$^{(3)}$ NVarley(18) (chsd ldrs: one pce fnl 2f) | s.h | **8** | 20/1 | 39 | 10 |
| $4686^{24}$ | **Rafters (48)** (JMBradley) **7-9-2b**$^{1}$ JFEgan(1) (b: led tl hdd & wknd over 2f out) | 3 | **9** | 33/1 | 39 | 10 |
| $4702^{2}$ | **Giftbox (USA) (52)** (SirMarkPrescott) **4-9-6** GDuffield(17) (lw: prom: outpcd 3f out: no imp after) | hd | **10** | 7/2$^{1}$ | 43 | 14 |
| $1696^{8}$ | **El Don (39)** (MJRyan) **4-8-7** GCarter(15) (in tch tl outpcd over 4f out) | 4 | **11** | 25/1 | 23 | — |
| $4582^{14}$ | **Surrey Dancer (60)** (MrsMReveley) **8-9-9**$^{(5)}$ SCopp(16) (bit bkwd: stdd s: nvr plcd to chal) | 1 | **12** | 20/1 | 43 | 14 |
| $4617^{20}$ | **Drummer Hicks (47)** (EWeymes) **7-9-1** MBirch(9) (hdwy on outside 5f out: wknd fnl 3f) | 4 | **13** | 11/1 | 24 | — |
| $4753^{11}$ | **Shamokin (43)** (FWatson) **4-8-11** NKennedy(12) (in tch tl wknd 3f out) | ¾ | **14** | 33/1 | 18 | — |
| $1025^{5}$ | **Hever Golf Queen (50)** (TJNaughton) **3-8-13** SSanders(2) (hld up: rdn over 3f out: n.d) | 5 | **15** | 20/1 | 17 | — |
| $4753^{12}$ | **Fairy Highlands (IRE) (50)** (JSHaldane) **3-8-8**$^{(5)}$ PFessey(7) (prom to st) | 1 | **16** | 33/1 | 16 | — |
| | **Birequest (52)** (DMoffatt) **5-9-3**$^{(3)}$ DarrenMoffatt(6) (a outpcd & bhd) | 5 | **17** | 25/1 | 10 | — |
| $4559^{18}$ | **Sizzling Symphony (50)** (RAFahey) **3-8-13** ACulhane(20) (chsd ldrs to st: sn bhd) | 8 | **18** | 33/1 | — | — |
| *$114^{6}$* | **Warhurst (IRE) (57)** (DNicholls) **5-9-11** AlexGreaves(19) (a bhd) | 17 | **19** | 12/1 | — | — |
| *$462^{8}$* | **French Ginger (58)** (WStorey) **5-9-12** JFanning(10) (bit bkwd: prom early: sn bhd) | 6 | **20** | 25/1 | — | — |
| | | | | (SP 140.3%) | **20 Rn** | |

**2m 11.7** (5.00) CSF £99.54 CT £898.81 TOTE £4.80: £1.20 £1.80 £3.10 £5.30 (£50.30) Trio £299.40; £253.04 to Newbury 24/10/96 OWNER Mr Dunstan French (MALTON) BRED Mrs S. Camacho
WEIGHT FOR AGE 3yo-5lb

**4686 Lapu-Lapu** has really improved of late and won this most authoritatively. (4/1)
**4000 Alfayza** was putting in some useful late work, but still left the impression that, if she really gave it her best, there is plenty more to come. (25/1)
**4323 Bold Enough** is certainly running better over these longer trips and perhaps nine furlongs would be ideal. (10/1)
**4559 Newbridge Boy** has yet to win on Turf, but is certainly off a useful mark at present. (14/1)
**4597 Advance East** spent most of the race swinging off the bit, but yet again failed to see it out. His new stable may yet find the answer with him. (10/1)
**4236 Gold Desire** is slipping back down the handicap and showed he is still in good heart by staying on well in the home straight. (14/1)
**4483 Lord Advocate** ran really well over a trip short of his best and obviously remains in good heart. (20/1)

## 4811 ASHINGTON H'CAP (0-85) (3-Y.O+) (Class D)

4-40 (4-45) **5f** £3,793.75 (£1,150.00: £562.50: £268.75) Stalls: High GOING minus 0.41 sec per fur (F)

| | Horse | Dist | Pos | SP | RR | SF |
|---|---|---|---|---|---|---|
| 4791* | **Stuffed (79)** (MWEasterby) **4-9-3**(5) 7x GParkin(1) (lw: b: racd far side: a.p: hdwy to ld ins fnl f: r.o) | — | **1** | 6/1[3] | 86 | 44 |
| 4616[8] | **Shadow Jury (60)** (DWChapman) **6-8-3b** LCharnock(8) (led far side tl hdd ins fnl f: kpt on) | 1 | **2** | 20/1 | 64 | 22 |
| 4772[10] | **Ziggy's Dancer (USA) (82)** (EJAlston) **5-9-11** KFallon(10) (in tch far side: drvn along ½-wy: kpt on wl fnl f) | nk | **3** | 11/2[2] | 85 | 43 |
| 4765[14] | **Able Sheriff (60)** (MWEasterby) **4-8-3b** JQuinn(6) (in tch far side: styd on wl fnl f) | nk | **4** | 16/1 | 62 | 20 |
| 4791[10] | **Jucea (68)** (JLSpearing) **7-8-11** SDrowne(5) (bhd far side: hdwy over 1f out: fin wl) | 1 | **5** | 14/1 | 67 | 25 |
| 4589[3] | **Middle East (71)** (TDBarron) **3-9-0** JFortune(13) (chsd ldrs stands' side: hdwy 2f out: styd on: nvr able to chal) | hd | **6** | 14/1 | 69 | 27 |
| 4616* | **Gone Savage (76)** (WJMusson) **8-9-5** DRMcCabe(3) (lw: bhd far side tl hdwy over 1f out: r.o) | ½ | **7** | 7/2[1] | 73 | 31 |
| 4765[15] | **Precious Girl (76)** (DMoffatt) **3-9-5** DeanMcKeown(7) (bhd far side tl styd on fnl 2f) | ¾ | **8** | 25/1 | 70 | 28 |
| 4356[14] | **Plum First (56)** (JLEyre) **6-7-13** TWilliams(17) (w ldrs stands' side tl rdn & btn 1f out) | ½ | **9** | 11/1 | 49 | 7 |
| 4765[8] | **Insider Trader (78)** (MrsJRRamsden) **5-9-2**(5) GFaulkner(2) (b.off fore: racd far side: drvn along ½-wy: sn btn) | 1¼ | **10** | 11/1 | 67 | 25 |
| 4791[3] | **French Grit (IRE) (74)** (MDods) **4-9-0**(3) CTeague(4) (chsd ldrs far side tl rdn & btn appr fnl f) | nk | **11** | 10/1 | 62 | 20 |
| 4687[17] | **Saint Express (79)** (MrsMReveley) **6-9-8b** ACulhane(12) (racd stands' side: in tch: rdn ½-wy: no imp) | nk | **12** | 11/1 | 66 | 24 |
| 4473[8] | **Six for Luck (54)** (DANolan) **4-7-8**(3) NVarley(11) (cl up far side tl wknd 1½f out) | ½ | **13** | 33/1 | 39 | — |
| 4772[11] | **Takadou (IRE) (79)** (MissLCSiddall) **5-9-8** JCarroll(15) (lw: racd stands' side: a rr div) | ½ | **14** | 8/1 | 63 | 21 |
| 4687[19] | **Stylish Ways (IRE) (82)** (MissSEHall) **4-9-11** MBirch(18) (racd stands' side: nvr wnt pce) | ½ | **15** | 20/1 | 64 | 22 |
| 4616[21] | **Stephensons Rocket (58)** (DNicholls) **5-8-1**ow1 JFEgan(14) (led stands' side 3f: sn wknd) | hd | **16** | 16/1 | 40 | — |
| 4589[8] | **River Tern (67)** (JBerry) **3-8-10v** GCarter(16) (b: dwlt: racd stands' side: a bhd) | ½ | **17** | 25/1 | 47 | 5 |
| *3419*[11] | **Takhlid (USA) (80)** (DWChapman) **5-9-9** GDuffield(9) (racd far side: sn bhd) | 6 | **18** | 33/1 | 41 | — |
| | | | | (SP 145.3%) | **18 Rn** | |

**59.99 secs** (1.59) CSF £125.49 CT £690.30 TOTE £6.60: £1.90 £7.60 £1.80 £4.50 (£136.60) Trio £745.80; £630.31 to Newbury 24/10/96
OWNER Early Morning Breakfast Syndicate (SHERIFF HUTTON) BRED Manor Grange Stud Co Ltd
**4791* Stuffed** found a 7lb penalty no problem and again won in useful style. (6/1: op 4/1)
**3338 Shadow Jury** has not won for some time, but this was a useful effort and he is back on a decent mark. (20/1)
**4554 Ziggy's Dancer (USA)** was always close enough if good enough and kept responding to pressure, but was never doing things quickly enough to offer a live threat. (11/2)
**4246* Able Sheriff** ran here as though he is coming back to form. (16/1)
**4616 Jucea**, like the winner, was having his second race of the week and, happier on this quicker ground, made useful late headway. (14/1)
**4589 Middle East** is difficult to weigh up, but he did run well here and his stable is now in cracking form. (14/1)
**4616* Gone Savage** found the ground a bit too fast early on and only got going when it was too late. (7/2)
**2238 Precious Girl** will be interesting if she gets soft ground before the end of the season. (25/1)

## 4812 CALDER PRINT H'CAP (0-60) (II) (3-Y.O+) (Class F)

5-10 (5-17) **1m 2f 32y** £2,563.00 (£718.00: £349.00) Stalls: Low GOING minus 0.41 sec per fur (F)

| | Horse | Dist | Pos | SP | RR | SF |
|---|---|---|---|---|---|---|
| 1624[8] | **Adamton (45)** (MrsJCecil) **4-9-0** JCarroll(19) (mde all: hld on wl fnl 2f) | — | **1** | 14/1 | 51 | 25 |
| 4609[6] | **Explosive Power (55)** (GCBravery) **5-9-5**(5) LNewton(18) (swtg: hld up: smooth hdwy over 2f out: chal ins fnl f: nt qckn towards fin) | ½ | **2** | 12/1 | 60 | 34 |
| 4489[10] | **Super High (52)** (PHowling) **4-9-7** KFallon(9) (a chsng ldrs: ev ch 3f out: r.o one pce appr fnl f) | 1 | **3** | 10/1 | 56 | 30 |
| 3808[8] | **Zahran (IRE) (36)** (JMBradley) **5-8-5** SDrowne(6) (lw: mid div: hdwy 3f out: styd on u.p: nvr able to chal) | 1¼ | **4** | 16/1 | 38 | 12 |
| 4455* | **Brambles Way (51)** (MrsMReveley) **7-9-1**(5) SCopp(13) (in tch: styd on u.p fnl 2f: no imp) | nk | **5** | 8/1[3] | 52 | 26 |
| 4497[11] | **Ottavio Farnese (55)** (AHide) **4-9-10** GCarter(8) (mid div: swtchd & styd on wl appr fnl f) | ½ | **6** | 20/1 | 55 | 29 |
| 4483[10] | **Elpidos (51)** (MDHammond) **4-9-3b**(3) FLynch(16) (lw: hld up: hdwy appr st: sn prom: rdn & no ex appr fnl f) | 2 | **7** | 3/1[1] | 48 | 22 |
| 4587[9] | **Bold Top (40)** (BSRothwell) **4-8-4b**(5) PRoberts(14) (bhd tl styd on fnl 3f: n.d) | 1½ | **8** | 16/1 | 35 | 9 |
| 4703[7] | **Oakbury (IRE) (37)** (MissLCSiddall) **4-8-6** NCarlisle(5) (broke wl: sn lost pl & bhd: sme hdwy fnl 3f: n.d) | 1½ | **9** | 16/1 | 30 | 4 |
| 4497[12] | **Hever Golf Eagle (45)** (TJNaughton) **3-8-9** JFortune(4) (lw: mid div & rdn along 4f out: n.d) | 3 | **10** | 20/1 | 33 | 2 |
| 4686[9] | **Cuban Reef (47)** (WJMusson) **4-9-2** DRMcCabe(17) (hld up & bhd: stdy hdwy 3f out: nvr plcd to chal) | nk | **11** | 7/2[2] | 34 | 8 |
| 3403[5] | **Rood Music (50)** (MGMeagher) **5-9-5** FNorton(2) (chsd ldrs: rdn over 2f out: sn wknd) | ½ | **12** | 12/1 | 37 | 11 |
| *4574*[8] | **Ihtimaam (FR) (37)** (MrsASwinbank) **4-8-6** JQuinn(7) (in tch to st) | 1 | **13** | 20/1 | 22 | — |
| 4497[16] | **Princely Affair (49)** (MBell) **3-8-6**(7) RMullen(3) (bhd: sn drvn along: n.d) | ½ | **14** | 10/1 | 33 | 2 |
| 4472[4] | **Tolepa (IRE) (40)** (JJO'Neill) **3-8-4** JFEgan(11) (chsd ldrs tl rdn & wknd 3f out) | 1 | **15** | 20/1 | 23 | — |
| 4587[16] | **My Millie (52)** (DWBarker) **3-9-2** DeanMcKeown(20) (prom tl wknd fnl 3f) | s.h | **16** | 16/1 | 35 | 4 |
| 4686[21] | **Habeta (USA) (44)** (JWWatts) **10-8-13** GDuffield(15) (a bhd) | s.h | **17** | 20/1 | 26 | — |
| 4344[4] | **Peep O Day (37)** (JLEyre) **5-8-6** RLappin(1) (lw: lost tch fnl 4f) | ½ | **18** | 14/1 | 19 | — |
| 3463[11] | **Deauville Dancer (IRE) (45)** (DNicholls) **4-9-0b**1 AlexGreaves(10) (lw: cl up tl wknd qckly 3f out) | 12 | **19** | 20/1 | 8 | — |
| | | | | (SP 157.3%) | **19 Rn** | |

**2m 11.9** (5.20) CSF £179.59 CT £1,638.66 TOTE £18.90: £4.60 £2.30 £4.30 £3.90 (£139.00) Trio £376.50; £477.36 to Newbury 24/10/96
OWNER Mrs J. Cecil (NEWMARKET) BRED Lady Murless
WEIGHT FOR AGE 3yo-5lb
**607 Adamton** swished his tail repeatedly under pressure, but still refused to give in. (14/1)
**4609 Explosive Power** travelled particularly well but, when it came down to a struggle, he was just found wanting. (12/1)
**4078 Super High** has yet to win on Turf, but there was nothing wrong with this effort. (10/1)
**3645 Zahran (IRE)** last won over a year ago and is certainly well handicapped, but is just short of a real turn of foot. (16/1)
**4455* Brambles Way**, put up 10lb for his Redcar win, had his chances, but the weight was always anchoring him. (8/1: 6/1-9/1)
**Ottavio Farnese** showed enough here to suggest that he is coming to hand. (20/1)

**Elpidos**, wearing his customary tongue-strap, was heavily gambled on and travelled well on the bridle but, once off it early in the straight, was then disappointing. (3/1: 10/1-5/2)
**4236* Cuban Reef** had a quiet run here and looks worth bearing in mind. (7/2)

T/Jkpt: Not won; £32,476.11 to Newbury 24/10/96. T/Plpt: £69.80 (213.37 Tckts). T/Qdpt: £20.50 (49.29 Tckts). WG

## 4258-YARMOUTH (L-H) (Good to firm)
## Wednesday October 23rd

WEATHER: fine WIND: fresh against

### 4813 RUNHAM MAIDEN STKS (3-Y.O) (Class D)

2-00 (2-00) **1m 3y** £3,893.85 (£1,162.80: £555.90: £252.45) Stalls: Low GOING minus 0.03 sec per fur (G)

| Form | Horse | Dist | Pos | SP | RR | SF |
|---|---|---|---|---|---|---|
| 4478[3] | **Medfee** (RCharlton) **3-8-9** KDarley(7) (hld up: hdwy over 2f out: led 1f out: rdn out) | — | **1** | 7/1 | 76 | 39 |
| 703[3] | **Catumbella (USA)** (JHMGosden) **3-8-9** LDettori(1) (trckd ldrs: nt clr run & lost pl 3f out: r.o fnl 2f: nt trble wnr) | 3 | **2** | 6/4[1] | 70 | 33 |
| 4615[10] | **Royal Action (73)** (JEBanks) **3-9-0** RCochrane(5) (trckd ldrs: rdn over 1f out: styd on same pce) | ¾ | **3** | 16/1 | 74 | 37 |
| 4591[2] | **Yukon Hope (USA) (73)** (RCharlton) **3-8-9** TSprake(8) (hld up: hdwy over 3f out: led over 1f out: sn hdd & btn) | 1½ | **4** | 11/2[3] | 66 | 29 |
| | **Two To Tango (IRE)** (JHMGosden) **3-8-9** GHind(2) (unf: in tch: no imp fnl 2f) | 1¼ | **5** | 20/1 | 63 | 26 |
| 4622[8] | **Questing Star** (GWragg) **3-8-9** MHills(6) (prom: led over 2f out tl over 1f out: btn whn nt clr run ins fnl f) | nk | **6** | 20/1 | 62 | 25 |
| 4690[3] | **Rash Gift** (LordHuntingdon) **3-8-9** DHarrison(4) (led over 5f: sn wknd) | 17 | **7** | 7/2[2] | 29 | — |
| 4622[10] | **Sufuf** (DMorley) **3-8-9** RHills(3) (w ldr tl wknd 3f out) | nk | **8** | 20/1 | 28 | — |

(SP 110.3%) **8 Rn**

**1m 40.2** (4.90) CSF £16.64 TOTE £9.30: £2.20 £1.30 £2.70 (£8.20) OWNER Mr K. Abdulla (BECKHAMPTON) BRED Juddmonte Farms
**4478 Medfee**, dropped back in trip, was ridden for speed and not stamina, but still won in convincing style. (7/1: 4/1-15/2)
**703 Catumbella (USA)** has clearly had her problems, but is much better than this suggests, for she got no run at all. (6/4)
**3704 Royal Action**, dropped back in trip, ran as if needing further, but is proving expensive to follow. (16/1)
**4591 Yukon Hope (USA)** was given time to find her stride before mounting a challenge, but did not last long once things got tough. (11/2: op 11/4)
**Two To Tango (IRE)**, a newcomer showing plenty of knee-action, did not threaten to take a hand once the race proper began. (20/1)
**Questing Star**, dropped in trip, was just beginning to struggle when her ground was taken. (20/1)
**4690 Rash Gift** (7/2: op 2/1)

### 4814 BILLOCKBY NURSERY H'CAP (0-85) (2-Y.O) (Class D)

2-30 (2-31) **1m 3y** £3,993.30 (£1,193.40: £571.20: £260.10) Stalls: Low GOING minus 0.03 sec per fur (G)

| Form | Horse | Dist | Pos | SP | RR | SF |
|---|---|---|---|---|---|---|
| 4516[4] | **Social Pillar (USA) (81)** (JHMGosden) **2-9-4** LDettori(5) (trckd ldrs: nt clr run over 2f out: rdn & ev ch fnl f: led post) | — | **1** | 13/8[1] | 81 | 42 |
| 4599[4] | **Polar Flight (84)** (MJohnston) **2-9-7** MRoberts(6) (lw: s.i.s: bhd & sn pushed along: gd hdwy 2f out: led 1f out: r.o: jst ct) | hd | **2** | 8/1[3] | 84 | 45 |
| 4440* | **Zaima (IRE) (84)** (JLDunlop) **2-9-7** KDarley(1) (chsd ldrs: rdn 3f out: swtchd ins 2f out: one pce fnl f) | 3 | **3** | 11/2[2] | 78 | 39 |
| 4607* | **Time Can Tell (70)** (CMurray) **2-8-7** MTebbutt(8) (b: chsd ldrs: led over 1f out: sn hdd: one pce ins fnl f) | s.h | **4** | 14/1 | 64 | 25 |
| 4601[8] | **Wobble (74)** (WJHaggas) **2-8-11** RHills(2) (w ldr: led 2f out: sn hdd & wknd) | 2½ | **5** | 10/1 | 63 | 24 |
| 4495[3] | **Irish Fiction (IRE) (66)** (DJSCosgrove) **2-7-12**(5) MartinDwyer(7) (swtg: in tch: rdn over 2f out: no imp) | 2 | **6** | 14/1 | 51 | 12 |
| 4500[4] | **Ink Pot (USA) (75)** (MRStoute) **2-8-12v** RCochrane(4) (chsd ldrs: rdn 2f out: fnd nil) | ¾ | **7** | 11/2[2] | 58 | 19 |
| 4694[11] | **Fancy A Fortune (IRE) (68)** (JPearce) **2-8-5v** GBardwell(9) (led 6f) | 5 | **8** | 25/1 | 41 | 2 |
| 4386[9] | **Bert (63)** (PTWalwyn) **2-8-0**ow1 TSprake(10) (plld hrd: in tch 5f) | 3 | **9** | 33/1 | 30 | — |
| 4188[6] | **Linden's Lad (IRE) (73)** (JRJenkins) **2-8-10** SWhitworth(3) (in tch 6f) | hd | **10** | 25/1 | 40 | 1 |

(SP 113.0%) **10 Rn**

**1m 40.8** (5.50) CSF £13.82 CT £54.00 TOTE £3.10: £1.40 £2.00 £2.30 (£9.10) Trio £9.40 OWNER Mr K. Abdulla (NEWMARKET) BRED Juddmonte Farms
**4516 Social Pillar (USA)**, just turning in his coat, was always travelling well, but seemed in trouble when short of room to make his move. Getting out approaching the final furlong, he got there just in time. (13/8)
**4599 Polar Flight**, keen to post, reared and lost half a dozen lengths as the stalls open. Pushed along to get in touch, he found a turn of speed to burst his way through the field to lead entering the final furlong. Just caught, he did not fail through lack of stamina. (8/1: 6/1-9/1)
**4440* Zaima (IRE)**, gone in her coat, needed to switch sharply to get a run, but still produced a challenge before being outpaced inside the final furlong. (11/2: 7/2-6/1)
**4607* Time Can Tell** looks the sort to go the right way and appreciated the galloping track, only giving best in the final furlong. (14/1)
**4383 Wobble** took a keen hold racing with the leader, but lasted rather better than in the past. (10/1: 7/1-12/1)
**4495 Irish Fiction (IRE)** got warm on this cool and windy day, failing to land a blow. (14/1: 8/1-16/1)
**4500 Ink Pot (USA)** (11/2: op 3/1)

### 4815 MARTHAM (S) H'CAP (0-60) (3-Y.O+) (Class G)

3-00 (3-01) **1m 3f 101y** £2,784.00 (£774.00: £372.00) Stalls: Low GOING minus 0.37 sec per fur (F)

| Form | Horse | Dist | Pos | SP | RR | SF |
|---|---|---|---|---|---|---|
| 4763[11] | **Petoskin (50)** (JPearce) **4-9-8** MWigham(15) (prom: hmpd 5f out: led over 1f out: rdn out) | — | **1** | 16/1 | 64 | 46 |
| 4626[16] | **Rock The Barney (IRE) (40)** (PBurgoyne) **7-8-9**(3) PMcCabe(8) (hmpd 5f out: hdwy 3f out: one pce ins fnl f) | 3 | **2** | 11/2[1] | 50 | 32 |
| 4703[3] | **Mcgillycuddy Reeks (IRE) (40)** (NTinkler) **5-8-12** KDarley(10) (swtg: chsd ldrs: hmpd 5f out: rdn 2f out: kpt on) | hd | **3** | 13/2[2] | 50 | 32 |
| 4236[9] | **Eskimo Kiss (IRE) (37)** (MJFetherston-Godley) **3-8-3b** DHarrison(17) (racd wd early: disp ld tl led over 3f out: hdd over 1f out: sn wknd) | 1¼ | **4** | 12/1 | 45 | 21 |
| 3968[6] | **Record Lover (IRE) (34)** (MCChapman) **6-8-1**(5) MartinDwyer(16) (led 10f out: hdd over 3f out: sn wknd) | 3½ | **5** | 14/1 | 37 | 19 |
| 4448[11] | **Junior Ben (IRE) (38)** (PHowling) **4-8-10** BDoyle(5) (nvr nrr) | 3 | **6** | 20/1 | 37 | 19 |
| 4603[3] | **Pat's Splendour (48)** (HJCollingridge) **5-9-6** MRimmer(7) (a.p: ev ch 3f out: sn wknd) | 1¼ | **7** | 8/1 | 45 | 27 |
| *2086*[9] | **Contrarie (38)** (MJRyan) **3-7-11**(7) AMcCarthy(11) (r.o fnl 2f: nvr trbld ldrs) | 1¾ | **8** | 25/1 | 33 | 9 |
| 4626[20] | **El Bardador (IRE) (57)** (WJarvis) **3-9-9b** MHills(14) (n.d) | 3½ | **9** | 12/1 | 47 | 23 |

4703[9] **Haute Cuisine (45)** (RJRWilliams) **3-8-11** TSprake(13) (bdly hmpd 5f out: nvr trbld ldrs) ....hd **10** 14/1 35 11
4597[8] **Spanish Stripper (USA) (52)** (MCChapman) **5-9-10** AMcGlone(18) (nvr nr to chal) ....½ **11** 20/1 41 23
4603* **Comedy River (51)** (NEBerry) **9-9-9** GHind(2) (chsd ldrs tl rdn & btn over 3f out) ....6 **12** 11/2[1] 32 14
4587[11] **Tee Tee Too (IRE) (35)** (MissMKMilligan) **4-8-0**(7) JennyBenson(9) (chsd ldrs tl bdly hmpd 5f out: no ch after) ....½ **13** 50/1 15 —
*4107*[4] **Yellow Dragon (IRE) (37)** (BAPearce) **3-8-3** StephenDavies(12) (swtg: s.s: a bhd) ....15 **14** 20/1 — —
*275*[6] **Shedansar (IRE) (28)** (RCSpicer) **4-8-0** JO'Reilly(20) (bit bkwd: rdn 7f out: sn bhd) ....hd **15** 50/1 — —
4337[14] **Media Express (40)** (PSFelgate) **4-8-12** JStack(19) (a bhd) ....9 **16** 40/1 — —
4724[12] **La Thuile (26)** (TJEtherington) **4-7-9**(3)ow2 MHenry(4) (plld hrd: bhd whn bdly hmpd & fell 5f out) .... **F** 50/1 — —
4515[7] **Quillwork (USA) (42)** (JPearce) **4-9-0** GBardwell(1) (bhd whn bdly hmpd & p.u 5f out) .... **P** 14/1 — —
3619[4] **Tirols Tyrant (IRE) (44)** (MJohnston) **3-8-10** MRoberts(3) (led over 1f: prom whn broke leg, struck into & uns rdr 5f out: dead) .... **U** 7/1[3] — —
2192[23] **Chilly Lad (46)** (MJRyan) **5-9-4b** RCochrane(6) (chsd ldrs tl clipped heels & stumbled 5f out: uns rdr) .... **U** 25/1 — —
(SP 139.3%) **20 Rn**

**2m 27.3** (4.30) CSF £103.76 CT £606.01 TOTE £22.90: £7.80 £1.70 £1.30 £2.60 (£80.80) Trio £103.60 OWNER Mr G Lowe; The Losers Owners Group (NEWMARKET) BRED James Wigan
WEIGHT FOR AGE 3yo-6lb
Bt in 4,000 gns

**4515 Petoskin**, whose useful two-year-old form included a third to Lammtarra, had shown precious little since, but bounced back to form on ground a little better than the official description. The word consistent can not be applied to his efforts this year. (16/1)
**4509 Rock The Barney (IRE)**, forced wide by the problems on the bend, then got to work and looked a big danger, but the effort was petering out as the line approached. This was the first time the Handicapper had really dropped the old horse all season, and it certainly had an effect. (11/2)
**4703 Mcgillycuddy Reeks (IRE)** looked short of any change of gear, but kept plugging away to the line. (13/2)
**3965 Eskimo Kiss (IRE)** looked well served by racing alone on the wide outside in the back straight, but does not quite seem to get this trip. (12/1)
**3638 Record Lover (IRE)**, back on the level after making the frame in two hurdles and a chase, tried to make full use of his stamina, but could not keep it up in the straight. (14/1)
**3141 Junior Ben (IRE)** got behind and only began to stay on when the race was over. (20/1)
**4603 Pat's Splendour** (8/1: 6/1-9/1)
**4603* Comedy River** (11/2: 4/1-6/1)

## 4816 MAUTBY CONDITIONS STKS (2-Y.O) (Class C)

3-30 (3-39) **6f 3y** £5,427.36 (£1,733.76: £830.88) Stalls: Low GOING minus 0.03 sec per fur (G)

SP RR SF
4383* **Intikhab (USA)** (DMorley) **2-9-2** RHills(3) (lw: trckd ldrs: led on bit over 1f out: pushed clr ins fnl f) ....— **1** 3/10[1] 87+ 41
4208[4] **Restless Spirit (USA)** (MJohnston) **2-8-11** LDettori(1) (led over 4f: no ch w wnr) ....3 **2** 3/1[2] 74 28
4762[8] **Turtle Moon** (MHTompkins) **2-8-11** KDarley(2) (hld up: rdn 2f out: no imp) ....7 **3** 20/1[3] 55 9
(SP 106.7%) **3 Rn**

**1m 14.9** (4.00) CSF £1.49 TOTE £1.30 (£1.10) OWNER Mr Hamdan Al Maktoum (NEWMARKET) BRED J. I. Racing Inc. and Marvin Little Jr
**4383* Intikhab (USA)** took this without barely turning a hair. (3/10)
**4208 Restless Spirit (USA)** might need further, but was being laughed at by the winner some way from home although, to his credit, he stuck to the task. (3/1)
**1453 Turtle Moon** travelled well enough until the pace quickened in the final quarter-mile. (20/1)

## 4817 WICKHAMPTON MAIDEN STKS (I) (2-Y.O) (Class D)

4-00 (4-14) **7f 3y** £3,357.05 (£1,000.40: £476.70: £214.85) Stalls: Low GOING minus 0.03 sec per fur (G)

SP RR SF
**Sekari** (DRLoder) **2-9-0** RHughes(9) (str: scope: bit bkwd: dwlt: hld up: led over 1f out: pushed out) ....— **1** 8/11[1] 72+ 55
**Alezal** (WJarvis) **2-9-0** AMcGlone(10) (leggy: scope: s.i.s: hdwy 3f out: no ex ins fnl f) ....¾ **2** 25/1 70 53
**Motet** (GWragg) **2-9-0** MHills(5) (w'like: scope: bkwd: hld up: hdwy over 1f out: r.o) ....3 **3** 20/1 63 46
4699[3] **Sporting Fellow** (MRStoute) **2-9-0** KDarley(11) (prom: rdn 3f out: unable qckn fnl f) ....¾ **4** 7/2[2] 62 45
**Irsal** (ACStewart) **2-9-0** RHills(3) (w'like: unf: hld up: hdwy 2f out: nt clr run 1f out: no ch after) ....1 **5** 10/1[3] 60 43
4242[6] **Harmony Hall** (JRFanshawe) **2-9-0** DHarrison(6) (lw: hld up & plld hrd: hdwy over 1f out: eased whn btn ins fnl f) ....hd **6** 33/1 59 42
**Farnese (IRE)** (LMCumani) **2-9-0** OUrbina(2) (w'like: bit bkwd: in tch: n.m.r over 2f out: no ch after) ....½ **7** 14/1 58 41
**Fatal Sahra (IRE)** (JHMGosden) **2-9-0** LDettori(8) (neat: scope: chsd ldr tl led 3f out: hdd over 1f out: sn wknd) ....¾ **8** 16/1 56 39
4516[10] **Kamin (USA)** (RWArmstrong) **2-9-0** RPrice(7) (prom: rdn over 2f out: eased whn btn ins fnl) ....s.h **9** 33/1 56 39
**Macaroni Beach** (CEBrittain) **2-8-9** BDoyle(4) (unf: a bhd) ....3 **10** 50/1 44 27
**Basic Impulse** (CMurray) **2-9-0** PBloomfield(1) (rangy: unf: led 4f: wknd 2f out) ....20 **11** 100/1 4 —
(SP 119.2%) **11 Rn**

**1m 27.6** (3.40) CSF £19.58 TOTE £1.60: £1.20 £8.80 £2.60 (£73.40) Trio £127.60 OWNER Sheikh Mohammed (NEWMARKET) BRED Sheikh Mohammed Bin Rashid Al Maktoum
**Sekari**, whose dam is a sister to Gone West, is sturdily-made and moved really well to post. Some way short of full fitness, this only became apparent once the race was already won. The pace he used to burst through once a run appeared stamps him as an exciting prospect. (8/11)
**Alezal**, cheaply bought and bred to need a trip, showed a fair amount of ability after missing the break. Moving up on the outside to challenge entering the final furlong, he did not impress with his head carriage, but stayed on well enough. (25/1)
**Motet** looked in need of the race, but finished as well as any. (20/1)
**4699 Sporting Fellow** looked fit this time and had quite a hard race, but never looked like quickening. (7/2: 3/1-9/2)
**Irsal**, a Nashwan newcomer who still looked well in his coat, travelled well in behind the others. Denied a run as his effort developed, he should have finished closer. (10/1: 7/1-12/1)
**4242 Harmony Hall** proved difficult to settle, but still had the ability when asked for his effort. His last two runs have come in decent maidens and the Handicapper may not be lenient. (33/1)

## 4818 WICKHAMPTON MAIDEN STKS (II) (2-Y.O) (Class D)

4-30 (4-41) **7f 3y** £3,326.50 (£991.00: £472.00: £212.50) Stalls: Low GOING minus 0.03 sec per fur (G)

SP RR SF
4516[2] **Courtship** (HRACecil) **2-9-0** AMcGlone(5) (w ldr: led over 1f out: drvn out) ....— **1** 8/15[1] 85 41

| | | | | SP | RR | SF |
|---|---|---|---|---|---|---|
| | **Judicial Supremacy** (JRFanshawe) **2-9-0** DHarrison(8) (w'like: scope: lw: hld up: hdwy over 1f out: r.o wl ins fnl f: jst failed) | s.h | **2** | 16/1 | 85 | 41 |
| 4508[3] | **Indium** (JHMGosden) **2-9-0** LDettori(7) (lw: prom: ev ch 1f out: no ex) | ¾ | **3** | 9/1[3] | 83 | 39 |
| 4451[11] | **Bicton Park** (DMorley) **2-9-0b[1]** JStack(1) (lw: led over 5f: wknd ins fnl f) | 1½ | **4** | 66/1 | 80 | 36 |
| | **Fayik** (HThomsonJones) **2-9-0** RHills(4) (scope: bkwd: a.p: one pce fnl f) | s.h | **5** | 7/2[2] | 80 | 36 |
| 4698[8] | **Doc Ryan's** (MJRyan) **2-9-0** GBardwell(3) (bit bkwd: prom tl wknd over 1f out) | 1 | **6** | 66/1 | 77 | 33 |
| | **Tyrolean Dream (IRE)** (MHTompkins) **2-8-11**(3) MHenry(10) (str: bkwd: in tch: rdn 3f out: no imp) | s.h | **7** | 33/1 | 77 | 33 |
| | **Enavius (IRE)** (MBell) **2-9-0** MFenton(6) (lengthy: scope: bit bkwd: hld up: effrt over 2f out: no imp) | 5 | **8** | 25/1 | 66 | 22 |
| 4605[12] | **Pirongia** (PHowling) **2-8-9** BDoyle(9) (a bhd) | 11 | **9** | 100/1 | 36 | — |
| *4585[5]* | ***Premier*** (MJohnston) **2-9-0** MHills(2) (Withdrawn not under Starter's orders: ref to ent stalls) | | **W** | 20/1 | — | — |

(SP 118.8%) **9 Rn**

**1m 28.8** (4.60) CSF £9.77 TOTE £1.40: £1.00 £4.00 £2.10 (£9.60) Trio £34.00 OWNER Lord Howard de Walden (NEWMARKET) BRED Lord Howard de Walden

OFFICIAL EXPLANATION **Silclare (IRE): her rider reported that the filly felt flat.**

**4516 Courtship** is not a speed horse like many of his family and took an eternity to get to the front. He nearly surrendered the lead on the line, and the time was much slower than the other division. (8/15)

**Judicial Supremacy** looked really well, but was ridden without irons once mounted in the paddock and did flash his tail. Bursting through inside the final furlong, he was the only one in the race to show a turn of foot, and was unlucky not to win. (16/1)

**4508 Indium** proved a Racereader's nightmare, as do so many of the trainer's horses, as he was only brought into the paddock after everything else had gone down. He does appear highly strung and not to have much heart for a battle. (9/1: op 6/1)

**Bicton Park** showed much more sparkle in first-time blinkers and, after being loaded last, only gave way inside the last furlong. (66/1)

**Fayik**, whose dam is a half-sister to White Muzzle, looked very burly and showed plenty of knee-action going down. Short of gears at the business end, there is some hope for him. (7/2)

**Doc Ryan's** still looked as though he would be better for the race but broke on terms, only to fade as soon as room became scarce on the far rail. (66/1)

## 4819 THRIGBY H'CAP (0-85) (3-Y.O+) (Class D)

5-00 (5-04) **1m 2f 21y** £4,457.40 (£1,336.20: £642.60: £295.80) Stalls: Low GOING minus 0.37 sec per fur (F)

| | | | | SP | RR | SF |
|---|---|---|---|---|---|---|
| 4422* | **Omara (USA) (76)** (HRACecil) **3-9-9** AMcGlone(5) (hld up gng wl: stdy hdwy to ld ins fnl f: rdn & r.o) | — | **1** | 7/2[1] | 89+ | 57 |
| 4489[2] | **Bubble Wings (FR) (67)** (SPCWoods) **4-9-5** KDarley(9) (hld up: nt clr run over 2f out: hdwy over 1f out: r.o wl fnl f) | ½ | **2** | 5/1[2] | 79 | 52 |
| 4702[9] | **Harvey White (IRE) (62)** (JPearce) **4-9-0** GBardwell(2) (prom: led over 1f out: hdd ins fnl f: unable qckn) | 1¾ | **3** | 14/1 | 71 | 44 |
| 4214[3] | **Hippy (75)** (CEBrittain) **3-9-8** BDoyle(10) (prom: rdn over 2f out: ev ch over 1f out: sn btn) | 1¼ | **4** | 13/2 | 83 | 51 |
| 4238[5] | **Sadler's Walk (72)** (GWragg) **5-9-10** MHills(4) (lw: hld up: hdwy 3f out: hmpd 1f out: nt rcvr) | 1½ | **5** | 11/2[3] | 77 | 50 |
| 4686[16] | **Lady of Leisure (USA) (72)** (MrsJCecil) **4-9-10** MFenton(7) (hld up: hdwy 5f out: rdn 3f out: sn btn) | ¾ | **6** | 10/1 | 76 | 49 |
| 4550[14] | **Polish Rhythm (IRE) (65)** (MHTompkins) **3-8-9**(3) MHenry(8) (lw: rdn 4f out: a bhd) | 2 | **7** | 25/1 | 66 | 34 |
| 4559[2] | **Melt The Clouds (CAN) (76)** (PWHarris) **3-9-9** GHind(3) (led: clr 7f out: hdd & wknd over 1f out) | hd | **8** | 9/1 | 77 | 45 |
| 4591[4] | **Family Man (72)** (JRFanshawe) **3-9-5** DHarrison(1) (plld hrd: chsd ldr tl rdn & wknd 2f out) | 7 | **9** | 5/1[2] | 62 | 30 |
| 4499* | **Zilclare (IRE) (72)** (EALDunlop) **3-9-5** SWhitworth(6) (lw: in tch: pushed along 4f out: sn bhd) | 10 | **10** | 5/1[2] | 46 | 14 |

(SP 130.5%) **10 Rn**

**2m 6.9** (2.50) CSF £22.82 CT £214.50 TOTE £5.40: £1.80 £1.70 £3.90 (£11.00) Trio £64.90 OWNER Mr F. Hinojosa (NEWMARKET) BRED Indian Creek, H. Lascelles, A. Stroud and W. B. Is

WEIGHT FOR AGE 3yo-5lb

OFFICIAL EXPLANATION **Zilclare (IRE): felt 'flat' throughout.**

**4422* Omara (USA)**, brought wide of the field, was given a cracker of a ride and was still cantering when put in front inside the final furlong. Shaken up, she found little as usual, but enough to hold on. (7/2)

**4489 Bubble Wings (FR)** is keeping her form admirably and has found her trip, for she struggled to get through, but stayed on really well in the final furlong. (5/1)

**4702 Harvey White (IRE)**, closely weighted with the runner-up on their last meeting, could not quicken enough in the final furlong when the chance of victory was there. (14/1)

**4214 Hippy**, stepping up in trip, looked to be getting outpaced when ridden along early in the straight, but battled away and was one of four in line at the final furlong, only then to fade. (13/2)

**4238 Sadler's Walk**, still fresher than most, looked in great shape and would have gone close with a trouble-free passage. (11/2)

**4387* Lady of Leisure (USA)** was one of the first in trouble, although she did keep trying. (10/1)

T/Plpt: £20.70 (483.03 Tckts). T/Qdpt: £9.20 (59.06 Tckts). Dk

# 4324-NEWBURY (L-H) (Soft)

## Thursday October 24th

WEATHER: overcast WIND: mod bhd

## 4820 VODAFONE BRITISH AND NORTHERN RACING SCHOOLS APPRENTICE H'CAP (0-80) (3-Y.O+) (Class F)

2-10 (2-11) **7f (straight)** £3,457.50 (£970.00: £472.50) Stalls: High GOING: 0.09 sec per fur (G)

| | | | | SP | RR | SF |
|---|---|---|---|---|---|---|
| 4775[3] | **Amber Fort (69)** (DRCElsworth) **3-9-2v** DGriffiths(24) (hld up in tch: led 1f out: r.o wl) | — | **1** | 9/1[1] | 80 | 58 |
| 4688[19] | **Sovereigns Court (64)** (MajorDNChappell) **3-8-11** RHavlin(21) (swtg: chsd ldrs: rdn & ev ch 1f out: unable qckn) | 2½ | **2** | 10/1[2] | 69 | 47 |
| 4550[4] | **Ca'd'oro (54)** (GBBalding) **3-8-1** IonaWands(10) (lw: mid div: hdwy 2f out: rdn over 1f out: r.o one pce ins fnl f) | hd | **3** | 14/1 | 59 | 37 |
| 4231[5] | **Proud Monk (73)** (GLMoore) **3-9-6v[1]** CWebb(20) (chsd ldrs: rdn & ev ch 1f out: one pce) | ½ | **4** | 20/1 | 77 | 55 |
| 3985[12] | **Tatika (74)** (GWragg) **6-9-9** GMilligan(26) (hld up in rr: hdwy 2f out: styd on ins fnl f) | 1 | **5** | 14/1 | 76 | 56 |
| 4592[4] | **Minoletti (72)** (EALDunlop) **3-9-5** PDoe(18) (b.nr hind: swtg: led: hdd 1f out: no ex) | 2½ | **6** | 16/1 | 68 | 46 |
| 4206[7] | **Winsome Wooster (61)** (PGMurphy) **5-8-10** SDrowne(15) (chsd ldrs: rdn 2f out: one pce) | 2½ | **7** | 14/1 | 51 | 31 |
| 4445[16] | **Anastina (79)** (NAGraham) **4-10-0** FLynch(1) (led far side: no ch w stands' side fnl 2f) | hd | **8** | 20/1 | 69 | 49 |
| 3680[4] | **Sagebrush Roller (65)** (JWWatts) **8-9-0** PFessey(7) (chsd ldrs far side: rdn 2f out: no hdwy) | s.h | **9** | 11/1[3] | 55 | 35 |
| 4784[3] | **Shontaine (61)** (MJohnston) **3-8-8** KSked(9) (in tch: rdn 2f out: grad wknd) | s.h | **10** | 16/1 | 51 | 29 |
| 4373[9] | **Jaazim (49)** (MMadgwick) **6-7-8**(4) CCarver(13) (prom tl wknd over 1f out) | ½ | **11** | 20/1 | 38 | 18 |

4689[12] **Ben Gunn (70)** (PTWalwyn) **4-9-1**(4) RCody-Boutcher(2) (chsd ldr far side: wknd 2f out)....1 **12** 33/1 56 36
4693[2] **Regal Splendour (CAN) (70)** (PFICole) **3-8-13**(4) AMcCarthy(25) (lw: nvr bttr than mid div)....1½ **13** 14/1 53 31
4376[8] **Press On Nicky (72)** (WRMuir) **3-9-5** JWilkinson(27) (w ldr tl over 2f out)....s.h **14** 20/1 55 33
4550* **Sea Danzig (65)** (JJBridger) **3-8-12** SCopp(11) (lw: prom to ½-wy)....1 **15** 16/1 46 24
1319[16] **Croagh Patrick (56)** (JCFox) **4-8-1**(4) PClarke(5) (racd far side: in tch 4f)....¾ **16** 33/1 35 15
3694[12] **Chili Heights (49)** (GBBalding) **6-7-8v**(4) JFowle(14) (a bhd)....3½ **17** 25/1 20 —
4775[14] **Knobbleeneeze (74)** (MRChannon) **6-9-9v** AEddery(4) (racd far side: chsd ldrs tl wknd 2f out)....3½ **18** 14/1 37 17
4688[26] **Barrel of Hope (75)** (JLEyre) **4-9-3**(7) RWinks(6) (racd far side: sn bhd)....2 **19** 14/1 33 13
3403[8] **Vanborough Lad (51)** (MJBolton) **7-7-10**(4)ow1 TField(3) (racd far side: in tch 4f)....s.h **20** 25/1 9 —
2229[12] **Hurtleberry (IRE) (70)** (LordHuntingdon) **3-8-13**(4) CCogan(8) (racd far side: prom over 4f)....1¼ **21** 33/1 25 3
2579[11] **Double March (76)** (PRWebber) **3-9-9** CTeague(17) (s.i.s: a bhd)....¾ **22** 14/1 30 8
*4778*[11] **Leigh Crofter (58)** (PDCundell) **7-8-7b** MBaird(22) (a bhd)....2 **23** 25/1 7 —
4504[4] **Green Bopper (USA) (73)** (MBell) **3-9-6v**[1] RMullen(23) (lw: bhd fr ½-wy)....hd **24** 20/1 22 —
3439[13] **Primelta (54)** (RAkehurst) **3-8-1** DDenby(12) (sn bhd)....1¾ **25** 25/1 — —
*180*[8] **Flashing Sabre (51)** (AJChamberlain) **4-7-10**(4) JMcAuley(16) (prom 4f)....2½ **26** 25/1 — —

(SP 143.6%) **26 Rn**

**1m 28.72** (4.22) CSF £96.98 CT £1,200.37 TOTE £6.40: £1.70 £2.80 £3.70 £4.40 (£37.80) Trio £173.40 OWNER The Caledonian Racing Society (WHITCOMBE) BRED Campbell Stud

WEIGHT FOR AGE 3yo-2lb

**4775 Amber Fort**, produced with a well-timed run, was ridden to perfection and found plenty. (9/1)
**4511 Sovereigns Court** seems to go well on a straight track as his only other placed run in seven outings was at Salisbury. (10/1)
**4550 Ca'd'oro** is worth another try back at a mile. (14/1)
**3806 Proud Monk**, returning to his best trip, was not disgraced. (20/1)
**3501* Tatika**, who really needs another furlong, ran encouragingly after a seven-week lay-off. (14/1)
**4592 Minoletti** has not quite got home in his two attempts at this trip, but in both cases he has been asked to make the running. (16/1)

## 4821 VODAFONE GROUP H'CAP (0-90) (3-Y.O+) (Class C)

2-40 (2-40) **2m** £6,154.00 (£1,852.00: £896.00: £418.00) Stalls: High GOING: 0.09 sec per fur (G)

SP RR SF

4365[4] **Bowcliffe Court (IRE) (58)** (BWHills) **4-7-10** JQuinn(9) (hld up: hdwy gng wl 4f out: led & edgd lft 2f out: rdn appr fnl f: r.o wl)....— **1** 6/1[3] 77 33
4750[2] **Upper Gallery (IRE) (80)** (PWChapple-Hyam) **3-8-8b**[1] JReid(2) (hld up in tch: chsd wnr fnl 2f: unable qckn)....2½ **2** 5/1[2] 97 43
4750[7] **Double Agent (70)** (MJohnston) **3-7-9**(3) MHenry(1) (prom: rdn & lost pl 7f out: rallied 3f out: kpt on one pce fnl 2f)....11 **3** 16/1 76 22
4673[3] **Benfleet (70)** (RWArmstrong) **5-8-8** RPrice(6) (hld up: hdwy 5f out: rdn & ev ch 2f out: wknd over 1f out)....3 **4** 9/1 73 29
4673[2] **Sea Freedom (60)** (GBBalding) **5-7-9v**(3) NVarley(5) (lw: rr: sn rdn along: effrt 6f out: hrd rdn fnl 3f: one pce)..6 **5** 10/1 57 13
4362* **Ginger Fox (USA) (88)** (HRACecil) **3-9-2** PatEddery(11) (lw: led: hdd 12f out: sn led again: hdd 2f out: sn wknd)....1 **6** 7/2[1] 84 30
3142[6] **Mirador (60)** (RCurtis) **5-7-12** GBardwell(13) (s.i.s: sn rcvrd & mid div: hrd rdn 6f out: no hdwy)....¾ **7** 16/1 55 11
4447[5] **Shining Dancer (62)** (SDow) **4-8-0**ow1 JFEgan(8) (hld up: hdwy ½-wy: wknd over 2f out)....5 **8** 9/1 52 7
4447[7] **Pearl Venture (72)** (SPCWoods) **4-8-10** KDarley(4) (hld up: hdwy 6f out: rdn over 3f out: wknd over 2f out) ....5 **9** 15/2 57 13
4612[4] **Ginka (58)** (JWMullins) **5-7-10** NCarlisle(12) (a bhd)....6 **10** 100/1 37 —
4673[15] **Muse (75)** (DRCElsworth) **9-8-13b**[1] BDoyle(14) (w ldr: led briefly 12f out: wknd 7f out: t.o)....3½ **11** 25/1 50 6
4673[11] **Sharaf (IRE) (70)** (WRMuir) **3-7-12** DeclanO'Shea(3) (prom tl rdn & wknd 4f out: t.o)....1¾ **12** 16/1 44 —
4673[12] **Mull House (58)** (GPEnright) **9-7-10** NAdams(10) (b: bhd fr ½-wy: t.o)....dist **13** 100/1 — —
4377[6] **Blaaziing Joe (IRE) (90)** (DLWilliams) **5-9-9**(5) DGriffiths(7) (a bhd: t.o fnl 6f)....dist **14** 66/1 — —

(SP 119.0%) **14 Rn**

**3m 36.44** (11.44) CSF £33.34 CT £420.50 TOTE £10.10: £2.80 £1.90 £7.30 (£20.90) Trio £184.60 OWNER Mr J. Hanson (LAMBOURN) BRED Crest Stud Ltd

LONG HANDICAP Ginka 5-8 Mull House 7-2

WEIGHT FOR AGE 3yo-10lb

**4365 Bowcliffe Court (IRE)**, well handicapped at present, was on his best behaviour and won readily. (6/1)
**4750 Upper Gallery (IRE)**, blinkered for the first time, travelled well during the race, but the winner found the better response. (5/1)
**4596 Double Agent** ran better here than he had at Catterick, but the first two left him standing. (16/1)
**4673 Benfleet** ran well in his previous race over this trip, but the searching gallop here stretched his stamina to the limit. (9/1)
**4673 Sea Freedom** continues to find it hard to overcome his lack of pace. (10/1)
**4362* Ginger Fox (USA)** ran rather freely in front and only succeeded in setting the race up for the others, while running himself into the ground. (7/2)

## 4822 VODAFONE HORRIS HILL STKS (Gp 3) (2-Y.O C & G) (Class A)

3-10 (3-14) **7f 64y (round)** £19,665.00 (£7,399.50: £3,587.25: £1,598.25) Stalls: High GOING: 0.09 sec per fur (G)

SP RR SF

4462[2] **Desert Story (IRE) (100)** (MRStoute) **2-8-9** JReid(1) (hld up: hdwy 2f out: rdn over 1f out: led wl ins fnl f: r.o)....— **1** 6/4[1] 101 62
4127* **Royal Amaretto (IRE) (91)** (BJMeehan) **2-8-9** MTebbutt(6) (chsd ldr: led 4f out: hdd 2f out: hrd rdn & ev ch wl ins fnl f: unable qckn)....¾ **2** 10/1 99 60
4684* **Hidden Meadow** (IABalding) **2-8-9** MHills(5) (chsd ldrs: led 2f out: hrd rdn 1f out: hdd wl ins fnl f: unable qckn)....hd **3** 5/1[3] 99 60
4065[3] **Starborough** (DRLoder) **2-8-9** KDarley(8) (hld up in rr: n.m.r over 3f out tl over 1f out: rdn appr fnl f: r.o one pce)....nk **4** 12/1 99 60
4303* **Bali Paradise (USA) (96)** (PFICole) **2-8-9** TQuinn(4) (swtg: sn led: hdd 4f out: wknd 3f out)....8 **5** 25/1 81 42
4681* **Andreyev (IRE) (100)** (RHannon) **2-8-9** DaneO'Neill(3) (lw: hld up: rdn over 4f out: wknd over 1f out)....½ **6** 6/1 80 41
4328[7] **General Song (IRE)** (KMcAuliffe) **2-8-9** JFEgan(2) (broke wl: stdd in mid div: rdn 3f out: wknd wl over 1f out)....¾ **7** 50/1 78 39
4700* **Showboat** (BWHills) **2-8-9** PatEddery(7) (hld up: rdn 4f out: wknd 3f out)....5 **8** 4/1[2] 67 28

(SP 113.5%) **8 Rn**

**1m 31.57** (3.47) CSF £15.43 TOTE £2.30: £1.10 £1.60 £2.30 (£10.50) OWNER Maktoum Al Maktoum (NEWMARKET) BRED Gainsborough Stud Management Ltd

**4462 Desert Story (IRE)**, the form horse of the race, won well without setting the world alight. Ridden below the distance, he got on top in the final 100 yards for a workmanlike success. (6/4)
**4127* Royal Amaretto (IRE)** ran a very game race. Taking it up early in the straight, he looked cooked when headed at the two-furlong pole but, to his credit, he battled on. Although ultimately no match for the winner, he grabbed second place near the line. (10/1)
**4684* Hidden Meadow** has quite a high reputation and went some way to justifying it here. Never far away, he led two furlongs out, but could not get away from his pursuers and was worn down late on. (5/1)
**4065 Starborough** was slightly unlucky not to finish closer. Short of room for much of the straight, he stayed on quite nicely in the final furlong and may have been second with a clear run. (12/1: op 6/1)
**4303* Bali Paradise (USA)** cut out the early pace, but was soon put in his place. (25/1)
**4681* Andreyev (IRE)** looked outstanding in the paddock, but his performance was a bit disappointing, being beaten halfway up the straight. (6/1)
**4700* Showboat** was most disappointing, dropping away early in the straight, and probably needs faster ground. (4/1: 3/1-9/2)

## 4823 GARDNER MERCHANT RATED STKS H'CAP (0-110) (3-Y.O+) (Class B)

3-40 (3-42) **6f 8y** £8,518.80 (£3,169.20: £1,534.60: £643.00: £271.50: £122.90) Stalls: High GOING: 0.09 sec per fur (G)

| | | | | SP | RR | SF |
|---|---|---|---|---|---|---|
| 2003[6] | **The Puzzler (IRE) (100)** (BWHills) **5-9-4** MHills(3) (b: stdd & swtchd rt s: hld up: gd hdwy 2f out: led wl ins fnl f: r.o wl) | — | **1** | 10/1 | 112 | 65 |
| 4679[7] | **Musical Season (89)** (TDBarron) **4-8-7** KDarley(10) (led: hdd wl ins fnl f: unable qckn) | ¾ | **2** | 9/2[2] | 99 | 52 |
| 4687[3] | **Bajan Rose (89)** (MBlanshard) **4-8-2**(5) ADaly(9) (chsd ldr: rdn over 1f out: one pce) | 2½ | **3** | 7/1 | 92 | 45 |
| 4485[8] | **Montendre (101)** (RJHodges) **9-9-5** TQuinn(8) (rr: rdn ½-wy: styd on ins fnl f) | 1¼ | **4** | 16/1 | 101 | 54 |
| 4774[14] | **Averti (IRE) (102)** (WRMuir) **5-9-6** DaneO'Neill(7) (a.p: rdn 2f out: one pce) | hd | **5** | 16/1 | 102 | 55 |
| 4554[2] | **Madly Sharp (101)** (JWWatts) **5-9-5** PatEddery(1) (hld up: rdn 2f out: one pce) | 1¼ | **6** | 5/1[3] | 98 | 51 |
| 4674[2] | **Russian Music (104)** (MissGayKelleway) **3-9-7** JReid(2) (mid div: rdn over 2f out: no hdwy) | ¾ | **7** | 8/1 | 99 | 51 |
| 4314[15] | **Hard to Figure (98)** (RJHodges) **10-9-2** SDrowne(6) (a bhd) | ½ | **8** | 16/1 | 91 | 44 |
| 4772[20] | **Repertory (96)** (MRChannon) **3-8-13** RPerham(5) (mid div: rdn over 2f out: sn wknd) | 1½ | **9** | 50/1 | 85 | 37 |
| 4444[22] | **World Premier (97)** (CEBrittain) **3-9-0** BDoyle(4) (lw: chsd ldrs tl rdn & wknd over 2f out) | 3 | **10** | 12/1 | 78 | 30 |
| 4679[15] | **Samwar (94)** (MissGayKelleway) **4-8-12** JQuinn(11) (b: chsd ldrs: rdn 2f out: sn wknd: eased whn btn ins fnl f) | ¾ | **11** | 7/2[1] | 73 | 26 |
| | | | | (SP 117.1%) | | **11 Rn** |

**1m 15.05** (3.25) CSF £50.84 CT £315.28 TOTE £8.90: £1.80 £2.00 £1.60 (£22.80) Trio £45.70 OWNER Lady Richard Wellesley (LAMBOURN)
LONG HANDICAP Bajan Rose 8-3
WEIGHT FOR AGE 3yo-1lb
OFFICIAL EXPLANATION **Samwar: was not suited by the soft ground.**
**2003 The Puzzler (IRE)** has bad legs and is well suited by plenty of cut. Held up in the rear, he looked the winner from the moment he made his challenge at the two-furlong pole. Brought with a well-timed run inside the final furlong, he won a shade cosily. (10/1)
**4314 Musical Season**, who showed the way, tried hard to burn his rivals off, but unfortunately for him found one too good. (9/2)
**4687 Bajan Rose** ran very well, but could not change pace when required. (7/1)
**4485 Montendre**, a proven mudlark, stayed on late to grab fourth. (16/1)
**4304 Averti (IRE)** proved one-paced in the closing stages. (16/1)
**4554 Madly Sharp** is best suited by a sounder surface. (5/1)
**4679 Samwar** was very disappointing, being beaten as soon as he was ridden approaching the two-furlong pole, and connections found he was unsuited by the conditions. (7/2: 9/4-4/1)

## 4824 PADDY HEFFERNAN MEMORIAL MAIDEN STKS (I) (3-Y.O) (Class D)

4-10 (4-12) **1m 2f 6y** £3,392.00 (£1,016.00: £488.00: £224.00) Stalls: High GOING: 0.09 sec per fur (G)

| | | | | SP | RR | SF |
|---|---|---|---|---|---|---|
| 4622[3] | **Enriched (IRE) (75)** (JHMGosden) **3-8-9** GHind(6) (hld up in tch: led over 1f out: pushed out) | — | **1** | 9/4[1] | 86 | 34 |
| 1326[8] | **Danish Rhapsody (IRE)** (LadyHerries) **3-9-0** DeclanO'Shea(11) (bit bkwd: a.p: led ½-wy tl over 1f out: r.o) | ½ | **2** | 33/1 | 90 | 38 |
| 4622[5] | **Tiutchev** (RCharlton) **3-9-0** RPerham(7) (a.p: rdn over 2f out: one pce) | 10 | **3** | 16/1 | 74 | 22 |
| 4611[3] | **Sea Wedding** (HRACecil) **3-8-9** AMcGlone(1) (mid div: rdn & lost pl 4f out: styd on again ins fnl f) | 1¼ | **4** | 9/4[1] | 67 | 15 |
| 4064[19] | **Phonetic (77)** (GBBalding) **3-9-0** JStack(3) (chsd ldrs: rdn over 2f out: one pce) | nk | **5** | 11/1[3] | 72 | 20 |
| 4611[2] | **Scarpetta (USA) (75)** (JWHills) **3-8-9** MTebbutt(4) (hld up in tch: rdn over 2f out: sn btn) | 5 | **6** | 11/2[2] | 59 | 7 |
| 4690[8] | **All Stand** (MajorDNChappell) **3-8-9** NCarlisle(14) (lw: prom: rdn over 2f out: grad wknd) | 2½ | **7** | 33/1 | 55 | 3 |
| 677[9] | **Mazurek** (PWChapple-Hyam) **3-9-0** NAdams(15) (bit bkwd: chsd ldrs: rdn over 2f out: sn btn) | 3½ | **8** | 12/1 | 54 | 2 |
| 3704[5] | **Sulawesi (IRE)** (WJarvis) **3-8-9** CNutter(12) (mid div: rdn ½-wy: no hdwy) | nk | **9** | 12/1 | 49 | — |
| 2855[2] | **Lavender Della (IRE) (63)** (MJFetherston-Godley) **3-8-9** CRutter(13) (rr: effrt 3f out: sn btn) | ¾ | **10** | 12/1 | 48 | — |
| | **Patiala (IRE)** (RWArmstrong) **3-8-9** RPrice(2) (lengthy: lt-f: sn rdn in rr: t.o) | 12 | **11** | 16/1 | 28 | — |
| 640[16] | **D J Cat** (WRMuir) **3-9-0** SDWilliams(5) (lw: a bhd: t.o) | 7 | **12** | 50/1 | 22 | — |
| 3767[5] | **Windrush Holly** (JRBosley) **3-8-9** StephenDavies(16) (dwlt: a bhd: t.o) | hd | **13** | 20/1 | 17 | — |
| 4548[11] | **Executive Officer** (RMFlower) **3-9-0** DBiggs(8) (sn led: hdd ½-wy: sn wknd: t.o) | ¾ | **14** | 50/1 | 21 | — |
| 3115[10] | **Bryanston Square (IRE)** (CREgerton) **3-9-0** NDay(10) (bit bkwd: a bhd: sn t.o) | 10 | **15** | 50/1 | 5 | — |
| 4379[9] | **Thatcham Island** (DLWilliams) **3-8-9** GBardwell(9) (a bhd: t.o) | 18 | **16** | 50/1 | — | — |
| | | | | (SP 138.6%) | | **16 Rn** |

**2m 12.19** (8.39) CSF £74.67 TOTE £3.10: £1.50 £4.70 £3.80 (£75.90) Trio £358.20; £312.88 to Doncaster 25/10/96 OWNER Sheikh Mohammed (NEWMARKET) BRED Sheikh Mohammed Bin Rashid Al Maktoum
**4622 Enriched (IRE)** got her reward for a couple of good efforts, but the runner-up made sure she had a race. (9/4)
**Danish Rhapsody (IRE)**, a strongly-made sort who has changed stables since his debut in May, looks a likely prospect for next season and possibly over hurdles as well. He cost a mere 1,300 guineas and looks to have been seriously under-priced. (33/1)
**4622 Tiutchev** was clearly outpointed by the leading pair and seems likely to settle down in handicap company. (16/1)
**4611 Sea Wedding**, who took an age to get going, did not appear to be over-endowed with speed, and longer trips are an obvious option. (9/4)
**3516 Phonetic** has ability, but is inconsistent and this trip may be a shade too far at present. (11/1)
**4611 Scarpetta (USA)** failed to confirm Nottingham form with Sea Wedding. (11/2)

## 4825 E.B.F. THEALE MAIDEN STKS (2-Y.O) (Class D)

4-40 (4-42) **6f 8y** £4,276.00 (£1,288.00: £624.00: £292.00) Stalls: High GOING: 0.09 sec per fur (G)

| | | | | SP | RR | SF |
|---|---|---|---|---|---|---|
| 4475[5] | **Za-Im** (BWHills) **2-9-0** MHills(12) (a.p: led gng wl over 1f out: pushed clr ins fnl f: comf) | — | **1** | 9/2[2] | 99+ | 42 |
| 2243[W] | **Soviet State (USA)** (PWChapple-Hyam) **2-9-0** JReid(18) (unf: lw: a.p: chsd wnr over 1f out: sn rdn: one pce) | 2 | **2** | 7/4[1] | 94 | 37 |

**Fly To The Stars** (MJohnston) **2-9-0** KDarley(19) (w'like: scope: lw: a.p: led 2f out: hdd wl over 1f out: one pce) ....2 **3** 14/1 88 31
4670[6] **Praeditus** (RHannon) **2-9-0** DaneO'Neill(20) (led to 2f out: hrd rdn over 1f out: one pce) ....4 **4** 12/1 78 21
4475[9] **Sweet Bettsie** (AGFoster) **2-8-9** MTebbutt(8) (led far side: no ch w stands' side fnl 2f) ....1¼ **5** 40/1 70 13
4601[6] **Dead Aim (IRE)** (IABalding) **2-9-0** BDoyle(17) (lw: hld up in rr: styd on fnl 2f: nvr nrr) ....s.h **6** 25/1 74 17
**Davids Revenge** (MajorDNChappell) **2-9-0** DeclanO'Shea(21) (str: scope: bit bkwd: hld up: hdwy 3f out: rdn over 2f out: one pce) ....hd **7** 40/1 74 17
**Arantxa** (MBell) **2-8-9** MFenton(15) (neat: mid div: rdn over 2f out: one pce) ....1¼ **8** 20/1 66 9
**Maypole (IRE)** (DRLoder) **2-8-11**(3) PMcCabe(23) (unf: lw: dwlt: styd on fr 2f out: nvr nrr) ....nk **9** 10/1[3] 70 13
**Smart Dominion** (LordHuntingdon) **2-9-0** GHind(6) (w'like: scope: bit bkwd: racd far side: prom: rdn over 2f out: one pce) ....hd **10** 20/1 70 13
**Mary Magdalene** (MBell) **2-8-9** TQuinn(10) (b.nr hind: leggy: a mid div) ....s.h **11** 16/1 65 8
4670[4] **Musharak** (JLDunlop) **2-9-0** PatEddery(3) (racd far side: hld up: effrt over 2f out: sn btn) ....2 **12** 9/2[2] 64 7
4461[8] **E-Mail (IRE)** (JMPEustace) **2-8-11**(3) FLynch(2) (racd far side: tk keen hld: in tch tl wknd over 2f out) ....nk **13** 33/1 64 7
**Yabint El Sultan** (BAMcMahon) **2-8-9** JQuinn(13) (w'like: scope: a bhd) ....1 **14** 40/1 56 —
4756[18] **Flying Thatch (IRE)** (RHannon) **2-9-0** RPerham(16) (chsd ldrs to ½-wy) ....hd **15** 33/1 61 4
4720[14] **Timothy George (IRE)** (GBBalding) **2-9-0** JStack(22) (mid div: rdn over 2f out: sn btn) ....1½ **16** 40/1 57 —
4461[11] **Purchasing Power (IRE)** (NACallaghan) **2-9-0** JFEgan(4) (racd far side: bhd fr ½-wy) ....2½ **17** 20/1 50 —
**Khafaaq** (MajorWRHern) **2-9-0** SWhitworth(9) (w'like: lw: racd far side: a bhd) ....nk **18** 10/1[3] 49 —
4599[5] **Thornton (USA)** (JHMGosden) **2-9-0** AMcGlone(7) (b: racd far side: prom 4f) ....¾ **19** 20/1 47 —
**Ardent** (CJBenstead) **2-9-0** DBiggs(5) (wl grwn: bit bkwd: racd far side: dwlt: a bhd) ....3½ **20** 40/1 38 —
**Hibernica (IRE)** (GBBalding) **2-8-9** SDrowne(14) (unf: bit bkwd: a bhd) ....1¼ **21** 33/1 30 —
3660[8] **Karen's Hat (USA)** (IABalding) **2-8-9** CRutter(11) (dwlt: a bhd) ....2 **22** 33/1 24 —
4512[19] **Top of The Green (IRE)** (PJMakin) **2-8-11**(3) RHavlin(1) (racd far side: prom to ½-wy) ....¾ **23** 33/1 27 —

(SP 160.9%) **23 Rn**

**1m 16.41** (4.61) CSF £14.96 TOTE £6.30: £2.10 £1.80 £4.30 (£7.70) Trio £40.30 OWNER Mr Hamdan Al Maktoum (LAMBOURN) BRED Shadwell Estate Company Limited

**4475 Za-Im**, all the better for his debut, continued the fine winning form of his stable's two-year-olds. (9/2)
**Soviet State (USA)**, a $275,000 son of Nureyev, was withdrawn at the start in a race here in June. He looked fit for this belated debut and ran with credit, but will be much stronger next season. (7/4)
**Fly To The Stars**, a 125,000 guinea yearling, looks the sort to do better next year, but the experience should have done him good. (14/1)
**4670 Praeditus** is making gradual progress and is the sort to have prospects as a three-year-old as long as he is kept to a realistic level. (12/1)
**Sweet Bettsie** ran a big race on the unfavoured side of the track, though her proximity to the placed horses does raise a few questions about the overall quality of the race. (40/1)
**4601 Dead Aim (IRE)**, a grand-looking sort, ran with promise and is one to note in handicaps now he is qualified. (25/1)
**Maypole (IRE)**, more sparely-made than most in this field, looked fit for this debut, but may be capable of some improvement. (10/1)
**4670 Musharak** (9/2: 3/1-5/1)

## 4826 ROUND OAK H'CAP (0-90) (3-Y.O+) (Class C)

5-10 (5-13) **1m 2f 6y** £6,417.50 (£1,940.00: £945.00: £447.50) Stalls: High GOING: 0.09 sec per fur (G)

SP RR SF

4675[9] **Edan Heights (72)** (SDow) **4-8-6**(5) ADaly(5) (lw: hld up mid div: hrd rdn & hdwy over 2f out: led wl ins fnl f: r.o) ....— **1** 9/1[3] 82 39
4617[7] **Gone for a Burton (IRE) (81)** (PJMakin) **6-9-6** PatEddery(18) (hld up in rr: rdn over 3f out: hdwy 2f out: led ins fnl f: sn hdd: unable qckn) ....1 **2** 7/1[1] 89 46
3760[4] **Nabhaan (IRE) (90)** (DMorley) **3-9-10** MFenton(13) (hld up: hdwy 4f out: ev ch wl ins fnl f: unable qckn) ....hd **3** 14/1 98 50
4675[11] **Bit on the Side (IRE) (82)** (NEBerry) **7-9-4**(3) PMcCabe(12) (hld up in rr: rdn 5f out: hdwy over 1f out: styd on ins fnl f) ....1¾ **4** 10/1 88 45
4568[4] **Another Time (80)** (SPCWoods) **4-9-5** DBiggs(17) (chsd ldrs: rdn over 1f out: one pce) ....hd **5** 10/1 85 42
4620[10] **Polar Eclipse (81)** (MJohnston) **3-9-1b**[1] MHills(16) (a.p: led over 3f out: hdd ins fnl f: no ex) ....1 **6** 20/1 85 37
4769[13] **Danegold (IRE) (74)** (MRChannon) **4-8-13v** TQuinn(19) (hld up: hdwy over 3f out: rdn 2f out: one pce) ....2½ **7** 20/1 74 31
4450[6] **Secret Aly (CAN) (83)** (CEBrittain) **6-9-8** BDoyle(1) (dwlt: rr: rdn 5f out: sme hdwy over 2f out: rdn over 1f out: sn btn) ....½ **8** 20/1 82 39
4568[19] **Game Ploy (POL) (89)** (DHaydnJones) **4-10-0** SWhitworth(20) (hld up in rr: hdwy 2f out: sn rdn: one pce) ....¾ **9** 8/1[2] 87 44
4568[26] **Champagne Prince (87)** (PWHarris) **3-9-7** GHind(15) (chsd ldrs tl wknd 2f out) ....3 **10** 16/1 80 32
4489[6] **Vola Via (USA) (81)** (IABalding) **3-8-8**(7) RFowley(8) (a mid div) ....1½ **11** 20/1 72 24
4583[8] **Therhea (IRE) (81)** (BRMillman) **3-9-1** SDrowne(14) (a mid div) ....5 **12** 12/1 64 16
4624[7] **Ten Past Six (82)** (MartynWane) **4-9-7** RPerham(22) (nvr nrr) ....2 **13** 33/1 61 18
4617[3] **Time for Action (IRE) (85)** (MHTompkins) **4-9-10** JReid(7) (lw: led tl over 3f out: sn wknd) ....¾ **14** 11/1 63 20
**Red Rainbow (84)** (BHanbury) **8-9-9** JStack(21) (lw: chsd ldrs tl wknd over 2f out) ....4 **15** 25/1 56 13
4686[6] **Shining Example (73)** (PJMakin) **4-8-12** KDarley(6) (bhd fnl 4f) ....6 **16** 11/1 35 —
4326[7] **Diminutive (USA) (82)** (JWHills) **3-8-13**(3) MHenry(10) (swtg: a bhd) ....1¾ **17** 20/1 41 —
**Shifting Moon (82)** (FJordan) **4-9-7** JQuinn(2) (bhd fnl 5f) ....1¼ **18** 33/1 39 —
4615[7] **Vaugrenier (IRE) (68)** (RHannon) **4-8-7** DaneO'Neill(11) (a bhd) ....nk **19** 10/1 25 —
4714[9] **Shehab (IRE) (84)** (PRHedger) **3-9-4** AMcGlone(4) (chsd ldr tl wknd 4f out) ....22 **20** 20/1 6 —
4580[6] **Debutante Days (66)** (CREgerton) **4-8-0**(5) SophieMitchell(9) (chsd ldrs: rdn over 3f out: sn wknd) ....4 **21** 14/1 — —

(SP 142.8%) **21 Rn**

**2m 11.7** (7.90) CSF £73.68 CT £846.36 TOTE £12.30: £2.70 £2.30 £3.20 £3.10 (£53.40) Trio £750.40 OWNER Mr T. R. Mountain (EPSOM) BRED T. R. Mountain
WEIGHT FOR AGE 3yo-5lb

**4326 Edan Heights** did not look the winner when coming under pressure some way from home, but he kept responding and got on top near the finish. (9/1)
**4617 Gone for a Burton (IRE)** likes this ground and put up his best performance this term. He can pick up a handicap before the season closes. (7/1)
**3760 Nabhaan (IRE)** had every chance, but gave the impression that he was not putting it all in. (14/1: 10/1-16/1)
**650* Bit on the Side (IRE)**, a real mudlark, made good headway to snatch fourth and will go close next time, given suitable conditions. (10/1)
**4568 Another Time** was never far away and ran a sound race. (10/1)
**2354 Polar Eclipse** led early in the straight, but had little more to give once headed. (20/1)

## 4827 PADDY HEFFERNAN MEMORIAL MAIDEN STKS (II) (3-Y.O) (Class D)

5-35 (5-41) **1m 2f 6y** £3,392.00 (£1,016.00: £488.00: £224.00) GOING: 0.09 sec per fur (G)

| | | | SP | RR | SF |
|---|---|---|---|---|---|
| $671^{5}$ | **Highland Gift (IRE)** (RCharlton) **3-8-9** RPerham(9) (hld up: hdwy 4f out: led gng wl 3f out: clr over 1f out: eased ins fnl f) .......... — | **1** | 9/2 $^{2}$ | 88+ | 27 |
| $1804^{2}$ | **Dancing Debut** (JHMGosden) **3-8-9** GHind(15) (hld up: hdwy 4f out: chsd wnr over 2f out: sn rdn: no imp) ....5 | **2** | 5/2 $^{1}$ | 80 | 19 |
| $4427^{9}$ | **Madame Steinlen (70)** (BWHills) **3-8-9** AMcGlone(14) (chsd ldrs: rdn & outpcd 3f out: styd on one pce ins fnl f) ..........5 | **3** | 11/1 | 72 | 11 |
| $4108^{4}$ | **Lacandona (USA)** (PWChapple-Hyam) **3-8-9** NAdams(16) (hld up: hdwy 4f out: hrd rdn 2f out: one pce) ....2½ | **4** | 8/1 | 68 | 7 |
| $4615^{6}$ | **Lady Joshua (IRE) (75)** (JLDunlop) **3-8-9b**$^{1}$ JStack(5) (took keen hld: chsd ldrs: rdn over 2f out: one pce)....hd | **5** | 15/2 $^{3}$ | 68 | 7 |
| $4617^{19}$ | **Forest Robin (84)** (RFJohnsonHoughton) **3-9-0** StephenDavies(11) (b: lw: chsd ldrs: rdn over 3f out: wknd over 2f out) ..........7 | **6** | 8/1 | 62 | 1 |
| | **Persuasion** (LordHuntingdon) **3-8-9** NCarlisle(1) (nvr nrr) ..........1 | **7** | 20/1 | 55 | — |
| | **Bold Buster** (IABalding) **3-9-0** CRutter(10) (unf: scope: bit bkwd: dwlt: nvr nrr) ..........8 | **8** | 20/1 | 47 | — |
| $4603^{6}$ | **Back By Dawn (47)** (DRCElsworth) **3-9-0** MTebbutt(8) (b.hind: a.p: led over 3f out: sn hdd: grad wknd) .......2½ | **9** | 50/1 | 43 | — |
| $576^{6}$ | **Tassili (IRE)** (LadyHerries) **3-9-0** NDay(12) (bit bkwd: a bhd) ..........3½ | **10** | 11/1 | 38 | — |
| $4613^{7}$ | **Alarico (FR)** (IPWilliams) **3-9-0** RPrice(3) (chsd ldrs tl wknd over 2f out) ..........8 | **11** | 66/1 | 25 | — |
| $4622^{6}$ | **Bonanza Peak (USA)** (MrsJCecil) **3-9-0** GBardwell(6) (lw: mid div: hrd rdn over 3f out: wknd over 2f out)....1¼ | **12** | 8/1 | 23 | — |
| | **Three Weeks** (WRMuir) **3-9-0** SDWilliams(4) (led tl over 3f out: sn wknd) ..........2½ | **13** | 66/1 | 19 | — |
| $4201^{10}$ | **Porlock Castle** (KRBurke) **3-9-0** DBiggs(7) (bhd fnl 5f: t.o) ..........18 | **14** | 66/1 | — | — |
| $2281^{W}$ | **Amazon Princess** (JFfitch-Heyes) **3-8-9** CNutter(13) (lt-f: a bhd: t.o) ..........dist | **15** | 66/1 | — | — |
| *$1656^{15}$* | ***Canadian Jive*** (DWPArbuthnot) **3-8-9** DeclanO'Shea(2) (b: b.hind: Withdrawn not under Starter's orders: burst out of stalls) .......... | **W** | 33/1 | — | — |
| | | | (SP 128.9%) | **15 Rn** | |

**2m 13.03** (9.23) CSF £15.86 TOTE £5.50: £2.30 £1.60 £1.70 (£4.90) Trio £20.40 OWNER Lord Weinstock/Exors of late S Weinstock (BECKHAMPTON) BRED Ballymacoll Stud Farm Ltd

**671 Highland Gift (IRE)**, the day's most impressive winner, was eased enormously in the final furlong and was probably value for three times the winning distance. She is still not the finished article and, bred to stay, should make up into a smart four-year-old. (9/2: op 3/1)
**1804 Dancing Debut**, although no match for the winner, still beat the rest emphatically and is improving. (5/2)
**4083 Madame Steinlen** kept on for third, but looked woefully one-paced. (11/1)
**4108 Lacandona (USA)** made a promising move early in the straight, but was making little progress in the final two furlongs. (8/1)
**4615 Lady Joshua (IRE)** was another to look slow. (15/2)
**4064 Forest Robin** is becoming increasingly disappointing and finds this trip stretching his stamina. (8/1)
**576 Tassili (IRE)** (11/1: 7/1-12/1)

T/Jkpt: £29,241.30 (0.39 Tckts); £25,122.89 to Doncaster 25/10/96. T/Plpt: £110.30 (233.23 Tckts). T/Qdpt: £10.80 (136.41 Tckts). SM

# 4607-NOTTINGHAM (L-H) (Good, Good to firm patches)

## Thursday October 24th

WEATHER: overcast WIND: almost nil

## 4828 KEGWORTH LIMITED STKS (0-65) (3-Y.O+) (Class F)

2-00 (2-01) **5f 13y** £2,381.00 (£656.00: £311.00) Stalls: High GOING minus 0.09 sec per fur (G)

| | | | SP | RR | SF |
|---|---|---|---|---|---|
| $4727^{7}$ | **Superbit (52)** (BAMcMahon) **4-9-3** SSanders(3) (chsd clr ldr: r.o u.p fnl f: led post) .......... — | **1** | 16/1 | 66 | 41 |
| 4727* | **Another Batchworth (61)** (EAWheeler) **4-9-3b** SWhitworth(6) (lw: led & sn clr: wknd fnl f: ct post)..........s.h | **2** | 5/2 $^{1}$ | 66 | 41 |
| *$4778^{3}$* | **Walk the Beat (64)** (MartynMeade) **6-8-13**(7) DSweeney(12) (lw: hdwy over 1f out: r.o wl fnl f) ..........s.h | **3** | 7/1 $^{3}$ | 69 | 44 |
| $4356^{2}$ | **Maraschino (42)** (BJMeehan) **3-8-11** GCarter(4) (chsd ldrs over 3f) ..........2 | **4** | 14/1 | 53 | 28 |
| $4610^{6}$ | **Lloc (49)** (CADwyer) **4-8-4**(7) JoHunnam(17) (b: led stands' side: rdn & edgd lft over 1f out: r.o) ..........½ | **5** | 9/1 | 52 | 27 |
| *$4776^{10}$* | **Smithereens (64)** (PTWalwyn) **3-8-11** JCarroll(15) (chsd ldrs stands' side: rdn & wnt lft 2f out: sn btn) .........1¾ | **6** | 14/1 | 46 | 21 |
| $4229^{7}$ | **Good To Talk (40)** (TDEasterby) **3-9-0** JFanning(7) (chsd ldrs: no imp fnl 2f) ..........½ | **7** | 25/1 | 48 | 23 |
| $4439^{5}$ | **Robellion (65)** (DWPArbuthnot) **5-9-6** TSprake(11) (b: prom 3f)..........hd | **8** | 11/1 | 53 | 28 |
| $4589^{2}$ | **Standown (65)** (JBerry) **3-9-3** JFortune(2) (in tch: no hdwy fnl 2f) ..........¾ | **9** | 15/2 | 48 | 23 |
| $4220^{4}$ | **Premium Gift (59)** (CBBBooth) **4-8-11** MBirch(9) (s.i.s: bhd tl r.o fnl f) ..........2 | **10** | 6/1 $^{2}$ | 36 | 11 |
| $3957^{10}$ | **Supreme Desire (23)** (MissJFCraze) **8-8-4**(7) CarolynBales(10) (bit bkwd: s.i.s: a bhd) ..........1¼ | **11** | 50/1 | 32 | 7 |
| $3937^{19}$ | **Polli Pui (37)** (WMBrisbourne) **4-8-4**(7) RFfrench(16) (a bhd)..........¾ | **12** | 50/1 | 29 | 4 |
| | **Carnival of Light (35)** (JSMoore) **4-9-0** DeanMcKeown(8) (bkwd: dwlt: a bhd) ..........¾ | **13** | 50/1 | 30 | 5 |
| $3957^{8}$ | **First Option (25)** (RBastiman) **6-8-13**(5)ow4 HBastiman(14) (t: a bhd)..........1¼ | **14** | 50/1 | 30 | 1 |
| *$3602^{5}$* | **Aljaz (64)** (MissGayKelleway) **6-9-3** KFallon(5) (b: in tch 3f) ..........4 | **15** | 10/1 | 16 | — |
| | **Grecian Garden (29)** (MrsLStubbs) **5-8-11** AClark(1) (bkwd: wnt lft s: racd alone far side: a bhd)..........5 | **16** | 50/1 | — | — |
| $4075^{23}$ | **Mister Sean (IRE) (35)** (JWPayne) **3-9-0b** RHughes(13) (swtg: virtually p.u fnl 2f)..........dist | **17** | 16/1 | — | — |
| | | | (SP 133.3%) | **17 Rn** | |

**61.7 secs** (3.10) CSF £56.43 TOTE £22.40: £5.20 £1.40 £4.70 (£29.10) Trio £82.60 OWNER Mr Neville Smith (TAMWORTH) BRED A. D. Bottomley

**4610 Superbit** had no right to reverse Redcar form with the runner-up on paper, but races are run on grass and his stamina proved decisive at the eleventh hour. (16/1)
**4727* Another Batchworth** again burnt her field off in the first couple of furlongs, but was flaking out in the final furlong and just failed to last home. This race took four seconds longer than the one at Redcar. (5/2)
**4778 Walk the Beat** does stay another furlong and found the post coming just too soon, despite putting in some sterling work. (7/1)
**4356 Maraschino** ran well here a second time, but was outpaced from the distance. (14/1)
**4610 Lloc** led the five on the stands' rail a merry dance, but was never living with the centre group. (9/1: op 14/1)
**4219 Smithereens** chased Lloc on the stands' rail until hanging as the pressure was applied. (14/1)

## 4829 RAINWORTH CLAIMING STKS (3-Y.O+) (Class F)

2-30 (2-34) **1m 54y** £2,381.00 (£656.00: £311.00) Stalls: Low GOING minus 0.09 sec per fur (G)

| | | | SP | RR | SF |
|---|---|---|---|---|---|
| $4691^{7}$ | **Holloway Melody (52)** (BAMcMahon) **3-8-9** GCarter(17) (bhd: hdwy 3f out: led ins fnl f: rdn out).......... — | **1** | 14/1 | 68 | 43 |

| Horse / Details | Dist | Pos | SP | RR | SF |
|---|---|---|---|---|---|
| 4691[11] **La Fille de Cirque (44)** (RJRWilliams) **4-8-6b[1]** RHills(3) (hdwy over 1f out: r.o wl ins fnl f) | 2½ | **2** | 20/1 | 57 | 35 |
| 4511[6] **Northern Celadon (IRE) (60)** (MJHeaton-Ellis) **5-8-11** AClark(15) (a.p: led over 4f out tl ins fnl f: no ex) | hd | **3** | 8/1 | 62 | 40 |
| 3808[11] **Absolute Ruler (IRE) (35)** (JLHarris) **5-8-7b** TSprake(6) (gd hdwy fnl 2f: r.o) | 1¾ | **4** | 25/1 | 55 | 33 |
| 1651[3] **Bold Angel (55)** (KAMorgan) **9-8-0**(7) RFfrench(1) (b: bkwd: swtg: prom: rdn 3f out: btn appr fnl f) | nk | **5** | 7/1[3] | 54 | 32 |
| 3978[8] **Paint It Black (65)** (RHannon) **3-8-10** SSanders(2) (swtg: in tch: rdn over 3f out: kpt on same pce) | 1½ | **6** | 10/1 | 57 | 32 |
| 4129[12] **Shanghai Lil (28)** (MJFetherston-Godley) **4-8-2** FNorton(13) (nvr nrr) | ½ | **7** | 50/1 | 45 | 23 |
| 4598[3] **Power Game (61)** (JBerry) **3-9-4b** JFortune(16) (nvr nrr) | ¾ | **8** | 9/2[1] | 63 | 38 |
| 4428[6] **Bold Habit (42)** (JPearce) **11-8-11v[1]** MBirch(12) (b.nr hind: r.o fnl 2f: nvr nrr) | ¾ | **9** | 20/1 | 51 | 29 |
| 4719[7] **Charlie Chang (IRE) (72)** (RHannon) **3-9-4** RHughes(7) (a.p: ev ch over 2f out: sn rdn: eased whn btn ins fnl f) | 2½ | **10** | 8/1 | 56 | 31 |
| 4686[27] **King Curan (USA) (66)** (DHaydnJones) **5-9-1b** LCharnock(9) (hdwy over 3f out: eased whn btn fnl f) | nk | **11** | 11/2[2] | 50 | 28 |
| 4701[16] **First Gold (54)** (JWharton) **7-8-13b** KFallon(10) (s.i.s: sme hdwy fnl 2f) | ½ | **12** | 20/1 | 47 | 25 |
| 2941[7] **Mystic Legend (IRE) (27)** (JJSheehan) **4-9-1** GDuffield(5) (swtg: stdd s: plld hrd: a bhd) | 3 | **13** | 50/1 | 43 | 21 |
| 4609[12] **Comeonup (50)** (JMBradley) **5-8-11** TWilliams(4) (b: chsd ldrs over 4f) | 4 | **14** | 20/1 | 31 | 9 |
| 4571[16] **Northern Judge (49)** (BHanbury) **3-9-0** MRimmer(18) (bhd: rdn over 3f out: nvr able to chal) | 2 | **15** | 8/1 | 33 | 8 |
| 4221[17] **Khattat (USA) (60)** (JAHarris) **6-8-11** DeanMcKeown(11) (prom tl wknd over 1f out: eased) | hd | **16** | 16/1 | 27 | 5 |
| 4082* **Richard House Lad (44)** (RHollinshead) **3-8-10** DHarrison(14) (lw: led over 3f: wknd over 1f out: eased) | 9 | **17** | 14/1 | 12 | — |
| 2971[12] **Daring Ryde (45)** (JPSmith) **5-8-13** JCarroll(8) (bit bkwd: bhd fnl 3f) | ¾ | **18** | 33/1 | 10 | — |
| | | | (SP 137.5%) | | **18 Rn** |

**1m 45.7** (4.40) CSF £258.58 TOTE £15.80: £3.00 £6.20 £2.90 (£154.10) Trio Not won; £314.23 to Doncaster 25/10/96 OWNER Mr R. Thornhill (TAMWORTH) BRED Robert Thornhill
WEIGHT FOR AGE 3yo-3lb
La Fille de Cirque clmd PHowling £5,000

**4360 Holloway Melody** failed to shine last time but, back over this course and distance, produced a good turn of foot to bounce back to her form of two outings ago. (14/1)
**2130 La Fille de Cirque**, quite keen in first-time blinkers, was settled in the rear. Quickening well towards the finish, the winner was already home and dry. (20/1)
**4511 Northern Celadon (IRE)**, whose best Turf form is all on softer ground, ran well on ground that appeared slightly slower than officially. (8/1)
**1828 Absolute Ruler (IRE)**, a poor mover, was putting in good work towards the finish as he does all too often, and remains a maiden. (25/1)
**1651 Bold Angel** looked to need this after nearly five months off, but often runs well fresh and showed up well for a long way. (7/1)
**3789 Paint It Black** looked well beaten when ridden along and slightly outpaced early in the straight, but kept plugging away until eased in the final strides. (10/1)
**4598 Power Game** (9/2: 4/1-6/1)
**4470 King Curan (USA)** (11/2: op 7/2)

## 4830 TOTE E.B.F. MAIDEN STKS (2-Y.O) (Class D)

3-00 (3-00) **1m 54y** £5,280.00 (£1,590.00: £770.00: £360.00) Stalls: Low GOING minus 0.09 sec per fur (G)

| Horse / Details | Dist | Pos | SP | RR | SF |
|---|---|---|---|---|---|
| 4204[3] **Over To You (USA)** (EALDunlop) **2-9-0** TSprake(11) (prom: edgd lft 2f out: led wl over 1f out: rdn out) | — | **1** | 14/1 | 77 | 35 |
| **Midnight Watch (USA)** (HRACecil) **2-9-0** KFallon(5) (lt-f: prom: led 2f out: sn hdd: r.o fnl f) | hd | **2** | 1/2[1] | 77 | 35 |
| 4723[18] **Nominator Lad** (BAMcMahon) **2-9-0** GCarter(6) (hdwy over 2f out: r.o ins fnl f) | 2½ | **3** | 14/1 | 72 | 30 |
| 4492[9] **Include Me Out** (JRFanshawe) **2-9-0** DHarrison(4) (swtg: rdn over 4f out: r.o fnl 2f: nt pce to chal) | 1¼ | **4** | 25/1 | 70 | 28 |
| **Lahab Nashwan** (MRChannon) **2-9-0** RHughes(8) (w'like: lengthy: prom: led over 4f out: hdd 2f out: eased whn btn ins fnl f) | 1¼ | **5** | 14/1 | 67 | 25 |
| 4508[2] **Nordic Crest (IRE)** (PWHarris) **2-9-0** AClark(9) (hdwy over 3f out: eased whn btn ins fnl f) | 5 | **6** | 13/2[3] | 57 | 15 |
| 4310[2] **Lawn Lothario** (MJohnston) **2-9-0** TWilliams(15) (swtg: led over 3f: rdn 3f out: wknd over 1f out) | 1 | **7** | 16/1 | 56 | 14 |
| **Little Acorn** (SCWilliams) **2-9-0** DRMcCabe(3) (w'like: bkwd: nvr nr to chal) | 1¼ | **8** | 33/1 | 53 | 11 |
| **Basman (IRE)** (BSmart) **2-9-0** SSanders(10) (leggy: unf: in tch: rdn over 3f out: sn btn) | 1¼ | **9** | 33/1 | 51 | 9 |
| 4584[3] **Mutabari (USA)** (DMorley) **2-9-0** RHills(14) (swtg: chsd ldrs: rdn & n.m.r 2f out: sn wknd) | ½ | **10** | 4/1[2] | 50 | 8 |
| 4756[17] **Secret Ballot (IRE)** (RHannon) **2-9-0** DeanMcKeown(1) (chsd ldrs over 3f) | 2 | **11** | 33/1 | 46 | 4 |
| 4700[6] **The Roundsills** (RFJohnsonHoughton) **2-9-0** GDuffield(12) (swtg: prom: rdn 3f out: sn wknd) | ¾ | **12** | 33/1 | 44 | 2 |
| **Crinolette (IRE)** (JHMGosden) **2-8-9** JCarroll(7) (lengthy: scope: s.s: a bhd) | 1¼ | **13** | 12/1 | 37 | — |
| 4705[11] **Keen Dancer** (MBell) **2-8-9**(5) GFaulkner(2) (plld hrd: bhd fnl 4f) | 3½ | **14** | 50/1 | 35 | — |
| **Pagel (IRE)** (RHollinshead) **2-9-0** JFortune(13) (lengthy: unf: bkwd: a bhd) | 13 | **15** | 33/1 | 10 | — |
| | | | (SP 154.1%) | | **15 Rn** |

**1m 47.0** (5.70) CSF £25.65 TOTE £16.30: £3.60 £1.20 £3.80 (£18.40) Trio £104.30 OWNER Maktoum Al Maktoum (NEWMARKET) BRED Charles Nuckols, Jr & Sons

**4204 Over To You (USA)** just got the better of a protracted duel with the runner-up, despite not entirely impressing with his attitude. (14/1)
**Midnight Watch (USA)**, a sparely-made daughter of May Hill Stakes winner Midnight Air, was being niggled along some way before striking the front. Quickly headed by the winner, she battled away and was coming back at the line. Given her lack of substance, she is not guaranteed to go on from this. (1/2)
**3919 Nominator Lad**, stepped up in trip, seemed to stay well, doing plenty of work in the last quarter-mile. (14/1)
**4261 Include Me Out** shaped like a horse who will do better over middle-distances. (25/1)
**Lahab Nashwan**, a rangy type who needs time, showed enough to suggest patience will be rewarded. (14/1)
**4508 Nordic Crest (IRE)** failed to progress from his first run, but was not knocked about. (13/2: op 10/1)
**4584 Mutabari (USA)** (4/1: op 7/1)
**Crinolette (IRE)** (12/1: op 8/1)

## 4831 NOTTINGHAM AMBASSADORS H'CAP (0-70) (3-Y.O+) (Class E)

3-30 (3-30) **1m 54y** £4,068.00 (£1,224.00: £592.00: £276.00) Stalls: Low GOING minus 0.09 sec per fur (G)

| Horse / Details | Dist | Pos | SP | RR | SF |
|---|---|---|---|---|---|
| 4436[6] **Polly Peculiar (60)** (BSmart) **5-9-4** TSprake(13) (hdwy over 3f out: led 1f out: qcknd & r.o wl) | — | **1** | 8/1[2] | 73 | 44 |
| 4238[14] **Myfontaine (63)** (KTIvory) **9-9-7** JCarroll(7) (b: gd hdwy over 1f out: fin wl) | 1¼ | **2** | 20/1 | 74 | 45 |
| 4202[8] **Kingchip Boy (63)** (MJRyan) **7-9-7v** AClark(17) (hld up: hdwy 4f out: ev ch over 2f out: one pce fnl f) | ¾ | **3** | 12/1 | 72 | 43 |
| 4674[9] **Baba Au Rhum (IRE) (61)** (IPWilliams) **4-8-12**(7) RFfrench(8) (chsd ldrs: outpcd over 2f out: r.o fnl f) | ½ | **4** | 16/1 | 69 | 40 |
| 4702[8] **Nosey Native (68)** (JPearce) **3-9-9** MWigham(18) (bhd tl r.o wl fnl f) | ¾ | **5** | 16/1 | 75 | 43 |
| 4560[4] **Tael of Silver (62)** (ABailey) **4-9-3**(3) DWright(14) (in tch: rdn 3f out: no imp) | 1 | **6** | 11/1 | 67 | 38 |

| Form | Horse / Details | Dist | Pos | SP | RR | SF |
|---|---|---|---|---|---|---|
| 4691[3] | **Kazimiera (IRE) (62)** (CWCElsey) **3-8-12**(5) GFaulkner(11) (swtg: a.p: led over 2f out to 1f out: one pce) | nk | **7** | 12/1 | 66 | 34 |
| 4582[4] | **Ron's Secret (67)** (JWPayne) **4-9-11** RHughes(1) (s.i.s: hdwy 3f out: nt clr run over 2f out: no ch after) | ¾ | **8** | 8/1[2] | 70 | 41 |
| 4550[15] | **Paojiunic (IRE) (65)** (LMCumani) **3-9-6** OUrbina(16) (lw: hld up: rdn 2f out: no rspnse) | hd | **9** | 12/1 | 68 | 36 |
| 4682[16] | **Balance of Power (70)** (RAkehurst) **4-10-0** SSanders(5) (swtg: in tch: lost pl & nt clr run 3f out: r.o fnl f) | 2½ | **10** | 12/1 | 68 | 39 |
| 4617[5] | **Apollono (69)** (JRFanshawe) **4-9-13** DHarrison(2) (hld up: hdwy over 3f out: n.m.r over 1f out: sn btn) | 2 | **11** | 6/1[1] | 63 | 34 |
| 4609[8] | **Euro Sceptic (IRE) (58)** (TDEasterby) **4-8-11**(5) GParkin(10) (prom over 6f) | 1 | **12** | 16/1 | 50 | 21 |
| 4606[9] | **Distinct Beauty (IRE) (64)** (WAO'Gorman) **3-9-5** EmmaO'Gorman(15) (swtg: in tch: c wd over 3f out: sn btn) | ¾ | **13** | 16/1 | 54 | 22 |
| 4098[5] | **Perilous Plight (64)** (MrsLStubbs) **5-9-8** KFallon(12) (in tch 6f: eased whn btn fnl f) | 2½ | **14** | 9/1[3] | 50 | 21 |
| 4775[21] | **Flying Pennant (IRE) (70)** (RHannon) **3-9-11** GCarter(6) (prom tl wknd wl over 1f out) | 1¼ | **15** | 14/1 | 53 | 21 |
| 4591[5] | **Brother Roy (66)** (TGMills) **3-9-7** JFortune(9) (bhd fnl 3f) | 1¼ | **16** | 10/1 | 47 | 15 |
| 2739[6] | **Spring Campaign (IRE) (67)** (MCPipe) **3-9-8** MBirch(4) (led tl hdd & wknd over 2f out) | 3 | **17** | 20/1 | 42 | 10 |
| 2320[12] | **Iceni (IRE) (64)** (HCandy) **3-9-5** GDuffield(3) (bit bkwd: plld hrd: prom tl n.m.r & wknd over 2f out) | 6 | **18** | 14/1 | 27 | — |

(SP 141.1%) **18 Rn**

**1m 46.5** (5.20) CSF £158.78 CT £1,838.27 TOTE £7.90: £3.70 £6.50 £5.40 £4.00 (£115.20) Trio £263.40; £189.24 to Doncaster 25/10/96 OWNER Miss Victoria Marshall (LAMBOURN) BRED Aston Park Stud

WEIGHT FOR AGE 3yo-3lb

**4436 Polly Peculiar**, off on terms this time, found a telling turn of foot once let down. (8/1)

**3981 Myfontaine** is a spring horse and has never won after June, but nearly broke that record here over an inadequate trip. (20/1)

**1685 Kingchip Boy**, having only his second race since June, moved poorly to post, but returned to form. (12/1)

**Baba Au Rhum (IRE)**, who began his career over hurdles, is lightly-raced and ought to find a race in this grade with normal improvement. (16/1)

**4559* Nosey Native**, over a shorter trip, only got going at the last moment, but finished as well as any. (16/1)

**4560 Tael of Silver**, forced to race quite wide throughout, could never land a blow. (11/1)

**4691 Kazimiera (IRE)**, cantering when she hit the front, soon came off the bridle and folded rather tamely once headed. (12/1)

## 4832 WOODBOROUGH H'CAP (0-80) (3-Y.O+) (Class D)

4-00 (4-00) **2m 9y** £4,305.00 (£1,290.00: £620.00: £285.00) Stalls: Low GOING minus 0.09 sec per fur (G)

| Form | Horse / Details | Dist | Pos | SP | RR | SF |
|---|---|---|---|---|---|---|
| 4750* | **Backwoods (59)** (WMBrisbourne) **3-8-2** 4x AGarth(2) (lw: hld up: hdwy over 3f out: led over 2f out: pushed out) | — | **1** | 6/1[3] | 71 | 15 |
| 4771[5] | **Sea Victor (75)** (JLHarris) **4-10-0** KFallon(5) (lw: a.p: rdn 3f out: ev ch fnl f: styd on) | hd | **2** | 9/2[1] | 87 | 41 |
| 4771[22] | **Paradise Navy (67)** (CREgerton) **7-9-6b** RHughes(4) (lw: hld up: hdwy over 3f out: chal on bit 1f out: nt qckn) | 1¼ | **3** | 12/1 | 78 | 32 |
| 4673[8] | **Izza (57)** (WStorey) **5-8-10** NKennedy(11) (hld up: plld hrd: hdwy over 2f out: r.o) | ¾ | **4** | 11/2[2] | 67 | 21 |
| 3922[5] | **Anglesey Sea View (56)** (ABailey) **7-8-6**(3) DWright(9) (s.i.s: sn prom: led over 3f out: hdd over 2f out: no ex) | 1¾ | **5** | 14/1 | 64 | 18 |
| 4604[8] | **Coleridge (50)** (JJSheehan) **8-8-3b** TWilliams(8) (s.s: hdwy after 4f: drvn along 6f out: sn lost pl: styd on appr fnl f) | 2 | **6** | 20/1 | 56 | 10 |
| 4365[5] | **The Swan (80)** (JLDunlop) **3-9-9** TSprake(12) (prom: plld hrd: rdn 3f out: wknd appr fnl f) | 2 | **7** | 9/1 | 84 | 28 |
| 4203[7] | **Classic Affair (USA) (64)** (RHarris) **3-8-7** AClark(3) (bhd: s.i.s: hld up: nvr nrr) | 1¼ | **8** | 14/1 | 67 | 11 |
| 4726* | **Broughtons Formula (46)** (WJMusson) **6-7-13b**ow1 4x DRMcCabe(7) (hld up: drvn along over 9f out: n.d) | 6 | **9** | 6/1[3] | 43 | — |
| 4596* | **Highfield Fizz (45)** (CWFairhurst) **4-7-12** LCharnock(13) (hld up: hdwy over 4f out: wknd over 2f out) | 2 | **10** | 12/1 | 40 | — |
| 3813[9] | **Tommy Cooper (43)** (MrsBarbaraWaring) **5-7-10** FNorton(1) (lw: prom: plld hrd: wknd 3f out) | ¾ | **11** | 33/1 | 37 | — |
| 4673[7] | **Mr Browning (USA) (65)** (RAkehurst) **5-9-4** SSanders(6) (led over 12f: sn rdn & btn) | 1¼ | **12** | 10/1 | 58 | 12 |
| 4476[3] | **Jelali (IRE) (58)** (DJGMurraySmith) **3-7-8**(7) RFfrench(14) (lw: mid div: rdn over 4f out: sn lost tch) | ¾ | **13** | 12/1 | 50 | — |
| *3422*[6] | **Mr Speculator (60)** (JEBanks) **3-8-3v** GDuffield(15) (hld up: hdwy 10f out: wknd over 2f out) | ½ | **14** | 20/1 | 52 | — |
| 4695[4] | **Diego (70)** (CEBrittain) **3-8-13** MBirch(10) (w ldr: rdn 4f out: sn lost pl) | 5 | **15** | 12/1 | 57 | 1 |

(SP 137.8%) **15 Rn**

**3m 36.5** (13.50) CSF £35.46 CT £311.53 TOTE £9.60: £3.40 £3.30 £2.70 (£31.30) Trio £90.20 OWNER Mr P. R. Kirk (NESSCLIFFE) BRED Sheikh Mohammed bin Rashid al Maktoum

LONG HANDICAP Tommy Cooper 7-7

WEIGHT FOR AGE 3yo-10lb

**4750* Backwoods** has done nothing but thrive since tackling a distance of ground. (6/1)

**4771 Sea Victor**, giving lots of weight away, lost nothing in defeat. (9/2)

**4604 Paradise Navy**, as he had done before, managed to turn victory into defeat. (12/1)

**4365 Izza** was never doing things quickly enough. (11/2)

**3922 Anglesey Sea View**, returning after a two-month break, just lacked another gear in the latter stages. (14/1)

**2857 Coleridge** retains ability, but is a moody individual. (20/1)

**4726* Broughtons Formula** was never travelling and may well have found the ground had too much cut for him. (6/1: op 4/1)

## 4833 ST ANNS MAIDEN STKS (3-Y.O+) (Class D)

4-30 (4-31) **1m 6f 15y** £4,175.00 (£1,250.00: £600.00: £275.00) Stalls: Low GOING minus 0.09 sec per fur (G)

| Form | Horse / Details | Dist | Pos | SP | RR | SF |
|---|---|---|---|---|---|---|
| 4722[2] | **Totem Dancer (70)** (JLEyre) **3-8-0**(7) RFfrench(14) (b.off hind: mid div: hdwy over 4f out: led 2f out: sn clr) | — | **1** | 9/1 | 82 | 44 |
| 2744[2] | **Sea of Stone (USA)** (LMCumani) **3-8-7** OUrbina(13) (hld up: stdy hdwy & nt clr run over 2f out: nvr plcd to chal: fin lame) | 10 | **2** | 6/1[2] | 71 | 33 |
| | **Dato Star (IRE) (89)** (JMJefferson) **5-9-7** KFallon(8) (lw: a.p: led over 2f out: sn hdd: eased whn btn fnl f) | hd | **3** | 6/5[1] | 76 | 47 |
| 4478[6] | **Mutanassib (IRE) (73)** (ACStewart) **3-8-12** RHills(1) (hld up: hdwy over 6f out: rdn & hung lft 2f out: no imp) | 1¾ | **4** | 12/1 | 74 | 36 |
| 4580[4] | **Bechstein (77)** (JLDunlop) **3-8-12b** GCarter(18) (hld up: nvr nr to chal) | 11 | **5** | 7/1[3] | 61 | 23 |
| 4613[4] | **Mr Wild (USA)** (BHanbury) **3-8-12** MRimmer(2) (b.nr hind: lw: led 1f: rdn & wknd over 2f out) | 1 | **6** | 12/1 | 60 | 22 |
| | **Siberian Henry** (BSmart) **3-8-12** SSanders(3) (hld up: hdwy over 3f out: wknd over 2f out) | 1¼ | **7** | 50/1 | 59 | 21 |
| 4429[5] | **Diamond Dance (IRE)** (JHMGosden) **3-8-7** JCarroll(11) (b: b.hind: trckd ldrs: rdn over 3f out: sn wknd) | 6 | **8** | 12/1 | 47 | 9 |
| 4070[17] | **Lady Swift (35)** (KWHogg) **5-8-9**(7) DSweeney(5) (nvr nrr) | 7 | **9** | 100/1 | 39 | 10 |
| 4613[3] | **Benning (USA)** (JHMGosden) **3-8-7** GDuffield(10) (b.hind: led after 1f: clr 10f out: hdd & wknd over 2f out) | 3 | **10** | 9/1 | 35 | — |

4615$^{5}$ **Annecy (USA) (70)** (HRACecil) **3-8-7** JFortune(4) (chsd ldrs: drvn along over 3f out: sn wknd)........................5 **11** 9/1 30 —
4611$^{5}$ **Magic Role (62)** (MAJarvis) **3-8-12** PBloomfield(12) (in tch: rdn over 4f out: wknd qckly over 2f out: t.o) ..........6 **12** 25/1 28 —
4763$^{9}$ **Lost Dream** (CADwyer) **7-9-2** CDwyer(16) (a bhd: t.o) ........................................................................¾ **13** 100/1 22 —
2610$^{11}$ **Filly Mignonne (IRE)** (BWHills) **3-8-4**$^{(3)}$ JDSmith(15) (lw: a bhd: t.o)............................................1½ **14** 20/1 20 —
**Come On In** (RDickin) **3-8-5**$^{(7)}$ PMundy(17) (a bhd: t.o).......................................................................dist **15** 100/1 — —
3584$^{8}$ **Young Rose (33)** (PatMitchell) **4-9-2** TSprake(9) (prom 6f: t.o)..................................................................dist **16** 100/1 — —
668$^{9}$ **Krasnik (IRE)** (MrsDHaine) **3-8-12** RHughes(7) (bhd fr ½-wy: virtually p.u fnl 2f: t.o)........................................19 **17** 100/1 — —
(SP 140.8%) **17 Rn**

**3m 5.7** (7.20) CSF £65.87 TOTE £8.80: £1.50 £3.10 £1.10 (£9.50) Trio £11.10 OWNER Diamond Racing Ltd (HAMBLETON) BRED Sheikh Mohammed Bin Rashid Al Maktoum
WEIGHT FOR AGE 3yo-9lb
STEWARDS' ENQUIRY Fallon susp. 2 & 4-5 & 7/11/96 (failure to obtain best possible placing).
**4722 Totem Dancer** is not very big, but gained due reward for some consistent performances. (9/1)
**2744 Sea of Stone (USA)**, returning after a lengthy break, only got going when the race was over, but unfortunately finished badly lame. (6/1)
**Dato Star (IRE)** looked fit enough beforehand and would have finished second but for his pilot dropping his hands. Even so, this was still disappointing. (6/5: 2/1-Evens)
**4478 Mutanassib (IRE)**, tackling his furthest trip to date, was still never doing things quickly enough. (12/1: op 8/1)
**4580 Bechstein** (7/1: op 9/2)

## 4834 HORSERACE BETTING LEVY BOARD MEDIAN AUCTION MAIDEN STKS (I) (2-Y.O) (Class F)
5-00 (5-00) **1m 1f 213y** £2,364.20 (£651.20: £308.60) Stalls: Low GOING minus 0.09 sec per fur (G)

SP RR SF
4041$^{2}$ **Supreme Sound** (PWHarris) **2-9-0** AClark(3) (trckd ldr: led over 3f out: sn clr: eased fnl f)............................— **1** 4/6$^{1}$ 67+ 6
4585$^{6}$ **Tommy Tortoise** (PFICole) **2-9-0** RHills(1) (lw: hld up: hdwy to chse wnr over 3f out: sn rdn: no imp)..........2½ **2** 5/2$^{2}$ 63 2
4599$^{9}$ **Tartan Party (65)** (PFICole) **2-9-0** KFallon(10) (s.i.s: pushed along 6f out: styd on appr fnl f: nvr nrr)..............3 **3** 7/1$^{3}$ 58 —
3874$^{8}$ **Le Grand Gousier (USA)** (RJRWilliams) **2-8-9**$^{(5)}$ LNewton(4) (chsd ldrs: rdn 3f out: styd on same pce)..........1 **4** 20/1 57 —
4361$^{9}$ **Foolish Flutter (IRE) (40)** (GROldroyd) **2-8-4v**$^{(5)}$ GParkin(7) (prom: rdn over 3f out: sn btn)..............................8 **5** 33/1 39 —
4599$^{11}$ **Such Presence** (KSBridgwater) **2-9-0** VSlattery(5) (hld up: rdn over 3f out: n.d)................................................3 **6** 33/1 39 —
4694$^{4}$ **Grovefair Lad (IRE) (57)** (BJMeehan) **2-9-0** SSanders(8) (led & sn clr: hdd over 3f out: sn rdn & wknd) ..........8 **7** 14/1 26 —
**Ryles Dancer** (DrJDScargill) **2-9-0** JFanning(6) (cmpt: bkwd: s.i.s: hld up: a in rr: t.o) ....................................10 **8** 20/1 10 —
(SP 123.1%) **8 Rn**

**2m 13.3** (10.80) CSF £3.14 TOTE £1.60: £1.00 £1.20 £2.80 (£2.30) Trio £3.30 OWNER Mrs P. W. Harris (BERKHAMSTED) BRED Pendley Farm
**4041 Supreme Sound** was made to look very good by some moderate opposition. (4/6)
**4585 Tommy Tortoise** is well named. (5/2)
**Tartan Party** owed his finishing position to his pilot, who was probably still smarting from the previous race. (7/1)
**Le Grand Gousier (USA)**, showing his first glimpse of form, will be sharper with this outing under his belt. He may need to drop to selling company to get off the mark. (20/1)

## 4835 HORSERACE BETTING LEVY BOARD MEDIAN AUCTION MAIDEN STKS (II) (2-Y.O) (Class F)
5-30 (5-30) **1m 1f 213y** £2,364.20 (£651.20: £308.60) Stalls: Low GOING minus 0.09 sec per fur (G)

SP RR SF
4625$^{16}$ **Indifferent Guy (80)** (CEBrittain) **2-9-0** DRMcCabe(1) (lw: led tl over 3f out: led over 2f out: all out) ..............— **1** 3/1$^{2}$ 68 4
4705$^{7}$ **High On Life** (ACStewart) **2-9-0** RHills(6) (hld up: hdwy over 2f out: ev ch fnl f: r.o) .........................................hd **2** 6/1$^{3}$ 68 4
4261$^{10}$ **Ramadour (IRE)** (JRFanshawe) **2-9-0** DHarrison(8) (bit bkwd: hld up: hdwy over 3f out: rdn & ev ch wl over 1f out: styd on same pce)........................................................................................................3 **3** 13/2 63 —
4508$^{7}$ **Walk On By** (RHannon) **2-9-0** JCarroll(3) (chsd wnr: led over 3f out: hdd over 2f out: no ex fnl f)......................½ **4** 9/1 62 —
**Abajany** (MRChannon) **2-9-0** RHughes(5) (cmpt: bkwd: s.i.s: hld up: hdwy over 2f out: styd on u.p)..............hd **5** 11/1 62 —
4106$^{11}$ **Dive Master (IRE) (52)** (CMurray) **2-9-0b**$^{1}$ JFortune(2) (chsd ldrs tl hrd rdn & wknd over 1f out) .....................nk **6** 20/1 62 —
4618$^{6}$ **Trooper** (PFICole) **2-9-0** TSprake(9) (lw: hld up: hdwy over 3f out: hrd rdn & ev ch 2f out: sn btn) ................d.h **6** 13/8$^{1}$ 62 —
4694$^{7}$ **Hopperetta (55)** (BPalling) **2-8-9** GDuffield(7) (mid div: hdwy over 4f out: wknd over 2f out) .............................3 **8** 33/1 52 —
4458$^{3}$ **Swiftway** (KWHogg) **2-8-7**$^{(7)}$ DSweeney(4) (prom: plld hrd: hung rt & rn out 7f out: sn p.u) ............................. **P** 8/1 — —
(SP 127.9%) **9 Rn**

**2m 13.5** (11.00) CSF £22.34 TOTE £3.60: £1.40 £2.00 £1.80 (£14.90) Trio £83.50 OWNER Mr W. J. Gredley (NEWMARKET) BRED Stetchworth Park Stud Ltd
**OFFICIAL EXPLANATION Swiftway: the bit slipped through the gelding's mouth.**
**4261 Indifferent Guy** clearly stays well, but will not forget this in a hurry. (3/1)
**High On Life**, having learnt from his debut, would have made it in another couple of strides. (6/1: op 4/1)
**Ramadour (IRE)** finished closer to the winner this time, but looked woefully one-paced in the latter stages. (13/2)
**Walk On By** may well still have needed this. (9/1)
**Abajany**, quite a stocky individual, has plenty of stamina in his pedigree. (11/1)

T/Plpt: £586.20 (17.59 Tckts). T/Qdpt: £22.30 (40.56 Tckts) Dk/KH

## 4836a-4845a (Irish Racing) - See Computer Raceform

# 4638a-CURRAGH (Newbridge, Ireland) (R-H) (Yielding to soft)
## Saturday October 19th

## 4846a JUDDMONTE BERESFORD STKS (Gp 3) (2-Y.O)
2-55 (2-58) **1m** £19,500.00 (£5,700.00: £2,700.00: £900.00) GOING: 0.53 sec per fur (GS)

SP RR SF
4398a$^{5}$ **Johan Cruyff** (APO'Brien,Ireland) **2-8-12**$^{ow1}$ CRoche (hld up: chal over 2f out: led wl over 1f out: pushed clr: r.o) ........................................................................................................— **1** 1/2$^{1}$ 92+ 43
**Cambodian (USA)** (JSBolger,Ireland) **2-8-11** KJManning (chsd ldrs: chal over 2f out: led briefly over 1f out: no ex fnl f) ........................................................................................................2 **2** 7/1$^{3}$ 87 39
4027a$^{3}$ **Quws** (KPrendergast,Ireland) **2-8-11** WJSupple (broke wl: hld up towards rr: chal over 1f out: 3rd 1f out: kpt on u.p) ........................................................................................................s.h **3** 8/1 87 39

4642a[5] **Moon Flower (IRE)** (APO'Brien,Ireland) **2-8-8** JAHeffernan (sn led: jnd & rdn over 2f out: hdd over 1f out: 4th & btn 1f out)....4 **4** 16/1 76 28
**Animagic (IRE)** (CCollins,Ireland) **2-8-11** SCraine (led briefly early: chsd ldr: chal & ev ch early st: rdn over 2f out: 4th & btn over 1f out)....2 **5** 5/1[2] 75 27
(SP 112.8%) **5 Rn**

**1m 44.3** (9.30) OWNER Mrs John Magnier (PILTOWN)
**4398a Johan Cruyff** accomplished a relatively simple task with some aplomb. Held up in fourth place, he challenged over two furlongs out and, leading 200 yards later, ran on well. He could make up into a very useful performer. (1/2: op 5/4)
**Cambodian (USA)** ran well for a maiden, considering he had only made his first appearance four days previously. Gaining the advantage briefly a furlong and a half out, he had no chance with the winner at these weights. (7/1: op 5/2)
**4027a Quws**, a real drifter in the market, could find no extra in third place throughout the final furlong. (8/1: op 3/1)
**4642a Moon Flower (IRE)** made the running, but was a beaten fourth with a furlong to run. (16/1)
**Animagic (IRE)**, who chased the leader, flattered briefly in the straight, but was a beaten fourth once the pressure was turned on over a furlong out. (5/1: op 2/1)

## 4848a WATERFORD TESTIMONIAL STKS (Listed) (3-Y.O+)
3-55 (3-56) **6f** £9,675.00 (£2,775.00: £1,275.00: £375.00) GOING: 0.53 sec per fur (GS)

SP RR SF

2459a[9] **Ger's Royale (IRE)** (PJFlynn,Ireland) **5-9-0** MJKinane (hld up: hdwy 2f out: chal over 1f out: led ins fnl f: rdn clr: r.o)....— **1** 100/30[2] 110+ 54
4649a[4] **Burden Of Proof (IRE)** (CO'Brien,Ireland) **4-8-11**ow1 CRoche (hmpd early: hld up: led over 1f out: hdd ins fnl f: no ex)....2½ **2** 2/1[1] 100 43
**Orange Grouse (IRE)** (LBrowne,Ireland) **3-8-6** JPSpencer (cl up: 4th ½-wy: rdn & ev ch fr 2f out: no ex 1f out: kpt on u.p)....nk **3** 20/1 96 39
4518[3] **Anzio (IRE)** (MissGayKelleway) **5-9-3b** RCochrane (chsd ldrs: 6th ½-wy: rdn over 1f out: n.m.r & kpt on ins fnl f)....1½ **4** 7/2[3] 102 46
4660a[10] **Ailleacht (USA)** (JSBolger,Ireland) **4-8-11** KJManning (prom: 2nd & rdn 2f out: no ex over 1f out)....3½ **5** 8/1 86 30
**Tinker Amelia** (JGMcDonnell,Ireland) **4-8-7** JoannaMorgan (sn led: hdd over 1f out: no ex)....¾ **6** 50/1 80 24
4396a[8] **Sir Silver Sox (USA)** (TStack,Ireland) **4-8-10b** PJSmullen (chsd ldrs: rdn & no imp over 1f out: kpt on)....s.h **7** 20/1 83 27
4396a* **Wandering Thoughts (IRE)** (PJFlynn,Ireland) **7-9-0** NGMcCullagh (cl up: 2nd ½-wy: rdn & btn over 1f out)....3½ **8** 8/1 78 22
(SP 112.3%) **8 Rn**

**1m 16.8** (6.30) OWNER Mrs Patrick Flynn (CARRICK-ON-SUIR)
**4644a* Ger's Royale (IRE)** gained his sixth course win in good style. In front early inside the last, he ran on strongly to go clear. (100/30)
**4649a Burden Of Proof (IRE)**, with everything in his favour, again disappointed. He got his head in front over a furlong out, but was totally outpaced by the winner. (2/1)
**Orange Grouse (IRE)** put up a much-improved performance, holding every chance from two furlongs out and battling on under pressure. (20/1)
**4518 Anzio (IRE)** had only two behind him at halfway and was being ridden to close within the leaders over a furlong out. He did not enjoy anything like a clear passage, although running on inside the last. (7/2)

## 4849a BLANDFORD STKS (Gp 2) (3-Y.O+)
4-30 (4-30) **1m 3f** £26,000.00 (£7,600.00: £3,600.00: £1,200.00) GOING: 0.53 sec per fur (GS)

SP RR SF

4268a* **Predappio** (JOxx,Ireland) **3-8-7** PShanahan (led briefly early: hld up in tch: 3rd & chal over 2f out: led over 1f out: rdn & styd on)....— **1** 9/2[3] 117 15
4371[4] **Sanoosea (USA)** (MRStoute) **4-9-0** RCochrane (sn chsng ldr: chal & ev ch 2f out: styd on)....1 **2** 7/2[2] 117 20
**Mohaajir (USA)** (JSBolger,Ireland) **5-9-0** KJManning (hld up in tch: 3rd 4f out: chal over 2f out: 3rd ins fnl f: styd on)....nk **3** 11/2 116 20
4654a[3] **Zafzala (IRE)** (JOxx,Ireland) **3-8-4** PJSmullen (hld up: hdwy & 6th over 3f out: chal 2f out: 3rd & u.p 1f out: kpt on same pce)....1 **4** 6/4[1] 111 10
4397a[5] **I'm Supposin (IRE)** (KPrendergast,Ireland) **4-9-0** WJSupple (hld up: 6th 4f out: nt rch ldrs over 1f out: styd on ins fnl f)....s.h **5** 7/1 115 19
4643a[9] **Gan Saru** (PJFlynn,Ireland) **3-8-7** NGMcCullagh (towards rr: rdn & lost tch over 2f out: no imp)....8 **6** 12/1 102 2
2474a[9] **Humbel (USA)** (DKWeld,Ireland) **4-9-0b**[1] MJKinane (sn led: hdd 2f out: rdn & wknd)....½ **7** 6/1 102 8
(SP 130.3%) **7 Rn**

**2m 30.3** (16.30) OWNER Sheikh Mohammed (CURRABEG)
**4268a* Predappio**, always in touch, led over a furlong out and stayed on well under pressure. His rider subsequently received a severe caution for his use of the whip. (9/2: op 3/1)
**4371 Sanoosea (USA)** raced in second place and challenged from two furlongs out. Holding every chance inside the last, he could just keep on at the one pace. (7/2)
**Mohaajir (USA)** threw down his challenge over the last quarter-mile and went third inside the last, but could not quicken. (11/2)
**4654a Zafzala (IRE)**, whose recent French efforts might have taken their toll, was under pressure in third place a furlong out and made to look very one-paced by her winning stable-companion. (6/4)
**4644a I'm Supposin (IRE)**, chasing the leaders when under pressure early in the straight, never looked likely to get on terms, despite staying on inside the last. He really does not seem to have an optimum distance. (7/1)

## 4851a DIAMOND STKS (Listed) (3-Y.O+ F & M)
5-30 (5-32) **1m 2f** £9,675.00 (£2,775.00: £1,275.00: £375.00)

SP RR SF

4738a* **French Ballerina (IRE)** (PJFlynn,Ireland) **3-8-12** MJKinane (hld up in tch: 3rd st: chal over 2f out: led over 1f out: sn drifted lft: rdn & r.o)....— **1** 4/5[1] 108 57
2825a[9] **Asmara (USA)** (JOxx,Ireland) **3-8-8** PJSmullen (cl up: led wl over 2f out: hdd, rdn & hmpd over 1f out: rallied ins fnl f: wnt 2nd cl home)....1½ **2** 9/1 102 51
4397a[8] **Viaticum (IRE)** (NMeade,Ireland) **4-9-0b** JoannaMorgan (hld up: hdwy on outside 4f out: chal over 2f out: disp ld & ev ch 1f out: no ex ins fnl f: kpt on same pce)....nk **3** 3/1[2] 102 56
4738a[2] **Inchacooley (IRE)** (MBrassil,Ireland) **4-9-0** KJManning (hld up towards rr: hdwy early st: chal 2f out: kpt on same pce fr over 1f out)....3½ **4** 7/1[3] 97 51
**Unassisted (IRE)** (VBowens,Ireland) **3-8-8** NGMcCullagh (chsd ldr early: cl up: 4th ½-wy: rdn & lost tch over 3f out: n.d)....13 **5** 50/1 75 24

| | | | | | SP | RR | SF |
|---|---|---|---|---|---|---|---|
| | **Cashel Princess (IRE)** (APO'Brien,Ireland) **3-8-8** JAHeffernan (led tl over 2f out: sn wknd) | ½ | **6** | | 16/1 | 74 | 23 |
| | | | | | (SP 110.9%) | | **6 Rn** |

**2m 14.2** (10.20) OWNER Mrs John Magnier (CARRICK-ON-SUIR)
**4738a* French Ballerina (IRE)**, challenging from over two furlongs out, drifted left over a furlong out and, despite inconveniencing the runner-up, was allowed to keep the race. She will stay further than this and could make an Irish St Leger filly next season. (4/5)
**1255a Asmara (USA)** had an unlucky run. In front in the straight, she was headed a furlong out and lost her place when hampered by the winner. Battling back under pressure, she stayed on to go second close home. (9/1: op 5/1)
**4644a Viaticum (IRE)** had every chance a furlong out, but found little inside the last. (3/1)
**4738a Inchacooley (IRE)** challenged two furlongs out, but finds this trip just a bit too far for her. (7/1)
NR

## 2476a-LYON PARILLY (Lyon, France) (Good)
### Monday October 14th

### 4852a PRIX GENY COURSES (Listed) (3-Y.O+)
3-15 (3-15) **1m 4f** £26,350.00 (£9,486.00: £4,743.00)

| | | | | SP | RR | SF |
|---|---|---|---|---|---|---|
| | **Trait De Genie (FR)** (ALyon,France) **4-8-13** MCesandri | — | **1** | | 118 | — |
| 3597[3] | **Taufan's Melody** (LadyHerries) **5-9-2** RCochrane | 2 | **2** | | 118 | — |
| | **Peckinpah's Soul (FR)** (DSmaga,France) **4-9-2** FHead | 1½ | **3** | | 116 | — |
| | | | | | | **14 Rn** |

**2m 30.0** P-M 7.90F: 4.30F 2.10F 2.40F (64.50F) OWNER Mr J. Bouchara BRED Comtesse Bertrand de Tarragon
**3597 Taufan's Melody**, carrying top weight, put up a good display here. However, he had no answer to the winner when challenged and had to admit defeat inside the final furlong. He may return to France for the Grand Prix de Nantes.

## FONTAINEBLEAU (France) (Soft)
### Tuesday October 15th

### 4853a PRIX NICEAS (Listed) (4-Y.O+)
3-15 (3-23) **1m 2f** £18,445.00 (£6,324.00: £3,953.00)

| | | | | SP | RR | SF |
|---|---|---|---|---|---|---|
| 4326[2] | **Inquisitor (USA)** (JHMGosden) **4-8-11** LDettori | — | **1** | /1 | 117 | — |
| | **Mister Alleged (USA)** (France) **5-8-11** CHanotel | 2½ | **2** | | 113 | — |
| 3386a[2] | **Diamond Mix (IRE)** (AFabre,France) **4-9-2** TJarnet | ¾ | **3** | | 117 | — |
| | | | | (SP 100.0%) | | **8 Rn** |

**0m** OWNER Mr K. Abdullah (NEWMARKET) BRED Juddmonte Farms
**4326 Inquisitor (USA)**, waited with at the head of the field, repelled all attacks in the straight. Given his liking for the soft ground, he has been hard to place and difficult to train. He is now off to the Sales. (/1)

## 3752a-GELSENKIRCHEN-HORST (Gelsenkirchen, Germany) (R-H) (Soft)
### Saturday October 19th

### 4854a NEREIDE-RENNEN (Listed) (3-Y.O+ F & M)
2-43 (2-44) **1m 2f** £9,009.00 (£3,604.00: £1,802.00)

| | | | | SP | RR | SF |
|---|---|---|---|---|---|---|
| | **First Smile (GER)** (HJentzsch,Germany) **3-8-13** PSchiergen | — | **1** | | 99 | — |
| 4297[4] | **Ground Game** (DRLoder) **3-8-5** DRMcCabe | hd | **2** | | 91 | — |
| | **Tippolina (GER)** (ALowe,Germany) **3-8-5** ABest | 3 | **3** | | 86 | — |
| | | | | | | **11 Rn** |

**2m 12.3** TOTE 32DM: 15DM 32DM 18DM OWNER Gestut Ittlingen BRED Gestut Hof Ittlingen
**4297 Ground Game** set the early pace and found extra when she was challenged from two furlongs out, but she was unable to keep up the pace and was headed in the final 25 yards.

## 4659a-DUSSELDORF (Germany) (R-H)
### Sunday October 20th

### 4855a PREIS DER SPIELBANKEN DES LANDES NORDRHEIN-WESTFALEN (Gp 3) (3-Y.O+)
3-40 (3-44) **1m 4f** £22,523.00

| | | | | SP | RR | SF |
|---|---|---|---|---|---|---|
| 4413a[2] | **Protektor (GER)** (ALowe,Germany) **7-9-6** THellier | — | **1** | | 123 | — |
| 4413a[6] | **Mongol Warrior (USA)** (LordHuntingdon) **3-8-12** DHarrison | 1¾ | **2** | | 120 | — |
| 4413a[7] | **Caballo (GER)** (HJentzsch,Germany) **5-8-11** PSchiergen | 6 | **3** | | 104 | — |
| | | | | | | **12 Rn** |

**2m 41.2** TOTE 28DM: 13DM 13DM 17DM OWNER Mr D. Joswich BRED Frau H. Liesten
**4413a Mongol Warrior (USA)** set the pace for the first furlong. Disputing the lead again from four furlongs out, he was headed a furlong out but ran on under pressure.

## 4742a-LONGCHAMP (Paris, France) (R-H) (Soft)
### Sunday October 20th

### 4856a PRIX DE CONSEIL DE PARIS (Gp 2) (3-Y.O+)
2-10 (2-10) **1m 4f** £39,526.00 (£15,810.00: £7,905.00: £3,953.00) GOING: 0.30 sec per fur (G)

| | | | | SP | RR | SF |
|---|---|---|---|---|---|---|
| 4654a* | **Annaba (IRE)** (JHMGosden) **3-8-10** LDettori (trckd ldr: rdn to ld 2½f out: r.o wl) | — | **1** | | 120 | 41 |

| | | | | | |
|---|---|---|---|---|---|
| 4040a[7] | **Poliglote** (MmeCHead,France) **4-9-6** FHead (led: qcknd 5f out: rdn & hdd 2½f out: styd on) ....2 | **2** | | 120 | 48 |
| 1577a[2] | **Rainbow Dancer (FR)** (PBary,France) **5-9-2** TJarnet (racd in 4th: styd on one pce fnl 2f) ....2½ | **3** | | 113 | 41 |
| 4656a[2] | **Percutant** (DSmaga,France) **5-9-4** DBoeuf (racd in 3rd: nvr able to chal) ....2 | **4** | | 112 | 40 |
| 3915a[6] | **Oliviero (FR)** (AVergeade,France) **3-8-9b** GMosse (in rr: swtchd lft 2f out: sn one pce) ....nk | **5** | | 110 | 31 |
| 4410a* | **Running Flame (FR)** (JEHammond,France) **4-9-4** SGuillot (hld up in rr: nvr nr to chal) ....1 | **6** | | 111 | 39 |
| 4656a[11] | **Punishment** (CEBrittain) **5-9-2** BDoyle (in rr: rdn & btn 2½f out) ....5 | **7** | | 102 | 30 |
| | | | | | **7 Rn** |

**2m 37.38** (11.38) P-M 2.10F: 1.40F 1.90F OWNER Sheikh Mohammed (NEWMARKET) BRED Sheikh Mohammed Bin Rashid Al Maktoum
**4654a* Annaba (IRE)** took over from the long-time leader Poliglote early in the straight and won comfortably. She has possibly finished for the season, but may stay in training. She is an autumn filly and appreciated the soft ground here.
**4656a Punishment** was never close enough to put in a challenge and was beaten some way out.

## 4857a PRIX DE LA FORET (Gp 1) (3-Y.O+ C & F)
2-45 (2-49) **7f** £65,876.00 (£26,350.00: £13,175.00: £6,588.00) GOING: 0.30 sec per fur (G)

| | | | SP | RR | SF |
|---|---|---|---|---|---|
| 4409a[2] | **A Magicman (FR)** (HSteguweit,Germany) **4-9-2** ASuborics (in rr: hdwy & 4th st: swtchd lft 2f out: led ins fnl f: jst hld on) ....— | **1** | 225/10 | 125 | 79 |
| 4057[7] | **Miesque's Son (USA)** (JEHammond,France) **4-9-2** CAsmussen (mid div: hdwy 2½f out: swtchd lft over 1f out: fin wl: jst failed) ....hd | **2** | 41/10[3] | 125 | 79 |
| 4664a[2] | **Shaanxi (USA)** (ELellouche,France) **4-8-13** OPeslier (mid div: rdn 1½f out: styd on wl fnl f: nt rch ldrs) ....¾ | **3** | 16/10[1] | 120 | 74 |
| 4417a* | **Zarannda (IRE)** (AdeRoyerDupre,France) **3-8-11** GMosse (hld up in rr: hdwy 3f out: n.m.r 1½f out: r.o wl fnl f: nvr nrr) ....1½ | **4** | 34/10[2] | 117 | 69 |
| 4378* | **Tagula (IRE)** (IABalding) **3-9-0** KDarley (a.p: disp ld ent st: led 2f out tl ins fnl f: one pce) ....1½ | **5** | 46/10 | 116 | 68 |
| 3083[6] | **Inzar (USA)** (PFICole) **4-9-2** TQuinn (trckd ldrs: disp ld 2½f out to 2f out: wknd fnl f) ....nk | **6** | 38/1 | 116 | 70 |
| 4664a[7] | **Blackwater (USA)** (MZilber,France) **3-9-0** LDettori (prom: rdn 1½f out: unable qckn) ....s.h | **7** | 14/1 | 115 | 67 |
| 1581a[7] | **General Monash (USA)** (CLaffon-Parias,France) **4-9-2** ODoleuze (mid div: rdn & one pce fnl 2f) ....3 | **8** | 24/1 | 109 | 63 |
| 4030a* | **Rising Colours** (PDemercastel,France) **3-9-0** AJunk (a in rr) ....3 | **9** | 20/1 | 102 | 54 |
| 4417a[2] | **Winning Smile (FR)** (TClout,France) **6-9-2b** SGuillot (a bhd) ....4 | **10** | 20/1 | 93 | 47 |
| | **Hamirpour (IRE)** (AdeRoyerDupre,France) **3-9-0** EAlloix (set str pce to 2½f out: wknd qckly) .... | **11** | 34/10[2] | — | — |
| | | | (SP 148.4%) | | **11 Rn** |

**1m 22.8** (3.80) P-M 23.50F: 3.60F 1.60F 1.30F (59.10F) OWNER Stall Dagobert BRED H. Voegele & Maria Koenig
**IN-FOCUS: For betting purposes Zarannda (IRE) and Hamipour (IRE) were cpld**
**4033a A Magicman (FR)** held on well in a close finish to give his trainer the first Group One success of his career. (225/10)
**4057 Miesque's Son (USA)** ran well and there were no excuses, but he may well have won in another stride. He now retires to stud. (41/10)
**4378* Tagula (IRE)** took the lead with two furlongs to run, but lacked the speed to take a hand in the finish. Connections believe the ground may have been a little soft for him. He may either go on to race in Hong Kong or be retired to stud. (46/10)
**3083 Inzar (USA)**, like Tagula, was up with the pace, but failed to find the necessary speed in the closing stages. (38/1)

# 4744a-SAN SIRO (Milan, Italy) (R-H) (Heavy)
## Sunday October 20th

## 4858a PREMIO BAGUTTA-MEMORIAL SERGIO CUMANI (Gp 3) (3-Y.O+ F & M)
2-15 (2-28) **1m** £26,674.00 (£12,454.00: £7,004.00)

| | | | SP | RR | SF |
|---|---|---|---|---|---|
| 2843a[9] | **Lara (GER)** (BSchutz,Germany) **4-8-11**ow1 AStarke ....— | **1** | | 108 | — |
| 4541a[10] | **Bemont Park (ITY)** (RBrogi,Italy) **5-8-12** GBietolini ....s.nk | **2** | | 109 | — |
| | **Niniska (GER)** (AWohler,Germany) **3-8-7** ABoschert ....1¼ | **3** | | 104 | — |
| 4312[4] | **Wardara** (CADwyer) **4-8-9** SDrowne (btn over 39l) .... | **9** | | — | — |
| | | | | | **9 Rn** |

**1m 43.3** (13.30) TOTE 28L: 14L 20L 26L (114L) OWNER Gestut Brummerhof BRED Dr C. Burmester
**4312 Wardara** raced in fifth place as the field turned into the straight, but soon weakened. She will stay in Italy to be trained by Valfredo Valiani.

## 4859a GRAN CRITERIUM (Gp 1) (2-Y.O C & F)
3-45 (3-56) **1m** £65,387.00 (£35,195.00: £21,082.00: £10,541.00)

| | | | SP | RR | SF |
|---|---|---|---|---|---|
| 4666a* | **Hello (IRE)** (JLDunlop) **2-8-11** FJovine (mid div: brought wd: led 2f out: r.o wl) ....— | **1** | | 98 | — |
| 4386* | **Panama City (USA)** (PWChapple-Hyam) **2-8-11** JReid (led 1f: 3rd st: lost pl wl over 2f out: r.o wl fnl f) ....3½ | **2** | | 91 | — |
| 4471[3] | **Ivan Luis (FR)** (MBell) **2-8-11v**[1] MRoberts (prom: led 4f out to 2f out: kpt on one pce) ....s.nk | **3** | | 91 | — |
| 4471* | **Further Outlook (USA)** (MRStoute) **2-8-11** KFallon (prom: wnt 2nd over 2f out: sn rdn & btn) ....3¾ | **4** | | 83 | — |
| 4661a[3] | **Family Tradition (IRE)** (APO'Brien,Ireland) **2-8-8** CRoche (hld up: nvr nr to chal) ....1½ | **5** | | 77 | — |
| | **Golden Aventura (IRE)** (GFratini,Italy) **2-8-11** GBietolini (led after 1f to 4f out: 2nd st: wknd over 2f out) ....6¾ | **6** | | 67 | — |
| | **Woods of Cisterna (IRE)** (LCamici,Italy) **2-8-11** MPasquale (prom 4f: 6th st: sn wknd) ....s.nk | **7** | | 66 | — |
| | **War Declaration (IRE)** (BGrizzetti,Italy) **2-8-11** MTellini (gd prog over 2f out: wknd qckly over 1f out) ....¾ | **8** | | 65 | — |
| | **Golden Blushing (USA)** (GFratini,Italy) **2-8-11** EBotti (a in rr) ....3 | **9** | | 59 | — |
| 4666a[3] | **Kingsinger (IRE)** (PCeriotti,Italy) **2-8-11** AParravani (a in rr) ....¾ | **10** | | 57 | — |
| | | | | | **10 Rn** |

**1m 44.6** (14.60) TOTE 21L: 14L 20L 34L (82L) OWNER Mr P. Wroughton (ARUNDEL) BRED H Volz
**4666a* Hello (IRE)** raced in mid-division and was in fifth place turning into the straight. He was brought wide and made steady progress to lead over two furlongs out and ran on well.
**4386* Panama City (USA)** led for the first furlong and raced in third place into the straight. He then lost his place well over two furlongs out, but ran on well in the final furlong. He will return to challenge for the Premio Guido Berardelli in Rome during November.
**4471 Ivan Luis (FR)** led from four furlongs out to two furlongs out, and kept on at one pace in the closing stages.
**4471* Further Outlook (USA)** raced in fourth position into the straight and took second place over two furlongs out, but was soon ridden and beaten.

## 4189-DONCASTER (L-H) (Good, St crse Good to firm patches)
**Friday October 25th**
WEATHER: overcast WIND: mod against

### 4860 OCTOBER APPRENTICE H'CAP (0-70) (3-Y.O) (Class E)
2-00 (2-04) **7f** £4,068.00 (£1,224.00: £592.00: £276.00) Stalls: High GOING minus 0.05 sec per fur (G)

| | Horse | Dist | Pos | SP | RR | SF |
|---|---|---|---|---|---|---|
| 4499[3] | **Really A Dream (IRE) (67)** (MRStoute) **3-9-4** FLynch(13) (lw: hld up stands' side: swtchd lft ½-wy: r.o to ld ins fnl f) | — | 1 | 11/1[3] | 81 | 41 |
| 4376[12] | **Waypoint (70)** (RCharlton) **3-9-2**(5) RBrisland(4) (mde most far side tl hdd & no ex ins fnl f) | 3 | 2 | 12/1 | 77 | 37 |
| 4430[18] | **Myttons Mistake (62)** (ABailey) **3-8-8**(5) RStudholme(8) (a chsng ldrs far side: nt qckn fnl f) | s.h | 3 | 33/1 | 69 | 29 |
| 4598[10] | **Polar Refrain (53)** (CADwyer) **3-8-1**(3) JoHunnam(5) (chsd ldrs far side: nt qckn appr fnl f) | ½ | 4 | 12/1 | 59 | 19 |
| 4701* | **Silver Harrow (59)** (AGNewcombe) **3-8-10** [6x] DGriffiths(6) (racd far side: hdwy 3f out: styd on) | 3 | 5 | 11/1[3] | 58 | 18 |
| 3973[5] | **Finisterre (IRE) (64)** (JJO'Neill) **3-9-1** DaneO'Neill(2) (prom far side: rdn over 2f out: btn over 1f out) | nk | 6 | 14/1 | 62 | 22 |
| 4768[8] | **Classy Chief (68)** (RBoss) **3-9-2**(3) GFaulkner(10) (dwlt: racd far side: sme late hdwy) | 3½ | 7 | 14/1 | 58 | 18 |
| 4323[17] | **Belbay Star (45)** (JLEyre) **3-7-5**(5) JBramhill(7) (disp ld far side to ½-wy: grad wknd fnl 2f) | hd | 8 | 25/1 | 35 | — |
| 4206[5] | **Marino Street (56)** (PDEvans) **3-8-2**(5) AnthonyBond(11) (racd far side: nvr trbld ldrs) | nk | 9 | 16/1 | 45 | 5 |
| 4598[2] | **The Barnsley Belle (IRE) (46)** (JLEyre) **3-7-11** PFessey(1) (racd far side: prom tl wknd fnl 2f) | 1 | 10 | 10/1[2] | 33 | — |
| 2914[5] | **Fancy Design (IRE) (45)** (PMitchell) **3-7-10** MHenry(3) (b.hind: dwlt: racd far side: hdwy & prom ½-wy: sn wknd) | 1 | 11 | 20/1 | 30 | — |
| 4793[16] | **Theatre Magic (55)** (SRBowring) **3-8-6** CTeague(14) (racd stands' side: chsd ldrs: edgd lft ½-wy: sn btn) | ¾ | 12 | 20/1 | 38 | — |
| 4505[4] | **Comic Fantasy (AUS) (60)** (JLEyre) **3-8-6b**(5) SBuckley(15) (racd stands' side: drifted lft ½-wy: n.d) | ½ | 13 | 16/1 | 42 | 2 |
| 4768[2] | **Stackattack (IRE) (60)** (PRWebber) **3-8-6**(5) DavidO'Neill(16) (lw: s.i.s: racd stands' side: hdwy ½-wy: n.d) | s.h | 14 | 6/1[1] | 42 | 2 |
| 4498[3] | **Just Millie (USA) (58)** (JEBanks) **3-8-6**(3) RMullen(12) (racd stands' side: drifted lft ½-wy: n.d) | hd | 15 | 16/1 | 40 | — |
| 4071[14] | **Dispol Diamond (60)** (GROldroyd) **3-8-11** ADaly(17) (racd stands' side: sme hdwy ½-wy: n.d) | 3½ | 16 | 25/1 | 34 | — |
| 4590[7] | **Marjaana (IRE) (65)** (PTWalwyn) **3-9-2v** DWright(21) (in tch stands' side: sn drvn along & no imp) | hd | 17 | 16/1 | 38 | — |
| 4486* | **Bataleur (61)** (MissJBower) **3-8-7**(5) RFfrench(19) (led stands' side: no ch fr ½-wy) | s.h | 18 | 10/1[2] | 34 | — |
| *3602*[9] | **Napoleon's Return (47)** (JLEyre) **3-7-7v**(5) JennyBenson(9) (hdwy far side over 3f out: sn btn) | 6 | 19 | 25/1 | 7 | — |
| 4598[15] | **Fairly Sure (IRE) (47)** (NEBerry) **3-7-7**(5)ow2 KerryBaker(22) (swtg: racd stands' side: n.d) | 3 | 20 | 25/1 | — | — |
| 4689[5] | **Blessingindisguise (66)** (MWEasterby) **3-9-3** GParkin(20) (racd stands' side: nvr wnt pce) | 1 | 21 | 10/1[2] | 17 | — |
| 4309[10] | **With The Tempo (IRE) (52)** (DrJDScargill) **3-8-3** MBaird(18) (racd stands' side: n.d) | ¾ | 22 | 16/1 | 1 | — |

(SP 144.2%) **22 Rn**

**1m 28.37** (4.77) CSF £140.43 CT £3,984.42 TOTE £10.00: £2.50 £4.30 £8.60 £4.40 (£55.20) Trio £647.50; £592.80 to Doncaster 26/10/96 OWNER Mr Peter Pritchard (NEWMARKET) BRED Tarworth Bloodstock Investments Ltd
LONG HANDICAP Belbay Star 7-7

**4499 Really A Dream (IRE)**, whose jockey realised that the stands' side was no good at halfway, switched to the far-side group and won really well. (11/1)
**676 Waypoint** put up a decent performance, but was easily picked off entering the last furlong. (12/1)
**3154 Myttons Mistake** has not won for some time, but this was a much better effort. (33/1)
**4259 Polar Refrain** has yet to win a race, but keeps showing bits of form to suggest that the ability is there. (12/1)
**4701* Silver Harrow** ran reasonably with a 6lb penalty, but was never good enough to offer a live threat. (11/1)
**3973 Finisterre (IRE)** was always close enough if good enough, but his absence for over seven weeks probably made the difference. (14/1)

### 4861 E.B.F. FLAXTON MAIDEN STKS (2-Y.O F) (Class D)
2-30 (2-33) **1m (round)** £3,801.50 (£1,142.00: £551.00: £255.50) Stalls: High GOING minus 0.05 sec per fur (G)

| | Horse | Dist | Pos | SP | RR | SF |
|---|---|---|---|---|---|---|
| 4363[2] | **Calypso Grant (IRE)** (PWHarris) **2-8-11** GHind(14) (hld up: effrt over 2f out: shkn up & qcknd to ld ins fnl f) | — | 1 | 5/1[3] | 88 | 58 |
| | **Summer Dance** (MRStoute) **2-8-11** JReid(9) (w'like: leggy: scope: trckd ldrs: smooth hdwy 2f out: led ins fnl f: sn hdd & nt qckn) | 1¾ | 2 | 5/2[1] | 85+ | 55 |
| 4608[2] | **Brave Kris (IRE)** (LMCumani) **2-8-11** OUrbina(13) (led tl hdd & no ex ins fnl f) | 2½ | 3 | 11/4[2] | 80 | 50 |
| 4564[2] | **Almi Ad (USA)** (DMorley) **2-8-11** RHills(7) (a chsng ldrs: effrt over 2f out: nt qckn appr fnl f) | 2½ | 4 | 6/1 | 75 | 45 |
| 4608[11] | **Agony Aunt** (MrsJCecil) **2-8-11** KDarley(12) (sn chsng ldrs: styd on one pce fnl 2f) | s.h | 5 | 20/1 | 74 | 44 |
| 4608[8] | **Thornby Park** (JLDunlop) **2-8-11** TSprake(8) (hld up: hdwy over 2f out: styd on wl) | 1½ | 6 | 16/1 | 71 | 41 |
| | **True Glory (IRE)** (JHMGosden) **2-8-11** AMcGlone(4) (b: b.hind: lengthy: s.s: hdwy ½-wy: nvr plcd to chal) | 1¾ | 7 | 14/1 | 68+ | 38 |
| | **Epworth** (ACStewart) **2-8-11** MRoberts(3) (leggy: scope: mid div: sn pushed along: kpt on fnl 2f) | ¾ | 8 | 11/1 | 66 | 36 |
| | **Move The Clouds** (JRFanshawe) **2-8-11** DHarrison(11) (w'like: leggy: scope: stdd s: hdwy ½-wy: n.d) | 6 | 9 | 25/1 | 54 | 24 |
| 4697[6] | **Inimitable** (JLDunlop) **2-8-11** MHills(5) (bit bkwd: hld up & bhd: nvr nr to chal) | 1 | 10 | 16/1 | 52 | 22 |
| 3988[9] | **Ceanothus (IRE)** (JHMGosden) **2-8-11** GDuffield(10) (prom tl wknd fnl 3f) | 5 | 11 | 14/1 | 42 | 12 |
| 4605[10] | **Teutonic Lass (IRE)** (PTWalwyn) **2-8-11** JStack(1) (chsd ldrs 5f: wknd) | 3½ | 12 | 50/1 | 35 | 5 |
| | **Damanka (IRE)** (MBell) **2-8-6**(5) GFaulkner(15) (w'like: leggy: racd wd: cl up to ½-wy: sn lost pl) | ¾ | 13 | 25/1 | 8 | 4 |
| | **Dear Drue** (CEBrittain) **2-8-11** BDoyle(6) (w'like: bkwd: s.i.s: a wl bhd) | 13 | 14 | 20/1 | 9 | — |
| | **Spriolo** (RWArmstrong) **2-8-11b**[1] RPrice(2) (cmpt: a outpcd & bhd) | 1 | 15 | 25/1 | 6 | — |

(SP 142.6%) **15 Rn**

**1m 39.65** (3.15) CSF £20.04 TOTE £7.30: £2.20 £2.00 £1.80 (£12.80) Trio £16.20 OWNER Mrs P. W. Harris (BERKHAMSTED) BRED Pendley Farm

**4363 Calypso Grant (IRE)** settled just off the pace and then picked up well when asked and won most authoritatively. She has a good turn of foot which will stand her in good stead. (5/1)
**Summer Dance** travelled as though the race was hers for the taking but, when it came down to a struggle, her lack of experience was the difference. (5/2)
**4608 Brave Kris (IRE)**, an excitable sort, attempted to make all, but was well tapped for speed late on. (11/4)
**4564 Almi Ad (USA)** had her chances, but was short of speed, and may prefer plenty of give in the ground. (6/1: op 4/1)
**4451 Agony Aunt**, who ran particularly well, was not overpunished when beaten and will obviously find her mark in due course. (20/1)
**Thornby Park** is improving and was picking up nicely at the end to show that, over further next year, better will be seen. (16/1)
**True Glory (IRE)** was very green indeed, but showed plenty of promise and, given more experience, better is likely. (14/1: 8/1-16/1)
**Epworth**, clueless for much of the trip, was continually being pushed along, but was beginning to realise what was required by the end. (11/1: 8/1-12/1)

## 4862 SPINAL INJURIES ASSOCIATION H'CAP (0-85) (3-Y.O+) (Class D)

3-00 (3-02) **1m 6f 132y** £4,077.50 (£1,220.00: £585.00: £267.50) Stalls: Low GOING minus 0.05 sec per fur (G)

| | | | | SP | RR | SF |
|---|---|---|---|---|---|---|
| 4448* | **Great Tern (47)** (NMBabbage) **4-7-6**$^{(7)}$ RFfrench(8) (a gng wl: led over 4f out: pushed along: r.o wl fnl 2f) | — | 1 | 9/1 | 62 | 43 |
| 4722$^{3}$ | **Deano's Beeno (70)** (MJohnston) **4-9-8** MRoberts(2) (lw: prom tl lost pl 9f out: styd on wl fnl 3f: no ch w wnr) | 4 | 2 | 12/1 | 81 | 62 |
| 4626$^{3}$ | **Karisma (IRE) (63)** (DenysSmith) **3-8-6**$^{ow1}$ KFallon(4) (lw: prom: drvn along 7f out: one pce fnl 3f) | ½ | 3 | 9/1 | 73 | 44 |
| 4683* | **Beaumont (IRE) (67)** (JEBanks) **6-9-5** JQuinn(9) (lw: bhd: hdwy 5f out: sn rdn: one pce fnl 3f) | 7 | 4 | 100/30$^{1}$ | 69 | 50 |
| 4297$^{7}$ | **Circled (USA) (72)** (BWHills) **3-9-1** MHills(10) (bhd: sme hdwy 4f out: n.d) | 14 | 5 | 12/1 | 59 | 31 |
| 4563$^{20}$ | **Shakiyr (FR) (50)** (RHollinshead) **5-7-13**$^{(3)ow4}$ FLynch(1) (drvn along & lost pl 8f out: styd on fnl 3f: n.d) | 3 | 6 | 20/1 | 34 | 11 |
| 4683$^{2}$ | **Midyan Blue (IRE) (74)** (JMPEustace) **6-9-7**$^{(5)}$ MartinDwyer(3) (chsd ldrs: drvn along 6f out: sn btn) | 1¾ | 7 | 5/1$^{3}$ | 56 | 37 |
| 4683$^{5}$ | **Turnpole (IRE) (70)** (MrsMReveley) **5-9-3**$^{(5)}$ GLee(11) (hld up & bhd: pushed along 9f out: n.d) | ¾ | 8 | 4/1$^{2}$ | 51 | 32 |
| 4457$^{4}$ | **Classic Eagle (85)** (RHarris) **3-10-0** RPrice(5) (led tl hdd over 4f out: sn wknd) | 1 | 9 | 33/1 | 65 | 37 |
| 4683$^{9}$ | **Meant to Be (65)** (LadyHerries) **6-9-3** AClark(7) (prom: effrt 5f out: wknd over 3f out) | nk | 10 | 14/1 | 45 | 26 |
| 3155$^{8}$ | **Ela-Yie-Mou (IRE) (78)** (SDow) **3-9-7** RHughes(6) (dwlt: a bhd: t.o) | dist | 11 | 16/1 | — | — |

(SP 115.4%) **11 Rn**

**3m 10.25** (6.05) CSF £97.29 CT £910.78 TOTE £11.00: £2.80 £1.90 £2.20 (£48.40) Trio £146.40 OWNER Mr John Cantrill (CHELTENHAM) BRED Theakston Stud

WEIGHT FOR AGE 3yo-9lb

**4448* Great Tern** could have taken this whenever she wanted. With her rider looking round continually, she won particularly well and should be able to follow up. (9/1)

**4722 Deano's Beeno** has only won one race and that was two years ago, but again showed here that he has ability. (12/1)

**4626 Karisma (IRE)** was off the bit a long way out, but he did keep on well, albeit in vain. He looks the sort to do well over hurdles. (9/1)

**4683* Beaumont (IRE)** failed to fire this time and was going nowhere in the last half-mile. (100/30)

**Circled (USA)** seems to have connections in a quandary as to what trip she wants and never really shed any light on the situation here. (12/1)

**3922 Shakiyr (FR)** was having his ears pushed off with a mile to go and never looked likely to get into it, despite staying on. (20/1)

**4683 Midyan Blue (IRE)** seems a funny customer these days and was never enjoying it. (5/1)

**4683 Turnpole (IRE)** ran far too badly to be true. (4/1)

## 4863 E.B.F. WHEATLEY PARK MAIDEN STKS (2-Y.O) (Class D)

3-30 (3-32) **7f** £4,295.50 (£1,294.00: £627.00: £293.50) Stalls: High GOING minus 0.05 sec per fur (G)

| | | | | SP | RR | SF |
|---|---|---|---|---|---|---|
| | **Sophomore** (BWHills) **2-9-0** MHills(8) (w'like: hld up: stdy hdwy ½-wy: led ins fnl f: r.o) | — | 1 | 5/2$^{1}$ | 80 | 33 |
| 4670$^{7}$ | **Labeq (IRE)** (PTWalwyn) **2-9-0** RHills(12) (cl up: led over 3f out tl ins fnl f: kpt on) | ¾ | 2 | 16/1 | 78 | 31 |
| | **Minersville (USA)** (JHMGosden) **2-9-0** GHind(4) (w'like: str: scope: bit bkwd: hld up: stdy hdwy 2f out: r.o strly towards fin: nvr plcd to chal) | 1 | 3 | 9/1 | 76+ | 29 |
| 4512$^{5}$ | **Great Child** (MRStoute) **2-9-0** KFallon(9) (sn wl bhd: stdy hdwy ½-wy: nvr plcd to chal) | 5 | 4 | 3/1$^{2}$ | 65+ | 18 |
| | **Arco Colora** (MRStoute) **2-8-9** JReid(11) (small: unf: trckd ldrs: effrt over 2f out: btn over 1f out) | 1 | 5 | 7/2$^{3}$ | 57 | 10 |
| 4127$^{8}$ | **Nemisto** (CEBrittain) **2-9-0** BDoyle(2) (chsd ldrs tl outpcd fnl 2f) | 3 | 6 | 25/1 | 55 | 8 |
| | **Rheinbold** (TJEtherington) **2-9-0** MTebbutt(5) (lengthy: bit bkwd: s.i.s: wl bhd: hdwy 3f out: nvr nr to chal) | 2½ | 7 | 50/1 | 50 | 3 |
| | **Blowing Away (IRE)** (MHTompkins) **2-8-6**$^{(3)}$ MHenry(1) (unf: sn pushed along: sme hdwy over 2f out: n.d) | nk | 8 | 25/1 | 44 | — |
| 4601$^{4}$ | **Present Chance** (BAMcMahon) **2-9-0** GCarter(3) (bit bkwd: led tl hdd over 3f out: wknd over 2f out) | ½ | 9 | 14/1 | 48 | 1 |
| | **Sea Ya Maite** (SRBowring) **2-9-0** SDWilliams(6) (leggy: w ldrs tl wknd 2f out) | 7 | 10 | 50/1 | 32 | — |
| | **Straffan Gold (USA)** (GWragg) **2-9-0** KDarley(10) (w'like: scope: bkwd: sn wl bhd & pushed along: n.d) | 5 | 11 | 7/1 | 21 | — |
| | **Pamela's Boy** (ASmith) **2-9-0** MBirch(7) (neat: bkwd: wandered & lost pl fr ½-wy: t.o) | 23 | 12 | 50/1 | — | — |

(SP 124.4%) **12 Rn**

**1m 28.74** (5.14) CSF £40.39 TOTE £3.40: £1.50 £3.30 £3.30 (£30.50) Trio £125.80 OWNER Mr K. Abdulla (LAMBOURN) BRED Juddmonte Farms

STEWARDS' ENQUIRY Hind susp. 4-5 & 7-8/11/96 Rule 151(failure to ensure best possible placing). Gosden fined £600 (schooling in public). Tebbutt & Etherington rescinded.

**Sophomore** won well here, despite showing signs of greenness, and no doubt there is plenty more to come. (5/2)

**Labeq (IRE)** has obviously learnt plenty from his debut and, although looking held in the final furlong, he did keep fighting back. (16/1)

**Minersville (USA)**, a decent sort, needed this and left the distinct impression that he should have won given a more enterprising ride. He looks one to watch. (9/1)

**4512 Great Child** had another educational and, tenderly handled, was picking up nicely as the race progressed. With time, he looks one to keep in mind. (3/1)

**Arco Colora** ran well until blowing up approaching the final furlong. (7/2)

**Nemisto** showed something this time, but was left struggling in the last couple of furlongs. (25/1)

**Rheinbold** had a quiet run, but was inclined to hang and was wisely not knocked about. (50/1)

**Straffan Gold (USA)** (7/1: op 4/1)

## 4864 SPINAL INJURIES NURSERY H'CAP (2-Y.O) (Class D)

4-00 (4-09) **1m (round)** £4,035.50 (£1,214.00: £587.00: £273.50) Stalls: High GOING minus 0.05 sec per fur (G)

| | | | | SP | RR | SF |
|---|---|---|---|---|---|---|
| 4672$^{8}$ | **I Can't Remember (77)** (PDEvans) **2-8-7** JFEgan(9) (cl up: led wl over 2f out: hld on wl) | — | 1 | 16/1 | 80 | 30 |
| 4625$^{5}$ | **Mr Bombastique (IRE) (83)** (BWHills) **2-8-13** MHills(3) (w ldrs: ev ch 1f out: kpt on) | nk | 2 | 11/2$^{2}$ | 85 | 35 |
| 4384* | **Southerly Wind (79)** (MrsJRRamsden) **2-8-9** KFallon(15) (lw: rr div: hdwy on outside 3f out: edgd lft: styd on u.p) | 1½ | 3 | 5/2$^{1}$ | 78 | 28 |
| 4361$^{8}$ | **Triple Term (75)** (JLDunlop) **2-8-5** KDarley(6) (lw: a.p: kpt on one pce fnl 2f) | hd | 4 | 12/1 | 74 | 24 |
| 4477$^{3}$ | **Drive Assured (82)** (CEBrittain) **2-8-12** BDoyle(1) (dwlt: sn in tch: effrt over 2f out: kpt on one pce fnl f) | 1 | 5 | 25/1 | 79 | 29 |
| 4760$^{9}$ | **Hello Dolly (IRE) (66)** (KRBurke) **2-7-3**$^{(7)}$ RFfrench(7) (sn trckng ldrs: effrt 2f out: nt qckn) | ¾ | 6 | 20/1 | 62 | 12 |
| 4565$^{7}$ | **Idrica (85)** (JHMGosden) **2-9-1** GHind(4) (bhd: hdwy & n.m.r over 2f out: styd on towards fin) | hd | 7 | 12/1 | 81 | 31 |
| 4482$^{3}$ | **Leviticus (IRE) (74)** (TPTate) **2-8-4** ACulhane(13) (led tl hdd wl over 2f out: one pce) | 1 | 8 | 10/1 | 68 | 18 |
| 4113$^{16}$ | **Top of The Wind (IRE) (76)** (JJO'Neill) **2-8-6** DaneO'Neill(14) (lw: mid div: effrt 3f out: no imp) | nk | 9 | 16/1 | 69 | 19 |
| 4298* | **Foxes Tail (79)** (MissSEHall) **2-8-6**$^{(3)}$ FLynch(12) (b: bhd: effrt & nt clr run over 2f out: n.d) | 1 | 10 | 6/1$^{3}$ | 70 | 20 |

| | | | | SP | RR | SF |
|---|---|---|---|---|---|---|
| 3835[13] | **Raven Master (USA) (91)** (PWChapple-Hyam) **2-9-7v** JReid(2) (bhd: styd on fnl 2f: n.d) | ½ | **11** | 20/1 | 81 | 31 |
| 4435[2] | **Pretty Sharp (70)** (APJarvis) **2-8-0** JQuinn(10) (s.i.s: sn in tch: effrt over 2f out: sn wknd) | 3 | **12** | 16/1 | 54 | 4 |
| 4602[18] | **Sudest (IRE) (73)** (IABalding) **2-7-12**(5) MartinDwyer(5) (bhd: effrt 3f out: n.d) | ¾ | **13** | 16/1 | 55 | 5 |
| 4127[15] | **Golden Melody (71)** (RHannon) **2-8-1**ow1 GCarter(11) (bhd & pushed along: n.d) | 1½ | **14** | 25/1 | 50 | — |
| 4790[4] | **Loch-Hurn Lady (67)** (KWHogg) **2-7-8**(3)ow1 DWright(16) (w ldrs to ½-wy: sn lost pl) | 7 | **15** | 33/1 | 32 | — |
| *4764[2]* | ***Gipsy Princess (67)*** (MWEasterby) **2-7-4b**(7) RMullen(8) (Withdrawn not under Starter's orders: uns rdr & bolted bef s) | | **W** | 8/1 | — | — |
| | | | | (SP 137.5%) | **15 Rn** | |

**1m 42.05** (5.55) CSF £98.04 CT £283.71 TOTE £14.70: £3.50 £2.60 £1.70 (£43.60) Trio £57.60 OWNER Peter Graham Racing (WELSHPOOL) BRED C. G. Reid

LONG HANDICAP Loch-Hurn Lady 7-4 Hello Dolly (IRE) 7-9

**4602 I Can't Remember** was having his seventeenth race of the season and was as enthusiastic as ever, but needed to show plenty of courage to hold on. (16/1)

**4625 Mr Bombastique (IRE)** ran a sound race and kept plugging away, but just found one too determined. (11/2)

**4384* Southerly Wind**, always struggling to make ground, tried to edge left under pressure and could never quicken enough to get in a real blow. (5/2)

**4361 Triple Term**, dropped back in trip, had his chances, but failed to quicken when it mattered. (12/1)

**4477 Drive Assured** obviously has ability, but is a bit of a character. (25/1)

**4602 Hello Dolly (IRE)** travels well but, when the button was pressed, failed to pick up sufficiently. (20/1)

**4565 Idrica** showed more enthusiasm this time and was staying on really well at the end, but she is not one to rely on. (12/1)

## 4865 SPROTBOROUGH CLAIMING STKS (3, 4 & 5-Y.O) (Class E)

4-30 (4-38) **7f** £3,756.00 (£1,128.00: £544.00: £252.00) Stalls: High GOING minus 0.05 sec per fur (G)

| | | | | SP | RR | SF |
|---|---|---|---|---|---|---|
| 3518[9] | **Thordis (68)** (PJMakin) **3-8-10v**[1] KDarley(17) (trckd ldrs: hdwy centre over 1f out: r.o wl) | — | **1** | 9/1 | 82 | 45 |
| 4606[13] | **Nineacres (46)** (NMBabbage) **5-8-0v**(7) RFfrench(5) (chsd ldrs far side: led over 2f out tl over 1f out: one pce) | 5 | **2** | 25/1 | 66 | 31 |
| 4590[5] | **Sharp Shuffle (IRE) (72)** (RHannon) **3-8-12** RHughes(9) (lw: outpcd & bhd far side: hdwy over 2f out: styd on wl) | nk | **3** | 9/4[1] | 72 | 35 |
| | **Perang Polly** (LordHuntingdon) **4-8-6** DHarrison(8) (sn outpcd & bhd far side: styd on wl fnl 2f) | hd | **4** | 10/1 | 64 | 29 |
| 4592[6] | **Gad Yakoun** (MGMeagher) **3-8-10** JReid(4) (trckd ldrs gng wl far side: ev ch over 1f out: wknd) | 1½ | **5** | 14/1 | 66 | 29 |
| 4688[17] | **Ochos Rios (IRE) (59)** (BSRothwell) **5-8-7**(3) FLynch(15) (lw: cl up centre: rdn ½-wy: one pce fnl 2f) | 3½ | **6** | 10/1 | 56 | 21 |
| 4701[4] | **Euphyllia (52)** (BobJones) **4-8-1** FNorton(3) (trckd ldrs far side: effrt over 2f out: wknd over 1f out) | nk | **7** | 9/2[2] | 47 | 12 |
| 4589[5] | **Oriel Lad (55)** (DonEnricoIncisa) **3-8-3** KimTinkler(18) (rdn ½-wy: styd on fnl f: nrst fin) | nk | **8** | 50/1 | 50 | 13 |
| 4436[12] | **Lady Silk (43)** (MissJFCraze) **5-8-6** DeanMcKeown(20) (bhd: drvn along centre: hdwy 2f out: no imp) | ½ | **9** | 33/1 | 50 | 15 |
| *3877[15]* | **Dahiyah (USA) (65)** (DLWilliams) **5-8-4v**(5)ow2 DGriffiths(19) (swtg: effrt u.p 3f out: n.d) | ½ | **10** | 20/1 | 52 | 15 |
| | **Lab Test (IRE)** (JPearce) **4-9-0** JQuinn(21) (n.d) | s.h | **11** | 10/1 | 57 | 22 |
| *607[9]* | **Sweet Mate (44)** (MartynMeade) **4-7-12**(7) TField(11) (prom far side over 4f) | 7 | **12** | 25/1 | 32 | — |
| 4592[11] | **Lawsimina** (MissJFCraze) **3-8-5** AMcGlone(1) (racd far side: led tl hdd & wknd over 2f out) | ½ | **13** | 50/1 | 32 | — |
| 4591[10] | **Great Chief (60)** (HRACecil) **3-9-2** KFallon(22) (lw: cl up centre tl wknd fnl 2f) | ½ | **14** | 6/1[3] | 42 | 5 |
| 4070[13] | **Cameron Edge (28)** (ABMulholland) **3-8-2**ow2 TSprake(10) (drvn along far side: no ch fr ½-wy) | 6 | **15** | 50/1 | 15 | — |
| *4081[9]* | **Niteowl Raider (IRE) (38)** (JAHarris) **3-8-3** JO'Reilly(14) (b.hind: w ldr centre tl wknd over 1f out) | 1 | **16** | 33/1 | 13 | — |
| 4436[26] | **Oh Susannah (35)** (JAHarris) **5-8-2v**[1] CRutter(7) (racd far side: n.d) | 2 | **17** | 50/1 | 6 | — |
| 3986[10] | **Grand Popo** (SEKettlewell) **3-8-3**(7) JennyBenson(16) (sn bhd) | s.h | **18** | 50/1 | 16 | — |
| 4221[20] | **Masai Man (USA) (35)** (MissJBower) **5-8-7b** TWilliams(13) (nvr trbld ldrs) | 1 | **19** | 50/1 | 8 | — |
| 4472[5] | **La Finale (45)** (DNicholls) **3-7-13b** NKennedy(6) (cl up far side 4f: wknd) | 2 | **20** | 16/1 | — | — |
| *3062[12]* | **Colebrook Leader** (JRBosley) **4-8-4**(3) DWright(12) (dwlt: sn drvn along: t.o) | dist | **21** | 50/1 | — | — |
| | | | | (SP 145.1%) | **21 Rn** | |

**1m 27.35** (3.75) CSF £209.21 TOTE £9.00: £2.50 £5.90 £1.70 (£398.70) Trio £208.90 OWNER Mr Barrie Whitehouse (MARLBOROUGH) BRED B. Whitehouse

WEIGHT FOR AGE 3yo-2lb

**2947 Thordis** had the visor on for the first time and, with the jockey using his brains and keeping well away from the slower stands' side, he won well. (9/1)

**4356 Nineacres**, from a yard in form, ran a sound race, but had no answer to the winner's turn of foot in the closing stages. (25/1)

**4590 Sharp Shuffle (IRE)** was struggling with the pace early on but, despite responding to pressure, lacked the speed to make any impression. (9/4)

**Perang Polly** had no idea in the early stages but, judging by the way she picked up late on, she should find a race in due course. (10/1)

**4592 Gad Yakoun** went well until failing to see out this trip. (14/1)

**3995* Ochos Rios (IRE)**, unlike the winner, was always finding the draw disadvantage too much. (10/1)

**4221 Oriel Lad**, poorly drawn, picked up well in the closing stages. (50/1)

## 4866 WESTWOODSIDE H'CAP (0-80) (3-Y.O) (Class D)

5-00 (5-08) **1m 2f 60y** £4,727.50 (£1,420.00: £685.00: £317.50) Stalls: Low GOING minus 0.05 sec per fur (G)

| | | | | SP | RR | SF |
|---|---|---|---|---|---|---|
| 4702[3] | **Blurred (IRE) (70)** (MHTompkins) **3-8-8**(3) MHenry(3) (trckd ldrs: nt clr run 3f out to 1f out: qcknd to ld wl ins fnl f) | — | **1** | 100/30[1] | 80 | 55 |
| 4216[6] | **Absolutelystunning (56)** (MrsBarbaraWaring) **3-7-8**(3) NVarley(7) (b: sn in tch: led appr fnl f: sn hdd & nt qckn) | 3 | **2** | 20/1 | 61 | 36 |
| 3876[8] | **Alicia (IRE) (71)** (JLDunlop) **3-8-12** KDarley(10) (bhd: hdwy 2f out: hung lft: styd on: nvr able to chal) | ½ | **3** | 20/1 | 76 | 51 |
| 4613[2] | **Raise A Prince (FR) (74)** (JWHills) **3-9-1** MHills(5) (bhd: nt clr run 3f out: swtchd & r.o wl appr fnl f) | 2½ | **4** | 9/1 | 75 | 50 |
| 4810[4] | **Newbridge Boy (56)** (MGMeagher) **3-7-11**ow1 FNorton(11) (led tl hdd over 1f out: one pce) | s.h | **5** | 14/1 | 57 | 31 |
| 4422[3] | **Seirenes (72)** (PTWalwyn) **3-8-13** TSprake(6) (rr div: hdwy on outside 3f out: nrst fin: lame) | ¾ | **6** | 16/1 | 71 | 46 |
| 4580[17] | **Exalted (IRE) (80)** (SirMarkPrescott) **3-9-7** GDuffield(8) (chsd ldrs: ev ch 2f out: wknd fnl f) | hd | **7** | 14/1 | 79 | 54 |
| 4682[10] | **Apache Len (USA) (68)** (RHannon) **3-8-9b** DaneO'Neill(1) (lw: prom: outpcd over 2f out: no imp after) | ½ | **8** | 11/1 | 67 | 42 |
| 4238[7] | **Chabrol (CAN) (65)** (TTClement) **3-8-1**(5) ADaly(2) (sn drvn along: hdwy over 2f out: n.d) | 1½ | **9** | 20/1 | 61 | 36 |
| 4691[16] | **Desert Lynx (IRE) (70)** (TRWatson) **3-8-11** TWilliams(14) (b.hind: bhd: gd hdwy on outside 3f out: hung lft 2f out: sn btn) | nk | **10** | 25/1 | 66 | 41 |
| 3926[13] | **Catherine's Choice (60)** (JDBethell) **3-8-1** SDrowne(16) (bhd: hdwy over 3f out: wknd wl over 1f out) | ½ | **11** | 25/1 | 55 | 30 |
| 4248[5] | **Mock Trial (IRE) (65)** (MrsJRRamsden) **3-8-6** KFallon(13) (bhd: gd hdwy 3f out: rdn & btn appr fnl f) | ½ | **12** | 12/1 | 59 | 34 |

| | | | SP | RR | SF |
|---|---|---|---|---|---|
| 3322[8] | **My Mariam (70)** (CREgerton) **3-8-11** RHughes(4) (mid div: effrt & nt clr run 3f out: n.d after) ... ¾ | **13** | 15/2[3] | 63 | 38 |
| 4513[7] | **Peppers (IRE) (64)** (KRBurke) **3-8-5** DHarrison(18) (trckd ldrs gng wl: effrt 3f out: sn btn) ... 4 | **14** | 20/1 | 51 | 26 |
| 4793[15] | **Le Sport (64)** (DNicholls) **3-8-5b[1]** JQuinn(12) (in tch: effrt 4f out: sn btn) ... 1½ | **15** | 25/1 | 48 | 23 |
| 4374[9] | **Divine (67)** (ACStewart) **3-8-8** MRoberts(17) (lw: cl up tl wknd over 2f out) ... ¾ | **16** | 10/1 | 50 | 25 |
| 4422[2] | **Kentucky Fall (FR) (68)** (LadyHerries) **3-8-9** AClark(9) (chsd ldrs tl wknd 3f out) ... 19 | **17** | 7/1[2] | 22 | — |
| | | | (SP 132.3%) | **17 Rn** | |

**2m 11.51** (4.51) CSF £67.35 CT £1,094.12 TOTE £4.00: £1.80 £3.80 £4.00 £2.30 (£75.70) Trio £350.00 OWNER Trafalgar Racing Club and Partners (NEWMARKET) BRED Dr Paschal Carmody

LONG HANDICAP Newbridge Boy 7-7

**4702 Blurred (IRE)** was short of room for most of the way up the straight but, once a gap appeared, he quickened immediately and the race was his in a couple of strides. (100/30)

**4216 Absolutelystunning** ran one of her better races, only to be outclassed in the closing stages. (20/1)

**3434 Alicia (IRE)** ran well after two months off and this trip was probably short of her best. (20/1)

**4613 Raise A Prince (FR)** appeared unlucky, but has yet to win a race, and may be a bit of a funny customer. (9/1)

**4810 Newbridge Boy** is running well at present and this was another sound effort. (14/1)

**4422 Seirenes** finished well, staying on up the outside of the field but, after passing the post, was found to be very lame. (16/1)

T/Jkpt: Not won; £31,871.06 to Doncaster 25/10/96. T/Plpt: £331.70 (63.56 Tckts). T/Qdpt: £42.40 (28.55 Tckts). AA

# 4860-DONCASTER (L-H) (Good)
## Saturday October 26th
WEATHER: fine WIND: str against

## 4867 'JOCK MURRAY MEMORIAL' NURSERY H'CAP (2-Y.O) (Class C)
1-40 (1-41) **7f** £6,020.50 (£1,804.00: £867.00: £398.50) Stalls: High GOING: 0.27 sec per fur (G)

| | | | SP | RR | SF |
|---|---|---|---|---|---|
| 4717[11] | **Broughtons Error (66)** (WJMusson) **2-7-11** JQuinn(3) (hld up & bhd: effrt & swtchd lft over 1f out: str run to ld wl ins fnl f) ... — | **1** | 10/1 | 68 | 17 |
| 4512[8] | **Effervescence (77)** (RHannon) **2-8-8** JReid(7) (lw: trckd ldrs: rdn to chal wl ins fnl f: r.o) ... ½ | **2** | 12/1 | 78 | 27 |
| 4764[4] | **The In-Laws (IRE) (83)** (SirMarkPrescott) **2-9-0** GDuffield(5) (hld up & bhd: gd hdwy ins fnl f: fin fast) ... s.h | **3** | 11/1 | 84+ | 33 |
| 4751[2] | **Erosion (IRE) (77)** (MJohnston) **2-8-8** JWeaver(8) (lw: led tl hdd wl ins fnl f) ... ¾ | **4** | 5/1[2] | 76 | 25 |
| 4672[4] | **Blue Goblin (USA) (90)** (LMCumani) **2-9-7** KDarley(2) (stdd s: sn chsng ldrs: ev ch over 1f out: unable qckn) ... s.h | **5** | 7/2[1] | 89 | 38 |
| 4760[10] | **Spaniard's Mount (65)** (MHTompkins) **2-7-3v[1](7)** RMullen(10) (hld up: effrt & n.m.r 2f out: r.o wl towards fin) ... ½ | **6** | 16/1 | 63 | 12 |
| 4764* | **Abstone Queen (70)** (PDEvans) **2-8-1v** JFEgan(4) (hld up: hdwy 2f out: rdn & one pce appr fnl f) ... 2½ | **7** | 10/1 | 62 | 11 |
| 4586[8] | **Barresbo (67)** (CWFairhurst) **2-7-7(5)** PFessey(9) (prom tl wknd over 1f out) ... 1½ | **8** | 20/1 | 56 | 5 |
| 4717[6] | **Heart Throb (81)** (WJHaggas) **2-8-9(3)** FLynch(6) (prom: rdn over 2f out: sn btn) ... 2 | **9** | 7/2[1] | 65 | 14 |
| 4672[2] | **Manikato (USA) (73)** (DJSCosgrove) **2-8-4v** CRutter(1) (lw: trckd ldrs: effrt & rdn over 2f out: wknd appr fnl f) ... s.h | **10** | 6/1[3] | 57 | 6 |
| | | | (SP 120.2%) | **10 Rn** | |

**1m 31.0** (7.40) CSF £110.53 CT £1,234.02 TOTE £16.50: £3.10 £3.20 £2.50 (£141.60) Trio £116.50 OWNER Broughton Thermal Insulation (NEWMARKET) BRED Broughton Bloodstock

LONG HANDICAP Spaniard's Mount 7-8

**3259 Broughtons Error** has shown little of note so far, but he was able to take advantage of his weight allowance here, and stormed through to take charge nearing the finish. (10/1)

**3128 Effervescence** looked to have timed his run to perfection when putting in his bid 200 yards out, but the winner was also in top gear and beat him to the punch in an all-out battle to the line. (12/1)

**4764 The In-Laws (IRE)** ran a most extraordinary race and for most of the way looked like to finish in the pack, but she sprouted wings when given the office inside the final furlong, and would have got there in another couple of strides. (11/1)

**4751 Erosion (IRE)** only just failed in this attempt to make all at this first try at the trip and does appear to be a progressive colt. (5/1)

**4672 Blue Goblin (USA)**, a bit of a handful in the preliminaries, is obviously not an easy ride, although he does appear to do too much too soon and keep very little in the locker. Experience should settle him. (7/2)

**4760 Spaniard's Mount** performed much better in the visor and, had he not found trouble in running, may well have made the frame. (16/1)

**4764* Abstone Queen** (10/1: 7/1-11/1)

**4717 Heart Throb** came off the bridle approaching the quarter-mile pole and, failing to respond to pressure, was soon in trouble and beaten. This longer trip would seem to have no bearing on the final outcome, for she was beaten too far out. (7/2)

## 4868 BREEDERS' CUP DAY CLAIMING STKS (3-Y.O+) (Class D)
2-10 (2-22) **1m 2f 60y** £4,597.50 (£1,380.00: £665.00: £307.50) Stalls: Low GOING: 0.10 sec per fur (G)

| | | | SP | RR | SF |
|---|---|---|---|---|---|
| 4763[3] | **Break the Rules (70)** (MrsMReveley) **4-9-4** KDarley(5) (lw: bhd: hdwy u.p 3f out: led appr fnl f: sn clr) ... — | **1** | 9/2[1] | 85 | 60 |
| 4354[10] | **Bernard Seven (IRE) (70)** (CEBrittain) **4-8-13b** MRoberts(10) (led tl appr fnl f: no ch w wnr) ... 5 | **2** | 11/1 | 72 | 47 |
| 4703[4] | **Taniyar (FR) (41)** (RHollinshead) **4-8-6(5)** DGriffiths(13) (trckd ldrs: rdn over 2f out: styd on one pce) ... 4 | **3** | 25/1 | 64 | 39 |
| 4580[14] | **Evezio Rufo (65)** (NPLittmoden) **4-8-13v** TGMcLaughlin(12) (chsd ldrs: hrd drvn 4f out: kpt on one pce) ... 1½ | **4** | 50/1 | 64 | 39 |
| 4826[13] | **Ten Past Six (82)** (MartynWane) **4-9-4** DeanMcKeown(6) (hdwy 3f out: hrd drvn over 1f out: kpt on same pce) ... 1 | **5** | 12/1 | 67 | 42 |
| 4775[13] | **Gymcrak Premiere (80)** (GHolmes) **8-9-1v** JQuinn(14) (b.nr fore: b.hind: hld up & bhd: effrt & swtchd 3f out: btn 2f out) ... 9 | **6** | 9/2[1] | 50 | 25 |
| 4513[11] | **Dark Truffle (63)** (MrsJCecil) **3-8-2ow1** GDuffield(15) (nvr trbld ldrs) ... 3½ | **7** | 6/1[2] | 37 | 6 |
| 4326[14] | **King Athelstan (USA) (78)** (BAMcMahon) **8-8-10(5)** LNewton(19) (prom: effrt 4f out: wknd over 2f out) ... 7 | **8** | 13/2[3] | 34 | 9 |
| *4092[8]* | **Tabriz (54)** (JDBethell) **3-8-2** SDrowne(3) (uns rdr bef s: mid div: no hdwy fnl 3f) ... 2½ | **9** | 16/1 | 22 | — |
| 4497[14] | **Wet Patch (IRE) (60)** (RHannon) **4-8-11** MHills(7) (hdwy 3f out: nt rch ldrs) ... 7 | **10** | 7/1 | 15 | — |
| 4427[11] | **Begger's Opera (22)** (PatMitchell) **4-8-5(3)** FLynch(8) (in tch over 6f) ... ¾ | **11** | 50/1 | 11 | — |
| 4703[18] | **Bianca's Son (BEL)** (JMPlasschaert,Belgium) **6-9-7** MKeogh(17) (chsd ldrs over 6f) ... 1 | **12** | 50/1 | 22 | — |
| | **Nantgarw** (DRCElsworth) **3-8-7** AMcGlone(1) (small: bit bkwd: s.s: a in rr) ... 1 | **13** | 33/1 | 12 | — |
| 4808[18] | **Haido'hart (42)** (BSRothwell) **4-8-7v** JStack(2) (chsd ldrs tl wknd over 3f out) ... ¾ | **14** | 50/1 | 6 | — |

| Form | Horse | Dist | Pos | SP | RR | SF |
|---|---|---|---|---|---|---|
| | **Master Foodbroker (IRE)** (WJMusson) **8-8-9** DRMcCabe(16) (bkwd: s.s: a bhd) | ½ | **15** | 33/1 | 7 | — |
| | **General Monty** (PatMitchell) **4-8-11**(7) VictoriaAppleby(20) (s.s: a bhd: t.o) | 6 | **16** | 50/1 | 6 | — |
| 4693[10] | **Fair Lady (BEL)** (JMPlasschaert,Belgium) **3-8-11** JO'Reilly(11) (mid div tl wknd fnl 4f: t.o) | 2 | **17** | 50/1 | 1 | — |
| 4690[9] | **New Technique (FR) (25)** (KMcAuliffe) **3-8-3** JFEgan(18) (bhd fnl 4f: t.o) | 7 | **18** | 50/1 | — | — |
| *3970[16]* | ***Lady Ploy (27)*** (MissLCSiddall) **4-8-2**[ow1] GHind(4) (Withdrawn not under Starter's orders: loose bef s) | | **W** | 50/1 | — | — |
| | | | | (SP 123.8%) | | **18 Rn** |

**2m 13.36** (6.36) CSF £46.94 TOTE £4.50: £1.80 £3.00 £4.80 (£22.70) Trio £121.90 OWNER P. D. Savill (SALTBURN) BRED Cleaboy Farms Co
WEIGHT FOR AGE 3yo-5lb
Break the Rules clmd ALomas £15,000

**4763 Break the Rules** won this very easily indeed, but he was hard at work and going nowhere early in the straight before his undoubted stamina came into play. Sold for £15,000, he will now join Martin Pipe. (9/2)
**2188 Bernard Seven (IRE)** quickened from the front soon after entering the straight and quickly had most of his rivals in trouble, but his stamina appeared to give out and he was down to a walk passing the furlong marker. (11/1)
**4703 Taniyar (FR)** was never far away, but he has nothing in the way of finishing speed and was fighting a losing battle from a long way out. (25/1)
**Evezio Rufo**, stepping down in class, ran one of his better races and, if kept at this grade, there could be another race to be won. (50/1)
**1867 Ten Past Six** is proving difficult to win with, but he was staying on under hard driving in the latter stages and may well find his mark on the All-Weather. (12/1)
**4620 Gymcrak Premiere** would have been a class apart at his best in this grade, but he has not really fired this season, and this extended trip may not have been in his best interest. (9/2: op 3/1)
**4236 Wet Patch (IRE)** (7/1: 12/1-13/2)

## 4869 DONCASTER WRITERS RATED STKS H'CAP (0-100) (3-Y.O+) (Class B)

2-40 (2-50) **5f** £8,110.20 (£3,001.80: £1,440.90: £589.50: £234.75: £92.85) Stalls: High GOING: 0.27 sec per fur (G)

| Form | Horse | Dist | Pos | SP | RR | SF |
|---|---|---|---|---|---|---|
| 4679[5] | **Shanghai Girl (85)** (DRLoder) **3-8-7v** DRMcCabe(3) (lw: trckd ldrs: led appr fnl f: sn clr: r.o wl) | — | **1** | 20/1 | 99 | 73 |
| 4679[2] | **To the Roof (IRE) (99)** (PWHarris) **4-9-7** GHind(11) (lw: a.p: led over 1f out: sn hdd: one pce) | 3½ | **2** | 6/1[3] | 102 | 76 |
| 4772[2] | **Lago Di Varano (87)** (RMWhitaker) **4-8-9v** DeanMcKeown(8) (lw: bhd: hdwy 2f out: edgd lft u.p: styd on) | 1½ | **3** | 11/2[2] | 85 | 59 |
| 4772[5] | **Tedburrow (89)** (MrsAMNaughton) **4-8-11** ACulhane(10) (bhd: hdwy ½-wy: rdn over 1f out: nt pce to chal) | ½ | **4** | 5/1[1] | 85 | 59 |
| 4772[7] | **Ansellman (85)** (JBerry) **6-8-7b** GCarter(13) (hdwy u.p over 3f out: r.o ins fnl f) | nk | **5** | 10/1 | 80 | 54 |
| 4554[11] | **Maid For The Hills (89)** (DRLoder) **3-8-11** KDarley(12) (trckd ldrs stands' side: drvn along 2f out: one pce) | ½ | **6** | 16/1 | 83 | 57 |
| 4765* | **Palacegate Touch (85)** (JBerry) **6-8-2b**(5) PFessey(9) (rdn & no imp fr ½-wy) | ¾ | **7** | 16/1 | 76 | 50 |
| 4772[9] | **Bowden Rose (90)** (MBlanshard) **4-8-12b** JQuinn(7) (w ldrs: rdn & wknd over 1f out) | hd | **8** | 14/1 | 81 | 55 |
| 4765[5] | **Eastern Prophets (85)** (TJNaughton) **3-8-0**(7) RFfrench(4) (lw: rdn along over 2f out: nt pce of ldrs) | 1½ | **9** | 33/1 | 71 | 45 |
| 4772[3] | **Swynford Dream (86)** (JFBottomley) **3-8-5**(3) FLynch(6) (s.s: sn in tch: rdn & wknd over 1f out) | hd | **10** | 15/2 | 72 | 46 |
| 4679* | **Tadeo (97)** (MJohnston) **3-9-5** JWeaver(2) (disp ld tl over 1f out: sn rdn & btn) | ¾ | **11** | 13/2 | 81 | 55 |
| 4772[6] | **Crofters Ceilidh (85)** (BAMcMahon) **4-8-7b** JReid(5) (lw: gd spd over 3f) | 2½ | **12** | 10/1 | 61 | 35 |
| 4772[4] | **Portelet (87)** (RGuest) **4-8-4**(5) DGriffiths(1) (disp ld over 3f: eased whn btn fnl f) | 1½ | **13** | 10/1 | 58 | 32 |
| | | | | (SP 124.8%) | | **13 Rn** |

**60.85 secs** (2.45) CSF £130.22 CT £728.87 TOTE £22.90: £5.90 £2.50 £1.90 (£76.10) Trio £208.00 OWNER Mr Wafic Said (NEWMARKET) BRED Addison Racing Ltd Inc
LONG HANDICAP Eastern Prophets 8-1 Shanghai Girl 8-1 Palacegate Touch 8-3

**4679 Shanghai Girl**, waiting on the leaders, found a rare burst of speed when set alight to lead approaching the final furlong, and scooted clear impressively. If she is seen out again, she could defy a penalty. (20/1)
**4679 To the Roof (IRE)** got the better of a tightly-packed group to nose ahead below the distance, but the winner pounced in next to no time and soon showed who was boss. (6/1)
**4772 Lago Di Varano** is not enjoying the best of fortune, but he ran his heart out once again and shows no signs of going over the top. (11/2)
**4772 Tedburrow** always seemed to have too much to do and, though he stuck on willingly under pressure, could not summon the pace to deliver a challenge. (5/1)
**4772 Ansellman** lacked the pace to get himself into the battle, but he did keep staying on and quite possibly needs more testing conditions these days. (10/1)
**3222 Maid For The Hills** has not got the speed to win at this minimum trip, but she ran well enough in defeat and could be ready to strike when put back over six furlongs. (16/1)
**4772 Swynford Dream** could not afford to give away ground at the start in such a hotly-contested sprint as this and this effort can safely be ignored. (15/2)

## 4870 RACING POST CONDITIONS STKS (3-Y.O+) (Class B)

3-10 (3-17) **7f** £8,319.00 (£3,081.00: £1,480.50: £607.50: £243.75: £98.25) Stalls: High GOING: 0.27 sec per fur (G)

| Form | Horse | Dist | Pos | SP | RR | SF |
|---|---|---|---|---|---|---|
| 4442* | **Diffident (FR) (113)** (SbinSuroor) **4-9-10** KDarley(4) (a.p: effrt 2f out: r.o u.p to ld wl ins fnl f) | — | **1** | 7/2[2] | 122 | 86 |
| 4774* | **Russian Revival (USA) (110)** (SbinSuroor) **3-9-6** JReid(2) (chsd ldr: led over 2f out tl wl ins fnl f: rallied u.p) | hd | **2** | 9/4[1] | 120 | 82 |
| 4800[6] | **Celestial Key (USA) (105)** (MJohnston) **6-8-12** JWeaver(3) (hld up: effrt appr fnl f: nt pce to chal) | 1½ | **3** | 9/2[3] | 106 | 70 |
| 4444[4] | **Ramooz (USA) (106)** (BHanbury) **3-9-8** MRimmer(6) (lw: hld up & bhd: hdwy 2f out: sn rdn: nvr able to chal) | 1¼ | **4** | 5/1 | 116 | 78 |
| 4595[4] | **Hi Nod (102)** (MJCamacho) **6-8-12** GDuffield(5) (hld up: rdn & wl outpcd appr fnl f) | 3 | **5** | 13/2 | 97 | 61 |
| 4378[6] | **Sergeyev (IRE) (112)** (RHannon) **4-8-12** MHills(1) (lw: led tl over 2f out: outpcd appr fnl f) | 3½ | **6** | 8/1 | 89 | 53 |
| | | | | (SP 112.3%) | | **6 Rn** |

**1m 27.31** (3.71) CSF £11.31 TOTE £4.20: £2.30 £1.70 (£3.10) OWNER Godolphin (NEWMARKET) BRED Haras d'Etreham & R Ades in France
WEIGHT FOR AGE 3yo-2lb

**4442* Diffident (FR)**, a very smart colt at his best, had enjoyed a relatively quiet season and, when the race was really on inside the distance, he showed his younger stable-companion how it should be done. (7/2)
**4774* Russian Revival (USA)** failed narrowly in his bid to complete a hat-trick, but he did go down with all guns blazing, and success at this trip is well within his grasp. (9/4)
**4800 Celestial Key (USA)** ran much better than he did in the mud at Chepstow earlier in the week, but he does have to struggle against younger rivals of this class and, in the circumstances, was not disgraced. (9/2)
**4444 Ramooz (USA)** could not produce the response needed when popped the question and, against rivals as useful as the principals, it is probably asking too much to allow them a start. (5/1)
**4595 Hi Nod** was out of his depth in this company, but he is weighted out of most handicaps and these races are the only alternatives. (13/2)

**4378 Sergeyev (IRE)** tried his luck at blazing a trail this time, but those tactics were doomed for failure once the principals were sent about their work. (8/1)

## 4871 RACING POST TROPHY STKS (Gp 1) (2-Y.O) (Class A)

3-40 (3-42) **1m (round)** £97,489.50 (£36,280.50: £17,577.75: £7,376.25: £3,125.63: £1,425.37) Stalls: High GOING: 0.10 sec per fur (G)

| | | | | SP | RR | SF |
|---|---|---|---|---|---|---|
| 4462[5] | **Medaaly (100)** (SbinSuroor) **2-9-0** GHind(6) (trckd ldrs: chal over 1f out: styd on gamely to ld ins fnl f) | — | **1** | 14/1 | 111 | 64 |
| 4578* | **Poteen (USA)** (LMCumani) **2-9-0** JWeaver(9) (hld up in rr: gd hdwy to ld over 1f out: hdd & no ex ins fnl f) | ½ | **2** | 13/2[3] | 110+ | 63 |
| 4462* | **Benny The Dip (USA) (100)** (JHMGosden) **2-9-0** JReid(7) (hld up: effrt & rdn 2f out: styd on wl fnl f) | 1¼ | **3** | 11/10[1] | 108 | 61 |
| 4462[3] | **Besiege (100)** (HRACecil) **2-9-0** MRoberts(5) (lw: chsd ldr: led over 2f out tl over 1f out: rdn & one pce fnl f) | 1¼ | **4** | 5/1[2] | 105 | 58 |
| 4488* | **Papua (100)** (IABalding) **2-9-0** GCarter(1) (rr: pushed along over 3f out: kpt on u.p fnl f) | 1½ | **5** | 14/1 | 102 | 55 |
| 4398a[8] | **Daylight In Dubai (USA) (100)** (PWChapple-Hyam) **2-9-0** KDarley(4) (led tl over 2f out: rdn & outpcd appr fnl f) | 2½ | **6** | 33/1 | 97 | 50 |
| 4488[5] | **Sandstone (IRE) (100)** (JLDunlop) **2-9-0** GDuffield(2) (a chsng ldrs: rdn over 2f out: one pce) | 2 | **7** | 12/1 | 93 | 46 |
| 4306[2] | **Solo Mio (IRE)** (BWHills) **2-9-0** MHills(3) (s.s: rdn ½-wy: no imp) | 3½ | **8** | 16/1 | 86 | 39 |
| 4492* | **Asas** (SbinSuroor) **2-9-0** RHills(8) (chsd ldrs: rdn 3f out: wknd over 2f out) | 3 | **9** | 13/2[3] | 80 | 33 |
| | | | | (SP 120.8%) | **9 Rn** | |

**1m 41.12** (4.62) CSF £95.92 TOTE £29.80: £4.80 £1.70 £1.30 (£139.80) Trio £44.30 OWNER Godolphin (NEWMARKET) BRED Sheikh Mohammed Bin Rashid Al Maktoum

**4462 Medaaly** caused quite an upset and proved his £15,000 supplementary fee a shrewd gamble with a very game success. His 2000 Guineas price has been halved to 20/1, and he is also well up in the Derby betting. (14/1)

**4578* Poteen (USA)** found the ground more lively than that on which he won on his debut at Haydock, but he showed he is going the right way with a very brave effort. He could be the one to improve most when the Classics come round next year. (13/2)

**4462* Benny The Dip (USA)**, waiting on the leaders travelling well, went from one extreme to the other when the tempo was stepped up a quarter of a mile out and, though he did stay on willingly under strong driving, he was always being comfortably held. (11/10)

**4462 Besiege** tried to kick clear after taking it up over two furlongs out, but the pursuing pack would not let him get away, and he had to admit them too strong in the battle to the finish. (5/1)

**4488* Papua** did well in the circumstances to finish so close, for he was at full stretch soon after halfway and was never going to take a hand in the outcome. (14/1)

**4398a Daylight In Dubai (USA)** came from off the pace when successful in Ireland, but he adopted forceful tactics on this occasion and they proved to be his undoing. (33/1)

## 4872 LADBROKE H'CAP (0-100) (3-Y.O+) (Class C)

4-15 (4-17) **1m 4f** £12,232.50 (£3,660.00: £1,755.00: £802.50) Stalls: Low GOING: 0.10 sec per fur (G)

| | | | | SP | RR | SF |
|---|---|---|---|---|---|---|
| 4385[4] | **Henry Island (IRE) (88)** (GWragg) **3-8-9**(7) GMilligan(15) (a.p: led 5f out: jst hld on) | — | **1** | 14/1 | 99 | 74 |
| 4580[7] | **Wild Rita (76)** (WRMuir) **4-8-11** JReid(9) (hld up: hdwy & hrd drvn over 2f out: str chal fnl f: jst failed) | s.h | **2** | 16/1 | 87 | 69 |
| 4580* | **Sugar Mill (77)** (MrsMReveley) **6-8-12** ACulhane(19) (hld up: hdwy 4f out: sn chsng ldrs: kpt on u.p) | 3½ | **3** | 10/1 | 83 | 65 |
| 4686* | **Dreams End (75)** (PBowen) **8-8-10** GHind(1) (hld up & bhd: gd hdwy on ins 3f out: hrd rdn appr fnl f: one pce) | 1 | **4** | 9/1[3] | 80 | 62 |
| 4568[21] | **Bold Amusement (73)** (WSCunningham) **6-8-1**(7)ow1 DSweeney(14) (hld up: hdwy over 2f out: nvr nrr) | nk | **5** | 33/1 | 77 | 59 |
| 4675[5] | **River Keen (IRE) (84)** (RWArmstrong) **4-9-5** RHills(2) (lw: hld up: hdwy on ins whn nt clr run 3f out: hmpd ins fnl f: nt rcvr) | nk | **6** | 10/1 | 88 | 70 |
| 4617[6] | **Fern's Governor (61)** (WJMusson) **4-7-10** JQuinn(16) (hld up: hdwy 4f out: one pce fnl 2f) | ½ | **7** | 12/1 | 65 | 47 |
| 4465[17] | **Zaralaska (92)** (LMCumani) **5-9-6**(7) RFfrench(13) (lw: a chsng ldrs: ev ch 4f out: one pce fnl 2f) | ¾ | **8** | 6/1[2] | 95 | 77 |
| 4556[8] | **Albaha (USA) (73)** (JEBanks) **3-7-8**(7) RMullen(8) (nvr nrr) | nk | **9** | 20/1 | 75 | 50 |
| 4673[6] | **Bob's Ploy (71)** (MHTompkins) **4-8-3**(3) FLynch(11) (nvr nr to chal) | nk | **10** | 16/1 | 73 | 55 |
| 4568[6] | **Fairywings (82)** (MrsJRRamsden) **3-8-10** GCarter(7) (hld up: effrt 3f out: rdn & nt trble ldrs) | ½ | **11** | 12/1 | 83 | 58 |
| 564[4] | **Penny a Day (IRE) (93)** (MrsMReveley) **6-10-0** KDarley(12) (bit bkwd: hld up: stdy hdwy over 3f out: nvr plcd to chal) | ¾ | **12** | 20/1 | 93 | 75 |
| 4753[3] | **Rasayel (USA) (64)** (PDEvans) **6-7-13**ow2 JFEgan(5) (hld up in tch: effrt to chse ldr 4f out: sn rdn: wknd over 2f out) | 3 | **13** | 20/1 | 60 | 40 |
| 4121[11] | **Proton (67)** (RAkehurst) **6-8-2** AMcGlone(10) (prom 7f: sn wknd) | 5 | **14** | 20/1 | 56 | 38 |
| 4753[4] | **Tessajoe (74)** (MJCamacho) **4-8-4**(5) GParkin(18) (b.hind: trckd ldrs: effrt 3f out: wknd wl over 1f out) | ½ | **15** | 20/1 | 63 | 45 |
| 4487[3] | **Ionio (USA) (90)** (CEBrittain) **5-9-11** MRoberts(6) (led 7f: rdn & wknd wl over 2f out) | s.h | **16** | 20/1 | 79 | 61 |
| 4615[2] | **Step Aloft (80)** (LordHuntingdon) **4-9-1** JWeaver(3) (chsd ldrs: rdn over 2f out: sn lost tch) | 3 | **17** | 5/1[1] | 65 | 47 |
| 4683[6] | **Domappel (72)** (MrsJCecil) **4-8-7** GDuffield(17) (prom on outside: reminders ent st: sn wknd: t.o) | 8 | **18** | 12/1 | 46 | 28 |
| 4716[7] | **Mystic Hill (86)** (GHarwood) **5-9-0**(7) GayeHarwood(4) (a bhd: t.o) | 1¼ | **19** | 20/1 | 58 | 40 |
| | | | | (SP 136.9%) | **19 Rn** | |

**2m 35.12** (5.12) CSF £215.48 CT £2,175.31 TOTE £20.20: £4.00 £2.20 £2.70 £2.50 (£63.40) Trio £529.60 OWNER Mr H. H. Morriss (NEWMARKET) BRED Mr and Mrs H. H. Morriss

LONG HANDICAP Fern's Governor 7-9

WEIGHT FOR AGE 3yo-7lb

OFFICIAL EXPLANATION **Step Aloft: was unable to act on the loose going.**

**4385 Henry Island (IRE)** came good at the first time of asking over this longer trip and also had far more use made of him. It would seem his future lies in middle-distance trips and beyond from now on. (14/1)

**4580 Wild Rita** has had a very light season and looked sure to land the spoils when joining issue 100 yards out, but the winner pulled out more and she was still half a stride down at the line. She has been well supported for the November Handicap. (16/1)

**4580* Sugar Mill** moved into a challenging position below the distance but, on ground not quite testing enough for him, was unable to conjure the pace to mount his bid. (10/1)

**4686* Dreams End** enjoyed a trouble-free run on the inside rail and had every chance entering the final furlong, but was unable to go through with his effort when the whips were cracking. (9/1)

**3344 Bold Amusement**, having his first try at this extended trip, turned in a very pleasing performance without his customary blinkers, and there is still time for him to make his mark this term. (33/1)

**4675 River Keen (IRE)** had a nightmare run on the inside when about to launch his bid early in the straight, and again had nowhere to go when renewing his challenge 200 yards out. The position had to be accepted, but he could be the one to be on if he takes his chance in the November Handicap. (10/1)

**4617 Fern's Governor** ran well from the bottom of the handicap and is capable of finding another opening before the season closes. (12/1)
**Zaralaska** was only having his sixth race in the last couple of seasons, but he was well supported and was certainly not disgraced in finishing up a close-up eighth. There could be a race in mind. (6/1)
**4615 Step Aloft** probably needs less use made of her over this trip, for she was in trouble over two furlongs out and proved most disappointing. (5/1)

## 4873 CHARLES SIDNEY MERCEDES BENZ DONCASTER STKS (Listed) (2-Y.O) (Class A)

4-45 (4-45) **6f** £9,300.00 (£3,450.00: £1,662.50: £687.50: £281.25: £118.75) Stalls: High GOING: 0.27 sec per fur (G)

| | | | | SP | RR | SF |
|---|---|---|---|---|---|---|
| 4570* | **Elegant Warning (IRE) (89)** (BWHills) **2-8-4** RHills(2) (hld up & bhd: nt clr run over 2f out: qcknd to ld appr fnl f: sn clr) | — | **1** | 9/4[1] | 108+ | 76 |
| 1148* | **Open Credit** (HRACecil) **2-8-4** AMcGlone(4) (lw: a.p: led 2f out tl hdd & one pce appr fnl f) | 5 | **2** | 5/2[2] | 95 | 63 |
| 4677[4] | **Omaha City (IRE) (100)** (BGubby) **2-8-9** JWeaver(7) (led 4f: rdn over 1f out: kpt on) | ¾ | **3** | 6/1 | 98 | 66 |
| 4723[10] | **Jhazi** (DRLoder) **2-8-9** KDarley(6) (hld up: hdwy 2f out: rdn & one pce fnl f) | 1¾ | **4** | 7/2[3] | 93 | 61 |
| 4677[5] | **Superior Premium (99)** (RAFahey) **2-8-9** ACulhane(3) (lw: chsd ldrs 4f: sn rdn & btn) | 1¼ | **5** | 16/1 | 90 | 58 |
| 4555[6] | **Johnny Staccato (100)** (JMPEustace) **2-8-9** GDuffield(5) (lost pl after 1f: rdn ½-wy: no imp) | 4 | **6** | 12/1 | 79 | 47 |
| 4490[8] | **Naked Poser (IRE) (87)** (RHannon) **2-8-4** DBiggs(1) (lw: prom on outside 4f) | 5 | **7** | 16/1 | 61 | 29 |
| | | | | (SP 115.3%) | **7 Rn** | |

**1m 13.57** (2.57) CSF £8.19 TOTE £3.20: £1.70 £1.50 (£3.00) OWNER Mr Pip Elson (LAMBOURN) BRED Charlton Down Stud
**4570* Elegant Warning (IRE)** is a very progressive filly and, in winning this readily, could be set to go places next term. She should get a mile. (9/4)
**1148* Open Credit**, returning after over five months out of action, coped with this step up in class admirably, but she had met a tartar in the winner and could only look on in amazement. (5/2)
**4677 Omaha City (IRE)** adopted more forceful tactics and battled on willingly after being headed, but he was firmly put in his place when the sprint to the line developed. (6/1)
**4723 Jhazi** may well have found this easier ground not in his favour, for he was never really happy and proved unable to land a blow. (7/2)
**4677 Superior Premium** sat in behind the leader travelling smoothly for the first half-mile but, once the tempo picked up, he quite simply had no answer. (16/1)

T/Jkpt: Not won; £42,939.68 to Wetherby 27/10/96. T/Plpt: £632.90 (48.09 Tckts). T/Qdpt: £17.80 (118.94 Tckts). IM

# 4820-NEWBURY (L-H) (Soft)
## Saturday October 26th

WEATHER: overcast WIND: almost nil

## 4874 FURLONG CLUB RATED STKS H'CAP (0-100) (3-Y.O+) (Class B)

1-30 (1-30) **1m 1f** £8,739.20 (£3,252.80: £1,576.40: £662.00: £281.00: £128.60) Stalls: High GOING: 0.64 sec per fur (GS)

| | | | | SP | RR | SF |
|---|---|---|---|---|---|---|
| 4680[2] | **Wilcuma (100)** (PJMakin) **5-9-7** AClark(9) (rdn over 3f out: hdwy over 1f out: led ins fnl f: r.o wl) | — | **1** | 5/1[2] | 113 | 66 |
| 4556* | **Najm Mubeen (IRE) (91)** (ACStewart) **3-8-8** DHarrison(2) (hld up: rdn over 2f out: led 1f out tl ins fnl f: unable qckn) | 2 | **2** | 7/2[1] | 100 | 49 |
| 4568[10] | **Star Manager (USA) (86)** (PFICole) **6-8-7** TQuinn(6) (rdn over 2f out: hdwy over 1f out: r.o wl ins fnl f) | 1¼ | **3** | 13/2[3] | 93 | 46 |
| 4704* | **Questonia (99)** (HRACecil) **3-9-2** KFallon(10) (led over 7f: one pce) | nk | **4** | 8/1 | 106 | 55 |
| 4568[25] | **Stone Ridge (IRE) (90)** (RHannon) **4-8-11** DaneO'Neill(5) (lw: hdwy 4f out: led over 1f out: sn hdd: wknd ins fnl f) | 1¼ | **5** | 10/1 | 95 | 48 |
| 4671[6] | **Nagnagnag (IRE) (95)** (SDow) **4-9-2** SSanders(7) (lw: rdn over 2f out: hdwy over 1f out: wknd fnl f) | 1¼ | **6** | 8/1 | 97 | 50 |
| 4769[7] | **Rebel County (IRE) (90)** (ABailey) **3-8-7** DBiggs(4) (s.s: rdn & hdwy over 2f out: wknd over 1f out) | 5 | **7** | 7/1 | 83 | 32 |
| 3503[6] | **Committal (IRE) (100)** (JHMGosden) **3-9-3** JCarroll(12) (lw: prom over 7f) | 1¼ | **8** | 16/1 | 91 | 40 |
| 4568[18] | **Secret Spring (FR) (86)** (PRHedger) **4-8-7** BDoyle(11) (a bhd) | 1¼ | **9** | 20/1 | 75 | 28 |
| | **Twilight Sleep (USA) (86)** (LordHuntingdon) **4-8-7** TSprake(3) (prom over 5f) | 6 | **10** | 33/1 | 64 | 17 |
| 4682[19] | **Night Wink (USA) (86)** (GLMoore) **4-8-0**(7) JDennis(1) (prom over 5f) | 10 | **11** | 33/1 | 47 | — |
| 3709[15] | **Desert Green (FR) (95)** (RHannon) **7-9-2** RHughes(8) (lw: bhd fnl 4f) | s.h | **12** | 33/1 | 55 | 8 |
| | | | | (SP 115.5%) | **12 Rn** | |

**2m 0.28** (9.98) CSF £20.97 CT £103.75 TOTE £5.20: £1.90 £1.70 £2.10 (£9.00) Trio £16.50 OWNER Mr T. G. Warner (MARLBOROUGH) BRED Red House Stud
LONG HANDICAP Star Manager (USA) 8-6 Twilight Sleep (USA) 8-6 Night Wink (USA) 8-6 Secret Spring (FR) 8-2
WEIGHT FOR AGE 3yo-4lb
**4680 Wilcuma**, second in this race last year, went one better here, picking up nicely from below the distance to settle the issue inside the final furlong. (5/1)
**4556* Najm Mubeen (IRE)**, who has never run on this ground before, seemed to have no problem coping with it. Poking a nostril in front a furlong out, he was soon passed by the winner. (7/2: 5/2-4/1)
**4568 Star Manager (USA)**, 5lb higher than he has ever won off before, put in some good work in the last furlong and a half to take third. (13/2)
**4704* Questonia**, who scrambled home in a five-runner Conditions Stakes recently, has been raised a steep 10lb since her last handicap outing. (8/1: 11/2-9/1)
**1330 Stone Ridge (IRE)**, who has disappointed badly since winning the Lincoln in soft ground in March, ran a lot better here on this easier surface. (10/1)
**4671 Nagnagnag (IRE)** made an effort below the distance, but was soon feeling the pinch. (8/1: 6/1-10/1)

## 4875 RADLEY STKS (Listed) (2-Y.O F) (Class A)

2-00 (2-03) **7f 64y (round)** £10,235.00 (£3,080.00: £1,490.00: £695.00) Stalls: High GOING: 0.64 sec per fur (GS)

| | | | | SP | RR | SF |
|---|---|---|---|---|---|---|
| 4488[8] | **Boojum (95)** (BWHills) **2-8-8** AClark(8) (a.p: rdn over 3f out: led wl ins fnl f: r.o wl) | — | **1** | 10/1 | 96 | 54 |
| 4565[2] | **Fernanda (100)** (JLDunlop) **2-8-8b** TSprake(5) (a.p: rdn over 3f out: r.o wl ins fnl f) | 1 | **2** | 7/1[3] | 94 | 52 |
| 4305* | **Etoile (FR) (89)** (PWChapple-Hyam) **2-8-11** RHughes(9) (led: rdn 2f out: hdd wl ins fnl f: unable qckn) | nk | **3** | 9/1 | 96 | 54 |
| 4605* | **Dragonada (USA)** (HRACecil) **2-8-8** KFallon(7) (lw: chsd ldr: rdn over 3f out: ev ch wl ins fnl f: one pce) | hd | **4** | 4/1[1] | 93 | 51 |
| 3251* | **Tumbleweed Pearl (93)** (BJMeehan) **2-8-8** MTebbutt(10) (hld up: rdn over 2f out: one pce) | 1¾ | **5** | 10/1 | 89 | 47 |
| 4133[4] | **Bint Baladee** (SbinSuroor) **2-8-8b[1]** JCarroll(6) (lw: nvr nr to chal) | 2½ | **6** | 4/1[1] | 84 | 42 |
| 4723[7] | **Blues Queen (82)** (MRChannon) **2-8-8** RPerham(4) (bhd fnl 3f) | 1½ | **7** | 16/1 | 80 | 38 |

| | | | Pos | SP | RR | SF |
|---|---|---|---|---|---|---|
| 4758[5] | **More Silver (USA)** (PFICole) **2-8-8** TQuinn(2) (s.s: plld hrd: a bhd) | 12 | **8** | 12/1 | 54 | 12 |
| 4723[4] | **Blane Water (USA)** (JRFanshawe) **2-8-8** DHarrison(3) (a bhd) | 4 | **9** | 11/2[2] | 45 | 3 |
| | | | | (SP 109.6%) | **9 Rn** | |

**1m 36.11** (8.01) CSF £67.18 TOTE £12.30: £2.50 £2.10 £2.10 (£27.20) Trio £93.60 OWNER Mrs A. D. Bourne (LAMBOURN) BRED W. H. F. Carson

**4488 Boojum** appreciated the easier ground and, with her stamina coming into play, she wore down the leader to get on top in the last 50 yards. (10/1)

**4565 Fernanda**, fractious leaving the paddock and very troublesome going into the stalls, ran on nicely to take second inside the final furlong, a position she has now filled four times in a row. (7/1)

**4305* Etoile (FR)** appeared to be travelling supremely well as her rivals, with the exception of Tumbleweed Pearl, were all off the bridle in the straight, but she was overhauled in the final 50 yards. (9/1)

**4605* Dragonada (USA)** had a nice battle with Etoile in the straight, but was unable to cope with the first two in the last 50 yards. (4/1)

**3251* Tumbleweed Pearl**, taking a step up in class, had never encountered this ground before but travelled well. However, she appeared to get stuck in the mud when asked for an effort and is obviously more effective on a faster surface. (10/1: 8/1-12/1)

**4133 Bint Baladee** was fitted with blinkers for the first time, but they failed to have the desired effect. (4/1: 3/1-9/2)

**4758 More Silver (USA)** (12/1: 8/1-14/1)

## 4876 PERPETUAL ST SIMON STKS (Gp 3) (3-Y.O+) (Class A)

2-30 (2-32) **1m 4f 5y** £21,660.00 (£8,118.00: £3,909.00: £1,713.00) Stalls: High GOING: 0.64 sec per fur (GS)

| | | | Pos | SP | RR | SF |
|---|---|---|---|---|---|---|
| 4441[2] | **Salmon Ladder (USA) (113)** (PFICole) **4-9-0** TQuinn(12) (lw: mde all: rdn out) | — | **1** | 11/2[2] | 121 | 85 |
| 4327* | **Kutta (103)** (RWArmstrong) **4-9-0** RPrice(7) (hdwy over 4f out: chsd wnr over 2f out: hrd rdn over 1f out: r.o) | ¾ | **2** | 6/1[3] | 120 | 84 |
| 4569[4] | **Eva Luna (USA) (108)** (HRACecil) **4-9-0** KFallon(6) (a.p: rdn over 3f out: unable qckn) | 5 | **3** | 6/1[3] | 113 | 77 |
| 4654a[2] | **Whitewater Affair (106)** (MRStoute) **3-8-4** AClark(4) (b: lw: hld up: rdn over 3f out: one pce) | ¾ | **4** | 6/1[3] | 109 | 66 |
| 4192[4] | **Mons (119)** (LMCumani) **3-8-7** OUrbina(9) (lw: rdn over 3f out: hdwy over 1f out: nvr nrr) | 1¼ | **5** | 4/1[1] | 111 | 68 |
| 3781[3] | **Summer Spell (USA) (103)** (RCharlton) **3-8-7** SSanders(10) (hld up: rdn over 2f out: wknd over 1f out) | 3½ | **6** | 25/1 | 106 | 63 |
| 4441[5] | **Kalabo (USA) (113)** (SbinSuroor) **4-9-0** JCarroll(8) (nvr nr to chal) | 12 | **7** | 14/1 | 90 | 54 |
| 4479[3] | **Story Line (96)** (BWHills) **3-8-4** RPerham(11) (b.hind: lw: prom over 9f) | nk | **8** | 25/1 | 87 | 44 |
| 4657a[3] | **Chief Contender (IRE) (109)** (PWChapple-Hyam) **3-8-7** DHarrison(5) (prom over 9f) | 2½ | **9** | 13/2 | 86 | 43 |
| 3728a[4] | **Murajja (USA) (110)** (PTWalwyn) **4-9-0** TSprake(3) (lw: prom 4f) | ¾ | **10** | 16/1 | 85 | 49 |
| 4441[7] | **Quakers Field (107)** (GLMoore) **3-8-7** DaneO'Neill(1) (prom 8f) | 1¼ | **11** | 33/1 | 84 | 41 |
| 4678[6] | **Asterita (98)** (DRLoder) **4-8-11** RHughes(2) (a bhd: t.o) | 30 | **12** | 33/1 | 41 | 5 |
| | | | | (SP 117.7%) | **12 Rn** | |

**2m 39.69** (9.69) CSF £35.60 TOTE £4.90: £1.60 £2.20 £1.90 (£8.90) Trio £21.00 OWNER Mr M. Arbib (WHATCOMBE) BRED Robert N. Clay and Michael J. & Mrs Ryan

WEIGHT FOR AGE 3yo-7lb

**4441 Salmon Ladder (USA)**, who did not sweat up in the paddock as he had done on his two previous outings, is as tough as old boots and, despite a string of hard races, put up a marvellous display, despite Quinn momentarily losing his reigns approaching the final furlong, to richly gain his first-ever Group success. (11/2)

**4327* Kutta** moved into second place over a quarter of a mile from home but, although he did keep on inside the final furlong, he never looked like overhauling the winner. (6/1)

**4569 Eva Luna (USA)**, who ran no sort of race last time, went better here, but found this trip too sharp, even with some cut. (6/1)

**4654a Whitewater Affair** lacks a turn of foot in top company and never looked like quickening up in the last three furlongs. (6/1)

**4192 Mons**, on ground that should have been to his liking, was very disappointing and, although staying on from below the distance, never threatened at any stage. (4/1)

**3781 Summer Spell (USA)**, whose only victory to date came with some cut, chased the leaders, but was hung out to dry below the distance. (25/1)

## 4877 PADDOCK PAVILIONS CLAIMING STKS (3-Y.O+) (Class D)

3-00 (3-05) **1m 4f 5y** £4,341.00 (£1,308.00: £634.00: £297.00) Stalls: High GOING: 0.64 sec per fur (GS)

| | | | Pos | SP | RR | SF |
|---|---|---|---|---|---|---|
| 4496[3] | **Royal Diversion (IRE) (67)** (JLDunlop) **3-8-6** TSprake(10) (a.p: led over 3f out: clr over 2f out: comf) | — | **1** | 6/1 | 80+ | 55 |
| 4669[2] | **Country Lover (68)** (LordHuntingdon) **5-8-12v** KFallon(8) (lw: hld up: rdn over 3f out: chsd wnr fnl 2f: no imp) | 14 | **2** | 100/30[1] | 60 | 42 |
| 4785[9] | **Sally's Twins (56)** (JSMoore) **3-8-0**(3) MHenry(7) (rdn over 3f out: hdwy over 2f out: r.o) | 1¼ | **3** | 33/1 | 57 | 32 |
| 4766[4] | **Forever Noble (IRE) (57)** (MRChannon) **3-7-12**(5) PPMurphy(12) (lost pl 8f out: rallied over 2f out: r.o ins fnl f) | hd | **4** | 16/1 | 57 | 32 |
| *4332*[8] | **Harbet House (FR) (55)** (CACyzer) **3-8-8** RPrice(15) (rdn over 3f out: hdwy over 1f out: nvr nrr) | 1½ | **5** | 20/1 | 60 | 35 |
| 4703* | **Te Amo (IRE) (63)** (MBell) **4-8-9** MFenton(14) (hld up: rdn over 3f out: sn wknd) | 4 | **6** | 5/1[3] | 48 | 30 |
| 4515[11] | **Domettes (IRE) (58)** (RHannon) **3-7-10** NAdams(2) (lw: led over 8f: wknd 2f out) | 1¼ | **7** | 10/1 | 41 | 16 |
| | **Memory's Music (42)** (MMadgwick) **4-8-5**(3) NVarley(11) (nvr nr to chal) | 6 | **8** | 33/1 | 38 | 20 |
| 4365[9] | **Tirolette (IRE) (52)** (RJRWilliams) **4-8-5b** DHarrison(4) (prom over 8f) | 2 | **9** | 16/1 | 32 | 14 |
| *228*[6] | **Tamandu** (CJames) **6-8-3** FNorton(6) (nvr nrr) | 9 | **10** | 33/1 | 18 | — |
| 4716[6] | **At Liberty (IRE) (82)** (RHannon) **4-9-6** DaneO'Neill(17) (lw: prom over 8f) | 7 | **11** | 9/2[2] | 26 | 8 |
| | **Adonisis** (DRCElsworth) **4-9-11** AProcter(5) (lw: bhd fnl 4f) | 1¾ | **12** | 33/1 | 28 | 10 |
| | **Derrybelle** (DLWilliams) **5-8-3** GBardwell(16) (bhd fnl 5f) | nk | **13** | 33/1 | 6 | — |
| *1970*[W] | **Frankly Fran (43)** (DWPArbuthnot) **4-7-12**(5) MartinDwyer(3) (bhd fnl 4f) | 18 | **14** | 33/1 | — | — |
| 4557[2] | **Lalindi (IRE) (72)** (DRCElsworth) **5-9-6b** TQuinn(1) (prom over 8f: virtually p.u fnl 2f) | 16 | **15** | 6/1 | — | — |
| 4674[12] | **Western Country (20)** (EAWheeler) **4-9-0** MTebbutt(13) (a bhd: t.o fnl 5f) | 5 | **16** | 50/1 | — | — |
| | | | | (SP 131.7%) | **16 Rn** | |

**2m 42.94** (12.94) CSF £26.66 TOTE £7.90: £2.00 £1.50 £13.50 (£26.66) Trio £296.30 OWNER Mr Peter Townsend (Susa Racing) (ARUNDEL) BRED Romanny Investments and Tipper House Stud

WEIGHT FOR AGE 3yo-7lb

Royal Diversion (IRE) clmd CBarnes £18,000, Country Lover clmd CBarnes £12,000.

**4496 Royal Diversion (IRE)** revelled in the soft ground and, appreciating the drop in class, absolutely scooted up. (6/1)

**4669 Country Lover**, whose only victory since his three-year-old days came in a claimer on softish ground in May, went in vain pursuit of the winner in the final quarter-mile. (100/30)

**Sally's Twins** ran her best race of the season but, despite running on for third, never threatened. (33/1)

**4509 Forever Noble (IRE)** did stay on again in the last three furlongs, only just failing to secure third. (16/1)
**4092 Harbet House (FR)** has been campaigned on the All-Weather for the majority of the season. (20/1)
**4703* Te Amo (IRE)**, claimed out of Reg Akehurst's stable for £6,000, could not cope with the ground. (5/1)
**4216 Domettes (IRE)** (10/1: op 6/1)

## 4878 DICK DAWSON NURSERY H'CAP (2-Y.O) (Class C)

3-30 (3-32) **6f 8y** £5,865.00 (£1,770.00: £860.00: £405.00) Stalls: High GOING: 0.64 sec per fur (GS)

| Form | Horse | Dist | Pos | SP | RR | SF |
|---|---|---|---|---|---|---|
| 4469* | **Yorkie George (82)** (LMCumani) **2-9-3** OUrbina(10) (b.off hind: hld up: rdn over 1f out: led ins fnl f: r.o wl) | — | **1** | 4/1$^{1}$ | 93+ | 52 |
| 4475$^{3}$ | **Just Nick (76)** (WRMuir) **2-8-11** KFallon(4) (hld up: rdn over 2f out: r.o ins fnl f) | 3 | **2** | 9/2$^{2}$ | 79 | 38 |
| 4510$^{4}$ | **Heavenly Miss (IRE) (75)** (JJBridger) **2-8-10** DHarrison(3) (a.p: rdn over 2f out: ev ch ins fnl f: one pce) | nk | **3** | 20/1 | 77 | 36 |
| 4672$^{6}$ | **Farewell My Love (IRE) (80)** (PFICole) **2-9-1** TQuinn(2) (b.off hind: a.p: rdn 2f out: ev ch ins fnl f: one pce) | 1¼ | **4** | 15/2$^{3}$ | 79 | 38 |
| 4425* | **Ellens Lad (IRE) (77)** (RHannon) **2-8-12** DaneO'Neill(7) (led tl ins fnl f: sn wknd) | 2½ | **5** | 8/1 | 69 | 28 |
| 4566$^{15}$ | **Dalmeny Dancer (80)** (BJMeehan) **2-9-1** BDoyle(5) (nvr nr to chal) | nk | **6** | 14/1 | 72 | 31 |
| 4723$^{12}$ | **Song of Skye (86)** (TJNaughton) **2-9-7** SSanders(6) (s.s: nvr nrr) | 1¼ | **7** | 12/1 | 74 | 33 |
| 3659$^{2}$ | **Aegean Sound (80)** (RHannon) **2-9-1** RHughes(12) (nvr nrr) | 2 | **8** | 12/1 | 63 | 22 |
| 4614$^{12}$ | **Levelled (78)** (MRChannon) **2-8-13** RPerham(11) (lw: nvr nrr) | 2 | **9** | 25/1 | 56 | 15 |
| 4614$^{4}$ | **Nostalgic Air (USA) (68)** (EWeymes) **2-7-12**$^{(5)}$ MartinDwyer(1) (prom over 3f) | nk | **10** | 20/1 | 45 | 4 |
| 4566$^{6}$ | **A Breeze (80)** (DMorris) **2-9-1v$^{1}$** TSprake(9) (hld up: rdn over 2f out: wknd over 1f out) | nk | **11** | 8/1 | 56 | 15 |
| 4717$^{16}$ | **Feel A Line (76)** (BJMeehan) **2-8-11** MTebbutt(8) (a bhd) | 1¾ | **12** | 25/1 | 47 | 6 |
| 2873$^{3}$ | **Baritone (85)** (JWWatts) **2-9-6** JCarroll(13) (lw: prom 4f) | ¾ | **13** | 11/1 | 54 | 13 |

(SP 119.8%) **13 Rn**

**1m 19.16** (7.36) CSF £21.13 CT £300.09 TOTE £4.00: £1.80 £2.40 £4.80 (£10.80) Trio £98.10 OWNER Mr M. J. Dawson (NEWMARKET) BRED Robert Charles Key

**4469* Yorkie George** put up a thoroughly convincing display and, woken up below the distance, shot into the lead inside the final furlong for a decisive success. (4/1)
**4475 Just Nick**, tucked in behind the leaders, ran on inside the final furlong to snatch second. (9/2)
**4510 Heavenly Miss (IRE)**, who has changed stables since her last outing, was 11lb higher than when she last won. (20/1)
**4672 Farewell My Love (IRE)** appreciated the return to six furlongs. (15/2)
**4425* Ellens Lad (IRE)** found six furlongs too much for him in the soft ground. (8/1: op 5/1)
**4034a Dalmeny Dancer** (14/1: 10/1-16/1)
**4299 Song of Skye** (12/1: 8/1-14/1)
**2873 Baritone** (11/1: 8/1-12/1)

## 4879 WHATCOMBE CONDITIONS STKS (2-Y.O) (Class C)

4-00 (4-00) **1m (straight)** £4,793.00 (£1,787.00: £868.50: £367.50: £158.75: £75.25) Stalls: High GOING: 0.64 sec per fur (GS)

| Form | Horse | Dist | Pos | SP | RR | SF |
|---|---|---|---|---|---|---|
| 4104$^{4}$ | **Tempting Prospect** (LordHuntingdon) **2-8-6** DHarrison(7) (rdn over 3f out: hdwy over 2f out: led over 1f out: edgd lft: r.o wl) | — | **1** | 8/1 | 90 | 33 |
| | **Badlesmere (USA)** (PFICole) **2-8-8** TQuinn(4) (leggy: scope: a.p: rdn over 3f out: unable qckn) | 2 | **2** | 10/1 | 88 | 31 |
| 4050$^{2}$ | **Captain Collins (IRE)** (PWChapple-Hyam) **2-8-8**$^{(3)}$ RHavlin(3) (led: rdn 2f out: hdd over 1f out: wknd ins fnl f) | 4 | **3** | 11/8$^{1}$ | 83 | 26 |
| 3499* | **Gonzaga (IRE)** (JLDunlop) **2-9-0** TSprake(5) (lost pl over 3f out: r.o one pce fnl f) | 3½ | **4** | 6/1$^{3}$ | 79 | 22 |
| 4507$^{10}$ | **Baubigny (USA)** (MRChannon) **2-8-11** RHughes(1) (hld up: rdn over 3f out: wknd 2f out) | ¾ | **5** | 50/1 | 75? | 18 |
| 4449* | **Myrtlebank** (HRACecil) **2-8-9** KFallon(2) (lw: a.p: rdn over 3f out: wknd wl over 1f out) | s.h | **6** | 9/4$^{2}$ | 72 | 15 |
| 4494$^{6}$ | **Serenade (IRE)** (MJHaynes) **2-8-11** SSanders(6) (a bhd) | 22 | **7** | 66/1 | 30 | — |

(SP 110.8%) **7 Rn**

**1m 47.76** (10.76) CSF £68.31 TOTE £8.10: £1.90 £4.40 (£36.90) OWNER The Queen (WEST ILSLEY) BRED The Queen

**IN-FOCUS: This success gave The Queen her six-hundredth winner.**

**4104 Tempting Prospect** came through to strike the front below the distance and, despite drifting left, kept on well. (8/1: op 12/1)
**Badlesmere (USA)**, quite a tall colt with room for development, made a pleasing debut and, although done no favours by the winner as she went across him, it made not the slightest bit of difference to the result. There is a race waiting for him. (10/1)
**4050 Captain Collins (IRE)** appeared to be travelling really well in front but, once let down, failed to find as much as expected. (11/8)
**3499* Gonzaga (IRE)** was very disappointing. He did struggle on to be a very moderate fourth, but the race was already well and truly over. (6/1)
**Baubigny (USA)** had been hung out to dry two furlongs from home. (50/1)
**4449* Myrtlebank** flopped in the soft ground after racing up with the pace. (9/4: 6/4-5/2)

## 4880 LEVY BOARD NURSERY H'CAP (0-85) (2-Y.O) (Class D)

4-30 (4-32) **7f 64y (round)** £3,701.00 (£1,118.00: £544.00: £257.00) Stalls: High GOING: 0.64 sec per fur (GS)

| Form | Horse | Dist | Pos | SP | RR | SF |
|---|---|---|---|---|---|---|
| 4566$^{14}$ | **Kaiser Kache (IRE) (75)** (KMcAuliffe) **2-9-0** OUrbina(20) (a.p: led over 1f out: edgd lft ins fnl f: rdn out) | — | **1** | 20/1 | 82 | 59 |
| 4717$^{4}$ | **Petite Danseuse (77)** (CADwyer) **2-8-9**$^{(7)}$ JoHunnam(3) (swtchd rt over 2f out: hdwy over 1f out: r.o wl ins fnl f) | ¾ | **2** | 8/1$^{3}$ | 82 | 59 |
| 4760$^{14}$ | **Heart Full of Soul (77)** (PFICole) **2-9-2** TQuinn(17) (lw: led over 2f: led over 3f out tl over 1f out: 2nd & btn whn nt clr run ins fnl f) | 2 | **3** | 9/1 | 78 | 55 |
| 4672$^{3}$ | **Merciless Cop (69)** (BJMeehan) **2-8-8b** MTebbutt(13) (rdn & hdwy over 2f out: unable qckn ins fnl f) | hd | **4** | 6/1$^{1}$ | 70 | 47 |
| 4715* | **River of Fortune (IRE) (69)** (MHTompkins) **2-8-5**$^{(3)}$ MHenry(8) (hdwy over 1f out: r.o ins fnl f) | 1 | **5** | 13/2$^{2}$ | 68 | 45 |
| 4375$^{5}$ | **Palaemon (69)** (GBBalding) **2-8-8** DHarrison(15) (hdwy over 1f out: nvr nrr) | s.h | **6** | 10/1 | 67 | 44 |
| 4715$^{6}$ | **Marsh Marigold (67)** (MartynMeade) **2-7-13**$^{(7)}$ TField(12) (lw: hdwy over 2f out: edgd lft over 1f out: one pce) | 2½ | **7** | 11/1 | 60 | 37 |
| 4672$^{7}$ | **Silca's My Key (IRE) (70)** (MRChannon) **2-8-9v** RPerham(18) (nvr nr to chal) | 7 | **8** | 14/1 | 48 | 25 |
| 4566$^{8}$ | **Homestead (66)** (RHannon) **2-8-5** DaneO'Neill(14) (nvr nrr) | 1¼ | **9** | 12/1 | 41 | 18 |
| 3998$^{6}$ | **Blue Movie (69)** (MBell) **2-8-8b$^{1}$** MFenton(9) (a mid div) | 7 | **10** | 12/1 | 29 | 6 |
| 4717$^{17}$ | **Lamorna (75)** (MRChannon) **2-8-9**$^{(5)}$ PPMurphy(6) (nvr nrr) | 1 | **11** | 20/1 | 32 | 9 |
| 4451$^{8}$ | **Chorus Song (USA) (79)** (PWChapple-Hyam) **2-9-1**$^{(3)}$ RHavlin(10) (prom over 4f) | 1¼ | **12** | 11/1 | 34 | 11 |
| 4614$^{5}$ | **Tailwind (68)** (WRMuir) **2-8-0**$^{(7)}$ PDoe(5) (a.p: led 5f out tl over 3f out: wknd over 2f out) | 2 | **13** | 14/1 | 18 | — |

| | | | | SP | RR | SF |
|---|---|---|---|---|---|---|
| $4672^{11}$ | **Oneknight With You (77)** (MJFetherston-Godley) **2-9-2** KFallon(11) (hdwy over 2f out: wknd over 1f out) | 2½ | **14** | 16/1 | 22 | — |
| $4625^{15}$ | **Shimazu (IRE) (82)** (JHMGosden) **2-9-7** JCarroll(19) (bhd fnl 3f) | s.h | **15** | 11/1 | 27 | 4 |
| $4330^{16}$ | **Bewitching Lady (65)** (DWPArbuthnot) **2-8-4** TSprake(7) (prom 4f) | 1½ | **16** | 20/1 | 6 | — |
| $4549^{4}$ | **Greenwich Fore (73)** (TGMills) **2-8-12** SSanders(1) (bhd fnl 2f) | ½ | **17** | 16/1 | 13 | — |
| $4359^{6}$ | **Indian Rapture (73)** (RHannon) **2-8-12** RHughes(2) (lw: a bhd) | 1¼ | **18** | 20/1 | 10 | — |
| $4495^{11}$ | **Mystic Quest (IRE) (71)** (KMcAuliffe) **2-8-10v** PBloomfield(4) (lw: bhd fnl 3f) | 2½ | **19** | 20/1 | 3 | — |

(SP 147.1%) **19 Rn**

**1m 36.16** (8.06) CSF £175.34 CT £1,470.44 TOTE £52.10: £11.20 £1.20 £3.10 £2.60 (£312.90) Trio £337.10 OWNER Mr Peter Barclay (LAMBOURN) BRED St Simon Foundation

**4024a Kaiser Kache (IRE)** bounced back to form. Striking the front below the distance, he was rousted along for victory. (20/1)

**4717 Petite Danseuse** has been a model of consistency this season and was not at all inconvenienced by the step up to seven furlongs. Indeed, she was putting in all her best work in the last furlong and a half. (8/1)

**4602* Heart Full of Soul** was held when done no favours by the winner inside the final furlong. (9/1)

**4672 Merciless Cop** almost got on terms entering the final furlong, before tapped for toe. (6/1)

**4715* River of Fortune (IRE)**, who finally got off the mark in a seller last time, did not run badly in this better-class race and stayed on nicely from below the distance. (13/2)

**4375 Palaemon** made up some late headway without ever posing a threat. (10/1: 7/1-11/1)

**4368* Silca's My Key (IRE)** (14/1: 10/1-16/1)

**2619 Shimazu (IRE)** (11/1: 8/1-12/1)

T/Plpt: £3,181.10 (7.71 Tckts). T/Qdpt: £252.40 (4.19 Tckts). AK

## 4698-**LEICESTER** (R-H) (Good, Good to firm patches bk st)
## Monday October 28th

WEATHER: unsettled WIND: str bhd

### 4881 THRUSSINGTON H'CAP (0-70) (I) (3-Y.O+) (Class E)

12-45 (12-53) **5f 218y** £3,263.90 (£975.20: £466.60: £212.30) Stalls: High GOING minus 0.51 sec per fur (F)

| | | | | SP | RR | SF |
|---|---|---|---|---|---|---|
| $4805^{7}$ | **Bayin (USA) (68)** (MDIUsher) **7-9-12** RStreet(10) (hld up: hdwy over 2f out: shkn up to ld ins fnl f) | — | **1** | 5/1 [1] | 78 | 33 |
| $4610^{8}$ | **Beau Venture (USA) (61)** (BPalling) **8-9-5** TSprake(11) (lw: led tl over 1f out: rallied u.p fnl f) | ¾ | **2** | 11/1 | 69 | 24 |
| $2931^{4}$ | **Madrina (60)** (JBerry) **3-9-3** KDarley(17) (a.p: ev ch & rdn 1f out: unable qckn) | ½ | **3** | 20/1 | 67 | 21 |
| $4799^{11}$ | **Sue Me (IRE) (59)** (WRMuir) **4-9-3** JReid(20) (racd far side: ev ch 1f out: no ex fnl f) | ¾ | **4** | 16/1 | 64 | 19 |
| $4206^{10}$ | **Rambold (62)** (NEBerry) **5-9-6** KFallon(12) (a.p: ev ch 1f out: unable qckn) | nk | **5** | 12/1 | 66 | 21 |
| $4460^{4}$ | **Dissentor (IRE) (40)** (JAGlover) **4-7-9b**[1](3) MBaird(22) (racd far side: led over 1f out tl ins fnl f) | hd | **6** | 15/2 [3] | 44 | — |
| $4805^{8}$ | **Another Nightmare (IRE) (52)** (RMMcKellar) **4-8-10** PatEddery(4) (trckd ldrs: no hdwy fnl 2f) | 1¼ | **7** | 10/1 | 52 | 7 |
| $4809^{12}$ | **Castlerea Lad (65)** (RHollinshead) **7-9-4**(5) DGriffiths(1) (nvr nrr) | d.h | **7** | 9/1 | 65 | 20 |
| *$4090^{6}$* | **Featherstone Lane (42)** (MissLCSiddall) **5-8-0v** NCarlisle(8) (trckd ldrs: rdn & no hdwy fnl 2f) | 1½ | **9** | 20/1 | 38 | — |
| $4312^{9}$ | **Bee Health Boy (69)** (MWEasterby) **3-9-7b**(5) GParkin(14) (lw: prom over 4f) | nk | **10** | 13/2 [2] | 64 | 18 |
| $4592^{13}$ | **Honeyhall (39)** (NBycroft) **3-7-7**(3) NVarley(7) (hdwy ½-wy: rdn & wknd 2f out) | 1¼ | **11** | 50/1 | 31 | — |
| $4765^{13}$ | **Colston-C (53)** (PDEvans) **4-8-11** JFEgan(9) (plld hrd: spd 4f) | nk | **12** | 8/1 | 44 | — |
| $4259^{17}$ | **Rapier Point (IRE) (46)** (CMurray) **5-8-4** GCarter(19) (b: bkwd: outpcd) | 1½ | **13** | 20/1 | 33 | — |
| *$4778^{12}$* | **Cheeky Chappy (66)** (DWChapman) **5-9-10b** ACulhane(5) (chsd ldrs: rdn ½-wy: wknd over 2f out) | s.h | **14** | 20/1 | 53 | 8 |
| $3643^{13}$ | **Mu-Arrik (48)** (GROldroyd) **8-7-13v**(7)ow10 ClaireWest(6) (bit bkwd: outpcd: a bhd) | ¾ | **15** | 40/1 | 33 | — |
| $4356^{10}$ | **Petraco (IRE) (59)** (NASmith) **8-8-10**(7) JBramhill(2) (outpcd) | s.h | **16** | 20/1 | 44 | — |
| $4828^{12}$ | **Polli Pui (39)** (WMBrisbourne) **4-7-4**(7)ow1 RMullen(15) (unruly bef s: a outpcd) | ¾ | **17** | 33/1 | 22 | — |
| *$4573^{5}$* | **Halbert (44)** (PBurgoyne) **7-8-2** GDuffield(3) (outpcd) | 3½ | **18** | 20/1 | 18 | — |
| $4323^{18}$ | **Lady Seren (IRE) (38)** (SEKettlewell) **4-7-3**(7) JennyBenson(13) (dwlt: a bhd) | nk | **19** | 33/1 | 11 | — |
| $4074^{16}$ | **Imperial Red (IRE) (39)** (HJCollingridge) **3-7-10** NAdams(16) (outpcd) | nk | **20** | 50/1 | 11 | — |
| $4430^{14}$ | **Maybank (IRE) (41)** (AStreeter) **4-7-13** JQuinn(21) (s.s: a bhd & outpcd: t.o) | 12 | **21** | 25/1 | — | — |

(SP 138.5%) **21 Rn**

**1m 12.4** (2.40) CSF £60.16 CT £997.61 TOTE £5.90: £2.00 £7.60 £5.50 £2.00 (£59.80) Trio £377.90; £479.11 to Leicester 29/10/96 OWNER Mr Trevor Barker (SWINDON) BRED David V. Hall

LONG HANDICAP Polli Pui 7-9 Mu-Arrik 7-4 Lady Seren (IRE) 7-9 Imperial Red (IRE) 7-6 Honeyhall 7-9

WEIGHT FOR AGE 3yo-1lb

**4805 Bayin (USA)**, a very in-and-out performer nowadays, returned to form in this low-grade event with a comfortable success and does at least always pay for his keep. (5/1)

**2976 Beau Venture (USA)** used to be a regular trail-blazer and tried to adopt these tactics again this time but, over a trip that he has not yet succeeded at, was being held nearing the line. (11/1)

**2931 Madrina**, returning to sprinting after a three-month lay-off, produced by far her best performance yet, and this is where her future lies. (20/1)

**1522 Sue Me (IRE)** has had a very lean time in the last couple of years, but he showed a bit of his old dash and still retains some ability. (16/1)

**3700 Rambold**, beginning to look wintry in her coat, went with the pace and was a live contender until tapped for toe in the dash to the line. (12/1)

**4460 Dissentor (IRE)**, with just Sue Me for company, made his way home up the far rail, but a turn of finishing speed was missing when it was most needed. (15/2: op 5/1)

### 4882 SEAGRAVE APPRENTICE CLAIMING H'CAP (0-70) (3-Y.O+) (Class G)

1-15 (1-16) **1m 8y** £2,263.00 (£643.00: £319.00) Stalls: High GOING minus 0.51 sec per fur (F)

| | | | | SP | RR | SF |
|---|---|---|---|---|---|---|
| $4808^{5}$ | **Desert Zone (USA) (46)** (JLHarris) **7-8-4**(3) CLowther(18) (hld up centre: hdwy to ld wl over 1f out: drvn clr fnl f) | — | **1** | 20/1 | 60 | 27 |
| $4307^{18}$ | **Arcatura (51)** (CJames) **4-8-7**(5) RCody-Boutcher(13) (a.p: kpt on u.p ins fnl f) | 4 | **2** | 25/1 | 57 | 24 |
| $4831^{4}$ | **Baba Au Rhum (IRE) (61)** (IPWilliams) **4-9-8** JDennis(12) (chsd ldrs: led 3f out tl wl over 1f out: one pce) | hd | **3** | 11/1 | 67 | 34 |
| $4455^{15}$ | **Yuppy Girl (IRE) (45)** (CaptJWilson) **3-7-10**(7) AngelaHartley(16) (trckd ldrs: kpt on u.p appr fnl f) | ¾ | **4** | 25/1 | 49 | 13 |
| $4691^{2}$ | **Cats Bottom (53)** (AGNewcombe) **4-8-9**(5) DavidO'Neill(11) (led 5f: rdn, edgd lft & wknd ins fnl f) | 3½ | **5** | 7/2 [1] | 50 | 17 |
| $4701^{12}$ | **Queen of Shannon (IRE) (49)** (AWCarroll) **8-8-5v**(5)ow3 RStudholme(19) (hld up: sme late hdwy: nvr nrr) | hd | **6** | 8/1 | 46 | 10 |

| | | | | SP | RR | SF |
|---|---|---|---|---|---|---|
| 4692$^{5}$ | **Just Harry (54)** (MJRyan) **5-8-10**(5) AMcCarthy(17) (lw: hdwy over 2f out: nrst fin) | hd | **7** | 10/1 | 51 | 18 |
| 4829$^{5}$ | **Bold Angel (55)** (KAMorgan) **9-9-2** DDenby(15) (b: sn racing alone far side: no hdwy fnl 2f) | 3½ | **8** | 8/1 | 45 | 12 |
| 4701$^{8}$ | **Super Park (51)** (JPearce) **4-8-5**(7) LisaMoncrieff(4) (nvr nr to chal) | 2 | **9** | 10/1 | 37 | 4 |
| 4808$^{6}$ | **Kowtow (49)** (MDIUsher) **3-8-2**(5) RBrisland(1) (hld up: hdwy 3f out: wknd wl over 1f out) | ½ | **10** | 20/1 | 34 | — |
| 4551$^{10}$ | **Adilov (46)** (JJBridger) **4-8-7** CWebb(20) (nvr nr ldrs) | hd | **11** | 33/1 | 31 | — |
| 4820$^{20}$ | **Vanborough Lad (50)** (MJBolton) **7-8-11** JWilkinson(9) (prom over 5f) | s.h | **12** | 25/1 | 35 | 2 |
| 4511$^{8}$ | **Proud Brigadier (IRE) (47)** (PBurgoyne) **8-8-1**(7) JBosley(7) (trckd ldrs over 5f: sn rdn & wknd) | 5 | **13** | 14/1 | 22 | — |
| 4808$^{2}$ | **Funky (43)** (DNicholls) **3-8-1** JBramhill(2) (prom stands' side 5f) | 1¼ | **14** | 11/2 2 | 15 | — |
| 4808$^{10}$ | **Butterwick Belle (IRE) (53)** (RAFahey) **3-8-4**(7) RWinston(5) (a in rr) | ¾ | **15** | 25/1 | 24 | — |
| 4059$^{8}$ | **Mubariz (IRE) (65)** (CSmith) **4-9-12** JEdmunds(14) (chsd ldrs 5f) | 2 | **16** | 25/1 | 32 | — |
| 4701$^{14}$ | **Speedy Snaps Pride (47)** (PDCundell) **4-8-1**(7) SCrawford(8) (t.o) | 17 | **17** | 14/1 | — | — |
| 4597$^{15}$ | **Western Venture (IRE) (54)** (RMMcKellar) **3-8-7**(5) JMcAuley(3) (bhd fnl 3f: t.o) | s.h | **18** | 12/1 | — | — |
| 4829$^{15}$ | **Northern Judge (49)** (BHanbury) **3-8-7b** PDoe(6) (a bhd: t.o) | 4 | **19** | 11/1 | — | — |
| 2000$^{7}$ | **Gadge (57)** (ABailey) **5-9-4v** AngelaGallimore(10) (b: bit bkwd: t.o) | 30 | **20** | 15/2 3 | — | — |

(SP 159.2%) **20 Rn**

**1m 37.1** (2.10) CSF £469.48 CT £5,246.80 TOTE £36.70: £5.50 £10.40 £2.50 £12.10 (£245.80) Trio Not won; £214.00 to Leicester 29/10/96
OWNER Lavender Hill Leisure Ltd (MELTON MOWBRAY) BRED Michael D. Baudhuin
WEIGHT FOR AGE 3yo-3lb

**4808 Desert Zone (USA)**, winning his first race since the spring of 1992, took control soon after entering the final quarter-mile and, set alight into the last furlong, quickly pulled clear to win going away. (20/1)
**3466 Arcatura**, stepping down in distance, ran one of his better races and, if he could be relied on to give a repeat performance, there could be a prize waiting to be won. (25/1)
**4831 Baba Au Rhum (IRE)**, brought out quickly after a promising effort five days earlier, turned in another good performance, despite being plenty high enough in the weights. He would seem to be about to strike. (11/1)
**3849 Yuppy Girl (IRE)** was struggling to hold her pitch below the distance, but she was finding her stride again towards the finish, and she does appear to need a stiffer test of stamina. (25/1)
**4691 Cats Bottom** gradually drifted over towards the stands' rail after holding the call for five furlongs and probably gave away almost as much ground as she was beaten by. (7/2)
**3694 Queen of Shannon (IRE)** only found her stride when the race was as good as over and is surely capable of winning another prize when in the mood. (8/1)

## 4883 JOHN O'GAUNT NURSERY H'CAP (0-85) (2-Y.O) (Class E)

1-45 (1-47) **7f 9y** £3,507.00 (£1,050.00: £504.00: £231.00) Stalls: High GOING minus 0.51 sec per fur (F)

| | | | | SP | RR | SF |
|---|---|---|---|---|---|---|
| 4602$^{14}$ | **Maraud (69)** (JLSpearing) **2-8-7**(3) FLynch(4) (a.p: led 4f out: hld on wl fnl f) | — | **1** | 14/1 | 75 | 33 |
| 4564$^{6}$ | **Swan Island (64)** (BPalling) **2-8-5** TSprake(8) (b: lw: in tch: hdwy u.p over 2f out: r.o wl towards fin) | ¾ | **2** | 25/1 | 68 | 26 |
| 4717$^{10}$ | **Return of Amin (62)** (JDBethell) **2-8-3** TWilliams(13) (chsd ldrs far side: effrt & ev ch over 1f out: one pce) | 2 | **3** | 9/2 1 | 62 | 20 |
| 4364$^{6}$ | **Pericles (80)** (MJohnston) **2-9-7** JWeaver(2) (chsd ldrs: rdn & one pce appr fnl f) | 2½ | **4** | 8/1 | 74 | 32 |
| 4700$^{3}$ | **Silver Secret (75)** (MJHeaton-Ellis) **2-9-2** JCarroll(6) (s.s: hdwy 3f out: rdn over 1f out: nt pce to chal) | s.h | **5** | 14/1 | 69 | 27 |
| 4792$^{5}$ | **Tinkerbell (78)** (WRMuir) **2-9-5v** JReid(5) (led 3f: rdn & wknd appr fnl f) | hd | **6** | 6/1 3 | 72 | 30 |
| *4780$^{2}$* | **Princess of Hearts (66)** (BJMeehan) **2-8-7b** GDuffield(9) (nvr nrr) | 2 | **7** | 11/2 2 | 55 | 13 |
| 3515$^{11}$ | **Dizzy Tilly (61)** (TJNaughton) **2-8-2** JFEgan(17) (nvr nr to chal) | 1 | **8** | 25/1 | 48 | 6 |
| 4049$^{8}$ | **Bluebell Miss (69)** (MJRyan) **2-8-10** KFallon(16) (prom: outpcd after 3f: rallied over 2f out: wknd over 1f out) | 2 | **9** | 7/1 | 51 | 9 |
| 4764$^{9}$ | **King Uno (60)** (MrsJRRamsden) **2-8-1** NAdams(10) (s.s: a in rr) | 2 | **10** | 12/1 | 38 | — |
| 4182$^{5}$ | **Petrel (64)** (LordHuntingdon) **2-8-2v**(3) MHenry(11) (prom over 4f) | 1 | **11** | 8/1 | 40 | — |
| 4764$^{14}$ | **Mirror Four Life (IRE) (77)** (MHTompkins) **2-8-11**(7) RMullen(14) (prom far side: rdn 2f out: sn btn) | ½ | **12** | 14/1 | 51 | 9 |
| *4251$^{2}$* | **Windborn (55)** (CNAllen) **2-7-10** NCarlisle(3) (a in rr) | 2 | **13** | 14/1 | 25 | — |
| 4795$^{16}$ | **Suave Star (58)** (CADwyer) **2-7-10**(3) NVarley(12) (mid div tl lost pl over 2f out) | ¾ | **14** | 14/1 | 26 | — |
| 4751$^{7}$ | **Cimmerian (58)** (MrsJRRamsden) **2-7-13** JQuinn(15) (a bhd) | s.h | **15** | 10/1 | 26 | — |
| 4384$^{9}$ | **Ninth Symphony (77)** (PCHaslam) **2-9-4** GCarter(1) (a bhd) | 2 | **16** | 14/1 | 41 | — |
| 4602$^{16}$ | **Interdream (72)** (RHannon) **2-8-13** PatEddery(7) (a bhd) | 2½ | **17** | 12/1 | 30 | — |

(SP 154.7%) **17 Rn**

**1m 24.6** (1.60) CSF £335.66 CT £1,762.95 TOTE £30.20: £9.00 £2.50 £1.10 £5.40 (£284.30) Trio £263.10; £303.93 to Leicester 29/10/96
OWNER Dr P. J. Doherty (ALCESTER) BRED L. H. J. Ward
LONG HANDICAP Windborn 7-8

**3943 Maraud** poked a nostril in front before halfway and showed his true grit to ward off a host of would-be challengers inside the distance. (14/1)
**3493 Swan Island,** ridden with more restraint in this first handicap, was fairly eating up ground at the finish and she is coming to herself fast at this late stage of the season. (25/1)
**4091 Return of Amin,** heavily supported in the Ring, was always in the firing-line, but his measure had been taken 200 yards out and he could only stay on at the one pace. He may well be better suited to a slightly longer trip. (9/2: op 8/1)
**4364 Pericles** has adopted forceful tactics in the past, but he had it all to do here with topweight and could never find the pace to deliver his challenge. (8/1)
**4700 Silver Secret** once again lost ground at the start and always had a mountain to climb, but he did keep staying on, and he has the ability once he gets his act together. (14/1)
**4792 Tinkerbell** has been kept pretty busy of late and this slightly disappointing effort could suggest she has had enough for the time being. (6/1)
**4780 Princess of Hearts** was tackling slightly better company than she has in her most recent outings, and her finishing position of seventh was as close as she could manage. (11/2: 4/1-6/1)
**1467* Bluebell Miss** (7/1: op 16/1)

## 4884 E.B.F. WIDMERPOOL MAIDEN STKS (2-Y.O) (Class D)

2-15 (2-17) **7f 9y** £4,272.50 (£1,280.00: £615.00: £282.50) Stalls: High GOING minus 0.51 sec per fur (F)

| | | | | SP | RR | SF |
|---|---|---|---|---|---|---|
| 4801$^{17}$ | **Ortelius** (RHannon) **2-9-0** RHughes(4) (lw: mde all: hld on gamely nr fin) | — | **1** | 40/1 | 68 | 28 |
| 4698$^{4}$ | **Prince of Denial** (DWPArbuthnot) **2-9-0** TSprake(8) (b.hind: a.p: hrd rdn & ev ch over 1f out: rallied nr fin) | nk | **2** | 12/1 | 67 | 27 |

Tanaasa (IRE) (MRStoute) 2-9-0 JReid(5) (b.hind: str: scope: s.s: hdwy 2f out: r.o wl ins fnl f)....s.h 3 4/1[2] 67+ 27
Just Grand (IRE) (MJohnston) 2-9-0 JWeaver(2) (lt-f: unf: lw: hld up: hdwy & rdn 2f out: r.o wl towards fin)....hd 4 5/1[3] 67+ 27
4514[10] **Sharpest** (JLDunlop) **2-9-0** GCarter(7) (hld up: effrt & swtchd rt 3f out: ev ch appr fnl f: one pce)....½ 5 33/1 66 26
**Memorise (USA)** (HRACecil) **2-9-0** PatEddery(6) (unf: scope: s.i.s: hld up: swtchd lft over 2f out: hrd rdn: no rspnse)....4 6 4/6[1] 57 17
4507[7] **Hartshorn** (JLDunlop) **2-9-0** KDarley(10) (spd far side over 4f)....2½ 7 25/1 51 11
4123[8] **Swinging The Blues (IRE)** (RAkehurst) **2-9-0** JQuinn(3) (prom tl rdn & wknd 2f out)....2 8 20/1 47 7
4050[7] **Freedom Chance (IRE)** (JWHills) **2-9-0** GDuffield(1) (hrd drvn 3f out: sn lost tch)....3 9 25/1 40 —
**Patina** (RHollinshead) **2-8-6**(3) FLynch(9) (lt-f: bit bkwd: prom: rdn & ev ch over 2f out: sn wknd: t.o)....11 10 40/1 10 —
(SP 124.6%) **10 Rn**

**1m 25.3** (2.30) CSF £407.89 TOTE £157.10: £15.50 £2.00 £1.90 (£85.40) Trio £129.20 OWNER Mr I. A. N. Wight (MARLBOROUGH) BRED Cheveley Park Stud Ltd

**Ortelius**, a half-brother to several winners who has been slow to come to hand, made every post a winning one and stuck his neck out to hold on in a fierce battle to the line. (40/1)

**4698 Prince of Denial** showed he is getting the hang of things with another improved performance and does look to be a progressive youngster. (12/1)

**Tanaasa (IRE)**, a May foal from a very smart family, looked a bag of nerves. Flat-footed as the stalls opened, he was gaining with every stride inside the final furlong, and was most unfortunate not to make a winning debut. (4/1: 5/2-9/2)

**Just Grand (IRE)**, who should improve as he strengthens up, turned in a good display on this debut and more will be heard of him next term. (5/1)

**Sharpest** ran much better on this occasion, and he was only forced to admit defeat inside the last 50 yards. (33/1)

**Memorise (USA)**, a highly thought-of colt with plenty of scope, did look very green and, after a tardy start, could never get himself into the action. Bred to need middle-distances, he should come to himself as a three-year-old. (4/6)

## 4885 WYSALL CONDITIONS STKS (3-Y.O+) (Class C)

2-45 (2-45) **7f 9y** £5,232.44 (£1,807.64: £865.82: £352.10) Stalls: High GOING minus 0.51 sec per fur (F)

SP RR SF

3255[4] **Mashmoum** (JHMGosden) **3-8-5** JCarroll(1) (prom: rdn 3f out: hung lft fnl 2f: r.o wl to ld nr fin)....— 1 10/1 93 21
**Applaud (USA) (110)** (DRLoder) **3-8-5** KDarley(4) (bit bkwd: led: rdn over 2f out: hdd nr fin)....½ 2 10/11[1] 92 20
4774[15] **Tumbleweed Ridge (104)** (BJMeehan) **3-8-10** PatEddery(5) (lw: chsd ldr: rdn 3f out: ev ch ins fnl f: r.o)....½ 3 3/1[2] 96 24
4800[2] **Welton Arsenal (90)** (MRChannon) **4-9-4** RHughes(3) (lw: hld up: hdwy over 1f out: ev ch ins fnl f: rdn & nt r.o)....1¼ 4 4/1[3] 99 29
(SP 106.5%) **4 Rn**

**1m 25.2** (2.20) CSF £18.53 TOTE £10.60 (£4.70) OWNER Sheikh Ahmed Al Maktoum (NEWMARKET) BRED Mrs John Trotter
WEIGHT FOR AGE 3yo-2lb

**3255 Mashmoum**, a half-sister to Chipaya, looked a tricky ride and, despite drifting right over to the stands' rail, managed to land the spoils at the death. (10/1)

**Applaud (USA)**, off the course since winning last season's Cherry Hinton, looked short of peak-fitness and her rider subsequently reported that he did not think she would stay a mile. (10/11)

**681 Tumbleweed Ridge** has been highly tried since finishing fifth in the Free Handicap. (3/1)

**4800 Welton Arsenal**, a really frustrating character, again failed to go through with his effort. (4/1)

## 4886 SQUIRREL CONDITIONS STKS (3-Y.O+) (Class C)

3-15 (3-16) **1m 3f 183y** £5,198.52 (£1,924.68: £924.34: £378.70: £151.35: £60.41) Stalls: Low GOING minus 0.51 sec per fur (F)

SP RR SF

3781[2] **Masehaab (IRE) (104)** (JLDunlop) **3-8-7** KDarley(2) (mde all: rdn over 2f out: sn clr: r.o wl)....— 1 4/1[3] 106 32
3689[4] **Harbour Dues (94)** (LadyHerries) **3-8-11** KFallon(4) (lw: hld up & bhd: hdwy 3f out: chsd wnr 2f out: sn rdn: no imp)....3 2 7/4[1] 106 32
4714[7] **Wahiba Sands** (JLDunlop) **3-8-7** TSprake(5) (plld hrd in rr: rdn 3f out: styd on fnl f)....5 3 10/1 95 21
3986* **Mohawk River (IRE)** (MRStoute) **3-8-11** JReid(6) (prom tl wknd wl over 1f out)....1 4 3/1[2] 98 24
4178[8] **Weet-A-Minute (IRE) (100)** (RHollinshead) **3-8-4**(3) FLynch(3) (chsd wnr: rdn over 3f out: wknd 2f out)....3 5 10/1 90 16
1076[4] **Dovaly** (HRACecil) **3-8-11** PatEddery(1) (bkwd: bhd fnl 3f: t.o)....19 6 4/1[3] 68 —
(SP 119.5%) **6 Rn**

**2m 32.0** (3.00) CSF £11.83 TOTE £6.60: £2.30 £1.70 (£3.90) OWNER Mr Hamdan Al Maktoum (ARUNDEL) BRED T. Newman and Mellon Stud

**3781 Masehaab (IRE)** made full use of his stamina, having finished second over a longer trip last time. (4/1)

**3689 Harbour Dues** was never going to bridge the gap once the chips were down. (7/4)

**Wahiba Sands** made a belated seasonal debut earlier in the month and did not switch off as well as his rider would have liked. (10/1)

**3986* Mohawk River (IRE)**, a half-brother to Breeders' Cup Turf winner In The Wings, had more to do here and is probably not so effective over this longer distance. (3/1: op 2/1)

**2677 Weet-A-Minute (IRE)** seems to be struggling to find a trip. (10/1: 12/1-8/1)

**1076 Dovaly** (4/1: op 9/4)

## 4887 E.B.F. FLECKNEY MAIDEN STKS (2-Y.O F) (Class D)

3-45 (3-48) **5f 218y** £3,947.50 (£1,180.00: £565.00: £257.50) Stalls: High GOING minus 0.51 sec per fur (F)

SP RR SF

4797[3] **Arapi** (SirMarkPrescott) **2-8-11** GDuffield(4) (a.p: led over 1f out: edgd rt ins fnl f: rdn out)....— 1 7/2[2] 75 38
4578[3] **Bea's Ruby (IRE)** (ABailey) **2-8-11** JWeaver(9) (b: led over 4f: r.o)....¾ 2 8/1[3] 73 36
4706[8] **Tajrebah (USA)** (PTWalwyn) **2-8-11** JCarroll(1) (hdwy 3f out: r.o ins fnl f)....2½ 3 25/1 66 29
4756[9] **Midnight Shift (IRE)** (RGuest) **2-8-11** JReid(3) (a.p: rdn over 1f out: one pce)....nk 4 9/1 66 29
**Passion** (TGMills) **2-8-11** KFallon(14) (unf: bkwd: nvr nrr)....3 5 20/1 58 21
4756[7] **Miss Golden Sands** (GWragg) **2-8-11** PatEddery(8) (bkwd: dwlt: sn rcvrd: rdn over 2f out: no hdwy)....nk 6 Evens[1] 57 20
**Finarts Bay** (MrsJCecil) **2-8-11** KDarley(5) (leggy: lt-f: hdwy over 2f out: wknd over 1f out)....nk 7 12/1 56 19
4706[5] **Come Together** (DWPArbuthnot) **2-8-11** GCarter(12) (nvr trbld ldrs)....3½ 8 33/1 47 10
4558[7] **Ruby Tuesday (75)** (BAMcMahon) **2-8-6**(5) LNewton(11) (prom 4f)....nk 9 12/1 46 9
4451[12] **Ocean Light** (ABailey) **2-8-8**(3) DWright(7) (dwlt: rdn over 2f out: sn bhd)....5 10 33/1 32 —
**Oxbane** (HCandy) **2-8-11** NAdams(13) (unf: scope: bkwd: bhd fnl 2f)....nk 11 16/1 32 —
**Trevor Mitchell** (JJBridger) **2-8-4**(7) RMullen(2) (lt-f: unf: bkwd: a bhd)....1½ 12 50/1 28 —

| | | | | SP | RR | SF |
|---|---|---|---|---|---|---|
| *4331*$^{9}$ | **Terry's Rose (62)** (RHollinshead) **2-8-8**$^{(3)}$ FLynch(10) (prom over 3f) | 1¾ | **13** | 33/1 | 23 | — |

(SP 134.0%) **13 Rn**

**1m 11.0** (1.00) CSF £33.54 TOTE £4.30: £2.40 £1.60 £8.00 (£9.80) Trio £51.70 OWNER Hesmonds Stud (NEWMARKET) BRED Hesmonds Stud Ltd

**4797 Arapi** was certainly not inconvenienced by this drop back to six. (7/2: 5/2-4/1)
**4578 Bea's Ruby (IRE)**, a half-sister to Distinct Beauty, lost nothing in defeat. (8/1: op 4/1)
**Tajrebah (USA)**, a half-sister to Alhawa and Jallad, got stuck in the mud at Haydock last time and will do better when reverting to further. (25/1)
**Midnight Shift (IRE)**, a 40,000 guinea half-sister to Owington and Common Counsel, seems to be going the right way. (9/1: op 5/1)
**Passion** was by no means disgraced and should come on considerably for this debut. (20/1)
**4756 Miss Golden Sands** did not live up to her skinny starting price. (Evens)

## 4888 THRUSSINGTON H'CAP (0-70) (II) (3-Y.O+) (Class E)

4-15 (4-17) **5f 218y** £3,263.90 (£975.20: £466.60: £212.30) Stalls: High GOING minus 0.51 sec per fur (F)

| | | | | SP | RR | SF |
|---|---|---|---|---|---|---|
| 4571$^{9}$ | **Oggi (65)** (PJMakin) **5-9-9** PatEddery(18) (a.p: led 3f out: drvn out) | — | **1** | 9/2$^{1}$ | 77 | 56 |
| 4791$^{13}$ | **Souperficial (54)** (JAGlover) **5-8-12v** NDay(20) (hld up: hdwy over 2f out: hrd rdn & ev ch over 1f out: unable qckn) | 1½ | **2** | 11/1 | 62 | 41 |
| 4610$^{14}$ | **Mansab (USA) (52)** (PGMurphy) **3-8-9** JFEgan(4) (chsd ldr: rdn over 1f out: unable qckn) | ¾ | **3** | 9/2$^{1}$ | 58 | 36 |
| 4809$^{5}$ | **Ballard Lady (IRE) (44)** (JSWainwright) **4-7-9**$^{(7)}$ JBramhill(16) (lw: chsd ldrs: rdn 2f out: one pce) | 1¼ | **4** | 10/1 | 47 | 26 |
| 4828$^{4}$ | **Maraschino (42)** (BJMeehan) **3-7-13** JQuinn(19) (a.p: rdn over 2f out: one pce) | ¾ | **5** | 10/1 | 43 | 21 |
| 4679$^{10}$ | **Scissor Ridge (66)** (JJBridger) **4-9-3**$^{(7)}$ RMullen(21) (prom far side: eased whn btn ins fnl f) | ¾ | **6** | 10/1 | 65 | 44 |
| 4376$^{7}$ | **Never Think Twice (65)** (KTIvory) **3-9-8b** JReid(22) (b: hdwy far side over 2f out: hrd rdn over 1f out: one pce) | 1¾ | **7** | 12/1 | 59 | 37 |
| 4356$^{16}$ | **Rockcracker (IRE) (58)** (GGMargarson) **4-9-2b** GCarter(11) (nvr nr to chal) | 1¾ | **8** | 25/1 | 47 | 26 |
| 4521$^{11}$ | **Sabaah Elfull (63)** (ACStewart) **3-9-6** JCarroll(14) (hdwy over 1f out: nt rch ldrs) | s.h | **9** | 14/1 | 52 | 30 |
| 2345$^{2}$ | **Jareer Do (IRE) (51)** (BPalling) **4-8-9** TSprake(3) (swtg: bit bkwd: led 3f: wknd 2f out) | 1¾ | **10** | 12/1 | 36 | 15 |
| *4577*$^{5}$ | **Prudent Princess (52)** (AHide) **4-8-3**$^{(7)}$ CWebb(1) (prom stands' side over 3f) | ¾ | **11** | 25/1 | 35 | 14 |
| *4778*$^{10}$ | **Allwight Then (IRE) (58)** (DJSCosgrove) **5-9-2** MRimmer(7) (prom over 3f) | 1¾ | **12** | 14/1 | 36 | 15 |
| 4788$^{W}$ | **Denbrae (IRE) (70)** (DJGMurraySmith) **4-10-0** GDuffield(13) (n.d) | 1½ | **13** | 9/1 | 44 | 23 |
| 4053$^{14}$ | **Redskin Lady (54)** (RJO'Sullivan) **3-8-11** KFallon(10) (prom over 3f) | 1 | **14** | 8/1$^{3}$ | 25 | 3 |
| 4701$^{10}$ | **Everset (FR) (55)** (ABailey) **8-8-10b**$^{(3)}$ DWright(8) (b: lw: a bhd) | ½ | **15** | 6/1$^{2}$ | 25 | 4 |
| 4809$^{15}$ | **Miss Aragon (38)** (MissLCSiddall) **8-7-10** NCarlisle(5) (lw: a bhd) | ¾ | **16** | 16/1 | 6 | — |
| 4581$^{22}$ | **Erupt (70)** (GBBalding) **3-9-13v** RHughes(15) (a bhd) | ¾ | **17** | 33/1 | 36 | 14 |
| 4693$^{9}$ | **Northern Clan (40)** (AJChamberlain) **3-7-11b**$^{ow1}$ NAdams(17) (b: a bhd) | nk | **18** | 100/1 | 5 | — |
| 4805$^{17}$ | **Magic Melody (58)** (JLSpearing) **3-8-12**$^{(3)}$ FLynch(9) (a bhd) | 1 | **19** | 20/1 | 20 | — |
| 4598$^{11}$ | **Rowlandsons Stud (IRE) (49)** (PBurgoyne) **3-7-13**$^{(7)}$ JBosley(2) (prom 3f) | ½ | **20** | 25/1 | 10 | — |
| | **Green Golightly (USA) (46)** (RMFlower) **5-8-1**$^{(3)}$ NVarley(6) (bkwd: prom 3f) | 1¼ | **21** | 50/1 | 4 | — |

(SP 164.2%) **21 Rn**

**1m 10.5** (0.50) CSF £64.90 CT £249.39 TOTE £3.60: £2.00 £2.30 £3.60 £2.20 (£21.80) Trio £184.70 OWNER Skyline Racing Ltd (MARLBOROUGH) BRED H. D. and M. J. Gee
LONG HANDICAP Northern Clan 7-8
WEIGHT FOR AGE 3yo-1lb

**4198 Oggi,** 7lb higher than when scoring at Haydock, probably found seven beyond his best last time. (9/2: op 3/1)
**4610 Souperficial**, 4lb higher than when winning over the minimum here last month, bounced back to form on this step up to six. (11/1)
**4356 Mansab (USA)**, a springer in the market, had dropped 22lb since first appearing in a handicap. (9/2)
**4809 Ballard Lady (IRE)** may have preferred a little more cut in the ground. (10/1)
**4828 Maraschino** has been raised 2lb for a couple of decent efforts in non-handicaps. (10/1)
**4372* Scissor Ridge** did not have much to race with on the far side and ran better than his finishing position suggests. (10/1)
**3162 Redskin Lady** (8/1: op 4/1)

T/Jkpt: Not won; £2,180.31 to Leicester 29/10/96. T/Plpt: £12,867.60 (0.56 Tckts); £7,651.06 to Leicester 29/10/96. T/Qdpt: £246.40 (4.19 Tckts). IM/KH

# 4544-LINGFIELD (L-H) (Turf Good to soft, Soft patches, AWT Standard)

## Monday October 28th

WEATHER: blustery WIND: v.str half bhd

## 4889 E.B.F. CEDAR MAIDEN STKS (I) (2-Y.O F) (Class D)

1-00 (1-01) **7f** £3,295.95 (£981.60: £467.30: £210.15) Stalls: High GOING: 0.40 sec per fur (GS)

| | | | | SP | RR | SF |
|---|---|---|---|---|---|---|
| 4756$^{2}$ | **Miss Sancerre** (GWragg) **2-8-11** MHills(11) (mde virtually all: comf) | — | **1** | 10/11$^{1}$ | 75+ | 34 |
| 4570$^{12}$ | **Kilshanny** (LMCumani) **2-8-11** OUrbina(5) (b.nr hind: lw: hld up: rdn over 2f out: r.o one pce ins fnl f) | 3 | **2** | 8/1 | 68 | 27 |
| 4725$^{4}$ | **Amaryllis (IRE)** (JHMGosden) **2-8-11** GHind(3) (a.p: rdn wl over 1f out: one pce) | s.h | **3** | 3/1$^{2}$ | 68 | 27 |
| 4797$^{14}$ | **Sound Appeal** (AGFoster) **2-8-11b**$^{1}$ RPerham(6) (a.p: rdn wl over 1f out: one pce) | nk | **4** | 33/1 | 67 | 26 |
| 4706$^{6}$ | **Star Precision** (GBBalding) **2-8-11** SDrowne(12) (lw: no hdwy fnl 2f) | 4 | **5** | 33/1 | 58 | 17 |
| 4797$^{12}$ | **Venetian Scene** (PFICole) **2-8-11** RHills(4) (a.p: rdn wl over 1f out: sn wknd) | 1¼ | **6** | 20/1 | 55 | 14 |
| | **La Chatelaine** (GLewis) **2-8-11** SWhitworth(8) (unf: bit bkwd: nvr nrr) | 7 | **7** | 20/1 | 39 | — |
| 4435$^{4}$ | **Tyrolean Dancer (IRE)** (SPCWoods) **2-8-11** DBiggs(10) (hld up: rdn 3f out: wknd 2f out) | ½ | **8** | 50/1 | 38 | — |
| 4605$^{7}$ | **Bobbitt** (WJarvis) **2-8-11** WRyan(1) (bhd fnl 2f) | 3½ | **9** | 20/1 | 30 | — |
| 3593$^{12}$ | **Snow Eagle (IRE)** (RHannon) **2-8-11** DaneO'Neill(2) (bit bkwd: a bhd) | 2½ | **10** | 7/1$^{3}$ | 25 | — |
| | **Flying Colours (IRE)** (CJBenstead) **2-8-11** AMcGlone(7) (str: bkwd: s.s: a bhd) | 2½ | **11** | 33/1 | 19 | — |

(SP 126.1%) **11 Rn**

**1m 29.42** (7.82) CSF £9.83 TOTE £1.90: £1.20 £3.30 £1.40 (£8.50) Trio £6.10 OWNER Mr J. L. C. Pearce (NEWMARKET) BRED J. L. C. Pearce

**4756 Miss Sancerre** confirmed the promise shown on her debut and needed only to be nudged along for a cosy success. (10/11: 4/6-11/10)
**Kilshanny**, who looked very well and was the pick of the paddock, left her initial run behind, staying on to snatch second right on the line. Staying is going to be her game. (8/1)
**4725 Amaryllis (IRE)** did not take the eye in the paddock. (3/1)

**3982 Sound Appeal** ran much better with the first-time blinkers on. (33/1)
**4706 Star Precision** was left standing in the last quarter-mile. (33/1)
**4797 Venetian Scene** played an active role until coming to the end of her tether approaching the final furlong. (20/1)

## 4890 E.B.F. CEDAR MAIDEN STKS (II) (2-Y.O F) (Class D)

1-30 (1-34) **7f** £3,295.95 (£981.60: £467.30: £210.15) Stalls: High GOING: 0.40 sec per fur (GS)

| Form | Horse | Dist | Pos | SP | RR | SF |
|---|---|---|---|---|---|---|
| 4697[2] | **Apache Star** (GWragg) **2-8-11** MHills(1) (lw: w ldr: led 1f out: rdn out) | — | **1** | 11/8[1] | 81 | 36 |
| 4605[3] | **Sweeten Up** (HRACecil) **2-8-11** WRyan(4) (lw: led: rdn over 2f out: hdd 1f out: unable qckn) | 1¾ | **2** | 9/4[2] | 77 | 32 |
| | **Melodica** (MRStoute) **2-8-11** DHarrison(11) (b.nr hind: leggy: unf: hld up: rdn 3f out: r.o one pce) | 4 | **3** | 10/1[3] | 68+ | 23 |
| 4211[7] | **Push A Venture** (SPCWoods) **2-8-11** AClark(7) (rdn over 2f out: hdwy over 1f out: nvr nrr) | 4 | **4** | 50/1 | 59 | 14 |
| 3988[12] | **Pointe Fine (FR)** (JWHills) **2-8-11** GHind(8) (hld up: rdn over 2f out: wknd over 1f out) | hd | **5** | 50/1 | 59 | 14 |
| | **Ladybird** (JHMGosden) **2-8-11** RHills(9) (unf: bit bkwd: a.p: rdn over 2f out: wknd over 1f out) | 1½ | **6** | 10/1[3] | 55 | 10 |
| | **Bint Rosie** (MJFetherston-Godley) **2-8-11** CRutter(6) (w'like: a bhd) | 6 | **7** | 50/1 | 41 | — |
| | **Slipstream Star** (IABalding) **2-8-6**(5) MartinDwyer(2) (leggy: unf: prom 4f) | 1¼ | **8** | 16/1 | 39 | — |
| 4357[7] | **Missfortuna** (SirMarkPrescott) **2-8-11** CNutter(10) (a bhd) | 3 | **9** | 20/1 | 32 | — |
| 2904[11] | **Tariff (IRE)** (NAGraham) **2-8-11** MRoberts(5) (hdwy over 5f out: wknd 4f out) | 20 | **10** | 33/1 | — | — |
| | ***Pennywell*** (RFJohnsonHoughton) **2-8-11** AMcGlone(3) (Withdrawn not under Starter's orders: ref to ent stalls) | | **W** | 25/1 | — | — |

(SP 114.4%) **10 Rn**

**1m 29.3** (7.70) CSF £4.37 TOTE £2.30: £1.00 £1.40 £3.50 (£2.30) Trio £3.60 OWNER Mr A. E. Oppenheimer (NEWMARKET) BRED Hascombe and Valiant Studs

**4697 Apache Star** confirmed the promise shown on her debut. (11/8)
**4605 Sweeten Up**, together with the winner, was the paddock pick and drew clear of the rest of the field, bar the winner, in the final quarter-mile. (9/4: 6/4-5/2)
**Melodica**, whose dam won the Italian Oaks and dead-heated for the Irish Oaks, never threatened to get on terms with the front two. (10/1: op 6/1)
**Push A Venture** ran better here and stayed on without posing a threat. (50/1)
**Pointe Fine (FR)** had been hung out to dry below the distance. (50/1)
**Ladybird** needed the run, and so it proved as she tired below the distance, having raced up with the pace from the outset. (10/1: op 6/1)

## 4891 E.B.F. WILLOW MAIDEN STKS (2-Y.O) (Class D)

2-00 (2-03) **7f** £4,079.20 (£1,222.60: £587.80: £270.40) Stalls: High GOING: 0.40 sec per fur (GS)

| Form | Horse | Dist | Pos | SP | RR | SF |
|---|---|---|---|---|---|---|
| 4700[2] | **Maylane** (ACStewart) **2-8-11** MRoberts(18) (racd stands' side: mde all: comf) | — | **1** | 9/2[2] | 83+ | 42 |
| | **Stamp (IRE)** (BSmart) **2-8-11** MTebbutt(2) (neat: lw: a.p: rdn over 2f out: unable qckn fnl f) | 7 | **2** | 14/1 | 67 | 26 |
| | **Royale Finale (IRE)** (HRACecil) **2-8-11** WRyan(15) (scope: lw: racd stands' side: hld up: rdn 3f out: r.o one pce) | 3 | **3** | 9/4[1] | 60+ | 19 |
| | **Young Precedent** (PWHarris) **2-8-11** GHind(4) (leggy: bit bkwd: rdn & hdwy over 2f out: one pce) | 1 | **4** | 13/2 | 58 | 17 |
| 4370[9] | **Utah (IRE)** (LMontagueHall) **2-8-6**(5) MartinDwyer(11) (racd stands' side: a.p: rdn over 2f out: wknd over 1f out) | 4 | **5** | 33/1 | 49 | 8 |
| 3245[3] | **Olivo (IRE)** (PFICole) **2-8-11** AClark(1) (a.p: rdn over 2f out: wknd over 1f out) | ½ | **6** | 11/2[3] | 48 | 7 |
| 4380[8] | **Cheval Roc** (RHannon) **2-8-11** DaneO'Neill(14) (racd stands' side: prom over 4f) | 2½ | **7** | 25/1 | 42 | 1 |
| | **Such Boldness** (RAkehurst) **2-8-11** DHarrison(8) (w'like: bit bkwd: prom over 5f) | 3 | **8** | 25/1 | 35 | — |
| 4700[4] | **Final Trial (IRE)** (GWragg) **2-8-11** MHills(3) (prom over 5f) | 5 | **9** | 13/2 | 24 | — |
| 4715[16] | **Zorro** (RMFlower) **2-8-11** DBiggs(17) (racd stands' side: nvr nrr) | ¾ | **10** | 50/1 | 22 | — |
| | **Mr Music** (KMcAuliffe) **2-8-11** OUrbina(12) (w'like: bit bkwd: a mid div) | ½ | **11** | 33/1 | 21 | — |
| 4516[15] | **Oliver (IRE)** (RWArmstrong) **2-8-11** RHills(10) (nvr nrr) | 2 | **12** | 20/1 | 16 | — |
| 4801[18] | **Euro Superstar (FR)** (SDow) **2-8-8**(3) AWhelan(16) (racd stands' side: bhd fnl 3f) | nk | **13** | 33/1 | 16 | — |
| 3829[8] | **Hippios** (SDow) **2-8-6**(5) ADaly(13) (bit bkwd: racd stands' side: a bhd) | hd | **14** | 50/1 | 15 | — |
| | **Jolly Jackson** (RAkehurst) **2-8-11** RPerham(7) (w'like: a bhd) | 1¾ | **15** | 33/1 | 11 | — |
| 4330[8] | **Klondike Charger (USA)** (BWHills) **2-8-8**(3) JDSmith(5) (mid div 5f) | hd | **16** | 10/1 | 11 | — |
| 4825[16] | **Timothy George (IRE)** (GBBalding) **2-8-11** SDrowne(9) (bhd fnl 3f) | ½ | **17** | 33/1 | 10 | — |
| 4369[14] | **Sylvan Jubilacion** (PMitchell) **2-8-11** SWhitworth(6) (b.hind: a bhd) | nk | **18** | 33/1 | 9 | — |

(SP 140.8%) **18 Rn**

**1m 28.76** (7.16) CSF £69.38 TOTE £5.40: £2.00 £3.10 £2.10 (£22.80) Trio £80.60 OWNER Sheikh Ahmed Al Maktoum (NEWMARKET) BRED Sheikh Ahmed Bin Rashid Al Maktoum

**4700 Maylane** was allowed to bowl along in front and that appeared to suit him down to the ground, as he comfortably had the measure of his rivals. (9/2)
**Stamp (IRE)** looked in good shape for this debut and won the battle on the far side. (14/1: op 33/1)
**Royale Finale (IRE)**, a 200,000 guinea individual who has room for development, took the eye in the paddock. (9/4: 5/4-5/2)
**Young Precedent** looked as though the run would do him good. (13/2: 10/1-6/1)
**Utah (IRE)**, always close up on the stands' side, had shot his bolt below the distance. (33/1)
**3245 Olivo (IRE)**, given a three-month break, set the pace on the far side but had burnt his boats below the distance. (11/2: 3/1-6/1)
**4700 Final Trial (IRE)** (13/2: 3/1-8/1)

## 4892 MCDOWELLS MEDIAN AUCTION MAIDEN STKS (3-Y.O) (Class E)

2-30 (2-31) **1m 5f (Equitrack)** £2,988.30 (£890.40: £424.20: £191.10) Stalls: Low GOING minus 0.48 sec per fur (FST)

| Form | Horse | Dist | Pos | SP | RR | SF |
|---|---|---|---|---|---|---|
| 4726[4] | **Hoofprints (IRE) (60)** (GHarwood) **3-9-0** AClark(7) (chsd ldr: led over 4f out: rdn out) | — | **1** | 9/4[2] | 68 | 42 |
| 4496[6] | **Matthias Mystique (55)** (MissBSanders) **3-8-9** DaneO'Neill(2) (hld up: rdn over 4f out: r.o one pce fnl 2f) | 1 | **2** | 6/1[3] | 62 | 36 |
| 4496[7] | **Coh Sho No (54)** (SDow) **3-8-9e** MRoberts(1) (a.p: rdn over 4f out: one pce) | 1½ | **3** | 6/1[3] | 60 | 34 |
| 4548[5] | **Shirley Venture (71)** (SPCWoods) **3-8-9** WRyan(6) (led over 8f: rdn & one pce) | ¾ | **4** | 2/1[1] | 59 | 33 |
| 4833[12] | **Magic Role (62)** (MAJarvis) **3-9-0** MHills(8) (hld up: rdn 4f out: chsd wnr over 2f out tl ins fnl f: sn wknd) | 1½ | **5** | 12/1 | 62 | 36 |
| 3942[6] | **Shoshone** (JHMGosden) **3-8-9** GHind(3) (a bhd) | 9 | **6** | 8/1 | 46 | 20 |
| 4506[10] | **Hallikeld (37)** (TJEtherington) **3-8-9b**[1] CRutter(5) (lw: a bhd: t.o fnl 4f) | 26 | **7** | 50/1 | 14 | — |
| 4752[9] | **Philgem (20)** (CWFairhurst) **3-8-9** NKennedy(4) (a bhd: t.o fnl 4f) | dist | **8** | 66/1 | — | — |

(SP 114.9%) **8 Rn**

**2m 46.16** (2.96) CSF £15.20 TOTE £3.00: £1.50 £1.70 £1.70 (£9.20) OWNER Mr Selwyn Lewis (PULBOROUGH) BRED Eamon Freaney

**IN-FOCUS: this was a dreadful contest with none of the horses inspiring confidence for the future.**

**4726 Hoofprints (IRE)**, with his jockey rousting him along in the straight, won unconvincingly. (9/4)
**4496 Matthias Mystique** railed well into the straight and stayed on to take second. She is very moderate indeed. (6/1)
**1614 Coh Sho No**, trying a longer trip, was made to looked very one-paced in the last half-mile. (6/1)
**4548 Shirley Venture**, collared over half a mile from home, could only do everything in her own time. (2/1: 5/4-9/4)
**4611 Magic Role**, collared for the runner-up berth inside the final furlong, had nothing more to give. (12/1: 10/1-16/1)
**Shoshone** (8/1: 6/1-10/1)

## 4893 BURR CONDITIONS STKS (2-Y.O) (Class C)

3-00 (3-00) **5f** £4,646.88 (£1,717.92: £822.96: £334.80: £131.40: £50.04) Stalls: High GOING: 0.40 sec per fur (GS)

| | | | | SP | RR | SF |
|---|---|---|---|---|---|---|
| 4579$^{2}$ | **Jennelle (100)** (CADwyer) **2-8-5**(7) JoHunnam(3) (a.p: rdn over 1f out: led ins fnl f: r.o wl) | — | **1** | 4/1$^{2}$ | 89 | 54 |
| 2070$^{6}$ | **Darb Alola (USA)** (MRStoute) **2-8-11** MHills(2) (led: rdn over 1f out: hung lft & hdd ins fnl f: r.o wl) | s.h | **2** | 11/4$^{1}$ | 88 | 53 |
| 3160$^{9}$ | **Joint Venture (IRE) (80)** (BJMeehan) **2-9-1** MTebbutt(8) (a.p: rdn over 1f out: unable qckn) | 2½ | **3** | 25/1 | 84 | 49 |
| 4247$^{4}$ | **Joza** (HCandy) **2-8-10** CRutter(9) (hld up: rdn over 2f out: one pce) | nk | **4** | 11/2 | 78 | 43 |
| 4754* | **Lady Diesis (USA)** (BWHills) **2-8-7**(3) JDSmith(6) (rdn & hdwy over 1f out: one pce) | ½ | **5** | 9/2$^{3}$ | 76 | 41 |
| 2712* | **Salty Behaviour (IRE) (85)** (RHannon) **2-8-11** DaneO'Neill(4) (lw: rdn & no hdwy fnl 2f) | nk | **6** | 10/1 | 76 | 41 |
| 4685$^{4}$ | **For Old Times Sake (100)** (JBerry) **2-9-4**(5) PRoberts(7) (nvr nr to chal) | nk | **7** | 10/1 | 87 | 52 |
| 4517$^{2}$ | **Hattab (IRE) (93)** (PTWalwyn) **2-9-1** RHills(5) (lw: rdn over 3f out: hdwy over 1f out: sn wknd) | 3 | **8** | 9/2$^{3}$ | 70 | 35 |
| | **Riverine** (GLewis) **2-8-3** GHind(1) (neat: s.s: a bhd) | 10 | **9** | 25/1 | 26 | — |
| | | | | (SP 124.3%) | **9 Rn** | |

**61.42 secs** (4.42) CSF £15.97 TOTE £4.80: £1.20 £2.20 £6.30 (£12.20) Trio £158.70 OWNER Mrs J. A. Cornwell (NEWMARKET) BRED Mrs A. J. Owen

**4579 Jennelle**, troublesome leaving the paddock, did nothing wrong in the race and held on in a very tight finish. (4/1)
**2070 Darb Alola (USA)** ran a first-class race. After making it, he stuck on really well and may even have got back in front in a few more strides. (11/4)
**1766 Joint Venture (IRE)**, off the course for three months, appreciated the easy ground. (25/1)
**4247 Joza**, fitted with a net-muzzle, never looked like finding that vital turn of foot in the last two furlongs. (11/2)
**4754* Lady Diesis (USA)** probably found the drop to five not in her favour. (9/2: 3/1-5/1)
**2712* Salty Behaviour (IRE)** looked in good shape for this first run in over three months. A return to six would probably help. (10/1)

## 4894 BYAS MOSLEY H'CAP (0-70) (3-Y.O+) (Class E)

3-30 (3-31) **1m 4f (Equitrack)** £3,206.70 (£957.60: £457.80: £207.90) Stalls: Low GOING minus 0.48 sec per fur (FST)

| | | | | SP | RR | SF |
|---|---|---|---|---|---|---|
| 4617$^{4}$ | **Manful (54)** (CWCElsey) **4-8-12b** NKennedy(14) (stdy hdwy over 4f out: led on bit over 3f out: rdn over 2f out: all out) | — | **1** | 7/2$^{1}$ | 64 | 36 |
| 4753$^{2}$ | **Almuhtaram (69)** (GLewis) **4-9-10b**(3) AWhelan(12) (hdwy over 3f out: chsd wnr over 2f out: rdn over 1f out: r.o wl ins fnl f) | s.h | **2** | 5/1$^{2}$ | 79 | 51 |
| *4779$^{5}$* | **Allstars Express (60)** (TJNaughton) **3-8-11** MHills(8) (led 2f: led 5f out tl over 3f out: wknd wl over 1f out) | 9 | **3** | 12/1 | 58 | 23 |
| *4575$^{6}$* | **Sweet Supposin (IRE) (68)** (JohnBerry) **5-9-12v** DHarrison(4) (lw: hdwy over 1f out: nvr nrr) | nk | **4** | 12/1 | 66 | 38 |
| 4603$^{2}$ | **Proud Image (50)** (GMMcCourt) **4-8-8** CRutter(3) (hld up: rdn over 3f out: wknd over 2f out) | 1¾ | **5** | 12/1 | 45 | 17 |
| 4702$^{11}$ | **Platinum Plus (50)** (CADwyer) **4-8-8** MRoberts(1) (prom 8f) | 5 | **6** | 12/1 | 39 | 11 |
| *4107$^{2}$* | **Awesome Power (53)** (JWHills) **10-8-11** AClark(5) (nvr nr to chal) | 1 | **7** | 7/1$^{3}$ | 40 | 12 |
| 4381$^{4}$ | **By The Bay (44)** (SDow) **4-7-11e**(5)ow2 ADaly(6) (hld up: rdn over 3f out: wknd over 2f out) | 1 | **8** | 8/1 | 30 | — |
| 4626$^{11}$ | **Double Echo (IRE) (52)** (JDBethell) **8-8-10** SDrowne(13) (hld up: rdn 3f out: sn wknd) | 9 | **9** | 9/1 | 26 | — |
| 3786$^{8}$ | **Our Eddie (62)** (BGubby) **7-9-6v** DaneO'Neill(2) (led 10f out to 5f out: wknd 4f out) | 2 | **10** | 12/1 | 33 | 5 |
| 4750$^{3}$ | **Arcady (57)** (PTWalwyn) **3-8-8** WRyan(7) (prom 8f) | 7 | **11** | 10/1 | 19 | — |
| 4789$^{13}$ | **Private Percival (47)** (JRPoulton) **3-7-12** GBardwell(10) (prom 8f) | ¾ | **12** | 50/1 | 8 | — |
| 4784$^{6}$ | **Apartments Abroad (47)** (KMcAuliffe) **3-7-12v** DeclanO'Shea(9) (b.hind: a bhd) | ½ | **13** | 33/1 | 7 | — |
| 4252$^{17}$ | **Little Wobbly (43)** (PCClarke) **6-7-8b**1(7)ow5 CherylBone(11) (bhd fnl 9f: t.o fnl 5f) | dist | **14** | 100/1 | — | — |
| | | | | (SP 125.9%) | **14 Rn** | |

**2m 33.44** (3.44) CSF £21.23 CT £181.68 TOTE £3.30: £1.80 £2.40 £7.80 (£10.30) Trio £106.30 OWNER Mr C. D. Barber-Lomax (MALTON) BRED John Rose
LONG HANDICAP Little Wobbly 6-11
WEIGHT FOR AGE 3yo-7lb

**4617 Manful**, rated 15lb lower on the All-Weather than on his last Turf run, cruised into the lead on the bridle over three furlongs out, which might have been a bit early. With the runner-up finishing to good effect, he found the line coming not a stride too soon. (7/2: 2/1-4/1)
**4753 Almuhtaram**, running on strongly, would certainly have prevailed in another stride. He is a winner without a penalty. (5/1)
**4551 Allstars Express**, collared over three furlongs out, tried grimly to hold on, but was left for dead turning into the straight. (12/1)
**4575 Sweet Supposin (IRE)**, the winner of eleven races on the All-Weather, is yet to win on Turf. A drop to claiming company would help. (12/1)
**4603 Proud Image** had given his all over two furlongs out. (12/1: 8/1-14/1)
**3952 Platinum Plus** (12/1: 6/1-16/1)
**3435* Our Eddie** (12/1: 7/1-14/1)

## 4895 FALLING LEAF LIMITED STKS (0-65) (3-Y.O+) (Class F)

4-00 (4-04) **7f (Equitrack)** £2,381.00 (£656.00: £311.00) Stalls: Low GOING minus 0.48 sec per fur (FST)

| | | | | SP | RR | SF |
|---|---|---|---|---|---|---|
| *4781$^{3}$* | **Twin Creeks (59)** (VSoane) **5-9-0** CRutter(4) (s.s: hdwy over 4f out: rdn over 1f out: led wl ins fnl f: r.o wl) | — | **1** | 16/1 | 68 | 29 |
| 4606$^{11}$ | **Dancing Heart (65)** (BJMeehan) **4-8-7**(7) GHannon(5) (led: hrd rdn over 1f out: hdd wl ins fnl f: unable qckn) | 1½ | **2** | 8/1 | 65 | 26 |
| *3877$^{4}$* | **Invocation (65)** (AMoore) **9-8-11**(3) AWhelan(16) (b.hind: a.p: rdn over 1f out: r.o) | nk | **3** | 12/1 | 64 | 25 |
| *4577$^{8}$* | **No Monkey Nuts (61)** (JBerry) **3-8-11**(5) PRoberts(14) (lw: hdwy over 1f out: r.o wl ins fnl f) | s.h | **4** | 16/1 | 68 | 27 |
| 4784$^{8}$ | **Mystical Maid (58)** (HThomsonJones) **3-8-9b** WRyan(11) (hdwy over 1f out: nvr nrr) | 1¼ | **5** | 16/1 | 58 | 17 |
| 4603$^{14}$ | **Samara Song (50)** (WGMTurner) **3-8-12b** DaneO'Neill(1) (lw: a.p: ev ch 2f out: wknd ins fnl f) | nk | **6** | 33/1 | 60 | 19 |
| 1532$^{7}$ | **Apollo Red (50)** (AMoore) **7-9-2** CandyMorris(15) (b.hind: hld up: rdn 2f out: sn wknd) | 3½ | **7** | 16/1 | 54 | 15 |
| 4373$^{11}$ | **Our Shadee (USA) (65)** (KTIvory) **6-9-0v** CScally(9) (b: nvr nrr) | 1 | **8** | 9/1 | 50 | 11 |
| 4788$^{3}$ | **Fresh Fruit Daily (65)** (PAKelleway) **4-8-11** DRMcCabe(8) (lw: nvr nrr) | 2½ | **9** | 5/1$^{1}$ | 41 | 2 |

| Form | Horse | Dist | Pos | SP | RR | SF |
|---|---|---|---|---|---|---|
| *$190^{5}$* | **Mr Frosty (65)** (WJarvis) **4-9-0** MHills(13) (a bhd) | ¾ | **10** | $7/1^{3}$ | 43 | 4 |
| $4206^{11}$ | **Time Clash (60)** (BPalling) **3-8-9** DHarrison(12) (bhd fnl 3f) | ¾ | **11** | 20/1 | 38 | — |
| $1964^{6}$ | **Agwa (63)** (RJO'Sullivan) **7-9-0** DBiggs(2) (prom over 4f) | 1¼ | **12** | 14/1 | 38 | — |
| *$4336^{2}$* | **What A Fuss (65)** (BHanbury) **3-8-12** JStack(7) (hld up: rdn over 3f out: sn wknd) | 6 | **13** | $6/1^{2}$ | 24 | — |
| $4690^{6}$ | **Hannalou (FR) (60)** (SPCWoods) **3-8-9** AClark(6) (bhd fnl 3f) | 2½ | **14** | 9/1 | 16 | — |
| $2179^{7}$ | **Miss Offset (61)** (MJohnston) **3-8-11b** MRoberts(10) (s.s: a wl bhd) | s.h | **15** | 9/1 | 17 | — |
| $4577^{9}$ | **Red Admiral (65)** (CMurray) **6-9-2** MTebbutt(3) (Withdrawn not under Starter's orders: ref to ent stalls) | | **W** | 12/1 | — | — |

(SP 137.8%) **15 Rn**

**1m 26.5** (2.50) CSF £129.19 TOTE £26.60: £7.00 £3.90 £2.90 (£158.70) Trio £404.50; £17.09 to Leicester 29/10/96 OWNER The Armchair Jockeys-Four Seasons Racing (ASTON ROWANT) BRED Crest Stud Ltd
WEIGHT FOR AGE 3yo-2lb

**4781 Twin Creeks** was bustled along from below the distance and managed to get on top in the last 50 yards. (16/1)
**4212 Dancing Heart** bounced back to form and gamely attempted to make all the running, only losing out in the last 50 yards. (8/1)
**3877 Invocation** has not won for nineteen months. (12/1)
**4044* No Monkey Nuts** put in some good work in the last furlong and a half, but found the line always beating him. (16/1)
**2636 Mystical Maid** stayed on in the last furlong and a half without posing a serious threat. (16/1)
**4082 Samara Song** had every chance entering the straight, but had come to the end of his tether inside the final furlong. (33/1)
**631* Agwa** (14/1: 10/1-16/1)
**4336 What A Fuss** (6/1: op 4/1)

T/Plpt: £20.20 (531.3 Tckts). T/Qdpt: £15.10 (58.29 Tckts). AK

## 4881-LEICESTER (R-H) (Good, Good to firm bk st)
## Tuesday October 29th

WEATHER: fine & sunny WIND: mod half bhd

### 4896 TUGBY MEDIAN AUCTION MAIDEN STKS (I) (2-Y.O) (Class F)

1-00 (1-00) **5f 218y** £2,530.80 (£698.80: £332.40) GOING minus 0.16 sec per fur (GF)

| Form | Horse | Dist | Pos | SP | RR | SF |
|---|---|---|---|---|---|---|
| $4600^{2}$ | **Triple Hay** (RHannon) **2-9-0** DaneO'Neill(7) (a.p: led wl over 2f out: sn clr: unchal) | — | **1** | $1/2^{1}$ | 73 | 32 |
| *$4572^{5}$* | **Canton Ron** (CADwyer) **2-9-0** TGMcLaughlin(8) (prom: chsd wnr fnl 2f: no imp) | 13 | **2** | 10/1 | 38 | — |
| $4783^{12}$ | **Always Alight (45)** (KRBurke) **2-9-0b** JFEgan(6) (swvd lft s: hld up in tch: effrt over 2f out: nt rch ldrs) | 1¼ | **3** | 33/1 | 35 | — |
| $4786^{8}$ | **Dancing Mystery** (EAWheeler) **2-8-9**(5) ADaly(1) (hdwy 2f out: nvr nr to chal) | 2 | **4** | 25/1 | 30 | — |
| | **Hermanus** (MAJarvis) **2-9-0** PBloomfield(12) (w'like: str: bit bkwd: s.s: wl bhd tl styd on appr fnl f) | 1½ | **5** | $7/1^{2}$ | 26 | — |
| $4061^{10}$ | **Wrn Princess** (BJMeehan) **2-8-9** MTebbutt(11) (trckd ldrs: effrt & rn green 2f out: no imp) | 2 | **6** | 10/1 | 15 | — |
| | **Ok Pal** (JAkehurst) **2-9-0** GDuffield(5) (w'like: str: bkwd: dwlt: hmpd s: a in rr) | ½ | **7** | $8/1^{3}$ | 19 | — |
| $4783^{10}$ | **Welcome Heights** (MJFetherston-Godley) **2-9-0** CRutter(3) (in tch tl rdn & outpcd fr ½-wy) | ½ | **8** | 10/1 | 18 | — |
| $4244^{12}$ | **Stakis Casinos Lad (IRE)** (MJohnston) **2-9-0** MRoberts(9) (bit bkwd: plld hrd: led over 3f: sn rdn & wknd) | 2 | **9** | 14/1 | 12 | — |
| $4368^{10}$ | **Municipal Girl (IRE) (54)** (BPalling) **2-8-9** TSprake(4) (disp ld 3f: sn rdn & wknd: t.o) | 12 | **10** | 14/1 | — | — |

(SP 137.7%) **10 Rn**

**1m 13.7** (3.70) CSF £9.02 TOTE £1.50: £1.30 £1.50 £39.10 (£4.20) Trio £39.90 OWNER The Broadgate Partnership (MARLBOROUGH) BRED S. C. Palmer

**4600 Triple Hay**, faced with an [illegible] task, accomplished the mission with considerable ease and will have trouble finding another contest as easy as this. (1/2)
**4572 Canton Ron**, who will be more the finished article next season, found the winner much too good for him. (10/1)
**Always Alight** did not fare badly after losing ground at the start and he has plenty of time on his side. (33/1)
**Dancing Mystery** still has a bit left to work on, but he is gaining experience all the time. (25/1)
**Hermanus**, closely-related to a couple of winners, lost his chance at the start, but he did stay on and will be much the wiser after this. (7/1: op 4/1)
**Wrn Princess** still has not got a grasp of what is needed and appears to be a slow learner. (10/1)
**Ok Pal** (8/1: 6/1-10/1)
**Welcome Heights** (10/1: 7/1-12/1)

### 4897 E.B.F. HOBY MAIDEN STKS (2-Y.O) (Class D)

1-30 (1-32) **1m 8y** £4,532.50 (£1,360.00: £655.00: £302.50) Stalls: High GOING minus 0.16 sec per fur (GF)

| Form | Horse | Dist | Pos | SP | RR | SF |
|---|---|---|---|---|---|---|
| $3706^{5}$ | **Musalsal (IRE)** (BWHills) **2-9-0** MHills(1) (lw: hld up: hdwy ½-wy: led 1f out: sn clr: easily) | — | **1** | $3/1^{1}$ | 91+ | 24 |
| | **Kyle Rhea** (HRACecil) **2-8-9** PatEddery(9) (lt-f: unf: a.p: led 3f out to 1f out: no ch w wnr) | 2½ | **2** | $7/2^{2}$ | 81 | 14 |
| | **Leading Note (USA)** (LMCumani) **2-8-9** OUrbina(12) (leggy: scope: dwlt: hdwy ½-wy: one pce ins fnl f) | 1 | **3** | 9/1 | 79+ | 12 |
| $4705^{12}$ | **Protocol (IRE)** (JWHills) **2-9-0** RHills(15) (in tch: effrt 3f out: no imp appr fnl f) | 5 | **4** | 33/1 | 74 | 7 |
| $4720^{10}$ | **City Hall (IRE)** (PWChapple-Hyam) **2-9-0** JReid(3) (hld up: hdwy 2f out: nvr nrr) | 1½ | **5** | $8/1^{3}$ | 71 | 4 |
| $4782^{7}$ | **Strictly Hard** (GCBravery) **2-8-9** DeclanO'Shea(4) (s.s: bhd tl r.o fnl 2f) | 1½ | **6** | 33/1 | 63 | — |
| $4801^{10}$ | **Brynkir** (DJGMurraySmith) **2-9-0** DHarrison(7) (chsd ldrs over 5f) | 1¼ | **7** | 50/1 | 66 | — |
| | **Naval Dispatch** (JHMGosden) **2-8-9** JCarroll(10) (unf: scope: bit bkwd: in tch: effrt 3f out: btn over 1f out) | nk | **8** | 14/1 | 60 | — |
| $4720^{5}$ | **Galibis (FR)** (PAKelleway) **2-9-0** AClark(14) (lw: prom: hrd rdn over 2f out: sn btn) | nk | **9** | $3/1^{1}$ | 64 | — |
| | **Stahr** (HCandy) **2-9-0** CRutter(13) (leggy: lt-f: s.s: a wl bhd) | 8 | **10** | 20/1 | 49 | — |
| $4481^{3}$ | **Moorbird (IRE)** (MJohnston) **2-9-0** MRoberts(5) (bhd fr ½-wy) | 1 | **11** | 14/1 | 47 | — |
| $4584^{7}$ | **Sand Cay (USA)** (RHannon) **2-9-0** DaneO'Neill(16) (w ldrs 5f: grad wknd) | ½ | **12** | 16/1 | 46 | — |
| $4188^{14}$ | **Chaluz** (MJohnston) **2-8-11**(3) MHenry(17) (bit bkwd: trckd ldrs 5f: sn lost tch) | 2½ | **13** | 20/1 | 41 | — |
| | **Three Cheers (IRE)** (JHMGosden) **2-9-0** AGarth(11) (w'like: scope: s.s: a wl bhd: t.o) | 8 | **14** | 20/1 | 25 | — |
| $4605^{13}$ | **Aquatic Queen** (RJWeaver) **2-8-4**(5) ADaly(2) (bit bkwd: trckd ldrs 5f: sn lost tch: t.o) | ½ | **15** | 50/1 | 19 | — |
| $3069^{9}$ | **The Real McCoy** (MRChannon) **2-9-0** RHughes(6) (bit bkwd: plld hrd: led 5f: wknd qckly: t.o) | 3½ | **16** | 16/1 | 17 | — |

(SP 142.5%) **16 Rn**

**1m 40.9** (5.90) CSF £15.76 TOTE £3.70: £2.40 £2.30 £3.10 (£5.00) Trio £21.40 OWNER Maktoum Al Maktoum (LAMBOURN) BRED Gainsborough Stud Management Ltd

**3706 Musalsal (IRE)**, faced with a much easier task over this longer trip, won without being asked a question and could prove a useful colt as a three-year-old. (3/1: op 2/1)

**Kyle Rhea**, an unfurnished half-sister to three winners, was getting her winter coat, but shaped promisingly and more will be heard of her next term. (7/2: op 2/1)
**Leading Note (USA)**, a well-grown, attractive filly with plenty left to work on, showed she possesses ability and should prove the point next season. (9/1: 6/1-10/1)
**Protocol (IRE)** found the principals much too good for him in the closing stages and was not persevered with when held. (33/1)
**City Hall (IRE)**, a long-backed colt who has gone in his coat, stayed on steadily inside the final quarter-mile and will not have much trouble in making the grade. (8/1)
**Strictly Hard** did well to finish so close after losing ground at the start and being well outpaced. (33/1)
**Naval Dispatch** (14/1: op 8/1)
**4720 Galibis (FR)**, hard at work to hold his pitch entering the final quarter-mile, found the task beyond him. (3/1)

## 4898 FOSSE WAY CLAIMING STKS (3-Y.O) (Class F)

2-00 (2-03) **1m 8y** £3,166.40 (£880.40: £423.20) Stalls: High GOING minus 0.16 sec per fur (GF)

| | | | | SP | RR | SF |
|---|---|---|---|---|---|---|
| 4829[8] | **Power Game (61)** (JBerry) **3-9-3b** MHills(18) (hld up: hdwy 2f out: rdn to ld wl ins fnl f) | — | 1 | 5/1[3] | 72 | 13 |
| 4799[4] | **Yeoman Oliver (70)** (BAMcMahon) **3-9-3b** GDuffield(13) (lw: led after 2f tl hdd wl ins fnl f) | ½ | 2 | 9/2[2] | 71 | 12 |
| 4296[11] | **Giddy (39)** (JHetherton) **3-8-2** NKennedy(10) (a.p: ev ch ins fnl f: unable qckn) | nk | 3 | 50/1 | 55 | — |
| 4815[4] | **Eskimo Kiss (IRE) (37)** (MJFetherston-Godley) **3-7-12b** CRutter(12) (lw: hld up: hdwy 2f out: kpt on u.p fnl f) | ½ | 4 | 16/1 | 50 | — |
| 4082[15] | **Zdenka (39)** (MBlanshard) **3-7-12** JQuinn(2) (led 2f: rdn & one pce appr fnl f) | ¾ | 5 | 20/1 | 49 | — |
| 4511[13] | **Whispering Dawn (63)** (MRChannon) **3-8-6** JReid(5) (swtg: unruly stalls: s.s: hdwy 3f out: no imp appr fnl f) | hd | 6 | 7/2[1] | 57 | — |
| 4808[7] | **Square Mile Miss (IRE) (42)** (PHowling) **3-8-4** AClark(6) (hld up in tch: effrt 2f out: one pce fnl f) | 1¼ | 7 | 33/1 | 52 | — |
| 2340[4] | **Alakhluki (46)** (GLewis) **3-7-13**(3) AWhelan(7) (lw: hld up: hdwy 3f out: sn rdn: nt pce to chal) | hd | 8 | 7/2[1] | 50 | — |
| *4781*[9] | **Red Rusty (USA) (47)** (DMorris) **3-8-6** NDay(19) (hdwy 3f out: rdn & one pce appr fnl f) | ½ | 9 | 14/1 | 53 | — |
| 4784[10] | **Sweet Amoret (47)** (PHowling) **3-7-13**(3) DWright(1) (lw: in tch: effrt 2f out: sn rdn: no imp) | ¾ | 10 | 25/1 | 48 | — |
| 4611[8] | **Ajkuit (IRE)** (JJSheehan) **3-8-13** AMorris(8) (in tch: rdn over 2f out: no imp) | 2 | 11 | 33/1 | 55 | — |
| 3860[4] | **Followthe Allstars (46)** (TJNaughton) **3-8-11b** TSprake(15) (sn pushed along: nvr bttr than mid div) | 1½ | 12 | 16/1 | 50 | — |
| 4693[7] | **Gay Breeze** (PSFelgate) **3-9-3** JStack(11) (w ldrs 4f: sn lost tch) | 5 | 13 | 33/1 | 46 | — |
| 4689[11] | **Air Wing (65)** (MHTompkins) **3-8-6**(3) MHenry(17) (hdwy 3f out: hrd rdn & wknd wl over 1f out) | 1¼ | 14 | 9/1 | 35 | — |
| 4341[15] | **Siberian Rose (30)** (JWharton) **3-7-12** NAdams(4) (a in rr) | 6 | 15 | 50/1 | 12 | — |
| 3881[9] | **Petite Heritiere (38)** (MJRyan) **3-7-9**(7) AMcCarthy(14) (trckd ldrs tl wknd wl over 2f out) | 5 | 16 | 33/1 | 6 | — |
| | **Dunmebrains (IRE)** (JSMoore) **3-8-12** JFEgan(9) (b: chsd ldrs over 4f: sn rdn & wknd: t.o) | 9 | 17 | 33/1 | — | — |
| 4387[8] | **Candy's Delight (36)** (MrsSJSmith) **3-8-1**(3)ow4 FLynch(3) (a bhd: t.o) | hd | 18 | 50/1 | — | — |
| 4589[11] | **Sarasota Ryde** (JEBanks) **3-8-1**(7) RMullen(16) (a bhd: t.o) | 22 | 19 | 33/1 | — | — |
| | | | | (SP 139.9%) | **19 Rn** | |

**1m 42.3** (7.30) CSF £29.26 TOTE £6.00: £2.20 £2.30 £24.10 (£12.90) Trio £241.20 OWNER Countrywide Racing (COCKERHAM) BRED Bearstone Stud
Zdenka clmd MPipe £3,000
**4598 Power Game** has really come good in the latter part of the season and, though he had to struggle here, was always going to win. (5/1)
**4799 Yeoman Oliver** runs best from the front and it was only well inside the final furlong that he was forced to give best. He is ready to return to form now, but may need to pay another visit to the All-Weather. (9/2: op 3/1)
**2780 Giddy** showed much-improved form here and she does seem to be getting it together. (50/1)
**4815 Eskimo Kiss (IRE)**, trying her luck at this shorter trip, could never get to terms, despite staying on. (16/1)
**2540 Zdenka**, in the firing-line all the way, found lack of stamina a problem approaching the final furlong. She was claimed for £3,000 by Martin Pipe. (20/1)
**595 Whispering Dawn**, lowered in class, misbehaved in the stalls and, flat-footed when they opened, was never quite able to recover the lost ground. (7/2)
**3761 Square Mile Miss (IRE)** tried to get into the action inside the distance, but could not muster the pace to mount a challenge. (33/1)
**Air Wing** (9/1: 9/2-10/1)

## 4899 BARSBY LIMITED STKS (0-70) (3-Y.O) (Class E)

2-30 (2-30) **1m 3f 183y** £3,042.90 (£907.20: £432.60: £195.30) Stalls: High GOING minus 0.16 sec per fur (GF)

| | | | | SP | RR | SF |
|---|---|---|---|---|---|---|
| 4427[2] | **Prospero (70)** (GHarwood) **3-9-0** JReid(4) (a.p: led 2f out: drvn clr fnl f) | — | 1 | 3/1[1] | 75+ | 39 |
| 4557[3] | **Full Throttle (69)** (MHTompkins) **3-9-1**(3) MHenry(3) (hld up & bhd: hdwy over 3f out: chsd wnr appr fnl f: no imp) | 5 | 2 | 4/1[3] | 72 | 36 |
| 4557[5] | **Ceilidh Star (IRE) (66)** (BWHills) **3-8-13** PatEddery(8) (b.hind: hld up & bhd: effrt 3f out: nvr nrr) | ½ | 3 | 7/2[2] | 67 | 31 |
| 4374[7] | **Kitty Kitty Cancan (66)** (LadyHerries) **3-8-8b**[1](3) FLynch(2) (chsd ldr: led 3f out to 2f out: sn rdn & btn) | 3½ | 4 | 6/1 | 60 | 24 |
| 4703[8] | **Precious Island (32)** (PTDalton) **3-8-11** NAdams(6) (in tch: drvn along over 3f out: no hdwy) | 1¼ | 5 | 66/1 | 58 | 22 |
| *2304*[6] | **Chik's Secret (42)** (BPalling) **3-8-11** TSprake(5) (bkwd: chsd ldrs: pushed along ½-wy: wknd 3f out) | ½ | 6 | 40/1 | 58 | 22 |
| 4752* | **Laazim Afooz (66)** (RTPhillips) **3-9-2** RPerham(1) (plld hrd: led 9f: wknd over 2f out: t.o) | 11 | 7 | 3/1[1] | 48 | 12 |
| 3849[9] | **Budding Annie (40)** (JRBosley) **3-8-11** CRutter(7) (lw: a bhd: t.o) | 20 | 8 | 66/1 | 16 | — |
| | | | | (SP 111.9%) | **8 Rn** | |

**2m 36.0** (7.00) CSF £14.23 TOTE £3.20: £1.20 £1.40 £2.00 (£6.40) OWNER Mrs Gaynor Scruton (PULBOROUGH) BRED Littleton Stud
**4427 Prospero**, always travelling comfortably, had little trouble in getting off the mark and there seems no reason why he can not follow up. (3/1)
**4557 Full Throttle** looks to be over the top, but he did his level best to make a race of it. (4/1: op 5/2)
**4557 Ceilidh Star (IRE)** began to stay on in the closing stages, but the progress was slow and she was never going to make it. (7/2)
**3657 Kitty Kitty Cancan**, blinkered for the first time and lowered in class, helped share the lead until fading below the distance. (6/1: 4/1-13/2)
**Precious Island** came off the bridle early in the straight and failed to make her presence felt. (66/1)
**4752* Laazim Afooz** found this much tougher than the maiden he won at Catterick and had been hung out to dry over two furlongs out. (3/1)

## 4900 CASTLE H'CAP (0-70) (3-Y.O+) (Class E)

3-00 (3-03) **1m 1f 218y** £3,916.50 (£1,176.00: £567.00: £262.50) Stalls: High GOING minus 0.16 sec per fur (GF)

| | | | | SP | RR | SF |
|---|---|---|---|---|---|---|
| 4669* | **Fairy Knight (66)** (RHannon) **4-9-12** PatEddery(6) (hld up: hdwy & swtchd lft over 1f out: str run to ld ins fnl f: readily) | — | 1 | 5/2[1] | 77 | 45 |

| | | | | SP | RR | SF |
|---|---|---|---|---|---|---|
| 3786[9] | **Renown (68)** (LordHuntingdon) **4-10-0** DHarrison(13) (lw: a.p: led over 1f out tl ins fnl f) | 1¾ | **2** | 14/1 | 76 | 44 |
| 4669[5] | **Rex Mundi (61)** (PDEvans) **4-9-7** JFEgan(9) (hld up: hdwy over 2f out: unable qckn ins fnl f) | ½ | **3** | 14/1 | 68 | 36 |
| 3635* | **Double Rush (IRE) (50)** (TGMills) **4-8-10** GDuffield(18) (hld up: effrt & nt clr run 2f out: r.o wl ins fnl f) | ½ | **4** | 6/1 [2] | 57 | 25 |
| *4779[3]* | **Troubadour Song (52)** (WWHaigh) **4-8-12** RHughes(5) (hld up: hdwy 2f out: r.o wl fnl f) | nk | **5** | 12/1 | 58 | 26 |
| 963* | **Eskimo Nel (IRE) (66)** (JLSpearing) **5-9-9**(3) FLynch(1) (hld up: hdwy 4f out: one pce fnl 2f) | ½ | **6** | 10/1 | 71 | 39 |
| 4785[2] | **Mimosa (61)** (SDow) **3-9-2** MRoberts(2) (prom: led over 3f out: sn rdn: hdd over 1f out: eased whn btn) | 2 | **7** | 6/1 [2] | 63 | 26 |
| 4719[8] | **Golden Touch (USA) (59)** (DJSCosgrove) **4-9-5** MRimmer(17) (prom: ev ch over 1f out: sn rdn & no ex) | 1¼ | **8** | 20/1 | 59 | 27 |
| 4753[8] | **Askern (60)** (DHaydnJones) **5-9-6** AClark(4) (trckd ldrs tl outpcd over 2f out) | 3 | **9** | 14/1 | 55 | 23 |
| 4609[14] | **Arzani (USA) (50)** (DJSCosgrove) **5-8-10** JQuinn(19) (dwlt: sn chsng ldrs: effrt on ins & n.m.r over 2f out: sn btn) | 1 | **10** | 33/1 | 44 | 12 |
| 4513[3] | **Princess Danielle (59)** (WRMuir) **4-9-5** JReid(8) (w ldrs: ev ch tl wknd ent fnl f) | 1¼ | **11** | 9/1 [3] | 51 | 19 |
| 4819[3] | **Harvey White (IRE) (62)** (JPearce) **4-9-8** GBardwell(15) (lw: in tch: rdn over 2f out: sn btn) | 1¾ | **12** | 10/1 | 51 | 19 |
| 4793[10] | **Name of Our Father (USA) (70)** (PBowen) **3-9-6**(5) PPMurphy(10) (led tl hdd & wknd over 2f out) | 2 | **13** | 33/1 | 56 | 19 |
| 3318[5] | **Augustan (55)** (SGollings) **5-9-1** DaneO'Neill(12) (s.i.s: a bhd) | hd | **14** | 20/1 | 41 | 9 |
| 4831[2] | **Myfontaine (63)** (KTIvory) **9-9-9** JCarroll(14) (b: hld up & bhd: effrt over 2f out: no imp) | 1 | **15** | 12/1 | 47 | 15 |
| 4551[5] | **No Pattern (66)** (GLMoore) **4-9-12** SWhitworth(7) (dwlt: hdwy 4f out: rdn & wknd wl over 1f out) | 2 | **16** | 25/1 | 47 | 15 |
| *4781[13]* | **North Ardar (60)** (TWall) **6-9-6** DeclanO'Shea(3) (s.i.s: a bhd) | 3 | **17** | 25/1 | 36 | 4 |
| 4768[11] | **Parliament Piece (55)** (CaptJWilson) **10-9-1** CRutter(16) (bhd fnl 4f: t.o) | 6 | **18** | 33/1 | 21 | — |
| *4373[13]* | ***Premier League (IRE) (53)*** (JELong) **6-8-6**(7) JWilkinson(11) (Withdrawn not under Starter's orders: bolted bef s) | | **W** | 33/1 | — | — |

(SP 149.7%) **18 Rn**

**2m 10.1** (6.40) CSF £42.88 CT £427.37 TOTE £3.30: £1.20 £3.60 £3.40 £2.50 (£32.90) Trio £415.30; £350.97 to Yarmouth 30/10/96 OWNER P & S Lever Partners (MARLBOROUGH) BRED Peter McCalmont

WEIGHT FOR AGE 3yo-5lb

**4669* Fairy Knight**, at the top of his form at this time of year, landed a substantial gamble with authority and has not stopped winning yet. (5/2)

**1660* Renown** ran up to his best from the top of the handicap and did not go down for the want of trying. (14/1)

**4669 Rex Mundi** is running well enough to pick up another race, but the season may come to an end before he has the chance to do so. (14/1)

**3635* Double Rush (IRE)** failed in his bid to complete a three-timer, but he did not enjoy the run of the race, otherwise he would have given the winner something to do. (6/1)

**4779 Troubadour Song** needs the All-Weather to produce his best, but this was a decent performance and his form is holding up. (12/1)

**963* Eskimo Nel (IRE)**, just in need of this first run in over five months, gave a good account of herself and is fresher than most at this time of year. (10/1)

**4785 Mimosa** ran much better than her finishing position would suggest and she will be worth keeping in mind for the All-Weather. (6/1)

## 4901 ERMINE STREET H'CAP (0-85) (3-Y.O+) (Class D)

3-35 (3-36) **1m 8y** £4,192.20 (£1,254.60: £601.80: £275.40) Stalls: High GOING minus 0.16 sec per fur (GF)

| | | | | SP | RR | SF |
|---|---|---|---|---|---|---|
| 4432[3] | **Pomona (79)** (PJMakin) **3-9-7** PatEddery(10) (hld up: hdwy over 2f out: led ent fnl f: jst hld on) | — | **1** | 7/2 [1] | 92 | 36 |
| 4688[8] | **Duello (69)** (MBlanshard) **5-9-0** JQuinn(15) (hld up: gd hdwy 2f out: str chal fnl f: jst failed) | s.h | **2** | 14/1 | 82 | 29 |
| 4590[9] | **Missile Toe (IRE) (58)** (JEBanks) **3-8-0** GBardwell(12) (lw: hld up: gd hdwy appr fnl f: fin strly) | 2½ | **3** | 12/1 | 66 | 10 |
| 4682[3] | **Fionn de Cool (IRE) (67)** (RAkehurst) **5-8-12** AClark(11) (a.p: ev ch fr 2f out: kpt on u.p) | s.h | **4** | 7/1 | 75 | 22 |
| 4692[3] | **Mustn't Grumble (IRE) (53)** (MissSJWilton) **6-7-5v**(7) JBramhill(5) (a.p: led over 2f out tl ent fnl f: sn rdn & no ex) | 1 | **5** | 11/2 [3] | 59 | 6 |
| 4686[7] | **Seventeens Lucky (77)** (BobJones) **4-9-8** MWigham(7) (prom: hrd rdn & one pce appr fnl f) | ¾ | **6** | 14/1 | 81 | 28 |
| 4309[5] | **Diamond Beach (75)** (BWHills) **3-9-3** MHills(14) (s.s: hdwy 2f out: nt rch ldrs) | 3 | **7** | 5/1 [2] | 73 | 17 |
| 4799[2] | **Embankment (IRE) (70)** (RHannon) **6-9-1** RHughes(4) (prom tl outpcd appr fnl f) | nk | **8** | 8/1 | 68 | 15 |
| 4719[4] | **Blatant Outburst (70)** (GCBravery) **6-9-1** JReid(1) (lw: chsd ldrs stands' side: no hdwy appr fnl f) | ¾ | **9** | 16/1 | 66 | 13 |
| 4444[15] | **Queenfisher (83)** (GLMoore) **4-10-0** GDuffield(18) (racd centre: led over 4f out tl over 2f out: wknd appr fnl f) | ¾ | **10** | 50/1 | 78 | 25 |
| 4691* | **Mystic Dawn (65)** (SDow) **3-8-7** MRoberts(13) (hld up & plld hrd: effrt over 2f out: eased whn btn appr fnl f) | ½ | **11** | 13/2 | 59 | 3 |
| 4800[3] | **Dee-Lady (70)** (WGMTurner) **4-8-8**(7) DSweeney(16) (b: w ldrs stands' side: ev ch tl wknd wl over 1f out) | ¾ | **12** | 16/1 | 62 | 9 |
| 4355[9] | **Delight of Dawn (62)** (RMStronge) **4-8-7** VSlattery(2) (nvr nr to chal) | 3½ | **13** | 33/1 | 47 | — |
| 4719[6] | **Hardy Dancer (81)** (GLMoore) **4-9-12** SWhitworth(6) (bhd fnl 3f) | ½ | **14** | 33/1 | 65 | 12 |
| 4769[9] | **Saifan (83)** (DMorris) **7-10-0b** NDay(3) (hld up in rr: hdwy over 2f out: wknd appr fnl f) | 1 | **15** | 14/1 | 65 | 12 |
| 4674[11] | **Show Faith (IRE) (75)** (RHannon) **6-9-6** DaneO'Neill(17) (prom tl rdn & wknd 3f out) | 1¼ | **16** | 20/1 | 55 | 2 |
| 4617[13] | **Queens Consul (IRE) (80)** (BSRothwell) **6-9-11** JStack(9) (led tl hdd & wknd qckly over 4f out) | 1½ | **17** | 20/1 | 57 | 4 |
| *4577[11]* | **Gulf Shaadi (59)** (EJAlston) **4-8-1**(3) DWright(19) (chsd ldr centre 5f) | ½ | **18** | 50/1 | 35 | — |
| 4802[14] | **Fly Tip (IRE) (79)** (BJMeehan) **3-9-7** MTebbutt(20) (prom to ½-wy: sn wknd) | 1¼ | **19** | 16/1 | 52 | — |
| *4682[20]* | ***Zajko (USA) (75)*** (LadyHerries) **6-9-3**(3) FLynch(8) (Withdrawn not under Starter's orders: by permission of Stewards) | | **W** | | — | — |

(SP 155.9%) **19 Rn**

**1m 40.3** (5.30) CSF £61.13 CT £553.03 TOTE £6.40: £3.40 £3.20 £4.60 £1.60 (£82.90) Trio £538.20 OWNER Skyline Racing Ltd (MARLBOROUGH) BRED R. Kent and Miss R. L. Birchall

WEIGHT FOR AGE 3yo-3lb

**4432 Pomona** kept up the stable's good recent run, hanging on gamely to open her account. This success was due to the strength of the man on top. (7/2)

**4571 Duello** does perform better when there is more give in the ground, but he gave it his best shot here and only just failed to peg back the winner. (14/1)

**4337 Missile Toe (IRE)** threw down a determined challenge inside the distance, but the principals were not stopping and he was just unable to get there. (12/1)

**4682 Fionn de Cool (IRE)** is not enjoying the best of fortune, but he has performed with credit in all his most recent outings and thoroughly deserves the rub of the green. (7/1)

**4692 Mustn't Grumble (IRE)** had more use made of him this time and only lost out in the battle to the line. He is running consistently well and he can also win on the All-Weather. (11/2)

**4686 Seventeens Lucky** sat much closer to the pace, but had kept little in hand for a late battle. (14/1)

**4309 Diamond Beach**, still to find an opening, lost ground at the start, probably by choice, and was noticed staying on well when it was all too late. (5/1: op 10/1)

## 4902 TUGBY MEDIAN AUCTION MAIDEN STKS (II) (2-Y.O) (Class F)

4-10 (4-11) **5f 218y** £2,530.80 (£698.80: £332.40) Stalls: High GOING minus 0.16 sec per fur (GF)

| Form | Horse | Dist | Pos | SP | RR | SF |
|---|---|---|---|---|---|---|
| $4330^{5}$ | **Refuse To Lose** (JMPEustace) **2-9-0** JCarroll(5) (a.p: led over 3f out: clr fnl f: eased nr fin) | — | 1 | 11/10[1] | 63+ | 23 |
| $4783^{6}$ | **Mr Paradise (IRE)** (TJNaughton) **2-9-0** RHughes(3) (lw: a.p: rdn over 1f out: kpt on towards fin) | 1¼ | 2 | 20/1 | 60 | 20 |
| $4562^{4}$ | **Fearless Cavalier (52)** (RHollinshead) **2-8-11**(3) FLynch(4) (a.p: effrt & rdn appr fnl f: r.o) | 1¼ | 3 | 20/1 | 56 | 16 |
| | **Occam (IRE)** (GWragg) **2-9-0** MHills(8) (w'like: unf: bit bkwd: s.s: hdwy over 1f out: nvr nrr) | 3½ | 4 | 10/1 | 47+ | 7 |
| $4481^{6}$ | **Blown-Over (50)** (ACStewart) **2-8-9b**[1] MRoberts(2) (led over 2f: wknd appr fnl f) | 3½ | 5 | 11/1 | 33 | — |
| $4599^{6}$ | **Myosotis (75)** (PJMakin) **2-9-0** GDuffield(12) (chsd ldrs: rdn & no imp fnl 2f) | 1 | 6 | 10/1 | 35 | — |
| $4330^{12}$ | **Mutasawwar** (EALDunlop) **2-9-0** RHills(1) (b: bit bkwd: plld hrd: hld up: nvr trbld ldrs) | ¾ | 7 | 9/2[2] | 33 | — |
| $2764^{2}$ | **Royal Emblem (62)** (AGFoster) **2-8-4**(5) CAdamson(10) (bit bkwd: chsd ldrs over 3f) | nk | 8 | 12/1 | 27 | — |
| *$4572^{7}$* | **Aspecto Lad (IRE)** (MJohnston) **2-8-11**(3) MHenry(11) (bit bkwd: in tch: rdn ½-wy: wknd fnl 2f) | hd | 9 | 20/1 | 32 | — |
| $4600^{8}$ | **Wing of A Prayer** (WJarvis) **2-9-0** JReid(7) (a in rr) | 2 | 10 | 13/2[3] | 27 | — |
| *$4777^{W}$* | **Sandkatoon (IRE)** (JSMoore) **2-8-9** NAdams(9) (in tch: drvn along ½-wy: sn wknd) | ½ | 11 | 33/1 | 20 | — |
| $4363^{9}$ | **Honourable Felix** (EJAlston) **2-9-0** JQuinn(6) (lw: trckd ldrs 4f: wknd qckly: t.o) | 9 | 12 | 50/1 | 1 | — |

(SP 132.5%) **12 Rn**

**1m 14.4** (4.40) CSF £26.30 TOTE £2.00: £1.90 £1.10 £3.20 (£171.20) Trio £144.70; £144.77 to Yarmouth 30/10/96 OWNER Mr J. C. Smith (NEWMARKET) BRED Britton House Stud

**4330 Refuse To Lose**, who unseated his jockey in the paddock, carries plenty of condition, but he won this with the minimum of fuss and his future looks bright. (11/10: Evens-5/4)

**Mr Paradise (IRE)** pushed the pace all the way and stayed on well towards the finish, but he is flattered to finish so close to the winner. (20/1)

**4562 Fearless Cavalier**, taking a step up in class, kept beavering away in the latter stages without ever looking likely to trouble the winner. (20/1)

**Occam (IRE)**, a smallish May colt who is closely related to several of the stable's winners, stood still as the stalls opened and lost quite a lot of ground. Given a quiet introduction, he was staying on well at the finish and the experience will not be lost. (10/1: op 5/1)

**4481 Blown-Over**, very free in the first-time blinkers, was feeling the strain below the distance and was soon beaten. (11/1: 7/1-12/1)

**4599 Myosotis**, stepping down from seven furlongs, found the pace too hot for him in the last quarter-mile. (10/1: op 6/1)

**Mutasawwar** (9/2: op 2/1)

**2764 Royal Emblem** (12/1: op 8/1)

T/Jkpt: £2,629.60 (2.7 Tckts). T/Plpt: £34.50 (679.33 Tckts). T/Qdpt: £15.10 (69.79 Tckts). IM

# 4721-REDCAR (L-H) (Good to firm)

## Tuesday October 29th

WEATHER: sunny & cool WIND: slt against

## 4903 LEVY BOARD NURSERY H'CAP (0-75) (2-Y.O) (Class E)

1-05 (1-05) **6f** £3,172.75 (£952.00: £458.50: £211.75) Stalls: Centre GOING minus 0.42 sec per fur (F)

| Form | Horse | Dist | Pos | SP | RR | SF |
|---|---|---|---|---|---|---|
| $4717^{9}$ | **Style Dancer (IRE) (70)** (RMWhitaker) **2-9-3** KFallon(5) (lw: hld up: hdwy to ld over 1f out: r.o) | — | 1 | 6/1 | 72 | 21 |
| $4803^{3}$ | **Mike's Double (IRE) (51)** (GLewis) **2-7-12b** NCarlisle(6) (b.hind: chsd ldrs: hdwy 2f out: sn ev ch: nt qckn fnl f) | 1½ | 2 | 3/1[1] | 49 | — |
| $4749^{7}$ | **William's Well (56)** (MWEasterby) **2-8-3b** GHind(3) (lw: led tl hdd over 1f out: no ex) | ½ | 3 | 11/2[3] | 53 | 2 |
| $4433^{7}$ | **Why O Six (64)** (RAFahey) **2-8-11** ACulhane(11) (chsd ldrs tl rdn & nt qckn fnl 2f) | 3 | 4 | 10/1 | 53 | 2 |
| $4867^{7}$ | **Abstone Queen (70)** (PDEvans) **2-8-10v**(7) RFfrench(10) (hdwy ½-wy: sn chsng ldrs & rdn: nt qckn appr fnl f) | nk | 5 | 6/1 | 58 | 7 |
| $2897^{7}$ | **Soda (68)** (TDBarron) **2-9-1** DeanMcKeown(1) (stdd s: hdwy 2f out: nvr plcd to chal) | 1½ | 6 | 33/1 | 52+ | 1 |
| $4764^{5}$ | **Contravene (IRE) (60)** (JBerry) **2-8-7** GCarter(9) (prom: effrt over 2f out: sn btn) | 3 | 7 | 5/1[2] | 36 | — |
| $4619^{6}$ | **Figlia (65)** (CBBBooth) **2-8-12b** JWeaver(8) (hld up: effrt over 2f out: sn btn) | s.h | 8 | 14/1 | 41 | — |
| $4751^{3}$ | **Janie's Boy (74)** (RGuest) **2-9-7** KDarley(7) (lw: spd 4f: sn wknd) | 2½ | 9 | 6/1 | 43 | — |
| $4764^{6}$ | **Tribal Mischief (66)** (DMoffatt) **2-8-10**(3) DarrenMoffatt(4) (bhd: hdwy u.p ½-wy: nvr able to chal) | s.h | 10 | 14/1 | 35 | — |
| $4207^{9}$ | **Mirror Four Sport (53)** (MJohnston) **2-8-0** TWilliams(2) (spd over 2f: sn wknd) | nk | 11 | 33/1 | 21 | — |

(SP 128.2%) **11 Rn**

**1m 13.4** (3.20) CSF £25.26 CT £100.68 TOTE £7.90: £2.10 £1.90 £2.40 (£8.00) Trio £109.40; £63.22 to Yarmouth 30/10/96 OWNER Mrs C. A. Hodgetts (LEEDS) BRED Noel Carter

**4614 Style Dancer (IRE)**, who took the eye in the paddock, won well and seems to really be getting it together. (6/1)

**4803 Mike's Double (IRE)**, from a yard that can do little right, had previously shown his best form on soft ground and, in the circumstances, this was not a bad effort. (3/1)

**4459 William's Well** has the ability, but is not really seeing it out as yet. (11/2)

**3941 Why O Six** ran a fair race and, with some give in the ground, should do better. (10/1)

**4764* Abstone Queen**, after an incredibly busy season, is still running well and is a credit to all concerned. (6/1)

**2562 Soda** has been gelded since his last outing and had a quiet run. In due course, he looks one to watch. (33/1)

## 4904 BRASS CASTLE CLAIMING STKS (3-Y.O+) (Class F)

1-35 (1-39) **1m 3f** £2,847.00 (£792.00: £381.00) Stalls: Low GOING minus 0.42 sec per fur (F)

| Form | Horse | Dist | Pos | SP | RR | SF |
|---|---|---|---|---|---|---|
| $4515^{2}$ | **Once More for Luck (IRE) (65)** (MrsMReveley) **5-9-7** ACulhane(3) (trckd ldrs: stdy hdwy to ld over 1f out: rdn & styd on) | — | 1 | 5/4[1] | 73 | 55 |
| $4703^{2}$ | **Loki (IRE) (62)** (GLewis) **8-8-11** KDarley(10) (lw: hld up: stdy hdwy 3f out: effrt to chse wnr ins fnl f: kpt on towards fin) | nk | 2 | 7/4[2] | 63 | 45 |
| $4815^{3}$ | **Mcgillycuddy Reeks (IRE) (38)** (NTinkler) **5-8-4** GCarter(12) (lw: cl up: led 4f out tl over 1f out: nt qckn) | 3½ | 3 | 7/1[3] | 51 | 33 |
| $4702^{7}$ | **Willy Star (BEL) (45)** (MrsSJSmith) **6-8-8**(5) GLee(11) (bhd: effrt 4f out: styd on: no imp) | 4 | 4 | 20/1 | 54 | 36 |
| $2776^{10}$ | **Elite Bliss (IRE) (38)** (MJCamacho) **4-8-8** KFallon(8) (lw: a.p: effrt over 3f out: btn appr fnl f) | hd | 5 | 12/1 | 49 | 31 |
| *$2168^{11}$* | **Radmore Brandy (37)** (PDEvans) **3-7-5**(7) RFfrench(5) (led 2f: chsd ldrs: n.m.r 3f out: sn outpcd) | 2½ | 6 | 12/1 | 41 | 17 |
| $1198^{12}$ | **Antarcticern (USA) (39)** (GROldroyd) **6-8-13** MMcAndrew(6) (dwlt: rdn 4f out: a bhd) | 6 | 7 | 100/1 | 41 | 23 |
| $3052^{14}$ | **Jimjareer (IRE) (49)** (CaptJWilson) **3-8-0**(5) PFessey(4) (lw: outpcd & bhd 4f out: n.d after) | ½ | 8 | 20/1 | 38 | 14 |

| | | | SP | RR | SF |
|---|---|---|---|---|---|
| 4763[4] | **Kashana (IRE) (43)** (WStorey) **4-7-9v**(7) IonaWands(9) (in tch tl rdn & wknd 4f out)......1 | **9** | 14/1 | 28 | 10 |
| | **Running Green** (DMoffatt) **5-8-8**(3) DarrenMoffatt(7) (b: led after 2f to 4f out: sn wknd)......¾ | **10** | 25/1 | 36 | 18 |
| *4868[W]* | ***Lady Ploy (27)*** (MissLCSiddall) **4-8-3**ow1 GHind(1) (Withdrawn not under Starter's orders: uns rdr & bolted leaving paddock)...... | **W** | 100/1 | — | — |

(SP 130.7%) **10 Rn**

**2m 20.3** (2.30) CSF £4.35 TOTE £2.40: £2.10 £1.00 £2.50 (£1.50) Trio £1.80 OWNER The Mary Reveley Racing Club (SALTBURN) BRED Kerr and Co Ltd

WEIGHT FOR AGE 3yo-6lb

**4515 Once More for Luck (IRE)**, under a good ride, did the business this time, but he had been in front long enough and the line came just in time. (5/4)

**4703 Loki (IRE)** sat in, waiting to pounce on the winner, but then took time to get going when first asked the question, and the line came a couple of strides too soon. (7/4)

**4815 Mcgillycuddy Reeks (IRE)** is running consistently well just now, but found the front pair too strong in the final furlong. (7/1)

**2941 Willy Star (BEL)** does not do anything quickly, but he does stay and will be interesting over hurdles. (20/1)

**1828 Elite Bliss (IRE)**, having her first outing for a while, ran well enough to suggest that she should be kept in mind for the winter game. (12/1)

**1451 Radmore Brandy**, having her first run for her new trainer, showed something and could well be one to watch on the All-Weather. (12/1)

## 4905 TELEPROMPTER LIMITED STKS (0-65) (3-Y.O+) (Class F)

2-10 (2-10) **1m 2f** £2,847.00 (£792.00: £381.00) Stalls: Low GOING minus 0.42 sec per fur (F)

| | | | SP | RR | SF |
|---|---|---|---|---|---|
| 4582[3] | **South Sea Bubble (IRE) (65)** (LMCumani) **4-9-0** KDarley(3) (lw: mde all: styd on strly fnl 2f)......— | **1** | 5/2[1] | 74 | 36 |
| 4626[10] | **Kalou (60)** (CWCElsey) **5-8-9**(5) PFessey(12) (hld up & bhd: effrt 4f out: styd on: nvr able to chal)......2½ | **2** | 14/1 | 70 | 32 |
| 4088[16] | **Master Millfield (IRE) (64)** (PDEvans) **4-9-3** ACulhane(11) (a.p: rdn over 3f out: styd on one pce appr fnl f)...½ | **3** | 11/1 | 72 | 34 |
| 4580[12] | **Mentalasanythin (63)** (DHaydnJones) **7-9-5** TWilliams(2) (chsd ldrs: effrt 3f out: one pce fnl 2f)......1 | **4** | 7/1 | 73 | 35 |
| 4692[6] | **Waft (USA) (63)** (BWHills) **3-8-9** KFallon(1) (prom tl outpcd 4f out: kpt on appr fnl f)......s.h | **5** | 4/1[2] | 68 | 25 |
| 4617[11] | **Daira (65)** (JDBethell) **3-8-11** SDrowne(4) (in tch: hdwy & prom 2f out: sn btn)......nk | **6** | 9/2[3] | 69 | 26 |
| 4724[6] | **Spanish Verdict (62)** (DenysSmith) **9-9-5** JWeaver(5) (lw: hld up & bhd: effrt 2f out: hrd rdn & no imp)......5 | **7** | 8/1 | 64 | 26 |
| 4691[12] | **Sistar Act (65)** (MRChannon) **3-8-6**(7) AEddery(6) (hld up & bhd: effrt 3f out: no imp)......nk | **8** | 6/1 | 63 | 20 |
| 4686[22] | **Elite Hope (USA) (60)** (NTinkler) **4-9-0** KimTinkler(7) (chsd ldrs tl wknd 3f out)......4 | **9** | 50/1 | 52 | 14 |
| 4257[9] | **Rubbiyati (51)** (CEBrittain) **4-9-2** WRyan(8) (trckd ldrs tl wknd fnl 3f)......2 | **10** | 14/1 | 51 | 13 |
| | **Kanat Lee (IRE) (25)** (MrsVAAconley) **5-9-0** GHind(10) (a rr div)......3½ | **11** | 200/1 | 43 | 5 |

(SP 128.8%) **11 Rn**

**2m 7.1** (3.50) CSF £37.47 TOTE £3.30: £2.60 £3.70 £6.60 (£63.80) Trio £167.80; £75.64 to Yarmouth 30/10/96 OWNER Lady Juliet De Chair (NEWMARKET) BRED Lady Juliet de Chair

WEIGHT FOR AGE 3yo-5lb

**4582 South Sea Bubble (IRE)** got it right this time and, given a most positive ride, was well on top in the final furlong. (5/2)

**4227 Kalou** probably just found this trip too short and, although finishing well, the effort was always too late. (14/1)

**3340 Master Millfield (IRE)**, over this much longer trip, ran much better. (11/1)

**4315 Mentalasanythin** has not won over a trip as short as this for some time and, despite running well, was tapped for toe in the last couple of furlongs. (7/1)

**4692 Waft (USA)**, stepping up in trip here, is either a funny customer or needs still further. (4/1)

**4556 Daira** has more ability that she sometimes cares to show, and cried enough approaching the final furlong. (9/2)

**4724 Spanish Verdict**, stepping up in trip, was given a most negative ride and, in the end, had a hardish race for nothing. (8/1)

## 4906 ELLERBY H'CAP (0-75) (3-Y.O+) (Class D)

2-40 (2-41) **1m** £3,951.00 (£1,188.00: £574.00: £267.00) Stalls: Centre GOING minus 0.42 sec per fur (F)

| | | | SP | RR | SF |
|---|---|---|---|---|---|
| 4793[7] | **Thatched (IRE) (49)** (REBarr) **6-7-12**(7)ow1 KSked(11) (hdwy over 2f out: r.o to ld towards fin)......— | **1** | 8/1 | 58 | 14 |
| 4724[4] | **Cee-Jay-Ay (53)** (JBerry) **9-8-4**(5) PRoberts(7) (dwlt: hdwy far side 3f out: led ins fnl f: hdd & no ex towards fin)......hd | **2** | 5/1[2] | 62 | 19 |
| 4597[11] | **Dispol Gem (61)** (GROldroyd) **3-9-0** KDarley(16) (chsd ldrs centre: chal 2f out: nt qckn ins fnl f)......1 | **3** | 10/1 | 68 | 22 |
| *4089[6]* | **Pc's Cruiser (IRE) (42)** (JLEyre) **4-7-12b** TWilliams(1) (a.p far side: led over 3f out tl ins fnl f: wknd)......4 | **4** | 12/1 | 41 | — |
| 3777[5] | **Grey Kingdom (42)** (MBrittain) **5-7-9**(3) NVarley(17) (led centre over 6f: grad wknd)......¾ | **5** | 10/1 | 39 | — |
| 4686[23] | **Darling Clover (72)** (RBastiman) **4-9-9**(5) HBastiman(15) (effrt centre ½-wy: styd on: nvr rchd ldrs)......1 | **6** | 14/1 | 67 | 24 |
| 4109[16] | **Shadow Casting (70)** (BWHills) **3-9-9** KFallon(6) (t: b: hdwy centre over 3f out: ev ch 2f out: sn rdn & btn)...1¾ | **7** | 4/1[1] | 62 | 16 |
| 4692[7] | **Johnnie the Joker (49)** (JPLeigh) **5-8-5b** DeanMcKeown(14) (chsd ldrs centre tl wknd fnl 2f)......¾ | **8** | 10/1 | 39 | — |
| 3314[10] | **Paronomasia (42)** (JLHarris) **4-7-5b**(7)ow2 RFfrench(9) (racd centre: drvn & bhd ½-wy: sme late hdwy)......s.h | **9** | 50/1 | 32 | — |
| 3974[5] | **Pleasure Trick (USA) (40)** (DonEnricoIncisa) **5-7-10** KimTinkler(3) (chsd ldrs far side tl wknd fnl 2½f)......4 | **10** | 14/1 | 22 | — |
| 4808* | **Diamond Crown (IRE) (51)** (MartynWane) **5-8-4**(3)ow1 6x RHavlin(12) (racd centre: n.d)......6 | **11** | 12/1 | 21 | — |
| *1487[7]* | **Carol Again (41)** (NBycroft) **4-7-11** NCarlisle(10) (racd centre: nvr trbld ldrs)......1¼ | **12** | 50/1 | 9 | — |
| 4701[3] | **Morocco (IRE) (58)** (MRChannon) **7-8-7**(7) AEddery(8) (trckd ldrs far side tl wknd over 2f out)......nk | **13** | 6/1[3] | 25 | — |
| 4348[10] | **Katie Komaite (43)** (CaptJWilson) **3-7-5b**1(5) PFessey(2) (led far side tl hdd & wknd over 3f out)......s.h | **14** | 25/1 | 10 | — |
| 4597[10] | **Vanadium Ore (57)** (JLEyre) **3-8-10v** MBirch(4) (racd far side: outpcd & bhd fnl 3f)......1¾ | **15** | 14/1 | 21 | — |
| 2209[9] | **Scorpius (42)** (TTClement) **6-7-12b**ow2 FNorton(13) (racd alone stands' side: wl bhd fr ½-wy)......15 | **16** | 16/1 | — | — |

(SP 138.4%) **16 Rn**

**1m 39.7** (4.00) CSF £50.46 CT £408.06 TOTE £7.70: £1.70 £1.70 £3.00 £3.10 (£22.50) Trio £126.40 OWNER Mr C. W. Marwood (MIDDLESBROUGH) BRED D. P. O'Brien

LONG HANDICAP Paronomasia 6-7 Katie Komaite 7-7 Pleasure Trick (USA) 7-9

WEIGHT FOR AGE 3yo-3lb

**4226* Thatched (IRE)** was in the right mood for a change and, well handled, produced a run to land it late on. (8/1)

**4724 Cee-Jay-Ay** is a character and a half and, after looking likely to trot up here, was just worried out of it. (5/1)

**3295 Dispol Gem** has run some decent races this season and this was another useful effort, but she proved short of toe in the closing stages. (10/1)

**4089 Pc's Cruiser (IRE)** is obviously in good form and should be kept in mind for a return to the All-Weather. (12/1)

**3777 Grey Kingdom** ran particularly well, but probably just needed this after over two months off. (10/1)

**4470 Darling Clover** is beginning to slip down the handicap and is running quite well. (14/1)

**2974 Shadow Casting** seems to have big gaps between her races and, although running reasonably here, she may well have a problem. (4/1)

**4808* Diamond Crown (IRE)** (12/1: op 8/1)
**4701 Morocco (IRE)** (6/1: 4/1-7/1)

## 4907 E.B.F. WILTON MEDIAN AUCTION MAIDEN STKS (2-Y.O) (Class F)

3-10 (3-11) **5f** £2,777.00 (£772.00: £371.00) Stalls: Centre GOING minus 0.42 sec per fur (F)

| | Horse | | Pos | SP | RR | SF |
|---|---|---|---|---|---|---|
| 4250[7] | **Morning Star** (MJohnston) **2-8-9** JWeaver(4) (mde most: reminders & hung lft after 1f: styd on strly fnl 2f) | — | 1 | 5/2[1] | 63+ | 6 |
| 4803[10] | **The Wyandotte Inn (65)** (RHollinshead) **2-8-9**(5) DGriffiths(5) (s.i.s: hdwy ½-wy: styd on: no ch w wnr) | 1¾ | 2 | 10/1 | 62 | 5 |
| 4767[3] | **Enchantica (65)** (JBerry) **2-8-9** GCarter(9) (w wnr: rdn ½-wy: one pce) | ½ | 3 | 3/1[2] | 56 | — |
| 4250[W] | **Red Romance (68)** (DenysSmith) **2-9-0** KFallon(3) (lw: chsd ldrs: rdn & one pce fnl 2f) | 1 | 4 | 5/1 | 58 | 1 |
| 4700[9] | **Ewar Arrangement** (CEBrittain) **2-9-0** WRyan(8) (lw: sn outpcd & wl bhd: r.o wl appr fnl f) | hd | 5 | 14/1 | 57 | — |
| 4807[12] | **Bright Gold** (ASmith) **2-9-0** DeanMcKeown(10) (in tch: wandered u.p 2f out: nt qckn) | hd | 6 | 100/1 | 57 | — |
| 4754[2] | **Fullopep** (MrsMReveley) **2-9-0** KDarley(7) (lw: hld up: sme hdwy ½-wy: nvr plcd to chal) | 2 | 7 | 9/2[3] | 51 | — |
| | **La Doyenne (IRE)** (CBBBooth) **2-8-9** MBirch(2) (neat: chsd ldrs: bmpd after 1f: wknd 2f out) | 3 | 8 | 9/2[3] | 36 | — |
| | **Redspet** (SRBowring) **2-8-9** SDWilliams(1) (lw: sltly hmpd after 1f: outpcd fr ½-wy) | 6 | 9 | 25/1 | 17 | — |

(SP 127.2%) **9 Rn**

**60.6 secs** (3.10) CSF £27.93 TOTE £3.60: £1.10 £3.70 £1.20 (£56.20) Trio £50.30 OWNER Mrs L. E. McKeown (MIDDLEHAM) BRED Zetland Stud

**Morning Star** needed some sharp reminders early on to get her to concentrate but, as the race progressed, she got better, and was well on top at the end. (5/2: 6/4-11/4)
**4079 The Wyandotte Inn** put in his best effort on Turf to show he has the ability. (10/1)
**4767 Enchantica** has the speed, but she is liable to beat herself. (3/1)
**3291 Red Romance** was having his first outing for almost three months, and that probably made the difference. (5/1)
**Ewar Arrangement** made it before stopping very quickly over seven furlongs last time, but was completely outpaced and tailed off over this minimum trip until suddenly picking up in the closing stages. He obviously has ability if he can be persuaded. (14/1)
**Bright Gold** showed something this time, but failed to keep a straight course when ridden. (100/1)

## 4908 CAPTAIN COOK CONDITIONS STKS (2-Y.O) (Class D)

3-45 (3-45) **7f** £3,281.50 (£982.00: £471.00: £215.50) Stalls: Centre GOING minus 0.42 sec per fur (F)

| | Horse | | Pos | SP | RR | SF |
|---|---|---|---|---|---|---|
| 4755* | **Squeak** (JHMGosden) **2-8-6** GHind(4) (hld up: qcknd to ld wl over 1f out: r.o wl) | — | 1 | 11/8[2] | 78+ | 19 |
| 4618* | **Cybertechnology** (BWHills) **2-9-3** KFallon(1) (led over 5f: kpt on u.p) | 2 | 2 | 6/5[1] | 84 | 25 |
| 4748* | **Kadeena** (MJohnston) **2-8-12** JWeaver(3) (cl up: outpcd 3f out: kpt on appr fnl f) | 1¾ | 3 | 9/2[3] | 75 | 16 |
| 4301[4] | **Coral Strand** (JWWatts) **2-8-6** WRyan(2) (lw: prom tl outpcd over 2f out: sn btn & eased) | 28 | 4 | 14/1 | 5 | — |

(SP 112.4%) **4 Rn**

**1m 26.1** (3.10) CSF £3.44 TOTE £2.20 (£1.50) OWNER Lord Hartington (NEWMARKET) BRED Side Hill Stud

**4755* Squeak**, a different proposition this time, won in useful style, and is obviously on the upgrade. (11/8)
**4618* Cybertechnology** made it, but probably did not go fast enough soon enough and the winner always had him for toe. (6/5)
**4748* Kadeena** needed a stronger pace and got left behind when things hotted up but, to her credit, she did keep on really well after looking beaten. (9/2)
**4301 Coral Strand** ran poorly, getting completely outpaced with over two furlongs to go, and was then eased when well beaten. (14/1)

## 4909 GANTON H'CAP (0-85) (3-Y.O+) (Class D)

4-15 (4-16) **7f** £4,055.00 (£1,220.00: £590.00: £275.00) Stalls: Centre GOING minus 0.42 sec per fur (F)

| | Horse | | Pos | SP | RR | SF |
|---|---|---|---|---|---|---|
| 4688[4] | **Pharmacy (70)** (JWWatts) **3-9-2** MBirch(11) (hld up: stdy hdwy over 2f out: led wl ins fnl f: all out) | — | 1 | 9/1 | 80 | 42 |
| 4688[5] | **Best of All (IRE) (58)** (JBerry) **4-8-6b** GCarter(9) (s.i.s: hdwy 3f out: r.o fnl f: jst failed) | hd | 2 | 7/1[2] | 68 | 32 |
| 4724[U] | **Quilling (72)** (MDods) **4-9-6** RLappin(18) (chsd ldrs: led over 2f out tl wl ins fnl f) | 1 | 3 | 8/1[3] | 80 | 44 |
| 4811[12] | **Saint Express (79)** (MrsMReveley) **6-9-13** KDarley(8) (chsd ldrs: chal 1f out: nt qckn) | ½ | 4 | 20/1 | 85 | 49 |
| 4688[20] | **Keston Pond (IRE) (75)** (MrsVAAconley) **6-9-9** MDeering(17) (dwlt: hdwy over 2f out: sn chsng ldrs: kpt on fnl f) | ½ | 5 | 9/1 | 80 | 44 |
| 4719[5] | **Ertlon (71)** (CEBrittain) **6-9-2**(3) PMcCabe(4) (hdwy ½-wy: sn in tch: nt qckn fnl f) | hd | 6 | 9/1 | 76 | 40 |
| 4769[10] | **Royal Ceilidh (IRE) (78)** (DenysSmith) **3-9-10** GHind(2) (a in tch: hdwy over 2f out: styd on: nvr able to chal) | hd | 7 | 9/1 | 83 | 45 |
| 4504* | **Divine Quest (76)** (HRACecil) **3-9-8** WRyan(16) (lw: effrt over 2f out: rdn & nvr trbld ldrs) | 3 | 8 | 2/1[1] | 74 | 36 |
| 4809* | **Saddlehome (USA) (72)** (TDBarron) **7-9-6** 6x DeanMcKeown(14) (sn pushed along: nvr trbld ldrs) | 1 | 9 | 9/1 | 68 | 32 |
| 4453[11] | **Mybotye (78)** (GROldroyd) **3-9-5**(5) GParkin(13) (in tch: effrt 3f out: no imp) | nk | 10 | 33/1 | 73 | 35 |
| 4724[10] | **Antarctic Storm (63)** (RAFahey) **3-8-9** FNorton(15) (prom 5f: wknd) | nk | 11 | 20/1 | 57 | 19 |
| 956[12] | **Ashgore (77)** (JLEyre) **6-9-11** TWilliams(10) (cl up: disp ld ½-wy tl over 2f out: wknd) | 2 | 12 | 10/1 | 67 | 31 |
| 4809[6] | **Cavers Yangous (61)** (MJohnston) **5-8-9v** JWeaver(6) (s.i.s: n.d) | 2½ | 13 | 9/1 | 45 | 9 |
| 4768[18] | **Superpride (63)** (MrsMReveley) **4-8-11** ACulhane(12) (bolted gng to s: chsd ldrs 5f) | 2½ | 14 | 20/1 | 41 | 5 |
| 4687[20] | **Benzoe (IRE) (78)** (MrsJRRamsden) **6-9-12** KFallon(7) (sn prom: hdwy to disp ld ½-wy: wknd fnl 2f) | 3 | 15 | 16/1 | 49 | 13 |
| 4765[20] | **Sihafi (USA) (70)** (JMCarr) **3-9-2** NCarlisle(5) (led to ½-wy: grad wknd) | nk | 16 | 100/1 | 41 | 3 |
| 4691[9] | **Gymcrak Flyer (64)** (GHolmes) **5-8-12** JFanning(3) (hdwy ½-wy: sn rdn: wknd 2f out) | nk | 17 | 20/1 | 34 | — |
| 4687[22] | **Antonias Melody (77)** (SRBowring) **3-9-9** SDWilliams(1) (cl up tl wknd over 2f out) | 3½ | 18 | 33/1 | 39 | 1 |

(SP 157.8%) **18 Rn**

**1m 24.9** (1.90) CSF £82.89 CT £535.98 TOTE £10.40: £2.20 £2.60 £2.00 £6.00 (£63.90) Trio £190.30 OWNER Lady Jane Kaplan (RICHMOND) BRED Stanley Estate and Stud Co

WEIGHT FOR AGE 3yo-2lb

**4688 Pharmacy** travelled well and, patiently ridden, was produced to lead in the closing stages. (9/1: 6/1-10/1)
**4688 Best of All (IRE)**, closely handicapped with the winner on their York run, put up another useful effort with the blinkers on. (7/1)
**4439* Quilling**, last into the stalls as he has to be, ran well to show he is still in good form. (8/1)
**4505 Saint Express**, trying a longer trip, had his chances, but failed to come up with the goods once the pressure was applied. (20/1)
**4504 Keston Pond (IRE)** is still running well and could be interesting if tried on the All-Weather again. (9/1)
**4719 Ertlon** showed his well-being and should be watched for on a return to the All-Weather. (9/1)
**4504* Divine Quest** looked tremendously well, but proved disappointing. (2/1: op 7/2)

T/Plpt: £95.70 (101.1 Tckts). T/Qdpt: £37.60 (20 Tckts). AA

# 4813-YARMOUTH (L-H) (Good)
## Wednesday October 30th
WEATHER: fine, cool WIND: mod across

### 4910 NEWPORT CLAIMING STKS (3-Y.O+) (Class F)
1-20 (1-20) **1m 6f 17y** £2,833.20 (£785.20: £375.60) Stalls: High GOING minus 0.07 sec per fur (G)

| Form | Horse / Trainer / Weight / Jockey (Comment) | Dist | Pos | SP | RR | SF |
|---|---|---|---|---|---|---|
| 4763[2] | **Cross Talk (IRE) (65)** (NTinkler) **4-9-0** KDarley(6) (a.p: led over 2f out: sn clr: rdn out) | — | 1 | 4/1[2] | 57 | 38 |
| 4794[5] | **Bobby's Dream (33)** (MHTompkins) **4-8-2**(3) MHenry(7) (chsd ldrs: rdn 3f out: edgd lft & chsd wnr appr fnl f: r.o) | 3 | 2 | 25/1 | 45 | 26 |
| 4766[9] | **Iota (51)** (JLHarris) **7-8-7** DeanMcKeown(3) (trckd ldrs: outpcd 3f out: hmpd over 1f out: r.o wl ins fnl f) | 2 | 3 | 5/1[3] | 44 | 25 |
| 4496[12] | **Lucy Tufty (35)** (JPearce) **5-8-5** GBardwell(1) (hld up & plld hrd: rdn 3f out: kpt on appr fnl f) | ¾ | 4 | 25/1 | 42 | 23 |
| 4358[2] | **Influence Pedler (62)** (CEBrittain) **3-8-13** MRoberts(5) (a.p: ev ch 4f out: sn rdn: btn appr fnl f) | 1 | 5 | 5/2[1] | 57 | 29 |
| 4794[11] | **Zeliba (35)** (MrsNMacauley) **4-8-6**(7) JoHunnam(4) (chsd ldrs: rdn over 1f out: edgd lft & sn btn) | ½ | 6 | 20/1 | 48 | 29 |
| 4815[6] | **Junior Ben (IRE) (38)** (PHowling) **4-8-12** KFallon(10) (led tl over 2f out: wknd fnl f) | 3 | 7 | 20/1 | 43 | 24 |
| 4252[16] | **Flight Master (58)** (PJMakin) **4-8-10** PatEddery(11) (t: chsd ldrs: lost pl over 4f out: rallied 4f out: eased whn btn fnl f) | 19 | 8 | 4/1[2] | 20 | 1 |
| *4092*[10] | **Well Arranged (IRE) (56)** (MJPolglase) **5-9-12** JWeaver(8) (lw: hld up: effrt & nt clr run 6f out: nvr rchd ldrs) | 3½ | 9 | 14/1 | 32 | 13 |
| 4877[13] | **Derrybelle** (DLWilliams) **5-8-7** DHarrison(9) (dwlt: bhd fnl 6f) | 5 | 10 | 50/1 | 7 | — |
| 1526[15] | **New Regime (IRE)** (PTDalton) **3-8-4** JFEgan(2) (prom tl wknd qckly over 4f out) | dist | 11 | 50/1 | — | — |

(SP 113.0%) **11 Rn**

**3m 9.4** (10.00) CSF £78.71 TOTE £4.90: £1.80 £2.40 £1.90 (£55.20) Trio £57.50 OWNER Elite Racing Club (MALTON) BRED Juddmonte Farms
WEIGHT FOR AGE 3yo-9lb
Influence Pedler clmd FWebber £10,000

**4763 Cross Talk (IRE)** took a good hold and was travelling best some way from home, scoring on his third outing for new connections. (4/1)
**4794 Bobby's Dream** did not keep straight in the last couple of furlongs, but still seemed to excel as she was on much worse than handicap terms with some of those behind. Having faith in her has proved expensive in the past though. (25/1)
**4203 Iota** really needs further and was getting outpaced when having to be snatched up, losing momentum, at the distance. The way she finished in the final furlong suggests she would have gone close with a clear run. (5/1)
**4236 Lucy Tufty** took a keen hold, but stuck to her task in the home straight and is worth keeping an eye on back over hurdles. (25/1)
**4358 Influence Pedler** gets further, and could never get on top when making his bid early in the home straight. (5/2)
**4612 Zeliba** would have had a much easier task in a handicap and ran respectably. (20/1)
**3849 Flight Master**, a tubed horse, seemed badly inconvenienced by the strong head-on breeze as he left the back straight. (4/1)

### 4911 CORTON CONDITIONS STKS (3-Y.O+) (Class C)
1-55 (1-55) **1m 2f 21y** £5,022.20 (£1,857.80: £890.90: £363.50: £143.75: £55.85) Stalls: Low GOING minus 0.07 sec per fur (G)

| Form | Horse / Trainer / Weight / Jockey (Comment) | Dist | Pos | SP | RR | SF |
|---|---|---|---|---|---|---|
| 4680[8] | **Medaille Militaire (102)** (JLDunlop) **4-9-2** KDarley(1) (trckd ldrs: chal 3f out: led wl over 1f out: sn pushed clr) | — | 1 | 5/1 | 115 | 48 |
| 4567[6] | **Miss Universal (IRE) (104)** (CEBrittain) **3-8-6** MRoberts(2) (set slow pce to 4f out: plld out over 1f out: r.o fnl f) | 3½ | 2 | 9/2[3] | 105 | 33 |
| 4714[3] | **Florid (USA) (110)** (HRACecil) **5-9-7** PatEddery(7) (lw: prom: led 4f out: rdn over 2f out: hdd wl over 1f out: one pce) | nk | 3 | 6/4[1] | 114 | 47 |
| 2706* | **Poddington (85)** (RAkehurst) **5-9-5** DHarrison(5) (bit bkwd: hld up & plld hrd: hdwy & n.m.r over 1f out: kpt on fnl f) | 1¾ | 4 | 14/1 | 109 | 42 |
| 1899[3] | **Anthelia (100)** (GWragg) **3-8-6** MHills(6) (trckd ldrs: rdn & kpt on fnl 2f) | ½ | 5 | 7/2[2] | 100 | 28 |
| 4622[7] | **Tumi (USA)** (JHMGosden) **3-8-6** LDettori(3) (stdd s: hld up: effrt over 3f out: wknd 2f out) | 7 | 6 | 25/1 | 89 | 17 |
| | **Steady Ready Go (IRE)** (JRPoulton) **4-9-2** AMorris(4) (b: bit bkwd: plld hrd: prom 4f: sddle slipped & virtually p.u) | dist | 7 | 40/1 | — | — |

(SP 110.0%) **7 Rn**

**2m 10.2** (5.80) CSF £24.74 TOTE £5.90: £2.40 £2.00 (£10.80) OWNER Mr James Hartnett (ARUNDEL) BRED Fares Stables Ltd
WEIGHT FOR AGE 3yo-5lb

**1131 Medaille Militaire**, a moderate mover, is a hard horse to place, but found the right race and was cruising all over these in the final three furlongs. (5/1: op 3/1)
**4567 Miss Universal (IRE)**, forced to set her own pace, was short of toe when the tempo picked up in the straight, but was rallying well as the line approached. (9/2)
**4714 Florid (USA)** looked well as usual but, once sent on, soon had the winner upsides him going twice as well. He was beginning to flag in the final furlong. (6/4)
**2706* Poddington** is very lightly-raced, but is likely to have ruined his advantageous handicap mark with a good run against this company. (14/1: 5/1-16/1)
**1899 Anthelia**, off since June, moved to post poorly and failed to run to her best. (7/2)
**4622 Tumi (USA)** got fractious just before the stalls opened, but was settled at the back before showing some promise early in the straight. She would have a chance in an ordinary maiden if her temperament does not get the better of her. (25/1)
**Steady Ready Go (IRE)** looked to have done plenty of work, despite still carrying condition. He was cheaply bought at the Sales, but the saddle slipped too early to make any assessment of how much ability he retains. (40/1)

### 4912 LOUND NURSERY H'CAP (0-85) (2-Y.O) (Class E)
2-30 (2-30) **5f 43y** £3,070.20 (£915.60: £436.80: £197.40) Stalls: Low GOING minus 0.07 sec per fur (G)

| Form | Horse / Trainer / Weight / Jockey (Comment) | Dist | Pos | SP | RR | SF |
|---|---|---|---|---|---|---|
| 4754[3] | **Dominant Air (72)** (SirMarkPrescott) **2-9-0** GDuffield(1) (mde all: rdn 1f out: jst hld on) | — | 1 | 7/1[3] | 75 | 26 |
| 4493* | **Royal Blackbird (64)** (JEBanks) **2-7-13**(7) RMullen(3) (dwlt: hdwy 2f out: r.o wl u.p fnl f: jst failed) | s.h | 2 | 7/1[3] | 67 | 18 |
| 4545[3] | **Nopalea (75)** (CEBrittain) **2-9-3** MRoberts(8) (lw: chsd ldrs: rdn over 1f out: kpt on fnl f) | 1¼ | 3 | 5/1[1] | 74 | 25 |
| 4234[12] | **Regal Equity (68)** (BJMeehan) **2-8-10** JWeaver(6) (w ldr: ev ch over 1f out: n.m.r & eased wl ins fnl f) | ½ | 4 | 16/1 | 66 | 17 |
| 4672[12] | **Sparkling Edge (55)** (CADwyer) **2-7-11** JQuinn(2) (chsd ldrs: rdn 2f out: wknd ins fnl f) | 2 | 5 | 12/1 | 46 | — |
| 4803[5] | **Expectation (IRE) (66)** (PRWebber) **2-8-8** DHarrison(9) (nvr nrr) | 1½ | 6 | 16/1 | 53 | 4 |
| 4767* | **Swift (65)** (MJPolglase) **2-8-7** KDarley(5) (lw: prom 3f) | ½ | 7 | 7/1[3] | 50 | 1 |

| | Horse | Dist | Pos | SP | RR | SF |
|---|---|---|---|---|---|---|
| 4749* | **Sarabi (69)** (JPearce) **2-8-11** KFallon(7) (chsd ldrs 3f) | hd | **8** | 6/1[2] | 54 | 5 |
| 4558[2] | **Fine Times (73)** (CWFairhurst) **2-9-1** DeanMcKeown(4) (dwlt: sn in tch: rdn 2f out: sn wknd) | nk | **9** | 10/1 | 57 | 8 |
| 2495[12] | **Manhattan Diamond (66)** (ABailey) **2-8-8b[1]** GCarter(10) (s.s: a bhd) | 1¼ | **10** | 16/1 | 46 | — |
| 4566[9] | **Stygian (USA) (79)** (BWHills) **2-9-7** PatEddery(11) (chsd ldrs 3f) | 6 | **11** | 5/1[1] | 41 | — |

(SP 119.5%) **11 Rn**

**64.6 secs** (4.10) CSF £51.78 CT £251.40 TOTE £9.00: £2.80 £2.40 £1.50 (£35.70) Trio £51.70 OWNER Mr Neil Greig (NEWMARKET) BRED W. N. Greig

**4754 Dominant Air** again moved down poorly and had got his winter coat, but belied his appearance by breaking fast and making all the running, despite drifting gradually to the centre of the course. He is rather small and would not appreciate much more weight. (7/1)
**4493* Royal Blackbird** was very keen on leaving the paddock and her young rider did really well to get her to post in such good order. Missing the start may have been deliberate, but it set her a task that she just failed to achieve. (7/1)
**4545 Nopalea** kept battling away in the last couple of furlongs without really closing on the winner. (5/1)
**3502 Regal Equity** had gone in his coat, but led the group in the centre of the course without every having the call over the winner. Connections clearly feel he is a sprinter, but he is bred to stay very much further. (16/1)
**3871 Sparkling Edge**, whose trip is proving hard to find, raced with the leaders until dropping away in the closing stages. (12/1)
**4803 Expectation (IRE)** looks to need further than this, but has the scope to win a race. (16/1)

## 4913 E.B.F. HERRINGFLEET MAIDEN STKS (2-Y.O) (Class D)

3-05 (3-09) **7f 3y** £3,980.00 (£1,190.00: £570.00: £260.00) Stalls: Low GOING minus 0.07 sec per fur (G)

| | Horse | Dist | Pos | SP | RR | SF |
|---|---|---|---|---|---|---|
| | **Happy Valentine** (SbinSuroor) **2-9-0** LDettori(13) (gd sort: mde all stands' side: clr over 1f out: easily) | — | **1** | 7/4[1] | 103++ | 61 |
| | **Silverani (IRE)** (LMCumani) **2-9-0** OUrbina(15) (leggy: unf: hld up stands' side: hdwy over 1f out: r.o fnl f) | 5 | **2** | 25/1 | 92+ | 50 |
| | **Shawm** (DRLoder) **2-9-0** RHughes(16) (scope: bit bkwd: hld up stands' side: hdwy 2f out: one pce fnl f) | 1½ | **3** | 8/1 | 88 | 46 |
| | **Darnaway** (HRACecil) **2-9-0** PatEddery(4) (leggy: scope: prom centre: chal 2f out: eased ins fnl f) | 1¼ | **4** | 6/1[3] | 85 | 43 |
| | **Gharib (USA)** (ACStewart) **2-9-0** MRoberts(2) (leggy: unf: bit bkwd: b.hind: prom centre: ev ch 2f out: eased whn btn fnl f) | 3 | **5** | 4/1[2] | 79 | 37 |
| | **Double Alleged (USA)** (MJohnston) **2-9-0** JWeaver(9) (leggy: scope: prom: one pce appr fnl f) | 1½ | **6** | 14/1 | 75 | 33 |
| 4705[8] | **Wathbat Nashwan** (LMCumani) **2-8-7**(7) RFfrench(3) (bit bkwd: stdy hdwy fnl 2f: nvr plcd to chal) | 1¾ | **7** | 50/1 | 71 | 29 |
| 4100[13] | **Crystal Gold** (MRStoute) **2-9-0** KBradshaw(6) (bit bkwd: hld up: effrt over 2f out: nvr nr to chal) | hd | **8** | 33/1 | 71 | 29 |
| 4782[4] | **Shalstayholy (IRE)** (GLMoore) **2-8-9** SWhitworth(10) (bhd tl r.o fnl 2f) | 1¼ | **9** | 50/1 | 63 | 21 |
| 4756[15] | **Alyportent** (WJHaggas) **2-9-0** GDuffield(12) (lw: w wnr stands' side 4f) | ¾ | **10** | 33/1 | 66 | 24 |
| 4584[4] | **Itatinga (USA)** (MRStoute) **2-8-9** KFallon(17) (trckd ldrs stands' side 5f) | s.h | **11** | 9/1 | 61 | 19 |
| 4698[6] | **Fabled Light (IRE)** (GWragg) **2-9-0** MHills(7) (led centre over 4f) | 1½ | **12** | 12/1 | 63 | 21 |
| | **Hulal** (ACStewart) **2-9-0** RHills(1) (w'like: s.s: a bhd) | 4 | **13** | 25/1 | 54 | 12 |
| 4494[15] | **Babe (IRE)** (MHTompkins) **2-8-6**(3) MHenry(11) (rdn & edgd rt over 2f out: nvr nr to chal) | 1 | **14** | 100/1 | 46 | 4 |
| 4756[22] | **Water Garden** (GWragg) **2-9-0** AClark(14) (s.i.s: racd stands' side: bhd fnl 2f) | ½ | **15** | 50/1 | 50 | 8 |
| | **Northern Angel (IRE)** (MrsJCecil) **2-9-0** KDarley(5) (unf: bkwd: effrt 3f out: a bhd) | hd | **16** | 33/1 | 50 | 8 |
| | **Salford Lad** (GWragg) **2-9-0** WRyan(8) (unf: scope: bkwd: virtually p.u fnl 2f) | 28 | **17** | 33/1 | — | — |
| *4756[20]* | ***Nor-Do-I*** (JMPEustace) **2-9-0** AMcGlone(18) (Withdrawn not under Starter's orders: reard & bolted bef s) | | **W** | 50/1 | — | — |

(SP 134.4%) **17 Rn**

**1m 26.9** (2.70) CSF £46.48 TOTE £2.60: £1.10 £12.30 £3.30 (£41.00) Trio £258.50 OWNER Godolphin (NEWMARKET) BRED Cheveley Park Stud Ltd

**Happy Valentine**, closely related to Blushing Flame from the family of many top-class horses including Salsabil, cost 600,000 guineas as a yearling and it is easy to see why. He has looked rather weak on the gallops during the summer, but has really come to himself in recent weeks and did this with little fuss. Making him second-favourite for the Derby on the basis of one maiden win seems premature but, with the winter in Dubai under his belt, he looks a fascinating prospect for the better races next year. (7/4)
**Silverani (IRE)**, not the greatest of movers, nevertheless shaped well, staying on in a manner that suggests he will stay further. (25/1)
**Shawm**, a newcomer, looked well in his coat, but tended to edge towards the centre of the course as he made his effort. (8/1: 6/1-10/1)
**Darnaway** moved to post nicely and was going as well as any with two furlongs left. Failing to pick up, he was not knocked about. (6/1)
**Gharib (USA)**, well supported, did not look quite ready, but ran well and was given an easy time in the final furlong. (4/1)
**Double Alleged (USA)** looks the sort to come into his own next year over a longer trip. (14/1: 20/1-33/1)
**Wathbat Nashwan** still looks weak and backward, but has plenty of scope to do better as he matures. (50/1)
**4584 Itatinga (USA)** (9/1: op 14/1)

## 4914 RANWORTH MAIDEN STKS (2-Y.O) (Class D)

3-40 (3-42) **1m 3y** £3,834.80 (£1,147.40: £550.20: £251.60) Stalls: Low GOING minus 0.07 sec per fur (G)

| | Horse | Dist | Pos | SP | RR | SF |
|---|---|---|---|---|---|---|
| 4461[10] | **Mandilak (USA)** (LMCumani) **2-9-0** OUrbina(11) (bit bkwd: trckd ldrs: rdn over 1f out: str run to ld wl ins fnl f) | — | **1** | 5/1 | 80 | 31 |
| | **Street General** (HRACecil) **2-9-0** WRyan(3) (unf: scope: bhd: hdwy 3f out: led ins fnl f: sn hdd & unable qckn) | 1 | **2** | 20/1 | 78 | 29 |
| 4069[5] | **Invermark** (JRFanshawe) **2-9-0** DHarrison(1) (bit bkwd: trckd ldrs: led over 2f out: rdn & edgd rt over 1f out: hdd ins fnl f) | 1½ | **3** | 20/1 | 75 | 26 |
| 4516[3] | **Red Guard** (GWragg) **2-9-0** MHills(9) (led 4f: ev ch 2f out: one pce) | 7 | **4** | 15/8[1] | 61 | 12 |
| 4697[9] | **Top Shelf** (CEBrittain) **2-8-9** MRoberts(13) (in tch: rdn 4f out: kpt on fnl 2f) | ½ | **5** | 33/1 | 55 | 6 |
| 4720[12] | **Fantail** (MHTompkins) **2-8-11**(3) MHenry(8) (lw: in tch: no hdwy fnl 2f) | ½ | **6** | 66/1 | 59 | 10 |
| 4705[2] | **Michael Venture** (SPCWoods) **2-9-0** KDarley(4) (lw: a.p: ev ch 2f out: sn wknd) | 1¼ | **7** | 100/30[2] | 57 | 8 |
| 4684[6] | **Hadidi** (DMorley) **2-9-0** RHills(12) (stdd s: a bhd) | 1¼ | **8** | 25/1 | 54 | 5 |
| | **Seattle Art (USA)** (HRACecil) **2-9-0** PatEddery(5) (lengthy: scope: b.hind: prom: shkn up 3f out: sn wknd) | 7 | **9** | 4/1[3] | 40 | — |
| | **Miracle Kid (USA)** (JHMGosden) **2-9-0** LDettori(2) (scope: bit bkwd: hld up: effrt 3f out: btn 2f out) | s.h | **10** | 10/1 | 40 | — |
| 4386[10] | **The Tig** (LRLloyd-James) **2-9-0** KFallon(10) (chsd ldrs 4f) | 2½ | **11** | 66/1 | 35 | — |
| 4756[12] | **Kweilo** (JWPayne) **2-9-0** AMcGlone(6) (w ldr: led 4f out tl over 2f out: sn wknd) | 2½ | **12** | 20/1 | 30 | — |
| | **Gold Clipper** (MJRyan) **2-9-0** AClark(7) (leggy: unf: lw: sn pushed along: a bhd) | 8 | **13** | 66/1 | 14 | — |

(SP 129.2%) **13 Rn**

**1m 41.2** (5.90) CSF £94.32 TOTE £9.10: £2.10 £3.10 £3.00 (£83.90) Trio £361.50; £458.36 to Nottingham 31/10/96 OWNER H H Aga Khan (NEWMARKET) BRED His Highness the Aga Khan's Studs S.C.

**IN-FOCUS: This was the Aga Khan's first winner in this country since he pulled out of British racing over the Aliysa affair.**

**Mandilak (USA)**, a good mover, found a useful turn of foot when let down, and will stay further next year. (5/1)
**Street General** took a while to find his feet, but stayed on strongly, although just denied. He should not be hard to place over middle distances. (20/1)
**4069 Invermark** was certainly more at home back on a galloping track, but did hang away form the whip when hitting the front. (20/1)
**4516 Red Guard** did not pay too many compliments to his Newmarket conquerors. (15/8: 5/4-2/1)
**Top Shelf** got outpaced at halfway, but was noted staying on towards the finish. (33/1)
**Fantail** never threatened to take a hand, but is going the right way. (66/1)
**4705 Michael Venture** (100/30: op 6/1)
**Seattle Art (USA)**, a tall, weak half-brother to several winners, looked in need of the race and was heavily bandaged behind. Going well with the leaders to halfway, he was given an easy time as his fitter rivals got the better of him. (4/1)

## 4915 CALIFORNIA H'CAP (0-70) (3-Y.O+) (Class E)
4-10 (4-16) **7f 3y** £3,725.40 (£1,117.20: £537.60: £247.80) Stalls: Low GOING minus 0.07 sec per fur (G)

| | | | | SP | RR | SF |
|---|---|---|---|---|---|---|
| 4788[5] | **Absolute Magic (70)** (WJHaggas) **6-10-0** MHills(5) (lw: trckd ldrs: led over 1f out: rdn out) | — | **1** | 16/1 | 80 | 63 |
| 4860[15] | **Just Millie (USA) (58)** (JEBanks) **3-8-7v**(7) RMullen(4) (rdn & hdwy over 1f out: r.o ins fnl f) | 1¼ | **2** | 25/1 | 65 | 46 |
| 4768[5] | **Sharp 'n' Shady (53)** (CFWall) **3-8-9** GDuffield(2) (rdn 2f out: hdwy over 1f out: r.o wl fnl f) | hd | **3** | 4/1[2] | 60 | 41 |
| 4768[13] | **Statistician (56)** (JohnBerry) **4-9-0b** KFallon(17) (prom: led over 2f out tl over 1f out: one pce) | hd | **4** | 25/1 | 63 | 46 |
| 4768* | **Allinson's Mate (IRE) (62)** (TDBarron) **8-8-13b**(7) VictoriaAppleby(14) (in tch: effrt 3f out: edgd lft & no ex fnl f) | 1¼ | **5** | 12/1 | 66 | 49 |
| 4820[15] | **Sea Danzig (65)** (JJBridger) **3-9-7** DHarrison(10) (prom: rdn over 3f out: ev ch over 2f out: one pce) | nk | **6** | 14/1 | 68 | 49 |
| 4768[6] | **Comanche Companion (60)** (TJNaughton) **6-9-4** JWeaver(1) (swtchd rt s: sn in tch: no imp appr fnl f) | nk | **7** | 10/1 | 63 | 46 |
| 4881[13] | **Rapier Point (IRE) (46)** (CMurray) **5-8-4** GCarter(18) (b: hdwy fnl 2f: nvr able to chal) | 1½ | **8** | 50/1 | 45 | 28 |
| 4829[12] | **First Gold (50)** (JWharton) **7-8-8b** KDarley(12) (hld up: effrt 2f out: no imp appr fnl f) | hd | **9** | 25/1 | 49 | 32 |
| 2345[8] | **Pusey Street Boy (39)** (JRBosley) **9-7-4**(7) RFfrench(6) (t: lw: prom: one pce fnl 3f) | 2 | **10** | 33/1 | 33 | 16 |
| 4624[9] | **Czarna (IRE) (70)** (CEBrittain) **5-10-0** MRoberts(7) (w ldrs: rdn 3f out: sn btn) | 3 | **11** | 12/1 | 57 | 40 |
| 4809[3] | **Don Pepe (62)** (RBoss) **5-9-1**(5) ADaly(20) (lw: in tch: rdn 2f out: no imp) | s.h | **12** | 11/2[3] | 49 | 32 |
| 4692[2] | **Bentico (53)** (MrsNMacauley) **7-8-8**(3) CTeague(15) (in tch: rdn 2f out: sn btn) | 1¼ | **13** | 7/2[1] | 37 | 20 |
| 4373[6] | **Soaking (50)** (PBurgoyne) **6-8-8** DRMcCabe(19) (lw: chsd ldrs 5f: eased whn btn) | 1¼ | **14** | 16/1 | 32 | 15 |
| *4895[8]* | **Our Shadee (USA) (47)** (KTIvory) **6-8-5v** CScally(3) (a bhd) | ½ | **15** | 20/1 | 28 | 11 |
| 4888[15] | **Everset (FR) (55)** (ABailey) **8-8-10b**(3) DWright(11) (b: bhd fnl 3f) | 3 | **16** | 16/1 | 29 | 12 |
| 4323* | **Komlucky (49)** (ABMulholland) **4-8-2v**(5) LNewton(16) (prom: n.m.r & wknd over 2f out) | hd | **17** | 14/1 | 22 | 5 |
| 4560[14] | **Summer Beauty (65)** (JHMGosden) **3-9-7** LDettori(13) (prom 4f) | hd | **18** | 12/1 | 38 | 19 |
| 2541[8] | **In The Highlands (45)** (DJSCosgrove) **3-8-1** FNorton(9) (b: bhd fnl 2f) | s.h | **19** | 50/1 | 18 | — |
| 1598[9] | **Hickory Blue (62)** (KAMorgan) **6-9-6b** RHughes(8) (led over 4f) | nk | **20** | 25/1 | 34 | 17 |
| | | | | (SP 147.8%) | | **20 Rn** |

**1m 27.8** (3.60) CSF £366.31 CT £1,209.34 TOTE £20.50: £4.00 £5.10 £1.50 £9.70 (£366.50) Trio £764.50 OWNER Mrs Barbara Bassett (NEWMARKET) BRED Glazeley Stud
WEIGHT FOR AGE 3yo-2lb
**4788 Absolute Magic** reaped the benefit of not having a hard season. (16/1)
**4498 Just Millie (USA)** stayed on well towards the finish and remains in good form. (25/1)
**4768 Sharp 'n' Shady**, keen to post, was held up at the back and got going rather too late. (4/1)
**4701 Statistician**, made plenty of use of this time, only gave best inside the final furlong. (25/1)
**4768* Allinson's Mate (IRE)**, a moderate mover who looked wintry, unshipped his pilot on the way to post, but still ran his race. (12/1)
**4550* Sea Danzig** could never get to the front and was fighting a losing battle a long way from home. (14/1)

T/Jkpt: Not won; £2,871.44 to Nottingham 31/10/96. T/Plpt: £4,726.00 (3.29 Tckts). T/Qdpt: £438.10 (3.65 Tckts). Dk

# 4828-NOTTINGHAM (L-H) (Good to soft becoming Soft)
## Thursday October 31st
WEATHER: rain WIND: slt against

## 4916 RUSHCLIFFE NURSERY H'CAP (0-85) (2-Y.O) (Class E)
1-00 (1-09) **6f 15y** £3,210.00 (£960.00: £460.00: £210.00) Stalls: High GOING: 0.53 sec per fur (GS)

| | | | | SP | RR | SF |
|---|---|---|---|---|---|---|
| 4600* | **Craigievar (84)** (JRFanshawe) **2-9-7** DHarrison(5) (lw: trckd ldrs centre: led ins fnl f: pushed clr) | — | **1** | 3/1[1] | 97+ | 61 |
| 4787* | **Sharp Return (60)** (MJRyan) **2-7-4**(7)ow1 7x AMcCarthy(4) (lw: chsd ldr: led 2f out tl hdd & no ex ins fnl f) | 5 | **2** | 16/1 | 60 | 27 |
| 4350* | **Balladoole Bajan (78)** (MJohnston) **2-9-1** JWeaver(10) (chsd ldrs centre: rdn over 2f out: kpt on one pce) | 2 | **3** | 6/1[2] | 73 | 39 |
| 4614[10] | **Step N Go (IRE) (67)** (MrsJRRamsden) **2-8-4** JQuinn(6) (trckd ldrs centre: rdn 2f out: one pce) | 4 | **4** | 14/1 | 51 | 19 |
| 4878[3] | **Heavenly Miss (IRE) (75)** (JJBridger) **2-8-5**(7) RMullen(2) (prom centre tl wknd over 1f out) | hd | **5** | 14/1 | 59 | 26 |
| 3293[4] | **Faringdon Future (83)** (BWHills) **2-9-6** MHills(9) (bit bkwd: in tch: effrt & rdn 2f out: nt rch ldrs) | 2½ | **6** | 13/2[3] | 60 | 27 |
| 1408* | **C-Harry (IRE) (71)** (RHollinshead) **2-8-5**(3) FLynch(3) (swtg: bkwd: led to 2f out: sn wknd) | ¾ | **7** | 20/1 | 46 | 15 |
| 4717[14] | **Puzzlement (62)** (CEBrittain) **2-7-13** DeclanO'Shea(15) (racd stands' side: rdn over 2f out: sn outpcd) | ½ | **8** | 20/1 | 36 | 5 |
| 4880[2] | **Petite Danseuse (77)** (CADwyer) **2-8-7**(7) JoHunnam(12) (racd stands' side: rdn & btn over 2f out) | ½ | **9** | 3/1[1] | 50 | 18 |
| 4512[9] | **Bold Spring (IRE) (77)** (RHannon) **2-9-0** DaneO'Neill(14) (outpcd: a bhd) | 3 | **10** | 10/1 | 42 | 10 |
| 4790[3] | **Sparkling Harry (66)** (MissLCSiddall) **2-8-3b**ow1 GHind(8) (racd stands' side: prom 4f) | ½ | **11** | 16/1 | 29 | — |
| 3128[12] | **Threeplay (IRE) (73)** (JAkehurst) **2-8-10v** GDuffield(1) (b.hind: bit bkwd: prom centre 4f: sn rdn & wknd: t.o) | 5 | **12** | 25/1 | 23 | — |
| 3259[20] | **Scarlet Lake (72)** (DRLoder) **2-8-9** LDettori(7) (led stands' side over 3f: sn lost tch: t.o) | 2½ | **13** | 12/1 | 16 | — |
| *4545[8]* | ***Myrmidon (80)*** (JLDunlop) **2-9-3** PatEddery(11) (Withdrawn not under Starter's orders: bolted bef s) | | **W** | 13/2[3] | — | — |
| | | | | (SP 146.2%) | | **13 Rn** |

**1m 16.8** (6.30) CSF £51.15 CT £276.50 TOTE £4.50: £2.20 £5.00 £3.40 (£56.50) Trio £135.00 OWNER Mr D. I. Russell (NEWMARKET) BRED C. R. and V. M. Withers
LONG HANDICAP Sharp Return 6-13
**4600* Craigievar** had no trouble handling this more testing ground and, let down to lead 200 yards out, quickly asserted his superiority. (3/1)
**4787* Sharp Return** pulled away with the winner inside the distance, but had no answer to the superior finishing speed of that rival. There was no disgrace in this defeat. (16/1)

**4350* Balladoole Bajan** was onto a hat-trick, but she did not appear to be very happy in this softer ground and was never going well enough to get to terms with the principals. (6/1)
**3250 Step N Go (IRE)** sat closer to the pace, but she did not find much when asked for an effort and was always being comfortably held. (14/1: 10/1-16/1)
**4878 Heavenly Miss (IRE)**, a very consistent filly, showed up with the pace in the centre of the track, but could not get her feet out of the mud in the latter stages, and could only keep on at the one speed. (14/1: 12/1-20/1)
**3293 Faringdon Future** just needed this after a three-month break, but he did not fare badly and his turn will come. (13/2)
**4880 Petite Danseuse**, very much on her toes, had the bad luck to be drawn on the slower stands' side and, driven along for all she was worth soon after halfway, could never get near the leaders. (3/1)

## 4917 SNEINTON CONDITIONS STKS (3-Y.O+) (Class C)

1-30 (1-34) **6f 15y** £5,038.20 (£1,873.80: £906.90: £379.50: £159.75: £71.85) Stalls: High GOING: 0.53 sec per fur (GS)

| | | | | SP | RR | SF |
|---|---|---|---|---|---|---|
| 4687$^{4}$ | **Astrac (IRE) (87)** (MissGayKelleway) **5-8-12** KFallon(7) (lw: a.p: led 2f out: clr ent fnl f: comf) | — | **1** | 8/1 | 98+ | 46 |
| 4304$^{8}$ | **Top Banana (95)** (HCandy) **5-8-5**(7) LJames(4) (hld up: hdwy over 1f out: r.o wl cl home) | 3 | **2** | 8/1 | 90 | 39 |
| 4823$^{4}$ | **Montendre (101)** (RJHodges) **9-8-12** JReid(6) (lw: hld up: effrt & rdn wl over 1f out: kpt on) | hd | **3** | 13/2$^{3}$ | 90 | 38 |
| 4774$^{3}$ | **Easy Option (IRE) (112)** (SbinSuroor) **4-8-7** LDettori(8) (lw: hld up: effrt & rdn wl over 1f out: nt pce to chal) | ½ | **4** | 10/11$^{1}$ | 84 | 32 |
| 4823* | **The Puzzler (IRE) (100)** (BWHills) **5-9-5** MHills(5) (b: hld up: gd hdwy over 2f out: wknd & eased ins fnl f) | 2 | **5** | 5/2$^{2}$ | 90 | 39 |
| 4616$^{16}$ | **The Happy Fox (IRE) (68)** (BAMcMahon) **4-8-12b** SSanders(1) (chsd ldrs over 4f: sn outpcd) | 4 | **6** | 50/1 | 73 | 23 |
| 4772$^{22}$ | **Willow Dale (IRE) (77)** (DRCElsworth) **3-8-6b**$^{1}$ DHarrison(3) (led ½-wy to 2f out: sn rdn & wknd) | ¾ | **7** | 50/1 | 66 | 15 |
| 3788$^{12}$ | **Hostile Native** (RGuest) **3-8-11** PBloomfield(2) (led to ½-wy: sn wknd: t.o) | 20 | **8** | 100/1 | 18 | — |

(SP 121.4%) **8 Rn**

**1m 17.3** (6.80) CSF £65.04 TOTE £6.90: £2.60 £2.40 £1.80 (£50.30) OWNER Mr Clive Titcomb (WHITCOMBE) BRED Miss Aisling O'Connell
WEIGHT FOR AGE 3yo-1lb
**4687 Astrac (IRE)** had the going in his favour for the first time this season, and showed what a useful individual he really is when conditions are suitable. (8/1)
**3946 Top Banana**, at his best on a sounder surface, has had quite a light season and, though he was never a threat to the winner, he was doing all his best work at the finish. (8/1: 4/1-9/1)
**4823 Montendre** looked assured of the runner-up prize until inside the last furlong, when Top Banana got the better of him in the dying strides. (13/2)
**4774 Easy Option (IRE)** is well suited by this easier ground, but was friendless in the market, and this below-par performance would suggest that all was not as it should be. (10/11: 2/5-Evens)
**4823* The Puzzler (IRE)** was going every bit like a winner when he took up a challenging position below the distance but, unable to go through with his effort, may well have aggravated his suspect legs again. (5/2)

## 4918 'JACK JENNINGS' CONDITIONS STKS (2-Y.O) (Class D)

2-00 (2-00) **6f 15y** £3,481.25 (£1,040.00: £497.50: £226.25) Stalls: High GOING: 0.53 sec per fur (GS)

| | | | | SP | RR | SF |
|---|---|---|---|---|---|---|
| 4816$^{2}$ | **Restless Spirit (USA)** (MJohnston) **2-8-11** JWeaver(8) (mde all: drvn clr ent fnl f) | — | **1** | 6/1 | 86 | 37 |
| 4681$^{6}$ | **Ursa Major** (PAKelleway) **2-8-11** JReid(1) (hld up: hdwy 2f out: chsd wnr fnl f: kpt on) | 2 | **2** | 8/1 | 81 | 32 |
| 4558$^{4}$ | **Savona (IRE)** (PJMakin) **2-8-6** MRoberts(4) (hld up: drvn along wl over 1f out: edgd lft: r.o) | 1¼ | **3** | 11/1 | 72 | 24 |
| 4807$^{2}$ | **Tal-Y-Llyn (IRE)** (BWHills) **2-8-11** PatEddery(3) (a.p: hrd drvn over 1f out: one pce) | ½ | **4** | 13/8$^{1}$ | 76 | 28 |
| 4311$^{9}$ | **Secret Combe (IRE) (84)** (PJMakin) **2-8-10** SSanders(9) (swtg: hld up: hdwy & rdn 2f out: nt pce to chal) | hd | **5** | 12/1 | 75 | 26 |
| 4790* | **Key Largo (IRE)** (MHTompkins) **2-9-1** KDarley(7) (lw: prom: drvn along 2f out: btn appr fnl f) | hd | **6** | 9/1 | 80 | 31 |
| 4723$^{14}$ | **Mujova (IRE) (85)** (RHollinshead) **2-9-3** LDettori(5) (hld up: effrt & rdn 2f out: no imp) | nk | **7** | 5/1$^{2}$ | 81 | 32 |
| 4723$^{21}$ | **The Gay Fox (86)** (BAMcMahon) **2-8-11** GDuffield(6) (trckd ldrs tl rdn & wknd wl over 1f out: t.o) | 7 | **8** | 11/2$^{3}$ | 56 | 10 |
| 4698$^{7}$ | **Boater** (DMorley) **2-8-11** GCarter(2) (bit bkwd: dwlt: a in rr: t.o) | ¾ | **9** | 20/1 | 54 | 8 |

(SP 126.3%) **9 Rn**

**1m 17.9** (7.40) CSF £52.13 TOTE £5.90: £1.80 £2.30 £1.70 (£21.60) Trio £145.50; £125.09 to Newmarket 1/11/96 OWNER Sheikh Mohammed (MIDDLEHAM) BRED Darley Stud Management Inc
**4816 Restless Spirit (USA)** put the emphasis on stamina by stretching his rivals from the start, and he had them all in trouble from some way out. (6/1: op 5/2)
**4461 Ursa Major**, stepping down in distance and tackling soft ground for the first time, stayed on pleasingly inside the final furlong, but the runner-up prize was the only issue at stake inside the final furlong. (8/1: 6/1-10/1)
**4558 Savona (IRE)** began to stay on approaching the final furlong, but she hung left under pressure and was always being comfortably held. She could make a useful three-year-old. (11/1: 8/1-12/1)
**4807 Tal-Y-Llyn (IRE)** had the easier ground he was thought to need, but he was always struggling to match the speed of the winner and was a spent force approaching the final furlong. (13/8)
**3468 Secret Combe (IRE)** could have found this ground more than she could cope with, but she never once stopped trying and there will be other days. (12/1: 8/1-14/1)
**4790* Key Largo (IRE)**, waiting on the leaders, was struggling to hold his pitch two furlongs out and, though he did keep battling on, he had met his match below the distance. (9/1: 5/1-10/1)
**4366 Mujova (IRE)** (5/1: op 8/1)

## 4919 DAVID WILSON HOMES H'CAP (0-80) (3-Y.O+) (Class D)

2-30 (2-31) **1m 6f 15y** £4,240.00 (£1,270.00: £610.00: £280.00) Stalls: Low GOING: 0.53 sec per fur (GS)

| | | | | SP | RR | SF |
|---|---|---|---|---|---|---|
| 4804* | **Sweetness Herself (71)** (MJRyan) **3-8-13**(3) 5x MBaird(5) (swtg: hld up in rr: hdwy 4f out: led wl over 1f out: styd on strly) | — | **1** | 5/2$^{1}$ | 84 | 46 |
| 4750$^{4}$ | **Siege Perilous (IRE) (65)** (SCWilliams) **3-8-10** KFallon(13) (hld up: hdwy 3f out: rdn & styd on wl ins fnl f) | 1½ | **2** | 10/1 | 76 | 39 |
| 4832$^{3}$ | **Paradise Navy (66)** (CREgerton) **7-9-1b**(5) SophieMitchell(18) (hld up: hdwy over 5f out: styd on u.p fnl f) | s.h | **3** | 16/1 | 77 | 48 |
| 4683$^{13}$ | **Compass Pointer (57)** (JMPEustace) **3-7-11**(5) MartinDwyer(10) (hld up: gd hdwy 3f out: styd on u.p fnl f) | nk | **4** | 16/1 | 68 | 31 |
| 4683$^{7}$ | **Ski For Gold (65)** (JLDunlop) **3-8-10** KDarley(9) (lw: hld up: hdwy over 3f out: ev ch 2f out: sn hrd rdn & no ex) | 1 | **5** | 9/1 | 75 | 37 |
| 4804$^{2}$ | **Taufan Boy (73)** (PWHarris) **3-9-4** GHind(16) (lw: chsd ldrs: hrd drvn over 2f out: r.o one pce) | nk | **6** | 9/1 | 82 | 45 |
| 4826$^{21}$ | **Debutante Days (66)** (CREgerton) **4-9-6b**$^{1}$ MRoberts(12) (hdwy 6f out: led over 3f out tl wl over 1f out: wknd appr fnl f) | ¾ | **7** | 16/1 | 75 | 46 |

| | | | Pos | SP | RR | SF |
|---|---|---|---|---|---|---|
| 4794* | **Lepikha (USA) (67)** (BWHills) **3-8-12** 5x MHills(8) (trckd ldrs tl rdn & wknd over 2f out) | nk | **8** | 9/1 | 75 | 38 |
| 4862[6] | **Shakiyr (FR) (49)** (RHollinshead) **5-8-0**(3)ow3 FLynch(1) (nvr nrr) | 1 | **9** | 25/1 | 56 | 29 |
| 4695[2] | **Trick (IRE) (74)** (LMCumani) **3-9-5** LDettori(4) (led over 2f: prom tl wknd over 3f out) | 4 | **10** | 11/2[2] | 77 | 40 |
| 4580[13] | **Johns Act (USA) (62)** (DHaydnJones) **6-9-2** DHarrison(7) (led 12f out tl over 4f out: grad wknd) | 2½ | **11** | 33/1 | 62 | 35 |
| 4761[6] | **Prince Kinsky (77)** (LordHuntingdon) **3-9-8** JWeaver(2) (trckd ldrs tl wknd 3f out) | ½ | **12** | 16/1 | 76 | 40 |
| 4832* | **Backwoods (67)** (WMBrisbourne) **3-8-12** 5x AGarth(11) (hld up: a in rr) | 3½ | **13** | 15/2 | 62 | 27 |
| 4771[25] | **Granby Bell (51)** (PHayward) **5-8-5** DaneO'Neill(6) (nvr nr to chal) | 2½ | **14** | 20/1 | 43 | 18 |
| 4872[10] | **Bob's Ploy (71)** (MHTompkins) **4-9-8**(3) MHenry(15) (lw: hld up in tch: hdwy to ld over 4f out: hdd over 3f out: sn rdn & wknd: t.o) | 14 | **15** | 16/1 | 47 | 23 |
| 4766[6] | **Children's Choice (IRE) (53)** (CNAllen) **5-8-7** PatEddery(17) (in tch tl wknd 4f out: t.o) | 13 | **16** | 12/1 | 15 | — |
| 4426[9] | **White Claret (55)** (RAkehurst) **4-8-9** SSanders(3) (chsd ldrs 10f: sn wknd: t.o) | 13 | **17** | 7/1[3] | 2 | — |

(SP 156.0%) **17 Rn**

**3m 15.7** (17.20) CSF £34.60 CT £368.17 TOTE £3.60: £1.50 £3.70 £2.20 £5.70 (£38.20) Trio £261.00 OWNER Mrs M. J. Lavell (NEWMARKET) BRED Stud-On-The-Chart

WEIGHT FOR AGE 3yo-9lb

**4804* Sweetness Herself** has come to herself in leaps and bounds this season, and defied her penalty with another very game performance. (5/2)

**4750 Siege Perilous (IRE)** stays this trip well, but he did not get going until far too late, and by then the filly had gone beyond recall. (10/1: 7/1-12/1)

**4832 Paradise Navy** does need a stiffer test of stamina, but he did put his best foot forward for his rider and still has the ability when he cares to put it to good use. (16/1)

**4448 Compass Pointer**, still struggling to get off the mark, was staying on strongly nearing the finish and it would be worth giving him a try over two miles. (16/1)

**4683 Ski For Gold**, fighting for the lead entering the last quarter-mile, did not fail for the lack of trying, but she does lack a turn of finishing pace. (9/1: 5/1-10/1)

**4804 Taufan Boy** should have had the beating of the winner on these better terms, but he was hard at work from some way out and, though he did keep staying on, he was unable to conjure up anything in the way of finishing speed. (9/1)

**4580 Debutante Days** did not appear to get home after leading the straight, but she ran well enough in the first-time blinkers and will be spot on when she returns to hurdles. (16/1)

**4794* Lepikha (USA)** (9/1: op 6/1)

**4695 Trick (IRE)** (11/2: 4/1-13/2)

**4766 Children's Choice (IRE)** (12/1: op 6/1)

**White Claret** (7/1: tchd 14/1)

## 4920 E.B.F. NETHERFIELD MAIDEN STKS (2-Y.O) (Class D)

3-00 (3-03) **1m 54y** £4,241.75 (£1,274.00: £614.50: £284.75) Stalls: Low GOING: 0.53 sec per fur (GS)

| | | | Pos | SP | RR | SF |
|---|---|---|---|---|---|---|
| 4492[4] | **Desert Horizon** (JHMGosden) **2-9-0** LDettori(9) (a.p: rdn to ld wl ins fnl f) | — | **1** | 9/4[1] | 89 | 51 |
| 4492[2] | **Jaunty Jack** (LMCumani) **2-9-0** OUrbina(6) (hld up in tch: hdwy to ld over 1f out: hdd nr fin) | ½ | **2** | 100/30[2] | 88 | 50 |
| 3987[9] | **Sioux** (CWThornton) **2-8-9** DeanMcKeown(8) (lw: hld up & bhd: hdwy 3f out: kpt on u.p ins fnl f) | 4 | **3** | 33/1 | 75 | 38 |
| 4175[7] | **Flirting Around (USA)** (MRStoute) **2-9-0** KDarley(5) (trckd ldrs: styd on u.p ins fnl f) | s.h | **4** | 11/2[3] | 80 | 43 |
| 4512[3] | **Eshtiaal (USA)** (JLDunlop) **2-9-0** RHills(12) (lw: hld up: hdwy 3f out: wknd ins fnl f) | 1 | **5** | 9/4[1] | 78 | 41 |
| 4706[2] | **Outflanker (USA)** (PWChapple-Hyam) **2-9-0** JReid(1) (led tl over 1f out: wknd ins fnl f) | 2 | **6** | 10/1 | 74 | 38 |
| 4830[3] | **Nominator Lad (85)** (BAMcMahon) **2-9-0** GCarter(3) (w ldrs over 4f: wknd over 2f out) | 10 | **7** | 20/1 | 55 | 21 |
| 4801[13] | **Ramike (IRE)** (MJohnston) **2-9-0** JWeaver(2) (in tch on ins: hrd rdn 4f out: wknd 2f out) | hd | **8** | 20/1 | 55 | 20 |
| 4720[11] | **Regait** (MAJarvis) **2-9-0** PBloomfield(13) (bit bkwd: a in rr) | nk | **9** | 20/1 | 54 | 20 |
| 4349[W] | **Fruitie O'Flarety** (CEBrittain) **2-9-0b**[1] MRoberts(14) (bit bkwd: s.s: hdwy on outside 4f out: wknd fnl 2f) | 1¾ | **10** | 25/1 | 51 | 17 |
| | **Trienta Mil** (PTDalton) **2-9-0** JFEgan(11) (w'like: leggy: s.i.s: a bhd) | 3 | **11** | 50/1 | 45 | 12 |
| 4796[12] | **T-N-T Express** (JLEyre) **2-9-0** RLappin(4) (prom to ½-wy: sn lost tch) | 1¼ | **12** | 50/1 | 43 | 10 |
| 4755[3] | **Kristopher** (JWHills) **2-9-0** MHills(7) (bit bkwd: s.i.s: a bhd: t.o) | 9 | **13** | 33/1 | 25 | — |
| | ***Charlotte's Dancer*** (MGMeagher) **2-8-9** JQuinn(10) (Withdrawn not under Starter's orders: ref to ent stalls) | | **W** | 50/1 | — | — |

(SP 139.0%) **13 Rn**

**1m 50.5** (9.20) CSF £11.58 TOTE £4.00: £1.70 £1.10 £10.20 (£8.20) Trio £211.20; £184.46 to Newmarket 1/11/96 OWNER Mr K. Abdulla (NEWMARKET) BRED Juddmonte Farms

**4492 Desert Horizon** turned the tables on the runner-up, but it was a close-run thing, and a lot of credit should go to his never-say-die partner. (9/4)

**4492 Jaunty Jack** looked to be going just the better when striking the front over a furlong out, but he could not shake off the winner and that rival proved the stronger inside the final 50 yards. (100/30)

**Sioux** is not short of stamina, for she was at full stretch over two furlongs out, but refused to give and was rewarded when she gained third prize right on the line. She could come into her own next year. (33/1)

**4175 Flirting Around (USA)** seemed likely to be suited by soft ground, but is beginning to look as though he is going backwards from his useful debut. (11/2: 4/1-6/1)

**4512 Eshtiaal (USA)**, closely-related to several winners, moved onto the heels of the leaders over two furlongs out, but he was tapped for toe when the principals took one another on, and he ran out of puff inside the distance. (9/4: 2/1-7/2)

**4706 Outflanker (USA)** adopted forceful tactics on this occasion, but was unable to go clear and was worn down below the distance. (10/1)

## 4921 WOODTHORPE H'CAP (0-70) (3-Y.O) (Class E)

3-30 (3-35) **1m 54y** £3,626.00 (£1,088.00: £524.00: £242.00) Stalls: Low GOING: 0.53 sec per fur (GS)

| | | | Pos | SP | RR | SF |
|---|---|---|---|---|---|---|
| 4590[3] | **Scenicris (IRE) (60)** (RHollinshead) **3-8-8**(3) FLynch(12) (hld up: stdy hdwy 3f out: led ent fnl f: drvn clr) | — | **1** | 8/1 | 71 | 51 |
| 4598[9] | **Agent (56)** (JLEyre) **3-8-7** LCharnock(15) (hld up: hdwy 3f out: kpt on u.p fnl f: no ch w wnr) | 3½ | **2** | 10/1 | 60 | 41 |
| 4691[4] | **Parsa (USA) (61)** (JLDunlop) **3-8-12** PatEddery(13) (hld up in tch: hdwy & ev ch 1f out: sn rdn: unable qckn) | nk | **3** | 100/30[1] | 65 | 45 |
| 4799[5] | **Belzao (60)** (DRCElsworth) **3-8-11** DaneO'Neill(9) (led tl ent fnl f: kpt on same pce) | 1 | **4** | 14/1 | 62 | 43 |
| 4898[16] | **Petite Heritiere (45)** (MJRyan) **3-7-10** GBardwell(6) (mid div: drvn along ½-wy: styd on appr fnl f) | 2½ | **5** | 40/1 | 42 | 24 |
| 4785* | **Mono Lady (IRE) (57)** (DHaydnJones) **3-8-8** 6x DHarrison(14) (swtg: chsd ldrs: ev ch 2f out: sn rdn: wknd appr fnl f) | 2½ | **6** | 11/2[3] | 49 | 31 |

| | | | | | | |
|---|---|---|---|---|---|---|
| 4598[14] | **Oriole (45)** (NTinkler) **3-7-10** KimTinkler(17) (mid div: rdn & one pce fnl 2f) ......¾ | **7** | 40/1 | 36 | 19 |
| 4591[7] | **Winnebago (60)** (CWThornton) **3-8-11** DeanMcKeown(10) (trckd ldrs: effrt & rdn over 2f out: no imp) ......1 | **8** | 8/1 | 49 | 31 |
| 1181[9] | **Queen's Insignia (USA) (65)** (PFICole) **3-9-2** CRutter(11) (nvr nr to chal) ......3½ | **9** | 8/1 | 47 | 30 |
| 4831[17] | **Spring Campaign (IRE) (67)** (MCPipe) **3-9-4b[1]** MRoberts(2) (prom: rdn over 2f out: sn btn) ......3 | **10** | 16/1 | 43 | 26 |
| 4429[14] | **Shirlaty (49)** (CWThornton) **3-8-0** FNorton(16) (a in rr) ......¾ | **11** | 33/1 | 24 | 9 |
| 4752[10] | **Nexsis Star (45)** (MrsSJSmith) **3-7-10** NCarlisle(7) (a in rr) ......nk | **12** | 40/1 | 19 | 4 |
| 4860[2] | **Waypoint (70)** (RCharlton) **3-9-7** TSprake(4) (trckd ldrs tl wknd wl over 1f out) ......1½ | **13** | 4/1 [2] | 41 | 25 |
| 4690[10] | **Eccentric Dancer (46)** (MPBielby) **3-7-11b**[ow1] NAdams(18) (s.s: a bhd) ......2 | **14** | 40/1 | 13 | — |
| 4799[8] | **Brighton Road (IRE) (70)** (GBBalding) **3-9-7** SDrowne(1) (dwlt: sn pushed along in rr: a bhd) ......1½ | **15** | 16/1 | 34 | 19 |
| 4437[12] | **Lomond Lassie (USA) (45)** (MissJFCraze) **3-7-5v[1](5)** PFessey(5) (lw: chsd ldr tl wknd over 3f out) ......nk | **16** | 40/1 | 9 | — |
| 1042[9] | **Guy's Gamble (50)** (JWharton) **3-8-1** JQuinn(3) (bit bkwd: a in rr: t.o fnl 3f) ......12 | **17** | 14/1 | — | — |
| *4437[14]* | ***Rothley Imp (IRE) (45)*** (JWharton) **3-7-7**(3) NVarley(8) (Withdrawn not under Starter's orders: bridle broke & uns rdr bef s) ...... | **W** | 33/1 | — | — |
| | | | (SP 144.1%) | | **17 Rn** |

**1m 50.2** (8.90) CSF £88.29 CT £301.97 TOTE £8.60: £2.20 £2.20 £1.90 £2.20 (£49.30) Trio £113.70 OWNER Mrs Christine Johnson (UPPER LONGDON) BRED Peter Deane and Peter O'Connor

LONG HANDICAP Oriole 7-5 Eccentric Dancer 6-4 Petite Heritiere 7-3 Lomond Lassie (USA) 6-11 Nexsis Star 7-3 Rothley Imp (IRE) 7-5

**4590 Scenicris (IRE)** has taken a long time to win a race but, relishing this ever-softening ground, won this with the minimum of fuss. In this form, she should be able to win again. (8/1)

**3810 Agent** followed the winner through, but he lacked the extra pace that she possessed and was soon fighting a losing battle. (10/1)

**4691 Parsa (USA)** moved up easily and may have led for a couple of strides before the winner but, once the tempo picked up, she was unable to respond. (100/30)

**4799 Belzao** tried hard to make it all and stuck on willingly when headed, but his legs turned to clay inside the last furlong. (14/1)

**Petite Heritiere** could not get near enough to pose a threat, but she did a lot of running in the last half-mile and obviously found the ground to her liking. (40/1)

**4785* Mono Lady (IRE)** was not ideally suited to this step down to a mile, but she got herself in with every chance passing the quarter-mile pole, before her penalty began to take its toll. (11/2)

**4860 Waypoint** (4/1: 3/1-9/2)

**280 Guy's Gamble** (14/1: 10/1-16/1)

T/Jkpt: Not won; £6,238.14 to Newmarket 1/11/96. T/Plpt: £985.50 (17.82 Tckts). T/Qdpt: £36.00 (42.06 Tckts). IM

## 4922a-4939a (Irish Racing) - See Computer Raceform

## 4029a-DEAUVILLE (France) (R-H) (Soft)
## Monday October 21st

### 4940a PRIX DE SAINT-CYR (Listed) (3-Y.O F)
3-20 (3-21) **7f** £18,445.00 (£6,324.00: £3,953.00)

| | | | SP | RR | SF |
|---|---|---|---|---|---|
| 720a[3] | **Blushing Gleam** (MmeCHead,France) **3-8-12** ODoleuze ......— | **1** | | 104 | — |
| | **Flurry (FR)** (JEPease,France) **3-8-12** MBoutin ......3 | **2** | | 97 | — |
| 4405a[3] | **Sherema (USA)** (AdeRoyerDupre,France) **3-9-2** GMosse ......½ | **3** | | 100 | — |
| 4595* | **Darling Flame (USA)** (JHMGosden) **3-8-12** TJarnet (btn over 9l) ...... | **9** | | — | — |
| | **Midnight Flame** (WJarvis) **3-8-12** GGuignard (btn over 10l) ...... | **10** | | — | — |
| | | | | | **10 Rn** |

**1m 28.6** (4.60) P-M 6.20F: 2.10F 2.50F 1.90F (18.10F) OWNER Wertheimer Brothers (CHANTILLY) BRED J.Wertheimer & Frere

**4595* Darling Flame (USA)** was well up for most of this race, but was in reverse gear by the furlong marker.

**Midnight Flame** was to the fore, but the seventh furlong was one too much for her. She will stay in training, but will go back to six furlongs.

### 4941a PRIX DES MONCEAUX APPRENTICE (4-Y.O+)
3-50 (3-46) **1m 2f** £7,246.00

| | | | SP | RR | SF |
|---|---|---|---|---|---|
| | **Ophira** (NClement,France) **4-8-11** CBrechon ......— | **1** | | 75 | — |
| | **Three Wizards (FR)** (France) **5-8-11** BMarchand ......s.nk | **2** | | 75 | — |
| | **Coup De Poker (FR)** (France) **5-8-11** WMessina ......½ | **3** | | 74 | — |
| 3388a[0] | **Cedez le Passage (FR)** (KOCunningham-Brown) **5-8-11** EWianny (btn over 1½l) ...... | **5** | | — | — |
| | | | | | **9 Rn** |

**2m 24.0** (19.00) P-M 4.70F: 1.70F 1.60F 1.60F (13.90F) OWNER P-N Rossier (CHANTILLY) BRED Juddmonte Farms

**3388a Cedez le Passage (FR)** raced in mid-division and found little room two furlongs from home. However, he stayed on in the final furlong to be nearest at the finish.

## 4940a-DEAUVILLE (France) (R-H) (Good to soft)
## Tuesday October 22nd

### 4942a PRIX DES RESERVOIRS (Gp 3) (2-Y.O F)
1-50 (2-09) **1m** £28,986.00 (£10,540.00: £5,270.00)

| | | | SP | RR | SF |
|---|---|---|---|---|---|
| | **Mousse Glacee (FR)** (JLesbordes,France) **2-8-9** SGuillot ......— | **1** | | 98 | — |
| 3748a[3] | **Queen Maud (IRE)** (JdeRoualle,France) **2-8-9** CAsmussen ......2½ | **2** | | 93 | — |
| | **Gazelle Royale (FR)** (JEHammond,France) **2-8-9** MBoutin ......2½ | **3** | | 88 | — |
| | | | | | **9 Rn** |

**1m 45.3** (9.30) P-M 3.60F: 1.70F 3.50F 4.20F (39.10F) OWNER Mr G. Biszantz BRED Claude Ankri & Robert Acton

**Mousse Glacee (FR)**, a top-class filly and probably the best of her sex in France, is not only good looking but already a very mature horse and this victory could not have been more impressive. She settled in behind the leaders before taking the lead by the final furlong and, without being touched by the whip, outclassed the field. She has endless scope and will certainly stay further, and is a nice Classic prospect, with the Epsom Oaks not having been ruled out.

**Queen Maud (IRE)** ran an honest sort of race and was putting in her best at the finish. Like the rest of the field though, she was no match for the winner.
**Gazelle Royale (FR)**, held up, made steady late progress and will do better over a longer distance.

## 4943a PRIX VULCAIN (Listed) (3-Y.O)
2-20 (2-22) **1m 4f 110y** £18,445.00 (£6,324.00: £3,953.00)

| | Horse | Dist | Pos | SP | RR | SF |
|---|---|---|---|---|---|---|
| | **Stretarez (FR)** (DSepulchre,France) **3-8-12** CAsmussen | — | 1 | | 107 | — |
| 2669a$^{2}$ | **Faucon Royal (FR)** (J-CRouget,France) **3-9-2** J-BEyquem | 2½ | 2 | | 108 | — |
| | **Si Seductor (USA)** (AFabre,France) **3-9-2** TJarnet | 1½ | 3 | | 106 | — |
| 2041$^{29}$ | **Henry The Fifth** (CEBrittain) **3-8-12** BDoyle (btn over 16l) | | 9 | | — | — |

**11 Rn**

**2m 46.7** (8.20) P-M 11.10F: 3.80F 3.60F 3.20F (9.40F) OWNER Mr J-L Lagardere BRED SNC Lagardere Elevage
**1389a Henry The Fifth**, in touch for most of the way, was ridden two furlongs from home, but failed to respond and soon weakened.

# 4942a-DEAUVILLE (France) (R-H) (Good)
## Wednesday October 23rd

## 4944a PRIX DE CROISSANVILLE (Claimer) (2-Y.O)
12-50 (12-50) **6f** £9,223.00: £922.00

| | Horse | Dist | Pos | SP | RR | SF |
|---|---|---|---|---|---|---|
| | **Malou Grand (FR)** (Jean-MarcCapitte,Belgium) **2-8-11** DBoeuf | — | 1 | | 87 | — |
| 3201a$^{6}$ | **Winter Brook (FR)** (France) **2-8-8** SGuillot | 1½ | 2 | | 80 | — |
| | **Pretty In Pink (USA)** (France) **2-8-8** TJarnet | s.h | 3 | | 80 | — |
| 4512$^{15}$ | **Village Pub (FR)** (KOCunningham-Brown) **2-8-11** FSanchez (btn over 3l) | | 5 | | 75 | — |

**10 Rn**

**1m 12.7** (4.70) P-M 21.30F: 4.60F 2.00F 1.40F (62.00F) OWNER Mr C. Fulgoni BRED Baron Guy de Rothschild
**4127 Village Pub (FR)** was dropped into a claimer after contesting maiden events. He may have finished down the order, but was only beaten about three lengths.

## 4945a PRIX ECLIPSE (Gp 3) (2-Y.O)
1-50 (1-47) **6f 110y** £28,986.00 (£10,540.00: £5,270.00)

| | Horse | Dist | Pos | SP | RR | SF |
|---|---|---|---|---|---|---|
| 4519$^{7}$ | **Hurricane State (USA)** (PWChapple-Hyam) **2-8-11** WRSwinburn | — | 1 | | 99 | — |
| 4285a$^{2}$ | **Heaven's Command** (NClement,France) **2-8-8** GMosse | nk | 2 | | 95 | — |
| 4661a$^{6}$ | **Dissertation (FR)** (MmeCHead,France) **2-8-8** FHead | 1½ | 3 | | 92 | — |
| 4677$^{6}$ | **Rudi's Pet (IRE)** (RHannon) **2-8-11** PatEddery (btn approx 8¼l) | | 5 | | — | — |

**6 Rn**

**1m 19.4** (4.40) P-M 2.00F: 1.50F 1.80F OWNER Mr R. E. Sangster (MARLBOROUGH) BRED Clovelly Farms, Division of Gnl Agri Services
**4519 Hurricane State (USA)** made virtually every yard of the running and hung on gamely to win after edging towards the bad ground on the rail a furlong out. The year might not be finished for him as he is due back in France for the Criterium at Evry.
**4285a Heaven's Command**, who raced in mid-division, then put in a determined challenge throughout the final furlong. She battled on gamely right up to the line, but is a most consistent filly who deserves success in a Group race.
**4291a Dissertation (FR)**, slightly disappointing having been held up for a late run, may have been feeling the effects of a hard race in the Marcel Boussac and will now be put away.
**4677 Rudi's Pet (IRE)**, close up for most of the way, weakened with over a furlong left to travel.

## 4946a COUPE DES POULICHES DU F.E.E. AUCTION (3-Y.O F)
2-50 (2-49) **1m 2f** £19,763.00

| | Horse | Dist | Pos | SP | RR | SF |
|---|---|---|---|---|---|---|
| | **Maroussie (FR)** (NClement,France) **3-8-12** J-MBreux | — | 1 | | 84 | — |
| | **Sing With Me (FR)** (France) **3-8-12** TJarnet | 2½ | 2 | | 80 | — |
| *4575$^{2}$* | **Tea Party (USA)** (KOCunningham-Brown) **3-8-12** FSanchez | ¾ | 3 | | 79 | — |

**5 Rn**

**2m 13.0** (8.00) P-M 2.40F: 1.20F 1.30F OWNER J-F Malle (CHANTILLY) BRED Mme Frauke Schlaudecker Herbig & Bruce McNall
**4575 Tea Party (USA)** led for some of the way, but was headed inside the final furlong and could find no more. However, she did finish best of the Cunningham-Brown raiders at this meeting and picked up £5,929 for her efforts.

## 4947a PRIX DE MEZIDON CLAIMING (3-Y.O)
3-20 (3-20) **1m** £6,588.00

| | Horse | Dist | Pos | SP | RR | SF |
|---|---|---|---|---|---|---|
| | **Battling Siki (FR)** (J-PPelat,France) **3-8-12** OPeslier | — | 1 | | 65 | — |
| | **Noble Note (FR)** (France) **3-8-12** DBoeuf | nse | 2 | | 65 | — |
| | **Marieavah (FR)** (France) **3-8-13** GMosse | 1½ | 3 | | 63 | — |
| 4603$^{7}$ | **Ewar Bold** (KOCunningham-Brown) **3-9-2** FSanchez (btn over 15l) | | 14 | | — | — |

**20 Rn**

**1m 47.2** (11.20) P-M 4.60F: 2.80F 2.50F 5.00F (22.60F) OWNER P. Krief BRED SCEA de la Fontaine
**2196 Ewar Bold**, who has generally raced over longer distances and finished last in a two-mile handicap at Nottingham in September, raced in mid-division. Ridden for an effort two furlongs from home, he soon weakened and was eased close home.

# 4856a-LONGCHAMP (Paris, France) (R-H) (Soft)
## Thursday October 24th

## 4948a PRIX CASIMIR DELAMARRE (Listed) (3-Y.O F)
3-30 (3-34) **1m 1f** £18,445.00 (£6,324.00: £3,953.00)

| | Horse | Dist | Pos | SP | RR | SF |
|---|---|---|---|---|---|---|
| 3568a$^{3}$ | **Contare** (JEPease,France) **3-9-0** FSanchez | — | 1 | | 103 | — |

| | | | | SP | RR | SF |
|---|---|---|---|---|---|---|
| 796a[4] | **Occupandiste (IRE)** (MmeCHead,France) **3-9-0** ODoleuze | nk | **2** | | 103 | — |
| 4671[4] | **Awaamir** (JHMGosden) **3-9-0** TJarnet | 2 | **3** | | 99 | — |
| 4671[3] | **Parrot Jungle (IRE)** (JLDunlop) **3-9-0** OPeslier (btn over 3¼l) | | **5** | | — | — |

**7 Rn**

**1m 52.5** (4.50) P-M 5.30F: 2.20F 1.40F OWNER Mr George Strawbridge (CHANTILLY) BRED George Strawbridge
**4671 Awaamir,** virtually always in third place, was probably somewhat out of her ground. She was putting in her best work at the finish.
**4671 Parrot Jungle (IRE)** certainly did not run up to her best. She was far too out of her ground and only started to run on when the race was virtually over. She is now likely to be retired to stud.

## 4651a-SAINT-CLOUD (France) (L-H) (Good to soft)
## Friday October 25th

### 4949a PRIX ISONOMY (Listed) (2-Y.O C & G)
2-55 (2-55) **1m** £18,445.00 (£6,324.00: £3,953.00)

| | | | | SP | RR | SF |
|---|---|---|---|---|---|---|
| | **Film Noir (USA)** (MmeCHead,France) **2-8-11** ODoleuze | — | **1** | | 112 | — |
| | **Samapour (IRE)** (AdeRoyerDupre,France) **2-8-11** GMosse | 2 | **2** | | 108 | — |
| | **Varxi (FR)** (DSmaga,France) **2-8-11** DBoeuf | ¾ | **3** | | 107 | — |
| 4488[7] | **Home Alone** (JHMGosden) **2-8-11** JCarroll (btn approx 11½l) | 2 | **7** | | 89 | — |

**8 Rn**

**1m 45.0** (6.50) P-M 8.00F: 1.70F 1.20F 1.70F (12.70F) OWNER Wertheimer Brothers (CHANTILLY) BRED Wertheimer et Frere
**4488 Home Alone,** taken down to the start early, became very nervous in the stalls. He led for much of the race, but was beaten early in the straight. He does not seem an easy colt to train.

## 4543a-WOODBINE (Toronto, Canada) (L-H) (Turf Good, Dirt Fast)
## Saturday October 26th

### 4950a BREEDERS' CUP JUVENILE FILLIES' (Gd 1) (2-Y.O F)
6-55 (6-52) **1m 110y (Dirt)** £335,484.00 (£129,032.00: £77,419.00: £36,129.00) GOING minus 0.50 sec per fur (FST)

| | | | | SP | RR | SF |
|---|---|---|---|---|---|---|
| | **Storm Song (USA)** (NZito,USA) **2-8-7** CPerret (hdwy ½-wy: qckn to ld over 1f out: sn clr: comf) | — | **1** | 16/10[1] | 111+ | 67 |
| | **Love That Jazz (USA)** (NZito,USA) **2-8-7** MSmith (sn led: clr ent st: rdn & hdd over 1f: no ch w wnr) | 4½ | **2** | 174/10 | 103 | 59 |
| | **Critical Factor (USA)** (MyungKwonCho,Japan) **2-8-7** ASolis (rr early: gd hdwy appr st: rdn & r.o wl) | 3¼ | **3** | 82/1 | 96 | 52 |
| | **Minister's Melody (USA)** (NMO'Callaghan,USA) **2-8-7** PDay (chsd ldrs: hdwy ½-wy: rdn 2f out: sn wknd) | 4½ | **4** | 375/10 | 88 | 44 |
| | **Larkwhistle (CAN)** (RAttfield,Canada) **2-8-7b[1]** MWalls (rr early: hdwy appr st: kpt on) | 2 | **5** | 55/1 | 84 | 40 |
| | **Runaway Mary (USA)** (TerranceDunlavy,Canada) **2-8-7** SHawley (s.s: sn bhd: r.o st) | ¾ | **6** | 56/1 | 83 | 39 |
| | **Hidden Reserve (USA)** (CMcGaughey,USA) **2-8-7** JVelasquez (trckd ldrs: hmpd 1st bnd: hdwy ½-wy: rdn & wknd 2f out) | 3½ | **7** | 17/1 | 76 | 32 |
| | **Cheyenne City (USA)** (DWLukas,USA) **2-8-7** GStevens (outpcd & a bhd) | 2 | **8** | 98/10[3] | 72 | 28 |
| | **Sharp Cat (USA)** (DWLukas,USA) **2-8-7** JBailey (prom: hmpd 1st bnd: 2nd ½-wy: rdn & lost pl ent st) | nk | **9** | 4/1[2] | 72 | 28 |
| | **City Band (USA)** (DWLukas,USA) **2-8-7** SSellers (trckd ldr: lost pl ½-wy: rdn & wknd over 2f out: eased) | 5½ | **10** | 98/10[3] | 62 | 18 |
| | **Dunbar Hill (USA)** (RMcAnally,USA) **2-8-7** CMcCarron (sn outpcd & bhd) | 5¼ | **11** | 11/1 | 52 | 8 |
| | **Barbed Wire (CAN)** (MrsBMinshall,USA) **2-8-7** ERamsammy (mid div: rdn 3f out: sn wknd) | 11½ | **12** | 17/1 | 30 | — |

(SP 109.2%) **12 Rn**

**1m 43.6** (-1.60) P-M $5.20 PL (1-2) $3.40 $12.20 SHOW (1-2-3) $3.00 $8.20 $10.20 OWNER Dogwood Stable BRED W.S.Farrish & O.M Phipps
IN-FOCUS: **For betting purposes Cheyenne City (USA) and City Band (USA) were cpld**
**Storm Song (USA),** off the pace as his rivals went too fast early on, came home clear of his legless rivals. (16/10)

### 4951a BREEDERS' CUP SPRINT (Gd 1) (3-Y.O+)
7-25 (7-27) **6f (Dirt)** £335,484.00 (£129,032.00: £77,419.00: £36,129.00) GOING minus 0.50 sec per fur (FST)

| | | | | SP | RR | SF |
|---|---|---|---|---|---|---|
| | **Lit de Justice (USA)** (JenineSahadi,USA) **6-9-0** CNakatani (dwlt: hdwy on ins 2f out: str run to ld cl home) | — | **1** | 4/1[1] | 134 | 100 |
| | **Paying Dues (USA)** (CSise,USA) **4-9-0** PDay (cl up on outside: hdwy & 3rd ½-wy: rdn st: r.o fnl f) | 1¼ | **2** | 31/1 | 131 | 97 |
| | **Honour And Glory (USA)** (DWLukas,USA) **3-8-11** GStevens (chsd ldr: rdn to ld ins fnl f: hdd & nt qckn cl home) | nk | **3** | 52/10[3] | 128 | 93 |
| | **Lord Carson (USA)** (DWLukas,USA) **4-9-0** SSellers (sn led: rdn over 1f out: hdd ins fnl f: wknd) | 1¼ | **4** | 545/10 | 127 | 93 |
| | **Lakota Brave (USA)** (BHeadley,Canada) **7-9-0** ASolis (rdn & hdwy 2f out: r.o one pce) | nk | **5** | 21/1 | 126 | 92 |
| 4057* | **Iktamal (USA)** (EALDunlop) **4-9-0** WRyan (dwlt: shkn up & mid div after 2f: r.o st: nt pce to chal) | 1½ | **6** | 22/1 | 122 | 88 |
| | **Capote Belle (USA)** (DPeitz,USA) **3-8-8** JVelasquez (trckd ldrs: rdn 2f out: r.o) | hd | **7** | 44/10[2] | 117 | 82 |
| | **Langfuhr (CAN)** (MKeogh,USA) **4-9-0** JChavez (outpcd early: rn wd st: nt pce to chal) | ½ | **8** | 68/10 | 120 | 86 |
| | **Boundless Moment (USA)** (KWalsh,USA) **4-9-0** KDesormeaux (mid div: rdn ½-wy: no imp) | nk | **9** | 29/1 | 119 | 85 |
| | **Appealing Skier (USA)** (BPerkins,USA) **3-8-11** MSmith (chsd ldr: outpcd st) | ¾ | **10** | 77/10 | 115 | 80 |
| | **Friendly Lover (USA)** (JHPierce,USA) **8-9-0** HMcCauley (sn bhd) | ¾ | **11** | 79/1 | 115 | 81 |
| | **Criollito (ARG)** (BBaffert,USA) **5-9-0** CMcCarron (a bhd) | 2½ | **12** | 13/1 | 109 | 75 |
| | **Jess C's Whirl (USA)** (JForbes,USA) **6-9-0** JulieKrone (outpcd & a in rr) | 4½ | **13** | 31/1 | 97 | 63 |

(SP 107.6%) **13 Rn**

**1m 8.6** (-3.00) P-M $10.00: PL (1-2) $5.90 $23.30 SHOW (1-2-3) $4.30 $8.90 $3.80 OWNER Evergreen Farms
IN-FOCUS: **For betting purposes Jess C's Whirl (USA) and Paying Dues (USA) were cpld as 'The Field'.**
**Lit de Justice (USA)** left his run too late last year, but everything went to plan this time as the grey blur swept from last to first. His trainer became the first woman to train a Breeders' Cup winner. (4/1)
**4057* Iktamal (USA)** put up a creditable performance, but was always up against it after missing the break. (22/1)

### 4952a BREEDERS' CUP DISTAFF (Gd 1) (3-Y.O+ F & M)
8-00 (8-01) **1m 1f (Dirt)** £335,484.00 (£129,032.00: £77,419.00: £36,129.00) GOING minus 0.50 sec per fur (FST)

| | | | | SP | RR | SF |
|---|---|---|---|---|---|---|
| | **Jewel Princess (USA)** (WDollase,USA) **4-8-11** CNakatani (hld up: hdwy on ins 3f out: rdn to ld ins fnl f: r.o wl) | — | **1** | 24/10[2] | 118 | 87 |

Serena's Song (USA) (DWLukas,USA) **4-8-11** GStevens (a.p: chal ent st: led over 1f out: r.o u.p) ..............1½ **2** 27/10[3] 115 84
Different (ARG) (RMcAnally,USA) **4-8-11** CMcCarron (chsd ldrs: rdn over 2f out: flashed tail u.p: r.o) .........1¾ **3** 13/10[1] 112 81
*1946a[3]* **My Flag (USA)** (CMcGaughey,USA) **3-8-7** JBailey (rr early: rdn & hdwy 3f out: nt rch ldrs) ..........................5¼ **4** 76/10 103 68
**Top Secret (USA)** (GArnold,USA) **3-8-7** MSmith (led: rdn & hdd ent st: sn btn) ...............................................¾ **5** 214/10 102 67
**Clear Mandate (USA)** (GArnold,USA) **4-8-11** CPerret (hld up: rdn over 2f: no imp) ........................................3¾ **6** 327/10 95 64
(SP 119.0%) **6 Rn**

**1m 48.4** (-3.40) P-M $6.80: PL (1-2) $3.50 $3.40 SHOW (1-2-3) $2.70 $2.30 $2.10 OWNER R & Martha Stephen & T'Bred Corp
**Jewel Princess (USA)**, completing a double for her jockey, was given a fine ride, sticking to the fence all the way. (24/10)

## 4953a BREEDERS' CUP MILE (Gd 1) (3-Y.O+)

8-35 (8-39) **1m (Turf)** £335,484.00 (£129,032.00: £77,419.00: £36,129.00) GOING minus 0.20 sec per fur (GF) SP RR SF

**Da Hoss (USA)** (MWDickinson,USA) **4-9-0** GStevens (hld up: gd hdwy on ins ½-wy: 2nd st: led 1f out: r.o strly) ........— **1** 85/10[3] 136 105
4165a[2] **Spinning World (USA)** (JEPease,France) **3-8-10** CAsmussen (trckd ldrs: hdwy gng wl over 1f out: nt pce of wnr) ........1½ **2** 80/10[2] 132 98
**Same Old Wish (USA)** (RBarbara,USA) **6-9-0** SSellers (hld up: in rr & rdn 3f out: hdwy over 1f out: fin wl)..2½ **3** 472/10 128 97
**Kiridashi (CAN)** (MrsBMinshall,USA) **4-9-0** MWalls (sn led: rdn & hdd over 1f out: wknd)..............................½ **4** 109/10 127 96
**Memories Of Silver (USA)** (JToner,USA) **3-8-10** JBailey (chsd ldrs: rdn & styd on) ........................................1½ **5** 86/10 123 89
**Helmsman (USA)** (WDollase,USA) **4-9-0** CNakatani (mid div: trckd ldrs ent st: rdn & no ex)..........................1½ **6** 19/1 121 90
4443* **Mark of Esteem (IRE)** (SbinSuroor) **3-8-10** LDettori (mid div: trckd ldrs ent st: rdn & one pce)......................1¼ **7** 13/10[1] 118 84
2840a* **Volochine (IRE)** (NMO'Callaghan,USA) **5-9-0** PDay (trckd ldrs: cl up over 1f out: rdn & wknd) ...................nse **8** 23/1 118 87
4718* **Charnwood Forest (IRE)** (SbinSuroor) **4-9-0** WRSwinburn (s.i.s: bhd: rdn & no hdwy st) ............................nk **9** 13/10[1] 118 87
**Urgent Request (IRE)** (CWhittingham,USA) **6-9-0** ASolis (a.p: rdn over 2f out: wknd).................................1¼ **10** 13/1 115 84
**Smooth Runner (USA)** (RMettee,USA) **5-9-0** CMcCarron (hld up in rr: effrt 2f out: no imp) ..............................4 **11** 11/1 107 76
**Dumaani (USA)** (KPMcLaughlin,UAE) **5-9-0** JulieKrone (mid div tl wknd st) ...................................................1¼ **12** 50/1 105 74
**Mighty Forum (CAN)** (MHennig,USA) **5-9-0** JVelasquez (a in rr) .......................................................................1½ **13** 50/1 102 71
**Chaposa Springs (USA)** (MWolfson,USA) **4-8-11** CPerret (prom early: 4th & rdn st: wknd qckly) ..................9 **14** 22/1 81 50
(SP 162.4%) **14 Rn**

**1m 35.8** (-2.00) P-M $18.90: PL (1-2) $7.80 $8.50 SHOW (1-2-3) $5.80 $6.80 $10.30 OWNER Prestonwood Farm Inc
IN-FOCUS: **For betting purposes Charnwood Forest (IRE) and Mark of Esteem (IRE) were cpld, as were Dumaani (USA) and Mighty Forum (CAN) cpld as 'The Field'.**
**Da Hoss (USA)**, who ran in the Sprint last year, used his speed to gain a good position turning in, but still had plenty left when required in the straight. He gave former master jump trainer Michael Dickinson his biggest Flat success. (85/10)
**4165a Spinning World (USA)** ran a terrific race. He looked the likely winner turning in, but could not quite get to Da Hoss. (80/10)
**4443* Mark of Esteem (IRE)** was yet another top European horse to run below-par at the Breeders' Cup. He looked unhappy on the left-hand bends, and never got to the leaders. He now retires to Stud. (13/10)
**4718* Charnwood Forest (IRE)** looked slightly out of his depth, and never reached the firing-line. (13/10)

## 4954a BREEDERS' CUP JUVENILE (Gd 1) (2-Y.O C & G)

9-10 (9-13) **1m 110y (Dirt)** £335,484.00 (£129,032.00: £77,419.00: £36,129.00: £12,903.00) GOING minus 0.50 sec per fur (FST) SP RR SF

**Boston Harbor (USA)** (DWLukas,USA) **2-8-10** JBailey (led: qcknd clr 3f out: hld on wl)...............................— **1** 24/10[2] 112 72
**Acceptable (USA)** (NZito,USA) **2-8-10** SSellers (prom on outside: rdn to chal 1f out: r.o wl) .........................nk **2** 126/10 111 71
**Ordway (USA)** (DDonk,USA) **2-8-10** JVelasquez (rr early: hdwy 3f out: r.o up)...............................................2½ **3** 14/10[1] 107 67
**Cash Deposit (USA)** (DanielVella,Canada) **2-8-10** TKabel (a.p: chsd ldr over 2f out: rdn ent st: wknd) .........2½ **4** 66/10[3] 102 62
4183* **Falkenham** (MichaelHarte,USA) **2-8-10** MWalls (rr early: hdwy on ins st: fin wl) ............................................nse **5** 53/1 102 62
**Gold Tribute (USA)** (DWLukas,USA) **2-8-10** GStevens (trckd ldrs: lost pl ½-wy: sme hdwy fnl 2f)..................hd **6** 7/1 102 62
**Zippersup (USA)** (BBaffert,USA) **2-8-10** CNakatani (prom tl rdn & wknd 2f out)..............................................3½ **7** 354/10 95 55
**Gun Fight (USA)** (MMoubarak,USA) **2-8-10** PDay (rr early: hdwy 3f out: rdn & no ex fnl 2f)............................nk **8** 129/10 95 55
**His Honor (USA)** (DavidVivian,USA) **2-8-10b[1]** CPerret (a in rr).......................................................................2 **9** 505/10 91 51
**Sal's Driver (USA)** (GuadalupePreciado,USA) **2-8-10b[1]** JChavez (prom: rdn over 2f out: wkng whn hmpd st) ........11 **10** 986/10 70 30
(SP 118.8%) **10 Rn**

**1m 43.4** (-1.80) P-M $6.80: PL (1-2) $4.10 $10.00 SHOW (1-2-3) $3.00 $5.40 $2.60 OWNER Overbrook Farm et al BRED Overbrook Farm
**Boston Harbor (USA)** put up a brave performance. He set a good pace and simply refused to let the runner-up pass. (24/10)
**4183* Falkenham**, formerly with Paul Cole, was having his first run on Dirt. He missed the break but, once he found his stride, came storming through. He could do very well for his new connections. (53/1)

## 4955a BREEDERS' CUP TURF (Gd 1) (3-Y.O+)

9-50 (9-54) **1m 4f (Turf)** £670,968.00 (£258,065.00: £154,839.00: £72,258.00) GOING minus 0.20 sec per fur (GF) SP RR SF

4662a[2] **Pilsudski (IRE)** (MRStoute) **4-9-0** WRSwinburn (lw: trckd ldrs: 3rd st: rdn to ld ins fnl f: gamely)..................— **1** 137/10 132 92
4543a* **Singspiel (IRE)** (MRStoute) **4-9-0** GStevens (trckd ldrs: 2nd ½-wy: led 3f out: rdn & hdd ins fnl f) ...............1¼ **2** 11/10[1] 130 90
4662a[4] **Swain (IRE)** (AFabre,France) **4-9-0** OPeslier (cl up: rdn over 2f out: r.o fnl f) ..........................................1¼ **3** 11/10[1] 129 89
4747a* **Shantou (USA)** (JHMGosden) **3-8-9** LDettori (bhd early: hdwy on outside over 2f out: styd on u.p) .............2½ **4** 11/10[1] 127 80
**Windsharp (USA)** (WDollase,USA) **5-8-11** CNakatani (mid div: hdwy to go 2nd ent st: rdn & wknd fnl f) ........¾ **5** 337/10 121 81
**Talloires (USA)** (RMandella,USA) **6-9-0** KDesormeaux (rr early: hdwy on ins over 2f out: r.o u.p st) ............nk **6** 69/10[3] 124 84
4192[2] **Dushyantor (USA)** (HRACecil) **3-8-9** PatEddery (mid div: hdwy over 2f out: hrd rdn & nt qckn st) ................1½ **7** 124/10 124 77
4441* **Wall Street (USA)** (SbinSuroor) **3-8-9** JSantos (mid div: rdn over 2f out: r.o one pce) ...................................2 **8** 11/10[1] 121 74
4652a[2] **Awad (USA)** (DDonk,USA) **6-9-0** CMcCarron (hld up in rr: effrt ent st: no imp)................................................nk **9** 49/10[2] 119 79
4662a[5] **Luna Wells (IRE)** (AFabre,France) **3-8-6** TJarnet (mid div: rdn & no imp fnl 2f).............................................nk **10** 296/10 118 71
4543a[2] **Chief Bearhart (CAN)** (MFrostad,Canada) **3-8-9** SHawley (mid div: rdn & hdwy 3f out: wknd).........................1 **11** 201/10 119 72
4652a* **Diplomatic Jet (USA)** (JPicou,USA) **4-9-0** JChavez (led to 3f out: wknd)...........................................................3¾ **12** 70/10 112 72
4652a[3] **Marlin (USA)** (DWLukas,USA) **3-8-9** SSellers (prom tl wknd 2f out) ..................................................................6 **13** 437/10 106 59
**Ricks Natural Star (USA)** (WLivingston,USA) **7-9-0** LisaMcFarland (prom early: wknd qckly ½-wy: sn t.o) .dist **14** 561/10 — —
(SP 261.7%) **14 Rn**

**2m 30.2** (-1.30) P-M $29.40: PL (1-2) $9.80 $3.00 SHOW (1-2-3) $7.50 $2.70 OWNER Lord Weinstock/Exors of late S Weinstock (NEWMARKET) BRED Ballymacoll Stud Co

IN-FOCUS: **For betting purposes Swain (IRE), Shantou (USA), Wall Street (USA) and Singspiel (IRE) were combined.**
**4662a Pilsudski (IRE)**, on good terms with himself despite his Longchamp exertions, was always moving well. He got an opening between the two leaders at just the right time and battled his way to the front. He is expected to stay in training, and should win more big races. (137/10)
**4543a* Singspiel (IRE)** almost repeated his recent course win. He did nothing wrong under a confident ride, but just failed to get home against a determined rival. (11/10)
**4662a Swain (IRE)** produced another good effort, but his lack of an extra gear found him out when the pace quickened turning in. (11/10)
**4747a* Shantou (USA)**, in good form at present, ran well again, but just lacked the speed to cope with these older rivals. (11/10)
**4192 Dushyantor (USA)** ran his usual genuine race, but is a little short of toe at the top level. (124/10)
**4441* Wall Street (USA)** is still improving, but found this big step up beyond him. There is more to come. (11/10)
**3916a* Luna Wells (IRE)** had every chance, but was out of her depth against the colts. (296/10)

## 4956a BREEDERS' CUP CLASSIC (Gd 1) (3-Y.O+)

10-35 (10-40) **1m 2f (Dirt)** £1,341,935.00 (£516,129.00: £309,677.00: £144,516.00) GOING minus 0.50 sec per fur (F)

| | | | | SP | RR | SF |
|---|---|---|---|---|---|---|
| | **Alphabet Soup (USA)** (DHofmans,USA) **5-9-0** CMcCarron (a cl up: rdn to ld ins fnl f: r.o wl) | — | 1 | 199/10 | 132 | 92 |
| *1391a** | **Louis Quatorze (USA)** (NZito,USA) **3-8-9** PDay (b.hind: a.p: rdn to chal 3f out: r.o gamely) | nse | 2 | 18/1 | 132 | 87 |
| *2842a** | **Cigar (USA)** (WMott,USA) **6-9-0** JBailey (b.hind: mid div: hdwy over 4f out: chal wd ent st: r.o gamely) | hd | 3 | 65/100[1] | 132 | 92 |
| | **Mt. Sassafras (CAN)** (MrsBMinshall,USA) **4-9-0** MWalls (cl up: led ent st: rdn & no ex ins fnl f) | ½ | 4 | 101/1 | 131 | 91 |
| | **Formal Gold (CAN)** (WPerry,USA) **3-8-9** MSmith (in rr early: hdwy fr 3f out: styd on) | 4 | 5 | 209/10 | 125 | 80 |
| 4281a[6] | **Tamayaz (CAN)** (SbinSuroor) **4-9-0** LDettori (trckd ldrs: rdn over 2f out: no ex) | hd | 6 | 703/10 | 124 | 84 |
| | **Will's Way (USA)** (HJBond,USA) **3-8-9** JChavez (sn bhd) | 1¼ | 7 | 8/1[3] | 122 | 77 |
| | **Atticus (USA)** (RMandella,USA) **4-9-0** CNakatani (led: hdd ent st: wknd) | hd | 8 | 76/10[2] | 122 | 82 |
| *2842a[2]* | **Dramatic Gold (USA)** (DHofmans,USA) **5-9-0** KDesormeaux (hld up: trckd ldrs 4f out: rdn 2f out: one pce) | ¾ | 9 | 179/10 | 121 | 81 |
| | **Mahogany Hall (USA)** (JBaker,USA) **5-9-0** SSellers (b: a bhd) | 3¾ | 10 | 209/10 | 115 | 75 |
| | **Dare And Go (USA)** (RMandella,USA) **5-9-0** ASolis (trckd ldrs early: rdn & lost pl 4f out) | 5 | 11 | 76/10[2] | 107 | 67 |
| *1946a** | **Editor's Note (USA)** (DWLukas,USA) **3-8-9** GStevens (mid div on outside: pushed along ½-wy: no hdwy) | 10 | 12 | 11/1 | 91 | 46 |
| 1952a[2] | **Taiki Blizzard (USA)** (KFujisawa,Japan) **5-9-0** YOkabe (hld up pllng hrd: lost pl & btn 4f out) | 1¼ | 13 | 205/10 | 89 | 49 |

(SP 134.8%) **13 Rn**

**2m 1.0** (-4.10) P-M $41.70: PL (1-2) $15.30 $13.00 SHOW (1-2-3) $6.80 $6.00 $2.40 OWNER Ridder Thoroughbred Stable
IN-FOCUS: **For betting purposes Dare And Go (USA) and Atticus (USA) were cpld, as were Formal Gold (CAN) and Mahogany Hall (USA) cpld as 'The Field'.**
**Alphabet Soup (USA)**, who is on a roll, gained a narrow victory in a terrific race. Always on the premises, he forced his way to the front in the straight, and refused to let his rivals pass. He has taken Cigar's crown, but can he now take over the mantle? (199/10)
**1391a* Louis Quatorze (USA)** has had a busy year, but the Preakness winner produced an ultra-game effort against older horses. He is one to put in the notebook for next year. (18/1)
**2842a* Cigar (USA)** ended his career with a defeat, but plenty of glory. Given a less-than-inspired ride, he came around the outside of his field to deliver his challenge. He always looked in trouble, but kept battling away, and was closest at the post. He has captured the imagination of American public and the whole of the racing world, and will be missed. (65/100)
**4281a Tamayaz (CAN)** performed creditably, but was taking on the very best here. (703/10)
AR/GM

# 4741a-COLOGNE (Germany) (R-H) (Soft)

## Sunday October 27th

## 4957a KOLNER-SPRINT-PREIS (Listed)

1-30 (1-40) **6f** £9,009.00 (£3,604.00: £1,802.00)

| | | | | SP | RR | SF |
|---|---|---|---|---|---|---|
| 4774[8] | **Branston Abby (IRE)** (MJohnston) **7-9-3** MRoberts | — | 1 | | 106 | — |
| 3045[9] | **My Cadeaux** (RGuest) **4-8-6** PBloomfield | nk | 2 | | 94 | — |
| 497a[3] | **Novize (GER)** (EGroschel,Germany) **5-9-7** LPyritz | 1¾ | 3 | | 105 | — |

**9 Rn**

**1m 13.52** (3.72) TOTE 21DM: 13DM 37DM 25DM OWNER Mr J. D. Abell (MIDDLEHAM) BRED John David Abell
**4774 Branston Abby (IRE)** lost a couple of places on the final turn. Rousted along by Roberts over two furlongs out, she came with her patented late burst to collar My Cadeaux in the final 30 yards. She runs in a Group Three in Milan at the beginning of November.
**1652* My Cadeaux** vindicated the decision to supplement her for this race with a fine performance. Never far off the pace, she took it up a furlong and a half out and stuck on gamely all the way to the line. She is difficult to train but clearly goes well fresh.

# 4948a-LONGCHAMP (Paris, France) (R-H) (Soft)

## Sunday October 27th

## 4958a PRIX DU PETIT COUVERT (Gp 3)

1-35 (1-34) **5f** £28,986.00 (£10,540.00: £5,270.00: £2,635.00)

| | | | | SP | RR | SF |
|---|---|---|---|---|---|---|
| 4660a[8] | **Don't Worry Me (IRE)** (GHenrot,France) **4-9-8** AJunk | — | 1 | | 115 | — |
| 4518* | **Croft Pool** (JAGlover) **5-9-11** GCarter | 2 | 2 | | 112 | — |
| 3914a[2] | **Titus Livius (FR)** (JEPease,France) **3-9-11** CAsmussen | 1 | 3 | | 108 | — |
| 4744a* | **Leap for Joy** (JHMGosden) **4-9-11** LDettori | ½ | 4 | | 107 | — |
| 4518[2] | **Blue Iris** (MAJarvis) **3-9-8** PatEddery | ½ | 5 | | 102 | — |
| 1911a[5] | **Millyant** (RGuest) **6-9-8** JReid (btn approx 7¼l) | | 7 | | — | — |

**9 Rn**

**57.4 secs** (2.90) P-M 13.20F: 3.30F 3.20F 1.80F (68.70F) OWNER Mr J. Gribomont BRED Irish National Stud Co Ltd
**4406a Don't Worry Me (IRE)** thoroughly deserved this victory as she has been thereabouts in Group company all season. This ex-English filly took the lead at the final furlong marker and ran on gamely. It is good news to know that she will be around again next year.
**4518* Croft Pool** was totally outpaced early on and did not really find his feet until halfway through the race. He fairly bolted the final furlong and was finishing so fast that victory would have been his in a further 50 yards. A game and consistent horse, he now goes for a sprint at Doncaster in early November.
**4744a* Leap for Joy**, held up at the rear of the field, was never in a position to challenge.

**4518 Blue Iris** struck the front two and a half furlongs out, but her effort was short-lived and she soon weakened.
**1911a Millyant** will now be retired to Stud as it seems she has lost her old sparkle.

## 4959a PRIX ROYAL-OAK (Gp 1) (3-Y.O+)

2-40 (2-40) **1m 7f 110y** £52,701.00 (£21,080.00: £10,540.00: £5,270.00)

| | Horse | Dist | Pos | SP | RR | SF |
|---|---|---|---|---|---|---|
| 438a[2] | **Red Roses Story** (MmePBarbe,France) **4-9-1** VVion (3rd st: rdn 2f out: hdwy on ins to ld ins fnl f: r.o wl) | — | **1** | 59/10 | 123 | — |
| 4655a[2] | **Moonax (IRE)** (BWHills) **5-9-4** PatEddery (disp ld tl led wl over 2f out: kpt on wl ins fnl f) | ½ | **2** | 7/10[1] | 126 | — |
| 3915a[4] | **Helen Of Spain** (AFabre,France) **4-9-1** TJarnet (disp ld: hdd wl over 2f out) | ¾ | **3** | 7/10[1] | 122 | — |
| 4655a* | **Nononito (FR)** (JLesbordes,France) **5-9-4** SGuillot (rdn st: nvr able to chal) | 1 | **4** | 2/1[2] | 124 | — |
| 4655a[3] | **Always Earnest (USA)** (MmeMBollack-Badel,France) **8-9-4b** ABadel (a in rr) | 5 | **5** | 41/10[3] | 119 | — |
| | | | | (SP 185.1%) | **5 Rn** | |

**3m 38.4** (22.40) P-M 6.90F: 2.40F 1.30F OWNER Mme P. Barbe BRED Shira Racing
**IN-FOCUS: For betting purposes Moonax (IRE) and Helen Of Spain (GB) were cpld**
**438a Red Roses Story** showed a good burst of speed to take the lead inside the final furlong and just hold off the persistent runner-up. (59/10)
**4655a Moonax (IRE)** was totally unsuited by the lack of pace and just stayed on in the final stages after sharing the lead throughout with Shiekh Mohammed's other runner, Helen of Spain, but only at a moderate gallop. The race was won in over 22 seconds outside the course record. Not the easiest of individuals, he will now be schooled over hurdles which might have a positive effect on his character, so he may be a live-wire for the Champion Hurdle next march. (7/10)
**3915a Helen Of Spain** shared the lead and sprinted with Moonax in the straight until they were both passed by the speedier winner. She is a consistent filly who would also have been unsuited by the way this race went. (7/10)
**4655a* Nononito (FR)** seemed to lack a little of his sparkle on this occasion and must surely have been another who was unsuited by the way this race was run. There are several people interested in buying this winner of the Prix du Cadran, so his future is in the balance for the moment. (2/1)
DS

# SANTA ANITA (Los Angeles, USA) (L-H) (Firm)
## Sunday October 27th

## 4960a MORVICH H'CAP (3-Y.O+)

10-30 (10-32) **6f 110y (Turf)** £42,000.00 (£12,903.00: £7,742.00)

| | Horse | Dist | Pos | SP | RR | SF |
|---|---|---|---|---|---|---|
| | **Comininalittlehot (USA)** (MMitchell,USA) **5-8-5** KDesormeaux | — | **1** | | 108 | — |
| | **Wild Zone (USA)** (USA) **6-8-4** EDelahoussaye | 1 | **2** | | 105 | — |
| | **Wavy Run (IRE)** (USA) **5-8-4** BBlanc | hd | **3** | | 104 | — |
| 2472a[10] | **America's Cup (IRE)** (DKWeld,Ireland) **4-8-5** LPincay (btn over 9l) | | **7** | | — | — |
| | | | | | | **7 Rn** |

**1m 11.57** P-M 8.00: PL (1-2) 4.60 6.40 SHOW (1-2-3) 3.60 5.60 5.40 OWNER Gary W & Timothy R Burke BRED Diane C. Kem
**America's Cup (IRE)** was never a factor.

# 4950a-WOODBINE (Toronto, Canada) (L-H) (Good)
## Sunday October 27th

## 4961a E P TAYLOR STKS (Gd 2) (3-Y.O+ F & M)

7-50 (7-58) **1m 2f (Turf)** £96,283.00 (£32,094.00: £17,652.00)

| | Horse | Dist | Pos | SP | RR | SF |
|---|---|---|---|---|---|---|
| 4567[5] | **Wandering Star (USA)** (JRFanshawe) **3-8-6** HMcCauley | — | **1** | | 115 | — |
| 4567[3] | **Flame Valley (USA)** (MRStoute) **3-8-6** GStevens | 1½ | **2** | | 113 | — |
| 4410a[2] | **Carling (FR)** (MmePBarbe,France) **4-8-11** TThulliez | nk | **3** | | 112 | — |
| 4663a[3] | **Sangria (USA)** (AFabre,France) **3-8-6** OPeslier | ¾ | **7** | | 111 | — |
| | | | | | | **8 Rn** |

**2m 4.6** P-M $37.50: PL (1-2) $20.10 $9.70 SHOW (1-2-3) $7.30 $5.60 $3.50 OWNER Mr J. Allen (NEWMARKET) BRED Mr and Mrs R. Lyons
**4567 Wandering Star (USA)**, getting her head in front turning for home, was driven out to score. She will continue her career in the United States.
**4567 Flame Valley (USA)**, after holding a good early pitch, was shuffled back and had trouble finding a run at the top of the straight. However, she got to within half a length of the winner approaching the furlong pole, so had no real excuses.

# 4769-NEWMARKET (R-H) (Good)
## Friday November 1st

Race 7 - hand-timed
WEATHER: fine WIND: fresh across

## 4962 E.B.F. RED LODGE MAIDEN STKS (2-Y.O) (Class D)

12-50 (12-51) **6f (Rowley)** £4,077.50 (£1,220.00: £585.00: £267.50) Stalls: Centre GOING minus 0.45 sec per fur (F)

| | Horse | Dist | Pos | SP | RR | SF |
|---|---|---|---|---|---|---|
| 4756[3] | **Kumait (USA) (88)** (SbinSuroor) **2-9-0** LDettori(10) (mde all: rdn & r.o wl fnl f) | — | **1** | 7/2[2] | 94 | 41 |
| 3706[4] | **Elnadim (USA)** (JLDunlop) **2-9-0** RHills(9) (plld hrd: trckd ldrs: rdn over 1f out: no ex ins fnl f) | 1¾ | **2** | Evens[1] | 89 | 36 |
| | **Zaahir (IRE)** (BWHills) **2-9-0** MHills(11) (w'like: bit bkwd: trckd ldrs: one pce fnl 2f) | 3 | **3** | 4/1[3] | 81+ | 28 |
| 4756[21] | **First Chance (IRE)** (DRCElsworth) **2-8-9** DaneO'Neill(7) (plld hrd: prom: rdn 2f out: no imp) | 4 | **4** | 33/1 | 66 | 13 |
| 3685[12] | **Blood Orange** (GGMargarson) **2-9-0** AClark(3) (wnt rt s: w ldrs 4f) | 2 | **5** | 50/1 | 65 | 12 |
| | **Supreme Maimoon** (MJPolglase) **2-9-0** OUrbina(8) (unf: bkwd: chsd ldrs tl rdn & wknd over 2f out) | nk | **6** | 50/1 | 65 | 12 |
| 4756[10] | **Rotor Man (IRE)** (JDBethell) **2-9-0** GCarter(6) (chsd ldrs: rdn 2f out: sn wknd) | 1¼ | **7** | 33/1 | 61 | 8 |
| | **Zest (USA)** (MBell) **2-8-9** MRoberts(4) (unf: a bhd) | ¾ | **8** | 25/1 | 54 | 1 |
| 2783[10] | **The Green Grey** (LordHuntingdon) **2-9-0** JReid(2) (hld up: nvr trbld ldrs) | 2½ | **9** | 33/1 | 53 | — |
| | **Hardiprincess** (MBell) **2-8-2**(7) RMullen(5) (small: unf: hmpd & dwlt s: a bhd) | 2½ | **10** | 25/1 | 41 | — |

| | | | | SP | RR | SF |
|---|---|---|---|---|---|---|
| | **Ioulios** (JEBanks) **2-9-0** JQuinn(1) (w'like: unf: bit bkwd: s.i.s: a bhd) | 9 | **11** | 33/1 | 22 | — |

(SP 115.6%) **11 Rn**

**1m 13.22** (1.42) CSF £6.87 TOTE £3.60: £1.10 £1.60 £1.80 (£2.10) Trio £1.70 OWNER Godolphin (NEWMARKET) BRED Darley Stud Management Inc

**4756 Kumait (USA)** again had his tongue tied down and finally came good in fine style. (7/2)
**3706 Elnadim (USA)**, off since his debut at York, showed some knee-action and did not catch the eye going down. He may have needed this more than it appeared, for his effort petered out in the last furlong. (Evens)
**Zaahir (IRE)**, a half-brother to the ill-fated Mubhij, is nothing like as sharp to look at. This was a respectable debut and he should stay further. (4/1: 3/1-9/2)
**First Chance (IRE)** again saw the wrong end of Kumait, but took a strong hold, both going down and in the early stages, showing much more than on her debut. (33/1)
**Blood Orange** improved from his debut, but still did not get home. (50/1)
**Supreme Maimoon** still has some filling out to do and was scratchy to post, even on this better ground. Lack of full fitness told late in the race, but he left the impression that he would not have been better than fourth. (50/1)

## 4963 NGK SPARK PLUGS SOHAM HOUSE CONDITIONS STKS (2-Y.O) (Class C)

1-20 (1-20) **1m (Rowley)** £4,927.68 (£1,702.08: £815.04: £331.20) Stalls: Centre GOING minus 0.45 sec per fur (F)

| | | | | SP | RR | SF |
|---|---|---|---|---|---|---|
| 4699[4] | **River Usk** (HRACecil) **2-8-13** WRyan(4) (hld up: plld out & hdwy 2f out: edgd lft: rdn & r.o wl to ld nr fin) | — | **1** | 6/1[3] | 102 | 33 |
| 4676[2] | **Barnum Sands (100)** (JLDunlop) **2-9-3** PatEddery(2) (trckd ldr: rdn to ld over 1f out: edgd lft ins fnl f: ct nr fin) | hd | **2** | 4/9[1] | 106 | 37 |
| 4705* | **Our People** (MJohnston) **2-8-13** JWeaver(3) (lw: led: hdd over 1f out: one pce) | 2½ | **3** | 7/2[2] | 97? | 28 |
| 4488[13] | **Get The Point** (RHollinshead) **2-8-11** LDettori(1) (prom: ev ch 3f out: rdn & wandered: sn btn) | 1½ | **4** | 20/1 | 92? | 23 |

(SP 110.5%) **4 Rn**

**1m 40.02** (2.72) CSF £9.24 TOTE £5.00: (£2.00) OWNER Mr K. Abdulla (NEWMARKET) BRED Juddmonte Farms

**4699 River Usk**, taken to post very early, looks is if he lives on his nerves. Sent about his task passing the Bushes, he brushed Get The Point as he moved through, but found his stride on hitting the rising ground. He is certainly worth another chance on faster ground. (6/1: op 7/2)
**4676 Barnum Sands** took an awful long time to get in front once asked for his effort and again did not run straight and true to the line, getting caught near the finish. (4/9)
**4705* Our People** moved well to post and did not go down without a fight, despite a somewhat high head carriage. (7/2: 5/2-4/1)
**3668 Get The Point** is bred to be useful, but looked green and hung left then right when the pressure was applied. (20/1)

## 4964 JAMES SEYMOUR STKS (Listed) (3-Y.O+) (Class A)

1-55 (1-55) **1m 2f (Rowley)** £11,366.20 (£4,205.80: £2,017.90: £824.50: £327.25: £128.35) Stalls: Centre GOING minus 0.45 sec per fur (F)

| | | | | SP | RR | SF |
|---|---|---|---|---|---|---|
| 4680* | **Proper Blue (USA) (96)** (TGMills) **3-8-10** SSanders(2) (hld up: hdwy 4f out: rdn & n.m.r over 2f out: r.o wl to ld ins fnl f) | — | **1** | 15/2 | 112 | 53 |
| 4622* | **Multicoloured (IRE) (92)** (MRStoute) **3-8-10** JReid(1) (lw: w ldrs: chal & edgd rt over 2f out: ev ch ins fnl f: unable qckn nr fin) | nk | **2** | 4/1[2] | 112 | 53 |
| 4568* | **Clifton Fox (96)** (JAGlover) **4-9-0** NDay(7) (a.p: ev ch ins fnl f: r.o) | nk | **3** | 5/1[3] | 111 | 56 |
| 4467[5] | **Balalaika (102)** (LMCumani) **3-8-5** LDettori(8) (racd alone far side: w ldrs: led over 2f out tl hdd & btn ins fnl f) | 1 | **4** | 5/1[3] | 104 | 45 |
| 4678[7] | **Roses In The Snow (IRE) (96)** (JWHills) **3-8-5** RHills(6) (in tch: effrt & swtchd lft over 2f out: no imp appr fnl f) | 5 | **5** | 20/1 | 96 | 37 |
| 4680[6] | **Ninia (USA) (93)** (MJohnston) **4-8-9** JWeaver(4) (led over 7f) | 2½ | **6** | 14/1 | 92 | 37 |
| 4714* | **Bright Water (110)** (HRACecil) **3-8-10** PatEddery(5) (trckd ldrs: rdn over 3f out: btn whn nt clr run over 2f out) | 2½ | **7** | 5/2[1] | 93 | 34 |
| 4595[3] | **General Academy (IRE) (100)** (PAKelleway) **3-8-10** DRMcCabe(3) (rdn 4f out: a bhd) | 5 | **8** | 33/1 | 85 | 26 |

(SP 108.0%) **8 Rn**

**2m 4.17** (0.57) CSF £33.08 TOTE £7.20: £2.20 £1.60 £1.50 (£18.20) OWNER Mr M. J. Legg (EPSOM) BRED Claiborne Farm and The Gamely Corporation

WEIGHT FOR AGE 3yo-4lb

STEWARDS' ENQUIRY Day susp.11 & 12-14/11/96 (excessive use of whip)

**4680* Proper Blue (USA)** has had an easy season and took this step up in class in his stride. He looked most enthusiastic in a driving finish. (15/2: 5/1-8/1)
**4622* Multicoloured (IRE)**, always with the pace in the centre of the track, might have led for a few strides when edging right passing the Bushes. Going down fighting, this was only his fourth start and he has the scope to progress. (4/1)
**4568* Clifton Fox** did not really get the pace he needs, but performed with great credit, the ground having come in his favour. (5/1: 4/1-6/1)
**4467 Balalaika**, taken to race alone, was always up with the pace, but she stays further and was just unable to hold on in the closing stages. It was though another good performance. (5/1: op 8/1)
**3836 Roses In The Snow (IRE)**, not over-raced this year, made her bid towards the stands' side and could never land a blow. (20/1)
**4680 Ninia (USA)** seems past her best for the year and, as such, performed with credit on her first run above handicap company. Her forcing style of racing could see black type coming her way when she is at the top of her form. (14/1: 10/1-16/1)
**4714* Bright Water** was not suited by the rain that had fallen and was one of the first beaten. Like so many others by Caerleon, he looks to need fast ground. (5/2)

## 4965 GEORGE STUBBS RATED STKS H'CAP (0-105) (Listed) (3-Y.O+) (Class A)

2-30 (2-31) **2m (Rowley)** £10,912.64 (£4,033.76: £1,931.88: £785.40: £307.70: £116.62) Stalls: Low GOING minus 0.45 sec per fur (F)

| | | | | SP | RR | SF |
|---|---|---|---|---|---|---|
| 4771[7] | **Orchestra Stall (90)** (JLDunlop) **4-8-7** TQuinn(6) (b: a.p: led over 3f out: rdn clr over 1f out: eased ins fnl f) | — | **1** | 7/2[1] | 102+ | 54 |
| 4465[11] | **Leonato (FR) (98)** (PDEvans) **4-9-1** JFEgan(9) (swtg: chsd ldrs: ev ch 2f out: rdn & hung rt: sn btn) | 1¾ | **2** | 25/1 | 108 | 60 |
| 4548* | **Zaforum (97)** (LMontagueHall) **3-8-5b** LDettori(4) (lw: led tl over 3f out: kpt on) | 2½ | **3** | 10/1 | 105 | 48 |
| 4761* | **Flamands (IRE) (90)** (LMCumani) **3-7-12** RFfrench(5) (swtg: hdwy 5f out: one pce fnl 3f) | ¾ | **4** | 5/1[3] | 97 | 40 |
| 4569[5] | **Old Rouvel (USA) (102)** (DJGMurraySmith) **5-9-5** MRoberts(8) (hld up: hdwy 3f out: nvr rchd ldrs) | ¾ | **5** | 20/1 | 108 | 60 |

| | | | SP | RR | SF |
|---|---|---|---|---|---|
| 4771[2] | **En Vacances (IRE) (90)** (AGFoster) **4-8-7** TSprake(10) (prom tl wknd over 3f out)....3 | 6 | 11/1 | 93 | 45 |
| 4761[2] | **Mount Pleasant (IRE) (90)** (PFICole) **3-7-12** JQuinn(7) (lw: prom: lost pl 7f out: n.d after)....2½ | 7 | 10/1 | 91 | 34 |
| 1336[3] | **Purple Splash (94)** (PJMakin) **6-8-11v** PatEddery(11) (bit bkwd: hld up: rdn 5f out: nvr trbld ldrs)....12 | 8 | 14/1 | 83 | 35 |
| 4771[12] | **Jiyush (100)** (HThomsonJones) **3-8-8** RHills(1) (a.p: ev ch 6f out tl wknd over 2f out)....9 | 9 | 7/1 | 80 | 23 |
| 4821[9] | **Pearl Venture (90)** (SPCWoods) **4-8-7** WRyan(2) (hld up & plld hrd: effrt 5f out: eased whn btn fnl 2f)....28 | 10 | 66/1 | 42 | — |
| 4112* | **Corradini (104)** (HRACecil) **4-9-7** KFallon(3) (nvr gng wl: a bhd: virtually p.u fnl 3f)....21 | 11 | 4/1[2] | 35 | — |

(SP 114.7%) **11 Rn**

**3m 23.58** (0.28) CSF £70.65 CT £727.24 TOTE £3.80: £1.80 £3.50 £3.40 (£56.60) Trio £721.90 OWNER Mr D. Sieff (ARUNDEL) BRED Alan Gibson

LONG HANDICAP Orchestra Stall 8-6 Pearl Venture 7-3 En Vacances (IRE) 8-3 Flamands (IRE) 7-11

WEIGHT FOR AGE 3yo-9lb

**4771 Orchestra Stall** may not have stayed in the Cesarewitch, for he soon had matters well in hand once given a couple of sharp reminders. He would have won by six lengths but for being eased. (7/2)

**3934 Leonato (FR)** looked well suited by the move up to two miles, but blotted his copybook by hanging when the chance of victory appeared. (25/1)

**4548* Zaforum** bowled along happily in front, but both Jiyush and the winner were snapping at his heels some way from home. Once headed, he could find no more. (10/1)

**4761* Flamands (IRE)**, a moderate mover, could not get to the leaders in the closing stages, but staying does appear to be his game. (5/1)

**4569 Old Rouvel (USA)** only got going when the race was almost over and needs even further to be at his best. (20/1)

**4771 En Vacances (IRE)** excelled herself last time and that hard race seemed to have left its mark. (11/1)

## 4966 EQUITY FINANCIAL COLLECTIONS NURSERY H'CAP (2-Y.O) (Class D)

3-05 (3-05) **5f (Rowley)** £3,655.00 (£1,090.00: £520.00: £235.00) Stalls: Centre GOING minus 0.45 sec per fur (F)

| | | | SP | RR | SF |
|---|---|---|---|---|---|
| 4878[5] | **Ellens Lad (IRE) (77)** (RHannon) **2-9-3** PatEddery(1) (trckd ldrs: r.o to ld wl ins fnl f)....— | 1 | 11/4[1] | 73 | 32 |
| 4749[8] | **Kilcullen Lad (IRE) (59)** (PMooney) **2-7-13v[1]** DRMcCabe(4) (lw: plld hrd: trckd ldrs: led over 1f out tl hdd & unable qckn wl ins fnl f)....½ | 2 | 6/1[3] | 53 | 12 |
| 4614[6] | **Gaelic Storm (81)** (MJohnston) **2-9-7** JWeaver(8) (lw: reard s: bhd tl hdwy 2f out: ev ch over 1f out: no ex fnl f)....1½ | 3 | 7/2[2] | 71 | 30 |
| 3299[W] | **Gopi (69)** (RHannon) **2-8-9** DaneO'Neill(2) (b.nr fore: chsd ldrs: rdn & ev ch over 1f out: one pce)....nk | 4 | 10/1 | 58 | 17 |
| 4234[10] | **Sous Le Nez (80)** (RGuest) **2-9-1**(5) DGriffiths(7) (prom: ev ch 1f out: one pce)....nk | 5 | 8/1 | 68 | 27 |
| 4912[7] | **Swift (65)** (MJPolglase) **2-8-5** MRoberts(3) (led tl over 2f out: sn wknd)....2 | 6 | 15/2 | 46 | 5 |
| 4517[8] | **Last Chance (73)** (CNAllen) **2-8-8**(5) MartinDwyer(5) (w ldr: ev ch over 1f out: sn wknd)....s.h | 7 | 10/1 | 54 | 13 |
| 4912[9] | **Fine Times (73)** (CWFairhurst) **2-8-13** DeanMcKeown(6) (reard s: a bhd)....4 | 8 | 12/1 | 41 | — |

(SP 111.9%) **8 Rn**

**60.51 secs** (1.81) CSF £17.74 CT £52.16 TOTE £3.00: £1.30 £1.80 £1.90 (£8.80) OWNER Mrs Chris Harrington (MARLBOROUGH) BRED Mrs Chris Harrington

**4878 Ellens Lad (IRE)** seems ideally suited by the minimum trip and, racing close to the stands' side, forged ahead in the dying strides. (11/4)

**4749 Kilcullen Lad (IRE)**, visored for the first time, was taken down steadily, but took a terrific hold in the race. Going for home in the Dip, he edged slightly right and raced far apart from the winner, only going down close home. (6/1)

**4614 Gaelic Storm** again missed the break, but did some good running to challenge in the Dip before the effort beat him. (7/2)

**3110 Gopi** ran well back at five, but could not change gear to take her chance from the Dip. (10/1)

**4034a Sous Le Nez**, a sharp sort, looked ready for this run in seven weeks, but could find no more after looking a danger to all in the Dip. (8/1)

**4767* Swift** got warm, but stretched the field until tying up on the hill. (15/2)

**4558 Fine Times** (12/1: 8/1-14/1)

## 4967 NGK SPARK PLUGS H'CAP (0-70) (3-Y.O+ F & M) (Class E)

3-40 (3-40) **1m 4f (Rowley)** £4,012.50 (£1,200.00: £575.00: £262.50) Stalls: Low GOING minus 0.45 sec per fur (F)

| | | | SP | RR | SF |
|---|---|---|---|---|---|
| 4766[3] | **Silvretta (IRE) (59)** (ACStewart) **3-9-3b[1]** MRoberts(12) (in tch: rdn & outpcd 5f out: styd on wl to ld ins fnl f)....— | 1 | 12/1 | 68 | 44 |
| 4804[6] | **Dalwhinnie (62)** (JWHills) **3-9-3**(3) MHenry(1) (s.i.s: hdwy 5f out: ev ch 3f out: r.o fnl f)....½ | 2 | 25/1 | 70 | 46 |
| 4702[10] | **Temptress (63)** (PTWalwyn) **3-9-7v** PatEddery(2) (hdwy 5f out: led over 3f out tl ins fnl f: unable qckn)....s.h | 3 | 14/1 | 71 | 47 |
| 4752[2] | **Totally Yours (IRE) (45)** (MRChannon) **3-8-3** JFEgan(5) (hld up: hdwy over 3f out: no imp appr fnl f)....nk | 4 | 6/1[2] | 53 | 29 |
| 4582[13] | **Kathryn's Pet (62)** (MrsMReveley) **3-9-6** ACulhane(9) (hdwy 4f out: ev ch over 2f out: no ex ins fnl f)....½ | 5 | 25/1 | 69 | 45 |
| *4779** | **Glow Forum (52)** (LMontagueHall) **5-8-11**(5) MartinDwyer(17) (b: w ldr: led 5f out tl over 3f out: wknd fnl f)...1½ | 6 | 5/1[1] | 57 | 39 |
| 4793[12] | **Your Most Welcome (57)** (DJSffrenchDavis) **5-9-2**(5) GParkin(7) (bhd: hdwy fnl 2f: nvr able to chal)....1 | 7 | 33/1 | 61 | 43 |
| 4810[2] | **Alfayza (43)** (JDBethell) **3-8-1** SDrowne(11) (hld up: hdwy 6f out: wknd fnl f)....1¾ | 8 | 9/1 | 45 | 21 |
| 4559[12] | **Calendula (64)** (DMorley) **3-9-8** GCarter(15) (lw: in tch: effrt 5f out: sn rdn: eased whn btn over 1f out)....11 | 9 | 10/1 | 51 | 27 |
| 1852[9] | **Pip's Dream (49)** (MJRyan) **5-8-13** AClark(10) (swtg: chsd ldrs: rdn over 3f out: sn btn)....1 | 10 | 10/1 | 35 | 17 |
| 4551[2] | **Roisin Clover (63)** (RRowe) **5-9-13** TQuinn(4) (racd wd: led 2f: wknd over 2f out)....¾ | 11 | 8/1 | 48 | 30 |
| 4793[4] | **Kristal Breeze (57)** (WRMuir) **4-9-7** JReid(14) (in tch: rdn over 3f out: sn btn)....s.h | 12 | 7/1[3] | 42 | 24 |
| 4866[2] | **Absolutelystunning (56)** (MrsBarbaraWaring) **3-8-11**(3) NVarley(16) (b: b.nr hind: prom 9f)....2 | 13 | 11/1 | 38 | 14 |
| 4691[14] | **Ember (49)** (RTPhillips) **3-8-7** RPerham(8) (s.i.s: nvr trbld ldrs)....nk | 14 | 33/1 | 30 | 6 |
| 4726[7] | **Needwood Epic (52)** (BCMorgan) **3-8-10v** SSanders(13) (lw: led after 2f to 5f out: wknd over 2f out)....2½ | 15 | 50/1 | 30 | 6 |
| 4497[18] | **Bellateena (36)** (HJCollingridge) **4-8-0** JQuinn(3) (chsd ldrs 9f: sn rdn & wknd)....12 | 16 | 50/1 | — | — |
| 4868[7] | **Dark Truffle (63)** (MrsJCecil) **3-9-7b[1]** KDarley(6) (prom tl rdn & wknd 4f out)....5 | 17 | 33/1 | 18 | — |

(SP 125.9%) **17 Rn**

**2m 33.74** (3.24) CSF £248.57 CT £3,836.89 TOTE £12.40: £2.40 £5.50 £3.40 £2.10 (£170.80) Trio £388.40 OWNER Sir Stephen Hastings (NEWMARKET) BRED Leo Collins

WEIGHT FOR AGE 3yo-6lb

**4766 Silvretta (IRE)** probably owes this victory to first-time blinkers, but they took an awful long time to work as she looked more likely to finish last than first with half a mile left. She continues to give the impression that extreme distances will be her forte. (12/1)

**4804 Dalwhinnie**, forced into a change of tactics by missing the break, put up an improved display as a result. (25/1)

**4513 Temptress** took much longer to get to the front than usual, but still looked to have done enough entering the final furlong. (14/1)

**4752 Totally Yours (IRE)** looked the likely winner when let loose, but her effort petered out tamely when the chance was there. (6/1)

**1023 Kathryn's Pet**, having her second run after a long break, finally admitted defeat in the Dip. (25/1)

**4779* Glow Forum** moved well enough to post and is much better on this surface than the All-Weather, but still could not prevail, tying up in the final furlong. (5/1)
**Bellateena** was going as well as any half a mile from home, but did not stay this longer trip. (50/1)

## 4968 AVENUE APPRENTICE H'CAP (0-70) (3-Y.O) (Class E)

4-15 (4-16) **1m 1f (Rowley)** £4,045.00 (£1,210.00: £580.00: £265.00) Stalls: Centre GOING minus 0.45 sec per fur (F)

| | | | | SP | RR | SF |
|---|---|---|---|---|---|---|
| 4898[6] | **Whispering Dawn (63)** (MRChannon) **3-9-4** PPMurphy(15) (hdwy 2f out: rdn to ld wl ins fnl f) | — | **1** | 14/1 | 73 | 51 |
| 4866[14] | **Peppers (IRE) (64)** (KRBurke) **3-9-5** RPainter(13) (s.i.s: hdwy over 1f out: fin fast) | nk | **2** | 25/1 | 74 | 52 |
| *4781*[2] | **Allstars Rocket (55)** (TJNaughton) **3-8-10** PFessey(17) (sn w ldr: led over 4f out: hdd over 1f out: edgd lft & kpt on) | ¾ | **3** | 12/1 | 63 | 41 |
| 4626[13] | **Dauphin (IRE) (41)** (WJMusson) **3-7-7**(3) IonaWands(19) (a.p: led over 1f tl ins fnl f: r.o) | ½ | **4** | 10/1[3] | 48 | 26 |
| 4480* | **Shouldbegrey (44)** (WRMuir) **3-7-13** AmandaSanders(5) (b: swtg: plld hrd: w ldrs: no ex appr fnl f) | ½ | **5** | 10/1[3] | 50 | 28 |
| 4496[8] | **Burning Flame (41)** (RMFlower) **3-7-10** CAdamson(7) (plld out 3f out: sn rdn: styd on fnl f) | 1½ | **6** | 33/1 | 45 | 23 |
| 4692[12] | **Night of Glass (59)** (DMorris) **3-8-11v**(3) AEddery(10) (prom: rdn 2f out: wknd fnl f) | 1¼ | **7** | 14/1 | 61 | 39 |
| 4071[10] | **Perpetual Light (55)** (JJQuinn) **3-8-10** GParkin(4) (in tch: no hdwy fnl 2f) | 1¾ | **8** | 25/1 | 53 | 31 |
| 4905[8] | **Sistar Act (65)** (MRChannon) **3-9-1v**[1](5) AMcCarthy(16) (wnt lft s: hdwy 6f out: ev ch 2f out: wknd fnl f) | s.h | **9** | 14/1 | 63 | 41 |
| 2592[9] | **Voodoo Rocket (60)** (JHMGosden) **3-9-1** MartinDwyer(2) (bit bkwd: prom tl wknd 2f out) | hd | **10** | 14/1 | 58 | 36 |
| 2026* | **Loch Style (50)** (RHollinshead) **3-8-2**(3) KSked(3) (bit bkwd: prom over 6f) | ½ | **11** | 7/1[1] | 47 | 25 |
| 4898[14] | **Air Wing (65)** (MHTompkins) **3-9-3v**[1](3) RMullen(21) (hld up: rdn over 3f out: hung lft & no imp) | s.h | **12** | 25/1 | 62 | 40 |
| 4000[17] | **Jean Pierre (55)** (JPearce) **3-8-7**(3) GMilligan(14) (n.d) | ¾ | **13** | 33/1 | 51 | 29 |
| 4480[4] | **One In The Eye (46)** (JRPoulton) **3-7-10**(5)ow1 TField(18) (dwlt: sn w ldrs: rdn & wknd over 2f out) | nk | **14** | 16/1 | 41 | 18 |
| 4606[5] | **Danlora (66)** (WJarvis) **3-9-7** DGriffiths(6) (b.hind: swtg: nvr trbld ldrs) | 3 | **15** | 10/1[3] | 56 | 34 |
| 4831[16] | **Brother Roy (66)** (TGMills) **3-9-7** ADaly(11) (led over 4f) | nk | **16** | 16/1 | 55 | 33 |
| 4866[9] | **Chabrol (CAN) (65)** (TTClement) **3-9-3**(3) JoHunnam(12) (in tch: rdn 4f out: sn btn) | 1¼ | **17** | 16/1 | 52 | 30 |
| 2945[9] | **Commin' Up (65)** (JWHills) **3-9-3**(3) RFfrench(9) (bit bkwd: s.i.s: sn prom: wknd 3f out) | 3 | **18** | 12/1 | 47 | 25 |
| 4606[7] | **Hadadabble (45)** (PatMitchell) **3-8-0**ow1 LNewton(8) (a bhd) | ½ | **19** | 20/1 | 26 | 3 |
| 4882[14] | **Funky (43)** (DNicholls) **3-7-12** MBaird(20) (bhd fnl 3f) | 1½ | **20** | 11/1 | 21 | — |
| 4480[3] | **Scimitar (53)** (PJMakin) **3-8-5**(3) DSweeney(1) (swtg: hld up: rdn over 3f out: eased whn btn) | 17 | **21** | 9/1[2] | 1 | — |
| | | | | (SP 140.0%) | **21 Rn** | |

**1m 52.6** (1.60) CSF £311.94 CT £3,948.09 TOTE £11.80: £2.80 £7.90 £2.80 £4.00 (£156.60) Trio £1,273.60 OWNER Mr W. H. Ponsonby (UPPER LAMBOURN) BRED R. Barber

LONG HANDICAP Burning Flame 7-6 Dauphin (IRE) 7-9

STEWARDS' ENQUIRY Murphy susp. 11-12/11/96 (excessive use of whip).

**4898 Whispering Dawn** got out on terms this time and burst through in the Dip to seal the issue. She missed the summer and so came here quite fresh. (14/1)
**Peppers (IRE)** missed the kick and was ridden with more restraint, but she was really flying in the closing stages and probably ought to have won. (25/1)
**4781 Allstars Rocket** seems to have found his ideal trip, sticking to his task in the final furlong without being able to quicken. (12/1)
**4042* Dauphin (IRE)**, dropped in trip, was wisely made plenty of use of and his winning bid only just failed. (10/1: 8/1-12/1)
**4480* Shouldbegrey** ruined his chance by pulling too hard in the early stages. He edged slightly left in the final furlong, but still stayed on. (10/1)
**2738 Burning Flame** does not seem to have a trip, for he was just getting going here having finished weakly over further in the past. (33/1)
**4582 Sistar Act** (14/1: 10/1-16/1)
**4480 Scimitar** (9/1: 16/1-8/1)

T/Jkpt: Not won; £10,650.09 to Newmarket 2/11/96. T/Plpt: £227.00 (71.43 Tckts). T/Qdpt: £28.80 (71.17 Tckts). Dk

# 4962-NEWMARKET (R-H) (Good)
## Saturday November 2nd

WEATHER: overcast, showers WIND: str across

## 4969 E.B.F. BALATON LODGE MAIDEN STKS (2-Y.O F) (Class D)

1-00 (1-01) **7f (Rowley)** £4,142.50 (£1,240.00: £595.00: £272.50) Stalls: Centre GOING minus 0.25 sec per fur (GF)

| | | | | SP | RR | SF |
|---|---|---|---|---|---|---|
| | **Palisade (USA)** (HRACecil) **2-8-11** WRyan(20) (unf: a.p: led over 2f out: rdn & r.o wl appr fnl f) | — | **1** | 12/1 | 85+ | 50 |
| | **Rebecca Sharp** (GWragg) **2-8-11** MHills(24) (unf: hld up: hdwy 3f out: sn ev ch: no imp appr fnl f) | 1¼ | **2** | 7/2[1] | 82+ | 47 |
| | **Coretta (IRE)** (LMCumani) **2-8-11** OUrbina(23) (b.nr hind: scope: hdwy over 1f out: r.o) | 1½ | **3** | 14/1 | 79+ | 44 |
| 4061[3] | **Silver Kristal** (RAkehurst) **2-8-11** TQuinn(16) (bit bkwd: hdwy 2f out: r.o) | ½ | **4** | 6/1[3] | 78 | 43 |
| | **St Blaine (CAN)** (DRLoder) **2-8-11** DRMcCabe(1) (w'like: scope: bit bkwd: prom stands' side: r.o wl fnl f) | hd | **5** | 25/1 | 77 | 42 |
| | **Gingersnap** (HRACecil) **2-8-11** PatEddery(21) (w'like: scope: led over 4f) | 1 | **6** | 5/1[2] | 75 | 40 |
| | **Beguine (USA)** (WJarvis) **2-8-11** JWeaver(3) (w'like: leggy: led stands' side: one pce fnl 2f) | s.h | **7** | 14/1 | 75 | 40 |
| | **Sharkiyah (IRE)** (RWArmstrong) **2-8-11** RHills(9) (unf: scope: chsd ldrs stands' side: rdn 2f out: no imp) | 1 | **8** | 14/1 | 73 | 38 |
| | **Doyella (IRE)** (DRLoder) **2-8-8**(3) PMcCabe(2) (unf: nvr nrr) | 1½ | **9** | 20/1 | 69 | 34 |
| | **Night Sceptre (IRE)** (RWArmstrong) **2-8-11** GCarter(17) (w'like: s.i.s: bhd tl rdn & r.o appr fnl f) | hd | **10** | 33/1 | 69 | 34 |
| | **Nubile** (BWHills) **2-8-8**(3) JDSmith(8) (w'like: lt-f: bit bkwd: nvr nrr) | hd | **11** | 33/1 | 69 | 34 |
| | **Russian Olive** (LMCumani) **2-8-11** JFortune(10) (b.hind: leggy: lt-f: prom stands' side over 4f) | 1 | **12** | 25/1 | 67 | 32 |
| | **Maroulla (IRE)** (MRStoute) **2-8-11** KDarley(13) (w'like: dwlt: sn prom: wknd over 2f out) | hd | **13** | 20/1 | 66 | 31 |
| 3706[8] | **Double Eight (IRE)** (BWHills) **2-8-11** GDuffield(7) (nvr nr to chal) | nk | **14** | 20/1 | 66 | 31 |
| | **Glacier** (LordHuntingdon) **2-8-11** DHarrison(11) (leggy: unf: sn prom: rdn over 2f out: wknd) | 2 | **15** | 25/1 | 61 | 26 |
| | **Marozia (USA)** (JHMGosden) **2-8-11** LDettori(4) (unf: scope: w ldrs stands' side 5f) | ½ | **16** | 9/1 | 60 | 25 |
| | **La Curamalal (IRE)** (GWragg) **2-8-11** AClark(5) (w'like: leggy: chsd ldrs stands' side: rdn over 2f out: sn wknd) | nk | **17** | 50/1 | 59 | 24 |
| 4798[5] | **Free As A Bird** (MRChannon) **2-8-11** JFEgan(19) (prom: rdn 3f out: sn wknd) | ½ | **18** | 25/1 | 58 | 23 |
| 4570[8] | **Blueygreen** (PWChapple-Hyam) **2-8-11** NDay(6) (chsd ldrs stands' side over 4f) | 2 | **19** | 16/1 | 54 | 19 |
| 4861[13] | **Damanka (IRE)** (MBell) **2-8-11** MFenton(15) (a bhd) | 1½ | **20** | 50/1 | 50 | 15 |
| 4697[10] | **Jucinda** (JPearce) **2-8-11** GBardwell(22) (prom 4f) | 1¼ | **21** | 50/1 | 47 | 12 |
| | **Pointelle** (AHide) **2-8-11** AMcGlone(18) (leggy: lt-f: wl bhd fnl 3f) | nk | **22** | 33/1 | 47 | 12 |

| | Horse | Dist | Pos | SP | RR | SF |
|---|---|---|---|---|---|---|
| | **Apple Brandy (USA)** (GLewis) **2-8-11** GHind(14) (leggy: s.i.s: a bhd: t.o) | 25 | **23** | 33/1 | — | — |
| | | | | (SP 144.1%) | | **23 Rn** |

**1m 26.59** (2.09) CSF £55.81 TOTE £16.00: £4.60 £1.80 £6.10 (£44.30) Trio £351.90; £158.62 to Southwell 4/11/96 OWNER Mr K. Abdulla (NEWMARKET) BRED Juddmonte Farms

**Palisade (USA)**, quite a taking filly, if still unfurnished, is out of a Cheshire Oaks winner but, given the jockey booking, had to have been the stable's second string. Moving well to post, she showed commendable resolution after being in front for quite some time. She is an interesting prospect for next year. (12/1: op 6/1)

**Rebecca Sharp** had been working well and was fancied if the market is any guide. A good, long-striding mover, she looked likely to win when starting her run, but could not get by the determined winner. There are races to be won with her and she should stay a little further. (7/2)

**Coretta (IRE)** did not take everyone's eye in the paddock but, considering her middle-distance pedigree, she showed plenty of promise by finishing so strongly, and is one to note. (14/1: 10/1-16/1)

**4061 Silver Kristal** did not break as well as some and did her running late this time. She still looks as if there is plenty left to work on. (6/1)

**St Blaine (CAN)** has plenty of scope for improvement and did not look ready, but came home really well and ought to win a race. (25/1)

**Gingersnap**, a very good mover, looked more in need of the race than her winning stable-companion and got tired in the last couple of furlongs. She has a pedigree that is hard to call, being a half-sister to the sprinter Leap For Joy but by a sire, Salse, who seems to impart more stamina than he had himself. (5/1: 3/1-11/2)

**Beguine (USA)**, a half-sister to the stable's former star Grand Lodge, is still on the leg, but ought to progress. He raced pleasingly throughout, close the stands' rail, where the ground has been at its slowest at recent meetings. (14/1)

**Sharkiyah (IRE)** shaped with some promise, but is not really bred to stay any further. (14/1: 10/1-16/1)

**Night Sceptre (IRE)**, who has plenty of stamina on her dam's side. was not helped by a sluggish start and only began to get going at the eleventh hour. (33/1)

**Marozia (USA)**, a fine mover who is not bred to stay middle-distances, showed up well for a long way. (9/1: 5/1-10/1)

## 4970 NGK SPARK PLUGS (S) STKS (2-Y.O) (Class E)

1-30 (1-35) **1m (Rowley)** £4,077.50 (£1,220.00: £585.00: £267.50) Stalls: Centre GOING minus 0.25 sec per fur (GF)

| | Horse | Dist | Pos | SP | RR | SF |
|---|---|---|---|---|---|---|
| 4715$^{5}$ | **Aficionado (IRE) (66)** (RFJohnsonHoughton) **2-8-11** GDuffield(19) (hdwy 4f out: rdn over 1f out: r.o to ld nr fin) | — | **1** | 10/1 | 71 | 35 |
| 4795$^{8}$ | **Hallmark (IRE) (67)** (RHannon) **2-8-11** DaneO'Neill(18) (mde all centre: led over 1f out: sn rdn: ct nr fin) | hd | **2** | 10/1 | 71 | 35 |
| 4795$^{9}$ | **Heggies (IRE) (57)** (CREgerton) **2-8-11** LDettori(7) (chsd ldrs: outpcd over 2f out: r.o wl fnl f) | 2½ | **3** | 20/1 | 66 | 30 |
| 4883$^{7}$ | **Princess of Hearts (66)** (BJMeehan) **2-8-9b** TQuinn(10) (led: hung rt over 2f out: hdd over 1f out: rallied ins fnl f) | 1 | **4** | 9/2$^{2}$ | 62 | 26 |
| 4041$^{11}$ | **Motcombs Club (68)** (NACallaghan) **2-8-11** PatEddery(5) (chsd ldrs: rdn over 2f out: wknd ins fnl f) | hd | **5** | 2/1$^{1}$ | 64 | 28 |
| 4715$^{4}$ | **Summerville Wood (63)** (PMooney) **2-8-11b**(3) PMcCabe(20) (chsd ldrs tl wknd appr fnl f) | 3 | **6** | 12/1 | 61 | 25 |
| 4792$^{6}$ | **Imperial Or Metric (IRE) (74)** (JBerry) **2-9-0** KDarley(2) (prom tl rdn & btn 2f out) | s.h | **7** | 9/1$^{3}$ | 61 | 25 |
| *4780$^{3}$* | **Royal Roulette (58)** (SPCWoods) **2-8-6** DBiggs(11) (nvr nrr) | 4 | **8** | 20/1 | 45 | 9 |
| 4756$^{16}$ | **Double-O** (WJarvis) **2-8-11** SSanders(14) (in tch: rdn 3f out: hung lft & sn btn) | ½ | **9** | 20/1 | 49 | 13 |
| | **Beveled Mill** (PDEvans) **2-8-6** JFEgan(3) (lt-f: nvr trbld ldrs) | 2 | **10** | 20/1 | 40 | 4 |
| | **Northern Touch** (SCWilliams) **2-8-6** DRMcCabe(8) (w'like: dwlt: nvr nrr) | 3½ | **11** | 40/1 | 33 | — |
| | **Santella Twinkle (IRE)** (DMorris) **2-8-6** NDay(4) (small: lt-f: prom 5f) | hd | **12** | 40/1 | 32 | — |
| *4091$^{9}$* | **Mellwood (IRE) (50)** (MHTompkins) **2-8-8**(3) MHenry(1) (bit bkwd: nvr nr to chal) | 1¼ | **13** | 40/1 | 35 | — |
| | **Ike's Pet** (MAJarvis) **2-8-6b$^{1}$** PBloomfield(6) (lt-f: prom tl rdn & btn 2f out) | nk | **14** | 20/1 | 29 | — |
| 4762$^{13}$ | **Flood's Hot Stuff (55)** (MRChannon) **2-8-7**ow1 RPerham(17) (dwlt: sn prom: wknd over 2f out) | 1¾ | **15** | 40/1 | 27 | — |
| | **Zafarelli** (SCWilliams) **2-8-11** GCarter(16) (leggy: bkwd: dwlt: a bhd) | 5 | **16** | 25/1 | 21 | — |
| 4790$^{13}$ | **Mechilie** (JWPayne) **2-8-6** MTebbutt(13) (bit bkwd: a bhd) | 5 | **17** | 33/1 | 6 | — |
| 4715$^{23}$ | **Sam's Yer Man** (SCWilliams) **2-8-11** GHind(12) (a bhd) | 1¾ | **18** | 25/1 | 7 | — |
| 4720$^{16}$ | **Rinca** (JPearce) **2-8-6** GBardwell(22) (sn wl bhd) | ½ | **19** | 25/1 | 1 | — |
| 4715$^{22}$ | **Prince Jordan** (ICampbell) **2-9-0**ow3 MWigham(15) (hdwy 5f out: wknd over 2f out) | 2½ | **20** | 40/1 | 4 | — |
| 4607$^{W}$ | **Don't Fool Me (IRE)** (PMooney) **2-8-11** SDWilliams(21) (s.s: a bhd) | 1½ | **21** | 40/1 | — | — |
| 4780$^{13}$ | **Sheeba** (MissAEEmbiricos) **2-7-13**(7) AMcCarthy(9) (Withdrawn not under Starter's orders: uns rdr & bolted bef s) | | **W** | 50/1 | — | — |
| | | | | (SP 142.3%) | | **21 Rn** |

**1m 41.18** (3.88) CSF £105.48 TOTE £11.70: £3.60 £3.20 £3.40 (£37.40) Trio £431.50 OWNER Mr Anthony Pye-Jeary (DIDCOT) BRED Hadi Al Tajir

No bid

**4715 Aficionado (IRE)** could not beat Princess of Hearts or Summerville Wood on their running over course and distance at the last meeting, but saw out this trip well. (10/1)

**4103 Hallmark (IRE)** led the group in the centre of the track, but took some time to gain the overall lead. Just collared in the shadow of the post, this does appear to be his trip. (10/1)

**1989 Heggies (IRE)** came out best of the stands'-side group after getting outpaced at a vital stage. She is bred to stay middle-distances next year. (20/1)

**4883 Princess of Hearts** blotted her copybook, for she looked to have this won when going a couple of lengths up on the bridle with most of those behind hard at work. However, she hung and surrendered the lead, only to run on again when all was lost. (9/2)

**Motcombs Club** ran his best race yet, but finally had to give best inside the final furlong. (2/1: 3/1-7/4)

**4715 Summerville Wood**, made more use of this time, did not run to his best. (12/1: op 7/1)

**4792 Imperial Or Metric (IRE)** (9/1: 6/1-10/1)

## 4971 EQUITY FINANCIAL COLLECTIONS CONDITIONS STKS (2 & 3-Y.O) (Class C)

2-05 (2-06) **6f (Rowley)** £4,801.80 (£1,774.20: £849.10: £344.50: £134.25: £50.15) Stalls: Centre GOING minus 0.25 sec per fur (GF)

| | Horse | Dist | Pos | SP | RR | SF |
|---|---|---|---|---|---|---|
| 4772$^{18}$ | **Saheeel (USA) (89)** (SbinSuroor) **3-9-8** LDettori(2) (lw: mde all: rdn & r.o wl ins fnl f) | — | **1** | 6/1 | 96 | 73 |
| 4418a$^{2}$ | **How Long (100)** (LMCumani) **3-9-8** OUrbina(8) (lw: chsd ldrs: chal over 1f out: unable qckn ins fnl f) | 1¼ | **2** | 3/1$^{2}$ | 93 | 70 |
| 4723$^{5}$ | **Vasari (IRE) (98)** (MRChannon) **2-8-8** TQuinn(7) (a.p: rdn over 1f out: one pce) | nk | **3** | 7/2$^{3}$ | 97 | 55 |
| 4592* | **Volley (IRE)** (JBerry) **3-9-3** GCarter(5) (outpcd: rdn over 2f out: r.o fnl f) | 1¼ | **4** | 11/2 | 84 | 61 |
| 4786* | **Unshaken (84)** (JRFanshawe) **2-8-5** DHarrison(3) (trckd ldrs over 4f: sn rdn & btn) | 3 | **5** | 9/4$^{1}$ | 83 | 41 |
| 4689$^{9}$ | **Naissant (75)** (RMMcKellar) **3-9-3** JCarroll(1) (prom 4f) | 2 | **6** | 33/1 | 70 | 47 |
| 4800$^{9}$ | **Agnella (IRE) (79)** (GLMoore) **3-9-3** GDuffield(6) (s.i.s: a bhd) | 3 | **7** | 33/1 | 62 | 39 |

4824[13] **Windrush Holly** (JRBosley) **3-9-0** CRutter(4) (reard s: sn outpcd & bhd) ....nk **8** 100/1 58 35
(SP 114.5%) **8 Rn**

**1m 12.63** (0.83) CSF £23.09 TOTE £5.80: £1.60 £1.50 £1.80 (£8.90) OWNER Godolphin (NEWMARKET) BRED Darley Stud Management
WEIGHT FOR AGE 2yo-19lb

**4561 Saheeel (USA)** returned to his best after a couple of modest efforts and proved a tough horse to pass. (6/1: 4/1-13/2)
**4418a How Long,** dropped to sprinting for the first time, was not made that much use of and could not quicken enough in the final furlong. He moved down poorly, but was the clear form choice for this race and trip and the tactics look to blame. (3/1)
**4723 Vasari (IRE)** has held his form well through autumn but, hard as he tried, he could not peg back the winner in the final furlong. (7/2: 5/2-4/1)
**4592* Volley (IRE)** shaped as if she needs a longer trip. (11/2)
**4786* Unshaken,** cruising close to the leaders to the Dip, has yet to prove she stays beyond five furlongs. (9/4)
**4485 Naissant** seems to have gone off the boil in recent weeks. (33/1)

## 4972 BEN MARSHALL STKS (Listed) (3-Y.O+) (Class A)

2-40 (2-40) **1m (Rowley)** £11,169.00 (£4,131.00: £1,980.50: £807.50: £318.75: £123.25) Stalls: Centre GOING minus 0.25 sec per fur (GF)

| | | | | SP | RR | SF |
|---|---|---|---|---|---|---|
| 4479* | **Ali-Royal (IRE) (114)** (HRACecil) **3-8-13** PatEddery(7) (swtg: trckd ldrs: led over 1f out: rdn & r.o strly) | — | **1** | 9/4[1] | 118 | 69 |
| 4757[2] | **Nijo (102)** (DRLoder) **5-8-12** DRMcCabe(1) (set stdy pce: rdn & hdd over 1f out: r.o ins fnl f) | 1¼ | **2** | 14/1 | 113 | 66 |
| 4671* | **Fatefully (USA) (108)** (SbinSuroor) **3-8-8** LDettori(3) (trckd ldrs: rdn over 2f out: one pce) | s.h | **3** | 7/2[2] | 110 | 61 |
| 4870[3] | **Celestial Key (USA) (105)** (MJohnston) **6-8-12** JWeaver(5) (plld hrd: trckd ldrs: no imp fnl 2f) | 2½ | **4** | 12/1 | 107 | 60 |
| 4718[3] | **My Branch (112)** (BWHills) **3-8-8** MHills(4) (lw: hld up: hdwy whn nt clr run over 1f out: nvr able to chal) | 1½ | **5** | 11/2 | 102 | 53 |
| 4649a[2] | **Cool Edge (IRE) (110)** (MHTompkins) **5-9-1** NDay(8) (lw: hld up & plld hrd: hdwy 3f out: rdn over 1f out: one pce) | hd | **6** | 12/1 | 107 | 60 |
| 4664a[8] | **Centre Stalls (IRE) (113)** (RFJohnsonHoughton) **3-8-13** SSanders(2) (hld up & plld hrd: hdwy 3f out: rdn & btn 2f out) | ¾ | **7** | 4/1[3] | 106 | 57 |
| 4757[10] | **Lionize (USA)** (PWChapple-Hyam) **3-8-10** DHarrison(6) (trckd ldr: rdn 3f out: sn btn) | 1¼ | **8** | 25/1 | 86 t | 51 |

(SP 114.3%) **8 Rn**

**1m 38.0** (0.70) CSF £28.67 TOTE £3.10: £1.40 £2.20 £1.50 (£23.70) OWNER Greenbay Stables Ltd (NEWMARKET) BRED C. H. WACKER III
WEIGHT FOR AGE 3yo-2lb

**4479* Ali-Royal (IRE)** did not take the eye in the paddock having got warm, but gave the sort of performance that will have had those who supported him through the summer tearing their hair out. What we learnt here was that he does get a mile in a slowly-run race, that he likes a bit of cut in the ground and that he loves Headquarters. After all, the run that brought him to everyone's attentions was over the course in May. (9/4)
**4757 Nijo,** allowed to wait in front once again, was suited by it and ran a sound race, coming back for more inside the final furlong. (14/1)
**4671* Fatefully (USA),** as usual, had her tongue tied down, but had turned in her coat. Moving well to post, she appeared to run her race out well enough, although unable to pick up sufficiently inside the final furlong. (7/2: 5/2-4/1)
**4870 Celestial Key (USA),** a surprise winner of this race last year, could not repeat the feat after refusing to settle at the dawdling early pace. (12/1)
**4718 My Branch** looked the part, but moved to post rather scratchily. She looked to have been set a huge task as she was still last when the pace quickened, and interference just afterwards ended all hope. (11/2)
**4649a Cool Edge (IRE)** took too strong a hold, but ran respectably and does still seem on the upgrade. (12/1)

## 4973 ZETLAND STKS (Listed) (2-Y.O) (Class A)

3-10 (3-10) **1m 2f (Rowley)** £9,522.80 (£3,525.20: £1,692.60: £693.00: £276.50: £109.90) Stalls: High GOING minus 0.25 sec per fur (GF)

| | | | | SP | RR | SF |
|---|---|---|---|---|---|---|
| 4585* | **Silver Patriarch (IRE) (84)** (JLDunlop) **2-8-11** PatEddery(9) (a.p: led 1f out: rdn out) | — | **1** | 9/2[2] | 91 | 43 |
| 4477* | **Eldorado (IRE)** (MJohnston) **2-8-11** JWeaver(8) (lw: a.p: ev ch over 2f out: r.o wl fnl f) | ¾ | **2** | 5/2[1] | 90 | 42 |
| 3668[4] | **Shadow Lead (96)** (LMCumani) **2-8-11** LDettori(7) (hld up: hdwy 2f out: r.o ins fnl f) | nk | **3** | 9/2[2] | 89 | 41 |
| 4565[5] | **Attitre (FR) (89)** (CEBrittain) **2-8-6** SSanders(1) (plld hrd: prom: led wl over 1f out: hdd 1f out: no ex) | ¾ | **4** | 16/1 | 83 | 35 |
| 4696[2] | **Atlantic Desire (IRE) (84)** (MJohnston) **2-8-6** RHills(3) (lw: ed over 8f: one pce) | 1 | **5** | 14/1 | 82 | 34 |
| 4696[3] | **Mister Pink (85)** (RFJohnsonHoughton) **2-8-11b** KDarley(4) (chsd ldrs 8f) | 3 | **6** | 20/1 | 82 | 34 |
| 4760* | **Bold Words (CAN) (90)** (EALDunlop) **2-9-0** WRyan(6) (lw: hld up: rdn 3f out: sn btn) | 1¼ | **7** | 11/1 | 83 | 35 |
| 4361* | **Swallow Breeze (67)** (DrJDScargill) **2-8-6** GBardwell(2) (in tch: rdn over 2f out: sn btn) | 3½ | **8** | 50/1 | 69 | 21 |
| 4213[2] | **Cinema Paradiso** (PFICole) **2-8-11** TQuinn(5) (lw: hld up & plld hrd: hdwy over 3f out: wknd & eased fnl 2f) | 3 | **9** | 14/1 | 69 | 21 |
| 4797* | **My Valentina (85)** (BWHills) **2-8-6** MHills(10) (trckd ldrs: rdn over 2f out: sn wknd & eased) | 6 | **10** | 7/1[3] | 55 | 7 |

(SP 111.7%) **10 Rn**

**2m 7.53** (3.93) CSF £14.69 TOTE £5.00: £1.50 £1.80 £1.80 (£5.30) Trio £11.90 OWNER Mr Peter Winfield (ARUNDEL) BRED Peter Winfield

**4585* Silver Patriarch (IRE),** already a distance winner, is bred to stay well and took this step up in class in his stride, holding on well in a driving finish. (9/2)
**4477* Eldorado (IRE)** showed a lovely action going down and was still running on strongly at the line after losing a good pitch going into the Dip. He looks a good prospect for next year. (5/2: 2/1-3/1)
**3668 Shadow Lead,** taking a big step up in trip, had not run since finishing behind Revoque and In Command at York over ten weeks ago. Looking fit, he weaved his way through to challenge inside the final furlong and is obviously very useful. (9/2)
**4565 Attitre (FR)** took a good grip and was made plenty of use of, but still seemed to stay the trip. (16/1)
**4696 Atlantic Desire (IRE)** went to post rather keenly and could do nothing extra once headed. (14/1)
**4696 Mister Pink,** stepping up in class, did not have the pace to compete in the last two furlongs. (20/1)
**4760* Bold Words (CAN)** (11/1: 6/1-12/1)
**4797* My Valentina** is not bred to get this trip and went to post far too keenly, so it was no surprise when her effort fizzled out with two furlongs left. (7/1: 9/2-15/2)

## 4974 LADBROKE AUTUMN H'CAP (0-100) (3-Y.O+) (Class C)

3-45 (3-46) **1m (Rowley)** £22,900.00 (£8,500.00: £4,100.00: £1,700.00: £700.00: £300.00) Stalls: Centre GOING minus 0.25 sec per fur (GF)

| | | | | SP | RR | SF |
|---|---|---|---|---|---|---|
| 4901[15] | **Saifan (83)** (DMorris) **7-8-13b** NDay(7) (hdwy 3f out: led over 1f out: drvn out) | — | **1** | 33/1 | 94 | 65 |
| 4674* | **Prince Babar (98)** (JEBanks) **5-9-7**(7) RMullen(11) (w ldrs: led wl over 1f out: sn hdd: r.o) | nk | **2** | 14/1 | 108 | 79 |

| Horse | Dist | Pos | SP | RR | SF |
|---|---|---|---|---|---|
| 4568[28] **Kayvee (97)** (GHarwood) **7-9-13** AClark(14) (hld up: hdwy 2f out: r.o) | ¾ | **3** | 25/1 | 106 | 77 |
| 4872[4] **Dreams End (75)** (PBowen) **8-8-5** GDuffield(19) (gd hdwy over 1f out: fin wl) | 1 | **4** | 20/1 | 82 | 53 |
| 4568[12] **Sky Dome (IRE) (88)** (MHTompkins) **3-9-2** TQuinn(2) (w ldr: led 4f out: hdd wl over 1f out: sn btn) | ½ | **5** | 20/1 | 94 | 63 |
| 4769[3] **Artful Dane (IRE) (73)** (MJHeaton-Ellis) **4-8-3v** SDrowne(8) (hdwy 3f out: ev ch 1f out: sn btn) | s.h | **6** | 25/1 | 79 | 50 |
| 4769[2] **High Premium (82)** (RAFahey) **8-8-12** ACulhane(12) (chsd ldrs: rdn 3f out: one pce fnl f) | ¾ | **7** | 10/1[2] | 86 | 57 |
| 4686[12] **Master Beveled (73)** (PDEvans) **6-8-3** JFEgan(3) (b.off hind: lw: led stands' side: outpcd over 2f out: r.o fnl f) | 1 | **8** | 25/1 | 75 | 46 |
| 4769[6] **Sandmoor Chambray (80)** (TDEasterby) **5-8-10b** MBirch(17) (chsd ldrs: rdn 3f out: kpt on same pce) | hd | **9** | 25/1 | 82 | 53 |
| 4769* **Hawksley Hill (IRE) (90)** (MrsJRRamsden) **3-9-4** JFortune(15) (hld up: hdwy 3f out: rdn & no imp fnl f) | 1¼ | **10** | 9/2[1] | 90 | 59 |
| 4901[2] **Duello (69)** (MBlanshard) **5-7-13** JQuinn(1) (trckd ldr stands' side: btn 3f out) | ¾ | **11** | 16/1 | 67 | 38 |
| 4769[16] **Flying North (IRE) (74)** (MrsMReveley) **3-8-2** DRMcCabe(13) (dwlt: nvr nrr) | 1 | **12** | 33/1 | 70 | 39 |
| 833[10] **Carburton (86)** (JAGlover) **3-9-0** SSanders(4) (led 4f: wknd 2f out) | ½ | **13** | 11/1[3] | 81 | 50 |
| 4688[25] **Royal Jade (69)** (BWHills) **3-7-4**(7) RFfrench(9) (b.hind: nvr rchd ldrs) | 1¾ | **14** | 16/1 | 61 | 30 |
| 4769[12] **Catch The Lights (81)** (RHannon) **3-8-9** DaneO'Neill(21) (prom over 4f: eased fnl f) | nk | **15** | 33/1 | 72 | 41 |
| 4775[7] **Delta Soleil (USA) (86)** (PWHarris) **4-9-2** GHind(25) (lw: s.i.s: a bhd) | 1¾ | **16** | 12/1 | 74 | 45 |
| 4682[12] **Tremplin (USA) (82)** (NACallaghan) **4-8-12** SWhitworth(5) (s.i.s: a bhd) | hd | **17** | 25/1 | 69 | 40 |
| 4719* **Saltando (IRE) (66)** (PatMitchell) **5-7-10** LCharnock(10) (nvr nr ldrs) | 1½ | **18** | 50/1 | 50 | 21 |
| 4874[8] **Committal (IRE) (96)** (JHMGosden) **3-9-10** LDettori(6) (lw: nvr nr to chal) | 6 | **19** | 25/1 | 68 | 37 |
| 4511* **Ashby Hill (IRE) (70)** (RRowe) **5-8-0**ow1 GCarter(18) (bhd fnl 3f) | 5 | **20** | 11/1[3] | 32 | 2 |
| 4769[11] **Gladys Althorpe (IRE) (72)** (JLEyre) **3-8-0** TWilliams(23) (bhd fnl 3f) | 3 | **21** | 16/1 | 28 | — |
| 4769[8] **Winston (70)** (JDBethell) **3-7-7**(5)ow1 MartinDwyer(24) (lw: prom: rdn 4f out: sn bhd) | 1¼ | **22** | 12/1 | 24 | — |
| 4682[2] **Alsahib (USA) (68)** (WRMuir) **3-7-10** DeclanO'Shea(20) (bhd fnl 3f) | 1 | **23** | 10/1[2] | 20 | — |
| 4885[4] **Welton Arsenal (90)** (MRChannon) **4-9-6v**1 CandyMorris(26) (lw: hld up & plld hrd: n.d) | nk | **24** | 50/1 | 41 | 12 |
| 4824[6] **Scarpetta (USA) (73)** (JWHills) **3-7-12**(3) MHenry(22) (chsd ldrs 5f) | s.h | **25** | 40/1 | 24 | — |
| 4826[15] **Red Rainbow (80)** (BHanbury) **8-8-10** WRyan(16) (t.o fnl 3f) | 9 | **26** | 50/1 | 13 | — |

(SP 142.5%) **26 Rn**

**1m 38.37** (1.07) CSF £429.15 CT £10,305.32 TOTE £56.50: £10.40 £3.90 £4.90 £4.80 (£489.80) Trio £2,197.10 OWNER Mrs L. Brook (NEWMARKET) BRED M. M. Nashar

LONG HANDICAP Saltando (IRE) 7-2

WEIGHT FOR AGE 3yo-2lb

**OFFICIAL EXPLANATION Saifan: Regarding the apparent improvement in form, the trainer stated that the gelding sat down in the stalls, missed the break and consequently lost interest on his last start.**

**4769 Saifan** is just the sort of inconsistent type bookmakers love to see in this type of handicap, although the key to him is the start - he gets worked up going into the stalls and often loses many lengths. Getting his best start in years, the others were going to struggle once he got to the front and, although he was tying up close home, he lasted out for his biggest success since winning the Rothmans North South Challenge Final over the course and distance in 1993. (33/1)

**4674* Prince Babar** did his trainer nothing but credit in these days where big handicap winners are often lightly-raced or laid out, and it is sad to see such an honest horse fail to land any of the big handicaps whilst consistently rising in the Ratings. (14/1)

**4444 Kayvee** ran to his best and looked a possible danger on meeting the rising ground, but just failed to maintain the effort. He often runs well here and it is extraordinary that he has failed to win in seventeen appearances at Headquarters. (25/1)

**4872 Dreams End** needs further and was just about last at halfway. Weaving his way through the pack, he finished with a tremendous flourish and remains in fine heart. (20/1)

**3805* Sky Dome (IRE)** ran a fine race without being able to dominate, as natural front-runners do not often thrive with company. (20/1)

**4769 Artful Dane (IRE)** ran another good race, although the Handicapper does seem to have his measure. (25/1)

**4769* Hawksley Hill (IRE)**, up 7lb for his recent win over course and distance, was again forced to work to close on the leaders, but this time the effort petered out in the Dip. (9/2)

**709 Carburton** looked as fit as he could have been made without a run, but the absence since April proved too big a burden. He should not be written off. (11/1: 8/1-12/1)

## 4975 BURROUGH GREEN H'CAP (0-80) (3-Y.O+) (Class D)

4-15 (4-22) **7f (Rowley)** £4,788.90 (£1,438.20: £693.60: £321.30) Stalls: Centre GOING minus 0.25 sec per fur (GF)

| Horse | Dist | Pos | SP | RR | SF |
|---|---|---|---|---|---|
| 4688* **Persian Fayre (79)** (JBerry) **4-9-13** KDarley(5) (w ldr: led over 3f out: rdn out) | — | **1** | 11/1 | 89 | 71 |
| 4805[3] **Indiahra (48)** (JLEyre) **5-7-3v**(7) RFfrench(17) (in tch: effrt & ev ch 2f out: unable qckn ins fnl f) | nk | **2** | 16/1 | 57 | 39 |
| 4686[5] **Broughton's Pride (IRE) (50)** (JLEyre) **5-7-12**ow2 TWilliams(1) (lw: a.p: one pce appr fnl f) | 1¾ | **3** | 16/1 | 55 | 35 |
| 4802[3] **Stoppes Brow (75)** (GLMoore) **4-9-9v** SWhitworth(15) (hdwy 3f out: no ex appr fnl f) | ¾ | **4** | 14/1 | 79 | 61 |
| 4775[6] **Broughtons Turmoil (77)** (WJMusson) **7-9-11** DRMcCabe(3) (hdwy over 1f out: fin wl) | nk | **5** | 12/1 | 80 | 62 |
| 4820* **Amber Fort (75)** (DRCElsworth) **3-9-3v**(5) DGriffiths(27) (r.o wl appr fnl f: nvr nrr) | 2 | **6** | 5/1[1] | 73 | 54 |
| 4581[12] **Tiler (IRE) (77)** (MJohnston) **4-9-11** JWeaver(13) (lw: chsd ldrs: rdn 2f out: one pce) | ½ | **7** | 33/1 | 74 | 56 |
| 4583[11] **Sualtach (IRE) (80)** (RHollinshead) **3-9-13** LDettori(4) (trckd ldrs: rdn 2f out: one pce) | 1¾ | **8** | 16/1 | 73 | 54 |
| 4000[12] **Bowcliffe (48)** (MrsAMNaughton) **5-7-10** NAdams(18) (bhd tl hdwy 2f out: nvr able to chal) | nk | **9** | 50/1 | 41 | 23 |
| 4595[6] **Mountgate (75)** (MPBielby) **4-9-9** DeanMcKeown(22) (hld up: effrt 2f out: no imp) | 1 | **10** | 25/1 | 65 | 47 |
| 4820[12] **Ben Gunn (67)** (PTWalwyn) **4-9-1** JCarroll(10) (lw: chsd ldrs tl wknd 3f out) | nk | **11** | 25/1 | 57 | 39 |
| 4769[4] **Impulsive Air (IRE) (65)** (EWeymes) **4-8-13** JQuinn(6) (lw: w ldrs over 4f) | 1 | **12** | 14/1 | 52 | 34 |
| 4820[18] **Knobbleeneeze (70)** (MRChannon) **6-9-4v** TQuinn(12) (chsd ldrs 5f) | hd | **13** | 20/1 | 57 | 39 |
| 4909[3] **Quilling (72)** (MDods) **4-9-3**(3) FLynch(29) (dwlt: effrt over 2f out: nvr rchd ldrs) | 1½ | **14** | 10/1[3] | 56 | 38 |
| 4453[2] **Oberon's Dart (IRE) (73)** (PJMakin) **3-9-6** AClark(19) (bhd tl sme late hdwy) | nk | **15** | 16/1 | 56 | 37 |
| 4888[4] **Ballard Lady (IRE) (48)** (JSWainwright) **4-7-10** LCharnock(23) (lw: n.d) | 1¼ | **16** | 33/1 | 28 | 10 |
| 554[6] **Jibereen (70)** (PHowling) **4-9-4** JFEgan(21) (chsd ldrs: rdn 3f out: sn wknd) | 1¾ | **17** | 16/1 | 46 | 28 |
| 4820[22] **Double March (72)** (PRWebber) **3-9-5** RPerham(8) (s.s: sn rdn & chsng ldrs: wknd over 2f out) | s.h | **18** | 50/1 | 48 | 29 |
| 4820[7] **Winsome Wooster (60)** (PGMurphy) **5-8-8** SDrowne(28) (nvr nr ldrs) | 1 | **19** | 20/1 | 34 | 16 |
| 4865[7] **Euphyllia (49)** (BobJones) **4-7-11** FNorton(9) (swtg: nvr nr to chal) | s.h | **20** | 20/1 | 23 | 5 |
| 4802* **Charlie Sillett (83)** (BWHills) **4-10-3** MHills(24) (hld up & plld hrd: effrt 3f out: sn btn) | nk | **21** | 8/1[2] | 56 | 38 |
| 4376[13] **Ruwy (75)** (CJBenstead) **3-9-8** RHills(11) (swtg: prom over 4f: eased fnl f) | 1¼ | **22** | 33/1 | 45 | 26 |
| 4198[13] **No Extras (IRE) (77)** (GLMoore) **6-9-4**(7) JDennis(25) (b.off hind: dwlt: plld hrd: n.d) | s.h | **23** | 33/1 | 47 | 29 |
| 4788[9] **Maristax (70)** (PJMakin) **3-9-3** SSanders(14) (dwlt: rdn 4f out: nvr nr ldrs) | 3 | **24** | 25/1 | 33 | 14 |
| 1799[9] **Al Reet (IRE) (73)** (MDHammond) **5-9-7** JFortune(26) (a bhd) | ¾ | **25** | 40/1 | 34 | 16 |
| 4498[5] **Classic Beauty (IRE) (65)** (RHarris) **3-8-12** DBatteate(2) (a bhd) | ½ | **26** | 50/1 | 25 | 6 |
| 4820[17] **Chili Heights (48)** (GBBalding) **6-7-7v**(3) NVarley(7) (s.i.s: a bhd) | 1¼ | **27** | 50/1 | 5 | — |

| | | | | SP | RR | SF |
|---|---|---|---|---|---|---|
| 4693* | **Alpine Hideaway (IRE) (76)** (BHanbury) **3-9-9b$^{1}$** JStack(16) (led over 3f: wknd 2f out) | 1¼ | **28** | 20/1 | 31 | 12 |
| | | | | (SP 148.3%) | **28 Rn** | |

**1m 26.05** (1.55) CSF £177.90 CT £2,642.24 TOTE £12.60: £3.00 £4.50 £7.40 £6.50 (£167.70) Trio £1,426.40 OWNER Mr Murray Grubb (COCKERHAM) BRED Aramstone Stud Co
LONG HANDICAP Indiahra 7-8 Bowcliffe 7-7 Ballard Lady (IRE) 7-5 Chili Heights 7-6 Broughton's Pride (IRE) 7-9
WEIGHT FOR AGE 3yo-1lb
**4688* Persian Fayre** does seem to like to get his toe in and proved a hardy battler up the hill. (11/1)
**4805 Indiahra**, stepped up in trip, saw it out well and the ability has always been there. (16/1)
**4686 Broughton's Pride (IRE)**, well to the fore throughout, does look likely to win again off this sort of mark. (16/1)
**4802 Stoppes Brow** looked a big threat in the Dip, but is probably marginally better at six furlongs. (14/1)
**4775 Broughtons Turmoil** remains in good form as do most of the stable, but his effort proved too little too late. (12/1)
**4820* Amber Fort** went down keenly, but had a mountain to climb by the two-furlong pole before finishing best of all. (5/1)
**2023 Bowcliffe**, dropped in trip, was given a rather conservative ride as he was not set alight until the last couple of furlongs. (50/1)

T/Jkpt: Not won; £16,727.49 to Southwell 4/11/96. T/Plpt: £545.10 (57.03 Tckts). T/Qdpt: £35.60 (90.47 Tckts). Dk

## 4776-WOLVERHAMPTON (L-H) (Standard)
### Saturday November 2nd
WEATHER: dry WIND: fresh bhd

### 4976 PENDEFORD MEDIAN AUCTION MAIDEN STKS (2-Y.O) (Class E)
7-00 (7-02) **6f (Fibresand)** £3,184.00 (£952.00: £456.00: £208.00) Stalls: Low

| | | | | SP | RR | SF |
|---|---|---|---|---|---|---|
| 4469$^{3}$ | **Trailblazer** (CWThornton) **2-9-0** DeanMcKeown(11) (lw: hld up: hdwy ½-wy. qcknd to ld ins fnl f: pushed clr) | — | **1** | 11/4$^{2}$ | 66 | 48 |
| 4807$^{4}$ | **Cee-N-K (IRE)** (MJohnston) **2-9-0** JFanning(4) (lw: led after 2f tl hdd & outpcd fnl f) | 3 | **2** | 9/4$^{1}$ | 58 | 40 |
| *1080$^{7}$* | **Colins Choice** (JLSpearing) **2-8-6**(3) FLynch(2) (outpcd: hdwy 2f out: styd on ins fnl f) | 5 | **3** | 25/1 | 40 | 22 |
| 4241$^{9}$ | **Mythical** (SirMarkPrescott) **2-8-9** GDuffield(6) (hld up & bhd: effrt & shkn up 2f out: kpt on) | ¾ | **4** | 10/1 | 38 | 20 |
| 2985$^{5}$ | **Harmony In Red (72)** (JBerry) **2-9-0** GCarter(12) (bit bkwd: led after 1f: sn hdd: rdn after 2f out: edgd rt: sn btn) | hd | **5** | 14/1 | 42 | 24 |
| 3464$^{11}$ | **Fly Me Home** (BAMcMahon) **2-8-9**(5) LNewton(10) (bkwd: sn drvn along: nvr gng pce of ldrs) | 1 | **6** | 50/1 | 40 | 22 |
| 4903$^{9}$ | **Janie's Boy (74)** (RGuest) **2-9-0b$^{1}$** JQuinn(5) (in tch: c wd ent st: sn wknd) | 1 | **7** | 10/1 | 37 | 19 |
| 4786$^{9}$ | **Lochinvar (56)** (JSMoore) **2-9-0** JFEgan(9) (led 1f: hrd rdn & wknd 2f out: t.o) | 10 | **8** | 50/1 | 10 | — |
| 3478$^{10}$ | **Chilling (56)** (PGMurphy) **2-8-9** SDrowne(8) (swtg: trckd ldrs over 3f: sn wknd: t.o) | 4 | **9** | 33/1 | — | — |
| 4715$^{21}$ | **Swynford Charmer** (JFBottomley) **2-9-0** LCharnock(7) (b.hind: prom: hrd drvn over 2f out: sn lost tch: t.o) | nk | **10** | 8/1 | — | — |
| | **Henley (USA)** (DRLoder) **2-9-0** DRMcCabe(13) (neat: str: bkwd: s.s: a wl bhd: t.o) | 8 | **11** | 7/2$^{3}$ | — | — |
| 4825$^{14}$ | **Yabint El Sultan** (BAMcMahon) **2-8-9** SSanders(3) (a wl bhd: t.o) | dist | **12** | 20/1 | — | — |
| | | | | (SP 131.1%) | **12 Rn** | |

**1m 14.4** (0.90 under 2y best) (3.00) CSF £10.08 TOTE £4.30: £2.20 £1.80 £3.60 (£4.90) Trio £51.80 OWNER Mr Guy Reed (MIDDLEHAM) BRED Bearstone Stud
**4469 Trailblazer** turned in a scintillating display on this first appearance on the Sand and could now be finding his way. (11/4)
**4807 Cee-N-K (IRE)** finished much closer to the winner than he did when they last met and would seem to be on the upgrade. (9/4)
**895 Colins Choice**, a poor mover, showed her appreciation for this slightly longer trip, but looks to need further still. (25/1)
**Mythical**, still carrying surplus condition, could not get herself into the action, but she did stay on, and is beginning to grasp what is needed. (10/1)
**2985 Harmony In Red**, a tall colt for such a sharp track, went with the pace and, had he not drifted over towards the stands' rail in the straight, he may well have made the frame. (14/1)
**Fly Me Home** is not yet the finished article and, off the bridle from the start, was never any nearer than at the finish. (50/1)
**Henley (USA)** (7/2: op 6/4)

### 4977 SHIFNAL CLAIMING STKS (3-Y.O+) (Class F)
7-30 (7-31) **1m 4f (Fibresand)** £2,243.00 (£618.00: £293.00) Stalls: Low

| | | | | SP | RR | SF |
|---|---|---|---|---|---|---|
| 4763$^{6}$ | **Pharly Dancer (66)** (WWHaigh) **7-9-1**(5) LNewton(6) (hld up: hdwy 4f out: hrd drvn to ld wl ins fnl f) | — | **1** | 4/1$^{2}$ | 83 | 58 |
| 4753$^{6}$ | **Mad Militant (IRE) (62)** (AStreeter) **7-9-3**(3) RHavlin(7) (lw: s.i.s: hld up: stdy hdwy ½-wy: led wl over 1f out: rdn & edgd lft: hdd wl ins fnl f) | 1½ | **2** | 2/1$^{1}$ | 81 | 56 |
| 2612$^{11}$ | **Princely Gait (73)** (MJPolglase) **5-9-6** MRimmer(5) (bit bkwd: a.p: led 4f out tl wl over 1f out: one pce) | 2½ | **3** | 4/1$^{2}$ | 78 | 53 |
| 4603$^{9}$ | **Hill Farm Dancer (53)** (WMBrisbourne) **5-8-10**(5) MartinDwyer(3) (trckd ldrs: effrt & rdn 3f out: nt pce to chal) | 7 | **4** | 7/1$^{3}$ | 63 | 38 |
| | **Mr Bean** (KRBurke) **6-8-11**(5) RPainter(4) (hld up: hdwy u.p 3f out: nt rch ldrs) | 3½ | **5** | 14/1 | 60 | 35 |
| 4691$^{17}$ | **Honestly (70)** (BSmart) **3-8-13** MTebbutt(1) (prom tl wknd over 3f out) | 3½ | **6** | 14/1 | 58 | 27 |
| 4437$^{9}$ | **Swynford Supreme (40)** (JFBottomley) **3-9-4** LCharnock(2) (led 8f: rdn & wknd wl over 2f out: t.o) | 13 | **7** | 40/1 | 46 | 15 |
| 4703$^{14}$ | **Hand of Straw (IRE) (54)** (PGMurphy) **4-9-2v** SDrowne(8) (prom: drvn along 3f out: sn wknd: t.o) | 2½ | **8** | 20/1 | 34 | 9 |
| *4574$^{10}$* | **Rousitto (50)** (RHollinshead) **8-8-7**(3) FLynch(9) (s.s: a in rr: t.o) | 3½ | **9** | 10/1 | 24 | — |
| 4703$^{5}$ | **Rose of Glenn (36)** (BPalling) **5-8-13** TSprake(10) (plld hrd: w ldrs tl wknd qckly over 4f out: t.o) | hd | **10** | 25/1 | 27 | 2 |
| | **Lochwood** (ABailey) **3-8-7** SSanders(11) (w'like: bkwd: b: a bhd: t.o) | 13 | **11** | 20/1 | 9 | — |
| 3252$^{8}$ | **Jon's Choice (30)** (BPreece) **8-8-8** VSlattery(12) (a bhd: t.o) | nk | **12** | 25/1 | 4 | — |
| | | | | (SP 127.9%) | **12 Rn** | |

**2m 38.3** (5.80) CSF £12.85 TOTE £6.30: £2.60 £1.70 £1.80 (£6.20) Trio £7.70 OWNER Mr A. Marucci (MALTON) BRED Stud-On-The-Chart
WEIGHT FOR AGE 3yo-6lb
**4763 Pharly Dancer** continues to pay his way, but he did have to work hard here to get the better of the favourite inside the final 100 yards. (4/1)
**4753 Mad Militant (IRE)** moved through easily to show in front on straightening up, but it was possibly too soon, for he edged over to the far rail when pressed and was well outpointed close home. (2/1)
**2304 Princely Gait** goes well on this surface, but he looked tubby for this first run in almost four months and, in the circumstances, performed extremely well. (4/1)
**3587 Hill Farm Dancer** could not muster the pace to deliver her challenge and was always being held. (7/1)
**Mr Bean** has done all his winning on the All-Weather, but he was ring-rusty for this seasonal debut and will be much sharper next time. (14/1)
**220 Honestly** found this extended trip more than she could manage and dropped away quickly after pressing the leaders for over a mile.(14/1)

## 4978 CHARLECOTE MEDIAN AUCTION MAIDEN STKS (3-Y.O) (Class E)

8-00 (8-01) **1m 100y (Fibresand)** £2,950.00 (£880.00: £420.00: £190.00) Stalls: Low

| Form | Horse | Dist | Pos | SP | RR | SF |
|---|---|---|---|---|---|---|
| 4813$^{5}$ | **Two To Tango (IRE)** (JHMGosden) **3-8-9** GHind(9) (hld up gng wl: led on bit wl over 1f out: comf) | — | 1 | 4/5$^{1}$ | 81+ | 46 |
| | **Sounds Legal** (PDEvans) **3-8-9** JFEgan(13) (unf: dwlt: hdwy 5f out: led 3f out tl wl over 1f out: no ch w wnr) | 2½ | 2 | 20/1 | 76 | 41 |
| 4592$^{5}$ | **Carreamia** (JLEyre) **3-8-9** RLappin(2) (led over 5f: sn drvn along: outpcd appr fnl f) | 7 | 3 | 11/4$^{2}$ | 63 | 28 |
| 4693$^{4}$ | **Balinsky (IRE) (55)** (JBerry) **3-8-4**$^{(5)}$ PRoberts(7) (prom tl rdn & wknd over 2f out) | 4 | 4 | 14/1 | 56 | 21 |
| 4900$^{13}$ | **Name of Our Father (USA) (68)** (PBowen) **3-8-9**$^{(5)}$ PPMurphy(10) (hld up: hdwy over 3f out: hrd drvn & wknd wl over 1f out) | 1½ | 5 | 6/1$^{3}$ | 58 | 23 |
| 4472$^{7}$ | **Cerise (IRE) (39)** (CWCElsey) **3-8-4b**$^{(5)}$ MartinDwyer(12) (trckd ldrs tl wknd u.p over 2f out) | ¾ | 6 | 50/1 | 51 | 16 |
| | **Stretching (IRE)** (ABailey) **3-9-0** WHollick(4) (leggy: scope: bkwd: b: outpcd: a in rr) | ½ | 7 | 25/1 | 55 | 20 |
| 4074$^{15}$ | **Soul Sister** (DHaydnJones) **3-8-9** MFenton(11) (bit bkwd: a in rr: t.o) | 11 | 8 | 50/1 | 29 | — |
| 4206$^{20}$ | **Smiling Bess (43)** (RHollinshead) **3-8-6**$^{(3)}$ FLynch(1) (swtg: sn chsng ldrs: rdn & wknd 3f out) | 1¾ | 9 | 50/1 | 26 | — |
| | **Daratown** (PDEvans) **3-9-0** JFortune(3) (w'like: leggy: sn drvn along: outpcd fr ½-wy) | 2½ | 10 | 33/1 | 26 | — |
| 4603$^{17}$ | **Inaminit (46)** (HJCollingridge) **3-9-0b** JQuinn(6) (s.s: sn in tch: hrd rdn wl over 2f out: wknd qckly: t.o) | 13 | 11 | 50/1 | 2 | — |
| | **Deri Sue** (BJLlewellyn) **3-8-9** TWilliams(5) (lt-f: bit bkwd: a wl bhd: t.o) | 13 | 12 | 50/1 | — | — |

(SP 124.5%) **12 Rn**

**1m 49.1** (4.10) CSF £17.83 TOTE £2.00: £1.20 £4.10 £1.60 (£21.30) Trio £81.10; £45.73 to Southwell 4/11/96 OWNER Mrs C. A. Waters (NEWMARKET) BRED Lordship and Egerton Studs Ltd

**4813 Two To Tango (IRE)**, much better suited to this easier surface, did not need to come off the bridle to succeed. She has certainly started her career at the bottom. (4/5)

**Sounds Legal**, an unfurnished half-sister to a couple of winners, ran a sound race in defeat and, if she can steer clear of such as the winner, she should be able to win races. (20/1)

**4592 Carreamia** is going the right way and will not have much of a problem in finding an opening. (11/4: 3/1-2/1)

**4693 Balinsky (IRE)** had plenty of use made of her and did not quite last the trip. (14/1)

**Name of Our Father (USA)**, who has been competing over longer trips, tried to get into the race on the home turn but, hard as he tried, failed to make any impression. (6/1: 4/1-13/2)

**2541 Cerise (IRE)** was flat to the boards before reaching the straight and quite possibly needs a sound surface. (50/1)

## 4979 CASTLECROFT H'CAP (0-70) (3-Y.O+) (Class E)

8-30 (8-30) **7f (Fibresand)** £3,210.00 (£960.00: £460.00: £210.00) Stalls: High

| Form | Horse | Dist | Pos | SP | RR | SF |
|---|---|---|---|---|---|---|
| *4077*$^{7}$ | **Jigsaw Boy (62)** (PGMurphy) **7-9-6** SDrowne(4) (trckd ldrs: led 3f out: rdn & styd on wl) | — | 1 | 12/1 | 75 | 39 |
| 3469$^{14}$ | **Sea Spouse (62)** (MBlanshard) **5-8-13**$^{(7)}$ KerryBaker(5) (a.p: effrt 2f out: kpt on wl towards fin) | 1¾ | 2 | 20/1 | 71 | 35 |
| *4895*$^{4}$ | **No Monkey Nuts (61)** (JBerry) **3-9-4** GCarter(11) (a w ldrs: rdn tl no ex fnl f) | 1½ | 3 | 7/1$^{2}$ | 67 | 30 |
| 4799$^{7}$ | **Bold Street (IRE) (62)** (ABailey) **6-9-3b**$^{(3)}$ DWright(10) (b: hld up: hdwy u.p 3f out: kpt on ins fnl f) | 1¼ | 4 | 9/1$^{3}$ | 65 | 29 |
| 4560$^{2}$ | **Princess Efisio (60)** (BAMcMahon) **3-9-3** SSanders(3) (lw: hld up: hdwy over 2f out: nvr able to chal) | s.h | 5 | 4/1$^{1}$ | 63 | 26 |
| 4769$^{5}$ | **Anonym (IRE) (64)** (DNicholls) **4-9-8b** AlexGreaves(6) (trckd ldrs: rdn over 2f out: nt pce to chal) | 1½ | 6 | 4/1$^{1}$ | 63 | 27 |
| 4768$^{16}$ | **Encore M'Lady (IRE) (66)** (FHLee) **5-9-10** ACulhane(1) (lw: hld up: effrt 3f out: nvr nr to chal) | 1¾ | 7 | 25/1 | 61 | 25 |
| 4799* | **Jimmy the Skunk (IRE) (62)** (PDEvans) **5-9-6** JFEgan(12) (led after 2f to 3f out: sn hrd drvn & wknd qckly wl over 1f out) | 6 | 8 | 4/1$^{1}$ | 44 | 8 |
| 4240$^{9}$ | **Four of Spades (65)** (RJHodges) **5-9-4v**$^{(5)}$ AmandaSanders(7) (b.off hind: chsd ldrs: sn drvn along: wknd over 3f out) | 2½ | 9 | 9/1$^{3}$ | 41 | 5 |
| 4788$^{2}$ | **Sharp 'n Smart (70)** (BSmart) **4-10-0** MTebbutt(8) (led 2f: wknd 3f out) | nk | 10 | 12/1 | 45 | 9 |
| 4860$^{5}$ | **Silver Harrow (53)** (AGNewcombe) **3-8-5**$^{(5)}$ DGriffiths(2) (outpcd fnl 3f) | hd | 11 | 9/1$^{3}$ | 28 | — |
| 2903$^{9}$ | **Respectable Jones (52)** (RHollinshead) **10-8-3**$^{(7)}$ LisaWatson(9) (outpcd: a bhd) | 2½ | 12 | 33/1 | 21 | — |

(SP 129.4%) **12 Rn**

**1m 29.5** (4.80) CSF £207.99 CT £1,693.74 TOTE £17.50: £3.60 £6.10 £1.50 (£243.10) Trio Not won; £147.08 to Southwell 4/11/96 OWNER The Jigsaw Puzzlers (BRISTOL) BRED Mrs J. A. Rawding

WEIGHT FOR AGE 3yo-1lb

**4077 Jigsaw Boy**, winning for the third time over course and distance this year, has found his form in the autumn in the past and, if he can be trusted, a follow up could be on the cards. (12/1)

**2428 Sea Spouse**, content to be given a lead, did look dangerous early in the straight, but he was never doing things fast enough to trouble the winner. Stronger handling could have made a difference. (20/1)

**4895 No Monkey Nuts** has yet to win at this trip or on this surface, but he did remain in the firing-line until feeling the strain inside the distance. (7/1)

**4778 Bold Street (IRE)** began to pick up turning in and battled on to the end, but a turn of finishing speed was the one thing that was missing. (9/1)

**4560 Princess Efisio** reserves her best for this track, but she took time to get into top gear and, when she did, the race was as good as over. (4/1)

**4769 Anonym (IRE)** travelled well behind the leaders but, when an effort was called for on the home turn, the response was somewhat limited. He does seem to need a faster surface than he had here. (4/1)

**4799* Jimmy the Skunk (IRE)** could never establish a clear lead and, at full stretch after being headed at the end of the back straight, soon called enough. (4/1)

**4788 Sharp 'n Smart** (12/1: op 8/1)

## 4980 MIDLAND BAR NURSERY (S) H'CAP (0-65) (2-Y.O) (Class F)

9-00 (9-02) **1m 100y (Fibresand)** £2,415.00 (£665.00: £315.00) Stalls: Low

| Form | Horse | Dist | Pos | SP | RR | SF |
|---|---|---|---|---|---|---|
| 3879$^{7}$ | **Barachois Lad (42)** (JJO'Neill) **2-8-2** JQuinn(3) (lw: mid div: drvn along 3f out: r.o strly to ld cl home) | — | 1 | 33/1 | 42 | 11 |
| 4694$^{12}$ | **Bali-Pet (57)** (WGMTurner) **2-8-10b**$^{(7)}$ DSweeney(12) (lw: hld up: hdwy to ld over 5f out: hdd over 1f out: led ins fnl f: ct post) | nk | 2 | 14/1 | 56 | 25 |
| 4347$^{5}$ | **Lycius Touch (49)** (MJohnston) **2-8-9** TWilliams(1) (lw: led over 2f: hrd rdn 3f out: led over 1f out tl ins fnl f: r.o) | hd | 3 | 6/1$^{3}$ | 48 | 17 |
| 4549$^{16}$ | **Running Free (IRE) (56)** (MJFetherston-Godley) **2-9-2b** JFortune(13) (hdwy 6f out: hrd drvn over 2f out: unable qckn ins fnl f) | ½ | 4 | 10/1 | 54 | 23 |
| 4562$^{18}$ | **Jingoist (IRE) (55)** (JLHarris) **2-9-1b** SSanders(2) (prom: hrd drvn fnl 2f: one pce) | 1½ | 5 | 4/1$^{2}$ | 51 | 20 |

| Form | Horse | Dist | Pos | SP | RR | SF |
|---|---|---|---|---|---|---|
| 4361[7] | **Spondulicks (IRE) (60)** (BPJBaugh) **2-8-13v[1]**(7) IonaWands(8) (lw: hld up: hdwy ½-wy: hrd drvn 2f out: no imp) | 1¼ | **6** | 12/1 | 53 | 22 |
| 4607[2] | **Verinder's Gift (53)** (DrJDScargill) **2-8-10**(3) FLynch(5) (effrt u.p: 3f out: nvr nr to chal) | ¾ | **7** | 5/2[1] | 45 | 14 |
| 4694[5] | **Ballydinero (IRE) (48)** (CaptJWilson) **2-8-8** DeanMcKeown(11) (s.s: hdwy 4f out: wknd 2f out) | 3½ | **8** | 9/1 | 33 | 2 |
| *4576*[9] | **Dancing Star (IRE) (46)** (PDEvans) **2-8-6** JFEgan(10) (chsd ldrs: pushed along ½-wy: sn lost tch) | ¾ | **9** | 14/1 | 30 | — |
| *4780*[9] | **Tazio Nuvolari (47)** (WGMTurner) **2-8-0**(7) DMcGaffin(9) (a in rr) | nk | **10** | 25/1 | 30 | — |
| 4790[8] | **Morritt Magic (40)** (CWThornton) **2-8-0** NCarlisle(4) (a bhd & outpcd) | 1¾ | **11** | 20/1 | 20 | — |
| *4780*[5] | **Grovefair Dancer (IRE) (61)** (MissSJWilton) **2-9-2**(5) LNewton(7) (a bhd & outpcd: t.o) | 6 | **12** | 11/1 | 29 | — |
| 3976[6] | **Neon Deion (IRE) (55)** (SCWilliams) **2-8-8b[1]**(7) DarrenWilliams(6) (a bhd: outpcd: t.o) | 2 | **13** | 25/1 | 20 | — |

(SP 126.7%) **13 Rn**

**1m 52.2** (7.20) CSF £397.70 CT £2,964.26 TOTE £63.70: £10.00 £5.80 £2.70 (£513.70) Trio Not won; £177.25 to Southwell 4/11/96 OWNER Mr J. D. Graham (PENRITH) BRED J. D. Graham

No bid

**2850 Barachois Lad** had to step up to a mile to get off the mark and, as he only just got there, it would seem he has been crying out for such a trip. (33/1)

**2750 Bali-Pet** proved a tough nut to wear down and was most unfortunate to be shaded right on the line. (14/1)

**4347 Lycius Touch**, subjected to a very punishing ride, showed her true grit to fight back and, if she recovers from this pasting, there are more prizes to be won. (6/1)

**3498 Running Free (IRE)**, hard at work entering the straight, put his head down and battled on and was still holding his own at the finish. (10/1)

**4223 Jingoist (IRE)** pushed the pace all the way, but she was getting the worst of the argument for the final quarter-mile and her measure had been taken. (4/1)

**4097 Spondulicks (IRE)** gives every indication that he is capable of winning races, but he does not appear to go through with his effort when the chips are down. (12/1)

**4607 Verinder's Gift** could never get himself close enough to cause concern and could well need a less testing surface to last this trip. (5/2: 7/2-9/4)

## 4981 WEST MIDLANDS H'CAP (0-60) (3-Y.O+) (Class F)

9-30 (9-32) **6f (Fibresand)** £2,208.00 (£608.00: £288.00) Stalls: Low

| Form | Horse | Dist | Pos | SP | RR | SF |
|---|---|---|---|---|---|---|
| 4881[14] | **Cheeky Chappy (56)** (DWChapman) **5-9-10b** ACulhane(13) (lw: broke smartly: sn wl clr: hld on gamely cl home) | — | **1** | 10/1 | 68 | 42 |
| 4802[13] | **How's Yer Father (56)** (RJHodges) **10-9-5**(5) AmandaSanders(5) (a chsng ldrs: r.o ins fnl f: nt rch wnr) | 1½ | **2** | 14/1 | 64 | 38 |
| *4573*[3] | **Dragonjoy (52)** (NPLittmoden) **3-9-6v** AMcGlone(4) (hdwy over 2f out: hrd rdn & kpt on ins fnl f) | ½ | **3** | 5/1[3] | 59 | 33 |
| *4577*[13] | **Delrob (55)** (DHaydnJones) **5-9-9b** MFenton(6) (lw: hdwy u.p 2f out: nvr nrr) | 1½ | **4** | 9/2[2] | 58 | 32 |
| *4333*[6] | **Anita's Contessa (IRE) (55)** (BPalling) **4-9-9** TSprake(3) (in tch: hrd drvn ½-wy: nvr nr ldrfs) | 1 | **5** | 14/1 | 55 | 29 |
| 4860[9] | **Marino Street (52)** (PDEvans) **3-9-6v** JFortune(12) (in tch: drvn along ½-wy: nt rch ldrs) | s.h | **6** | 10/1 | 52 | 26 |
| 4486[4] | **Disco Boy (54)** (PDEvans) **6-9-8** JFEgan(7) (sn drvn along: a outpcd) | 1¾ | **7** | 3/1[1] | 49 | 23 |
| *4776*[5] | **Playmaker (54)** (DNicholls) **3-9-8** AlexGreaves(10) (lw: trckd ldrs 4f: sn wknd) | 5 | **8** | 12/1 | 36 | 10 |
| 4860[4] | **Polar Refrain (53)** (CADwyer) **3-9-7** CDwyer(1) (outpcd: a bhd) | 2 | **9** | 7/1 | 30 | 4 |
| 4206[13] | **Galacia (IRE) (52)** (WGMTurner) **4-8-13**(7) DSweeney(9) (a bhd & outpcd) | 3 | **10** | 25/1 | 21 | — |
| 1688[6] | **Incatinka (58)** (JLSpearing) **3-9-12** SDrowne(8) (a bhd & outpcd) | 4 | **11** | 16/1 | 16 | — |
| *4776*[11] | **Lady Eclat (53)** (JAGlover) **3-9-7b** SDWilliams(2) (lw: chsd wnr 4f: sn drvn along & wknd) | ½ | **12** | 20/1 | 10 | — |
| 4882[18] | **Western Venture (IRE) (54)** (RMMcKellar) **3-9-8** TWilliams(11) (a bhd & outpcd) | 1¼ | **13** | 16/1 | 7 | — |

(SP 131.9%) **13 Rn**

**1m 15.5** (4.10) CSF £137.00 CT £760.00 TOTE £9.00: £3.10 £4.10 £1.90 (£18.70) Trio £95.70 OWNER Mrs Jeanne Chapman (YORK) BRED Ian W. Glenton

**4577 Cheeky Chappy** only just lasts home over this trip, but his trail-blazing tactics had all his rivals in deep trouble soon after the start, and he kept going long enough to get back to winning ways. (10/1)

**4701 How's Yer Father**, having his first try on Fibresand, ran his usual game race and an extra furlong could be in his favour. (14/1)

**4573 Dragonjoy** found this trip much too sharp, but he did stick to the task in hand and all is not lost yet. (5/1)

**3602* Delrob**, flat out from the start, did keep persevering under pressure, but the task was always hopeless. (9/2)

**2308 Anita's Contessa (IRE)**, racing in midfield but always at full stretch, did keep staying on, but could not get within striking range of the winner. (14/1)

**4206 Marino Street**, driven along to stay in touch at halfway, stuck to her task, but was always doomed to failure. (10/1)

**4486 Disco Boy** can usually hold a prominent pitch just behind the leaders, but he was outpaced all the way on this occasion and was never a factor. (3/1)

T/Plpt: £390.50 (27.14 Tckts). T/Qdpt: £185.80 (1.9 Tckts). IM

# 4089-SOUTHWELL (L-H) (Standard)

## Monday November 4th

WEATHER: overcast WIND: fresh half bhd

## 4982 SOLOMAN H'CAP (0-60) (I) (3-Y.O+) (Class F)

12-45 (12-46) **1m (Fibresand)** £2,031.00 (£556.00: £261.00) Stalls: Low GOING minus 0.06 sec per fur (STD)

| Form | Horse | Dist | Pos | SP | RR | SF |
|---|---|---|---|---|---|---|
| 4898[3] | **Giddy (39)** (JHetherton) **3-8-5** NKennedy(12) (in tch: rdn over 2f out: styd on to ld wl ins fnl f) | — | **1** | 8/1 | 52 | 19 |
| 4789[10] | **Ilandra (IRE) (43)** (RAkehurst) **4-8-11** SSanders(6) (lw: a.p: led over 2f out tl wl ins fnl f) | ½ | **2** | 12/1 | 55 | 24 |
| 4865[9] | **Lady Silk (48)** (MissJFCraze) **5-9-2** SDWilliams(5) (hld up mid div: styd on fnl 2f: nvr nrr) | 5 | **3** | 16/1 | 50 | 19 |
| 4906[4] | **Pc's Cruiser (IRE) (48)** (JLEyre) **4-9-2b** TWilliams(11) (s.i.s: sn pushed along & racd wd: hdwy over 2f out: nt rch ldrs) | 2 | **4** | 7/1 | 46 | 15 |
| *4778*[5] | **Legal Issue (IRE) (59)** (WWHaigh) **4-9-13** SWhitworth(1) (lw: trckd ldrs: effrt over 2f out: wknd fnl f) | 1 | **5** | 13/2[3] | 55 | 24 |
| 4900[17] | **North Ardar (52)** (TWall) **6-9-3**(3) PMcCabe(2) (s.i.s: hdwy fnl 2f: nvr nrr) | hd | **6** | 8/1 | 48 | 17 |
| 3257[16] | **Bad News (37)** (JMBradley) **4-8-5** LCharnock(9) (chsd ldrs over 5f) | 3½ | **7** | 33/1 | 26 | — |
| 4827[13] | **Three Weeks (42)** (WRMuir) **3-8-3**(5) PFessey(15) (bhd: styng on whn n.m.r & swtchd 1f out) | s.h | **8** | 25/1 | 31 | — |
| 4815[11] | **Spanish Stripper (USA) (39)** (MCChapman) **5-8-7** DRMcCabe(14) (bhd: sme late hdwy: n.d) | 1 | **9** | 14/1 | 26 | — |
| 3645[10] | **Return To Brighton (43)** (JMBradley) **4-8-11** SDrowne(10) (in tch: drvn along ½-wy: btn 3f out) | 7 | **10** | 16/1 | 16 | — |

1072[9] **Roussi (USA) (59)** (DNicholls) **4-9-13** AlexGreaves(16) (lw: chsd ldrs to ½-wy: sn lost tch) ....1½ **11** 10/1 29 —
4881[21] **Maybank (IRE) (59)** (AStreeter) **4-9-10**(3) RHavlin(8) (a bhd) ....1½ **12** 16/1 26 —
4829* **Holloway Melody (52)** (BAMcMahon) **3-9-4** GCarter(3) (trckd ldrs tl rdn & wknd over 2f out) ....1 **13** 5/1[1] 17 —
*4781[4]* **People Direct (60)** (KMcAuliffe) **3-9-12** DaneO'Neill(4) (b.hind: chsd ldrs tl wknd qckly over 2f out) ....5 **14** 6/1[2] 15 —
*2934[16]* **Roar on Tour (60)** (MrsMReveley) **7-10-0b** ACulhane(7) (bit bkwd: led tl over 2f out: eased whn btn over 1f out) ....hd **15** 8/1 15 —
4881[19] **Lady Seren (IRE) (37)** (SEKettlewell) **4-8-5** JFEgan(13) (a bhd: t.o) ....5 **16** 33/1 — —
(SP 140.9%) **16 Rn**

**1m 46.7** (6.70) CSF £104.79 CT £1,471.28 TOTE £12.50: £2.50 £3.10 £2.50 £1.50 (£75.90) Trio £216.80; £216.88 to Redcar 5/11/96 OWNER Mr C. D. Barber-Lomax (MALTON) BRED Side Hill Stud and Earl of Halifax
WEIGHT FOR AGE 3yo-2lb

**4898 Giddy** looked to be in trouble turning in, but she answered her jockey's every call to get on top inside the last 100 yards. (8/1)
**Ilandra (IRE)** ran her best race yet on this step down in distance and looked all over the winner until worn down nearing the finish. (12/1: op 6/1)
**4323 Lady Silk** is a sprinter and it is proving expensive to run her over trips much further than she requires. This is the best way to sicken her. (16/1)
**4906 Pc's Cruiser (IRE)** did not relish having his ears pushed off him all the way and could have won this if his pilot knew the meaning of sitting still. (7/1)
**4778 Legal Issue (IRE)**, a seven-furlong specialist, had every chance, but tied up quickly entering the final furlong. (13/2)
**4484 North Ardar**, once again sluggish leaving the stalls, was doing all his best work when it was all too late. (8/1)
**4781 People Direct** (6/1: 4/1-7/1)
**2934 Roar on Tour** needed this after over three months on the sidelines, but he forced the pace for over five furlongs before being eased when all chance had gone. He will not be long in getting back to winning ways. (8/1: op 5/1)

## 4983 ALEX LAWRIE H'CAP (0-70) (I) (3-Y.O+) (Class E)

1-15 (1-15) **6f (Fibresand)** £2,881.70 (£857.60: £407.80: £182.90) Stalls: Low GOING minus 0.06 sec per fur (STD)

SP RR SF

*4895[15]* **Miss Offset (61)** (MJohnston) **3-9-6b** JWeaver(13) (lw: hld up in tch: hdwy on outside over 2f out: led ent fnl f: sn clr) ....— **1** 8/1 75 33
4860[10] **The Barnsley Belle (IRE) (47)** (JLEyre) **3-8-6**ow1 RLappin(1) (bhd: hdwy & swtchd rt 2f out: r.o strly fnl f) ....4 **2** 9/1 50 7
4881[3] **Madrina (60)** (JBerry) **3-9-0**(5) PFessey(12) (lw: led: clr 2f out: wknd & hdd 1f out: one pce) ....1¾ **3** 7/2[1] 59 17
4888[16] **Miss Aragon (37)** (MissLCSiddall) **8-7-10** NCarlisle(14) (s.i.s: gd hdwy on outside over 2f out: kpt on wl fnl f) ....3 **4** 16/1 28 —
*4981** **Cheeky Chappy (63)** (DWChapman) **5-9-8b** 7x ACulhane(2) (chsd ldr: sn drvn along: one pce appr fnl f) ....1¼ **5** 4/1[2] 50 8
4610[15] **Margaretrose Anna (42)** (BPJBaugh) **4-7-8**(7) IonaWands(9) (mid div: kpt on wl fnl 2f) ....s.h **6** 33/1 29 —
4456[8] **Time To Fly (39)** (BWMurray) **3-7-12**ow1 TWilliams(11) (chsd ldrs tl wknd over 1f out) ....½ **7** 20/1 25 —
4237[14] **Anaxagoras (37)** (SGollings) **6-7-10** JQuinn(10) (mid div: effrt over 2f out: no imp) ....1¼ **8** 40/1 20 —
3883[7] **Katy-Q (IRE) (42)** (PCalver) **3-7-12b**(3) DarrenMoffatt(16) (racd wd: in tch: effrt over 2f out: no real imp) ....nk **9** 14/1 24 —
4805[12] **Bent Raiwand (USA) (50)** (DonEnricoIncisa) **3-8-9** KimTinkler(7) (b.hind: sn bhd) ....3½ **10** 33/1 22 —
4460[11] **Ragazzo (IRE) (40)** (JSWainwright) **6-7-13b** LCharnock(15) (a in rr) ....hd **11** 25/1 12 —
4828[15] **Aljaz (47)** (MissGayKelleway) **6-8-6** SSanders(5) (b: mid div: drvn along 3f out: no imp) ....s.h **12** 6/1[3] 19 —
4341[7] **Havana Miss (38)** (BPalling) **4-7-11** NAdams(3) (chsd ldrs to ½-wy: sn wknd) ....1 **13** 14/1 7 —
4768[9] **Dancing Sioux (65)** (DNicholls) **4-9-10b** MWigham(6) (s.i.s: a in rr) ....½ **14** 10/1 33 —
4486[10] **Henry the Hawk (45)** (MDods) **5-8-4b**1 AClark(8) (b: chsd ldrs 4f: sn lost tch: t.o) ....6 **15** 10/1 — —
(SP 131.9%) **15 Rn**

**1m 18.4** (4.90) CSF £77.99 CT £287.56 TOTE £7.10: £2.70 £4.00 £2.00 (£33.10) Trio £86.10 OWNER Hertford Offset Ltd (MIDDLEHAM) BRED J. Coombes and E. Henshaw
LONG HANDICAP Miss Aragon 7-9 Anaxagoras 7-9

**897 Miss Offset**, returning to sprinting and ridden with restraint, won this very much as she pleased and it will come as something of a surprise if she can not defy a penalty. (8/1)
**4598 The Barnsley Belle (IRE)** could not get within striking range of the winner, but she made up all of six lengths inside the distance and that elusive first success can not be too far away. (9/1)
**4881 Madrina** cut her own throat by winning the duel with the confirmed front-runner and then going clear in the straight, but she was down to a walk on reaching the final furlong. (7/2)
**4486 Miss Aragon**, a mere shadow of her old self, did stay on well in the closing stages and there could still be a race in her. (16/1)
**4981* Cheeky Chappy**, who needs to dictate to show his true form, was always being denied that here and the penalty for his success on Saturday night was taking its toll in the latter stages. (4/1: 11/4-9/2)
**167 Margaretrose Anna**, still to get off the mark, kept plugging away in the latter stages and a return to seven furlongs could be what she requires. (33/1)

## 4984 BOUNTY AMATEUR H'CAP (0-70) (3-Y.O+) (Class F)

1-45 (1-46) **1m 6f (Fibresand)** £2,381.00 (£656.00: £311.00) Stalls: High GOING minus 0.06 sec per fur (STD)

SP RR SF

4794[2] **Onefourseven (45)** (JLEyre) **3-9-3** MissDianaJones(9) (hld up: hdwy 5f out: led over 1f out: edgd lft: styd on strly) ....— **1** 5/4[1] 52 15
4789[4] **Stalled (IRE) (58)** (PTWalwyn) **6-10-5**(5) MarchionessBlandford(1) (a.p: drvn along to ld wl over 1f out: sn hdd: one pce) ....3½ **2** 7/1[3] 61 32
4669[7] **Golden Hadeer (45)** (MJRyan) **5-9-6**(5)ow5 MrSLavallin(10) (hld up: hdwy 6f out: sn pushed along: one pce fnl 2f) ....3 **3** 14/1 45 11
4789[5] **Sharp Command (50)** (PEccles) **3-9-3**(5) MissEJJones(4) (a.p: led 7f out tl wl over 1f out: wknd fnl f) ....1¾ **4** 16/1 48 11
73[5] **Mudlark (46)** (JNorton) **4-9-7v**1(5)ow8 MrJMBrown(7) (chsd ldrs: no hdwy fnl 2f) ....12 **5** 25/1 30 —
4771[24] **Witney-de-Bergerac (IRE) (46)** (JSMoore) **4-9-7**(5) MrsSMoore(2) (wl bhd: styd on fnl 3f: nvr nrr) ....nk **6** 10/1 30 1
*3066[3]* **Greek Night Out (IRE) (50)** (JLEyre) **5-9-11**(5) MrsCWilliams(11) (outpcd & bhd tl styd on fnl 3f) ....4 **7** 11/1 29 —
4789[16] **Kadiri (IRE) (58)** (JRBosley) **5-10-10** MrsSBosley(12) (hld up: hdwy over 5f out: rdn & wknd ent st) ....6 **8** 20/1 30 1
4815[5] **Record Lover (IRE) (38)** (MCChapman) **6-8-13**(5)ow1 MrVLukaniuk(14) (led 3f: wknd over 3f out) ....nk **9** 14/1 10 —
*4779[8]* **Claque (57)** (DWChapman) **4-10-9b** MissRClark(5) (a in rr) ....nk **10** 20/1 28 —
4238[10] **Gold Blade (69)** (JPearce) **7-11-7** MrsLPearce(13) (lw: hld up: hdwy 5f out: wknd 3f out) ....½ **11** 5/1[2] 40 11
4794[15] **Mr Moriarty (IRE) (38)** (SRBowring) **5-8-13**(5) MrsMMorris(15) (b: swtg: led after 3f to 7f out: wknd fnl 5f: t.o) ....10 **12** 12/1 — —

| Form | Horse | Dist | Pos | SP | RR | SF |
|---|---|---|---|---|---|---|
| *2936[7]* | **Jean de Florette (USA) (34)** (RCSpicer) **5-8-9b**(5) MrSRutherford(8) (lw: mid div: drvn along 9f out: grad wknd: t.o) | 1½ | **13** | 33/1 | — | — |
| | **Dormston Boyo (56)** (TWall) **6-10-3**(5)ow22 MrDBRoberts(3) (bkwd: swtg: lost pl after 5f: t.o) | dist | **14** | 50/1 | — | — |

(SP 136.2%) **14 Rn**

**3m 13.9** (14.90) CSF £12.41 CT £96.30 TOTE £2.20: £1.30 £2.40 £3.50 (£9.10) Trio £86.20 OWNER Mr J. Roundtree (HAMBLETON) BRED Peter Storey
LONG HANDICAP Jean de Florette (USA) 8-6 Dormston Boyo 8-4
WEIGHT FOR AGE 3yo-8lb

**4794 Onefourseven**, always galloping all over these rivals, hardly needed to let himself down to win with any amount in hand. (5/4)
**4789 Stalled (IRE)**, a consistent performer in these events, does appear to need all of this trip, but he found the concession of 16lb just too much of a handicap on this occasion. (7/1)
**2989 Golden Hadeer** ran up to his mark at this first attempt at the trip, but he had to admit the leading pair much too good for him. (14/1)
**4789 Sharp Command** tried hard to slip his field early in the straight, but he failed to get away and the trip as much as anything took its toll inside the last quarter-mile. (16/1)
**Mudlark** pushed the pace from the start, but he was feeling the strain entering the straight and could do little more than stay on at the one pace. (25/1)
**2385 Witney-de-Bergerac (IRE)**, virtually tailed off down the back straight, did well to finish so close and it would seem he has the ability when he cares to use it. (10/1)

## 4985 MIDWAY MEDIAN AUCTION MAIDEN STKS (2-Y.O) (Class F)
2-15 (2-15) **1m (Fibresand)** £2,381.00 (£656.00: £311.00) Stalls: Low GOING minus 0.06 sec per fur (STD)

| Form | Horse | Dist | Pos | SP | RR | SF |
|---|---|---|---|---|---|---|
| 4748[3] | **Bonnie Lassie (72)** (CWThornton) **2-8-9** DeanMcKeown(3) (mde virtually all: clr ent st: unchal) | — | **1** | 2/1[2] | 77 | 20 |
| 4748[6] | **Ziggy's Viola (IRE)** (MrsMReveley) **2-8-9** ACulhane(5) (a.p: chsd wnr over 2f out: no imp) | 10 | **2** | 5/1[3] | 57 | — |
| 4801[15] | **Wesley's Lad (IRE)** (JNeville) **2-9-0** AClark(6) (sn pushed along: hdwy ½-wy: styd on one pce fnl 2f) | 3 | **3** | 12/1 | 56 | — |
| 4599[2] | **Rhapsody In White (IRE)** (MAJarvis) **2-9-0** PBloomfield(1) (sn drvn along: lost pl after 2f: n.d after) | 13 | **4** | Evens[1] | 30 | — |
| 4607[11] | **Macari** (BPJBaugh) **2-9-0** RPerham(7) (trckd ldrs 5f: sn outpcd) | ¾ | **5** | 33/1 | 29 | — |
| 4594[11] | **Pupil Master (IRE)** (DenysSmith) **2-9-0** LCharnock(4) (outpcd in rr: effrt 2f out: no imp) | 1½ | **6** | 20/1 | 26 | — |
| 4700[10] | **Dunston Gold** (PJBevan) **2-9-0** NCarlisle(8) (sn drvn along: a outpcd: t.o) | 8 | **7** | 33/1 | 10 | — |
| 4834[8] | **Ryles Dancer** (DrJDScargill) **2-9-0** JFanning(2) (w wnr tl wknd qckly 3f out: t.o) | 4 | **8** | 33/1 | 2 | — |
| 4796[13] | **Impish (IRE) (45)** (TJEtherington) **2-9-0** MTebbutt(9) (chsd ldrs tl rdn & wknd over 2f out: t.o) | 1¾ | **9** | 25/1 | — | — |

(SP 125.1%) **9 Rn**

**1m 46.9** (6.90) CSF £13.17 TOTE £3.50: £1.90 £2.10 £4.40 (£5.30) Trio £20.10 OWNER Mr Guy Reed (MIDDLEHAM) BRED M. J. Paver

**4748 Bonnie Lassie**, appreciating this step up to a mile, has been performing well and was not winning out of turn. (2/1)
**4748 Ziggy's Viola (IRE)** finished further behind the winner than she did on her recent outing and she will need to avoid confrontation again if she is to win a race. (5/1)
**4477 Wesley's Lad (IRE)**, off the bridle all the way, did keep staying on, but very much in his own time. (12/1: 8/1-14/1)
**4599 Rhapsody In White (IRE)** took an instant dislike to having sand kicked in his face and wanted no part of it. (Evens)
**Macari** performed better than he did on his debut and is getting to know what it is all about. (33/1)

## 4986 WEATHERBYS DATA SERVICES LIMITED STKS (0-55) (3-Y.O+) (Class F)
2-45 (2-46) **1m 3f (Fibresand)** £2,952.20 (£819.20: £392.60) Stalls: Low GOING minus 0.06 sec per fur (STD)

| Form | Horse | Dist | Pos | SP | RR | SF |
|---|---|---|---|---|---|---|
| *4089[9]* | **No Submission (USA) (55)** (DWChapman) **10-9-2v** ACulhane(7) (bhd: hdwy 7f out: led 1f out: hld on wl towards fin) | — | **1** | 16/1 | 62 | 17 |
| 4726[9] | **Arc of The Diver (IRE) (53)** (JBerry) **3-8-6b**(5) PRoberts(14) (lw: trckd ldrs: ev ch fnl f: nt qckn nr fin) | nk | **2** | 10/1 | 62 | 12 |
| 4812[13] | **Ihtimaam (FR) (52)** (MrsASwinbank) **4-9-4** JFortune(15) (trckd ldrs: led over 3f out to 1f out: one pce) | 2 | **3** | 16/1 | 61 | 16 |
| 4587[14] | **In the Money (IRE) (55)** (RHollinshead) **7-9-1**(3) FLynch(2) (hld up: hdwy 4f out: sn rdn: one pce) | 8 | **4** | 16/1 | 49 | 4 |
| 4603[13] | **Araboybill (52)** (JNeville) **5-9-2b** SDrowne(9) (chsd ldrs: led over 6f out tl over 3f out: sn wknd) | ¾ | **5** | 25/1 | 46 | 1 |
| 4752[3] | **Basood (USA) (52)** (SPCWoods) **3-8-1b**(7) CWebb(1) (bhd: sme hdwy 4f out: nvr nr ldrs) | 13 | **6** | 7/1[2] | 24 | — |
| 4810[10] | **Giftbox (USA) (52)** (NBycroft) **4-9-4** JQuinn(6) (mid div: rdn 4f out: n.d) | 2½ | **7** | 9/1[3] | 25 | — |
| 4812[6] | **Ottavio Farnese (53)** (AHide) **4-9-2** AMcGlone(4) (lw: hld up: sme hdwy 3f out: n.d) | 4 | **8** | 7/1[2] | 18 | — |
| 4726[15] | **Rainelle (50)** (JWWatts) **4-8-13v[1]** GDuffield(10) (b: chsd ldrs: drvn along 8f out: lost pl 4f out) | s.h | **9** | 25/1 | 15 | — |
| 4785[4] | **Nawaji (USA) (45)** (WRMuir) **3-8-8** DaneO'Neill(11) (in tch tl lost pl 5f out) | ¾ | **10** | 12/1 | 13 | — |
| | **Jemima Puddleduck (51)** (AStreeter) **5-8-10v[1]**(3) RHavlin(13) (lw: a bhd) | ½ | **11** | 9/1[3] | 13 | — |
| *4334[7]* | **Last Roundup (48)** (CWThornton) **4-9-2** DeanMcKeown(3) (chsd ldrs: shkn up 4f out: grad wknd) | hd | **12** | 20/1 | 16 | — |
| *319[5]* | **Tadellal (IRE) (55)** (WGMTurner) **5-8-6**(7) DSweeney(12) (bkwd: s.s: a wl bhd) | 2 | **13** | 14/1 | 10 | — |
| 4810* | **Lapu-Lapu (56)** (MJCamacho) **3-8-12** LCharnock(16) (hld up: stdy hdwy 7f out: ev ch 4f out: hung lft & eased over 2f out) | 1¼ | **14** | 3/1[1] | 12 | — |
| 2415[3] | **Silver Hunter (USA) (52)** (GCBravery) **5-8-11**(5) LNewton(5) (bkwd: in tch tl lost pl ½-wy: sn bhd) | 14 | **15** | 7/1[2] | — | — |
| 4752[5] | **Noir Esprit (47)** (JMCarr) **3-8-11b** PBloomfield(8) (led tl over 6f out: lost pl over 4f out) | 1½ | **16** | 14/1 | — | — |

(SP 142.7%) **16 Rn**

**2m 31.2** (11.20) CSF £175.11 TOTE £20.10: £4.30 £3.20 £5.00 (£73.50) Trio £347.40; £352.34 to Redcar 5/11/96 OWNER Mr T. S. Redman (YORK) BRED Mr. Francis X. Weber
WEIGHT FOR AGE 3yo-5lb

**776 No Submission (USA)**, fresh and well after a break, came from the back to record his fifteenth win here. (16/1)
**4587 Arc of The Diver (IRE)** put a poor effort on grass behind him last time and was only just denied. (10/1)
**2935* Ihtimaam (FR)**, who had shown little since winning a claimer here in July, travelled strongly, but could only stay on at the one pace in the final furlong. (16/1)
**3865 In the Money (IRE)** has two ways of running. (16/1)
**4810* Lapu-Lapu**, stepping up slightly in distance, moved up onto the heels of the leaders travelling strongly but, once in line for home, hung left and looked in some discomfort. Her rider sensibly eased her up as something was clearly amiss. (3/1)

## 4987 ALEX LAWRIE H'CAP (0-70) (II) (3-Y.O+) (Class E)
3-15 (3-18) **6f (Fibresand)** £2,854.40 (£849.20: £403.60: £180.80) Stalls: Low GOING minus 0.06 sec per fur (STD)

| Form | Horse | Dist | Pos | SP | RR | SF |
|---|---|---|---|---|---|---|
| 4768[4] | **Naughty Pistol (USA) (51)** (PDEvans) **4-8-10v** JFEgan(2) (mde virtually all: hung rt ins fnl f: hld on wl) | — | **1** | 11/2[2] | 62 | 23 |
| *4094** | **Elton Ledger (IRE) (70)** (MrsNMacauley) **7-10-1v** SSanders(9) (b: hld up: n.m.r & swtchd rt over 2f out: hung lft & styd on fnl f: nt rch wnr) | 1¾ | **2** | 5/1[1] | 76 | 37 |

| | | | | | |
|---|---|---|---|---|---|
| 4778[8] **Bold Aristocrat (IRE) (57)** (RHollinshead) **5-8-13**(3) FLynch(5) (hld up: hdwy over 3f out: chsd wnr over 1f out: no imp) ....1½ | **3** | 11/2[2] | 59 | 20 |
| 4881[11] **Honeyhall (38)** (NBycroft) **3-7-11** JQuinn(16) (sn prom: kpt on one pce fnl 2f) ....1¾ | **4** | 33/1 | 36 | — |
| 4865[13] **Lawsimina (48)** (MissJFCraze) **3-8-7** SDrowne(12) (racd wd: mid div: kpt on fnl 2f: nvr nr to chal) ....nk | **5** | 16/1 | 45 | 6 |
| 4811[9] **Plum First (52)** (JLEyre) **6-8-11v** RLappin(3) (a in tch: drvn along over 2f out: nvr nr to chal) ....¾ | **6** | 8/1[3] | 47 | 8 |
| 4888[21] **Green Golightly (USA) (40)** (RMFlower) **5-7-13e** FNorton(4) (bhd: hdwy over 2f out: styd on fnl f) ....¾ | **7** | 33/1 | 33 | — |
| 4811[16] **Stephensons Rocket (54)** (DNicholls) **5-8-13** AlexGreaves(13) (lw: nvr rchd ldrs) ....½ | **8** | 12/1 | 46 | 7 |
| 4888[7] **Never Think Twice (65)** (KTIvory) **3-9-10b** CScally(8) (b: s.i.s: bhd tl sme hdwy fnl 2f: n.d) ....hd | **9** | 12/1 | 56 | 17 |
| 4820[9] **Sagebrush Roller (63)** (JWWatts) **8-9-8** GDuffield(7) (s.i.s: bhd: styng on whn nt clr run over 2f out: kpt on) ....½ | **10** | 8/1[3] | 53 | 14 |
| 4550[13] **School Boy (64)** (TJNaughton) **3-9-9** JFortune(6) (chsd wnr tl wknd over 1f out) ....1¾ | **11** | 12/1 | 49 | 10 |
| 4372[19] **Into Debt (37)** (JRPoulton) **3-7-10** GBardwell(11) (bhd: effrt over 2f out: sn wknd) ....4 | **12** | 20/1 | 12 | — |
| 4909[13] **Cavers Yangous (66)** (MJohnston) **5-9-11v** TWilliams(1) (sn chsng ldrs: sn drvn along: lost pl over 1f out: eased) ....nk | **13** | 9/1 | 40 | 1 |
| 4909[16] **Sihafi (USA) (70)** (JMCarr) **3-10-1** AClark(15) (racd wd: trckd ldrs tl lost pl 3f out) ....5 | **14** | 33/1 | 31 | — |
| *1606*[5] **Square Deal (FR) (63)** (SRBowring) **5-9-8** SDWilliams(10) (bkwd: chsd ldrs tl hung lft & wknd over 2f out) ...s.h | **15** | 10/1 | 23 | — |
| 4550[17] **Mrs McBadger (57)** (BSmart) **3-9-2b** MTebbutt(14) (chsd ldrs tl lost pl over 3f out) ....2½ | **16** | 25/1 | 11 | — |
| | | (SP 135.1%) **16 Rn** | | |

**1m 18.4** (4.90) CSF £34.46 CT £158.70 TOTE £10.70: £3.10 £2.00 £1.80 £7.00 (£30.60) Trio £43.90 OWNER Mr Colin Booth (WELSHPOOL) BRED Brereton C. Jones

LONG HANDICAP Into Debt 7-8

**4768 Naughty Pistol (USA)** is running well at present and had this won some way from home. (11/2)
**4094* Elton Ledger (IRE)** invariably gives a good account of himself. After having to switch to get a run, he hung under pressure and was never going to reach the winner. (5/1)
**4577 Bold Aristocrat (IRE)** has four wins to his credit, all recorded here. (11/2)
**Honeyhall** seemed to run easily her best race so far. (33/1)
**4094 Lawsimina** is settling down with racing. (16/1)
**3844 Never Think Twice** (12/1: op 8/1)

## 4988 BONIN (S) STKS (2-Y.O) (Class G)

3-45 (3-48) **7f (Fibresand)** £2,070.00 (£570.00: £270.00) Stalls: Low GOING minus 0.06 sec per fur (STD)

| | | SP | RR | SF |
|---|---|---|---|---|
| 4896[9] **Stakis Casinos Lad (IRE)** (MJohnston) **2-8-4**(7) KSked(5) (chsd ldrs: led over 1f out: hld on towards fin) ....— | **1** | 14/1 | 57 | — |
| 4607[4] **Slightly Oliver (IRE)** (GLewis) **2-8-8b**(3) AWhelan(8) (swtg: chsd ldrs: hdwy & ev ch 1f out: nt qckn nr fin) ....nk | **2** | 7/2[2] | 56 | — |
| 4097[13] **Ginny Wossername (58)** (WGMTurner) **2-8-4b**(7) DSweeney(6) (led: clr 3f out: edgd rt & hdd over 1f out: sn wknd) ....7 | **3** | 9/1[3] | 40 | — |
| 4715[24] **Racing Carr (40)** (TJNaughton) **2-8-6** SSanders(7) (bhd: styd on fnl 2f: nvr nr to chal) ....5 | **4** | 33/1 | 24 | — |
| 4435[5] **Diamond Eyre** (JLEyre) **2-8-6** RLappin(9) (sn outpcd & bhd: styd on fnl 2f: n.d) ....2 | **5** | 10/1 | 19 | — |
| 4041[14] **Cool Grey** (JJO'Neill) **2-8-6** JQuinn(13) (b.hind: sn in tch: drvn along over 3f out: no imp) ....s.h | **6** | 14/1 | 19 | — |
| 4796[2] **Night Chorus (75)** (BSRothwell) **2-8-11** JStack(3) (lw: s.i.s: bhd: sme hdwy 2f out: n.d) ....5 | **7** | 5/4[1] | 13 | — |
| 4835[8] **Hopperetta (54)** (BPalling) **2-8-6** GDuffield(4) (swtg: sn wl bhd) ....7 | **8** | 10/1 | — | — |
| 4721[8] **Rising Glory (45)** (MissJFCraze) **2-8-11** SDWilliams(12) (in tch tl lost tch over 2f out) ....¾ | **9** | 33/1 | — | — |
| 4607[9] **Mustang Scally** (JMackie) **2-8-6** JFanning(2) (bit bkwd: chsd ldrs tl wknd qckly over 2f out) ....nk | **10** | 20/1 | — | — |
| 4806[7] **Whirl Pool** (MJCamacho) **2-8-6** LCharnock(1) (in tch tl lost tch over 2f out) ....1¼ | **11** | 16/1 | — | — |
| *3954*[11] **Woodland Dove** (KGWingrove) **2-8-6** GBardwell(10) (sltly hmpd s: sn prom: rdn & lost pl over 4f out) ....hd | **12** | 33/1 | — | — |
| 4621[6] **Sodelk** (JHetherton) **2-8-7**ow1 MBirch(11) (sn wl bhd: virtually p.u over 1f out) ....dist | **13** | 10/1 | — | — |
| | | (SP 136.7%) **13 Rn** | | |

**1m 34.9** (8.10) CSF £66.95 TOTE £24.10: £3.90 £1.80 £2.80 (£56.10) Trio £100.50 OWNER Mark Johnston Racing Ltd (MIDDLEHAM) BRED Vincent and Joseph Fitzpatrick

No bid

**Stakis Casinos Lad (IRE)**, who had shown precious little on his first two outings, did just enough to get home in a race that was poor even by seller standards. (14/1)
**4607 Slightly Oliver (IRE)** misbehaved on the way to the start. After moving up and looking sure to win, he seemed reluctant to go past. (7/2)
**3976 Ginny Wossername** went into a clear lead soon after halfway. Edging towards the stands' side, her stride shortened in the final furlong. (9/1)
**Racing Carr** showed her first glimmer of ability. (33/1)
**4796 Night Chorus** seemed to get messed about at the start and could never get into the contest. (5/4: 11/10-Evens)

## 4989 SOLOMAN H'CAP (0-60) (II) (3-Y.O+) (Class F)

4-15 (4-15) **1m (Fibresand)** £2,031.00 (£556.00: £261.00) Stalls: Low GOING minus 0.06 sec per fur (STD)

| | | SP | RR | SF |
|---|---|---|---|---|
| 4882* **Desert Zone (USA) (48)** (JLHarris) **7-9-5** SSanders(13) (b: chsd ldrs: chal over 1f out: styd on u.p to ld towards fin) ....— | **1** | 11/2[1] | 60 | 47 |
| *4781*[7] **Domino Flyer (55)** (MrsASwinbank) **3-9-10** JFortune(12) (chsd ldrs: led over 2f out tl wl ins fnl f) ....½ | **2** | 11/2[1] | 66 | 51 |
| 4812[4] **Zahran (IRE) (39)** (JMBradley) **5-8-10** SDrowne(11) (bit bkwd: a chsng ldrs: one pce appr fnl f) ....2½ | **3** | 8/1[3] | 45 | 32 |
| 4906[10] **Pleasure Trick (USA) (39)** (DonEnricoIncisa) **5-8-10** KimTinkler(16) (s.i.s: bhd tl styd on wl fnl 2f) ....2½ | **4** | 20/1 | 40 | 27 |
| 3292[4] **Ya Marhaba (40)** (JWPayne) **3-8-9** AMcGlone(8) (bit bkwd: hld up: hdwy over 2f out: kpt on: nvr nr to chal) ....5 | **5** | 11/2[1] | 31 | 16 |
| *4077*[6] **Fiaba (40)** (MrsNMacauley) **8-8-8v**(3) CTeague(1) (bit bkwd: swtchd outside & hdwy over 3f out: kpt on: nvr nr to chal) ....1¾ | **6** | 10/1 | 28 | 15 |
| *4781*[11] **Sandmoor Denim (52)** (SRBowring) **9-9-9** DeanMcKeown(3) (led 1f: chsd ldrs: outpcd fnl 3f) ....4 | **7** | 12/1 | 32 | 19 |
| 4820[23] **Leigh Crofter (52)** (PDCundell) **7-9-9b** GDuffield(7) (led after 1f tl over 2f out: wknd over 1f out) ....hd | **8** | 20/1 | 31 | 18 |
| 4812[10] **Hever Golf Eagle (52)** (TJNaughton) **3-9-7** JWeaver(6) (lw: in tch: drvn along over 3f out: sn btn) ....hd | **9** | 11/1 | 31 | 16 |
| 4810[14] **Shamokin (38)** (FWatson) **4-8-9** JQuinn(9) (s.i.s: bhd: sme hdwy 2f out: n.d) ....hd | **10** | 25/1 | 17 | 4 |
| 4824[14] **Executive Officer (40)** (RMFlower) **3-8-9** DBiggs(14) (s.i.s: a bhd) ....2 | **11** | 10/1 | 15 | — |
| 4692[15] **Nicola's Princess (51)** (BAMcMahon) **3-9-6** GCarter(4) (chsd ldrs tl lost pl 3f out) ....9 | **12** | 8/1[3] | 8 | — |
| *4076*[8] **Juba (40)** (DrJDScargill) **4-8-11** JFanning(5) (chsd ldrs tl lost pl over 3f out) ....3 | **13** | 16/1 | — | — |
| 4824[12] **D J Cat (48)** (WRMuir) **3-9-3** DaneO'Neill(15) (bit bkwd: a in rr) ....3 | **14** | 14/1 | — | — |
| 4784* **Corniche Quest (IRE) (54)** (MRChannon) **3-9-9** JFEgan(10) (sn chsng ldrs: drvn along 3f out: wknd over 1f out: eased) ....3½ | **15** | 6/1[2] | — | — |

4808[17] **Fiery Footsteps (38)** (SWCampion) **4-8-6b**[(3)] FLynch(2) (trckd ldrs tl lost pl over 2f out: eased & sn wl bhd: virtually p.u)....20 **16** 33/1 — —
(SP 145.7%) **16 Rn**

**1m 45.1** (5.10) CSF £40.23 CT £198.75 TOTE £6.50: £2.30 £2.10 £2.10 £3.00 (£29.00) Trio £55.80 OWNER Lavender Hill Leisure Ltd (MELTON MOWBRAY) BRED Michael D. Baudhuin
WEIGHT FOR AGE 3yo-2lb

**4882* Desert Zone (USA)**, who was ending a long losing sequence at Leicester, stuck on under pressure to gain the upper hand near the line. (11/2)
**2934 Domino Flyer**, who shows plenty of knee-action, is obviously well suited by soft going on Turf and the All-Weather. He showed the right sort of spirit, but had to give best near the line. (11/2)
**4812 Zahran (IRE)**, who presumably needed it last time after two months off, had every chance. (8/1)
**3974 Pleasure Trick (USA)**, who has lost his way since winning a claimer at Pontefract, came from off the pace to finish best of all. (20/1)
**3292 Ya Marhaba**, a keen-going type, settled off the pace. Making ground once in line for home, he was soon flat out and unable to take a hand. (11/2)
**4784* Corniche Quest (IRE)** (6/1: op 7/2)

T/Jkpt: Not won; £20,826.61 to Redcar 5/11/96. T/Plpt: £386.80 (30.04 Tckts). T/Qdpt: £71.90 (18.09 Tckts). IM/WG

## 4903-REDCAR (L-H) (Good to firm, Firm patches)
## Tuesday November 5th
WEATHER: fine but windy WIND: fresh half against

### 4990 BEECH NURSERY H'CAP (0-75) (2-Y.O) (Class E)
1-35 (1-38) **1m** £3,309.25 (£994.00: £479.50: £222.25) Stalls: Centre GOING minus 0.41 sec per fur (F)

| | | | | SP | RR | SF |
|---|---|---|---|---|---|---|
| 4319[7] | **Epic Stand (56)** (MrsJRRamsden) **2-8-2**[(3)ow2] FLynch(10) (s.i.s: hdwy ½-wy: led ins fnl f: r.o wl) | — | **1** | 8/1[3] | 63 | 30 |
| 4795* | **Double Espresso (IRE) (70)** (MJohnston) **2-9-5** JWeaver(8) (cl up: led 3f out tl ins fnl f: r.o) | 1 | **2** | 5/2[1] | 75 | 44 |
| 4787[2] | **Castles Burning (USA) (55)** (CACyzer) **2-8-4** GCarter(11) (lw: a chsng ldrs: ev ch fnl 3f: kpt on) | 1¼ | **3** | 10/1 | 58 | 27 |
| 4814[4] | **Time Can Tell (70)** (CMurray) **2-9-5** MTebbutt(16) (b: in tch: hdwy 3f out: ev ch 1f out: kpt on) | hd | **4** | 10/1 | 72 | 41 |
| 4715[9] | **Gresatre (59)** (CADwyer) **2-8-8** LDettori(3) (bhd: effrt ½-wy: styd on: nvr trbld ldrs) | 5 | **5** | 8/1[3] | 51 | 20 |
| 4795[6] | **Dee Pee Tee Cee (IRE) (59)** (MWEasterby) **2-8-3**[(5)] GParkin(14) (mid div: hdwy u.p ½-wy: styd on: no imp) | ½ | **6** | 25/1 | 50 | 19 |
| 4721[3] | **Select Star (IRE) (67)** (APJarvis) **2-9-2** WRyan(13) (trckd ldrs: effrt 3f out: outpcd fnl 2f) | 2½ | **7** | 9/1 | 53 | 22 |
| 4564[3] | **Smart Spirit (IRE) (72)** (MrsMReveley) **2-9-7** ACulhane(18) (hld up & bhd: hdwy over 2f out: nvr plcd to chal) | nk | **8** | 20/1 | 58+ | 27 |
| 4715[12] | **Island Prince (50)** (NACallaghan) **2-7-13** JQuinn(7) (led 5f: sn wknd) | 1¾ | **9** | 9/2[2] | 32 | 1 |
| 4602[12] | **Chairmans Daughter (65)** (JPearce) **2-9-0v**[1] MBirch(6) (w ldrs tl wknd over 2f out) | 4 | **10** | 20/1 | 39 | 8 |
| 4562[6] | **Broctune Line (50)** (MrsMReveley) **2-7-13** LCharnock(9) (bhd & rdn ½-wy: n.d) | 4 | **11** | 12/1 | 16 | — |
| 4594[10] | **Ibn Masirah (60)** (MrsMReveley) **2-8-4**[(5)] SCopp(15) (a rr div) | ¾ | **12** | 33/1 | 25 | — |
| *4980*[9] | **Dancing Star (IRE) (53)** (PDEvans) **2-8-2**[ow6] JFEgan(12) (prom 5f) | 2½ | **13** | 33/1 | 13 | — |
| 3326[4] | **Aurelian (65)** (MBell) **2-9-0** MFenton(5) (cl up 5f) | hd | **14** | 14/1 | 25 | — |
| 4570[13] | **Perfect Angel (IRE) (54)** (MHTompkins) **2-8-0**[(3)] MHenry(4) (outpcd fr ½-wy) | 2½ | **15** | 20/1 | 9 | — |
| 4084[7] | **Salabatni (70)** (EALDunlop) **2-9-5** KDarley(2) (cl up over 5f) | 2 | **16** | 16/1 | 21 | — |
| 4764[12] | **Jonfy (IRE) (55)** (BWHills) **2-8-4**[ow1] JCarroll(17) (wl bhd fr ½-wy) | ½ | **17** | 33/1 | 5 | — |
| 4749[16] | **Compact Disc (IRE) (55)** (MJohnston) **2-8-4** TWilliams(1) (spd to ½-wy) | 3½ | **18** | 33/1 | — | — |

(SP 147.3%) **18 Rn**

**1m 38.1** (2.40) CSF £31.22 CT £206.69 TOTE £8.60: £2.60 £1.10 £2.10 £2.40 (£36.20) Trio £199.80 OWNER Mr Colin Webster (THIRSK) BRED Cleaboy Farms Co
LONG HANDICAP Dancing Star (IRE) 7-8

**3969 Epic Stand**, trying his longest trip to date, was well supported and not surprisingly put up his best performance to date to win in useful style. (8/1: op 14/1)
**4795* Double Espresso (IRE)**, up 7lb for a win last time, was again in top form and beat all but the dark horse. (5/2)
**4787 Castles Burning (USA)** has slipped down the handicap and is running well, but was short of toe in the final furlong. (10/1)
**4814 Time Can Tell** is a good, honest and consistent sort who stays well, but he was just short of speed in the closing stages. (10/1)
**4262 Gresatre** seems to have his own ideas, but was persuaded to run in the closing stages, albeit too late. (8/1: op 5/1)
**4795 Dee Pee Tee Cee (IRE)** may need further, but he is certainly a hard ride and may have a mind of his own. (25/1)
**4564 Smart Spirit (IRE)** had another educational and never got in a blow. Time will see better from her. (20/1)
**Island Prince** (9/2: op 8/1)

### 4991 E.B.F. BIRCH MAIDEN STKS (2-Y.O) (Class D)
2-05 (2-07) **7f** £3,666.75 (£1,104.00: £534.50: £249.75) Stalls: Centre GOING minus 0.41 sec per fur (F)

| | | | | SP | RR | SF |
|---|---|---|---|---|---|---|
| 4756[4] | **Tayseer (USA)** (EALDunlop) **2-9-0** WRyan(6) (lw: hld up: hdwy to ld over 2f out: r.o wl) | — | **1** | 4/1[3] | 88 | 50 |
| 4825[3] | **Fly To The Stars** (MJohnston) **2-9-0** KDarley(15) (lw: trckd ldrs: effrt over 2f out: r.o wl towards fin) | 1 | **2** | 3/1[1] | 86 | 48 |
| 4770[5] | **Russian Ruler (IRE)** (APJarvis) **2-9-0** SDrowne(7) (in tch: hdwy 3f out: styd on towards fin) | 2 | **3** | 10/1 | 81 | 43 |
| | **Song of Freedom** (JHMGosden) **2-9-0** JCarroll(11) (w'like: str: bit bkwd: in tch: hdwy over 2f out: nt qckn ins fnl f) | nk | **4** | 25/1 | 81+ | 43 |
| 4817[7] | **Farnese (IRE)** (LMCumani) **2-9-0** JWeaver(2) (w ldrs: effrt over 2f out: kpt on one pce appr fnl f) | nk | **5** | 11/2 | 80 | 42 |
| 4797[2] | **Catria (IRE) (80)** (JHMGosden) **2-8-9** LDettori(17) (w ldr: led ½-wy: hdd over 2f out: wknd over 1f out) | 9 | **6** | 4/1[3] | 54 | 16 |
| 4046[11] | **My Saltarello (IRE)** (ABMulholland) **2-9-0** MBirch(16) (lw: w ldrs 4f: wknd) | 2 | **7** | 100/1 | 55 | 17 |
| 4796[9] | **Anetta** (MissSEHall) **2-8-9** DaneO'Neill(12) (led to ½-wy: sn wknd) | 1¼ | **8** | 20/1 | 47 | 9 |
| 4105[4] | **Viva Verdi (IRE)** (JLDunlop) **2-8-9** TSprake(10) (plld hrd: effrt 3f out: sn btn) | 2 | **9** | 100/30[2] | 42 | 4 |
| 4818[8] | **Enavius (IRE)** (MBell) **2-9-0** MFenton(8) (outpcd & bhd tl styd on fnl 2f) | 1¾ | **10** | 25/1 | 43 | 5 |
| | **Panooras Lord (IRE)** (JSWainwright) **2-9-0** LCharnock(4) (cmpt: bkwd: outpcd fr ½-wy) | 3 | **11** | 200/1 | 36 | — |
| 4807[8] | **Whitegate's Son** (BEllison) **2-9-0** JQuinn(1) (prom to ½-wy) | s.h | **12** | 200/1 | 36 | — |
| | **Six Shooter** (EWeymes) **2-8-9** DeanMcKeown(14) (unf: scope: prom over 4f) | ½ | **13** | 50/1 | 30 | — |
| 4684[10] | **Polarize** (TDBarron) **2-9-0** JFortune(5) (s.i.s: nvr nr to chal) | 1¼ | **14** | 50/1 | 32 | — |
| 4706[10] | **Hit The Flag (IRE)** (ABMulholland) **2-9-0** JFEgan(3) (sn outpcd & wl bhd) | 11 | **15** | 100/1 | 7 | — |
| 4807[11] | **Toon Flyer** (WStorey) **2-9-0** NKennedy(9) (a outpcd & wl bhd) | ¾ | **16** | 100/1 | 5 | — |

46844 *Noirie* (MBrittain) **2-9-0** MWigham(13) (Withdrawn not under Starter's orders: permission of Stewards) ........... **W** — —
(SP 132.9%) **16 Rn**

**1m 24.1** (1.10) CSF £16.94 TOTE £4.80: £1.80 £1.60 £3.10 (£13.40) Trio £35.00 OWNER Mr Hilal Salem (NEWMARKET) BRED Gainsborough Farm Inc
**4756 Tayseer (USA)**, appreciating this trip, won really well and would seem to be improving fast. (4/1)
**4825 Fly To The Stars** either needs softer ground or further still, as he took an age to get going. There is better to come. (3/1)
**4770 Russian Ruler (IRE)** has improved a good deal from his first run and should not be hard to place next year. (10/1)
**Song of Freedom**, a useful-looking type, needed this, but showed plenty of promise, and is well worth noting for the future. (25/1)
**Farnese (IRE)** was really taught his job here and ran well. This should stand him in good stead. (11/2)
**4797 Catria (IRE)** was ultra-fit and had her chances, but was disappointing once off the bit. (4/1)

## 4992 SYCAMORE H'CAP (0-80) (3-Y.O) (Class D)

2-35 (2-36) **1m 3f** £3,665.00 (£1,100.00: £530.00: £245.00) Stalls: Low GOING minus 0.53 sec per fur (F)

| | | | | SP | RR | SF |
|---|---|---|---|---|---|---|
| 4548³ | **Renzo (IRE) (77)** (GHarwood) **3-9-4** AClark(4) (lw: s.i.s: drvn along & sn rcvrd: hdwy over 3f out: hung lft fnl 2f: styd on wl: fin 2nd, nk: awrdd r) | — | **1** | 14/1 | 89 | 49 |
| 4761⁷ | **Traceability (80)** (SCWilliams) **3-9-4**(3) FLynch(8) (led after 2f: rdn over 2f out: styd on: jst ct: fin 3rd, hd: plcd 2nd) | | **2** | 10/1 | 91 | 51 |
| 4824* | **Enriched (IRE) (77)** (JHMGosden) **3-9-4** LDettori(7) (trckd ldrs: chal over 3f out: sn rdn: btn whn hmpd ins fnl f: fin 4th, 3l: plcd 3rd) | | **3** | 7/4 1 | 84 | 44 |
| 4866* | **Blurred (IRE) (77)** (MHTompkins) **3-9-1**(3) MHenry(6) (lw: trckd ldrs: nt clr run fr 3f out tl squeezed thro ins fnl f: led cl home: fin 1st: disq: plcd 4th) | | **4** | 7/2 2 | 89+ | 49 |
| 4580⁵ | **Rusk (74)** (JPearce) **3-9-1** MWigham(2) (lw: hld up: effrt 3f out: no imp) | ½ | **5** | 10/1 | 80 | 40 |
| 2558* | **Florentino (IRE) (72)** (BWHills) **3-8-13** JCarroll(9) (lw: bhd: effrt over 3f out: wandered & nvr rchd ldrs) | 3 | **6** | 10/1 | 74 | 34 |
| 4866³ | **Alicia (IRE) (71)** (JLDunlop) **3-8-12** KDarley(5) (bhd: drvn along 4f out: styd on: n.d) | 1¾ | **7** | 8/1 3 | 70 | 30 |
| 4695⁶ | **General Glow (61)** (PDEvans) **3-8-2**ow1 JFEgan(10) (effrt over 4f out: sn rdn & wknd) | 13 | **8** | 20/1 | 42 | 1 |
| 4827⁶ | **Forest Robin (80)** (MrsJRRamsden) **3-9-7** WRyan(3) (in tch tl lost pl over 3f out) | 1¾ | **9** | 20/1 | 58 | 18 |
| 4217² | **Ballpoint (74)** (GMMoore) **3-9-1** JFortune(1) (led 2f: w ldr tl wknd over 3f out) | 8 | **10** | 16/1 | 40 | — |

(SP 119.0%) **10 Rn**

**2m 19.4** (1.40) CSF £131.33 CT £334.83 TOTE £11.00: £2.70 £2.50 £1.20 (£49.90) Trio £30.70 OWNER Mr K. J. Buchanan (PULBOROUGH) BRED K. J. and Mrs Buchanan
STEWARDS' ENQUIRY Henry susp. 14-16,18-19 & 22/11/96 (careless riding). Clark susp. 14-15/11/96 (careless riding). (Careless Riding)
**4548 Renzo (IRE)** was fortunate to get this in the Stewards' Room as he caused a fair bit of trouble himself, and he was also well outpointed by the winner. (14/1)
**3997 Traceability**, happier at this trip, put up a decent show and, if anything, was the one who deserved to get the race in the Stewards' Room. (10/1)
**4824* Enriched (IRE)** had her chances, but was not good enough and being hampered made no difference. (7/4)
**4866* Blurred (IRE)** should have won this, but his young rider found the other jockeys not helping him at all, and he eventually pushed his way through. Easily the best horse in the race, he had to lose it as the Rules stand. (7/2)
**4580 Rusk** always found this trip on this fastish surface too short. (10/1)
**2558* Florentino (IRE)**, after four months off, was ring-rusty. (10/1)
**4866 Alicia (IRE)** never took the slightest interest. (8/1: 6/1-9/1)

## 4993 POPLAR H'CAP (0-70) (3-Y.O+) (Class E)

3-05 (3-08) **1m 2f** £3,400.25 (£1,022.00: £493.50: £229.25) Stalls: Low GOING minus 0.53 sec per fur (F)

| | | | | SP | RR | SF |
|---|---|---|---|---|---|---|
| 4900⁹ | **Askern (60)** (DHaydnJones) **5-9-4** AClark(6) (trckd ldrs: led wl over 2f out & qcknd clr: jst hld on) | — | **1** | 16/1 | 71 | 53 |
| 4793⁶ | **Shaffishayes (62)** (MrsMReveley) **4-9-6** LDettori(7) (lw: hld up: effrt over 3f out: hrd rdn & r.o appr fnl f: jst failed) | hd | **2** | 11/2 2 | 73 | 55 |
| 4900³ | **Rex Mundi (61)** (PDEvans) **4-9-5** JFEgan(8) (a.p: hrd rdn fnl 2½f: styd on wl) | nk | **3** | 8/1 3 | 71 | 53 |
| 4793¹⁴ | **Calder King (62)** (JLEyre) **5-9-6b** RLappin(5) (hdwy over 3f out: edgd lft over 1f out: styd on) | ¾ | **4** | 20/1 | 71 | 53 |
| 4967⁷ | **Your Most Welcome (57)** (DJSffrenchDavis) **5-8-10b1**(5) GParkin(12) (chsd ldrs: wandered u.p fnl 2f: btn whn hmpd towards fin) | ¾ | **5** | 12/1 | 65 | 47 |
| 4624³ | **Leif the Lucky (USA) (61)** (MissSEHall) **7-9-5** DaneO'Neill(15) (hld up: stdy hdwy 3f out: effrt & hung lft over 1f out: nt qckn) | 1 | **6** | 8/1 3 | 67 | 49 |
| 4900¹⁴ | **Augustan (55)** (SGollings) **5-8-13** JQuinn(3) (bhd: styd on fnl 3f: nrst fin) | 1 | **7** | 25/1 | 60 | 42 |
| 4793¹¹ | **Essayeffsee (58)** (MrsMReveley) **7-9-2** KDarley(2) (nvr nr to chal) | 1 | **8** | 11/1 | 61 | 43 |
| 4872⁷ | **Fern's Governor (59)** (WJMusson) **4-9-3** DRMcCabe(11) (hld up & bhd: hdwy & n.m.r 2f out: too much to do) | s.h | **9** | 9/2 1 | 62 | 44 |
| 4906* | **Thatched (IRE) (52)** (REBarr) **6-8-3**(7) 5x KSked(14) (hld up: effrt on outside 3f out: n.d) | nk | **10** | 12/1 | 55 | 37 |
| 4905⁴ | **Mentalasanythin (63)** (DHaydnJones) **7-9-7** LCharnock(1) (pushed along over 4f out: n.d) | 3 | **11** | 9/1 | 61 | 43 |
| 4812⁵ | **Brambles Way (51)** (MrsMReveley) **7-8-4v**(5) SCopp(9) (chsd ldrs tl rdn & wknd over 2f out) | 2½ | **12** | 12/1 | 45 | 27 |
| 4724² | **Mr Teigh (67)** (MrsJRRamsden) **4-9-11** JFortune(10) (led tl hdd & wknd wl over 2f out) | 1½ | **13** | 8/1 3 | 58 | 40 |
| 3509⁷ | **Domitia (USA) (65)** (MBell) **4-9-9** MFenton(17) (b: lost tch fnl 4f) | 4 | **14** | 16/1 | 50 | 32 |
| 4905⁷ | **Spanish Verdict (62)** (DenysSmith) **9-9-6** JWeaver(16) (cl up tl wknd over 3f out) | 2½ | **15** | 20/1 | 43 | 25 |
| 4753⁹ | **Blackpatch Hill (60)** (NTinkler) **7-9-4** KimTinkler(4) (a bhd) | 2 | **16** | 100/1 | 38 | 20 |
| 4810²⁰ | **French Ginger (53)** (WStorey) **5-8-11** NKennedy(13) (sn bhd: t.o) | 30 | **17** | 50/1 | — | — |

(SP 136.4%) **17 Rn**

**2m 4.3** (0.70) CSF £103.87 CT £727.90 TOTE £25.10: £4.10 £2.00 £1.80 £4.40 (£79.10) Trio £442.10; £137.02 to Newton Abbot 6/10/96 OWNER Mr Hugh O'Donnell (PONTYPRIDD) BRED Highclere Stud Ltd
**4484 Askern**, given a good opportunist ride, went for home approaching the final two furlongs and stole just enough to last out. (16/1)
**4793 Shaffishayes** runs when in the mood and his rider eventually persuaded him in the final furlong, but the line came that half stride too soon. (11/2)
**4900 Rex Mundi** is probably better over a bit further but he did keep answering his rider's calls all the way to the line. (8/1)
**4431 Calder King** gives the impression that if he really put his mind to it, he has more ability. (20/1)
**4597* Your Most Welcome**, in blinkers for the first time, had her chances but failed to go through with the effort. (12/1)
**4624 Leif the Lucky (USA)** appeared to be cantering three furlongs out but when asked for an effort, there was no response. (8/1)
**4872 Fern's Governor**, set an impossible task, never saw enough daylight to do anything about it. (9/2)

## 4994 ASH H'CAP (0-95) (3-Y.O+) (Class C)
3-35 (3-40) **6f** £6,784.50 (£2,046.00: £993.00: £466.50) Stalls: Centre GOING minus 0.41 sec per fur (F)

| | | | | SP | RR | SF |
|---|---|---|---|---|---|---|
| 4791[7] | **Cretan Gift (73)** (NPLittmoden) **5-8-7b** TGMcLaughlin(6) (trckd ldrs far side: stdy hdwy 2f out: hrd rdn fnl f to ld cl home) | — | **1** | 14/1 | 87 | 59 |
| 4975[7] | **Tiler (IRE) (77)** (MJohnston) **4-8-11** JWeaver(13) (lw: led centre group: ev ch ins fnl f: kpt on wl) | s.h | **2** | 16/1 | 91 | 63 |
| 4689[3] | **Daawe (USA) (72)** (MrsVAAconley) **5-8-6** MDeering(2) (racd far side: led tl hrd rdn & no ex cl home) | ½ | **3** | 12/1 | 85 | 57 |
| 4909[4] | **Saint Express (77)** (MrsMReveley) **6-8-11** KDarley(21) (a chsng ldrs: nt qckn fnl f) | 2½ | **4** | 10/1[3] | 83 | 55 |
| 4811[11] | **French Grit (IRE) (73)** (MDods) **4-8-7** AClark(1) (a chsng ldrs far side: nt qckn fnl 2f) | nk | **5** | 16/1 | 78 | 50 |
| 4687[5] | **Palo Blanco (76)** (TDBarron) **5-8-10** JFortune(18) (trckd ldrs: effrt 2f out: nt qckn) | ½ | **6** | 7/1[1] | 80 | 52 |
| 4623[3] | **Primo Lara (88)** (PWHarris) **4-9-8** LDettori(3) (lw: prom far side: nt qckn fnl 2f) | 1¼ | **7** | 10/1[3] | 88 | 60 |
| 4811[14] | **Takadou (IRE) (79)** (MissLCSiddall) **5-8-13** RLappin(20) (lw: bhd: hdwy 2f out: nrst fin) | s.h | **8** | 25/1 | 79 | 51 |
| 4772[13] | **Mr Bergerac (IRE) (85)** (BPalling) **5-9-5** TSprake(19) (a in tch: no hdwy fnl 2f) | nk | **9** | 14/1 | 85 | 57 |
| 4788[6] | **Prima Silk (67)** (MJRyan) **5-8-1** GBardwell(12) (sme hdwy fnl 2f) | ½ | **10** | 25/1 | 65 | 37 |
| 4687[12] | **Double Blue (90)** (MJohnston) **7-9-3**(7) KSked(26) (racd stands' side: swtchd centre ½-wy: n.d) | nk | **11** | 33/1 | 87 | 59 |
| 4802[5] | **So Intrepid (IRE) (77)** (JMBradley) **6-8-11** SDrowne(5) (lw: in tch far side: effrt over 2f out) | nk | **12** | 12/1 | 74 | 46 |
| 4571[4] | **Thwaab (70)** (FWatson) **4-8-4b** NKennedy(11) (lw: effrt over 2f out: no imp) | s.h | **13** | 12/1 | 66 | 38 |
| 4823[3] | **Bajan Rose (85)** (MBlanshard) **4-9-5** JQuinn(24) (trckd ldrs tl wknd fnl 2f) | hd | **14** | 9/1[2] | 81 | 53 |
| 4881[7] | **Castlerea Lad (64)** (RHollinshead) **7-7-12** NCarlisle(16) (nvr trbld ldrs) | hd | **15** | 25/1 | 60 | 32 |
| 4687[10] | **Garnock Valley (84)** (JBerry) **6-9-4** GCarter(8) (in tch over 3f) | ½ | **16** | 16/1 | 79 | 51 |
| 4788[7] | **Be Warned (62)** (MDods) **5-7-10b** FNorton(17) (a in rr) | s.h | **17** | 50/1 | 56 | 28 |
| 4689[10] | **Miss Waterline (70)** (PDEvans) **3-8-4** JFEgan(15) (a bhd) | 1 | **18** | 25/1 | 62 | 34 |
| 4909[9] | **Saddlehome (USA) (71)** (TDBarron) **7-8-5** JCarroll(4) (hld up: effrt 2f out: sn btn) | ½ | **19** | 14/1 | 61 | 33 |
| 4869[6] | **Maid For The Hills (87)** (DRLoder) **3-9-7** DRMcCabe(23) (racd stands' side: prom: rdn ½-wy: btn over 1f out) | 1¾ | **20** | 16/1 | 73 | 45 |
| 4811[15] | **Stylish Ways (IRE) (78)** (MissSEHall) **4-8-12** MBirch(9) (hld up: effrt ½-wy: no rspnse) | ½ | **21** | 14/1 | 62 | 34 |
| 4909[5] | **Keston Pond (IRE) (75)** (MrsVAAconley) **6-8-9** WRyan(10) (prom: sn drvn along: wknd 2f out) | 1¾ | **22** | 16/1 | 55 | 27 |
| 4805[5] | **Barato (68)** (MrsJRRamsden) **5-8-2** NAdams(22) (b.nr hind: reard s: racd stands' side tl swtchd ½-wy: a bhd) | 1¾ | **23** | 20/1 | 43 | 15 |
| 4811[18] | **Takhlid (USA) (77)** (DWChapman) **5-8-11** ACulhane(7) (sn outpcd & bhd) | ¾ | **24** | 50/1 | 50 | 22 |
| 4809[14] | **Halmanerror (63)** (MrsJRRamsden) **6-7-11** LCharnock(25) (racd stands' side: prom 4f: wknd) | 1¾ | **25** | 20/1 | 31 | 3 |

(SP 151.6%) **25 Rn**

**1m 10.0** (-0.20) CSF £230.48 CT £2,613.78 TOTE £29.10: £4.40 £3.40 £4.70 £2.70 (£260.60) Trio £1,752.50; £1,777.23 to Newton Abbot 6/11/96 OWNER Mr T. Clarke (WOLVERHAMPTON) BRED Hesmonds Stud Ltd
LONG HANDICAP Be Warned 7-8

**4312* Cretan Gift** was back to his best here and travelled well. When the pressure was on, he found just enough. (14/1)
**3296 Tiler (IRE)** is back to his best and well-handicapped, but unless he can find opportunities on the All-Weather it would all seem to be in vain. (16/1)
**4689 Daawe (USA)** ran another cracking race but despite a valiant effort, was just touched off. (12/1)
**4909 Saint Express** is running well but is not quite doing enough when it matters. (10/1)
**4791 French Grit (IRE)** keeps showing up well but is just short of dash. (16/1)
**4687 Palo Blanco** looked to be going quite well, but failed to pick up when asked for a serious effort in the last couple of furlongs. (7/1)
**4561 Takadou (IRE)** seems to still have the ability but seems to have his own ideas these days. (25/1)

## 4995 OAK LIMITED STKS (0-75) (3-Y.O+) (Class D)
4-05 (4-06) **5f** £3,535.00 (£1,060.00: £510.00: £235.00) Stalls: Centre GOING minus 0.41 sec per fur (F)

| | | | | SP | RR | SF |
|---|---|---|---|---|---|---|
| 4765[19] | **Palacegate Jack (IRE) (73)** (CADwyer) **5-9-1** JCarroll(1) (mde all: all out) | — | **1** | 8/1 | 81 | 58 |
| 4802[11] | **Friendly Brave (USA) (70)** (MissGayKelleway) **6-9-7** JWeaver(8) (b.hind: hld up & bhd: hdwy whn n.m.r 1f out: r.o wl towards fin) | nk | **2** | 10/1 | 86 | 63 |
| 4802[4] | **Splicing (73)** (WJHaggas) **3-8-6**(3) FLynch(4) (cl up: rdn 2f out: edgd rt appr fnl f: kpt on) | ¾ | **3** | 3/1[1] | 72 | 49 |
| 4765[10] | **Lady Sheriff (74)** (RHollinshead) **5-8-2**(7) KSked(3) (a chsng ldrs: rdn 2f out: nt qckn) | hd | **4** | 9/2[3] | 71 | 48 |
| 4811[10] | **Insider Trader (75)** (MrsJRRamsden) **5-9-1** JFortune(7) (b.off fore: prom tl rdn & wknd appr fnl f) | ¾ | **5** | 4/1[2] | 75 | 52 |
| 4791[17] | **Wollstonecraft (IRE) (74)** (JHMGosden) **3-8-9** LDettori(2) (prom: rdn ½-wy: hung lft over 1f out: sn btn) | 1 | **6** | 7/1 | 66 | 43 |
| 4791[6] | **Sally Slade (68)** (CACyzer) **4-8-12** GCarter(6) (in tch: rdn ½-wy: no imp) | ½ | **7** | 9/2[3] | 67 | 44 |
| 4791[5] | **Tropical Beach (63)** (JBerry) **3-9-4** KDarley(5) (outpcd ½-wy: n.d after) | 2 | **8** | 12/1 | 67 | 44 |

(SP 121.8%) **8 Rn**

**57.8 secs** (0.30) CSF £76.43 TOTE £9.40: £3.00 £2.50 £2.10 (£37.60) OWNER Binding Matters Ltd (NEWMARKET) BRED Brendan and Sheila Powell

**4342 Palacegate Jack (IRE)** always had the edge on these for speed and showed fine courage to last out. (8/1)
**4581 Friendly Brave (USA)** would have won this with any luck at all and was given a terrific ride, but things just went wrong through no fault of his own. (10/1)
**4802 Splicing** had her chances but was inclined to hang when the pressure was on, throwing all chances away. (3/1)
**3602 Lady Sheriff** ran well and will no doubt earn her keep on the All Weather. (9/2)
**4765 Insider Trader** has put in some useful efforts without the headgear this season, but almost all his victories have come with either blinkers or a visor. (4/1)

T/Jkpt: Not won; £26,175.27 to Newton Abbot 6/11/96. T/Plpt: £247.00 (75.39 Tckts). T/Qdpt: £77.40 (17.76 Tckts). AA/WG

# 4889-LINGFIELD (L-H) (Standard)
## Thursday November 7th
WEATHER: unsettled WIND: mod half bhd

## 4996 TAURUS H'CAP (0-70) (I) (3-Y.O+) (Class E)
12-30 (12-33) **5f (Equitrack)** £2,690.60 (£798.80: £378.40: £168.20) Stalls: High GOING minus 0.54 sec per fur (FST)

| | | | | SP | RR | SF |
|---|---|---|---|---|---|---|
| *4776** | **Ramsey Hope (65)** (CWFairhurst) **3-9-9v** JReid(4) (led over 2f: led ins fnl f: rdn out) | — | **1** | 13/2[2] | 75 | 49 |

4828$^{2}$ **Another Batchworth (63)** (EAWheeler) **4-9-7b** SWhitworth(2) (dwlt: hdwy 3f out: led over 2f out tl ins fnl f: unable qckn)....1½ **2** 6/4$^{1}$ 68 42
*4776$^{4}$* **Napier Star (57)** (MrsNMacauley) **3-8-12v**$^{(3)}$ CTeague(5) (rn v.wd & lost pl bnd wl over 1f out: rallied fnl f: r.o wl)....1 **3** 9/1$^{3}$ 59 33
4215$^{9}$ **Lift Boy (USA) (68)** (AMoore) **7-9-12** CandyMorris(1) (hdwy over 1f out: r.o ins fnl f)....1 **4** 16/1 67 41
4610$^{16}$ **Kalar (61)** (DWChapman) **7-9-5b** TQuinn(6) (a.p: rdn over 1f out: one pce)....nk **5** 13/2$^{2}$ 59 33
*4573$^{10}$* **Bashful Brave (50)** (BPJBaugh) **5-8-8** RPerham(7) (a.p: one pce fnl 2f)....s.h **6** 10/1 48 22
4205$^{13}$ **Windrush Boy (54)** (JRBosley) **6-8-12** CRutter(3) (a.p: rdn over 1f out: wknd ins fnl f)....1¾ **7** 14/1 46 20
4428$^{5}$ **Mystery Matthias (48)** (MissBSanders) **3-8-6v** SSanders(9) (a bhd)....2 **8** 16/1 34 8
4881$^{6}$ **Dissentor (IRE) (53)** (JAGlover) **4-8-11b** SDWilliams(8) (bhd fnl 2f)....1 **9** 12/1 36 10
1512$^{W}$ **Distant Dynasty (49)** (BAPearce) **6-8-7** StephenDavies(10) (a bhd)....2 **10** 25/1 25 —
(SP 115.7%) **10 Rn**

**58.65 secs** (0.65) CSF £15.82 CT £81.37 TOTE £9.20: £2.70 £1.10 £2.10 (£9.40) Trio £18.80 OWNER Mr C. D. Barber-Lomax (MIDDLEHAM) BRED Norton Grove Stud Ltd
STEWARDS' ENQUIRY Davies fined £80 under Rule 150(vi) (failing to parade his mount in front of stands).
**4776* Ramsey Hope**, a surprise winner on the Sand three weeks ago, showed that to be no fluke. (13/2)
**4828 Another Batchworth**, in tremendous form at present, failed to get her customary fast start, which probably cost her the race. Losses are only lent. (6/4)
**4776 Napier Star** raced up with the pace but ran extremely wide on the home turn, conceding a tremendous amount of ground. Had she handled the bend better, the result may have been different. (9/1)
**3864 Lift Boy (USA)** has gained four of his seven victories to date on Sand, but needs to drop into selling or claiming company to be seen at his best. (16/1)
**4473 Kalar** is rated 2lb lower than when winning here in March and should be able to find a handicap before long on the Sand, especially if he can dominate. (13/2)
**3146 Bashful Brave** has been out of form on Turf recently, but ran better. (10/1: 12/1-20/1)

## 4997 A-PLANT POWERED ACCESS MAIDEN STKS (I) (3-Y.O) (Class D)
1-00 (1-01) **7f (Equitrack)** £3,206.80 (£951.40: £450.20: £199.60) Stalls: Low GOING minus 0.54 sec per fur (FST)

SP RR SF
1651$^{12}$ **Lancashire Legend (60)** (SDow) **3-8-9**$^{(5)}$ ADaly(9) (a.p: led over 1f out: hrd rdn: r.o wl)....— **1** 10/1$^{3}$ 68 37
2432$^{3}$ **Woodbury Lad (USA) (80)** (WRMuir) **3-9-0** JReid(3) (w ldr: led over 4f out tl over 1f out: unable qckn fnl f)....3 **2** 4/6$^{1}$ 61 30
*4978$^{4}$* **Balinsky (IRE) (55)** (JBerry) **3-8-4**$^{(5)}$ PRoberts(8) (hdwy over 1f out: r.o one pce)....3½ **3** 10/1$^{3}$ 48 17
4813$^{6}$ **Questing Star (62)** (GWragg) **3-8-2**$^{(7)}$ GMilligan(7) (hdwy over 1f out: nvr nrr)....1¼ **4** 3/1$^{2}$ 45 14
4340$^{5}$ **Areish (IRE) (35)** (JFfitch-Heyes) **3-8-9b$^{1}$** DHarrison(6) (a.p: rdn over 3f out: wknd over 1f out)....1¼ **5** 50/1 42 11
*4336$^{7}$* **Bellacardia (40)** (AMoore) **3-8-9** CandyMorris(1) (bhd fnl 4f)....14 **6** 50/1 10 —
*4776$^{12}$* **Il Doria (IRE) (50)** (AHide) **3-8-9** AMcGlone(4) (led over 2f: wknd over 2f out)....1¼ **7** 20/1 8 —
758$^{9}$ **First Gallery** (RMFlower) **3-8-9** DBiggs(2) (bhd fnl 4f)....5 **8** 50/1 — —
**Jendali Princess** (MJPolglase) **3-8-9** SSanders(5) (s.s: a wl bhd)....9 **9** 50/1 — —
(SP 115.8%) **9 Rn**

**1m 25.4** (1.40) CSF £16.67 TOTE £8.80: £1.90 £1.00 £2.60 (£6.00) Trio £10.90 OWNER Bryan Taker & David Wilson (EPSOM) BRED Peter Nash
**352 Lancashire Legend** may have been out of form on Turf this year, but he ran well to be placed on the Equitrack last winter and put that experience to good use. (10/1: 9/2-12/1)
**2432 Woodbury Lad (USA)**, placed in ordinary maidens in the summer, was returning from a four-month break and making his All-Weather debut. He finished clear of the remainder and should soon lose his maiden tag. (4/6)
**4978 Balinsky (IRE)** is a very poor performer. (10/1)
**4813 Questing Star** did not show much on Turf and gave little encouragement on this surface either. (3/1: op 2/1)
**Areish (IRE)** has very little ability. (50/1)

## 4998 LEO CLAIMING STKS (3-Y.O+) (Class F)
1-30 (1-31) **1m 4f (Equitrack)** £2,381.00 (£656.00: £311.00) Stalls: Low GOING minus 0.54 sec per fur (FST)

SP RR SF
4669$^{15}$ **Persian Conquest (IRE) (67)** (RIngram) **4-9-9b** AMcGlone(4) (chsd ldr: led 4f out: rdn out)....— **1** 12/1 76 48
4904$^{2}$ **Loki (IRE) (62)** (GLewis) **8-9-0**$^{(3)}$ AWhelan(11) (hdwy 6f out: chsd wnr over 3f out: unable qckn fnl 2f)....3 **2** 15/8$^{1}$ 66 38
*4894$^{5}$* **Proud Image (50)** (GMMcCourt) **4-9-6** CRutter(12) (hdwy 6f out: rdn over 2f out: one pce)....½ **3** 8/1 68 40
*4894$^{10}$* **Our Eddie (62)** (BGubby) **7-9-0v** RHughes(13) (hdwy 6f out: wknd over 2f out)....9 **4** 11/2$^{3}$ 50 22
4898$^{12}$ **Followthe Allstars (46)** (TJNaughton) **3-9-0b** TSprake(9) (hdwy 8f out: rdn over 3f out: sn wknd)....1½ **5** 20/1 54 20
4703$^{12}$ **Shuttlecock (37)** (MrsNMacauley) **5-9-3**$^{(3)}$ CTeague(7) (nvr nr to chal)....½ **6** 33/1 54 26
3965$^{9}$ **Efficacious (IRE) (44)** (AMoore) **3-7-11**$^{(3)}$ MHenry(3) (led 8f)....2 **7** 14/1 37 3
3849$^{4}$ **Tablets of Stone (IRE) (40)** (JRBosley) **3-8-8**$^{(3)}$ DWright(2) (nvr nrr)....15 **8** 20/1 28 —
4603$^{11}$ **Chesteine (41)** (PJMakin) **3-8-6** SSanders(6) (bhd fnl 4f)....5 **9** 33/1 16 —
4426$^{15}$ **Emnala (IRE) (43)** (EAWheeler) **4-8-10**$^{(5)}$ ADaly(10) (bhd fnl 6f)....hd **10** 33/1 19 —
4868$^{12}$ **Bianca's Son (BEL)** (JMPlasschaert,Belgium) **6-9-12** MKeogh(8) (prom 6f)....10 **11** 50/1 17 —
**Nordic Spree (IRE)** (AMoore) **4-9-12** AClark(1) (bhd fnl 7f: t.o)....dist **12** 33/1 — —
*4977$^{3}$* **Princely Gait (73)** (MJPolglase) **5-9-12** MRimmer(5) (prom 6f: t.o whn fell 4f out: dead).... **F** 7/2$^{2}$ — —
(SP 121.1%) **13 Rn**

**2m 32.33** (2.33) CSF £33.35 TOTE £21.80: £5.60 £1.30 £2.70 (£21.80) Trio £90.70 OWNER Mr C. G. Adams (EPSOM) BRED Louis A. Walshe
WEIGHT FOR AGE 3yo-6lb
**Persian Conquest (IRE)**, whose three victories to date have all come on the All-Weather, showed nothing on Turf this year but bounced back to form on his favoured surface. (12/1: 8/1-14/1)
**4904 Loki (IRE)** failed to find the necessary turn of foot in the straight. This seems to be his grade nowadays. (15/8)
**4894 Proud Image** failed to find the necessary turn of foot in the straight. This is his grade. (8/1: op 5/1)
**3435* Our Eddie** has gained all five victories here over a mile and a quarter and this extra two furlongs is beyond him. (11/2)
**3860 Followthe Allstars**, in a handy position early on the final circuit, had given his all three furlongs out. (20/1)

## 4999 SCORPIO NURSERY H'CAP (0-75) (2-Y.O) (Class E)
2-00 (2-01) **5f (Equitrack)** £3,015.60 (£898.80: £428.40: £193.20) Stalls: High GOING minus 0.54 sec per fur (FST)

SP RR SF
4762$^{7}$ **Fruitana (IRE) (75)** (JBerry) **2-9-2**$^{(5)}$ PRoberts(4) (mde virtually all: rdn out)....— **1** 11/2$^{2}$ 85 39

| | | | Pos | SP | RR | SF |
|---|---|---|---|---|---|---|
| 4966[2] | **Kilcullen Lad (IRE) (59)** (PMooney) **2-8-5v** DRMcCabe(2) (hdwy over 1f out: r.o wl ins fnl f) | 1 | **2** | 9/4[1] | 66 | 20 |
| 4244[11] | **Melbourne Princess (57)** (RMWhitaker) **2-8-3** FNorton(6) (a.p: hrd rdn over 1f out: unable qckn) | 1¼ | **3** | 16/1 | 60 | 14 |
| 4749[17] | **Suite Factors (66)** (KRBurke) **2-8-12v[1]** SSanders(9) (a.p: hrd rdn over 1f out: one pce) | 1¼ | **4** | 11/1 | 65 | 19 |
| 4749[6] | **Come Too Mamma's (65)** (JBerry) **2-8-11** MRoberts(3) (a.p: rdn over 1f out: wknd ins fnl f) | 2½ | **5** | 6/1[3] | 56 | 10 |
| 4912[5] | **Sparkling Edge (55)** (CADwyer) **2-7-8**(7) JoHunnam(10) (nvr nr to chal) | 2½ | **6** | 12/1 | 38 | — |
| 4803[8] | **Will To Win (62)** (PGMurphy) **2-8-8** SDrowne(5) (a bhd) | 1½ | **7** | 12/1 | 40 | — |
| 4748[5] | **Brazilia (66)** (PTWalwyn) **2-8-12** TQuinn(1) (bhd fnl 3f) | ½ | **8** | 13/2 | 42 | — |
| 4425[8] | **Statuette (60)** (BPalling) **2-8-6** TSprake(7) (prom over 3f) | ¾ | **9** | 25/1 | 34 | — |
| 4787[4] | **Suite Addition (IRE) (50)** (CAHorgan) **2-7-10** NAdams(8) (bhd fnl 3f) | 2½ | **10** | 15/2 | 16 | — |

(SP 119.0%) **10 Rn**

**59.11 secs** (0.16 under 2y best) (1.11) CSF £17.82 CT £174.06 TOTE £6.10: £3.60 £1.10 £5.40 (£11.10) Trio £124.40; £3.50 to Doncaster 8/11/96 OWNER Comerford Brothers Ltd (COCKERHAM) BRED Paul Hyland

**4762 Fruitana (IRE)** made virtually all the running to lose his maiden tag, despite topweight. (11/2)

**4966 Kilcullen Lad (IRE)**, without the pricker he wore when running so well at Newmarket last week, put in some really good work in the last furlong and a half, but found the line was always going to beat him. He should soon be winning but, on a fast, sharp track like this, he might be better off over six. (9/4)

**3879 Melbourne Princess** was always to the fore but, despite her rider's efforts, failed to quicken from below the distance. (16/1)

**4230 Suite Factors** was tapped for toe in the last furlong and a half. (11/1: 8/1-12/1)

**2635* Come Too Mamma's**, winner of two Fibresand sellers, played an active role, but had come to the end of her tether inside the final furlong. (6/1)

## 5000 TAURUS H'CAP (0-70) (II) (3-Y.O+) (Class E)

2-30 (2-31) **5f (Equitrack)** £2,663.30 (£790.40: £374.20: £166.10) Stalls: High GOING minus 0.54 sec per fur (FST)

| | | | Pos | SP | RR | SF |
|---|---|---|---|---|---|---|
| 4341[8] | **Mister Raider (48)** (EAWheeler) **4-8-1**(5) ADaly(9) (a.p: led over 2f out: r.o wl) | — | **1** | 10/1 | 57 | 20 |
| 4521[7] | **Step On Degas (60)** (MJFetherston-Godley) **3-8-11**(7) RFfrench(4) (hld up: rdn over 1f out: r.o wl ins fnl f) | hd | **2** | 100/30[1] | 69 | 32 |
| 4881[9] | **Featherstone Lane (65)** (MissLCSiddall) **5-9-9v** DRMcCabe(7) (hdwy over 1f out: r.o wl ins fnl f) | ¾ | **3** | 16/1 | 71 | 34 |
| *4983[5]* | **Cheeky Chappy (63)** (DWChapman) **5-9-7b** 7x TQuinn(2) (hld up: n.m.r over 1f out: unable qckn) | nk | **4** | 7/2[2] | 68 | 31 |
| *4895[3]* | **Invocation (65)** (AMoore) **9-9-9** SSanders(6) (hdwy over 1f out: r.o one pce) | hd | **5** | 10/1 | 70 | 33 |
| 4828[5] | **Lloc (55)** (CADwyer) **4-8-6**(7) JoHunnam(10) (prom over 3f) | 3 | **6** | 8/1 | 50 | 13 |
| *4778[7]* | **Dieci Anno (IRE) (67)** (BPalling) **3-9-11** TSprake(8) (nvr nr to chal) | ¾ | **7** | 16/1 | 60 | 23 |
| *1971[6]* | **Midnight Cookie (51)** (BAPearce) **3-8-9** SDrowne(3) (led over 2f) | 4 | **8** | 25/1 | 31 | — |
| *4776[13]* | **Gi La High (50)** (JBerry) **3-8-3**(5) PRoberts(5) (hdwy & hmpd on ins over 1f out: nt rcvr) | 1¾ | **9** | 7/1[3] | 25 | — |
| *4776[7]* | **Risking (52)** (GLewis) **3-8-7**(3) AWhelan(1) (prom over 3f) | 3½ | **10** | 10/1 | 15 | — |

(SP 111.8%) **10 Rn**

**59.42 secs** (1.42) CSF £39.23 CT £490.20 TOTE £11.20: £2.50 £1.30 £3.90 (£28.60) Trio £161.50; £47.77 to Doncaster 8/11/96 OWNER Raiders Partnership (PANGBOURNE) BRED Alan Hogan

**3661 Mister Raider**, whose only previous success came here in February, just managed to hold off the strong run of the runner-up. (10/1: 7/1-12/1)

**4094 Step On Degas** may have only one win to her name, but she ran on really strongly inside the final furlong, only to find the line just beating her. (100/30)

**4090 Featherstone Lane** put in some really good work, but he has won just twice from sixty-five starts. (16/1)

**4983 Cheeky Chappy**, making a quick reappearance, found himself behind a wall of horses below the distance but, when a gap did appear, he was unable to find the necessary turn of foot. (7/2)

**4895 Invocation** found this trip too sharp. A real Equitrack specialist - four of his five victories have come here - he has done all his winning over five or six furlongs, and needs to step up in trip. (10/1)

**4828 Lloc** (8/1: 11/2-10/1)

**1684 Risking** (10/1: 8/1-12/1)

## 5001 A-PLANT POWERED ACCESS MAIDEN STKS (II) (3-Y.O) (Class D)

3-00 (3-01) **7f (Equitrack)** £3,206.80 (£951.40: £450.20: £199.60) Stalls: Low GOING minus 0.54 sec per fur (FST)

| | | | Pos | SP | RR | SF |
|---|---|---|---|---|---|---|
| 4828[6] | **Smithereens (60)** (PTWalwyn) **3-8-9** TQuinn(5) (mde virtually all: clr 2f out: r.o wl) | — | **1** | 7/1 | 77 | 34 |
| 4693[5] | **The Fugative** (PMitchell) **3-8-9** SSanders(4) (outpcd: hdwy 1f out: swtchd rt ins fnl f: r.o wl) | 9 | **2** | 9/2[3] | 56 | 13 |
| 4592[7] | **Daisy Bates (IRE)** (PWHarris) **3-8-9** AClark(8) (a.p: chsd wnr over 2f out: unable qckn) | ½ | **3** | 3/1[2] | 55 | 12 |
| 3831[7] | **Misky Bay (68)** (DJSCosgrove) **3-9-0** DRMcCabe(6) (wl bhd over 5f: gd hdwy fnl f: r.o wl) | s.h | **4** | 13/2 | 60 | 17 |
| 4921[4] | **Belzao (57)** (DRCElsworth) **3-9-0** DaneO'Neill(2) (a.p: hrd rdn over 1f out: wknd fnl f) | 1 | **5** | 2/1[1] | 58 | 15 |
| | **Zelaya (IRE)** (GLMoore) **3-8-9** SWhitworth(7) (outpcd) | 1½ | **6** | 12/1 | 50 | 7 |
| 4784[13] | **Madison's Touch** (RMFlower) **3-8-9** DBiggs(1) (s.s: a wl bhd) | 15 | **7** | 40/1 | 15 | — |
| 4868[17] | **Fair Lady (BEL)** (JMPlasschaert,Belgium) **3-8-9** StephenDavies(3) (prom over 3f) | 16 | **8** | 40/1 | — | — |

(SP 114.9%) **8 Rn**

**1m 25.21** (1.21) CSF £35.81 TOTE £6.50: £2.60 £1.90 £1.10 (£11.50) OWNER Major & Mrs Kennard and Partners (LAMBOURN) BRED Mrs R. B. Kennard

**4828 Smithereens** at last came good at the tenth attempt and forged clear with the minimum of fuss turning for home to win going away. (7/1)

**4693 The Fugative**, unable to go the fast pace, ran on in the final furlong to finish a very moderate second. (9/2)

**4592 Daisy Bates (IRE)**, taken down early, went in vain pursuit of the winner over a quarter of a mile out and was caught for the runner-up berth near the line. (3/1: 7/4-100/30)

**3681 Misky Bay**, formerly with John Gosden, totally failed to go the pace and was tailed off by halfway. Still in a different parish entering the straight, he absolutely flew in the final furlong and would probably have taken second in a few more strides. He needs further. (13/2)

**4921 Belzao** has had plenty of chances - he has been beaten three times in maidens when odds-on. (2/1)

## 5002 GEMINI H'CAP (0-80) (3-Y.O+) (Class D)

3-30 (3-31) **7f (Equitrack)** £4,159.05 (£1,244.40: £596.70: £272.85) Stalls: Low GOING minus 0.54 sec per fur (FST)

| | | | Pos | SP | RR | SF |
|---|---|---|---|---|---|---|
| 4354[3] | **Mr Nevermind (IRE) (73)** (GLMoore) **6-9-7** SWhitworth(8) (hdwy over 2f out: rdn over 1f out: led wl ins fnl f: r.o wl) | — | **1** | 10/1 | 80 | 51 |
| 3696[6] | **Kings Harmony (IRE) (70)** (PJMakin) **3-9-3** SSanders(15) (a.p: led over 1f out tl wl ins fnl f: r.o) | nk | **2** | 16/1 | 76 | 46 |
| 4831[14] | **Perilous Plight (65)** (MrsLStubbs) **5-8-8**(5) PRoberts(14) (hdwy over 2f out: r.o one pce) | 1¼ | **3** | 12/1 | 69 | 40 |

| | Dist | Pos | SP | RR | SF |
|---|---|---|---|---|---|
| 4909[6] **Ertlon (71)** (CEBrittain) **6-9-5** MRoberts(13) (a.p: led over 3f out tl over 1f out: one pce) | 2 | **4** | 5/1[2] | 70 | 41 |
| 4799[3] **Milos (73)** (TJNaughton) **5-9-7** DaneO'Neill(11) (hdwy over 1f out: r.o wl ins fnl f) | 1 | **5** | 11/1 | 70 | 41 |
| 4775[22] **My Gallery (IRE) (77)** (ABailey) **5-9-4**(7) AngelaGallimore(2) (hdwy over 1f out: nvr nrr) | ½ | **6** | 9/2[1] | 73 | 44 |
| 4768[15] **Desert Invader (IRE) (71)** (DWChapman) **5-9-5** TQuinn(3) (prom over 5f) | hd | **7** | 20/1 | 66 | 37 |
| *502*[*] **Carol's Dream (USA) (72)** (JWHills) **4-9-3**(3) MHenry(9) (nvr nrr) | 2 | **8** | 10/1 | 63 | 34 |
| 4769[27] **Slip Jig (IRE) (78)** (RHannon) **3-9-11** RHughes(7) (prom over 5f) | ½ | **9** | 20/1 | 68 | 38 |
| 4329[13] **Shamrock Fair (IRE) (66)** (LordHuntingdon) **4-9-0** DHarrison(10) (a mid div) | 1½ | **10** | 16/1 | 52 | 23 |
| 4568[30] **Autumn Cover (75)** (PRHedger) **4-9-9** DBiggs(4) (bhd fnl 2f) | nk | **11** | 5/1[2] | 60 | 31 |
| **Bon Secret (IRE) (66)** (TJNaughton) **4-8-11**(3) JDSmith(6) (a bhd) | 1¼ | **12** | 33/1 | 49 | 20 |
| 4682[17] **Blue Flyer (IRE) (79)** (RIngram) **3-9-12** AMcGlone(16) (a bhd) | 5 | **13** | 16/1 | 50 | 20 |
| **Tom Morgan (75)** (PTWalwyn) **5-9-9** TSprake(5) (led over 3f) | nk | **14** | 25/1 | 45 | 16 |
| 4552[8] **Kind of Light (70)** (RGuest) **3-9-3** JReid(1) (prom over 3f) | 1¾ | **15** | 7/1[3] | 36 | 6 |
| 4550[18] **Moi Canard (73)** (BAPearce) **3-9-6** DRMcCabe(12) (bhd fnl 4f) | 5 | **16** | 20/1 | 28 | — |

(SP 136.9%) **16 Rn**

**1m 24.7** (0.70) CSF £158.73 CT £1,881.25 TOTE £8.50: £1.60 £2.20 £2.70 £1.50 (£49.10) Trio £105.60 OWNER Pennine Partners (EPSOM) BRED Robert Corridan

WEIGHT FOR AGE 3yo-1lb

**4354 Mr Nevermind (IRE)** loves it round here - he has won four times and managed to get up in the closing stages. (10/1)
**3696 Kings Harmony (IRE)**, given an eleven-week break, ran a fine race. (16/1)
**4098 Perilous Plight**, five times a winner round here, stayed on for third prize. (12/1)
**4909 Ertlon** is not very consistent. (5/1)
**4799 Milos** is much better on Sand and has won four times here - three over this distance. (11/1)
**4571 My Gallery (IRE)**, winner of nine races this year, never looked like making it ten. (9/2)

## 5003 ARIES AMATEUR H'CAP (0-65) (3-Y.O+) (Class G)

4-00 (4-00) **1m 2f (Equitrack)** £2,070.00 (£570.00: £270.00) Stalls: Low GOING minus 0.54 sec per fur (FST)

| | Dist | Pos | SP | RR | SF |
|---|---|---|---|---|---|
| 4900[10] **Arzani (USA) (50)** (DJSCosgrove) **5-10-11** MissEJohnsonHoughton(6) (hdwy over 2f out: led ins fnl f: r.o wl) | — | **1** | 25/1 | 59 | 49 |
| *4894*[3] **Allstars Express (60)** (TJNaughton) **3-10-12**(5) MrsJNaughton(11) (hdwy over 1f out: r.o wl ins fnl f) | hd | **2** | 7/1 | 69 | 55 |
| 4551[8] **Father Dan (IRE) (58)** (MissGayKelleway) **7-11-0**(5) MrNMoran(4) (hld up: rdn fnl f: unable qckn) | 2 | **3** | 5/1[3] | 64 | 54 |
| 4669[16] **Montone (IRE) (58)** (JRJenkins) **6-11-5v** DrMMannish(7) (a.p: led over 3f out tl ins fnl f: one pce) | ¾ | **4** | 6/1 | 62 | 52 |
| 4793[17] **Our Main Man (50)** (RMWhitaker) **6-10-11** MissRClark(12) (hdwy over 1f out: nvr nrr) | 2 | **5** | 33/1 | 51 | 41 |
| 3980[*] **Don't Drop Bombs (USA) (41)** (DTThom) **7-10-2v** MissJFeilden(3) (led over 6f: wknd ins fnl f) | 1½ | **6** | 7/2[2] | 40 | 30 |
| **Can Can Charlie (60)** (JPearce) **6-11-7** MrsLPearce(5) (nvr nr to chal) | 2½ | **7** | 12/1 | 55 | 45 |
| 3860[5] **She Said No (49)** (AMoore) **4-10-5**(5) MrsJMoore(2) (prom 8f) | 1½ | **8** | 25/1 | 41 | 31 |
| 4815[U] **Chilly Lad (65)** (MJRyan) **5-11-7b**(5)ow13 MrMEmmanuel(1) (a bhd) | hd | **9** | 50/1 | 57 | 34 |
| 4436[19] **Love Legend (42)** (DWPArbuthnot) **11-10-3** MrsDArbuthnot(13) (prom over 7f) | 6 | **10** | 20/1 | 25 | 15 |
| 4513[16] **Mapengo (55)** (JCullinan) **5-10-11**(5) MissEmmaGarley(8) (a wl bhd) | 2 | **11** | 50/1 | 35 | 25 |
| 4125[11] **Mister O'Grady (IRE) (50)** (RAkehurst) **5-10-11** MrTMcCarthy(9) (mid div whn p.u 8f out: dead) | | **P** | 5/2[1] | — | — |

(SP 121.3%) **12 Rn**

**2m 7.99** (3.69) CSF £177.37 CT £944.22 TOTE £40.40: £5.50 £2.80 £2.40 (£692.60) Trio £146.80; £70.31 to Doncaster 8/11/96 OWNER Mr Derrick Yarwood (NEWMARKET) BRED Eaton and Thorne and Robert N. Clay

WEIGHT FOR AGE 3yo-4lb

**Arzani (USA)** had shown nothing in three runs this year, but held on well to lose his maiden tag. (25/1)
**4894 Allstars Express** got into top gear from below the distance but, despite running on strongly, found the line always just beating him. (7/1)
**4355 Father Dan (IRE)** was going nicely on the heels of the principals entering the straight but, when his pilot rousted him along in the final furlong, he could not find the necessary turn of foot. (5/1)
**4503* Montone (IRE)** gets on really well with this rider - the combination have won five times this year together. (6/1)
**Our Main Man** has shown nothing in three runs this year, but picked up ground in the last furlong and a half to be nearest at the line. (33/1)
**3980* Don't Drop Bombs (USA)** goes well in these type of events. (7/2)
**Can Can Charlie** (12/1: op 5/1)

T/Plpt: £19.90 (419.3 Tckts). T/Qdpt: £24.50 (26.5 Tckts). AK

# 4343-MUSSELBURGH (R-H) (Good to soft, Soft patches)
## Thursday November 7th

WEATHER: fine WIND: almost nil

## 5004 LADBROKE ON-COURSE H'CAP (0-70) (I) (3-Y.O+) (Class E)

1-10 (1-10) **1m 16y** £3,160.00 (£955.00: £465.00: £220.00) Stalls: High GOING: 0.37 sec per fur (GS)

| | Dist | Pos | SP | RR | SF |
|---|---|---|---|---|---|
| 4769[17] **Scaraben (70)** (SEKettlewell) **8-10-0** JFortune(10) (s.i.s: bhd tl hdwy 3f out: r.o wl to ld last stride) | — | **1** | 8/1[3] | 83 | 65 |
| 4975[3] **Broughton's Pride (IRE) (47)** (JLEyre) **5-8-5** TWilliams(13) (cl up: led 3f out tl ct last stride) | s.h | **2** | 7/1[2] | 60 | 42 |
| *4989*[*] **Desert Zone (USA) (49)** (JLHarris) **7-8-7** 5x DeanMcKeown(5) (bhd: styd on wl fnl 3f: nrst fin) | 2 | **3** | 8/1[3] | 58 | 40 |
| 4968[*] **Whispering Dawn (63)** (MRChannon) **3-9-0**(5) PPMurphy(1) (in tch: effrt 3f out: nt qckn fnl f) | ½ | **4** | 8/1[3] | 71 | 51 |
| 4831[3] **Kingchip Boy (63)** (MJRyan) **7-9-0v**(7) AMcCarthy(12) (led to 3f out: r.o one pce) | 2 | **5** | 12/1 | 67 | 49 |
| 4831[7] **Kazimiera (IRE) (61)** (CWCElsey) **3-8-12**(5) PFessey(8) (bhd: hdwy over 2f out: nvr rchd ldrs) | s.h | **6** | 20/1 | 65 | 45 |
| 4831[6] **Tael of Silver (61)** (ABailey) **4-9-5v**[1] KDarley(4) (in tch tl outpcd fnl 2½f) | 4 | **7** | 12/1 | 57 | 39 |
| 4829[3] **Northern Celadon (IRE) (57)** (MJHeaton-Ellis) **5-9-1** GDuffield(6) (in tch: hdwy 3f out: wknd appr fnl f) | s.h | **8** | 11/1 | 53 | 35 |
| 4975[9] **Bowcliffe (47)** (MrsAMNaughton) **5-8-5**ow2 JCarroll(3) (s.i.s: racd wd & hdwy to jn ldrs after 2f: grad wknd fnl 3f) | 3 | **9** | 12/1 | 37 | 17 |
| 4909[2] **Best of All (IRE) (58)** (JBerry) **4-9-2b** GCarter(7) (bhd: hdwy 3f out: btn appr fnl f) | nk | **10** | 11/4[1] | 47 | 29 |
| 4808[9] **Miss Pigalle (41)** (MissLAPerratt) **5-7-6b**(7) JBramhill(11) (cl up tl wknd over 2f out) | 2½ | **11** | 50/1 | 25 | 7 |
| 4436[23] **Prudent Pet (46)** (CWFairhurst) **4-8-4** LCharnock(9) (prom 5f: wknd) | 3 | **12** | 50/1 | 24 | 6 |
| *4981*[13] **Western Venture (IRE) (54)** (RMMcKellar) **3-8-7**(3) RHavlin(2) (bhd fnl 3f) | 1 | **13** | 66/1 | 30 | 10 |

4793[8] **In Good Faith (60)** (JJQuinn) **4-9-4** JQuinn(14) (in tch: racd alone far side st: wknd fnl 3f)..........10 **14** 9/1 17 —
(SP 124.1%) **14 Rn**

**1m 46.1** (7.50) CSF £60.15 CT £445.16 TOTE £10.50: £3.80 £2.10 £3.60 (£28.80) Trio £168.60 OWNER Mr J. Tennant (MIDDLEHAM) BRED Burton Agnes Stud Co Ltd
WEIGHT FOR AGE 3yo-2lb

**4190 Scaraben** is not as good as he was on the Flat, but he showed here that he can still do the business in the right company. He is obviously one to keep on the right side at the winter game. (8/1)
**4975 Broughton's Pride (IRE)** is obviously in good form. Although she has previously shown little on the All-Weather, that was over too long a trip, and a return to that surface would be interesting. (7/1)
**4989* Desert Zone (USA)** is keeping his form really well and a return to the All-Weather should bring further success. (8/1)
**4968* Whispering Dawn** had a hard race when winning last time and that might have just taken the edge off her. (8/1)
**4831 Kingchip Boy** raced a bit too freely for his own good, but he is obviously well, and is useful on the Sand. (12/1)
**4831 Kazimiera (IRE)** failed to impress on looks, but again showed that, if she ever decides to go through with it, she has the ability. (20/1)
**4909 Best of All (IRE)** was a shade edgy beforehand and never found things going her way. (11/4)

## 5005 DRYBURN NURSERY (S) H'CAP (0-65) (2-Y.O) (Class F)

1-40 (1-41) **5f** £2,840.00 (£860.00: £420.00: £200.00) Stalls: High GOING: 0.37 sec per fur (GS)

| Form | Horse / details | Dist | Pos | SP | RR | SF |
|---|---|---|---|---|---|---|
| 4902[3] | **Fearless Cavalier (52)** (RHollinshead) **2-8-5**(3) FLynch(3) (outpcd tl hdwy & swtchd over 1f out: r.o to ld cl home) | — | **1** | 7/4[1] | 56 | 36 |
| *4777*[12] | **Imperial Garden (IRE) (57)** (PCHaslam) **2-8-13** JFortune(9) (chsd ldrs: led ins fnl f: hrd drvn, hdd & nt qckn towards fin) | nk | **2** | 10/1 | 60 | 40 |
| 4907[3] | **Enchantica (65)** (JBerry) **2-9-7** GCarter(2) (cl up: led over 1f out tl ins fnl f: kpt on wl) | hd | **3** | 5/1[2] | 68 | 48 |
| *4251*[3] | **Tinker's Surprise (IRE) (58)** (JBalding) **2-9-0** JFanning(1) (led tl hdd over 1f out: sn btn) | 5 | **4** | 6/1[3] | 45 | 25 |
| *4251*[11] | **Face It (42)** (WGMTurner) **2-7-12** LCharnock(8) (in tch: kpt on fnl f: no imp) | 1¼ | **5** | 12/1 | 25 | 5 |
| 4787[8] | **Le Shuttle (55)** (MHTompkins) **2-8-4**(7) RMullen(11) (outpcd: hdwy ½-wy: sn btn) | 3 | **6** | 6/1[3] | 28 | 8 |
| 4762[12] | **Waltz Time (57)** (MissLAPerratt) **2-8-13** JWeaver(7) (outpcd & bhd: hdwy ½-wy: sn wknd) | hd | **7** | 7/1 | 30 | 10 |
| *4572*[10] | **Jay Tee Ef (IRE) (46)** (BAMcMahon) **2-8-2b**[1]ow1 GDuffield(10) (sn drvn along & nvr trbld ldrs) | s.h | **8** | 33/1 | 19 | — |
| *4988*[9] | **Rising Glory (45)** (MissJFCraze) **2-7-10b**[1](5) PFessey(4) (in tch tl outpcd fr ½-wy) | ¾ | **9** | 33/1 | 15 | — |
| 4796[11] | **Thewrightone (IRE) (47)** (GROldroyd) **2-8-3b** JQuinn(6) (nvr wnt pce) | 1 | **10** | 33/1 | 14 | — |
| 4594[20] | **Cantsaynowt (41)** (RMMcKellar) **2-7-4**(7)ow1 JMcAuley(5) (dwlt: a wl bhd) | ¾ | **11** | 20/1 | 6 | — |

(SP 124.5%) **11 Rn**

**62.8 secs** (5.10) CSF £20.05 CT £71.56 TOTE £3.00: £1.40 £3.80 £2.70 (£65.10) Trio £55.20 OWNER The Three R's (UPPER LONGDON) BRED Longdon Stud Ltd
LONG HANDICAP Cantsaynowt 7-5
No bid

**4902 Fearless Cavalier**, despite the shorter trip, appreciated the slower ground and, getting stronger as the race progressed, won nicely. (7/4)
**3950* Imperial Garden (IRE)** did well from his draw and, but for that, would probably have won. (10/1)
**4907 Enchantica** ran her usual race, only to be worried out of it in the closing stages. (5/1)
**4251 Tinker's Surprise (IRE)**, after seven weeks off and a change of stables, ran quite well and will probably find opportunities on the All-Weather. (6/1)
**1097 Face It** was always struggling to overcome her draw and lacked the pace to make it. (12/1: op 8/1)
**4787 Le Shuttle** ran well from an impossible draw. (6/1)

## 5006 E.B.F. RATING RELATED MAIDEN STKS (0-70) (2-Y.O) (Class E)

2-10 (2-10) **7f 15y** £3,046.25 (£920.00: £447.50: £211.25) Stalls: High GOING: 0.37 sec per fur (GS)

| Form | Horse / details | Dist | Pos | SP | RR | SF |
|---|---|---|---|---|---|---|
| 4867[6] | **Spaniard's Mount (63)** (MHTompkins) **2-8-7v**(7) RMullen(5) (hld up: smooth hdwy ent st: led wl over 2f out: hung lft: eased towards fin) | — | **1** | 7/2[3] | 65 | 47 |
| 4764[3] | **Zorba (65)** (CWThornton) **2-9-0** DeanMcKeown(4) (lw: a chsng ldrs: ev ch over 1f out: hrd drvn: styd on wl towards fin) | s.h | **2** | 6/1 | 65 | 47 |
| 4751[6] | **I'm Still Here (60)** (JBerry) **2-9-0** KDarley(3) (led tl wl over 2f out: r.o one pce) | 5 | **3** | 16/1 | 54 | 36 |
| 4830[7] | **Lawn Lothario (69)** (MJohnston) **2-9-0** JWeaver(2) (lw: prom: outpcd 3f out: no imp after) | ½ | **4** | 3/1[2] | 52 | 34 |
| 4786[6] | **Forcing Bid (69)** (SirMarkPrescott) **2-9-0** GDuffield(1) (outpcd ent st: hrd drvn & no imp after) | 1¼ | **5** | 6/4[1] | 50 | 32 |
| 4907[4] | **Red Romance (68)** (DenysSmith) **2-9-0** LCharnock(6) (w ldr tl wknd fnl 2½f) | 16 | **6** | 16/1 | 13 | — |

(SP 113.3%) **6 Rn**

**1m 32.5** (7.00) CSF £21.83 TOTE £4.30: £1.90 £1.40 (£15.20) OWNER Mr B. Schmidt-Bodner (NEWMARKET) BRED Whitsbury Manor Stud

**4867 Spaniard's Mount** travelled well and would have won more decisively but for his rider dropping his hands in the last few strides. (7/2: op 6/1)
**4764 Zorba** had his chances, but he seemed reluctant to go through with it, although he almost stole it. (6/1: op 7/2)
**3648 I'm Still Here** gave the impression that he will improve as he strengthens next year. (16/1)
**4310 Lawn Lothario** has not the best of actions and, after getting outpaced entering the straight, was no further danger. (3/1: op 2/1)
**4786 Forcing Bid** was most disappointing, but this track on this ground did not suit. (6/4)

## 5007 GIFFORD WATER H'CAP (0-65) (3-Y.O+ F & M) (Class F)

2-40 (2-40) **1m 4f 31y** £2,814.00 (£852.00: £416.00: £198.00) Stalls: High GOING: 0.37 sec per fur (GS)

| Form | Horse / details | Dist | Pos | SP | RR | SF |
|---|---|---|---|---|---|---|
| 4812[18] | **Peep O Day (35)** (JLEyre) **5-8-1** TWilliams(8) (lw: mde all: rdn & styd on wl fnl 3f) | — | **1** | 25/1 | 48 | 29 |
| 4872[13] | **Rasayel (USA) (62)** (PDEvans) **6-10-0** JFEgan(13) (a.p: kpt on u.p fnl 2f: nt pce to chal) | 2 | **2** | 6/1[3] | 72 | 53 |
| *3086*[3] | **Moonlight Calypso (42)** (MartynWane) **5-8-8** JFortune(2) (lw: chsd ldrs: outpcd appr st: kpt on fnl 2f) | 1¼ | **3** | 12/1 | 51 | 32 |
| 4815[8] | **Contrarie (36)** (MJRyan) **3-7-3**(7) AMcCarthy(9) (a.p: rdn 3f out: styd on: nvr able to chal) | 2 | **4** | 20/1 | 42 | 17 |
| 4752[7] | **Sing And Dance (41)** (EWeymes) **3-8-1** LCharnock(7) (lw: cl up: rdn 3f out: wknd appr fnl f) | 3½ | **5** | 20/1 | 43 | 18 |
| 4967[4] | **Totally Yours (IRE) (45)** (MRChannon) **3-8-0**(5) PPMurphy(3) (in tch: effrt ent st: no imp fnl 3f) | 3 | **6** | 11/2[2] | 43 | 18 |
| 4967[5] | **Kathryn's Pet (62)** (MrsMReveley) **3-9-8** ACulhane(10) (bhd: effrt ent st: nvr rchd ldrs) | 1 | **7** | 5/1[1] | 58 | 33 |
| 4249[15] | **Hutchies Lady (35)** (RMMcKellar) **4-7-8**(7) JMcAuley(1) (b.hind: bhd: effrt over 3f out: n.d) | ½ | **8** | 16/1 | 31 | 12 |
| 4766[2] | **Miss Prism (51)** (JLDunlop) **3-8-11** KDarley(4) (cl up tl rdn & wknd over 3f out) | 3½ | **9** | 5/1[1] | 42 | 17 |
| 4967[10] | **Pip's Dream (49)** (MJRyan) **5-9-1** GCarter(11) (lost tch fnl 4f) | 14 | **10** | 10/1 | 22 | 3 |
| 4906[12] | **Carol Again (41)** (NBycroft) **4-8-7** JQuinn(12) (in tch tl wknd over 3f out) | 1¾ | **11** | 12/1 | 11 | — |
| 4437* | **Dunrowan (54)** (MrsMReveley) **3-9-0** JWeaver(5) (a bhd) | 2½ | **12** | 8/1 | 21 | — |

| | | | | SP | RR | SF |
|---|---|---|---|---|---|---|
| 4474[9] | **Ragtime Cowgirl (40)** (DANolan) **3-7-11**(3) NVarley(6) (effrt ent st: sn btn) | nk | **13** | 20/1 | 7 | — |

(SP 122.6%) **13 Rn**

**2m 46.2** (13.20) CSF £158.72 CT £1,760.46 TOTE £48.40: £8.50 £1.90 £2.30 (£268.60) Trio £234.30; £300.36 to Doncaster 8/11/96 OWNER Mr John Holdroyd (HAMBLETON) BRED G. E. Peace
LONG HANDICAP Contrarie 7-9
WEIGHT FOR AGE 3yo-6lb
**4344 Peep O Day**, back to a trip that suits on ground she likes, did it well. (25/1)
**4753 Rasayel (USA)** ran well under topweight on ground softer than she really prefers. (6/1)
**3086 Moonlight Calypso** has changed stables and ran well after getting outpaced at a vital stage. (12/1)
**Contrarie** had her chances and kept staying on, but was basically short of toe. (20/1)
**2486 Sing And Dance** looked and ran well, but may just have found this trip beyond her. (20/1)
**4967 Totally Yours (IRE)** (11/2: 4/1-6/1)
**4967 Kathryn's Pet** tried to come from some way behind and was never good enough to get in a blow. (5/1)

## 5008 MUSSELBURGH NOVEMBER H'CAP (0-70) (3-Y.O+) (Class E)

3-10 (3-12) **1m 7f 16y** £3,598.75 (£1,090.00: £532.50: £253.75) Stalls: High GOING: 0.37 sec per fur (GS)

| | | | | SP | RR | SF |
|---|---|---|---|---|---|---|
| 4506[9] | **Northern Motto (47)** (JSGoldie) **3-8-6** JQuinn(11) (hld up: gd hdwy ent st: led wl over 2f out: r.o) | — | **1** | 8/1 | 60 | 22 |
| 4832[5] | **Anglesey Sea View (55)** (ABailey) **7-9-8b[1]** GCarter(17) (trckd ldrs: led 4f out tl wl over 2f out: kpt on) | 2½ | **2** | 7/1[3] | 65 | 35 |
| 4919[9] | **Shakiyr (FR) (45)** (RHollinshead) **5-8-9**(3) FLynch(6) (bhd: hdwy appr st: chsng wnr over 1f out: no ex) | nk | **3** | 7/1[3] | 55 | 25 |
| *4986[2]* | **Arc of The Diver (IRE) (53)** (JBerry) **3-8-7b**(5) PFessey(7) (lw: a chsng ldrs: one pce fnl 3f) | 2 | **4** | 14/1 | 61 | 23 |
| 4810[8] | **Lord Advocate (40)** (DANolan) **8-8-4b**(3) NVarley(14) (prom tl lost pl 6f out: styd on fnl 3f: nrst fin) | 1¼ | **5** | 20/1 | 47 | 17 |
| 4832[10] | **Highfield Fizz (45)** (CWFairhurst) **4-8-12** KDarley(15) (bhd: hdwy 3f out: styd on: no imp) | 2 | **6** | 20/1 | 50 | 20 |
| 4766* | **Los Alamos (62)** (CWThornton) **3-9-7** DeanMcKeown(16) (led to 4f out: sn outpcd) | 1¾ | **7** | 6/1[2] | 65 | 27 |
| 4794[6] | **Arian Spirit (IRE) (52)** (JLEyre) **5-9-5** RLappin(10) (effrt ent st: nvr nr to chal) | hd | **8** | 9/2[1] | 55 | 25 |
| | **Cornet (30)** (DenysSmith) **10-7-11** LCharnock(13) (prom tl grad wknd fnl 3f) | 1½ | **9** | 100/1 | 31 | 1 |
| 4483[6] | **Swandale Flyer (35)** (NBycroft) **4-7-9**(7) JBramhill(1) (lw: hdwy ent st: n.d) | hd | **10** | 33/1 | 36 | 6 |
| 620[8] | **Eurotwist (42)** (SEKettlewell) **7-8-9** JFortune(4) (outpcd 6f out: n.d after) | 14 | **11** | 16/1 | 28 | — |
| 4563[15] | **Havana Heights (IRE) (44)** (JLEyre) **3-8-3** TWilliams(3) (chsd ldrs tl outpcd ent st: sn wknd) | 6 | **12** | 20/1 | 24 | — |
| 4910[3] | **Iota (51)** (JLHarris) **7-9-4** JWeaver(12) (lw: outpcd appr st: sn bhd) | ½ | **13** | 10/1 | 30 | — |
| *4894[6]* | **Platinum Plus (51)** (CADwyer) **4-9-4** JCarroll(2) (lw: chsd ldrs tl wknd over 3f out) | 1¼ | **14** | 10/1 | 29 | — |
| 3878[6] | **Chantry Beath (41)** (CWThornton) **5-8-8** GDuffield(9) (lw: chsd ldrs: outpcd 6f out: sn wknd) | 2½ | **15** | 20/1 | 16 | — |
| 4484[5] | **Latvian (57)** (RAllan) **9-9-10** ACulhane(8) (reluctant to r after 5f: sn t.o & virtually p.u) | dist | **16** | 33/1 | — | — |
| 4832[14] | **Mr Speculator (57)** (JEBanks) **3-9-2v** GBardwell(5) (lw: sn pushed along & bhd: hdwy whn slipped & uns rdr ent st) | | **U** | 25/1 | — | — |

(SP 129.1%) **17 Rn**

**3m 29.3** (18.80) CSF £61.30 CT £390.63 TOTE £8.70: £2.10 £1.80 £1.60 £3.20 (£46.30) Trio £176.40 OWNER Mr D. Callaghan (GLASGOW) BRED Exors of the late Sir Robin McAlpine
WEIGHT FOR AGE 3yo-8lb
**3242 Northern Motto** has been promising to do this and got it right here after changing stables again, and was nicely on top in the final stages. (8/1)
**4832 Anglesey Sea View** is in fine form and should be kept in mind if trying either the All-Weather or hurdles this winter. (7/1)
**4862 Shakiyr (FR)** has plenty of ability, but seems to save his best for the Sand. (7/1)
**4986 Arc of The Diver (IRE)** keeps running well without winning and is probably his own worst enemy, but no doubt opportunities will come his way on the All-Weather. (14/1)
**4810 Lord Advocate** did not like being shut in here and dropped himself out at halfway. Despite flying at the finish, he never had a hope. (20/1)
**4596* Highfield Fizz** stays well but, on this occasion, lacked the pace to make it. (20/1)
**4766* Los Alamos** looked well in here, but proved disappointing, dropping out once collared in the straight. (6/1)
**4794 Arian Spirit (IRE)** (9/2: 3/1-5/1)

## 5009 E.B.F. MAIDEN STKS (2-Y.O) (Class D)

3-40 (3-41) **1m 16y** £3,582.50 (£1,085.00: £530.00: £252.50) Stalls: High GOING: 0.37 sec per fur (GS)

| | | | | SP | RR | SF |
|---|---|---|---|---|---|---|
| 4801[4] | **Wellaki (USA)** (JHMGosden) **2-9-0** JCarroll(6) (lw: a cl up: rdn to ld ins fnl f: styd on wl) | — | **1** | 5/4[1] | 80 | 27 |
| 4818[6] | **Doc Ryan's** (MJRyan) **2-9-0** GCarter(4) (w ldr: led over 3f out tl ins fnl f: kpt on) | 1½ | **2** | 16/1 | 77 | 24 |
| 4863[4] | **Great Child** (MRStoute) **2-9-0** DeanMcKeown(3) (trckd ldrs: outpcd 3f out: kpt on u.p) | 3 | **3** | 11/8[2] | 71 | 18 |
| | **One For Baileys** (MJohnston) **2-9-0** JWeaver(5) (leggy: bit bkwd: in tch: outpcd ½-wy: kpt on wl fnl 2f) | 2 | **4** | 12/1[3] | 67 | 14 |
| 4481[2] | **Lightning Rebel** (CWThornton) **2-9-0** GDuffield(2) (prom: outpcd ent st: no imp after) | 3½ | **5** | 12/1[3] | 60 | 7 |
| | **Touch'n'go** (MJohnston) **2-9-0** JFanning(1) (neat: dwlt: a wl bhd) | 4 | **6** | 20/1 | 52 | — |
| 4751[8] | **Freedom of Troy** (JLEyre) **2-9-0** TWilliams(7) (b: led tl over 3f out: wknd 2f out) | 10 | **7** | 16/1 | 32 | — |

(SP 118.5%) **7 Rn**

**1m 48.7** (10.10) CSF £19.22 TOTE £2.00: £1.00 £7.90 (£14.50) OWNER Mr Mohammed Bin Hendi (NEWMARKET) BRED Golden Gate Stud and Henry Mastey
**4801 Wellaki (USA)** had to work to win this, but was nicely on top by the end. (5/4)
**4818 Doc Ryan's** ran well and will no doubt find plenty of opportunities next season. (16/1)
**4863 Great Child** did not appear suited by this track and looked short of pace. (11/8)
**One For Baileys** ran a useful first race and experience should improve him no end. (12/1: op 8/1)
**4481 Lightning Rebel** took time to get going when the pace increased at halfway, and failed to offer a threat. Next year and over further he should come into his own. (12/1)
**Touch'n'go** needed this and, after a slow start, was wisely not knocked about. (20/1)

## 5010 LADBROKE ON-COURSE H'CAP (0-70) (II) (3-Y.O+) (Class E)

4-10 (4-11) **1m 16y** £3,143.75 (£950.00: £462.50: £218.75) Stalls: High GOING: 0.37 sec per fur (GS)

| | | | | SP | RR | SF |
|---|---|---|---|---|---|---|
| 4915* | **Absolute Magic (72)** (WJHaggas) **6-9-13**(3) 5x FLynch(4) (lw: hdwy 3f out: led 1f out: sn clr) | — | **1** | 11/4[1] | 84 | 56 |
| 4296[3] | **Broctune Gold (65)** (MrsMReveley) **5-9-9** ACulhane(12) (led to 1f out: kpt on one pce) | ¾ | **2** | 11/2[2] | 76 | 48 |
| 4905[3] | **Master Millfield (IRE) (64)** (PDEvans) **4-9-8** JFEgan(5) (chsd ldrs: chal 3f out: one pce appr fnl f) | hd | **3** | 7/1[3] | 74 | 46 |

$4827^{5}$ **Lady Joshua (IRE) (70)** (JLDunlop) **3-9-12b** KDarley(2) (lw: hdwy ½-wy: chal 3f out: rdn & wknd over 1f out) ....2½ **4** $7/1^{3}$ 75 45
$4882^{20}$ **Gadge (57)** (ABailey) **5-9-1** GCarter(8) (b: hmpd & lost pl appr st: styd on fnl 2f: nrst fin)....1 **5** $7/1^{3}$ 60 32
$4906^{11}$ **Diamond Crown (IRE) (49)** (MartynWane) **5-8-7** JFortune(1) (bhd tl styd on fnl 3f)....1 **6** 20/1 50 22
$4898^{2}$ **Yeoman Oliver (70)** (BAMcMahon) **3-9-12b** GDuffield(11) (lw: cl up tl wknd fnl 2f)....¾ **7** 12/1 70 40
$4882^{12}$ **Vanborough Lad (47)** (MJBolton) **7-8-5** JQuinn(6) (prom tl outpcd 3f out)....1¾ **8** 20/1 43 15
$4881^{7}$ **Another Nightmare (IRE) (49)** (RMMcKellar) **4-8-7** TWilliams(3) (bhd: effrt ½-wy: n.d)....¾ **9** 20/1 44 16
$4808^{3}$ **Harvest Reaper (46)** (JLHarris) **4-8-4**ow1 DeanMcKeown(7) (nvr bttr than mid div)....1 **10** 20/1 39 10
$4805^{4}$ **Mister Westsound (57)** (MissLAPerratt) **4-9-1b** JCarroll(13) (bhd: hmpd appr st: sme hdwy over 2f out: sn wknd)....2½ **11** 14/1 45 17
$4820^{10}$ **Shontaine (58)** (MJohnston) **3-9-0** JWeaver(10) (cl up tl wknd over 3f out)....4 **12** 12/1 38 8
$2682^{4}$ **Northern Spark (49)** (MissLAPerratt) **8-8-4**(3)ow1 RHavlin(9) (b: outpcd & bhd fnl 3f)....s.h **13** 25/1 29 —
$4455^{7}$ **Raindeer Quest (45)** (JLEyre) **4-8-3** RLappin(14) (bhd & pushed along: n.d)....2 **14** 20/1 21 —
(SP 129.3%) **14 Rn**

**1m 47.2** (8.60) CSF £18.89 CT £97.03 TOTE £4.40: £1.80 £2.80 £2.40 (£12.40) Trio £40.50 OWNER Mrs Barbara Bassett (NEWMARKET) BRED Glazeley Stud
WEIGHT FOR AGE 3yo-2lb
**4915* Absolute Magic** had to work to get there but, once in front, it was all over in a few strides. (11/4)
**4296 Broctune Gold** loves this track, but was well outclassed in the closing stages. (11/2)
**4905 Master Millfield (IRE)** had his chances, but lacked a turn of foot to take them. He will certainly appreciate further. (7/1)
**4827 Lady Joshua (IRE)** was always well enough placed but, when an effort was required, she failed to respond. (7/1)
**1872 Gadge** met with trouble on the home turn and that cost him his chance. (7/1)
**4808* Diamond Crown (IRE)** is a law unto himself, but he was noted finishing quite well here. (20/1)
**4805 Mister Westsound** (14/1: op 8/1)

T/Jkpt: Not won; £2,250.31 to Doncaster 8/11/96. T/Plpt: £1,499.80 (9.21 Tckts). T/Qdpt: £110.70 (9.12 Tckts). AA

## 5011a-5013a (Irish Racing) - See Computer Raceform

## 1105a-LEOPARDSTOWN (Dublin, Ireland) (L-H) (Soft)
## Monday October 28th

### 5014a BORD GAIS KILLAVULLAN STKS (Gp 3) (2-Y.O)
2-15 (2-17) **7f** £16,250.00 (£4,750.00: £2,250.00: £750.00) GOING: 0.37 sec per fur (GS)

SP RR SF
**Shell Ginger (IRE)** (APO'Brien,Ireland) **2-8-7** JAHeffernan (mde all: sn clr: styd on wl)....— **1** 10/1 104+ 21
**Lil's Boy (USA)** (JSBolger,Ireland) **2-8-10** KJManning (hld up: mod 5th 2f out: 2nd, rdn & no imp 1f out)....12 **2** $6/1^{3}$ 80 —
**Carlisle Bay (IRE)** (JOxx,Ireland) **2-8-10** JPMurtagh (hld up towards rr: wnt mod 4th 2f out: kpt on same pce)....2 **3** $9/2^{2}$ 75 —
**No Slouch (IRE)** (APO'Brien,Ireland) **2-8-10** CRoche (hld up: wnt mod 2nd ½-wy: rdn & no imp)....3½ **4** $4/6^{1}$ 67 —
**Blushing Minstrel (IRE)** (JCHarley,Ireland) **2-8-7** RMBurke (chsd wnr early: mod 3rd ½-wy: 5th & btn under 2f out)....3 **5** 8/1 57 —
**Go Thunder (IRE)** (WPMullins,Ireland) **2-8-10** JoannaMorgan (chsd wnr to ½-wy: dropped bhd bef st)....dist **6** 16/1 — —
*$4280a^{6}$* ***Really Chuffed*** (WPMullins,Ireland) **2-8-10** NGMcCullagh (Withdrawn not under Starter's orders).... **W** 10/1 — —
(SP 127.6%) **6 Rn**

**1m 33.7** (8.70) OWNER Mrs John Magnier (PILTOWN)
**Shell Ginger (IRE)** had stretched into a clear lead before the others realised the fact. Holding an unassailable advantage turning into the straight, she kept on the inner and won virtually unchallenged. (10/1)
**Lil's Boy (USA)**, steadied early on, had only one behind him turning into the straight and, although keeping on to go second inside the last, never had any chance of getting on terms with the winner. (6/1: op 3/1)
**Carlisle Bay (IRE)**, not the quickest away, was soon settled and, although in fourth place turning into the straight, was never in a position to get on terms. (9/2: op 3/1)
**No Slouch (IRE)** was another quite content to settle early on. Roche realised that the stable-companion had stolen a march and he went second at halfway. Ridden and making no impression when coming wide into the straight, he weakened in the last furlong. (4/6)
**Blushing Minstrel (IRE)**, in third place turning into the straight, soon weakened. (8/1)

### 5015a NATURAL GAS ENERGY RATED HOME TRIGO STKS (Listed) (3-Y.O+)
3-45 (3-45) **1m 2f** £11,287.50 (£3,237.50: £1,487.50: £437.50) GOING: 0.37 sec per fur (GS)

SP RR SF
$4851a^{2}$ **Asmara (USA)** (JOxx,Ireland) **3-8-7** PJSmullen (hld up in tch: wnt 3rd 4f out: chal st: led u.p over 1f out: kpt on)....— **1** 5/1 107 35
$4849a^{5}$ **I'm Supposin (IRE)** (KPrendergast,Ireland) **4-9-1** SCraine (hld up in tch: 3rd st: chal 2f out: ev ch u.p tl no ex ins fnl f: kpt on)....1 **2** $3/1^{2}$ 108 41
$4738a^{3}$ **Oriane** (JOxx,Ireland) **3-8-9**ow2 JPMurtagh (hld up towards rr: 4th, chsd ldrs & nt clr run 2f out: swtchd & 4th u.p 1f out: kpt on: no ex nr fin)....s.h **3** $7/2^{3}$ 107 33
$4026a^{2}$ **Escrito (USA)** (DKWeld,Ireland) **3-8-10** PShanahan (hld up: 6th 3f out: chal 2f out: ev ch over 1f out: no ex ins fnl f)....½ **4** 5/1 108 36
**Akhiyar (IRE)** (MJPO'Brien,Ireland) **5-9-1** CRoche (disp ld early: chsd ldr: led 3f out: jnd u.p over 1f out: sn hdd: no ex)....6 **5** 16/1 98 31
**Little Musgrave (IRE)** (JEMulhern,Ireland) **5-9-1** TEDurcan (hld up: 5th & chsd ldrs 3f out: rdn & no imp over 1f out)....5½ **6** 14/1 89 22
$4849a^{3}$ **Mohaajir (USA)** (JSBolger,Ireland) **5-9-8** KJManning (disp ld early: sn led: jnd 4f out: hdd 3f out: wknd qckly st)....15 **7** $11/4^{1}$ 72 5
(SP 119.8%) **7 Rn**

**2m 14.8** (10.80) OWNER H H Aga Khan (CURRABEG)
**4851a Asmara (USA)**, the outsider of the Oxx runners, gained her first success of the season. Going second into the straight, she took it up a furlong and a half out and stayed on well. (5/1)
**4849a I'm Supposin (IRE)** put in his sustained challenge from a furlong and a half out, but could only keep on a the one pace. (3/1: op 2/1)

**4738a Oriane** did not enjoy any luck in the straight, having to be switched out with two furlongs left. Disputing the lead in the straight from over a furlong out, she was never nearer than at the line. She could still make a good filly next year. (7/2: op 2/1)
**4026a Escrito (USA)** held every chance in second place over a furlong out, but could not quicken. (5/1)
**4849a Mohaajir (USA)** was a surprise favourite and was sent off in front, despite hating the ground. He dropped away quickly before the straight and finished tailed off, being reported clinically abnormal after the race. (11/4: op 5/1)

## 5016a-5017a (Irish Racing) - See Computer Raceform

## 4285a-EVRY (France) (R-H) (Good to soft)
### Tuesday October 29th

### 5018a PRIX PHIL DRAKE (Listed) (4-Y.O+)
2-10 (2-10) **1m** £18,445.00 (£6,324.00: £3,953.00)

| | | | | SP | RR | SF |
|---|---|---|---|---|---|---|
| 4739a* | **Decorated Hero** (JHMGosden) **4-9-2** LDettori | — | 1 | | 121 | — |
| | **Serviable (IRE)** (MmeCHead,France) **4-8-11** FHead | nk | 2 | | 115 | — |
| 4623* | **Verzen (IRE)** (DRLoder) **4-8-11** DRMcCabe | 3 | 3 | | 109 | — |
| | | | | | | **6 Rn** |

**1m 40.9** (3.90) P-M 1.30F: 1.10F 1.10F OWNER Mr H. Allen (NEWMARKET) BRED Reg Griffin and Jim McGrath
**4739a* Decorated Hero** looked to have this race sewn up a furlong and a half out when he took the lead, but he began to tire inside the final furlong, only just holding on. Apparently short of a gallop here, this was his second listed victory in France and he may return for the Prix Perth.
**4623* Verzen (IRE)** attempted to make all the running and stuck to his guns to the bitter end, but is not quite up to this class.

## PARC-BORELY (Marseille, France) (Good to firm)
### Wednesday October 30th

### 5019a PRIX ANDRE BABOIN GRAND PRIX DES PROVINCES (Gp 3) (3-Y.O+)
2-30 (2-40) **1m 2f** £28,986.00 (£10,540.00: £5,270.00)

| | | | | SP | RR | SF |
|---|---|---|---|---|---|---|
| 4290a* | **Artan (IRE)** (H-APantall,France) **4-9-8** PSchiergen | — | 1 | | 125 | — |
| 3386a* | **Bulington (FR)** (H-APantall,France) **4-9-4** CAsmussen | ¾ | 2 | | 120 | — |
| | **Brisby (FR)** (JBernard,France) **3-8-3** FBlondel | 3½ | 3 | | 104 | — |
| 4463* | **Amrak Ajeeb (IRE)** (BHanbury) **4-8-11** MRimmer (btn approx 6l) | | 6 | | — | — |
| | | | | | | **8 Rn** |

**2m 8.0** P-M 3.50F: 1.30F 1.20F 1.10F (3.20F) OWNER Stall Brandenburg BRED J. Brennen
**4290a* Artan (IRE)** is a very smart performer, giving weight to the rest of the field and winning with more in hand than the margin suggests. He retires for the season, but will be back next year when he is sure to make his presence felt in top-class company, especially when the ground is good or firmer.
**3386a* Bulington (FR)** was no match for the winner. He rarely puts in a bad run, but needs ten furlongs, a right-handed track and a sound surface to give his best. He probably goes on to the Grand Prix de Marseilles later in the month.
**Brisby (FR)** was putting in his best work at the finish, but is probably only listed class.
**4463* Amrak Ajeeb (IRE)** pulled hard and took them along, but his early exertions seemed to take their toll in the straight. He did not seem to handle this tight track and was never on an even keel, changing legs throughout, so this should be forgotten.

## 4958a-LONGCHAMP (Paris, France) (R-H) (Soft)
### Thursday October 31st

### 5020a PRIX DE L'UNIVERSITE (Claimer) (3-Y.O)
2-00 (2-02) **1m 7f** £7,905.00

| | | | | SP | RR | SF |
|---|---|---|---|---|---|---|
| 1757a15 | **Hoist To Heaven (USA)** (CLaffon-Parias,France) **3-7-13**(5) MPoirier | — | 1 | | 63 | — |
| | **Negra (FR)** (France) **3-7-9**(5) MSautjeau | nk | 2 | | 59 | — |
| | **Special Effect (FR)** (France) **3-8-9** SGuillot | ½ | 3 | | 67 | — |
| 4947a14 | **Ewar Bold** (KOCunningham-Brown) **3-9-2** FSanchez (btn over 13½l) | | 10 | | 60 | — |
| | | | | | | **13 Rn** |

**3m 27.3** (21.30) P-M 5.80F: 2.30F 3.70F 4.20F (50.10F) OWNER Mr J. Gispert (CHANTILLY)
**4947a Ewar Bold,** making his second French appearance in just over a week, was over a longer distance here. Holding the lead in the straight, he was headed over a furlong out and faded disappointingly.

### 5021a PRIX DU RANELAGH (Listed) (3-Y.O C & G)
2-30 (2-32) **1m** £18,445.00 (£6,324.00: £3,953.00)

| | | | | SP | RR | SF |
|---|---|---|---|---|---|---|
| | **Precious Ring (USA)** (MmeCHead,France) **3-8-11b1** FHead | — | 1 | | 114 | — |
| | **Alamo Bay (USA)** (AFabre,France) **3-8-11** OPeslier | 1½ | 2 | | 111 | — |
| | **Going Green (USA)** (MmeCHead,France) **3-8-11** ODoleuze | 2 | 3 | | 107 | — |
| 46202 | **Hal's Pal** (DRLoder) **3-8-11** RHughes (btn approx 13l) | | 8 | | 81 | — |
| | | | | | | **12 Rn** |

**1m 45.5** (10.50) P-M 5.60F: 1.80F 1.70F 1.80F (9.90F) OWNER Maktoum Al Maktoum (CHANTILLY) BRED Societe Aland
**4620 Hal's Pal** took very little part. He never recovered from his outside draw and was always too far from the leaders to take a hand in the finish. This is best forgotten.

### 5022a PRIX DE LA TABLE H'CAP (4-Y.O+)
3-00 (3-04) **1m 2f** £18,445.00

| | | | | SP | RR | SF |
|---|---|---|---|---|---|---|
| | **Danish Field (IRE)** (TClout,France) **5-8-6** ASanglard | — | 1 | | 77 | — |

| | | | | SP | RR | SF |
|---|---|---|---|---|---|---|
| | **Le Conquet (FR)** (France) **8-8-7** CTellier | s.nk | **2** | | 78 | — |
| | **Un Solitaire (USA)** (France) **4-8-6** GGuignard | 1½ | **3** | | 74 | — |
| 4941a[5] | **Cedez le Passage (FR)** (KOCunningham-Brown) **5-9-2** FSanchez (btn over 9½l) | | **13** | | 69 | — |
| | | | | | | **18 Rn** |

**2m 14.5** (14.50) P-M 17.60F: 4.80F 2.20F 3.80F (38.20F) OWNER K. Watanabe BRED Biddestone Stud
**4941a Cedez le Passage (FR)**, who raced in mid-division, went about his work two furlongs out. Lacking the pace to put in a serious challenge, he was already beaten when hampered a furlong from home.
DS

# TESIO (Turin, Italy) (R-H) (Good to soft)
## Friday November 1st

### 5023a ST LEGER ITALIANO - MEMORIAL GIANNI FERRARIS (3-Y.O+)
3-35 (3-43) **1m 6f 110y** £32,480.00 (£14,292.00: £7,796.00)

| | | | | SP | RR | SF |
|---|---|---|---|---|---|---|
| | **Duke of Flight (USA)** (RRossini,Italy) **3-8-6** GForte | — | **1** | | 118 | — |
| 4413a[5] | **Lear White (USA)** (PAKelleway) **5-8-13** FJovine | 1½ | **2** | | 115 | — |
| | **Radames (IRE)** (GBotti,Italy) **4-8-13** EBotti | 5 | **3** | | 110 | — |
| | | | | | | **9 Rn** |

**3m 10.6** TOTE 201L: 25L 11L 15L (122L) OWNER Allevamento Cavallin Nero BRED David's Farm
**IN-FOCUS: This event is now a Classic in name only.**
**4413a Lear White (USA)** should have won this in a canter on all his form this year but, after quickening to lead two furlongs out, he had no answer to the winner's finishing kick. He may have been feeling the effects of a long, hard season, in which he has now earned over £80,000 without winning a race.

# 4949a-SAINT-CLOUD (France) (L-H) (Very Soft)
## Saturday November 2nd

### 5024a CRITERIUM DE SAINT-CLOUD (Gp 1) (2-Y.O C & F)
1-50 (1-46) **1m 2f** £52,701.00 (£21,080.00: £10,540.00: £5,270.00)

| | | | | SP | RR | SF |
|---|---|---|---|---|---|---|
| | **Shaka** (J-CRouget,France) **2-9-0** J-BEyquem (mid div: gd hdwy 2f out: led ins fnl f: r.o wl) | — | **1** | 67/10 | 105 | — |
| | **Daylami (IRE)** (AdeRoyerDupre,France) **2-9-0** GMosse (in rr: 6th st: rdn 2f out: hdwy to ld over 1f out: hdd ins fnl f) | ¾ | **2** | 4/5[1] | 104 | — |
| | **Sendoro (IRE)** (AdeRoyerDupre,France) **2-9-0** CAsmussen (led tl over 1f out: one pce) | 2 | **3** | 4/5[1] | 101 | — |
| 4653a* | **New Frontier (IRE)** (AFabre,France) **2-9-0** OPeslier (racd in 4th: 5th st: rdn 2f out: one pce) | 2½ | **4** | 33/10[2] | 97 | — |
| 4370* | **Voyagers Quest (USA)** (PWChapple-Hyam) **2-9-0** JReid (prom: rdn 2f out: one pce) | 2 | **5** | 143/10 | 93 | — |
| 4415a* | **Fine Fellow (IRE)** (MmeCHead,France) **2-9-0** FHead (prom: rdn over 2f out: no imp) | nk | **6** | 58/10[3] | 93 | — |
| | **Alcalali (USA)** (PAKelleway) **2-8-11** ODoleuze (mid div: one pce fnl 2f) | ¾ | **7** | 283/10 | 89 | — |
| | **Kaldoun Choice (FR)** (RCollet,France) **2-9-0** CHanotel (plld hrd mid div: hdwy st: sn wknd) | s.nk | **8** | 27/1 | 91 | — |
| | **Reef D'Irlande (FR)** (RMongil,France) **2-9-0** AJunk (a bhd) | 15 | **9** | 80/1 | 67 | — |
| | **Keroub (FR)** (PBary,France) **2-9-0** SGuillot (a bhd) | 4 | **10** | 199/10 | 61 | — |
| | | | | (SP 181.6%) | | **10 Rn** |

**2m 15.8** (12.30) P-M 7.70F: 2.30F 1.30F 2.30F (10.10F) OWNER Mr R. Bousquet (PAU) BRED Petra Bloodstack Agency Ltd
**IN-FOCUS: For betting purposes, Daylami (IRE) and Sendoro (IRE) were cpld.**
**Shaka**, the pick of the paddock, is a fine-looking colt. Racing in mid-division before being brought to challenge up the middle of the track, he hit the front just over a furlong out and was unnecessarily hard ridden in the final stages by his jockey. This might have been a sub-standard renewal, but he won in good style, and he still has room for improvement, and looks as if he could stay further. Providing he is successful at the trials, he will be aimed at the Prix du Jockey-Club. (67/10)
**Daylami (IRE)**, held up in the early stages, was brought through to lead with a furlong and a half to run. He stayed on well, but did not have the speed to go with the winner. He is still inexperienced and has scope for further improvement. (4/5)
**Sendoro (IRE)** attempted to make all the running and stayed on well to the bitter end. He is another who is sure to improve. (4/5)
**4653a* New Frontier (IRE)** was fourth virtually throughout, but lacked speed in the final furlong. (33/10)
**4370* Voyagers Quest (USA)** was always well up, but could not go with the others when pace was injected in the straight. (143/10)
**Alcalali (USA)** looked well and did not run badly, considering she was making her debut in such exalted company. She never looked likely to take a hand in the finish, but will have benefited from the outing. (283/10)

### 5025a PRIX DE FLORE (Gp 3) (3-Y.O+ F & M)
2-25 (2-19) **1m 2f 110y** £28,986.00 (£10,540.00: £5,270.00)

| | | | | SP | RR | SF |
|---|---|---|---|---|---|---|
| 4654a[4] | **Dance Treat (USA)** (DSepulchre,France) **4-9-1b**[1] CAsmussen | — | **1** | | 116 | — |
| 1750a[6] | **Dapprima (GER)** (BSchutz,Germany) **3-8-8** AStarke | 2½ | **2** | | 109 | — |
| 4654a[8] | **Blue Water (FR)** (JEHammond,France) **4-8-11** MBoutin | hd | **3** | | 108 | — |
| 4678[5] | **Altamura (USA)** (JHMGosden) **3-8-8** JReid (btn over 5l) | | **6** | | 101 | — |
| | | | | | | **14 Rn** |

**2m 18.2** (8.20) P-M 10.50F: 3.60F 7.40F 6.90F (126.20F) OWNER Mr P. Pritchard BRED John C. and Mrs Mabee
**4654a Dance Treat (USA)**, something of a course specialist, took her second Group event here, having been supplemented by her trainer instead of going for the Yellow Ribbon Stakes at Santa Anita. Coming through with a sweeping late run to lead at the furlong pole, she was going away in good style at the end, and will now either go to stud or be raced in America.
**1060a Dapprima (GER)** opened at a long price, considering her decent form in Germany. She was going as well as the winner halfway up the straight, but just stayed on in the final furlong. She is a decent sort who has come to hand at the end of the season.
**Blue Water (FR)**, held up early on, moved up into a challenging position in the straight. When she was let down, she kept on one-paced without being able to challenge the first two. She too opened a big price and is probably only listed class.
**4678 Altamura (USA)** set the pace to the straight, but had no response when passed at the furlong marker. She looks like she has had enough for the season.
DS

## 4858a-SAN SIRO (Milan, Italy) (R-H) (Good to soft)
### Saturday November 2nd

### 5026a PREMIO GIOVANNI FALCK (Listed) (3-Y.O+ F & M)
1-30 (1-47) **1m 4f** £20,300.00 (£8,932.00: £4,872.00)

| | | | | SP | RR | SF |
|---|---|---|---|---|---|---|
| 4678[3] | **Ninotchka (USA)** (JLDunlop) **3-8-6** FJovine | — | 1 | | 107 | — |
| 4539a[3] | **Truly Generous (IRE)** (RCollet,France) **3-8-6** GGuignard | 3½ | 2 | | 102 | — |
| | **Reine Wells (IRE)** (PBary,France) **3-8-6** GForte | nk | 3 | | 102 | — |
| | | | | | | 6 Rn |

**2m 33.4** (13.40) TOTE 15L: 11L 14L (22L) OWNER Miss K. Rausing (ARUNDEL) BRED Swettenham Stud, RonCon 1 and Binfield House
**4678 Ninotchka (USA)** bowed out with the easiest of victories. Soon at the head of affairs, she quickened clear two furlongs out and won easing down. From Nijinsky's last crop, she looks a good broodmare prospect.

### 5027a PREMIO CHIUSURA (Gp 3)
2-50 (3-12) **7f** £26,723.00 (£12,491.00: £7,028.00)

| | | | | SP | RR | SF |
|---|---|---|---|---|---|---|
| 4743a[2] | **Macanal (USA)** (HJentzsch,Germany) **4-9-8** PSchiergen | — | 1 | | 114 | — |
| 4774[4] | **Lucky Lionel (USA)** (RHannon) **3-9-8** RHughes | ½ | 2 | | 114 | — |
| 4957a* | **Branston Abby (IRE)** (MJohnston) **7-9-5** MRoberts | 1¾ | 3 | | 106 | — |
| | | | | | | 12 Rn |

**1m 25.5** (6.60) TOTE 52L: 18L 18L 25L (90L) OWNER Gestut Fahrhof BRED Bruce Hundley in USA
**3572a* Macanal (USA)** made all the running to hold off the British raiders.
**4774 Lucky Lionel (USA)**, always prominent, stayed the extra furlong well, but could never peg back the winner.
**4957a* Branston Abby (IRE)** came with her usual late run without ever threatening the front two. Softer ground would have helped.

## 4541a-CAPANNELLE (Rome, Italy) (R-H) (Good to soft)
### Sunday November 3rd

### 5028a PREMIO FIUGGI (2-Y.O)
2-50 (3-27) **1m** £28,420.00 (£12,505.00: £6,821.00)

| | | | | SP | RR | SF |
|---|---|---|---|---|---|---|
| 4859a[6] | **Golden Aventura (IRE)** (GFratini,Italy) **2-8-13**ow2 RCangiano | — | 1 | | 67 | — |
| 4859a[8] | **War Declaration (IRE)** (BGrizzetti,Italy) **2-8-11** MTellini | nse | 2 | | 65 | — |
| 4745a[2] | **Passi d'Orlando (IRE)** (JLDunlop) **2-8-7** FJovine | 3 | 3 | | 55 | — |
| | | | | | | 13 Rn |

**1m 38.8** TOTE 86L: 24L 20L 21L (156L) OWNER Scuderia Golden Horse SRL
**4745a Passi d'Orlando (IRE)** stayed on from out of the pack to take third a furlong out without threatening the leaders.

## 1750a-MULHEIM (Mulheim-Ruhr, Germany) (Heavy)
### Sunday November 3rd

### 5029a BUCHMACHER KOTTKAMP SILBERNES BAND DER RUHR (Listed) (3-Y.O+)
2-15 (2-19) **2m 4f** £13,513.00 (£5,405.00: £2,703.00)

| | | | | SP | RR | SF |
|---|---|---|---|---|---|---|
| 4741a[3] | **Diktys (GER)** (HBlume,Germany) **4-9-0** THellier | — | 1 | | 107 | — |
| 4855a[3] | **Caballo (GER)** (HJentzsch,Germany) **5-9-0** PSchiergen | 1¾ | 2 | | 106 | — |
| 4741a[2] | **Lord Jim (IRE)** (LordHuntingdon) **4-9-2** DHarrison | hd | 3 | | 108 | — |
| | | | | | | 5 Rn |

**4m 59.57** TOTE 39DM: 13DM 16DM (85DM) OWNER Stall Kaiserberg BRED Getsut Rottgen
**4741a Lord Jim (IRE)** made the running in an attempt to bring his stamina into play, but ended up giving the principals a handy lead. Headed two furlongs out, he stayed on dourly and almost regained second when Caballo tied up in the closing stages. There are races to be won with him.

## 2669a-NANTES (France) (L-H) (Soft)
### Sunday November 3rd

### 5030a GRAND PRIX DE LA VILLE DE NANTES (Listed) (3-Y.O+)
1-30 (1-30) **1m 4f** £30,303.00 (£11,067.00: £5,534.00)

| | | | | SP | RR | SF |
|---|---|---|---|---|---|---|
| 4943a* | **Stretarez (FR)** (DSepulchre,France) **3-9-0** FSanchez | — | 1 | | 126 | — |
| 4852a[2] | **Taufan's Melody** (LadyHerries) **5-9-0** JReid | 3 | 2 | | 116 | — |
| 4852a[3] | **Peckinpah's Soul (FR)** (DSepulchre,France) **4-9-1** FHead | ¾ | 3 | | 116 | — |
| | | | | | | 6 Rn |

**2m 33.0** P-M 3.40F: 1.50F 1.50F OWNER Mr J-L Lagardere BRED SNC Lagardere Elevage
**4852a Taufan's Melody**, who won this race last year, raced prominently, but had little in reserve when the winner went for home. This was a good performance and he was simply beaten by a better horse.

## 5026a-SAN SIRO (Milan, Italy) (R-H) (Soft)
### Sunday November 3rd

### 5031a PREMIO CARCANO (2-Y.O)
1-35 (1-40) **1m** £10,150.00 (£4,466.00: £2,436.00)

| | | | | SP | RR | SF |
|---|---|---|---|---|---|---|
| 4253[5] | **Yavlensky (IRE)** (JLDunlop) **2-9-0** MRoberts | — | 1 | | 66+ | — |

| | Horse | Dist | Pos | SP | RR | SF |
|---|---|---|---|---|---|---|
| | **Royal Aty (IRE)** (PAKelleway) **2-9-0** RHughes | 1¼ | **2** | | 64 | — |
| | **Archipova (IRE)** (PBary,France) **2-8-11** GForte | 5 | **3** | | 51 | — |

**6 Rn**

**1m 41.7** (11.70) TOTE 35L: 18L 16L (32L) OWNER Allevamento Annarosa (ARUNDEL) BRED Allevamento Annarosa di V. Schirone
**4253 Yavlensky (IRE)** broke his duck comfortably enough, showing a decent turn of foot when quickening into the lead at the two-furlong pole.
**Royal Aty (IRE)** saw out the mile well and seems to have the ability to at least win a race of this nature.

# 4960a-SANTA ANITA (Los Angeles, USA) (L-H) (Firm)
## Sunday November 3rd

## 5032a YELLOW RIBBON STKS (Gp 1) (3-Y.O+ F & M)
**1m 2f** £232,258.00 (£77,419.00: £46,452.00)

| | Horse | Dist | Pos | SP | RR | SF |
|---|---|---|---|---|---|---|
| 4663a* | **Donna Viola** (CFWall) **4-8-10** GStevens | — | **1** | | 119 | — |
| | **Real Connection (USA)** (MStute,USA) **5-8-10** GAlmeida | ½ | **2** | | 118 | — |
| | **Dixie Pearl (USA)** (RMandella,USA) **4-8-10** RDouglas | hd | **3** | | 118 | — |

**8 Rn**

**2m 0.62** P-M 21.80: PL (1-2) 12.00 12.40 SHOW (1-2-3) 7.40 7.00 9.60 OWNER Mr G. Tanaka (NEWMARKET) BRED Lady Juliet de Chair
**4663a* Donna Viola** was given a brilliant ride by Stevens, who was sitting on her for the very first time. In what turned out to be a rough race, she raced in fourth before showing great bravery to quicken up between horses in the straight. She will remain in California to be trained by Ben Cecil.

# 4867-DONCASTER (L-H) (Soft)
## Friday November 8th
Race 3: hand-timed
WEATHER: sunny WIND: mod against

## 5033 E.B.F. DRANSFIELD NOVELTY COMPANY MAIDEN STKS (2-Y.O) (Class D)
1-00 (1-02) **7f** £4,534.25 (£1,364.00: £659.50: £307.25) Stalls: High GOING: 0.46 sec per fur (GS)

| | Horse | Dist | Pos | SP | RR | SF |
|---|---|---|---|---|---|---|
| | **Handsome Ridge** (JHMGosden) **2-9-0** JCarroll(10) (w'like: bit bkwd: chsd ldrs far side: led wl over 1f out: r.o) | — | **1** | 20/1 | 91+ | 43 |
| | **Ninth Chord** (JHMGosden) **2-9-0** WRyan(8) (lengthy: scope: hld up far side: hdwy 3f out: styd on wl) | 1 | **2** | 7/1[3] | 89+ | 41 |
| 4875[6] | **Bint Baladee (97)** (SbinSuroor) **2-8-9b** LDettori(1) (lw: cl up far side: led 4f out tl wl over 1f out: kpt on) | hd | **3** | 11/4[1] | 84 | 36 |
| 4797[5] | **Toi Toi (IRE)** (DWPArbuthnot) **2-8-9** SWhitworth(9) (hld up: hdwy far side to chse ldrs over 2f out: nt qckn appr fnl f) | 4 | **4** | 14/1 | 74 | 26 |
| | **Nash Point** (IABalding) **2-9-0** TQuinn(17) (lt-f: racd stands' side: hdwy 3f out: styd on: no ch w far side) | 1¼ | **5** | 14/1 | 77 | 29 |
| 4720[4] | **Valagalore** (BWHills) **2-8-9** MHills(15) (lw: racd stands' side: prom: kpt on fnl 2f: no ch w ldrs far side) | ½ | **6** | 5/1[2] | 70 | 22 |
| | **Winter Garden** (LMCumani) **2-9-0** OUrbina(13) (w'like: scope: bit bkwd: dwlt & swtchd far side: styd on fnl 3f: nrst fin) | 1½ | **7** | 14/1 | 72 | 24 |
| | **Royal Castle (IRE)** (MajorWRHern) **2-9-0** TSprake(3) (w'like: scope: bit bkwd: chsd ldrs far side tl outpcd fnl 2f) | ½ | **8** | 10/1 | 71 | 23 |
| | **Purist** (MRStoute) **2-9-0** JReid(18) (w'like: scope: racd stands' side: in tch over 4f) | ¾ | **9** | 7/1[3] | 69 | 21 |
| 4884[4] | **Just Grand (IRE)** (MJohnston) **2-9-0** JWeaver(16) (lw: led stands' side tl wl outpcd fnl 3f) | ½ | **10** | 8/1 | 68 | 20 |
| 4897[10] | **Stahr** (HCandy) **2-9-0** CRutter(7) (dwlt: racd far side: drvn along ½-wy: n.d) | ¾ | **11** | 33/1 | 66 | 18 |
| | **Fife Major (USA)** (BWHills) **2-9-0** RStreet(12) (neat: scope: dwlt: racd stands' side: hld up: effrt ½-wy: n.d) | 1¼ | **12** | 20/1 | 63 | 15 |
| | **Awash** (BWHills) **2-9-0** RHills(14) (leggy: scope: racd stands' side: trckd ldrs tl outpcd fnl 3f) | nk | **13** | 10/1 | 63 | 15 |
| | **Briggs Turn** (WJarvis) **2-9-0** MTebbutt(6) (wl grwn: unf: unruly leaving paddock: racd far side: n.d) | 9 | **14** | 25/1 | 42 | — |
| 4514[18] | **Chief Predator (USA)** (RHannon) **2-9-0** DaneO'Neill(2) (chsd ldrs far side to ½-wy: wknd qckly) | 1 | **15** | 33/1 | 40 | — |
| 3941[9] | **Silver Button** (MissSEHall) **2-9-0** AMcGlone(11) (racd far side: hld up: effrt & lost tch fnl 3f) | 1½ | **16** | 33/1 | 36 | — |
| 4907[5] | **Ewar Arrangement** (CEBrittain) **2-9-0** MRoberts(20) (cl up stands' side 4f: wknd) | 2 | **17** | 20/1 | 32 | — |
| | **Hever Golf Magic (IRE)** (MJohnston) **2-8-9** TWilliams(19) (scope: bit bkwd: cl up stands' side over 4f) | 2 | **18** | 20/1 | 22 | — |
| | **Tarradale** (CBBBooth) **2-9-0** MBirch(4) (str: bit bkwd: led far side 3f: sn wknd) | 4 | **19** | 33/1 | 18 | — |
| | **Shades of Love** (VSoane) **2-9-0** SSanders(5) (w'like: bkwd: racd far side: wl bhd fr ½-wy) | 13 | **20** | 16/1 | — | — |

(SP 158.2%) **20 Rn**

**1m 31.46** (7.86) CSF £173.28 TOTE £43.10: £13.00 £3.80 £1.50 (£121.50) Trio £92.40 OWNER Platt Promotions Ltd (NEWMARKET) BRED Mrs Willa Harford
**Handsome Ridge**, a useful type, looked sure to benefit from this and did the job well. Over further next year, there should be plenty to come. (20/1)
**Ninth Chord**, given time to find his stride, was finishing in good style and looks the sort to improve a fair bit as he strengthens. (7/1)
**4875 Bint Baladee** again had her chances, but failed to come up with the goods when the pressure was on. (11/4)
**4797 Toi Toi (IRE)** put in another useful effort until running out of fuel approaching the final furlong, from which point she was not given too hard a time. (14/1)
**Nash Point** ran well from a poor draw, and the experience should stand him in good stead. (14/1)
**4720 Valagalore** ran a fine race from a bad draw and is certainly going the right way. (5/1)
**Winter Garden** shaped well after a poor start and should have learnt plenty. (14/1)
**Purist**, a brother to Pure Grain, is a particularly nice sort. He needed this and, from an impossible draw, ran well enough to suggest that next year plenty more will be seen of him. (7/1: op 4/1)

## 5034 E.B.F. GIBSON BOOTH MAIDEN STKS (2-Y.O) (Class D)
1-30 (1-35) **6f** £3,978.50 (£1,193.00: £574.00: £264.50) Stalls: High GOING: 0.46 sec per fur (GS)

| | Horse | Dist | Pos | SP | RR | SF |
|---|---|---|---|---|---|---|
| 4825[2] | **Soviet State (USA)** (PWChapple-Hyam) **2-9-0** JReid(2) (lw: mde all: drew clr fnl 2f) | — | **1** | 6/5[1] | 95+ | 49 |

4913[W] **Nor-Do-I** (JMPEustace) **2-9-0b[1]** PBloomfield(13) (plld hrd: hdwy 2f out: hung lft & styd on wl) ....3 **2** 33/1 87 41
**Wild Sky (IRE)** (MJHeaton-Ellis) **2-9-0** SDrowne(9) (w'like: scope: effrt over 2f out: styd on wl: nvr able to chal) ....1¼ **3** 20/1 84 38
4807[3] **Nariskin (IRE)** (JLDunlop) **2-9-0** TQuinn(16) (lw: in tch: hdwy 2f out: kpt on wl) ....hd **4** 6/1[3] 83 37
4918[3] **Savona (IRE)** (PJMakin) **2-8-9** KDarley(5) (lw: chsd ldrs: effrt over 2f out: wknd over 1f out) ....2½ **5** 10/1 72 26
1896[10] **Share Delight (IRE)** (BWHills) **2-9-0** MHills(3) (stdd s: effrt 2f out: styd on one pce) ....s.h **6** 8/1 77 31
**Jay-Owe-Two (IRE)** (RMWhitaker) **2-9-0** ACulhane(14) (rangy: scope: bit bkwd: s.i.s: bhd tl sme late hdwy) ....2½ **7** 33/1 70 24
4818[4] **Bicton Park (77)** (DMorley) **2-9-0b** JStack(15) (lw: chsd ldrs 4f) ....hd **8** 20/1 70 24
4782[10] **Ella Lamees** (WJMusson) **2-8-9** DRMcCabe(17) (hld up & bhd: stdy hdwy 2f out: nvr plcd to chal) ....½ **9** 33/1 63 17
3475[8] **Sally Green (IRE)** (CFWall) **2-8-9** GDuffield(10) (in tch: nt qckn fnl 2f) ....3½ **10** 33/1 54 8
4891[2] **Stamp (IRE)** (BSmart) **2-9-0** MTebbutt(6) (lw: cl up 4f: sn btn) ....1¾ **11** 9/2[2] 54 8
**Van Chino** (BAMcMahon) **2-9-0** SSanders(7) (b.off hind: neat: scope: chsd ldrs 4f: sn wknd) ....1 **12** 33/1 52 6
4825[15] **Flying Thatch (IRE)** (RHannon) **2-9-0** DaneO'Neill(12) (chsd ldrs: sn pushed along: wknd 2f out) ....½ **13** 20/1 50 4
4806[2] **Kippilaw** (MJohnston) **2-8-9** JWeaver(18) (lw: gd spd 4f: wknd) ....3 **14** 14/1 37 —
4907[6] **Bright Gold** (ASmith) **2-9-0** DeanMcKeown(8) (in tch 4f: wknd) ....1¾ **15** 33/1 38 —
4046[15] **Crosby Nod** (EWeymes) **2-9-0** JQuinn(4) (bit bkwd: spd to ½-wy: wknd qckly) ....2½ **16** 33/1 31 —
4720[15] **Gadroon** (PCHaslam) **2-9-0** JFortune(11) (unruly & s.s: drvn along ½-wy: sn bhd) ....1 **17** 20/1 28 —
*4863[10] **Sea Ya Maite** (SRBowring) 2-9-0 SDWilliams(1) (Withdrawn not under Starter's orders: ref to ent stalls)* .... W 33/1 — —
(SP 147.4%) **17 Rn**

**1m 17.22** (6.22) CSF £54.55 TOTE £2.10: £1.10 £15.20 £5.80 (£48.30) Trio £353.10; £452.65 to Doncaster 9/11/96 OWNER Mr R. E. Sangster (MARLBOROUGH) BRED Echo Valley Horse Farm and Swettenham Stud

**4825 Soviet State (USA)** turned this into a precession in the last two furlongs, and this should have done him no end of good. (6/5: 4/5-5/4)
**Nor-Do-I** pulled extremely hard in the first-time blinkers, but he did finish well, albeit without having a chance. If he should ever learn to settle, he has the ability. (33/1)
**Wild Sky (IRE)** put in a decent first effort and was taught his job well. He looks a progressive type. (20/1)
**4807 Nariskin (IRE)**, having her third run, showed plenty. Now eligible for handicaps, she should make her mark next year. (6/1: op 7/2)
**4918 Savona (IRE)** had her chances but, when the pressure was on, she proved a bit disappointing. (10/1)
**Share Delight (IRE)** had an educational and the experience should have done him good. (8/1: 5/1-9/1)
**Jay-Owe-Two (IRE)**, a backward-looking sort, took time to realise what was required, but did pick up well at the end. Plenty of improvement is likely in time. (33/1)
**Ella Lamees**, from an impossible draw, had a nice quiet run and should have learnt plenty. (33/1)
**Sally Green (IRE)** never made an impression, but showed enough to suggest that she will do better in due course. (33/1)

## 5035 COAL PRODUCTS GROUP CONDITIONS STKS (3-Y.O+) (Class C)

2-00 (2-00) **1m 6f 132y** £4,939.90 (£1,782.40: £856.20: £351.00: £140.50) Stalls: Low GOING: 0.46 sec per fur (GS)

SP RR SF

3934[9] **Prussian Blue (USA) (98)** (HRACecil) **4-9-7** WRyan(1) (lw: trckd ldr: rdn to chal 2f out: styd on to ld nr fin) ....— **1** 11/4[1] 110 64
4569[6] **Poltarf (USA) (103)** (JHMGosden) **5-9-0** LDettori(3) (lw: led: rdn over 2f out: kpt on wl: jst ct) ....s.h **2** 11/4[1] 103 57
4569[7] **Further Flight (108)** (BWHills) **10-9-5** MHills(5) (b.hind: hld up: effrt over 3f out: sn rdn: ev ch appr fnl f: no ex) ....3 **3** 11/4[1] 105 59
4965[8] **Purple Splash (94)** (PJMakin) **6-9-0v** AClark(4) (chsd ldrs: effrt over 3f out: btn appr fnl f) ....5 **4** 3/1[2] 94 48
4824[11] **Patiala (IRE)** (RWArmstrong) **3-8-1** GCarter(2) (drvn along 8f out: sn lost pl: t.o) ....dist **5** 33/1[3] — —
(SP 107.9%) **5 Rn**

**3m 17.7** (14.10) CSF £9.72 TOTE £3.30: £1.70 £1.70 (£4.30) OWNER Mr L. Marinopoulos (NEWMARKET) BRED E. A. Cox Jnr
WEIGHT FOR AGE 3yo-8lb

**2352 Prussian Blue (USA)** likes cut in the ground and, although he does not do anything quickly, he is game. Responding to pressure, he wore down the leader near the line. (11/4)
**4569 Poltarf (USA)** made this a real test in very sticky ground but, despite a valiant effort, just failed to last out. (11/4)
**4569 Further Flight** would have kicked these out of the way at his best, but this holding ground, coupled with his years, found him out. (11/4)
**1336 Purple Splash** ran pretty well, but found things beyond him, despite the ground being in his favour. (3/1)

## 5036 RJB MINING CONDITIONS STKS (3-Y.O+ F & M) (Class C)

2-30 (2-31) **1m 2f 60y** £4,976.00 (£1,844.00: £887.00: £365.00: £147.50: £60.50) Stalls: Low GOING: 0.46 sec per fur (GS)

SP RR SF

4678[8] **Russian Snows (IRE) (111)** (SbinSuroor) **4-8-12** LDettori(2) (swtg: mde all: qcknd on bit over 3f out: rdn & styd on wl appr fnl f) ....— **1** 5/2[1] 104 60
4874[4] **Questonia (98)** (HRACecil) **3-9-4** KFallon(8) (a.p: pushed along over 4f out: chsd wnr fnl 2f: no imp) ....3½ **2** 10/1 109 61
4827* **Highland Gift (IRE)** (RCharlton) **3-8-12** KDarley(1) (lw: trckd ldrs tl rdn & wknd 2f out) ....6 **3** 5/2[1] 93 45
4948a[5] **Parrot Jungle (IRE) (100)** (JLDunlop) **3-8-8** TQuinn(3) (lw: in tch: rdn over 4f out: lost pl: styd on fnl 2f) ....s.h **4** 11/2[2] 89 41
4876[8] **Story Line (96)** (BWHills) **3-8-8** RHills(9) (b.hind: bhd: effrt 4f out: styd on: n.d) ....1½ **5** 20/1 87 39
2991[2] **Papaha (FR) (100)** (HRACecil) **3-8-12** WRyan(5) (b: hld up: effrt over 3f out: hung lft & no imp) ....nk **6** 9/1 90 42
4911[2] **Miss Universal (IRE) (104)** (CEBrittain) **3-8-8** MRoberts(7) (chsd ldrs tl outpcd 4f out: sn lost pl) ....nk **7** 8/1[3] 86 38
4567[8] **Berenice (97)** (GWragg) **3-8-12** MHills(6) (hdwy & prom 6f out: rdn over 3f out: wknd over 2f out) ....9 **8** 12/1 76 28
4819* **Omara (USA) (82)** (HRACecil) **3-8-12** AMcGlone(4) (lw: hld up: effrt over 4f out: sn outpcd & bhd) ....23 **9** 14/1 40 —
(SP 121.9%) **9 Rn**

**2m 16.24** (9.24) CSF £26.65 TOTE £3.10: £1.10 £2.60 £1.30 (£19.40) Trio £10.40 OWNER Godolphin (NEWMARKET) BRED Kilfrush Stud Ltd
WEIGHT FOR AGE 3yo-4lb

**4467 Russian Snows (IRE)**, given a fine ride, picked up the pace over three furlongs out and immediately had her rivals in trouble. (5/2)
**4874 Questonia** was off the bit some way out. To her credit, she did keep struggling on, but she was always short of the necessary pace. (10/1)
**4827* Highland Gift (IRE)** had her chances, but had her limitations exposed in the last two furlongs. (5/2)
**4948a Parrot Jungle (IRE)** was caught flat-footed early in the straight and, despite struggling on, never had a hope. (11/2)
**4479 Story Line**, who looked pretty slow, did keep staying on all the way up the straight but without ever having a chance. (20/1)
**2991 Papaha (FR)** gave problems by hanging left when the pressure was on. (9/1)
**4911 Miss Universal (IRE)** again looked a frustrating character. (8/1)

## 5037 AMCO CORPORATION PLC NURSERY H'CAP (0-85) (2-Y.O) (Class D)

3-00 (3-05) **5f** £3,489.50 (£1,046.00: £503.00: £231.50) Stalls: High GOING: 0.46 sec per fur (GS)

| Form | Horse | Dist | Pos | SP | RR | SF |
|---|---|---|---|---|---|---|
| 4916$^{W}$ | **Myrmidon (80)** (JLDunlop) **2-9-2** LDettori(2) (lw: unruly gng to s: trckd ldrs: led over 1f out: r.o) | — | **1** | 7/1 | 90 | 60 |
| 4903$^{8}$ | **Figlia (65)** (CBBBooth) **2-8-1b** LCharnock(4) (trckd ldrs: disp ld 2f out: sn hdd: kpt on u.p) | 3 | **2** | 25/1 | 65 | 35 |
| 4912$^{2}$ | **Royal Blackbird (62)** (JEBanks) **2-7-5**(7) RMullen(13) (lw: s.i.s: hdwy stands' side ½-wy: hung lft & r.o wl) | 1 | **3** | 7/2$^{1}$ | 59 | 29 |
| 4903$^{3}$ | **William's Well (61)** (MWEasterby) **2-7-6b**(5)ow1 MartinDwyer(1) (lw: cl up: disp ld 2f out: sn hdd & nt qckn) | 1¼ | **4** | 14/1 | 54 | 23 |
| 4364$^{12}$ | **Nomore Mr Niceguy (79)** (EJAlston) **2-9-1** JFortune(5) (lw: s.i.s: hdwy 2f out: styd on wl) | hd | **5** | 20/1 | 72 | 42 |
| 4966$^{5}$ | **Sous Le Nez (80)** (RGuest) **2-8-11**(5) DGriffiths(11) (racd stands' side: effrt ½-wy: nvr trbld ldrs) | ½ | **6** | 14/1 | 71 | 41 |
| 4912$^{8}$ | **Sarabi (69)** (JPearce) **2-8-5** JQuinn(3) (led 3f: wknd) | 1¾ | **7** | 12/1 | 55 | 25 |
| 4762$^{4}$ | **Mungo Park (75)** (MrsJRRamsden) **2-8-11** KFallon(7) (lw: stdd s: sn wl bhd: r.o appr fnl f) | d.h | **7** | 13/2$^{3}$ | 61 | 31 |
| 4749$^{3}$ | **Express Girl (77)** (DMoffatt) **2-8-10**(3) DarrenMoffatt(9) (racd stands' side: spd over 3f) | 1 | **9** | 5/1$^{2}$ | 60 | 30 |
| 4912$^{4}$ | **Regal Equity (68)** (BJMeehan) **2-8-4** SSanders(14) (spd stands' side 3f) | nk | **10** | 12/1 | 50 | 20 |
| 4893$^{6}$ | **Salty Behaviour (IRE) (85)** (RHannon) **2-9-7** DaneO'Neill(8) (lw: racd stands' side: effrt ½-wy: no imp) | ½ | **11** | 7/1 | 65 | 35 |
| 4749$^{15}$ | **Molly Drummond (62)** (CWCElsey) **2-7-7b**(5) PFessey(12) (led stands' side to ½-wy: sn wknd) | s.h | **12** | 25/1 | 42 | 12 |
| 3508$^{4}$ | **Whisper Low (IRE) (69)** (RHollinshead) **2-8-2**(3) FLynch(6) (prom to ½-wy: sn lost pl) | 4 | **13** | 16/1 | 36 | 6 |

(SP 124.3%) **13 Rn**

**63.05 secs** (4.65) CSF £147.05 CT £678.56 TOTE £7.90: £3.10 £8.30 £1.80 (£122.60) Trio £420.60 OWNER Mr Ian Pilkington (ARUNDEL) BRED M. J. Worth

LONG HANDICAP William's Well 7-6

**3924 Myrmidon** again gave problems on the way to the start, but there was little wrong with this performance as he scored most convincingly. (7/1)

**4619 Figlia** had her chances, but failed to pick up under vigorous driving approaching the final furlong. (25/1)

**4912 Royal Blackbird**, poorly drawn, just missed the break and, by the time she picked up, it was always too late. (7/2: 3/1-9/2)

**4903 William's Well** has ability, but as yet fails to see it out. (14/1)

**2700 Nomore Mr Niceguy** missed the kick and then took a hefty knock, but he was noted finishing well. (20/1)

**4966 Sous Le Nez** raced towards the slower stands' side and, in the circumstances, ran well. (14/1)

**4762 Mungo Park** had another educational, and finished well after being set an impossible task. (13/2)

## 5038 CO-OPERATIVE BANK PLC CONDITIONS STKS (2-Y.O) (Class C)

3-30 (3-33) **1m (straight)** £4,593.20 (£1,698.80: £814.40: £332.00: £131.00: £50.60) Stalls: High GOING: 0.46 sec per fur (GS)

| Form | Horse | Dist | Pos | SP | RR | SF |
|---|---|---|---|---|---|---|
| 4706* | **Catienus (USA) (86)** (MRStoute) **2-9-1** KDarley(1) (lw: cl up: led ½-wy: hld on wl fnl f) | — | **1** | 5/2$^{2}$ | 89 | 70 |
| 4792$^{4}$ | **Sunbeam Dance (USA) (99)** (SbinSuroor) **2-9-1** JReid(2) (lw: trckd ldrs: hdwy over 2f out: chal over 1f out: kpt on wl) | hd | **2** | 7/1$^{3}$ | 89 | 70 |
| 4880* | **Kaiser Kache (IRE) (80)** (KMcAuliffe) **2-8-11** OUrbina(6) (lw: chsd ldrs: rdn 2f out: r.o one pce) | 6 | **3** | 7/1$^{3}$ | 73 | 54 |
| | **Bold Demand** (SbinSuroor) **2-8-8** LDettori(3) (gd sort: scope: hld up: hdwy 3f out: wknd fnl 2f) | ½ | **4** | 5/6$^{1}$ | 69+ | 50 |
| 4801$^{8}$ | **Night Mirage (USA)** (MJohnston) **2-8-6** MRoberts(5) (in tch: wandered bdly u.p 2f out: no imp) | s.h | **5** | 14/1 | 67 | 48 |
| 4607$^{W}$ | **Cathies Flower** (JAHarris) **2-8-3b$^{1}$** JO'Reilly(4) (lt-f: unf: led to ½-wy: wknd qckly: sn t.o) | dist | **6** | 50/1 | — | — |

(SP 116.7%) **6 Rn**

**1m 43.51** (6.51) CSF £18.40 TOTE £2.70: £1.70 £2.70 (£9.70) OWNER Sheikh Mohammed (NEWMARKET) BRED Darley Stud Management Inc

**4706* Catienus (USA)** loves cut in the ground and stays well. That won him the day. (5/2)

**4792 Sunbeam Dance (USA)**, back to form, had a real tussle with the winner throughout the last furlong and a half but, despite trying hard, was never quite up to it. (7/1)

**4880* Kaiser Kache (IRE)** ran pretty well in this company, but was firmly put in his place in the last couple of furlongs. (7/1)

**Bold Demand**, a really nice type, looked likely to be all the better for it, and was wisely not knocked about when beaten. (5/6)

**Night Mirage (USA)**, still very green, looks to have ability when she finds out what the game is about. (14/1)

## 5039 C.I.S.W.O. H'CAP (0-80) (3-Y.O+) (Class D)

4-00 (4-02) **5f** £4,272.50 (£1,280.00: £615.00: £282.50) Stalls: High GOING: 0.46 sec per fur (GS)

| Form | Horse | Dist | Pos | SP | RR | SF |
|---|---|---|---|---|---|---|
| 4802$^{15}$ | **High Domain (IRE) (64)** (JLSpearing) **5-8-12** JWeaver(13) (a chsng ldrs: led ins fnl f: drvn out) | — | **1** | 20/1 | 71 | 54 |
| 4765$^{6}$ | **Chadwell Hall (65)** (SRBowring) **5-8-10b**(3) CTeague(19) (chsd ldrs: hdwy over 1f out: sn ev ch: kpt on towards fin) | hd | **2** | 20/1 | 72 | 55 |
| 4865$^{2}$ | **Nineacres (62)** (NMBabbage) **5-8-3v**(7) RFfrench(20) (lw: s.i.s: hdwy stands' side over 1f out: fin wl) | nk | **3** | 20/1 | 68 | 51 |
| 4765$^{3}$ | **Spender (74)** (PWHarris) **7-9-8** GDuffield(21) (lw: bhd: hdwy over 1f out: hrd rdn & r.o wl towards fin) | ½ | **4** | 16/1 | 78 | 61 |
| 4768$^{7}$ | **Fame Again (59)** (MrsJRRamsden) **4-8-7** KFallon(6) (bhd: hdwy ½-wy: hrd rdn appr fnl f: kpt on) | hd | **5** | 6/1$^{1}$ | 63 | 46 |
| 4869$^{9}$ | **Eastern Prophets (79)** (TJNaughton) **3-9-13** JFortune(22) (lw: hdwy ½-wy: styd on u.p fnl f: nvr able to chal) | d.h | **5** | 25/1 | 83 | 66 |
| 4727$^{2}$ | **Midnight Spell (68)** (JWHills) **4-8-13**(3) MHenry(12) (spd over 3f) | ½ | **7** | 14/1 | 70 | 53 |
| 4765$^{9}$ | **Goretski (IRE) (60)** (NTinkler) **3-8-8** KimTinkler(5) (mde most tl hdd ins fnl f) | nk | **8** | 25/1 | 61 | 44 |
| 4828$^{3}$ | **Walk the Beat (64)** (MartynMeade) **6-8-12** JReid(3) (s.i.s: hdwy over 1f out: r.o wl towards fin) | ½ | **9** | 11/1 | 64 | 47 |
| 4811$^{7}$ | **Gone Savage (76)** (WJMusson) **8-9-10** JStack(2) (b: bhd: hdwy 2f out: nt qckn ins fnl f) | ½ | **10** | 6/1$^{1}$ | 74 | 57 |
| 4994$^{3}$ | **Daawe (USA) (72)** (MrsVAAconley) **5-9-6** MDeering(11) (disp ld tl wknd appr fnl f) | 1½ | **11** | 10/1 | 65 | 48 |
| 4995$^{3}$ | **Splicing (73)** (WJHaggas) **3-9-4**(3) FLynch(8) (a chsng ldrs: effrt 2f out: nt qckn fnl f) | ¾ | **12** | 9/1$^{3}$ | 64 | 47 |
| 4312$^{22}$ | **Master of Passion (70)** (JMPEustace) **7-9-4** MTebbutt(15) (bhd: effrt ½-wy: no imp) | 1 | **13** | 25/1 | 58 | 41 |
| 4811$^{2}$ | **Shadow Jury (62)** (DWChapman) **6-8-10b** LCharnock(7) (chsd ldrs: rdn ½-wy: sn btn) | 4 | **14** | 12/1 | 37 | 20 |
| 4616$^{14}$ | **Johayro (55)** (JSGoldie) **3-8-3** JQuinn(18) (cl up tl wknd over 1f out) | nk | **15** | 25/1 | 29 | 12 |
| 3693$^{13}$ | **Chemcast (68)** (JLEyre) **3-9-2** RLappin(17) (outpcd & bhd fr ½-wy) | 1 | **16** | 25/1 | 39 | 22 |
| 2349$^{7}$ | **Perfect Brave (57)** (JBalding) **5-8-5** NCarlisle(16) (unruly s: s.i.s: hdwy & prom 2f out: sn wknd) | ½ | **17** | 25/1 | 26 | 9 |
| 4727$^{5}$ | **Sing With the Band (62)** (BAMcMahon) **5-8-10** SSanders(10) (w ldrs tl wknd appr fnl f) | hd | **18** | 8/1$^{2}$ | 31 | 14 |
| 4881$^{10}$ | **Bee Health Boy (69)** (MWEasterby) **3-8-12b**(5) GParkin(14) (lw: outpcd & wl bhd fnl 3f) | hd | **19** | 12/1 | 37 | 20 |
| 4995$^{4}$ | **Lady Sheriff (74)** (RHollinshead) **5-9-8** LDettori(4) (chsd ldrs tl wknd appr fnl f) | nk | **20** | 12/1 | 42 | 25 |
| 4791$^{4}$ | **Brecongill Lad (68)** (MissSEHall) **4-9-2** ACulhane(9) (lw: chsd ldrs tl wknd 1½f out) | ½ | **21** | 14/1 | 34 | 17 |
| 4765$^{17}$ | **Cross The Border (80)** (DNicholls) **3-10-0** KDarley(1) (prom 3f: sn lost pl) | 1¾ | **22** | 25/1 | 40 | 23 |

(SP 150.6%) **22 Rn**

**63.17 secs** (4.77) CSF £355.60 CT £7,267.46 TOTE £25.70: £6.30 £5.60 £3.30 £4.70 (£271.90) Trio £2,375.20; £2,074.18 to Doncaster 9/11/96 OWNER Mr Stephen Borsberry (ALCESTER) BRED Shannon Holdings Ltd

**2508 High Domain (IRE)** enjoyed this easy ground and needed all his courage to hold on in a desperate finish. (20/1)
**4610 Chadwell Hall** did really well from his draw, and kept answering his rider's calls in the final furlong, but just failed to quicken enough. (20/1)
**4865 Nineacres** raced towards the much slower stands' side and ran a cracking race, finishing like a train. He is in top form should he go on to the All-Weather. (20/1)
**4765 Spender** ran well, making up a terrific amount of ground in the final furlong. He is even better on the All-Weather. (16/1)
**3510 Fame Again** is a frustrating character and, although staying on strongly under pressure, always found this trip too sharp. (6/1)
**4765 Eastern Prophets** took time to get going, but he did finish well to put up a really good performance from his draw. (25/1)
**4811 Shadow Jury** (12/1: op 8/1)
**4727 Sing With the Band** (8/1: op 14/1)

T/Jkpt: £7,100.00 (0.1 Tckts); £4,851.60 to Doncaster 9/11/96. T/Plpt: £26.70 (536.63 Tckts). T/Qdpt: £10.70 (103.37 Tckts). AA

# 5033-DONCASTER (L-H) (Soft)
## Saturday November 9th
WEATHER: unsettled

## 5040 B.O.C. SUREFLOW MEDIAN AUCTION MAIDEN STKS (I) (2-Y.O) (Class E)
12-20 (12-22) **1m (straight)** £2,911.00 (£868.00: £414.00: £187.00) Stalls: High GOING minus 0.44 sec per fur (F)

| | | | | SP | RR | SF |
|---|---|---|---|---|---|---|
| 4814[2] | **Polar Flight (88)** (MJohnston) **2-9-0** JWeaver(13) (lw: cl up: led after 3f: strly chal over 1f out: kpt on wl towards fin) | — | **1** | 3/1[2] | 93 | 61 |
| 4913[2] | **Silverani (IRE)** (LMCumani) **2-9-0** OUrbina(5) (a.p: rdn to chal over 1f out: nt qckn wl ins fnl f) | ½ | **2** | 7/4[1] | 92 | 60 |
| 4897[3] | **Leading Note (USA)** (LMCumani) **2-8-9** JFortune(12) (chsd ldrs: effrt 2f out: edgd lft & no ex ins fnl f) | 6 | **3** | 13/2 | 75 | 43 |
| 4225[3] | **Perfect Poppy** (JRFanshawe) **2-8-9** DHarrison(8) (hld up: stdy hdwy over 3f out: chsd ldrs over 2f out: one pce) | ½ | **4** | 6/1[3] | 74 | 42 |
| | **Brand New Dance** (DWPArbuthnot) **2-9-0** TQuinn(7) (leggy: scope: dwlt: hdwy 3f out: rdn 2f out: sn outpcd) | .5 | **5** | 25/1 | 69 | 37 |
| 4760[11] | **Supply And Demand (84)** (GLMoore) **2-9-0** SWhitworth(9) (hld up & bhd: stdy hdwy fnl 2f: nvr plcd to chal) | 1 | **6** | 11/1 | 67+ | 35 |
| 4920[10] | **Fruitie O'Flarety** (CEBrittain) **2-9-0** MRoberts(15) (lw: cl up: rdn 3f out: wknd fnl 2f) | 7 | **7** | 25/1 | 53 | 21 |
| 4798[9] | **Bisquet-de-Bouche** (RDickin) **2-8-9** DaneO'Neill(10) (rr div: effrt over 3f out: sn outpcd) | 10 | **8** | 50/1 | 28 | — |
| | **Eternal Host (IRE)** (RHollinshead) **2-8-11**(3) FLynch(14) (cmpt: mid div & effrt ½-wy: wknd fnl 3f) | 1 | **9** | 25/1 | 31 | — |
| | **Mogul** (NAGraham) **2-9-0** AMcGlone(2) (w'like: chsd ldrs tl wknd fr wl over 3f out) | 1¾ | **10** | 16/1 | 28 | — |
| 4796[4] | **Spicetress** (JLSpearing) **2-8-9** SDrowne(1) (prom to ½-wy: sn rdn & lost pl) | 2½ | **11** | 33/1 | 18 | — |
| 4891[11] | **Mr Music** (KMcAuliffe) **2-9-0** JFEgan(4) (prom over 4f) | 1¾ | **12** | 33/1 | 19 | — |
| | **Quarterstaff** (CFWall) **2-9-0** GDuffield(16) (lengthy: w'like: bkwd: s.i.s: swtchd lft after s: a bhd) | nk | **13** | 16/1 | 18 | — |
| 4834[6] | **Such Presence** (KSBridgwater) **2-9-0** CRutter(3) (chsd ldrs to ½-wy: sn lost pl) | ½ | **14** | 50/1 | 17 | — |
| 4913[17] | **Salford Lad** (GWragg) **2-9-0** MHills(6) (led 3f: prom tl rdn & btn over 2f out) | 9 | **15** | 14/1 | — | — |
| 4803[16] | **Highland Pass (IRE) (63)** (PBurgoyne) **2-9-0** DRMcCabe(11) (bhd & drvn along ½-wy: t.o) | 26 | **16** | 33/1 | — | — |
| | | | | (SP 140.0%) | **16 Rn** | |

**1m 44.08** (7.08) CSF £9.55 TOTE £3.40: £1.60 £1.40 £2.00 (£3.60) Trio £4.90 OWNER The Middleham Partnership (MIDDLEHAM) BRED P. and Mrs Venner
STEWARDS' ENQUIRY Whitworth susp. 18-19 & 22 & 25-26 & 29-30/11 (failing to ride out mount). Moore fined £1,000 under Rule 151 (iii) (schooling in public). Supply And Demand susp. 10/11-9/1
**4814 Polar Flight** refused to be denied when strongly pressed and saw out his race in tremendous style. (3/1)
**4913 Silverani (IRE)** looked likely to prevail entering the final furlong, but found the winner too tough towards the finish. (7/4)
**4897 Leading Note (USA)**, who floundered in the ground when let down, will appreciate the winter to furnish and strengthen to his large frame. (13/2)
**4225 Perfect Poppy** looked likely to be involved in the finish entering the final quarter-mile, but could then do no more. (6/1)
**Brand New Dance** showed signs of ability before weakening in the final two furlongs. (25/1)
**4369 Supply And Demand**, dropped out at the back, stayed on through beaten horses in the last two furlongs, with his rider virtually sitting motionless. The Stewards took a dim view and fined the trainer £1,000, suspended the jockey for seven days, and banned the horse for thirty days. (11/1)

## 5041 B.O.C. SUREFLOW MEDIAN AUCTION MAIDEN STKS (II) (2-Y.O) (Class E)
12-50 (12-56) **1m (straight)** £2,885.00 (£860.00: £410.00: £185.00) Stalls: High GOING: 0.44 sec per fur (GS)

| | | | | SP | RR | SF |
|---|---|---|---|---|---|---|
| | **Moon River (IRE)** (JLDunlop) **2-9-0** TSprake(10) (wl grwn: bit bkwd: hld up: smooth hdwy over 2f out: shkn up & led over 1f out: sn clr: easily) | — | **1** | 8/1[3] | 88+ | 34 |
| 4818[7] | **Tyrolean Dream (IRE)** (MHTompkins) **2-8-11**(3) MHenry(8) (chsd ldrs: led 2f out tl over 1f out: no ch w wnr) | 2½ | **2** | 14/1 | 83 | 29 |
| 4801[3] | **Percy Isle (IRE)** (MRStoute) **2-9-0** KFallon(2) (lw: chsd ldrs: pushed along bef ½-wy: one pce u.p fnl 2f) | 4 | **3** | 15/8[1] | 75 | 21 |
| 4969[12] | **Russian Olive** (LMCumani) **2-8-9** OUrbina(7) (mid div: effrt & hdwy ½-wy: styd on same pce fnl 2f) | hd | **4** | 6/1[2] | 70 | 16 |
| | **Zinzari (FR)** (DRLoder) **2-9-0** DRMcCabe(15) (w'like: lw: cl up: led ½-wy tl rdn & hdd 2f out: no ex) | 2½ | **5** | 6/1[2] | 70 | 16 |
| 4253[4] | **Here's To Howie (USA)** (RHannon) **2-9-0** DaneO'Neill(11) (in tch: rdn wl over 2f out: btn over 1f out) | ¾ | **6** | 12/1 | 68 | 14 |
| 4798[10] | **Ginger Rogers** (DWPArbuthnot) **2-8-9** CRutter(12) (bhd: rdn along ½-wy: sme late hdwy: n.d) | 10 | **7** | 33/1 | 43 | — |
| | **Belle Bijou** (MJohnston) **2-8-9** JWeaver(5) (lt-f: unf: sn chsng ldrs: rdn over 2f out: hung lft & wknd wl over 1f out) | 1½ | **8** | 11/1 | 40 | — |
| | **Pinchincha (FR)** (DMorris) **2-9-0** NDay(13) (w'like: unf: bhd: rdn along bef ½-wy: nt pce to chal) | 2 | **9** | 25/1 | 41 | — |
| 4969[21] | **Jucinda** (JPearce) **2-8-9** JQuinn(14) (rr div: effrt over 3f out: no imp) | 3 | **10** | 33/1 | 30 | — |
| 4890[6] | **Ladybird** (JHMGosden) **2-8-9** LDettori(3) (led to ½-wy: sn rdn & lost pl) | 2½ | **11** | 6/1[2] | 25 | — |
| 4897[6] | **Strictly Hard** (GCBravery) **2-8-9** DeclanO'Shea(1) (prom to ½-wy: sn bhd) | 1½ | **12** | 25/1 | 22 | — |
| 4863[11] | **Straffan Gold (USA)** (GWragg) **2-9-0** KDarley(6) (trckd ldrs tl lost pl fr ½-wy) | 2½ | **13** | 14/1 | 22 | — |
| 4684[8] | **Arisaig (IRE)** (PCalver) **2-9-0** MBirch(9) (bhd: sn pushed along: a outpcd) | s.h | **14** | 33/1 | 22 | — |
| *4861[9]* | ***Move The Clouds*** (JRFanshawe) **2-8-9** DHarrison(4) (Withdrawn not under Starter's orders: uns rdr & bolted bef s) | | **W** | 16/1 | — | — |
| | | | | (SP 140.5%) | **14 Rn** | |

**1m 46.72** (9.72) CSF £114.17 TOTE £9.20: £2.50 £4.30 £1.50 (£88.60) Trio £296.70 OWNER Mr Benny Andersson (ARUNDEL) BRED Liscannor Stud Ltd

**Moon River (IRE)**, a well-grown half-brother to Moonax, looked on the backward side beforehand, but won in the style of a useful horse, and can hardly have known he had a race. He looks an interesting prospect for next year. (8/1)
**Tyrolean Dream (IRE)** stepped up on his debut effort to finish a clear second best, but had no chance with the easy winner when the chips were down. (14/1)
**4801 Percy Isle (IRE)** was never travelling with any real fluency, and was left for dead in the final quarter-mile. Longer distances will be required as a three-year-old. (15/8)
**Russian Olive** ran a respectable race and should find oppurtunities in her second season. (6/1)
**Zinzari (FR)**, who looked pretty fit from his debut, showed up well before fading in the last two furlongs. He will doubtless do better in time. (6/1)
**4253 Here's To Howie (USA)** came to the end of his tether when the race began in earnest from the two-furlong pole. (12/1)

## 5042 TOTE CHAMPIONSHIP LADIES' H'CAP (0-80) (3-Y.O+) (Class E)

1-20 (1-25) **1m (straight)** £4,175.00 (£1,250.00: £600.00: £275.00) Stalls: High GOING minus 0.44 sec per fur (F)

| Form | Horse | Dist | Pos | SP | RR | SF |
|---|---|---|---|---|---|---|
| 4590* | **Mels Baby (IRE) (61)** (JLEyre) **3-10-1** MissDianaJones(9) (hld up & bhd far side: hdwy over 2f out: rdn to ld ins fnl f: kpt on) | — | **1** | 6/1$^{2}$ | 74 | 43 |
| 4974$^{9}$ | **Sandmoor Chambray (79)** (TDEasterby) **5-11-2b**(5) MissADeniel(6) (trckd ldrs far side: led ½-wy: rdn over 1f out: hdd ins fnl f: one pce) | 1¼ | **2** | 12/1 | 90 | 61 |
| 4831* | **Polly Peculiar (65)** (BSmart) **5-10-2**(5) MissVMarshall(15) (chsd ldrs stands' side: effrt over 2f out: kpt on fnl f) | 2½ | **3** | 8/1$^{3}$ | 71 | 42 |
| 4906$^{3}$ | **Dispol Gem (61)** (GROldroyd) **3-10-1** MrsDKettlewell(3) (hdwy far side over 3f out: kpt on fr over 1f out: nt pce to chal) | 1¼ | **4** | 16/1 | 64 | 33 |
| 4813$^{2}$ | **Catumbella (USA) (74)** (JHMGosden) **3-11-0** MrsLPearce(8) (prom far side tl rdn & outpcd fr over 1f out) | 2 | **5** | 11/4$^{1}$ | 73 | 42 |
| 4860$^{14}$ | **Stackattack (IRE) (63)** (MrsJRRamsden) **3-9-12**(5) MissERamsden(1) (led far side to ½-wy: rdn & edgd lft over 2f out: no ex) | ½ | **6** | 12/1 | 61 | 30 |
| 4906$^{6}$ | **Darling Clover (70)** (RBastiman) **4-10-7**(5) MissRBastiman(19) (racd stands' side: hdwy over 2f out: kpt on fnl f) | 2 | **7** | 20/1 | 64 | 35 |
| | **Express Gift (60)** (MrsMReveley) **7-10-2** MrsSBosley(4) (effrt & hdwy far side over 2f out: nt rch ldrs) | 1¾ | **8** | 20/1 | 51 | 22 |
| 4868$^{8}$ | **King Athelstan (USA) (72)** (BAMcMahon) **8-10-9**(5) MissEJJones(11) (lw: led stands' side tl rdn & wknd fr over 2f out) | nk | **9** | 20/1 | 62 | 33 |
| 4909$^{10}$ | **Mybotye (75)** (GROldroyd) **3-10-10**(5) MrsCWilliams(22) (swtchd lft after s: sltly hmpd 3f out: hung lft & kpt on wl fnl f) | nk | **10** | 25/1 | 64 | 33 |
| 4820$^{4}$ | **Proud Monk (73)** (GLMoore) **3-10-8v**(5) MrsJMoore(12) (lw: in tch centre: rdn over 3f out: no imp) | nk | **11** | 9/1 | 62 | 31 |
| 4909$^{7}$ | **Royal Ceilidh (IRE) (78)** (DenysSmith) **3-10-13**(5) MissMCarson(13) (chsd ldrs stands' side: no imp fr wl over 2f out) | 1 | **12** | 16/1 | 65 | 34 |
| 4597$^{13}$ | **Absolute Utopia (USA) (64)** (NEBerry) **3-9-13**(5) MissEFolkes(17) (chsd ldrs stands' side over 4f) | ¾ | **13** | 25/1 | 49 | 18 |
| 4975$^{11}$ | **Ben Gunn (62)** (PTWalwyn) **4-9-13**(5) MarchionessBlandford(16) (prom stands' side tl wknd over 3f out) | 1¼ | **14** | 25/1 | 45 | 16 |
| 629$^{2}$ | **Dances With Hooves (77)** (DJSffrenchDavis) **4-11-5** MissJAllison(10) (hdwy far side ½-wy: rdn & wknd over 2f out) | 2 | **15** | 8/1$^{3}$ | 56 | 27 |
| 4769$^{20}$ | **Maple Bay (IRE) (77)** (ABailey) **7-11-0**(5) MissBridgetGatehouse(21) (a bhd stands' side) | 1¼ | **16** | 16/1 | 53 | 24 |
| 4901$^{17}$ | **Queens Consul (IRE) (78)** (BSRothwell) **6-11-1**(5) MrsDMcHale(7) (hld up far side: effrt ½-wy: sn bhd) | 1 | **17** | 16/1 | 52 | 23 |
| *4895*$^{10}$ | **Mr Frosty (62)** (WJarvis) **4-10-4** MissEJohnsonHoughton(2) (cl up far side to ½-wy) | 6 | **18** | 14/1 | 24 | — |
| 4994$^{24}$ | **Takhlid (USA) (77)** (DWChapman) **5-11-5** MissRClark(5) (prom far side 4f) | 5 | **19** | 20/1 | 29 | — |
| 4624$^{8}$ | **Northern Fan (IRE) (69)** (NTinkler) **4-10-11** MissPJones(20) (t.o) | 14 | **20** | 25/1 | — | — |
| 4504$^{3}$ | **Knotty Hill (73)** (RCraggs) **4-11-1** MissPRobson(14) (in tch centre: rdn & wkng whn fell 3f out) | | **F** | 25/1 | — | — |

(SP 157.0%) **21 Rn**

**1m 47.24** (10.24) CSF £84.07 CT £573.97 TOTE £6.60: £1.50 £3.80 £2.00 £4.10 (£31.50) Trio £195.40 OWNER Mr John Roberts (Wakefield) (HAMBLETON) BRED A. F. O'Callaghan
WEIGHT FOR AGE 3yo-2lb
STEWARDS' ENQUIRY Moore susp. 18-19&22/11/96 (careless riding).
**4590* Mels Baby (IRE)** completed her hat-trick in fine style, coming from a long way off the pace to settle the issue late in the day. She was very well handled. (6/1)
**4769 Sandmoor Chambray** ran a solid race but, despite receiving every assistance, was simply unable to concede so much weight to such an in-form rival. (12/1)
**4831* Polly Peculiar** raced with the stands'-side group and did well to get so close to the first two, who had the advantage of racing towards the favoured far side of the course. (8/1)
**4906 Dispol Gem** ran another good race but, despite staying on, was unable to peg back the leaders inside the final furlong. (16/1)
**4813 Catumbella (USA)**, having only her fourth career start, showed up prominently before gradually fading inside the final quarter-mile. (11/4)
**4768 Stackattack (IRE)**, always in the firing-line on the far side, was found wanting from over a furlong out. (12/1)
**2754 Mybotye**, drawn on the stands' side, moved across to the centre and was slightly hampered by a faller three furlongs out. Despite hanging left, which carried him to the far side of the course, he stayed on strongly in the closing stages and did well to finish so close. (25/1)

## 5043 CIU NSPCC APPEAL NURSERY H'CAP (2-Y.O) (Class D)

1-50 (1-53) **7f** £4,066.25 (£1,220.00: £587.50: £271.25) Stalls: High GOING: 0.44 sec per fur (GS)

| Form | Horse | Dist | Pos | SP | RR | SF |
|---|---|---|---|---|---|---|
| 4303$^{2}$ | **Jeffrey Anotherred (86)** (KMcAuliffe) **2-8-11** RHughes(1) (trckd ldrs gng wl: led & qcknd wl over 1f out: hld on wl towards fin) | — | **1** | 8/1$^{3}$ | 96 | 47 |
| 4782$^{2}$ | **Don Sebastian (73)** (WJHaggas) **2-7-5**(7) RMullen(7) (lw: hld up & bhd: effrt & gd hdwy over 2f out: edgd lft & chal ins fnl f: kpt on: jst failed) | s.h | **2** | 9/1 | 83 | 34 |
| 4878* | **Yorkie George (91)** (LMCumani) **2-9-2** LDettori(11) (b.off hind: lw: hld up & racd keenly: hdwy 2f out: sn rdn & one pce) | 6 | **3** | 7/4$^{1}$ | 87 | 38 |
| 4864* | **I Can't Remember (81)** (PDEvans) **2-8-6** JFEgan(6) (rr div: effrt over 2f out: kpt on fr over 1f out) | 2 | **4** | 11/1 | 73 | 24 |
| 4807* | **Rihan (USA) (88)** (SbinSuroor) **2-8-13** RHills(8) (lw: led tl wl over 1f out: sn wknd) | 2½ | **5** | 7/1$^{2}$ | 74 | 25 |
| 4864$^{9}$ | **Top of The Wind (IRE) (74)** (JJO'Neill) **2-7-13** JQuinn(10) (lw: chsd ldrs: rdn & lost pl over 2f out: sme late hdwy) | 3 | **6** | 10/1 | 53 | 4 |
| 4723$^{20}$ | **Out of Sight (IRE) (83)** (BAMcMahon) **2-8-8** SSanders(12) (chsd ldrs tl rdn & wknd fnl 2f) | nk | **7** | 16/1 | 61 | 12 |
| 4817$^{6}$ | **Harmony Hall (80)** (JRFanshawe) **2-8-5** DHarrison(4) (b: bmpd sn after s: hdwy 2f out: ch wl over 1f out: sn wknd) | nk | **8** | 14/1 | 58 | 9 |

4912$^{10}$ **Manhattan Diamond (71)** (ABailey) **2-7-3**$^{(7)}$ IonaWands(3) (chsd ldrs tl lost pl bef ½-wy: n.d after)..............1¼ **9** 33/1 46 —
4867$^{2}$ **Effervescence (78)** (RHannon) **2-8-3** DaneO'Neill(13) (in tch tl rdn & wknd over 2f out)..............1½ **10** 11/1 49 —
2375$^{2}$ **Passiflora (83)** (JLDunlop) **2-8-8** TQuinn(5) (in tch: effrt & hdwy over 2f out: btn & eased fnl f)..............nk **11** 8/1$^{3}$ 54 5
4131$^{13}$ **For Your Eyes Only (96)** (TDEasterby) **2-9-7** MBirch(9) (b: bhd: rdn along bef ½-wy: nvr wnt pce)..............nk **12** 20/1 66 17
4787$^{10}$ **The Four Isles (71)** (DHaydnJones) **2-7-10** FNorton(2) (cl up tl wknd wl over 2f out)..............1 **13** 33/1 39 —
(SP 130.0%) **13 Rn**

**1m 30.71** (7.11) CSF £77.53 CT £176.36 TOTE £11.70: £2.90 £2.70 £1.40 (£59.90) Trio £37.90 OWNER Highgrove Developments Ltd (LAMBOURN) BRED John Rose
LONG HANDICAP Manhattan Diamond 6-12 The Four Isles 6-6
**4303 Jeffrey Anotherred**, an admirably consistent gelding, held on gamely towards the finish to notch his third win of the season. (8/1)
**4782 Don Sebastian** threw down a strong challenge inside the final furlong but, having edged to his left, his rider put down his whip and pushed him out to the finish. The effort was not quite enough though. (9/1)
**4878* Yorkie George** ran a fraction too freely off the pace in the early stages and was found wanting when let down inside the final quarter-mile. (7/4)
**4864* I Can't Remember**, racing off a 4lb higher mark than last time, did all his best work late on, but could never get into the thick of the action. (11/1)
**4807* Rihan (USA)**, stepping up in distance, attempted to make all the running, but was left for dead from over a furlong out. (7/1)
**3835 Top of The Wind (IRE)**, despite carrying her head slightly high, stayed on again in the closing stages after losing her pitch. (10/1)

## 5044 WENTWORTH STKS (Listed) (3-Y.O+) (Class A)

2-25 (2-26) **6f** £11,798.00 (£4,382.00: £2,116.00: £880.00: £365.00: £159.00) Stalls: High GOING: 0.44 sec per fur (GS)

SP RR SF

4917* **Astrac (IRE) (87)** (MissGayKelleway) **5-8-11** KFallon(14) (lw: bhd: hmpd after 1f: hdwy ½-wy: r.o u.p to ld nr fin)..............— **1** 8/1 117 69
4870* **Diffident (FR) (113)** (SbinSuroor) **4-9-6** KDarley(9) (trckd ldrs: rdn to ld ins fnl f: jst ct)..............s.h **2** 5/1$^{2}$ 126 78
4870$^{2}$ **Russian Revival (USA) (113)** (SbinSuroor) **3-9-0** LDettori(1) (lw: trckd ldrs: led 2f out tl ins fnl f: kpt on)..............½ **3** 4/1$^{1}$ 119 71
4774$^{7}$ **Carranita (IRE) (107)** (BPalling) **6-8-9** TSprake(7) (lw: chsd ldrs: effrt 2f out: r.o one pce)..............1¼ **4** 5/1$^{2}$ 110 62
4869$^{11}$ **Tadeo (97)** (MJohnston) **3-8-11** MRoberts(10) (cl up: effrt over 2f out: nt qckn)..............1¼ **5** 16/1 109 61
4869* **Shanghai Girl (94)** (DRLoder) **3-8-6v** DRMcCabe(16) (bhd: hdwy over 1f out: r.o wl towards fin)..............nk **6** 9/1 103 55
4917$^{5}$ **The Puzzler (IRE) (104)** (BWHills) **5-8-11** MHills(12) (b: bhd: effrt over 2f out: styd on u.p: nvr able to chal)..............1¼ **7** 11/1 105 57
4743a$^{4}$ **Warning Star (98)** (BWHills) **4-8-6** RHills(4) (prom: effrt over 2f out: btn over 1f out)..............5 **8** 14/1 86 38
4958a$^{2}$ **Croft Pool (107)** (JAGlover) **5-9-0** GCarter(13) (lw: drvn along ½-wy: n.d)..............1¾ **9** 10/1 90 42
2072$^{17}$ **Keepers Dawn (IRE) (100)** (RFJohnsonHoughton) **3-8-6** SSanders(11) (in tch: rdn ½-wy: sn btn)..............3½ **10** 33/1 72 24
4994$^{8}$ **Takadou (IRE) (79)** (MissLCSiddall) **5-8-11** DHarrison(6) (lw: in tch: effrt over 2f out: sn btn)..............nk **11** 66/1 77 29
4774$^{6}$ **Royale Figurine (IRE) (105)** (MJFetherston-Godley) **5-8-6** TQuinn(15) (spd over 3f: sn lost pl)..............nk **12** 6/1$^{3}$ 71 23
4772$^{15}$ **Double Quick (IRE) (85)** (MJohnston) **4-8-6v$^{1}$** JWeaver(2) (led 4f: sn rdn & btn)..............1¾ **13** 33/1 66 18
4802$^{9}$ **Montserrat (74)** (LGCottrell) **4-8-6v** MFenton(3) (chsd ldrs 4f: sn btn)..............1¼ **14** 33/1 63 15
1075$^{6}$ **Paris Babe (93)** (DMorris) **4-8-6** NDay(5) (spd to ½-wy: sn bhd)..............2 **15** 50/1 58 10
4823$^{5}$ **Averti (IRE) (100)** (WRMuir) **5-8-11** DaneO'Neill(8) (lw: sn outpcd & bhd: eased fnl 2f)..............dist **16** 25/1 — —
(SP 134.8%) **16 Rn**

**1m 15.51** (4.51) CSF £49.17 TOTE £9.60: £2.30 £2.40 £2.40 (£50.30) Trio £19.90 OWNER Mr T. L. Beecroft (WHITCOMBE) BRED Miss Aisling O'Connell
**4917* Astrac (IRE)** again had the soft ground he loves. Although poorly drawn, he was given a cracking ride and showed fine courage. (8/1)
**4870* Diffident (FR)** has had three hard races in a row and showed just as much enthusiasm here but, despite a valiant effort, was just touched off. (5/1)
**4870 Russian Revival (USA)** has possibly looked at his best on faster ground, but he put up a fine show here and kept fighting back when all looked lost. (4/1)
**3759* Carranita (IRE)** was trying to win this for the second year running and put up a good performance, but just found the opposition too classy. (5/1)
**4679* Tadeo** is at his best over the minimum trip and, in the circumstances, this was a useful effort. (16/1)
**4869* Shanghai Girl**, stepping up in class, showed that she is in good heart at present, running well from a very poor draw. (9/1)
**4917 The Puzzler (IRE)** likes the soft ground and loves to come from off the pace, but had his limitations exposed here. (11/1)

## 5045 CO-OPERATIVE BANK SERLBY STKS (Listed) (3-Y.O+) (Class A)

2-55 (3-02) **1m 4f** £10,928.00 (£4,052.00: £1,951.00: £805.00: £327.50: £136.50) Stalls: Low GOING: 0.44 sec per fur (GS)

SP RR SF

4911* **Medaille Militaire (102)** (JLDunlop) **4-8-13** KDarley(3) (lw: a gng wl: led over 2f out: shkn up over 1f out: r.o)— **1** 6/1$^{3}$ 120 66
4876$^{3}$ **Eva Luna (USA) (108)** (HRACecil) **4-9-2** KFallon(9) (lw: a.p: slt ld over 2f out: sn rdn & hdd: kpt on wl)..............¾ **2** 100/30$^{2}$ 122 68
4876$^{7}$ **Kalabo (USA) (113)** (SbinSuroor) **4-8-13** LDettori(4) (swtg: bhd: effrt over 3f out: styd on: no imp)..............8 **3** 8/1 108 54
2113$^{8}$ **Election Day (IRE) (115)** (MRStoute) **4-9-4v$^{1}$** PatEddery(10) (pushed along 7f out: hdwy u.p to chse ldrs over 3f out: sn btn)..............5 **4** 2/1$^{1}$ 107 53
4678$^{9}$ **Poppy Carew (IRE) (106)** (PWHarris) **4-8-8** GDuffield(1) (lw: trckd ldrs: n.m.r ent st: one pce fnl 3f)..............½ **5** 11/1 96 42
4886$^{5}$ **Weet-A-Minute (IRE) (100)** (RHollinshead) **3-8-7** FLynch(8) (cl up: led 6f out tl over 2f out: sn wknd)..............4 **6** 50/1 96 36
4421a$^{4}$ **Freequent (103)** (LMCumani) **3-8-7** OUrbina(5) (hld up: effrt over 4f out: sn btn)..............18 **7** 14/1 72 12
4465$^{2}$ **Sheer Danzig (IRE) (102)** (RWArmstrong) **4-8-13** MHills(7) (led to 6f out: sn wknd)..............10 **8** 13/2 58 4
4856a$^{7}$ **Punishment (115)** (CEBrittain) **5-8-13** MRoberts(2) (chsd ldrs tl wknd over 3f out)..............9 **9** 14/1 46 —
(SP 118.8%) **9 Rn**

**2m 39.9** (9.90) CSF £25.61 TOTE £6.30: £2.10 £1.50 £2.60 (£10.80) Trio £24.60 OWNER Mr James Hartnett (ARUNDEL) BRED Fares Stables Ltd
WEIGHT FOR AGE 3yo-6lb
**OFFICIAL EXPLANATION Averti (IRE): finished distressed.**
**4911* Medaille Militaire**, stepping up in trip and trying much softer ground, was as good as ever and always had the situation in hand. (6/1)
**4876 Eva Luna (USA)** was second best from a long way out, but she is game beyond belief and would not give in. (100/30)
**4441 Kalabo (USA)** got very warm beforehand and never ran any sort of race, despite keeping on when it was all over. (8/1)
**2113 Election Day (IRE)**, tried in a visor this time, needed a lot of help from the saddle to get into it and then quickly threw in the towel. (2/1)
**4290a Poppy Carew (IRE)** got cramped for room when the others, who had been racing wide, joined her on the home turn, and she then looked to be struggling in these soft conditions. (11/1)
**4886 Weet-A-Minute (IRE)** has lost his form altogether in the second half of the season. (50/1)

## 5046 TOTE CREDIT NOVEMBER H'CAP (3-Y.O+) (Class B)

3-30 (3-32) **1m 4f** £26,670.00 (£9,930.00: £4,815.00: £2,025.00: £862.50: £397.50) Stalls: Low GOING: 0.44 sec per fur (GS)

| Form | Horse | Dist | Pos | SP | RR | SF |
|---|---|---|---|---|---|---|
| 4964[3] | **Clifton Fox (96)** (JAGlover) **4-8-10** NDay(14) (hld up & bhd: swtchd & hdwy over 2f out: hung bdly lft: r.o wl to ld cl home) | — | **1** | 9/1 | 111 | 61 |
| 4876[2] | **Kutta (103)** (RWArmstrong) **4-9-3** RHills(10) (lw: trckd ldrs: smooth hdwy to ld over 2f out: drvn fnl f: jst ct) | nk | **2** | 5/2[1] | 118 | 68 |
| 4826[3] | **Nabhaan (IRE) (92)** (DMorley) **3-8-0**ow2 GCarter(2) (lw: trckd ldrs: effrt on ins 3f out: ev ch wl over 1f out: swtchd, edgd rt & nt qckn fnl f) | 1¾ | **3** | 14/1 | 104 | 46 |
| 4833[3] | **Dato Star (IRE) (89)** (JMJefferson) **5-8-3** DaneO'Neill(4) (lw: trckd ldrs: effrt 3f out: sn rdn: one pce whn hmpd ins fnl f) | ½ | **4** | 7/1[2] | 101 | 51 |
| 4872[3] | **Sugar Mill (82)** (MrsMReveley) **6-7-7**(3) DWright(8) (s.i.s & pushed along: hdwy ½-wy: kpt on u.p fnl 3f: nvr able to chal) | 5 | **5** | 16/1 | 87 | 37 |
| 4675[3] | **Dance So Suite (90)** (PFICole) **4-8-4** TQuinn(16) (lw: hdwy 5f out: chsng ldrs & rdn over 2f out: r.o one pce) | 2 | **6** | 20/1 | 92 | 42 |
| 4675* | **Shadow Leader (82)** (CREgerton) **5-7-10** LCharnock(11) (lw: plld hrd: a.p: effrt 4f out: nt qckn fnl 3f) | 1 | **7** | 16/1 | 83 | 33 |
| 4548[4] | **Heart (88)** (MRStoute) **3-7-3**(7) RFfrench(12) (chsd ldrs tl wknd fnl 3f) | ½ | **8** | 33/1 | 88 | 32 |
| 4617[14] | **Far Ahead (83)** (JLEyre) **4-7-11** TWilliams(3) (in tch: effrt over 3f out: r.o one pce) | 2 | **9** | 33/1 | 81 | 31 |
| 4695* | **Present Arms (USA) (88)** (PFICole) **3-7-10** 4x JQuinn(7) (lw: led tl hdd & wknd over 2f out) | 2 | **10** | 8/1[3] | 83 | 27 |
| 4872[2] | **Wild Rita (82)** (WRMuir) **4-7-3**(7) PDoe(23) (lw: bhd: effrt over 4f out: n.d) | 1½ | **11** | 14/1 | 75 | 25 |
| 4826[9] | **Game Ploy (POL) (89)** (DHaydnJones) **4-8-3** SSanders(9) (chsd ldrs tl wknd fnl 3f) | ¾ | **12** | 20/1 | 81 | 31 |
| 4826* | **Edan Heights (87)** (SDow) **4-7-10**(5)ow5 4x ADaly(21) (nvr trbld ldrs) | nk | **13** | 25/1 | 79 | 24 |
| 4716[3] | **Romios (IRE) (84)** (PFICole) **4-7-12** CRutter(19) (bhd: effrt over 4f out: n.d) | 1¼ | **14** | 14/1 | 74 | 24 |
| 4714[4] | **Overbury (IRE) (114)** (SbinSuroor) **5-10-0** LDettori(15) (trckd ldrs tl wknd fnl 3f) | nk | **15** | 25/1 | 104 | 54 |
| 4626* | **Voila Premiere (IRE) (83)** (MHTompkins) **4-7-4**(7)ow1 RMullen(5) (sme hdwy u.p over 3f out: sn btn) | 2 | **16** | 25/1 | 70 | 19 |
| 4385[3] | **Celestial Choir (91)** (JLEyre) **6-8-5** JFortune(13) (effrt over 4f out: rdn & n.d) | s.h | **17** | 20/1 | 78 | 28 |
| 4771[14] | **Better Offer (IRE) (106)** (GHarwood) **4-9-6** PatEddery(20) (a rr div) | 1½ | **18** | 16/1 | 91 | 41 |
| 4826[2] | **Gone for a Burton (IRE) (82)** (PJMakin) **6-7-10** NCarlisle(22) (n.m.r appr st: n.d) | 4 | **19** | 12/1 | 61 | 11 |
| 4862[7] | **Midyan Blue (IRE) (82)** (JMPEustace) **6-7-10** NKennedy(1) (in tch: hdwy ent st: wknd 3f out) | 1¼ | **20** | 33/1 | 60 | 10 |
| 4872[12] | **Penny a Day (IRE) (93)** (MrsMReveley) **6-8-7** KDarley(24) (bhd: pushed along & hdwy 7f out: wknd fnl 4f) | ¾ | **21** | 12/1 | 70 | 20 |
| 4868[5] | **Ten Past Six (82)** (MartynWane) **4-7-10** FNorton(17) (a bhd) | nk | **22** | 50/1 | 58 | 8 |
| | | | | (SP 151.8%) | **22 Rn** | |

**2m 40.19** (10.19) CSF £35.08 CT £332.25 TOTE £13.10: £3.50 £2.00 £3.60 £2.30 (£27.60) Trio £383.50 OWNER P and S Partnership (WORKSOP) BRED Crest Stud Ltd

LONG HANDICAP Edan Heights 7-0 Heart 7-2 Sugar Mill 7-5 Voila Premiere (IRE) 6-10 Wild Rita 7-4 Gone for a Burton (IRE) 7-9 Midyan Blue (IRE) 7-2 Present Arms (USA) 7-3

WEIGHT FOR AGE 3yo-6lb

**4964 Clifton Fox**, trying a longer trip, put up an incredible performance and, had he not persisted in hanging left, he would have scored comfortably. (9/1)

**4876 Kutta** looked the winner for much of the race but, when the pressure was on, he was inclined to hang left for a few strides and was beaten fair and square. (5/2)

**4826 Nabhaan (IRE)** had his chances if good enough, but Kutta crossed him at a vital stage, and he then hung badly right himself and threw any hopes away. (14/1)

**4833 Dato Star (IRE)** went well for much of the trip but, asked to pick up early in the straight, he seemed short of a change of gear. His future lies over jumps. (7/1)

**4872 Sugar Mill**, who needed encouragement to get him going early on, was always having to fight for a position, and was never good enough to make a real impression. (16/1)

**4675 Dance So Suite** keeps running consistently well, but is just short of that vital turn of speed. (20/1)

**4675* Shadow Leader** beat himself by pulling too hard. (16/1)

**4695* Present Arms (USA)** has been doing all his winning on much faster ground and found this a different proposition. (8/1)

## 5047 COALITE DRAGON H'CAP (0-95) (3-Y.O+) (Class C)

4-05 (4-06) **2m 110y** £7,830.00 (£2,340.00: £1,120.00: £510.00) Stalls: Low GOING: 0.44 sec per fur (GS)

| Form | Horse | Dist | Pos | SP | RR | SF |
|---|---|---|---|---|---|---|
| 4919* | **Sweetness Herself (76)** (MJRyan) **3-7-11**(3) MBaird(10) (lw: trckd ldrs: hdwy on ins to ld over 3f out: hld on wl) | — | **1** | 11/2 | 89 | 27 |
| 4965* | **Orchestra Stall (98)** (JLDunlop) **4-10-3** TQuinn(2) (lw: hld up: hdwy 5f out: sn trckng ldrs & nt clr run: hdwy over 1f out: ev ch tl nt qckn nr fin) | ½ | **2** | 9/2[2] | 111 | 58 |
| 4821* | **Bowcliffe Court (IRE) (66)** (RAkehurst) **4-7-13** JQuinn(4) (trckd ldrs: squeezed thro 3f out: ev ch ins fnl f: nt qckn towards fin) | hd | **3** | 4/1[1] | 78 | 25 |
| 4919[3] | **Paradise Navy (67)** (CREgerton) **7-7-7b**(7) RMullen(15) (hld up & bhd: hdwy 4f out: effrt 3f out: styd on towards fin) | 10 | **4** | 11/1 | 70 | 17 |
| 4588[4] | **Shirley Sue (72)** (MJohnston) **3-7-10** FNorton(11) (w ldrs: effrt over 4f out: one pce fnl 2½f) | s.h | **5** | 12/1 | 75 | 13 |
| 4112[8] | **Generosa (87)** (HCandy) **3-8-11** CRutter(16) (hld up: stdy hdwy ent st: ev ch 3f out: one pce fnl 2f) | 2½ | **6** | 14/1 | 87 | 25 |
| 4919[8] | **Lepikha (USA) (72)** (BWHills) **3-7-10** NCarlisle(3) (trckd ldrs: nt clr run 3f out: sn rdn & btn) | 6 | **7** | 14/1 | 66 | 4 |
| | **Outset (IRE) (63)** (MDHammond) **6-7-7**(3) DWright(8) (bit bkwd: led after 6f tl over 3f out: sn outpcd) | 3½ | **8** | 50/1 | 54 | 1 |
| 4832[4] | **Izza (63)** (WStorey) **5-7-10** NKennedy(9) (effrt on outside 4f out: rdn & no imp) | s.h | **9** | 14/1 | 54 | 1 |
| 961[7] | **Executive Design (76)** (MrsMReveley) **4-8-9** KDarley(17) (bhd: hdwy 6f out: sn in tch: rdn & one pce fnl 3f) | ½ | **10** | 20/1 | 67 | 14 |
| 4832[2] | **Sea Victor (78)** (JLHarris) **4-8-11** LDettori(5) (led 6f: cl up tl wknd fnl 3f) | nk | **11** | 5/1[3] | 68 | 15 |
| 4862[3] | **Karisma (IRE) (72)** (DenysSmith) **3-7-3**(7) RFfrench(1) (chsd ldrs tl wknd over 4f out) | ½ | **12** | 25/1 | 62 | — |
| 4722[4] | **Uncle Doug (65)** (MrsMReveley) **5-7-12** LCharnock(13) (lw: hld up: effrt 4f out: sn wknd) | 24 | **13** | 10/1 | 32 | — |
| 4919[7] | **Debutante Days (66)** (CREgerton) **4-7-10b**(3)ow2 MHenry(12) (sn wl bhd: gd hdwy 6f out: sn btn) | 3½ | **14** | 25/1 | 29 | — |
| 4365[14] | **Noufari (FR) (70)** (RHollinshead) **5-8-0**(3) FLynch(14) (bhd: hdwy 5f out: sn wknd) | hd | **15** | 14/1 | 33 | — |
| 573[14] | **Torch Vert (IRE) (75)** (NJHWalker) **4-8-8** JStack(7) (prom tl outpcd fnl 3½f) | 4 | **16** | 33/1 | 34 | — |
| 4877[15] | **Lalindi (IRE) (72)** (RChampion) **5-8-5** AMcGlone(6) (lw: wl bhd fnl 4f) | ½ | **17** | 20/1 | 31 | — |
| | | | | (SP 144.1%) | **17 Rn** | |

**3m 48.36** (19.36) CSF £33.62 CT £111.40 TOTE £6.30: £1.80 £1.90 £1.90 £2.10 (£13.60) Trio £19.80 OWNER Mrs M. J. Lavell (NEWMARKET) BRED Stud-On-The-Chart

LONG HANDICAP Izza 7-4 Shirley Sue 7-8 Karisma (IRE) 6-13 Lepikha (USA) 7-4 Outset (IRE) 6-10

WEIGHT FOR AGE 3yo-9lb

**4919* Sweetness Herself** loves the soft ground and, although shooting up the weights, she is game, and would not be denied once in front. (11/2)
**4965* Orchestra Stall** had trouble in getting a run but, when he did, he quickened to have his chance, only to find his weight and these testing conditions anchoring him late on. (9/2: op 3/1)
**4821* Bowcliffe Court (IRE)** likes plenty of give and is on good terms with himself since changing stables, but just failed to see it out this time. (4/1)
**4919 Paradise Navy** runs when in the mood and, after travelling on the bit as usual, took far too long to get going. (11/1)
**4588 Shirley Sue** has run her socks off this season, but was left struggling here halfway up the straight. (12/1)
**3699* Generosa**, returning here after two months off, ran as though it was needed. (14/1)
**4794* Lepikha (USA)** was going well when shut in but, when a gap came, he lacked a change of gear. (14/1)
**Outset (IRE)** had a good blow and should be kept in mind over jumps. (50/1)
**961 Executive Design** blew up. (20/1)

T/Jkpt: Not won; £8,898.07 to Wolverhampton 11/11/96. T/Plpt: £21.30 (1,072.12 Tckts). T/Qdpt: £11.10 (153.85 Tckts). O'R/AA

# 4782-FOLKESTONE (R-H) (Soft, Heavy patches)
## Monday November 11th

WEATHER: overcast WIND: almost nil

### 5048 BEEWOOD COACHES NURSERY H'CAP (0-75) (2-Y.O) (Class E)
12-50 (12-51) **6f 189y** £3,206.70 (£957.60: £457.80: £207.90) Stalls: Low GOING: 1.15 sec per fur (S)

| | | | SP | RR | SF |
|---|---|---|---|---|---|
| 4883[3] | **Return of Amin (61)** (JDBethell) **2-8-8** TQuinn(1) (lw: a.p: led over 1f out: rdn out) —- | **1** | 7/1 | 63 | 35 |
| 4549[2] | **Silk St John (74)** (MJRyan) **2-9-7** AClark(4) (hdwy over 1f out: r.o wl ins fnl f) 3 | **2** | 6/1[3] | 69 | 41 |
| 5006* | **Spaniard's Mount (69)** (MHTompkins) **2-8-13v**(3) 6x MHenry(11) (lw: led over 5f: unable qckn) hd | **3** | 3/1[1] | 64 | 36 |
| 4782* | **Havago (72)** (RHannon) **2-9-5** DaneO'Neill(2) (lw: chsd ldr: rdn over 2f out: wknd over 1f out) 9 | **4** | 7/2[2] | 46 | 18 |
| 4495[8] | **Run Lucy Run (66)** (MissGayKelleway) **2-8-13** GDuffield(10) (nvr nr to chal) 12 | **5** | 25/1 | 12 | — |
| 4721[2] | **Rake Hey (68)** (RFJohnsonHoughton) **2-9-1b** JReid(6) (hld up: rdn 3f out: wknd over 2f out) 3½ | **6** | 7/1 | 6 | — |
| 4787[5] | **Battle Ground (IRE) (54)** (NACallaghan) **2-8-1** SDrowne(8) (lw: bhd fnl 5f) nk | **7** | 7/1 | — | — |
| 4796[6] | **Tom Pladdey (60)** (RBastiman) **2-8-7** DHolland(3) (bhd fnl 5f) ½ | **8** | 20/1 | — | — |
| 4368[7] | **Bapsford (64)** (GLMoore) **2-8-11v** RPerham(5) (stdy hdwy 3f out: wknd 2f out) 5 | **9** | 25/1 | — | — |
| *4780*[8] | **Mujadil Express (IRE) (49)** (JSMoore) **2-7-7**(3) NVarley(9) (bhd fnl 4f) 3 | **10** | 25/1 | — | — |
| 4803[4] | **Wild Nettle (52)** (JCFox) **2-7-13** DeclanO'Shea(7) (swtg: bhd fnl 3f) 9 | **11** | 14/1 | — | — |
| | | | (SP 122.0%) | **11 Rn** | |

**1m 34.2** (12.60) CSF £46.81 CT £140.89 TOTE £8.60: £1.80 £2.30 £1.30 (£49.80) Trio £57.60 OWNER Sheikh Amin Dahlawi (MIDDLEHAM) BRED Al Dahlawi Stud Co Ltd
LONG HANDICAP Mujadil Express (IRE) 7-9
**4883 Return of Amin** has been crying out for these conditions all year according to his owner's representative. Pushed along to assert, he gained a cosy success. (7/1)
**4549 Silk St John** raced at the back of the field, but put in some sterling work in the final furlong and a half. He needs further. (6/1)
**5006* Spaniard's Mount** took the field along until collared below the distance. He likes easier ground. (3/1)
**4782* Havago** was nicely placed entering the short home straight, but the writing was soon on the wall. (7/2)
**4787 Battle Ground (IRE)** (7/1: 5/1-15/2)
**4368 Bapsford** travelled sweetly racing down the hill, but seven is beyond him on this ground. (25/1)
**4803 Wild Nettle** (14/1: op 8/1)

### 5049 DOUG WOOD CONDITIONS STKS (2-Y.O) (Class C)
1-20 (1-20) **5f** £4,688.64 (£1,733.76: £830.88: £338.40: £133.20: £51.12) Stalls: Low GOING: 0.90 sec per fur (S)

| | | | SP | RR | SF |
|---|---|---|---|---|---|
| 5037[11] | **Salty Behaviour (IRE) (90)** (RHannon) **2-8-11** DaneO'Neill(4) (led tl ins fnl f: hrd rdn: led nr fin) —- | **1** | 9/2[3] | 76 | 48 |
| 5037[6] | **Sous Le Nez (78)** (RGuest) **2-8-11** PBloomfield(3) (a.p: rdn over 1f out: led ins fnl f: hdd nr fin) hd | **2** | 9/2[3] | 76 | 48 |
| 4918[6] | **Key Largo (IRE)** (MHTompkins) **2-8-8**(3) MHenry(1) (lw: chsd ldrs: rdn 3f out: r.o one pce fnl 2f) 5 | **3** | 4/1[2] | 60 | 32 |
| 4825[13] | **E-Mail (IRE)** (JMPEustace) **2-8-11** MTebbutt(5) (dwlt: hld up: rdn over 2f out: wknd over 1f out) 3 | **4** | 7/2[1] | 50 | 22 |
| 4547[5] | **Daintree (IRE)** (HJCollingridge) **2-8-7**ow1 JReid(6) (b.hind: chsd wnr over 3f) hd | **5** | 9/2[3] | 46 | 17 |
| 4790[W] | **Loganlea (IRE)** (WJMusson) **2-8-6** DRMcCabe(7) (leggy: rdn over 2f out: sme hdwy over 1f out: sn wknd) 1¼ | **6** | 7/1 | 41 | 13 |
| | **Falcon Ridge** (JCFox) **2-8-11** SWhitworth(2) (w'like: scope: bkwd: dwlt: a bhd) 1¼ | **7** | 33/1 | 42 | 14 |
| 4330[24] | **Carlton (IRE)** (GLewis) **2-8-11** AClark(8) (lw: a bhd) 2 | **8** | 20/1 | 35 | 7 |
| | | | (SP 117.0%) | **8 Rn** | |

**64.8 secs** (7.20) CSF £23.89 TOTE £4.90: £1.50 £1.90 £2.20 (£9.50) OWNER Mr J. R. Shannon (MARLBOROUGH) BRED Airlie Stud
**4893 Salty Behaviour (IRE)**, making a quick reappearance, set the pace, but was marginally headed inside the final furlong. To his credit, he refused to give way and got back in front near the finish. (9/2: op 3/1)
**5037 Sous Le Nez**, making a quick reappearance, is not very big, but may well have been unlucky not to have won as her off-fore shoe had all but fallen off. (9/2: 5/2-5/1)
**4918 Key Largo (IRE)** found this trip too sharp even in these conditions and, pushed along for a lot of the race, only stayed on in the closing stages. (4/1: 5/2-9/2)
**E-Mail (IRE)** has been running out of his depth and chased the leaders until giving best below the distance. (7/2: op 6/1)
**Loganlea (IRE)** (7/1: 12/1-5/1)

### 5050 E.B.F. KATHY TANNER (CORALS) MEDIAN AUCTION MAIDEN STKS (I) (2-Y.O) (Class E)
1-50 (1-51) **6f** £2,799.80 (£832.40: £395.20: £176.60) Stalls: Low GOING: 0.90 sec per fur (S)

| | | | SP | RR | SF |
|---|---|---|---|---|---|
| 4825[8] | **Arantxa** (MBell) **2-8-9** MFenton(9) (racd far side: chsd ldr: led 2f out: rdn out) —- | **1** | 7/2[2] | 71+ | 27 |
| 4902[2] | **Mr Paradise (IRE) (69)** (TJNaughton) **2-9-0** DHolland(2) (hld up: hrd rdn over 1f out: r.o one pce) 4 | **2** | 2/1[1] | 65 | 21 |
| 4896[3] | **Always Alight (60)** (KRBurke) **2-9-0b** SDrowne(4) (lw: a.p: hrd rdn over 1f out: one pce) 2½ | **3** | 25/1 | 59 | 15 |
| 4944a[5] | **Village Pub (FR) (70)** (KOCunningham-Brown) **2-9-0b[1]** JReid(7) (racd far side: led 4f) 1½ | **4** | 7/1 | 55 | 11 |
| 4408a[2] | **Tetris (IRE)** (CFWall) **2-8-9** GDuffield(6) (unf: jinked lft s: racd far side: chsd ldrs: rdn over 2f out: wknd over 1f out) 5 | **5** | 4/1[3] | 36 | — |
| | **Lights of Home** (RHannon) **2-9-0** DaneO'Neill(8) (w'like: bit bkwd: racd far side: a bhd) 7 | **6** | 7/1 | 23 | — |

| | | | | SP | RR | SF |
|---|---|---|---|---|---|---|
| 4601[9] | **Prix de Clermont (IRE)** (GLewis) **2-9-0** AClark(1) (lw: bhd fnl 3f) | 3½ | **7** | 20/1 | 13 | — |
| *4976*[8] | **Lochinvar (56)** (JSMoore) **2-9-0** DRMcCabe(3) (spd over 4f) | 2 | **8** | 33/1 | 8 | — |
| | **Muara Bay** (MissGayKelleway) **2-9-0** TQuinn(5) (w'like: bkwd: carried lft s: a bhd) | 13 | **9** | 9/1 | — | — |
| | | | | (SP 122.1%) | **9 Rn** | |

**1m 20.3** (10.10) CSF £11.18 TOTE £3.80: £1.10 £1.70 £3.70 (£9.40) Trio £25.20 OWNER Mrs Anne Yearley (NEWMARKET) BRED Mrs A. Yearley

**Arantxa** was well suited by the mud and, sent to the front two furlongs out on the far side, soon asserted. (7/2)

**4902 Mr Paradise (IRE)** did manage to win the battle on the stands' side, but never looked like coping with the winner. (2/1)

**4896 Always Alight** had a battle for the lead with the runner-up on the stands' side in the final quarter mile, but lost out. (25/1)

**4944a Village Pub (FR)**, in blinkers of the first time, had overall control on the far side but, headed by the winner two furlongs out, was soon left for dead. (7/1: op 4/1)

**4408a Tetris (IRE)** (4/1: op 5/2)

**Muara Bay** (9/1: 6/1-10/1)

## 5051 E.B.F. KATHY TANNER (CORALS) MEDIAN AUCTION MAIDEN STKS (II) (2-Y.O) (Class E)

2-20 (2-20) **6f** £2,799.80 (£832.40: £395.20: £176.60) Stalls: Low GOING: 0.90 sec per fur (S)

| | | | | SP | RR | SF |
|---|---|---|---|---|---|---|
| 4878[2] | **Just Nick (78)** (WRMuir) **2-9-0** JReid(7) (mde all: swvd bdly lft wl ins fnl f: drvn out) | — | **1** | 4/5[1] | 74 | 33 |
| | **Khairun Nisaa** (MJPolglase) **2-8-9** TGMcLaughlin(8) (unf: a.p: rdn 2f out: ev ch whn hung lft wl ins fnl f: r.o) | nk | **2** | 33/1 | 68 | 27 |
| | **Roffey Spinney (IRE)** (RHannon) **2-9-0** RPerham(3) (unf: lw: racd stands' side: outpcd: hdwy over 2f out: r.o ins fnl f) | 1¾ | **3** | 9/1 | 69 | 28 |
| 4913[9] | **Shalstayholy (IRE) (64)** (GLMoore) **2-8-9** SWhitworth(6) (a.p: rdn 2f out: unable qckn) | nk | **4** | 9/2[2] | 63 | 22 |
| 4893[9] | **Riverine** (GLewis) **2-8-6**(3) AWhelan(1) (a bhd) | 24 | **5** | 20/1 | — | — |
| | **Havana Reserve** (RHannon) **2-9-0** DaneO'Neill(5) (leggy: unf: lw: a bhd) | 3½ | **6** | 5/1[3] | — | — |
| 4897[16] | **The Real McCoy** (MRChannon) **2-9-0** RHughes(2) (lw: racd stands' side: prom over 3f) | 4 | **7** | 7/1 | — | — |
| 4962[10] | **Hardiprincess** (MBell) **2-8-9** MFenton(4) (dwlt: a wl bhd) | 20 | **8** | 12/1 | — | — |
| | | | | (SP 128.3%) | **8 Rn** | |

**1m 20.2** (10.00) CSF £26.12 TOTE £1.70: £1.00 £8.60 £4.90 (£14.80) OWNER Mr D. G. Clarke (LAMBOURN) BRED B. Minty

**4878 Just Nick**, the clear form selection, was in command when all but throwing the race away by swerving badly left in the closing stages. (4/5)

**Khairun Nisaa** had every chance when she followed the winner's erratic course in the closing stages. (33/1)

**Roffey Spinney (IRE)**, totally outpaced on the stands' side, stayed on nicely in the second half of the race and will probably be better suited by further. (9/1)

**4782 Shalstayholy (IRE)**, nicely placed a quarter of a mile out, then failed to find the necessary turn of foot. (9/2: 3/1-5/1)

**Havana Reserve** (5/1: 4/1-6/1)

**Hardiprincess** (12/1: 8/1-14/1)

## 5052 ELMTREE PACKAGING LTD. CLAIMING H'CAP (0-65) (3-Y.O+) (Class F)

2-50 (2-51) **2m 93y** £2,785.60 (£771.60: £368.80) Stalls: Low GOING: 1.15 sec per fur (S)

| | | | | SP | RR | SF |
|---|---|---|---|---|---|---|
| 3870[3] | **No More Hassle (IRE) (37)** (MrsMReveley) **3-7-7**(3) DWright(9) (hdwy over 5f out: led over 2f out: edgd lft ins fnl f: drvn out) | — | **1** | 3/1[1] | 49 | 1 |
| 4821[10] | **Ginka (28)** (JWMullins) **5-7-7**(3) NVarley(10) (rdn over 8f out: hdwy 5f out: chsd wnr over 1f out: carried lft ins fnl f: unable qckn) | ¾ | **2** | 7/2[2] | 39 | — |
| 4703[10] | **Aydigo (38)** (JPearce) **3-7-11**ow1 FNorton(12) (led over 2f: rdn over 3f out: one pce) | 9 | **3** | 20/1 | 41 | — |
| 5007[4] | **Contrarie (37)** (MJRyan) **3-7-7**(3) MBaird(7) (hld up: ev ch over 2f out: wknd over 1f out) | ¾ | **4** | 5/1[3] | 39 | — |
| 4603[8] | **Petros Pride (46)** (MJBolton) **3-8-5**ow1 PBloomfield(4) (rdn & hdwy over 3f out: wknd over 2f out) | 15 | **5** | 33/1 | 33 | — |
| 4910[2] | **Bobby's Dream (41)** (MHTompkins) **4-8-6**(3) MHenry(3) (lw: stdy hdwy over 7f out: led 4f out tl over 2f out: sn wknd) | 3 | **6** | 7/2[2] | 25 | — |
| 4868[15] | **Master Foodbroker (IRE) (60)** (WJMusson) **8-10-0** DRMcCabe(8) (nvr nr to chal) | 17 | **7** | 8/1 | 28 | — |
| *4894*[12] | **Private Percival (42)** (JRPoulton) **3-8-1**ow2 SDrowne(11) (prom over 11f) | ¾ | **8** | 33/1 | 9 | — |
| *4998*[10] | **Emnala (IRE) (43)** (EAWheeler) **4-8-8b**[1](3) JDSmith(1) (led 14f out to 4f out: sn wknd) | 24 | **9** | 20/1 | — | — |
| 668[14] | **Sussex Gorse (33)** (JELong) **5-8-1**ow5 LeesaLong(5) (prom over 10f: t.o) | dist | **10** | 50/1 | — | — |
| 2891[17] | **Peggy Ess (37)** (APJames) **3-7-3**(7) IonaWands(6) (b: a bhd: t.o fnl 6f) | dist | **11** | 50/1 | — | — |
| | | | | (SP 116.6%) | **11 Rn** | |

**4m 7.1** (36.10) CSF £13.14 CT £158.02 TOTE £2.90: £1.10 £1.10 £8.20 (£7.00) Trio £66.70 OWNER The No Hassle Partnership (SALTBURN) BRED Declan MacPartlin

LONG HANDICAP No More Hassle (IRE) 7-7 Aydigo 7-5 Contrarie 7-8 Sussex Gorse 7-5 Peggy Ess 6-7

WEIGHT FOR AGE 3yo-9lb

**3870 No More Hassle (IRE)** moved to the front over a quarter of a mile out and, despite drifting left in the closing stages, held on to win an appalling race. (3/1)

**4612 Ginka** was done no favours by the drifting winner in the closing stages, but was second best on the day. (7/2)

**Aydigo**, in a handy position throughout, failed to quicken in the straight. (20/1)

**5007 Contrarie**, making a quick reappearance, had every chance entering the short straight before sending out distress signals. (5/1: 3/1-11/2)

**4910 Bobby's Dream** appeared to be going sweetly as she struck the front over half a mile from home but, collared over a quarter of a mile from home, was soon in trouble. (7/2: op 7/4)

## 5053 ALAN DREW STOCKTAKING (S) H'CAP (0-60) (3-Y.O+) (Class G)

3-20 (3-23) **1m 4f** £2,616.00 (£726.00: £348.00) Stalls: Low GOING: 1.15 sec per fur (S)

| | | | | SP | RR | SF |
|---|---|---|---|---|---|---|
| 4910[4] | **Lucy Tufty (35)** (JPearce) **5-8-6** FNorton(8) (hld up: chsd wnr over 1f out: led ins fnl f: drvn out) | — | **1** | 5/1[2] | 50 | 3 |
| 4789[14] | **Nothing Doing (IRE) (37)** (WJMusson) **7-8-8** SWhitworth(14) (hdwy 2f out: rdn over 1f out: r.o wl ins fnl f) | ¾ | **2** | 9/2[1] | 51 | 4 |
| *1967*[8] | **Zesti (40)** (TTClement) **4-8-11** JStack(4) (hld up: led 3f out tl ins fnl f: sn wknd) | 7 | **3** | 20/1 | 45 | — |
| 4815[9] | **El Bardador (IRE) (55)** (WJarvis) **3-9-6b** JReid(1) (hdwy 3f out: one pce fnl 2f) | ¾ | **4** | 12/1 | 59 | 6 |
| 4236[12] | **Nautical Jewel (46)** (MDIUsher) **4-9-3** DaneO'Neill(5) (hld up: rdn over 2f out: one pce) | 1½ | **5** | 16/1 | 48 | 1 |
| *4998*[8] | **Tablets of Stone (IRE) (45)** (JRBosley) **3-8-7**(3) DWright(10) (lw: nvr nr to chal) | hd | **6** | 16/1 | 47 | — |
| *240*[9] | **Harry (46)** (DBurchell) **6-9-3** SDrowne(12) (led 9f: wknd over 1f out) | 1½ | **7** | 16/1 | 46 | — |
| 4815[7] | **Pat's Splendour (45)** (HJCollingridge) **5-8-9**(7) JoHunnam(18) (prom 10f) | hd | **8** | 8/1[3] | 44 | — |

| | | | | SP | RR | SF |
|---|---|---|---|---|---|---|
| *5003*[9] | **Chilly Lad (46)** (MJRyan) **5-9-3b** AClark(6) (lw: hdwy over 7f out: wknd over 1f out) | 1¼ | **9** | 20/1 | 44 | — |
| 5020a[10] | **Ewar Bold (55)** (KOCunningham-Brown) **3-9-6b** RHughes(16) (w ldr 9f: wknd over 1f out) | 1¼ | **10** | 20/1 | 51 | — |
| 4860[22] | **With The Tempo (IRE) (48)** (DrJDScargill) **3-8-13** DHolland(17) (a mid div) | 2½ | **11** | 14/1 | 41 | — |
| 4877[8] | **Memory's Music (42)** (MMadgwick) **4-8-10**(3) NVarley(13) (lw: prom over 9f) | 1 | **12** | 14/1 | 33 | — |
| | **Persian Bud (IRE) (35)** (JRBosley) **8-8-6** RPerham(15) (b: hdwy 3f out: wknd over 2f out) | nk | **13** | 25/1 | 26 | — |
| 4497[19] | **Moving Up (IRE) (42)** (TEPowell) **3-8-0**(7) IonaWands(2) (a bhd) | ½ | **14** | 25/1 | 32 | — |
| 2488[6] | **Yet Again (44)** (MissGayKelleway) **4-9-1** TQuinn(7) (bit bkwd: a bhd) | hd | **15** | 9/1 | 34 | — |
| 4815* | **Petoskin (54)** (JPearce) **4-9-11** MWigham(3) (prom over 9f: t.o) | dist | **16** | 9/2 1 | — | — |
| 3353[12] | **Etoile du Nord (35)** (HJCollingridge) **4-8-3**(3) MHenry(11) (b: bhd fnl 7f: t.o) | 20 | **17** | 25/1 | — | — |
| 3220[14] | **Foreign Judgement (USA) (50)** (WJMusson) **3-9-1** DRMcCabe(9) (s.s: a bhd: t.o) | 4 | **18** | 20/1 | — | — |

(SP 143.4%) **18 Rn**

**2m 58.5** (27.30) CSF £30.31 CT £410.24 TOTE £8.20: £1.50 £1.90 £6.60 £2.70 (£19.70) Trio £155.00 OWNER Mr G. H. Tufts (NEWMARKET) BRED C. R. Franks

WEIGHT FOR AGE 3yo-6lb

No bid

**4910 Lucy Tufty** moved into second below the distance and, coming through to lead inside the final furlong, held on well. (5/1)

**4509* Nothing Doing (IRE)** really found his feet in the straight and ran on strongly, only to find the line coming too soon. (9/2)

**125 Zesti**, having his first run in five months, went on three furlongs out, but lack of a run told and he was collared inside the final furlong. He should he kept in mind for the All-Weather. (20/1)

**4237* El Bardador (IRE)** could only go up and down in the same place in the short home straight. (12/1)

## 5054 DENISE MACKLIN H'CAP (0-70) (3-Y.O+) (Class E)

3-50 (3-51) **1m 4f** £3,643.50 (£1,092.00: £525.00: £241.50) Stalls: Low GOING: 1.15 sec per fur (S)

| | | | | SP | RR | SF |
|---|---|---|---|---|---|---|
| 4497[17] | **Tonka (54)** (PJMakin) **4-8-12** DHarrison(12) (hdwy over 2f out: led over 1f out: hrd rdn & edgd rt ins fnl f: r.o wl) | — | **1** | 20/1 | 66 | 21 |
| 4919[4] | **Compass Pointer (57)** (JMPEustace) **3-8-9** MTebbutt(8) (hdwy on ins 2f out: chsd wnr over 1f out: 2nd & btn whn nt clr run on ins ins fnl f) | 1½ | **2** | 10/1 | 67 | 16 |
| 4919[2] | **Siege Perilous (IRE) (66)** (SCWilliams) **3-9-4** DaneO'Neill(3) (rdn 5f out: gd hdwy over 1f out: r.o wl) | 4 | **3** | 3/1 1 | 71 | 20 |
| 4900* | **Fairy Knight (71)** (RHannon) **4-10-1** RHughes(16) (stdy hdwy 3f out: rdn over 1f out: one pce) | 2 | **4** | 6/1 2 | 73 | 28 |
| 4810[12] | **Surrey Dancer (57)** (MrsMReveley) **8-8-10**(5) SCopp(1) (lw: rdn over 4f out: hdwy over 1f out: nvr nrr) | 2½ | **5** | 12/1 | 56 | 11 |
| *4892*[6] | **Shoshone (58)** (JHMGosden) **3-8-10** JReid(9) (lw: rdn over 4f out: hdwy over 1f out: nvr nrr) | 5 | **6** | 12/1 | 50 | — |
| *4984*[3] | **Golden Hadeer (38)** (MJRyan) **5-7-7**(3) MBaird(5) (lw: hld up: rdn over 4f out: wknd over 1f out) | nk | **7** | 12/1 | 30 | — |
| 4868[4] | **Evezio Rufo (60)** (NPLittmoden) **4-9-4v** TGMcLaughlin(14) (a.p: led over 2f out tl over 1f out: wknd fnl f) | hd | **8** | 16/1 | 52 | 7 |
| 4753* | **Typhoon Eight (IRE) (70)** (BWHills) **4-10-0** DHolland(17) (led 1f: taken wd bk st: rdn over 4f out: wknd over 1f out) | 3 | **9** | 9/1 | 58 | 13 |
| 4905[2] | **Kalou (61)** (CWCElsey) **5-9-2**(3) DWright(18) (hdl up: rdn over 4f out: wknd over 2f out) | 2 | **10** | 12/1 | 46 | 1 |
| *132*[4] | **Wildfire (SWI) (50)** (RAkehurst) **5-8-8** TQuinn(2) (b: led 11f out tl over 2f out: wknd over 1f out) | 1 | **11** | 8/1 3 | 34 | — |
| 4900[12] | **Harvey White (IRE) (62)** (JPearce) **4-9-6** FNorton(4) (a bhd) | 1¼ | **12** | 12/1 | 44 | — |
| 4968[16] | **Brother Roy (62)** (TGMills) **3-9-0** StephenDavies(15) (b: lw: prom over 9f) | 21 | **13** | 20/1 | 16 | — |
| *4332*[10] | **Bayrak (USA) (56)** (GLMoore) **6-9-0** SWhitworth(10) (b: lw: stdy hdwy 7f out: wknd over 2f out) | ¾ | **14** | 16/1 | 9 | — |
| 4967[2] | **Dalwhinnie (63)** (JWHills) **3-8-12**(3) MHenry(11) (bhd fnl 5f) | 1½ | **15** | 12/1 | 14 | — |
| 4793[3] | **North Reef (IRE) (70)** (JPearce) **5-10-0** GDuffield(13) (bhd fnl 4f) | 2½ | **16** | 10/1 | 18 | — |
| 4877[6] | **Te Amo (IRE) (63)** (MBell) **4-9-7v**1 MFenton(6) (prom 7f) | nk | **17** | 12/1 | 10 | — |

(SP 153.7%) **17 Rn**

**2m 56.5** (25.30) CSF £229.23 CT £734.98 TOTE £39.70: £7.80 £2.90 £1.30 £2.00 (£345.20) Trio £482.70 OWNER Mrs J. M. West (MARLBOROUGH) BRED Mrs J. Murray-Smith and N. Bowyer

LONG HANDICAP Golden Hadeer 7-8

WEIGHT FOR AGE 3yo-6lb

STEWARDS' ENQUIRY Harrison susp. 22 & 25/11/96 (careless riding).

**87 Tonka** was very fresh, this being only his third run of the year. Sent on below the distance, despite hanging away from the whip, he was the best horse on the day. (20/1)

**4919 Compass Pointer** came through for second below the distance and, although not helped by the winner in the final furlong, would not have beaten his rival. (10/1)

**4919 Siege Perilous (IRE)** found this trip too sharp, but made giant strides in the last furlong and a half, if never looking like getting there in time. (3/1: op 5/1)

**4900* Fairy Knight** appeared to be going really well in the home straight, but his rider let the winner get first run on him and he could only plod on at one pace. (6/1: op 4/1)

**Surrey Dancer**, going nowhere at the back of the field running down the hill, stayed on to be nearest at the line. (12/1)

**Shoshone** made up late headway without posing a threat. (12/1: 8/1-14/1)

**4793 North Reef (IRE)** (10/1: 7/1-12/1)

T/Plpt: £32.80 (277.6 Tckts). T/Qdpt: £8.70 (100.57 Tckts). AK

# 4976-WOLVERHAMPTON (L-H) (Standard)

## Monday November 11th

WEATHER: fine

## 5055 THORPE VERNON LIMITED STKS (0-60) (I) (3-Y.O+) (Class F)

12-40 (12-42) **7f (Fibresand)** £2,169.00 (£594.00: £279.00) Stalls: High GOING minus 0.09 sec per fur (STD)

| | | | | SP | RR | SF |
|---|---|---|---|---|---|---|
| *4989*[8] | **Leigh Crofter (52)** (PDCundell) **7-9-0b** JWeaver(4) (mde virtually all: hrd drvn fnl f: jst hld on) | — | **1** | 14/1 | 61 | 39 |
| 5004[10] | **Best of All (IRE) (62)** (JBerry) **4-8-11e** GCarter(11) (s.i.s: sn wl outpcd: gd hdwy 2f out: str chal fnl f: jst failed) | hd | **2** | 3/1 2 | 58 | 36 |
| 4915[4] | **Statistician (59)** (JohnBerry) **4-9-0b** TWilliams(9) (chsd ldrs: rdn 2f out: r.o ins fnl f) | 1¾ | **3** | 10/1 | 57 | 35 |
| *4981*[2] | **How's Yer Father (57)** (RJHodges) **10-8-12**(5) AmandaSanders(10) (hld up: hdwy over 2f out: r.o wl nr fin) | nk | **4** | 5/1 3 | 59 | 37 |
| 4968[11] | **Loch Style (53)** (RHollinshead) **3-8-13**(3) FLynch(1) (trckd ldrs: drvn along over 2f out: no hdwy) | 1¼ | **5** | 11/1 | 56 | 33 |
| 4881[4] | **Sue Me (IRE) (55)** (WRMuir) **4-8-7**(7) JWilkinson(5) (w ldrs: ev ch 2f out: sn rdn: wknd ins fnl f) | 1¼ | **6** | 7/1 | 50 | 28 |

| | | | | SP | RR | SF |
|---|---|---|---|---|---|---|
| 4968$^{3}$ | **Allstars Rocket (55)** (TJNaughton) **3-9-2** TSprake(3) (w ldrs: ev ch 2f out: sn rdn: wknd fnl f) | 1½ | **7** | 11/4$^{1}$ | 50 | 27 |
| 3316$^{3}$ | **Have a Nightcap (40)** (NPLittmoden) **7-8-9b**$^{(5)}$ DGriffiths(2) (lw: disp ld tl wknd over 1f out: eased whn btn) | 2 | **8** | 20/1 | 42 | 20 |
| *4981*$^{10}$ | **Galacia (IRE) (45)** (WGMTurner) **4-8-5**$^{(7)ow1}$ DMcGaffin(6) (outpcd) | 1 | **9** | 33/1 | 38 | 15 |
| 4382$^{14}$ | **Thick as Thieves (47)** (RonaldThompson) **4-9-0** JQuinn(8) (outpcd) | 1¾ | **10** | 33/1 | 36 | 14 |
| 4805$^{16}$ | **Present 'n Correct (43)** (CBBBooth) **3-9-2** LCharnock(7) (lw: chsd ldrs 4f: sn rdn & wknd: t.o) | 15 | **11** | 14/1 | 5 | — |
| 3883$^{13}$ | **Daffodil Express (IRE) (41)** (MJRyan) **3-8-10** DBiggs(12) (bit bkwd: sn bhd & outpcd: t.o) | 17 | **12** | 16/1 | — | — |
| | | | | (SP 128.1%) | **12 Rn** | |

**1m 29.1** (4.40) CSF £56.79 TOTE £13.40: £4.30 £1.50 £2.20 (£26.70) Trio £158.80; £8.95 to Lingfield 12/11/96 OWNER Mr P. D. Cundell (NEWBURY) BRED Richard Castle

WEIGHT FOR AGE 3yo-1lb

**1521 Leigh Crofter** probably finds this trip ideal nowadays and, steering clear of sand being kicked into his face, held on with not an ounce to spare. (14/1: 8/1-16/1)

**5004 Best of All (IRE)** was sluggish as the stalls opened and soon well outpaced, but almost did the impossible and came from another parish to fail narrowly. (3/1)

**4915 Statistician** ran a genuine race and plugged away willingly in the closing stages without being able to muster the speed for a challenge. (10/1)

**4981 How's Yer Father** always had far too much to do, but he stuck to the task in hand, and was pegging back the principals with every stride nearing the finish. (5/1: 3/1-11/2)

**2026* Loch Style** had his full quota of weight and ran as one would as expect, but the task was always beyond him. (11/1: 7/1-12/1)

**4881 Sue Me (IRE)** did promise to make a race of it two furlongs out, but he flattered to deceive when the pressure was on and failed to go through with his effort. (7/1: 5/1-8/1)

**4968 Allstars Rocket** had plenty of use made of him, but was unable to respond when the pace lifted, and obviously finds this trip short of his best. (11/4)

## 5056 WIMPEY HOMES H'CAP (0-70) (I) (3-Y.O+) (Class E)

1-10 (1-10) **1m 1f 79y (Fibresand)** £2,948.60 (£876.80: £416.40: £186.20) Stalls: Low GOING minus 0.09 sec per fur (STD)

| | | | | SP | RR | SF |
|---|---|---|---|---|---|---|
| *4779*$^{9}$ | **Shahik (USA) (60)** (DHaydnJones) **6-9-7** LCharnock(7) (a.p: slt ld over 3f out: clr appr fnl f: r.o) | — | **1** | 5/1$^{3}$ | 71 | 52 |
| 5010$^{3}$ | **Master Millfield (IRE) (63)** (PDEvans) **4-9-10** JFEgan(11) (plld hrd early: rdn 5f out: gd hdwy over 2f out: r.o: nt rch wnr) | 1 | **2** | 3/1$^{1}$ | 72 | 53 |
| 4860$^{12}$ | **Theatre Magic (63)** (SRBowring) **3-9-7** DeanMcKeown(13) (prom: led 5f out tl over 3f out: wknd appr fnl f) | 7 | **3** | 10/1 | 60 | 38 |
| *2304*$^{10}$ | **Queens Stroller (IRE) (36)** (REPeacock) **5-7-6**$^{(5)ow1}$ PFessey(8) (hld up: effrt over 3f out: kpt on one pce fnl 2f) | nk | **4** | 33/1 | 33 | 13 |
| *4977*$^{8}$ | **Hand of Straw (IRE) (47)** (PGMurphy) **4-8-8v** TWilliams(3) (prom 6f) | 7 | **5** | 16/1 | 32 | 13 |
| 4968$^{2}$ | **Peppers (IRE) (65)** (KRBurke) **3-9-4**$^{(5)}$ RPainter(6) (sn wl bhd: rdn ½-wy: sme late hdwy) | 1¼ | **6** | 4/1$^{2}$ | 48 | 26 |
| 4829$^{14}$ | **Comeonup (42)** (JMBradley) **5-7-10**$^{(7)}$ RFfrench(12) (b: bhd: sn drvn along: no imp) | nk | **7** | 16/1 | 24 | 5 |
| | **River Run (IRE) (56)** (RHollinshead) **4-9-0**$^{(3)}$ FLynch(9) (bkwd: a bhd) | 2½ | **8** | 14/1 | 34 | 15 |
| 2563$^{11}$ | **Greek Gold (IRE) (37)** (DWBarker) **7-7-5**$^{(7)}$ JBramhill(2) (bit bkwd: led over 4f: wkng whn n.m.r on ins 4f out) | .5 | **9** | 20/1 | 6 | — |
| *4982** | **Giddy (48)** (JHetherton) **3-8-6** 5x NKennedy(10) (bhd: hdwy over 3f out: wknd over 2f out) | ¾ | **10** | 4/1$^{2}$ | 16 | — |
| 4921$^{14}$ | **Eccentric Dancer (46)** (MPBielby) **3-8-4b** JQuinn(4) (trckd ldrs: sn lost tch) | 1½ | **11** | 14/1 | 12 | — |
| 2563$^{7}$ | **Crystal Warrior (53)** (DNicholls) **3-8-11** CRutter(5) (prom 4f: sn rdn & lost pl: t.o) | 22 | **12** | 14/1 | — | — |
| 4888$^{18}$ | **Northern Clan (38)** (AJChamberlain) **3-7-10v**$^{1}$ NCarlisle(1) (b: a in rr: t.o fnl 3f) | 3½ | **13** | 33/1 | — | — |
| | | | | (SP 133.2%) | **13 Rn** | |

**2m 1.3** (5.30) CSF £21.64 CT £142.38 TOTE £5.10: £2.70 £1.10 £2.40 (£12.70) Trio £46.30 OWNER Mr S. Hunter (PONTYPRIDD)

LONG HANDICAP Northern Clan 7-4

WEIGHT FOR AGE 3yo-3lb

**4513* Shahik (USA)** has had a very chequered career with success in Dubai as well as Ireland, and he thoroughly deserved this initial success on Sand. (5/1: op 3/1)

**5010 Master Millfield (IRE)** has not yet won over further than seven, but he delivered a strong, late challenge here, and he is certainly happy on this surface. (3/1)

**4575 Theatre Magic** is not yet seeing out the trip and could benefit from a more patient ride. (10/1: 8/1-12/1)

**Queens Stroller (IRE)** showed a glimpse of her old form this time and could be coming to herself. (33/1)

**4315 Hand of Straw (IRE)** has been competing over longer trips of late, and was in trouble at the end of the back straight and easily shaken off. (16/1)

**4968 Peppers (IRE)** tried for a repeat of her promising run at Newmarket, but she would not face the kick-back and was well adrift until staying on when it was as good as over. (4/1)

**River Run (IRE)** (14/1: op 8/1)

**4982* Giddy** should have been thereabouts if she had produced her most recent form, but she failed to fire at all this time and was always out with the washing. (4/1: op 2/1)

## 5057 WOLVERHAMPTON CHAMBER NURSERY H'CAP (0-75) (2-Y.O) (Class E)

1-40 (1-40) **1m 100y (Fibresand)** £3,273.60 (£976.80: £466.40: £211.20) Stalls: Low GOING minus 0.09 sec per fur (STD)

| | | | | SP | RR | SF |
|---|---|---|---|---|---|---|
| 4864$^{6}$ | **Hello Dolly (IRE) (63)** (KRBurke) **2-8-5**$^{(7)}$ RFfrench(2) (a.p: led 3f out tl wl over 1f out: rallied to ld ins fnl f) | — | **1** | 12/1 | 65 | 33 |
| 4795$^{14}$ | **Skelton Sovereign (IRE) (60)** (RHollinshead) **2-8-6**$^{(3)}$ FLynch(4) (lw: hld up: hdwy on outside to ld wl over 1f out: hdd & no ex ins fnl f) | ¾ | **2** | 12/1 | 61 | 29 |
| 4880$^{17}$ | **Greenwich Fore (69)** (TGMills) **2-9-4** JQuinn(11) (hld up: hdwy over 3f out: styd on u.p ins fnl f) | s.h | **3** | 16/1 | 70 | 38 |
| 4970* | **Aficionado (IRE) (68)** (RFJohnsonHoughton) **2-9-3** SSanders(8) (a.p: ev ch 2f out: outpcd fnl f) | 3½ | **4** | 5/1$^{3}$ | 62 | 30 |
| 4803$^{7}$ | **Muliere (62)** (MJohnston) **2-8-11** JWeaver(7) (prom 5f: sn rdn & lost tch) | 10 | **5** | 9/2$^{2}$ | 37 | 5 |
| *4777*$^{6}$ | **Our Kevin (65)** (KMcAuliffe) **2-9-0v** JFEgan(9) (prom: ev ch 2f out: sn rdn & btn) | s.h | **6** | 14/1 | 40 | 8 |
| *4780** | **Bonne Ville (62)** (BPalling) **2-8-11** TSprake(5) (lw: led 3f: wknd over 2f out) | 1½ | **7** | 6/1 | 34 | 2 |
| 4471$^{4}$ | **Ben's Ridge (72)** (PCHaslam) **2-9-7** GCarter(6) (lw: led 5f out to 3f out: rdn & wknd fnl f) | s.h | **8** | 11/4$^{1}$ | 44 | 12 |
| 4970$^{3}$ | **Heggies (IRE) (63)** (CREgerton) **2-8-7b**$^{1(5)}$ SophieMitchell(1) (lw: led after 3f to 5f out: sn rdn & wknd) | 1¾ | **9** | 7/1 | 32 | — |
| 4435$^{6}$ | **Dance Melody (48)** (GROldroyd) **2-7-11** NKennedy(10) (sn drvn along mid div: bhd fnl 4f) | 1¾ | **10** | 20/1 | 13 | — |
| 4883$^{14}$ | **Suave Star (54)** (CADwyer) **2-7-10**$^{(7)}$ RMullen(12) (swtg: hld up in tch: wknd 3f out) | 4 | **11** | 10/1 | 12 | — |
| | | | | (SP 130.1%) | **11 Rn** | |

**1m 50.9** (5.90) CSF £141.68 CT £2,186.56 TOTE £14.50: £4.00 £3.00 £5.60 (£43.10) Trio £124.40; £87.66 to Lingfield 12/11/96 OWNER Mr Nigel Shields (WANTAGE) BRED Rathasker Stud

**4864 Hello Dolly (IRE)** looked to have shot her bolt when headed early in the straight, but it was probably just the spur she needed, for she fought back grimly and held on close home. (12/1: op 8/1)
**4694* Skelton Sovereign (IRE)** is not short of stamina and promised to come away after taking control soon after straightening up, but the winner was in no mood to accept defeat, and she proved the stronger in the battle to the post. (12/1: op 8/1)
**4549 Greenwich Fore**, ridden from off the pace, produced a sustained challenge up the stands' rail inside the distance and only just failed to reel in the leading pair. A race of this description is well within his grasp. (16/1)
**4970* Aficionado (IRE)** found this step up in class just too much for him and he was treading water once inside the final furlong. (5/1)
**4454 Muliere** failed to cut any ice on this first attempt on the surface, and it would seem this trip is beyond her at this stage of her career. (9/2: op 7/1)
**3523 Our Kevin** is not much better than the average selling plater, but he performed with credit for over six furlongs before having to admit this company far too good for him. He will be worth bearing in mind when he returns to his own grade. (14/1)
**4471 Ben's Ridge**, a winner on his previous appearance here, tried hard to follow up, but was already in deep trouble before the final furlong sapped his reserves. (11/4)
**4970 Heggies (IRE)** (7/1: op 4/1)

## 5058 TAYLOR & CO. ACCOUNTANTS MEDIAN AUCTION MAIDEN STKS (3-Y.O) (Class E)

2-10 (2-10) **1m 100y (Fibresand)** £3,097.50 (£924.00: £441.00: £199.50) Stalls: Low GOING minus 0.09 sec per fur (STD)

| | | | SP | RR | SF |
|---|---|---|---|---|---|
| 4322[13] **Mighty Keen (70)** (MJohnston) **3-9-0** JWeaver(7) (lw: led 3f: led 4f out: rdn & kpt on fnl f) | — | **1** | 5/1[2] | 72 | 51 |
| 4921[2] **Agent (67)** (JLEyre) **3-9-0** DeanMcKeown(5) (lw: a.p: hrd rdn over 3f out: ev ch over 1f out: unable qckn fnl f) | 1½ | **2** | 5/2[1] | 69 | 48 |
| *4987[11]* **School Boy (64)** (TJNaughton) **3-9-0** TSprake(11) (a chsng ldrs: rdn over 1f out: sn outpcd) | 6 | **3** | 6/1[3] | 58 | 37 |
| 4591[12] **Surf City (57)** (WWHaigh) **3-9-0** JQuinn(9) (led over 5f out to 4f out: rdn & wknd over 2f out) | 6 | **4** | 12/1 | 47 | 26 |
| 2432[6] **Ruby Angel** (HCandy) **3-8-9** CRutter(10) (bit bkwd: chsd ldrs over 5f: sn outpcd) | 3 | **5** | 5/1[2] | 36 | 15 |
| *4978[10]* **Daratown** (PDEvans) **3-9-0** JFEgan(4) (nvr nr ldrs) | 2½ | **6** | 33/1 | 36 | 15 |
| *4978[7]* **Stretching (IRE)** (ABailey) **3-9-0** WHollick(12) (nvr plcd to chal) | 1 | **7** | 16/1 | 34 | 13 |
| *651[5]* **Cashaplenty** (NPLittmoden) **3-8-9**(5) DGriffiths(13) (b.hind: hdwy 5f out: sn drvn along: wknd wl over 2f out) | nk | **8** | 33/1 | 34 | 13 |
| 4422[7] **Bianca Cappello (IRE) (25)** (PSFelgate) **3-8-9b[1]** NAdams(1) (a bhd) | 1½ | **9** | 50/1 | 26 | 5 |
| *4978[3]* **Carreamia** (JLEyre) **3-8-9** RLappin(3) (in rr & drvn along ½-wy: no imp) | 4 | **10** | 5/1[2] | 18 | — |
| 4075[11] **Petarina (39)** (TJEtherington) **3-8-9** LCharnock(8) (mid div: hrd rdn & wknd 3f out) | 5 | **11** | 20/1 | 9 | — |
| 4591[14] **Dunston Star (IRE)** (PJBevan) **3-9-0** NCarlisle(6) (prom tl rdn & wknd over 4f out: t.o) | 6 | **12** | 50/1 | 2 | — |
| 4784[12] **Timely Times** (CADwyer) **3-8-9** SSanders(2) (a bhd: t.o) | 18 | **13** | 25/1 | — | — |
| | | | (SP 124.8%) | **13 Rn** | |

**1m 49.2** (4.20) CSF £17.74 TOTE £8.00: £1.50 £2.40 £1.50 (£6.00) Trio £12.50 OWNER Greenland Park Ltd (MIDDLEHAM) BRED Laharna Ltd
**3642 Mighty Keen** has only been lightly-raced and it is questionable whether he was fully wound up after six weeks off, but he was intent on making this a thorough test of stamina and he worried the favourite out of it in the last 100 yards. (5/1: op 5/2)
**4921 Agent** ran another good race and showed what a real trier he is, but once again he was forced to give best. When things do eventually go his way, it will not be out of turn. (5/2)
**3317 School Boy** was always poised to challenge but, once the leading pair took one another on, he was tapped for toe, and may well have failed through lack of stamina. (6/1)
**2432 Surf City** took the leaders on, but only succeeded in running himself into the ground. (12/1)
**2432 Ruby Angel**, having only her second look at a racecourse, found the four-month break since her last outing taking its toll from the turn into the straight. She did appear to take to the surface and there are races to be won. (5/1: op 3/1)
**Daratown** still needs time, but stayed on to reach his final placing and is getting to know what the game is all about. (33/1)
**4978 Carreamia** (5/1: 3/1-11/2)

## 5059 THORPE VERNON LIMITED STKS (0-60) (II) (3-Y.O+) (Class F)

2-40 (2-41) **7f (Fibresand)** £2,169.00 (£594.00: £279.00) Stalls: High GOING minus 0.09 sec per fur (STD)

| | | | SP | RR | SF |
|---|---|---|---|---|---|
| 4323[3] **Sis Garden (53)** (JCullinan) **3-8-9b**(7) RFfrench(1) (lw: mde all: rdn out) | — | **1** | 7/1[2] | 67 | 35 |
| 4905[9] **Elite Hope (USA) (55)** (NTinkler) **4-8-11** LCharnock(5) (w wnr: hrd rdn over 1f out: r.o one pce) | 1 | **2** | 10/1[3] | 59 | 28 |
| *4981[3]* **Dragonjoy (52)** (NPLittmoden) **3-9-0v**(5) DGriffiths(6) (hdwy 3f out: hrd rdn 2f out: nt rch ldrs) | 6 | **3** | 5/1[1] | 54 | 22 |
| 4915[17] **Komlucky (49)** (ABMulholland) **4-8-9v**(5) LNewton(12) (bhd: sn rdn along: hdwy over 3f out: nt rch ldrs) | 1½ | **4** | 5/1[1] | 45 | 14 |
| 4968[10] **Voodoo Rocket (55)** (JHMGosden) **3-8-10** AMcGlone(3) (bhd tl r.o fnl 2f: nvr nrr) | nk | **5** | 5/1[1] | 41 | 9 |
| 3812[13] **Caddy's First (60)** (SMellor) **4-9-0v[1]** JQuinn(10) (bhd tl r.o fnl 2f: nrst fin) | s.h | **6** | 20/1 | 44 | 13 |
| *4983[11]* **Ragazzo (IRE) (40)** (JSWainwright) **6-9-0** DeanMcKeown(11) (nvr trbld ldrs) | 3 | **7** | 25/1 | 37 | 6 |
| 4231[7] **Miss Pickpocket (IRE) (49)** (MissGayKelleway) **3-8-10** SSanders(4) (prom: hrd rdn & wknd over 3f out) | 1¾ | **8** | 5/1[1] | 30 | — |
| **River Seine (FR) (50)** (SGKnight) **4-8-11** VSlattery(9) (bkwd: plld hrd early: chsd ldrs: wkng whn hmpd over 3f out) | 1¾ | **9** | 33/1 | 26 | — |
| 4784[15] **Miss Carottene (48)** (MJRyan) **3-8-10** DBiggs(7) (prom over 3f: t.o) | 12 | **10** | 12/1 | — | — |
| *1096[11]* **Skelton Countess (IRE) (59)** (RHollinshead) **3-8-7**(3) FLynch(2) (a bhd: t.o) | 7 | **11** | 14/1 | — | — |
| 2185[18] **Penny's Wishing (40)** (CSmith) **4-8-11** CRutter(8) (s.i.s: a bhd: t.o) | hd | **12** | 33/1 | — | — |
| | | | (SP 117.1%) | **12 Rn** | |

**1m 29.6** (4.90) CSF £67.33 TOTE £10.40: £2.20 £2.20 £1.20 (£97.70) Trio £51.70 OWNER Alan Spargo Ltd Toolmakers (AYLESBURY) BRED Mrs J. Mackie and Major W. R. Paton Smith
WEIGHT FOR AGE 3yo-1lb
**4323 Sis Garden**, on the inside, was inclined to hang into the rail on the home turn and it was probably a good thing she was going left-handed. (7/1)
**3800 Elite Hope (USA)**, making her debut on the Sand, was the only one to really make a race of it. (10/1)
**4981 Dragonjoy** was stepping back up to a more suitable trip, but his two wins here have come over the extended mile. (5/1)
**4323* Komlucky** was 3lb better off with the winner than when narrowly beaten by her at Catterick last month. (5/1)
**2158 Voodoo Rocket** had disappointed when tried on the Equitrack at Lingfield in June. (5/1: op 3/1)
**Caddy's First** never threatened to take a hand in the first-time visor. (20/1)
**131* Miss Carottene** (12/1: op 8/1)

## 5060 WIMPEY HOMES H'CAP (0-70) (II) (3-Y.O+) (Class E)

3-10 (3-13) **1m 1f 79y (Fibresand)** £2,948.60 (£876.80: £416.40: £186.20) Stalls: Low GOING minus 0.09 sec per fur (STD)

| | | | SP | RR | SF |
|---|---|---|---|---|---|
| *4781[5]* **Slievenamon (41)** (JEBanks) **3-7-7**(7) RMullen(11) (led over 5f out tl over 2f out: led ins fnl f: r.o) | — | **1** | 10/1 | 52 | 30 |

| Form | Horse | Dist | Pos | SP | RR | SF |
|---|---|---|---|---|---|---|
| 4900[8] | **Golden Touch (USA) (60)** (DJSCosgrove) **4-9-8** GCarter(6) (hld up: hdwy on ins 5f out: led over 2f out tl ins fnl f) | nk | **2** | 5/2[1] | 71 | 52 |
| *4989*[7] | **Sandmoor Denim (52)** (SRBowring) **9-9-0** DeanMcKeown(9) (hdwy 6f out: rdn & r.o one pce fnl 2f) | 3 | **3** | 6/1[2] | 57 | 38 |
| *2934*[11] | **Chadleigh Lane (USA) (62)** (RHollinshead) **4-9-5**(5) DGriffiths(8) (bit bkwd: hld up: hdwy 3f out: one pce fnl 2f) | 1¾ | **4** | 8/1[3] | 64 | 45 |
| 4381[7] | **Runic Symbol (41)** (MBlanshard) **5-8-3** JQuinn(1) (hdwy 5f out: wknd over 2f out) | 10 | **5** | 9/1 | 26 | 7 |
| 4427[7] | **Classic Romance (65)** (RHarris) **3-9-10** DBatteate(12) (hdwy over 5f out: wknd over 2f out) | 1¼ | **6** | 12/1 | 48 | 26 |
| 4808[16] | **Great Bear (40)** (DWChapman) **4-8-2** LCharnock(10) (prom over 6f) | 1½ | **7** | 12/1 | 21 | 2 |
| *4895*[11] | **Time Clash (50)** (BPalling) **3-8-9** TSprake(2) (led 4f: sn wknd) | nk | **8** | 6/1[2] | 30 | 8 |
| *4982*[7] | **Bad News (37)** (JMBradley) **4-7-6**(7) RFfrench(7) (bhd fnl 3f) | 2½ | **9** | 33/1 | 13 | — |
| *4575*[12] | **Our Tom (60)** (JWharton) **4-9-8b** NCarlisle(13) (b: lw: prom tl rdn & wknd over 3f out) | 7 | **10** | 14/1 | 24 | 5 |
| *4982*[11] | **Roussi (USA) (59)** (DNicholls) **4-9-7** CRutter(5) (prom 4f) | 1¼ | **11** | 14/1 | 21 | 2 |
| 4785[14] | **Note of Caution (USA) (53)** (NAGraham) **3-8-12** AMcGlone(4) (w ldrs tl wknd qckly over 4f out: t.o) | 17 | **12** | 10/1 | — | — |

(SP 128.1%) **12 Rn**

**2m 1.5** (5.50) CSF £36.04 CT £160.74 TOTE £14.40: £3.00 £1.40 £2.10 (£37.10) Trio £47.30 OWNER Mr P. Cunningham (NEWMARKET) BRED Mrs Celia Miller

WEIGHT FOR AGE 3yo-3lb

**4781 Slievenamon**, backed from 16/1 to 8/1 with Sean Graham in Ireland, surprisingly opened at 33/1 on course. 9lb lower than his comeback race after having finished lame at Windsor in the spring, he relished this longer trip. (10/1)
**4068 Golden Touch (USA)** did little wrong, but came up against something of a buzzer in the winner. (5/2)
**4089 Sandmoor Denim** kept on to secure the minor berth without threatening the two principals. (6/1)
**836 Chadleigh Lane (USA)** found lack of a recent outing taking its toll in the battle for third. (8/1: op 5/1)
**1121 Time Clash** (6/1: op 4/1)
**Roussi (USA)** (14/1: op 7/1)
**58 Note of Caution (USA)** (10/1: 8/1-12/1)

## 5061 YVONNE AULTON (S) STKS (2-Y.O F) (Class F)

3-40 (3-41) **6f (Fibresand)** £2,519.00 (£694.00: £329.00) Stalls: Low GOING minus 0.09 sec per fur (STD)

| Form | Horse | Dist | Pos | SP | RR | SF |
|---|---|---|---|---|---|---|
| *4777*[3] | **Robec Girl (IRE) (67)** (JBerry) **2-8-9**(5) PFessey(6) (led after 1f: rdn out) | — | **1** | 8/11[1] | 66 | 42 |
| 4762[10] | **Lightning Bolt (IRE)** (MJohnston) **2-8-9** JWeaver(12) (led 1f: chsd wnr: hrd rdn & r.o ins fnl f) | 1¼ | **2** | 10/1[3] | 57 | 34 |
| 4970[4] | **Princess of Hearts (66)** (BJMeehan) **2-9-0** SSanders(9) (hdwy over 3f out: wknd over 1f out: styd on ins fnl f) | 5 | **3** | 3/1[2] | 49 | 25 |
| 4748[10] | **Silent Valley (48)** (BJMeehan) **2-8-9b** CRutter(11) (a.p: one pce fnl 2f) | 2½ | **4** | 20/1 | 37 | 14 |
| *4976*[9] | **Chilling (47)** (PGMurphy) **2-8-9** TWilliams(5) (chsd ldrs: rdn over 3f out: no hdwy) | 3½ | **5** | 33/1 | 28 | 4 |
| *4988*[3] | **Ginny Wossername (58)** (WGMTurner) **2-8-7**(7) DSweeney(2) (nvr nr to chal) | nk | **6** | 14/1 | 32 | 9 |
| 4896[10] | **Municipal Girl (IRE) (48)** (BPalling) **2-8-9** TSprake(3) (nvr nr ldrs) | 1¼ | **7** | 16/1 | 24 | — |
| 4902[11] | **Sandkatoon (IRE)** (JSMoore) **2-8-9** NAdams(10) (chsd ldrs over 3f) | nk | **8** | 33/1 | 23 | — |
| *4572*[6] | **Morning Line (IRE)** (RJRWilliams) **2-8-9** DBiggs(4) (bit bkwd: outpcd) | s.h | **9** | 10/1[3] | 23 | — |
| 4787[12] | **Pretty Sally (IRE) (58)** (DJGMurraySmith) **2-8-6**(3) FLynch(1) (a bhd: t.o) | 10 | **10** | 20/1 | — | — |
| *4780*[6] | **Skyers Tryer (55)** (RonaldThompson) **2-9-0** JQuinn(7) (s.i.s: sn prom: wknd over 2f out: t.o) | 7 | **11** | 16/1 | — | — |

(SP 134.9%) **11 Rn**

**1m 14.9** (3.50) CSF £11.15 TOTE £2.00: £1.20 £2.30 £1.20 (£11.70) Trio £10.80 OWNER Highgrove Developments Ltd (COCKERHAM) BRED Michael Fleming
Bt in 7,200 gns

**4777 Robec Girl (IRE)** always seemed in command, but had to be kept up to her work towards the finish to see off the persistent runner-up. (8/11)
**4468 Lightning Bolt (IRE)** responded to some liberal use of the whip in the last 200 yards. (10/1: op 6/1)
**4970 Princess of Hearts** had the blinkers left off for this return to sprinting. (3/1: op 7/4)
**4594 Silent Valley**, without the headgear, fared better than when running over course and distance at the end of August. (20/1)
**4572 Morning Line (IRE)** (10/1: 7/1-12/1)

## 5062 DISPLACEMENT DESIGN APPRENTICE H'CAP (0-65) (3-Y.O+) (Class G)

4-10 (4-11) **1m 4f (Fibresand)** £2,243.00 (£618.00: £293.00) Stalls: Low GOING minus 0.09 sec per fur (STD)

| Form | Horse | Dist | Pos | SP | RR | SF |
|---|---|---|---|---|---|---|
| *4977*[4] | **Hill Farm Dancer (53)** (WMBrisbourne) **5-9-8**(3) RMullen(9) (s.i.s: hdwy 6f out: led over 2f out: pushed out) | — | **1** | 11/4[1] | 68 | 49 |
| *4984*[4] | **Sharp Command (50)** (PEccles) **3-8-13**(3) RFfrench(12) (a.p: led over 4f out tl over 2f out: one pce) | 5 | **2** | 5/1[3] | 58 | 33 |
| 4515[6] | **State Approval (62)** (APJarvis) **3-9-9**(5) CCarver(3) (led over 7f: one pce fnl 2f) | ¾ | **3** | 4/1[2] | 69 | 44 |
| 2120[7] | **Tremendisto (38)** (CaptJWilson) **6-8-3**(7) AngelaHartley(11) (bkwd: prom tl wknd 2f out) | 4 | **4** | 20/1 | 40 | 21 |
| *4986*[4] | **In the Money (IRE) (55)** (RHollinshead) **7-9-13** DGriffiths(1) (hld up: stdy hdwy 6f out: wknd over 3f out) | 1 | **5** | 7/1 | 56 | 37 |
| *512*[4] | **Pontynyswen (37)** (DBurchell) **8-8-6v**(3) KSked(4) (bkwd: chsd ldrs tl wknd over 4f out) | 2½ | **6** | 12/1 | 34 | 15 |
| 4753[10] | **Colosse (48)** (JLEyre) **4-9-1**(5) SBuckley(5) (s.s: nvr nr ldrs) | s.h | **7** | 8/1 | 45 | 26 |
| 4563[6] | **Charlie Bigtime (46)** (RHarris) **6-9-4** CAdamson(7) (b.hind: sn rdn along: a bhd) | 11 | **8** | 8/1 | 29 | 10 |
| *4986*[5] | **Araboybill (52)** (JNeville) **5-9-10b** AmandaSanders(6) (prom over 7f) | ¾ | **9** | 20/1 | 34 | 15 |
| *4092*[6] | **Drama King (42)** (SRBowring) **4-9-0b** HBastiman(2) (bhd fnl 7f: t.o) | 10 | **10** | 10/1 | 10 | — |
| *4332*[5] | **Miss Pravda (49)** (BJLlewellyn) **3-8-10**(5) JBramhill(8) (bhd: rdn 7f out: sn t.o) | 21 | **11** | 20/1 | — | — |
| *4575*[11] | **Flowing Ocean (50)** (DWChapman) **6-9-5**(3) DSweeney(10) (bkwd: w ldr tl wknd 6f out: sn t.o) | 11 | **12** | 10/1 | — | — |

(SP 138.2%) **12 Rn**

**2m 40.5** (8.00) CSF £19.27 CT £53.82 TOTE £4.30: £1.10 £3.50 £3.30 (£15.00) Trio £84.20 OWNER Mr M. E. Hughes (NESSCLIFFE) BRED D. Newton

WEIGHT FOR AGE 3yo-6lb

**4977 Hill Farm Dancer**, a well-backed favourite, put up a good performance in registering her fourth course and distance win. (11/4: op 5/1)
**4984 Sharp Command** found the winner much too strong in the short home straight. (5/1)
**4515 State Approval** bounced back to form on this return to Sand. (4/1)
**1478 Tremendisto**, dropped 9lb, looks on a useful mark and will be all the better for the run. (20/1)
**4986 In the Money (IRE)** was 5lb lower than when running here in September. (7/1: 5/1-8/1)
**512 Pontynyswen**, usually visored over jumps, was having his first run in one on the Flat. (12/1)

T/Jkpt: Not won; £10,799.43 to Lingfield 12/11/96. T/Plpt: £192.40 (43.76 Tckts). T/Qdpt: £36.80 (22.91 Tckts). IM/KH

# 1216a-LEOPARDSTOWN (Dublin, Ireland) (L-H) (Yielding)
## Sunday November 10th

### 5063a EYREFIELD STKS (Listed) (2-Y.O)
12-30 (12-33) **1m 1f** £9,675.00 (£2,775.00: £1,275.00: £375.00) GOING: 0.44 sec per fur (GS)

| | Horse | | SP | RR | SF |
|---|---|---|---|---|---|
| | **Strawberry Roan (IRE)** (APO'Brien,Ireland) **2-8-12** CRoche (chsd ldrs: led 2f out: rdn & kpt on wl)..............— | 1 | 1/2 1 | 80 | 63 |
| | **Buddy Marvel (IRE)** (JJMcLoughlin,Ireland) **2-8-13** NGMcCullagh (chsd ldrs: 4th st: kpt on wl ins fnl f) .......1½ | 2 | 10/1 | 78 | 61 |
| | **Mingling Glances (USA)** (APO'Brien,Ireland) **2-8-7** RMBurke (hld up in rr: hdwy st: 3rd over 1f out: r.o) .....3½ | 3 | 20/1 | 66+ | 49 |
| | **Dr Johnson (USA)** (CO'Brien,Ireland) **2-8-10** GDuffield (chsd ldrs: lost pl 4f out: r.o fr over 1f out)..................5 | 4 | 8/1 3 | 60 | 43 |
| 4023a6 | **Menja (USA)** (APO'Brien,Ireland) **2-8-10** JAHeffernan (led tl hdd 1f out: sn btn) ..................................3 | 5 | 12/1 | 55 | 38 |
| | **Storm Master (IRE)** (APO'Brien,Ireland) **2-8-13** PShanahan (rn 2nd to st: sn btn)......................................4½ | 6 | 16/1 | 50 | 33 |
| 4639a6 | **Daffodil Dale (IRE)** (KPrendergast,Ireland) **2-8-10** SCraine (hld up: 5th st: no imp fr 2f out)............................½ | 7 | 16/1 | 46 | 29 |
| 4846a2 | **Cambodian (USA)** (JSBolger,Ireland) **2-8-13** KJManning (hld up: progress 4f out: rdn 3f out: sn btn)............12 | 8 | 3/1 2 | 28 | 11 |
| | **Celtic Link (IRE)** (JEMulhern,Ireland) **2-8-7** WJSmith (s.s: a bhd) ..................................................................3½ | 9 | 33/1 | 15 | — |
| | | | (SP 139.0%) | | **9 Rn** |

**1m 58.2** (7.70) OWNER Mrs John Magnier (PILTOWN)

**Strawberry Roan (IRE)**, tremendously impressive at Navan previously, did not exactly sparkle. A nice unimpeded path was made for her turning into the straight and she led two furlongs out and, despite hitting a bit of plastic rail with her foot inside the last, she was never in any trouble. A half-sister to Generous, she could make a nice filly next season and will stay. (1/2)

**Buddy Marvel (IRE)** chased the winner unavailingly from over a furlong and a half out to be nearest at the end. (10/1)

**Mingling Glances (USA)**, a stable-companion of the winner, made eyecatching progress from the rear in the straight. Going third over a furlong out, she ran as green as grass with her head in the air. She is certainly one to look for next season. (20/1)

**4846a Cambodian (USA)** was being pushed along after halfway and at no stage looked a possibility. (3/1)

### 5065a KNOCKAIRE STKS (Listed) (3-Y.O+)
1-30 (1-34) **7f** £9,675.00 (£2,775.00: £1,275.00: £375.00) GOING: 0.44 sec per fur (GS)

| | Horse | | SP | RR | SF |
|---|---|---|---|---|---|
| 4649a* | **Wizard King** (SirMarkPrescott) **5-9-7** GDuffield (mde all: r.o wl) ...................................................................— | 1 | 100/30 1 | 119 | 60 |
| 4857a6 | **Inzar (USA)** (PFICole) **4-9-7** TQuinn (always 2nd: rdn along bef st: kpt on wl: nt trble wnr)..............................2 | 2 | 6/1 3 | 114 | 55 |
| 4848a3 | **Orange Grouse (IRE)** (LBrowne,Ireland) **3-8-11** SCraine (hdwy st: 5th over 1f out: r.o to go 3rd last 100y).....5 | 3 | 16/1 | 94 | 34 |
| 4649a3 | **Idris (IRE)** (JSBolger,Ireland) **6-9-7** KJManning (in tch: 3rd after 2f out: rdn & no imp fr over 1½f out) ..........1½ | 4 | 7/2 2 | 100 | 41 |
| | **Dancing Hours (USA)** (JGBurns,Ireland) **3-8-11** NGMcCullagh (towards rr: r.o fnl 2f: nrst fin)............................¾ | 5 | 20/1 | 89 | 29 |
| 4848a2 | **Burden Of Proof (IRE)** (CO'Brien,Ireland) **4-9-5** CRoche (hld up: progress bef st: 4th & btn 1½f out)............nk | 6 | 6/1 3 | 95 | 36 |
| 5015a6 | **Little Musgrave (IRE)** (JEMulhern,Ireland) **5-8-12b1** JFEgan (in tch: lost pl over 4f out: no imp st)..................3 | 7 | 25/1 | 81 | 22 |
| | **Maldinion** (LBrowne,Ireland) **3-8-8b** JPSpencer (bhd: r.o wl fnl f)........................................................................nk | 8 | 33/1 | 78 | 18 |
| 4848a* | **Ger's Royale (IRE)** (PJFlynn,Ireland) **5-9-5** MDuffy (n.d)..........................................................................2½ | 9 | 100/30 1 | 82 | 23 |
| 48745 | **Stone Ridge (IRE)** (RHannon) **4-8-12** DaneO'Neill (prom: rdn after 2f: sn lost pl) ...............................................½ | 10 | 16/1 | 74 | 15 |
| | **Analisa (IRE)** (JSBolger,Ireland) **3-8-8b** JoannaMorgan (outpcd: n.d)...................................................................2 | 11 | 33/1 | 66 | 6 |
| | **Roblexie (IRE)** (APO'Brien,Ireland) **3-8-11** JAHeffernan (bhd: n.d) ......................................................................hd | 12 | 25/1 | 69 | 9 |
| | | | (SP 127.0%) | | **12 Rn** |

**1m 31.9** (6.90) OWNER Sh Ahmed Bin Saeed Al Maktoum (NEWMARKET) BRED Sheikh Mohammed bin Rashid al Maktoum

**4649a* Wizard King** made all the running. Ridden along through the last furlong and a half, he was never in any danger of being caught. (100/30)

**4857a Inzar (USA)**, chasing the winner throughout, flattered briefly a furlong and a half out, but just could not get on challenging terms. (6/1)

**4848a Orange Grouse (IRE)** ran on to go third well inside the last furlong. (16/1)

**4649a Idris (IRE)** was showing signs of a long season and, although third two furlongs out, was not capable of making any impression. (7/2)

**4848a Burden Of Proof (IRE)** made some headway to go fourth a furlong and a half out, but this was too competitive for him. (6/1)

**4848a* Ger's Royale (IRE)** never showed with a chance and the Curragh is his track. (100/30)

**4874 Stone Ridge (IRE)** was never in contention. (16/1)

### 5066a-5067a (Irish Racing) - See Computer Raceform

# 5018a-EVRY (France) (R-H) (Good to Soft)
## Tuesday November 5th

### 5068a PRIX DE L'ECOUTE S'IL PLEUT H'CAP (3-Y.O+)
3-00 (3-03) **6f** £22,398.00

| | Horse | | SP | RR | SF |
|---|---|---|---|---|---|
| | **Tommelise (FR)** (JEHammond,France) **4-8-10** GMosse ..................................................................— | 1 | | 93 | — |
| | **Meadow Leader (USA)** (France) **6-8-7b1** OPeslier ................................................................1½ | 2 | | 86 | — |
| | **Bid for Blue** (France) **5-7-13** NPerret ..................................................................................¾ | 3 | | 76 | — |
| 446613 | **Bold Effort (FR)** (KOCunningham-Brown) **4-9-8** FSanchez (btn over 5l)............................................... | 11 | | — | — |
| | | | | | **18 Rn** |

**1m 12.45** (2.45) P-M 11.60F: 4.60F 5.10F 3.60F (101.70F) OWNER Mrs J. Ramsden (CHANTILLY) BRED Darley Stud Management Inc

**4411a* Bold Effort (FR)** held the early lead but, when asked to sustain his effort, he was headed with a furlong left to race and quickly faded.

# FLEMINGTON (Melbourne, Australia) (L-H) (Good)
## Tuesday November 5th

### 5069a FOSTER'S MELBOURNE CUP H'CAP (Gd 1) (3-Y.O+)
4-20 (4-21) **2m** £684,211.00 (£210,526.00: £94,737.00)

| | Horse | | SP | RR | SF |
|---|---|---|---|---|---|
| | **Saintly (AUS)** (JBCummings,Australia) **4-8-10** DBeadman ..................................................................— | 1 | | 127 | — |
| | **Count Chivas (NZ)** (DLFreedman,Australia) **5-9-0** SKing ..............................................................2¼ | 2 | | 129 | — |
| | **Skybeau (NZ)** (LJSmith,Australia) **4-7-13** JHolder ...........................................................................nk | 3 | | 113 | — |
| 36734 | **Grey Shot** (IABalding) **4-8-9** PatEddery (btn nearly 5l)............................................................ | 7 | | — | — |

| | | | | SP | RR | SF |
|---|---|---|---|---|---|---|
| 4662a[3] | **Oscar Schindler (IRE)** (KPrendergast,Ireland) **4-8-12** MJKinane (btn over 7½l) | | **15** | | — | — |
| 4434[2] | **Court of Honour (IRE)** (PWChapple-Hyam) **4-8-12** SDMarshall (btn over 12½l) | | **20** | | — | — |
| | | | | | | **22 Rn** |

**3m 18.8** TOTE 6.80: 2.40 10.00 19.60 (125.70) OWNER J B Cummings et al BRED J. B. Cummings
**Saintly (AUS)** became trainer Bart Cummings' tenth winner of Australia's biggest race, and he now goes for the Japan Cup.
**3673 Grey Shot** ran best of the European challengers. He made the running, but could not quicken when the winner went by. His jockey felt he may have won on easier ground and he could be back next year.
**4662a Oscar Schindler (IRE)** was as usual held up, but he could not find an extra gear in the straight. His owner was rueing the decision to run here instead of in the Breeders' Cup Turf.
**4434 Court of Honour (IRE)** pulled hard early on and was in trouble turning in. He will stay in Australia to be trained by Peter Hayes.

## 5024a-SAINT-CLOUD (France) (L-H) (Good)
### Friday November 8th

### 5070a PRIX SEA BIRD (3-Y.O)
1-40 (1-39) **1m 2f** £23,715.00

| | | | | SP | RR | SF |
|---|---|---|---|---|---|---|
| | **Missing Link (FR)** (PDemercastel,France) **3-9-2** AJunk | — | **1** | | 109 | — |
| 2845a[2] | **Grisellito (FR)** (France) **3-9-2** TThulliez | 2 | **2** | | 106 | — |
| | **Pretty Ears (FR)** (France) **3-8-8** PCoppin | s.nk | **3** | | 98 | — |
| 4943a[9] | **Henry The Fifth** (CEBrittain) **3-9-2** FSanchez (btn over 17½l) | | **9** | | — | — |
| | | | | | | **10 Rn** |

**2m 17.0** (13.50) P-M 24.60F: 4.90F 3.80F 8.10F (89.40F) OWNER Ecurie Fabien Ouaki BRED Petra Bloodstock Agency
**4943a Henry The Fifth** held the early lead and set a good pace but, after being headed inside the final furlong, he soon weakened.

## 5068a-EVRY (France) (R-H) (Soft)
### Saturday November 9th

### 5071a CRITERIUM DES DEUX ANS (Gp 2) (2-Y.O)
1-30 (1-36) **6f 110y** £46,113.00 (£18,445.00: £9,223.00: £4,611.00)

| | | | | SP | RR | SF |
|---|---|---|---|---|---|---|
| 2607[8] | **Deadly Dudley (IRE)** (RHannon) **2-8-11** OPeslier (bhd: rdn 2f out: r.o strly to ld nr fin) | — | **1** | | 106 | — |
| 3201a[3] | **Sheer Reason (USA)** (MmeCHead,France) **2-8-8** FHead (prom: rdn wl over 1f out: qcknd to ld ins fnl f: hdd nr line) | ¾ | **2** | | 101 | — |
| 4945a* | **Hurricane State (USA)** (PWChapple-Hyam) **2-8-11** JReid (led: gng wl 2f out: sn rdn: hdd ins fnl f: no ex) | 1½ | **3** | | 101 | — |
| 4945a[2] | **Heaven's Command** (NClement,France) **2-8-8** GMosse (mid div: rdn 2f out: styd on ins fnl f) | nse | **4** | | 97 | — |
| 4723* | **Proud Native (IRE)** (APJarvis) **2-8-11** WRyan (mid div: rdn 2f out: kpt on one pce) | 2 | **5** | | 96 | — |
| 4875* | **Boojum** (BWHills) **2-8-8** AClark (prom: rdn to chal 2f out: outpcd) | nse | **6** | | 92 | — |
| 4661a[10] | **Shigeru Summit** (CBoutin,France) **2-8-8** MBoutin (in rr: nvr plcd to chal) | 2 | **7** | | 88 | — |
| | **Luminosity** (JEPease,France) **2-8-8** FSanchez (a in rr) | 2 | **8** | | 83 | — |
| | | | | | | **8 Rn** |

**1m 20.11** (4.41) P-M 14.10F: 2.70F 1.40F 1.60F (22.90F) OWNER Lucayan Stud Ltd (MARLBOROUGH) BRED John Kent
**2607 Deadly Dudley (IRE)**, behind early, was brought with a perfectly-timed challenge to collar the favourite inside the final furlong and was running on at the finish. He had not been seen out since July, so a lot of credit must go to his trainer. He was given time to mature over the summer as he did not appreciate the firm ground. Judging by the way he finished, he will stay further, so may line up for next year's Greenham Stakes at Newbury. He certainly acts well on soft ground and is going the right way.
**Sheer Reason (USA)**, always well up, took the lead inside the final furlong, but could not hold the late challenge of the winner. She is a little below top-class, but has been placed in a pair of Group Two events this season. Although she possesses plenty of speed, her breeding suggests that racing over further could be to her advantage.
**4945a* Hurricane State (USA)** ran his usual brave race. He was quickly into the lead and held that position until inside the final furlong, but was one-paced in the final stages. A genuine sort, he might be better suited by further.
**4723* Proud Native (IRE)**, rather nervous before the race, was virtually always in fifth place and made a little progress. It was his first time on soft ground, and the distance probably led to his failure to finish in the first four.
**4875* Boojum**, quickly away and well up for much of the race, was beaten by the furlong marker.

### 5072a PRIX SOLITUDE (Listed) (3-Y.O F)
2-30 (2-32) **1m** £18,445.00 (£6,324.00: £3,953.00)

| | | | | SP | RR | SF |
|---|---|---|---|---|---|---|
| 4948a* | **Contare** (JEPease,France) **3-9-2** FSanchez | — | **1** | | 104 | — |
| 1949a[10] | **Whenby (USA)** (MmeCHead,France) **3-8-12** FHead | nse | **2** | | 100 | — |
| 3391a[4] | **Ecoute (USA)** (MmeCHead,France) **3-9-2** GGuignard | s.h | **3** | | 104 | — |
| 4738a[4] | **Tsarnista** (JLDunlop) **3-8-12** JReid (btn approx 1½l) | | **6** | | — | — |
| 4671[2] | **Scarlet Plume** (JLDunlop) **3-8-12** OPeslier (btn approx 2l) | | **7** | | — | — |
| | | | | | | **13 Rn** |

**1m 42.26** (5.26) P-M 10.30F: 3.20F 4.40F 2.60F (54.10F) OWNER Mr G. Strawbridge (CHANTILLY) BRED George Strawbridge
**4738a Tsarnista**, in mid-division, ran on in the final stages, if rather one-paced.
**4671 Scarlet Plume** raced in third position before challenging for the lead early in the straight. Her effort petered out a little later and she just stayed on at the finish.

## 5028a-CAPANNELLE (Rome, Italy) (R-H) (Good to firm)
### Sunday November 10th

### 5073a PREMIO ROMA (Gp 1) (3-Y.O+ C & F)
2-10 (2-39) **1m 2f** £90,417.00 (£46,416.00: £27,263.00: £13,632.00)

| | | | | SP | RR | SF |
|---|---|---|---|---|---|---|
| 4656a* | **Flemensfirth (USA)** (JHMGosden) **4-9-3** LDettori (in tch: hdwy & wnt lft 3f out: led over 2f out: rdn out) | — | **1** | | 121 | — |

| | Horse | Btn | Pos | SP | RR | SF |
|---|---|---|---|---|---|---|
| 4747a[4] | **Hollywood Dream (GER)** (UOstmann,Germany) **5-9-0** CAsmussen (hld up in rr: hdwy 3f out: ev ch over 1f out: no ex cl home) | nk | 2 | | 118 | — |
| 4650a[7] | **Needle Gun (IRE)** (CEBrittain) **6-9-3** MRoberts (led: wnt wd st: hdd over 2f out: ev ch 1f out: r.o one pce) | 1 | 3 | | 119 | — |
| 4650a* | **Oxalagu (GER)** (BSchutz,Germany) **4-9-3** AStarke (a in tch: hdwy on outside & ev ch 1f out: one pce) | ¾ | 4 | | 118 | — |
| 4421a[3] | **Snake Snap** (VCaruso,Italy) **3-9-1** FJovine (hld up: effrt & ev ch 2f out: wknd 1f out) | 3½ | 5 | | 114 | — |
| 4747a[5] | **Slicious** (VCaruso,Italy) **4-9-3** MEsposito (unruly s: in tch tl over 2f out) | 3½ | 6 | | 107 | — |
| 4849a[2] | **Sanoosea (USA)** (MRStoute) **4-9-3** JReid (prom: btn wl over 2f out) | 5 | 7 | | 99 | — |
| 1580a[5] | **Dancer Mitral** (LBrogi,Italy) **3-9-1** VMezzatesta (mid div st: sn wknd) | 3 | 8 | | 96 | — |

**8 Rn**

**2m 0.8** TOTE 15L: 12L 15L 28L (27L) OWNER Sheikh Mohammed (NEWMARKET) BRED Mill Ridge Farm Ltd in USA
**4656a* Flemensfirth (USA)**, having his first run since recapturing the Prix Dollar, is a credit to his trainer. He may start next year in either the Dubai World Cup or the Prix Ganay.
**4650a Needle Gun (IRE)**, a well-travelled individual, ran his best race since the early summer. Prominent throughout, he was still on terms a furlong out, but had only the one pace.
**4849a Sanoosea (USA)** is a consistent performer, but has only won once. He is not up to this level, but this ground was against him.

## 5074a PREMIO RIBOT (Gp 2) (3-Y.O+)

2-35 (3-07) **1m** £31,006.00 (£14,445.00: £8,114.00: £4,057.00)

| | Horse | Btn | Pos | SP | RR | SF |
|---|---|---|---|---|---|---|
| | **Taxi de Nuit (USA)** (AVerdesi,Italy) **4-9-2** LDettori (mde all: clr 1f out: r.o wl) | — | 1 | | 108 | — |
| | **Golden Agos** (GFratini,Italy) **3-9-1** CAsmussen (prom: chal over 2f out: sn outpcd: rallied cl home) | 3½ | 2 | | 102 | — |
| 903a[3] | **Dungeon Master (IRE)** (LBrogi,Italy) **3-9-1** VMezzatesta (mid div: hdwy 3f out: outpcd 2f out: styd on fnl f) | ½ | 3 | | 101 | — |
| 4667a[3] | **Morigi** (ITellini,Italy) **5-9-2** MTellini (gd hdwy 3f out: ev ch 2f out: wknd fnl f) | 1¼ | 4 | | 98 | — |
| 4667a[2] | **Gothenberg (IRE)** (MJohnston) **3-9-1** JWeaver (prom & brought wd st: one pce fnl 2f) | ½ | 5 | | 98 | — |
| | **Zero Problemo (IRE)** (Germany) **3-9-1** AStarke (prom st: nvr able to chal) | 1½ | 6 | | 95 | — |
| 1759a[4] | **Lake Storm (IRE)** (Italy) **5-9-2** MEsposito (prom 5f) | ½ | 7 | | 93 | — |
| 4667a[4] | **Ravier (ITY)** (Italy) **5-9-2** FJovine (mid div st: nvr able to chal) | 3¼ | 8 | | 86 | — |
| | **Robins (IRE)** (Italy) **4-9-2** OFancera (in tch st: nvr able to chal) | s.nk | 9 | | 86 | — |
| 4858a[2] | **Bemont Park (ITY)** (Italy) **5-8-13** GBietolini (n.d) | 1¼ | 10 | | 80 | — |
| 4416a[3] | **Acharne** (CEBrittain) **3-9-1** MRoberts (n.d) | 2 | 11 | | 80 | — |
| | **Kierkegaard** (Italy) **3-9-1** JCaro (prom 4f) | 4 | 12 | | 72 | — |
| | **Oxford Line (IRE)** (Italy) **4-9-2** MPasquale (bhd fnl 3f) | 3 | 13 | | 65 | — |

**13 Rn**

**1m 35.3** TOTE 56L: 27L 114L 89L (1109L) OWNER Gerecon Italia BRED Le Haras Inc
**Taxi de Nuit (USA)** put up an impressive display and broke the course-record set by Lucky Ring in 1986.
**4667a Gothenberg (IRE)**, never able to land a blow in the straight, has had a busy season.
**4416a Acharne** found this ground far too firm. He will have better opportunities.

# LA ZARZUELA (Madrid, Spain) (L-H) (Good to firm)

### Sunday November 10th

## 5075a GRAN PREMIO MEMORIAL DUQUE DE TOLEDO (Gp 3) (3-Y.O+)

4-40 (4-43) **1m 4f** £26,545.00 (£10,618.00: £5,309.00)

| | Horse | Btn | Pos | SP | RR | SF |
|---|---|---|---|---|---|---|
| 4855a[2] | **Mongol Warrior (USA)** (LordHuntingdon) **3-8-11** DHarrison | — | 1 | | 100 | — |
| | **Leonard Quercus (FR)** (FBedouret,Spain) **4-9-1** BGalebert | 3½ | 2 | | 93 | — |
| | **Wild Park (SPA)** (J-LdeSalas,Spain) **3-8-11** MDiaz | s.nk | 3 | | 95 | — |

**8 Rn**

**2m 43.54** TOTE 300PS: 300PS 780PS (6760PS) OWNER H De Kwiatkowski (WEST ILSLEY) BRED Kennelot Stables Limited
**4855a Mongol Warrior (USA)**, who has only won when the ground has been good or soft, handled these conditions well and proved too good for these.

# 5031a-SAN SIRO (Milan, Italy) (R-H) (Heavy)

### Sunday November 10th

## 5076a PREMIO PALAZZETTO (2-Y.O)

1-10 (1-13) **1m** £8,120.00

| | Horse | Btn | Pos | SP | RR | SF |
|---|---|---|---|---|---|---|
| | **Livergod (USA)** (MCiciarelli,Italy) **2-8-10** AParravani | — | 1 | | — | — |
| | **Barba Papa (IRE)** (LMCumani) **2-8-10** LPanici | 1 | 2 | | — | — |
| | **Rossi Osvaldo (ITY)** (Italy) **2-8-10** MLatorre | 8 | 3 | | — | — |
| | **Stillet (IRE)** (LMCumani) **2-8-10** MDemuro (btn over 16l) | | 6 | | — | — |

**7 Rn**

**1m 48.0** (18.00) TOTE 62L: 33L 37L (273L) OWNER Scuderia Briantea BRED Bruce Hundley
**Barba Papa (IRE)** finished the better of the two Cumani raiders, beating his favoured stable-companion and earning £3,573 for his effort.
**Stillet (IRE)** started favourite, but was disappointing.

# 5070a-SAINT-CLOUD (France) (L-H) (Good to soft)

### Monday November 11th

## 5077a PRIX THOMAS BRYON (Gp 3) (2-Y.O)

1-30 (1-28) **1m** £28,986.00 (£10,540.00: £5,270.00)

| | Horse | Btn | Pos | SP | RR | SF |
|---|---|---|---|---|---|---|
| 4949a[3] | **Varxi (FR)** (DSmaga,France) **2-8-9** DBoeuf | — | 1 | | 105+ | — |
| | **Aneysar (IRE)** (AdeRoyerDupre,France) **2-8-9** GMosse | 5 | 2 | | 95 | — |

| | | | | SP | RR | SF |
|---|---|---|---|---|---|---|
| | **Keos (USA)** (JEHammond,France) **2-8-9** CAsmussen | 2 | **3** | | 91 | — |

**6 Rn**

**1m 53.8** (15.30) P-M 20.70F: 5.20F 2.20F OWNER Baron Thierry Van Zuylen (LAMORLAYE) BRED Baron T de Zuylen
**Varxi (FR)** revelled in the heavy ground. He surged into the lead a furlong and a half out and drew away in the final furlong, making his five rivals look rather ordinary. His previous run was below-par because he became very nervous when being loaded for the races at his stable. This probably was not a very high-class Group event, but he is sure to be a tough opponent whenever the ground is testing.
**Aneysar (IRE)** attempted to make all the running, but had nothing to offer when the winner took the lead halfway up the straight. He would probably prefer better ground.
**Keos (USA)** was given every possible chance and just stayed on on ground that was certainly not to his liking.

## 5078a PRIX PERTH (Gp 3) (3-Y.O+)
2-00 (1-56) **1m** £28,986.00 (£10,540.00: £5,270.00: £2,635.00)

| | | | | SP | RR | SF |
|---|---|---|---|---|---|---|
| 4664a5 | **River Bay (USA)** (JEHammond,France) **3-8-12** TJarnet | — | **1** | | 121 | — |
| 5018a* | **Decorated Hero** (JHMGosden) **4-9-0** LDettori | 1½ | **2** | | 118 | — |
| 4940a* | **Blushing Gleam** (MmeCHead,France) **3-8-8** ODoleuze | 1½ | **3** | | 111 | — |
| 41328 | **Royal Philosopher** (JWHills) **4-9-0** RHills | 3 | **4** | | 109 | — |

**10 Rn**

**1m 52.4** (13.90) P-M 2.70F: 1.30F 1.40F 1.50F (6.40F) OWNER Ecurie Chalhoub (CHANTILLY) BRED Rosemont Farm Inc.
**River Bay (USA)** is an extremely decent horse in the making. He challenged at the furlong marker and then showed good stamina in the final 50 yards. He has gone from strength to strength and is particularly effective when there is cut in the ground. A bright prospect for next season, he may be aimed at the Prix d'Harcourt, which could be followed by the Prix Ganay.
**5018a* Decorated Hero** lost nothing in defeat. He took command halfway up the straight, but could not hold the lead. He has had an extremely successful autumn campaign in France and certainly looks capable of winning a Group Three next year.
**720a Blushing Gleam** was waited with and put in her best work at the finish, but her effort came too late. She was probably too far out of her ground, bearing in mind the state of the track. She is probably also suited to better ground.
**4132 Royal Philosopher** tried to make all the running. He stuck to his task until the bitter end, but was one-paced in the final furlong.
DS

## 1995 RACEFORM ANNUAL ERRATA

**Race 840**: **Elburg (IRE)** has been disqualified (prohibited substances (caffeine, theobromine, Theophylline and paraxanthine) in urine). **Brandon Prince (IRE)** awrdd r, **Kadiri (IRE)** plcd 2nd, **Grace Card** plcd 3rd and **Cristal Springs** plcd 4th.

**Race 2492**: **Ashkernazy (IRE)** has been disqualified (prohibited substances (procaine & sulphadimidine) found in urine). **Southern Dominion** awrdd r, **King Rambo** plcd 2nd, **La Belle Dominique** plcd 3rd, **Most Uppity** plcd 4th and **Featherstone Lane** plcd 5th.

**Race 2784**: **Pretty Average** has been disqualified (ran at an unrecognised meeting). **Dante's Rubicon (IRE)** awrdd r, **Panther (IRE)** plcd 2nd, **Murray's Mazda (IRE)** and **Brookhead Lady** plcd 3rd.

**Race 3687a**: **Titus Livius (FR)** has been disqualified (prohibited substance (dembrexine) found in urine). **Ella Nico (IRE)** awrdd r and **Branston Jewel (IRE)** plcd 2nd.

**Race 3898 4128**: Due to mistaken identity, the horse that ran as **Hong Kong Dollar** was in fact the unraced **Ela-Ment (IRE)**. Runs stand for Handicapping purposes. Pearce fined £750.

**Race 4119**: **Croft Pool** has been disqualified and plcd last (prohibited substance (flunixin) found in urine). **Takadou (IRE)** awrdd r, **Snowing** plcd 2nd, **Jawlaat (USA)** plcd 3rd, **Ziggy's Dancer** (USA) plcd 4th, **Don't Worry Me (IRE)** plcd 5th and **Mr Bergerac (IRE)** plcd 6th.

# INDEX TO MEETINGS



† abandoned * All-Weather

# INDEX TO FLAT RACING

Figure following the horse's name indicates its **age**. The figures following the pedigree refer to the numbers of the races (*all-weather are in italics*) in which the horse has run; parentheses () indicate a win; small figures [2,3,4] etc denote other placings. Foreign races are denoted by the suffix 'a'. Horses withdrawn (not under orders) are shown with the suffix 'w'. The figure within arrows eg. **>100<** indicate Raceform Private Handicap MASTER rating. The ratings are based on a scale of 0-140. The following symbols are used: 'a' all-weather rating, 'f' turf rating, '+' on the upgrade, 'd' disappointing, '?' questionable form, 't' tentative rating based on time.

2208[2] **>80f<**
**Afarka (IRE) 3** b f Kahyasi-Afasara *4643a[5]* ***>86f<***
**Affidavit (USA) 4** b c Affirmed (USA)-Narwala (Darshaan) 902a[4] 1397a[7] **>115f<**
**Aficionado (IRE) 2** b g Marju (IRE)-Haneena (Habitat) 1445[3] 1774[3] 2112[8] 2734[3] 3128[8] 4546[6] 4715[5] (4970) *5057[4]* **>62a 71f<**
**Afisiak 3** b f Efisio-Maestrette (Manado) 539[4] 638[14] 867[16] **>59a 51f<**
**Afon Alwen 3** ch f Henbit (USA)-Brenig (Horage) *3626[3] (3966)* 4209[3] 4702[12] **>49a 66f<**
**African Chimes 9** b h Kampala-Rynville (Ballymore) **1995:** *4362[7]* **>67a 75f<**
**African-Pard (IRE) 4** b g Don't Forget Me-Petite Realm (Realm) *979[17] 1457[3] 1613[5]* 2577[10] 2785[3] 2994[2] 3139[5] 3340[9] *3627[13]* **>65a 70f<**
**African Sun (IRE) 3** b g Mtoto-Nuit D'Ete (USA) (Super Concorde (USA)) 1174[9] *1456[5] 1676[8]* 1999[4] 2297[5] **>32a 58df<**
**After Hours 2** b f Polar Falcon (USA)-Tarasova (USA) (Green Forest (USA)) 4798[11] **>44f<**
**Against The Clock 4** b g Puissance-Sara Sprint (Formidable (USA)) *265[8]*
**Again Together 3** b f Then Again-Starawak (Star Appeal) *464[2] 897[6] 1876[12]* 2016[4] 2202[4] 2738[2] 2768[5] **>61a 64f<**
**Agdistis 3** b f Petoski-Kannbaniya (Mouktar) 2326[7] 2794[2] 3108[2] 3459[9] 4216[9] **>69f<**
**Agent 3** ch g Anshan-Maria Cappuccini (Siberian Express (USA)) **1995:** *4408[2]* **1996:** *102[2] 161[3] 237[3] 2805[4]* 3424[10] 3810[6] 4598[9] 4921[2] *5058[2]* **>69a 60f<**
**Agent Mulder 2** b g Kylian (USA)-Precious Caroline (IRE) (The Noble Player (USA)) 4514[17] **>29f<**
**Age of Reality (USA) 3** b f Alleged (USA)-Isticanna (USA) (Far North (CAN)) 707[8] 2715[6] 3109[2] 3333[10] 3500[6] 3825[10] **>61f<**
**Aggies Dream 5** ch g Librate-Achnahuaigh (Known Fact (USA)) *247[9] 305[6]* **>34f<**
**Agnella (IRE) 3** b f Polish Patriot (USA)-Annaberta (GER) (Alpenkonig (GER)) 1493[3] 3945[11] 4214[9] 4800[9] 4971[7] **>85?f<**
**Agnelli 3** b c Surumu (GER)-Aragosta (GER) (Nebos (GER)) 1751a[2] 2668a[15] 3574a[4] 4040a[5] 4542a[3] **>116f<**
**Agoer 4** ch f Hadeer-Abuzz (Absalom) **1995:** *4479[8] 4515[7]* **1996:** *66[10] 166[6] 257[7]* **>41a 56f<**
**Agony Aunt 2** b f Formidable (USA)-Loch Clair (IRE) (Lomond (USA)) 4451[4] 4608[11] 4861[5] **>74f<**
**Agwa 7** b g Local Suitor (USA)-Meissarah (USA) (Silver Hawk (USA)) **1995:** *4441[9]* **1996:** *163[6] 205[10] 243[11] (631)* 1073[8] 1536[9] 1715[9] 1964[6] *4895[12]* **>63a 59f<**
**Ahjay 6** br g Tina's Pet-City Link Rose (Lochnager) *582[24]* 846[6] 1121[9] 1521[7] 1856[13] 2209[6] 2412[8] 4240[12] **>33f<**
**Ahkaam (USA) 3** ch c Riverman (USA)-Rare Mint (USA) (Key To The Mint (USA)) 1249a[5] 2839a[6] **>118f<**
**Ailesbury Hill (USA) 3** ch f Woodman (USA)-Golden Oriole (USA) (Northern Dancer) 593[8] 731[8] 2246[3] 2599[7] 2943[5] 4117[10] **>76f<**
**Ailleacht (USA) 4** b or br f Chief's Crown (USA)-Poster Beauty (Codex (USA)) 1911a[2] 2115[14] 2472a[6] (2816a) 4280a[2] 4660a[10] 4848a[5] **>115?f<**
**Aim For Stardom 4** b c Polish Precedent (USA)-Aim for the Top (USA) (Irish River (FR)) 495[7] 645[4] 820[17] **>76df<**
**Aim Seven 2** b c Pursuit of Love-Figini (Glint of Gold) 2243[7] 2758[2] 2972[5] 3697[4] 4547[3] **>70f<**
**Airborne Harris (IRE) 3** ch g Persian Heights-Excuse Slip (USA) (Damascus (USA)) 566[5] **>63f<**
**Air Command (BAR) 6** br g Concorde Hero (USA)-Hubbardair (Town And Country) **1995:** *4534[12]* **1996:** *208[8] 1449[21]* 1778[10] 2155[11] 2709[10] **>19a 41f<**
**Air Commodore (IRE) 5** b g Elegant Air-Belle Enfant (Beldale Flutter (USA)) 3933[18] 4136[8] 4329[3] **>92f<**
**Air Express (IRE) 2** b c Salse (USA)-Ibtisamm (USA) (Caucasus (USA)) 1694[2] 2607[3] 3143[4] 3927[3] (4258) 4462[6] 4759[3] **>105f<**
**Airman (TUR) 4** b c Bachelors Party (TUR)-Puma (TUR) 4289a[2] **>112f<**
**Air Of Distinction (IRE) 2** br f Distinctly North (USA)-Kaysama (FR) (Kenmare (FR)) (4027a) 4159a[7] **>91f<**
**Air of Mystery 4** ch f Ballad Rock-Keep Looking (USA) (Mr Prospector (USA)) **1995:** *4351[11]* **1996:** *201[8] 328[13]* **>17a 16f<**
**Airport (USA) 5** b h Lear Fan (USA)-Vague Prospect (USA) (Vaguely Noble) *(396a) 435a[3]* **>107a 116f<**
**Air Quest 3** b c Rainbow Quest (USA)-Aryenne (FR) (Green Dancer (USA)) (707) 986[5] **>98f<**
**Air Wing 3** ch c Risk Me (FR)-Greenstead Lass (Double-U-Jay) 1006[8] 1628[10] 4521[9] 4616[20] 4689[11] 4898[14] 4968[12] **>62f<**
**Aiyana (GER) 3** f 1750a[7] **>84f<**
**Ajaad Aljaree (IRE) 3** b c Sadler's Wells (USA)-Impudent Miss (Persian Bold) 677[12] **>54f<**
**Ajayib (USA) 2** b f Riverman (USA)-Maplejinsky (USA) (Nijinsky (CAN)) 2315[2] 3449[2] (3820) **>88f<**
**Ajdar 5** b g Slip Anchor-Loucoum (FR) (Iron Duke (FR)) *(72) 279[2] 303[5] 635[2]* 759[4] 1019[4] 1514[14] 1803[10] 2440[5] 2941[6] **>51a 54f<**
**Ajkuit (IRE) 3** b c Persian Heights-Hazar (IRE) (Thatching) 4611[8] 4898[11] **>58f<**
**Ajnad (IRE) 2** b c Efisio-Lotte Lenta (Gorytus (USA)) 3807[14] **>40f<**
**Akalim 3** b c Petong-Tiszta Sharok (Song) 692[8] 992[6] 2017[7] 2518[8] **>62f<**
**Akhiyar (IRE) 5** gr g Doyoun-Akishka (Nishapour (FR)) 5015a[5] **>107f<**
**Akhla (USA) 3** ch f Nashwan (USA)-Beautiful River (USA) (Irish River (FR)) 1508[4] (1804) **>86f<**
**Akil (IRE) 4** b c Cyrano de Bergerac-Nonnita (Welsh Saint) 728[17] 809[13] 967[5] 2053[23] 2328[7] 2623[14] 3612[2] (3782) **>97f<**
**Akiymann (USA) 6** b g El Gran Senor (USA)-Akila (FR) (Top Ville) *2182[2]* 2494[5] 2737[8] **>63f<**
**Akola Angel 4** ch f Indian Ridge-Heavenly Note (Chief Singer) *34[12]* **>33a 42f<**
**Alabang 5** ch g Valiyar-Seleter (Hotfoot) 991[14] (1502) 1633[2] 1821[4] (2296) 2701[4] 2803[2] (3109) 3412[5] **>74f<**
**Alabastro (IRE) 3** b c Fairy King (USA)-Fatal Charm (USA) (Sham (USA)) 722a[2] 903a[6] (4418a) **>106f<**
**Al Abraq (IRE) 3** b c Reprimand-Dazzling Maid (IRE) (Tate Gallery (USA)) 808[6] 2041[11] 2621[4] 3211[13] **>98f<**
**Alaflak (IRE) 5** b h Caerleon (USA)-Safe Haven (Blakeney) 1894[2] (2525) 3205[5] 3710[10] 4067[P] **>90f<**
**Alajyal (IRE) 3** ch f Kris-Yaqut (USA) (Northern Dancer) 710[17] 1350[8] 1649[7] 2251[17] 3286[8] **>35f<**
**Alakhluki 3** b f Aragon-Hawaiian Bloom (USA) (Hawaii) 644[12] 862[16] 2340[4] 4898[8] **>58f<**
**Alambar (IRE) 3** b c Fairy King (USA)-Lightino (Bustino) 788[6] 1000[2] (1671) 2001[2] 2894[4] 3521[3] 4187[5] 4559[14] **>85f<**
**Alamein (USA) 3** ch g Roi Danzig (USA)-Pollination (Pentotal) *714[3]* (1608) (1648) 2041[6] 2501[3] **>90f<**
**Alami (USA) 4** br c Danzig (USA)-Alchaasibiyeh (USA) (Seattle Slew (USA)) *286a[3] 375a[5] 432a[2]* **>93a 104f<**
**Alamo Bay (USA) 3** b c Nureyev (USA)-Albertine (FR) (Irish River (FR)) 5021a[2] **>111f<**
**Alana's Ballad (IRE) 3** b f Be My Native (USA)-Radalgo (Ballad Rock) 957[9] 1451[8] **>10f<**
**Alaraby (IRE) 4** b f Caerleon (USA)-Circo (High Top) 753[20] **>80f<**
**Alarico (FR) 3** ch g Kadrou (FR)-Calabria (FR) (Vitiges (FR)) 4613[7] 4827[11] **>56f<**
**Alaska 3** b f Polar Falcon (USA)-Priceless Bond (USA) (Blushing Groom (FR)) *4336[12] 4590[12]* ***>62df<***
**Al Ava Consonant 2** b f Reprimand-Dragonist (Dragonara Palace (USA)) 2755[6] 3121[3] 3687[13] 4364[10] **>60f<**
**Al Azhar 2** b c Alzao (USA)-Upend (Main Reef) 3319[2] (3821) (4131) **>88f<**
**Albaha (USA) 3** br g Woodman (USA)-Linda's Magic (USA) (Far North (CAN)) 575[12] 842[5] 1327[12] 1473[2] 1693[7] 1994[3] 2299[4] 2514[7] 4556[8] 4872[9] **>75f<**
**Albaran (GER) 3** b c Sure Blade (USA)-Araqueen (GER) (Konigsstuhl (GER)) 2668a[3] 4542a[6] **>108f<**
**Alberelle 2** b f Rudimentary (USA)-Desert Ditty (Green Desert (USA)) 2664a[3] **>73f<**
**Albert The Bear 3** b g Puissance-Florentynna Bay (Aragon) 1340[8] 1985[2] (2222) 2705[2] 3210[5] 3920[3] **>23a 85f<**
**Albinor (IRE) 4** b c Danehill (USA)-Schwanensee (USA) (Mr Leader (USA)) **1995:** 4401a[2] **>95f<**
**Al Blu (IRE) 2** br c Exit To Nowhere (USA)-Kiri (Kris) 4163a[6] 4514[7] **>75f< (DEAD)**
**Alcalali (USA) 2** 5024a[7] **>89f<**
**Al Corniche (IRE) 4** b f Bluebird (USA)-Naxos (USA) (Big Spruce (USA)) **1995:** *4530[12]* **>48a 51f<**
**Aldaneh 4** ch f Indian Ridge-Maiyaasah (Kris) *888[10]* 988[9] 2246[7] **>62f<**
**Aldevonie 4** b f Green Desert (USA)-Kintail (Kris) 982[7] **>81f<**
**Alessandra 3** ch f Generous (IRE)-Kiss (Habitat) 813[2] 1004[4] (1895) 2069[7] 3571a[4] 4467[6] **>102f<**
**Alessia 4** b f Caerleon (USA)-Kiss (Habitat) *960[9]* 1770[9] 4800[11] **>74f<**
**Alexandre Farnese (FR) 3** gr c Caerwent-Coincidence (Fereed (FR)) 4031a[2] **>108f<**
**Alezal 2** b c Anshan-Dance On The Stage (Dancing Brave (USA)) *4817[2]* ***>70f<***
**Alfahaal (IRE) 3** b c Green Desert (USA)-Fair of the Furze (Ela-Mana-Mou) 934[9] **>51f<**
**Alfahad 3** b c Doyoun-Moogie (Young Generation) 1434[13] 2124[8] **>42f<**
**Alfayza 3** b f Danehill (USA)-Dahlawise (IRE) (Caerleon (USA)) 739[8] *859[7] 1850[11]* 2241[6] 2592[10] 3289[6] 3812[4] 4000[9] 4810[2] 4967[8] **>27a 51f<**
**Alfredo Alfredo (USA) 4** b c Miswaki (USA)-Alleged Queen (USA) (Alleged (USA)) 2510[4] 2718[6] 3425[5] **>67f<**
**Algonquin (IRE) 3** 799a[9]
**Alhaarth (IRE) 3** b c Unfuwain (USA)-Irish Valley (USA) (Irish River (FR)) 695[2] 926[4] 1791[5] 2473a[9] 3144[3] 3784[3] (4664a) **>128f<**
**Alhawa (USA) 3** ch c Mt Livermore (USA)-Petrava (NZ) (Imposing (AUS)) (1051) 1440[7] 2041[7] 2299[6] 2621[11] 3926[7] 4682[14] **>87f<**
**Al Helal 4** b c In The Wings-Rosia Bay (High Top) *4574[6]* **>46a 70f<**
**Alicia (IRE) 3** b br f Darshaan-Tribal Rite (Be My Native (USA)) 845[9] 1123[4] 2430[2] 3434[5] 3876[8] 4866[3] 4992[7] **>76f<**
**Alifandango (IRE) 2** b f Alzao (USA)-Fandangerina (USA) (Grey Dawn II) 4720[8] **>62f<**
**A Likely Tale (USA) 3** b c Alleged (USA)-Thatsallshewrote (USA) (Graustark) 494[3] **>80f<**

**Alikhlas 2** b br f Lahib (USA)-Mathaayl (USA) (Shadeed (USA)) 3433$^{2}$ 4062$^{11}$ **>83f<**
**Alimerjam 2** b f Thowra (FR)-Sicilian Vespers (Mummy's Game) 807$^{8}$ 910$^{4}$ 1331$^{5}$ 1954$^{8}$ 3803$^{10}$ 3964$^{6}$ **>46f<**
**Alioli 4** br f Nishapour (FR)-Allegra (Niniski (USA)) **1995:** *4412$^{10}$* **>55f<**
**Alips (FR) 2** ch f Beaudelaire (USA)-New Miss (FR) (New Chapter (FR)) (3029a) **>78f<**
**Ali-Royal (IRE) 3** b c Royal Academy (USA)-Alidiva (Chief Singer) 736$^{3}$ (1151) 2050$^{5}$ 3144$^{7}$ 3712$^{2}$ 4181$^{2}$ (4479) (4972) **>119f<**
**Alisadara 2** b f Nomination-Nishara (Nishapour (FR)) *1026$^{4}$ 1360$^{4}$* 1583$^{4}$ 2025$^{10}$ 2122$^{8}$ 2875$^{5}$ 3082$^{6}$ 3241$^{6}$ 3423$^{13}$ **>47f<**
**Alisidora (IRE) 4** ch f Nashwan (USA)-Christabelle (USA) (Northern Dancer) 2474a$^{10}$ **>106f<**
**Alis Princess 3** ch f Sayf El Arab (USA)-Princess Zeddera (English Prince) 2026$^{16}$
**Alistover 3** b f Zalazl (USA)-Song of Gold **1995:** *4373$^{5}$ 4443$^{6}$* **>33a 22f<**
**Alisura 3** br f Lead on Time (USA)-Iosifa (Top Ville) 2036$^{5}$ 2439$^{5}$ 3225$^{3}$ 4203$^{11}$ 4448$^{16}$ **>68f<**
**Aljaz 6** b g Al Nasr (FR)-Santa Linda (USA) (Sir Ivor) **1995:** *4428$^{8}$* **1996:** *1020$^{10}$ 2308$^{4}$ (3416) 3602$^{5}$ 4828$^{15}$ 4983$^{12}$* **>49a 23f<**
**Alkarine 4** gr g Alias Smith (USA)-Colly Cone (Celtic Cone) *369$^{7}$*
**Alkateb 4** ch g Rock City-Corley Moor (Habitat) **1995:** *4404a$^{5}$* **1996:** 4680$^{3}$ **>96f<**
**All Apologies (IRE) 4** b g Common Grounds-Living Rough (Wolverlife) *86$^{8}$ 234$^{5}$ (310) 399$^{8}$ 418$^{10}$ 652$^{10}$ 1460$^{10}$ 1810$^{6}$* **>40a f<**
**Alleged Challenge (USA) 3** b c Alleged (USA) 326a$^{2}$ **>62f<**
**Allegro 2** b c Night Shift (USA)-Merry Rous (Rousillon (USA)) 3631$^{2}$ 4469$^{7}$ **>57f<**
**Allez Cyrano (IRE) 5** b g Alzao (USA)-Miss Bergerac (Bold Lad (IRE)) *(356) 409$^{4}$ 485$^{6}$ 649$^{2}$* 756$^{8}$ 971$^{7}$ **>65a 74?f<**
**Allez Pablo 6** b g Crisp-Countess Mariga (Amboise) 1465$^{7}$ 1996$^{11}$ 2594$^{6}$ 4252$^{12}$ 4509$^{12}$ **>24f<**
**Allied Academy 2** ch c Royal Academy (USA)-Tsungani (Cure The Blues (USA)) 4200$^{6}$ 4547$^{6}$ **>64f<**
**All In Good Time 3** b g Shadeed (USA)-Good Thinking (USA) *428$^{9}$ 537$^{11}$* 2683$^{7}$ 3104$^{7}$ **>30f<**
**All In Leather 2** b f Saddlers' Hall (IRE)-Ivana (IRE) (Taufan (USA)) 3773$^{3}$ 4253$^{3}$ 4697$^{3}$ **>80f<**
**Allinson's Mate (IRE) 8** b g Fayruz-Piney Pass (Persian Bold) *282$^{6}$ 331$^{4}$ 357$^{7}$ 413$^{5}$ 479$^{5}$* 629$^{13}$ 827$^{9}$ 935$^{11}$ 1313$^{10}$ 1609$^{4}$ 1789$^{4}$ 2047$^{6}$ 2149$^{7}$ 2357$^{4}$ (2391) 2566$^{3}$ 2630$^{6}$ 3151$^{7}$ 3306$^{4}$ 3460$^{4}$ 3578$^{6}$ (4768) 4915$^{5}$ **>60a 67f<**
**All Is Fair 2** b f Selkirk (USA)-Allegra (Niniski (USA)) 3433$^{3}$ (3647) 4052$^{7}$ **>76f<**
**Allmosa 7** b m Alleging (USA)-Wimosa (Mossborough) *1194$^{13}$* 1439$^{11}$ 1835$^{9}$ 3850$^{7}$ **>69a 41f<**
**All On 5** ch m Dunbeath (USA)-Fresh Line (High Line) 2756$^{5}$ *4334$^{2}$ (4574) 4753$^{5}$* ***>61++a*** **43f<**
**All Stand 3** ch f Dominion-Now In Session (USA) (Diesis) 1333$^{7}$ 1709$^{5}$ 4690$^{8}$ 4824$^{7}$ **>59f<**
**Allstars Dancer 3** b f Primo Dominie-Danzig Harbour (USA) (Private Account (USA)) **1995:** *4365$^{7}$ 4538$^{9}$* **1996:** *143$^{5}$ 307$^{4}$ 3606$^{9}$* 3863$^{8}$ 4075$^{14}$ **>37a 29f<**
**Allstars Express 3** b c Rambo Dancer (CAN)-Aligote (Nebbiolo) 577$^{10}$ *856$^{3}$ 1535$^{3}$* (1996) 2159$^{3}$ 2378$^{5}$ 2768$^{2}$ (2905) 3079$^{4}$ 3284$^{3}$ 3634$^{4}$ 3830$^{6}$ 4551$^{4}$ *4779$^{5}$ 4894$^{3}$ 5003$^{2}$* **>69a 70f<**
**Allstars Rocket 3** b c Puissance-Sally Delight (Homing) 1994$^{14}$ 2197$^{12}$ 2557$^{12}$ 3138$^{4}$ (3492) 3681$^{8}$ 3977$^{5}$ *4781$^{2}$ 4968$^{3}$ 5055$^{7}$* **>69a 63f<**
**All the Joys 5** b or br m Adbass (USA)-Joytime (John de Coombe) *165$^{4}$ 260$^{5}$ 759$^{8}$* 1953$^{5}$ 2066$^{9}$ (2599) **>45a 50f<**
**All the Vowels (IRE) 5** g Ela-Mana-Mou-Irena (Bold Lad (IRE)) 4643a$^{13}$ **>75f<**
**Alltime Dancer (IRE) 4** b g Waajib-Dance On Lady (Grundy) 4125$^{13}$ **>64f<**
**Allwight Then (IRE) 5** gr g Dancing Dissident (USA)-Abergwrle (Absalom) *407$^{8}$ 601$^{15}$* 742$^{2}$ 862$^{14}$ 1049$^{5}$ 1708$^{11}$ 2064$^{9}$ 3932$^{15}$ 4259$^{4}$ 4430$^{5}$ *4778$^{10}$ 4888$^{12}$* ***>48a 66f<***
**Allyana (IRE) 4** b f Thatching-Miss Loving (Northfields (USA)) *846$^{11}$* 1049$^{12}$ **>68df<**
**Ally Camp (USA) 3** f 794a$^{4}$ **>100f<**
**Alma Latina (IRE) 2** b f Persian Bold-Celestial Melody (USA) (The Minstrel (CAN)) 1910a$^{5}$ **>73f<**
**Almapa 4** ch g Absalom-More Fun (Malicious) 470$^{6}$ 636$^{15}$ 887$^{13}$ 1170$^{3}$ 1348$^{2}$ 1085$^{9}$ 1992$^{5}$ 2079$^{5}$ 2405$^{6}$ **>54f<**
**Almasi (IRE) 4** b f Petorius-Best Niece (Vaigly Great) 480$^{9}$ 749$^{7}$ (868) 1157$^{2}$ (1786) 1991$^{3}$ 2431$^{4}$ 2860$^{2}$ 3152$^{7}$ 3758$^{3}$ 4198$^{12}$ 4571$^{13}$ **>75f<**
**Al Masroor (USA) 2** b c Red Ransom (USA)-Gaye's Delight (USA) (Imperial Falcon (CAN)) 2972$^{10}$ 3615$^{10}$ 4208$^{5}$ **>77f<**
**Almaty (IRE) 3** b c Dancing Dissident (USA)-Almaaseh (IRE) (Dancing Brave (USA)) 1911a$^{4}$ 2115$^{3}$ 3126$^{11}$ **>115f<**
**Almi Ad (USA) 2** b f Silver Hawk (USA)-Mashaarif (USA) (Mr Prospector (USA)) 4564$^{2}$ 4861$^{4}$ **>75f<**
**Al Mohaajir (USA) 5** ch h Cadeaux Genereux-Lady in White (Shareef Dancer (USA)) 1252a$^{2}$ 1575a$^{7}$ 1938a$^{3}$ 2839a$^{4}$ 4396a$^{4}$ **>110f<**
**Almond Rock 4** b g Soviet Star (USA)-Banket (Glint of Gold) *809$^{2}$* 3516$^{2}$ (3842) 4290a$^{5}$ 4568$^{36}$ **>105f<**
**Al Muallim (USA) 2** b c Theatrical-Gerri N Jo Go (USA) (Top Command (USA)) 4547$^{4}$ (4751) **>70f<**
**Almuhimm (USA) 4** b g Diesis-Abeesh (USA) (Nijinsky (CAN)) 842$^{3}$ 1045$^{2}$ 1442$^{5}$ (2134) (2328) 2623$^{4}$ 3158$^{7}$ 3445$^{11}$ 4196$^{6}$ 4444$^{8}$ **>90f<**
**Almuhtaram 4** b g Rambo Dancer (CAN)-Mrs Mainwaring (FR) (Home Guard (USA)) **1995:** *(4526)* **1996:** *18$^{4}$ 132$^{2}$ 233$^{2}$ 306$^{5}$ 439$^{4}$* 2203$^{4}$ 2378$^{7}$ 2613$^{4}$ (2776) 3000$^{4}$ 3113$^{8}$ 3412$^{2}$ 3819$^{3}$ 4427$^{D}$ 4753$^{2}$ *4894$^{2}$* **>79a 78f<**
**Almushtarak (IRE) 3** b c Fairy King (USA)-Exciting (Mill Reef (USA)) (1615) 1796$^{3}$ 2050$^{4}$ (2704) 3083$^{8}$ **>113f<**
**Al Nufooth (IRE) 4** b g Green Desert (USA)-Reine Maid (USA) (Mr Prospector (USA)) 1334$^{12}$ **>92f<**
**Alphabet 2** b f Saddlers' Hall (IRE)-A-to-Z (IRE) (Ahonoora) 4052$^{2}$ 4211$^{2}$ 4608$^{7}$ **>78f<**
**Alphabet Soup (USA) 5** ro h Cozzene (USA)-Illiterate (USA) (Arts And Letters) (4956a) **>132f<**
**Alpha Plus (USA) 2** dk c Mr Prospector (USA)-Danzante (USA) (Danzig (USA)) 3032a$^{2}$ (4029a) 4415a$^{2}$ **>95f<**
**Alpheton Prince 3** b g Prince of Cill Dara-Batsam Lady (Battle Hymn) **1995:** *4408$^{13}$ 4485$^{6}$* **1996:** *46$^{8}$ 271$^{8}$ 637$^{5}$* 1067$^{11}$ **>34a 45f<**
**Alpine Hideaway (IRE) 3** b c Tirol-Arbour (USA) (Graustark) 566$^{2}$ 755$^{2}$ 987$^{9}$ 1171$^{2}$ 1901$^{13}$ 2532$^{3}$ 3519$^{2}$ 4044$^{5}$ 4591$^{6}$ (4693) 4975$^{28}$ **>77f<**
**Alpine Joker 3** b g Tirol-Whitstar (Whitstead) 660$^{3}$ 851$^{5}$ 914$^{2}$ 1025$^{3}$ **>64f<**
**Alpine Music (IRE) 2** b g Tirol-Holy Devotion (Commanche Run) 4127$^{17}$ 4475$^{11}$ **>40f<**
**Alpine Panther (IRE) 3** b c Tirol-Kentucky Wildcat (Be My Guest (USA)) 448$^{6}$ 583$^{11}$ 669$^{7}$ 1089$^{3}$ 1345$^{3}$ **>68f<**
**Alpine Storm (IRE) 4** b f Al Hareb (USA)-Alpine Dance (USA) (Apalachee (USA)) **1995:** *4420$^{6}$ 4507$^{3}$* **1996:** *54$^{4}$ 85$^{3}$ 154$^{4}$ 275$^{4}$* **>35a 44f<**
**Alpine Time (IRE) 2** b f Tirol-Millie Musique (Miller's Mate) (1036) 1419$^{2}$ (1831) 2063$^{4}$ **>82f<**
**Alpine Twist (USA) 3** b f Seattle Dancer (USA)-Polar Bird (Thatching) (648) 966$^{9}$ 1481$^{2}$ **>97f<**
**Alpride (IRE) 5** b m Alzao (USA)-Roberts Pride (Roberto (USA)) 3907a$^{3}$ **>119f<**
**Alrayyih (USA) 3** b br c Mr Prospector (USA)-Cheval Volant (USA) (Kris S (USA)) 1690$^{5}$ 3226$^{3}$ 3519$^{4}$ 4053$^{9}$ **>60f<**
**Alreeh (IRE) 3** b f Priolo (USA)-Fleeting (USA) (Lear Fan (USA)) 873$^{6}$ 1155$^{3}$ (1504) 1883$^{3}$ 2246$^{2}$ (2486) **>83f<**
**Al Reet (IRE) 5** b m Alzao (USA)-Reet Petite (Thatching) 455$^{7}$ 610$^{18}$ 876$^{23}$ 1322$^{9}$ 1799$^{9}$ 4975$^{25}$ **>67f<**
**Alriffa 5** b h Danehill (USA)-Sweet Soprano (High Line) **1996:** *4403a$^{6}$* ***>116f<*** **(DEAD)**
**Alsahah (IRE) 3** b f Unfuwain (USA)-Princess Sucree (USA) (Roberto (USA)) 3441$^{6}$ **>67f<**
**Alsahib (USA) 3** b g Slew O' Gold (USA)-Khwlah (USA) (Best Turn (USA)) 892$^{10}$ 1434$^{5}$ 2027$^{4}$ 4582$^{7}$ 4682$^{2}$ 4974$^{23}$ **>73f<**
**Al's Alibi 3** b c Alzao (USA)-Lady Kris (IRE) (Kris) 447$^{6}$ 593$^{5}$ (731) 1002$^{7}$ 1175$^{5}$ **>81f<**
**Al Shaati (FR) 6** b m Lead on Time (USA)-With You All (Free Round (USA)) **1995:** *4484$^{6}$ 4502$^{9}$* **1996:** *41$^{8}$ 120$^{8}$ 273$^{10}$ 3686$^{8}$* 4130$^{4}$ **>30a 35f<**
**Al Shadeedah (USA) 3** br f Nureyev (USA)-Copperama (AUS) (Comeram (FR)) 1181$^{6}$ (2188) 2621$^{17}$ 4238$^{4}$ **>90f<**
**Al Shafa 3** b c Midyan (USA)-Thundercloud (Electric) 575$^{7}$ (701) 937$^{4}$ 1432$^{8}$ (2001) 2608$^{2}$ 3145$^{12}$ 3691$^{14}$ 4385$^{10}$ **>101f<**
**Altamura (USA) 3** b f El Gran Senor (USA)-Narwala (Darshaan) *1359$^{3}$* (3298) (3497) 3836$^{4}$ (4467) 4678$^{5}$ 5025a$^{6}$ **>115f<**
**Alte Kunst (IRE) 2** 4035a$^{5}$ **>75f<**
**Altermeera 8** br g Noalto-Mac's Melody (Wollow) 753$^{16}$ **>4f<**
**Alumisiyah (USA) 2** b br f Danzig (USA)-Mathkurh (USA) (Riverman (USA)) (3282) 3990$^{3}$ **>75f<**
**Alvilde 2** b f Alzao (USA)-Volida (Posse (USA)) 4043$^{5}$ 4357$^{6}$ 4762$^{5}$ **>63f<**
**Alwarqa 3** b f Old Vic-Ostora (USA) (Blushing Groom (FR)) 526$^{11}$ 668$^{6}$ 1317$^{5}$ 1591$^{2}$ (1877) 2204$^{4}$ 3056$^{3}$ 3117$^{7}$ *3600$^{6}$ 4302$^{8}$* (4588) 4794$^{9}$ **>36a 71f<**
**Always Alight 2** ch g Never so Bold-Fire Sprite (Mummy's Game) 869$^{9}$ 3682$^{15}$ *4079$^{11}$ 4783$^{12}$* 4896$^{3}$ 5050$^{3}$ **>24a 59f<**
**Always Aloof (USA) 5** b h Alleged (USA)-Miranda (USA) (Forli (ARG)) 875$^{3}$ 1397a$^{3}$ 2071$^{4}$ 3673$^{2}$ (4167a) 4655a$^{6}$ **>125f<**
**Always Earnest (USA) 8** b g Alleged (USA)-Nettie Cometti (USA) (Giacometti) 1397a$^{5}$ 4655a$^{3}$ 4959a$^{5}$ **>124f<**
**Always Grace 4** b f Never so Bold-Musical Sally (USA) (The Minstrel (CAN)) **1995:** *4371$^{11}$* **1996:** *368$^{6}$ 418$^{5}$ 592$^{5}$* 893$^{15}$ 981$^{8}$ (1536) 1689$^{3}$ 2686$^{11}$ (3096) 3313$^{5}$ 3702$^{6}$ 3989$^{10}$ **>50a 63f<**
**Always Happy 3** ch f Sharrood (USA)-Convivial (Nordance (USA)) 763$^{6}$ 1069$^{14}$ 1687$^{6}$ (2133) **>73f<**
**Always On My Mind 2** b f Distant Relative-Fleur Rouge (Pharly (FR)) 4062$^{4}$ **>69f<**
**Al Widyan (IRE) 4** b c Slip Anchor-Rafha (Kris) 193a$^{12}$ **>108f<**
**Alyportent 2** b c Warning-Alilisa (USA) (Alydar (USA)) 4756$^{15}$ 4913$^{10}$ **>66f<**
**Alzabella (IRE) 3** b f Alzao (USA)-Believer (Blakeney) 719a$^{3}$ (908a) 1335$^{5}$ 2069$^{4}$ 2886$^{4}$

4031a[4] 4114[6] **>100f<**

**Alzanti 3** b c Alzao (USA)-Mumtaz Flyer (USA) (Al Hattab (USA)) 891[3] **>87f<**

**Alzeus (IRE) 3** b c Alzao (USA)-Rentina (Adonijah) 892[2] (1182) **>83f<**

**Alzoomo (IRE) 4** b g Alzao (USA)-Fandangerina (USA) (Grey Dawn II) **1995:** *4506[3]* **1996:** *33[2] 124[3] 333[4] 402[4]* **>74a 73f<**

**Alzotic (IRE) 3** b g Alzao (USA)-Exotic Bride (USA) (Blushing Groom (FR)) **1995:** *4410[4]* **1996:** *775[12]* 995[13] 1418[7] 2397[6] 2627[10] 4321[10] **>70a 40f<**

**Amadour (IRE) 3** b c Contract Law (USA)-Truly Flattering (Hard Fought) 1470[2] 2326[2] 2876[3] 4216[5] (4496) 4626[19] **>72f<**

**A Magicman (FR) 4** dk br c The Wonder (FR)-Ayanapa (FR) (Pharly (FR)) (2271a) 2843a[8] 3573a[6] 4033a[3] 4409a[2] (4857a) **>123f<**

**Amahsan (IRE) 4** ch g Nashamaa-Singing Filly (Relkino) *357[12] 496[10]* 582[25] 750[12] **>8f<**

**Amanita 3** ch f Lead on Time (USA)-Amana River (USA) (Raise A Cup (USA)) 824[10] 1340[11] **>77f<**

**Amaniy (USA) 3** b f Dayjur (USA)-Muhbubh (USA) (Blushing Groom (FR)) 966[6] 3524[8] 4122[9] **>79f<**

**Amarella (IRE) 2** ch f Soviet Lad (USA)-Eight Mile Rock (Dominion) 1871[13] 3159[9] 3787[4] **>62f<**

**Amaryllis (IRE) 2** b f Sadler's Wells (USA)-Heartbreak (USA) (Stage Door Johnny) 4725[4] 4889[3] **>68f<**

**Amaze 7** b g Natroun (FR)-Entrancing (Posse (USA)) *963[7]* *>53f<*

**Amazing Bay 3** b f Mazilier (USA)-Petriece (Mummy's Pet) 1146[9] 2143[10] 2698[2] 3126[12] 3495[2] 3875[7] 4115[2] 4304[3] 4466[15] **>99f<**

**Amazing Grace (IRE) 3** b f Polish Patriot (USA)-Sepideh (Habitat) *921[14]*

***Amazon Princess* 3** b f Inca Chief (USA)-Forest Nymph (Native Bazaar) 2281[W] 4827[15]

**Ambassador (USA) 3** b c Hansel (USA)-Taba (ARG) (Table Play) 448[5] 677[4] 985[6] (1668) (2350) 3145[9] 3689[12] **>100f<**

**Ambassadori (USA) 3** b c Lear Fan (USA)-Czar's Bride (USA) (Northern Dancer) 1090[4] 1359[6] 2135[7] 3594[12] 3983[19] 4216[10] 4550[7] 4598[12] **>50f<**

**Amber Fort 3** gr g Indian Ridge-Lammastide (Martinmas) **1995:** *4383[3]* **1996:** *644[5]* 887[5] 1101[8] 1671[4] 2013[5] *(2325) 2621[13]* 4256[2] 4550[2] 4775[3] (4820) 4975[6] **>66a 80f<**

**Amber Ring 3** ch f Belmez (USA)-Ring of Pearl (Auction Ring (USA)) 813[12] 964[8] 1123[10] 1839[11] 2506[7] 2958[7] **>41f<**

**Ambidextrous (IRE) 4** b c Shareef Dancer (USA)-Amber Fizz (USA) (Effervescing (USA)) **1995:** *4510[11]* **1996:** *221[5] 547[6]* 1019[5] 1418[9] 1544[5] (2024) (2177) 2356[2] 2390[3] 2847[3] 3220[10] 3346[3] 3587[4] 3649[4] 3878[4] 4102[9] **>57a 60f<**

**Ameer Alfayaafi (IRE) 3** b g Mujtahid (USA)-Sharp Circle (IRE) (Sure Blade (USA)) 583[10] 732[8] 978[11] 2501[6] 2705[5] 4186[8] 4702[6] 4785[7] **>55f<**

**Amelanchier 3** ch f Cigar-Frost In Summer (Busted) 1614[16] 1857[6] 2529[6] 2617[13] **>65f<**

**Ameliajill 3** ch f Aragon-Crackerjill (Sparkler) 648[9] 1033[8] 1422[10] 2255[6] 2528[8] 2946[10] 3399[4] 3698[9] **>51f<**

**Amercius 4** ch g Old Vic-Elarrih (USA) (Sharpen Up) 753[17] 872[10] **>9a 35f<**

**American Whisper 2** b c Dixieland Band (USA)-Only A Rumour (Ela-Mana-Mou) 3499[3] 4127[6] **>76f<**

**America's Cup (IRE) 4** b g Fairy King (USA)-Boat Race (USA) (Seattle Slew (USA)) 1235a[5] 2472a[10] 4960a[7] **>107f<**

**Amfortas (IRE) 3** b c Caerleon (USA)-High Spirited (Shirley Heights) 684[7] 830[7] 1180[10] (2116) 2473a[13] **>118f<**

**Amiarge 6** b g Reference Point-Scotia Rose (Tap On Wood) 972[5] 1150[4] 1784[5] 2319[9] 3335[5] 3463[6] 3928[7] 4365[2] (4612) 4794[8] **>55f<**

**Amiarma (IRE) 3** b f Unfuwain (USA)-Chepstow Vale (USA) (Key To The Mint (USA)) **1995:** (4494a) **1996:** 791a[3] 1388a[2] **>98f<**

**Amico 2** b c Efisio-Stormswept (USA) (Storm Bird (CAN)) 3994[14] 4578[9] **>55f<**

**Amid Albadu (USA) 2** b c Sheikh Albadou-Dream Play (USA) (Blushing Groom (FR)) 2353[2] 3349[2] (3919) (4699) **>84f<**

**Amid The Stars 2** b f Midyan (USA)-Celebrity (Troy) 2315[4] 2863[9] **>76f<**

**Amington Lass 3** ch f Cree Song-Millfields House (Record Token) 3999[6] 4219[4] **>68f<**

**Amlah (USA) 4** gr c Storm Bird (CAN)-Old Mother Hubbard (USA) (Al Hattab (USA)) 1816[5] 2341[8] **>64f<**

**Amnesia (IRE) 5** b m Don't Forget Me-Amboselli (Raga Navarro (ITY)) 884[14] 1311[6] 1866[7] 2024[8] 2177[7] **>40a 35df<**

**Amnesty Bay 4** b f Thatching-Sanctuary Cove (Habitat) **1995:** *4388[14]* **1996:** *749[17]* 1121[12] 1468[13] 1893[8] 1979[13] **>44f<**

**Amocachi (IRE) 2** b c Classic Secret (USA)-Cleo Modena (IRE) (Dalsaan) *4024a[23]* ***>65f<***

**Amoeba (IRE) 3** b f Distinctly North (USA)-Lady Ingrid (Taufan (USA)) **1995:** *4375[6]* **1996:** *(517) 606[5] 781[6] 1635[5]* 1885[2] 2139[9] 2212[4] **>62da 60f<**

**Amontillado (IRE) 4** b c Toca Madera-Rosebran Ruby 2472a[17] **>81f<**

**Amor's Princess (USA) 3** ch f Sanglamore (USA)-Paddy's Princess (St Paddy) 3202a[3] **>96f<**

**Amrak Ajeeb (IRE) 4** b c Danehill (USA)-Noble Dust (USA) (Dust Commander (USA)) 679[14] 925[11] 967[6] (1190) 1944a[2] 2053[13] 2248[5] 2724[8] (3691) 3996[9] (4463) 5019a[6] **>111f<**

**Amron 9** b g Bold Owl-Sweet Minuet (Setay) 589[14] 814[6] 956[8] 1588[2] 1781[7] 2005[16] 2329[12] 2421[3] 2725[7] 2911[8] 3937[5] 4246[3] 4312[18] 4805[2] **>61f<**

**Amusing Aside (IRE) 3** ch f In The Wings-Most Amusing (Blushing Groom (FR)) 826[6] 1189[5] 1670[4] 2536[7] 3134[7] *4076[4]* **>62a 70f<**

**Amy 2** b f Timeless Times (USA)-Rion River (IRE) (Taufan (USA)) *984[6]* 1105[5] 1987[P] 2772[W] 3250[9] 3423[12] *3604[10]* **>2a 35f<**

**Amyas (IRE) 2** b c Waajib-Art Duo (Artaius (USA)) 3494[5] 4118[6] (4318) (4614) 4717[8] **>84f<**

**Amy Leigh (IRE) 3** b f Imperial Frontier (USA)-Hollyberry (IRE) (Runnett) 443[5] 559[9] 773[10] 4130[12] 4367[13] 4610[17] 4809[9] **>70a 46f<**

**Amylou 3** b f Dunbeath (USA)-La Chiquita (African Sky) 2492[2] 2680[W] **>31?f<**

**Anabaa (USA) 4** b c Danzig (USA)-Balbonella (FR) (Gay Mecene (USA)) **1995:** 4469a[3] **1996:** (790a) (1056a) (1581a) (2622) (3573a) 4660a[2] **>129+f<**

**Anak-Ku 3** ch c Efisio-City Link Lass (Double Jump) *67[6] 161[2] 241[3] 1671[5]* 2235[2] 2760[3] (2931) 3284[2] **>68a 77f<**

**Analisa (IRE) 3** b f Don't Forget Me-Volnost (USA) 5065a[11] **>84f<**

**Analogue (IRE) 4** b g Reference Point-Dancing Shadow (Dancing Image (USA)) *222[7] 666[16]* ***>38a 66df<***

**Anastina 4** ch f Thatching-Nikitina (Nijinsky (CAN)) *(234) 371[2] (491)* 728[12] 1296a[7] 4308[7] 4445[16] 4820[8] **>75a 79f<**

**Anatomic 2** b f Deerhound (USA)-Bouncing Slew (USA) (Seattle Slew (USA)) *465[9]* 2125[5]

**Anaxagoras 6** b g Mtoto-I'll Try (Try My Best (USA)) 4237[14] *4983[8]* **>20a 35f<**

**Anchor Clever 4** b c Slip Anchor-Mountain Bluebird (USA) (Clever Trick (USA)) 3673[5] 3972[3] 4178[9] **>105df<**

**Anchorena 4** b f Slip Anchor-Canna (Caerleon (USA)) *33[10] 85[6] 169[11] 198[11] 402[13] 508[2]* 690[5] 787[4] (1159) *1487[2] 1803[7]* 2165[8] 2217[3] *2936[13] 3086[4]* **>50a 59f<**

**Anchor Venture 3** b c Slip Anchor-Ski Michaela (USA) (Devil's Bag (USA)) 717[4] 1200[5] 1647[5] *1997[4] 2205[3]* 2505[10] **>54a 67f<**

**Ancient Quest 3** b c Rainbow Quest (USA)-Racquette (Ballymore) *985[8]* 1153[2] 1587[2] 1957[6] **>81df<**

**Andreyev (IRE) 2** ch c Presidium-Missish (Mummy's Pet) 1130[4] (1653) (3931) 4328[4] 4519[8] (4681) 4822[6] **>102f<**

**Android (USA) 3** dk c Riverman (USA)-Action Francaise (USA) (Nureyev (USA)) (1754a) 2276a[3] 3746a[2] 4416a[2] **>120f<**

**Andsome Boy 3** ch g Out of Hand-My Home (Homing) *893[14]* 1099[6] 1464[7] 1594[11] 1891[5] 2180[15] **>21a 48f<**

**Andy Coin 5** ch m Andy Rew-Legal Coin (Official) *3473[9]* 3849[13] 3970[15] **>17f<**

**Anetta 2** ch f Aragon-Pronetta (USA) (Mr Prospector (USA)) 4796[9] 4991[8] **>47f<**

**Aneysar (IRE) 2** 5077a[2]

**Angaar (IRE) 3** b c Fairy King (USA)-Decadence (Vaigly Great) (716) 1006[5] 1628[6] 2301[6] (2968) 3322[2] 3790[4] **>89f<**

**Angel Chimes 3** ch f Most Welcome-Bell Toll (High Line) (917) **>84f<**

**Angel Face (USA) 3** b f Zilzal (USA)- Touching Love (Touching Wood (USA)) 2675[4] 3255[8] 4206[24] **>48f<**

**Anglesey Sea View 7** gr m Seymour Hicks (FR)-Lexham View (Abwah) 563[6] 647[8] 1005[11] 1529[4] 1802[4] 2042[17] 2697[8] 3149[4] 3463[5] 3922[5] 4832[5] 5008[2] **>66f<**

**Angus-G 4** br g Chief Singer-Horton Line (High Line) 613[5] 879[3] 1476[7] 2164[3] (3043) (3447) 3947[2] 4193[2] 4568[3] **>90f<**

**Angus McCoatup (IRE) 3** ch c Mac's Imp (USA)-In For More (Don) **1995:** *4365[4] 4431[2] 4509[5]* **1996:** *448[14]* 992[5] 1435[9] 1707[8] 1986[5] *2303[4] 2672[6] 3089[5] 3354[8] 4076[2] 4336[3] 4693[3] 4781[8]* **>65a 62f<**

**Animagic (IRE) 2** b c Simply Great (FR)-Waterstown Girl 4846a[5] **>96f<**

**Animation 3** ch f Superlative-What A Looker (USA) (Raise A Native) 1301[7] *2168[12] 2752[11]* 3315[5] 3832[W] 4356[W] **>50f<**

**Anistop 4** b c Nomination-Pounelta (Tachypous) **1995:** *(4390)* **1996:** *13[5] 113[2] 333[5] 401[2] 504[7] 520[2] 853[3] 1031[14] 1309[11]* **>69a 55f<**

**Anita's Contessa (IRE) 4** b f Anita's Prince-Take More (GER) (Frontal) **1995:** *4413[4] 4479[7] 4508[5]* **1996:** *893[9]* 1624[10] *2308[3] 3602[8] 4098[13] 4333[6] 4981[5]* **>58a 52f<**

**Anjomajasa 4** b f Teenoso (USA)-Captain Bonnie (Captain James) **1995:** *4350[13]* **>6a 47f<**

**Anjou 4** b g Saumarez-Bourbon Topsy (Ile de Bourbon (USA)) **1995:** *4416[6] (4530)* **1996:** *97[4] 339[5]* **>75a 75f<**

**Annaba (IRE) 3** ch f In The Wings-Anna Matrushka (Mill Reef (USA)) (2036) 3231[3] 3711[5] 4218[5] (4654a) (4856a) **>119f<**

**Anna Soleil (IRE) 3** b g Red Sunset-Flying Anna (Roan Rocket) 560[2] 804[3] **>65f<**

**Annecy (USA) 3** b f Mr Prospector (USA)-Lake Country (CAN) (Caucasus (USA)) 813[8] 1434[3] 2601[7] 3521[5] 4615[5] 4833[11] **>79f<**

**Ann Hill (IRE) 6** ch m Bob Back (USA)-Yuma (USA) (Caro) **1995:** *4448[8] 4474[3] 4516[7]* **>36a 42f<**

**Anno Luce 3** ch f Old Vic-Anna Paola (GER)

(Prince Ippi (GER)) 1750a$^{3}$ 2478a$^{2}$ (4164a) 4542a$^{7}$ **>112f<**

**Ann's Pearl (IRE) 5** br m Cyrano de Bergerac-Pariscene (Dragonara Palace (USA)) *1064$^{3}$* 1501$^{11}$ 1985$^{13}$ 2311$^{6}$ **>77df<**

**Annus Mirabilis (FR) 4** b c Warning-Anna Petrovna (FR) (Wassl) *435a$^{4}$ 1575a$^{3}$* 2113$^{2}$ 2583$^{3}$ 3070$^{5}$ (3798) (4668a) **>87a 121f<**

**Anokato 2** b g Tina's Pet-High Velocity (Frimley Park) 2413$^{6}$ 2792$^{3}$ 3170$^{4}$ 3478$^{3}$ 3792$^{6}$ 4043$^{14}$ 4234$^{3}$ (4424) 4517$^{3}$ **>71f<**

**Anonym (IRE) 4** b g Nashamaa-Bonny Bertha (Capistrano) 451$^{15}$ 610$^{21}$ 718$^{11}$ 827$^{7}$ 1341$^{4}$ 1650$^{5}$ 2047$^{8}$ 2426$^{4}$ (2566) 2874$^{6}$ 3060$^{3}$ 3254$^{6}$ 3854$^{9}$ 4070$^{4}$ 4190$^{4}$ 4439$^{3}$ 4609$^{5}$ 4769$^{5}$ *4979$^{6}$* **>63a 71f<**

**Anorak (USA) 6** b g Storm Bird (CAN)-Someway Somehow (USA) (What Luck (USA)) 2136$^{5}$ 2394$^{10}$ 3309$^{8}$ **>54da 56f<**

**Another Batchworth 4** b f Beveled (USA)-Batchworth Dancer (Ballacashtal (CAN)) **1995:** *4358$^{7}$ 4407$^{3}$ 4447$^{7}$* **1996:** *2129$^{2}$* 2280$^{2}$ 2403$^{7}$ 2745$^{13}$ 3097$^{2}$ 3506$^{7}$ 3864$^{3}$ *4081$^{13}$ 4205$^{2}$* (4610) (4727) 4828$^{2}$ *4996$^{2}$* **>68a 71f<**

**Another Episode (IRE) 7** b g Drumalis-Pasadena Lady (Captain James) *1545$^{8}$* 1865$^{8}$ 2119$^{8}$ 2386$^{9}$ 2523$^{10}$ 2680$^{8}$ **>56a 34f<**

**Another Fiddle (IRE) 6** b g Waajib-Elmar (Lord Gayle (USA)) *2736$^{4}$* ***>73f<***

**Another Monk (IRE) 5** br g Supreme Leader-Royal Demon (Tarboosh (USA)) **1995:** *4489$^{4}$* **>24a 25f<**

**Another Night (IRE) 2** ch c Waajib-Little Me (Connaught) 3499$^{2}$ 3695$^{2}$ 4118$^{3}$ **>77f<**

**Another Nightmare (IRE) 4** b f Treasure Kay-Carange (Known Fact (USA)) 617$^{10}$ 997$^{9}$ 1163$^{7}$ 1545$^{4}$ 1889$^{10}$ 2391$^{7}$ 2421$^{4}$ 2680$^{5}$ 2910$^{2}$ 2962$^{3}$ 3139$^{13}$ (3644) 3680$^{6}$ 3883$^{5}$ (3937) 4058$^{2}$ 4206$^{4}$ 4259$^{6}$ 4430$^{21}$ 4486$^{8}$ 4805$^{8}$ 4881$^{7}$ 5010$^{9}$ **>1a 52f<**

**Anotherone to Note 5** ch g Beveled (USA)-Dame Nellie (Dominion) **1995:** *4362$^{9}$ 4540$^{5}$* **1996:** *43$^{3}$ 90$^{9}$ 179$^{9}$ 246$^{4}$ 299$^{5}$* **>41a 47f<**

**Another Picea 3** b g Picea-Atoka (March Past) 2419$^{5}$ **>9f<**

**Another Quarter (IRE) 3** b f Distinctly North (USA)-Numidia (Sallust) 870$^{8}$ 1155$^{6}$ 1589$^{3}$ *2169$^{4}$ 2297$^{2}$* 2594$^{4}$ 2915$^{2}$ *(3090) (3638)* 4750$^{8}$ **>72a 57f<**

**Another Sky-Lark (IRE) 8** b g Muscatite-Another Deb (African Sky) 2472a$^{5}$ **>88f<**

**Another Time 4** ch g Clantime-Another Move (Farm Walk) *641$^{8}$* 853$^{2}$ 1450$^{6}$ (2068) 2593$^{5}$ (3272) 3856$^{7}$ 4125$^{3}$ 4568$^{4}$ 4826$^{5}$ **>87f<**

**Ansal Boy 4** b c Robellino (USA)-Son Et Lumiere (Rainbow Quest (USA)) *177$^{10}$ 261$^{6}$ 308$^{9}$ 413$^{9}$* **>53a 21f<**

**Ansellman 6** gr g Absalom-Grace Poole (Sallust) 475$^{7}$ 587$^{15}$ (862) 1064$^{6}$ 1473$^{8}$ (2381) 2615$^{2}$ 3216$^{D}$ 3783$^{11}$ 4116$^{8}$ 4452$^{5}$ 4561$^{2}$ 4772$^{7}$ 4869$^{5}$ **>91f<**

**Answers-To-Thomas 3** b g Komaite (USA)-Launde Abbey (Absalom) *1612$^{3}$* 1888$^{9}$ 2215$^{8}$ **>49df<**

**Antapoura (IRE) 4** b f Bustino-Aneyza (USA) (Blushing Groom (FR)) 4643a$^{3}$ **>71f<**

**Antarctic Storm 3** b g Emarati (USA)-Katie Scarlett (Lochnager) 528$^{8}$ 756$^{10}$ (2032) 4724$^{10}$ 4909$^{11}$ **>68df<**

**Antares 2** b c Governor General-Eucharis (Tickled Pink) 848$^{8}$ 975$^{10}$ 1632$^{3}$ 1827$^{9}$ 2781$^{9}$ 2926$^{2}$ 3224$^{9}$ 3448$^{14}$ *3604$^{9}$* **>10a 65f<**

**Antartictern (USA) 6** b g Arctic Tern (USA)-False Image (USA) (Danzig (USA)) *251$^{4}$ 504$^{8}$* 1198$^{12}$ 4904$^{7}$ **>38a 41f<**

**Anthelia 3** b f Distant Relative-Confection (Formidable (USA)) 572$^{9}$ 952$^{2}$ 1187$^{3}$ 1899$^{3}$ 4911$^{5}$ **>105f<**

**Anticolano (IRE) 3** c **1995:** 4424a$^{8}$ **1996:** 1580a$^{13}$

**Antiguan Jane 3** b f Shirley Heights-Dabbiana (CAN) (Fappiano (USA)) **1995:** *4414$^{3}$* **1996:** *813$^{9}$* ***>62a 77f<***

**Antonia Bin (IRE) 3** gr f Sadler's Wells (USA)-Lady Capulet (USA) (Sir Ivor) 2439$^{7}$ 2739$^{3}$ **>56f<**

**Antonia's Choice 2** ch f Music Boy-Mainly Sunset (Red Sunset) 585$^{3}$ (1014) **>72f<**

**Antonias Melody 3** b f Rambo Dancer (CAN)-Ayodessa (Lochnager) *686$^{6}$* (824) 1181$^{7}$ 1628$^{2}$ 2078$^{8}$ 4581$^{15}$ 4687$^{22}$ 4909$^{18}$ **>83f<**

**Any Colour 3** b f Anshan-Council Rock (General Assembly (USA)) 613$^{14}$ *859$^{9}$ 1363$^{14}$* ***>6a 46f<***

**Anytime Baby 4** b f Bairn (USA)-Cindys Gold (Sonnen Gold) **1995:** *(4358) 4407$^{11}$ 4459$^{4}$ 4487$^{4}$* **1996:** *63$^{11}$ 178$^{10}$ 203$^{W}$* **>48a 61f<**

**Anzio (IRE) 5** b g Hatim (USA)-Highdrive (Ballymore) **1995:** *(4421) 4539$^{15}$* **1996:** *55$^{9}$ 121$^{10}$ (185) (451)* 582$^{9}$ (711) (1016) (1911a) 2114$^{17}$ (4115) 4518$^{3}$ 4848a$^{4}$ **>78a 111f<**

**Anziyan (USA) 3** b c Danzig (USA)-Razyana (USA) (His Majesty (USA)) 798a$^{4}$ 3387a$^{3}$ **>102f<**

**Apache Len (USA) 3** br c Rahy (USA)-Shining Skin (USA) (Fappiano (USA)) 894$^{12}$ 1485$^{4}$ 1872$^{6}$ 2549$^{8}$ 3681$^{13}$ 3929$^{2}$ 4125$^{8}$ 4379$^{3}$ 4682$^{10}$ 4866$^{8}$ **>77f<**

**Apache Raider 4** br g Dancing Brave (USA)-Calandra (USA) (Sir Ivor) 1782$^{10}$ **>29f<**

**Apache Star 2** b f Arazi (USA)-Wild Pavane (Dancing Brave (USA)) 4697$^{2}$ (4890) **>81+f<**

**Apartments Abroad 3** b f Prince Sabo-La Graciosa (Comedy Star (USA)) **1995:** *(4538)* **1996:** *11$^{4}$ 123$^{10}$ 262$^{4}$ 344$^{6}$ 376$^{3}$ 1312$^{5}$* 1497$^{8}$ 2345$^{5}$ 2753$^{6}$ 2971$^{14}$ 3166$^{9}$ 4784$^{6}$ *4894$^{13}$* **>52a 42f<**

**Apia (USA) 3** 1751a$^{7}$ **>37f<**

**Apicella 3** ch c Pharly (FR)-Sixslip (USA) (Diesis) 677$^{14}$ 845$^{10}$ **>67f<**

**Apiculate (IRE) 2** b c Exactly Sharp (USA)-Reine de Chypre (FR) (Habitat) 880$^{5}$ 1362$^{6}$ 1543$^{5}$ 2161$^{8}$ 2387$^{2}$ 2850$^{4}$ 2959$^{6}$ 3678$^{6}$ 4223$^{10}$ 4501$^{9}$ **>53f<**

**Apollono 4** b g Cyrano de Bergerac-Daima (Dominion) 633$^{2}$ 1018$^{10}$ 1819$^{7}$ 2206$^{2}$ 2862$^{5}$ 3272$^{5}$ 4121$^{6}$ 4438$^{5}$ 4617$^{5}$ 4831$^{11}$ **>79f<**

**Apollo Red 7** ch g Dominion-Woolpack (Golden Fleece (USA)) **1995:** *4357$^{3}$ 4421$^{7}$ 4456$^{2}$* **1996:** *41$^{10}$ 261$^{3}$ 273$^{4}$ 340$^{3}$ 408$^{9}$ 631$^{3}$* (742) (1074) 1532$^{7}$ *4895$^{7}$* **>62a 63f<**

**Appeal Again (IRE) 3** br g Mujtahid (USA)-Diva Encore (Star Appeal) 509$^{9}$ 688$^{7}$ 784$^{4}$ 849$^{6}$ **>54f<**

**Appealing Skier (USA) 2** b c Baldski (USA)-Jealous Appeal (USA) (Nijinsky (CAN)) *4951a$^{10}$* **>115a f<**

**Appearance Money (IRE) 5** b m Dancing Dissident (USA)-Fussy Budget (Wolver Hollow) *787$^{18}$*

***Applaud (USA) 3*** ch f Rahy (USA)-Band (USA) (Northern Dancer) *4885$^{2}$* ***>106f<***

**Applausi (IRE) 2** b c Bluebird (USA)-Plaidoirie (ITY) (Malacate (USA)) 4745a$^{3}$ **>69f<**

**Apple Brandy (USA) 2** ch f Cox's Ridge (USA)-Channel Three (USA) (Tri Jet (USA)) 4969$^{23}$

**Apprehension 2** b c In The Wings-First Kiss (Kris) (4060) **>84+f<**

**April In Paris 2** b f Inca Chief (USA)-Plectrum (Adonijah) 2343$^{7}$ 3110$^{8}$ **>23f<**

**April Jackson 2** b f Petong-Raintree Venture (Good Times (ITY)) 1413$^{5}$ 1664$^{10}$ 2538$^{9}$ **>48f<**

**April's Joy 3** b f Mazilier (USA)-Ziobia (Tribal Chief) 478$^{4}$ *606$^{11}$ 1039$^{11}$* 2777$^{10}$ 2964$^{7}$ **>51a 31f<**

**April The Eighth 3** b c Statoblest-Miami Melody (Miami Springs) 722a$^{5}$ 1431$^{2}$ 2072$^{10}$ 2436$^{4}$ 3672$^{15}$ 3984$^{12}$ 4194$^{4}$ 4352$^{3}$ 4620$^{3}$ **>97f<**

**Aquado 7** b g Green Desert (USA)-Meliora (Crowned Prince (USA)) *50$^{5}$ 84$^{4}$ 115$^{9}$ 155$^{10}$ 199$^{11}$ 1157$^{6}$* 1423$^{10}$ (1541) 1765$^{2}$ 2005$^{5}$ 2185$^{7}$ 2518$^{5}$ 2757$^{5}$ 2903$^{2}$ 3973$^{8}$ 4058$^{R}$ **>44a 60f<**

**Aqua Star (IRE) 3** br g Village Star (FR)-First Water (FR) (Margouillat (FR)) 1656$^{14}$ 1873$^{11}$ **>48f<**

**Aquatic Queen 2** b f Rudimentary (USA)-Aquarula (Dominion) 4605$^{13}$ 4897$^{15}$ **>19f<**

**Aquavita 2** b gr f Kalaglow-Aigua Blava (USA) (Solford (USA)) 4261$^{13}$ **>47f<**

**Arabian Design 4** b g Shareef Dancer (USA)-Classic Design (Busted) 1701$^{6}$ 2080$^{8}$ 4296$^{12}$ **>49f<**

**Arabian Flight 4** ch c Sayf El Arab (USA)-Smooth Flight (Sandhurst Prince) *836$^{11}$ 883$^{15}$* ***>46f<***

**Arabian Heights 3** ch g Persian Heights-Arabian Rose (USA) (Lyphard (USA)) *458$^{9}$ 529$^{4}$ 662$^{10}$* 1042$^{3}$ 1641$^{7}$ 2066$^{W}$ (2348) 2397$^{9}$ 2866$^{4}$ 3117$^{8}$ 3220$^{11}$ 3589$^{5}$ **>47a 58f<**

**Arabian Story 3** gr c Sharrood (USA)-Once Upon a Time (Teenoso (USA)) 689$^{2}$ (2576) 3145$^{6}$ (3828) (3997) 4465$^{14}$ 4716$^{2}$ **>110f<**

**Araboybill 5** b g Aragon-Floral (Floribunda) *30$^{5}$ 61$^{7}$ 100$^{6}$ 195$^{4}$ 305$^{4}$ 1012$^{2}$* 1661$^{5}$ 1894$^{6}$ 2056$^{11}$ 4603$^{13}$ *4986$^{5}$ 5062$^{9}$* **>52a 58f<**

**Arabride 4** ch f Unfuwain (USA)-Model Bride (USA) (Blushing Groom (FR)) *3945$^{4}$* 4160a$^{4}$ **>106f<**

**Arak (USA) 8** b g Clever Trick (USA)-Twilight Flight (USA) (Quack (USA)) *4237$^{11}$* 4503$^{11}$ *4781$^{10}$* **>34a 45f<**

**Aramon 6** b g Aragon-Princess Mona (Prince Regent (FR)) 3664$^{5}$ **>25f< (DEAD)**

**Arantxa 2** b f Sharpo-Amalancher (USA) (Alleged (USA)) 4825$^{8}$ (5050) **>71+f<**

**Arapi 2** b f Arazi (USA)-Princess Pati (Top Ville) 4514$^{5}$ 4797$^{3}$ (4887) **>75f<**

**Arasong 4** b f Aragon-Songstead (Song) 3774$^{7}$ 3957$^{11}$ *4094$^{7}$* **>44a 59f<**

**Aratikos (GER) 5** b h Konigsstuhl (GER)-Aratika (FR) (Zino) 1138a$^{3}$ **>115f<**

**Aravinda (IRE) 3** b f Superpower-Surmise (USA) (Alleged (USA)) 2399$^{9}$ 2744$^{12}$ **>51f<**

**Arbatax (IRE) 3** br c Mtoto-Caprarola (FR) (Bellypha) 621a$^{2}$ (1057a) 1757a$^{10}$ 3746a$^{7}$ 4293a$^{5}$ **>116f<**

**Arcady 3** b f Slip Anchor-Elysian (Northfields (USA)) **1995:** *4365$^{6}$* **1996:** *863$^{3}$* 1585$^{5}$ 1852$^{8}$ 2202$^{2}$ 2709$^{5}$ 2953$^{3}$ 3283$^{3}$ 3855$^{11}$ (4086) *4332$^{2}$ 4574$^{2}$ 4750$^{3}$ 4894$^{11}$* **>65a 65f<**

**Arcatura 4** b g Beveled (USA)-Bar Gold (Lucky Brief) **1995:** *4372$^{4}$ 4503$^{5}$* **1996:** *18$^{7}$ 817$^{5}$* 1196$^{6}$ 3048$^{3}$ 3466$^{4}$ 3849$^{7}$ 4307$^{18}$ 4882$^{2}$ **>65a 58f<**

**Arc Bright (IRE) 6** b h Trempolino (USA)-Brillante (FR) (Green Dancer (USA)) *4203$^{16}$* 4588$^{11}$ **>73a 56f<**

**Arch Angel (IRE) 3** ch f Archway (IRE)-Saintly Guest (What A Guest) **1995:** *4361$^{12}$ 4389$^{5}$ 4509$^{9}$* **1996:** *46$^{2}$ 89$^{2}$ 123$^{8}$ 258$^{2}$ 329$^{5}$ 344$^{5}$ 404$^{8}$ 3951$^{9}$ 4784$^{11}$* ***>39a 28f<***

**Archello (IRE) 2** b f Archway (IRE)-Golden Room (African Sky) 4228$^{2}$ 4454$^{3}$ **>72f<**

**Arch Enemy (IRE) 3** gr c Archway (IRE)-Rosserk (Roan Rocket) 949$^{6}$ 1429$^{9}$ 1667$^{10}$ 3257$^{18}$ **>62f<**

**Archipova (IRE) 2** b f Ela-Mana-Mou-Anna Comnena (IRE) (Shareef Dancer (USA)) 5031a$^{3}$ **>51f<**

**Arc Lamp 10** b g Caerleon (USA)-Dazzling Light (Silly Season) *418$^{11}$ 534$^{5}$ 592$^{8}$* 704$^{12}$ 991$^{17}$ 1423$^{14}$ **>35a 31f<**

**Arco Colora 2** b f Rainbow Quest (USA)-Bella Colora (Bellypha) 4863$^{5}$ **>57f<**

**Arc of The Diver (IRE) 3** ch g Archway (IRE)-Inner Pearl (Gulf Pearl) 3228$^{7}$ 3591$^{2}$ 3882$^{5}$ 4042$^{5}$ 4317$^{2}$ 4484$^{3}$ 4587$^{2}$ 4726$^{9}$ *4986$^{2}$ 5008$^{4}$* ***>62a 61f<***

**Arctic Fancy (USA) 3** ch c Arctic Tern (USA)-Fit And Fancy (USA) (Vaguely Noble) 932[3] 1407[2] (1782) 2074[16] 2882[2] 3504[7] 3983[9] **>91f<**

**Arctic Romancer (IRE) 3** b c Distinctly North (USA)-Kowalski (IRE) (Cyrano de Bergerac) **1995:** *4383[2] (4453) (4528)* **>84a 79f<**

**Arctic Starry (FR) 4** ch f Star Maite (FR)-Arrow Blue (FR) (Gairloch) 3910a[2] **>79f<**

**Arctic Thunder (USA) 5** b g Far North (CAN)-Flying Cloud (USA) (Roberto (USA)) 1176[5] 1767[6] 2250[3] **>99df<**

**Arctiid (USA) 3** b br c Silver Hawk (USA)-Arctic Eclipse (USA) (Northern Dancer) 1180[4] (1530) 2350[2] 2724[3] **>98+f<**

**Ardent 2** b c Aragon-Forest of Arden (Tap On Wood) 4825[20] **>38f<**

**Ardilan (IRE) 3** dk c Kings Lake (USA)-Akelei (GER) (Orofino (GER)) (904a) 4290a[8] **>96f<**

**Arecibo (FR) 4** ch g Dancing Spree (USA)-Anahita (FR) (Gay Mecene (USA)) *34[8] 111[5] 239[11] 328[4] 426[7] 508[13] 602[6] 752[20]* 1037[15] **>36a 30f<**

**Areed Al Ola (USA) 3** b c Chief's Crown (USA)-Ballerina Princess (USA) (Mr Prospector (USA)) 684[20] **>42f<**

**Areish (IRE) 3** b f Keen-Cool Combination (Indian King (USA)) 1956[7] *2325[7] 2740[6]* 4340[5] *4997[5]* **>42a 34f<**

**Arel (FR) 3** f 2277a[4] **>104f<**

**Aren't We Lucky (IRE) 3** b c Project Manager-Keshia (Buckskin (FR)) 1434[11] 1973[4] 2591[4] 4042[P] 4321[9] **>57f<**

**Arethusa 2** ch f Primo Dominie-Downeaster Alexa (USA) (Red Ryder (USA)) (841) 1143[2] 2070[7] 3707[2] (4065) 4491[5] **>97f<**

**Argyle Cavalier (IRE) 6** b g Simply Great (FR)-Fete Champetre (Welsh Pageant) 3037[14] 4365[15] **>76a 71?f<**

**Ar Hyd Y Knos 2** b f Alzao (USA)-Top Table (Shirley Heights) 3494[9] 4061[7] **>62f<**

**Arian Spirit (IRE) 5** b m High Estate-Astral Way (Hotfoot) *365[7] (474)* 625[2] 852[5] (1091) (1478) 3149[2] (3428) 3772[3] 4794[6] 5008[8] **>44a 63f<**

**Arietta's Way (IRE) 3** b f Darshaan-Captive Island (Northfields (USA) 820[9] 1117[5] 1644[5] 2140[5] **>88f<**

**Arisaig (IRE) 2** ch g Ela-Mana-Mou-Glasson Lady (GER) (Priamos (GER)) 4684[8] 5041[14] **>58f<**

**Arkady (IRE) 5** ch h Tate Gallery (USA)-Veruschka (Lorenzaccio) (3384a) **>74a 68f<**

**Arktikos (IRE) 3** b c Sadler's Wells (USA)-Arctic Heroine (USA) (Arctic Tern (USA)) 1530[7] 1957[4] 2318[6] 2627[12] 2952[3] 3249[10] (3611) 3876[5] 4252[10] **>74f<**

**Arlington Lady 3** b f Prince Sabo-Flitcham (Elegant Air) *488[3] 503[6] 780[6] 1642[11]* 1691[10] 2405[7] **>44a 27f<**

**Arnhem 3** b c Damister (USA)-Baltic Leap (USA) (Northern Dancer) 447[2] 576[3] 985[4] (1153) 2054[8] 2620[3] 3155[3] **>101f<**

**Arnie (IRE) 4** b g Double Schwartz-The Moneys Gone (Precocious) **1995:** *4385[11]* **>10a 42f<**

**Around Fore Alliss 2** b c Reprimand-Artistic Licence (High Top) 3695[5] 4123[5] 4383[8] **>69f<**

**Arriving 2** br f Most Welcome-Affirmation (Tina's Pet) 3454[4] **>55f<**

**Arruhan (IRE) 2** b f Mujtahid (USA)-Wakayi (Persian Bold) (2230) 2770[3] 3990[4] **>81f<**

**Artan (IRE) 4** b c Be My Native (USA)-Cambridge Lodge (Tower Walk) 1948a[4] 2479a[3] 2843a[4] 3395a[6] (3905a) (4290a) (5019a) **>125f<**

**Arterxerxes 3** b c Anshan-Hanglands (Bustino) 583[5] (755) 1843[5] 2160[2] 2630[2] 2907[2] 3322[3] 4136[19] **>87f<**

**Artful Dane (IRE) 4** b c Danehill (USA)-Art Age (Artaius (USA)) 527[11] 1856[4] *2170[7] 2526[8]* 3052[13] (3340) 3501[8] 3991[7] 4186[11] (4329) 4682[5] 4769[3] 4974[6] **>55a 79f<**

**Arthur's Seat 2** b c Salse (USA)-Abbey Strand (USA) (Shadeed (USA)) 3494[14] **>19f<**

**Artic Bay 4** b g Arctic Lord-Galley Bay (Welsh Saint) 1461[5] 1839[7] 2124[6] (2711) 3471[6] 3828[4] 4121[5] (4551) 4669[9] **>78f<**

**Artic Courier 5** gr g Siberian Express (USA)-La Reine de France (Queen's Hussar) 439[5] 647[9] (968) 1792[4] (2401) 2969[4] 3351[2] 3683[5] 4067[3] 4320[2] 4675[15] **>91f<**

**Art Tatum 5** b g Tate Gallery (USA)-Rose Chanelle (Welsh Pageant) *654[12]* **>4a 68f<**

**Arzani (USA) 5** ch h Shahrastani (USA)-Vie En Rose (USA) (Blushing Groom (FR)) 4428[15] 4609[14] 4900[10] *(5003)* **>59a 60df<**

**Asas 2** b c Nashwan (USA)-Oumaldaaya (USA) (Nureyev (USA)) (4492) 4871[9] **>93++f<**

**As Friendly 2** b c Arazi (USA)-Zawaahy (USA) (El Gran Senor (USA)) 3319[10] *4331[3]* **>78a 66f<**

**Ashanti Dancer (IRE) 3** b f Dancing Dissident (USA)-Shanntabariya (IRE) (Shernazar) 1007[8] 1326[6] 1615[6] 1986[4] 3832[4] 4550[16] **>69f<**

**Ashbal (USA) 3** ch c Elmaamul (USA)-Hooriah (USA) (Northern Dancer) 1938a[7] 3021a[4] **>114f<**

**Ashby Hill (IRE) 5** ch m Executive Perk-Petite Deb (Cure The Blues (USA)) (760) 1145[5] 1462[12] (1682) 2000[4] 2574[12] 2784[3] 3205[3] (3496) 3947[6] (4186) (4511) 4974[20] **>75f<**

**Ashdren 9** b g Lochnager-Stellaris (Star Appeal) *255[5] 372[6]* **>32a 36f<**

**Ashgore 6** b g Efisio-Fair Atlanta (Tachypous) **1995:** *4368[8]* **1996:** *(20) 270[11] 311[2] 409[3] 427[2] 513[2] 629[4] 778[3] 956[12]* 4909[12] **>88a 81f<**

**Ashik (IRE) 3** b g Marju (IRE)-Wakayi (Persian Bold) 566[10] 648[13] 2496[12] **>19f<**

**Ashjar (USA) 3** b c Kris-Jathibiyah (USA) (Nureyev (USA)) 709[4] (1172) 1820[5] 2705[6] 3271[3] 3833[6] **>92f<**

**Ashkalani (IRE) 3** ch c Soviet Star (USA)-Ashtarka (Dalsaan) (798a) (1141a) 2039[2] (4165a) 4443[5] **>132f<**

**Ashkernazy (IRE) 5** ch m Salt Dome (USA)-Eskaroon (Artaius (USA)) *1307[10] 1455[7] (3661)* 3993[14] 4130[2] 4372[14] **>50a 47f<**

**Ashover 6** gr g Petong-Shiny Kay (Star Appeal) *(124) 196[4] 612[9]* 3939[12] 3968[5] 4073[14] 4249[11] 4483[7] 4587[3] 4626[6] 4789[11] **>82a 55f<**

**Ashtina 11** b g Tina's Pet-Mrewa (Runnymede) **1995:** *4441[14] 4488[4]* **1996:** *812[16]* 1016[10] 1073[11] 1446[9] 1630[10] 1777[11] **>55a 54f<**

**As-Is 2** b c Lomond (USA)-Capriati (USA) (Diesis) 4245[5] 4451[7] 4807[6] **>61f<**

**Askern 5** gr g Sharrood (USA)-Silk Stocking (Pardao) 690[11] 920[3] 999[13] 1870[2] 2342[3] 2558[3] 2953[2] (3242) (3346) 3710[13] 4176[10] 4326[6] 4484[2] 4753[8] 4900[9] (4993) **>71f<**

**Asking For Kings (IRE) 3** b g Thatching-Lady Donna (Dominion) 146a[13] 192a[4] 289a[3] 322a[8] 471[7] 575[8] 873[16] 1338[2] 1523[4] **>63f<**

**Asmara (USA) 3** b f Lear Fan (USA)-Anaza (Darshaan) 1255a[3] 1567a[8] 2825a[9] 4851a[2] (5015a) **>107f<**

**Aspecto Lad (IRE) 2** ch g Imp Society (USA)-Thatcherite (Final Straw) 4228[14] *4572[7] 4902[9]* ***>44a 32f<***

**Assessor (IRE) 7** b h Niniski (USA)-Dingle Bay (Petingo) 751[2] 1397a[4] 1482[2] 2071[7] 3751a[5] 4134[6] **>117f<**

**Assignment 10** b g Known Fact (USA)-Sanctuary (Welsh Pageant) **1995:** *4464[7] 4521[13]* **1996:** *41[4] 117[12] 133[6] 203[12] 981[19]* 1170[7] 1992[13] 2286[17] **>43a 33f<**

**Assume (USA) 2** br c Known Fact (USA)-Free Spirit (USA) (Avatar (USA)) 1989[2] 2782[2] **>69f<**

**Assumpta 2** b f Superpower-Russell Creek (Sandy Creek) *2371[6] (3604)* **>60a f<**

**Asterita 4** b f Rainbow Quest (USA)-Northshiel (Northfields (USA)) **1995:** 4470a[2] **1996:** 1128[5] 1988[6] 2533[9] 4377[2] 4678[6] 4876[12] **>105f<**

**Asterix 8** ch g Prince Sabo-Gentle Gael (Celtic Ash) *632[13]* 749[10] 983[11] 1196[15] 1449[9] 1658[3] 1890[10] 2185[5] (2344) 2379[2] 2577[12] 2796[7] 2994[8] 3118[4] **>19a 54f<**

**Aston Manor (IRE) 4** b g Cyrano de Bergerac-Mamie's Joy (Prince Tenderfoot (USA)) *41[5] 64[7]* **>61a 70f< (DEAD)**

**Astor Place (IRE) 3** b c Sadler's Wells (USA)-Broadway Joan (USA) (Bold Arian (USA)) 1125[3] 1757a[8] (2144) 3035a[3] **>112f<**

**Astrac (IRE) 5** b g Nordico (USA)-Shirleen (Daring Display (USA)) 679[6] 1107[7] 2114[7] 2497[5] 3232[19] 4466[6] 4687[4] (4917) (5044) **>117f<**

**Astral Invader (IRE) 4** ch g Astronef-Numidia (Sallust) 582[21] 1351[3] 1536[5] 1715[W] 2286[12] 2561[3] 2713[7] 2791[2] 2957[5] 3304[3] 3606[4] 3694[7] 4128[12] **>58df<**

**Astral's Chance 3** ch g Risk Me (FR)-Astral Suite (On Your Mark) *867[14]* 959[7] 1364[15] 1592[8] *2684[4] 3384a[4]* 3686[13] **>40a 42f<**

**Astral Weeks (IRE) 5** ch g Astronef-Doon Belle (Ardoon) (477) 541[2] 619[3] 972[7] 4483[14] **>70f<**

**Astra Martin 3** ch f Doc Marten-Bertrade (Homeboy) 761[11] 890[12] **>26f<**

**Astrojoy (IRE) 4** ch f Astronef-Pharjoy (FR) (Pharly (FR)) **1995:** *4350[8] 4362[11] 4418[W] 4447[8] 4515[14]* **1996:** *33[16]* **>33a 51f<**

**Astrolabe 4** b g Rainbow Quest (USA)-Sextant (Star Appeal) *647[12]* 753[18] 2182[10] **>48f<**

**Ath Cheannaithe (FR) 4** ch g Persian Heights-Pencarreg (Caerleon (USA)) 1314[19] **>4f<**

**Athenian Alliance 7** ch m Ayyabaan-Springaliance (Reliance II) 2345[10] 3258[14] 3339[9] **>19f<**

**Athenry 3** b c Siberian Express (USA)-Heresheis (Free State) (588) (1110) 2054[2] 2620[2] **>112f<**

**Atherton Green (IRE) 6** ch g Shy Groom (USA)-Primacara (Rusticaro (FR)) 2060[3] 2516[3] 2756[8] 4203[18] **>50a 58f<**

**Athinar 4** b f Tina's Pet-Highland Rossie (Pablond) *776[7] 1099[17]* ***>42a 7f<*** **(DEAD)**

**Atienza (USA) 3** ch f Chief's Crown (USA)-Hattab Voladora (USA) (Dewan (USA)) 921[12] 1200[8] 1600[5] 2424[3] 2928[2] *3605[6] 4203[5]* 4496[15] 4612[16] **>30a 57f<**

**Atlantic Desire (IRE) 2** b f Ela-Mana-Mou-Bold Miss (Bold Lad (IRE)) 4100[7] (4349) 4696[2] 4973[5] **>82f<**

**Atlantic Mist 3** ch g Elmaamul (USA)-Overdue Reaction (Be My Guest (USA)) 471[4] 594[D] 731[6] (1100) (1507) 1894[3] 2377[11] 2998[6] 3657[2] 4042[7] 4216[8] **>70f<**

**Atlantic Storm 3** b g Dowsing (USA)-Tatouma (USA) (The Minstrel (CAN)) 577[7] 1301[W] 2760[2] 2987[2] 3609[5] **>70df<**

**At Liberty (IRE) 4** b c Danehill (USA)-Music of The Night (USA) (Blushing Groom (FR)) **1995:** *4481[7]* **1996:** *580[13]* 682[8] 925[6] 1767[8] 2055[3] 2534[8] 2882[9] (3233) 3710[8] 4326[5] 4465[9] 4716[6] 4877[11] **>81a 87df<**

**Atnab (USA) 2** b br f Riverman (USA)-Magic Slipper (Habitat) 4547[8] 4797[8] **>66f<**

**Atomic Shell (CAN) 3** ch c Geiger Counter (USA)-In Your Sights (USA) (Green Dancer (USA)) 3262[12] **>44f<**

**Atraf 3** b c Clantime-Flitteriss Park (Beldale Flutter (USA)) (548) 737[2] 1146[2] (1628) (2072) 3083[9]

3759[2] 4406a[8] 4774[13] >**120f**<

**Attalos 3** ch c Cadeaux Genereux-Messaria (Ile de Bourbon (USA)) 1530[10] 1963[4] >**55f**<

**Attarikh (IRE) 3** b c Mujtahid (USA)-Silly Tune (IRE) (Coquelin (USA)) *1350[5]* 1649[4] 2033[6] 2526[3] >**75f**<

**At the Savoy (IRE) 5** gr g Exhibitioner-Hat And Gloves (Wolver Hollow) **1995:** *4430[3] 4493[10]* **1996:** *42[5] 76[2] 121[14] 168[5] 255[2] 330[2] 347[8] 427[4] 805[3] 896[7] 1030[6] 2056[21]* >***58?a 53f***<

**Atticus (USA) 4** ch c Nureyev (USA)-Athyka (USA) (Secretariat (USA)) 4956a[8] >**122f**<

**Attimo Fuggente (IRE) 3** b c Roi Danzig (USA)-Pepi Image (USA) (National) **1995:** 4424a[11] **1996:** 793a[3] >**87f**<

**Attitre (FR) 2** b f Mtoto-Aquaglow (Caerleon (USA)) 3264[W] 3454[W] 4133[10] (4359) 4565[5] 4973[4] >**83f**<

**Attitude 2** b g Priolo (USA)-Parfum D'Automne (FR) (Sharpen Up) 4233[8] (4698) >**76f**<

**Attribute 2** b f Warning-Victoriana (USA) (Storm Bird (CAN)) 3269[4] 3660[7] 3988[10] 4222[2] 4495[14] >**73f**<

**Attune (FR) 6** ch h Cariellor (FR)-Silver Lightning (FR) (Luthier) (3744a) >**100f**<

**Auckland Castle 5** b g Chilibang-Palace Tor (Dominion) *85[11] 328[15]* >**35f**< **(DEAD)**

**Auction Hall 2** b f Saddlers' Hall (IRE)-Single Bid (Auction Ring (USA)) *1664[8]* 2315[5] 3581[5] 4361[5] 4625[6] >**74f**<

**Aude la Belle (FR) 8** ch m Ela-Mana-Mou-Arjona (GER) (Caracol (FR)) 469[8] 573[11] 666[11] 2401[9] 2697[5] 3037[19] 3476[4] 4426[10] >**51?a 54f**<

**Audencia (IRE) 2** b f Arazi (USA)-Celtic Assembly (USA) (Secretariat (USA)) 3956[4] >**52+f**<

**Audrey Grace 5** b m Infantry-Fair Nic (Romancero) 2285[5] 2605[5] 3167[3] 3443[8] 3991[5] >**33a 51f**<

**Auenadler (GER) 4** b c Big Shuffle (USA)-Auenmaid (Luciano) (1394a) >**114f**<

**Augustan 5** b g Shareef Dancer (USA)-Krishnagar (Kris) **1995:** *4472[10]* **1996:** *1198[15]* 1450[5] 1696[5] 1803[5] 1977[3] 2183[3] 2319[6] 2628[2] 2776[6] 2896[4] (2989) 3318[5] 4900[14] 4993[7] >**64da 63f**<

**Aunt Daphne 2** b f Damister (USA)-Forbearance (Bairn (USA)) 4797[10] >**59f**<

**Aunty Jane 3** b f Distant Relative-Aloha Jane (USA) (Hawaii) 710[2] (1007) 1770[P] 2354[D] 2585[10] 3568a[6] >**99f**<

**Aurelian 2** ch g Ron's Victory (USA)-Rive-Jumelle (IRE) (M Double M (USA)) 2600[11] 2977[3] 3326[4] 4990[14] >**69f**<

**Autobabble (IRE) 3** b g Glenstal (USA)-Almalat (Darshaan) **1995:** *4417[2] 4491[12] 4528[4]* **1996:** *381[7] 471[5] 555[5] 1012[7]* >***57da 45f***<

**Autoberry 3** b g Autobird (FR)-Sister Racine (Dom Racine (FR)) 458[W] 783[W]

**Autofyr 3** br f Autobird (FR)-Fyrish (Mr Fluorocarbon) 539[9] *605[12] 885[7]* >***33f***<

**Autumn (FR) 3** ch f Rainbow Quest (USA)-River Nomad (Gorytus (USA)) *137[9] 245[9]* >**37a 54f**<

**Autumn Affair 4** b f Lugana Beach-Miss Chalk (Dominion) 455[20] 810[8] 1193[13] 2465a[4] 3158[13] 3709[13] >**94f**<

**Autumn Cover 4** gr g Nomination-Respray (Rusticaro (FR)) *487[3] (636)* (747) 879[4] (2000) 2483[9] 2784[2] (3123) 3805[13] (4184) 4463[4] 4568[30] *5002[11]* >**60a 80f**<

**Avant Huit 4** ch f Clantime-Apres Huit (Day Is Done) *1028[14] 2308[13] 2684[9] 4229[11]* >***12a 12f***<

**Avanti Blue 2** b c Emarati (USA)-Dominion Blue (Dominion) 4127[11] 4700[8] >**58f**<

**Avenue Foch (IRE) 7** gr g Saint Estephe (FR)-Marie d'Irlande (FR) (Kalamoun) **1995:** *4503[10]* **1996:** *18[6] 97[8]* >**53a f**<

**Averring (USA) 3** b f Alleged (USA)-Chinguetti (Green Dancer (USA)) 1949a[4] >**112f**<

**Averti (IRE) 5** b h Warning-Imperial Jade (Lochnager) 1621[4] 2114[W] (2498) 2880[7] 4304[6] 4442[10] 4774[14] 4823[5] 5044[16] >**102f**<

**Avinalarf 2** ch f Fools Holme (USA)-Pure Formality (Forzando) (2254) 3057[5] 3343[2] 3962[12] >**61f**<

**A Votre Sante (USA) 3** ch f Irish River (FR)-Mrs Jenney (USA) (The Minstrel (CAN)) 1140a[4] 1949a[9] >**104f**<

**Awaamir 3** b f Green Desert (USA)-Kadwah (USA) (Mr Prospector (USA)) (3640) 3945[7] 4671[4] 4948a[3] >**99f**<

**Awad (USA) 6** b h Caveat (USA)-Dancer's Candy (USA) **1995:** 4471a[5] **1996:** 3912a[2] 4652a[2] 4955a[9] >**125f**<

**Awafeh 3** b g Green Desert (USA)-Three Piece (Jaazeiro (USA)) *780[2] 1490[2] 1721[7] 2158[5] 3089[16] 3628[8]* >**45a 48f**<

**Awash 2** b c Reprimand-Wave Dancer (Dance In Time (CAN)) 5033[13] >**63f**<

**Awasha (IRE) 4** b f Fairy King (USA)-Foliage (Thatching) **1995:** *4451[3] 4543[3]* **1996:** *36[2] 155[3] 178[3] 231[2] (292) (931)* 1199[5] 1446[4] >**65a 66f**<

**Awesome Power 10** b g Vision (USA)-Majestic Nurse (On Your Mark) **1995:** *(4438) 4490[2]* **1996:** *27[6] 145[10] 318[2] (499) 1411[11]* 2192[18] *3435[3] 4107[2] 4894[7]* >**61a 31f**<

**Awesome Venture 6** b g Formidable (USA)-Pine Ridge (High Top) *50[2] 88[2] 127[4] 168[2] 213[8] 259[4] 302[2] 343[2] 368[2] 399[2] 431[3] 479[4] (521) 607[3] 713[8] (778) 991[11] 1029[3] (1094) 1674[3]* 1860[5] 2047[5] 2412[4] 2947[2] 3172[2] 3443[6] 3702[5] 4098[8] 4240[8] 4259[7] 4436[2] 4597[12] >**79a 61f**<

**Awestruck 6** b g Primo Dominie-Magic Kingdom (Kings Lake (USA)) **1995:** *4364[6] 4370[10] 4455[6]* **1996:** *3952[10]* >**30a 46f**<

**Awfully Risky 5** b m Risk Me (FR)-Gemma Kaye (Cure The Blues (USA)) **1995:** *4388[12]* >**36a 50f**<

**Axed Again 4** b f Then Again-Axe Valley (Royben) **1995:** *4372[13]* >**1f**<

**Axeman (IRE) 4** b g Reprimand-Minnie Tudor (Tudor Melody) 2874[7] 2963[4] 3254[7] 3985[22] >**46f**<

**Axford (USA) 3** ch c Woodman (USA)-Timely (Kings Lake (USA)) 687[2] 847[2] 970[3] 3709[18] 4124[3] 4591[3] >**85f**<

**Aybeegirl 2** b f Mazilier (USA)-So it Goes (Free State) 1036[2] 1404[8] 1683[5] 2059[3] 2323[4] (2699) 2965[8] 3975[6] 4207[2] 4364[4] 4717[12] >**71f**<

**Aydigo 3** b g Aydimour-Briglen (Swing Easy (USA)) 4317[7] 4613[9] 4703[10] 5052[3] >**41f**<

**Aye Ready 3** ch g Music Boy-Cindy's Princess (Electric) 473[7] *606[15] 881[4]* 1342[11] 1547[6] 2179[8] 2417[8] 2914[7] 3236[9] >**34f**<

**Aylesbury (IRE) 3** ch c Lycius (USA)-Ayah (USA) (Secreto (USA)) 1235a[4] >**82f**<

**Ayunli 5** b m Chief Singer-Tsungani (Cure The Blues (USA)) *1811[8] 2300[9]* 3500[5] 3710[16] (3968) 4048[2] (4345) (4426) (4483) 4551[3] >**70a 82f**<

**Azizzi 4** ch g Indian Ridge-Princess Silca Key (Grundy) (840) 1623[2] >**105f**<

**Azra (IRE) 2** b f Danehill (USA)-Easy to Please (What A Guest) (1910a) (3018a) 3561a[6] 4027a[4] 4159a[3] 4398a[3] 4642a[4] >**104f**<

**Aztec Flyer (USA) 3** b g Alwasmi (USA)-Jetta J (USA) (Super Concorde (USA)) 3816[3] 4248[4] 4506[8] >**61f**<

**Aztec Traveller 2** b g Timeless Times (USA)-Chief Dancer (Chief Singer) (568) 984[5] 1471[2] (1858) 2063[5] 2595[6] 3408[9] 3523[5] >**69f**<

**Azwah (USA) 3** b f Danzig (USA)-Magic Slipper (Habitat) 962[4] 2529[4] 3518[7] 3844[7] 4788[4] >**69f**<

**B**

**Baaderah (IRE) 4** ch f Cadeaux Genereux-Labwa (USA) (Lyphard (USA)) **1995:** 4425a[2] >**108df**<

**Baaheth (USA) 2** ch c Seeking the Gold (USA)-Star Glimmer (USA) (General Assembly (USA)) 3757[5] 4261[11] >**79f**<

**Baasm 3** br g Polar Falcon (USA)-Sariah (Kris) 1593[6] >**65f**<

**Baba Au Rhum (IRE) 4** b g Baba Karam-Spring About (Hard Fought) 4129[7] 4499[6] 4674[9] 4831[4] 4882[3] >**69f**<

**Baba Thong (USA) 4** b g Nureyev (USA)-Madame Premier (USA) (4651a) >**83f**<

**Babe (IRE) 2** b f Treasure Kay-Nujoom (USA) (Halo (USA)) 4105[6] 4494[15] 4913[14] >**54f**<

**Babinda 3** b c Old Vic-Babita (Habitat) 1015[4] 1580a[10] 3597[4] 3797[5] >**105f**<

**Babsy Babe 3** b f Polish Patriot (USA)-Welcome Break (Wollow) 966[4] 1321[4] 1628[5] 1975[6] (2532) 4314[16] 4552[7] >**100f**<

**Baby Jane 2** b f Old Vic-Sutosky (Great Nephew) 1808[4] 3454[5] 3820[5] >**69f**<

**Babyshooz 3** b f Efisio-Payvashooz (Ballacashtal (CAN)) 1405[14] 2049[16] >**22f**<

**Bacchereto (IRE) 2** b c Danehill (USA)-Berbera (Tierceron (ITY)) 4038a[2]

**Bachelors Pad 2** b c Pursuit of Love-Note Book (Mummy's Pet) 3245[2] (4380) 4555[5] >**96f**<

**Back By Dawn 3** b g Risk Me (FR)-Moonlight Princess (Alias Smith (USA)) *2711[11]* 3505[10] 3785[16] 4603[6] 4827[9] >**53f**<

**Backdrop (IRE) 3** b c Scenic-Knapping (Busted) (763) (1002) 1580a[2] 2054[5] 2330[6] >**112f**<

**Backgammon 5** b g Midyan (USA)-Messaria (Ile de Bourbon (USA)) 941[3] 1336[2] (1767) >**101f**< **(DEAD)**

**Backhander (IRE) 4** b g Cadeaux Genereux-Chevrefeuille (Ile de Bourbon (USA)) *328[9] 517[2] 562[2]* 740[4] *834[5] 1416[12]* 1764[2] 2167[4] 2358[4] 2520[7] 2902[6] 3228[4] 3414[8] 3644[11] >**52a 62f**<

**Back In The Ussr (IRE) 2** ch c Soviet Lad (USA)-Bilander (High Line) 1869[4] 2174[4] 2387[3] 3448[10] >**57f**<

**Backview 4** ch g Backchat (USA)-Book Review (Balidar) **1995:** *4526[12]* **1996:** *60[7] 97[5] 222[3] (333) 392[7] (422) 532[3] 647[5] 1082[3] 2221[4]* 2717[9] >**81a 65f**<

**Backwoods 3** ch g In The Wings-Kates Cabin (Habitat) 566[8] 821[7] 1002[13] 1498[8] 3459[4] *3630[5] (3952) 4563[11]* (4750) (4832) 4919[13] >**65a 71f**<

**Badawi (FR) 6** ch g Script Ohio (USA)-Beautiful Bedouin (USA) (His Majesty (USA)) *60[3] (169) 283[9]* >**54a 42f**<

**Bad Bertrich Again (IRE) 3** b c Dowsing (USA)-Ajuga (USA) (The Minstrel (CAN)) 1751a[9] 2668a[11] (3574a) >**115f**<

**Baddamix (FR) 3** b c Linamix (FR)-Baddaba (FR) (Roi Dagobert) (4031a) >**108f**<

**Badger Bay (IRE) 3** b f Salt Dome (USA)-Legit (IRE) (Runnett) *118[4] 276[2] 377[4] 488[6] 692[14]* 1693[11] 1908[3] 2320[11] 2805[2] 3525[6] 3609[4] >**53a 68df**<

**Badius (IRE) 3** b f Sadler's Wells (USA)-Bay Shade (USA) (Sharpen Up) 957[10]

**Badlesmere (USA) 2** b c Geiger Counter (USA)-Arising (USA) (Secreto (USA)) 4879[2] >**88f**<

**Bad News 4** ch f Pharly (FR)-Phylae (Habitat) *201[6] 645[3]* 979[19] 1416[3] 1691[14] 2313[12] 2716[10] 3257[16] *4982[7] 5060[9]* >**26a 35f**<

**Bag And A Bit 3** b f Distant Relative-Vaigrant Wind (Vaigly Great) 524[9] 591[7] 665[5] (1836) 2026[6] 2411[2] 2777[3] >**57f**<

**Bagby Boy** 4 b g Puissance-Miss Milton (Young Christopher) 2124$^{10}$ 2706$^{6}$ 3274$^{14}$ **>40f<**

**Bag of Tricks (IRE)** 6 br g Chief Singer-Bag Lady (Be My Guest (USA)) *214$^{4}$ 296$^{6}$ 489$^{3}$ (745)* 1011$^{8}$ 1347$^{17}$ 1534$^{3}$ 1839$^{8}$ **>60a 63f<**

**Bagshot** 5 b h Rousillon (USA)-Czar's Bride (USA) (Northern Dancer) **1995:** *4435$^{3}$ 4476$^{3}$* **1996:** *450$^{11}$* 633$^{5}$ 1314$^{4}$ 1506$^{6}$ **>84a 73f<**

**Bahamian Bounty** 2 ch c Cadeaux Genereux-Clarentia (Ballad Rock) 2624$^{2}$ (2951) (3750a) (4519) 4759$^{4}$ **>109f<**

**Bahamian Knight (CAN)** 3 b br c Ascot Knight (CAN)-Muskoka Command (USA) (Top Command (USA)) 736$^{2}$ 918$^{2}$ 1114$^{7}$ (1580a) 2480a$^{8}$ 3124$^{9}$ 3911a$^{9}$ **>113f<**

**Bahamian Sunshine (USA)** 5 ch g Sunshine Forever (USA)-Pride of Darby (USA) (Danzig (USA)) *965$^{2}$* 1482$^{5}$ 2117$^{4}$ 2723$^{4}$ 3972$^{4}$ **>100f<**

**Baher (USA)** 7 b g Damister (USA)-Allatum (USA) (Alleged (USA)) *236$^{2}$ 283$^{4}$ 369$^{3}$ 398$^{4}$ 603$^{5}$* **>50da f<**

**Bahhare (USA)** 2 b c Woodman (USA)-Wasnah (USA) (Nijinsky (CAN)) (2580) (3243) (4179) **>111f<**

**Bahrain Queen (IRE)** 8 ch m Caerleon (USA)-Bahrain Vee (CAN) (Blushing Groom (FR)) *2310$^{7}$* ***>44a 15f<***

**Baileys First (IRE)** 3 b f Alzao (USA)-Maiden Concert (Condorcet (FR)) 714$^{2}$ 785$^{7}$ 1324$^{3}$ 1666$^{6}$ 2536$^{8}$ 2962$^{4}$ 3152$^{4}$ 3256$^{9}$ 3424$^{7}$ 3703$^{11}$ **>74f<**

**Baileys Imp (IRE)** 2 ch g Imp Society (USA)-Best Academy (USA) (Roberto (USA)) 1884$^{7}$ 2219$^{6}$ 4383$^{7}$ **>56f<**

**Baileys Sunset (IRE)** 4 b g Red Sunset-Stradey Lynn (Derrylin) *407$^{10}$ 631$^{2}$* (750) 862$^{9}$ 1307$^{3}$ 1598$^{15}$ **>73a 64f< (DEAD)**

**Bailieborough Boy (IRE)** 2 ch g Shalford (IRE)-Salique (Sallust) 950$^{3}$ 1479$^{3}$ 4318$^{9}$ **>65f<**

**Bailiwick** 3 b g Dominion-Lady Barkley (Habitat) *(171) 220$^{3}$ 314$^{3}$ 515$^{2}$ 1100$^{8}$* 1498$^{10}$ *2086$^{8}$* **>56a 46f<**

**Bairn Atholl** 3 ch f Bairn (USA)-Noble Mistress (Lord Gayle (USA)) 4589$^{9}$ 4784$^{7}$ **>43f<**

**Baize** 3 ch f Efisio-Bayonne (Bay Express) 673$^{12}$ 966$^{2}$ **>103+f<**

**Bajan (IRE)** 5 b g Taufan (USA)-Thatcherite (Final Straw) 3944$^{12}$ 4669$^{14}$ **>70df<**

**Bajan Frontier (IRE)** 4 ch f Imperial Frontier (USA)-Sajanjal (Dance In Time (CAN)) **1995:** *4358$^{8}$ (4484)* **1996:** *63$^{10}$ 139$^{8}$ 587$^{19}$* 704$^{13}$ *1028$^{16}$ 2555$^{7}$ 2748$^{11}$ 3420$^{13}$* **>35a 39f<**

**Bajan Rose** 4 b f Dashing Blade-Supreme Rose (Frimley Park) 814$^{16}$ 1521$^{2}$ (1708) 1974$^{4}$ 2220$^{9}$ 3618$^{3}$ 3946$^{8}$ 4314$^{12}$ 4552$^{2}$ 4687$^{3}$ 4823$^{3}$ 4994$^{14}$ **>94f<**

**Baked Alaska** 2 b f Green Desert (USA)-Snowing (USA) (Icecapade (USA)) (4756) **>89+f<**

**Baker** 3 b g Cigar-Bread 'N Honey (Goldhills Pride) *52$^{7}$ 637$^{11}$* 1009$^{9}$ 1839$^{12}$ **>32f<**

**Bakers Daughter** 4 ch f Bairn (USA)-Tawnais (Artaius (USA)) **1995:** *4385$^{9}$ 4452$^{12}$ 4532$^{3}$* **1996:** *53$^{2}$ 153$^{7}$ 239$^{3}$ 308$^{3}$ 366$^{10}$ 2000$^{3}$* 2313$^{3}$ 2743$^{3}$ (3111) *(3608) 3947$^{5}$* 4125$^{15}$ 4513$^{5}$ **>59a 59f<**

**Bakers' Gate (USA)** 4 b br c Danzig (USA)-Alydaress (USA) (Alydar (USA)) 613$^{8}$ 2128$^{5}$ 2701$^{10}$ **>78df<**

**Bakheta** 4 b f Persian Bold-Vielle (Ribero) **1995:** *4415$^{11}$ 4476$^{11}$* **1996:** *1145$^{3}$* (1486) (1841) 2127$^{3}$ (2246) 2536$^{5}$ **>39a 72f<**

**Bakiya (USA)** 3 b f Trempolino (USA)-Banque Privee (USA) (Private Account (USA)) 2102a$^{5}$ 3021a$^{9}$ **>91f<**

**Balalaika** 3 b f Sadler's Wells (USA)-Bella Colora (Bellypha) (1614) 1899$^{5}$ 2886$^{2}$ 3711$^{7}$ 4218$^{2}$ 4467$^{5}$ 4964$^{4}$ **>106f<**

**Balance of Power** 4 b g Ballacashtal (CAN)-Moreton's Martha (Derrylin) 1073$^{7}$ 1442$^{7}$ 2229$^{11}$ 2981$^{3}$ (3139) 3686$^{11}$ (3861) 3967$^{2}$ 4354$^{6}$ 4682$^{16}$ 4831$^{10}$ **>79f<**

**Balasara (IRE)** 6 ch g Don't Forget Me-Tameen (FR) (Pharly (FR)) **1995:** *4356$^{8}$* **1996:** *879$^{22}$* ***>31a 86f<***

**Balata Bay** 5 ch g Chief Singer-Lets Fall In Love (USA) (Northern Baby (CAN)) 883$^{14}$ 1069$^{15}$ **>49a 28f<**

**Bal Des Sirenes (IRE)** 3 b f Warning-Save Me The Waltz 287a$^{2}$ **>70f<**

**Bal Harbour** 5 b h Shirley Heights-Balabina (USA) (Nijinsky (CAN)) (1817) (2227) 2881$^{4}$ 3749a$^{2}$ 4178$^{5}$ 4371$^{5}$ **>113f<**

**Balinsky (IRE)** 3 b f Skyliner-Ballinacurra (King's Troop) 2393$^{7}$ 3058$^{3}$ 3832$^{7}$ 4693$^{4}$ *4978$^{4}$ 4997$^{3}$* **>56a 58f<**

**Balios (IRE)** 3 b g Be My Guest (USA)-Clifden Bottoms (Wolver Hollow) **1995:** *4480$^{2}$* **1996:** *(197) 348$^{3}$ 594$^{9}$* 738$^{6}$ 2355$^{4}$ *2747$^{2}$ 2922$^{3}$* ***>69a 68f<***

**Bali Paradise (USA)** 2 b g Red Ransom (USA)-Dream Creek (USA) (The Minstrel (CAN)) (958) 1437$^{3}$ 3684$^{6}$ (4303) 4822$^{5}$ **>91f<**

**Bali-Pet** 2 b c Tina's Pet-Baligay (Balidar) *2307$^{6}$ 2750$^{2}$ 2977$^{5}$ 3417$^{9}$ 4694$^{12}$ 4980$^{2}$* **>56a 49f<**

**Bali Tender** 5 ch g Balidar-Highest Tender (Prince Tenderfoot (USA)) 440$^{7}$ 558$^{8}$ **>22a 42f<**

**Ballade Viennoise (FR)** 2 dk f Dancing Spree (USA)-Heracleia (FR) (Kenmare (FR)) (3748a) 4285a$^{3}$ **>94f<**

**Balladoole Bajan** 2 b f Efisio-Rectitude (Runnymede) 2781$^{3}$ 3241$^{2}$ (3464) (4350) 4916$^{3}$ **>82f<**

**Ballad Ruler** 10 ch g Ballad Rock-Jessamy Hall (Crowned Prince (USA)) *54$^{12}$ 240$^{10}$* **>16a 51?f<**

**Balladur (USA)** 3 b c Nureyev (USA)-Ballinderry (Irish River (FR)) (2333) 2608$^{13}$ **>82f<**

**Ballard Lady (IRE)** 4 ch f Ballad Rock-First Blush (Ela-Mana-Mou) 491$^{3}$ 586$^{5}$ 884$^{7}$ *1096$^{10}$ 1665$^{4}$* 2045$^{4}$ 2340$^{7}$ (2428) 2672$^{4}$ (3424) 3680$^{5}$ 4206$^{12}$ 4809$^{5}$ 4888$^{4}$ 4975$^{16}$ **>48f<**

**Ballerina's Dream** 2 b f Suave Dancer (USA)-Our Reverie (USA) (J O Tobin (USA)) 4600$^{10}$ **>33f<**

**Ballet de Cour** 3 b g Thowra (FR)-Chaleureuse (Final Straw) 2062$^{7}$ 2591$^{5}$ 2961$^{4}$ **>49f<**

**Ballet High (IRE)** 3 b c Sadler's Wells (USA)-Marie D'Argonne (FR) (Jefferson) 3209$^{3}$ 3505$^{4}$ 4110$^{2}$ 4362$^{3}$ **>77f<**

**Ball Gown** 6 b m Jalmood (USA)-Relatively Smart (Great Nephew) (925) 1131$^{6}$ 2145$^{8}$ 2502$^{12}$ 3125$^{5}$ 3248$^{4}$ 3447$^{4}$ (3791) 4066$^{6}$ **>106f<**

**Ballpoint** 3 ch c Indian Ridge-Ballaquine (Martinmas) 1615$^{7}$ 2000$^{2}$ 2574$^{19}$ 3165$^{3}$ 3456$^{4}$ (3831) 3981$^{4}$ 4217$^{2}$ 4992$^{10}$ **>82f<**

**Ballydinero (IRE)** 2 b c Ballacashtal (CAN)-Nutwood Emma (Henbit (USA)) 1166$^{9}$ 1537$^{14}$ 2519$^{4}$ 2932$^{5}$ 3848$^{15}$ 4319$^{9}$ 4694$^{5}$ *4980$^{8}$* **>33a 50f<**

**Ballykissangel** 3 ro g Hadeer-April Wind (Windjammer (USA)) *857$^{6}$ 1363$^{16}$* 2154$^{12}$ 3492$^{9}$ 4322$^{12}$ 4474$^{10}$ **>30a 25f<**

**Ballymac Girl** 8 gr m Niniski (USA)-Alruccaba (Crystal Palace (FR)) **1995:** *(4370) 4387$^{9}$ (4449) 4506$^{5}$* **1996:** *19$^{7}$ 97$^{3}$* **>65a 63f<**

**Ballymoney (IRE)** 3 b c Fayruz-Blunted (Sharpen Up) **1995:** *4408$^{3}$ 4461$^{2}$ 4491$^{3}$* **>70a 49f<**

**Ballymote** 2 b g Chilibang-Be My Honey (Bustino) *1404$^{12}$* 1705$^{4}$ 2076$^{2}$ (2781) 3224$^{5}$ 4024a$^{21}$ (4346) **>73f<**

**Ballynakelly** 4 ch g Deploy-Musical Charm (USA) (The Minstrel (CAN)) **1995:** *(4452) (4489)* **1996:** *(38) (2319)* (2707) (2973) (3504) (4327) 4771$^{6}$ **>77+a 90f<**

**Ballyrag (USA)** 5 ch g Silver Hawk (USA)-Dancing Rags (USA) (Nijinsky (CAN)) *114$^{4}$ 235$^{5}$ 284$^{3}$ 384$^{11}$ 440$^{18}$* ***>58da 20f<* (DEAD)**

**Ballysokerry (IRE)** 5 b h Hatim (USA)-Wonder Woman (Horage) *1530$^{17}$* 1860$^{8}$ 2058$^{12}$ *2555$^{9}$*

**Bally Souza (IRE)** 2 b f Alzao (USA)-Cheese Soup (USA) (Spectacular Bid (USA)) 4208$^{10}$ 4363$^{3}$ 4725$^{5}$ **>76f<**

**Balmoral Princess** 3 b f Thethingaboutitis (USA)-Fair Balmoral (Hasty Word) **1995:** *4365$^{9}$* **1996:** *655$^{7}$ 899$^{11}$ 1814$^{8}$ 2751$^{10}$* **>16a f<**

**Baloustar (USA)** 3 b f Green Forest (USA)-Ballerina Star (USA) (Forli (ARG)) 678$^{9}$ 1119$^{14}$ **>63f<**

**Balpare** 3 ch f Charmer-Balinese (Balidar) **1995:** *4383$^{7}$ 4462$^{3}$* **1996:** *131$^{8}$ 1806$^{6}$* 1881$^{7}$ 2209$^{3}$ 2373$^{6}$ 2507$^{12}$ 3257$^{4}$ (3358) 3443$^{4}$ **>56a 52f<**

**Baltic Dream (USA)** 3 b f Danzig Connection (USA)-Ascot Princess (USA) (Vanlandingham (USA)) 833$^{12}$ 2576$^{8}$ 3522$^{9}$ **>60f<**

**Bandit Girl** 3 b f Robellino (USA)-Manx Millenium (Habitat) 1195$^{3}$ 1617$^{8}$ (2235) 2710$^{W}$ 2945$^{6}$ 3167$^{6}$ (3456) 3655$^{3}$ **>76f<**

**Band on the Run** 9 ch h Song-Sylvanecte (FR) (Silver Shark) **1995:** *4482$^{9}$* **1996:** *442$^{6}$* 728$^{6}$ 960$^{3}$ 1112$^{6}$ 1406$^{2}$ 1800$^{4}$ 2497$^{2}$ 3153$^{5}$ 3612$^{12}$ 3933$^{13}$ 4190$^{20}$ 4769$^{21}$ **>66a 80f<**

**Bandore (IRE)** 2 ch c Salse (USA)-Key tothe Minstrel (USA) (The Minstrel (CAN)) 1960$^{5}$ (4253) 4488$^{16}$ **>73f<**

**Bang in Trouble (IRE)** 5 b g Glenstal (USA)-Vaguely Deesse (USA) (Vaguely Noble) 4563$^{2}$ **>66f<**

**Bangles** 6 ch m Chilibang-Vague Lass (Vaigly Great) 1853$^{10}$ 2244$^{7}$ 2561$^{4}$ 3049$^{3}$ 3360$^{3}$ (3652) **>63a 68f<**

**Bankers Order** 2 b c Prince Sabo-Bad Payer (Tanfirion) 1779$^{8}$

**Banneret (USA)** 3 b c Imperial Falcon (CAN)-Dashing Partner (Formidable (USA)) 730$^{7}$ 1301$^{4}$ **>65f<**

**Banzhaf (USA)** 3 ch c Rare Performer (USA)-Hang On For Effer (USA) (Effervescing (USA)) **1995:** *(4414) 4492$^{4}$* **1996:** *(28) (164) 232$^{4}$ 692$^{9}$* 1073$^{5}$ 1327$^{8}$ 1820$^{2}$ 2705$^{3}$ 3210$^{6}$ **>85a 75f<**

**Bapsford** 2 b c Shalford (IRE)-Bap's Miracle (Track Spare) 569$^{6}$ 1622$^{9}$ 1982$^{4}$ 3803$^{5}$ 4049$^{5}$ 4368$^{7}$ 5048$^{9}$ **>61f<**

**Barachois Lad** 2 b g Nomination-Barachois Princess (USA) (Barachois (CAN)) 2850$^{6}$ 3082$^{8}$ 3576$^{6}$ 3879$^{7}$ *(4980)* **>42a 37f<**

**Baranov (IRE)** 3 b g Mulhollande (USA)-Silojoka (Home Guard (USA)) *67$^{5}$ 217$^{2}$ 310$^{5}$ 377$^{2}$ 503$^{5}$ 1518$^{P}$* 1689$^{12}$ (2506) 2736$^{3}$ 2905$^{4}$ 4804$^{8}$ **>61a 72f<**

**Baraqueta** 4 b c Sayf El Arab (USA)-Coqueta (Coquelin (USA)) 974$^{6}$ 1530$^{5}$ 1863$^{3}$ 2366$^{9}$ 2988$^{9}$ 3780$^{14}$ 4070$^{11}$ **>60f<**

**Barato** 5 ch g Efisio-Tentraco Lady (Gay Fandango (USA)) *475$^{3}$* 582$^{8}$ 749$^{3}$ 806$^{7}$ 1040$^{2}$ 1412$^{3}$ 1781$^{6}$ (2029) 2329$^{7}$ 2524$^{2}$ 2911$^{10}$ 3328$^{7}$ 3639$^{7}$ 3973$^{3}$ 4430$^{3}$ (4460) 4805$^{5}$ 4994$^{23}$ **>72f<**

**Barba Papa (IRE)** 2 b c Mujadil (USA)-Baby's Smile (Shirley Heights) 5076a$^{2}$

**Barbara's Jewel** 4 b g Rakaposhi King-Aston Lass (Headin' Up) 2420$^{7}$ 2913$^{6}$ 3425$^{7}$ **>62f<**

**Barbaroja** 5 ch g Efisio-Bias (Royal Prerogative) 455$^{3}$ 580$^{17}$ 988$^{8}$ 1406$^{7}$ **>88df<**

**Barbason** 4 ch g Polish Precedent (USA)-Barada (USA) (Damascus (USA)) *175$^{3}$ (320) 363$^{7}$ 464$^{5}$ 664$^{11}$* 4497$^{5}$ **>58a 53f<**

**Barbed Wire (CAN)** 2 f *4950a$^{12}$* **>30a f<**

**Barbrallen** 4 b f Rambo Dancer (CAN)-Barrie Baby (Import) **1995:** *4351$^{7}$* **1996:** *2945$^{12}$* 3304$^{W}$

3585$^{5}$ 3812$^{14}$ 4212$^{9}$ **>27a 40?f<**

**Bardia 6** b m Jalmood (USA)-Bauhinia (Sagaro) 1088$^{13}$ 1418$^{13}$ 1832$^{5}$ 2136$^{6}$ 2776$^{7}$ *3086$^{9}$ 3412$^{7}$* 3638$^{4}$ **>49f<**

**Bardon Hill Boy (IRE) 4** br g Be My Native (USA)-Star With A Glimer (Montekin) *223$^{4}$ 306$^{3}$ 410$^{6}$ (1066)* 1353$^{2}$ 1700$^{2}$ 2008$^{6}$ 2331$^{2}$ 2612$^{9}$ (3248) 3791$^{4}$ 4120$^{9}$ 4326$^{16}$ **>88a 97f<**

**Bareeq 2** b c Nashwan (USA)-Urjwan (USA) (Seattle Slew (USA)) (3319) 3684$^{7}$ 4056$^{5}$ **>89f<**

**Barford Sovereign 4** b f Unfuwain (USA)-Barford Lady (Stanford) 811$^{4}$ 1439$^{5}$ 2131$^{6}$ ***>77f<***

**Bargash 4** ch g Sharpo-Anchor Inn (Be My Guest (USA)) (479) 592$^{3}$ 662$^{7}$ 718$^{5}$ 935$^{4}$ 1609$^{5}$ 1781$^{9}$ 2426$^{8}$ 4430$^{12}$ *4573$^{6}$* **>38a 65f<**

**Barik (IRE) 6** b g Be My Guest (USA)-Smoo (Kris) 1311$^{10}$ 4808$^{19}$ **>27a 4f<**

**Baritone 2** b c Midyan (USA)-Zinzi (Song) 1424$^{3}$ 1849$^{3}$ 2873$^{3}$ 4878$^{13}$ **>71f<**

**Bark'n'bite 4** b g Reprimand-Tree Mallow (Malicious) 542$^{8}$ 4612$^{5}$ 4794$^{P}$ **>48f<**

**Barlovento (GER) 3** b c Dowsing (USA)-Bebe Eliza (GER) (Esclavo (FR)) 1395a$^{3}$ **>92f<**

**Barnburgh Boy 2** ch c Shalford (IRE)-Tuxford Hideaway (Cawston's Clown) 1038$^{5}$ 1583$^{5}$ 2873$^{6}$ 3250$^{4}$ 3814$^{4}$ **>67f<**

**Barnum Sands 2** b c Green Desert (USA)-Circus Plume (High Top) 3131$^{4}$ (3873) (4213) 4676$^{2}$ 4963$^{2}$ **>106f<**

**Barnwood Crackers 2** ch c Be My Chief (USA)-Tartique Twist (USA) (Arctic Tern (USA)) 1626$^{8}$ (1880) (2759) 3762$^{6}$ 3943$^{6}$ **>59f<**

**Baroness Blixen 3** b f Cyrano de Bergerac-Provocation (Kings Lake (USA)) 2765$^{6}$ **>21f<**

**Baroness Gold 3** ch f Ron's Victory (USA)-Baroness Gymcrak (Pharly (FR)) *1526$^{18}$* ***>37f<*** **(DEAD)**

**Baron Hrabovsky 3** ch g Prince Sabo-Joli's Girl (Mansingh (USA)) 2597$^{8}$ 2859$^{3}$ 3320$^{5}$ *3630$^{11}$ 4373$^{5}$* 4703$^{11}$ **>20a 59f<**

**Baroud d'Honneur (FR) 3** gr c Highest Honor (FR)-Petite Soeur (FR) (Lyphard (USA)) (4416a) **>119f<**

**Barrack Yard 3** b c Forzando-Abbotswood (Ahonoora) 842$^{12}$ 1319$^{10}$ *(1972) 2577$^{5}$ (3089)* **>67a 59f<**

**Barranak (IRE) 4** b g Cyrano de Bergerac-Saulonika (Saulingo) 664$^{9}$ 951$^{3}$ 1512$^{8}$ 2129$^{12}$ 2378$^{14}$ 2902$^{3}$ 3146$^{8}$ 3506$^{4}$ (3624) 3793$^{4}$ 4180$^{20}$ 4342$^{6}$ **>70f<**

**Barrel of Hope 4** b c Distant Relative-Musianica (Music Boy) **1995:** *4427$^{8}$* **1996:** *77$^{3}$ 153$^{6}$ 450$^{14}$* 589$^{2}$ (850) 935$^{3}$ 956$^{13}$ 1186$^{19}$ 4136$^{16}$ 4581$^{4}$ 4688$^{26}$ 4820$^{19}$ **>60a 86f<**

**Barresbo 2** b c Barrys Gamble-Bo' Babbity (Strong Gale) 2211$^{7}$ 2720$^{6}$ 4318$^{4}$ 4586$^{8}$ 4867$^{8}$ **>57f<**

**Barricade (USA) 3** b c Riverman (USA)-Balletta (Lyphard (USA)) 1141a$^{6}$ 4030a$^{3}$ 4664a$^{6}$ **>113f<**

**Barrier King (USA) 2** b c Sovereign Dancer (USA)-Coastal Jewel (IRE) (Kris) 1626$^{2}$ 1892$^{2}$ 2073$^{9}$ (2323) **>74f<**

**Bartok (IRE) 5** b h Fairy King (USA)-Euromill (Shirley Heights) **1995:** *4402a$^{6}$* **1996:** 327a$^{11}$ *378$^{2}$* **>84a 111f<**

**Bashaayeash (IRE) 4** b c Fairy King (USA)-Queen Cake (Sandhurst Prince) 2271a$^{2}$ 3914a$^{3}$ **>117f<**

**Bashful Brave 5** ch g Indian Ridge-Shy Dolly (Cajun) (632) 846$^{13}$ 1680$^{5}$ 2017$^{3}$ 2508$^{7}$ 3146$^{5}$ 3579$^{10}$ 4430$^{17}$ *4573$^{10}$ 4996$^{6}$* **>48a 76f<**

**Bashtheboards 3** b g Dancing Dissident (USA)-Vilanika (FR) (Top Ville) 786$^{W}$ 962$^{9}$ 1359$^{10}$ *1719$^{16}$ 4472$^{10}$* ***>60f<***

**Basic Impulse 2** b c Rudimentary (USA)-Double Finesse (Double Jump) 4817$^{11}$ **>4f<**

**Basman (IRE) 2** b c Persian Heights-Gepares (IRE) (Mashhor Dancer (USA)) 4830$^{9}$ **>51f<**

**Basood (USA) 3** b f Woodman (USA)-Basoof (USA) (Believe It (USA)) 468$^{2}$ 761$^{5}$ 1589$^{4}$ 3703$^{7}$ *4076$^{7}$ 4496$^{4}$* 4752$^{3}$ *4986$^{6}$* **>58?a 61f<**

**Bataleur 3** b g Midyan (USA)-Tinkerbird (Music Boy) 2777$^{8}$ 3100$^{3}$ 3624$^{12}$ (4486) 4860$^{18}$ **>62f<**

**Bathe In Light (USA) 2** ch f Sunshine Forever (USA)-Ice House (Northfields (USA)) 2245$^{6}$ 4233$^{10}$ **>61f<**

**Bathilde (IRE) 3** ch f Generous (IRE)-Bex (USA) (Explodent (USA)) (1111) 2069$^{5}$ 2991$^{3}$ 3711$^{4}$ 4063$^{4}$ **>107f<**

**Bath Knight 3** b g Full Extent (USA)-Mybella Ann (Anfield) **1995:** *4360$^{5}$ 4439$^{U}$ 4485$^{2}$ 4528$^{7}$* **1996:** *40$^{3}$ 119$^{2}$ 175$^{2}$ 241$^{4}$ 355$^{7}$ 2015$^{2}$* 2326$^{6}$ *2689$^{13}$ 3474$^{9}$ 4076$^{11}$* **>46a 59f<**

**Batoutoftheblue 3** br g Batshoof-Action Belle (Auction Ring (USA)) 472$^{4}$ 763$^{5}$ 1600$^{4}$ 1973$^{3}$ 2067$^{4}$ 3249$^{8}$ *(4092) (4332) 4722$^{5}$* ***>73a 64f<***

**Batsman 2** b c Batshoof-Lady Bequick (Sharpen Up) 3581$^{2}$ 4043$^{7}$ **>66f<**

**Battery Boy 4** b g K-Battery-Bonny's Pet (Mummy's Pet) *855$^{8}$ 1411$^{13}$* 1778$^{15}$ 2162$^{8}$ **>30f<**

**Battle Colours (IRE) 7** b g Petorius-Streamertail (Shirley Heights) *518$^{7}$ 688$^{14}$ 776$^{4}$ 884$^{12}$* 1417$^{8}$ 1830$^{7}$ *2081$^{14}$ 2520$^{8}$* 2898$^{5}$ 3410$^{6}$ 3481$^{7}$ 3854$^{7}$ **>49a 41f<**

**Battle Ground (IRE) 2** b g Common Grounds-Last Gunboat (Dominion) 877$^{6}$ 1331$^{3}$ *1489$^{9}$ 3523$^{6}$* 4234$^{9}$ 4715$^{3}$ 4787$^{5}$ 5048$^{7}$ **>10a 69f<**

**Battleship Bruce 4** b g Mazilier (USA)-Quick Profit (Formidable (USA)) 470$^{4}$ 527$^{2}$ 817$^{7}$ 1338$^{3}$ 3825$^{6}$ 3944$^{6}$ **>73a 70f<**

**Battle Spark (USA) 3** b g Gold Seam (USA)-Flick Your Bick (USA) (Bicker (USA)) 730$^{12}$ 934$^{4}$ 1180$^{5}$ 1465$^{3}$ 1627$^{3}$ 2124$^{4}$ *2552$^{11}$* **>36a 72f<**

**Battling Siki (FR) 3** b g Sicyos (USA)-Sweet Suki (FR) (Matahawk) (4947a) **>65f<**

**Baubigny (USA) 2** b c Shadeed (USA)-Pearl Essence (USA) (Conquistador Cielo (USA)) 4306$^{9}$ 4507$^{10}$ 4879$^{5}$ **>75?f<**

**Baujes (IRE) 6** b h Taufan (USA)-Benguela (IRE) (Pampapaul) 1392a$^{3}$ 3917a$^{3}$ **>103f<**

**Baxworthy Lord 5** b g Arctic Lord-Sugar Pea (Bold As Brass) 1465$^{6}$ **>33f<**

**Bay Bob (IRE) 7** b h Bob Back (USA)-Princess Peppy (Pitskelly) *106$^{8}$* **>9a f<**

**Baydah 3** b f Green Desert (USA)-Al Theraab (USA) (Roberto (USA)) 1901$^{9}$ **>60f<**

**Bayford Thrust 2** ro g Timeless Times (USA)-Gem of Gold (Jellaby) 975$^{2}$ (1308) (2317) 2726$^{2}$ 3771$^{5}$ 4723$^{22}$ **>87f<**

**Bayin (USA) 7** b g Caro-Regatela (USA) (Dr Fager) 928$^{20}$ 1178$^{8}$ 1473$^{4}$ 1853$^{2}$ 2329$^{3}$ 2725$^{2}$ (2856) 3219$^{4}$ 3672$^{17}$ 3810$^{7}$ 4198$^{15}$ 4342$^{3}$ 4687$^{21}$ 4765$^{11}$ 4805$^{7}$ (4881) **>78f<**

**Bayrak (USA) 6** b g Bering-Phydilla (FR) (Lyphard (USA)) 816$^{2}$ 886$^{7}$ (1544) 1788$^{3}$ 1839$^{3}$ 2066$^{7}$ 2377$^{3}$ 2549$^{9}$ 2798$^{4}$ 3878$^{7}$ *4092$^{4}$ 4332$^{10}$ 5054$^{14}$* ***>62a 63f<***

**Beacon Hill Lady 3** b f Golden Lahab (USA)-Homing Hill (Homing) 1526$^{13}$ 1828$^{8}$ *3601$^{13}$* **>24f<**

**Beaconscot 2** b f Sheikh Albadou-Model Village (Habitat) 2758$^{3}$ 3663$^{4}$ **>61f<**

**Beacontree 3** ch c Lycius (USA)-Beaconaire (USA) (Vaguely Noble) 974$^{3}$ 1201$^{5}$ **>83df<**

**Beano Script 3** b g Prince Sabo-Souadah (USA) (General Holme (USA)) 3353$^{11}$ 4074$^{W}$ 4456$^{3}$ 4591$^{9}$ **>76f<**

**Bear Hug 3** b c Polar Falcon (USA)-Tender Loving Care (Final Straw) 2579$^{4}$ **>72f<**

**Bear To Dance 3** b f Rambo Dancer (CAN)-Pooh Wee (Music Boy) *276$^{4}$ 381$^{8}$ 1009$^{11}$* ***>39a 40f<***

**Beas River (IRE) 3** b g Classic Music (USA)-Simple Annie (Simply Great (FR)) 453$^{8}$ 676$^{7}$ **>78f<**

**Bea's Ruby (IRE) 2** b f Fairy King (USA)-Beautiful Secret (USA) (Secreto (USA)) 3588$^{4}$ 4578$^{3}$ 4887$^{2}$ **>73f<**

**Beat of Drums 5** b h Warning-Nyoka (USA) (Raja Baba (USA)) **1995:** *(4425a)* **1996:** (1136a) **>118f<**

**Beau Bruno 3** b g Thatching-Lady Lorelei (Derring-Do) 922$^{2}$ 1319$^{13}$ 1438$^{8}$ 1617$^{3}$ *1809$^{3}$ 3406$^{6}$* ***>75a 73f<***

**Beauchamp Jade 4** gr f Kalaglow-Beauchamp Buzz (High Top) *580$^{4}$* (941) (1426) 2055$^{4}$ (2969) 3689$^{2}$ 4114$^{3}$ 4465$^{6}$ **>105f<**

**Beauchamp Jazz 4** ch c Nishapour (FR)-Afariya (FR) (Silver Shark) 455$^{6}$ 680$^{8}$ 1484$^{8}$ 2053$^{7}$ 2544$^{9}$ 3072$^{5}$ 3709$^{7}$ 4194$^{10}$ **>106f<**

**Beauchamp Kate 3** b f Petoski-Beauchamp Buzz (High Top) 1101$^{17}$ 1594$^{12}$ 2376$^{12}$ 2799$^{4}$ 3456$^{5}$ 3852$^{11}$ **>46f<**

**Beauchamp King 3** gr c Nishapour (FR)-Afariya (FR) (Silver Shark) (695) 926$^{5}$ 1574a$^{3}$ 2039$^{4}$ 2546$^{7}$ 3784$^{7}$ **>121df<**

**Beauchamp Knight 3** ch g Chilibang-Beauchamp Cactus (Niniski (USA)) 892$^{8}$ 1142$^{16}$ 2794$^{7}$ **>65f<**

**Beauchamp Lion 2** ch c Be My Chief (USA)-Beauchamp Cactus (Niniski (USA)) 3615$^{16}$ 4204$^{8}$ 4705$^{10}$ **>47f<**

**Beauchief 4** br g Kind of Hush-Firdale Rosie (Town Crier) *401$^{6}$ 426$^{13}$* **>21a 39f<**

**Beauman 6** b g Rainbow Quest (USA)-Gliding (Tudor Melody) *18$^{2}$ 43$^{4}$ 70$^{3}$ 124$^{6}$* **>68a 68f<**

**Beau Matelot 4** ch g Handsome Sailor-Bellanoora (Ahonoora) 853$^{7}$ **>61a 58f<**

**Beaumont (IRE) 6** br g Be My Native (USA)-Say Yes (Junius (USA)) **1995:** *4390$^{4}$ (4475)* **1996:** *70$^{6}$ (184) 222$^{2}$ 979$^{2}$* 1647$^{2}$ 2046$^{5}$ 3983$^{3}$ (4365) (4683) 4862$^{4}$ **>72a 75f<**

**Beau Quest 9** b g Rainbow Quest (USA)-Elegant Tern (USA) (Sea Bird II) **1995:** *4507$^{12}$*

**Beau Roberto 2** b c Robellino (USA)-Night Jar (Night Shift (USA)) 3119$^{3}$ 3837$^{11}$ 4060$^{6}$ 4298$^{7}$ **>56f<**

**Beautiful Ballad (IRE) 3** b f Ballad Rock-Delightful Time (Manado) 548$^{6}$ 959$^{4}$ **>76f<**

**Beautiful Fire (IRE) 2** ro c Selkirk (USA)-Beautiful France (Sadler's Wells (USA)) 4023a$^{3}$ 4398a$^{9}$ **>100f<**

**Beauty To Petriolo (IRE) 3** b f Scenic-Overspent (Busted) (794a) 1396a$^{4}$ 4541a$^{8}$ **>105f<**

**Beau Venture (USA) 8** ch h Explodent (USA)-Old Westbury (USA) (Francis S) *587$^{6}$* 735$^{17}$ 931$^{9}$ (1985) 2156$^{4}$ 2548$^{2}$ 2976$^{6}$ 3338$^{7}$ 3618$^{10}$ 3932$^{12}$ 4180$^{17}$ 4610$^{8}$ 4881$^{2}$ **>69f<**

**Beaver Brook 6** gr g Baim (USA)-Lucky Song (Lucky Wednesday) 982$^{17}$ **>26f<**

**Bebeto (IRE) 3** 3574a$^{6}$ **>69f<**

**Bechstein 3** ch c Rainbow Quest (USA)-Anegada (Welsh Pageant) 730$^{6}$ 1180$^{2}$ 1644$^{8}$ 3398$^{7}$ 4580$^{4}$ 4833$^{5}$ **>84f<**

**Becky Boo 6** b m White Mill-Aber Cothi (Dominion) *520$^{8}$* **>26f<**

**Bedazzle 5** b g Formidable (USA)-Wasimah (Caerleon (USA)) (561) 662$^{6}$ 1001$^{14}$ 1546$^{7}$ 2075$^{2}$ 2313$^{6}$ 2481$^{2}$ 2573$^{7}$ 3592$^{6}$ 3812$^{10}$ **>31a 49f<**

**Bedfort (FR) 6** dk g Damister (USA)-Miss Persia (Persian Bold) 3388a$^{3}$ **>57f<**

**Bedouin Honda 2** b br c Mtoto-Bedouin Veil (USA) (Shareef Dancer (USA)) 2972$^{8}$ **>56f<**

**Bee Dee Best (IRE) 5** b g Try My Best (USA)-Eloquent Charm (USA) (Private Account (USA))

1642$^{3}$ **>40a 41f<**

**Bee Health Boy 3** b g Superpower-Rekindle (Relkino) *780$^{9}$ 857$^{7}$ 1527$^{11}$* (2427) 2778$^{5}$ (3154) 3465$^{2}$ (3758) 4198$^{18}$ 4312$^{9}$ 4881$^{10}$ 5039$^{19}$ **>30a 72f<**

**Beeny 3** b g Lugana Beach-Child Star (Precocious) **1995:** *4383$^{12}$ 4437$^{3}$ 4473$^{11}$* **1996:** *461$^{5}$ 749$^{15}$* 861$^{11}$ 1663$^{7}$ 2286$^{23}$ **>66a 49f<**

**Begger's Opera 4** ch g North Briton-Operelle (Music Boy) **1995:** *4363$^{11}$ 4418$^{8}$* **1996:** *820$^{14}$* 991$^{15}$ 1411$^{12}$ 1691$^{15}$ 1803$^{13}$ 2284$^{13}$ 4427$^{11}$ 4868$^{11}$ **>14a 13f<**

**Begorrat (IRE) 2** ch g Ballad Rock-Hada Rani (Jaazeiro (USA)) 4330$^{4}$ 4494$^{11}$ **>51f<**

**Beguine (USA) 2** br f Green Dancer (USA)-La Papagena (Habitat) 4969$^{7}$ **>75f<**

**Behaviour 4** b c Warning-Berry's Dream (Darshaan) 580$^{14}$ 878$^{2}$ 1112$^{13}$ 1768$^{2}$ 2691$^{3}$ (3071) 3798$^{5}$ 4313$^{3}$ 4757$^{8}$ **>109f<**

**Belacqua (USA) 3** gr f Northern Flagship (USA)-Wake The Town (FR) (Kalamoun) *156$^{6}$ 238$^{7}$ 329$^{9}$ 459$^{4}$ 522$^{4}$ 859$^{10}$ 1503$^{11}$* 1887$^{10}$ *2168$^{9}$ 2563$^{5}$* 3059$^{13}$ 3104$^{6}$ *3422$^{8}$* **>20a 34df<**

**Belbay Star 3** b f Belfort (FR)-Gavea (African Sky) 2048$^{4}$ 2899$^{6}$ 3255$^{7}$ 3578$^{8}$ 4323$^{17}$ 4860$^{8}$ **>49f<**

**Beldray Park (IRE) 3** b br c Superpower-Ride Bold (USA) (J O Tobin (USA)) (467) 539$^{6}$ 1805$^{7}$ 3937$^{17}$ 4109$^{18}$ **>62f<**

**Belfry Green (IRE) 6** ro g Doulab (USA)-Checkers (Habat) (1775) **>100f<**

**Belgravia 2** b c Rainbow Quest (USA)-Affection Affirmed (USA) (Affirmed (USA)) (1130) 2073$^{3}$ 2503$^{4}$ 3143$^{8}$ **>95f<**

**Believe Me 3** b c Beveled (USA)-Pink Mex (Tickled Pink) *574$^{9}$* 694$^{11}$ 1432$^{3}$ 1771$^{4}$ 2041$^{22}$ 2502$^{9}$ 3211$^{9}$ 3445$^{5}$ 3782$^{P}$ **>104f< (DEAD)**

**Belinda Blue 4** b f Belfort (FR)-Carrula (Palm Track) 587$^{9}$ 762$^{2}$ 868$^{10}$ *1455$^{2}$ 1702$^{4}$ 2308$^{5}$ 3416$^{6}$ 3602$^{12}$ 4075$^{22}$* ***>49a 49f<***

**Bellacardia 3** b f Law Society (USA)-Clarista (USA) (Riva Ridge (USA)) 1171$^{7}$ 1876$^{7}$ *2170$^{11}$ 2577$^{16}$* 3985$^{17}$ *4336$^{7}$ 4997$^{6}$* **>40a 61f<**

**Bella Coola 4** b f Northern State (USA)-Trigamy (Tribal Chief) 559$^{13}$ 1876$^{8}$ 2185$^{12}$ 2507$^{8}$ *2636$^{6}$ 2940$^{9}$ 3236$^{2}$* ***>13a 29f<***

**Bella Daniella 2** br f Prince Daniel (USA)-Danse D'Esprit (Lidhame) 3848$^{13}$ 3982$^{20}$ **>24f<**

**Bellaf 2** gr g Belfort (FR)-Gavea (African Sky) 975$^{7}$ 1183$^{6}$ 1607$^{2}$ 2696$^{6}$ 2797$^{6}$ 2926$^{9}$ 3092$^{6}$ **>49f<**

**Bella Michela (IRE) 3** ch f Superpower-Lumiere (USA) (Northjet) 794a$^{14}$ **>75f<**

**Bellaphento 3** b f Lyphento (USA)-Nautical Belle (Kind of Hush) 1104$^{12}$ 2015$^{5}$ **>54f<**

**Bellara** 4 b f Thowra (FR)-Sicilian Vespers (Mummy's Game) *(642)* (944) 3850$^{5}$ 4476$^{8}$ **>28a 68f<**

**Bella Sedona 4** ch f Belmez (USA)-My Surprise (Welsh Pageant) 546$^{4}$ 753$^{11}$ *1095$^{3}$ 1454$^{3}$ 4574$^{12}$* **>64a 61f<**

**Bellas Gate Boy 4** b g Doulab (USA)-Celestial Air (Rheingold) 469$^{2}$ *1601$^{7}$ 1953$^{11}$* 2440$^{7}$ 2885$^{10}$ 3702$^{7}$ 3980$^{7}$ 4249$^{4}$ **>40a 56f<**

**Bella's Legacy 3** b f Thowra (FR)-Miss Lawsuit (Neltino) 949$^{10}$ 1333$^{16}$ 2013$^{10}$ 2286$^{7}$ 2578$^{14}$ 3166$^{3}$ 3458$^{4}$ 3698$^{14}$ **>46f<**

**Bellateena 4** b f Nomination-Bella Travaille (Workboy) **1995:** *4379$^{2}$* **1996:** *851$^{14}$* 1414$^{15}$ 2378$^{13}$ 2577$^{15}$ 4497$^{18}$ 4967$^{16}$ **>49a 38f<**

**Bellator 3** b g Simply Great (FR)-Jupiter's Message (Jupiter Island) 575$^{2}$ 1002$^{4}$ (1407) 1783$^{6}$ 4580$^{3}$ 4804$^{3}$ **>82f<**

**Belle Bijou 2** ch f Midyan (USA)-Pushkar (Northfields (USA)) 5041$^{8}$ **>40f<**

**Belle Dancer 2** b f Rambo Dancer (CAN)-Warning Bell (Bustino) 596$^{10}$ *838$^{8}$*

**Belle's Boy 3** b g Nalchik (USA)-Ty-With-Belle (Pamroy) **1995:** *(4480)* **1996:** *56$^{7}$ 348$^{9}$ 522$^{2}$* (599) 890$^{7}$ *2936$^{8}$ 3872$^{7}$* **>56a 69f<**

**Belle Vue 2** b f Petong-Bellyphax (Bellypha) 950$^{4}$ *(1489)* **>60a 63f<**

**Bellflower (FR) 3** f (719a) 1393a$^{8}$ 4541a$^{7}$ **>97f<**

**Bello Carattere 3** b c Caerleon (USA)-Hyabella (Shirley Heights) 1142$^{12}$ 3788$^{11}$ 4309$^{8}$ **>60f<**

**Bellroi (IRE) 5** b g Roi Danzig (USA)-Balela (African Sky) *2530$^{4}$* (3641) 3801$^{10}$ **>56f<**

**Bells of Holland 3** b f Belmez (USA)-Annie Albright (USA) (Verbatim (USA)) **1995:** *4477$^{6}$* **1996:** *28$^{2}$ 68$^{5}$ 129$^{3}$ 293$^{5}$ 310$^{4}$* **>63da 65f<**

**Bells of Longwick 7** b m Myjinski (USA)-Bells of St Martin (Martinmas) **1995:** *4394$^{12}$ 4413$^{5}$* **>50a 57f<**

**Belmarita (IRE) 3** ch f Belmez (USA)-Congress Lady (General Assembly (USA)) 1631$^{3}$ 1875$^{4}$ 2505$^{3}$ 2961$^{2}$ 3218$^{2}$ 3441$^{4}$ 3983$^{8}$ 4548$^{2}$ 4761$^{5}$ **>77f<**

**Belmontee 2** b c Belmez (USA)-Annie Albright (USA) (Verbatim (USA)) 2335$^{8}$ **>67f<**

**Below The Red Line 3** b g Reprimand-Good Try (Good Bond) *1027$^{11}$ 1497$^{11}$ 3064$^{8}$ 3761$^{18}$* ***>33a f<***

**Bel Promise (IRE) 7** ch m Soughaan (USA)-Linbel (Linacre) *318$^{5}$* **>14a f<**

**Belzao 3** b c Alzao (USA)-Belle Enfant (Beldale Flutter (USA)) 740$^{5}$ 1984$^{4}$ 2235$^{8}$ 4799$^{5}$ 4921$^{4}$ *5001$^{5}$* **>58a 62f<**

**Bemont Park (ITY) 5** br m Love the Groom (USA)-Boscher Queen (Ela-Mana-Mou) **1995:** 4402a$^{7}$ **1996:** 4419a$^{2}$ 4541a$^{10}$ 4858a$^{2}$ 5074a$^{10}$ **>110f<**

**Bemont Track (ITY) 5** b m Love the Groom (USA)-Boscher Queen (Ela-Mana-Mou) (1951a) **>109f<**

**Be My Bird 3** b f Be My Chief (USA)-Million Heiress (Auction Ring (USA)) *11$^{5}$ 25$^{5}$ 89$^{4}$ 171$^{6}$ 280$^{8}$* **>53da 61f<**

**Benatom (USA) 3** gr c Hawkster (USA)-Dance Til Two (USA) (Sovereign Dancer (USA)) (717) 1002$^{5}$ 1407$^{4}$ 2054$^{9}$ (2612) (3155) 3673$^{6}$ 4761$^{8}$ **>101f<**

**Ben'a'vachei Boy 3** gr g Rock City-Vacherin (USA) (Green Dancer (USA)) *118$^{8}$ 281$^{4}$ 463$^{5}$* **>53a 62f<**

**Ben Bowden 3** br g Sharrood (USA)-Elegant Rose (Noalto) 819$^{5}$ 1100$^{18}$ 1594$^{W}$ 2032$^{14}$ 2407$^{5}$ 4252$^{15}$ **>25f<**

**Bend Wavy (IRE) 4** ch c Kefaah (USA)-Prosodie (FR) (Relko) 1319$^{2}$ 2128$^{3}$ (2483) 3158$^{8}$ **>90f<**

**Beneficial 6** b h Top Ville-Youthful (FR) (Green Dancer (USA)) 4410a$^{5}$ 4757$^{9}$ **>105f<**

**Benfleet 5** ch h Dominion-Penultimate (Final Straw) **1995:** *4419$^{2}$* **1996:** *38$^{5}$ 130$^{3}$ 682$^{12}$* 1528$^{7}$ 1792$^{6}$ 2055$^{16}$ 2697$^{11}$ 2973$^{4}$ 3504$^{8}$ 3689$^{13}$ 3983$^{17}$ 4673$^{3}$ 4821$^{4}$ **>88a 84f<**

**Ben Gunn 4** b g Faustus (USA)-Pirate Maid (Auction Ring (USA)) 3995$^{24}$ 4689$^{12}$ 4820$^{12}$ 4975$^{11}$ 5042$^{14}$ **>57f<**

**Benjamins Law 5** b or br g Mtoto-Absaloute Service (Absalom) **1995:** *4350$^{7}$ (4378) 4415$^{3}$ 4432$^{2}$ (4503)* **1996:** *18$^{5}$ 77$^{2}$ (84) 122$^{4}$ 184$^{4}$ 1449$^{6}$* 1685$^{4}$ 1803$^{17}$ 2159$^{5}$ 2573$^{4}$ 2896$^{14}$ **>76a 56f<**

**Benjarong 4** ch f Sharpo-Rose And The Ring (Welsh Pageant) **1995:** *4390$^{14}$* **1996:** *319$^{7}$ 561$^{7}$* ***>48a 48f<***

**Benning (USA) 3** b f Manila (USA)-Belle Pensee (USA) 4613$^{3}$ 4833$^{10}$ **>74f<**

**Benny The Dip (USA) 2** b br c Silver Hawk (USA)-Rascal Rascal (USA) (Ack Ack (USA)) 1960$^{2}$ (2335) (4111) (4462) 4871$^{3}$ **>109f<**

**Ben's Ridge 2** b c Indian Ridge-Fen Princess (IRE) (Trojan Fen) 699$^{9}$ 996$^{3}$ 1869$^{3}$ 2122$^{3}$ *2746$^{4}$ 2923$^{D}$ (3417)* 3678$^{2}$ 3835$^{11}$ (3880) 4471$^{4}$ *5057$^{8}$* **>65+a 80f<**

**Bentico 7** b g Nordico (USA)-Bentinck Hotel (Red God) **1995:** *4392$^{5}$ 4476$^{7}$ 4539$^{6}$* **1996:** *14$^{2}$ 120$^{3}$ 181$^{7}$ 249$^{6}$ 1088$^{7}$* 1807$^{10}$ 1996$^{6}$ *(2170) 2552$^{6}$ 2773$^{5}$* 3274$^{5}$ *3419$^{2}$ 3623$^{16}$* 3703$^{5}$ *4078$^{3}$ 4226$^{6}$* 4337$^{3}$ *4573$^{2}$ 4692$^{2}$* 4915$^{13}$ **>78a 73f<**

**Bentnose 2** b c Saddlers' Hall (IRE)-Blonde Prospect (USA) (Mr Prospector (USA)) 4370$^{10}$ **>57f<**

**Bent Raiwand (USA) 3** b f Cadeaux Genereux-Raiwand (Tap On Wood) 1438$^{11}$ 1667$^{4}$ 2208$^{9}$ 4229$^{9}$ 4592$^{8}$ 4805$^{12}$ *4983$^{10}$* **>22a 52f<**

**Benzoe (IRE) 6** b g Taufan (USA)-Saintly Guest (What A Guest) 475$^{10}$ 610$^{22}$ 814$^{13}$ 991$^{8}$ (1157) 1186$^{2}$ 1974$^{15}$ 2137$^{3}$ 2725$^{3}$ 3055$^{2}$ (3223) 3672$^{13}$ 4314$^{10}$ 4581$^{17}$ 4687$^{20}$ 4909$^{15}$ **>86f<**

**Bequeath 4** ch c Rainbow Quest (USA)-Balabina (USA) (Nijinsky (CAN)) (1863) (2336) 2583$^{5}$ **>120+f<**

**Berenice 3** b f Groom Dancer (USA)-Belle Arrivee (Bustino) 578$^{3}$ 1004$^{6}$ 1409$^{3}$ 1804$^{3}$ 2318$^{2}$ (2869) 4063$^{5}$ 4218$^{2}$ 4567$^{8}$ 5036$^{8}$ **>106f<**

**Berge (IRE) 5** b h Most Welcome-Miss Blitz (Formidable (USA)) **1995:** *(4428)* **1996:** *(86) 135$^{2}$ (255) 338$^{3}$ (500) 592$^{14}$ (2637) (3601)* **>85a 68+f<**

**Berkeley Bounder (USA) 4** b g Diesis-Top Socialite (USA) (Topsider (USA)) 3401$^{6}$ 3939$^{13}$ **>39f<**

**Berlin Blue 3** b g Belmez (USA)-Blue Brocade (Reform) 1530$^{8}$ 1797$^{6}$ 2333$^{5}$ (2570) (2912) 3669$^{9}$ **>86f<**

**Bernard Seven (IRE) 4** b g Taufan (USA)-Madame Nureyev (USA) (Nureyev (USA)) **1995:** *4392$^{14}$ 4520$^{5}$* **1996:** *(61) 132$^{9}$ 181$^{9}$ 312$^{7}$ 410$^{7}$ 920$^{10}$* 1322$^{7}$ 2188$^{2}$ 2526$^{9}$ 3123$^{17}$ 3765$^{7}$ 4354$^{10}$ 4868$^{2}$ **>81a 72f<**

**Berry Bird (IRE) 3** **1995:** 4422a$^{3}$

**Bert 2** b c Mujtahid (USA)-Keswa (Kings Lake (USA)) 3468$^{5}$ 3809$^{10}$ 4386$^{9}$ 4814$^{9}$ **>58f<**

**Beryllium 2** b g Tragic Role (USA)-Flower Princess (Slip Anchor) 2335$^{7}$ 3499$^{8}$ 4060$^{3}$ (4363) 4621$^{3}$ 4792$^{7}$ **>88f<**

**Be Satisfied 3** ch g Chilibang-Gentalyn (Henbit (USA)) **1995:** *4352$^{9}$ 4417$^{4}$ 4519$^{5}$* **1996:** *304$^{2}$ 460$^{5}$ 663$^{11}$* ***>51a 34f<***

**Bescaby (IRE) 5** ch g Dominion Royale-Elegant Act (USA) (Shecky Greene (USA)) *47$^{4}$ 125$^{5}$ 235$^{8}$* **>33a f<**

**Besiege 2** b c Rainbow Quest (USA)-Armeria (USA) (Northern Dancer) (3779) (4056) 4462$^{3}$ 4871$^{4}$ **>105f<**

**Bestelina 2** b f Puissance-Brittle Grove (Bustino) 3105$^{6}$ 3454$^{10}$ **>51f<**

**Best Kept Secret 5** b g Petong-Glenfield Portion (Mummy's Pet) *59$^{4}$ 109$^{6}$ 135$^{6}$ 190$^{9}$ 315$^{5}$ 389$^{3}$ 661$^{5}$* 769$^{2}$ 1020$^{2}$ 1163$^{12}$ 1610$^{5}$ 1685$^{15}$ 2212$^{3}$ 2392$^{3}$ 2672$^{7}$ 2981$^{8}$ 3285$^{7}$ 3304$^{6}$ 4221$^{2}$ 4337$^{11}$ **>55a 62f<**

**Best of All (IRE) 4** b f Try My Best (USA)-Skisette (Malinowski (USA)) *450$^{19}$* 802$^{7}$ 1092$^{3}$ 1585$^{7}$ 2149$^{8}$ 2428$^{4}$ 2679$^{3}$ 2874$^{5}$ *2934$^{10}$ 3426$^{12}$* 4560$^{7}$ 4688$^{5}$ 4909$^{2}$ 5004$^{10}$ *5055$^{2}$* **>58a 68f<**

**Best of Bold 4** ch g Never so Bold-I'll Try (Try My Best (USA)) **1995:** *4450$^{9}$* **1996:** *2550$^{5}$* **>41a 66f<**

**Besweetome 3** b f Mtoto-Actraphane (Shareef Dancer (USA)) 550$^{16}$ **>19f<**

**Beton Lucky (USA) 2** dk c Lucky North (USA)-Beton Gail (ITY) (Maxistar (ITY)) 2667a$^{3}$

**Be True 2** b c Robellino (USA)-Natchez Trace (Commanche Run) 1622$^{10}$ 2702$^{9}$ 3269$^{6}$ 3631$^{3}$ 3962$^{11}$ **>66f<**

**Betterbebob (IRE) 5** b m Bob Back (USA)-Rare

Girl 4643a[21] **>62f<**
**Better Be Sure (USA) 2** ch f Diesis-Nutbush One (USA) 4639a[9] **>67f<**
**Bettergeton 4** ch c Rakaposhi King-Celtic Tore (IRE) (Torus) **1995:** *4481[8]* **>70+a 100f<**
**Better Offer (IRE) 4** b g Waajib-Camden's Gift (Camden Town) 925[8] 1336[5] (3073) 3212[3] 3689[7] (4465) 4771[14] 5046[18] **>111f<**
**Bettynouche 2** b f Midyan (USA)-Colourful (FR) (Gay Mecene (USA)) (643) 1815[3] 2504[5] **>57f<**
**Beveled Crystal 2** ro f Beveled (USA)-Countess Mariga (Amboise) 4061[11] **>53f<**
**Beveled Mill 2** b f Beveled (USA)-Lonely Shore (Blakeney) 4970[10] **>40f<**
**Beverly Hills 3** b f Shareef Dancer (USA)-Debbie Harry (USA) (Alleged (USA)) **1995:** *4443[7]* **>36a 53f<**
**Be Warned 5** b g Warning-Sagar (Habitat) **1995:** *(4392) 4432[4]* **1996:** *554[13]* 876[18] 1192[3] 1588[10] 1958[8] 2228[4] 2376[8] 2860[5] 3442[9] 4788[7] 4994[17] **>85a 67f<**
**Bewitching (USA) 3** ch f Imp Society (USA)-Mrs Magnum (USA) (Northjet) (1639) 2050[3] 2704[3] 3127[11] 3517[6] **>109df<**
**Bewitching Lady 2** ch f Primo Dominie-Spirit of India (Indian King (USA)) 2879[13] 3269[3] 3620[6] 4330[16] 4880[16] **>75f<**
**Bex Hill 4** ch f Grey Desire-Pour Moi (Bay Express) **1995:** *4508[11]* **1996:** *29[8] 57[7] 86[5] 135[9]* **>30a 39f<**
**Beyond Calculation (USA) 2** ch c Geiger Counter (USA)-Placer Queen (Habitat) 3069[4] **>85tf<**
**Beyond Doubt 4** ch f Belmez (USA)-Highbrow (Shirley Heights) 455[13] 925[7] 3073[2] 4114[5] 4487[4] 4675[7] **>88f<**
**Beyond Our Reach 8** br g Reach-Over Beyond (Bold Lad (IRE)) 1893[6] 2192[11] 2556[8] **>52f<**
**Bianca Cappello (IRE) 3** b f Glenstal (USA) - Idara (Top Ville) 3655[9] 3852[12] 4422[7] *5058[9]* **>26a 33f<**
**Bianca Nera 2** b f Salse (USA)-Birch Creek (Carwhite) (3508) (3707) (4159a) 4661a[4] **>106f<**
**Bianca's Son (BEL) 6** ch h Bacalao (USA)-Bianca Girl (McIndoe) 4703[18] 4868[12] *4998[11]* **>17a 22f<**
**Biased View 4** ch g Beveled (USA)-Scenic Villa (Top Ville) **1995:** *4420[12]* **>35f<**
**Biba (IRE) 2** ch f Superlative-Fahrenheit (Mount Hagen (FR)) *1489[8] 3259[21]* 4241[8] **>13a 49f<**
**Bicton Park 2** b c Distant Relative-Merton Mill (Dominion) 4188[11] 4451[11] 4818[4] 5034[8] **>80f<**
**Bid for Blue 5** ch h Primo Dominie-Single Bid (Auction Ring (USA)) 5068a[3] **>92f<**
**Biff-Em (IRE) 2** ch c Durgam (USA)-Flash The Gold (Ahonoora) 996[8] 1583[3] (1632) **>62f<**
**Big Bands Are Back (USA) 4** b g Alleged (USA)-Jetta J (USA) (Super Concorde (USA)) **1995:** *4382[6]* **>62a 68f<**
**Big Bang 2** b c Superlative-Good Time Girl (Good Times (ITY)) 3821[6] 4801[14] **>66f<**
**Big Ben 2** ch c Timeless Times (USA)-Belltina (Belfort (FR)) *1531[8]* (2995) (3436) 3692[4] 3940[3] 4510[5] 4579[5] **>93f<**
**Big River (ITY) 4** c 1135a[9]
**Bigwig (IRE) 3** ch c Thatching-Sabaah (USA) (Nureyev (USA)) 3262[17] 3656[13] **>28f<**
**Bijou d'Inde 3** ch c Cadeaux Genereux-Pushkar (Northfields (USA)) 926[3] 1574a[4] (2039) 2546[2] 3670[3] 4443[6] **>129f<**
**Biko Pegasus (USA) 5** b h Danzig (USA)-Condessa (Condorcet (FR)) **1995:** 4563a[2]
**Bilko 2** gr c Risk Me (FR)-Princess Tara (Prince Sabo) (551) 877[2] **>84f<**
**Billaddie 3** b g Touch of Grey-Young Lady (Young Generation) *(11) 119[3] 277[4]* **>59a 60f<**
**Bill Moon 10** ch g Nicholas Bill-Lunar Queen (Queen's Hussar) 4436[17] **>32da 30f<**
**Billyback 6** b g Absalom-Petit Secret (Petingo) *777[8]*
**Billy Bushwacker 5** b g Most Welcome-Secret Valentine (Wollow) *455[22]* 953[2] 1476[2] 1867[2] 2724[7] 3071[6] 3447[8] 3691[12] 4193[3] 4568[24] **>98f<**
**Billycan (IRE) 2** b c Mac's Imp (USA)-Sassalin (Sassafras (FR)) 2043[10] 2429[6] *2750[7] 2959[10]* 3651[8] **>28a 13f<**
**Biloela 6** ch m Nicholas Bill-Maple Syrup (Charlottown) 787[7] 972[2] **>67f<**
**Binary 3** ch f Rainbow Quest (USA)-Balabina (USA) (Nijinsky (CAN)) 3570a[2] 4654a[10] **>107f<**
**Binba Star (TUR) 6** h 4289a[8]
**Binlaboon (IRE) 5** b or br h Polish Precedent (USA)-Aldhabyih (General Assembly (USA)) 1691[16] **>24a 35f<**
**Binneas (IRE) 2** bb f Roi Danzig (USA)-Lady Celina (FR) (Crystal Palace (FR)) 4024a[20] **>82f<**
**Bin Rosie 4** b g Distant Relative-Come on Rosi (Valiyar) **1995:** 4405a[8] **1996:** 818[4] 2337[3] 2839a[2] (3199a) (3596) 4132[2] 4664a[3] **>121f<**
**Bint Albaadiya (USA) 2** ch f Woodman (USA)-Pixie Erin (Golden Fleece (USA)) (4547) **>67+f<**
**Bintang Timor (USA) 2** ch c Mt Livermore (USA)-Frisky Kitten (USA) (Isopach (USA)) 4670[2] 4770[4] **>79tf<**
**Bint Baladee 2** b f Nashwan (USA)-Sahara Baladee (USA) (Shadeed (USA)) 3756[2] 4133[4] 4875[6] 5033[3] **>84f<**
**Bint Rosie 2** b f Exit To Nowhere (USA)-Butterfly Rose (USA) (Iron Ruler (USA)) 4890[7] **>41f<**
**Bint Salsabil (USA) 3** ch f Nashwan (USA)-Salsabil (Sadler's Wells (USA)) *674[2]* 939[7] 1769[11] (3409) 3916a[2] 4292a[9] 4567[4] **>113f<**
**Bint Shadayid (USA) 3** gr f Nashwan (USA)-Shadayid (USA) (Shadeed (USA)) 939[3] 1567a[12] 3916a[3] 4218[6] **>112df<**
**Bint Zamayem (IRE) 4** b f Rainbow Quest (USA)-Zamayem (Sadler's Wells (USA)) **1995:** *4481[9]* **>44a 80f<**
**Birchwood Sun 6** b g Bluebird (USA)-Shapely Test (USA) (Elocutionist (USA)) *505[16]* 589[16] 814[12] 882[13] 1040[7] 1538[12] 1635[P] **>54f<**
**Birequest 5** ch g Rainbow Quest (USA)-Artic Mistral (CAN) (Briartic (CAN)) 4810[17] **>84a 10f<**
**Birthday Boy (IRE) 4** b g Scenic-Thank You Note (What A Guest) 1514[4] 2148[12] 3584[6] **>57f<**
**Biscay 3** b f Unfuwain (USA)-Bay Bay (Bay Express) 840[3] *3064[4] 3421[4] 4064[8]* 4453[6] **>58a 68f<**
**Bishop of Cashel 4** b c Warning-Ballet Classique (USA) (Sadler's Wells (USA)) 810[9] 3153[2] 3784[2] (4132) 4664a[4] 4718[2] **>122f<**
**Bishops Court 2** ch g Clantime-Indigo (Primo Dominie) 4228[3] (4468) **>78+f<**
**Bisquet-de-Bouche 2** ch f Most Welcome-Larive (Blakeney) 4798[9] 5040[8] **>49f<**
**Bitch 4** ch f Risk Me (FR)-Lightning Legend (Lord Gayle (USA)) *154[9] 239[14] 302[5] 700[10]* **>38a 43f<**
**Bites 3** b f Risk Me (FR)-Sundaysport Splash (Lord Gayle (USA)) *1969[7] 2303[13] 2939[8]* **>19a 48f<**
**Bite the Bullet 5** ch g Ballacashtal (CAN)-Longgoe (Lorenzaccio) **1995:** *4534[13]* **1996:** *1685[13]* 2560[6] **>20f<**
**Bit of Bother (IRE) 3** b g Millfontaine-Mother White (Jukebox) *35[9] 112[4] 194[2] 237[2] (300) (344) 382[3] 415[2] 595[10] 776[2] 1027[5]* **>75da 57f<**
**Bit on the Side (IRE) 7** b m Vision (USA)-Mistress (USA) (Damascus (USA)) *(650)* 1353[7] 4675[11] 4826[4] **>88f<**
**Bitter Moon 5** b m Rambling River-Elitist (Keren) *1847[F]*
***Blaaziing Joe (IRE)* 5** b g Alzao (USA)-Beijing (USA) (Northjet) *4377[6]* 4821[14] **>98?f<**
**Black And Amber 4** ch f Weldnaas (USA)-Palimony (Communication) *337[6] 390[8] 414[3] 592[17]* **>44a f<**
**Black and Blues 10** b g Music Boy-Blackeye (Busted) 2678[7] 2851[12] 3490[2] 4249[19] **>29f<**
**Black Boy (IRE) 7** br g Auction Ring (USA)-Relic Spirit (Relic) *834[4] 1030[11]* **>40a 57f<**
**Black Ice Boy (IRE) 5** b g Law Society (USA)-Hogan's Sister (USA) (Speak John) **1995:** *4387[10]* **>2a 60f<**
**Blackpatch Hill 7** br g Efisio-Myrtlegrove (Scottish Rifle) 825[9] 1426[6] 4580[18] 4615[11] 4753[9] 4993[16] **>47f<**
**Blackwater (USA) 3** b c Irish River (FR)-Fruhlingstag (FR) (Orsini) 1756a[3] 2276a[5] 4664a[7] 4857a[7] **>110f<**
**Black Wood (USA) 3** f 1393a[10] **>74f<**
**Blade Ae (USA) 2** c 3390a[4] **>84f<**
**Blain 5** gr h Roaring Riva-Miss Colenca (Petong) 1309[15] **>33df<**
**Blakenmor 3** b g No Evil-Kinz (Great Nephew) 4129[15] **>25f<**
**Blanchland 7** gr g Bellypha-Premier Rose (Sharp Edge) 1124[5] 2511[4] 2717[12] **>68a 44f<**
**Blane Water (USA) 2** b f Lomond (USA)-Triode (USA) (Sharpen Up) (4061) 4488[6] 4723[4] 4875[9] **>91f<**
**Blasted 4** ch g Statoblest-Apprila (Bustino) **1995:** *4351[6]* **1996:** *27[5] 84[8] 206[7]* **>48a 74df<**
**Blatant Outburst 6** b g War Hero-Miss Metro (Upper Case (USA)) 2181[4] 2439[4] 2706[2] 2876[2] 3521[6] 3933[9] 4499[4] 4719[4] 4901[9] **>82f<**
**Blaze Away (USA) 5** b h Polish Navy (USA)-Battle Drum (USA) (Alydar (USA)) 449[3] 1005[7] 1428[6] 3948[4] 4199[5] 4476[9] 4771[17] **>82f<**
**Blaze of Oak (USA) 5** ch g Green Forest (USA)-Magic Robe (USA) (Grey Dawn II) 650[13] 4125[10] 4237[3] 4337[8] 4603[12] **>56f<**
**Blaze of Song 4** ch c Jester-Intellect (Frimley Park) 809[10] 1469[2] 2053[26] 2603[12] 3430[6] 3765[6] 4329[7] 4432[8] 4568[31] 4769[19] **>77f<**
**Blazing Castle 2** gr g Vague Shot-Castle Cary (Castle Keep) 800[3] *1603[4] (2485)* 2965[7] 3299[2] 3478[8] **>57a 82f<**
**Blazing Imp (USA) 3** ch g Imp Society (USA)-Marital (USA) (Marine Patrol (USA)) 2150[5] 2333[8] 2987[3] 3453[12] **>40f<**
**Blazon of Troy 7** b g Trojan Fen-Mullet (Star Appeal) 1436[5] 1826[3] 2319[5] 2884[6] **>59f<**
**Blending Element (IRE) 3** ch f Great Commotion (USA)-Blue Wedding (USA) (Irish River (FR)) 1573a[4] 2102a[4] **>91f<**
**Blenheim Terrace 3** b g Rambo Dancer (CAN)-Boulevard Girl (Nicholas Bill) 849[15] 1089[4] 1850[4] (2356) 2627[2] 3249[2] 3459[2] 3878[2] 4683[8] **>48a 76f<**
**Blessed Spirit 3** ch f Statoblest-Kukri (Kris) 467[2] 758[3] 1171[4] 1608[2] 2425[6] 2945[2] (3133) 3926[2] 4214[5] 4590[4] **>87+f<**
**Blessingindisguise 3** b g Kala Shikari-Blowing Bubbles (Native Admiral (USA)) 610[8] 1340[4] 2007[14] 2532[4] 3296[16] 4180[11] 4453[12] 4689[5] 4860[21] **>70f<**
**Blockade (USA) 7** b g Imperial Falcon (CAN)-Stolen Date (USA) (Sadair) *1154[8]* 1638[3] 2234[3] (2438) 2885[9] (2981) **>67f<**
**Blomberg (IRE) 4** b c Indian Ridge-Daniella Drive (USA) (Shelter Half (USA)) 679[5] 878[7] (1484) (1768) 2053[31] 3731a[4] 4194[7] 4409a[11] 4757[4] **>113f<**
**Blondane 3** b g Danehill (USA)-Whos The Blonde (Cure The Blues (USA)) *344[12] 390[11]* **>16a f<**

**Blonde Rock** 2 ch f Rock City-Golden Scissors (Kalaglow) 1424[5] 1645[4] 1845[2] **>51f<**

**Blood Orange** 2 ch c Ron's Victory (USA)-Little Bittern (USA) (Riva Ridge (USA)) 3685[12] 4962[5] **>65f<**

**Blooming Amazing** 2 b c Mazilier (USA)-Cornflower Blue (Tyrnavos) 3462[2] 3837[6] 3982[7] 4614[7] **>80f<**

**Bloomsy Babe** 2 b f Batshoof-Mia Fillia (Formidable (USA)) 2025[7] 2519[5] 3105[8] 3576[5] 3769[W] **>43f<**

**Blossom Dearie** 3 b f Landyap (USA)-Jose Collins (Singing Bede) 949[4] 1301[9] 1840[12] 2255[10] **>45f<**

**Blossomville** 3 gr f Petong-Ruthenia (IRE) (Taufan (USA)) 1882[7] 2208[8] 2794[6] 3314[9] *4076[12]* **>13a 54f<**

**Blow Dry (IRE)** 6 b g Glenstal (USA)-Haco (Tribal Chief) 749[22] 882[6] 1040[10] 1196[8] *1966[11] 2391[5]* 3306[14] 4486[7] **>22a 48f<**

**Blowing Away (IRE)** 2 b br f Last Tycoon-Taken By Force (Persian Bold) 4863[8] **>44f<**

**Blown-Over** 2 ch f Ron's Victory (USA)-Woodwind (FR) (Whistling Wind) 3438[6] 3685[8] 4481[6] 4902[5] **>33f<**

**Blow Up (TUR)** 3 f 4289a[6]

**Blue Adelaide** 3 b f Puissance-Dominion Blue (Dominion) **1995:** *4429[14] 4529[7]* **>27a 65f<**

**Blue And Royal (IRE)** 4 b g Bluebird (USA)-Cat Girl (USA) (Grey Dawn II) *4334[6] 4612[18]* ***>37a 35f<***

**Bluebell Miss** 2 b f High Kicker (USA)-Mio Mementa (Streak) 1346[8] (1467) 3467[12] 4049[8] 4883[9] **>71f<**

**Blueberry Fields** 3 gr f Shernazar-Be Easy (Be Friendly) *188[4] 555[2] 1100[8]* 1641[10] **>55a 57f<**

**Blue Bomber** 5 b g Tina's Pet-Warm Wind (Tumble Wind (USA)) 589[13] 1609[3] 1829[9] 2005[18] (2392) (2963) (3278) 3578[9] **>75f<**

**Blue Danish** 2 b f Prince Sabo-Real Party (Realm) (4037a) **>75f<**

**Blue Drifter (IRE)** 7 b g Bluebird (USA)-Sea Swallow (FR) 4537b[6] **>51f<**

**Blue Duck (IRE)** 3 ch g Magical Wonder (USA)-Grave Error (Northern Treat (USA)) **1995:** *4541[5]* **>21a f<**

**Blue Duster (USA)** 3 b f Danzig (USA)-Blue Note (FR) (Habitat) (2919) 3573a[5] 4057[2] **>120f<**

**Blue Flyer (IRE)** 3 b g Bluebird (USA)-Born to Fly (IRE) (Last Tycoon) **1995:** *4461[3] 4509[8] 4528[3]* **1996:** *56[6] 67[2] (188) (232) 352[2] 692[5]* 1615[12] (3696) 4064[11] 4212[5] 4254[3] 4682[17] *5002[13]* **>78a 74f<**

**Blue Goblin (USA)** 2 gr c Trempolino (USA)-Blue Daisy (USA) (Shahrastani (USA)) 2413[2] 3757[3] 4127[2] 4672[4] 4867[5] **>89f<**

**Blue Grit** 10 b g Thatching-Northern Wisdom (Northfields (USA)) 662[8] 764[3] 850[6] 971[10] 1474[4] 2030[4] 2391[9] 2898[7] 3410[7] **>32a 56f<**

**Blue Hopper** 2 b f Rock Hopper-Kimble Blue (Blue Refrain) 2714[3] 2967[2] 3454[13] **>67f<**

**Blue Imperial (FR)** 2 gr c Bluebird (USA)-Real Gold (Yankee Gold) 4512[14] 4698[9] **>50f<**

**Blue Iris** 3 b f Petong-Bo' Babbity (Strong Gale) *927[7]* 1616[3] 2270a[4] 3562a[7] (3693) 4115[4] 4518[2] 4958a[5] **>107f<**

**Blue Jazz (IRE)** 2 b f Bluebird (USA)-Laser Show *4024a[12]* ***>78f<***

**Blue Jumbo (IRE)** 3 b f Bluebird (USA)-Finalist (Star Appeal) 1350[10] 1667[12] 4309[11] **>41f<**

**Blue Lamp (USA)** 2 ch f Shadeed (USA)-Matter of Time (Habitat) 2611[7] **>58f<**

**Blue Lugana** 4 b g Lugana Beach-Two Friendly (Be Friendly) *425[7] 534[4] 607[14] 704[8]* 1001[17] 1500[6] 1702[6] 2316[13] 2421[5] 2732[9] 3624[10] 3937[13] **>22a 29f<**

**Blue Movie** 2 ch c Bluebird (USA)-Zoom Lens (IRE) (Caerleon (USA)) (476) 698[4] 1437[4] 2965[9] 3659[7] 3998[6] 4880[10] **>70f<**

**Blue Ridge** 2 ch c Indian Ridge-Souadah (USA) (General Holme (USA)) 1774[8] (1959) 3156[6] 3750a[5] 4677[7] **>91f<**

**Blue River (IRE)** 2 ch c River Falls-Royal Resident (Prince Regent (FR)) 2543[5] 2783[4] (3407) (3762) 4183[5] 4676[5] **>88f<**

**Blueshaan (IRE)** 3 c 1389a[4] **>102f<**

**Blue Sioux** 4 b f Indian Ridge-Blues Indigo (Music Boy) **1995:** *4413[12] 4484[5]* **>63a 57f<**

**Blues Queen** 2 b f Lahib (USA)-Queens Welcome (Northfields (USA)) 2854[3] 3050[4] 3475[2] 4113[5] (4311) 4490[13] 4723[7] 4875[7] **>90f<**

**Blue Suede Hoofs** 3 br g Nomination-Massive Powder (Caerleon (USA)) 692[13] 992[4] 1101[15] 1304[6] 1657[2] 2013[11] 4215[10] **>57f<**

**Blue Water (FR)** 4 dk b br f Bering-Shining Water (USA) (Riverman (USA)) 4654a[8] 5025a[3] **>109f<**

**Blueygreen** 2 b f Green Desert (USA)-Bluebook (USA) (Secretariat (USA)) 4570[8] 4969[19] **>58f<**

**Blue Zulu (IRE)** 4 gr f Don't Forget Me-Aldern Stream (Godswalk (USA)) 967[8] 1476[14] 2544[8] 2704[5] 3148[3] 4352[9] **>90f<**

**Blu Meltimi (ITY)** 3 4541a[11] **>50f<**

**Blu Metemi (ITY)** 3 dk f Star Shareef-Antoniette Pagnini (ITY) (Scouting Miller) 1393a[2] **>105f<**

**Bluntswood Hall** 3 b g Governor General-Miss Sarajane (Skyliner) *58[8] 156[5] 269[7] 2751[7]* **>24a f<**

**Blurred (IRE)** 3 ch g Al Hareb (USA)-I'll Take Paris (USA) (Vaguely Noble) 691[3] 1035[3] 1470[6] 2570[6] 3134[2] 3348[7] 4702[3] (4866) 4992[4] **>89+f<**

**Blush** 2 b f Gildoran-Rather Warm (Tribal Chief) *4694[3]* ***>52+f<***

**Blushing Desert** 2 b f Green Desert (USA)-Blushing Storm (USA) (Blushing Groom (FR)) 4670[5] **>63tf<**

**Blushing Flame (USA)** 5 b h Blushing Groom (FR)-Nearctic Flame (Sadler's Wells (USA)) *726[6]* 1988[4] (2474a) 4397a[7] **>114f<**

**Blushing Gleam** 3 ch f Caerleon (USA) 720a[3] (4940a) 5078a[3] **>99f<**

**Blushing Grenadier (IRE)** 4 ch g Salt Dome (USA)-La Duse (Junius (USA)) 649[9] 981[17] 1642[6] (2376) 2602[7] 3151[14] 3686[14] 4128[14] 4430[7] **>63?f<**

**Blushing Minstrel (IRE)** 2 b f Nicholas (USA)-Motley (Rainbow Quest (USA)) 5014a[5] **>79f<**

**Blu Tascheta (ITY)** 3 4541a[5] **>98f<**

**Blu Taxidoo (USA)** 3 c **1995:** 4399a[7] 4424a[5] **1996:** (722a) 903a[7] **>95f<**

**Blu Tuama (USA)** 3 b f Northern Prospect (USA)-Fulvous Gold 794a[3] **>100f<**

**Blyton Star (IRE)** 8 b g Horage-Saintly Angel (So Blessed) *203[11] 259[8] 341[6] 389[7]* **>30a f<**

**Boater** 2 b c Batshoof-Velvet Beret (IRE) (Dominion) 4698[7] 4918[9] **>54f<**

**Bobaluna** 3 b c Inca Chief (USA)-Davemma (Tachypous) *835[13] 1030[14] 1456[11]*

**Bobanlyn (IRE)** 4 b f Dance of Life (USA)-Sheer Innocence (Shirley Heights) 628[8] 787[14] 883[9] 1411[2] 1676[2] 1977[2] (2355) (2390) (2565) **>71f<**

**Bobbitt** 2 b f Reprimand-Pleasuring (Good Times (ITY)) 4233[9] 4605[7] 4889[9] **>63f<**

**Bobby Blue (IRE)** 5 gr g Bob Back (USA)-Yuma (USA) (Caro) *128[7] 275[7] 398[6] 603[6] 2203[6]* ***>32a 32f<***

**Bobby's Dream** 4 b f Reference Point-Kiralyi (FR) (Kings Lake (USA)) *33[14] 108[14] 642[10]* 1611[3] 2182[14] 4203[10] 4515[8] 4794[5] 4910[2] 5052[6] **>45f<**

**Bobinski** 4 br c Polish Precedent (USA)-Cockade (Derring-Do) 907a[3] **>117f<**

**Bob's Ploy** 4 b g Deploy-Santa Magdalena (Hard Fought) 682[14] 941[9] 2055[20] 2603[7] 2862[10] 3948[3] 4365[6] 4673[6] 4872[10] 4919[15] **>79f<**

**Bob The Broker (IRE)** 2 b c Bob Back (USA)-Java Jive (Hotfoot) 2073[8] **>74f<**

**Boccadirosa (IRE)** 3 b f Waajib-Atreides (Simply Great (FR)) 794a[11] **>85f<**

**Boffy (IRE)** 3 ch c Mac's Imp (USA)-No Dowry (Shy Groom (USA)) *21[4] (101) 183[2] (224) 272[2] 394[5] 525[8]* 644[11] 1405[7] 1707[9] *2171[10] 2634[6] 3350[5]* 3652[9] *3953[9] 4045[15]* ***>77da 34f<***

**Bogart** 5 gr g Belfort (FR)-Larnem (Meldrum) **1995:** *4371[2] 4512[5]* **1996:** *77[9] 153[9] 589[9]* ***>56a 62df<***

**Bog Wild (USA)** 3 c **1995:** 4424a[6] **1996:** 794a[10] 1393a[3] 4541a[3] **>104f<**

**Bold Acre** 6 ch g Never so Bold-Nicola Wynn (Nicholas Bill) **1995:** *4366[9]* **1996:** *124[5]* **>37a 64f<**

**Bold African** 2 b g Emarati (USA)-White African (Carwhite) 608[5] 829[4] 1003[7] 1046[3] 1479[2] 1705[2] 1884[2] 2138[2] 2309[3] 2726[8] (2846) (3224) 3299[3] (3590) 3940[2] 3975[4] 4247[8] **>82f<**

**Bold Amusement** 6 ch g Never so Bold-Hysterical (High Top) *211[13] 802[11]* 1502[2] 1633[5] 2077[6] 3344[2] 3646[9] 4568[21] 4872[5] **>79f<**

**Bold Angel** 9 b g Lochnager-Lobela (Lorenzaccio) 1156[3] 1651[3] 4829[5] 4882[8] **>66a 57f<**

**Bold Aristocrat (IRE)** 5 b g Bold Arrangement-Wyn Mipet (Welsh Saint) **1995:** *4371[6] 4388[9] 4428[7] 4502[13]* **1996:** *59[9] 126[8] (168) 250[6] 282[5] 330[3] (342) 431[9] 607[5] 806[8] 896[8] 4090[4] 4577[2] 4778[8] 4987[3]* **>62a 47f<**

**Bold Brief** 2 b c Tina's Pet-Immodest Miss (Daring Display (USA)) 699[7] 975[6] 1827[5] (2118) 2364[6] 2872[5] 3577[7] **>63f<**

**Bold Buster** 3 b g Bustino-Truly Bold (Bold Lad (IRE)) 4827[8] **>47f<**

**Bold Catch (USA)** 2 ch c Diesis-Social Wish (USA) (Lyphard's Wish (FR)) 841[4] 1118[5] (1822) 2703[4] 3792[3] **>79f<**

**Bold Classic (IRE)** 3 b c Persian Bold-Bay Street (Grundy) 1079[7] 1461[4] 2205[2] (2952) 3476[2] 3850[8] 4476[6] **>86f<**

**Bold Demand** 2 b c Rainbow Quest (USA)-Dafrah (USA) (Danzig (USA)) 5038[4] **>69+f<**

**Bold Effort (FR)** 4 b g Bold Arrangement-Malham Tarn (Riverman (USA)) 876[22] 1621[10] 2114[29] 2497[6] 2856[9] 3232[22] (3569a) 3910a[3] 4116[7] (4411a) 4466[13] 5068a[11] **>80a 86f<**

**Bold Elect** 8 b g Electric-Famous Band (USA) (Banderilla (USA)) *60[8] 625[8]* 767[8] 886[11] 1676[3] 2066[2] (2165) (2360) **>19a 60+f<**

**Bold Engagement** 2 b f Never so Bold-Diamond House (Habitat) *4594[17]* ***>9f<***

**Bold Enough** 3 ch f Bold Arrangement-Sweet Enough (Caerleon (USA)) **1995:** *4431[12]* **1996:** *978[10]* 1152[4] 1526[3] 2016[5] 2253[8] 4323[6] 4497[7] 4810[3] **>56f<**

**Bolder Still** 3 ch g Never so Bold-Glenfinlass (Lomond (USA)) 2744[11] 3519[6] **>49f<**

**Bold Future (IRE)** 3 b g Treasure Kay-Mother Courage (Busted) 1539[11] 3619[16] **>27f< (DEAD)**

**Bold Gayle** 2 ch f Never so Bold-Storm Gayle (IRE) (Sadler's Wells (USA)) 3956[5] 4228[8] **>51+f<**

**Bold Gem** 5 b m Never so Bold-Precious Jade (Northfields (USA)) **1995:** *4377[5] 4413[8] 4450[8]* **>58a 56f<**

**Bold Habit** 11 ch g Homing-Our Mother (Bold Lad (IRE)) 1074[13] 2581[18] 3084[11] 3585[11] *3955[7] 4089[12] 4428[6]* 4829[9] **>53a 51f<**

**Bold Joker** 5 b g Jester-Bold Difference (Bold Owl) *248[6] 2183[12]* 2537[11] 2848[10] **>10a 20f<**

**Bold Motion** 2 b f Anshan-Fast Motion (Midsummer Night II) 2606[12] 2948[3] *3954[10] 4694[16]*

**>18a 40f<**

**Bold Oriental (IRE) 2** b c Tirol-Miss Java (Persian Bold) 1191$^{7}$ 1583$^{2}$ 1878$^{3}$ 2624$^{10}$ 3046$^{4}$ 3259$^{6}$ 3975$^{2}$ 4262$^{7}$ (4375) **>76f<**

**Bold Patriot (IRE) 3** b c Polish Patriot (USA)-Don't Be Cruel (Persian Bold) 663$^{5}$ (1000) 1785$^{6}$ **>78f<**

**Bold Pursuit (IRE) 7** b g Thatching-Pursue (Auction Ring (USA)) *196$^{6}$ 254$^{5}$ 333$^{6}$ (504)* 609$^{4}$ *855$^{P}$* **>48a 52f< (DEAD)**

**Bold Resolution (IRE) 8** b g Shardari-Valmarine (FR) (Val de Loir) 2002$^{2}$ **>82f<**

**Bold Revival 4** b f Never so Bold-Convivial (Nordance (USA)) 549$^{8}$ **>51df< (DEAD)**

**Bold Risk 2** b c Midyan (USA)-Madam Bold (Never so Bold) 1344$^{3}$ 1801$^{5}$ **>63f<**

**Bold Saint (IRE) 2** b c Persian Bold-St Clair Star (Sallust) 3695$^{6}$ 4069$^{7}$ **>63f<**

**Bold Spring (IRE) 2** b c Never so Bold-Oasis (Valiyar) 1191$^{8}$ 1892$^{4}$ 2527$^{3}$ 3478$^{6}$ 3829$^{2}$ 4512$^{9}$ 4916$^{10}$ **>76f<**

**Bold Street (IRE) 6** ch g Shy Groom (USA)-Ferry Lane (Dom Racine (FR)) **1995:** *4447$^{3}$ 4502$^{7}$* **1996:** *1781$^{2}$* 2386$^{4}$ 2431$^{7}$ *3953$^{6}$ 4333$^{9}$ 4778$^{2}$ 4799$^{7}$ 4979$^{4}$* **>67a 66f<**

**Bold Time Monkey 5** ch m Bold Owl-Play For Time (Comedy Star (USA)) *388$^{10}$ 836$^{12}$ 981$^{18}$* 1642$^{19}$ *1809$^{12}$* **>24f<**

**Bold Tina (IRE) 2** b f Persian Bold-Tinas Image (He Loves Me) 2614$^{2}$ 2782$^{3}$ 3475$^{3}$ 4061$^{5}$ 4697$^{12}$ **>68f<**

**Bold Top 4** ch g Bold Owl-Whirlygigger (Taufan (USA)) 504$^{3}$ 609$^{8}$ 625$^{10}$ 872$^{19}$ 1697$^{3}$ 2922$^{7}$ 3348$^{2}$ 3780$^{9}$ 3970$^{3}$ 4355$^{5}$ 4587$^{9}$ 4812$^{8}$ **>48f<**

**Bold Welcome 2** ch c Most Welcome-Song's Best (Never so Bold) 523$^{5}$ 869$^{2}$ 1987$^{4}$ **>73f<**

**Bold Words (CAN) 2** ch c Bold Ruckus (CAN)-Trillium Woods (USA) (Briartic (CAN)) 3682$^{9}$ 4242$^{7}$ (4507) (4760) 4973$^{7}$ **>91f<**

**Bolero Boy 2** b c Rambo Dancer (CAN)-Barrie Baby (Import) 557$^{5}$ 699$^{D}$ 930$^{2}$ (1344) 1699$^{4}$ 2063$^{3}$ 3674$^{4}$ 3835$^{16}$ 4311$^{2}$ 4621$^{2}$ **>92f<**

**Bolivar (IRE) 4** b g Kahyasi-Shuss (USA) (Princely Native (USA)) *968$^{10}$* 1511$^{7}$ 1710$^{4}$ (2148) (3037) 3760$^{5}$ **>81df<**

**Bollero (IRE) 2** b f Topanoora-Charo (Mariacci (FR)) 910$^{2}$ *1093$^{3}$ 1632$^{2}$* (1869) 3400$^{7}$ 3620$^{4}$ 4024a$^{27}$ 4195$^{10}$ **>54a 62f<**

**Bollin Dorothy 3** b f Rambo Dancer (CAN)-Bollin Harriet (Lochnager) *1155$^{7}$* 1527$^{14}$ (2393) 2729$^{8}$ 3154$^{5}$ 3844$^{11}$ 4058$^{6}$ 4560$^{5}$ **>62f<**

**Bollin Frank 4** b c Rambo Dancer (CAN)-Bollin Emily (Lochnager) 713$^{5}$ 851$^{2}$ 1069$^{2}$ (1406) (1799) 2164$^{5}$ 2693$^{7}$ 3623$^{3}$ 3842$^{2}$ 4190$^{12}$ 4769$^{24}$ **>79f<**

**Bollin Harry 4** b c Domynsky-Bollin Harriet (Lochnager) 475$^{2}$ 587$^{5}$ (749) 850$^{2}$ 1186$^{17}$ (1829) 2363$^{5}$ 3432$^{19}$ 3672$^{14}$ 4312$^{12}$ 4581$^{13}$ 4765$^{12}$ **>79f<**

**Bollin Jacob 3** b c Efisio-Bollin Emily (Lochnager) 705$^{8}$ 774$^{4}$ 934$^{7}$ 1155$^{8}$ 1539$^{3}$ 1780$^{6}$ 2027$^{11}$ **>65f<**

**Bollin Joanne 3** b f Damister (USA)-Bollin Zola (Alzao (USA)) 768$^{2}$ 1007$^{4}$ 1475$^{2}$ 2011$^{2}$ 2497$^{3}$ (2987) (3296) 3622$^{5}$ 4314$^{9}$ (4687) **>100f<**

**Bollin Terry 2** b c Terimon-Bollin Zola (Alzao (USA)) 3131$^{7}$ 3620$^{5}$ 4041$^{5}$ **>60f<**

**Bolshoi (IRE) 4** br g Royal Academy (USA)-Mainly Dry (The Brianstan) *451$^{8}$* 850$^{4}$ (951) 1598$^{2}$ 1829$^{2}$ 2137$^{5}$ 2349$^{4}$ (2518) 2889$^{7}$ (3038) 3232$^{4}$ 3622$^{4}$ 4116$^{5}$ 4314$^{8}$ (4466) 4679$^{4}$ 4772$^{8}$ **>104f<**

**Bombay Sapphire 3** b f Be My Chief (USA)-Ginny Binny (Ahonoora) 710$^{14}$ 1007$^{12}$ 1709$^{6}$ **>56f<**

**Bonanza Peak (USA) 3** b c Houston (USA)-Bunnicula (USA) (Shadeed (USA)) *4622$^{6}$* 4827$^{12}$ **>71f<**

**Bonarelli (IRE) 3** b c Dancing Dissident (USA)-Sovereign Dona (Sovereign Path) 694$^{9}$ 1015$^{5}$ 3153$^{7}$ 3811$^{2}$ 4181$^{7}$ **>99f<**

**Bon Guest (IRE) 2** ch c Kefaah (USA)-Uninvited Guest (Be My Guest (USA)) 3502$^{11}$ 4380$^{10}$ 4700$^{7}$ **>71f<**

**Bon Jovi (GER) 3** bl c Konigsstuhl (GER)-Book Of Love (GER) (Formidable (USA)) 2109a$^{3}$ 2668a$^{12}$ **>89f<**

**Bon Luck (IRE) 4** ch g Waajib-Elle Va Bon (Tanfirion) 496$^{5}$ 2526$^{2}$ 3120$^{2}$ 3765$^{4}$ 4329$^{4}$ **>76f<**

**Bonne Etoile 4** b f Diesis-Bonne Ile (Ile de Bourbon (USA)) 3071$^{11}$ **>98f<**

**Bonne Ville 2** gr f Good Times (ITY)-Ville Air (Town Crier) 4041$^{13}$ 4477$^{5}$ *(4780) 5057$^{7}$* **>71a 56f<**

**Bonnie Lassie 2** gr f Efisio-Normanby Lass (Bustino) 1632$^{5}$ 4046$^{3}$ 4748$^{3}$ *(4985)* **>77a 77f<**

**Bonny Melody 5** b m Sizzling Melody-Bonny Quiver (Gorytus (USA)) **1995:** *4358$^{6}$ 4464$^{10}$* **1996:** *180$^{7}$ 466$^{3}$* **>42a 43f<**

**Bon Secret (IRE) 4** b g Classic Secret (USA)-Bon Retour (Sallust) **1995:** *4362$^{10}$* **1996:** *5002$^{12}$* **>49a 32f<**

**Bonsiel 2** b f Skyliner-Shawiniga (Lyphard's Wish (FR)) *2371$^{9}$ 2938$^{2}$ 3087$^{6}$ 3448$^{12}$* **>45a 35f<**

**Boogie Bopper (IRE) 7** b or br g Taufan (USA)-Mey (Canisbay) *3066$^{9}$ 3437$^{P}$*

**Boojum 2** b f Mujtahid (USA)-Haboobti (Habitat) (2184) 2619$^{2}$ 3566a$^{4}$ 4488$^{8}$ (4875) 5071a$^{6}$ **>96f<**

**Boost 4** b g Superpower-Sirene Bleu Marine (USA) (Secreto (USA)) *106$^{6}$ 179$^{5}$ 782$^{5}$ 1500$^{8}$* 2056$^{23}$ 3358$^{6}$ **>24a 46df<**

**Boozeroo 3** ch g Never so Bold-Show Home (Music Boy) 4451$^{5}$

**Born A Lady 3** ch f Komaite (USA)-Lucky Candy (Lucky Wednesday) *160$^{4}$ 224$^{6}$ 606$^{3}$ 748$^{7}$* 868$^{13}$ *1028$^{12}$ 1598$^{10}$* 1908$^{7}$ 2075$^{11}$ 2180$^{3}$ 2507$^{3}$ 2752$^{5}$ 3059$^{3}$ 3254$^{4}$ *3602$^{7}$ 3808$^{17}$* 4226$^{13}$ 4340$^{4}$ **>54a 58f<**

**Born On The Wild 3** b f Golden Lahab (USA)-First Born (Be My Native (USA)) *4074$^{17}$* 4322$^{9}$ **>46f<**

**Bosra Sham (USA) 3** ch f Woodman (USA)-Korveya (USA) (Riverman (USA)) (708) (939) 4443$^{2}$ (4773) **>134f<**

**Boston Harbor (USA) 2** b c Capote (USA)-Harbor Springs (CAN) (Vice Regent (CAN)) *(4954a)* **>112a f<**

**Boston Rock (IRE) 4** ch g Ballad Rock-Miss Boston (FR) (River River (FR)) 613$^{6}$ 786$^{8}$ 1190$^{13}$ 1953$^{2}$ 2251$^{6}$ **>68f<**

**Boston Tea Party 3** b f Rambo Dancer (CAN)-Tea-Pot (Ragstone) **1995:** *4360$^{8}$* **1996:** *1012$^{6}$* 1514$^{15}$ *1997$^{5}$ 2978$^{7}$* **>50a 27f<**

**Bouche Bee (USA) 4** b f Naevus (USA)-Miss Henderson Co (USA) (Silver Hawk (USA)) *1056a$^{2}$* 2072$^{11}$ 3199a$^{3}$ **>105f<**

**Boundary Bird (IRE) 3** b g Tirol-Warning Sound (Red Alert) **1995:** *4410$^{9}$* **1996:** *616$^{8}$* 1539$^{6}$ *1809$^{11}$ 2168$^{10}$ 3287$^{6}$* 3427$^{13}$ 4344$^{6}$ **>54a 46f<**

**Boundary Express 4** b g Sylvan Express-Addison's Jubilee (Sparkler) 1044$^{12}$ **>51a 63f<**

**Boundless Moment (USA) 5** ch g Crafty Prospector (USA)-Mysterious Gift (USA) (Great Mystery (USA)) *4951a$^{9}$* **>119a f<**

**Bourbonist (FR) 3** b g Soviet Star (USA)-Bourbon Topsy (Ile de Bourbon (USA)) 1690$^{10}$ **>62f<**

**Bourdonner 4** b g Pharly (FR)-Buzzbomb (Bustino) *268$^{6}$ 2756$^{11}$* **>34a f<**

**Bout 2** br f Batshoof-Reyah (Young Generation) 4104$^{8}$ 4449$^{6}$ **>65f<**

**Bouton d'Or 3** b f Mazilier (USA)-Cow Pastures (Homing) **1995:** *4483$^{12}$ 4541$^{2}$* **1996:** *51$^{3}$ 78$^{3}$ 160$^{2}$ 292$^{6}$ 644$^{13}$* 1170$^{12}$ 1688$^{7}$ *2305$^{4}$ 3061$^{4}$* **>35a 18f<**

**Bowcliffe 5** b g Petoski-Gwiffina (Welsh Saint) 612$^{11}$ 999$^{11}$ (1546) 2023$^{7}$ 2567$^{10}$ 4000$^{12}$ 4975$^{9}$ 5004$^{9}$ **>56df<**

**Bowcliffe Court (IRE) 4** b g Slip Anchor-Res Nova (USA) (Blushing Groom (FR)) 753$^{5}$ 1116$^{7}$ 1611$^{2}$ 2547$^{2}$ 3598$^{7}$ 3855$^{6}$ 4365$^{4}$ (4821) 5047$^{3}$ **>78f<**

**Bowcliffe Grange (IRE) 4** b g Dominion Royale-Cala-Vadella (Mummy's Pet) *259$^{11}$ 278$^{6}$ 806$^{9}$* 1020$^{6}$ 1500$^{2}$ *1606$^{6}$ (1702)* 1889$^{3}$ (2156) 2324$^{3}$ 2496$^{11}$ (2745) (2771) 2849$^{3}$ 3146$^{12}$ *3416$^{5}$ 3864$^{6}$* **>42a 56f<**

**Bowden Rose 4** ch f Dashing Blade-Elegant Rose (Noalto) 711$^{13}$ 928$^{8}$ 1178$^{4}$ 1630$^{2}$ 1790$^{10}$ 2232$^{4}$ 2381$^{2}$ 2889$^{6}$ 3296$^{5}$ (3495) 3875$^{2}$ 3984$^{13}$ 4304$^{9}$ 4466$^{17}$ 4772$^{9}$ 4869$^{8}$ **>95f<**

**Bowland Park 5** b m Nicholas Bill-Macusla (Lighter) *346$^{7}$ 1159$^{11}$* 1596$^{7}$ 2162$^{12}$ 2522$^{5}$ **>42f<**

**Bowled Over 3** b g Batshoof-Swift Linnet (Wolver Hollow) 528$^{2}$ 677$^{10}$ 985$^{3}$ 1461$^{3}$ (1973) 2233$^{3}$ 2665a$^{5}$ 3669$^{10}$ 3923$^{8}$ 4117$^{4}$ 4327$^{11}$ 4617$^{18}$ **>78df<**

**Bowlers Boy 3** ch g Risk Me (FR)-Snow Wonder (Music Boy) 626$^{3}$ 824$^{7}$ 973$^{5}$ 1527$^{7}$ 2029$^{2}$ *2305$^{3}$ (2870)* 3844$^{13}$ 3959$^{2}$ (4382) 4689$^{7}$ **>43a 75f<**

**Boy Blakeney 3** b g Blakeney-Sarah Bear (Mansingh (USA)) *2026$^{10}$* 2297$^{4}$ 2568$^{9}$ *3090$^{4}$ 3325$^{4}$* **>20a 44f<**

**Boyfriend 6** b g Rolfe (USA)-Lady Sweetapples (Super Song) *175$^{5}$* **>37a 65f<**

**Braes'O'Shieldhill 3** ch f Music Maestro-Dalchroy (Hotfoot) 3427$^{11}$ **>13a 18f<**

**Brafferton Bella 4** ch f Sylvan Express-Janie-O (Hittite Glory) *167$^{8}$ 252$^{9}$*

**Braille (IRE) 5** br g Vision (USA)-Winning Feature (Red Alert) *963$^{2}$* 1019$^{8}$ **>80f<**

**Bramble Bear 2** b f Beveled (USA)-Supreme Rose (Frimley Park) *977$^{5}$* 1118$^{7}$ 2343$^{3}$ (2956) 3160$^{11}$ 3924$^{7}$ 4517$^{6}$ **>67f<**

**Brambles Way 7** ch g Clantime-Streets Ahead (Ovid) *479$^{10}$* 805$^{7}$ 1041$^{3}$ 1417$^{2}$ 1538$^{4}$ 1665$^{15}$ 2801$^{7}$ 3645$^{5}$ (4455) 4812$^{5}$ 4993$^{12}$ **>55f<**

**Brand New Dance 2** b g Gildoran-Starawak (Star Appeal) 5040$^{5}$

**Brandon Court (IRE) 5** b g Law Society (USA)-Dance Date (IRE) (Sadler's Wells (USA)) 2549$^{5}$ 2884$^{5}$ **>86f<**

**Brandon Jack 2** ch c Cadeaux Genereux-Waitingformargaret (Kris) 2993$^{3}$ 3312$^{3}$ (3809) (4182) 4364$^{3}$ **>84f<**

**Brandon Magic 3** ch c Primo Dominie-Silk Stocking (Pardao) 936$^{5}$ 1395a$^{5}$ 1768$^{8}$ 2041$^{9}$ 2544$^{5}$ 2888$^{9}$ 3594$^{2}$ 3997$^{5}$ 4326$^{13}$ 4556$^{7}$ **>101f<**

**Brandon Prince (IRE) 8** b g Shernazar-Chanson de Paris (USA) (The Minstrel (CAN)) *647$^{4}$* 852$^{8}$ 1063$^{12}$ **>74df<**

**Brandonville 3** b c Never so Bold-Enduring (Sadler's Wells (USA)) 714$^{5}$ 976$^{8}$ 1301$^{8}$ 2630$^{5}$ 2968$^{4}$ 3414$^{9}$ **>55f<**

**Branston Abby (IRE) 7** ch m Risk Me (FR)-Tuxford Hideaway (Cawston's Clown) **1995:** 4469a$^{2}$ 4523a$^{10}$ **1996:** 673$^{8}$ 818$^{3}$ 889$^{5}$ 1075$^{4}$ 1129$^{2}$ 1566a$^{7}$ (1629) 1800$^{2}$ 2072$^{15}$ 2332$^{6}$ (2436) 2692$^{4}$ 2880$^{14}$ 3083$^{3}$ (3394a) 3752a$^{4}$ 3712$^{8}$ 4442$^{7}$ (4743a) 4774$^{8}$ (4957a) 5027a$^{3}$ **>113f<**

**Branston Danni 3** b f Ron's Victory (USA)-Softly Spoken (Mummy's Pet) 2137$^{8}$ 2571$^{7}$ 3774$^{5}$ 3959$^{8}$ 4206$^{21}$ 4589$^{12}$ 4765$^{7}$ **>45f<**

**Branston Jewel (IRE) 3** ch f Prince Sabo-Tuxford Hideaway (Cawston's Clown) 3085$^{15}$ **>93f<**

**Branston Kristy 4** b f Hallgate-Bare Spectacle (Welsh Pageant) *63$^{13}$ 212$^{6}$ 248$^{9}$ 255$^{6}$ 328$^{5}$ 368$^{4}$ 399$^{7}$ 631$^{8}$* 1517$^{8}$ 1642$^{16}$ 1702$^{3}$ 1859$^{8}$ 2757$^{20}$ **>24a 32f<**

**Brass Tacks 4** br f Prince Sabo-Brassy Nell (Dunbeath (USA)) *2737$^{7}$* 2981$^{4}$ **>10a 57f<**

**Brave Act** 2 b c Persian Bold-Circus Act (Shirley Heights) (2416) (2629) 3150$^{2}$ (3927) **>107f<**

**Brave Edge** 5 b g Beveled (USA)-Daring Ditty (Daring March) *711$^{5}$* 940$^{5}$ 1113$^{2}$ (1616) 1818$^{6}$ 2114$^{24}$ 2545$^{8}$ 3126$^{9}$ 3232$^{24}$ 3875$^{4}$ 4115$^{3}$ 4518$^{4}$ 4744a$^{2}$ **>107f<**

**Brave Envoy** 2 b c High Estate-Restless Anna (Thatching) 4514$^{14}$ **>50f<**

**Braveheart (IRE)** 2 br g Mujadil (USA)-Salonniere (FR) (Bikala) 815$^{4}$ (930) 1103$^{2}$ 1303$^{3}$ 1362$^{4}$ 3931$^{3}$ 4258$^{5}$ **>90f<**

**Brave Indigo** 3 b c Rainbow Quest (USA)-Nyoka (USA) (Raja Baba (USA)) **1995:** (4424a)

**Brave Kris (IRE)** 2 b f Kris-Famosa (Dancing Brave (USA)) 3988$^{7}$ 4608$^{2}$ 4861$^{3}$ **>81f<**

**Brave Montgomerie** 2 ch c Most Welcome-Just Precious (Ela-Mana-Mou) 2153$^{2}$ 2416$^{3}$ (4245) **>77f<**

**Brave Patriarch (IRE)** 5 gr g Alzao (USA)-Early Rising (USA) (Grey Dawn II) 628$^{9}$ 816$^{5}$ 1150$^{6}$ **>78f<**

**Brave Princess** 4 b f Dancing Brave (USA)-Princess Zena (Habitat) **1995:** *4378$^{5}$* **>74a 75f<**

**Brave Spy** 5 b g Law Society (USA)-Contralto (Busted) *206$^{W}$ 312$^{5}$ 422$^{7}$ 546$^{16}$ 855$^{3}$ 1095$^{7}$ 1488$^{7}$* **>62a 65f<**

**Bravo Star (USA)** 11 b g The Minstrel (CAN)-Stellarette (CAN) (Tentam (USA)) 2385$^{7}$ 2556$^{12}$ **>30f<**

**Brawling Springs** 2 b g Belfort (FR)-Oyster Gray (Tanfirion) 1036$^{6}$ 1184$^{5}$ 1858$^{8}$ **>43f<**

**Braydon Forest** 4 b g Presidium-Sleekit (Blakeney) 546$^{19}$ 1655$^{16}$ 2377$^{5}$ 2784$^{9}$ 3471$^{2}$ **>55f<**

**Brazilia** 2 b f Forzando-Dominio (IRE) (Dominion) 2956$^{4}$ 3438$^{3}$ 3859$^{2}$ *4572$^{3}$ 4748$^{5}$ 4999$^{8}$* **>56a 69f<**

**Break the Rules** 4 b g Dominion-Surf Bird (Shareef Dancer (USA)) *537$^{4}$* 871$^{8}$ 1417$^{3}$ 2068$^{2}$ 2390$^{2}$ (2673) 3856$^{4}$ 4073$^{11}$ 4483$^{4}$ 4582$^{2}$ 4763$^{3}$ (4868) **>85f<**

**Brecongill Lad** 4 b g Clantime-Chikala (Pitskelly) 451$^{11}$ 610$^{15}$ 1186$^{8}$ 1501$^{9}$ 2005$^{13}$ 2431$^{8}$ 3152$^{5}$ (3482) 3868$^{2}$ 4312$^{17}$ 4616$^{6}$ 4791$^{4}$ 5039$^{21}$ **>70f<**

**Breezed Well** 10 b g Wolverlife-Precious Baby (African Sky) *219$^{12}$ 341$^{10}$ 752$^{5}$* 1074$^{11}$ 1449$^{15}$ 1890$^{7}$ 3510$^{3}$ 4307$^{8}$ 4436$^{4}$ 4551$^{7}$ **>44a 58f<**

**Breffni (IRE)** 2 b f Mac's Imp (USA)-Bon Retour (Sallust) 2611$^{15}$ 2951$^{3}$ 3169$^{2}$ 3311$^{2}$ *3604$^{4}$ 4207$^{7}$* 4339$^{5}$ **>43a 58f<**

**Brentability (IRE)** 3 b g Dancing Dissident (USA)-Stanerra's Song (USA) (Seattle Song (USA)) 578$^{7}$ 730$^{10}$ 1050$^{8}$ 1641$^{11}$ *2086$^{5}$ 4086$^{12}$* ***>43a 61df<***

**Bresil (USA)** 7 ch g Bering-Clever Bidder (USA) (Bold Bidder) **1995:** *4434$^{10}$ 4516$^{9}$* **1996:** *642$^{4}$ 898$^{11}$ 1347$^{18}$* 1803$^{16}$ 2282$^{5}$ 2537$^{2}$ 2556$^{5}$ 2891$^{5}$ 3273$^{4}$ 3520$^{7}$ 4509$^{9}$ **>29a 43f<**

**Breydon** 3 ch g Be My Guest (USA)-Palmella (USA) (Grundy) *526$^{12}$* 640$^{15}$ 820$^{12}$ 1514$^{6}$ 2493$^{3}$ *2936$^{2}$ 3249$^{3}$* 3882$^{2}$ **>46a 62f<**

**Brick Court (IRE)** 4 ch f Bluebird (USA)-Palmyra (GER) (Arratos (FR)) **1995:** *4416$^{7}$* **1996:** *642$^{7}$* 1347$^{12}$ *1444$^{6}$ 2556$^{11}$* 4548$^{8}$ **>32a 53f<**

**Bride's Reprisal** 2 b f Dunbeath (USA)-Matching Lines (Thatching) (1884) 2112$^{10}$ 2872$^{2}$ (2930) 3128$^{3}$ 3400$^{3}$ 3613$^{5}$ 3990$^{6}$ **>93?f<**

**Bridlington Bay** 3 b g Roscoe Blake-City Sound (On Your Mark) **1995:** *4501$^{7}$* **1996:** *89$^{7}$ 281$^{7}$ 4484$^{7}$* ***>33a 19f<***

**Brief Glimpse (IRE)** 4 b or br f Taufan (USA)-Mini Look (FR) (In Fijar (USA)) 1177$^{7}$ 1629$^{6}$ 2609$^{7}$ 3127$^{9}$ 3517$^{8}$ 4378$^{8}$ **>99f<**

**Briganoone** 3 b g Cyrano de Bergerac-Zareeta (Free State) **1995:** *4473$^{9}$* **1996:** *32$^{3}$ (102) 157$^{5}$ 313$^{3}$ 525$^{10}$* 882$^{15}$ 1068$^{12}$ **>53a 36f<**

**Briggs Turn** 2 b g Rudimentary (USA)-Turnabout (Tyrnavos) 5033$^{14}$ **>42f<**

**Brighstone** 3 ch c Cadeaux Genereux-High Fountain (High Line) 830$^{9}$ 1441$^{7}$ 2436$^{6}$ **>99df<**

**Bright Desert** 3 b c Green Desert (USA)-Smarten Up (Sharpen Up) *786$^{9}$* 3425$^{10}$ **>24f<**

**Bright Diamond** 3 b f Never so Bold-Diamond House (Habitat) 595$^{11}$ 819$^{11}$ 3518$^{5}$ 3702$^{8}$ 4098$^{10}$ 4337$^{10}$ 4690$^{4}$ 4805$^{6}$ **>69f<**

**Bright Eclipse (USA)** 3 br g Sunny's Halo (CAN)-Miss Lantana (USA) (Danzig Connection (USA)) *555$^{3}$ 763$^{8}$* 1119$^{4}$ 1535$^{2}$ *2158$^{4}$ 2358$^{3}$* 2489$^{5}$ **>58a 65df<**

**Brighter Byfaah (IRE)** 3 ch g Kefaah (USA)-Bright Landing (Sun Prince) **1995:** *4439$^{6}$* **1996:** *560$^{6}$* 890$^{9}$ 1503$^{6}$ (3104) **>49f<**

**Bright Gold** 2 ch g Clantime-Miss Brightside (Crofthall) 4807$^{12}$ 4907$^{6}$ 5034$^{15}$ **>38f<**

**Brighton Road (IRE)** 3 b br g Pennine Walk-Share The Vision (Vision (USA)) 646$^{12}$ 1485$^{2}$ 2526$^{11}$ 3516$^{12}$ 3786$^{5}$ 3926$^{9}$ 4799$^{8}$ 4921$^{15}$ **>67f<**

**Bright Paragon (IRE)** 7 b or br g Treasure Kay-Shining Bright (USA) (Bold Bidder) **1995:** *4406$^{15}$* **1996:** *762$^{7}$* ***>38a 36f<***

**Bright Pet** 3 ch f Anshan-Morica (Moorestyle) 703$^{11}$ 994$^{10}$ 1160$^{8}$ 2563$^{10}$ 3048$^{8}$ 3325$^{5}$ **>40f<**

**Bright Water** 3 b c Caerleon (USA)-Shining Water (Kalaglow) 725$^{4}$ (4714) 4964$^{7}$ **>114f<**

**Brilliant Red** 3 b c Royal Academy (USA)-Red Comes Up (USA) (Blushing Groom (FR)) *2853$^{6}$* 3067$^{5}$ 3594$^{9}$ **>99f<**

**Brindle** 3 b c Polar Falcon (USA)-Blade of Grass (Kris) 3387a$^{2}$ **>103f<**

**Brin-Lodge (IRE)** 3 b f Doubletour (USA)-Nordico's Dream (Nordico (USA)) *2632$^{9}$ 2966$^{13}$ 3420$^{7}$ 3851$^{13}$ 4090$^{7}$ 4229$^{13}$* ***>34a 15f<***

**Brisas** 9 ch g Vaigly Great-Legal Sound (Legal Eagle) *74$^{5}$ 250$^{5}$ 1541$^{13}$* 2964$^{10}$ 3252$^{W}$ **>39a 43df<**

**Brisby (FR)** 3 b f Courtroom (FR)-Belle Caro (FR) (Caro) 5019a$^{3}$ **>104f<**

**Briska (IRE)** 2 b f River Falls-Calash (Indian King (USA)) 1626$^{5}$ 1871$^{3}$ (2187) 3208$^{6}$ 4490$^{11}$ **>76f<**

**Broadgate Flyer (IRE)** 2 b g Silver Kite (USA)-Fabulous Pet (Somethingfabulous (USA)) 1842$^{6}$ 2044$^{5}$ 3259$^{11}$ 3498$^{3}$ **>67f<**

**Broad River (USA)** 2 b c Broad Brush (USA)-Monture Creek (USA) (Stop The Music (USA)) 3994$^{13}$ **>57f<**

**Broadstairs Beauty (IRE)** 6 ch g Dominion Royale-Holy Water (Monseigneur (USA)) **1995:** *(4394)* **1996:** *475$^{5}$* 1199$^{10}$ 2586$^{11}$ **>83a 75f<**

**Brockville Bairn** 3 b g Tina's Pet-Snow Chief (Tribal Chief) *332$^{4}$* **>40a 40f<**

**Broctune Bay** 7 b g Midyan (USA)-Sweet Colleen (Connaught) 4683$^{4}$ **>57f<**

**Broctune Gold** 5 b g Superpower-Golden Sunlight (Ile de Bourbon (USA)) 971$^{2}$ (1162) 1474$^{7}$ (2022) 2426$^{5}$ (2851) 3109$^{7}$ (3481) 3815$^{5}$ 4296$^{3}$ 5010$^{2}$ **>49a 76f<**

**Broctune Line** 2 ch c Safawan-Ra Ra (Lord Gayle (USA)) 2519$^{7}$ 3099$^{5}$ 3423$^{10}$ 4440$^{8}$ 4562$^{6}$ 4990$^{11}$ **>42f<**

**Brodessa** 10 gr g Scallywag-Jeanne du Barry (Dubassoff (USA)) 1847$^{2}$ (2182) 2626$^{2}$ (3507) **>66da 72f<**

**Brogans Brush** 3 ch c Jendali (USA)-Sweet 'n' Sharp (Sharpo) *537$^{10}$* 1762$^{4}$ 2175$^{9}$ 4317$^{10}$ **>34a 35f<**

**Broken Innate (IRE)** 2 br f Broken Hearted-Innate (Be My Native (USA)) 4024a$^{28}$ **>44f<**

**Bromfylde Fayemaid (IRE)** 4 b f Treasure Kay-Fayes Ben (Don) *1099$^{20}$* 1681$^{6}$ **>2f<**

**Bronhallow** 3 b g Belmez (USA)-Grey Twig (Godswalk (USA)) 821$^{10}$ 1142$^{17}$ 1496$^{10}$ 2709$^{9}$ 3113$^{11}$ 3333$^{12}$ **>51f<**

**Bronze Maquette (IRE)** 6 b m Ahonoora-Working Model (Ile de Bourbon (USA)) 635$^{10}$ 866$^{3}$ 1047$^{5}$ 1414$^{11}$ 1874$^{4}$ 2155$^{7}$ 2226$^{5}$ 2409$^{6}$ **>37a 42f<**

**Bronze Runner** 12 b or ro g Gunner B-Petingalyn (Petingo) 1821$^{10}$ 2056$^{10}$ 2192$^{6}$ 2556$^{7}$ 2716$^{8}$ 2941$^{9}$ 3204$^{8}$ 3944$^{11}$ 4236$^{11}$ **>35a 52?f<**

**Brookhead Lady** 5 b m Petong-Lewista (Mandrake Major) **1995:** *4486$^{7}$* **1996:** *59$^{3}$ 342$^{2}$ 388$^{8}$ 511$^{6}$ 764$^{4}$* 1885$^{6}$ 2212$^{5}$ *2550$^{9}$ 2748$^{6}$ 3252$^{7}$* 3345$^{5}$ 3700$^{7}$ 4045$^{9}$ 4486$^{16}$ **>43a 46f<**

**Broom Isle** 8 b m Damister (USA)-Vynz Girl (Tower Walk) *1458$^{8}$ 1967$^{6}$ 2935$^{5}$ 3066$^{P}$* **>50a 60df<**

**Brother Roy** 3 b c Prince Sabo-Classic Heights (Shirley Heights) 4379$^{5}$ 4591$^{5}$ 4831$^{16}$ 4968$^{16}$ 5054$^{13}$ **>70f<**

**Broughtons Champ** 4 b g Dowsing (USA)-Knees Up (USA) (Dancing Champ (USA)) 4515$^{W}$ **>42f<**

**Broughtons Error** 2 ch c Most Welcome-Eloquent Charm (USA) (Private Account (USA)) 2374$^{5}$ 2606$^{8}$ 3259$^{4}$ 3796$^{13}$ 4717$^{11}$ (4867) **>68f<**

**Broughtons Formula** 6 b g Night Shift (USA)-Forward Rally (Formidable (USA)) **1995:** *4442$^{4}$ (4516) (4546)* **1996:** *69$^{9}$ 2226$^{11}$* 2866$^{8}$ 3260$^{9}$ 3802$^{11}$ 3928$^{8}$ (4203) 4321$^{3}$ 4604$^{3}$ (4726) 4832$^{9}$ **>67a 52f<**

**Broughton's Port** 6 b g Reesh-Tawnais (Artaius (USA)) *43$^{7}$ 122$^{8}$* **>25a 39f<**

**Broughton's Pride (IRE)** 5 b m Superpower-French Quarter (Ile de Bourbon (USA)) 508$^{6}$ 787$^{12}$ (1416) 1650$^{P}$ 2801$^{16}$ 4071$^{8}$ 4686$^{5}$ 4975$^{3}$ 5004$^{2}$ **>36a 60f<**

**Broughtons Turmoil** 7 b g Petorius-Rustic Stile (Rusticaro (FR)) *1190$^{15}$* 1775$^{6}$ 2134$^{3}$ 2229$^{3}$ 2722$^{4}$ 3139$^{3}$ 3274$^{3}$ (3686) 3861$^{10}$ 4463$^{9}$ 4571$^{2}$ 4775$^{6}$ 4975$^{5}$ **>68a 82f<**

**Browbeat** 2 ch c Diesis-Gentle Persuasion (Bustino) 3615$^{17}$ **>42f<**

**Brown Eyed Girl** 4 ch f Sharpo-Ella Mon Amour (Ela-Mana-Mou) *424$^{11}$ 469$^{13}$* 598$^{7}$ 752$^{6}$ 866$^{13}$ 1468$^{9}$ 3849$^{10}$ 3970$^{10}$ 4426$^{13}$ **>1a 35f<**

**Brownie's Promise** 3 b g Grey Desire-Telegraph Callgirl (Northern Tempest (USA)) *1864$^{7}$* 2026$^{7}$ 2212$^{11}$ 2780$^{10}$ 3619$^{18}$ 4340$^{8}$ 4624$^{11}$ **>13f<**

**Brume La Voile** 3 b c Puissance-Bali Lady (Balidar) **1995:** *4501$^{8}$* **>30a f<**

**Brutal Fantasy (IRE)** 2 b g Distinctly North (USA)-Flash Donna (USA) (Well Decorated (USA)) (1543) 2237$^{2}$ 3771$^{2}$ 3969$^{3}$ 4586$^{7}$ 4749$^{12}$ **>68f<**

**Bruz** 5 b g Risk Me (FR)-My Croft (Crofter (USA)) 1165$^{4}$ 1637$^{6}$ **>43a 37f<**

**Bryan Robson (USA)** 5 b g Topsider (USA)-Queen's Visit (Top Command (USA)) *582$^{7}$* 893$^{17}$ 1777$^{10}$ 2005$^{22}$ **>46f<**

**Bryanston Square (IRE)** 3 b g Taufan (USA)-Noble Treasure (USA) (Vaguely Noble) 3115$^{10}$ 4824$^{15}$ **>31f<**

**Brynkir** 2 b c Batshoof-Felinwen (White Mill) 4508$^{6}$ 4801$^{10}$ 4897$^{7}$ **>66f<**

**Bubble Gum Fellow (JPN)** 3 b c Sunday Silence (USA)-Bubble Company (FR) (Lyphard (USA)) 4668a$^{3}$ **>119f<**

**Bubble Wings (FR)** 4 b f In The Wings-Bubble Prospector (USA) (Miswaki (USA)) **1995:** *(4543)* **1996:** *530$^{5}$ 1074$^{2}$* (1533) 1825$^{5}$ (2592) 2917$^{3}$ 4059$^{3}$ 4489$^{2}$ 4819$^{2}$ **>61a 79f<**

**Bubbly** 2 b c Rudimentary (USA)-Champagne Season (USA) (Vaguely Noble) 3319$^{5}$ **>74f<**

**Buckley Boys** 5 gr m Grey Desire-Strip Fast (Virginia Boy) **1995:** *4412[2] 4513[10]* **1996:** *360[9] 604[11]* **>42da 57f<**

**Budby** 3 ch f Rock City-Lustrous (Golden Act (USA)) *768[3]* 1301[3] 1641[3] 2743[2] (3138) 3655[4] 4059[2] **>76f<**

**Budding Annie** 3 b f Lord Bud-Gold Paper (FR) (Rheingold) 982[13] 2855[6] 3333[14] 3849[9] 4899[8] **>53f<**

**Budding Prospect** 2 b f Rudimentary (USA)-City Link Rose (Lochnager) 1827[11] **>28f<**

**Buddy Marvel (IRE)** 2 b c Law Society (USA)-Rosa Van Fleet (Sallust) 5063a[2] **>78f<**

**Buddy's Friend (IRE)** 8 ch h Jester-Hasta (Skymaster) *645[12] 778[8] 920[12]* 1691[8] 2075[6] 2507[6] **>62da 42f<**

**Bud's Bet (IRE)** 8 b g Reasonable (FR)-Pearl Creek (Gulf Pearl) 2537[13] **>50a 36f<**

**Built for Comfort (IRE)** 4 b f Nordico (USA)-Dewan's Niece (USA) (Dewan (USA)) *210[12] 301[13]* **>69f<**

**Bulington (FR)** 4 br c Sicyos (USA)-Barbra (FR) (Le Fabuleux) 2273a[2] (3386a) 5019a[2] **>122f<**

**Bullfinch** 3 b c Anshan-Lambay (Lorenzaccio) *574[10]* 833[5] 1126[10] 1484[10] 2041[10] **>91f<**

**Bullpen Belle** 3 b f Relief Pitcher-Hopeful Waters (Forlorn River) **1995:** *4380[5]* **1996:** *754[10]* 955[6] 1689[11] 2344[6] **>53a 45f<**

**Bulsara** 4 b g Dowsing (USA)-Taiga (Northfields (USA)) 1846[6] 2023[4] 2214[3] (2803) (3081) 3280[4] 3623[8] 4470[5] 4597[9] **>1a 61f<**

**Bumblefoot (IRE)** 3 b f Cyrano de Bergerac-La Vosgienne (Ashmore (FR)) **1995:** *4433[6] 4477[5]* **1996:** *46[4] 171[2] 258[4] 281[5] 314[2] 329[3] 404[7]* **>59a 56f<**

**Bunty Bagshaw** 3 b f Arctic Lord-Sarah Carter (Reesh) 3472[16] 4129[16] **>1f< (DEAD)**

**Bunty Boo** 7 b m Noalto-Klairove (Averof) 2698[5] 3126[13] 3495[4] **>90f<**

**Burberry Quest** 2 gr f Thornberry (USA)-Flying Joker (Kalaglow) 465[8] *895[11]* **>8f<**

**Burden Of Proof (IRE)** 4 b c Fairy King (USA)-Belle Passe (Be My Guest (USA)) 1235a[2] 1566a[9] 2092a[2] 2471a[5] 4396a[3] 4649a[4] 4848a[2] 5065a[6] **>110f<**

**Burj** 3 b g Aragon-Aspark (Sparkler) *488[7] 655[11]* **>30a 67f<**

**Burkes Manor** 2 b g Presidium-Miss Nelski (Most Secret) 1827[3] (2138) 2726[3] 2875[4] 3224[4] 3792[4] 3969[2] 4311[3] 4614[3] *(4777)* **>81a 81f<**

**Burlesque** 2 b c Old Vic-Late Matinee (Red Sunset) 3423[6] 4069[12] **>68f<**

**Burlington House (USA)** 2 b c Housebuster (USA)-Queluz (USA) (Saratoga Six (USA)) 829[3] 1003[5] *(1603) 1795[5]* 3674[5] (3969) 4182[4] 4566[3] 4717[5] **>70a 89f<**

**Burning (USA)** 4 b c Bering-Larnica (USA) (Alydar (USA)) *580[10]* 941[10] 2055[18] 2603[11] 3073[10] 3806[5] **>82f<**

**Burning Flame** 3 b f Robellino (USA)-No Islands (Lomond (USA)) 1350[11] 1617[12] 1857[10] 2409[13] 2738[4] *3437[11] 4068[9]* 4496[8] 4968[6] **>47f<**

**Burning Truth (USA)** 2 ch c Known Fact (USA)-Galega (Sure Blade (USA)) 4512[10] **>67f<**

**Burnt Offering** 3 b c Old Vic-Burnt Amber (Balidar) *228[3] (351) 444[7]* 702[3] 1071[4] 1175[4] 1771[5] 2608[10] **>59a 84df<**

**Burnt Sienna (IRE)** 4 b f Don't Forget Me-Ribot Ann (Kampala) **1995:** *4544[6]* **1996:** *53[10] 141[7] 1099[13]* 1651[10] 1821[9] 1979[9] 2507[9] 2981[9] **>38a 41f<**

**Burnt Toast (IRE)** 2 b f Night Shift (USA)-House of Queens (IRE) (King of Clubs) 4639a[8] **>76f<**

**Burntwood Melody** 5 gr g Merdon Melody-Marwick (Roan Rocket) *47[6]* **>38a 8f<**

**Burooj** 6 br h Danzig (USA)-Princess Sucree (USA) (Roberto (USA)) 919[2] **>122f<**

**Burrough Hill Lass** 6 b m Northern State (USA)-Hawthorne Vale (Richboy) *47[10]* **>22f<**

**Bursul Lady** 3 b f Be My Chief (USA)-Neverdown (Never so Bold) 3320[8] 3466[6] **>14f<**

**Burundi (IRE)** 2 b c Danehill (USA)-Sofala (Home Guard (USA)) 4306[8] 4508[W] 4601[2] **>88f<**

**Bushehr (IRE)** 4 b c Persian Bold-Shejrah (USA) (Northjet) *138[9] 208[9]* **>75f<**

**Busy Flight** 3 br c Pharly (FR)-Bustling Nelly (Bustino) 830[6] 1791[18] (3841) (4178) (4553) **>121f<**

**But Not For Me (IRE)** 6 b h Flash of Steel-Anglo Irish (Busted) (193a)

**Butterwick Belle (IRE)** 3 b f Distinctly North (USA)-Forest Berries (IRE) (Thatching) 2320[8] 2715[5] 3959[7] 4486[17] *4577[10] 4808[10]* 4882[15] **>27a 54f<**

**But Why** 2 ch g Then Again-Pleasure Island (Dalsaan) 697[5] 869[5] (1494) **>59f<**

**Buzzards Hall** 6 ch m Buzzards Bay-Nikoola Eve (Roscoe Blake) *33[11] 85[13]* **>8a 36f<**

**Buzzby** 2 b c Buzzards Bay-Capricious Lady (IRE) (Capricorn Line) 1519[5] 1959[8] (2606) **>71f<**

**Buzzby Babe** 2 b f Presidium-Aposse Ad Esse (Record Run) 4380[13] **>57f<**

**Bybus (FR)** 5 gr h Courtroom (FR)-Belle Caro (FR) (Caro) (151a) 324a[2] **>89f<**

**By The Bay** 4 b f Shareef Dancer (USA)-Beryl's Jewel (Siliconn) **1995:** *4385[4] 4456[6] 4521[6]* **1996:** *172[5] 337[4] 4381[4] 4894[8]* **>40a 56f<**

**Byzantium (USA)** 3 b c Gulch (USA)-Bravemie (Nureyev (USA)) (721a)

**C**

**Caballo (GER)** 5 br h Konigsstuhl (GER)-Carmelita (GER) (Surumu (GER)) 1138a[9] 3203a[7] 3753a[8] 4413a[7] 4855a[3] 5029a[2] **>106f<**

**Caballus (USA)** 3 b c Danzig Connection (USA)-Rutledge Place (USA) (Caro) *1957[3]* 2601[W] 2786[2] 3209[4] 3598[9] **>74f<**

**Cabaret (IRE)** 3 b f Sadler's Wells (USA)-Chamonis (USA) (Affirmed (USA)) (1201) 1899[4] 2533[7] 3836[5] 4445[9] **>107f<**

**Cabcharge Blue** 4 b f Midyan (USA)-Mashobra (Vision (USA)) **1995:** *4390[16] 4458[9] 4515[8]* **1996:** *37[4] 104[8] (166) 213[11] 301[4] 336[4] 417[6] 518[11]* **>58a 76f<**

**Cabcharge Gemini** 2 b c High Kicker (USA)-Miss Noname (High Top) 3269[11] **>9f<**

**Cacharro** 5 b g Aragon-Jalopy (Jalmood (USA)) 661[14] 1541[12] 1885[9] **>58?a 20f<**

**Cachet Noir (USA)** 3 b c Theatrical-Irish Wisdom (USA) (Turkoman (USA)) 1139a[5] (2108a) 2665a[3] **>103f<**

**Cadbury Castle** 2 b f Midyan (USA)-Orange Hill (High Top) 4200[4] 4508[12] **>59f<**

**Caddy's First** 4 b g Petong-Love Scene (Carwhite) 3469[9] 3812[13] *5059[6]* **>44a 47f<**

**Cadeau Elegant** 3 ch f Cadeaux Genereux-Wasimah (Caerleon (USA)) 672[11] 1994[7] 2861[5] **>70+f<**

**Cadeaux Cher** 2 ch c Cadeaux Genereux-Home Truth (Known Fact (USA)) 829[7] 1822[2] 1959[2] 4425[4] **>67f<**

**Cadeaux Tryst** 4 b c Cadeaux Genereux-Trystero (Shareef Dancer (USA)) 442[5] 728[3] 1296a[2] 2053[6] 3153[4] (4289a) 4739a[4] **>112f<**

**Ca'd'oro** 3 ch g Cadeaux Genereux-Palace Street (USA) (Secreto (USA)) 648[10] 893[13] 1856[5] 3162[8] (3474) 3852[6] 4186[7] 4376[4] 4550[4] 4820[3] **>63f<**

**Caerfilly Dancer** 2 ch f Caerleon (USA)-Darnelle (Shirley Heights) (3206) 4189[7] 4565[4] **>83f<**

**Cafe Glace** 4 b f Beldale Flutter (USA)-Little White Star (Mill Reef (USA)) **1995:** *4449[6]* **>3a 44f<**

**Caherass Court (IRE)** 5 b m Taufan (USA)-Grass Court (Thatch (USA)) *59[10] 347[9] 1966[12] 2636[9]* **>15a 50f<**

**Cairn Dhu** 2 ch g Presidium-My Precious Daisy (Sharpo) 2727[5] 3291[5] 3464[10] 4195[11] 4433[4] **>54f<**

**Cajun Sunset (IRE)** 2 b g Red Sunset-Carcajou (High Top) 2044[9] 2396[8] 2606[7] 2959[3] 3324[5] 3678[3] 4097[4] (4482) **>61f<**

**Cala-Holme (IRE)** 2 b f Fools Holme (USA)-Calaloo Sioux (USA) (Our Native (USA)) 1086[11] 1845[6] 2043[7] **>30f<**

**Calamander (IRE)** 2 b f Alzao (USA)-Local Custom (IRE) (Be My Native (USA)) 1590[8] 2404[4] 3475[6] 3962[10] **>58f<**

**Calandrella** 3 b f Sizzling Melody-Maravilla (Mandrake Major) 3115[7] 3262[11] 3442[11] 3698[5] 4206[14] 4480[15] **>43f<**

**Calcando** 4 b f Teenoso (USA)-Musical Princess (Cavo Doro) *1168[4]* 1784[8] 2120[9] 3329[6] 3870[11] **>26f<**

**Calchou** 2 bl f Barrys Gamble-Ping Pong (Petong) *848[9] 1080[3] 1760[5] (1968) 2317[6]* **>55a 55f<**

**Calder King** 5 ch g Rakaposhi King-Name the Game (Fair Season) **1995:** *4378[3] 4475[3]* **1996:** *72[2] 210[2] 345[2] 392[3] 440[13]* (541) 619[4] 853[9] (912) 1024[9] 1418[5] 1647[4] 1763[2] 2066[6] 4000[3] 4249[2] 4431[8] 4617[9] 4793[14] 4993[4] **>75a 71f<**

**Calendula** 3 b f Be My Guest (USA)-Sesame (Derrylin) 3441[8] 3942[5] 4110[5] 4559[12] 4967[9] **>67f<**

**Calgary Girl** 4 ch f Weld-Calgary (Run The Gantlet (USA)) **1995:** *4451[6] 4527[12]* **1996:** *79[16]* **>6a 24f<**

**Callaloo** 3 b c Mtoto-Catawba (Mill Reef (USA)) 2943[10] **>59f<**

**Calling Jamaica** 4 b f Elmaamul (USA)-Tolstoya (Northfields (USA)) *246[10]* **>52f< (DEAD)**

**Call Me** 3 b f Most Welcome-Stylish Sister (Great Nephew) *(516) 659[6] 859[2] (1345)* 1771[6] 2593[3] 2855[3] (3238) 3327[3] **>69a 77f<**

**Call Me Albi (IRE)** 5 ch g Glenstal (USA)-Albeni (Great Nephew) **1995:** *4530[4]* **1996:** *108[4] 265[3] 365[5]* **>55a 65f<**

**Call Me Flash** 4 ch g Presidium-Relkisha (Relkino) *372[9] 401[7]* **>25a 51f<**

**Call Me I'm Blue (IRE)** 6 b g Reasonable (FR)-Bluebutton (Blue Cashmere) *589[20]* 735[11] 931[15] 1505[7] 2005[W] 2590[7] 3152[9] 3477[3] *3602[11]* **>41a 59f< (DEAD)**

**Call My Guest (IRE)** 6 b g Be My Guest (USA)-Overcall (Bustino) *656[5] 811[9]* 1063[11] 1835[8] **>42a 58f<**

**Callonescy (IRE)** 4 b g Royal Academy (USA)-Take Your Mark (USA) (Round Table) *24[5] 79[4] 103[3] 260[8] 274[8]* **>61a 4f<**

**Call Tophorse** 4 b g Today and Tomorrow-Sum Star (Comedy Star (USA)) *134[4] 217[8] (334) 501[12]* **>48a f<**

**Call to the Bar (IRE)** 7 b g Kafu-Papun (USA) (Mount Hagen (FR)) *762[10]* 997[5] 1342[4] 1541[2] 1889[6] 2212[P] **>52a 61df< (DEAD)**

**Caltroom (FR)** 3 gr c Courtroom (FR)-Caline de Mars (Kaldoun (FR)) (287a) **>79f<**

**Calypso Grant (IRE)** 2 b f Danehill (USA)-Why so Silent (Mill Reef (USA)) 3988[2] 4363[2] (4861) **>88f<**

**Calypso Lady (IRE)** 2 ch f Priolo (USA)-Taking Steps (Gay Fandango (USA)) (4062) 4305[3] **>89f<**

**Cambodian (USA)** 2 b c Roanoke (USA)-September Kaper (USA) 4846a[2] 5063a[8] **>87f<**

**Cambridge Ball (IRE)** 2 b f Royal Academy (USA)-Boat Race (USA) (Seattle Slew (USA)) 3129[2] 3462[4] 3809[2] 4234[5] 4790[5] **>75f<**

**Camden's Ransom (USA)** 9 b g Hostage (USA)-Camden Court (USA) (Inverness Drive (USA)) **1995:**

4490$^{4}$ **1996:** 3786$^{7}$ 4107$^{13}$ **>62a 53f<**

**Cameron Edge 3** ch f Komaite (USA)-Rapid Action (Gunner B) 2572$^{7}$ 3048$^{9}$ 3325$^{6}$ 4070$^{13}$ 4865$^{15}$ **>25f<**

**Camille (FR) 3** b f Bikala-Jemifa (FR) (Fabulous Dancer (USA)) 791a$^{2}$ 1388a$^{3}$ 4292a$^{10}$ 4663a$^{9}$ **>101f<**

**Camionneur (IRE) 3** b g Cyrano de Bergerac-Fact of Time (Known Fact (USA)) 824$^{15}$ 1068$^{4}$ 1500$^{7}$ 1674$^{13}$ 1860$^{6}$ 2236$^{4}$ 2316$^{4}$ 2427$^{4}$ 2571$^{3}$ 2732$^{2}$ (2902) 3135$^{3}$ 3453$^{4}$ 3465$^{7}$ 3937$^{9}$ 4205$^{4}$ 4246$^{8}$ 4460$^{6}$ 4809$^{4}$ **>56f<**

**Campaspe 4** b f Dominion-Lady River (FR) (Sir Gaylord) (1034) 1542$^{3}$ 1826$^{8}$ 2775$^{2}$ 2988$^{2}$ 3267$^{2}$ 3600$^{5}$ 3878$^{3}$ (4227) 4726$^{6}$ **>22a 59f<**

**Camp David (GER) 6** b h Surumu (GER)-Capitolina (GER) (Empery (USA)) (1054a) (1752a) (4032a) 4655a$^{4}$ **>123f<**

**Camp Follower 3** b c Warrshan (USA)-House Maid (Habitat) 793a$^{2}$ 1990$^{3}$ 2250$^{4}$ **>81f<**

**Camphar 3** ch f Pharly (FR)-Camomilla (Targowice (USA)) 1350$^{12}$ **>20f<**

**Camporese (IRE) 3** b f Sadler's Wells (USA)-Campestral (USA) (Alleged (USA)) (957) 1769$^{4}$ 3392a$^{2}$ 4654a$^{6}$ **>112f<**

**Canadian Fantasy 2** b c Lear Fan (USA)-Florinda (CAN) (Vice Regent (CAN)) 2057$^{3}$ 2295$^{2}$ 2727$^{2}$ 3237$^{4}$ 4245$^{2}$ 4585$^{3}$ **>74f<**

**Canadian Jive 3** b f Dominion-Ural Dancer (Corvaro (USA)) 1656$^{15}$ 4827$^{W}$

**Canary Blue (IRE) 5** b m Bluebird (USA)-Norfolk Bonnet (Morston (FR)) 3580$^{7}$ 3870$^{7}$ **>5a 23f<**

**Canary Falcon 5** ch g Polish Precedent (USA)-Pumpona (USA) (Sharpen Up) **1995:** 4421$^{8}$ 4445$^{2}$ 4503$^{8}$ **1996:** 87$^{8}$ 145$^{7}$ 219$^{3}$ 306$^{8}$ 366$^{6}$ 469$^{15}$ 1674$^{10}$ 2155$^{6}$ 2587$^{5}$ 2628$^{6}$ **>60a 56f<**

**Can Can Charlie 6** gr g Vaigly Great-Norton Princess (Wolver Hollow) 5003$^{7}$ **>55a 53f<**

**Can Can Lady 2** ch f Anshan-Agama (USA) (Nureyev (USA)) 2211$^{4}$ (2519) 2797$^{4}$ 3128$^{7}$ 4113$^{8}$ (4262) 4384$^{5}$ **>71f<**

**Candle Light (IRE) 2** b f Petorius-Alberjas (IRE) (Sure Blade (USA)) 865$^{7}$ 1026$^{5}$ 3629$^{6}$ **>16a 29f<**

**Candle Smile (USA) 4** b c Pleasant Colony (USA)-Silent Turn (USA) (Silent Cal (USA)) 845$^{5}$ 974$^{2}$ 1168$^{2}$ (1587) 2042$^{3}$ 3266$^{4}$ 4112$^{2}$ (4377) 4771$^{23}$ **>103f<**

**Candle Smoke (USA) 3** b br g Woodman (USA)-Light the Lights (FR) (Shirley Heights) 668$^{8}$ (2739) 3149$^{3}$ 3486$^{5}$ (3667) 3928$^{2}$ 4199$^{4}$ **>79f<**

**Candrika 3** b f High Estate-Chevisaunce (Fabulous Dancer (USA)) 2318$^{7}$ 2591$^{6}$ 3441$^{7}$ 4170a$^{3}$ **>64f<**

**Candy's Delight 3** b f Dunbeath (USA)-Simply Candy (IRE) (Simply Great (FR)) 4340$^{6}$ 4387$^{8}$ 4898$^{18}$ **>32f<**

**Cane Them 3** ch c Risk Me (FR)-She's A Sport (Jalmood (USA)) 663$^{12}$ 3162$^{13}$ 3665$^{6}$ **>28f<**

**Cannizaro (IRE) 4** b f Gallic League-Paradise Regained (North Stoke) 174$^{7}$ 393$^{8}$ **>30a 43f<**

**Canon Can (USA) 3** ch g Green Dancer (USA)-Lady Argyle (USA) (Don B (USA)) 2036$^{3}$ 2601$^{4}$ (3404) (3972) 4771$^{3}$ **>115?f<**

**Canovas Heart 7** b g Balidar-Worthy Venture (Northfields (USA)) (601) 814$^{3}$ 911$^{5}$ (1512) (1974) 2548$^{7}$ 3432$^{7}$ 3827$^{6}$ (4220) **>59a 79f<**

**Can She Can Can 4** b f Sulaafah (USA)-Dominance (Dominion) 236$^{12}$ 400$^{7}$ 504$^{5}$ 609$^{13}$ 1070$^{13}$ 1542$^{6}$ 2182$^{9}$ 2310$^{13}$ **>1a 36f<**

**Cante Chico 4** b c Reference Point-Flamenco Wave (USA) (Desert Wine (USA)) (1697) 2008$^{11}$ 2513$^{5}$ 3944$^{16}$ **>63f<**

**Canton Ron 2** ch c Ron's Victory (USA)-Briery Fille (Sayyaf) 4204$^{9}$ 4572$^{5}$ 4896$^{2}$ **>55a 38f<**

**Canton Venture 4** ch g Arctic Tern (USA)-Ski Michaela (USA) (Devil's Bag (USA)) 898$^{2}$ (1098) (1514) (1837) (2046) 2221$^{2}$ (2331) 2613$^{6}$ (2767) 2921$^{3}$ (3302) 3587$^{2}$ 4073$^{8}$ 4176$^{6}$ **>76a 80f<**

**Cantsaynowt 2** b f Rambo Dancer (CAN)-Petiller (Monsanto (FR)) 733$^{3}$ 838$^{9}$ 1645$^{2}$ 1869$^{8}$ 2018$^{4}$ 2416$^{6}$ 2681$^{6}$ 2872$^{6}$ 3648$^{7}$ 3840$^{12}$ 4244$^{15}$ 4343$^{W}$ 4594$^{20}$ 5005$^{11}$ **>56f<**

**Canyon Creek (IRE) 3** b c Mr Prospector (USA)-River Memories (USA) (Riverman (USA)) (4591) **>86+f<**

**Cape Cross (IRE) 2** b c Green Desert (USA)-Park Appeal (Ahonoora) 3757$^{4}$ (4175) **>104+f<**

**Cape Merino 5** ch m Clantime-Laena (Roman Warrior) (864) **>107f<**

**Cape Pigeon (USA) 11** ch g Storm Bird (CAN)-Someway Somehow (USA) (What Luck (USA)) 645$^{8}$ (1314) 1651$^{5}$ 2373$^{2}$ (3115) 3469$^{3}$ 3786$^{4}$ 4129$^{3}$ **>73f<**

**Capias (USA) 5** b h Alleged (USA)-Smooth Bore (USA) (His Majesty (USA)) **1995:** 4482$^{5}$ **>96a 114f<**

**Capilano Princess 3** b f Tragic Role (USA)-Lady Capilano (Nebbiolo) 888$^{8}$ (1181) 1785$^{2}$ 2146$^{8}$ 3153$^{6}$ 3926$^{11}$ **>61a 86f<**

**Capitaine Achab (FR) 4** dk g Kendor (FR)-La Bandolera (FR) (Thatching) 4411a$^{3}$ **>75f<**

**Cap Juluca (IRE) 4** b c Mtoto-Tabyan (USA) (Topsider (USA)) 2038$^{11}$ **>122+f<**

**Capote Belle (USA) 3** b f Capote (USA)-Rythmical (USA) (Fappiano (USA)) 4951a$^{7}$ **>117a f<**

**Capstone 3** b f Shirley Heights-Doumayna (Kouban (FR)) 687$^{7}$ 980$^{7}$ **>59f<**

**Captain Carat 5** gr g Handsome Sailor-Gem of Gold (Jellaby) 475$^{4}$ 587$^{4}$ (762) 850$^{7}$ 956$^{6}$ (1364) 1588$^{5}$ 1848$^{9}$ 2329$^{6}$ 2523$^{2}$ 2590$^{6}$ 2771$^{4}$ 2867$^{3}$ 3106$^{5}$ 3352$^{3}$ 3482$^{9}$ 3868$^{12}$ 3973$^{6}$ 4382$^{2}$ 4505$^{7}$ 4791$^{14}$ **>62a 66f<**

**Captain Carparts 2** b c Hubbly Bubbly (USA)-Choir (High Top) 3779$^{7}$ 4578$^{7}$ **>57f<**

**Captain Collins (IRE) 2** gr c El Gran Senor (USA)-Kanmary (FR) (Kenmare (FR)) 4050$^{2}$ 4879$^{3}$ **>83f<**

**Captain Flint 2** b br g Bedford (USA)-Sun Yat Chen (Chou Chin Chow) 2422$^{5}$ 4594$^{13}$ 4694$^{7}$ **>48f<**

**Captain Horatius (IRE) 7** b h Taufan (USA)-One Last Glimpse (Relko) 581$^{3}$ 909a$^{5}$ (1355) 2730$^{4}$ 3431$^{3}$ **>118f<**

**Captain Marmalade 7** ch g Myjinski (USA)-Lady Seville (Orange Bay) 9$^{2}$ 83$^{8}$ 186$^{4}$ 400$^{6}$ 440$^{9}$ (485) 666$^{12}$ 898$^{6}$ 1095$^{8}$ **>54a 56f<**

**Captain Picard 2** b c Today and Tomorrow-Nimble Dancer (Northern Wizard) 1093$^{8}$ 1513$^{11}$

***Captain's Day* 4** ch g Ballacashtal (CAN)-Seymour Ann (Krayyan) 650$^{10}$ 1354$^{7}$ 1659$^{6}$ 2130$^{8}$ 2201$^{10}$ 3052$^{11}$ 3161$^{12}$ 4129$^{5}$ 4373$^{16}$ **>45a 63f<**

**Captain's Guest (IRE) 6** b g Be My Guest (USA)-Watership (USA) (Foolish Pleasure (USA)) 3797$^{6}$ 4377$^{5}$ 4771$^{26}$ **>81f<**

**Captain Tandy (IRE) 7** ch g Boyne Valley-Its All A Dream (Le Moss) 613$^{10}$ **>22a 48f<**

**Captain William (IRE) 2** b c Shernazar-Our Galadrial (Salmon Leap (USA)) 2783$^{6}$ 3423$^{2}$ 3904a$^{2}$ **>82f<**

**Captive Song (IRE) 4** b c Danehill (USA)-Tony Award (USA) (Kirtling) 495$^{9}$

**Capture The Moment 3** b f Keen-Shaieef (IRE) (Shareef Dancer (USA)) **1995:** 4383$^{14}$ **1996:** 646$^{6}$ 955$^{7}$ 1152$^{8}$ 1761$^{7}$ 1991$^{10}$ 2133$^{5}$ 2286$^{22}$ 2411$^{5}$ **>45f<**

**Cara Alanna (IRE) 9** br m Dalsaan-Dinsero 4537b$^{8}$ **>10f<**

**Carati 2** b f Selkirk (USA)-Clytie (USA) (El Gran Senor (USA)) 2147$^{4}$ (3105) 3990$^{2}$ 4491$^{8}$ **>81f<**

**Carburton 3** b c Rock City-Arminda (Blakeney) 709$^{3}$ 833$^{10}$ 4974$^{13}$ **>89?f<**

**Care And Comfort 4** ch f Most Welcome-Whipp's Cross (Kris) 661$^{10}$ 822$^{7}$ 971$^{8}$ 1474$^{13}$ 3645$^{12}$ **>35f<**

**Careful (IRE) 3** gr f Distinctly North (USA)-Caring (Crowned Prince (USA)) 1719$^{8}$ 2528$^{7}$ 2994$^{11}$ 3991$^{14}$ 4506$^{11}$ **>34a 54f<**

**Cariad Cymru 2** b br g Welsh Captain-Daddy's Darling (Mummy's Pet) 1062$^{5}$ **>60f<**

**Caribbean Dancer 3** b f Shareef Dancer (USA)-Deposit (Thatch (USA)) 786$^{5}$ (1155) 1666$^{5}$ **>71f<**

**Caribbean Quest 3** b f Rainbow Quest (USA)-Jammaayil (IRE) (Lomond (USA)) 1899$^{6}$ 3497$^{9}$ **>96f<**

**Caribbean Star 2** b f Soviet Star (USA)-Whos The Blonde (Cure The Blues (USA)) 1467$^{3}$ 1954$^{4}$ 3787$^{2}$ 4578$^{6}$ **>66f<**

**Caribbee Beach (IRE) 2** ch f Magical Strike (USA)-Madam John (Ballad Rock) 741$^{6}$ **>10f<**

**Caricature (IRE) 3** b g Cyrano de Bergerac-That's Easy (Swing Easy (USA)) 646$^{8}$ 833$^{8}$ 1127$^{3}$ 1820$^{9}$ 3210$^{8}$ 3612$^{11}$ 3926$^{5}$ 4109$^{4}$ 4376$^{5}$ 4687$^{23}$ 4802$^{2}$ **>84f<**

**Carling (FR) 4** b f Garde Royale-Corraleja (FR) (Carvin (FR)) **1995:** 4471a$^{11}$ **1996:** 622a$^{2}$ 906a$^{9}$ 2480a$^{9}$ (3749a) 4165a$^{5}$ 4410a$^{2}$ 4961a$^{3}$ **>121f<**

**Carlisle Bay (IRE) 2** b c Darshaan-My Potters (USA) 5014a$^{3}$ **>76f<**

**Carlito Brigante 4** b g Robellino (USA)-Norpella (Northfields (USA)) 440$^{10}$ 628$^{2}$ (690) 953$^{3}$ 1816$^{4}$ 2010$^{2}$ 2164$^{4}$ 2350$^{8}$ 2724$^{4}$ **>89f<**

**Carlton (IRE) 2** ch c Thatching-Hooray Lady (Ahonoora) 1626$^{6}$ 4330$^{24}$ 5049$^{8}$ **>46f<**

**Carlton Express (IRE) 6** b g Persian Heights-Snow Finch (Storm Bird (CAN)) 508$^{17}$ 752$^{2}$ 995$^{5}$ 1088$^{5}$ 1421$^{3}$ 2136$^{P}$ **>42?a 50f<**

**Carlys Quest 2** ch c Primo Dominie-Tuppy (USA) (Sharpen Up) 3625$^{8}$ 3963$^{4}$ 4331$^{7}$ 4602$^{P}$ **>57a 65f<**

**Carmarthen Bay 3** ch c Prionsaa-Pattie's Grey (Valiyar) **1995:** (4519) **1996:** 182$^{9}$ 321$^{2}$ (352) 391$^{5}$ 2687$^{7}$ 2974$^{5}$ 3926$^{12}$ 4202$^{4}$ 4376$^{2}$ 4498$^{7}$ **>81a 75f<**

**Carmenoura (IRE) 4** ch f Carmelite House (USA)-Flower Petals (Busted) 328$^{11}$ 619$^{9}$ 1600$^{11}$ 2565$^{6}$ 3414$^{7}$ 3492$^{10}$ **>12f<**

**Carmine Lake (IRE) 2** ch f Royal Academy (USA)-Castilian Queen (USA) (Diesis) (683) 984$^{3}$ (3213) 3707$^{4}$ 4660a$^{5}$ **>104f<**

**Carmosa (USA) 3** ch f Blushing John (USA)-Bobbinette (Whitstead) **1995:** 4414$^{4}$ 4483$^{3}$ **1996:** 453$^{12}$ 562$^{5}$ 660$^{2}$ 1764$^{3}$ 2019$^{7}$ 3225$^{9}$ **>62a 60df<**

**Carnival of Light 4** b f Squill (USA)-June Fayre (Sagaro) 4828$^{13}$ **>6a 30f<**

**Carol Again 4** b f Kind of Hush-Lady Carol (Lord Gayle (USA)) 43$^{2}$ 87$^{2}$ 124$^{4}$ 239$^{9}$ 328$^{2}$ 367$^{3}$ 426$^{5}$ (604) (777) 898$^{8}$ 1098$^{5}$ 1487$^{7}$ 4906$^{12}$ 5007$^{11}$ **>54da 24f<**

**Carol's Dream (USA) 4** ch c Risen Star (USA)-Merle Halton (USA) (Rattle Dancer) (502) 5002$^{8}$ **>80+a 83f<**

**Carranita (IRE) 6** b m Anita's Prince-Take More (GER) (Frontal) (507) (737) 889$^{4}$ 1075$^{2}$ 1800$^{3}$ 2332$^{4}$ (2692) 3127$^{7}$ (3759) 4442$^{11}$ 4774$^{7}$ 5044$^{4}$ **>114f<**

**Carreamia 3** b f Weldnaas (USA)-Carribean Tyme (Tyrnavos) 4592$^{5}$ 4978$^{3}$ 5058$^{10}$ **>63da 70f<**

**Carrolls Marc (IRE) 8** b g Horage-Rare Find (Rarity) **1995:** 4507$^{9}$ **1996:** (104) (140) 240$^{2}$ 309$^{5}$ 349$^{6}$ **>61a 57f<**

**Cartouche** 2 gr g Terimon-Emblazon (Wolver Hollow) 3099$^{7}$ 3312$^{5}$ 3848$^{9}$ **>65f<**
**Carwyn's Choice** 3 b f Then Again-Over My Head (Bay Express) **1995:** *4533$^{8}$* **1996:** *102$^{8}$ 3286$^{9}$* 3606$^{13}$ 3965$^{R}$ **>24a 24f<**
**Cashaplenty** 3 ch g Ballacashtal (CAN)-Storm of Plenty (Billion (USA)) *651$^{5}$ 5058$^{8}$* **>34a f<**
**Cash Deposit (USA)** 2 b br c Deposit Ticket (USA)-Aneka (USA) (Believe It (USA)) *4954a$^{4}$* **>102a f<**
**Cashel Princess (IRE)** 3 ch f Fayruz-House of Queens (IRE) (King of Clubs) 4851a$^{6}$ **>82f<**
**Cashmere Lady** 4 b f Hubbly Bubbly (USA)-Choir (High Top) **1995:** *(4372) (4479)* **1996:** *115$^{2}$ 285$^{5}$ (416) 739$^{4}$* 1505$^{4}$ *1601$^{2}$ 1868$^{5}$* 2045$^{2}$ 2351$^{3}$ 2679$^{4}$ 3770$^{4}$ 4316$^{5}$ 4686$^{17}$ **>90a 81f<**
**Cashmirie** 4 b f Domynsky-Betrothed (Aglojo) **1995:** *4391$^{5}$ 4448$^{5}$* **>36a 60f<**
**Casino Chip** 3 br c Daring March-Important Guest (Be My Guest (USA)) **1995:** *4353$^{7}$* **1996:** *460$^{7}$ 1806$^{10}$* 3661$^{12}$ **>27a 3f<**
**Caspian Beluga** 8 b g Persian Bold-Miss Thames (Tower Walk) *38$^{9}$ 116$^{11}$* **>36a 70f<**
**Caspian Morn** 2 b f Lugana Beach-Parijoun (Manado) 3129$^{3}$ (3438) 3620$^{7}$ 4182$^{9}$ 4440$^{9}$ 4546$^{4}$ **>77f<**
**Cassimere** 4 ch f Clantime-Poshteen (Royal Smoke) 943$^{5}$ 1351$^{5}$ 1964$^{8}$ 3167$^{13}$ **>46f<**
**Castan (IRE)** 3 b g Persian Bold-Erzsi (Caerleon (USA)) *756$^{6}$* 1447$^{4}$ 1780$^{4}$ (2013) 2602$^{3}$ 2925$^{3}$ (4609) 4775$^{19}$ **>81f<**
**Castel Rosselo** 6 br h Rousillon (USA)-On The House (FR) (Be My Guest (USA)) **1995:** *4368$^{12}$ 4476$^{16}$* **1996:** *358$^{9}$ 455$^{19}$* 537$^{5}$ 679$^{9}$ 933$^{12}$ 1051$^{6}$ 1473$^{10}$ 2058$^{7}$ 2403$^{8}$ **>88a 63f<**
**Castle Ashby Jack** 2 gr c Chilibang-Carly-B (IRE) (Commanche Run) *1080$^{2}$ 1315$^{3}$* 1653$^{7}$ 1822$^{3}$ 2323$^{3}$ 2600$^{9}$ 2951$^{2}$ **>62a 64f<**
**Castle Governor** 3 b g Governor General-Sorcha (IRE) (Shernazar) *32$^{4}$ (68) 81$^{5}$ 112$^{10}$ 271$^{6}$* **>51a 54f<**
**Castle House** 2 b c Risk Me (FR)-Moonlight Princess (Alias Smith (USA)) 639$^{2}$ (741) 946$^{4}$ 1437$^{7}$ 1713$^{5}$ 3478$^{9}$ 3871$^{7}$ 3975$^{9}$ 4493$^{5}$ *4576$^{4}$* **>43a 68f<**
**Castlerea Lad** 7 b h Efisio-Halo (Godswalk (USA)) 451$^{4}$ 610$^{5}$ 737$^{5}$ 928$^{11}$ 1186$^{14}$ 1334$^{7}$ 1652$^{9}$ 1829$^{3}$ 2329$^{8}$ 2363$^{13}$ 3045$^{7}$ 3639$^{11}$ 4058$^{4}$ 4198$^{10}$ 4342$^{5}$ 4460$^{5}$ 4689$^{6}$ 4809$^{12}$ 4881$^{7}$ 4994$^{15}$ **>68f<**
**Castles Burning (USA)** 2 b br g Minshaanshu Amad (USA)-Major Overhaul (Known Fact (USA)) 1531$^{4}$ 1774$^{7}$ 2335$^{9}$ 3821$^{7}$ 4106$^{4}$ 4262$^{10}$ 4549$^{3}$ 4787$^{2}$ 4990$^{3}$ **>58f<**
**Castle Secret** 10 b g Castle Keep-Baffle (Petingo) **1995:** *4411$^{7}$* **1996:** *1488$^{2}$ 1981$^{2}$* 2385$^{2}$ **>60a 66f<**
**Castletown Count** 4 b g Then Again-Pepeke (Mummy's Pet) 822$^{2}$ 1697$^{4}$ **>64f<**
**Cast the Line** 6 b g Pharly (FR)-Off The Reel (USA) (Silent Screen (USA)) **1995:** *4412$^{12}$* **>77f<**
**Casual Cottage (IRE)** 2 b f Thatching-Non Casual (Nonoalco (USA)) 1308$^{3}$ 1595$^{6}$ 2569$^{6}$ 2930$^{4}$ **>54f<**
**Casual Water (IRE)** 5 b g Simply Great (FR)-Top Nurse (High Top) 1109$^{11}$ 1792$^{5}$ 2300$^{7}$ 2534$^{6}$ 2884$^{4}$ (3235) 3828$^{3}$ **>79f<**
**Catalyst (IRE)** 3 b f Sadler's Wells (USA)-Welsh Love 2474a$^{7}$ **>87f<**
**Catchable** 2 b c Pursuit of Love-Catawba (Mill Reef (USA)) 4492$^{6}$ 4720$^{2}$ **>80f<**
**Catch The Blues (IRE)** 4 b f Bluebird (USA)-Dear Lorraine (FR) (Nonoalco (USA)) 1566a$^{2}$ 2072$^{2}$ 3562a$^{5}$ 3708$^{5}$ 4057$^{3}$ 4280a$^{3}$ **>117f<**
**Catch The Lights** 3 b f Deploy-Dream Chaser (Record Token) **1995:** *(4380)* **1996:** *1121$^{11}$* 1820$^{7}$ 2126$^{4}$ (2526) (2710) (2974) 3148$^{9}$ 3516$^{11}$ 3989$^{4}$ 4329$^{8}$ 4769$^{12}$ 4974$^{15}$ **>75+a 87f<**
**Catechism (USA)** 2 b br f St Jovite (USA)-Sunday Best (USA) (Halo (USA)) 2892$^{2}$ 3206$^{2}$ (3593) 4113$^{7}$ 4490$^{10}$ **>85f<**
**Cathedral (IRE)** 2 b c Prince Sabo-Choire Mhor (Dominion) 1519$^{3}$ **>90+f<**
**Catherine's Choice** 3 ch g Primo Dominie-Bambolona (Bustino) **1995:** *4485$^{5}$* **1996:** *17$^{P}$ 445$^{4}$* 701$^{6}$ 1654$^{12}$ *(2934) 3426$^{15}$ 3603$^{3}$ 3926$^{13}$* 4866$^{11}$ **>74a 57f<**
**Cathies Flower** 2 b f Rock Hopper-Deflowered (Red God) *4607$^{W}$* 5038$^{6}$
**Catienus (USA)** 2 b br c Storm Cat (USA)-Diamond City (USA) (Mr Prospector (USA)) 4050$^{5}$ 4301$^{3}$ (4706) (5038) **>89f<**
**Catoki (USA)** 3 b c Storm Cat (USA)-Matoki (USA) (Hail To Reason) 795a$^{3}$ **>77f<**
**Catria (IRE)** 2 br f Caerleon (USA)-Embla (Dominion) 1954$^{6}$ 4547$^{7}$ 4797$^{2}$ 4991$^{6}$ **>83f<**
**Cats Bottom** 4 ch f Primo Dominie-Purple Fan (Dalsaan) 981$^{13}$ 1423$^{7}$ 1613$^{4}$ 1703$^{6}$ 2312$^{7}$ 2342$^{7}$ 3991$^{18}$ 4256$^{11}$ 4373$^{2}$ 4691$^{2}$ 4882$^{5}$ **>65f<**
**Catumbella (USA)** 3 ch f Diesis-Benguela (USA) (Little Current (USA)) 703$^{3}$ 4813$^{2}$ 5042$^{5}$ **>74f<**
**Catwalk** 2 b f Shirley Heights-Moogie (Young Generation) 2863$^{6}$ (3444) 4133$^{9}$ 4676$^{4}$ **>91f<**
**Catwalk Girl** 3 b f Skyliner-Pokey's Pet (Uncle Pokey) 1610$^{6}$ 2049$^{12}$ 2481$^{8}$ 2983$^{12}$ **>47f<**
**Cauda Equina** 2 gr c Statoblest-Sea Fret (Habat) 1328$^{3}$ 1525$^{7}$ 3807$^{7}$ **>66f<**
**Causley** 11 br g Swing Easy (USA)-Four Lawns (Forlorn River) *2303$^{11}$ 2507$^{15}$* 2709$^{11}$ 3067$^{11}$ **>26a 42f<**
**Caution** 2 b f Warning-Fairy Flax (IRE) (Dancing Brave (USA)) 3853$^{2}$ 4043$^{3}$ (4250) **>79f<**
**Cavendish Rose** 5 ch m Music Boy-Afef John (Monseigneur (USA)) *427$^{W}$* **>48f<**
**Cavers Yangous** 5 b g Daring March-Rapid Lady (Rapid River) 2874$^{4}$ 3328$^{3}$ 3639$^{10}$ 3817$^{3}$ 3973$^{11}$ 4136$^{10}$ 4460$^{3}$ *4778$^{9}$ 4809$^{6}$* 4909$^{13}$ *4987$^{13}$* **>48a 64f<**
**Caviar And Candy** 2 b f Soviet Star (USA)-Blue Brocade (Reform) 465$^{3}$ 557$^{4}$ 639$^{3}$ 733$^{6}$ *895$^{7}$ 1494$^{3}$* 1713$^{3}$ 1880$^{2}$ 2125$^{4}$ 2435$^{4}$ **>37a 54f<**
**Caviar Royale (IRE)** 2 ch c Royal Academy (USA)-Petite Liqueurelle (IRE) (Shernazar) 950$^{2}$ (1046) 1795$^{3}$ 2112$^{5}$ 3128$^{2}$ 3468$^{2}$ **>95f<**
**Cavonnier (USA)** 3 dk g Batonnier (USA)-Direwarning (USA) (Caveat (USA)) *1055a$^{2}$* **>126a f<**
**Cayman Kai (IRE)** 3 ch c Imperial Frontier (USA)-Safiya (USA) (Riverman (USA)) (681) 1141a$^{4}$ 2039$^{5}$ 3144$^{8}$ **>119f<**
**Cayumanque (CHI)** 7 br h El Morgon (USA)-Recoleta (CHI) (Sun Sun) *397a$^{3}$* **>92f<**
**Cd Super Targeting (IRE)** 3 ch f Polish Patriot (USA)-Hazy Bird (Ballymore) 550$^{11}$ 678$^{15}$ 1523$^{2}$ (1589) 1714$^{5}$ 4472$^{6}$ **>67f<**
**Ceanothus (IRE)** 2 ch f Bluebird (USA)-Golden Bloom (Main Reef) 3988$^{9}$ 4861$^{11}$ **>67f<**
**Cebwob** 3 br f Rock City-Island Ruler (Ile de Bourbon (USA)) 1152$^{11}$ *2325$^{11}$ 3244$^{4}$* 3654$^{2}$ 3882$^{3}$ **>33a 62f<**
**Cedar Dancer** 4 b f Rambo Dancer (CAN)-Nonasalome (Absalom) *545$^{4}$* 631$^{4}$ 862$^{8}$ 981$^{12}$ 1302$^{13}$ *1970$^{8}$ 2286$^{6}$* 2743$^{12}$ 3473$^{2}$ 4082$^{12}$ **>39a 41f<**
**Cedar Girl** 4 b f Then Again-Classic Times (Dominion) *231$^{5}$ 278$^{9}$* 2598$^{7}$ 2745$^{10}$ *2937$^{3}$ 2994$^{7}$* 3306$^{10}$ **>45a 41f<**
**Cedez le Passage (FR)** 5 b h Warning-Microcosme (Golden Fleece (USA)) **1995:** 4498a$^{6}$ **1996:** 455$^{8}$ 580$^{15}$ 1792$^{12}$ 2053$^{27}$ 3388a$^{0}$ 4941a$^{5}$ 5022a$^{13}$ **>95a 73f<**
**Cee-Jay-Ay** 9 gr g Free State-Raffinrula (Raffingora) *399$^{9}$ 505$^{6}$* 598$^{8}$ 851$^{9}$ 1037$^{7}$ 1302$^{5}$ 1538$^{5}$ 1704$^{5}$ 2214$^{7}$ 2521$^{2}$ 2672$^{3}$ 2868$^{10}$ (3289) 3510$^{2}$ 3777$^{6}$ 3867$^{4}$ 4226$^{12}$ 4436$^{3}$ 4597$^{3}$ 4724$^{4}$ 4906$^{2}$ **>62a 64f<**
**Cee-N-K (IRE)** 2 b c Thatching-Valois (Lyphard (USA)) 4469$^{8}$ 4807$^{4}$ *4976$^{2}$* **>58a 68f<**
**Ceilidh Star (IRE)** 3 b f Soviet Star (USA)-Highland Ball (Bold Lad (IRE)) 738$^{3}$ 1669$^{2}$ 1900$^{3}$ 3276$^{2}$ (3819) 4042$^{3}$ 4216$^{15}$ 4557$^{5}$ 4899$^{3}$ **>70f<**
**Ceirseach (IRE)** 3 br f Don't Forget Me-Beparoejojo (Lord Gayle (USA)) 1249a$^{4}$ 2102a$^{2}$ 2069$^{8}$ 2465a$^{6}$ 3021a$^{3}$ 3531a$^{6}$ 4268a$^{4}$ 4738a$^{8}$ **>105f<**
**Celandine** 3 b f Warning-Silly Bold (Rousillon (USA)) *182$^{6}$ 335$^{6}$ 1199$^{7}$* 1829$^{10}$ **>69a 83f<**
**Celebrant** 2 b f Saddlers' Hall (IRE)-Cathedra (So Blessed) 3105$^{2}$ 3515$^{4}$ 3796$^{5}$ **>74f<**
**Celebration Cake (IRE)** 4 b g Mister Majestic-My Louise (Manado) 2567$^{7}$ 2679$^{2}$ (3344) 3426$^{2}$ (3592) 3985$^{18}$ 4300$^{5}$ (4316) 4470$^{7}$ **>82f<**
**Celeric** 4 b g Mtoto-Hot Spice (Hotfoot) 941$^{6}$ (1116) 1976$^{2}$ (2330) (2723) (3673) 4134$^{2}$ (4569) **>119+f<**
**Celestial Choir** 6 b m Celestial Storm (USA)-Choir (High Top) **1995:** *4367$^{2}$ 4476$^{9}$* **1996:** *(13) (75) 181$^{4}$ 392$^{4}$ 450$^{5}$* 765$^{2}$ 933$^{15}$ 1198$^{13}$ 2008$^{2}$ 2350$^{3}$ 2674$^{2}$ (3134) (3710) 4193$^{14}$ 4385$^{3}$ 5046$^{17}$ **>89a 103f<**
**Celestial Dollar** 5 b g Celestial Storm (USA)-Pennies to Pounds (Ile de Bourbon (USA)) 2989$^{14}$ 3474$^{14}$ **>13a 46f<**
**Celestial Fire** 4 gr g Celestial Storm (USA)-Fiery Gal (CAN) (Explodent (USA)) 2740$^{4}$ **>54f<**
**Celestial Key (USA)** 6 br g Star de Naskra (USA)-Casa Key (USA) (Cormorant (USA)) **1995:** *4482$^{8}$* **1996:** *3996$^{5}$* 4196$^{4}$ 4325$^{3}$ 4444$^{26}$ 4623$^{2}$ 4800$^{6}$ 4870$^{3}$ 4972$^{4}$ **>70a 109f<**
**Celestial Waters** 4 b f Monsanto (FR)-Hopeful Waters (Forlorn River) **1995:** *4418$^{W}$* **>10f< (DEAD)**
**Celestial Way (USA)** 5 ch g Diesis-Stellaria (USA) (Roberto (USA)) 3388a$^{2}$ **>76f<**
**Celia's Rainbow** 3 gr f Belfort (FR)-Mrs Skinner (Electric) 705$^{12}$ 1201$^{6}$ **>28f<**
**Celtic Lady** 5 b m Kabour-Lady Gilly (Remainder Man) 1435$^{13}$ *1810$^{7}$*
**Celtic Lilley** 6 ch m Celtic Cone-Pal Alley (Pals Passage) *1717$^{9}$*
**Celtic Link (IRE)** 2 b f Toca Madera-Ali Mo Gra 5063a$^{9}$ **>15f<**
**Celtic Lore** 4 b g Caerleon (USA)-Slender Style (USA) (Alleged (USA)) 4643a$^{14}$ **>91f<**
**Censor** 3 b c Kris-Mixed Applause (USA) (Nijinsky (CAN)) 808$^{5}$ 1193$^{6}$ 2621$^{3}$ 3229$^{5}$ **>95f<**
**Cent Plaisirs (FR)** 3 f b Priolo (USA)-Centriste (FR) (Miswaki (USA)) (3389a) **>75f<**
**Centre Stalls (IRE)** 3 b c In The Wings-Lora's Guest (Be My Guest (USA)) 574$^{2}$ 694$^{8}$ (3503) (4051) 4664a$^{8}$ 4972$^{7}$ **>121df<**
**Cerbera** 7 b g Caruso-Sealed Contract (Runnymede) *302$^{4}$ 386$^{5}$ 414$^{P}$ 511$^{7}$* **>43a f<**
**Cerdan (USA)** 3 ch c Zilzal (USA)-Vie En Rose (USA) (Blushing Groom (FR)) 1195$^{5}$ 2718$^{2}$ 2918$^{3}$ 3272$^{4}$ **>89f<**
**Cerise (IRE)** 3 b f Red Sunset-Noble Nancy (Royal And Regal (USA)) 595$^{2}$ 1042$^{11}$ 1363$^{15}$ 1908$^{6}$ 2541$^{4}$ 2780$^{8}$ 3102$^{13}$ 4472$^{7}$ *4978$^{6}$* **>51a 51f<**
**Certain Magic** 2 ch c Faustus (USA)-Dependable (Formidable (USA)) 3685$^{5}$ (3941) 4303$^{6}$ **>77f<**
**Certain Way (IRE)** 6 ch h Sure Blade (USA)-Ruffling Point (Gorytus (USA)) **1995:** *(4377) 4390$^{9}$ 4505$^{6}$ (4512)* **1996:** *57$^{5}$* **>68a 56?f<**

**Cezanne** 7 b h Ajdal (USA)-Reprocolor (Jimmy Reppin) *375a$^{4}$ 436a$^{2}$ 535a$^{2}$ 1135a$^{6}$* 2038$^{5}$ 4066$^{4}$ **>112a 120f<**

**Chabrol (CAN)** 3 b c El Gran Senor (USA)-Off The Record (USA) (Chas Conerly (USA)) 684$^{6}$ 985$^{5}$ 1357$^{4}$ 3041$^{7}$ (3357) 3623$^{13}$ 4238$^{7}$ 4866$^{9}$ 4968$^{17}$ **>71f<**

**Chadleigh Lane (USA)** 4 ch g Imp Society (USA)-Beauty Hour (USA) (Bold Hour) **1995:** *4445$^{7}$* **1996:** *76$^{6}$ (111) (207) 249$^{4}$ 270$^{3}$ 356$^{4}$ (417) 513$^{5}$ 654$^{3}$ 778$^{5}$ 836$^{4}$ 2934$^{11}$ 5060$^{4}$* **>68a 56f<**

**Chadwell Hall** 5 b h Kala Shikari-Cherrywood Blessin (Good Times (ITY)) *16$^{2}$ 63$^{4}$ (139) 315$^{2}$ 394$^{7}$ 601$^{2}$* (704) 1708$^{5}$ 2005$^{4}$ (2508) 2725$^{13}$ 3432$^{10}$ 3618$^{6}$ 3932$^{7}$ 4180$^{16}$ 4382$^{6}$ 4610$^{3}$ 4765$^{6}$ 5039$^{2}$ **>81a 72f<**

**Chain Reaction (IRE)** 2 b f Fayruz-Timiya (High Top) 1531$^{3}$ 1987$^{3}$ 3502$^{5}$ (3859) 4222$^{8}$ **>72f<**

**Chairmans Choice** 6 ch g Executive Man-Revida Girl (Habat) **1995:** *(4374) 4476$^{2}$* **1996:** *358$^{7}$ 713$^{3}$* 1337$^{4}$ (1658) 2285$^{3}$ 3123$^{12}$ **>84a 75f<**

**Chairmans Daughter** 2 b f Unfuwain (USA)-Ville Sainte (FR) (Saint Estephe (FR)) 2758$^{4}$ 3499$^{9}$ 3663$^{7}$ (4097) 4361$^{2}$ 4602$^{12}$ 4990$^{10}$ **>66f<**

**Chai-Yo** 6 b h Rakaposhi King-Ballysax Lass (Main Reef) 4800$^{8}$ **>71f<**

**Chakalak** 8 b g Damister (USA)-Wig And Gown (Mandamus) 666$^{7}$ 852$^{2}$ 1070$^{5}$ *(1444) 1679$^{3}$* 1981$^{3}$ *(2322) 2717$^{5}$* 3149$^{10}$ **>65a 56f<**

**Chakra** 2 gr c Mystiko (USA)-Maracuja (USA) (Riverman (USA)) 1339$^{9}$ **>16f<**

**Chalamont (IRE)** 3 ch f Kris-Durtal (Lyphard (USA)) 1146$^{8}$ **>89f<**

**Chalcuchima** 3 gr g Reprimand-Ica (Great Nephew) **1995:** *4480$^{5}$* **1996:** *4216$^{14}$* 4448$^{18}$ **>65a 61f<**

**Chalice** 3 b f Governor General-Eucharis (Tickled Pink) 714$^{6}$ *779$^{4}$ 1028$^{11}$ (1429)* 2867$^{7}$ 3135$^{4}$ 3465$^{10}$ 4382$^{10}$ 4521$^{12}$ **>48a 70f<**

**Chalk Dust (USA)** 3 b f Unbridled (USA)-Charmie Carmie (USA) (Lyphard (USA)) *3255$^{2}$* 3446$^{7}$ **>68f<**

**Chalky Dancer** 4 br g Adbass (USA)-Tiny Feet (Music Maestro) **1995:** *4363$^{14}$* **1996:** *84$^{9}$ 4098$^{17}$* 4263$^{5}$ 4503$^{2}$ 4692$^{10}$ **>16a 49f<**

**Challenger (IRE)** 3 b g Nordico (USA)-Sweet Miyabi (JPN) (Royal Ski (USA)) 583$^{16}$ 1535$^{9}$ 2326$^{5}$ 2574$^{20}$ **>50f<**

**Chaluz** 2 b c Night Shift (USA)-Laluche (USA) (Alleged (USA)) 3637$^{6}$ 4188$^{14}$ 4897$^{13}$ **>43f<**

**Chamber Music** 3 ch f Music Boy-Piccadilly Etta (Floribunda) **1995:** *4375$^{13}$* **>41a 57f<**

**Champagne Grandy** 6 ch m Vaigly Great-Monstrosa (Monsanto (FR)) *497a$^{0}$* (554) 633$^{9}$ 2497$^{8}$ 2722$^{11}$ 2856$^{10}$ 3265$^{3}$ 3440$^{5}$ 3639$^{9}$ 3920$^{8}$ 4136$^{7}$ 4316$^{3}$ 4463$^{24}$ **>83f<**

**Champagne N Dreams** 4 b f Rambo Dancer (CAN)-Pink Sensation (Sagaro) 1502$^{6}$ 1665$^{6}$ 2045$^{3}$ 2573$^{10}$ 2851$^{7}$ 3253$^{3}$ 3621$^{9}$ **>51f<**

**Champagne On Ice** 2 b f Efisio-Nip In The Air (USA) (Northern Dancer) 568$^{9}$ 1014$^{7}$ 3105$^{7}$ 3330$^{2}$ 3651$^{4}$ 3976$^{7}$ 4562$^{11}$ **>53f<**

**Champagne Prince** 3 b c Prince Sabo-Champagne Season (USA) (Vaguely Noble) 2774$^{5}$ 3207$^{5}$ 3594$^{8}$ 3923$^{3}$ 4120$^{4}$ 4568$^{26}$ 4826$^{10}$ **>95f<**

**Champagne Toast** 2 ch c Mazilier (USA)-Saraswati (Mansingh (USA)) 1453$^{7}$ 3259$^{13}$ 3685$^{3}$ 4131$^{12}$ 4715$^{10}$ **>66f<**

**Champagne Warrior (IRE)** 3 b f Waajib-Late Swallow (My Swallow) 614$^{6}$ 849$^{2}$ 1325$^{3}$ *2086$^{4}$ 2397$^{2}$* 2683$^{5}$ 4317$^{4}$ **>39a 54f<**

**Chancancook** 3 ch f Hubbly Bubbly (USA)-Majuba Road (Scottish Rifle) 4317$^{5}$ 4703$^{13}$ **>37f<**

**Chancey Fella** 5 ch g Sylvan Express-Musical Piece (Song) *27$^{8}$* **>38a 67f<**

**Changed To Baileys (IRE)** 2 b c Distinctly North (USA)-Blue Czarina (Sandhurst Prince) 958$^{7}$ 2327$^{5}$ 3956$^{3}$ 4468$^{3}$ 4517$^{5}$ **>65f<**

**Chanson d'Amour (IRE)** 2 b f High Estate-Wind of Change (FR) (Sicyos (USA)) 1543$^{4}$ 2118$^{3}$ 2491$^{6}$ 3880$^{9}$ 4245$^{7}$ 4347$^{7}$ 4482$^{7}$ **>45f<**

**Chant d'Alouette** 3 b f Buzzards Bay-Singing Lark (Sir Lark) 2579$^{16}$ 3273$^{6}$ **>26f<**

**Chantry Beath** 5 ch g Dunbeath (USA)-Sallametti (USA) (Giacometti) *152$^{4}$ 251$^{9}$ 2988$^{7}$* 3297$^{9}$ 3575$^{8}$ 3878$^{6}$ 5008$^{15}$ **>50a 44f<**

**Chapel Annie** 4 ch f Tinoco-The Suestan (Ballyciptic) **1995:** *4363$^{9}$ 4474$^{4}$ 4516$^{14}$* **>23a f<**

**Chaposa Springs (USA)** 4 b f Baldski (USA)-La Chaposa (USA) 4953a$^{14}$ **>81f<**

**Charcol** 3 b f Nicholas Bill-Dutch Princess (Royalty) 3656$^{10}$ **>39f<**

**Charisse Dancer** 3 b f Dancing Dissident (USA)-Cadisa (Top Ville) *2597$^{5}$* 2970$^{3}$ 3525$^{3}$ 3800$^{4}$ 3966$^{4}$ 4263$^{15}$ **>54f<**

**Charita (IRE)** 2 ch f Lycius (USA)-Seme de Lys (USA) (Slew O' Gold (USA)) 4642a$^{6}$ **>76f<**

**Charlie Bigtime** 6 b g Norwick (USA)-Sea Aura (Roi Soleil) *373$^{3}$ 422$^{5}$ 542$^{11}$ 898$^{3}$ 1150$^{7}$ 1458$^{9}$ 1514$^{7}$* 1803$^{6}$ *2173$^{3}$ 2372$^{7}$ 3094$^{4}$* 3302$^{5}$ *3952$^{4}$ 4563$^{6}$ 5062$^{8}$* **>57a 44f<**

**Charlie Chang (IRE)** 3 b g Don't Forget Me-East River (FR) (Arctic Tern (USA)) **1995:** *(4381)* **1996:** *917$^{4}$* 1126$^{4}$ 1337$^{5}$ 2581$^{15}$ 2994$^{6}$ 3107$^{2}$ 3322$^{6}$ 3402$^{4}$ 4719$^{7}$ 4829$^{10}$ **>73a 64f<**

**Charlie-Don't Surf** 4 b c Reprimand-Miami Melody (Miami Springs) **1995:** *4415$^{13}$ 4445$^{3}$ 4515$^{12}$* **>48a 22f<**

**Charlie Sillett** 4 ch g Handsome Sailor-Bystrouska (Gorytus (USA)) 876$^{19}$ 1334$^{6}$ 1898$^{6}$ 4581$^{8}$ 4775$^{11}$ (4802) 4975$^{21}$ **>54a 88f<**

**Charlock (IRE)** 3 ch f Nureyev (USA)-Charmante (USA) (Alydar (USA)) 3530a$^{3}$ 4160a$^{3}$ **>107f<**

**Charlotte Corday** 3 b f Kris-Dancing Rocks (Green Dancer (USA)) 678$^{3}$ 1007$^{2}$ (1857) 2608$^{4}$ **>89f<**

**Charlotte's Dancer** 2 b f Kris-Sextant (Star Appeal) 4920$^{W}$

**Charlton Imp (USA)** 3 b f Imp Society (USA)-Percentage (USA) (Vaguely Noble) 550$^{6}$ 732$^{12}$ 1101$^{7}$ 1466$^{9}$ 1654$^{5}$ 2033$^{8}$ (2380) 3257$^{14}$ (3473) 3812$^{2}$ 3989$^{6}$ 4373$^{8}$ **>64f<**

**Charlton Spring (IRE)** 2 ch f Masterclass (USA)-Relankina (IRE) (Broken Hearted) 2031$^{2}$ 2343$^{8}$ 2596$^{6}$ 3110$^{2}$ (3467) 3674$^{7}$ 3969$^{8}$ **>71f<**

**Charm Dancer** 4 b f Rambo Dancer (CAN)-Skelton (Derrylin) *216$^{5}$ 249$^{3}$ 334$^{5}$* **>71a 61f<**

**Charmed Again** 3 b f Midyan (USA)-Charming (Glenstal (USA)) 3849$^{14}$

**Charmed Life** 7 b g Legend of France (USA)-Tanagrea (Blakeney) *474$^{10}$ 602$^{7}$* **>29f<**

**Charming Admiral (IRE)** 3 b g Shareef Dancer (USA)-Lilac Charm (Bustino) *576$^{9}$* 717$^{5}$ 1100$^{13}$ 2120$^{3}$ 2433$^{2}$ 3768$^{2}$ **>72f<**

**Charming Bride** 3 b f Charmer-Loredana (Grange Melody) *(276) 686$^{8}$* 978$^{7}$ 1092$^{5}$ 3959$^{3}$ 4323$^{14}$ 4701$^{13}$ **>55a 52f<**

**Charm The Stars** 2 ch f Roi Danzig (USA)-Deloraine (Pharly (FR)) 2611$^{14}$ 2967$^{8}$ **>51f<**

**Charnwood Forest (IRE)** 4 b or br c Warning-Dance of Leaves (Sadler's Wells (USA)) 1177$^{2}$ (2037) 3144$^{2}$ 3745a$^{4}$ 4443$^{4}$ (4718) 4953a$^{9}$ **>128f<**

**Charnwood Jack (USA)** 3 ch c Sanglamore (USA)-Hyroglyph (USA) (Northern Dancer) 684$^{15}$ 820$^{10}$ 1668$^{10}$ **>66f<**

**Charnwood Meg (IRE)** 3 ch f Scenic-Cathryn's Song (Prince Tenderfoot (USA)) *3418$^{8}$* **>10a f<**

**C-Harry (IRE)** 2 ch c Imperial Frontier (USA)-Desert Gale (Taufan (USA)) 476$^{4}$ 568$^{3}$ 639$^{10}$ 770$^{2}$ *895$^{3}$ (1084) 1320$^{2}$* (1408) 4916$^{7}$ **>55a 55f<**

**Charter** 5 b h Reference Point-Winter Queen (Welsh Pageant) 751$^{4}$ 1065$^{2}$ 1508$^{7}$ 3205$^{12}$ **>79f<**

**Charterhouse Xpres** 3 b c Clantime-Uptown Girl (Caruso) **1995:** *4473$^{3}$ 4533$^{3}$* **1996:** *(10)* **>70a 78f<**

**Chasetown Flyer (USA)** 2 b c Thorn Dance (USA)-Thought Provoker (USA) (Exceller (USA)) 1537$^{9}$ 2059$^{10}$ 4790$^{6}$ **>51f<**

**Chastleton** 4 b f Presidium-Double Stitch (Wolver Hollow) *393$^{10}$* **>57a 30f<**

**Chateauherault (IRE)** 2 b g Contract Law (USA)-Secret Hideaway (USA) (Key To The Mint (USA)) 1849$^{11}$ 2044$^{10}$ 4046$^{12}$ 4361$^{4}$ **>55f<**

**Chatham Island** 8 ch g Jupiter Island-Floreal (Formidable (USA)) *392$^{6}$ 439$^{15}$* 816$^{7}$ 1862$^{2}$ 2046$^{2}$ 2401$^{3}$ 2921$^{2}$ 3073$^{8}$ (3355) **>93a 80f<**

**Chato (USA)** 4 b c Local Talent (USA)-Quick Blush (USA) (Blushing Groom (FR)) **1995:** 4405a$^{5}$ **1996:** 1052a$^{4}$ 4409a$^{4}$ 4659a$^{4}$ **>114f<**

**Chauvelin (IRE)** 3 ch c Durgam (USA)-Kaliala (FR) (Pharly (FR)) **1995:** *4439$^{4}$* **1996:** *(314) 515$^{4}$* **>55a 46f<**

**Checkpoint Charlie** 11 b g Artaius (USA)-Clouded Issue (Manado) 1159$^{6}$ 1534$^{10}$ **>44f<**

**Check The Band (USA)** 2 gr c Dixieland Band (USA)-Check Bid (USA) (Grey Dawn II) 2470a$^{2}$ 2607$^{5}$ 3018a$^{2}$ 3561a$^{8}$ 4156a$^{3}$ (4639a) 4677$^{2}$ **>108+f<**

**Cheek To Cheek** 2 b f Shavian-Intoxication (Great Nephew) 3787$^{7}$ **>50f<**

**Cheeky Chappy** 5 b g Sayf El Arab (USA)-Guilty Guest (USA) (Be My Guest (USA)) **1995:** *(4459) (4488) 4542$^{3}$* **1996:** *(22) 63$^{2}$ 139$^{5}$ 231$^{7}$ 315$^{6}$ 394$^{2}$ 407$^{7}$ 704$^{6}$* 1020$^{5}$ (1163) *1492$^{7}$ 1865$^{3}$* (2185) 2376$^{3}$ 2403$^{2}$ (2434) (2598) 2867$^{5}$ 2911$^{3}$ (2964) 3055$^{3}$ (3106) 3168$^{4}$ 3223$^{3}$ 3424$^{12}$ *3602$^{15}$ 3639$^{12}$ 4081$^{11}$ 4180$^{19}$* 4460$^{7}$ 4505$^{13}$ *4577$^{3}$ 4778$^{12}$ 4881$^{14}$ (4981) 4983$^{5}$ 5000$^{4}$* **>68a 71f<**

**Cheerful Aspect (IRE)** 3 b g Cadeaux Genereux-Strike Home (Be My Guest (USA)) (689) 863$^{4}$ 1862$^{4}$ 2164$^{6}$ 2418$^{5}$ 3856$^{3}$ 4489$^{7}$ **>83f<**

**Cheerful Groom (IRE)** 5 ch g Shy Groom (USA)-Carange (Known Fact (USA)) *127$^{15}$ 199$^{10}$ 247$^{2}$ 431$^{6}$ 521$^{9}$ 839$^{5}$ (991)* 1538$^{11}$ 2481$^{10}$ **>43a 48f<**

**Chelsea (USA)** 3 ch f Miswaki (USA)-Prodigious **1995:** 4494a$^{3}$

**Chelwood** 4 b f Kala Shikari-Cherrywood Blessin (Good Times (ITY)) 1787$^{7}$ 2498$^{6}$ 3100$^{8}$ 4075$^{15}$ 4348$^{11}$ **>48?f<**

**Chemcast** 3 ch g Chilibang-Golden October (Young Generation) **1995:** *4533$^{9}$* **1996:** *32$^{8}$ (142) (160) 443$^{17}$* 1646$^{4}$ 1823$^{5}$ (2021) 2395$^{4}$ 2849$^{7}$ 3135$^{6}$ 3215$^{4}$ 3350$^{3}$ 3693$^{13}$ 5039$^{16}$ **>71a 65f<**

**Cher Laskar (FR)** 4 b c Lashkari-Coimbra (FR) (Fabulous Dancer (USA)) 148a$^{2}$ **>71f<**

**Cherokee Flight** 2 b g Green Desert (USA)-Totham (Shernazar) 2485$^{4}$ 2897$^{4}$ (3050) 3674$^{8}$ 4195$^{13}$ 4433$^{5}$ **>63f<**

**Cherry Blossom (IRE)** 2 br f Primo Dominie-Varnish (Final Straw) (729) 1318$^{4}$ **>79f<**

**Cherry Garden (IRE)** 3 b g Treasure Kay-Door To Door (USA) (Nureyev (USA)) *460$^{4}$ 516$^{3}$ 1317$^{9}$* 1992$^{4}$ 2180$^{6}$ 2402$^{4}$ 2594$^{8}$ 3831$^{3}$ *4107$^{3}$* **>54a 59f<**

**Cherry Muna** 3 ch f Say Primula-Muna (Thatch (USA)) 1434$^{15}$ 1638$^{12}$ 1847$^{9}$ **>17f<**

**Chesteine** 3 ch f Soviet Lad (USA)-Makalu (Godswalk (USA)) 2197$^{9}$ 2529$^{9}$ 3472$^{9}$ 3966$^{5}$ 4603$^{11}$ *4998$^{9}$* **>16a 44f<**

**Chesters Quest** 4 ch g Domynsky-Chess Mistress (USA) (Run The Gantlet (USA)) 3298$^{8}$ 3480$^{6}$ **>22?f<**

**Chevalier (USA)** 4 b br c Danzig (USA)-Royal Touch (Tap On Wood) *$402^{2}$ $532^{6}$ $650^{15}$ $1602^{3}$ $1811^{11}$ $2304^{4}$ $2553^{4}$ $2935^{4}$ $3630^{3}$ $4095^{2}$ $4575^{10}$* **>65a 73f<**

**Cheval Roc** 2 ch c Keen-Gentle Gain (Final Straw) $4188^{10}$ $4380^{8}$ $4891^{7}$ **>75f<**

**Cheveley Dancer (USA)** 8 b g Northern Baby (CAN)-Alwah (USA) (Damascus (USA)) *$214^{9}$ $752^{4}$* $1347^{19}$ $1803^{4}$ $2587^{9}$ $2711^{4}$ $2989^{8}$ $3314^{2}$ **>36f<**

**Chewit** 4 gr g Beveled (USA)-Sylvan Song (Song) **1995:** *$4441^{3}$ $4517^{4}$* **1996:** *(55) (338) $582^{15}$* $1621^{6}$ $2017^{5}$ $2548^{4}$ $2976^{9}$ (4109) (4254) $4378^{7}$ **>94+a 90f<**

**Cheyenne City (USA)** 2 f *$4950a^{8}$* **>72a f<**

**Cheyenne Spirit** 4 ch f Indian Ridge-Bazaar Promise (Native Bazaar) $940^{9}$ $1629^{4}$ $1879^{2}$ **>112f<**

**Chez Catalan** 5 b h Niniski (USA)-Miss Saint-Cloud (Nonoalco (USA)) **1995:** *$4530^{3}$* **1996:** *$23^{9}$ $206^{8}$ $1679^{5}$* $4426^{14}$ **>31a 27f<**

**Chickamauga (USA)** 2 gr ro f Wild Again (USA)-Gray And Red (USA) (Wolf Power (SA)) $4512^{17}$ **>21f<**

**Chickawicka (IRE)** 5 b h Dance of Life (USA)-Shabby Doll (Northfields (USA)) *$600^{4}$* $933^{3}$ $1018^{4}$ $1962^{7}$ $2053^{19}$ (2400) $3263^{2}$ $3920^{5}$ $4136^{11}$ $4775^{5}$ $4800^{5}$ **>93f<**

**Chief Bearhart (CAN)** 3 ch c Chief's Crown (USA)-Amelia Beaarhart (CAN) (Bold Hour) $4543a^{2}$ $4955a^{11}$ **>119f<**

**Chief Bee** 5 b m Chief's Crown (USA)-Lady Be Mine (USA) (Sir Ivor) **1995:** $4470a^{6}$ **>95f<**

**Chief Burundi (USA)** 4 b g Alleged (USA)-Lantana Lady (CAN) (Vice Regent (CAN)) (1160) $1484^{3}$ $2502^{19}$ $3125^{11}$ $4051^{5}$ **>111df<**

**Chief Contender (IRE)** 3 b c Sadler's Wells (USA)-Minnie Hauk (USA) (Sir Ivor) $671^{9}$ (948) (1120) $1791^{9}$ (2669a) $3124^{2}$ $3751a^{3}$ $4657a^{3}$ $4876^{9}$ **>122f<**

**Chief Island** 2 b f Be My Chief (USA)-Clare Island (Connaught) $2708^{7}$ **>64f<**

**Chief Mouse** 3 b g Be My Chief (USA)-Top Mouse (High Top) *(390) $593^{10}$* $980^{6}$ **>77a 60f<**

**Chief Predator (USA)** 2 ch c Chief's Crown (USA)-Tsavorite (USA) (Halo (USA)) $4127^{18}$ $4514^{18}$ $5033^{15}$ **>40f<**

**Chief's Lady** 4 b f Reprimand-Pussy Foot (Red Sunset) *$255^{8}$ $387^{11}$ $408^{4}$ $461^{9}$ $631^{7}$* $1013^{4}$ $1500^{11}$ $1642^{4}$ $2075^{7}$ $2507^{11}$ $2801^{13}$ $3257^{12}$ **>53a 42f<**

**Chief's Song** 6 b g Chief Singer-Tizzy (Formidable (USA)) $573^{18}$ $3802^{10}$ **>54f<**

**Chieftain's Crown (USA)** 5 ch g Chief's Crown (USA)-Simple Taste (USA) (Sharpen Up) $1821^{7}$ (1903) $2203^{2}$ $2409^{8}$ **>47f<**

**Chik's Secret** 3 ch f Nalchik (USA)-Lana's Secret (Most Secret) $1600^{9}$ *$2082^{4}$ $2304^{6}$ $4899^{6}$* ***>51a 58f<***

**Children's Choice (IRE)** 5 b m Taufan (USA)-Alice Brackloon (USA) (Melyno) *$309^{11}$ $3218^{5}$* (3520) $3813^{2}$ $3983^{11}$ $4307^{4}$ $4563^{3}$ $4604^{5}$ $4766^{6}$ $4919^{16}$ **>57a 63f<**

**Chilibang Bang** 3 b f Chilibang-Quenlyn (Welsh Pageant) **1995:** *$4509^{2}$* **1996:** *$102^{5}$ (157) $194^{5}$ (332) $383^{2}$ $421^{7}$ $473^{4}$* $4768^{19}$ **>66a 51f<**

**Chili Bouchier (USA)** 2 br f Stop The Music (USA)-Low Approach (Artaius (USA)) $4446^{5}$ **>50f<**

**Chili Concerto** 2 ro f Chilibang-Whirling Words (Sparkler) $2230^{2}$ (3114) **>84f<**

**Chili Heights** 6 gr g Chilibang-Highest Tender (Prince Tenderfoot (USA)) $2858^{6}$ $3518^{14}$ $3694^{12}$ $4820^{17}$ $4975^{27}$ **>37f<**

**Chili-Wah-Wah** 5 ch g Chilibang-Abalone (Abwah) $4110^{10}$ $4237^{18}$ $4362^{7}$ **>48f< (DEAD)**

**Chillam** 3 ch g Chilibang-Tissue Paper (Touch Paper) *$112^{7}$ $194^{6}$ $209^{8}$ $292^{5}$ $478^{9}$* $750^{10}$ **>39a 33f<**

**Chilled Wine** 2 gr f Chilibang-Persian Joy (Persian Bold) $481^{5}$ *$533^{6}$ $590^{3}$* $624^{4}$ $733^{8}$ *$1097^{8}$ $1320^{8}$* ***>8a 36f<***

**Chilli Boom** 2 gr f Chilibang-Silent Sun (Blakeney) $3114^{13}$ $3438^{8}$ $3685^{16}$ $4495^{10}$ **>47f<**

**Chilling** 2 gr f Chilibang-Appealing (Star Appeal) $1590^{2}$ $2527^{6}$ $2942^{8}$ $3478^{10}$ *$4976^{9}$ $5061^{5}$* **>28a 43f<**

**Chillington** 3 gr g Chilibang-Saskia's Pride (Giacometti) $599^{6}$ *$651^{7}$ $899^{9}$ $1498^{18}$* ***>29a 21f<***

**Chilly Lad** 5 ch g High Kicker (USA)-Miss Poll Flinders (Swing Easy (USA)) $508^{3}$ $690^{7}$ $884^{5}$ $1347^{14}$ $1496^{6}$ *$1970^{6}$ $2082^{7}$ $2192^{23}$* $4815^{U}$ *$5003^{9}$ $5053^{9}$* ***>57a 51f<***

**Chilly Looks** 3 b f Siberian Express (USA)-Exceptional Beauty (Sallust) $971^{14}$ $1608^{6}$ $2075^{17}$ $2393^{6}$ $2893^{6}$ **>37f<**

**Chimanimani** 5 b g Petong-La Primavera (Northfields (USA)) $2866^{7}$ $3253^{6}$ **>44f<**

**China Castle** 3 b g Sayf El Arab (USA)-Honey Plum (Kind of Hush) **1995:** *$4389^{13}$* **1996:** *(35) (56) (137) $176^{4}$ $285^{4}$ (329) $385^{3}$ $444^{16}$ $3063^{8}$ $3246^{7}$ $3419^{3}$ $3649^{3}$ $4078^{11}$ $4575^{7}$ $4779^{4}$* **>76a 60f<**

**China Girl (IRE)** 2 b f Danehill (USA)-Chamonis (USA) (Affirmed (USA)) (2327) $3068^{8}$ (3697) **>87f<**

**China Hand (IRE)** 4 ch g Salt Dome (USA)-China Blue (Ahonoora) *$559^{10}$* $704^{10}$ $1547^{5}$ $1702^{7}$ $2316^{12}$ $2395^{2}$ $2732^{4}$ $2933^{2}$ $3310^{7}$ $3643^{12}$ $4075^{5}$ **>36f<**

**China Red (USA)** 2 br c Red Ransom (USA)-Akamare (FR) (Akarad (FR)) $2887^{4}$ $3588^{2}$ $3987^{4}$ **>80f<**

**Chinensis (IRE)** 3 ch c Lycius (USA)-Chinese Justice (USA) (Diesis) $544^{5}$ $640^{7}$ $1435^{3}$ $1659^{2}$ $1955^{5}$ (2573) (2805) $3123^{13}$ (3634) **>85f<**

**Chingachgook** 2 b c Superlative-Petomania (Petong) $2057^{4}$ $2600^{12}$ $3757^{11}$ $3975^{5}$ $4350^{5}$ $4586^{W}$ **>66f<**

**Chipalata** 3 b g Derrylin-Kirsheda (Busted) $637^{8}$ $784^{8}$ $1067^{8}$ $3507^{9}$ **>30f<**

**Chipet** 2 b f Tina's Pet-Chinese Princess (Sunny Way) $4607^{8}$ **>25f<**

**Chirico (USA)** 3 b c Danzig (USA)-Colour Chart (USA) (Mr Prospector (USA)) $1617^{11}$ $1797^{4}$ $2197^{15}$ $2617^{5}$ (4598) **>82f<**

**Chita Rivera** 5 b m Chief Singer-Shirley Superstar (Shirley Heights) **1995:** *$4463^{7}$* **>33a 50f<**

**Chivalric (IRE)** 2 b c Arazi (USA)-Air Distingue (USA) (Sir Ivor) $4242^{2}$ $4492^{5}$ **>81f<**

**Chloella** 4 b f Shaadi (USA)-Echoing (Formidable (USA)) *$74^{8}$ $127^{10}$ $342^{4}$ $425^{8}$ $517^{5}$* **>26a 38f<**

**Chloe Nicole (USA)** 2 b f Personal Flag (USA)-Balakhna (FR) (Tyrant (USA)) $2854^{4}$ **>79f<**

**Chloe's Mark** 2 b f Crowning Honors (CAN)-Junuh (Jalmood (USA)) $1543^{6}$ $2174^{6}$ $2387^{5}$ **>7f<**

**Chloezymp (IRE)** 2 b f Mac's Imp (USA)-Genzyme Gene (Riboboy (USA)) *$858^{7}$ $1097^{9}$*

**Chocolate Chip** 4 b g Hard Fought-Roses Galore (USA) (Stage Door Johnny) **1995:** *$4354^{11}$* **>50f<**

**Chocolate Ice** 3 b g Shareef Dancer (USA)-Creake (Derring-Do) $640^{8}$ $826^{3}$ $1153^{3}$ $1631^{5}$ $2067^{7}$ $2673^{3}$ $3077^{4}$ $3283^{4}$ *$3610^{5}$ $3831^{4}$* $4086^{8}$ $4217^{4}$ $4427^{10}$ **>41a 68f<**

**Chopin (IRE)** 2 b g Classic Music (USA)-La Toulzanie (FR) (Sanctus II) $639^{5}$ $741^{4}$ $3312^{7}$ $3662^{7}$ $3924^{8}$ $4097^{10}$ **>56f<**

**Chorus Boy** 11 br g Sonnen Gold-Toccata (USA) (Mr Leader (USA)) **1995:** *$4434^{12}$*

**Chorus Song (USA)** 2 b f Alleged (USA)-Performing Arts (The Minstrel (CAN)) $3593^{5}$ $4105^{2}$ $4451^{8}$ $4880^{12}$ **>78f<**

**Chris's Lad** 5 b g Thowra (FR)-Stockline (Capricorn Line) $1835^{6}$ $2042^{22}$ *$3066^{4}$ (3163) $3437^{2}$ $3772^{2}$* (3928) $4771^{16}$ **>56a 74f<**

**Christian Flight (IRE)** 7 b m Fayruz-Opening Flight (Falcon) $2185^{16}$ $2434^{5}$ $2757^{8}$ $2771^{8}$ *$2940^{10}$ $2992^{6}$* $3525^{11}$ *$4094^{9}$* **>27a 39f<**

**Christian Warrior** 7 gr g Primo Dominie-Rashah (Blakeney) *$3420^{12}$ $3825^{14}$* ***>9a 24f<***

**Christmas Kiss** 4 b f Taufan (USA)-Ancestry (Persepolis (FR)) $554^{7}$ $679^{7}$ $1075^{3}$ $1770^{10}$ $2298^{7}$ **>97df<**

**Christmas Rose** 2 gr f Absalom-Shall We Run (Hotfoot) $3454^{12}$ $4087^{12}$ **>34f<**

**Chucklestone** 13 b g Chukaroo-Czar's Diamond (Queen's Hussar) **1995:** *$4530^{14}$* **1996:** *$2310^{12}$* $2958^{4}$ (3476) $3801^{11}$ **>43f<**

**Chynna** 2 b f Golden Heights-What A Present (Pharly (FR)) $2413^{3}$ **>57f<**

**Cicerone** 6 br g Tina's Pet-Emma Royale (Royal And Regal (USA)) **1995:** *$4378^{6}$ $4409^{6}$* **1996:** *$30^{6}$ $527^{5}$* (545) $983^{W}$ (1196) **>48a 72f<**

**Cigar (USA)** 6 b h Palace Music (USA)-Solar Slew (USA) (Seattle Slew (USA)) *(536a) (2842a) $4956a^{3}$* ***>138+a 132f<***

**Cim Bom Bom (IRE)** 4 b c Dowsing (USA)-Nekhbet (Artaius (USA)) $728^{19}$ $960^{12}$ $1314^{6}$ $1506^{5}$ $1807^{8}$ $2340^{3}$ (2590) $2860^{3}$ $3045^{5}$ $3639^{3}$ $3758^{8}$ **>79f<**

**Cimmerian** 2 ch f Risk Me (FR)-Dark Kristal (IRE) (Gorytus (USA)) $4208^{7}$ $4454^{5}$ $4751^{7}$ $4883^{15}$ **>63f<**

**Cindy Kate (IRE)** 3 br f Sayf El Arab (USA)-Marton Maid (Silly Season) *$118^{9}$ $264^{3}$ $1356^{5}$* $1840^{11}$ **>50a 59f<**

**Cinema Paradiso** 2 b c Polar Falcon (USA)-Epure (Bellypha) (2852) $4213^{2}$ $4973^{9}$ **>94f<**

**Cinnamon Stick (IRE)** 3 ch g Don't Forget Me-Gothic Lady (Godswalk (USA)) $525^{12}$ $1067^{6}$ *$1970^{10}$ $2180^{19}$* ***>44a 41f<***

**Ciracusa (IRE)** 4 b g Kahyasi-Miranisa (Habitat) *$603^{4}$ $753^{2}$* $872^{3}$ $2221^{3}$ $2798^{P}$ **>54a 74f< (DEAD)**

**Circled (USA)** 3 gr f Cozzene (USA)-Hold The Hula (USA) (Hawaii) **1995:** $4499a^{5}$ **1996:** $1111^{W}$ $1854^{5}$ $4297^{7}$ $4862^{5}$ **>67f<**

**Circle of Magic** 2 gr f Midyan (USA)-Miss Witch (High Line) $2614^{7}$ $3515^{5}$ $3796^{8}$ $4207^{8}$ $4795^{7}$ **>61f<**

**Circus Star** 3 b g Soviet Star (USA)-Circus Act (Shirley Heights) (2895) $4431^{10}$ **>77f<**

**Ciro's Pearl (IRE)** 2 b f Petorius-Cut it Fine (USA) (Big Spruce (USA)) $3105^{5}$ $3454^{2}$ $4024a^{24}$ **>72f<**

**Ciserano (IRE)** 3 ch f Mujtahid (USA)-Blue Persian (Majority Blue) *$468^{8}$* $540^{4}$ $743^{2}$ $1122^{7}$ $1356^{6}$ (1592) $1707^{7}$ $1840^{8}$ $2029^{4}$ $2215^{5}$ $2500^{8}$ $2719^{2}$ $2929^{5}$ $3166^{5}$ **>64df< (DEAD)**

**City Band (USA)** 2 f *$4950a^{10}$* **>62a f<**

**City Gambler** 2 b f Rock City-Sun Street (Ile de Bourbon (USA)) $3859^{3}$ $4241^{4}$ $4369^{8}$ $4602^{2}$ **>75f<**

**City Hall (IRE)** 2 b c Generous (IRE)-City Fortress (Troy) $4720^{10}$ $4897^{5}$ **>71f<**

**Civil Liberty** 3 b c Warning-Libertine (Hello Gorgeous (USA)) $583^{2}$ $1452^{2}$ $2041^{20}$ (3262) $3658^{4}$ $4185^{7}$ $4352^{4}$ **>95?f<**

**Claire's Dancer (IRE)** 3 b g Classic Music (USA)-Midnight Patrol (Ashmore (FR)) $894^{14}$ (1443) $1687^{5}$ $3205^{8}$ $3876^{6}$ $4216^{13}$ $4626^{18}$ **>67f<**

**Claireswan (IRE)** 4 ch g Rhoman Rule (USA)-Choclate Baby (Kashiwa) $4626^{F}$ $4771^{20}$ **>70a 62f<**

**Clan Ben (IRE)** 4 ch c Bluebird (USA)-Trina's Girl (Nonoalco (USA)) $728^{11}$ $967^{2}$ $1112^{3}$ $3071^{5}$ $3691^{5}$ $4120^{2}$ $4326^{8}$ $4568^{23}$ (4800) **>104f<**

**Clancassie** 3 b f Clantime-Casbar Lady (Native Bazaar) *$1422^{13}$* $2048^{8}$ $2777^{14}$ **>15f<**

**Clan Chief** 3 b g Clantime-Mrs Meyrick (Owen Dudley) $1844^{5}$ $2156^{2}$ $2244^{2}$ (2500) (2999) (3215)

3693$^{2}$ (4198) **>87f<**
**Clancy's Express 5** b g Faustus (USA)-Pink Pumpkin (Tickled Pink) *843$^{12}$ >27f<*
**Claque 4** ch c Kris-Mixed Applause (USA) (Nijinsky (CAN)) **1995:** *4366$^{8}$ 4411$^{9}$* **1996:** *33$^{13}$ 145$^{9}$ (206) 236$^{4}$ (279) (303) 392$^{10}$ 440$^{23}$* 508$^{11}$ 752$^{17}$ 1022$^{8}$ *(2173) 2553$^{2}$ 3428$^{6}$ 3952$^{8}$ 4092$^{13}$ 4779$^{8}$ 4984$^{10}$* **>51a 42f<**
**Clara Bliss (IRE) 2** b f Fayruz-Kinosium (Relkino) 729$^{6}$ 823$^{6}$ (1645) 2879$^{11}$ 3975$^{3}$ (4230) 4350$^{4}$ 4517$^{9}$ 4749$^{5}$ **>77f<**
**Clarion Call (IRE) 5** b g Don't Forget Me-Hillbrow (Swing Easy (USA)) **1995:** *4435$^{9}$* **>56f<**
**Clash of Swords 3** b c Shaadi (USA)-Swept Away (Kris) *826$^{12}$* 1090$^{7}$ 1359$^{9}$ 1850$^{12}$ 2570$^{5}$ 3297$^{6}$ 3580$^{2}$ 3870$^{6}$ 4321$^{13}$ **>63f<**
**Class Distinction (IRE) 2** ch c Masterclass (USA)-Brook's Dilemma (Known Fact (USA)) *815$^{8}$* 1622$^{2}$ (1827) 2252$^{3}$ 2879$^{8}$ 4350$^{7}$ 4614$^{9}$ **>73f<**
**Classic Affair (USA) 3** ch f Trempolino (USA)-Coupole (USA) (Vaguely Noble) 1174$^{6}$ 1515$^{10}$ 1804$^{11}$ *1993$^{8}$ 2368$^{3}$ 2988$^{5}$* (3335) 3598$^{6}$ 3850$^{4}$ *4092$^{5}$ 4203$^{7}$* 4832$^{8}$ **>54a 71f<**
**Classical Risk (IRE) 2** b f Fairy King (USA)-Aldhabiyh 2834a$^{6}$ **>76f<**
**Classic Ballet (FR) 3** b f Fabulous Dancer (USA)-Tyranesque (USA) (Key To The Mint (USA)) 575$^{4}$ 754$^{3}$ 1100$^{3}$ 1498$^{4}$ (1908) 2206$^{4}$ 2605$^{6}$ 3522$^{8}$ 3830$^{7}$ 4609$^{17}$ **>61f<**
**Classic Beauty (IRE) 3** b f Fairy King (USA)-Working Model (Ile de Bourbon (USA)) *364$^{3}$ 390$^{4}$ 415$^{4}$ 740$^{2}$* 934$^{6}$ 1995$^{3}$ *2168$^{8}$ 2602$^{10}$* (3490) 3664$^{6}$ 4498$^{5}$ 4975$^{26}$ **>66a 71df<**
**Classic Cliche (IRE) 4** b c Salse (USA)-Pato (High Top) (1128) (2071) 3070$^{2}$ 4662a$^{15}$ **>130f<**
**Classic Colleen (IRE) 3** b f Sadler's Wells (USA)-Nawara (Welsh Pageant) 804$^{4}$ 1631$^{2}$ 2080$^{3}$ 2533$^{10}$ 2952$^{2}$ 3486$^{8}$ **>84f<**
**Classic Colours (USA) 3** ch g Blushing John (USA)-All Agleam (USA) (Gleaming (USA)) *528$^{4}$* 788$^{2}$ 955$^{2}$ 1496$^{5}$ 1666$^{3}$ 3111$^{13}$ 3819$^{4}$ *4089$^{15}$* **>69f<**
**Classic Daisy 3** b f Prince Sabo-Bloom of Youth (IRE) (Last Tycoon) **1995:** *4375$^{7}$ 4433$^{14}$* **1996:** *427$^{7}$ 781$^{5}$ 1416$^{14}$* 2180$^{20}$ **>38a 43f<**
**Classic Dame (FR) 3** gr f Highest Honor (FR)-Reem El Fala (FR) (Fabulous Dancer (USA)) 2918$^{6}$ 3818$^{3}$ 4110$^{3}$ 4582$^{15}$ **>70f<**
**Classic Defence (IRE) 3** b c Cyrano de Bergerac-My Alanna (Dalsaan) (660) 851$^{7}$ 1594$^{3}$ (1955) 2558$^{2}$ 3161$^{18}$ 3786$^{F}$ **>82f<**
**Classic Delight (USA) 3** b f Green Forest (USA)-Weather Girl (USA) (One For All (USA)) *387$^{10}$ 1721$^{10}$ 3333$^{13}$ 4107$^{10}$* **>43a 40f<**
**Classic Eagle 3** b c Unfuwain (USA)-La Lutine (My Swallow) 736$^{7}$ 986$^{6}$ 1791$^{11}$ 3145$^{8}$ 3822$^{6}$ 4457$^{4}$ 4862$^{9}$ **>65f<**
**Classic Find (USA) 3** b br c Lear Fan (USA)-Reve de Reine (USA) (Lyphard (USA)) 820$^{7}$ (1090) 1712$^{3}$ **>92f<**
**Classic Flyer (IRE) 3** b f Alzao (USA)-Sea Harrier (Grundy) 938$^{5}$ 1071$^{2}$ *4078$^{6}$ 4117$^{6}$* 4559$^{19}$ **>78a 87f<**
**Classic Form (IRE) 3** b f Alzao (USA)-Formulate (Reform) 3058$^{2}$ 4422$^{W}$ 4611$^{4}$ **>59f<**
**Classic Lady 2** ch f Ron's Victory (USA)-Lady St Lawrence (USA) (Bering) *1459$^{5}$ 1813$^{6}$* **>11a f<**
**Classic Leader 3** b c Thatching-Tenderetta (Tender King) 669$^{6}$ 994$^{2}$ 1469$^{3}$ 1807$^{5}$ 2079$^{3}$ **>81f<**
**Classic Line 2** b f Last Tycoon-Classic Beam (Cut Above) 2892$^{7}$ 3245$^{9}$ 3988$^{13}$ **>64f<**
**Classic Look (IRE) 3** b br f Classic Music (USA)-Mini Look (FR) (In Fijar (USA)) *1333$^{6}$* 1711$^{13}$ 2710$^{8}$ 4128$^{5}$ 4232$^{8}$ **>52f<**
**Classic Lover (IRE) 3** b f Taufan (USA)-Sound Pet (Runnett) 447$^{4}$ 541$^{8}$ 702$^{5}$ 819$^{14}$ 2198$^{6}$ 3703$^{4}$ **>56f<**
**Classic Mystery (IRE) 2** ch g Classic Secret (USA)-Mystery Bid (Auction Ring (USA)) 706$^{12}$ 1842$^{9}$ 2184$^{4}$ *3417$^{8}$ 3616$^{10}$ >20a 55f<*
**Classic Parisian (IRE) 3** b f Persian Bold-Gay France (FR) (Sir Gaylord) 957$^{3}$ 1711$^{8}$ 2135$^{2}$ 2383$^{3}$ 2601$^{6}$ 3942$^{2}$ 4320$^{3}$ 4580$^{8}$ **>79f<**
**Classic Park 2** b f Robellino (USA)-Wanton (Kris) 1565a$^{3}$ 1910a$^{2}$ 2051$^{6}$ 2834a$^{4}$ 4156a$^{2}$ 4639a$^{7}$ 4723$^{13}$ **>82f<**
**Classic Partygoer 2** ch g Prince Sabo-Star Arrangement (Star Appeal) 452$^{5}$ 568$^{5}$ 685$^{12}$ 1183$^{8}$ 3227$^{10}$ 4072$^{6}$ 4223$^{13}$ 4562$^{23}$ **>55f<**
**Classic Pet (IRE) 4** b f Petorius-Checkers (Habat) *36$^{6}$ 203$^{9}$ 1958$^{9}$* 2156$^{8}$ 2286$^{16}$ 2735$^{5}$ 2787$^{9}$ 3261$^{8}$ 3469$^{15}$ 3585$^{9}$ 3698$^{15}$ **>33a 41f<**
**Classic Ribbon (IRE) 3** b f Persian Bold-House Tie (Be Friendly) 4322$^{5}$ **>66f<**
**Classic Romance 3** b f Cadeaux Genereux-What A Pity (Blakeney) 739$^{9}$ 2202$^{5}$ 2384$^{2}$ 2603$^{16}$ 3800$^{7}$ 4427$^{7}$ *5060$^{6}$* **>48a 54f<**
**Classic Royale (USA) 3** b f Chief's Crown (USA)-Cuidado (USA) (Damascus (USA)) *678$^{10}$* 2996$^{10}$ 3353$^{8}$ *3877$^{6}$ 4095$^{7}$ 4263$^{14}$ >46a 61f<*
**Classic Services 2** br g Totem (USA)-Loving Doll (Godswalk (USA)) 770$^{6}$ 990$^{7}$ 2031$^{9}$ 2509$^{7}$ *2635$^{8}$* **>40f<**
**Classic Sky (IRE) 5** b g Jareer (USA)-Nawadder (Kris) *1898$^{W}$* **>104f<**
**Classic Victory 3** b g Puissance-Seattle Mama (USA) (Seattle Song (USA)) *383$^{8}$ 403$^{7}$ 418$^{13}$ 540$^{2}$ 839$^{12}$ 1456$^{8}$ 1497$^{10}$* 1806$^{9}$ **>30a 59df<**
**Classic Warrior 3** b g Sharpo-Petty Purse (Petingo) 3446$^{14}$ 3832$^{11}$ 4108$^{15}$ **>44f<**
**Classy Chief 3** b g Be My Chief (USA)-Jalopy (Jalmood (USA)) 833$^{7}$ 1319$^{5}$ 1662$^{5}$ 2603$^{18}$ 3656$^{6}$ 3876$^{10}$ 4186$^{14}$ 4609$^{2}$ 4768$^{8}$ 4860$^{7}$ **>76f<**
**Clear Mandate (USA) 4** ch f Deputy Minister (CAN)-Dream Deal (USA) (Sharpen Up) *4952a$^{6}$* **>95a f<**
**Clear The Air 2** ch f Salse (USA)-Belle Enfant (Beldale Flutter (USA)) 3615$^{14}$ 3820$^{8}$ 4096$^{3}$ **>44f<**
**Cledeschamps 7** b m Doc Marten-Cape Farewell (Record Run) 545$^{7}$ *2085$^{7}$* **>42da 36f<**
**Clemente 3** b br c Robellino (USA)-Gravad Lax (Home Guard (USA)) 575$^{3}$ 947$^{2}$ 1317$^{4}$ 1507$^{8}$ 4804$^{7}$ **>79f<**
**Clerkenwell (USA) 3** b c Sadler's Wells (USA)-Forlene (Forli (ARG)) 578$^{2}$ 717$^{3}$ 1712$^{2}$ 2054$^{7}$ (2505) (3689) 4657a$^{7}$ **>112f<**
**Clever Caption (IRE) 2** b c Topanoora-Findraiser (FR) (Welsh Saint) (3903a) **>97f<**
**Clever Cliche 3** b c Danehill (USA)-Beacon Hill (Bustino) (640) 918$^{4}$ 2038$^{10}$ **>107f<**
**Cliburnel News (IRE) 6** b m Horage-Dublin Millennium (Dalsaan) 546$^{2}$ 690$^{6}$ 872$^{5}$ 993$^{5}$ 1472$^{6}$ 1640$^{6}$ 2060$^{6}$ **>55a 64f<**
**Clifton Fox 4** b g Deploy-Loveskate (USA) (Overskate (CAN)) 547$^{8}$ 765$^{3}$ (913) 1322$^{2}$ 2483$^{4}$ 2862$^{6}$ 3248$^{3}$ 3947$^{3}$ (4193) (4568) 4964$^{3}$ (5046) **>111f<**
**Clifton Game 6** b g Mummy's Game-Brave Maiden (Three Legs) (3705) 3928$^{4}$ **>49a 49f<**
**Clincher Club 3** b f Polish Patriot (USA)-Merry Rous (Rousillon (USA)) 1646$^{7}$ 2518$^{10}$ (2753) *3062$^{4}$ 3288$^{2}$* 3442$^{4}$ **>57a 58f<**
**Clint 3** b c Colmore Row-Eastwood Heiress (Known Fact (USA)) **1995:** *4360$^{12}$* **>41f<**
**Clonavon Girl (IRE) 2** b f Be My Guest (USA)-Welcome Addition (Habitat) 823$^{7}$ 975$^{9}$ 1360$^{6}$ 2161$^{3}$ 2512$^{2}$ *2938$^{5}$ 3512$^{7}$* 4097$^{14}$ **>56f<**
**Close Conflict (USA) 5** b h High Estate-Catopetl (USA) (Northern Dancer) **1995:** *4500a$^{6}$* **>117f<**
**Close Relative (IRE) 2** b c Distant Relative-Jamaican Punch (IRE) (Shareef Dancer (USA)) 1774$^{2}$ (2057) 2607$^{4}$ 3156$^{7}$ 3931$^{2}$ **>97f<**
**Clouds Hill (FR) 3** b c Sarhoob (USA)-Dana Dana (FR) (Pharly (FR)) 578$^{10}$ 969$^{5}$ 1175$^{9}$ 2688$^{4}$ **>73df<**
**Clover Girl 5** bl m Spin of a Coin-Byerley Rose (Rolfe (USA)) *3090$^{7}$ 3305$^{6}$*
***Club Elite 4*** b f Salse (USA)-Little Bittern (USA) (Riva Ridge (USA)) *1717$^{6}$ 2310$^{11}$* 2537$^{4}$ 2891$^{6}$ 3305$^{5}$ **>37a 29f<**
**Clued Up 3** b f Beveled (USA)-Scharade (Lombard (GER)) 2506$^{11}$ *2751$^{6}$ 3228$^{5}$* (3451) 3591$^{5}$ 3808$^{6}$ 4217$^{3}$ 4497$^{13}$ 4603$^{18}$ **>32a 63f<**
**Clytha Hill Lad 5** b g Domitor (USA)-Quae Supra (On Your Mark) *204$^{8}$ 248$^{5}$ 613$^{16}$* 2056$^{9}$ 2313$^{7}$ 2716$^{5}$ **>41a 41f<**
**Coachella 3** b f Warning-Cockatoo Island (High Top) *(58) (242) 572$^{8}$* 674$^{11}$ 2742$^{6}$ 3248$^{P}$ **>69a 85f< (DEAD)**
**Coalisland 6** br g Kind of Hush-Hit The Line (Saulingo) *2286$^{21}$* 4215$^{13}$ **>38?a 5f<**
**Coal To Diamonds 2** b f Merdon Melody-Dubitable (Formidable (USA)) 3137$^{3}$ 4104$^{12}$ 4607$^{14}$
**Coastal Bluff 4** gr g Standaan (FR)-Combattente (Reform) 2114$^{13}$ (2694) (3232) (4314) **>121+f<**
**Coast Along (IRE) 4** b g Satco (FR)-Golden Flats (Sonnen Gold) **1995:** *4448$^{6}$* **1996:** *2173$^{11}$* **>26a 48f<**
**Coastguards Hero 3** ch g Chilibang-Aldwick Colonnade (Kind of Hush) *134$^{3}$ (209) 405$^{5}$ 421$^{5}$ 857$^{5}$ 1122$^{4}$* 1592$^{10}$ 1776$^{2}$ 1956$^{2}$ 2402$^{5}$ **>51a 61f<**
**Cockney Lad (IRE) 7** ch g Camden Town-Big Bugs Bomb (Skymaster) *2055$^{17}$* 2825a$^{7}$ **>89f<**
**Cocoloba (IRE) 2** b f Distinctly North (USA)-Born to Fly (IRE) (Last Tycoon) 1822$^{8}$ **>26f<**
**Cocoon (IRE) 3** b f Cyrano de Bergerac-Arena (Sallust) *123$^{7}$ 171$^{7}$ 237$^{5}$ 1721$^{9}$ 2180$^{9}$* 4437$^{5}$ **>28a 39f<**
**Code 2** b g Mystiko (USA)-Farewell Letter (USA) (Arts And Letters) 3110$^{5}$ **>31f< (DEAD)**
**Code Red 3** b c Warning-For Action (USA) (Assert) 578$^{8}$ 847$^{6}$ 1305$^{5}$ 1833$^{3}$ 2120$^{5}$ 2952$^{5}$ 3928$^{11}$ **>72f<**
**Coeur Francais (FR) 4** b g Hero's Honor (USA)-Marie d'Anjou (FR) (Free Round (USA)) *2637$^{8}$ 3074$^{7}$* **>42a 66df<**
**Coh Sho No 3** b f Old Vic-Castle Peak (Darshaan) 1614$^{5}$ 1895$^{7}$ 3258$^{7}$ 4496$^{7}$ *4892$^{3}$* **>60a 60f<**
**Cointosser (IRE) 3** b f Nordico (USA)-Sure Flyer (IRE) (Sure Blade (USA)) *58$^{3}$ 1518$^{2}$* 2133$^{2}$ (2411) (2893) (2966) 3592$^{4}$ 3852$^{3}$ (4129) **>56a 72f<**
**Cois Na Farraige (IRE) 3** b c Nashamaa-Persian Sparkler (Persian Bold) 4315$^{9}$ 4580$^{16}$ **>80df<**
**Cold Lazarus 2** br g Warning-Indian Pink (USA) (Seattle Slew (USA)) 4599$^{8}$ **>69f<**
**Cold Steel 2** b c Warrshan (USA)-Rengaine (FR) (Music Boy) 4698$^{5}$ **>64f<**
**Colebrook Leader 4** b g Governor General-Sharp Reality (Dreams to Reality (USA)) *3062$^{12}$ 4865$^{21}$*
**Colebrook Willie** *3* br g Dowsing (USA)-A Little Hot (Petong) 2197$^{16}$ 2706$^{7}$ 3849$^{15}$ 4202$^{15}$ **>38f<**
**Coleridge 8** gr g Bellypha-Quay Line (High Line) **1995:** *4355$^{3}$ 4411$^{2}$ (4455) 4530$^{6}$* **1996:** *12$^{2}$ 83$^{2}$ 130$^{2}$ 339$^{2}$ 449$^{11}$* (1063) 1679$^{S}$ 2042$^{20}$ 2511$^{3}$ 2857$^{3}$ 3142$^{8}$ 4604$^{8}$ 4832$^{6}$ **>67a 62f<**
**Colins Choice 2** ch f Risk Me (FR)-Give Me a Day (Lucky Wednesday) *895$^{5}$ 1080$^{7}$ 4976$^{3}$* **>44a f<**
**College Don 5** gr g Kalaglow-Westerlake (Blakeney) 3486$^{P}$ **>70?f<**
**College Night (IRE) 4** b f Night Shift (USA)-

Gertrude Lawrence (Ballymore) 508[18] 636[2] 747[2] 1010[3] 1533[4] 1659[7] 2130[11] 2437[5] 4263[7] 4480[5] **>51f<**

**College Princess 2** b f Anshan-Tinkers Fairy (Myjinski (USA)) 4600[15] 4786[11] **>33f<**

**Colombia (IRE) 2** ch f Mujtahid (USA)-Camarat (Ahonoora) (2531) 2944[2] 3164[3] 3826[4] **>79f<**

**Colonel's Pride 2** ch c Superpower-Yankeedoodledancer (Mashhor Dancer (USA)) 1036[8] 2076[7] 2562[2] 3050[6] 4586[W] **>56?f<**

**Colorful Ambition 6** b g Slip Anchor-Reprocolor (Jimmy Reppin) *18[10] 4073[18]* 4320[9] 4438[R] **>36a 50?f<**

**Colosse 4** b f Reprimand-French Cutie (USA) (Vaguely Noble) **1995:** *4366[6] 4416[5] 4537[7]* **1996:** *90[7] (309) 349[3] (489) 620[14]* 4587[5] 4753[10] *5062[7]* **>49a 50f<**

**Colour Counsellor 3** gr g Touch of Grey-Bourton Downs (Philip of Spain) *277[8] 364[7] 1047[12]* (1534) 1877[5] 2282[7] 2407[4] 2978[5] 3303[5] 3635[8] (3965) 4307[17] **>37a 53f<**

**Colour Key (USA) 2** b c Red Ransom (USA)-Trend (USA) (Ray's Word (USA)) 3873[8] **>65f<**

**Colston-C 4** gr g Belfort (FR)-Grand Occasion (Great Nephew) **1995:** *4464[3] 4487[7] 4514[11]* **1996:** *109[10] 1985[8]* 2347[6] 2791[7] 4130[9] 4382[12] 4765[13] 4881[12] **>52a 44f<**

**Colt D'Or 4** ch g Beldale Lark-Nijinsgayle (FR) (Nice Havrais (USA)) 2953[5] **>55f< (DEAD)**

**Columella (ITY) 2** b c Law Society (USA)-Canadian Guest (Be My Guest (USA)) 4171a[2]

**Colway Bridge 3** b g Colway Radial-Bell Bridge Girl (Coded Scrap) 4437[15] **>18f<**

**Colway Rake 5** b g Salse (USA)-Barely Hot (Bold Lad (IRE)) *587[8]* 956[9] 1364[4] 1588[9] 1848[6] 2431[6] 2911[6] **>74da 64f<**

**Colway Rock (USA) 6** b g Irish River (FR)-Petite Diable (USA) (Sham (USA)) *2077[W]* ***>65df<*** **(DEAD)**

**Comanche Companion 6** b m Commanche Run-Constant Companion (Pas de Seul) 455[23] *854[6] 2400[7]* 2544[10] 3123[15] 3516[8] 3799[8] 4682[11] 4768[6] 4915[7] **>66a 74f<**

**Come Dancing 2** b f Suave Dancer (USA)-Cominna (Dominion) 4318[6] 4593[5] **>49f<**

**Comedie Arrete (FR) 4** b f Old Vic-Seattle Siren (USA) (Seattle Slew (USA)) 994[13] *1717[10] 2439[8] 2935[9] 3090[3] 3605[10]* **>33a f<**

**Comedy River 9** br g Comedy Star (USA)-Hopeful Waters (Forlorn River) *353[10] 843[7]* 1037[3] 1411[4] 1633[6] 2056[2] *(4107) (4603)* 4815[12] **>56a 56f<**

**Come On In 3** b g Most Welcome-Lominda (IRE) (Lomond (USA)) 4833[15]

**Comeonup 5** b g Most Welcome-Scarlet Veil (Tyrnavos) 4430[19] 4609[12] 4829[14] *5056[7]* **>26a 41f<**

**Come Together 2** b f Mtoto-Pfalz (Pharly (FR)) *4210[10]* 4706[5] 4887[8] **>59f<**

**Come Too Mamma's 2** ch f La Grange Music-Purchased by Phone (IRE) (Wolverlife) *838[3] 1026[2] (1097) 1408[4] 1813[4] 2031[3] 2371[3] (2635) 4749[6] 4999[5]* **>58a 58f<**

**Comic Fantasy (AUS) 3** b f Rory's Jester (AUS)-Enchanted Dream (NZ) (Danzatore (CAN)) 700[6] 1823[4] 2151[3] 2425[5] 2778[4] 3055[11] 3350[4] 3465[4] 3774[10] 3844[10] 4071[13] 4382[7] 4505[4] 4860[13] **>64f<**

**Comic Opera (IRE) 2** b f Royal Academy (USA)-Miss Toshiba (USA) (Sir Ivor) 4797[15] **>25f<**

**Comic's Future (USA) 3** b c Carnivalay (USA)-Destiny's Hour (USA) (Fit To Fight (USA)) 588[4] 1180[12]

**Cominenalittlehot (USA) 5** dk g Just The Time (USA)-Isle Of View (USA) (Burd Alane (USA)) *(4960a)* ***>108f<***

**Commanche Court (IRE) 3** ch c Commanche Run-Sorceress (FR) (Fabulous Dancer (USA)) (2275a) **>97f<**

**Commanchero 9** gr g Telsmoss-Count On Me (No Mercy) *1861[3]* **>13a 46f<**

**Commander Glen (IRE) 4** b g Glenstal (USA)-Une Parisienne (FR) (Bolkonski) 480[13] 662[9] 1037[2] 1313[13] (1538) 1830[2] 1886[5] 2058[9] 2366[2] 2587[6] 2678[6] 3084[7] 3348[9] 4249[12] **>69f<**

**Commander Jones (IRE) 2** b g Common Grounds-Play A Golden Disc (Ashmore (FR)) 1959[9] 2219[3] 2559[7] 2772[4] (4046) 4364[5] (4546) *4777[5]* **>41a 78f<**

**Commin' Up 3** b f Primo Dominie-Ridalia (Ridan (USA)) 1181[2] 1615[11] 2162[5] 2945[9] 4968[18] **>67f<**

**Committal (IRE) 3** b c Lycius (USA)-Just Cause (Law Society (USA)) 3153[10] 3503[6] 4874[8] 4974[19] **>95f<**

**Common Divine (IRE) 3** b f Common Grounds-Day Dress (Ashmore (FR)) **1995:** *4519[6]* **1996:** *101[11] 215[4] 3059[15]* ***>31a f<***

**Commoner (USA) 4** b c Far North (CAN)-Searching Around (USA) (Round Table) **1995:** *4522a[6]* **1996:** 726[5] 919[5] 1065[W] 1509[6] 2336[2] **>115f<**

**Common Rock (IRE) 2** b f Common Grounds-Quatre Femme (Petorius) 2025[11] *(2938) 3417[10]* **>46a f<**

**Compact Disc (IRE) 2** b f Royal Academy (USA)-Sharp Circle (IRE) (Sure Blade (USA)) 2755[5] 3050[7] 3941[5] 4343[3] 4749[16] 4990[18] **>58f<**

**Compass Pointer 3** gr c Mazilier (USA)-Woodleys (Tyrnavos) *593[12]* 1100[4] 1498[2] 2247[9] 3113[14] 3459[7] 3948[2] 4448[7] 4683[13] 4919[4] 5054[2] **>68f<**

**Compatibility (IRE) 2** b c Common Grounds-Nikki's Groom (Shy Groom (USA)) 2624[8] **>61f<**

**Compton Place 2** ch c Indian Ridge-Nosey (Nebbiolo) (1980) 2504[2] (3164) 3690[2] 4191[2] **>111f<**

**Comtec's Legend 6** ch m Legend of France (USA)-Comtec Princess (Gulf Pearl) **1995:** *4416[9] (4507)* **1996:** *72[3] 152[6] 267[3] 422[2] 512[5] (609) 898[7] 1070[8]* ***>48a 34f<***

**Concepcion (GER) 6** br h Acatenango (GER)-Comprida (GER) (Windwurf (GER)) 1135a[4] 2479a[8] 3754a[3] 4172a[2] 4747a[8] **>119f<**

**Concer Un 4** ch g Lord Bud-Drudwen (Sayf El Arab (USA)) *1625[9]* (1983) (2312) (2544) 3072[12] (3709) (3920) 4329[9] 4769[15] **>55a 104f<**

**Condition Red 3** b f Sayf El Arab (USA)-Forever Mary (Red Alert) 4704[5] **>18f<**

**Condor Ridge 3** b g Inca Chief (USA)-Second Flower (Indian Ruler (USA)) *577[12]* 761[9] *856[10] 1956[3] 2325[10] 2411[10]* ***>23a 54f<***

**Coneybury (IRE) 6** b h Last Tycoon-Jackie Berry (Connaught) 1138a[8] **>113?f<**

**Confronter 7** ch g Bluebird (USA)-Grace Darling (USA) (Vaguely Noble) 148a[7] 191a[4] 288a[4] 290a[2] 324a[5] 809[8] 1051[4] 1819[14] 2312[4] 2761[3] 3123[6] 3805[8] 4243[7] 4463[19] 4609[10] **>79a 70f<**

**Congo Man 3** b c Rainbow Quest (USA)-African Dance (USA) (El Gran Senor (USA)) 3042[5] (4235) **>80f<**

**Conic Hill (IRE) 5** ch g Lomond (USA)-Krisalya (Kris) *187[6] 309[9] 920[9]* 1414[6] 1696[7] 2159[2] 2409[14] 2896[10] 3220[8] **>51a 55f<**

**Connemara (IRE) 2** b f Mujadil (USA)-Beechwood (USA) (Blushing Groom (FR)) (596) (984) 2051[4] 2582[9] 3213[2] **>95f<**

**Conon Falls (IRE) 2** b c Sadler's Wells (USA)-Cocotte (Troy) 3407[8] 3925[3] **>89f<**

**Conquistajade (USA) 3** b br f Conquistador Cielo (USA)-Uncut Jade (CAN) (Vice Regent (CAN)) **1995:** *4501[3]* **1996:** *17[9] 119[6] 188[8] 277[7] 300[7] 483[9]* ***>47da 49df<***

**Considerable Charm 4** ch f Charmer-Leap in Time (Dance In Time (CAN)) **1995:** *4540[7]* **1996:** *179[11] 409[6] 1099[7]* 1661[7] **>36a 36f<**

**Consordino 3** b f Alzao (USA)-Consolation (Troy) 676[9] 1481[6] 2142[7] (4470) 4559[13] **>93f<**

**Consort 3** b c Groom Dancer (USA)-Darnelle (Shirley Heights) 669[2] (3519) 3926[3] 4136[5] 4444[7] 4682[4] **>91f<**

**Conspicuous (IRE) 6** b g Alzao (USA)-Mystery Lady (USA) (Vaguely Noble) 988[7] 1440[10] 1793[4] 2145[3] 3072[4] 3516[10] (3806) 4184[8] 4568[27] **>60+a 90f<**

**Conspiracy 2** b f Rudimentary (USA)-Roussalka (Habitat) 1346[2] (1998) 2484[3] 3823[2] (4247) **>91f<**

**Constance Do 3** ch f Risk Me (FR)-The Boozy News (USA) (L'Emigrant (USA)) (150a) **>78f<**

**Contare 3** b f Shirley Heights-Balenare (FR) (Pharly (FR)) 3568a[3] (4948a) (5072a) **>103f<**

**Contentment (IRE) 2** b c Fairy King (USA)-Quality Of Life (Auction Ring (USA)) 3807[9] 4123[7] 4318[2] **>64f<**

**Contract Bridge (IRE) 3** b f Contract Law (USA)-Mystery Bid (Auction Ring (USA)) **1995:** *4431[13]* **1996:** *348[4] 1042[6]* (1539) 1850[8] 2356[3] 2752[6] 3354[5] 3484[4] (3845) 4474[5] **>29a 54f<**

**Contrafire (IRE) 4** b g Contract Law (USA)-Fiery Song (Ballad Rock) 598[4] 738[4] 1173[4] 1696[2] (2988) 3290[4] 3828[5] **>76a 73f<**

**Contrarie 3** b f Floose-Chanita (Averof) **1995:** *4393[14] 4433[11]* **1996:** *1498[7] 2086[9] 4815[8]* 5007[4] 5052[4] **>11a 42f<**

**Contravene (IRE) 2** b f Contract Law (USA)-Vieux Carre (Pas de Seul) 446[4] *533[2] (624)* 990[3] 1164[3] *1459[4] 3343[5]* (3648) 3879[5] 4046[2] *(4335) 4764[5]* 4903[7] **>65a 66f<**

**Control Freak 2** b f Inca Chief (USA)-Forest Nymph (Native Bazaar) 3663[8] 4359[7] 4607[5] **>35f<**

**Convent Guest (IRE) 3** ch f Be My Guest (USA)-Point of View (FR) (Sharpman) *10[6] 158[6]* **>61a f<**

**Conwy 3** ch f Rock City-Degannwy (Caerleon (USA)) 1508[16] **>53f<**

**Coochie 7** b m King of Spain-York Street (USA) (Diamond Shoal) 2310[6] 2556[10] **>28f<**

**Cool Caper 3** b c Inca Chief (USA)-Rekindled Flame (IRE) (Kings Lake (USA)) 545[3] *856[8]* **>52a 51f<**

**Cool Edge (IRE) 5** ch g Nashamaa-Mochara (Last Fandango) *(450)* 728[2] (960) 1484[4] (3612) 3782[3] 4649a[2] 4972[6] **>110f<**

**Cool Fire 3** b c Colmore Row-Into the Fire (Dominion) *(460) 819[2]* 1185[11] 1773[9] *3627[7] 4078[5] 4329[16]* 4769[25] **>73a 56f<**

**Cool Grey 2** gr f Absalom-Crisp Air (Elegant Air) *4041[14] 4988[6]* **>19a 23f<**

**Cool Jazz 5** b h Lead on Time (USA)-Amber Fizz (USA) (Effervescing (USA)) **1995:** 4523a[14] **1996:** 457[3] 673[5] (927) 1483[9] 2072[12] 2622[9] 3126[4] 3708[7] 4057[10] 4442[12] **>111f<**

**Coolowen Flash (IRE) 5** gr m Standaan (FR)-Little Cynthia (Wolver Hollow) 559[12] 1865[6] 2757[19] 3777[10] 4205[5] 4473[11] **>39f<**

**Copperbeech (IRE) 2** ch f Common Grounds-Caimanite (Tap On Wood) 729[2] 1179[6] 4545[6] 4803[13] **>68f<**

**Copper Bright 3** b g Mon Tresor-Arabian Nymph (Sayf El Arab (USA)) *10[4] 28[4] 51[2] 78[5] 160[5] (215) (271) 383[6] 430[4]* **>67a 47f<**

**Copper Shell 2** ch g Beveled (USA)-Luly My Love (Hello Gorgeous (USA)) 2972[9] **>54f<**

**Coral Island 2** b g Charmer-Misowni (Niniski (USA)) 3941[7] 4481[4] 4618[12] **>53f<**

**Coral Reef (ITY) 3** b c Big Reef-All the Crown (Chief's Crown (USA)) **1995:** 4399a[5] **1996:** (1058a) 1580a[3] 4421a[2] 4747a[6] **>118f<**

**Coral Springs (USA)** 2 b br f Minshaanshu Amad (USA)-Distinctiveness (USA) (Distinctive (USA)) 2044[8] 2942[7] **>43f<**

**Coral Strand** 2 ch f Indian Ridge-Sea Venture (FR) (Diatome) 3349[7] 4301[4] 4908[4] **>72f<**

**Coretta (IRE)** 2 b f Caerleon (USA)-Free At Last (Shirley Heights) 4969[3] **>79+f<**

**Corinchili** 2 ch f Chilibang-Corinthia (USA) (Empery (USA)) 490[5] **>45f<**

**Corinthian (IRE)** 2 b c Lycius (USA)-Royal Recreation (USA) (His Majesty (USA)) 4507[4] 4801[7] **>65f<**

**Corky's Girl** 4 b f Today and Tomorrow-Rectory Maid (Tina's Pet) 2931[5] 3239[4]

**Corncrake (IRE)** 2 b f Nordico (USA)-Lemon Balm (High Top) 2614[5] 2764[3] 2995[5] 3467[7] 3769[3] *3954[4] 4607[3]* ***>55a 59f<***

**Cornet** 10 b g Coquelin (USA)-Corny Story (Oats) 5008[9] **>31f<**

**Corniche Quest (IRE)** 3 b f Salt Dome (USA)-Angel Divine (Ahonoora) (1535) 1806[5] 2139[7] 2255[3] 2411[D] 2713[6] 2983[9] 3167[10] 3427[3] 3761[4] 3977[4] (4259) 4598[7] (4784) *4989[15]* **>60f<**

**Cornish Snow (USA)** 3 br c Storm Cat (USA)-Pleasantly Free (USA) (Pleasant Colony (USA)) *(217) (321) 2436[5]* ***>85a 68f<***

**Coro (SWI)** 4 ch c Aguarico (GER)-Concisely (Connaught) 4414a[2] **>90f<**

**Corona Gold** 6 b g Chilibang-Miss Alkie (Noalcoholic (FR)) *2971[15] 3089[15] 3306[17]* 3460[8] 3777[8] **>45a 27f<**

**Corporal Nym (USA)** 3 gr g Cozzene (USA)-Fiji Fan (USA) (Danzig (USA)) 4108[10] 4309[6] 4581[16] **>69f<**

**Corradini** 4 b c Rainbow Quest (USA)-Cruising Height (Shirley Heights) 712[3] 1005[3] 1428[4] (1976) (2352) 3689[3] (4112) 4965[11] **>113f<**

**Corrina Corrina** 3 b f Risk Me (FR)-Dona Krista (King of Spain) 949[11] **>18f<**

**Corsini** 2 b f Machiavellian (USA)-Dangora (USA) (Sovereign Dancer (USA)) (4105) 4446[2] **>89f<**

**Cortes** 3 ch f Roi Danzig (USA)-Jumra (Thatch (USA)) 1656[13] **>46f<**

**Coscoroba (IRE)** 2 ch f Shalford (IRE)-Tameeza (USA) (Shahrastani (USA)) 3082[3] **>40f<**

**Cosmic Prince (IRE)** 2 b c Teenoso (USA)-Windmill Princess (Gorytus (USA)) 3407[6] 4100[3] (4494) **>86f<**

**Cossack Count** 3 ch c Nashwan (USA)-Russian Countess (USA) (Nureyev (USA)) 1235a[10] 2472a[15] **>90f<**

**Cottage Prince (IRE)** 3 b g Classic Secret (USA)-Susan's Blues (Cure The Blues (USA)) 1830[11] 2563[13] 2752[7] 3354[3] 3780[5] 3961[3] **>25a 48f<**

**Couchant (IRE)** 5 b g Petoski-Be Easy (Be Friendly) *1102[10]* 1454[9] **>68df<**

**Count Basie** 3 b c Batshoof-Quiet Harbour (Mill Reef (USA)) 845[2] 1180[3] (1656) 2074[18] 2690[7] **>88f<**

**Count Chivas (NZ)** 5 b g Lord Ballina (AUS)-Inquisit (NZ) (Imposing (AUS)) 5069a[2]

**Countdown (FR)** 4 ch g Galetto-Comtesse Du Barry (191a) **>79f<**

**Countess of Cadiz (USA)** 3 b f Badger Land (USA)-Cokebutton (Be My Guest (USA)) *2062[9]* 2365[8] 3108[9] **>12f<**

**Countless Times** 2 ch c Timeless Times (USA)-Arroganza (Crofthall) 569[8] 2374[8] 2600[10] 2942[6] **>50f<**

**Count of Flanders (IRE)** 6 b g Green Desert (USA)-Marie de Flandre (FR) (Crystal Palace (FR)) 3981[9] **>44f<**

**Count Roberto (USA)** 2 ch c El Gran Senor (USA)-Numeral (USA) (Alleged (USA)) 3595[4] 3919[3] 4123[6] (4586) **>88f<**

**Country Lover** 5 ch g Thatching-Fair Country (Town And Country) 151a[5] 227a[9] 325a[5] 450[9] 879[14] 1102[4] (1338) 1792[8] 2883[9] 3470[5] 4669[2] 4877[2] **>86?a 76f<**

**Country Thatch** 3 b c Thatching-Alencon (Northfields (USA)) 3162[7] 3513[10] 4053[15] 4232[10] **>61f<**

**Count Tony** 2 ch c Keen-Turtle Dove (Gyr (USA)) *3625[4] 4069[13]* 4261[7] **>56a 63f<**

**Coup De Poker (FR)** 5 b h Saint Cyrien (FR)-Cagliari (Djakao (FR)) 4941a[3] **>74f<**

**Courageous Dancer (IRE)** 4 b f Cadeaux Genereux-Hafwah (Gorytus (USA)) 1149[3] 1354[8] 1799[5] 2220[8] 2693[6] 3521[2] 3799[6] 3974[2] 4432[7] 4775[17] **>84f<**

**Courageous Knight** 7 gr g Midyan (USA)-Little Mercy (No Mercy) 2994[9] **>64da 46f<**

**Courbaril** 4 b g Warrshan (USA)-Free on Board (Free State) *187[4] 309[7] 635[3]* 759[2] 1063[3] 1439[7] 2155[8] 2711[R] 2978[2] 3466[2] **>60a 64f<**

**Coureur** 7 b g Ajdal (USA)-Nihad (Alleged (USA)) *440[11]* 827[13] (1069) 1337[2] 1672[3] 4300[15] **>79f<**

**Courroux (FR)** 5 b h Foolish Pleasure (USA)-Mediation (Fabulous Dancer (USA)) 193a[2]

**Course Fishing** 5 ch g Squill (USA)-Migoletty (Oats) 2214[6] 2574[8] 2896[9] (3297) 3621[5] 3825[4] 4563[18] 4726[10] **>17a 54f<**

**Court Express** 2 b c Then Again-Moon Risk (Risk Me (FR)) 4060[5] 4363[7] 4807[5] **>66f<**

**Court House** 2 b c Reprimand-Chalet Girl (Double Form) *895[8] 1489[5] 2361[7]* 3848[6] **>44a 62f<**

**Courting Danger** 3 b g Tina's Pet-Court Town (Camden Town) 445[3] 917[11] **>73f<**

**Courting Newmarket** 8 b g Final Straw-Warm Wind (Tumble Wind (USA)) *649[12]* 981[6] 1658[11] 2602[14] **>57a 47f<**

**Court Jester** 5 gr g Petong-First Experience (Le Johnstan) *4107[8] 4203[20]* ***>25a 27f<***

**Court of Honour (IRE)** 4 b c Law Society (USA)-Captive Island (Northfields (USA)) 1128[3] 1482[3] 4434[2] 5069a[20] **>122f<**

**Courtship** 2 b c Groom Dancer (USA)-Dance Quest (FR) (Green Dancer (USA)) 4516[2] (4818) **>85f<**

**Cousin Bull (USA)** 3 543a[3]

**Coven Moon** 6 ch m Crofthall-Mayspark (Stanford) **1995:** *4385[6]* **1996:** *2058[5]* 2409[11] 2438[5] 2766[7] **>39a 37f<**

**Covered Girl (IRE)** 3 b f Thatching-Tootle (Main Reef) 710[9] 1007[9] 1617[14] *2934[15] 4480[10]* ***>52f<***

**Cowboy Dreams (IRE)** 3 b g Nashamaa-Shahrazad (Young Emperor) 851[11] 1518[4] 2489[6] **>48f<**

**Cowrie** 2 b f Efisio-Bawbee (Dunbeath (USA)) *(1643)* 2051[W] 3990[5] 4258[4] 4566[11] **>94f<**

**Cowtharee** 2 ch f Arazi (USA)-Hawait Al Barr (Green Desert (USA)) 3663[3] **>62f<**

**Coyote Bluff (IRE)** 3 gr c Fayruz-Ikala (Lashkari) 611[3] (785) **>78a 91f<**

**Crabbie's Pride** 3 ch g Red Sunset-Free Rein (Sagaro) 566[4] 985[7] 1434[6] 2001[6] 3918[8] *4336[9] 4448[15]* ***>21a 63f<***

**Craigie Boy** 6 b g Crofthall-Lady Carol (Lord Gayle (USA)) 505[10] 587[12] 617[6] (882) 1020[3] 1423[11] 1634[2] 2490[6] 2725[18] 3424[6] 3937[11] 4473[5] 4486[11] 4805[10] **>29a 50f<**

**Craigievar** 2 b c Mujadil (USA)-Sweet Home (Home Guard (USA)) 2195[4] (4600) (4916) **>97+f<**

**Craigmore Magic (USA)** 3 br g Simply Majestic (USA)-Some Rehearsal (USA) (Halo (USA)) *1043[3]* 1363[7] *1721[14] 2026[5]* 3780[11] 4752[13] **>43a 44f<**

**Craignairn** 3 b g Merdon Melody-Bri-Ette (Brittany) 453[13] 1475[7] (2236) 2417[10] 2870[4] 3278[9] 3959[4] 4430[23] 4768[20] **>50f<**

**Crambella (IRE)** 4 b f Red Sunset-Simbella (Simbir) 3353[9] 3480[4] 3638[3] 4345[4] **>40f<**

**Crandon Boulevard** 3 b c Niniski (USA)-Last Clear Chance (USA) (Alleged (USA)) 1305[8] 2739[2] 3699[4] **>72f<**

**Craven Cottage** 3 b g Inca Chief (USA)-Seymour Ann (Krayyan) 819[15] 1074[14] 1689[13] 2281[5] 3166[8] 3633[3] **>36f<**

**Craven Hill (IRE)** 2 gr g Pursuit of Love-Crodelle (IRE) (Formidable (USA)) 4516[11] **>54f<**

**Crazy Chief** 3 b c Indian Ridge-Bizarre Lady (Dalsaan) 577[5] 669[3] 892[4] (1319) 1464[2] 1843[4] 3039[2] 3923[7] **>85f<**

**Credit Controller (IRE)** 7 b g Dromod Hill-Fotopan (Polyfoto) *2551[12] 3699[5]* ***>1a 6f<***

**Credite Risque** 3 b f Risk Me (FR)-Lompoa (Lomond (USA)) 638[10] **>43f<**

**Creeking** 3 b f Persian Bold-Miller's Creek (USA) (Star de Naskra (USA)) **1995:** *4519[2]* **1996:** *67[4] 143[2] 277[2] 300[4] 2019[5]* 2242[2] 2358[6] 2979[4] 3304[2] 3881[4] 4263[8] **>66a 59f<**

**Crested Knight (IRE)** 4 gr g Night Shift (USA)-Casual (USA) (Caro) *636[12]* 844[4] 1150[9] 1618[4] 3514[8] 4086[7] (4373) **>64f<**

**Crest Wing (USA)** 3 b c Storm Bird (CAN)-Purify (USA) (Fappiano (USA)) 1182[12] 1593[8] 2876[4] **>52f<**

**Cretan Gift** 5 ch g Cadeaux Genereux-Caro's Niece (USA) (Caro) **1995:** *4392[7] 4508[2]* **1996:** *20[4] 88[3] 170[4] 270[2] 357[2] 592[2]* 718[8] *(835) 896[6] 956[2]* 1412[13] *1810[2] 2005[2] (2171) 2376[4]* 2725[6] 3152[3] 3265[6] 3639[6] 3810[4] 3932[10] 4058[5] (4205) (4312) 4687[14] 4791[7] (4994) **>92a 87f<**

**Crimson And Clover** 3 gr f Midyan (USA)-Carose (Caro) **1995:** *4360[2]* **>72a 66f<**

**Crimson Rosella** 3 b br f Polar Falcon (USA)-Double Finesse (Double Jump) 669[8] 1050[6] 1995[6] 2542[8] 2738[3] 2952[7] *3422[7]* **>59f<**

**Crimson Tide (IRE)** 2 b c Sadler's Wells (USA)-Sharata (IRE) (Darshaan) 4514[2] (4770) **>92f<**

**Crinolette (IRE)** 2 b f Sadler's Wells (USA)-Organza (High Top) 4830[13] **>37f<**

**Criollito (ARG)** 5 ch h Candy Stripes (USA)-Greek Filly (USA) (Greek Waters (USA)) *4951a[12]* **>109a f<**

**Crissem (IRE)** 3 b f Thatching-Deer Emily (Alzao (USA)) 773[13] **>69f<**

**Cristin (ITY)** 2 b f Luge-Sartagna (ITY) (Jalmood (USA)) 4420a[3] (4745a) **>73f<**

**Critical Factor (USA)** 2 dk f Star de Naskra (USA)-Stormy Spell (CAN) (Tsunami Slew (USA)) *4950a[3]* **>96a f<**

**Croa (IRE)** 3 b f Alzao (USA)-Crodas (Shirley Heights) 4170a[2] **>68f<**

**Croagh Patrick** 4 b g Faustus (USA)-Pink Pumpkin (Tickled Pink) 842[11] 1045[10] 1319[16] 4820[16] **>59f<**

**Croeso Cynnes** 3 ch f Most Welcome-Miss Taleca (Pharly (FR)) 1634[4] 1840[2] 2186[4] (2578) 2799[2] 2946[4] (3323) 3844[4] 4044[9] **>74f<**

**Crofters Ceilidh** 4 ch f Scottish Reel-Highland Rowena (Royben) 1974[7] 2381[4] 2694[10] 3038[8] 3618[11] 3932[9] 4304[4] (4367) 4561[3] 4772[6] 4869[12] **>92f<**

**Croft Pool** 5 b g Crofthall-Blackpool Belle (The Brianstan) **1995:** *4368[10]* **1996:** *1321[7]* 1630[3] 2270a[2] 2545[3] 3126[3] 3524[7] (4101) 4115[5] 4466[3] (4518) 4958a[2] 5044[9] **>84a 112f<**

**Cromaboo Crown** 5 b m Crowning Honors (CAN)-La Belle Epoque (Tachypous) *3090[6]*

**Crosby Nod** 2 b g Shalford (IRE)-Kirkby Belle (Bay Express) 3941[15] 4046[15] 5034[16] **>31f<**

**Crossillion** 8 b g Rousillon (USA)-Croda Rossa

(ITY) (Grey Sovereign) 1018[7] **>83f<**

**Cross of Valour 3** b g Never so Bold-X-Data (On Your Mark) 1709[9] (2281) 2950[2] 3210[15] 3518[12] 4044[2] 4308[12] **>86f<**

**Cross Talk (IRE) 4** b g Darshaan-Liaison (USA) (Blushing Groom (FR)) *113[8] 169[12] 187[5] 222[4] 256[7] 297[5] 400[4] (482)* 771[7] *855[4] 1095[6] 1542[4]* 1763[5] 2394[7] 2988[8] *4332[9] 4763[2]* (4910) **>67da 68f<**

**Cross The Border 3** b g Statoblest-Brave Advance (USA) (Bold Laddie (USA)) 832[2] 959[5] 1394a[10] 2003[7] 3085[12] 4581[21] 4765[17] 5039[22] **>67f<**

**Crowded Avenue 4** b g Sizzling Melody-Lady Bequick (Sharpen Up) 1016[8] 1818[3] 2003[3] 2292[9] 3126[5] 3432[18] (3946) 4466[7] **>108f<**

**Crown And Cushion 3** b g High Adventure-Soulieana (Manado) *1456[7] 1602[8] 2189[12]* 2895[8] **>24a 9f<**

**Crown Court (USA) 3** b c Chief's Crown (USA)-Bold Courtesan (USA) (Bold Bidder) 942[6] 1182[6] 1701[3] (2581) 3211[3] 4568[20] **>92f<**

**Crowning Tino 4** b f Crowning Honors (CAN)-Tino Reppin (Neltino) **1995:** *4540[9]* **1996:** *44[8] 85[14] 207[11] 868[20]* 1474[16] **>24df<**

**Crown of Light 2** b f Mtoto-Russian Countess (USA) (Nureyev (USA)) *(3454)* **>72f<**

**Crowther Homes 6** br m Neltino-Fair Sara (McIndoe) **1995:** *4391[11]* **>30f<**

**Crumpton Hill (IRE) 4** b g Thatching-Senane (Vitiges (FR)) 967[3] 2053[3] (2623) 3445[3] **>99f<**

**Cruz Santa 3** b f Lord Bud-Linpac Mapleleaf (Dominion) 2393[2] 3255[6] 3624[7] 3973[15] 4323[10] **>53f<**

**Cry Baby 3** b c Baim (USA)-Estonia (Kings Lake (USA)) 597[6] 849[7] (1451) 1828[5] 2388[3] 2915[5] **>37a 49f<**

**Cryhavoc 2** b c Polar Falcon (USA)-Sarabah (IRE) (Ela-Mana-Mou) 2559[11] 2852[4] 3114[3] (4123) (4717) **>96f<**

**Crystal Crossing (IRE) 2** b f Royal Academy (USA)-Never so Fair (Never so Bold) 2245[2] (2877) 4159a[6] **>101f<**

**Crystal Falls (IRE) 3** b r Alzao (USA)-Honourable Sheba (USA) (Roberto (USA)) *589[7]* **>79f<**

**Crystal Fast (USA) 3** b g Fast Play (USA)-Crystal Cave (USA) (Nearctic) *17[5] 188[5] 376[2] 447[9]* 637[10] *899[6] 1067[5]* 1691[18] 2753[8] 3217[8] **>62a 42df<**

**Crystal Gift 4** b g Dominion-Grain Lady (USA) (Greinton) **1995:** *4363[3] 4386[9]* **>60a 64f<**

**Crystal Gold 2** ch c Arazi (USA)-Crystal Land (Kris) 4100[13] 4913[8] **>71f<**

**Crystal Hearted 2** b c Broken Hearted-Crystal Fountain (Great Nephew) 4233[4] (4601) **>92+f<**

**Crystal Heights (FR) 8** ch g Crystal Glitters (USA)-Fahrenheit (Mount Hagen (FR)) **1995:** *4421[2] 4531[11]* **1996:** *42[2] 121[11] 177[3] 244[5] (363) 633[6]* 744[7] 1010[9] 1532[3] 2229[8] (2763) (2982) (3313) 3783[7] **>75a 76f<**

**Crystal Hills (IRE) 2** b c Darshaan-Lustre (USA) (Halo (USA)) 4507[9] **>42f<**

**Crystal Loop 4** b f Dowsing (USA)-Gipping (Vision (USA)) **1995:** *4368[11] 4508[8]* **1996:** *139[F]* **>76a 72f<** **(DEAD)**

**Crystal Warrior 3** b f Warrshan (USA)-Crystal's Solo (USA) (Crystal Water (USA)) 445[11] 763[4] 1089[10] 2027[7] 2563[7] *5056[12]* **>56f<**

**Cuango (IRE) 5** b or br h Mtoto-Barinia (Corvaro (USA)) **1995:** *4370[2] 4411[5]* **1996:** *(15) 83[3] (296) 392[5] 411[2] 439[6]* 546[7] 642[3] 753[4] (872) 1524[5] 1802[5] 2060[4] **>75a 67f<**

**Cuban Nights (USA) 4** b g Our Native (USA)-Havana Moon (USA) (Cox's Ridge (USA)) *402[6] 419[2] (512) 898[5] (1031) 1458[5] 1778[9]* 2707[5] **>71a 54f<**

**Cuban Reef 4** b f Dowsing (USA)-Cox's Pippin (USA) (Cox's Ridge (USA)) 879[28] 1449[20] 1613[3] 2032[8] 2743[7] 3334[2] 3592[5] 3800[5] 4000[4] (4236) 4686[9] 4812[11] **>32a 56f<**

**Cuckmere Venture 6** br m King of Spain-Kala Nashan (Kala Shikari) **1995:** *4450[10]* **>14a 34f<**

**Cuff Link (IRE) 6** ch g Caerleon (USA)-Corinth Canal (Troy) 1176[7] **>113f<**

**Cugina 2** b f Distant Relative-Indubitable (Sharpo) 4061[8] 4512[6] 4797[7] **>77f<**

**Culrain 5** b g Hadeer-La Vie En Primrose (Henbit (USA)) *837[7] 898[10]* **>36a 36f<**

**Cultural Icon (USA) 4** b g Kris S (USA)-Sea Prospector (USA) (Mr Prospector (USA)) *106[5] 228[7] 402[11] 4202[13]* **>40a 29f<**

**Cumbrian Maestro 3** b g Puissance-Flicker Toa Flame (USA) (Empery (USA)) 509[10] 976[11] 1185[8] 1477[5] 1783[9] (3484) 3845[2] 4000[6] 4249[10] **>66f<**

**Cumbrian Quest 2** b g Be My Chief (USA)-Tinkerbird (Music Boy) 1801[6] 2295[8] **>15f< (DEAD)**

**Cumbrian Rhapsody 6** ch m Sharrood (USA)-Bustellina (Busted) 3297[3] **>71f<**

**Cumbrian Waltzer 11** ch g Stanford-Mephisto Waltz **1995:** *4432[9]* **>32a 80f<**

**Cupla Focail 3** b f Inca Chief (USA)-Lizzie Bee (Kind of Hush) *40[6]* **>7a 21f<**

**Current Leader 3** b g Primo Dominie-Trelissick (Electric) 1533[13] 2033[9] 2253[6] 2373[14] 3316[6] **>36f<**

**Current Speech (IRE) 5** b g Thatching-Lady Aladdin (Persian Bold) *1198[5]* 1476[6] **>76f<**

**Curtelace 6** ch g Nishapour (FR)-Khandjar (Kris) *439[20]* 690[2] 853[5] 1661[6] 2010[14] 2178[4] **>67f<**

**Curzon Street 2** b f Night Shift (USA)-Pine Ridge (High Top) 3269[2] 3593[8] 4104[11] 4469[5] **>79df<**

**Cutthroat Kid (IRE) 6** b g Last Tycoon-Get Ahead (Silly Season) *541[5]* 620[11] 886[3] *1488[3] 2423[2]* 2804[4] 3428[8] 3676[3] **>66a 72df<**

**Cybertechnology 2** b c Environment Friend-Verchinina (Star Appeal) 4461[7] (4618) 4908[2] **>84f<**

**Cycladic (USA) 4** ch c Nureyev (USA)-Carnet Solaire (USA) (Sharpen Up) (290a) **>77f<**

**Cyclone (IRE) 5** b g Treasure Kay-Pallachine (FR) (Lichine (USA)) 649[6] 745[9] **>4a 29f<**

**Cymbalo 5** ch g Sharpo-Cynomis (Shergar) 617[15]

**Cypress Avenue (IRE) 4** b g Law Society (USA)-Flying Diva (Chief Singer) 573[13] 712[7] 811[10] 2505[6] 2560[4] 3142[7] 3801[9] **>64f<**

**Cyprus Point 5** b m Unfuwain (USA)-Sunshine Coast (Posse (USA)) **1995:** *4379[10]* **>31a 57f<**

**Cyrano's Lad (IRE) 7** b or br g Cyrano de Bergerac-Patiala (Crocket) 940[6] 1149[4] 1630[6] (1975) (2220) 3232[29] 3524[4] 3672[4] 3984[2] 4116[19] 4687[6] 4774[10] **>105f<**

**Cyrillic 3** ch f Rock City-Lariston Gale (Pas de Seul) 572[6] 674[9] **>92f<**

**Czarna (IRE) 5** b g Polish Precedent (USA)-Noble Dust (USA) (Dust Commander (USA)) 728[18] 1149[2] 1898[3] 2053[9] 2497[4] 2623[10] 3125[7] 3521[4] 4184[15] 4624[9] 4915[11] **>82df<**

**D**

**Daaniera (IRE) 6** gr g Standaan (FR)-Right Cash (Right Tack) **1995:** *4358[5] 4460[7] 4542[6]* **1996:** *16[7] 231[4] 362[7] 652[9] 900[6] 1492[9] 1971[4]* **>36a 23f<**

**Daawe (USA) 5** b h Danzig (USA)-Capo Di Monte (Final Straw) *44[6] 90[5] (127) 207[2] 259[7] 282[7] (368) 431[7] 749[2]* (956) 1157[4] *(1492) (2005)* 2725[8] 3223[5] 3424[4] 3622[12] 4180[3] 4452[10] 4616[19] 4689[3] 4994[3] 5039[11] **>63a 85f<**

**Dacha (IRE) 4** b c Soviet Star (USA)-Shadywood (Habitat) 2036[2] (2591) 3710[4] (4055) 4465[3] **>105f<**

**Dacoit (USA) 2** b c Red Ransom (USA)-Krishka (CAN) (Drone) (4514) 4681[2] **>92f<**

**Daffodil Dale (IRE) 2** b f Cyrano de Bergerac-Supreme Crown (USA) (Chief's Crown (USA)) 1565a[7] 4639a[6] 5063a[7] **>79f<**

**Daffodil Express (IRE) 3** b f Skyliner-Miss Henry (Blue Cashmere) 686[11] 1840[4] 3525[9] 3698[13] 3883[13] *5055[12]* **>45f<**

**Dahiyah (USA) 5** b g Ogygian (USA)-Sticky Prospect (USA) (Mr Prospector (USA)) *26[9] 133[2] (178) 266[3] 316[6] 380[5] 631[5] 896[9] 1992[3]* (2286) 3049[9] 3285[3] *3877[15] 4865[10]* **>64a 70f<**

**Da Hoss (USA) 4** b g Gone West (USA)-Jolly Saint (USA) *(4953a)* **>57a 136f<**

**Daily Risk 3** ch g Risk Me (FR)-Give Me a Day (Lucky Wednesday) 149a[6] 226a[7] 326a[12] 595[5] 819[13] 1009[4] 1122[D] 1348[14] *1993[10]* **>4a 70f<**

**Daily Sport Girl 7** b m Risk Me (FR)-Net Call (Song) 1462[5] 1640[2] 1870[3] *2173[10]* **>34a 56f<**

**Daintree (IRE) 2** b f Tirol-Aunty Eileen (Ahonoora) 4104[7] 4547[5] 5049[5] **>67f<**

**Daira 3** br f Daring March-Ile de Reine (Ile de Bourbon (USA)) *803[13]* 1324[2] (1600) 2067[12] 3225[2] 3923[2] 4297[2] 4556[5] 4617[11] 4905[6] **>43a 71f<**

**Daisy Bates (IRE) 3** b f Danehill (USA)-Martha Stevens (USA) (Super Concorde (USA)) 4074[4] 4229[W] 4592[7] *5001[3]* **>55a 65f<**

**Dajraan (IRE) 7** b h Shirley Heights-Sugarbird (Star Appeal) 2117[10] **>52?f<**

**Dakota (GER) 3** f 1750a[11]

**Dalcross 5** gr m Nishapour (FR)-Pomade (Luthier) **1995:** *4385[13] 4457[13]* **>26a 41f<**

**Dallai (IRE) 5** b g Dance of Life (USA)-Wavetree (Realm) **1995:** *4455[8]* **>56a 55f<**

**Dally Boy 4** b g Efisio-Gay Hostess (FR) (Direct Flight) **1995:** *4378[4] 4412[4]* **1996:** *474[8]* **>47a 43f<**

**Dalmeny Dancer 2** b c Batshoof-Greek Goddess (Young Generation) 697[4] 865[2] (1531) 1795[6] 2073[5] 2503[2] 2702[5] 3164[2] 4034a[5] 4131[16] 4566[15] 4878[6] **>92f<**

**Dalwhinnie 3** b f Persian Bold-Land Line (High Line) 1180[6] 1804[9] 2247[3] 3500[13] *4095[15] 4448[9]* 4804[6] 4967[2] 5054[15] **>70f<**

**Damancher 4** b c Damister (USA)-Amalancher (USA) (Alleged (USA)) 2474a[3] **>118f<**

**Damanka (IRE) 2** b f Slip Anchor-Doumayna (Kouban (FR)) 4861[13] 4969[20] **>50f<**

**Damarita 5** ch m Starry Night (USA)-Sirenivo (USA) (Sir Ivor) *866[5]* 2408[8] 3586[3] **>37f<**

**Dame D'Harvard (USA) 2** gr f Quest for Fame-Bridge Table (FR) (Riva Ridge (USA)) 3908a[2] 4294a[4] 4661a[12] **>103f<**

**Dame Laura (IRE) 2** b f Royal Academy (USA)-Aunty (FR) (Riverman (USA)) 683[2] (916) 1653[2] 2051[2] 2582[8] 4133[2] **>91f<**

**Danamich (IRE) 3** b g Fayruz-Galapagos (Pitskelly) 458[10] **>25f<**

**Dana Point (IRE) 4** br g Phardante (FR)-Wallpark Princess (Balidar) *477[6]* 527[4] 690[8] 853[4] 999[6] (4763) **>71f<**

**Danccini (IRE) 2** b f Dancing Dissident (USA)-Fantoccini (Taufan (USA)) 3018a[6] **>78f<**

**Dance a Dream 4** b f Sadler's Wells (USA)-Exclusive Order (USA) (Exclusive Native (USA)) 1017[5] 2113[6] 2336[3] **>113f<**

**Dance Band (USA) 4** b c Dixieland Band (USA)-Brief Remarks (USA) (Talc (USA)) *433a[2]* **>103a 98f<**

**Dance Clear (IRE) 3** b f Marju (IRE)-Dance Ahead (Shareef Dancer (USA)) 1246a[3] **>89f<**

**Dance Design (IRE) 3** b f Sadler's Wells (USA)-Elegance in Design (Habitat) 1567a[2] 2052[3] (2465a) (2837a) 4281a[2] **>119f<**

**Dance d'Ore (SWE) 4** br c Ore-La Grande Danseuse (USA) (North Pole (CAN)) 2117[5] **>84f<**

**Dance King 4** b g Rambo Dancer (CAN)-Northern Venture (St Alphage) *340[5] 553[8] 598[11]* 1625[4]

(1965) 2130[14] 2482[5] 2673[4] 3220[5] **>46a 72df<**

**Dance Melody 2** b f Rambo Dancer (CAN)-Cateryne (Ballymoss) 1664[9] 3448[6] 4041[12] 4435[6] *5057[10]* **>13a 44f<**

**Dance Model 3** b f Unfuwain (USA)-Bourgeonette (Mummy's Pet) 847[9] 1117[10] 1614[18] 4426[12] 4612[9] **>50f<**

**Dance Motion 4** b g Damister (USA)-Tantalizing Song (CAN) (The Minstrel (CAN)) *4291[10]* **>42?a 22f<**

**Dance of Joy 4** b f Shareef Dancer (USA)-Lady Habitat (Habitat) *62[13] (586)* 739[7] 787[15] 1088[8] 1311[7] 1821[14] 2898[3] **>14a 39f<**

**Dance On A Cloud (USA) 3** b f Capote (USA)-Sharp Dance (USA) (Dancing Czar (USA)) *693[6]* 969[7] 1955[8] **>82f<**

**Dance on Sixpence 8** b g Lidhame-Burning Ambition (Troy) *62[12] 184[9]* **>27a 52f<**

**Dance Parade (USA) 2** ch f Gone West (USA)-River Jig (USA) (Irish River (FR)) (1105) (1673) (2051) 4661a[11] **>94f<**

**Dancer Mitral 3** c Shareef Dancer (USA)-Almitra (Targowice (USA)) **1995:** 4399a[8] **1996:** 722a[3] (903a) 1580a[5] 5073a[8] **>102f<**

**Dance Sequence (USA) 3** ch f Mr Prospector (USA)-Dancing Tribute (USA) (Nureyev (USA)) 939[6] 2072[8] 2337[6] 3083[2] 3524[2] 4135[3] **>110df<**

**Dance So Suite 4** b g Shareef Dancer (USA)-Three Piece (Jaazeiro (USA)) **1995:** *4356[3]* **1996:** *(1147)* (1792) 2055[11] 3125[6] 3691[3] 4465[4] 4675[3] 5046[6] **>58a 97f<**

**Dance Star 3** b f Damister (USA)-Glen Dancer (Furry Glen) 4117[8] 4450[4] **>74f<**

**Dances With Dreams 2** b f Be My Chief (USA)-Oh So Well (IRE) (Sadler's Wells (USA)) (4670) **>76tf<**

**Dances With Hooves 4** b c Dancing Dissident (USA)-Princesse Legere (USA) (Alleged (USA)) *450[3]* 629[2] 5042[15] **>82f<**

**Dancethenightaway 2** gr f Efisio-Dancing Diana (Raga Navarro (ITY)) 2956[3] (3475) 3697[2] 4049[2] 4324[4] **>81f<**

**Dance Treat (USA) 4** ch f Nureyev (USA)-Office Wife (USA) (Secretariat (USA)) (2273a) 4654a[4] (5025a) **>119f<**

**Dancing Beggar (USA) 4** ch c Nureyev (USA)-Alydariel (USA) (Alydar (USA)) *396a[2]* **>114f<**

**Dancing Cavalier 3** b g Nalchik (USA)-Miss Admington (Double Jump) **1995:** *4389[8] 4433[12] 4504[6]* **1996:** *46[3] (123) (280) 329[2] 348[2] 385[4] 444[3]* 483[3] *519[2] 594[2]* 1415[6] 2433[3] 3459[3] 4358[4] **>74a 70f<**

**Dancing Debut 3** b f Polar Falcon (USA)-Exclusive Virtue (USA) (Shadeed (USA)) 1804[2] 4827[2] **>84f<**

**Dancing Destiny 4** b f Dancing Brave (USA)-Tender Loving Care (Final Straw) **1995:** *4406[9]* **1996:** *2066[12]* 2440[9] 2776[2] 3173[6] **>42a 51f<**

**Dancing Drop 2** b f Green Desert (USA)-Moon Drop (Dominion) 1480[2] 2051[9] 2504[3] (2741) 3444[3] (3990) 4565[3] **>87f<**

**Dancing Fire (FR) 2** ch f Dancing Spree (USA)-Firyal (Nonoalco (USA)) 4661a[13]

**Dancing Fred (USA) 3** b c Fred Astaire (USA)-Grand Couture (USA) (Miswaki (USA)) 2275a[2] 3911a[3] **>111f<**

**Dancing Heart 4** b g Thowra (FR)-Miss Lawsuit (Neltino) **1995:** *(4351) 4441[10] 4527[3] 4539[10]* **1996:** *1074[7]* 1536[6] 1677[6] *1810[4] 2034[2]* 2193[5] 2228[7] 2602[15] 4212[4] 4606[11] *4895[2]* **>73a 71f<**

**Dancing Hours (USA) 3** b f Seattle Dancer (USA)-Rolfette 5065a[5] **>89f<**

**Dancing Image 3** ch g Salse (USA)-Reflection (Mill Reef (USA)) 1119[2] 1420[3] (1872) (2065) 2501[2] 3210[2] **>85f<**

**Dancing Jack 3** ch c Clantime-Sun Follower (Relkino) **1995:** *4383[9] (4437) 4492[3] 4545[3]* **1996:** *39[2] 78[4] 142[2] 354[5] 488[2] 743[4]* 1049[7] 1536[8] 1844[11] 2200[6] 2500[9] **>63a 42f<**

**Dancing Jazztime 5** b m Clantime-Dance in Spain (King of Spain) **1995:** *4428[12]* **1996:** *1864[9]* 2392[8] 2902[12] 3774[11] **>7f<**

**Dancing Lawyer 5** b g Thowra (FR)-Miss Lawsuit (Neltino) **1995:** *(4435) 4520[7]* **1996:** *13[6] (174) 379[10] 747[7]* 1010[B] 3339[6] 3599[9] *3953[13] 4354[11] 4573[9]* **>62a 56f<**

**Dancing Man 3** ch g Executive Man-Lyne Dancer (Be My Native (USA)) *943[10]* 1356[8] **>42f<**

**Dancing Mystery 2** b g Beveled (USA)-Batchworth Dancer (Ballacashtal (CAN)) *4786[8]* 4896[4] **>48f<**

**Dancing Queen (IRE) 2** b f Sadler's Wells (USA)-Bay Shade (USA) (Sharpen Up) 3036[4] 3449[3] **>76tf<**

**Dancing Rainbow 3** b f Rambo Dancer (CAN)-Heemee (On Your Mark) *1028[10] 1674[14]* 2238[8] 2359[9] **>21a 36f<**

**Dancing Sioux 4** b g Nabeel Dancer (USA)-Sutosky (Great Nephew) **1995:** *4374[6] 4421[6] 4521[12]* **1996:** *(253) (291) 357[9] 662[5] 1094[3] 1609[11] 3419[8] 3601[10] 3995[13] 4077[4] 4573[8] 4768[9] 4983[14]* **>68a 57f<**

**Dancing Star (IRE) 2** b f Waajib-Havana Blade (USA) (Blade (USA)) *533[4] 590[2]* 733[5] *838[5] 895[10] 2172[7] 2406[4] 2635[3] 3065[6] 3448[7]* 3455[2] 3763[6] 4207[13] 4339[7] *4576[9] 4980[9] 4990[13]* **>45a 44f<**

**Dancing Zena (IRE) 6** b h Dancing Brave (USA)-Princess Zena (Habitat) *435a[2]* **>101a f<**

**Dande Flyer 3** b br c Clantime-Lyndseylee (Swing Easy (USA)) 989[10] 1304[5] 1597[3] 1985[3] 2143[4] 2301[4] 2999[4] 3215[5] 3465[11] **>80f<**

**Dandy Regent 2** b g Green Desert (USA)-Tahilla (Moorestyle) 4188[13] **>46f<**

**Danegold (IRE) 4** b g Danehill (USA)-Cistus (Sun Prince) 1793[14] 2312[6] 2536[2] 2603[5] 2883[10] 4125[9] 4329[5] 4450[3] 4682[15] 4769[13] 4826[7] **>67a 81f<**

**Danehill Dancer (IRE) 3** b c Danehill (USA)-Mira Adonde (USA) (Sharpen Up) (727) 926[6] 1141a[9] 2622[5] 3573a[3] 4057[11] **>121f<**

**Danehill Prince 2** b g Danehill (USA)-Santarem (USA) (El Gran Senor (USA)) 3848[17] 3976[3] 4230[2] **>68f< (DEAD)**

**Danehill Princess (IRE) 2** b f Danehill (USA)-Top Glad (USA) (I'm Glad (ARG)) 608[4] 1014[3] 1413[4] 1664[4] 2025[2] 2211[2] 2531[3] 2696[5] 2865[2] 3264[3] 3462[5] 4207[5] 4339[4] 4586[15] **>69f<**

**Daneskaya 3** b f Danehill (USA)-Boubskaia (FR) (Niniski (USA)) 3909a[2] **>98f<**

**Danetime (IRE) 2** b c Danehill (USA)-Allegheny River (USA) (Lear Fan (USA)) *4043[4]* (4502) 4770[2] **>93f<**

**Danewin (AUS) 5** h **1995:** 4471a[9] **1996:** *536a[10]* **>95a 117f<**

**Dangerous Waters 3** b f Risk Me (FR)-Queen's Lake (Kings Lake (USA)) **1995:** *4365[8] 4480[10]* **>33a 10f<**

**Danico 3** ch g Most Welcome-Spica (USA) (Diesis) *460[6] 660[4]* 784[3] 885[2] (914) 1152[7] *1456[2] 1806[8]* 1836[8] 2180[8] *2368[4]* **>61a 47f<**

**Daniel Deronda 2** b c Danehill (USA)-Kilvarnet (Furry Glen) 4584[2] **>74f<**

**Danish Ayr 2** b f Danehill (USA)-Cumbrian Melody (Petong) 2741[8] 2995[6] **>57f<**

**Danish Circus (IRE) 3** b c Danehill (USA)-Circus Maid (IRE) (High Top) 2197[4] **>74f<**

**Danish Field (IRE) 5** gr g Danehill (USA)-Pizzini (Artaius (USA)) (5022a) **>77f<**

**Danish Melody (IRE) 3** b c Danehill (USA)-Cajun Melody (Cajun) 146a[3] 149a[3] 226a[3] (326a) **>78f<**

**Danish Rhapsody (IRE) 3** b g Danehill (USA)-Ardmelody (Law Society (USA)) 1326[8] 4824[2] **>90f<**

**Danjing (IRE) 4** b g Danehill (USA)-Beijing (USA) (Northjet) 2547[3] 3266[2] 3834[8] 4771[19] **>97f<**

**Danka 2** gr c Petong-Angel Drummer (Dance In Time (CAN)) 3147[7] 3499[6] 3873[7] 4440[4] **>68f<**

**Dankeston (USA) 3** b c Elmaamul (USA)-Last Request (Dancers Image (USA)) **1995:** 4399a[6] **1996:** 574[5] 903a[2] 1754a[3] 2038[4] (3034a) 3671[6] **>115?f<**

**Danlora 3** b f Shareef Dancer (USA)-Loreef (Main Reef) 3446[5] 3767[9] 4322[2] 4606[5] 4968[15] **>68f<**

**Dannistar 4** br f Puissance-Loadplan Lass (Nicholas Bill) **1995:** *4372[2] (4444) 4503[6]* **1996:** *57[8] 1605[4] 3849[2] 4080[9] 4455[12]* **>63da 54f<**

**Danseur Landais 6** b h Damister (USA)-Rise and Fall (Mill Reef (USA)) 1947a[3] 3035a[4] **>114f<**

**Dantean 4** b g Warning-Danthonia (USA) (Northern Dancer) *337[3] 366[9] 487[9] 636[14]* 1013[5] 2286[14] 2617[7] 3316[4] **>54a 34f<**

**Dantesque (IRE) 3** b c Danehill (USA)-I Want My Say (USA) (Tilt Up (USA)) 3262[5] 3788[5] **>81f<**

**Dante's Rubicon (IRE) 5** ch g Common Grounds-Dromorehill (Ballymore) **1995:** *4390[3]* **>55a 52f<**

**Dapprima (GER) 3** br f Shareef Dancer (USA)-Diaspora (GER) (Sparkler) 1060a[2] 1750a[6] 5025a[2] **>109f<**

**Daralbayda (IRE) 3** fb f Doyoun-Daralinsha (USA) (Empery (USA)) 3031a[3] **>105f<**

**Daratown 3** b g Tragic Role (USA)-Darakah (Doulab (USA)) *4978[10] 5058[6]* **>36a f<**

**Daraydala (IRE) 4** b f Royal Academy (USA)-Daralinsha (USA) (Empery (USA)) **1995:** 4423a[3] **>113f<**

**Daraydan (IRE) 4** b c Kahyasi-Delsy (Abdos) 456[2] 875[4] 1005[2] 1752a[8] 2330[10] 3157[4] **>113f<**

**Darazari (IRE) 3** fb c Sadler's Wells (USA)-Darara (Top Ville) (3035a) 4293a[2] 4662a[11] **>122f<**

**Darb Alola (USA) 2** b c Nureyev (USA)-Kristana (Kris) 1519[2] 2070[6] 4893[2] **>92f<**

**Darbonne (USA) 6** b h Danzig (USA)-Bon Debarras (CAN) (Ruritania (USA)) 374a[5]

**Darby Flyer 3** ch c Dominion Royale-Shining Wood (Touching Wood (USA)) **1995:** *4519[3]* **1996:** *51[6] 131[12]* **>44a 30f<**

**Darcey Bussell 4** b f Green Desert (USA)-Docklands (On Your Mark) 991[7] (1610) 1825[4] (2045) (2130) 2209[4] **>73f<**

**Dare And Go (USA) 5** b h Alydar (USA)-Partygoer (USA) (Secretariat (USA)) *4956a[11]* ***>115f<***

**Darerock 3** b g Daring March-Marock Morley (Most Secret) 473[11] 540[6] **>21f<**

**Dargo 2** b c Formidable (USA)-Mountain Memory (High Top) *3099[2]* 3423[5] **>75f<**

**Darika Lad 8** gr g Belfort (FR)-Lindrake's Pride (Mandrake Major) *124[10] 159[8]* **>26f<**

**Daring Destiny 5** b m Daring March-Raunchy Rita (Brigadier Gerard) 457[7] 711[3] 960[6] (2298) 2692[2] 2880[12] (3562a) (4033a) 4442[9] 4718[8] **>118?f<**

**Daring Flight (USA) 2** b c Danzig (USA)-Life At the Top (Habitat) 3637[4] 3994[4] 4475[10] 4717[15] **>76f<**

**Daring Ryde 5** b g Daring March-Mini Myra (Homing) *1196[18]* 1468[17] 1638[6] 2345[6] 2971[12] 4829[18] **>54df<**

**Daring Venture 3** b f Dowsing (USA)-Berberana (Never so Bold) *526[8]* 758[5] 1412[17] 2578[18] **>44f<**

**Dark Deed (USA) 3** ch f Known Fact (USA)-Sin Lucha (USA) (Northfields (USA)) 783[3] (1667) 2584[9] 3219[7] **>84f<**

**Dark Green (USA) 2** ch c Green Dancer (USA)-Ardisia (USA) (Affirmed (USA)) 2543[3] 4492[3] **>87f<**

**Dark Lady (GER) 3** f 1750a$^{P}$

**Dark Menace 4** br g Beveled (USA)-Sweet and Sure (Known Fact (USA)) 1715$^{12}$ 2286$^{19}$ (2765) 3096$^{6}$ 3698$^{8}$ 4256$^{7}$ **>53f<**

**Dark Mile (USA) 2** b f Woodman (USA)-Fateful (USA) (Topsider (USA)) 3660$^{2}$ **>82+f<**

**Dark Nile (USA) 3** b c Riverman (USA) 1057a$^{2}$ 1757a$^{14}$ **>103f<**

**Dark Shot (IRE) 4** b g Rock City-Jeanne Avril (Music Boy) 2524$^{5}$ *3089$^{13}$ 3420$^{4}$ 4070$^{8}$* 4221$^{9}$ **>57a 50f<**

**Dark Sound (IRE) 3** b g Darshaan-Second Guess (Ela-Mana-Mou) 932$^{13}$ **>23f< (DEAD)**

**Dark Truffle 3** br f Deploy-River Dove (USA) (Riverman (USA)) 3262$^{3}$ 3949$^{8}$ 4513$^{11}$ 4868$^{7}$ 4967$^{17}$ **>55f<**

**Dark Waters (IRE) 3** b c Darshaan-Grecian Sea (FR) (Homeric) 3656$^{7}$ **>75f<**

**Darling Clover 4** ch f Minster Son-Lady Clementine (He Loves Me) (787) 1072$^{2}$ 1418$^{8}$ (2513) (2924) 3509$^{2}$ (3981) 4238$^{6}$ 4470$^{6}$ 4686$^{23}$ 4906$^{6}$ 5042$^{7}$ **>61a 67f<**

**Darling Flame (USA) 3** b f Capote (USA)-My Darling One (USA) (Exclusive Native (USA)) 674$^{6}$ 1441$^{8}$ 4445$^{7}$ (4595) 4940a$^{9}$ **>100+f<**

**Darnaway 2** b c Green Desert (USA)-Reuval (Sharpen Up) 4913$^{4}$ **>85f<**

**Darnay 5** br h Darshaan-Flawless Image (USA) (The Minstrel (CAN)) *(433a)* **>113a 121f<**

**Darter (IRE) 4** b c Darshaan-Mamouna (USA) (Vaguely Noble) (811) **>85f<**

**Daryabad (IRE) 4** b c Thatching-Dayanata (Shirley Heights) 1193$^{11}$ 1484$^{13}$ 1793$^{12}$ 2134$^{8}$ 2351$^{7}$ 3271$^{5}$ (3817) 4212$^{8}$ 4463$^{18}$ **>79f<**

**Dashing Blue 3** ch c Dashing Blade-Blubella (Balidar) (832) 1431$^{3}$ 2007$^{7}$ 2584$^{6}$ 3038$^{4}$ 3232$^{25}$ 3693$^{3}$ 3946$^{2}$ **>107f<**

**Dashing Dancer (IRE) 5** ch g Conquering Hero (USA)-Santa Maria (GER) (Literat) 749$^{9}$ 981$^{2}$ 1624$^{13}$ 2228$^{5}$ 2604$^{6}$ 3140$^{4}$ *4336$^{10}$* **>63da 53f<**

**Dashing Invader (USA) 3** ch c Pirate Army (USA)-Cherie's Hope (USA) (Flying Paster (USA)) 578$^{13}$ 1100$^{14}$ 1498$^{13}$ 1874$^{14}$ 2511$^{7}$ 3249$^{4}$ 3584$^{3}$ 3813$^{7}$ **>57f<**

**Dashing Rocksville 2** b f Rock City-Dash (Connaught) 1179$^{5}$ (1537) 1980$^{5}$ 2509$^{4}$ 2984$^{3}$ (3227) 3498$^{11}$ 3826$^{7}$ **>61f<**

**Dasul 2** ch f Risk Me (FR)-Bocas Rose (Jalmood (USA)) 1513$^{12}$

**Dato Star (IRE) 5** br g Accordion-Newgate Fairy (Flair Path) *4833$^{3}$* 5046$^{4}$ **>101f<**

**Datum (USA) 3** br g Dayjur (USA)-My Ballerina (USA) (Sir Ivor) 1667$^{13}$ **>34f<**

**Daubigny (GER) 3** 1751a$^{5}$ **>59f<**

**Daunt 4** b g Darshaan-Minute Waltz (Sadler's Wells (USA)) 728$^{20}$ 2350$^{7}$ (2883) 3125$^{3}$ 3710$^{5}$ 4176$^{2}$ 4465$^{10}$ 4680$^{5}$ **>103f<**

**Daunting Destiny (BEL) 3** b c Formidable (USA)-Heavy Land (FR) (Recitation (USA)) 693$^{4}$ 863$^{6}$ 1955$^{2}$ 2608$^{12}$ (3039) (3401) **>86f< (DEAD)**

**Daunting Times 2** b f Timeless Times (USA)-Dauntless Flight (Golden Mallard) *4435$^{8}$* **>23f<**

**Dauntless Fort 5** gr m Belfort (FR)-Dauntless Flight (Golden Mallard) *2367$^{9}$ 2940$^{12}$ 3091$^{12}$* **>20a 39f<**

**Dauphin (IRE) 3** b br g Astronef-Va Toujours (Alzao (USA)) *118$^{6}$ 230$^{5}$ 597$^{9}$* 1821$^{15}$ 2130$^{12}$ 2587$^{10}$ 3249$^{12}$ 3584$^{2}$ (4042) 4307$^{13}$ 4626$^{13}$ 4968$^{4}$ **>53a 49f<**

**David James' Girl 4** b f Faustus (USA)-Eagle's Quest (Legal Eagle) **1995:** *4413$^{7}$ 4447$^{5}$ 4486$^{3}$* **1996:** *166$^{4}$ 295$^{5}$ 356$^{5}$ (372) 417$^{3}$ 521$^{3}$ 654$^{7}$ 1081$^{2}$ 1602$^{4}$ 1811$^{6}$ 1966$^{3}$ (2085) 2369$^{8}$ 2550$^{3}$ 2672$^{9}$ 3603$^{6}$ 3761$^{15}$ 4080$^{5}$* **>69a 52df<**

**Davids Revenge 2** b c Reprimand-Tribal Lady (Absalom) 4825$^{7}$ **>74f<**

**Davis Rock 2** ch f Rock City-Sunny Davis (USA) (Alydar (USA)) *3088$^{2}$ 3869$^{2}$ 4091$^{2}$ (4572)* **>69a 51f<**

**Davoski 2** b gr c Niniski (USA)-Pamela Peach (Habitat) 3595$^{3}$ 4720$^{6}$ **>84f<**

**Dawadar (USA) 9** b g Exceller (USA)-Damana (FR) (Crystal Palace (FR)) *4683$^{17}$* 4794$^{19}$ **>45f<**

**Dawalib (USA) 6** ch g Danzig Connection (USA)-Centavos (USA) (Scout Leader (USA)) *554$^{15}$* 756$^{7}$ 876$^{15}$ 1018$^{15}$ 1354$^{2}$ 1522$^{3}$ 1789$^{8}$ 2034$^{11}$ 2907$^{4}$ 3151$^{5}$ 3518$^{16}$ 3991$^{6}$ 4128$^{2}$ 4256$^{10}$ 4511$^{14}$ **>73a 62f<**

**Dawam Allail 2** b g Night Shift (USA)-Veronica (Persian Bold) 2335$^{6}$ 2802$^{3}$ 3277$^{4}$ 4380$^{5}$ **>79f<**

**Dawawin (USA) 3** b f Dixieland Band (USA)-Stalwart Moment (USA) (Stalwart (USA)) 550$^{8}$ (4360) 4671$^{12}$ **>81f<**

**Dawna 3** b f Polish Precedent (USA)-Welsh Daylight (Welsh Pageant) 870$^{2}$ 1160$^{2}$ (1690) (2142) 2609$^{4}$ 3127$^{12}$ **>105f<**

**Dawn Flight 7** b g Precocious-Sea Kestrel (Sea Hawk II) 2377$^{8}$ **>36a 52f<**

**Dawn Summit 2** ch c Salse (USA)-Bereeka (Main Reef) 3757$^{12}$ 4383$^{9}$ **>50f<**

**Daydream Island 3** ch f Never so Bold-La Belle Vie (Indian King (USA)) *1855$^{12}$* 2347$^{8}$ 2791$^{9}$ **>3f<**

**Daylami (IRE) 2** gr c Doyoun-Daltawa (IRE) (Miswaki (USA)) 5024a$^{2}$ **>104f<**

**Daylight Dreams 2** b f Indian Ridge-Singing Nelly (Pharly (FR)) (823) 3707$^{7}$ 3843$^{7}$ 4113$^{22}$ **>79f<**

**Daylight In Dubai (USA) 2** ch c Twilight Agenda (USA)-Lady Godolphin (USA) (Son Ange (USA)) *(706)* 1510$^{3}$ 2040$^{2}$ (2470a) 4398a$^{8}$ 4871$^{6}$ **>104f<**

**Dayrella 2** ch f Beveled (USA)-Divissima (Music Boy) 2245$^{8}$ 4357$^{8}$ 4545$^{7}$ 4717$^{18}$ **>56f<**

**Daytona Beach (IRE) 6** ch g Bluebird (USA)-Water Spirit (USA) (Riverman (USA)) 4609$^{15}$ **>72a 64f<**

**Dayville (USA) 2** b f Dayjur (USA)-Chain Fern (USA) (Blushing Groom (FR)) 1980$^{3}$ 2404$^{3}$ *(2746) 4433$^{2}$* **>69a 82f<**

**Dazzle 2** b br f Gone West (USA)-Belle et Deluree (USA) (The Minstrel (CAN)) (2112) (2582) 4491$^{4}$ 4758$^{2}$ **>112f<**

**Dazzle Me 4** ch f Kalaglow-Defy Me (Bustino) 4205$^{18}$ **>26df<**

**Dazzling 3** b f Rambo Dancer (CAN)-Azaiyma (Corvaro (USA)) 3093$^{4}$ 3258$^{4}$ *3421$^{5}$ 3630$^{12}$* **>38a 75?f<**

**Dazzling Star 3** gr f Thatching-Dazzlingly Radiant (Try My Best (USA)) 549$^{5}$ 637$^{3}$ 748$^{5}$ 861$^{6}$ **>47f<**

**Dazzling Stone 2** b c Mujtahid (USA)-Lady In Green (Shareef Dancer (USA)) 3647$^{2}$ **>79+f<**

**D-Day-Smoke 2** ch c Cigar-Little Pockthorpe (Morston (FR)) *533$^{5}$* **>15a f<**

**Dead Aim (IRE) 2** b g Sadler's Wells (USA)-Dead Certain (Absalom) 4363$^{6}$ 4601$^{6}$ 4825$^{6}$ **>74f<**

**Deadline Time (IRE) 3** b c Fayruz-Cut it Fine (USA) (Big Spruce (USA)) 444$^{2}$ 483$^{2}$ 1002$^{11}$ (1349) 1507$^{6}$ 2128$^{2}$ *(3063) 3926$^{10}$* 4117$^{11}$ **>91a 91f<**

**Deadly Dudley (IRE) 2** gr c Great Commotion (USA)-Renzola (Dragonara Palace (USA)) (1328) (1510) 2040$^{3}$ 2607$^{8}$ (5071a) **>106f<**

**Deaken Dancer 3** b f Rambo Dancer (CAN)-Une Emigree (USA) (L'Emigrant (USA)) **1995:** *4360$^{10}$ 4462$^{W}$* **>28a 37f<**

**Deano's Beeno 4** b g Far North (CAN)-Sans Dot (Busted) *1198$^{6}$* 1450$^{9}$ 1700$^{3}$ 1862$^{3}$ 2190$^{3}$ 2547$^{9}$ 3434$^{2}$ 3834$^{7}$ 4112$^{6}$ 4315$^{8}$ 4722$^{3}$ 4862$^{2}$ **>81f<**

**Deardaw 4** b f Tina's Pet-Faw (Absalom) 949$^{9}$ 1170$^{10}$ 1642$^{21}$ 1844$^{9}$ 1985$^{9}$ 2129$^{10}$ 2286$^{9}$ 2561$^{2}$ 2787$^{12}$ 2791$^{4}$ 4075$^{24}$ *4094$^{8}$ 4205$^{12}$* 4372$^{13}$ **>20a 43f<**

**Dear Drue 2** b f Jupiter Island-Top and Tail (USA) (Tilt Up (USA)) 4861$^{14}$ **>9f<**

**Dear Life (USA) 3** b f Lear Fan (USA)-Charming Life (NZ) (Sir Tristram) 826$^{2}$ 957$^{7}$ 1804$^{6}$ (2202) 2688$^{2}$ (3290) 3683$^{7}$ 3997$^{3}$ (4121) (4487) 4716$^{4}$ **>101f<**

**Deauville Dancer (IRE) 4** ch g Al Hareb (USA)-Bru Ri (FR) (Sir Gaylord) 2847$^{6}$ 3463$^{11}$ 4812$^{19}$ **>26f<**

**Debonair 2** b f Batshoof-Celestial Air (Rheingold) 2025$^{6}$ 2252$^{4}$ 4380$^{16}$ 4715$^{13}$ **>50f<**

**Debutante Days 4** ch f Dominion-Doogali (Doon) *2793$^{4}$* 4580$^{6}$ 4826$^{21}$ 4919$^{7}$ 5047$^{14}$ **>75f<**

**Decision Maker (IRE) 3** b c Taufan (USA)-Vain Deb (Gay Fandango (USA)) 526$^{4}$ 709$^{5}$ 1349$^{5}$ 2036$^{6}$ 2557$^{7}$ **>82f<**

**Decorated Hero 4** b g Warning-Bequeath (USA) (Lyphard (USA)) 600$^{3}$ 810$^{12}$ (4194) (4444) (4739a) (5018a) 5078a$^{2}$ **>121+f<**

**Deedeejay 3** b f Cigar-Miss Patdonna (Starch Reduced) **1995:** *4369$^{11}$* **>21a 15f<**

**Deed of Love (USA) 3** b c Shadeed (USA)-Widaad (USA) (Mr Prospector (USA)) (1247a) 1574a$^{9}$ **>103f<**

**Dee-Lady 4** b f Deploy-Bermuda Lily (Dunbeath (USA)) **1995:** *4419$^{5}$ 4451$^{4}$* **1996:** *1520$^{5}$* 1775$^{8}$ 4297$^{5}$ 4432$^{14}$ 4615$^{8}$ 4800$^{3}$ 4901$^{12}$ **>51a 87f<**

**Dee Pee Tee Cee (IRE) 2** b g Tidaro (USA)-Silver Glimpse (Petingo) (1845) 3251$^{6}$ 3577$^{6}$ 3998$^{5}$ 4298$^{5}$ 4602$^{17}$ 4795$^{6}$ 4990$^{6}$ **>61f<**

**Deep Finesse 2** b c Reprimand-Babycham Sparkle (So Blessed) (1453) 1653$^{3}$ (2269a) (2664a) 3213$^{3}$ 4191$^{3}$ 4519$^{5}$ 4677$^{10}$ **>103f<**

**Deeply Vale (IRE) 5** b g Pennine Walk-Late Evening (USA) (Riverman (USA)) **1995:** *4502$^{2}$ 4512$^{3}$ 4539$^{7}$* **1996:** *65$^{3}$ 126$^{4}$ 291$^{4}$ (388) 413$^{8}$ 549$^{W}$* (664) 4788$^{W}$ **>72a 71f<**

**Deep Water (USA) 2** b c Diesis-Water Course (USA) (Irish River (FR)) 4705$^{3}$ **>81f<**

**Deerly 3** b f Hadeer-Grafitti Gal (USA) (Pronto (ARG)) *1412$^{15}$* 1876$^{5}$ *2308$^{6}$ 2858$^{F}$* 3844$^{17}$ 3973$^{13}$ 4128$^{7}$ 4206$^{9}$ **>51a 50f<**

**Deevee 7** b h Hallgate-Lady Woodpecker (Tap On Wood) 879$^{27}$ 1625$^{6}$ 1819$^{12}$ 2581$^{12}$ 3469$^{11}$ 4511$^{11}$ 4719$^{10}$ **>62df<**

**Defined Feature (IRE) 3** ch f Nabeel Dancer (USA)-Meissarah (USA) (Silver Hawk (USA)) 2919$^{4}$ 3445$^{12}$ 4122$^{4}$ 4552$^{3}$ **>95f<**

**Definite Article 4** b c Indian Ridge-Summer Fashion (Moorestyle) (1252a) (1575a) 2546$^{5}$ 4040a$^{4}$ 4652a$^{6}$ **>124f<**

**Degree 3** b f Warning-Krill (Kris) 894$^{3}$ 2589$^{2}$ 3457$^{9}$ **>75f<**

**Delegate 3** ch c Polish Precedent (USA)-Dangora (USA) (Sovereign Dancer (USA)) 721a$^{2}$

**Delight of Dawn 4** b f Never so Bold-Vogos Angel (Song) 633$^{7}$ 850$^{12}$ (1099) 1841$^{7}$ 2379$^{6}$ 2796$^{6}$ 2994$^{5}$ 3281$^{4}$ 3340$^{4}$ 3944$^{7}$ 4202$^{9}$ 4355$^{9}$ 4901$^{13}$ **>71f<**

**Delilah (IRE) 2** b f Bluebird (USA)-Courtesane (USA) (Majestic Light (USA)) 4451$^{3}$ **>73+f<**

**Della Casa (IRE) 3** ch f Royal Academy (USA)-Diamond Spring (USA) (Vaguely Noble) 2540$^{6}$ 3249$^{14}$ **>61f<**

**Delmour 5** b g Seymour Hicks (FR)-Delbounty (Bounteous) 983$^{21}$ **>15a 29f<**

**Delphine 3** b br f Formidable (USA)-Archaic (Relic) 1171$^{3}$ 1475$^{6}$ 1692$^{2}$ 2167$^{3}$ **>71f< (DEAD)**

**Delrob 5** b m Reprimand-Stoneydale (Tickled Pink) **1995:** *4484$^{10}$ 4502$^{10}$* **1996:** *36$^{U}$ 63$^{5}$ 315$^{8}$*

601[10] 893[11] 1083[4] 1455[5] 1606[9] 1716[3] 1971[3] (2308) 2555[2] 2745[8] (3602) 4577[13] 4981[4] **>58a 42f<**
**Delta Soleil (USA)** **4** b c Riverman (USA)-Sunny Roberta (USA) (Robellino (USA)) 455[5] 876[8] 1425[4] 4775[7] 4974[16] **>94f<**
**Demoiselle** **4** b f Midyan (USA)-Little Mercy (No Mercy) 3601[7] **>48a 36+f<**
**Demolition Man** **2** br c Primo Dominie-Town Lady (Town Crier) 1344[4] (2495) 3247[2] 3674[2] 3835[2] **>84f<**
**Denbrae (IRE)** **4** b g Sure Blade (USA)-Fencing (Viking (USA)) 496[4] 582[20] 893[3] 1073[3] 1334[4] 1680[2] 1958[4] 2129[4] (2347) 2713[10] 4058[13] 4312[5] 4788[W] 4888[13] **>69a 75f<**
**Denomination (USA)** **4** br g Danzig Connection (USA)-Christchurch (FR) (So Blessed) 502[8] 598[2] 690[12] 853[13] 1506[3] 2506[17] **>52a 71f<**
**Densben** **12** b g Silly Prices-Eliza de Rich (Spanish Gold) 617[14] 806[10] 1040[9] 1634[5] 1848[5] 2030[6] 2680[3] 3289[8] 3453[2] 3817[4] 4045[6] (4430) 4724[7] **>55f<**
**Denton Lad** **2** b c Prince Sabo-Dahlawise (IRE) (Caerleon (USA)) 2897[5] 3293[6] 3588[7] 3969[7] 4764[10] **>61f<**
**Depiction** **3** b g Hadeer-Depict (Derring-Do) 448[3] 779[3] 934[5] 1356[9] 2281[3] **>61a 71df<**
**Depreciate** **3** ch c Beveled (USA)-Shiny Penny (Glint of Gold) 945[4] 1628[9] **>89f<**
**De Quest** **4** b c Rainbow Quest (USA)-De Stael (USA) (Nijinsky (CAN)) 907a 1794[3] 2480a[6] **>117f<**
**Derek's Bo** **3** b f Rambo Dancer (CAN)-Mother Hubbard (Mummy's Pet) 35[13] **>27a 38f<**
**Deri Sue** **3** b f Relief Pitcher-Royal Rabble (Rabdan) 4978[12]
**Derrybelle** **5** ch m Derrylin-Pokey's Belle (Uncle Pokey) 4877[13] 4910[10] **>7f<**
**Desert Beauty (IRE)** **2** b f Green Desert (USA)-Hellenic (Darshaan) 4052[8] **>67f<**
**Desert Boy (IRE)** **3** br c Green Desert (USA)-City Fortress (Troy) 681[6] 1015[2] 2116[2] 2844a[3] 3124[7] 4192[11] **>117f<**
**Desert Calm (IRE)** **7** br g Glow (USA)-Lancette (Double Jump) 505[15] 666[13] 887[3] 1190[16] 1685[6] 1953[8] 2234[5] 2577[4] 2784[6] 3694[5] 4128[13] **>58f<**
**Desert Cat (IRE)** **3** b c Green Desert (USA)-Mahabba (USA) (Elocutionist (USA)) 987[13] 1872[7] **>76f<**
**Desert Challenger (IRE)** **6** b g Sadler's Wells (USA)-Verily (Known Fact (USA)) 4669[11] **>25a 8f<**
**Desert Dunes** **3** b c Unfuwain (USA)-Palm Springs (Top Ville) 576[8] 948[4] 1631[4] 3948[5] 4506[7] **>80f<**
**Desert Ease (IRE)** **2** bb f Green Desert (USA)-Easy to Copy (USA) (Affirmed (USA)) (4156a) 4639a[5] **>86f<**
**Desert Fighter** **5** b g Green Desert (USA)-Jungle Rose (Shirley Heights) 482[8] 4073[13] 4193[13] 4438[3] **>83?a 77f<**
**Desert Force (IRE)** **7** b g Lomond (USA)-St Padina (St Paddy) 504[4] 625[15] 852[11] **>16a 37f<**
**Desert Frolic (IRE)** **3** b f Persian Bold-Try To Catch Me (USA) (Shareef Dancer (USA)) 1701[4] (2141) (2239) (2418) (2522) (2674) 2969[2] 3689[14] 3934[5] **>100f<**
**Desert Green (FR)** **7** b g Green Desert (USA)-Green Leaf (USA) (Alydar (USA)) **1995:** 4482[10] **1996:** 809[4] (967) 1484[12] 2053[11] 3158[10] 3709[15] 4874[12] **>61a 101f<**
**Desert Harvest** **4** b g Green Desert (USA)-Mill on the Floss (Mill Reef (USA)) 968[15] 1099[4] 2169[5] **>66a 51f<**
**Desert Horizon** **2** b c Danehill (USA)-Sand Grouse (USA) (Arctic Tern (USA)) 4492[4] (4920) **>89f<**
**Desert Invader (IRE)** **5** br g Lead on Time (USA)-Aljood (Kris) **1995:** 4367[9] 4428[3] 4514[3] **1996:** 57[10] 76[4] 212[4] (341) 368[3] 388[2] 425[2] 718[15] 882[3] 1024[10] 1094[2] 1601[9] 2030[5] 2171[4] 2552[5] 3089[2] 3419[10] 3601[4] 3627[6] 3953[5] 4486[2] 4768[15] 5002[7] **>74a 56f<**
**Desert King (IRE)** **2** b c Danehill (USA)-Sabaah (USA) (Nureyev (USA)) (4398a) 4759[6] **>101f<**
**Desert Lore** **5** b g Green Desert (USA)-Chinese Justice (USA) (Diesis) 372[4] 518[4] 662[11] **>40a 44f<**
**Desert Lynx (IRE)** **3** b f Green Desert (USA)-Sweeping (Indian King (USA)) (973) 1340[9] 2427[3] 3152[6] 4071[3] 4243[12] 4453[3] 4560[3] 4691[16] 4866[10] **>73f<**
**Desert Man** **5** b g Green Desert (USA)-Grayfoot (Grundy) 195[6] 255[7] 299[7] 372[5] 427[9] **>37a f<**
**Desert Power** **7** b g Green Desert (USA)-Rivers Maid (Rarity) **1995:** 4503[13] **1996:** 184[8] **>13a 73f<**
**Desert President** **5** ch g Polish Precedent (USA)-Majestic Kahala (USA) (Majestic Prince (USA)) 275[5] 1717[5] **>18a 49f<**
**Desert Scout** **3** b g Picea-Queens Pearl (Queen's Hussar) 2197[19] 2601[13] 3609[6] 4129[19] 4340[11] **>34f<**
**Desert Serenade (USA)** **3** b f Green Desert (USA)-Sanctuary (Welsh Pageant) 3162[F] 3767[8] **>55f<**
**Desert Shot** **6** b g Green Desert (USA)-Out of Shot (Shirley Heights) 680[6] 2038[7] 2730[3] 3409[3] 4178[4] 4313[2] 4714[2] **>114f<**
**Desert Skimmer (USA)** **3** ch f Shadeed (USA)-Massorah (FR) (Habitat) 710[11] 921[11] 1422[7] 3700[8] 4075[8] **>49f<**
**Desert Spring** **4** b c Green Desert (USA)-Little Loch Broom (Reform) 963[6] 1414[10] 1832[6] **>64f<**
**Desert Story (IRE)** **2** b c Green Desert (USA)-Aliysa (Darshaan) (3794) 4111[2] 4462[2] (4822) **>108f<**
**Desert Style (IRE)** **4** b c Green Desert (USA)-Organza (High Top) **1995:** 4523a[2] **>124f<**
**Desert Tiger** **3** br f Green Desert (USA)-Desert Bride (USA) (Key to the Kingdom (USA)) 1974[13] 2078[9] **>88f<**
**Desert Track** **2** b c Green Desert (USA)-Mill Path (Mill Reef (USA)) 4100[5] **>70f<**
**Desert Warrior (IRE)** **2** b c Fairy King (USA)-Highland Girl (USA) (Sir Ivor) 4380[17] **>52f<**
**Desert Water (IRE)** **4** b g Green Desert (USA)-Ozone Friendly (USA) (Green Forest (USA)) **1995:** 4418[3] 4525[10] 4543[5] **1996:** 163[10] 203[8] 217[5] 273[5] 2745[12] **>46a 25f<**
**Desert Zone (USA)** **7** ch g Affirmed (USA)-Deloram (CAN) (Lord Durham (CAN)) 3089[14] 3849[6] 3974[9] 4237[7] 4808[5] (4882) (4989) 5004[3] **>60a 60f<**
**Designer Lines** **3** ch g Beveled (USA)-Parrot Fashion (Pieces of Eight) 2597[6] 3162[11] (3609) 4064[16] **>81f<**
**Despina** **2** ch f Waajib-Staiconme (USA) (Pancho Villa (USA)) 4330[19] **>31f<**
**Detachment (USA)** **3** b c Night Shift (USA)-Mumble Peg (General Assembly (USA)) 1435[5] 1667[5] 2041[28] 2687[5] 3424[14] 4606[4] **>68f<**
**De-Veers Currie (IRE)** **4** b f Glenstal (USA)-Regent Star (Prince Regent (FR)) 801[5] (998) 3968[8] 4334[12] 4484[8] **>59df<**
**Devil River Peek (USA)** **4** c Silver Hawk (USA)-Black Tulip (FR) (Fabulous Dancer (USA)) 1755a[3] (2274a) 2843a[2] 3395a[5] 3905a[2] 4409a[3] **>122f<**
**Devilry** **6** b g Faustus (USA)-Ancestry (Persepolis (FR)) 4227[13] **>60?f<**
**Devil's Dance (FR)** **3** b g Mujtahid (USA)-Dance of Leaves (Sadler's Wells (USA)) 640[10] 894[11] 2365[4] 3459[10] **>62f<**
**Devon Peasant** **4** b f Deploy-Serration (Kris) 820[6] 3148[W] **>71f<**
**Dewhurst House** **3** ch f Emarati (USA)-Spring In Rome (USA) (Forli (ARG)) 4074[3] 4229[6] 4592[10] **>54f<**
**Deynawari (IRE)** **3** b c Doyoun-Denizliya 1247a[4] **>105f< (DEAD)**
**Dhes-C** **3** b f Lochnager-Keep Cool (FR) (Northern Treat (USA)) **1995:** 4501[9] **1996:** 21[6] 101[4] 183[3] 220[5] 271[3] 359[3] (423) 515[6] 780[7] 1455[11] 2308[11] 2968[5] **>46da 31f<**
**Dhulikhel** **3** b f Reprimand-Travel Storm (Lord Gayle (USA)) **1995:** 4509[10] **1996:** (597) 863[5] 1100[17] 1490[12] 2558[6] 3300[3] 3608[2] 4374[8] **>45a 55f< (DEAD)**
**Dia Georgy** **5** b h Reesh-Carpadia (Icecapade (USA)) **1995:** 4385[12] 4532[5] **1996:** 23[4] 159[7] 201[4] 353[11] **>44da 60f<**
**Diamond Bangle** **4** b f Chilibang-My Diamond Ring (Sparkling Boy) **1995:** 4354[10] 4418[10] 4460[6] **1996:** 74[9] 203[13] 273[9] 592[15] 1351[6] 1516[9] **>25a 18f<**
**Diamond Beach** **3** b c Lugana Beach-Cannon Boy (USA) (Canonero II (USA)) 1709[3] 2146[2] 2760[5] 3609[2] 4231[4] 4309[5] 4901[7] **>86f<**
**Diamond Crown (IRE)** **5** ch g Kris-State Treasure (USA) (Secretariat (USA)) 1411[3] 1676[9] 2165[10] 2356[4] 2568[3] 2731[5] 2988[10] 3289[3] 4102[5] 4355[3] 4455[4] (4808) 4906[11] 5010[6] **>17a 50f<**
**Diamond Cut (FR)** **8** b g Fast Topaze (USA)-Sasetto (FR) (St Paddy) 2494[4] 2711[7] **>59f< (DEAD)**
**Diamond Dance (IRE)** **3** b f Sadler's Wells (USA)-Diamond Field (USA) (Mr Prospector (USA)) 3949[6] 4429[5] 4833[8] **>65f<**
**Diamond Eyre** **2** ch f Then Again-Renira (Relkino) 4435[5] 4988[5] **>19a 49f<**
**Diamond Lil** **2** b f Environment Friend-Cataclysmic (Ela-Mana-Mou) 2195[12] 2734[6] **>32f<**
**Diamond Market** **4** gr g Absalom-The Victor Girls (Crofthall) **1995:** 4372[3] **1996:** 2303[12] **>63da 57tf<**
**Diamond Mix (IRE)** **4** gr c Linamix (FR)-Diamond Seal (Persian Bold) 438a[4] 906a[6] 2273a[3] 3386a[2] 4853a[3] **>122f<**
**Diamond Pro** **5** b h Diamond Prospect (USA)-French Cutie **1995:** (4466a)
**Diamonds Are** **2** b f Touch of Grey-H R Micro (High Award) 4572[11] 4715[27]
***Diasafina*** **3** b f Safawan-Diana Dee (Blakeney) **1995:** 4393[10] **1996:** 129[9] 197[4] 280[5] 1503[9] 1814[5] **>35a 26f<**
**Dicentra** **3** b f Rambo Dancer (CAN)-Be Noble (Vaguely Noble) **1995:** 4408[9] 4480[9] **1996:** 826[13] 1310[4] **>46a 43f<**
**Dickie Bird (IRE)** **2** ch c Shalford (IRE)-Peace In The Woods (Tap On Wood) 2575[7] 2852[6] (3214) 3674[6] 4182[6] 4303[9] **>76f<**
**Dick Turpin (USA)** **2** br c Red Ransom (USA)-Turn To Money (USA) (Turn To Mars (USA)) 3615[6] **>76f<**
**Dictation (USA)** **4** b g Dayjur (USA)-Mofida (Right Tack) 882[11] 1364[10] 2005[21] 3424[11] 3973[9] 4312[13] 4809[11] **>62f<**
**Diebiedale** **4** b f Dominion-Welwyn (Welsh Saint) 868[11] 1049[14] 2305[5] 2745[9] 4263[2] 4480[6] **>23a 50f<**
**Dieci Anno (IRE)** **3** b f Classic Music (USA)-Moira My Girl (Henbit (USA)) 4778[7] 5000[7] **>60a 70f<**
**Diego** **3** b c Belmez (USA)-True Queen (USA) (Silver Hawk (USA)) (175) 263[5] 444[18] 788[10] 1002[12] 1523[3] (1788) 2148[10] 2570[11] 2998[2] 3434[3] 4252[2] 4695[4] 4832[15] **>71a 76f<**
**Diesel Dan (IRE)** **3** b g Mac's Imp (USA)-Elite Exhibition 2472a[14] **>77f<**

**Diet** **10** b g Starch Reduced-Highland Rossie (Pablond) 561$^{5}$ 617$^{7}$ (661) 1020$^{9}$ 1041$^{2}$ 1163$^{4}$ 1313$^{9}$ 1635$^{9}$ 1885$^{7}$ 2005$^{19}$ 2154$^{13}$ 2178$^{2}$ 2391$^{14}$ 2566$^{2}$ 2680$^{6}$ **>57f<**

**Different (ARG)** **4** ch f Candy Stripes (USA)-Diferente (ARG) (Procipio (ARG)) *4952a$^{3}$* **>112a f<**

**Diffident (FR)** **4** b c Nureyev (USA)-Shy Princess (USA) (Irish River (FR)) *(374a)* 1129$^{8}$ 2337$^{9}$ (4442) (4870) 5044$^{2}$ **>126f<**

**Digital Option (IRE)** **2** b g Alzao (USA)-Elevated (Shirley Heights) *4331$^{8}$ 4594$^{12}$* ***>38a 55f<***

**Digpast (IRE)** **6** ch g Digamist (USA)-Starlit Way (Pall Mall) **1995:** *4386$^{7}$ 4539$^{8}$* **1996:** *13$^{2}$ (190) 21$^{9}$ 306$^{6}$ 670$^{7}$* 1047$^{11}$ 1173$^{5}$ 1953$^{16}$ 2577$^{6}$ **>80a 57f<**

**Digwana (IRE)** **3** b g Digamist (USA)-Siwana (IRE) (Dom Racine (FR)) **1995:** *4360$^{U}$* **1996:** *129$^{6}$ 522$^{7}$ 1721$^{13}$ 2281$^{6}$* ***>50a 36f<***

**Dijon** **2** ro c Chilibang-Princess Fair (Crowned Prince (USA)) 2967$^{13}$

**Diktys (GER)** **4** b c Kamiros II-Danae (Nebos (GER)) 4741a$^{3}$ (5029a) **>107f<**

**Dilazar (USA)** **3** ch g Zilzal (USA)-Dictina (FR) (Dictus (FR)) 894$^{2}$ 1142$^{10}$ 2197$^{3}$ 3770$^{2}$ 4238$^{8}$ (4724) **>95f<**

**Dil Dil** **3** b f Puissance-My Croft (Crofter (USA)) 571$^{9}$ 868$^{16}$ 1119$^{11}$ 1840$^{9}$ 2179$^{6}$ 2507$^{7}$ 2893$^{2}$ 3059$^{4}$ 3491$^{2}$ 3694$^{6}$ 4486$^{13}$ **>52f<**

**Diligent Dodger (IRE)** **5** b g Posen (USA)-Crannog (Habitat) 2472a$^{4}$ **>91f<**

**Dimakya (USA)** **3** b f Dayjur (USA)-Reloy (USA) (Liloy (FR)) 870$^{4}$ 1540$^{3}$ **>89df<**

**Diminuet** **3** b f Dominion-Primulette (Mummy's Pet) 775$^{P}$ **>76df<**

**Diminutive (USA)** **3** b c Diesis-Graceful Darby (USA) (Darby Creek Road (USA)) 669$^{5}$ 1190$^{6}$ (1649) 2041$^{24}$ 2701$^{5}$ (2955) (3521) 3766$^{3}$ 4120$^{5}$ 4326$^{7}$ 4826$^{17}$ **>89f<**

**Dino's Mistral** **3** b g Petong-Marquessa d'Howfen (Pitcairn) *2751$^{9}$ 2931$^{6}$* 4437$^{4}$ 4752$^{11}$ **>53f<**

**Diodeme (FR)** **6** b h Fabulous Dancer (USA)-Desertine (FR) (Arctic Tern (USA)) *2840a$^{3}$* ***>107f<***

**Diogene Laerzio (ITY)** **3** b c Horage-Nagarook (ITY) (Brook) 1578a$^{2}$ **>83f<**

**Diplomatic Jet (USA)** **4** ch c Roman Diplomat (USA)-Precious Jet (USA) (Tri Jet (USA)) (4288a) (4652a) 4955a$^{12}$ **>129f<**

**Dirab** **3** ch g Groom Dancer (USA)-Double Celt (Owen Dudley) *58$^{5}$ 123$^{6}$ (348)* 1309$^{9}$ 1647$^{7}$ 2067$^{6}$ (2627) 2804$^{3}$ (3772) 4248$^{7}$ **>63a 84f<**

**Direct Dial (USA)** **4** br c Phone Trick (USA)-Jig Jig (USA) (Never Bend) *1448$^{8}$ 3705$^{9}$* ***>34a 53f<***

**Disallowed (IRE)** **3** b f Distinctly North (USA)-Miss Allowed (USA) (Alleged (USA)) 588$^{2}$ 969$^{10}$ *1719$^{7}$ 2001$^{3}$* 2399$^{5}$ (2899) 3246$^{6}$ 3470$^{6}$ 3800$^{8}$ 4232$^{7}$ 4606$^{3}$ 4691$^{6}$ **>62da 76f<**

**Disco Boy** **6** b g Green Ruby (USA)-Sweet And Shiny (Siliconn) *534$^{2}$ 653$^{3}$ 762$^{9}$ 900$^{7}$ 1460$^{6}$ 1606$^{8}$ 2185$^{14}$ 2940$^{2}$ 3602$^{2}$ 3937$^{4}$* 4486$^{4}$ *4981$^{7}$* **>56a 46f<**

**Disc of Gold (USA)** **3** ch f Silver Hawk (USA)-Equal Change (USA) (Arts And Letters) *(370) 1407$^{6}$* ***>68+a 79f<***

**Discorsi** **4** b g Machiavellian (USA)-Bustara (Busted) *79$^{7}$ 228$^{5}$ 265$^{7}$* **>50a 71f<**

**Dismissed (USA)** **3** b c Dayjur (USA)-Bemissed (USA) (Nijinsky (CAN)) 1076$^{5}$ 1580a$^{7}$ 1768$^{7}$ **>98f<**

**Dispol Agenda** **3** b f Jendali (USA)-Welsh Fashion (Welsh Saint) 717$^{7}$ 784$^{7}$ 1196$^{17}$ **>23f<**

**Dispol Conqueror (IRE)** **3** b c Conquering Hero (USA)-Country Niece (Great Nephew) 522$^{8}$ 586$^{7}$ 1089$^{7}$ 2163$^{5}$ 2348$^{9}$ 2397$^{10}$ **>41f<**

**Dispol Dancer** **5** ch g Salse (USA)-High Quail (USA) (Blushing Groom (FR)) **1995:** *4387$^{13}$* **1996:** *1034$^{10}$ 1095$^{9}$ 2936$^{9}$ 4766$^{8}$* ***>6a 24f<***

**Dispol Diamond** **3** b f Sharpo-Fabulous Rina (FR) (Fabulous Dancer (USA)) 768$^{7}$ 962$^{8}$ 1323$^{3}$ 1675$^{3}$ 2079$^{4}$ 2514$^{8}$ 2805$^{3}$ 3133$^{7}$ 3854$^{4}$ 4071$^{14}$ 4860$^{16}$ **>62df<**

**Dispol Duchess** **3** b f Rock City-Antum (Hittite Glory) 626$^{9}$ 748$^{16}$ 867$^{9}$ 2393$^{4}$ 3102$^{7}$ 3354$^{11}$ 4070$^{7}$ **>42f<**

**Dispol Gem** **3** b f Rambo Dancer (CAN)-Andbracket (Import) 584$^{9}$ 703$^{5}$ 786$^{4}$ 976$^{4}$ 1470$^{8}$ 2572$^{3}$ 2899$^{3}$ 3295$^{5}$ 3845$^{7}$ 4436$^{8}$ 4597$^{11}$ 4906$^{3}$ 5042$^{4}$ **>68f<**

**Disputed** **3** b c Common Grounds-Family At War (USA) (Explodent (USA)) 2861$^{3}$ (3446) 3790$^{11}$ **>84f<**

**Dissentor (IRE)** **4** b g Dancing Dissident (USA)-Helen's Dynasty (Habitat) **1995:** *4430$^{5}$ 4521$^{5}$* **1996:** *16$^{6}$ (71) 127$^{5}$ 155$^{7}$ 259$^{6}$ 347$^{2}$ 403$^{2}$ 425$^{3}$ 592$^{7}$* 850$^{11}$ *3602$^{16}$ 4259$^{5}$* 4460$^{4}$ 4881$^{6}$ *4996$^{9}$* **>52a 45f<**

**Dissertation (FR)** **2** ch f Sillery (USA)-Devalois (Nureyev (USA)) 4291a$^{2}$ 4661a$^{6}$ 4945a$^{3}$ **>100f<**

**Dissington Times** **2** ch g Timeless Times (USA)-Zam's Slave (Zambrano) 1537$^{15}$ *2938$^{6}$*

**Distant Dynasty** **6** br g Another Realm-Jianna (Godswalk (USA)) **1995:** *4542$^{2}$* **1996:** *26$^{7}$ 64$^{2}$ 139$^{7}$ 173$^{6}$ 231$^{8}$ 316$^{10}$ 362$^{6}$ 464$^{8}$ 664$^{15}$* 1512$^{W}$ *4996$^{10}$* **>41a 53f<**

**Distant Oasis (USA)** **3** b f Green Desert (USA)-Just You Wait (Nonoalco (USA)) *(874)* 1567a$^{4}$ 3784$^{5}$ 4132$^{4}$ 4567$^{9}$ **>114f<**

**Distant Princess** **4** b f Distant Relative-Sojourn (Be My Guest (USA)) **1995:** *4377$^{9}$* **>44a 75f<**

**Distant Storm** **3** ch g Pharly (FR)-Candle in the Wind (Thatching) 3094$^{5}$ 3305$^{2}$ **>45f<**

**Distinct Beauty (IRE)** **3** ch f Pancho Villa (USA)-Beautiful Secret (USA) (Secreto (USA)) **1995:** *4365$^{2}$* **1996:** *(119) 164$^{2}$ 176$^{6}$ 754$^{5}$ (1096) 1448$^{3}$ 4606$^{9}$* 4831$^{13}$ **>77a 63f<**

**Distinctive Dream (IRE)** **2** b c Distinctly North (USA)-Green Side (USA) (Green Dancer (USA)) 3807$^{11}$ 3982$^{21}$ 4546$^{16}$ 4787$^{7}$ **>64f<**

**Distinctly Swingin (IRE)** **3** b f Distinctly North (USA)-Swoon Along (Dunphy) 1608$^{13}$ 2123$^{8}$ 2359$^{5}$ 2902$^{11}$ 2933$^{4}$ **>29f<**

**Distinctly West (IRE)** **2** b g Distinctly North (USA)-Card Queen (Lord Gayle (USA)) 4024a$^{8}$ **>78f<**

**Ditty Box** **2** b f Northern State (USA)-Upholder (Young Generation) *2172$^{8}$ 2371$^{10}$* **>8a f<**

**Dive Master (IRE)** **2** ch c Masterclass (USA)-Perle's Fashion (Sallust) 1086$^{3}$ 1453$^{6}$ 1531$^{6}$ 4106$^{11}$ 4835$^{6}$ **>62f<**

**Divide And Rule** **2** b c Puissance-Indivisible (Remainder Man) 1525$^{3}$ 1849$^{5}$ (2076) 2965$^{5}$ 3224$^{8}$ 3590$^{3}$ **>78f<**

**Divina Luna** **3** b f Dowsing (USA)-Famosa (Dancing Brave (USA)) (1301) 1648$^{2}$ 2146$^{3}$ (2687) (2907) (3322) 3920$^{4}$ 4445$^{5}$ **>94f<**

**Divine** **3** b f Dowsing (USA)-Rectitude (Runnymede) 2004$^{4}$ 2393$^{3}$ 3173$^{2}$ (3960) 4374$^{9}$ 4866$^{16}$ **>76f<**

**Divine Miss-P** **3** ch f Safawan-Faw (Absalom) 626$^{2}$ 768$^{9}$ **>67f<**

**Divine Quest** **3** ch f Kris-Dance Quest (FR) (Green Dancer (USA)) 710$^{3}$ 964$^{5}$ 1662$^{4}$ 3246$^{2}$ (3525) 3833$^{4}$ 4231$^{2}$ (4504) 4909$^{8}$ **>90f<**

**Dixie Jamboree (USA)** **2** b br c Dixie Brass (USA)-Glimmering (Troy) 3221$^{9}$ 3757$^{8}$ 4204$^{6}$ 4549$^{17}$ **>65f<**

**Dixie Pearl (USA)** **4** dk f Dixieland Band (USA)-Pleasantly Free (USA) (Pleasant Colony (USA)) 5032a$^{3}$ **>118f<**

**Dizzy Dancer** **2** gr f Rambo Dancer (CAN)-Fancy Flight (FR) (Arctic Tern (USA)) 1014$^{5}$ 1197$^{5}$ **>48f<**

**Dizzy Tilly** **2** b f Anshan-Nadema (Artaius (USA)) 1851$^{6}$ 2187$^{4}$ *3088$^{3}$ 3515$^{11}$* 4883$^{8}$ **>35a 62f<**

**Djais (FR)** **7** ch g Vacarme (USA)-Dame de Carreau (FR) (Targowice (USA)) 929$^{3}$ 1176$^{6}$ 2117$^{7}$ **>99f<**

**D J Cat** **3** b g Ballad Rock-Four-Legged Friend (Aragon) 526$^{10}$ 640$^{16}$ 4824$^{12}$ *4989$^{14}$* **>40f<**

**D'naan (IRE)** **3** b g Royal Academy (USA)-Festive Season (USA) (Lypheor) 575$^{11}$ 788$^{9}$ 1317$^{10}$ 2027$^{8}$ 2366$^{8}$ 2896$^{12}$ 3348$^{6}$ 3520$^{6}$ **>76a 50f<**

**Docklands Carriage (IRE)** **2** b c Anita's Prince-Zestino (Shack (USA)) 657$^{2}$ 869$^{7}$ 1086$^{6}$ 1537$^{5}$ (2043) (2588) 2875$^{3}$ 3275$^{7}$ 3687$^{15}$ 3969$^{10}$ **>70f<**

**Docklands Courier** **4** b g Dominion-High Quail (USA) (Blushing Groom (FR)) **1995:** *4355$^{13}$ 4452$^{10}$* **1996:** *2251$^{7}$* 2440$^{4}$ *3074$^{2}$ 3412$^{6}$ 3955$^{11}$* **>54a 50f<**

**Docklands Limo** **3** b c Most Welcome-Bugle Sound (Bustino) **1995:** *4535$^{5}$* **1996:** *(304) 444$^{4}$* (754) 969$^{6}$ 1714$^{2}$ **>65a 92f<**

**Dockmaster** **5** b g Dominion-Surf Bird (Shareef Dancer (USA)) 4794$^{16}$ **>32?f<**

**Doc Ryan's** **2** b c Damister (USA)-Jolimo (Fortissimo) 4698$^{8}$ 4818$^{6}$ 5009$^{2}$ **>77f<**

**Doctor Bravious (IRE)** **3** b c Priolo (USA)-Sharp Slipper (Sharpo) *(17) 646$^{4}$* 4582$^{8}$ 4702$^{13}$ **>71a 72f<**

**Doctor Green (FR)** **3** b g Green Desert (USA)-Highbrow (Shirley Heights) 691$^{7}$ 826$^{8}$ 1415$^{5}$ 1984$^{2}$ 2141$^{4}$ **>70f<**

**Doctor Leckter (USA)** **2** b c Key to the Kingdom (USA)-Clothes Horse (ITY) (Proudest Roman (USA)) 2671a$^{2}$ **>90f<**

**Doctor's Remedy** **10** br g Doc Marten-Champagne Party (Amber Rama (USA)) 542$^{12}$ 4321$^{15}$ **>33?f<**

**Doddington Flyer** **4** b c Distant Relative-Tino-Ella (Bustino) **1995:** *4355$^{7}$ 4463$^{2}$* **1996:** *69$^{3}$* **>68a 81f<**

**Dodgy Dancer** **6** b g Shareef Dancer (USA)-Fluctuate (Sharpen Up) 752$^{14}$ **>1a 47f<**

**Dolliver (USA)** **4** b g Northern Baby (CAN)-Mabira (Habitat) 847$^{7}$ 2603$^{8}$ 2953$^{7}$ **>64df<**

**Dolly Dolittle** **5** ch m Infantry-Lost Moment (Hotfoot) *1314$^{17}$* 2192$^{17}$ 2592$^{13}$ 2941$^{14}$ **>30a 24f<**

**Domain (GER)** **3** b c Mondrian (GER)-Dimdl (Dschingis Khan) (4741a) **>102f<**

**Domak Amaam (IRE)** **3** b c Dominion-La Courant (USA) (Little Current (USA)) *484$^{2}$ 692$^{4}$* 1178$^{2}$ 1475$^{4}$ 2597$^{3}$ *3064$^{5}$ 3679$^{3}$* ***>68a 68f<***

**Domappel** **4** b g Domynsky-Appelania (Star Appeal) 598$^{5}$ 738$^{2}$ 968$^{6}$ 1109$^{7}$ (1647) 1837$^{2}$ 4683$^{6}$ 4872$^{18}$ **>81f<**

**Dombey** **3** b c Dominion-Arderelle (FR) (Pharly (FR)) *(419) (575)* (1106) 1476$^{10}$ **>83a 92f<**

**Dome Patrol** **5** gr g Dominion-Tranquility Base (Roan Rocket) *1460$^{5}$ 1970$^{13}$ 3062$^{3}$ 3435$^{2}$* **>50a 43f<**

**Domettes (IRE)** **3** ch f Archway (IRE)-Superetta (Superlative) *25$^{6}$ 171$^{9}$ 376$^{5}$ 545$^{5}$* 761$^{4}$ 1100$^{6}$ 1999$^{3}$ 2975$^{2}$ 3320$^{2}$ (3654) 3825$^{5}$ 4216$^{2}$ 4515$^{11}$ 4877$^{7}$ **>50a 62f<**

**Domicksky** **8** b g Dominion-Mumruffin (Mummy's Pet) 466$^{6}$ 559$^{2}$ 601$^{16}$ 667$^{7}$ 762$^{6}$ 882$^{9}$ 911$^{4}$ **>67a 54f< (DEAD)**

**Dominant Air** **2** b g Primo Dominie-Area Girl (Jareer (USA)) 4228$^{6}$ 4475$^{8}$ 4754$^{3}$ (4912) **>75f<**

**Dominelle** **4** b f Domynsky-Gymcrak Lovebird (Taufan (USA)) 931$^{14}$ 1040$^{11}$ 1364$^{7}$ 1541$^{10}$ (1859) 2186$^{2}$ 2518$^{3}$ 2757$^{2}$ 3055$^{5}$ 3252$^{3}$ 3352$^{10}$ 3415$^{2}$ 3868$^{4}$ 4045$^{4}$ 4206$^{2}$ 4430$^{16}$ 4610$^{2}$ **>32a 62f<**

**Domino Flyer** **3** b c Warrshan (USA)-Great Dilemma (Vaigly Great) *345$^{5}$ 616$^{3}$ (782) (1025) 2086$^{6}$ 2552$^{8}$ 2934$^{4}$ 4575$^{9}$ 4781$^{7}$ 4989$^{2}$* **>66a 69f<**

**Domino Style** **2** b f Primo Dominie-Corman-Style

(Ahonoora) 4069$^{10}$ 4806$^{4}$ **>55f<**

**Domitia (USA) 4** ch f Arctic Tern (USA)-Fast Trek (FR) (Trepan (FR)) **1995:** 4366$^{3}$ **1996:** 920$^{7}$ (1072) 1440$^{2}$ 1486$^{8}$ 1816$^{9}$ 2924$^{6}$ 3248$^{7}$ 3509$^{7}$ 4993$^{14}$ **>56a 66f<**

**Domoor 3** b g Dominion-Corley Moor (Habitat) **1995:** (4446) **1996:** 56$^{2}$ 137$^{5}$ 230$^{2}$ 245$^{2}$ (277) 294$^{6}$ 463$^{2}$ 503$^{2}$ 605$^{7}$ 976$^{10}$ 2391$^{13}$ 3059$^{7}$ 3427$^{12}$ **>66a 46f<**

**Dom Ruinart (IRE) 2** b c Cyrano de Bergerac-Dazzling Maid (IRE) (Tate Gallery (USA)) 3515$^{9}$ 4079$^{10}$ 4210$^{11}$ 4614$^{11}$ **>26a 57f<**

**Domulla 6** br h Dominion-Ulla Laing (Mummy's Pet) 457$^{8}$ 940$^{4}$ 1621$^{7}$ **>111f<**

**Domusky 3** ch f Domynsky-Roches Roost (Pauper) 550$^{17}$ 1474$^{15}$ 2026$^{8}$ 2368$^{5}$ 3358$^{11}$ 3881$^{5}$ **>39f<**

**Dona Filipa 3** ch f Precocious-Quisissanno (Be My Guest (USA)) 2672$^{10}$ 2902$^{9}$ 3256$^{6}$ 4074$^{12}$ 4456$^{6}$ 4598$^{6}$ **>50f<**

**Don Bosio (USA) 3** b c El Gran Senor (USA)-Celtic Loot (USA) (Irish River (FR)) 892$^{12}$ 1142$^{6}$ 1593$^{2}$ 2041$^{15}$ 2501$^{5}$ 3472$^{3}$ 4108$^{3}$ (4322) (4376) 4554$^{7}$ **>102f<**

**Done Well (USA) 4** b g Storm Bird (CAN)-Suspicious Toosome (USA) (Secretariat (USA)) 4313$^{6}$ **>65f<**

**Donia (USA) 7** ch m Graustark-Katrinka (USA) (Sovereign Dancer (USA)) **1995:** 4406$^{12}$ **1996:** 45$^{8}$ 140$^{10}$ **>48a f<**

**Donington Park 3** ch f Risk Me (FR)-Small Double (IRE) (Double Schwartz) 1840$^{15}$ 2185$^{17}$ 2684$^{6}$ **>45a 20f<**

**Don Micheletto 3** b c Machiavellian (USA)-Circe's Isle (Be My Guest (USA)) 1141a$^{8}$ (1329) 1757a$^{4}$ 2473a$^{10}$ **>113f<**

**Donna's Dancer (IRE) 2** ch c Magical Wonder (USA)-Ice On Fire (Thatching) 2361$^{8}$ 2625$^{4}$ 4046$^{9}$ 4346$^{2}$ 4459$^{2}$ 4586$^{5}$ 4749$^{2}$ **>74f<**

**Donna Viola 4** b f Be My Chief (USA)-Countess Olivia (Prince Tenderfoot (USA)) 809$^{6}$ 1193$^{3}$ (1770) 2053$^{4}$ 2609$^{3}$ (4160a) (4663a) (5032a) **>119f<**

**Don Pepe 5** br g Dowsing (USA)-Unique Treasure (Young Generation) 662$^{12}$ 1010$^{6}$ 1313$^{12}$ (1715) 1905$^{2}$ 2005$^{7}$ 2285$^{10}$ 2729$^{5}$ 2929$^{2}$ 3306$^{8}$ 3666$^{3}$ 3758$^{2}$ 4088$^{10}$ (4240) 4571$^{7}$ 4809$^{3}$ 4915$^{12}$ **>71f<**

**Don Sebastian 2** b c Indian Ridge-Sunley Stars (Sallust) 1118$^{6}$ 1683$^{4}$ 4545$^{5}$ 4782$^{2}$ 5043$^{2}$ **>83f<**

**Don't Care (IRE) 5** b m Nordico (USA)-Eyeliner (USA) (Raise A Native) 4314$^{23}$ 4581$^{11}$ 4687$^{18}$ **>76f<**

**Don't Cry 8** b m Dominion-Black Veil (Blakeney) 609$^{14}$ 886$^{9}$ 1542$^{8}$ 1611$^{6}$ 1847$^{8}$ 2423$^{10}$ 2779$^{9}$ **>32?f<**

**Don't Drop Bombs (USA) 7** ch g Fighting Fit (USA)-Promised Star (USA) (Star de Naskra (USA)) **1995:** 4364$^{12}$ 4465$^{8}$ **1996:** 15$^{2}$ 83$^{9}$ 116$^{3}$ (219) 279$^{3}$ 406$^{2}$ 440$^{22}$ 1449$^{14}$ 1816$^{6}$ 2284$^{2}$ (2440) 2587$^{4}$ 3443$^{9}$ 3575$^{2}$ (3980) 5003$^{6}$ **>46a 49f<**

**Don't Fool Me (IRE) 2** ch g Don't Forget Me-Foolish Passion (USA) (Secretariat (USA)) 4331$^{10}$ 4607$^{W}$ 4970$^{21}$ **>27a f<**

**Dont Forget Curtis (IRE) 4** b g Don't Forget Me-Norse Lady (Viking (USA)) 541$^{6}$ 625$^{14}$ 4726$^{14}$ **>78a 68f<**

**Dontforget Insight (IRE) 5** b g Don't Forget Me-Starlust (Sallust) 1154$^{5}$ 1517$^{4}$ **>67f<**

**Don't Forget Shoka (IRE) 2** br f Don't Forget Me-Shoka (FR) (Kaldoun (FR)) 446$^{5}$ 569$^{5}$ 741$^{5}$ 1084$^{2}$ (1463) 3046$^{12}$ 3092$^{4}$ 3455$^{3}$ 3582$^{8}$ 3943$^{12}$ **>44a 46f<**

**Don't Get Caught (IRE) 4** b f Danehill (USA)-Be Discreet (Junius (USA)) **1995:** 4382$^{3}$ 4464$^{8}$ 4512$^{7}$ **1996:** 50$^{4}$ 115$^{8}$ 217$^{3}$ 261$^{4}$ 320$^{4}$ 839$^{7}$ 3812$^{3}$ (4098) 4212$^{2}$ 4354$^{2}$ (4571) 4738a$^{11}$ **>56a 79f<**

**Don't Give Up 8** b h Nomination-Tug Along (Posse (USA)) **1995:** 4355$^{14}$ **>40a 41f<**

**Dont Shoot Fairies 4** ch c Vague Shot-Fairy Fans (Petingo) 682$^{5}$ 968$^{5}$ 1147$^{11}$ 1524$^{4}$ 1965$^{4}$ **>56a 76f<**

**Don't Tell Anyone 3** gr g Petong-Glenfield Portion (Mummy's Pet) **1995:** 4369$^{8}$ **1996:** 183$^{5}$ 272$^{4}$ 423$^{4}$ 652$^{6}$ 750$^{6}$ 989$^{5}$ 1761$^{W}$ **>60a 58f<**

**Don't Tell Vicki 3** b f Mazilier (USA)-Jans Contessa (Rabdan) **1995:** 4437$^{8}$ 4511$^{12}$ **1996:** 1715$^{10}$ 2193$^{10}$ 2686$^{13}$ **>34a 35f<**

**Don't Worry Me (IRE) 4** b f Dancing Dissident (USA)-Diva Encore (Star Appeal) 1581a$^{5}$ 2270a$^{3}$ 2841a$^{3}$ 4406a$^{2}$ 4660a$^{8}$ (4958a) **>115f<**

**Don't Worry Mike 2** ch c Forzando-Hat Hill (Roan Rocket) 2122$^{9}$ 3588$^{8}$ 4069$^{6}$ 4501$^{4}$ 4795$^{19}$ **>59f<**

**Don Vito 3** ch c Generous (IRE)-Dance by Night (Northfields (USA)) (691) 2116$^{6}$ 2677$^{2}$ 3124$^{11}$ **>113f<**

**Doodies Pool (IRE) 6** b g Mazaad-Barncogue (Monseigneur (USA)) **1995:** 4379$^{14}$ 4409$^{13}$ **1996:** 1651$^{11}$ 1893$^{17}$ 2056$^{6}$ 2313$^{10}$ 2507$^{14}$ 2971$^{17}$ **>44a 45f<**

**Dorado Beach 2** b f Lugana Beach-Cannon Boy (USA) (Canonero II (USA)) 4547$^{9}$ 4697$^{11}$ **>45f<**

**Doreen's Delight 10** ch h Bay Express-Elizabeth Howard (Sharpen Up) 995$^{12}$ 1472$^{P}$ **>42a 16f<**

**Dorlando 5** ch g Kris-Diana Dance (CAN) (Northern Dancer) 3394a$^{3}$ **>97f<**

**Dormston Boyo 6** b g Sula Bula-March at Dawn (Nishapour (FR)) 4984$^{14}$ **>8a 6f<**

**Dormy Three 6** b g Morston (FR)-Dominant (Behistoun) 844$^{6}$ 1124$^{9}$ 1450$^{3}$ 1686$^{4}$ 1874$^{14}$ 2203$^{5}$ 2342$^{6}$ 2953$^{4}$ 3466$^{3}$ 3824$^{5}$ **>65a 72f<**

**Dosses Dan (IRE) 4** b c Danehill (USA)-Flyaway Bride (USA) (Blushing Groom (FR)) 390$^{12}$ **>28a 74f<**

**Doth Protest (IRE) 4** br f Dancing Dissident (USA)-Star of Victoria (What A Guest) 949$^{12}$ 1994$^{8}$ 2346$^{6}$ **>42f<**

**Dots Dee 7** ch m Librate-Dejote (Bay Express) 609$^{3}$ 866$^{8}$ 1047$^{9}$ 1778$^{13}$ 2284$^{9}$ (2556) 2906$^{3}$ 2941$^{5}$ 2989$^{5}$ 3507$^{6}$ 4509$^{6}$ **>38f<**

**Double Action 2** br c Reprimand-Final Shot (Dalsaan) 699$^{3}$ 958$^{4}$ (1184) 1699$^{3}$ **>80f<**

**Double Agent 3** ch g Niniski (USA)-Rexana (Relko) (1783) (1826) 2247$^{5}$ 3486$^{4}$ 4596$^{6}$ 4750$^{7}$ 4821$^{3}$ **>80f<**

**Double Alleged (USA) 2** b br c Alleged (USA)-Danseuse Etoile (USA) (Buckpasser) 4913$^{6}$ **>75f<**

**Double Blue 7** ch g Town And Country-Australia Fair (AUS) (Without Fear (FR)) 737$^{4}$ 940$^{7}$ 1107$^{8}$ 1623$^{4}$ 1975$^{3}$ 2328$^{8}$ 2704$^{2}$ 2920$^{4}$ 3271$^{7}$ 3622$^{16}$ 3984$^{14}$ 4687$^{12}$ 4994$^{11}$ **>89f<**

**Double Bluff (IRE) 3** gr g Sharrood (USA)-Timely Raise (USA) (Raise A Man (USA)) 732$^{6}$ 1127$^{4}$ 1432$^{7}$ 2004$^{5}$ (2326) (2742) 3211$^{10}$ 3791$^{3}$ 4120$^{3}$ 4568$^{8}$ **>97f<**

**Double Bounce 6** b g Interrex (CAN)-Double Gift (Cragador) 1853$^{9}$ 2114$^{3}$ (2329) 3232$^{2}$ 3672$^{6}$ 4314$^{17}$ 4444$^{13}$ **>95f<**

**Double Dash (IRE) 3** gr g Darshaan-Safka (USA) (Irish River (FR)) 1587$^{4}$ 2560$^{5}$ 2804$^{7}$ **>49a 70f<**

**Double Diamond (IRE) 3** b c Last Tycoon-State Treasure (USA) (Secretariat (USA)) **1995:** (4389) 4410$^{6}$ 4528$^{5}$ **1996:** 391$^{4}$ 611$^{2}$ (1059a) 1106$^{5}$ 2041$^{5}$ 2459a$^{6}$ 3158$^{16}$ **>84a 101f<**

**Double Echo (IRE) 8** br g Glow (USA)-Piculet (Morston (FR)) 1874$^{8}$ 2226$^{6}$ 2423$^{6}$ 2884$^{2}$ 3434$^{7}$ 3813$^{6}$ 4073$^{17}$ (4307) 4489$^{5}$ 4626$^{11}$ 4894$^{9}$ **>26a 57f<**

**Double Eclipse (IRE) 4** b c Ela-Mana-Mou-Solac (FR) (Gay Lussac (ITY)) (563) (902a) (1397a) **>123f<**

**Double-E-I-B-A 2** br g Reprimand-Doppio (Dublin Taxi) 4233$^{13}$ 4492$^{12}$ 4715$^{20}$ **>54f<**

**Double Eight (IRE) 2** b f Common Grounds-Boldabsa (Persian Bold) 3706$^{8}$ 4969$^{14}$ **>66f<**

**Double Espresso (IRE) 2** b f Taufan (USA)-Kilcoy (USA) (Secreto (USA)) 3080$^{7}$ 3982$^{2}$ 4331$^{4}$ (4795) 4990$^{2}$ **>66a 75f<**

**Double Flight 2** b f Mtoto-Sariah (Kris) 3277$^{3}$ 3756$^{8}$ (4310) 4760$^{12}$ **>73f<**

**Double Glow 4** b f Presidium-Glow Again (The Brianstan) **1995:** 4407$^{10}$ 4430$^{6}$ **1996:** 71$^{12}$ 127$^{14}$ 172$^{6}$ 207$^{5}$ 253$^{7}$ 259$^{9}$ 342$^{7}$ 368$^{9}$ 1492$^{13}$ 1859$^{12}$ 2395$^{3}$ 2564$^{4}$ 2771$^{7}$ 2910$^{10}$ 2960$^{6}$ 3091$^{11}$ 3310$^{5}$ 3460$^{9}$ 3774$^{12}$ 3957$^{6}$ **>19a 30f<**

**Double Gold 2** b f Statoblest-Adriya (Vayrann) 1851$^{11}$ 2714$^{2}$ (2904) (3616) 3835$^{15}$ 4113$^{21}$ **>72f<**

**Double Impression (IRE) 3** b f Mac's Imp (USA)-Thalssa (Rusticaro (FR)) 292$^{7}$ 1592$^{6}$ 1964$^{5}$ 2359$^{8}$ 2800$^{6}$ 3317$^{4}$ **>23a 54f<**

**Double-J (IRE) 2** b c Fayruz-Farriers Slipper (Prince Tenderfoot (USA)) 1191$^{3}$ 1453$^{5}$ 2323$^{2}$ 2527$^{2}$ (2755) 3483$^{2}$ 4065$^{6}$ 4723$^{24}$ **>89f<**

**Double Jeopardy 5** b g Polish Precedent (USA)-Infamy (Shirley Heights) **1995:** 4540$^{6}$ **1996:** 79$^{9}$ 175$^{6}$ **>45a 77f<**

**Double Leaf 3** b c Sadler's Wells (USA)-Green Leaf (USA) (Alydar (USA)) 830$^{4}$ 1114$^{5}$ 1791$^{10}$ 3797$^{2}$ 3992$^{3}$ 4351$^{2}$ **>115f<**

**Double March 3** b g Weldnaas (USA)-Double Gift (Cragador) 1350$^{2}$ 2004$^{7}$ 2579$^{11}$ 4820$^{22}$ 4975$^{18}$ **>71f<**

**Double Matt (IRE) 4** b g Double Schwartz-Kasarose (Owen Dudley) 956$^{4}$ 1078$^{5}$ 1354$^{11}$ **>78f<**

**Double Niner (USA) 3** br c Forty Niner (USA)-Sure Locked (USA) 2135$^{11}$ **>57f<**

**Double-O 2** b c Sharpo-Ktolo (Tolomeo) 4756$^{16}$ 4970$^{9}$ **>49f<**

**Double Or Bust 3** ch f Presidium-Defy Me (Bustino) **1995:** 4533$^{6}$ **1996:** 142$^{7}$ 1663$^{6}$ 2156$^{13}$ 2528$^{5}$ 3166$^{12}$ 4372$^{18}$ **>41a 32f<**

**Double Oscar (IRE) 3** ch g Royal Academy (USA)-Broadway Rosie (Absalom) **1995:** 4504$^{4}$ **1996:** 1628$^{13}$ 1707$^{4}$ 1836$^{3}$ 1891$^{2}$ 2022$^{3}$ 2520$^{3}$ 2898$^{9}$ 3278$^{4}$ 4430$^{6}$ 4598$^{8}$ **>46a 51f<**

**Double-O-Seven 3** b c Tirol-Anneli Rose (Superlative) (143) 232$^{2}$ 1185$^{10}$ 2325$^{4}$ 2551$^{9}$ 2935$^{8}$ **>55da 42f<**

**Double Park (FR) 2** b f Lycius (USA)-Just Pretty (USA) (Danzig (USA)) 608$^{2}$ 715$^{2}$ 1760$^{2}$ (2875) (3230) 3908a$^{8}$ 4183$^{3}$ **>94f<**

**Double Quick (IRE) 4** b f Superpower-Haraabah (USA) (Topsider (USA)) 927$^{8}$ 1483$^{7}$ 1616$^{2}$ 1818$^{5}$ (2003) 2115$^{15}$ 2472a$^{8}$ 2545$^{10}$ 3038$^{5}$ 3946$^{12}$ 4116$^{17}$ 4466$^{10}$ 4772$^{15}$ 5044$^{13}$ **>82f<**

**Double Rush (IRE) 4** b g Doulab (USA)-Stanza Dancer (Stanford) **1995:** (4385) 4420$^{7}$ **1996:** 635$^{9}$ 1173$^{15}$ 1515$^{11}$ 2159$^{6}$ 2689$^{9}$ 3141$^{10}$ (3314) (3635) 4900$^{4}$ **>65a 62f<**

**Double Splendour (IRE) 6** b g Double Schwartz-Princess Pamela (Dragonara Palace (USA)) (592) 814$^{4}$ 1186$^{5}$ 1442$^{2}$ 2329$^{2}$ (2725) 3672$^{2}$ 3984$^{3}$ 4314$^{4}$ 4687$^{2}$ **>45a 104f<**

**Double Trigger (IRE) 5** ch h Ela-Mana-Mou-Solac (FR) (Gay Lussac (ITY)) (875) (1482) 2071$^{2}$ (4134) 4655a$^{5}$ **>128f<**

**Double Up 3** ch f Weldnaas (USA)-Bel Esprit (Sagaro) 860$^{6}$ (1447) 1641$^{14}$ 2384$^{5}$ 2780$^{2}$ 3111$^{6}$ 3452$^{2}$ 4000$^{14}$ 4257$^{4}$ **>76f<**

**Doubleyoubeay 3** ch c Beveled (USA)-Hollia (Touch Boy) **1995:** 4389$^{10}$ **>61a 57f<**

**Doubly-H (IRE) 2** b g Be My Guest (USA)-Pursue (Auction Ring (USA)) 1626$^{10}$ 2887$^{7}$ 3259$^{18}$ 3405$^{5}$

>49f<

**Douce Maison (IRE)** 5 b m Fools Holme (USA)-Cardomine (Dom Racine (FR)) 283$^{6}$ >68a 67f<

**Doug's Folly** 3 ch f Handsome Sailor-Stern Lass (Bold Lad (IRE)) 762$^{14}$ 973$^{6}$ 1405$^{4}$ 1780$^{12}$ 2215$^{3}$ 2983$^{7}$ 3292$^{6}$ 3937$^{3}$ 4589$^{16}$ 4598$^{16}$ 4805$^{19}$ >46f<

**Dovaly** 3 b c Lycius (USA)-Sedova (USA) (Nijinsky (CAN)) (677) 1076$^{4}$ 4886$^{6}$ >98f<

**Dovebrace** 3 b g Dowsing (USA)-Naufrage (Main Reef) 1431$^{5}$ 1800$^{9}$ 2328$^{9}$ 3984$^{15}$ 4185$^{8}$ 4485$^{9}$ >88f<

**Dovedon Lad** 4 ch c Statoblest-Miss Petella (Dunphy) **1995:** 4454$^{7}$ >21a 21f<

**Dover Straits (USA)** 5 b or br h Riverman (USA)-Sahsie (USA) 375a$^{3}$ 535a$^{12}$ >50a 99f<

**Dowdency** 4 b f Dowsing (USA)-Tendency (Ballad Rock) **1995:** 4388$^{5}$ 4444$^{4}$ 4505$^{7}$ >55a 60f<

**Down The Yard** 3 b f Batshoof-Sequin Lady (Star Appeal) 112$^{6}$ 158$^{3}$ 238$^{6}$ 280$^{11}$ 344$^{7}$ 404$^{3}$ 605$^{2}$ 1068$^{15}$ 1110$^{5}$ 1721$^{3}$ 2320$^{10}$ 2937$^{5}$ 3354$^{7}$ >47a 39f<

**Dowry** 2 b f Rudimentary (USA)-Priceless Bond (USA) (Blushing Groom (FR)) 569$^{4}$ 683$^{4}$ 2382$^{2}$ 2696$^{4}$ 3046$^{2}$ 3408$^{10}$ (3871) 4046$^{5}$ 4423$^{5}$ 4546$^{3}$ 4586$^{2}$ 4803$^{15}$ >70f<

**Doyella (IRE)** 2 b f Doyoun-Santella Bell (Ballad Rock) 4969$^{9}$ >69f<

**Dozen Roses** 2 b f Rambo Dancer (CAN)-Andbracket (Import) 465$^{7}$ 590$^{8}$ 1720$^{5}$ 2279$^{4}$ 2764$^{4}$ 3075$^{3}$ 3311$^{4}$ 3763$^{2}$ 3976$^{5}$ 4207$^{10}$ 4493$^{7}$ >5a 59f<

**Dragonada (USA)** 2 b f Nureyev (USA)-Don't Sulk (USA) (Graustark) 4357$^{2}$ (4605) 4875$^{4}$ >93f<

**Dragonflight** 5 b h Formidable (USA)-Lappet (Kampala) **1995:** 4362$^{12}$ 4390$^{15}$ >65a 17f<

**Dragon Green** 5 gr g Green Desert (USA)-Dunoof (Shirley Heights) **1995:** 4362$^{5}$ **1996:** 65$^{5}$ 177$^{9}$ >54a 50f<

**Dragonjoy** 3 b g Warrshan (USA)-Nazakat (Known Fact (USA)) **1995:** 4433$^{2}$ 4462$^{6}$ **1996:** 49$^{3}$ (158) (238) 404$^{2}$ 540$^{5}$ (1456) 1811$^{9}$ (2169) 2551$^{5}$ 2637$^{5}$ 2934$^{13}$ 3063$^{11}$ 3628$^{5}$ 3951$^{6}$ 4077$^{9}$ 4337$^{7}$ 4573$^{3}$ 4981$^{3}$ 5059$^{3}$ >62a 61f<

**Dragon Rose** 4 ch g Grey Desire-The Shrew (Relko) 2181$^{10}$ 2553$^{10}$ >4a 27f<

**Dragon's Back (IRE)** 3 ch c Digamist (USA)-Classic Choice (Patch) 1530$^{3}$ 1955$^{4}$ 2183$^{11}$ 4432$^{11}$ >78f<

**Drama King** 4 b g Tragic Role (USA)-Consistent Queen (Queen's Hussar) 2936$^{4}$ 3297$^{12}$ (3630) 3952$^{2}$ 4092$^{6}$ 5062$^{10}$ >48a 19f<

**Dramatic Act** 3 gr f Tragic Role (USA)-Curious Feeling (Nishapour (FR)) 892$^{14}$ 1301$^{6}$ 1641$^{13}$ 1956$^{4}$ 4804$^{13}$ >54f<

**Dramatic Gold (USA)** 5 b h Slew O' Gold (USA)-American Drama (USA) (Danzig (USA)) 2842a$^{2}$ 4956a$^{9}$ >127a 128f<

**Dramatic Moment** 3 b f Belmez (USA)-Drama School (Young Generation) 1357$^{3}$ 1682$^{2}$ (2251) 2855$^{5}$ 3500$^{8}$ >75f<

**Dr Beat (IRE)** 3 b g Distinctly North (USA)-Milly's Song 2459a$^{4}$ >85f<

**Dr Caligari (IRE)** 4 b g My Generation-Mallabee (Pall Mall) **1995:** 4377$^{4}$ 4406$^{2}$ 4510$^{4}$ **1996:** 50$^{8}$ 167$^{7}$ >61da 70f<

**Dream Carrier (IRE)** 8 b g Doulab (USA)-Dream Trader (Auction Ring (USA)) **1995:** 4427$^{9}$ 4512$^{4}$ **1996:** 57$^{11}$ 190$^{3}$ 219$^{4}$ 341$^{5}$ 412$^{3}$ 440$^{20}$ 854$^{9}$ 1449$^{19}$ >51a 36f<

**Dream of My Life (USA)** 3 gr g Danzatore (CAN)-Sureya (Sharpen Up) **1995:** 4501$^{10}$ **1996:** 17$^{8}$ 494$^{5}$ 599$^{5}$ >15a 23f<

**Dream of Nurmi** 2 ch c Pursuit of Love-Finlandaise (FR) (Arctic Tern (USA)) 2802$^{4}$ 3119$^{2}$ 3625$^{2}$ >75a 79f<

**Dreams And Schemes (IRE)** 3 ch f Mujtahid (USA)-Continuite (FR) (Pharly (FR)) 2777$^{2}$ 3288$^{F}$ >58f< (DEAD)

**Dreams End** 8 ch h Rainbow Quest (USA)-Be Easy (Be Friendly) 2008$^{4}$ 2145$^{11}$ 2724$^{9}$ 3689$^{18}$ 3983$^{18}$ 4626$^{2}$ (4686) 4872$^{4}$ 4974$^{4}$ >85f<

**Dr Edgar** 4 b g Most Welcome-African Dancer (Nijinsky (CAN)) 641$^{10}$ 816$^{6}$ 1072$^{7}$ 1345$^{7}$ 1650$^{3}$ 2077$^{3}$ 2152$^{4}$ 2357$^{5}$ 2701$^{8}$ 2988$^{3}$ 3242$^{5}$ 3575$^{7}$ >68f<

**Drift** 2 b g Slip Anchor-Norgabie (Northfields (USA)) 2538$^{10}$ 2702$^{7}$ 2967$^{7}$ >64f<

**Driftholme** 3 b f Safawan-Avahra (Sahib) 459$^{3}$ 899$^{8}$ 1534$^{14}$ 3965$^{7}$ >27a 26f<

**Drimard (IRE)** 5 ch g Ela-Mana-Mou-Babilla (USA) **1995:** (4387) >51a 33f<

**Drive Assured** 2 gr c Mystiko (USA)-Black Ivor (USA) (Sir Ivor) 2132$^{6}$ 3668$^{7}$ 4233$^{6}$ 4477$^{3}$ 4864$^{5}$ >79f<

**Dr Johnson (USA)** 2 ch c Woodman (USA)-Russian Ballet (USA) 5063a$^{4}$ >73f<

**Dr Massini (IRE)** 3 b c Sadler's Wells (USA)-Argon Laser (Kris) (970) (1125) 2473a$^{7}$ >113+f<

**Droit Divin (FR)** 5 b h Diamond Prospect (USA)-Munsingen (FR) (Emerson (BRA)) 3200a$^{3}$ >120f<

**Drum Battle** 4 ch c Bold Arrangement-Cannon Boy (USA) (Canonero II (USA)) 184$^{7}$ >41a 70f<

**Drumgor Prince** 2 b c Robellino (USA)-Victoria Mill (Free State) 4584$^{5}$ 4801$^{6}$ >67f<

**Drummer Hicks** 7 b or br h Seymour Hicks (FR)-Musical Princess (Cavo Doro) **1995:** 4472$^{6}$ **1996:** 124$^{8}$ 477$^{3}$ 558$^{5}$ 853$^{6}$ 999$^{3}$ 1585$^{3}$ (1778) 3401$^{4}$ 4617$^{20}$ 4810$^{13}$ >22a 60f<

**Dr Woodstock** 2 br c Rock City-Go Tally-Ho (Gorytus (USA)) 706$^{10}$ >39f<

**Dry Point** 10 ch g Sharpo-X-Data (On Your Mark) 632$^{10}$ 744$^{8}$ 1853$^{13}$ 2228$^{8}$ >55f<

**Dry Rocks (ITY)** 3 b c Shernazar-Kashna (USA) (Blushing Groom (FR)) (799a)

**Dry Sea** 5 b g Green Desert (USA)-Prickle (Sharpen Up) 1305$^{9}$ >67f< (DEAD)

**Dtoto** 4 b g Mtoto-Deposit (Thatch (USA)) 1981$^{6}$ 2342$^{8}$ 2613$^{7}$ 4086$^{11}$ >54f<

**Dubai College (IRE)** 3 b c Old Vic-Murooj (USA) (Diesis) 663$^{4}$ 955$^{4}$ 1363$^{4}$ 2209$^{2}$ 2501$^{12}$ 2946$^{5}$ 3603$^{14}$ 3702$^{9}$ >5a 77f<

**Dublin Indemnity (USA)** 7 b g Alphabatim (USA)-Sailongal (USA) (Sail On-Sail On) **1995:** 4472$^{11}$ **1996:** 29$^{9}$

**Dublin River (USA)** 3 b c Irish River (FR)-Vivre Libre (USA) (Honest Pleasure (USA)) 3822$^{5}$ 4181$^{8}$ >91f<

**Duc De Zoz (FR)** 3 b c Legend of France (USA)-Queen Margaret (Val de L'Orne (FR)) (322a)

**Duchesse de Berri (USA)** 3 ch f Diesis-Berry Berry Good (USA) (Shadeed (USA)) 1855$^{3}$ >74f<

**Ducking** 4 b f Reprimand-Gliding (Tudor Melody) **1995:** 4366$^{7}$ >43a 74f<

**Duel At Dawn** 3 ch c Nashwan (USA)-Gayane (Nureyev (USA)) 1452$^{3}$ 1667$^{2}$ (1994) 2584$^{4}$ 3232$^{13}$ 3946$^{13}$ 4466$^{4}$ >93f<

**Duello** 5 b g Sure Blade (USA)-Royal Loft (Homing) 496$^{2}$ 765$^{15}$ 1190$^{11}$ (1522) 1703$^{3}$ 1962$^{3}$ 2249$^{2}$ 2885$^{6}$ 3985$^{4}$ 4186$^{4}$ (4308) 4571$^{3}$ 4688$^{8}$ 4901$^{2}$ 4974$^{11}$ >71a 82f<

**Duet** 3 b f Loch Pearl-Double Song (Double Form) 861$^{13}$ 1122$^{9}$ 1592$^{7}$ 2561$^{9}$ 2966$^{4}$ 3458$^{12}$ 4784$^{9}$ >37f<

**Duffertoes** 4 ch g High Kicker (USA)-Miss Poll Flinders (Swing Easy (USA)) 496$^{12}$ 887$^{15}$ 1469$^{6}$ 1856$^{P}$ >49f<

**Duggan** 9 b g Dunbeath (USA)-Silka (ITY) (Lypheor) **1995:** 4455$^{5}$ 4507$^{6}$ **1996:** 54$^{3}$ 104$^{5}$ 138$^{6}$ 186$^{8}$ >37a 42f<

**Duke of Flight (USA)** 3 b c Alleged (USA)-Stage Flight (ITY) (Lord Durham (CAN)) (5023a) >118f<

**Duke Valentino** 4 br c Machiavellian (USA)-Aldhabyih (General Assembly (USA)) **1995:** (4354) (4386) 4421$^{13}$ 4520$^{2}$ (4539) **1996:** 14$^{7}$ 121$^{7}$ 205$^{2}$ 243$^{3}$ 409$^{2}$ 450$^{12}$ 629$^{16}$ 765$^{18}$ 1048$^{2}$ 1406$^{10}$ 3403$^{2}$ 3592$^{3}$ 3650$^{9}$ 4128$^{16}$ 4432$^{4}$ >83a 67f<

**Dulas Bay** 2 b g Selkirk (USA)-Ivory Gull (USA) (Storm Bird (CAN)) 2512$^{7}$ 2923$^{7}$ 4807$^{9}$ >52f<

**Dulcinea** 2 ch f Selkirk (USA)-Ahohoney (Ahonoora) 4305$^{8}$ >48f<

**Dulford Lad** 5 b h In Fijar (USA)-Highsplasher (USA) (Bucksplasher (USA)) 1944a$^{3}$ 3754a$^{2}$ 4174a$^{2}$ >115f<

**Dumaani (USA)** 5 gr h Danzig (USA)-Desirable (Lord Gayle (USA)) 4953a$^{12}$ >118f<

**Dummer Golf Time** 3 ch c Clantime-Chablisse (Radetzky) 134$^{2}$ (264) 571$^{6}$ 824$^{4}$ 2228$^{10}$ 2578$^{3}$ 2785$^{5}$ 2968$^{2}$ (3650) 4054$^{2}$ 4232$^{5}$ 4688$^{22}$ >61+a 75f<

**Dunbar Hill (USA)** 2 f 4950a$^{11}$ >52a f<

**Duncombe Hall** 3 b g Salse (USA)-Springs Welcome (Blakeney) 1357$^{7}$ 1644$^{10}$ 3284$^{4}$ 3584$^{5}$ 3872$^{4}$ 3965$^{3}$ 4358$^{3}$ 4612$^{17}$ >38a 48f<

**Dundel (IRE)** 2 gr f Machiavellian (USA)-Dunoof (Shirley Heights) 1664$^{6}$ 3159$^{6}$ >71+f<

**Dune River** 7 b g Green Desert (USA)-River Spey (Mill Reef (USA)) 2722$^{8}$ >95a 79f<

**Dungeon Master (IRE)** 3 ch c Polish Patriot (USA)-Etty (Relko) 903a$^{3}$ 5074a$^{3}$ >99f<

**Dungeon Princess (IRE)** 3 b f Danehill (USA)-Taplow (Tap On Wood) 445$^{13}$ 492$^{2}$ 562$^{4}$ 616$^{6}$ 761$^{3}$ 914$^{4}$ 1025$^{2}$ 1119$^{17}$ 1908$^{2}$ (2019) 2567$^{4}$ 2980$^{8}$ 3165$^{9}$ 4098$^{12}$ 4550$^{11}$ >52f<

**Dunmebrains (IRE)** 3 ch f Rich Charlie-Branch Out (Star Appeal) 4898$^{17}$ >54f<

**Dunrowan** 3 b f Dunbeath (USA)-Sun Lamp (Pall Mall) 3960$^{3}$ (4437) 5007$^{12}$ >58f<

**Dunston Gold** 2 ch c Risk Me (FR)-Maria Whittaker (Cure The Blues (USA)) 4584$^{11}$ 4700$^{10}$ 4985$^{7}$ >10a 36f<

**Dunston Knight** 3 ch c Proud Knight (USA)-Lucy Johnston's (IRE) (Burslem) 4703$^{20}$

**Dunston Queen** 3 ch f Proud Knight (USA)-Alto Dancer (Noalto) 4429$^{15}$

**Dunston Star (IRE)** 3 b c Poet's Dream (IRE)-Cherry Glory (Final Straw) 4591$^{14}$ 5058$^{12}$ >2a f<

**Duo Master** 3 b g Primo Dominie-Musical Sally (USA) (The Minstrel (CAN)) 584$^{12}$ 873$^{15}$ 2417$^{5}$ 3426$^{13}$ 3677$^{9}$ 4045$^{22}$ 4221$^{7}$ 4701$^{17}$ >69df<

**Duralock Fencer** 3 b g General Wade-Madame Laffitte (Welsh Pageant) 387$^{3}$ 515$^{8}$ 863$^{12}$ 1506$^{9}$ 1809$^{9}$ 4480$^{16}$ >52a 45f<

**Durham** 5 ch g Caerleon (USA)-Sanctuary (Welsh Pageant) 108$^{9}$ 369$^{4}$ 485$^{2}$ 573$^{7}$ 656$^{3}$ 944$^{3}$ 1063$^{5}$ (2060) 2322$^{2}$ 2556$^{2}$ 2788$^{3}$ 3130$^{4}$ (3273) 3480$^{2}$ (4048) (4315) 4447$^{11}$ 4683$^{3}$ >56a 76f<

**Durshan (USA)** 7 ch g Shahrastani (USA)-Dukayna (Northfields (USA)) 2547$^{10}$ 3204$^{7}$ 3801$^{4}$ 4673$^{14}$ >43f<

**Dushyantor (USA)** 3 b c Sadler's Wells (USA)-Slightly Dangerous (USA) (Roberto (USA)) (923) 1114$^{2}$ 1791$^{2}$ 2473a$^{4}$ (3671) 4192$^{2}$ 4955a$^{7}$ >125f<

**Dusk in Daytona** 4 b f Beveled (USA)-Mount of Light (Sparkler) **1995:** 4362$^{3}$ 4457$^{9}$ **1996:** 65$^{8}$ 133$^{5}$ 218$^{6}$ 278$^{7}$ >55da 68f<

**Dust Dancer** 2 ch f Suave Dancer (USA)-Galaxie Dust (USA) (Blushing Groom (FR)) 4052$^{5}$ 4446$^{3}$ >73f<

**Duston Boy** 2 ch c Beveled (USA)-Julie's Star (IRE) (Thatching) 3349$^{11}$ 3807$^{12}$ 4091$^{12}$ >58f<

**Dusty Ocean (USA)** 5 ch h Chief's Crown (USA)-

Dusty Dollar (Kris) 151a$^{3}$ (288a) **>79f<**
**Dutosky 6** b m Doulab (USA)-Butosky (Busted) 1515$^{12}$ 4257$^{11}$ 4587$^{13}$ **>53a 51f<**
**Duty Sergeant (IRE) 7** b g Pennine Walk-Plainsong (FR) (Amen (FR)) 1347$^{8}$ (1472) 1874$^{9}$ 2341$^{5}$ 2574$^{22}$ 2871$^{7}$ 3802$^{5}$ *4332$^{4}$* *4563$^{10}$* ***>60a 33f<***
**Duveen (IRE) 6** b g Tate Gallery (USA)-Wish You Were Here (USA) (Secretariat (USA)) **1995:** *4525$^{7}$* **1996:** *37$^{3}$* *128$^{5}$* *198$^{10}$* **>57a f< (DEAD)**
**Dvorak (IRE) 5** b g Darshaan-Grace Note (FR) (Top Ville) **1995:** *4366$^{12}$* *4506$^{8}$* **1996:** *12$^{5}$* *69$^{8}$* *97$^{6}$* *365$^{10}$* *738$^{9}$* 852$^{12}$ **>59da 75f<**
**Dwingeloo (IRE) 3** b f Dancing Dissident (USA)-Thank One's Stars (Alzao (USA)) 846$^{9}$ 1512$^{6}$ **>76f<**
**Dyanko 3** b g Midyan (USA)-Regain (Relko) 1122$^{8}$ 1594$^{8}$ 1984$^{7}$ 2541$^{9}$ 3852$^{13}$ 3978$^{12}$ **>32df<**
**Dyhim Diamond (IRE) 2** ch c Night Shift (USA)-Happy Landing (FR) (Homing) (3032a) 3390a$^{2}$ 4035a$^{3}$ **>96f<**
**E**
**Eager To Please 2** ch g Keen-Ackcontent (USA) (Key To Content (USA)) 706$^{7}$ 930$^{6}$ 1537$^{11}$ *(2172)* *2199$^{2}$* 2685$^{4}$ *3087$^{3}$* *3455$^{6}$* *(4251)* *(4423)* 4549$^{7}$ 4803$^{11}$ **>70a 65f<**
**Eagle Canyon (IRE) 3** b br c Persian Bold-Chrism (Baptism) *364$^{5}$* *444$^{14}$* 575$^{14}$ *(1027)* *1152$^{2}$* 1345$^{2}$ 1773$^{4}$ (2067) 2549$^{2}$ 3073$^{4}$ 3617$^{4}$ 3997$^{10}$ 4431$^{11}$ 4673$^{16}$ **>78a 81f<**
**Eagle Day (USA) 5** b h Phone Trick (USA)-Ellen L (USA) (To Market) **1995:** *4421$^{11}$* **>53a 82f<**
**Early Peace (IRE) 4** b g Bluebird (USA)-Everything Nice (Sovereign Path) 1314$^{12}$ (1506) 3828$^{12}$ 3947$^{19}$ 4121$^{8}$ 4426$^{6}$ 4588$^{6}$ 4766$^{5}$ **>61f<**
**Early Warning 3** br f Warning-Ile de Danse (Ile de Bourbon (USA)) 1855$^{11}$ 2529$^{8}$ 2718$^{7}$ *3608$^{9}$* *4068$^{10}$* ***>12a 41f<***
**East Barns (IRE) 8** gr g Godswalk (USA)-Rocket Lass (Touch Paper) *43$^{8}$* *87$^{6}$* *239$^{13}$* *257$^{5}$* *297$^{7}$* *384$^{9}$* *440$^{19}$* 496$^{7}$ 527$^{9}$ 688$^{12}$ 4240$^{5}$ 4808$^{13}$ **>33a 41f<**
**Eastern Eagle (IRE) 2** b c Polish Patriot (USA)-Lady's Turn (Rymer) 4782$^{5}$ **>61f<**
**Eastern Firedragon (IRE) 2** b f Shalford (IRE)-Doobie Do (Derring-Do) 2138$^{5}$ 2361$^{6}$ 3462$^{11}$ 3941$^{10}$ **>58f<**
**Eastern Prophets 3** b g Emarati (USA)-Four Love (Pas de Seul) 565$^{5}$ 790a$^{3}$ 989$^{9}$ 1820$^{12}$ 2007$^{10}$ 2143$^{14}$ 4505$^{8}$ 4765$^{5}$ 4869$^{9}$ 5039$^{5}$ **>83f<**
**Eastleigh 7** b g Efisio-Blue Jane (Blue Cashmere) **1995:** *4378$^{8}$* *4406$^{5}$* *4457$^{11}$* *4493$^{4}$* *4525$^{6}$* **1996:** *30$^{7}$* *62$^{5}$* *114$^{5}$* *174$^{4}$* *412$^{4}$* *501$^{4}$* *545$^{9}$* 3981$^{10}$ *4573$^{4}$* **>55a 31f<**
**East Sheen 4** b f Salse (USA)-Madam Cody (Hot Spark) 1173$^{10}$ 1655$^{13}$ 3141$^{12}$ **>47f<**
**Easycall 2** b c Forzando-Up And Going (FR) (Never so Bold) (1987) (2890) (3156) 3690$^{4}$ (4191) 4519$^{6}$ (4677) **>112f<**
**Easy Choice (USA) 4** b c Easy Goer (USA)-Monroe (USA) (Sir Ivor) **1995:** *(4418)* *(4451)* *(4520)* **1996:** *61$^{12}$* *243$^{2}$* *263$^{3}$* *809$^{18}$* 1078$^{8}$ 1440$^{14}$ 1623$^{7}$ 1841$^{13}$ 3991$^{10}$ 4121$^{9}$ 4351$^{4}$ **>79a 54f<**
**Easy Dollar 4** ch g Gabitat-Burglars Girl (Burglar) 579$^{2}$ 673$^{4}$ 818$^{2}$ 1129$^{7}$ 1879$^{3}$ 2880$^{2}$ 3573a$^{8}$ 3759$^{7}$ **>112f<**
**Easy Jet (POL) 4** b c Robellino (USA)-Etourdie (USA) (Arctic Tern (USA)) *1154$^{2}$* 1902$^{2}$ 2312$^{3}$ 2858$^{3}$ 4329$^{12}$ 4769$^{26}$ **>74f<**
**Easy Listening (USA) 4** b g Easy Goer (USA)-Queen of Song (USA) (His Majesty (USA)) 581$^{11}$ 1066$^{3}$ 2603$^{2}$ 3073$^{6}$ **>93f<**
**Easy Number (USA) 3** ch f Easy Goer (USA)-Treizieme (USA) (The Minstrel (CAN)) 2529$^{12}$
**Easy Option (IRE) 4** ch f Prince Sabo-Brazen Faced (Bold And Free) *1581a$^{2}$* 4660a$^{4}$ 4774$^{3}$ 4917$^{4}$ **>117f<**
**Eaton Park (IRE) 2** ch c Mac's Imp (USA)-Pepilin (Coquelin (USA)) 1046$^{2}$ 1445$^{4}$ 1871$^{12}$ 4182$^{10}$ 4350$^{6}$ **>65f<**
**Eau de Cologne 4** b g Persian Bold-No More Rosies (Warpath) *(619)* 816$^{10}$ 1022$^{5}$ 3939$^{5}$ 4483$^{3}$ 4683$^{15}$ **>67f<**
**Eben Naas (USA) 3** b c Dayjur (USA)-Regal State (USA) (Affirmed (USA)) **1995:** *4538$^{8}$* **1996:** *134$^{5}$* *234$^{3}$* *300$^{2}$* *(562)* (819) 1001$^{10}$ 1363$^{17}$ 2179$^{5}$ **>54a 63df< (DEAD)**
**Ebony Boy 3** bl c Sayf El Arab (USA)-Actress (Known Fact (USA)) **1995:** *4431$^{6}$* *4509$^{4}$* **1996:** *35$^{5}$* *280$^{9}$* *382$^{5}$* *1780$^{W}$* 2061$^{11}$ *2367$^{10}$* **>47a 38f<**
**Ebony T-A-P-S 3** bl f Adbass (USA)-August Seventeenth (Sharpo) *2234$^{8}$* ***>20f<***
**Eccentric Dancer 3** b f Rambo Dancer (CAN)-Lady Eccentric (IRE) (Magical Wonder (USA)) 595$^{18}$ 686$^{12}$ 1068$^{11}$ *1456$^{3}$* *1850$^{14}$* 2026$^{9}$ 3059$^{9}$ *3626$^{2}$* *4690$^{10}$* 4921$^{14}$ *5056$^{11}$* **>51a 47f<**
**Ecoute (USA) 3** b f Manila (USA)-Soundings (USA) (Mr Prospector (USA)) 905a$^{2}$ 1396a$^{3}$ 3030a$^{2}$ 3391a$^{4}$ 5072a$^{3}$ **>105f<**
**Ectomorph (IRE) 3** ch f Sharp Victor (USA)-Hail To You (USA) (Kirtling) 1508$^{W}$ 2297$^{6}$ **>8f<**
**Edan Heights 4** b g Heights of Gold-Edna (Shiny Tenth) 439$^{9}$ 968$^{11}$ 2226$^{8}$ (2549) 3125$^{U}$ 3447$^{2}$ 3947$^{13}$ 4326$^{4}$ 4675$^{9}$ (4826) 5046$^{13}$ **>82f<**
**Eden Dancer 4** b g Shareef Dancer (USA)-Dash (Connaught) 995$^{19}$ 3297$^{13}$ 4345$^{5}$ **>41f<**
**Edessa (IRE) 4** b f Tirol-Damia (Vision (USA)) 4410a$^{3}$ **>113f<**
**Edgar Kirby 5** ch g Caerleon (USA)-Martha Stevens (USA) (Super Concorde (USA)) *713$^{4}$* 1074$^{8}$ 1533$^{3}$ *2081$^{10}$* **>43a 65f<**
**Edipo Re 4** b c Slip Anchor-Lady Barrister (Law Society (USA)) 2250$^{2}$ 4434$^{4}$ **>91f<**
**Editor's Note (USA) 3** ch c Forty Niner (USA)-Beware of the Cat (USA) (Caveat (USA)) *1391a$^{3}$* *(1946a)* *4956a$^{12}$* ***>128a 116f<***
**Ed's Folly (IRE) 3** b c Fayruz-Tabriya (Nishapour (FR)) 443$^{9}$ 571$^{8}$ 978$^{3}$ 1172$^{6}$ 1624$^{11}$ **>62f<**
**Eduardo (ITY) 3** 4542a$^{8}$ **>83f<**
**Efaad (IRE) 5** b g Shaadi (USA)-Krismas River (Kris) *1031$^{6}$* *1488$^{6}$* *1717$^{7}$* **>29a 68f<**
**Effectual 3** b c Efisio-Moharabuiee (Pas de Seul) 892$^{7}$ 1104$^{3}$ 1465$^{2}$ 1656$^{4}$ **>78f<**
**Effervescence 2** ch c Efisio-Petite Elite (Anfield) 2243$^{6}$ 2559$^{4}$ 2699$^{2}$ 2942$^{2}$ 3128$^{5}$ 4043$^{8}$ 4512$^{8}$ 4867$^{2}$ 5043$^{10}$ **>78f<**
**Efficacious (IRE) 3** ch f Efisio-Bushti Music (Bustino) **1995:** *4462$^{5}$* **1996:** *597$^{5}$* 761$^{2}$ 1654$^{20}$ 1883$^{4}$ 2191$^{6}$ 2409$^{15}$ 2768$^{3}$ 2979$^{6}$ 3303$^{2}$ 3965$^{9}$ *4998$^{7}$* **>44a 55f<**
**Efficacy 5** b m Efisio-Lady Killane (Reform) **1995:** *4447$^{6}$* **1996:** *259$^{5}$* *282$^{10}$* *356$^{2}$* *413$^{3}$* *653$^{4}$* *769$^{4}$* 862$^{10}$ 1715$^{6}$ 2154$^{14}$ *3420$^{2}$* *4081$^{8}$* **>61a 40f<**
**Efharisto 7** b g Dominion-Excellent Alibi (USA) (Exceller (USA)) *766$^{5}$* 913$^{5}$ 2055$^{12}$ **>78f<**
**Efipetite 3** ch f Efisio-Petite Elite (Anfield) **1995:** *4375$^{3}$* *4433$^{10}$* **1996:** *32$^{7}$* *49$^{4}$* *123$^{5}$* *171$^{3}$* *237$^{4}$* *258$^{3}$* *(281)* *332$^{2}$* *344$^{3}$* *404$^{4}$* *531$^{3}$* *605$^{3}$* *781$^{4}$* *1027$^{6}$* *1490$^{5}$* 1721$^{8}$ *2417$^{9}$* 3059$^{12}$ 3427$^{7}$ 3619$^{14}$ 3866$^{12}$ **>44a 36f<**
**Efizia 6** b m Efisio-Millie Grey (Grey Ghost) 1698$^{3}$ 2152$^{5}$ 3452$^{5}$ **>67f<**
**Efra 7** b g Efisio-Ra Ra (Lord Gayle (USA)) 846$^{2}$ 1442$^{6}$ 4788$^{11}$ **>69f<**
**Egeo (FR) 3** ch c Kris-Robertiya (FR) (Don Roberto (USA)) 797a$^{2}$ **>106f<**
**Eight Sharp (IRE) 4** b g Sure Blade (USA)-Octavia Girl (Octavo (USA)) *439$^{21}$* 589$^{18}$ **>79df<**
**Eire Leath-Sceal 9** b g Legend of France (USA)-Killarney Belle (USA) (Irish Castle (USA)) *1977$^{13}$* ***>67f<***
**Ejeer (IRE) 2** b g Jareer (USA)-Precious Egg (Home Guard (USA)) 3685$^{7}$ **>27f<**
**Ekaterini Paritsi 2** b f Timeless Times (USA)-Wych Willow (Hard Fought) 741$^{3}$ 869$^{3}$ 1021$^{2}$ 1164$^{2}$ *1459$^{2}$* *1645$^{7}$* *2750$^{5}$* **>54a 60f<**
**Ela Agapi Mou (USA) 3** b g Storm Bird (CAN)-Vaguar (USA) (Vaguely Noble) 860$^{11}$ 1079$^{10}$ 1338$^{5}$ *2322$^{6}$* *3860$^{3}$* 3965$^{2}$ 4551$^{11}$ **>38a 60f<**
**Ela-Aristokrati (IRE) 4** b c Danehill (USA)-Dubai Lady (Kris) 831$^{11}$ (1793) 2546$^{4}$ 3431$^{2}$ 4066$^{3}$ **>118f<**
**Ela Man Howa 5** b g Mtoto-Top Treat (USA) (Topsider (USA)) 1019$^{7}$ 1788$^{4}$ 2779$^{8}$ 2871$^{6}$ 3218$^{7}$ 3463$^{4}$ 3928$^{5}$ 4315$^{6}$ 4365$^{13}$ **>59da 56f<**
**Ela-Ment (IRE) 4** b g Ela-Mana-Mou-Dorado Llave (USA) (Well Decorated (USA)) *37$^{8}$* *745$^{8}$* 1174$^{10}$ *1444$^{9}$* **>26a 23f<**
**El Angelo (USA) 4** b c El Gran Senor (USA)-Angela Serra (Arctic Tern (USA)) 4656a$^{3}$ **>120f<**
**Ela Patricia (IRE) 2** ch f Shalford (IRE)-Alice Brackloon (USA) (Melyno) 2712$^{9}$ 3848$^{14}$ 4096$^{5}$ **>30f<**
**Elashath (USA) 3** b c El Gran Senor (USA)-Gorgeoso (USA) (Damascus (USA)) 687$^{10}$ 1668$^{6}$ (2163) (2780) 3220$^{4}$ 4257$^{2}$ 4438$^{2}$ **>75f<**
**El Atrevido (FR) 6** ch g Rainbow Quest (USA)-Majestic Peck (USA) (Majestic Light (USA)) **1995:** *4419$^{8}$* **1996:** *216$^{3}$* *318$^{7}$* **>72a 16f<**
**Ela-Yie-Mou (IRE) 3** ch c Kris-Green Lucia (Green Dancer (USA)) 731$^{7}$ 993$^{3}$ (1415) 1783$^{3}$ 2233$^{4}$ 3155$^{8}$ 4862$^{11}$ **>85df<**
**Elbaaha 2** ch f Arazi (USA)-Gesedeh (Ela-Mana-Mou) 3206$^{3}$ 3764$^{2}$ 4608$^{3}$ **>75f<**
**El Bailador (IRE) 5** b g Dance of Life (USA)-Sharp Ego (USA) (Sharpen Up) *(254)* *429$^{4}$* **>62a 71f<**
**El Bardador (IRE) 3** b g Thatching-Osmunda (Mill Reef (USA)) 1797$^{7}$ 2181$^{9}$ 3442$^{12}$ 3780$^{4}$ *4095$^{8}$* *(4237)* 4626$^{20}$ 4815$^{9}$ 5053$^{4}$ **>61f<**
**Elburg (IRE) 6** b g Ela-Mana-Mou-Iosifa (Top Ville) *265$^{5}$* *449$^{16}$* ***>63a 74f<***
**El Ceremonioso (SPA) 4** gr c Glauco (SPA)-Krone (SPA) (Crystal Palace (FR)) 3747a$^{2}$ **>116f<**
**El Don 4** b g High Kicker (USA)-Madam Gerard (Brigadier Gerard) **1995:** *4420$^{11}$* **1996:** *1416$^{6}$* 1472$^{8}$ 1696$^{8}$ 4810$^{11}$ **>16a 44f<**
**Eldorado (IRE) 2** b c Ela-Mana-Mou-Happy Tidings (Hello Gorgeous (USA)) (4477) 4973$^{2}$ **>90f<**
**Eleanor May 3** b br f Crofthall-Melaura Belle (Meldrum) *524$^{7}$* 626$^{7}$ 1608$^{12}$ **>34f<**
**Election Day (IRE) 4** b c Sadler's Wells (USA)-Hellenic (Darshaan) (687) 1017$^{2}$ (1176) 2113$^{8}$ 5045$^{4}$ **>120f<**
**Elegant Dance 2** ch f Statoblest-Furry Dance (USA) (Nureyev (USA)) 3159$^{8}$ **>64f<**
**Elegantissima 3** b f Polish Precedent (USA)-Ela Meem (USA) (Kris) **1995:** *4535$^{4}$* **1996:** *320$^{5}$* *550$^{15}$* *859$^{W}$* *1356$^{7}$* 1890$^{18}$ **>57a 37f<**
**Elegant Warning (IRE) 2** b f Warning-Dance It (USA) (Believe It (USA)) 3234$^{2}$ 3593$^{3}$ (4570) (4873) **>108f<**
**Elementary 13** b g Busted-Santa Vittoria (Ragusa) **1995:** *4442$^{8}$* **>73a 82f<**
**Elfin Queen (IRE) 3** b f Fairy King (USA)-West of Eden (Crofter (USA)) *131$^{5}$* *183$^{6}$* *292$^{4}$* *359$^{6}$* *405$^{13}$* **>53a 70f<**
**Elhafid (USA) 2** ch c Nureyev (USA)-Shy Dame (USA) (Damascus (USA)) 2224$^{7}$ 2708$^{9}$ 4370$^{7}$ **>68f<**

**Elinor Dashwood (IRE)** 2 br f Fools Holme (USA)-Nordic Pride (Horage) 4024a$^{30}$ **>56f<**
**Elite Bliss (IRE)** 4 b f Tirol-Krismas River (Kris) 1159$^{3}$ 1596$^{3}$ 1828$^{4}$ 2348$^{8}$ 2776$^{10}$ 4904$^{5}$ **>49f<**
**Elite Force (IRE)** 3 b g Fairy King (USA)-La Petruschka (Ballad Rock) 584$^{3}$ 774$^{2}$ 987$^{12}$ 3599$^{6}$ 4231$^{6}$ 4724$^{11}$ **>76f<**
**Elite Hope (USA)** 4 ch f Moment of Hope (USA)-Chervil (USA) (Greenough (USA)) 809$^{16}$ 1018$^{13}$ 1962$^{6}$ 2722$^{9}$ 3800$^{6}$ 4432$^{16}$ 4686$^{22}$ 4905$^{9}$ 5059$^{2}$ **>59a 64f<**
**Elite Justice** 4 ch g Absalom-Persian Express (Persian Bold) 48$^{11}$ 87$^{9}$ 124$^{12}$ 1698$^{6}$ **>39a 66f<**
**Elite Racing** 4 b f Risk Me (FR)-Hot Stone (Hotfoot) 629$^{17}$ (1311) 1665$^{12}$ 2507$^{4}$ 2716$^{14}$ 3257$^{13}$ 3645$^{7}$ **>43f<**
**Elite Reg** 7 b g Electric-Coppice (Pardao) 2385$^{5}$ **>37f<**
**Eliza** 2 ch f Shavian-One Degree (Crooner) 4798$^{8}$ **>51f<**
**Ella Lamees** 2 b f Statoblest-Lamees (USA) (Lomond (USA)) 4782$^{10}$ 5034$^{9}$ **>63f<**
**Elle Est Revenue (IRE)** 2 b f Night Shift (USA)-Shelbiana (USA) (Chieftain II) 3390a$^{3}$ **>85f<**
**Ell Ell Eff** 3 ch f Pharly (FR)-Yen (AUS) (Biscay (AUS)) 1104$^{W}$ 1999$^{7}$ 2297$^{7}$ **>12f<**
**Elle Mac** 3 b f Merdon Melody-Tripolitaine (FR) (Nonoalco (USA)) 3058$^{6}$ 3451$^{8}$ **>31?f<**
**Ellens Lad (IRE)** 2 b c Polish Patriot (USA)-Lady Ellen (Horage) 1896$^{8}$ 3114$^{7}$ 3615$^{12}$ 4230$^{3}$ (4425) 4878$^{5}$ (4966) **>73f<**
**Elle Shaped (IRE)** 6 b g Treasure Kay-Mamie's Joy (Prince Tenderfoot (USA)) **1995:** 4536$^{10}$ **>24a 89f<**
**Ellie Ardensky** 4 b f Slip Anchor-Circus Ring (High Top) 1793$^{5}$ 2145$^{2}$ 2533$^{8}$ 3125$^{12}$ 3836$^{7}$ 4063$^{2}$ 4467$^{7}$ **>105f<**
**Ellway Lady (IRE)** 2 br f Be My Native (USA)-Scaravie (IRE) (Drumalis) 2942$^{9}$ 3438$^{4}$ 3685$^{11}$ 4384$^{4}$ **>69f<**
**Elly Fleetfoot (IRE)** 4 b f Elmaamul (USA)-Fleetwood Fancy (Taufan (USA)) **1995:** 4366$^{11}$ 4415$^{12}$ **1996:** 37$^{6}$ 165$^{6}$ 216$^{9}$ 319$^{4}$ 1462$^{8}$ 1682$^{8}$ 1979$^{11}$ 2740$^{2}$ 2941$^{3}$ 3113$^{2}$ 3260$^{7}$ 3435$^{10}$ 4236$^{14}$ **>50a 62f<**
**Elmi Elmak (IRE)** 3 b c Fairy King (USA)-Ascensiontide (Ela-Mana-Mou) 1617$^{2}$ (2913) (3430) **>101f<**
**Elnadim (USA)** 2 b br c Danzig (USA)-Elle Seule (USA) (Exclusive Native (USA)) 3706$^{4}$ 4962$^{2}$ **>95f<**
**El Nido** 8 ch g Adonijah-Seleter (Hotfoot) **1995:** 4391$^{4}$ **1996:** 73$^{3}$ 138$^{3}$ 284$^{4}$ 369$^{2}$ **>56a 53f<**
**El Opera (IRE)** 3 b f Sadler's Wells (USA)-Ridge The Times (USA) (Riva Ridge (USA)) (1662) (2715) 3568a$^{5}$ 3836$^{6}$ 4126$^{4}$ **>107f<**
**El Penitente (IRE)** 3 b c Ela-Mana-Mou-Penny Habit (Habitat) (982) 4520$^{9}$ **>89f<**
**Elpida (USA)** 4 b g Trempolino (USA)-All For Hope (USA) (Sensitive Prince (USA)) **1995:** 4455$^{7}$ **1996:** 1109$^{10}$ 1655$^{12}$ (2014) 2183$^{10}$ 2408$^{7}$ **>58a 66f<**
**Elpidos** 4 ch g Bold Arrangement-Thalassa (IRE) (Appiani II) 629$^{10}$ 1069$^{10}$ 3815$^{8}$ 3937$^{20}$ 4190$^{23}$ 4483$^{10}$ 4812$^{7}$ **>48f<**
**El Presidente** 3 b c Presidium-Spanish Princess (King of Spain) 1656$^{9}$ 2383$^{8}$ 4124$^{7}$ 4513$^{10}$ 4785$^{8}$ **>66f<**
**Elraas (USA)** 4 b g Gulch (USA)-Full Card (USA) (Damascus (USA)) 2130$^{17}$ 2340$^{13}$ 2745$^{7}$ 3097$^{6}$ 3420$^{8}$ **>32a 5f<**
**Elrayahin** 2 ch f Riverman (USA)-Gracious Beauty (USA) (Nijinsky (CAN)) 2315$^{3}$ 3159$^{4}$ 3764$^{3}$ 4084$^{3}$ 4384$^{11}$ **>84f<**
**Elriyadh (USA)** 2 b c Time For A Change (USA)-All My Memories (USA) (Little Current (USA)) 3407$^{2}$ 3779$^{3}$ **>70f<**
**Elsaleet (USA)** 3 b br c Storm Cat (USA)-Blushing Redhead (USA) (Blushing Groom (FR)) (672) 936$^{6}$ **>95f<**
**Elshabiba (USA)** 3 b br c Dayjur (USA)-Sweet Roberta (USA) (Roberto (USA)) 574$^{3}$ **>97f<**
**Eltish (USA)** 4 b c Cox's Ridge (USA)-Nimble Feet (USA) (Danzig (USA)) 2842a$^{3}$ **>116a 122f<**
**Elton Ledger (IRE)** 7 b g Cyrano de Bergerac-Princess of Nashua (Crowned Prince (USA)) **1995:** 4427$^{10}$ **1996:** 88$^{8}$ 126$^{7}$ 168$^{3}$ 218$^{8}$ 257$^{4}$ (425) (518) 607$^{4}$ 1029$^{2}$ 1094$^{5}$ 1492$^{4}$ 1716$^{2}$ (1971) 2084$^{4}$ 3089$^{3}$ 3601$^{6}$ (4094) 4987$^{2}$ **>77a 53f<**
**Elusive Star** 6 b m Ardross-Star Flower (Star Appeal) 174$^{6}$ **>41a f<**
**El Volador** 9 br g Beldale Flutter (USA)-Pharjoy (FR) (Pharly (FR)) **1995:** 4506$^{4}$ **1996:** 80$^{3}$ (128) 296$^{2}$ (411) 498$^{3}$ 3141$^{11}$ 3520$^{3}$ 4048$^{8}$ **>80a 58f<**
**E-Mail (IRE)** 2 b c High Estate-Water Pixie (IRE) (Dance of Life (USA)) 4461$^{8}$ 4825$^{13}$ 5049$^{4}$ **>64f<**
**Embankment (IRE)** 6 b or br g Tate Gallery (USA)-Great Leighs (Vaigly Great) 728$^{13}$ 967$^{9}$ 1190$^{12}$ 1843$^{3}$ 2010$^{8}$ 2883$^{7}$ 3123$^{10}$ 3786$^{3}$ (4059) 4202$^{2}$ 4463$^{7}$ 4799$^{2}$ 4901$^{8}$ **>71a 84f<**
**Ember** 3 b f Nicholas (USA)-Cinderwench (Crooner) 921$^{8}$ 1171$^{8}$ 1692$^{4}$ 2251$^{15}$ 4513$^{8}$ 4691$^{14}$ 4967$^{14}$ **>48f<**
**Embezzler** 4 b g Emarati (USA)-Double Touch (FR) (Nonoalco (USA)) 2316$^{14}$ **>57a 43df<**
**Embroidered** 3 br f Charmer-Emblazon (Wolver Hollow) 1657$^{7}$ 1995$^{10}$ 2405$^{9}$ 3435$^{8}$ 3977$^{10}$ 4499$^{11}$ **>28a 29f<**
**Embryonic (IRE)** 4 b c Prince Rupert (FR)-Belle Viking (FR) (Riverman (USA)) 753$^{3}$ 1436$^{2}$ 1529$^{2}$ 1802$^{8}$ 2330$^{4}$ 2912$^{4}$ 3266$^{3}$ 3486$^{2}$ 3834$^{2}$ 4112$^{7}$ 4447$^{6}$ 4771$^{10}$ **>86f<**
**Emei Shan** 3 br f Inca Chief (USA)-Tricata (Electric) 4323$^{16}$ **>26f<**
**Emerging Market** 4 b g Emarati (USA)-Flitteriss Park (Beldale Flutter (USA)) 679$^{4}$ 876$^{4}$ 1149$^{6}$ (2114) 2623$^{11}$ 3232$^{16}$ 4314$^{6}$ 4554$^{9}$ **>107f<**
**Emily-Jayne** 2 b f Absalom-Tearful Reunion (Pas de Seul) 975$^{8}$ 2161$^{4}$ 2606$^{9}$ **>56f<**
**Emilyjill** 2 b f Emarati (USA)-Crackerjill (Sparkler) 643$^{5}$ 1036$^{5}$ 1413$^{6}$ 2685$^{2}$ 3075$^{4}$ 3330$^{8}$ 3651$^{7}$ **>59f<**
**Emily-Mou (IRE)** 4 b f Cadeaux Genereux-Sarajill (High Line) 1145$^{18}$ 1450$^{8}$ 1625$^{2}$ 1775$^{11}$ 1983$^{4}$ 2412$^{5}$ 2581$^{2}$ 2743$^{4}$ **>47a 78f<**
**Emmas Breeze** 2 ch f Anshan-Baby Flo (Porto Bello) 590$^{6}$ 1531$^{7}$ 1904$^{5}$ (2207) 2795$^{7}$ 3169$^{7}$ **>54f<**
**Emma's Risk** 2 b f Risk Me (FR)-Lana's Pet (Tina's Pet) 1968$^{7}$ 2199$^{3}$ 2406$^{3}$ 4576$^{10}$ 4777$^{9}$ **>21a 42f<**
**Emnala (IRE)** 4 b f Contract Law (USA)-African Light (Kalaglow) 4426$^{15}$ 4998$^{10}$ 5052$^{9}$ **>19a 17f<**
**Emperors Wood** 5 b g Then Again-Silver Empress (Octavo (USA)) 103$^{8}$ 845$^{13}$ 1319$^{17}$ 1893$^{W}$ **>11a 30f<**
**Emy Coasting (USA)** 3 b f El Gran Senor (USA)-Coast Patrol (USA) (Cornish Prince) 710$^{10}$ 966$^{3}$ 1333$^{9}$ 1787$^{2}$ **>86df<**
**Enamel Tiger** 3 ch g Risk Me (FR)-Dancing Belle (Dance In Time (CAN)) 2718$^{11}$ 2918$^{9}$ 3089$^{11}$ **>23a 48f<**
**Enavius (IRE)** 2 b c Lycius (USA)-Enaya (Caerleon (USA)) 4818$^{8}$ 4991$^{10}$ **>43f<**
**Enchanted Guest (IRE)** 3 ch f Be My Guest (USA)-Last Blessing (Final Straw) 550$^{13}$ 663$^{9}$ 934$^{2}$ (1340) 1805$^{4}$ 2228$^{11}$ 3419$^{13}$ **>77f<**
**Enchantica** 2 ch f Timeless Times (USA)-North Pine (Import) 596$^{4}$ 823$^{2}$ 1062$^{2}$ 1760$^{3}$ 2699$^{4}$ 4767$^{3}$ 4907$^{3}$ 5005$^{3}$ **>68f<**
**Enchanting Eve** 2 ch f Risk Me (FR)-Red Sails (Town And Country) (506) 715$^{6}$ 996$^{7}$ 1471$^{4}$ (1720) (1813) 2382$^{4}$ **>70a 66f<**
**Encore M'Lady (IRE)** 5 b m Dancing Dissident (USA)-Diva Encore (Star Appeal) **1995:** 4484$^{4}$ (4502) **1996:** 88$^{11}$ 127$^{2}$ 170$^{7}$ 1786$^{9}$ (2030) 2363$^{11}$ (2929) 3101$^{5}$ 3650$^{6}$ 4071$^{7}$ 4226$^{14}$ 4692$^{16}$ 4768$^{16}$ 4979$^{7}$ **>75da 59f<**
**Endaxi Sam** 3 b c St Enodoc-Stos (IRE) (Bluebird (USA)) 2579$^{P}$ 2918$^{8}$ 3472$^{14}$ 4674$^{13}$ **>41f<**
**Endless Fantasy** 4 b f Kalaglow-Headrest (Habitat) **1995:** 4355$^{6}$ 4463$^{3}$ 4530$^{11}$ **1996:** 140$^{6}$ **>61da 41f<**
**Endowment** 4 ch g Cadeaux Genereux-Palm Springs (Top Ville) 184$^{10}$ 4176$^{7}$ 4431$^{15}$ **>61f<**
**Eneldo (SPA)** 3 b c Luth Dancer (USA)-La Ribert (SPA) (Brabant (SPA)) 3755a$^{2}$ **>101f<**
**Energy Man** 3 b g Hadeer-Cataclysmic (Ela-Mana-Mou) 614$^{14}$ 1363$^{11}$ 1674$^{15}$ 3102$^{16}$ **>55df<**
**English Invader** 5 b h Rainbow Quest (USA)-Modica (Persian Bold) 647$^{11}$ 1336$^{6}$ 2690$^{8}$ **>94df<**
**Enriched (IRE)** 3 b f Generous (IRE)-Embla (Dominion) 707$^{7}$ 4235$^{3}$ 4622$^{3}$ (4824) 4992$^{3}$ **>86f<**
**Entice (FR)** 2 b f Selkirk (USA)-Loure (USA) (Lyphard (USA)) 4305$^{7}$ (4512) (4792) **>88f<**
**Entrepreneur** 2 b c Sadler's Wells (USA)-Exclusive Order (USA) (Exclusive Native (USA)) 3221$^{4}$ (3682) (4366) **>95+f<**
**En Vacances (IRE)** 4 b f Old Vic-Welcome Break (Wollow) 449$^{9}$ 647$^{10}$ 1194$^{2}$ 1710$^{2}$ 2042$^{24}$ (3598) 3983$^{15}$ 4771$^{2}$ 4965$^{6}$ **>72a 93f<**
**Environmentalist (IRE)** 5 b g Sure Blade (USA)-Vielle (Ribero) **1995:** 4370$^{5}$ 4463$^{P}$ **>64a 69f< (DEAD)**
**Epaulette** 2 b f Warrshan (USA)-Dame Helene (USA) (Sir Ivor) 538$^{5}$ **>30f<**
**Epic Stand** 2 b c Presidium-Surf Bird (Shareef Dancer (USA)) 1884$^{5}$ 2211$^{6}$ 3637$^{9}$ 3969$^{6}$ 4319$^{7}$ (4990) **>63f<**
**Eponine** 2 ch f Sharpo-Norska (Northfields (USA)) 2531$^{5}$ 2712$^{6}$ 3919$^{5}$ 4449$^{3}$ **>75f<**
**Epsilon** 2 b f Environment Friend-Girette (USA) (General Assembly (USA)) 3663$^{6}$ **>48f<**
**Epworth** 2 b f Unfuwain (USA)-Positive Attitude (Red Sunset) 4861$^{8}$ **>66f<**
**Equal Rights (IRE)** 2 b c Royal Academy (USA)-Lady Liberty (NZ) (Noble Bijou (USA)) 2580$^{2}$ (2909) 3143$^{3}$ (4023a) 4462$^{4}$ **>107f<**
**Equerry** 5 b g Midyan (USA)-Supreme Kingdom (Take A Reef) 1505$^{2}$ (1672) (2293) 2552$^{7}$ (3101) 3430$^{8}$ 3833$^{9}$ 3981$^{3}$ 4136$^{9}$ (4296) **>68a 88?f<**
**Equilibrium** 4 b f Statoblest-Allander Girl (Miralgo) **1995:** 4444$^{9}$ **>46a 58f<**
**Eric's Bett** 3 b g Chilibang-Mira Lady (Henbit (USA)) 1072$^{8}$ 1341$^{10}$ 2188$^{6}$ 2514$^{2}$ 3461$^{5}$ 3805$^{11}$ **>66f<**
**Erin Bird (FR)** 5 b m Bluebird (USA)-Maid of Erin (USA) (Irish River (FR)) **1995:** 4497a$^{2}$ **>116f<**
**Erlemo** 7 b g Mummy's Game-Empress Catherine (Welsh Pageant) 2182$^{5}$ 3335$^{10}$ **>44f<**
**Erlking (IRE)** 6 b g Fairy King (USA)-Cape of Storms (Fordham (USA)) (23) 69$^{5}$ **>45a f<**
**Erosion (IRE)** 2 b c Green Desert (USA)-Swept Away (Kris) 3773$^{5}$ 4318$^{3}$ 4751$^{2}$ 4867$^{4}$ **>76f<**
**Errant** 4 b c Last Tycoon-Wayward Lass (USA) (Hail the Pirates (USA)) **1995:** 4382$^{4}$ 4540$^{2}$ **1996:** 24$^{4}$ 106$^{2}$ 179$^{10}$ 296$^{5}$ (337) (486) 553$^{6}$ 920$^{6}$ 1440$^{13}$ 1655$^{7}$ 1996$^{3}$ **>71a 64df<**
**Ertlon** 6 b g Shareef Dancer (USA)-Sharpina (Sharpen Up) **1995:** 4482$^{12}$ **1996:** 223$^{7}$ 357$^{11}$ 554$^{11}$ 744$^{3}$ 876$^{24}$ 1048$^{5}$ 1962$^{8}$ 2283$^{3}$ 2729$^{9}$ 3265$^{4}$

3445$^{14}$ 3833$^{10}$ 4240$^{D}$ 4463$^{11}$ 4719$^{5}$ 4909$^{6}$ *5002$^{4}$* **>74a 82f<**

**Erupt 3** b g Beveled (USA)-Sparkling Sovereign (Sparkler) *571$^{4}$* 4058$^{15}$ 4581$^{22}$ 4888$^{17}$ **>74f<**

**Erzadjan (IRE) 6** b g Kahyasi-Ezana (Ela-Mana-Mou) *811$^{6}$* ***>88f<***

**Esbooain (FR) 7** b h Rainbow Quest (USA)-Wind Spring (FR) (Baldric) *436a$^{3}$* **>96a f<**

**Escobar (IRE) 3** br c Cyrano de Bergerac-Gale Force Seven (Strong Gale) 775$^{17}$ **>54f<**

**Escrito (USA) 3** b c Cox's Ridge (USA)-Lyphard's Starlite (USA) 4026a$^{2}$ 5015a$^{4}$ **>108f<**

**E Sharp (USA) 2** b f Diesis-Elvia (USA) (Roberto (USA)) 1433$^{5}$ **>43f<**

**Eshtiaal (USA) 2** b br c Riverman (USA)-Lady Cutlass (USA) (Cutlass (USA)) 4512$^{3}$ 4920$^{5}$ **>85f<**

**Eskimo Kiss (IRE) 3** b f Distinctly North (USA)-Felicitas (Mr Fluorocarbon) 522$^{9}$ 890$^{10}$ 1534$^{7}$ 1979$^{3}$ 2192$^{4}$ 2716$^{6}$ 3633$^{2}$ 3965$^{4}$ 4236$^{9}$ 4815$^{4}$ 4898$^{4}$ **>50f<**

**Eskimo Nel (IRE) 5** ch m Shy Groom (USA)-North Lady (Northfields (USA)) (508) 547$^{5}$ (641) 787$^{2}$ (963) 4900$^{6}$ **>24a 71f<**

**Espartero (IRE) 4** ch c Ballad Rock-Elabella (Ela-Mana-Mou) 940$^{3}$ 1483$^{5}$ 1800$^{5}$ 2114$^{27}$ 2880$^{4}$ 3232$^{18}$ 4101$^{3}$ 4485$^{6}$ **>110df<**

**Esperto 3** b g Risk Me (FR)-Astrid Gilberto (Runnett) (522) **>59f<**

**Esquiline (USA) 3** ch f Gone West (USA)-Ville Eternelle (USA) (Slew O' Gold (USA)) 705$^{13}$ 1614$^{8}$ 2079$^{5}$ *2636$^{11}$ 3608$^{10}$* **>8a 60f<**

**Essayeffsee 7** b g Precocious-Floreal (Formidable (USA)) *1418$^{3}$* (1698) 2077$^{2}$ 2296$^{3}$ 2628$^{5}$ 2803$^{4}$ (3348) 4102$^{6}$ 4438$^{4}$ 4597$^{5}$ 4793$^{11}$ 4993$^{8}$ **>64f<**

**Essesstee (FR) 5** h Perrault-Insistance (USA) (Sir Gaylord) 1390a$^{4}$

**Esta Maria (IRE) 3** b f High Estate-Maria Stuarda (Royal And Regal (USA)) *351$^{5}$ 364$^{6}$ 668$^{12}$* ***>42a 20f<***

**Estragon (SPA) 3** ch c Luth Dancer (USA)-Plum Run (USA) 3755a$^{3}$ **>94f<**

**Eternal Host (IRE) 2** b c Be My Guest (USA)-To The Limit (Junius (USA)) 5040$^{9}$ **>31f<**

**Eternally Grateful 3** b f Picea-Carpadia (Icecapade (USA)) **1995:** *4414$^{11}$* **1996:** *1908$^{10}$* ***>23f<***

**Eternity Range (USA) 3** b c Majestic Light (USA)-Northern Eternity 798a$^{2}$ 1141a$^{7}$ **>109f<**

**Ethbaat (USA) 5** b or br g Chief's Crown (USA)-Alchaasibiyeh (USA) (Seattle Slew (USA)) 1775$^{15}$ 1983$^{6}$ *2169$^{3}$ (2551) 2632$^{2}$ (3062) 3419$^{6}$ 3627$^{12}$ 4125$^{12}$* 4355$^{10}$ **>83a 62f<**

**Etna 2** b f Salse (USA)-Top Sovereign (High Top) 3206$^{5}$ 4570$^{3}$ **>78f<**

**Etoile (FR) 2** gr f Kris-La Luna (USA) (Lyphard (USA)) 2611$^{9}$ 4104$^{3}$ (4305) 4875$^{3}$ **>96f<**

**Etoile du Nord 4** b or br g Tragic Role (USA)-Daisy Topper (Top Ville) 3353$^{12}$ 5053$^{17}$

**Etterby Park (USA) 3** b g Silver Hawk (USA)-Bonita Francita (CAN) (Devil's Bag (USA)) 614$^{8}$ 1089$^{9}$ (1887) 2067$^{3}$ (2397) *(2553) (2631) 2900$^{2}$* 3037$^{13}$ 3653$^{6}$ 3939$^{3}$ (4248) 4344$^{2}$ 4447$^{8}$ 4761$^{3}$ **>73+a 83f<**

**Eulogy (FR) 9** b or br g Esprit du Nord (USA)-Louange (Green Dancer (USA)) *(73) 169$^{4}$ 268$^{4}$ (369) 429$^{2}$ 474$^{11}$ 603$^{3}$ 1488$^{4}$ 2082$^{2}$* **>71da 44f<**

**Euphonic 6** br g Elegant Air-Monalda (FR) (Claude) 3802$^{4}$ 4048$^{3}$ 4203$^{15}$ **>67f<**

**Euphoric Illusion 5** ch g Rainbow Quest (USA)-High and Bright (Shirley Heights) 3776$^{5}$ 4360$^{12}$ **>42f<**

**Euphyllia 4** b f Superpower-Anse Chastanet (Cavo Doro) **1995:** *4525$^{8}$* **1996:** *2437$^{6}$* 3151$^{6}$ 3761$^{13}$ 4098$^{11}$ 4256$^{12}$ 4701$^{4}$ 4865$^{7}$ 4975$^{20}$ **>43a 58f<**

**Eurobox Boy 3** ch g Savahra Sound-Princess Poquito (Hard Fought) *655$^{5}$ 756$^{9}$* 1099$^{19}$ 1497$^{2}$ 1651$^{2}$ 2123$^{5}$ 2617$^{6}$ (2859) 3456$^{2}$ (3655) 3985$^{9}$ 4240$^{2}$ 4597$^{7}$ **>40a 65f<**

**Euro Express 3** ch g Domynsky-Teresa Deevey (Runnett) 775$^{19}$ 3578$^{11}$ 4070$^{14}$ **>53f<**

**Eurolink Excaliber (USA) 2** b c Red Ransom (USA)-Queen's Warning (USA) (Caveat (USA)) 1896$^{2}$ 2224$^{2}$ 2923$^{2}$ 3835$^{8}$ **>84f<**

**Eurolink Profile 2** b f Prince Sabo-Taiga (Northfields (USA)) *4241$^{11}$* ***>44f<***

**Eurolink Rascal (IRE) 2** b c Lycius (USA)-Villota (Top Ville) 4594$^{19}$

**Eurolink Spartacus 2** b gr c High Estate-Princess Eurolink (Be My Guest (USA)) 2720$^{3}$ 3269$^{5}$ 3807$^{4}$ 4303$^{4}$ (4594) **>81f<**

**Eurolink the Rebel (USA) 4** ch g Timeless Native (USA)-Seeing Stars (USA) (Unconscious (USA)) *580$^{19}$* 953$^{7}$ **>88df<**

**Eurolink Windsong (IRE) 2** ch f Polish Patriot (USA)-Delvecchia (Glint of Gold) 3129$^{11}$ **>49f<**

**Europex 3** bl g Dunbeath (USA)-Afrabela (African Sky) 971$^{15}$ **>44f<**

**Euroquest 2** b g Ron's Victory (USA)-Raaya (Be My Guest (USA)) 4754$^{6}$ **>20f<**

**Euro Sceptic (IRE) 4** ch g Classic Secret (USA)-Very Seldom (Rarity) (1037) 1341$^{11}$ 1502$^{11}$ 1672$^{4}$ 1861$^{4}$ 2296$^{4}$ 2573$^{6}$ 2925$^{2}$ 3120$^{6}$ 3287$^{2}$ (3460) 3510$^{4}$ (3777) 3995$^{23}$ 4300$^{17}$ 4609$^{8}$ 4831$^{12}$ **>57f<**

**Euro Superstar (FR) 2** b c Rock City-Douceur (USA) (Shadeed (USA)) 3874$^{7}$ 4801$^{18}$ 4891$^{13}$ **>49f<**

**Eurotwist 7** b g Viking (USA)-Orange Bowl (General Assembly (USA)) (542) 620$^{8}$ 5008$^{11}$ **>40a 52f<**

**Eurynome (GER) 3** ch f Acatenango (GER)-Eidothea (GER) (Teotepec (GER)) (3202a) **>98f<**

**Eva Luna (USA) 4** b f Alleged (USA)-Media Luna (Star Appeal) (2786) (3711) (4114) 4569$^{4}$ 4876$^{3}$ 5045$^{2}$ **>122f<**

**Evan 'elp Us 4** ch g Executive Man-Recent Events (Stanford) **1995:** *4374$^{5}$* **1996:** *480$^{2}$* 718$^{P}$ **>46a 68f<**

**Evening Brigadier 5** bl g Al Amead-Evening Horizon (Evening All) *1081$^{6}$ 1460$^{7}$ 1638$^{13}$* ***>30a 27f<***

**Evening In Paris 3** ch f Be My Chief (USA)-Photo Call (Chief Singer) 4429$^{12}$

**Eveningperformance 5** b m Night Shift (USA)-Classic Design (Busted) 927$^{6}$ 2115$^{10}$ (2545) 3126$^{6}$ 3708$^{2}$ (4280a) 4660a$^{6}$ **>124f<**

**Evensong (ITY) 2** ch c Shalford (IRE)-Romina Girl (ITY) (Pilgrim (USA)) 4407a$^{3}$

**Even Top (IRE) 3** br c Topanoora-Skevena (Niniski (USA)) 926$^{2}$ 1791$^{13}$ 3671$^{5}$ (3996) 4773$^{4}$ **>131f<**

**Ever Friends 4** ch g Crever-Cappuccilli (Lorenzaccio) *520$^{7}$ 635$^{15}$* 852$^{14}$ 3303$^{4}$ 3507$^{7}$ *4080$^{11}$* **>37a 41f<**

**Everglades (IRE) 8** b g Green Desert (USA)-Glowing With Pride (Ile de Bourbon (USA)) 889$^{2}$ 1107$^{9}$ (1898) 2623$^{16}$ 2853$^{2}$ 4554$^{10}$ **>108f<**

**Everset (FR) 8** b g Green Desert (USA)-Eversince (USA) (Foolish Pleasure (USA)) **1995:** *4525$^{5}$* **1996:** *20$^{9}$ 135$^{3}$ 223$^{8}$ 270$^{5}$ 357$^{5}$ 480$^{10}$ 513$^{3}$ 645$^{6}$* 661$^{2}$ 4129$^{11}$ 4701$^{10}$ 4888$^{15}$ 4915$^{16}$ **>80a 66f<**

**Ever so Lyrical 6** b h Never so Bold-Lyra (Blakeney) 641$^{12}$ 827$^{12}$ 879$^{15}$ 1302$^{10}$ 1515$^{14}$ 1830$^{9}$ **>61f<**

**Evezio Rufo 4** b g Blakeney-Empress Corina (Free State) **1995:** *4481$^{11}$* **1996:** *358$^{8}$ 449$^{8}$* 563$^{5}$ 767$^{14}$ 1005$^{18}$ 4580$^{14}$ 4868$^{4}$ 5054$^{8}$ **>46a 64f<**

**Evidence In Chief 3** b f Be My Chief (USA)-Ominous (Dominion) 1682$^{7}$ 2246$^{8}$ 2711$^{3}$ (2975) 3318$^{7}$ 3500$^{11}$ (4515) 4726$^{3}$ 4789$^{3}$ **>66f<**

**Ewar Arrangement 2** b c Bold Arrangement-Emily Allan (IRE) (Shirley Heights) 4547$^{12}$ 4700$^{9}$ 4907$^{5}$ 5033$^{17}$ **>57f<**

**Ewar Bold 3** b c Bold Arrangement-Monaneigue Lady (Julio Mariner) 570$^{5}$ 707$^{6}$ 1023$^{3}$ 1591$^{6}$ 2196$^{6}$ 3028a$^{8}$ 4358$^{6}$ 4513$^{18}$ 4603$^{7}$ 4947a$^{14}$ 5020a$^{10}$ 5053$^{10}$ **>53f<**

**Ewar Imperial 4** b g Legend of France (USA)-Monaneigue Lady (Julio Mariner) 1833$^{5}$ *1997$^{7}$* **>57df<**

**Ewar Sunrise 3** ch f Shavian-Sunset Reef (Mill Reef (USA)) 550$^{5}$ 686$^{15}$ 1692$^{3}$ 2049$^{8}$ *2325$^{5}$ 3027a$^{2}$* 2945$^{7}$ **>39a 67df<**

**Exactly (IRE) 3** b f Taufan (USA)-Not Mistaken (USA) (Mill Reef (USA)) *402$^{7}$ 444$^{6}$* 754$^{2}$ 954$^{5}$ (1200) 1669$^{6}$ 2570$^{9}$ (3276) 3621$^{4}$ 3983$^{7}$ **>41a 78f<**

**Exalted (IRE) 3** b c High Estate-Heavenward (USA) (Conquistador Cielo (USA)) 1175$^{8}$ 1619$^{7}$ 1798$^{2}$ 2006$^{5}$ 2674$^{5}$ 3039$^{3}$ 3211$^{11}$ *4078$^{7}$ 4580$^{17}$* 4866$^{7}$ **>71a 86df<**

**Excelled (IRE) 7** gr m Treasure Kay-Excelling Miss (USA) (Exceller (USA)) 2192$^{8}$ **>28a 55f<**

**Exclusion 7** ch g Ballad Rock-Great Exception (Grundy) *196$^{3}$ 246$^{8}$ 256$^{6}$ 429$^{6}$ 542$^{W}$* 3346$^{4}$ **>43a 48f<**

**Exclusive Assembly 4** ch g Weldnaas (USA)-Pretty Pollyanna (General Assembly (USA)) **1995:** *4377$^{3}$ 4457$^{5}$ 4493$^{5}$* **1996:** *200$^{7}$ 1085$^{9}$* **>60da 54f<**

**Executive Design 4** b g Unfuwain (USA)-Seven Seas (FR) (Riverman (USA)) 961$^{7}$ 5047$^{10}$ **>88df<**

**Executive Officer 3** b g Be My Chief (USA)-Caro's Niece (USA) (Caro) 847$^{11}$ 4548$^{11}$ 4824$^{14}$ *4989$^{11}$* **>15a 46f<**

**Exemption 5** ch g Ballad Rock-Great Exception (Grundy) *3496$^{7}$* 3947$^{15}$ 4073$^{12}$ 4227$^{12}$ **>58f<**

**Exhibit Air (IRE) 6** b m Exhibitioner-Airy Queen (USA) (Sadair) **1995:** *4355$^{4}$ 4442$^{2}$* **1996:** *844$^{11}$* 1011$^{6}$ **>70a 54f<**

**Exit To Rio (CAN) 2** ch c Mining (USA)-Miami Vacation (USA) (Far North (CAN)) 698$^{3}$ (800) 1115$^{4}$ 1419$^{5}$ 2726$^{4}$ 3247$^{4}$ 3936$^{4}$ 4131$^{10}$ **>90f<**

**Expansive Runner (USA) 4** b c Explodent (USA)-Scissors (USA) (Blade (USA)) *4574$^{4}$ 4766$^{12}$* ***>53a 42?f<***

**Expectation (IRE) 2** b f Night Shift (USA)-Phantom Row (Adonijah) 2531$^{4}$ 2879$^{14}$ 4043$^{10}$ 4803$^{5}$ 4912$^{6}$ **>63f<**

**Expeditious Way (GR) 3** br c Wadood (USA)-Maid of Milan (Home Guard (USA)) *263$^{7}$ 378$^{5}$ 570$^{7}$* 819$^{12}$ 1119$^{12}$ **>74a 48f<**

**Expensive Taste 3** b f Cadeaux Genereux-Um Lardaff (Mill Reef (USA)) *917$^{10}$* (1619) 2006$^{4}$ 2294$^{4}$ 3923$^{4}$ **>94f<**

**Explosive Power 5** br h Prince Sabo-Erwarton Seabreeze (Dunbeath (USA)) **1995:** *4537$^{2}$* **1996:** *(66) 189$^{3}$ 303$^{3}$ (424) 469$^{11}$* 636$^{7}$ 817$^{17}$ 4609$^{6}$ 4812$^{2}$ **>81a 60f<**

**Export Mondial 6** b g Night Shift (USA)-Star Face (African Sky) **1995:** *4457$^{12}$* **>31a 44f<**

**Express Gift 7** br g Bay Express-Annes Gift (Ballymoss) *5042$^{8}$* ***>70?f<***

**Express Girl 2** b f Sylvan Express-Oh My Oh My (Ballacashtal (CAN)) (618) (996) 2484$^{5}$ 2728$^{5}$ 4113$^{20}$ 4749$^{3}$ 5037$^{9}$ **>81f<**

**Express Routing 4** b c Aragon-San Marguerite (Blakeney) *1522$^{7}$* 1856$^{6}$ 2251$^{12}$ *2749$^{12}$ 4499$^{10}$* ***>57f<***

**Extra Hour (IRE) 3** b g Cyrano de Bergerac-Renzola (Dragonara Palace (USA)) *758$^{7}$* 1657$^{4}$ 2235$^{7}$ 2528$^{10}$ *2634$^{7}$ 2893$^{7}$* ***>22a 50f<***

**Extremely Friendly 3** ch g Generous (IRE)-Water Woo (USA) (Tom Rolfe) **1995:** *4380$^{6}$* **1996:** *4252$^{14}$*

**>57a 50f<**

**Eye Shadow 2** ch f Mujtahid (USA)-Piney River (Pharly (FR)) 1834$^{5}$ (2059) 2338$^{3}$ 2582$^{4}$ 3068$^{7}$ 3444$^{6}$ 3707$^{6}$ 3990$^{7}$ 4758$^{6}$ **>82f<**

**Ezekiel 5** ch g Be My Guest (USA)-Judeah (Great Nephew) *202$^{7}$ 273$^{7}$ 342$^{10}$* **>7a 36f<**

**F**

**Faateq 3** b c Caerleon (USA)-Treble (USA) (Riverman (USA)) (788) 1361$^{2}$ (2164) 2401$^{5}$ **>93f<**

**Fabiana Sciumbata 2** ch f Polar Falcon (USA)-Melodic (Song) 4286a$^{2}$

**Fabillion 4** ch c Deploy-Kai (Kalamoun) 546$^{5}$ (753) 886$^{5}$ 1150$^{2}$ 1802$^{7}$ 2697$^{6}$ **>46a 79f<**

**Fable 2** ch f Absalom-Fiction (Dominion) 4105$^{9}$ 4369$^{12}$ **>47f<**

**Fabled Light (IRE) 2** b c Alzao (USA)-Fabled Lifestyle (Kings Lake (USA)) 4698$^{6}$ 4913$^{12}$ **>63f<**

**Fablinix (FR) 4** gr c Linamix (FR)-Fabliau (FR) (Slew O' Gold (USA)) 1059a$^{3}$ **>84f<**

**Fabulous Mtoto 6** b h Mtoto-El Fabulous (FR) (Fabulous Dancer (USA)) **1995:** *4376$^{6}$* **1996:** *108$^{7}$ 1063$^{6}$* 1454$^{4}$ (1655) 1965$^{2}$ 2226$^{4}$ 2558$^{4}$ (2866) 3113$^{4}$ 3302$^{3}$ 3479$^{7}$ 3611$^{6}$ 3980$^{8}$ **>41a 62f<**

**Face It 2** b f Interrex (CAN)-Facetious (Malicious) 465$^{6}$ 538$^{3}$ 770$^{3}$ *1097$^{5}$ 3846$^{9}$ 4251$^{11}$ 5005$^{5}$* **>38a 47f<**

**Face the Future 7** ch g Ahonoora-Chiltern Red (Red God) **1995:** *4351$^{10}$* **1996:** *582$^{3}$* 749$^{6}$ 3666$^{5}$ 3930$^{8}$ 4259$^{14}$ **>37a 54f<**

**Faez 6** b g Mtoto-Ghanimah (Caerleon (USA)) *29$^{3}$ 62$^{2}$ 105$^{10}$ 389$^{P}$* **>66a f< (DEAD)**

**Fag End (IRE) 3** b f Treasure Kay-Gauloise Bleue (USA) (Lyphard's Wish (FR)) 1060a$^{11}$ 1335$^{7}$ 1770$^{8}$ **>87f<**

**Fahal (USA) 4** b c Silver Hawk (USA)-By Land By Sea (USA) (Sauce Boat (USA)) 1355$^{4}$ 2038$^{6}$ 2730$^{5}$ 3797$^{4}$ **>115f<**

**Fahim 3** b c Green Desert (USA)-Mahrah (USA) (Vaguely Noble) (1701) (2621) (3211) 3691$^{2}$ 4371$^{3}$ **>113f<**

**Fahris (IRE) 2** ch c Generous (IRE)-Janbiya (IRE) (Kris) (3695) 4792$^{2}$ **>92f<**

**Fahs (USA) 4** b br c Riverman (USA)-Tanwi (Vision (USA)) 682$^{4}$ 1019$^{3}$ 1524$^{6}$ 1841$^{3}$ 1961$^{2}$ 2603$^{9}$ 3043$^{2}$ 3205$^{9}$ 3947$^{9}$ 4193$^{6}$ 4326$^{3}$ **>78f<**

**Failed To Hit 3** b c Warrshan (USA)-Missed Again (High Top) 2970$^{2}$ *3418$^{4}$ (3665)* 4559$^{17}$ 4724$^{9}$ **>70a 73f<**

**Failte Ro 4** bl f Macmillion-Safe Passage (Charlottown) *301$^{8}$* **>64a 52f<**

**Fair and Fancy (FR) 5** b g Always Fair (USA)-Fancy Star (FR) (Bellypha) **1995:** *4387$^{2}$* **>48a 66f<**

**Fair Attraction 4** ch g Charmer-Fairfields (Sharpen Up) *140$^{12}$* **>10a 54f<**

**Fairelaine 4** b f Zalazl (USA)-Blue and White (Busted) *403$^{6}$ 1689$^{5}$* 2032$^{12}$ 3220$^{6}$ 3991$^{15}$ **>34a 55f<**

**Fairey Firefly 5** b m Hallgate-Tremellick (Mummy's Pet) **1995:** *4413$^{14}$ 4502$^{5}$* **1996:** *(74) 127$^{13}$ 259$^{10}$ 368$^{7}$* **>60da 54f<**

**Fair Lady (BEL) 3** b f Bacalao (USA)-Bianca Girl (McIndoe) 4693$^{10}$ 4868$^{17}$ *5001$^{8}$* **>17f<**

**Fairly Sure (IRE) 3** b f Red Sunset-Mirabiliary (USA) (Crow (FR)) 2326$^{4}$ 2752$^{4}$ 3286$^{4}$ (3606) 3852$^{5}$ 4240$^{14}$ 4598$^{15}$ 4860$^{20}$ **>5a 43f<**

**Fair Relation 2** b f Distant Relative-Gold Flair (Tap On Wood) 3454$^{11}$ 4605$^{11}$ 4694$^{6}$ **>55f<**

**Fairy Highlands (IRE) 3** b f Fairy King (USA)-Breyani (Commanche Run) *355$^{2}$ 428$^{3}$ 531$^{7}$ 1888$^{4}$* 2019$^{3}$ 2358$^{2}$ 3348$^{10}$ 3575$^{4}$ 4042$^{11}$ 4753$^{12}$ 4810$^{16}$ **>59a 48f<**

**Fairy Knight 4** b c Fairy King (USA)-Vestal Flame (Habitat) **1995:** *4481$^{10}$* **1996:** *440$^{16}$* 598$^{6}$ 871$^{13}$ 1066$^{8}$ 1874$^{10}$ 2763$^{7}$ 3161$^{4}$ 3496$^{4}$ 3828$^{2}$ 4067$^{7}$ 4257$^{6}$ (4669) (4900) 5054$^{4}$ **>40a 77f<**

**Fairy Lake (IRE) 3** b f Fairy King (USA)-Inisfree (USA) (Hoist The Flag (USA)) 4738a$^{6}$ **>87f<**

**Fairy Path (USA) 4** ch f Irish River (FR)-Pointed Path **1995:** *4405a$^{7}$* **>109f<**

**Fairy Prince (IRE) 3** b g Fairy King (USA)-Danger Ahead (Mill Reef (USA)) *638$^{15}$* 862$^{13}$ 1888$^{3}$ (2215) 2500$^{2}$ 2719$^{4}$ 2790$^{6}$ 3292$^{2}$ 3583$^{3}$ **>66f<**

**Fairy Ring (IRE) 2** b f Fairy King (USA)-Emmuska (USA) (Roberto (USA)) 4250$^{10}$ 4469$^{2}$ **>61f<**

**Fairy Song (IRE) 2** b f Fairy King (USA)-Arcade 4024a$^{4}$ 4639a$^{2}$ **>90f<**

**Fairy Wind (IRE) 4** b f Fairy King (USA)-Decadence (Vaigly Great) (1113) 1483$^{6}$ 1616$^{6}$ **>101f<**

**Fairywings 3** b f Kris-Fairy Flax (IRE) (Dancing Brave (USA)) 613$^{11}$ 1092$^{2}$ (1324) 1666$^{2}$ (1861) 2294$^{5}$ 2773$^{7}$ 2924$^{3}$ 3118$^{3}$ (3509) 3815$^{2}$ 4297$^{3}$ 4568$^{6}$ 4872$^{11}$ **>89f<**

**Faith Alone 3** b f Safawan-Strapless (Bustino) **1995:** *4414$^{2}$ (4491)* **1996:** *1101$^{12}$* (1805) 2200$^{9}$ 4689$^{13}$ **>74a 71f<**

**Fakih (USA) 4** b c Zilzal (USA)-Barakat (Bustino) 879$^{5}$ 1198$^{11}$ 2412$^{10}$ **>78f<**

**Falak (USA) 2** b c Diesis-Tafrah (IRE) (Sadler's Wells (USA)) 3682$^{2}$ (4050) 4555$^{3}$ **>93f<**

**Falcon Ridge 2** ch g Seven Hearts-Glen Kella Manx (Tickled Pink) 5049$^{7}$ **>42f<**

**Falcon's Flame (USA) 3** b br g Hawkster (USA)-Staunch Flame (USA) (Bold Forbes (USA)) *428$^{4}$ 4581$^{2}$* 774$^{8}$ 1312$^{4}$ 1477$^{9}$ 1669$^{8}$ 2061$^{9}$ 2486$^{8}$ (2752) 3102$^{6}$ 3354$^{2}$ 3592$^{2}$ 4047$^{9}$ 4226$^{17}$ 4590$^{10}$ **>50a 61f<**

**Falkenham 2** b c Polar Falcon (USA)-Barsham (Be My Guest (USA)) (1339) (2252) 3927$^{2}$ (4183) *4954a$^{5}$* **>102a 107f<**

**Fallah 2** b c Salse (USA)-Alpine Sunset (Auction Ring (USA)) 3615$^{7}$ 4306$^{7}$ **>75f<**

**Fallal (IRE) 4** b f Fayruz-Lady Bidder (Auction Ring (USA)) **1995:** *4354$^{5}$ 4407$^{13}$* **1996:** *41$^{7}$* **>33a 55f<**

**Falls O'Moness (IRE) 2** b f River Falls-Sevens Are Wild (Petorius) 1197$^{2}$ 1499$^{2}$ 2396$^{9}$ 2733$^{3}$ 3230$^{2}$ 4024a$^{18}$ 4224$^{10}$ **>68f<**

**Faltaat (USA) 6** b h Mr Prospector (USA)-Epitome (USA) (Summing (USA)) (286a) 374a$^{3}$ **>119f<**

**Fame Again 4** b f Then Again-Starawak (Star Appeal) 455$^{12}$ 765$^{13}$ 933$^{7}$ 1018$^{12}$ 1186$^{4}$ 1425$^{3}$ 1829$^{6}$ 2329$^{5}$ 2363$^{6}$ 3045$^{2}$ 3219$^{4}$ 3510$^{5}$ 3833$^{12}$ 4054$^{14}$ 4316$^{11}$ 4560$^{11}$ 4688$^{11}$ 4768$^{7}$ 5039$^{5}$ **>63f<**

**Family Man 3** ch g Indian Ridge-Auntie Gladys (Great Nephew) 544$^{6}$ 4360$^{4}$ 4591$^{4}$ 4819$^{9}$ **>75f<**

**Family Tradition (IRE) 2** b f Sadler's Wells (USA)-Sequel 4159a$^{8}$ 4661a$^{3}$ 4859a$^{5}$ **>102f<**

**Famous (FR) 3** dk f Tropular-Famous Horse (FR) (Labus (FR)) 3389a$^{3}$ **>74f<**

**Fanadiyr (IRE) 4** b g Kahyasi-Fair Fight (Fine Blade (USA)) 620$^{12}$ 2120$^{4}$ 2331$^{4}$ **>52f<**

**Fancy A Fortune (IRE) 2** b c Fools Holme (USA)-Fancy's Girl (FR) (Nadjar (FR)) 2132$^{8}$ 2396$^{3}$ 2708$^{11}$ 3423$^{8}$ 3632$^{2}$ 3962$^{8}$ 4347$^{4}$ 4694$^{11}$ 4814$^{8}$ **>61f<**

**Fancy Clancy 3** b f Clantime-Bold Sophie (Bold Owl) 1787$^{4}$ 2176$^{6}$ 2732$^{11}$ 2970$^{8}$ 3135$^{8}$ 4075$^{18}$ 4727$^{10}$ **>31f<**

**Fancy Design (IRE) 3** b f Cyrano de Bergerac-Crimson Robes (Artaius (USA)) 2597$^{7}$ 2914$^{5}$ 4860$^{11}$ **>41f<**

**Fancy Heights 3** b f Shirley Heights-Miss Fancy That (USA) (The Minstrel (CAN)) 1644$^{3}$ 2223$^{2}$ (3434) 3669$^{4}$ **>97f<**

**Fanion de Fete (FR) 5** b h **1995:** 4500a$^{2}$ **>114f<**

**Fanny's Choice (IRE) 2** b f Fairy King (USA)-Gaychimes (Steel Heart) *1998$^{3}$* (2375) 2879$^{5}$ 3613$^{7}$ **>84f<**

**Fan of Vent-Axia 2** b c Puissance-Miss Milton (Young Christopher) *452$^{4}$* 685$^{8}$ *858$^{3}$ 1904$^{3}$* 2606$^{4}$ 3046$^{8}$ 4262$^{9}$ 4795$^{11}$ **>35a 62f<**

**Fantail 2** b c Taufan (USA)-Eleganza (IRE) (Kings Lake (USA)) 4516$^{13}$ 4720$^{12}$ 4914$^{6}$ **>59f<**

**Fantastic Fellow (USA) 2** b c Lear Fan (USA)-Chateaubaby (USA) (Nureyev (USA)) (3987) 4398a$^{4}$ 4519$^{4}$ **>106f<**

**Fantastic Gold (FR) 3** ch g Goldneyev-Our Charmer (USA) (Our Michael (USA)) 226a$^{2}$ **>68f<**

**Fantasy Flight 2** b f Forzando-Ryewater Dream (Touching Wood (USA)) 3773$^{8}$ **>26f<**

**Fantasy Girl (IRE) 2** br f Marju (IRE)-Persian Fantasy (Persian Bold) 3493$^{11}$ 4253$^{10}$ **>52f<**

**Fantasy Racing (IRE) 4** b f Tirol-Highland Girl (USA) (Sir Ivor) *451$^{12}$* 582$^{16}$ 735$^{6}$ 744$^{4}$ 2508$^{6}$ 2725$^{11}$ 2976$^{7}$ 3112$^{6}$ 3216$^{7}$ 3424$^{3}$ 3622$^{3}$ 3783$^{6}$ 3932$^{5}$ 4058$^{18}$ **>81f<**

**Far Ahead 4** b g Soviet Star (USA)-Cut Ahead (Kalaglow) **1995:** *4367$^{6}$ (4419) 4481$^{3}$* **1996:** *48$^{4}$ 120$^{7}$ 1861$^{6}$* 2152$^{3}$ 2487$^{2}$ 2900$^{3}$ (3253) 3587$^{3}$ (4073) 4315$^{3}$ 4617$^{14}$ 5046$^{9}$ **>83a 89f<**

**Farasan (IRE) 3** b c Fairy King (USA)-Gracieuse Majeste (FR) (Saint Cyrien (FR)) (684) (1427) 2276a$^{6}$ 3070$^{6}$ 3671$^{4}$ 4197$^{3}$ **>114f<**

**Far Atlantic 3** b f Phardante (FR)-Atlantic View (Crash Course) 4217$^{9}$ **>28f<**

**Faraway Lass 3** b f Distant Relative-Vague Lass (Vaigly Great) 868$^{4}$ (1412) 1991$^{2}$ (2255) 2434$^{3}$ 3599$^{2}$ 3989$^{2}$ 4308$^{11}$ (4689) **>83f<**

**Faraway Waters 3** ch f Pharly (FR)-Gleaming Water (Kalaglow) 938$^{2}$ 1335$^{8}$ 1769$^{7}$ 3067$^{4}$ 3836$^{10}$ **>96df<**

**Far Dawn (USA) 3** b c Sunshine Forever (USA)-Dawn's Reality (USA) (In Reality) 892$^{6}$ 1319$^{7}$ 2744$^{5}$ 3161$^{10}$ 3470$^{7}$ (4083) 4374$^{6}$ 4580$^{11}$ **>75f<**

**Farewell My Love (IRE) 2** b f Waajib-So Long Boys (FR) (Beldale Flutter (USA)) 2343$^{2}$ (2562) 3128$^{6}$ (3803) 4113$^{14}$ 4672$^{6}$ 4878$^{4}$ **>79f<**

**Farfen 4** ch g Vague Shot-Shirlstar Investor (Some Hand) 3048$^{11}$

**Farfeste 3** b f Jester-Our Horizon (Skyliner) **1995:** *4491$^{11}$* **1996:** *595$^{8}$* 1691$^{9}$ 2339$^{7}$ 3357$^{4}$ 3655$^{8}$ 3761$^{14}$ 4221$^{15}$ **>36a 41f<**

**Farhan (USA) 2** b c Lear Fan (USA)-Mafatin (IRE) (Sadler's Wells (USA)) 4189$^{5}$ 4451$^{2}$ 4599$^{2}$ **>81f<**

**Farhana 3** b f Fayruz-Fahrenheit (Mount Hagen (FR)) (638) (945) (1431) 3562a$^{2}$ **>109f<**

**Farida Seconda 3** gr f Green Ruby (USA)-Faridetta (Good Bond) 783$^{6}$ 1592$^{9}$ 1684$^{5}$ 1995$^{8}$ 3166$^{11}$ **>44f<**

**Faringdon Future 2** b c Distant Relative-Lady Dowery (USA) (Manila (USA)) 1896$^{7}$ 2873$^{2}$ 3293$^{4}$ 4916$^{6}$ **>79f<**

**Farmer's Tern (IRE) 4** ch f Sharrood (USA)-Winter Tern (USA) (Arctic Tern (USA)) **1995:** *4374$^{7}$ 4412$^{9}$* **>36a 61f<**

**Farmost 3** ch g Pharly (FR)-Dancing Meg (USA) (Marshua's Dancer (USA)) **1995:** *4529$^{2}$* **1996:** *(134) 976$^{5}$* (1485) (1532) (1677) *1718$^{2}$ (2980)* 3076$^{2}$ *3877$^{2}$ (3955)* **>81a 87f<**

**Farnese (IRE) 2** b c Alzao (USA)-Flaxen Hair (Thatch (USA)) 4817$^{7}$ 4991$^{5}$ **>80f<**

**Faro Flyer 3** b c Shere Khan-Midyanzie (Midyan (USA)) 4129$^{18}$ 4340$^{12}$ 4592$^{P}$ **(DEAD)**

**Farringdon Hill 5** b g Minster Son-Firgrove (Relkino) 1618$^{6}$ (2002) 2319$^{11}$ 2973$^{5}$ 3355$^{2}$ 4187$^{4}$ 4476$^{11}$ **>85f<**

**Fascinating Rhythm 2** b f Slip Anchor-Pick of the Pops (High Top) (4608) **>84+f<**

**Fascination Waltz 9** b m Shy Groom (USA)-Cuckoo Weir **1995:** *4359$^{6}$ 4413$^{10}$ 4464$^{9}$* **>41a 58f<**

**Fasih** 4 b c Rock City-Nastassia (FR) (Noble Decree (USA)) 537$^{8}$ 771$^{P}$ **>76df< (DEAD)**

**Fasil (IRE)** 3 ch c Polish Patriot (USA)-Apple Peel (Pall Mall) 732$^{10}$ 1326$^{3}$ 1508$^{6}$ (2128) 3594$^{11}$ (4374) 4675$^{8}$ **>92f<**

**Fassan (IRE)** 4 br g Contract Law (USA)-Persian Susan (USA) (Herbager) 619$^{8}$ **>35f<**

**Fast Forward Fred** 5 gr g Sharrood (USA)-Sun Street (Ile de Bourbon (USA)) 760$^{2}$ 1514$^{9}$ 1826$^{12}$ 2739$^{5}$ 3514$^{5}$ **>51f<**

**Fastini Gold** 4 b g Weldnaas (USA)-La Carlotta (Ela-Mana-Mou) **1995:** *4379$^{5}$ 4416$^{8}$* **1996:** *760$^{9}$* 979$^{13}$ 1347$^{7}$ 1522$^{4}$ *1719$^{11}$ 2192$^{9}$* 2574$^{6}$ 3111$^{9}$ 3257$^{7}$ 3474$^{7}$ 3808$^{10}$ 4480$^{11}$ **>47a 47f<**

**Fastnet** 2 ch f Forzando-Lambay (Lorenzaccio) 2323$^{7}$ **>29f<**

**Fastnet View (IRE)** 2 b f Soviet Lad (USA)-Classic Dilemma (Sandhurst Prince) 4159a$^{9}$ **>81f<**

**Fast Spin** 2 b c Formidable (USA)-Topwinder (USA) (Topsider (USA)) 848$^{6}$ 2122$^{7}$ *2370$^{4}$ 3324$^{6}$* ***>48a 48f<***

**Fatal Baraari** 2 b c Green Desert (USA)-Possessive (Posse (USA)) 4050$^{W}$ 4233$^{3}$ **>71f<**

**Fatal Sahra (IRE)** 2 ch c Caerleon (USA)-Ploy (Posse (USA)) 4817$^{8}$ **>56f<**

**Fatefully (USA)** 3 b f Private Account (USA)-Fateful (USA) (Topsider (USA)) 921$^{2}$ 1333$^{10}$ (1882) 3133$^{2}$ (4214) (4445) (4671) 4972$^{3}$ **>110f<**

**Fatehalkhair (IRE)** 4 ch g Kris-Midway Lady (USA) (Alleged (USA)) 1530$^{12}$ 2023$^{9}$ *2369$^{2}$ 2749$^{5}$ 3306$^{13}$ 3603$^{13}$* **>48a 47f<**

**Father Dan (IRE)** 7 ch g Martin John-Sonia John (Main Reef) **1995:** *4364$^{2}$ 4472$^{5}$* **1996:** *116$^{8}$ 152$^{8}$ 4236$^{7}$* 4355$^{2}$ 4551$^{8}$ *5003$^{3}$* **>64a 65f<**

**Father Eddie** 2 b c Aragon-Lady Philippa (IRE) (Taufan (USA)) 1086$^{13}$ 1583$^{6}$ 3423$^{9}$ **>48f<**

**Fattash (USA)** 4 ch g Tejano (USA)-Green Pompadour (USA) (Green Dancer (USA)) **1995:** *4516$^{12}$* **1996:** *9$^{9}$ 1839$^{10}$* 2310$^{9}$ **>15a 47f<**

**Faucon Royal (FR)** 3 b c Nikos-Aliscafi (FR) (Caro) 2669a$^{2}$ 4943a$^{2}$ **>108f<**

**Faugeron** 7 ch g Niniski (USA)-Miss Longchamp (Northfields (USA)) *1700$^{5}$* 2182$^{13}$ 2499$^{7}$ (2626) 3273$^{2}$ 3507$^{2}$ **>68f<**

**Fauna (IRE)** 2 b f Taufan (USA)-Labwa (USA) (Lyphard (USA)) 4105$^{8}$ 4748$^{4}$ **>71f<**

**Faustino** 4 gr g Faustus (USA)-Hot Case (Upper Case (USA)) *4086$^{13}$* ***>58a 59f<***

**Favourite Prince (IRE)** 5 b h Prince Rupert (FR)-Fete Champetre (Welsh Pageant) 4290a$^{11}$ **>120f<**

**Faydini (IRE)** 7 b g Fayruz-Windini (Windjammer (USA)) 2459a$^{10}$ **>72f<**

**Fayik** 2 ch c Arazi (USA)-Elfaslah (IRE) (Green Desert (USA)) 4818$^{5}$ **>80f<**

**Fayre Holly (IRE)** 3 b f Fayruz-Holly Bird (Runnett) 1876$^{10}$ *2636$^{10}$* **>8a 64f<**

**Fay Wray (FR)** 6 ch m Primo Dominie-Canaletto (USA) (Iron Duke (FR)) **1995:** 4500a$^{3}$ **>103f<**

**Fearless Cavalier** 2 b g Bold Arrangement-Gold Belt (IRE) (Bellypha) 1845$^{3}$ 2043$^{6}$ *2172$^{4}$ 2307$^{4}$ 2926$^{4}$* 3082$^{2}$ 3330$^{6}$ 3651$^{3}$ 3840$^{8}$ 4562$^{4}$ 4902$^{3}$ (5005) **>52a 56f<**

**Fearless Sioux** 2 b f Formidable (USA)-Washita (Valiyar) 4751$^{5}$ **>42f<**

**Fearless Wonder** 5 b g Formidable (USA)-Long View (Persian Bold) *2494$^{7}$* 2626$^{3}$ 2891$^{10}$ (3305) 3638$^{7}$ **>62a 61f<**

**Featherstone Lane** 5 b g Siberian Express (USA)-Try Gloria (Try My Best (USA)) *16$^{3}$ 63$^{3}$ 139$^{3}$ 225$^{2}$ (315) 362$^{2}$ 394$^{10}$ 407$^{5}$ 559$^{6}$* 704$^{11}$ 1364$^{3}$ 1541$^{4}$ 2119$^{6}$ 2244$^{4}$ 2496$^{4}$ 2586$^{9}$ 3223$^{9}$ 3331$^{7}$ 3652$^{5}$ *3953$^{7}$ 4090$^{6}$ 4881$^{9}$ 5000$^{3}$* **>71a 42f<**

**February** 3 b f Full Extent (USA)-Foligno (Crofter (USA)) 2029$^{9}$ 3847$^{5}$ 3977$^{11}$ *4077$^{12}$ 4129$^{13}$* 4337$^{U}$ **>32a 31f<**

**Federico (USA)** 4 b c Known Fact (USA)-Illusive Icicle (USA) (Far North (CAN)) 2843a$^{5}$ (3754a) 4656a$^{9}$ **>110f<**

**Feel A Line** 2 b c Petong-Cat's Claw (USA) (Sharpen Up) 2624$^{13}$ 2887$^{6}$ 3282$^{2}$ 3687$^{7}$ 3924$^{3}$ 4717$^{16}$ 4878$^{12}$ **>79f<**

**Feeling Hope** 5 ch m Hadeer-Bonnie Hope (USA) (Nijinsky (CAN)) *104$^{15}$* **>5a 28f<**

**Feet On Fire** 3 b f Nomination-Peregrine Falcon (Saulingo) 591$^{9}$ 768$^{13}$ **>8f<**

**Fellwah (IRE)** 2 b f Sadler's Wells (USA)-Continual (USA) (Damascus (USA)) 4225$^{4}$ **>65f<**

**Femme Savante** 4 b f Glenstal (USA)-Femme Formidable (Formidable (USA)) 1629$^{8}$ 2694$^{18}$ 2889$^{11}$ 3207$^{7}$ **>79f<**

**Fencer's Quest (IRE)** 3 ch c Bluebird (USA)-Fighting Run (Runnett) 4108$^{9}$ **>56f<**

**Fen Terrier** 4 b f Emarati (USA)-Kinz (Great Nephew) *210$^{9}$* **>62da 62f<**

**Fergal (USA)** 3 ch g Inishpour-Campus (USA) (Minnesota Mac) *405$^{11}$ 483$^{7}$* 594$^{8}$ 2162$^{13}$ 3780$^{15}$ 4042$^{12}$ **>19a 23f<**

**Fernanda** 2 b f Be My Chief (USA)-Flaming Rose (USA) (Upper Nile (USA)) (1413) (1978) 2997$^{7}$ 3444$^{2}$ 3804$^{2}$ 4133$^{W}$ 4565$^{2}$ 4875$^{2}$ **>94f<**

**Fern's Governor** 4 b f Governor General-Sharp Venita (Sharp Edge) 853$^{10}$ 1496$^{8}$ 2183$^{4}$ 3220$^{3}$ (3471) 3802$^{7}$ 4068$^{2}$ (4355) 4617$^{6}$ 4872$^{7}$ 4993$^{9}$ **>65f<**

**Fernway** 3 ch f Handsome Sailor-Redgrave Design (Nebbiolo) *783$^{10}$* 1033$^{12}$ **>40f<**

**Ferny Hill (IRE)** 2 b c Danehill (USA)-Miss Allowed (USA) (Alleged (USA)) 3701$^{4}$ *4331$^{2}$ 4494$^{4}$* ***>80a 80f<***

**Fervent Fan (IRE)** 3 b f Soviet Lad (USA)-Shannon Lady (Monsanto (FR)) 978$^{13}$ 1420$^{9}$ 1825$^{8}$ 2209$^{8}$ **>68a 53f<**

**Fiaba** 8 b m Precocious-Historia (Northfields (USA)) **1995:** *4407$^{2}$ 4479$^{4}$* **1996:** *53$^{7}$ 334$^{6}$ 521$^{11}$ 2169$^{7}$ 2551$^{7}$ (2940) 3700$^{10}$ 4077$^{6}$ 4989$^{6}$* **>41a 35f<**

**Fiasco** 3 ch f Dunbeath (USA)-Rainbow Trout (Comedy Star (USA)) 974$^{5}$ 1359$^{11}$ 1526$^{14}$ 2493$^{4}$ **>52f<**

**Fiddles Delight** 3 b f Colmore Row-Nutwood Emma (Henbit (USA)) 3474$^{17}$ **>12a 52f<**

**Field of Vision (IRE)** 6 b g Vision (USA)-Bold Meadows (Persian Bold) **1995:** *4440$^{2}$ 4457$^{10}$ 4531$^{3}$* **1996:** *42$^{7}$ (136) (181) 306$^{4}$ 358$^{6}$ 392$^{8}$ 410$^{5}$ (537)* 1022$^{3}$ 1198$^{4}$ *1602$^{2}$ 1811$^{4}$ 2552$^{9}$ 2803$^{3}$* 3056$^{2}$ 3487$^{3}$ 3677$^{4}$ **>75a 81f<**

**Fieldridge** 7 ch g Rousillon (USA)-Final Thought (Final Straw) *1440$^{4}$* 1793$^{8}$ 2127$^{6}$ 2502$^{18}$ 3922$^{8}$ **>79f<**

**Fiello (GER)** 6 ch h Vacarme (USA)-Fair Abode (Habitat) 2843a$^{11}$ **>114f<**

**Fiery Footsteps** 4 ro f Chilibang-Dancing Daughter (Dance In Time (CAN)) **1995:** *4407$^{12}$ 4486$^{2}$ 4515$^{10}$* **1996:** *36$^{3}$ 107$^{10}$ 155$^{6}$ 203$^{10}$ 347$^{5}$ 386$^{6}$ 388$^{7}$ 3851$^{14}$* 4045$^{21}$ 4808$^{17}$ *4989$^{16}$* **>31a 7f<**

**Fife Major (USA)** 2 b c Gone West (USA)-Fife (IRE) (Lomond (USA)) 5033$^{12}$ **>63f<**

**Fifire (GER)** 4 2843a$^{12}$ **>96f<**

**Fighter Squadron** 7 ch g Primo Dominie-Formidable Dancer (Formidable (USA)) *389$^{4}$ 653$^{6}$ 1348$^{15}$* 1890$^{9}$ 2047$^{9}$ 2344$^{7}$ 2735$^{3}$ *2940$^{3}$ 3252$^{5}$* ***>29a 32f<***

**Fighting Times** 4 b g Good Times (ITY)-Duellist (Town Crier) **1995:** *4465$^{9}$* **1996:** *690$^{4}$* 817$^{2}$ 993$^{4}$ 1353$^{5}$ 1618$^{12}$ 1874$^{11}$ 2603$^{14}$ 3111$^{8}$ 4683$^{11}$ **>43?a 62df<**

**Figlia** 2 b f Sizzling Melody-Fiorini (Formidable (USA)) 3508$^{8}$ 3838$^{5}$ 4619$^{6}$ 4903$^{8}$ 5037$^{2}$ **>65f<**

**Fig Tree Bay** 3 b g Puissance-Rose Barton (Pas de Seul) 1787$^{8}$ 2197$^{18}$ 2604$^{8}$ 3331$^{8}$ **>28f<**

**Fig Tree Drive (USA)** 2 b f Miswaki (USA)-Rose O'Riley (USA) (Nijinsky (CAN)) (2245) **>85f<**

**Fiji** 2 b f Rainbow Quest (USA)-Island Jamboree (USA) (Explodent (USA)) (4211) **>80+f<**

**Fijon (IRE)** 3 b f Doyoun-Tasskeen (FR) (Lyphard (USA)) *955$^{3}$* 1589$^{5}$ 1984$^{5}$ 2189$^{8}$ 2537$^{5}$ *4080$^{6}$ 4563$^{17}$* ***>47a 57f<***

**Fikra (USA)** 3 b br f Gulch (USA)-Bolt From The Blue (USA) (Blue Times (USA)) 788$^{7}$ 955$^{5}$ 2540$^{4}$ *2751$^{5}$ 3173$^{9}$* ***>42a 60f<***

**Filial (IRE)** 3 b c Danehill (USA)-Sephira (Luthier) 2996$^{3}$ (3505) 3947$^{12}$ 4121$^{10}$ 4695$^{5}$ **>81f<**

**Fill the Bill (IRE)** 4 b c Bob Back (USA)-Neat Dish (CAN) (Stalwart (USA)) 2474a$^{2}$ 3021a$^{2}$ 3531a$^{4}$ 3728a$^{5}$ 4268a$^{3}$ 4397a$^{9}$ **>109f<**

**Filly Mignonne (IRE)** 3 ch f Nashwan (USA)-Christabelle (USA) (Northern Dancer) 1530$^{11}$ 2610$^{11}$ 4833$^{14}$ **>56f<**

**Film Noir (USA)** 2 b c Alleged (USA)-Black Princess (FR) (Prince Mab (FR)) (4949a) **>112f<**

**Filmore West** 3 b c In The Wings-Sistabelle (Bellypha) **1995:** *4485$^{3}$* **1996:** *3986$^{2}$* (4379) **>63+a 90f<**

**Final Stab (IRE)** 3 b c Kris-Premier Rose (Sharp Edge) 2293$^{5}$ 2621$^{18}$ **>79f<**

**Final Trial (IRE)** 2 b c Last Tycoon-Perfect Alibi (Law Society (USA)) 4700$^{4}$ 4891$^{9}$ **>77f<**

**Finarts Bay** 2 b f Aragon-Salinas (Bay Express) 4887$^{7}$ **>56f<**

**Finder's Fortune (USA)** 7 b h Buckfinder (USA)-Isle of Fortune **1995:** 4523a$^{3}$

**Fine Detail (IRE)** 3 b f Shirley Heights-De Stael (USA) (Nijinsky (CAN)) (3441) **>81f<**

**Fine Fellow (IRE)** 2 b c Bluebird (USA)-Majieda (Kashmir II) 3748a$^{2}$ (4415a) 5024a$^{6}$ **>96f<**

**Fine Gachette (FR)** 3 b f Kadrou (FR)-Soicaline (Olmeto) 150a$^{2}$ **>77f<**

**Finestatetobein** 3 ch f Northern State (USA)-Haywain (Thatching) *2393$^{8}$* 3309$^{7}$ 4763$^{8}$ **>32f<**

**Fine Times** 2 b c Timeless Times (USA)-Marfen (Lochnager) *950$^{6}$* 1086$^{5}$ 1537$^{6}$ 2792$^{4}$ 3224$^{7}$ 4558$^{2}$ 4912$^{9}$ 4966$^{8}$ **>71f<**

**Finisterre (IRE)** 3 b g Salt Dome (USA)-Inisfail (Persian Bold) **1995:** *4369$^{7}$* **1996:** *478$^{8}$* 740$^{6}$ 881$^{3}$ 1039$^{3}$ 1163$^{10}$ (1527) 2005$^{12}$ 2222$^{2}$ 2729$^{4}$ 2870$^{2}$ 3973$^{5}$ 4860$^{6}$ **>42a 70f<**

**Finjan** 9 b g Thatching-Capriconia (Try My Best (USA)) 645$^{13}$ 1468$^{19}$ **>44a 35f<**

**Finlana** 3 b f Alzao (USA)-Insaf (USA) (Raise A Native) *820$^{5}$* 1123$^{6}$ **>65f<**

**Finsbury Flyer (IRE)** 3 ch g Al Hareb (USA)-Jazirah (Main Reef) (1891) 2231$^{4}$ 2618$^{3}$ 2955$^{3}$ **>77f<**

**Fiona Shann (USA)** 3 b f Phone Trick (USA)-Aminata (Glenstal (USA)) 595$^{4}$ 2542$^{3}$ 3225$^{4}$ 3813$^{8}$ 3979$^{7}$ **>57f<**

**Fionn de Cool (IRE)** 5 b g Mazaad-Pink Fondant (Northfields (USA)) 1775$^{12}$ 2285$^{8}$ 2605$^{7}$ 3123$^{4}$ 3516$^{3}$ 3765$^{5}$ 4184$^{14}$ 4511$^{2}$ 4682$^{3}$ 4901$^{4}$ **>75f<**

**Fiorenz (USA)** 4 ch f Chromite (USA)-Christi Dawn (USA) (Grey Dawn II) *125$^{7}$* **>2a f<**

**Firbur** 3 b g Be My Chief (USA)-La Masse (High Top) 892$^{13}$ 1711$^{7}$ 2300$^{5}$ 3039$^{P}$ **>77f< (DEAD)**

**Fire Dome (IRE)** 4 ch c Salt Dome (USA)-Penny Habit (Habitat) *(457)* 818$^{5}$ 1410$^{2}$ **>113f<**

**Firefighter** 7 ch g Sharpo-Courtesy Call (Northfields (USA)) 642$^{11}$ 872$^{15}$ (1167) 1472$^{7}$ **>59f<**

**Fire on Ice (IRE)** 4 b c Sadler's Wells (USA)-

Foolish Lady (USA) (Foolish Pleasure (USA)) 581$^{7}$ 1520$^{3}$ **>101f<**

**Firle Phantasy 3** ch g Pharly (FR)-Shamasiya (FR) (Vayrann) 3051$^{2}$ 3461$^{W}$ 3974$^{15}$ 4226$^{19}$ 4598$^{20}$ **>33f<**

**Firm Contract (IRE) 4** b g Double Schwartz-Glass Goblet (USA) (Storm Bird (CAN)) 2604$^{9}$ 3442$^{10}$ **>60f<**

**First Chance (IRE) 2** b f Lahib (USA)-Honagh Lee (Main Reef) 4756$^{21}$ 4962$^{4}$ **>66f<**

**First Gallery 3** b f Charmer-Hound Song (Jukebox) 758$^{9}$ 4997$^{8}$

**First Gold 7** gr g Absalom-Cindys Gold (Sonnen Gold) **1995:** 4390$^{8}$ 4514$^{4}$ **1996:** 29$^{4}$ (76) 115$^{4}$ 211$^{12}$ 255$^{4}$ 372$^{3}$ 545$^{6}$ 971$^{5}$ (1041) 1474$^{5}$ 1638$^{7}$ 2081$^{13}$ 2369$^{11}$ 4701$^{16}$ 4829$^{12}$ 4915$^{9}$ **>57a 64f<**

**First Hello (GER) 4** dk c Nebos (GER)-First Love (GER) (Limbo (GER)) 1138a$^{5}$ 1752a$^{2}$ **>120f<**

**First Island (IRE) 4** ch c Dominion-Caymana (FR) (Bellypha) (442) 680$^{3}$ 810$^{5}$ (1112) (2038) (3144) 3670$^{2}$ 4443$^{3}$ 4773$^{5}$ **>129f<**

**First Law 3** ch f Primo Dominie-Barsham (Be My Guest (USA)) 1617$^{15}$ 1994$^{6}$ 2529$^{5}$ 3138$^{7}$ 3473$^{8}$ **>62f<**

**First Maite 3** b g Komaite (USA)-Marina Plata (Julio Mariner) 32$^{2}$ 112$^{5}$ (237) (282) 357$^{6}$ 453$^{2}$ 773$^{2}$ 3622$^{13}$ 3844$^{5}$ 4044$^{4}$ 4453$^{14}$ **>84a 75f<**

**First Option 6** ch g Primo Dominie-Merrywren (Julio Mariner) 126$^{13}$ 225$^{7}$ 347$^{11}$ 1541$^{14}$ 1889$^{7}$ 2064$^{10}$ 2212$^{6}$ 2523$^{7}$ 2757$^{16}$ 3168$^{9}$ 3294$^{11}$ 3643$^{9}$ 3957$^{8}$ 4828$^{14}$ **>62a 30f<**

**First Page 2** b f Rudimentary (USA)-Miss Paige (AUS) (Luskin Star (AUS)) 1678$^{7}$ 4062$^{12}$ 4423$^{10}$ **>33f<**

**First Smile (GER) 3** b f Surumu (GER)-First Love (GER) (Limbo (GER)) (4854a)

**Fishin Cabin (IRE) 4** b g Gone Fishin-Reign Of Swing 4643a$^{25}$ **>65f<**

**Fisiostar 3** b g Efisio-Sweet Colleen (Connaught) 1526$^{17}$ 2179$^{4}$ 2752$^{10}$ 3102$^{4}$ 3228$^{3}$ 3881$^{3}$ 4348$^{14}$ **>46f<**

**Fistral Flame 2** ch f Superlative-Northern Empress (Northfields (USA)) 2252$^{7}$ 3498$^{8}$ 4507$^{13}$ **>43f<**

**Fit For The Job (IRE) 2** ch g Mac's Imp (USA)-Jolly Dale (IRE) (Huntingdale) 1093$^{5}$ 1320$^{4}$ 1491$^{3}$ 4093$^{7}$ 4576$^{6}$ **>54a 26f<**

**Fitzwilliam (USA) 3** b g Rahy (USA)-Early Lunch (USA) (Noble Table (USA)) 1668$^{3}$ (2365) 2882$^{5}$ 4067$^{4}$ 4487$^{2}$ **>94f<**

**Five Live 2** b f Pharly (FR)-Manageress (Mandamus) 1858$^{4}$ 2361$^{5}$ 2569$^{2}$ **>66f<**

**Five-O-Fifty 2** b br c Anshan-Wyns Vision (Vision (USA)) 3332$^{2}$ 3853$^{9}$ 4208$^{14}$ 4749$^{10}$ **>65f<**

**Five to Seven (USA) 7** br g Little Missouri (USA)-French Galaxy (USA) (Majestic Light (USA)) **1995:** 4387$^{6}$ **>63a 76df<**

**Fizzy Boy (IRE) 3** b g Contract Law (USA)-Generation Gap (Young Generation) 3425$^{9}$ 3960$^{5}$ **>28f<**

**Flag Fen (USA) 5** b br g Riverman (USA)-Damascus Flag (USA) (Damascus (USA)) 537$^{3}$ 628$^{7}$ 752$^{16}$ 843$^{4}$ 983$^{18}$ 1522$^{8}$ 1775$^{13}$ 2431$^{5}$ 2903$^{4}$ 3060$^{2}$ 3274$^{2}$ 3592$^{7}$ 4068$^{16}$ 4432$^{13}$ **>67f<**

**Flagship 2** ch f Rainbow Quest (USA)-Bireme (Grundy) 4507$^{2}$ 4801$^{5}$ **>69f<**

**Flagstaff (USA) 3** b g Personal Flag (USA)-Shuffle Up (USA) **1995:** 4365$^{10}$ 4529$^{8}$ **1996:** 183$^{4}$ 834$^{2}$ 1013$^{2}$ 2013$^{2}$ 2765$^{5}$ 3304$^{5}$ 3316$^{8}$ **>58a 61f<**

**Flahive's First 2** ch g Interrex (CAN)-Striking Image (IRE) (Flash of Steel) 4210$^{14}$ 4607$^{12}$ **>34f<**

**Flahuil 3** b f Generous (IRE)-Sipsi Fach (Prince Sabo) **1995:** 4492$^{6}$ **1996:** 176$^{5}$ 522$^{12}$ **>48a 60df<**

**Flair Lady 5** gr m Chilibang-Flair Park (Frimley Park) **1995:** 4456$^{5}$ 4505$^{10}$ **1996:** 105$^{11}$ 3257$^{17}$ **>23a 21f<**

**Flamanda 3** b f Niniski (USA)-Nemesia (Mill Reef (USA)) 1668$^{5}$ 4099$^{4}$ 4478$^{8}$ **>62f<**

**Flamands (IRE) 3** b f Sadler's Wells (USA)-Fleur Royale (Mill Reef (USA)) 3042$^{2}$ 3441$^{2}$ (3935) (4761) 4965$^{4}$ **>97f<**

**Flamboro 4** ch g Handsome Sailor-Scottish Legend (Legend of France (USA)) **1995:** 4514$^{12}$ **1996:** 342$^{5}$ 661$^{7}$ 801$^{2}$ 971$^{16}$ **>38a 55f<**

**Flame of Athens (IRE) 3** b c Royal Academy (USA)-Flame of Tara (Artaius (USA)) 1296a$^{6}$ 1574a$^{10}$ 3731a$^{6}$ **>104f<**

**Flame of Hope 3** b f Marju (IRE)-Tweedling (USA) (Sir Ivor) 640$^{9}$ 1100$^{11}$ 1655$^{15}$ 2159$^{4}$ 2541$^{3}$ 3165$^{10}$ **>62f<**

**Flame Valley (USA) 3** b f Gulch (USA)-Lightning Fire (Kris) 813$^{4}$ 1077$^{2}$ 1899$^{10}$ (3258) 3497$^{4}$ 3836$^{2}$ (4218) 4567$^{3}$ 4961a$^{2}$ **>113f<**

**Flaming June (USA) 3** ch f Storm Bird (CAN)-Affirmative Fable (USA) (Affirmed (USA)) 3986$^{9}$ 4590$^{11}$ **>61f<**

**Flaming Miracle (IRE) 6** b g Vision (USA)-Red Realm (Realm) 753$^{12}$ 852$^{13}$ **>37f<**

**Flamingo Garden (GER) 3** b c Rainbow Quest (USA)-Fabula Dancer (Northern Dancer) 1751a$^{3}$ 2668a$^{14}$ 3574a$^{3}$ **>106f<**

**Flamingo Paradise 5** ch h Rainbow Quest (USA)-Fabula Dancer (Northern Dancer) 1054a$^{2}$ 4032a$^{3}$ 4655a$^{9}$ **>112f<**

**Flaming West (USA) 2** ch c Gone West (USA)-Flaming Torch (Rousillon (USA)) 2243$^{2}$ (2695) 3150$^{4}$ **>94?f<**

**Flamma Vestalis (IRE) 2** b f Waajib-Splendid Chance (Random Shot) 2559$^{6}$ 3054$^{5}$ **>57f<**

**Flashfeet 6** b g Rousillon (USA)-Miellita (King Emperor (USA)) 257$^{6}$ 341$^{9}$ 1601$^{5}$ 1966$^{6}$ **>42a 40f<**

**Flashing Sabre 4** b g Statoblest-Placid Pet (Mummy's Pet) **1995:** 4542$^{10}$ **1996:** 59$^{13}$ 126$^{14}$ 180$^{8}$ 4820$^{26}$ **>9a 9?f<**

**Flash In The Pan (IRE) 3** ch f Bluebird (USA)-Tomona (Linacre) 914$^{3}$ 1025$^{4}$ 1457$^{6}$ 1814$^{6}$ 4789$^{15}$ **>45a 54f<**

**Flashman 6** b g Flash of Steel-Proper Madam (Mummy's Pet) 83$^{6}$ 656$^{4}$ **>39a 39f<**

**Flashy's Son 8** b or br g Balidar-Flashy Looker (Good Bond) 1342$^{3}$ 1598$^{4}$ 1885$^{4}$ 2329$^{13}$ 3460$^{7}$ 4356$^{17}$ 4460$^{14}$ 4809$^{19}$ **>46f<**

**Flaunt (IRE) 4** bb g Persian Bold-Fuchsia Belle 2459a$^{2}$ **>83f<**

**Fleeting Footsteps 4** b c Komaite (USA)-Hyperion Palace (Dragonara Palace (USA)) 1452$^{11}$ 1994$^{13}$ 2181$^{12}$ **>21f<**

**Fleet River (USA) 2** b f Riverman (USA)-Nimble Feet (USA) (Danzig (USA)) (3787) **>87f<**

**Flemensfirth (USA) 4** b c Alleged (USA)-Etheldreda (USA) (Diesis) (4656a) (5073a) **>128f<**

**Fletcher 2** b g Salse (USA)-Ballet Classique (USA) (Sadler's Wells (USA)) (697) 2040$^{7}$ 2364$^{4}$ 2878$^{4}$ 3792$^{12}$ 4084$^{2}$ 4625$^{11}$ **>92f<**

**Fleur de Tal 5** b m Primitive Rising (USA)-Penset (Red Sunset) **1995:** 4463$^{5}$ **>49a 43df<**

**Fleuve d'Or (IRE) 2** gr f Last Tycoon-Aldern Stream (Godswalk (USA)) 4600$^{13}$ 4783$^{11}$ **>35f<**

**Flight Master 4** ch g Master Willie-Mumtaz Mayfly (Tap On Wood) 1965$^{6}$ 2378$^{8}$ (2788) 3303$^{3}$ 3849$^{3}$ 4252$^{16}$ 4910$^{8}$ **>65f<**

**Flint And Steel 3** b g Rock City-Brassy Nell (Dunbeath (USA)) 943$^{4}$ 4511$^{10}$ **>58f<**

**Flirting Around (USA) 2** b c Silver Hawk (USA)-Dancing Grass (USA) (Northern Dancer) 3757$^{2}$ 4175$^{7}$ 4920$^{4}$ **>83f<**

**Flirty Gertie 4** ch f Prince Sabo-Red Tapsi (Tap On Wood) (110) 177$^{8}$ 2605$^{9}$ 3167$^{9}$ 3601$^{11}$ 4206$^{17}$ **>68a 55f<**

**Floating Devon 2** br g Simply Great (FR)-Devon Dancer (Shareef Dancer (USA)) 1849$^{4}$ 2370$^{5}$ 2633$^{7}$ 3099$^{4}$ 3512$^{6}$ 4625$^{9}$ **>45a 61f<**

**Floating Line 8** ch g Bairn (USA)-County Line (High Line) 1116$^{8}$ 2068$^{4}$ 2239$^{4}$ 2697$^{7}$ 2884$^{3}$ 3297$^{2}$ 3487$^{5}$ 3710$^{14}$ 3922$^{2}$ 4315$^{2}$ (4557) 4771$^{4}$ **>83f<**

**Flocheck (USA) 3** ch c Hansel (USA)-Eurobird (Ela-Mana-Mou) 687$^{5}$ 954$^{2}$ (1591) 1783$^{2}$ 4260$^{2}$ 4447$^{15}$ (4673) **>100f<**

**Flood's Fancy 3** b gr f Then Again-Port Na Blath (On Your Mark) **1995:** 4483$^{5}$ 4511$^{5}$ **1996:** 21$^{7}$ 183$^{7}$ 531$^{6}$ 1780$^{11}$ 4045$^{19}$ **>54a 62f<**

**Flood's Flyer (IRE) 2** ch f Silver Kite (USA)-Al Shany (Burslem) 624$^{6}$ 910$^{5}$ 1164$^{4}$ **>7f<**

**Flood's Hot Stuff 2** gr f Chilibang-Tiszta Sharok (Song) 3593$^{19}$ 4593$^{6}$ 4762$^{13}$ 4970$^{15}$ **>38f<**

**Florentine Diamond (IRE) 2** b f Primo Dominie-Poplina (USA) (Roberto (USA)) 3282$^{6}$ 3475$^{9}$ 3807$^{17}$ 4343$^{7}$ **>47f<**

**Florentino (IRE) 3** b br c Machiavellian (USA)-Helens Dreamgirl (Caerleon (USA)) 445$^{7}$ 577$^{9}$ (1515) 1838$^{3}$ (2558) 4992$^{6}$ **>80f<**

**Floresta (FR) 3** b f Kaldoun (FR)-Belle du Bresil (Akarad (FR)) **1995:** (4496a) **1996:** 720a$^{4}$ **>100f<**

**Florid (USA) 5** ch h The Minstrel (CAN)-Kenanga (Kris) 581$^{4}$ 726$^{4}$ (929) 1620$^{3}$ 1988$^{3}$ 4714$^{3}$ 4911$^{3}$ **>116f<**

**Florismart 4** b g Never so Bold-Spoilt Again (Mummy's Pet) **1995:** 4510$^{10}$ **1996:** 420$^{7}$ 1778$^{11}$ 2989$^{B}$ 3507$^{8}$ **>16a 31f<**

**Florrie'm 3** ch f Tina's Pet-Rosie Dickins (Blue Cashmere) 49$^{8}$ 129$^{8}$ 1500$^{14}$ 2061$^{8}$ 2966$^{7}$ 3481$^{9}$ 3761$^{9}$ **>16a 42df<**

**Flo's Choice (IRE) 2** b f Dancing Dissident (USA)-Miss Siddons (Cure The Blues (USA)) 1197$^{10}$ 1525$^{5}$ 2315$^{7}$ 3293$^{9}$ 3582$^{10}$ 4079$^{7}$ **>32a 54f<**

**Flotilla 2** b c Saddlers' Hall (IRE)-Aim for the Top (USA) (Irish River (FR)) 1038$^{6}$ 1603$^{2}$ 1892$^{7}$ 2984$^{2}$ 3417$^{11}$ 4602$^{10}$ **>59a 73f<**

**Flourishing Way 2** b f Sadler's Wells (USA)-Darayna (IRE) (Shernazar) 3593$^{11}$ 4062$^{2}$ 4225$^{2}$ **>75f<**

**Flow Back 4** gr g Royal Academy (USA)-Flo Russell (USA) (Round Table) 982$^{15}$ 1448$^{6}$ 1772$^{7}$ (2372) **>65a 44f<**

**Flower Hill Lad (IRE) 2** b c Sizzling Melody-Persian Tapestry (Tap On Wood) 2596$^{10}$ 2967$^{4}$ 3462$^{6}$ 3982$^{19}$ **>70f<**

**Flowing Fortune 2** b c Kenmare (FR)-Green Flower (USA) (Fappiano (USA)) 4755$^{2}$ **>60tf<**

**Flowing Ocean 6** ch h Forzando-Boswellia (Frankincense) 3951$^{13}$ 4077$^{11}$ 4575$^{11}$ 5062$^{12}$ **>8a 65?f<**

**Fluidity (USA) 8** b g Robellino (USA)-Maple River (USA) (Clandestine) 1685$^{7}$ **>33a 50f<**

**Flurry (FR) 3** b f Groom Dancer (USA)-Snowtop (Thatching) 4940a$^{2}$ **>97f<**

**Flyaway Blues 4** b g Bluebird (USA)-Voltigeuse (USA) (Filiberto (USA)) 589$^{10}$ 690$^{10}$ 998$^{3}$ 1474$^{12}$ 1847$^{7}$ 2075$^{3}$ 3958$^{7}$ 4226$^{16}$ **>55f<**

**Flyaway Hill (FR) 2** b f Danehill (USA)-Flyaway Bride (USA) (Blushing Groom (FR)) 4104$^{5}$ 4512$^{16}$ **>71f<**

**Fly Down To Rio (IRE) 2** ch f Silver Kite (USA)-Brazilian Princess (Absalom) 1531$^{5}$ 1683$^{7}$ 3405$^{7}$ 3820$^{7}$ 3976$^{8}$ 4223$^{11}$ 4562$^{12}$ 4780$^{7}$ **>27a 57f<**

**Flyfisher (IRE) 3** b c Batshoof-Inveraven (Alias Smith (USA)) 725$^{2}$ 1580a$^{8}$ 2227$^{3}$ 2620$^{6}$ 4313$^{5}$

4800$^{10}$ **>97f<**

**Fly Fishing (USA) 3** ch c Miswaki (USA)-Sharp Flick (USA) (Sharpen Up) 509$^{7}$ **>73f<**

**Fly For Fame 3** b f Shaadi (USA)-Fly Me (FR) (Luthier) 2669a$^{3}$ **>98f<**

**Fly-Girl 2** ch f Clantime-Lyndseylee (Swing Easy (USA)) 2699$^{6}$ 3050$^{8}$ **>36f<**

**Flying Colours (IRE) 2** b f Fairy King (USA)-Crazed Rainbow (USA) (Graustark) 4889$^{11}$ **>19f<**

**Flying Flowers 3** ch f Thatching-Flying Fairy (Bustino) 2208$^{7}$ 2785$^{8}$ 3334$^{14}$ **>54f<**

**Flying Green (FR) 3** ch g Persian Bold-Flying Sauce (Sauce Boat (USA)) (2557) 3071$^{7}$ 3594$^{14}$ **>90f<**

**Flying Harold 3** b c Gildoran-Anytime Anywhere (Daring March) 1901$^{15}$ 2235$^{6}$ 2617$^{11}$ 3048$^{5}$ 3165$^{5}$ 3286$^{2}$ 3492$^{2}$ 3852$^{15}$ 4263$^{17}$ **>53f<**

**Flying Legend (USA) 3** b c Alleged (USA)-L'Extravagante (USA) (Le Fabuleux) 1644$^{4}$ (2080) (3760) 4192$^{9}$ **>103+f<**

**Flying North (IRE) 3** b g Distinctly North (USA)-North Kildare (USA) (Northjet) 689$^{3}$ 937$^{10}$ 2894$^{3}$ 3134$^{6}$ 3640$^{4}$ 3974$^{8}$ 4190$^{13}$ 4470$^{2}$ 4769$^{16}$ 4974$^{12}$ **>83f<**

**Flying Pennant (IRE) 3** ch c Waajib-Flying Beckee (IRE) (Godswalk (USA)) 640$^{12}$ 730$^{9}$ (1122) 1348$^{4}$ 1594$^{2}$ 1902$^{3}$ 2577$^{2}$ 4775$^{21}$ 4831$^{15}$ **>78f<**

**Flying Squaw 3** b f Be My Chief (USA)-Sea Fret (Habat) 708$^{9}$ **>96f<**

**Flying Thatch (IRE) 2** b c Thatching-More Candy (Ballad Rock) 4756$^{18}$ 4825$^{15}$ 5034$^{13}$ **>50f<**

**Fly Me Home 2** ch c Efisio-My Croft (Crofter (USA)) 3464$^{11}$ *4976$^{6}$* **>40a 34f<**

**Fly Tip (IRE) 3** b f Bluebird (USA)-Sharp Deposit (Sharpo) *1146$^{7}$* 1493$^{4}$ 3989$^{13}$ 4802$^{14}$ 4901$^{19}$ **>79f<**

**Fly To The Stars 2** b c Bluebird (USA)-Rise and Fall (Mill Reef (USA)) 4825$^{3}$ 4991$^{2}$ **>88f<**

**Fog City 3** b c Damister (USA)-Front Line Romance (Caerleon (USA)) 3810$^{13}$ 3973$^{17}$ **>83a 72f<**

**Foist 4** b g Efisio-When The Saints (Bay Express) *(431) (534) (607) 806$^{5}$* 1364$^{8}$ 2154$^{5}$ 3995$^{3}$ 4226$^{3}$ 4686$^{11}$ **>64+a 51f<**

**Folgore (USA) 2** ch f Irish River (USA)-Florie (FR) (Gay Mecene (USA)) (2666a) 4039a$^{2}$ (4420a) 4746a$^{9}$

**Folle Tempete (FR) 3** dk f Fabulous Dancer (USA)-Belle Tempete (FR) **1995:** 4400a$^{3}$ **1996:** 3568a$^{2}$ 4405a$^{2}$ **>102f<**

**Followmegirls 7** b m Sparkling Boy-Haddon Anna (Dragonara Palace (USA)) 466$^{7}$ 601$^{14}$ 812$^{8}$ 1039$^{7}$ 2186$^{U}$ **>47f<**

**Followthe Allstars 3** ch c Anshan-Angel's Sing (Mansingh (USA)) *528$^{10}$* 634$^{6}$ 2124$^{7}$ 2506$^{16}$ 2979$^{10}$ 3300$^{2}$ 3473$^{11}$ 3860$^{4}$ 4898$^{12}$ *4999$^{5}$* **>54a 65f<**

**Folly Foot Fred 2** b g Crisp-Wessex Kingdom (Vaigly Great) (590) 877$^{4}$ 1331$^{6}$ 1980$^{6}$ 2509$^{5}$ **>50f<**

**Fond Embrace 3** b f Emarati (USA)-Detente (Dominion) (591) (959) 3693$^{7}$ 3875$^{3}$ 4115$^{9}$ **>98f<**

**Fontcaudette (IRE) 2** b f River Falls-Lune de Miel (Kalamoun) 3171$^{5}$ 3963$^{7}$ 4241$^{12}$ **>63f<**

**Fonzy 2** b g Phountzi (USA)-Diavalezza (Connaught) *(1026) (1183)* 1360$^{5}$ 1543$^{3}$ 2125$^{2}$ (2174) (2389) 2846$^{W}$ **>54a 74f<**

**Foolish Flutter (IRE) 2** b br f Fools Holme (USA)-Thornbeam (Beldale Flutter (USA)) 608$^{7}$ 1197$^{12}$ 2512$^{10}$ 2850$^{3}$ 2959$^{7}$ 4097$^{12}$ 4361$^{9}$ 4834$^{5}$ **>40f<**

**Fools of Pride (IRE) 4** ch f Al Hareb (USA)-I'll Take Paris (USA) (Vaguely Noble) **1995:** *4449$^{4}$ 4530$^{9}$* **1996:** *34$^{7}$ 73$^{4}$ 138$^{4}$ 186$^{12}$ 365$^{9}$* **>36a 49f<**

**Foot Battalion (IRE) 2** b c Batshoof-Roxy Music (IRE) (Song) 490$^{4}$ (685) 984$^{2}$ 1115$^{6}$ 1419$^{7}$ 2317$^{2}$ 2700$^{3}$ 3150$^{3}$ 3268$^{2}$ 4621$^{5}$ 4723$^{25}$ **>87f<**

**Foothill (IRE) 3** b g Tirol-Threshold (Alleged (USA)) *167$^{9}$ 1104$^{16}$* ***>40f<* (DEAD)**

**Force of Will (USA) 3** ch c Diesis-Clear Issue (USA) (Riverman (USA)) 1253a$^{3}$ 1296a$^{5}$ 2092a$^{4}$ **>100f<**

**Forcing Bid 2** b c Forzando-Cox's Pippin (USA) (Cox's Ridge (USA)) 4468$^{4}$ 4600$^{3}$ 4786$^{6}$ 5006$^{5}$ **>61f<**

**Forecast 3** b g Formidable (USA)-Princess Matilda (Habitat) *606$^{8}$ 781$^{9}$ (867)* 973$^{16}$ *2367$^{7}$ 2777$^{6}$* 3458$^{13}$ 3789$^{9}$ 3970$^{17}$ 4589$^{15}$ **>32a 32f<**

**Foreign Judgement (USA) 3** b g El Gran Senor (USA)-Numeral (USA) (Alleged (USA)) 2135$^{12}$ 2744$^{9}$ 3220$^{14}$ 5053$^{18}$ **>56df<**

**Foreign Relation (IRE) 3** b f Distant Relative-Nicola Wynn (Nicholas Bill) 3624$^{4}$ 4074$^{5}$ 4229$^{2}$ 4550$^{10}$ 4692$^{11}$ **>57f<**

**Foreman 3** b g Timeless Times (USA)-Skiddaw Bird (Bold Owl) **1995:** *4383$^{8}$ 4431$^{4}$ 4453$^{6}$* **1996:** *123$^{4}$ 157$^{4}$ 194$^{4}$ 238$^{3}$ (317) 340$^{4}$ 1009$^{5}$* 3285$^{6}$ **>62a 57f<**

**Forentia 3** b f Formidable (USA)-Clarentia (Ballad Rock) *966$^{7}$* 1628$^{11}$ 1962$^{10}$ 2548$^{9}$ 4044$^{3}$ 4552$^{9}$ **>72f<**

**Forest Boy 3** b g Komaite (USA)-Khadine (Astec) 458$^{7}$ (616) (775) (915) 976$^{6}$ 1523$^{7}$ **>68a 76f<**

**Forest Buck (USA) 3** ch c Green Forest (USA)-Perlee (FR) (Margouillat (FR)) *(4177)* 4757$^{3}$ **>114f<**

**Forest Cat (IRE) 4** b f Petorius-Forest of Arden (Tap On Wood) *1481$^{4}$* 1800$^{6}$ 3127$^{2}$ 3712$^{3}$ 4135$^{5}$ **>104f<**

**Forest Fantasy 3** b f Rambo Dancer (CAN)-Another Treat (Derring-Do) 819$^{4}$ 1089$^{6}$ 1477$^{3}$ 2067$^{8}$ 2776$^{3}$ (3414) 3655$^{2}$ 3938$^{4}$ 4438$^{8}$ **>66f<**

**Forest Heights 3** b f Slip Anchor-Forest Blossom (USA) (Green Forest (USA)) 813$^{7}$ (1644) 1990$^{4}$ 3398$^{3}$ **>92f<**

**Forest Robin 3** ch c Formidable (USA)-Blush Rambler (IRE) (Blushing Groom (FR)) 577$^{8}$ 833$^{2}$ 969$^{3}$ 2041$^{14}$ 3298$^{3}$ 3799$^{4}$ 4064$^{2}$ 4617$^{19}$ 4827$^{6}$ 4992$^{9}$ **>87df<**

**Forest Star (USA) 7** b g Green Forest (USA)-Al Madina (USA) (Round Table) **1995:** *4546$^{8}$* **1996:** *9$^{8}$ 553$^{14}$* **>34a f<**

**Foreverfree 3** b f Sylvan Express-Lady Homily (Homing) *3064$^{12}$ 4090$^{11}$*

**Forever Noble (IRE) 3** b g Forzando-Pagan Queen (Vaguely Noble) 746$^{3}$ 948$^{8}$ 1839$^{5}$ 2251$^{4}$ 2736$^{5}$ 4448$^{3}$ 4509$^{11}$ 4766$^{4}$ 4877$^{4}$ **>57f<**

**Forgetful 7** br m Don't Forget Me-Peak Squaw (USA) (Icecapade (USA)) **1995:** *4507$^{8}$* **1996:** *116$^{6}$ 240$^{8}$* **>30a 38f<**

**Forget Paris (IRE) 3** gr f Broken Hearted-Miss Deauville (Sovereign Path) 1196$^{7}$ 1526$^{10}$ *2082$^{6}$ 2540$^{8}$* 2587$^{14}$ 3481$^{8}$ **>46a 43f<**

**Forget To Remindme 2** b f Forzando-Sandy Looks (Music Boy) 4783$^{4}$ **>44f<**

**Forgie (IRE) 3** b g Don't Forget Me-Damia (Vision (USA)) 614$^{10}$ 803$^{3}$ (1503) 1783$^{7}$ 2165$^{4}$ 3329$^{2}$ 3641$^{2}$ 4506$^{2}$ 4596$^{8}$ **>74f<**

**Forgotten Dancer (IRE) 5** ch g Don't Forget Me-Dancing Diana (Raga Navarro (ITY)) 664$^{10}$ 983$^{15}$ 1517$^{5}$ 1658$^{8}$ 3698$^{12}$ **>36a 51f<**

**Forgotten Empress 4** b f Dowsing (USA)-Vynz Girl (Tower Walk) *77$^{13}$ 211$^{7}$ 1341$^{15}$* 2331$^{5}$ 2565$^{4}$ **>52a 51f<**

**Forgotten Times (USA) 2** ch f Nabeel Dancer (USA)-Etoile D'Amore (USA) (The Minstrel (CAN)) 4208$^{6}$ 4697$^{4}$ **>75f<**

**For Lara (IRE) 2** ch f Soviet Star (USA)-On the Staff (USA) (Master Willie) 3796$^{6}$ **>45f<**

**Forliando 3** b g Forzando-Lucky Orphan (Derrylin) 471$^{15}$ *655$^{6}$ 1451$^{5}$* 1979$^{10}$ 3474$^{15}$ *3872$^{11}$* **>33a 34f<**

**Forlorn Point (IRE) 2** ch f General Assembly (USA)-Romantic Feeling (Shirley Heights) 4024a$^{29}$ **>41f<**

**Formal Gold (CAN) 3** b br c Black Tie Affair-Ingoldsby (USA) (Screen King (USA)) 4956a$^{5}$ **>125f<**

**Formentiere 3** gr f Sharrood (USA)-Me Spede (Valiyar) 820$^{15}$ 1196$^{16}$ 1836$^{7}$ 2180$^{16}$ 2556$^{14}$ 3116$^{6}$ **>36f<**

**Formidable Flame 3** ch g Formidable (USA)-Madiyla (Darshaan) 732$^{9}$ 821$^{8}$ 1508$^{14}$ 4559$^{8}$ 4804$^{12}$ **>69f<**

**Formidable Lass 5** ch m Formidable (USA)-Stock Hill Lass (Air Trooper) *133$^{10}$* **>37f<**

**Formidable Liz 6** ch m Formidable (USA)-Areej (Rusticaro (FR)) 1848$^{8}$ 2064$^{8}$ 2363$^{2}$ 2590$^{4}$ *2937$^{4}$ 3223$^{8}$* (3639) 4071$^{11}$ 4206$^{3}$ 4323$^{8}$ **>52a 69f<**

**Formidable Partner 3** b c Formidable (USA)-Brush Away (Ahonoora) 840$^{7}$ 1319$^{12}$ 1654$^{2}$ 2000$^{5}$ 2603$^{3}$ 3043$^{7}$ 3653$^{4}$ 3986$^{11}$ **>76f<**

**Formidable Spirit 2** ch c Formidable (USA)-Hicklam Millie (Absalom) 3581$^{6}$ **>24f<**

**For Old Times Sake 2** ch c Efisio-Blue Birds Fly (Rainbow Quest (USA)) 685$^{10}$ *(858) (1032)* (1303) 1699$^{5}$ (2484) 2890$^{4}$ 3247$^{5}$ (3483) (3940) 4247$^{5}$ 4685$^{4}$ 4893$^{7}$ **>57a 97?f<**

**For the Present 6** b g Then Again-Axe Valley (Royben) 735$^{13}$ 928$^{24}$ 1501$^{7}$ 1974$^{10}$ (2137) 2694$^{15}$ 2911$^{12}$ 3085$^{3}$ 3232$^{23}$ 3622$^{15}$ 3810$^{3}$ 4116$^{6}$ 4314$^{14}$ **>92f<**

**Fortis Pavior (IRE) 6** b g Salt Dome (USA)-Heather Lil (Ballymore) **1995:** *4427$^{11}$* **1996:** *76$^{9}$ 155$^{14}$* **>20a f<**

**Fort Knox (IRE) 5** b g Treasure Kay-Single Viking (Viking (USA)) **1995:** *(4350) 4385$^{5}$ 4456$^{3}$ 4531$^{5}$* **1996:** *26$^{2}$ 36$^{4}$ 107$^{2}$ 121$^{3}$ 163$^{8}$ (406) (464) 487$^{6}$ 1658$^{2}$* 1953$^{3}$ 2283$^{5}$ 2581$^{13}$ 2761$^{2}$ 2982$^{5}$ *3078$^{4}$ 3281$^{2}$* 3443$^{5}$ 3861$^{4}$ 3967$^{7}$ **>72a 67f<**

**Fort Lamy 3** b g 3387a$^{4}$ **>97f<**

**Fort Nottingham (USA) 3** b c Alleged (USA)-Aletta Maria (USA) (Diesis) 1139a$^{3}$ 2276a$^{9}$ **>109f<**

**Fortuitious (IRE) 3** b f Polish Patriot (USA)-Echo Cove (Slip Anchor) *35$^{11}$ 1903$^{8}$* 2594$^{9}$ **>35f<**

**Fortunes Course (IRE) 7** b m Crash Course-Night Rose (Sovereign Gleam) 1123$^{9}$ 1462$^{9}$ (2530) 4612$^{8}$ **>55f<**

**Forward Miss 2** b f Bold Arrangement-Maiden Bidder (Shack (USA)) 4544$^{12}$

**For Your Eyes Only 2** b c Pursuit of Love-Rivers Rhapsody (Dominion) 848$^{3}$ (1197) (1699) 2070$^{9}$ 3247$^{6}$ 3690$^{6}$ 3843$^{4}$ 4131$^{13}$ 5043$^{12}$ **>92f<**

**Forza Figlio 3** b c Warning-Wish You Well (Sadler's Wells (USA)) *732$^{2}$* 894$^{4}$ (1326) 1619$^{3}$ 2616$^{5}$ **>88f<**

**Forzair 4** b g Forzando-Persian Air (Persian Bold) **1995:** *4510$^{2}$* **1996:** *77$^{5}$ (125) 184$^{6}$ 477$^{5}$ (520) 612$^{5}$* 738$^{8}$ 1034$^{2}$ 1637$^{4}$ 2488$^{5}$ 2568$^{8}$ 2731$^{6}$ *3955$^{9}$ 4563$^{9}$ 4779$^{12}$* **>73a 62f<**

**Forzara 3** ch f Risk Me (FR)-Valldemosa (Music Boy) 1787$^{6}$ 2176$^{4}$ *2305$^{8}$ 2732$^{7}$* (2933) 3331$^{11}$ **>53f<**

**Foundry Lane 5** b g Mtoto-Eider (Niniski (USA)) 2330$^{7}$ 3689$^{19}$ 3983$^{6}$ **>89f<**

**Fourdaned (IRE) 3** b c Danehill (USA)-Pro Patria (Petingo) 705$^{2}$ 3067$^{6}$ 3353$^{5}$ 3788$^{9}$ 4047$^{10}$ **>68f<**

**Four Lane Flyer 4** b f Sayf El Arab (USA)-Collegian (Stanford) 586$^{17}$ 734$^{7}$ 1421$^{15}$ 1596$^{12}$ 1846$^{7}$ **>41f<**

**Four of Spades 5** ch g Faustus (USA)-Fall To Pieces (USA) (Forli (ARG)) **1995:** *4394$^{13}$ 4457$^{2}$ 4502$^{3}$ (4531)* **1996:** *20$^{7}$ 55$^{4}$ 121$^{13}$ 144$^{2}$ 177$^{7}$ 190$^{2}$ 851$^{6}$ 1048$^{4}$ 1088$^{3}$ 1448$^{2}$ 1604$^{2}$ 1812$^{3}$ 2032$^{4}$*

2201$^{4}$ 3578$^{2}$ 3877$^{7}$ 4240$^{9}$ 4979$^{9}$ **>64a 61f<**

**Fourofus** 7 b g Wassl-Que Sera (Music Boy) 15$^{13}$

**Four Weddings (USA)** 3 b g Runaway Groom (CAN)-Kitty's Best (USA) (Amen (FR)) 56$^{8}$ 483$^{5}$ 599$^{2}$ (849) 1900$^{10}$ 2613$^{3}$ **>44a 58f<**

**Fox Chapel** 9 b g Formidable (USA)-Hollow Heart (Wolver Hollow) 268$^{3}$ 398$^{3}$ 422$^{12}$ **>63a f<**

**Foxes Tail** 2 gr g Batshoof-Secret Gill (Most Secret) 2495$^{3}$ (2932) 3512$^{5}$ 3835$^{10}$ (4298) 4864$^{10}$ **>77f<**

**Foxford Lad** 2 b g Akid (USA)-Spring Rose (Blakeney) 4368$^{9}$ **>28f<**

**Fraise du Roi (IRE)** 4 b f Roi Danzig (USA)-Stolen Fruit (Bold Lad (IRE)) 79$^{8}$ 138$^{2}$ **>71a f<**

**Framed (IRE)** 6 b g Tate Gallery (USA)-Golden Thread (Glint of Gold) **1995:** 4428$^{9}$ **1996:** 479$^{9}$ 688$^{4}$ 979$^{9}$ 4263$^{4}$ **>43a 56f<**

**Frances Mary** 3 ch f Sylvan Express-Maydrum (Meldrum) **1995:** 4369$^{2}$ (4375) **>67a 55?f<**

**Frandickbob** 2 b c Statoblest-Crimson Ring (Persian Bold) 2083$^{8}$ 2413$^{8}$ **>19a f<**

**Fran Godfrey** 3 b f Taufan (USA)-One Last Glimpse (Relko) **1995:** 4352$^{2}$ **1996:** 646$^{15}$ 4109$^{17}$ 4438$^{9}$ **>60a 65f<**

**Frankie** 2 b c Shalford (IRE)-Twilight Secret (Vaigly Great) 3794$^{6}$ **>49f<**

**Franklinsboy** 4 b g Clantime-Sky Fighter (Hard Fought) 1081$^{9}$ **>45a 3f<**

**Frankly Fran** 4 b f Petorius-Sunita (Owen Dudley) 495$^{4}$ 604$^{8}$ 817$^{12}$ 1462$^{11}$ 1970$^{W}$ 4877$^{14}$ **>10a 56f<**

**Frans Lad** 4 ch g Music Boy-Moberry (Mossberry) **1995:** 4388$^{7}$ **>57a 63f<**

**Freckles Kelly** 4 b f Shavian-Choke Cherry (Connaught) 1028$^{7}$ 1157$^{7}$ (1455) (1716) 1971$^{W}$ **>59a 47f< (DEAD)**

**Freddie's Recall** 3 b f Warrshan (USA)-Coir 'a' Ghaill (Jalmood (USA)) 2557$^{10}$ 3108$^{7}$ 3466$^{7}$ **>33f<**

**Frederick James** 2 b c Efisio-Rare Roberta (USA) (Roberto (USA)) 4619$^{8}$ **>46f<**

**Fredrik The Fierce (IRE)** 2 b g Puissance-Hollia (Touch Boy) 441$^{4}$ 865$^{4}$ 1184$^{2}$ (2219) 2879$^{7}$ (3160) 3692$^{5}$ 4191$^{7}$ **>94f<**

**Fred's Delight (IRE)** 5 b g Law Society (USA)-Madame Nureyev (USA) (Nureyev (USA)) 426$^{8}$ 521$^{7}$ 1029$^{7}$ 1718$^{7}$ **>25a 35df<**

**Free As A Bird** 2 b f Robellino (USA)-Special Guest (Be My Guest (USA)) 4798$^{5}$ 4969$^{18}$ **>58f<**

**Freedom Chance (IRE)** 2 ch c Lahib (USA)-Gentle Guest (IRE) (Be My Guest (USA)) 4050$^{7}$ 4884$^{9}$ **>54f<**

**Freedom Flame** 3 b f Darshaan-Fire and Shade (USA) (Shadeed (USA)) 2318$^{3}$ (2608) 2742$^{4}$ 3211$^{14}$ **>87f<**

**Freedom of Troy** 2 b c Puissance-Wing of Freedom (Troy) 4383$^{10}$ 4751$^{8}$ 5009$^{7}$ **>36f<**

**Freedom Run** 3 b c Polish Precedent (USA)-Ausherra (USA) (Diesis) 67$^{11}$

**Freequent** 3 ch c Rainbow Quest (USA)-Free Guest (Be My Guest (USA)) 583$^{3}$ (786) (1469) 1771$^{8}$ 2608$^{6}$ (3145) 3781$^{4}$ 4421a$^{4}$ 5045$^{7}$ **>108f<**

**Free To Speak (IRE)** 4 ch g Be My Guest (USA)-Love For Poetry (Lord Gayle (USA)) 1252a$^{6}$ 1912a$^{2}$ 2459a$^{8}$ **>99f<**

**French Ballerina (IRE)** 3 b f Sadler's Wells (USA)-Filia Ardross (Ardross) 2837a$^{5}$ (4738a) (4851a) **>108f<**

**French Ginger** 5 ch m Most Welcome-French Plait (Thatching) 337$^{2}$ 409$^{7}$ 462$^{8}$ 4810$^{20}$ 4993$^{17}$ **>57a 37f<**

**French Grit (IRE)** 4 b g Common Grounds-Charbatte (FR) (In Fijar (USA)) 610$^{6}$ 716$^{2}$ 928$^{22}$ 1652$^{8}$ 2911$^{7}$ 3639$^{4}$ 3793$^{6}$ 4058$^{3}$ 4460$^{2}$ 4689$^{2}$ 4791$^{3}$ 4811$^{11}$ 4994$^{5}$ **>78f<**

**French Ivy (USA)** 9 ch g Nodouble (USA)-Lierre (USA) (Gummo (USA)) 1070$^{11}$ 1343$^{6}$ 2148$^{3}$ (2516) 3037$^{6}$ 3329$^{4}$ (3801) 4199$^{2}$ **>76f<**

**French Mist** 2 b f Mystiko (USA)-Flambera (FR) (Akarad (FR)) 2147$^{9}$ 2611$^{10}$ 3159$^{5}$ 3764$^{6}$ 4211$^{5}$ 4488$^{22}$ **>75f<**

**Fresh Fruit Daily** 4 b f Reprimand-Dalmally (Sharpen Up) **1995:** 4543$^{2}$ **1996:** 24$^{3}$ 141$^{4}$ 204$^{3}$ 2124$^{5}$ 2437$^{7}$ 4360$^{7}$ 4788$^{3}$ 4895$^{9}$ **>77da 69f<**

**Fresh Look (IRE)** 4 b f Alzao (USA)-Bag Lady (Be My Guest (USA)) **1995:** 4416$^{10}$ 4506$^{10}$ **1996:** 760$^{7}$ 1414$^{8}$ 1821$^{3}$ 2896$^{15}$ **>5a 51f<**

**Fret (USA)** 6 b g Storm Bird (CAN)-Windy and Mild (USA) (Best Turn (USA)) 73$^{13}$ **>67f<**

**Frezeliere** 3 b f Be My Chief (USA)-Anna Karietta (Precocious) (746) 947$^{2}$ 2608$^{3}$ 3039$^{6}$ 3947$^{17}$ 4297$^{6}$ 4617$^{16}$ **>89df<**

**Friar Street (IRE)** 6 b g Carmelite House (USA)-Madam Slaney (Prince Tenderfoot (USA)) 363$^{6}$ **>41a 54f<**

**Friendly Brave (USA)** 6 b g Well Decorated (USA)-Companionship (USA) (Princely Native (USA)) **1995:** (4359) **1996:** 266$^{4}$ 315$^{4}$ 380$^{9}$ 407$^{4}$ 601$^{7}$ (667) 742$^{3}$ 862$^{3}$ 1049$^{4}$ 1351$^{2}$ 1512$^{5}$ 1777$^{5}$ (1958) 2129$^{7}$ (2280) 2586$^{3}$ 2976$^{2}$ 3146$^{7}$ (3338) 4367$^{5}$ 4581$^{5}$ 4689$^{8}$ 4802$^{11}$ 4995$^{2}$ **>71a 86f<**

**Friendly Dreams (IRE)** 3 gr f Midyan (USA)-Friendly Thoughts (USA) (Al Hattab (USA)) 849$^{14}$ 1451$^{P}$ 1497$^{12}$ 2060$^{10}$ 2362$^{6}$ 2537$^{9}$ 2775$^{8}$ 2891$^{16}$ **>31f<**

**Friendly Knight** 6 b g Horage-Be A Dancer (Be Friendly) 620$^{13}$ **>40f<**

**Friendly Lover (USA)** 8 b h Cutlass (USA)-Glide Along (USA) (Great Above (USA)) 4951a$^{11}$ **>118a f<**

**Fro** 3 b f Salse (USA)-Silent Sun (Blakeney) 528$^{9}$ 1462$^{10}$ 4496$^{10}$ 4612$^{D}$ 4794$^{4}$ **>56f<**

**Frog** 3 b f Akarad (FR)-Best Girl Friend (Sharrood (USA)) **1995:** 4383$^{10}$ **1996:** (2542) (2688) (2768) (2855) (3056) 3145$^{11}$ 4385$^{7}$ **>31++a 88f<**

**Frontier Flight (USA)** 6 b g Flying Paster (USA)-Sly Charmer (USA) (Valdez (USA)) 2173$^{12}$ 3149$^{7}$ 3463$^{10}$ **>34a 51f<**

**Frontman (IRE)** 3 ch g Imperial Frontier (USA)-Countess Kildare (Dominion) **1995:** 4429$^{3}$ **1996:** 458$^{3}$ 591$^{5}$ 779$^{2}$ 997$^{10}$ 1492$^{10}$ 1527$^{15}$ **>66a 61f< (DEAD)**

**Frost King** 2 gr g Northern State (USA)-Celtic Image (Welsh Saint) 2972$^{7}$ 3682$^{7}$ 4200$^{9}$ **>60f<**

**Frozen Sea (USA)** 5 ch h Diesis-Ocean Ballad (Grundy) (1695) 2707$^{4}$ 3355$^{5}$ **>72df<**

**Fruitana (IRE)** 2 b g Distinctly North (USA)-Tadjnama (USA) (Exceller (USA)) 1849$^{6}$ 2491$^{2}$ 3250$^{2}$ 3429$^{3}$ 4043$^{2}$ 4558$^{11}$ 4762$^{7}$ (4999) **>85a 73f<**

**Fruitful Lady** 3 b f Puissance-Tamango Lady (Shack (USA)) 768$^{14}$ **(DEAD)**

**Fruitie O'Flarety** 2 gr c Environment Friend-Dame Margot (USA) (Northern Dancer) 4175$^{8}$ 4349$^{W}$ 4920$^{10}$ 5040$^{7}$ **>77f<**

**Fruit Town (IRE)** 7 b g Camden Town-Fruitful (Oats) 4674$^{14}$

**Frutina** 3 b f Risk Me (FR)-Queen's Piper (Song) 3862$^{4}$ 4074$^{14}$ 4221$^{14}$ **>42f<**

**Frutti Tutti (FR)** 5 b h Le Glorieux-Lignita (FR) (Amen (FR)) 193a$^{3}$ **>107f<**

**Fujiyama Crest (IRE)** 4 b g Roi Danzig (USA)-Snoozy Time (Cavo Doro) 825$^{3}$ 1005$^{5}$ 1439$^{3}$ 2042$^{9}$ 2330$^{12}$ (4447) **>100f<**

**Fujiyama Kenzan (JPN)** 8 b h Lucky Cast (JPN)-Waka Suzuran (JPN) (Contrite (USA)) **1995:** (4524a)

**Full of Tricks** 8 ch g Mossberry-Duchess of Hayling VII (Damsire Unregistered) 175$^{9}$ 260$^{9}$

**Fullopep** 2 b g Dunbeath (USA)-Suggia (Alzao (USA)) 4578$^{10}$ 4754$^{2}$ 4907$^{7}$ **>60f<**

**Full Quiver** 11 br g Gorytus (USA)-Much Pleasure (Morston (FR)) 546$^{9}$ 1655$^{14}$ 1826$^{9}$ **>53f<**

**Full Throttle** 3 br g Daring March-Wheatley (Town Crier) 1656$^{7}$ 1873$^{10}$ 2135$^{13}$ 2506$^{3}$ 3611$^{2}$ (3878) (3961) 4557$^{3}$ 4899$^{2}$ **>75f<**

**Full Traceability (IRE)** 2 b f Ron's Victory (USA)-Miss Petella (Dunphy) 506$^{2}$ (657) 996$^{9}$ 1183$^{3}$ 1491$^{5}$ 1645$^{3}$ 2174$^{2}$ 2429$^{8}$ 4562$^{20}$ **>47a 58f<**

**Fully Booked** 2 b f Midyan (USA)-Vielle (Ribero) 3475$^{11}$ 3807$^{16}$ **>32f<**

**Funchal Way** 4 b g One Man Band-Dusky Nancy (Red Sunset) 2853$^{7}$ **>58?f<**

**Fun Galore (USA)** 2 b c Gone West (USA)-Ma Petite Jolie (USA) (Northern Dancer) (1897) (2291) 3143$^{7}$ **>82+f<**

**Fun Harbour (FR)** 3 ch c Funambule (USA)-Clef des Ondes 149a$^{2}$ **>82f<**

**Funky** 3 ch f Classic Music (USA)-Foreno (Formidable (USA)) 3100$^{4}$ 3461$^{6}$ 4323$^{11}$ 4808$^{2}$ 4882$^{14}$ 4968$^{20}$ **>49f<**

**Funny Rose** 6 b m Belfort (FR)-Scottish Rose (Warpath) 537$^{6}$ 661$^{6}$ 1309$^{7}$ 2024$^{6}$ 2565$^{8}$ 2682$^{5}$ 3242$^{6}$ 3645$^{9}$ **>25f<**

**Funny Wave** 3 b f Lugana Beach-Comedy Lady (Comedy Star (USA)) 842$^{8}$ **>56f<**

**Fuoco Stellare (ITY)** 3 c **1995:** 4424a$^{7}$

**Furnish** 2 b f Green Desert (USA)-Eternal (Kris) 4111$^{3}$ 4461$^{3}$ **>80f<**

**Fursan (USA)** 3 b c Fred Astaire (USA)-Ancient Art (USA) (Tell (USA)) 528$^{3}$ 701$^{4}$ 947$^{6}$ 1504$^{4}$ 2247$^{2}$ **>76f<**

**Further Flight** 10 gr g Pharly (FR)-Flying Nelly (Nelcius) (751) 1017$^{6}$ 2352$^{3}$ 4569$^{7}$ 5035$^{3}$ **>113f<**

**Further Future (IRE)** 3 br g Doubletour (USA)-Tamara's Reef (Main Reef) 370$^{4}$ 402$^{9}$ (459) **>59a 17+f<**

**Further Outlook (USA)** 2 gr c Zilzal (USA)-Future Bright (USA) (Lyphard's Wish (FR)) 3131$^{2}$ (3485) 4056$^{3}$ (4471) 4859a$^{4}$ **>96f<**

**Future Perfect** 2 b g Efisio-True Ring (High Top) (4584) **>77f<**

**Future Prospect (IRE)** 2 b c Marju (IRE)-Phazania (Tap On Wood) 1404$^{2}$ (1801) 2040$^{13}$ 2834a$^{5}$ 3940$^{6}$ **>83f<**

**Future's Trader** 3 b c Alzao (USA)-Awatef (Ela-Mana-Mou) 821$^{9}$ 1711$^{11}$ 3249$^{16}$ 4496$^{11}$ **>64f<**

**Fyors Gift (IRE)** 3 b f Cadeaux Genereux-Miss Fyor (USA) (Danzig (USA)) 768$^{4}$ 897$^{4}$ 1028$^{15}$ 1455$^{9}$ (1688) **>44a 70f<**

**G**

**Gablesea** 2 b c Beveled (USA)-Me Spede (Valiyar) 2044$^{7}$ 2993$^{2}$ 4600$^{7}$ 4790$^{9}$ **>49f<**

**Gabr** 6 b h Green Desert (USA)-Ardassine (Ahonoora) 680$^{4}$ (810) 1177$^{5}$ 2037$^{9}$ (2337) **>129f< (DEAD)**

**Gabrielle Gerard** 4 ch f Roaring Riva-Mr Chris Cakemaker (Hotfoot) 994$^{W}$

***Gabriel's Lady*** 5 b m Valiyar-Autumn Harvest (Martinmas) 351$^{7}$ **>35f<**

**Gadge** 5 br g Nomination-Queenstyle (Moorestyle) 765$^{11}$ 1613$^{6}$ 1775$^{9}$ 1872$^{5}$ 2000$^{7}$ 4882$^{20}$ 5010$^{5}$ **>35a 61f<**

**Gadroon** 2 ch c Cadeaux Genereux-Greensward Blaze (Sagaro) 4720$^{15}$ 5034$^{17}$ **>41f<**

**Gad Yakoun** 3 ch g Cadeaux Genereux-Summer Impressions (USA) (Lyphard (USA)) 4229$^{3}$ 4592$^{6}$ 4865$^{5}$ **>73f<**

**Gaelic Storm** 2 b c Shavian-Shannon Princess (Connaught) 3637$^{3}$ 3853$^{4}$ (4210) 4614$^{6}$ 4966$^{3}$

**>92f<**

**Gagajulu** 3 b f Al Hareb (USA)-Rion River (IRE) (Taufan (USA)) 63$^{9}$ 142$^{6}$ 272$^{3}$ 394$^{6}$ 773$^{12}$ 931$^{18}$ 1823$^{6}$ 2029$^{5}$ 2238$^{6}$ 2757$^{11}$ 3135$^{10}$ 3331$^{6}$ 3863$^{10}$ **>59a 61f<**

**Gain Line (USA)** 3 b c Dayjur (USA)-Safe Play (USA) (Sham (USA)) 892$^{11}$ 1174$^{5}$ **>65f<**

**Galacia (IRE)** 4 br f Gallic League-Little Wild Duck (Great Heron (USA)) 4206$^{13}$ 4981$^{10}$ 5055$^{9}$ **>38a 46f<**

**Galaka** 3 b f Slip Anchor-Golden Glint (Vitiges (FR)) 3656$^{9}$ 3986$^{7}$ 4448$^{17}$ **>70f<**

**Galapino** 3 b c Charmer-Carousella (Rousillon (USA)) 137$^{4}$ 245$^{3}$ (294) (313) 391$^{2}$ 693$^{10}$ 1507$^{5}$ 1861$^{5}$ 2334$^{6}$ 3220$^{13}$ 3484$^{5}$ 3703$^{6}$ 4128$^{11}$ 4497$^{4}$ **>82a 57f<**

**Galb Alasad (IRE)** 3 b c Royal Academy (USA)-Soleiade (Posse (USA)) 3472$^{6}$ 3788$^{4}$ **>72f<**

**Galibis (FR)** 2 b c Groom Dancer (USA)-Damasquine (USA) (Damascus (USA)) 4720$^{5}$ 4897$^{9}$ **>73f<**

**Galine** 3 b f Most Welcome-Tarasova (USA) (Green Forest (USA)) **1995:** (4429) **1996:** (692) 812$^{7}$ 1805$^{2}$ 2078$^{4}$ (2301) 2584$^{5}$ 2889$^{4}$ 3047$^{2}$ 3693$^{11}$ 4552$^{5}$ **>78a 96f<**

**Gallardini (IRE)** 7 b g Nordico (USA)-Sweet (Pitskelly) 440$^{4}$ 508$^{14}$ 1159$^{8}$ 1529$^{8}$ 1676$^{6}$ 1977$^{6}$ 2183$^{8}$ 2348$^{7}$ 2568$^{11}$ **>48f<**

**Gallic Victory (IRE)** 5 b g Gallic League-Sally St Clair (Sallust) **1995:** 4527$^{5}$ **1996:** 82$^{3}$ 162$^{6}$ 233$^{5}$ 334$^{P}$ **>64da f< (DEAD)**

**Galloping Guns (IRE)** 4 ch g Conquering Hero (USA)-Jillette (Fine Blade (USA)) 2747$^{5}$ 3473$^{12}$ **>16f<**

**Galtee (IRE)** 4 b c Be My Guest (USA)-Gandria (Charlottown) (327a) 4172a$^{3}$ 4650a$^{2}$ **>116f<**

**Galway Blade** 3 b g Faustus (USA)-Slipperose (Persepolis (FR)) 890$^{5}$ 1498$^{15}$ 1655$^{8}$ 1874$^{12}$ **>63f<**

**Game Ploy (POL)** 4 b g Deploy-Guestimate (FR) (Be My Guest (USA)) 1145$^{13}$ 1894$^{4}$ (2378) (2574) (2701) 2883$^{3}$ 3947$^{11}$ 4125$^{2}$ (4326) 4568$^{19}$ 4826$^{9}$ 5046$^{12}$ **>94f<**

**Ganador** 4 gr f Weldnaas (USA)-Shakana (Grundy) 106$^{3}$ 189$^{8}$ 254$^{7}$ 351$^{6}$ 412$^{6}$ **>49a 48f<**

**Gan Ainm (IRE)** 2 b f Mujadil (USA)-Allorette (Ballymore) 4639a$^{3}$ **>92f<**

**Ganga (IRE)** 2 ch f Generous (IRE)-Congress Lady (General Assembly (USA)) 3756$^{7}$ **>52f<**

**Gan Saru** 3 ch c Never so Bold-Ravaro (Raga Navarro (ITY)) 4643a$^{9}$ 4849a$^{6}$ **>102f<**

**Garlandhayes** 4 b f Adbass (USA)-Not Alone (Pas de Seul) 1661$^{9}$

**Garnock Valley** 6 b g Dowsing (USA)-Sunley Sinner (Try My Best (USA)) 617$^{3}$ (659) 911$^{6}$ (1545) 1588$^{8}$ (2119) 2911$^{5}$ 3868$^{14}$ 4058$^{8}$ 4312$^{11}$ 4444$^{16}$ (4581) 4687$^{10}$ 4994$^{16}$ **>75a 94f<**

**Gay Breeze** 3 b g Dominion-Judy's Dowry (Dragonara Palace (USA)) 4229$^{12}$ 4693$^{7}$ 4898$^{13}$ **>46f<**

**Gazelle Royale (FR)** 2 b f Garde Royale-Beautyuwal (FR) (Magwal (FR)) 4942a$^{3}$ **>88f<**

**Gee Bee Boy** 2 ch c Beveled (USA)-Blue and White (Busted) 4330$^{9}$ **>59f<**

**Gee Bee Dream** 2 ch f Beveled (USA)-Return to Tara (Homing) 3129$^{8}$ 3593$^{10}$ 3807$^{2}$ 4113$^{15}$ 4490$^{7}$ **>71f<**

**Gee Gee Tee** 3 ch g Superlative-Glorietta (USA) (Shadeed (USA)) 470$^{9}$ 1314$^{7}$ 1970$^{4}$ 2716$^{17}$ **>43a 54f<**

**Gelinim (TUR)** 5 m 4289a$^{5}$

**Gemini Dream** 3 br g Green Ruby (USA)-Dream Again (Blue Cashmere) 4074$^{W}$ 4499$^{12}$ 4693$^{W}$ **>4f<**

**General Academy (IRE)** 3 c Royal Academy (USA)-Hastening (Shirley Heights) **1995:** 4424a$^{9}$ **1996:** 797a$^{5}$ 1329$^{8}$ 2050$^{6}$ 2844a$^{7}$ 4595$^{3}$ 4964$^{8}$ **>104f<**

**General Alan (FR)** 3 ch c Genereux Genie-Sweet Charlotte (USA) (Hul A Hul) 1581a$^{3}$ **>107f<**

**General Equation** 3 b g Governor General-Logarithm (King of Spain) 224$^{3}$ 359$^{4}$ (430) 478$^{3}$ 644$^{9}$ 1716$^{8}$ 1971$^{9}$ 2940$^{14}$ **>73da 65df<**

**General Glow** 3 b g Presidium-Glow Again (The Brianstan) 483$^{8}$ 594$^{7}$ 803$^{6}$ 2120$^{8}$ (2979) (3283) 3484$^{3}$ (3589) 4047$^{3}$ 4248$^{3}$ 4695$^{6}$ 4992$^{8}$ **>67f<**

**General Haven** 3 ch g Hadeer-Verchinina (Star Appeal) **1995:** 4439$^{11}$ 4491$^{9}$ **1996:** 209$^{3}$ 264$^{2}$ 298$^{3}$ (377) 405$^{3}$ 873$^{4}$ 1000$^{3}$ 1993$^{5}$ 2253$^{5}$ (2577) 2689$^{4}$ 4702$^{4}$ 4793$^{9}$ **>73a 75f<**

**General Henry** 3 b g Belmez (USA)-Western Star (Alcide) **1995:** 4352$^{10}$ 4518$^{12}$ **1996:** 67$^{10}$ 262$^{5}$ **>10a f<**

**General Jimbo (IRE)** 4 b g King Luthier-The Saltings (FR) (Morston (FR)) 251$^{12}$

**General Macarthur** 3 b c Alzao (USA)-Royal Climber (Kings Lake (USA)) (593) (1071) 1712$^{5}$ 3710$^{3}$ 3997$^{4}$ 4327$^{5}$ 4761$^{4}$ **>100f<**

**General Monash (USA)** 4 b c Thorn Dance (USA)-Zummerudd (Habitat) 673$^{9}$ 960$^{2}$ 1581a$^{7}$ 4857a$^{8}$ **>105f<**

**General Monty** 4 b g Vague Shot-State Free (Free State) 4868$^{16}$ **>6f<**

**General Mouktar** 6 ch g Hadeer-Fly The Coop (Kris) 844$^{2}$ 968$^{3}$ 1147$^{8}$ 1618$^{3}$ 1660$^{2}$ 1837$^{3}$ 1874$^{6}$ 2401$^{D}$ 2711$^{2}$ 2762$^{2}$ 2989$^{7}$ 3073$^{11}$ 3683$^{8}$ **>67f<**

**General Shirley (IRE)** 5 b g Shirley Heights-Adjala (Northfields (USA)) 14$^{9}$ 53$^{6}$ 353$^{4}$ 2574$^{17}$ **>48a 52df<**

**General Song (IRE)** 2 b c Fayruz-Daybreaker (Thatching) (4287a) 4328$^{7}$ 4822$^{7}$ **>84f<**

**General's Star** 2 b c Night Shift (USA)-Colorsnap (Shirley Heights) 1779$^{3}$ 2370$^{6}$ 2802$^{6}$ (3678) (3998) 4131$^{8}$ 4625$^{13}$ **>11a 80f<**

**Generosa** 3 b f Generous (IRE)-Hotel Street (USA) (Alleged (USA)) 578$^{4}$ 847$^{3}$ 1409$^{2}$ 2233$^{2}$ 2882$^{3}$ (3699) 4112$^{8}$ 5047$^{6}$ **>96f<**

**Generosus (FR)** 3 ch c Generous (IRE)-Minya (USA) (Blushing Groom (FR)) 677$^{3}$ (974) 1427$^{7}$ **>93+f<**

**Generous Gift** 2 ch c Generous (IRE)-Barari (USA) (Blushing Groom (FR)) 1339$^{8}$ 2580$^{10}$ 4069$^{2}$ **>86f<**

**Generous Libra** 2 b c Generous (IRE)-Come on Rosi (Valiyar) 4770$^{3}$ **>84f<**

**Generous Present** 3 ch g Cadeaux Genereux-Dance Move (Shareef Dancer (USA)) 562$^{8}$ 1363$^{9}$ 1850$^{10}$ (2241) (2679) 3287$^{3}$ 4064$^{15}$ 4232$^{9}$ 4785$^{6}$ **>54f<**

**Genesis Four** 6 b g Dreams to Reality (USA)-Relma (Relko) 45$^{4}$ 159$^{5}$ 207$^{4}$ 252$^{3}$ 297$^{2}$ 373$^{7}$ 424$^{5}$ 426$^{6}$ 801$^{4}$ 1602$^{6}$ 1788$^{2}$ 2182$^{3}$ 2322$^{12}$ 2891$^{7}$ 3335$^{9}$ 3507$^{3}$ 3638$^{6}$ **>46a 60f<**

**Genevra (IRE)** 2 b g Danehill (USA)-Astra Adastra (Mount Hagen (FR)) 4746a$^{2}$

**Gentilhomme** 3 ch c Generous (IRE)-Bold Flawless (USA) (Bold Bidder) 3997$^{8}$ **>102f<**

**Gentle Fan (USA)** 7 b h Lear Fan (USA)-Gay Bentley (USA) (Riverman (USA)) 1136a$^{3}$ **>109f<**

**Gentle Gambler** 5 b m Risk Me (FR)-Queen's Lake (Kings Lake (USA)) 1159$^{10}$ **>37f<**

**Gentle Irony** 4 b f Mazilier (USA)-Irenic (Mummy's Pet) **1995:** 4479$^{5}$ 4510$^{9}$ **1996:** 172$^{8}$ 244$^{8}$ 319$^{6}$ 1302$^{6}$ 1533$^{7}$ (1856) (2016) 2320$^{6}$ 2577$^{3}$ 2763$^{2}$ **>52da 67f<**

**Gentleman Sid** 6 b g Brotherly (USA)-Eugenes Chance (Flashback) 208$^{4}$ 449$^{15}$ 811$^{12}$ 1063$^{14}$ 1835$^{10}$ 2148$^{11}$ 2385$^{6}$ 3037$^{16}$ **>32a 47f<**

**Gentleman's Word (USA)** 2 b br c Red Ransom (USA)-Attacat (USA) (Advocator) 3069$^{8}$ 3919$^{4}$ 4242$^{9}$ 4760$^{6}$ **>72f<**

**Genuine Leader** 4 b g Formidable (USA)-Glorietta (USA) (Shadeed (USA)) 60$^{10}$

**Geoffreys Gamble** 2 gr c Barrys Gamble-Palace Pet (Dragonara Palace (USA)) 3332$^{R}$ 3511$^{12}$ **>4f<**

**Geolly (IRE)** 4 b g Formidable (USA)-Four-Legged Friend (Aragon) **1995:** 4382$^{9}$ **1996:** 50$^{6}$ **>42a 39f< (DEAD)**

**Geordie Lad** 2 ch g Tina's Pet-Edraianthus (Windjammer (USA)) 1822$^{7}$ 2309$^{9}$ 4210$^{8}$ **>63f<**

**George Bull** 4 b g Petoski-Firgrove (Relkino) 844$^{3}$ 1414$^{4}$ 4209$^{2}$ **>74f<**

**George Dillingham** 6 b g Top Ville-Premier Rose (Sharp Edge) 771$^{6}$ **>94f<**

**Georgie Boy (USA)** 3 b br c Zilzal (USA)-Stealthy Lady (USA) (J O Tobin (USA)) 320$^{7}$ 445$^{12}$ 672$^{10}$ **>17a 31f<**

**Georgina (IRE)** 2 b f Lycius (USA)-Princess Nawaal (USA) (Seattle Slew (USA)) 3988$^{5}$ **>74f<**

**Germano** 3 b c Generous (IRE)-Gay Fantastic (Ela-Mana-Mou) 1427$^{5}$ 2116$^{4}$ 2668a$^{18}$ **>108f<**

**Germany (USA)** 5 b h Trempolino (USA)-Inca Princess (USA) (Big Spruce (USA)) (1948a) 2479a$^{2}$ 3395a$^{2}$ 4040a$^{2}$ **>125f<**

**Germignaga (ITY)** 3 4541a$^{4}$ **>98f<**

**Germignana (ITY)** 3 b f Miswaki Tern (USA)-Guida Centrale (ITY) (Teenoso (USA)) 794a$^{5}$ (1393a) **>106f<**

**Gersey** 2 ch f Generous (IRE)-River Spey (Mill Reef (USA)) 3756$^{6}$ **>55f<**

**Ger's Royale (IRE)** 5 ch g Dominion Royale-Sister Dympna (Grundy) 1252a$^{4}$ 2053$^{29}$ 2459a$^{9}$ (4848a) 5065a$^{9}$ **>110f<**

**Get Away With It (IRE)** 3 b c Last Tycoon-Royal Sister II (Claude) 677$^{13}$ 821$^{2}$ 1090$^{2}$ 2074$^{14}$ 2549$^{7}$ 3457$^{3}$ 3653$^{2}$ **>84f<**

**Get The Point** 2 b c Sadler's Wells (USA)-Tolmi (Great Nephew) 3668$^{6}$ 4488$^{13}$ 4963$^{4}$ **>92f<**

**Get Tough** 3 b c Petong-Mrs Waddilove (Bustino) 468$^{4}$ 616$^{2}$ 873$^{12}$ (1773) 1955$^{3}$ 2486$^{6}$ 3111$^{11}$ 3611$^{4}$ 4216$^{7}$ **>71f<**

**Gharib (USA)** 2 b c Dixieland Band (USA)-The Way We Were (USA) (Avatar (USA)) 4913$^{5}$ **>79f<**

**Ghataas** 2 b c Sadler's Wells (USA)-Harmless Albatross (Pas de Seul) 4578$^{2}$ **>86+f<**

**Ghayyur (USA)** 2 ch f Riverman (USA)-New Trends (USA) (Lyphard (USA)) 2531$^{2}$ 2863$^{5}$ 3778$^{2}$ **>80f<**

**Ghostly Apparition** 3 gr g Gods Solution-Tawny (Grey Ghost) 39$^{3}$ 81$^{8}$ 131$^{4}$ 157$^{7}$ 253$^{8}$ 377$^{7}$ **>55a 52f<**

**Ghusn** 3 b c Warning-North Page (FR) (Northfields (USA)) 821$^{12}$ 1305$^{7}$ 1668$^{7}$ 2033$^{11}$ **>55f<**

**Giant Nipper** 3 b f Nashwan (USA)-Flamingo Pond (Sadler's Wells (USA)) 1614$^{14}$ **>51f<**

**Gibb's Beach (IRE)** 2 ch f Shalford (IRE)-Kuwaiti (Home Guard (USA)) 2132$^{9}$ 2714$^{6}$ 4423$^{9}$ **>36f<**

**Giddy** 3 b br f Polar Falcon (USA)-Spin Turn (Homing) 678$^{16}$ 1174$^{7}$ 1654$^{8}$ 2133$^{4}$ 2780$^{4}$ 3084$^{10}$ 3344$^{7}$ 3426$^{11}$ 4296$^{11}$ 4898$^{3}$ (4982) 5056$^{10}$ **>52a 55f<**

**Giftbox (USA)** 4 b c Halo (USA)-Arewehavingfunyet (USA) (Sham (USA)) 134$^{6}$ 217$^{7}$ 234$^{6}$ (883) 999$^{4}$ 1903$^{4}$ 2282$^{3}$ (2489) 2678$^{U}$ 2749$^{2}$ 3344$^{6}$ 3603$^{4}$ 4483$^{8}$ 4702$^{2}$ 4810$^{10}$ 4986$^{7}$ **>61a 60f<**

**Gift Token** 2 b f Batshoof-Visible Form (Formidable (USA)) 3848$^{3}$ 4369$^{7}$ 4798$^{4}$ **>74f<**

**Giggleswick Girl** 5 b m Full Extent (USA)-Foligno

(Crofter (USA)) 592[6] 664[5] 742[4] 1351[8] **>46a 61f<**

**Gi La High** 3 gr f Rich Charlie-Gem of Gold (Jellaby) **1995:** *4473[5] (4533)* **1996:** *10[3] 142[4] (272) 335[7] 430[2] 478[5] 4776[13] 5000[9]* **>55a 66?f<**

**Gilding The Lily (IRE)** 2 b f High Estate-Millingdale Lillie (Tumble Wind (USA)) 3137[2] 3675[3] 4069[9] **>53f<**

**Gildoran Palace** 5 ch g Gildoran-Hyperion Palace (Dragonara Palace (USA)) *1967[10]*

**Gildoran Sound** 3 b f Gildoran-Sound of Laughter (Hasty Word) 804[W] 932[10] 1409[7] **>34f<**

**Gilling Dancer (IRE)** 3 b g Dancing Dissident (USA)-Rahwah (Northern Baby (CAN)) 873[11] 1185[9] 2019[4] 2162[7] (2521) 2801[15] 3107[6] 3354[13] **>62df<**

**Ginas Girl** 3 gr f Risk Me (FR)-Grey Cree (Creetown) **1995:** *4429[15]* **1996:** *209[5] 298[W] 3350[6]* 3789[5] 4045[18] 4221[11] **>20a 48f<**

**Ginger Fox (USA)** 3 ch c Diesis-Over Your Shoulder (USA) (Graustark) 1508[3] 1873[5] 3042[3] (4362) 4821[6] **>92f<**

**Ginger Hodgers** 3 ch f Crofthall-Jarrettelle (All Systems Go) 775[18] 1089[14] 1363[18] 1887[6] 2362[2] 3116[5] **>33f<**

**Ginger Jim** 5 ch g Jalmood (USA)-Stratch (FR) (Thatch (USA)) *309[10]* **>62a 76f<**

**Ginger Rogers** 2 ch f Gildoran-Axe Valley (Royben) 4798[10] 5041[7] **>47f<**

**Gingersnap** 2 ch f Salse (USA)-Humble Pie (Known Fact (USA)) 4969[6] **>75f<**

**Ginka** 5 b m Petoski-Pine (Supreme Sovereign) 1012[9] 1347[6] 3801[3] 4509[3] 4612[4] 4821[10] 5052[2] **>31a 39f<**

**Ginny Wossername** 2 br f Prince Sabo-Leprechaun Lady (Royal Blend) *1166[5]* 1494[2] *1813[5] (2509)* 2959[4] 3662[3] 3976[4] 4097[13] *4988[3] 5061[6]* **>40a 56f<**

**Ginzbourg** 2 b g Ferdinand (USA)-Last Request (Dancers Image (USA)) 4601[5] (4783) **>81f<**

**Gipsy Princess** 2 b f Prince Daniel (USA)-Gypsy's Barn Rat (Balliol) 930[8] 1036[3] 1595[4] 2588[6] 4072[3] (4319) 4625[2] 4764[2] 4864[W] **>66f<**

**Girl of My Dreams (IRE)** 3 b f Marju (IRE)-Stylish Girl (USA) (Star de Naskra (USA)) 3624[11] 3832[8] 4108[7] 4348[6] 4691[13] **>55f<**

**Give And Take** 3 ch c Generous (IRE)-Starlet (Teenoso (USA)) 1508[13] 2786[3] 3841[5] 4496[5] **>62f<**

**Give Me A Ring (IRE)** 3 b c Be My Guest (USA)-Annsfield Lady (Red Sunset) 509[6] 1868[4] *2201[2] (2514)* (2693) (3295) 4300[3] 4568[11] **>74a 96f<**

**Glacier** 2 b f Polish Precedent (USA)-Graphite (USA) (Mr Prospector (USA)) 4969[15] **>61f<**

**Gladys Althorpe (IRE)** 3 b f Posen (USA)-Gortadoo (USA) (Sharpen Up) 686[13] (3450) 3640[6] (3866) (4190) 4432[2] 4769[11] 4974[21] **>79f<**

**Glen Garnock (IRE)** 4 gr g Danehill (USA)-Inanna (Persian Bold) 2913[3] 3624[6] 4348[5] 4686[14] **>56f<**

**Glenlivet (SWE)** 8 ch g Grant's (DEN)-Skyline (SWE) (Jimmy Reppin) 4033a[4] **>116f<**

**Glen Parker (IRE)** 3 ch c Bluebird (USA)-Trina's Girl (Nonoalco (USA)) 1142[14] 2579[6] 3353[2] (3642) **>86f<**

**Glenvally** 5 gr m Belfort (FR)-Hivally (High Line) *239[10] 301[11] 586[9]* 1034[5] 1418[10] 1665[7] 2348[5] 2513[7] **>55da 27f<**

**Glide Path (USA)** 7 ch h Stalwart (USA)-Jolly Polka (USA) (Nice Dancer (CAN)) 580[16] 1066[5] 2825a[6] 3351[4] 3754a[6] 4174a[9] 4431[14] **>87f<**

**Glimmering Hope (IRE)** 2 b g Petorius-Angevin (English Prince) 4363[10]

**Global Dancer** 5 b g Night Shift (USA)-Early Call (Kind of Hush) **1995:** *4384[6]* **1996:** *1792[11]* 2401[10] 2737[6] 3095[3] 3471[9] **>77a 69f<**

**Globe Runner** 3 b c Adbass (USA)-Scenic Villa (Top Ville) 827[20] 1042[15] 1635[8] *1812[6] 2308[12] 2524[6]* 2780[5] (3059) 3289[7] 3427[5] 3958[5] **>45a 55f<**

**Globetrotter (IRE)** 2 b c Polish Patriot (USA)-Summer Dreams (CAN) (Victoria Park) 3941[12] 4046[14] 4224[3] 4586[14] 4764[8] **>76f<**

**Gloria Imperator (IRE)** 3 b c Imperial Frontier (USA)-English Lily (Runnett) 591[10] 783[12] 934[10] **>43f<**

**Gloriana** 4 b f Formidable (USA)-Tudor Pilgrim (Welsh Pageant) *844[14]* 1102[5] 1515[6] 1894[7] (3403) 4243[13] 4582[6] 4686[20] **>76f<**

**Glorious Aragon** 4 b f Aragon-Gloria Maremmana (King Emperor (USA)) *812[3]* 1016[6] 1171[10] 1430[6] (3618) 3932[6] 4367[10] **>90f<**

**Glorious Island** 6 ch g Jupiter Island-Gloria Maremmana (King Emperor (USA)) 1691[12] **>27f<**

**Glory of Dancer** 3 b c Shareef Dancer (USA)-Glory of Hera (Formidable (USA)) **1995:** (4399a) **1996:** 830[2] (1114) 1791[4] 2276a[2] 3431[4] 3912a[4] 4281a[3] 4773[6] **>127f<**

**Glow Forum** 5 b m Kalaglow-Beau's Delight (USA) (Lypheor) **1995:** *4452[5] 4516[2]* **1996:** *(1347)* 1803[9] *(3086) (3600) 3876[2] (4334) 4626[5] (4779) 4967[6]* ***>83a 57f<***

**Glowing Jade** 6 b m Kalaglow-Precious Jade (Northfields (USA)) 527[6] (739) 879[25] 3052[7] 4212[3] 4439[2] 4520[8] **>52a 76f<**

**Glowing Reeds** 3 ch f Kalaglow-No Jazz (Jaazeiro (USA)) 671[10] *1081[7] 1814[4] 2204[2]* 2530[7] *3086[7] 3667[6]* ***>41a 50f<***

**Go Between (FR)** 3 b c Highest Honor (FR)-Ruffle 621a[5] **>99f<**

**Go Britannia** 3 b c Machiavellian (USA)-Chief Celebrity (USA) (Chief's Crown (USA)) 1690[9] 2004[2] (2510) 2888[5] 3447[5] **>94f<**

**Godmersham Park** 4 b g Warrshan (USA)-Brown Velvet (Mansingh (USA)) *4053[6]* 4256[3] 4511[9] 4768[12] **>72f<**

**Go For Green** 2 br f Petong-Guest List (Be My Guest (USA)) 3809[9] 4435[3] 4697[8] **>59f<**

**Go For Salt (USA)** 2 b f Hawkster (USA)-Wall St Girl (USA) (Rich Cream (USA)) *3873[2]* ***>74f<***

**Go-Go-Power-Ranger** 3 ch g Golden Lahab (USA)-Nibelunga (Miami Springs) 477[7] 658[2] (803) 1325[2] 1778[12] 1887[8] 3308[6] 3459[8] **>52f<**

**Go Hever Golf** 4 ch g Efisio-Sweet Rosina (Sweet Revenge) *928[12]* 1790[16] 3038[9] 3338[8] 4198[8] 4367[2] 4651a[2] 4679[14] 4802[17] **>100?a 87f<**

**Going For Broke** 2 b g Simply Great (FR)-Empty Purse (Pennine Walk) 1036[7] 1360[2] *2370[9] 3275[2] 3417[2] 3762[5]* 4501[2] **>57a 61f<**

**Going Green (USA)** 3 dk c Green Dancer (USA)-Partygoer (USA) (Secretariat (USA)) 5021a[3] **>107f<**

**Golborne Lad** 3 ch g Jester-Taskalady (Touching Wood (USA)) *529[6] 606[10] 783[11]* ***>32a 32f<***

**Gold Blade** 7 ch g Rousillon (USA)-Sharp Girl (FR) (Sharpman) *116[2] (152) 279[6] (752)* 1778[2] 2066[4] 2487[3] (2587) (2678) (2871) (3118) (3575) 4067[13] 4238[10] *4984[11]* **>73a 74f<**

**Gold Clipper** 2 b c High Kicker (USA)-Ship of Gold (Glint of Gold) 4914[13] **>14f<**

**Gold Delivery (USA)** 5 b h Java Gold (USA)-Tremor (Tromos) *151a[2]* 227a[3] **>88f<**

**Gold Desire** 6 b g Grey Desire-Glory Gold (Hittite Glory) 477[11] 558[2] 1034[4] 1309[2] 1418[4] 1548[4] 1676[7] 2020[6] (3220) 3346[5] 3412[3] (4000) 4236[5] 4626[8] 4686[18] 4810[6] **>18a 53f<**

**Gold Disc (USA)** 3 ch c Slew O' Gold (USA)-Singing (USA) (The Minstrel (CAN)) 808[7] (1666) 2074[11] 2608[11] 3248[11] (3923) 4193[10] 4556[10] **>95f<**

**Gold Edge** 2 ch f Beveled (USA)-Golden October (Young Generation) 3853[5] 4087[6] 4244[2] 4493[3] 4787[6] **>62f<**

**Golden Ace (IRE)** 3 ch c Archway (IRE)-Gobolino (Don) *(732)* 1495[5] **>83f<**

**Golden Agos** 3 5074a[6]

**Golden Arrow (IRE)** 5 ch g Glint of Gold-Sheer Luck (Shergar) 439[3] 573[4] 712[6] 1116[2] 1511[4] 2042[5] 3037[2] (3850) 4260[6] **>90f<**

**Golden Aventura (IRE)** 2 4859a[6] (5028a) **>67f<**

**Golden Blushing (USA)** 2 4859a[9]

**Golden Fact (USA)** 2 b c Known Fact (USA)-Cosmic Sea Queen (USA) (Determined Cosmic (USA)) 1315[2] 1519[4] 2702[4] 3230[5] 3616[4] 3792[10] **>79f<**

**Golden Fawn** 3 ch f Crowning Honors (CAN)-Hill of Fare (Brigadier Gerard) 2744[8] 3402[2] 3966[2] 4496[13] 4752[8] **>60f<**

**Golden Filigree** 4 ch f Faustus (USA)-Muarij (Star Appeal) 668[13] 821[15] *1081[4]* **>51a 37f<**

**Golden Goddess** 2 ch f Formidable (USA)-Tame Duchess (Saritamer (USA)) 3593[14] 4798[12] **>58f<**

**Golden Hadeer** 5 ch h Hadeer-Verchinina (Star Appeal) 2482[6] 2989[4] 3348[8] 3471[11] 4669[7] *4984[3] 5054[7]* ***>45a 34f<***

**Golden Melody** 2 b f Robellino (USA)-Rose Chanelle (Welsh Pageant) 2404[8] 3787[5] 4127[15] 4864[14] **>57f<**

**Golden Perform (USA)** 4 b c Once Wild (USA)-Barely Rarely (USA) (Rare Performer (USA)) **1995:** 4402a[9] **>100f<**

**Golden Pond (IRE)** 3 b f Don't Forget Me-Golden Bloom (Main Reef) 493[2] 571[3] 917[2] 1181[3] 1615[2] (1825) (2146) 2544[2] 3158[9] (4405a) **>102f<**

**Golden Pound (USA)** 4 b g Seeking the Gold (USA)-Coesse Express (USA) (Dewan (USA)) *14[3] 99[2] 204[2] 234[2] 450[4]* 554[4] (714) 1078[6] 1178[6] 1521[3] 1790[7] 2232[3] (2403) 2856[5] 3219[2] 3406[3] 3672[9] 4314[18] **>77a 91f<**

**Golden Punch (USA)** 5 b g Seattle Song (USA)-Pagan Winter (USA) (Pago Pago (AUS)) **1995:** *4543[9]* **1996:** *24[9] 103[4] 169[6] 365[4]* **>33a f<**

**Golden Quint (ITY)** 3 903a[13] **>64f<**

**Golden Silver** 3 b f Precious Metal-Severals Princess (Formidable (USA)) *2528[13]* 3166[2] **>42f<**

**Golden Thunderbolt (FR)** 3 b c Persian Bold-Carmita (Caerleon (USA)) 1319[6] 1690[4] 2124[3] 2572[2] 3123[8] 4124[4] 4499[2] 4690[5] **>84f<**

**Golden Torque** 9 br g Taufan (USA)-Brightelmstone (Prince Regent (FR)) **1995:** *4376[7]* **>44a 65f<**

**Golden Touch (USA)** 4 ch c Elmaamul (USA)-Tour D'Argent (USA) (Halo (USA)) *243[5] 308[7] 424[2] 462[3] (654) (843)* (920) 988[5] 1440[5] 1625[7] 1996[5] 4068[6] 4257[12] 4719[8] 4900[8] *5060[2]* **>71a 64f<**

**Golden Turk (IRE)** 3 b c Fairy King (USA)-Golden Concorde **1995:** 4397a[3]

**Golden Tyke (IRE)** 3 b g Soviet Lad (USA)-Golden Room (African Sky) *529[5] 780[4] 881[8]* ***>52a 33f<***

**Gold Kicker** 3 b c High Kicker (USA)-Ship of Gold (Glint of Gold) **1995:** *4380[9]* **>14a 60f< (DEAD)**

**Gold Lance (USA)** 3 ch g Seeking the Gold (USA)-Lucky State (USA) (State Dinner (USA)) 1508[10] 1670[8] **>73f<**

**Gold Lining (IRE)** 3 ch f Magical Wonder (USA)-Muntaz (ARG) (Search Tradition (USA)) 870[9] 1099[12] 1434[10] 2433[5] 2683[9] 3354[14] 3591[7] 4348[12] **>37f<**

**Goldrill** 3 ch c Never so Bold-Irish Impulse (USA) (Irish River (FR)) 1033[10] 1422[9] **>54f<**

**Goldsearch (IRE)** 3 ch f Fayruz-Win For Me (Bonne Noel) **1995:** *4353[3] 4437[5]* **>47a 62f<**

**Gold Spats (USA)** 3 b c Seeking the Gold (USA)-Foot Stone (USA) (Cyane) *808[2]* 1142[2] (1617) 3709[10] 4444[12] **>86f<**

**Gold Tribute (USA)** 2 b c Mr Prospector (USA)-

Dancing Tribute (USA) (Nureyev (USA)) *4954a$^{6}$* **>102a f<**

**Gollaccia 2** gr f Mystiko (USA)-Millie Grey (Grey Ghost) 4454$^{6}$ 4593$^{7}$ 4806$^{8}$ **>34f<**

**Gondo 9** br g Mansingh (USA)-Secret Valentine (Wollow) 1040$^{12}$ 1598$^{11}$ 1708$^{8}$ 2496$^{5}$ 2523$^{8}$ 2564$^{3}$ 2849$^{6}$ 2910$^{6}$ 3294$^{10}$ 3352$^{9}$ 4367$^{3}$ 4791$^{16}$ **>31a 59f<**

**Gone for a Burton (IRE) 6** ch g Bustino-Crimbourne (Mummy's Pet) 4326$^{15}$ 4617$^{7}$ 4826$^{2}$ 5046$^{19}$ **>89f<**

**Gone Savage 8** b g Nomination-Trwyn Cilan (Import) *812$^{5}$* 928$^{15}$ 1351$^{4}$ 1844$^{3}$ 2193$^{8}$ 2586$^{7}$ 2787$^{2}$ 2976$^{4}$ (3261) 3506$^{3}$ 3930$^{2}$ 4180$^{2}$ 4452$^{2}$ (4616) 4811$^{7}$ 5039$^{10}$ **>81f<**

**Gone to Heaven 4** b g Aragon-Divine Fling (Imperial Fling (USA)) 1087$^{13}$ 1342$^{8}$ 1598$^{16}$ **>41f<**

**Gonzaga (IRE) 2** ro c Pistolet Bleu (IRE)-Gay Spring (FR) (Free Round (USA)) *(3499)* 4879$^{4}$ **>79f<**

**Good (IRE) 4** b g Persian Heights-Tres Bien (Pitskelly) 4099$^{7}$ **>26a 54f<**

**Goodbye Gatemen (IRE) 2** gr c Soviet Lad (USA)-Simple Love (Simply Great (FR)) 4786$^{13}$ **>14f<**

**Goodbye Millie 6** b or br m Sayf El Arab (USA)-Leprechaun Lady (Royal Blend) 558$^{9}$ 609$^{10}$ 1159$^{4}$ 1544$^{4}$ 1676$^{10}$ **>37a 43f<**

**Good Day 2** gr c Petong-Courtesy Call (Northfields (USA)) 2495$^{10}$ 3293$^{7}$ *4091$^{4}$ 4433$^{6}$* 4795$^{10}$ **>56a 59f<**

**Good Hand (USA) 10** ch g Northjet-Ribonette (USA) (Ribot) (1847) 2148$^{8}$ 3149$^{9}$ 3428$^{4}$ (4302) (4457) 4771$^{13}$ **>81+f<**

**Good Judge (IRE) 2** b c Law Society (USA)-Cuirie (Main Reef) 3982$^{18}$ 4224$^{5}$ 4684$^{11}$ **>62f<**

**Good News (IRE) 2** ch f Ajraas (USA)-Blackeye (Busted) 3282$^{5}$ 3660$^{5}$ 4061$^{13}$ **>65f<**

**Good so Fa (IRE) 4** b g Taufan (USA)-Future Shock (Full Out (USA)) **1995:** *4374$^{10}$ 4438$^{4}$* **1996:** *82$^{10}$ 140$^{13}$ 661$^{9}$* 1047$^{8}$ 1665$^{9}$ 1826$^{13}$ 2159$^{14}$ **>38a 32f<**

**Good To Talk 3** b g Weldnaas (USA)-Kimble Blue (Blue Refrain) 1612$^{8}$ 2238$^{4}$ 2359$^{2}$ 2800$^{8}$ 2983$^{10}$ 3256$^{10}$ 3294$^{2}$ 3774$^{4}$ 4075$^{7}$ 4229$^{7}$ 4828$^{7}$ **>48f<**

**Goodwood Lass (IRE) 2** b f Alzao (USA)-Cutleaf (Kris) 1339$^{6}$ (2967) 3616$^{8}$ 4375$^{9}$ **>79f<**

**Goodwood Rocket 3** ch c Midyan (USA)-Feather-in-Her-Cap (Primo Dominie) 575$^{13}$ 819$^{6}$ 1594$^{15}$ 1986$^{8}$ **>67f<**

**Gool Lee Shay (USA) 3** b br c Explodent (USA)-Titled Miss (USA) (Sir Ivor) 717$^{6}$ 826$^{9}$ 994$^{7}$ 1420$^{8}$ 1504$^{10}$ 3052$^{8}$ 3228$^{2}$ 3354$^{4}$ 3492$^{4}$ 3777$^{4}$ 3995$^{25}$ 4263$^{13}$ **>57f<**

**Gooseberry Pie 3** b f Green Desert (USA)-Supper Time (Shantung) 1180$^{11}$ 1614$^{7}$ 1855$^{9}$ 3107$^{3}$ 3474$^{4}$ 3967$^{9}$ **>69f<**

**Gopi 2** b f Marju (IRE)-Chandni (IRE) (Ahonoora) 1590$^{4}$ 1834$^{2}$ 2854$^{5}$ 3110$^{3}$ 3299$^{W}$ 4966$^{4}$ **>71f<**

**Gordi (USA) 3** ch c Theatrical-Royal Alydar (USA) (Alydar (USA)) (2054) 4192$^{10}$ 4397a$^{6}$ **>113f<**

**Gore Hill 2** b f Be My Chief (USA)-Hollow Heart (Wolver Hollow) 4514$^{16}$ 4797$^{16}$ **>12f<**

**Goretski (IRE) 3** b c Polish Patriot (USA)-Celestial Path (Godswalk (USA)) 539$^{2}$ 638$^{11}$ (773) 862$^{4}$ 881$^{2}$ 1597$^{2}$ 1663$^{2}$ 2151$^{6}$ 3844$^{12}$ 4246$^{22}$ 4505$^{12}$ 4765$^{9}$ 5039$^{8}$ **>61f<**

**Gormire 3** ro f Superlative-Lady of the Lodge (Absalom) 783$^{2}$ 1033$^{9}$ 1356$^{4}$ 1761$^{8}$ *2367$^{11}$ 4430$^{22}$ 4577$^{12}$* **>38a 65f<**

**Gothenberg (IRE) 3** b c Polish Patriot (USA)-Be Discreet (Junius (USA)) *574$^{8}$* 681$^{4}$ (1253a) 1141a$^{10}$ 2271a$^{3}$ (2471a) 2622$^{10}$ 3745a$^{7}$ 3784$^{6}$ 4132$^{5}$ 4667a$^{2}$ 5074a$^{5}$ **>119f<**

**Go Thunder (IRE) 2** b g Nordico (USA)-Moving Off 5014a$^{6}$ **>80f<**

**Gotla Bird 3** b f Petong-Addison's Jubilee (Sparkler) **1995:** *4408$^{F}$* **>51f< (DEAD)**

**Governance (IRE) 3** b f Imperial Frontier (USA)-La Padma (Sassafras (FR)) 669$^{12}$ 1709$^{10}$ 2557$^{11}$ *3955$^{12}$* **>37f<**

**Governor's Bid 3** b g Governor General-Maiden Bidder (Shack (USA)) 758$^{8}$ 1518$^{6}$ 1994$^{9}$ 2405$^{11}$ 2946$^{14}$ 3300$^{6}$ **>21f<**

**Governors Dream 3** b f Governor General-Friendly Miss (Be Friendly) **1995:** *4429$^{12}$* **1996:** *51$^{4}$ 118$^{11}$ 524$^{W}$* **>37a 25f<**

**Go With The Wind 3** b c Unfuwain (USA)-Cominna (Dominion) *484$^{4}$ 803$^{4}$* 1600$^{3}$ 1877$^{2}$ 2120$^{11}$ 2482$^{2}$ 2927$^{2}$ 3218$^{6}$ 3667$^{8}$ 4086$^{4}$ (4358) 4506$^{4}$ **>49a 73f<**

**Graceful Lady 6** br m Bold Arrangement-Northern Lady (The Brianstan) **1995:** *4413$^{W}$* **1996:** *179$^{12}$* **>39f<**

**Graceful Lass 2** b f Sadler's Wells (USA)-Hi Lass (Shirley Heights) 4608$^{5}$ **>72f<**

**Gracious Gretclo 3** gr f Common Grounds-Gratclo (Belfort (FR)) **1995:** *4389$^{6}$ 4473$^{4}$ 4492$^{2}$ 4509$^{12}$ 4533$^{5}$* **1996:** *131$^{11}$ 2528$^{11}$* 3661$^{11}$ **>53a 38f<**

**Graduated (IRE) 4** b g Royal Academy (USA)-Saviour (USA) (Majestic Light (USA)) 4026a$^{4}$ **>86f<**

**Granby Bell 5** b g Ballacashtal (CAN)-Betbellof (Averof) 753$^{6}$ 944$^{5}$ 1194$^{8}$ (1524) 1710$^{6}$ 4771$^{25}$ 4919$^{14}$ **>61f<**

**Grand Applause (IRE) 6** gr g Mazaad-Standing Ovation (Godswalk (USA)) 3471$^{7}$ **>62a 53f<**

**Grand Chapeau (IRE) 4** b g Ballad Rock-All Hat (Double Form) 1588$^{6}$ 2005$^{11}$ 2722$^{12}$ 3055$^{10}$ (3973) 4198$^{11}$ 4246$^{7}$ 4616$^{13}$ 4805$^{11}$ **>60f<**

**Grand du Lac (USA) 4** ch c Lac Ouimet (USA)-Vast Domain (CAN) (Vice Regent (CAN)) 878$^{5}$ 1193$^{12}$ 1484$^{9}$ **>93f<**

**Grandes Oreilles (IRE) 4** b f Nordico (USA)-Top Knot (High Top) 745$^{2}$ 1124$^{8}$ 1534$^{11}$ 2056$^{20}$ 3824$^{7}$ **>53a 32f<**

**Grand Lad (IRE) 2** ch c Mujtahid (USA)-Supportive (IRE) (Nashamaa) 924$^{3}$ (1525) 2070$^{5}$ 4258$^{2}$ 4677$^{3}$ **>103f<**

**Grand Musica 3** b g Puissance-Vera Musica (USA) (Stop The Music (USA)) 3262$^{2}$ 3472$^{2}$ (3832) 4196$^{2}$ 4620$^{4}$ **>98f<**

**Grandpa Lex (IRE) 2** gr c Kalaglow-Bustling Nelly (Bustino) 4200$^{8}$ **>49f< (DEAD)**

**Grand Popo 3** b c Salse (USA)-Rose Cordial (USA) (Blushing Groom (FR)) 3642$^{8}$ 3986$^{10}$ 4865$^{18}$ **>36f<**

**Grand Selection (IRE) 4** b g Cricket Ball (USA)-Sine Labe (USA) (Vaguely Noble) *358$^{4}$ 988$^{6}$* 1476$^{15}$ 2128$^{6}$ (2603) (3125) 3691$^{6}$ 4055$^{9}$ **>81a 93f<**

**Grand Splendour 3** b f Shirley Heights-Mayaasa (FR) (Green Desert (USA)) 1895$^{4}$ 3656$^{5}$ 4429$^{2}$ 4622$^{2}$ **>82f<**

**Grand Time 7** ch g Clantime-Panay (Arch Sculptor) 2561$^{10}$ **>43da 34f<**

**Granique (BEL) 4** b g Rabbi (BEL)-Gall (BEL) (Sea Bomb) **1995:** *(4436)* **>63a f< (DEAD)**

**Granny's Pet 2** ch c Selkirk (USA)-Patsy Western (Precocious) 706$^{2}$ 1328$^{2}$ (1766) 2070$^{8}$ 2504$^{4}$ 4488$^{3}$ 4681$^{4}$ **>95f<**

**Grapeshot (USA) 2** b c Hermitage (USA)-Ardy Arnie (USA) (Hold Your Peace (USA)) 2302$^{3}$ (2624) 3143$^{2}$ (4555) **>107f<**

**Grape Tree Road 3** b c Caerleon (USA)-One Way Street (Habitat) 1757a$^{7}$ (2276a) 3670$^{4}$ 4293a$^{4}$ **>126f<**

**Grapevine (IRE) 2** b f Sadler's Wells (USA)-Gossiping (USA) (Chati (USA)) 4608$^{6}$ **>71f<**

**Grate Times 2** b c Timeless Times (USA)-Judys Girl (IRE) (Simply Great (FR)) 800$^{4}$ 930$^{5}$ 1166$^{3}$ 2044$^{3}$ (2396) 2517$^{2}$ 2984$^{10}$ 3307$^{3}$ 3512$^{3}$ 3936$^{7}$ 3998$^{4}$ 4364$^{2}$ 4672$^{13}$ 4764$^{11}$ **>80f<**

**Great Bear 4** ch g Dominion-Bay Bay (Bay Express) **1995:** *4394$^{17}$ 4430$^{7}$ 4508$^{9}$* **1996:** *43$^{6}$ 159$^{6}$ 211$^{9}$ 366$^{8}$ 479$^{13}$* 822$^{9}$ 1546$^{9}$ 2630$^{7}$ 2954$^{2}$ (3084) 3172$^{4}$ 3340$^{7}$ 3958$^{14}$ 4436$^{25}$ 4503$^{10}$ 4808$^{16}$ *5060$^{7}$* **>31a 27f<**

**Great Chief 3** ch c Be My Chief (USA)-Padelia (Thatching) 1690$^{11}$ 2181$^{7}$ 4591$^{10}$ 4865$^{14}$ **>54f<**

**Great Child 2** b c Danehill (USA)-Charmina (FR) (Nonoalco (USA)) 4512$^{5}$ 4863$^{4}$ 5009$^{3}$ **>82f<**

**Great Easeby (IRE) 6** ch g Caerleon (USA)-Kasala (USA) (Blushing Groom (FR)) 825$^{2}$ 1158$^{2}$ 1343$^{3}$ 2042$^{14}$ 2612$^{2}$ 2857$^{2}$ 3834$^{10}$ (4199) **>69f<**

**Greatest 5** b g Superlative-Pillowing (Good Times (ITY)) 1337$^{10}$ 1819$^{10}$ 2312$^{2}$ 2761$^{5}$ 3516$^{7}$ **>73a 65f<**

**Great Hall 7** gr g Hallgate-Lily of France (Monsanto (FR)) *496$^{8}$* 664$^{6}$ 893$^{18}$ 1121$^{13}$ 1473$^{5}$ 1642$^{17}$ 1902$^{7}$ *2940$^{7}$ 3089$^{7}$ 3442$^{6}$* 3599$^{8}$ 3694$^{11}$ *4077$^{10}$* **>39a 45f<**

**Great Lord (IRE) 7** b h Last Tycoon-Mummy's Favourite (Mummy's Pet) **1995:** 4561a$^{3}$

**Great Oration (IRE) 7** b or br g Simply Great (FR)-Spun Gold (Thatch (USA)) **1995:** *4411$^{6}$* **1996:** *625$^{7}$* 767$^{4}$ 852$^{3}$ 1070$^{7}$ 1784$^{3}$ (2028) 2423$^{3}$ (2697) 3037$^{5}$ 3486$^{3}$ 4302$^{3}$ 4588$^{3}$ **>27a 65f<**

**Great Ovation (IRE) 2** b c High Estate-Wild Applause (IRE) (Sadler's Wells (USA)) (2414) (3684) 3927$^{6}$ (4621) **>97f<**

**Great Simplicity 9** ch g Simply Great (FR)-Affaire D'Amour (Tudor Music) 4307$^{21}$ 4476$^{12}$ **>10f<**

**Great Tern 4** b f Simply Great (FR)-La Neva (FR) (Arctic Tern (USA)) *654$^{9}$ 866$^{6}$* 1496$^{7}$ *2631$^{4}$ 4252$^{4}$* (4448) (4862) **>37a 62f<**

**Grecian Garden 5** b m Sharrood (USA)-Greek Goddess (Young Generation) *4828$^{16}$* **>37da 14f<**

**Greek Gold (IRE) 7** b g Rainbow Quest (USA)-Gay Hellene (Ela-Mana-Mou) **1995:** *4390$^{6}$ 4537$^{9}$* **1996:** *210$^{7}$ 246$^{2}$ 1548$^{5}$* 1821$^{5}$ 2024$^{5}$ 2056$^{5}$ 2394$^{8}$ 2563$^{11}$ *5056$^{9}$* **>40a 48f<**

**Greek Icon 3** b f Thatching-Rosie Potts (Shareef Dancer (USA)) **1995:** 4397a$^{4}$ **1996:** 1753a$^{9}$ 2498$^{5}$ **>84f<**

**Greek Night Out (IRE) 5** b m Ela-Mana-Mou-Ce Soir (Northern Baby (CAN)) **1995:** *4370$^{3}$* **1996:** *(154) 208$^{2}$ 360$^{3}$ 373$^{4}$ 482$^{4}$ (602)* 767$^{2}$ 872$^{8}$ (1784) 2028$^{5}$ *3066$^{3}$ 4984$^{7}$* **>59a 54f<**

**Green Apache 4** b g Green Desert (USA)-Can Can Girl (Gay Fandango (USA)) *43$^{10}$* **>25f<**

**Green Barries 3** b c Green Desert (USA)-Barari (USA) (Blushing Groom (FR)) *(458)* 571$^{7}$ 773$^{5}$ 1693$^{2}$ 2007$^{5}$ 2137$^{2}$ (2501) (2754) (3210) 3445$^{8}$ 4444$^{6}$ **>97f<**

**Green Bentley (IRE) 3** b f Green Desert (USA)-Lady Bentley (Bellypha) 2529$^{7}$ 2945$^{10}$ 3800$^{10}$ **>75f<**

**Green Bopper (USA) 3** b c Green Dancer (USA)-Wayage (USA) (Mr Prospector (USA)) 472$^{3}$ (584) 937$^{15}$ 1127$^{12}$ 3799$^{9}$ 4504$^{4}$ 4820$^{24}$ **>73f<**

**Green Boulevard (USA) 2** ch f Green Forest (USA)-Assez Cuite (USA) (Graustark) 3502$^{7}$ **>52f<**

**Green Card (USA) 2** br c Green Dancer (USA)-Dunkellin (USA) (Irish River (FR)) 4516$^{7}$ **>68f<**

**Green Gem (BEL) 3** b f Pharly (FR)-Batalya (BEL) (Boulou) **1995:** *4461$^{4}$ 4529$^{6}$* **1996:** *156$^{2}$ 230$^{3}$ 382$^{4}$ (468)* 775$^{4}$ 915$^{2}$ 1181$^{8}$ 1539$^{4}$ 2241$^{8}$ **>62a 73f<**

**Green Golightly (USA) 5** b g Green Dancer (USA)-Polly Daniels (USA) (Clever Trick (USA)) **1995:** *4351$^{9}$ 4379$^{7}$ 4415$^{9}$ 4458$^{11}$ 4527$^{9}$* **1996:** *4888$^{21}$ 4987$^{7}$* **>33a 47f<**

**Green Green Desert (FR)** **5** b g Green Desert (USA)-Green Leaf (USA) (Alydar (USA)) 878[3] 1112[2] 2053[18] 2544[3] 3067[2] 3158[4] **>116f<**
**Green Jewel** **2** gr f Environment Friend-Emeraude (Kris) 1346[3] (1851) 2073[6] 2575[2] 3936[2] **>84f<**
**Green Lady (IRE)** **2** b f Green Desert (USA)-Fawaayid (USA) (Vaguely Noble) (3566a) 3908a[3] 4661a[7] **>98f<**
**Green Land (BEL)** **4** b f Hero's Honor (USA)-Heavy Land (FR) (Recitation (USA)) 993[9] 1150[10] 1462[7] 1695[4] 2020[3] 2239[5] 2866[3] 3653[8] **>67f<**
**Green Perfume (USA)** **4** b c Naevus (USA)-Pretty Is (USA) (Doonesbury (USA)) 1112[8] 1330[2] (1623) 2114[4] (2691) (2853) 3596[8] 4122[3] 4520[7] **>116df<**
**Green Power** **2** b c Green Desert (USA)-Shaft of Sunlight (Sparkler) 2302[5] 3494[3] **>72f<**
**Green's Bid** **6** gr g Siberian Express (USA)-Arianna Aldini (Habitat) **1995:** *4377[10] 4390[12] 4458[4] 4484[8] 4512[10]* **1996:** *16[5] 45[7] 71[4] 253[4] 343[5] 412[8] 607[P]* **>50a 64df< (DEAD)**
**Green's le Sidaner (USA)** **8** b g Ziggy's Boy (USA)-Matriarchal (USA) (Pronto (ARG)) (3385a) **>47f<**
**Greenspan (IRE)** **4** b c Be My Guest (USA)-Prima Ballerina (FR) (Nonoalco (USA)) *(251) 532[4] (855) 963[5] 1082[7]* **>80a 78f<**
**Greenstead (USA)** **3** b c Green Dancer (USA)-Evening Air (USA) (J O Tobin (USA)) 2318[5] (2610) 3153[8] (3594) 4055[11] **>103f<**
**Greenwich Again** **4** b g Exodal (USA)-What a Challenge (Sallust) **1995:** *4440[7] 4525[4]* **1996:** *13[7] 82[4] (284) 349[4] 486[2] 546[18]* 1347[11] *1605[2] 2014[6]* (2762) 3094[6] 3664[2] 4048[12] 4252[8] **>70a 68+f<**
**Greenwich Fore** **2** b c Formidable (USA)-What a Challenge (Sallust) 3269[7] 3874[4] 4069[8] 4253[9] 4549[4] 4880[17] *5057[3]* **>70a 75f<**
**Grenadier (FR)** **3** ch g Saint Andrews (FR)-Whitegun (FR) (Carwhite) (226a) 323a[3] 2845a[3] **>104f<**
**Gresatre** **2** gr c Absalom-Mild Deception (IRE) (Glow (USA)) 490[6] 639[7] 916[9] 1471[3] 2797[3] *3417[4] 3982[4]* 4106[6] 4262[6] 4384[7] 4715[9] 4990[5] **>34a 65f<**
**Gresham Flyer** **3** b g Clantime-Eleanor Cross (Kala Shikari) **1995:** *4429[16]* **1996:** *35[12] 112[11] 637[6]* 849[10] **>30f<**
**Gretel** **2** ch f Hansel (USA)-Russian Royal (USA) (Nureyev (USA)) (2543) 2997[6] 4133[3] 4464[8] **>91f<**
**Gretna Green (USA)** **3** b f Hansel (USA)-Greenland Park (Red God) 1667[11] **>33f<**
**Grey Again** **4** gr f Unfuwain (USA)-Grey Goddess (Godswalk (USA)) *44[5] (87) 181[6] 254[2] 301[5] 429[7] 629[15]* 787[16] **>65a 33f<**
**Grey Charmer (IRE)** **7** gr h Alzao (USA)-Sashi Woo (Rusticaro (FR)) **1995:** *4421[9] 4502[8]* **1996:** *71[7] 127[12] 155[13] 3257[8]* 3473[10] 3698[16] **>33a 45f<**
**Greycoat Boy** **4** br g Pragmatic-Sirdar Girl (Milford) 1194[10] 1439[4] 1784[4] 2042[19] **>73f<**
**Grey Galava** **3** gr f Generous (IRE)-Galava (CAN) (Graustark) 732[14] *857[2] 1096[3] 2014[3]* 2217[2] (2424) **>61a 65f<**
**Grey Kingdom** **5** gr g Grey Desire-Miss Realm (Realm) *604[12] 1037[6]* 1414[12] 1502[10] 1674[2] (1860) 2023[3] 2357[7] (3151) 3344[4] 3777[5] 4906[5] **>49f<**
**Grey Legend** **3** gr c Touch of Grey-Northwold Star (USA) (Monteverdi) *1073[14]* 1172[13] **>40f<**
**Grey Risk (FR)** **3** gr c Kendor (FR)-Swiss Risk (FR) (Last Tycoon) (3033a) 3745a[5] 4165a[7] **>124f<**
**Grey Shot** **4** gr g Sharrood (USA)-Optaria (Song) *875[2]* 1128[4] 1752a[5] (3157) 3673[4] 5069a[7] **>121f<**
**Grey Sonata** **9** gr m Horage-The Grey (GER) (Pentathlon) 3507[4] 3775[9] **>42f<**
**Greystyle** **6** b g Grey Desire-Riverstyle (River Knight (FR)) *1070[10]* 1165[2] 1472[4] 1826[10] 3580[5] 3855[7] **>40f<**
**Grey Way (USA)** **3** gr f Cozzene (USA)-Northern Dancer (ITY) (Nureyev (USA)) 723a[2] 1393a[5] (4170a) (4541a) **>111f<**
**Grief (IRE)** **3** ch g Broken Hearted-Crecora (Royal Captive) 4026a[6] **>88f<**
**Griega (IRE)** **2** b f Danehill (USA)-French Flair (USA) (Bering) (4034a)
**Griffin's Girl** **4** ch f Bairn (USA)-All That Crack (Stanford) *3944[15]* 4237[17] **>21a 31f<**
**Grindstone (USA)** **3** dk c Unbridled (USA)-Buzz My Bell (USA) (Drone) *(1055a)* **>126a f<**
**Grisellito (FR)** **3** b c Galetto (FR)-Grisellina (FR) (River River (FR)) 2845a[2] 5070a[2] **>106f<**
**Grooms Gold (IRE)** **4** ch c Groom Dancer (USA)-Gortynia (FR) (My Swallow) 440[25] **>64f<**
**Groom's Gordon (FR)** **2** b c Groom Dancer (USA)-Sonoma (FR) (Habitat) 1779[4] (2184) (2503) 4023a[4] 4488[11] **>100f<**
**Ground Game** **3** b f Gildoran-Running Game (Run The Gantlet (USA)) (955) 1145[2] 1669[3] (3938) 4297[4] 4854a[2] **>66a 90f<**
**Grovefair Dancer (IRE)** **2** ch f Soviet Lad (USA)-Naval Artiste (Captain's Gig (USA)) 1494[5] 2012[2] *(2307) 2554[2] 4339[8] 4780[5] 4980[12]* **>55a 55f<**
**Grovefair Flyer (IRE)** **2** b c Astronef-Hitness (Hittite Glory) 706[8] *838[2] (990)* 1103[3] 1713[7] 2606[10] 2759[5] 3169[4] 3299[5] **>50a 70f<**
**Grovefair Lad (IRE)** **2** b g Silver Kite (USA)-Cienaga (Tarboosh (USA)) *916[11]* 1871[8] 2161[5] 3311[3] 3498[7] *3629[2] 3662[4]* 3943[9] 4694[4] 4834[7] **>58a 55f<**
**Grovefair Maiden (IRE)** **2** ch f Red Sunset-Coffee Bean (Doulab (USA)) *1346[13]* 2435[2] (2685) 2959[9] 3092[2] **>55f<**
**Grovefair Venture** **2** ch c Presidium-Miramede (Norwick (USA)) 2600[13] 3259[16] 3464[12] 3976[10] **>43f<**
**Gryada** **3** b f Shirley Heights-Grimpola (GER) (Windwurf (GER)) *1004[7]* 3497[8] 3836[11] **>89df<**
**Guards Brigade** **5** b g Bustino-Light Duty (Queen's Hussar) 999[10] 1165[5] **>30a 38df<**
**Guesstimation (USA)** **7** b g Known Fact (USA)-Best Guess (USA) (Apalachee (USA)) 827[16] 1515[8] 1841[6] 2068[5] 2568[2] 2737[2] (3000) 3136[5] 3635[5] (3849) 3970[4] 4236[8] **>51a 63f<**
**Guest Alliance (IRE)** **4** ch g Zaffaran (USA)-Alhargah (Be My Guest (USA)) **1995:** *4364[9] (4463) 4530[7]* **1996:** *260[2] 339[7] 498[2] 635[6]* 1660[4] 4252[9] **>68a 54f<**
**Gulf of Gdansk (USA)** **6** b g Danzig Connection (USA)-Unique Millie *374a[6] 432a[4]* **>55a f<**
**Gulf of Siam** **3** ch g Prince Sabo-Jussoli (Don) *703[9]* 976[9] 1477[7] 2163[2] 2752[2] 3238[3] 3490[3] 4226[15] **>67f<**
**Gulf Shaadi** **4** b g Shaadi (USA)-Ela Meem (USA) (Kris) **1995:** *4520[9]* **1996:** *181[12] 211[11] 270[10] 4577[11] 4901[18]* **>40a 62f<**
**Gulliver** **3** b c Rainbow Quest (USA)-Minskip (USA) (The Minstrel (CAN)) 684[13] 845[8] 3505[3] 3986[4] 4362[6] **>82f<**
**Gumair (USA)** **3** ch c Summer Squall (USA)-Finisterre (AUS) (Biscay (AUS)) 1507[10] 1900[4] 2616[4] 3155[6] 4353[6] **>81f<**
**Gunboat Diplomacy (FR)** **5** b h Dominion-Singapore Girl (FR) (Lyphard (USA)) (438a) 622a[6] 1749a[2] **>125f<**
**Gun Fight (USA)** **2** b c Fit To Fight (USA)-Lady Turk (USA) (Turkoman (USA)) *4954a[8]* **>95a f<**
**Gunfire (IRE)** **2** ch c Great Commotion (USA)-West Chazy (USA) 4024a[11] **>84f<**
**Gunmaker** **7** ch g Gunner B-Lucky Starkist (Lucky Wednesday) *73[6] 1717[2] 2028[3]* 2530[9] **>48a 34f<**
**Gunner B Special** **3** ch g Gunner B-Sola Mia (Tolomeo) **1995:** *4433[9]* **1996:** *3845[5]* 4563[7] 4612[14] **>39a 42f<**
**Gunners Glory** **2** b c Aragon-Massive Powder (Caerleon (USA)) (2942) 3436[3] 3871[2] 3975[7] **>80f<**
**Guy's Gamble** **3** ch g Mazilier (USA)-Deep Blue Sea (Gulf Pearl) **1995:** *4511[10]* **1996:** *(49) 123[3] 280[4] 1042[9]* 4921[17] **>63a 39f<**
**Gwespyr** **3** ch g Sharpo-Boozy (Absalom) 525[6] 638[12] 881[5] 1597[7] 1761[4] 2021[3] 2151[7] (2496) 2676[3] 2790[4] (3049) 3215[6] 4616[23] **>67f<**
**Gymcrak Flyer** **5** b m Aragon-Intellect (Frimley Park) *739[3]* 1069[4] 1423[8] 1538[10] (2242) (2630) (2947) 3817[9] 4560[13] 4691[9] 4909[17] **>54a 72f<**
**Gymcrak Gem (IRE)** **3** b f Don't Forget Me-Santa Patricia (IRE) (Taufan (USA)) 1429[6] 2029[3] 4075[4] 4356[8] **>64f<**
**Gymcrak Gorjos** **2** b br f Rock Hopper-Bit O' May (Mummy's Pet) 3982[16] **>31f<**
**Gymcrak Hero (IRE)** **4** b g Taufan (USA)-Jamie's Girl (Captain James) **1995:** *4409[16]* **1996:** *609[18]* 713[16] 1611[7] **>29df<**
**Gymcrak Jareer (IRE)** **4** b g Jareer (USA)-Katzarah (IRE) (Pharly (FR)) 3489[8] **>46df<**
**Gymcrak Jester** **2** b g Derrylin-Emerin (King Emperor (USA)) 4796[14] **>6f<**
**Gymcrak Premiere** **8** ch g Primo Dominie-Oraston (Morston (FR)) 876[9] 1322[3] 2053[30] 3709[11] 3933[12] 4190[17] 4620[5] 4775[13] 4868[6] **>80f<**
**Gymcrak Watermill (IRE)** **2** b br f River Falls-Victorian Pageant (Welsh Pageant) 3508[6] **>33f<**

**H**

**Habeta (USA)** **10** ch h Habitat-Prise (Busted) 827[11] 1037[5] 1502[3] (1830) (2214) 2868[4] 3344[5] 3812[11] 3958[13] 4436[7] 4686[21] 4812[17] **>49f<**
**Hachiyah (IRE)** **2** b br f Generous (IRE)-Himmah (USA) (Habitat) 3837[7] 4188[W] **>56f<**
**Hadadabble** **3** ch f Hadeer-Magnifica (Sandy Creek) **1995:** *4431[10]* **1996:** *471[16]* 937[14] *1096[2] 1416[17] 1719[4] 1969[5] 2369[5] 2687[6] 2937[6] 3274[11]* 3586[5] 3655[5] 3929[5] 4212[7] 4422[6] 4606[7] 4968[19] **>46a 56df<**
**Hadawah (USA)** **2** ch f Riverman (USA)-Sajjaya (USA) (Blushing Groom (FR)) 2147[7] 2741[6] 3663[5] 3962[7] **>61f<**
**Haddit** **3** b g Thowra (FR)-Ocean Hound (Main Reef) *4083[8]* 4478[10] 4703[17] **>13f<**
**Hadidi** **2** b c Alzao (USA)-Sesame (Derrylin) 4242[12] 4684[6] 4914[8] **>60f<**
**Hagwah (USA)** **4** b f Dancing Brave (USA)-Saraa Ree (USA) (Caro) 726[9] 941[D] 1476[8] 1770[2] 2465a[5] (3530a) (3836) 4160a[2] (4371) 4663a[6] 4757[6] **>115f<**
**Haido'hart** **4** b g Pharly (FR)-Try Vickers (USA) (Fuzzbuster (USA)) *993[15]* 1198[8] 1674[9] 2162[4] 2379[4] 2731[7] 4808[18] 4868[14] **>40f<**
**Hajat** **2** ch f Mujtahid (USA)-Nur (USA) (Diesis) 4545[4] 4762[3] **>64f<**
**Hakiki (IRE)** **4** b c Ballad Rock-Salvationist (Mill Reef (USA)) 1943a[3] 4173a[4] **>102f<**
**Hakkaniyah** **2** b f Machiavellian (USA)-Mousaiha (USA) (Shadeed (USA)) 1413[2] (1808) 2877[4] **>83f<**
**Halbert** **7** b g Song-Stoneydale (Tickled Pink) **1995:** *4458[6] 4542[5]* **1996:** *41[2] 107[4] 163[4] 231[3] 466[12]* 632[9] 812[17] 1049[6] 1351[10] *1716[5] 1844[8]* 2244[8] 4130[13] 4342[7] *4573[5] 4881[18]* **>49a 50f<**
**Halcon** **3** c Rainbow Quest (USA)-Teresa (SPA) (Rheffissimo (FR)) 1057a[4] **>96f<**
**Haleakala (IRE)** **3** ch f Kris-Haiati (USA) (Alydar (USA)) (2223) 3992[2] 4178[7] 4377[3] **>104f<**
**Halebid** **3** b c Dowsing (USA)-Pink Robber (USA) (No Robbery) 1535[5] *(2168) (2749) 3063[2] 3295[3]* (3681) **>84a 75f<**
**Halfabob (IRE)** **4** ch g Broken Hearted-Hasten

(Northfields (USA)) **1995:** $4363^{6}$ **1996:** $84^{5}$ **>37a 69f<**

**Half An Inch (IRE) 3** gr g Petoski-Inch (English Prince) $833^{9}$ $978^{9}$ $1104^{4}$ $1317^{6}$ $1523^{6}$ $2339^{3}$ (2402) $2689^{10}$ $2766^{5}$ $3785^{17}$ $3978^{10}$ **>42a 62f<**

**Half Tone 4** gr c Touch of Grey-Demilinga (Nishapour (FR)) **1995:** (4460) (4487) $4536^{6}$ **1996:** $173^{3}$ $316^{4}$ (362) $1049^{15}$ $1512^{3}$ $1777^{4}$ $2034^{9}$ $2129^{3}$ $2280^{3}$ $2586^{4}$ $2598^{2}$ $3146^{2}$ (3506) **>71a 60f<**

**Hal Hoo Yaroom 3** b c Belmez (USA)-Princess Nawaal (USA) (Seattle Slew (USA)) $702^{7}$ (2205) (2407) $2697^{10}$ $3404^{3}$ **>90f<**

**Halleluja Time 4** b g Risk Me (FR)-Warm Wind (Tumble Wind (USA)) $133^{11}$ **>16a 36f<**

**Halliard 5** b g Hallgate-Princess Blanco (Prince Regent (FR)) **1995:** $4358^{4}$ $4484^{7}$ **1996:** $308^{6}$ $470^{5}$ $636^{11}$ $879^{29}$ $981^{5}$ (1170) (1446) $1716^{10}$ $2156^{10}$ $2324^{6}$ $3236^{10}$ **>54a 67f< (DEAD)**

**Hallikeld 3** ch f Bustino-Spring Sparkle (Lord Gayle (USA)) $763^{9}$ $3053^{6}$ $3463^{9}$ $3961^{5}$ $4344^{7}$ $4506^{10}$ $4892^{7}$ **>14a 47f<**

**Halling (USA) 5** ch h Diesis-Dance Machine (Green Dancer (USA)) (434a) $536a^{11}$ (1749a) (2546) (3670) $4773^{2}$ **>130+a 134f<**

**Hallmark (IRE) 2** b c Shalford (IRE)-Cryptic Gold (Glint of Gold) $3234^{6}$ $3515^{6}$ $3809^{3}$ $4103^{3}$ $4795^{8}$ $4970^{2}$ **>71f<**

**Hallstar 4** b f Hallgate-Star Route (Owen Dudley) $86^{7}$ $235^{7}$ **>15a 24f<**

**Halmanerror 6** gr g Lochnager-Counter Coup (Busted) $589^{6}$ $850^{9}$ $1609^{6}$ $1829^{7}$ $2030^{2}$ $2213^{3}$ $2363^{4}$ $2590^{5}$ (3152) $3639^{5}$ $3817^{5}$ $4058^{9}$ $4460^{13}$ $4688^{9}$ $4809^{14}$ $4994^{25}$ **>60f<**

**Halowing (USA) 2** b f Danzatore (CAN)-Halo Ho (USA) (Halo (USA)) $1510^{5}$ $1878^{2}$ $2338^{5}$ (2703) $3707^{9}$ $4113^{4}$ $4301^{2}$ $4565^{6}$ **>85f<**

**Hal's Pal 3** br c Caerleon (USA)-Refinancing (USA) (Forli (ARG)) $640^{2}$ $937^{8}$ (3418) (3627) $4194^{6}$ $4463^{2}$ $4620^{2}$ $5021a^{8}$ **>95a 103f<**

**Haltarra (USA) 2** ch c Zilzal (USA)-Snow Bride (USA) (Blushing Groom (FR)) $3987^{2}$ $4306^{3}$ **>89f<**

**Hamilton Gold 3** ch f Safawan-Golden Della (Glint of Gold) $1667^{8}$ $1972^{7}$ $2732^{8}$ $3310^{3}$ $4205^{16}$ $4486^{18}$ **>7a 47f<**

**Hamilton Silk 4** b g K-Battery-Silver's Girl (Sweet Monday) $1655^{5}$ $2155^{4}$ **>57f<**

**Hamirpour (IRE) 3** $4857a^{11}$

**Hamlet (IRE) 3** b c Danehill (USA)-Blasted Heath (Thatching) $428^{2}$ $693^{7}$ (1477) $1712^{4}$ (2294) $2608^{7}$ **>71a 88f<**

**Hammerstein 3** b c Kris-Musical Bliss (USA) (The Minstrel (CAN)) (934) $1187^{2}$ $1484^{7}$ (3067) (3229) $3596^{5}$ $4051^{4}$ $4520^{5}$ **>112f<**

**Ham N'Eggs 5** b g Robellino (USA)-Rose And The Ring (Welsh Pageant) $450^{20}$ $3098^{3}$ $3253^{5}$ **>78f<**

**Hampi (USA) 3** b f Runaway Groom (CAN)-Foresighted Lady (USA) (Vent Du Nord) **1995:** $4535^{8}$ **>37a f<**

**Hanan (USA) 2** b f Twilight Agenda (USA)-Maikai (USA) (Never Bend) $2147^{5}$ $3201a^{5}$ **>71tf<**

**Hanbitooh (USA) 3** b c Hansel (USA)-Bitooh (Seattle Slew (USA)) $495^{3}$ $668^{4}$ $890^{11}$ $1072^{3}$ $1418^{6}$ $1591^{7}$ **>74df<**

**Hand Craft (IRE) 4** b g Dancing Dissident (USA)-Fair Flutter (Beldale Flutter (USA)) $765^{9}$ $1018^{16}$ $1190^{18}$ $1841^{5}$ $4385^{11}$ $4617^{12}$ **>81+a 82f<**

**Handmaiden 6** gr m Shardari-Flyaway Bride (USA) (Blushing Groom (FR)) **1995:** $4434^{9}$ **>24a 34f<**

**Hand of Straw (IRE) 4** b g Thatching-Call Me Miss (Hello Gorgeous (USA)) (62) $105^{3}$ $162^{7}$ $261^{5}$ $384^{2}$ $424^{10}$ (598) $979^{3}$ $1450^{4}$ $1686^{7}$ $1838^{4}$ $3825^{8}$ $4125^{14}$ $4315^{5}$ $4574^{11}$ $4703^{14}$ $4977^{8}$ $5056^{5}$ **>34a 56f<**

**Handsome Ridge 2** ch c Indian Ridge-Red Rose Garden (Electric) (5033) **>91+f<**

**Handsome Squaw 4** ch f Handsome Sailor-Brave Squaw (High Top) **1995:** $4388^{15}$ **>27f<**

**Hang a Right 9** b g Enchantment-Martina's Magic (Martinmas) $1012^{3}$ $1411^{22}$ $1658^{6}$ $2130^{15}$ $2763^{10}$ $2940^{11}$ $3281^{3}$ **>18a 42f<**

**Hangoninthere 5** b g Rakaposhi King-Dusky Nancy (Red Sunset) $2551^{10}$ $3130^{6}$ $3849^{12}$ $4129^{17}$ **>18a 45f<**

**Hangover Square (IRE) 2** ch c Jareer (USA)-Dancing Line (High Line) $706^{5}$ $916^{4}$ $1766^{2}$ $1987^{5}$ $2879^{9}$ $3429^{5}$ $4234^{2}$ $4545^{2}$ $4786^{5}$ **>83f<**

**Hang Ten 7** b h Kris-Broken Wave (Bustino) $1454^{10}$

**H'Ani 4** b f Woodman (USA)-African Dance (USA) (El Gran Senor (USA)) **1995:** $4416^{2}$ $4452^{3}$ **>64a 65f<**

**Hank-a-chief 3** b c Inca Chief (USA)-Be Sharp (Sharpen Up) $605^{9}$ $1010^{8}$ $2251^{11}$ $2542^{10}$ **>35a 43f<**

**Hannahs Bay 3** b f Buzzards Bay-Hi-Hannah (Red Sunset) **1995:** $4477^{3}$ **1996:** $1970^{7}$ $2397^{7}$ **>44a 34f<**

**Hannah's Usher 4** b g Marching On-La Pepper (Workboy) **1995:** $4517^{5}$ **1996:** $55^{6}$ $88^{4}$ $117^{7}$ $173^{5}$ $202^{3}$ $386^{3}$ (511) $652^{2}$ $951^{6}$ $1412^{16}$ $1598^{8}$ $2084^{6}$ $2481^{9}$ $2929^{7}$ **>76a 57f<**

**Hannalou (FR) 3** b f Shareef Dancer (USA)-Litani River (USA) (Irish River (FR)) $921^{9}$ $1323^{2}$ $1864^{2}$ $2687^{3}$ $2861^{6}$ $3832^{2}$ $4108^{6}$ $4456^{2}$ $4690^{6}$ $4895^{14}$ **>16a 73f<**

**Happy 2** b c Rock City-Joyful Thought (Green Desert (USA)) $4544^{7}$ **>33f<**

**Happy Boy 3** ch c Time For A Change (USA)-Happy Gini (Ginistrelli (USA)) $1395a^{6}$ **>99f<**

**Happy Dancer (USA) 2** b f Seattle Dancer (USA)-Happy Result (USA) (Diesis) (4746a)

**Happy Go Lucky 2** ch f Teamster-Meritsu (IRE) (Lyphard's Special (USA)) $2559^{8}$ $3159^{3}$ (3764) $4760^{15}$ **>78f<**

**Happy Minstral (USA) 2** b c Alleged (USA)-Minstrelete (USA) (Round Table) $2909^{2}$ (4204) **>75f<**

**Happy Partner (IRE) 3** b c Nabeel Dancer (USA)-Dublah (USA) (Private Account (USA)) (51) **>66a 52f<**

**Happy Taipan (IRE) 3** b g Keen-Eastern View (IRE) (Persian Bold) $1973^{5}$ **>58f<**

**Happy Traveller (IRE) 3** b c Treasure Kay-Elegant Owl (Tumble Wind (USA)) **1995:** $4529^{5}$ **1996:** $3446^{12}$ $3624^{8}$ $3867^{6}$ **>57a 54f<**

**Happy Tycoon (IRE) 3** br c Polish Patriot (USA)-Art Age (Artaius (USA)) $1597^{8}$ $3955^{U}$ **>51f<**

**Happy Valentine 2** b c Rainbow Quest (USA)-Nearctic Flame (Sadler's Wells (USA)) (4913) **>103++f<**

**Happy Venturer (IRE) 3** br g Petorius-Primacara (Rusticaro (FR)) $1535^{6}$ $1972^{8}$ $2326^{W}$ $2915^{6}$ $3316^{9}$ **>43df<**

**Haramayda (FR) 3** $4654a^{13}$

**Harbet House (FR) 3** b g Bikala-Light of Hope (USA) (Lyphard (USA)) $576^{14}$ $856^{7}$ $932^{9}$ $1415^{8}$ $1814^{3}$ (2086) $2372^{2}$ $2553^{6}$ $3872^{8}$ $4092^{3}$ $4332^{8}$ $4877^{5}$ **>66a 62f<**

**Harbour Dues 3** b c Slip Anchor-Quillotern (USA) (Arctic Tern (USA)) (1180) (1712) $2074^{3}$ $3689^{4}$ $4886^{2}$ **>106f<**

**Harbour Island 4** b c Rainbow Quest (USA)-Quay Line (High Line) $1700^{6}$ $1976^{6}$ $3834^{3}$ $4199^{7}$ $4673^{4}$ $4771^{8}$ **>89f<**

**Harding 5** b g Dowsing (USA)-Orange Hill (High Top) $4669^{8}$ **>54f<**

**Hardiprincess 2** b f Keen-Hardiheroine (Sandhurst Prince) $4962^{10}$ $5051^{8}$ **>41f<**

**Hard Love 4** b f Rambo Dancer (CAN)-Djimbaran Bay (Le Levanstell) **1995:** $4505^{4}$ $4544^{5}$ **1996:** $15^{10}$ $114^{3}$ $297^{4}$ $400^{2}$ $449^{6}$ **>61a 69df<**

**Hard to Figure 10** gr g Telsmoss-Count On Me (No Mercy) $457^{4}$ (579) $864^{7}$ $1332^{3}$ $1621^{8}$ $2114^{23}$ $2853^{3}$ $3232^{26}$ $3782^{5}$ $3984^{7}$ $4314^{15}$ $4823^{8}$ **>96f<**

**Hardy Dancer 4** ch c Pharly (FR)-Handy Dancer (Green God) $410^{8}$ $580^{3}$ $925^{2}$ $988^{3}$ $1793^{6}$ $2055^{13}$ $2502^{20}$ $3947^{10}$ $4120^{10}$ $4326^{10}$ $4719^{6}$ $4901^{14}$ **>45a 77f<**

**Hareb (USA) 3** b c Diesis-All At Once (USA) (Dixieland Band (USA)) $684^{5}$ $970^{8}$ $1319^{4}$ $2126^{6}$ (3074) $3327^{5}$ $3918^{2}$ $4387^{4}$ **>80a 74f<**

**Harghar (USA) 3** gr c El Gran Senor (USA)-Harouniya (Siberian Express (USA)) $1249a^{2}$ $1573a^{2}$ (2459a) **>108f<**

**Harik 2** ch c Persian Bold-Yaqut (USA) (Northern Dancer) $4492^{10}$ **>65f<**

**Harlequin Walk (IRE) 5** ch m Pennine Walk-Taniokey (Grundy) (318) $485^{4}$ $1534^{6}$ (2594) $2793^{2}$ $3314^{4}$ **>58a 48f<**

**Harlestone Heath 3** gr f Aragon-Harlestone Lake (Riboboy (USA)) $4379^{6}$ **>45f<**

**Harmony Hall 2** ch c Music Boy-Fleeting Affair (Hotfoot) $2195^{10}$ $4242^{6}$ $4817^{6}$ $5043^{8}$ **>66f<**

**Harmony In Red 2** ch c Rock Hopper-Lucky Song (Lucky Wednesday) $1884^{4}$ $2295^{6}$ $2985^{5}$ $4976^{5}$ **>42a 72f<**

**Harpoon Louie (USA) 6** b g Eskimo (USA)-Twelfth Pleasure (USA) (Fappiano (USA)) **1995:** $4520^{4}$ **>75a 83f<**

**Harriet's Beau 3** b g Superpower-Pour Moi (Bay Express) $525^{14}$ $762^{15}$ $1527^{12}$ $2163^{9}$ $2902^{5}$ $3097^{3}$ $3317^{5}$ $3774^{8}$ $4075^{16}$ **>35f<**

**Harry 6** ch g Risk Me (FR)-Relko's Pride (Relko) $104^{3}$ $198^{9}$ $240^{9}$ $5053^{7}$ **>55a 46f<**

**Harry's Coming 12** b g Marching On-Elegant Star (Star Moss) $750^{9}$ **>62f<**

**Harry's Treat 4** b f Lochnager-Megara (USA) (Thatching) $328^{8}$ $562^{12}$ $734^{3}$ $851^{10}$ $1196^{4}$ $1821^{U}$ **>29a 63f<**

**Harry Welsh (IRE) 4** gr g Treasure Kay-Excelling Miss (USA) (Exceller (USA)) **1995:** $4370^{11}$ **>23a 70f<**

**Harry Wolton 2** b c Distant Relative-Tashinsky (USA) (Nijinsky (CAN)) $3994^{2}$ (4242) **>82+f<**

**Harsh Times 3** ch f Efisio-Larnem (Meldrum) $427^{8}$ $2481^{6}$ $2568^{12}$ $3306^{12}$ $3854^{3}$ $3951^{12}$ $4472^{9}$ **>52a 53f<**

**Hartfields Boy 3** b g Shavian-Fallen Angel (Quiet Fling (USA)) $1012^{12}$ **>40f< (DEAD)**

**Hartshorn 2** br c Warning-Roxy Hart (High Top) $4100^{12}$ $4507^{7}$ $4884^{7}$ **>51f<**

**Harvest Reaper 4** gr g Bairn (USA)-Real Silver (Silly Season) **1995:** $4456^{7}$ $4505^{13}$ **1996:** $1416^{7}$ $1500^{15}$ $3761^{12}$ $4808^{3}$ $5010^{10}$ **>43a 46f<**

**Harvey White (IRE) 4** b or br g Petorius-Walkyria (Lord Gayle (USA)) **1995:** $4364^{8}$ **1996:** $469^{4}$ $641^{5}$ $871^{2}$ (979) $1686^{3}$ $1838^{5}$ $1903^{3}$ $2784^{4}$ $3161^{3}$ $3470^{4}$ $3785^{8}$ (4068) $4489^{3}$ $4686^{8}$ $4702^{9}$ $4819^{3}$ $4900^{12}$ $5054^{12}$ **>53a 71f<**

**Hasta la Vista 6** b g Superlative-Falcon Berry (FR) (Bustino) $612^{4}$ (771) $972^{4}$ $1116^{6}$ $1611^{5}$ $2423^{4}$ $3297^{8}$ $4092^{7}$ $4626^{12}$ **>50a 57f<**

**Hathor Eria (FR) 3** b f Legend of France (USA)-Money Can't Buy (FR) (Thatching) $4739a^{3}$ **>107f<**

**Hats of to Hilda 4** b f Aragon-Incarnadine (Hot Spark) $586^{13}$ $1092^{8}$ $1665^{18}$ $2565^{9}$ $2891^{15}$ **>19f<**

**Hattaafeh (IRE) 5** b m Mtoto-Monongelia (Welsh Pageant) **1995:** $4376^{9}$ **1996:** $666^{2}$ $811^{5}$ $1124^{2}$

$1618^{2}$ $1792^{3}$ $3037^{4}$ **>68a 72f<**

**Hattab (IRE) 2** b c Marju (IRE)-Funun (USA) (Fappiano (USA)) $3069^{5}$ $3494^{4}$ (4043) $4517^{2}$ $4893^{8}$ **>92f<**

**Hatta Breeze 4** b f Night Shift (USA)-Jouvencelle (Rusticaro (FR)) **1995:** *$4386^{10}$* **>67a 73+f<**

**Hatta River (USA) 6** b g Irish River (FR)-Fallacieuse (Habitat) $504^{10}$ $1454^{7}$ $2511^{8}$ $2989^{13}$ **>47f<**

**Hatta Sunshine (USA) 6** b g Dixieland Band (USA)-Mountain Sunshine (USA) (Vaguely Noble) *(201) $243^{4}$ $366^{3}$ $412^{2}$ $501^{5}$ $553^{7}$ $4381^{6}$* $4789^{7}$ **>55a 44f<**

**Haute Cuisine 3** b g Petong-Nevis (Connaught) $566^{7}$ *$782^{16}$ $1764^{5}$* $1888^{W}$ $4340^{2}$ $4703^{9}$ $4815^{10}$ **>53f<**

**Havago 2** b c Risk Me (FR)-Sporting Lass (Blakeney) $2538^{6}$ $3941^{11}$ (4782) $5048^{4}$ **>72f<**

**Havana Heights (IRE) 3** ch f Persian Heights-Havana Blade (USA) (Blade (USA)) **1995:** *$4443^{5}$* **1996:** *$46^{6}$ $101^{8}$ $329^{6}$ $370^{3}$ $3605^{7}$ $3775^{4}$* (4317) $4563^{15}$ $5008^{12}$ **>38a 45f<**

**Havana Miss 4** b f Cigar-Miss Patdonna (Starch Reduced) $4045^{8}$ $4341^{7}$ *$4983^{13}$* **>29a 49f<**

**Havana Reserve 2** ch g Cigar-Shy Hiker (Netherkelly) $5051^{6}$

**Have a Nightcap 7** ch g Night Shift (USA)-Final Orders (USA) (Prince John) *$2085^{2}$ $2391^{6}$ $2632^{3}$ $2903^{7}$* $3316^{3}$ *$5055^{8}$* **>51a 39f<**

**Hawa Al Nasamaat (USA) 4** b g Houston (USA)-Barrera Miss (USA) (Barrera (USA)) $496^{11}$ $3106^{3}$ (3216) $3440^{3}$ $4314^{26}$ **>85f<**

**Hawaii Storm (FR) 8** b g Plugged Nickle (USA)-Slewvindaloo (USA) (Seattle Slew (USA)) **1995:** *$4386^{2}$ $4420^{8}$ $4440^{3}$ $4493^{6}$ (4515)* **1996:** *$42^{6}$ $121^{2}$ $177^{2}$ $244^{6}$ $291^{6}$ $645^{9}$* $887^{14}$ *$1048^{8}$ $1302^{14}$ $2934^{7}$ $3078^{3}$ $3877^{5}$ $4089^{5}$ $4186^{15}$ $4781^{6}$* **>57a 35f<**

**Hawait (IRE) 2** gr c Green Desert (USA)-Hayati (Hotfoot) $924^{4}$ $1130^{3}$ (3269) $3674^{9}$ $4311^{4}$ **>86f<**

**Hawanafa 3** b f Tirol-Woodland View (Precipice Wood) $1142^{18}$ $1689^{6}$ $1856^{12}$ $2286^{11}$ $2743^{13}$ $3108^{3}$ $3500^{9}$ $4082^{9}$ **>53f<**

**Hawkish (USA) 7** b g Silver Hawk (USA)-Dive Royal (USA) (Inverness Drive (USA)) *$817^{3}$* $1496^{9}$ $2348^{2}$ $2776^{4}$ $3297^{5}$ $4102^{2}$ **>41a 57f<**

**Hawksley Hill (IRE) 3** ch g Rahy (USA)-Gaijin (Caerleon (USA)) **1995:** *$4429^{13}$* **1996:** *(605) (658)* (1089) $1418^{2}$ (2541) (2885) $3279^{2}$ $3640^{2}$ $4190^{6}$ $4300^{2}$ $4568^{5}$ (4769) $4974^{10}$ **>57a 96f<**

**Hawwam 10** b g Glenstal (USA)-Hone (Sharpen Up) **1995:** *$4388^{2}$ $4476^{13}$ $4503^{7}$* **1996:** *$29^{2}$ $111^{4}$ $198^{8}$ $210^{4}$ $251^{3}$ $284^{5}$ $688^{11}$* $883^{7}$ $1167^{6}$ $1468^{3}$ $1866^{8}$ *$2304^{9}$ $2521^{8}$* $2567^{3}$ (2731) (2801) $3084^{9}$ $3217^{3}$ $3403^{6}$ $3623^{11}$ $4190^{18}$ $4455^{8}$ $4769^{18}$ $4810^{7}$ **>68a 57f<**

**Hayaain 3** b c Shirley Heights-Littlefield (Bay Express) $1873^{3}$ (2314) $2576^{7}$ $2882^{12}$ **>87f<**

**Haya Ya Kefaah 4** b g Kefaah (USA)-Hayat (IRE) (Sadler's Wells (USA)) *$221^{2}$ (439)* $546^{10}$ (993) $3683^{2}$ $4067^{10}$ (4431) **>71a 72f<**

**Haydn James (USA) 2** ch c Danzig Connection (USA)-Royal Fi Fi (USA) (Conquistador Cielo (USA)) $3615^{4}$ $4233^{7}$ **>83f<**

**Haydown (IRE) 4** b or br g Petorius-Hay Knot (Main Reef) $2711^{8}$ $3076^{4}$ $3471^{5}$ $3944^{10}$ **>54f<**

**Hayling-Billy 3** ch c Captain Webster-Mistress Royal (Royalty) $4548^{7}$ $4611^{9}$ **>60f<**

**Haysong (IRE) 3** ch f Ballad Rock-Hay Knot (Main Reef) $2432^{12}$ $2572^{10}$ $2777^{13}$ **>34f<**

**Hazard a Guess (IRE) 6** ch g Digamist (USA)-Guess Who (Be My Guest (USA)) $440^{2}$ (580) $628^{3}$ $1198^{3}$ $1793^{7}$ $2010^{9}$ $2164^{2}$ $2350^{6}$ $2502^{7}$ $2724^{5}$ (3280) $3509^{8}$ $3691^{9}$ (4624) **>91f<**

**Hazel 4** ro f Risk Me (FR)-Sir Tangs Gift (Runnett) $4108^{5}$ $4428^{12}$ **>61f<**

**Hazy Dayz 2** gr f Today and Tomorrow-Mossaka (Targowice (USA)) *$1720^{6}$*

**Head Gardener (IRE) 2** b br c Be My Chief (USA)-Silk Petal (Petorius) $1960^{7}$ $2224^{4}$ $2702^{8}$ **>73f<**

**Head Girl (IRE) 2** ch f Masterclass (USA)-Rebecca's Girl (IRE) (Nashamaa) $3080^{3}$ $3326^{2}$ $3687^{4}$ $4072^{5}$ $4796^{5}$ **>66f<**

**Head Over Heels (IRE) 2** b f Pursuit of Love-Proudfoot (IRE) (Shareef Dancer (USA)) $2230^{5}$ (2614) $2879^{3}$ (3170) (3613) $3903a^{2}$ $4191^{4}$ $4299^{2}$ $4677^{8}$ **>99f<**

**Heart 3** ch f Cadeaux Genereux-Recipe (Bustino) $1359^{4}$ $1804^{5}$ $3935^{2}$ $4362^{2}$ $4548^{4}$ $5046^{8}$ **>88f<**

**Heart Full of Soul 2** ch c Primo Dominie-Scales of Justice (Final Straw) $841^{8}$ $1118^{8}$ $4188^{12}$ $4495^{2}$ (4602) $4760^{14}$ $4880^{3}$ **>78f<**

**Heart Lake 5** ch h Nureyev (USA)-My Darling One (USA) (Exclusive Native (USA)) $286a^{2}$ $374a^{2}$ (1134a) $1952a^{12}$ $3144^{9}$ **>123f<**

**Heart of Armor 2** b c Tirol-Hemline (Sharpo) $3682^{3}$ $3964^{3}$ $4118^{4}$ **>75f<**

**Heart of Gold (IRE) 2** ch c Broken Hearted-Originality (Godswalk (USA)) $4041^{6}$ $4618^{7}$ **>66+f<**

**Heart Throb 2** b f Statoblest-Lets Fall In Love (USA) (Northern Baby (CAN)) $4210^{2}$ (4545) $4717^{6}$ $4867^{9}$ **>87f<**

**Heathyards Boy 6** b g Sayf El Arab (USA)-French Cooking (Royal And Regal (USA)) *$333^{W}$* **>20a f<**

**Heathyards Jade 3** b f Damister (USA)-French Cooking (Royal And Regal (USA)) *$209^{7}$ $314^{5}$* **>10a f<**

**Heathyards Lady (USA) 5** b m Mining (USA)-Dubiously (USA) (Jolie Jo (USA)) **1995:** *$4367^{5}$ $4427^{6}$* **1996:** *$1830^{6}$ $2306^{5}$ $2749^{3}$ $2925^{5}$* $2994^{4}$ $3334^{8}$ *$3627^{9}$ $3955^{3}$ $4078^{4}$ $4575^{4}$* **>77a 63f<**

**Heathyards Magic (IRE) 4** b g Magical Strike (USA)-Idle Gossip (Runnett) $479^{11}$ $537^{2}$ $805^{5}$ $884^{13}$ $1596^{6}$ $1866^{5}$ $2066^{8}$ $2394^{6}$ $2731^{8}$ *$3062^{8}$* **>63da 49f<**

**Heathyards Pearl (USA) 2** gr ro f Mining (USA)-Dance Dance Dance (IRE) (Dance of Life (USA)) $1978^{4}$ $2495^{4}$ $3588^{6}$ $4364^{11}$ **>70f<**

**Heathyards Rock 4** br g Rock City-Prudence (Grundy) **1995:** *$4481^{6}$* **1996:** *(235) (299) (401) $420^{2}$ $603^{2}$* **>87da 86f<**

**Heathyards Rose (IRE) 3** b f Conquering Hero (USA)-Another Gayle (Tumble Wind (USA)) *$134^{9}$ $516^{7}$ $856^{9}$* **>15a f<**

**Heavenly Dancer 2** b f Warrshan (USA)-High Halo (High Top) $3454^{8}$ $3662^{2}$ *$4091^{6}$ $4694^{14}$* ***>34a 57f<***

**Heavenly Miss (IRE) 2** b f Anita's Prince-Heavenly Blessed (Monseigneur (USA)) $596^{7}$ $1463^{2}$ $2685^{6}$ *$3065^{2}$ (3651)* $3846^{8}$ (4207) $4510^{4}$ $4878^{3}$ $4916^{5}$ **>47a 77f<**

**Heavenly Ray (USA) 2** ch f Rahy (USA)-Highest Truth (USA) (Alydar (USA)) *$3269^{8}$* ***>61f<***

**Heaven's Command 2** b f Priolo (USA)-Heavenly Music (FR) (Seattle Song (USA)) $4285a^{2}$ $4945a^{2}$ $5071a^{4}$ **>97f<**

**Heaven Sent (IRE) 3** b f Fayruz-Folle Remont (Prince Tenderfoot (USA)) *$230^{6}$* **>47f<**

**Heboob Alshemaal (IRE) 4** b f Nordico (USA)-Royal Climber (Kings Lake (USA)) **1995:** *(4363) $4419^{3}$ $4481^{P}$* **>81?a 80f<**

**Hee's a Dancer 4** b g Rambo Dancer (CAN)-Heemee (On Your Mark) *$3780^{6}$* ***>41f<***

**Heggies (IRE) 2** b c High Estate-Princess Pavlova (IRE) (Sadler's Wells (USA)) $1404^{10}$ $1622^{W}$ $1989^{5}$ *$2633^{12}$ $4795^{9}$* $4970^{3}$ *$5057^{9}$* **>32a 66f<**

**Heighth of Fame 5** b g Shirley Heights-Land of Ivory (USA) (The Minstrel (CAN)) **1995:** *$4376^{2}$* **1996:** *$33^{8}$ $60^{6}$ $104^{4}$ (186) $275^{2}$ $349^{2}$ $365^{12}$ $2304^{3}$ $2631^{2}$ $3066^{6}$ (4080) $4779^{2}$* **>79a 52f<**

**Heights of Love 3** b f Persian Heights-Lets Fall In Love (USA) (Northern Baby (CAN)) *$1049^{16}$* $1304^{8}$ $3862^{7}$ $3977^{13}$ $4356^{20}$ **>28f<**

**Helen Of Spain 4** b f Sadler's Wells (USA)-Port Helene (Troy) $902a^{3}$ (3392a) $3915a^{4}$ $4959a^{3}$ **>122f<**

**Helette 2** ch f Be My Chief (USA)-Miss Butterfield (Cure The Blues (USA)) $4037a^{2}$ **>73f<**

**Helios 8** br g Blazing Saddles (AUS)-Mary Sunley (Known Fact (USA)) *$243^{10}$ $554^{10}$* $747^{8}$ $983^{12}$ $1302^{11}$ (1659) (1902) $2058^{4}$ $3274^{8}$ (3694) $3978^{3}$ $4129^{6}$ $4354^{7}$ $4511^{4}$ **>39a 71f<**

**Helissio (FR) 3** b c Fairy King (USA)-Helice (Slewpy) (621a) (1139a) $1757a^{5}$ (2480a) (4293a) (4662a) **>136+f<**

**Hello (IRE) 2** b c Lycius (USA)-Itqan (IRE) (Sadler's Wells (USA)) *(1424)* $2040^{5}$ $2878^{2}$ $3927^{4}$ $4183^{2}$ (4666a) (4859a) **>102f<**

**Hello Dolly (IRE) 2** b f Mujadil (USA)-Great Leighs (Vaigly Great) *$446^{2}$* $596^{3}$ $685^{6}$ $757^{2}$ *$895^{4}$ (1360)* $1713^{4}$ $3632^{4}$ $3880^{2}$ $4602^{3}$ $4760^{9}$ $4864^{6}$ *(5057)* **>65a 65f<**

**Hello Hobson's (IRE) 6** b m Fayruz-Castleforbes (Thatching) **1995:** *$4407^{5}$ $4502^{12}$* **>38a 55f<**

**Hello Mister 5** b h Efisio-Ginnies Petong (Petong) *$864^{6}$* $940^{11}$ $1107^{5}$ $1332^{6}$ $1621^{9}$ **>83a 101f<**

**Hello Peter (IRE) 4** b g Taufan (USA)-Apple Rings (Godswalk (USA)) *$34^{6}$* **>41a 59f<**

**Hello There 2** b g Picea-Estonia (Kings Lake (USA)) $4072^{9}$ $4383^{11}$ $4502^{5}$ **>36f<**

**Helmsman (USA) 4** b c El Gran Senor (USA)-Sacred Journey (USA) (King's Bishop (USA)) $4953a^{6}$ **>121f<**

**Helsingor (IRE) 3** b c Danehill (USA)-Assya (Double Form) $2050^{7}$ **>91f<**

**Hencarlam (IRE) 3** b g Astronef-War Ballad (FR) (Green Dancer (USA)) $576^{15}$ **>56f<**

**Hen Harrier 2** ch f Polar Falcon (USA)-Circus Feathers (Kris) $1808^{2}$ (2404) $3057^{2}$ $3408^{3}$ $4084^{5}$ $4490^{12}$ **>83f<**

**Henley (USA) 2** b c Salem Drive (USA)-Leap of The Heart (USA) (Nijinsky (CAN)) *$4976^{11}$*

**Henry Cooper 3** b g Distant Relative-Miss Echo (Chief Singer) **1995:** *$4380^{8}$* **>3a f<**

**Henry Island (IRE) 3** ch c Sharp Victor (USA)-Monterana (Sallust) **1995:** *$4501^{4}$* **1996:** *$526^{3}$* $703^{2}$ (1470) $2041^{21}$ $2608^{5}$ $3071^{8}$ $3791^{2}$ $4385^{4}$ (4872) **>41++a 99f<**

**Henry Otis 3** ch g Savahra Sound-Seenachance (King of Clubs) $983^{17}$ $1172^{10}$ $1613^{13}$ $2768^{4}$ $3141^{13}$ **>53f<**

**Henry The Fifth 3** b c Village Star (FR)-Microcosme (Golden Fleece (USA)) **1995:** $4496a^{5}$ **1996:** $574^{4}$ $727^{4}$ $1389a^{3}$ $2041^{29}$ $4943a^{9}$ $5070a^{9}$ **>102f<**

**Henry the Hawk 5** b g Doulab (USA)-Plum Blossom (USA) (Gallant Romeo (USA)) (806) (1020) $1163^{5}$ $1635^{6}$ $1765^{4}$ $1865^{5}$ $2047^{11}$ $2964^{4}$ $3236^{8}$ $3957^{2}$ $4486^{10}$ *$4983^{15}$* **>9a 48f<**

**Henry Weston 4** b c Statoblest-Young Tearaway (Young Generation) **1995:** *$4458^{14}$ $4515^{15}$* **1996:** *$110^{11}$* **>54f<**

**Herbshan Dancer 2** b c Warrshan (USA)-Herbary (USA) (Herbager) $1513^{9}$ $2254^{6}$ $2904^{5}$ $3312^{6}$ $3848^{10}$ **>58f<**

**Here Comes a Star 8** b g Night Shift (USA)-Rapidus (Sharpen Up) *$716^{3}$* $931^{11}$ $1161^{3}$ $1321^{6}$ $1781^{3}$ $2064^{4}$ $2349^{6}$ $2518^{4}$ $2725^{9}$ $3055^{7}$ $3223^{4}$ $3579^{3}$ $3868^{13}$ $4616^{17}$ $4727^{3}$ $4809^{16}$ **>63f<**

**Here Comes Herbie 4** ch g Golden Lahab (USA)-

Megan's Move (Move Off) *586$^{11}$* 971$^{6}$ 1309$^{5}$ 1548$^{2}$ (1763) 1977$^{4}$ 2522$^{2}$ 3297$^{4}$ 3649$^{6}$ **>48f<**

**Herecomestheknight 2** b g Thatching-Storm Riding (USA) (Storm Bird (CAN)) (569) 698$^{2}$ 946$^{2}$ 1766$^{P}$ **>73f< (DEAD)**

**Here's Honour (IRE) 4** ch g King of Clubs-Coronea (High Line) *76$^{13}$*

**Here's To Howie (USA) 2** b c Hermitage (USA)-Choice Comment (USA) (Rich Cream (USA)) 3963$^{3}$ 4253$^{4}$ 5041$^{6}$ **>68f<**

**Heretical Miss 6** br m Sayf El Arab (USA)-Silent Prayer (Queen's Hussar) *1996$^{10}$* 2282$^{U}$ 2556$^{9}$ **>31a 37f<**

**Heritage 2** b c Danehill (USA)-Misty Halo (High Top) 4370$^{4}$ **>77f<**

**Hermanus 2** b g Lugana Beach-Hitravelscene (Mansingh (USA)) 4896$^{5}$ **>26f<**

**Hernando (FR) 6** b h Niniski (USA)-Whakilyric (USA) (Miswaki (USA)) **1995:** 4471a$^{3}$ **>128f<**

**Herodian (USA) 3** b br c Housebuster (USA)-Try Something New (USA) (Hail the Pirates (USA)) (566) 952$^{4}$ 3295$^{4}$ 4054$^{3}$ 4352$^{10}$ 4583$^{9}$ **>96f<**

**Heron Island (IRE) 3** b c Shirley Heights-Dalawara (IRE) (Top Ville) 694$^{6}$ (891) 1076$^{2}$ 1580a$^{11}$ (3597) 4192$^{8}$ 4553$^{4}$ **>114f<**

**Heronwater (IRE) 3** b f Ela-Mana-Mou-Water Girl (FR) (Faraway Son (USA)) 1409$^{4}$ 1782$^{3}$ **>78f<**

**Herr Trigger 5** gr g Sharrood (USA)-Four-Legged Friend (Aragon) *462$^{2}$* **>83a 80f<**

**He's a King (USA) 6** b g Key to the Kingdom (USA)-She's A Jay (USA) (Honey Jay (USA)) 944$^{7}$ **>59f< (DEAD)**

**He's Got Wings (IRE) 3** b c In The Wings-Mariella (Sir Gaylord) 526$^{9}$ 1100$^{12}$ 1503$^{7}$ *2168$^{5}$ 2716$^{2}$* 2979$^{5}$ (3325) 4249$^{5}$ (4506) 4588$^{7}$ **>34a 63f<**

**He's My Love (IRE) 3** ch c Be My Guest (USA)-Taken By Force (Persian Bold) 677$^{11}$ 1045$^{5}$ 1323$^{6}$ 3985$^{19}$ **>60f<**

**Hever Golf Charger (IRE) 2** b c Silver Kite (USA)-Peace Carrier (IRE) (Doulab (USA)) 2157$^{W}$ 3114$^{11}$ 3515$^{10}$ 3803$^{3}$ 3963$^{5}$ 4423$^{2}$ 4546$^{11}$ **>65f<**

**Hever Golf Classic 3** b br c Bustino-Explosiva (USA) (Explodent (USA)) 730$^{11}$ 1963$^{5}$ 2505$^{9}$ **>54f<**

**Hever Golf Dancer 2** b c Distant Relative-Blue Rag (Ragusa) *1842$^{12}$* 2538$^{4}$ 2734$^{5}$ **>65f<**

**Hever Golf Diamond 3** b g Nomination-Cadi Ha (Welsh Pageant) **1995:** *4491$^{14}$* **1996:** *46$^{5}$ 158$^{9}$ 752$^{10}$ 899$^{2}$ 1012$^{8}$ 1444$^{7}$ 2440$^{3}$* 2628$^{8}$ *3090$^{8}$ 3605$^{5}$ 3965$^{6}$* **>38a 54f<**

**Hever Golf Eagle 3** b g Aragon-Elkie Brooks (Relkino) *118$^{10}$ 161$^{5}$ 167$^{3}$ 300$^{3}$ 381$^{2}$ 463$^{6}$ 914$^{5}$* 1956$^{8}$ 4497$^{12}$ 4812$^{10}$ *4989$^{9}$* **>58a 51f<**

**Hever Golf Express 3** b g Primo Dominie-Everdene (Bustino) *182$^{2}$ 272$^{5}$ 1776$^{4}$* 1891$^{3}$ 2578$^{10}$ (3339) 3636$^{3}$ 3851$^{6}$ **>80da 69f<**

**Hever Golf Lady 4** b f Dominion-High Run (HOL) (Runnymede) **1995:** *4355$^{8}$ 4463$^{4}$ 4530$^{8}$* **1996:** *108$^{3}$ 1816$^{2}$* 2042$^{16}$ 2511$^{5}$ 2599$^{2}$ **>59a 66f<**

**Hever Golf Lily 2** ch f Efisio-Teresa Deevey (Runnett) 639$^{6}$ 1851$^{4}$ 2025$^{3}$ **>60f<**

**Hever Golf Lover (IRE) 2** b f Taufan (USA)-Anagall (USA) (Irish River (FR)) 4210$^{9}$ 4600$^{9}$ *4777$^{8}$* **>21a 59f<**

**Hever Golf Magic (IRE) 2** ch f Ballad Rock-Track Twenty Nine (IRE) (Standaan (FR)) 5033$^{18}$ **>22f<**

**Hever Golf Mover 2** ch f Efisio-Joyce's Best (Tolomeo) 3581$^{4}$ 4123$^{9}$ 4762$^{11}$ **>48f<**

**Hever Golf Queen 3** b f Efisio-Blue Jane (Blue Cashmere) **1995:** 4494a$^{9}$ *4504$^{5}$* **1996:** *232$^{6}$ 1025$^{5}$* 4810$^{15}$ **>35a 28f<**

**Hever Golf Rose 5** b m Efisio-Sweet Rosina (Sweet Revenge) 927$^{11}$ 1943a$^{2}$ 1945a$^{2}$ 2115$^{4}$ 2663a$^{2}$ 2622$^{3}$ 3126$^{2}$ 3708$^{3}$ 4033a$^{2}$ 4057$^{4}$ 4304$^{2}$ 4660a$^{3}$ 4744a$^{3}$ **>111a 120df<**

**Hever Golf Star 4** b g Efisio-Truly Bold (Bold Lad (IRE)) **1995:** *4394$^{2}$* **1996:** *(173) 407$^{3}$* **>79a 72f<**

**Hever Golf Stormer (IRE) 2** b c Mujadil (USA)-Clogher Head (Sandford Lad) 1842$^{10}$ 2059$^{7}$ 2374$^{9}$ 2846$^{2}$ 3075$^{5}$ 3332$^{3}$ 3488$^{3}$ 3607$^{3}$ *4093$^{6}$ 4251$^{5}$* **>33a 64f<**

**Hey Up Dolly (IRE) 4** b f Puissance-I Don't Mind (Swing Easy (USA)) 615$^{8}$ 739$^{12}$ 912$^{5}$ **>49a 45f< (DEAD)**

**Hibernate (IRE) 2** ch c Lahib (USA)-Ministra (USA) (Deputy Minister (CAN)) 4200$^{3}$ **>80f<**

**Hibernica (IRE) 2** b br f Law Society (USA)-Brave Ivy (Decoy Boy) 4825$^{21}$ **>30f<**

**Hickleton Miss 3** ch f Timeless Times (USA)-Honest Opinion (Free State) 762$^{13}$ *1028$^{13}$ 1340$^{5}$* 1527$^{20}$ 1859$^{5}$ 2029$^{6}$ 2427$^{6}$ 2964$^{8}$ 4356$^{19}$ **>9a 55f<**

**Hickory Blue 6** ch g Clantime-Blueit (FR) (Bold Lad (IRE)) 1412$^{12}$ 1598$^{9}$ 4915$^{20}$ **>50a 68f<**

**Hidden Meadow 2** b c Selkirk (USA)-Spurned (USA) (Robellino (USA)) 2708$^{5}$ (4684) 4822$^{3}$ **>99f<**

**Hidden Oasis 3** b c Green Desert (USA)-Secret Seeker (USA) (Mr Prospector (USA)) 936$^{2}$ 1441$^{6}$ 2041$^{4}$ 2888$^{11}$ **>103f<**

**Hidden Reserve (USA) 2** f *4950a$^{7}$* **>76a f<**

**High Atlas 3** b f Shirley Heights-Balliasta (USA) (Lyphard (USA)) 2135$^{W}$ 3699$^{3}$ **>67f<**

**High Baroque (IRE) 3** b c High Estate-Alpine Symphony (Northern Dancer) (526) (725) (986) 1757a$^{9}$ 3915a$^{8}$ **>110f<**

**Highborn (IRE) 7** b or br g Double Schwartz-High State (Free State) 451$^{19}$ 610$^{3}$ (1018) 1703$^{4}$ 2220$^{4}$ 2722$^{2}$ 3622$^{8}$ 3920$^{10}$ 4054$^{9}$ (4554) 4623$^{5}$ **>83a 98f<**

**High Commotion (IRE) 4** b f Taufan (USA)-Bumble-Bee (High Line) 645$^{5}$ **>70+f<**

**High Cut 3** b f Dashing Blade-High Habit (Slip Anchor) 1435$^{2}$ 3513$^{4}$ 3949$^{11}$ **>72df<**

**High Desire (IRE) 3** b f High Estate-Sweet Adelaide (USA) (The Minstrel (CAN)) **1995:** *4361$^{8}$* **1996:** *890$^{3}$* 1044$^{4}$ 1498$^{11}$ 1874$^{2}$ 2196$^{2}$ 2377$^{4}$ 3318$^{10}$ **>24a 63f<**

**High Domain (IRE) 5** b h Dominion Royale-Recline (Wollow) 981$^{16}$ (1351) *1606$^{7}$ (1781)* 1853$^{3}$ 2137$^{7}$ 2508$^{4}$ 2725$^{17}$ 4058$^{16}$ 4581$^{9}$ 4802$^{15}$ (5039) **>56a 71f<**

**High Extreme (IRE) 2** b c Danehill (USA)-Rustic Lawn (Rusticaro (FR)) 3147$^{6}$ 3499$^{4}$ 4349$^{3}$ 4602$^{13}$ **>77f<**

**Highfield Fizz 4** b f Efisio-Jendor (Condorcet (FR)) *1778$^{14}$ 2082$^{9}$ 2628$^{9}$* 3402$^{5}$ 3938$^{7}$ 3970$^{6}$ 4321$^{11}$ (4596) 4832$^{10}$ 5008$^{6}$ **>28a 50f<**

**Highfield Pet 3** b g Efisio-Jendor (Condorcet (FR)) 1160$^{6}$ 1504$^{9}$ **>57f<**

**High Flown (USA) 4** b g Lear Fan (USA)-Isticanna (USA) (Far North (CAN)) 609$^{15}$ 2537$^{8}$ 3130$^{7}$ 3303$^{9}$ **>64da 45f<**

**Highflying 10** br g Shirley Heights-Nomadic Pleasure (Habitat) 1116$^{9}$ 1428$^{5}$ 1802$^{10}$ 2008$^{13}$ 2330$^{9}$ (2900) 3434$^{6}$ (3816) 4112$^{5}$ 4457$^{3}$ 4683$^{19}$ **>87f<**

**High Hope Henry (USA) 3** b c Known Fact (USA)-Parquill (USA) (One For All (USA)) 4254$^{2}$ 4571$^{10}$ **>78f<**

**High Intrigue (IRE) 2** b br c Shirley Heights-Mild Intrigue (USA) (Sir Ivor) 4705$^{6}$ **>60f<**

**Highland Fawn 3** ch f Safawan-Highland Rowena (Royben) *58$^{10}$ 134$^{13}$ 234$^{11}$ 298$^{7}$ (359) 762$^{17}$ 900$^{9}$ 1455$^{12}$ 1859$^{6}$* 2186$^{7}$ *2555$^{8}$ 2800$^{12}$* **>38a 34f<**

**Highland Gift (IRE) 3** b f Generous (IRE)-Scots Lass (Shirley Heights) 671$^{5}$ (4827) 5036$^{3}$ **>93f<**

**Highland Pass (IRE) 2** b g Petorius-Whatawoman (Tumble Wind (USA)) 452$^{7}$ 685$^{5}$ 841$^{6}$ 4803$^{16}$ 5040$^{16}$ **>61f<**

**Highland Rhapsody (IRE) 3** ch f Kris-Farewell Song (USA) (The Minstrel (CAN)) 1333$^{5}$ 1901$^{2}$ 2346$^{8}$ (3162) 3599$^{4}$ 3989$^{12}$ **>82f<**

**Highland Spin 5** ch g Dunbeath (USA)-In a Spin (Windjammer (USA)) *393$^{6}$* **>16a f<**

**Highlights 3** ch f Phountzi (USA)-Idella's Gold (FR) (Glint of Gold) *40$^{4}$ 161$^{4}$ 269$^{3}$ 471$^{9}$* **>50a 33f<**

**Highly Motivated 3** b f Midyan (USA)-Spin Dry (High Top) 1246a$^{5}$ 4396a$^{9}$ **>81f<**

**Highly Prized 2** b c Shirley Heights-On The Tiles (Thatch (USA)) 4720$^{9}$ **>59f<**

**Highly Spirited 3** b c Lochnager-Soudley Lady (Glenstal (USA)) 3115$^{12}$ 3519$^{10}$

**High Note 3** b f Shirley Heights-Soprano (Kris) 1825$^{2}$ 2146$^{6}$ **>82f<**

**High On Life 2** b c Mazilier (USA)-Tina Rosa (Bustino) 4705$^{7}$ 4835$^{2}$ **>68f<**

**High Patriarch (IRE) 4** b g Alzao (USA)-Freesia (Shirley Heights) *19$^{2}$* **>95a 94f<**

**High Premium 8** b g Forzando-High Halo (High Top) *20$^{2}$ 61$^{6}$ 136$^{4}$ 211$^{3}$ (371) (513) 589$^{4}$* 933$^{4}$ 1406$^{4}$ *(1810) 3933$^{10}$* 4190$^{5}$ 4296$^{2}$ (4432) (4682) 4769$^{2}$ 4974$^{7}$ **>88a 88f<**

**High Priority (IRE) 3** b c Marju (IRE)-Blinding (IRE) (High Top) 579$^{5}$ 3759$^{9}$ 3875$^{9}$ 4116$^{21}$ **>83f<**

**High Pyrenees 4** b g Shirley Heights-Twyla (Habitat) 1428$^{7}$ 2008$^{10}$ **>73f<**

**High Roller (IRE) 2** b c Generous (IRE)-Helpless Haze (USA) (Vaguely Noble) (4261) (4676) **>106f<**

**High Romance 6** b or br m Today and Tomorrow-Nahawand (High Top) *342$^{P}$* **(DEAD)**

**High Shot 6** b g Darshaan-Nollet (High Top) 818$^{6}$ 1065$^{3}$ **>77f<**

**Highspeed (IRE) 4** ch g Double Schwartz-High State (Free State) *341$^{11}$ (1001)* (1586) 1846$^{2}$ 2803$^{6}$ 3426$^{4}$ 3646$^{8}$ **>6a 64f<**

**High Spirits (IRE) 2** b g Great Commotion (USA)-Spoilt Again (Mummy's Pet) 800$^{6}$ 975$^{3}$ 1404$^{7}$ **>62f<**

**High Summer 6** b g Green Desert (USA)-Beacon Hill (Bustino) *4327$^{10}$* 4673$^{12}$ **>40f<**

**High Summer (USA) 3** ch f Nureyev (USA)-Miss Summer (Luthier) 1901$^{3}$ (2718) 3210$^{13}$ (3989) 4135$^{2}$ 4444$^{20}$ **>103df<**

**High Tower (ITY) 3** f b Bound for Honour (USA)-Rural Like (USA) (Temperence Hill (USA)) 901a$^{2}$

**Hightown-Princess (IRE) 8** gr m King Persian-Ambient (Amber Rama (USA)) 3824$^{6}$ **>37f<**

**Highway 2** gr c Salse (USA)-Ivory Lane (USA) (Sir Ivor) 4060$^{4}$ 4301$^{6}$ **>67f<**

**Highway Robber (IRE) 2** b c Robellino (USA)-High Habit (Slip Anchor) 2353$^{4}$ 3269$^{10}$ *3625$^{5}$ 4625$^{14}$* **>54a 51f<**

**Hi Hoh (IRE) 3** ch f Fayruz-Late Date (Goldhill) **1995:** *4483$^{11}$* **1996:** *10$^{W}$* **>38a 41f<**

**Hilaala (USA) 3** ch f Elmaamul (USA)-Halholah (USA) (Secreto (USA)) *(1464)* (1714) 2128$^{4}$ 3799$^{2}$ 4184$^{10}$ 4620$^{9}$ **>91f<**

**Hill Farm Blues 3** b f Mon Tresor-Loadplan Lass (Nicholas Bill) *2747$^{4}$ 3309$^{4}$* 3854$^{8}$ *4095$^{10}$* **>43a 51f<**

**Hill Farm Dancer 5** ch m Gunner B-Loadplan Lass (Nicholas Bill) **1995:** *4376$^{3}$ 4507$^{4}$* **1996:** *140$^{2}$ 186$^{7}$ (360) (420) 532$^{2}$ 771$^{9}$* 866$^{4}$ 3267$^{3}$ 3476$^{3}$ 3587$^{5}$ 3922$^{9}$ *4092$^{12}$ 4603$^{9}$ 4977$^{4}$ (5062)* **>68a 54f<**

**Hill Farm Katie 5** b m Derrylin-Kate Brook (Nicholas Bill) **1995:** *4513$^{5}$* **1996:** *138$^{10}$ 189$^{10}$ 512$^{3}$ 598$^{12}$ 836$^{6}$ 2428$^{8}$ 2550$^{12}$* **>38a 23f<**

**Hill House Teacher 4** b f Komaite (USA)-Shakira Grove (Hot Grove) 4074$^{19}$

**Hill Silver (USA) 3** b f Alysheba (USA)-Hot Silver (FR) (Nureyev (USA)) (3568a) 4663a$^5$ **>114f<**
**Hill Society (IRE) 4** br g Law Society (USA)-Sun Screen (Caerleon (USA)) (4026a) **>82f<**
**Hillswick 5** ch g Norwick (USA)-Quite Lucky (Precipice Wood) *1534$^5$* 2191$^9$ **>33f<**
**Hillzah (USA) 8** ch g Blushing Groom (FR)-Glamour Girl (ARG) (Mysolo) *136$^{10}$ 222$^6$ 312$^9$ 482$^2$* 753$^8$ 825$^5$ *1082$^2$* **>78a 87f<**
**Hil Rhapsody 2** ch f Anshan-Heavenly Note (Chief Singer) (815) 1352$^4$ 1897$^3$ 2575$^3$ 2797$^5$ 3467$^8$ 4084$^9$ 4311$^6$ 4586$^{16}$ **>82f<**
**Hiltons Executive (IRE) 2** b f Petorius-Theatral (Orchestra) 585$^8$ 910$^6$ 4072$^{10}$ 4343$^4$ *4576$^5$ 4790$^{11}$* ***>35a 48f<***
**Hindsight (IRE) 2** br c Don't Forget Me-Vian (USA) (Far Out East (USA)) 2783$^2$ 3264$^2$ (4481) **>82f<**
**Hi Nod 6** b h Valiyar-Vikris (Viking (USA)) (1425) 1898$^2$ 2691$^2$ 3083$^7$ 3709$^9$ 4194$^2$ 4444$^{25}$ 4595$^4$ 4870$^5$ **>109f<**
**Hint 2** b c Warning-Throw Away Line (USA) (Assert) 4306$^6$ **>76f<**
**Hint Of Humour (USA) 3** b f Woodman (USA)-High Competence 3530a$^7$ **>85f<**
**Hinton Rock (IRE) 4** ch g Ballad Rock-May Hinton (Main Reef) 1016$^9$ 1430$^{10}$ 1708$^4$ *2171$^{12}$ 3106$^6$* 3216$^3$ 3851$^{11}$ **>28a 78f<**
**Hio Nod 2** b g Precocious-Vikris (Viking (USA)) 4807$^W$
**Hippios 2** b br c Formidable (USA)-Miss Doody (Gorytus (USA)) 3829$^8$ 4891$^{14}$ **>15f<**
**Hippy 3** b f Damister (USA)-Breakaway (Song) 678$^{12}$ 1508$^9$ 1876$^3$ (2208) 2437$^2$ 2585$^7$ 4064$^5$ 4214$^3$ 4819$^4$ **>85f<**
**Hippy Chick 2** b f Ron's Victory (USA)-Enchanted Tale (USA) (Told (USA)) 3582$^6$ **>38f<**
**Hirasah (IRE) 2** b f Lahib (USA)-Mayaasa (USA) (Lyphard (USA)) (3044) **>59f<**
**Hi Rock 4** ch f Hard Fought-Miss Racine (Dom Racine (FR)) **1995:** *4502$^6$* **1996:** *44$^3$ 213$^2$ 247$^8$ 331$^6$ 1040$^8$* 1196$^2$ *1718$^{13}$ 2075$^{18}$* 3481$^4$ 3970$^5$ 4355$^7$ 4455$^5$ **>51a 48f<**
**His Excellence (USA) 3** b c El Gran Senor (USA)-Hail The Lady (USA) (Hail the Pirates (USA)) 1580a$^{15}$ 1938a$^3$ 2473a$^3$ 3196a$^6$ 3911a$^{10}$ **>118f<**
**Hishi Akebono (USA) 4** dk c Woodman (USA)-Mysteries (USA) (Seattle Slew (USA)) **1995:** (4563a) **1996:** 1952a$^3$ **>124f<**
**Hishi Amazon (USA) 5** dk m Theatrical-Katies (Nonoalco (USA)) **1995:** 4471a$^2$ **>121f<**
**His Honor (USA) 2** b b c Honor Grades (USA)-Unsanctioned (USA) (Star Gallant (USA)) *4954a$^9$* **>91a f<**
**Hismagicmoment (USA) 3** b c Proud Birdie (USA)-Affirmed Ambience (USA) (Affirmed (USA)) 684$^4$ 860$^5$ 1142$^3$ 1662$^2$ 2333$^3$ **>84f<**
**Histoire D'Amour (ITY) 3** b f Groom Dancer (USA)-Biograph (USA) (Riverman (USA)) 792a$^3$
**Hit Or Miss 2** ch f Be My Chief (USA)-Jennies' Gem (Sayf El Arab (USA)) (446) 715$^3$ 996$^5$ 3321$^5$ (3488) 3687$^{18}$ 4207$^3$ 4346$^4$ *4777$^{11}$* **>62f<**
**Hit the Canvas (USA) 5** ch g At The Threshold (USA)-Also Royal (USA) (Native Royalty (USA)) *852$^9$* 2516$^4$ **>71a 73df<**
**Hit The Flag (IRE) 2** b c Jurado (USA)-Janeswood (IRE) (Henbit (USA)) 4706$^{10}$ 4991$^{15}$ **>7f<**
**Hobbs Choice 3** b f Superpower-Excavator Lady (Most Secret) 473$^6$ (539) 638$^5$ 775$^{14}$ 1527$^8$ 2139$^5$ 2489$^2$ 3938$^8$ **>50f<**
**Hoh Dancer 2** ch f Indian Ridge-Alteza Real (Mansingh (USA)) 2995$^2$ 3429$^4$ 3796$^{14}$ **>76f<**
**Hoh Down (IRE) 2** b f Fairy King (USA)-Tintomara (IRE) (Niniski (USA)) 3848$^{11}$ **>40f<**
**Hoh Express 4** b g Waajib-Tissue Paper (Touch Paper) 455$^{14}$ 728$^{15}$ 1193$^5$ 1484$^6$ 1793$^3$ 2145$^9$ 3071$^2$ 3691$^8$ 4036a$^3$ 4184$^9$ 4680$^4$ **>100f<**
**Hoh Flyer (USA) 2** b f Northern Flagship (USA)-Beautiful Bedouin (USA) (His Majesty (USA)) 3438$^7$ (3685) 4113$^{10}$ **>66f<**
**Hoh Magic 4** ch f Cadeaux Genereux-Gunner's Belle (Gunner B) 600$^5$ **>113df< (DEAD)**
**Hoh Majestic (IRE) 3** b g Soviet Lad (USA)-Sevens Are Wild (Petorius) *773$^6$* 1006$^6$ 1340$^3$ 1527$^{17}$ 1599$^6$ 2123$^6$ 3278$^5$ 3399$^5$ 3959$^D$ *4090$^3$ 4341$^2$* 4473$^{10}$ 4486$^{12}$ 4589$^7$ **>53a 56f<**
**Hoh Returns (IRE) 3** b c Fairy King (USA)-Cipriani (Habitat) 672$^6$ (992) 1628$^3$ 2007$^{15}$ 2143$^3$ **>93f<**
**Hoh Surprise (IRE) 2** b f Mac's Imp (USA)-Musical Gem (USA) (The Minstrel (CAN)) 1595$^2$ 2569$^5$ 3075$^2$ 3582$^3$ (3795) 3962$^6$ 4423$^6$ 4562$^5$ **>67f<**
**Hoist To Heaven (USA) 3** 797a$^6$ 1757a$^{15}$ (5020a) **>63f<**
**Holiday Island 7** ch g Good Times (ITY)-Green Island (St Paddy) *190$^{12}$* **>18a 52f<**
**Holloway Melody 3** ch f Cree Song-Holloway Wonder (Swing Easy (USA)) **1995:** *4393$^6$ 4433$^4$* **1996:** *605$^4$ 834$^3$ 1041$^7$* 3458$^3$ 3591$^6$ 4360$^5$ 4691$^7$ (4829) *4982$^{13}$* **>48a 69f<**
**Hollywood Dream (GER) 5** ch m Master Willie-Holly (GER) (Cortez (GER)) **1995:** 4403a$^2$ **1996:** (1135a) 1948a$^5$ 2479a$^4$ (3203a) 3753a$^2$ 4413a$^3$ 4747a$^4$ 5073a$^2$ **>121f<**
**Home Alone 2** b c Groom Dancer (USA)-Quiet Week-End (Town And Country) 3245$^{11}$ (4200) 4488$^7$ 4949a$^7$ **>89f<**
**Home Cookin' 3** b f Salse (USA)-Home Fire (Firestreak) *515$^7$ 1806$^2$* 2162$^9$ 2380$^3$ 2507$^{18}$ 2966$^3$ 3929$^3$ **>40a 64f<**
**Home Counties (IRE) 7** ch g Ela-Mana-Mou-Safe Home (Home Guard (USA)) 1585$^6$ 2418$^6$ 3401$^5$ 3587$^6$ 4626$^9$ **>66f<**
**Homecrest 4** b g Petoski-Homing Hill (Homing) **1995:** *4372$^7$* **>41a 59f<**
**Ho Mei Surprise 4** ch c Hadeer-By Surprise (Young Generation) *387$^9$ 389$^5$ 414$^8$ 514$^5$ 834$^7$ 3294$^{14}$* ***>38a 4f<***
**Homeland 3** b c Midyan (USA)-Little Loch Broom (Reform) **1995:** *4373$^3$ 4431$^5$ 4462$^2$ 4528$^8$* **>71a 62f<**
**Homestead 2** ch c Indian Ridge-Bertrade (Homeboy) 3069$^7$ 3615$^9$ 3821$^5$ 4303$^7$ 4566$^8$ 4880$^9$ **>70f<**
**Homing Pigeon (USA) 6** dk h Magloira (USA)-Bird House (USA) (Yukon Eagle (USA)) 3906a$^2$ **>109f<**
**Homme D'Honneur (FR) 4** 3035a$^5$ **>109f<**
**Hondero (GER) 6** b h Damister (USA)-Hone (Sharpen Up) 1948a$^6$ 2479a$^7$ 3395a$^8$ **>115f<**
**Honest Guest (IRE) 3** b f Be My Guest (USA)-Good Policy (IRE) (Thatching) 674$^3$ 939$^5$ 1769$^8$ 2609$^9$ 3916a$^4$ 4168a$^3$ 4467$^8$ **>107df<**
**Honestly 3** ch f Weldnaas (USA)-Shadha (Shirley Heights) **1995:** *4365$^3$ 4485$^4$ (4509)* **1996:** *102$^4$ 220$^6$ 3977$^9$* 4691$^{17}$ *4977$^6$* **>77a 29f<**
**Honey Colour (IRE) 2** ch c Night Shift (USA)-Honey Stage (USA) (Stage Door Johnny) (2667a)
**Honeyhall 3** b f Crofthall-Attila the Honey (Connaught) 3624$^{13}$ 4074$^{10}$ 4456$^7$ 4592$^{13}$ 4881$^{11}$ *4987$^4$* **>36a 45f<**
**Honey Mount 5** b g Shirley Heights-Honeybeta (Habitat) *19$^{10}$* **>42a 84f<**
**Honeyshan 4** b f Warrshan (USA)-Divissima (Music Boy) 2996$^8$ 3505$^{12}$ **>43f<**
**Honey Trader 4** b g Beveled (USA)-Lizzie Bee (Kind of Hush) *514$^6$ 653$^7$* **>33a 68f<**
**Hong Kong Designer 4** br g Dunbeath (USA)-Pokey's Pet (Uncle Pokey) *268$^8$ 1421$^{13}$* 1665$^{19}$ 2165$^{13}$ **>54a 57f<**
**Hong Kong Dollar 4** b g Superpower-Daleside Ladybird (Tolomeo) **1995:** *4359$^8$ 4418$^7$ 4456$^{10}$* **1996:** *2201$^{11}$ 2735$^7$* 3439$^{14}$ 3661$^{13}$ **>20a 42df<**
**Hong Kong Express (IRE) 2** b f Distinctly North (USA)-North Kildare (USA) (Northjet) 1525$^{10}$ 2416$^4$ 2727$^3$ 3080$^8$ 3647$^4$ 3941$^8$ **>59f<**
**Honorable Estate (IRE) 3** b f High Estate-Holy Devotion (Commanche Run) 888$^2$ 1324$^9$ 1523$^5$ (1776) 2032$^6$ 2339$^8$ 2710$^5$ 3115$^3$ (3458) 3686$^{10}$ 3991$^2$ 4256$^9$ 4550$^8$ 4691$^{15}$ **>71f<**
**Honourable Felix 2** b c Wace (USA)-Lady Gilly (Remainder Man) *1525$^{12}$* 4363$^9$ 4902$^{12}$ **>31f<**
**Honour And Glory (USA) 3** b c Relaunch (USA)-Fair To All (USA) (Al Nasr (FR)) *4951a$^3$*
**Hoofprints (IRE) 3** b c Distinctly North (USA)-Sweet Reprieve (Shirley Heights) *847$^8$* 1104$^{10}$ 4086$^6$ 4252$^5$ 4426$^5$ 4596$^7$ 4726$^4$ *(4892)* **>68a 70f<**
**Hope Chest 2** ch f Kris-Hopeful Search (USA) (Vaguely Noble) 4105$^3$ **>77f<**
**Hopesay 2** b f Warning-Tatouma (USA) (The Minstrel (CAN)) 3807$^3$ 4062$^3$ 4330$^2$ **>79f<**
**Hopperetta 2** b f Rock Hopper-Can Can Girl (Gay Fandango (USA)) *2938$^3$ 3629$^3$ 3871$^5$* 4097$^9$ *4335$^7$ 4694$^7$* 4835$^8$ *4988$^8$* **>51a 52f<**
**Horesti 4** b c Nijinsky (CAN)-Sushila (Petingo) 668$^3$ 1019$^{10}$ 1961$^7$ 2226$^9$ 2882$^{13}$ 3705$^3$ **>57f<**
**Hornbeam 2** b c Rich Charlie-Thinkluckybelucky (Maystreak) 2782$^4$ 3156$^5$ **>91?f<**
**Hornpipe 4** b g Handsome Sailor-Snake Song (Mansingh (USA)) *521$^{10}$ 782$^3$ 1457$^2$ 1719$^{13}$ 2082$^5$* **>64a f<**
**Horsetrader 4** b g Aragon-Grovette (Derring-Do) **1995:** *4448$^{10}$* **>38a 47f<**
**Hostile Native 3** b g Formidable (USA)-Balatina (Balidar) 3446$^{13}$ 3788$^{12}$ 4917$^8$ **>51?f<**
**Hotcake 3** b g Sizzling Melody-Bold Cookie (Never so Bold) 2777$^7$ 4074$^{13}$ **>41f<**
**Hot Dogging 3** b f Petoski-Mehtab (Touching Wood (USA)) *1035$^4$* 1530$^{15}$ *2158$^2$ 2592$^4$* 3306$^6$ **>49a 42f<**
**Hotlips Houlihan 3** b f Risk Me (FR)-Lana's Pet (Tina's Pet) **1995:** *4431$^{15}$* **1996:** *11$^3$ 119$^4$ 176$^7$ 277$^6$ 2903$^8$* 3244$^7$ 3761$^{17}$ **>56da 35f<**
**Hot Shot 2** gr g Chilibang-Free Rein (Sagaro) 2759$^7$
**Hotspur Street 4** b g Cadeaux Genereux-Excellent Alibi (USA) (Exceller (USA)) 474$^3$ 625$^{12}$ 1070$^6$ 1421$^9$ 2046$^6$ **>59a 71f<**
**Hotstepper 3** ch f Never so Bold-Brilliant Timing (USA) (The Minstrel (CAN)) *4309$^{12}$* 4690$^{13}$ **>9f<**
**Houghton Venture (USA) 4** ch c Groom Dancer (USA)-Perle Fine (USA) (Devil's Bag (USA)) *510$^3$ 817$^{13}$* 1024$^{11}$ *2170$^8$ 2934$^5$ 3078$^5$ 3358$^5$* 3970$^7$ **>53a 41f<**
**Housa Dancer (FR) 3** b f Fabulous Dancer (USA)-Housatonic (USA) (Riverman (USA)) 1140a$^8$ 3030a$^3$ 3391a$^3$ **>106f<**
**Housamix (FR) 4** b c Linamix (FR)-Housatonic (USA) (Riverman (USA)) 622a$^3$ **>121f<**
**House of Dreams 4** b c Darshaan-Helens Dreamgirl (Caerleon (USA)) 482$^6$ 619$^6$ 771$^2$ **>66f<**
**House of Riches 3** b g Shirley Heights-Pelf (USA) (Al Nasr (FR)) 567$^2$ 772$^4$ 3791$^6$ 4431$^5$ 4580$^{15}$ **>91f<**
**Howard the Duck 6** ch g Baron Blakeney-One More Try (Kemal (FR)) *822$^{10}$*
***How Could-I (IRE)* 3** br f Don't Forget Me-Shikari Rose (Kala Shikari) 1067$^3$ 1503$^{10}$ *1721$^{11}$ 2026$^2$*

2162$^{3}$ (2180) 2541$^{2}$ 2592$^{5}$ 2801$^{10}$ 2893$^{3}$ 3300$^{5}$ **>52f<**

**How Long 3** b c Alzao (USA)-Fresh (High Top) 1137a$^{4}$ 1797$^{2}$ (2004) 2248$^{3}$ 2623$^{5}$ 2888$^{4}$ 3158$^{12}$ 3712$^{7}$ 4418a$^{2}$ 4971$^{2}$ **>104f<**

**How Long (FR) 3** b c Diamond Prospect (USA)-Sorredja (Try My Best (USA)) (192a) **>71f<**

**Howqua River 4** b g Petong-Deep Blue Sea (Gulf Pearl) *400$^{5}$ 1472$^{3}$* 2060$^{5}$ (4587) 4789$^{6}$ **>46a 54f<**

**How's Yer Father 10** b g Daring March-Dawn Ditty (Song) 711$^{11}$ 846$^{4}$ 1073$^{2}$ 1178$^{7}$ 1334$^{10}$ 1684$^{2}$ 2347$^{3}$ 2615$^{7}$ 3339$^{5}$ 3783$^{10}$ 3973$^{10}$ (4221) 4701$^{7}$ 4802$^{13}$ *4981$^{2}$ 5055$^{4}$* **>64a 65f<**

**Hugwity 4** ch c Cadeaux Genereux-Nuit D'Ete (USA) (Super Concorde (USA)) *687$^{4}$* (820) (988) (1330) 1793$^{16}$ **>89f<**

**Huish Cross 4** ch f Absalom-Sixslip (USA) (Diesis) **1995:** *4534$^{11}$* **>21a 53df<**

**Hulal 2** b c Arazi (USA)-Almarai (USA) (Vaguely Noble) 4913$^{13}$ **>54f<**

**Hula Prince (IRE) 2** b c Lead on Time (USA)-Hud Hud (USA) (Alydar (USA)) (1086) (1362) 2040$^{4}$ 2607$^{7}$ 3690$^{7}$ **>102f<**

**Hullbank 6** b g Uncle Pokey-Dubavarna (Dubassoff (USA)) *113$^{4}$ 482$^{7}$* 625$^{3}$ 872$^{7}$ 1070$^{3}$ 1542$^{2}$ 2165$^{5}$ 2516$^{2}$ (2756) 4321$^{2}$ 4588$^{10}$ **>57a 69f<**

**Hulm (IRE) 3** ch f Mujtahid (USA)-Sunley Princess (Ballad Rock) *1007$^{3}$* 1540$^{2}$ 2208$^{3}$ 3093$^{2}$ (3413) **>79f<**

**Humbel (USA) 4** b c Theatrical-Claxton's Slew (USA) (Seattle Slew (USA)) 1938a$^{8}$ 2474a$^{9}$ 4849a$^{7}$ **>114f<**

**Humbert's Landing (IRE) 5** b h Cyrano de Bergerac-Bilander (High Line) 4173a$^{2}$ **>103f<**

**Humourless 3** ch c Nashwan (USA)-Sans Blague (USA) (The Minstrel (CAN)) (766) 1106$^{2}$ **>94+f<**

**Hunter Field (FR) 4** dk c Huntercombe-Maelstrom Dance (Maelstrom Lake) (325a) 3744a$^{2}$ **>92f<**

**Hunters of Brora (IRE) 6** b m Sharpo-Nihad (Alleged (USA)) 3709$^{12}$ 3836$^{8}$ **>102f<**

**Hunza Story 4** b f Rakaposhi King-Sense of Occasion (Artaius (USA)) **1995:** *4445$^{6}$ 4513$^{7}$ 4546$^{7}$* **1996:** *54$^{10}$ 145$^{6}$ 586$^{16}$* 822$^{8}$ 1411$^{17}$ 1665$^{13}$ 1828$^{6}$ 2189$^{7}$ 2366$^{5}$ 2592$^{11}$ 2716$^{3}$ 2906$^{5}$ 3314$^{8}$ 3849$^{8}$ 3970$^{9}$ 4355$^{13}$ **>29a 40f<**

**Hurgill Dancer 2** b c Rambo Dancer (CAN)-Try Vickers (USA) (Fuzzbuster (USA)) 1197$^{7}$ *2370$^{2}$ 2909$^{3}$* 4298$^{6}$ 4625$^{7}$ 4795$^{3}$ **>60a 69f<**

**Hurgill King (IRE) 2** gr c Ajraas (USA)-Winter Lady (Bonne Noel) *4091$^{11}$ 4347$^{10}$* 4594$^{15}$ **>40f<**

**Hurgill Lady 2** ch f Emarati (USA)-Gitee (FR) (Carwhite) 3941$^{2}$ 4250$^{6}$ 4468$^{2}$ 4749$^{9}$ **>68f<**

**Hurgill Minstrel 2** gr c Absalom-Sabonis (USA) (The Minstrel (CAN)) 1360$^{8}$

**Hurgill Times 2** b c Timeless Times (USA)-Crimson Dawn (Manado) 2295$^{4}$ 2865$^{3}$ 3423$^{7}$ 4049$^{6}$ 4482$^{5}$ 4721$^{4}$ **>60f<**

**Hurricane Horn (IRE) 3** ch c Kefaah (USA)-Musical Horn (Music Boy) **1995:** *4360$^{11}$ 4439$^{5}$* **>52a 65f<**

**Hurricane State (USA) 2** ch c Miswaki (USA)-Regal State (USA) (Affirmed (USA)) *3837$^{2}$* (4188) 4519$^{7}$ (4945a) 5071a$^{3}$ **>99f<**

**Hurtleberry (IRE) 3** b f Tirol-Allberry (Alzao (USA)) 2229$^{12}$ 4820$^{21}$ **>77f<**

**Husun (USA) 2** b f Sheikh Albadou-Tadwin (Never so Bold) 3660$^{6}$ **>64f<**

**Hutchies Lady 4** b f Efisio-Keep Mum (Mummy's Pet) (884) 1024$^{4}$ 1313$^{4}$ 1546$^{2}$ 1633$^{4}$ 1867$^{6}$ 2023$^{8}$ *2303$^{8}$ 2678$^{4}$* 3426$^{10}$ 4249$^{15}$ 5007$^{8}$ **>27a 40f<**

**Hyde Park (IRE) 2** b c Alzao (USA)-Park Elect (Ahonoora) 4558$^{5}$ 4762$^{2}$ **>71f<**

**Hylters Girl 4** b f Dominion-Jolimo (Fortissimo) **1995:** *4363$^{7}$* **>28a 37f<**

**Hype Energy 2** b f Tina's Pet-Stoneydale (Tickled Pink) 3796$^{16}$ 4087$^{2}$ 4210$^{5}$ **>78f<**

**I**

**Iamus 3** ch c Most Welcome-Icefern (Moorestyle) 526$^{2}$ 705$^{4}$ 1127$^{6}$ 1452$^{4}$ 1820$^{10}$ (2181) 2888$^{6}$ 3211$^{12}$ 4479$^{6}$ **>80f<**

**Iberian Dancer (CAN) 3** b f El Gran Senor (USA)-Cutty (USA) (Smart) 1007$^{5}$ 1614$^{2}$ (2124) 2576$^{5}$ 3148$^{2}$ 3806$^{7}$ 4117$^{9}$ 4704$^{4}$ **>86f<**

**Ibin St James 2** b c Salse (USA)-St James's Antigua (IRE) (Law Society (USA)) 2887$^{8}$ 3485$^{4}$ 4175$^{9}$ 4760$^{17}$ **>77f<**

**Iblis (IRE) 4** b c Danehill (USA)-In Unison (Bellypha) *3842$^{6}$* ***>94f<***

**Ibn Masirah 2** b c Crowning Honors (CAN)-Masirah (Dunphy) 4069$^{15}$ 4347$^{3}$ 4594$^{10}$ 4990$^{12}$ **>58f<**

**Icanspell 5** b g Petoski-Bewitched (African Sky) *1784$^{9}$* ***>56da 2f<***

**I Can't Remember 2** br g Petong-Glenfield Portion (Mummy's Pet) 590$^{5}$ 770$^{10}$ (2422) 2795$^{2}$ 2965$^{2}$ 3128$^{4}$ (3268) 3478$^{5}$ 3659$^{4}$ 3880$^{5}$ (3936) 4195$^{9}$ 4298$^{4}$ 4384$^{2}$ 4602$^{5}$ 4672$^{8}$ (4864) 5043$^{4}$ **>80f<**

**Ice Age 2** gr c Chilibang-Mazarine Blue (Bellypha) (950) 1699$^{6}$ **>80f<**

**Ice and Glacial (IRE) 4** b c Law Society (USA)-What A Candy (USA) (Key To The Mint (USA)) 909a$^{2}$ **>103f<**

**Ice Cream (GER) 3** f 1750a$^{12}$

**Ice Magic 9** ch g Red Sunset-Free Rein (Sagaro) 1778$^{7}$ 2066$^{10}$ 2587$^{13}$ **>29f<**

**Iceni (IRE) 3** b br f Distinctly North (USA)-Princess Galicia (Welsh Pageant) (1050) 1820$^{11}$ 2320$^{12}$ 4831$^{18}$ **>70f<**

**Ichor 3** b f Primo Dominie-Adeebah (USA) (Damascus (USA)) 1624$^{W}$ **>36df<**

**Icy Guest (USA) 2** b br f Clever Trick (USA)-Minstrel Guest (Be My Guest (USA)) 2892$^{6}$ **>56f<**

**Identify (IRE) 3** b f Persian Bold-Nordic Pride (Horage) *(1573a)* 1769$^{9}$ 2275a$^{3}$ 4738a$^{13}$ **>111f<**

**Idle Fancy 3** b f Mujtahid (USA)-Pizzin (Artaius (USA)) 1855$^{7}$ 2197$^{2}$ 4738a$^{7}$ **>85f<**

**Idrica 2** b f Rainbow Quest (USA)-Idraak (Kris) (4096) 4565$^{7}$ 4864$^{7}$ **>81f<**

**Idris (IRE) 6** b h Ahonoora-Idara (Top Ville) *(1235a)* (1296a) 1566a$^{5}$ (1912a) (2092a) 2471a$^{4}$ (3196a) (3731a) 4281a$^{5}$ 4649a$^{3}$ 5065a$^{4}$ **>122f<**

**Iechyd-Da (IRE) 2** b g Sharp Victor (USA)-Key Partner (Law Society (USA)) (490) (552) 1419$^{4}$ 2629$^{2}$ 4369$^{11}$ **>84f<**

**Ihtimaam (FR) 4** b g Polish Precedent (USA)-Haebeh (USA) (Alydar (USA)) 1309$^{14}$ 1474$^{11}$ 1596$^{10}$ 2214$^{9}$ 2356$^{7}$ *(2935) 4574$^{8}$ 4812$^{13}$ 4986$^{3}$* **>61a 29f<**

**Ihtiram (IRE) 4** b c Royal Academy (USA)-Welsh Love *375a$^{7}$ 535a$^{7}$* **>72a 117f<**

**Ihtiraz 6** ch h Soviet Star (USA)-Azyaa (Kris) **1995:** 4561a$^{2}$ **1996:** 374a$^{4}$

**Ihtiyati (USA) 2** ch c Chief's Crown (USA)-Native Twine (Be My Native (USA)) 1897$^{6}$ 2702$^{10}$ (4599) **>84f<**

**Ijab (CAN) 6** b g Ascot Knight (CAN)-Renounce (USA) (Buckpasser) **1995:** *4391$^{2}$ 4434$^{2}$* **1996:** *(400) 422$^{4}$* **>62a 50f<**

**Ijtinab 2** b c Green Desert (USA)-Nahilah (Habitat) 4619$^{7}$ **>48f<**

**Ikatania 2** b c Highest Honor (FR)-Lady Liska (USA) (Diesis) 1339$^{4}$ 2543$^{4}$ 3319$^{6}$ 4384$^{3}$ 4760$^{13}$ **>74f<**

**Ikdam (USA) 2** b br f Dayjur (USA)-Orca (ARG) (Southern Halo (USA)) 2245$^{3}$ (2892) (3468) **>95f<**

**Ike's Pet 2** ch f Tina's Pet-Cold Blow (Posse (USA)) 4970$^{14}$ **>29f<**

**Ikhtiraa (USA) 6** b g Imperial Falcon (CAN)-True Native (USA) (Raise A Native) **1995:** *4364$^{3}$ 4530$^{2}$* **1996:** *12$^{3}$ (130) 206$^{3}$ 265$^{2}$ 339$^{6}$ 635$^{7}$* 759$^{3}$ 1063$^{13}$ **>66a 47f<**

**Ikhtisar (USA) 2** b br f Slew O' Gold (USA)-Halholah (USA) (Secreto (USA)) 4725$^{6}$ **>47f<**

**Iktamal (USA) 4** ch c Danzig Connection (USA)-Crystal Cup (USA) (Nijinsky (CAN)) 457$^{6}$ 673$^{2}$ (889) 1621$^{2}$ 2072$^{5}$ 2332$^{5}$ 2622$^{4}$ (3083) 3573a$^{4}$ (4057) *4951a$^{6}$* **>122a 126f<**

**Ilandra (IRE) 4** b f Roi Danzig (USA)-Island Goddess (Godswalk (USA)) *15$^{11}$ 66$^{7}$ 145$^{5}$ 214$^{8}$ 353$^{8}$ 1450$^{10}$* 4789$^{10}$ *4982$^{2}$* **>55a 32f<**

**Ilanga (IRE) 3** b f Common Grounds-Golden Leap 3530a$^{8}$ **>87f<**

**Il Doria (IRE) 3** ch f Mac's Imp (USA)-Pasadena Lady (Captain James) 3665$^{3}$ 4521$^{13}$ *4776$^{12}$ 4997$^{7}$* **>8a 59f<**

**Ile Distinct (IRE) 2** b g Dancing Dissident (USA)-Golden Sunlight (Ile de Bourbon (USA)) 1626$^{7}$ 2211$^{3}$ 4618$^{10}$ **>64f<**

**Il Furetto 4** b g Emarati (USA)-Irresistable **1995:** *4354$^{7}$ 4459$^{7}$* **>20a 25f<**

**I'll Be Bound 5** b g Beveled (USA)-Treasurebound (Beldale Flutter (USA)) *47$^{5}$ 125$^{4}$ 236$^{11}$* **>31a 59f<**

**Illegally Yours 3** br f Be My Chief (USA)-Legal Precedent (Star Appeal) **1995:** *4491$^{10}$* **1996:** *129$^{4}$ 245$^{6}$ 1591$^{3}$ 1997$^{2}$ 3077$^{5}$ 3872$^{6}$* **>52a 52df<**

**Illuminate 3** b c Marju (IRE)-Light Bee (USA) (Majestic Light (USA)) 860$^{3}$ 1711$^{5}$ 2074$^{12}$ 3341$^{4}$ 3818$^{5}$ **>77f<**

**Il Principe (IRE) 2** b g Ela-Mana-Mou-Seattle Siren (USA) (Seattle Slew (USA)) 4228$^{13}$ 4754$^{7}$ **>15f<**

**Il Trastevere (FR) 4** b c L'Emigrant (USA)-Ideas At Work (Persepolis (FR)) 809$^{11}$ 967$^{11}$ 1198$^{9}$ 1775$^{14}$ **>81f<**

**Ilustre (IRE) 4** ch g Al Hareb (USA)-Time For Pleasure (Tower Walk) *53$^{11}$ 328$^{14}$* **>56f<**

**Ilyazia 5** b m Governor General-Tina's Beauty (Tina's Pet) **1995:** *4362$^{14}$*

**Imad (USA) 6** b or br g Al Nasr (FR)-Blue Grass Field (Top Ville) 767$^{10}$ 2042$^{26}$ **>71f<**

**Image Maker (IRE) 3** gr f Nordico (USA)-Dream Trader (Auction Ring (USA)) **1995:** *4373$^{4}$ 4446$^{4}$ 4477$^{4}$ 4511$^{7}$* **1996:** *35$^{8}$ 385$^{5}$ 415$^{5}$ 2631$^{7}$* **>34a 52f<**

**I'm a Nut Man 5** b h Shardari-Zahiah (So Blessed) 609$^{17}$ 752$^{3}$ 995$^{14}$ 1167$^{2}$ 1468$^{2}$ 1979$^{5}$ **>22a 49f<**

**Imlak (IRE) 4** ch g Ela-Mana-Mou-Mashteen (USA) (Majestic Prince (USA)) 546$^{12}$ 642$^{6}$ 759$^{7}$ 1472$^{11}$ **>61f<**

**Impala 2** ch g Interrex (CAN)-Raleigh Gazelle (Absalom) 1463$^{4}$ *1720$^{2}$ 2512$^{5}$* 4787$^{11}$ **>44a 53f<**

**Impending Danger 3** ch g Fearless Action (USA)-Crimson Sol (Crimson Beau) *3474$^{13}$* ***>37a 26f<***

**Imperial Bid (FR) 8** b or br g No Pass No Sale (FR)-Tzaritsa (USA) (Young Emperor) *256$^{3}$* **>60a 63f<**

**Imperial Garden (IRE) 2** ch g Imperial Frontier (USA)-Spindle Berry (Dance In Time (CAN)) *1093$^{9}$ 2926$^{10}$ (3950) 4195$^{12}$* 4459$^{6}$ *4777$^{12}$ 5005$^{2}$* ***>63a 60f<***

**Imperial Or Metric (IRE) 2** b g Prince Rupert (FR)-Caroline's Mark (On Your Mark) 1537$^{13}$ 2044$^{6}$ 2396$^{6}$ 2932$^{2}$ 3462$^{3}$ 3687$^{9}$ 4024a$^{25}$ (4347) 4625$^{10}$ 4792$^{6}$ 4970$^{7}$ **>71f<**

**Imperial President 2** b c Known Fact (USA)-Houseproud (USA) (Riverman (USA)) *1892$^{3}$* (2517) (2878) 3143$^{5}$ 3925$^{2}$ 4555$^{7}$ **>102f<**

**Imperial Prospect (USA) 4** b f Imperial Falcon

(CAN)-One Tough Lady (USA) (Mr Prospector (USA)) *1508[11]* ***>67f<***

**Imperial Red (IRE)** **3** ch g Mac's Imp (USA)-Bluemore (Morston (FR)) *3350[7]* 3609[9] 4074[16] 4881[20] **>11f<**

**Imperial Scholar (IRE)** **2** b f Royal Academy (USA)-Last Ball (IRE) (Last Tycoon) 3794[2] **>82f<**

**Impetuous Air** **2** b f Warning-Hardihostess (Be My Guest (USA)) 1115[5] 1673[2] (2122) 2997[4] 3444[5] **>79f<**

**Impetuous Lady (USA)** **3** b f Imp Society (USA)-Urakawa (USA) (Roberto (USA)) 2528[4] 2994[10] 4480[14] **>47f<**

**Imp Express (IRE)** **3** b c Mac's Imp (USA)-Fair Chance (Young Emperor) 443[18] 587[17] 773[7] 973[17] 1199[9] 1541[9] 1761[3] 2021[5] 2757[6] 2960[8] 3294[13] **>50f<**

**Impington (IRE)** **3** b f Mac's Imp (USA)-Ultra (Stanford) **1995:** *4437[4] 4483[4] 4541[3]* **1996:** *39[4] 101[6] 160[8] 224[4] 264[5] 430[3]* **>55a 68f<**

**Impish (IRE)** **2** ch g Imp Society (USA)-Halimah (Be My Guest (USA)) 1827[14] *2083[10] 3429[9]* 4562[19] 4796[13] *4985[9]* **>15f<**

**Imposing Time** **5** b g Music Boy-Jandell (NZ) (Shifnal) 3261[6] 3477[W] 3661[2] 3864[2] 3993[8] 4130[3] *4333[2] (4778)* **>76a 66f<**

**Imprevedibile (IRE)** **6** b h Bluebird (USA)-Corozal (Corvaro (USA)) (1053a) 1136a[4] **>115f<**

**Impromptu Melody (IRE)** **3** b f Mac's Imp (USA)-Greek Music (Tachypous) 775[15] 867[15] **>52f<**

**Impulsif (USA)** **2** ch c Diesis-High Sevens (Master Willie) 1038[2] 1831[4] 2184[3] 2559[5] (4495) 4764[7] **>80f<**

**Impulsion (IRE)** **2** b c Imp Society (USA)-Verthumna (Indian King (USA)) *551[5]* 1713[2] 2699[5] 3336[6] 4244[10] **>54f<**

**Impulsive Air (IRE)** **4** b g Try My Best (USA)-Tracy's Sundown (Red Sunset) 1412[5] 1610[9] (2213) 2679[5] (3279) 3646[3] 4190[2] 4686[15] 4769[4] 4975[12] **>73f<**

**Impy Fox (IRE)** **2** ch f Imp Society (USA)-Rusty Goddess (Hard Fought) *3582[4] (3954) 4207[4]* 4495[13] **>65a 58f<**

**Imroz (USA)** **2** b f Nureyev (USA)-All At Sea (USA) (Riverman (USA)) *(2611)* 3068[5] (4338) **>90f<**

**I'm Still Here** **2** gr g Skyliner-Miss Colenca (Petong) 476[2] 618[2] 880[4] *1080[6] 3648[2]* 3880[7] 4751[6] 5006[3] **>50a 68?f<**

**I'm Supposin (IRE)** **4** b c Posen (USA)-Robinia (USA) (Roberto (USA)) 1235a[9] 1252a[3] 1912a[3] (2825a) 3531a[2] 3728a[2] 4268a[2] 4397a[5] 4849a[5] 5015a[2] **>116f<**

**I'm Your Lady** **5** ch m Risk Me (FR)-Impala Lass (Kampala) **1995:** *4394[7]* **1996:** *610[11]* 814[5] (935) 1703[7] *2306[3] 2860[4]* 3106[4] 3296[7] *3601[5] 4077[2]* **>76a 78f<**

**Inaminit** **3** gr g Timeless Times (USA)-Dolly Bevan (Another Realm) *1045[9]* 1518[3] 2049[15] 3650[8] 4053[10] 4603[17] *4978[11]* **>2a 44f<**

**In a Moment (USA)** **5** ch g Moment of Hope (USA)-Teenage Fling (USA) (Laomedonte (USA)) *236[8] 482[12]* ***>57a 44f<***

**I Nanu (TUR)** **4** f 4289a[4] **>108f<**

**In A Tizzy** **3** b f Sizzling Melody-Tizzy (Formidable (USA)) 3490[4] 3780[7] 4075[12] **>38a 44f<**

**Inca Bird** **3** b f Inca Chief (USA)-Polly Oligant (Prince Tenderfoot (USA)) *606[9] 748[12] 1081[8] 2180[18]* 2753[9] 2966[12] **>19a 18f<**

**In Cahoots** **3** gr c Kalaglow-Royal Celerity (USA) (Riverman (USA)) 861[12] 1067[7] *1456[6] 1979[7]* 3808[20] 3965[8] (4340) 4603[15] **>36a 55f<**

**Incandescent** **2** b f Inca Chief (USA)-Heavenly State (Enchantment) 1590[6] 1954[7] *3088[7]* **>62f<**

**Incapol** **3** b c Inca Chief (USA)-Miss Poll Flinders (Swing Easy (USA)) *644[P]* ***>29a 66f<*** **(DEAD)**

**Incatime** **2** b c Inca Chief (USA)-Parrot Fashion (Pieces of Eight) 2942[3] 3502[4] **>64f<**

**Incatinka** **3** gr f Inca Chief (USA)-Encore L'Amour (USA) (Monteverdi) 943[7] 1688[6] *4981[11]* **>16a 65f<**

**Inchacooley (IRE)** **4** b f Rhoman Rule (USA)-Blue Cashmere (USA) 4026a[8] 4738a[2] 4851a[4] **>102f<**

**Inchcailloch (IRE)** **7** b g Lomond (USA)-Glowing With Pride (Ile de Bourbon (USA)) 4199[12] 4476[2] (4604) (4771) **>84f<**

**Inchella** **3** b f Inca Chief (USA)-Sandy Cap (Sandy Creek) *4472[12]*

***Inchrory*** ***3*** b c Midyan (USA)-Applecross (Glint of Gold) 4174a[3] **>113f<**

**Inchyre** **3** b f Shirley Heights-Inchmurrin (Lomond (USA)) (3847) 4218[4] 4467[4] **>106f<**

**Inclination** **2** b f Beveled (USA)-Pallomere (Blue Cashmere) *3493[2]* 3874[2] 4330[6] **>73f<**

**Include Me Out** **2** ch c Old Vic-Tafila (Adonijah) 4261[6] 4492[9] 4830[4] **>70f<**

**In Command (IRE)** **2** b c Sadler's Wells (USA)-Flying Melody (Auction Ring (USA)) (3147) 3668[3] 4179[2] 4519[3] (4759) **>106f<**

**Indiahra** **5** b m Indian Ridge-Mavahra (Mummy's Pet) **1995:** *4413[2] 4447[10]* **1996:** *74[4] 88[6] 115[3] 153[3] 166[3] 213[5] 301[7] 331[8] 3310[4]* 3868[7] 4805[3] 4975[2] **>52a 57f<**

**Indiana Princess** **3** b f Warrshan (USA)-Lovely Greek Lady (Ela-Mana-Mou) *3298[5]* 3642[6] 3818[6] 4227[6] 4448[5] 4726[2] **>65f<**

**Indian Blaze** **2** ch c Indian Ridge-Odile (Green Dancer (USA)) *3319[12]* 3773[2] 4188[4] 4578[5] **>68f<**

**Indian Brave** **2** b c Indian Ridge-Supreme Kingdom (Take A Reef) 4502[2] 4619[3] **>89f<**

**Indian Jockey** **4** b g Indian Ridge-Number Eleven (Local Suitor (USA)) *1953[6]* (2313) 2577[17] 2737[10] **>70f<**

**Indian Nectar** **3** b f Indian Ridge-Sheer Nectar (Piaffer (USA)) *1061[4]* 1614[11] 2943[4] 3496[11] *4095[9] 4513[15]* ***>2a 68f<***

**Indian Rapture** **2** ch f Be My Chief (USA)-Moments Joy (Adonijah) 3820[6] 4211[6] 4359[6] 4880[18] **>63f<**

**Indian Relative** **3** b f Distant Relative-Elegant Tern (USA) (Sea Bird II) 870[7] 1126[11] 1608[3] (2167) (2311) 2571[8] 3168[2] 3758[5] 4198[2] 4312[7] 4791[9] **>75a 83f<**

**Indian Rhapsody** **4** b f Rock City-Indian Love Song (Be My Guest (USA)) 1121[14] *1460[8] 1821[18]* 1893[4] 2121[5] (3217) 3442[13] 4296[6] **>18a 60f<**

**Indian Rocket** **2** b c Indian Ridge-Selvi (Mummy's Pet) 1445[2] (1892) 2700[2] (3400) (3843) (4328) 4519[10] **>108f<**

**Indian Serenade** **5** ch g Mansingh (USA)-La Melodie (Silly Season) 1533[15] 1893[12] *2201[8] 2405[10]* ***>46a 42f<***

**Indian Spark** **2** ch c Indian Ridge-Annes Gift (Ballymoss) (441) 1115[2] **>85f<**

**Indian Sunset** **3** ch c Indian Ridge-Alanood (Northfields (USA)) 2718[8] 3341[3] *3630[10]* **>40a 53f<**

**Indian Treasure (IRE)** **4** b f Treasure Kay-Arminiya **1995:** *4387[14]* **>14f<**

**Indian Wolf** **3** ch c Indian Ridge-Red Riding Hood (FR) (Mummy's Pet) 860[15] 1099[18] 1465[5] 1891[11] 3258[11] 3474[12] 4202[17] **>36f<**

**Indifferent Guy** **2** b c Environment Friend-Sarah's Love (Caerleon (USA)) 3221[7] 3685[6] 3925[5] 4261[3] 4625[16] (4835) **>83f<**

**Indihash (USA)** **2** b br f Gulch (USA)-Linda's Magic (USA) (Far North (CAN)) 2611[4] 3756[5] (4104) **>81+f<**

**Indiphar** **3** ch f Weld-Spring Drill (Blushing Scribe (USA)) 705[10] 994[8] 1201[4] 1887[4] 2120[10] *2751[4] 4752[14]* ***>41a 54f<***

**Indira** **3** b f Indian Ridge-Princess Rosananti (IRE) (Shareef Dancer (USA)) 2061[5] 2743[16] 3333[9] (3824) *4080[8] 4217[7]* ***>36a 63f<***

**Indiscreet (CAN)** **2** b c St Jovite (USA)-Imprudent Love (USA) (Foolish Pleasure (USA)) (3706) **>101++f<**

**Indium** **2** b c Groom Dancer (USA)-Gold Bracelet (Golden Fleece (USA)) 4253[7] 4508[3] 4818[3] **>83f<**

**Indonesian (IRE)** **4** b or br g Alzao (USA)-Miss Garuda (Persian Bold) *649[11]* 2077[7] 2366[6] 2900[8] **>66f<**

**Indrapura (IRE)** **4** b g Gallic League-Stella Ann (Ahonoora) **1995:** *4531[9]* **1996:** *1685[12]* 2032[10] 2229[10] (2345) 2796[5] 2981[6] **>74a 59f<**

**Induna Mkubwa** **3** ch c Be My Chief (USA)-Hyatti (Habitat) *248[8] 932[8]* 1319[15] 1641[8] 3249[11] *3422[3] 4042[2]* 4249[14] **>40a 53f<**

**Infamous (USA)** **3** ch c Diesis-Name And Fame (USA) (Arts And Letters) (494) 731[2] 1407[7] 1712[7] 2041[18] 2576[2] 2905[2] 3155[7] 3791[11] 4117[3] **>89f<**

**Infantry Dancer** **3** ch f Infantry-Electropet (Remainder Man) 2540[7] *3086[12] 3334[4]* 3525[8] 4082[16] **>56f<**

**Infatuation** **3** b g Music Boy-Fleeting Affair (Hotfoot) 2996[6] 4201[4] 4429[3] **>83f<**

**Infiel** **3** b f Luge-Indocina (Indian King (USA)) *794a[13]* ***>79f<***

**Infiraaj (USA)** **4** b g Dayjur (USA)-Capricorn Belle (Nonoalco (USA)) *248[4] 356[6] 517[6] 2185[19]* ***>48a 4f<***

**Inflation** **2** b f Primo Dominie-Fluctuate (Sharpen Up) 2741[3] 3436[2] **>76f<**

**Influence Pedler** **3** b g Keen-La Vie En Primrose (Henbit (USA)) **1995:** *4410[8]* **1996:** *348[7] 471[8]* 594[3] (954) 1415[4] 1679[2] (2204) 2407[2] 3077[2] 3667[4] 4358[2] 4910[5] **>11a 69f<**

**In Good Faith** **4** b g Beveled (USA)-Dulcidene (Behistoun) *3426[14]* 4793[8] 5004[14] **>67f<**

**In Good Nick** **2** b f Nicholas (USA)-Better Still (IRE) (Glenstal (USA)) 1183[7] 1858[3] 3511[3] 3687[10] 3969[4] 4195[3] 4501[5] **>63f<**

**Ingrina** **3** b f Warning-Naswara (USA) (Al Nasr (FR)) 1079[6] 1530[9] **>48f<**

**Inherent Magic (IRE)** **7** ch m Magical Wonder (USA)-Flo Kelly (Florescence) **1995:** *4368[5] 4517[2]* **1996:** *64[3] 185[2] 202[4]* **>77a 98f<**

**Inimitable** **2** b f Polish Precedent (USA)-Saveur (Ardross) 4697[6] 4861[10] **>67f<**

**Inishmann (IRE)** **5** ch g Soughaan (USA)-Danova (FR) (Dan Cupid) *54[13]* **>6a f<**

**Injazaat (USA)** **2** b br f Dayjur (USA)-Basma (USA) (Grey Dawn II) 3593[6] 4061[12] 4544[2] **>76f<**

**Ink Pot (USA)** **2** ch f Green Dancer (USA)-Refill (Mill Reef (USA)) 3159[12] 4069[3] 4500[4] 4814[7] **>78f<**

**Inkwell** **2** b c Relief Pitcher-Fragrant Hackette (Simply Great (FR)) 4600[12] 4782[11] **>40f<**

**Inn At the Top** **4** b g Top Ville-Woolpack (Golden Fleece (USA)) *3335[8] 3605[3] 3813[3] 4092[11]* **>61a 67f<**

**Inner Circle (USA)** **3** ch f El Gran Senor (USA)-Conquistress (USA) (Conquistador Cielo (USA)) (550) 794a[9] 1410[4] 1639[6] **>96df<**

**Inovar** **6** b g Midyan (USA)-Princess Cinders (King of Spain) *33[9] 85[5] (367) 429[8] 558[13] 2372[9]* **>35a 34f<**

**In Question** **2** br b c Deploy-Questionable (Rainbow Quest (USA)) 3595[2] 4041[4] **>86f<**

**Inquisitor (USA)** **4** b c Alleged (USA)-Imperturbable Lady (CAN) (Northern Dancer) 581[6] 3658[3] 4326[2] (4853a) **>113?f<**

**Insatiable (IRE)** **3** b c Don't Forget Me-Petit Eclair (Major Portion) 1807[3] 2041[2] **>96+f<**

**Insideout** 3 b g Macmillion-Parijoun (Manado) 2753$^{7}$ 3288$^{4}$ 3579$^{12}$ **>33f<**

**Insider Trader** 5 b g Dowsing (USA)-Careless Whisper (Homing) **1995:** *4394$^{11}$* **1996:** *587$^{18}$* 735$^{14}$ 931$^{6}$ 1113$^{10}$ 1199$^{4}$ 1501$^{3}$ 1646$^{2}$ (2064) 2349$^{10}$ 2694$^{7}$ 3085$^{2}$ 3432$^{11}$ 3932$^{3}$ 4180$^{5}$ 4246$^{10}$ 4505$^{2}$ 4616$^{9}$ 4765$^{8}$ 4811$^{10}$ 4995$^{5}$ **>63a 75f<**

**Insiyabi (USA)** 3 b c Mr Prospector (USA)-Ashayer (USA) (Lomond (USA)) (445) 3229$^{9}$ 3503$^{7}$ **>96f<**

**Instantaneous** 4 b f Rock City-Mainmast (Bustino) **1995:** *4376$^{8}$* **1996:** *777$^{6}$ 1487$^{9}$ 1676$^{13}$* 2046$^{3}$ 2775$^{5}$ 3117$^{5}$ 3412$^{8}$ **>39a 45f<**

**Inteabadun** 4 ch g Hubbly Bubbly (USA)-Madam Taylor (Free State) *398$^{8}$ 512$^{8}$* **>23a f<**

**Intendant** 4 b g Distant Relative-Bunduq (Scottish Rifle) **1995:** *4531$^{6}$* **1996:** *851$^{3}$* 1024$^{2}$ 1341$^{2}$ 1650$^{2}$ 2483$^{8}$ 2929$^{4}$ 3592$^{10}$ **>47a 65f<**

**Intention (USA)** 6 b g Shahrastani (USA)-Mimi Baker (USA) (What Luck (USA)) *12$^{4}$ 108$^{10}$* **>51a 71f<**

**Interdream** 2 b g Interrex (CAN)-Dreamtime Quest (Blakeney) 3848$^{12}$ (3963) 4303$^{11}$ 4602$^{16}$ 4883$^{17}$ **>69f<**

**Interregnum** 2 ch f Interrex (CAN)-Lillicara (FR) (Caracolero (USA)) 2863$^{11}$ **>30f<**

**In The Band** 3 b f Sharrood (USA)-Upper Caen (High Top) *40$^{2}$ 248$^{3}$ 385$^{7}$ 2762$^{5}$* 3318$^{8}$ 4068$^{4}$ 4236$^{13}$ **>62a 47f<**

**In The Evening (IRE)** 3 b f Distinctly North (USA)-Selkis 1246a$^{7}$ **>58f<**

**In The Highlands** 3 gr f Petong-Thevetia (Mummy's Pet) 964$^{9}$ 1422$^{8}$ 1994$^{5}$ 2541$^{8}$ 4915$^{19}$ **>44f<**

**In the Money (IRE)** 7 b h Top Ville-Rensaler (USA) (Stop The Music (USA)) **1995:** *4534$^{9}$* **1996:** *267$^{6}$ 512$^{2}$ (532) (898) 993$^{7}$ 1458$^{4}$ (1640) 2173$^{5}$ 2553$^{3}$ 2674$^{3}$* 2969$^{3}$ 3117$^{6}$ 3653$^{9}$ 3865$^{3}$ *4334$^{8}$ 4587$^{14}$ 4986$^{4}$ 5062$^{5}$* **>56a 58f<**

**Intiaash (IRE)** 4 br f Shaadi (USA)-Funun (USA) (Fappiano (USA)) *513$^{6}$ 582$^{17}$ 835$^{2}$ (896) 1178$^{3}$* 1466$^{4}$ *2306$^{4}$ 2615$^{5}$* **>81a 76f<**

**Intidab (USA)** 3 b c Phone Trick (USA)-Alqwani (USA) (Mr Prospector (USA)) (3058) 3430$^{2}$ 3709$^{16}$ **>102f<**

**Intikhab (USA)** 2 b c Red Ransom (USA)-Crafty Example (USA) (Crafty Prospector (USA)) 3293$^{2}$ (4383) (4816) **>87+f<**

**Intimation** 3 b f Warning-It's Terrific (Vaguely Noble) 3519$^{3}$ 3832$^{5}$ 4360$^{8}$ **>66f<**

**Intisab** 3 b f Green Desert (USA)-Ardassine (Ahonoora) 672$^{W}$ **>64f<**

**Into Debt** 3 b f Cigar-Serious Affair (Valiyar) *377$^{8}$ 1171$^{12}$* 1518$^{W}$ 1891$^{12}$ 3636$^{5}$ 3698$^{2}$ 3863$^{11}$ 4372$^{19}$ *4987$^{12}$* **>27a 36f<**

**Intrepid Fort** 7 gr g Belfort (FR)-Dauntless Flight (Golden Mallard) 1610$^{10}$ 2075$^{16}$ 2162$^{10}$ 2348$^{6}$ 2513$^{6}$ 2587$^{8}$ 3414$^{5}$ **>28a 37f<**

**In Tune** 3 b c Prince Sabo-Singing Nelly (Pharly (FR)) 583$^{6}$ 842$^{9}$ **>63f< (DEAD)**

**Invermark** 2 b c Machiavellian (USA)-Applecross (Glint of Gold) 3615$^{8}$ 4069$^{5}$ 4914$^{3}$ **>75f<**

**Invest Wisely** 4 ch g Dashing Blade-Saniette (Crystal Palace (FR)) 1109$^{9}$ 1428$^{8}$ 1976$^{4}$ 2330$^{8}$ 2612$^{4}$ 2857$^{6}$ 3142$^{9}$ 3850$^{9}$ **>89f<**

**Invigilate** 7 ch g Viking (USA)-Maria da Gloria (St Chad) *769$^{11}$* 1364$^{11}$ 1646$^{5}$ (1848) 2154$^{11}$ 2523$^{5}$ 2757$^{18}$ 2964$^{6}$ 3252$^{6}$ 4460$^{17}$ 4486$^{14}$ 4610$^{10}$ **>45f<**

**Invocation** 9 ch g Kris-Royal Saint (USA) (Crimson Satan) **1995:** *4350$^{4}$ 4421$^{4}$ 4457$^{4}$ 4531$^{8}$* **1996:** *109$^{2}$ 121$^{8}$ 163$^{2}$ 205$^{6}$ 244$^{2}$ 380$^{6}$ 461$^{4}$ 556$^{2}$ 632$^{6}$* 1334$^{11}$ 1715$^{4}$ 1958$^{3}$ 2129$^{8}$ 3146$^{4}$ 3439$^{8}$ *3877$^{4}$ 4895$^{3}$ 5000$^{5}$* **>71a 57f<**

**In Your Dreams (IRE)** 2 b f Suave Dancer (USA)-By Charter (Shirley Heights) 4208$^{11}$ **>54f<**

**Inzar (USA)** 4 b c Warning-Czar's Bride (USA) (Northern Dancer) 810$^{11}$ 1621$^{3}$ (1800) 2337$^{2}$ 2880$^{8}$ 3083$^{6}$ 4857a$^{6}$ 5065a$^{2}$ **>119df<**

**Iolanta (IRE)** 2 f Danehill (USA)-Kifenia 2272a$^{4}$ **>61f<**

**Ionio (USA)** 5 ch g Silver Hawk (USA)-Private View (USA) (Mr Prospector (USA)) 456$^{4}$ 878$^{8}$ 1620$^{4}$ 2055$^{9}$ 2534$^{4}$ 3212$^{8}$ 3791$^{9}$ 4055$^{7}$ 4487$^{3}$ 4872$^{16}$ **>96a 95f<**

**Iota** 7 b or br m Niniski (USA)-Iosifa (Top Ville) *268$^{7}$ 360$^{5}$ 422$^{9}$ (656) 753$^{7}$* 872$^{11}$ *1082$^{4}$ 1826$^{5}$* 2165$^{6}$ (2423) 2717$^{7}$ *3066$^{5}$ 4203$^{3}$ 4332$^{7}$ 4604$^{9}$* 4766$^{9}$ 4910$^{3}$ 5008$^{13}$ **>65a 59f<**

**Ioulios** 2 ch c Shavian-Touch of White (Song) 4962$^{11}$ **>22f<**

**Ipponatte (ITY)** 2 ro c Siberian Express (USA)-Idyll Secret (ITY) (Cormorant (USA)) 4407a$^{2}$

**Irchester Lass** 4 ch f Presidium-Fool's Errand (Milford) **1995:** *4413$^{9}$ 4430$^{2}$ 4479$^{2}$* **1996:** *71$^{5}$ 122$^{5}$ (172) 518$^{6}$ 839$^{4}$ 1085$^{6}$ 1423$^{13}$* 1674$^{12}$ 1905$^{8}$ **>51a 35f<**

**I Recall (IRE)** 5 b g Don't Forget Me-Sable Lake (Thatching) 752$^{11}$ 843$^{3}$ 1145$^{14}$ 1522$^{5}$ *2158$^{12}$* **>60a 62f<**

**Irie Mon (IRE)** 4 b g Waajib-Achafalaya (USA) (Apalachee (USA)) *413$^{6}$ 521$^{8}$ 629$^{8}$* 1832$^{3}$ 2183$^{15}$ 2366$^{12}$ 2898$^{8}$ **>50a 60f<**

**Irish Academy (IRE)** 4 ch g Royal Academy (USA)-Rosa Mundi (USA) (Secretariat (USA)) 2459a$^{7}$ **>65f<**

**Irish Accord (USA)** 2 b br c Cahill Road (USA)-Dimples (USA) (Smile (USA)) (3349) 3971$^{4}$ **>80f<**

**Irish Fiction (IRE)** 2 b g Classic Music (USA)-Wasmette (IRE) (Wassl) 490$^{2}$ 551$^{2}$ 618$^{3}$ 869$^{4}$ 1032$^{2}$ (1904) 2509$^{2}$ 3046$^{7}$ 3227$^{4}$ 3523$^{2}$ 3803$^{9}$ (3976) 4495$^{3}$ 4814$^{6}$ **>63f<**

**Irish Groom** 9 b g Shy Groom (USA)-Romany Pageant (Welsh Pageant) 979$^{16}$ **>42da 52f<**

**Irish Kinsman** 3 b g Distant Relative-Inesdela (Wolver Hollow) **1995:** *4519$^{8}$* **1996:** *1452$^{6}$* 2346$^{5}$ 3470$^{8}$ 3852$^{10}$ 4587$^{12}$ **>17a 54f<**

**Irish Oasis (IRE)** 3 b g Mazaad-Alpenwind (Tumble Wind (USA)) 1067$^{2}$ 1477$^{6}$ 1762$^{8}$ 2362$^{3}$ 3451$^{2}$ 3777$^{12}$ 3970$^{11}$ 4437$^{11}$ **>32a 51f<**

**Irish Pet** 2 br f Petong-Crystal's Solo (USA) (Crystal Water (USA)) 4608$^{9}$ **>65f<**

**Irish Sea (USA)** 3 b g Zilzal (USA)-Dunkellin (USA) (Irish River (FR)) 1530$^{2}$ 1711$^{6}$ 2314$^{3}$ 3451$^{4}$ 3481$^{5}$ 3623$^{17}$ 4217$^{5}$ 4237$^{5}$ 4587$^{15}$ **>64df<**

**Irish Stamp (IRE)** 7 b g Niniski (USA)-Bayazida (Bustino) 2804$^{9}$ **>52?f<**

**Irish Wildcard (NZ)** 8 b g Lyphard's Trick (USA)-Courageous Mahoney (NZ) (Rocky Mountain (FR)) 645$^{10}$ **>62f<**

**Irish Woman (FR)** 3 ch f Assert-Irish Beauty (FR) (Irish River (FR)) 2108a$^{3}$ 2665a$^{2}$ 3202a$^{5}$ **>99f<**

**Iron And Steel** 3 ch g Dominion-Fairy Fortune (Rainbow Quest (USA)) *4081$^{0}$* **>25a 28f<**

**Iron Gent (USA)** 5 b g Greinton-Carrot Top (High Hat) 1847$^{5}$ **>59f<**

**Ironheart** 3 b c Lycius (USA)-Inshirah (USA) (Caro) 840$^{5}$ **>66f<**

**Iron N Gold** 4 b g Heights of Gold-Southern Dynasty (Gunner B) **1995:** *4546$^{2}$* **1996:** *12$^{6}$ (69) 279$^{4}$ 411$^{8}$* **>56a 58f<**

**Irrepressible (IRE)** 5 b g Don't Forget Me-Lady of Shalott (Kings Lake (USA)) 1411$^{7}$ (1691) 2032$^{3}$ 2344$^{4}$ 2525$^{6}$ 2785$^{4}$ 2994$^{3}$ 3274$^{7}$ 4240$^{4}$ **>54f<**

**Irsal** 2 ch c Nashwan (USA)-Amwag (USA) (El Gran Senor (USA)) 4817$^{5}$ **>60f<**

**Irtifa** 2 ch f Lahib (USA)-Thaidah (CAN) (Vice Regent (CAN)) 2559$^{2}$ (2944) 3467$^{5}$ 3998$^{7}$ **>76f<**

**I Say Dancer (IRE)** 3 b f Distinctly North (USA)-Lady Marigot (Lord Gayle (USA)) 4429$^{13}$

**Isca Maiden** 2 b f Full Extent (USA)-Sharp N' Easy (Swing Easy (USA)) 4330$^{23}$ 4600$^{14}$ 4798$^{15}$ **>23f<**

**Isit Izzy** 4 b f Crofthall-Angie's Girl (Dubassoff (USA)) 2515$^{4}$ 3353$^{10}$ **>42f<**

**Isitoff** 3 b c Vague Shot-Plum Blossom (USA) (Gallant Romeo (USA)) *377$^{5}$ 634$^{3}$ 856$^{4}$ (1317)* 1477$^{2}$ 1783$^{5}$ 2247$^{6}$ 2688$^{3}$ 3484$^{2}$ 4068$^{15}$ **>56a 79f<**

**Isla Del Rey (USA)** 4 ch f Nureyev (USA)-Priceless Pearl (USA) (Alydar (USA)) (1075) 2072$^{6}$ 3127$^{14}$ **>104f<**

**Isla Glen** 3 b f Be My Chief (USA)-Serration (Kris) 1857$^{11}$ 2197$^{13}$ 2540$^{9}$ 3825$^{11}$ **>45f<**

**Island Cascade** 4 b f Hadeer-Island Mill (Mill Reef (USA)) 993$^{13}$ 1159$^{12}$ 1697$^{5}$ *2372$^{11}$ 2522$^{3}$* 2756$^{10}$ **>30f<**

**Island Jewel** 8 ch g Jupiter Island-Diamond Talk (Counsel) *251$^{W}$*

**Island Prince** 2 ch g Prince Sabo-Island Mead (Pharly (FR)) 4330$^{20}$ 4516$^{12}$ 4715$^{12}$ 4990$^{9}$ **>54f<**

**Islay Brown (IRE)** 3 b f Petorius-Speedy Action (Horage) 453$^{14}$ 976$^{7}$ 1155$^{9}$ 1636$^{2}$ 2027$^{9}$ 2542$^{7}$ 2776$^{11}$ 4436$^{18}$ **>50f<**

**Isle of Corregidor (USA)** 2 b c Manila (USA)-Comtesse de Loir (FR) (Val de Loir) (1878) 3251$^{4}$ 4111$^{5}$ 4510$^{6}$ **>77f<**

**Isle of Man (USA)** 2 b c Manila (USA)-Princess of Man (Green God) 2600$^{2}$ (2783) **>75+f<**

**Ism** 4 b g Petong-Brigado (Brigadier Gerard) *2032$^{11}$* 2376$^{11}$ *3089$^{8}$* **>71a 65f<**

**Ismeno** 5 b g Ela-Mana-Mou-Seattle Siren (USA) (Seattle Slew (USA)) **1995:** *4355$^{11}$* **>37a 67f<**

**Istabraq (IRE)** 4 b c Sadler's Wells (USA)-Betty's Secret (USA) (Secretariat (USA)) 1802$^{2}$ **>96f<**

**Istinsaar (USA)** 5 b h Crafty Prospector (USA)-Kalista (Bellypha) *(435a)* **>105a 81f<**

**Italian Symphony (IRE)** 2 b c Royal Academy (USA)-Terracotta Hut (Habitat) *2802$^{5}$* 3349$^{4}$ 3588$^{5}$ 3880$^{6}$ 4319$^{6}$ 4594$^{3}$ **>77f<**

**Itatinga (USA)** 2 b f Riverman (USA)-Ivrea (Sadler's Wells (USA)) 4584$^{4}$ 4913$^{11}$ **>61f<**

**It Is Now** 4 ch g Blow the Whistle-Final Game (Pardao) **1995:** *4359$^{10}$* **>33a 33f<**

**Itkan (IRE)** 3 b f Marju (IRE)-Boldabsa (Persian Bold) 2346$^{4}$ 3847$^{4}$ 4201$^{7}$ 4785$^{15}$ **>54f<**

**It's Academic** 4 b f Royal Academy (USA)-It's Terrific (Vaguely Noble) 491$^{2}$ 802$^{9}$ 935$^{8}$ 1157$^{10}$ 1423$^{4}$ 1609$^{9}$ 1786$^{6}$ 1991$^{4}$ 2320$^{2}$ 2426$^{2}$ **>70f<**

**Itsinthepost** 3 b f Risk Me (FR)-Where's the Money (Lochnager) **1995:** *(4383) 4453$^{3}$ 4509$^{7}$* **1996:** *1466$^{11}$* 2578$^{11}$ *2937$^{9}$ 3602$^{3}$ 4081$^{3}$ 4333$^{10}$ 4788$^{10}$* **>65a 55f<**

**It's So Easy** 5 b m Shaadi (USA)-Carmelina (Habitat) **1995:** *4521$^{3}$* **1996:** *30$^{9}$ 109$^{8}$* **>32a 57f<**

**It'sthebusiness** 4 b g Most Welcome-Douceur (USA) (Shadeed (USA)) 636$^{5}$ 817$^{16}$ 1047$^{7}$ (1173) 1515$^{3}$ 1660$^{6}$ 1996$^{4}$ 2574$^{21}$ 3314$^{6}$ 4513$^{4}$ 4603$^{5}$ **>63f<**

**Ivan Luis (FR)** 2 b c Lycius (USA)-Zivania (IRE) (Shernazar) 2122$^{5}$ 2702$^{6}$ 3779$^{2}$ (4069) 4471$^{3}$ 4859a$^{3}$ **>91f<**

**Ivan the Terrible (IRE)** 8 ch g Siberian Express (USA)-Chrisanthy (So Blessed) *3089$^{10}$ 3457$^{7}$* **>42a 32f<**

**Ivor's Deed** 3 b c Shadeed (USA)-Gena Ivor (USA) (Sir Ivor) **1995:** *4417$^{5}$ 4491$^{7}$* **1996:** *614$^{11}$* 1068$^{2}$ 1527$^{5}$ (1764) 1995$^{2}$ 2179$^{3}$ 4098$^{4}$ 4240$^{10}$ 4590$^{8}$ **>41a 58f<**

**Ivor's Flutter** 7 b g Beldale Flutter (USA)-Rich Line (High Line) *1439$^{6}$* 1710$^{3}$ 2117$^{6}$ (3948) 4199$^{3}$ 4447$^{4}$ 4771$^{21}$ **>94f<**

**Ivory Dawn** 2 b f Batshoof-Cradle of Love (USA) (Roberto (USA)) 2600$^{8}$ 2904$^{3}$ 3171$^{6}$ **>60f<**

**Ivory's Grab Hire** 3 b g Shavian-Knees Up (USA) (Dancing Champ (USA)) 468$^{5}$ *503$^{4}$ 597$^{4}$* 761$^{6}$ *1027$^{13}$ 1152$^{3}$* 1654$^{10}$ 1776$^{3}$ (1995) 2034$^{4}$ 2578$^{5}$ 2763$^{3}$ 3172$^{7}$ 3244$^{3}$ 3301$^{2}$ 3458$^{6}$ 3789$^{12}$ 4128$^{3}$ 4256$^{18}$ 4356$^{3}$ 4598$^{5}$ **>55a 62f<**

**Ivy Lilian (IRE)** 4 b f Cyrano de Bergerac-Catherine Clare (Sallust) *514$^{10}$ 762$^{12}$ 835$^{10}$ 1598$^{5}$ 1716$^{7}$ 2496$^{9}$* 2561$^{6}$ **>30a 30f<**

**Izza** 5 b m Unfuwain (USA)-Wantage Park (Pas de Seul) (852) 1070$^{2}$ 2028$^{4}$ 2516$^{5}$ (2804) (2986) 3598$^{2}$ (3922) 4365$^{3}$ 4673$^{8}$ 4832$^{4}$ 5047$^{9}$ **>67f<**

**J**

**Jaazim** 6 ch g Night Shift (USA)-Mesmerize (Mill Reef (USA)) *107$^{5}$ 133$^{4}$ 218$^{10}$ 316$^{9}$ 406$^{6}$ 636$^{8}$* 887$^{2}$ 1121$^{2}$ 1533$^{5}$ 1856$^{2}$ 2285$^{2}$ 2604$^{5}$ 3096$^{4}$ 3469$^{5}$ 3694$^{2}$ 3991$^{4}$ 4373$^{9}$ 4820$^{11}$ **>59a 56f<**

**Jabaroot (IRE)** 5 b g Sadler's Wells (USA)-Arctic Heroine (USA) (Arctic Tern (USA)) 537$^{9}$ 1044$^{10}$ 1309$^{13}$ 1544$^{7}$ 1866$^{10}$ 2487$^{7}$ 2682$^{6}$ 2871$^{9}$ 3428$^{10}$ 3575$^{5}$ 3649$^{8}$ 3855$^{9}$ 3878$^{5}$ 4237$^{15}$ 4344$^{5}$ **>38f<**

**Jackatack (IRE)** 4 b g Astronef-Redwood Hut (Habitat) **1995:** *4493$^{8}$ 4515$^{9}$* **1996:** *14$^{10}$* **>63da 55f<**

**Jack Brown** 2 gr c Robellino (USA)-Crispahan (Critique (USA)) 3796$^{12}$ *4331$^{6}$ 4585$^{8}$* ***>63a 66f<***

**Jack Flush (IRE)** 2 b g Broken Hearted-Clubhouse Turn (IRE) (King of Clubs) 1197$^{6}$ 2044$^{4}$ 2538$^{3}$ 3411$^{2}$ 4024a$^{19}$ 4440$^{5}$ 4795$^{12}$ **>71f<**

**Jack Jennings** 3 ch c Deploy-Lareyna (Welsh Pageant) *694$^{3}$* 1114$^{3}$ 1791$^{7}$ **>77a 119f<**

**Jack Says** 2 b g Rambo Dancer (CAN)-Madam Cody (Hot Spark) 1479$^{4}$ *1968$^{3}$ 2083$^{2}$ 2396$^{10}$* 3982$^{9}$ 4298$^{8}$ 4594$^{9}$ **>55a 61f<**

**Jackson Falls** 2 ch g Dunbeath (USA)-Hysteria (Prince Bee) 2720$^{2}$ 4245$^{4}$ 4310$^{3}$ **>66f<**

**Jackson Hill** 3 b c Priolo (USA)-Orange Hill (High Top) (444) 693$^{5}$ (947) **>99f<**

**Jackson Park** 3 gr g Domynsky-Hysteria (Prince Bee) (483) 702$^{2}$ 803$^{10}$ 1200$^{6}$ 2067$^{11}$ 2397$^{8}$ 3855$^{10}$ **>60df<**

**Jack The Lad (IRE)** 2 b c Shalford (IRE)-Indian Honey (Indian King (USA)) 1842$^{3}$ 2040$^{12}$ 2904$^{8}$ 3411$^{3}$ 3796$^{4}$ 4072$^{4}$ **>72f<**

**Jade Age** 6 b g Forzando-Emma's Whisper (Kind of Hush) **1995:** 4524a$^{3}$

**Jade's Gem** 2 b f Sulaafah (USA)-Jadebelle (Beldale Flutter (USA)) 4062$^{13}$ 4208$^{13}$ 4368$^{8}$ **>47f<**

**Jades Shadow** 3 gr c General Wade-Gellifawr (Saulingo) 840$^{13}$ 3162$^{15}$ 3472$^{18}$ 3930$^{15}$

**Jade Venture** 5 b m Never so Bold-Our Shirley (Shirley Heights) *103$^{2}$* **>53a 72f<**

**Jady's Dream (IRE)** 5 b m Dreams to Reality (USA)-Lemon Balm (High Top) *140$^{8}$ 210$^{10}$* **>36a 40f<**

**Jagellon (USA)** 5 b h Danzig Connection (USA)-Heavenlyspun (USA) (His Majesty (USA)) *3125$^{10}$* 3447$^{12}$ 3791$^{5}$ 4176$^{11}$ **>84f<**

**Jahangir (IRE)** 7 ch g Ballad Rock-Marsh Benham (Dragonara Palace (USA)) **1995:** *4421$^{15}$ 4490$^{7}$* **>31a 32f< (DEAD)**

**Jahid (USA)** 4 ch c Diesis-Hot Topic (USA) (The Minstrel (CAN)) 286a$^{4}$ **>111f<**

**Jalb (IRE)** 2 b c Robellino (USA)-Adjacent (IRE) (Doulab (USA)) 3245$^{6}$ 3794$^{5}$ 4100$^{8}$ **>76f<**

**Jalcanto** 6 ch g Jalmood (USA)-Bella Canto (Crooner) *236$^{5}$ 1091$^{4}$* 1529$^{3}$ 1847$^{3}$ 2804$^{5}$ 3149$^{5}$ (3775) 4203$^{12}$ **>48a 62f<**

**Jalmaid** 4 ch f Jalmood (USA)-Misowni (Niniski (USA)) **1995:** *(4409) 4503$^{3}$* **1996:** *153$^{4}$ 199$^{8}$ 301$^{2}$ 384$^{12}$ 527$^{8}$ 1096$^{7}$ 1487$^{3}$ 1821$^{12}$ 2082$^{U}$ 2372$^{8}$ 3062$^{5}$ 3334$^{6}$* ***>60a 38f<***

**Jalore** 7 gr g Jalmood (USA)-Lorelene (FR) (Lorenzaccio) 2217$^{4}$ **>3a 41df<**

**Jamaican Flight (USA)** 3 b c Sunshine Forever (USA)-Kalamona (USA) (Hawaii) 1050$^{4}$ 1771$^{10}$ 2141$^{5}$ (2927) 3329$^{3}$ 3667$^{2}$ **>71f<**

**Jambo** 3 b f Rambo Dancer (CAN)-Nicholess (Nicholas Bill) 973$^{14}$ 1885$^{8}$ (2567) 3102$^{2}$ (3334) **>70f<**

**James Is Special (IRE)** 8 b g Lyphard's Special (USA)-High Explosive (Mount Hagen (FR)) 546$^{20}$ **>26f<**

**Jamrat Jumairah (IRE)** 3 b f Polar Falcon (USA)-Coryana (Sassafras (FR)) (3353) **>91+f<**

**Jamrat Samya (IRE)** 2 b f Sadler's Wells (USA)-Samya's Flame (Artaius (USA)) 4570$^{5}$ **>71f<**

**Jandeel (IRE)** 4 b c Last Tycoon-Pizziri (Artaius (USA)) *434a$^{3}$* **>88a 106f<**

**Janglynyve** 2 ch f Sharpo-Wollow Maid (Wollow) *1021$^{4}$* 1513$^{10}$ 3171$^{4}$ 3632$^{3}$ 4106$^{15}$ **>65f<**

**Janib (USA)** 2 ch c Diesis-Shicklah (USA) (The Minstrel (CAN)) 958$^{4}$ (3250) (3692) 4191$^{5}$ **>105f<**

**Janie's Boy** 2 b c Persian Bold-Cornelian (Great Nephew) 924$^{5}$ 4380$^{12}$ 4751$^{3}$ 4903$^{9}$ *4976$^{7}$* **>37a 70f<**

**Janies Girl (IRE)** 3 ch f Persian Heights-Lovat Spring (USA) (Storm Bird (CAN)) 1485$^{11}$ 4701$^{18}$ **>48f<**

**Jaraab** 5 b g Sure Blade (USA)-Ostora (USA) (Blushing Groom (FR)) **1995:** *(4355) (4384) 4442$^{5}$* **1996:** *296$^{4}$ (339) 474$^{9}$ (603) (837) 1343$^{7}$ (1488)* **>91a 39f<**

**Jarah (USA)** 3 b c Forty Niner (USA)-Umniyatee (Green Desert (USA)) 1824$^{5}$ (2354) 3071$^{9}$ 4194$^{3}$ 4479$^{5}$ 4620$^{6}$ **>106f<**

**Jareer Do (IRE)** 4 b f Jareer (USA)-Shining Bright (USA) (Bold Bidder) *1689$^{4}$* 2345$^{2}$ 4888$^{10}$ **>40a 67f<**

**Jari (USA)** 5 b g Dixieland Band (USA)-Dusty Heart (USA) (Run Dusty Run (USA)) **1995:** *4416$^{13}$ 4476$^{15}$* **1996:** *18$^{11}$* **>72f<**

**Jarrow** 5 ch g Jalmood (USA)-Invite (Be My Guest (USA)) **1995:** *4370$^{6}$ 4506$^{7}$* **1996:** *87$^{7}$ 604$^{6}$* **>18a 48f<**

**Jarvey (IRE)** 4 ch g Jareer (USA)-Blue Czarina (Sandhurst Prince) *553$^{12}$ 1012$^{10}$* ***>8a 16f<***

**Jaseur (USA)** 3 b c Lear Fan (USA)-Spur Wing (USA) (Storm Bird (CAN)) 1434$^{4}$ **>77f<**

**Jashin (IRE)** 3 c 1395a$^{8}$ **>83f<**

**Jato** 7 b g Pharly (FR)-Minsden's Image (Dancers Image (USA)) *4202$^{7}$* 4428$^{9}$ **>3a 74f<**

**Jaunty Jack** 2 b c Midyan (USA)-Juliette Marny (Blakeney) 4163a$^{2}$ 4492$^{2}$ 4920$^{2}$ **>88+f<**

**Java Bay** 2 b f Statoblest-Flopsy (Welsh Pageant) 3796$^{9}$ 4087$^{10}$ 4783$^{5}$ **>50f<**

**Java Red (IRE)** 4 b g Red Sunset-Coffee Bean (Doulab (USA)) *853$^{12}$* 1830$^{5}$ *2369$^{16}$ 3958$^{4}$* ***>57?a 60f<***

**Jawaal** 6 ch g Soviet Star (USA)-Pencil Sharpener (USA) (Sharpen Up) 728$^{8}$ 876$^{14}$ 1112$^{12}$ 1484$^{11}$ 3782$^{6}$ 4308$^{5}$ 4444$^{19}$ 4620$^{7}$ **>86f<**

**Jawhari** 2 b c Lahib (USA)-Lady of the Land (Wollow) 2852$^{2}$ 3794$^{4}$ **>87f<**

**Jayannpee** 5 ch g Doulab (USA)-Amina (Brigadier Gerard) 711$^{8}$ (928) (1107) 1818$^{9}$ 2114$^{10}$ (2880) 3232$^{9}$ 3759$^{4}$ (4173a) 4442$^{8}$ **>113f<**

**Jay-Gee-Em** 2 b f Aragon-Mana (GER) (Windwurf (GER)) *(3092)* (3343) 4037a$^{11}$ **>61f<**

**Jay-Owe-Two (IRE)** 2 b g Distinctly North (USA)-Fiery Song (Ballad Rock) 5034$^{7}$ **>70f<**

**Jay Tee Ef (IRE)** 2 br c Mac's Imp (USA)-Arachosia (Persian Bold) *3604$^{7}$ 3950$^{6}$ 4572$^{10}$ 5005$^{8}$* ***>36a 19f<***

**Jazz King** 3 br g Kalaglow-Sabrine (Mount Hagen (FR)) (2015) 2576$^{3}$ 3155$^{4}$ 3669$^{8}$ **>85f<**

**Jean de Florette (USA)** 5 b g Our Native (USA)-The Branks (USA) (Hold Your Peace (USA)) *604$^{4}$ 760$^{3}$ 1031$^{2}$ 1472$^{9}$* 1965$^{7}$ 2165$^{11}$ *2936$^{7}$ 4984$^{13}$* **>34a 42f<**

**Jeanne Cutrona** 3 b f Risk Me (FR)-Veuve Perrin (Legend of France (USA)) 1692$^{6}$ **>4f<**

**Jean Pierre** 3 b c Anshan-Astolat (Rusticaro (FR)) 693$^{9}$ 2067$^{10}$ 2506$^{2}$ 3341$^{2}$ 3586$^{9}$ 4000$^{17}$ 4968$^{13}$ **>61f<**

**Jebi (USA)** 6 b g Phone Trick (USA)-Smokey Legend (USA) (Hawaii) *320$^{6}$ 351$^{3}$ 499$^{10}$ 2316$^{5}$* 2566$^{4}$ 2933$^{5}$ **>49a 42df<**

**Jedi Knight** 2 b c Emarati (USA)-Hannie Caulder (Workboy) 2865$^{4}$ 3250$^{3}$ 3464$^{4}$ **>67f<**

**Jeffrey Anotherred** 2 b g Emarati (USA)-First Pleasure (Dominion) 2614$^{3}$ (3241) 3577$^{3}$ (4049) 4303$^{2}$ (5043) **>96f<**

**Jelali (IRE)** 3 b g Last Tycoon-Lautreamont (Auction Ring (USA)) 894$^{15}$ 1641$^{17}$ 1833$^{4}$ *4095$^{12}$ 4476$^{3}$* 4832$^{13}$ **>69f<**

**Jellaby Askhir** 4 b c Salse (USA)-Circus Act (Shirley Heights) 875$^{8}$ **>108f<**

**Jemima Puddleduck** 5 ch m Tate Gallery (USA)-Tittlemouse (Castle Keep) **1995:** *(4412)* **1996:** *4986$^{11}$* **>49a 52f<**

**Jemsilverthorn (IRE)** 3 b g Maelstrom Lake-Fairy Don (Don) **1995:** *4353$^{6}$ 4439$^{7}$ 4491$^{6}$ 4518$^{7}$ 4538$^{7}$* **1996:** *10$^{2}$ 118$^{5}$ 264$^{4}$ 2427$^{8}$ 3091$^{8}$ 3602$^{14}$ 3957$^{9}$* ***>44a 41f<***

**Jendali Princess** 3 ro f Jendali (USA)-Hyperion Princess (Dragonara Palace (USA)) *4997$^{9}$*

**Jennelle** 2 b f Nomination-Its A Romp (Hotfoot) (465) (715) 2051$^{12}$ (2595) 2890$^{2}$ 3903a$^{3}$ 4285a$^{4}$ 4579$^{2}$ (4893) **>89f<**

**Jenny's Charmer** 3 ch c Charmer-Jenny Wyllie (Nishapour (FR)) 1527$^{13}$ 1761$^{9}$ 3102$^{14}$ 3256$^{11}$ **>17a 34f<**

**Jeopardize** 3 b f Polish Patriot (USA)-Extra Cost (USA) (Vaguely Noble) 2572$^{5}$ 2996$^{9}$ 3986$^{12}$ 4263$^{16}$ **>56f<**

**Jermyn Street (USA)** 5 b h Alleged (USA)-My Mother Mary (USA) (Boldnesian) *682$^{9}$* 1426$^{2}$ 2882$^{6}$ 3037$^{7}$ **>79f<**

**Jerry Cutrona (IRE)** 3 br g Distinctly North (USA)-Foulkesmills (Tanfirion) **1995:** *4361$^{3}$* **1996:** *676$^{5}$* 756$^{5}$ 937$^{11}$ (1693) 1805$^{3}$ 2754$^{4}$ 3045$^{4}$ (3271) (3461) 3790$^{3}$ 4463$^{22}$ 4556$^{3}$ **>62a 97f<**

**Jersey Belle** 4 b f Distant Relative-Hong Kong Girl (Petong) **1995:** *4357$^{8}$ 4486$^{4}$* **1996:** *76$^{7}$ 163$^{7}$ 203$^{2}$ (273)* **>52a 53f<**

**Jess C's Whirl (USA)** 6 br h Island Whirl (USA)-Proud Woman (USA) (Proudest Roman (USA)) *4951a$^{13}$* **>97a f<**

**Jessica's Song** 3 b f Colmore Row-Sideloader Special (Song) 743$^{6}$ 861$^{10}$ 1170$^{5}$ 1592$^{4}$ 2286$^{20}$ *2684$^{8}$* **>51a 58f<**

**Jewel Princess (USA)** 4 b f Key To The Mint (USA)-Jewell Ridge (USA) (Melyno) *(4952a)* **>118a f<**

**Jezyah (USA)** 3 ch f Chief's Crown (USA)-Empress Jackie (USA) (Mount Hagen (FR)) 2585$^{6}$ 3148$^{W}$ 4238$^{13}$ **>81f<**

**Jhazi** 2 b c Arazi (USA)-Shoot Clear (Bay Express) (4228) 4723$^{10}$ 4873$^{4}$ **>97f<**

**Jibereen** 4 b g Lugana Beach-Fashion Lover (Shiny Tenth) 554$^{6}$ 4975$^{17}$ **>51f<**

**Jib Jab** 2 br g Jendali (USA)-No Rejection (Mummy's Pet) 733$^{2}$ 800$^{5}$ 3057$^{6}$ 3227$^{7}$ 3969$^{12}$ **>67f<**

**Jigsaw Boy** 7 ch g Homeboy-Chiparia (Song) **1995:** *4377$^{2}$ (4447) 4502$^{4}$ 4514$^{6}$* **1996:** *59$^{6}$ 135$^{4}$ (311) 356$^{3}$ 806$^{6}$* 893$^{5}$ 981$^{9}$ 1348$^{10}$ *(1460) 1812$^{5}$ 3953$^{10}$ 4077$^{7}$ (4979)* **>75a 60f<**

**Jilly Beveled** 4 b f Beveled (USA)-Karens Valentine (Daring March) *3474$^{5}$* 3761$^{5}$ 4082$^{4}$ 4480$^{2}$ **>47f<**

**Jilly Woo 2** gr f Environment Friend-William's Bird (USA) (Master Willie) *1590$^{3}$* 1851$^{5}$ 2429$^{5}$ 4230$^{7}$ 4546$^{15}$ 4715$^{7}$ 4787$^{3}$ **>60f<**

**Jimbo 5** b h Salse (USA)-Damelle (Shirley Heights) *186$^{15}$* **>7a 39f<**

**Jimjareer (IRE) 3** br c Jareer (USA)-Onthecomet (Chief Singer) 769$^{10}$ 1042$^{5}$ *1490$^{10}$ 1721$^{4}$ 2241$^{3}$* 2521$^{7}$ 3052$^{14}$ 4904$^{8}$ **>50a 57f<**

**Jimmy-S (IRE) 3** b g Marju (IRE)-Amber Fizz (USA) (Effervescing (USA)) 3425$^{11}$ 3882$^{8}$

**Jimmy the Skunk (IRE) 5** b g Fayruz-Very Seldom (Rarity) 3384a$^{3}$ (4799) *4979$^{8}$* **>52a 70f<**

**Jingoist (IRE) 2** b f Polish Patriot (USA)-Hot Curry (USA) (Sharpen Up) *895$^{6}$ 1166$^{7}$ 1491$^{6}$ 2207$^{2}$* 2795$^{5}$ *3087$^{2}$ (3455)* 3648$^{5}$ 4097$^{2}$ 4223$^{2}$ 4562$^{18}$ *4980$^{5}$* **>51a 57f<**

**Jive Boogie 2** b br c Nomination-Jive Music (Music Boy) *4244$^{16}$*

***Jiyush* 3** b c Generous (IRE)-Urjwan (USA) (Seattle Slew (USA)) 845$^{3}$ 1461$^{2}$ 2601$^{2}$ 3504$^{2}$ (3983) (4260) 4771$^{12}$ 4965$^{9}$ **>109f<**

**Jobber's Fiddle 4** b f Sizzling Melody-Island Mead (Pharly (FR)) *37$^{2}$ 82$^{9}$ 104$^{13}$* **>40a 55f<**

**Jobie 6** b g Precocious-Lingering (Kind of Hush) 1715$^{3}$ 1958$^{10}$ 2976$^{8}$ 3278$^{7}$ 3585$^{8}$ **>67f<**

**Jo Coleman 2** b f Puissance-Miss Echo (Chief Singer) 4546$^{17}$ **>20f<**

**Joe Jagger (IRE) 5** b g Petorius-Seapoint (Major Point) 4726$^{13}$ **>6a 34f<**

**Johan Cruyff 2** b c Danehill (USA)-Teslemi (USA) (Ogygian (USA)) 4398a$^{5}$ (4846a) **>92f<**

**Johayro 3** ch g Clantime-Arroganza (Crofthall) *335$^{4}$ 407$^{9}$ 443$^{16}$* 773$^{8}$ 1823$^{9}$ 2561$^{8}$ 2791$^{5}$ 3883$^{2}$ 4246$^{17}$ 4367$^{6}$ 4616$^{14}$ 5039$^{15}$ **>68a 59f<**

**John Emms (IRE) 2** ch c Shalford (IRE)-Miss Lee Ann (Tumble Wind (USA)) 1315$^{5}$ 3994$^{8}$ **>71f<**

**Johnnie the Joker 5** gr g Absalom-Magic Tower (Tower Walk) **1995:** *4392$^{6}$ 4432$^{5}$ 4476$^{10}$* **1996:** *282$^{8}$ 371$^{5}$ 480$^{5}$ 778$^{2}$ (1423)* 1674$^{8}$ *2084$^{5}$ (2306) 2552$^{2}$ 2749$^{7}$ 3419$^{5}$ 4078$^{12}$ 4240$^{3}$* 4692$^{7}$ 4906$^{8}$ **>80a 56f<**

**Johnny Staccato 2** b g Statoblest-Frasquita (Song) (3796) 4065$^{4}$ 4555$^{6}$ 4873$^{6}$ **>97f<**

**John O'Dreams 11** b g Indian King (USA)-Mississipi Shuffle (Steel Heart) *601$^{19}$* 700$^{3}$ 862$^{5}$ 951$^{5}$ 1684$^{7}$ (2244) 2586$^{10}$ 2787$^{6}$ 2992$^{3}$ 3323$^{6}$ 3930$^{6}$ 4088$^{3}$ 4372$^{3}$ **>56f<**

**Johns Act (USA) 6** b g Late Act (USA)-Deluxe Type (USA) (Singh (USA)) *19$^{6}$ 75$^{5}$ 312$^{2}$ 392$^{11}$ 647$^{7}$* 712$^{5}$ 1524$^{8}$ 4580$^{13}$ 4919$^{11}$ **>72a 62f<**

**Johns Joy 11** b g Martin John-Saybya (Sallust) 1772$^{6}$ 1953$^{15}$ 2192$^{5}$ 2574$^{24}$ **>37f<**

**John's Law (IRE) 3** b g Contract Law (USA)-Vieux Carre (Pas de Seul) *637$^{14}$* 2970$^{4}$ 3506$^{10}$ 3937$^{18}$ 4045$^{5}$ 4430$^{13}$ **>52f<**

**John-T 3** b c Thatching-Ower (IRE) (Lomond (USA)) 544$^{10}$ 1142$^{7}$ 1714$^{6}$ *3063$^{7}$ 3457$^{8}$* 4322$^{10}$ 4559$^{15}$ **>65a 54f<**

**John Tufty 5** ch g Vin St Benet-Raffles Virginia (Whistling Deer) 2192$^{16}$ 2537$^{15}$ **>16f<**

**Joint Venture (IRE) 2** b c Common Grounds-Renata's Ring (IRE) (Auction Ring (USA)) 441$^{2}$ 523$^{4}$ 841$^{2}$ 1008$^{2}$ (1404) 1766$^{3}$ 2965$^{10}$ 3160$^{9}$ 4893$^{3}$ **>84f<**

**Jolis Absent 6** b m Primo Dominie-Jolimo (Fortissimo) *4509$^{20}$* ***>32a 31f<***

**Joli's Great 8** ch m Vaigly Great-Jolimo (Fortissimo) *508$^{12}$* 2192$^{22}$ **>17f<**

**Jolis Present 3** b c Prince Sabo-Jolimo (Fortissimo) 893$^{16}$ 1512$^{11}$ *1721$^{P}$* **>58f< (DEAD)**

**Joli's Prince 2** b g Superlative-Joli's Girl (Mansingh (USA)) 4261$^{9}$ 4720$^{17}$ **>60f<**

**Jolly Hokey 4** b g Dominion-Judy's Dowry (Dragonara Palace (USA)) *517$^{3}$ 782$^{11}$* **>37a 45f<**

**Jolly Jackson 2** br c Primo Dominie-Pounelta (Tachypous) 4891$^{15}$ **>11f<**

**Jolto 7** b g Noalto-Joytime (John de Coombe) 2000$^{8}$ 2347$^{5}$ 3076$^{5}$ *3601$^{8}$ 3877$^{13}$ 4573$^{7}$ 4789$^{12}$* ***>63a 59f<***

**Jo Maximus 4** b g Prince Sabo-Final Call (Town Crier) *633$^{3}$* 744$^{2}$ 876$^{10}$ 1790$^{5}$ 2400$^{8}$ 2981$^{10}$ (3967) **>81f<**

**Jo Mell 3** b g Efisio-Militia Girl (Rarity) *701$^{9}$* 935$^{10}$ 1127$^{8}$ 1432$^{2}$ 1785$^{4}$ 2328$^{3}$ 2722$^{5}$ 3833$^{3}$ 3933$^{2}$ 4583$^{4}$ 4688$^{3}$ **>89f<**

**Jona Holley 3** b g Sharpo-Spurned (USA) (Robellino (USA)) 669$^{9}$ 887$^{18}$ 1416$^{10}$ 1999$^{5}$ 2192$^{7}$ **>56f<**

**Jonfy (IRE) 2** b g Waajib-Hyland Rose (Steel Heart) 2614$^{6}$ 2852$^{11}$ 2942$^{10}$ 4764$^{12}$ 4990$^{17}$ **>48f<**

**Jonny's Joker 2** b c Precocious-Mardessa (Ardross) 4228$^{15}$

**Jon's Choice 8** b g Andy Rew-Whangarei (Gold Rod) **1995:** *4377$^{7}$ 4456$^{11}$ 4512$^{9}$* **1996:** *30$^{4}$ 190$^{8}$ 219$^{7}$ 343$^{7}$ 393$^{9}$ 418$^{3}$ 653$^{5}$ 981$^{4}$ 1083$^{2}$ 1460$^{4}$ 1606$^{4}$ 1789$^{10}$ 2085$^{10}$ 2550$^{11}$ 2632$^{7}$ 3252$^{8}$ 4977$^{12}$* **>20a 28f<**

**Jovian 2** gr f Petong-What A Pet (Mummy's Pet) *4570$^{11}$* ***>46f<***

**Jovie King (IRE) 4** ch g Salt Dome (USA)-Jovial Josie (USA) (Sea Bird II) 844$^{13}$ *1095$^{10}$ 1468$^{18}$* 1613$^{7}$ *1719$^{9}$ 2285$^{7}$* ***>14a 39f<***

**Joyeuse Entree 2** gr f Kendor (FR)-Cape Of Good Hope (FR) (Crystal Glitters (USA)) 2269a$^{2}$ (4291a) **>104f<**

**Joyful Joy 2** b f River God (USA)-Joyfulness (FR) (Cure The Blues (USA)) 2043$^{9}$ 2429$^{7}$ 3121$^{8}$ **>31f<**

**Joyful Times 4** br f Doc Marten-Time for Joy (Good Times (ITY)) *76$^{14}$ 295$^{6}$ 342$^{9}$* **>36da 24f<**

**Joy of Glory (USA) 7** b h General Holme (USA)-Joy Returned (USA) (Big Spruce (USA)) 3906a$^{3}$ **>110f<**

**Joza 2** b f Marju (IRE)-Gold Runner (Runnett) (3660) 4247$^{4}$ 4893$^{4}$ **>84f<**

**Juba 4** b f Dowsing (USA)-Try the Duchess (Try My Best (USA)) **1995:** *4382$^{5}$* **1996:** *1030$^{4}$ 1314$^{10}$ 1719$^{15}$ 4076$^{8}$ 4989$^{13}$* **>45a 45f<**

**Jubilee Place (IRE) 3** br f Prince Sabo-Labelon Lady (Touching Wood (USA)) *888$^{11}$* 1181$^{13}$ 1805$^{6}$ 2320$^{9}$ 2785$^{7}$ 3167$^{14}$ 3585$^{6}$ **>52f<**

**Jucea 7** b m Bluebird (USA)-Appleby Park (Bay Express) 601$^{12}$ 862$^{2}$ 1064$^{4}$ (1307) (1501) 1829$^{8}$ 2381$^{6}$ 2548$^{3}$ 2976$^{3}$ 3432$^{14}$ 3482$^{5}$ 3930$^{3}$ 4088$^{4}$ 4452$^{11}$ 4616$^{5}$ 4791$^{10}$ 4811$^{5}$ **>67f<**

**Jucinda 2** gr f Midyan (USA)-Catch The Sun (Kalaglow) 4697$^{10}$ 4969$^{21}$ 5041$^{10}$ **>53f<**

**Judgement Call 9** b g Alzao (USA)-Syllabub (Silly Season) 846$^{10}$ (1049) 1446$^{5}$ 1777$^{9}$ 2156$^{5}$ 2434$^{7}$ 2787$^{10}$ 3442$^{7}$ 4045$^{7}$ 4259$^{11}$ **>51f<**

**Judicial Field (IRE) 7** b g Law Society (USA)-Bold Meadows (Persian Bold) 625$^{11}$ 767$^{9}$ 1022$^{7}$ **>68f<**

**Judicial Supremacy 2** b c Warning-Song Test (USA) (The Minstrel (CAN)) 4818$^{2}$ **>85f<**

**Juicy Ting 2** ch g Hatim (USA)-Floating Note (Music Boy) 2755$^{7}$ 3687$^{11}$ 3840$^{3}$ 4319$^{2}$ 4482$^{6}$ **>62f<**

**Jukebox Jive 2** ch f Scottish Reel-My Sweet Melody (Music Boy) 3848$^{7}$ 3982$^{15}$ **>52f<**

**Juliasdarkinvader 6** br g Lidhame-Una Donna (GER) (Windwurf (GER)) *(275) 365$^{6}$ 485$^{3}$ 666$^{4}$ 1444$^{3}$ 1772$^{5}$ 3610$^{P}$* **>47a 52f< (DEAD)**

**Julia's Relative 2** b f Distant Relative-Alkion (Fordham (USA)) 4756$^{19}$ **>47f<**

**Julietta Mia (USA) 2** ch f Woodman (USA)-Just Juliet (USA) (What A Pleasure (USA)) 2611$^{11}$ 2985$^{4}$ 3493$^{8}$ 4106$^{2}$ (4501) 4760$^{2}$ 4795$^{2}$ **>73f<**

**Jumairah Sunset 3** ch f Be My Guest (USA)-Catalonda (African Sky) 2004$^{3}$ 2529$^{3}$ (4108) 4432$^{15}$ **>76f<**

**Jumilla (USA) 4** b f El Gran Senor (USA)-Refill (Mill Reef (USA)) *396a$^{4}$* **>111f<**

**Jump The Lights 3** b g Siberian Express (USA)-Turtle Dove (Gyr (USA)) 471$^{6}$ *(651) 954$^{6}$* 1325$^{4}$ **>60a 63f<**

**Junction Twentytwo 6** ch g Local Suitor (USA)-Pollinella (Charlottown) *152$^{10}$* **>57f<**

**Jundi (IRE) 5** b g Sadler's Wells (USA)-Royal Sister II (Claude) 1478$^{10}$ 1784$^{7}$ 2117$^{9}$ *2936$^{5}$ 3855$^{5}$* 4321$^{8}$ **>36a 56f<**

**Jungle Fresh 3** b g Rambo Dancer (CAN)-Report 'em (USA) (Staff Writer (USA)) 2589$^{4}$ 3425$^{W}$ 4322$^{6}$ 4429$^{11}$ **>52f<**

**Jungle Patrol (IRE) 4** ch c Night Shift (USA)-Jungle Rose (Shirley Heights) *181$^{11}$ 299$^{2}$ 318$^{3}$ 393$^{2}$ 765$^{10}$* 991$^{10}$ 1341$^{5}$ 1698$^{5}$ 1886$^{6}$ *2085$^{6}$ 2212$^{7}$* ***>58a 60f<***

**Junie (IRE) 2** ch f Astronef-Numidia (Sallust) 4062$^{7}$ 4380$^{6}$ 4756$^{13}$ **>74f<**

**Junior Ben (IRE) 4** b g Tirol-Piney Pass (Persian Bold) 1421$^{4}$ 1655$^{4}$ 2191$^{7}$ 2549$^{6}$ 2952$^{4}$ 3141$^{6}$ 3584$^{10}$ 4237$^{10}$ 4448$^{11}$ 4815$^{6}$ 4910$^{7}$ **>45f<**

**Jupiter (IRE) 2** b c Astronef-Native Flower (Tumble Wind (USA)) *(2083) 2607$^{9}$* 3436$^{5}$ 3924$^{6}$ **>65+a 68f<**

**Jural 4** ch f Kris-Just Cause (Law Society (USA)) *535a$^{4}$ 929$^{2}$* 2227$^{2}$ 2886$^{5}$ **>76a 101f<**

**Just A Guess (IRE) 5** ch g Classic Secret (USA)-Wild Justice (Sweet Revenge) 2626$^{6}$ **>15f<**

**Just a Single (IRE) 5** b g Adbass (USA)-Sniggy (Belfort (FR)) **1995:** *4362$^{13}$ 4416$^{12}$* **>38a 49f<**

**Just Bob 7** b g Alleging (USA)-Diami (Swing Easy (USA)) 475$^{6}$ 601$^{9}$ 659$^{3}$ 762$^{11}$ (911) (997) (1039) 1161$^{2}$ **>56a 75+f<**

**Just by Chance 4** b g Teenoso (USA)-Skerryvore (Kalaglow) **1995:** *4448$^{11}$* **>22f<**

**Just Dissident (IRE) 4** b g Dancing Dissident (USA)-Betty Bun (St Chad) 610$^{10}$ 735$^{9}$ 956$^{5}$ 1161$^{5}$ 1538$^{13}$ 2005$^{10}$ 2185$^{9}$ 2366$^{13}$ 2518$^{2}$ 2757$^{3}$ (2867) 3085$^{10}$ 3352$^{5}$ 3482$^{3}$ 3643$^{4}$ (3868) 4180$^{13}$ 4246$^{18}$ 4382$^{5}$ **>64f<**

**Juste Ciel (FR) 4** 4655a$^{10}$

**Just Flamenco 5** ch g Scorpio (FR)-Suzannah's Song (Song) **1995:** *4390$^{5}$ 4445$^{5}$ 4537$^{8}$* **1996:** *196$^{10}$ 688$^{10}$* 883$^{13}$ **>53a 56f<**

**Justforthercord 4** br f Forzando-Classical Vintage (Stradavinsky) **1995:** *4363$^{8}$* **>28a 42f<**

**Just Grand (IRE) 2** b c Green Desert (USA)-Aljood (Kris) 4884$^{4}$ 5033$^{10}$ **>68f<**

**Just Harry 5** ch h High Kicker (USA)-Dorame (Music Boy) 2577$^{7}$ 2796$^{2}$ 3052$^{5}$ 3469$^{7}$ 3606$^{2}$ 3694$^{10}$ *4078$^{10}$ 4337$^{5}$* 4692$^{5}$ 4882$^{7}$ **>84da 58f<**

**Justinianus (IRE) 4** ch c Try My Best (USA)-Justitia (Dunbeath (USA)) *65$^{7}$ 117$^{11}$ 229$^{3}$ 295$^{3}$ 334$^{4}$ 406$^{10}$ 511$^{8}$ 1030$^{7}$ 1094$^{10}$ 1516$^{3}$* 1992$^{9}$ 2286$^{15}$ 2577$^{14}$ 2785$^{10}$ 3140$^{6}$ 3274$^{6}$ 3661$^{8}$ *3877$^{10}$ 4202$^{12}$* ***>44a 45f<***

**Just Lady 3** b f Emarati (USA)-Just Run (IRE) (Runnett) 1646$^{W}$ 2021$^{9}$ 2186$^{8}$ 3261$^{5}$ 3579$^{4}$ 3883$^{W}$ *4090$^{12}$ 4372$^{20}$* ***>50f<***

**Just Lex 3** b g Ballacashtal (CAN)-Mio Mementa (Streak) 3320$^{9}$

**Just Loui 2** gr g Lugana Beach-Absaloui (Absalom) *895$^{9}$ (1080)* 1471$^{6}$ 2174$^{3}$ *2635$^{U}$ 3604$^{2}$ 3823$^{5}$* 4230$^{6}$ *4777$^{2}$* **>68a 63f<**

**Just Lucky (IRE) 4** b g Fools Holme (USA)-Miss Victoria (Auction Ring (USA)) **1995:** *4388$^{11}$ 4448$^{4}$* **1996:** *206$^{9}$ 246$^{11}$ 520$^{4}$ 656$^{8}$* **>43a 37f<**

**Just-Mana-Mou (IRE) 4** b g Caerleon (USA)-Clarista (USA) (Riva Ridge (USA)) **1995:** *4420$^{3}$ 4452$^{2}$ 4516$^{5}$ 4546$^{3}$* **>62a 60f<**

**Just Millie (USA) 3** ch f Elmaamul (USA)-La Plus Belle (USA) (Robellino (USA)) 641[14] 1172[9] 1648[5] 1908[8] 2133[3] 2592[3] 2766[3] 3591[3] 3849[11] (3977) 4240[13] 4498[3] 4860[15] 4915[2] **>65f<**

**Just Nick 2** b c Nicholas (USA)-Just Never Know (USA) (Riverman (USA)) 865[3] 1822[4] 4475[3] 4878[2] (5051) **>79f<**

**Just Typical 2** ch f Timeless Times (USA)-Mayor (Laxton) 823[11]

**Just Visiting 2** b f Superlative-Just Julia (Natroun (FR)) *(1093) 1831[2]* 2872[3] 3251[2] (3620) 3843[3] 4113[19] **>60a 85f<**

**Juwwi 2** ch c Mujtahid (USA)-Nouvelle Star (AUS) (Luskin Star (AUS)) 2057[2] (2243) 2607[2] **>104f<**

**Juyush (USA) 4** b c Silver Hawk (USA)-Silken Doll (USA) (Chieftain II) *(456)* 919[8] 1706[3] 2117[8] **>119f<**

## K

**Kaafih Homm (IRE) 5** b g Kefaah (USA)-Shereeka (Shergar) **1995:** *4451[2] 4544[2]* **1996:** *13[3] 2130[10]* 2300[4] 2736[2] 2862[4] (2921) 3136[2] 3509[5] (3802) 3944[2] 4515[W] **>77a 78f<**

**Kabalevsky (USA) 3** b c Nureyev (USA)-Beautiful Aly (USA) (Alydar (USA)) 2432[11] **>25f<**

**Kabcast 11** b g Kabour-Final Cast (Saulingo) *2395[5]* 2518[6] 2910[11] (3294) 3352[6] 3643[10] 3868[10] 3957[5] 4473[9] **>13a 39f<**

**Kadamann (IRE) 4** b c Doyoun-Kadissya (USA) (Blushing Groom (FR)) 1193[10] 1767[9] **>80f<**

**Kadari 7** b m Commanche Run-Thoughtful (Northfields (USA)) 1019[9] 1529[10] 1828[7] **>29f<**

**Kadastrof (FR) 6** ch h Port Etienne (FR)-Kadastra (FR) (Stradavinsky) 647[2] (712) 1005[16] 1194[15] 1976[7] 4683[18] **>91df<**

**Kadeena 2** b f Never so Bold-Alencon (Northfields (USA)) (4748) 4908[3] **>75f<**

**Kadiri (IRE) 5** b g Darshaan-Kadissya (USA) (Blushing Groom (FR)) **1995:** *4411[11] 4434[4]* **1996:** *4789[16] 4984[8]* **>60a 67?f<**

**Kafaf (USA) 2** b br f Zilzal (USA)-Alqwani (USA) (Mr Prospector (USA)) 3499[7] 4052[4] 4500[2] **>80f<**

**Kaffir (IRE) 2** b c Alzao (USA)-Kenitra (ITY) (Head for Heights) (4171a)

**Kafhar 3** b c In The Wings-Ittisaal (Caerleon (USA)) **1995:** 4424a[3] **1996:** 1580a[6]

**Kafil (USA) 2** b br c Housebuster (USA)-Alchaasibiyeh (USA) (Seattle Slew (USA)) 4514[13] 4756[8] **>80f<**

**Kahal 2** b c Machiavellian (USA)-Just a Mirage (Green Desert (USA)) *4100[2]* (4461) 4759[5] **>102f<**

**Kahir Almaydan (IRE) 3** b c Distinctly North (USA)-Kilfenora (Tribal Chief) 727[2] 1141a[5] 2271a[5] 3083[4] 3524[5] **>116f<**

**Kairine (IRE) 3** b f Kahyasi-Reamur (Top Ville) 1305[10] 1656[12] 2015[4] **>47f<**

**Kaiser Kache (IRE) 2** b c Treasure Kay-Poka Poka (FR) (King Of Macedon) 2040[14] 2309[5] 2904[2] 3237[2] (3659) 4024a[17] 4131[14] 4566[14] (4880) 5038[3] **>82f<**

**Kai's Lady (IRE) 3** b f Jareer (USA)-Rathnaleen (Scorpio (FR)) *197[5] 329[7] 522[11]* 1665[16] **>9f<**

**Kaitak (IRE) 5** ch g Broken Hearted-Klairelle (Klairon) 2534[5] 3710[21] **>46a 79f<**

**Kalabo (USA) 4** b c Trempolino (USA)-Kalikala (Darshaan) (1706) (2864) 3157[6] 4178[2] 4441[5] 4876[7] 5045[3] **>117f<**

**Kalamata 4** ch c Kalaglow-Good Try (Good Bond) **1995:** *(4366)* **1996:** *75[6]* **>81da 72f<**

**Kala Noire 3** gr c Kalaglow-Noire Small (USA) (Elocutionist (USA)) *3042[4]* ***>81f<***

**Kalao Tua (IRE) 3** b f Shaadi (USA)-Lisa's Favourite (Gorytus (USA)) 964[7] 2032[7] 2412[11] **>61f<**

**Kalar 7** b g Kabour-Wind And Reign (Tumble Wind (USA)) **1995:** *4359[2] 4394[8] 4460[2] 4487[3] 4517[7]* **1996:** *139[10] 225[6] 316[3] 362[5] 500[5] 559[8]* 704[9] 931[3] 1161[9] 1545[5] *1971[8] 2064[2]* 2386[2] 2564[6] 2960[2] 3252[2] (3310) 3774[2] 3883[3] 4246[15] 4473[4] 4610[16] *4996[5]* **>59a 59f<**

**Kala Sunrise 3** ch c Kalaglow-Belle of the Dawn (Bellypha) 785[6] 1432[4] 1798[8] 2041[23] 2621[6] 3039[9] 3710[11] 3996[6] 4181[4] 4300[10] (4620) **>101?f<**

**Kalatos (GER) 4** ch c Big Shuffle (USA)-Kardia (GER) (Mister Rock's (GER)) 1755a[2] 3397a[3] 4409a[7] **>113f<**

**Kaldoun Choice (FR) 2** 5024a[8] **>91f<**

**Kaldou Star 2** ch c Kaldoun (FR)-Loisaida (FR) (Sicyos (USA)) 4653a[3] **>89f<**

**Kalimat 2** b f Be My Guest (USA)-Kantado (Saulingo) 3259[8] 3675[2] 4748[2] **>75f<**

**Kalinini (USA) 2** ch c Seattle Dancer (USA)-Kaiserfahrt (GER) (Frontal) 3987[10] 4386[3] 4618[4] **>73f<**

**Kalinka (IRE) 2** b f Soviet Star (USA)-Tralthee (USA) (Tromos) 2147[3] (2714) 4369[2] **>86f<**

**Kalisko (FR) 6** b g Cadoudal (FR)-Mista (FR) (Misti IV) *221[7]*

**Kalko 7** b g Kalaglow-Salchow (Niniski (USA)) *1167[13]* 1544[8] 2563[9] 2871[8] **>23a 19f<**

**Kalmoss (FR) 3** b c Kaldoun (FR)-Mossma (FR) (Tip Moss (FR)) **1995:** 4499a[2] **1996:** 1133a[2] 1756a[4] **>104f<**

**Kalou 5** b m K-Battery-Louise Moulton (Moulton) *4073[3]* 4227[8] 4626[10] 4905[2] 5054[10] **>70f<**

**Kalousion 2** b g K-Battery-Louise Moulton (Moulton) 4502[4] 4584[10] **>30f<**

**Kamari (USA) 3** ch c Woodman (USA)-Karri Valley (USA) (Storm Bird (CAN)) 982[2] 1174[2] (2166) 2693[5] 3295[2] 3923[9] 4352[6] **>93f<**

**Kama Simba 4** b g Lear Fan (USA)-Dance It (USA) (Believe It (USA)) 752[22] 1099[11] 2373[9] 2788[5] 3048[7] **>43a 54f< (DEAD)**

**Kamikaze 6** gr g Kris-Infamy (Shirley Heights) 712[2] 852[4] 1194[7] **>74f<**

**Kamin (USA) 2** b c Red Ransom (USA)-Sweet Rhapsody (USA) (Sea Bird II) 4516[10] 4817[9] **>56f<**

**Kammtarra (USA) 3** ch c Zilzal (USA)-Snow Bride (USA) (Blushing Groom (FR)) *942[2]* 1427[3] (2197) 3229[3] (4181) 4568[15] **>111f<**

**Kanat Lee (IRE) 5** b m Salse (USA)-Badiya (USA) (Sir Ivor) 4905[11] **>43f<**

**Kanawa 2** b f Beveled (USA)-Kiri Te (Liboi (USA)) 4208[15] **>46f<**

**Karawan 2** ch f Kris-Sweetly (FR) (Lyphard (USA)) 3593[13] 4754[4] **>48f<**

**Karaylar (IRE) 4** b g Kahyasi-Karamana (Habitat) *1530[13]* 1649[6] 2077[9] 2988[6] 3329[5] 3580[6] 3870[2] **>55f<**

**Karen's Hat (USA) 2** ch f Theatrical-Miss Carlotita (ARG) (Masqued Dancer (USA)) 3660[8] 4825[22] **>55f<**

**Karinska 6** b m Master Willie-Kaiserchronik (GER) (Cortez (GER)) *30[3] 122[6] 166[2] 239[4] 301[6] 341[3] 505[11]* 933[8] 1069[5] 1832[4] 2351[5] 2581[6] 3447[10] **>69a 68f<**

**Karisma (IRE) 3** b g Tirol-Avra (FR) (Mendez (FR)) *826[5]* 1361[6] 2067[9] 2570[4] 4626[3] 4862[3] 5047[12] **>73f<**

**Karlaska 3** f Lashkari-Kariya (USA) (Irish River (FR)) 1393a[4] 3571a[3] **>103f<**

**Karla Wyller (ITY) 3** ch f Salse (USA)-Calder Hall (Grundy) 723a[3]

**Karpacka (IRE) 5** b m Rousillon (USA)-Lutoviska (Glenstal (USA)) 4541a[2] **>106f<**

**Karttikeya (FR) 5** br g Darshaan-Karosa (FR) (Caro) **1995:** *4472[7]* **>40a 84f<**

**Kasamir (GER) 2** 4035a[6] **>57f<**

**Kashana (IRE) 4** b f Shahrastani (USA)-Kashna (USA) (Blushing Groom (FR)) 472[7] 691[8] 805[6] 1341[14] 2423[9] 2804[8] 3308[9] 3463[7] 4763[4] 4904[9] **>51f<**

**Kass Alhawa 3** b c Shirley Heights-Silver Braid (USA) (Miswaki (USA)) 691[2] 932[5] *3418[7] 3626[8] 4076[13] 4322[8]* 4456[5] 4753[13] **>24a 60f<**

**Kassani (IRE) 4** b c Alleged (USA)-Kassiyda (Mill Reef (USA)) **1995:** 4426a[2] **1996:** (3751a) 4167a[2] 4655a[8] **>128f<**

**Kassbaan (USA) 6** b g Alydar (USA)-Ma Biche (USA) (Key to the Kingdom (USA)) 3984[5] **>100f<**

**Kates Choice (IRE) 4** b f Taufan (USA)-Global Princess (USA) 2825a[5] **>79f<**

**Kathryn's Pet 3** b f Blakeney-Starky's Pet (Mummy's Pet) 494[4] 687[6] 763[3] 1023[5] 4582[13] 4967[5] 5007[7] **>69f<**

**Katie Is My Love (USA) 3** ch f Talinum (USA)-Familiar (USA) (Diesis) *3421[8]* **>9a f<**

**Katie Komaite 3** b f Komaite (USA)-City to City (Windjammer (USA)) *421[6] 595[14]* 873[10] 1068[8] 1610[4] 1888[8] 2320[5] 2851[8] 3403[3] 4348[10] 4906[14] **>33a 50f<**

**Katie Oliver 4** b f Squill (USA)-Shih Ching (USA) (Secreto (USA)) *125[2]* **>58a 76f<**

**Katun (FR) 3** c 1057a[5] **>95f<**

**Katy-Q (IRE) 3** b f Taufan (USA)-Swift Chorus (Music Boy) *1599[8]* 2021[4] 2238[3] 2427[10] 3292[7] 3643[8] 3883[7] *4983[9]* **>24a 55f<**

**Kavin (GER) 3** 2668a[9] **>88f<**

**Kawa-Ib (IRE) 2** b f Nashwan (USA)-Awayed (USA) (Sir Ivor) 4798[3] **>81f<**

**Kawanin 3** ch f Generous (IRE)-Nahilah (Habitat) 1333[13] 1614[12] 1895[2] 2223[3] **>86f<**

**Kayaara (IRE) 4** b c Kahyasi-Ilyaara (Huntercombe) 1575a[R]

**Kayartis 7** b m Kaytu-Polyartis (Artaius (USA)) 666[14] 866[11] **>9f<**

**Kaye's Secret 3** b f Failiq (FR)-Another-Kaye (Jimmy The Singer) 3776[6] 4099[8] 4763[13] **>8f<**

**Kayf 3** ch f Nashwan (USA)-Northshiel (Northfields (USA)) 1530[16]

**Kayvee 7** gr g Kaldoun (FR)-Secret Life (USA) (Elocutionist (USA)) 455[17] 679[8] 876[7] 1112[9] 2053[12] 2544[4] 3072[8] 3207[2] 3612[4] (3811) 4184[11] 4444[2] 4568[28] 4974[3] **>106f<**

**Kayzee (IRE) 2** b f River Falls-Northern Amber (Shack (USA)) 3438[9] 3829[6] **>38f<**

**Kazimiera (IRE) 3** b f Polish Patriot (USA)-Cartier Bijoux (Ahonoora) **1995:** *4473[6]* **1996:** *566[6]* 701[2] 987[5] 1185[3] 2065[4] 2514[4] 2754[3] 3133[8] 4071[4] 4243[5] 4453[7] 4691[3] 4831[7] 5004[6] **>65a 73f<**

**Kealbra Lady 3** b f Petong-Greensward Blaze (Sagaro) 2557[13] 2893[8] 3851[12] 3977[12] 4372[17] **>22f<**

**Keen Dancer 2** ch g Keen-Royal Shoe (Hotfoot) 4705[11] 4830[14] **>41f<**

**Keen Sally 3** ch f Keen-Super Sally (Superlative) 4456[9]

**Keen To Please 2** ch f Keen-Tasseled (USA) (Tate Gallery (USA)) *2932[3]* 3241[3] (3838) 4195[14] 4459[3] 4749[4] 4767[2] **>58f<**

**Keen To The Last (FR) 4** ch g Keen-Derniere Danse (Gay Mecene (USA)) 620[9] 4073[16] 4302[7] 4588[9] **>54f<**

**Keen Waters 2** b f Keen-Miss Oasis (Green Desert (USA)) 2712[7] 2995[3] 4087[4] 4339[6] 4424[2] 4749[13] **>64f<**

**Keep Battling 6** b g Hard Fought-Keep Mum (Mummy's Pet) 558[3] 612[3] 999[2] 1548[3] (2020) 2152[2] **>58f<**

**Keepers Dawn (IRE) 3** b f Alzao (USA)-Keepers Lock (USA) (Sunny's Halo (CAN)) *708[2]* 939[13] 1441[9] 2072[17] 5044[10] **>102df<**

**Keeping The Faith (IRE)** **2** b f Ajraas (USA)-Felicitas (Mr Fluorocarbon) 4024a[7] **>80f<**
**Keep Quiet** **4** b f Reprimand-Silent Pool (Relkino) *85[15] 1803[20]* ***>31a f<***
**Keepsake (IRE)** **2** b f Distinctly North (USA)-Souveniers (Relko) 4475[12] 4684[7] 4748[7] **>58f<**
**Kellaire Girl (IRE)** **4** b f Gallic League-Frensham Manor (Le Johnstan) **1995:** *4418[2] 4493[9] 4515[11]* **1996:** *204[4] 274[8] 319[3] 502[4] 746[7] 4107[14]* **>55a 46f<**
**Kelly Mac** **6** b g Precocious-Ridalia (Ridan (USA)) 469[5] 968[12] 1522[12] **>75a 59f<**
**Keltoi 3** b c Soviet Star (USA)-Celtic Assembly (USA) (Secretariat (USA)) 962[2] (1142) 1824[7] 3248[9] **>96f<**
**Kemo Sabo** **4** b g Prince Sabo-Canoodle (Warpath) *802[4]* ***>88f<***
**Kenaftor (IRE)** **2** gr c Kenmare (FR)-Afternoon Nap (USA) (Key To Content (USA)) 4024a[26] **>61f<**
**Kenesha (IRE)** **6** br m Don't Forget Me-Calvino (Relkino) *559[5]* 1163[6] **>39f<**
**Kenilworth Dancer** **3** br g Shareef Dancer (USA)-Reltop (High Top) *370[5] 428[10]* **>5a 46f<**
**Kennemara Star (IRE)** **2** ch c Kenmare (FR)-Dawn Star (High Line) 2708[10] 3874[5] 4584[6] **>69f<**
**Kentavrus Way (IRE)** **5** b g Thatching-Phantom Row (Adonijah) **1995:** *4355[9] 4379[8]* **1996:** *140[7] 279[8] 353[7] 499[4]* **>50a 55f<**
**Kentford Conquista** **3** b f El Conquistador-Notinhand (Nearly A Hand) *2529[11]* 3699[6] **>21f<**
**Kentucky Fall (FR)** **3** b f Lead on Time (USA)-Autumn Tint (USA) (Roberto (USA)) 1857[4] 3949[4] 4422[2] 4866[17] **>72f<**
**Kenwood Melody** **2** ch c Lead on Time (USA)-Baddi Baddi (USA) (Sharpen Up) 1531[2] 1878[5] 2195[5] 2703[2] **>74f<**
**Kenyatta (USA)** **7** b g Mogambo (USA)-Caranga (USA) (Caro) **1995:** *4438[5] 4516[6] 4534[3]* **1996:** *54[8] 1534[9]* 2155[9] *2322[7]* **>54da 8f< (DEAD)**
**Kenzo (GER)** **5** 2479a[6] **>106f<**
**Keos (USA)** **2** dk c Riverman (USA)-Konafa (USA) (Damascus (USA)) 5077a[3]
**Kernof (IRE)** **3** b g Rambo Dancer (CAN)-Empress Wu (High Line) 827[18] 1068[9] 1363[13] 1850[7] 2177[2] (2366) 2486[5] **>56f<**
**Keroub (FR)** **2** 5024a[10] **>61f<**
**Kerrier (IRE)** **4** ch c Nashwan (USA)-Kerrera (Diesis) 1314[11] *1602[7] 2373[12]* 2851[10] **>12a 38f<**
**Kerry Jane** **6** gr m Nestor-Quaife Sport (Quayside) *98[7]* **>6a f<**
**Kerry Ring** **3** b f Sadler's Wells (USA)-Kerrera (Diesis) 678[4] (3767) 4376[6] 4571[14] **>82f<**
**Kesanta** **6** b m The Dissident-Nicaline (High Line) 3775[2] 4203[13] **>44f<**
**Keston Pond (IRE)** **6** b g Taufan (USA)-Maria Renata (Jaazeiro (USA)) *956[10]* 1425[9] 1848[2] *2084[2] 2351[8]* (2722) 3328[2] 3833[2] 4136[4] 4312[8] 4504[2] 4688[20] 4909[5] 4994[22] **>73a 87f<**
**Ketabi (USA) 5** ch g Alydar (USA)-Ivory Fields (USA) (Sir Ivor) *411[9] 469[14]* 650[8] 2159[10] *3435[4] 3473[4]* 3785[10] (3860) 3978[5] 4129[9] 4603[10] **>50a 66df<**
**Ketchican** **4** b g Joligeneration-Fair Melys (FR) (Welsh Pageant) **1995:** *4537[13]* **>30a 38f<**
**Kevasingo** **4** b g Superpower-Katharina (Frankincense) 670[9] 1348[6] 1685[3] 1890[15] 2284[7] 3980[5] 4355[4] 4455[3] 4603[4] 4808[8] **>55a 57f<**
**Kewarra** **2** b g Distant Relative-Shalati (FR) (High Line) 841[7] 1892[5] 2734[4] 3823[4] **>68f<**
**Key Change (IRE)** **3** b f Darshaan-Kashka (USA) (The Minstrel (CAN)) (1249a) 2069[2] 2837a[3] (3688) 4397a[2] **>118f<**
**Key Largo (IRE)** **2** b c Priolo (USA)-Pamiers (Huntercombe) (4790) 4918[6] 5049[3] **>80f<**
**Key of Luck (USA)** **5** b or br h Chief's Crown (USA)-Balbonella (FR) (Gay Mecene (USA)) *(535a)* **>131a 107f<**
**Key to My Heart (IRE)** **6** b h Broken Hearted-Originality (Godswalk (USA)) *(1131)* 1706[2] (2534) 3431[5] 3614[5] (4313) 4553[2] **>116f<**
**Khabar** **3** b g Forzando-Ella Mon Amour (Ela-Mana-Mou) 640[11] 824[16] 1068[16] 1539[10] 2979[2] 3961[9] 4597[16] **>67?f<**
**Khafaaq** **2** b c Green Desert (USA)-Ghanimah (Caerleon (USA)) *4825[18]* ***>49f<***
**Khairun Nisaa** **2** b f Never so Bold-Sea Clover (IRE) (Ela-Mana-Mou) 5051[2] **>68f<**
**Khalisa (IRE)** **3** b f Persian Bold-Khaiyla (Mill Reef (USA)) (1388a) 1949a[6] (3030a) 3907a[4] 4663a[4] **>117f<**
**Kharir (IRE)** **2** b c Machiavellian (USA)-Alkaffeyeh (IRE) (Sadler's Wells (USA)) (3701) 3971[3] 4366[2] **>90f<**
**Kharizmi (FR)** **3** ro c Lashkari-Khariyda (FR) (Shakapour) 3202a[2] 4657a[2] **>116f<**
**Khassah** **2** b f Green Desert (USA)-Kadwah (USA) (Mr Prospector (USA)) (2147) 2582[6] (4085) 4464[2] **>108f<**
**Khattat (USA)** **6** ch g El Gran Senor (USA)-Don't Joke (USA) (Shecky Greene (USA)) 3510[W] 4221[17] 4829[16] **>69f<**
**Khayrapour (IRE)** **6** b g Kahyasi-Khayra (FR) (Zeddaan) 3158[17] **>95?f<**
**Ki Chi Saga (USA)** **4** ch c Miswaki (USA)-Cedilla (USA) (Caro) 600[7] 878[6] 1520[6] 3072[6] 3450[9] 3856[10] 4184[17] 4470[8] **>80f<**
**Kickonsun (IRE)** **2** b g High Estate-Damezao (Alzao (USA)) 2802[8] 3769[6] **>45f<**
**Kid Ory** **5** ch g Rich Charlie-Woomargama (Creetown) 480[15] 629[7] 991[3] 1423[3] 1789[7] 2047[3] 2426[3] 2773[3] 3052[9] 3328[6] 3817[8] 4439[6] **>28a 66f<**
**Kidston Lass (IRE)** **3** b f Alzao (USA)-Anthis (IRE) (Ela-Mana-Mou) 1117[4] 2557[3] 3041[3] **>76f<**
**Kierchem (IRE)** **5** b g Mazaad-Smashing Gale (Lord Gayle (USA)) *609[12]* 883[3] 1024[7] **>63a 51f<**
**Kierkegaard** **3** 5074a[12]
**Kilcoran Bay** **4** b g Robellino (USA)-Catkin (USA) (Sir Ivor) 944[4] 1194[9] **>71f<**
**Kilcullen Lad (IRE)** **2** b c Fayruz-Royal Home (Royal Palace) 2031[7] (2199) 4049[9] 4339[2] (4459) 4749[8] 4966[2] *4999[2]* **>66a 53f<**
**Kildee Lad** **6** b g Presidium-National Time (USA) (Lord Avie (USA)) *1307[7]* 1446[2] 1777[7] 1985[4] 2311[4] (2799) (2957) 3338[4] 3810[2] 4198[16] **>86f<**
**Kilernan** **5** ch g K-Battery-Lekuti (Le Coq d'Or) (558) **>56f<**
**Killatty Lark (IRE)** **3** ch f Noalto-Killatty Sky (IRE) (Drumalis) *123[15] 1876[9]* 2180[10] **>36f<**
**Kill the Crab (IRE)** **4** b f Petorius-Final Decision (Tap On Wood) 2843a[6] (4174a) **>112f<**
**Kilmeena Lady** **2** b f Inca Chief (USA)-Kilmeena Glen (Beveled (USA)) 4798[13] **>34f<**
**Kilnamartyra Girl** **6** b m Arkan-Star Cove (Porto Bello) *4226[10]* 4436[24] **>23a 40f<**
**Kilshanny** **2** b f Groom Dancer (USA)-Kiliniski (Niniski (USA)) 4570[12] 4889[2] **>68f<**
**Kilvine** **3** b c Shaadi (USA)-Kilavea (USA) (Hawaii) 575[6] 833[6] 1327[7] 1820[4] 2065[3] 2754[2] 3207[6] **>88f<**
**Kindakoola** **5** b or br g Kind of Hush-Nikoola Eve (Roscoe Blake) *34[11]* **>14a 46df< (DEAD)**
**Kind of Light** **3** b f Primo Dominie-Kind Thoughts (Kashmir II) **1995:** *(4393) 4504[3]* **1996:** *10[7] 112[3] 194[3] 2578[16]* (2860) (3112) 3270[3] 3810[14] 4255[4] 4552[8] *5002[15]* **>69a 84f<**
**Kindred Greeting** **4** b g Most Welcome-Red Berry (Great Nephew) *284[6] 1717[8] 2165[15]* 2182[7] 2626[5] 2779[2] 2891[2] 3297[10] 3335[12] 3641[5] **>23a 44f<**
**King Alex** **3** b c Rainbow Quest (USA)-Alexandrie (USA) (Val de L'Orne (FR)) (821) 1125[2] **>108f<**
**King Athelstan (USA)** **8** b g Sovereign Dancer (USA)-Wimbledon Star (USA) (Hoist The Flag (USA)) 2862[11] 3071[4] 3509[10] 3791[7] 4326[14] 4868[8] 5042[9] **>67f<**
**Kingchip Boy** **7** b g Petong-Silk St James (Pas de Seul) *77[8] (90) (122) (159) 199[2] 249[2] 285[2] 645[2]* 670[2] *(854) 1047[6]* 1348[7] 1449[3] *1601[8] 1685[5]* 4202[8] 4831[3] 5004[5] **>75a 72f<**
**King Curan (USA)** **5** b g Lear Fan (USA)-Runaway Lady (USA) (Caucasus (USA)) 440[26] 619[7] 817[19] 1868[7] 2679[6] (2729) 2954[6] 3344[9] 3646[2] (3958) 4300[11] 4316[4] 4470[3] 4686[27] 4829[11] **>75f<**
**Kingdom Emperor** **2** b c Forzando-Wrangbrook (Shirley Heights) 1849[9] 2295[7] 2512[9] **>48f<**
**Kingdom Princess** **3** br f Forzando-Song of Hope (Chief Singer) **1995:** *4429[5]* **1996:** *58[6] (156) (220) 391[6] 509[3]* **>68da 70f<**
**Kingfisher Brave** **3** b g Rock City-Lambada Style (IRE) (Dancing Brave (USA)) 1420[7] 2027[10] 2536[4] *3063[10] 3918[9]* 4042[9] **>66a 66f<**
**Kingfisher Mill (USA)** **2** ch c Riverman (USA)-Charming Life (NZ) (Sir Tristram) 3319[7] **>72f<**
**King Kato** **3** b g Unfuwain (USA)-Sharmood (USA) (Sharpen Up) 4099[3] 4478[2] **>85f<**
**King of Babylon (IRE)** **4** b g Persian Heights-My My Marie (Artaius (USA)) *553[9]* **>46a 76f<**
**King of Munster (AUS)** **4** gr g Kenmare (FR)-Artistic Princess (AUS) (Luskin Star (AUS)) 943[9] 1446[10] *1718[10]* **>24a 77df<**
**King of Peace (IRE)** **3** b g Persian Bold-Pickety Place (Prince Tenderfoot (USA)) *344[11] 405[9]* **>35a 71f<**
**King of Peru** **3** b c Inca Chief (USA)-Julie's Star (IRE) (Thatching) *579[6]* 945[3] 1127[10] (1327) 1796[7] 2248[7] 3524[9] 4185[5] 4485[2] 4595[5] **>99f<**
**King of Show (IRE)** **5** b g Green Desert (USA)-Don't Rush (USA) (Alleged (USA)) 2566[5] (2732) (2849) 3345[2] 3868[11] 4312[24] 4805[18] **>27a 63f<**
**King of Sparta** **3** b c Kefaah (USA)-Khaizaraan (CAN) (Sham (USA)) 845[6] 1104[2] 1973[2] 2557[2] 2899[2] 3161[7] (3633) 4117[7] **>84f<**
**King of The East (IRE)** **3** b c Fairy King (USA)-Rising Tide (Red Alert) *1146[4]* (1493) 2050[9] 2545[12] 2880[11] 3759[6] 3875[5] 4485[3] **>99f<**
**King of Tunes (FR)** **4** b c Chief Singer-Marcotte (Nebos (GER)) *(132) 306[2] 1775[4]* 2127[2] **>78a 84f<**
**King Parrot (IRE)** **8** br g King of Spain-Red Lory (Bay Express) *(133) 426[3] (887)* (1992) (2994) 4373[4] **>63da 61f<**
**King Rambo 5** b g Rambo Dancer (CAN)-Infanta Maria (King of Spain) *139[2] 180[2] 225[4] 835[8]* **>74a 79f<**
**King Rat (IRE)** **5** ch g King of Clubs-Mrs Tittlemouse (Nonoalco (USA)) **1995:** *4482[6]* **1996:** *2722[10]* 3106[7] 3639[8] 3817[2] 3933[17] 4136[14] 4300[13] 4439[8] *(4573)* **>83a 81f<**
**King Rufus** **3** ch c No Evil-Djanila (Fabulous Dancer (USA)) 821[4] 1079[9] 1180[7] 1773[6] *2689[12]* **>14a 71f<**
**King's Academy (IRE)** **3** b c Royal Academy (USA)-Regal Beauty (USA) (Princely Native (USA)) 1182[10] 1711[3] 2135[5] (2572) (3815) 4238[15] **>92f<**
**Kings Assembly** **4** b c Presidium-To The Point (Sharpen Up) 580[5] (871) 1440[3] 1961[4] 3791[10] 4193[15] 4617[17] **>84f<**
**Kings Cay (IRE)** **5** b g Taufan (USA)-Provocation (Kings Lake (USA)) 872[18] 1436[6] 1647[6] 1676[4] 1861[7] 2024[2] (2066) (2217) 2239[2] (2487) 2779[3] 2900[5] 3235[6] **>69f<**
**Kingsdown Trix (IRE)** **2** b c Contract Law (USA)-Three of Trumps (Tyrnavos) 3685[9] 3963[6] 4210[12]

4494[12] **>58f<**
**Kings Harmony (IRE) 3** b g Nordico (USA)-Kingston Rose (Tudor Music) **1995:** *(4408)* **1996:** *638[6]* (743) 1412[4] 1823[8] 2578[2] 2974[3] (3301) 3696[6] *5002[2]* **>76a 77f<**
**Kingsinger (IRE) 2** b c Fairy King (USA)-Silly Tune (IRE) (Coquelin (USA)) (452) 552[2] 877[3] (946) 1565a[2] (2671a) 4666a[3] 4859a[10] **>95f<**
**Kings Nightclub 3** b f Shareef Dancer (USA)-Troy Moon (Troy) 1305[11] 2314[5] 3053[8] 3965[5] **>48f<**
**King Sound 2** br c Caerleon (USA)-Flood (USA) (Riverman (USA)) 4050[4] (4306) 4742a[3] **>96f<**
**King's Theatre (IRE) 5** b h Sadler's Wells (USA)-Regal Beauty (USA) (Princely Native (USA)) 1520[2] 2111a[3] **>130f<**
**Kings Witness (USA) 3** b c Lear Fan (USA)-Allison's Deeds (Sassafras (FR)) 2194[4] 2535[5] 2881[6] 4674[3] **>96f<**
**King Ubad (USA) 7** ch g Trempolino (USA)-Glitter (FR) (Reliance II) *1347[15]* 1511[8] 2310[4] 2958[6] **>37f<**
**King Uno 2** b c Be My Chief (USA)-The Kings Daughter (Indian King (USA)) 3637[8] *4091[7]* *4318[5]* 4586[9] 4764[9] 4883[10] **>27a 53f<**
**King William 11** b g Dara Monarch-Norman Delight (USA) (Val de L'Orne (FR)) *3801[7]* 4612[11] **>25a 34f<**
**Kinlochewe 3** b f Old Vic-Reuval (Sharpen Up) (826) 1111[2] 1899[9] 3658[2] 4063[3] **>105f<**
**Kinnescash (IRE) 3** ch g Persian Heights-Gayla Orchestra (Lord Gayle (USA)) *530[7]* *731[11]* 863[13] 1451[6] 1654[14] 1893[14] **>48a 52f<**
**Kinship (IRE) 2** ch c In The Wings-Happy Kin (USA) (Bold Hitter (USA)) 2878[5] 4507[12] **>54f<**
**Kintwyn 6** b g Doulab (USA)-Harriet Emma (USA) (Secretariat (USA)) **1995:** *4356[7]* *4440[6]* **1996:** *61[3]* *136[3]* *(233)* *358[3]* *410[4]* *979[5]* 1496[14] *2552[10]* *3113[12]* ***>76a 51f<***
**Kippilaw 2** ch f Selkirk (USA)-Contralto (Busted) 3837[9] 4806[2] 5034[14] **>64f<**
**Kira 6** b m Starry Night (USA)-Irish Limerick (Try My Best (USA)) **1995:** *4407[7]* *4464[2]* **1996:** *71[2]* *(155)* *(225)* *282[2]* *354[4]* *(394)* *418[6]* *(587)* 762[5] 868[8] 3223[2] (3415) (3643) 3774[3] 3973[2] 4180[4] 4452[8] 4616[15] **>79a 78f<**
**Kiridashi (CAN) 4** b c Bold Ruckus (CAN)-Sharp Briar (USA) (Briartic (CAN)) 4953a[4] **>127f<**
**Kirkadian 6** b m Norwick (USA)-Pushkar (Northfields (USA)) *1717[12]* *1967[9]*
**Kirov Lady (IRE) 3** b f Soviet Lad (USA)-Cestrefeld (Capistrano) *378[4]* *833[14]* 3133[6] 3634[5] 3926[6] 4214[7] **>69a 82f<**
**Kirov Protege (IRE) 4** b g Dancing Dissident (USA)-Still River (Kings Lake (USA)) 979[11] 1468[16] 2282[4] 2594[3] 3606[14] 3808[23] 3860[8] **>63a 29f<**
**Kirov Royale 5** b m Rambo Dancer (CAN)-Gay Princess (Lord Gayle (USA)) *4511[17]* ***>14?f<***
**Kirsberry (GER) 3** f 1060a[5] 1750a[5] **>89f<**
**Kismetim 6** b g Dowsing (USA)-Naufrage (Main Reef) *198[2]* *252[5]* *401[5]* *420[6]* *426[11]* *558[10]* 886[12] 1472[12] 1548[8] *1718[12]* *1966[10]* *2082[8]* *2322[9]* *3297[11]* ***>32a 12f<***
**Kissel 4** b f Warning-Ice Chocolate (USA) (Icecapade (USA)) 1410[5] 1867[5] 2332[9] 2901[6] 3974[14] **>66f<**
**Kissing Gate (USA) 3** ch f Easy Goer (USA)-Love's Reward (Nonoalco (USA)) **1995:** *(4501)* **1996:** *56[10]* *471[13]* ***>65a 53f<***
**Kiss Me Again (IRE) 3** b f Cyrano de Bergerac-Now Serving (Super Concorde (USA)) 1521[5] 1652[3] 2146[4] 4560[12] 4802[10] **>76f<**
**Kistena (FR) 3** ro f Miswaki (USA)-Mabrova (Prince Mab (FR)) (2270a) 2841a[2] (3914a) (4406a) (4660a) **>125f<**
**Kitty Galore (IRE) 2** b f Silver Kite (USA)-Sudbury (IRE) (Auction Ring (USA)) 2043[5] 2519[3] 3082[9] 3576[W] 4501[8] 4594[16] **>53f<**
**Kitty Kitty Cancan 3** b f Warrshan (USA)-Kittycatoo Katango (USA) (Verbatim (USA)) 1656[2] 2601[9] 3148[10] 3657[5] 4374[7] 4899[4] **>76f<**
**Kiwud 3** ch f Superlative-Mimining (Tower Walk) *644[15]* 762[16] 868[19] *1492[17]* *1761[2]* 2156[9] 2359[7] 2386[10] **>11a 45f<**
**Klinsman (IRE) 2** gr c Danehill (USA)-Faakirah (Dragonara Palace (USA)) 4639a[4] **>91f<**
**Klipspinger 3** ch f Formidable (USA)-Distant Relation (Great Nephew) *(1030)* *1490[8]* *1606[2]* *1812[2]* *2084[3]* *2518[9]* *4094[5]* *4333[11]* **>72a 33f<**
**Klondike Charger (USA) 2** b c Crafty Prospector (USA)-Forever Waving (USA) (Hoist The Flag (USA)) 3319[9] 4330[8] 4891[16] **>69f<**
**Knave 3** b c Prince Sabo-Royal Agnes (Royal Palace) **1995:** *4389[3]* **1996:** *453[5]* 595[13] 1312[8] 1548[9] 1866[4] **>58a 54f<**
**Knobbleeneeze 6** ch g Aragon-Proud Miss (USA) (Semi-Pro) *450[7]* 480[7] 935[12] 1354[6] 1522[2] (1703) 1902[4] 2188[5] 3426[3] 3612[5] 3933[8] 4054[10] 4308[4] 4571[12] 4688[21] 4775[14] 4820[18] 4975[13] **>67f<**
**Knotally Wood (USA) 4** b f Woodman (USA)-Countess Tully (Hotfoot) **1995:** *4366[2]* *4465[6]* **>71a 72f<**
**Knotty Hill 4** b g Green Ruby (USA)-Esilam (Frimley Park) 1160[5] 1649[2] 2420[6] 3101[3] 3279[10] 3842[7] 4504[3] 5042[F] **>81f<**
**Known Secret (USA) 3** ch g Known Fact (USA)-Loa (USA) (Hawaii) 472[5] 873[20] **>43f<**
**Koathary (USA) 5** b g Capote (USA)-Jeffo (USA) (Ridan (USA)) *817[4]* 979[4] 1486[3] 1965[9] 2574[7] (3161) (3765) (4381) **>86f<**
**Koli 3** b f Sayf El Arab (USA)-Miss Willow (Horage) 3942[7] **>52f<**
**Komasta 2** b c Komaite (USA)-Sky Fighter (Hard Fought) *1026[3]* *1537[10]* 1827[4] *2083[3]* **>53a 55f<**
**Komiamaite 4** b g Komaite (USA)-Mia Scintilla (Blazing Saddles (AUS)) **1995:** *4444[5]* **1996:** *(30)* *90[3]* *153[5]* *198[6]* *239[7]* *343[3]* *424[8]* **>63a 52f<**
**Komlucky 4** b f Komaite (USA)-Sweet And Lucky (Lucky Wednesday) *195[3]* *426[9]* *661[11]* 764[5] *839[2]* *1087[2]* 1642[9] *1812[12]* *2075[10]* *2550[2]* *3289[4]* 3410[2] 3761[2] (4323) 4915[17] *5059[4]* **>45a 57f<**
**Komodo (USA) 4** ch g Ferdinand (USA)-Platonic Interest (USA) (Drone) **1995:** *4386[12]* *4456[8]* *4493[11]* **1996:** *82[13]* *879[30]* 1102[12] 1314[9] 1516[5] 1893[15] **>29da 51df<**
**Komreyev Dancer 4** b g Komaite (USA)-L'Ancressaan (Dalsaan) *61[4]* *136[7]* *181[2]* *223[5]* *462[4]* *(628)* 988[15] (1198) 1861[3] 2145[10] 2299[3] 2502[6] 2862[2] 3081[6] **>88a 85f<**
**Konic (ITY) 3** c **1995:** 4424a[4]
**Koordinaite 2** b f Komaite (USA)-Fair Dino (Thatch (USA)) 3110[7] 3871[8] 4046[17] **>21f<**
**Koraloona (IRE) 3** b g Archway (IRE)-Polynesian Charm (USA) (What A Pleasure (USA)) *2859[7]* 3115[6] 3262[7] 4068[17] 4785[11] **>51f<**
**Korambi 4** ch g Kris-Green Lucia (Green Dancer (USA)) 925[12] 1767[3] 4465[20] **>102f<**
**Kornado 6** ch h Superlative-K-Sera (Lord Gayle (USA)) 789a[3] 1948a[7] **>115f<**
**Kosevo (IRE) 2** b c Shareef Dancer (USA)-Kallista (Zeddaan) 4458[5]
**Kossolian 3** b f Emarati (USA)-Cwm Deri (IRE) (Alzao (USA)) 1101[11] 1307[13] **>56f<**
**Kowtow 3** b f Forzando-Aim to Please (Gunner B) 710[16] 921[10] 1061[5] 2617[9] 2793[7] 3112[7] *4336[11]* *4478[9]* 4808[6] 4882[10] **>40f<**
**Kralingen 4** ch f Move Off-Elitist (Keren) 3428[9] **>9f<**
**Krasnik (IRE) 3** br g Roi Danzig (USA)-Kermesse (IRE) (Reference Point) 668[9] 4833[17] **>58f<**
**Kratz (IRE) 3** b g Prince Rupert (FR)-Some Spice (Horage) **1995:** *4433[8]* **1996:** *89[5]* *158[7]* **>51da 60f<**
**Krayyalei (IRE) 5** gr m Krayyan-Garland Song 2472a[12] **>79f<**
**Kriscliffe 3** ch c Kris-Lady Norcliffe (USA) (Norcliffe (CAN)) 969[2] 1432[6] *2306[10]* *2603[4]* 3073[9] 3947[16] 4559[16] **>4a 90df<**
**Krissante (USA) 3** b f Kris-Vallee Dansante **1995:** 4400a[2]
**Kristal Breeze 4** ch f Risk Me (FR)-Mistral's Dancer (Shareef Dancer (USA)) 477[10] 822[4] 1347[2] (1468) 2563[6] (2941) 3267[5] (3500) (4497) 4626[14] 4793[4] 4967[12] **>19a 64f<**
**Kristal Diva 5** ch m Kris-Dame Ashfield (Grundy) **1995:** *4391[12]* **>16a 61df<**
**Kristal's Paradise (IRE) 4** b f Bluebird (USA)-Kristal's Pride (Kris) **1995:** *4470a[3]* **1996:** 563[4] 1054a[10] 2723[2] 3972[2] 4665a[2] **>108f<**
**Kristopher 2** ch c Kris-Derniere Danse (Gay Mecene (USA)) 4755[3] 4920[13] **>39tf<**
**Krystal Davey (IRE) 2** b g Classic Music (USA)-Robin Red Breast (Red Alert) 2076[6] **>56f<**
**Krystal Max (IRE) 3** b g Classic Music (USA)-Lake Isle (IRE) (Caerleon (USA)) **1995:** *(4473)* *(4545)* **1996:** *(39)* *(293)* *443[6]* 1006[10] 2078[5] 2425[8] **>88a 75f<**
**Kuala Lipis (USA) 3** b c Lear Fan (USA)-Caerna (USA) (Caerleon (USA)) 732[5] 845[4] (2011) 3211[6] **>87f<**
**Kuantan (USA) 3** b g Gone West (USA)-Cuddly Doll (USA) (Bold Hour) 1332[4] 1495[3] 1824[8] 2248[6] **>104f<**
**Kuda 2** b f Classic Secret (USA)-Deverells Walk (IRE) (Godswalk (USA)) *770[8]* 1360[7] **>15f<**
**Kudos Blue 3** b f Elmaamul (USA)-Don't Be Shy (IRE) (Kafu) 703[15] 1067[14] 1474[10] 2752[9] **>42f<**
**Kulshi Momken 3** ch g In The Wings-Gesedeh (Ela-Mana-Mou) 1434[14] 2510[10] 3638[8] **>18f<**
**Kumait (USA) 2** b br c Danzig (USA)-Colour Chart (USA) (Mr Prospector (USA)) 2040[8] 2624[3] 3757[6] 4188[2] 4502[3] 4756[3] (4962) **>94f<**
**Kummel King 8** b g Absalom-Louise (Royal Palace) *549[7]* 801[8] 1650[8] 1830[13] 2520[9] **>14f<**
**Kung Frode 4** ch c Interrex (CAN)-Harmony Heights (Music Boy) *1716[4]* *1971[5]* *4081[7]* *4333[7]* **>66a 65f<**
**Kunucu (IRE) 3** ch f Bluebird (USA)-Kunuz (Ela-Mana-Mou) 565[3] 966[8] (1188) 2143[13] 3693[10] 3946[11] 4304[5] 4485[4] 4561[6] 4772[17] **>88f<**
**Kury Girl 3** b f Superlative-Azubah (Castle Keep) *51[5]* *209[9]* **>36a f<**
**Kustom Kit (IRE) 3** ch c Timeless Times (USA)-Friendly Song (Song) *773[11]* *1492[16]* *2064[11]* *2634[8]* *3061[7]* **>35a 44f<**
**Kustom Kit Xpres 2** gr f Absalom-Miss Serlby (Runnett) 1643[2] 1834[4] 2245[5] **>66f<**
**Kutan (IRE) 6** ch g Mansooj-Lady Fandet (Gay Fandango (USA)) *898[9]* **>30a f< (DEAD)**
**Kutman (USA) 3** b c Seattle Slew (USA)-Ouro Verde (USA) (Cool Moon (CAN)) 732[13] 4360[2] 4478[4] **>80f<**
**Kutta 4** b c Old Vic-Ardassine (Ahonoora) 2724[13] (4327) 4876[2] 5046[2] **>120f<**
**Kuwam (IRE) 3** b g Last Tycoon-Inshad (Indian King (USA)) 1168[3] 1498[14] 2402[7] 2915[3] 3217[7] 3358[4] **>50df<**
**Kweilo 2** b g Mtoto-Hug Me (Shareef Dancer (USA)) 2184[6] 4756[12] 4914[12] **>68+f<**
**Kyle Rhea 2** b f In The Wings-Rynechra (Blakeney) 4897[2] **>81f<**
**Kymin (IRE) 4** b f Kahyasi-Akila (FR) (Top Ville) *79[2]* *130[5]* *268[2]* *339[9]* *422[10]* *1454[6]* 1835[5] 2182[8] 2530[6] 2958[5] **>71a 60f<**

L

**Laafee 3** gr g Machiavellian (USA)-Al Sylah (Nureyev (USA)) 832[7] 1188[3] 2007[4] 2920[2] 3612[7] 3933[16] **>105f<**

**Laal (USA) 4** b g Shirley Heights-Afaff (USA) (Nijinsky (CAN)) *520[5]* **>23a 63f<**

**Laazim Afooz 3** b c Mtoto-Balwa (USA) (Danzig (USA)) 4110[6] 4353[3] (4752) 4899[7] **>79f<**

**Labeed (USA) 3** b c Riverman (USA)-Gracious Beauty (USA) (Nijinsky (CAN)) 863[8] 995[17] (1984) 2511[2] 4199[P] **>76f< (DEAD)**

**La Belle Affair (USA) 2** gr f Black Tie Affair-Away's Halo (USA) (Sunny's Halo (CAN)) 3988[15] **>26f<**

**La Belle Dominique 4** b f Dominion-Love Street (Mummy's Pet) *466[14]* 632[8] 667[4] 862[6] 1064[7] 1446[7] 1688[8] 3261[2] (3864) 4119[6] 4372[15] **>49a 59f<**

**La Belle Shyanne 5** ch m Shy Groom (USA)-Defy Me (Bustino) 1979[12] 2313[11] 2556[4] 2891[8] 3808[14] **>36f<**

**Labeq (IRE) 2** b c Lycius (USA)-Ahbab (IRE) (Ajdal (USA)) 4670[7] 4863[2] **>78f<**

**La Blue (GER) 3** dk f Bluebird (USA)-La Luganese (Surumu (GER)) (1060a) 1750a[4] 3395a[3] (4028a) 4663a[2] **>123f<**

**La Bossette (IRE) 4** b f Cyrano de Bergerac-Bosquet (Queen's Hussar) **1995:** *4359[9] 4458[12] 4537[12]* **1996:** *37[9]* **>8a 53f<**

**La Brief 4** b f Law Society (USA)-Lady Warninglid (Ela-Mana-Mou) **1995:** *4355[2] (4391) (4411)* **1996:** *4563[8]* ***>77a 63f<***

**Lab Test (IRE) 4** ch g Doulab (USA)-Princess Reema (USA) (Affirmed (USA)) *4865[11]* ***>57f<***

**Labudd (USA) 6** ch h Deputy Minister (CAN)-Delightful Vie (USA) (Barbs Delight) **1995:** *4438[3]* **1996:** *(14) 120[3] 189[6] 243[7] 363[4] 487[8] 501[7] 690[14]* 979[18] 1314[14] 1533[6] 2159[7] 2377[2] 2574[11] 3141[5] **>62a 54f<**

**Lacandona (USA) 3** b f Septieme Ciel (USA)-Grand Luxe (USA) (Sir Ivor) 4108[4] 4827[4] **>68f<**

**La Chatelaine 2** b f Then Again-La Domaine (Dominion) 4889[7] **>39f<**

**Lachesis 3** ch f Lycius (USA)-Chance All (FR) (Glenstal (USA)) 1160[3] 1864[4] 2316[8] 2675[3] 3107[5] 3458[7] 4693[6] **>57f<**

**Lacinia 3** b f Groom Dancer (USA)-Pretty Lady (High Top) 3021a[5] **>106f<**

**Lacryma Cristi (IRE) 3** b c Green Desert (USA)-L'Anno d'Oro (Habitat) 2498[3] **>93f<**

**La Curamalal (IRE) 2** b f Rainbow Quest (USA)-North Telstar (Sallust) 4969[17] **>59f<**

**La Dama (USA) 4** ch f Known Fact (USA)-Cypria Sacra (USA) (Sharpen Up) *212[3] 342[6] 427[5] 545[8]* 661[4] *839[10] 1546[11]* ***>55a 40f<***

**La Dolce Vita 2** b f Mazilier (USA)-Actress (Known Fact (USA)) 4043[9] 4244[7] (4762) **>70f<**

**Ladoni 4** b c Danehill (USA)-Lilac Charm (Bustino) 4409a[6] **>113f<**

**La Doyenne (IRE) 2** ch f Masterclass (USA)-Sainthill (St Alphage) 4907[8] **>36f<**

**Lady Bankes (IRE) 3** b f Alzao (USA)-Never so Fair (Never so Bold) 755[4] 1061[3] 1671[2] (2593) 2924[4] 3500[10] 4209[5] **>73f<**

**Lady Benson (IRE) 3** b f Pennine Walk-Sit Elnaas (USA) (Sir Ivor) 763[12] 2579[15] 3051[4] 3334[11] **>52f<**

**Lady Bi (IRE) 2** b f Alzao (USA)-Kallopina (ITY) (Targowice (USA)) 4420a[2]

**Ladybird 2** b f Polar Falcon (USA)-Classic Heights (Shirley Heights) 4890[6] 5041[11] **>55f<**

**Ladybower (IRE) 4** b f Pennine Walk-Eimkar (Junius (USA)) *(43) 201[2] 336[2] 983[9] 2085[8] 2743[8]* ***>51a 40f<***

**Lady Carla 3** b f Caerleon (USA)-Shirley Superstar (Shirley Heights) (1077) (1769) 2837a[4] **>120df<**

**Lady Caroline Lamb (IRE) 3** b f Contract Law (USA)-Tuft Hill (Grundy) 443[2] (478) 644[3] (665) 1761[W] 3360[6] 3643[7] 3883[10] **>42a 52f<**

**Lady Diesis (USA) 2** b f Diesis-Sedulous (Tap On Wood) 4570[6] (4754) 4893[5] **>76f<**

**Lady Dignity (IRE) 3** b f Nordico (USA)-Royal Respect (Kings Lake (USA)) **1995:** *4443[2] 4491[4]* **1996:** *35[6] 137[3] (382) (463) 1096[6] 1594[6]* 2541[6] *4575[8]* **>73a 68df<**

**Lady Eclat 3** b f Nomination-Romantic Saga (Prince Tenderfoot (USA)) **1995:** *(4483) 4511[3] 4533[2]* **1996:** *32[9] 4776[11] 4981[12]* **>55da 50f<**

**Lady Elizabeth (FR) 4** b f Bold Arrangement-Top Fille (FR) (Top Ville) *79[14] 125[6] 175[7] 291[10] 360[8] 393[11] 547[12]* ***>11a 19f<***

**Lady Godiva 2** b f Keen-Festival Fanfare (Ile de Bourbon (USA)) 1960[8] 2252[2] 3171[3] 3762[2] (3982) 4490[4] **>72f<**

**Lady Grovefair (IRE) 2** ch f Shalford (IRE)-Zinovia (USA) (Ziggy's Boy (USA)) 3651[6] 3795[5] **>50f<**

**Lady Highfield 5** br m High Kicker (USA)-Judy Burton **1995:** *4385[8] 4406[7]* **>54a 63f<**

**Lady Isabell 3** b f Rambo Dancer (CAN)-Warning Bell (Bustino) 2760[4] 3093[5] 3686[12] **>63f<**

**Lady Joshua (IRE) 3** ch f Royal Academy (USA)-Claretta (USA) (Roberto (USA)) 2610[2] 3441[3] 4615[6] 4827[5] 5010[4] **>75f<**

**Lady Kate (USA) 4** ch f Trempolino (USA)-Glitter (FR) (Reliance II) **1995:** *4382[10]* **>21a 13f<**

**Ladykirk 3** b f Slip Anchor-Lady Day (FR) (Lightning (FR)) 766[3] 1361[5] 2430[7] 3280[5] 4059[7] **>66f<**

**Lady Lacey 9** b m Kampala-Cecily (Prince Regent (FR)) *267[7]* **>24a 55f<**

**Lady Louise (IRE) 2** b f Lord Americo-Louisa Anne (Mummy's Pet) 3343[6]

**Lady Lucre (IRE) 3** b f Last Tycoon-Queen Helen (Troy) 1804[4] **>77f<**

**Lady Magnum (IRE) 3** b f Eve's Error-Illiney Girl (Lochnager) 1895[6] 2383[7] 2557[9] 3165[8] 3473[7] 3978[9] 4082[14] **>67f<**

**Lady Mail (IRE) 2** b f Pursuit of Love-Wizardry (Shirley Heights) 2503[6] (2802) 3444[4] 4183[4] **>89f<**

**Lady Nash 4** b f Nashwan (USA)-Je Comprend (USA) (Caerleon (USA)) **1995:** *4409[2]* **1996:** *179[3]* **>50a 72f<**

**Lady of Leisure (USA) 4** b f Diesis-Lyrebird (USA) (Storm Bird (CAN)) 613[7] 820[4] 994[6] 1504[2] 2949[4] 3819[5] (4209) (4387) 4686[16] 4819[6] **>77f<**

**Lady of The Lake 2** b f Caerleon (USA)-Llyn Gwynant (Persian Bold) 3988[3] 4359[4] 4697[7] **>82df<**

**Lady Ploy 4** b f Deploy-Quisissanno (Be My Guest (USA)) 2320[13] 2540[10] 3151[13] 3460[11] 3970[16] 4868[W] 4904[W] **>21f<**

**Lady Poly 8** b m Dunbeath (USA)-First Temptation (USA) (Mr Leader (USA)) *83[13] 232[11] 2711[10]* ***>18?f<***

**Lady Rambo 3** b f Rambo Dancer (CAN)-Albaciyna (Hotfoot) 1891[9] *2169[12]* **>13a 7f<**

**Lady Risk Me 7** gr m Risk Me (FR)-Donrae (Don (ITY)) *109[12]*

**Lady Sabina 6** ch m Bairn (USA)-Calibina (Caliban) *145[11] 440[21]* 787[6] 1449[4] 1696[4] 2203[7] 2574[15] 2896[5] 3111[4] 3785[4] 4236[6] **>33a 42f<**

**Lady Sadie (IRE) 2** b f Red Sunset-Eimkar (Junius (USA)) 1062[9]

**Lady Salome 2** gr f Absalom-Lady River (FR) (Sir Gaylord) 1827[10] 3080[10] 4072[8] **>48f<**

**Lady Seren (IRE) 4** gr f Doulab (USA)-Princess Pamela (Dragonara Palace (USA)) *1649[8]* 2913[4] 3100[7] 4323[18] 4881[19] *4982[16]* **>33f<**

**Lady Sheriff 5** b m Taufan (USA)-Midaan (Sallust) **1995:** *4394[5]* **1996:** *653[2] 735[3] (900) 1016[4]* 1113[5] 1501[6] 1708[2] 1974[8] 2220[6] 2694[4] 3296[10] 3432[8] *3602[6] 3953[11] 4116[20]* 4679[9] 4765[10] 4995[4] 5039[20] **>65a 79f<**

**Lady Shirl (IRE) 2** b f Fayruz-Christmas Show (Petorius) 4600[6] 4796[3] **>65f<**

**Lady Silk 5** ch m Prince Sabo-Adduce (USA) (Alleged (USA)) **1995:** *4409[3] 4479[6]* **1996:** *159[U] 505[12]* 1546[6] 1866[6] *2081[9] (2367) 2940[5] 3089[6] 3995[21] 4077[8] 4206[8]* 4323[5] 4436[12] 4865[9] *4982[3]* **>50a 51f<**

**Lady Swift 5** ch m Jalmood (USA)-Appealing (Star Appeal) 4070[17] 4833[9] **>39f<**

**Lady Woodstock 4** b f Chilibang-Vent du Soir (Main Reef) *116[12] 260[7] 343[9] 745[6]* ***>7a 26f<***

**La Fandango (IRE) 3** b f Taufan (USA)-Cursory Look (USA) (Nijinsky (CAN)) *859[11] 2486[9]* 3059[6] 3225[7] 3619[15] 3761[7] **>43f<**

**La Fille de Cirque 4** ch f Cadeaux Genereux-Lady of the Land (Wollow) 2130[4] 2801[14] 3205[11] 4691[11] 4829[2] **>38a 57f<**

**La Finale 3** ch f Dunbeath (USA)-Jamarj (Tyrnavos) **1995:** *4393[3] 4433[3]* **1996:** *3256[5]* 3288[3] 4075[6] 4206[19] 4323[4] 4472[5] 4865[20] **>48a 54f<**

**La Fra Angelico (FR) 5** b m Tip Moss (FR)-Fragrance (FR) (Shakapour) 3199a[2] 4739a[2] **>106f<**

**L'Africain Bleu (FR) 3** b c Saint Cyrien (FR)-Afrique Bleu Azur (FR) 1757a[11] **>105f<**

**Lagan 3** b g Shareef Dancer (USA)-Lagta (Kris) **1995:** *4389[9]* **1996:** *1490[15] 1671[7]* 1986[10] 2163[8] 2506[18] 2627[7] 3053[7] 3335[13] 3619[11] *3872[10]* **>42a 50f<**

**Lago Di Varano 4** b g Clantime-On the Record (Record Token) 600[8] (700) 1016[2] 1113[11] 1790[14] 2137[4] (2349) 2694[5] 2889[2] 3232[12] 3432[5] 3618[4] 3946[4] 3984[4] 4116[3] 4314[11] 4679[12] 4772[2] 4869[3] **>93f<**

**La Grande Ourse (FR) 3** ch f Mansonnien-Sanhia (Sanhedrin (FR)) 150a[3] **>72f<**

**Laguna Bay (IRE) 2** b f Arcane (USA)-Meg Daughter (IRE) (Doulab (USA)) 3159[10] 3449[4] 4052[10] **>66?f<**

**Lahab Nashwan 2** ch c Nashwan (USA)-Shadha (USA) (Devil's Bag (USA)) 4830[5] **>67f<**

**La Haye Sainte 3** ch f Rock City-Billante (USA) (Graustark) 522[10] *655[9] 983[14]* ***>40a 38f<***

**Lahik (IRE) 3** b g Lycius (USA)-Sangala (FR) (Jim French (USA)) 528[11] 761[7] 980[8] 1099[14] 1152[10] 1514[13] 1907[5] *2322[5] 2594[11]* 2983[11] 3059[11] **>27a 41f<**

**Laid Back Lucy 3** b br f Prince Daniel (USA)-Granny's Birthday (Young Generation) **1995:** *4393[13] 4477[7]* **>14a 7f<**

**Lajatta 2** ch c Superlative-Lady Keyser (Le Johnstan) 4171a[6] 4242[14] 4544[9] **>43f<**

**Lakeline Legend (IRE) 3** ch c Caerleon (USA)-Bottom Line (Double Jump) 671[8] 1668[2] (2135) 2724[11] 3145[3] 3689[16] 4465[7] **>104f<**

**Lake Spring (IRE) 2** b g Shalford (IRE)-Isla Bonita (Kings Lake (USA)) 3110[9] 3336[5] *4251[9]* **>6a f<**

**Lake Storm (IRE) 5** b h Maelstrom Lake-Our Duck (The Go-Between) **1995:** 4402a[2] **1996:** 1759a[4] 5074a[7] **>118f<**

**Lakota Brave (USA) 7** b g Northern Prospect (USA)-Norene's Nemesis (CAN) (King Emperor (USA)) *4951a[5]* **>126a f<**

**Lalindi (IRE) 5** b m Cadeaux Genereux-Soemba (General Assembly (USA)) *449[7]* 573[15] 647[6] 944[2] 1063[2] 1306[2] 1852[4] (2155) 2321[W] (2430) 2612[7] 2882[14] 4327[8] 4557[2] 4877[15] 5047[17] **>79a 80df<**

**Lallans (IRE)** 3 b c Old Vic-Laluche (USA) (Alleged (USA)) (804) $923^{2}$ $1110^{3}$ $2054^{11}$ **>98f<**
**La Mafarr (USA)** 3 b c Mr Prospector (USA)-Sense of Unity (USA) (Northern Dancer) $3446^{6}$ $4456^{4}$ **>76f<**
**Lamarita** 2 b f Emarati (USA)-Bentinck Hotel (Red God) $1622^{4}$ $2195^{2}$ $2495^{6}$ **>70f<**
**La Menorquina (USA)** 6 b m Woodman (USA)-Hail The Lady (USA) (Hail the Pirates (USA)) $169^{7}$ $2717^{10}$ $3335^{4}$ **>54da 40f<**
**L'Ami Louis (USA)** 3 ch c Easy Goer (USA)-Jadana (Pharly (FR)) $548^{4}$ (1187) **>109f<**
**La Modiste** 3 b f Most Welcome-Dismiss (Daring March) $1327^{11}$ $1771^{11}$ $2225^{3}$ $2705^{7}$ $2980^{6}$ **>72f<**
**Lamorna** 2 ch f Shavian-Malibasta (Auction Ring (USA)) (1683) $2112^{9}$ $2696^{3}$ $3046^{5}$ $3478^{7}$ (3687) $3936^{5}$ $4324^{3}$ $4566^{16}$ $4717^{17}$ $4880^{11}$ **>77f<**
**Lancashire Knight** 2 b c High Estate-Just a Treat (IRE) (Glenstal (USA)) $1445^{7}$ $1989^{11}$ **>14f<**
**Lancashire Legend** 3 gr g Belfort (FR)-Peters Pet Girl (Norwick (USA)) $188^{2}$ $304^{3}$ $352^{3}$ $467^{9}$ $746^{5}$ $1010^{12}$ $1301^{10}$ $1651^{12}$ (4997) **>68a 45f<**
**Lancashire Life (IRE)** 5 b g Petorius-Parlais (Pardao) $615^{12}$ $1043^{7}$ $1156^{9}$ **>28a 31f<**
**Landfall** 3 b g Most Welcome-Sextant (Star Appeal) $2062^{8}$ $2368^{7}$ **>23f<**
**Landlord** 4 b g Be My Chief (USA)-Pubby (Doctor Wall) **1995:** $4364^{14}$ (4490) **1996:** $27^{9}$ $66^{12}$ $130^{8}$ $2953^{6}$ **>66a 67f<**
**Lando (GER)** 6 b h Acatenango (GER)-Laurea (Sharpman) **1995:** (4471a) **>127f<**
**Landsome Dove (FR)** 3 b c Lashkari-Leontine (Kashmir II) $322a^{3}$
**Langfuhr (CAN)** 4 b c Danzig (USA)-Sweet Briar Too (USA) (Briartic (CAN)) $4951a^{8}$ **>120a f<**
**Langtonian** 7 br g Primo Dominie-Yankee Special (Bold Lad (IRE)) **1995:** $4377^{6}$ $4390^{10}$ **1996:** $341^{8}$ $418^{8}$ $431^{8}$ $586^{3}$ $806^{11}$ $1088^{11}$ $1311^{2}$ $1665^{11}$ $2391^{8}$ $2481^{5}$ $2678^{3}$ $3252^{9}$ $3452^{4}$ $3808^{13}$ $4503^{5}$ **>30a 29f<**
**L'Annee Folle (FR)** 3 b f Double Bed (FR) $1396a^{5}$ (3031a) **>110f<**
**La Pellegrina (IRE)** 3 b f Be My Guest (USA)-Spanish Habit (Habitat) $678^{8}$ $1117^{3}$ $1508^{8}$ $1902^{8}$ $2945^{5}$ $3479^{6}$ $3918^{7}$ $4779^{11}$ **>19a 69f<**
**La Perruche (IRE)** 3 b f Cyrano de Bergerac-Red Lory (Bay Express) **1995:** $4461^{8}$ $4519^{7}$ **1996:** $320^{3}$ $421^{4}$ $859^{5}$ **>50a f<**
**La Petite Fusee** 5 br m Cigar-Little Missile (Ile de Bourbon (USA)) **1995:** (4371) $4394^{9}$ **1996:** $846^{3}$ $1334^{3}$ $1777^{2}$ $2228^{3}$ (2615) (3518) $3783^{15}$ $4312^{3}$ $4802^{19}$ **>78a 85f<**
**Lap of Luxury** 7 gr m Sharrood (USA)-Lap of Honour (Final Straw) $810^{7}$ $1112^{10}$ $1623^{3}$ $3153^{9}$ $3503^{4}$ $3945^{5}$ $4289a^{3}$ **>111f<**
**Lapu-Lapu** 3 b f Prince Sabo-Seleter (Hotfoot) $626^{5}$ $857^{4}$ $1405^{13}$ $2316^{10}$ $2902^{7}$ (3354) $3866^{4}$ $4071^{5}$ $4686^{4}$ (4810) $4986^{14}$ **>53a 62f<**
**Lara (GER)** 4 b f Sharpo-La Salina **1995:** $4398a^{2}$ **1996:** $1951a^{2}$ $2843a^{9}$ (4858a) **>107f<**
**Largesse** 2 b c Cadeaux Genereux-Vilanika (FR) (Top Ville) $1842^{2}$ (2361) $2700^{6}$ $3483^{4}$ $4303^{12}$ **>84f<**
**Larissa (IRE)** 3 b f Soviet Star (USA)-Pipitina (Bustino) $710^{12}$ $1627^{4}$ $1906^{4}$ $2895^{4}$ $3600^{7}$ **>35a 62f<**
**Larkwhistle (CAN)** 2 f $4950a^{5}$ **>84a f<**
**Larn Fort** 6 gr g Belfort (FR)-Larnem (Meldrum) **1995:** $4472^{2}$ $4513^{6}$ **1996:** $70^{5}$ $508^{7}$ $2573^{9}$ $2868^{11}$ $3645^{13}$ **>57a 46f<**
**Laroche (GER)** 5 br h Nebos (GER)-Laurea (Sharpman) (1138a) **>125f<**
**Larrocha (IRE)** 4 b f Sadler's Wells (USA)-Le Melody (Levmoss) (397a) $536a^{9}$ **>96a 113f<**
**Larry Lambrusco** 3 b g Executive Man-Freudenau (Wassl) $1969^{8}$ **>51a 47f<**
**Larrylukeathugh** 3 b g Prince Sabo-Hidden Asset (Hello Gorgeous (USA)) $479^{3}$ $539^{10}$ $661^{12}$ $4045^{20}$ **>41f<**
**Lasco With'Em (ITY)** 3 ch f Welsh Guide-Danzatrice () (Scorpio (FR)) $792a^{2}$
**Laser Light Lady** 4 b f Tragic Role (USA)-Raina Perera (Tyrnavos) $162^{8}$ $1605^{8}$ **>17a f<**
**La Sorrela (IRE)** 4 ch f Cadeaux Genereux-Miss Silca Key (Welsh Saint) **1995:** $4540^{W}$
**Last Ambition (IRE)** 4 b f Cadeaux Genereux-Fabulous Rina (FR) (Fabulous Dancer (USA)) $2941^{15}$ $3331^{4}$ **>30f<**
**Last But Not Least** 3 b f Dominion-Almadaniyah (Dunbeath (USA)) **1995:** $4429^{4}$ **1996:** (78) $142^{5}$ $335^{5}$ $665^{3}$ **>68da 61f<**
**Last Chance** 2 b c River Falls-Little Red Hut (Habitat) $1815^{4}$ (1982) $2210^{2}$ $3803^{2}$ $4230^{5}$ $4517^{8}$ $4966^{7}$ **>73f<**
**Last Hero (FR)** 3 ch c Hero's Honor (USA)-Waterford (Crystal Palace (FR)) **1995:** (4397a)
**Last Roundup** 4 b g Good Times (ITY)-Washita (Valiyar) $530^{4}$ $654^{10}$ $4334^{7}$ $4986^{12}$ **>55a 71f<**
**Last Second (IRE)** 3 gr f Alzao (USA)-Alruccaba (Crystal Palace (FR)) $2052^{2}$ (3231) (4567) **>121f<**
**Last Spin** 4 b f Unfuwain (USA)-Spin (High Top) $787^{17}$ $1838^{7}$ $2340^{12}$ $2599^{10}$ **>12a 36f<**
**Last World** 4 b f Puissance-Flicker Toa Flame (USA) (Empery (USA)) **1995:** $4362^{15}$ $4430^{8}$ $4508^{13}$ **>5a 40f< (DEAD)**
**La Suquet** 4 b f Puissance-Persian Case (Upper Case (USA)) $475^{12}$ $587^{3}$ $700^{2}$ $735^{8}$ $951^{7}$ $1430^{8}$ $1598^{3}$ $1964^{3}$ $2492^{3}$ $2694^{9}$ **>34a 66f<**
**Latahaab (USA)** 5 b h Lyphard (USA)-Eye Drop (USA) (Irish River (FR)) $1428^{2}$ $2071^{5}$ $2723^{3}$ $3673^{7}$ $3992^{4}$ **>57a 101df<**
**La Tansani (IRE)** 3 b c High Estate-Hana Marie (Formidable (USA)) $747^{6}$ $928^{18}$ $1719^{2}$ $1809^{2}$ $2501^{8}$ $2578^{9}$ $2934^{2}$ $3078^{2}$ **>69a 63f<**
**Latching (IRE)** 4 ch f Thatching-Keepers Lock (USA) (Sunny's Halo (CAN)) (582) $735^{12}$ (846) $1178^{11}$ $2114^{12}$ $2363^{8}$ $3106^{2}$ $3612^{8}$ $4774^{11}$ **>91f<**
**Latch Key Lady (USA)** 4 b f Tejano (USA)-Key To The Heart (USA) (Arts And Letters) $508^{16}$ **>41a 18f<**
**Late Parade (IRE)** 5 b h Astronef-Skisette (Malinowski (USA)) (3393a) **>116f<**
**La Thuile** 4 b f Statoblest-Mild Wind (Porto Bello) $4360^{11}$ $4724^{12}$ $4815^{F}$ **>40f<**
**Latin Leader** 6 b g Primo Dominie-Ravaro (Raga Navarro (ITY)) **1995:** $4378^{11}$ **>52a 70f<**
**Latin Lover (GER)** 3 br g Roi Danzig (USA)-Lago Real (Kings Lake (USA)) $705^{14}$ $2365^{7}$ **>39f<**
**Latin Master (IRE)** 2 ch c Priolo (USA)-Salustrina (Sallust) $916^{5}$ $1339^{2}$ (1842) **>73f<**
**Latin Quarter (USA)** 3 b c Zilzal (USA)-Artiste (Artaius (USA)) $3788^{8}$ $4201^{6}$ $4499^{5}$ **>71f<**
**Latin Reign (USA)** 3 b br c El Gran Senor (USA)-Love Bunny (USA) (Exclusive Native (USA)) **1995:** $4424a^{2}$ **>87f<**
**L A Touch** 3 b f Tina's Pet-Silvers Era (Balidar) $2800^{2}$ $3135^{2}$ $3345^{4}$ $3700^{2}$ $4206^{23}$ **>19a 63f<**
**Latvian** 9 gr g Rousillon (USA)-Lorelene (FR) (Lorenzaccio) (972) $1159^{7}$ $1544^{3}$ $2020^{7}$ $2239^{6}$ $2682^{2}$ $2986^{2}$ $3329^{7}$ $3676^{2}$ (3865) $4344^{8}$ $4484^{5}$ $5008^{16}$ **>69f<**
**Latzio** 3 b f Arrasas (USA)-Remould (Reform) **1995:** $4461^{10}$ $4533^{7}$ **1996:** $317^{8}$ $361^{3}$ $459^{7}$ $755^{10}$ **>30da 49?f<**
**Laughing Buccaneer** 3 ch g Weldnaas (USA)-Atlantic Line (Capricorn Line) **1995:** $4352^{4}$ $4437^{7}$ $4453^{4}$ **1996:** $595^{12}$ $863^{9}$ $1119^{9}$ $1821^{8}$ $3681^{3}$ $4068^{8}$ $4334^{9}$ **>55a 47f<**
**Laurel Delight** 6 ch m Presidium-Foudroyer (Artaius (USA)) $735^{18}$ $864^{5}$ $1113^{8}$ $1630^{9}$ $2349^{3}$ $2694^{3}$ (3085) $3432^{15}$ **>92f<**
**Lavender Bloom (IRE)** 3 ch f Broken Hearted-African Bloom (African Sky) **1995:** $4519^{4}$ $4541^{4}$ **>48a 63f<**
**Lavender Della (IRE)** 3 gr f Shernazar-All In White (FR) (Carwhite) $1589^{2}$ $2251^{16}$ $2855^{2}$ $4824^{10}$ **>67f<**
**Lavinia Fontana (IRE)** 7 ch m Sharpo-Belle Origine (USA) (Exclusive Native (USA)) **1995:** $4425a^{6}$ **>113f<**
**Lavirco (GER)** 3 bl c Konigsstuhl (GER)-La Virginia (GER) (Surumu (GER)) $795a^{2}$ (1395a) (2109a) (2668a) $3574a^{2}$ (4413a) **>126f<**
**La Volta** 3 b f Komaite (USA)-Khadino (Relkino) $1193^{9}$ $2774^{6}$ $3430^{9}$ **>71f<**
**Law Commission** 6 ch g Ela-Mana-Mou-Adjala (Northfields (USA)) $1064^{9}$ $1192^{4}$ (1680) $2114^{14}$ (2604) $2856^{4}$ (3207) $3782^{2}$ $4196^{W}$ $4554^{5}$ $4775^{16}$ **>96f<**
**Law Dancer (IRE)** 3 b c Alzao (USA)-Judicial (USA) (Law Society (USA)) $355^{4}$ (510) $593^{6}$ (836) $1447^{6}$ $1780^{9}$ $2170^{2}$ $2552^{4}$ $2980^{3}$ $3205^{4}$ $3496^{6}$ $3856^{9}$ $4257^{7}$ **>81a 76f<**
**Lawful Find (IRE)** 2 gr c Contract Law (USA)-Mrs Mutton (Dancers Image (USA)) (533) $590^{7}$ (838) $1032^{3}$ $1183^{2}$ (1471) $1858^{2}$ **>57a 64f<**
**Lawful Love (IRE)** 6 b g Law Society (USA)-Amata (USA) (Nodouble (USA)) $1640^{11}$ $2355^{2}$ **>40f<**
**Lawn Lothario** 2 ch c Pursuit of Love-Blade of Grass (Kris) $4069^{11}$ $4310^{2}$ $4830^{7}$ $5006^{4}$ **>67f<**
**Lawn Order** 3 b f Efisio-Zebra Grass (Run The Gantlet (USA)) $686^{9}$ $859^{6}$ $1363^{8}$ $1850^{6}$ $1887^{7}$ $2366^{3}$ (2683) $2871^{5}$ $3347^{4}$ $3845^{10}$ **>21a 50f<**
**Lawnswood Captain (IRE)** 3 ro c Maelstrom Lake-Morgiana (Godswalk (USA)) $1156^{4}$ $1665^{8}$ **>51f<**
**Lawnswood Junior** 9 gr g Bairn (USA)-Easymede (Runnymede) $246^{5}$ $2056^{12}$ **>46a 46f<**
**Lawsimina** 3 b f Silly Prices-Star of the Sea (Absalom) $4094^{6}$ $4592^{11}$ $4865^{13}$ $4987^{5}$ **>45a 34f<**
**Layik (IRE)** 3 b c Be My Guest (USA)-Forest Lair (Habitat) $3021a^{6}$ **>99f<**
**Lay The Blame** 3 b c Reprimand-Rose And The Ring (Welsh Pageant) $1799^{7}$ $2041^{26}$ $3322^{5}$ $3833^{7}$ $3920^{12}$ **>81f<**
**Lazali (USA)** 3 ch c Zilzal (USA)-Leyali (Habitat) $544^{11}$ $705^{3}$ $894^{9}$ $1773^{15}$ $2417^{4}$ **>74f<**
**L'Carriere (USA)** 5 b g Carr de Naskra (USA)-Northern Sunset (USA) (Northfields (USA)) $536a^{3}$ **>134a f<**
**Lead Him On (USA)** 3 b c Cahill Road (USA)-Wicked Ways (USA) (Devil's Bag (USA)) $578^{5}$ $821^{6}$ $1079^{4}$ $1780^{8}$ $2934^{12}$ **>13a 74f<**
**Leading Note (USA)** 2 ch f Blushing John (USA)-Beat (USA) (Nijinsky (CAN)) $4897^{3}$ $5040^{3}$ **>79f<**
**Leading Princess (IRE)** 5 gr m Double Schwartz-Jenny Diver (USA) (Hatchet Man (USA)) **1995:** $4407^{4}$ **1996:** $559^{11}$ $617^{13}$ $659^{7}$ $882^{10}$ $997^{6}$ $1020^{8}$ $1163^{11}$ (1889) $2119^{2}$ $2154^{7}$ $2386^{W}$ $2564^{8}$ $2849^{2}$ $2960^{7}$ (3345) $3644^{3}$ $3883^{6}$ $4246^{21}$ $4486^{5}$ (4805) **>41a 54f<**
**Leading Spirit (IRE)** 4 b g Fairy King (USA)-Shopping (FR) (Sheshoon) $641^{7}$ $1019^{2}$ (1618) $2674^{4}$ $3073^{3}$ $3683^{3}$ (4067) **>56a 93f<**
**Lead Story (IRE)** 3 br g Lead on Time (USA)-Mashmoon (USA) (Habitat) $1182^{7}$ $1530^{6}$ $2036^{10}$ $2493^{8}$ **>60f<**
**Leap for Joy** 4 ch f Sharpo-Humble Pie (Known Fact (USA)) $1053a^{2}$ $1483^{4}$ $3126^{14}$ $3562a^{3}$ $3914a^{4}$ $4442^{3}$ (4744a) $4958a^{4}$ **>111f<**
**Leap in the Dark (IRE)** 7 br h Shadeed (USA)-

Star Guide (FR) (Targowice (USA)) 2060$^{9}$ 2366$^{7}$ 2537$^{10}$ 2941$^{10}$ 3204$^{10}$ 3968$^{7}$ **>38f<**

**Lear Dancer (USA) 5** b or br g Lear Fan (USA)-Green Gown (Green Dancer (USA)) **1995:** *4384$^{3}$ 4455$^{4}$* **1996:** *(19) (60) 422$^{11}$ 811$^{13}$* 1158$^{5}$ **>81da 79df<**

**Lear Express (USA) 3** b c Lear Fan (USA)-Sheer Enchantment (USA) (Siberian Express (USA)) 2135$^{4}$ 2439$^{2}$ (2949) 3351$^{3}$ **>85f<**

**Lear Jet (USA) 3** b c Lear Fan (USA)-Lajna (Be My Guest (USA)) (860) 1120$^{3}$ 1619$^{2}$ 1798$^{9}$ 2975$^{5}$ 3320$^{3}$ **>92f<**

**Learmont (USA) 6** b h Lear Fan (USA)-Wistoral (USA) (Exceller (USA)) *397a$^{2}$ 724a$^{4}$* ***>100f<***

**Learning Curve (IRE) 3** gr f Archway (IRE)-Children's Hour (Mummy's Pet) **1995:** *4369$^{3}$ 4429$^{9}$* **1996:** *203$^{5}$ 307$^{6}$ 383$^{9}$* **>42a 9f<**

**Lear White (USA) 5** b h Lear Fan (USA)-White Water (FR) (Pharly (FR)) 581$^{8}$ 680$^{9}$ 831$^{5}$ 1355$^{3}$ 2113$^{4}$ 2480a$^{4}$ 2583$^{4}$ 3157$^{2}$ 3753a$^{3}$ 4134$^{3}$ 4413a$^{5}$ 5023a$^{2}$ **>119f<**

**Le Bal 4** b f Rambo Dancer (CAN)-Skarberg (FR) (Noir Et Or) *30$^{15}$ 126$^{10}$ 347$^{4}$ 431$^{4}$* **>37a 44f<**

**Le Bam Bam 4** ch c Emarati (USA)-Lady Lustre (On Your Mark) 626$^{8}$ 840$^{6}$ 1319$^{11}$ *1809$^{7}$ 2081$^{6}$ 2602$^{12}$* ***>55a 64f<***

**Lebedinski (IRE) 3** ch f Soviet Lad (USA)-Excavate (Nishapour (FR)) 1067$^{4}$ 1451$^{7}$ 2568$^{5}$ 3048$^{10}$ 3619$^{8}$ **>48f<**

**Le Conquet (FR) 8** b h Pink (FR)-Miss Kit (FR) (Tourangeau (FR)) *5022a$^{2}$* ***>113f<***

**Le Destin (FR) 3** b c Zayyani-My Darling (Arctic Slave) 1757a$^{3}$ 3035a$^{6}$ 3746a$^{5}$ 4293a$^{8}$ 4662a$^{6}$ **>125f<**

**Ledgendry Line 3** b g Mtoto-Eider (Niniski (USA)) 447$^{3}$ 691$^{9}$ 974$^{4}$ 1361$^{4}$ 1783$^{4}$ 4559$^{7}$ **>77f<**

**Leedons Park 4** br g Precocious-Scottish Rose (Warpath) *153$^{10}$* **>47f<**

**Leeds (IRE) 4** b c Law Society (USA)-Miss Persia (Persian Bold) 2476a$^{2}$ 3035a$^{2}$ 3915a$^{5}$ 4295a$^{3}$ 4662a$^{8}$ **>123f<**

**Lees Please (IRE) 4** b c Glenstal (USA)-Perfect Choice (Bold Lad (IRE)) **1995:** *4379$^{12}$* **>10a 42f<**

**Legal Brief 4** b g Law Society (USA)-Ahonita (Ahonoora) 786$^{6}$ 1037$^{17}$ 1196$^{19}$ 2056$^{22}$ 2801$^{19}$ **>29df<**

**Legal Drama (USA) 4** ch f Turkoman (USA)-Sworn Statement (USA) (Believe It (USA)) *24$^{8}$ 116$^{10}$ 155$^{15}$ 670$^{14}$* 1449$^{8}$ 1953$^{10}$ 2155$^{14}$ 2284$^{10}$ 3944$^{14}$ **>51f<**

**Legal Issue (IRE) 4** b c Contract Law (USA)-Natuschka (Authi) *44$^{4}$ 122$^{2}$ 199$^{7}$ 505$^{4}$* 713$^{9}$ 1069$^{13}$ 1610$^{3}$ (1789) (2426) 2630$^{8}$ 3995$^{22}$ 4688$^{23}$ *4778$^{5}$ 4982$^{5}$* **>55a 74f<**

**Legal Right (USA) 3** b c Alleged (USA)-Rose Red (USA) (Northern Dancer) (985) 1329$^{4}$ 2116$^{7}$ 2845a$^{5}$ 3145$^{10}$ **>105f<**

**Legatee 5** ch m Risk Me (FR)-Legal Sound (Legal Eagle) **1995:** *4413$^{13}$ 4479$^{10}$ 4502$^{11}$* **1996:** *86$^{6}$ 126$^{9}$ 168$^{4}$ 195$^{5}$* **>39a 31f<**

**Leg Beforum (IRE) 2** b c Distinctly North (USA)-Paulines Girl (Hello Gorgeous (USA)) 2374$^{12}$

**Legendary Leap 6** b m Legend of France (USA)-Leap in Time (Dance In Time (CAN)) 3989$^{9}$ **>50f<**

**Legend Dulac (IRE) 7** b g Legend of France (USA)-Westerlake (Blakeney) **1995:** *4390$^{13}$* **>51da 53f<**

**Legend of Aragon 2** b f Aragon-Legendary Dancer (Shareef Dancer (USA)) *639$^{4}$* 823$^{4}$ (975) 1362$^{5}$ **>62f<**

**Le Grand Gousier (USA) 2** ch c Strawberry Road (AUS)-Sandy Baby (USA) (Al Hattab (USA)) *3625$^{7}$ 3874$^{8}$* 4834$^{4}$ **>57f<**

**Leguard Express (IRE) 8** b g Double Schwartz-All Moss (Prince Tenderfoot (USA)) 983$^{3}$ (1302) 1613$^{2}$ 1685$^{8}$ **>11a 42f<**

**Leif the Lucky (USA) 7** ch g Lemhi Gold (USA)-Corvine (USA) (Crow (FR)) *61$^{8}$ 211$^{10}$ 1322$^{11}$* 2010$^{11}$ 2536$^{3}$ 3081$^{5}$ 3939$^{8}$ 4624$^{3}$ 4993$^{6}$ **>61a 67f<**

**Leigh Crofter 7** ch g Son of Shaka-Ganadora (Good Times (ITY)) **1995:** *4368$^{2}$ 4394$^{6}$* **1996:** *88$^{9}$ 170$^{8}$ 282$^{3}$ 315$^{3}$ 394$^{9}$ 418$^{4}$ 466$^{13}$* 749$^{20}$ 814$^{10}$ *1083$^{6}$ 1348$^{11}$* 1442$^{3}$ 1521$^{4}$ *4081$^{10}$ 4333$^{13}$ 4778$^{11}$ 4820$^{23}$ 4989$^{8}$ (5055)* **>61a 62f<**

**Leith Academy (USA) 3** b f Academy Award (USA)-Uvula (USA) (His Majesty (USA)) 2576$^{9}$ 2943$^{7}$ 3244$^{5}$ *3608$^{5}$* **>51a 62f<**

**Leitrim Lodge (IRE) 2** b f Classic Music (USA)-Gentle Freedom (Wolver Hollow) 1808$^{3}$ 2031$^{10}$ (2406) 2606$^{5}$ **>64f<**

**Le Khoumf (FR) 5** ch g Son of Silver-Bentry (FR) (Ben Trovato (FR)) 613$^{4}$ 821$^{5}$ 982$^{8}$ 1198$^{7}$ 1504$^{5}$ 2077$^{8}$ **>72f<**

**Lennox Lewis 4** b c Superpower-Song's Best (Never so Bold) 610$^{9}$ 711$^{7}$ 812$^{12}$ 1334$^{5}$ 1790$^{15}$ 2856$^{7}$ 3232$^{20}$ 3622$^{14}$ 3783$^{8}$ 4198$^{19}$ 4215$^{4}$ **>89f<**

**Lentini 5** 3753a$^{4}$ **>116f<**

**Leonard Quercus (FR) 4** b c Hero's Honour (SPA)-Money Can't Buy (FR) (Thatching) 5075a$^{2}$

**Leonato (FR) 4** b g Law Society (USA)-Gala Parade (Alydar (USA)) 1824$^{6}$ 2194$^{5}$ 2730$^{6}$ 3934$^{2}$ 4055$^{10}$ 4465$^{11}$ 4965$^{2}$ **>109f<**

**Leonila (IRE) 3** b f Caerleon (USA)-Dinalina (FR) (Top Ville) 1942a$^{4}$ 2277a$^{2}$ 3031a$^{2}$ 3392a$^{5}$ 4292a$^{4}$ 4662a$^{9}$ **>119f<**

**Leonine (IRE) 3** gr c Danehill (USA)-Inanna (Persian Bold) 926$^{9}$ 2050$^{16}$ **>102+f<**

**Lepikha (USA) 3** ch f El Gran Senor (USA)-Hortensia (FR) (Luthier) 684$^{11}$ 1711$^{10}$ 2080$^{5}$ 3398$^{8}$ 4086$^{3}$ 4227$^{2}$ 4448$^{4}$ (4794) 4919$^{8}$ 5047$^{7}$ **>76f<**

**Les Boyer 5** b h Midyan (USA)-Debutante *4667a$^{5}$* ***>121f<***

**Le Shuttle 2** b f Presidium-Petitesse (Petong) 1622$^{7}$ 2157$^{4}$ 2865$^{11}$ 3169$^{3}$ 3582$^{2}$ 3763$^{4}$ 3879$^{3}$ 4493$^{2}$ 4787$^{8}$ 5005$^{6}$ **>61f<**

**Le Silencieux (IRE) 4** b c Shaadi (USA)-Silent Hill **1995:** (4404a) **>103f<**

**Le Sport 3** b g Dowsing (USA)-Tendency (Ballad Rock) **1995:** *(4504)* **1996:** *137$^{7}$ 294$^{5}$ (383) (391) 416$^{2}$ 453$^{10}$* 987$^{6}$ 1703$^{9}$ *2170$^{6}$ 3063$^{6}$ 3265$^{9}$ 3419$^{7}$ 3627$^{10}$ 4078$^{9}$ 4688$^{14}$* 4793$^{15}$ 4866$^{15}$ **>78a 57f<**

**Le Temeraire 10** b g Top Ville-La Mirande (FR) (Le Fabuleux) **1995:** *4387$^{8}$* **1996:** *603$^{7}$ 855$^{7}$* **>10a 47f<**

**Le Teteu (FR) 3** b c Saint Andrews (FR)-Nouvelle Star (USA) (Star de Naskra (USA)) 668$^{11}$ 820$^{8}$ 1100$^{16}$ (1780) 3039$^{8}$ 3456$^{7}$ 4583$^{3}$ **>67f<**

**Letluce 3** b f Aragon-Childish Prank (Teenoso (USA)) 572$^{5}$ 960$^{D}$ 1127$^{5}$ **>102f<**

**Le Topolino (USA) 2** 4742a$^{8}$ **>70f<**

**Le Tourron (FR) 3** b c Kaldoun (FR)-Orangerie **1995:** 4562a$^{2}$

**Le Triton (USA) 3** b c El Gran Senor (USA)-La Tritona (Touching Wood (USA)) 1139a$^{4}$ (1756a) 2276a$^{4}$ 3745a$^{8}$ 4165a$^{8}$ **>115f<**

**Let's Get Lost 7** ch g Chief Singer-Lost in France (Northfields (USA)) **1995:** *4475$^{4}$* **1996:** *187$^{7}$* **>56a 72f< (DEAD)**

**Let's Hang On (IRE) 3** b f Petorius-Madam Slaney (Prince Tenderfoot (USA)) **1995:** *4393$^{12}$* **>2a f<**

**Letterluna 4** ch f Shavian-Alteza Real (Mansingh (USA)) *419$^{5}$* **>31a 55f<**

**Levelled 2** b g Beveled (USA)-Baino Charm (USA) (Diesis) 2374$^{3}$ (3869) 4614$^{12}$ 4878$^{9}$ **>58f<**

**Leviticus (IRE) 2** b g Law Society (USA)-Rubbiera (IRE) (Pitskelly) 2695$^{4}$ 3131$^{5}$ 3423$^{4}$ 3982$^{13}$ 4482$^{3}$ 4864$^{8}$ **>77f<**

**Lexus (IRE) 8** b g Gorytus (USA)-Pepi Image (USA) (National) 609$^{11}$ **>44a 39f<**

**Lia Fail (IRE) 3** b f Soviet Lad (USA)-Sympathy (Precocious) *383$^{4}$ 529$^{2}$ (834) 3626$^{7}$ 4692$^{18}$* ***>56a 43f<***

**Liberatrice (FR) 3** b f Assert-Liberale (FR) (Fabulous Dancer (USA)) 687$^{9}$ 1079$^{11}$ 4086$^{14}$ **>51f<**

**Lidanna 3** b f Nicholas (USA)-Shapely Test (USA) (Elocutionist (USA)) (1566a) 2115$^{8}$ **>109f<**

**Lidhama (USA) 4** b f Sword Dance-Running Melody (Rheingold) 1965$^{W}$ *2173$^{2}$ 2401$^{F}$* ***>70a 73f<*** **(DEAD)**

**Liefling (USA) 3** b f Alleged (USA)-Mata Cara (Storm Bird (CAN)) 2610$^{5}$ (3209) 3669$^{5}$ 4675$^{13}$ **>86f<**

**Life Is Precious (IRE) 4** b f Shernazar-Neelam (USA) (Arctic Tern (USA)) *18$^{9}$ 135$^{10}$ 247$^{4}$ 311$^{5}$ 389$^{6}$ 518$^{8}$ 868$^{F}$* ***>44a f<*** **(DEAD)**

**Life On The Street 2** b f Statoblest-Brave Advance (USA) (Bold Laddie (USA)) *729$^{5}$* 910$^{3}$ 1834$^{3}$ 2374$^{10}$ 3494$^{10}$ 3823$^{3}$ 3962$^{3}$ 4207$^{W}$ **>69f<**

**Life's a Breeze 7** b g Aragon-Zahira (What A Guest) **1995:** *4514$^{10}$* **>35da 25f<**

**Life's A Roar (IRE) 2** b g Roaring Riva-Wolviston (Wolverlife) *1471$^{7}$ 4251$^{10}$ 4546$^{18}$* ***>5a 14f<***

**Liffre (IRE) 2** b f Sadler's Wells (USA)-Liffey Lass (USA) (Irish River (FR)) 4608$^{4}$ **>73f<**

**Lift Boy (USA) 7** b g Fighting Fit (USA)-Pressure Seat (USA) (Ginistrelli (USA)) **1995:** *4464$^{5}$* **1996:** *(64) 117$^{6}$ 185$^{3}$ (202) 316$^{5}$ (389) 407$^{6}$ 667$^{6}$* 1170$^{2}$ 1512$^{4}$ (1681) 1992$^{7}$ 3864$^{4}$ 4215$^{9}$ *4996$^{4}$* **>72a 56f<**

**Light Fantastic 4** gr f Deploy-La Nureyeva (USA) (Nureyev (USA)) **1995:** *4454$^{5}$* **>40a 72f<**

**Light Movement (IRE) 6** br g Thatching-Annie Albright (USA) (Verbatim (USA)) **1995:** *4358$^{9}$ 4428$^{10}$* **>24a 48f<**

**Lightning Bolt (IRE) 2** b f Magical Strike (USA)-Killyhevlin (Green God) 4468$^{5}$ 4762$^{10}$ *5061$^{2}$* **>57a 68f<**

**Lightning Rebel 2** b g Rambo Dancer (CAN)-Ozra (Red Alert) 3809$^{5}$ 4481$^{2}$ 5009$^{5}$ **>71?f<**

**Lights of Home 2** b c Deploy-Dream Chaser (Record Token) 5050$^{6}$ **>23f<**

**Lilac Rain 4** b f Petong-Dame Corley (L'Enjoleur (CAN)) **1995:** *4409$^{7}$ 4448$^{7}$* **1996:** *31$^{2}$ 84$^{2}$ 166$^{8}$ (336) 416$^{5}$ 501$^{10}$ 776$^{3}$ 1613$^{8}$ 2081$^{8}$ 2234$^{7}$* 2989$^{U}$ 3257$^{10}$ *3435$^{9}$* **>50a 28f<**

**Lila Pedigo (IRE) 3** b f Classic Secret (USA)-Miss Goldie Locks (Dara Monarch) *183$^{11}$ 405$^{12}$ 973$^{13}$* 1449$^{5}$ 2180$^{2}$ 2507$^{5}$ 3059$^{2}$ 3333$^{5}$ (3619) 3845$^{3}$ 4209$^{6}$ 4355$^{12}$ **>51a 66f<**

**Lililo (IRE) 4** b g Vision (USA)-Persian Royale (Persian Bold) 3318$^{9}$ **>40f<**

**Lillibella 3** b f Reprimand-Clarandal (Young Generation) 648$^{5}$ 1688$^{3}$ 2013$^{3}$ 2255$^{4}$ 2528$^{2}$ 2769$^{3}$ 3700$^{6}$ 4206$^{18}$ **>70f<**

**Lilli Claire 3** ch f Beveled (USA)-Lillicara (FR) (Caracolero (USA)) 572$^{13}$ (888) 1190$^{7}$ 1770$^{7}$ 2126$^{2}$ (2585) 3210$^{11}$ 3516$^{14}$ 4185$^{6}$ **>93f<**

**Lill Niagara (IRE) 2** b f Dancing Dissident (USA)-Eskaroon (Artaius (USA)) 2272a$^{3}$

**Lil's Boy (USA) 2** b c Danzig (USA)-Kentucky Lill (USA) (Raise A Native) 5014a$^{2}$ **>101f<**

**Lily Jaques 2** b f Petong-Scossa (USA) (Shadeed (USA)) 1467$^{5}$ 2057$^{6}$ 2575$^{6}$ **>64f<**

**Lima 2** b f Distant Relative-Lady Kris (IRE) (Kris) (2734) (3971) **>90f<**

**Limerick Princess (IRE) 3** ch f Polish Patriot (USA)-Princess of Nashua (Crowned Prince (USA))

773$^{4}$ *(897) 1039$^{4}$* (1405) (1599) 1820$^{8}$ 2078$^{6}$ 2571$^{6}$ **>73+a 74f<**

**L'Imperialis (FR) 3** b f Apeldoorn (FR)-Pali Dancer (Green Dancer (USA)) 322a$^{2}$

**Limyski 3** b g Petoski-Hachimitsu (Vaigly Great) 2961$^{5}$ **>29f<**

**Lincon Twenty One 3** ch f Sharpo-Angels Are Blue (Stanford) *292$^{9}$ 665$^{4}$* 1122$^{12}$ 1776$^{12}$ 2324$^{7}$ **>12a 46f<**

**Linda's Joy (IRE) 3** b f Classic Secret (USA)-Enaam (Shirley Heights) 1104$^{5}$ 1310$^{3}$ (1806) 2163$^{7}$ 2798$^{2}$ 2978$^{R}$ **>66df<**

**Linden's Lad (IRE) 2** b c Distinctly North (USA)-Make Or Mar (Daring March) 2600$^{15}$ 3147$^{5}$ 4188$^{6}$ 4814$^{10}$ **>65f<**

**Lindisfarne Lady 4** b f Jupiter Island-Harifa (Local Suitor (USA)) 972$^{8}$ 1478$^{9}$ 2779$^{10}$ 3297$^{15}$ **>33f<**

**Line Dancer 3** b c Shareef Dancer (USA)-Note Book (Mummy's Pet) **1995:** 4399a$^{2}$ **1996:** 574$^{6}$ 1389a$^{5}$ 2839a$^{7}$ **>111f<**

**Linpac West 10** b h Posse (USA)-North Page (FR) (Northfields (USA)) 456$^{6}$ 1005$^{14}$ **>71f< (DEAD)**

**Lionel Edwards (IRE) 3** b g Polish Patriot (USA)-Western Heights (Shirley Heights) 646$^{13}$ 1152$^{5}$ 1356$^{2}$ 1599$^{3}$ (1709) (1986) **>74a 81f<**

**Lionize (USA) 3** ch c Storm Cat (USA)-Pedestal (High Line) (696) 4757$^{10}$ 4972$^{8}$ **>86f<**

**Listed Account (USA) 2** b f Private Account (USA)-Sypharina (FR) (Lyphard (USA)) 4211$^{3}$ 4564$^{7}$ **>74+f<**

**Lit de Justice (USA) 6** gr h El Gran Senor (USA)-Kanmary (FR) (Kenmare (FR)) *(4951a)* **>134a 107f<**

**Literary 2** b f Woodman (USA)-Book Collector (USA) (Irish River (FR)) 2611$^{6}$ 3044$^{2}$ 3444$^{7}$ **>77f<**

**Literary Society (USA) 3** ch c Runaway Groom (CAN)-Dancing Gull (USA) (Northern Dancer) 672$^{8}$ 1101$^{18}$ 2244$^{3}$ (2769) 3215$^{2}$ (3465) 3693$^{9}$ 4180$^{8}$ 4521$^{2}$ 4616$^{4}$ **>73f<**

**Lithe Spirit (IRE) 4** b f Dancing Dissident (USA)-Afternoon Nap (USA) (Key To Content (USA)) *298$^{6}$ 414$^{6}$ 517$^{7}$ 1156$^{8}$* ***>24a 37f<***

**Little Acorn 2** b c Unfuwain (USA)-Plaything (High Top) 4830$^{8}$ **>53f<**

**Little Black Dress (USA) 3** b f Black Tie Affair-Seattle Kat (USA) (Seattle Song (USA)) 550$^{9}$ 888$^{5}$ 1775$^{10}$ 2384$^{6}$ **>70f<**

**Little Blue (IRE) 2** b f Bluebird (USA)-Winter Tern (USA) (Arctic Tern (USA)) 1595$^{5}$ *2083$^{4}$ 2371$^{4}$ 2728$^{4}$* 3121$^{9}$ (3448) 4195$^{5}$ (4244) 4459$^{5}$ **>43a 70f<**

**Little Gent (IRE) 5** b g Jareer (USA)-Arfjah (Taufan (USA)) 1170$^{9}$ 1658$^{10}$ 1992$^{12}$ 2982$^{8}$ **>26f<**

**Little Ibnr 5** b g Formidable (USA)-Zalatia (Music Boy) **1995:** *4368$^{3}$ 4392$^{9}$ (4508)* **1996:** *20$^{8}$ 117$^{10}$ 270$^{12}$ 315$^{7}$ 394$^{8}$ 511$^{5}$ (653) 749$^{18}$ 896$^{5}$ 1018$^{8}$* 1708$^{9}$ *2171$^{7}$ 2719$^{6}$* 2799$^{5}$ 3265$^{8}$ 3579$^{6}$ **>72a 54f<**

**Little Kenny 3** b f Warning-Tarvie (Swing Easy (USA)) 983$^{19}$ 1122$^{3}$ 1594$^{5}$ *2636$^{4}$ 2971$^{4}$* 3257$^{3}$ 3474$^{6}$ 3654$^{3}$ **>38a 52f<**

**Little Kris (FR) 2** ch c Shining Steel-Little Grise (FR) (Solicitor (FR)) 4034a$^{2}$

**Little Luke (IRE) 5** b h Somethingfabulous (USA)-Yours Sincerely (USA) (Stalwart (USA)) 1449$^{12}$ 1655$^{11}$ 2716$^{9}$ 3471$^{8}$ **>49da 36f<**

**Little Millie 3** b f Colmore Row-Little Kraker (Godswalk (USA)) 709$^{7}$ 887$^{20}$ *1993$^{11}$ 4428$^{16}$* 4692$^{19}$ **>42f<**

**Littlemissmischief (IRE) 5** b m Nashamaa-Swan Upping (Lord Gayle (USA)) *3531$^{3}$* **>27a 41f<**

**Little Miss Rocker 2** b f Rock Hopper-Drama School (Young Generation) 4105$^{7}$ 4386$^{5}$ **>62f<**

**Little Murray 3** b c Mon Tresor-Highland Daisy (He Loves Me) 1319$^{14}$ 1627$^{7}$ **>49f<**

**Little Musgrave (IRE) 5** gr h Toca Madera-Avital (Pitskelly) 5015a$^{6}$ 5065a$^{7}$ **>89f<**

**Little Noggins (IRE) 3** b f Salt Dome (USA)-Calash (Indian King (USA)) *(443)* 571$^{11}$ 773$^{9}$ 1707$^{10}$ *2171$^{13}$ 4044$^{6}$* 4589$^{4}$ 4788$^{8}$ **>8a 66f<**

**Little Pilgrim 3** b g Precocious-Bonny Bright Eyes (Rarity) 527$^{12}$ 943$^{8}$ 1844$^{12}$ **>42f<**

**Little Progress 2** b c Rock City-Petite Hester (Wollow) 3259$^{19}$ 3807$^{19}$ 4380$^{15}$ 4786$^{12}$ **>62f<**

**Little Red 5** b g Dreams to Reality (USA)-Qualitairess (Kampala) 1159$^{14}$ 1596$^{11}$ 2136$^{11}$ 2521$^{11}$ **>24f<**

**Little Redwing 4** ch f Be My Chief (USA)-Forward Rally (Formidable (USA)) 1587$^{5}$ 1866$^{9}$ 2175$^{5}$ 2423$^{5}$ 2848$^{4}$ 2986$^{3}$ **>40f<**

**Little Saboteur 7** ch m Prince Sabo-Shoot To Win (FR) (Rabdan) **1995:** *4359$^{7}$ 4441$^{12}$* **1996:** *461$^{10}$ 652$^{3}$ 835$^{5}$ 1028$^{4}$ 1455$^{4}$ 1681$^{4}$ 2684$^{7}$* **>55a 60df<**

**Little Scarlett 4** b f Mazilier (USA)-Scarlett Holly (Red Sunset) **1995:** *4378$^{10}$ 4436$^{5}$ (4510)* **1996:** *62$^{4}$ 166$^{7}$ 336$^{3}$ 501$^{9}$* **>58da 29f<**

**Little Smart (GER) 4** b c 1752a$^{3}$ 3753a$^{6}$ **>111f<**

**Littlestone Rocket 2** ch c Safawan-Miss Hocroft (Dominion) 1774$^{9}$ *2633$^{11}$ 4545$^{10}$* ***>19a 26f<***

**Little Wobbly 6** ch m Cruise Missile-Jameena (Absalom) 1517$^{7}$ 1839$^{13}$ 2981$^{12}$ 3694$^{14}$ 4252$^{17}$ *4894$^{14}$* **>16df<**

**Lituus (USA) 3** gr g El Gran Senor (USA)-Liturgism (USA) (Native Charger (USA)) 970$^{5}$ 1142$^{19}$ 1771$^{7}$ 2001$^{5}$ 4243$^{4}$ 4379$^{4}$ **>85f<**

**Lively Mount (JPN) 5** b h Green Mount-Shinano Kachidoki *536a$^{6}$* **>108a f<**

**Live Project (IRE) 4** b g Project Manager-Saturday Live (Junius (USA)) **1995:** *4386$^{4}$ 4421$^{14}$ 4512$^{8}$* **1996:** *57$^{2}$ 121$^{15}$* **>69a 44f<**

**Livergod (USA) 2** ch c Mt Livermore (USA)-Igmaar (ITY) (Don Roberto (USA)) (5076a)

**Livio (USA) 5** b g Lyphard (USA)-Make Change (USA) (Roberto (USA)) 767$^{13}$ **>40f<**

**Lizapet (IRE) 4** b f Petorius-Sybaris (Crowned Prince (USA)) *545$^{11}$* 649$^{14}$

**Lizium 4** b f Ilium-Lizaway (Casino Boy) 845$^{12}$ 1050$^{7}$ 1123$^{11}$ 3500$^{14}$ 3785$^{15}$ **>42f<**

**Lloc 4** b f Absalom-Nosey (Nebbiolo) *(466)* 601$^{11}$ 1049$^{3}$ 1512$^{12}$ *2555$^{3}$ 2598$^{5}$ 2748$^{2}$ 3360$^{2}$* 3793$^{10}$ 4205$^{8}$ 4382$^{8}$ 4610$^{6}$ 4828$^{5}$ *5000$^{6}$* **>58a 52f<**

**Llyswen 3** ch c Generous (IRE)-Llyn Gwynant (Persian Bold) *2197$^{10}$* 2744$^{3}$ 3041$^{5}$ 3425$^{6}$ 3657$^{8}$ **>75f<**

**Lochangel 2** ch f Night Shift (USA)-Peckitts Well (Lochnager) 4061$^{2}$ (4446) **>88f<**

**Lochbuie 4** ch g Forzando-Nigel's Dream (Pyjama Hunt) *110$^{7}$ 204$^{9}$* **>40a 19f< (DEAD)**

**Loch Dibidale 2** b f Robellino (USA)-Carn Maire (Northern Prospect (USA)) 807$^{7}$ 1315$^{4}$ 1645$^{6}$ *2371$^{2}$ 3230$^{8}$* 3582$^{11}$ *3954$^{7}$* **>49a 42f<**

**Loch-Hurn Lady 2** b f Lochnager-Knocksharry (Palm Track) *823$^{10}$* 975$^{11}$ 2865$^{5}$ 3080$^{11}$ 3121$^{4}$ 3429$^{2}$ 4072$^{7}$ 4790$^{4}$ 4864$^{15}$ **>64f<**

**Lochinvar 2** b c Lochnager-Starchy Cove (Starch Reduced) *2031$^{11}$* 4546$^{7}$ 4786$^{9}$ *4976$^{8}$ 5050$^{8}$* ***>10a 47f<***

**Lochlass (IRE) 2** b f Distinctly North (USA)-Littleton Song (Song) *4079$^{6}$ 4570$^{10}$* ***>46a 48f<***

**Lochlore 2** b f Lochnager-Severals Princess (Formidable (USA)) 2792$^{7}$ *3065$^{7}$*

**Lochon 5** br g Lochnager-Sky Mariner (Julio Mariner) **1995:** *4459$^{W}$ 4488$^{3}$* **1996:** *16$^{9}$ (163) 218$^{3}$ 388$^{4}$ 425$^{4}$ 769$^{6}$* 1541$^{7}$ 1765$^{10}$ 2386$^{8}$ *2748$^{9}$* **>53a 44f<**

**Loch Patrick 6** b g Beveled (USA)-Daisy Loch (Lochnager) 889$^{3}$ (1332) 1621$^{5}$ 2115$^{7}$ 2545$^{4}$ 3232$^{8}$ 3517$^{3}$ 4122$^{5}$ 4466$^{8}$ **>108f<**

**Loch Style 3** b g Lochnager-Simply Style (Bairn (USA)) **1995:** *4408$^{6}$ 4480$^{4}$ 4511$^{4}$* **1996:** *47$^{7}$ 158$^{5}$ 238$^{5}$ 355$^{6}$ 655$^{3}$ 781$^{3}$ 985$^{9}$* (2026) 4968$^{11}$ *5055$^{5}$* **>56a 61f<**

**Lochwood 3** b f Lochnager-Soltago (Touching Wood (USA)) *4977$^{11}$* **>9a f<**

**Locket 3** b f Precocious-Bracelet (Balidar) 3108$^{10}$ 3656$^{15}$ 4201$^{11}$

**Locorotondo (IRE) 5** b m Broken Hearted-Rahwah (Northern Baby (CAN)) *181$^{10}$ 486$^{6}$ 598$^{3}$* 690$^{3}$ *1458$^{2}$ 2173$^{6}$ 2536$^{10}$* ***>69a 75f<***

**Lofty Deed (USA) 6** b g Shadeed (USA)-Soar Aloft (USA) (Avatar (USA)) 1803$^{22}$ **>24a 18f<**

**Loganlea (IRE) 2** br f Petong-White's Pet (Mummy's Pet) 4790$^{W}$ 5049$^{6}$ **>41f<**

**Logic 2** b f Slip Anchor-Docklands (On Your Mark) 2863$^{4}$ 3129$^{7}$ 4253$^{2}$ 4464$^{5}$ **>100?f<**

**Logica (IRE) 2** b f Priolo (USA)-Salagangai (Sallust) 2147$^{8}$ 2702$^{2}$ 3159$^{14}$ 3873$^{6}$ 4211$^{4}$ 4746a$^{8}$ **>74f<**

**Logie 4** ch g Prince Sabo-Ashdown (Pharly (FR)) *1516$^{6}$* ***>63a 37f<***

**Logie Pert Lad 4** b g Green Ruby (USA)-Rhazya (Rousillon (USA)) 3506$^{12}$ 3864$^{7}$ 4130$^{10}$ **>28f<**

**Logstown (IRE) 4** b f Keen-No Distractions (Tap On Wood) 4738a$^{10}$ **>80f<**

**Loki (IRE) 8** ch g Thatching-Sigym (Lord Gayle (USA)) **1995:** *(4364) 4416$^{4}$* **1996:** *3233$^{2}$* 3470$^{9}$ 3828$^{6}$ 4073$^{9}$ 4121$^{4}$ 4515$^{4}$ 4703$^{2}$ 4904$^{2}$ *4998$^{2}$* **>73a 75f<**

**Lombardic (USA) 5** b h Private Account (USA)-If Winter Comes (USA) (Dancing Champ (USA)) *(564)* 941$^{11}$ 1353$^{8}$ 2055$^{15}$ 3710$^{7}$ 4055$^{4}$ **>95f<**

**Lomberto 3** b c Robellino (USA)-Lamees (USA) (Lomond (USA)) 727$^{7}$ 3409$^{5}$ 3658$^{5}$ 4066$^{7}$ 4680$^{7}$ **>99f<**

**Lomond Lassie (USA) 3** b f Lomond (USA)-Herbivorous (USA) (Northern Jove (CAN)) 2080$^{7}$ 2318$^{9}$ 2591$^{8}$ 3580$^{13}$ 3866$^{7}$ 4209$^{7}$ 4437$^{12}$ 4921$^{16}$ **>35f<**

**Lone Eagle (IRE) 3** b c Alzao (USA)-Cellophane (Coquelin (USA)) 1573a$^{6}$ **>96f<**

**Lonely Heart 2** b f Midyan (USA)-Take Heart (Electric) 4330$^{7}$ 4605$^{6}$ 4797$^{4}$ **>74f<**

**Lonely Leader (IRE) 3** ch c Royal Academy (USA)-Queen To Conquer (USA) (King's Bishop (USA)) (2346) 3517$^{4}$ 4185$^{4}$ 4325$^{6}$ **>104f<**

**Lonely Man (USA) 2** b c Woodman (USA)-Lonely Bird (USA) (Storm Bird (CAN)) (4408a)

**Lonely Vigil (FR) 4** b f Noblequest (FR)-Castaway (FR) (Filiberto (USA)) *117$^{13}$ 174$^{W}$ 317$^{9}$ 356$^{8}$*

**Longano Bay (IRE) 3** b c Contract Law (USA)-Mettle (USA) (Pretendre) 3051$^{6}$ 3466$^{8}$ **>4f<**

**Longcroft 4** ch f Weldnaas (USA)-Najariya (Northfields (USA)) 1676$^{12}$ 1784$^{6}$ 1847$^{4}$ 2756$^{4}$ 4321$^{12}$ **>12a 49f<**

**Longhill Boy 3** b g Statoblest-Summer Eve (Hotfoot) 468$^{9}$ 525$^{22}$ 748$^{19}$ 2373$^{15}$ **>42df<**

**Longwick Lad 3** ro c Chilibang-Bells of St Martin (Martinmas) 1429$^{2}$ 3162$^{5}$ 3446$^{10}$ 3652$^{2}$ 3827$^{9}$ 3930$^{4}$ (4088) 4220$^{2}$ 4521$^{6}$ **>78f<**

**Lookingforarainbow (IRE) 8** ch g Godswalk (USA)-Bridget Folly (Crofter (USA)) 547$^{2}$ 641$^{4}$ 933$^{5}$ 1476$^{5}$ 2008$^{9}$ 2131$^{2}$ 2300$^{2}$ 2724$^{10}$ 3161$^{6}$ 4683$^{12}$ **>78a 78f<**

**Lookout 2** b f Salse (USA)-Sea Pageant (Welsh Pageant) 4175$^{5}$ **>85f<**

**Look Who's Calling (IRE) 3** b c Al Hareb (USA)-House Call (Artaius (USA)) 640$^{6}$ 774$^{6}$ 962$^{5}$ 1422$^{3}$ **>84f<**

**Loophole (FR) 3** b f Groom Dancer (USA)-Luvia (FR) (Cure The Blues (USA)) 4539a$^{2}$ **>104f<**

**Loose Talk 3** ch f Thatching-Brazen Faced (Bold And Free) 458$^{6}$ 524$^{2}$ 626$^{4}$ 1466$^{8}$ **>59f<**

**Lorcan (GER)** 3 1751a$^{6}$ **>48f<**

**Lorcanjo** 5 b m Hallgate-Perfect Double (Double Form) *2191$^{11}$* 2530$^{11}$ **>47da 41df<**

**Lord Advocate** 8 br g Law Society (USA)-Kereolle (Riverman (USA)) 542$^{9}$ 558$^{6}$ 620$^{5}$ (1022) 1044$^{6}$ 1165$^{3}$ (1309) (1870) 2020$^{2}$ 2390$^{5}$ 2418$^{3}$ 2487$^{5}$ 2847$^{4}$ 3098$^{2}$ 3242$^{3}$ 3290$^{3}$ 3487$^{6}$ 3649$^{2}$ 3878$^{11}$ 3958$^{12}$ 4315$^{7}$ 4483$^{5}$ 4810$^{8}$ 5008$^{5}$ **>32a 47f<**

**Lord Barnard (IRE)** 6 gr g Toca Madera-Avital (Pitskelly) **1995:** *4430$^{10}$* **1996:** *29$^{6}$ 79$^{15}$* **>13a f<**

**Lord Carson (USA)** 4 b c Carson City (USA)-Bedgays Lady (USA) (Lord Gaylord (USA)) *4951a$^{4}$* **>127a f<**

**Lord Cornelious** 3 b c Lochnager-Title (Brigadier Gerard) *1023$^{6}$* 1168$^{6}$ 1547$^{7}$ 2021$^{7}$ 2732$^{5}$ 3100$^{9}$ 3292$^{8}$ 3342$^{8}$ **>33f<**

**Lord Discord** 2 b g Primo Dominie-Busted Harmony (Busted) 2138$^{6}$ 2517$^{4}$ 3462$^{8}$ 4319$^{3}$ 4482$^{4}$ **>62f<**

**Lord Ellangowan (IRE)** 3 ch c Astronef-Gossip (Sharp Edge) **1995:** *4352$^{8}$* **1996:** *67$^{9}$ 176$^{2}$ 245$^{8}$ 351$^{4}$ 361$^{2}$ 502$^{9}$ 760$^{10}$* 1514$^{10}$ 1963$^{8}$ 3929$^{8}$ **>50a 48f<**

**Lord Hastie (USA)** 8 b g Affirmed (USA)-Sheika (USA) (Minnesota Mac) 508$^{5}$ (620) 886$^{2}$ 1109$^{4}$ 1421$^{6}$ 1637$^{5}$ 3710$^{6}$ 3828$^{7}$ 4431$^{6}$ 4683$^{10}$ **>23a 73f<**

**Lord High Admiral (CAN)** 8 b g Bering-Baltic Sea (CAN) (Danzig (USA)) 451$^{7}$ 711$^{10}$ 1430$^{9}$ (1964) 2292$^{3}$ (2548) 3085$^{7}$ 3432$^{12}$ 3618$^{7}$ 4215$^{2}$ (4452) **>93f<**

**Lord Jim (IRE)** 4 b g Kahyasi-Sarah Georgina (Persian Bold) **1995:** *4481$^{4}$* **1996:** *1976$^{5}$* (2250) (3531a) 4032a$^{2}$ 4741a$^{2}$ 5029a$^{3}$ **>89a 108f<**

**Lord of The Manor** 3 b c Simply Great (FR)-Wharton Manor (Galivanter) *1090$^{3}$* (1310) 1669$^{11}$ 2570$^{12}$ **>67f<**

**Lord Olivier (IRE)** 6 b g The Noble Player (USA)-Burkina (African Sky) *711$^{9}$* 928$^{10}$ 1334$^{9}$ 2220$^{10}$ (3140) (3399) 3672$^{5}$ 4255$^{3}$ 4687$^{11}$ **>82f<**

**Lord Palmerston (USA)** 4 b g Hawkster (USA)-First Minister (USA) (Deputy Minister (CAN)) *122$^{13}$* **>73f<**

**Lord President (USA)** 6 br h Danzig Connection (USA)-A Surprise (USA) (Bold Bidder) **1995:** 4402a$^{11}$ **>68f<**

**Lord Sky** 5 b g Emarati (USA)-Summer Sky (Skyliner) **1995:** *4394$^{4}$ 4517$^{6}$* **1996:** *63$^{6}$ 139$^{9}$ 270$^{9}$ 331$^{3}$ 394$^{4}$ 418$^{2}$ 461$^{2}$ 500$^{4}$ 997$^{7}$* 1307$^{11}$ *1492$^{12}$ 1765$^{5}$ 1812$^{10}$* **>56a 26f<**

**Lorelei Lee (IRE)** 4 ch f Old Vic-Most Amusing (Blushing Groom (FR)) **1995:** *4407$^{16}$* **>62df<**

**Lorins Gold** 6 ch g Rich Charlie-Woolcana (Some Hand) 893$^{7}$ (1013) 1536$^{2}$ 1890$^{4}$ 2193$^{2}$ 3096$^{5}$ 3439$^{5}$ 3661$^{6}$ 3861$^{5}$ **>43f<**

**Los Alamos** 3 b f Keen-Washita (Valiyar) **1995:** *4410$^{3}$ 4446$^{3}$* **1996:** *346$^{2}$ 402$^{3}$ 1023$^{2}$ 2368$^{2}$ (2747) 3309$^{2}$* 3459$^{6}$ 3855$^{4}$ (4766) 5008$^{7}$ **>70a 70f<**

**Lost Dream** 7 gr m Niniski (USA)-Rocketina (Roan Rocket) 4763$^{9}$ 4833$^{13}$ **>36f<**

**Lost Lagoon (USA)** 4 ch c Riverman (USA)-Lost Virtue (USA) (Cloudy Dawn (USA)) 613$^{2}$ 4360$^{3}$ **>84?f<**

**Lost Realm** 4 b g Reprimand-Clarandal (Young Generation) *2788$^{7}$* 3273$^{3}$ **>46f<**

**Lostris (IRE)** 5 b m Pennine Walk-Herila (FR) (Bold Lad (USA)) 612$^{6}$ 886$^{6}$ 1044$^{2}$ 1478$^{6}$ 2028$^{2}$ 2530$^{3}$ 4588$^{2}$ 4794$^{18}$ **>46f<**

**Lothlorien (USA)** 3 ch f Woodman (USA)-Fairy Dancer (USA) (Nijinsky (CAN)) 813$^{6}$ 1434$^{2}$ 1895$^{3}$ (3839) 4539a$^{7}$ **>86f<**

**Lotties Bid** 4 b f Ring Bidder-Gleneagle (Swing Easy (USA)) *1460$^{12}$* **>45a f< (DEAD)**

**Lough Erne** 4 b f Never so Bold-Laugharne (Known Fact (USA)) 1781$^{8}$ 2316$^{2}$ (3439) (3810) 4136$^{3}$ 4581$^{3}$ 4775$^{15}$ **>85f<**

**Louisiana Purchase** 3 b g Macmillion-My Charade (Cawston's Clown) 637$^{13}$ 1591$^{9}$ **>39f<**

**Louis Quatorze (USA)** 3 b c Sovereign Dancer (USA)-On To Royalty (USA) (On To Glory (USA)) *(1391a) 4956a$^{2}$* ***>126a 132f<***

**Louis' Queen (IRE)** 4 b f Tragic Role (USA)-Bourbon Queen (Ile de Bourbon (USA)) **1995:** 4398a$^{3}$ **1996:** 1770$^{5}$ (2248) 2704$^{7}$ **>106f<**

**Louisville Belle (IRE)** 7 ch m Ahonoora-Lomond Fairy (Lomond (USA)) *814$^{14}$* 1064$^{10}$ 1178$^{5}$ 1466$^{7}$ 1985$^{6}$ 2193$^{3}$ 2376$^{6}$ **>42a 47f<**

**Loup Solitaire (USA)** 3 b c Lear Fan (USA)-Louveterie (USA) (Nureyev (USA)) 1139a$^{2}$ **>113f<**

**Love And Kisses** 3 ch f Salse (USA)-Soba (Most Secret) 1333$^{11}$ 1614$^{17}$ 2610$^{9}$ 3249$^{9}$ *(3605) 3922$^{6}$* ***>70a 69f<***

**Love Bateta (IRE)** 3 b br f Caerleon (USA)-Marie Noelle (FR) (Brigadier Gerard) 921$^{6}$ 1117$^{11}$ 2197$^{7}$ 2399$^{6}$ 3657$^{3}$ 3979$^{9}$ 4559$^{4}$ *4779$^{6}$* **>60a 74f<**

**Love Bird (IRE)** 3 b g Bluebird (USA)-Top Glad (USA) (I'm Glad (ARG)) **1995:** *4361$^{4}$* **1996:** *67$^{3}$ 175$^{8}$* **>68a 78f< (DEAD)**

**Love Has No Pride (USA)** 2 gr c El Prado (IRE)-Chili Lee (USA) (Belted Earl (USA)) 2543$^{6}$ 2708$^{6}$ (3631) 4049$^{12}$ 4375$^{2}$ (4625) 4760$^{7}$ **>83f<**

**Love Legend** 11 ch g Glint of Gold-Sweet Emma (Welsh Saint) **1995:** *4374$^{9}$ 4406$^{4}$ 4440$^{5}$* **1996:** *30$^{10}$ 190$^{4}$ 219$^{10}$ 341$^{2}$ 406$^{3}$ 854$^{7}$ 1074$^{6}$* 1449$^{13}$ 1890$^{11}$ 3443$^{W}$ 4436$^{19}$ *5003$^{10}$* **>45a 42f<**

**Lovely Morning** 3 b f Thowra (FR)-Sweet Pleasure (Sweet Revenge) *3418$^{9}$ 3847$^{3}$* 3966$^{6}$ 4480$^{17}$ **>10a 57f<**

**Lovely Prospect** 3 b f Lycius (USA)-Lovely Lagoon (Mill Reef (USA)) 689$^{4}$ 1092$^{7}$ 4257$^{15}$ 4387$^{5}$ 4692$^{17}$ **>56f<**

**Lovely Smile (BEL)** 3 ch f River Smile (USA)-Love Ballad (Song) *232$^{7}$*

**Love Me Do (USA)** 2 b c Minshaanshu Amad (USA)-I Assume (USA) (Young Emperor) *2967$^{3}$* 4386$^{4}$ 4618$^{11}$ 4795$^{18}$ **>73+f<**

**Lovescape** 5 b m Precocious-Alpine Damsel (Mountain Call) *99$^{7}$ 360$^{10}$* **>65a f<**

**Love That Jazz (USA)** 2 b f Dixieland Band (USA)-Love From Mom (USA) (Mr Prospector (USA)) *4950a$^{2}$* **>103a f<**

**Love The Blues** 4 ch f Bluebird (USA)-Love Match (USA) (Affiliate (USA)) *642$^{2}$* 4365$^{7}$ **>73f<**

**Loveyoumillions (IRE)** 4 b g Law Society (USA)-Warning Sound (Red Alert) **1995:** *4368$^{6}$ 4392$^{4}$* **1996:** *338$^{2}$ 357$^{8}$ 496$^{6}$* 771$^{5}$ 913$^{4}$ 1159$^{2}$ 1506$^{2}$ 2121$^{4}$ **>85a 76df<**

**Loving And Giving** 2 b f Sharpo-Pretty Poppy (Song) (4087) 4579$^{4}$ **>75f<**

**Lower Egypt (USA)** 6 b h Silver Hawk (USA)-Naughty Nile (USA) (Upper Nile (USA)) 1824$^{2}$ **>114f<**

**Loxley's Girl (IRE)** 2 b f Lahib (USA)-Samnaun (USA) (Stop The Music (USA)) 733$^{7}$ 848$^{7}$ 1645$^{8}$ **>30f<**

**Lubaba (USA)** 3 b br f Woodman (USA)-Minifah (USA) (Nureyev (USA)) 870$^{3}$ 1333$^{8}$ (1906) 2945$^{8}$ 3334$^{9}$ **>67f<**

**Lucayan Beach** 2 gr g Cyrano de Bergerac-Mrs Gray (Red Sunset) 706$^{4}$ 815$^{2}$ 1130$^{5}$ **>68f<**

**Lucayan Prince (USA)** 3 br c Fast Play (USA)-Now That's Funny (USA) (Saratoga Six (USA)) 727$^{6}$ 952$^{3}$ 1495$^{2}$ (2050) 2622$^{2}$ 4057$^{5}$ 4442$^{2}$ 4718$^{5}$ **>124f<**

**Lucitino** 3 ch f Bustino-Lucky Fingers (Hotfoot) *390$^{7}$ 484$^{5}$ 763$^{11}$ 1487$^{12}$ 1721$^{15}$* **>37a f<**

**Lucky Archer** 3 b c North Briton-Preobrajenska (Double Form) 445$^{6}$ 730$^{5}$ 936$^{3}$ 1796$^{5}$ 2004$^{6}$ 2584$^{8}$ 3210$^{10}$ 3446$^{3}$ 3790$^{5}$ 4124$^{2}$ 4231$^{3}$ 4352$^{8}$ 4571$^{11}$ 4690$^{2}$ **>88f<**

**Lucky Bea** 3 b g Lochnager-Knocksharry (Palm Track) *473$^{3}$* 539$^{3}$ 827$^{5}$ (976) 1089$^{5}$ 1200$^{7}$ 1526$^{2}$ 2123$^{3}$ 2152$^{7}$ 2573$^{3}$ 2752$^{8}$ 3461$^{8}$ *4089$^{10}$ 4436$^{15}$* 4808$^{15}$ **>47a 57f<**

**Lucky Begonia (IRE)** 3 br f Simply Great (FR)-Hostess (Be My Guest (USA)) 942$^{8}$ 1470$^{5}$ 1690$^{6}$ 2378$^{11}$ **>64f<**

**Lucky Coin** 4 b f Hadeer-Lucky Omen (Queen's Hussar) *968$^{14}$* 1695$^{2}$ 2002$^{8}$ 2415$^{2}$ 2707$^{7}$ 3520$^{5}$ 3802$^{12}$ 3979$^{4}$ 4203$^{8}$ **>65f<**

**Lucky Di (USA)** 4 b c Diesis-Lucky Song (USA) (Seattle Song (USA)) (581) 1509$^{2}$ 2038$^{9}$ **>121f<**

**Lucky Dip** 2 b f Tirol-Miss Loving (Northfields (USA)) 1346$^{7}$ 2708$^{4}$ 3159$^{13}$ **>67f<**

**Lucky Hoof** 3 b f Batshoof-Lucky Omen (Queen's Hussar) 2399$^{7}$ 3356$^{2}$ 4110$^{7}$ 4448$^{14}$ **>73df<**

**Lucky Lionel (USA)** 3 ch c Mt Livermore (USA)-Crafty Nan (USA) (Crafty Prospector (USA)) *681$^{7}$* 927$^{2}$ 1129$^{4}$ 2115$^{12}$ 2622$^{8}$ 3126$^{10}$ 3596$^{6}$ 4442$^{5}$ 4774$^{4}$ 5027a$^{2}$ **>114f<**

**Lucky Oakwood (USA)** 2 ch f Elmaamul (USA)-Fair Sousanne (Busted) 1086$^{4}$ *1968$^{8}$ (3088) 3307$^{2}$* 3408$^{8}$ 4049$^{3}$ 4222$^{3}$ 4566$^{7}$ **>65a 76f<**

**Lucky Parkes** 6 b m Full Extent (USA)-Summerhill Spruce (Windjammer (USA)) 507$^{6}$ 927$^{9}$ 1321$^{2}$ 1616$^{4}$ 1818$^{2}$ (2698) 3126$^{8}$ (3875) 4115$^{7}$ 4412a$^{3}$ 4540a$^{11}$ **>103f<**

**Lucky Power (IRE)** 3 2668a$^{17}$ **>75f<**

**Lucky Revenge** 3 b f Komaite (USA)-Sweet And Lucky (Lucky Wednesday) 1709$^{2}$ 1901$^{7}$ 2255$^{7}$ 2686$^{4}$ 2946$^{2}$ 3055$^{4}$ (3228) 3240$^{4}$ 3758$^{6}$ 4070$^{2}$ 4221$^{3}$ 4376$^{14}$ 4691$^{10}$ **>2a 59f<**

**Lucky Tucky** 5 b g Alleging (USA)-Romana (Roman Warrior) **1995:** *4409$^{8}$* **1996:** *45$^{3}$ 145$^{4}$* **>43a 68f<**

**Lucybod** 2 ch f Night Shift (USA)-Splintering (Sharpo) 452$^{9}$ 568$^{8}$ 3349$^{10}$ 3637$^{10}$ 3840$^{11}$ 4562$^{21}$ **>38f<**

**Lucy of Arabia (IRE)** 2 b f Mujadil (USA)-Fleur-de-Luce (Tumble Wind (USA)) 2230$^{8}$ 2596$^{7}$ 3259$^{10}$ **>56f<**

**Lucy's Gold** 5 b m Efisio-Hinton Rose (Frimley Park) *1085$^{10}$ 2058$^{11}$ 2636$^{7}$ 2891$^{14}$ 3086$^{8}$ 3601$^{12}$* **>5a 26df<**

**Lucy Tufty** 5 b m Vin St Benet-Manor Farm Toots (Royalty) 4236$^{4}$ 4496$^{12}$ 4910$^{4}$ (5053) **>50f<**

**Ludgate (USA)** 4 b f Lyphard (USA)-Hatton Gardens (Auction Ring (USA)) **1995:** *4495a$^{2}$* ***>99f<***

**Ludo** 2 br gr c Petong-Teacher's Game (Mummy's Game) 2852$^{9}$ 3044$^{4}$ 3493$^{10}$ **>67f<**

**Luisa Di Camerata (IRE)** 2 b f Marju (IRE)-Dignified Air (FR) (Wolver Hollow) 1910a$^{6}$ **>79f<**

**Lulu** 2 b f Polar Falcon (USA)-Cap Camarat (CAN) (Miswaki (USA)) 4547$^{10}$ **>39f<**

**Luminosity** 2 5071a$^{8}$

**Luna Mareza** 4 b f Saumarez-Luna Maya (FR) (Gay Mecene (USA)) 1947a$^{2}$ **>114f<**

**Lunar Gris** 3 gr f Absalom-Sliprail (USA) (Our Native (USA)) *4340$^{9}$* ***>25a 24f<***

**Lunar Mist** 3 b f Komaite (USA)-Sugar Token (Record Token) 3495$^{6}$ 3693$^{18}$ 3920$^{11}$ **>90?f<**

**Lunar Music** 2 b f Komaite (USA)-Lucky Candy (Lucky Wednesday) 770$^{9}$ 1320$^{3}$ (3075) 3321$^{4}$ 3590$^{5}$ 3687$^{5}$ (3879) 4195$^{8}$ 4459$^{7}$ **>80f<**

**Lunar Prince** 6 b g Mansingh (USA)-Lunate (Faraway Times (USA)) *353$^{14}$* **>8a 12f<**

**Lunar Risk** 6 b g Risk Me (FR)-Moonlight Princess (Alias Smith (USA)) *69$^{10}$ 635$^{8}$* ***>39f<***

**Luna Wells (IRE)** 3 b f Sadler's Wells (USA)-

Lunadix (FR) (Breton) **1995:** 4468a[2] **1996:** (905a) (1396a) 1949a[7] (3916a) 4292a[6] 4662a[5] 4955a[10] **>123f<**

**Lunch Party** 4 b g Beveled (USA)-Crystal Sprite (Crystal Glitters (USA)) (1156) 2963[2] 3623[10] 3995[7] 4486[9] **>59f<**

**Lunda (IRE)** 3 b f Soviet Star (USA)-Lucayan Princess (High Line) 710[8] 1004[8] 1690[8] **>66?f<**

**Luso** 4 b c Salse (USA)-Lucayan Princess (High Line) (680) 906a[2] (1579a) 2111a[2] 3070[6] (3753a) 4413a[4] **>129f<**

**Lycility (IRE)** 2 b f Lycius (USA)-She's the Tops (Shernazar) *(1664)* 2051[10] 2582[7] 2997[3] 3835[20] 4488[20] **>75f<**

**Lycius Touch** 2 b f Lycius (USA)-Homely Touch (Touching Wood (USA)) 585[6] (1021) 2728[6] 2926[8] *3087[4] 3648[3]* 3943[10] 4223[5] 4347[5] *4980[3]* **>48a 65f<**

**Lydhurst (USA)** 3 b c Runaway Groom (CAN)-Release The Lyd (USA) (Lydian (FR)) 4289a[11] **>61f<**

**Lyford Law (IRE)** 4 b c Contract Law (USA)-Kilboy Concorde (African Sky) **1995:** *(4367)* **>89a 81f<**

**Lynton Lad** 4 b g Superpower-House Maid (Habitat) 450[2] 650[11] 879[19] 1522[10] **>81f<**

**Lyrical Bid (USA)** 2 b br f Lyphard (USA)-Doctor Bid (USA) (Spectacular Bid (USA)) (4225) **>75f<**

**Lyzia (IRE)** 3 ch f Lycius (USA)-Zia (USA) (Shareef Dancer (USA)) 676[10] **>70f<**

**M**

**Ma Belle Poule** 3 b f Slip Anchor-The Kings Daughter (Indian King (USA)) 3949[13] **>67f<**

**Macanal (USA)** 4 b c Northern Flagship (USA)-Magnala (ARG) (Mount Athos) *1136a[2]* 2663a[3] (3572a) 4743a[2] (5027a) **>117f<**

**Macari** 2 gr g Arzanni-View Halloa (Al Sirat (USA)) *4607[11] 4985[5]* **>29a 22f<**

**Macaroni Beach** 2 ch f Jupiter Island-Real Princess (Aragon) 4817[10] **>44f<**

**Macaroon Lady** 5 b m Prince Sabo-Cookie Time (Posse (USA)) *44[7] 84[10] 1846[9]*

***Macfarlane*** 8 br g Kala Shikari-Tarvie (Swing Easy (USA)) 582[19] 711[W] 1708[6] 1974[16] **>50a 68f<**

**Macmorris (USA)** 3 b c Silver Hawk (USA)-Andover Cottage (USA) (Affiliate (USA)) 578[11] 668[5] 890[2] 1415[2] 1782[4] 2990[2] 4110[4] **>79f<**

**Mac Oates** 3 b g Bairn (USA)-Bit of a Lass (Wassl) 1654[15] 2033[10] 2994[12] 3317[2] 3862[6] 3993[13] **>55f<**

**Macs Clan** 3 ch f Clantime-Kabella (Kabour) *4229[14]* 4693[11]

**Mac's Delight** 2 b c Machiavellian (USA)-Bashoosh (USA) (Danzig (USA)) 1424[7] 2414[3] **>54tf<**

**Mac's Taxi** 4 b g Komaite (USA)-Orange Silk (Moulton) *42[14] 109[4] 121[16] 189[4] 200[4]* **>53a 74f<**

**Mad About The Girl (IRE)** 4 b f Cyrano de Bergerac-Makalu (Godswalk (USA)) 1881[8] 3358[10] **>28f<**

**Madame Chinnery** 2 b f Weldnaas (USA)-Bel Esprit (Sagaro) 1643[5] 1871[2] 2187[2] (4222) 4490[5] 4760[4] **>77f<**

**Madame Steinlen** 3 b f Steinlen-Equadif (FR) (Abdos) 570[3] 1071[3] 2223[4] 4083[2] 4427[9] 4827[3] **>72f<**

**Madam Lucy** 2 ch f Efisio-Our Aisling (Blakeney) 1858[9] 2161[11] 2512[6] **>48f<**

**Madam Marash (IRE)** 3 b f Astronef-Ballybannon (Ballymore) 761[12] 3824[8] **>59f<**

**Madam Pigtails** 3 ch f Rich Charlie-School Dinners (Sharpo) **1995:** *4369[12]* **>11a 24f<**

**Madam Poppy** 2 b f Risk Me (FR)-Egnoussa (Swing Easy (USA)) 1595[9] 1904[6] **>20f<**

**Madam Zando** 3 ch f Forzando-Madam Trilby (Grundy) *32[5] 112[8] 167[5] 973[2]* 1405[9] 1612[2] 1761[5] 1888[5] 2902[4] 3256[4] 3700[9] 3844[6] 4323[13] 4356[21] **>31a 50f<**

**Made Bold** 2 b f Never so Bold-Classical Vintage (Stradavinsky) 4357[3] **>74f<**

**Madison's Touch** 3 b f Touch of Grey-Cabinet Shuffle (Thatching) 4784[13] *5001[7]* **>15a f<**

**Madison Welcome (IRE)** 2 b c Be My Guest (USA)-Subtle Change (IRE) (Law Society (USA)) 2495[11] 2727[4] 2985[8] 3577[5] 4319[5] **>59f<**

**Madly Sharp** 5 ch g Sharpo-Madison Girl (Last Fandango) (940) 1107[2] 2114[18] 2332[7] 2880[10] 4554[2] 4823[6] **>107f<**

**Mad Militant (IRE)** 7 b g Vision (USA)-Ullapool (Dominion) 4320[4] 4626[4] 4753[6] *4977[2]* **>81a 59f<**

**Madonna da Rossi** 3 b f Mtoto-Granny's Bank (Music Boy) *403[8] 637[4]* 2026[15] 2391[11] 2777[9] 2963[3] 3427[2] 3881[7] **>51da 48f<**

**Madrileno (IRE)** 4 gr c Common Grounds-Legs And Things (Three Legs) 3747a[3] 4656a[7] **>115f<**

**Madrina** 3 b f Waajib-Mainly Sunset (Red Sunset) *524[6]* 783[8] 1429[5] 1688[5] 2048[3] 2358[5] 2931[4] 4881[3] *4983[3]* **>59a 67f<**

**Maestro Time (USA)** 3 br g Fred Astaire (USA)-Time For Muir (USA) (Sham (USA)) **1995:** *4480[6]* **>62a f< (DEAD)**

**Maftool** 2 ch c Machiavellian (USA)-Majmu (USA) (Al Nasr (FR)) 1896[11] 3221[5] 4363[4] **>78f<**

**Maftun (USA)** 4 ch c Elmaamul (USA)-Allesheny (Be My Guest (USA)) 771[10] 1072[6] 1504[8] 2077[5] 2493[2] (3098) 3290[5] 3939[9] 4726[11] **>56f<**

**Mafuta (IRE)** 4 b f Mtoto-Chrism (Baptism) **1995:** *4442[11] 4489[9]* **1996:** *23[7] 54[5] 104[12] 866[12]* ***>39a 51f<***

**Magarah (IRE)** 3 b f Magical Strike (USA)-Zurarah (Siberian Express (USA)) 1255a[P] **(DEAD)**

**Magellan (USA)** 3 b c Hansel (USA)-Dabaweyaa (Shareef Dancer (USA)) 2881[3] 3409[2] 3596[3] (4351) 4714[6] **>117f<**

**Maggi For Margaret** 3 b f Shavian-Feather Flower (Relkino) 3393a[3] **>102f<**

**Magical Lady (IRE)** 4 b f Magical Strike (USA)-Usance (GER) (Kronenkranich (GER)) 4643a[22] **>32f<**

**Magical Midnight** 3 ch f Timeless Times (USA)-Mayor (Laxton) 525[18] *605[11] 867[6]* 1042[13] 1888[10] 2780[9] 3960[4] 4437[10] **>34a 34f<**

**Magical Mill** 3 ch f Prince Sabo-Mimram Melody (Music Boy) **1995:** *4393[9]* **>35a 7f<**

**Magical Times** 2 ch c Timeless Times (USA)-Meadmore Magic (Mansingh (USA)) 452[2] 916[2] (1622) 1815[2] 2484[2] 2879[4] (3792) (4189) 4510[3] 4723[16] **>101f<**

**Magication** 6 b m Nomination-Gundreda (Gunner B) **1995:** *4412[3] 4507[10]* **1996:** *34[9]* **>39a 42f<**

**Magic Blue (IRE)** 2 b c Bluebird (USA)-Sallymiss (Tanfirion) 452[10] 800[7] 958[6] 1404[3] 1801[3] (1989) 2364[7] 3400[8] **>71f<**

**Magic Carousel** 3 b f Mtoto-Lap of Honour (Final Straw) *(1540) >76f<* **(DEAD)**

**Magic Combination (IRE)** 3 b g Scenic-Etage (Ile de Bourbon (USA)) 4643a[7] **>86f<**

**Magic Heights** 3 gr c Deploy-Lady Regent (Wolver Hollow) 1649[5] *1969[4] 4095[5]* **>49a 57f<**

**Magic Junction (USA)** 5 b h Danzig Connection (USA)-Sleeping Beauty (Mill Reef (USA)) **1995:** *4356[4]* **1996:** *48[9] (100)* **>85a 84f<**

**Magic Lake** 3 b f Primo Dominie-Magic Kingdom (Kings Lake (USA)) 1185[12] 1986[9] 2428[12] *2634[4] (2914)* 3102[12] 3680[2] 3881[6] 3995[27] 4486[3] 4769[23] **>48a 47f<**

**Magic Leader (IRE)** 4 b or br g Architect (USA)-Magic Rotation (USA) (His Majesty (USA)) *190[10] 343[4] 487[10] 854[8]* **>22a 47f<**

**Magic Mahal (GER)** 3 1751a[8] **>36f<**

**Magic Mail** 3 b c Aragon-Blue Rhythm (Blue Cashmere) *458[8]* 783[5] 1101[14] 2244[9] 2548[5] (2787) 2999[6] 3930[11] **>71df<**

**Magic Melody** 3 b f Petong-Miss Rossi (Artaius (USA)) *3341[7]* 3654[6] 4805[17] 4888[19] **>37a 38f<**

**Magic Pearl** 6 gr m Belfort (FR)-Oyster Gray (Tanfirion) *180[5] 315[W]* **>46a 76df<**

**Magic Rama (ITY)** 3 (543a)

**Magic Role** 3 b g Tragic Role (USA)-Athens by Night (USA) (London Bells (CAN)) 4099[6] 4429[9] 4611[5] 4833[12] *4892[5]* **>62a 64f<**

**Magic Solution (IRE)** 3 b f Magical Wonder (USA)-Brook's Dilemma (Known Fact (USA)) *2432[8]* 2970[6] **>37f<**

**Magic Times** 5 b g Good Times (ITY)-Young Wilkie (Callernish) 1044[11] 1165[6] *1605[6]* **>31a 32f<**

**Magnificient Style (USA)** 3 b f Silver Hawk (USA)-Mia Karina (USA) (Icecapade (USA)) (576) 938[3] (1108) 2069[6] **>110f<**

**Magnolia** 2 gr f Petong-Daffodil Fields (Try My Best (USA)) 807[4] 977[6] **>59f<**

**Magyar Titok (IRE)** 2 b c Treasure Kay-Aliyna (FR) (Vayrann) 2951[4] 3757[13] 3853[8] *4576[3] 4796[7] >47a 63f<*

**Mahalia (IRE)** 3 b f Danehill (USA)-Maresca (Mill Reef (USA)) (720a)

**Mahogany Hall (USA)** 5 ch h Woodman (USA)-Glimpse of Heaven (USA) (Majestic Light (USA)) 4956a[10] **>115f<**

**Mahool (USA)** 7 b g Alydar (USA)-Tax Dodge (USA) (Seattle Slew (USA)) 3817[7] 3985[20] **>92a 65f<**

**Maid By The Fire (USA)** 2 gr f El Gran Senor (USA)-Mist A Risin (USA) (Raise A Native) 1179[2] 1467[2] 1954[5] 2219[2] 2728[2] (3478) **>83f<**

**Maiden Castle** 3 b c Darshaan-Noble Destiny (Dancing Brave (USA)) (495) 725[5] 4177[5] 4487[5] **>101f<**

**Maid For Baileys (IRE)** 3 b f Marju (IRE)-Island Time (USA) (Bold Hour) 2924[2] 3081[7] 3401[2] 3509[3] 3806[2] 4117[5] (4354) 4590[6] **>86f<**

**Maid For The Hills** 3 b f Indian Ridge-Stinging Nettle (Sharpen Up) 674[5] 939[12] 1431[4] 1629[5] 2698[6] 3047[3] 3222[3] 3445[9] 4554[11] 4869[6] 4994[20] **>90f<**

**Maidment** 5 b m Insan (USA)-Lady Gerardina (Levmoss) 1509[10] **>92f<**

**Maid O'Cannie** 5 b m Efisio-Ichnusa (Bay Express) 480[12] 610[14] 704[5] 868[2] 1092[6] 1501[8] (2431) 2799[3] 3622[11] 3937[14] **>66a 62f<**

**Maid of Cadiz** 6 b m King of Spain-Maureen Mhor (Taj Dewan) 746[8] 982[18] **>21f<**

**Maid Of Honor (FR)** 4 br f Highest Honor (FR)-Scottish Bride (FR) (Owen Dudley) 1577a[3] **>115f<**

**Maid To Last** 3 b f Groom Dancer (USA)-Derniere Danse (Gay Mecene (USA)) 792a[6] 1434[12] 1797[11] **>39f<**

**Maid Welcome** 9 br m Mummy's Pet-Carolyn Christensen (Sweet Revenge) **1995:** *4371[10] 4421[16] 4515[2]* **1996:** *42[13] 200[8] 291[3] 340[6]* **>58da 59f<**

**Maiteamia** 3 ch g Komaite (USA)-Mia Scintilla (Blazing Saddles (AUS)) *(405) 421[2] 525[11] (780) (881)* 1405[2] (1597) 1823[2] 2571[2] 3672[8] **>79+a 76f<**

**Majal (IRE)** 7 b g Caerleon (USA)-Park Special (Relkino) *771[8]* 993[10] **>60a 46f<**

**Majaro** 2 b g Merdon Melody-Bri-Ette (Brittany) 452[8] **>20f<**

**Majboor Yafooz (USA)** 6 b g Silver Hawk (USA)-Forced To Fly (USA) (Accipiter (USA)) *251[8]* **>33a 73f<**

**Majdak Jereeb (IRE)** 3 b c Alzao (USA)-Aunty

(FR) (Riverman (USA)) 1349[4] 1687[3] 2002[4] 2140[4] 3283[6] 3699[2] 3928[10] **>77f<**

**Major Change 4** gr c Sharrood (USA)-May the Fourteenth (Thatching) *925[3]* 1193[2] (1961) 2055[7] 2502[15] 3791[12] 4120[6] **>97f<**

**Major Dundee (IRE) 3** b c Distinctly North (USA)-Indigo Blue (IRE) (Bluebird (USA)) *576[12]* 746[2] 1045[3] (1174) 1619[6] 2525[5] 3398[2] 3768[3] 4374[3] **>81f<**

**Majorien 2** ch c Machiavellian (USA)-Green Rosy (USA) (Green Dancer (USA)) 4166a[2] 4742a[2] **>104f<**

**Major Quality 3** b c Sizzling Melody-Bonne de Berry (Habitat) (783) 959[2] 2007[11] **>95f<**

**Major Snugfit 4** b g Tina's Pet-Sequoia (Sassafras (FR)) *77[7] 85[4] 152[5]* **>45da 48f<**

**Major Twist (IRE) 2** b c Dancing Dissident (USA)-Kafsa (IRE) (Vayrann) 3796[18] 4423[7] **>39f<**

**Makaskamina 3** b br g Mtoto-Flying Flo Jo (USA) (Aloma's Ruler (USA)) **1995:** *4352[7]* **>40a 52f<**

**Make a Note (USA) 5** b g Northern Flagship (USA)-Deep Powder (USA) (Researching (USA)) *61[13] 98[2] 136[5] 268[5]* **>81a 91f<**

**Make a Stand 5** ch g Master Willie-Make A Signal (Royal Gunner (USA)) *1803[2]* (2008) 2226[2] 2882[11] **>82f<**

**Make Ready 2** b f Beveled (USA)-Prepare (IRE) (Millfontaine) *1491[2] 1968[6] (2371) 3604[3] (4093)* **>57a f<**

**Makhbar 2** ch c Rudimentary (USA)-Primulette (Mummy's Pet) (2132) 2619[5] 3128[9] 3697[3] **>79f<**

**Maladerie (IRE) 2** b g Thatching-Native Melody (Tudor Music) 1774[4] 2009[2] (2195) 2503[3] 3904a[4] 3925[4] **>93f<**

**Maldinion 3** b f Dominion-Raffle (Balidar) 5065a[8] **>83f<**

**Male-Ana-Mou (IRE) 3** ch g Ela-Mana-Mou-Glasson Lady (GER) (Priamos (GER)) 892[3] 1319[3] (1711) 2074[9] 2608[8] 3124[8] 3689[11] **>107?f<**

**Malibu Man 4** ch c Ballacashtal (CAN)-National Time (USA) (Lord Avie (USA)) *466[2]* 601[7] 862[12] 1521[6] 1844[2] *2084[8] 2496[3]* 2787[3] 2992[2] 3261[W] 3930[W] (4130) 4372[7] 4616[18] **>77+a 71f<**

**Malik (IRE) 2** b c Sadler's Wells (USA)-Radiant (USA) (Foolish Pleasure (USA)) 4261[4] 4801[16] **>73f<**

**Mallia 3** b g Statoblest *571[5]* 1340[2] (2007) 2329[10] **>90f<**

**Mallooh 3** gr c Niniski (USA)-Kalisha (Rainbow Quest (USA)) 1670[7] 1963[3] 2318[4] 2901[5] **>74f<**

**Malou Grand (FR) 2** b c Caerwent-Malouna (FR) (General Holme (USA)) (4944a) **>87f<**

**Malquet (FR) 3** gr c Kendor (FR)-Mi Longa **1995:** (4499a) **>97f<**

**Malzoom 4** b g Statoblest-Plum Bold (Be My Guest (USA)) *387[12] 782[15] 1001[4]* 1502[12] 1992[U] **>32da 29f<**

**Mamlouk 4** gr g Distant Relative-Nelly Do Da (Derring-Do) 2136[10] 2683[10] **>26f<**

**Mamnoon (USA) 5** b g Nijinsky (CAN)-Continual (USA) (Damascus (USA)) *1094[8] 1411[21]* **>40a 28f<**

**Mam'selle Bergerac (IRE) 3** b f Cyrano de Bergerac-Miss Merryweather (Sexton Blake) 755[9] 1074[15] 2945[11] 4373[12] **>48f<**

**Manabar 4** b g Reprimand-Ring of Pearl (Auction Ring (USA)) *13[10] 105[7] 136[9] 177[4] 223[3] 261[2] 331[7] 549[3]* 670[3] 817[15] 920[4] 1154[6] 1345[5] 1870[7] 2192[20] 3471[14] 3985[15] 4129[10] **>72a 42f<**

**Manaloj (USA) 3** ch c Gone West (USA)-Deviltante (USA) (Devil's Bag (USA)) 684[14] (894) 1427[8] 2041[31] 4583[7] **>86f<**

**Mancini 3** b br g Nomination-Roman Blue (Charlottown) 1106[7] 1771[12] 2146[9] 2621[16] 3113[6] 3514[4] **>71f<**

**Mandarina (USA) 4** ch f El Gran Senor (USA)-Oriental Mystique (Kris) **1995:** 4495a[3] **>99f<**

**Manderella 3** b f Clantime-Ascot Lass (Touching Wood (USA)) 1521[8] 1840[6] 2193[11] *2637[P]* **>59f< (DEAD)**

**Mandilak (USA) 2** b c El Gran Senor (USA)-Madiriya (Diesis) 4461[10] (4914) **>80f<**

**Mandy's Bet (USA) 4** ch f Elmaamul (USA)-Dols Jaminque (USA) (Kennedy Road (CAN)) *162[5]* **>37a f<**

**Manful 4** b g Efisio-Mandrian (Mandamus) **1995:** *4385[2] 4416[3] 4452[11] 4507[2] 4534[2]* **1996:** *48[7] 113[5] 256[5] (440)* 541[3] 752[13] (999) 1309[4] 2020[8] 2296[2] 3081[8] 3939[7] 4176[8] (4484) 4617[4] *(4894)* **>64a 76f<**

**Mangus (IRE) 2** b c Mac's Imp (USA)-Holly Bird (Runnett) 877[5] 1622[5] *2633[4] 2942[4]* 3581[3] **>60a 61f<**

**Manhattan Diamond 2** ch f Primo Dominie-June Fayre (Sagaro) 1014[6] 1433[2] 1705[5] 2495[12] 4912[10] 5043[9] **>62f<**

**Man Howa (IRE) 2** ch c Lycius (USA)-Almuhtarama (IRE) (Rainbow Quest (USA)) 2302[2] (2887) **>88f<**

**Manikato (USA) 2** b c Clever Trick (USA)-Pasampsi (USA) (Crow (FR)) 2317[4] 2865[10] 3282[4] 3846[4] 4103[2] 4234[4] 4488[12] 4672[2] 4867[10] **>69f<**

**Manila Bay (USA) 6** b g Manila (USA)-Betty Money (USA) (Our Native (USA)) *111[6]* **>7a 52f<**

**Manileno 2** ch g K-Battery-Andalucia (Rheingold) 4310[4] 4481[5] **>34f<**

**Mankab (MOR) 4** b c The Wonder (FR)-Tabula Rasa (GER) (Gyr (USA)) 3569a[2] **>84f<**

**Mannagar (IRE) 4** ch g Irish River (FR)-Meadow Glen Lady (USA) (Believe It (USA)) 1079[12] 1338[8] 1651[14] *2551[11] 3606[15]* **>6a f<**

**Manninamix 3** gr c Linamix (FR)-Mrs Annie (FR) (Bolkonski) 1754a[2] **>110f<**

**Man of May 4** b c High Kicker (USA)-Faldwyn (Mr Fluorocarbon) *22[6] 59[7] 110[9]* **>41a f<**

**Man of Wit (IRE) 3** b g Fayruz-Laughing Matter (Lochnager) 648[6] 758[4] 1049[10] 2151[4] 2528[9] 3410[3] *3628[11]* **>4a 57f<**

**Manolo (FR) 3** b g Cricket Ball (USA)-Malouna (FR) (General Holme (USA)) 1033[11] 2392[7] 2849[4] 3883[11] 4075[2] (4229) 4727[4] **>68f<**

**Man On A Mission 3** ch g Hatim (USA)-Colly Cone (Celtic Cone) 4322[11] **>37f<**

**Manoy 3** b g Precocious-Redcross Miss (Tower Walk) 584[5] 851[8] 1000[5] 1200[3] 1503[4] (1636) 1887[9] 2196[3] 2433[4] 2627[11] 3098[6] 3346[8] 3426[8] 4249[9] **>60f<**

**Mansab (USA) 3** b g Housebuster (USA)-Epitome (USA) (Summing (USA)) 448[2] 755[3] 3765[9] 4053[17] 4356[5] 4610[14] 4888[3] **>58f<**

**Mans Passion 4** gr g Jupiter Island-Roybirdie (Mansingh (USA)) (1132a) **>42f<**

**Mansur (IRE) 4** b g Be My Chief (USA)-Moorish Idol (Aragon) 1862[5] *2372[3] 2952[6]* 3703[10] *(4095) (4575) 4793[2]* **>82a 70f<**

**Mantles Prince 2** ch c Emarati (USA)-Miami Mouse (Miami Springs) *841[3]* 1424[2] 1774[5] 4195[6] 4350[2] **>86f<**

**Mantovani (IRE) 2** b c Treasure Kay-Dream Of Spring (3561a) **>108f<**

**Manuetti (IRE) 2** b f Sadler's Wells (USA)-Rosefinch (USA) (Blushing Groom (FR)) 2863[7] **>76f<**

**Manwal (IRE) 2** b c Bluebird (USA)-My My Marie (Artaius (USA)) 3407[11] 3701[5] 4601[10] **>80f<**

**Manzoni (GER) 4** dk b c Solarstern-Manege (Neckar) 1135a[5] 1950a[2] (2843a) 4656a[5] **>119f<**

**Mapengo 5** b g Salse (USA)-Premiere Cuvee (Formidable (USA)) *2188[8] 3952[11] 4513[16] 5003[11]* **>35a 30f<**

**Ma Petite Anglaise 4** b f Reprimand-Astolat (Rusticaro (FR)) 739[11] 1102[3] 1462[3] 1792[7] 2945[4] 3173[7] 3635[3] 4068[18] **>81f<**

**Maple Bay (IRE) 7** b g Bold Arrangement-Cannon Boy (USA) (Canonero II (USA)) **1995:** *4374[4] 4512[2]* **1996:** *(18) (57) (77) 100[2] 136[2] 211[2] (358) 371[6] (527)* 615[7] 1019[6] (1341) *2170[9] (2357)* 2526[4] 2954[3] 3084[4] 3279[5] 3450[4] *3627[5] 3640[3]* (3812) 3933[4] (3974) 4054[8] 4190[22] 4432[6] 4682[6] 4769[20] 5042[16] **>86a 81f<**

**Maple Burl 3** b g Dominion-Cam Maire (Northern Prospect (USA)) *28[6] 68[3] 118[2] 218[9] (307) 493[5] 556[3] 743[5]* 861[9] 2954[7] **>71a 57f<**

**Maradata (IRE) 4** ch f Shardari-Maridana (USA) (Nijinsky (CAN)) *98[8] 235[6] 299[3] 384[8] 424[6] 477[4]* 547[4] 787[3] 995[2] (1418) 1502[8] (1704) 2010[15] 2701[7] 3785[6] 4125[7] 4226[2] 4337[9] 4617[15] (4793) **>44a 69f<**

**Maradi (IRE) 2** b c Marju (IRE)-Tigora (Ahonoora) 2335[10] 2580[6] 2923[3] 3485[3] 3998[3] 4262[3] 4625[17] **>73f<**

**Maralinga (IRE) 4** ch c Simply Great (FR)-Bellinzona (Northfields (USA)) **1995:** *4482[4]* **1996:** *831[9]* 1793[9] 2274a[3] 2840a[10] 3386a[9] (3658) 3996[4] 4194[9] 4479[4] **>100a 105f<**

**Mara River 2** b f Efisio-Island Mill (Mill Reef (USA)) 2600[4] 3259[W] 4127[5] **>64f<**

**Maraschino 3** ch f Lycius (USA)-Mystery Ship (Decoy Boy) 1908[9] 2235[10] *3061[3] 3420[10] 3789[11]* 4130[6] 4356[2] 4828[4] 4888[5] **>29a 55f<**

**Maratana (IRE) 2** b f Don't Forget Me-Zenga (Try My Best (USA)) 4156a[6] **>91f<**

**Marathon Maid 2** gr f Kalaglow-El Rabab (USA) (Roberto (USA)) (585) 1115[3] (1419) 2073[7] 3068[6] 4723[11] **>84f<**

**Maraud 2** ch c Midyan (USA)-Peak Squaw (USA) (Icecapade (USA)) 697[6] 1694[3] 1960[9] 3405[3] 3769[2] 3943[2] 4602[14] (4883) **>75f<**

**Marchant Ming (IRE) 4** br g Persian Bold-Hot Curry (USA) (Sharpen Up) 3939[11] 4315[10] 4683[16] **>56a 47f<**

**Marchman 11** b g Daring March-Saltation (Sallust) (1411) 2183[5] 2408[5] 2906[2] 3808[21] **>56f<**

**March Star (IRE) 2** b f Mac's Imp (USA)-Grade a Star (IRE) (Alzao (USA)) 729[3] 916[3] (1179) 1510[4] 2051[5] **>80f<**

**Marco Magnifico (USA) 6** b or br g Bering-Viscosity (USA) (Sir Ivor) 482[9] **>70a 47f<**

**Mardi Gras (IRE) 2** b c Danehill (USA)-Gracieuse Majeste (FR) (Saint Cyrien (FR)) 3615[5] 4200[2] 4508[5] **>82f<**

**Maremma 2** b f Robellino (USA)-Maiden Way (Shareef Dancer (USA)) 1845[5] 2161[7] 3454[7] 4501[6] 4594[8] 4721[7] **>50f<**

**Marengo 2** b c Never so Bold-Born to Dance (Dancing Brave (USA)) 3234[3] 3685[17] 4123[15] **>76tf<**

**Margaretrose Anna 4** b f Handsome Sailor-Be Bold (Bustino) *22[8] 63[12] 167[2] 253[9] 343[6] 587[16] 1455[13] 4610[15] 4983[6]* **>36a 37f<**

**Margi Boo 3** ch f Risk Me (FR)-Louisianalightning (Music Boy) *269[5] 314[6] 402[8] 459[6]* **>43a 46f<**

**Maria di Castiglia 2** b f Danehill (USA)-Macrina Pompea (Don Roberto (USA)) 1467[7] 2254[2] 2539[2] **>63f<**

**Marieavah (FR) 3** gr f Kadrou (FR)-Labonoise (FR) (Jaazeiro (USA)) 4947a[3] **>63f<**

**Marie de Ken (FR) 4** b f Kendor (FR)-Marie de Vez (FR) (Crystal Palace (FR)) **1995:** (4423a) **1996:** 1052a[5] **>114f<**

**Marigliano (USA) 3** b c Riverman (USA)-Mount Holyoke (Golden Fleece (USA)) 942[3] (1323) 1785[3]

**>93f<**

**Marildo (FR) 9** b h Romildo-Marike (FR) (Nasram II) **1995:** 4403a[7] **1996:** 622a[4] 906a[8] **>124f<**

**Marino Casino (USA) 3** b f Alleged (USA)-In Hot Pursuit (USA) (Bold Ruler) 1409[6] **>50f<**

**Marino Street 3** b f Totem (USA)-Demerger (Dominion) **1995:** *4461[5] 4511[2] 4545[5]* **1996:** *21[2] 52[3] 101[2] 271[5] 310[2] 359[2] 414[5] 423[3] 515[5] 531[8] 2236[3]* 2393[5] 2791[3] (2970) 2982[6] 3292[5] 3652[4] 4130[14] 4206[5] 4860[9] *4981[6]* **>52a 63f<**

**Maristax 3** b f Reprimand-Marista (Mansingh (USA)) 1986[7] 2715[4] 4550[5] 4788[9] 4975[24] **>73f<**

**Marjaana (IRE) 3** b f Shaadi (USA)-Funun (USA) (Fappiano (USA)) 785[5] 1327[5] 1648[4] 2729[2] 3167[8] 4214[8] 4590[7] 4860[17] **>70f<**

**Marjan (IRE) 5** ch m Classic Secret (USA)-Powder Lass (Tap On Wood) **1995:** *4406[14] 4449[5]* **>6a 9f<**

**Marjorie Rose (IRE) 3** b f Magical Strike (USA)-Arrapata (Thatching) 443[14] 524[4] 1007[10] 1405[11] 1859[10] 2359[4] 2777[5] 2910[7] *(3061) 3416[4] (3957) 4081[4] 4577[7]* **>62a 60f<**

**Mark of Esteem (IRE) 3** b c Darshaan-Homage (Ajdal (USA)) (926) 2039[8] (3784) (4443) 4953a[7] **>138f<**

**Marl 3** ch f Lycius (USA)-Pamela Peach (Habitat) 548[2] 674[10] 1146[5] 1818[4] 2545[6] 3038[7] 3672[3] 4122[2] 4445[6] 4674[6] **>92f<**

**Marlin (USA) 3** b c Sword Dancer (USA)-Syrian Summer (USA) (Damascus (USA)) (3911a) 4288a[3] 4652a[3] 4955a[13] **>127f<**

**Maronetta 4** ch f Kristian-Suzannah's Song (Song) **1995:** *4387[12] 4546[11]* **1996:** *54[11] 666[15]* ***>30a 53f<***

**Maroulla (IRE) 2** ch f Caerleon (USA)-Mamaluna (USA) (Roberto (USA)) 4969[13] **>66f<**

**Maroussie (FR) 3** br f Saumarez-Madiyma (FR) (Top Ville) (4946a) **>84f<**

**Marowins 7** ch g Sweet Monday-Top Cover (High Top) *18[8]* **>73a 53f<**

**Marozia (USA) 2** ch f Storm Bird (CAN)-Make Change (USA) (Roberto (USA)) 4969[16] **>60f<**

**Marqueta (USA) 4** ch f Woodman (USA)-Russian Ballet (USA) 1255a[4] 1912a[4] 3530a[5] **>93f<**

**Marsad (IRE) 2** ch c Fayruz-Broad Haven (IRE) (Be My Guest (USA)) 1896[6] 2195[3] 2600[3] 3259[2] 3829[4] 4566[10] 4786[2] **>75f<**

**Marsayas (IRE) 3** ch g Classic Music (USA)-Babiana (CAN) (Sharpen Up) 614[9] 803[12] 1887[2] 2175[4] 2627[4] 2804[2] 3053[2] (3580) 4321[4] 4750[5] **>42a 63f<**

**Marshall Pindari 6** b h Son of Shaka-Off The Pill (Marshal Pil) *2169[11]* **>12a f<**

**Marsh Marigold 2** br f Tina's Pet-Pulga (Blakeney) 2389[3] 2685[3] 3169[5] 3241[4] 3498[2] 3943[5] 4223[6] 4368[2] (4562) 4715[6] 4880[7] **>65f<**

**Marsh's Law 9** br g Kala Shikari-My Music (Sole Mio (USA)) 4436[28]

**Marsul (USA) 2** b br c Cozzene (USA)-Beside (USA) (Sportin' Life (USA)) 4261[12] **>56f<**

**Martindale (IRE) 3** b g Fairy King (USA)-Whist Awhile (Caerleon (USA)) 3832[10] 4690[12] **>37f<**

**Martine 2** ch f Clantime-Marcroft (Crofthall) 2772[3] 3464[8] 3660[3] 3921[4] 4311[11] **>66f<**

**Martiniquais (IRE) 3** ch c Simply Great (FR)-Majolique (Irish River (FR)) (1133a) 1756a[2] 2276a[10] 4656a[6] **>114f<**

**Martinosky 10** b g Martinmas-Bewitched (African Sky) 632[11] 981[10] (1516) 1881[6] 2185[3] 2340[11] 2713[8] 3585[7] **>40a 54f<**

**Martins Folly 3** ch f Beveled (USA)-Millingdale (Tumble Wind (USA)) **1995:** *4501[12]* **1996:** *849[16]* ***>5a 28f<***

**Mary Culi 2** gr f Liboi (USA)-Copper Trader (Faustus (USA)) 4104[9] 4798[6] **>56f<**

**Marylebone (IRE) 2** ch c River Falls-Pasadena Lady (Captain James) 2485[2] 2873[4] 3637[2] 4749[11] **>74f<**

**Mary Macblain 7** b m Damister (USA)-Tzarina (USA) (Gallant Romeo (USA)) **1995:** *4362[8] 4436[4] 4537[11]* **1996:** *1037[12]* 1502[9] 1665[10] 2357[6] **>44a 31f<**

**Mary Magdalene 2** b f Night Shift (USA)-Indian Jubilee (Indian King (USA)) 4825[11] **>65f<**

**Marytavy 2** b f Lycius (USA)-Rose Parade (Thatching) 3494[8] 3773[6] 4061[9] **>59f<**

**Masafah (USA) 4** ch f Cadeaux Genereux-Tatwij (USA) (Topsider (USA)) *1885[3]* 2328[12] 2680[7] **>58df<**

**Masai Man (USA) 5** ch g Riverman (USA)-Green Oasis (FR) (Green Dancer (USA)) 3335[17] 4074[11] 4221[20] 4865[19] **>41df<**

**Masai Mara (GER) 3** f 1060a[6] 1750a[10] **>82f<**

**Masbro Bird 3** b f Midyan (USA)-Grinning (IRE) (Bellypha) 4202[16] **>39f<**

**Masehaab (IRE) 3** b c Mujtahid (USA)-Firefly Night (Salmon Leap (USA)) 926[7] 1329[7] 2144[3] 2864[2] 3781[2] (4886) **>106f<**

**Maserati Monk 2** b c Emarati (USA)-Abbotswood (Ahonoora) 1118[2] (1445) 2040[10] 3478[2] 3792[8] 4065[2] 4328[8] **>100f<**

**Mashhaer (USA) 2** b br c Nureyev (USA)-Life's Magic (USA) (Cox's Ridge (USA)) *(4516)* ***>83+f<***

**Mashkorah (USA) 2** ch f Miswaki (USA)-Tom's Lassie (USA) (Tom Rolfe) 4797[11] **>55f<**

**Mashmoum 3** ch f Lycius (USA)-Flaming Rose (USA) (Upper Nile (USA)) 2718[12] 3255[4] (4885) **>93f<**

**Masimara Music 5** ch m Almushmmir-Native Chant (Gone Native) 2345[11]

**Mask Flower (USA) 3** b f Dayjur (USA)-Nom de Plume (USA) (Nodouble (USA)) **1995:** *4429[2] (4461)* **1996:** *340[2] (857) 1340[10]* ***>72a 74f<***

**Masnun (USA) 11** gr g Nureyev (USA)-Careless Kitten (USA) (Caro) **1995:** *(4357) 4525[3]* **1996:** *82[2] (105) (162) 216[2] 305[3] (350) 498[4]* **>72da 68f< (DEAD)**

**Masruf (IRE) 4** b c Taufan (USA)-Queen's Share (Main Reef) 2860[7] 3151[15] 3518[15] 4259[18] **>52f<**

**Massada 3** f 1060a[4] 1750a[9] **>90f<**

**Master Beveled 6** b g Beveled (USA)-Miss Anniversary (Tachypous) *120[2] 199[6] 650[4]* 843[5] 1102[9] 3805[6] 3985[11] 4193[9] 4463[8] (4582) (4606) 4686[12] 4974[8] **>72a 80f<**

**Master Blade (GER) 3** 2668a[6] **>98f<**

**Master Boots 3** br c Warning-Arpero (Persian Bold) 684[8] (774) (1410) 1800[7] 4739a[6] **>109f<**

**Master Charter 4** ch g Master Willie-Irene's Charter (Persian Bold) *(589)* (765) 876[2] 1807[2] 1961[5] (2299) 3072[2] 3640[5] 4190[9] 4568[22] **>91f<**

**Master Foley 2** ch c Cigar-Sultans Gift (Homing) *1080[8] 1453[8] 4572[9]* **>24a 34f<**

**Master Fontenaille (FR) 6** dk g Comrade in Arms-Miss Fontenailles 148a[3] (324a) **>67f<**

**Master Foodbroker (IRE) 8** br g Simply Great (FR)-Silver Mantle (Bustino) 4868[15] 5052[7] **>28f<**

**Master Glen 8** ch g Rabdan-Rage Glen (Grey Mirage) **1995:** *4411[10]* **>5a f<**

**Master Hyde (USA) 7** gr g Trempolino (USA)-Sandspur (USA) (Al Hattab (USA)) 2848[3] 3290[2] 3621[7] 4073[5] 4320[7] 4626[B] **>66a 67f<**

**Master M-E-N (IRE) 4** ch g My Generation-Secret Lightning (USA) (Secretariat (USA)) *995[3]* 1414[2] 1894[5] 3000[7] 3333[11] (3991) 4337[6] **>36a 64f<**

**Master Millfield (IRE) 4** b g Prince Rupert (FR)-Calash (Indian King (USA)) **1995:** *4392[12] 4478[8] 4510[3] 4539[9]* **1996:** *107[8] 177[5] 291[5] 308[10] 1985[10]* 2311[3] 2526[10] 3340[5] 3518[8] 4088[16] 4905[3] 5010[3] *5056[2]* **>72a 74f<**

**Master of Passion 7** b g Primo Dominie-Crime of Passion (Dragonara Palace (USA)) 812[4] 1186[7] 1630[11] 2114[9] 2548[8] 2694[21] 3232[21] 4180[14] 4312[22] 5039[13] **>46a 70df<**

**Master Ofthe House 10** b g Kind of Hush-Miss Racine (Dom Racine (FR)) *303[9] 439[17]* 586[6] 615[3] 752[7] 822[3] 1196[5] 2066[11] 2922[5] 3348[11] **>28a 54f<**

**Master Planner 7** b g Night Shift (USA)-Shaky Puddin (Ragstone) *1107[6]* ***>97f<***

**Masterstroke 2** b g Timeless Times (USA)-Fauve (Dominion) 569[3] (630) 996[6] (2797) 3208[4] 3659[W] 4195[15] 4546[5] 4586[4] **>68f<**

**Matam 3** b f Cyrano de Bergerac-Tasmim (Be My Guest (USA)) 870[13] 1033[4] 1429[3] 1671[6] 3938[10] **>64f<**

**Matamoros 4** gr c Kalaglow-Palama (USA) (Blushing Groom (FR)) 3944[8] **>81f<**

**Matarun (IRE) 8** b h Commanche Run-Miss Mat (Matahawk) **1995:** *(4500a)* **1996:** 3915a[9] **>117f<**

**Mathon (IRE) 3** b g High Estate-Sunley Saint (Artaius (USA)) 821[14] 948[9] 1180[9] 1591[8] 1762[2] 1907[2] 2216[4] **>57df<**

**Matikanetannhauser (JPN) 7** ch h Northern Taste (CAN)-Kuri Pussy (JPN) (Arrow Express (JPN)) **1995:** 4471a[12] **>115f<**

**Matisse 5** b m Shareef Dancer (USA)-Late Matinee (Red Sunset) **1995:** *4409[11]* **>26a 49f<**

**Matiya (IRE) 3** b f Alzao (USA)-Purchasepaperchase (Young Generation) 939[2] (1567a) 1949a[3] 3144[10] 4663a[10] **>117f<**

**Matoaka 2** b f Be My Chief (USA)-Echoing (Formidable (USA)) 1513[4] **>50f<**

**Mattawan 3** ch c Nashwan (USA)-Sweet Mover (USA) (Nijinsky (CAN)) (1168) 1990[2] 2620[5] 4055[3] (4414a) **>93f<**

**Matthew David 6** ch h Indian Forest (USA)-Mazurkanova (Song) **1995:** *4428[4] 4484[2] 4508[6]* **1996:** *71[6]* **>49a 34f<**

**Matthias Mystique 3** gr f Sharrood (USA)-Sheznice (IRE) (Try My Best (USA)) **1995:** *4414[7]* **1996:** *1773[11]* 4353[2] 4496[6] *4892[2]* **>62a 75?f<**

**Mattimeo (IRE) 3** b g Prince Rupert (FR)-Herila (FR) (Bold Lad (USA)) *364[2] 460[2] (3333)* 3710[15] 4067[11] 4374[4] **>52a 77f<**

**Matula (USA) 4** ch c Dixieland Band (USA)-Manduria (USA) (Aloma's Ruler (USA)) (4412a) 4540a[3] **>109f<**

**Maurangi 5** b g Warning-Spin Dry (High Top) *2428[13]* 2801[11] 3280[6] 3589[7] 4692[9] 4808[12] **>49f<**

**Ma Vielle Pouque (IRE) 2** ch f Fayruz-Aussie Aisle (IRE) (Godswalk (USA)) 4087[5] **>63f<**

**Mawared (IRE) 3** ch c Nashwan (USA)-Harmless Albatross (Pas de Seul) 732[7] 970[7] 1201[3] 4695[3] 4804[11] **>76f<**

**Mawhiba (USA) 2** b br f Dayjur (USA)-Histoire (FR) (Riverman (USA)) 3593[9] **>71+f<**

**Mawingo (IRE) 3** b c Taufan (USA)-Tappen Zee (Sandhurst Prince) **1995:** *4491[5]* **1996:** *663[6]* (978) 1126[5] (1807) (2334) 3211[5] 4556[6] **>69a 86f<**

**Mawjud 3** b c Mujtahid (USA)-Elfaslah (IRE) (Green Desert (USA)) 3811[3] 4051[8] **>97f<**

**Mawwal (USA) 3** ch c Elmaamul (USA)-Dish Dash (Bustino) 694[7] 2436[3] **>101f< (DEAD)**

**Maybank (IRE) 4** gr g Contract Law (USA)-Katysue (King's Leap) *110[5] 234[4] (298) 431[2] 592[9] 1029[4] 1473[11] 1718[6] 2084[7] 4430[14]* 4881[21] *4982[12]* **>65a 31f<**

**Mayfair 2** b f Green Desert (USA)-Emaline (FR) (Empery (USA)) (3036) 3804[5] 4621[4] **>86tf<**

**Mayflower 2** b f Midyan (USA)-Chesnut Tree (USA) (Shadeed (USA)) 2854[2] 3807[5] 4208[3] 4605[5] **>83f<**

**May King Mayhem 3** ch g Great Commotion (USA)-Queen Ranavalona (Sure Blade (USA)) 1009[7]

$1497^{4}$ $2159^{9}$ $3845^{8}$ $4587^{6}$ $4766^{11}$ **>45f<**

**Maylane** 2 b c Mtoto-Possessive Dancer (Shareef Dancer (USA)) $4451^{5}$ $4700^{2}$ (4891) **>83+f<**

**Maypole (IRE)** 2 ch g Mujtahid (USA)-Dance Festival (Nureyev (USA)) $4825^{9}$ **>70f<**

**May Queen Megan** 3 gr f Petorius-Siva (FR) (Bellypha) $468^{6}$ $525^{17}$ $686^{4}$ $1013^{6}$ $1466^{10}$ $1836^{6}$ $2200^{2}$ (2686) $2946^{12}$ $3270^{4}$ **>58f<**

**Maysimp (IRE)** 3 ch f Mac's Imp (USA)-Splendid Yankee (Yankee Gold) $867^{10}$ $1405^{3}$ $2049^{10}$ $2496^{10}$ $2777^{11}$ $3399^{6}$ $3591^{9}$ **>33f<**

**Mazamet (USA)** 3 b g Elmaamul (USA)-Miss Mazepah (USA) $4643a^{17}$ **>75f<**

**Mazara (IRE)** 2 b f High Estate-Shy Jinks (Shy Groom (USA)) $4449^{10}$ **>10f<**

**Mazcobar** 3 ch c Mazilier (USA)-Barbary Court (Grundy) $873^{3}$ (1312) $1773^{7}$ (2061) (2126) $3107^{4}$ $3501^{2}$ $3830^{2}$ $4329^{15}$ **>85f<**

**Mazeed (IRE)** 3 ch c Lycius (USA)-Maraatib (IRE) (Green Desert (USA)) $737^{7}$ $1327^{6}$ $2950^{3}$ $3790^{16}$ **>88f<**

**Mazil** 2 b g Mazilier (USA)-Gymcrak Lovebird (Taufan (USA)) $2485^{5}$ $2720^{8}$ $2897^{2}$ $3275^{6}$ $3464^{6}$ $3969^{11}$ $4562^{9}$ $4749^{14}$ **>58f<**

**Mazilla** 4 b f Mazilier (USA)-Mo Ceri (Kampala) **1995:** *$4376^{11}$ $4409^{10}$ $4444^{2}$ $4505^{9}$ $4510^{7}$* **1996:** *$90^{8}$ $122^{9}$ $210^{8}$ (252) (297) $333^{9}$ $360^{6}$ $979^{12}$ $1098^{7}$ $1411^{9}$* $1468^{5}$ $1665^{5}$ $1838^{9}$ (2056) $2366^{4}$ (2716) (2896) (3173) $3452^{3}$ $4226^{5}$ $4355^{16}$ $4513^{12}$ **>45a 65f<**

**Mazirah** 5 b g Mazilier (USA)-Barbary Court (Grundy) $1348^{8}$ $1890^{14}$ $3220^{7}$ *$3630^{7}$ $4186^{16}$* ***>44a 38f<***

**Mazurek** 3 b c Sadler's Wells (USA)-Maria Waleska (Filiberto (USA)) $677^{9}$ $4824^{8}$ **>61f<**

**Mazzarello (IRE)** 6 ch g Hatim (USA)-Royal Demon (Tarboosh (USA)) **1995:** *$4488^{8}$* **1996:** *$466^{16}$* $601^{20}$ $664^{3}$ $862^{17}$ $1049^{2}$ $1512^{13}$ $1777^{12}$ $2286^{24}$ $3146^{11}$ $3323^{9}$ **>9a 26f<**

**Mbulwa** 10 ch g Be My Guest (USA)-Bundu (FR) (Habitat) **1995:** *$4374^{11}$* **1996:** *$851^{13}$* $1474^{3}$ (1819) $2164^{8}$ $2351^{2}$ $2693^{4}$ $3985^{23}$ $4190^{15}$ **>43a 71f<**

**Mcgillycuddy Reeks (IRE)** 5 b m Kefaah (USA)-Kilvarnet (Furry Glen) $1167^{8}$ $1548^{6}$ $1803^{11}$ $4070^{6}$ $4237^{4}$ $4455^{6}$ $4703^{3}$ $4815^{3}$ $4904^{3}$ **>16a 51f<**

**McKellar (IRE)** 7 b h Lomond (USA)-Local Belle (Ballymore) **1995:** *$4447^{9}$* **1996:** *$71^{8}$ (387) $403^{3}$* **>70a f<**

**Md Thompson** 4 ch f Siberian Express (USA)-Zipperti Do (Precocious) *$206^{10}$ $1001^{18}$* ***>54a 57f<***

**Mdudu** 5 b h Mtoto-Golden Pampas (Golden Fleece (USA)) (3747a) **>118f<**

**Meadow Blue** 3 b f Northern State (USA)-Cornflower (USA) (Damascus (USA)) $2589^{6}$ $2794^{11}$ $3226^{6}$ $3592^{12}$ $4345^{6}$ **>26f<**

**Meadow Foods** 4 ch g Handsome Sailor-Stern Lass (Bold Lad (IRE)) *$346^{P}$* **(DEAD)**

**Meadow Leader (USA)** 6 ro h Meadowlake (USA)-Tobriand (FR) (Mr Leader (USA)) $5068a^{2}$

**Meant to Be** 6 b m Morston (FR)-Lady Gerardina (Levmoss) $449^{19}$ $4199^{10}$ $4447^{13}$ $4683^{9}$ $4862^{10}$ **>78a 71f<**

**Me Cherokee** 4 br f Persian Bold-Siouan (So Blessed) *$172^{7}$ $303^{7}$ $367^{4}$ $542^{2}$* $620^{6}$ $912^{4}$ $1637^{3}$ *$2173^{8}$ $2493^{6}$* ***>49a 52f<***

**Mechilie** 2 b f Belmez (USA)-Tundra Goose (Habitat) $4790^{13}$ $4970^{17}$ **>6f<**

**Mecke (USA)** 4 b c Maudlin (USA) (3912a) $4288a^{2}$ $4543a^{3}$ **>128f<**

**Medaaly** 2 gr c Highest Honor (FR)-Dance of Leaves (Sadler's Wells (USA)) $2543^{2}$ (3131) (3925) $4462^{5}$ (4871) **>111f<**

**Medaille Militaire** 4 gr c Highest Honor (FR)-Lovely Noor (USA) (Fappiano (USA)) $581^{12}$ $831^{10}$ $1131^{2}$ $4680^{8}$ (4911) (5045) **>120f<**

**Medfee** 3 b f Alzao (USA)-Liaison (USA) (Blushing Groom (FR)) $4309^{4}$ $4478^{3}$ (4813) **>76f<**

**Media Express** 4 b g Sayf El Arab (USA)-Far Claim (USA) (Far North (CAN)) *$295^{4}$ $372^{8}$ $690^{9}$* $817^{18}$ $971^{13}$ $4098^{19}$ $4337^{14}$ $4815^{16}$ **>63da 37df<**

**Media Messenger** 7 b g Hadeer-Willow Court (USA) (Little Current (USA)) **1995:** *$4507^{11}$ $4534^{8}$* **1996:** *$30^{13}$ $72^{7}$ $140^{11}$* **>37a 40f<**

**Mediate (IRE)** 4 b g Thatching-Unheard Melody (Lomond (USA)) **1995:** *$4457^{3}$ $4510^{8}$* **1996:** *$53^{9}$ $120^{5}$ $636^{13}$* $1625^{11}$ $2032^{15}$ $2587^{12}$ $3217^{4}$ $4221^{13}$ **>67a 51f<**

**Medieval Lady** 3 ch f Efisio-Ritsurin (Mount Hagen (FR)) (1901) $2142^{3}$ $4682^{9}$ **>88f<**

**Medland (IRE)** 6 ch g Imperial Frontier (USA)-Miami Dancer (Miami Springs) *$3951^{2}$ $4107^{12}$* **>58a 36f<**

**Megan Carew** 2 ch f Gunner B-Molly Carew (Jimmy Reppin) $2211^{8}$ $4041^{8}$ $4435^{7}$ **>37f<**

**Megaron (FR)** 3 b c Le Glorieux-Mer D'Huille (Kenmare (FR)) *(146a)* (289a) $2476a^{3}$ **>115f<**

**Mega Tid** 4 b g Old Vic-Dunoof (Shirley Heights) *$1031^{7}$ $1098^{10}$ $1803^{19}$* $2155^{13}$ **>30a 48f<**

**Meghdoot** 4 b f Celestial Storm (USA)-Greenhills Joy (Radetzky) $682^{7}$ $1145^{11}$ $1426^{3}$ **>32a 73f<**

**Meglio Che Posso (IRE)** 5 b m Try My Best (USA)-Knapping (Busted) $2459a^{3}$ **>86f<**

**Meg's Memory (IRE)** 3 b f Superlative-Meanz Beanz (High Top) (863) $1317^{7}$ $1883^{5}$ $2133^{7}$ $2558^{5}$ $2793^{6}$ $3337^{3}$ $3667^{7}$ *$3872^{9}$* **>29a 64f<**

**Melbourne Princess** 2 ch f Primo Dominie-Lurking (Formidable (USA)) $823^{8}$ $2361^{3}$ $2625^{9}$ $3224^{6}$ $3488^{4}$ $3879^{2}$ $4244^{11}$ *$4999^{3}$* **>60a 63f<**

**Meldorf** 3 ch c Lycius (USA)-Melanoura (Imperial Fling (USA)) *$232^{3}$ $833^{11}$* ***>69a 87+f<***

**Meliksah (IRE)** 2 ch c Thatching-Lady of Shalott (Kings Lake (USA)) (1479) $2112^{7}$ $2575^{5}$ $3940^{5}$ (4324) (4517) $4677^{11}$ **>98f<**

**Melina Mou (IRE)** 3 b f Persian Bold-Gold Necklace (FR) $1949a^{11}$

**Mellaby (USA)** 8 ch g Nureyev (USA)-Hitting Irish (USA) (Irish Ruler (USA)) $2008^{5}$ **>95f<**

**Melleray (IRE)** 2 b f Danehill (USA)-Twany Angel $4024a^{5}$ $4642a^{2}$ **>88+f<**

**Mellors (IRE)** 3 b c Common Grounds-Simply Beautiful (IRE) (Simply Great (FR)) $595^{15}$ $734^{4}$ $1068^{3}$ (1612) $1905^{7}$ *$2308^{9}$ $2982^{2}$* $3313^{2}$ $3636^{2}$ $4799^{6}$ **>40a 71f<**

**Mellottie** 11 b or br g Meldrum-Lottie Lehmann (Goldhill) $2350^{4}$ $2862^{9}$ $3115^{2}$ $3402^{3}$ $3854^{2}$ $3981^{2}$ (4385) **>101f<**

**Mellow Master** 3 b c Royal Academy (USA)-Upward Trend (Salmon Leap (USA)) $943^{3}$ $1171^{9}$ $1452^{8}$ $1780^{7}$ $2061^{W}$ **>60f<**

**Mellwood (IRE)** 2 b c Maledetto (IRE)-Traminer (Status Seeker) $3259^{17}$ $3687^{16}$ *$4091^{9}$ $4970^{13}$* ***>8a 38f<***

**Melodica** 2 b f Machiavellian (USA)-Melodist (USA) (The Minstrel (CAN)) $4890^{3}$ **>68f<**

**Melodic Squaw** 2 b f Merdon Melody-Young Whip (Bold Owl) *$4806^{W}$*

***Melody Wheel*** 4 b f Merdon Melody-Spare Wheel (Track Spare) *$517^{4}$ $649^{10}$* ***>35a 57f<***

**Melomania (USA)** 4 b c Shadeed (USA)-Medley of Song (USA) (Secretariat (USA)) $1465^{4}$ $2036^{8}$ $2505^{7}$ $3947^{20}$ *$4076^{10}$* **>23a 60f<**

**Melos** 3 b f Emarati (USA)-Double Stretch (Double-U-Jay) $595^{19}$ **>12a 45f<**

**Mels Baby (IRE)** 3 br g Contract Law (USA)-Launch The Raft (Home Guard (USA)) *$516^{2}$ $660^{6}$* $748^{4}$ *$1029^{8}$ $1156^{2}$* $1610^{2}$ $1888^{6}$ $2162^{2}$ $2425^{2}$ $2752^{2}$ $3414^{3}$ $4000^{5}$ (4436) (4590) (5042) **>46a 74f<**

**Meltemison** 3 b g Charmer-Salchow (Niniski (USA)) *$241^{2}$ $346^{3}$ $402^{5}$ $593^{11}$* $1047^{3}$ $1477^{8}$ (2321) $4695^{7}$ **>66a 74f<**

**Melt The Clouds (CAN)** 3 ch c Diesis-Population (General Assembly (USA)) $786^{2}$ $982^{4}$ $1323^{4}$ $1901^{5}$ $2510^{2}$ $2918^{2}$ $3472^{4}$ $3986^{5}$ $4257^{5}$ $4559^{2}$ $4819^{8}$ **>82f<**

**Members Welcome (IRE)** 3 b g Eve's Error-Manuale Del Utente (Montekin) $748^{2}$ $861^{4}$ $1612^{4}$ $1891^{4}$ $2578^{8}$ $2800^{5}$ $3294^{7}$ $3339^{4}$ $3644^{7}$ $4045^{13}$ $4259^{12}$ $4809^{17}$ **>45f<**

**Memories Of Silver (USA)** 3 b f Silver Hawk (USA)-All My Memories (USA) (Little Current (USA)) $4953a^{5}$ **>123f<**

**Memorise (USA)** 2 b c Lyphard (USA)-Shirley Valentine (Shirley Heights) $4884^{6}$ **>57f<**

**Memory's Music** 4 b c Dance of Life (USA)-Sheer Luck (Shergar) $4877^{8}$ $5053^{12}$ **>57a 38f<**

**Memphis Beau (IRE)** 3 ch g Ballad Rock-Texly (FR) (Lyphard (USA)) $1709^{8}$ $2011^{6}$ $2510^{6}$ $2765^{3}$ (3317) $3863^{7}$ $4498^{4}$ $4799^{12}$ **>69f<**

**Menas Gold** 4 b f Heights of Gold-Tolomena (Tolomeo) *$580^{6}$* $1440^{6}$ $1961^{9}$ $3805^{14}$ $4184^{7}$ $4489^{9}$ **>79f<**

**Mendoza** 2 b g Rambo Dancer (CAN)-Red Poppy (IRE) (Coquelin (USA)) $2596^{9}$ $4100^{9}$ $4349^{5}$ $4602^{15}$ **>59f<**

**Mengaab (USA)** 2 b c Silver Hawk (USA)-Cherie's Hope (USA) (Flying Paster (USA)) $3987^{3}$ **>87+f<**

**Menja (USA)** 2 b f Lomond (USA)-Suvla Bay (IRE) (Kemal (FR)) $4023a^{6}$ $5063a^{5}$ **>93f<**

**Menoo Hal Batal (USA)** 3 b c Gone West (USA)-Bank On Love (USA) (Gallant Romeo (USA)) $577^{4}$ $774^{3}$ $987^{7}$ $1485^{3}$ $1820^{3}$ $2065^{2}$ $2754^{W}$ *$3421^{2}$ (3818)* ***>78a 90f<***

**Menoo Who (IRE)** 4 ch g Keen-Flying Anna (Roan Rocket) *$4448^{19}$*

***Mentalasanythin*** 7 b g Ballacashtal (CAN)-Lafrowda (Crimson Beau) *$184^{2}$ $210^{6}$ (222) $251^{2}$ $392^{9}$ $439^{10}$* $482^{13}$ $619^{2}$ $2784^{8}$ $3347^{2}$ $3487^{2}$ (3649) $4193^{4}$ $4249^{7}$ $4315^{4}$ $4483^{11}$ $4580^{12}$ $4905^{4}$ $4993^{11}$ **>80a 73f<**

**Mental Pressure** 3 ch g Polar Falcon (USA)-Hysterical (High Top) $932^{6}$ $1200^{2}$ $1647^{3}$ $2140^{2}$ $2570^{2}$ $3155^{2}$ $3669^{3}$ **>96f<**

**Meranti** 3 b g Puissance-Sorrowful (Moorestyle) **1995:** *$4361^{9}$* **1996:** *$525^{5}$* $893^{2}$ $1101^{4}$ $1615^{10}$ $2200^{4}$ $2578^{17}$ $3139^{14}$ $4341^{9}$ **>22a 55df<**

**Merciless Cop** 2 ch c Efisio-Naturally Bold (Bold Lad (IRE)) $1191^{12}$ $1453^{3}$ $3494^{7}$ $3962^{9}$ $4303^{5}$ $4375^{4}$ (4549) $4672^{3}$ $4880^{4}$ **>71f<**

**Mercury (IRE)** 3 b g Contract Law (USA)-Monrovia (FR) (Dancers Image (USA)) $1608^{10}$ *(1969) $2514^{9}$ $2749^{11}$* **>77?a 34f<**

**Meribel (IRE)** 3 b f Nashwan (USA)-Dark Lomond (Lomond (USA)) $1077^{4}$ $1409^{5}$ **>85df<**

**Merit (IRE)** 4 b c Rainbow Quest (USA)-Fur Hat (Habitat) *(1005)* $2042^{6}$ **>78+a 93f<**

**Merlin's Honour** 3 ch f Crowning Honors (CAN)-Miss Merlin (Manacle) *$81^{7}$ $119^{7}$* **>26a 31f<**

**Merrie le Bow** 4 b f Merdon Melody-Arch Sculptress (Arch Sculptor) *$583^{15}$ $782^{10}$ $868^{3}$ $1028^{9}$ $1412^{6}$* (1624) $1715^{5}$ $1881^{3}$ $2193^{6}$ $2340^{10}$ $2686^{7}$ $3439^{4}$ $3700^{2}$ $3930^{7}$ (4206) $4259^{2}$ $4356^{11}$ $4788^{P}$ **>26a 64f< (DEAD)**

**Merrily** 3 gr f Sharrood (USA)-Babycham Sparkle (So Blessed) $1475^{5}$ $1667^{3}$ $2778^{3}$ $3154^{8}$ $3624^{2}$ $3844^{14}$ $4592^{9}$ **>57f<**

**Merryhill Mariner** 2 ch c Superlative-Merryhill Maid (IRE) (M Double M (USA)) $3502^{12}$ $3840^{7}$ *$4091^{10}$* **>1a 36f<**

**Meshhed (USA)** 2 ch f Gulch (USA)-Umniyatee (Green Desert (USA)) $4570^{2}$ (4725) **>85+f<**

**Messalina (IRE)** 3 b f Un Desperado (FR)-Seven

Hills (FR) (Reform) 2048[6] 2333[7] 2680[W] **>33f<**
**Metal Badge (IRE) 3** b c Doyoun-Sharaya (USA) (Youth (USA)) *402[12] 419[7]* **>1a f<**
**Metal Boys 9** b g Krayyan-Idle Gossip (Runnett) 1039[10] 1342[7] 1364[2] 1964[4] 2787[8] 2867[8] 3506[6] 3930[10] **>58f<**
**Metaphor (USA) 3** 4165a[9] **>72f<**
**Metastasio (IRE) 4** b c Petoski-Top of the League (High Top) 4643a[15] **>56f<**
**Metaxas 3** b c Midyan (USA)-Miller's Melody (Chief Singer) (4036a) **>95f<**
**Met Mech Nich (FR) 3** ch f Assert-Honorariat (FR) (Roi Lear (FR)) 1942a[3] 2277a[U] 3202a[4] 3571a[2] (4539a) **>105f<**
**Mezaan (IRE) 4** ch c Royal Academy (USA)-Arctic Heroine (USA) (Arctic Tern (USA)) 941[4] **>101f<**
**Meznh (IRE) 3** ch f Mujtahid (USA)-Johara (USA) (Exclusive Native (USA)) 3255[5] 3767[2] 3999[7] 4453[13] **>81f<**
**Mezzanotte (IRE) 3** b c Midyan (USA)-Late Evening (USA) (Riverman (USA)) 1901[8] 2197[6] 2589[3] 3679[2] 4453[4] (4775) **>87f<**
**Mezzogiorno 3** b f Unfuwain (USA)-Aigue (High Top) 674[7] (1144) 1769[3] 2277a[5] 3231[5] 3688[3] 4654a[11] **>111f<**
**Mezzoramio 4** ch g Cadeaux Genereux-Hopeful Search (USA) (Vaguely Noble) *122[3] 213[4] (328) 426[10] 778[6] 983[10]* 1411[5] *2369[14] (2796)* 3084[2] (3443) 3786[10] 4355[14] **>50a 55f<**
**Mhemeanles 6** br g Jalmood (USA)-Folle Idee (USA) (Foolish Pleasure (USA)) 983[16] **>7a 55df<**
**Miami Banker 10** ch g Miami Springs-Banking Coyne (Deep Diver) *862[11]* 1049[11] 1512[10] 1844[6] 2156[14] 2244[6] *2555[4]* **>39a 54f<**
**Michael Venture 2** b c Shirley Heights-Ski Michaela (USA) (Devil's Bag (USA)) 4492[11] 4705[2] 4914[7] **>83f<**
**Michelle's Ella (IRE) 4** b f Ela-Mana-Mou-Bustina (FR) (Busted) 932[12] 1099[21] **>28f<**
**Mick's Love (IRE) 3** b c Law Society (USA)-Flute (FR) (Luthier) *(918)* **>103f<**
**Midas Man 5** ch g Gold Claim-Golden Starfish (Porto Bello) 2420[9] 2731[11] 4484[10]
**Midatlantic 2** b c Midyan (USA)-Secret Waters (Pharly (FR)) 1118[10] 2243[4] 2708[12] 3230[6] 4084[11] 4549[8] **>64f<**
**Midday Cowboy (USA) 3** b c Houston (USA)-Perfect Isn't Easy (USA) (Saratoga Six (USA)) 2718[3] 3353[7] 3513[2] 3818[4] 4064[6] 4109[13] 4499[9] **>72f<**
**Middle East 3** b g Beveled (USA)-Godara (Bustino) 997[11] 2049[2] (2778) 3154[6] 3844[3] 4312[27] 4589[3] 4811[6] **>77f<**
**Midnight Blue 3** br f Be My Chief (USA)-Guyum (Rousillon (USA)) (4485) **>89+f<**
**Midnight Cookie 3** b c Midyan (USA)-Midnight's Reward (Night Shift (USA)) **1995:** *4437[2]* **1996:** *648[8]* 742[6] 862[19] 1446[11] 1663[5] *1971[6] 5000[8]* **>33a 27f<**
**Midnight Escape 3** b g Aragon-Executive Lady (Night Shift (USA)) (1316) (2143) 3693[15] 4116[10] 4466[11] (4772) **>100f<**
**Midnight Flame 10** gr g Kalaglow-Midnight Flit (Bold Lad (IRE)) 4940a[10]
**Midnight Legend 5** b h Night Shift (USA)-Myth (Troy) 919[4] 1620[2] (1988) 2336[4] 2583[8] 3212[2] 3689[21] **>119f<**
**Midnight Romance 2** b f Inca Chief (USA)-Run Amber Run (Run The Gantlet (USA)) 4725[7] **>40f<**
**Midnight Shift (IRE) 2** b f Night Shift (USA)-Old Domesday Book (High Top) 4488[23] 4756[9] 4887[4] **>73f<**
**Midnight Spell 4** ch f Night Shift (USA)-Bundled Up (USA) (Sharpen Up) 1154[7] 1701[5] 2316[9] 2769[2] (3097) 3360[4] (3477) 3827[3] 4119[4] 4727[2] 5039[7] **>65a 71f<**
**Midnight Times 2** b f Timeless Times (USA)-Midnight Lass (Today and Tomorrow) *1097[7] 1622[11]* 2956[5] 3282[7] **>22a 38f<**
**Midnight Watch (USA) 2** b c Capote (USA)-Midnight Air (USA) (Green Dancer (USA)) 4830[2] **>77f<**
**Midyan Blue (IRE) 6** ch g Midyan (USA)-Jarretiere (Star Appeal) *816[3]* 1116[4] 1511[6] 2002[3] 2499[4] 2912[6] 3983[2] 4327[6] 4683[2] 4862[7] 5046[20] **>63a 83f<**
**Midyan Queen 2** b f Midyan (USA)-Queen of Aragon (Aragon) 1779[7] 2699[3] 4558[3] 4762[6] **>62f<**
**Midyans Song 2** ch f Midyan (USA)-Diva Madonna (Chief Singer) 557[8] 1595[3] 1869[9] 4223[12] **>61f<**
**Miesque's Son (USA) 4** b c Mr Prospector (USA)-Miesque (USA) (Nureyev (USA)) (2841a) 3573a[2] 4057[7] 4857a[2] **>122f<**
**Mighty Flyer (IRE) 2** ch f Mujtahid (USA)-Brentsville (USA) (Arctic Tern (USA)) 4547[11] **>35f<**
**Mighty Forum (CAN) 5** b h Presidium-Mighty Flash (Rolfe (USA)) 4953a[13] **>102f<**
**Mighty Keen 3** ch c Keen-Mary Martin (Be My Guest (USA)) 3413[3] 3642[2] 4322[13] *(5058)* **>72a 65f<**
**Mighty Phantom (USA) 3** b f Lear Fan (USA)-Migiyas (Kings Lake (USA)) 755[6] 1773[5] *(1997) 2407[3]* (2775) 3155[5] *3610[2] 3983[4]* 4457[2] **>74a 82f<**
**Migwar 3** b c Unfuwain (USA)-Pick of the Pops (High Top) 576[2] 804[2] (953) (1476) 2074[19] **>101f<**
**Mihriz (IRE) 4** b g Machiavellian (USA)-Ghzaalh (USA) (Northern Dancer) *450[15]* 1843[6] 2283[4] 3072[7] 3439[9] 3805[12] 4463[13] **>74f<**
**Mijas 3** ch f Risk Me (FR)-Out of Harmony (Song) (1171) 1652[6] *2171[8] 2705[P]* 2999[5] 3406[5] 4521[15] **>52a 69f<**
**Mike's Double (IRE) 2** br c Cyrano de Bergerac-Glass Minnow (IRE) (Alzao (USA)) 815[6] 1008[4] 3796[17] 4234[11] 4803[3] 4903[2] **>49f<**
**Mile High 2** b c Puissance-Jobiska (Dunbeath (USA)) 2993[4] 3147[2] **>97f<**
**Miletrian City 3** gr g Petong-Blueit (FR) (Bold Lad (IRE)) 448[13] 774[7] 1042[14] 1584[4] 2019[6] 2380[4] 2898[4] 2983[2] (3288) 3427[4] 3491[3] 3881[2] 4212[6] **>21a 65f<**
**Miletrian Fit-Out 3** b g Most Welcome-White Domino (Sharpen Up) 821[16] 1035[6] 1644[11]
**Miletrian Refurb (IRE) 3** b br g Anita's Prince-Lady of Man (So Blessed) *(473)* 638[4] 861[2] 973[8] 1592[2] 1761[W] **>69f<**
**Milford Sound 3** b c Batshoof-Nafis (USA) (Nodouble (USA)) 2333[4] 2579[3] (3051) 3640[10] 4326[11] 4559[3] **>74f<**
**Milford Track (IRE) 3** 2276a[8] **>100f<**
**Miliardaire (IRE) 2** ch c Night Shift (USA)-Measuring (Moorestyle) 2671a[3] **>88f<**
**Mill Boy (FR) 7** b h Moulin-Safari Girl (Faraway Son (USA)) 147a[3] 191a[3] 288a[3] **>82f<**
**Mill Dancer (IRE) 4** b f Broken Hearted-Theatral (Orchestra) *87[5] 124[7] 172[4] 615[9]* 787[8] 1417[6] 1546[5] 1828[9] 3410[5] 3592[9] 3645[11] 4070[10] **>41a 36f<**
**Millemay 6** br m Respect-Ravenscraig (Impecunious) 882[4] 1001[6] 1163[14] 1634[6] **>35f<**
**Mill End Boy 2** ch g Clantime-Annaceramic (Horage) 800[8] 930[3] 1086[7] 2396[4] 2984[7] 3275[5] 3771[4] 4586[10] **>62f<**
**Mill End Girl 2** ch f Superpower-Estefan (Taufan (USA)) 538[4] 624[5] (733) (770) 3687[20] **>58f<**
**Mill End Lady 3** b f Tina's Pet-Azelly (Pitskelly) *562[14]* 1526[12] 2481[7] 3059[8] (3256) 3453[13] 3937[7] *4090[8]* **>27a 50f<**
**Millesime (IRE) 4** ch g Glow (USA)-Persian Myth (Persian Bold) 2976[10] 3261[10] 3477[5] 3993[15] **>47f<**
**Mill Force 5** b g Forzando-Milinetta (Milford) *2868[7]* 3081[U] **>66f<**
**Mill House Boy (IRE) 3** b g Astronef-Avantage Service (IRE) (Exactly Sharp (USA)) 2362[7] 2780[11] 3309[10] **>24df<**
**Milliardaire (IRE) 2** ch c Night Shift (USA)-Measuring (Moorestyle) (4163a)
**Mill King (GER) 3** b c Dashing Blade-Marcasita (GER) (Mille Balles (FR)) 2843a[3] 4028a[3] 4659a[3] **>112f<**
**Millroy (USA) 2** ch c Carnivalay (USA)-Royal Millinery (USA) (Regal And Royal (USA)) 2132[3] 2619[6] 2890[3] 3706[6] 4131[17] 4328[9] **>88f<**
**Milltown Classic (IRE) 4** b f Classic Secret (USA)-Houwara (IRE) (Darshaan) *520[6] 604[3] 855[5] 1098[8] 1487[5] 2366[U]* (2563) 2896[3] 3118[2] 3412[4] 3808[7] 4102[10] 4703[15] **>26a 42f<**
**Millyant 6** ch m Primo Dominie-Jubilee Song (Song) *1056a[4]* 1911a[5] 4958a[7] **>116f<**
**Milngavie (IRE) 6** ch g Pharly (FR)-Wig And Gown (Mandamus) **1995:** *4489[5] 4530[10]* **1996:** *(12) 97[2] 169[9] 206[2] 240[3] 275[3] 1444[2] (3066)* **>53a 43f<**
**Milos 5** b g Efisio-Elkie Brooks (Relkino) **1995:** *4350[2] 4357[2] 4539[11]* **1996:** *26[6] 109[5] (117) 170[3] (195) 270[8] 311[3] 350[5] 413[2] 511[4] 981[3]* 1516[4] 1684[F] 3501[7] 3765[2] 3991[11] 4128[9] 4430[8] 4799[3] *5002[5]* **>75a 66f<**
**Miltak 4** b f Risk Me (FR)-Tralee Maiden (IRE) (Persian Bold) **1995:** *4412[5]* **1996:** *54[2] 104[2] 186[2] 240[4]* **>53a 49f<**
**Milton 3** ch g Groom Dancer (USA)-Gold Flair (Tap On Wood) **1995:** *4380[3]* **1996:** *2383[4]* ***>75a 77f<***
**Miltonfield 7** ch g Little Wolf-Kingsfold Flash (Warpath) (4643a) **>86f<**
**Mim-Lou-and 4** b g Glacial Storm (USA)-Tina's Melody (Tina's Pet) 1826[4] 2717[11] **>35a 51f<**
**Mimosa 3** ch f Midyan (USA)-Figini (Glint of Gold) 550[10] 813[14] 1333[14] 1613[10] 1685[11] 1953[7] (2253) 2710[7] 3161[5] 3496[5] 4064[14] 4674[4] 4785[2] 4900[7] **>71f<**
**Min Alhawa (USA) 3** b f Riverman (USA)-Saffaanh (USA) (Shareef Dancer (USA)) *1899[2]* 2533[6] 2991[4] 3497[2] (4126) 4445[17] **>111f<**
**Minarello (USA) 2** b c Blushing John (USA)-Inuvik (ITY) (Herat (USA)) 2667a[2]
**Mind Games 4** b c Puissance-Aryaf (CAN) (Vice Regent (CAN)) (1483) 2115[2] 2622[7] 3708[4] 4057[6] **>126f<**
**Mindrace 3** b g Tina's Pet-High Velocity (Frimley Park) 467[14] 832[6] 1101[16] 1693[10] 1995[4] 2500[4] 2745[4] (2790) 2999[2] 3477[4] 3693[17] 4372[8] 4521[4] **>15a 69f<**
**Minds Music (USA) 4** ch c Silver Hawk (USA)-Misinskie (USA) (Nijinsky (CAN)) 1017[3] 1176[2] 3597[2] 4178[3] **>119f<**
**Mineral Water 3** ch g Weldnaas (USA)-Joud (Dancing Brave (USA)) 2591[9] **>4f<**
**Minersville (USA) 2** b c Forty Niner (USA)-Angel Fever (USA) (Danzig (USA)) 4863[3] **>76+f<**
**Ming Dynasty (IRE) 5** b g Sadler's Wells (USA)-Marie Noelle (FR) (Brigadier Gerard) (3200a) 3751a[4] 4167a[3] **>123f<**
**Mingling Glances (USA) 2** b f Woodman (USA)-Last Glance (USA) 5063a[3] **>66f<**
**Minister's Melody (USA) 2** f *4950a[4]* **>88a f<**
**Minnehaha (FR) 3** b f Groom Dancer (USA)-Mondialite (FR) (Habitat) 287a[3] **>66f<**
**Minneola 4** ch f Midyan (USA)-High Halo (High Top) 4083[9] **>36f<**

**Minnie The Minx** 5 b m Then Again-Sahara Shadow (Formidable (USA)) *1605$^{7}$ 2169$^{9}$* **>14a f<**

**Minnisam** 3 ch c Niniski (USA)-Wise Speculation (USA) (Mr Prospector (USA)) 471$^{2}$ 594$^{4}$ 980$^{3}$ 1984$^{6}$ (2408) 3079$^{5}$ 3514$^{7}$ **>77f<**

**Minoletti** 3 b g Emarati (USA)-French Plait (Thatching) 4074$^{2}$ 4322$^{3}$ 4592$^{4}$ 4820$^{6}$ **>76f<**

**Minster Glory** 5 b g Minster Son-Rapid Glory (Hittite Glory) 3589$^{3}$ 3780$^{2}$ (3918) 4000$^{2}$ **>30a 57f<**

**Mint Condition** 2 ch c Superlative-Penny Mint (Mummy's Game) 2926$^{11}$ 3332$^{4}$ 4072$^{11}$ **>37f<**

**Miracle Kid (USA)** 2 b c Red Ransom (USA)-Fan Mail (USA) (Zen (USA)) 4914$^{10}$ **>40f<**

**Mirador** 5 b m Town And Country-Wild Jewel (Great Heron (USA)) 2042$^{2}$ (2385) 3142$^{6}$ 4821$^{7}$ **>67f<**

**Mirani (IRE)** 3 b f Danehill (USA)-Alriyaah (Shareef Dancer (USA)) *(2632) 3062$^{13}$* **>73a f<**

**Mironov** 3 b c Marju (IRE)-Marquina 454$^{2}$ 903a$^{8}$ 1125$^{6}$ **>93f<**

**Miroswaki (USA)** 6 br g Miswaki (USA)-Miroswava (FR) (In Fijar (USA)) **1995:** *4455$^{2}$* **1996:** *(79) 4199$^{8}$* 4447$^{3}$ **>76a 75f<**

**Mirror Four Life (IRE)** 2 b f Treasure Kay-Gazettalong (Taufan (USA)) *(869)* 1980$^{4}$ 2375$^{4}$ 2595$^{5}$ (2984) 4764$^{14}$ 4883$^{12}$ **>73f<**

**Mirror Four Sport** 2 ch f Risk Me (FR)-Madison Girl (Last Fandango) 2491$^{4}$ *2746$^{5}$ 3088$^{6}$ 4207$^{9}$* 4903$^{11}$ **>49a 46f<**

**Mirus** 3 ch g Tina's Pet-Water Stock (Roscoe Blake) 2166$^{3}$ 2966$^{14}$

**Mischief Star** 3 b f Be My Chief (USA)-Star Face (African Sky) 1873$^{8}$ 2251$^{10}$ 2709$^{7}$ 2927$^{3}$ 3337$^{5}$ *(3872) (4252)* 4604$^{7}$ **>67a 69f<**

**Misellina (FR)** 2 b f Polish Precedent (USA)-Misallah (IRE) (Shirley Heights) 4564$^{5}$ **>52f<**

**Mishaweer** 3 b f Primo Dominie-Ideal Home (Home Guard (USA)) 768$^{5}$ 2231$^{5}$ 2528$^{6}$ 3052$^{12}$ **>55f<**

**Mish Mish** 2 ch f Groom Dancer (USA)-Kirsten (Kris) 4105$^{12}$ **>30f<**

**Misinterrex** 5 1132a$^{3}$ **>14f<**

**Miskin Heights (IRE)** 2 ch f Sharp Victor (USA)-Nurse Jo (USA) (J O Tobin (USA)) 1595$^{8}$ 1842$^{11}$ **>35f<**

**Misky Bay** 3 b c Shareef Dancer (USA)-Rain Date (Rainbow Quest (USA)) 584$^{7}$ 786$^{3}$ 1002$^{10}$ 1798$^{7}$ 2514$^{10}$ 3681$^{4}$ 3831$^{7}$ *5001$^{4}$* **>60a 69df<**

**Mislemani (IRE)** 6 b g Kris-Meis El-Reem (Auction Ring (USA)) **1995:** *4388$^{3}$ 4432$^{3}$* **1996:** *159$^{2}$ 243$^{8}$ 285$^{3}$ 384$^{3}$ 1613$^{9}$* 1819$^{16}$ 2345$^{3}$ 2763$^{9}$ 3139$^{12}$ **>59a 55f<**

**Misrule (USA)** 3 b f Miswaki (USA)-Crowning Ambition (USA) (Chief's Crown (USA)) 1617$^{6}$ 1882$^{5}$ 2675$^{2}$ 3167$^{12}$ 3525$^{5}$ (4498) 4768$^{10}$ **>67f<**

**Miss Alice** 2 b f Komaite (USA)-Needle Sharp (Kris) 2781$^{6}$ *3088$^{4}$ 3809$^{7}$* 4223$^{F}$ 4562$^{14}$ **>31a 41f<**

**Miss Aragon** 8 b m Aragon-Lavenham Blue (Streetfighter) *1040$^{13}$* 1157$^{12}$ 1786$^{5}$ 4058$^{10}$ 4206$^{16}$ 4460$^{10}$ 4486$^{6}$ 4809$^{15}$ 4888$^{16}$ *4983$^{4}$* **>28a 37f<**

**Miss Barcelona (IRE)** 2 b f Mac's Imp (USA)-National Ballet (Shareef Dancer (USA)) 916$^{13}$ 1331$^{2}$ 1513$^{8}$ 1869$^{5}$ *1968$^{5}$ 2279$^{2}$* 2596$^{3}$ 2792$^{2}$ 2995$^{4}$ 3405$^{4}$ 3803$^{4}$ 4049$^{14}$ 4424$^{4}$ 4549$^{12}$ **>14a 61f<**

**Miss Bigwig** 3 b f Distinctly North (USA)-Jacqui Joy (Music Boy) *443$^{15}$* 989$^{6}$ 1188$^{4}$ 1597$^{5}$ 3465$^{5}$ 4088$^{14}$ 4246$^{4}$ 4452$^{13}$ 4727$^{6}$ **>70f<**

**Miss Carottene** 3 b f Siberian Express (USA)-Silk St James (Pas de Seul) **1995:** *4545$^{8}$* **1996:** *81$^{4}$ (131) 194$^{7}$ 4691$^{19}$* 4784$^{15}$ *5059$^{10}$* **>52a 36f<**

**Miss Cashtal (IRE)** 5 b m Ballacashtal (CAN)-Midnight Mistress (Midsummer Night II) *79$^{5}$ 128$^{4}$ 198$^{7}$* **>45a f<**

**Miss Charlie** 6 ch m Pharly (FR)-Close to You (Nebbiolo) *839$^{8}$ (1043)* 1638$^{5}$ 2242$^{4}$ 4691$^{18}$ **>39a 60f<**

**Miss Clonteen (IRE)** 2 br f Tirol-Kottna (USA) (Lyphard (USA)) 1480$^{5}$ 1590$^{9}$ **>33f<**

**Miss Darling** 2 b f Clantime-Slipperose (Persepolis (FR)) 3075$^{6}$ 3336$^{W}$ **>48f<**

**Miss Ebene (FR)** 3 f **1995:** 4496a$^{2}$ **>97f<**

**Missed the Boat (IRE)** 6 b g Cyrano de Bergerac-Lady Portobello (Porto Bello) **1995:** *4546$^{9}$* **1996:** *23$^{8}$ 108$^{11}$ 2341$^{6}$* 3141$^{4}$ **>24a 50f<**

**Missel** 4 b c Storm Bird (CAN)-Miss Demure (Shy Groom (USA)) *2862$^{8}$* 3447$^{6}$ **>99f<**

**Miss Electra** 4 b f Superpower-Apocalypse (Auction Ring (USA)) *1314$^{20}$* ***>20f<***

**Miss Express (BEL)** 3 gr f Siberian Express (USA)-Landing Power (Hill's Forecast) 2026$^{14}$ 2189$^{11}$ 2626$^{4}$ 3775$^{8}$ **>49f<**

**Missfortuna** 2 b f Priolo (USA)-Lucky Round (Auction Ring (USA)) *4241$^{7}$* 4357$^{7}$ 4890$^{9}$ **>61f<**

**Miss Fugit Penance** 2 br f Puissance-Figment (Posse (USA)) 3332$^{W}$ 3879$^{6}$ 4043$^{12}$ 4244$^{14}$ **>35f<**

**Miss Golden Sands** 2 ch f Kris-Miss Kuta Beach (Bold Lad (IRE)) 4756$^{7}$ 4887$^{6}$ **>57f<**

**Miss Haversham** 4 b f Salse (USA)-Rustic Stile (Rusticaro (FR)) 2246$^{6}$ 2693$^{9}$ *3074$^{6}$ 3419$^{12}$ 3608$^{3}$ 3711$^{10}$ 3877$^{9}$ 3979$^{11}$* ***>67a 65df<***

**Missile** 3 b g Rock City-Fast Chick (Henbit (USA)) (1126) 2502$^{8}$ (2888) 3158$^{2}$ 3996$^{3}$ 4568$^{2}$ **>115f<**

**Missile Toe (IRE)** 3 b c Exactly Sharp (USA)-Debach Dust (Indian King (USA)) 571$^{10}$ 676$^{13}$ 1693$^{6}$ 1905$^{5}$ 2200$^{8}$ 2598$^{8}$ 3650$^{5}$ 3852$^{4}$ 4243$^{2}$ 4337$^{2}$ 4590$^{9}$ 4901$^{3}$ **>59a 69f<**

**Miss Impulse** 3 b f Precocious-Dingle Belle (Dominion) *2753$^{2}$* 2983$^{13}$ *3628$^{10}$ 4340$^{10}$* ***>32a 40f<***

**Missing Link (FR)** 3 b c Saumarez-Mistreat (Gay Mecene (USA)) (5070a)

**Miss Iron Heart (USA)** 4 b f Minshaanshu Amad (USA)-Iron Franco (USA) (Barrera (USA)) 562$^{10}$ 739$^{5}$ 979$^{14}$ 1682$^{6}$ 2016$^{6}$ 2344$^{5}$ **>17a 33f<**

**Miss Jemmima** 4 b f Night Shift (USA)-Jenny Mere (Brigadier Gerard) **1995:** *4406$^{10}$* **>51a 64f<**

**Miss Kalaglow** 2 b f Kalaglow-Dame du Moulin (Shiny Tenth) 4359$^{8}$ 4618$^{9}$ **>49f<**

**Miss Kive** 10 b m Kabour-Final Cast (Saulingo) *388$^{9}$*

**Miss Laughter** 4 b f Sulaafah (USA)-Miss Comedy (Comedy Star (USA)) 888$^{7}$ 1533$^{9}$ (1893) 2313$^{13}$ 3217$^{6}$ 3785$^{13}$ 4129$^{8}$ **>62f<**

**Miss Mary Garden (FR)** 3 b f Assert-Heavenly Pearl (FR) (Graustark) 3028a$^{3}$

**Miss Mercy (IRE)** 4 b f Law Society (USA)-Missing You (Ahonoora) **1995:** *4350$^{10}$ 4388$^{13}$* **>33a 71f<**

**Miss Mezzanine** 2 b f Norton Challenger-Forest Fawn (FR) (Top Ville) 4801$^{19}$ **>5f<**

**Miss Michelle** 6 ch m Jalmood (USA)-Southern Dynasty (Gunner B) *3086$^{13}$*

**Miss Offset** 3 ch f Timeless Times (USA)-Farinara (Dragonara Palace (USA)) *1231$^{4}$ 245$^{5}$ (347) 383$^{5}$ 405$^{4}$ (421) 531$^{4}$ 661$^{3}$ 781$^{2}$ (859) 897$^{3}$ 1068$^{13}$* 1312$^{10}$ 1405$^{5}$ 2179$^{7}$ *4895$^{15}$ (4983)* **>75a 37f<**

**Miss Parkes** 7 ch m Mummy's Game-Bonne Baiser (Most Secret) **1995:** *4416$^{11}$ 4455$^{9}$* **>1a f<**

**Miss Pickpocket (IRE)** 3 b f Petorius-Fingers (Lord Gayle (USA)) **1995:** *4360$^{3}$ (4541)* **1996:** *21$^{3}$ 78$^{2}$ 423$^{5}$ 4231$^{7}$ 5059$^{8}$* **>60da 74f<**

**Miss Pigalle** 5 b m Good Times (ITY)-Panayr (Faraway Times (USA)) *1001$^{3}$* 1313$^{3}$ 1538$^{8}$ 2023$^{2}$ 2391$^{12}$ 2851$^{4}$ 3306$^{3}$ 3680$^{3}$ 4045$^{17}$ 4316$^{9}$ 4808$^{9}$ 5004$^{11}$ **>53f<**

**Miss Pravda** 3 ch f Soviet Star (USA)-Miss Paige (AUS) (Luskin Star (AUS)) 703$^{12}$ (922) 1061$^{7}$ 1682$^{4}$ 2014$^{5}$ 2542$^{6}$ 2989$^{P}$ 3104$^{4}$ *3630$^{4}$ 4095$^{16}$ 4332$^{5}$ 5062$^{11}$* **>52a 51f<**

**Miss Prism** 3 b f Niniski (USA)-Reflected Glory (SWE) (Relko) 703$^{13}$ 1514$^{8}$ 2191$^{4}$ 3053$^{3}$ 3335$^{14}$ *3872$^{2}$ 4086$^{2}$* 4426$^{2}$ 4612$^{10}$ 4766$^{2}$ 5007$^{9}$ **>57a 61f<**

**Miss Riviera** 3 b f Kris-Miss Beaulieu (Northfields (USA)) 627$^{2}$ 874$^{4}$ 1111$^{6}$ 2142$^{2}$ 2585$^{2}$ 3210$^{3}$ 3909a$^{3}$ 4405a$^{3}$ 4704$^{2}$ **>101f<**

**Miss Riviera Rose** 2 ch f Niniski (USA)-Miss Beaulieu (Northfields (USA)) 3234$^{5}$ 4062$^{10}$ **>61f<**

**Miss Romance (IRE)** 3 b f Cyrano de Bergerac-Trysting Place (He Loves Me) 2579$^{7}$ 3041$^{9}$ 3451$^{3}$ 3929$^{6}$ **>62f<**

**Miss Sancerre** 2 b f Last Tycoon-Miss Bergerac (Bold Lad (IRE)) 4756$^{2}$ (4889) **>75+f<**

**Miss Stamper (IRE)** 2 b f Distinctly North (USA)-June Goddess (Junius (USA)) 1842$^{8}$ (2343) (2879) (3247) (4024a) 4299$^{3}$ **>103f<**

**Miss St Kitts** 2 ch f Risk Me (FR)-So Beguiling (USA) (Woodman (USA)) 1834$^{6}$ 2279$^{6}$ 3075$^{7}$ **>37f<**

**Miss Tahiti (IRE)** 3 b f Tirol-Mini Luthe (FR) (Luthier) 796a$^{3}$ 1396a$^{2}$ 1949a$^{2}$ 4292a$^{3}$ 4567$^{7}$ **>116f<**

**Miss Ticklepenny** 4 b f Distant Relative-Aphrosina (Known Fact (USA)) **1995:** *4363$^{13}$ 4418$^{9}$* **>12a 42f<**

**Miss Toffee Nose (IRE)** 4 b f Cyrano de Bergerac-Sweet Reprieve (Shirley Heights) *1416$^{15}$* ***>9a 4f<***

**Miss Tri Colour** 4 b f Shavian-Bourgeonette (Mummy's Pet) *782$^{4}$ 1030$^{5}$* **>44a 26f<**

**Miss Universal (IRE)** 3 ch f Lycius (USA)-Madame Nureyev (USA) (Nureyev (USA)) 572$^{3}$ 708$^{4}$ 939$^{9}$ 1144$^{3}$ 1639$^{2}$ 2052$^{5}$ 2502$^{2}$ 3231$^{7}$ 3945$^{2}$ 4126$^{2}$ 4567$^{6}$ 4911$^{2}$ 5036$^{7}$ **>105f<** .

**Miss Walsh** 3 b f Distant Relative-Andbell (Trojan Fen) 3839$^{4}$ 4221$^{8}$ 4589$^{14}$ **>44f<**

**Miss Waterline** 3 br f Rock City-Final Shot (Dalsaan) *686$^{10}$* 850$^{14}$ 1101$^{2}$ 1505$^{6}$ 2363$^{12}$ 4180$^{15}$ 4312$^{6}$ 4560$^{8}$ 4689$^{10}$ 4994$^{18}$ **>77f<**

**Miss Zanzibar** 4 b f Kefaah (USA)-Circe (Main Reef) *62$^{3}$ 111$^{7}$ 257$^{3}$ 521$^{6}$ 836$^{3}$ 999$^{8}$* 1596$^{4}$ 2075$^{4}$ *2303$^{7}$ 2801$^{2}$* 3410$^{4}$ 3460$^{6}$ **>50a 59df<**

**Mister** 4 ch g Risk Me (FR)-Beauvoir (Artaius (USA)) *103$^{6}$ 221$^{9}$ 347$^{10}$ 835$^{6}$ 1492$^{13}$* **>52a f<**

**Mister Alleged (USA)** 5 b h Alleged (USA)-Rich and Riotous (Empery (USA)) 4853a$^{2}$

**Mister Aspecto (IRE)** 3 b g Caerleon (USA)-Gironde (USA) (Raise A Native) *17$^{4}$ 228$^{2}$ (274) (381) (519) 575$^{10}$* 788$^{5}$ 980$^{5}$ 1325$^{5}$ 1887$^{3}$ 2175$^{2}$ 2360$^{3}$ (3117) (3487) 3816$^{4}$ 4227$^{11}$ 4506$^{3}$ 4750$^{6}$ **>75a 77f<**

**Mister Fire Eyes (IRE)** 4 b g Petorius-Surfing (Grundy) **1995:** *4441$^{2}$ (4478)* **1996:** *358$^{2}$ 450$^{8}$* 876$^{20}$ 1078$^{2}$ 1192$^{6}$ 1853$^{14}$ 2134$^{15}$ 2858$^{5}$ **>98a 66f<**

**Mister Jay** 2 b c Batshoof-Portvasco (Sharpo) 3234$^{7}$ 3874$^{6}$ 4508$^{9}$ **>53f<**

**Mister Joel** 3 b g Risk Me (FR)-Net Call (Song) 824$^{5}$ 1340$^{7}$ (1761) 2151$^{5}$ 2427$^{5}$ 2968$^{3}$ 3774$^{6}$ 3844$^{8}$ 3995$^{18}$ 4382$^{17}$ 4791$^{12}$ 4809$^{7}$ **>56f<**

**Mister Jolson** 7 br g Latest Model-Impromptu (My Swanee) 451$^{13}$ 582$^{4}$ (812) 928$^{23}$ 1064$^{8}$ 1652$^{2}$ 1853$^{8}$ (2232) 2856$^{3}$ 3146$^{9}$ 3672$^{16}$ 3810$^{9}$ **>84f<**

**Mister Lawson** 10 ch g Blushing Scribe (USA)-Nonpareil (FR) (Pharly (FR)) **1995:** *4391$^{13}$* **1996:** *73$^{10}$ 186$^{6}$ 318$^{9}$* **>29a f<**

**Mister O'Grady (IRE)** 5 b g Mister Majestic-Judy O'Grady (Whistler) 2525$^{4}$ (2784) 3111$^{12}$ 3635$^{2}$ 4125$^{11}$ *5003$^{P}$* **>39a 67f< (DEAD)**

**Mister Pink** 2 ch gr c Absalom-Blush Rambler

(IRE) (Blushing Groom (FR)) 1339$^{5}$ 1513$^{3}$ 1683$^{2}$ 2224$^{3}$ 2708$^{3}$ (3408) 3616$^{3}$ 4131$^{7}$ 4696$^{3}$ 4973$^{6}$ **>82f<**

**Mister Raider 4** ch g Ballacashtal (CAN)-Martian Melody (Enchantment) **1995:** *4484$^{9}$ 4542$^{8}$* **1996:** *36$^{7}$ 179$^{7}$ (203) 253$^{5}$ 291$^{7}$ 3331$^{5}$* 3661$^{3}$ 4341$^{8}$ *(5000)* **>57a 50f<**

**Mister Rm 4** b g Dominion-La Cabrilla (Carwhite) *871$^{11}$* 1198$^{10}$ 1522$^{13}$ 1890$^{17}$ 2134$^{13}$ *(2303) (2550)* **>69a 66f<**

**Mister Sean (IRE) 3** b g Mac's Imp (USA)-Maid of Mourne (Fairy King (USA)) 3661$^{15}$ 3851$^{10}$ 4075$^{23}$ 4828$^{17}$ **>22f<**

**Mister Westsound 4** b g Cyrano de Bergerac-Captivate (Mansingh (USA)) *617$^{2}$* 956$^{3}$ 1040$^{5}$ 1588$^{3}$ 1635$^{4}$ 2005$^{3}$ 2149$^{5}$ 2729$^{6}$ 2911$^{9}$ 3424$^{5}$ 3489$^{6}$ 4058$^{14}$ 4312$^{U}$ 4460$^{9}$ 4688$^{7}$ 4805$^{4}$ 5010$^{11}$ **>61f<**

**Mister Woodstick (IRE) 3** b g Distinctly North (USA)-Crannog (Habitat) 467$^{11}$ 616$^{7}$ (1042) 1172$^{3}$ (1846) 2130$^{6}$ 2917$^{7}$ 3456$^{3}$ 4098$^{6}$ 4432$^{10}$ **>66f<**

**Mistinguett (IRE) 4** b f Doyoun-Sidama (FR) (Top Ville) **1995:** *4481$^{5}$* **>68a 82f<**

**Mistle Cat (USA) 6** gr h Storm Cat (USA)-Mistle Toe (USA) (Maribeau) **1995:** 4402a$^{4}$ **1996:** 810$^{3}$ (1582a) 2037$^{3}$ 3144$^{6}$ 3596$^{2}$ (4667a) >**122f<** **(DEAD)**

**Mistroy 6** gr m Damister (USA)-Troja (Troy) 3580$^{11}$ **>34?a 12f< (DEAD)**

**Misty Cay (IRE) 2** b f Mujadil (USA)-Quai des Brumes (USA) (Little Current (USA)) 1008$^{3}$ 1331$^{4}$ (2012) 2797$^{2}$ 3230$^{3}$ (3498) 3826$^{5}$ 4084$^{6}$ 4222$^{5}$ 4495$^{15}$ **>67f<**

**Misty Rain 2** br f Polar Falcon (USA)-Ballerine (USA) (Lyphard's Wish (FR)) 4330$^{11}$ **>53f<**

**Misty View 7** ch m Absalom-Long View (Persian Bold) 3471$^{12}$ 4236$^{16}$ **>18f<**

**Miswaki Dancer (USA) 6** ch g Miswaki (USA)-Simply Divine (USA) (Danzig (USA)) 995$^{11}$ 1486$^{6}$ 2226$^{3}$ 2779$^{5}$ 3802$^{3}$ **>60f<**

**Mitch (USA) 3** b c Jade Hunter (USA)-Ottomwa (USA) (Strawberry Road (AUS)) 1253a$^{5}$ 2472a$^{16}$ 2816a$^{4}$ **>89f<**

**Mithak (USA) 2** b c Silver Hawk (USA)-Kapalua Butterfly (USA) (Stage Door Johnny) 2335$^{3}$ 3615$^{3}$ **>84+f<**

**Mithraic (IRE) 4** b g Kefaah (USA)-Persian's Glory (Prince Tenderfoot (USA)) 1596$^{5}$ 2136$^{2}$ 2394$^{2}$ 2563$^{2}$ (2682) (2847) 3109$^{10}$ 3309$^{5}$ **>65f<**

**Mixed Mood 4** br f Jalmood (USA)-Cool Combination (Indian King (USA)) *76$^{10}$ 114$^{7}$ 4573$^{12}$* **>7a 32f<**

**Mizyan (IRE) 8** b g Melyno-Maid of Erin (USA) (Irish River (FR)) *19$^{5}$ 130$^{4}$ 169$^{3}$ 759$^{5}$* 1695$^{3}$ 2190$^{5}$ 2717$^{2}$ 3335$^{3}$ 3850$^{6}$ 4203$^{6}$ 4588$^{8}$ 4794$^{10}$ **>75a 60f<**

**Mnemonic 4** b f Mtoto-Neenah (Bold Lad (IRE)) **1995:** *4420$^{4}$* **>50a 53f<**

**Mo-Addab (IRE) 6** b g Waajib-Tissue Paper (Touch Paper) 879$^{11}$ 1190$^{4}$ 1625$^{10}$ 2053$^{10}$ 2581$^{8}$ 3640$^{8}$ 4329$^{2}$ 4463$^{12}$ **>84f<**

**Mobile King 3** ch g Colmore Row-Donosa (Posse (USA)) 748$^{20}$ **>11a 40df<**

**Moccasin (IRE) 2** b f Lahib (USA)-Karine (Habitat) 2538$^{8}$ 4798$^{14}$ **>43f<**

**Mock Trial (IRE) 3** b g Old Vic-Test Case (Busted) 448$^{10}$ 577$^{13}$ 786$^{7}$ 1185$^{6}$ 1584$^{2}$ (1676) 2866$^{2}$ 3641$^{7}$ 3968$^{2}$ 4248$^{5}$ 4866$^{12}$ **>71f<**

**Modest Hope (USA) 9** b g Blushing Groom (FR)-Key Dancer (USA) (Nijinsky (CAN)) **1995:** *4434$^{3}$ 4513$^{3}$* **1996:** *(70) 113$^{6}$ 152$^{2}$ 196$^{2}$ 256$^{10}$ 4092$^{17}$* **>56a 56f<**

**Mofasa 3** b c Shardari-Round Midnight (Star Appeal) *156$^{7}$* **>11a f<**

**Mogin 3** ch f Komaite (USA)-Misdevious (USA) (Alleged (USA)) *118$^{7}$ 161$^{6}$ 203$^{4}$ 242$^{4}$ 405$^{8}$ 529$^{3}$ 3115$^{4}$* 3686$^{7}$ (3862) *4089$^{8}$ 4186$^{12}$* ***>45a 57f<***

**Mogul 2** b g Formidable (USA)-Madiyla (Darshaan) 5040$^{10}$ **>28f<**

**Mohaajir (USA) 5** b h Sadler's Wells (USA)-Very Charming (USA) (Vaguely Noble) 4849a$^{3}$ 5015a$^{7}$ **>118f<**

**Mohannad (IRE) 3** b c Royal Academy (USA)-Pudibunda (Bold Lad (IRE)) 677$^{8}$ 1090$^{6}$ 1906$^{2}$ **>72f<**

**Mohawk River (IRE) 3** b c Polish Precedent (USA)-High Hawk (Shirley Heights) 707$^{4}$ (3986) 4886$^{4}$ **>98f<**

**Moi Canard 3** ch c Bold Owl-Royal Scots Greys (Blazing Saddles (AUS)) **1995:** *(4353) 4383$^{4}$ 4453$^{2}$ 4492$^{5}$* **1996:** *177$^{6}$ 218$^{2}$ (230) 293$^{2}$ 321$^{3}$ (503) 632$^{5}$* 887$^{12}$ 978$^{4}$ 1172$^{8}$ *1601$^{10}$ 4428$^{13}$* 4550$^{18}$ *5002$^{16}$* **>76a 51f<**

**Mokuti 4** b c Green Desert (USA)-Marie D'Argonne (FR) (Jefferson) 554$^{5}$ (802) 1440$^{11}$ 2206$^{3}$ **>83f<**

**Mollily 2** ch f Ballacashtal (CAN)-Foligno (Crofter (USA)) 630$^{7}$ 757$^{8}$ **>13f<**

**Molly Drummond 2** b f Sizzling Melody-Miss Drummond (The Brianstan) 585$^{5}$ 930$^{9}$ (1433) 1978$^{5}$ 2728$^{7}$ 4459$^{9}$ 4749$^{15}$ 5037$^{12}$ **>62f<**

**Molly Music 2** b f Music Boy-Carlton Glory (Blakeney) 465$^{4}$ 551$^{3}$ 643$^{3}$ 865$^{6}$ *1093$^{4}$ 3467$^{6}$* 4343$^{2}$ **>30a 64f<**

**Moltaire (GER) 4** c Kaldoun (FR)-Monasia (GER) (Authi) 1054a$^{3}$ **>121f<**

**Moments of Fortune (USA) 4** b g Timeless Moment (USA)-How Fortunate (USA) (What Luck (USA)) *809$^{3}$* 960$^{5}$ 1131$^{4}$ 2053$^{20}$ 2544$^{13}$ 3709$^{3}$ 4308$^{8}$ 4385$^{8}$ 4568$^{14}$ 4800$^{7}$ **>104f<**

**Monaassib 5** ch g Cadeaux Genereux-Pluvial (Habat) *679$^{2}$* 1112$^{5}$ 1623$^{6}$ 2114$^{8}$ 2436$^{2}$ 2623$^{15}$ (3524) 4169a$^{2}$ 4595$^{2}$ **>110f<**

**Monaco Gold (IRE) 4** b g Durgam (USA)-Monaco Ville (Rheingold) 1478$^{5}$ (2120) 2779$^{4}$ (3347) 3878$^{10}$ 4321$^{6}$ **>49f<**

**Monarch 4** b c Sadler's Wells (USA)-Bint Pasha (USA) (Affirmed (USA)) 963$^{3}$ 3447$^{6}$ 3689$^{20}$ **>77a 92f<**

**Monarch's Pursuit 2** b c Pursuit of Love-Last Detail (Dara Monarch) 2495$^{5}$ 3080$^{6}$ **>54f<**

**Mon Bruce 2** ch c Beveled (USA)-Pendona (Blue Cashmere) 3807$^{6}$ 4188$^{5}$ *4572$^{2}$ 4803$^{12}$* ***>69a 69f<***

**Mondragon 6** b g Niniski (USA)-La Lutine (My Swallow) 449$^{13}$ 625$^{4}$ 825$^{6}$ 1091$^{3}$ 1343$^{4}$ 1611$^{4}$ 3641$^{4}$ **>74df<**

**Moneghetti 5** ch g Faustus (USA)-The Victor Girls (Crofthall) *1718$^{3}$ 2081$^{5}$ 2303$^{9}$ 3306$^{11}$* ***>49a 27f<***

**Mongol Warrior (USA) 3** b c Deputy Minister (CAN)-Surely Georgie's (USA) (Alleged (USA)) (149a) 323a$^{2}$ 904a$^{2}$ (1751a) (2110a) 4413a$^{6}$ 4855a$^{2}$ (5075a) **>107f<**

**Monis (IRE) 5** ch g Waajib-Gratify (Grundy) **1995:** *4508$^{4}$* **1996:** *50$^{3}$ 88$^{5}$ 155$^{2}$ 247$^{3}$ 368$^{5}$ 718$^{9}$* 991$^{6}$ *1029$^{5}$ 2367$^{4}$ 2748$^{3}$ 2940$^{4}$ 3151$^{10}$ 3420$^{6}$* **>54a 49f<**

**Monkey Face 5** gr m Clantime-Charming View (Workboy) 1087$^{6}$ 1162$^{4}$ **>40f<**

**Monkey's Wedding 5** b g Skyliner-Munequita (Marching On) *76$^{11}$ 126$^{11}$* **>36a f< (DEAD)**

**Monkey Trouble (USA) 3** c **1995:** 4399a$^{4}$ 4424a$^{10}$ **>99f<**

**Monkey Zanty (IRE) 3** b f Distinctly North (USA)-Achafalaya (USA) (Apalachee (USA)) **1995:** *4369$^{4}$ 4483$^{6}$ (4511) 4545$^{6}$* **1996:** *101$^{7}$ 160$^{D}$ 272$^{6}$ 525$^{9}$ 606$^{4}$ 1162$^{5}$* 2799$^{6}$ **>55a 44f<**

**Mono Lady (IRE) 3** b f Polish Patriot (USA)-Phylella (Persian Bold) 1654$^{11}$ 2033$^{4}$ 3852$^{8}$ 3961$^{6}$ (4785) 4921$^{6}$ **>63f<**

**Monopolize (AUS) 6** b g Rubiton-Gay Rosalind **1995:** (4523a)

**Mon Pere 3** b g Belfort (FR)-Lady Ever-so-Sure (Malicious) 885$^{9}$ 1612$^{7}$ **>28f<**

**Mon Performer 2** ch g Mon Tresor-Hot Performer (Hotfoot) 1849$^{10}$ 2802$^{7}$ 4618$^{14}$ 4754$^{5}$ **>50f<**

**Mons 3** b c Deploy-Morina (USA) (Lyphard (USA)) *830$^{3}$* 3124$^{4}$ 3671$^{2}$ 4192$^{4}$ 4876$^{5}$ **>117f<**

**Monsieur Culsyth 3** b g Mon Tresor-Regal Salute (Dara Monarch) 539$^{7}$ *780$^{8}$ 1624$^{12}$* ***>37a 43f<***

**Montague Dawson (IRE) 4** ch g Doulab (USA)-Annacloy (Majority Blue) **1995:** *4430$^{4}$ 4478$^{6}$* **1996:** *26$^{10}$ 107$^{7}$ 155$^{9}$ 749$^{23}$ 1030$^{15}$* **>43a 47f<**

**Monte Cavo 5** b g Bustino-Dance Festival (Nureyev (USA)) *562$^{9}$* 1024$^{8}$ 2130$^{7}$ 2567$^{9}$ 3297$^{7}$ 3589$^{2}$ 3780$^{3}$ 4563$^{13}$ **>61a 36f<**

**Montecristo 3** br g Warning-Sutosky (Great Nephew) *56$^{4}$ (245) 294$^{2}$ (361) 385$^{6}$ 471$^{3}$* 593$^{3}$ (784) 1002$^{D}$ 2074$^{6}$ **>76a 79f<**

**Monte Felice (IRE) 3** ch g Be My Guest (USA)-Elabella (Ela-Mana-Mou) 3258$^{12}$ 3472$^{17}$ 4083$^{6}$ 4603$^{19}$ **>36f<**

**Montendre 9** b g Longleat (USA)-La Lutine (My Swallow) *457$^{5}$* 889$^{7}$ 1332$^{2}$ 2072$^{13}$ 2498$^{2}$ 2880$^{9}$ 3822$^{3}$ 4485$^{8}$ 4823$^{4}$ 4917$^{3}$ **>101f<**

**Montfort (USA) 2** b c Manila (USA)-Sable Coated (Caerleon (USA)) 4801$^{9}$ **>58f<**

**Montjoy (USA) 4** b c Manila (USA)-Wendy's Ten (USA) (Tentam (USA)) **1995:** 4403a$^{3}$ **1996:** 1135a$^{3}$ 1749a$^{4}$ 2038$^{2}$ (2730) 3395a$^{4}$ 4288a$^{4}$ **>126f<**

**Montone (IRE) 6** b g Pennine Walk-Aztec Princess (Indian King (USA)) **1995:** *4351$^{3}$ 4415$^{5}$ 4465$^{5}$ 4526$^{9}$* **1996:** *116$^{4}$ 190$^{D}$ 219$^{5}$ 279$^{9}$ 353$^{3}$ 412$^{5}$ 501$^{2}$ 670$^{4}$ 854$^{2}$ 1047$^{2}$* (1449) (1685) *(1966) 2081$^{2}$ (2284)* 2628$^{3}$ 3111$^{7}$ 3348$^{4}$ 3786$^{6}$ *4089$^{4}$ 4355$^{8}$* (4503) 4669$^{16}$ *5003$^{4}$* **>67a 74f<**

**Montrestar 3** ch g Mon Tresor-Wing of Freedom (Troy) *180$^{6}$ 478$^{2}$* 644$^{2}$ 735$^{4}$ 824$^{2}$ 931$^{10}$ 1006$^{11}$ 1405$^{12}$ 4460$^{16}$ **>35a 61f<**

**Mont Royal 2** ch c Polar Falcon (USA)-Half a Dozen (USA) (Saratoga Six (USA)) 4287a$^{3}$

**Montserrat 4** b f Aragon-Follow the Stars (Sparkler) 451$^{3}$ 582$^{5}$ 673$^{13}$ 928$^{6}$ (1334) 2298$^{4}$ 4198$^{14}$ 4581$^{2}$ 4802$^{9}$ 5044$^{14}$ **>82f<**

**Monty 4** ch g Colmore Row-Sussarando (Music Boy) **1995:** *4382$^{8}$ 4457$^{15}$* **1996:** *782$^{13}$ 979$^{15}$* 1524$^{7}$ 2740$^{3}$ 3825$^{12}$ **>55da 50f<**

**Monty Royale (IRE) 7** b g Montelimar (USA)-Atlanta Royale (Prince Tenderfoot (USA)) *2341$^{7}$* 2891$^{13}$ **>38f<**

**Monument 4** ch g Cadeaux Genereux-In Perpetuity (Great Nephew) 1506$^{4}$ (2234) 2525$^{7}$ (2943) 3260$^{5}$ 3496$^{14}$ 4125$^{6}$ 4483$^{12}$ **>71f<**

**Monza (USA) 2** b c Woodman (USA)-Star Pastures (Northfields (USA)) 3040$^{3}$ (3615) 4653a$^{2}$ **>90f<**

**Moody 4** ch f Risk Me (FR)-Bocas Rose (Jalmood (USA)) *42$^{12}$ 86$^{4}$ 172$^{3}$ 301$^{12}$ 343$^{8}$ 426$^{12}$* **>48a 66f<**

**Moody's Cat (IRE) 3** b f Alzao (USA)-Zamayem (Sadler's Wells (USA)) 723a$^{4}$ 1077$^{3}$ 1769$^{5}$ **>97f<**

**Moofaji 5** b g Night Shift (USA)-Three Piece (Jaazeiro (USA)) 3460$^{10}$ 3645$^{3}$ 4345$^{7}$ 4484$^{6}$ 4808$^{11}$ **>45f<**

**Moonax (IRE) 5** ch h Caerleon (USA)-Moonsilk (Solinus) *726$^{3}$* (4434) 4655a$^{2}$ 4959a$^{2}$ **>126f<**

**Moonbi Range (IRE) 5** b m Nordico (USA)-Pheopotstown 3530a$^{4}$ **>93f<**

**Moon Blast 2** gr c Reprimand-Castle Moon (Kalamoun) 2783$^{3}$ 3319$^{W}$ 3499$^{5}$ **>77f<**

**Mooncusser 3** b g Forzando-Ragged Moon (Raga Navarro (ITY)) *167$^{4}$ 238$^{2}$ 281$^{3}$ 348$^{6}$* **>62a 59f<**

**Moon Flower (IRE) 2** b f Sadler's Wells (USA)-Mill

Princess (Mill Reef (USA)) 4642a$^{5}$ 4846a$^{4}$ **>76f<**
**Moon Is Up (USA) 3** b f Woodman (USA)-Miesque **1995:** 4494a$^{2}$ **1996:** (3909a) 4406a$^{3}$ 4664a$^{10}$ **>98f<**
**Moon King (IRE) 4** ch c Cadeaux Genereux-Moon Drop (Dominion) **1995:** 4405a$^{6}$ **>108f<**
**Moonlight Air 5** b m Bold Owl-Havon Air (Celtic Cone) *221$^{6}$* **>31a 53df<**
**Moonlight Calypso 5** ch m Jupiter Island-Moonlight Bay (Palm Track) 1870$^{6}$ *3086$^{3}$ 5007$^{3}$* ***>36a 51f<***
**Moonlight Invader (IRE) 2** br c Darshaan-Mashmoon (USA) (Habitat) 4386$^{6}$ 4706$^{9}$ **>66f<**
**Moonlight Paradise (USA) 2** b f Irish River (FR)-Ottomwa (USA) (Strawberry Road (AUS)) (1954) (2338) 3068$^{2}$ 4491$^{2}$ (4758) **>107f<**
**Moonlight Quest 8** gr g Nishapour (FR)-Arabian Rose (USA) (Lyphard (USA)) (2415) (2857) **>89f<**
**Moon Mischief 3** b c Be My Chief (USA)-Castle Moon (Kalamoun) 892$^{5}$ 2610$^{6}$ 3209$^{2}$ **>80f<**
**Moonraker (IRE) 2** b g Classic Secret (USA)-Moona (USA) (Lear Fan (USA)) *3604$^{12}$*
**Moonraking 3** gr g Rusticaro (FR)-Lunaire (Try My Best (USA)) *1608$^{11}$ 1972$^{2}$ 2432$^{9}$ 2751$^{2}$ 3630$^{6}$* **>60a 40f<**
**Moon River (IRE) 2** ch c Mujtahid (USA)-Moonsilk (Solinus) (5041) **>88+f<**
**Moonshell (IRE) 4** b f Sadler's Wells (USA)-Moon Cactus (Kris) *396a$^{3}$ 919$^{9}$* ***>116f<***
**Moon Shine (TUR) 6** h 4289a$^{9}$
**Moonshine Dancer 6** b g Northern State (USA)-Double Birthday (Cavo Doro) *208$^{5}$* **>41a 52f<**
**Moonshine Girl (USA) 2** ch f Shadeed (USA)-Fly to the Moon (USA) (Blushing Groom (FR)) (1480) 2051$^{3}$ 3707$^{5}$ 4065$^{5}$ **>93f<**
**Moonshiner (USA) 2** b c Irish River (FR)-Marling (IRE) (Lomond (USA)) 3245$^{10}$ 4380$^{2}$ 4619$^{2}$ **>87f<**
**Moonspell 2** b f Batshoof-Shimmer (Bustino) 2783$^{7}$ 3820$^{3}$ 4508$^{8}$ **>69f<**
**Moon Strike (FR) 6** b or br g Strike Gold (USA)-Lady Lamia (USA) (Secreto (USA)) 1074$^{5}$ (1517) 1789$^{9}$ 2022$^{2}$ (3793) 3993$^{6}$ 4198$^{5}$ **>85a 85f<**
**Moorbird (IRE) 2** b c Law Society (USA)-Heather Lark (Red Alert) 4224$^{8}$ 4481$^{3}$ 4897$^{11}$ **>59f<**
**Moor Hall Princess 2** gr f Chilibang-Forgiving (Jellaby) 1607$^{5}$ *2172$^{6}$ 2509$^{6}$* 3582$^{7}$ *3954$^{8}$* **>23a 38f<**
**More Bills (IRE) 4** b g Gallic League-Lady Portobello (Porto Bello) **1995:** *4452$^{13}$* **1996:** *79$^{13}$* **>40da 43f<**
**More Risk (IRE) 3** b f Fayruz-La Mortola (Bold Lad (IRE)) 2472a$^{9}$ **>83f<**
**More Silver (USA) 2** b f Silver Hawk (USA)-Dancing Lt (USA) (San Feliou (FR)) (1143) 2051$^{7}$ 4758$^{5}$ 4875$^{8}$ **>87f<**
**More Than You Know (IRE) 3** ch f Kefaah (USA)-Foston Bridge (Relkino) 874$^{6}$ 1075$^{5}$ 1639$^{5}$ 2006$^{7}$ 4675$^{12}$ **>91f<**
**Morigi 5** b h Rousillon (USA)-Ibtidaar (USA) (Danzig (USA)) **1995:** 4402a$^{3}$ **1996:** (1759a) 4667a$^{3}$ 5074a$^{4}$ **>117f<**
**Morning Line (IRE) 2** b f Mac's Imp (USA)-Sally Fay (IRE) (Fayruz) *4572$^{6}$ 5061$^{9}$* **>44a f<**
**Morning Master 4** b g Jupiter Island-Hound Song (Jukebox) **1995:** *4379$^{9}$* **>33a 51f<**
**Morning Queen (GER) 3** f 1750a$^{8}$ **>82f<**
**Morning Sir 3** b g Southern Music-Morning Miss (Golden Dipper) 894$^{6}$ 1104$^{11}$ 1496$^{12}$ 1894$^{8}$ 2506$^{19}$ 3165$^{12}$ **>59df<**
**Morning Star 2** b f Statoblest-Moushka (Song) 4250$^{7}$ (4907) **>63+f<**
**Morning Surprise 3** b br f Tragic Role (USA)-Fleur de Foret (USA) (Green Forest (USA)) *464$^{6}$ 775$^{7}$* 868$^{5}$ 1689$^{2}$ 1876$^{2}$ 2149$^{9}$ 3458$^{8}$ 3995$^{11}$ 4221$^{5}$ 4598$^{13}$ 4784$^{5}$ **>68a 52f<**
**Morocco (IRE) 7** b g Cyrano de Bergerac-Lightning Laser (Monseigneur (USA)) 1001$^{11}$ (1121) 1348$^{5}$ 1532$^{10}$ 2047$^{12}$ 3473$^{5}$ 3686$^{5}$ 3867$^{5}$ 4098$^{9}$ (4256) 4428$^{3}$ 4609$^{4}$ 4701$^{3}$ 4906$^{13}$ **>68f<**
**Morritt Magic 2** ch f Absalom-Vernair (USA) (Super Concorde (USA)) 506$^{6}$ 823$^{5}$ 1645$^{10}$ 4790$^{8}$ *4980$^{11}$* **>20a 43f<**
**Mosconi (IRE) 2** b c Last Tycoon-Volnost (USA) 1565a$^{4}$ 2470a$^{4}$ 4156a$^{4}$ **>95f<**
**Moscow Dynamo 9** br g Siberian Express (USA)-County Line (High Line) *417$^{8}$*
**Moscow Mist (IRE) 5** b g Soviet Star (USA)-Ivory Dawn (USA) (Sir Ivor) *1190$^{14}$* 1464$^{8}$ 2581$^{4}$ (3158) 3450$^{10}$ 4463$^{15}$ **>91f<**
**Most Uppitty 4** gr f Absalom-Hyatti (Habitat) **1995:** *(4430) 4478$^{5}$* **1996:** *74$^{10}$ 127$^{8}$ 155$^{11}$ 1492$^{8}$ 1786$^{8}$* 1889$^{8}$ 2154$^{3}$ *2367$^{2}$ 2490$^{2}$* 2686$^{8}$ **>48a 53f<**
**Most Wanted (IRE) 3** ch f Priolo (USA)-Dewan's Niece (USA) (Dewan (USA)) 957$^{8}$ 1123$^{8}$ 1497$^{6}$ 1836$^{4}$ 4000$^{19}$ 4323$^{15}$ 4474$^{11}$ **>45df<**
**Most Welcome News 4** b g Most Welcome-In the Papers (Aragon) *328$^{7}$ 521$^{13}$ 664$^{14}$* ***>47a 51df<***
**Motakabber (IRE) 4** b c Sadler's Wells (USA)-High Spirited (Shirley Heights) *535a$^{8}$* **>72a 90++f<**
**Motcombs Club 2** ch c Deploy-Unique Treasure (Young Generation) 2783$^{9}$ 3807$^{8}$ 4041$^{11}$ 4970$^{5}$ **>65f<**
**Motet 2** b c Mtoto-Guest Artiste (Be My Guest (USA)) 4817$^{3}$ **>63f<**
**Motrib (USA) 3** b g Thorn Dance (USA)-Disco Singer (CAN) (Lord Durham (CAN)) 892$^{16}$ 1122$^{13}$ 1638$^{15}$
**Motzki (FR) 3** f 905a$^{4}$ 1060a$^{9}$ **>94f<**
**Moujeeb (USA) 6** b h Riverman (USA)-Capricorn Belle (Nonoalco (USA)) **1995:** *4441$^{13}$ 4458$^{7}$* **1996:** *667$^{2}$* 846$^{7}$ 1073$^{12}$ 1412$^{14}$ 1512$^{7}$ **>62a 64f<**
**Mountain Dream 3** b c Batshoof-Echoing (Formidable (USA)) **1995:** *4352$^{5}$ 4439$^{8}$* **1996:** *982$^{6}$* 2794$^{3}$ 3260$^{W}$ 3657$^{9}$ **>43a 75f<**
**Mountain Holly 3** b f Shirley Heights-Ela Romara (Ela-Mana-Mou) 2383$^{5}$ 3841$^{4}$ **>71f<**
**Mountains of Mist (IRE) 4** b f Shirley Heights-Magic of Life (USA) (Seattle Slew (USA)) **1995:** 4423a$^{10}$ **>97f<**
**Mountgate 4** b g Merdon Melody-Young Whip (Bold Owl) 1069$^{16}$ 1528$^{5}$ 1807$^{6}$ 2134$^{2}$ 2328$^{10}$ (3254) 3445$^{4}$ 3805$^{7}$ 3985$^{7}$ 4190$^{19}$ 4444$^{23}$ 4595$^{6}$ 4975$^{10}$ **>73f<**
**Mount Holly (USA) 2** b c Woodman (USA)-Mount Helena (Danzig (USA)) 3837$^{5}$ **>67f<**
**Mount Kamet 2** b c Seattle Dancer (USA)-Kalikala (Darshaan) 2414$^{2}$ (2923) 3927$^{5}$ **>99f<**
**Mount Pleasant (IRE) 3** b c Danehill (USA)-Remoosh (Glint of Gold) 3656$^{3}$ 3841$^{3}$ 3999$^{2}$ (4353) 4761$^{2}$ 4965$^{7}$ **>99f<**
**Mount Row 3** b f Alzao (USA)-Temple Row (Ardross) 957$^{4}$ (1434) 2742$^{5}$ (3398) 3934$^{4}$ **>96f<**
**Mourne Mountains 3** b c Scenic-Orlaith (Final Straw) 2610$^{7}$ 3656$^{8}$ **>73f<**
**Mousehole 4** b g Statoblest-Alo Ez (Alzao (USA)) 592$^{13}$ 814$^{9}$ 1307$^{5}$ 1512$^{2}$ (1844) 1881$^{2}$ 2034$^{3}$ 3219$^{6}$ 3432$^{17}$ 3793$^{5}$ 3993$^{2}$ **>82f<**
**Mousse Glacee (FR) 2** b f Mtoto-Madame Est Sortie (FR) (Longleat (USA)) (4942a) **>98f<**
**Move Smartly (IRE) 6** b h Smarten (USA)-Key Maneuver (USA) (Key To Content (USA)) 586$^{8}$ 1156$^{6}$ 1474$^{2}$ 2075$^{5}$ **>47a 67f<**
**Move The Clouds 2** gr f Environment Friend-Che Gambe (USA) (Lyphard (USA)) 4861$^{9}$ 5041$^{W}$ **>54f<**
**Move With Edes 4** b g Tragic Role (USA)-Good Time Girl (Good Times (ITY)) 1099$^{2}$ 1348$^{9}$ 1532$^{6}$ (2520) 3060$^{4}$ *(3628)* **>70a 73f<**
**Moving Arrow 5** ch g Indian Ridge-Another Move (Farm Walk) 455$^{10}$ 1799$^{2}$ 2053$^{22}$ 2544$^{7}$ (2862) 3691$^{10}$ 3842$^{5}$ **>104f<**
**Moving Up (IRE) 3** ch f Don't Forget Me-Our Pet (Mummy's Pet) *11$^{9}$ 501$^{11}$ 1443$^{3}$* 1893$^{16}$ 2192$^{14}$ 2594$^{7}$ 2978$^{4}$ 3303$^{10}$ 4497$^{19}$ 5053$^{14}$ **>48f<**
**Mowjood (USA) 2** b c Mr Prospector (USA)-Bineyah (IRE) (Sadler's Wells (USA)) 3245$^{8}$ 3837$^{10}$ **>57f<**
**Mowlaie 5** ch g Nashwan (USA)-Durrah (USA) (Nijinsky (CAN)) **1995:** *4370$^{9}$ 4434$^{5}$ 4513$^{8}$* **1996:** *256$^{4}$* **>59a 75f<**
**Moylough Rebel 3** ch g Hotfoot-Stellajoe (Le Dauphin) 1776$^{7}$ 1956$^{6}$ 2785$^{9}$ 3115$^{9}$ 3609$^{7}$ **>48f<**
**Mr Bean 6** b g Salse (USA)-Goody Blake (Blakeney) **1995:** *4366$^{5}$* **1996:** *4977$^{5}$* **>67a 75f<**
**Mr Bergerac (IRE) 5** b g Cyrano de Bergerac-Makalu (Godswalk (USA)) **1995:** *(4368) 4392$^{3}$* **1996:** *1853$^{7}$* 2114$^{19}$ 2381$^{5}$ 2856$^{2}$ (3045) 3406$^{2}$ 4314$^{2}$ 4687$^{8}$ 4772$^{13}$ 4994$^{9}$ **>92a 96f<**
**Mr Black (TUR) 6** h 4289a$^{7}$
**Mr Blue 4** b g Sylvan Express-Footstool (Artaius (USA)) 2718$^{15}$ 2898$^{11}$ 2987$^{5}$ *4094$^{11}$ 4341$^{17}$* ***>8a 12f<***
**Mr Bombastique (IRE) 2** b c Classic Music (USA)-Duende (High Top) 1896$^{5}$ (2527) 3243$^{4}$ 4625$^{5}$ 4864$^{2}$ **>85f<**
**Mr Browning (USA) 5** br g Al Nasr (FR)-Crinoline (Blakeney) 2549$^{10}$ 3235$^{2}$ 3876$^{7}$ 4067$^{15}$ 4427$^{4}$ 4673$^{7}$ 4832$^{12}$ **>47a 72f<**
**Mr Christie 4** b g Doulab (USA)-Hi There (High Top) 972$^{6}$ 1150$^{8}$ **>39f<**
**Mr Copyforce 6** gr g Sharrood (USA)-Cappuccilli (Lorenzaccio) **1995:** *4530$^{13}$* **1996:** *279$^{5}$ 365$^{3}$ (1679)* (1981) 2190$^{4}$ 2385$^{3}$ 2707$^{2}$ 3163$^{4}$ 4426$^{4}$ **>56a 56f<**
**Mr Cube (IRE) 6** ch h Tate Gallery (USA)-Truly Thankful (CAN) (Graustark) *887$^{16}$* 1010$^{4}$ 1074$^{9}$ 1609$^{12}$ 1890$^{8}$ 2032$^{2}$ 2188$^{3}$ 2405$^{5}$ 2903$^{5}$ 2954$^{5}$ 3606$^{5}$ 3812$^{12}$ 3991$^{3}$ 4240$^{7}$ (4428) 4511$^{15}$ **>41a 60f<**
**Mr Dominie (ITY) 7** b h Primo Dominie-Princess Home 437a$^{3}$
**Mr Fortywinks (IRE) 2** ch c Fools Holme (USA)-Dream on (Absalom) 441$^{5}$ 699$^{10}$ 3869$^{3}$ 4244$^{8}$ **>45f<**
**Mr Frosty 4** b g Absalom-Chadenshe (Taufan (USA)) **1995:** *4350$^{3}$ 4386$^{3}$* **1996:** *190$^{5}$ 4895$^{10}$ 5042$^{18}$* ***>70a 60?f<***
**Mr Gold (IRE) 3** b g Toledo (USA)-Liangold (Rheingold) 1668$^{11}$ 2166$^{2}$ **>10f<**
**Mr Hacker 3** b g Shannon Cottage (USA)-Aosta (Shack (USA)) *1350$^{9}$* 2004$^{8}$ 2744$^{7}$ 3469$^{12}$ 3852$^{14}$ **>51f<**
**Mr Majica 2** b c Rudimentary (USA)-Pellinora (USA) (King Pellinore (USA)) 4330$^{15}$ **>52f<**
**Mr Martini (IRE) 6** b h Pennine Walk-Arab Art (Artaius (USA)) **1995:** *4402a$^{8}$ 4482$^{7}$* **1996:** *1768$^{3}$* 2037$^{6}$ **>80a 108f<**
**Mr Medley 4** b g Merdon Melody-Hsian (Shantung) **1995:** *4418$^{6}$ 4527$^{8}$* **>50a 80df<**
**Mr Moriarty (IRE) 5** ch g Tate Gallery (USA)-Bernica (FR) (Caro) *(33) 70$^{2}$ 154$^{2}$ (196) 236$^{6}$ 333$^{2}$ 367$^{5}$ 777$^{5}$ 883$^{8}$ 1098$^{9}$ 2550$^{6}$ 3812$^{9}$ 3955$^{5}$ 4794$^{15}$ 4984$^{12}$* **>39a 40f<**
**Mr Music 2** ch g La Grange Music-Golden (Don) 4891$^{11}$ 5040$^{12}$ **>21f<**
**Mr Nevermind (IRE) 6** b g The Noble Player (USA)-Salacia (Seaepic (USA)) **1995:** *4362$^{2}$ (4454) (4527)* **1996:** *105$^{2}$ 141$^{3}$ 174$^{3}$ 350$^{2}$ (409) 462$^{6}$ 636$^{4}$* 747$^{5}$ 1314$^{8}$ 1532$^{2}$ 1890$^{12}$ 3861$^{7}$ (3978) 4354$^{3}$ *(5002)* **>84a 73f<**

**Mr Oscar 4** b g Belfort (FR)-Moushka (Song) *1016$^{7}$* 1113$^{12}$ 1818$^{10}$ 2292$^{7}$ **>97f<**

**Mr Paradise (IRE) 2** b g Salt Dome (USA)-Glowlamp (IRE) (Glow (USA)) 4330$^{18}$ 4783$^{6}$ 4902$^{2}$ 5050$^{2}$ **>65f<**

**M R Poly 2** b c Green Desert (USA)-Report 'em (USA) (Staff Writer (USA)) 3515$^{7}$ 3796$^{11}$ 3963$^{8}$ 4123$^{11}$ 4210$^{13}$ 4494$^{8}$ 4782$^{6}$ **>64f<**

**Mr Rough 5** b g Fayruz-Rheinbloom (Rheingold) 636$^{6}$ 995$^{10}$ 1173$^{6}$ 1704$^{4}$ 1830$^{12}$ 2130$^{3}$ 2412$^{2}$ 2868$^{3}$ 3161$^{14}$ 3469$^{10}$ 3703$^{3}$ 4186$^{6}$ **>55a 69f<**

**Mrs Drummond (IRE) 3** br f Dromod Hill-Dear France (USA) (Affirmed (USA)) 3320$^{6}$ *3626$^{4}$ 4237$^{8}$* 4437$^{8}$ **>40a 43f<**

**Mrs Jawleyford (USA) 8** b m Dixieland Band (USA)-Did She Agree (USA) (Restless Native) **1995:** *4434$^{7}$* **1996:** *60$^{5}$ 208$^{7}$ 236$^{10}$* **>43da 51f<**

**Mrs Keen 3** b f Beveled (USA)-Haiti Mill (Free State) *2380$^{5}$* 2978$^{6}$ 3286$^{7}$ **>41f<**

**Mr Slick 4** ch g Sharpo-Taj Victory (Final Straw) 4771$^{4}$ **>52a 46f<**

**Mrs McBadger 3** ch f Weldnaas (USA)-Scottish Lady (Dunbeath (USA)) 467$^{5}$ 1466$^{5}$ 2255$^{11}$ *3064$^{6}$ 4550$^{17}$ 4987$^{16}$* **>43a 56f<**

**Mrs Miniver (USA) 2** b f Septieme Ciel (USA)-Becomes A Rose (CAN) (Deputy Minister (CAN)) 2580$^{4}$ 3131$^{3}$ 4133$^{11}$ 4464$^{6}$ **>97?f<**

**Mr Speaker (IRE) 3** ch g Statoblest-Casting Vote (USA) (Monteverdi) 819$^{9}$ 1185$^{7}$ 1654$^{18}$ (2528) 2946$^{7}$ 3322$^{4}$ 3790$^{13}$ **>37a 66f<**

**Mr Speculator 3** ch g Kefaah (USA)-Humanity (Ahonoora) 994$^{12}$ 1174$^{8}$ 1696$^{9}$ 2191$^{5}$ (2511) 2717$^{8}$ *3422$^{6}$ 4832$^{14}$* 5008$^{U}$ **>23a 66f<**

**Mr Streaky 5** gr g Sizzling Melody-Cawstons Prejudice (Cawston's Clown) *217$^{9}$ 363$^{9}$* **>27a 46f<**

**Mr Tamburino (USA) 2** b c Alleged (USA)-Prancing Queen (ITY) (Sovereign Dancer (USA)) 4538a$^{2}$

**Mr Teddy 3** gr g Absalom-Chadenshe (Taufan (USA)) **1995:** *4417$^{6}$* **>25a 56f<**

**Mr Teigh 4** b g Komaite (USA)-Khadino (Relkino) *(261) 1048$^{6}$ 1464$^{3}$ (1811) (2552) 2701$^{3}$* 4059$^{4}$ 4724$^{2}$ 4993$^{13}$ **>82a 74f<**

**Mr Titch 3** b g Totem (USA)-Empress Nicki (Nicholas Bill) 1311$^{9}$ 1762$^{6}$ 2026$^{12}$ 2521$^{10}$ **>36f<**

**Mr Towser 5** b g Faustus (USA)-Saltina (Bustino) *48$^{6}$ 100$^{7}$ 251$^{7}$* **>84a 73f<**

**Mr Wild (USA) 3** b g Wild Again (USA)-Minstress (USA) (The Minstrel (CAN)) 4235$^{4}$ 4613$^{4}$ 4833$^{6}$ **>79f<**

**Ms Jones (IRE) 3** ch f Headin' Up-Deep Joy (Deep Run) **1995:** *4433$^{16}$*

**Ms Ziman 2** b f Mystiko (USA)-Leave Her Be (USA) (Known Fact (USA)) 2611$^{17}$ 3171$^{7}$ 3662$^{6}$ **>52f<**

**Mt. Sassafras (CAN) 4** ch g Mt Livermore (USA)-Charming Sassafras (USA) (Sassafras (FR)) 4956a$^{4}$ **>131f<**

**M T Vessel 2** b c Risk Me (FR)-Brown Taw (Whistlefield) 441$^{7}$ 697$^{3}$ 869$^{8}$ 1315$^{6}$ 1959$^{7}$ 3075$^{8}$ **>54f<**

**Muara Bay 2** gr c Absalom-Inca Girl (Tribal Chief) 5050$^{9}$

**Mu-Arrik 8** b or br h Aragon-Maravilla (Mandrake Major) 617$^{11}$ 806$^{2}$ 882$^{7}$ 1040$^{4}$ 1423$^{12}$ 1642$^{14}$ 2185$^{8}$ 2757$^{13}$ 3453$^{7}$ 3643$^{13}$ 4881$^{15}$ **>7a 33f<**

**Mua-Tab 3** ch f Polish Precedent (USA)-Alsabiha (Lord Gayle (USA)) 1326$^{5}$ 1857$^{3}$ 2384$^{4}$ 2855$^{7}$ 3479$^{8}$ 3979$^{10}$ 4804$^{5}$ **>65f<**

**Mubarhin (USA) 3** br c Silver Hawk (USA)-Upper Dancer (USA) (Upper Nile (USA)) 684$^{12}$ **>71f<**

**Mubariz (IRE) 4** b g Royal Academy (USA)-Ringtail (Auction Ring (USA)) 1675$^{2}$ 2181$^{2}$ 2420$^{4}$ 3067$^{12}$ 3413$^{4}$ 3770$^{6}$ 4059$^{8}$ 4882$^{16}$ **>81f<**

**Mubhij (IRE) 3** ch c Mujtahid (USA)-Abhaaj (Kris) 1129$^{12}$ 2115$^{11}$ 2545$^{5}$ 3047$^{F}$ **>108f< (DEAD)**

**Much Commended 2** b f Most Welcome-Glowing With Pride (Ile de Bourbon (USA)) *(4357)* 4723$^{3}$ **>87f<**

**Muchea 2** ch c Shalford (IRE)-Bargouzine (Hotfoot) 441$^{3}$ (481) (698) 2070$^{3}$ 3561a$^{2}$ (4035a) 4519$^{2}$ **>109f<**

**Much Sought After 7** b g Adonijah-Lady Clementine (He Loves Me) *38$^{10}$ 439$^{18}$* ***>37a 39f<***

**Much Too High 4** b g Salse (USA)-Hi-Li (High Top) *85$^{9}$* **>26a 63f<**

**Mudflap 2** b f Slip Anchor-River's Rising (FR) (Mendez (FR)) 2404$^{5}$ *2746$^{2}$ (3625) 3835$^{5}$* 3998$^{10}$ **>76a 81f<**

**Mudlark 4** b g Salse (USA)-Mortal Sin (USA) (Green Forest (USA)) *331$^{2}$ 73$^{5}$ 4984$^{5}$* **>34a 51f<**

**Muhandam (IRE) 3** b c Common Grounds-Unbidden Melody (USA) (Chieftain II) 1709$^{7}$ *2305$^{6}$* **>35a 74f<**

**Muhandis 3** b c Persian Bold-Night At Sea (Night Shift (USA)) (2918) 4453$^{5}$ **>83f<**

**Muhassil (IRE) 3** ch g Persian Bold-Nouvelle Star (AUS) (Luskin Star (AUS)) 994$^{4}$ **>71f<**

**Muhtadi (IRE) 3** br c Marju (IRE)-Moon Parade (Welsh Pageant) (614) 803$^{15}$ 1415$^{7}$ 1900$^{9}$ 2342$^{5}$ **>69f<**

**Mujadil Express (IRE) 2** b f Mujadil (USA)-Peace Mission (Dunbeath (USA)) 2252$^{8}$ 3336$^{3}$ 3582$^{5}$ *3954$^{3}$ 4335$^{3}$ 4694$^{10}$ 4780$^{8}$ 5048$^{10}$* ***>61a 39f<***

**Mujazi (IRE) 2** ch c Mujtahid (USA)-Leaping Salmon (Salmon Leap (USA)) 3701$^{6}$ 4242$^{16}$ **>45f<**

**Mujova (IRE) 2** b c Mujadil (USA)-Kirsova (Absalom) 441$^{6}$ 523$^{3}$ 1003$^{3}$ 1705$^{3}$ 1987$^{2}$ 2219$^{5}$ 2755$^{4}$ (3080) 3620$^{2}$ 4024a$^{6}$ 4301$^{5}$ 4366$^{4}$ 4723$^{14}$ 4918$^{7}$ **>83f<**

**Mujtahida (IRE) 3** b f Mujtahid (USA)-Domino's Nurse (Dom Racine (FR)) *921$^{13}$* 1614$^{15}$ *3064$^{7}$ 3608$^{4}$* **>52a 51f<**

**Mukaddar (USA) 2** ch c Elmaamul (USA)-Both Sides Now (USA) (Topsider (USA)) (3494) 4050$^{3}$ 4488$^{2}$ **>96f<**

**Mukeed 3** b c Be My Chief (USA)-Rimosa's Pet (Petingo) 1359$^{13}$ 1711$^{12}$ 2080$^{4}$ 2570$^{7}$ (3218) **>78f<**

**Mukhlles (USA) 3** b c Diesis-Serenely (USA) (Alydar (USA)) 730$^{3}$ **>78f<**

**Mulhollande Lad (IRE) 3** ch g Mulhollande (USA)-La Kumbha (FR) (Critique (USA)) **1995:** *4389$^{14}$ 4433$^{7}$* **1996:** *46$^{7}$ 197$^{W}$* **>31a 28f<**

**Muliere 2** b f Mujtahid (USA)-Shojoon (USA) (Danzig (USA)) 3994$^{10}$ 4228$^{5}$ 4554$^{4}$ 4803$^{7}$ *5057$^{5}$* **>37a 58f<**

**Mullagh Hill Lad (IRE) 3** b c Cyrano de Bergerac-Fantasise (FR) (General Assembly (USA)) **1995:** *(4369) 4473$^{2}$* **1996:** *525$^{19}$* 638$^{13}$ 1068$^{7}$ 1527$^{4}$ 2215$^{6}$ 2578$^{6}$ 3937$^{8}$ 4356$^{22}$ 4589$^{6}$ **>74a 59f<**

**Mull House 9** b g Local Suitor (USA)-Foudre (Petingo) *3163$^{8}$* 4673$^{12}$ 4821$^{13}$ **>46f<**

**Mullitover 6** ch g Interrex (CAN)-Atlantic Air (Air Trooper) 2623$^{3}$ 3158$^{6}$ 3612$^{13}$ 4444$^{18}$ **>65a 97f<**

**Multan 4** b g Indian Ridge-Patchinia (Patch) *577$^{17}$* 812$^{10}$ 1473$^{7}$ 2345$^{4}$ 4053$^{11}$ 4497$^{9}$ **>54f<**

**Multicoloured (IRE) 3** b c Rainbow Quest (USA)-Greektown (Ela-Mana-Mou) 3656$^{2}$ 3841$^{2}$ (4622) 4964$^{2}$ **>112f<**

**Multi Franchise 3** ch g Gabitat-Gabibti (IRE) (Dara Monarch) **1995:** *4518$^{8}$* **1996:** *254 129$^{2}$ (262) 1661$^{2}$* 1979$^{4}$ 2594$^{10}$ (3300) 3978$^{7}$ *4107$^{9}$* **>65a 65f<**

**Multitone 2** b g Saddlers' Hall (IRE)-Warning Light (High Top) 2132$^{7}$ 2503$^{5}$ (3277) **>88f<**

**Mumkin 2** b c Reprimand-Soon to Be (Hot Spark) (3259) 3620$^{3}$ 4189$^{8}$ **>79f<**

**Munaadee (USA) 4** b c Green Dancer (USA)-Aliysa (Darshaan) *(402)* **>77a 74f<**

**Munaaji (USA) 5** b h Storm Cat (USA)-Growth Rate (USA) (Blushing Groom (FR)) **1995:** 4425a$^{3}$ **1996:** 1945a$^{3}$ 4033a$^{6}$ 4412a$^{2}$ 4540a$^{2}$ **>116f<**

**Muncie (IRE) 4** b f Sadler's Wells (USA)-Martingale (Luthier) 906a$^{5}$ 1947a$^{5}$ **>119f<**

**Mungo Park 2** b c Selkirk (USA)-River Dove (USA) (Riverman (USA)) 4208$^{8}$ 4558$^{10}$ 4762$^{4}$ 5037$^{7}$ **>61f<**

**Municipal Girl (IRE) 2** b f Mac's Imp (USA)-Morning Welcome (IRE) (Be My Guest (USA)) 1982$^{5}$ *3604$^{6}$ 3840$^{4}$* 4368$^{10}$ 4896$^{10}$ *5061$^{7}$* **>29a 50f<**

**Munif (IRE) 4** ch c Caerleon (USA)-Forest Lair (Habitat) 4268a$^{5}$ **>99f<**

**Muntafi 5** b g Unfuwain (USA)-Princess Sucree (USA) (Roberto (USA)) 3948$^{10}$ **>80df<**

**Muppet 2** b f Law Society (USA)-Shaadin (USA) (Sharpen Up) 643$^{4}$ 757$^{7}$ 1021$^{5}$ **>54f<**

**Murajja (USA) 4** ch c Silver Hawk (USA)-Halholah (USA) (Secreto (USA)) *726$^{7}$* (1520) 3728a$^{4}$ 4876$^{10}$ **>121f<**

**Murheb 3** b g Mtoto-Masarrah (Formidable (USA)) 544$^{4}$ (845) 1785$^{7}$ 2544$^{6}$ 3211$^{2}$ 3594$^{5}$ **>97f<**

**Murphy's Gold (IRE) 5** ch g Salt Dome (USA)-Winter Harvest (Grundy) 505$^{13}$ 713$^{6}$ 879$^{23}$ 1037$^{13}$ 1674$^{4}$ 1860$^{2}$ 2925$^{4}$ 3120$^{8}$ 4226$^{4}$ 4503$^{7}$ **>27a 59f<**

**Murray Grey 2** gr f Be My Chief (USA)-Couleur de Rose (Kalaglow) 4224$^{11}$ 4584$^{9}$ 4806$^{6}$ **>46f<**

**Murray's Mazda (IRE) 7** ch g M Double M (USA)-Lamya (Hittite Glory) **1995:** *4371$^{5}$* **1996:** *(1313)* 1674$^{5}$ (2047) 2149$^{3}$ 2590$^{2}$ 2725$^{12}$ 4316$^{10}$ 4439$^{4}$ 4724$^{8}$ **>50a 52f<**

**Murron Wallace 2** gr f Reprimand-Fair Eleanor (Saritamer (USA)) 3956$^{6}$ 4250$^{5}$ 4594$^{5}$ 4795$^{5}$ **>54f<**

**Musalsal (IRE) 2** b c Sadler's Wells (USA)-Ozone Friendly (USA) (Green Forest (USA)) 3706$^{5}$ (4897) **>91+f<**

**Muscatana 2** b f Distant Relative-Sauhatz (GER) (Alpenkonig (GER)) 2559$^{9}$ 3475$^{7}$ 3803$^{6}$ 4223$^{15}$ **>44f<**

**Muse 9** ch g High Line-Thoughtful (Northfields (USA)) 1194$^{11}$ 4673$^{15}$ 4821$^{11}$ **>59f<**

**Musetta (IRE) 4** b f Cadeaux Genereux-Monaiya (Shareef Dancer (USA)) 581$^{10}$ 1770$^{6}$ (2194) 2730$^{2}$ 3905a$^{3}$ 4410a$^{4}$ **>107f<**

**Museum (IRE) 5** b g Tate Gallery (USA)-Go Anywhere (Grundy) *113$^{7}$ 256$^{2}$ 303$^{8}$ 2136$^{7}$* ***>70a 70f<***

**Mushahid (USA) 3** b c Wild Again (USA)-Playful Queen (USA) (Majestic Prince (USA)) 454$^{3}$ 833$^{4}$ (1785) 2041$^{12}$ (2774) 3211$^{7}$ 3709$^{14}$ **>104f<**

**Musharak 2** b c Mujtahid (USA)-Mahasin (USA) (Danzig (USA)) 4670$^{4}$ 4825$^{12}$ **>71tf<**

**Musheer (USA) 2** b c Known Fact (USA)-Summer Trip (USA) (L'Emigrant (USA)) 2416$^{2}$ (3040) 4179$^{3}$ **>98f<**

**Musical Dancer (USA) 2** ch c Dixieland Band (USA)-Parrish Empress (USA) (His Majesty (USA)) 2580$^{5}$ (3119) 3684$^{2}$ 3971$^{6}$ 4338$^{2}$ 4555$^{2}$ **>102f<**

**Musical Heights (IRE) 3** b f Roaring Riva-Littleton Song (Song) *430$^{7}$* **>4a 1f<**

**Musical Pursuit 2** b c Pursuit of Love-Gay Music (FR) (Gay Mecene (USA)) 2624$^{5}$ (3245) 4759$^{2}$ **>106f<**

**Musical Season 4** b g Merdon Melody-Earles-Field (Wolverlife) 610$^{24}$ 1430$^{7}$ 1975$^{5}$ (4116) 4314$^{7}$ 4679$^{7}$ 4823$^{2}$ **>99f<**

**Musical Vocation (IRE) 5** ch m Orchestra-Kentucky Calling (Pry) *138$^{7}$* **>10a f<**

**Music Express (IRE) 2** b f Classic Music (USA)-Hetty Green (Bay Express) 2025$^{5}$ 2932$^{4}$ **>50f<**

**Music Gold (IRE) 3** b br c Taufan (USA)-Nonnita (Welsh Saint) *565$^4$* 1316$^4$ 4518$^5$ **>93f<**

**Music In Motion 3** b f Batshoof-Falaka (Sparkler) 2915$^7$ **>12f<**

**Musick House (IRE) 3** b c Sadler's Wells (USA)-Hot Princess (Hot Spark) 732$^3$ (962) 1574a$^8$ 2050$^{10}$ 4714$^8$ **>94f<**

**Music Mistress (IRE) 3** ch f Classic Music (USA)-Blue Scholar (Hotfoot) *52$^5$ 131$^{10}$ 242$^5$ 637$^9$* 867$^4$ 1170$^{15}$ 2500$^{10}$ 3761$^{16}$ **>30a 46f<**

**Music of Dance (IRE) 5** b m Roi Danzig (USA)-Betty Bun (St Chad) **1995:** 4467a$^2$ **>29a 57f<**

**Muskat (GER) 5** dk h Konigsstuhl (GER)-Musette (Tudor Music) 327a$^3$

**Mustahil (IRE) 7** gr g Sure Blade (USA)-Zumurrudah (USA) (Spectacular Bid (USA)) 1651$^9$ 1893$^{11}$ 2310$^{10}$ **>48f<**

**Mustang 3** ch c Thatching-Lassoo (Caerleon (USA)) 566$^9$ **>60f<**

**Mustang Scally 2** b f Makbul-Another Scally (Scallywag) 4607$^9$ *4988$^{10}$* **>23f<**

**Mustard 3** ch f Keen-Tommys Dream (Le Bavard (FR)) 870$^{12}$ 2079$^7$ 2572$^{13}$ **>22f<**

**Mustn't Grumble (IRE) 6** b g Orchestra-Gentle Heiress (Prince Tenderfoot (USA)) 479$^2$ *511$^2$ 592$^4$* 749$^4$ *896$^4$ 1094$^6$ 1890$^6$ 2308$^7$ 2637$^2$ 3062$^6$ 4129$^2$* (4337) 4609$^{13}$ 4692$^3$ 4901$^5$ **>59a 70f<**

**Mutabari (USA) 2** ch c Seeking the Gold (USA)-Cagey Exuberance (USA) (Exuberant (USA)) 2057$^5$ 4584$^3$ 4830$^{10}$ **>74f<**

**Mutadarra (IRE) 3** ch c Mujtahid (USA)-Silver Echo (Caerleon (USA)) 696$^2$ 934$^3$ (1422) 2501$^{11}$ 3106$^8$ **>86df<**

**Mu-Tadil 4** ch g Be My Chief (USA)-Inveraven (Alias Smith (USA)) 4083$^5$ 4476$^{10}$ **>42?f<**

**Mutahadeth 2** ch c Rudimentary (USA)-Music in My Life (IRE) (Law Society (USA)) 2224$^{12}$ 3485$^8$ 3964$^5$ 4375$^6$ **>61f<**

**Mutakddim (USA) 5** ch h Seeking the Gold (USA)-Oscillate (USA) (Seattle Slew (USA)) **1995:** 4405a$^3$ **>120f<**

**Mutamanni (USA) 3** b c Caerleon (USA)-Mathkurh (USA) (Riverman (USA)) 672$^4$ 1078$^4$ 1799$^4$ **>82f<**

**Mutanassib (IRE) 3** b c Mtoto-Lightning Legacy (USA) (Super Concorde (USA)) 3704$^6$ 4099$^2$ 4478$^6$ 4833$^4$ **>74f<**

**Mutasarrif (IRE) 3** b c Polish Patriot (USA)-Bouffant (High Top) 1171$^{11}$ **>40f<**

**Mutasawwar 2** ch c Clantime-Keen Melody (USA) (Sharpen Up) 4330$^{12}$ 4902$^7$ **>58f<**

**Mutazz (USA) 4** b c Woodman (USA)-Ghashtah (USA) (Nijinsky (CAN)) 753$^{14}$ **>71f<**

**Mutee (IRE) 3** b f Mujtahid (USA)-Cum Laude (Shareef Dancer (USA)) **1995:** *4519$^9$* **1996:** *89$^8$*

**Mutinique 5** br m General Wade-Little Visitor (Tina's Pet) **1995:** *4350$^9$ 4357$^{10}$ 4420$^{10}$ 4436$^8$ 4465$^{10}$* **>21a 50f<**

**Mutribah (USA) 2** b f Silver Hawk (USA)-Pattimech (USA) (Nureyev (USA)) 3663$^2$ 4096$^2$ **>63f<**

**Muzrak (CAN) 5** ch g Forty Niner (USA)-Linda North (USA) (Northern Dancer) 482$^{10}$ **>65f<**

**My Achates 3** b f Prince Sabo-Persian Air (Persian Bold) 3350$^W$

**My Archie 3** b c Silver Arch-My Alma (IRE) (Reasonable (FR)) *370$^6$ 428$^{11}$* **>20f<**

**Myasha (USA) 7** b g Imp Society (USA)-Mauna Loa (USA) (Hawaii) **1995:** *4517$^8$* **1996:** *1681$^2$* ***>54a 47f<***

**My Beautiful Dream 3** gr f Kalaglow-Cinderella Derek (Hittite Glory) 634$^4$ 1012$^{11}$ **>49df<**

**My Beloved (IRE) 2** b f Polish Patriot (USA)-Arbour (USA) (Graustark) 1169$^5$ 1467$^4$ (2309) 3046$^3$ **>79f<**

**My Best Valentine 6** b h Try My Best (USA)-Pas de Calais (Pas de Seul) *(744)* 1186$^{11}$ 1354$^5$ 1790$^2$ 2400$^2$ 3232$^6$ 3783$^{13}$ 3920$^2$ 4196$^5$ 4352$^7$ 4444$^5$ 4775$^{20}$ **>50a 96f<**

**My Betsy 2** gr f Absalom-Formidable Task (Formidable (USA)) 3080$^5$ 3840$^9$ **>55f<**

**My Bonus 6** b m Cyrano de Bergerac-Dress in Spring (Northfields (USA)) **1995:** *4542$^9$* **1996:** *42$^{15}$* **>35a 56df<**

**Mybotye 3** br c Rambo Dancer (CAN)-Sigh (Highland Melody) 638$^3$ 785$^3$ 1126$^9$ 1829$^5$ (2139) 2754$^6$ 4453$^{11}$ 4909$^{10}$ 5042$^{10}$ **>73f<**

**My Branch 3** b f Distant Relative-Pay the Bank (High Top) *939$^4$* 1567a$^3$ 2050$^8$ 3127$^{13}$ (4135) 4378$^4$ 4718$^3$ 4972$^5$ **>109f<**

**My Brave Girl 4** b f Never so Bold-Souadah (USA) (General Holme (USA)) *688$^{18}$ 855$^{10}$* **>50f<**

**My Cadeaux 4** ch f Cadeaux Genereux-Jubilee Song (Song) (1652) 2692$^8$ 3045$^9$ 4957a$^2$ **>94f<**

**My Cherrywell 6** br m Kirchner-Cherrywood Blessin (Good Times (ITY)) **1995:** *(4413) 4486$^9$* **1996:** *74$^3$ 127$^3$ 259$^3$ 762$^3$* 911$^2$ *1028$^2$ 1492$^5$ 1716$^9$ 4473$^3$* ***>60a 56f<***

**My Dear Watson 2** b f Chilibang-Mrs Bacon (Balliol) 2025$^9$ 2531$^6$ **>24f<**

**My Dutch Girl 4** b f Midyan (USA)-Double Dutch (Nicholas Bill) *79$^{12}$* **>20a 46f<**

**My Emma 3** b f Marju (IRE)-Pato (High Top) 2533$^5$ (3042) 3570a$^3$ (4292a) **>117f<**

**Myfanwy Bethesda 3** b f Relief Pitcher-Take a Break (Take A Reef) 2181$^{13}$ 2383$^{10}$ 2557$^{14}$ **>12f<**

**My Flag (USA) 3** ch f Easy Goer (USA)-Personal Ensign (USA) (Private Account (USA)) *1946a$^3$ 4952a$^4$* **>116a 110tf<**

**Myfontaine 9** b h Persepolis (FR)-Mortefontaine (FR) (Polic) 650$^3$ 817$^8$ 979$^8$ (1450) 1686$^5$ 1841$^4$ 2574$^{14}$ 2943$^8$ 3457$^5$ 3785$^7$ 3981$^5$ 4238$^{14}$ 4831$^2$ 4900$^{15}$ **>74f<**

**My Gallery (IRE) 5** ch m Tate Gallery (USA)-Sententious (Kautokeino (FR)) **1995:** *4371$^9$ 4407$^6$* **1996:** *247$^5$ 291$^2$ (343) (403) (413) (617)* 662$^3$ 1001$^2$ *1601$^3$ 1674$^6$* 1825$^3$ (1890) 1983$^3$ 2149$^6$ 2240$^2$ 2428$^3$ 2672$^2$ (2874) 2954$^4$ (3265) (3426) 3805$^4$ (3933) *4078$^8$ 4194$^5$* 4316$^6$ 4444$^{11}$ 4571$^5$ 4775$^{22}$ *5002$^6$* **>74a 92f<**

**My Girl 2** b f Mon Tresor-Lady of Itatiba (BEL) (King Of Macedon) 2018$^3$ 2569$^7$ 2926$^6$ 3241$^5$ 3448$^{13}$ *3950$^3$ 4093$^9$ 4562$^{10}$* ***>43a 42f<***

**My Girl Lucy 2** b f Picea-English Mint (Jalmood (USA)) 2404$^6$ **>29f<**

**My Godson 6** br g Valiyar-Blessit (So Blessed) **1995:** *4409$^{15}$* **1996:** *207$^6$ 704$^7$* 882$^8$ (971) 1162$^2$ 1474$^{14}$ (2481) 2964$^3$ 3252$^4$ (3306) 3777$^3$ 3985$^{16}$ 4226$^{18}$ 4768$^{14}$ **>19a 63f<**

**My Handsome Prince 4** b g Handsome Sailor-My Serenade (USA) (Sensitive Prince (USA)) 688$^2$ 983$^5$ 1411$^8$ 1893$^9$ *2303$^5$ 2551$^8$ 2868$^5$* 3403$^7$ 3808$^{16}$ *3951$^7$* **>45a 40f<**

**My Handy Man 5** ch g Out of Hand-My Home (Homing) *341$^7$ 477$^9$* 561$^9$ 615$^5$ **>64a 49f<**

**My Happy Guest (IRE) 3** gr c Be My Guest (USA)-Rarely Irish (USA) (Irish Tower (USA)) 2109a$^5$ 2668a$^{10}$ 4290a$^{10}$ **>87f<**

**My Hero (IRE) 2** b f Bluebird (USA)-Risacca (ITY) (Sir Gaylord) 3036$^5$ 3319$^4$ 4508$^{10}$ **>73f<**

**My Irish 6** b h Assert-Cremets (Mummy's Pet) **1995:** 4470a$^5$ **>118f<**

**Myjinka 6** gr m Myjinski (USA)-Royal Bat (Crowned Prince (USA)) **1995:** *4351$^8$ (4464) 4521$^2$* **1996:** *(36) 278$^4$ 308$^4$ 366$^7$ 406$^8$* **>53a 29f<**

**My Kind 3** ch f Mon Tresor-Kind of Shy (Kind of Hush) 748$^{10}$ 885$^4$ 1067$^{10}$ 1526$^7$ 1806$^4$ 2180$^7$ 2966$^9$ 3451$^7$ 3654$^4$ **>36a 54f<**

**My King (GER) 3** br c Fairy King (USA)-Monamira (Kashmir II) 1753a$^2$ 3752a$^2$ **>104f<**

**My Learned Friend 5** b or br g Broken Hearted-Circe (Main Reef) 925$^9$ 1147$^7$ 2055$^2$ 2690$^3$ 3689$^{10}$ 4067$^6$ 4465$^{13}$ 4675$^{10}$ **>90df<**

**My Lewicia (IRE) 3** b f Taufan (USA)-Christine Daae (Sadler's Wells (USA)) 964$^2$ (1438) 2888$^2$ 3229$^6$ **>106df<**

**Mylordmayor 9** ch g Move Off-Sharenka (Sharpen Up) 2341$^{10}$ **>15f<**

**My Mariam 3** ch f Salse (USA)-Birch Creek (Carwhite) *2722$^7$* 2974$^6$ 3322$^8$ 4866$^{13}$ **>68f<**

**My Melody Parkes 3** b f Teenoso (USA)-Summerhill Spruce (Windjammer (USA)) 674$^4$ 939$^8$ 1629$^2$ 2072$^9$ 2498$^4$ 3495$^3$ **>98df<**

**My Millie 3** ch f Midyan (USA)-Madam Millie (Milford) 1665$^{20}$ 2013$^9$ 2316$^7$ 3166$^7$ 4323$^{12}$ 4437$^2$ 4587$^{16}$ 4812$^{16}$ **>57f<**

**My Mother's Local (USA) 3** b f Local Talent (USA)-My Mother's Eyes (FR) (Saint Cyrien (FR)) **1995:** *4491$^{13}$ 4529$^9$* **1996:** *67$^7$ 123$^{12}$ 597$^{12}$* 669$^{11}$ 861$^8$ 1512$^{14}$ 1836$^9$ **>11a 43f<**

**Myosotis 2** ch g Don't Forget Me-Ella Mon Amour (Ela-Mana-Mou) 3259$^{15}$ 3615$^{15}$ 4599$^6$ 4902$^6$ **>71f<**

**My Precious 2** ch f Mon Tresor-Nipotina (Simply Great (FR)) 1346$^{11}$ 1851$^8$ 2187$^5$ 2904$^9$ 3311$^5$ **>61f<**

**Myrmidon 2** b c Midyan (USA)-Moorish Idol (Aragon) 1191$^2$ 1774$^6$ 2495$^2$ 3924$^4$ 4545$^8$ 4916$^W$ (5037) **>90f<**

**My Rossini 7** b g Ardross-My Tootsie (Tap On Wood) 872$^{14}$ **>53a 60f<**

**Myrtle 3** b f Batshoof-Greek Goddess (Young Generation) *572$^{10}$* ***>97f<***

**Myrtlebank 2** ch f Salse (USA)-Magical Veil (Majestic Light (USA)) (4449) 4879$^6$ **>91f<**

**My Saltarello (IRE) 2** b c Salt Dome (USA)-Daidis (Welsh Pageant) 3869$^4$ 4046$^{11}$ 4991$^7$ **>55f<**

**Myself 4** ch f Nashwan (USA)-Pushy (Sharpen Up) 810$^6$ 1582a$^2$ 2609$^5$ 3712$^4$ **>107f<**

**Mysterium 2** gr c Mystiko (USA)-Way to Go (Troy) *3349$^{13}$ 3625$^6$* **>12a 6f<**

**Mystery 2** b f Mystiko (USA)-Dismiss (Daring March) 1328$^4$ 1678$^2$ 1954$^9$ 4062$^{14}$ 4514$^9$ 4787$^9$ **>59f<**

**Mystery Matthias 3** b f Nicholas (USA)-Devils Dirge (Song) **1995:** *4361$^{11}$ 4381$^5$* **1996:** *81$^6$ 131$^3$ 230$^4$ 1840$^3$* 2193$^4$ 2500$^6$ 2686$^2$ 2946$^6$ 3139$^6$ 3316$^7$ 4428$^5$ *4996$^8$* **>51a 56f<**

**Mystical City (IRE) 6** ch m The Noble Player (USA)-Felicitas (Mr Fluorocarbon) 4537b$^2$ 4643a$^{23}$ **>86f<**

**Mystical Island 2** b f Deploy-Do Run Run (Commanche Run) 1851$^{10}$ **>10f<**

**Mystical Maid 3** b f Aragon-Persistent Girl (Superlative) 1122$^2$ 1776$^8$ *2325$^2$ 2636$^3$ 3244$^8$* 4098$^{20}$ 4784$^8$ *4895$^5$* **>58a 38f<**

**Mystical Mind 3** gr g Emarati (USA)-Spanish Chestnut (Philip of Spain) 3058$^5$ 3226$^7$ **>26f<**

**Mystic Circle (IRE) 2** ch f Magical Wonder (USA)-Rozala (USA) (Roberto (USA)) 1664$^5$ 2396$^2$ (3326) 3814$^3$ 4113$^{17}$ 4566$^{12}$ **>66f<**

**Mystic Dawn 3** b f Aragon-Ahonita (Ahonoora) 888$^4$ 1119$^5$ 1654$^6$ 2016$^3$ 2605$^3$ 3634$^7$ 4064$^4$ 4186$^2$ 4337$^4$ (4691) 4901$^{11}$ **>77f<**

**Mystic Hill 5** b g Shirley Heights-Nuryana (Nureyev (USA)) 1440$^8$ 1767$^5$ 2131$^3$ (2882) 3760$^7$ 4055$^6$ 4716$^7$ 4872$^{19}$ **>97df<**

**Mystic Knight 3** b c Caerleon (USA)-Nuryana (Nureyev (USA)) 725$^3$ (1076) 1791$^6$ **>121f<**

**Mystic Legend (IRE) 4** gr g Standaan (FR)-Mandy

Girl (Manado) *217$^{10}$ 409$^{9}$ 498$^{5}$ 670$^{11}$* 1099$^{10}$ 1655$^{18}$ 2711$^{9}$ 2941$^{7}$ 4829$^{13}$ **>34a 43f<**
**Mystic Maid (IRE) 3** b f Mujtahid (USA)-Dandizette (Danzig (USA)) 768$^{10}$ 1033$^{3}$ **>70f<**
**Mystic Quest (IRE) 2** b c Arcane (USA)-Tales of Wisdom (Rousillon (USA)) *1489$^{3}$ 2396$^{7}$* 2733$^{4}$ 3312$^{2}$ 3848$^{4}$ 4106$^{14}$ *(4331) 4495$^{11}$* 4880$^{19}$ **>83a 70f<**
**Mystic Ridge 2** ch c Mystiko (USA)-Vallauris (Faustus (USA)) 1519$^{6}$ **>68f<**
**Mystic Tempo (USA) 3** ch f El Gran Senor (USA)-Doubling Time (USA) (Timeless Moment (USA)) *(21) (183) 271$^{2}$ 383$^{3}$ 423$^{2}$* **>70a 79?f<**
**Mystictich 4** b f Germont-Bauhinia (Sagaro) **1995:** *4388$^{16}$ 4444$^{10}$*
**Mystic Times 3** b f Timeless Times (USA)-Chikala (Pitskelly) 867$^{8}$ 1527$^{16}$ 1761$^{10}$ 2185$^{10}$ 2481$^{12}$ 3427$^{10}$ (3645) 3866$^{5}$ 3961$^{4}$ 4472$^{8}$ **>45f<**
**Mystique Air (IRE) 2** b f Mujadil (USA)-Romany Pageant (Welsh Pageant) 4245$^{3}$ 4684$^{5}$ **>67f<**
**Mystique Smile 3** ch f Music Boy-Jay Gee Ell (Vaigly Great) *644$^{8}$* 1527$^{9}$ 1663$^{3}$ 2021$^{6}$ 2238$^{7}$ **>49f<**
**Mythical 2** gr f Mystiko (USA)-Geryea (USA) (Desert Wine (USA)) 4241$^{9}$ *4976$^{4}$* **>38a 47f<**
**Myttons Mistake 3** b g Rambo Dancer (CAN)-Hi-Hunsley (Swing Easy (USA)) **1995:** *4509$^{3}$* **1996:** *102$^{3}$ 182$^{3}$ 220$^{2}$ 335$^{3}$ 503$^{3}$ 1006$^{2}$* 1708$^{7}$ 2078$^{7}$ 2222$^{5}$ 2676$^{4}$ 3154$^{3}$ 3465$^{9}$ 3793$^{7}$ 3932$^{8}$ 4246$^{20}$ 4430$^{18}$ 4860$^{3}$ **>76a 69f<**
**My Valentina 2** b f Royal Academy (USA)-Imperial Jade (Lochnager) 4305$^{2}$ (4797) 4973$^{10}$ **>85f<**
**My West End Girl 3** b f Dunbeath (USA)-Carnfield (Anfield) **1995:** *4408$^{14}$* **1996:** *101$^{10}$* **>19a f<**

**N**

**Naaman (IRE) 3** b br f Marju (IRE)-Shaiybaniyda (He Loves Me) 1319$^{8}$ 1690$^{7}$ **>60f<**
**Naazeq 3** ch f Nashwan (USA)-Gharam (USA) (Green Dancer (USA)) (4429) 4678$^{11}$ **>83?f<**
**Nabeel Moon (IRE) 3** b c Nabeel Dancer (USA)-Lunaris () (High Top) 799a$^{2}$
**Nabhaan (IRE) 3** b c In The Wings-Miss Gris (USA) (Hail the Pirates (USA)) 593$^{2}$ (702) 1175$^{3}$ 1712$^{6}$ 2534$^{3}$ 3760$^{4}$ 4826$^{3}$ 5046$^{3}$ **>104f<**
**Nabjelsedr 6** b g Never so Bold-Klewraye (Lord Gayle (USA)) 887$^{19}$ 1468$^{12}$ 2344$^{3}$ 2971$^{8}$ 3694$^{4}$ **>48f<**
**Nador 3** ch c Rainbow Quest (USA)-Nadma (USA) (Northern Dancer) *570$^{6}$* 947$^{4}$ 1175$^{2}$ 2074$^{5}$ (2616) 3145$^{7}$ **>100f<**
**Nadwaty (IRE) 4** b f Prince Sabo-Faisalah (Gay Mecene (USA)) **1995:** *4413$^{W}$ 4478$^{7}$* **1996:** *126$^{6}$ 750$^{5}$* 951$^{8}$ *1028$^{6}$ 1642$^{12}$* ***>55a 46f<***
**Nagnagnag (IRE) 4** b f Red Sunset-Rubina Park (Ashmore (FR)) 1112$^{7}$ 1484$^{14}$ 1770$^{3}$ 2477a$^{5}$ 3709$^{5}$ 4194$^{11}$ 4352$^{2}$ 4568$^{33}$ 4671$^{6}$ 4874$^{6}$ **>101f<**
**Nahrawali (IRE) 5** b g Kahyasi-Nashkara (Shirley Heights) *37$^{10}$* **>13a f<**
**Nails Tails 3** b c Efisio-Northern Dynasty (Breeders Dream) 2036$^{12}$ **>45f<**
**Naissant 3** b f Shaadi (USA)-Nophe (USA) (Super Concorde (USA)) 987$^{10}$ 1323$^{5}$ 1666$^{8}$ 3240$^{3}$ 3424$^{15}$ 3489$^{5}$ 3644$^{2}$ (3844) (3867) 3995$^{10}$ 4312$^{20}$ 4453$^{10}$ 4485$^{5}$ 4689$^{9}$ 4971$^{6}$ **>80f<**
**Naivasha 2** gr f Petong-Nevis (Connaught) 2138$^{4}$ 3054$^{3}$ 3508$^{5}$ (3840) 4311$^{10}$ **>71f<**
**Najiya 3** b f Nashwan (USA)-The Perfect Life (IRE) (Try My Best (USA)) 708$^{7}$ 1639$^{4}$ 3127$^{4}$ 3945$^{10}$ 4445$^{13}$ **>101f<**
**Najm Almaydaan (USA) 5** b or br h Nureyev (USA)-Teacher's Joy (USA) (Daryl's Joy (NZ)) *395a$^{3}$ 535a$^{5}$* **>78a 68df<**
**Najm Mubeen (IRE) 3** b c Last Tycoon-Ah Ya Zein (Artaius (USA)) *(4556)* 4874$^{2}$ **>102f<**
**Nakami 4** b g Dashing Blade-Dara's Bird (Dara Monarch) 3162$^{4}$ 3930$^{13}$ 4430$^{15}$ **>63f<**
**Nakayama Express (IRE) 3** b c Warning-Bluebook (USA) (Secretariat (USA)) 2472a$^{2}$ **>84f<**
**Naked Emperor 3** b g Dominion Royale-Torville Gold (Aragon) **1995:** *4417$^{7}$* **1996:** *25$^{7}$ 171$^{7}$* **>18a 52f<**
**Naked Poser (IRE) 2** b f Night Shift (USA)-Art Age (Artaius (USA)) (1352) 2338$^{6}$ 4113$^{2}$ 4490$^{8}$ 4873$^{7}$ **>82f<**
**Naked Welcome 4** ch c Most Welcome-Stripanoora (Ahonoora) *831$^{3}$* 919$^{7}$ 1767$^{4}$ 2055$^{10}$ 2881$^{5}$ 3689$^{9}$ **>113f<**
**Nakhal 3** b c Puissance-Rambadale (Vaigly Great) 468$^{3}$ 734$^{5}$ 1172$^{7}$ 2409$^{9}$ 2710$^{4}$ *3074$^{3}$ 3165$^{4}$* 3456$^{14}$ *4076$^{9}$* **>59a 59f<**
**Namaste 8** b g Petoski-View (Shirley Heights) *260$^{3}$ 369$^{6}$* **>47a 51f< (DEAD)**
**Nameless 3** ch f Doc Marten-Opuntia (Rousillon (USA)) *359$^{7}$* **>59a 59f<**
**Name of Our Father (USA) 3** b g Northern Baby (CAN)-Ten Hail Marys (USA) (Halo (USA)) 754$^{11}$ 4793$^{10}$ 4900$^{13}$ *4978$^{5}$* **>58a 75f<**
**Name That Tune 4** ch f Fayruz-Gandoorah (Record Token) **1995:** *4407$^{14}$* **>31a 49f<**
**Name the Tune 5** b h Chief Singer-Try to Remember (Music Boy) **1995:** *4394$^{10}$* **>67a 91f<**
**Namoodaj 3** b g Polish Precedent (USA)-Leipzig (Relkino) 1670$^{9}$ 3505$^{7}$ 4083$^{3}$ (4450) 4669$^{3}$ **>82f<**
**Namouna (IRE) 3** b f Sadler's Wells (USA)-Amaranda (USA) (Bold Lad (IRE)) *1614$^{6}$* 3041$^{4}$ **>65f<**
**Nampara Bay 2** b f Emarati (USA)-Dewberry (Bay Express) *1093$^{6}$ 1513$^{7}$* ***>15a 22f<***
**Nanda 3** ch f Nashwan (USA)-Pushy (Sharpen Up) 957$^{6}$ 1201$^{2}$ (2399) **>84f<**
**Naninja (USA) 3** ch c Alysheba (USA)-Nijinsky's Lover (USA) (Nijinsky (CAN)) 4417a$^{3}$ **>106f<**
**Nanny-B 3** br f Chilibang-Carly-B (IRE) (Commanche Run) 2915$^{4}$ 3654$^{8}$ 4070$^{18}$ 4221$^{16}$ **>32f<**
**Nanshan (IRE) 3** b f Nashwan (USA)-Pass the Peace (Alzao (USA)) *269$^{2}$ 2919$^{3}$* ***>55a 90f<***
**Nantgarw 3** b f Teamster-Dikay (IRE) (Anita's Prince) 4868$^{13}$ **>12f<**
**Nanton Point (USA) 4** b g Darshaan-Migiyas (Kings Lake (USA)) *1194$^{6}$* ***>88f<***
**Nant Y Gamer (FR) 2** b c Warning-Norfolk Lily (Blakeney) 2211$^{5}$ *2633$^{8}$ (3237)* 3577$^{2}$ 3846$^{3}$ 4298$^{10}$ **>41a 72f<**
**Napier Star 3** b f Inca Chief (USA)-America Star (Norwick (USA)) **1995:** *4408$^{5}$ 4535$^{7}$* **1996:** *49$^{11}$ 158$^{4}$ 258$^{5}$ 405$^{14}$ 524$^{8}$ (779) 897$^{5}$ 1455$^{3}$ 1716$^{6}$ 2084$^{9}$ (2555) 2748$^{5}$ 3061$^{2}$ 3416$^{2}$ 3602$^{4}$ 4081$^{2}$ 4333$^{8}$ 4577$^{4}$ 4776$^{4}$ 4996$^{3}$* **>61a 24f<**
**Napoleon's Return 3** gr g Daring March-Miss Colenca (Petong) 586$^{18}$ 769$^{13}$ 1087$^{11}$ 1312$^{3}$ 1527$^{18}$ 2023$^{10}$ (2123) 2241$^{2}$ 2417$^{2}$ 2914$^{9}$ 2983$^{8}$ *3602$^{9}$ 4860$^{19}$* ***>54a 56df<***
**Napoleon Star (IRE) 5** ch g Mulhollande (USA)-Lady Portobello (Porto Bello) *461$^{7}$ 654$^{8}$ 1010$^{7}$* 1302$^{17}$ 1533$^{8}$ 1856$^{10}$ **>51a 61f<**
**Narbonne 5** b m Rousillon (USA)-Historical Fact (Reform) 3800$^{11}$ 4186$^{20}$ **>64df<**
**Nariskin (IRE) 2** b c Danehill (USA)-Nurah (USA) (Riverman (USA)) 4670$^{3}$ 4807$^{3}$ 5034$^{4}$ **>83f<**
**Narita Brian (JPN) 5** h **1995:** 4471a$^{6}$ **>121f<**
**Narrabeth (IRE) 3** bl c Shaadi (USA)-Nocturna (IRE) (Diu Star) 3913a$^{2}$ 4542a$^{4}$ **>108f<**
**Naseem Alsahar 3** ch f Nashwan (USA)-El Fabulous (FR) (Fabulous Dancer (USA)) 845$^{7}$ 1123$^{3}$ 2208$^{5}$ 2955$^{2}$ 3356$^{3}$ 3845$^{11}$ 4387$^{7}$ **>74f<**
**Naseer (USA) 7** b g Hero's Honor (USA)-Sweet Delilah (USA) (Super Concorde (USA)) 1454$^{W}$ 2056$^{18}$ 2556$^{6}$ 2978$^{3}$ **>42f<**
**Nashaat (USA) 8** b g El Gran Senor (USA)-Absentia (USA) (Raise A Cup (USA)) **1995:** *(4427) 4476$^{6}$* **1996:** *48$^{8}$ 88$^{7}$ 211$^{4}$ 255$^{3}$ (331) 371$^{7}$ 480$^{6}$* 718$^{3}$ 935$^{7}$ 1069$^{6}$ 1638$^{8}$ 1789$^{2}$ 2047$^{2}$ (2209) (2962) (3172) 3445$^{13}$ 3702$^{2}$ **>77a 83f<**
**Nashcash (IRE) 3** ch c Nashamaa-Six Penny Express (Bay Express) 1253a$^{4}$ 1566a$^{3}$ 2143$^{6}$ **>103f<**
**Nash House (IRE) 3** b c Nashwan (USA)-River Dancer (Irish River (FR)) (730) 1114$^{4}$ 3431$^{7}$ **>114f<**
**Nash Point 2** b c Robellino (USA)-Embroideress (Stanford) 5033$^{5}$ **>77f<**
**Naskramar 3** f 794a$^{12}$ **>82f<**
**Nasrudin (USA) 3** b c Nureyev (USA)-Sunshine O'My Life (USA) (Graustark) (2079) 2621$^{20}$ 3072$^{9}$ 3430$^{4}$ 4583$^{12}$ **>82f<**
**Nasscina 2** b f Weldnaas (USA)-Runcina (Runnett) 1346$^{W}$
**Natalia Bay (IRE) 2** b f Dancing Dissident (USA)-Bayazida (Bustino) (1103) 1352$^{2}$ 2338$^{4}$ **>80f<**
**Nataliana 3** ch f Surumu (GER)-Nathia (GER) (Athenagoras (GER)) 2478a$^{3}$ **>104f<**
**Natal Ridge 3** b g Indian Ridge-Song Grove (Song) 648$^{7}$ 840$^{8}$ 2347$^{7}$ 2528$^{15}$ **>57f<**
**Natatarl (IRE) 3** ch f Roi Danzig (USA)-Little Me (Connaught) *859$^{8}$ 1100$^{19}$* 1891$^{6}$ 2180$^{14}$ 2373$^{11}$ **>19a 41f<**
**National Treasure 3** b f Shirley Heights-Brocade (Habitat) *2601$^{8}$* 3441$^{5}$ 3942$^{4}$ **>69f<**
**Native Chieftan 7** b g Trojan Fen-Habituee (Habitat) **1995:** *4489$^{10}$* **>19a f<**
**Native Lass (IRE) 7** ch m Be My Native (USA)-Fun Frolic (Sexton Blake) 4337$^{15}$
**Native Princess (IRE) 2** ch f Shalford (IRE)-Jealous One (USA) (Raise A Native) 4061$^{6}$ 4225$^{5}$ 4748$^{8}$ **>64f<**
**Native Rhythm (IRE) 2** ch f Lycius (USA)-Perfect Time (IRE) (Dance of Life (USA)) 1664$^{2}$ **>63f<**
**Native Song 3** b f Hatim (USA)-Ivors Melody (Music Maestro) **1995:** *4538$^{6}$* **1996:** *188$^{6}$ 364$^{8}$ 471$^{12}$* 1174$^{12}$ 1651$^{8}$ 1999$^{6}$ 2297$^{3}$ 2599$^{8}$ 4509$^{13}$ **>42a 50f<**
**Nattie 2** b c Almoojid-Defy Me (Bustino) *446$^{7}$* 590$^{4}$ 1032$^{5}$ 1463$^{3}$ **>49f<**
**Nattier 3** b f Prince Sabo-Naturally Fresh (Thatching) 1033$^{6}$ 1429$^{7}$ 1608$^{5}$ 1888$^{2}$ 2236$^{2}$ 2982$^{4}$ *3602$^{13}$ 3867$^{7}$* ***>23a 61f<***
**Natural Eight (IRE) 2** b c In The Wings-Fenny Rough (Home Guard (USA)) 4720$^{3}$ **>78f<**
**Natural Key 3** ch f Safawan-No Sharps Or Flats (USA) (Sharpen Up) 617$^{17}$ 749$^{19}$ 931$^{20}$ 1163$^{3}$ 1865$^{10}$ (2680) (3240) 3342$^{4}$ 3489$^{3}$ (3959) 4246$^{5}$ 4316$^{8}$ (4473) **>74f<**
**Natural Path 5** b m Governor General-Cuba Libre (Rum (USA)) *255$^{9}$ 4436$^{27}$* ***>4f<***
**Naughty Pistol (USA) 4** ch f Big Pistol (USA)-Naughty Nile (USA) (Upper Nile (USA)) 1087$^{10}$ 1417$^{5}$ 1684$^{6}$ 2240$^{6}$ *2748$^{4}$ 2940$^{8}$ 3453$^{5}$* 4045$^{16}$ (4341) 4430$^{10}$ 4768$^{4}$ *(4987)* **>62a 59f<**
**Nautical Jewel 4** b g Handsome Sailor-Kopjes (Bay Express) **1995:** *4370$^{8}$* **1996:** *239$^{2}$ 346$^{6}$ 510$^{4}$ 604$^{5}$ 4236$^{12}$* 5053$^{5}$ **>59a 48f<**
**Nautical Pet (IRE) 4** b c Petorius-Sea Mistress (Habitat) *1235a$^{8}$* ***>111f<*** **(DEAD)**
**Nautiker (GER) 5** h (4540a) **>105f<**
**Naval Dispatch 2** b f Slip Anchor-Speed Writing (USA) (Secretariat (USA)) 4897$^{8}$ **>60f<**
**Naval Gazer (IRE) 3** b f Sadler's Wells (USA)-Naval Light (USA) (Majestic Light (USA)) 766$^{4}$ 2430$^{3}$ 2924$^{7}$ 3522$^{5}$ (3979) 4580$^{10}$ **>81f<**

**Naval Hunter (USA) 3** ch c Jade Hunter (USA)-Navy Light (USA) (Polish Navy (USA)) *(428) 575$^{15}$* 1872$^{11}$ **>73a 48f<**

**Navigate (USA) 3** ch c Diesis-Libras Shiningstar (USA) (Gleaming (USA)) 593$^{7}$ 1615$^{4}$ 1983$^{2}$ 2501$^{9}$ (2861) 4044$^{7}$ **>87f<**

**Nawaji (USA) 3** b f Trempolino (USA)-Nobile Decretum (USA) (Noble Decree (USA)) 813$^{13}$ 1326$^{9}$ 3472$^{12}$ 3845$^{13}$ 4785$^{4}$ *4986$^{10}$* **>13a 54f<**

**Nawal (FR) 2** b f Homme de Loi (IRE)-Lute String (FR) (No Lute (FR)) 4291a$^{3}$ 4661a$^{9}$ **>99f<**

**Nawar (FR) 6** b g Kahyasi-Nabita (FR) (Akarad (FR)) 1005$^{15}$ **>78f<**

**Nawasib (IRE) 2** b f Warning-Tanouma (USA) (Miswaki (USA)) 3129$^{5}$ 3787$^{6}$ 4725$^{2}$ **>77f<**

**Nayib 3** b c Bustino-Nicholas Grey (Track Spare) 717$^{2}$ 1359$^{8}$ 1782$^{8}$ **>67f<**

**Nayil 4** b c Unfuwain (USA)-Rose Cordial (USA) (Blushing Groom (FR)) 2459a$^{5}$ 4026a$^{10}$ 4643a$^{6}$ **>89f<**

**Nazmi (IRE) 4** b g Doyoun-Nawazish (Run The Gantlet (USA)) *4537b$^{3}$* ***>64f<***

**Ndaba 5** b g Mtoto-Lightning Legacy (USA) (Super Concorde (USA)) **1995:** *4445$^{8}$* **>26a f<**

**Nebrangus (IRE) 4** ch g Nashamaa-Choral Park (Music Boy) *33$^{15}$ 85$^{12}$ 152$^{9}$* **>24f<**

**Nec Plus Ultra (FR) 5** b h Kendor (FR)-Quintefolle (FR) (Luthier) **1995:** *(4405a)* **1996:** 1052a$^{2}$ (1950a) 2271a$^{4}$ 3033a$^{2}$ **>124f<**

**Ned's Bonanza 7** b g Green Ruby (USA)-Miss Display (Touch Paper) *931$^{12}$* 1157$^{15}$ 1364$^{12}$ 1646$^{6}$ 2005$^{17}$ 2029$^{8}$ 2154$^{4}$ 2523$^{3}$ (2757) 2787$^{7}$ 3055$^{8}$ 3352$^{2}$ 3482$^{6}$ 3643$^{3}$ 3868$^{5}$ 3993$^{3}$ 4088$^{2}$ 4382$^{3}$ 4505$^{5}$ 4791$^{15}$ **>64f<**

**Ned's Contessa (IRE) 3** ch f Persian Heights-Beechwood (USA) (Blushing Groom (FR)) 775$^{10}$ 1312$^{7}$ 1416$^{13}$ (2179) 2425$^{7}$ 2914$^{4}$ 2983$^{4}$ 3427$^{9}$ **>6a 52f<**

**Needle Gun (IRE) 6** b or br h Sure Blade (USA)-Lucayan Princess (High Line) **1995:** *4522a$^{2}$* **1996:** *536a$^{7}$ 1135a$^{2}$* (1938a) 2038$^{12}$ 3395a$^{7}$ 3912a$^{7}$ 4650a$^{7}$ 5073a$^{3}$ **>106a 122f<**

**Needle Match 3** ch c Royal Academy (USA)-Miss Tatting (USA) (Miswaki (USA)) *528$^{5}$* 687$^{8}$ 1119$^{8}$ 2235$^{5}$ 3052$^{10}$ 3698$^{7}$ 4045$^{12}$ **>58f<**

**Needwood Epic 3** b f Midyan (USA)-Epure (Bellypha) 1641$^{18}$ 2506$^{10}$ *4574$^{7}$ 4726$^{7}$* 4967$^{15}$ **>55a 56f<**

**Needwood Fantasy 3** b f Rolfe (USA)-Needwood Nymph (Bold Owl) *1602$^{9}$ 2180$^{11}$* 2362$^{5}$ 3619$^{10}$ 4340$^{7}$ **>29f<**

**Needwood Legend 3** b br c Rolfe (USA)-Enchanting Kate (Enchantment) 4611$^{7}$ **>58f<**

**Needwood Limelight 3** b c Rolfe (USA)-Lime Brook (Rapid River) 4341$^{5}$ **>43f< (DEAD)**

**Needwood Muppet 9** b g Rolfe (USA)-Sea Dart (Air Trooper) 4365$^{8}$ 4612$^{12}$ **>45f<**

**Needwood Native 8** b g Rolfe (USA)-The Doe (Alcide) *4515$^{13}$*

***Needwood Nutkin 3*** b f Rolfe (USA)-Needwood Nut (Royben) 4613$^{8}$ **>50f<**

**Need You Badly 3** b f Robellino (USA)-Persian Tapestry (Tap On Wood) 1532$^{9}$ 2176$^{3}$ 2500$^{5}$ 2598$^{6}$ *(2748) 3091$^{2}$ 3416$^{3}$ 3602$^{10}$ 3937$^{12}$ 4776$^{9}$* **>61a 56f<**

**Nefertiti 2** b f Superpower-Vico Equense (Absalom) *858$^{6}$ 1968$^{9}$ 2207$^{4}$*

***Negra (FR) 3*** b f Tropular-Chesnebop (FR) (R B Chesne) 5020a$^{2}$ **>59f<**

**Nellie North 3** b f Northern State (USA)-Kimble Princess (Kala Shikari) 1101$^{3}$ 1304$^{4}$ 1715$^{8}$ 2186$^{5}$ 2743$^{14}$ 3112$^{3}$ 3810$^{5}$ 3993$^{12}$ 4356$^{18}$ **>62f<**

**Nelly's Cousin 3** b f Distant Relative-Glint of Victory (Glint of Gold) *419$^{4}$ 502$^{5}$ 1614$^{13}$* 1903$^{2}$ 2033$^{5}$ 2506$^{15}$ (2737) 3043$^{4}$ (3284) 3357$^{3}$ 3657$^{4}$ 3831$^{2}$ **>55a 69f<**

**Nemisto 2** b c Mystiko (USA)-Nemesia (Mill Reef (USA)) 4127$^{8}$ 4863$^{6}$ **>55f<**

**Nenna (IRE) 4** 4541a$^{6}$ **>95f<**

**Neon Deion (IRE) 2** b c Alzao (USA)-Sharnazad (IRE) (Track Barron (USA)) 657$^{4}$ 916$^{12}$ *2633$^{10}$ 3762$^{7}$* 3976$^{6}$ *4980$^{13}$* **>32a 48f<**

**Nereus 3** b c Shareef Dancer (USA)-Lady of the Sea (Mill Reef (USA)) 576$^{11}$ 2557$^{6}$ (2876) 3155$^{10}$ 4067$^{8}$ 4320$^{5}$ **>87f<**

**Nero Zilzal (USA) 3** b c Zilzal (USA)-Golden Bowl (USA) (Vaguely Noble) 4162a$^{2}$ **>111f<**

**Nervous Rex 2** b c Reprimand-Spinner (Blue Cashmere) 452$^{6}$ 523$^{2}$ 685$^{4}$ 2595$^{4}$ 2879$^{W}$ 3590$^{8}$ 3823$^{6}$ 4103$^{4}$ **>65f<**

**Nesbet 2** b c Nicholas (USA)-Brera (IRE) (Tate Gallery (USA)) 3919$^{6}$ *4079$^{12}$* **>21a f<**

**Nessun Doro 4** b g Hallgate-Bamdoro (Cavo Doro) **1995:** *4372$^{5}$* **>65a 71f<**

**Neuwest (USA) 4** b c Gone West (USA)-White Mischief (Dance In Time (CAN)) **1995:** *4435$^{2}$* **1996:** *20$^{6}$ 379$^{4}$ 450$^{18}$* 633$^{4}$ 879$^{17}$ (1078) 1680$^{3}$ 1962$^{2}$ (2283) 2623$^{8}$ 3271$^{2}$ (3440) 3612$^{9}$ **>84a 91f<**

**Nevada (IRE) 2** gr c Marju (IRE)-Silver Singing (USA) (Topsider (USA)) 2834a$^{2}$ 3018a$^{3}$ 4191$^{6}$ **>93f<**

**Never Come Back (GER) 3** 4033a$^{8}$ **>88f<**

**Neverneyev (USA) 6** b h Nureyev (USA)-River Rose (FR) (Riverman (USA)) **1995:** 4405a$^{2}$ **>121f<**

**Never Say so 4** ch f Prince Sabo-So Rewarding (Never so Bold) *2937$^{15}$ 3310$^{8}$* 4473$^{13}$ **>37?a 14f<**

**Never so Brave 6** ch g Never so Bold-Another Move (Farm Walk) 2066$^{15}$ 2587$^{3}$ **>37f<**

**Never So Rite (IRE) 4** b f Nordico (USA)-Nephrite (Godswalk (USA)) **1995:** *4385$^{3}$ 4420$^{9}$ 4537$^{5}$* **1996:** *23$^{2}$ 80$^{5}$ 165$^{2}$ 214$^{2}$* **>56a 66f<**

**Never so True 5** b m Never so Bold-Cottage Pie (Kalamoun) 2394$^{9}$ 2522$^{4}$ 2776$^{9}$ 3287$^{5}$ 3645$^{2}$ 3866$^{11}$ **>37da 43f<**

**Never Such Bliss 4** b f Shavian-Donna Bold (Never so Bold) **1995:** *4413$^{6}$ 4479$^{11}$* **>35a 54f<**

**Never Think Twice 3** b g Never so Bold-Hope and Glory (USA) (Well Decorated (USA)) 644$^{14}$ 758$^{6}$ 1594$^{13}$ 2034$^{10}$ 2411$^{3}$ 2604$^{4}$ (2946) 3168$^{3}$ 3270$^{5}$ (3583) 3844$^{2}$ 4058$^{17}$ 4376$^{7}$ 4888$^{7}$ *4987$^{9}$* **>56a 73f<**

**Never Time (IRE) 4** b g Simply Great (FR)-Islet Time (Burslem) **1995:** *4391$^{7}$* **1996:** *47$^{9}$ 208$^{6}$ 504$^{2}$* 1034$^{7}$ 1600$^{7}$ 1676$^{14}$ *1967$^{7}$ 2423$^{8}$* 2683$^{4}$ 3348$^{5}$ 3575$^{3}$ 4355$^{11}$ 4587$^{10}$ **>28a 41f<**

**New Albion (USA) 5** b or br g Pleasant Colony (USA)-Grand Bonheur (USA) (Blushing Groom (FR)) *308$^{2}$ 1486$^{12}$* 2214$^{8}$ 2678$^{2}$ 2851$^{6}$ 3081$^{3}$ 3280$^{3}$ 3677$^{8}$ **>73a 65f<**

**Newbridge Boy 3** b g Bustino-Martyrdom (USA) (Exceller (USA)) 994$^{11}$ 1434$^{8}$ *1969$^{2}$ 2683$^{2}$ (2751) 3422$^{4}$ 4334$^{11}$ 4559$^{5}$* 4810$^{4}$ 4866$^{5}$ **>63a 59f<**

**Newbury Coat 6** b g Chilibang-Deanta in Eirinn (Red Sunset) **1995:** *4358$^{10}$ 4484$^{13}$* **1996:** *3384a$^{2}$* ***>51a 60f<***

**New Century (USA) 4** gr g Manila (USA)-Casessa (USA) (Caro) 450$^{6}$ 765$^{7}$ (933) 1703$^{2}$ 2053$^{16}$ (2351) 3158$^{18}$ 3709$^{17}$ **>100df<**

**New Frontier (IRE) 2** b c Sadler's Wells (USA)-Diamond Field (USA) (Mr Prospector (USA)) (4653a) 5024a$^{4}$ **>97f<**

**Newgate Hush 4** ch f Kind of Hush-Mummys Colleen (Mummy's Pet) **1995:** *4412$^{8}$ 4474$^{6}$* **1996:** *299$^{8}$ 1037$^{16}$* 2587$^{15}$ 2801$^{17}$ **>18f<**

**New Herald (IRE) 7** b h Heraldiste (USA)-New Mary (New Model (FR)) 623a$^{3}$ 909a$^{3}$ **>108f<**

**Newington Butts (IRE) 6** br m Dowsing (USA)-Cloud Nine (Skymaster) **1995:** *4377$^{8}$ 4413$^{3}$ 4460$^{3}$ 4487$^{8}$* **1996:** *16$^{4}$ 107$^{3}$ 178$^{5}$ (278) 388$^{6}$ 461$^{8}$ 601$^{18}$ (1606) 1812$^{9}$* **>53a 41f<**

**New Inn 5** b g Petoski-Pitroyal (Pitskelly) *196$^{8}$ 254$^{4}$* **>63da 57f<**

**Newlands Corner 3** b f Forzando-Nice Lady (Connaught) 747$^{9}$ 893$^{8}$ 1314$^{18}$ 1642$^{13}$ 2286$^{8}$ 2902$^{2}$ 3256$^{2}$ (3292) (3698) (3863) **>60f<**

**Newport Knight 5** ch g Bairn (USA)-Clara Barton (Youth (USA)) 1486$^{10}$ 1965$^{12}$ (2377) (3113) 3479$^{2}$ 4669$^{10}$ **>78f<**

**New Regime (IRE) 3** b f Glenstal (USA)-Gay Refrain (Furry Glen) 1323$^{9}$ 1526$^{15}$ 4910$^{11}$ **>11f<**

**New Spain (USA) 4** br c Seeking the Gold (USA)-Trunk (USA) (Danzig (USA)) 2346$^{3}$ **>58f< (DEAD)**

**New Technique (FR) 3** br f Formidable (USA)-Dolly Bea Sweet (USA) (Super Concorde (USA)) *1969$^{6}$ 2325$^{12}$ 2632$^{8}$ 4094$^{10}$ 4690$^{9}$* 4868$^{18}$ **>29a 42f<**

**New York (GER) 2** ch f Greinton-Noble House (GER) (Siberian Express (USA)) 3396a$^{2}$ **>82f<**

**New York New York (FR) 3** c 1057a$^{6}$ **>95f<**

**Nexsis Star 3** ch g Absalom-The High Dancer (High Line) 1435$^{12}$ 1670$^{10}$ 3642$^{5}$ 4070$^{16}$ 4227$^{10}$ 4752$^{10}$ 4921$^{12}$ **>36f<**

**Nezool Almatar (IRE) 3** b f Last Tycoon-Rowa (Great Nephew) 2579$^{8}$ *3418$^{6}$* **>31a 60f<**

**Nice Nature (JPN) 8** b h Nice Dancer (CAN)-Urakawa Miyuki (JPN) (Habitony) **1995:** 4471a$^{13}$ **>114f<**

**Nichol Fifty 2** b g Old Vic-Jawaher (IRE) (Dancing Brave (USA)) 4782$^{8}$ **>55f<**

**Nick of Time 2** b f Mtoto-Nikitina (Nijinsky (CAN)) 4305$^{9}$ 4797$^{9}$ **>62f<**

**Nick the Biscuit 5** b g Nicholas Bill-Maryland Cookie (USA) (Bold Hour) *47$^{3}$ 221$^{4}$ 656$^{6}$* **>59a 69f<**

**Nicola's Princess 3** b f Handsome Sailor-Barachois Princess (USA) (Barachois (CAN)) 524$^{5}$ 768$^{6}$ 1007$^{11}$ 1689$^{8}$ *2308$^{10}$ 2636$^{5}$ 3062$^{2}$ 3421$^{6}$ (4076) 4692$^{15}$ 4989$^{12}$* **>60a 52f<**

**Nifty Norman 2** b g Rock City-Nifty Fifty (IRE) (Runnett) 1086$^{8}$ 1827$^{2}$ 2118$^{2}$ 2625$^{7}$ 3853$^{3}$ **>62f<**

**Nigels Choice 4** gr g Teenoso (USA)-Warm Winter (Kalaglow) 745$^{3}$ **>64f<**

**Nigel's Lad (IRE) 4** b g Dominion Royale-Back To Earth (FR) (Vayrann) *61$^{9}$ 132$^{10}$ 455$^{18}$* 628$^{5}$ 913$^{6}$ 1322$^{6}$ 2164$^{9}$ 2331$^{3}$ 3939$^{2}$ 4073$^{15}$ 4193$^{16}$ 4568$^{17}$ *4779$^{7}$* **>59a 82f<**

**Nightbird (IRE) 2** b f Night Shift (USA)-Pippas Song (Reference Point) (977) 1143$^{4}$ (4113) (4490) (4685) **>95f<**

**Night Chorus 2** b c Most Welcome-Choral Sundown (Night Shift (USA)) 3994$^{16}$ 4228$^{10}$ 4796$^{2}$ *4988$^{7}$* **>13a 75f<**

**Night City 5** b g Kris-Night Secret (Nijinsky (CAN)) (1193) 1520$^{7}$ 2248$^{4}$ 4325$^{7}$ 4800$^{4}$ **>109f<**

**Night Dance 4** ch c Weldnaas (USA)-Shift Over (USA) (Night Shift (USA)) **1995:** *4482$^{11}$* **1996:** *455$^{11}$* 728$^{7}$ 967$^{13}$ 1330$^{10}$ 4682$^{22}$ **>59a 88f<**

**Night Edition 6** b g Night Shift (USA)-New Chant (CAN) (New Providence) **1995:** *4452$^{9}$* **1996:** *12$^{8}$* **>44a 54f<**

**Night Excellence 4** b g Night Shift (USA)-Briar Creek (Busted) **1995:** *4357$^{15}$* **>29a 33f<**

**Night Flight 2** gr c Night Shift (USA)-Ancestry (Persepolis (FR)) 1344$^{2}$ 2897$^{3}$ 3277$^{5}$ 3956$^{2}$ 4311$^{7}$ **>72f<**

**Night Harmony (IRE) 3** ch c Digamist (USA)-Quaver (Song) 525$^{3}$ 4215$^{6}$ 4356$^{9}$ 4430$^{9}$ 4610$^{4}$ *4776$^{2}$* **>55a 66f<**

**Night in a Million 5** br g Night Shift (USA)-Ridalia (Ridan (USA)) *1337$^{11}$* ***>68a 31f<***

**Nightingale Song** 2 b f Tina's Pet-Songlines (Night Shift (USA)) 630[3] 715[5] 1404[9] 1982[2] 2309[4] 2795[4] (3110) 3659[3] 4244[3] **>65f<**

**Nightlark (IRE)** 2 b f Night Shift (USA)-Overcall (Bustino) 4359[2] **>71f<**

**Night Mirage (USA)** 2 b f Silver Hawk (USA)-Colony Club (USA) (Tom Rolfe) 4801[8] 5038[5] **>67f<**

**Night of Glass** 3 b g Mazilier (USA)-Donna Elvira (Chief Singer) 873[13] 1119[16] 1995[5] *2158[10] 2966[2]* 4053[3] (4263) 4692[12] 4968[7] **>21a 64f<**

**Night Parade (USA)** 3 b c Rory's Jester (AUS)-Nocturnal Song (USA) (Northern Dancer) 692[7] 989[2] **>88f<**

**Night Petticoat (GER)** 3 b f Petoski-Nightrockette (GER) (Rocket) (1750a) 2478a[6] 3203a[6] 4164a[3] 4542a[2] **>109f<**

**Night Sceptre (IRE)** 2 b f Night Shift (USA)-Spire (Shirley Heights) 4969[10] **>69f<**

**Night Spell (IRE)** 3 b f Fairy King (USA)-Moonsilk (Solinus) 3530a[9] **>80f<**

**Nightswimming (IRE)** 3 b g Mac's Imp (USA)-Kilnahard (Steel Heart) 1171[15] 1681[7] 2281[7] **>26f<**

**Night Time** 4 b g Night Shift (USA)-Gathering Place (USA) (Hawaii) *99[4] 198[3] 251[6] 373[5] 688[8] 836[8] 1031[9]* **>62a 66f<**

**Night Watch (USA)** 3 b c Night Shift (USA)-Christchurch (FR) (So Blessed) 2844a[5] 3746a[6] **>111f<**

**Night Wink (USA)** 4 ch g Rahy (USA)-Lady in White (Shareef Dancer (USA)) 450[13] 589[5] 802[5] 1322[4] 1425[7] 2400[9] (2761) 3123[16] 3450[5] (3786) 4184[2] 4352[5] 4682[19] 4874[11] **>91f<**

**Nigrasine** 2 b c Mon Tresor-Early Gales (Precocious) (1849) (2364) 3690[5] 3971[2] 4189[4] 4723[2] **>98f<**

**Nijmegen** 8 b g Niniski (USA)-Petty Purse (Petingo) *75[4] 1194[14]* 1529[5] **>55a 67f<**

**Nijo** 5 b g Top Ville-Nibabu (FR) (Nishapour (FR)) **1995:** *4482[W]* **1996:** *810[10]* 4132[7] 4479[2] 4757[2] 4972[2] **>113f<**

**Nikita's Star (IRE)** 3 ch g Soviet Lad (USA)-Sally Chase (Sallust) **1995:** *4361[10]* **1996:** *(269) 313[2] (385) 471[11]* 1317[8] 1900[7] *(2368) (2738)* 2998[5] 3117[2] 3283[5] 4216[4] 4551[12] **>75a 73f<**

**Niknaks Nephew** 4 br g Tragic Role (USA)-Bubulina (Dunphy) (1145) **>82f<**

**Nile Valley (IRE)** 2 b f Royal Academy (USA)-Sphinx (GER) (Alpenkonig (GER)) 3820[2] 4449[4] 4605[8] **>74f<**

**Nilgiri Hills (IRE)** 3 ch c Indian Ridge-Our Resolution (Caerleon (USA)) 453[6] 646[5] 2431[2] 3446[2] 4312[23] 4592[3] 4802[8] **>84f<**

**Nimble (IRE)** 3 b f Danehill (USA)-Sierra Leone (ITY) (Weimar) 543a[2] (901a) 1144[4] **>94f<**

**Nineacres** 5 b g Sayf El Arab (USA)-Mayor (Laxton) 3851[7] 4130[16] 4356[6] 4606[13] 4865[2] 5039[3] **>62a 68f<**

**Ninety-Five** 4 ch f Superpower-Vanishing Trick (Silly Season) *1028[3] 1161[4]* (1547) 1844[7] (2395) 2771[6] 3122[2] (3883) **>60a 73f<**

**Ninia (USA)** 4 ch f Affirmed (USA)-Lajna (Be My Guest (USA)) 1313[7] (1528) 2134[12] 2351[4] 2581[10] 3158[11] 3450[6] (3623) (3947) (4120) 4193[12] 4300[4] 4445[11] 4680[6] 4964[6] **>52a 99f<**

**Niniska (GER)** 3 dk f Niniski (USA)-Nona (GER) (Cortez (GER)) 4858a[3]

**Ninotchka (USA)** 3 b f Nijinsky (CAN)-Puget Sound (High Top) 813[3] (1409) 2069[9] 2533[3] 3711[8] 4678[3] (5026a) **>108f<**

**Ninth Chord** 2 gr c Alzao (USA)-Jazz (Sharrood (USA)) 5033[2] **>89+f<**

**Ninth Symphony** 2 ch g Midyan (USA)-Good as Gold (IRE) (Glint of Gold) 1197[9] 1424[6] 1779[2] 2588[5] (3046) 3408[5] 3674[3] 3835[12] 4384[9] 4883[16] **>73f<**

**Nirvana Prince** 7 ch g Celestial Storm (USA)-Princess Sunshine (Busted) 3298[6] 3776[4] **>72a 64?f<**

**Nita's Choice** 6 b m Valiyar-What's the Matter (High Top) 3314[11] 3808[9] **>28f<**

**Niteowl Raider (IRE)** 3 ch g Standaan (FR)-Havana Moon (Ela-Mana-Mou) **1995:** *4480[7]* **1996:** *49[7] 342[3] (414) 478[7] (606) 835[12] 1030[10] 1642[10] 2084[11] 2185[13]* 3294[12] 3331[10] 3583[10] *4081[9] 4865[16]* ***>70da 27f<***

**Nitwitty** 2 b g Nomination-Dawn Ditty (Song) 4512[18] **>25f<**

**Nivasha** 4 b f Shavian-Rheinza (Rheingold) **1995:** *4363[12] 4450[4] 4515[13]* **1996:** *41[3] 107[9] 203[3] 278[5] 334[2] 406[11] 499[5] 1719[6] 2158[3] 2594[5] 3074[8]* **>42a 52f<**

**Nizaal (USA)** 5 ch h Diesis-Shicklah (USA) (The Minstrel (CAN)) 505[14] 610[20] 851[12] 884[9] 3344[13] 3677[6] 3958[11] 4503[4] **>40f<**

**Nkapen Rocks (SPA)** 3 b g Risk Me (FR)-Debutina Park (Averof) 562[3] 775[9] 1539[8] *1809[5] 2179[2]* 2931[2] 3102[8] 4054[13] 4432[17] **>49a 69f<**

**No-Aman** 3 b c Nashwan (USA)-Ghanimah (Caerleon (USA)) *703[7]* 894[7] 1326[2] 1773[2] 2036[4] **>87f<**

**No Animosity (IRE)** 3 ch c Ajraas (USA)-Arctic Ford (FR) (Arctic Tern (USA)) 1235a[6] 1247a[5] 4396a[7] **>96f<**

**Nobby Barnes** 7 b g Nordance (USA)-Loving Doll (Godswalk (USA)) *521[14] 827[2]* 883[2] 1024[6] 1341[8] 1633[7] *2369[9] 2521[4]* 3052[6] 3333[6] 3623[12] 3958[8] 3985[6] 4624[6] **>37a 51f<**

**Nobleata** 4 ch f Dunbeath (USA)-Lobela (Lorenzaccio) 820[16] **>14f<**

**Noble Canonire** 4 b f Gunner B-Lucky Candy (Lucky Wednesday) *196[5] (246) 303[2] 360[4] 508[4]* 612[7] *836[2] 1096[5] 1487[4]* **>61a 51f<**

**Noble Colours** 3 b g Distinctly North (USA)-Kentucky Tears (USA) (Cougar (CHI)) 3410[9] 4070[9] 4437[R] **>25a 36f<**

**Noble Dancer (IRE)** 2 b c Imperial Frontier (USA)-Que Sera (Music Boy) 1184[4] **>59f<**

**Noble Dane (IRE)** 2 b f Danehill (USA)-Noble Dust (USA) (Dust Commander (USA)) 4052[3] (4564) **>75f<**

**Noble Hero** 2 b c Houston (USA)-Noble Devorcee (USA) (Vaguely Noble) 2252[5] 2712[4] 4370[8] 4602[9] **>62f<**

**Noble Investment** 2 b c Shirley Heights-Noble Destiny (Dancing Brave (USA)) 3407[10] 3837[4] 4242[5] 4488[14] **>74f<**

**Noble Lord** 3 ch g Lord Bud-Chasers' Bar (Oats) 849[3] 1963[9] 2197[8] 3260[8] 3470[10] **>62f<**

**Noble Neptune** 4 b g Governor General-Calibina (Caliban) *132[12] 233[6] 713[13]* 1190[17] 1515[13] 2577[8] **>47a 64df<**

**Noble Note (FR)** 3 ch f Noblequest-Note Bleue (FR) (Posse (USA)) 4947a[2] **>65f<**

**Noble Society** 8 b g Law Society (USA)-Be Noble (Vaguely Noble) 1695[6] **>35a 41f<**

**Noble Sprinter (IRE)** 4 b c The Noble Player (USA)-Daybreaker (Thatching) 580[9] 766[2] 879[7] 1145[4] 1486[5] 2127[4] (2536) 3248[8] 3683[4] **>83f<**

**Noble Story** 2 br f Last Tycoon-Certain Story (Known Fact (USA)) 3660[4] 4570[W] **>66f<**

**No Class** 2 ch f Keen-Plie (Superlative) 1513[13] 2059[9] 3438[5] 3848[8] *4079[9]* **>26a 66f<**

**No Cliches** 3 ch c Risk Me (FR)-Always on a Sunday (Star Appeal) 593[9] 833[13] 1337[9] 2294[6] 4232[2] 4387[2] 4590[2] 4719[9] **>82f<**

**No Comment** 2 b c Puissance-Safidar (Roan Rocket) 1626[9] 3637[5] 3829[7] 4549[14] **>51+f<**

**No Dancer (GER)** 5 b h Shareef Dancer (USA)-Nice Gold (Pentathlon) 4290a[9] **>111f<**

**No Dunce (IRE)** 6 b m Nordance (USA)-Dundovail 4643a[18] **>69f<**

**Noeprob (USA)** 6 b m Majestic Shore (USA)-Heat Haze (USA) (Jungle Savage (USA)) 469[9] 549[2] 688[9] 1302[3] (1651) 1890[3] 2373[3] 2743[15] 2971[9] **>30a 66f<**

**No Extradition** 2 b g Midyan (USA)-Honey Pot (Hotfoot) 2327[4] 2897[6] 3250[5] 3590[9] 3969[13] **>56+f<**

**No Extras (IRE)** 6 b g Efisio-Parkland Rose (Sweet Candy (VEN)) *2880[16]* 3140[7] 3618[12] 3783[12] 4198[13] 4975[23] **>77f<**

**No Hiding Place** 3 ch c Nabeel Dancer (USA)-Blushing Pink (USA) (Blushing Groom (FR)) *779[6] 943[11]* 1470[3] 2049[17] 2528[12] **>7a 57f<**

**Noir Esprit** 3 br c Prince Daniel (USA)-Danse D'Esprit (Lidhame) *826[10]* 1325[8] 3878[12] 4227[9] 4752[5] *4986[16]* **>49f<**

**Noirie** 2 br c Warning-Callipoli (USA) (Green Dancer (USA)) 4451[6] 4684[4] 4991[W] **>64f<**

**Noisette** 2 ch f Nashwan (USA)-Nadma (USA) (Northern Dancer) 4449[7] **>55f<**

**Nomadic Dancer (IRE)** 4 b f Nabeel Dancer (USA)-Loveshine (USA) (Gallant Romeo (USA)) *388[5] 466[8] 534[7] 652[7] 1013[7]* 2376[9] **>46a 23f<**

**Nombre Premier** 2 gr c Kendor (FR)-Sabiola (FR) (The Wonder (FR)) 2269a[3] 2664a[2] 3201a[2] (4166a) 4742a[6] **>92f<**

**Nominator Lad** 2 b c Nomination-Ankara's Princess (USA) (Ankara (USA)) 2057[7] 3919[2] 4723[18] 4830[3] 4920[7] **>72f<**

**No Monkey Nuts** 3 ch g Clantime-Portvally (Import) 737[6] 992[3] 1087[3] 1707[6] *2084[10] 2427[2]* (2777) 3154[2] 3350[2] 3672[12] *3953[4] (4044)* 4255[7] *4577[8] 4895[4] 4979[3]* **>68a 87f<**

**No More Hassle (IRE)** 3 ch g Magical Wonder (USA)-Friendly Ann (Artaius (USA)) 2241[9] 2563[8] 3104[2] 3507[5] 3870[3] (5052) **>49f<**

**Nomore Mr Niceguy** 2 b c Rambo Dancer (CAN)-Lariston Gale (Pas de Seul) 1003[8] 1166[2] 2219[4] (2491) 2700[4] 3247[8] 3590[6] 4364[12] 5037[5] **>76f<**

**Nononito (FR)** 5 b h Nikos-Feuille D'Automne (FR) (Crystal Palace (FR)) *1397a[2]* 2071[3] 3751a[2] (4655a) 4959a[4] **>127f<**

**Non Vintage (IRE)** 5 ch g Shy Groom (USA)-Great Alexandra (Runnett) *196[7] 2319[8]* 3117[9] 3404[2] 3855[8] 3983[14] 4260[8] 4794[13] **>63a 58f<**

**Nopalea** 2 b f Warrshan (USA)-Nophe (USA) (Super Concorde (USA)) 2741[4] 3593[2] 4123[3] 4357[4] 4545[3] 4912[3] **>74f<**

**No Pattern** 4 ch c Rock City-Sunfleet (Red Sunset) *378[6] 411[7] 771[3]* 968[8] 4067[16] 4327[9] 4427[3] 4551[5] 4900[16] **>78a 68f<**

**Norbreck House** 2 b g Rambo Dancer (CAN)-Close the Deal (Nicholas Bill) 3057[4] 3291[4] 3576[2] 3769[5] 4594[18] 4796[10] **>62f<**

**Nordan Raider** 8 ch m Domynsky-Vikris (Viking (USA)) **1995:** *4368[9]* **1996:** *88[10] 282[4] 356[7] 511[3] 610[17]* ***>68a 64f<***

**Nordansk** 7 ch g Nordance (USA)-Free on Board (Free State) 968[2] 1640[4] (2226) 3801[8] 4048[4] **>61f<**

**Nordic Breeze (IRE)** 4 b or br g Nordico (USA)-Baby Clair (Gulf Pearl) 988[12] 1072[4] 1625[16] 1672[2] 1799[6] 3623[7] 3646[7] **>79f<**

**Nordic Colours (IRE)** 5 b m Nordico (USA)-Gorm (Majority Blue) *65[9]* **>16a f<**

**Nordic Crest (IRE)** 2 b c Danehill (USA)-Feather Glen (Glenstal (USA)) 4508[2] 4830[6] **>83f<**

**Nordic Doll (IRE)** 4 ch f Royal Academy (USA)-

**Maculatus (USA)** (Sharpen Up) **1995:** 4454$^{2}$ 4527$^{6}$ **>58a 77f<**

**Nordic Flash 9** b g Nordico (USA)-Rosemore (Ashmore (FR)) 1314$^{13}$ **>37f<**

**Nordic Gift (DEN) 3** ch g Bold Arrangement-Nordic Rose (DEN) (Drumhead) 703$^{14}$ 934$^{14}$ 2150$^{4}$ 2420$^{8}$ 2851$^{13}$ **>36f<**

**Nordic Hero (IRE) 3** b g Nordico (USA)-Postscript (Final Straw) 651$^{3}$ 804$^{6}$ 899$^{4}$ 3630$^{8}$ 4095$^{13}$ **>54a 8f<**

**Nordico Melody (IRE) 2** b g Nordico (USA)-Musical Essence (Song) 2044$^{11}$ **>20f<**

**Nordico Princess 5** b m Nordico (USA)-Try Vickers (USA) (Fuzzbuster (USA)) **1995:** 4460$^{4}$ 4487$^{6}$ **>74a 58f<**

**Nordic Spree (IRE) 4** b g Nordico (USA)-Moonsilk (Solinus) 4998$^{12}$

**Nordic Sun (IRE) 8** gr g Nordico (USA)-Cielsoleil (USA) (Conquistador Cielo (USA)) **1995:** 4506$^{6}$ **1996:** 169$^{13}$ 267$^{2}$ 767$^{11}$ **>69a 25f<**

**Nordinex (IRE) 4** b g Nordico (USA)-Debbie's Next (USA) (Arctic Tern (USA)) **1995:** 4476$^{14}$ 4539$^{14}$ **1996:** 132$^{11}$ (308) 379$^{8}$ 879$^{26}$ 2581$^{5}$ 2885$^{4}$ 3123$^{7}$ 3765$^{3}$ 4078$^{13}$ 4568$^{38}$ **>73da 83f<**

**Nordisk Legend 4** b g Colmore Row-Nordic Rose (DEN) (Drumhead) 613$^{15}$ 687$^{12}$ 1313$^{11}$ 1541$^{11}$ 2421$^{7}$ 2849$^{8}$ **>24f<**

**Nord Lys (IRE) 5** b g Nordico (USA)-Beach Light (Bustino) **1995:** 4448$^{9}$ **1996:** 57$^{13}$ 1778$^{6}$ 1979$^{8}$ 2513$^{8}$ 2801$^{8}$ 3306$^{15}$ **>25f<**

**Nor-Do-I 2** ch g Primo Dominie-True Nora (Ahonoora) 4756$^{20}$ 4913$^{W}$ 5034$^{2}$ **>87f<**

**Norling (IRE) 6** ch g Nashamaa-Now Then (Sandford Lad) 2713$^{9}$ 3339$^{8}$ 3583$^{6}$ 3698$^{17}$ **>36f<**

**Norman Conquest (USA) 2** ch c Miswaki (USA)-Grand Luxe (USA) (Sir Ivor) 3040$^{5}$ 3499$^{10}$ 4508$^{4}$ **>78f<**

**Normanton 2** gr c Petong-Mehtab (Touching Wood (USA)) 3293$^{10}$ **>20f<**

**Norsong 4** b g Northern State (USA)-Winsong Melody (Music Maestro) 1074$^{10}$ 1515$^{4}$ 1816$^{7}$ 2284$^{5}$ 2767$^{3}$ 3141$^{2}$ (3514) 3948$^{11}$ 4048$^{14}$ 4252$^{11}$ **>58f<**

**North Ardar 6** b g Ardar-Langwaite (Seaepic (USA)) (1596) (1828) (2136) (2568) 2731$^{2}$ (3239) 3480$^{3}$ 3981$^{6}$ (4089) 4296$^{4}$ 4484$^{4}$ 4781$^{13}$ 4900$^{17}$ 4982$^{6}$ **>63a 69f<**

**North Bear 4** b g North Briton-Sarah Bear (Mansingh (USA)) 2682$^{3}$ 2922$^{2}$ 3130$^{3}$ (3480) 4766$^{7}$ **>64f<**

**Northern Angel (IRE) 2** b c Waajib-Angel Divine (Ahonoora) 4913$^{16}$ **>50f<**

**Northern Ballet (IRE) 3** b f Sadler's Wells (USA)-Miranisa (Habitat) 860$^{10}$ 1326$^{7}$ **>60f<**

**Northern Celadon (IRE) 5** b h Classic Secret (USA)-Exemplary (Sovereign Lord) (645) 836$^{5}$ 1314$^{16}$ 1464$^{6}$ 2169$^{6}$ 2551$^{2}$ 3062$^{7}$ 3603$^{12}$ 4511$^{6}$ 4829$^{3}$ 5004$^{8}$ **>66a 63f<**

**Northern Chief 6** b g Chief Singer-Pacific Gull (USA) (Storm Bird (CAN)) 747$^{10}$ 836$^{10}$ 1454$^{8}$ **>37a 48f<**

**Northern Chief (FR) 5** gr h Law Society (USA)-Southern Maid (USA) (Northern Dancer) 1392a$^{2}$ **>103f<**

**Northern Clan 3** b g Clantime-Northern Line (Camden Town) 525$^{13}$ 784$^{5}$ 1034$^{6}$ 1363$^{10}$ 1500$^{4}$ 2989$^{15}$ 3422$^{9}$ 3657$^{10}$ 4693$^{9}$ 4888$^{18}$ 5056$^{13}$ **>34df<**

**Northern Falcon 3** gr f Polar Falcon (USA)-Bishah (USA) (Balzac (USA)) 782$^{12}$ 1089$^{12}$ 1850$^{5}$ 2397$^{4}$ 2780$^{7}$ **>7a 40f<**

**Northern Fan (IRE) 4** b g Lear Fan (USA)-Easy Romance (USA) (Northern Jove (CAN)) (1085) (1601) 4136$^{18}$ 4624$^{8}$ 5042$^{20}$ **>89a 43f<**

**Northern Fleet 3** b c Slip Anchor-Kamkova (USA) (Northern Dancer) 668$^{2}$ 948$^{3}$ 2576$^{4}$ (3776) 4447$^{2}$ 4673$^{5}$ **>92f<**

**Northern Girl (IRE) 2** b f Distinctly North (USA)-Auction Maid (IRE) (Auction Ring (USA)) 596$^{8}$ 3454$^{3}$ 3515$^{2}$ 3796$^{3}$ 4087$^{3}$ 4210$^{4}$ 4493$^{4}$ 4777$^{4}$ **>27a 70f<**

**Northern Grey 4** gr g Puissance-Sharp Anne (Belfort (FR)) **1995:** 4354$^{4}$ 4409$^{4}$ 4540$^{4}$ **1996:** 57$^{6}$ 110$^{8}$ 195$^{2}$ 250$^{7}$ 298$^{5}$ 1337$^{8}$ 1691$^{2}$ 1992$^{6}$ 2130$^{16}$ 4082$^{13}$ 4263$^{3}$ 4436$^{13}$ **>51a 52f<**

**Northern Judge 3** ch g Highest Honor (FR)-Nordica (Northfields (USA)) 962$^{7}$ 1668$^{8}$ 1836$^{2}$ 2283$^{8}$ 2573$^{11}$ 2975$^{6}$ 3442$^{2}$ 3628$^{6}$ (3789) 4571$^{16}$ 4829$^{15}$ 4882$^{19}$ **>34a 69f<**

**Northern Law 4** gr c Law Society (USA)-Pharland (FR) (Bellypha) 2862$^{12}$ 3043$^{6}$ 3404$^{6}$ **>59f<**

**Northern Miracle (IRE) 3** b f Distinctly North (USA)-Danny's Miracle (Superlative) 143$^{4}$ 215$^{6}$ **>34a f<**

**Northern Motto 3** b g Mtoto-Soulful (FR) (Zino) 444$^{8}$ 593$^{4}$ 752$^{9}$ 1309$^{10}$ 1669$^{7}$ 2056$^{4}$ 2418$^{2}$ 3242$^{8}$ 4506$^{9}$ (5008) **>60f<**

**Northern Pass (USA) 2** ch f Crowning (USA)-North To Pine Pass (USA) (Holy War (USA)) 3873$^{3}$ 4052$^{11}$ 4512$^{13}$ **>68f<**

**Northern Princess 2** b f Nomination-Glenstal Princess (Glenstal (USA)) 1499$^{5}$ 3099$^{6}$ 3433$^{4}$ **>42f<**

**Northern Saga (IRE) 3** b g Distinctly North (USA)-Saga's Humour (Bustino) 2373$^{10}$ 2716$^{13}$ 3473$^{3}$ 3681$^{7}$ 4480$^{9}$ 4703$^{16}$ **>36a 47f<**

**Northern Sal 2** ch f Aragon-Sister Sal (Baim (USA)) (538) 715$^{4}$ 3823$^{7}$ 4234$^{8}$ 4459$^{8}$ **>55f<**

**Northern Singer 6** ch g Norwick (USA)-Be Lyrical (Song) 82$^{11}$ **>10a f<**

**Northern Soul (USA) 3** b c Tasso (USA)-Wajibird (USA) (Storm Bird (CAN)) 2110a$^{3}$ **>86f<**

**Northern Spark 8** b g Trojan Fen-Heavenly Spark (Habitat) **1995:** 4447$^{4}$ 4514$^{2}$ **1996:** 480$^{8}$ 561$^{3}$ 661$^{8}$ 806$^{15}$ 1001$^{12}$ 1538$^{9}$ (1866) 2121$^{6}$ 2296$^{5}$ 2488$^{3}$ 2682$^{4}$ 5010$^{13}$ **>53a 57f<**

**Northern Spruce (IRE) 4** ch g Astronef-Perle's Fashion (Sallust) 649$^{7}$ 760$^{11}$ 1338$^{6}$ **>43f<**

**Northern Sun 2** b c Charmer-Princess Dancer (Alzao (USA)) (2977) 3400$^{5}$ (3632) 3826$^{3}$ 3936$^{6}$ 4375$^{3}$ 4625$^{8}$ 4760$^{16}$ **>80f<**

**Northern Touch 2** b f Warrshan (USA)-Shirley's Touch (Touching Wood (USA)) 4970$^{11}$ **>33f<**

**Northern Trial (USA) 8** b g Far North (CAN)-Make An Attempt (USA) (Nashua) 82$^{5}$ 128$^{2}$ 186$^{3}$ 240$^{6}$ 318$^{0}$ 373$^{2}$ 420$^{5}$ 499$^{2}$ 2321$^{3}$ 2394$^{5}$ **>59a 51f< (DEAD)**

**Northern Trove (USA) 4** b c Northern Jove (CAN)-Herbivorous (USA) (Northern Jove (CAN)) 24$^{10}$ **>64f<**

**Northern Union (CAN) 5** b h Alwasmi (USA)-Loving Cup (USA) (Big Spruce (USA)) (312) 392$^{2}$ **>96a 88f<**

**North Esk (USA) 7** ch g Apalachee (USA)-Six Dozen (USA) (What A Pleasure (USA)) **1995:** 4386$^{8}$ 4450$^{7}$ 4532$^{7}$ **1996:** 334$^{3}$ **>53a 63f<**

**Northgate Chief 4** ch g Indian Forest (USA)-Warthill Lady (Hittite Glory) 1435$^{8}$ 1598$^{13}$ 1789$^{11}$ 2481$^{14}$ **>46f<**

**North Reef (IRE) 5** b h Danehill (USA)-Loreef (Main Reef) 3272$^{2}$ 3401$^{3}$ 3856$^{11}$ 4354$^{5}$ 4606$^{6}$ 4793$^{3}$ 5054$^{16}$ **>79a 77f<**

**North Song 3** b c Anshan-Norfolk Serenade (Blakeney) 544$^{2}$ 1035$^{2}$ (1357) (2041) 2334$^{2}$ 2888$^{3}$ 3709$^{2}$ 4184$^{3}$ 4568$^{13}$ **>103f<**

**North to Glory 5** b m Northern State (USA)-Mummy's Glory (Mummy's Pet) 747$^{11}$ 1011$^{11}$ **>14a 3f<**

**Norton Sound (USA) 5** b h Bering-Shining Water (USA) (Riverman (USA)) 290a$^{3}$ **>106f<**

**No Rush 2** b g Puissance-Practical (Ballymore) 1320$^{5}$ 1543$^{2}$ 1720$^{4}$ 2237$^{3}$ 2389$^{4}$ **>14a 60f<**

**Norwegian Blue (IRE) 3** b c Mac's Imp (USA)-Opening Day (Day Is Done) 571$^{2}$ 832$^{4}$ 1493$^{6}$ 2007$^{9}$ 3232$^{28}$ 3693$^{8}$ 4581$^{10}$ 4802$^{20}$ **>82f<**

**Nose No Bounds (IRE) 3** b g Cyrano de Bergerac-Damezao (Alzao (USA)) **1995:** 4361$^{6}$ **1996:** 614$^{2}$ 702$^{6}$ 738$^{7}$ 1490$^{9}$ 1861$^{2}$ 2027$^{3}$ 2294$^{2}$ 2487$^{4}$ 2689$^{2}$ 2749$^{6}$ 3063$^{5}$ 3238$^{2}$ 3295$^{6}$ 3677$^{7}$ **>71a 82f< (DEAD)**

**Nosey Native 3** b g Cyrano de Bergerac-Native Flair (Be My Native (USA)) 731$^{5}$ 1175$^{7}$ 1669$^{5}$ 2033$^{7}$ 2189$^{6}$ 2394$^{3}$ 2711$^{12}$ 2989$^{6}$ 3149$^{6}$ 3428$^{2}$ 3520$^{4}$ 4307$^{F}$ (4559) 4702$^{8}$ 4831$^{5}$ **>77f<**

**No Slouch (IRE) 2** b c Royal Academy (USA)-Hastening (Shirley Heights) 5014a$^{4}$ **>83+f<**

**No Speeches (IRE) 5** b g Last Tycoon-Wood Violet (USA) (Riverman (USA)) **1995:** 4415$^{2}$ 4465$^{2}$ 4544$^{3}$ **1996:** 13$^{9}$ (80) 486$^{3}$ **>70a 63f<**

**No Spoken Word (IRE) 5** ch m Hawaiian Return (USA)-Lucky Fiver 4537b$^{9}$

**Nostalgic Air (USA) 2** gr f El Prado (IRE)-Jane Scott (USA) (Copelan (USA)) 585$^{7}$ 975$^{5}$ 1489$^{2}$ (2025) 2588$^{4}$ 3057$^{3}$ 3275$^{3}$ 3835$^{18}$ 3969$^{15}$ 4614$^{4}$ 4878$^{10}$ **>47a 68f<**

**No Submission (USA) 10** b h Melyno-Creeping Kate (USA) (Stop The Music (USA)) **1995:** 4388$^{4}$ 4472$^{8}$ **1996:** 31$^{3}$ 62$^{7}$ 111$^{2}$ (198) 249$^{5}$ 254$^{3}$ 333$^{8}$ 372$^{2}$ (393) 417$^{2}$ 477$^{8}$ 499$^{7}$ 561$^{6}$ 586$^{2}$ 776$^{6}$ 854$^{10}$ 1167$^{7}$ 1411$^{19}$ 1468$^{11}$ 2081$^{11}$ 3603$^{10}$ 4089$^{9}$ (4986) **>62a 36f<**

**No Sympathy 3** ch f Ron's Victory (USA)-Ackcontent (USA) (Key To Content (USA)) **1995:** 4437$^{6}$ 4545$^{4}$ **1996:** 131$^{7}$ 293$^{3}$ (1009) 1536$^{10}$ 1658$^{5}$ 2253$^{9}$ 3863$^{9}$ **>54a 47f<**

**Notaire (IRE) 3** b g Law Society (USA)-La Toulzanie (FR) (Sanctus II) 1963$^{7}$ 2314$^{4}$ 2601$^{12}$ 3785$^{18}$ **>66f< (DEAD)**

**Not A Lot 2** ch g Emarati (USA)-Spanish Chestnut (Philip of Spain) 1849$^{7}$ 2389$^{2}$ 2865$^{7}$ 3324$^{8}$ 3511$^{4}$ 3838$^{4}$ 4223$^{U}$ 4384$^{6}$ 4795$^{17}$ **>71f<**

**Notcomplainingbut (IRE) 5** b m Supreme Leader-Dorcetta (Condorcet (FR)) 4643a$^{2}$ **>79f<**

**Note of Caution (USA) 3** b f Diesis-Silver Dollar (Shirley Heights) **1995:** 4538$^{3}$ **1996:** 58$^{4}$ 188$^{7}$ 3979$^{13}$ 4785$^{14}$ 5060$^{12}$ **>60da 10f<**

**Nothing Doing (IRE) 7** b g Sarab-Spoons (Orchestra) 1874$^{16}$ 2372$^{6}$ 2941$^{2}$ 3113$^{3}$ 3649$^{5}$ (4509) 4789$^{14}$ 5053$^{2}$ **>29a 51f<**

**Not Out Lad 2** b c Governor General-Sorcha (IRE) (Shernazar) 1871$^{14}$

**Not Quite Grey 3** gr g Absalom-Strawberry Song (Final Straw) 754$^{9}$ 4427$^{8}$ 4752$^{15}$ **>52f<**

**Nottonitejosephine 3** ch f Be My Chief (USA)-Josephine Gibney (High Top) **1995:** 4360$^{9}$ **>31a 51?f<**

**Noufari (FR) 5** b g Kahyasi-Noufiyla (Top Ville) 563$^{3}$ 837$^{3}$ 1005$^{8}$ 1428$^{3}$ 2042$^{18}$ 2330$^{5}$ 2612$^{8}$ 3834$^{4}$ 4365$^{14}$ 5047$^{15}$ **>85a 83f<**

**Novize (GER) 5** dk b h Zampano (GER)-Nombreuse (Nebos (GER)) 497a$^{3}$ 4957a$^{3}$ **>105f<**

**Noyan 6** ch g Northern Baby (CAN)-Istiska (FR) (Irish River (FR)) 19$^{4}$ 449$^{2}$ 767$^{5}$ 852$^{10}$ **>50a 64f<**

**Nubile 2** b f Pursuit of Love-Trojan Lady (USA) (Irish River (FR)) 4969$^{11}$ **>69f<**

**Nukud (USA) 4** b g Topsider (USA)-Summer Silence (USA) (Stop The Music (USA)) 479$^{8}$ 2898$^{6}$ 3306$^{9}$ 3970$^{14}$ **>44df<**

**Nullahs Pet 4** b br f Tina's Pet-Nullah (Riverman (USA)) 1452$^{10}$ 1667$^{14}$ **>24f<**

**Nunsharpa 3** b f Sharpo-Missed Blessing (So Blessed) 678$^{5}$ 1617$^{4}$ 2229$^{5}$ 2974$^{2}$ 3167$^{3}$ 3518$^{10}$

4109[5] (4453) 4688[13] **>87f<**
**Nushka Babushka 4** b f Nishapour (FR)-Jessamine (Jalmood (USA)) *2322[10]* **>39f<**
**Nutcracker 3** b f Rambo Dancer (CAN)-Fair Madame (Monseigneur (USA)) **1995:** *4393[11]* **>29a 58f<**
**Nutcracker Suite (IRE) 4** b f Dancing Dissident (USA)-Carlyle Suite (USA) (Icecapade (USA)) 1500[17] 1764[4] 2236[5] 2902[8] 3256[12] 4348[8] **>36f<**
**Nuthatch (IRE) 4** b f Thatching-New Edition (Great Nephew) *133[3] 201[5] 334[7]* **>37a 37f<**
**Nuzu (IRE) 3** b c Belmez (USA)-Nutria (GER) (Tratteggio) 684[16] 847[5] 1957[2] (2140) 2612[10] 3617[3] 3983[12] (4476) **>93f<**
**Nwaamis (USA) 4** b c Dayjur (USA)-Lady Cutlass (USA) (Cutlass (USA)) 442[3] 810[4] 1177[6] **>118f<**
**O**
**Oakbrook Rose 2** b f Forzando-Oakbrook Tern (USA) (Arctic Tern (USA)) 3105[4] 3685[13] 4783[9] **>62f<**
**Oakbury (IRE) 4** ch g Common Grounds-Doon Belle (Ardoon) *439[14]* 612[8] 690[18] 872[17] 995[18] 2573[12] 2731[9] 3402[6] 3808[2] 4703[7] 4812[9] **>37a 48f<**
**Oaken Wood (IRE) 2** ch c Lycius (USA)-Little Red Rose (Precocious) 4233[15] 4720[13] **>44f<**
**Oakley Folly 3** b f Puissance-Brown's Cay (Formidable (USA)) *134[10] 258[7]*
**Oare Budgie 3** ch f Midyan (USA)-Portvasco (Sharpo) 1539[9] 1850[17] *2368[6] 2902[10]* 3256[13] 3458[10] **>30f<**
**Oatey 3** ch f Master Willie-Oatfield (Great Nephew) *531[5] 769[7]* 2592[12] (3135) 3292[3] 3465[3] 3643[2] (3774) 4180[7] 4312[21] **>38a 67f<**
**Obelos (USA) 5** ch g Diesis-Fair Sousanne (Busted) 641[3] 871[4] 4193[7] 4450[2] 4617[2] **>79f<**
**Oberons Boy (IRE) 3** b g Fairy King (USA)-Bold Starlet (Precocious) 2041[27] 2544[12] 2753[4] 2975[3] 3320[4] 3657[6] *3955[10]* **>39a 78df<**
**Oberon's Dart (IRE) 3** b g Fairy King (USA)-Key Maneuver (USA) (Key To Content (USA)) **1995:** *4408[4]* **1996:** *962[6] (1809) 2306[2] 3168[5] 3953[3] 4453[2]* 4975[15] **>80a 76f<**
**Oblomov 3** b c Most Welcome-Flambera (FR) (Akarad (FR)) **1995:** *4361[2]* **>77a 78f<**
**Obsessive (USA) 3** b br f Seeking the Gold (USA)-Secret Obsession (USA) (Secretariat (USA)) *936[4]* 1108[3] 2465a[7] 3945[8] 4126[3] **>106f<**
**Occam (IRE) 2** ch c Sharp Victor (USA)-Monterana (Sallust) 4902[4] **>47+f<**
**Occupandiste (IRE) 3** b f Kaldoun (FR)-Only Seule 796a[4] 4948a[2] **>103f<**
**Ocean Breeze 2** ch g Most Welcome-Sea Power (Welsh Pageant) 3687[19] 4458[4] **>35f<**
**Ocean Grove (IRE) 3** b f Fairy King (USA)-Leyete Gulf (IRE) (Slip Anchor) 676[11] 959[3] 1898[5] 2585[8] 3426[5] 3920[13] 4453[9] 4802[12] **>84f<**
**Ocean Light 2** ch f Anshan-Waveguide (Double Form) 4451[12] 4887[10] **>37f<**
**Ocean Park 5** b g Dominion-Chiming Melody (Cure The Blues (USA)) **1995:** *4374[2]* **1996:** *(99) 181[5] (306) (410) (547)* 879[10] 3947[14] (4427) 4617[10] **>90a 72f<**
**Ocean Ridge (USA) 2** b f Storm Bird (CAN)-Polar Bird (Thatching) (1896) 2582[2] (3201a) 3561a[4] 4491[3] **>100f<**
**Ocean Sea (USA) 3** 2109a[6] 2668a[4] 3574a[5] **>104f<**
**Ocean Stream (IRE) 3** b c Waajib-Kilboy Concorde (African Sky) **1995:** *4414[5]* **1996:** *414[4] 448[12]* 584[8] **>66da 68f<**
**Ochos Rios (IRE) 5** br g Horage-Morgiana (Godswalk (USA)) **1995:** *4427[3] 4476[12]* **1996:** *505[8]* 629[6] 718[2] 1423[2] 1610[8] 2005[9] 2293[3] 2722[3] 3151[4] 3450[7] 3623[15] (3995) 4136[13] 4688[17] 4865[6] **>62a 65f<**
**Ocker (IRE) 2** br c Astronef-Violet Somers (Will Somers) 916[7] 1537[8] 2985[2] 3247[7] 3792[2] **>71f<**
**O'Connor (IRE) 4** b c Ela-Mana-Mou-Orillia (Red God) 3753a[7] **>104f<**
**Octavia Hill 3** ch f Prince Sabo-Clara Barton (Youth (USA)) 3162[12] 3446[11] 3832[6] 4550[9] **>60f<**
**Oddfellows Girl 2** b f Nomination-Kaleidophone (Kalaglow) 1499[6] *2938[4] 3087[5] 3576[4]* 3769[8] 3982[22] 4207[6] 4594[14] 4790[10] **>40a 44f<**
**Office Hours 4** b g Danehill (USA)-Charmina (FR) (Nonoalco (USA)) *132[14] 217[6] 380[7] 424[13] 756[3]* 1010[11] 1532[5] 1856[14] 2014[8] 3316[2] 3583[7] 3978[4] 4263[9] 4373[19] **>49a 64f<**
**Off the Air (IRE) 5** b m Taufan (USA)-Milly Daydream (Hard Fought) *62[6] 98[6] 141[5] 252[10]* **>48a 36f<**
**Off The Rails 2** b f Saddlers' Hall (IRE)-Sliprail (USA) (Our Native (USA)) 3988[6] **>71f<**
**Oggi 5** gr g Efisio-Dolly Bevan (Another Realm) *592[10]* 893[10] 1178[13] 2005[20] (4058) 4198[3] 4571[9] (4888) **>77f<**
**Ohio Royale 2** ch g Shalford (IRE)-Jupiter's Message (Jupiter Island) 3293[11] 3511[11] *4331[12]* **>16f<**
**Ohnonotagain 4** b f Kind of Hush-Dear Glenda (Gold Song) *213[10] 700[9]* 805[4] 1162[7] *2085[9] 2801[12]* 3460[5] **>15a 25f<**
**Oh So Handy 8** b g Nearly A Hand-Geordie Lass (Bleep-Bleep) *9[5] 130[7] 265[6]* **>30a 47f<**
**Oh Susannah 5** b m Rousillon (USA)-Sue Grundy (Grundy) *3442[14]* 3812[7] 4356[12] 4436[26] 4865[17] **>39f<**
**Oh Whataknight 3** b f Primo Dominie-Carolside (Music Maestro) 2007[13] 3799[11] 4453[15] 4589[18] **>35f<**
**Okawango (SPA) 3** b c Don Roberto (USA)-Noche Gris (SPA) (Blue Skyer (SPA)) (3755a) **>102f<**
**Okay Baby (IRE) 4** b f Treasure Kay-Miss Tuko (Good Times (ITY)) **1995:** *4486[10]* **1996:** *4082[18]* 4808[20] **>19a 10?f<**
**Okeedokee (FR) 6** gr g Kaldoun (FR)-Multitude (USA) (Lyphard (USA)) 437a[2]
**Ok Pal 2** b c Interrex (CAN)-Rockery (Track Spare) 4896[7] **>19f<**
**Old Colony 2** b f Pleasant Colony (USA)-Annoconnor (USA) (Nureyev (USA)) 4449[5] 4608[13] **>66f<**
**Old Gold N Tan 3** ch g Ballacashtal (CAN)-Raleigh Gazelle (Absalom) *376[6] 467[8] 555[7] 1013[8]* 1681[5] 1992[10] 3274[15] **>24a 17f<**
**Old Hook (IRE) 5** b or br h Digamist (USA)-Day Dress (Ashmore (FR)) **1995:** *4351[4] (4440)* **1996:** *205[9] 243[9]* **>78a f<**
**Old Hush Wing (IRE) 3** b g Tirol-Saneena (Kris) 626[10] 700[8] 885[3] 1539[7] *4076[6] 4574[3]* **>54a 55f<**
**Old Irish 3** gr c Old Vic-Dunoof (Shirley Heights) 691[6] 826[4] (1124) 1524[2] 1854[2] 2612[5] **>92f<**
**Old Provence 6** b h Rainbow Quest (USA)-Orange Hill (High Top) **1995:** *(4448) 4505[8]* **1996:** *(98) (268) 449[20]* 682[13] *837[4] 1717[P]* **>76a 64f<** **(DEAD)**
**Old Roma (IRE) 3** b f Old Vic-Romantic Past (USA) (Miswaki (USA)) 1422[2] 1797[9] 2079[6] 2366[11] **>50f<**
**Old Rouvel (USA) 5** b h Riverman (USA)-Marie de Russy (FR) (Sassafras (FR)) 563[2] 875[5] 1752a[4] 2117[3] 4032a[6] 4134[5] 4569[5] 4965[5] **>67a 112f<**
**Old School House 3** ch c Polar Falcon (USA)-Farewell Letter (USA) (Arts And Letters) 760[4] 912[3] *(1814) 2086[2] 2155[2] 3066[2] (3149)* (3337) 3504[4] *(3610)* **>79a 78f<**
**Oleana (IRE) 3** b f Alzao (USA)-Buraida (Balidar) *2231[2]* **>84f<**
**Olifantsfontein 8** b g Thatching-Taplow (Tap On Wood) 3055[9] 3252[11] 3289[12] **>49a 18f<**
**Olimpia Dukakis (ITY) 4** b f Isopach (USA)-Jaana (Cure The Blues (USA)) **1995:** 4403a[5] **>115f<**
**Oliver (IRE) 2** b c Priolo (USA)-Daniella Drive (USA) (Shelter Half (USA)) 4516[15] 4891[12] **>16f<**
**Oliver Rock 3** b g Shareef Dancer (USA)-Short Rations (Lorenzaccio) 731[9] 1100[10] 2709[6] **>62f<**
**Oliviero (FR) 3** dk b c Vaguely Pleasant (FR)-My Green Eyes (USA) (Big Spruce (USA)) 621a[3] 797a[4] 1057a[8] 1757a[5] 2276a[7] 2480a[5] 3746a[8] 3915a[6] 4856a[5] **>118f<**
**Olivo (IRE) 2** ch c Priolo (USA)-Honourable Sheba (USA) (Roberto (USA)) 2852[3] 3245[3] 4891[6] **>85f<**
**Olympic Majesty (FR) 2** b c Law Society (USA)-Bella Senora (USA) (Northern Dancer) 4742a[7] **>75f<**
**Olympic Spirit 2** b f Puissance-Stripanoora (Ahonoora) 1622[3] (1834) 2112[3] (2700) 3213[5] 3613[2] 3921[2] 4299[4] 4579[6] **>92f<**
**Omaha City (IRE) 2** b g Night Shift (USA)-Be Discreet (Junius (USA)) *(1705)* 2877[2] 3213[4] 3843[2] 4035a[2] 4328[6] 4677[4] 4873[3] **>98f<**
**Omara (USA) 3** b f Storm Cat (USA)-Alamosa (Alydar (USA)) 672[3] 1033[5] 1882[3] 2208[4] 2399[3] 3148[8] 3522[2] 3938[5] (4422) (4819) 5036[9] **>89f<**
**Omidjoy (IRE) 6** ch m Nishapour (FR)-Fancy Finish (Final Straw) *275[8]* **>38f<**
**Once More for Luck (IRE) 5** b g Petorius-Mrs Lucky (Royal Match) 3043[3] 4073[4] 4320[6] 4515[2] (4904) **>73f<**
**One Dream 3** b g Weldnaas (USA)-Superb Lady (Marcus Superbus) 3162[10] 3665[4] **>58f<**
**One For Baileys 2** b c Unfuwain (USA)-Three Stars (Star Appeal) 5009[4] **>67f<**
**One for Jeannie 4** b f Clantime-Miss Henry (Blue Cashmere) *4094[4] 4367[12]* 4610[9] **>72a 56f<**
**Onefortheditch (USA) 3** gr f With Approval (CAN)-Wee Dram (USA) (Nostrum (USA)) 1171[5] 3832[3] 4256[6] 4597[4] 4691[5] **>74f<**
**Onefourseven 3** b g Jumbo Hirt (USA)-Dominance (Dominion) *123[9] 280[6] 348[5] 415[3] 522[6]* 3870[4] (4321) 4506[5] 4794[2] *(4984)* **>52a 63f<**
**One In The Eye 3** br c Arrasas (USA)-Mingalles (Prince de Galles) 1050[3] 1901[14] 3656[11] 3860[6] *4107[5] 4480[4]* 4968[14] **>39a 51f<**
**Oneknight With You 2** gr f Rudimentary (USA)-Inshirah (USA) (Caro) 1643[4] 2245[7] 2559[3] 3160[5] 3475[4] 4113[3] 4672[11] 4880[14] **>72f<**
**One Lady 2** gr f Mazilier (USA)-Ashbocking (Dragonara Palace (USA)) *2746[7] 3330[5]* 4228[9] **>38a 44f<**
**One Life To Live (IRE) 3** gr c Classic Music (USA)-Fine Flame (Le Prince) **1995:** *4389[7] 4431[14]* **1996:** *614[4]* 1363[6] 1850[15] **>55a 53f<**
**Onemoretime 2** b f Timeless Times (USA)-Dear Glenda (Gold Song) 3773[10] 4228[11] 4767[4] **>31f<**
**One Off the Rail (USA) 6** b h Rampage (USA)-Catty Queen (USA) (Tom Cat) **1995:** *4356[5] 4442[7]* **1996:** *80[6] (214) 296[3] (349) 3635[7]* **>76a 46f<**
**Oneoftheoldones 4** b g Deploy-Waveguide (Double Form) 547[13] 713[14] *3603[15] 3939[10]* **>66a 45f<**
**One Pound 3** b g Shareef Dancer (USA)-Beloved Visitor (USA) (Miswaki (USA)) 863[10] (1833) 2067[2] 2570[10] 3667[5] 3802[9] **>78f<**
**One Shot (IRE) 3** b g Fayruz-La Gravotte (FR) (Habitat) 595[16] 1122[5] 1526[6] 1776[5] 1891[7] **>44f<**
**One So Wonderful 2** b f Nashwan (USA)-Someone Special (Habitat) (4052) **>86+f<**
**One Voice (USA) 6** ch h Affirmed (USA)-Elk's Ellie (USA) (Vaguely Noble) 2973[9] **>72a 66f<**

**Only (USA)** 3 ch c Rahy (USA)-Stay With Bruce (USA) (Grey Dawn II) **1995:** *4535$^{6}$* **1996:** *448$^{7}$* 544$^{12}$ 1956$^{5}$ 2133$^{10}$ 2234$^{6}$ 2313$^{8}$ 2971$^{6}$ 3217$^{5}$ 3698$^{18}$ **>57f<**

**On the Carpet (IRE)** 3 f **1995:** 4422a$^{2}$ **>52f<**

**On The Green** 3 br f Pharly (FR)-Regal Wonder (Stupendous) 4613$^{6}$ **>53f<**

**On The Home Run** 3 b f Governor General-In the Papers (Aragon) 1061$^{8}$ 1333$^{12}$ 1883$^{6}$ 2411$^{7}$ 2946$^{9}$ 3244$^{9}$ **>27f<**

**On The Nose** 3 ch f Sharpo-Wollow Maid (Wollow) *577$^{15}$ >20f<*

**On The Piste** 3 gr f Shirley Heights-Snowing (USA) (Icecapade (USA)) 1895$^{5}$ **>76f<**

**On The Wildside** 3 ch f Charmer-No Control (Bustino) 2197$^{14}$ 2380$^{2}$ 2979$^{8}$ **>60f<**

**On Y Va (USA)** 9 ch m Victorious (USA)-Golden Moony (Northfields (USA)) **1995:** *4432$^{6}$* **>44da 71f<**

**Ood Dancer (USA)** 3 b c Night Shift (USA)-Homemade Cookie (USA) (Our Native (USA)) *663$^{10}$* 842$^{9}$ 982$^{3}$ 1443$^{2}$ (1675) 2126$^{3}$ (2705) 3210$^{18}$ 4054$^{11}$ **>91f<**

**Oops Pettie** 3 ch f Machiavellian (USA)-Miquette (FR) (Fabulous Dancer (USA)) 1508$^{5}$ 1873$^{9}$ (2383) 3039$^{5}$ 3248$^{5}$ (4117) 4556$^{2}$ **>98f<**

**Oozlem (IRE)** 7 b g Burslem-Fingers (Lord Gayle (USA)) **1995:** *4527$^{4}$* **1996:** *66$^{5}$ 105$^{8}$ (200) 261$^{7}$ 308$^{5}$ 1613$^{12}$ 2689$^{11}$ 3257$^{2}$* 3501$^{9}$ **>45a 48f<**

**Opalette** 3 b f Sharrood (USA)-Height of Folly (Shirley Heights) 3656$^{4}$ 4201$^{2}$ 4559$^{11}$ **>78f<**

**Opal Jewel** 3 b f Sadler's Wells (USA)-Optimistic Lass (USA) (Mr Prospector (USA)) 3103$^{2}$ (3425) **>81f<**

**Opaque** 4 b g Shirley Heights-Opale (Busted) 668$^{7}$ 872$^{2}$ (1150) 1529$^{6}$ 2060$^{7}$ **>77f<**

**Open Affair** 3 ch f Bold Arrangement-Key to Enchantment (Key To Content (USA)) 2121$^{3}$ 2975$^{4}$ 3233$^{3}$ 3785$^{12}$ 4000$^{16}$ 4373$^{18}$ **>65f<**

**Open Credit** 2 ch f Magical Wonder (USA)-Forest Treasure (USA) (Green Forest (USA)) 977$^{2}$ (1148) 4873$^{2}$ **>95f<**

**Opening Chorus** 3 ch g Music Boy-One Sharper (Dublin Taxi) *443$^{12}$* 973$^{15}$ 2049$^{4}$ 2215$^{4}$ 2490$^{5}$ 4784$^{4}$ **>52f<**

**Opening Range** 5 b m Nordico (USA)-Waveguide (Double Form) *204$^{7}$ 328$^{12}$ 412$^{9}$ 1117$^{12}$* 1416$^{11}$ 1658$^{12}$ **>39a 21f<**

**Opera Buff (IRE)** 5 br g Rousillon (USA)-Obertura (USA) (Roberto (USA)) **1995:** *(4376) (4416) (4442)* **1996:** *38$^{2}$ 100$^{3}$ 682$^{3}$* 1005$^{10}$ 1353$^{4}$ 1524$^{3}$ 2002$^{7}$ **>93a 81f<**

**Ophira** 4 b f Old Vic-Sephira (Luthier) (4941a) **>75f<**

**Options Open** 4 b c Then Again-Zahiah (So Blessed) (1417) 1824$^{4}$ 2328$^{5}$ 2544$^{11}$ 3072$^{11}$ 3430$^{3}$ 3622$^{2}$ (3672) (3984) **>105f<**

**Opulent** 5 b g Robellino (USA)-One Half Silver (CAN) (Plugged Nickle (USA)) 4238$^{3}$ 4489$^{11}$ **>81f<**

**Orange And Blue** 3 br f Prince Sabo-Mazarine Blue (Bellypha) **1995:** *4375$^{8}$ 4483$^{9}$* **1996:** *1312$^{11}$ 1966$^{5}$ 2367$^{3}$ 2800$^{4}$ 3091$^{7}$ 3294$^{6}$* 3579$^{13}$ 3957$^{7}$ 4589$^{17}$ **>41a 33f<**

**Orange Extreme** 5 b or br m Superlative-Suddenly Amber (USA) (Quiet Fling (USA)) *1081$^{W}$* **>56a 52f<**

**Orange Grouse (IRE)** 3 b f Taufan (USA)-Winter Tern (USA) (Arctic Tern (USA)) 4848a$^{3}$ 5065a$^{3}$ **>96f<**

**Orange Order (IRE)** 3 ch c Generous (IRE)-Fleur D'Oranger (Northfields (USA)) 2706$^{5}$ (3320) **>76f<**

**Orange Place (IRE)** 5 ch g Nordance (USA)-Little Red Hut (Habitat) **1995:** *4392$^{15}$* **1996:** *263$^{6}$ 350$^{4}$ 480$^{3}$* 744$^{6}$ 1010$^{5}$ 1314$^{3}$ (1354) 1703$^{12}$ 1962$^{11}$ **>61a 80f<**

**Orchard Gold** 5 b g Glint of Gold-On The Top (High Top) 2192$^{12}$ (2507) 2785$^{2}$ 3052$^{2}$ 3340$^{3}$ *4574$^{9}$* **>26a 56f<**

**Orchestral Designs (IRE)** 5 b g Fappiano (USA)-Elegance in Design (Habitat) *136$^{11}$ 2556$^{15}$ >1a f<*

**Orchestra Stall** 4 b g Old Vic-Blue Brocade (Reform) 495$^{2}$ (825) 1194$^{4}$ (3834) 4771$^{7}$ (4965) 5047$^{2}$ **>111f<**

**Orchidarma** 4 b g Reprimand-My Fair Orchid (Roan Rocket) *239$^{6}$ 303$^{10}$* **>45a 62f<**

**Ordained** 3 b f Mtoto-In the Habit (USA) (Lyphard (USA)) **1995:** *4504$^{7}$* **1996:** *129$^{5}$ 262$^{3}$ 614$^{6}$* 803$^{7}$ 914$^{9}$ 1089$^{2}$ 1641$^{5}$ (1850) 2163$^{3}$ 2294$^{7}$ 2780$^{3}$ 3249$^{6}$ (3412) 3621$^{6}$ 3677$^{2}$ 3961$^{7}$ 4438$^{7}$ 4559$^{10}$ **>51a 67f<**

**Ordway (USA)** 2 dk c Salt Lake (USA)-Priceless Countess (USA) (Vaguely Noble) *4954a$^{3}$* **>107a f<**

**Orfijar (FR)** 6 dk b h In Fijar (USA) (3397a) 4409a$^{5}$ 4659a$^{5}$ **>116f<**

**Oriane** 3 ch f Nashwan (USA)-Rappa Tap Tap (FR) (Tap On Wood) 4738a$^{3}$ 5015a$^{3}$ **>107f<**

**Oriel Lad** 3 b g Colmore Row-Consistent Queen (Queen's Hussar) *313$^{6}$ 344$^{8}$ 421$^{9}$ 1006$^{12}$* 2139$^{2}$ 2425$^{9}$ 2725$^{16}$ 3301$^{4}$ 3644$^{9}$ 4221$^{4}$ 4341$^{13}$ 4589$^{5}$ 4865$^{8}$ **>44a 58f<**

**Orinoco River (USA)** 3 ch c El Gran Senor (USA)-Miss Lilian (Sandford Lad) 578$^{9}$ 788$^{8}$ (1019) 1147$^{6}$ (1669) 2074$^{15}$ 2912$^{2}$ 3155$^{11}$ **>94f<**

**Oriole** 3 b g Mazilier (USA)-Odilese (Mummy's Pet) **1995:** *4389$^{12}$* **1996:** *453$^{7}$* 973$^{7}$ 1363$^{12}$ 1527$^{10}$ 1846$^{3}$ 2139$^{4}$ (2417) 2914$^{6}$ 3102$^{11}$ 3456$^{12}$ 4098$^{16}$ 4598$^{14}$ 4921$^{7}$ **>18a 36f<**

**Orontes (USA)** 2 b c Lomond (USA)-Chateau Princess (USA) (Majestic Prince (USA)) 3147$^{3}$ (3493) 3925$^{6}$ 4672$^{9}$ **>85f<**

**Orsay** 4 b c Royal Academy (USA)-Bellifontaine (FR) (Bellypha) 3123$^{2}$ 3799$^{3}$ 4184$^{6}$ 4444$^{10}$ **>85f<**

**Ortelius** 2 b c Rudimentary (USA)-Third Movement (Music Boy) 4233$^{11}$ 4801$^{17}$ (4884) **>68f<**

**Orthorhombus** 7 b g Aragon-Honeybeta (Habitat) 470$^{11}$ 561$^{12}$ 679$^{13}$ **>64a 58f<**

**Ortolan** 3 gr c Prince Sabo-Kala Rosa (Kalaglow) *1146$^{6}$* (1356) 2604$^{7}$ (3166) (3244) (3442) 3696$^{2}$ 4198$^{7}$ 4376$^{9}$ (4589) **>89f<**

**Oscar Rose** 3 b g Aragon-Mossy Rose (King of Spain) 1416$^{4}$ 2251$^{14}$ 3060$^{7}$ 3474$^{11}$ 3681$^{12}$ **>45f<**

**Oscar Schindler (IRE)** 4 ch c Royal Academy (USA)-Saraday (Northfields (USA)) (1017) (2113) 3070$^{4}$ (4397a) 4662a$^{3}$ 5069a$^{15}$ **>130f<**

**Oscilights Gift** 4 b f Chauve Souris-Oscilight (Swing Easy (USA)) *1658$^{13}$* 2016$^{7}$ 2255$^{8}$ 2745$^{3}$ 3331$^{3}$ 3506$^{5}$ 4215$^{12}$ **>36f<**

**Osomental** 2 gr g Petong-Proper Madam (Mummy's Pet) 996$^{4}$ 1404$^{4}$ 1653$^{5}$ 1869$^{2}$ (2728) (2965) 3792$^{9}$ 3931$^{4}$ 4189$^{6}$ 4247$^{7}$ 4723$^{23}$ **>90f<**

**Ostia** 3 b f Slip Anchor-Sarsina (Forli (ARG)) 4591$^{11}$ **>39f<**

**Otaiti (IRE)** 4 b f Sadler's Wells (USA)-Ode (USA) (Lord Avie (USA)) (4168a) 4654a$^{5}$ **>109f<**

**Otaru (IRE)** 4 b f Indian Ridge-Radiant (USA) (Foolish Pleasure (USA)) *99$^{8}$*

**Other Club** 2 ch c Kris-Tura (Northfields (USA)) 4507$^{6}$ 4770$^{6}$ **>66f<**

**Ottavio Farnese** 4 ch g Scottish Reel-Sense of Pride (Welsh Pageant) 1145$^{17}$ 2127$^{11}$ 4497$^{11}$ 4812$^{6}$ *4986$^{8}$* **>18a 55f<**

**Otto E Mezzo** 4 bl c Persian Bold-Carolside (Music Maestro) 1355$^{6}$ 1867$^{3}$ 2194$^{7}$ 3071$^{10}$ 3233$^{5}$ 3442$^{8}$ 3754a$^{7}$ 4431$^{12}$ 4675$^{6}$ **>74f<**

**Our Adventure** 3 ch f Green Adventure (USA)-Honey Dipper (Golden Dipper) 2383$^{9}$ **>26f<**

**Our Albert (IRE)** 3 b g Durgam (USA)-Power Girl (Tyrant (USA)) 3333$^{15}$ 4598$^{17}$ 4809$^{8}$ **>41f<**

**Our Eddie** 7 ch g Gabitat-Ragusa Girl (Morston (FR)) *499$^{6}$ 1448$^{4}$ (3435) 3786$^{8}$ 4894$^{10}$ 4998$^{4}$* **>69a 21f<**

**Our Future (IRE)** 2 b c Imp Society (USA)-Petite Realm (Realm) 618$^{4}$ 685$^{11}$ 1583$^{7}$ 2588$^{3}$ 3324$^{2}$ 3678$^{7}$ **>64f<**

**Our Highness (FR)** 3 gr f Highest Honor (FR)-Admiration (Kashmir II) 3028a$^{2}$

**Our Home Land (USA)** 2 b c Red Ransom (USA)-What Not To Do (USA) (What Luck (USA)) 1344$^{7}$ (2985) **>75f<**

**Our Kevin** 2 gr g Chilibang-Anse Chastanet (Cavo Doro) 630$^{4}$ 880$^{3}$ *1080$^{4}$ 1494$^{4}$* (1607) 1904$^{2}$ *2172$^{2}$ 2382$^{6}$* 2606$^{2}$ *(2750) 3046$^{10}$* 3408$^{6}$ 3523$^{3}$ 4586$^{11}$ *4777$^{6}$ 5057$^{6}$* **>64a 64f<**

**Our Kris** 4 b c Kris-Our Reverie (USA) (J O Tobin (USA)) *2042$^{21}$* 2717$^{4}$ 3163$^{3}$ **>76f<**

**Our Little Lady** 4 b f Queen's Soldier (USA)-Charlotte's Pearl (Monsanto (FR)) 1515$^{15}$ 2373$^{8}$ 2766$^{6}$ **>11a 59df<**

**Our Main Man** 6 ch g Superlative-Ophrys (Nonoalco (USA)) **1995:** *4376$^{4}$ 4475$^{6}$* **1996:** *690$^{17}$* 4686$^{26}$ 4793$^{17}$ *5003$^{5}$* **>56a 35f<**

**Our People** 2 ch c Indian Ridge-Fair and Wise (High Line) 4500$^{3}$ (4705) 4963$^{3}$ **>97f<**

**Our Robert** 4 b g Faustus (USA)-Duck Soup (Decoy Boy) *110$^{3}$ 159$^{4}$ 256$^{8}$* **>60a 68f<**

**Our Shadee (USA)** 6 b g Shadeed (USA)-Nuppence (Reform) **1995:** *4357$^{4}$ 4464$^{6}$ 4515$^{3}$ 4536$^{5}$* **1996:** *14$^{8}$ 42$^{11}$ 212$^{5}$ 273$^{2}$ 317$^{3}$ (354) 380$^{2}$ (408) 461$^{3}$ (556) 601$^{6}$* 749$^{16}$ 812$^{9}$ *1030$^{3}$ 1307$^{4}$* 1624$^{3}$ 1684$^{4}$ 1905$^{6}$ 2602$^{4}$ 3139$^{7}$ (3274) 3469$^{6}$ 3606$^{6}$ *3877$^{11}$ 3995$^{5}$* 4098$^{7}$ 4256$^{5}$ 4373$^{11}$ *4895$^{8}$ 4915$^{15}$* **>75a 58f<**

**Our Tom** 4 br g Petong-Boa (Mandrake Major) **1995:** *4378$^{9}$ 4503$^{4}$* **1996:** *(48) 100$^{8}$ 210$^{5}$ 384$^{6}$ 469$^{10}$* 1414$^{13}$ 2058$^{10}$ *4575$^{12}$ 5060$^{10}$* **>68a 44f<**

**Our Way** 2 ch f Forzando-Hanglands (Bustino) 3438$^{2}$ 3706$^{7}$ 4241$^{2}$ 4490$^{14}$ **>75f<**

**Our Worley (IRE)** 3 b f Mac's Imp (USA)-Castleforbes (Thatching) *748$^{6}$* 867$^{12}$ **>50df<**

**Outflanker (USA)** 2 b br c Danzig (USA)-Lassie's Lady (USA) (Alydar (USA)) 4706$^{2}$ 4920$^{6}$ **>74f<**

**Out Line** 4 gr f Beveled (USA)-Free Range (Birdbrook) 949$^{8}$ 1099$^{16}$ 1994$^{4}$ 2255$^{2}$ 2686$^{3}$ 3767$^{3}$ 4053$^{7}$ 4372$^{6}$ **>75f<**

**Out of Sight (IRE)** 2 ch c Salse (USA)-Starr Danias (USA) (Sensitive Prince (USA)) 1404$^{5}$ 3293$^{5}$ 3668$^{5}$ 3994$^{6}$ 4723$^{20}$ 5043$^{7}$ **>78f<**

**Out on a Promise (IRE)** 4 b c Night Shift (USA)-Lovers' Parlour (Beldale Flutter (USA)) *564$^{7}$* 682$^{11}$ 871$^{7}$ 1450$^{12}$ **>68a 78f<**

**Outset (IRE)** 6 ch g Persian Bold-It's Now Or Never (High Line) *5047$^{8}$ >74?f<*

**Outstayed Welcome** 4 b g Be My Guest (USA)-Between Time (Elegant Air) **1995:** *4364$^{5}$ 4489$^{2}$ 4546$^{4}$* **1996:** *1081$^{3}$ 439$^{2}$* 612$^{2}$ 993$^{2}$ 1837$^{5}$ 2066$^{3}$ 2717$^{13}$ 2989$^{3}$ 3297$^{14}$ 4048$^{11}$ 4307$^{6}$ 4551$^{6}$ **>56a 60f<**

**Out West (USA)** 2 br f Gone West (USA)-Chellingoua (USA) (Sharpen Up) (3778) 4111$^{4}$ **>90f<**

**Ovation** 2 ch f Generous (IRE)-Bint Pasha (USA) (Affirmed (USA)) (2863) 4085$^{2}$ 4464$^{7}$ **>93f<**

**Overbury (IRE)** 5 br h Caerleon (USA)-Overcall (Bustino) (724a) 3386a$^{7}$ 4174a$^{4}$ 4371$^{2}$ 4714$^{4}$ 5046$^{15}$ **>123f<**

**Overpower** 12 b g Try My Best (USA)-Just A Shadow (Laser Light) 1691$^{7}$ **>60f<**

**Overruled (IRE)** 3 b f Last Tycoon-Overcall (Bustino) 1002$^{8}$ 1407$^{5}$ (2384) 3134$^{8}$ **>86f<**

**Oversman** 3 b c Keen-Jamaican Punch (IRE)

(Shareef Dancer (USA)) **1995:** *4431$^{11}$* **1996:** *197$^{2}$ (346) 1002$^{3}$* **>75a 78f<**

**Over To You (USA) 2** ch c Rubiano (USA)-Overnight (USA) (Mr Leader (USA)) 4204$^{3}$ (4830) **>77f<**

**Owdbetts (IRE) 4** b f High Estate-Nora Yo Ya (Ahonoora) **1995:** *4505$^{5}$ 4526$^{3}$* **1996:** *120$^{6}$ 219$^{11}$ 1496$^{13}$* (1979) 2284$^{3}$ 2599$^{11}$ 3048$^{6}$ *3435$^{6}$* **>65a 64f<**

**Owen Meany (FR) 4** b g Cricket Ball (USA)-Up And Going (FR) (Never so Bold) (3910a) **>89f<**

**Oxalagu (GER) 4** gr c Lagunas-Oxalis (GER) (Ashmore (FR)) (789a) 1138a$^{4}$ 1948a$^{2}$ 2479a$^{5}$ (4650a) 5073a$^{4}$ **>122f<**

**Oxbane 2** b f Soviet Star (USA)-Oxslip (Owen Dudley) 4887$^{11}$ **>32f<**

**Oxford Line (IRE) 4** b c Caerleon (USA)-Lorenza Bertini (Star Appeal) 5074a$^{13}$ **>103f<**

**Oxgang (IRE) 3** b g Taufan (USA)-Casla (Lomond (USA)) *234$^{10}$ 370$^{2}$ 483$^{6}$* 1363$^{5}$ 1821$^{17}$ 2348$^{10}$ *2935$^{7}$ 3492$^{8}$* **>50a 46f<**

**Ozark (IRE) 2** 4658a$^{3}$

**Ozzie Jones 5** b g Formidable (USA)-Distant Relation (Great Nephew) *3335$^{16}$* ***>51a 34?f<***

**P**

**Pab's Choice 5** ch m Telsmoss-Dido (Full of Hope) **1995:** *4457$^{7}$* **1996:** *55$^{11}$ 2188$^{4}$* 2605$^{8}$ 3139$^{10}$ **>56a 57f<**

**Pacific Girl (IRE) 4** b f Emmson-Power Girl (Tyrant (USA)) **1995:** *4362$^{6}$ 4406$^{11}$ 4450$^{6}$* **1996:** *53$^{12}$ 76$^{5}$* **>40a 48f<**

**Pacific Grove 3** b f Persian Bold-Dazzling Heights (Shirley Heights) **1995:** 4400a$^{8}$ **1996:** 2991$^{6}$ **>93f<**

**Packitin 3** b g Rich Charlie-Sound Type (Upper Case (USA)) 2777$^{15}$

**Padauk 2** b c Warrshan (USA)-Free on Board (Free State) 3682$^{8}$ 4050$^{6}$ 4370$^{5}$ 4681$^{5}$ **>77f<**

**Paddy Hurry 2** b c Silver Kite (USA)-Little Preston (IRE) (Pennine Walk) *4715$^{26}$* ***>28f<***

**Paddy Lad (IRE) 2** b br c Anita's Prince-Lady of Man (So Blessed) *1489$^{6}$ 3349$^{5}$* (3502) 4024a$^{2}$ 4258$^{3}$ **>26a 98f<**

**Paddy's Rice 5** ch g Hadeer-Requiem (Song) (1689) 1856$^{8}$ 2285$^{9}$ 2602$^{5}$ 2903$^{3}$ 3274$^{4}$ 3686$^{2}$ 4128$^{8}$ 4256$^{17}$ **>66f<**

**Pageboy 7** b g Tina's Pet-Edwin's Princess (Owen Dudley) *(26) 55$^{2}$ 107$^{6}$ 117$^{5}$ 2586$^{5}$* 2757$^{7}$ 3045$^{8}$ (3489) 3639$^{2}$ 3758$^{4}$ 3973$^{7}$ *(4081) 4246$^{2}$* 4382$^{13}$ 4473$^{6}$ **>71a 75f<**

**Pagel (IRE) 2** b g Polish Patriot (USA)-Fanfan (IRE) (Taufan (USA)) 4830$^{15}$ **>10f<**

**Painted Hall (USA) 4** br g Imperial Falcon (CAN)-Moon O'Gold (USA) (Slew O' Gold (USA)) *941$^{12}$* 1145$^{6}$ 1486$^{9}$ **>73f<**

**Paint It Black 3** ch c Double Schwartz-Tableaux (FR) (Welsh Pageant) 917$^{7}$ 1127$^{11}$ 2041$^{19}$ 2334$^{7}$ 2618$^{2}$ 2980$^{5}$ 3518$^{13}$ 3789$^{4}$ 3978$^{8}$ 4829$^{6}$ **>65f<**

**Pair of Jacks (IRE) 6** ch g Music Boy-Lobbino (Bustino) **1995:** *4350$^{11}$* **1996:** *133$^{7}$ 406$^{9}$ 2286$^{10}$* 2405$^{4}$ **>37da 31f<**

**Palacegate Chief 3** b g Inca Chief (USA)-Sports Post Lady (IRE) (M Double M (USA)) 1707$^{11}$ *2169$^{13}$* **>16a 25f<**

**Palacegate Gold (IRE) 7** b g Sarab-Habilite (Habitat) **1995:** *4521$^{10}$ 4537$^{10}$* **1996:** *201$^{3}$ 347$^{3}$ 412$^{10}$ 470$^{8}$* 549$^{6}$ **>26a 37f<**

**Palacegate Jack (IRE) 5** gr g Neshad (USA)-Pasadena Lady (Captain James) 864$^{8}$ 1016$^{11}$ 1708$^{3}$ 2508$^{3}$ 3146$^{13}$ *(4090) 4215$^{3}$* 4342$^{2}$ 4581$^{20}$ 4765$^{19}$ (4995) **>81a 83f<**

**Palacegate Jo (IRE) 5** b m Drumalis-Welsh Rhyme (Welsh Term) **1995:** *4479$^{9}$* **1996:** *77$^{6}$ 285$^{6}$ 424$^{7}$ 1487$^{11}$ 1970$^{2}$ 2321$^{5}$ 3600$^{9}$* **>39a 20f<**

**Palacegate Touch 6** gr g Petong-Dancing Chimes (London Bells (CAN)) 610$^{16}$ (805) *896$^{2}$ 1043$^{5}$ 1094$^{4}$ 1810$^{3}$ 2171$^{8}$ 2392$^{4}$ (2684) (2908)* 3140$^{3}$ (3579) 3851$^{2}$ *4094$^{3}$ (4215)* 4505$^{9}$ 4679$^{6}$ (4765) 4869$^{7}$ **>83a 84f<**

**Palace of Gold 6** b g Slip Anchor-Salacious (Sallust) *474$^{6}$* 542$^{3}$ 620$^{3}$ 886$^{4}$ 1022$^{4}$ 4302$^{5}$ **>46a 47f<**

**Palaemon 2** b c Slip Anchor-Palace Street (USA) (Secreto (USA)) 1437$^{5}$ 3319$^{11}$ 3493$^{7}$ 4106$^{3}$ 4375$^{5}$ 4880$^{6}$ **>67f<**

**Palamon (USA) 3** ch c Sanglamore (USA)-Gantlette (Run The Gantlet (USA)) 1182$^{3}$ 1711$^{2}$ 2601$^{5}$ (2794) **>84f<**

**Palatal (USA) 3** b c Lyphard's Wish (FR)-Nickle Lady (FR) 4293a$^{10}$ **>104f<**

**Paldost 2** b c Efisio-Fishki (Niniski (USA)) 2416$^{5}$ 3349$^{12}$ 3773$^{9}$ **>29f<**

**Paley Prince (USA) 10** b h Tilt Up (USA)-Apalachee Princess (USA) (Apalachee (USA)) 3261$^{9}$ 3323$^{8}$ 3506$^{9}$ 3661$^{14}$ 4088$^{12}$ 4130$^{5}$ 4372$^{16}$ **>48a 49f<**

**Palio Sky 2** b c Niniski (USA)-Live Ammo (Home Guard (USA)) 3423$^{3}$ (4041) **>80f<**

**Palisade (USA) 2** b f Gone West (USA)-Peplum (USA) (Nijinsky (CAN)) (4969) **>85+f<**

**Palisander (IRE) 2** ch c Conquering Hero (USA)-Classic Choice (Patch) 1437$^{6}$ 2195$^{7}$ 2600$^{5}$ 4118$^{9}$ **>64f<**

**Pallium (IRE) 8** b g Try My Best (USA)-Jungle Gardenia (Nonoalco (USA)) 1342$^{9}$ 1889$^{5}$ 2154$^{9}$ 2386$^{7}$ 2523$^{4}$ 2757$^{9}$ 2910$^{3}$ 3278$^{2}$ 3294$^{9}$ 3579$^{7}$ 4246$^{13}$ 4460$^{8}$ **>51a 59f<**

**Palo Blanco 5** b m Precocious-Linpac Mapleleaf (Dominion) 931$^{13}$ 1199$^{6}$ (1588) 1786$^{2}$ 2363$^{3}$ 2725$^{15}$ 4312$^{15}$ 4687$^{5}$ 4994$^{6}$ **>81f<**

**Paloma Bay (IRE) 3** b f Alzao (USA)-Adventurine (Thatching) 572$^{4}$ 708$^{5}$ 4218$^{7}$ 4445$^{18}$ **>96f<**

**Pamela's Boy 2** ch c UT'Clantime-Allez-Oops (Moulin) 4863$^{12}$

**Pampasa (FR) 2** br f Pampabird (FR)-Dounasa (FR) (Kaldoun (FR)) 2741$^{7}$ **>57f<**

**Pampas Breeze (IRE) 4** b f Darshaan-Pampas Miss (USA) (Pronto (ARG)) **1995:** *4387$^{11}$* **>29a 74f<**

**Panama City (USA) 2** b c El Gran Senor (USA)-Obeah (Cure The Blues (USA)) 3821$^{2}$ (4386) 4859a$^{2}$ **>81f<**

**Panama Jive (IRE) 3** ch f Dancing Spree (USA)-Straw Beret (USA) (Chief's Crown (USA)) *(89) 530$^{6}$ 658$^{4}$* 803$^{14}$ 1067$^{13}$ **>55a 44f<**

**Panata (IRE) 3** b f Tirol-Rince Deas (IRE) (Alzao (USA)) 1452$^{5}$ (1692) (2618) (3148) 4184$^{4}$ 4445$^{8}$ **>89f<**

**Pandiculation 2** ch c Statoblest-Golden Panda (Music Boy) 685$^{7}$ 869$^{6}$ 1038$^{4}$ 1537$^{3}$ (1779) 2063$^{6}$ 2629$^{P}$ **>62f< (DEAD)**

**Pandora's Gift 3** b f Zalazl (USA)-Lady Clementine (He Loves Me) *899$^{7}$ 1605$^{9}$* **>16a f<**

**Pangeran (USA) 4** ch g Forty Niner (USA)-Smart Heiress (USA) (Vaguely Noble) *234$^{9}$ 402$^{W}$* **>21a f<**

**Panooras Lord (IRE) 2** b c Topanoora-Ladyship (Windjammer (USA)) 4991$^{11}$ **>36f<**

**Panther (IRE) 6** ch g Primo Dominie-High Profile (High Top) **1995:** *4409$^{9}$ 4450$^{5}$* **1996:** *155$^{8}$ 253$^{6}$ 291$^{8}$ 617$^{4}$* (769) 882$^{2}$ (1087) *1460$^{3}$ 1635$^{3}$* (1684) 2034$^{6}$ 3399$^{2}$ *3628$^{4}$ (3932)* 4180$^{6}$ 4246$^{14}$ 4367$^{9}$ **>50a 75f<**

**Panto Queen 5** b m Lepanto (GER)-Tyqueen (Tycoon II) 1839$^{9}$ 2036$^{9}$ 2189$^{13}$ **>55df<**

**Paojiunic (IRE) 3** ch c Mac's Imp (USA)-Audenhove (GER) (Marduk (GER)) *2597$^{4}$* 2861$^{4}$ 3215$^{8}$ 4053$^{4}$ 4243$^{8}$ 4550$^{15}$ 4831$^{9}$ **>76f<**

**Papaha (FR) 3** b f Green Desert (USA)-Turban (Glint of Gold) 550$^{2}$ (2515) 2991$^{2}$ 5036$^{6}$ **>105f<**

**Papalma (USA) 3** f 1396a$^{6}$

**Paper Cloud 4** b f Lugana Beach-Sweet Enough (Caerleon (USA)) *2711$^{6}$* 2989$^{9}$ 4307$^{19}$ **>58f<**

**Papering (IRE) 3** b f Shaadi (USA)-Wrapping (Kris) 939$^{11}$ 1335$^{3}$ (2991) 3231$^{2}$ 3688$^{2}$ 4292a$^{2}$ 4678$^{4}$ **>117f<**

**Paper Maze 3** b f Mazilier (USA)-Westonepaperchase (USA) (Accipiter (USA)) 1435$^{11}$ 2587$^{18}$ 2899$^{7}$ 3354$^{9}$ 3592$^{11}$ 4229$^{10}$ **>50a 30f<**

**Papita (IRE) 2** b f Law Society (USA)-Fantasise (FR) (General Assembly (USA)) 2741$^{5}$ (3129) 3444$^{9}$ 4065$^{7}$ 4369$^{6}$ 4672$^{10}$ **>88f<**

**Pappa Reale 3** ch f Indian Ridge-Daffodil Fields (Try My Best (USA)) 794a$^{6}$ **>99f<**

**Papua 2** ch c Green Dancer (USA)-Fairy Tern (Mill Reef (USA)) 1896$^{4}$ (2702) (3150) 4029a$^{2}$ (4488) 4871$^{5}$ **>102f<**

**Parade Sauvage (FR) 3** gr f Kenmare (FR)-Fairy Gold (Golden Fleece (USA)) 1140a$^{9}$ **>97f<**

**Paradise Navy 7** b g Slip Anchor-Ivory Waltz (USA) (Sir Ivor) **1995:** *4411$^{4}$* **1996:** *811$^{8}$* 1439$^{9}$ 1835$^{3}$ 2042$^{13}$ 2148$^{4}$ 2547$^{13}$ 2709$^{4}$ (2958) 3142$^{4}$ *(3437) 3610$^{3}$ 3801$^{6}$* 4260$^{7}$ 4426$^{3}$ 4604$^{4}$ 4771$^{22}$ 4832$^{3}$ 4919$^{3}$ 5047$^{4}$ **>72a 78f<**

**Paradise Waters 4** gr f Celestial Storm (USA)-Gleaming Water (Kalaglow) 635$^{4}$ (866) 1147$^{2}$ (1306) (1874) 2131$^{4}$ **>74f<**

**Parellie 3** b f Inca Chief (USA)-Parklands Belle (Stanford) **1995:** *4511$^{13}$*

**Parfait Glace (FR) 4** b c Pampabird (FR)-Star System **1995:** 4404a$^{3}$ **>102f<**

**Parijazz (IRE) 2** b f Astronef-Brandywell (Skyliner) 2993$^{5}$ 3796$^{2}$ 4087$^{8}$ 4250$^{2}$ (4796) **>69f<**

**Paris Babe 4** b f Teenoso (USA)-Kala's Image (Kala Shikari) 1075$^{6}$ 5044$^{15}$ **>95df<**

**Paris Circus (ITY) 3** b c Most Welcome-False Look (USA) (Alleged (USA)) 799a$^{3}$

**Parklife (IRE) 4** ch g Double Schwartz-Silk Trade (Auction Ring (USA)) *33$^{4}$ 85$^{2}$ 116$^{7}$ 328$^{3}$ 604$^{9}$ 4604$^{2}$* ***>44a 49f<***

**Park Petard 3** gr f Petong-What A Pet (Mummy's Pet) 4738a$^{9}$ **>87f<**

**Park Ridge 4** b g Indian Ridge-Aspark (Sparkler) 504$^{6}$ *602$^{8}$ 745$^{4}$* 1655$^{17}$ 3861$^{9}$ 4082$^{8}$ 4497$^{15}$ **>25f<**

**Parliament Piece 10** ch g Burslem-Sallywell (Manado) 589$^{11}$ 1018$^{9}$ 1088$^{4}$ 1423$^{9}$ 2121$^{2}$ 2313$^{5}$ 3481$^{6}$ 3640$^{11}$ 4609$^{11}$ 4768$^{11}$ 4900$^{18}$ **>55a 61f<**

**Paronomasia 4** b g Precocious-The Crying Game (Manor Farm Boy) *53$^{3}$ 71$^{10}$ 179$^{8}$ 200$^{5}$ 412$^{12}$ 527$^{7}$ 604$^{7}$ 995$^{6}$* 1309$^{12}$ 1414$^{7}$ 2060$^{8}$ 2165$^{12}$ 2360$^{5}$ 2511$^{11}$ 3314$^{10}$ 4906$^{9}$ **>34a 32f<**

**Parquet 2** ch f Lead on Time (USA)-Tocaronte (FR) (Kris) *4251$^{8}$ 4493$^{8}$* ***>5a 11f<***

**Parrot Jungle (IRE) 3** b f High Estate-Palm Dove (USA) (Storm Bird (CAN)) 572$^{2}$ 794a$^{7}$ 1899$^{8}$ 3497$^{5}$ 4671$^{3}$ 4948a$^{5}$ 5036$^{4}$ **>103f<**

**Parrot's Hill (IRE) 3** b g Nashamaa-Cryptic Gold (Glint of Gold) 763$^{10}$ 982$^{14}$ 1656$^{10}$ 2424$^{2}$ 3260$^{4}$ 3584$^{9}$ 3705$^{5}$ 4587$^{7}$ **>56f<**

**Parsa (USA) 3** b f Risen Star (USA)-Pallanza (USA) (Lyphard (USA)) 1104$^{14}$ (1641) 1883$^{2}$ 2486$^{2}$ 3173$^{3}$ 3459$^{5}$ 4513$^{6}$ 4691$^{4}$ 4921$^{3}$ **>72f<**

**Parsis (USA) 3** b c Diesis-Par Excellance (CAN) (L'Enjoleur (CAN)) 1594$^{14}$ 1797$^{3}$ **>70f<**

**Partipral (USA) 7** b h Procida (USA)-Partition (FR) (Top Ville) **1995:** (4522a) **>121f<**

**Partita 3** b f Polish Precedent (USA)-Pharian (USA) (Diesis) 2529$^{10}$ 2949$^{5}$ 4611$^{10}$ **>47f<**

**Party Poll (USA) 3** b c Bering-Spark of Success (USA) (Topsider (USA)) 1253a$^{6}$ 1296a$^{8}$ **>79+f<**

**Party Poser 3** b f Presidium-Pooka (Dominion)

479$^{14}$

**Party Romance (USA) 2** gr c Black Tie Affair-Tia Juanita (USA) (My Gallant (USA)) 2073$^{4}$ 2335$^{4}$ 2972$^{3}$ 3998$^{2}$ 4578$^{4}$ **>92f<**

**Pas De Reponse (USA) 2** b f Danzig (USA)-Soundings (USA) (Mr Prospector (USA)) 3750a$^{3}$ (4285a) (4491) **>105f<**

**Pash 4** b f Hallgate-Pashmina (Blue Cashmere) **1995:** *4379$^{13}$* **1996:** *561$^{13}$* 586$^{10}$ 827$^{19}$ 883$^{6}$ (1024) 1196$^{14}$ 1468$^{7}$ 1633$^{8}$ **>5a 47f<**

**Pasi Kali (FR) 3** b c Shining Steel-Miss Kabreez (FR) (Sir Tor) (3028a)

**Passage Creeping (IRE) 3** b f Persian Bold-Tiptoe (Dance In Time (CAN)) 921$^{7}$ 1438$^{5}$ 1986$^{2}$ 2412$^{6}$ 2980$^{2}$ 3173$^{4}$ 3800$^{12}$ **>79f<**

**Passi d'Orlando (IRE) 2** ch c Persian Bold-When Lit (Northfields (USA)) 2667a$^{5}$ 3695$^{3}$ (4538a) 4745a$^{2}$ 5028a$^{3}$ **>75f<**

**Passiflora 2** ch f Night Shift (USA)-Pineapple (Superlative) (1678) 2375$^{2}$ 5043$^{11}$ **>83f<**

**Passing Strangers (USA) 3** b c Lyphard (USA)-The Way We Were (USA) (Avatar (USA)) 2718$^{13}$ 3333$^{8}$ 3611$^{3}$ **>66f<**

**Passion 2** ch f Risk Me (FR)-Gotcher (Jalmood (USA)) 4887$^{5}$ **>58f<**

**Passion For Life 3** br g Charmer-Party Game (Red Alert) 443$^{3}$ (571) (673) 1129$^{6}$ (1945a) 2271a$^{6}$ 2663a$^{12}$ 4774$^{2}$ **>121f<**

**Passionnee (USA) 4** b f Woodman (USA)-Pallanza (USA) (Lyphard (USA)) **1995:** *(4495a)* *>100f<*

**Passion Sunday 5** ch g Bairn (USA)-Holy Day (Sallust) **1995:** *4505$^{12}$* **>22a 47f<**

**Pasternak 3** b c Soviet Star (USA)-Princess Pati (Top Ville) 915$^{5}$ 2894$^{2}$ 3161$^{8}$ 4201$^{3}$ (4478) (4617) **>91f<**

**Patch Of Blue 3** ch f Siberian Express (USA)-Plume Bleu Pale (FR) (El Gran Senor (USA)) 1758a$^{2}$ **>109f<**

**Pater Noster (USA) 7** b h Stately Don (USA)-Sainera (USA) (Stop The Music (USA)) *438a$^{9}$* 3811$^{4}$ **>109df<**

**Pathaze 3** b f Totem (USA)-Stilvella (Camden Town) 748$^{13}$ 973$^{3}$ 1405$^{10}$ 2049$^{3}$ 2151$^{2}$ 2215$^{2}$ 2571$^{4}$ 2778$^{6}$ 2914$^{3}$ 3240$^{2}$ 3342$^{3}$ 3489$^{2}$ 3680$^{7}$ 3959$^{5}$ **>54f<**

**Patiala (IRE) 3** b f Nashwan (USA)-Catherine Parr (USA) (Riverman (USA)) 4824$^{11}$ 5035$^{5}$ **>28f<**

**Patina 2** ch f Rudimentary (USA)-Appledorn (Doulab (USA)) 4884$^{10}$ **>10f<**

**Patrio (IRE) 3** b f Polish Patriot (USA)-Fleetwood Fancy (Taufan (USA)) **1995:** *4365$^{5}$* **1996:** *1096$^{8}$ 1612$^{6}$* 1995$^{7}$ *2325$^{6}$ 2411$^{9}$* 3059$^{10}$ 3761$^{10}$ **>31a 49f<**

**Patrita Park 2** br f Flying Tyke-Bellinote (FR) (Noir Et Or) 4046$^{W}$ 4228$^{7}$ 4558$^{12}$ 4806$^{5}$ **>47f<**

**Pat Said No (IRE) 2** b f Last Tycoon-Fiddle-Faddle (Silly Season) *2157$^{2}$* 2538$^{5}$ **>60f<**

**Patscilla 5** b or br m Squill (USA)-Fortune Teller (Troy) 2891$^{11}$ *3086$^{10}$* **>26f<**

**Pats Delight 4** ch f Crofthall-Petroc Concert (Tina's Pet) *134$^{7}$ 207$^{7}$ 267$^{8}$ 386$^{7}$ 527$^{10}$* 981$^{14}$ **>20a 29f<**

**Pats Folly 5** bl m Macmillion-Cavo Varka (Cavo Doro) *1638$^{14}$* 4362$^{8}$ **>12f<**

**Pat's Splendour 5** b m Primitive Rising (USA)-Northern Venture (St Alphage) **1995:** *4364$^{11}$ 4489$^{3}$* **1996:** *12$^{7}$ 2896$^{11}$* 3173$^{5}$ 3466$^{5}$ 3785$^{2}$ 4068$^{14}$ 4603$^{3}$ 4815$^{7}$ 5053$^{8}$ **>38a 53f<**

**Patsy Grimes 6** b m Beveled (USA)-Blue Angel (Lord Gayle (USA)) **1995:** *4441$^{6}$ 4536$^{3}$* **1996:** *42$^{3}$ 121$^{12}$ 178$^{2}$ 270$^{4}$ 338$^{4}$ (893)* 1186$^{15}$ (1466) 1853$^{5}$ (2437) 2623$^{9}$ 3127$^{8}$ (3599) 4314$^{19}$ 4444$^{14}$ **>70a 97f<**

**Pay Homage 8** ch g Primo Dominie-Embraceable Slew (USA) (Seattle Slew (USA)) *879$^{13}$* 1330$^{4}$ 1819$^{6}$ 2010$^{10}$ 2312$^{5}$ 2525$^{3}$ 3161$^{13}$ 3786$^{2}$ 4125$^{5}$ 4381$^{3}$ **>82f<**

**Paying Dues (USA) 4** ch g Cure The Blues (USA)-Far Too Young (Young Generation) *4951a$^{2}$* **>131a f<**

**Pay Me Back (IRE) 6** ch h Master Willie-Princess Reema (USA) (Affirmed (USA)) *1579a$^{3}$* 2111a$^{4}$ 3917a$^{2}$ **>118f<**

**Pc's Cruiser (IRE) 4** b g Homo Sapien-Ivy Holme (Silly Season) *159$^{3}$ 219$^{8}$ 239$^{5}$ 353$^{9}$ 521$^{4}$ 662$^{2}$* 1088$^{2}$ 1538$^{15}$ 1789$^{5}$ *1966$^{4}$ 2369$^{3}$ 2868$^{13}$ 3089$^{9}$ (3603) 3958$^{10}$ 4089$^{6}$ 4906$^{4}$ 4982$^{4}$* **>54a 41f<**

**Peacefull Reply (USA) 6** b h Hold Your Peace (USA)-Drone Answer (USA) (Drone) **1995:** *4406$^{3}$ 4444$^{8}$* **1996:** *62$^{8}$ 124$^{9}$ 518$^{2}$ 776$^{9}$ 1029$^{10}$ 1162$^{8}$* 2075$^{9}$ *2550$^{10}$ 2929$^{8}$* 4436$^{11}$ 4503$^{9}$ **>49da 31f<**

**Peace House (IRE) 3** ch f Magical Strike (USA)-Theda (Mummy's Pet) 467$^{12}$ 648$^{16}$ 786$^{12}$ 1500$^{16}$

**Peace Melody (IRE) 2** b f Classic Music (USA)-Manntika (Kalamoun) 4159a$^{9}$ **>81f<**

**Peace Offering (IRE) 3** b f Fairy King (USA)-Commanche Belle (Shirley Heights) 1249a$^{3}$ **>95f< (DEAD)**

**Peace Prize (IRE) 3** ch c Polish Precedent (USA)-Sizes Vary (Be My Guest (USA)) 3731a$^{3}$ 4396a$^{5}$ **>118f<**

**Pearl Anniversary (IRE) 3** ch g Priolo (USA)-Tony Award (USA) (Kirtling) 822$^{6}$ *(899) 1167$^{9}$ 1444$^{4}$ (1605) 1814$^{2}$ 2204$^{5}$ 2322$^{4}$ 3104$^{5}$ 3422$^{2}$ 3872$^{3}$ 4080$^{2}$ 4332$^{5}$* **>65a 50f<**

**Pearl Dawn (IRE) 6** b m Jareer (USA)-Spy Girl (Tanfirion) **1995:** *4359$^{5}$* **1996:** *163$^{9}$ 203$^{7}$ 278$^{10}$ 2017$^{2}$* 2129$^{9}$ 2311$^{5}$ 2403$^{4}$ 2763$^{5}$ (2766) 2981$^{5}$ 3139$^{8}$ 3285$^{4}$ 4428$^{7}$ 4692$^{4}$ 4701$^{9}$ 4799$^{9}$ **>41a 61f<**

**Pearl d'Azur (USA) 3** b c Dayjur (USA)-Priceless Pearl (USA) (Alydar (USA)) 2011$^{3}$ *(3064) (3406)* 3946$^{5}$ 4687$^{13}$ **>82a 92df<**

**Pearls of Thought (IRE) 3** b f Persian Bold-Miss Loving (Northfields (USA)) *473$^{8}$* 5391$^{3}$ 885$^{6}$ 1041$^{10}$ **>33f<**

**Pearl Venture 4** b f Salse (USA)-Our Shirley (Shirley Heights) 455$^{21}$ 809$^{7}$ 953$^{6}$ 1322$^{10}$ 1875$^{2}$ 2190$^{2}$ (2547) 3266$^{9}$ 3504$^{5}$ 4260$^{4}$ 4447$^{7}$ 4821$^{9}$ 4965$^{10}$ **>83f<**

**Peartree House (IRE) 2** b c Simply Majestic (USA)-Fashion Front (Habitat) 1897$^{4}$ (2153) 2575$^{4}$ (3307) 4131$^{6}$ **>83f<**

**Peckinpah's Soul (FR) 4** b c Zino-Nashra (Brustolon) *4852a$^{3}$* 5030a$^{3}$ **>118f<**

**Peco's Bill (IRE) 4** b c Royal Academy (USA)-Vernon Hills (Hard Fought) **1995:** 4401a$^{3}$ **>79f<**

**Pedaltothemetal (IRE) 4** b f Nordico (USA)-Full Choke (Shirley Heights) *360$^{2}$ 1098$^{6}$ 1618$^{7}$* 1679$^{B}$ 1981$^{4}$ 2560$^{2}$ 2848$^{5}$ 2973$^{8}$ **>51a 55df<**

**Peep O Day 5** b m Domynsky-Betrothed (Aglojo) *3391$^{0}$ 4344$^{4}$* 4812$^{18}$ (5007) **>48f<**

**Peetsie (IRE) 4** b f Fairy King (USA)-Burning Ambition (Troy) 1117$^{8}$ 1461$^{6}$ **>60f<**

**Peggy Ess 3** b f Seymour Hicks (FR)-Daffodil (Welsh Pageant) *2380$^{7}$* 2891$^{17}$ 5052$^{11}$ **>3f<**

**Peggy Spencer 4** ch f Formidable (USA)-Careful Dancer (Gorytus (USA)) **1995:** *(4407) (4450) 4478$^{2}$* **1996:** *44$^{2}$ 77$^{12}$ (270) 357$^{4}$ 480$^{4}$* 1001$^{16}$ **>72a 61f<**

**Pegram (IRE) 3** b c Cadeaux Genereux-Pertinent (Persepolis (FR)) 696$^{4}$ 942$^{5}$ **>68f<**

**Pegwood (IRE) 3** gr f High Estate-Spindle Berry (Dance In Time (CAN)) 1246a$^{4}$ 2102a$^{6}$ **>88f<**

**Peintre Celebre (USA) 2** ch c Nureyev (USA)-Peinture Bleue (USA) (Alydar (USA)) 4166a$^{3}$ **>90f<**

**Pelham (IRE) 2** b c Archway (IRE)-Yavarro (Raga Navarro (ITY)) 706$^{9}$ (865) 1303$^{2}$ 1795$^{4}$ (2210) 2877$^{5}$ 3321$^{2}$ 4024a$^{3}$ 4369$^{3}$ 4723$^{8}$ **>96f<**

**Penbola (IRE) 4** b g Pennine Walk-Sciambola (Great Nephew) 625$^{16}$ **>40a 27f<**

**Pendley Rose 3** ch f Prince Sabo-Rose Bouquet (General Assembly (USA)) 739$^{6}$ 2743$^{11}$ 3165$^{11}$ 3583$^{5}$ 3863$^{4}$ 4075$^{13}$ 4259$^{8}$ **>45a 49f<**

**Pendolino (IRE) 5** b g Thatching-Pendulina (Prince Tenderfoot (USA)) 1977$^{8}$ 2077$^{4}$ 2183$^{6}$ 2390$^{4}$ 3117$^{4}$ **>48f<**

**Pengamon 4** b c Efisio-Dolly Bevan (Another Realm) **1995:** *4367$^{12}$ 4435$^{4}$ 4539$^{12}$* **1996:** *20$^{3}$ 270$^{7}$ (379) 455$^{16}$* 600$^{2}$ 809$^{5}$ 1018$^{6}$ 1425$^{2}$ 2053$^{24}$ **>85a 96df<**

**Penlop 2** b c Mac's Imp (USA)-Marton Maid (Silly Season) 2580$^{11}$ 3259$^{5}$ 4253$^{11}$ **>68f<**

**Penmar 4** b g Reprimand-Latakia (Morston (FR)) **1995:** *4432$^{7}$* **1996:** *1085$^{5}$ (1457) 1811$^{5}$ 2304$^{8}$ 2372$^{4}$ 2631$^{5}$ 3603$^{9}$ 4575$^{5}$* **>66a 61f<**

**Pennine Ridge (USA) 5** b h Cure The Blues (USA)-La Rouquine (Silly Season) (3906a) **>108f<**

**Pennine Wind (IRE) 4** b g Pennine Walk-Wintina (Tumble Wind (USA)) 546$^{17}$ 1640$^{14}$ 2127$^{8}$ 2284$^{8}$ 2482$^{7}$ 3586$^{6}$ **>60a 52f<**

**Penny a Day (IRE) 6** b g Supreme Leader-Mursuma (Rarity) 456$^{3}$ 564$^{4}$ 4872$^{12}$ 5046$^{21}$ **>102f<**

**Penny Drops 7** b m Sharpo-Darine (Nonoalco (USA)) 442$^{4}$ 623a$^{4}$ 3905a$^{6}$ **>115f<**

**Penny Parkes 3** ch f Clantime-Bonne Baiser (Most Secret) *769$^{5}$* 973$^{9}$ 1634$^{3}$ 1859$^{9}$ (2359) (2492) 2800$^{10}$ *3061$^{5}$ 3957$^{12}$* 4045$^{W}$ **>39a 60df<**

**Penny Peppermint 4** b br f Move Off-Cheeky Pigeon (Brave Invader (USA)) 2922$^{6}$ 3309$^{9}$ 3865$^{6}$ 4321$^{14}$ **>35f<**

**Pennys From Heaven 2** gr c Generous (IRE)-Heavenly Cause (USA) (Grey Dawn II) 3221$^{8}$ 3682$^{4}$ 4370$^{3}$ **>85f<**

**Penny's Wishing 4** b f Clantime-Lady Pennington (Blue Cashmere) *480$^{16}$* 592$^{11}$ 704$^{3}$ 868$^{14}$ 997$^{3}$ 1364$^{13}$ 1635$^{10}$ 1859$^{11}$ 2185$^{18}$ *5059$^{12}$* **>19a 19f<**

**Pennywell 2** b f Nicholas (USA)-Fee (Mandamus) 4890$^{W}$

**Penprio (IRE) 2** b c Priolo (USA)-Pennine Mist (IRE) (Pennine Walk) 3941$^{4}$ **>64f< (DEAD)**

**Pension Fund 2** b g Emperor Fountain-Navarino Bay (Averof) 1086$^{10}$ 1344$^{5}$ 1827$^{12}$ (2625) 3483$^{3}$ (3674) 3835$^{6}$ **>76f<**

**Pentire 4** b c Be My Guest (USA)-Gull Nook (Mill Reef (USA)) *536a$^{4}$ 2546$^{3}$* (3070) 4295a$^{2}$ 4662a$^{10}$ **>122a 132+f<**

**Penygarn Guv'nor 3** b g Governor General-Alumia (Great Nephew) 703$^{8}$ 1035$^{5}$ *1456$^{4}$* **>45a 58f<**

**People Direct 3** ch f Ron's Victory (USA)-Ayr Classic (Local Suitor (USA)) **1995:** *4393$^{4}$ (4477) 4528$^{6}$* **1996:** *(46) 89$^{3}$ (258) 281$^{2}$ (404) 654$^{6}$ (781) 859$^{3}$ 1027$^{2}$ 1490$^{6}$ 1993$^{7}$ 2402$^{6}$ (3951) 4077$^{3}$ 4781$^{4}$ 4982$^{14}$* **>70a 43f<**

**Pepitist 5** b g Bold Owl-Misoptimist (Blakeney) 1977$^{7}$ 2482$^{4}$ 2628$^{4}$ 2871$^{2}$ 3428$^{5}$ **>48f<**

**Peppers (IRE) 3** b f Bluebird (USA)-Pepilin (Coquelin (USA)) 4513$^{7}$ 4866$^{14}$ 4968$^{2}$ *5056$^{6}$* **>49a 74f<**

**Peppito (GER) 3** c 1395a$^{4}$ 4659a$^{6}$ **>86f<**

**Pep Talk (USA) 3** ch c Lyphard (USA)-Peplum (USA) (Nijinsky (CAN)) 994$^{5}$ 1174$^{3}$ 3818$^{2}$ 3942$^{3}$ 4622$^{4}$ **>79f<**

**Perang Polly 4** br f Green Ruby (USA)-Perang Peggy (Bay Express) 4865$^{4}$ **>64f<**

**Perchance To Dream (IRE) 2** b f Bluebird (USA)-Foliage (Thatching) 2852$^{12}$ 3593$^{15}$ 4475$^{7}$ **>58f<**

**Perche No (FR) 4** dk c Akarad (FR)-Dancing Star

**1995:** (4426a) **>114f<**

**Percussion Bird 4** b f Bold Owl-Cymbal (Ribero) *$105^{12}$ $186^{17}$* **>8a 42tf<**

**Percutant 5** br h Perrault-Estada (FR) (Luthier) *(907a)* $1390a^{3}$ $1947a^{4}$ $3749a^{3}$ $3915a^{3}$ $4656a^{2}$ $4856a^{4}$ **>124f<**

**Percy Braithwaite (IRE) 4** b g Kahyasi-Nasseem (FR) (Zeddaan) $580^{18}$ $802^{2}$ $1069^{9}$ $2010^{4}$ $2145^{5}$ $2483^{5}$ (2901) $3073^{7}$ **>90f<**

**Percy Isle (IRE) 2** br c Doyoun-Percy's Girl (IRE) (Blakeney) $4492^{7}$ $4801^{3}$ $5041^{3}$ **>77f<**

**Percy Park (USA) 3** br g Rajab (USA)-Clayton's Miss (USA) (Distinctive (USA)) $638^{16}$ $775^{16}$ $1196^{20}$ $1500^{5}$ $1846^{4}$ $2163^{4}$ $3151^{9}$ **>42f<**

**Percy Parrot 4** b g Lochnager-Soltago (Touching Wood (USA)) **1995:** *$4372^{9}$ $4409^{14}$* **1996:** *$738^{11}$* $883^{11}$ $999^{12}$ (1665) $1830^{3}$ $2075^{14}$ $2428^{6}$ $2567^{5}$ $2868^{2}$ $3120^{10}$ $3358^{9}$ $3460^{2}$ **>39a 53f<**

**Perfect Angel (IRE) 2** b f Maledetto (IRE)-Blue Infanta (Chief Singer) $4104^{10}$ $4242^{15}$ $4570^{13}$ $4990^{15}$ **>42f<**

**Perfect Arc (USA) 4** b f Brown Arc (USA)-Podeica (USA) (Petronisi (USA)) $3907a^{2}$ **>116f<**

**Perfect Bear 2** b g Wing Park-Sarah Bear (Mansingh (USA)) $2364^{5}$ **>35f<**

**Perfect Bliss 2** ch f Superlative-Nikatino (Bustino) $481^{3}$ $1404^{6}$ *$1813^{3}$ $2750^{4}$ (3082)* (3275) $3467^{2}$ (3523) (3577) (3771) $3971^{5}$ $4113^{12}$ **>52a 72f<**

**Perfect Brave 5** b g Indian Ridge-Perfect Timing (Comedy Star (USA)) **1995:** *$4359^{3}$ $4421^{12}$* **1996:** *$418^{7}$ $607^{2}$ $900^{2}$ $1161^{6}$ $1492^{2}$ $2349^{7}$* $5039^{17}$ **>79a 57f<**

**Perfect Gift 3** ch f Generous (IRE)-Knight's Baroness (Rainbow Quest (USA)) *$1061^{6}$* $1600^{2}$ $2424^{5}$ $2762^{3}$ $3337^{4}$ $3667^{3}$ $4086^{9}$ $4496^{16}$ **>63f<**

**Perfect Paradigm (IRE) 2** b c Alzao (USA)-Brilleaux (Manado) $4261^{8}$ $4585^{2}$ $4801^{2}$ **>78f<**

**Perfect Poppy 2** b f Shareef Dancer (USA)-Benazir (High Top) $4225^{3}$ $5040^{4}$ **>74f<**

**Pericles 2** b c Primo Dominie-Egalite (FR) (Luthier) $3080^{2}$ $3647^{3}$ $3848^{2}$ *(4079) $4364^{6}$* $4883^{4}$ **>77a 74f<**

**Perilous Plight 5** ch g Siberian Express (USA)-Loveskate (USA) (Overskate (CAN)) **1995:** *$4357^{5}$ $4440^{4}$* **1996:** *$65^{2}$ $105^{4}$ $144^{3}$ $216^{6}$ (295) $311^{4}$ (1010)* $1302^{16}$ $1532^{4}$ $1659^{4}$ *$1993^{2}$ (2178)* $2438^{3}$ $2763^{8}$ $3217^{2}$ (3410) $3650^{3}$ $3867^{3}$ $4098^{5}$ $4831^{14}$ *$5002^{3}$* **>77a 70f<**

**Permission 2** b f Rudimentary (USA)-Ask Mama (Mummy's Pet) $1346^{4}$ $3820^{4}$ $3988^{11}$ $4433^{10}$ $4564^{4}$ $4696^{5}$ **>69f<**

**Perpetual 2** ch f Prince Sabo-Brilliant Timing (USA) (The Minstrel (CAN)) $2076^{8}$ $2343^{4}$ $2491^{3}$ $2875^{6}$ *(3087) $3511^{2}$* (3823) $3924^{2}$ (3975) $4247^{6}$ $4425^{3}$ **>58a 71f<**

**Perpetual Hope 3** b f Dowsing (USA)-Woodfold (Saritamer (USA)) $4108^{13}$ $4422^{9}$ $4690^{11}$ **>43f<**

**Perpetual Light 3** b f Petoski-Butosky (Busted) $705^{6}$ *(856) $1487^{10}$ (2081) $2486^{7}$* $3845^{9}$ $4071^{10}$ $4968^{8}$ **>74a 62f<**

**Perryston View 4** b c Primo Dominie-Eastern Ember (Indian King (USA)) $928^{3}$ $1186^{16}$ $2694^{17}$ $3296^{4}$ $3622^{7}$ $4116^{14}$ $4505^{11}$ **>91f<**

**Perseo (ITY) 3** b c Jung-Persian Dream (Persian Bold) $1058a^{3}$ **>81f<**

**Persephone 3** ch f Lycius (USA)-Elarrih (USA) (Sharpen Up) $870^{11}$ $1174^{11}$ $1696^{10}$ $2016^{8}$ $2130^{2}$ $2340^{8}$ *$2937^{12}$ $3138^{6}$* $3456^{11}$ **>53f<**

**Persian Affair (IRE) 5** b g Persian Heights-Lady Chesterfield (USA) (In Reality) *$843^{10}$* $887^{6}$ $1074^{12}$ $1533^{10}$ (1953) $2127^{9}$ $2577^{13}$ **>79a 68f< (DEAD)**

**Persian Blue 2** b f Persian Bold-Swift Pursuit (Posse (USA)) $4105^{11}$ **>34f<**

**Persian Bud (IRE) 8** b or br g Persian Bold-Awakening Rose (Le Levanstell) *$5053^{13}$* ***>27a 43?f<***

**Persian Butterfly 4** b f Dancing Dissident (USA)-Butterfly Kiss (Beldale Flutter (USA)) $648^{4}$ $1178^{9}$ $2034^{5}$ $2376^{7}$ $2617^{18}$ $3112^{10}$ $3168^{10}$ $3825^{7}$ $4186^{18}$ **>66f<**

**Persian Conquest (IRE) 4** b g Don't Forget Me-Alaroos (IRE) (Persian Bold) $1173^{8}$ $1618^{14}$ $3470^{11}$ $3785^{19}$ $4669^{15}$ *(4998)* **>84a 55df<**

**Persian Dawn 3** br f Anshan-Visible Form (Formidable (USA)) $1857^{12}$ $3258^{9}$ $4186^{13}$ $4341^{11}$ $4674^{7}$ **>58f<**

**Persian Elite (IRE) 5** ch g Persian Heights-Late Sally (Sallust) $3828^{11}$ $4320^{8}$ **>59f<**

**Persian Fayre 4** b g Persian Heights-Dominion Fayre (Dominion) *$827^{6}$* $1018^{2}$ $1313^{2}$ $1586^{2}$ $1703^{11}$ $3279^{3}$ (3833) $4054^{4}$ $4316^{7}$ (4688) (4975) **>89f<**

**Persian Flower 4** b f Persian Heights-Edraianthus (Windjammer (USA)) **1995:** *$4364^{13}$ $4406^{8}$ $4444^{6}$* **>47a 56f<**

**Persian Gusher (IRE) 6** gr g King Persian-Magnanimous (Runnymede) *$135^{8}$ $207^{9}$ $273^{8}$* **>36a 22f<**

**Persian Haze (IRE) 7** ch g Bold Arrangement-Crufty Wood (Sweet Revenge) **1995:** *$4475^{8}$* **1996:** *$15^{12}$ $83^{14}$ $489^{5}$* **>26a f<**

**Persian Punch (IRE) 3** ch g Persian Heights-Rum Cay (USA) (Our Native (USA)) (1104) (1854) $2054^{3}$ (2620) $3157^{3}$ $4569^{3}$ **>115f<**

**Persian Secret (FR) 3** b f Persian Heights-Rahaam (USA) (Secreto (USA)) $1187^{5}$ **>87f<**

**Persian Smoke 5** b m Persian Bold-Gauloise (Welsh Pageant) (1044) $1150^{5}$ $1826^{7}$ $2511^{10}$ **>48f<**

**Persian Symphony (IRE) 5** ch m Persian Heights-River Serenade (USA) (Riverman (USA)) *$2565^{5}$ $2936^{10}$* **>12a 36f<**

**Personal Love (USA) 3** b f Diesis-Personal Glory (USA) (Danzig (USA)) $1060a^{7}$ (3752a) $4378^{5}$ **>108f<**

**Personimus 6** b g Ballacashtal (CAN)-Sea Charm (Julio Mariner) *$30^{2}$ $884^{2}$ $1098^{3}$ $1418^{11}$* $1633^{3}$ $2177^{5}$ **>46a 44f<**

**Persuasion 3** b f Batshoof-Primetta (Precocious) $4827^{7}$ **>55f<**

**Pertemps Flyer 5** b g Presidium-Brilliant Future (Welsh Saint) **1995:** *$4436^{6}$ $4527^{7}$* **>46a 56df<**

**Pertemps Mission 2** b c Safawan-Heresheis (Free State) $3982^{14}$ $4175^{6}$ $4585^{7}$ **>84f<**

**Peruke (IRE) 5** ch m Thatching-Really Sharp (Sharpen Up) $3562a^{8}$ **>22f<**

**Petarina 3** gr f Petong-Katharina (Frankincense) $1422^{6}$ $1787^{5}$ $2572^{11}$ *$3091^{10}$ $3331^{9}$* $3624^{9}$ $4075^{11}$ *$5058^{11}$* **>23a 43df<**

**Peter Monamy 4** ch g Prince Sabo-Revisit (Busted) $1772^{4}$ **>40a 56f<**

**Peter Perfect 2** gr c Chilibang-Misdevious (USA) (Alleged (USA)) $4233^{12}$ $4494^{13}$ $4786^{7}$ **>51f<**

**Peter Quince 6** b h Kris-Our Reverie (USA) (J O Tobin (USA)) $2131^{9}$ $2690^{9}$ **>35f<**

**Peterrex 3** b g Interrex (CAN)-Standard Rose (Ile de Bourbon (USA)) **1995:** *$4518^{11}$* **1996:** *$11^{7}$ $40^{5}$* **>22a 53f<**

**Peters Folly 3** b f King Among Kings-Santo Star (Monsanto (FR)) *$21^{8}$* **>40a 40f<**

**Pet Express 2** b g Petoski-Hush it Up (Tina's Pet) *$2083^{9}$*

**Petite Annie 3** b f Statoblest-Kuwait Night (Morston (FR)) **1995:** *$4417^{10}$* **1996:** *$131^{9}$ $281^{8}$ $1122^{11}$* $1516^{8}$ **>36a 70df<**

**Petite Danseuse 2** b f Aragon-Let Her Dance (USA) (Sovereign Dancer (USA)) $815^{5}$ (1062) (1318) $1673^{4}$ $2726^{7}$ $2965^{6}$ $3160^{7}$ $3321^{3}$ $3687^{3}$ $4195^{2}$ $4350^{3}$ $4546^{2}$ $4717^{4}$ $4880^{2}$ $4916^{9}$ **>82f<**

**Petite Fantasy 4** b f Mansooj-Ride Bold (USA) (J O Tobin (USA)) $1566a^{4}$ **>107f<**

**Petite Heritiere 3** b f Last Tycoon-Arianna Aldini (Habitat) $595^{9}$ $914^{8}$ *$2081^{15}$ $3583^{9}$* $3881^{9}$ $4898^{16}$ $4921^{5}$ **>27a 42f<**

**Petite Juliette 3** b f Salse (USA)-Cascade (Shirley Heights) **1995:** *$4393^{7}$* **>15a 70f<**

**Petite Princess (USA) 2** b f Dayjur (USA)-Classy Women $2834a^{3}$ $4639a^{10}$ **>90f<**

**Petite Risk 2** ch f Risk Me (FR)-Technology (FR) (Top Ville) $2781^{10}$ $2926^{12}$ $3082^{10}$ **>22f<**

**Petit Flora 4** b f Lord Bud-Pretty Soon (Tina's Pet) $2515^{6}$ $2572^{12}$ $2794^{9}$ $3580^{10}$ **>38f<**

**Petitjean (IRE) 5** b g Last Tycoon-Working Model (Ile de Bourbon (USA)) **1995:** *$4513^{11}$* **>7a 36f< (DEAD)**

**Petit Point (IRE) 3** b f Petorius-Minnie Tudor (Tudor Melody) $678^{13}$ $949^{2}$ $1181^{4}$ (1840) $1991^{9}$ $2705^{8}$ $3112^{5}$ **>76df<**

**Petoskin 4** b g Petoski-Farcical (Pharly (FR)) *$379^{7}$ $450^{17}$* $650^{7}$ $844^{8}$ $2131^{7}$ $2921^{4}$ $4515^{5}$ $4763^{11}$ (4815) $5053^{16}$ **>72a 64f<**

**Petraco (IRE) 8** b g Petorius-Merrie Moira (Bold Lad (IRE)) *$601^{3}$* $667^{3}$ $762^{4}$ $806^{12}$ $1307^{9}$ $1412^{10}$ $1844^{4}$ $2029^{7}$ $2286^{5}$ $2745^{6}$ $3216^{9}$ $3698^{3}$ $3851^{5}$ (4045) $4215^{8}$ $4356^{10}$ $4881^{16}$ **>64a 66f<**

**Petrel 2** gr f Petong-Brise de Mer (USA) (Bering) $2195^{9}$ $3454^{6}$ $3873^{5}$ $4182^{5}$ $4883^{11}$ **>66f<**

**Petrico 4** b c Petong-Balearica (Bustino) **1995:** *$4372^{12}$* **>4a 13f<**

**Petrine Gray 2** gr f St Ninian-Nellie Bly (Dragonara Palace (USA)) $1183^{5}$ $2512^{4}$ $3448^{4}$ $3840^{5}$ *$4093^{13}$ $4562^{13}$* $4594^{7}$ **>5a 51f<**

**Petrolio (IRE) 3** b c Scenic-Petrolea Girl (Connaught) $671^{W}$

**Petros Pride 3** b f Safawan-Hala (Persian Bold) *$863^{14}$* $4124^{8}$ $4353^{5}$ $4603^{8}$ $5052^{5}$ **>50f<**

**Petsong 2** b br c Petong-Petriece (Mummy's Pet) $4514^{15}$ **>44f<**

**Petula Boy 2** gr g Nicholas (USA)-Tulapet (Mansingh (USA)) $706^{6}$ $950^{7}$ *$1489^{7}$ $2370^{7}$ $2967^{12}$* ***>21a 54f<***

**Peutetre 4** ch c Niniski (USA)-Marchinella (Daring March) $3457^{10}$ $3653^{10}$ *$3951^{10}$ $4355^{15}$* ***>22a 34f<***

**P Grayco Choice 3** b f Bold Fox-Unjha (Grey Desire) *$376^{7}$ $409^{10}$ $502^{10}$ $635^{16}$* ***>19a f<***

**P G Tips (IRE) 5** ch g Don't Forget Me-Amenaide (Known Fact (USA)) *$136^{12}$ $2082^{P}$* **>56a 81f<**

**Phanan 10** ch g Pharly (FR)-L'Ecossaise (Dancers Image (USA)) **1995:** *$4434^{6}$ $4465^{7}$ $4513^{9}$ $4526^{8}$* **1996:** *$72^{5}$ $152^{7}$ $279^{7}$ $3149^{11}$* $3944^{9}$ **>33a 56f<**

**Phantom Dancer (IRE) 3** b g Distinctly North (USA)-Angel of Music (Burslem) $540^{7}$ $586^{15}$ $784^{2}$ *$1457^{10}$ $1762^{3}$* $2024^{7}$ **>28a 58f<**

**Phantom Gold 4** b f Machiavellian (USA)-Trying for Gold (USA) (Northern Baby (CAN)) *$1509^{9}$* $2113^{5}$ $2533^{2}$ $3203a^{5}$ (3614) **>121f<**

**Phantom Haze 3** gr g Absalom-Caroline Lamb (Hotfoot) $614^{3}$ $1089^{15}$ $2027^{2}$ $2397^{3}$ $2895^{3}$ $3492^{7}$ **>71f<**

**Phantom Quest 3** b c Rainbow Quest (USA)-Illusory (Kings Lake (USA)) $732^{4}$ (942) $1574a^{6}$ $2774^{2}$ $3153^{3}$ $3503^{2}$ (4325) $4520^{4}$ **>110f<**

**Pharaoh's Dancer 9** b g Fairy King (USA)-Marie Louise (King Emperor (USA)) **1995:** *$4350^{6}$ $4441^{11}$* **1996:** *$127^{11}$* **>58a 74f<**

**Pharaoh's Joy 3** b f Robellino (USA)-Joyce's Best (Tolomeo) $525^{21}$ $686^{14}$ $1840^{10}$ (2238) $2571^{5}$ $2999^{3}$ (3360) $3993^{4}$ $4246^{16}$ $4610^{12}$ **>66f<**

**Phar Closer 3** br f Phardante (FR)-Forever Together (Hawaiian Return (USA)) $588^{3}$ $849^{11}$ $885^{8}$ $1359^{14}$ $1503^{2}$ $1548^{7}$ $1636^{3}$ $2388^{5}$ $2848^{9}$ $2928^{3}$ $3775^{6}$ **>35f<**

**Pharly Dancer 7** b g Pharly (FR)-Martin-Lavell Mail (Dominion) **1995:** *4411[8]* **1996:** *98[3] 235[3] 284[2] 401[3] 1544[2]* 1763[3] *(1967) (2394)* (2494) 3309[3] 4483[9] 4596[5] 4763[6] *(4977)* **>83?a 64f<**

**Pharly Reef 4** b g Pharly (FR)-Hay Reef (Mill Reef (USA)) **1995:** *4366[10] 4510[12]* **1996:** *510[5]* **>21a 63f<**

**Pharmacy 3** b f Mtoto-Anodyne (Dominion) 987[3] 2328[11] 2773[4] 3154[7] 4312[19] 4688[4] (4909) **>80f<**

**Phase One (IRE) 6** b m Horage-Fayes Ben (Don) 508[9] 1423[5] 1778[4] 2240[4] 2592[7] **>26a 58f<**

**Philgem 3** b f Precocious-Andalucia (Rheingold) *826[11]* 998[6] 1311[5] 2753[5] 3427[8] 3619[5] 3882[6] 4249[17] 4317[6] 4474[7] 4752[9] *4892[8]* **>36f<**

**Philgun 7** b g K-Battery-Andalucia (Rheingold) *2008[7]* 2487[6] 2989[F] **>64a 56f< (DEAD)**

**Philidor 7** b h Forzando-Philgwyn (Milford) (1944a) **>99f<**

**Philip's Glorie (BEL) 5** b m Saint-Philippe (BEL)-Gardegan **1995:** 4467a[3]

**Philistar 3** ch c Baim (USA)-Philgwyn (Milford) 1121[7] 1420[5] 1773[10] *2201[5] (2689) 3063[3] 3627[11]* **>75a 69f<**

**Philmist 4** b f Hard Fought-Andalucia (Rheingold) **1995:** *4387[3]* **1996:** *333[3] 367[2] 422[8] 542[5]* 620[4] 1022[2] *(1487) 1637[2]* 2066[5] 2565[2] 2871[4] 4302[11] **>56a 57f<**

**Philosopher (IRE) 3** b c Royal Academy (USA)-Flyaway Bride (USA) (Blushing Groom (FR)) 566[3] 970[4] 1593[4] 1819[9] 2687[4] 4124[5] **>83f<**

**Philosophic 2** b g Be My Chief (USA)-Metaphysique (FR) (Law Society (USA)) 2184[5] 3631[5] 3837[13] 4106[7] **>49f<**

**Phoenix House 3** ch c Formidable (USA)-Ladysave (Stanford) **1995:** *4360[7]* **>38a 66f<**

**Phone Fee (USA) 3** 1581a[6] **>103f<**

**Phonetic 3** b g Shavian-So True (So Blessed) 894[13] 1438[3] 2557[5] 3516[4] 4064[19] 4824[5] **>80f<**

**Phylida 2** b f Mazilier (USA)-May the Fourteenth (Thatching) 3502[8] 3859[4] 4514[6] 4790[2] **>67f<**

**Pibarnon (FR) 6** h 1397a[6] **>105f<**

**Pickens (USA) 4** b g Theatrical-Alchi (USA) (Alleged (USA)) 682[10] 825[7] 993[14] 1436[4] (2922) 3130[5] **>65f<**

**Pierrot Solaire (FR) 3** ch c Dancing Spree (USA)-Mare Aux Fees (Kenmare (FR)) (793a) 1580a[9] **>83f<**

**Pietro Bembo (IRE) 2** b g Midyan (USA)-Cut No Ice (Great Nephew) 4253[6] 4383[5] 4544[8] (4721) **>67f<**

**Pigalle Wonder 8** br g Chief Singer-Hi-Tech Girl (Homeboy) **1995:** *4507[5]* **1996:** *62[9]* **>43a 35f<**

**Pigeon Hole 3** b f Green Desert (USA)-Cubby Hole (Town And Country) 768[8] 1033[7] 1532[8] **>54f<**

**Pike Creek (USA) 3** b f Alwasmi (USA)-Regal Heights (USA) (Forli (ARG)) (3315) 3711[9] 4176[4] 4447[10] 4673[10] **>91f<**

**Pillow Talk (IRE) 5** b m Taufan (USA)-Concave (Connaught) 2056[19] 2355[5] **>64a 46df<**

**Pilsudski (IRE) 4** b c Polish Precedent (USA)-Cocotte (Troy) 831[2] (1509) 2038[8] (3728a) (4040a) 4662a[2] (4955a) **>132f<**

**Pimsboy 9** b g Tender King-Hitopah (Bustino) *3480[5]* ***>40f<***

**Pinchincha (FR) 2** b g Priolo (USA)-Western Heights (Shirley Heights) 5041[9] **>41f<**

**Pine Essence (USA) 5** ch m Green Forest (USA)-Paradise Coffee (Sharpo) **1995:** *4420[5] 4532[6]* **1996:** *162[4] (301) 336[6] (426) 527[3]* 688[13] *2081[W]* **>59a 53f<**

**Pine Needle 3** ch f Kris-Fanny's Cove (Mill Reef (USA)) 788[3] (1361) 2131[5] 2547[5] (2998) **>90f<**

**Pine Ridge Lad (IRE) 6** gr g Taufan (USA)-Rosserk (Roan Rocket) **1995:** *(4388) 4503[2]* **1996:** *18[3] 86[2] (211) 331[2] (357) (505)* 713[7] (2672) 2962[2] 3254[5] 3815[3] 3995[16] 4688[16] 4793[18] **>85a 72f<**

**Ping-Pong Ball 3** b f Statoblest-Desert Ditty (Green Desert (USA)) *292[10] 430[8] 1761[12]*

***Pininfarina*** **2** b f Fairy King (USA)-Kaiserlinde (GER) (Frontal) 3114[9] **>23f<**

**Pinkerton Polka 4** b f Shareef Dancer (USA)-Holy Day (Sallust) *213[6] 297[9] 345[9] 636[3]* 787[10] 1022[9] 1691[12] 1903[9] 2284[12] 2481[4] *3074[5] 3414[10]* 4455[13] 4763[10] **>39a 52f<**

**Pinkerton's Pal 5** ch g Dominion-White Domino (Sharpen Up) *679[12]* 1018[11] 1330[8] 1476[9] 1793[11] 2674[6] **>85f<**

**Pink Petal 4** gr f Northern Game-Gratclo (Belfort (FR)) *2192[13]* 2716[11] **>27a 15f<**

**Pioneerhifidelity 3** gr f Handsome Sailor-Vico Equense (Absalom) 3108[4] 3847[2] **>63f<**

**Pipers Glen 4** ch g Domynsky-Linanhot (Hot Spark) 4249[16] **>40df<**

**Pip's Dream 5** b m Glint of Gold-Arabian Rose (USA) (Lyphard (USA)) **1995:** *4544[7]* **1996:** *23[5] 69[7] (546)* (612) 760[6] 866[9] 1514[3] 1640[3] 1852[9] 4967[10] 5007[10] **>25a 62df<**

**Pirate's Girl 2** b f Mtoto-Maritime Lady (USA) (Polish Navy (USA)) 3227[3] **>60f<**

**Pirongia 2** b f Wing Park-Gangawayhame (Lochnager) 4105[13] 4605[12] 4818[9] **>36f<**

**Pistol (IRE) 6** ch g Glenstal (USA)-First Wind (Windjammer (USA)) *469[12]* 879[18] 1124[6] 1337[12] 1996[2] (2409) (2736) (2953) 3205[2] (3479) 4067[5] **>84f<**

**Pistols At Dawn (USA) 6** b g Al Nasr (FR)-Cannon Run (USA) (Cannonade (USA)) **1995:** *4448[2] (4513)* **1996:** *15[8] 70[7] 235[4] 420[4]* **>71da 57f<**

**Pivotal 3** ch c Polar Falcon (USA)-Fearless Revival (Cozzene (USA)) (2115) 2622[6] (3708) **>128f<**

**Place de L'Opera 3** b f Sadler's Wells (USA)-Madame Dubois (Legend of France (USA)) 957[2] (1189) (1990) 2886[3] 4467[9] **>100f<**

**Plaisir d'Amour (IRE) 2** b f Danehill (USA)-Mira Adonde (USA) (Sharpen Up) 4446[4] 4593[2] 4751[4] **>66f<**

**Plan For Profit (IRE) 2** b c Polish Patriot (USA)-Wild Sable (IRE) (Kris) 699[5] 975[4] 1537[7] 2327[2] (2681) 2728[3] 3160[6] 3792[5] 4195[4] 4440[2] **>72f<**

**Platinum Plus 4** ch c Hadeer-Verchinina (Star Appeal) *3115[8]* 3479[5] *3952[9] 4334[5] 4702[11] 4894[6] 5008[14]* ***>40a 62f<***

**Playful Juliet (CAN) 8** b m Assert-Running Around (USA) (What A Pleasure (USA)) *2530[10]* ***>13f<***

**Playmaker 3** b g Primo Dominie-Salacious (Sallust) 1485[6] 1805[5] 2301[7] 3055[6] 3223[7] 3937[16] 3995[20] 4180[9] 4382[18] *4776[5] 4981[8]* **>42a 65f<**

**Play The Tune 3** b c Music Boy-Stepping Gaily (Gay Fandango (USA)) 648[14] 1617[13] 1709[11] 2427[9] **>50f<**

**Pleading 3** b c Never so Bold-Ask Mama (Mummy's Pet) (949) (1473) 2007[2] 2584[7] **>98f<**

**Pleasant Surprise 3** b g Cadeaux Genereux-Quiet Week-End (Town And Country) 1002[2] 1106[4] (1798) 2074[4] 2502[17] 3997[9] 4176[12] **>102f<**

**Please Suzanne 3** b f Cadeaux Genereux-Aquaglow (Caerleon (USA)) 708[8] (966) 2050[12] 2692[5] 2880[6] 3271[6] 4196[3] **>102f<**

**Pleasureland (IRE) 3** ch g Don't Forget Me-Elminya (IRE) (Sure Blade (USA)) 595[17] 2251[13] *2751[3] 3437[3] 3872[5] 4448[10]* ***>61a 54f<***

**Pleasure Time 3** ch c Clantime-First Experience (Le Johnstan) 773[3] 989[8] 1188[5] 1493[5] 1597[4] 1823[3] 2301[5] 2500[7] 3049[5] 3135[7] **>68f<**

**Pleasure Trick (USA) 5** br g Clever Trick (USA)-Pleasure Garden (USA) (Foolish Pleasure (USA)) 1860[7] 2573[8] 2868[6] 3120[7] 3578[7] 3974[5] 4906[10] *4989[4]* **>40a 45f<**

**Plein Gaz (FR) 3** ch c Lesotho (USA)-Gazzara (USA) (Irish River (FR)) **1995:** *4518[2]* **1996:** *10[5] 52[4]* **>75a f<**

**Plinth 5** b g Dowsing (USA)-Pedestal (High Line) *2574[18]* ***>62a 66f<***

**Plum First 6** b g Nomination-Plum Bold (Be My Guest (USA)) 507[2] 587[2] 659[4] 850[10] 1157[3] 1364[9] 1765[3] 1848[4] 2005[15] 2329[11] 2518[7] 4356[14] 4811[9] *4987[6]* **>47a 51f<**

**Plutarch Angel 2** b c King Among Kings-Heavenly Pet (Petong) 1583[8] 1869[6] 3779[5] 3982[W] 4224[6] 4347[8] **>61f<**

**Poddington 5** b g Crofthall-Bold Gift (Persian Bold) *(2706)* 4911[4] **>109f<**

**Poetic Dance (USA) 3** ch c Seattle Dancer (USA)-French Poem (USA) (Sharpen Up) 3788[6] 4047[6] 4474[8] **>69df<**

**Poetry (IRE) 3** gr f Treasure Kay-Silver Heart (Yankee Gold) *560[4]* 663[2] (1333) (1505) (2160) 2585[5] 3322[7] 3790[14] **>88df<**

**Poignant (IRE) 2** b g Priolo (USA)-Ah Ya Zein (Artaius (USA)) 2708[15] 2923[8] 3227[9] **>30f<**

**Pointe Fine (FR) 2** b f Homme de Loi (IRE)-Pointe Argentee (Pas de Seul) 3988[12] 4890[5] **>62f<**

**Pointelle 2** b f Sharpo-Clymene (Vitiges (FR)) 4969[22] **>47f<**

**Pointer 4** b g Reference Point-Greenhill Lass (Upper Case (USA)) *417[5] 508[15]* 664[4] 893[6] (1348) 1658[7] 1856[3] (2193) (2713) 2957[4] 3518[2] 3686[6] 3995[8] **>41a 64f<**

**Poker Princess 2** br f Waajib-Mory Kante (USA) (Icecapade (USA)) 2792[6] 3259[7] 3660[9] 4459[10] **>59f<**

**Polar Champ 3** b g Polar Falcon (USA)-Ceramic (USA) (Raja Baba (USA)) 1627[5] 1906[2] 2198[4] 2610[8] *3418[2] 3704[2]* (4099) 4487[8] **>91a 77f<**

**Polar Eclipse 3** ch c Polar Falcon (USA)-Princess Zepoli (Persepolis (FR)) 1151[4] 1573a[5] 2354[2] 2888[8] 3229[7] 4385[6] 4620[10] 4826[6] **>91f<**

**Polar Flight 2** br c Polar Falcon (USA)-Fine Honey (USA) (Drone) 4204[7] 4383[2] 4599[4] 4814[2] (5040) **>93f<**

**Polaris Flight (USA) 3** b c Northern Flagship (USA)-Anytimeatall (USA) (It's Freezing (USA)) **1995:** 4399a[3] **1996:** 695[3] 903a[9] 1757a[2] 2473a[2] 4293a[9] 4662a[F] **>118f< (DEAD)**

**Polarize 2** ch g Polar Falcon (USA)-Comhail (USA) (Nodouble (USA)) 4684[10] 4991[14] **>54f<**

**Polar Prince (IRE) 3** b c Distinctly North (USA)-Staff Approved (Teenoso (USA)) 709[2] 937[3] 1432[5] (1820) 2623[7] (3445) 3712[6] (4185) 4378[9] 4718[6] **>111f<**

**Polar Prospect 3** b g Polar Falcon (USA)-Littlemisstrouble (USA) (My Gallant (USA)) 1195[2] 1438[9] (1864) 2501[4] 2621[14] 3594[4] 3830[8] 3985[14] 4583[6] **>79f<**

**Polar Refrain 3** ch f Polar Falcon (USA)-Cut No Ice (Great Nephew) 473[2] 3352[8] 3525[7] 4045[3] 4259[3] 4598[10] 4860[4] *4981[9]* **>30a 61f<**

**Polar Spirit 3** ch f Polar Falcon (USA)-Spirit of India (Indian King (USA)) **1995:** *4373[2]* **>50a 68f<**

**Poliglote 4** b c Sadler's Wells (USA)-Alexandrie (USA) (Val de L'Orne (FR)) (1577a) (1947a) 2480a[3] 4040a[7] 4856a[2] **>121f<**

**Polinesso 3** b c Polish Precedent (USA)-Lypharita (FR) (Lightning (FR)) 445[2] (613) 1824[3] 2248[2] 2774[4] 3594[6] **>107f<**

**Polish Lady (IRE) 3** b f Posen (USA)-Dame Ross (Raga Navarro (ITY)) 445[9] 561[14] 2979[9] 3461[7] 3578[3] 3817[10] 4348[9] **>47f<**

**Polish Rhythm (IRE) 3** b f Polish Patriot (USA)-Clanjingle (Tumble Wind (USA)) 3262[6] 3446[8] 3949[5]

4550[14] 4819[7] **>68f<**
**Polish Romance (USA) 2** b f Danzig (USA)-Some Romance (USA) (Fappiano (USA)) 4570[4] 4756[5] **>80f<**
**Polish Saga 3** ch f Polish Patriot (USA)-Sagar (Habitat) 638[2] 973[11] 1500[10] *1809[10] 2417[7]* 3059[5] 3591[8] 3882[7] **>17a 47f<**
**Polish Spring (IRE) 3** ch f Polish Precedent (USA)-Diavolina (USA) (Lear Fan (USA)) 917[8] (1127) 2142[8] **>90f<**
**Polish Warrior (IRE) 2** ch c Polish Patriot (USA)-Opuntia (Rousillon (USA)) 3164[4] 3494[2] 3829[3] (4234) **>83f<**
**Polish Widow 3** b f Polish Precedent (USA)-Widows Walk (Habitat) 544[8] 678[11] 2334[3] 2855[9] **>76f<**
**Polli Pui 4** b f Puissance-Wing of Freedom (Troy) **1995:** *4413[11]* **1996:** *834[11] 983[6]* 1041[8] 1307[2] 1500[12] 1642[15] 1893[7] 3937[19] 4828[12] 4881[17] **>27a 42f<**
**Polly Golightly 3** ch f Weldnaas (USA)-Polly's Teahouse (Shack (USA)) 443[7] 989[4] 1064[11] 1652[5] 1823[7] 2222[4] 2715[3] 3112[4] 3323[7] 3652[3] 3863[3] 4058[12] 4205[9] 4606[12] **>66f<**
**Polly Peculiar 5** b m Squill (USA)-Pretty Pollyanna (General Assembly (USA)) **1995:** *4503[11]* **1996:** *553[3] 752[8]* 888[6] (3510) (4202) 4436[6] (4831) 5042[3] **>52a 73f<**
**Polo Kit (IRE) 5** b g Trempolino (USA)-Nikitina (Nijinsky (CAN)) 3948[12] 4199[11] **>55f<**
**Polonaise Prince (USA) 3** b c Alleged (USA)-La Polonaise (USA) (Danzig (USA)) 578[14] 3942[10] **>51f<**
**Polska (USA) 3** b f Danzig (USA)-Aquaba (USA) (Damascus (USA)) 3517[5] 4135[4] 4445[12] **>100f<**
**Poltarf (USA) 5** b h Alleged (USA)-La Polonaise (USA) (Danzig (USA)) 3597[6] 3934[7] 4434[3] 4569[6] 5035[2] **>103f<**
**Poly By Staufan (IRE) 3** b f Taufan (USA)-Ana Gabriella (USA) (Master Derby (USA)) **1995:** *4369[10] 4414[10]* **>27a 60f<**
**Polydamas 4** b c Last Tycoon-Graecia Magna (USA) (Private Account (USA)) *925[4]* 1109[2] 4465[16] 4675[2] 4716[10] **>93f<**
**Poly Dancer 2** b f Suave Dancer (USA)-Blink Naskra (USA) (Naskra (USA)) 2025[8] 2708[14] 2850[5] 3092[5] 4694[9] **>41f<**
**Polygueza (FR) 3** ch f Be My Guest (USA)-Polifontaine (FR) 4738a[12] **>77f<**
**Polykala (FR) 2** b f Kaldoun (FR)-Belle du Bresil (Akarad (FR)) 3566a[2] **>85f<**
**Poly Moon 2** b f Mujtahid (USA)-Ragged Moon (Raga Navarro (ITY)) 729[4] 823[3] 990[2] 2759[4] (2959) 3512[9] 3795[2] 3943[7] 4097[7] *4251[6] 4495[9]* 4562[7] *4780[11]* **>27a 65f<**
**Poly My Son (IRE) 3** ch c Be My Guest (USA)-Green Memory (USA) (Forli (ARG)) 447[10] 599[4] 849[5] (1067) 1317[W] 1514[2] 2196[8] 2975[P] **>64df<**
**Pommard (IRE) 3** b c Darshaan-Pont-Aven (Try My Best (USA)) 695[4] 4181[6] **>93f<**
**Pomona 3** b f Puissance-Plum Bold (Be My Guest (USA)) 710[15] 982[9] 1333[2] 3167[11] 3800[2] 4432[3] (4901) **>92f<**
**Pompier 3** ch c Be My Chief (USA)-Fire Risk (Thatch (USA)) *820[13]* 1153[4] **>60f<**
**Pontynyswen 8** b g Ballacashtal (CAN)-Tropingay (Cawston's Clown) *154[7] 512[4] 5062[6]* **>42a f<**
**Poplar Bluff (IRE) 4** b c Dowsing (USA)-Bleu Pale (FR) (El Gran Senor (USA)) 3573a[9] **>123f<**
**Poppy Carew (IRE) 4** b f Danehill (USA)-Why so Silent (Mill Reef (USA)) *581[5]* 831[7] 1017[4] 1509[5] 1988[5] 3409[4] 3711[6] (4063) 4290a[7] 4678[9] 5045[5] **>107f<**
**Poppy Dancer 2** b f Nalchik (USA)-Zoomar (Legend of France (USA)) *2371[8]* **>14a f<**
**Poppy My Love 3** ch f Clantime-Yankeedoodledancer (Mashhor Dancer (USA)) **1995:** *4369[6] 4433[13]* **1996:** *2970[5]* ***>37a 37f<***
**Porlock Castle 3** b g Thowra (FR)-Miss Melmore (Nishapour (FR)) 3505[9] 4201[10] 4827[14] **>55f<**
**Portelet 4** b f Night Shift (USA)-Noirmant (Dominion) 1113[15] 3618[8] (3827) 4119[3] 4220[3] (4505) 4679[17] 4772[4] 4869[13] **>53a 93f<**
**Portend 4** b g Komaite (USA)-Token of Truth (Record Token) *451[10]* 610[19] 716[4] 850[13] (1199) 1501[2] 1974[2] *2171[6] 2548[6]* 2694[13] 3783[3] 3933[7] 4198[17] 4687[15] **>79a 96f<**
**Portite Sophie 5** b m Doulab (USA)-Impropriety (Law Society (USA)) *609[6]* 1167[15] 2024[9] 2563[4] *(2636) 2937[10]* **>38a 34f<**
**Portolano (FR) 5** b g Reference Point-Kottna (USA) (Lyphard (USA)) 2891[9] **>38a 23f<**
**Porto Novo (FR) 3** gr c Highest Honor (FR) 4031a[3] **>102f<**
**Portuguese Lil 3** ch f Master Willie-Sabonis (USA) (The Minstrel (CAN)) 939[10] 1324[5] 1791[20] 3255[3] 3640[9] 3830[9] **>75f<**
**Poseidon 2** b c Polar Falcon (USA)-Nastassia (FR) (Noble Decree (USA)) (4407a)
**Posen Gold (IRE) 3** b f Posen (USA)-Golden Sunlight (Ile de Bourbon (USA)) **1995:** *4443[4]* **1996:** *11[2] (40)* **>62a 61f<**
**Posidonas 4** b c Slip Anchor-Tamassos (Dance In Time (CAN)) 1176[3] 2113[3] (2583) 3203a[2] 3614[2] 4397a[4] 4652a[10] **>129f<**
**Possessive Artiste 3** b f Shareef Dancer (USA)-Possessive (Posse (USA)) 1438[4] 1714[4] 2706[4] 2980[4] 3522[3] (4110) **>75f<**
**Poteen (USA) 2** b c Irish River (FR)-Chaleur (CAN) (Rouge Sang (USA)) *(4578)* 4871[2] **>110f<**
**Pourquoi Pas (IRE) 4** b f Nordico (USA)-Mystery Lady **1995:** 4403a[10] **>101f<**
**Powder River 2** b c Alzao (USA)-Nest (Sharpo) 946[3] 1191[4] 1960[3] (2398) 2703[5] 3595[5] **>80f<**
**Power Don 3** ch g Superpower-Donalee (Don) *3601[9]* **>49a 64f<**
**Power Game 3** b g Puissance-Play the Game (Mummy's Game) *1101[9]* 1527[2] 1780[3] 2034[8] 2213[2] 2618[4] 3123[14] (3591) 3789[3] *3951[11] (4070)* 4296[7] (4472) 4598[3] 4829[8] (4898) **>22a 72f<**
**Power Princess 3** b f Superpower-Hyde Princess (Touch Paper) 768[12] 1991[7] 2180[12] 3166[4] 3458[5] **>34f<**
**Pow Wow 2** b c Efisio-Mill Hill (USA) (Riva Ridge (USA)) 2614[4] 3114[14] 3637[7] **>50f<**
**Pradilla (GER) 3** f 1750a[13]
**Praeditus 2** b c Cadeaux Genereux-Round Midnight (Star Appeal) 4670[6] 4825[4] **>78f<**
**Prague Spring 4** b f Salse (USA)-Wassl's Sister (Troy) 1841[10] 2377[6] 2756[3] 3598[5] 3801[5] 4203[9] **>69f<**
**Prairie Falcon (IRE) 2** b c Alzao (USA)-Sea Harrier (Grundy) 3214[3] 3682[5] **>63f<**
**Prairie Minstrel (USA) 2** b c Regal Intention (CAN)-Prairie Sky (USA) (Gone West (USA)) 1191[6] 2252[6] 3931[6] 4361[10] **>58f<**
**Prancing 3** br f Prince Sabo-Valika (Valiyar) 2298[3] 2692[3] 3127[5] 4445[3] 4671[9] **>102f<**
**Precedency 4** b g Polish Precedent (USA)-Allegedly Blue (USA) (Alleged (USA)) 2140[6] 2494[6] 2737[P] *2935[2] 3605[2] 3952[6] 4095[11] 4515[12]* ***>69a*** **46f<**
**Precious Caroline (IRE) 8** b m The Noble Player (USA)-What A Breeze (Whistling Wind) *70[9]* **(DEAD)**
**Precious Girl 3** ch f Precious Metal-Oh My Oh My (Ballacashtal (CAN)) 997[4] 1340[6] (2151) 2238[5] 4044[8] 4765[15] 4811[8] **>70f<**
**Precious Island 3** b f Jupiter Island-Burmese Ruby (Good Times (ITY)) 1644[13] 2380[6] 4703[8] 4899[5] **>58f<**
**Precious Ring (USA) 3** b c Bering-Most Precious (USA) (Nureyev (USA)) (5021a) **>114f<**
**Precious Topaze (FR) 5** b h Fast Topaze (USA)-Abasted (Busted) (3388a) **>68f<**
**Predappio 3** b c Polish Precedent (USA)-Khalafiya (Darshaan) 3196a[2] 3728a[3] (4268a) (4849a) **>117f<**
**Premazing 4** ch g Precocious-Amazing Journey (USA) (Spectacular Bid (USA)) *745[7]* ***>22a 33f<***
**Premier 2** b c Rainbow Quest (USA)-Formosanta (USA) (Believe It (USA)) 4585[5] 4818[W] **>73f<**
**Premier Bay 2** b c Primo Dominie-Lydia Maria (Dancing Brave (USA)) (1191) 1795[2] 2364[2] **>93f<**
**Premier Censure 3** b f Reprimand-Mrs Thatcher (Law Society (USA)) 550[4] 1104[9] 2135[10] **>72f<**
**Premier Dance 9** ch g Bairn (USA)-Gigiolina (King Emperor (USA)) **1995:** *4370[7] 4387[5] 4442[6] (4506)* **1996:** *38[6] (113) (267) 4391[2]* 620[7] *837[5] (1458) 2341[3]* 3113[7] **>80a 52f<**
**Premier Generation (IRE) 3** b g Cadeaux Genereux-Bristle (Thatch (USA)) 892[9] 1119[6] 3246[8] 3785[11] 4047[5] 4511[5] **>64f<**
**Premier League (IRE) 6** gr g Don't Forget Me-Kilmara (USA) (Caro) *5531[1] 6701[0]* 1102[6] 1655[3] 1996[9] 2378[2] 2574[4] 2784[10] 3111[5] 4068[5] 4373[13] 4900[W] **>41a 72f<**
**Premier Night 3** b f Old Vic-Warm Welcome (General Assembly (USA)) 964[4] 1357[5] 1857[2] 2706[3] 4804[10] **>76f<**
**Premium Gift 4** ch f Most Welcome-Emerald Eagle (Sandy Creek) *868[7]* 956[11] 1786[3] 2349[2] 2694[12] 3049[6] 3482[4] 4220[4] 4828[10] **>61f<**
**Prends Ca (IRE) 3** b f Reprimand-Cri de Coeur (USA) (Lyphard (USA)) *646[7]* (987) 1481[3] 1796[4] 2142[5] 2585[4] 3210[12] 3920[6] 4122[6] (4552) **>99f<**
**Prerogative 6** ch g Dominion-Nettle (Kris) 1011[4] 1124[7] 2182[11] 2958[8] 3303[8] **>50f<**
**Present Arms (USA) 3** b c Affirmed (USA)-Au Printemps (USA) (Dancing Champ (USA)) 1687[2] 1900[2] (3103) (3657) (4695) 5046[10] **>89f<**
**Present Chance 2** ch c Cadeaux Genereux-Chance All (FR) (Glenstal (USA)) 4601[4] 4863[9] **>75f<**
**Present Generation 3** ch c Cadeaux Genereux-Penny Mint (Mummy's Game) 1142[15] 1438[2] 2346[2] 2861[2] **>81f<**
**Presentiment 2** b c Puissance-Octavia (Sallust) *1603[7] 2495[9]* 2865[6] 3821[W] 4041[7] 4223[7] 4482[2] 4795[15] **>37a 62f<**
**Present Imperfect 3** ch f Cadeaux Genereux-Scarcely Blessed (So Blessed) 3446[9] 4229[4] **>61f<**
**Present 'n Correct 3** ch g Cadeaux Genereux-Emerald Eagle (Sandy Creek) 1422[12] 2026[13] 2316[3] *2940[16] (4075)* 4805[16] *5055[11]* **>5a 51f<**
**Present Situation 5** ch g Cadeaux Genereux-Storm Warning (Tumble Wind (USA)) **1995:** *4351[2] 4392[8] 4539[3]* **1996:** *(177) 363[2] 513[4] (2285)* 3123[5] 3805[2] 4463[16] (4692) **>76a 77+f<**
**Preskidul (IRE) 2** b f Silver Kite (USA)-Dul Dul (USA) (Shadeed (USA)) 807[5] 1062[4] 1331[7] 3467[11] 3969[9] 4046[8] 4368[6] **>64f<**
**Press Again 4** ch f Then Again-Silver Empress (Octavo (USA)) 2706[W] 3472[7] 3800[9] 4068[11] **>48f<**
**Press On Nicky 3** b f Nicholas (USA)-Northern Empress (Northfields (USA)) 1333[3] 1855[8] *3064[W] 3262[W]* (3513) 3790[6] 4064[9] 4308[2] 4376[8] 4820[14] **>75f<**
**Prestige Lad 4** ch g Weldnaas (USA)-Chic

Antique (Rarity) *$31^{8}$ $103^{9}$* **>18a f<**

**Prestige Lass 3** ch f Weldnaas (USA)-Monalda (FR) (Claude) $1104^{8}$ $1656^{8}$ $2124^{9}$ $4789^{17}$ **>61f<**

**Presuming Ed (IRE) 3** b c Nordico (USA)-Top Knot (High Top) **1995:** *$4381^{7}$ $4439^{12}$*

**Pretty Ears (FR) 3** b f Top Ville-Aytana (FR) (Riverman (USA)) 5070a$^{3}$

**Pretty In Pink (USA) 2** ch f Elmaamul (USA)-La Plus Belle (USA) (Robellino (USA)) 4944a$^{3}$ **>80f<**

**Pretty Sally (IRE) 2** b f Polish Patriot (USA)-Sally Chase (Sallust) $1989^{9}$ *$2633^{6}$ $2746^{6}$ $4787^{12}$ $5061^{10}$* **>46a 24f<**

**Pretty Scarce 5** ch m Handsome Sailor-Not Enough (Balinger) **1995:** *$4357^{12}$ $4445^{9}$* **1996:** *$154^{8}$* **>27a f<**

**Pretty Sharp 2** ch f Interrex (CAN)-To The Point (Sharpen Up) 3159$^{W}$ $3764^{5}$ $4242^{4}$ $4435^{2}$ $4864^{12}$ **>62f<**

**Pricket (USA) 3** ch f Diesis-Cacti (USA) (Tom Rolfe) (938) $1769^{2}$ **>108f<**

**Priddy Fair 3** b f North Briton-Rainbow Ring (Rainbow Quest (USA)) $4808^{14}$ **>27a 27f<**

**Pride of Brixton 3** b c Dominion-Caviar Blini (What A Guest) *$467^{3}$* $591^{2}$ $716^{7}$ (989) $1113^{13}$ $1630^{7}$ $3693^{5}$ $3946^{10}$ $4367^{8}$ $4765^{2}$ **>89f<**

**Pride of Hayling (IRE) 5** ch m Bold Arrangement-Malham Tarn (Riverman (USA)) *$1446^{6}$* $1777^{3}$ $2286^{3}$ (2735) $2982^{3}$ (3636) $3967^{6}$ $4198^{20}$ $4372^{2}$ $4610^{7}$ $4788^{12}$ **>17a 69f<**

**Pride of Kashmir 3** gr g Petong-Proper Madam (Mummy's Pet) $470^{2}$ $562^{7}$ $873^{14}$ $1119^{7}$ $1594^{4}$ $2013^{7}$ $2409^{5}$ $2979^{3}$ $3314^{3}$ $3845^{6}$ $4186^{9}$ $4497^{6}$ **>56f<**

**Pride of May (IRE) 5** b g Law Society (USA)-Aztec Princess (Indian King (USA)) *$169^{8}$ $3641^{6}$* ***>40a 29f<***

**Pride of Pendle 7** ro m Grey Desire-Pendle's Secret (Le Johnstan) *$935^{5}$* $1069^{12}$ $1341^{6}$ $1609^{8}$ $1819^{8}$ $2962^{5}$ $3161^{16}$ $3279^{6}$ $3985^{8}$ $4071^{2}$ $4190^{3}$ (4300) $4463^{14}$ $4686^{19}$ $4769^{22}$ **>80f<**

**Pride of Whalley (IRE) 3** b f Fayruz-Wilderness (Martinmas) *$748^{3}$* $867^{2}$ $1039^{6}$ $1500^{9}$ **>51a 54f<**

**Priena (IRE) 2** ch f Priolo (USA)-Isabena (Star Appeal) (4435) **>78+f<**

**Prima Cominna 4** ch f Unfuwain (USA)-Cominna (Dominion) $679^{10}$ $1078^{7}$ $1149^{5}$ *$1601^{4}$ $2201^{7}$* **>62a 71f<**

**Prima Silk 5** b m Primo Dominie-Silk St James (Pas de Seul) **1995:** *(4432)* **1996:** *$144^{6}$ $211^{8}$ $632^{12}$* $868^{6}$ (1073) $1307^{6}$ $1624^{2}$ $1680^{4}$ $1786^{7}$ $2311^{2}$ $2363^{9}$ $3112^{8}$ $3339^{2}$ *$3601^{2}$ $3810^{10}$* $3989^{5}$ $4109^{9}$ $4430^{2}$ $4788^{6}$ $4994^{10}$ **>80a 71f<**

**Prima Verde 3** b f Leading Counsel (USA)-Bold Green (FR) (Green Dancer (USA)) $3949^{9}$ **>55f<**

**Prima Volta 3** b f Primo Dominie-Femme Formidable (Formidable (USA)) $945^{6}$ $1481^{5}$ $2045^{6}$ $3799^{7}$ (3929) $4296^{9}$ $4498^{6}$ **>71f<**

**Prime Light 3** ch c Primo Dominie-Flopsy (Welsh Pageant) $696^{3}$ $1350^{3}$ $1617^{5}$ **>71f<**

**Primelta 3** b f Primo Dominie-Pounelta (Tachypous) $3112^{9}$ $3439^{13}$ $4820^{25}$ **>29f<**

**Prime Partner 3** b g Formidable (USA)-Baileys by Name (Nomination) $1101^{10}$ $1527^{19}$ *$2158^{9}$ $2325^{3}$ $2617^{10}$ $4577^{6}$* **>53a 35f<**

**Prime Property (IRE) 4** b f Tirol-Busker (Bustino) *$425^{9}$ $850^{15}$* $868^{12}$ $971^{9}$ $1087^{12}$ $1650^{9}$ $1848^{7}$ $1859^{7}$ $2496^{7}$ $2757^{14}$ $3252^{12}$ **>7a 30f<**

**Prim Lass 5** b m Reprimand-Vague Lass (Vaigly Great) *$782^{14}$ $1156^{7}$* $1411^{14}$ **>30a 45f<**

**Primo Lad 3** b c Primo Dominie-Zinzi (Song) *$665^{2}$* $764^{8}$ *$1456^{10}$ $2085^{11}$ $2176^{7}$* ***>15a 65df<***

**Primo Lara 4** ch c Primo Dominie-Clara Barton (Youth (USA)) $505^{3}$ (629) (718) $933^{13}$ $1898^{4}$ $2328^{2}$ $2725^{14}$ (4054) $4444^{21}$ $4623^{3}$ $4994^{7}$ **>49a 93f<**

**Primrose Path 3** b f Shaadi (USA)-Crimson Conquest (USA) (Diesis) $1324^{10}$ **>71f<**

**Primula Bairn 6** b m Bairn (USA)-Miss Primula (Dominion) *$16^{8}$ $71^{11}$ $126^{5}$ (180) $225^{5}$ (386) $514^{3}$ $4090^{2}$ $4220^{8}$* ***>64a 50f<***

**Prince Arthur (IRE) 4** b c Fairy King (USA)-Daniela Samuel (USA) (No Robbery) $831^{8}$ $1355^{5}$ **>120f<**

**Prince Aslia 3** b c Aragon-Aslia (Henbit (USA)) $565^{6}$ $1127^{14}$ **>93df<**

**Prince Babar 5** b g Fairy King (USA)-Bell Toll (High Line) $600^{6}$ $876^{3}$ $2114^{2}$ $3158^{3}$ $3445^{2}$ $4314^{3}$ $4444^{9}$ (4674) $4974^{2}$ **>108f<**

**Prince Danzig (IRE) 5** ch g Roi Danzig (USA)-Veldt (High Top) **1995:** *$4419^{4}$* **1996:** *$38^{3}$ $100^{4}$ (187) $263^{4}$ $312^{10}$ $411^{5}$ (1011)* $1660^{3}$ $2002^{5}$ $2401^{7}$ $2767^{4}$ $3094^{2}$ $3302^{4}$ $3876^{4}$ **>82a 73f<**

**Prince de Berry 5** ch g Ballacashtal (CAN)-Hoonah (FR) (Luthier) $1655^{20}$ $1953^{12}$ $2155^{3}$ $2530^{12}$ $3204^{3}$ **>42f<**

**Prince de Loir 2** b c Be My Chief (USA)-Princesse Vali (FR) (Val de L'Orne (FR)) $3407^{13}$ **>27f<**

**Prince Dome (IRE) 2** ch c Salt Dome (USA)-Blazing Glory (IRE) (Glow (USA)) $2138^{7}$ $2985^{6}$ $3464^{2}$ **>65f<**

**Prince Equiname 4** gr g Dominion-Moments Peace (Adonijah) *$297^{10}$ $625^{9}$* ***>59a 57f<***

**Prince Jordan 2** ch g Keen-Diami (Swing Easy (USA)) $4599^{10}$ $4715^{22}$ $4970^{20}$ **>46f<**

**Prince Kinsky 3** ch c Master Willie-Princess Lieven (Royal Palace) *(555) $1798^{6}$* $2616^{3}$ $4761^{6}$ $4919^{12}$ **>67a 86f<**

**Princely Affair 3** b g Prince Sabo-Shillay (Lomond (USA)) $597^{7}$ $890^{8}$ *$1490^{3}$ (1696)* $1850^{2}$ *$2086^{3}$ $2321^{2}$* $2440^{6}$ $4236^{10}$ $4497^{16}$ $4812^{14}$ **>47a 52f<**

**Princely Gait 5** b g Darshaan-Roussalka (Habitat) **1995:** *$4384^{4}$* **1996:** *$2304^{2}$ $2612^{11}$ $4977^{3}$ 4998$^{F}$* **>80a 55f< (DEAD)**

**Princely Hush (IRE) 4** b c Prince Sabo-So Kind (Kind of Hush) $3875^{8}$ $4485^{10}$ **>82f<**

**Princely Sound 3** b c Prince Sabo-Sound of the Sea (Windjammer (USA)) *(118) $182^{4}$ (335) $443^{8}$* $692^{6}$ (1006) $1316^{7}$ $1599^{5}$ $2676^{5}$ $2950^{4}$ $3844^{16}$ $4088^{8}$ $4382^{11}$ **>79a 59f<**

**Prince of Andros (USA) 6** b h Al Nasr (FR)-Her Radiance (USA) (Halo (USA)) **1995:** 4403a$^{4}$ *(4482)* **1996:** *$831^{6}$* $1509^{11}$ 1938a$^{2}$ 2273a$^{4}$ (2677) 3196a$^{4}$ 3912a$^{9}$ **>111a 118f<**

**Prince of Denial 2** b c Soviet Star (USA)-Gleaming Water (Kalaglow) $4514^{12}$ $4698^{4}$ $4884^{2}$ **>67f<**

**Prince of Fortune 2** b c Prince Sabo-Beautiful Orchid (Hays) $1896^{12}$ **>55+f<**

**Prince of India 4** b c Night Shift (USA)-Indian Queen (Electric) **1995:** 4497a$^{8}$ **1996:** $2037^{7}$ $2337^{7}$ 3755a$^{5}$ **>108f<**

**Prince of My Heart 3** ch c Prince Daniel (USA)-Blue Room (Gorytus (USA)) $570^{2}$ (772) $986^{3}$ $1791^{19}$ $3798^{4}$ $4177^{3}$ $4568^{9}$ $4714^{5}$ **>110f<**

**Prince of Parkes 2** b c Full Extent (USA)-Summerhill Spruce (Windjammer (USA)) $608^{8}$ $1583^{10}$ **>36f<**

**Prince of Spades 4** ch g Shavian-Diamond Princess (Horage) *$1655^{19}$* $2525^{8}$ **>58df<**

**Prince of Thieves (USA) 3** ch c Hansel (USA)-Fall Aspen (USA) (Pretense (USA)) *1055a$^{3}$* **>120a f<**

**Prince Rooney (IRE) 8** b h Dayeem (USA)-Fourth Degree (Oats) *$389^{8}$ $1449^{11}$* $1677^{10}$ **>20a 37f<**

**Prince Rudolf (IRE) 4** b g Cyrano de Bergerac-Princess Raisa (Indian King (USA)) *36$^{U}$ $203^{6}$ $273^{6}$ $336^{7}$ $688^{17}$* $2022^{5}$ $2075^{15}$ $2507^{10}$ $2766^{4}$ $3095^{4}$ $3358^{7}$ **>45a 52f<**

**Princess Belfort 3** b f Belfort (FR)-Domino Rose (Dominion) $750^{11}$ *$1030^{12}$* **>14a 6f<**

**Princess Danielle 4** b f Prince Daniel (USA)-Bells of St Martin (Martinmas) *$440^{3}$* $641^{2}$ $888^{9}$ $2127^{7}$ $2574^{5}$ $2943^{3}$ $3111^{2}$ $3470^{3}$ $3938^{2}$ $4238^{11}$ $4513^{3}$ $4900^{11}$ **>70f<**

**Princess Efisio 3** b f Efisio-Cutlass Princess (USA) (Cutlass (USA)) $591^{6}$ $783^{7}$ *$1028^{5}$ $1412^{9}$* $1688^{4}$ *(2305) (2634) $2937^{2}$ $3419^{9}$ $4560^{2}$ $4979^{5}$* **>69a 67f<**

**Princesse Lyphard 3** gr f Keen-Bercheba (Bellypha) $2133^{8}$ $2568^{10}$ $2981^{7}$ $3286^{6}$ $3301^{3}$ **>46f<**

**Princess Ferdinand (IRE) 2** b f Roi Danzig (USA)-Silvera (Ribero) $1346^{9}$ $1683^{6}$ $2031^{6}$ *$2633^{9}$ 3336$^{P}$* $3607^{4}$ **>34a 41f<**

**Princess of Hearts 2** b f Prince Sabo-Constant Delight (Never so Bold) $1664^{7}$ $2219^{7}$ $2413^{4}$ (3662) $4084^{4}$ $4213^{3}$ $4361^{11}$ $4602^{7}$ $4715^{2}$ *$4780^{2}$ $4883^{7}$* $4970^{4}$ *$5061^{3}$* **>75a 75f<**

**Princess Pamgaddy 3** gr f Petong-Edwin's Princess (Owen Dudley) *$776^{5}$ $1027^{3}$ $1167^{5}$ $1487^{8}$ (1721) $2016^{2}$* $2133^{6}$ (2339) $2743^{9}$ $3286^{3}$ $3681^{5}$ $4071^{6}$ **>52a 62f<**

**Princess Parrot (IRE) 5** br m Roi Danzig (USA)-Red Lory (Bay Express) *$145^{12}$ $200^{6}$* **>26a 39f<**

**Princess Renata (IRE) 3** ch f Maelstrom Lake-Sajanjal (Dance In Time (CAN)) *$896^{10}$* **>45f<**

**Princess Tallulah 5** b m Chief Singer-Nuts and Brazen (Bold Lad (IRE)) *$400^{8}$ $558^{11}$* ***>21f<***

**Princess Topaz 2** b f Midyan (USA)-Diamond Princess (Horage) $2741^{2}$ $3054^{2}$ $3807^{10}$ $4131^{3}$ $4625^{4}$ **>80f<**

**Princess Tycoon (IRE) 3** br f Last Tycoon-Scoby Lass (Prominer (FR)) 1567a$^{11}$ **>69f<**

**Prince Zizim 3** b c Shareef Dancer (USA)-Possessive Lady (Dara Monarch) $942^{7}$ $1416^{18}$ $1654^{13}$ $2542^{9}$ $3249^{15}$ $3456^{6}$ $3780^{16}$ $4102^{12}$ **>52f<**

**Principal Boy (IRE) 3** br g Cyrano de Bergerac-Shenley Lass (Prince Tenderfoot (USA)) **1995:** *$4473^{7}$* **1996:** *$209^{2}$ (247) $313^{5}$ $405^{2}$ $421^{8}$ $780^{5}$ $857^{3}$ (1029) $1490^{7}$ $1718^{4}$ $4805^{15}$* ***>58a 37f<***

**Principal Player (USA) 6** br g Chief Singer-Harp Strings (FR) (Luthier) $1022^{6}$ **>46f<**

**Printers Quill 4** b g Squill (USA)-On Impulse (Jellaby) $1102^{11}$ $1618^{13}$ $2560^{7}$ (3341) $3825^{9}$ $4257^{3}$ $4489^{8}$ $4726^{8}$ **>59f<**

**Priolina (IRE) 3** b f Priolo (USA)-Salustrina (Sallust) 3531a$^{3}$ $3711^{3}$ $4441^{3}$ $4678^{10}$ **>112f<**

**Priory Belle (IRE) 3** ch f Priolo (USA)-Ingabelle (Taufan (USA)) 1255a$^{5}$ 1567a$^{5}$ $2052^{7}$ **>104f<**

**Priory Gardens (IRE) 2** b c Broken Hearted-Rosy O'Leary (Majetta) $2527^{7}$ $3809^{8}$ $4242^{17}$ $4803^{9}$ **>38f<**

**Private Audience (USA) 3** b c Private Account (USA)-Monroe (USA) (Sir Ivor) $1153^{5}$ **>52f<**

**Private Despatch (USA) 6** ch h Private Account (USA)-Soft Dawn **1995:** 4466a$^{2}$

**Private Encore (IRE) 5** b m Niniski (USA)-Muffitys (Thatch (USA)) 4643a$^{11}$ **>56f<**

**Private Fixture (IRE) 5** ch g The Noble Player (USA)-Pennyala (Skyliner) **1995:** *$4514^{9}$* **1996:** *$645^{11}$ $1460^{9}$* **>51a 58f<**

**Private Percival 3** b c Arrasas (USA)-Romacina (Roman Warrior) *$2579^{12}$* $2786^{5}$ $4548^{10}$ $4789^{13}$ *$4894^{12}$ $5052^{8}$* ***>8a 47df<***

**Private Song (USA) 3** b c Private Account (USA)-Queen of Song (USA) (His Majesty (USA)) $576^{7}$ $860^{2}$ (1305) $2074^{2}$ 2473a$^{8}$ $3669^{7}$ $4385^{9}$ **>97f<**

**Privilege (IRE) 5** b g Last Tycoon-Spire (Shirley Heights) 724a$^{3}$

**Prix de Clermont (IRE) 2** b c Petorius-Sandra's Choice (Sandy Creek) $4601^{9}$ $5050^{7}$ **>73f<**

**Prizefighter 5** b g Rambo Dancer (CAN)-Jaisalmer (Castle Keep) **1995:** *(4493)* **1996:** *14[6] (257) 2962[7]* (3287) 3501[5] **>72a 70f<**

**Prize Giving 3** ch c Most Welcome-Glowing With Pride (Ile de Bourbon (USA)) (693) (1015) 1329[2] 2116[5] 2844a[4] 4197[4] **>114f<**

**Prize Pupil (IRE) 4** b c Royal Academy (USA)-Bestow (Shirley Heights) *871[3]* 1109[8] 1486[4] 2145[4] 3516[9] 3765[8] **>74f<**

**Progression 5** b h Reprimand-Mainmast (Bustino) *132[6] 187[2] 312[4] 411[3] (682)* 941[5] 1109[5] 1353[9] **>75a 89f< (DEAD)**

**Projection (USA) 3** b c Topsider (USA)-Image of Reality (USA) (In Reality) 454[5] 681[2] (936) 1151[6] 2092a[3] **>103f<**

**Promise Fulfilled (USA) 5** b m Bet Twice (USA)-Kind Prospect (USA) (Mr Prospector (USA)) *59[5] 135[5]* **>71da 78df<**

**Promissory 3** b f Caerleon (USA)-Tricky Note (Song) 583[7] 938[7] 1335[9] 2197[11] 2855[8] **>61f<**

**Prompt 3** b f Old Vic-In Perpetuity (Great Nephew) *555[4]* **>42a f<**

**Promptly (IRE) 3** b f Lead on Time (USA)-Ghariba (Final Straw) (768) 1126[13] 2007[6] 2328[13] **>91f<**

**Propellant 2** b c Formidable (USA)-Kirsheda (Busted) 4046[18] 4584[8] 4807[7] **>48f<**

**Proper Blue (USA) 3** b c Proper Reality (USA)-Blinking (USA) (Tom Rolfe) 4325[5] (4680) (4964) **>112f<**

**Proposing (IRE) 4** b c Rainbow Quest (USA)-La Romance (USA) (Lyphard (USA)) (965) 1176[8] **>98a 96f<**

**Prospector's Cove 3** b g Dowsing (USA)-Pearl Cove (Town And Country) (570) 694[10] 2350[9] **>92f<**

**Prospero 3** b g Petong-Pennies to Pounds (Ile de Bourbon (USA)) 3505[6] 4201[5] 4427[2] (4899) **>77f<**

**Protaras Bay 2** b c Superpower-Vivid Impression (Cure The Blues (USA)) 924[7] 1424[8] 2600[14] **>58f<**

**Protektor (GER) 7** b h Acatenango (GER)-Prioritat (FR) (Frontal) 1138a[2] (2479a) 3203a[3] 4040a[6] 4413a[2] (4855a) **>123f<**

**Protocol (IRE) 2** ch c Taufan (USA)-Ukraine's Affair (USA) (The Minstrel (CAN)) 4705[12] 4897[4] **>74f<**

**Proton 6** b g Sure Blade (USA)-Banket (Glint of Gold) 573[17] 844[12] 1486[13] 3073[5] 3828[10] 4121[11] 4872[14] **>76f<**

**Pro Trader (USA) 3** b c Lyphard (USA)-Fuerza (USA) 1247a[2] 2825a[2] 3911a[5] **>111f<**

**Proud Brigadier (IRE) 8** b g Auction Ring (USA)-Naughty One Gerard (Brigadier Gerard) 3115[5] 3469[4] 4373[17] 4511[8] 4882[13] **>58f<**

**Proud Fact (USA) 3** f 3391a[5] **>93f<**

**Proud Image 4** b g Zalazl (USA)-Fleur de Foret (USA) (Green Forest (USA)) 545[2] 645[14] (801) 1041[4] 2426[6] 2737[5] 3139[15] *3951[4] 4603[2] 4894[5] 4998[3]* **>68a 71f<**

**Proud Look 3** b c Dayjur (USA)-Very Charming (USA) (Vaguely Noble) 458[2] 663[3] 1901[17] 4322[7] **>71f<**

**Proud Monk 3** gr g Aragon-Silent Sister (Kind of Hush) **1995:** *4389[11]* **1996:** *554[2]* 646[2] 987[8] 1819[4] 2146[11] 3806[3] 4064[12] 4231[5] 4820[4] 5042[11] **>40a 77f<**

**Proud Native (IRE) 2** b c Imp Society (USA)-Karamana (Habitat) (608) (1115) (1795) 3156[4] 3690[9] 4328[2] (4723) 5071a[5] **>101f<**

**Proud Titania (IRE) 3** b f Fairy King (USA)-Dignified Air (FR) (Wolver Hollow) (1255a) 3530a[2] 4160a[5] **>108f<**

**Prove The Point (IRE) 3** b f Maelstrom Lake-In Review (Ela-Mana-Mou) 3832[9] 4124[9] **>47f<**

**Province 3** b g Dominion-Shih Ching (USA) (Secreto (USA)) (3788) 4351[3] **>88f<**

**Prudent Pet 4** b f Distant Relative-Philgwyn (Milford) **1995:** *4378[13]* **1996:** *629[9]* 827[17] 1092[4] 1502[7] 2045[5] 2592[6] 2793[5] 3443[2] *3603[16] 3866[13] 4089[14] 4323[9]* 4436[23] 5004[12] **>67a 48f<**

**Prudent Princess 4** b f Puissance-Princess Story (Prince de Galles) **1995:** *4372[6]* **1996:** *782[8] 1096[4] 1449[17] 1719[10] 2937[7] 3937[10] 4577[5] 4888[11]* **>59a 59f<**

**Prussia 5** b h Roi Danzig (USA)-Vagrant Maid (USA) (Honest Pleasure (USA)) *872[4]* 993[12] **>51f<**

**Prussian Blue (USA) 4** b c Polish Navy (USA)-Lit'l Rose (USA) (Mr Prospector (USA)) 828[2] (1336) 2352[2] 3689[8] 3934[9] (5035) **>110f<**

**Psicossis 3** b c Slip Anchor-Precious Jade (Northfields (USA)) 1873[6] **>74f<**

**Psp Lady 3** b f Ballacashtal (CAN)-Sunshine Gal (Alto Volante) 2794[13] 3273[5] 3824[9] **>17f<**

**Public Way (IRE) 6** b g Common Grounds-Kilpeacon (Florescence) 883[P] 1309[8] 1763[4] *1966[8] 2513[4]* 2587[16] 3426[9] 3854[5] **>23a 49f<**

**Puce 3** b f Darshaan-Souk (IRE) (Ahonoora) 1142[11] 2124[2] (2589) 3235[3] (4615) **>89f<**

**Pulga Circo 3** b f Tina's Pet-Pulga (Blakeney) 1526[9] *1721[12] 2180[17] 2553[9]* **>27a 44df<**

**Pumpkin Pie (IRE) 4** b f Jareer (USA)-Sauntry (Ballad Rock) *114[9]*

**Pun 2** b f Batshoof-Keen Wit (Kenmare (FR)) 2132[2] (2720) 3512[4] 3835[7] **>80f<**

**Punch 4** b g Reprimand-Cartooness (USA) (Achieved) 767[12] 1044[7] 1676[11] 2177[6] 3308[3] 3775[5] **>42f<**

**Punishment 5** b h Midyan (USA)-In the Shade (Bustino) 831[4] 1390a[2] 1794[4] 2113[7] 2583[6] 3670[6] 3996[7] 4656a[11] 4856a[7] 5045[9] **>102f<**

**Punkah (USA) 3** b c Lear Fan (USA)-Gentle Persuasion (Bustino) *(364) 731[4]* 947[5] (2033) **>53a 77f<**

**Pupil Master (IRE) 2** b g Masterclass (USA)-Lamya (Hittite Glory) 4244[9] 4594[11] *4985[6]* **>26a 48f<**

**Purchasing Power (IRE) 2** b c Danehill (USA)-Purchasepaperchase (Young Generation) 4461[11] 4825[17] **>50f<**

**Pure Grain 4** b f Polish Precedent (USA)-Mill Line (Mill Reef (USA)) **1995:** 4471a[10] **>120f<**

**Purist 2** b c Polish Precedent (USA)-Mill Line (Mill Reef (USA)) 5033[9] **>69f<**

**Purple Fling 5** ch g Music Boy-Divine Fling (Imperial Fling (USA)) 1334[2] 1853[6] 2615[3] 3518[4] 3930[5] 4215[5] 4581[14] (4788) **>73a 76f<**

**Purple Memories 3** b c Don't Forget Me-Tyrian Belle (Enchantment) 1597[6] 2222[6] 4430[20] 4692[20] **>53f<**

**Purple Splash 6** b g Ahonoora-Quay Line (High Line) (647) (961) 1336[3] 4965[8] 5035[4] **>102f<**

**Purple Sun (GER) 3** f 1750a[14]

**Pursuance (IRE) 4** b c Glenstal (USA)-Pocket (Tumble Wind (USA)) *22[5] 74[6]* **>55a 51f< (DEAD)**

**Pusey Street Boy 9** ch g Vaigly Great-Pusey Street (Native Bazaar) 1449[10] 2075[12] 2345[8] 4915[10] **>52a 52f<**

**Pusey Street Girl 3** ch f Gildoran-Pusey Street (Native Bazaar) *842[13]* 982[10] (1452) 2078[3] **>87f<**

**Push A Venture 2** b f Shirley Heights-Push a Button (Bold Lad (IRE)) 3593[17] 4211[7] 4890[4] **>59f<**

**Pushka Fair 5** b g Salse (USA)-Orient (Bay Express) **1995:** *4543[10]* **1996:** *110[10] 248[7] 3256[7]* **>11a 27f<**

**Putra (USA) 2** ch c Dixie Brass (USA)-Olatha (USA) (Miswaki (USA)) *(1960)* (3143) **>113+f<**

**Puzzlement 2** gr c Mystiko (USA)-Abuzz (Absalom) *924[6]* 1191[5] 3837[8] 4131[9] 4262[5] 4717[14] 4916[8] **>61f<**

**Pytchley Dawn 6** b m Welsh Captain-Cawston's Arms (Cawston's Clown) 2345[7] 2617[17] *3420[11]* **>20a 34f<**

**Q**

**Qasida (IRE) 3** b c Lycius (USA)-Arab Heritage (Great Nephew) 671[7] 918[5] 1305[2] 2054[12] (2439) 3691[11] 3997[11] **>87f<**

**Q Factor 4** br f Tragic Role (USA)-Dominiana (Dominion) **1995:** *4367[7] 4392[11]* **1996:** *55[8] 77[4] 211[5] 301[3] 345[4] 649[3]* 1406[9] (2058) 2526[5] (2945) 3469[8] (3800) (4560) 4802[6] **>71a 85f<**

**Quadrant 7** b g Shirley Heights-Sextant (Star Appeal) *104[11] 186[11] 240[5]* **>53a 27f<**

**Quakers Field 3** b c Anshan-Nosey (Nebbiolo) 1441[5] 2274a[7] 2677[5] 3124[5] 3997[2] 4441[7] 4876[11] **>113f<**

**Qualitair Beauty 3** b f Damister (USA)-Mac's Princess (USA) (Sovereign Dancer (USA)) *1969[9]*

**Quality (IRE) 3** b c Rock City-Queens Welcome (Northfields (USA)) **1995:** *(4361) 4410[2] 4462[4]* **1996:** *263[2] (378) 444[9]* 567[3] 646[3] 1066[4] 2146[5] 2334[5] 3246[3] (3702) 3967[4] 4064[13] 4376[3] **>85+a 84f<**

**Quango 4** b g Charmer-Quaranta (Hotfoot) 1476[13] 3710[20] 4450[7] **>71+a 70f<**

**Quarterstaff 2** b c Charmer-Quaranta (Hotfoot) 5040[13] **>18f<**

**Queen Bee 3** ch f Royal Academy (USA)-Honey Bridge (Crepello) 1182[4] 1711[9] 2601[10] 3283[2] 3705[6] **>70f<**

**Queenbird 5** b or br m Warning-Song Test (USA) (The Minstrel (CAN)) **1995:** *4374[12]* **>2a 69f<**

**Queenfisher 4** b or br f Scottish Reel-Mavahra (Mummy's Pet) *889[9]* 2704[6] 4444[15] 4901[10] **>87f<**

**Queen Maud (IRE) 2** b f Akarad (FR)-Modiyna (Nishapour (FR)) 3748a[3] 4942a[2] **>93f<**

**Queen of All Birds (IRE) 5** b m Bluebird (USA)-Blue Bouquet (Cure The Blues (USA)) *14[5] (120) 223[2] 379[2] 491[6]* 1051[3] 1625[5] 1825[6] 4381[8] 4560[10] **>88a 77df<**

**Queen of Shannon (IRE) 8** b m Nordico (USA)-Raj Kumari (Vitiges (FR)) 1893[2] 2344[8] 2716[15] *3062[9] (3257)* 3694[3] 4373[7] 4701[12] 4882[6] **>24a 58+f<**

**Queen Sceptre (IRE) 2** b f Fairy King (USA)-Happy Smile (IRE) (Royal Match) (2035) 2338[2] 3068[4] 3613[3] 3804[4] (4299) 4491[6] **>95f<**

**Queen's Charter 3** b f Welsh Captain-Sussex Queen (Music Boy) 1836[W]

**Queens Check 3** b f Komaite (USA)-Ski Baby (Petoski) *478[6] (1028) 2757[15] (3091) 3930[9] 4333[12] 4776[3]* **>68a 45f<**

**Queens Consul (IRE) 6** gr m Kalaglow-Queens Connection (Bay Express) 491[5] 629[5] 739[2] 1322[5] (1609) 1799[3] 2010[6] 2351[10] 2483[7] 2693[2] 3265[7] 3430[7] (3770) 3920[7] 4190[24] 4300[7] 4617[13] 4901[17] 5042[17] **>59a 87f<**

**Queens Fancy 3** ch f Infantry-Sagareina (Sagaro) **1995:** *4417[8]* **1996:** *2794[10]* 3258[13] 3785[14] 4422[8] **>11a 36f<**

**Queen's Insignia (USA) 3** b f Gold Crest (USA)-Years (USA) (Secretariat (USA)) 1181[9] 4921[9] **>47f<**

**Queen's Pageant 2** ch f Risk Me (FR)-Mistral's Dancer (Shareef Dancer (USA)) 1480[3] 3994[5] (4558) 4723[17] **>79f<**

**Queens Stroller (IRE) 5** b m Pennine Walk-Mount Isa (Miami Springs) **1995:** *4445[4]* **1996:** *66[8] 124[11] 512[7] 1411[18] 2169[10] 2304[10] 5056[4]* **>35a 47f<**

**Quertier (IRE) 2** ch c Bluebird (USA)-Ganna (ITY) (Molvedo) 3214[4] 3695[7] 3976[11] **>22f<**

**Quest Again 5** ch g Then Again-Eagle's Quest (Legal Eagle) *1826[6]* 2155[10] 4252[P] **>74?f<**

**Quest Express** 2 ch c Rudimentary (USA)-Swordlestown Miss (USA) (Apalachee (USA)) (1694) 2607[6] 3243[3] 4023a[5] **>102f<**

**Quest For Best (USA)** 2 b br f Quest for Fame-Chic Monique (USA) (Halo (USA)) 3874[3] **>73f<**

**Questing Star** 3 ch f Rainbow Quest (USA)-Guest Artiste (Be My Guest (USA)) 4379[8] 4622[8] 4813[6] *4997[4]* **>45a 62f<**

**Questonia** 3 b f Rainbow Quest (USA)-Danthonia (USA) (Northern Dancer) 1359[2] 1644[2] (2579) 3791[8] 4445[4] (4704) 4874[4] 5036[2] **>109f<**

**Quezon City** 2 ch c Keen-Calachuchi (Martinmas) 4807[10] **>24f<**

**Quibbling** 2 b f Salse (USA)-Great Exception (Grundy) 2230[7] 4797[6] **>71f<**

**Quick Million** 5 b m Thowra (FR)-Miss Quick (Longleat (USA)) **1995:** *4534[7]* **1996:** *15[9] 104[14]* **>56da 41f<**

**Quick Silver Boy** 6 gr g Kalaglow-Safidar (Roan Rocket) 752[15] **>50a 44f<**

**Quiet Amusement (USA)** 5 ch m Regal And Royal (USA)-My Little Guest (Be My Guest (USA)) **1995:** *4516[13]* **>28a 62f<**

**Quiet Arch (IRE)** 3 b g Archway (IRE)-My Natalie (Rheingold) 544[9] 672[9] 860[12] *1490[4] (1993) 2201[3] 2689[5] 3603[8] 3929[4]* 4374[5] 4515[3] 4624[2] 4785[3] **>75a 73f<**

**Quiet Moments (IRE)** 3 b g Ron's Victory (USA)-Saint Cynthia (Welsh Saint) 597[8] 803[9] 1498[12] 4042[10] **>28f<**

**Quilling** 4 ch g Thatching-Quillotern (USA) (Arctic Tern (USA)) 765[19] 935[15] 1505[5] 1789[6] 2149[2] 2630[3] 2729[7] 2874[3] 3120[3] 3328[4] 3623[5] 3815[4] 3985[3] (4136) 4300[8] (4439) 4688[10] 4724[U] 4909[3] 4975[14] **>80f<**

**Quillwork (USA)** 4 b f Val de L'Orne (FR)-Quaff (USA) (Raise A Cup (USA)) *547[7]* 690[16] 4237[9] 4515[7] 4815[P] **>53a 48f<**

**Quinella** 3 b f Generous (IRE)-Bempton (Blakeney) 2365[5] 3042[7] **>52f<**

**Quinntessa** 3 ch f Risk Me (FR)-Nannie Annie (Persian Bold) **1995:** *4429[7] 4483[2] 4511[9]* **1996:** *21[9] 129[7] 209[4] 344[4] 427[6] 492[3]* 3650[7] 4045[14] 4341[10] **>46a 57f<**

**Quinta Boy** 3 b g Puissance-Figment (Posse (USA)) 591[11] 2960[9] 3331[12] **>12f<**

**Quintellina** 2 b f Robellino (USA)-High Quinta (High Line) 2611[3] (3159) 4133[7] 4471[5] **>83f<**

**Quintus Decimus** 4 b g Nordico (USA)-Lemon Balm (High Top) *876[13]* 1464[5] 1680[7] 4109[11] 4511[16] **>47f<**

**Quinze** 3 b g Charmer-Quaranta (Hotfoot) (2760) 3067[7] 3634[6] 4059[6] 4513[9] **>72f<**

**Quinzii Martin** 8 b g Song-Quaranta (Hotfoot) **1995:** *4377[12] 4421[10] 4503[9] 4531[2]* **1996:** *42[9] 115[7] 213[3] 363[3] 393[3] 654[2] 839[3] 1085[8] 1460[2] 1604[4] 1718[5] 2081[3] 2303[6] 2550[4] 3628[7] 3951[3]* **>63a 51f<**

**Quivira** 5 ch m Rainbow Quest (USA)-Nobly Born (USA) (The Minstrel (CAN)) *181[8] 968[9]* 1852[7] 2300[3] 2900[7] **>63a 74df<**

**Quota** 3 b f Rainbow Quest (USA)-Armeria (USA) (Northern Dancer) (813) 1144[2] 3688[8] **>102f<**

**Quws** 2 b c Robellino (USA)-Fleeting Rainbow (Rainbow Quest (USA)) 2470a[3] 4027a[3] 4846a[3] **>99f<**

**R**

**Raaha** 2 b f Polar Falcon (USA)-Ostora (USA) (Blushing Groom (FR)) 4570[7] **>67f<**

**Raased** 4 b g Unfuwain (USA)-Sajjaya (USA) (Blushing Groom (FR)) 1417[7] 1866[3] 3344[12] 3646[6] **>51f<**

**Rabican (IRE)** 3 b c Distinctly North (USA)-Kaysama (FR) (Kenmare (FR)) *1151[2]* 2623[2] **>112f<**

**Racing Brenda** 5 b m Faustus (USA)-Icecapped (Caerleon (USA)) *1825[7]* 2592[8] 3052[4] 3334[3] 3812[5] 3958[2] 4603[16] **>78a 53f<**

**Racing Carr** 2 ch f Anshan-Bamian (USA) (Topsider (USA)) 3129[14] 3803[12] 4715[24] *4988[4]* **>24a 40f<**

**Racing Hawk (USA)** 4 ch g Silver Hawk (USA)-Lorn Lady (Lorenzaccio) *532[7] 1011[10]* 1347[10] 1651[4] 2251[3] (2540) 2896[6] 3496[12] 3991[13] **>66a 56f<**

**Racing Heart** 2 b f Pursuit of Love-Hearten (Hittite Glory) 3593[16] 3988[8] 4127[13] 4549[11] **>67f<**

**Racing Telegraph** 6 b g Claude Monet (USA)-Near Enough (English Prince) **1995:** *4515[6]* **1996:** *53[4] 201[7] 3139[4]* 3686[3] 4186[5] 4240[11] 4497[3] **>29a 44f<**

**Radames (IRE)** 4 b g Law Society (USA)-Sphinx (GER) (Alpenkonig (GER)) 5023a[3] **>110f<**

**Radanpour (IRE)** 4 b g Kahyasi-Rajpoura (Kashmir II) 4643a[20] **>62f<**

**Radar O'Reilly** 2 b c Almoojid-Travel Bye (Miller's Mate) 639[9] **>36f<**

**Radevore** 3 ch c Generous (IRE)-Bioudan **1995:** 4468a[3] **1996:** 797a[3] (1389a) 1757a[13] (2844a) 4293a[3] 4662a[12] **>120f<**

**Radiant Star** 3 b c Rainbow Quest (USA)-Miss Kuta Beach (Bold Lad (IRE)) 677[7] 1125[5] 2135[3] 2610[3] 3986[6] **>81f<**

**Radical Exception (IRE)** 6 b g Radical-A Stoir (Camden Town) 3115[11] 3472[15] 3860[7] **>24f<**

**Radmore Brandy** 3 b f Derrylin-Emerin (King Emperor (USA)) *49[9] 134[8] 269[6] 300[6] 522[3] 651[4] 849[9]* 1451[2] 1821[11] *2168[11] 4904[6]* **>33a 44f<**

**Raed** 3 b c Nashwan (USA)-Awayed (USA) (Sir Ivor) *847[4]* 1687[4] 3295[7] 3985[4] 4257[13] 4606[2] 4724[5] **>75f<**

**Raffles Rooster** 4 ch g Galetto (FR)-Singapore Girl (FR) (Lyphard (USA)) **1995:** *4540[3]* **1996:** *24[6] 583[14]* 691[11] 1426[4] 2499[3] 4673[9] **>57a 66f<**

**Rafter-J** 5 b or br g Petoski-Coming Out (Fair Season) *34[13] 84[7] 247[7] 311[6]* **>33a 55f<**

**Rafters** 7 b g Celestial Storm (USA)-Echoing (Formidable (USA)) *4686[24]* 4810[9] **>39f<**

**Ragazzo (IRE)** 6 b g Runnett-Redecorate (USA) (Hatchet Man (USA)) *806[17]* 991[16] 2356[8] 2801[18] 3453[6] 3643[5] 3957[3] 4460[11] *4983[11] 5059[7]* **>37a 33f<**

**Ragmar (FR)** 3 ch c Tropular-Reggae (FR) (New Chapter (FR)) (797a) (1757a) 2480a[7] **>116f<**

**Ragsak Jameel (USA)** 3 b g Northern Baby (CAN)-Dream Play (USA) (Blushing Groom (FR)) 1305[4] 1782[9] 2141[2] 2378[4] 2896[2] (3094) 3333[2] (3653) **>85f<**

**Ragtime Cowgirl** 3 ch f Aragon-Echo Chamber (Music Boy) 473[10] *606[12] 748[8] 2168[3] (2362)* 2565[3] 3116[3] 3325[3] 3619[3] 3808[3] (3882) 4313[7] 4474[9] 5007[13] **>42a 47f<**

**Raheefa (USA)** 3 b br f Riverman (USA)-Oogie Poogie (USA) (Storm Bird (CAN)) *3505[8]* (4201) **>78f<**

**Raheen (USA)** 3 b c Danzig (USA)-Belle de Jour (USA) (Speak John) 703[4] **>83f<**

**Rahona (IRE)** 2 b f Sharp Victor (USA)-Hail To You (USA) (Kirtling) *446[3]* 506[7] 990[6] *1097[4] 1459[3] 1645[5]* 2161[6] *4093[8] 4223[9]* **>49a 46f<**

**Rainbow Blues (IRE)** 3 b c Bluebird (USA)-Tudor Loom (Sallust) 1235a[3] 1253a[2] 1574a[2] 2473a[5] 2839a[3] **>123f<**

**Rainbow Dancer (FR)** 5 b h Rainbow Quest (USA)-Ramanouche (FR) 907a[2] 1577a[2] 4856a[3] **>116f<**

**Rainbow Rain (USA)** 2 b c Capote (USA)-Grana (USA) (Miswaki (USA)) 1003[4] 1197[3] 3987[7] 4311[5] 4717[2] **>84f<**

**Rainbow Road** 5 b g Shareef Dancer (USA)-Chalkey Road (Relko) *252[4]* **>47a 66f< (DEAD)**

**Rainbows Rhapsody** 5 b m Handsome Sailor-Rainbow Trout (Comedy Star (USA)) *50[7] 208[12] 236[15] 239[14]* 2567[2] 2743[4] 2851[5] *2937[13] 3460[3]* 3866[6] 4071[12] 4348[4] 4436[9] **>11a 36f<**

**Rainbow Top** 4 b c Rainbow Quest (USA)-Aigue (High Top) *(24) (263) 1706[4]* 2723[5] (3402) 3854[6] 3981[11] **>82a 104f<**

**Rainbow Walk (IRE)** 6 ch g Rainbow Quest (USA)-Widows Walk (Habitat) *136[8] 198[12]* **>66da 70df<**

**Raindancing (IRE)** 2 b f Tirol-Persian Song (Persian Bold) 1179[4] 1954[2] (2600) 3068[3] 4133[5] 4488[18] **>88f<**

**Raindeer Quest** 4 ch f Hadeer-Rainbow Ring (Rainbow Quest (USA)) 561[4] (688) 827[3] 883[4] 1546[10] 1830[4] 2587[2] 3333[3] 3589[4] 4455[7] 5010[14] **>51f<**

**Rainelle** 4 ch f Rainbow Quest (USA)-Dame Ashfield (Grundy) 4588[12] 4726[15] *4986[9]* **>15a 42f<**

**Rainwatch** 2 b c Rainbow Quest (USA)-Third Watch (Slip Anchor) 4306[5] **>81f<**

**Rainy Day Song** 3 br f Persian Bold-Sawaki (Song) 4108[12] 4499[8] **>64f<**

**Raisa Point** 5 ch m Raised Socially (USA)-To The Point (Sharpen Up) 862[15] *1971[2] 2186[3]* 2745[11] **>46a 31f<**

**Raise A Prince (FR)** 3 b c Machiavellian (USA)-Enfant D'Amour (USA) (Lyphard (USA)) 730[4] 1690[12] 3298[2] 3923[5] 4429[4] 4613[2] 4866[4] **>81f<**

**Raise A Ripple** 3 b c Primitive Rising (USA)-Bonnybrook (Tanfirion) 705[9] 934[8] 1168[5] 2679[9] 2847[8] **>49f<**

**Raisonnable** 3 b f Common Grounds-Salvora (USA) (Spectacular Bid (USA)) 796a[2] 1140a[7] **>101f<**

**Raivue** 2 ch g Beveled (USA)-Halka (Daring March) 4706[7] **>42f<**

**Raiyoun (IRE)** 3 b c Doyoun-Raymouna (High Top) 2839a[5] 3731a[2] 4396a[6] **>117f<**

**Rajah** 3 b br g Be My Chief (USA)-Pretty Thing (Star Appeal) *167[6] 234[7] 298[4] (515) 658[3] 1490[14]* **>52a 52f<**

**Rake Hey** 2 gr c Petong-Dancing Daughter (Dance In Time (CAN)) 706[11] 829[5] 1003[9] 4060[7] 4721[2] 5048[6] **>66f<**

**Rakis (IRE)** 6 b or br g Alzao (USA)-Bristle (Thatch (USA)) **1995:** *(4514)* **1996:** *(42) (121) (144) (205) 744[5]* 935[6] 1337[7] 1775[3] (1962) 2134[9] 2400[4] 3833[8] 4109[3] (4212) 4432[5] 4688[15] **>91a 83f<**

**Ralitsa (IRE)** 4 b g Nordico (USA)-Bold-E-Be (Persian Bold) *4596[9]* **>48f<**

**Ramadour (IRE)** 2 b c Rambo Dancer (CAN)-Minwah (USA) (Diesis) 4261[10] 4835[3] **>63f<**

**Rambling Bear** 3 ch c Sharrood (USA)-Supreme Rose (Frimley Park) 889[6] (1146) (1621) 2072[14] 2880[5] (3126) 3759[3] 4057[8] 4660a[9] **>120f<**

**Rambold** 5 b m Rambo Dancer (CAN)-Boldie (Bold Lad (IRE)) 1466[3] (1634) 1991[8] 2185[2] 2719[7] 2957[3] (3168) 3439[3] 3599[3] 3700[4] 4088[13] 4206[10] 4881[5] **>61a 66f<**

**Rambo's Hall** 11 b g Crofthall-Murton Crags (No Argument) **1995:** *4476[5]* **1996:** *48[2]* **>87a 90f<**

**Rambo's Rumtime** 4 b f Rambo Dancer (CAN)-Errol Emerald (Dom Racine (FR)) 3289[13] 3490[6] **>24f<**

**Rambo Tango** 2 b g Rambo Dancer (CAN)-Jumra (Thatch (USA)) *3629[7]* **>13a f<**

**Rambo Waltzer** 4 b g Rambo Dancer (CAN)-Vindictive Lady (USA) (Foolish Pleasure (USA)) **1995:** *4367[4]* **1996:** *(29) 61[5] 105[6] (135) 211[6] 505[2]*

(615) (713) (827) 933$^{11}$ 1069$^{7}$ 3623$^{14}$ 3933$^{15}$ 3974$^{10}$ 4190$^{16}$ 4432$^{9}$ 4686$^{13}$ 4769$^{14}$ **>84a 62f<**

**Ramike (IRE) 2** b c Caerleon (USA)-Marie Noelle (FR) (Brigadier Gerard) 4801$^{13}$ 4920$^{8}$ **>55f<**

**Ramooz (USA) 3** b c Rambo Dancer (CAN)-My Shafy (Rousillon (USA)) (736) 918$^{3}$ (1796) 2050$^{2}$ 2337$^{5}$ 4051$^{6}$ 4396a$^{2}$ 4444$^{4}$ 4870$^{4}$ **>116f<**

**Ramsey Hope 3** b c Timeless Times (USA)-Marfen (Lochnager) 443$^{13}$ 587$^{14}$ 824$^{12}$ 1157$^{16}$ 1599$^{2}$ 2049$^{11}$ 2193$^{12}$ 2238$^{2}$ 2427$^{7}$ 2950$^{5}$ 3085$^{13}$ 3122$^{7}$ 3342$^{5}$ *4081$^{5}$ 4246$^{19}$* 4356$^{13}$ *(4776) (4996)* **>75a 78f<**

**Ramsey Pride 2** b f Timeless Times (USA)-Lindrake's Pride (Mandrake Major) 506$^{5}$ 557$^{7}$ 823$^{9}$ *1097$^{6}$ 1845$^{7}$* 4748$^{11}$ **>22a 35f<**

**Random 5** ch m Beveled (USA)-Martian Melody (Enchantment) **1995:** *4357$^{6}$ 4441$^{5}$* **1996:** *26$^{8}$ (107) 178$^{6}$ 354$^{3}$ 461$^{6}$ 1536$^{3}$* 1958$^{6}$ 2129$^{6}$ 2713$^{5}$ 3216$^{4}$ **>56a 71f<**

**Random Kindness 3** b g Alzao (USA)-Lady Tippins (USA) (Star de Naskra (USA)) 860$^{14}$ 1305$^{3}$ 1670$^{3}$ 2080$^{2}$ 2601$^{11}$ **>80f<**

**Ranger Sloane 4** ch g Gunner B-Lucky Amy (Lucky Wednesday) *97$^{7}$ 138$^{11}$ 983$^{20}$* 1821$^{16}$ **>51a 24f<**

**Rankaidade 5** b m Governor General-Keep Cool (FR) (Northern Treat (USA)) *607$^{11}$ 700$^{7}$* 750$^{7}$ 882$^{14}$ 1087$^{8}$ 1364$^{14}$ 1598$^{12}$ 1848$^{10}$ *2367$^{12}$ 2910$^{5}$ 3091$^{9}$ 3294$^{5}$* 3579$^{11}$ **>6a 28f<**

**Ranuncolo (ITY) 3** ch c Be My Guest (USA)-Rocca Delle Macie (Be My Native (USA)) 1058a$^{2}$ 1580a$^{4}$ **>84f<**

**Raphane (USA) 2** b c Rahy (USA)-Fast Nellie (USA) (Ack Ack (USA)) (1565a) 2070$^{2}$ (2834a) 3156$^{2}$ 3561a$^{7}$ **>103f<**

**Rapiddima (IRE) 5** b m Drumalis-Snow Storm (ITY) (Ercolano (USA)) (4419a) **>89f<**

**Rapid Liner 3** b g Skyliner-Stellaris (Star Appeal) 638$^{17}$ *834$^{10}$ 978$^{12}$* 1301$^{11}$ **>16a 57df<**

**Rapid Mover 9** ch g Final Straw-Larive (Blakeney) 541$^{7}$ 558$^{7}$ 615$^{6}$ 1024$^{3}$ 1309$^{6}$ 1546$^{12}$ 1633$^{9}$ 1868$^{8}$ 2023$^{11}$ 2356$^{6}$ 3242$^{4}$ 3346$^{7}$ 3646$^{5}$ 3878$^{9}$ **>36f<**

**Rapid Retreat (FR) 3** ch f Polish Precedent (USA)-Rapide Pied (USA) (Raise A Native) 3262$^{16}$ 3519$^{7}$ **>30f<**

**Rapier 2** b c Sharpo-Sahara Breeze (Ela-Mana-Mou) 3794$^{3}$ (3964) 4366$^{3}$ **>85f<**

**Rapier Point (IRE) 5** gr g Cyrano de Bergerac-Renzola (Dragonara Palace (USA)) 4259$^{17}$ 4881$^{13}$ 4915$^{8}$ **>43a 45f<**

**Raqib 5** b g Slip Anchor-Reine Maid (USA) (Mr Prospector (USA)) *1063$^{8}$* **>54f<**

**Rasayel (USA) 6** b m Bering-Reham (Mill Reef (USA)) *836$^{9}$ (995)* 1306$^{3}$ *1487$^{6}$ 1778$^{3}$* 2348$^{4}$ 2793$^{3}$ (3267) 3500$^{2}$ 3918$^{5}$ 4000$^{7}$ 4365$^{10}$ 4753$^{3}$ 4872$^{13}$ 5007$^{2}$ **>31a 72f<**

**Rash Gift 3** ch f Cadeaux Genereux-Nettle (Kris) 4690$^{3}$ 4813$^{7}$ **>70f<**

**Rasin Charge 5** b g Governor General-Airlanka (Corvaro (USA)) 3226$^{5}$ 3413$^{5}$ **>31df<**

**Rasmi (CAN) 5** ch h Riverman (USA)-Snow Blossom (CAN) (The Minstrel (CAN)) **1995:** *4442$^{10}$* **1996:** *872$^{20}$* 1173$^{14}$ 1533$^{14}$ *2085$^{13}$ 2868$^{12}$* 3172$^{8}$ **>40f<**

**Rasmussen (IRE) 2** b c Sadler's Wells (USA)-Arctic Heroine (USA) (Arctic Tern (USA)) 3493$^{5}$ 3821$^{4}$ 4204$^{5}$ 4760$^{8}$ **>71f<**

**Rattle 3** b g Mazilier (USA)-Snake Song (Mansingh (USA)) 473$^{5}$ 540$^{3}$ 616$^{5}$ 849$^{8}$ 998$^{2}$ 1167$^{4}$ 1584$^{3}$ *1814$^{9}$ 2493$^{5}$* 2847$^{5}$ **>43a 57f<**

**Raven Master (USA) 2** b c Shalford (IRE)-Face The Facts (Lomond (USA)) 1003$^{2}$ (1519) 2070$^{10}$ 2671a$^{5}$ 3616$^{5}$ 3835$^{13}$ 4864$^{11}$ **>90f<**

**Raven's Roost (IRE) 5** b g Taufan (USA)-Al Zumurrud (Be My Guest (USA)) 1685$^{2}$ 1893$^{18}$ **>60f<**

**Ravier (ITY) 5** gr h Highest Honor (FR)-Revarola (ITY) (Marracci) **1995:** 4402a$^{5}$ **1996:** 1759a$^{2}$ 4667a$^{4}$ 5074a$^{8}$ **>117f<**

**Raw Deal 3** ch f Domynsky-Close the Deal (Nicholas Bill) *1027$^{12}$* **>2a f<**

**Rawi 3** ch g Forzando-Finally (Final Straw) **1995:** *4389$^{4}$ 4431$^{16}$ 4453$^{7}$ 4509$^{11}$* **1996:** *25$^{2}$ 81$^{2}$ 143$^{3}$ 188$^{3}$ 242$^{2}$ 949$^{5}$ 2158$^{6}$ 2617$^{14}$* 2769$^{4}$ 3863$^{6}$ 3977$^{3}$ *4336$^{8}$* **>56a 61f<**

**React 3** b f Reprimand-Shehana (USA) (The Minstrel (CAN)) 987$^{2}$ 1629$^{3}$ 2007$^{12}$ **>95f<**

**Read Your Contract (IRE) 2** ch g Imp Society (USA)-Princess of Nashua (Crowned Prince (USA)) 1479$^{7}$ 2122$^{10}$ *2554$^{6}$ 3629$^{5}$ 4046$^{16}$* **>28a 42f<**

**Ready Teddy (IRE) 3** b f Fayruz-Racey Naskra (USA) (Star de Naskra (USA)) *539$^{11}$* 881$^{6}$ 1547$^{2}$ 2021$^{8}$ 2176$^{2}$ 2359$^{3}$ 2732$^{3}$ 2800$^{7}$ **>52f<**

**Ready to Draw (IRE) 7** ch g On Your Mark-Mitsubishi Art (Cure The Blues (USA)) *489$^{2}$ 666$^{10}$ 1717$^{3}$ 1967$^{2}$ 2631$^{3}$* **>57a 31f<**

**Reaganesque (USA) 4** b g Nijinsky (CAN)-Basoof (USA) (Believe It (USA)) 642$^{8}$ 811$^{11}$ 1124$^{4}$ 1837$^{4}$ (2191) (2341) 2973$^{7}$ 3318$^{2}$ (3587) **>57f<**

**Real Connection (USA) 5** gr m Vigors (USA)-Right Connection (USA) (Unconscious (USA)) 5032a$^{2}$ **>118f<**

**Real Estate 2** b c High Estate-Haitienne (FR) (Green Dancer (USA)) 2302$^{6}$ 4720$^{7}$ **>67f<**

**Real Fire (IRE) 2** b c Astronef-Golden Arum (Home Guard (USA)) *1166$^{6}$* 1827$^{7}$ *2746$^{8}$ 4041$^{10}$* 4384$^{12}$ 4562$^{17}$ 4790$^{7}$ **>27a 49f<**

**Real Gem 3** b f Formidable (USA)-Emerald Ring (Auction Ring (USA)) 2528$^{3}$ *3061$^{6}$ 3166$^{13}$* 3698$^{11}$ 4373$^{20}$ **>45a 59df<**

**Real Guest (IRE) 3** b f Be My Guest (USA)-You Make Me Real (USA) 4643a$^{10}$ **>75f<**

**Really A Dream (IRE) 3** br f Last Tycoon-Ancestry (Persepolis (FR)) *678$^{2}$* 874$^{5}$ 2888$^{10}$ 3353$^{3}$ 3767$^{4}$ 4109$^{6}$ 4499$^{3}$ (4860) **>81f<**

**Really Chuffed 2** b g Shavian-Oriental Splendour (Runnett) 4280a$^{6}$ 5014a$^{W}$ **>78f<**

**Real Madrid 5** b g Dreams to Reality (USA)-Spanish Princess (King of Spain) **1995:** *4466a$^{4}$* (4467a) *4537$^{3}$* **1996:** *66$^{2}$ 122$^{7}$ (145) 189$^{9}$ 309$^{2}$ 349$^{5}$ 1448$^{7}$ 1903$^{6}$* 2203$^{8}$ **>50a 34f<**

**Realms of Glory (IRE) 3** b c Reprimand-Wasaif (IRE) (Lomond (USA)) *467$^{7}$* 1119$^{18}$ *1721$^{5}$ 2158$^{11}$ 2542$^{11}$* 2913$^{7}$ 4624$^{10}$ **>51a 12f<**

**Reams of Verse (USA) 2** ch f Nureyev (USA)-Modena (USA) (Roberto (USA)) 2863$^{2}$ (3756) (4133) (4464) **>110f<**

**Rebecca Sharp 2** b f Machiavellian (USA)-Nuryana (Nureyev (USA)) 4969$^{2}$ **>82+f<**

**Rebel County (IRE) 3** b f Maelstrom Lake-Haven Bridge (Connaught) 453$^{11}$ 676$^{6}$ 917$^{5}$ (1152) (1497) 1659$^{3}$ 1999$^{2}$ (2218) 2536$^{6}$ 2677$^{8}$ 2701$^{9}$ 3403$^{4}$ 3634$^{2}$ (3830) 3933$^{3}$ 3989$^{3}$ 4190$^{14}$ (4297) 4463$^{5}$ (4583) 4769$^{7}$ 4874$^{7}$ **>94f<**

**Rebounder 3** b g Reprimand-So Bold (Never so Bold) *1030$^{13}$ 1311$^{11}$* 2380$^{8}$ **>1a 1f<**

**Rebuke 2** b g Reprimand-Lyra (Blakeney) 569$^{7}$ 685$^{9}$ 757$^{4}$ 2254$^{5}$ 3405$^{6}$ 4795$^{13}$ **>49f<**

**Recall To Mind 3** b g Don't Forget Me-Northern Notion (USA) (Northern Baby (CAN)) 1089$^{17}$ 1669$^{10}$ 2136$^{8}$ **>43f<**

**Recessions Over 5** b g Komaite (USA)-Lucky Councillor (Lucky Wednesday) **1995:** *4508$^{7}$* **1996:** *29$^{7}$* **>14a f<**

**Rechullin 2** ch f Niniski (USA)-Rechanit (IRE) (Local Suitor (USA)) 4783$^{3}$ **>69f<**

**Recluse 5** b g Last Tycoon-Nomadic Pleasure (Habitat) *620$^{15}$* 1167$^{17}$ 2175$^{10}$ **>8f<**

**Recondite (IRE) 2** b c Polish Patriot (USA)-Recherchee (Rainbow Quest (USA)) 800$^{2}$ (1038) 1419$^{3}$ (2619) 4023a$^{2}$ 4462$^{8}$ **>103f<**

**Record Lover (IRE) 6** b g Alzao (USA)-Spun Gold (Thatch (USA)) *113$^{3}$ 154$^{3}$ (208) 283$^{7}$ 602$^{4}$ 1031$^{8}$ 1095$^{4}$ 1717$^{4}$ 2028$^{6}$* 3638$^{2}$ 3968$^{6}$ 4815$^{5}$ *4984$^{9}$* **>40a 50f<**

**Recourse (USA) 2** b c Alleged (USA)-Queens Only (USA) (Marshua's Dancer (USA)) 4175$^{4}$ 4500$^{5}$ **>94?f<**

**Red Acuisle (IRE) 3** br c Soviet Lad (USA)-Scottish Gaelic (USA) (Highland Park (USA)) **1995:** *4353$^{2}$ 4389$^{2}$ 4461$^{6}$ 4518$^{10}$* **1996:** *21$^{5}$ 59$^{8}$ 101$^{3}$ 160$^{3}$ 209$^{6}$ 359$^{5}$* **>64da 63f<**

**Red Adair (IRE) 4** ch g Waajib-Little Red Hut (Habitat) *274$^{10}$ 1691$^{17}$* **>20f<**

**Red Admiral 6** ch g Formidable (USA)-Dancing Meg (USA) (Marshua's Dancer (USA)) *1905$^{4}$* 2280$^{4}$ 2434$^{2}$ 2947$^{3}$ 3096$^{2}$ 3168$^{6}$ 3313$^{6}$ *4081$^{6}$ (4333) 4577$^{9}$ 4895$^{W}$* **>72a 67f<**

**Redbrook Lady 3** ch f Clantime-Silently Yours (USA) (Silent Screen (USA)) 1087$^{14}$ **>5a 39f<**

**Red Camellia 2** b f Polar Falcon (USA)-Cerise Bouquet (Mummy's Pet) (2211) (2997) (3804) 4464$^{4}$ **>111f<**

**Red Carnival (USA) 4** b f Mr Prospector (USA)-Seaside Attraction (USA) (Seattle Slew (USA)) 4325$^{4}$ 4671$^{8}$ **>109df<**

**Red Channel (IRE) 6** b g Import-Winscarlet North (Garland Knight) **1995:** *4543$^{6}$* **1996:** *103$^{7}$* **>39a f<**

**Reddish Creek (USA) 3** f **1995:** (4422a)

**Red Embers 2** gr f Saddlers' Hall (IRE)-Kala Rosa (Kalaglow) *(1590)* 2375$^{5}$ **>79f<**

**Red Five 5** b g Clantime-Miami Dolphin (Derrylin) **1995:** *4371$^{12}$* **1996:** *1163$^{2}$* **>29a 56f< (DEAD)**

**Red Garter (IRE) 2** b f Common Grounds-Red Magic (Red God) 481$^{2}$ 807$^{2}$ 946$^{5}$ 1479$^{5}$ 2051$^{13}$ 2309$^{10}$ 3771$^{6}$ 3826$^{6}$ *4079$^{5}$ 4230$^{10}$* **>45a 62f<**

**Red Guard 2** ch c Soviet Star (USA)-Zinzara (USA) (Stage Door Johnny) 4242$^{13}$ 4516$^{3}$ 4914$^{4}$ **>78f<**

**Red Hot Risk 4** b g Risk Me (FR)-Hot Sunday Sport (Star Appeal) *77$^{10}$* **>60f<**

**Red Indian 10** ch g Be My Native (USA)-Martialette (Welsh Saint) *777$^{7}$ 855$^{6}$ 1031$^{10}$* **>30a 50f<**

**Red Leo (USA) 3** b c Crafty Prospector (USA)-Lucky Brook (USA) (What Luck (USA)) 648$^{12}$ **>30f<**

**Red Light 4** b g Reprimand-Trull (Lomond (USA)) 1695$^{5}$ **>66df<**

**Red March Hare 5** b m Daring March-Happy Harriet (Red Sunset) 3399$^{7}$ 3592$^{8}$ 4348$^{2}$ **>33a 38f<**

**Red Nymph 3** b f Sharpo-Red Gloves (Red God) *1493$^{2}$* 2007$^{16}$ 3222$^{4}$ 3783$^{4}$ 3984$^{6}$ 4581$^{18}$ **>96f<**

**Red O'Reilly 4** ch g Hubbly Bubbly (USA)-Name the Game (Fair Season) *401$^{8}$* **>19a 53f<**

**Red Phantom (IRE) 4** ch g Kefaah (USA)-Highland Culture (Lomond (USA)) *898$^{12}$ 1458$^{3}$ 1967$^{3}$ 2082$^{3}$ 2304$^{5}$ 4669$^{13}$* **>72a 24f<**

**Red Rainbow 8** b h Rainbow Quest (USA)-Red Berry (Great Nephew) 4826$^{15}$ 4974$^{26}$ **>56f<**

**Red Raja 3** b c Persian Heights-Jenny Splendid (John Splendid) 4307$^{11}$ 4604$^{6}$ 4804$^{9}$ **>68f<**

**Red Robbo (CAN) 3** b c Red Ransom (USA)-Aunt Jobiska (USA) (What Luck (USA)) 808$^{3}$ 1015$^{7}$ **>91f<**

**Red Romance 2** b g Prince Daniel (USA)-Rio Piedras (Kala Shikari) 1038$^{3}$ 1308$^{2}$ 1869$^{7}$ 2681$^{2}$ 2930$^{3}$ 3291$^{2}$ 4250$^{W}$ 4907$^{4}$ 5006$^{6}$ **>60f<**

**Red Roses Story 4** ch f Pink-Roses For The Star

438a$^{2}$ (4959a) **>123f<**

**Red Rusty (USA)** 3 ch g The Carpenter (USA)-Super Sisters (AUS) (Call Report (USA)) **1995:** *4501$^{2}$ (4535)* **1996:** *676$^{12}$ 836$^{7}$ 1993$^{3}$ 2541$^{5}$ 2689$^{6}$ 2934$^{6}$ 4216$^{12}$ 4781$^{9}$ 4898$^{9}$* **>65a 53f<**

**Redskin Lady** 3 ch f Indian Ridge-Meritsu (IRE) (Lyphard's Special (USA)) 1617$^{9}$ 1857$^{9}$ 2432$^{5}$ 2765$^{4}$ 2946$^{3}$ 3162$^{2}$ 3513$^{9}$ 4053$^{14}$ 4888$^{14}$ **>68df<**

**Red Sky Delight (IRE)** 3 b f Skyliner-Blazing Sunset (Blazing Saddles (AUS)) *1012$^{13}$* 1677$^{8}$ 2284$^{14}$ **>26f<**

**Red Spectacle (IRE)** 4 b g Red Sunset-Buz Kashi (Bold Lad (IRE)) *9$^{3}$ 69$^{4}$ 108$^{8}$ 187$^{3}$ 267$^{4}$ 1478$^{7}$* 1870$^{5}$ 2165$^{14}$ 2355$^{3}$ 2848$^{8}$ 3347$^{3}$ 3487$^{4}$ **>57a 58f<**

**Redspet** 2 ch f Tina's Pet-Manabel (Manado) 4907$^{9}$ **>17f<**

**Redstella (USA)** 7 ch h Theatrical-Orange Squash (Red God) *1421$^{7}$* 1977$^{5}$ 2418$^{4}$ *2936$^{6}$* **>47a 63f<**

**Red Test (USA)** 2 b g Glitterman (USA)-Cut Test (USA) (Relaunch (USA)) *1603$^{5}$ 1968$^{2}$ 2076$^{3}$* 3436$^{4}$ *3604$^{8}$* **>52a 68f<**

**Red Tie Affair (USA)** 3 b c Miswaki (USA)-Quiet Rendezvous (USA) (Nureyev (USA)) 1901$^{11}$ 2048$^{5}$ 2506$^{6}$ *2751$^{8}$ 3000$^{3}$* 3584$^{11}$ 4355$^{6}$ 4474$^{6}$ **>17a 55f<**

**Red Time** 3 br g Timeless Times (USA)-Crimson Dawn (Manado) *390$^{9}$ 861$^{5}$* 1009$^{3}$ 1356$^{3}$ 1535$^{7}$ 3166$^{10}$ 3477$^{6}$ 3698$^{6}$ 3862$^{5}$ 3993$^{7}$ 4372$^{11}$ **>30a 53f<**

**Red Valerian** 5 b g Robellino (USA)-Fleur Rouge (Pharly (FR)) *2214$^{U}$* 2593$^{4}$ (3452) 3856$^{2}$ **>90a 79f< (DEAD)**

**Red Viper** 4 b c Posen (USA)-Within A Whisper (Welsh Pageant) 2015$^{3}$ 2194$^{8}$ 2510$^{9}$ 3067$^{13}$ 3471$^{10}$ 3694$^{8}$ **>51f<**

**Redwing** 2 b g Reprimand-Bronzewing (Beldale Flutter (USA)) 3221$^{3}$ (3837) 4471$^{6}$ **>82f<**

**Reed My Lips (IRE)** 5 br g Thatching-Taunsa (Nishapour (FR)) *479$^{11}$* 645$^{7}$ 1638$^{10}$ 1830$^{10}$ 2218$^{4}$ **>52da 39f<**

**Reefa's Mill (IRE)** 4 b g Astronef-Pharly's Myth (Pharly (FR)) 817$^{10}$ 979$^{7}$ 1698$^{4}$ 2189$^{10}$ 3340$^{10}$ **>61df<**

**Reef D'Irlande (FR)** 2 5024a$^{9}$ **>67f<**

**Reef Raider** 3 gr g Siberian Express (USA)-Superior Quality (Star Appeal) 522$^{15}$ 594$^{10}$ **>44f<**

**Reem Fever (IRE)** 3 b f Fairy King (USA)-Jungle Jezebel (Thatching) 4053$^{12}$ 4202$^{10}$ 4356$^{23}$ 4785$^{12}$ **>52f<**

**Reeves (IRE)** 4 b g Caerleon (USA)-Kalkeen (Sheshoon) 4537b$^{7}$ **>64f<**

**Referendum (IRE)** 2 b c Common Grounds-Final Decision (Tap On Wood) 706$^{3}$ 1130$^{2}$ (3807) 4398a$^{2}$ 4742a$^{4}$ **>95f<**

**Refuse To Lose** 2 ch c Emarati (USA)-Petrol (Troy) 4330$^{5}$ (4902) **>63+f<**

**Regait** 2 b c In The Wings-Rowa (Great Nephew) 4720$^{11}$ 4920$^{9}$ **>54f<**

**Regal Academy (IRE)** 2 b f Royal Academy (USA)-Polistatic (Free State) 4104$^{6}$ **>67f<**

**Regal Archive (IRE)** 3 b c Fairy King (USA)-Marseillaise (Artaius (USA)) (577) (808) (1441) 1756a$^{5}$ (3387a) 3911a$^{8}$ **>111f<**

**Regal Discovery (CAN)** 4 *535a$^{9}$* **>62a f<**

**Regal Dynasty (IRE)** 2 b f Royal Academy (USA)-Reality (Known Fact (USA)) (4286a)

**Regal Eagle** 3 b c Shirley Heights-On The Tiles (Thatch (USA)) *1182$^{9}$* 1434$^{7}$ 1900$^{5}$ 2247$^{7}$ 3471$^{13}$ **>76df<**

**Regal Equity** 2 b c Keen-Nazmiah (Free State) 2852$^{10}$ 2977$^{6}$ 3502$^{3}$ 4049$^{10}$ 4234$^{12}$ 4912$^{4}$ 5037$^{10}$ **>66f<**

**Regal Fanfare (IRE)** 4 b f Taufan (USA)-Tender Time (Tender King) 742$^{5}$ 1041$^{9}$ 1629$^{7}$ 2524$^{3}$ 3168$^{7}$ 3578$^{4}$ 4323$^{2}$ 4768$^{17}$ **>62f<**

**Regal Patrol** 2 b c Red Ransom (USA)-River Patrol (Rousillon (USA)) 1694$^{4}$ 1960$^{4}$ **>72f<**

**Regal Reprimand** 2 b c Reprimand-Queen Caroline (USA) (Chief's Crown (USA)) 4599$^{7}$ 4801$^{11}$ **>70f<**

**Regal Splendour (CAN)** 3 ch c Vice Regent (CAN)-Seattle Princess (USA) (Seattle Slew (USA)) 3788$^{10}$ 4108$^{2}$ 4360$^{10}$ 4693$^{2}$ 4820$^{13}$ **>75?f<**

**Regal Thunder (USA)** 2 b c Chief's Crown (USA)-Summertime Showers (USA) (Raise A Native) 4516$^{5}$ **>70f<**

**Regiment (IRE)** 3 gr c Shaadi (USA)-Rossaldene (Mummy's Pet) *(574)* 926$^{13}$ **>101+f<**

**Rehaab** 3 b f Mtoto-Top Treat (USA) (Topsider (USA)) 2789$^{2}$ (3108) 3522$^{7}$ 3979$^{5}$ **>69f<**

**Rehearsal (IRE)** 2 b c Royal Academy (USA)-Yashville (Top Ville) 2243$^{3}$ 2580$^{9}$ 2695$^{3}$ **>84f<**

**Rehlat Farah (USA)** 5 b h Pleasant Colony (USA)-Venus Bound (USA) (Conquistador Cielo (USA)) *535a$^{10}$* **>62a 94f<**

**Reimei** 7 b g Top Ville-Brilliant Reay (Ribero) 1421$^{5}$ (2300) 2882$^{10}$ 4447$^{16}$ 4675$^{14}$ **>73f<**

**Reinaldo (FR)** 4 b c Green Desert (USA)-Ghariba (Final Straw) 1053a$^{3}$ **>105f<**

**Reine Wells (IRE)** 3 b f Sadler's Wells (USA)-Rivoltade (USA) (Sir Ivor) 5026a$^{3}$ **>102f<**

**Reinhardt (IRE)** 3 b g Bluebird (USA)-Rhein Bridge (Rheingold) 544$^{3}$ 772$^{3}$ 982$^{5}$ 2234$^{4}$ 2581$^{14}$ 3056$^{4}$ 3280$^{7}$ 3344$^{8}$ 3780$^{13}$ 4437$^{6}$ **>66f<**

**Reiterate** 3 b f Then Again-Indubitable (Sharpo) 813$^{11}$ 1117$^{9}$ 1852$^{11}$ 3113$^{10}$ 3500$^{12}$ **>50df<**

**Rejoicing (IRE)** 2 b f Damister (USA)-Rocket Alert (Red Alert) 3245$^{4}$ 3359$^{2}$ 3701$^{3}$ **>78f<**

**Relatively High** 5 b m Persian Heights-Kissin' Cousin (Be Friendly) 2344$^{10}$ **>16f<**

**Reliquary (USA)** 2 b c Zilzal (USA)-Reloy (USA) (Liloy (FR)) *(3588)* 4179$^{4}$ 4685$^{3}$ **>85f<**

**Remaadi Sun** 4 gr g Cadeaux Genereux-Catch The Sun (Kalaglow) **1995:** *4435$^{7}$ 4454$^{3}$ 4503$^{12}$* **1996:** *451$^{18}$* 547$^{3}$ 641$^{6}$ (853) (1109) 1426$^{5}$ 2055$^{6}$ 2330$^{13}$ 2690$^{4}$ 3266$^{8}$ 3689$^{5}$ 4055$^{5}$ 4327$^{4}$ 4465$^{18}$ **>51a 94f<**

**Remember Star** 3 ch f Don't Forget Me-Star Girl Gay (Lord Gayle (USA)) *550$^{14}$* 707$^{11}$ 1009$^{8}$ 1347$^{16}$ **>54f<**

**Remontant (IRE)** 4 ch f Al Hareb (USA)-Red Red Rose (USA) (Blushing Groom (FR)) 609$^{7}$ *1457$^{11}$ 1697$^{6}$* 1828$^{2}$ 2028$^{7}$ 2191$^{8}$ **>43a 48f<**

**Remski** 2 b c Risk Me (FR)-Dona Krista (King of Spain) 815$^{10}$ **>14f<**

**Renata's Prince (IRE)** 3 b g Prince Rupert (FR)-Maria Renata (Jaazeiro (USA)) 4511$^{18}$ 4702$^{14}$ **>60df<**

**Rennyholme** 5 ch g Rich Charlie-Jacqui Joy (Music Boy) **1995:** *4430$^{11}$ 4488$^{6}$* **1996:** *22$^{4}$ 127$^{7}$ 292$^{2}$ 386$^{2}$ 394$^{3}$ (514) 601$^{17}$ 835$^{7}$ 900$^{3}$ 1492$^{3}$ 1716$^{11}$* **>57a 27f<**

**Reno's Treasure (USA)** 3 ch f Beau Genius (CAN)-Ligia M (USA) (Noholme Jr (USA)) 2411$^{8}$ 2893$^{5}$ 3108$^{5}$ 3357$^{5}$ 3808$^{19}$ **>46f<**

**Renown** 4 b g Soviet Star (USA)-Starlet (Teenoso (USA)) **1995:** *4386$^{5}$ (4544)* **1996:** *132$^{7}$ (462) 871$^{12}$* (1660) 3786$^{9}$ 4900$^{2}$ **>79a 76f<**

**Renzo (IRE)** 3 b c Alzao (USA)-Watership (USA) (Foolish Pleasure (USA)) 576$^{4}$ 2383$^{2}$ 2601$^{3}$ 4379$^{2}$ 4548$^{3}$ (4992) **>89f<**

**Repertory** 3 b g Anshan-Susie's Baby (Balidar) 565$^{2}$ 832$^{9}$ 945$^{7}$ 4772$^{20}$ 4823$^{9}$ **>85f<**

**Reploy** 3 gr f Deploy-Nelly Do Da (Derring-Do) **1995:** *4352$^{6}$* **1996:** *17$^{2}$ 197$^{3}$ 4766$^{10}$* **>62a 56df<**

**Requested** 9 b g Rainbow Quest (USA)-Melody Hour (Sing Sing) 1511$^{5}$ 2148$^{2}$ 3037$^{15}$ 3813$^{4}$ 4048$^{10}$ 4203$^{2}$ **>58f<**

**Requin Bleu (IRE)** 3 b c Thatching-Robertet (USA) (Roberto (USA)) 2050$^{15}$ **>90f< (DEAD)**

**Rescue Time (IRE)** 3 b c Mtoto-Tamassos (Dance In Time (CAN)) 1249a$^{6}$ 4026a$^{9}$ **>83f<**

**Resounder (USA)** 3 b c Explodent (USA)-Rub Al Khali (USA) (Mr Prospector (USA)) 3132$^{4}$ 3524$^{6}$ 3822$^{4}$ 4196$^{7}$ 4554$^{12}$ **>95f<**

**Respectable Jones** 10 ch g Tina's Pet-Jonesee (Dublin Taxi) **1995:** *4456$^{4}$ 4512$^{11}$* **1996:** *65$^{4}$ 117$^{3}$ 273$^{3}$ 317$^{7}$ 1889$^{11}$* 2212$^{12}$ 2392$^{6}$ 2903$^{9}$ *4979$^{12}$* **>56a 24f<**

**Respect A Secret** 4 ch f Respect-Pendle's Secret (Le Johnstan) 1092$^{9}$ (1500) 1859$^{3}$ 2047$^{13}$ **>46f< (DEAD)**

**Respecting** 3 b g Respect-Pricey (Silly Prices) 804$^{5}$ 1090$^{8}$ 2420$^{3}$ 3102$^{15}$ **>70f<**

**Restate (IRE)** 5 b m Soviet Star (USA)-Busca (USA) (Mr Prospector (USA)) *99$^{3}$ 204$^{5}$* **>57a f<**

**Restiv Star (FR)** 4 b f Soviet Star (USA)-Restiver **1995:** 4423a$^{2}$ **1996:** 3392a$^{4}$ **>113f<**

**Restless Mixa (IRE)** 3 b f Linamix (FR)-Restless Girl (FR) (Bolkonski) 1949a$^{12}$

**Restless Spirit (USA)** 2 b c Sheikh Albadou-Wayward Lass (USA) (Hail the Pirates (USA)) 4208$^{4}$ 4816$^{2}$ (4918) **>86f<**

**Restructure (IRE)** 4 b c Danehill (USA)-Twine (Thatching) 680$^{5}$ (1824) 2037$^{2}$ (2839a) 3144$^{5}$ 3784$^{4}$ 4132$^{3}$ 4409a$^{12}$ 4520$^{2}$ **>121f<**

**Retender (USA)** 7 br g Storm Bird (CAN)-Dandy Bury (FR) (Exbury) **1995:** *4465$^{3}$ 4526$^{5}$* **1996:** *83$^{10}$ 309$^{8}$* **>59da 70f<**

**Ret Frem (IRE)** 3 b g Posen (USA)-New Light (Reform) 595$^{7}$ 1317$^{3}$ (1654) 1872$^{2}$ 2214$^{4}$ (2773) 4300$^{14}$ **>76f<**

**Reticent** 3 b c Sadler's Wells (USA)-Shy Princess (USA) (Irish River (FR)) 1906$^{5}$ 3505$^{5}$ 3986$^{8}$ 4478$^{7}$ **>72df<**

**Retoto** 2 ch f Totem (USA)-Responder (Vitiges (FR)) 2043$^{2}$ (2435) 3046$^{11}$ 3582$^{9}$ **>58f<**

**Return of Amin** 2 ch c Salse (USA)-Ghassanah (Pas de Seul) 1344$^{6}$ 3245$^{7}$ *4091$^{3}$ 4717$^{10}$* 4883$^{3}$ (5048) **>63a 63f<**

**Return To Brighton** 4 b f Then Again-Regency Brighton (Royal Palace) 1638$^{2}$ (2075) 2313$^{4}$ 2801$^{5}$ 2971$^{10}$ 3257$^{5}$ 3645$^{10}$ *4982$^{10}$* **>16a 53f<**

**Reunion (IRE)** 2 br f Be My Guest (USA)-Phylella (Persian Bold) (1499) 4338$^{3}$ **>83f<**

**Reverand Thickness** 5 b g Prince Sabo-Wollow Maid (Wollow) *270$^{6}$ 384$^{7}$ 470$^{14}$* (649) 1406$^{3}$ 1704$^{U}$ **>71a 76f< (DEAD)**

**Reveuse de Jour (IRE)** 3 b f Sadler's Wells (USA)-Magic of Life (USA) (Seattle Slew (USA)) *583$^{4}$* 842$^{2}$ **>70f<**

**Revoque (IRE)** 2 b c Fairy King (USA)-La Bella Fontana (Lafontaine (USA)) (3069) (3668) (4294a) (4742a) **>114+f<**

**Rex Mundi** 4 b g Gunner B-Rose Standish (Gulf Pearl) 691$^{10}$ 2036$^{11}$ 2540$^{2}$ 3109$^{3}$ 3580$^{4}$ (4249) 4431$^{4}$ 4669$^{5}$ 4900$^{3}$ 4993$^{3}$ **>71f<**

**Rhapsody In White (IRE)** 2 b g Contract Law (USA)-Lux Aeterna (Sandhurst Prince) 4330$^{13}$ 4599$^{2}$ *4985$^{4}$* **>30a 81f<**

**Rheinbold** 2 br g Never so Bold-Rheinbloom (Rheingold) 4863$^{7}$ **>50f<**

**Rhythmic Ball** 3 ch f Classic Music (USA)-Chrisanthy (So Blessed) 638$^{8}$ 973$^{10}$ 1405$^{8}$ 1692$^{5}$ 2061$^{6}$ 2752$^{14}$ **>28a 54f< (DEAD)**

**Rhythmic Dancer** 8 b g Music Boy-Stepping Gaily (Gay Fandango (USA)) 2421$^{W}$ **>78a 71f<**

**Ricasso** 2 b c Kris-Chicarica (USA) (The Minstrel (CAN)) *2633$^{2}$ 2985$^{3}$* 3282$^{3}$ 3792$^{11}$ 4566$^{4}$ **>69a**

**76f<**

**Riccarton** 3 b c Nomination-Legendary Dancer (Shareef Dancer (USA)) 613[13] 703[10] 1160[7] 1780[5] 2425[3] 2851[3] 3289[2] 3958[3] 4263[6] **>56f<**

**Richard House Lad** 3 b c Warrshan (USA)-Sirenivo (USA) (Sir Ivor) **1995:** *4380[7]* **1996:** *528[7] 651[6] 1526[4]* 1638[11] 2061[4] 2180[5] 3354[6] 3474[8] 3619[6] (4082) 4829[17] **>41a 45f<**

**Richard of York** 6 b h Rainbow Quest (USA)-Triple First **1995:** *4403a[8]* ***>118f<***

**Rich Glow** 5 b g Rich Charlie-Mayglow (Sparkling Boy) *475[8]* 610[23] 806[14] 928[9] 1186[13] 1588[7] 2005[14] 2119[3] (2421) 2586[6] 2694[11] 2911[4] 3085[5] (3352) 3482[8] 3868[6] 4058[11] 4246[6] 4367[7] 4505[10] **>22a 61f<**

**Rich Ground** 2 gr c Common Grounds-Gratclo (Belfort (FR)) *1197[11]* (2295) (2607) 3750a[4] 4519[9] **>104f<**

**Rich In Love (IRE)** 2 b f Alzao (USA)-Chief's Quest (USA) (Chief's Crown (USA)) 1148[2] (2063) 2582[5] 2997[5] 3243[2] 3835[4] 4488[19] **>94f<**

**Ricks Natural Star (USA)** 7 ch g Natural Native (USA)-Malaysian Star (USA) (Crimson Star (USA)) 4955a[14]

**Ricky Ticky Tavie (USA)** 2 b c Dixieland Band (USA)-Save The Doe (USA) (Spend A Buck (USA)) 4461[2] **>90+f<**

**Ride Sally Ride (IRE)** 2 ch c Shalford (IRE)-Sally St Clair (Sallust) 848[4] (1166) 1510[6] 1980[2] 2364[3] 3032a[3] **>91f<**

**Rififi** 3 ch c Aragon-Bundled Up (USA) (Sharpen Up) 755[7] 1101[5] 1412[W] 1536[4] 1693[9] 2500[W] **>62f<**

**Righteous Gent** 3 b g Superpower-Golden (Don) **1995:** *4433[5] 4518[4]* **1996:** *25[3] 245[7] 364[4] 2631[8] 3089[12] 3422[5]* **>29a 51f<**

**Right Man** 2 gr c Robellino (USA)-High Matinee (Shirley Heights) 3829[5] 4123[14] 4380[14] **>62f<**

**Right Tune** 2 b f Green Desert (USA)-Triste Oeil (USA) (Raise A Cup (USA)) 2611[8] (3221) 3762[4] 4182[2] **>83f<**

**Right Win (IRE)** 6 br h Law Society (USA)-Popular Win (Lorenzaccio) 456[5] **>115df<**

**Right Wing (IRE)** 2 b c In The Wings-Nekhbet (Artaius (USA)) 4706[3] **>63f<**

**Righty Ho** 2 b g Reprimand-Challanging (Mill Reef (USA)) 3796[7] 3982[8] 4224[4] 4602[8] **>73f<**

**Rihan (USA)** 2 b br f Dayjur (USA)-Sweet Roberta (USA) (Roberto (USA)) 2051[8] 2611[2] (4807) 5043[5] **>78f<**

**Rinca** 2 b f Unfuwain (USA)-Branitska (Mummy's Pet) 4720[16] 4970[19] **>34f<**

**Ring of Vision (IRE)** 4 br g Scenic-Circus Lady (High Top) 993[11] 1821[D] 2066[14] (2628) 3220[2] 4000[10] 4249[6] 4626[15] **>61f<**

**Ring the Chief** 4 b g Chief Singer-Lomond Ring (Lomond (USA)) **1995:** *4464[11]* **1996:** *518[10] 654[5] 1085[7] 1809[6] 1966[2] 2085[5] 2303[3] 2574[3]* ***>43a 45f<***

**Rinus Manor (IRE)** 5 b g Ballad Rock-Never Never Land (Habitat) 617[8] 806[13] 911[3] 1039[5] 1547[4] 1865[4] 2240[7] 2732[6] 3100[5] 3489[7] 4809[13] **>38a 38f<**

**Rio Duvida** 3 ch c Salse (USA)-Fluctuate (Sharpen Up) *695[5]* 1329[5] 1768[5] 2354[3] 3906a[9] **>102f<**

**Rio Napo (IRE)** 2 b c Law Society (USA)-My Southern love (ITY) (Southern Arrow (USA)) 4287a[2]

**Riparius (USA)** 5 b g Riverman (USA)-Sweet Simone (FR) (Green Dancer (USA)) (816) 1147[5] 1802[3] 2401[8] 2900[6] 3457[6] 3653[7] **>88f<**

**Ripsnorter (IRE)** 7 ch g Rousillon (USA)-Formulate (Reform) **1995:** *4406[13] 4440[8] 4526[11]* **1996:** *1449[22]* 2032[5] *2369[10] 3496[15]* ***>27a 35f<***

**Riscatto (USA)** 2 b c Red Ransom (USA)-Ultima Cena (USA) (Leonardo da Vinci (FR)) 1445[6] *2307[2] 2554[4] 3616[11]* 3943[13] **>58a 35f<**

**Rise 'n Shine** 2 ch f Night Shift (USA)-Clunk Click (Star Appeal) 1678[6] 1998[2] 2230[3] 2398[2] 2595[2] 4210[3] 4425[7] **>79f<**

**Rise Up Singing** 8 ch g Noalto-Incarnadine (Hot Spark) *846[12]* 1423[15] 1872[10] 2340[2] 2885[11] 3076[3] 3606[11] **>55f<**

**Risiat (IRE)** 2 4658a[2]

**Rising Colours** 3 gr c Rusticaro (FR)-Galina (FR) (Bon Sang (FR)) (4030a) 4857a[9] **>112f<**

**Rising Dough (IRE)** 4 br g Dowsing (USA)-Shortning Bread (Blakeney) 670[8] 1618[9] (1816) 2401[4] 2767[2] 3136[3] 3944[4] 4121[7] **>75f<**

**Rising Glory** 2 b g Absalom-Glow Again (The Brianstan) *1968[W] 3941[14] 4079[13] 4347[6]* 4607[13] 4721[8] *4988[9] 5005[9]* ***>22a 37f<***

**Rising Spray** 5 ch g Waajib-Rose Bouquet (General Assembly (USA)) 1965[5] 2506[14] 2707[3] 3037[20] 3204[6] (3584) (3664) 3825[2] 4307[2] **>68f<**

**Rising Stream** 3 b f Pharly (FR)-River's Rising (FR) (Mendez (FR)) **1995:** *4353[5] 4375[4] 4492[7]* **>56a 28f<**

**Riskie Things** 5 ch m Risk Me (FR)-Foolish Things (Song) **1995:** *4542[7]* **1996:** *36[8] 133[9]* **>51da 47f<**

**Risking** 3 b f Risk Me (FR)-Dark Kristal (IRE) (Gorytus (USA)) *1333[15]* 1684[3] 1964[7] *4776[7] 5000[10]* **>35a 52f<**

**Risky Baby** 4 ch f Risk Me (FR)-Gemma Kaye (Cure The Blues (USA)) 982[16] 1171[13] 1876[11] **>63a 35f<**

**Risky Flight** 2 ch c Risk Me (FR)-Stairway to Heaven (IRE) (Godswalk (USA)) 452[12] 2485[6] 2781[8] *4093[11] 4228[12]* ***>26f<***

**Risky Missile** 2 b f Risk Me (FR)-Veuve Perrin (Legend of France (USA)) 4600[4] 4786[3] **>64f<**

**Risky Romeo** 4 b g Charmer-Chances Are (He Loves Me) **1995:** *4367[10] 4451[5] 4520[6]* **1996:** *(983)* 1010[10] 1449[23] 1807[11] 2709[8] **>68a 53f<**

**Risky Rose** 4 b f Risk Me (FR)-Moharabuiee (Pas de Seul) 1828[U] 2056[16] 2189[2] (2537) 2891[4] 2989[12] 3305[3] 4455[10] **>40a 50df<**

**Risky Royal** 4 ch g Risk Me (FR)-Royal Clover (Mansingh (USA)) **1995:** *4354[9]* **>59a 40f<**

**Risky Tu** 5 ch m Risk Me (FR)-Sarah Gillian (USA) (Zen (USA)) **1995:** *4391[3] 4475[2] 4534[4]* **1996:** *27[4] 353[5] 635[5]* 787[5] 1011[3] 2415[4] 2775[7] 3314[5] 3979[6] **>49a 47f<**

**Riston Lady (IRE)** 6 b m Salt Dome (USA)-Trompe D'Oeil (Longleat (USA)) **1995:** *4484[11]* **>40a 53df<**

**Rithab** 3 b f Shaadi (USA)-Lawahed (USA) 1255a[6] **>85f<**

**Ritto** 6 b g Arctic Tern (USA)-Melodrama (Busted) 3504[W] **>96?f<**

**Riva La Belle** 2 b f Ron's Victory (USA)-Haunting (Lord Gayle (USA)) 1086[14] 1494[6] 1904[4] 4097[15] 4361[12] 4694[13] **>44f<**

**Rival Bid (USA)** 8 b g Cannonade (USA)-Love Triangle (USA) (Nodouble (USA)) **1995:** *4537[4]* **1996:** *(27) 66[3] 184[5] 214[6] 547[9]* 843[9] (1838) 2183[7] *2553[5] 2689[8] 3272[7]* 3457[4] 3812[8] 4102[3] 4209[4] 4427[5] (4702) 4793[5] **>60a 76f<**

**Rival Queen (IRE)** 4 ch f Royal Academy (USA)-Maria Stuarda (Royal And Regal (USA)) *299[6] 440[24] 520[3] 1034[9]* ***>41a 53f<***

**Riva Rock** 6 b g Roaring Riva-Kivulini (Hotfoot) *2282[6]* ***>23a 43f<***

**Riva's Book (USA)** 5 b g Mari's Book (USA)-Riva's Revenge (USA) (Riva Ridge (USA)) 1167[16] **>48f<**

**River Bay (USA)** 3 ch c Irish River (FR)-Buckeye Gal **1995:** 4562a[3] **1996:** 4664a[5] (5078a) **>116f<**

**Riverbourne (USA)** 3 b c Riverman (USA)-Umaimah (USA) (Halo (USA)) 458[5] 3519[9] **>56f<**

**River Captain (USA)** 3 ch c Riverman (USA)-Katsura (USA) (Northern Dancer) 578[12] **>54f<**

**Rivercare (IRE)** 3 b c Alzao (USA)-Still River (Kings Lake (USA)) *415[6] 471[10]* 594[5] 731[3] 954[4] 1110[4] 1507[2] 1655[9] *1997[6] 2505[4]* 2570[8] 3768[6] 3928[9] 4365[11] 4509[7] 4612[7] **>37a 52f<**

**River Foyle (USA)** 2 ch c Irish River (FR)-Katsura (USA) (Northern Dancer) 4069[4] **>81f<**

**River Garnock** 4 br g Dowsing (USA)-Duboff (So Blessed) 559[16] 769[8] 1586[4] *1718[9] 2023[5]* 2421[6] **>16a 49f<**

**Riverine** 2 ch f Risk Me (FR)-Celtic River (IRE) (Caerleon (USA)) 4893[9] 5051[5] **>26f<**

**River Keen (IRE)** 4 ch c Keen-Immediate Impact (Caerleon (USA)) **1995:** *(4356) (4481)* **1996:** *(392) 573[16]* 4675[5] 4872[6] **>100a 88f<**

**River King** 2 b c River Falls-Sialia (IRE) (Bluebird (USA)) 2783[8] 3131[8] 3493[9] 4084[10] 4361[6] **>63f<**

**River North (IRE)** 6 ch g Lomond (USA)-Petillante (USA) (Riverman (USA)) 1575a[5] 1948a[3] 2194[3] 3212[9] 3597[5] **>113f<**

**River of Fortune (IRE)** 2 b f Lahib (USA)-Debach Delight (Great Nephew) 1871[6] 2187[3] 2596[2] 3171[2] 3826[2] 4072[2] 4224[2] 4364[7] 4594[2] (4715) 4880[5] **>73f<**

**River Run (IRE)** 4 b c Nordico (USA)-Irish Call (USA) (Irish River (FR)) *5056[8]* **>36a 52f<**

**River Seine (FR)** 4 b f Shining Steel-River Sans Retour (FR) (Vacarme (USA)) *5059[9]* **>40a 39f<**

**Riverside Girl (IRE)** 2 b f River Falls-Ballywhat (IRE) (Be My Native (USA)) 4607[6] 4715[25] **>34f<**

**Rivers Magic** 3 b g Dominion-Rivers Maid (Rarity) 1901[10] (2432) 4674[8] 4802[16] **>88f<**

**River's Source (USA)** 2 b c Irish River (FR)-Singing (USA) (The Minstrel (CAN)) 4514[4] 4698[2] **>81f<**

**River Tern** 3 b g Puissance-Millaine (Formidable (USA)) *1604[5] 2167[2]* 2732[10] 3399[3] 3624[3] (4074) 4341[12] 4589[8] 4811[17] **>44a 47f<**

**River Usk** 2 b c Caerleon (USA)-Shining Water (Kalaglow) (4451) 4699[4] (4963) **>102f<**

**River Wye (IRE)** 4 b g Jareer (USA)-Sun Gift (Guillaume Tell (USA)) **1995:** *4371[8] 4409[5]* **1996:** *4480[13]* ***>49a 49f<***

**Riviere Rouge** 3 ch f Forzando-Furry Dance (USA) (Nureyev (USA)) **1995:** *4353[8] 4417[9]* **>16a 21f<**

**Rivonia (USA)** 2 ch f Irish River (FR)-Princess Ivy (USA) (Lyphard's Wish (FR)) 1197[4] 2138[3] 3050[5] 3275[4] 3512[8] 4244[5] 4594[4] 4795[4] **>61f<**

**Riyadian** 4 ch c Polish Precedent (USA)-Knight's Baroness (Rainbow Quest (USA)) (919) **>125+f<**

**Rizal (USA)** 4 ch g Zilzal (USA)-Sigy (FR) (Habitat) *134[12] 204[11] 337[9]* **>23a f<**

**Road Racer (IRE)** 3 br g Scenic-Rally (Relko) 2181[8] 2572[8] 3226[4] 3461[4] 4000[11] 4227[3] 4474[4] 4587[8] **>57f<**

**Roar on Tour** 7 b g Dunbeath (USA)-Tickled Trout (Red Alert) *30[14] 199[9] 257[8] 527[13]* 884[6] 1088[9] 2075[13] *(2369) 2934[16] 4982[15]* **>68da 29f<**

**Robamaset (IRE)** 3 b g Caerleon (USA)-Smageta (High Top) *677[5]* 1058a[5] 3413[2] (4690) **>87f<**

**Robec Girl (IRE)** 2 ch f Masterclass (USA)-Resiusa (ITY) (Niniski (USA)) 1021[3] (1595) 2035[2] 2681[3] 2872[4] 3160[8] 3838[3] 4244[4] *(4576) 4777[3] (5061)* **>66a 80f<**

**Robellion** 5 b g Robellino (USA)-Tickled Trout (Red Alert) **1995:** *4441[7] 4531[4]* **1996:** *14[4] (53) 109[3] (189) 233[3] 306[10] 410[3] 553[5] 1872[8]* 2283[7] 2713[2]

(2992) (3219) 3323$^{4}$ 3622$^{10}$ 3810$^{8}$ 3973$^{4}$ 4088$^{6}$ 4255$^{5}$ 4439$^{5}$ 4828$^{8}$ **>75a 70f<**

**Robereva (IRE) 3** b f Red Sunset-Gay Reign (Lord Gayle (USA)) (723a) 1393a$^{6}$ **>101f<**

**Roberto Riva 3** b c Shirley Heights-Rustle of Silk (General Assembly (USA)) 4429$^{8}$ **>58f<**

**Robingo (IRE) 7** b g Bob Back (USA)-Mill's Girl (Le Levanstell) *961$^{2}$* ***>87f<***

**Robins (IRE) 4** b c Scenic-Roman Walk (Petorius) 5074a$^{9}$ **>106f<**

**Roblexie (IRE) 3** br c Dominion-Takhiyra (Vayrann) 5065a$^{12}$ **>84f<**

**Robo Magic (USA) 4** b g Tejano (USA)-Bubble Magic (USA) (Clever Trick (USA)) **1995:** *4362$^{4}$ 4441$^{8}$ 4487$^{2}$ (4536)* **1996:** *55$^{3}$ 144$^{4}$ (218) (266) 338$^{5}$ 1351$^{7}$* 1624$^{7}$ 1958$^{7}$ 2228$^{6}$ 2735$^{4}$ 2976$^{11}$ 3439$^{10}$ **>80a 54f<**

**Robreva (IRE) 3** 4541a$^{9}$ **>75f<**

**Robsera (IRE) 5** b g Robellino (USA)-Que Sera (Music Boy) *3985$^{21}$* ***>62a 75f<***

**Robusta (IRE) 3** b f Batshoof-Loucoum (FR) (Iron Duke (FR)) 684$^{9}$ 1104$^{F}$ **>75f< (DEAD)**

**Rochea 2** br f Rock City-Pervenche (Latest Model) 4241$^{6}$ 4383$^{4}$ *4572$^{4}$* **>50a 64f<**

**Rock And Reign 2** b f Rock City-Reina (Homeboy) 4127$^{16}$ **>28f< (DEAD)**

**Rockaroundtheclock 2** b g Rock City-Times (Junius (USA)) 958$^{3}$ 1166$^{8}$ 1779$^{5}$ 4339$^{3}$ *4572$^{8}$ 4803$^{14}$* ***>35a 61f<***

**Rockcracker (IRE) 4** ch g Ballad Rock-Forest Blaze (USA) (Green Forest (USA)) **1995:** *4531$^{10}$* **1996:** *26$^{3}$ 107$^{12}$ 178$^{9}$ 466$^{5}$* 632$^{4}$ 862$^{7}$ (981) 1039$^{2}$ 1307$^{8}$ 1624$^{9}$ 2209$^{5}$ (2719) 2964$^{5}$ 3352$^{7}$ 3810$^{12}$ 4088$^{9}$ 4356$^{16}$ 4888$^{8}$ **>55da 68f<**

**Rock Daisy 3** b br f Rock City-New Pastures (Formidable (USA)) *1776$^{11}$* 1956$^{9}$ **>41f<**

**Rocket Grounds (IRE) 3** b f Common Grounds-Ginosa (Amen (FR)) **1995:** *4483$^{10}$* **>39a 49f<**

**Rock Fantasy 2** b f Keen-Runelia (Runnett) 1808$^{5}$ 2132$^{4}$ 2863$^{10}$ 3408$^{7}$ 4049$^{11}$ 4262$^{12}$ **>55f<**

**Rock Group 4** b g Rock City-Norska (Northfields (USA)) 439$^{7}$ 546$^{3}$ 666$^{6}$ 886$^{10}$ 1150$^{3}$ 1511$^{3}$ 1679$^{4}$ **>64f<**

**Rock Oyster 4** b g Ballad Rock-Bombshell (Le Levanstell) **1995:** *4374$^{8}$* **1996:** *83$^{11}$* **>19a 59f<**

**Rock Symphony 6** ch g Ballad Rock-Shamasiya (FR) (Vayrann) *812$^{6}$* 928$^{16}$ 1186$^{10}$ 1829$^{4}$ 2220$^{7}$ 2363$^{7}$ 3216$^{4}$ 3296$^{12}$ 3783$^{16}$ **>88f<**

**Rock The Barney (IRE) 7** b h Coquelin (USA)-Lady Loire (Wolverlife) *1472$^{5}$* 1655$^{6}$ 1965$^{11}$ 2226$^{7}$ 4236$^{2}$ 4509$^{15}$ 4626$^{16}$ 4815$^{2}$ **>59f<**

**Rock The Casbah 2** ch c Rock City-Romantic Saga (Prince Tenderfoot (USA)) 2720$^{4}$ 3080$^{9}$ 3423$^{11}$ *3950$^{7}$* **>25a 62f<**

**Rock To The Top (IRE) 2** b c Rudimentary (USA)-Well Bought (IRE) (Auction Ring (USA)) 4380$^{9}$ 4494$^{14}$ 4782$^{13}$ **>71f<**

**Rockusa 4** b f Rock City-Miss Derby (USA) (Master Derby (USA)) 3274$^{13}$ 4496$^{14}$ 4703$^{19}$ **>19f<**

**Rockville Pike (IRE) 4** b g Glenstal (USA)-Sound Pet (Runnett) **1995:** *4536$^{9}$* **1996:** *55$^{13}$ 451$^{21}$ 499$^{12}$ (549)* 631$^{9}$ 879$^{31}$ 1099$^{5}$ 1314$^{5}$ 1517$^{3}$ 1992$^{14}$ 2507$^{19}$ **>37a 61f<**

**Rocky Forum 4** ch f Deploy-Beau's Delight (USA) (Lypheor) 811$^{2}$ (1194) (1439) 1511$^{2}$ 2042$^{7}$ **>48a 83f< (DEAD)**

**Rocky Melody 4** b g Music Boy-Summer Posy (Posse (USA)) **1995:** *4382$^{11}$* **>5a 23f<**

**Rocky Oasis (USA) 3** b c Gulch (USA)-Knoosh (USA) (Storm Bird (CAN)) 1508$^{2}$ **>102f<**

**Rocky's Meteor 3** b c Emarati (USA)-Hoop la (Final Straw) 1435$^{6}$ 1780$^{10}$ **>36a 57f<**

**Rocky Stream 3** b f Reprimand-Pebble Creek (IRE) (Reference Point) 768$^{11}$ 934$^{13}$ 1422$^{11}$ 1702$^{5}$ 2061$^{7}$ 2417$^{3}$ *2937$^{16}$ 3427$^{6}$* 3780$^{10}$ 4341$^{6}$ **>50f<**

**Rocky Two 5** b g Cree Song-Holloway Wonder (Swing Easy (USA)) **1995:** *4358$^{3}$ 4460$^{5}$ 4488$^{7}$* **1996:** *231$^{10}$ 330$^{5}$ 363$^{8}$ 409$^{5}$ 470$^{12}$* 764$^{6}$ 991$^{12}$ 1170$^{6}$ 2992$^{8}$ 3473$^{13}$ **>48a 41f<**

**Rocky Waters (USA) 7** b or br g Rocky Marriage (USA)-Running Melody (Rheingold) 582$^{10}$ 749$^{12}$ 1010$^{2}$ 1533$^{2}$ 1872$^{9}$ *2551$^{4}$ 2766$^{2}$* 2971$^{5}$ 3304$^{4}$ *3877$^{3}$ 4186$^{10}$* 4373$^{10}$ **>65a 60f<**

**Rocquaine Bay 9** b m Morston (FR)-Queen's Royale (Tobrouk (FR)) 1852$^{5}$ 2226$^{W}$ 2599$^{4}$ 3141$^{7}$ 3500$^{4}$ 3664$^{4}$ 3979$^{8}$ 4252$^{6}$ 4476$^{7}$ **>45f<**

**Rodeo Star (USA) 10** ch g Nodouble (USA)-Roundup Rose (USA) (Minnesota Mac) *1343$^{10}$* ***>46f<***

**Roderick Hudson 4** b g Elmaamul (USA)-Moviegoer (Pharly (FR)) *876$^{17}$* 3612$^{10}$ 3827$^{11}$ **>67f<**

**Roditano (USA) 6** b h Dixieland Band (USA)-Table One (Round Table) 327a$^{2}$

**Roebuck (FR) 2** b c Cricket Ball (USA)-Tisaniere (FR) (Lightning (FR)) 3029a$^{3}$ **>69f<**

**Roffey Spinney (IRE) 2** ch c Masterclass (USA)-Crossed Line (Thatching) 5051$^{3}$ **>69f<**

**Rogue Trader (IRE) 3** b g Mazaad-Ruby Relic (Monseigneur (USA)) 1152$^{9}$ **>8f<**

**Roi de la Mer (IRE) 5** b h Fairy King (USA)-Sea Mistress (Habitat) 649$^{4}$ 817$^{11}$ 1173$^{7}$ 2058$^{3}$ 2526$^{7}$ (2898) 3205$^{10}$ 3694$^{13}$ 3991$^{12}$ 4237$^{2}$ 4373$^{15}$ 4701$^{5}$ **>62f<**

**Roi du Nord (FR) 4** b g Top Ville-Ridja (FR) (Djakao (FR)) 3353$^{6}$ 3704$^{3}$ 3942$^{8}$ 4238$^{9}$ 4387$^{6}$ **>72df<**

**Roi Ho (FR) 5** br h Holst (USA)-Reine Ka (FR) (Kaldoun (FR)) (147a) **>90f<**

**Roisin Clover 5** ch m Faustus (USA)-Valiyen (Valiyar) *(844)* 1792$^{9}$ 3073$^{12}$ 3235$^{5}$ 3828$^{9}$ 4067$^{9}$ 4252$^{3}$ 4551$^{2}$ 4967$^{11}$ **>72f<**

**Roka 4** br f Rock City-Kalandariya (Kris) *582$^{13}$* 887$^{17}$ 1302$^{15}$ 1624$^{14}$ **>32df<**

**Rokeby Bowl 4** b c Salse (USA)-Rose Bowl (USA) (Habitat) 2742$^{3}$ 3125$^{4}$ 3212$^{5}$ **>98f<**

**Romalito 6** b g Robellino (USA)-Princess Zita (Manado) *236$^{7}$ 1063$^{7}$* ***>47a 37f<***

**Roman Gold (IRE) 3** b c Petorius-Saffron (FR) (Fabulous Dancer (USA)) **1995:** *(4352) (4410)* **1996:** *(567)* 731$^{10}$ 4184$^{16}$ 4583$^{10}$ **>84+a 86f<**

**Roman Imp (IRE) 2** ch c Imp Society (USA)-Luvi Ullmann (Thatching) 699$^{2}$ (829) 1510$^{2}$ 2070$^{4}$ 3156$^{3}$ **>94f<**

**Roman Reel (USA) 5** ch g Sword Dance-Our Mimi (USA) (Believe It (USA)) *200$^{2}$ 219$^{2}$ 295$^{2}$ 366$^{4}$ 827$^{15}$* (1012) (1661) 2344$^{2}$ 2440$^{8}$ 3635$^{6}$ 3860$^{2}$ 3980$^{3}$ 4702$^{16}$ **>68a 68f<**

**Romantic Warrior 3** b g Welsh Captain-Romantic Melody (Battle Hymn) 4360$^{14}$ 4611$^{6}$ **>59f<**

**Romios (IRE) 4** ch c Common Grounds-Domino's Nurse (Dom Racine (FR)) 580$^{12}$ 728$^{14}$ 988$^{14}$ 1440$^{9}$ 2008$^{3}$ 2690$^{2}$ 2862$^{3}$ 3683$^{6}$ 4055$^{2}$ 4465$^{8}$ 4716$^{3}$ 5046$^{14}$ **>96f<**

**Ronken (IRE) 2** ch f Kenmare (FR)-Rontry (ITY) (Try My Best (USA)) (4039a)

**Ronquista d'Or 2** b c Ron's Victory (USA)-Gild the Lily (Ile de Bourbon (USA)) *3625$^{9}$ 4801$^{20}$*

***Rons Revenge* 2** b br g Midyan (USA)-Nip (Bay Express) *1093$^{10}$ 1463$^{5}$ 1720$^{3}$ (2512)* 2759$^{6}$ 2948$^{5}$ 3512$^{10}$ 3943$^{11}$ 4106$^{13}$ **>17a 59f<**

**Ron's Round 2** ch c Ron's Victory (USA)-Magical Spirit (Top Ville) 3515$^{12}$ **>51f<**

**Ron's Secret 4** br f Efisio-Primrose Bank (Charlottown) 809$^{17}$ 1190$^{10}$ 1625$^{14}$ 1841$^{8}$ 2603$^{17}$ 3148$^{5}$ 3623$^{4}$ 4184$^{5}$ 4243$^{6}$ 4582$^{4}$ 4831$^{8}$ **>76f<**

**Rood Music 5** ro g Sharrood (USA)-Rose Music (Luthier) **1995:** *4378$^{2}$ (4476)* **1996:** *2679$^{8}$* 3403$^{5}$ 4812$^{12}$ **>82a 51f<**

**Rookery Girl 4** b f Pharly (FR)-Persian Grey (Persepolis (FR)) *2378$^{10}$* 2737$^{9}$ **>60df<**

**Rory 5** b g Dowsing (USA)-Crymlyn (Welsh Pageant) 765$^{6}$ 933$^{17}$ (2077) 2603$^{10}$ 3134$^{3}$ 4238$^{2}$ 4381$^{5}$ **>83f<**

**Roseate Lodge 10** b g Habitat-Elegant Tern (USA) (Sea Bird II) *440$^{15}$* 827$^{14}$ 1069$^{8}$ 1449$^{7}$ 1890$^{13}$ 2075$^{8}$ 2567$^{6}$ (3236) 3306$^{2}$ 3443$^{3}$ 3644$^{6}$ 3958$^{6}$ 4070$^{3}$ 4296$^{10}$ **>80a 61df<**

**Roseberry Avenue (IRE) 3** b c Sadler's Wells (USA)-Lady's Bridge (USA) (Sir Ivor) 3249$^{5}$ (3768) 3928$^{3}$ 4248$^{2}$ **>83f<**

**Roseberry Topping 7** gr g Nicholas Bill-Habitab (Sovereign Path) **1995:** *4472$^{3}$* **1996:** *33$^{7}$* **>59a 63f<**

**Rose Bourbon (USA) 3** b f Woodman (USA)-River Rose (FR) (Riverman (USA)) 720a$^{2}$

**Rose Carnival 2** b f Salse (USA)-Jungle Rose (Shirley Heights) 3593$^{7}$ (4072) 4490$^{9}$ **>74f<**

**Rose Chime (IRE) 4** b or br f Tirol-Repicado Rose (USA) (Repicado (CHI)) **1995:** *4390$^{11}$* **1996:** *34$^{10}$ 128$^{6}$ 252$^{7}$ 787$^{11}$* 1159$^{5}$ 1472$^{10}$ 2537$^{12}$ *3086$^{11}$ 3358$^{8}$* ***>25a 18f<***

**Rosenkavalier (IRE) 2** b c Classic Music (USA)-Top Bloom (Thatch (USA)) 1062$^{8}$ 3807$^{18}$ 4188$^{9}$ 4602$^{19}$ **>57f<**

**Rose of Glenn 5** b m Crofthall-May Kells (Artaius (USA)) **1995:** *4387$^{7}$ (4474) 4546$^{6}$* **1996:** *9$^{4}$ 73$^{9}$ 186$^{10}$ 398$^{9}$ 3813$^{10}$ 4092$^{14}$ 4426$^{7}$* 4509$^{2}$ 4703$^{5}$ *4977$^{10}$* **>36a 52f<**

**Rose of Siberia (USA) 3** gr f Siberian Express (USA)-Exuberine (FR) (Be My Guest (USA)) *44$^{12}$* 954$^{8}$ **>66f<**

**Rose Sharp 2** b f Forzando-Katie Scarlett (Lochnager) 4359$^{9}$ **>6f<**

**Roses In The Snow (IRE) 3** gr f Be My Guest (USA)-Desert Bluebell (Kalaglow) (1061) 2142$^{6}$ 2585$^{9}$ 3039$^{7}$ 3836$^{2}$ 4678$^{7}$ 4964$^{5}$ **>103f<**

**Rose Tint (IRE) 3** b f Salse (USA)-Sally Rose (Sallust) 840$^{9}$ 3949$^{12}$ 4480$^{7}$ **>51f<**

**Rosevear (IRE) 4** b f Contract Law (USA)-Caimanite (Tap On Wood) **1995:** *4376$^{12}$* **>47a 49f<**

**Rosi Zambotti (IRE) 4** b f 3392a$^{6}$ **>100f<**

**Rossel (USA) 3** b g Blushing John (USA)-Northern Aspen (USA) (Northern Dancer) 663$^{8}$ 873$^{17}$ 2141$^{3}$ (2388) 2912$^{5}$ 3276$^{4}$ 3487$^{7}$ 3649$^{7}$ **>71f<**

**Rossi Osvaldo (ITY) 2** b c Big Reef-Roll on (Nabirpour (USA)) 5076a$^{3}$

**Rostaq 3** b c Keen-American Beauty (Mill Reef (USA)) *419$^{3}$ 519$^{4}$ 863$^{11}$ 1457$^{7}$* **>62da 52f<**

**Rosy Outlook (USA) 2** b br f Trempolino (USA)-Rosyphard (USA) (Lyphard (USA)) 4062$^{6}$ 4363$^{8}$ **>60f<**

**Rotherfield Park (IRE) 4** b f High Estate-Alriyaah (Shareef Dancer (USA)) **1995:** *4407$^{15}$* **1996:** *762$^{8}$* 1541$^{6}$ 1642$^{5}$ 1859$^{2}$ 2185$^{4}$ 2757$^{4}$ 3294$^{4}$ 3482$^{7}$ **>43a 40f<**

**Rotherfield Queen (IRE) 2** b f Mac's Imp (USA)-Blazing Success (Blazing Saddles (AUS)) 2374$^{11}$ 2741$^{10}$ 3259$^{14}$ **>12f<**

**Rothley Imp (IRE) 3** b f Mac's Imp (USA)-Valediction (Town Crier) *32$^{6}$ 102$^{7}$ 525$^{15}$* 748$^{15}$ 4098$^{14}$ 4259$^{16}$ 4437$^{14}$ 4921$^{W}$ **>38a 33f<**

**Rotor Man (IRE) 2** b c River Falls-Need For Cash (USA) (Raise A Native) *4330$^{14}$* 4756$^{10}$ 4962$^{7}$ **>61f<**

**Roufontaine 5** gr m Rousillon (USA)-Bellifontaine (FR) (Bellypha) *(221) 312$^{8}$ (1462)* (1894) (2342) 2883$^{4}$ 3205$^{6}$ (3944) 4125$^{4}$ 4385$^{5}$ 4669$^{12}$ **>70a 88f<**

**Rouge Rancon (USA) 3** b f Red Ransom (USA)-

Lady O'Lyph (Lyphard (USA)) $1111^{3}$ **>96f<**

**Roushan 3** ch c Anshan-Fleur Rouge (Pharly (FR)) $696^{5}$ $962^{3}$ $1326^{11}$ $1469^{4}$ $1686^{W}$ (3679) $4064^{3}$ (4231) $4554^{8}$ **>95f<**

**Rousitto 8** ch g Rousillon (USA)-Helenetta (Troy) **1995:** *$4366^{4}$ $4391^{6}$ $4513^{2}$* **1996:** *$4574^{10}$ $4977^{9}$* **>69a 50f<**

**Roussi (USA) 4** b g Nureyev (USA)-Iva Reputation (USA) (Sir Ivor) $477^{12}$ $613^{9}$ $1072^{9}$ *$4982^{11}$ $5060^{11}$* **>29a 64f<**

**Roving Minstrel 5** ch h Cree Song-Klairove (Averof) $455^{2}$ $679^{3}$ $876^{11}$ $960^{10}$ **>62a 103f<**

**Rowlandsons Charm (IRE) 3** b f Fayruz-Magic Gold (Sallust) **1995:** *$4360^{6}$ $4491^{2}$ $4518^{3}$* **1996:** *(25) $52^{2}$ (129) $262^{2}$ $294^{4}$ (376) $463^{3}$ $531^{2}$ $1099^{9}$* $4785^{10}$ **>71a 43f<**

**Rowlandsons Stud (IRE) 3** b br g Distinctly North (USA)-Be My Million (Taufan (USA)) **1995:** *$4461^{7}$ $4533^{4}$* **1996:** *$68^{2}$ $118^{3}$ $215^{3}$ $292^{3}$ $307^{2}$ $408^{6}$ (488) $743^{3}$* $861^{7}$ $1446^{8}$ $2286^{13}$ $4130^{8}$ *$4333^{4}$ $4598^{11}$* $4888^{20}$ **>67a 44f<**

**Roxane (IRE) 3** b f Cyrano de Bergerac-Janet Oliphant (Red Sunset) **1995:** *$4443^{9}$* **1996:** *$58^{11}$ $134^{11}$ $514^{9}$ $648^{15}$* $1598^{14}$ **>11a 6f<**

**Royal Abjar (USA) 5** b h Gone West (USA)-Encorelle (FR) (Arctic Tern (USA)) $3397a^{2}$ **>122f<**

**Royal Acclaim 11** ch g Tender King-Glimmer (Hot Spark) *$190^{7}$ $252^{8}$ $384^{5}$ $752^{18}$ $854^{3}$ $1778^{8}$* $2284^{6}$ $2379^{7}$ **>37a 34f<**

**Royal Action 3** b c Royal Academy (USA)-Ivor's Honey (Sir Ivor) $640^{5}$ $826^{7}$ $1690^{3}$ $2197^{5}$ $2949^{2}$ $3704^{4}$ $4176^{13}$ $4615^{10}$ $4813^{3}$ **>74f<**

**Royal Amaretto (IRE) 2** b c Fairy King (USA)-Melbourne Miss (Chaparral (FR)) $2580^{3}$ $2972^{4}$ (4127) $4822^{2}$ **>99f<**

**Royal Applause 3** b c Waajib-Flying Melody (Auction Ring (USA)) $926^{10}$ $2115^{6}$ (3132) $4057^{9}$ **>112f<**

**Royal Aty (IRE) 2** b c Royal Academy (USA)-Atyaaf (USA) (Irish River (FR)) $5031a^{2}$ **>64f<**

**Royal Blackbird 2** br f Most Welcome-Thulium (Mansingh (USA)) $2195^{11}$ (4493) $4912^{2}$ $5037^{3}$ **>67f<**

**Royal Born 2** ch c Prince Sabo-Shernborne (Kalaglow) $4380^{4}$ $4601^{3}$ $4783^{8}$ **>79f<**

**Royal Canaska 3** ch c Royal Academy (USA)-North Telstar (Sallust) (544) $808^{4}$ $1476^{12}$ $2041^{8}$ $3210^{14}$ **>94f<**

**Royal Carlton (IRE) 4** b g Mulhollande (USA)-Saintly Angel (So Blessed) $2982^{7}$ $3583^{8}$ **>40f<**

**Royal Castle (IRE) 2** b c Caerleon (USA)-Sun Princess (English Prince) $5033^{8}$ **>71f<**

**Royal Ceilidh (IRE) 3** b f Prince Rupert (FR)-Isa (Dance In Time (CAN)) $686^{3}$ $824^{6}$ (1185) $1648^{3}$ $2065^{6}$ $3461^{2}$ $3770^{3}$ $3985^{2}$ $4190^{11}$ $4769^{10}$ $4909^{7}$ $5042^{12}$ **>83f<**

**Royal Circus 7** b g Kris-Circus Ring (High Top) *$15^{4}$ $83^{4}$ (116) $140^{5}$ $214^{5}$ $365^{8}$ $1835^{2}$* $2060^{2}$ $2239^{3}$ $2511^{6}$ $2756^{7}$ **>50a 52f<**

**Royal Comedian 7** gr m Jester-Royal Huntress (Royal Avenue) *$1417^{9}$* $2047^{7}$ $2428^{2}$ $2672^{5}$ **>32a 46f<**

**Royal Court (IRE) 3** b c Sadler's Wells (USA)-Rose of Jericho (USA) (Alleged (USA)) (1461) (2535) $3671^{3}$ $4441^{4}$ **>119f<**

**Royal Crown (IRE) 2** b c Sadler's Wells (USA)-Rose of Jericho (USA) (Alleged (USA)) $4492^{8}$ **>66f<**

**Royal Crusade (USA) 2** b c Diesis-Sainte Croix (USA) (Nijinsky (CAN)) (4720) **>86f<**

**Royal Dancer 4** ch f Dancing Dissident (USA)-Aquarula (Dominion) *$45^{9}$ $167^{10}$ $368^{10}$ $402^{14}$ $491^{7}$* ***>7a 30?f<***

**Royal Diversion (IRE) 3** b f Marju (IRE)-Royal Recreation (USA) (His Majesty (USA)) $550^{3}$ $969^{8}$ $1349^{3}$ $1773^{13}$ $3148^{6}$ $3944^{3}$ $4216^{3}$ $4496^{3}$ (4877) **>80+f<**

**Royal Dome (IRE) 4** b g Salt Dome (USA)-Brook's Dilemma (Known Fact (USA)) $735^{2}$ $1113^{9}$ $1199^{8}$ $2119^{4}$ $2349^{9}$ $2867^{2}$ (3122) $3152^{2}$ (3432) $3672^{20}$ $3868^{9}$ $4180^{18}$ $4452^{3}$ $4616^{12}$ $4679^{13}$ **>18a 76f<**

**Royale Figurine (IRE) 5** ch m Dominion Royale-Cree's Figurine (Creetown) $1129^{3}$ $2115^{5}$ $2841a^{6}$ (3222) $4442^{6}$ $4679^{8}$ $4774^{6}$ $5044^{12}$ **>107f<**

**Royale Finale (IRE) 2** ch c Royal Academy (USA)-Final Farewell (USA) (Proud Truth (USA)) $4891^{3}$ **>60f<**

**Royal Emblem 2** gr f Presidium-Lily of France (Monsanto (FR)) $630^{2}$ $807^{3}$ $2527^{5}$ $2764^{2}$ $4902^{8}$ **>61f<**

**Royal Expose (USA) 3** ch c Unzipped (USA)-Royal Tasha (USA) (Northern Prospect (USA)) $677^{16}$ $948^{5}$ $1773^{P}$ $2341^{4}$ $2762^{4}$ $3109^{8}$ $3459^{11}$ **>63f<**

**Royal Expression 4** b g Sylvan Express-Edwin's Princess (Owen Dudley) *$214^{3}$ (1070)* $1343^{2}$ (1542) $1784^{2}$ **>60a 79f<**

**Royal Intrusion 3** ch g Roman Warrior-Image of War (Warpath) $2036^{15}$ $3166^{6}$ $3458^{9}$ $4337^{13}$ **>45f<**

**Royal Jade 3** b f Last Tycoon-Imperial Jade (Lochnager) $921^{5}$ $1882^{2}$ $2208^{10}$ (4456) $4688^{25}$ $4974^{14}$ **>76f<**

**Royal Legend 4** b g Fairy King (USA)-Legend of Arabia (Great Nephew) *$79^{3}$ $3704^{7}$* $3974^{13}$ $4345^{3}$ **>54a 62f<**

**Royal Mark (IRE) 3** b c Fairy King (USA)-Take Your Mark (USA) (Round Table) *$937^{5}$* $1127^{2}$ $2041^{17}$ $2584^{3}$ $3210^{16}$ $3920^{14}$ $4136^{W}$ $4775^{18}$ **>93df<**

**Royal Orchid (IRE) 2** ch f Shalford (IRE)-Indigo Blue (IRE) (Bluebird (USA)) $1105^{2}$ $2230^{6}$ $3129^{4}$ $3433^{5}$ $4605^{4}$ $4798^{16}$ **>76f<**

**Royal Philosopher 4** b c Faustus (USA)-Princess Lucy (Local Suitor (USA)) (728) $960^{11}$ $1484^{2}$ (2477a) $3033a^{3}$ $4030a^{4}$ $4132^{8}$ $5078a^{4}$ **>110f<**

**Royal Print (IRE) 7** ch g Kings Lake (USA)-Reprint (Kampala) *$79^{6}$ $140^{4}$ $228^{4}$ $260^{6}$* **>68a 44f<**

**Royal Rapport 3** ch g Rich Charlie-Miss Camellia (Sonnen Gold) $522^{13}$ $637^{2}$ *$1027^{9}$ $1497^{7}$ $1719^{5}$ $2637^{6}$ $3420^{5}$* **>53a 58df<**

**Royal Result (USA) 3** b br c Gone West (USA)-Norette (Northfields (USA)) $583^{8}$ $705^{5}$ $2996^{2}$ (3226) $4184^{12}$ $4470^{4}$ $4724^{3}$ **>86f<**

**Royal Rigger 3** gr f Reprimand-Overdraft (Bustino) $3780^{12}$ $3965^{10}$ $4472^{11}$ **>29a 21f<**

**Royal Roulette 2** ch f Risk Me (FR)-Princess Lily (Blakeney) $3685^{14}$ *$4331^{5}$ $4608^{12}$ $4780^{3}$ $4970^{8}$* ***>61a 45f<***

**Royal Scimitar (USA) 4** ch c Diesis-Princess of Man (Green God) **1995:** $4426a^{14}$ **1996:** (1065) $1353^{3}$ $1976^{3}$ $2534^{2}$ $3212^{7}$ (3934) **>105f<**

**Royal Snack (AUS) 7** b g Lunchtime-Queen Gipsy **1995:** $4522a^{3}$

**Royal Thimble (IRE) 5** b m Prince Rupert (FR)-Tootsie Roll (Comedy Star (USA)) *$1685^{14}$* $1996^{8}$ $2226^{13}$ (2793) $2896^{7}$ $3109^{4}$ $3340^{6}$ $3980^{2}$ **>63f<**

**Royal Vacation 7** b g King of Spain-Crane Beach (High Top) *(2216)* $2804^{6}$ $3641^{3}$ **>60f<**

**Roy Boy 4** b g Emarati (USA)-Starky's Pet (Mummy's Pet) $1504^{6}$ $1763^{6}$ **>59f<**

**Royce and Royce (JPN) 6** b h Toby Bin-That's My Pal (USA) (Key To The Mint (USA)) **1995:** $4471a^{7}$ **>125f<**

**Royrace 4** b g Wace (USA)-Royal Tycoon (Tycoon II) $546^{6}$ $738^{10}$ $1044^{9}$ $1454^{5}$ $4612^{13}$ $4794^{17}$ **>45f<**

**Rubadub 5** b m Kalaglow-Ravens Peak (High Top) *$189^{11}$ $246^{7}$ $305^{5}$* **>3a 52f<**

**Rubbiyati 4** ch f Cadeaux Genereux-Ibtisamm (USA) (Caucasus (USA)) *$320^{2}$ $390^{6}$ $502^{7}$ $2405^{3}$* (2743) $2945^{3}$ $4257^{9}$ $4905^{10}$ **>48a 60f<**

**Ruby Angel 3** ch f Superlative-Queen Angel (Anfield) $2432^{6}$ *$5058^{5}$* **>36a 56f<**

**Ruby Plus 5** b m Energy Plus-Irish Grace (Home Guard (USA)) *$782^{7}$ $1088^{12}$* $1500^{13}$ $1665^{14}$ *$1970^{12}$* **>12f<**

**Ruby Princess (IRE) 2** b f Mac's Imp (USA)-Princess Raisa (Indian King (USA)) $1453^{2}$ **>70f<**

**Ruby Tuesday 2** b f Al Nasr (FR)-Habibay (Habitat) $1014^{4}$ $1433^{3}$ $3921^{3}$ $4558^{7}$ $4887^{9}$ **>67?f<**

**Rude Awakening 2** b c Rudimentary (USA)-Final Call (Town Crier) $569^{2}$ $697^{2}$ (848) $1419^{6}$ $1766^{4}$ $4555^{8}$ **>83f<**

**Rudimental 2** b c Rudimentary (USA)-Full Orchestra (Shirley Heights) *$2370^{3}$ (2633)* **>70a f<**

**Rudi's Pet (IRE) 2** ch c Don't Forget Me-Pink Fondant (Northfields (USA)) *$1653^{4}$* $2195^{6}$ (2374) $2726^{5}$ $3160^{4}$ $3692^{3}$ (3924) $4677^{6}$ $4945a^{5}$ **>93f<**

**Rumba Rhythm (CAN) 3** ch f Thorn Dance (USA)-Skoblikova (USA) (Phone Trick (USA)) $2134^{7}$ $2437^{4}$ $2860^{6}$ **>68f<**

**Rumbustious 2** b f Rambo Dancer (CAN)-Persian Alexandra (Persian Bold) $1871^{11}$ $3405^{2}$ (3607) (3962) $4106^{8}$ $4549^{5}$ $4803^{6}$ **>65f<**

**Rum Lad 2** gr c Efisio-She's Smart (Absalom) $1184^{3}$ $1525^{6}$ $2076^{4}$ $2588^{2}$ $4433^{8}$ $4586^{6}$ **>69f<**

**Runaway Mary (USA) 2** f *$4950a^{6}$* **>83a f<**

**Runaway Pete (USA) 6** b g Runaway Groom (CAN)-Pete's Damas (USA) (Cutlass (USA)) $1835^{7}$ $4771^{18}$ **>65f<**

**Runforaction (IRE) 4** b f Contract Law (USA)-Prissy Miss (Free State) *$367^{7}$ $2550^{7}$ $2937^{11}$ $3289^{11}$* ***>32a 21f<***

**Run For Us (IRE) 2** b f Runnett-Blue Elver (Kings Lake (USA)) *$506^{4}$* $630^{5}$ $770^{7}$ *$1084^{4}$ $1595^{7}$* $2207^{3}$ *$4093^{10}$ $4251^{12}$ $4335^{5}$ $4576^{7}$ $4715^{19}$* ***>22a 43f<***

**Runic Symbol 5** b g Warning-Pagan Deity (Brigadier Gerard) $983^{2}$ $1302^{4}$ $1496^{3}$ (2183) $2574^{2}$ $2784^{5}$ $3111^{3}$ $3333^{7}$ $3496^{10}$ $4381^{7}$ *$5060^{5}$* **>26a 50f<**

**Run Lucy Run 2** b f Risk Me (FR)-Pat Or Else (Alzao (USA)) $757^{5}$ *$858^{2}$ $1097^{2}$ (1459) $2984^{4}$* $3324^{3}$ $3678^{4}$ (3943) *$4335^{6}$ $4495^{8}$* $5048^{5}$ **>54a 57f<**

**Running Flame (FR) 4** b c Assert-Fanning The Flame (FR) (Commanche Run) $3567a^{3}$ (4410a) $4856a^{6}$ **>119f<**

**Running Free (IRE) 2** b g Waajib-Selchis (Main Reef) $2600^{16}$ $2967^{11}$ $3498^{4}$ $4084^{8}$ $4549^{16}$ *$4980^{4}$* **>54a 61f<**

**Running Green 5** b g Green Desert (USA)-Smeralda (GER) (Dschingis Khan) *$4904^{10}$* ***>57f<***

**Runs in the Family 4** b f Distant Relative-Stoneydale (Tickled Pink) $2745^{5}$ *$3091^{3}$ $3146^{3}$* $3661^{4}$ $3783^{9}$ $3937^{6}$ $4372^{12}$ **>52a 57f<**

**Run With Pride 3** b f Mandrake Major-Kirkby (Midsummer Night II) $3591^{10}$ $3865^{5}$ **>27f<**

**Rupert (FR) 3** b c Kendor (FR)-Rudolfina (Pharly (FR)) $1133a^{3}$ $1756a^{6}$ (4162a) **>111f<**

**Rupert Manners 3** b g Mazilier (USA)-Entourage (Posse (USA)) *$3413^{6}$* $3642^{9}$ $4074^{18}$

**Rupert's Double (IRE) 2** ch g Silver Kite (USA)-Perfect Guest (What A Guest) $1896^{13}$ $2195^{13}$ **>29f<**

**Rupert's Princess (IRE) 4** b f Prince Rupert (FR)-Llanelli (Welsh Saint) *$76^{12}$ $126^{12}$ $347^{7}$* **>59a 57f<**

**Rupiana (IRE) 4** b f Prince Rupert (FR)-Webbiana (African Sky) *$1092^{10}$* $1533^{11}$ $2056^{17}$ $2906^{6}$ $3163^{7}$ **>33f<**

**Rural Lad 7** b g Town And Country-French Plait (Thatching) *$1081^{F}$* **>55da f< (DEAD)**

**Rushcutter Bay 3** br c Mon Tresor-Llwy Bren (Lidhame) $1316^{6}$ $1628^{7}$ (1823) $2143^{7}$ $2301^{2}$ $2790^{5}$

3219$^{3}$ 3432$^{4}$ 3693$^{4}$ 3984$^{8}$ 4116$^{18}$ **>41a 93f<**

**Rushen Raider 4** br g Reprimand-Travel Storm (Lord Gayle (USA)) 871$^{9}$ 995$^{9}$ 1072$^{5}$ (2798) (3130) (3309) (3486) 4112$^{4}$ 4302$^{4}$ **>79f<**

**Rusk 3** b c Pharly (FR)-Springwell (Miami Springs) 677$^{6}$ 2062$^{2}$ 3710$^{18}$ 3939$^{4}$ 4431$^{3}$ 4580$^{5}$ 4992$^{5}$ **>81f<**

**Russian Aspect 2** br c Al Nasr (FR)-Bourbon Topsy (Ile de Bourbon (USA)) 4451$^{10}$ 4684$^{9}$ **>56f<**

**Russian Music 3** b g Forzando-Sunfleet (Red Sunset) (1045) 1327$^{2}$ 2041$^{3}$ 3067$^{3}$ 3229$^{2}$ 3517$^{2}$ 3822$^{2}$ 4185$^{2}$ 4444$^{3}$ 4674$^{2}$ 4823$^{7}$ **>106f<**

**Russian Olive 2** b f Primo Dominie-Cottonwood (Teenoso (USA)) 4969$^{12}$ 5041$^{4}$ **>70f<**

**Russian Rascal (IRE) 3** b g Soviet Lad (USA)-Anglo Irish (Busted) *1126$^{6}$* 1363$^{2}$ 1666$^{7}$ 2065$^{5}$ 2514$^{5}$ **>72f<**

**Russian Request (IRE) 3** b f Soviet Star (USA)-I Want to Be (USA) (Roberto (USA)) 1627$^{2}$ 1963$^{2}$ 2399$^{4}$ 3253$^{4}$ 4257$^{10}$ **>73f<**

**Russian Revival (USA) 3** ch c Nureyev (USA)-Memories (USA) (Hail the Pirates (USA)) 1574a$^{7}$ 2050$^{11}$ 3132$^{2}$ 3759$^{8}$ (4239) (4774) 4870$^{2}$ 5044$^{3}$ **>120f<**

**Russian Rose (IRE) 3** b f Soviet Lad (USA)-Thornbeam (Beldale Flutter (USA)) 1104$^{15}$ 1508$^{12}$ (2062) 3938$^{9}$ **>68f<**

**Russian Roulette 3** b f Niniski (USA)-Gaucherie (USA) (Sharpen Up) 2591$^{7}$ 2961$^{6}$ **>27f<**

**Russian Ruler (IRE) 2** b c Bering-Whitecairn (Sure Blade (USA)) 4770$^{5}$ 4991$^{3}$ **>81f<**

**Russian Sable 2** b f Statoblest-Princess Zita (Manado) 1346$^{14}$ (1713) 2035$^{3}$ 2254$^{3}$ 2382$^{5}$ 3803$^{8}$ 3871$^{3}$ 4046$^{6}$ 4182$^{8}$ 4423$^{3}$ 4546$^{8}$ **>72f<**

**Russian Snows (IRE) 4** b f Sadler's Wells (USA)-Arctique Royale (Royal And Regal (USA)) *395a$^{2}$ 3688$^{6}$* 4114$^{4}$ 4467$^{3}$ 4678$^{8}$ (5036) **>113f<**

**Rustic League (IRE) 5** b g Gallic League-Walnut Lass (Tap On Wood) *350$^{6}$* **>36a 35f<**

**Rustic Song (IRE) 3** b f Fayruz-Red Note (Rusticaro (FR)) 525$^{20}$ 638$^{9}$ 1416$^{16}$ *1809$^{4}$ 2636$^{12}$ 2940$^{13}$* **>37a 36f<**

**Rusty (IRE) 2** ch f Shalford (IRE)-Karoi (IRE) (Kafu) 3121$^{6}$ (3511) 3803$^{11}$ 4230$^{8}$ *4576$^{11}$* **>15a 59f<**

**Ruth's Gamble 8** b g Kabour-Hilly's Daughter (Hillandale) *760$^{12}$ 2369$^{12}$* **>28a 7f<**

**Ruwy 3** b f Soviet Star (USA)-Psylla (Beldale Flutter (USA)) 1050$^{2}$ 1882$^{4}$ 3513$^{8}$ (3949) 4376$^{13}$ 4975$^{22}$ **>75f<**

**Ruznama (USA) 3** ch f Forty Niner (USA)-Last Feather (USA) (Vaguely Noble) 938$^{4}$ 1108$^{4}$ (3153) (3712) 4132$^{6}$ **>106f<**

**Ryafan (USA) 2** b f Lear Fan (USA)-Carya (USA) (Northern Dancer) (2315) 4159a$^{2}$ (4661a) **>107f<**

**Ryles Dancer 2** ch c Chilibang-Bee Dee Dancer (Ballacashtal (CAN)) 4834$^{8}$ *4985$^{8}$* **>2a 10f<**

**Rymer's Rascal 4** b g Rymer-City Sound (On Your Mark) 589$^{15}$ **>21a 59f<**

**S**

**Saabga (USA) 2** ch f Woodman (USA)-Catopetl (USA) (Northern Dancer) 3159$^{2}$ **>77+f<**

**Saafeya (IRE) 2** b f Sadler's Wells (USA)-Safa (Shirley Heights) 4684$^{3}$ **>71f<**

**Saafi (IRE) 5** b g Primo Dominie-Baby's Smile (Shirley Heights) 4604$^{12}$ **>55?f<**

**Sabaah Elfull 3** ch f Kris-Putupon (Mummy's Pet) 1901$^{12}$ (3100) 3465$^{8}$ 4202$^{6}$ 4521$^{11}$ 4888$^{9}$ **>69f<**

**Sabina 2** b f Prince Sabo-High Savannah (Rousillon (USA)) 4330$^{3}$ (4475) 4677$^{9}$ **>60f<**

**Sabot 3** b c Polar Falcon (USA)-Power Take Off (Aragon) 840$^{2}$ (2048) 2691$^{4}$ 3263$^{4}$ 4444$^{17}$ **>92f<**

**Sabotini 2** b f Prince Sabo-Low Line (High Line) (807) 1103$^{5}$ 3208$^{7}$ **>67f<**

**Sabrak (IRE) 3** b c Fairy King (USA)-Embryo (Busted) 962$^{10}$ 1326$^{4}$ 2011$^{4}$ (2420) 2621$^{15}$ 3594$^{7}$ 3830$^{5}$ **>96f<**

**Sacho (IRE) 3** b c Sadler's Wells (USA)-Oh So Sharp (Kris) 677$^{2}$ **>82+f<**

**Sacrament 5** b h Shirley Heights-Blessed Event (Kings Lake (USA)) 680$^{7}$ 919$^{3}$ (1390a) (4066) 4397a$^{3}$ 4747a$^{2}$ **>124f<**

**Sacred Loch (USA) 3** ch c Lomond (USA)-Cypria Sacra (USA) (Sharpen Up) 4201$^{9}$ 4622$^{9}$ **>59f<**

**Sacred Mirror (IRE) 5** b m Shaadi (USA)-Heavenly Abode (FR) (Habitat) *(165) 206$^{6}$ 254$^{8}$ 365$^{11}$ 1640$^{12}$* (2282) 2408$^{2}$ 2599$^{5}$ 3267$^{4}$ **>58a 65df<**

**Sacristan 2** gr c Warning-Sacristy (Godswalk (USA)) 4294a$^{5}$

**Saddlehome (USA) 7** b g Aragon-Kesarini (USA) (Singh (USA)) 475$^{11}$ 587$^{11}$ 735$^{15}$ 928$^{19}$ 1113$^{7}$ 1974$^{12}$ 2119$^{7}$ 4180$^{12}$ 4430$^{4}$ 4616$^{11}$ 4791$^{8}$ (4809) 4909$^{9}$ 4994$^{19}$ **>85a 75f<**

**Saddlers' Hope 2** b f Saddlers' Hall (IRE)-Hope and Glory (USA) (Well Decorated (USA)) 3319$^{3}$ 3764$^{4}$ **>77+f<**

**Sadler's Blaze (IRE) 2** b c Alzao (USA)-Christine Daae (Sadler's Wells (USA)) 4127$^{14}$ **>38f<**

**Sadler's Realm 3** b c Sadler's Wells (USA)-Rensaler (USA) (Stop The Music (USA)) 860$^{7}$ 1079$^{2}$ 1361$^{7}$ 3677$^{3}$ **>77f<**

**Sadler's Walk 5** b g Sadler's Wells (USA)-Widows Walk (Habitat) 766$^{7}$ 1476$^{16}$ 3447$^{9}$ 4238$^{5}$ 4819$^{5}$ **>80f<**

**Sadly Sober (IRE) 4** b f Roi Danzig (USA)-Overcall (Bustino) **1995:** *4354$^{2}$ 4386$^{6}$ 4486$^{5}$* **>65a 65f<**

**Sad Mad Bad (USA) 2** b c Sunny's Halo (CAN)-Quite Attractive (USA) (Well Decorated (USA)) 3326$^{3}$ (3874) 4131$^{15}$ **>80f<**

**Saeta Rubia (USA) 5** ch m Trempolino (USA)-Tuca Tuca (USA) (Miswaki (USA)) 4665a$^{3}$ **>99f<**

**Safa (USA) 3** b f Green Dancer (USA)-Romanette (USA) (Alleged (USA)) 677$^{15}$ 3776$^{2}$ 4110$^{8}$ 4588$^{13}$ **>71f<**

**Safa Dancer 3** b f Safawan-Dalby Dancer (Bustiki) *1972$^{3}$ 2181$^{11}$ 2551$^{6}$ 3456$^{10}$* 3970$^{13}$ 4129$^{14}$ **>48a 20f<**

**Safecracker 3** ch g Sayf El Arab (USA)-My Polished Corner (IRE) (Tate Gallery (USA)) *460$^{2}$ (761)* 1089$^{11}$ 2196$^{7}$ 3681$^{11}$ **>52a 59f<**

**Safety (USA) 9** b g Topsider (USA)-Flare Pass (USA) (Buckpasser) 1953$^{9}$ 2310$^{14}$ 2941$^{13}$ 3067$^{9}$ **>58f<**

**Safey Ana (USA) 5** b g Dixieland Band (USA)-Whatsoraire (USA) (Mr Prospector (USA)) 876$^{12}$ 2134$^{11}$ 2285$^{6}$ 3219$^{8}$ 3650$^{2}$ 3702$^{4}$ 3995$^{4}$ 4308$^{10}$ 4609$^{9}$ **>66f<**

**Safflower (IRE) 3** ch f Camden Town-The Saltings (FR) (Morston (FR)) 1573a$^{7}$ **>59f<**

**Saffron Rose 2** b f Polar Falcon (USA)-Tweedling (USA) (Sir Ivor) 3515$^{8}$ 3848$^{5}$ 4127$^{4}$ 4364$^{8}$ 4549$^{10}$ **>67f<**

**Safio 3** ch c Efisio-Marcroft (Crofthall) 824$^{9}$ 1185$^{W}$ 1495$^{4}$ 1648$^{6}$ 2501$^{10}$ 2754$^{5}$ 3424$^{9}$ **>69f<**

**Sagar Pride (IRE) 3** br f Jareer (USA)-Sagar Island (USA) (Sagace) 794a$^{2}$ 1140a$^{3}$ 1758a$^{5}$ 4419a$^{3}$ 4663a$^{7}$ 4738a$^{5}$ **>106f<**

**Sagebrush Roller 8** br g Sharpo-Sunita (Owen Dudley) *589$^{3}$* 801$^{3}$ 971$^{4}$ 1703$^{5}$ 2149$^{4}$ 2874$^{2}$ 3265$^{5}$ 3680$^{4}$ 4820$^{9}$ *4987$^{10}$* **>53a 73f<**

**Sahara River (USA) 2** b f Riverman (USA)-Sahara Forest (Green Desert (USA)) 3593$^{4}$ **>81+f<**

**Saheeel (USA) 3** b c Dayjur (USA)-Qirmazi (USA) (Riverman (USA)) 943$^{2}$ (4219) 4561$^{4}$ 4772$^{18}$ (4971) **>96f<**

**Sahhar 3** ch c Sayf El Arab (USA)-Native Magic (Be My Native (USA)) **1995:** *4439$^{3}$ 4535$^{2}$* **1996:** *381$^{6}$ 428$^{6}$ 2936$^{12}$ 3705$^{4}$ 4080$^{4}$* **>65da 57f<**

**Sahm (USA) 2** b br c Mr Prospector (USA)-Salsabil (Sadler's Wells (USA)) (2009) (2721) 3143$^{D}$ 4398a$^{7}$ **>112f<**

**Saifan 7** ch g Beveled (USA)-Superfrost (Tickled Pink) 809$^{12}$ 879$^{20}$ 1190$^{3}$ (1625) 1807$^{4}$ 2134$^{6}$ 2581$^{19}$ (2917) 3450$^{2}$ 3815$^{7}$ 4329$^{6}$ 4769$^{9}$ 4901$^{15}$ (4974) **>94f<**

**Sailormaite 5** ch g Komaite (USA)-Marina Plata (Julio Mariner) **1995:** *4368$^{4}$ 4392$^{2}$* **1996:** *20$^{5}$ 711$^{4}$* 814$^{11}$ 1178$^{14}$ (1430) 1630$^{R}$ 3432$^{6}$ 3622$^{17}$ 3810$^{11}$ 4452$^{6}$ 4581$^{6}$ 4688$^{U}$ 4791$^{2}$ **>93a 83f<**

**Sails Legend 5** b h Hotfoot-Miss Polly Peck (March Past) 944$^{8}$ 1347$^{13}$ **>31f<**

**Saint Amigo 4** gr g Presidium-Little Token (Shack (USA)) **1995:** *4412$^{7}$ 4458$^{10}$* **1996:** *4259$^{13}$* 4727$^{9}$ **>10a 40f<**

**Saint Express 6** ch g Clantime-Redgrave Design (Nebbiolo) *2292$^{8}$* 2694$^{19}$ 2889$^{9}$ 3085$^{11}$ 3296$^{13}$ 3672$^{11}$ 4116$^{11}$ 4505$^{3}$ 4687$^{17}$ 4811$^{12}$ 4909$^{4}$ 4994$^{4}$ **>85f<**

**Saintly (AUS) 4** ch g Sky Chase (AUS)-All Grace (AUS) (Sir Tristram) (5069a)

**Saint Rosalina 3** b f Common Grounds-Saint Systems (Uncle Pokey) **1995:** *4353$^{9}$* **>50a 49f<**

**Saint Who (USA) 2** b g Hooched (USA)-Saint Pea (USA) (Christopher R (USA)) 3349$^{9}$ 3651$^{2}$ 3757$^{10}$ 3962$^{2}$ (4103) 4566$^{13}$ **>76?f<**

**Sakeen 3** ch c Keen-Santa's Queen (USA) (Sovereign Dancer (USA)) **1995:** *4352$^{11}$*

**Sakharov 7** b g Bay Express-Supreme Kingdom (Take A Reef) (1474) 1893$^{10}$ 2212$^{2}$ 2481$^{3}$ 2573$^{5}$ **>60a 68f<**

**Salabatni 2** b f Rainbow Quest (USA)-Balwa (USA) (Danzig (USA)) 1467$^{6}$ 2413$^{7}$ 3493$^{3}$ 4084$^{7}$ 4990$^{16}$ **>70f<**

**Salaman (FR) 4** b g Saumarez-Merry Sharp (Sharpen Up) *449$^{14}$* 573$^{8}$ 1439$^{10}$ 2148$^{7}$ 3142$^{5}$ 3598$^{3}$ 4199$^{9}$ **>89f<**

**Salamander King 4** b g Distant Relative-Spirit of The Wind (USA) (Little Current (USA)) 1782$^{5}$ **>62f<**

**Saleemah (USA) 3** ch f Storm Bird (CAN)-Retire (USA) (Secretariat (USA)) 678$^{6}$ 964$^{3}$ 1855$^{4}$ 2432$^{2}$ (2789) (3076) (3516) 3842$^{4}$ 4194$^{8}$ 4704$^{3}$ **>98f<**

**Salford Lad 2** b c Don't Forget Me-Adjusting (IRE) (Busted) 4913$^{17}$ 5040$^{15}$

**Sally Green (IRE) 2** b f Common Grounds-Redwood Hut (Habitat) 2611$^{16}$ 3475$^{8}$ 5034$^{10}$ **>54f<**

**Sallyoreally (IRE) 5** b m Common Grounds-Prosapia (USA) (Our Native (USA)) 477$^{15}$ 586$^{14}$ 801$^{7}$ 971$^{3}$ 1157$^{5}$ 1364$^{6}$ 1500$^{3}$ 1650$^{4}$ 1846$^{5}$ 3236$^{7}$ 3453$^{10}$ 4075$^{17}$ **>41f<**

**Sally Slade 4** b f Dowsing (USA)-Single Gal (Mansingh (USA)) 582$^{18}$ 812$^{13}$ 931$^{5}$ 1466$^{6}$ (1777) 2064$^{5}$ 2232$^{5}$ 3783$^{14}$ 3827$^{8}$ 3930$^{14}$ 4220$^{5}$ 4616$^{7}$ 4791$^{6}$ 4995$^{7}$ **>69a 72f<**

**Sally's Twins 3** b f Dowsing (USA)-Bird of Love (Ela-Mana-Mou) 1900$^{6}$ 2377$^{9}$ 4785$^{9}$ 4877$^{3}$ **>57f<**

**Sally Weld 4** ch f Weldnaas (USA)-Sallytude (Tudor Music) **1995:** *4457$^{8}$ 4521$^{4}$* **>56a 62f<**

**Salmis 3** b f Salse (USA)-Misguided (Homing) 611$^{4}$ 1798$^{10}$ 2334$^{4}$ (3107) 3926$^{8}$ 4560$^{6}$ **>81f<**

**Salmon Ladder (USA) 4** b c Bering-Ballerina Princess (USA) (Mr Prospector (USA)) (1867) (2145) 2502$^{10}$ 2881$^{2}$ (3212) 3798$^{2}$ 4066$^{2}$ 4441$^{2}$ (4876) **>121f<**

**Salome 2** ch f Risk Me (FR)-Dancing Belle (Dance In Time (CAN)) 551$^{4}$ *858$^{4}$* **>7a 10f<**

**Salonrolle (IRE) 3** b f Tirol-Salesiana (Alpenkonig (GER)) 1060a$^{3}$ **>96f<**

**Sal's Driver (USA)** **2** b br c Salem Drive (USA)-Dame's Double (USA) (Double Leader (USA)) *4954a$^{10}$* **>70a f<**

**Salsee Lad** **2** b c Salse (USA)-Jamarj (Tyrnavos) 4516$^{16}$

**Salsian** **3** b f Salse (USA)-Phylae (Habitat) 705$^{11}$ 914$^{6}$ 1325$^{9}$ *1814$^{10}$ 2168$^{7}$ 2388$^{4}$* **>29a 48f<**

**Salska** **5** b m Salse (USA)-Anzeige (GER) (Soderini) 1778$^{5}$ 1826$^{2}$ 2165$^{7}$ 2319$^{3}$ (2717) (2779) **>41a 63+f<**

**Saltando (IRE)** **5** b g Salt Dome (USA)-Ange de Feu (Double Form) **1995:** *(4406) 4472$^{4}$* **1996:** *682$^{15}$* 879$^{6}$ 1496$^{2}$ 1640$^{15}$ 1803$^{8}$ 2000$^{6}$ *2081$^{7}$ 3220$^{9}$* 3703$^{9}$ 4209$^{8}$ 4674$^{10}$ (4719) 4974$^{18}$ **>66?a 65f<**

**Saltimbanco** **2** ch c Green Forest (USA)-Tea and Scandals (USA) (Key to the Kingdom (USA)) 3069$^{6}$ 3807$^{13}$ 4544$^{3}$ 4717$^{13}$ **>75f<**

**Saltis (IRE)** **4** ch g Salt Dome (USA)-Mrs Tittlemouse (Nonoalco (USA)) **1995:** *4457$^{14}$ 4526$^{7}$* **1996:** *24$^{7}$ 1600$^{10}$* 2056$^{14}$ 2310$^{8}$ **>50a 32f<**

**Salty Behaviour (IRE)** **2** ch c Salt Dome (USA)-Good Behaviour (Artaius (USA)) 552$^{3}$ (2712) 4893$^{6}$ 5037$^{11}$ (5049) **>76f<**

**Salty Girl (IRE)** **3** b f Scenic-Sodium's Niece (Northfields (USA)) 754$^{7}$ 1504$^{3}$ 2141$^{6}$ 4763$^{5}$ **>71f<**

**Salty Jack (IRE)** **2** b c Salt Dome (USA)-Play The Queen (IRE) (King of Clubs) 1118$^{9}$ 2398$^{3}$ 2712$^{3}$ (3515) 4182$^{3}$ 4303$^{3}$ **>78f<**

**Salutation (IRE)** **5** b g Salt Dome (USA)-Salvationist (Mill Reef (USA)) *2165$^{16}$* 2537$^{16}$ **>32a f<**

**Saluting Walter (USA)** **8** b g Verbatim (USA)-Stage Hour (USA) (Stage Director (USA)) **1995:** *4438$^{7}$* **>35a 15f<**

**Salvatore Grillo (IRE)** **7** b h Ahonoora-Diaphanese *(437a)*

***Samaka Hara (IRE)*** **4** b g Taufan (USA)-Aunt Hester (IRE) (Caerleon (USA)) *353$^{6}$* **>43a 64f<**

**Samana Cay** **4** ch f Pharly (FR)-Brown's Cay (Formidable (USA)) *77$^{11}$ 172$^{9}$ 210$^{11}$ 283$^{8}$ 360$^{7}$* **>6a 46f<**

**Samapour (IRE)** **2** b c Kahyasi-Samneeza (FR) (Storm Bird (CAN)) 4949a$^{2}$ **>108f<**

**Samara (IRE)** **3** ch f Polish Patriot (USA)-Smeralda (GER) (Dschingis Khan) (873) (1420) 2142$^{4}$ **>102+f<**

**Samara Song** **3** ch g Savahra Sound-Hosting (Thatching) *1457$^{8}$ 1651$^{6}$* 1836$^{5}$ *2637$^{4}$ 2966$^{5}$* 3285$^{5}$ 4082$^{2}$ 4480$^{12}$ 4603$^{14}$ *4895$^{6}$* **>60a 43f<**

**Sambac (USA)** **2** b f Mr Prospector (USA)-Kingscote (Kings Lake (USA)) 1954$^{3}$ (2413) (2770) (3921) 4328$^{5}$ 4758$^{4}$ **>91f<**

**Sambakonig (GER)** **3** c 1395a$^{9}$ **>83f<**

**Samba Sharply** **5** b g Rambo Dancer (CAN)-Sharper Still (Sharpen Up) *765$^{14}$* 879$^{2}$ 1330$^{11}$ 2010$^{12}$ 2249$^{3}$ 2581$^{9}$ 3974$^{12}$ **>80f<**

**Same Old Wish (USA)** **6** b g Lyphard's Wish (FR)-Olden Roberta (USA) (Roberto (USA)) *4953a$^{3}$* ***>128f<***

**Samim (USA)** **3** b c Nureyev (USA)-Histoire (FR) (Riverman (USA)) 444$^{11}$ 567$^{5}$ 702$^{4}$ 1200$^{4}$ 4193$^{17}$ 4450$^{5}$ 4559$^{6}$ 4624$^{5}$ **>68f<**

**Samiri (FR)** **5** b h Lashkari-Samirza (USA) (Riverman (USA)) 902a$^{2}$ **>106f<**

**Samorelle** **3** ch f High Kicker (USA)-Lemelasor (Town Crier) 3262$^{9}$ 3472$^{11}$ 3609$^{3}$ 3780$^{17}$ **>56f<**

**Sam Peeb** **2** b g Keen-Lutine Royal (Formidable (USA)) 2865$^{9}$ 3941$^{13}$ 4224$^{12}$ **>36f<**

**Samraan (USA)** **3** br c Green Dancer (USA)-Sedra (Nebbiolo) (578) 923$^{3}$ (1175) (2074) 2535$^{4}$ 3124$^{6}$ 3614$^{4}$ (3992) 4192$^{3}$ 4542a$^{5}$ **>120f<**

**Sam Rockett** **3** b g Petong-Art Deco (Artaius (USA)) *583$^{12}$* 730$^{13}$ 894$^{8}$ 1773$^{16}$ 3681$^{10}$ 3965$^{11}$ 4509$^{4}$ 4669$^{6}$ **>51f<**

**Samsolom** **8** b g Absalom-Norfolk Serenade (Blakeney) *338$^{6}$ 380$^{8}$ 451$^{20}$* 582$^{14}$ 850$^{5}$ 1073$^{6}$ 1186$^{9}$ 1412$^{7}$ 1881$^{5}$ 1905$^{3}$ 2129$^{11}$ 2193$^{9}$ 2870$^{3}$ 3151$^{2}$ 3328$^{5}$ 3585$^{10}$ 3702$^{3}$ 3995$^{19}$ 4109$^{14}$ 4136$^{12}$ 4259$^{15}$ **>61a 66df<**

**Samspet** **2** ch g Pharly (FR)-Almond Blossom (Grundy) 1183$^{9}$ 1845$^{4}$ 2161$^{9}$ *2307$^{5}$ 3082$^{5}$* 4347$^{12}$ 4562$^{8}$ **>36a 53f<**

**Samsung Lovelylady (IRE)** **4** b f Petorius-Kentucky Wildcat (Be My Guest (USA)) *562$^{13}$* 617$^{5}$ 868$^{17}$ 3310$^{6}$ 3644$^{10}$ 3937$^{15}$ 4075$^{9}$ **>33a 25f<**

**Samsung Spirit** **2** b f Statoblest-Sarong (Taj Dewan) (1583) 1978$^{3}$ 2291$^{2}$ 3150$^{5}$ 4685$^{5}$ **>66f<**

**Sam's Yer Man** **2** b c Full Extent (USA)-Falls of Lora (Scottish Rifle) 4423$^{8}$ 4715$^{23}$ 4970$^{18}$ **>41f<**

**Samuel Scott** **3** b g Shareef Dancer (USA)-Revisit (Busted) 894$^{10}$ 1045$^{8}$ 1498$^{6}$ 1783$^{8}$ **>64f<**

**Samwar** **4** b g Warning-Samaza (USA) (Arctic Tern (USA)) **1995:** *(4540)* **1996:** *876$^{6}$* 1018$^{18}$ 2725$^{4}$ (3622) 3783$^{2}$ 4466$^{2}$ 4679$^{15}$ 4823$^{11}$ **>76+a 95f<**

**Sandabar** **3** b c Green Desert (USA)-Children's Corner (FR) (Top Ville) (669) **>81f<**

**Sandbaggedagain** **2** b c Prince Daniel (USA)-Paircullis (Tower Walk) 1525$^{8}$ 2396$^{5}$ 2926$^{3}$ 3227$^{2}$ 3982$^{3}$ 4131$^{2}$ 4298$^{3}$ 4625$^{3}$ **>72f<**

**Sandblaster** **3** ch f Most Welcome-Honeychurch (USA) (Bering) 775$^{6}$ 1042$^{2}$ 1363$^{3}$ 1539$^{2}$ 2163$^{6}$ 2521$^{6}$ 2924$^{5}$ 3118$^{5}$ 3981$^{12}$ **>51f<**

**Sand Cay (USA)** **2** ch c Geiger Counter (USA)-Lily Lily Rose (USA) (Lypheor) 4200$^{7}$ 4584$^{7}$ 4897$^{12}$ **>50f<**

**Sandhill (IRE)** **3** b f Danehill (USA)-Sand Grouse (USA) (Arctic Tern (USA)) 710$^{4}$ 1007$^{6}$ (1435) 2050$^{13}$ 3127$^{10}$ 3830$^{4}$ 4214$^{2}$ **>99f<**

**Sandicliffe (USA)** **3** b f Imp Society (USA)-Sad Song (USA) (Roberto (USA)) 448$^{8}$ 1614$^{10}$ 2062$^{5}$ 2506$^{9}$ 3053$^{4}$ 3335$^{15}$ 3813$^{11}$ **>58f<**

**Sandkatoon (IRE)** **2** br f Archway (IRE)-Indian Sand (Indian King (USA)) 916$^{10}$ *4777$^{W}$ 4902$^{11}$ 5061$^{8}$* **>23a 20f<**

**Sandmoor Chambray** **5** ch g Most Welcome-Valadon (High Line) *933$^{2}$* 1322$^{8}$ 1528$^{2}$ 1819$^{3}$ (2010) 2293$^{2}$ 2483$^{2}$ 3081$^{9}$ 3623$^{2}$ 3856$^{5}$ 4190$^{7}$ 4463$^{25}$ 4769$^{6}$ 4974$^{9}$ 5042$^{2}$ **>90f<**

**Sandmoor Denim** **9** b g Red Sunset-Holemzaye (Sallust) **1995:** *4367$^{3}$ 4390$^{2}$ 4427$^{5}$* **1996:** *778$^{4}$ 884$^{10}$ 1081$^{3}$ 1196$^{12}$ (1602) 2169$^{8}$ 2551$^{3}$ 2749$^{9}$ 2935$^{6}$ 4089$^{7}$ 4781$^{11}$ 4989$^{7}$ 5060$^{3}$* **>57a 64f<**

**Sandmoor Zoe** **2** b f Puissance-Chiquitita (Reliance II) 2495$^{7}$ 3082$^{4}$ 3982$^{23}$ **>51f<**

**Sandomierz (IRE)** **2** b f Nordico (USA)-Sure Flyer (IRE) (Sure Blade (USA)) 4024a$^{16}$ **>71f<**

**Sandpiper** **3** b f Green Desert (USA)-Sojourn (Be My Guest (USA)) 1319$^{9}$ 3519$^{8}$ **>42f<**

**Sandpit (BRA)** **7** ch h Baynoun-Sand Dancer (FR) (Green Dancer (USA)) **1995:** 4471a$^{8}$ **1996:** 3912a$^{3}$ **>122f<**

**Sandra Dee (IRE)** **4** ch f Be My Guest (USA)-Adventurine (Thatching) 2617$^{16}$ 2799$^{7}$ *3420$^{9}$ 3694$^{9}$* ***>26a 21f<***

**Sand Reef** **5** b h Reference Point-Reine D'Egypte (USA) (Val de L'Orne (FR)) **1995:** 4498a$^{2}$ **>114f<**

**Sand Star** **4** b f Lugana Beach-Overseas (Sea Hawk II) **1995:** *4371$^{3}$ (4486) 4539$^{2}$* **1996:** *379$^{3}$ 935$^{13}$* 1121$^{3}$ 1481$^{7}$ 1962$^{12}$ 2134$^{14}$ 3989$^{11}$ 4428$^{2}$ 4609$^{16}$ **>77a 62f<**

**Sandstone (IRE)** **2** b c Green Desert (USA)-Rose De Thai (USA) (Lear Fan (USA)) (2708) 3684$^{5}$ 4056$^{2}$ 4488$^{5}$ 4871$^{7}$ **>93f<**

**Sandweld** **2** b c Weldnaas (USA)-Scottish Lady (Dunbeath (USA)) 3429$^{7}$ *3950$^{4}$ 4578$^{8}$* ***>43a 57f<***

**Sandy Floss (IRE)** **3** b c Green Desert (USA)-Mill on the Floss (Mill Reef (USA)) 640$^{3}$ 842$^{4}$ 1349$^{2}$ 1798$^{3}$ **>83f<**

**Sandystones** **2** b f Selkirk (USA)-Sharanella (Shareef Dancer (USA)) 3407$^{9}$ **>39f<**

**Sang d'Antibes (FR)** **2** ch f Sanglamore (USA)-Baratoga (USA) (Bering) 4469$^{4}$ 4751$^{9}$ **>51f<**

**Sangria (USA)** **3** ch f El Gran Senor (USA)-Champagne Cocktail (Roberto (USA)) (3570a) 4663a$^{3}$ 4961a$^{7}$ **>116f<**

**Sanmartino (IRE)** **4** b c Salse (USA)-Oscura (USA) (Caro) (675) 875$^{6}$ 2055$^{5}$ 3212$^{4}$ 3673$^{3}$ 4569$^{2}$ **>118f<**

**Sanoosea (USA)** **4** b c Storm Bird (CAN)-Nobiliare (USA) (Vaguely Noble) *1131$^{3}$* 1575a$^{4}$ 4371$^{4}$ 4849a$^{2}$ 5073a$^{7}$ **>117f<**

**Sanquillo (BEL)** **8** ch h Queen's Champion-Sainte Devote **1995:** 4466a$^{3}$

**Santa Rosa (IRE)** **2** b f Lahib (USA)-Bequeath (USA) (Lyphard (USA)) 3756$^{4}$ 4593$^{4}$ 4806$^{3}$ **>64f<**

**Santella Cape** **3** b c Alzao (USA)-Kijafa (USA) (Chief's Crown (USA)) 707$^{10}$ 948$^{10}$ **>26f<**

**Santella Katie** **3** ch f Anshan-Mary Bankes (USA) (Northern Baby (CAN)) 1901$^{6}$ 2529$^{2}$ 2996$^{4}$ 3341$^{5}$ **>73f<**

**Santella Twinkle (IRE)** **2** b f Jareer (USA)-Hellicroft (High Line) 4970$^{12}$ **>32f<**

**Santillana (USA)** **3** ch c El Gran Senor (USA)-Galway (FR) (Irish River (FR)) (611) (830) **>118f<**

**Sapio (NZ)** **5** br g Vice Regal (NZ)-Saga (Allgrit (USA)) 724a$^{2}$

**Sapphire Son (IRE)** **4** ch g Maelstrom Lake-Gluhwein (Ballymoss) *1517$^{2}$* 1691$^{5}$ *2081$^{4}$ 2405$^{2}$* 2602$^{9}$ 3585$^{4}$ 3761$^{11}$ 4428$^{4}$ **>57a 57f<**

**Sarabi** **2** b f Alzao (USA)-Sure Enough (IRE) (Diesis) 3114$^{12}$ 3475$^{5}$ 4087$^{11}$ 4586$^{13}$ (4749) 4912$^{8}$ 5037$^{7}$ **>72f<**

**Sarah's Guest (IRE)** **3** ch f Be My Guest (USA)-Lady Bennington (Hot Grove) 1255a$^{8}$ **>75f<**

**Sarasi** **4** ch g Midyan (USA)-Early Call (Kind of Hush) **1995:** *4388$^{6}$ 4427$^{7}$ (4505)* **1996:** *34$^{3}$ 57$^{3}$ 114$^{2}$ (223) 416$^{8}$* **>74a 61f<**

**Sarasonia** **5** b m Dunbeath (USA)-La Graciosa (Comedy Star (USA)) **1995:** *4436$^{9}$ 4458$^{13}$* **>14a 21f<**

**Sarasota Ryde** **3** gr f Komaite (USA)-Freedom Line (Absalom) 4589$^{11}$ 4898$^{19}$ **>42f<**

**Sarasota Storm** **4** b g Petoski-Challanging (Mill Reef (USA)) 641$^{9}$ 995$^{8}$ 1450$^{11}$ (2175) 2516$^{6}$ (2848) 3037$^{12}$ 3355$^{4}$ 4048$^{7}$ (4344) **>64f<**

**Saratoga Red (USA)** **2** ch c Saratoga Six (USA)-Wajibird (USA) (Storm Bird (CAN)) *1603$^{3}$ 1831$^{3}$* 2040$^{11}$ 3757$^{9}$ **>58a 76f<**

**Sarawat** **8** b g Slip Anchor-Eljazzi (Artaius (USA)) 439$^{13}$ 482$^{5}$ 620$^{2}$ (886) 1116$^{5}$ **>75f<**

**Sarayir (USA)** **2** b f Mr Prospector (USA)-Height of Fashion (FR) (Bustino) (3988) (4565) **>99f<**

**Sardonic** **3** b f Kris-Sardegna (Pharly (FR)) *(1123)* (1899) 2609$^{6}$ 3231$^{6}$ 3497$^{7}$ 4218$^{8}$ **>109df<**

**Sarmatian (USA)** **5** br g Northern Flagship (USA)-Tracy L (USA) (Bold Favorite (USA)) *913$^{3}$* 1198$^{2}$ (1585) 2164$^{7}$ 2350$^{5}$ 3120$^{9}$ **>74f<**

**Sarteano** **2** ch f Anshan-Daisy Girl (Main Reef) 3054$^{6}$ 3778$^{3}$ **>43f<**

**Sarum** **10** b g Tina's Pet-Contessa (HUN) (Peleid) *366$^{5}$ 393$^{4}$ (412) 487$^{5}$ 501$^{6}$ 553$^{10}$ 778$^{7}$ 1048$^{7}$ 1348$^{16}$* 1677$^{7}$ 1953$^{14}$ 2284$^{11}$ *4089$^{11}$ 4202$^{14}$* ***>55a 52f<***

**Saseedo (USA)** **6** ch g Afleet (CAN)-Barbara's Moment (USA) (Super Moment (USA)) **1995:** *4427$^{4}$* **1996:** *679$^{11}$* 928$^{6}$ (1149) 2114$^{11}$ (2363) (2497) 2623$^{13}$ 3445$^{5}$ 3782$^{7}$ 4554$^{3}$ 4775$^{10}$ **>80a 96f<**

**Sassetta (IRE)** **3** ch f Soviet Lad (USA)-Sun Gift

(Guillaume Tell (USA)) $614^{13}$ $784^{6}$ **>22f<**

**Sassiver (USA) 6** b g Riverman (USA)-Sassabunda (Sassafras (FR)) $108^{6}$ $140^{3}$ $206^{5}$ **>52da 42f<**

**Sassy Street (IRE) 3** b g Danehill (USA)-Sassy Lane (Sassafras (FR)) **1995:** $4414^{9}$ **>44a f<**

**Sasuru 3** b c Most Welcome-Sassalya (Sassafras (FR)) $671^{2}$ $986^{4}$ (1359) (2006) (3746a) **>115f<**

**Satin Bell 3** b f Midyan (USA)-Silk Petal (Petorius) (710) $874^{3}$ $3127^{6}$ $3909a^{5}$ $4445^{15}$ $4671^{10}$ **>94f<**

**Satin Lover 8** ch g Tina's Pet-Canoodle (Warpath) $449^{17}$ $961^{4}$ $1091^{2}$ (1436) $1802^{6}$ $2319^{4}$ **>83f<**

**Saucy Soul 3** ch g Ballacashtal (CAN)-Ninotchka (Niniski (USA)) $943^{12}$ $1305^{12}$ **>14f<**

**Saunders Wren 2** b f Handsome Sailor-Saunders Lass (Hillandale) (1315) $2051^{11}$ $2375^{3}$ $2595^{7}$ (2926) $3511^{10}$ **>74f<**

**Sausalito Bay 2** b c Salse (USA)-Cantico (Green Dancer (USA)) $4507^{5}$ (4801) **>79f<**

**Savage (IRE) 3** b f Polish Patriot (USA)-Special Meeting (Persian Bold) $1395a^{7}$ **>92f<**

**Savanna Blue 3** b f Moor House-Lady Havana Bay VII (Damsire Unregistered) $89^{6}$ $258^{6}$ $430^{6}$ **>18a f<**

**Saving Power 3** b g Superlative-Scented Goddess (IRE) (Godswalk (USA)) $2718^{10}$ $3513^{11}$ $4074^{7}$ $4809^{18}$ **>43f<**

**Savona (IRE) 2** b f Cyrano de Bergerac-Shannon Lady (Monsanto (FR)) $4558^{4}$ $4918^{3}$ $5034^{5}$ **>72f<**

**Sawa-Id 3** b br c Anshan-Bermuda Lily (Dunbeath (USA)) $2899^{4}$ $3258^{5}$ (3586) (4047) $4381^{2}$ **>84f<**

**Saxon Bay 4** ch g Cadeaux Genereux-Princess Athena (Ahonoora) $4360^{9}$ **>49f<**

**Saxonbury 2** b c Shirley Heights-Dancing Vaguely (USA) (Vaguely Noble) $4508^{11}$ **>29f<**

**Saxon Maid 5** b m Sadler's Wells (USA)-Britannia's Rule **1995:** $4470a^{4}$ **>111f<**

**Sayeh (IRE) 4** b c Fools Holme (USA)-Piffle (Shirley Heights) $2677^{7}$ $4184^{13}$ **>93f<**

**Sayitagain 4** b c Bering-Casey (Caerleon (USA)) $495^{6}$ $816^{11}$ $844^{7}$ $1486^{11}$ $1803^{21}$ **>47f<**

**Scandator (IRE) 3** b c Danehill (USA)-Rustic Lawn (Rusticaro (FR)) $447^{7}$ $576^{10}$ $826^{14}$ $1100^{W}$ **>57f<**

**Scaraben 8** b g Dunbeath (USA)-Varushka (Sharpen Up) $589^{8}$ $765^{8}$ $933^{9}$ $967^{10}$ $1528^{3}$ $1868^{3}$ $2293^{4}$ $2573^{2}$ (2868) $3084^{3}$ $3279^{4}$ $4190^{10}$ $4300^{12}$ $4769^{17}$ (5004) **>83f<**

**Scarlet Crescent 2** b f Midyan (USA)-Scarlet Veil (Tyrnavos) $3105^{3}$ $3515^{3}$ (3848) $4222^{7}$ **>67f<**

**Scarlet Lake 2** b f Reprimand-Stinging Nettle (Sharpen Up) $2343^{5}$ $2783^{5}$ $3259^{20}$ $4916^{13}$ **>51f<**

**Scarlet Plume 3** b f Warning-Circus Plume (High Top) $938^{6}$ $1335^{4}$ $2991^{7}$ $3836^{9}$ $4671^{2}$ $5072a^{7}$ **>104f<**

**Scarpetta (USA) 3** ch f Seattle Dancer (USA)-Pump (USA) (Forli (ARG)) $921^{4}$ $3949^{10}$ $4309^{2}$ $4611^{2}$ $4824^{6}$ $4974^{25}$ **>75f<**

**Scarrots 2** b c Mazilier (USA)-Bath (Runnett) $639^{8}$ $2733^{5}$ $3227^{8}$ $3498^{6}$ (4223) $4602^{4}$ **>64f<**

**Scathebury 3** b g Aragon-Lady Bequick (Sharpen Up) $515^{3}$ $747^{4}$ $1085^{4}$ $1516^{2}$ $2325^{8}$ $2578^{4}$ $2748^{8}$ $3274^{9}$ $3458^{2}$ $3666^{4}$ (3881) $3995^{12}$ $4232^{11}$ $4428^{11}$ $4589^{10}$ $4784^{2}$ **>54a 60f<**

**Scboo 7** b g Full Extent (USA)-Maygo (Maystreak) **1995:** $4357^{9}$ **1996:** $59^{11}$ $229^{5}$ $318^{8}$ **>42a 6f<**

**Scene Stealer 3** b f Scenic-Sindos (Busted) $599^{7}$ **>15f<**

**Scenic Dancer 8** b g Shareef Dancer (USA)-Bridestones (Jan Ekels) $1011^{5}$ $1655^{2}$ $1803^{14}$ $2008^{14}$ $2798^{P}$ **>56f<**

**Scenicris (IRE) 3** b f Scenic-Princesse Smile (Balidar) **1995:** $4443^{3}$ $4491^{8}$ **1996:** $17^{3}$ $137^{6}$ $300^{5}$ $344^{9}$ $605^{8}$ $740^{3}$ $1324^{8}$ $1689^{9}$ $2222^{3}$ $2672^{8}$ $3102^{10}$ $3591^{4}$ $3866^{3}$ $4296^{5}$ $4590^{3}$ (4921) **>57a 71f<**

**Scent of Power 6** b g Fairy King (USA)-Agreloui (Tower Walk) $43^{5}$ $84^{6}$ $145^{13}$ **>27a 38f<**

**Scharnhorst 4** b g Tacheron-Stardyn (Star Appeal) **1995:** $4356^{P}$ **1996:** $406^{7}$ (496) $554^{8}$ (756) $1018^{5}$ (1442) $1962^{9}$ $2623^{12}$ $3216^{10}$ $4255^{6}$ **>55a 75f<**

**Scherma 3** b f Green Desert (USA)-Escrime (USA) (Sharpen Up) $3767^{6}$ $3949^{3}$ **>70f<**

**Schisandra 2** b f Petong-Volcalmeh (Lidhame) $2852^{7}$ $3454^{9}$ $3687^{17}$ $4549^{15}$ **>54f<**

**School Boy 3** b c Aragon-Grovehurst (Homing) $414^{2}$ $510^{2}$ $819^{3}$ $987^{11}$ $1457^{9}$ $1986^{3}$ $2013^{6}$ $2617^{2}$ $2765^{2}$ $3210^{17}$ $3317^{3}$ $4550^{13}$ $4987^{11}$ $5058^{3}$ **>58a 64f<**

**School of Science 6** b g Then Again-Girl's Brigade (Brigadier Gerard) $558^{12}$ $1544^{6}$ $2493^{7}$ $2931^{3}$ $3239^{3}$ $3425^{8}$ $3490^{5}$ **>38f<**

**Scimitar 3** ch c Prince Sabo-Siokra (Kris) $732^{11}$ $1045^{6}$ $1350^{6}$ $2253^{7}$ $3681^{9}$ $4053^{16}$ $4480^{3}$ $4968^{21}$ **>58f<**

**Scissor Ridge 4** ch g Indian Ridge-Golden Scissors (Kalaglow) **1995:** $4356^{10}$ $4421^{5}$ $4450^{2}$ (4521) **1996:** $556^{5}$ $664^{2}$ $887^{8}$ $1029^{6}$ $1121^{8}$ $1715^{2}$ $1958^{5}$ (2129) $2285^{4}$ $2713^{3}$ $2735^{2}$ $3216^{8}$ $3439^{2}$ $3583^{2}$ $3666^{2}$ $4198^{4}$ (4372) $4679^{10}$ $4888^{6}$ **>53a 68f<**

**Scored Again 6** b g Music Boy-Thorner Lane (Tina's Pet) $1492^{11}$ $1812^{7}$ $2555^{5}$ $2992^{5}$ $3261^{3}$ $3416^{6}$ $3652^{6}$ $4045^{10}$ $4372^{10}$ **>51a 50f<**

**Scorpius 6** b h Soviet Star (USA)-Sally Brown (Posse (USA)) $205^{W}$ $505^{5}$ $884^{4}$ $979^{6}$ $1173^{13}$ $1625^{8}$ $1778^{16}$ $2209^{9}$ $4906^{16}$ **>46f<**

**Scorribanda (ITY) 2** b f Law Society (USA)-Somalia (Formidable (USA)) $4039a^{3}$

**Scotmail Lass 2** b f Clantime-Sapphirine (Trojan Fen) $2491^{5}$ $3121^{5}$ $3648^{6}$ **>38f<**

**Scottish Bambi 8** ch g Scottish Reel-Bambolona (Bustino) (670) $817^{9}$ $1047^{4}$ $1414^{5}$ **>65f<**

**Scottish Hero 3** b c North Briton-Tartan Pimpernel (Blakeney) $845^{11}$ $2036^{7}$ $2205^{4}$ $3249^{13}$ **>67df<**

**Scottish Mist (IRE) 2** gr f Digamist (USA)-Morgiana (Godswalk (USA)) $1565a^{5}$ $1910a^{3}$ $3561a^{9}$ **>82f<**

**Scottish Park 7** ch m Scottish Reel-Moss Agate (Alias Smith (USA)) $57^{9}$ $162^{3}$ $216^{7}$ $549^{4}$ $1196^{3}$ $1411^{6}$ (1638) $2379^{3}$ $2716^{4}$ $2788^{6}$ **>49a 54f<**

**Scott's Risk 6** b g Risk Me (FR)-Madam de Seul (Pas de Seul) $1162^{9}$ $1787^{9}$ $2185^{11}$ **>19f<**

**Scribano 6** b h Pharly (FR)-Biograph (USA) (Riverman (USA)) $1392a^{3}$ $2278a^{2}$ $2670a^{2}$ **>108f<**

**Script 5** b g Squill (USA)-Vitry (Vitiges (FR)) $349^{8}$ **>22a f<**

**Sea-Ayr (IRE) 6** ch m Magical Wonder (USA)-Kunuz (Ela-Mana-Mou) $505^{7}$ $718^{12}$ $1037^{9}$ **>30a 41f<**

**Sea Buck 10** b g Simply Great (FR)-Heatherside (Hethersett) $4203^{14}$ **>48f<**

**Sea Dane 3** b c Danehill (USA)-Shimmering Sea (Slip Anchor) $727^{8}$ (2332) $2880^{15}$ $3759^{11}$ $3984^{9}$ $4116^{13}$ $4466^{5}$ $4774^{9}$ **>105f<**

**Sea Danzig 3** ch g Roi Danzig (USA)-Tosara (Main Reef) $525^{2}$ $692^{10}$ $873^{9}$ $1155^{5}$ $2000^{9}$ $2061^{10}$ $2316^{6}$ $2578^{15}$ $3270^{2}$ $3519^{5}$ $3930^{12}$ $4053^{5}$ $4256^{4}$ $4376^{10}$ (4550) $4820^{15}$ $4915^{6}$ **>72f<**

**Sea-Deer 7** ch g Hadeer-Hi-Tech Girl (Homeboy) $117^{4}$ $180^{3}$ $202^{5}$ $250^{4}$ $302^{3}$ $389^{2}$ $700^{3}$ $764^{2}$ $951^{2}$ $1087^{4}$ (1342) (1598) (1881) (1905) $2228^{2}$ $2694^{6}$ $2889^{3}$ (3047) $3296^{8}$ $3432^{3}$ $3618^{2}$ (3953) $4116^{12}$ $4314^{21}$ $4581^{7}$ $4772^{14}$ **>83a 87f<**

**Sea Devil 10** gr g Absalom-Miss Poinciana (Averof) $76^{8}$ $126^{2}$ (212) $250^{2}$ $479^{7}$ $764^{7}$ $1030^{2}$ $1094^{9}$ **>68a 51f<**

**Sea Freedom 5** b h Slip Anchor-Rostova (Blakeney) $449^{5}$ $573^{10}$ $647^{3}$ $944^{6}$ $1439^{2}$ $1782^{2}$ $2042^{11}$ $2530^{5}$ $3163^{2}$ $3428^{3}$ $3801^{2}$ $3928^{6}$ $4476^{4}$ $4673^{2}$ $4821^{5}$ **>72f<**

**Sea God 5** ch g Rainbow Quest (USA)-Sea Pageant (Welsh Pageant) **1995:** $4428^{5}$ **1996:** $44^{W}$ $90^{4}$ $115^{5}$ $153^{2}$ $199^{4}$ (256) $303^{6}$ $429^{5}$ $440^{W}$ $508^{8}$ $2206^{6}$ $2348^{3}$ $4102^{4}$ $4753^{7}$ **>58a 50f<**

**Sea Idol (IRE) 3** br f Astronef-Pharjoy (FR) (Pharly (FR)) $1171^{14}$ $1535^{8}$ **>47f<**

**Sea Mist (IRE) 2** ch f Shalford (IRE)-Somnifere (USA) (Nijinsky (CAN)) $596^{9}$ $3475^{10}$ $4118^{7}$ $4495^{6}$ $4764^{13}$ **>63f<**

**Seamus 2** ch c Almoojid-Royal Celerity (USA) (Riverman (USA)) $452^{11}$

**Sea of Stone (USA) 3** ch f Sanglamore (USA)-Ocean Ballad (Grundy) $1690^{2}$ $2744^{2}$ $4833^{2}$ **>71f<**

**Sea Plane 7** gr h Nishapour (FR)-Pirogue (Reliance II) $4771^{15}$ **>66f<**

**Seaside (IRE) 2** b f Salt Dome (USA)-Cipriani (Habitat) $741^{2}$ (880) $1362^{3}$ $2879^{10}$ $3411^{5}$ **>68f<**

**Seasonal Splendour (IRE) 6** b m Prince Rupert (FR)-Snoozy Time (Cavo Doro) $573^{6}$ $1005^{9}$ $1194^{16}$ $2042^{15}$ $2499^{5}$ **>86f<**

**Sea Spouse 5** ch g Jalmood (USA)-Bambolona (Bustino) **1995:** $4505^{3}$ **1996:** $34^{5}$ $199^{3}$ (239) $345^{3}$ $416^{3}$ (470) $887^{11}$ $1029^{9}$ $1604^{3}$ (1718) $2428^{7}$ $3469^{14}$ $4979^{2}$ **>71a 51f<**

**Sea Spray (IRE) 3** b f Royal Academy (USA)-Sailor's Mate (Shirley Heights) (572) $1108^{5}$ $2069^{10}$ **>102f<**

**Sea Thunder 4** gr f Salse (USA)-Money Moon (Auction Ring (USA)) $850^{8}$ $1354^{10}$ $1790^{10}$ $2005^{8}$ $2229^{6}$ **>65f<**

**Seattle Alley (USA) 3** b g Seattle Dancer (USA)-Alyanaabi (USA) (Roberto (USA)) $453^{9}$ $646^{11}$ $819^{7}$ $995^{4}$ (1832) (2027) **>74f<**

**Seattle Art (USA) 2** b c Seattle Slew (USA)-Artiste (Artaius (USA)) $4914^{9}$ **>40f<**

**Seattle Saga (USA) 3** b c Seattle Dancer (USA)-Sid's Kate (USA) (Chieftain II) (228) $2673^{2}$ $2990^{3}$ **>58a 74df<**

**Seattle Swing 2** b f Saddlers' Hall (IRE)-Sweet Slew (USA) (Seattle Slew (USA)) $4359^{5}$ **>63f<**

**Sea Victor 4** b g Slip Anchor-Victoriana (USA) (Storm Bird (CAN)) **1995:** $4384^{2}$ $4481^{2}$ **1996:** $816^{9}$ $1005^{12}$ $1158^{3}$ $1529^{7}$ (1717) (1875) $2042^{4}$ $2330^{11}$ $2697^{4}$ $3142^{2}$ (3266) $3486^{6}$ $3834^{9}$ $4447^{18}$ $4596^{4}$ $4771^{5}$ $4832^{2}$ $5047^{11}$ **>87a 89f<**

**Sea Wedding 3** ch f Groom Dancer (USA)-Cruising Height (Shirley Heights) $4611^{3}$ $4824^{4}$ **>69f<**

**Sea Ya Maite 2** b g Komaite (USA)-Marina Plata (Julio Mariner) $4863^{10}$ $5034^{W}$ **>32f<**

**Second Barrage 3** b c Royal Academy (USA)-Proudfoot (IRE) (Shareef Dancer (USA)) (1578a) $2231^{6}$ **>56f<**

**Second Colours (USA) 6** b or br g Timeless Moment (USA)-Ruffled Silk (USA) (Our Hero (USA)) **1995:** $4444^{3}$ $4525^{2}$ **1996:** $61^{10}$ (141) (249) $371^{3}$ $2218^{2}$ $2483^{3}$ $2868^{9}$ $3279^{8}$ $3918^{4}$ **>85a 70f<**

**Secondment 3** b c Shernazar-Designate (USA) (Nureyev (USA)) $932^{11}$ $1104^{17}$ $1530^{4}$ $2062^{3}$ $2366^{10}$ **>66f<**

**Seconds Away 5** b g Hard Fought-Keep Mum (Mummy's Pet) $207^{10}$ $997^{2}$ $1163^{13}$ $1313^{5}$ $1545^{7}$ $1635^{11}$ $2154^{6}$ $2391^{3}$ $2851^{2}$ $3236^{4}$ $3344^{10}$ $3492^{3}$ $3645^{4}$ $3878^{8}$ $4296^{8}$ $4503^{6}$ **>19a 35f<**

**Secret Aly (CAN) 6** b g Secreto (USA)-Bouffant (USA) (Alydar (USA)) **1995:** $4476^{4}$ **1996:** $306^{7}$ $379^{9}$ $580^{7}$ $844^{5}$ $988^{4}$ $2010^{13}$ $2299^{2}$ $2724^{12}$ $3447^{11}$ (4238) $4450^{6}$ $4826^{8}$ **>90a 90f<**

**Secretary of State 10** b g Alzao (USA)-Colonial Line (USA) (Plenty Old (USA)) *27$^{2}$ 598$^{9}$* 752$^{21}$ **>61a 46f<**
**Secret Ballot (IRE) 2** b c Taufan (USA)-Ballet Society (FR) (Sadler's Wells (USA)) 2195$^{8}$ 4756$^{17}$ 4830$^{11}$ **>54f<**
**Secret Combe (IRE) 2** b f Mujadil (USA)-Crimbourne (Mummy's Pet) 2309$^{2}$ (2596) 2879$^{6}$ 3468$^{4}$ 4311$^{9}$ 4918$^{5}$ **>84f<**
**Secret Gift 3** ch f Cadeaux Genereux-Triste Oeil (USA) (Raise A Cup (USA)) 1670$^{6}$ 2140$^{3}$ 2365$^{3}$ **>76f<**
**Secret Lear (USA) 3** c **1995:** 4399a$^{9}$ **>83f<**
**Secret Miss 4** ch f Beveled (USA)-Zamindara (Crofter (USA)) **1995:** *4371$^{7}$ 4407$^{8}$* **1996:** *342$^{8}$ 466$^{15}$* 601$^{4}$ 667$^{5}$ 862$^{18}$ 1170$^{4}$ 2186$^{6}$ 2561$^{11}$ **>44a 59f<**
**Secret Pass (USA) 2** ch c Diesis-Mlle Lyphard (USA) (Lyphard (USA)) *1445$^{5}$* 3485$^{6}$ 4123$^{12}$ 4495$^{16}$ **>59f<**
**Secret Pleasure (IRE) 3** ch f Classic Secret (USA)-Abbessingh (Mansingh (USA)) 470$^{13}$ 2686$^{6}$ 3167$^{7}$ 3585$^{3}$ 3977$^{2}$ 4128$^{6}$ 4480$^{8}$ 4692$^{13}$ **>62f<**
**Secret Service (IRE) 4** b g Classic Secret (USA)-Mystery Bid (Auction Ring (USA)) *532$^{5}$ 972$^{3}$* 1436$^{3}$ 1524$^{9}$ 1875$^{3}$ 2330$^{3}$ 2912$^{7}$ 3983$^{5}$ 4431$^{7}$ 4771$^{11}$ **>59a 79f<**
**Secret Spring (FR) 4** b g Dowsing (USA)-Nordica (Northfields (USA)) *24$^{2}$ (204) (243) 379$^{5}$ 4308$^{6}$* 4568$^{18}$ 4874$^{9}$ **>89a 83f<**
**Secret Voucher 3** b c Vouchsafe-Welsh Secret (Welsh Captain) 443$^{4}$ (644) 989$^{7}$ 2007$^{F}$ **>77f<** **(DEAD)**
**Sedbergh (USA) 3** b g Northern Flagship (USA)-Crumbaugh Pike (USA) (Within Hail (USA)) 444$^{15}$ 560$^{3}$ *651$^{2}$ 1023$^{4}$* 1498$^{16}$ (1762) (1907) 2627$^{5}$ **>59a 79f<**
**Sedvicta 4** b g Primitive Rising (USA)-Annes Gift (Ballymoss) 4448$^{8}$ 4563$^{14}$ 4794$^{14}$ **>32f<**
**Seebe (USA) 2** b f Danzig (USA)-Annie Edge (Nebbiolo) (2782) (3068) 3707$^{3}$ 4328$^{3}$ **>102f<**
**Seeking Destiny (IRE) 3** b g Two Timing (USA)-Heads We Called (IRE) (Bluebird (USA)) **1995:** *4410$^{7}$* **1996:** *35$^{3}$ (112) (194) 282$^{9}$ 405$^{7}$ 518$^{5}$ 605$^{5}$ 780$^{3}$ 1030$^{8}$ 1721$^{2}$ 2027$^{6}$ 2369$^{13}$ 3089$^{4}$ 3354$^{10}$* 4217$^{10}$ **>50a 46f<**
**Seeking Fortune (USA) 3** b f Seeking the Gold (USA)-Gabfest (USA) (Tom Rolfe) 2181$^{3}$ 2744$^{4}$ 3133$^{5}$ 3522$^{4}$ 4232$^{6}$ **>75f<**
**Seenthelight 4** ch f Rich Charlie-Ackabarrow (Laser Light) *59$^{12}$ 537$^{12}$* ***>43f<***
**See You Again 4** b c Then Again-Down the Valley (Kampala) **1995:** *4372$^{8}$* **1996:** *140$^{9}$* **>49a 63f<** **(DEAD)**
**See You Soon 2** b c Distant Relative-Our Resolution (Caerleon (USA)) 4046$^{19}$ **>1f<**
**Segala (IRE) 5** b g Petorius-Cerosia (Pitskelly) 690$^{15}$ 802$^{10}$ 884$^{11}$ 1165$^{7}$ **>80a 46f<**
**Seigneurial 4** b g Primo Dominie-Spinner (Blue Cashmere) (582) 928$^{5}$ 1186$^{6}$ 3672$^{7}$ 3946$^{6}$ (4255) 4554$^{6}$ 4687$^{7}$ 4775$^{9}$ **>94f<**
**Seirenes 3** b f Formidable (USA)-Seriema (Petingo) 921$^{3}$ 1123$^{2}$ 1656$^{11}$ 4422$^{3}$ 4866$^{6}$ **>74df<**
**Sejaal (IRE) 4** b g Persian Heights-Cremets (Mummy's Pet) *809$^{15}$* 3799$^{10}$ 4109$^{15}$ 4354$^{8}$ **>67f<**
**Sekari 2** b c Polish Precedent (USA)-Secret Seeker (USA) (Mr Prospector (USA)) (4817) **>72+f<**
**Selberry 2** b g Selkirk (USA)-Choke Cherry (Connaught) *4619$^{4}$* ***>81f<***
**Select Choice (IRE) 2** b c Waajib-Stella Ann (Ahonoora) *1871$^{5}$* 3147$^{8}$ 3690$^{8}$ 4188$^{3}$ 4380$^{3}$ 4783$^{2}$ **>84f<**
**Select Few 3** b c Alzao (USA)-Elect (USA) (Vaguely Noble) *693$^{3}$* 1145$^{8}$ (1843) 2146$^{10}$ (3926) 4556$^{9}$ **>92f<**
**Select Lady 2** b f Presidium-Child Star (Precocious) 2153$^{3}$ 3336$^{4}$ *4777$^{10}$* **>31f<**
**Select Star (IRE) 2** b c Arcane (USA)-Chevrefeuille (Ile de Bourbon (USA)) 2122$^{2}$ 2967$^{9}$ 3821$^{3}$ 3982$^{17}$ 4262$^{2}$ 4375$^{7}$ 4721$^{3}$ 4990$^{7}$ **>74f<**
**Self Expression 8** b g Homing-Subtlety (Grundy) 505$^{9}$ 586$^{12}$ 688$^{6}$ 1088$^{10}$ **>59a 49f<**
**Selhurstpark Flyer (IRE) 5** b g Northiam (USA)-Wisdom to Know (Bay Express) 718$^{4}$ (1040) 1186$^{3}$ (1790) 2114$^{15}$ 2220$^{2}$ 3232$^{17}$ 3618$^{5}$ (4122) 4314$^{22}$ 4485$^{7}$ **>100f<**
**Sellette (IRE) 2** ch f Selkirk (USA)-Near the End (Shirley Heights) 4127$^{7}$ 4359$^{3}$ 4507$^{3}$ **>65f<**
**Selmeston (IRE) 4** b g Double Schwartz-Baracuda (FR) (Zeddaan) **1995:** *4428$^{11}$ 4508$^{12}$* **1996:** *45$^{5}$ 85$^{7}$ 221$^{3}$ 346$^{5}$ 367$^{W}$ (398) 474$^{7}$* 625$^{13}$ *1095$^{11}$ 1488$^{9}$* **>52da 46f<**
**Semper (IRE) 3** b c Soviet Lad (USA)-Classic Dilemma (Sandhurst Prince) 903a$^{14}$ **>76f<**
**Senador (IRE) 4** b g Alzao (USA)-Congress Lady (General Assembly (USA)) 4033a$^{7}$ **>95f<**
**Senate Swings 2** gr c Timeless Times (USA)-Heaven-Liegh-Grey (Grey Desire) 568$^{6}$ 2125$^{3}$ 2435$^{3}$ *3604$^{5}$ 3795$^{3}$ 4079$^{4}$ 4562$^{16}$* ***>63a 61f<***
**Sendmetomary 2** b f Efisio-Dreams to Riches (Busted) 2512$^{11}$ **>29f<**
**Sendoro (IRE) 2** b c Shahrastani (USA)-Sendana (FR) (Darshaan) 5024a$^{3}$ **>101f<**
**Senebrova 5** b m Warning-Stemegna (Dance In Time (CAN)) **1995:** (4398a) **>108f<**
**Senorita Matilda (USA) 2** b f El Gran Senor (USA)-Copperama (AUS) (Comeram (FR)) 1513$^{6}$ 2611$^{5}$ **>70f<**
**Sensation 3** b f Soviet Star (USA)-Outstandingly (USA) (Exclusive Native (USA)) (1758a) (2609) 3745a$^{9}$ **>114+f<**
**Sense of Priority 7** ch g Primo Dominie-Sense of Pride (Welsh Pageant) *(59) 76$^{3}$ 135$^{7}$ 212$^{2}$ 229$^{4}$ (250) (302) 317$^{6}$ 1087$^{7}$* 1342$^{5}$ 2154$^{8}$ (2212) 2392$^{2}$ 2492$^{B}$ 2870$^{5}$ 3223$^{6}$ 3278$^{6}$ *3420$^{3}$* **>72da 72f<**
**Senso (IRE) 5** b g Persian Heights-Flosshilde (Rheingold) *284$^{7}$* **>6a 68?f<**
**Separate Lives (SWE) 5** b g Ela-Mana-Mou-Much Blest (Mummy's Pet) 4655a$^{7}$ **>109f<**
**Sepoy (IRE) 3** ch c Common Grounds-Song of The Glens (Horage) *790a$^{2}$* ***>95f<***
**Septieme Brigade (USA) 3** b c Septieme Ciel (USA)-Brigade Speciale **1995:** 4496a$^{3}$ **>98f<**
**Serape 3** b f Primo Dominie-Absaloute Service (Absalom) 1452$^{7}$ 2718$^{9}$ 3162$^{6}$ 3439$^{7}$ **>56f<**
**Serenade (IRE) 2** gr g Classic Music (USA)-Friendly Thoughts (USA) (Al Hattab (USA)) 4233$^{14}$ 4494$^{6}$ 4879$^{7}$ **>65f<**
**Serena's Song (USA) 4** b f Rahy (USA)-Imagining (USA) (Northfields (USA)) *4952a$^{2}$* **>115a 114f<**
**Serendipity (FR) 3** b c Mtoto-Bint Damascus (USA) (Damascus (USA)) 584$^{10}$ (1035) 1666$^{4}$ 2074$^{8}$ 2603$^{15}$ 3123$^{3}$ 3805$^{9}$ 4193$^{5}$ 4463$^{23}$ 4719$^{3}$ **>88f<**
**Serene Swing (USA) 3** b f Seattle Dancer (USA)-Alyannock (USA) 2102a$^{7}$ **>75f<**
**Serenity 2** b f Selkirk (USA)-Mystery Ship (Decoy Boy) 2887$^{5}$ (3293) (4566) 4758$^{3}$ **>94f<**
**Serenus (USA) 3** b c Sunshine Forever (USA)-Curl And Set (USA) (Nijinsky (CAN)) 1711$^{3}$ 2439$^{3}$ 3041$^{2}$ 4353$^{4}$ **>82f<**
**Seretse's Nephew 2** b c Chilibang-Bunnyloch (Lochnager) 4368$^{5}$ 4493$^{6}$ 4715$^{15}$ **>50f<**
**Sergeyev (IRE) 4** ch c Mulhollande (USA)-Escape Path (Wolver Hollow) 3132$^{U}$ 3524$^{3}$ 3712$^{5}$ 4051$^{7}$ 4239$^{2}$ 4378$^{6}$ 4870$^{6}$ **>103f<**
**Sergio (IRE) 4** ch g Doubletour (USA)-Shygate (Shy Groom (USA)) *70$^{8}$* **>35a 42f<**
**Serious 6** b g Shadeed (USA)-Azallya (FR) (Habitat) 1775$^{2}$ 2053$^{8}$ 2477a$^{4}$ 3158$^{14}$ **>103f<**
**Serious Account (USA) 3** b c Danzig (USA)-Topicount (USA) (Private Account (USA)) 970$^{9}$ **>65f<**
**Serious Fact 4** b g Aragon-Plain Tree (Wolver Hollow) **1995:** *4458$^{5}$* **1996:** *74$^{2}$ 127$^{6}$ (179) 207$^{3}$ 336$^{5}$ 1043$^{6}$ 1606$^{10}$* **>47a 39f<**
**Serious Hurry 8** ch g Forzando-Lady Bequick (Sharpen Up) *316$^{8}$ 559$^{15}$* 659$^{8}$ 1541$^{5}$ 1865$^{2}$ 1889$^{4}$ 2523$^{9}$ 2960$^{4}$ 3342$^{6}$ 3793$^{9}$ 3868$^{8}$ 4205$^{10}$ **>54a 49f<**
**Serious Option (IRE) 5** b g Reprimand-Top Bloom (Thatch (USA)) *80$^{7}$ 887$^{10}$* 1145$^{20}$ **>42a 73f<**
**Serious Sensation 3** ch g Be My Chief (USA)-Maiyaasah (Kris) 2420$^{5}$ 2579$^{10}$ *3064$^{2}$ (3421) 3627$^{2}$ 3770$^{5}$* 4202$^{3}$ 4550$^{3}$ 4799$^{10}$ **>89a 70f<**
**Serious Trust 3** b c Alzao (USA)-Mill Line (Mill Reef (USA)) (890) 2024$^{4}$ 2627$^{3}$ 3077$^{3}$ *3437$^{7}$* **>41a 68f<**
**Serviable (IRE) 4** b c Royal Academy (USA)-Habituee (Habitat) 5018a$^{2}$ **>115f<**
**Set Adrift 3** b c Slip Anchor-Cephira (FR) (Abdos) 707$^{2}$ 948$^{6}$ (2198) **>91f<**
**Set-Em-Alight 6** b g Relkino-Dragon Fire (Dragonara Palace (USA)) *635$^{W}$* ***>14?f<***
**Setmatt 2** b c Rudimentary (USA)-Persian Air (Persian Bold) 4538a$^{3}$
**Set the Fashion 7** br g Green Desert (USA)-Prelude (Troy) **1995:** *4350$^{12}$* **1996:** *1902$^{5}$* 2155$^{5}$ 2342$^{4}$ 2513$^{2}$ (3052) 3161$^{11}$ 3812$^{6}$ 3991$^{17}$ 4203$^{17}$ (4740a) **>80a 65f<**
**Seva (IRE) 2** b f Night Shift (USA)-Swallowcliffe (Caerleon (USA)) 1413$^{3}$ 1678$^{3}$ 4208$^{9}$ 4721$^{5}$ **>69df<**
**Seven Crowns (USA) 3** b c Chief's Crown (USA)-Ivory Dance (USA) (Sir Ivor) 1654$^{16}$ 1714$^{3}$ 2251$^{8}$ 2408$^{3}$ 2613$^{5}$ 3113$^{13}$ 3141$^{8}$ 4086$^{10}$ **>75f<**
**Seventeens Lucky 4** gr g Touch of Grey-Westminster Waltz (Dance In Time (CAN)) **1995:** *4526$^{4}$* **1996:** *80$^{2}$ 100$^{5}$ 440$^{6}$* 1440$^{12}$ (1613) 1819$^{11}$ 2010$^{3}$ 2724$^{15}$ 3123$^{11}$ 3501$^{3}$ 3799$^{5}$ (3985) 4463$^{10}$ 4686$^{7}$ 4901$^{6}$ **>79a 84f<**
**Seventh Edition 3** b g Classic Music (USA)-Funny-Do (Derring-Do) 820$^{11}$ 1079$^{8}$ 1182$^{5}$ 1641$^{9}$ 1826$^{11}$ 2794$^{4}$ 2989$^{11}$ *3421$^{7}$* **>29a 67f<**
**Severn Mill 5** ch g Librate-Staryllis Girl (Star Moss) 1452$^{9}$ 2036$^{13}$ 2181$^{5}$ 2617$^{15}$ 3341$^{6}$ 3991$^{16}$ 4263$^{10}$ **>32f<**
**Sexman (POL) 3** b c Graf (USA)-Sexonia (CZE) (Beauvallon (FR)) 4740a$^{3}$ **>55f<**
**Shaamit (IRE) 3** b c Mtoto-Shomoose (Habitat) (1791) 3070$^{3}$ 4281a$^{4}$ 4662a$^{7}$ **>129f<**
**Shaanxi (USA) 4** ch f Zilzal (USA)-Rich and Riotous (Empery (USA)) **1995:** 4524a$^{8}$ **1996:** 1134a$^{7}$ 1952a$^{15}$ (3391a) 3745a$^{3}$ 4165a$^{6}$ 4664a$^{2}$ 4857a$^{3}$ **>124f<**
**Shaarid (USA) 8** b g El Gran Senor (USA)-Summer Silence (USA) (Stop The Music (USA)) *15$^{6}$* **>61a 72f<**
**Shaa Spin 4** b f Shaadi (USA)-Tight Spin (High Top) *2162$^{11}$* 2316$^{11}$ *2937$^{8}$ 3236$^{6}$* 3345$^{6}$ 3492$^{6}$ 4348$^{7}$ 4455$^{14}$ **>61a 45f<**
**Shabanaz 11** b g Imperial Fling (USA)-Claironcita (Don Carlos) **1995:** *4436$^{3}$* **1996:** *1772$^{2}$* 2152$^{6}$ 2494$^{3}$ (2740) (3095) (3466) 3824$^{2}$ 3970$^{2}$ 4237$^{6}$ 4515$^{9}$ 4703$^{6}$ **>67a 58f<**
**Shaddad (USA) 2** b c Shadeed (USA)-Desirable (Lord Gayle (USA)) 2624$^{11}$ 3245$^{5}$ **>81f<**
**Shaded (IRE) 2** b c Night Shift (USA)-Sarsaparilla (FR) (Shirley Heights) 3837$^{12}$ *4091$^{5}$ 4318$^{8}$* ***>50a 37f<***

**Shades of Love** 2 b c Pursuit of Love-Shadiliya (Red Alert) 5033[20]

**Shadirwan (IRE)** 5 b h Kahyasi-Shademah (Thatch (USA)) (449) 712[8] 1439[8] 2042[8] 2547[8] 3266[6] **>89f<**

**Shadow Casting** 3 b f Warning-Fanciful (FR) (Gay Mecene (USA)) 1593[5] (2529) 2974[4] 4109[16] 4906[7] **>74f<**

**Shadow Jury** 6 ch g Doulab (USA)-Texita (Young Generation) **1995:** *4394[3] 4432[8] 4517[3]* **1996:** *(63) 386[4] 475[13]* 587[10] 735[10] 1157[11] 1501[4] 1646[3] 1974[6] 2064[7] 2349[5] 2508[2] (2586) 2694[16] 2957[2] 3085[9] 3338[2] 3432[13] 3793[8] 4382[15] 4616[8] 4811[2] 5039[14] **>76a 64f<**

**Shadow Lead** 2 b c Midyan (USA)-Shadow Bird (Martinmas) 2624[4] (2993) 3668[4] 4973[3] **>89f<**

**Shadow Leader** 5 br g Tragic Role (USA)-Hush it Up (Tina's Pet) 2055[8] 2882[8] 4431[9] (4675) 5046[7] **>86f<**

**Shady Deed (USA)** 4 ch f Shadeed (USA)-Sum Sharp Lady (USA) (Sharpen Up) **1995:** *4415[7]* **>30a 72f<**

**Shady Girl (IRE)** 3 b f Shaadi (USA)-Octavia Girl (Octavo (USA)) 714[4] 1155[4] 1776[9] *2201[6] 4047[4]* 4381[9] **>47a 72f<**

**Shaffishayes** 4 ch g Clantime-Mischievous Miss (Niniski (USA)) *(851)* 1341[3] 1502[4] 4686[10] 4793[6] 4993[2] **>73f<**

**Shaft of Light** 4 gr g Sharrood (USA)-Reflection (Mill Reef (USA)) 4716[8] **>75a 92f<**

**Shaha** 3 b c Polish Precedent (USA)-Height of Passion (Shirley Heights) 1182[8] 1641[2] 1773[8] 2033[2] (2196) 3235[4] 4121[12] **>74f<**

**Shahboor (USA)** 2 b c Zilzal (USA)-Iva Reputation (USA) (Sir Ivor) 4461[9] **>50f<**

**Shahid** 4 b c Green Desert (USA)-Roussalka (Habitat) *433a[3]* **>105a 113f<**

**Shahik (USA)** 6 b g Spectacular Bid (USA)-Sham Street (USA) (Sham (USA)) *100[9] 135[11] 3628[3] 3955[2] 4073[7]* (4513) *4779[9] (5056)* **>71a 74f<**

**Shahrani** 4 b g Lear Fan (USA)-Windmill Princess (Gorytus (USA)) 635[11] 872[9] 1063[10] 3037[11] **>47f<**

**Shahrur (USA)** 3 b br c Riverman (USA)-Give Thanks (Relko) *684[19]* ***>56f<***

**Shaka** 2 b c Exit To Nowhere (USA)-Serafica (FR) (No Pass No Sale (FR)) (5024a) **>105f<**

**Shaken Up** 2 b c Kendor (FR)-Oshawa (Alzao (USA)) 1871[7] 2596[8] 3462[7] 4721[6] **>67f<**

**Shake the Yoke** 3 b f Caerleon (USA)-Bermuda Classic (Double Form) (796a) 1140a[2] (2052) 4165a[3] **>126f<**

**Shakiyr (FR)** 5 gr g Lashkari-Shakamiyn (Nishapour (FR)) **1995:** *4506[2]* **1996:** *19[3] 60[2] (97) 312[6] 449[12]* 625[6] 767[6] 961[5] *1082[6] 2697[3]* 2986[4] 3922[4] 4563[20] 4862[6] 4919[9] 5008[3] **>78a 56f<**

**Shalaal (USA)** 2 b c Sheikh Albadou-One Fine Day (USA) (Quadratic (USA)) 3682[6] 4233[5] 4488[17] **>73f<**

**Shalateeno** 3 b f Teenoso (USA)-Shalati (FR) (High Line) 710[7] 860[4] 1117[7] 1462[6] 1591[4] 1833[2] 2378[6] 2565[7] 3165[6] 3496[3] (3825) 4047[2] 4374[10] **>72f<**

**Shall We Go (IRE)** 2 b f Shalford (IRE)-Grapette (Nebbiolo) 1851[7] 2309[7] 2712[5] 2904[10] (3405) (3826) 4364[9] 4549[6] **>68f<**

**Shalstayholy (IRE)** 2 ch f Shalford (IRE)-Saintly Guest (What A Guest) 4087[7] 4782[4] 4913[9] 5051[4] **>63f<**

**Shalta Chief** 4 b g Be My Chief (USA)-Shalta (FR) (Targowice (USA)) 1864[6] 2515[5] 3918[6] 4606[14] **>39f<**

**Shamadara (IRE)** 3 b f Kahyasi-Shamarzana (Darshaan) (2277a) 2837a[2] 3688[4] 4292a[7] **>113f<**

**Shamand (USA)** 3 br g Minshaanshu Amad (USA)-Rose And Betty (USA) (Dare To Command (USA)) 471[17] 599[3] 849[12] *899[3] 1591[10] 1814[7] 1907[3]* 2537[14] **>56a 44f<**

**Shamanic** 4 b c Fairy King (USA)-Annie Albright (USA) (Verbatim (USA)) 940[10] 1186[20] 1790[4] 2400[3] 2856[8] 3232[11] 3612[6] 4122[8] 4314[27] **>90f<**

**Shambo** 9 b h Lafontaine (USA)-Lucky Appeal (Star Appeal) 1017[7] **>122f<**

**Shamikh** 2 b c Unfuwain (USA)-Narjis (USA) (Blushing Groom (FR)) (2073) **>96+f<**

**Shamokin** 4 b g Green Desert (USA)-Shajan (Kris) 2333[6] 2913[5] 3492[5] 4753[11] 4810[14] *4989[10]* **>17a 44f<**

**Shamrock Fair (IRE)** 4 ch f Shavian-Fair Country (Town And Country) 3516[5] 3933[11] 4329[13] *5002[10]* **>52a 72f<**

**Shanaladee** 3 b c Darshaan-Sahara Baladee (USA) (Shadeed (USA)) (1963) 2677[4] 3781[6] **>108f<**

**Shandana** 2 b f Merdon Melody-Thabeh (Shareef Dancer (USA)) 1032[4] *1813[2] 2161[12] 3065[4] 3455[4] 3954[5] 4097[8]* **>54a 46f<**

**Shanghai Girl** 3 b f Distant Relative-Come on Rosi (Valiyar) *304[4] (1475)* 2078[2] 2950[6] 3432[8] 3790[10] 4552[6] 4679[5] (4869) 5044[6] **>28a 103f<**

**Shanghai Lil** 4 b f Petong-Toccata (USA) (Mr Leader (USA)) *166[5] 534[6] 2303[2] 3334[15]* 3473[6] 4129[12] 4829[7] **>48a 45f<**

**Shank (RUS)** 3 c 4289a[10]

**Shanoora (IRE)** 3 gr f Don't Forget Me-Shalara (Dancers Image (USA)) **1995:** *4360[4] 4393[5] 4483[7]* **1996:** *35[10] 277[5] 459[5] 606[6] 781[8] 2637[7]* **>33a 57f<**

**Shantarskie (IRE)** 2 b c Mujadil (USA)-Bay Supreme (Martinmas) 4250[4] **>66f<**

**Shantou (USA)** 3 b c Alleged (USA)-Shaima (USA) (Shareef Dancer (USA)) 684[3] 985[2] (1508) 1791[3] 2116[3] 2535[2] (3797) (4192) (4747a) 4955a[4] **>128f<**

**Sharaf (IRE)** 3 b c Sadler's Wells (USA)-Marie de Flandre (FR) (Crystal Palace (FR)) 494[2] (668) 1407[3] 2547[4] 3155[9] 3398[4] 4327[7] 4557[4] 4673[11] 4821[12] **>77f<**

**Sharaf Kabeer** 3 ch c Machiavellian (USA)-Sheroog (USA) (Shareef Dancer (USA)) 1182[2] (1873) 2473a[11] (3781) 4192[7] 4553[3] **>114f<**

**Sharazamataz** 2 b f Shareef Dancer (USA)-Phylae (Habitat) 2059[8] 2435[5] 2733[6] 2948[2] 3467[9] **>53f<**

**Sharazi (USA)** 5 ch h Shahrastani (USA)-Rio Rita (USA) (Secretariat (USA)) **1995:** *4391[10]* **>42a 75f<**

**Share Delight (IRE)** 2 b c Common Grounds-Dorado Llave (USA) (Well Decorated (USA)) 1896[10] 5034[6] **>77f<**

**Shared Risk** 4 ch g Risk Me (FR)-Late Idea (Tumble Wind (USA)) *4089[13]* **>66da 40f<**

**Shareef Allah** 2 f 4286a[4]

**Sharemono (USA)** 2 br c Woodman (USA)-Perfect Circle (Caerleon (USA)) 3018a[5] 4027a[2] **>78f<**

**Shareoftheaction** 5 gr g Sharrood (USA)-Action Belle (Auction Ring (USA)) *586[4] 839[6] 1001[13]* 1196[13] **>32a 50f<**

**Shark (IRE)** 3 b c Tirol-Gay Appeal (Star Appeal) 1438[10] **>47f<**

**Sharkashka (IRE)** 6 ch m Shardari-Kashka (USA) (The Minstrel (CAN)) 2482[3] 2776[8] 3098[4] **>55f<**

**Sharkiyah (IRE)** 2 ch f Polish Precedent (USA)-Peace Girl (Dominion) 4969[8] **>73f<**

**Sharmoor** 4 b f Shardari-Linpac North Moor (Moorestyle) 542[10] 642[12] **>9f<**

**Sharp But Fair** 2 gr f Sharpo-Fair Minded (Shareef Dancer (USA)) 977[4] 1183[4] *1491[4] 2371[5]* **>45a 53f<**

**Sharp Cat (USA)** 2 f *4950a[9]* **>72a f<**

**Sharp Command** 3 ch g Sharpo-Bluish (USA) (Alleged (USA)) 528[6] 663[7] 932[7] 1641[16] *1993[4] 4047[7] 4336[5] 4789[5] 4984[4] 5062[2]* **>58a 52f<**

**Sharp Consul (IRE)** 4 br g Exactly Sharp (USA)-Alicia Markova (Habat) 843[6] 1145[12] (1496) 1872[3] 2342[2] 2883[8] (3470) 3856[6] **>85f<**

**Sharp Deed (IRE)** 2 ch g Sharp Victor (USA)-Fabulous Deed (USA) (Shadeed (USA)) 4601[7] 4796[8] **>49f<**

**Sharpest** 2 ch c Sharpo-Anna Karietta (Precocious) 4330[22] 4514[10] 4884[5] **>66f<**

**Sharp Falcon (IRE)** 5 gr m Shaadi (USA)-Honey Buzzard (Sea Hawk II) **1995:** *4472[9]* **>34a 81f<**

**Sharp Gazelle** 6 ch m Beveled (USA)-Shadha (Shirley Heights) *34[4] (114) 198[4] 602[5] 1012[5]* (3808) 3980[9] **>63a 48f<**

**Sharp Hat** 2 ch c Shavian-Madam Trilby (Grundy) 2708[8] 2977[2] 3494[11] (3846) (4195) 4566[2] 4717[7] **>89f<**

**Sharp Holly (IRE)** 4 b f Exactly Sharp (USA)-Children's Hour (Mummy's Pet) **1995:** *4354[8]* **1996:** *1702[8] 2305[7] 2550[8] 2903[6]* 3281[5] 3474[16] **>29a 43?f<**

**Sharpical** 4 b g Sharpo-Magical Spirit (Top Ville) 1154[3] *(1448) 2068[3]* 2593[2] (3205) (3457) 3947[4] 4568[16] **>80a 87f<**

**Sharp Imp** 6 b g Sharpo-Implore (Ile de Bourbon (USA)) **1995:** *4458[2] 4488[2] 4515[4]* **1996:** *(41) 109[7] 266[2] 278[2] 354[2] 380[4] 1073[10]* 1536[7] 1715[7] 1881[3] (2017) 2405[8] 2763[6] 3096[3] (3304) 3313[3] 3636[4] *3877[12] 3967[3]* 4109[8] 4256[8] **>60a 66f<**

**Sharp Monty** 3 b g Mon Tresor-Sharp Anne (Belfort (FR)) 458[11] 492[4] *606[7] 1405[6]* (1642) 2496[2] 2778[2] 3135[5] 3655[6] 3844[15] 4098[2] **>29a 66f<**

**Sharp Move** 4 ch f Night Shift (USA)-Judeah (Great Nephew) 3686[9] 4108[8] 4382[16] 4805[14] **>51f<**

**Sharp 'n' Shady** 3 b f Sharpo-Shadiliya (Red Alert) **1995:** *4408[8]* **1996:** *470[7]* 775[3] 1181[10] 2868[8] 4768[5] 4915[3] **>23a 60f<**

**Sharp 'n Smart** 4 ch g Weldnaas (USA)-Scottish Lady (Dunbeath (USA)) **1995:** *4454[4]* **1996:** *(244) 354[6] 554[9]* 1073[9] 1522[11] 1680[6] 4109[7] 4788[2] *4979[10]* **>74a 74f<**

**Sharp Pearl** 3 ch g Sharpo-Silent Pearl (USA) (Silent Screen (USA)) 949[7] 1304[2] (1663) 2143[11] 2403[10] 2790[3] 3215[9] 3864[5] 4342[4] 4521[8] **>72f<**

**Sharp Poppet** 2 ch f Statoblest-Razor Blade (Sharp Edge) 2195[14] 2741[9] 3330[P] **>32f<**

**Sharp Prod (USA)** 6 ch h Sharpo-Gentle Persuasion (Bustino) **1995:** (4469a) **1996:** 1394a[3] 3394a[2] 4033a[9] **>111f<**

**Sharp Progress** 3 b c Inca Chief (USA)-Sharp Venita (Sharp Edge) 1593[7] 1957[5] 2794[8] 3204[11] **>65f<**

**Sharp Prospect** 6 ch h Sharpo-Sabatina (USA) (Verbatim (USA)) *455[24]* 3811[5] 4054[7] 4300[16] 4688[18] **>83f<**

**Sharp Rebuff** 5 b h Reprimand-Kukri (Kris) **1995:** *4392[13]* **1996:** *876[5]* 1354[4] 1775[5] 2229[2] (2605) **>4a 87f<**

**Sharp Reproach** 3 903a[12] 1137a[3] 4418a[3] **>102f<**

**Sharp Return** 2 b c Sharpo-Langtry Lady (Pas de Seul) 1169[4] 1694[7] 1989[7] 3590[7] 3846[6] 4106[12] 4562[3] (4787) 4916[2] **>60f<**

**Sharp Sensation** 6 ch g Crofthall-Pink Sensation (Sagaro) 1421[10] 1478[2] 2165[9] 2175[3] 2360[2] 2848[2] 3308[5] 3463[3] 3772[4] **>47a 49f<**

**Sharp Shuffle (IRE)** 3 ch g Exactly Sharp (USA)-Style (Homing) *1613[11]* 2617[3] 2859[2] 3138[2] 3474[2] 3655[7] (4053) 4590[5] 4865[3] **>80f<**

**Sharp Stock 3** b c Tina's Pet-Mrewa (Runnymede) 467[13] 1101[13] **>67f<**

**Sharp Thrill 5** ch g Squill (USA)-Brightelmstone (Prince Regent (FR)) **1995:** *4448[3]* **1996:** *54[6] 104[6] 154[6]* **>44a 47f<**

**Sharvic (IRE) 3** b g Sharp Victor (USA)-Binnissima (USA) (Tilt Up (USA)) 458[15] *606[14] 1342[13]*

***Shashi (IRE) 4*** br f Shaadi (USA)-Homely Touch (Touching Wood (USA)) 716[8] 956[7] 1609[7] 1786[4] 2137[6] (2524) 3049[2] 3122[5] 4206[15] 4439[10] 4560[9] 4805[13] **>53f<**

**Shavinsky 3** b c Shavian-Alteza Real (Mansingh (USA)) 684[17] 1627[6] 1797[10] *2158[8] 2597[2]* 2946[13] 3665[2] 4074[6] 4219[5] **>49a 73f<**

**Shawaf (USA) 2** b c Mr Prospector (USA)-Shadayid (USA) (Shadeed (USA)) 3069[3] **>85t+f<**

**Shawanni 3** gr f Shareef Dancer (USA)-Negligent (Ahonoora) 1140a[6] 1899[W] **>102f<**

**Shawm 2** b c Alzao (USA)-Flute (USA) (Woodman (USA)) 4913[3] **>88f<**

**Shaya 2** ch c Nashwan (USA)-Gharam (USA) (Green Dancer (USA)) 4175[2] **>102+f<**

**Shayim (USA) 4** b or br c Storm Cat (USA)-Bundler (USA) (Raise A Native) 1625[12] 1775[7] 1962[4] 2134[16] **>76f<**

**Shaynes Domain 5** b g Dominion-Glen Na Smole (Ballymore) **1995:** *4521[8]* **1996:** *42[10] 53[8] 163[5] 178[7] 664[8]* 1047[10] 1348[3] 1715[11] 1856[7] **>33a 46f<**

**Shedansar (IRE) 4** b g In The Wings-Evening Kiss (Kris) **1995:** *4525[11]* **1996:** *23[10] 54[7] 186[16] 240[7] 275[6] 4815[15]* ***>35a 19f<***

**Sheeba 2** ch f Meqdaam (USA)-Normanby Damsel (High Line) *4780[13] 4970[W]*

***Sheecky 5*** b g Green Ruby (USA)-Beth of Houndhill (Filiberto (USA)) **1995:** *4412[11]* **>22a 14f<**

**Sheemore (IRE) 3** b g Don't Forget Me-Curie Abu (Crofter (USA)) **1995:** *4439[9]* **1996:** *355[8] 614[5]* ***>30a 49f<***

**Sheer Danzig (IRE) 4** b c Roi Danzig (USA)-Sheer Audacity (Troy) *580[8]* 1193[8] 1961[3] (2502) 3071[3] 3710[2] 4066[5] 4465[2] 5045[8] **>73a 111f<**

**Sheer Face 2** b c Midyan (USA)-Rock Face (Ballad Rock) 1960[6] 2224[5] (3312) 3616[2] (4084) 4369[4] 4676[3] **>90f<**

**Sheer Folly (USA) 2** ch c Woodman (USA)-Why So Much (USA) (Northern Baby (CAN)) (2224) **>88+f<**

**Sheer Reason (USA) 2** b f Danzig (USA)-Hiaam (USA) (Alydar (USA)) 3201a[3] 5071a[2] **>82f<**

**Sheffield (USA) 3** b f Dayjur (USA)-Formidable Lady (Formidable (USA)) 4160a[6] **>96f<**

**Sheffield Shark (IRE) 2** b c Alzao (USA)-Settlement (USA) (Irish River (FR)) 4370[11] 4507[11] 4715[17] **>49f<**

**Shehab (IRE) 3** b g Persian Bold-Fenjaan (Trojan Fen) 1701[2] (1999) 4714[9] 4826[20] **>89+f<**

**Sheilana (IRE) 3** b f Bluebird (USA)-Shadia (USA) (Naskra (USA)) 496[9] 1172[12] 1654[17] 2203[3] 2409[10] 2979[7] 3284[5] 3780[8] **>59f<**

**Sheilas Dream 3** b f Inca Chief (USA)-Windlass (Persian Bold) *484[6] 655[2] 781[7] 3481[2]* ***>46a 56f<***

**She Knew the Rules (IRE) 6** ch m Jamesmead-Falls of Lora (Scottish Rifle) *656[9]*

**Shell Ginger (IRE) 2** ch f Woodman (USA)-Truly Bound (USA) (In Reality) (5014a) **>104+f<**

**Shemozzle (IRE) 3** b f Shirley Heights-Reactress (USA) (Sharpen Up) 1004[3] 1335[2] 2069[3] 2533[4] (2886) 3688[7] **>109f<**

**Shenango (IRE) 3** b g Shernazar-Pipina (USA) (Sir Gaylord) **1995:** *4538[2]* **1996:** *269[4] 1656[3]* 2074[17] 2674[8] 3398[6] 4227[14] **>81f<**

**Shepherds Dean (IRE) 3** b f Tirol-Royal Episode (Royal Match) **1995:** *4393[8] 4443[8]* **1996:** *1526[11]* 3414[6] 3619[12] **>28a 19f<**

**Shepherds Rest (IRE) 4** b g Accordion-Mandy's Last (Krayyan) *777[3]* **>35a 53f<**

**Sherabi (IRE) 2** b f Shernazar-Majesty's Nurse 4024a[13] **>78f<**

**Sheraka (IRE) 3** b f Doyoun-Sherzana (Great Nephew) (1246a) 1567a[7] 1938a[5] 2825a[3] 4026a[5] **>112f<**

**Sheraton Girl 2** b f Mon Tresor-Sara Sprint (Formidable (USA)) 1308[5] 2569[3] 3121[10] 3343[4] 3488[5] *3950[5] 4097[5]* 4223[4] 4347[11] **>36a 57f<**

**Sheraz (IRE) 4** b c Persian Bold-Miss Siddons (Cure The Blues (USA)) 472[6] 738[5] 988[13] 1159[9] 1435[7] *(1719) 1993[6] 2428[5]* 2536[9] *2934[8]* **>65a 61f<**

**Sheregori (IRE) 6** b g Darshaan-Sherzana (Great Nephew) 4537b[4] **>59f<**

**Sherema (USA) 3** b f Riverman (USA)-Sherarda (FR) (Glenstal (USA)) 4405a[3] 4940a[3] **>101f<**

**Sheriff 5** b g Midyan (USA)-Daisy Warwick (USA) (Ribot) *(260) 1454[2]* 1710[5] *3437[4]* **>62a 64f<**

**Shermood 3** b f Shere Khan-Jalebird Blues (Jalmood (USA)) *516[5] 1089[13]* 1806[7] 2017[6] 2411[4] 2859[8] 2983[5] 3474[3] *3608[6] 3761[3]* 4082[11] 4240[16] 4598[19] **>32a 45df<**

**Sherna (IRE) 3** ch f Eurobus-Zulu Hut (Shack (USA)) 1357[6] 1957[7] 3320[7] **>38f<**

**Sheroot 4** b c Cigar-Act of Treason (Absalom) *57[12] 207[12] 561[8]* 883[12] 998[5] **>4a 37f<**

**Sherpas (IRE) 3** b c Shirley Heights-Ala Mahlik (Ahonoora) (671) 2054[10] **>94+f<**

**Sherzetto 2** b f Classic Music (USA)-Lake Isle (IRE) (Caerleon (USA)) 2600[7] (3054) 3467[4] **>78f<**

**She's A Cracker 2** b f Deploy-Red Secret (IRE) (Valiyar) 4261[15] **>34f<**

**She Said No 4** ch f Beveled (USA)-She Said Yes (Local Suitor (USA)) *424[12] 553[13] 1468[6] 3608[7] 3860[5] 5003[8]* **>41a 51f<**

**She's a Madam 5** b m Kabour-Mrs Buzby (Abwah) *4090[9] 4727[12]* ***>36a 18f<***

**She's A Winner (IRE) 3** ch f Classic Music (USA)-Eyre Square (IRE) (Flash of Steel) (540) 885[5] 1345[6] 1866[12] 2121[7] **>49f<**

**She's Dawan (IRE) 2** b f Taufan (USA)-Bellinzona (Northfields (USA)) 4605[9] **>63f<**

**She's My Love 3** ch f Most Welcome-Stripanoora (Ahonoora) *937[2]* 1324[7] 2146[7] 2621[5] 2885[7] 3790[15] 4775[8] **>79df<**

**She's Simply Great (IRE) 3** b f Simply Great (FR)-Petrine (IRE) (Petorius) 1310[2] 1636[4] 1850[9] 2241[7] 2592[2] 2851[9] 3619[2] 3938[6] **>60f<**

**Shift Again (IRE) 4** b f Siberian Express (USA)-Pushkinia (FR) (Pharly (FR)) 1145[9] 1462[13] 1874[5] **>71df<**

**Shifting Moon 4** b g Night Shift (USA)-Moonscape (Ribero) 4826[18] **>93?f<**

**Shifting Time 2** b f Night Shift (USA)-Timely Raise (USA) (Raise A Man (USA)) 3234[4] 4330[10] 4547[2] **>67f<**

**Shigeru Summit 2** b f Be My Chief (USA)-Riveryev (USA) (Irish River (FR)) 3201a[4] (3908a) 4661a[10] 5071a[7] **>102f<**

**Shii-Take 2** b c Deploy-Super Sally (Superlative) 3069[2] 3615[2] (4118) 4681[3] **>99f<**

**Shikari's Son 9** br g Kala Shikari-Have Form (Haveroid) 631[6] 889[8] 1078[9] 1334[13] 1790[9] 2114[25] 2403[5] 2725[5] 3232[14] **>82f<**

**Shimazu (IRE) 2** b c Darshaan-Shamshir (Kris) 2132[5] *(2370) 2619[4]* 4625[15] 4880[15] **>78a 69f<**

**Shine 3** ch f Sharrood (USA)-Varnish (Final Straw) *710[13]* 1617[10] 1891[8] **>53f<**

**Shinerolla 4** b g Thatching-Primrolla (Relko) *357[3] 455[4]* 728[10] 1406[8] **>84a 80f<**

**Shining Cloud 3** ch f Indian Ridge-Hardiheroine (Sandhurst Prince) 3162[9] 3767[7] (4356) 4521[3] **>71f<**

**Shining Dancer 4** b f Rainbow Quest (USA)-Strike Home (Be My Guest (USA)) **1995:** *4364[16] 4463[6]* **1996:** *1117[6]* (1841) 2246[10] 3141[3] 3500[3] 3876[3] 4121[2] 4447[5] 4821[8] **>38a 70f<**

**Shining Example 4** ch g Hadeer-Kick the Habit (Habitat) 871[6] (1102) 1618[5] 2943[6] 4686[6] 4826[16] **>80f<**

**Shining Silk (FR) 3** ch f Shining Steel-Sweet Cashmere (FR) (Kashmir II) (3027a)

**Shinkoh Rose (FR) 4** 227a[7]

**Ship's Dancer 3** b f Shareef Dancer (USA)-Sunderland (Dancers Image (USA)) 597[11] 890[4] 1503[5] 1877[3] 2204[6] 2927[4] 3225[6] 3580[8] 3961[8] 4317[8] 4506[6] **>48f<**

**Shirlaty 3** b f Shirley Heights-Jameelaty (USA) (Nureyev (USA)) *4429[14]* 4921[11] **>24f<**

**Shirley Sue 3** b f Shirley Heights-Dame Ashfield (Grundy) **1995:** *4381[4]* **1996:** *660[7]* 2191[10] (2493) 2627[6] *(2936) 3086[2] (3329)* (3463) 3598[4] 3855[2] 3922[7] 4199[6] 4302[2] 4588[4] 5047[5] **>75a 78f<**

**Shirley Venture 3** b f Be My Chief (USA)-Our Shirley (Shirley Heights) 932[2] 1189[3] 1769[10] 2505[5] 3355[3] 3776[3] 4548[5] *4892[4]* **>59a 80?f<**

**Shock Value (IRE) 2** b c Danehill (USA)-Rince Deas (IRE) (Alzao (USA)) (1626) 2040[6] 4555[4] **>98f<**

**Shoemaker Levy 3** b f Bedford (USA)-Little Missile (Ile de Bourbon (USA)) 746[9] 1061[10] 1711[14] 2159[12] 3077[6] **>35f<**

**Shoja 3** ch g Persian Bold-Dancing Berry (Sadler's Wells (USA)) 4437[13] 4763[12] **>22f<**

**Shonara's Way 5** b m Slip Anchor-Favorable Exchange (USA) (Exceller (USA)) 4315[11] **>40f<**

**Shontaine 3** b g Pharly (FR)-Hinari Televideo (Caerleon (USA)) *68[4] 157[6] 824[11]* 1805[8] 2139[3] 2417[6] 2929[2] (2983) 3102[3] 3151[12] 3424[13] 3578[5] *4333[3] 4784[3]* 4820[10] 5010[12] **>66a 64df<**

**Shoodah (IRE) 5** ch g Common Grounds-Tunguska (Busted) **1995:** *4451[7] 4532[13]* **1996:** *66[14]* **>30f<**

**Shoofk 5** ch g Dunbeath (USA)-River Reem (USA) (Irish River (FR)) 4497[10] **>44f<**

**Shooting Light (IRE) 3** b g Shernazar-Church Light (Caerleon (USA)) *763[2]* (1023) 1415[3] 1854[3] 3768[4] 3948[9] 4447[17] **>81f<**

**Shoot The Minstrel 3** ch c Brotherly (USA)-Shoot To Win (FR) (Rabdan) **1995:** *4501[13]* **1996:** *21[10] 101[9] 183[9] 224[5] 271[9]* **>43a f<**

**Shoshone 3** ch f Be My Chief (USA)-Bridestones (Jan Ekels) 3656[12] 3942[6] *4892[6] 5054[6]* ***>46a 52f<***

**Shotley Again 6** b g Then Again-Sweet Candice (African Sky) *30[11] 45[2] 72[4] 90[6] 154[5] 252[6]* **>35a 31df<**

**Shotley Princess 2** ch f Risk Me (FR)-Miss Camellia (Sonnen Gold) 1408[6] *1968[4] 2371[10] 3838[W]* 4046[13] *4093[15] 4244[13]* 4459[11] **>18a 27f<**

**Shouk 2** b f Shirley Heights-Souk (IRE) (Ahonoora) 2863[8] 3221[2] **>77f<**

**Shouldbegrey 3** ch g Siberian Express (USA)-Miss Magnetism (Baptism) 445[10] 669[10] 1195[4] 1594[9] 1654[4] *2168[4] 2540[U]* 3000[5] 3165[13] 4082[3] (4480) 4968[5] **>41a 51f<**

**Shoumatara (USA) 2** ch c Seeking the Gold (USA)-Crown Quest (USA) (Chief's Crown (USA)) 2695[5] 2972[2] 3277[2] 3674[10] **>87f<**

**Showboat 2** b c Warning-Boathouse (Habitat) (4700) 4822[8] **>93f<**

**Showcase 2** b f Shareef Dancer (USA)-Perfolia (USA) (Nodouble (USA)) 4363[5] 4494[9] **>68f<**

**Show Faith (IRE)** **6** ch g Exhibitioner-Keep the Faith (Furry Glen) *455$^{15}$* 765$^{12}$ 4568$^{31}$ 4674$^{11}$ 4901$^{16}$ **>67f<**

**Show Off** **2** ch f Efisio-Brazen Faced (Bold And Free) 807$^{6}$ 3054$^{4}$ 3660$^{13}$ 4424$^{5}$ **>66f<**

**Showtime Blues (IRE)** **7** b g Kafu-Susan's Blues (Cure The Blues (USA)) *99$^{6}$ 337$^{7}$ 390$^{13}$ 414$^{7}$* **>33a f<**

**Shturm (RUS)** **3** ch c Raut-Askanija (RUS) 1059a$^{2}$ 2110a$^{2}$ 4414a$^{3}$ **>93f<**

**Shu Fly (NZ)** **12** ch g Tom's Shu (USA)-Alycone (NZ) (Philoctetes) *343$^{10}$* **>3a f<**

**Shu Gaa (IRE)** **3** ch g Salse (USA)-River Reem (USA) (Irish River (FR)) (528) 1145$^{7}$ 1477$^{4}$ 2549$^{3}$ 2998$^{4}$ 4582$^{10}$ **>76f<**

**Shuttlecock** **5** ch g Pharly (FR)-Upper Sister (Upper Case (USA)) *31$^{6}$ 261$^{8}$ 521$^{5}$ 776$^{8}$ 1468$^{15}$* 1691$^{11}$ 2056$^{3}$ 2192$^{10}$ *2369$^{6}$ 2896$^{13}$ 3603$^{11}$ 3808$^{15}$* 4703$^{12}$ *4998$^{6}$* **>54a 39f<**

**Shuwaikh** **2** b c Puissance-Femme Formidable (Formidable (USA)) 2624$^{6}$ 3147$^{4}$ 3259$^{3}$ 4049$^{7}$ 4495$^{12}$ **>78f<**

**Shycock (FR)** **3** ch c Sicyos (USA)-Ordea Mare (FR) (Sparkler) 3389a$^{2}$ **>75f<**

**Shy Lady (FR)** **2** b f Kaldoun (FR)-Shy Danceuse (FR) (Groom Dancer (USA)) (3396a) 4035a$^{4}$ **>90f<**

**Shy Mystic** **6** ch m Shy Groom (USA)-Misowni (Niniski (USA)) *79$^{17}$*

**Shy Paddy (IRE)** **4** b g Shy Groom (USA)-Griqualand (Connaught) 546$^{11}$ 1514$^{16}$ **>54a 53f<**

**Sian Wyn** **6** ch m Hotfoot-Curzon House (Green God) 439$^{16}$ 3385a$^{2}$ **>53a 17f<**

**Siberian Henry** **3** b g Siberian Express (USA)-Semperflorens (Don) 4833$^{7}$ **>59f<**

**Siberian Mystic** **3** gr f Siberian Express (USA)-Mystic Crystal (IRE) (Caerleon (USA)) 761$^{10}$ 3474$^{10}$ (3780) **>42f<**

**Siberian Rose** **3** b f Siberian Express (USA)-Deanta in Eirinn (Red Sunset) 3458$^{11}$ 3789$^{7}$ 4341$^{15}$ 4898$^{15}$ **>14f<**

**Sibor Star** **2** b g Man Among Men (IRE)-My Ratbag (Main Reef) *2554$^{5}$* **>39a f<**

**Sicarian** **4** b g Kris-Sharka (Shareef Dancer (USA)) 2572$^{6}$ *2936$^{14}$ 4448$^{6}$* 4563$^{19}$ **>55f<**

**Side Note** **3** b c Warning-Sarah Siddons (FR) (Le Levanstell) (892) 1329$^{6}$ 3797$^{3}$ **>111f<**

**Sidney The Kidney** **2** b f Mystiko (USA)-Martin-Lavell Mail (Dominion) 4782$^{3}$ **>56f<**

**Siege Perilous (IRE)** **3** b g Taufan (USA)-Carado (Manado) (471) *519$^{3}$ (594)* 803$^{2}$ 954$^{3}$ 4042$^{6}$ 4750$^{4}$ 4919$^{2}$ 5054$^{3}$ **>58a 76f<**

**Siesta Time (USA)** **6** ch m Cure The Blues (USA)-Villa Rose (USA) (Key To The Mint (USA)) 2189$^{3}$ 2373$^{5}$ 2788$^{2}$ 3095$^{2}$ 3303$^{6}$ 3824$^{3}$ *4334$^{10}$* **>59f<**

**Sigama (USA)** **10** ch g Stop The Music (USA)-Lady Speedwell (USA) (Secretariat (USA)) *22$^{9}$ 1342$^{10}$* **>62a 51f<**

**Signs And Wonders** **2** b f Danehill (USA)-Front Line Romance (Caerleon (USA)) 2398$^{4}$ 2734$^{2}$ 3129$^{6}$ 3436$^{7}$ **>74f<**

**Signs R Us (IRE)** **3** b g Al Hareb (USA)-O La Bamba (IRE) (Commanche Run) *176$^{9}$* **>6a 26f<**

**Sihafi (USA)** **3** ch g Elmaamul (USA)-Kit's Double (USA) (Spring Double) *458$^{4}$* 548$^{5}$ 1033$^{2}$ 1608$^{4}$ 2281$^{2}$ 3844$^{18}$ 4765$^{20}$ 4909$^{16}$ *4987$^{14}$* **>31a 77f<**

**Silca Blanka (IRE)** **4** b c Law Society (USA)-Reality (Known Fact (USA)) 1112$^{11}$ 1755a$^{6}$ 1768$^{4}$ 2471a$^{W}$ 3397a$^{5}$ 3905a$^{9}$ 4028a$^{6}$ 4036a$^{8}$ **>104f<**

**Silca Key Silca** **2** ch f Polar Falcon (USA)-Night Transaction (Tina's Pet) 683$^{3}$ 3114$^{5}$ (3675) 4324$^{5}$ 4425$^{2}$ **>72f<**

**Silca's My Key (IRE)** **2** b c Persian Bold-Cloud Peak (USA) (Storm Bird (CAN)) 2224$^{11}$ 2512$^{3}$ 2606$^{3}$ (2948) 3208$^{2}$ 3324$^{7}$ 3408$^{2}$ 3678$^{5}$ 3962$^{5}$ 4106$^{5}$ 4262$^{11}$ (4368) 4672$^{7}$ 4880$^{8}$ **>64f<**

**Silent Expression** **6** gr m Siberian Express (USA)-Silent Sun (Blakeney) 1790$^{12}$ 2114$^{16}$ 2298$^{2}$ 2623$^{6}$ 2856$^{6}$ 3045$^{3}$ 3207$^{3}$ 3271$^{4}$ 3442$^{5}$ 3672$^{W}$ 3989$^{W}$ **>86a 93f< (DEAD)**

**Silent Guest (IRE)** **3** b g Don't Forget Me-Guest House (What A Guest) **1995:** *4431$^{7}$* **1996:** *914$^{7}$ 1490$^{11}$ 2014$^{9}$* 2419$^{3}$ **>52a 42f<**

**Silent Lake (GER)** **5** ch h Kings Lake (USA)-*3034a$^{3}$* 4290a$^{6}$ **>111f<**

**Silently** **4** b g Slip Anchor-Land of Ivory (USA) (The Minstrel (CAN)) 650$^{6}$ 1066$^{6}$ 1486$^{2}$ 1686$^{2}$ 1961$^{6}$ 2401$^{2}$ 2857$^{5}$ 3235$^{7}$ 3617$^{2}$ 3828$^{8}$ 4447$^{12}$ 4615$^{3}$ **>87f<**

**Silent Miracle (IRE)** **2** b f Night Shift (USA)-Curie Point (USA) (Sharpen Up) 4062$^{9}$ **>57f<**

**Silent System (IRE)** **3** gr c Petong-Light Thatch (Thatch (USA)) **1995:** *4408$^{10}$ 4501$^{11}$* **1996:** *4090$^{10}$ 4598$^{18}$* **>19a 7f<**

**Silent Valley** **2** b f Forzando-Tremmin (Horage) 3498$^{12}$ *3954$^{9}$ 3976$^{2}$* 4207$^{11}$ 4495$^{7}$ 4594$^{6}$ 4748$^{10}$ *5061$^{4}$* **>37a 53f<**

**Silent Wells** **2** b f Saddlers' Hall (IRE)-Silent Plea (Star Appeal) *2370$^{10}$ 2802$^{9}$* 3330$^{4}$ 3648$^{8}$ **>43f<**

**Silhouette (IRE)** **3** gr f Standaan (FR)-Frill (Henbit (USA)) *1122$^{10}$* 1497$^{5}$ 1776$^{6}$ 2255$^{9}$ **>62f<**

**Silk Cottage** **4** b g Superpower-Flute Royale (Horage) *931$^{19}$* 1157$^{14}$ 1547$^{3}$ 2064$^{5}$ *2305$^{2}$ 2421$^{2}$* (2564) 2771$^{3}$ 2960$^{5}$ 3122$^{3}$ 3342$^{2}$ 3477$^{2}$ 3661$^{7}$ 3883$^{12}$ 3932$^{14}$ 4205$^{17}$ 4473$^{7}$ 4765$^{4}$ **>66a 57f<**

**Silk Masque (USA)** **3** b f Woodman (USA)-Silk Slippers (USA) (Nureyev (USA)) *708$^{6}$* 1335$^{6}$ 2225$^{4}$ 2991$^{5}$ **>96f<**

**Silk St John** **2** b c Damister (USA)-Silk St James (Pas de Seul) 1989$^{6}$ 3407$^{5}$ 4242$^{11}$ 4549$^{2}$ 5048$^{2}$ **>74f<**

**Silktail (IRE)** **4** b f Jalmood (USA)-Silky (USA) (Nijinsky (CAN)) **1995:** *4489$^{6}$* **1996:** *309$^{3}$ 353$^{2}$ 411$^{4}$ 440$^{14}$* 2008$^{12}$ 2282$^{2}$ (2709) 2973$^{3}$ 3163$^{5}$ 3979$^{3}$ **>54a 75f<**

**Silky Smooth (IRE)** **3** b f Thatching-Smoo (Kris) 1690$^{13}$ 1994$^{11}$

**Sil Sila (IRE)** **3** b f Marju (IRE)-Porto Alegre (Habitat) 572$^{7}$ 708$^{3}$ 1108$^{2}$ (1949a) 3688$^{9}$ **>117f<**

**Silverani (IRE)** **2** b c High Estate-Rose Society (Caerleon (USA)) 4913$^{2}$ 5040$^{2}$ **>92+f<**

**Silver Blade (FR)** **3** b c Dashing Blade-Sankt Johanna (GER) (High Game) 4036a$^{2}$ **>91f<**

**Silver Button** **2** b g Silver Kite (USA)-Klairover (Smackover) 3687$^{8}$ 3941$^{9}$ 5033$^{16}$ **>57f<**

**Silverdale Count** **4** b g Nomination-Its My Turn (Palm Track) 1611$^{P}$ **>57f<**

**Silverdale Knight** **3** b c Nomination-Its My Turn (Palm Track) 453$^{3}$ 509$^{5}$ 873$^{2}$ 976$^{2}$ 1068$^{6}$ 1641$^{6}$ 1698$^{2}$ 1850$^{3}$ 1887$^{5}$ 2776$^{5}$ 3109$^{6}$ 3308$^{2}$ 3398$^{5}$ 4248$^{6}$ **>68f<**

**Silver Dome (USA)** **3** b br c Silver Hawk (USA)-Pink Topaze (FR) (Djakao (FR)) 830$^{5}$ **>106f<**

**Silver Groom (IRE)** **6** gr g Shy Groom (USA)-Rustic Lawn (Rusticaro (FR)) 2299$^{5}$ 2502$^{4}$ 3125$^{2}$ 3791$^{13}$ 4568$^{37}$ **>87f<**

**Silver Harrow** **3** ch g Belmez (USA)-Dancing Diana (Raga Navarro (ITY)) 545$^{10}$ 861$^{3}$ 1172$^{2}$ 1615$^{5}$ 2347$^{4}$ 2710$^{3}$ 2761$^{4}$ 3138$^{3}$ *4076$^{5}$ 4129$^{4}$* (4701) 4860$^{5}$ *4979$^{11}$* **>55a 65f<**

**Silver Hunter (USA)** **5** b g Silver Hawk (USA)-Martha Queen (USA) (Nijinsky (CAN)) *1098$^{2}$ 1514$^{5}$* 1965$^{3}$ 2177$^{3}$ 2415$^{3}$ *4986$^{15}$* **>58a 56f<**

**Silvering (FR)** **4** b c Polish Precedent (USA)-Silvermine (FR) (Bellypha) 1052a$^{3}$ 4656a$^{8}$ **>111f<**

**Silver Irene** **3** 719a$^{2}$

**Silver Jubilee** **2** b f Sylvan Express-Addison's Jubilee (Sparkler) *858$^{5}$*

**Silver Kristal** **2** gr f Kris-Reine D'Beaute (Caerleon (USA)) 4061$^{3}$ 4969$^{4}$ **>78f<**

**Silver Lining** **2** b c Beveled (USA)-Seymour Ann (Krayyan) (2795) 3251$^{5}$ 3763$^{7}$ 4546$^{10}$ **>77f<**

**Silver Moon** **2** gr f Environment Friend-High and Bright (Shirley Heights) *3088$^{5}$ 3330$^{7}$ 3954$^{6}$ 4562$^{22}$* ***>38a 40f<***

**Silver Patriarch (IRE)** **2** gr c Saddlers' Hall (IRE)-Early Rising (USA) (Grey Dawn II) 3682$^{11}$ 4204$^{4}$ (4585) (4973) **>91f<**

**Silver Prey (USA)** **3** b c Silver Hawk (USA)-Truly My Style (USA) (Mount Hagen (FR)) 4185$^{3}$ 4520$^{6}$ **>101f<**

**Silver Purse** **2** ch f Interrex (CAN)-Money Supply (Brigadier Gerard) (2559) 2944$^{3}$ 3613$^{9}$ **>75f<**

**Silver Raj** **2** gr g Rope Trick-Pilar (Godswalk (USA)) 481$^{4}$ 557$^{9}$ 1360$^{3}$ 1607$^{6}$ 2932$^{6}$ 3455$^{7}$ 3576$^{3}$ 3769$^{9}$ 4223$^{14}$ 4347$^{9}$ **>55f<**

**Silver Samurai** **7** b g Alleging (USA)-Be My Lady (Be My Guest (USA)) 440$^{17}$ 752$^{R}$ 1159$^{R}$ **>18?a 25?f<**

**Silver Sands** **2** gr f Chilibang-Sayida-Shahira (Record Run) 3159$^{15}$ 4105$^{5}$ 4544$^{10}$ **>66f<**

**Silver Secret** **2** ro c Absalom-Secret Dance (Sadler's Wells (USA)) 3259$^{12}$ 3494$^{13}$ 4700$^{3}$ 4883$^{5}$ **>80f<**

**Silver Showers (USA)** **3** ch f Zilzal (USA)-Katies First (USA) (Kris) 842$^{6}$ 1061$^{2}$ **>71f<**

**Silver Sign** **3** 2668a$^{8}$ **>88f<**

**Silver Singer** **4** gr f Pharly (FR)-Bustling Nelly (Bustino) **1995:** *4363$^{2}$ 4415$^{10}$ 4449$^{2}$* **>58a 71f<**

**Silver Sleeve (IRE)** **4** b g Taufan (USA)-Sable Coated (Caerleon (USA)) 871$^{10}$ 1037$^{10}$ 2851$^{11}$ **>51f<**

**Silver Spell** **2** gr f Aragon-Silver Berry (Lorenzaccio) 1987$^{6}$ 2309$^{8}$ 2606$^{11}$ (2764) 3160$^{10}$ 3523$^{7}$ 3962$^{13}$ **>62f<**

**Silversword (FR)** **3** b f Highest Honor (FR)-Silver Cobra (FR) (Silver Hawk (USA)) 1942a$^{2}$ **>97?f<**

**Silver Tzar** **4** gr g Dominion-Altaia (FR) (Sicyos (USA)) 2034$^{12}$ *3435$^{5}$ 4107$^{7}$* **>51a 76+f<**

**Silver Welcome** **3** ch g Most Welcome-Silver Ore (FR) (Silver Hawk (USA)) 775$^{2}$ 973$^{4}$ *1460$^{11}$ 1610$^{7}$* 2047$^{4}$ 2240$^{3}$ (2425) **>11a 67f<**

**Silver Widget (USA)** **2** ch c Silver Hawk (USA)-Nijit (USA) (Nijinsky (CAN)) 1626$^{3}$ 2708$^{2}$ 3040$^{4}$ **>91f<**

**Silver Wing (USA)** **3** b f Silver Hawk (USA)-Cojinx (USA) (Crafty Prospector (USA)) 627$^{3}$ 980$^{4}$ 1447$^{2}$ 1619$^{4}$ **>76f<**

**Silvestrini (IRE)** **2** b c Maledetto (IRE)-Law Student (Precocious) 1565a$^{6}$ **>72f<**

**Silvia Carpio (ITY)** **3** ch f 901a$^{3}$

**Silvian Bliss (USA)** **4** ch g Green Forest (USA)-Welcome Proposal (Be My Guest (USA)) 2053$^{14}$ **>89f<**

**Silvretta (IRE)** **3** br f Tirol-Lepoushka (Salmon Leap (USA)) 3353$^{4}$ 3788$^{7}$ 4201$^{8}$ 4474$^{3}$ 4766$^{3}$ (4967) **>68f<**

**Simafar (IRE)** **5** b g Kahyasi-Sidama (FR) (Top Ville) *283$^{5}$ 625$^{17}$* ***>52a 60f<***

**Simand** **4** b f Reprimand-Emmylou (Arctic Tern (USA)) **1995:** *4486$^{11}$* **1996:** *1041$^{6}$* 1196$^{10}$ 1596$^{2}$ 1866$^{11}$ 2178$^{3}$ 2394$^{4}$ 3048$^{4}$ 3481$^{3}$ **>25a 52f<**

**Simple Logic** **2** ch f Aragon-Dancing Chimes (London Bells (CAN)) 1179$^{3}$ (1871) 2619$^{3}$ 3444$^{10}$ **>67f<**

**Simply (IRE)** **7** b g Simply Great (FR)-Be A Dancer (Be Friendly) 2707$^{D}$ **>33f<**

**Simply a Sequel (IRE)** **5** ch g Simply Great (FR)-Salique (Sallust) 649$^{13}$ **>44df<**

**Simply Blessed** **2** gr f Ballacashtal (CAN)-Lucky

Starkist (Lucky Wednesday) *3065[5]* **>24a f<**
**Simply Katie 3** ch f Most Welcome-Rechanit (IRE) (Local Suitor (USA)) *(241) (627)* ***>64a 90+f<***
**Simply Miss Chief (IRE) 3** b f Mac's Imp (USA)-Wolverhants (Wolver Hollow) **1995:** *4375[10]* **>40a 55f<**
**Simply Seven 3** b g Seven Hearts-Simply Spim (Simply Great (FR)) 1009[10] 1651[15]
**Simply Times (USA) 2** b f Dodge (USA)-Nesian's Burn (USA) (Big Burn (USA)) 683[F]
**Sinclair Lad (IRE) 8** ch g Muscatite-Kitty Frisk (Prince Tenderfoot (USA)) 1347[5] 1534[8] *1967[4] 2192[3]* 2409[3] 2594[12] **>39a 43f<**
**Sinecure (USA) 2** br c Explodent (USA)-Caithness (USA) (Roberto (USA)) 1959[3] (2353) 3400[6] 3936[3] 4262[4] 4602[6] **>80f<**
**Sing And Dance 3** b f Rambo Dancer (CAN)-Musical Princess (Cavo Doro) 1668[9] 2123[2] 2486[3] 4047[8] 4297[8] 4591[13] 4752[7] 5007[5] **>45f<**
**Singapore Sting (USA) 3** br f Dayjur (USA)-Ambassador of Luck (USA) (What Luck (USA)) 678[7] (994) 1528[6] 1785[5] 3133[4] 3974[7] 4606[10] **>73f<**
**Singforyoursupper 2** ch f Superlative-Suzannah's Song (Song) *630[6]* 1760[4] 1989[10] 2404[11] 3299[4] 3523[4] (3763) 3846[7] *4093[4] 4222[6]* ***>39a 61f<***
**Singspiel (IRE) 4** b c In The Wings-Glorious Song (CAN) (Halo (USA)) (831) 1794[2] 2583[2] (4197) (4543a) 4955a[2] **>131f<**
**Sing Up 4** b g Sizzling Melody-Hellene (Dominion) **1995:** *4454[6] 4521[7]* **1996:** *893[4]* 1412[2] 1624[5] 1853[4] 2604[3] **>42a 67f< (DEAD)**
**Sing With Me (FR) 3** b f Hero's Honor (USA)-Live With Me (Free State) 4946a[2] **>80f<**
**Sing With the Band 5** b m Chief Singer-Ra Ra Girl (Shack (USA)) **1995:** *4508[3]* **1996:** *601[13]* 749[8] 931[2] 1430[2] 1708[10] 1991[6] *2171[3] (2186)* 2496[6] 2867[6] 3432[2] *3953[2] 4180[21]* 4452[9] 4727[5] 5039[18] **>78a 62f<**
**Sinking Sun 3** gr f Danehill (USA)-Oscura (USA) (Caro) 584[6] 3425[4] 3704[8] 4387[3] 4804[15] **>73f<**
**Sinyar 4** b or br c (1755a) 2843a[7] 4028a[2] 4409a[10] **>121f<**
**Sioux 2** ch f Kris-Lassoo (Caerleon (USA)) 3987[9] 4920[3] **>75f<**
**Siouxrouge 2** b g Indian Ridge-Scarlett Holly (Red Sunset) 1525[11] 3293[3] *3625[3]* **>59a 71f<**
**Sipowitz 2** b g Warrshan (USA)-Springs Welcome (Blakeney) 4261[14] **>40f<**
**Sir Alidaf 2** b c Broadsword (USA)-Bolton Flyer (Aragon) 1303[4]
**Sir Arthur Hobbs 9** b g Lyphard's Special (USA)-Song Grove (Song) *1866[2]* (2121) (2488) (3060) 4503[3] 4808[4] **>61f<**
**Sir Joey (USA) 7** ch g Honest Pleasure (USA)-Sougoli (Realm) 451[9] 582[11] 812[2] 928[2] 1064[5] 1178[12] (1853) 2114[5] 2381[3] 3232[3] 3783[5] 4116[9] 4314[24] 4679[3] 4772[19] **>90f<**
**Sir King (GER) 4** dk b c Konigsstuhl (GER)-Shirbella (Shirley Heights) 789a[2] 1138a[6] **>119f<**
**Sir Norman Holt (IRE) 7** b g Ela-Mana-Mou-Ploy (Posse (USA)) **1995:** *4526[6]* **1996:** *38[4] (108)* **>79a 62f<**
**Sir Oliver (IRE) 7** b g Auction Ring (USA)-Eurorose (Busted) **1995:** *4379[11] 4435[8] 4515[16]* **1996:** *2159[8]* 3469[13] **>12a 43f<**
**Sir Ricky (USA) 2** b c Woodman (USA)-Opera Queen (IRE) (Sadler's Wells (USA)) 3615[13] **>50f<**
**Sir Silver Sox (USA) 4** gr g Corwyn Bay-Sox In The Box (USA) (Cresta Rider (USA)) *1235a[7]* 1566a[6] 2114[20] 2472a[13] 4396a[8] 4848a[7] **>101f<**
**Sir Talbot 2** b c Ardross-Bermuda Lily (Dunbeath (USA)) 4512[4] 4618[5] **>83f<**
**Sir Tasker 8** b h Lidhame-Susie's Baby (Balidar) **1995:** *4394[14] 4441[4] 4536[7]* **1996:** *59[2] 126[3] 180[4] 218[4] 250[3] 266[5] 317[4] 408[8] 534[3] 750[4] 900[5] 1157[8]* 1473[9] 1642[20] **>51a 58df<**
**Sir Thomas Beecham 6** b g Daring March-Balinese (Balidar) **1995:** *4546[10]* **1996:** *83[12] 130[6] (265) 339[8] 365[2] 666[8]* 872[13] **>61a 56f<**
**Sir Warren (IRE) 3** b c Warning-Sistadari (Shardari) 904a[3] 1751a[4] 2668a[16] 3034a[2] 4290a[2] 4650a[3] **>113f<**
**Si Seductor (USA) 3** b c Diesis-Miss Evans (FR) (Nijinsky (CAN)) 4943a[3] **>106f<**
**Sis Garden 3** b f Damister (USA)-Miss Nanna (Vayrann) 740[7] 1042[16] 1600[8] *1970[3] 2168[2] 2369[7] 2636[2] 2898[2]* 3059[14] 3228[8] (3427) 3866[8] *(4077) 4323[3] (5059)* **>67a 54f<**
**Sistar Act 3** b f Salse (USA)-Unsuitable (Local Suitor (USA)) 448[11] (637) 978[6] (1594) 1654[9] (1883) 2027[5] 2241[5] 2621[19] 3845[4] 3866[9] 4232[4] 4513[14] 4582[5] 4691[12] 4905[8] 4968[9] **>76f<**
**Sister Chouchou (FR) 2** b f Lesotho (USA)-Sho Biz (FR) (Solicitor (FR)) 4037a[3] **>70f<**
**Sister Kit (IRE) 3** b f Glacial Storm (USA)-Good Holidays (Good Times (ITY)) *447[8]* 597[10] 1839[6] 2577[11] *2747[3]* **>47a 58f<**
**Six Clerks (IRE) 3** b g Shadeed (USA)-Skidmore Girl (USA) (Vaguely Noble) **1995:** *4410[5] 4528[2]* **1996:** *248[2] 444[5]* 803[8] 1089[8] 1539[5] **>64a 62f<**
**Six for Luck 4** b g Handsome Sailor-Fire Sprite (Mummy's Game) 559[7] 659[5] 1039[9] 1545[6] 1865[9] 2386[5] 2564[5] 2849[5] 3236[3] 3345[3] 3424[2] 3883[9] 4246[12] 4473[8] 4811[13] **>52f<**
**Six Shooter 2** b f Damister (USA)-Ten to Six (Night Shift (USA)) 4991[13] **>30f<**
**Sixties Melody 2** b c Merdon Melody-Balidilemma (Balidar) 4698[10] **>25f<**
**Siyadah (USA) 2** ch f Mr Prospector (USA)-Roseate Tern (Blakeney) 3787[3] 4305[5] **>78f<**
**Sizzling 4** b g Sizzling Melody-Oriental Splendour (Runnett) 749[13] 893[12] 1073[13] 1958[2] 2129[5] 2713[4] 2976[5] **>67f<**
**Sizzling Romp 4** b f Sizzling Melody-Its A Romp (Hotfoot) *3091[13] 3360[5]* 3525[12] 4075[20] **>35a 51df<**
**Sizzling Serenade 3** gr f Sizzling Melody-Trynova (Tyrnavos) **1995:** *4483[13]* **1996:** *2541[7]* 2752[12] 3789[10] **>31a 17f<**
**Sizzling Symphony 3** b g Sizzling Melody-Polly Worth (Wolver Hollow) 718[13] 873[18] 4559[18] 4810[18] **>39f<**
**Skedaddle 4** b f Formidable (USA)-Norfolk Serenade (Blakeney) **1995:** *4474[2] 4546[5]* **1996:** *85[10]* **>42da 60f<**
**Skelton Countess (IRE) 3** ch f Imperial Frontier (USA)-Running Brook (Run The Gantlet (USA)) *870[6] 1096[11] 5059[11]* **>4a 56f<**
**Skelton Sovereign (IRE) 2** b c Contract Law (USA)-Mrs Lucky (Royal Match) *1080[5] 1603[8] 1884[6]* 2904[4] 3324[4] 3512[2] 3835[14] 3936[8] 4384[10] 4602[11] (4694) 4795[14] *5057[2]* **>61a 63f<**
**Sketch Pad 2** br f Warning-Scribbling (USA) (Secretariat (USA)) 1105[3] 1480[P] **>71f<**
**Ski Academy (IRE) 3** b g Royal Academy (USA)-Cochineal (USA) (Vaguely Noble) 2006[8] 2233[5] 3923[6] 4121[13] 4804[16] **>80df<**
**Ski For Gold 3** b f Shirley Heights-Quest (USA) (The Minstrel (CAN)) 754[4] 1498[3] 3855[3] 4683[7] 4919[5] **>75f<**
**Ski Iberia (ARG) 4** 4663a[8] **>101f<**
**Skillington (USA) 3** b c Danzig (USA)-Annie Edge (Nebbiolo) 1180[8] (1670) 2006[2] 2502[16] 3145[5] 3710[19] 4193[11] 4385[2] **>105f<**
**Skip Away (USA) 3** gr c Skip Trial (USA)-Ingot Way (USA) (Diplomat Way) *1391a[2] 1946a[2]* **>127a 121f<**
**Skipman (IRE) 3** b g Posen (USA)-Near Miracle (Be My Guest (USA)) **1995:** *4501[6]* **1996:** *58[9] 197[6]* **>34a f< (DEAD)**
**Skippy Was A Kiwi (IRE) 2** b f River Falls-Hit For Six (Tap On Wood) 2118[4] 3448[2] 3651[5] **>57f<**
**Skram 3** b g Rambo Dancer (CAN)-Skarberg (FR) (Noir Et Or) 1669[9] 2574[23] **>58f<**
**Skybeau (NZ) 4** b g Daher (AUS)-Beaumont Babe (AUS) (Sky Diver) 5069a[3]
**Sky Commander (USA) 2** b br c Storm Bird (CAN)-Fairy Footsteps (Mill Reef (USA)) 3701[2] **>89+f<**
**Sky Dome (IRE) 3** ch c Bluebird (USA)-God Speed Her (Pas de Seul) (676) 917[6] 1126[7] 2621[7] (3246) (3805) 4463[17] 4568[12] 4974[5] **>95f<**
**Skyers Flyer (IRE) 2** b br f Magical Wonder (USA)-Siwana (IRE) (Dom Racine (FR)) 446[6] 770[4] (1320) 1607[3] 1673[3] 2484[4] 2770[2] 2965[4] 3251[3] (3299) 3483[5] 4113[9] 4311[8] 4699[5] *4777[7]* **>25a 72df<**
**Skyers Tryer 2** b f Lugana Beach-Saltina (Bustino) 3250[8] 3511[5] 3840[6] (4343) *4576[8] 4780[6] 5061[11]* **>40a 70f<**
**Skylight 3** ch g Domynsky-Indian Flower (Mansingh (USA)) 1323[7] 1608[14] 3642[7] **>51f<**
**Slapy Dam 4** b g Deploy-Key to the River (USA) (Irish River (FR)) *512[6] 816[8]* 1421[8] 1640[9] 2319[7] 2866[6] 3333[4] 3653[5] 4000[15] 4455[9] **>60da 56f<**
**Slayjay (IRE) 3** ch f Mujtahid (USA)-Fire Flash (Bustino) 1911a[6] 2472a[3] 2816a[3] 3693[12] **>92f<**
**Sleepless 2** b f Night Shift (USA)-Late Evening (USA) (Riverman (USA)) 3036[2] 3508[3] 4305[4] **>81f<**
**Sleepy Boy 3** br g Zero Watt (USA)-Furnace Lass VII (Damsire Unregistered) 2568[13] 3325[7] **>11f<**
**Sleepytime (IRE) 2** b f Royal Academy (USA)-Alidiva (Chief Singer) (4233) 4464[3] **>107+f<**
**Sliabh Bawn (USA) 3** b f Compliance (USA)-Andy's Bonus (USA) 1246a[6] **>76f<**
**Slicious 4** b c Slip Anchor-Precious Jade (Northfields (USA)) **1995:** (4403a) **1996:** (623a) 906a[10] 1135a[7] (4172a) 4747a[5] 5073a[6] **>126+f<**
**Slievenamon 3** br c Warning-Twice A Fool (USA) (Foolish Pleasure (USA)) 684[18] 982[12] 1319[18] *4781[5] (5060)* **>52a 56f<**
**Slightly Oliver (IRE) 2** b g Silver Kite (USA)-Red Note (Rusticaro (FR)) 4349[6] 4607[4] *4988[2]* **>56a 50f<**
**Slightly Speedy (IRE) 3** b c Prince Rupert (FR)-Moutalina (Ela-Mana-Mou) 2041[16] 2472a[11] **>88f<**
**Sliparis 3** b f Slip Anchor-Parisian Express (FR) (Siberian Express (USA)) 2505[11] 3505[14] 4353[7] 4509[19] **>7f<**
**Slip Jig (IRE) 3** b c Marju (IRE)-Taking Steps (Gay Fandango (USA)) 1142[8] (1350) 2231[3] 2621[12] 3248[6] 3830[3] 4329[14] 4769[27] *5002[9]* **>68a 79f<**
**Slippery Fin 4** b f Slip Anchor-Finyska (FR) (Niniski (USA)) *1605[3] 1717[11] 3090[2]* **>59a f<**
**Slipstream Star 2** b f Slip Anchor-Alsiba (Northfields (USA)) 4890[8] **>39f<**
**Slip The Net (IRE) 2** b c Slip Anchor-Circus Ring (High Top) 4306[4] 4477[2] **>82f<**
**Slivovitz 6** b g Petoski-Hiding (So Blessed) **1995:** *4350[5] 4458[8]* **1996:** *36[F]* **>53a 61f< (DEAD)**
**Slmaat 5** ch m Sharpo-Wasslaweyeh (USA) (Damascus (USA)) *19[8] 48[10] 124[13] 372[7] 429[9]* **>53a 69f<**
**Sloe Brandy 6** b m Hotfoot-Emblazon (Wolver Hollow) *1803[3]* 2066[13] **>16a 37f<**
**Sly Lady 4** b f Rambo Dancer (CAN)-Countess of Honour (USA) (Troy) 1159[13] 2589[5] 2963[6] **>34f<**
**Small Risk 2** b f Risk Me (FR)-Small Double (IRE) (Double Schwartz) 506[3] 624[2] *838[7]* **>25a 42f<**

**Smart Alec 4** b c Diesis-Ahead (Shirley Heights) 680$^{2}$ 1177$^{4}$ **>121f<**
**Smart Boy (IRE) 2** ch c Polish Patriot (USA)-Bouffant (High Top) (1169) 2210$^{3}$ 3046$^{9}$ **>60f<**
**Smart Dominion 2** b c Sharpo-Anodyne (Dominion) 4825$^{10}$ **>70f<**
**Smarter Charter 3** br c Master Willie-Irene's Charter (Persian Bold) 648$^{11}$ 851$^{4}$ (1068) 1185$^{2}$ 1420$^{2}$ 2293$^{6}$ 2514$^{3}$ 2593$^{6}$ 3084$^{6}$ (3120) 3246$^{5}$ 3327$^{4}$ **>81f<**
**Smart Guest 4** ch g Be My Guest (USA)-Konbola (Superlative) *31$^{5}$ 450$^{21}$* (764) 1018$^{17}$ **>45a 68f<**
**Smart Play (USA) 3** gr c Sovereign Dancer (USA)-Casessa (USA) (Caro) 707$^{5}$ (932) 1427$^{4}$ 4178$^{6}$ 4487$^{9}$ **>106df<**
**Smart Prospect 2** b g Superpower-Bustilly (Busted) 3499$^{11}$ 3848$^{16}$ *4091$^{8}$* **>27a 23f<**
**Smart Spirit (IRE) 2** b f Persian Bold-Sharp Ego (USA) (Sharpen Up) 3982$^{11}$ 4449$^{8}$ 4564$^{3}$ 4990$^{8}$ **>58+f<**
**Smile Forever (USA) 3** b f Sunshine Forever (USA)-Awenita (Rarity) *782$^{9}$ 1119$^{15}$* 4422$^{5}$ 4496$^{9}$ **>24a 56f<**
**Smiley Face 4** b g Colmore Row-Count On Me (No Mercy) *189$^{12}$* **>44f<**
**Smiling Bess 3** b f Salse (USA)-Wanda (Taufan (USA)) 2869$^{4}$ 4206$^{20}$ *4978$^{9}$* **>26a 28f<**
**Smilin N Wishin (USA) 3** b f Lyphard's Wish (FR)-Smilin Michele (USA) (Sharpen Up) 707$^{3}$ 1004$^{5}$ 1656$^{5}$ (4611) **>86f<**
**Smithereens 3** ch f Primo Dominie-Splintering (Sharpo) 648$^{3}$ 1652$^{7}$ 2615$^{8}$ 4219$^{3}$ 4521$^{14}$ *4776$^{10}$ 4828$^{6}$ (5001)* **>77a 70f<**
**Smocking 6** ch m Night Shift (USA)-Sue Grundy (Grundy) **1995:** *4442$^{9}$ 4452$^{8}$ 4532$^{4}$* **1996:** *1965$^{14}$ 2201$^{12}$* **>25a 43f<**
**Smokebush 2** gr c Petong-Kimberley Park (Try My Best (USA)) 1959$^{6}$ 4380$^{11}$ 4700$^{5}$ **>68f<**
**Smoke'n'jo (IRE) 2** ch c Masterclass (USA)-Alpine Dance (USA) (Apalachee (USA)) 1849$^{12}$ 2625$^{6}$ 2923$^{5}$ 3462$^{9}$ 3779$^{6}$ **>49f<**
**Smokey From Caplaw 2** b g Sizzling Melody-Mary From Dunlow (Nicholas Bill) 930$^{7}$ (1164) 2984$^{9}$ 3590$^{2}$ 3880$^{8}$ **>66f<**
**Smokey Pete 2** gr c Petong-Quick Profit (Formidable (USA)) (877) 1115$^{7}$ 2877$^{6}$ **>78f<**
**Smooth Asset (IRE) 3** b f Fairy King (USA)-Sofala (Home Guard (USA)) 840$^{4}$ 1333$^{4}$ 2913$^{2}$ 3123$^{9}$ 4499$^{7}$ *4778$^{6}$* **>56a 68f<**
**Smooth Runner (USA) 5** b br h Local Talent (USA)-Silken Ripples (USA) (Roberto (USA)) 4953a$^{11}$ **>107f<**
**Smuggler's Point (USA) 6** b g Lyphard (USA)-Smuggly (USA) (Caro) 4789$^{8}$ **>56?f<**
**Smugurs (IRE) 2** ch f Masterclass (USA)-Blue Vista (IRE) (Pennine Walk) 1851$^{2}$ 2538$^{2}$ 2733$^{2}$ 2904$^{6}$ 3685$^{4}$ 3982$^{6}$ (4364) 4625$^{12}$ **>62f<**
**Smurda (USA) 3** 903a$^{10}$ **>88f<**
**Snake Plissken (IRE) 5** ch g Reasonable (FR)-Shalie (Windjammer (USA)) **1995:** *4514$^{5}$ 4537$^{6}$* **1996:** *53$^{5}$ 90$^{2}$ 136$^{6}$ 615$^{2}$* 1001$^{9}$ 1167$^{10}$ **>59da 51f<**
**Snake Snap 3** b c Shareef Dancer (USA)-Clare Court (Glint of Gold) (2670a) 4421a$^{3}$ 5073a$^{5}$ **>114f<**
**Snap Crackle Pop (IRE) 2** b f Statoblest-Spinelle (Great Nephew) 2879$^{12}$ 3121$^{2}$ (3429) 3613$^{4}$ 4247$^{3}$ 4491$^{7}$ 4723$^{9}$ **>83f<**
**Snappy Girl (IRE) 2** b f Caerleon (USA)-Don't Rush (USA) (Alleged (USA)) 4797$^{13}$ **>43f<**
**Snipe Hall 5** b m Crofthall-Geopelia (Raffingora) 3672$^{21}$ 4452$^{15}$ **>82?f<**
**Snitch 3** ch g Blow the Whistle-Whispering Sea (Bustino) **1995:** *4408$^{12}$ 4429$^{8}$ 4473$^{12}$* **1996:** *762$^{W}$* 861$^{16}$ 1598$^{7}$ 1761$^{6}$ 2176$^{5}$ 2359$^{6}$ 2800$^{11}$ **>39a 35f<**
**Snow Domino (IRE) 3** ch g Habyom-Magic Picture (Deep Diver) **1995:** *4485$^{7}$* **1996:** *171$^{5}$* **>44a f<**
**Snow Eagle (IRE) 2** b f Polar Falcon (USA)-Icefern (Moorestyle) 3593$^{12}$ 4889$^{10}$ **>63f<**
**Snow Falcon 3** b g Polar Falcon (USA)-Cameroun (African Sky) *355$^{5}$ 1152$^{6}$* 1693$^{4}$ 1986$^{6}$ 2434$^{6}$ (2915) (3249) 3657$^{7}$ 3968$^{3}$ 4073$^{10}$ 4374$^{2}$ 4596$^{3}$ 4726$^{5}$ **>46a 71f<**
**Snow Partridge (USA) 2** ch c Arctic Tern (USA)-Lady Sharp (FR) (Sharpman) 3040$^{2}$ 4618$^{3}$ **>91f<**
**Snowpoles 3** b f High Estate-Bronzewing (Beldale Flutter (USA)) 1857$^{7}$ 2346$^{7}$ 3225$^{8}$ 3845$^{12}$ **>59df<**
**Snow Princess (IRE) 4** b f Ela-Mana-Mou-Karelia (USA) (Sir Ivor) (1428) 2330$^{2}$ 3689$^{17}$ 3934$^{3}$ (4665a) **>109f<**
**Snowy Mantle 3** b f Siberian Express (USA)-Mollified (Lombard (GER)) *1972$^{4}$ 2869$^{3}$* 4099$^{5}$ 4691$^{8}$ **>27a 54f<**
**Soaked 3** b c Dowsing (USA)-Water Well (Sadler's Wells (USA)) 842$^{7}$ 1438$^{6}$ 2135$^{9}$ 2339$^{4}$ 2577$^{18}$ **>67f<**
**Soaking 6** b g Dowsing (USA)-Moaning Low (Burglar) *(109) 205$^{4}$ 363$^{5}$ 470$^{16}$* 636$^{10}$ 991$^{5}$ 1302$^{12}$ 1856$^{9}$ (2602) 3151$^{8}$ 4128$^{15}$ 4373$^{6}$ 4915$^{14}$ **>74a 57f<**
**So Amazing 4** b f Hallgate-Jussoli (Don) *(44) (115) (153) (427) 629$^{11}$* 1157$^{9}$ 1528$^{4}$ 2320$^{7}$ **>84a 61f<**
**Soba Up 6** ch m Persian Heights-Soba (Most Secret) 1421$^{14}$ 1647$^{9}$ 2020$^{9}$ (2221) 2697$^{9}$ 3098$^{5}$ 3621$^{8}$ 4345$^{2}$ 4483$^{2}$ 4580$^{9}$ **>76f<**
**Sobeloved 4** gr g Beveled (USA)-Miss Solo (Runnymede) 1302$^{18}$ 2159$^{11}$ 2345$^{9}$ 2785$^{6}$ 3274$^{12}$ 3473$^{14}$ **>29f<**
**Social Pillar (USA) 2** b c Gone West (USA)-Social Column (USA) (Swoon's Son) 3221$^{6}$ 4060$^{2}$ 4516$^{4}$ (4814) **>81f<**
**Society Girl 3** b f Shavian-Sirene Bleu Marine (USA) (Secreto (USA)) *119$^{5}$ 220$^{4}$ 242$^{3}$ 344$^{2}$ 403$^{5}$ 464$^{7}$ (1526)* 1886$^{4}$ 2241$^{4}$ (2419) 2780$^{6}$ (3491) 3866$^{2}$ (4071) 4226$^{11}$ **>57a 67f<**
**Society Magic (USA) 3** b g Imp Society (USA)-Lady Kirtling (USA) (Kirtling) 892$^{15}$ 1416$^{8}$ 1689$^{10}$ (4348) 4550$^{12}$ **>65f<**
**Society Rose 2** b f Saddlers' Hall (IRE)-Ruthless Rose (USA) (Conquistador Cielo (USA)) *(4806)* **>73+f<**
**Soda 2** gr g Belfort (FR)-Bella Seville (King of Spain) 2327$^{3}$ 2562$^{3}$ 2897$^{7}$ 4903$^{6}$ **>55df<**
**Soda Pop (IRE) 2** b c River Falls-Riviere Salee (FR) (Luthier) 2243$^{5}$ 4127$^{10}$ **>55f<**
**Sodelk 2** ch f Interrex (CAN)-Summoned by Bells (Stanford) *4621$^{6}$ 4988$^{13}$* **>43f<**
**Soden (IRE) 2** b f Mujadil (USA)-Elminya (IRE) (Sure Blade (USA)) 2404$^{9}$ 2892$^{3}$ 3159$^{7}$ (3449) 3616$^{7}$ 3998$^{11}$ 4262$^{8}$ **>77f<**
**So Factual (USA) 6** b h Known Fact (USA)-Sookera (USA) (Roberto (USA)) **1995:** 4563a$^{3}$ **>127f<**
**So Intrepid (IRE) 6** ch h Never so Bold-Double River (USA) (Irish River (FR)) *(418) 464$^{3}$ 610$^{7}$* (814) 1073$^{4}$ 1199$^{3}$ 1473$^{3}$ 1781$^{5}$ (2034) (2228) 2725$^{10}$ 3038$^{6}$ 3296$^{9}$ 4198$^{6}$ 4312$^{14}$ 4802$^{5}$ 4994$^{12}$ **>64a 84f<**
**So Keen 3** ch g Keen-Diana's Bow (Great Nephew) 1434$^{9}$ 1797$^{8}$ 2062$^{6}$ 2223$^{5}$ 3870$^{12}$ 4448$^{13}$ **>47f<**
**Solar Crystal (IRE) 3** b f Alzao (USA)-Crystal Spray (Beldale Flutter (USA)) 1004$^{2}$ 1949a$^{8}$ 2677$^{3}$ 3231$^{8}$ 3945$^{6}$ **>103f<**
**Solatium (IRE) 4** b g Rainbow Quest (USA)-Consolation (Troy) 1640$^{10}$ 2042$^{10}$ 2310$^{2}$ 2530$^{8}$ **>67f<**
**Soldier Blue 3** ch g Infantry-Greenhil Jazz Time (Music Boy) 3505$^{11}$ 4083$^{7}$ 4429$^{10}$ **>50f<**
**Soldier Cove (USA) 6** ch g Manila (USA)-Secret Form (Formidable (USA)) *3978$^{6}$* 4226$^{8}$ 4436$^{14}$ 4563$^{12}$ **>49f<**
**Soldier Mak 3** ch g Infantry-Truly Blest (So Blessed) 734$^{2}$ 1042$^{7}$ 1507$^{3}$ 1984$^{3}$ 2204$^{3}$ 3705$^{2}$ 4042$^{4}$ 4496$^{2}$ 4752$^{4}$ **>67f<**
**Soldier's Song 3** b f Infantry-Top Soprano (High Top) 1857$^{8}$ 2198$^{5}$ 2510$^{7}$ **>57f<**
**Solfegietto 2** b f Music Boy-Maria Isabella (FR) (Young Generation) 1148$^{3}$ 3508$^{2}$ (3956) 4299$^{6}$ **>69f<**
**Solid Illusion (USA) 5** b h Cozzene (USA)-Polly's Harde (FR) (Lyphard (USA)) 4656a$^{10}$ **>120f<**
**Solo Mio (IRE) 2** b c Sadler's Wells (USA)-Marie de Flandre (FR) (Crystal Palace (FR)) 3987$^{8}$ 4306$^{2}$ 4871$^{8}$ **>89f<**
**Solo Prize 4** b g Chief Singer-Raffle (Balidar) **1995:** *4478$^{11}$* **1996:** *31$^{7}$ 109$^{11}$* **>22da 40f<**
**Solo Symphony (IRE) 3** ch f Fayruz-Keen Note (Sharpo) 524$^{3}$ 591$^{4}$ 783$^{4}$ 1657$^{5}$ *2684$^{3}$ 3061$^{8}$* **>48a 56f<**
**Solo Volumes 7** ch g Ballacashtal (CAN)-Miss Solo (Runnymede) *3505$^{15}$*
***Sombreffe* 4** b f Polish Precedent (USA)-Somfas (USA) (What A Pleasure (USA)) **1995:** *(4382) 4478$^{4}$* **>72a 71f<**
**Some Horse (IRE) 3** ch g Astronef-Daniela Lepida (ITY) (El-Muleta) 1432$^{10}$ 2497$^{7}$ 2883$^{11}$ 4300$^{18}$ **>21a 79df<**
**Somerton Boy (IRE) 6** b h Thatching-Bonnie Bess (Ardoon) **1995:** *4392$^{10}$* **1996:** *589$^{19}$* 935$^{9}$ 1425$^{8}$ (2149) 2328$^{6}$ 2729$^{3}$ 3254$^{3}$ 3933$^{6}$ 4190$^{25}$ 4688$^{6}$ **>43a 77f<**
**Something Blue 2** b f Petong-Blueit (FR) (Bold Lad (IRE)) 3508$^{7}$ 4558$^{8}$ 4762$^{14}$ **>33f<**
**Something Speedy (IRE) 4** b f Sayf El Arab (USA)-Fabulous Pet (Somethingfabulous (USA)) *114$^{8}$* **>50da 37f<**
**Sommersby (IRE) 5** b g Vision (USA)-Echoing (Formidable (USA)) **1995:** *4376$^{10}$* **1996:** *251$^{10}$ 1031$^{11}$ 2173$^{7}$ 2631$^{6}$ 3955$^{4}$ 4334$^{3}$* **>55a 54f<**
**So Natural (IRE) 4** ch f Sharpo-Sympathy (Precocious) *161$^{0}$ 110$^{6}$ 179$^{4}$ 310$^{3}$ 387$^{7}$ 834$^{6}$ 882$^{16}$* 1612$^{9}$ *2308$^{8}$* **>48a 1f<**
**Sondalo (IRE) 3** b c Bluebird (USA)-Staffa Speciale (ITY) (Vision (USA)) 1137a$^{2}$ **>70f<**
**Sonderise 7** br g Mummy's Game-Demderise (Vaigly Great) 466$^{4}$ 559$^{4}$ 806$^{3}$ 1040$^{3}$ 1364$^{5}$ (1765) 2030$^{3}$ 2185$^{6}$ 2719$^{3}$ 3352$^{4}$ 3643$^{D}$ 4058$^{21}$ **>60f<**
**Sondos 3** b f Dowsing (USA)-Krameria (Kris) *(529) 686$^{5}$* 1181$^{5}$ *2937$^{14}$* **>65+a 65f<**
**Song For Jess (IRE) 3** b f Accordion-Ritual Girl (Ballad Rock) 2314$^{6}$ 2798$^{5}$ **>46f<**
**Song Mist (IRE) 2** gr f Kenmare (FR)-Farewell Song (USA) (The Minstrel (CAN)) 2035$^{4}$ 2404$^{2}$ (2758) 3846$^{5}$ 4113$^{6}$ 4490$^{6}$ **>75f<**
**Song of Freedom 2** ch c Arazi (USA)-Glorious Song (CAN) (Halo (USA)) 4991$^{4}$ **>81+f<**
**Song of Peace (GER) 3** f 1060a$^{8}$ **>78f<**
**Song of Skye 2** b f Warning-Song of Hope (Chief Singer) (2854) 3170$^{2}$ 4299$^{5}$ 4723$^{12}$ 4878$^{7}$ **>88f<**
**Song of Tara (IRE) 4** b c Sadler's Wells (USA)-Flame of Tara (Artaius (USA)) 1509$^{3}$ 3196a$^{3}$ 3614$^{3}$ **>119f<**
**Song Of The Sword 3** b g Kris-Melodist (USA) (The Minstrel (CAN)) 2825a$^{4}$ 3021a$^{8}$ **>98f<**
**Songsheet 3** b f Dominion-Songstead (Song) (861) 1316$^{5}$ 1985$^{5}$ 2410$^{2}$ *2684$^{2}$ 3339$^{3}$* 3661$^{5}$

3883$^4$ 4130$^7$ *4776$^6$* **>59a 71f<**

**Song Song Blue (IRE) 3** b br g Ballad Rock-Bluethroat (Ballymore) 637$^7$ **>26f<**

**Sonic Mail 3** b g Keen-Martin-Lavell Mail (Dominion) 692$^{15}$ 992$^7$ **>70f<**

**Son of Sharp Shot (IRE) 6** b or br h Sharp Shot-Gay Fantasy (Troy) 941$^8$ 1767$^2$ 2055$^{14}$ (2690) 3212$^6$ 3754a$^9$ 4465$^{15}$ 4716$^5$ **>106f<**

**Soojama (IRE) 6** b g Mansooj-Pyjama Game (Cavo Doro) 666$^9$ 1514$^{12}$ (1803) 2547$^{11}$ 3037$^{18}$ 3204$^2$ *3437$^5$* **>37a 57f<**

**Sooty Tern 9** br h Wassl-High Tern (High Line) *416$^4$ 487$^4$ 654$^4$ 843$^2$* 933$^6$ *(1048) 1528$^8$* 1659$^5$ 1983$^7$ 3120$^5$ 3340$^8$ (3646) 3861$^2$ 4243$^{10}$ 4432$^{12}$ **>55a 80f<**

**Sophie Lockett 3** b f Mon Tresor-Silverdale Rose (Nomination) *2798$^6$* 3108$^6$ 3402$^7$ **>46f<**

**Sophie May 5** b m Glint of Gold-Rosana Park (Music Boy) *9$^7$* **>34a 41f<**

**Sophism (USA) 7** b g Al Nasr (FR)-Over The Waves (Main Reef) 1835$^4$ 2310$^3$ 2560$^3$ **>49f<**

**Sophomore 2** b c Sanglamore (USA)-Livry (USA) (Lyphard (USA)) (4863) **>80f<**

**Sopran Benda (ITY) 3** b f Danehill (USA)-Bengeula () (Pampapaul) 908a$^2$ 1393a$^9$ **>96f<**

**Sopran Big Bir (ITY) 2** b f Big Reef-Amazing Bir (ITY) (Storm Bird (CAN)) 4171a$^3$

**Sopran Glasik 2** b c Sikeston (USA)-Glauce (Superlative) (4038a)

**Sopran Mariduff 2** dk f Persian Bold-Marina Duff (Caerleon (USA)) 4746a$^3$

**Sorara 3** ch f Aragon-Sorebelle (Prince Tenderfoot (USA)) 3679$^4$ **>40?f<**

**Sorbie Tower (IRE) 3** b c Soviet Lad (USA)-Nozet (Nishapour (FR)) (448) (646) (833) 1441$^2$ 2039$^3$ 3144$^4$ 4417a$^7$ **>124f<**

**Sorisky 4** ch g Risk Me (FR)-Minabella (Dance In Time (CAN)) **1995:** *4534$^6$* **1996:** *15$^5$ (54) 83$^7$ 186$^5$ 279$^{10}$ 1444$^5$ 2226$^{10}$* **>46a 45f<**

**Sotoboy (IRE) 4** b c Danehill (USA)-Fire Flash (Bustino) 450$^W$ 809$^9$ 1051$^5$ 1486$^7$ 1841$^{11}$ *2201$^9$* **>46a 76f<**

**Sotonian (HOL) 3** br g Statoblest-Visage (Vision (USA)) 1429$^8$ *2325$^9$ 2794$^{12}$* 4058$^{20}$ 4205$^{14}$ 4610$^{19}$ **>25a 19f<**

**Soufriere (IRE) 3** b br f Caerleon (USA)-Shelbiana (USA) (Chieftain II) 1855$^{10}$ 2318$^8$ **>46f<**

**Soul of the Matter (USA) 5** dk b h Private Terms (USA)-Soul Light (USA) (T.V.Commercial (USA)) *536a$^2$* **>137a 126f<**

**Soul Sister 3** b f Distant Relative-Lappet (Kampala) 3847$^6$ 4074$^{15}$ *4978$^8$* **>29a 23f<**

**Sound Appeal 2** b f Robellino (USA)-Son Et Lumiere (Rainbow Quest (USA)) 3159$^{11}$ 3982$^5$ 4797$^{14}$ 4889$^4$ **>67f<**

**Sound Check 3** b f Formidable (USA)-Imperatrice (USA) (Kings Lake (USA)) 819$^{10}$ (1119) 1447$^5$ 1654$^3$ 2061$^3$ 2253$^4$ 2501$^7$ 2710$^6$ **>61f<**

**Sounds Legal 3** b f Rich Charlie-Legal Sound (Legal Eagle) *4978$^2$* **>76a f<**

**Sound the Trumpet (IRE) 4** b g Fayruz-Red Note (Rusticaro (FR)) *431$^5$ 514$^2$ 607$^{12}$ 749$^5$* 981$^7$ *1083$^5$ 1642$^2$* 2286$^4$ 2757$^{10}$ 3453$^W$ **>59da 58f<**

**Sound Trick (USA) 4** b f Phone Trick (USA)-Lettre d'Amour (USA) (Caro) **1995:** *4354$^6$ 4456$^9$* **>19a 33f<**

**Souperficial 5** gr g Petong-Duck Soup (Decoy Boy) *629$^{12}$* 718$^{14}$ 1423$^{16}$ *1812$^{11}$ 2030$^7$* 2496$^8$ *2637$^3$ 2934$^{14}$ 3091$^4$ (3331)* 3453$^{11}$ *4090$^5$ 4205$^6$* (4342) 4610$^{11}$ 4791$^{13}$ 4888$^2$ **>61a 62f<**

**Soura (USA) 2** ch f Beau Genius (CAN)-First Division (CHI) (Domineau (USA)) 2073$^{10}$ 3129$^9$ **>54f<**

**Source of Light 7** b g Rainbow Quest (USA)-De Stael (USA) (Nijinsky (CAN)) 751$^3$ 1336$^4$ 1767$^7$ 2534$^7$ **>109f<**

**Sous Le Nez 2** b f Midyan (USA)-Miss Swansong (Young Generation) 2374$^2$ (2772) 3170$^3$ 3590$^4$ 4034a$^3$ 4234$^{10}$ 4966$^5$ 5037$^6$ 5049$^2$ **>76f<**

**South Eastern Fred 5** b h Primo Dominie-Soheir (Track Spare) **1995:** *4356$^2$ 4520$^8$* **1996:** *61$^2$ 132$^5$ 181$^3$ 312$^3$ 358$^5$ 411$^6$ 462$^7$ 1515$^5$* 1841$^9$ 2409$^2$ 3220$^{12}$ *3627$^4$ (4078) 4226$^7$* **>79a 57f<**

**Southerly Wind 2** b c Slip Anchor-Karavina (Karabas) 2361$^{11}$ (2865) 4131$^5$ 4298$^2$ (4384) 4864$^3$ **>78f<**

**Southern Chief 2** b g Be My Chief (USA)-Southern Sky (Comedy Star (USA)) *4331$^{11}$ 4477$^6$* **>25f<**

**Southern Dominion 4** ch g Dominion-Southern Sky (Comedy Star (USA)) **1995:** *(4441) 4458$^3$ 4488$^5$ 4536$^2$* **1996:** *139$^4$ 170$^5$ 202$^2$ 266$^8$ 354$^7$ 408$^7$ 559$^{14}$* 631$^{10}$ 1156$^5$ 4428$^{14}$ 4701$^{11}$ **>53a 51f<**

**Southern Power (IRE) 5** b g Midyan (USA)-Tap The Line (Tap On Wood) *1147$^3$* (2042) 2612$^3$ (3142) 4377$^4$ **>96f<**

**Southern Ridge 5** b g Indian Ridge-Southern Sky (Comedy Star (USA)) *190$^{11}$* **>27a 70f<**

**South Pagoda (IRE) 3** b g Distinctly North (USA)-Lamya (Hittite Glory) 1530$^{14}$ 1608$^9$ 2139$^8$ 2486$^{10}$ **>36f<**

**South Salem (USA) 3** b c Salem Drive (USA)-Azzurrina (Knightly Manner (USA)) 830$^8$ 1427$^2$ *1946a$^P$* **>104f<**

**South Sea Bubble (IRE) 4** b f Bustino-Night At Sea (Night Shift (USA)) 687$^{11}$ 2246$^9$ 2901$^3$ 3621$^3$ 4227$^5$ 4582$^3$ (4905) **>75f<**

**South Wind 3** b f Tina's Pet-Warm Wind (Tumble Wind (USA)) 1614$^9$ 2062$^4$ 2326$^3$ 3079$^3$ 3315$^3$ *3600$^4$* **>44a 64f<**

**Sovereign Crest (IRE) 3** gr g Priolo (USA)-Abergwrle (Absalom) 3262$^{10}$ 3472$^8$ 4201$^F$ 4379$^7$ **>49f<**

**Sovereign Magic (USA) 3** b c Magic Prospect (USA)-Truly Sovereign (USA) (Sovereign Dancer (USA)) (1137a) **>74f<**

**Sovereign Page (USA) 7** ch g Caro-Tashinsky (USA) (Nijinsky (CAN)) *920$^5$* 1198$^{14}$ (1686) 2010$^5$ (2206) 2525$^9$ **>87f<**

**Sovereign Prince (IRE) 3** b c Bluebird (USA)-Everything Nice (Sovereign Path) **1995:** *4381$^6$ 4485$^9$ 4545$^7$* **1996:** *(81) 164$^3$ 176$^3$ 245$^4$ 2339$^6$* **>57a 39++f<**

**Sovereigns Court 3** ch g Statoblest-Clare Celeste (Coquelin (USA)) 1617$^7$ 1901$^{16}$ 3513$^5$ 4053$^{13}$ 4511$^3$ 4688$^{19}$ 4820$^2$ **>70f<**

**Soviet Bride (IRE) 4** b f Soviet Star (USA)-Nihad (Alleged (USA)) 866$^2$ 1124$^3$ 1618$^8$ 2943$^2$ (3136) 3272$^6$ 3635$^4$ (4125) **>79f<**

**Soviet King (IRE) 3** b c Soviet Lad (USA)-Finessing (Indian King (USA)) 616$^4$ 2130$^5$ 2540$^3$ 2739$^4$ **>60f<**

**Soviet Lady (IRE) 2** b f Soviet Lad (USA)-La Vosgienne (Ashmore (FR)) 975$^{12}$ 2043$^3$ 2315$^6$ *2750$^3$ 3227$^5$* 3448$^5$ (3769) 4223$^3$ **>51a 59f<**

**Soviet Line (IRE) 6** b g Soviet Star (USA)-Shore Line (High Line) *673$^7$* 810$^2$ (1177) 2037$^5$ 4443$^7$ 4664a$^9$ **>128f<**

**Soviet Sakti (IRE) 3** b c Soviet Lad (USA)-Hill's Realm (USA) (Key to the Kingdom (USA)) *2716$^{16}$* 2971$^{18}$ **>47f<**

**Soviet Shore 4** b c Soviet Star (USA)-Shore Line (High Line) *502$^2$* **>70a 77+f<**

**Soviet State (USA) 2** b c Nureyev (USA)-Absentia (USA) (Raise A Cup (USA)) 2243$^W$ 4825$^2$ (5034) **>95f<**

**Soy Soy (FR) 4** ch g Sicyos (USA)-Noujoud (Home Guard (USA)) 325a$^3$ **>74f<**

**Spa Lane 3** ch g Presidium-Sleekit (Blakeney) 1416$^2$ (1821) 2542$^4$ 2905$^3$ (3813) **>64f<**

**Spandrel 4** ch f Pharly (FR)-Oxslip (Owen Dudley) 840$^{10}$ 1667$^7$ 2193$^7$ 3112$^2$ 3686$^{15}$ **>57f<**

**Spaniards Close 8** b g King of Spain-Avon Belle (Balidar) 1964$^2$ 2604$^2$ **>83+a 102f<**

**Spaniards Inn 2** ch c Dominion-Zelda (USA) (Sharpen Up) 829$^6$ 1339$^7$ 1626$^4$ (3321) **>81f<**

**Spaniard's Mount 2** b c Distant Relative-Confection (Formidable (USA)) 3044$^5$ 3349$^8$ 4100$^{11}$ 4760$^{10}$ 4867$^6$ (5006) 5048$^3$ **>65f<**

**Spanish Falls 3** ch f Belmez (USA)-Flamenco Wave (USA) (Desert Wine (USA)) (1942a) 2277a$^3$ 4654a$^9$ **>106f<**

**Spanish Knot (USA) 2** b f El Gran Senor (USA)-Ingenuity (Clever Trick (USA)) 4062$^5$ 4494$^2$ 4705$^5$ **>78f<**

**Spanish Luck 3** b f Mazilier (USA)-Spanish Heart (King of Spain) **1995:** *4375$^{11}$* **>44a 49f<**

**Spanish Steps (IRE) 4** b g Danehill (USA)-Belle Enfant (Beldale Flutter (USA)) 477$^{13}$ 713$^{12}$ (1088) 1341$^{12}$ 1538$^2$ 2428$^{11}$ **>66f<**

**Spanish Stripper (USA) 5** b g El Gran Senor (USA)-Gourmet Dinner (USA) (Raise A Cup (USA)) *1966$^7$ 2209$^7$ 2367$^8$ 3168$^8$* 3703$^2$ 3995$^{26}$ 4221$^{10}$ 4259$^9$ 4439$^9$ 4597$^8$ 4815$^{11}$ *4982$^9$* **>33a 56f<**

**Spanish Verdict 9** b g King of Spain-Counsel's Verdict (Firestreak) 480$^{11}$ 802$^8$ 933$^{14}$ 1341$^{13}$ 1538$^7$ (1650) 1886$^2$ 2214$^2$ 3084$^8$ 3287$^4$ 3623$^9$ 3842$^3$ 3974$^{11}$ 4300$^9$ 4438$^6$ 4597$^2$ 4724$^6$ 4905$^7$ 4993$^{15}$ **>71f<**

**Spanish Warrior 2** b c Warrshan (USA)-Spanish Heart (King of Spain) 3685$^{15}$

**Sparkling Edge 2** b f Beveled (USA)-Sparkalot (USA) (Duel) (3582) 3871$^6$ 4234$^7$ 4672$^{12}$ 4912$^5$ *4999$^6$* **>38a 64f<**

**Sparkling Harry 2** ch c Tina's Pet-Sparkling Hock (Hot Spark) 2327$^6$ 2699$^7$ 3429$^6$ 3853$^7$ 4043$^{11}$ 4558$^6$ 4790$^3$ 4916$^{11}$ **>62f<**

**Sparkling Roberta 5** b m Kind of Hush-Hitesca **1995:** *4415$^4$ 4486$^6$* **>40a 45f<**

**Sparky 2** b g Warrshan (USA)-Pebble Creek (IRE) (Reference Point) 1320$^6$ 2043$^4$ 2161$^{10}$ 2984$^8$ (3311) (3512) 3998$^9$ 4384$^8$ 4586$^3$ **>65f<**

**Sparrowhawk (IRE) 4** b f Doyoun-Sparrow's Air (USA) (Assert) **1995:** *4419$^7$* **>46a 80df<**

**Spartan Girl (IRE) 2** ch f Ela-Mana-Mou-Well Head (IRE) (Sadler's Wells (USA)) 4706$^4$ **>58f<**

**Spartan Heartbeat 3** b c Shareef Dancer (USA)-Helen's Dream (Troy) 820$^3$ 1079$^3$ 1361$^3$ 1791$^{14}$ 2473a$^6$ 3157$^5$ **>113f<**

**Special Beat 4** b f Bustino-Special Guest (Be My Guest (USA)) *1977$^9$* (2560) 2958$^2$ **>69f<**

**Special Dawn (IRE) 6** ch g Be My Guest (USA)-Dawn Star (High Line) *580$^2$* 925$^5$ 2502$^{13}$ 2742$^2$ 3125$^9$ 4026a$^3$ 4326$^{17}$ **>96f<**

**Special Effect (FR) 3** ch g Groom Dancer (USA)-Hollywood Trick (FR) (Caro) 5020a$^3$ **>67f<**

**Specialize 4** b g Faustus (USA)-Scholastika (GER) (Alpenkonig (GER)) 612$^{10}$ **>17a 44df<**

**Special-K 4** br f Treasure Kay-Lissi Gori (FR) (Bolkonski) *991$^4$* 1341$^7$ 1674$^{11}$ 1860$^4$ 2693$^3$ 3134$^5$ 3450$^8$ 3623$^6$ 3867$^2$ 4071$^9$ 4226$^9$ 4323$^7$ **>67f<**

**Special Risk (IRE) 6** br g Simply Great (FR)-Ahonita (Ahonoora) 4236$^{15}$ 4604$^{11}$ **>55?a 40f<**

**Spectacle Jim 7** b g Mummy's Game-Welsh Blossom (Welsh Saint) **1995:** *4358$^2$ 4459$^6$* **1996:** *582$^6$* 846$^8$ 981$^{15}$ 1449$^{18}$ 1677$^5$ 2286$^{18}$ 2403$^9$ *3078$^7$* **>52da 54f<**

**Spectrum (IRE) 4** b c Rainbow Quest (USA)-River Dancer (Irish River (FR)) 906a$^4$ 1177$^3$ 3670$^5$ **>128f<**

**Speedball (IRE)** 2 b c Waajib-Lady Taufan (IRE) (Taufan (USA)) 3994[3] (4330) 4510[2] 4723[15] **>87f<**
**Speedboat (USA)** 2 ch c Diesis-Ocean Ballad (Grundy) 4494[3] **>83f<**
**Speedfit** 2 gr c Mystiko (USA)-Softly Spoken (Mummy's Pet) 841[9] 1191[10] **>47f<**
**Speedfriend (GER)** 2 gr c Unfuwain (USA)-Batchelor's Button (FR) (Kenmare (FR)) 4029a[3] 4415a[3] **>92f<**
**Speed On** 3 b g Sharpo-Pretty Poppy (Song) 648[2] (1033) 2003[2] 3132[3] 4115[6] 4466[14] **>104f<**
**Speed Rahy (USA)** 5 ch h Rahy (USA)-Spring Tour (USA) (Ack Ack (USA)) 2670a[3] **>106f<**
**Speed to Lead (IRE)** 4 b f Darshaan-Instant Desire (USA) (Northern Dancer) 682[2] 811[3] (1710) 2117[2] 3834[6] **>93f<**
**Speedy Classic (USA)** 7 br g Storm Cat (USA)-Shadows Lengthen (Star Appeal) **1995:** *4459[2] 4536[4]* **1996:** *26[4] 117[8] (229) 408[3] 632[2]* 981[11] 1844[10] 2376[10] 2719[5] 3439[12] *(3877) (4128)* 4356[4] 4571[6] **>80a 63f<**
**Speedy Snaps Image** 5 ch g Ballacashtal (CAN)-Lillicara (FR) (Caracolero (USA)) 1506[10] 1992[11] **>48a 30f<**
**Speedy Snaps Pride** 4 gr g Hallgate-Pineapple's Pride (John de Coombe) *74[7] 179[6] 213[7] 239[12] 387[6] 470[10]* 670[6] 1411[16] 1468[4] *1719[3] 2796[3]* 2971[11] 3442[3] (3761) 4045[11] 4701[14] 4882[17] **>33a 54f<**
**Spencer's Revenge** 7 ch g Bay Express-Armour of Light (Hot Spark) **1995:** *(4525)* **1996:** *(31) 86[3] 141[2] 174[2] 427[3] 479[6]* 649[5] *(776) 1081[5]* **>82a 79df<**
**Spencer Stallone** 3 b g Rambo Dancer (CAN)-Armour of Light (Hot Spark) *856[5] 1470[4]* 2373[13] 2966[5] **>46a 52f<**
**Spender** 7 b or br g Last Tycoon-Lady Hester (Native Prince) *55[7] 173[2] 266[7] 380[3] (407) 500[6] 1853[11]* 2324[2] 2586[2] 2889[8] 3338[3] 3993[16] 4220[6] 4765[3] 5039[4] **>93a 78f<**
**Speransella (FR)** 6 b m Miller's Mate-Serenella (FR) (Arctic Tern (USA)) 3744a[3] **>112df<**
**Sphinx Levelv (IRE)** 3 ch g Digamist (USA)-Fantoccini (Taufan (USA)) *463[4] 614[15] 1027[8] 2971[13]* ***>48a 36f<***
**Spice and Sugar** 6 ch m Chilibang-Pretty Miss (So Blessed) *1411[15]* 2189[9] 2906[4] 4102[8] **>40a 35f<**
**Spicetress** 2 gr f Chilibang-Foreign Mistress (Darshaan) 4600[11] 4796[4] 5040[11] **>62f<**
**Spillo** 3 b c Midyan (USA)-Myth (Troy) 509[4] (634) 920[2] 1147[4] 2006[3] 2616[2] 3145[4] 3710[9] (4176) 4487[6] **>102f<**
**Spinario (USA)** 5 ch h Miswaki (USA)-Spadina (USA) (Sharpen Up) (148a) 191a[2] 227a[2] 288a[2] **>88f<**
**Spinning Mouse** 3 b f Bustino-Minute Waltz (Sadler's Wells (USA)) **1995:** *4414[8]* **1996:** *1100[7]* 1498[5] 3079[2] (3308) 3520[2] 4321[5] 4551[9] **>46a 68f<**
**Spinning World (USA)** 3 ch c Nureyev (USA)-Imperfect Circle (USA) (Riverman (USA)) **1995:** (4468a) **1996:** 798a[3] 1141a[2] (1574a) 2039[6] (3745a) 4165a[2] 4953a[2] **>132f<**
**Spiral Flyer (IRE)** 3 b br f Contract Law (USA)-Souveniers (Relko) *377[6] 761[8]* 1119[10] 1594[10] 2313[9] 3681[6] 4082[10] **>38a 43f<**
**Spirit of Sport** 3 b f Forzando-What's the Matter (High Top) *281[6] 355[10] 591[W]* ***>28a f<***
**Spirito Libro (USA)** 3 b f Lear Fan (USA)-Teeming Shore (USA) (L'Emigrant (USA)) *561[2]* 662[4] (937) 1126[3] (1771) 2001[4] 2502[3] 2724[2] **>97f<**
**Spitfire Bridge (IRE)** 4 b g Cyrano de Bergerac-Maria Renata (Jaazeiro (USA)) **1995:** *(4379) (4420) 4452[6] 4490[5]* **1996:** *486[5] 690[13]* 1411[20] 1979[6] **>64a 60f<**
**Splashed** 2 gr f Absalom-Riverain (Bustino) 3773[4] 4593[3] **>64f<**
**Splicing** 3 ch f Sharpo-Soluce (Junius (USA)) (524) (686) *897[2] 1327[10] 2171[11] 2532[2] 2634[3] 3296[14]* 3693[19] 4581[19] 4802[4] 4995[3] 5039[12] **>89a 74f<**
**Splinter (IRE)** 3 b c Warning-Sharpthorne (USA) (Sharpen Up) 716[6] 3270[6] 3693[20] **>80f<**
**Spondulicks (IRE)** 2 b g Silver Kite (USA)-Greek Music (Tachypous) 452[3] 568[2] 1036[4] 1471[5] 2254[4] 2606[6] 2759[2] 3498[5] 3662[5] 3943[4] 4097[3] 4361[7] *4980[6]* **>53a 61f<**
**Sporting Fantasy** 3 b g Primo Dominie-Runelia (Runnett) **1995:** *4511[8]* **1996:** *171[4] 280[10] 314[4] 404[6] 2359[10]* ***>44a 57df<***
**Sporting Fellow** 2 ch c Groom Dancer (USA)-Shameem (USA) (Nureyev (USA)) 4699[3] 4817[4] **>62f<**
**Sporting Risk** 4 b g Risk Me (FR)-Sunday Sport's Pet (Mummy's Pet) *341[4] 406[5] 1085[2] 1457[13] 1638[9]* (2159) 2513[3] 3052[3] 3606[7] *4089[3] 4373[21]* ***>47a 56f<***
**Spotted Eagle** 3 ch g Risk Me (FR)-Egnoussa (Swing Easy (USA)) 458[14] (758) 1628[8] 2007[U] 2532[7] 4802[18] **>78f<**
**Spout** 4 b f Salse (USA)-Arderelle (FR) (Pharly (FR)) (726) 2474a[6] (2533) 3392a[3] 4567[2] 4678[2] **>115f<**
**Spread The Word** 4 b f Deploy-Apply (Kings Lake (USA)) *1147[10]* 2505[8] 2989[2] 3471[3] 3802[6] 4086[5] 4509[5] 4789[2] **>57f<**
**Spring Campaign (IRE)** 3 b c Sayaarr (USA)-March The Second (Millfontaine) 2183[9] 2383[6] 2739[6] 4831[17] 4921[10] **>74df<**
**Spring Dance (FR)** 2 f 4661a[8] **>94f<**
**Spring Silhouette** 3 b f Kind of Hush-Hasland (Aragon) **1995:** *4433[15]* **>34f<**
**Spring Sunrise** 6 b m Robellino (USA)-Saniette (Crystal Palace (FR)) *72[6]* **>20a 47f<**
**Spring to Glory** 9 b g Teenoso (USA)-English Spring (USA) (Grey Dawn II) *4509[8]* ***>25f<***
**Spriolo** 2 b f Priolo (USA)-Springtime Sugar (USA) (Halo (USA)) 4861[15] **>6f<**
**Spumante** 4 ch g Executive Man-Midler (Comedy Star (USA)) **1995:** *4543[7]* **1996:** *635[13]* 3801[14] **>43a 36f<**
**Spy Knoll** 2 b c Shirley Heights-Garden Pink (FR) (Bellypha) 4516[6] 4705[4] **>74f<**
**Squandamania** 3 b c Ela-Mana-Mou-Garden Pink (FR) (Bellypha) 4515[W] **>52f<**
**Squared Away** 4 b c Blakeney-Maureen Mhor (Taj Dewan) 613[12] 786[10] 994[9] 1414[14] 1803[18] (2162) 2440[2] 3067[8] 3991[9] 4436[5] 4597[14] **>59f<**
**Square Deal (FR)** 5 b g Sharpo-River Dove (USA) (Riverman (USA)) *110[2] (167) 257[2] 345[7] 371[4] 399[5] 416[6] 592[12] 1492[15] 1606[5] 4987[15]* **>55a 35f<**
**Square Mile Miss (IRE)** 3 b f Last Tycoon-Call Me Miss (Hello Gorgeous (USA)) 2208[6] 2610[12] 2918[7] 3456[9] 3761[6] 4221[12] 4808[7] 4898[7] **>52f<**
**Squeak** 2 ch f Selkirk (USA)-Santa Linda (USA) (Sir Ivor) (4755) (4908) **>78+f<**
**Squire Corrie** 4 b g Distant Relative-Fast Car (FR) (Carwhite) *55[10] 163[11] 749[11]* 1049[8] 1512[9] 2156[11] 2340[9] 2602[11] 2787[5] (2976) 3323[5] 3506[2] 3793[3] (3930) (3993) 4198[9] 4372[4] 4616[3] **>64a 73f<**
**Squire's Occasion (CAN)** 3 b g Black Tie Affair-Tayana (USA) (Wajima (USA)) 4064[17] **>62f<**
**Stackattack (IRE)** 3 b c Salt Dome (USA)-Must Hurry (Kampala) 2579[13] *3064[3] 3513[6]* 3985[10] 4059[5] 4513[13] 4768[2] 4860[14] 5042[6] **>69a 68f<**
**St Adele (USA)** 3 b f Pleasant Colony (USA)-Northern Sunset (USA) (Northfields (USA)) 2198[3] 2439[6] **>66f<**
**Stage Fright** 5 b g Sure Blade (USA)-First Act (Sadler's Wells (USA)) *1782[7]* ***>59f<***
**Stage Pass** 3 ch c In The Wings-Sateen (FR) (Round Table) *1057a[3]* 2108a[2] **>102f<**
**Stahr** 2 b c Liboi (USA)-Celia Brady (Last Tycoon) 4897[10] 5033[11] **>66f<**
**Stakis Casinos Lad (IRE)** 2 ch c Red Sunset-Stradey Lynn (Derrylin) *4244[12]* 4896[9] *(4988)* **>57a 33f<**
**Stalled (IRE)** 6 b g Glenstal (USA)-Chauffeuse (Gay Fandango (USA)) **1995:** *4385[7] (4434) 4513[4] (4534)* **1996:** *15[3] 83[5] 440[8]* 573[5] 666[3] 961[3] 1194[12] 1803[12] 4048[9] 4307[3] 4563[5] 4789[4] *4984[2]* **>65a 60f<**
**Stamp (IRE)** 2 ch c Sharpo-Likeness (Young Generation) 4891[2] 5034[11] **>67f<**
**Standing Ovation (ITY)** 2 b f Law Society (USA)-Stand By Me (Home Guard (USA)) 2666a[3]
**Standown** 3 b g Reprimand-Ashdown (Pharly (FR)) *(652) 824[14]* 1592[5] (1707) 2005[6] 2200[3] *2634[5] 2867[4]* 3140[5] 3844[9] 4430[11] 4589[2] 4828[9] **>75a 75f<**
**Stand Tall** 4 b g Unfuwain (USA)-Antilla (Averof) **1995:** *4427[2] (4458)* **1996:** *71[3] (170) 259[2] (330) (380) 500[2] 704[4]* 850[3] 1588[4] 1635[2] 1781[4] *2171[5] (2490)* 3995[17] **>87a 66f<**
**Stanton Harcourt (USA)** 2 b c Sovereign Dancer (USA)-Island Style (USA) (Manila (USA)) 3407[3] 3987[6] 4370[2] **>92f<**
**Star And Garter** 3 ch f Soviet Star (USA)-On Show (Welsh Pageant) 1615[9] 2438[4] **>75f<**
**Star Anise** 4 ch f Prince Daniel (USA)-Elmajarrah (CAN) (Caro) 2036[14] 2599[3] 3218[3] **>46f<**
**Starborough** 2 ch c Soviet Star (USA)-Flamenco Wave (USA) (Desert Wine (USA)) (3773) 4065[3] 4822[4] **>99f<**
**Star Dancer** 3 ch f Groom Dancer (USA)-Pencarreg (Caerleon (USA)) 1043[8]
**Star Defector (IRE)** 5 ch g Soviet Star (USA)-Citissima (Simbir) 4643a[12] **>76f<**
**Star Entry** 2 b f In The Wings-Top Berry (High Top) 4241[5] **>57f<**
**Star Fairy (IRE)** 2 b f Fairy King (USA)-Mrs Foodbroker (Home Guard (USA)) (2272a)
**Star Fighter** 4 gr c Siberian Express (USA)-Eezepeeze (Alzao (USA)) 1655[10] 1874[13] **>54a 54f<**
**Starlight Flyer** 9 b g In Fijar (USA)-Nareen (USA) (The Minstrel (CAN)) **1995:** *4434[11]* **1996:** *54[14]* **>30da 45?f<**
**Starlight Waltzer** 3 b g Arzanni-Marchiness Drake (Marechal Drake) 4613[10] **>30f<**
**Star Manager (USA)** 6 b g Lyphard (USA)-Angel Clare (FR) (Mill Reef (USA)) (809) 967[4] 1193[4] 2053[5] 3709[6] 4120[7] 4568[10] 4874[3] **>93f<**
**Starmaniac (USA)** 3 b c Septieme Ciel (USA)-Silver Lane (USA) (Silver Hawk (USA)) *721a[4]* ***>106f<***
**Star of Gold** 4 b g Night Shift (USA)-Sure Gold (Glint of Gold) *1966[9] (2405)* 2602[8] (2954) 3340[2] **>37a 81f<**
**Star of Ring (IRE)** 3 b c Taufan (USA)-Karine (Habitat) 640[14] **>71df<**
**Star of The Road** 2 b c Risk Me (FR)-Astrid Gilberto (Runnett) 1479[6] **>56f<**
**Star of Zilzal (USA)** 4 b g Zilzal (USA)-Tell Me Sumthing (USA) (Summing (USA)) 2853[4] 3263[3] 3691[13] (4196) (4352) 4623[7] **>109f<**
**Star Parade (FR)** 4 b g Be My Guest (USA)-Stapara (Mill Reef (USA)) 324a[3] **>65f<**
**Star Performer (IRE)** 5 b g Petorius-Whitstar (Whitstead) *210[3] 3605[4] (3870) 4092[2] 4302[9]* 4588[5]

**>55a 59f<**

**Star Precision 2** ch f Shavian-Accuracy (Gunner B) 4514[11] 4706[6] 4889[5] **>58f<**

**Star Profile (IRE) 2** b f Sadler's Wells (USA)-Sandhurst Goddess (Sandhurst Prince) 3561a[5] 4159a[5] **>103f<**

**Star Rage (IRE) 6** b g Horage-Star Bound (Crowned Prince (USA)) *837[2]* **>81a 91f<**

**Star Selection 5** b g Rainbow Quest (USA)-Selection Board (Welsh Pageant) 581[2] 828[4] 1509[8] 3996[8] **>113df<**

**Star Talent (USA) 5** b h Local Talent (USA)-Sedra (Nebbiolo) *(65) 185[4] 229[2] 317[5] 350[3] 442[7]* (633) 728[5] 935[2] 1330[3] 1354[9] 1819[2] 2053[28] 3207[4] 3696[4] **>75a 90f<**

**Startingo 3** b c Rustingo-Spartan's Girl (Spartan General) 3262[14] **>26f<**

**Star Turn (IRE) 2** ch c Night Shift (USA)-Ringtail (Auction Ring (USA)) 3796[15] 4600[5] 4782[9] **>53f<**

**Statajack (IRE) 8** b g King of Clubs-Statira (Skymaster) *378[3] 410[9] 682[6]* 920[11] 1066[7] 1338[4] (1772) 1839[2] (2127) 2299[7] 2737[4] *2939[2]* **>74a 87f<**

**State Approval 3** b g Pharly (FR)-Tabeeba (Diesis) 803[5] *1031[4] 1100[2]* 1507[7] 2120[2] 3053[5] (3318) *(3422) 3768[5]* 4217[6] 4515[6] *5062[3]* **>74a 70f<**

**State Circus 3** b f Soviet Star (USA)-Wily Trick (USA) (Clever Trick (USA)) *390[2] 502[3] 1644[6]* 2366[P] **>71a 73f< (DEAD)**

**State Fair 2** b c Shirley Heights-Lobinda (Shareef Dancer (USA)) 1896[3] 2073[2] (3264) (3595) 4462[7] **>98+f<**

**Stately Dancer 3** b f Be My Guest (USA)-Wild Pavane (Dancing Brave (USA)) 576[5] 813[10] (1117) 1852[10] 3248[10] (3522) 4067[14] 4617[8] **>78f<**

**State of Caution 3** b c Reprimand-Hithermoor Lass (Red Alert) 577[2] 785[4] 1327[3] 1709[4] 3839[3] 4591[8] **>83f<**

**State of Gold (IRE) 2** b c High Estate-Mawaal Habeebee (Northfields (USA)) 3682[12] 4253[8] 4494[10] **>60f<**

**Statesman 2** b c Doyoun-Affair of State (IRE) (Tate Gallery (USA)) (699) (1437) 2040[15] 3396a[3] 3927[7] **>88f<**

**State Theatre (IRE) 3** b c Sadler's Wells (USA)-Fruition (Rheingold) 1644[9] 1854[4] 2247[4] 3037[3] **>82f<**

**Static Love 3** b f Statoblest-Run for Love (Runnett) **1995:** *4369[W]* **1996:** *750[13]* 1039[12] 2133[9] **>7a 21f<**

**Station Express (IRE) 8** b g Rusticaro (FR)-Vallee d'O (FR) (Polyfoto) 2182[12] **>3f<**

**Statistician 4** b g Statoblest-Sharp Lady (Sharpen Up) 2410[4] 2908[4] 3152[10] 3406[4] 3758[7] 3973[W] 4436[20] 4701[2] 4768[13] 4915[4] *5055[3]* **>57a 65f<**

**Statoyork 3** b c Statoblest-Ultimate Dream (Kafu) *672[5]* 1657[D] (2150) 3232[30] 4136[15] 4376[11] 4571[15] **>62f<**

**Statuette 2** b f Statoblest-La Pirouette (USA) (Kennedy Road (CAN)) 1046[4] (3336) 3975[10] 4207[12] 4425[8] *4999[9]* **>34a 61f<**

**Stayerka (FR) 3** b f Tagel (USA)-River Note (FR) (River River (FR)) 3027a[3]

**St Blaine (CAN) 2** b f St Jovite (USA)-Blaine (USA) (Lyphard's Wish (FR)) 4969[5] **>77f<**

**Steadfast Elite (IRE) 5** b m Glenstal (USA)-Etching (Auction Ring (USA)) 477[2] 541[4] 1167[3] (1548) 1832[2] 2177[4] 2390[6] 2430[5] *3062[11]* **>2a 52f<**

**Steady Ready Go (IRE) 4** b g Night Shift (USA)-Smeralda (GER) (Dschingis Khan) *4911[7]* ***>105f<***

**Steal 'Em 3** b f Efisio-Eastern Ember (Indian King (USA)) *2555[6] (2675)* 3210[9] 3790[12] **>47a 67f<**

**Steamroller Stanly 3** b g Shirley Heights-Miss Demure (Shy Groom (USA)) **1995:** *4352[3]* **1996:** *578[6]* (2247) 2665a[4] 3504[6] 4187[3] 4260[5] 4615[9] **>60a 86f<**

**Steel Sovereign 5** gr g Nishapour (FR)-Perioscope (Legend of France (USA)) 971[12] 1087[9] 1765[9] 2030[8] 2212[8] 2520[4] 2801[9] 2898[10] 3410[8] **>11a 43f<**

**Stellar Line (USA) 3** ch g Zilzal (USA)-Stellaria (USA) (Roberto (USA)) 746[4] 2572[4] 3999[4] 4322[4] 4613[5] **>78f<**

**Step Aloft 4** b f Shirley Heights-Pas de Deux (Nijinsky (CAN)) 2591[2] 2882[7] 3766[2] (4489) 4615[2] 4872[17] **>87f<**

**Stephensons Rocket 5** ch g Music Boy-Martian Princess (Cure The Blues (USA)) *418[12] 475[14]* 610[12] 735[5] 931[7] 4205[7] 4246[9] 4473[2] 4616[21] 4811[16] *4987[8]* **>46a 61f<**

**Step N Go (IRE) 2** b f Alzao (USA)-River Jet (USA) (Lear Fan (USA)) 1822[5] 2772[2] 3250[6] 4614[10] 4916[4] **>62f<**

**Step On Degas 3** b f Superpower-Vivid Impression (Cure The Blues (USA)) (1688) 2244[5] 2790[7] 3215[7] 3661[10] *4094[2] 4521[7] 5000[2]* **>74a 53f<**

**Sterin 3** b f Chauve Souris-Sweet Lore (Law Society (USA)) 3656[14] 4108[14] **>42f<**

**Sterling Fellow 3** b c Pharly (FR)-Favorable Exchange (USA) (Exceller (USA)) **1995:** *4439[2]* **1996:** *56[9] 890[6]* 1347[4] 1591[5] 2191[3] (3077) 3337[2] 3514[2] 3813[5] 4426[11] 4612[3] 4794[3] **>33a 71f<**

**Sternkonig (IRE) 6** gr h Kalaglow-Sternwappen **1995:** (4470a) **>123f<**

**Stevie's Wonder (IRE) 6** ch g Don't Forget Me-Azurai (Dance In Time (CAN)) **1995:** *4475[7]* **1996:** *(138) 235[2] 837[6] 1063[9] 1458[7] 1640[13] 2304[7] 2553[7] 2939[3] 3066[8]* **>57a 53f<**

**St Honorine (IRE) 4** b f Ela-Mana-Mou-Taken By Force (Persian Bold) 4362[5] 4515[10] 4763[7] **>56f<**

**Sticks and Stones (IRE) 4** b g Waajib-Maiacourt (Malacate (USA)) 2249[5] **>83f<**

**Stillet (IRE) 2** 5076a[6]

**Still Here (IRE) 3** b g Astronef-Covey's Quick Step (Godswalk (USA)) *49[6] 381[4] (415) 522[14]* 1067[9] 1903[5] 2192[15] *2689[7] 3257[11]* ***>60a 48f<***

**Stilly Night (IRE) 3** b f Martin John-Syndikos (USA) (Nashua) *49[5] 112[9]* **>42a f<**

**Stinging Reply 4** ch f Belmez (USA)-Nettle (Kris) *223[6]* **>54a 81f<**

**Stitched Up (IRE) 7** ch h Ahonoora-Needlewoman (Moorestyle) 4651a[3] **>72f<**

**St Lawrence (CAN) 2** gr c With Approval (CAN)-Mingan Isle (USA) (Lord Avie (USA)) 3682[13] 3964[2] 4386[2] **>76f<**

**St Lucinda (CAN) 2** b f St Jovite (USA)-Majestic Nature (USA) (Majestic Prince (USA)) (4454) **>75f<**

**St Mawes (FR) 3** ch c Shahrastani (USA)-Exemina (USA) (Slip Anchor) 694[2] 986[2] 1329[3] 1791[17] (3124) 4192[5] 4441[6] **>115f< (DEAD)**

**Stock Hill Dancer 2** ch f Interrex (CAN)-Stocktina (Tina's Pet) 3502[6] 4123[13] 4786[4] **>56f<**

**Stoleamarch 3** br g Daring March-Pennine Star (IRE) (Pennine Walk) *1850[16]* 2388[2] 3116[4] *3605[8] 3865[4]* ***>21a 53f<***

**Stolen Kiss (IRE) 4** b or br f Taufan (USA)-Sweet Goodbye (Petorius) (475) 716[5] 1113[14] 1501[5] 2694[20] 4452[14] 4616[22] **>77df<**

**Stolen Melody 4** b f Robellino (USA)-Song of Hope (Chief Singer) 554[12] 814[7] 1074[4] 1876[4] 2283[6] **>68f<**

**Stolen Music (IRE) 3** b f Taufan (USA)-Causa Sua (Try My Best (USA)) 3949[14] 4309[9] **>54f<**

**Stompin 5** b g Alzao (USA)-Celebrity (Troy) 1147[9] (1454) (1835) 2042[25] 3149[8] 3850[3] **>58a 85f<**

**Stone Cross (IRE) 4** b g Pennine Walk-Micro Mover (Artaius (USA)) 1417[4] *2939[4] 3580[12]* ***>49a 52f<***

**Stone Flower (USA) 2** b f Storm Bird (CAN)-Lively Living (USA) (Key To The Mint (USA)) 2147[6] (2872) 3468[3] 3921[5] 4113[13] 4717[3] **>90f<**

**Stonehaven (IRE) 2** b c Night Shift (USA)-Assya (Double Form) 4156a[5] 4398a[10] **>80f<**

**Stone Island 3** b g Rambo Dancer (CAN)-Single Gal (Mansingh (USA)) 1050[5] 1326[10] 1518[4] 1657[3] 2126[5] 3165[P] 3300[7] 3606[12] **>54f<**

**Stone Ridge (IRE) 4** b c Indian Ridge-Cut in Stone (USA) (Assert) (455) 728[16] 1330[5] 1793[15] 2053[15] 4568[25] 4874[5] 5065a[10] **>95f<**

**Stoney End (USA) 3** b c High Brite (USA)-Cranareen (USA) (Nice Dancer (CAN)) 730[14] 1171[6] 1422[5] (1657) 2021[2] 2301[8] 2705[4] 2999[7] 3122[4] 3518[11] **>76f<**

**Stony Bay (NZ) 5** h **1995:** *4471a[14]* ***>114f<***

**Stoppes Brow 4** b g Primo Dominie-So Bold (Never so Bold) **1995:** *4368[7]* **1996:** *338[7] 407[2] 582[23]* 887[4] 1018[14] 1354[3] (1521) 1677[3] 4088[7] 4312[16] 4802[3] 4975[4] **>96a 80f<**

**Stop Play (IRE) 3** b f Distinctly North (USA)-Church Mountain (Furry Glen) 1485[7] 1693[3] **>72f< (DEAD)**

**Stories To Tell (USA) 2** ch c Shadeed (USA)-Million Stories (USA) (Exclusive Native (USA)) *2802[2]* 3485[2] **>86f<**

**Stormaway (ITY) 4** ch c Glenstal (USA)-Smurfiusa (USA) (Sharpen Up) **1995:** 4402a[10] **>71f<**

**Storm Bid (USA) 4** b br g Storm Cat (USA)-Slam Bid (USA) (Forli (ARG)) 554[14] 935[14] **>87f<**

**Stormless 5** b g Silly Prices-Phyl's Pet (Aberdeen) 999[9] 1345[4] 1585[2] (2152) 3346[2] (3677) 4249[3] 4582[11] **>60f<**

**Storm Master (IRE) 2** b c Generous (IRE)-Storm Weaver (USA) (Storm Bird (CAN)) 5063a[6] **>65f<**

**Storm Song (USA) 2** b f Summer Squall (USA)-Hum Along (CAN) (Fappiano (USA)) *(4950a)* **>111+a f<**

**Storm Trooper (USA) 3** b c Diesis-Stormette (USA) (Assert) (694) 926[11] 1114[6] 1791[15] 3124[3] 3798[3] 4177[2] **>118f<**

**Storm Wind (IRE) 3** ch g Digamist (USA)-Hilton Gateway (Hello Gorgeous (USA)) 1523[8] 4317[9] **>34f<**

**Story Line 3** ch f In The Wings-Known Line (Known Fact (USA)) 891[2] 1393a[7] 4479[3] 4876[8] 5036[5] **>100df<**

**Stowaway 2** b c Slip Anchor-On Credit (FR) (No Pass No Sale (FR)) (4500) **>93+f<**

**Straffan Gold (USA) 2** b c Lear Fan (USA)-Oro Bianco (USA) (Lyphard's Wish (FR)) 4863[11] 5041[13] **>22f<**

**Straight Thinking (USA) 3** ch c Bering-Sharp Perception (USA) (Sharpen Up) **1995:** *4538[5]* **1996:** *17[7] 1416[5]* 1654[21] 2133[11] 4307[20] 4436[22] 4551[14] 4701[15] **>57a 38f<**

**Strata Florida 3** b g Fearless Action (USA)-Fair Seas (General Assembly (USA)) 3103[4]

**Strategic Choice (USA) 5** b h Alleged (USA)-Danlu (USA) (Danzig (USA)) 1128[2] (2111a) 3070[8] (3915a) 4747a[3] **>128f<**

**Strategic Ploy 3** b f Deploy-Wryneck (Niniski (USA)) 444[10] 614[12] 788[4] 1034[3] (1325) (1421) (1498) 2300[10] 2775[4] 3434[4] **>70f<**

**Strathmore Clear 2** b c Batshoof-Sunflower Seed (Mummy's Pet) *1339[3]* 2073[11] **>65f<**

**Strathtore Dream (IRE) 5** b or br m Jareer (USA)-Beyond Words (Ballad Rock) *607[8] 661[13]*

806[16] 884[8] 1311[8] 1586[6] **>22a 28f<**
**Strat's Legacy 9** b g Chukaroo-State Romance (Free State) **1995:** *4364[4] 4465[4] 4530[5]* **1996:** *15[7] 108[12] 2341[9]* 3218[4] 3802[2] 4121[3] 4307[12] 4587[4] 4789[9] **>52a 51f<**
**Strat's Quest 2** b f Nicholas (USA)-Eagle's Quest (Legal Eagle) 2343[6] 2527[4] 2792[5] 3408[4] 4106[10] 4303[8] (4803) **>64f<**
**Stravano 2** b f Handsome Sailor-La Stravaganza (Slip Anchor) *1827[15] 2307[8] 2781[7]* 3511[9] **>1a 26f<**
**Strawberry Roan (IRE) 2** b f Sadler's Wells (USA)-Doff the Derby (USA) (Master Derby (USA)) (5063a) **>80f<**
**Strazo (IRE) 3** b c Alzao (USA)-Ministra (USA) (Deputy Minister (CAN)) 1142[5] (1465) (2231) 2621[10] **>90f<**
**Streaky Hawk (USA) 4** b g Hawkster (USA)-Veroom Maid (USA) (Distinctive (USA)) **1995:** *4534[5]* **1996:** *154[10] 274[3]* **>64a 71df<**
**Streamline (IRE) 2** ch c River Falls-Kowalski (IRE) (Cyrano de Bergerac) 829[9] 3964[7] 4369[10] 4782[12] **>60f<**
**Street General 2** b c Generous (IRE)-Hotel Street (USA) (Alleged (USA)) 4914[2] **>78f<**
**Street Kendra (FR) 4** b f Kendor (FR)-Street Opera (Sadler's Wells (USA)) 4800[13] **>38f<**
**Strelitza (IRE) 2** b f Taufan (USA)-Strident Note (The Minstrel (CAN)) 2076[9] 2361[9] 3853[6] *4093[3] 4440[3]* ***>39a 52f<***
**Stretarez (FR) 3** b c Saumarez-Street Opera (Sadler's Wells (USA)) (4943a) (5030a) **>126f<**
**Stretching (IRE) 3** br g Contract Law (USA)-Mrs Mutton (Dancers Image (USA)) *4978[7] 5058[7]* **>55a f<**
**Strictly Hard 2** b f Reprimand-Formidable Dancer (Formidable (USA)) 4782[7] 4897[6] 5041[12] **>63f<**
**Stride 2** b f Batshoof-The Strid (IRE) (Persian Bold) 1148[4] 1678[4] (2161) (2387) (2696) 2984[6] 3444[8] 3616[6] 3880[4] (4106) 4298[9] **>75f<**
**Striffolino 4** b g Robellino (USA)-Tizona (Pharly (FR)) 1996[7] 2189[5] **>73df<**
**Strimmer 8** ch h Sharpo-Toppeshamme (USA) (Topsider (USA)) *4411a[2]* ***>71f<***
**Strip Cartoon (IRE) 8** ch g Tate Gallery (USA)-Reveal (Pitskelly) *74[11]* **>26a f<**
**St Rita 3** gr f Bustino-Able Mabel (Absalom) 821[3] 1189[4] 1782[6] 2767[5] **>74df<**
**Struggler 4** b c Night Shift (USA)-Dreamawhile (Known Fact (USA)) 673[3] 927[4] (1321) 1483[2] 2115[16] 3393a[2] 3708[6] (4304) 4660a[7] 4774[12] **>115f<**
**Studio Thirty 4** gr g Rock City-Chepstow Vale (USA) (Key To The Mint (USA)) **1995:** *4379[6] (4415) 4490[3] 4510[6]* **1996:** *752[19]* 853[15] 1496[16] 1696[3] 1903[7] *2081[12] 3611[5]* 3825[13] 4509[16] **>66a 43f<**
**Stuffed 4** ch g Clantime-Puff Pastry (Reform) 587[7] (735) 928[4] 1199[2] 1974[5] 2329[4] 3672[10] 4312[10] 4616[2] (4791) (4811) **>86f<**
**Stunning Prospect (USA) 3** b c Gold Seam (USA)-Stunning Native (USA) (Our Native (USA)) **1995:** *4381[8]* **>49f<**
**Sturgeon (IRE) 2** ch c Caerleon (USA)-Ridge The Times (USA) (Riva Ridge (USA)) 1191[11] 2335[2] 2695[2] **>93f<**
**Stygian (USA) 2** ch f Irish River (FR)-Sin Lucha (USA) (Northfields (USA)) 3129[10] (3581) 4113[18] (4339) 4566[9] 4912[11] **>77f<**
**Style Dancer (IRE) 2** b c Dancing Dissident (USA)-Showing Style (Pas de Seul) 950[8] 3464[7] 3994[11] 4228[4] 4346[3] 4614[2] 4717[9] (4903) **>72f<**
**Stylish Gent 9** br g Vitiges (FR)-Squire's Daughter (Bay Express) *254[9] 284[8] 504[11]* ***>1f<***
**Stylish Ways (IRE) 4** b g Thatching-Style Of Life (USA) (The Minstrel (CAN)) 1107[4] 1975[4] 2114[21] 3296[15] 3984[10] 4687[19] 4811[15] 4994[21] **>78f<**
**Sualtach (IRE) 3** b c Marju (IRE)-Astra Adastra (Mount Hagen (FR)) *391[7] (453)* 676[8] 785[2] 987[4] 1127[7] *(1604) 2170[5] 2532[5]* 2621[8] 3101[2] 3295[8] 3920[9] 4583[11] 4975[8] **>87a 89?f<**
**Suave Star 2** ch f Suave Dancer (USA)-Princess Arabella (Crowned Prince (USA)) 1408[2] *1603[6] 2429[3]* 4495[4] 4795[16] 4883[14] *5057[11]* **>33a 54f<**
**Suave Tern (USA) 5** b h Arctic Tern (USA)-Suavite (USA) (Alleged (USA)) 1138a[7] **>118f<**
**Subfusk 3** b f Lugana Beach-Hush it Up (Tina's Pet) *652[4] 769[12] 835[9] 1455[10]* **>61a 60df<**
**Subterfuge 3** br f Machiavellian (USA)-Sandy Island (Mill Reef (USA)) 4063[6] 4675[4] **>88f<**
**Subtle One (IRE) 3** b f Polish Patriot (USA)-Subtle Change (IRE) (Law Society (USA)) *531[9] 2193[13]* ***>9a 33f<***
**Subzero 4** b c Thatching-Cut No Ice (Great Nephew) 4173a[3] **>101f<**
**Such Boldness 2** b c Persian Bold-Bone China (IRE) (Sadler's Wells (USA)) 4891[8] **>35f<**
**Such Presence 2** ch g Arzanni-Marchiness Drake (Marechal Drake) 4599[11] 4834[6] 5040[14] **>39f<**
**Sudden Spin 6** b g Doulab (USA)-Lightning Legacy (USA) (Super Concorde (USA)) **1995:** *4374[3]* **1996:** *48[5] 474[5]* (625) 1070[4] 3308[7] 3463[8] **>70a 56f<**
**Sudest (IRE) 2** b c Taufan (USA)-Frill (Henbit (USA)) 2972[6] 3494[6] 4118[5] 4602[18] 4864[13] **>74f<**
**Suedoro 6** b m Hard Fought-Bamdoro (Cavo Doro) 617[16] 882[12] 1020[4] 1163[9] 1635[7] 2964[9] **>42f<**
**Sue Me (IRE) 4** b or br g Contract Law (USA)-Pink Fondant (Northfields (USA)) *475[9]* 554[16] 617[12] *1083[7] 1522[6]* 1799[8] 2228[9] 4799[11] 4881[4] *5055[6]* **>50a 64f<**
**Sue's Artiste 5** b m Damister (USA)-Sedova (USA) (Nijinsky (CAN)) **1995:** 4423a[9] **>102f<**
**Sue's Return 4** b f Beveled (USA)-Return to Tara (Homing) 802[6] 1330[7] 1819[15] 2693[8] 2858[2] 3158[5] 3805[3] (4243) 4463[20] 4568[35] **>87f<**
**Sufuf 3** b br f Caerleon (USA)-Deira (NZ) (Sir Tristram) 4360[6] 4622[10] 4813[8] **>68f<**
**Sugarfoot 2** ch c Thatching-Norpella (Northfields (USA)) *(2873)* ***>82+f<***
**Sugarland Express (IRE) 5** br h Roi Danzig (USA)-Island Time (USA) (Bold Hour) **1995:** 4403a[9] **1996:** 1579a[4] **>117f<**
**Sugar Mill 6** b g Slip Anchor-Great Tom (Great Nephew) 2499[6] 2884[7] (3621) (3939) 4431[2] (4580) 4872[3] 5046[5] **>87f<**
**Sugar Plum 2** br f Primo Dominie-Ile de Danse (Ile de Bourbon (USA)) 2611[12] **>43f<**
**Suite Addition (IRE) 2** ch f Common Grounds-Mint Addition (Tate Gallery (USA)) 4787[4] *4999[10]* **>16a 46f<**
**Suite Factors 2** b g Timeless Times (USA)-Uptown Girl (Caruso) 1822[6] 2059[2] 2361[4] 2625[2] 3050[3] (3332) 3803[7] 4230[4] 4425[6] 4749[17] *4999[4]* **>65a 74f<**
**Suitor 3** b c Groom Dancer (USA)-Meliora (Crowned Prince (USA)) 576[13] 2141[7] 3258[10] 3580[3] 3870[5] **>55f<**
**Suivez 6** b g Persian Bold-Butterfly Kiss (Beldale Flutter (USA)) *87[4] 1091[6]* ***>64a 64f<***
**Suivez La (USA) 4** ch f Trempolino (USA)-Arisen (USA) (Mr Prospector (USA)) *1052a[6]* ***>110f<***
**Sujud (IRE) 4** b br f Shaadi (USA)-Sit Elnaas (USA) (Sir Ivor) 767[3] 852[6] 1343[5] 3870[8] **>54f<**
**Sulawesi (IRE) 3** b f In The Wings-Royal Loft (Homing) 3472[5] 3704[5] 4824[9] **>66f<**
**Summer Beauty 3** ch f Cadeaux Genereux-Try the Duchess (Try My Best (USA)) 2996[5] 3513[7] 3949[7] 4560[14] 4915[18] **>72f<**
**Summer Dance 2** b f Sadler's Wells (USA)-Hyabella (Shirley Heights) 4861[2] **>85+f<**
**Summerhill Special (IRE) 5** b m Roi Danzig (USA)-Special Thanks (Kampala) 968[7] 1353[6] 1819[13] 2127[5] 2246[4] 2743[6] 3516[13] 3698[10] 4000[18] 4128[10] 4252[7] 4509[10] (4789) **>61f<**
**Summerosa (USA) 2** ch f Woodman (USA)-Rose Red (USA) (Northern Dancer) 3036[3] 3613[6] 4798[2] **>81tf<**
**Summer Princess 3** ch f Prince Sabo-Lafrowda (Crimson Beau) 591[8] 626[6] 748[14] **>37f<**
**Summer Queen 2** b f Robellino (USA)-Carolside (Music Maestro) 1118[3] 1590[5] *2633[3] 3417[5]* **>62a 62f<**
**Summer Risotto 2** ch f Forzando-Indian Summer (Young Generation) 465[5] 1062[7] 1842[4] 2012[4] (2539) 2797[7] 3659[5] 3871[4] *4093[12] 4423[4]* 4546[12] 4803[2] **>9a 49f<**
**Summer Spell (USA) 3** b br c Alleged (USA)-Summertime Lady (USA) (No Robbery) (447) 1110[2] 3124[10] 3781[3] 4876[6] **>106f<**
**Summer Villa 4** b f Nomination-Maravilla (Mandrake Major) **1995:** *4486[12]* **1996:** *30[8] 111[3] 2320[4]* 2489[3] 2521[5] 2801[6] 3252[10] 3289[9] **>47a 46f<**
**Summerville Wood 2** b c Nomination-Four Love (Pas de Seul) 2279[3] 3114[8] (3330) 3632[5] 3943[3] 4106[16] 4368[3] 4607[7] 4715[4] 4970[6] **>74f<**
**Sun Ballet (IRE) 3** ch f In The Wings-Sunset Village (USA) (Spectacular Bid (USA)) 1573a[3] 2102a[3] 2474a[5] 3531a[5] **>100f<**
**Sunbeam Dance (USA) 2** b c Gone West (USA)-Encorelle (FR) (Arctic Tern (USA)) 2132[W] (4100) 4461[4] 4792[4] 5038[2] **>89f<**
**Sun Circus 4** b f Statoblest-Carmen Maria (Bold Lad (IRE)) *1450[13]* 2162[14] **>48f<**
**Sunday Maelstrom (IRE) 3** b f Distinctly North (USA)-Make Your Mark (On Your Mark) 1000[6] **>38f<**
**Sunday Mail Too (IRE) 4** b f Fayruz-Slick Chick (Shiny Tenth) *607[10] 882[5]* 997[8] 1020[7] 1311[4] 1546[4] (1635) 1865[7] 2023[6] 2154[2] 2490[4] (2910) 3236[5] 3424[8] 3644[8] 3957[4] 4246[11] 4473[12] 4486[15] 4809[10] **>1a 45f<**
**Sunday Market (USA) 2** b c Lear Fan (USA)-Sunday Bazaar (USA) (Nureyev (USA)) 2708[13] 3874[9] **>43f<**
**Sungrove's Best 9** ch g Buzzards Bay-Judann (Some Hand) *654[11] 855[9] 1496[15]* 1651[13] **>7f<**
**Sunless (IRE) 3** b f Bluebird (USA)-Pheopotstown 3021a[7] **>93f<**
**Sunley Secure 3** b g Warrshan (USA)-Brown Velvet (Mansingh (USA)) 448[9] 634[2] 755[8] (885) 1000[4] 1099[8] 1451[4] 1661[3] (1956) 2253[3] 2402[3] 2710[2] 2914[8] **>64f<**
**Sunley Sparkle 8** b m Sunley Builds-Royal Darwin (Royal Palm) *1132a[2]* ***>42f<***
**Sunny Sample (IRE) 2** ch c Royal Academy (USA)-Sentimental Mood (ITY) (Dunbeath (USA)) 4038a[3]
**Sun O'Tirol (IRE) 2** b c Tirol-Nous (Le Johnstan) 865[5] 1191[9] 2224[8] (2733) 3230[4] 3616[9] 3762[8] 4375[10] **>68f<**
**Sunset Harbour (IRE) 3** br f Prince Sabo-City Link Pet (Tina's Pet) *131[2] 142[3] 218[5] 307[3] 335[2] 488[5] 644[7]* 888[12] 1172[11] 1840[13] 2500[3] 2578[7] (2800) 2910[4] 3415[3] 3883[8] **>63a 51f<**
**Sunset Reigns (IRE) 3** b f Taufan (USA)-More Candy (Ballad Rock) 1911a[3] (2472a) 2816a[2] 3562a[6] 4280a[5] **>108f<**
**Sunset Wells (USA) 3** b f Sadler's Wells (USA)-

Alysunset (USA) (Alydar (USA)) 820[2] 1189[2] 2610[4] *3063[9]* **>57a 75f<**
**Sunshack 5** b h Rainbow Quest (USA)-Suntrap (USA) (Roberto (USA)) *3567a[2]* 4040a[3] **>126f<**
**Sun Sweet (ITY) 2** b c Primo Dominie-Elettra (ITY) (L'Emigrant (USA)) 4163a[3]
**Supamova (USA) 3** b f Seattle Slew (USA)-Maximova (FR) (Green Dancer (USA)) 1901[4] 2399[2] 3935[3] (4124) 4445[14] **>84f<**
**Suparoy 3** b g Midyan (USA)-Champ d'Avril (Northfields (USA)) **1995:** *4439[13] 4538[4]* **1996:** *11[6] 56[5] 280[2] 348[8] 459[2] 849[13] 1444[10]* **>49a 55df<**
**Superbelle 2** b f Damister (USA)-Nell of The North (USA) (Canadian Gil (CAN)) 4242[3] 4605[2] **>79f<**
**Super Benz 10** ch g Hello Gorgeous (USA)-Investiture (Welsh Pageant) **1995:** *4432[11] 4539[4]* **1996:** *(88) 121[5] (259) (340) (480)* (610) 1425[10] **>76a 82f<**
**Superbird 3** b f Superpower-Gymcrak Lovebird (Taufan (USA)) *1474[8]* 1762[7] 2026[11] **>44f<**
**Superbit 4** b g Superpower-On A Bit (Mummy's Pet) **1995:** *4371[4] 4428[6] 4484[3]* **1996:** *122[12] 2748[7] 3152[8]* 3331[2] 3851[3] (4045) 4205[3] 4356[15] 4610[5] 4727[7] (4828) **>52a 66f<**
**Superboots 2** b f Superpower-Wellington Bear (Dragonara Palace (USA)) 1858[5] *2371[7] 2926[7]* 3448[11] 4223[8] 4562[15] **>33a 42f<**
**Supercal 2** gr f Environment Friend-Sorayah (Persian Bold) 916[6] 1346[6] (1513) (1815) 2073[12] **>64f<**
**Supercharmer 2** ch g Charmer-Surpassing (Superlative) 829[8] 1989[3] 2210[4] 3687[6] 3962[4] 4182[7] 4495[5] **>69f<**
**Supercool 5** ch g Superlative-Florentynna Bay (Aragon) **1995:** *4357[11] 4378[7]* **1996:** *207[8] 246[9] 328[6]* **>21a 68f<**
**Superensis 6** ch g Sayf El Arab (USA)-Superlife (USA) (Super Concorde (USA)) 4237[13] **>40f<**
**Superfrills 3** b f Superpower-Pod's Daughter (IRE) (Tender King) 1429[4] 1761[11] 2151[8] 3100[2] 3624[5] 4075[21] 4610[13] **>10a 56f<**
**Super Gascon 4** b c Lesotho (USA)-Superstition (Touching Wood (USA)) 2477a[2] **>114f<**
**Super Gift (IRE) 3** b f Darshaan-Speciality Package 794a[8] **>97f<**
**Supergold (IRE) 3** ch c Keen-Superflash (Superlative) **1995:** *4485[8]* **1996:** *234[8]* **>32a f<**
**Super Hero 4** ch g Superlative-Beaute Fatale (Hello Gorgeous (USA)) *549[9]* 2617[8] 2971[2] **>42f<**
**Super High 4** b g Superlative-Nell of The North (USA) (Canadian Gil (CAN)) 879[12] 1418[12] *1811[3] 2170[3] 2574[16] (3419) 3627[3] 4078[2] 4489[10]* 4812[3] **>83a 56f<**
**Superhoo 5** b g Superlative-Boo Hoo (Mummy's Pet) 1803[15] 2423[7] 4321[7] **>27f<**
**Superior Force 3** ch g Superlative-Gleeful (Sayf El Arab (USA)) 583[13] 1074[3] 1485[5] 1654[7] 2032[13] *(2158) 2253[2] 2689[3] 3136[6]* 3501[6] *3877[8] 3991[8]* (4232) 4354[9] 4682[21] **>69a 66f<**
**Superior Premium 2** br c Forzando-Devils Dirge (Song) (639) 996[2] 1699[2] 2112[6] 2726[6] 4247[2] (4579) 4677[5] 4873[5] **>90f<**
**Superlao (BEL) 4** b f Bacalao (USA)-Princess of Import (Import) **1995:** *4525[12]* **1996:** *41[6] 64[6] 117[9] 202[6] 231[9] 514[8] 664[13]* 1681[3] 2156[3] 2324[4] 2686[9] 2787[4] 3261[7] 3506[8] 3698[4] 3993[17] **>51a 46f<**
**Supermick 5** ch g Faustus (USA)-Lardana (Burglar) 2251[8] 2556[3] (2891) (3141) 3318[3] *4092[16] 4307[5]* 4563[16] **>49a 44f<**
**Supermister 3** br g Damister (USA)-Superfina (USA) (Fluorescent Light (USA)) 734[6] 1042[17] 3102[9] 3289[10] 3780[18] **>45f<**
**Supermodel 4** ch f Unfuwain (USA)-Well Off (Welsh Pageant) *73[2] 2794[5]* 3356[4] *4332[3]* **>62a 61f<**
**Super Monarch 2** ch c Cadeaux Genereux-Miss Fancy That (USA) (The Minstrel (CAN)) 3757[7] **>73f<**
**Superoo 10** b g Superlative-Shirleen (Daring Display (USA)) **1995:** *(4362) (4457) 4539[13]* **1996:** *121[6]* **>72a 75f<**
**Super Park 4** b g Superpower-Everingham Park (Record Token) *854[12] 1677[4]* 2047[10] 2434[4] 2763[4] 2925[6] 3606[3] 3967[8] 4240[15] 4701[8] 4882[9] **>55f<**
**Superpride 4** b g Superpower-Lindrake's Pride (Mandrake Major) 806[4] 991[13] 1538[6] 1848[3] 2154[10] 2524[4] 2901[4] 3161[15] (3680) 3817[6] 4316[2] 4688[24] 4768[18] 4909[14] **>71f<**
**Superquest 2** ch c Superlative-More or Less (Morston (FR)) *1489[4] 1683[3]* 1878[4] 3046[6] 3208[5] *3417[6]* **>42a 57f<**
**Super Rocky 7** b g Clantime-Starproof (Comedy Star (USA)) **1995:** *(4542)* **1996:** *(16) 173[4] 316[7] 700[5]* 750[2] 951[4] 1161[8] *1492[6] 2410[3]* 2598[3] 2908[2] 3122[6] 3851[8] **>72a 70f<**
**Super Saint 2** b g Superpower-Martyrdom (USA) (Exceller (USA)) 557[6] *2083[5] 2781[4]* 3577[4] 3771[3] 4319[4] 4440[7] **>33a 61f<**
**Super Scravels 2** ch f Superlative-Scravels Saran (IRE) (Indian King (USA)) 1169[7] 1880[3] *2083[7] 2512[8]* 2850[2] 3092[3] 3455[5] 3943[8] 4783[7] **>12a 46f<**
**Super Serenade 7** b g Beldale Flutter (USA)-Super Melody (Song) 1890[5] 2284[4] (2379) 2678[8] 3084[5] 3471[4] 3802[8] 3980[6] **>65f<**
**Super Sheriff 2** b c Superpower-Spinney Hill (Dominion) 990[5] 1086[9] 1320[7] **>46f<**
**Super Sonata 4** b f Interrex (CAN)-Super Lady (Averof) *2748[10] 3294[15]* 3579[5] 3883[14] *4094[12] 4130[15]* ***>39da 42f<***
**Supertop 8** b or br g High Top-Myth (Troy) 4249[8] **>61?f<**
**Suplizi (IRE) 5** b h Alzao (USA)-Sphinx (GER) (Alpenkonig (GER)) (828) 1176[4] **>106f<**
**Supply And Demand 2** b g Belmez (USA)-Sipsi Fach (Prince Sabo) 4118[2] 4369[5] 4494[5] 4760[11] 5040[6] **>91f<**
**Supreme Commander (FR) 3** b c Saumarez-Autocratic (Tyrant) **1995:** (4562a) **1996:** 621a[4] 1057a[7] 2844a[6] **>108f<**
**Supreme Desire 8** gr m Grey Desire-Fire Mountain (Dragonara Palace (USA)) 2386[6] 3049[8] 3579[9] 3957[10] 4828[11] **>1a 34df<**
**Supreme Illusion (AUS) 3** ch f Rory's Jester (AUS)-Counterfeit Coin (AUS) (Comeram (FR)) *160[7] 224[7] 458[13] 859[4] 1027[7] 1443[4]* 1721[6] *1992[8]* ***>38a 31f<***
**Supreme Maimoon 2** b c Jareer (USA)-Princess Zena (Habitat) 4962[6] **>65f<**
**Supreme Power 3** ch c Superpower-Spinner (Blue Cashmere) **1995:** *4361[5] 4383[6] 4518[6]* **>62a 75f<**
**Supreme Scholar 3** b f Superpower-Double Decree (Sayf El Arab (USA)) 473[12]
**Supreme Sound 2** b c Superlative-Sing Softly (Luthier) 3682[10] 4041[2] (4834) **>76f<**
**Supreme Star (USA) 5** b g Gulch (USA)-Just A Game (Tarboosh (USA)) **1995:** *4411[3] 4455[3]* **1996:** *1710[7]* 2547[12] 2709[2] 2973[6] 3260[6] 3514[6] 4048[6] **>63a 74f<**
**Supreme Thought 4** b f Emarati (USA)-Who's That Girl (Skyliner) 3167[5] 3993[5] 4802[7] **>62f<**
**Supremism 2** b c Be My Chief (USA)-Ever Welcome (Be My Guest (USA)) 2335[5] 2887[3] **>79f<**
**Surako (GER) 3** bl c Konigsstuhl (GER)-Surata (GER) (Lagunas) (795a) 2109a[2] 2668a[2] 3203a[4] 3913a[3] **>117f<**
**Suranom (IRE) 4** b c Alzao (USA)-Gracieuse Majeste (FR) (Saint Cyrien (FR)) 828[3] (1392a) 1706[5] (2278a) 2864[3] 3917a[5] **>109f<**
**Sure Care 5** ch m Caerleon (USA)-Sure Gold (Glint of Gold) **1995:** *4449[7]* **>72f<**
**Suresnes (USA) 4** b c Lomond (USA)-Saison (USA) (L'Enjoleur (CAN)) **1995:** 4404a[2] **>102f<**
**Surf City 3** ch g Rock City-Waveguide (Double Form) 774[5] 934[12] 1435[4] 2139[6] 2432[4] 3973[16] 4591[12] *5058[4]* **>47a 69f<**
**Surprise Event 2** b c Tragic Role (USA)-Eleckydo (Electric) 1892[8] 2382[3] 2759[3] 2948[4] *3629[4] 3795[6]* ***>46a 60f<***
**Surprise Guest (IRE) 5** ch g Be My Guest (USA)-Olderfleet (Steel Heart) *104[9]* **>60da 46f<**
**Surprise Mission 4** ch g Clantime-Indigo (Primo Dominie) 735[16] 1430[5] 1974[3] 2349[8] 2694[14] 3085[8] (4180) 4452[4] 4616[10] 4791[11] **>81f<**
**Surrey Dancer 8** b g Shareef Dancer (USA)-Juliette Marny (Blakeney) 4582[14] 4810[12] 5054[5] **>75a 56f<**
**Sussex Gorse 5** ch g Arrasas (USA)-Testarossa (Tower Walk) *337[11] 409[11] 485[P] 668[14]* 5052[10] **>16f<**
**Suvalu (USA) 4** b g Woodman (USA)-Danlu (USA) (Danzig (USA)) *(248) 333[7] 416[7] 853[14]* 1037[14] 1418[14] **>65a 79f<**
**Sveltana 4** b f Soviet Star (USA)-Sally Brown (Posse (USA)) 765[16] 2862[7] 3148[11] 3856[8] **>81df<**
**Swain (IRE) 4** b c Nashwan (USA)-Love Smitten (CAN) (Key To The Mint (USA)) 906a[3] (1794) 2480a[2] (4295a) 4662a[4] 4955a[3] **>129f<**
**Swallow Breeze 2** b f Salse (USA)-Pica (Diesis) 2404[10] 2967[5] 3312[4] 3762[3] (4361) 4973[8] **>69f<**
**Swallows Dream (IRE) 5** ch g Bluebird (USA)-Gay Fantasy (Troy) *650[2]* 953[5] 2128[7] **>82f<**
**Swan At Whalley 4** b g Statoblest-My Precious Daisy (Sharpo) *514[4] 652[8] 750[3] 835[11] 911[7]* 1342[2] 1545[2] 1889[2] (2386) 2395[W] 2564[2] 2908[3] 2960[W] 3352[W] 4610[18] 4727[8] 4765[18] **>44a 46f<**
**Swandale Flyer 4** ch g Weldnaas (USA)-Misfire (Gunner B) *345[8] 399[6] 1585[4]* 1977[11] 3426[6] 3589[6] 3677[5] 4249[13] 4483[6] 5008[10] **>12a 37f<**
**Swan Hunter 3** b c Sharrood (USA)-Cache (Bustino) (560) 772[2] 2576[6] 3760[6] 4067[17] **>82f<**
**Swan Island 2** ch f Hubbly Bubbly (USA)-Green's Cassatt (USA) (Apalachee (USA)) 3493[6] 4100[10] 4370[W] 4564[6] 4883[2] **>68f<**
**Swedish Invader 5** b g Jareer (USA)-Nihad (Alleged (USA)) 1685[16] 2313[14] **>39f<**
**Sweeping Stakes (ITY) 2** ch f Miswaki Tern (USA)-Sweeping Away (ITY) (Captain James) 4408a[3]
**Sweeping Statement 2** b f Statoblest-Sweep Along (IRE) (Persian Bold) *2153[4]* 2387[4] *2750[6] (2850)* 3227[6] **>27a 52f<**
**Sweet Allegiance 6** b m Alleging (USA)-Child of Grace (King's Leap) **1995:** *4409[12]* **1996:** *106[4] 1173[12]* 3274[10] 3606[10] 3861[8] 4422[10] **>48a 29f<**
**Sweet Amoret 3** b f Forzando-Primrose Way (Young Generation) 522[5] *(655) 899[5] 1490[13] 2303[10] 2859[6]* 3244[6] 3358[2] 3654[5] 4070[12] 4237[12] 4784[10] 4898[10] **>53a 55f<**
**Sweet Bettsie 2** b f Presidium-Sweet and Sure (Known Fact (USA)) 4475[9] 4825[5] **>70f<**
**Sweet Disorder (IRE) 6** br m Never so Bold-Mists of Avalon (USA) (Nureyev (USA)) **1995:** *4444[7] 4506[11]* **1996:** *23[6] 82[8]* **>36a 68f<**
**Sweet Emmaline 2** b f Emarati (USA)-Chapelfell (Pennine Walk) *(557)* 1103[4] 1318[3] 1653[6] 2595[8] **>62f<**
**Sweeten Up 2** b f Shirley Heights-Honeybeta (Habitat) 4605[3] 4890[2] **>77f<**
**Sweet Magic 5** ch g Sweet Monday-Charm Bird

(Daring March) 928[13] 1113[4] 1630[5] 1790[17] 2292[12] 4220[7] **>88df<**
**Sweet Mate** **4** ch g Komaite (USA)-Be My Sweet (Galivanter) **1995:** *4447[2] 4478[3] 4512[6]* **1996:** *155[4] (213) 253[2] 403[4] 413[4] 607[9] 4865[12]* **>65a 50f<**
**Sweet Nature (IRE)** **3** b f Classic Secret (USA)-So Kind (Kind of Hush) 525[4] 686[7] *897[7]* **>69a 72f<**
**Sweetness Herself** **3** ch f Unfuwain (USA)-No Sugar Baby (FR) (Crystal Glitters (USA)) 687[3] 915[4] 1324[4] 1773[14] 2943[9] (3459) (4563) (4804) (4919) (5047) **>89f<**
**Sweet Noble (IRE)** **7** ch g The Noble Player (USA)-Penny Candy (Tamerlane) 852[15]
**Sweet Pavlova (USA)** **4** b f Zilzal (USA)-Meringue Pie (USA) (Silent Screen (USA)) 1066[9] 3094[3] 3496[9] **>61f<**
**Sweet Romeo** **6** ch g Local Suitor (USA)-Ladoucette (Bustino) **1995:** *4516[11]* **>37a f<**
**Sweet Seranade (IRE)** **3** b f Ballad Rock-Little Honey (Prince Bee) *428[8] 655[10]* **>7a f<**
**Sweet Seventeen** **3** gr f Touch of Grey-Westminster Waltz (Dance In Time (CAN)) 2970[7] 3665[5] 3851[9] **>35f<**
**Sweet Supposin (IRE)** **5** b h Posen (USA)-Go Honey Go (General Assembly (USA)) **1995:** *4390[7] (4445) 4527[2]* **1996:** *61[11] 105[5] 162[2] (216) (305) 379[6] (498) 641[15] (1081) 2169[2] 2749[4] 3955[8] 4575[6] 4894[4]* **>78a 67df<**
**Sweet Times** **3** ch f Riverman (USA)-Affection Affirmed (USA) (Affirmed (USA)) 2718[4] *3078[6]* **>28a 64f<**
**Sweet Wilhelmina** **3** b f Indian Ridge-Henpot (IRE) (Alzao (USA)) **1995:** *(4365) (4462)* **1996:** *3830[10]* 4109[12] 4498[2] **>78+a 59f<**
**Swift** **2** ch c Sharpo-Three Terns (USA) (Arctic Tern (USA)) 3407[12] 4118[8] 4210[7] 4517[6] (4767) 4912[7] 4966[6] **>66f<**
**Swift Fandango (USA)** **3** b c Lear Fan (USA)-Danlu (USA) (Danzig (USA)) 1329[9] 2888[7] 3229[4] 3594[15] **>97f<**
**Swift Gulliver (IRE)** **2** ch c Gulch (USA)-Aminata (Glenstal (USA)) 4023a[7] **>85f<**
**Swift Maiden** **3** gr f Sharrood (USA)-Gunner Girl (Gunner B) *873[7]* 995[16] 1302[9] (1523) **>79f<**
**Swift Move** **4** ch f Move Off-Phyl's Pet (Aberdeen) *3960[6]*
***Swift Refusal*** **2** ch f Emarati (USA)-Dark Hush (Kind of Hush) 465[2] 1014[2] 1959[4] 2323[6] 3129[13] 4230[9] 4545[9] 4786[10] **>63f<**
**Swiftway** **2** ch g Anshan-Solemn Occasion (USA) (Secreto (USA)) 4245[6] 4458[3] 4835[P] **>58f<**
**Swifty Nifty (IRE)** **3** b f Runnett-Swift Verdict (My Swallow) *881[7]* 1312[9] 1608[8] 2049[14] 2176[8] 2800[3] 3135[9] 3256[3] 3453[8] 4075[10] 4229[8] 4460[15] 4727[11] **>31f<**
**Swinging Sixties (IRE)** **5** b g Fairy King (USA)-La Bella Fontana (Lafontaine (USA)) (469) 547[10] 912[2] **>73f<**
**Swinging The Blues (IRE)** **2** b c Bluebird (USA)-Winsong Melody (Music Maestro) 4123[8] 4884[8] **>47f<**
**Swings'N'Things (USA)** **4** b f Shernazar-Quickshine (USA) (The Minstrel (CAN)) *4092[15]* **>59f<**
**Swing West (USA)** **2** b c Gone West (USA)-Danlu (USA) (Danzig (USA)) 4801[12] **>54f<**
**Swino** **2** b g Forzando-St Helena (Monsanto (FR)) 490[3] 557[2] 685[2] 848[2] 1003[6] 1801[2] 2361[2] 2755[2] (3291) 3792[7] **>79f<**
**Swiss Coast (IRE)** **2** b c Mujadil (USA)-Rose A Village (River Beauty) 1537[2] 2295[5] 2755[3] 3224[3] 3411[4] 3687[2] 3963[2] 4224[7] **>80f<**
**Swiss Law** **2** b c Machiavellian (USA)-Seductress (Known Fact (USA)) 3706[2] 4488[10] **>93f<**
**Swith Water (IRE)** **2** b f Classic Music (USA)-Snow Storm (ITY) (Ercolano (USA)) 2666a[2]
**Sword Arm** **2** b c Be My Guest (USA)-Gai Bulga (Kris) 3493[4] 3873[4] 4204[2] **>72f<**
**Swordking (IRE)** **7** ch g Kris-Reine Mathilde (USA) (Vaguely Noble) *60[9] 236[3] 283[3] 367[6] 400[3] 422[3] 602[2] 656[2] 1095[5]* **>46a 46f<**
**Swynford Charmer** **2** ch g Charmer-Qualitairess (Kampala) 4715[21] *4976[10]* **>44f<**
**Swynford Dream** **3** b g Statoblest-Qualitair Dream (Dreams to Reality (USA)) 832[8] 1188[2] 1501[10] 1818[12] 2694[8] 3085[14] 3693[6] 3932[2] (4521) 4679[11] 4772[3] 4869[10] **>92f<**
**Swynford Flyer** **7** b m Valiyar-Qualitairess (Kampala) **1995:** *4388[8] 4438[2] 4532[12] 4544[4]* **1996:** *66[4] 82[6] 116[5] 165[7] 186[9] 246[6]* **>31a 39f<**
**Swynford Supreme** **3** ch g Statoblest-Comtec Princess (Gulf Pearl) 2899[5] 3103[3] 3298[7] 3619[17] 4437[9] *4977[7]* **>46a 60f<**
**Sycamore Boy (USA)** **2** ch c Woodman (USA)-Kafiyah (USA) (Shadeed (USA)) 2852[5] **>79f<**
**Sycamore Lodge (IRE)** **5** ch g Thatching-Bell Tower (Lyphard's Wish (FR)) 451[2] 496[3] 629[3] 827[4] *854[4] 991[2]* 1425[5] 1789[3] 1962[5] 2162[6] (2316) 2722[6] **>61a 73f<**
**Sylvan Celebration** **5** b m Sylvan Express-Footstool (Artaius (USA)) *542[7]* 609[9] **>15a 22f<**
**Sylvan Dancer (IRE)** **2** b br f Dancing Dissident (USA)-Unspoiled (Tina's Pet) *3114[2]* 3464[3] 4062[8] 4762[9] **>60f<**
**Sylvan Heights** **3** b c Reprimand-Shibui (Shirley Heights) 1711[15] 2579[14] 2786[4] **>49f<**
**Sylvania Lights** **2** b f Emarati (USA)-Harmony Park (Music Boy) 465[W] *2635[7] 2795[9]* 3336[W] **>15a 24f<**
**Sylvan Jubilacion** **2** b c Sylvan Express-This Sensation (Balidar) 4369[14] 4891[18] **>31f<**
**Sylvan Princess** **3** b f Sylvan Express-Ela-Yianni-Mou (Anfield) 560[5] 998[7] 1691[6] 1908[4] 2130[W] 2320[3] (2785) (3102) (3165) 3246[4] (3286) 3634[3] (3703) 3995[6] 4064[7] 4329[10] **>72f<**
**Sylvan Sabre (IRE)** **7** b g Flash of Steel-Flute (FR) (Luthier) *2628[7]* 3443[10] 3808[22] **>67a 44f<**
**Sylva Paradise (IRE)** **3** b c Dancing Dissident (USA)-Brentsville (USA) (Arctic Tern (USA)) 646[14] 978[2] 1327[4] 1615[3] 2143[2] (2950) 3038[2] 3232[15] 4116[2] 4314[28] 4442[4] **>112f<**
**Sylvella** **3** b f Lear Fan (USA)-Suprematie (FR) (Gay Mecene (USA)) *1182[11]* 1908[5] 2542[5] 2859[4] 3357[2] 3705[7] *4080[3] 4437[3]* 4752[12] **>55a 56f<**
**Symboli Kildare (IRE)** **3** b c Kaldoun (FR)-Quiche (Formidable (USA)) 4280a[4] **>107f<**
**Symmetrical** **7** ch g Kris-Flawless Image (USA) (The Minstrel (CAN)) *3877[16]*
**Symonds Inn** **2** ch c In The Wings-Shining Eyes (USA) (Mr Prospector (USA)) 3349[3] 3668[2] 4792[3] **>91f<**

**T**

**Taahhub (IRE)** **6** b g Nordico (USA)-Undiscovered (Tap On Wood) *312[11]* **>53a 52f< (DEAD)**
**Ta Awun (USA)** **3** b f Housebuster (USA)-Barakat (Bustino) 1357[2] (3041) 3497[3] 4063[7] 4467[10] **>104df<**
**Tabl (IRE)** **3** b f Nashwan (USA)-Idle Gossip (USA) (Lyphard (USA)) 1160[4] 1670[5] 2789[3] **>64f<**
**Tablets of Stone (IRE)** **3** b g Contract Law (USA)-Remember Mulvilla (Ballad Rock) **1995:** *4439[10]* **1996:** *3074[4] 3586[7]* 3849[4] *4998[8] 5053[6]* ***>46a 54f<***
**Tabriz** **3** b f Persian Heights-Faisalah (Gay Mecene (USA)) *(509)* 693[8] 915[3] 1185[W] 1526[5] 1861[8] 3133[9] *3600[2] 3882[4] 4092[8] 4868[9]* ***>59a 60f<***
**Tachycardia** **4** ch f Weldnaas (USA)-Gold Ducat (Young Generation) *2156[12]* 2686[5] 3097[4] 3993[10] 4372[9] **>44a 49f<**
**Tadellal (IRE)** **5** ch m Glint of Gold-Meissarah (USA) (Silver Hawk (USA)) **1995:** *4376[5] 4452[4]* **1996:** *27[7] 319[5] 4986[13]* **>42a 63f<**
**Tadeo** **3** ch g Primo Dominie-Royal Passion (Ahonoora) 989[3] 1974[9] 2143[8] 2292[5] 2676[2] 2889[12] 3296[11] 3432[21] 4452[7] (4561) (4679) 4869[11] 5044[5] **>109f<**
**Tael of Silver** **4** b f Today and Tomorrow-Schula (Kala Shikari) *155[12] 218[7] 601[5]* 868[9] *1083[8] (2320)* 2773[2] 3148[4] 3334[12] 3833[5] 3995[15] 4560[4] 4831[6] 5004[7] **>34a 67f<**
**Tafahhus** **4** b g Green Desert (USA)-Mileeha (USA) (Blushing Groom (FR)) **1995:** *4478[9] 4508[10] 4536[8]* **1996:** *14[11] 120[9] 170[6] 178[4] 225[3] 266[6] 451[14]* 632[3] 711[12] 928[21] 2017[4] 2403[6] (2791) 2957[6] 3140[2] (3285) 3313[7] 3827[10] 4215[7] 4341[3] **>55a 70f<**
**Tagatay** **3** b g Nomination-Salala (Connaught) **1995:** *4408[11]* **1996:** *516[6] 1042[10]* (3116) **>26a 47f<**
**Tagula (IRE)** **3** b c Taufan (USA)-Twin Island (IRE) (Standaan (FR)) 727[3] 1141a[3] 1574a[5] (4378) 4857a[5] **>119f<**
**Taharqa (IRE)** **3** b c Sadler's Wells (USA)-Too Phar (Pharly (FR)) 2365[2] 2744[6] 3042[6] 3398[9] 4448[2] **>80f<**
**Tahya (USA)** **3** ch f Elmaamul (USA)-Tatwij (USA) (Topsider (USA)) **1995:** *4529[3]* **1996:** *67[8] 276[3] 377[3] 463[7]* **>50a 62f<**
**Taiki Blizzard (USA)** **5** b h Seattle Slew (USA)-Tree of Knowledge (Sassafras (FR)) **1995:** 4471a[4] **1996:** 1134a[2] 1952a[2] 4956a[13] **>125f<**
**Tailwind** **2** ch c Clantime-Casbar Lady (Native Bazaar) *1982[6]* 2374[7] 3502[10] 4049[4] 4324[2] 4424[3] 4614[5] 4880[13] **>68f<**
**Taipan (IRE)** **4** b c Last Tycoon-Alidiva (Chief Singer) (564) 941[2] (1353) (2476a) **>112f<**
**Tajrebah (USA)** **2** b f Dayjur (USA)-Petrava (NZ) (Imposing (AUS)) 4570[9] 4706[8] 4887[3] **>66f<**
**Takaddum (USA)** **8** ch h Riverman (USA)-Lyphard's Holme (USA) (Lyphard (USA)) 497a[2] **>104f<**
**Takadou (IRE)** **5** br h Double Schwartz-Taka (Blakeney) 927[10] 1321[3] 1630[8] 2292[10] 2545[7] 3946[9] 4466[16] 4561[5] 4687[9] 4772[11] 4811[14] 4994[8] 5044[11] **>85f<**
**Takapuna (IRE)** **3** ch f Be My Native (USA)-Tenoria (Mansingh (USA)) **1995:** *4375[9] 4477[2] 4518[9]* **>52a 67f<**
**Take Note (IRE)** **3** b c Don't Forget Me-Verthumna (Indian King (USA)) **1995:** *4529[4]* **1996:** *11[8] 637[12]* 1514[17] **>58da 52f<**
**Take Notice** **3** b c Warning-Metair (Laser Light) 3262[4] 3472[10] 3788[3] 4108[11] 4592[12] **>80df<**
**Takeshi (IRE)** **4** b f Cadeaux Genereux-Taplow (Tap On Wood) **1995:** *4382[2] 4457[6] 4493[7]* **1996:** *109[9] 217[4] 328[10]* **>66a 68f<**
**Take Two** **8** b g Jupiter Island-Dancing Daughter (Dance In Time (CAN)) **1995:** *4526[10]* **1996:** *2847[2]* 3309[6] 3575[6] **>45a 47f<**
**Takhlid (USA)** **5** b h Nureyev (USA)-Savonnerie (USA) (Irish River (FR)) *3419[11] 4811[18]* 4994[24] 5042[19] **>59a 50f<**
**Takin (GER)** **5** b h Formidable (USA)-Tosca Rhea (GER) (Song) 3572a[3] (4169a) 4409a[9] 4743a[3] **>111f<**
**Taking Liberties (IRE)** **3** b f Royal Academy (USA)-Lady Liberty (NZ) (Noble Bijou (USA)) 710[6] **>55f<**
**Takkatamm (USA)** **4** ch c Forty Niner (USA)-Relasure (USA) (Relaunch (USA)) 1410[3] 1768[6]

**>108f<**

**Talalathath (FR) 4** b g Soviet Star (USA)-Mashmoon (USA) (Habitat) 495[5] 641[13] 887[9] 1190[8] 1625[3] 2340[5] 2412[3] 2917[2] (3281) (3469) 3861[3] 4243[3] 4463[6] 4686[3] **>79f<**

**Talented Ting (IRE) 7** ch g Hatim (USA)-An Tig Gaelige (Thatch (USA)) **1995:** *4356[6] 4516[4]* **1996:** *23[12] 80[8] 440[27]* 537[7] 615[10] 1037[11] 1868[2] 2014[2] 2678[5] 2901[7] 3111[14] 3646[4] 3958[15] **>50da 66f<**

**Talib (USA) 2** b c Silver Hawk (USA)-Dance For Lucy (USA) (Dance Bid (USA)) 4261[5] 4500[6] **>71f<**

**Talisman (IRE) 2** b c Silver Kite (USA)-Sports Post Lady (IRE) (M Double M (USA)) 1169[6] 1766[5] 2398[5] 4303[10] 4375[8] **>56f<**

**Talloires (USA) 6** ch h Trempolino (USA)-Logiciel (Known Fact (USA)) *4955a[6]* ***>124f<***

**Tallulah Belle 3** b f Crowning Honors (CAN)-Fine a Leau (USA) (Youth (USA)) *529[7] 655[8] 834[9] 1043[2]* 1162[6] 2026[3] 2180[4] 2507[17] 2893[4] 3257[9] 3286[5] 3606[8] 3852[7] 3966[3] 4497[2] **>19a 54f<**

**Tal-Y-Llyn (IRE) 2** ch c Common Grounds-Welsh Fantasy (Welsh Pageant) 4619[5] 4807[2] 4918[4] **>80f<**

**Tamandu 6** b m Petoski-Gohar (USA) (Barachois (CAN)) *37[5] 228[6] 4877[10]* ***>45a 18f<***

**Tamayaz (CAN) 4** b c Gone West (USA)-Minstrelsy (USA) (The Minstrel (CAN)) *(375a) (436a) 536a[5] 1509[4]* 2038[3] 2471a[3] (3431) 4281a[6] 4956a[6] **>119a 126+f<**

**Tame Deer 4** ch c Hadeer-Ever Welcome (Be My Guest (USA)) *110[4] (126) 330[4] 368[8] 425[5] 718[7]* 995[15] 1665[3] 1830[8] *2085[4] 2369[4] 2940[6] 3091[5] 3601[3] (3854)* 3981[8] **>69a 55f<**

**Tamhid (USA) 3** b c Gulch (USA)-Futuh (USA) (Diesis) 736[4] 1187[4] 2050[14] 3503[3] 3996[2] 4325[2] **>107f<**

**Tamim (USA) 7** gr h Topsider (USA)-Passamaquoddy (USA) (Drone) *432a[3]* **>74a f<**

**Tamnia 3** br f Green Desert (USA)-Tanouma (USA) (Miswaki (USA)) 572[12] 1060a[10] 2225[2] 3127[3] 4135[6] 4520[3] 4757[7] **>106f<**

**Tamure (IRE) 4** b c Sadler's Wells (USA)-Three Tails (Blakeney) 4662a[14] **>128f<**

**Tanaasa (IRE) 2** b c Sadler's Wells (USA)-Mesmerize (Mill Reef (USA)) 4884[3] **>67f<**

**Tancia (ITY) 3** ch f Welsh Guide-Terza Luna (ITY) (Brook) 908a[3]

**Tancred Mischief 5** b m Northern State (USA)-Mischievous Miss (Niniski (USA)) *558[4]* 1070[W] 1542[5] 1847[6] 2216[5] **>44f<**

**Tandridge (IRE) 4** gr f Kefaah (USA)-Roof (Thatch (USA)) *409[8] 499[11] 1533[12]* ***>15a 40f<***

**Tango King 2** b c Suave Dancer (USA)-Be My Queen (Be My Guest (USA)) 3615[11] 4050[9] 4386[7] **>62f<**

**Tango Teaser 3** b br f Shareef Dancer (USA)-Ever Genial (Brigadier Gerard) 1864[5] *3064[11]* **>6a 48f<**

**Tangshan (CAN) 2** ch f Zilzal (USA)-Manzanares (USA) (Sir Ivor) 4697[5] **>68f<**

**Taniyar (FR) 4** b g Glenstal (USA)-Taeesha (Mill Reef (USA)) **1995:** *4418[4]* **1996:** *79[11] 175[4] 221[8] 274[5] 387[4] 1809[8] 2506[5]* 2756[9] *2939[5] 3630[9] 4000[8]* 4703[4] 4868[3] **>39a 64f<**

**Tanseeq 5** b g Green Desert (USA)-Kawkeb (USA) (Vaguely Noble) *4781[12]* **>28a 64f<**

**Taome (IRE) 2** b f Roi Danzig (USA)-Blue Bell Lady (Dunphy) 1499[3] 1989[8] (2237) 2539[3] **>66f<**

**Tap On Tootsie 4** b f Faustus (USA)-My Tootsie (Tap On Wood) **1995:** *4449[3] 4516[10]* **1996:** *254[6] 346[4] 373[8] 398[7]* **>51da 60f<**

**Tappeto 4** b g Liboi (USA)-Persian Carpet (FR) (Kalamoun) 650[14] 1102[7] 1450[7] 1874[7] 2341[2] 3479[3] 4067[12] 4307[9] **>76f<**

**Taragona 3** b f Handsome Sailor-Queen of Aragon (Aragon) *1667[9]* ***>47f<***

**Tarator (USA) 3** ch c Green Dancer (USA)-Happy Gal (FR) (Habitat) (2665a) 3915a[2] 4293a[6] (4657a) **>121f<**

**Tarawa (IRE) 4** br g Caerleon (USA)-Sagar (Habitat) **1995:** *4482[3]* **1996:** *(679)* (878) 1112[4] 2053[17] 2471a[6] 4196[8] 4568[7] (4757) **>100a 116f<**

**Tarf (USA) 3** ch f Diesis-Tadwin (Never so Bold) 1321[5] 1818[8] 2143[12] 4119[7] 4561[7] **>83df<**

**Tarhelm (IRE) 4** br c Helm Reef-Tarabella (Dance In Time (CAN)) 623a[2] (909a) 1135a[8] (3917a) 4747a[7] **>113f<**

**Tarian (USA) 4** b g Lyphard (USA)-Chain Fern (USA) (Blushing Groom (FR)) *495[8]* 577[11] 887[7] 1416[9] 1686[6] 2251[2] 2506[13] 2540[11] **>56f<**

**Ta Rib (USA) 3** ch f Mr Prospector (USA)-Madame Secretary (USA) (Secretariat (USA)) *(921)* (1140a) 2052[4] 2609[2] 3596[4] **>118f<**

**Tariff (IRE) 2** b f Common Grounds-Tasskeen (FR) (Lyphard (USA)) 2904[11] 4890[10] **>21f<**

**Tarneem (USA) 3** b f Zilzal (USA)-Willowy Mood (USA) (Will Win (USA)) 937[6] 1127[9] 2079[2] 2420[2] (3093) 3440[2] 3806[4] 4214[6] **>81f<**

**Taroudant 9** b g Pharly (FR)-Melbourne Miss (Chaparral (FR)) *825[8]* 1005[17] **>74a 55f<**

**Tarradale 2** br g Interrex (CAN)-Encore L'Amour (USA) (Monteverdi) 5033[19] **>18f<**

**Tarry 3** b f Salse (USA)-Waitingformargaret (Kris) 819[8] 1100[5] 1324[6] 3109[5] **>63f<**

**Tarski 2** ch c Polish Precedent (USA)-Illusory (Kings Lake (USA)) (2972) 3684[4] **>88f<**

**Tart 3** b f Tragic Role (USA)-Fee (Mandamus) **1995:** *4381[2] (4485)* **1996:** *1641[4]* (4216) 4804[14] **>66+a 78f<**

**Tart (FR) 3** br f Warning-Sharp Girl (FR) (Sharpman) 640[4] 1117[2] 2869[2] 3260[3] 3461[3] 3938[3] (4217) **>77f<**

**Tart and a Half 4** b f Distant Relative-Vaigrant Wind (Vaigly Great) 632[7] 812[14] 1064[2] 1178[10] 1630[4] 1974[14] 2232[2] 2508[5] 2889[14] 3338[6] 3618[9] 3827[4] 3993[9] 4119[2] 4312[26] **>87f<**

**Tartan Express (IRE) 3** b g New Express-Running Feud (Prince Tenderfoot (USA)) **1995:** *4535[9]* **1996:** *56[11] 176[10] 361[4] 471[14]* 635[14] **>20a 30f<**

**Tartan Gem (IRE) 5** ch h Lomond (USA)-Red Jade (Red God) **1995:** *4505[2]* **1996:** *(34) (37) 75[3] 80[4] 128[3] 369[5] 420[3] 439[11]* ***>75a 68f<*** **(DEAD)**

**Tartan Party 2** gr c Environment Friend-Northern Scene (Habitat) 3982[12] 4369[9] 4599[9] 4834[3] **>58f<**

**Tarte Aux Pommes (USA) 4** br f Local Talent (USA)-My Mother's Eyes (FR) (Saint Cyrien (FR)) 1817[7] 2248[8] 3503[8] 4177[6] 4489[13] **>90?f<**

**Tarthooth (IRE) 5** ch g Bob Back (USA)-Zoly (USA) (Val de L'Orne (FR)) 4643a[16] **>76f<**

**Tasdid 3** ch c In The Wings-Ghaadah (USA) (Linkage (USA)) 1247a[3] 1296a[4] 1791[12] 2474a[8] 3196a[5] **>114f<**

**Tashjir (USA) 3** ch f Slew O' Gold (USA)-Mashaarif (USA) (Mr Prospector (USA)) 955[P] 1325[7] 1763[7] **>52f<**

**Tashkent 4** b g Thowra (FR)-Royal Bat (Crowned Prince (USA)) *2510[8]* ***>30f<***

**Tashtaiya 3** b f Totem (USA)-Bonita Estrella (Macmillion) *779[5] 3064[9] 3421[8]* **>32a f<**

**Tasik Chini (USA) 2** b br c St Jovite (USA)-Ten Hail Marys (USA) (Halo (USA)) *2702[3]* 3131[6] 3407[7] 3835[17] **>80f<**

**Tasliya (USA) 3** ch f Gulch (USA)-Aghani (USA) (Blushing Groom (FR)) 689[5] 978[15] **>71df<**

**Tassili (IRE) 3** b g Old Vic-Topsy (Habitat) 576[6] 4827[10] **>68f<**

**Tatas 3** 1759a[5] **>96f<**

**Tathmin 3** b g Weldnaas (USA)-Alcassa (FR) (Satingo) 1104[13] 2557[8] *3418[5] 4551[13]* ***>68a 57f<***

**Tatika 6** ch g Tate Gallery (USA)-Independentia (Home Guard (USA)) **1995:** *4367[8] 4493[7] 4539[5]* **1996:** *(199) (285) 988[10]* 1406[5] 1868[6] 2412[7] (3501) 3985[12] 4820[5] **>84a 77f<**

**Tauber 12** b g Taufan (USA)-Our Bernie (Continuation) 466[9] 582[22] 1446[3] 1624[6] **>42a 46f<**

**Taufan Boy 3** b c Taufan (USA)-Lydia Maria (Dancing Brave (USA)) 701[3] 1955[6] *2552[3] 2701[2]* 3205[7] 3479[4] 3939[6] 4227[7] 4615[4] 4804[2] 4919[6] **>80a 85f<**

**Taufan Rookie (IRE) 2** b c Taufan (USA)-Royal Wolff (Prince Tenderfoot (USA)) 924[2] 2112[4] 2916[3] **>88f<**

**Taufan's Melody 5** b g Taufan (USA)-Glorious Fate (Northfields (USA)) **1995:** 4426a[3] **1996:** (1620) 1988[2] 3200a[4] 3597[3] 4852a[2] 5030a[2] **>121f<**

**Taufeliane 5** b m Taufan (USA)-Sweet Eliane (Birdbrook) 504[12] **>13a f<**

**Taunt 2** b c Robellino (USA)-Minute Waltz (Sadler's Wells (USA)) 3837[3] **>81f<**

**Taurean Fire 3** ch g Tina's Pet-Golden Decoy (Decoy Boy) 1001[5] 1500[18] 1765[8] 2391[10] 3256[8] **>25f<**

**Tauten (IRE) 6** br m Taufan (USA)-Pitaka (Pitskelly) 1314[2] *1719[14] 1965[13]* 2192[19] 2373[7] 2740[5] 3067[10] 3257[6] 4202[5] 4307[14] **>1a 60?f<**

**Tawaaded (IRE) 3** ch f Nashwan (USA)-Thaidah (CAN) (Vice Regent (CAN)) (678) 874[2] 1151[7] 2142[9] 2920[3] 3989[7] **>82f<**

**Tawafek (USA) 3** br c Silver Hawk (USA)-Tippy Tippy Toe (USA) (Nureyev (USA)) 544[7] 705[7] 969[9] **>69f<**

**Tawafij (USA) 7** ch g Diesis-Dancing Brownie (USA) (Nijinsky (CAN)) *589[17]* 1425[6] 1609[13] 2328[4] 2581[7] 2773[6] 3101[4] 3445[7] **>83f<**

**Tawkil (USA) 3** b c Riverman (USA)-Lyphette (FR) (Lyphard (USA)) 694[5] 1015[6] 1817[5] 3691[7] 4181[3] **>100f<**

**Taxi de Nuit (USA) 4** dk c Runaway Groom (CAN)-Mot d'Amour **1995:** (4401a) **1996:** (5074a) **>87f<**

**Taylors Revival 5** b m Sizzling Melody-Taylors Pet (Tina's Pet) *292[8] 337[8] 393[12] 853[11]* 2978[8] **>21a 3f<**

**Tayovullin (IRE) 2** ch f Shalford (IRE)-Fifth Quarter (Cure The Blues (USA)) 4087[9] 4475[6] **>65f<**

**Tayseer (USA) 2** ch c Sheikh Albadou-Millfit (USA) (Blushing Groom (FR)) 4383[3] 4756[4] (4991) **>88f<**

**Tazibari 2** b f Barrys Gamble-Jersey Maid (On Your Mark) 538[2] (910) 2681[5] 4767[5] **>56f<**

**Tazio Nuvolari 2** b f Weldnaas (USA)-Ty High (IRE) (High Line) *838[6] 1084[3] 4780[9] 4980[10]* **>37a f<**

**Te Amo (IRE) 4** b c Waajib-Avebury Ring (Auction Ring (USA)) *580[11]* 988[11] 1506[8] 1839[4] *2082[10] 2737[3]* 3260[2] 3653[3] 3948[6] (4703) 4877[6] 5054[17] **>33a 68f<**

**Tea Party (USA) 3** b f Night Shift (USA)-Meringue Pie (USA) (Silent Screen (USA)) 1174[4] 1614[4] 2399[8] 2855[4] 3165[7] *4076[3] (4336) 4575[2] 4946a[3]* ***>83a 79f<***

**Tear White (IRE) 2** b c Mac's Imp (USA)-Exemplary (Sovereign Lord) 930[R] 1169[3] 1632[6] 2758[5] (2897) 3160[2] 3299[6] 3924[5] 4234[6] 4425[5] **>74f<**

**Technicolour (IRE) 2** b f Rainbow Quest (USA)-Grecian Urn (Ela-Mana-Mou) (4798) **>81+f<**

**Tedburrow 4** b g Dowsing (USA)-Gwiffina (Welsh

Saint) *1186[12]* 1430[4] 1975[2] 2292[4] 2694[2] (2889) 3038[3] 3432[16] 3946[7] 4116[4] 4314[20] 4687[16] 4772[5] 4869[4] **>94f<**

**Teddy's Bow (IRE) 2** b br f Archway (IRE)-Gale Force Seven (Strong Gale) *2076[5]* 2569[4] **>53f<**

**Tee-Emm 6** b g Lidhame-Tower Glades (Tower Walk) **1995:** *4359[4] 4459[3] 4487[5]* **1996:** *652[5] 835[4] 900[4] 2156[7]* ***>55a 45f<***

**Teejay'n'aitch (IRE) 4** b g Maelstrom Lake-Middle Verde (USA) (Sham (USA)) 562[6] 1001[7] 1586[3] 2024[3] 2120[6] 2357[8] 2563[12] **>42df<**

**Teen Jay 6** b g Teenoso (USA)-Spoilt Again (Mummy's Pet) 1496[11] 1685[10] 1965[8] 2183[13] 2697[2] 2756[2] 3335[2] *3437[10] 3801[12] 3952[7] 4092[9] 4203[19]* 4476[5] (4722) **>63a 65f<**

**Tee Tee Too (IRE) 4** ch g Hatim (USA)-Scottish Welcome (Be My Guest (USA)) 713[15] 805[8] 883[10] 1001[15] 4455[11] 4587[11] 4815[13] **>61?a 31f<**

**Telemania (IRE) 2** b f Mujtahid (USA)-African Dance (USA) (El Gran Senor (USA)) 2892[4] (4208) 4490[3] **>86f<**

**Telephus 7** b g Efisio-Mrs Bizz (Status Seeker) **1995:** *4364[15] 4507[7] 4516[8]* **1996:** *9[6] 54[9] 104[7] 489[4]* **>35a 49f<**

**Telloff 2** b f Reprimand-La Primavera (Northfields (USA)) 4488[21] 4748[9] **>61f<**

**Temerity (IRE) 3** b f Last Tycoon-Pallas's Blue (Pitskelly) 4643a[19] **>72f<**

**Tempering 10** b g Kris-Mixed Applause (USA) (Nijinsky (CAN)) **1995:** *4475[5]* **1996:** *70[4] 152[3] (210) 251[5] 297[6] (373) 398[2] 429[3] 602[3] 777[2] 855[2] 1031[3] 2372[10]* **>63a 26f<**

**Tempting (IRE) 4** b f Waajib-Balela (African Sky) *34[14]* **>63f<**

**Tempting Prospect 2** b f Shirley Heights-Trying for Gold (USA) (Northern Baby (CAN)) 4104[4] (4879) **>90f<**

**Temptress 3** br f Kalaglow-Circe (Main Reef) (1584) (1900) 2430[6] 2775[3] 3249[7] 3522[6] 4216[11] 4513[2] 4702[10] 4967[3] **>72f<**

**Tenor 5** b g Music Boy-Songstead (Song) *63[8] 107[11] 127[9] 231[6] (316) 362[3] 500[3] 559[3]* 659[2] 735[7] 931[8] 1039[8] 2757[17] 2910[9] **>64a 51f<**

**Ten Past Six 4** ch g Kris-Tashinsky (USA) (Nijinsky (CAN)) 913[2] 988[2] 1131[5] 1867[4] 2331[6] 4624[7] 4826[13] 4868[5] 5046[22] **>67f<**

**Teofilio (IRE) 2** ch c Night Shift (USA)-Rivoltade (USA) (Sir Ivor) 4261[2] 4684[2] **>84+f<**

**Teoroma 6** ch h Teofane-Poppy Kelly (Netherkelly) 2537[6] 2891[12] 3870[10] **>33a 19f<**

**Teraab 2** b c Primo Dominie-Valika (Valiyar) 3044[6] **>37f<**

**Terdad (USA) 3** ch c Lomond (USA)-Istiska (FR) (Irish River (FR)) 584[2] **>88f<**

**Tereshkova (USA) 4** b f Mr Prospector (USA)-Lypatia (FR) (Lyphard (USA)) 1770[4] 2337[8] 4671[11] **>104df<**

**Termon 3** b f Puissance-Alipura (Anfield) 1312[2] 2019[2] 2123[4] (2358) 2962[8] 3238[4] 3491[5] 3881[8] 4472[3] **>66f<**

**Terry's Rose 2** br f Nomination-Moharabuiee (Pas de Seul) 1433[4] 3349[6] *4331[9] 4887[13]* ***>28a 49f<***

**Tertium (IRE) 4** b g Nordico (USA)-Nouniya (Vayrann) 802[3] 933[18] 1069[3] (1322) 1476[4] 1793[2] 2053[2] 2724[17] 3430[5] 3509[6] 3709[8] 4190[8] 4300[6] 4568[29] 4620[8] **>94f<**

**Tessajoe 4** ch g Clantime-Busted Love (Busted) 564[6] (738) 963[4] 1700[4] 3276[3] 3710[17] 4073[2] (4320) 4753[4] 4872[15] **>79f<**

**Test The Water (IRE) 2** ch c Maelstrom Lake-Baliana (CAN) (Riverman (USA)) 2624[9] 3502[2] 3685[2] 4123[2] 4250[3] (4672) **>90f<**

**Tethys (USA) 5** b m Topsider (USA)-Tide (USA) (Coastal (USA)) **1995:** *(4465)* **>86a 96f<**

**Tetris (IRE) 2** b f Nordico (USA)-Firefly Night (Salmon Leap (USA)) 4408a[2] 5050[5] **>36f<**

**Teutonic Lass (IRE) 2** b f Night Shift (USA)-Highness Lady (GER) (Cagliostro (GER)) 4061[14] 4605[10] 4861[12] **>61f<**

**Thahabyah (USA) 2** b f Sheikh Albadou-Golden Cap (USA) (Hagley (USA)) 3675[4] 4241[3] (4454) **>75f<**

**Thai Morning 3** gr c Petong-Bath (Runnett) *466[11]* 644[6] 824[3] 1101[6] 3506[11] 3863[5] 3973[14] 4128[4] 4511[7] *(4781)* **>84+a 59f<**

**Thaki 3** b g Distant Relative-Highly Polished (High Top) 786[11]

**Thaleros 6** b g Green Desert (USA)-Graecia Magna (USA) (Private Account (USA)) *426[2] 521[2] 854[5] 1088[6]* 1672[5] 1862[R] **>63a 56f<**

**Thaljanah (IRE) 4** ch g In The Wings-Dawn is Breaking (Import) 564[5] 675[3] 1005[13] 1194[3] 1710[8] **>94f<**

**Thames Side 5** gr g Beveled (USA)-Free Range (Birdbrook) 1337[3] 1953[4] 2605[2] (2883) 3161[9] **>45a 73f< (DEAD)**

**Thatcham Island 3** ch f Jupiter Island-Floreal (Formidable (USA)) *4379[9]* 4824[16]

**Thatched (IRE) 6** b g Thatching-Shadia (USA) (Naskra (USA)) *713[11]* 1037[8] 1313[6] 1886[3] 2214[5] 2357[3] 2801[3] (2925) 3060[5] 3344[3] 3777[2] 3974[4] (4226) 4436[10] 4503[8] 4793[7] (4906) 4993[10] **>58f<**

**Thatcherella 5** br m Thatching-Ella Mon Amour (Ela-Mana-Mou) 928[16] (1178) 1790[13] 2329[9] 2615[6] 3599[7] **>71f<**

**Thatcher's Era (IRE) 4** ch f Never so Bold-Prima Domina (FR) (Dominion) *33[3] 85[8] 169[10]* **>61da 69f<**

**Thatchmaster (IRE) 5** b g Thatching-Key Maneuver (USA) (Key To Content (USA)) *1121[6]* 1337[6] 1992[2] 2507[2] (2971) 3496[2] (3785) 4186[3] **>64f<**

**That Man Again 4** ch g Prince Sabo-Milne's Way (The Noble Player (USA)) *864[4]* 1332[7] 1818[7] 2003[4] 2292[11] 3875[6] 4116[15] 4466[9] 4772[16] **>73a 91f<**

**That Old Feeling (IRE) 4** b g Waajib-Swift Reply (He Loves Me) 4682[24] **>92f<**

**Thats Logic (IRE) 2** b g Cyrano de Bergerac-Allberry (Alzao (USA)) 4024a[10] **>81f<**

**Thea (USA) 3** br f Marju (IRE)-Switched on (Known Fact (USA)) *(583)* 3945[9] 4135[7] **>88f<**

**Theano (IRE) 3** b f Thatching-Akamantis (Kris) 2465a[3] 3731a[5] **>103f<**

**The Atheling (IRE) 6** b g Taufan (USA)-Shady Glade (Sun Prince) 1516[7] 2488[4] **>54f<**

**Theatre Magic 3** b g Sayf El Arab (USA)-Miss Orient (Damister (USA)) **1995:** *(4431)* **1996:** *35[2] 137[2] 182[5] 453[4]* 509[2] 701[5] 973[12] 1527[21] *2934[3] 3456[8] 3603[2] 4333[5] 4575[3] 4793[16]* 4860[12] *5056[3]* **>71a 43f<**

**Theatre's Dream (IRE) 3** b c Danehill (USA)-Habituee (Habitat) 3262[15] 3654[7] **>43f<**

**Theatreworld (IRE) 4** b g Sadler's Wells (USA)-Chamonis (USA) (Affirmed (USA)) (4537b) 4643a[8] **>85f<**

**The Barnsley Belle (IRE) 3** b f Distinctly North (USA)-La Tanque (USA) (Last Raise (USA)) **1995:** *4473[8]* **1996:** *1068[5]* 1312[6] 2983[6] 3289[5] 4348[3] 4598[2] 4860[10] *4983[2]* **>50a 54f<**

**The Bee Man 2** br g Superpower-Puffin Point (Ballad Rock) 608[6] 699[8] 733[4] 2959[5] 3448[3] 3577[8] **>59f<**

**The Black Dubh (IRE) 3** b g Classic Secret (USA)-Coral Cave (Ashmore (FR)) 2966[8] 3619[9] **>31f<**

**The Blade (GER) 3** ch f Sure Blade (USA)-Thea (GER) (Surumu (GER)) 4164a[2] **>109f<**

**The Boozing Brief (USA) 3** b g Turkoman (USA)-Evening Silk (USA) (Damascus (USA)) *821[11]* 1100[15] 1669[4] 2549[4] 2779[7] 3584[4] *4095[6] 4474[2]* ***>33a 70f<***

**The Bower (IRE) 7** br g Don't Forget Me-Nyama (USA) (Pretense (USA)) 2472a[7] **>100f<**

**The Butterwick Kid 3** ch g Interrex (CAN)-Ville Air (Town Crier) 525[7] 824[8] 1042[8] 1658[4] 2049[5] 2215[9] 4317[3] (4474) 4563[4] 4794[7] **>56f<**

**The Cape Doctor (IRE) 4** b g Distant Relative-Yldizlar (Star Appeal) *244[9] 303[4] 373[9] 499[8] 635[12]* ***>45a 42f<***

**The Commodore (IRE) 2** b c Common Grounds-Hinari Disk Deck (Indian King (USA)) 3796[10] 4369[15] 4546[13] **>41f<**

**The Cottonwool Kid 4** b g Blakeney-Relatively Smart (Great Nephew) **1995:** *4411[13]* **1996:** *3968[9]* ***>40a 29f<***

**The Deejay (IRE) 2** ch c Desse Zenny (USA)-White Jasmin (Jalmood (USA)) 1827[13] 2044[2] 2519[2] 2696[2] (3099) 3208[3] 3835[19] 4131[11] 4440[6] **>65f<**

**The Dilettanti (USA) 3** br c Red Ransom (USA)-Rich Thought (USA) (Rich Cream (USA)) 730[2] 942[4] (1593) 2006[9] 2621[9] 3211[4] 3691[15] **>92f<**

**The Dubious Goose 2** b g Yaheeb (USA)-Dunnington (Risk Me (FR)) 3511[8] 3687[14] 4607[10] **>43f<**

**The Faraway Tree 2** b f Suave Dancer (USA)-Sassalya (Sassafras (FR)) (4241) **>80+f<**

**The Fed 6** ch g Clantime-Hyde Princess (Touch Paper) *388[3] 418[9] 425[6] 514[7] 750[8]* 1170[8] 2185[15] **>38a 45f<**

**The Fly 2** gr c Pharly (FR)-Nelly Do Da (Derring-Do) 2580[7] (3423) (3835) 4131[4] **>88f<**

**The Four Isles 2** b g Never so Bold-Far Claim (USA) (Far North (CAN)) *1408[3]* 1842[7] 2059[6] 2374[6] 2681[4] 3647[5] 4195[6] 4787[10] 5043[13] **>58f<**

**The Frisky Farmer 3** b g Emarati (USA)-Farceuse (Comedy Star (USA)) **1995:** *4437[10]* **1996:** *102[6] 182[7] 215[2] 271[7] 317[2] 408[5] (492) 606[2] 748[11]* 867[3] 1304[3] 1707[5] 2392[5] 4589[13] **>69a 71f<**

**The Fugative 3** b f Nicholas (USA)-Miss Runaway (Runnett) 4309[7] 4693[5] *5001[2]* **>56a 58f<**

**The Fullbangladesh 3** ch f Hubbly Bubbly (USA)-Oakhurst (Mandrake Major) **1995:** *4480[8]* **1996:** *183[8] 344[10] 605[6] 658[5]* 1600[6] 2362[4] **>43a 40f<**

**The Gay Fox 2** b gr c Never so Bold-School Concert (Music Boy) 608[3] 958[2] 3940[4] 4208[2] 4566[5] 4723[21] 4918[8] **>79?f<**

**The Great Flood 3** ch g Risk Me (FR)-Yukosan (Absalom) 1470[7] 1675[4] 2365[6] 2928[4] *4077[5] 4336[4]* **>62a 49?f<**

**The Green Grey 2** gr c Environment Friend-Pea Green (Try My Best (USA)) 2600[6] 2783[10] 4962[9] **>57f<**

**The Grey Weaver 3** gr c Touch of Grey-Foggy Dew (Smoggy) *840[12]* 1050[9] 1350[13] 1995[9] 3609[8] 4498[8] **>3f<**

**The Happy Fox (IRE) 4** ch c Ballad Rock-Amanzi (African Sky) *451[17]* 1016[5] 1790[8] 2114[22] 2363[10] 2889[5] 3232[27] 3579[2] 3851[4] 3868[3] 4058[7] 4367[11] 4616[16] 4917[6] **>76a 73f<**

**The In-Laws (IRE) 2** ch f Be My Guest (USA)-Amboselli (Raga Navarro (ITY)) (3663) 4133[8] 4471[7] 4764[4] 4867[3] **>84f<**

**The Institute Boy 6** b g Fairy King (USA)-To Oneiro (Absalom) *22[2] 139[6] (231) 278[3] 316[2] 362[4] (461) 556[4] 769[3] 900[8] 1545[3]* 1765[7] 2564[7] 2745[2] 2771[5] (2960) 3261[4] 3310[2] 3652[8] **>70a 53f<**

**The Jolly Barmaid (IRE) 3** b f Don't Forget Me-Gay Broad (Gay Fandango (USA)) 870[10] 1089[16] 1821[13] 2397[5] 3104[3] **>41f<**

**The Lad** 7 b g Bold Owl-Solbella (Starch Reduced) *309$^{4}$ (365) 398$^{5}$ (759)* 1063$^{4}$ (2613) 3037$^{9}$ *3437$^{6}$ 4048$^{13}$* **>38a 58f<**
**The Lambton Worm** 2 b c Superpower-Springwell (Miami Springs) 1086$^{2}$ 1849$^{2}$ 2295$^{3}$ (2727) 3400$^{4}$ 3843$^{6}$ 4247$^{9}$ **>77f<**
**The Legions Pride** 3 b c Rambo Dancer (CAN)-Immaculate Girl (Habat) 2895$^{6}$ 3315$^{2}$ 3705$^{8}$ **>60f<**
**The Little Ferret** 6 ch g Scottish Reel-Third Movement (Music Boy) **1995:** *4386$^{11}$ 4436$^{2}$ 4490$^{6}$ 4525$^{9}$* **1996:** *82$^{7}$ 1012$^{4}$* 1173$^{9}$ 1534$^{4}$ 2014$^{7}$ **>57a 52f< (DEAD)**
**The Man** 3 b c Marju (IRE)-Mirkan Honey (Ballymore) **1995:** 4397a$^{2}$ **>86f<**
**Theme Arena** 3 b f Tragic Role (USA)-Sea Siesta (Vaigly Great) *3626$^{5}$ 4110$^{9}$* 4548$^{12}$ **>42a 50f<**
**The Mestral** 4 br f Formidable (USA)-Lariston Gale (Pas de Seul) **1995:** *4486$^{8}$ 4510$^{5}$ 4515$^{5}$* **1996:** *66$^{9}$ 84$^{3}$ 153$^{8}$ 172$^{2}$ 213$^{9}$ 247$^{6}$ 301$^{9}$* **>44da 50f<**
**The Noble Oak (IRE)** 8 ch g The Noble Player (USA)-Sea Palace (Huntercombe) *1049$^{9}$* 1170$^{11}$ 1715$^{13}$ 2598$^{4}$ 2745$^{14}$ 3661$^{9}$ 3978$^{11}$ **>45a 24f<**
**Thenorthernplayboy (IRE)** 3 gr c Distinctly North (USA)-Monetary Wish (Wishing Star) *58$^{7}$ 651$^{8}$* **>35a 22f<**
**The Oddfellow** 3 b c Efisio-Agnes Jane (Sweet Monday) *1526$^{W}$ 1972$^{6}$ 2419$^{4}$* ***>12a 22f<***
**The Orraman (IRE)** 2 b c Taufan (USA)-Miss Pennine (IRE) (Pennine Walk) *1166$^{10}$* 1583$^{9}$ **>23f<**
**The Polymath** 3 ch g Sharpo-Nisha (Nishapour (FR)) 2181$^{6}$ 3262$^{8}$ **>53f<**
**The Puzzler (IRE)** 5 b or br g Sharpo-Enigma (Ahonoora) 457$^{2}$ 579$^{3}$ 1483$^{8}$ 2003$^{6}$ (4823) 4917$^{5}$ 5044$^{7}$ **>112f<**
**The Real McCoy** 2 b c Deploy-Mukhayyalah (Dancing Brave (USA)) 3069$^{9}$ 4897$^{16}$ 5051$^{7}$ **>43tf<**
**The Real Whizzbang (IRE)** 5 b or br h New Express-Gail's Crystal (Crofter (USA)) **1995:** *4484$^{12}$* **1996:** *22$^{3}$ 63$^{7}$* **>52a 41f<**
**Therhea (IRE)** 3 b g Pennine Walk-Arab Art (Artaius (USA)) 493$^{4}$ (709) 1126$^{8}$ 2041$^{25}$ 4583$^{8}$ 4826$^{12}$ **>83f<**
**The Roundsills** 2 ch c Handsome Sailor-Eye Sight (Roscoe Blake) 4700$^{6}$ 4830$^{12}$ **>67f<**
**The Scythian** 4 ch g Komaite (USA)-City to City (Windjammer (USA)) 610$^{13}$ 931$^{4}$ 1186$^{18}$ 1781$^{10}$ 3323$^{2}$ 3622$^{6}$ 4312$^{25}$ 4689$^{4}$ **>77f< (DEAD)**
**The Stager (IRE)** 4 b c Danehill (USA)-Wedgewood Blue (USA) (Sir Ivor) 756$^{2}$ (1154) 1505$^{3}$ 2145$^{6}$ 2351$^{6}$ **>81f<**
**The Substitute** 4 b f Colmore Row-Snow Chief (Tribal Chief) *337$^{10}$* **(DEAD)**
**The Swan** 3 ch f Old Vic-El Vino (Habitat) 1507$^{4}$ (2433) (2990) 3486$^{7}$ 3922$^{3}$ 4365$^{5}$ 4832$^{7}$ **>88f<**
**The Tig** 2 b c Tigani-The Ranee (Royal Palace) 4386$^{10}$ 4914$^{11}$ **>44f<**
**The Wad** 3 b g Emarati (USA)-Fair Melys (FR) (Welsh Pageant) *17$^{6}$ 35$^{4}$ 123$^{13}$ 238$^{4}$ 298$^{2}$ 383$^{7}$ (748)* 1527$^{3}$ 1599$^{4}$ 1707$^{2}$ 2049$^{9}$ 2425$^{4}$ (2571) 2777$^{4}$ 3482$^{10}$ 3672$^{19}$ **>49a 73df<**
**The West (USA)** 2 ch c Gone West (USA)-Lady for Two (USA) (Storm Bird (CAN)) (3234) 3690$^{3}$ 4294a$^{2}$ 4759$^{7}$ **>107f<**
**Thewrightone (IRE)** 2 b f Fayruz-Vote Barolo (Nebbiolo) 930$^{10}$ 1086$^{12}$ 1645$^{9}$ 2846$^{W}$ 2926$^{5}$ 3291$^{3}$ 3511$^{7}$ *4093$^{14}$ 4343$^{5}$* 4796$^{11}$ 5005$^{10}$ **>47f<**
**The Wyandotte Inn** 2 ch c Ballacashtal (CAN)-Carolynchristensen (Sweet Revenge) 2361$^{10}$ *2633$^{5}$ 2746$^{3}$ 2967$^{10}$ 3950$^{2}$ 4079$^{3}$ 4803$^{10}$* 4907$^{2}$ **>59a 62f<**
**Thick as Thieves** 4 b g Shavian-Vivienda (Known Fact (USA)) **1995:** *4394$^{15}$ 4478$^{10}$ 4542$^{4}$* **1996:** *36$^{5}$ 133$^{8}$ 278$^{8}$ 592$^{16}$* 769$^{9}$ 1598$^{6}$ 1889$^{9}$ 2481$^{11}$ 4382$^{14}$ *5055$^{10}$* **>40a 43f<**
**Third Party** 2 gr f Terimon-Party Game (Red Alert) 977$^{3}$ 1480$^{4}$ 2230$^{4}$ 2703$^{3}$ **>64f<**
**Thisonesforalice** 8 b g Lochnager-Bamdoro (Cavo Doro) 561$^{10}$ **>45f<**
**Thomas Crown (IRE)** 4 ch c Last Tycoon-Upward Trend (Salmon Leap (USA)) *291$^{9}$ 353$^{12}$ 393$^{5}$ 417$^{7}$* **>26a 67f<**
**Thomire** 4 ch c Be My Chief (USA)-Timarete (ITY) (Green Dancer (USA)) 4667a$^{6}$ **>104f<**
**Thordis** 3 b g Mazilier (USA)-Doppio (Dublin Taxi) 992$^{2}$ 2200$^{5}$ 2615$^{4}$ 2947$^{5}$ 3518$^{9}$ (4865) **>64a 82f<**
**Thornby Park** 2 b f Unfuwain (USA)-Wantage Park (Pas de Seul) 4608$^{8}$ 4861$^{6}$ **>71f<**
**Thorniwama** 5 b m Hadeer-Hidden Asset (Hello Gorgeous (USA)) *82$^{12}$ 274$^{7}$ 337$^{5}$ 464$^{4}$ 499$^{3}$ (553) 670$^{12}$* 866$^{10}$ *1098$^{11}$ 2203$^{9}$* 2941$^{11}$ **>48a 20f<**
**Thornton (USA)** 2 b c Woodman (USA)-Dolsk (Danzig (USA)) 3994$^{9}$ 4599$^{5}$ 4825$^{19}$ **>77f<**
**Thorntoun Estate (IRE)** 3 b g Durgam (USA)-Furry Friend (USA) (Bold Bidder) **1995:** *(4439)* **1996:** *56$^{3}$ (176) 280$^{7}$ 294$^{3}$ 385$^{2}$ 483$^{4}$* 542$^{4}$ 803$^{11}$ 886$^{13}$ 954$^{7}$ **>64a 67df<**
**Thorntoun House (IRE)** 3 b g Durgam (USA)-Commanche Song (Commanche Run) 2876$^{5}$ 3305$^{4}$ **>35f<**
**Thorntoun Jewel (IRE)** 3 b f Durgam (USA)-Blue Bouquet (Cure The Blues (USA)) *606$^{13}$ 1087$^{5}$* 1474$^{9}$ 1642$^{7}$ 2022$^{6}$ 2212$^{9}$ **>42f<**
**Thorny Bishop** 5 b g Belfort (FR)-Hill of Fare (Brigadier Gerard) *65$^{10}$ 141$^{8}$ 185$^{5}$ 1074$^{16}$* 1170$^{13}$ **>34a 6f<**
**Thor's Phantom** 3 ch g Weldnaas (USA)-La Carlotta (Ela-Mana-Mou) 3472$^{13}$ 3789$^{8}$ 3929$^{7}$ **>38f<**
**Threadneedle (USA)** 3 b g Danzig Connection (USA)-Sleeping Beauty (Mill Reef (USA)) 526$^{7}$ (4309) 4682$^{23}$ **>81f<**
**Three Arch Bridge** 4 ch f Sayf El Arab (USA)-Alanood (Northfields (USA)) 739$^{10}$ 884$^{3}$ 1024$^{5}$ 1538$^{3}$ (1633) (1674) *1811$^{2}$ 1860$^{3}$* (1886) 2188$^{7}$ 2357$^{9}$ 2679$^{7}$ 3120$^{4}$ 3279$^{7}$ **>69a 75f<**
**Three Card Trick (IRE)** 2 ch f Shalford (IRE)-Tricky (Song) 3129$^{12}$ 3807$^{15}$ 3976$^{9}$ **>46f<**
**Three Cheers (IRE)** 2 b br c Slip Anchor-Three Tails (Blakeney) 4897$^{14}$ **>25f<**
**Three For A Pound** 2 b c Risk Me (FR)-Lompoa (Lomond (USA)) 1989$^{4}$ **>53f<**
**Three Hills** 3 b c Danehill (USA)-Three Stars (Star Appeal) 447$^{5}$ 693$^{2}$ 1002$^{9}$ 1670$^{2}$ (2318) 2690$^{5}$ 3710$^{22}$ 4176$^{5}$ 4326$^{12}$ 4716$^{9}$ **>89f<**
**Threeplay (IRE)** 2 b c Mac's Imp (USA)-Houwara (IRE) (Darshaan) 1842$^{5}$ 2374$^{4}$ 2596$^{5}$ 2965$^{3}$ 3128$^{12}$ 4916$^{12}$ **>63f<**
**Three Rivers** 3 b g Warrshan (USA)-Gentle Stream (Sandy Creek) 4643a$^{24}$ **>75f<**
**Threesocks** 3 ch f Weldnaas (USA)-Jeethgaya (USA) (Critique (USA)) *156$^{4}$ 329$^{4}$* **>46a 72f<**
**Threesome (USA)** 3 ch f Seattle Dancer (USA)-Triode (USA) (Sharpen Up) 689$^{6}$ 1825$^{9}$ **>81df<**
**Three Weeks** 3 ch g Formidable (USA)-Zilda (FR) (Zino) 4827$^{13}$ *4982$^{8}$* **>31a 19f<**
**Three Wizards (FR)** 5 b h The Wonder (FR)-Orbit (USA) (Snob (USA)) 4941a$^{2}$ **>75f<**
**Thrilling Day** 3 b f Groom Dancer (USA)-Pushoff (USA) (Sauce Boat (USA)) (674) 1129$^{11}$ 2052$^{6}$ (3127) 3596$^{7}$ 4378$^{3}$ 4718$^{4}$ **>112f<**
**Thrower** 5 b g Thowra (FR)-Atlantic Line (Capricorn Line) *60$^{4}$* **>48a 50f<**
**Thrushwood** 4 b f Move Off-Spring Garden (Silly Prices) 801$^{9}$ *1970$^{11}$ 3306$^{18}$* ***>12f<***
**Thunderous** 5 b g Green Desert (USA)-Mixed Applause (USA) (Nijinsky (CAN)) **1995:** *4490$^{8}$* **1996:** *65$^{6}$ 103$^{5}$ 140$^{14}$* **>38a 59f<**
**Thunder River (IRE)** 6 ch g Thatching-In For More (Don) *827$^{10}$* 991$^{9}$ 3172$^{6}$ **>63f<**
**Thurstaston (IRE)** 3 b c Thatching-Bell Tower (Lyphard's Wish (FR)) 2996$^{12}$ 3262$^{13}$ **>44f< (DEAD)**
**Thwaab** 4 b g Dominion-Velvet Habit (Habitat) **1995:** *4406$^{6}$* **1996:** *518$^{9}$ 805$^{2}$* 971$^{11}$ 1041$^{5}$ 1538$^{14}$ 1885$^{5}$ (2154) 2490$^{3}$ (2911) 2964$^{2}$ (3453) 3639$^{13}$ 4312$^{2}$ 4571$^{4}$ 4994$^{13}$ **>49a 74f<**
**Tiama (IRE)** 3 b f Last Tycoon-Soyata (Bustino) 840$^{11}$ 1181$^{11}$ 1682$^{5}$ 2768$^{6}$ *3074$^{9}$ 3584$^{7}$* ***>39a 48f<***
**Tiana (ITY)** 4 b c Bound for Honour (USA)-Tanah Lot (ITY) (Scouting Miller) 1579a$^{2}$ 2278a$^{3}$ **>115f<**
**Tiaphena** 5 b m Derrylin-Velda (Thatch (USA)) 642$^{5}$ 767$^{7}$ *1095$^{2}$ (1611)* 2028$^{8}$ **>52a 51f<**
**Tibbi Blues** 9 b m Cure The Blues (USA)-Tiberly (FR) (Lyphard (USA)) 2520$^{2}$ 3239$^{2}$ 3579$^{8}$ 3866$^{10}$ **>47f<**
**Ticka Ticka Timing** 3 b c Timeless Times (USA)-Belltina (Belfort (FR)) *35$^{7}$ 158$^{8}$ 405$^{10}$* **>20a 44f<**
**Tickntima** 2 ch c Precocious-Stolon Time (Good Times (ITY)) 1525$^{4}$ 1884$^{3}$ 2317$^{5}$ 2873$^{5}$ **>69f<**
**Tidjani (IRE)** 4 b g Alleged (USA)-Tikarna (FR) (Targowice (USA)) 4643a$^{26}$ **>43f<**
**Tifasi (IRE)** 6 b g Shardari-Tikrara (USA) (Assert) *73$^{12}$*
**Tiger Lake** 3 ch c Nashwan (USA)-Tiger Flower (Sadler's Wells (USA)) 1359$^{5}$ (1957) 2054$^{14}$ **>79f<**
**Tiger Shoot** 9 b g Indian King (USA)-Grand Occasion (Great Nephew) *256$^{9}$ 546$^{21}$ 1031$^{13}$* **>67da 63f<**
**Tigrello** 2 ch c Efisio-Prejudice (Young Generation) 1959$^{5}$ 4475$^{2}$ 4756$^{6}$ **>81f<**
**Tilaal (USA)** 4 ch c Gulch (USA)-Eye Drop (USA) (Irish River (FR)) 613$^{3}$ 879$^{9}$ **>83f<**
**Tiler (IRE)** 4 br g Ballad Rock-Fair Siobahn (Petingo) *451$^{5}$* 554$^{3}$ 610$^{4}$ 928$^{14}$ 1609$^{10}$ 1703$^{8}$ 2220$^{3}$ 2431$^{9}$ 2911$^{2}$ (3055) 3216$^{2}$ 3296$^{2}$ 3672$^{18}$ 4116$^{16}$ 4314$^{25}$ 4581$^{12}$ 4975$^{7}$ 4994$^{2}$ **>41a 91?f<**
**Tillyard (IRE)** 3 b f Caerleon (USA)-Royal Heroine (Lypheor) 1007$^{7}$ 1855$^{2}$ 3093$^{3}$ **>81f<**
**Tillyboy** 6 b g Little Wolf-Redgrave Creative (Swing Easy (USA)) 1587$^{3}$ **>76f<**
**Tilly Owl** 5 b m Formidable (USA)-Tilly Tavi (Welsh Pageant) **1995:** *4479$^{3}$* **1996:** *345$^{6}$ 413$^{7}$ 518$^{3}$ 607$^{7}$ 839$^{9}$* **>43a 38f<**
**Tilston** 5 b g Dunbeath (USA)-Cribyn (Brigadier Gerard) 3942$^{9}$ **>40f<**
**Timarida (IRE)** 4 gr f Kalaglow-Triumphant (Track Spare) 1575a$^{2}$ 2037$^{8}$ 2471a$^{2}$ (3395a) (3907a) (4281a) 4773$^{3}$ **>128f<**
**Time Allowed** 3 b f Sadler's Wells (USA)-Time Charter (Saritamer (USA)) 1873$^{2}$ (2601) 3145$^{2}$ 3711$^{2}$ 4114$^{2}$ 4467$^{2}$ (4678) **>112f<**
**Time Can Tell** 2 ch g Sylvan Express-Stellaris (Star Appeal) 815$^{9}$ 916$^{8}$ 3769$^{4}$ 4097$^{6}$ 4347$^{2}$ (4607) 4814$^{4}$ 4990$^{4}$ **>72f<**
**Time Clash** 3 b f Timeless Times (USA)-Ash Amour (Hotfoot) **1995:** *4431$^{9}$ (4492) 4545$^{2}$* **1996:** *28$^{3}$ 775$^{13}$* 1121$^{4}$ 1599$^{7}$ *3877$^{14}$ 3977$^{7}$* 4206$^{11}$ *4895$^{11}$ 5060$^{8}$* **>38a 59df<**
**Time for Action (IRE)** 4 b g Alzao (USA)-Beyond Words (Ballad Rock) 925$^{10}$ 2131$^{8}$ (3351) 3689$^{15}$ 4055$^{12}$ 4176$^{3}$ 4465$^{19}$ 4617$^{3}$ 4826$^{14}$ **>93f<**
**Time For A Glass** 3 b f Timeless Times (USA)-Marie Zephyr (Treboro (USA)) *2212$^{10}$* 2419$^{2}$ 2731$^{4}$ 3225$^{5}$ 3451$^{5}$ **>49f<**
**Time For Tea (IRE)** 3 ch f Imperial Frontier (USA)-Glowing Embers (Nebbiolo) **1995:** *4383$^{5}$* **1996:** *846$^{5}$* 1013$^{3}$ 1615$^{8}$ 1840$^{7}$ 2340$^{6}$ 2686$^{10}$ 2980$^{7}$ 3918$^{3}$ 4217$^{8}$ 4428$^{10}$ **>67a 71f<**
**Time Goes On** 4 b f Latest Model-Impromptu (My

Swanee)) 2510$^{11}$ 3162$^{14}$ 3339$^{7}$ 4341$^{16}$ **>18f<**

**Time Lapse 7** ch m The Noble Player (USA)-Low Line (High Line) 3385a$^{3}$ **>63df<**

**Time Leader 4** ch g Lead on Time (USA)-Green Leaf (USA) (Alydar (USA)) *4686$^{25}$* ***>71df<***

**Timeless 4** b f Royal Academy (USA)-Glory of Hera (Formidable (USA)) *412$^{7}$* **>52a 65f<**

**Timely Example (USA) 5** ch h Timeless Moment (USA)-Dearest Mongo (USA) (Mongo) *62$^{11}$ 98$^{4}$ 299$^{4}$ 369$^{8}$ 688$^{16}$ 1605$^{5}$* **>38a 35?f<**

**Timely Times 3** ch f Timeless Times (USA)-Times (Junius (USA)) 4219$^{6}$ 4784$^{12}$ *5058$^{13}$* **>29f<**

**Timely Touch 2** ch f Timeless Times (USA)-Miss Sherbrooke (Workboy) 2237$^{4}$ 2422$^{3}$ 2795$^{8}$ 3448$^{9}$ 3576$^{7}$ **>39f<**

**Time of Night (USA) 3** gr ro f Night Shift (USA)-Tihama (USA) (Sassafras (FR)) 646$^{10}$ 873$^{19}$ 1155$^{2}$ 1649$^{3}$ 2617$^{4}$ 3228$^{6}$ 3334$^{7}$ 3800$^{3}$ 4053$^{2}$ **>75f<**

**Time of Trouble (FR) 4** b f Warning-Invite (Be My Guest (USA)) 3569a$^{3}$ **>81f<**

**Times of Times (IRE) 3** b f Distinctly North (USA)-Lady Fandet (Gay Fandango (USA)) **1995:** *4383$^{13}$* **1996:** *1693$^{12}$* 1985$^{11}$ (2410) 2578$^{12}$ 2586$^{8}$ 2686$^{12}$ 2946$^{11}$ (3270) 3439$^{6}$ 3700$^{5}$ *4081$^{12}$ 4109$^{10}$* 4206$^{22}$ **>53a 72f<**

**Time Ticks On 3** b g Timeless Times (USA)-Miss Sherbrooke (Workboy) 2392$^{9}$ 2777$^{12}$ 2987$^{4}$ 3294$^{16}$ 4075$^{19}$ **>31f<**

**Time To Fly 3** b c Timeless Times (USA)-Dauntless Flight (Golden Mallard) *1612$^{5}$* 1888$^{7}$ 2757$^{12}$ *3091$^{6}$ 3774$^{9}$* 4456$^{8}$ *4983$^{7}$* **>40a 49f<**

**Time To Tango 3** b f Timeless Times (USA)-Tangalooma (Hotfoot) 1787$^{3}$ (2176) (2523) 3085$^{6}$ 3415$^{4}$ **>74f<**

**Timothy George (IRE) 2** b c Don't Forget Me-Ward of Court (IRE) (Law Society (USA)) 4720$^{14}$ 4825$^{16}$ 4891$^{17}$ **>57f<**

**Tina Katerina 3** ch f Executive Man-Tria Romantica (Another Realm) **1995:** *4375$^{12}$ 4446$^{2}$* **1996:** *123$^{11}$ 2859$^{9}$ 3626$^{6}$* **>38a 52f<**

**Tinashaan (IRE) 4** b f Darshaan-Catina (Nureyev (USA)) 929$^{4}$ 2352$^{4}$ 2690$^{6}$ **>101f<**

**Tinker Amelia 4** b f Damister (USA)-Miss Primula (Dominion) *4848a$^{6}$* ***>49a 80f<***

**Tinkerbell 2** ch f Sharpo-Chasing Moonbeams (Final Straw) *1046$^{5}$* 1892$^{6}$ *(2554) 2984$^{5}$ 3417$^{3}$ (3629) 3846$^{2}$ 4335$^{2}$ 4490$^{2}$* 4792$^{5}$ 4883$^{6}$ **>62a 79f<**

**Tinker Osmaston 5** br m Dunbeath (USA)-Miss Primula (Dominion) 582$^{12}$ 812$^{11}$ 1064$^{12}$ 1466$^{2}$ 1777$^{8}$ 1985$^{12}$ 2376$^{4}$ 2992$^{4}$ 3146$^{10}$ **>62f<**

**Tinker's Surprise (IRE) 2** b g Cyrano de Bergerac-Lils Fairy (Fairy King (USA)) 490$^{7}$ 2031$^{4}$ (2125) 2279$^{5}$ 2406$^{5}$ *2635$^{4}$ 3763$^{5}$* 3838$^{2}$ 4046$^{7}$ *4093$^{2}$ 4251$^{3}$ 5005$^{4}$* ***>54a 69f<***

**Tinklers Folly 4** ch g Bairn (USA)-Lucky Straw (Tumble Wind (USA)) 615$^{4}$ (662) 1001$^{8}$ 1313$^{8}$ 1546$^{8}$ (2023) (2240) 2357$^{2}$ 2630$^{9}$ (3328) 3510$^{6}$ 3833$^{11}$ 4439$^{7}$ **>70f<**

**Tintara (IRE) 3** b f Caerleon (USA)-Justsayno (USA) (Dr Blum (USA)) **1995:** *4381$^{3}$* **1996:** *597$^{3}$ (980) 2553$^{8}$ 2936$^{11}$ 2990$^{4}$* ***>52a 72df<***

**Tiny Astro 3** b g Superpower-Moonwalker (Night Shift (USA)) 473$^{9}$ **>21f<**

**Tip it In 7** gr g Le Solaret (FR)-Alidante (Sahib) *1719$^{12}$ 1967$^{P}$* **>2a f<**

**Tipperary Sunset (IRE) 2** gr c Red Sunset-Chapter And Verse (Dancers Image (USA)) 4468$^{6}$ **>10f<**

**Tippolina (GER) 3** b f Bayliss (GER)-Tarragona (GER) (Luciano) 4854a$^{3}$

**Tipsy Creek (USA) 2** b c Dayjur (USA)-Copper Creek (Habitat) (1118) (2070) 3213$^{6}$ 3692$^{2}$ **>109f<**

**Tip the Dove 7** br m Riberetto-Nimble Dove (Starch Reduced) 449$^{10}$ **>58?f< (DEAD)**

**Tirage 2** ch c Charmer-Maid of Essex (Bustino) 2224$^{10}$ 2720$^{7}$ 3485$^{5}$ 4041$^{3}$ 4242$^{10}$ 4549$^{9}$ **>72f<**

**Tirlie (IRE) 4** b g Tirol-Lisa's Favourite (Gorytus (USA)) 995$^{20}$ *2939$^{7}$ 3090$^{9}$* **>44f<**

**Tirolette (IRE) 4** b f Tirol-Etage (Ile de Bourbon (USA)) 993$^{8}$ 1306$^{7}$ 3204$^{4}$ *3600$^{3}$ 4048$^{5}$* 4365$^{9}$ 4877$^{9}$ **>48a 61f<**

**Tirol Hope (IRE) 3** b f Tirol-Salique (Sallust) 1246a$^{2}$ 1255a$^{7}$ **>103f<**

**Tirol's Treasure (IRE) 2** b f Tirol-Lisa's Favourite (Gorytus (USA)) 2948$^{6}$ 3169$^{8}$ 3795$^{7}$ **>12f<**

**Tirols Tyrant (IRE) 3** b g Tirol-Justitia (Dunbeath (USA)) *390$^{10}$ 445$^{14}$* 2242$^{3}$ 2567$^{8}$ 2683$^{8}$ 3451$^{6}$ 3619$^{4}$ 4815$^{U}$ **>30a 61f< (DEAD)**

**Tirra-Lirra (IRE) 4** b f Tirol-Run My Beauty (Runnett) *310$^{6}$ 390$^{3}$ 419$^{6}$ 4098$^{15}$* 4360$^{13}$ 4789$^{18}$ **>67da 33f<**

**Tisima (FR) 2** ch f Selkirk (USA)-Georgia Stephens (USA) (The Minstrel (CAN)) 1897$^{5}$ **>52f<**

**Tissisat (USA) 7** ch g Green Forest (USA)-Expansive (Exbury) 853$^{8}$ 1145$^{16}$ **>62f<**

**Tissue of Lies (USA) 3** b br g Ascot Knight (CAN)-Choral Group (CAN) (Lord Durham (CAN)) **1995:** *4380$^{2}$* **1996:** *920$^{8}$* 1361$^{8}$ 1671$^{3}$ 2061$^{2}$ 2514$^{6}$ 2917$^{5}$ 3242$^{2}$ 3327$^{2}$ 3426$^{7}$ 4582$^{12}$ **>76a 76f<**

**Titanium Honda (IRE) 5** gr g Doulab (USA)-Cumbrian Melody (Petong) 470$^{15}$ *556$^{6}$ 839$^{11}$ 1348$^{13}$ 1718$^{8}$* **>42da 41f<**

**Titchwell Lass 3** ch f Lead on Time (USA)-Bodham (Bustino) 1806$^{3}$ (2297) 3173$^{8}$ 4793$^{19}$ **>64f<**

**Tithcar 2** b f Cadeaux Genereux-Miznah (IRE) (Sadler's Wells (USA)) 4756$^{11}$ **>67f<**

**Titta Ruffo 2** b c Reprimand-Hithermoor Lass (Red Alert) 4514$^{3}$ **>81+f<**

**Titus Livius (FR) 3** ch c Machiavellian (USA)-Party Doll (Be My Guest (USA)) 721a$^{3}$ 1581a$^{4}$ 2115$^{9}$ 3914a$^{2}$ 4958a$^{3}$ **>112f<**

**Tiutchev 3** b g Soviet Star (USA)-Cut Ahead (Kalaglow) 4429$^{6}$ 4622$^{5}$ 4824$^{3}$ **>74f<**

**Tivolio (FR) 3** ch c Cricket Ball (USA)-Chirrup (FR) (Chief Singer) 146a$^{2}$ **>61f<**

**T-N-T Express 2** b c Sizzling Melody-Lady Minstrel (Tudor Music) 1827$^{16}$ 4796$^{12}$ 4920$^{12}$ **>43f<**

**Toat Chieftain 4** b g Puissance-Tribal Lady (Absalom) **1995:** *4363$^{4}$ 4412$^{6}$ 4436$^{7}$* **>59da 55f<**

**Toby Brown 3** b g Arzanni-Forest Nymph (NZ) (Oak Ridge (FR)) 4110$^{11}$ 4548$^{13}$ **>40f<**

**Tocco Jewel 6** br m Reesh-Blackpool Belle (The Brianstan) 1314$^{15}$ 2594$^{2}$ 2716$^{7}$ 2941$^{8}$ **>41da 29f<**

**Todd (USA) 5** b g Theatrical-Boldara (USA) (Alydar (USA)) **1995:** *4419$^{6}$ 4452$^{7}$* **1996:** *33$^{5}$ (103) 189$^{5}$ 424$^{4}$ 469$^{6}$* 670$^{5}$ 1514$^{11}$ 3785$^{5}$ 3948$^{7}$ *4334$^{4}$* **>60a 50f<**

**Toe Tappin Music (USA) 3** b g Show Dancer (USA)-Miss Garrett (USA) (Speak John) 539$^{5}$ 740$^{8}$ 861$^{14}$ 1891$^{10}$ **>46f<**

**Toffee 3** ch f Midyan (USA)-Vaula (Henbit (USA)) *1096$^{9}$* **>15a 80?f<**

**Toi Toi (IRE) 2** b f In The Wings-Walliser (Niniski (USA)) 4797$^{5}$ 5033$^{4}$ **>74f<**

**Token Gesture (IRE) 2** b f Alzao (USA)-Temporary Lull (USA) (Super Concorde (USA)) (4642a) **>81f<**

**Tolepa (IRE) 3** b f Contract Law (USA)-Our Investment (Crofter (USA)) 2731$^{10}$ 3058$^{4}$ *3951$^{8}$ 4249$^{18}$* 4472$^{4}$ 4812$^{15}$ **>30a 40f<**

**Tomal 4** b g King Among Kings-Jacinda (Thatching) **1995:** *4521$^{11}$* **1996:** *23$^{3}$ 66$^{13}$ 240$^{11}$ 334$^{8}$ 2313$^{2}$* 2761$^{6}$ 2971$^{3}$ 3314$^{7}$ 3469$^{2}$ 4082$^{5}$ 4257$^{8}$ 4455$^{W}$ **>42a 52f<**

**Tomba 2** ch c Efisio-Indian Love Song (Be My Guest (USA)) 3114$^{6}$ 3588$^{3}$ (3829) 4189$^{2}$ (4510) 4723$^{6}$ **>97f<**

**Tommelise (FR) 4** dk f Dayjur (USA)-Norland (FR) (Gay Mecene (USA)) (5068a)

**Tom Mi Dah 2** b c Superlative-Queensbury Star (Wishing Star) 2353$^{5}$ 2485$^{3}$ 3250$^{7}$ 3814$^{2}$ 4319$^{8}$ **>57f<**

**Tom Morgan 5** b g Faustus (USA)-Pirate Maid (Auction Ring (USA)) *5002$^{14}$* **>45a 84f<**

**Tommy Cooper 5** br h Macmillion-My Charade (Cawston's Clown) 3813$^{9}$ 4832$^{11}$ **>50f<**

**Tommyknocker (IRE) 4** ch g Woodman (USA)-Repercutionist (USA) (Beaudelaire (USA)) 1534$^{12}$ **>25f<**

**Tommy Tempest 7** ch g Northern Tempest (USA)-Silently Yours (USA) (Silent Screen (USA)) **1995:** *4460$^{8}$* **1996:** *22$^{7}$ 64$^{8}$ 386$^{8}$ 1170$^{16}$* 1307$^{12}$ 1708$^{12}$ *1971$^{7}$ 2156$^{6}$* 2324$^{5}$ 2561$^{5}$ *2684$^{5}$ 2791$^{6}$* 2992$^{7}$ *3416$^{8}$* **>28a 46f<**

**Tommy Tortoise 2** b c Rock Hopper-Wish You Well (Sadler's Wells (USA)) 4349$^{2}$ 4585$^{6}$ 4834$^{2}$ **>70f<**

**Tom Pladdey 2** ch c Clantime-Croft Original (Crofthall) *2083$^{6}$ 2596$^{4}$* 3462$^{10}$ 4796$^{6}$ 5048$^{8}$ **>21a 63f<**

**Tom Swift (IRE) 3** b g Law Society (USA)-Debbie's Next (USA) (Arctic Tern (USA)) 1104$^{7}$ 1641$^{12}$ 2895$^{7}$ 4237$^{16}$ **>67df<**

**Tom Tailor (GER) 2** b c Beldale Flutter (USA)-Thoughtful (Northfields (USA)) 3319$^{8}$ 3695$^{4}$ 4330$^{17}$ 4760$^{3}$ **>73f<**

**Tondres (USA) 5** br g Chief's Crown (USA)-Icing (Prince Tenderfoot (USA)) *274$^{2}$ 349$^{7}$* **>72a 79f<**

**Tonga Island (ITY) 2** b f Classic Music (USA)-Masriyana (ITY) (Riverman (USA)) 2272a$^{2}$

**Tonic Chord 3** b f La Grange Music-Tight (Lochnager) 2281$^{4}$ 2718$^{5}$ 3051$^{5}$ 3525$^{10}$ 3862$^{2}$ 4070$^{5}$ 4263$^{10}$ **>49f<**

**Tonka 4** b g Mazilier (USA)-Royal Meeting (Dara Monarch) *87$^{3}$ 4497$^{17}$* (5054) **>45a 66f<**

**Tonto 3** b g Nomination-Brigado (Brigadier Gerard) *856$^{6}$ 1969$^{3}$ 2521$^{9}$* ***>52a 9f<***

**Tony's Delight (IRE) 8** b g Krayyan-Tinas Image (He Loves Me) 2378$^{12}$ **>6a 43f<**

**Tonys Gift 4** b f Midyan (USA)-Harmonical (USA) (Lyphard's Wish (FR)) 1852$^{3}$ (2190) 2717$^{3}$ 3163$^{6}$ **>75f<**

**Tony's Mist 6** b g Digamist (USA)-Tinas Image (He Loves Me) *98$^{5}$ 752$^{12}$* 843$^{11}$ 1411$^{10}$ 1449$^{16}$ 1638$^{4}$ 1893$^{3}$ 2344$^{9}$ 2507$^{16}$ 2971$^{16}$ **>78da 52df<**

**Too Easy (IRE) 2** ch c Shalford (IRE)-Royal Episode (Royal Match) 4639a$^{11}$ **>58f<**

**Tooele 2** b g Full Extent (USA)-Little Madam (Habat) 2422$^{6}$ 2959$^{11}$

**Too Hasty 3** b g Dunbeath (USA)-Suggia (Alzao (USA)) 589$^{12}$ 689$^{7}$ 824$^{13}$ 1068$^{14}$ 1185$^{5}$ 1650$^{7}$ 2049$^{7}$ 3102$^{5}$ 3306$^{7}$ 4598$^{4}$ **>55f<**

**Toon Flyer 2** b g Shirley Heights-Caroline Lady (JPN) (Caro) 4807$^{11}$ 4991$^{16}$ **>5f<**

**Topaglow (IRE) 3** ch g Topanoora-River Glow (River Knight (FR)) 4358$^{5}$ **>43f<**

**Topanga 4** b g Dancing Brave (USA)-Trampship (High Line) 668$^{10}$ *2173$^{9}$* **>54a 81df<**

**Topanoora Bay (IRE) 3** b g Topanoora-Life's Chance (IRE) (Wolverlife) *344$^{13}$ 427$^{10}$ 588$^{5}$*

***Topatori (IRE) 2*** ch f Topanoora-Partygoer (General Assembly (USA)) 848$^{5}$ 1513$^{2}$ 2018$^{2}$ **>59f<**

**Top Banana 5** ch g Pharly (FR)-Oxslip (Owen Dudley) 711$^{2}$ 1107$^{3}$ (1630) 2114$^{28}$ 2880$^{13}$ 3946$^{3}$ 4304$^{8}$ 4917$^{2}$ **>99f<**

**Top Cees 6** b g Shirley Heights-Sing Softly (Luthier) 2547$^{7}$ (2884) 3266$^{7}$ 3689$^{6}$ **>96f<**

**Top Glory (FR)** **3** b g Le Glorieux-Top Slipper (Top Ville) (323a) 1389a$^{2}$ 3386a$^{3}$ 3746a$^{9}$ **>118f<**

**Top of The Form (IRE)** **2** ch f Masterclass (USA)-Haraabah (USA) (Topsider (USA)) 930$^{4}$ (2018) 2317$^{3}$ (2726) 3160$^{3}$ 4024a$^{15}$ 4517$^{4}$ **>81f<**

**Top of The Green (IRE)** **2** b c Common Grounds-Grayfoot (Grundy) 4512$^{19}$ 4825$^{23}$ **>27f<**

**Top of The Wind (IRE)** **2** b f Silver Kite (USA)-Domino's Nurse (Dom Racine (FR)) 585$^{2}$ 950$^{5}$ 1105$^{4}$ 2875$^{2}$ (3324) 3835$^{9}$ 4113$^{16}$ 4864$^{9}$ 5043$^{6}$ **>73f<**

**Top Pet (IRE)** **6** br g Petong-Pounelta (Tachypous) *366$^{11}$ 393$^{3}$ 417$^{4}$ 501$^{8}$* **>52a 56f<**

**Top Prize** **8** b g High Top-Raffle (Balidar) 474$^{2}$ 625$^{18}$ 852$^{7}$ 1044$^{8}$ *(1095) 1478$^{8}$ 2372$^{5}$ 2516$^{7}$ 2936$^{3}$ 3775$^{3}$* 4588$^{14}$ **>41a 40f<**

**Topps Trio** **2** ch f Risk Me (FR)-Ramz (IRE) (The Minstrel (CAN)) 2559$^{10}$ 3494$^{12}$ 4105$^{14}$ **>30f<**

**To Prove a Point** **4** b g Weldnaas (USA)-Run Little Lady (USA) (J O Tobin (USA)) 537$^{13}$ 801$^{6}$ **>34f<**

**Top Royal** **7** br g High Top-Maria Isabella (FR) (Young Generation) 753$^{13}$ 872$^{12}$ **>61f<**

**Top Secret (USA)** **3** b br f Afleet (CAN)-Half Secret (USA) (Upper Nile (USA)) *4952a$^{5}$* **>102a f<**

**Top Shelf** **2** b f Warning-Troy Moon (Troy) 4052$^{9}$ 4697$^{9}$ 4914$^{5}$ **>62f<**

**Top Skipper (IRE)** **4** b g Nordico (USA)-Scarlet Slipper (Gay Mecene (USA)) 3958$^{9}$ 4070$^{15}$ **>42f<**

**Top Titfer** **2** ch f Cap Diamant (USA)-Top Yard (Teekay) 1471$^{8}$ 2254$^{7}$ 3498$^{9}$ 4097$^{11}$ **>32f<**

**Topup** **3** b g Weldnaas (USA)-Daisy Topper (Top Ville) 2432$^{13}$ 2744$^{10}$ 3051$^{3}$ 4263$^{18}$ **>62f<**

**Torch Vert (IRE)** **4** b g Law Society (USA)-Arctic Winter (CAN) (Briartic (CAN)) 449$^{18}$ 573$^{14}$ 5047$^{16}$ **>84?f<**

**Tormount (USA)** **3** b c Local Talent (USA)-Virginia Hills (USA) (Tom Rolfe) *67$^{12}$ (161) 294$^{7}$ 4606$^{8}$* 4793$^{13}$ **>68a 64f<**

**Toronto** **2** b c Puissance-Impala Lass (Kampala) 1779$^{6}$ 3050$^{2}$ 3464$^{5}$ 4318$^{7}$ 4558$^{9}$ 4764$^{15}$ **>63f<**

**Torremolinos (USA)** **3** ch c Trempolino (USA)-Honor Guard (USA) (Vaguely Noble) 3986$^{3}$ 4235$^{2}$ (4613) **>87f<**

**Torrential (USA)** **4** b c Gulch (USA)-Killaloe (USA) (Dr Fager) *434a$^{2}$ 536a$^{8}$* **>116a 118f<**

**Torrey Pines (IRE)** **4** b g Red Sunset-Yukon Baby (USA) (Northern Dancer) *267$^{5}$ 373$^{6}$* **>59a 61f<**

**Torrismondo (USA)** **5** b or br h Tasso (USA)-Miss Cabell Co (USA) (Junction (USA)) 1579a$^{5}$ **>103f<**

**Toskano** **4** b g Salse (USA)-Kukri (Kris) *116$^{9}$* **>39a 55f<**

**Tossup (USA)** **3** br f Gone West (USA)-Tovalop (USA) (Northern Dancer) 1567a$^{9}$ 2609$^{8}$ 3530a$^{6}$ **>105f<**

**Total Aloof** **3** b f Groom Dancer (USA)-Bashoosh (USA) (Danzig (USA)) (626) 1006$^{7}$ (1304) 1646$^{8}$ 2301$^{3}$ 2790$^{8}$ **>78df<**

**Totally Different** **3** b c Totem (USA)-Bold Difference (Bold Owl) 1864$^{8}$ 2540$^{12}$ 2752$^{13}$ 3354$^{12}$ 3619$^{13}$ **>15f<**

**Totally Yours (IRE)** **3** b f Classic Music (USA)-Dominia (Derring-Do) 1526$^{8}$ 1651$^{7}$ 1776$^{10}$ 2251$^{5}$ 4340$^{3}$ 4752$^{2}$ 4967$^{4}$ 5007$^{6}$ **>59df<**

**Total Rach (IRE)** **4** b f Nordico (USA)-Miss Kelly (Pitskelly) **1995:** *4379$^{3}$ 4452$^{14}$ (4532)* **1996:** *27$^{3}$ 145$^{8}$ 233$^{4}$ 319$^{2}$ 499$^{9}$ 688$^{15}$* 879$^{24}$ 1011$^{9}$ 1515$^{9}$ 1691$^{4}$ 1893$^{5}$ (2373) 2507$^{13}$ **>56a 57f<**

**Totem Dancer** **3** b f Mtoto-Ballad Opera (Sadler's Wells (USA)) 2591$^{3}$ 2961$^{3}$ 3298$^{4}$ 3819$^{2}$ 3961$^{2}$ 4227$^{4}$ 4596$^{2}$ 4722$^{2}$ (4833) **>82f<**

**To the Roof (IRE)** **4** b g Thatching-Christine Daae (Sadler's Wells (USA)) 451$^{5}$ (559) 610$^{2}$ 814$^{2}$ (1064) (1186) (1818) 2114$^{6}$ 2545$^{9}$ 3232$^{10}$ 4466$^{12}$ 4679$^{2}$ 4869$^{2}$ **>65a 103f<**

**To The Whire** **3** br f Rock City-Free Dance (FR) (Green Dancer (USA)) **1995:** *4453$^{5}$* **1996:** *164$^{4}$ 3301$^{5}$* 3977$^{8}$ 4257$^{14}$ **>56a 52f<**

**Toto le Moko (IRE)** **3** b c Marju (IRE)-Shyoushka (Shy Groom (USA)) (4421a) **>118f<**

**Tot Ou Tard (IRE)** **6** b h Robellino (USA)-She's My Lovely (Sharpo) 438a$^{3}$ 622a$^{5}$ 906a$^{7}$ 3200a$^{2}$ **>121f<**

**Touch a Million (USA)** **4** b c Mr Prospector (USA)-Magic Gleam (USA) (Danzig (USA)) 547$^{11}$ 765$^{17}$ 1069$^{11}$ **>88f<**

**Touch Judge (USA)** **3** b c Nijinsky (CAN)-Hush Dear 1580a$^{14}$ 2474a$^{4}$ **>104f<**

**Touch'n'go** **2** b c Rainbow Quest (USA)-Mary Martin (Be My Guest (USA)) 5009$^{6}$ **>52f<**

**Touch of Fantasy** **3** b f Never so Bold-Brera (IRE) (Tate Gallery (USA)) **1995:** *4369$^{5}$ 4437$^{9}$* **1996:** *101$^{12}$ 430$^{5}$* **>41a 49f<**

**Touch of Snow** **3** b f Touch of Grey-Snow Huntress (Shirley Heights) *102$^{9}$* **>14a 4f<**

**Tough Act** **2** b c Be My Chief (USA)-Forelino (USA) (Trempolino (USA)) 841$^{5}$ 4233$^{2}$ 4514$^{8}$ 4760$^{5}$ **>82f<**

**Tough Leader** **2** b c Lead on Time (USA)-Al Guswa (Shernazar) 1169$^{2}$ 1424$^{4}$ 1801$^{4}$ (2044) 2517$^{3}$ **>71f<**

**Toujours Riviera** **6** ch g Rainbow Quest (USA)-Miss Beaulieu (Northfields (USA)) **1995:** *4520$^{3}$* **1996:** *132$^{13}$ 1807$^{9}$* 2134$^{10}$ 2400$^{6}$ 2581$^{11}$ 2885$^{2}$ 3072$^{10}$ 3501$^{4}$ 3806$^{6}$ 3981$^{7}$ 4243$^{9}$ 4682$^{7}$ 4719$^{2}$ **>83a 81f<**

**Toulston Lady (IRE)** **4** b f Handsome Sailor-Rainbow Lady (Jaazeiro (USA)) 2136$^{4}$ 2515$^{3}$ 2572$^{9}$ 2988$^{4}$ 3308$^{8}$ **>61f<**

**Tout A Coup (IRE)** **3** b f Ela-Mana-Mou-Coupe D'Hebe (Ile de Bourbon (USA)) (1004) (2102a) 2837a$^{6}$ **>103f<**

**Tout de Val** **7** b m Tout Ensemble-Julie Emma (Farm Walk) 2159$^{13}$ 2537$^{7}$ (2978) 3303$^{7}$ 3808$^{18}$ **>17a 33f<**

**Tovarich** **5** b g Soviet Star (USA)-Pretty Lucky (Shirley Heights) *4779$^{10}$* **>72da 63f<**

**Toyo Lyphard (JPN)** **6** ch h Relaunch (USA)-Thunderdome (USA) (Lyphard (USA)) 4668a$^{2}$ **>119f<**

**Toy Princess (USA)** **4** b f Arctic Tern (USA)-Princess Toy (Prince Tenderfoot (USA)) *222$^{5}$ 296$^{8}$ 422$^{6}$ (666)* 811$^{7}$ 1194$^{5}$ 1792$^{10}$ 2319$^{2}$ 3037$^{8}$ 3598$^{8}$ 4260$^{3}$ **>71a 84df<**

**Traceability** **3** b g Puissance-Miss Petella (Dunphy) *937$^{7}$* 1185$^{4}$ 1476$^{11}$ (1687) 2074$^{20}$ (3766) 3997$^{7}$ 4431$^{13}$ 4761$^{7}$ 4992$^{2}$ **>91f<**

**Traci's Castle (IRE)** **3** b f Ajraas (USA)-Mia Gigi (Hard Fought) 577$^{16}$ **>24f<**

**Tracks of My Tears** **2** gr f Damister (USA)-Carose (Caro) 4096$^{4}$ 4585$^{9}$ 4694$^{2}$ **>53f<**

**Trade Wind** **5** br g Rambo Dancer (CAN)-Cadasi (Persian Bold) *2189$^{4}$* 2494$^{2}$ 2674$^{7}$ 2788$^{4}$ **>62f<**

**Trading Aces** **2** b f Be My Chief (USA)-Corn Futures (Nomination) 585$^{4}$ 1622$^{6}$ 2323$^{5}$ 3230$^{7}$ 4106$^{9}$ (4433) 4672$^{5}$ **>74f<**

**Trafalgar Lady (USA)** **3** b f Fairy King (USA)-Tremulous (USA) (Gregorian (USA)) 3045$^{6}$ 3599$^{5}$ 3790$^{2}$ 4054$^{5}$ 4583$^{5}$ **>84f<**

**Tragic Hero** **4** b g Tragic Role (USA)-Pink Mex (Tickled Pink) *219$^{9}$ 2165$^{3}$* 2709$^{3}$ **>43a 74f<**

**Trailblazer** **2** b c Efisio-Flicker Toa Flame (USA) (Empery (USA)) 4043$^{6}$ 4469$^{3}$ *(4976)* **>66a 63f<**

**Trainglot** **9** ch g Dominion-Mary Green (Sahib) 1005$^{6}$ 3983$^{10}$ 4365$^{12}$ 4771$^{9}$ **>87f<**

**Trait De Genie (FR)** **4** ch g Diamond Prospect (USA)-Garmeritte (FR) (Garde Royale) (4852a)

**Trapped (IRE)** **2** ch f River Falls-Surprise Move 4642a$^{8}$ **>77f<**

**Trapper Norman** **4** b g Mazilier (USA)-Free Skip (Free State) **1995:** *4540$^{8}$* **1996:** *2041$^{10}$ 746$^{6}$* 1010$^{13}$ 2602$^{13}$ 3316$^{10}$ 4252$^{13}$ **>30a 23f<**

**Travelmate** **2** b c Persian Bold-Ustka (Lomond (USA)) 4242$^{8}$ **>61f<**

**Treasured Spirit (IRE)** **2** b f Treasure Kay-Thread of Gold (Huntercombe) *3604$^{11}$*

**Treasure Hill (IRE)** **2** ch c Roi Danzig (USA)-Grass Court (Thatch (USA)) 4024a$^{9}$ **>82f<**

**Treasure Touch (IRE)** **2** b g Treasure Kay-Bally Pourri (IRE) (Law Society (USA)) 990$^{W}$ 1308$^{4}$ 3941$^{3}$ 4250$^{8}$ **>70f<**

**Tregaron (USA)** **5** b h Lyphard (USA)-Klarifi (Habitat) (879) 1190$^{5}$ (2249) 3158$^{15}$ 3612$^{3}$ 3709$^{4}$ **>99f<**

**Tremendisto** **6** b g Petoski-Misty Halo (High Top) **1995:** *4370$^{4}$ 4434$^{8}$* **1996:** *33$^{6}$ 169$^{5}$ 260$^{4}$ 767$^{15}$* 961$^{6}$ 1478$^{3}$ 2120$^{7}$ *5062$^{4}$* **>45a 56f<**

**Tremplin (USA)** **4** b c Trempolino (USA)-Stresa (Mill Reef (USA)) *929$^{5}$* 1520$^{8}$ 4120$^{8}$ 4682$^{12}$ 4974$^{17}$ **>85f<**

**Trendy Auctioneer (IRE)** **8** b g Mazaad-Trendy Princess (Prince Tenderfoot (USA)) *760$^{13}$*

***Tres Heureux (GER)*** ***6*** *b h* Konigsstuhl (GER)-Tres Magnifique 1759a$^{3}$ 2843a$^{10}$ 4409a$^{8}$ 4659a$^{2}$ **>115f<**

**Trevor Mitchell** **2** b f Backchat (USA)-Versaillesprincess (Legend of France (USA)) 4887$^{12}$ **>28f<**

**Tria Kemata** **3** b c Kris-Third Watch (Slip Anchor) 570$^{4}$ 3517$^{7}$ **>93f<**

**Trial City (USA)** **3** dk c Red Ransom (USA)-Willow Runner (USA) (Alydar (USA)) 3911a$^{2}$ **>124f<**

**Trianna** **3** b f General Holme (USA)-Triemma (IRE) (M Double M (USA)) 467$^{6}$ *655$^{4}$ 1497$^{3}$ 2168$^{6}$* **>39a 45f<**

**Triarius (USA)** **6** ch h Trempolino (USA)-Noble Decretum (USA) (Noble Decree (USA)) **1995:** 4524a$^{10}$ **1996:** *535a$^{6}$* **>78a 119+f<**

**Tribal Mischief** **2** br f Be My Chief (USA)-Lammastide (Martinmas) 557$^{3}$ 880$^{2}$ 1166$^{4}$ 2122$^{6}$ 2781$^{5}$ (3853) 4764$^{6}$ 4903$^{10}$ **>64f<**

**Tribal Moon (IRE)** **3** b c Ela-Mana-Mou-Silk Blend (Busted) 707$^{9}$ 847$^{10}$ **>55f<**

**Tribal Peace (IRE)** **4** ch g Red Sunset-Mirabiliary (USA) (Crow (FR)) **1995:** *4476$^{8}$ 4526$^{2}$* **1996:** *13$^{8}$ (82) 132$^{8}$ 817$^{14}$* 1102$^{13}$ **>78a 71f<**

**Trible Pet** **3** b f Petong-Fire Sprite (Mummy's Game) *293$^{4}$ 376$^{4}$* **>54da 60f<**

**Trick (IRE)** **3** b f Shirley Heights-Hocus (High Top) 2610$^{10}$ 3041$^{6}$ (3704) 4193$^{8}$ 4489$^{4}$ 4695$^{2}$ 4919$^{10}$ **>77f<**

**Trickledown** **3** b f Dowsing (USA)-Pillowing (Good Times (ITY)) **1995:** *4375$^{2}$ 4473$^{10}$* **1996:** *49$^{12}$* **>60?a 65f<**

**Trienta Mil** **2** b c Prince Sabo-Burmese Ruby (Good Times (ITY)) 4920$^{11}$ **>45f<**

**Trilby** **3** b f In The Wings-Fur Hat (Habitat) 1644$^{7}$ 1857$^{5}$ 2246$^{5}$ 2384$^{3}$ 2895$^{2}$ (3225) *3610$^{4}$ 4626$^{7}$* 4804$^{4}$ **>50a 74f<**

**Trioming** **10** b g Homing-Third Generation (Decoy Boy) **1995:** *4377$^{11}$* **>38da 44f<**

**Triple (FR)** **4** b f General Holme (USA)-Triemma (IRE) (M Double M (USA)) **1995:** *4527$^{11}$* **1996:** *778$^{9}$* **>26a f<**

**Triple Hay** **2** ch c Safawan-Davinia (Gold Form) 4050$^{8}$ 4600$^{2}$ (4896) **>73f<**

**Triple Leap** **3** b c Sadler's Wells (USA)-Three Tails (Blakeney) 3041$^{8}$ 3425$^{2}$ (3942) **>86+f<**

**Triple Term** 2 br c Terimon-Triple Reef (Mill Reef (USA)) $2977^{4}$ $3485^{7}$ $3964^{4}$ $4361^{8}$ $4864^{4}$ **>74f<**

**Triple Tie (USA)** 5 ch m The Minstrel (CAN)-Tea And Roses (USA) (Fleet Nasrullah) *$1031^{12}$ $1306^{6}$* $1640^{8}$ $1965^{10}$ $3334^{5}$ **>38f<**

**Tristano** 4 b c Colmore Row-Tura (Northfields (USA)) $3752a^{3}$ **>110f<**

**Tristan's Comet** 9 br g Sayf El Arab (USA)-Gleneagle (Swing Easy (USA)) *$73^{7}$* **>66a 34f<**

**Trivellino (FR)** 3 c $1057a^{9}$ **>85f<**

**Troia (IRE)** 2 b f Last Tycoon-Dubai Lady (Kris) $2714^{5}$ **>42f<**

**Troika (IRE)** 3 ch f Roi Danzig (USA)-Trojan Relation (Trojan Fen) $584^{11}$ $804^{7}$ $1359^{12}$ $1850^{13}$ **>52f<**

**Trojan Risk** 3 ch g Risk Me (FR)-Troyes (Troy) $575^{9}$ $863^{2}$ (969) $1771^{2}$ $2033^{3}$ $4117^{2}$ $4326^{9}$ $4686^{2}$ **>66a 88f<**

**Trojan Sea (USA)** 5 b h Bering-Trojan Miss (Troy) $4030a^{2}$ **>111f<**

**Trood** 3 ch c Sharrood (USA)-Nesting Time (Dance In Time (CAN)) $1578a^{3}$

**Troon** 6 gr h Beveled (USA)-Cestrefeld (Capistrano) $4718^{7}$ **>103f<**

**Trooper** 2 b g Rock Hopper-Silica (USA) (Mr Prospector (USA)) $4507^{8}$ $4618^{6}$ $4835^{6}$ **>67f<**

**Tropical Beach** 3 b g Lugana Beach-Hitravelscene (Mansingh (USA)) *$605^{10}$ $775^{8}$ $1030^{9}$ $1342^{6}$* $1541^{3}$ (1865) $2049^{13}$ $2215^{7}$ $2386^{3}$ $2680^{4}$ (3252) (3342) $3489^{4}$ $3644^{5}$ $3793^{2}$ $4180^{10}$ $4382^{4}$ $4521^{10}$ $4791^{5}$ $4995^{8}$ **>41a 67f<**

**Tropical Dance (USA)** 3 ch f Thorn Dance (USA)-Missuma (USA) (Procida (USA)) $960^{8}$ $1628^{12}$ $1790^{3}$ $2332^{10}$ $3222^{2}$ $3984^{11}$ $4122^{7}$ $4552^{4}$ **>94f<**

**Tropical Lass (IRE)** 2 ch f Ballad Rock-Minnie Tudor (Tudor Melody) $4024a^{22}$ **>65f<**

**Trot Thunder (JPN)** 7 b h Dyna Cosmos (JPN)-La Seine Wonder (JPN) (Tesco Boy) $1134a^{3}$ (1952a) **>125f<**

**Troubadour Song** 4 b g King of Clubs-Silver Singing (USA) (Topsider (USA)) *$34^{2}$ $822^{5}$* $1596^{9}$ *(2082) (2304) (2939) $3280^{2}$* $4000^{13}$ *$4779^{3}$ $4900^{5}$* ***>85a 60f<***

**Trouble's Brewing** 5 gr m Hubbly Bubbly (USA)-Chemin de Guerre (Warpath) *$1810^{5}$* **>15a f<**

**Troysend** 3 b g Dowsing (USA)-Way to Go (Troy) $1296a^{3}$ $2041^{30}$ **>104f<**

**Truancy** 3 b g Polar Falcon (USA)-Zalfa (Luthier) $917^{9}$ $1126^{12}$ $1798^{4}$ $2006^{6}$ $2339^{5}$ $4327^{12}$ **>84df<**

**True Bird (IRE)** 4 b f In The Wings-I Want My Say (USA) (Tilt Up (USA)) $625^{5}$. **>69f<**

**True Flare (USA)** 3 b f Capote (USA)-Proflare (USA) (Mr Prospector (USA)) $1140a^{5}$ $1758a^{3}$ **>107f<**

**True Glory (IRE)** 2 b f In The Wings-Truly Special (Caerleon (USA)) $4861^{7}$ **>68+f<**

**True Joy (IRE)** 3 ch f Zilzal (USA)-Foreign Courier (USA) (Sir Ivor) $1882^{6}$ **>63f<**

**True Perspective** 2 b c Presidium-Madam Muffin (Sparkler) $3511^{6}$ $3879^{8}$ $4383^{12}$ **>50f<**

**True Vision** 2 ch f Interrex (CAN)-Lysithea (Imperial Fling (USA)) *$2307^{7}$ $2685^{5}$* ***>6a 25f<***

**Truly Bay** 3 b g Reprimand-Daymer Bay (Lomond (USA)) $2048^{7}$ $2150^{3}$ $2432^{10}$ $4348^{13}$ **>36f<**

**Trulyfan (IRE)** 2 b br f Taufan (USA)-Whateveryousay (USA) (Verbatim (USA)) $2059^{5}$ $3050^{9}$ $3956^{7}$ $4343^{6}$ **>59f<**

**Truly Generous (FR)** 3 $4654a^{7}$ **>108f<**

**Truly Generous (IRE)** 3 ch f Generous (IRE)-Arctique Royale (Royal And Regal (USA)) $4539a^{3}$ $5026a^{2}$ **>104f<**

**Truly Parched (USA)** 2 b c Known Fact (USA)-Drought (IRE) (Rainbow Quest (USA)) $4461^{6}$ $4723^{19}$ **>78f<**

**Trumble** 4 b g Tragic Role (USA)-Sideloader Special (Song) *$104^{10}$ $198^{5}$ $246^{3}$ $384^{4}$ $426^{4}$ $1970^{5}$ $2056^{7}$* $2377^{7}$ **>46a 49f<**

**Trumped (IRE)** 4 b f Last Tycoon-Sweetbird (Ela-Mana-Mou) $998^{4}$ $1167^{14}$ $1309^{3}$ $2020^{5}$ $2175^{7}$ $2563^{3}$ $3346^{6}$ (3676) $3865^{2}$ **>67?f<**

**Truth** 3 b f Prince Sabo-Pursuit of Truth (USA) (Irish River (FR)) **1995:** *(4417)* **1996:** *$1840^{14}$* $2929^{6}$ $3301^{6}$ **>65a 44f<**

**Truth Or Dare** 3 b c Royal Academy (USA)-Rose De Thai (USA) (Lear Fan (USA)) $1938a^{6}$ $2473a^{12}$ **>115f<**

**Try For Ever (IRE)** 4 b f Try My Best (USA)-Dame Ross (Raga Navarro (ITY)) $2825a^{8}$ **>108f<**

**Try-Haitai (IRE)** 5 ch g Colmore Row-Grain of Sand (Sandford Lad) **1995:** *$4357^{13}$* **>47f<**

**Try My Segnor** 3 b c Tirol-Carillon Miss (USA) (The Minstrel (CAN)) $903a^{11}$ **>78f<**

**Tryph** 4 b f Pharly (FR)-Troja (Troy) $2683^{6}$ *$3086^{6}$* **>10a 41f<**

**Try Prospect (USA)** 4 b c Allen's Prospect (USA)-Golden Triad *(432a)* **>106a f<**

**Tsarina** 2 b f Rudimentary (USA)-Dance a Jig (Dance In Time (CAN)) $3660^{11}$ **>48f<**

**Tsarnista** 3 b f Soviet Star (USA)-Princess Genista (Ile de Bourbon (USA)) $709^{6}$ $937^{13}$ $2687^{2}$ $3133^{3}$ $3926^{4}$ $4214^{4}$ $4738a^{4}$ $5072a^{6}$ **>99f<**

**Tsarskaya (USA)** 3 ch f Elmaamul (USA)-Wyandra (So Blessed) $894^{5}$ $1855^{5}$ $2196^{5}$ $2506^{12}$ **>63f< (DEAD)**

**Tsimtsoum (FR)** 3 ch c Fabulous Dancer (USA)-Belgaum (FR) (Dictus (FR)) $192a^{3}$ **>62f<**

**Ttyfran** 6 b g Petong-So it Goes (Free State) $2218^{3}$ $2537^{3}$ $2891^{3}$ $3117^{3}$ $3335^{11}$ $3775^{7}$ **>29a 43df<**

**Tuareg Blu (ITY)** 3 $903a^{4}$ **>99f<**

**Tudor Falcon** 3 b g Midyan (USA)-Tudorealm (USA) (Palace Music (USA)) *$763^{7}$ $1027^{4}$ $1497^{9}$* ***>64a 47f<***

**Tudor Flight** 5 b m Forzando-Tudor Pilgrim (Welsh Pageant) **1995:** *$4532^{10}$* **1996:** *$23^{13}$ $1534^{13}$* ***>16a 26f<***

**Tudor Island** 7 b g Jupiter Island-Catherine Howard (Tower Walk) $1802^{9}$ $2973^{2}$ $3504^{3}$ $3760^{2}$ $4112^{3}$ $4447^{14}$ **>93f<**

**Tuigamala** 5 b g Welsh Captain-Nelliellamay (Super Splash (USA)) **1995:** *$4385^{10}$ (4456) $4514^{8}$* **1996:** *$42^{4}$ $121^{4}$ $205^{5}$ $244^{4}$ (366) $406^{4}$ $486^{4}$ $4102^{7}$* $4497^{8}$ **>64a 37f<**

**Tukapa** 2 b g Risk Me (FR)-Haddon Anna (Dragonara Palace (USA)) $3502^{9}$ $4043^{13}$ **>48f<**

**Tulipa (USA)** 3 b f Alleged (USA)-Black Tulip (FR) (Fabulous Dancer (USA)) (791a) $1750a^{2}$ (2069) $4292a^{8}$ **>111f<**

**Tulsa (IRE)** 2 b c Priolo (USA)-Lagrion (USA) (Diesis) $2224^{13}$ $4369^{13}$ $4546^{9}$ **>48f<**

**Tulu** 5 ch m Nicholas Bill-Falcrello (Falcon) $450^{10}$ $650^{12}$ $816^{4}$ $993^{6}$ $1421^{12}$ (1862) **>53+a 78f<**

**Tumbleweed Pearl** 2 b f Aragon-Billie Blue (Ballad Rock) $2245^{4}$ (2792) (3251) $4875^{5}$ **>89f<**

**Tumbleweed Ridge** 3 ch c Indian Ridge-Billie Blue (Ballad Rock) $681^{5}$ $926^{12}$ $2072^{16}$ $4774^{15}$ $4885^{3}$ **>105df<**

**Tumi (USA)** 3 ch f Diesis-Carotene (CAN) (Great Nephew) $4622^{7}$ $4911^{6}$ **>89f<**

**Turbo North** 3 b g Nordico (USA)-Turbo Rose (Taufan (USA)) *$660^{8}$* $867^{13}$ $1067^{12}$ $1526^{16}$ **>38df<**

**Turgenev (IRE)** 7 b g Sadler's Wells (USA)-Tilia (ITY) (Dschingis Khan) *$196^{11}$ $546^{15}$* $619^{5}$ $886^{8}$ $1116^{3}$ (1802) $2499^{2}$ $3037^{10}$ **>73f<**

**Turia** 3 b f Slip Anchor-Tura (Northfields (USA)) $1123^{5}$ $1873^{4}$ $2430^{4}$ $3500^{7}$ **>75f<**

**Turning Wheel (USA)** 3 b f Seeking the Gold (USA)-Misinskie (USA) (Nijinsky (CAN)) $3258^{2}$ (3656) $4671^{7}$ **>94+f<**

**Turnpole (IRE)** 5 br g Satco (FR)-Mountain Chase (Mount Hagen (FR)) $4683^{5}$ $4862^{8}$ **>77f<**

**Turtle Moon** 2 gr c Absalom-Port Na Blath (On Your Mark) $1453^{4}$ $4762^{8}$ $4816^{3}$ **>65f<**

**Tuscan Dawn** 6 ch g Clantime-Excavator Lady (Most Secret) (1161) $1430^{3}$ $1974^{11}$ $2292^{6}$ $3146^{6}$ $3827^{5}$ $3932^{11}$ (4119) $4367^{4}$ $4765^{16}$ **>82f<**

**Tuscany** 2 b c Pursuit of Love-Jhansi Ki Rani (USA) (Far North (CAN)) (1774) $2040^{9}$ $2721^{2}$ $3684^{3}$ **>90f<**

**Tutu Sixtysix** 5 br m Petong-Odilese (Mummy's Pet) *$868^{18}$* $1040^{6}$ $1157^{13}$ $1541^{8}$ $1859^{4}$ $2523^{6}$ $3151^{11}$ $3453^{9}$ $3643^{11}$ $4205^{11}$ **>31f<**

**Twice as Sharp** 4 ch c Sharpo-Shadiliya (Red Alert) $812^{15}$ $1113^{3}$ $1334^{8}$ $1790^{6}$ (2292) $2694^{22}$ $3618^{13}$ $3827^{7}$ $4119^{5}$ $4452^{12}$ $4772^{21}$ **>89f<**

**Twice Purple (IRE)** 4 b g Then Again-Tyrian Belle (Enchantment) $1121^{10}$ $1442^{4}$ $1624^{4}$ *$1812^{8}$ $2286^{2}$* $2617^{12}$ **>41a 65f<**

**Twice Removed** 3 b f Distant Relative-Nigel's Dream (Pyjama Hunt) $2718^{14}$ $3140^{8}$ $3655^{10}$ **>45f<**

**Twice the Groom (IRE)** 6 b g Digamist (USA)-Monaco Lady (Manado) *$656^{7}$ $2697^{13}$* ***>5a 66f<***

**Twilight Sleep (USA)** 4 b g Shadeed (USA)-Sleeping Beauty (Mill Reef (USA)) *$4874^{10}$* ***>83f<***

**Twin Creeks** 5 b g Alzao (USA)-Double River (USA) (Irish River (FR)) *$122^{10}$ $199^{5}$ (345) $424^{9}$ $713^{10}$ $854^{11}$ $3628^{2}$ $3861^{6}$ $4089^{2}$ $4256^{16}$ $4781^{3}$ (4895)* **>68a 50f<**

**Twin Falls (IRE)** 5 b g Trempolino (USA)-Twice A Fool (USA) (Foolish Pleasure (USA)) *$1542^{7}$* ***>55f<***

**Twist Again (GER)** 3 b f Turfkonig (GER)-Twistqueen (ITY) (Athenagoras (GER)) (792a)

**Two Bills** 2 b g Totem (USA)-Chess Mistress (USA) (Run The Gantlet (USA)) $2538^{7}$ $3809^{6}$ $4208^{12}$ **>54f<**

**Two On The Bridge** 2 b c Chilibang-Constant Companion (Pas de Seul) $1537^{4}$ $2625^{3}$ **>62f<**

**Two Socks** 3 ch g Phountzi (USA)-Mrs Feathers (Pyjama Hunt) *$355^{11}$ $502^{6}$ $1301^{5}$* $1661^{4}$ $2191^{2}$ $2542^{2}$ (3079) $3611^{7}$ $4513^{17}$ $4702^{17}$ **>56a 65f<**

**Two Timer** 3 ch c Clantime-Two's Up (Double Jump) **1995:** *$4431^{8}$* **>32a 48f<**

**Two To Tango (IRE)** 3 ch f Anshan-Marie de Sologne (Lashkari) $4813^{5}$ *(4978)* **>81+a f<**

**Tycoon Girl (IRE)** 2 b f Last Tycoon-Forest Berries (IRE) (Thatching) $4357^{5}$ (4593) **>73f<**

**Tycoon King (IRE)** 4 b c Last Tycoon-Park Express (Ahonoora) $325a^{2}$ **>77f<**

**Tycoon Lady (IRE)** 5 b m Last Tycoon-Tumblella (Tumble Wind (USA)) $1951a^{3}$ **>105f<**

**Tycoon Tina** 2 b f Tina's Pet-Royal Tycoon (Tycoon II) *$2172^{5}$ $4564^{8}$ $4780^{10}$* **>23a 32f<**

**Tycoon Todd (USA)** 2 gr c Cozzene (USA)-Thirty Below (USA) (It's Freezing (USA)) (3994) **>84++f<**

**Tykeyvor (IRE)** 6 b g Last Tycoon-Ivoronica (Targowice (USA)) $766^{6}$ $1109^{3}$ (1700) (2055) **>93f<**

**Tymeera** 3 b f Timeless Times (USA)-Dear Glenda (Gold Song) *(525)* $644^{4}$ $868^{15}$ $1412^{8}$ *$1812^{4}$ $2049^{6}$* $3863^{2}$ $4130^{11}$ *$4776^{8}$* **>50a 58f<**

**Typhoon Eight (IRE)** 4 b c High Estate-Dance Date (IRE) (Sadler's Wells (USA)) $573^{9}$ $844^{9}$ $1450^{2}$ $1618^{10}$ $2574^{10}$ $4307^{7}$ (4753) $5054^{9}$ **>77f<**

**Typhoon Lad** 3 ch c Risk Me (FR)-Muninga (St Alphage) $2198^{2}$ $2557^{4}$ $3315^{4}$ $4354^{12}$ **>73df<**

**Tyrian Purple (IRE)** 8 b h Wassl-Sabrine (Mount Hagen (FR)) **1995:** *$4531^{12}$* **1996:** *$41^{9}$ $64^{4}$* **>60da 62f<**

**Tyrolean Dancer (IRE)** 2 b f Tirol-Waffling (Lomond (USA)) $3988^{14}$ $4435^{4}$ $4889^{8}$ **>83f<**

**Tyrolean Dream (IRE)** 2 b c Tirol-Heavenly Hope (Glenstal (USA)) $4818^{7}$ $5041^{2}$ **>77f<**

U

**Ultimate Warrior 6** b g Master Willie-Fighting Lady (Chebs Lad) *145[2] 1772[3]* 2128[8] 3233[4] 3785[9] 3824[4] *4107[11]* **>64a 68f<**

**Ultra Barley 3** ch g Beveled (USA)-Chapter One (Hello Gorgeous (USA)) **1995:** *(4518)* **1996:** *(52) 182[8]* **>93a 74+f<**

**Ultra Beet 4** b g Puissance-Cassiar (Connaught) **1995:** *4394[16] 4517[9]* **1996:** *55[5] 64[5] 117[2] 163[3] 205[8] 513[7] 617[9]* 931[17] 1163[8] 1474[6] 2680[2] 3278[3] *(3420) 3644[4] 3953[8]* **>63a 59f<**

**Ultra Boy 2** b g Music Boy-Golden Award (Last Tycoon) *1827[8]* 2495[8] 3044[3] 3247[3] (3411) **>76f<**

**Umberston (IRE) 3** b c Nabeel Dancer (USA)-Pivotal Walk (IRE) (Pennine Walk) 1498[9] 2067[5] 2627[9] 3204[5] **>55f<**

**Unalloyed (USA) 3** b f Silver Hawk (USA)-Copperhead (USA) (Hawaii) 813[5] 3505[2] 4422[4] **>84df<**

**Unassailable 3** ch f Hadeer-Penny In My Shoe (USA) (Sir Ivor) 4235[5] 4353[W] **>28f<**

**Unassisted (IRE) 3** b f Digamist (USA)-Velia *4851a[5]* **>75f<**

**Unchanged 4** b f Unfuwain (USA)-Favorable Exchange (USA) (Exceller (USA)) 675[2] 825[4] 1005[4] 1306[5] 2042[23] 2857[4] 3142[3] **>82f<**

**Uncharted Waters 5** b m Celestial Storm (USA)-Try the Duchess (Try My Best (USA)) *165[5] 214[7] (635)* 666[5] 866[7] 1011[2] 1306[4] 1462[2] 1640[5] 1852[2] 2148[9] 2408[4] 2599[6] **>43a 63f<**

**Uncle Doug 5** b g Common Grounds-Taqa (Blakeney) 753[10] 872[6] (1158) 1529[9] 2165[2] 2612[6] 3463[2] (3855) 4302[D] 4722[4] 5047[13] **>72f<**

**Uncle George 3** ch g Anshan-Son Et Lumiere (Rainbow Quest (USA)) 937[9] 1469[5] 2339[2] 2412[9] 2753[3] 2859[5] 2981[2] 3217[9] 3244[2] 3300[4] 3789[2] 3881[10] 4221[6] **>80f<**

**Uncle Oswald 5** ch g Nashwan (USA)-Riviere Bleue (Riverman (USA)) *2935[3]* **>65a 92f<**

**Unconditional Love (IRE) 3** b f Polish Patriot (USA)-Thatcherite (Final Straw) 832[3] 945[2] 2585[3] 2919[2] 3210[4] 4444[24] **>102f<**

**Undawaterscubadiva 4** ch g Keen-Northern Scene (Habitat) *782[6] 1094[7] 1457[5] 2056[13] 2939[6] 3090[5] 3970[8]* **>35a 40f<**

**Undercover Agent (IRE) 2** b f Fairy King (USA)-Audenhove (GER) (Marduk (GER)) 2887[2] (3171) 4113[11] **>80f<**

**Under Pressure 2** ch f Keen-Cal Norma's Lady (IRE) (Lyphard's Special (USA)) 1499[4] 1827[6] 2025[4] (2569) 2930[2] 3224[2] 3411[6] **>73f<**

**Unforeseen 4** ch c Unfuwain (USA)-Eversince (USA) (Foolish Pleasure (USA)) **1995:** *4378[12] 4416[14]* **>49da 64f<**

**Union Town (IRE) 2** b c Generous (IRE)-Exclusive Life (USA) (Exclusive Native (USA)) *2370[8] (2538)* (3057) (3208) 4056[4] **>91f<**

**Unitus (IRE) 3** b c Soviet Star (USA)-Unite (Kris) 1797[5] 2333[2] (2744) 3124[12] **>84f<**

**Unknown Territory (IRE) 2** ch g Imperial Frontier (USA)-Lilac Lass (Virginia Boy) 3214[5] 3607[2] 3840[2] 4195[16] 4694[15] **>69f<**

**U-No-Harry (IRE) 3** b c Mansooj-Lady Roberta (USA) (Roberto (USA)) 443[11] 638[7] 748[18] 867[11] 1707[3] (2049) (2200) 2431[3] (2676) 3154[4] 3465[6] 3693[14] 4521[5] **>61a 68f<**

**Unreal City (IRE) 3** b c Rock City-Tolmi (Great Nephew) (703) 1441[4] **>102f<**

**Unshaken 2** b c Environment Friend-Reel Foyle (USA) (Irish River (FR)) 4516[8] (4786) 4971[5] **>86f<**

**Un Solitaire (USA) 4** b c Bering-Holy Tobin (USA) (J O Tobin (USA)) 5022a[3] **>74f<**

**Unspoken Prayer 3** br f Inca Chief (USA)-Dancing Doll (USA) (Buckfinder (USA)) **1995:** *4461[9] 4509[6]* **1996:** *1594[7]* 1840[5] 2013[8] 3358[3] 3761[8] **>42a 47f<**

**Unsuspicious (IRE) 6** ch g Caerleon (USA)-Lady's Bridge (USA) (Sir Ivor) *1082[5] 1444[8]* **>33a 55f<**

**Uoni 3** ch f Minster Son-Maid of Essex (Bustino) **1995:** *4417[3] 4480[3]* **1996:** *176[8] 280[3] 381[3] 597[2]* 980[2] 1325[6] 1877[4] 2511[9] 2738[5] *3600[8] 3965[12]* **>58da 56f<**

**Upex le Gold Too 4** ch g Precocious-Restless Star (Star Appeal) *1846[8]* 3060[6] 3306[5] 3453[3] 4436[16] **>40a 31f<**

**Up in Flames (IRE) 5** br h Nashamaa-Bella Lucia (Camden Town) 629[14] 814[15] 933[10] 1406[6] 1819[5] 2010[7] 2351[9] 2483[6] 3254[2] 3344[11] 3815[6] **>78f<**

**Uplift 3** ch f Bustino-Relatively Easy (Relkino) *2216[2]* 2356[5] (3053) 3337[P] **>60f<**

**Upper Club (IRE) 4** b f Taufan (USA)-Sixpenny (English Prince) *4095[14] 4509[14]* **>20f<**

**Upper Gallery (IRE) 3** b c Sadler's Wells (USA)-Elevate (Ela-Mana-Mou) 1668[4] 3258[3] 3425[3] 3850[2] 4447[9] 4750[2] 4821[2] **>97f<**

**Upper Heights (GER) 8** b h Head for Heights-Utika (GER) (Frontal) 1948a[8] **>86f<**

**Upper Mount Clair 6** b m Ela-Mana-Mou-Sun Street (Ile de Bourbon (USA)) **1995:** *4355[5]* **1996:** *169[2] (236) (283) 449[4]* 573[3] (767) 1091[5] 2071[6] 3266[5] **>68a 78f<**

**Urban Dancing (USA) 7** ch g Nureyev (USA)-Afifa (USA) (Dewan (USA)) 1044[3] 1343[9] **>50f<**

**Urban Lily 6** ch m Town And Country-Laval (Cheval) *1967[5]* **>8a f<**

**Urgent Request (IRE) 6** gr h Rainbow Quest (USA)-Oscura (USA) (Caro) 4953a[10] **>125f<**

**Urgent Swift 3** ch g Beveled (USA)-Good Natured (Troy) 575[5] 754[8] 3161[2] 3414[2] 4068[3] (4438) 4582[9] **>77f<**

**Ursa Major 2** b c Warning-Double Entendre (Dominion) 4461[5] 4681[6] 4918[2] **>81f<**

**Utah (IRE) 2** b c High Estate-Easy Romance (USA) (Northern Jove (CAN)) 4370[9] 4891[5] **>49f<**

**Utmost Zeal (USA) 3** b c Cozzene (USA)-Zealous Lady (USA) (Highland Blade (USA)) 894[16] 1142[20] 1693[8] 2229[9] 3139[11] (3585) 3777[7] 4109[2] 4428[8] 4768[3] **>64f<**

V

**Vadsa Honor (FR) 3** gr f Highest Honor (FR)-Vadsa (FR) (Halo (USA)) (3571a) 4654a[12] **>105f<**

**Vagabond Chanteuse 2** ch f Sanglamore (USA)-Eclipsing (IRE) (Baillamont (USA)) 1664[3] 3080[4] (3462) 3835[3] 4133[6] **>77f<**

**Vain Prince 9** b g Sandhurst Prince-Vain Deb (Gay Fandango (USA)) 1070[9] 1158[4] 1478[4] 2175[6] 2360[4] 2756[6] 4344[3] **>55f<**

**Valagalore 2** b f Generous (IRE)-Victoria Cross (USA) (Spectacular Bid (USA)) 4720[4] 5033[6] **>71f<**

**Valanour (IRE) 4** b c Lomond (USA)-Vearia (Mill Reef (USA)) (622a) (906a) 2546[6] 3912a[8] **>129f<**

**Val D'Arbois (FR) 4** c **1995:** 4405a[4] (4497a) **>120f<**

**Val Di Taro (GER) 3** 2668a[13] **>84f<**

**Valedictory 3** b c Slip Anchor-Khandjar (Kris) 671[3] (1631) 2054[6] 2620[4] **>108f<**

**Valencia 2** b f Kenmare (FR)-De Stael (USA) (Nijinsky (CAN)) 4449[2] **>89+f<**

**Valentina Crown (USA) 2** dk f Chief's Crown (USA)-Shining Tiara (ITY) (Halo (USA)) 4286a[3]

**Valentine Fairy 2** b f Access Travel-Forest Fairy (Faustus (USA)) 2951[5] 3330[3] 3660[10] **>56f< (DEAD)**

**Vales Ales 3** b g Dominion Royale-Keep Mum (Mummy's Pet) *5391[2]* 2914[10] **>14f<**

**Valesan (CZE) 4** dk c Super Moment (USA)-Vikona Nelson (CZE) 4740a[2] **>59f<**

**Valiant Dash 10** b g Valiyar-Dame Ashfield (Grundy) *3428[7]* **>23f<**

**Valiant Man 5** br g Valiyar-Redcross Miss (Tower Walk) 1043[4] 1162[3] 1642[8] *2085[3] 2367[6] 2632[5] 3777[9]* **>47a 44f<**

**Valise 3** b f Salse (USA)-Secret Valentine (Wollow) *1504[7]* 1762[5] 1907[4] **>48f<**

**Valisky 6** gr m Valiyar-Rocket Trip (Tyrnavos) *79[10]* **>33a f<**

**Valjess 3** b f Today and Tomorrow-Emmer Green (Music Boy) *217[11] 329[8] 468[7] 859[12]* **>12a 34f<**

**Valley of Gold (FR) 4** dk b f Shirley Heights-Lustre (USA) (Halo (USA)) *(395a) 535a[3] 919[6]* 2194[2] **>92a 108f<**

**Vanadium Ore 3** b c Precious Metal-Rockefillee (Tycoon II) 3226[2] 3642[4] 3960[2] 4559[9] 4597[10] 4906[15] **>57f<**

**Vanborough Lad 7** b g Precocious-Lustrous (Golden Act (USA)) *2885[8]* 3403[8] 4820[20] 4882[12] 5010[8] **>43f<**

**Van Chino 2** b c Suave Dancer (USA)-Atlantic Flyer (USA) (Storm Bird (CAN)) 5034[12] **>52f<**

**Van Gurp 3** ch c Generous (IRE)-Atlantic Flyer (USA) (Storm Bird (CAN)) 736[5] 1125[4] 1432[9] 2774[3] 3229[8] 3788[2] (3999) 4181[9] 4674[5] **>93df<**

**Vanishing Trick (USA) 2** ch f Gone West (USA)-Wand (IRE) (Reference Point) 4100[6] (4697) **>82f<**

**Varxi (FR) 2** gr c Kaldoun (FR)-Girl Of France 4949a[3] (5077a) **>107f<**

**Vasari (IRE) 2** ch c Imperial Frontier (USA)-Why Not Glow (IRE) (Glow (USA)) 829[2] (1003) 4328[10] 4579[3] 4723[5] 4971[3] **>97f<**

**Vasiliev 8** b g Sadler's Wells (USA)-Poquito Queen (CAN) (Explodent (USA)) *251[11]* **>67df<**

**Vaugrenier (IRE) 4** b g Scenic-Church Mountain (Furry Glen) *439[8]* 564[3] 844[10] 4487[7] 4615[7] 4826[19] **>71f<**

**Vax New Way 3** gr g Siberian Express (USA)-Misty Arch (Starch Reduced) 644[10] *(1083) 1765[6] 2171[2] 2306[7] 2634[2] 3049[4] 3953[12] 4341[4]* 4809[2] **>73a 65f<**

**Vax Star 2** gr f Petong-Vax Lady (Millfontaine) *1525[2]* (1760) 2112[2] (2504) 3213[7] **>89f<**

**Veerapong (IRE) 2** b f Royal Academy (USA)-Persian Solitare (IRE) (Persian Bold) 1184[6] 1525[9] 1858[6] 2429[2] 3082[6] 3687[12] 4433[9] 4562[2] *4780[4]* **>52a 60f<**

**Veesey 3** b f Rock City-Travel On (Tachypous) 525[16] 664[16] **>60f<**

**Veiled Dancer (IRE) 3** b f Shareef Dancer (USA)-Fatal Distraction (Formidable (USA)) 1804[7] 2247[8] 4448[12] 4726[12] **>58f<**

**Veiled Threat (IRE) 2** f 4661a[5] **>98f<**

**Velmez 3** ch g Belmez (USA)-Current Raiser (Filiberto (USA)) 691[4] 932[4] 1631[6] *3063[13]* **>25a 75f<**

**Velour 2** b f Mtoto-Silk Braid (USA) (Danzig (USA)) 2863[2] (3359) 3804[3] **>94f<**

**Velvet Appeal (IRE) 2** b f Petorius-Sugarbird (Star Appeal) 4159a[4] 4642a[7] **>104f<**

**Velvet Jones 3** b gr g Sharrood (USA)-Cradle of Love (USA) (Roberto (USA)) **1995:** *4361[7]* **1996:** *664[12]* 1009[2] 1662[3] 2013[4] 2235[4] 3138[5] 3316[5] 3862[3] 3977[6] 4373[3] 4692[8] **>52a 62f<**

**Vendetta 3** b f Belmez (USA)-Storm Warning (Tumble Wind (USA)) 1123[7] 1873[7] 2506[8] 2895[5] **>66f<**

**Venetian Scene 2** ch f Night Shift (USA)-Revisit (Busted) 1643[3] 4797[12] 4889[6] **>60f<**

**Veni Vidi Vici (IRE) 3** b c Fayruz-Divine Apsara (Godswalk (USA)) *1972[5] 2306[9] (3852)* (4064) 4453[8] 4609[7] **>21a 70f<**

**Ventiquattrofogli (IRE)** 6 b h Persian Bold-India Atlanta (Ahonoora) **1995:** 4524a$^{2}$ **>116f<**

**Venture Capitalist** 7 ch g Never so Bold-Brave Advance (USA) (Bold Laddie (USA)) 507$^{3}$ 737$^{3}$ 940$^{2}$ (1129) 1800$^{8}$ 2072$^{7}$ 2332$^{2}$ 2545$^{2}$ 2880$^{3}$ 3232$^{7}$ 3759$^{10}$ **>119f<**

**Venture Connect** 2 ch g Interrex (CAN)-Tricata (Electric) *4079$^{2}$* **>64a f<**

**Venture Fourth** 7 b g Hotfoot-Four Lawns (Forlorn River) 1697$^{7}$ 2394$^{P}$ **>32da 44f<**

**Venus Victorious (IRE)** 5 ch m Tate Gallery (USA)-Persian Royale (Persian Bold) *2520$^{5}$* 2981$^{11}$ 3252$^{R}$ 4221$^{18}$ **>60a 42f<**

**Vera's First (IRE)** 3 b f Exodal (USA)-Shades of Vera (Precocious) **1995:** *(4360) 4393$^{2}$ 4483$^{8}$* **1996:** *293$^{6}$ 340$^{7}$* **>72da 72f<**

**Verde Luna** 4 b g Green Desert (USA)-Mamaluna (USA) (Roberto (USA)) *204$^{6}$ 296$^{7}$ 4086$^{15}$* **>47a 71f<**

**Verglas (IRE)** 2 gr c Highest Honor (FR)-Rahaam (USA) (Secreto (USA)) (2040) 3561a$^{3}$ 4398a$^{6}$ **>109f<**

**Veridian** 3 b g Green Desert (USA)-Alik (FR) (Targowice (USA)) 1142$^{4}$ 2011$^{5}$ 2579$^{9}$ 3258$^{6}$ 3586$^{2}$ (3876) **>81f<**

**Verinder's Gift** 2 ch g Chilibang-A Nymph Too Far (IRE) (Precocious) *4079$^{8}$ 4251$^{7}$ 4607$^{2}$ 4980$^{7}$* **>45a 52f<**

**Veronica Franco** 3 b f Darshaan-Maiden Eileen (Stradavinsky) 691$^{5}$ 948$^{7}$ 1507$^{9}$ 4110$^{12}$ 4426$^{16}$ 4548$^{9}$ 4785$^{13}$ **>53f<**

**Verro (USA)** 9 ch g Irish River (FR)-Royal Rafale (USA) (Reneged) *116$^{13}$ 186$^{14}$ 1718$^{11}$ 1890$^{16}$ 2367$^{5}$ 2632$^{6}$ 2940$^{15}$* **>23a 16f<**

**Verzen (IRE)** 4 ch c Salse (USA)-Virelai (Kris) **1995:** *4482$^{2}$* **1996:** *925$^{13}$* 2477a$^{3}$ (2920) 3445$^{10}$ 4051$^{3}$ (4623) 5018a$^{3}$ **>103a 113f<**

**Veshca Lady (IRE)** 3 b f Contract Law (USA)-Genzyme Gene (Riboboy (USA)) *775$^{11}$* 1068$^{10}$ 2026$^{4}$ 2180$^{13}$ 2568$^{4}$ 2731$^{3}$ 2922$^{4}$ 3116$^{2}$ 3491$^{4}$ **>53f<**

**Vetheuil (USA)** 4 ch c Riverman (USA)-Venise (1052a) 1749a$^{3}$ 1950a$^{3}$ 3745a$^{2}$ 4165a$^{4}$ **>129f<**

**Viardot (IRE)** 7 b g Sadler's Wells (USA)-Vive La Reine (Vienna) 1697$^{2}$ 2182$^{6}$ **>67a 63f<**

**Viaticum (IRE)** 4 gr f Scenic-Pete's Money (USA) (Caucasus (USA)) 1252a$^{5}$ 1296a$^{9}$ 1575a$^{6}$ 1912a$^{5}$ 4397a$^{8}$ 4851a$^{3}$ **>102f<**

**Via Verbano (IRE)** 2 b f Caerleon (USA)-Closette (FR) (Fabulous Dancer (USA)) 1910a$^{4}$ 2470a$^{5}$ 3018a$^{4}$ **>82f<**

**Vicki Romara** 2 ch f Old Vic-Romara () (Bold Lad (IRE)) 4585$^{4}$ 4696$^{4}$ **>71f<**

**Vickys Double** 2 b f Mazilier (USA)-Mrs Waddilove (Bustino) 2031$^{5}$ 2199$^{4}$ 2795$^{6}$ 3455$^{8}$ 3498$^{13}$ **>46f<**

**Vicomtesse Mag (FR)** 3 gr f Highest Honor (FR)-Vigoorine (FR) (Shakapour) 4168a$^{2}$ **>107f<**

**Vicoumtess Brave (IRE)** 2 (4658a)

**Victim of Love** 3 b f Damister (USA)-Tantalizing Song (CAN) (The Minstrel (CAN)) **1995:** *4380$^{4}$ (4443) 4504$^{2}$* **1996:** *28$^{5}$ 137$^{8}$ 313$^{4}$ 391$^{3}$ 421$^{3}$ (531) 692$^{12}$* 1181$^{12}$ **>73a 54f<**

**Victoria Day** 4 b f Reference Point-Victoress (USA) (Conquistador Cielo (USA)) 1070$^{12}$ 2717$^{6}$ 3335$^{7}$ 3580$^{9}$ 3870$^{9}$ 4612$^{15}$ **>35f<**

**Victorian Style** 3 ch f Nashwan (USA)-Victoriana (USA) (Storm Bird (CAN)) 1593$^{3}$ (1797) (2894) 3148$^{7}$ 3516$^{6}$ **>92f<**

**Victoria's Dream (IRE)** 2 b f Royal Academy (USA)-Woodland Garden (Godswalk (USA)) *1590$^{7}$* 1871$^{9}$ 2059$^{4}$ 2309$^{6}$ (2429) 3659$^{6}$ 4715$^{7}$ **>65f<**

**Victoria Sioux** 3 ch f Ron's Victory (USA)-Blues Indigo (Music Boy) *101$^{5}$ 183$^{10}$ 224$^{2}$ 271$^{4}$ 332$^{3}$ 405$^{6}$ 423$^{6}$ 867$^{5}$* 1013$^{9}$ 1684$^{8}$ **>59a 40f<**

**Victoria's Secret (IRE)** 4 b f Law Society (USA)-Organdy (Blakeney) 491$^{4}$ 546$^{8}$ 642$^{13}$ 1852$^{6}$ 2046$^{4}$ 2506$^{4}$ 2613$^{2}$ 2847$^{7}$ (2928) 3113$^{9}$ **>58f<**

**Victor Laszlo** 4 b g Ilium-Report 'em (USA) (Staff Writer (USA)) **1995:** *4391$^{8}$* **1996:** *(1165)* 1870$^{8}$ 2390$^{7}$ 2848$^{7}$ 3346$^{9}$ 4483$^{13}$ **>21a 29f<**

**Victory At Hart** 2 ch g Ron's Victory (USA)-Ceramic (USA) (Raja Baba (USA)) 1880$^{4}$ 2435$^{6}$ 3110$^{6}$ 3169$^{6}$ **>41f<**

**Victory Bound (USA)** 3 ch c Bering-Furajet (USA) (The Minstrel (CAN)) *484$^{3}$ 584$^{4}$* 994$^{3}$ 1420$^{4}$ **>57a 77f<**

**Victory Commander** 3 b g Efisio-Gay Hostess (FR) (Direct Flight) *123$^{16}$ 867$^{7}$* 1356$^{10}$ 1658$^{9}$ **>38f<**

**Victory Dancer** 2 b g Ron's Victory (USA)-Villajoyosa (FR) (Satingo) 1982$^{3}$ (2157) (2575) 2877$^{3}$ 3400$^{2}$ 3748a$^{4}$ 3931$^{5}$ 4685$^{2}$ **>87f<**

**Victory Team (IRE)** 4 b g Danehill (USA)-Hogan's Sister (USA) (Speak John) *366$^{2}$ (487) (501) 747$^{3}$* 1121$^{5}$ 2229$^{7}$ 2376$^{2}$ 2602$^{2}$ 3271$^{8}$ 3696$^{5}$ **>78a 75df<**

**Viennese Dancer** 3 b f Prince Sabo-Harmony Park (Music Boy) 4341$^{14}$ 4693$^{8}$ 4784$^{14}$ **>25f<**

**Vilayet** 3 ch c Machiavellian (USA)-Vilikaia (USA) (Nureyev (USA)) 1056a$^{3}$ **>90f<**

**Village King (IRE)** 3 b c Roi Danzig (USA)-Honorine (USA) (Blushing Groom (FR)) 445$^{8}$ 1656$^{6}$ 2135$^{6}$ (2233) 2570$^{3}$ 2998$^{3}$ 3617$^{5}$ 3710$^{12}$ 3876$^{9}$ **>82f<**

**Village Native (FR)** 3 ch c Village Star (FR)-Zedative (FR) (Zeddaan) **1995:** *4383$^{11}$* **1996:** *2200$^{7}$* 2602$^{6}$ 2946$^{8}$ 3389a$^{6}$ **>41a 76df<**

**Village Opera** 3 gr f Rock City-Lucky Song (Lucky Wednesday) 1092$^{11}$ 1503$^{12}$ *2082$^{11}$* **>41f<**

**Village Pub (FR)** 2 ch c Village Star (FR)-Sloe Berry (Sharpo) 4127$^{9}$ 4380$^{7}$ 4512$^{15}$ 4944a$^{5}$ 5050$^{4}$ **>75f<**

**Village Storm (FR)** 6 ch h Village Star (FR)-Purple Rain (FR) (Zino) (4659a) **>116f<**

**Villarica (IRE)** 2 b f Fairy King (USA)-Bolivia (GER) (Windwurf (GER)) 4061$^{4}$ **>76f<**

**Villeggiatura** 3 b c Machiavellian (USA)-Hug Me (Shareef Dancer (USA)) 947$^{7}$ 1106$^{6}$ 1619$^{5}$ 1798$^{11}$ 2206$^{5}$ 2803$^{5}$ 3081$^{2}$ 3253$^{2}$ 3816$^{2}$ 3983$^{16}$ **>80f<**

**Vindaloo** 4 ch g Indian Ridge-Lovely Lagoon (Mill Reef (USA)) 3509$^{9}$ 3691$^{16}$ 3947$^{18}$ 4238$^{16}$ **>74a 77f<**

**Vintage Red** 6 b g Sulaafah (USA)-Armonit (Town Crier) **1995:** *4527$^{10}$* **>32a f<**

**Vintage Taittinger (IRE)** 4 b g Nordico (USA)-Kalonji (Red Alert) *620$^{10}$* 1167$^{11}$ **>50a 27f<**

**Vinza (USA)** 4 *433a$^{4}$* **>90a f<**

**V I P Charlie** 2 b c Risk Me (FR)-Important Guest (Be My Guest (USA)) 2942$^{5}$ 3259$^{9}$ 4123$^{10}$ 4549$^{13}$ **>59f<**

**Viridis (USA)** 3 b f Green Dancer (USA)-Vachti (FR) (Crystal Palace (FR)) *1090$^{5}$* 1508$^{15}$ 1875$^{5}$ 2599$^{9}$ **>66f<**

**Vision Of Spirit (USA)** 2 ch c Chief's Crown (USA)-Viendra (USA) (Raise A Native) 3904a$^{3}$ **>73f<**

**Vitus** 4 b c Dancing Brave (USA)-Sancta (So Blessed) 821$^{13}$ **>85f<**

**Viva Verdi (IRE)** 2 b f Green Desert (USA)-Vaison la Romaine (Arctic Tern (USA)) 4105$^{4}$ 4991$^{9}$ **>77+f<**

**Vivora** 2 ch f Risk Me (FR)-Valldemosa (Music Boy) 1408$^{5}$ 2031$^{8}$ 2187$^{6}$ **>38f<**

**Vladivostok** 6 gr g Siberian Express (USA)-Tsungani (Cure The Blues (USA)) **1995:** *4354$^{3}$ 4428$^{2}$ 4464$^{4}$* **1996:** *36$^{9}$ 71$^{9}$* **>50a 30f<**

**Vocal Command** 4 b g Chief Singer-To Oneiro (Absalom) **1995:** *4388$^{10}$* **1996:** *62$^{10}$* **>39a 59f<**

**Voices in the Sky** 5 b m Petoski-Saltation (Sallust) *37$^{7}$ 106$^{7}$ 983$^{8}$ 1457$^{4}$ 1979$^{2}$* (2192) 3136$^{4}$ (3204) 3302$^{2}$ 3825$^{3}$ 3979$^{2}$ 4307$^{10}$ 4626$^{17}$ **>29a 57f<**

**Voila Premiere (IRE)** 4 b g Roi Danzig (USA)-Salustrina (Sallust) 1414$^{9}$ 1625$^{15}$ 2378$^{3}$ 2525$^{2}$ 2901$^{2}$ 3447$^{3}$ 4580$^{2}$ (4626) 5046$^{16}$ **>82f<**

**Volare** 3 b f Prince Sabo-Nazmiah (Free State) 943$^{6}$ 1061$^{9}$ 1181$^{14}$ 1663$^{4}$ 1840$^{16}$ 2528$^{14}$ 2578$^{13}$ **>41f< (DEAD)**

**Vola Via (USA)** 3 b br g Known Fact (USA)-Pinking Shears (USA) (Sharpen Up) 646$^{9}$ 1193$^{7}$ 1771$^{3}$ 2608$^{9}$ 2883$^{5}$ 3272$^{3}$ 3470$^{2}$ 4489$^{6}$ 4826$^{11}$ **>92df<**

**Volley (IRE)** 3 b f Al Hareb (USA)-Highdrive (Ballymore) (4592) 4971$^{4}$ **>84f<**

**Volochine (IRE)** 5 ch h Soviet Star (USA)-Harmless Albatross (Pas de Seul) **1995:** 4524a$^{5}$ **1996:** *535a$^{11}$ (2840a)* 4953a$^{8}$ **>52a 122f<**

**Volunteer (IRE)** 4 b g Midyan (USA)-Sistabelle (Bellypha) **1995:** *4489$^{8}$* **1996:** *3683$^{9}$* **>37a 64f<**

**Voodoo Rocket** 3 ch f Lycius (USA)-Vestal Flame (Habitat) 583$^{9}$ 1045$^{7}$ 1350$^{7}$ *2158$^{7}$ 2592$^{9}$* 4968$^{10}$ *5059$^{5}$* **>56a 58f<**

**Voyagers Quest (USA)** 2 b br c Dynaformer (USA)-Orange Sickle (USA) (Rich Cream (USA)) 4175$^{3}$ (4370) 5024a$^{5}$ **>96f<**

**W**

**Wacky (IRE)** 5 b or br m Petorius-Zany (Junius (USA)) 2963$^{5}$ 3060$^{8}$ 3306$^{16}$ **>7a 7f<**

**Wadada** 5 b or br g Adbass (USA)-No Rejection (Mummy's Pet) *2173$^{4}$ (2310)* 2958$^{3}$ 3335$^{6}$ *3952$^{5}$* **>39a 52f<**

**Waders Dream (IRE)** 7 b g Doulab (USA)-Sea Mistress (Habitat) 664$^{7}$ 2410$^{5}$ 2735$^{6}$ 3285$^{2}$ 3583$^{4}$ (3666) 3967$^{5}$ 4259$^{10}$ 4356$^{7}$ 4701$^{6}$ **>39a 54f<**

**Wafayt (IRE)** 5 b h Danehill (USA)-Diamond Field (USA) (Mr Prospector (USA)) **1995:** *(4561a)* **1996:** *375a$^{6}$* **>110f<**

**Wafir (IRE)** 4 b c Scenic-Taniokey (Grundy) *628$^{6}$* 953$^{4}$ 1476$^{3}$ 2055$^{19}$ 2724$^{14}$ 3081$^{4}$ 3621$^{2}$ (3856) 4073$^{6}$ 4450$^{9}$ **>89f<**

**Waft (USA)** 3 ch f Topsider (USA)-Gliding By (USA) (Tom Rolfe) **1995:** *4414$^{6}$* **1996:** *730$^{8}$* 982$^{11}$ 4609$^{3}$ 4692$^{6}$ 4905$^{5}$ **>50a 71f<**

**Wagga Moon (IRE)** 2 b c Mac's Imp (USA)-Faapette (Runnett) 476$^{3}$ 1632$^{4}$ 2720$^{5}$ 3969$^{14}$ **>58f<**

**Wagon Load** 11 . g Bustino-Noble Girl (Be Friendly) 1677$^{9}$ 1953$^{13}$ **>28f<**

**Wahab** 3 b c Unfuwain (USA)-Mileeha (USA) (Blushing Groom (FR)) *4221$^{19}$* **>3f<**

**Wahem (IRE)** 6 b g Lomond (USA)-Pro Patria (Petingo) **1995:** *4420$^{2}$ 4532$^{8}$* **1996:** *69$^{6}$ 138$^{8}$ (240) 309$^{6}$* **>49a 45f<**

**Wahiba Sands** 3 b g Pharly (FR)-Lovely Noor (USA) (Fappiano (USA)) *4714$^{7}$* 4886$^{3}$ **>102f<**

**Waikiki Beach (USA)** 5 ch g Fighting Fit (USA)-Running Melody (Rheingold) **1995:** *4435$^{5}$* **1996:** *487$^{2}$ (530) 756$^{4}$ 1048$^{3}$ 2170$^{4}$ (2201) 3419$^{4}$ 3627$^{8}$* **>86+a 70f<**

**Wait For Rosie** 2 b f Reprimand-Turbo Rose (Taufan (USA)) 596$^{2}$ 685$^{3}$ (1008) 1318$^{2}$ 1352$^{3}$ 3268$^{4}$ 3467$^{10}$ **>83f<**

**Waiting Game (IRE)** 2 b c Reprimand-Walesiana (GER) (Star Appeal) *(4091) 4471$^{2}$* **>82+a 96f<**

**Wakeel (USA)** 4 b g Gulch (USA)-Raahia (CAN) (Vice Regent (CAN)) 147a$^{2}$ (227a) 325a$^{4}$ 967$^{7}$ 1330$^{6}$ 1793$^{10}$ 3072$^{3}$ 3744a$^{10}$ 4682$^{13}$ **>91f<**

**Waky Nao** 3 b c Alzao (USA)-Waky Na (GER) (Ahonoora) (1753a) (2663a) 3572a$^{2}$ 4033a$^{5}$ **>114f<**

**Walking Possession** 7 b h Faustus (USA)-Pepeke (Mummy's Pet) (497a) >**104f**<

**Walk In The Wild** 4 b f Bold Owl-Tripolitaine (FR) (Nonoalco (USA)) **1995:** 4372$^{11}$ **1996:** 1488$^{8}$ 4484$^{9}$ >**15a 26df**<

**Walk On By** 2 gr c Terimon-Try G's (Hotfoot) 4508$^{7}$ 4835$^{4}$ >**62f**<

**Walk the Beat** 6 b g Interrex (CAN)-Plaits (Thatching) 1777$^{6}$ 2034$^{7}$ (2324) (2561) 2787$^{11}$ 3323$^{3}$ 3477$^{7}$ 4088$^{11}$ 4372$^{5}$ (4577) 4778$^{3}$ 4828$^{3}$ 5039$^{9}$ >**71a 69f**<

**Wall Street (USA)** 3 ch c Mr Prospector (USA)-Wajd (USA) (Northern Dancer) 970$^{2}$ (1627) 2039$^{7}$ (2881) 3746a$^{4}$ 4197$^{2}$ (4441) 4955a$^{8}$ >**121f**<

**Waltz Time** 2 b f Rambo Dancer (CAN)-Kiveton Komet (Precocious) 4244$^{6}$ 4469$^{6}$ 4762$^{12}$ 5005$^{7}$ >**46f**<

**Walworth Lady** 5 gr m Belfort (FR)-Manna Green (Bustino) 609$^{5}$ (822) 999$^{5}$ 1167$^{12}$ >**49a 59f**<

**Wandering Star (USA)** 3 b f Red Ransom (USA)-Beautiful Bedouin (USA) (His Majesty (USA)) 1614$^{3}$ (1855) (2225) (3945) 4567$^{5}$ (4961a) >**115f**<

**Wandering Thoughts (IRE)** 7 ch g Boyne Valley-Moves Well (Green God) (4396a) 4848a$^{8}$ >**106f**<

**Wannaplantatree** 5 b m Niniski (USA)-Cataclysmic (Ela-Mana-Mou) (573) 2002$^{6}$ >**61a 79df**<

**Wanstead (IRE)** 4 ch g Be My Native (USA)-All The Same (Cajun) 2408$^{6}$ >**39f**<

**Warbrook** 3 b c Warrshan (USA)-Bracey Brook (Gay Fandango (USA)) 1175$^{6}$ 2074$^{13}$ 3669$^{6}$ 3997$^{6}$ 4556$^{4}$ 4683$^{14}$ >**91f**<

**Wardara** 4 ch f Sharpo-Ward One (Mr Fluorocarbon) **1995:** 4531$^{13}$ **1996:** 466$^{10}$ 749$^{21}$ 896$^{3}$ 1083$^{3}$ 1455$^{8}$ 1606$^{3}$ (1812) (1991) (2084) 2347$^{2}$ 2590$^{3}$ (3700) 3793$^{11}$ 3937$^{2}$ 4136$^{2}$ 4312$^{4}$ 4858a$^{9}$ >**79a 79f**<

**War Declaration (IRE)** 2 4859a$^{8}$ 5028a$^{2}$ >**65f**<

**Warhurst (IRE)** 5 b g Nordance (USA)-Pourboire (Star Appeal) 31$^{4}$ (45) 57$^{4}$ 114$^{6}$ 4810$^{19}$ >**62a 62f**<

**Warm Hearted (USA)** 4 ch g Known Fact (USA)-Lovin' Lass (USA) (Cutlass (USA)) **1995:** 4382$^{7}$ 4543$^{4}$ **1996:** 26$^{5}$ 155$^{5}$ 2347$^{9}$ >**59a f**<

**Warming Trends** 3 b g Warning-Sunny Davis (USA) (Alydar (USA)) 917$^{3}$ 4054$^{12}$ 4583$^{2}$ 4688$^{2}$ 4775$^{2}$ >**101f**<

**Warm Spell** 6 b g Northern State (USA)-Warm Wind (Tumble Wind (USA)) 38$^{8}$ 573$^{12}$ 759$^{6}$ 4068$^{12}$ 4669$^{4}$ >**78a 57f**<

**Warning Reef** 3 b c Warning-Horseshoe Reef (Mill Reef (USA)) 567$^{4}$ 833$^{3}$ 970$^{6}$ 1106$^{3}$ 1771$^{9}$ 2074$^{7}$ 2314$^{2}$ 2505$^{2}$ >**86f**<

**Warning Shot** 4 b g Dowsing (USA)-Warning Bell (Bustino) 469$^{7}$ 561$^{11}$ 1893$^{13}$ >**25a 44f**<

**Warning Star** 4 b f Warning-Blade of Grass (Kris) 864$^{3}$ 1566a$^{8}$ (1879) 2332$^{3}$ 2692$^{6}$ 3914a$^{8}$ 4743a$^{4}$ 5044$^{8}$ >**100f**<

**Warning Time** 3 b c Warning-Ballad Island (Ballad Rock) 673$^{11}$ 1146$^{3}$ 1796$^{2}$ 2007$^{8}$ 2853$^{5}$ 3047$^{4}$ >**102f**<

**Warren Knight** 3 b c Weldnaas (USA)-Trigamy (Tribal Chief) 577$^{6}$ 1438$^{7}$ 4064$^{18}$ 4256$^{15}$ >**67f**<

**War Requiem (IRE)** 6 b g Don't Forget Me-Ladiz (Persian Bold) 3785$^{3}$ 4509$^{17}$ >**37a 43f**<

**Warring** 2 b g Warrshan (USA)-Emerald Ring (Auction Ring (USA)) 3682$^{14}$ 4127$^{12}$ 4512$^{11}$ 4715$^{11}$ >**60f**<

**Warrlin** 2 b c Warrshan (USA)-Lahin (Rainbow Quest (USA)) 1197$^{8}$ 2122$^{4}$ 2923$^{4}$ 3982$^{10}$ 4361$^{3}$ 4585$^{10}$ >**62f**<

**War Shanty** 3 b f Warrshan (USA)-Daring Ditty (Daring March) 4478$^{5}$ >**60f**<

**Warspite** 6 b g Slip Anchor-Valkyrie (Bold Lad (IRE)) 2226$^{12}$ 2574$^{9}$ 3141$^{9}$ 3496$^{8}$ 4095$^{4}$ 4509$^{18}$ >**40a 46f**<

**Warwick Mist (IRE)** 4 ch f Digamist (USA)-Flash Donna (USA) (Well Decorated (USA)) **1995:** 4479$^{12}$ **1996:** 2521$^{W}$ 2683$^{3}$ 3242$^{7}$ 3676$^{4}$ >**35a 35f**<

**Wasblest** 4 b f Statoblest-Safety First (Wassl) 835$^{3}$ 1028$^{8}$ 1455$^{6}$ 2022$^{4}$ 2240$^{5}$ 2520$^{6}$ >**60a 53f**<

**Washington Reef (USA)** 3 b g Seattle Dancer (USA)-Broken Wave (Bustino) 640$^{13}$ 1503$^{8}$ 1997$^{3}$ 2216$^{3}$ 2530$^{2}$ >**54a 63f**<

**Wasp Ranger (USA)** 2 b c Red Ransom (USA)-Lady Climber (USA) (Mount Hagen (FR)) 3706$^{3}$ 3987$^{5}$ 4512$^{2}$ >**93f**<

**Watch Me (IRE)** 3 b f Green Desert (USA)-Fenny Rough (Home Guard (USA)) 672$^{2}$ (943) 2072$^{3}$ 3222$^{5}$ >**114f**<

**Watch Me Go (IRE)** 7 b g On Your Mark-Nighty Night (Sassafras (FR)) **1995:** 4532$^{2}$ **1996:** 609$^{2}$ 995$^{7}$ 1098$^{4}$ 1534$^{2}$ 2322$^{3}$ >**47a 47f**<

**Watch The Fire** 3 b f Statoblest-Thulium (Mansingh (USA)) 591$^{3}$ 758$^{2}$ (2597) 3112$^{11}$ >**69f**<

**Water Chestnut** 3 ch g Most Welcome-Water Pageant (Welsh Pageant) 899$^{10}$ >**24a f**<

**Watercolour (IRE)** 2 b f Groom Dancer (USA)-River Nomad (Gorytus (USA)) 1346$^{10}$ 1683$^{8}$ 2404$^{7}$ >**35f**<

**Water Garden** 2 ch c Most Welcome-On Show (Welsh Pageant) 4756$^{22}$ 4913$^{15}$ >**50f**<

**Water Hazard (IRE)** 4 b g Maelstrom Lake-Simply Inch (Simply Great (FR)) **1995:** 4364$^{10}$ 4534$^{10}$ **1996:** 23$^{11}$ >**62a 59f**<

**Waterlord (IRE)** 6 b g Bob Back (USA)-Ringtail (Auction Ring (USA)) 615$^{11}$ 688$^{3}$ 827$^{8}$ 883$^{5}$ 1546$^{3}$ 1674$^{7}$ 2075$^{19}$ >**46a 46f**<

**Waterperry (USA)** 4 535a$^{13}$ >**42a f**<

**Water Poet (IRE)** 3 b c Sadler's Wells (USA)-Love Smitten (CAN) (Key To The Mint (USA)) 1757a$^{12}$ (2845a) (3567a) 3915a$^{7}$ 4293a$^{7}$ >**114f**<

**Waterspout (USA)** 2 b c Theatrical-Water Angel (USA) (Halo (USA)) 4127$^{3}$ 4370$^{6}$ >**76f**<

**Waterville Boy (IRE)** 2 ch c Don't Forget Me-East River (FR) (Arctic Tern (USA)) 4188$^{8}$ 4349$^{4}$ 4544$^{4}$ 4715$^{18}$ >**59f**<

**Wathbat Nashwan** 2 ch c Nashwan (USA)-Alwathba (USA) (Lyphard (USA)) 4705$^{8}$ 4913$^{7}$ >**71f**<

**Wathik (USA)** 6 ch h Ogygian (USA)-Copper Creek (Habitat) **1995:** 4561a$^{4}$ **1996:** 375a$^{2}$ 436a$^{4}$ >**90a f**<

**Waverley Star** 11 br g Pitskelly-Quelle Blague (Red God) 1342$^{12}$ 1642$^{18}$ 2910$^{8}$ 3278$^{8}$ 3294$^{8}$ 3957$^{13}$ >**41da 18f**<

**Wavian** 4 b c Warning-Vian (USA) (Far Out East (USA)) 579$^{4}$ 673$^{10}$ 864$^{2}$ 1332$^{5}$ 1818$^{11}$ 2115$^{13}$ 2381$^{7}$ 2545$^{11}$ >**102f**<

**Wavy Run (IRE)** 5 Commanche Run-Wavy Reef (Kris) 4960a$^{3}$ >**104f**<

**Wayne County (IRE)** 6 b h Sadler's Wells (USA)-Detroit (FR) (Riverman (USA)) 726$^{2}$ 1509$^{7}$ 1817$^{6}$ 2583$^{7}$ 3614$^{7}$ >**68a 97f**<

**Waypoint** 3 b f Cadeaux Genereux-Princess Athena (Ahonoora) (484) 676$^{4}$ 4376$^{12}$ 4860$^{2}$ 4921$^{13}$ >**67a 79f**<

**Wedding Gift (FR)** 3 b f Always Fair (USA)-Such Style (Sassafras (FR)) **1995:** (4400a) **1996:** 905a$^{3}$ 1949a$^{5}$ >**109f**<

**Wedding Music** 2 b f Music Boy-Diamond Wedding (USA) (Diamond Shoal) 1093$^{7}$ 2635$^{5}$ 3110$^{4}$ 3488$^{2}$ 3763$^{8}$ 3879$^{4}$ 4093$^{5}$ >**32a 54f**<

**Wee Dram** 2 ch f Most Welcome-Scottish Legend (Legend of France (USA)) 2712$^{8}$ 4210$^{6}$ 4475$^{4}$ >**72f**<

**Weeheby (USA)** 7 ch g Woodman (USA)-Fearless Dame (USA) (Fearless Knight) 4574$^{5}$ >**59a f**<

**Wee Hope (USA)** 3 b c Housebuster (USA)-Tell Me Sumthing (USA) (Summing (USA)) 783$^{9}$ 1422$^{4}$ (1787) >**78f**<

**Weet A Bit (IRE)** 2 b c Archway (IRE)-Aridje (Mummy's Pet) 568$^{7}$ >**44f**<

**Weet-A-Minute (IRE)** 3 ro c Nabeel Dancer (USA)-Ludovica (Bustino) 694$^{4}$ 1015$^{3}$ 2144$^{4}$ 2535$^{3}$ 2677$^{6}$ 3431$^{6}$ 3781$^{7}$ 4178$^{8}$ 4886$^{5}$ 5045$^{6}$ >**104f**<

**Weet Ees Girl (IRE)** 2 ro f Common Grounds-Kastiliya (Kalamoun) (523) 984$^{4}$ 2700$^{5}$ 3268$^{3}$ 3483$^{6}$ 3921$^{6}$ >**80f**<

**Wee Tinkerbell** 3 ch f Timeless Times (USA)-Kiveton Komet (Precocious) 1456$^{9}$ >**66f**<

**Weetman's Weigh (IRE)** 3 b c Archway (IRE)-Indian Sand (Indian King (USA)) (32) 112$^{2}$ 157$^{2}$ (182) (493) 692$^{3}$ 1006$^{3}$ >**80a 84f**<

**Welcome Brief** 3 b f Most Welcome-Lawful (Law Society (USA)) 1099$^{15}$ 1435$^{10}$ 1608$^{7}$ 2636$^{8}$ 2966$^{11}$ 3676$^{5}$ >**18a 32f**<

**Welcome Heights** 2 b g Most Welcome-Mount Ida (USA) (Conquistador Cielo (USA)) 4330$^{21}$ 4783$^{10}$ 4896$^{8}$ >**18f**<

**Welcome Home** 2 b f Most Welcome-Miss Cindy (Mansingh (USA)) 4041$^{9}$ 4449$^{9}$ >**38f**<

**Welcome Lu** 3 ch f Most Welcome-Odile (Green Dancer (USA)) 428$^{7}$ 516$^{4}$ 604$^{10}$ 1027$^{10}$ 1905$^{9}$ 2800$^{9}$ 2983$^{3}$ (3316) (3578) 3777$^{11}$ 4098$^{18}$ >**36a 49f**<

**Welcome Parade** 3 b c Generous (IRE)-Jubilee Trail (Shareef Dancer (USA)) 2949$^{3}$ (3356) (3683) 3983$^{13}$ >**95f**<

**Welcome Royale (IRE)** 3 ch g Be My Guest (USA)-Kirsova (Absalom) 444$^{13}$ 978$^{8}$ 1654$^{19}$ 2934$^{9}$ 3586$^{4}$ 3968$^{4}$ >**27a 56f**< **(DEAD)**

**Wellaki (USA)** 2 ch c Miswaki (USA)-Wellomond (FR) (Lomond (USA)) 4801$^{4}$ (5009) >**80f**<

**Well Arranged (IRE)** 5 ch h Bold Arrangement-Eurynome (Be My Guest (USA)) 753$^{9}$ (1082) 1458$^{6}$ 2884$^{8}$ 3437$^{8}$ 3801$^{13}$ 3952$^{3}$ 4092$^{10}$ 4910$^{9}$ >**70a 64df**<

**Wellcome Inn** 2 ch c Most Welcome-Mimining (Tower Walk) 4175$^{10}$ >**31f**<

**Well Done** 2 gr f Petong-Mrs Darling (Mummy's Pet) 4105$^{10}$ 4357$^{9}$ 4544$^{11}$ >**38f**<

**Well Drawn** 3 b c Dowsing (USA)-Classic Design (Busted) **1995:** 4535$^{3}$ **1996:** (67) >**70a 64f**<

**Welliran** 3 ch g Hadeer-Iranian (Indian King (USA)) 448$^{4}$ >**68f**<

**Well Suited** 6 b g Elegant Air-Gay Appeal (Star Appeal) 485$^{7}$ 983$^{7}$ 1534$^{15}$ 1838$^{8}$ 2408$^{9}$ >**24a 31f**<

**Well Warned** 2 b f Warning-Well Beyond (IRE) (Don't Forget Me) 2147$^{2}$ 2582$^{3}$ (3433) 3707$^{8}$ >**89f**<

**Welsh Emblem (IRE)** 3 b c Mujtahid (USA)-David's Star (Welsh Saint) 1350$^{4}$ 1667$^{6}$ 1994$^{10}$ 3421$^{3}$ >**64a 66f**<

**Welsh Liberty (IRE)** 7 b h Caerleon (USA)-Bernica (FR) (Caro) **1995:** (4402a) **1996:** 1759a$^{6}$ >**118f**<

**Welsh Melody** 3 b f Merdon Melody-Young Whip (Bold Owl) **1995:** 4375$^{5}$ 4431$^{3}$ **1996:** 49$^{2}$ 158$^{2}$ 404$^{5}$ >**60da 31f**<

**Welsh Mill (IRE)** 7 b g Caerleon (USA)-Gay Milly (FR) (Mill Reef (USA)) 1421$^{2}$ (1637) 1870$^{4}$ (2499) 2912$^{3}$ 3404$^{4}$ 3834$^{5}$ >**85f**<

**Welsh Mist** 5 b m Damister (USA)-Welwyn (Welsh Saint) 673$^{6}$ 940$^{8}$ 1129$^{9}$ 2298$^{5}$ 2692$^{7}$ 2889$^{13}$ 3126$^{7}$ 3495$^{5}$ >**99f**<

**Welsh Mountain** 3 b c Welsh Captain-Miss Nelski (Most Secret) 443$^{10}$ 571$^{13}$ 1693$^{5}$ 1985$^{7}$ 4205$^{15}$ 4460$^{12}$ 4805$^{9}$ >**61f**<

**Welton Arsenal** 4 b g Statoblest-Miller's Gait (Mill

Reef (USA)) 455[9] (600) 728[4] 1623[5] 4623[6] 4775[12] 4800[2] 4885[4] 4974[24] **>100f<**

**Welville 3** b c Most Welcome-Miss Top Ville (FR) (Top Ville) 676[2] **>100f<**

**Wendals Touch 5** gr m Touch of Grey-Snow Huntress (Shirley Heights) **1995:** *4357[14]* **>36f<**

**Wentbridge Lad (IRE) 6** b g Coquelin (USA)-Cathryn's Song (Prince Tenderfoot (USA)) **1995:** *4367[11]* **1996:** *513[8] 713[2]* 765[4] 879[8] 933[16] 1018[3] 1449[2] *1602[5] 1704[2] 1811[7] 1890[2]* 2351[F] 2701[6] 2796[4] 3125[8] 3265[2] 3450[3] 3805[5] **>82?a 73f<**

**We're Joken 4** b f Statoblest-Jay Gee Ell (Vaigly Great) **1995:** *4407[9]* **1996:** *155[16] 170[9]* **>25a 57f<**

**Wesley's Lad (IRE) 2** b br c Classic Secret (USA)-Galouga (FR) (Lou Piguet (FR)) 4477[4] 4801[15] *4985[3]* **>56a 61f<**

**Westcourt Magic 3** b g Emarati (USA)-Magic Milly (Simply Great (FR)) (565) 927[3] 1129[10] 2332[8] 3759[5] 4115[8] **>109f<**

**Westcourt Princess 4** b f Emarati (USA)-Petrol (Troy) 628[4] 787[9] 1037[4] **>41a 55f< (DEAD)**

**Western Country 4** ch g Beveled (USA)-Country Singer (Town And Country) 4360[15] 4674[12] 4877[16] **>27df<**

**Western Dynasty 10** ch g Hotfoot-Northern Dynasty (Breeders Dream) *546[14]* 753[15] 1524[10] **>42f<**

**Western General 5** ch g Cadeaux Genereux-Patsy Western (Precocious) 440[12] 765[5] 1341[9] (1868) **>77f<**

**Western Horizon (USA) 4** ch f Gone West (USA)-Norette (Northfields (USA)) 787[13] 1034[8] 1343[8] 1696[6] 2130[13] 2409[7] **>33a 36f<**

**Western Hour (USA) 2** b f Gone West (USA)-Out On The Town (USA) (Spend A Buck (USA)) 4052[6] 4725[3] **>72f<**

**Western Playboy 4** b g Law Society (USA)-Reine D'Beaute (Caerleon (USA)) 1079[5] 1305[6] 1640[16] **>65f<**

**Western Sal 4** b f Salse (USA)-Patsy Western (Precocious) *1496[4]* 1704[3] (2131) 2300[6] 2900[4] 3404[5] 3760[3] 3948[8] **>77f<**

**Western Sonata (IRE) 3** b f Alzao (USA)-Musique Classique (USA) (Exclusive Native (USA)) 150a[6] 287a[7] *355[3]* **>56a 59f<**

**Western Venture (IRE) 3** ch g Two Timing (USA)-Star Gazing (IRE) (Caerleon (USA)) 978[14] 1485[10] 3789[6] 3978[2] 4472[2] 4597[15] 4882[18] *4981[13] 5004[13]* ***>7a** **63f<**

**Westfield 4** b g Lyphento (USA)-Wessex Flyer (Pony Express) **1995:** *4412[13]*

**West-Hatch-Spirit 3** b f Forzando-Fairy Ballerina (Fairy King (USA)) 3108[8] **>9f<**

**West Humble 3** ch f Pharly (FR)-Humble Pie (Known Fact (USA)) (842) 1151[5] 1639[3] **>96f<**

**Westminster (IRE) 4** ch g Nashamaa-Our Galadrial (Salmon Leap (USA)) 641[11] (1839) 2020[4] 2300[8] 2798[3] 3130[2] **>72f<**

**West River (USA) 2** ch f Gone West (USA)-Rixe River (USA) (Irish River (FR)) 2611[13] **>41f<**

**West Side Story 2** b c Fabulous Dancer (USA)-Ruffle (FR) (High Line) 4024a[14] **>80f<**

**Wet Patch (IRE) 4** b or br g Common Grounds-Disco Girl (FR) (Green Dancer (USA)) **1995:** *(4537)* **1996:** *38[7] 66[11] 469[3] 553[4] 1173[2]* 1515[7] 1838[2] 2014[4] 2378[9] 3095[5] 4068[7] 4236[3] 4497[14] 4868[10] **>70a 70f<**

**Wey River Mist 3** b f General Wade-Donroya (Don) 1994[12] 2197[17]

**Whackford Squeers 4** ch g Komaite (USA)-Manhunt (Posse (USA)) *30[12] 50[9] 122[11] 1650[6]* ***>45a 55f<***

**What A Fuss 3** b g Great Commotion (USA)-Hafwah (Gorytus (USA)) 2610[13] 3258[8] *3418[3] 3703[8] 4336[2] 4895[13]* **>84a 54f<**

**What a Nightmare (IRE) 4** gr g Petorius-Mysterious Lady (Melyno) **1995:** *4531[7]* **1996:** *174[5] 331[5] 371[8] 2306[6] 2632[4] 3062[10] 3628[9]* **>47a 69f<**

**Whatashowman (IRE) 4** b g Exhibitioner-Whatawoman (Tumble Wind (USA)) *1196[9]* 1596[8] 2136[9] **>45f<**

**Whatever's Right (IRE) 7** b g Doulab (USA)-Souveniers (Relko) **1995:** *4421[3] 4493[2]* **1996:** *876[21]* 1145[15] 2032[9] (2903) *(3078) 3585[2]* 3686[4] 4256[14] **>70a 69f<**

**What Happened Was 2** b f Deploy-Berberana (Never so Bold) 1062[3] 1143[3] 1513[5] 1871[4] 2712[2] 2781[2] (3121) 3478[4] (4301) **>84f<**

**What Jim Wants (IRE) 3** b g Magical Strike (USA)-Sally Gone (IRE) (Last Tycoon) 542[6] 849[4] 1503[3] 2424[4] 2627[8] 2848[6] 3325[2] 4042[8] 4794[12] **>43f<**

**What's Secreto (USA) 4** gr g Secreto (USA)-What A Shack (USA) (Al Hattab (USA)) **1995:** *4355[10]* **>58a 62f<**

**What's That Amy 2** b f Sizzling Melody-Lady Pennington (Blue Cashmere) 3840[10] *4091[13]*

**What's the Verdict (IRE) 4** b g Law Society (USA)-Cecina (Welsh Saint) *75[2]* **>75a 81f<**

**Whenby (USA) 3** ch f Bering-Nether Poppleton (USA) (Deputy Minister (CAN)) 1949a[10] 5072a[2] **>97f<**

**Where's Wally (IRE) 2** ch g Archway (IRE)-Zanskar (Godswalk (USA)) *1607[8]* 2043[8] 2422[2] 3488[6] **>34f<**

**Whicksey Perry 3** b g Presidium-Phamilla (IRE) (Bellypha) 959[6] **>74f<**

**Whirlawhile (USA) 2** b c Silver Hawk (USA)-My Turbulent Beau (USA) (Beau's Eagle (USA)) 4386[8] **>31f<**

**Whirl Pool 2** b f Superpower-Rainbow Trout (Comedy Star (USA)) 4806[7] *4988[11]* **>21f<**

**Whispered Melody 3** b f Primo Dominie-Sing Softly (Luthier) 710[5] 870[5] 1359[7] *3063[4] 3650[4]* 4206[6] 4382[9] **>66a 65f<**

**Whispering Dawn 3** b f Then Again-Summer Sky (Skyliner) 595[3] 701[8] 4511[13] 4898[6] (4968) 5004[4] **>73f<**

**Whisper Low (IRE) 2** ch f Shalford (IRE)-Idle Gossip (Runnett) *3121[7]* 3429[8] 3508[4] 5037[13] **>36f<**

**Whitechapel (USA) 8** br g Arctic Tern (USA)-Christchurch (FR) (So Blessed) 3614[6] 4055[8] 4327[3] 4465[12] **>99f<**

**White Claret 4** b g Alzao (USA)-Vivid Impression (Cure The Blues (USA)) 1618[11] 4426[9] 4919[17] **>54f<**

**White Emir 3** b g Emarati (USA)-White African (Carwhite) 571[12] 832[5] 945[5] 1628[4] 2143[5] 2584[2] 2790[2] 3215[3] 3790[8] 4255[2] 4679[16] **>91f<**

**Whitegate's Son 2** ch g Minster Son-Whitegates Lady (Le Coq d'Or) 4754[8] 4807[8] 4991[12] **>36f<**

**White Gulch 2** b c Gulch (USA)-White Wisteria (ITY) (Ahonoora) 4666a[2] **>83f<**

**White Hare 3** b f Indian Ridge-Pomade (Luthier) 962[11] 3642[3] 4074[9] 4560[15] **>52f<**

**White Heat 4** b f Last Tycoon-Sweeping (Indian King (USA)) *141[6] 186[18]* **>47a 47f<**

**White Hot 2** b c Weldnaas (USA)-Glowing Reference (Reference Point) 2353[3] 2624[12] (4224) (4369) **>99f<**

**White Lady 5** ch m Risk Me (FR)-Cassiar (Connaught) **1995:** *4412[14]* **>20a 68f<**

**Whitelock Quest 8** b g Rainbow Quest (USA)-Sagar (Habitat) *384[10]* **>45a 20f<**

**White Nemesis (IRE) 2** b f Sillery (USA)-Top The Rest (Top Ville) *838[10]*

**White Plains (IRE) 3** b c Nordico (USA)-Flying Diva (Chief Singer) 493[3] 676[3] 775[5] 1172[5] 1515[2] 1773[3] (2203) 2486[4] 3039[4] (3327) 3947[7] (4102) (4257) 4489[12] **>81f<**

**White Sea (IRE) 3** ch f Soviet Lad (USA)-Bilander (High Line) 1462[4] (1852) 2202[3] 3235[W] **>85f<**

**White Settler 3** b g Polish Patriot (USA)-Oasis (Valiyar) 1304[7] 1773[11] 2235[3] (2617) 3165[2] 3518[3] 3995[9] **>75f<**

**White Sorrel 5** ro h Chilibang-Midnight Imperial (Night Shift (USA)) **1995:** *4432[10]* **1996:** *(50) 170[2] 357[10] 587[13]* 718[6] 935[W] 1186[21] 1423[6] 3973[12] **>77a 59f<**

**Whitewater Affair 3** ch f Machiavellian (USA)-Much Too Risky (Bustino) 684[2] (964) (1335) 1769[6] 3231[4] 3688[5] 4654a[2] 4876[4] **>114f<**

**White Willow 7** br g Touching Wood (USA)-Dimant Blanche (USA) (Gummo (USA)) 474[4] **>90a 76f<**

**Whitley Grange Boy 3** b g Hubbly Bubbly (USA)-Choir (High Top) **1995:** *4429[11]* **1996:** *390[5] 509[8]* 1477[10] **>67a 62f<**

**Whittle Rock 3** b f Rock City-Lurking (Formidable (USA)) *548[7]* 686[2] 1006[9] 1127[13] (2078) 2532[6] 2911[11] 3296[6] (3790) 3933[14] **>91f<**

**Whittle Times 2** ch f Timeless Times (USA)-La Pepper (Workboy) 1433[6] 1607[7] 2174[5] *2635[6] 2846[3]* ***>23a 30f<***

**Whizz Kid 2** b f Puissance-Panienka (POL) (Dom Racine (FR)) 757[6] *1093[2] 1352[5]* (2031) 2595[3] 2944[4] 3128[10] 3613[8] 3975[8] *4251[4] 4368[4]* ***>50a 67f<***

**Who (IRE) 2** b br g Don't Forget Me-Femme de Fer (USA) (Mr Leader (USA)) 2959[8] 3448[8] 3769[7] **>46f<**

**Who's the Best (IRE) 6** b g Wassl-Rip Roaring (Royal And Regal (USA)) **1995:** *4391[9] 4411[12] 4474[P]* **>57a 33f< (DEAD)**

**Whothehellisharry 3** ch g Rich Charlie-Ballagarrow Girl (North Stoke) 3414[4] 3831[6] 4437[7] **>51a 48f<**

**Who Told Vicky (IRE) 2** b f Anita's Prince-Little Club (King of Clubs) 757[3] *895[2] 1097[3] (1491) 2012[3]* 3299[7] **>55a 45f<**

**Whynotriskme 2** b f Risk Me (FR)-Spirit Away (Dominion) *1513[14]* 3405[8]

**Why O Six 2** b c Efisio-Scotch Imp (Imperial Fling (USA)) 2625[8] 2865[8] 3941[6] 4433[7] 4903[4] **>59f<**

**Wickins 6** b g Petong-Bo' Babbity (Strong Gale) 3974[6] 4236[17] **>69f<**

**Wicklow Boy (IRE) 5** b g Roi Danzig (USA)-Pickety Place (Prince Tenderfoot (USA)) *275[9] 299[R]* **>17a 44?f<**

**Widar 2** b c Soviet Star (USA)-Waseela (IRE) (Ahonoora) (3904a) **>90f<**

**Wigberto (IRE) 4** ch c Old Vic-Royal Loft (Homing) **1995:** *4392[16]* **1996:** *451[16]* ***>76a 88?f<***

**Wight 3** gr f Sharrood (USA)-Wrangbrook (Shirley Heights) 454[4] 1144[5] 3497[6] 4176[9] **>93f<**

**Wijara (IRE) 4** b c Waajib-Nawara (Welsh Pageant) 442[2] 581[9] 878[4] 1355[2] 1520[4] 4177[4] **>113f<**

**Wilawander 3** ch c Nashwan (USA)-Wilayif (USA) (Danzig (USA)) 671[4] 948[2] 1863[2] 2054[4] (2961) 3669[2] 4192[6] **>112f<**

**Wilcuma 5** b g Most Welcome-Miss Top Ville (FR) (Top Ville) 728[9] 1484[5] 2502[5] (2724) 4680[2] (4874) **>113f<**

**Wild City (USA) 2** b br c Wild Again (USA)-Garvin's Gal (USA) (Seattle Slew (USA)) 1424[9] **>17f<**

**Wildfire (SWI) 5** br g Beldale Flutter (USA)-Little

White Star (Mill Reef (USA)) **1995:** 4387$^{4}$ (4472) 4516$^{3}$ **1996:** 48$^{3}$ 132$^{4}$ 5054$^{11}$ **>58a 44f<**

**Wild Hadeer** **2** ch c Hadeer-Wild Moon (USA) (Arctic Tern (USA)) 4544$^{6}$ 4790$^{12}$ **>41f<**

**Wildmoor** **2** ch c Common Grounds-Impropriety (Law Society (USA)) 2865$^{12}$ 3277$^{6}$ 3779$^{4}$ 4361$^{13}$ 4501$^{7}$ **>58f<**

**Wild Nettle** **2** ch f Beveled (USA)-Pink Pumpkin (Tickled Pink) 3114$^{10}$ 3436$^{6}$ 3660$^{12}$ 3975$^{11}$ 4803$^{4}$ 5048$^{11}$ **>50f<**

**Wild Palm** **4** b c Darshaan-Tarasova (USA) (Green Forest (USA)) 462$^{5}$ 650$^{9}$ 879$^{16}$ 1154$^{4}$ 1412$^{11}$ 1807$^{7}$ 2134$^{5}$ (2340) (2412) 2947$^{4}$ 3172$^{3}$ 3603$^{5}$ 3995$^{2}$ 4308$^{9}$ 4571$^{8}$ **>71a 79f<**

**Wild Park (SPA)** **3** ch c Silver Cape (SPA)-Reve de Vol (SPA) (Lashkari) 5075a$^{3}$

**Wild Prospect** **8** b g Homing-Cappuccilli (Lorenzaccio) 3578$^{10}$ **>23f<**

**Wild Rice** **4** b g Green Desert (USA)-On Show (Welsh Pageant) 876$^{16}$ 1078$^{3}$ 1703$^{10}$ 2053$^{21}$ 4136$^{6}$ 4775$^{4}$ **>82+a 98f<**

**Wild Rita** **4** ch f Risk Me (FR)-Ma Pierrette (Cawston's Clown) (3260) 4067$^{2}$ 4187$^{2}$ 4580$^{7}$ 4872$^{2}$ 5046$^{11}$ **>87f<**

**Wild Rumour (IRE)** **3** b f Sadler's Wells (USA)-Gossiping (USA) (Chati (USA)) 674$^{8}$ 1111$^{4}$ 3934$^{6}$ **>87f<**

**Wild Sky (IRE)** **2** br c Warning-Erwinna (USA) (Lyphard (USA)) 5034$^{3}$ **>84f<**

**Wild Strawberry** **7** ro m Ballacashtal (CAN)-Pts Fairway (Runnymede) (83) 108$^{2}$ 165$^{3}$ 339$^{4}$ **>77a 73f<**

**Wild Thyme (USA)** **2** 4742a$^{9}$ **>65f<**

**Wildwood Flower** **3** b f Distant Relative-Tolstoya (Northfields (USA)) 692$^{2}$ 1006$^{4}$ (1101) 1316$^{2}$ 2007$^{3}$ (2584) 3232$^{5}$ (3783) 4314$^{5}$ 4774$^{5}$ **>105f<**

**Wild Zone (USA)** **6** b h Wild Again (USA)-Music Zone (USA) (The Minstrel (CAN)) 4960a$^{2}$ **>105f<**

**Wilfull Lad (IRE)** **3** b g Distinctly North (USA)-Lisa's Music (Abwah) 978$^{5}$ 1119$^{3}$ 1485$^{8}$ 1902$^{6}$ 2713$^{11}$ 3443$^{W}$ 3496$^{13}$ 4082$^{6}$ **>51f<**

**Will Do** **3** br g Weldnaas (USA)-Philogyny (Philip of Spain) 467$^{10}$ 949$^{3}$ 4690$^{7}$ **>77f<**

**William's Well** **2** ch c Superpower-Catherines Well (Junius (USA)) 2985$^{7}$ 3293$^{8}$ 3464$^{9}$ 3773$^{7}$ 4069$^{14}$ 4459$^{3}$ 4749$^{7}$ 4903$^{3}$ 5037$^{4}$ **>54f<**

**William Wallace** **2** b c Rudimentary (USA)-Irish Impulse (USA) (Irish River (FR)) 1871$^{10}$ 2224$^{6}$ 2967$^{6}$ 3237$^{3}$ **>63f<**

**Willie Conquer** **4** ch g Master Willie-Maryland Cookie (USA) (Bold Hour) 1961$^{8}$ 2742$^{7}$ 3248$^{2}$ (3617) (4187) 4465$^{5}$ (4716) **>98f<**

**Willie Miles** **3** b g Dancing Dissident (USA)-Madam Bold (Never so Bold) 1475$^{3}$ 2432$^{7}$ 3064$^{10}$ 4058$^{19}$ **>13a 79f<**

**Willie Rushton** **3** ch f Master Willie-Amberush (No Rush) 277$^{3}$ 381$^{5}$ 863$^{7}$ 1317$^{2}$ 1900$^{8}$ **>59a 64f<**

**Willisa** **3** ch f Polar Falcon (USA)-Ghassanah (Pas de Seul) (740) 937$^{12}$ 1527$^{6}$ 1820$^{6}$ 2885$^{5}$ 4064$^{10}$ **>72f<**

**Willow Dale (IRE)** **3** b f Danehill (USA)-Miss Willow Bend (USA) (Willow Hour (USA)) 572$^{11}$ 966$^{5}$ 1316$^{3}$ 1853$^{12}$ 2143$^{9}$ 4772$^{22}$ 4917$^{7}$ **>70f<**

**Willrack Farrier** **4** b f Lugana Beach-Bonny Bright Eyes (Rarity) 14$^{12}$ 55$^{12}$ 178$^{8}$ 1307$^{14}$ **>33a 66f<**

**Willskip (USA)** **2** b g Minshaanshu Amad (USA)-Eighty Lady (USA) (Flying Lark (USA)) 3588$^{9}$ 3869$^{5}$ 4224$^{9}$ **>56f<**

**Will's Way (USA)** **3** b c Easy Goer (USA)-Willamae (USA) (Tentam (USA)) 4956a$^{7}$ **>122f<**

**Will To Win** **2** b f Mazilier (USA)-Adana (FR) (Green Dancer (USA)) 596$^{5}$ 1118$^{4}$ 1851$^{3}$ 2157$^{3}$ 3128$^{13}$ 3336$^{2}$ 3763$^{3}$ 4046$^{10}$ 4576$^{2}$ 4803$^{8}$ 4999$^{7}$ **>59a 59f<**

**Will You Dance** **2** b f Shareef Dancer (USA)-Padelia (Thatching) 4305$^{6}$ 4618$^{2}$ **>78f<**

**Willy Star (BEL)** **6** b g Minstrel Star-Landing Power (Hill's Forecast) 2136$^{3}$ 2488$^{2}$ 2568$^{6}$ 2941$^{4}$ 3443$^{7}$ 3638$^{5}$ 4702$^{7}$ 4904$^{4}$ **>59f<**

**Windborn** **2** b f Superpower-Chablisse (Radetzky) 596$^{6}$ 815$^{3}$ 1062$^{6}$ 1346$^{5}$ 1590$^{10}$ 2406$^{2}$ 3128$^{11}$ 3954$^{2}$ 4251$^{2}$ 4883$^{13}$ **>60a 63f<**

**Wind Cheetah (USA)** **2** b br c Storm Cat (USA)-Won't She Tell (USA) (Banner Sport (USA)) 3994$^{6}$ (4544) 4759$^{8}$ **>96f<**

**Windmachine (SWE)** **5** b m River Scape (USA)-Miami Flyer (Miami Springs) (1943a) 3708$^{8}$ **>101f<**

**Wind Of Chance (GER)** **3** 2668a$^{7}$ 3753a$^{5}$ 4290a$^{4}$ **>113f<**

**Windrush Boy** **6** br g Dowsing (USA)-Bridge Street Lady (Decoy Boy) **1995:** 4459$^{5}$ **1996:** 1049$^{13}$ 1161$^{W}$ 2908$^{5}$ 3049$^{7}$ 3338$^{5}$ 3652$^{7}$ (3851) 3993$^{11}$ 4205$^{13}$ 4996$^{7}$ **>52a 63f<**

**Windrush Holly** **3** br f Gildoran-Bridge Street Lady (Decoy Boy) 3767$^{5}$ 4824$^{13}$ 4971$^{8}$ **>66f<**

**Windsharp (USA)** **5** b br m Lear Fan (USA)-Yes She's Sharp (USA) (Sharpen Up) 4955a$^{5}$ **>121f<**

**Windsor Castle** **2** b c Generous (IRE)-One Way Street (Habitat) (4458) (4696) **>87f<**

**Windswept (IRE)** **3** b f Taufan (USA)-Sutica (Don) 873$^{8}$ 1302$^{7}$ 1876$^{6}$ 2255$^{5}$ 2715$^{2}$ 3439$^{11}$ 3852$^{2}$ 4098$^{3}$ 4256$^{13}$ **>65f<**

**Windward Ariom** **10** ch g Pas de Seul-Deja Vu (FR) (Be My Guest (USA)) 482$^{11}$ **>22a 38f<**

**Windyedge (USA)** **3** ch c Woodman (USA)-Abeesh (USA) (Nijinsky (CAN)) 860$^{9}$ 1963$^{6}$ 3000$^{2}$ 3308$^{4}$ 3705$^{10}$ **>60f<**

**Wing And A Prayer (IRE)** **2** ch f Shalford (IRE)-God Speed Her (Pas de Seul) 3593$^{18}$ 3988$^{4}$ 4241$^{10}$ **>77f<**

**Winged Prince** **3** b g Prince Daniel (USA)-Phyl (Ballad Rock) 1145$^{10}$ 1498$^{17}$ 1835$^{11}$ **>54f<**

**Wingnut (IRE)** **3** ch f Digamist (USA)-Royal Cloak (Hardicanute) **1995:** 4353$^{4}$ **1996:** 11$^{10}$ 52$^{6}$ 131$^{6}$ 215$^{5}$ 242$^{6}$ 748$^{9}$ 861$^{15}$ 1009$^{6}$ 1451$^{3}$ 1661$^{8}$ 2402$^{2}$ 3831$^{5}$ **>47a 53f<**

**Wing of A Prayer** **2** b c Statoblest-Queen Angel (Anfield) 4600$^{8}$ 4902$^{10}$ **>46f<**

**Winn Caley** **3** ch f Beveled (USA)-Responder (Vitiges (FR)) 934$^{11}$ 1323$^{8}$ 1540$^{4}$ 3600$^{10}$ **>49?f<**

**Winnebago** **3** b f Kris-Siouan (So Blessed) 3999$^{5}$ 4429$^{7}$ 4591$^{7}$ 4921$^{8}$ **>70f<**

**Winning Smile (FR)** **6** br h Never so Bold-Funny Reef (FR) (Mill Reef (USA)) 4417a$^{2}$ 4857a$^{10}$ **>108f<**

**Winning Wonder** **4** b f Charmer-Salchow (Niniski (USA)) 1651$^{16}$

**Winsome Wooster** **5** ch m Primo Dominie-Bertrade (Homeboy) 1473$^{6}$ 1991$^{5}$ 2229$^{4}$ 2577$^{9}$ 2858$^{4}$ (3167) 3518$^{6}$ 3696$^{3}$ 4088$^{5}$ 4206$^{7}$ 4820$^{7}$ 4975$^{19}$ **>65f<**

**Winston** **3** b g Safawan-Lady Leman (Pitskelly) 428$^{5}$ (595) 976$^{3}$ (1363) 1586$^{5}$ 2294$^{3}$ 2621$^{2}$ 3279$^{9}$ 4190$^{21}$ 4769$^{8}$ 4974$^{22}$ **>46a 72f<**

**Winter Brook (FR)** **2** 3201a$^{6}$ 4944a$^{2}$ **>64f<**

**Wintered Out** **2** b f Digamist (USA)-Record Song (Indian King (USA)) 4756$^{14}$ **>59f<**

**Winter Garden** **2** ch c Old Vic-Winter Queen (Welsh Pageant) 5033$^{7}$ **>72f<**

**Winter Romance** **3** ch c Cadeaux Genereux-Island Wedding (USA) (Blushing Groom (FR)) 1126$^{2}$ (1432) 2041$^{13}$ 2502$^{14}$ 2724$^{6}$ 4162a$^{3}$ 4757$^{5}$ **>110f<**

**Winter Scout (USA)** **8** ch g It's Freezing (USA)-His Squaw (USA) (Tom Rolfe) 749$^{14}$ 893$^{19}$ 1348$^{12}$ 1689$^{7}$ (1885) 2213$^{4}$ 2428$^{10}$ 3817$^{11}$ 4202$^{11}$ 4307$^{16}$ **>18+a 66f<**

**Wire Act (USA)** **3** gr g Gate Dancer (USA)-Giovanelli (USA) (Monteverdi) 562$^{11}$ 634$^{5}$ 731$^{12}$ 1592$^{3}$ 1702$^{2}$ (1888) 2428$^{9}$ 4550$^{6}$ 4692$^{14}$ **>60a 64f<**

**Wisam** **3** b g Shaadi (USA)-Moon Drop (Dominion) 548$^{3}$ 736$^{6}$ 1327$^{9}$ 2704$^{4}$ 3210$^{7}$ 3790$^{9}$ 4136$^{17}$ **>95f<**

**Witching Hour (IRE)** **2** b f Alzao (USA)-Itching (IRE) (Thatching) (1346) 1978$^{2}$ **>84+f<**

**Witch of Fife (USA)** **3** b f Lear Fan (USA)-Fife (IRE) (Lomond (USA)) 1899$^{7}$ 2250$^{5}$ **>94f<**

**With A Will** **2** b g Rambo Dancer (CAN)-Henceforth (Full of Hope) 3809$^{4}$ 4188$^{7}$ 4544$^{5}$ **>64f<**

**With Care** **3** b f Warning-Benazir (High Top) 2918$^{5}$ (3255) 3790$^{7}$ 3989$^{8}$ 4688$^{12}$ **>78f<**

**Witherkay** **3** b g Safawan-High Heather (Shirley Heights) 1142$^{13}$ 1535$^{4}$ 2234$^{2}$ 2784$^{7}$ 3852$^{9}$ 4232$^{3}$ 4511$^{12}$ 4624$^{4}$ **>63f<**

**Without a Flag (USA)** **6** ch g Stately Don (USA)-Northerly Cheer (USA) (Northjet) 2377$^{12}$ **>51f<**

**Without Friends (IRE)** **2** b c Thatching-Soha (USA) (Dancing Brave (USA)) (757) (1331) 1713$^{D}$ (2382) 3029a$^{8}$ **>71f<**

**With The Tempo (IRE)** **3** b f Last Tycoon-Starlust (Sallust) 2515$^{2}$ 2919$^{5}$ 4309$^{10}$ 4860$^{22}$ 5053$^{11}$ **>61f<**

**Witney-de-Bergerac (IRE)** **4** b g Cyrano de Bergerac-Spy Girl (Tanfirion) **1995:** 4364$^{7}$ **1996:** 440$^{5}$ 573$^{2}$ 712$^{4}$ 944$^{9}$ 2008$^{8}$ 2148$^{5}$ 2385$^{4}$ 2711$^{5}$ 4771$^{24}$ 4984$^{6}$ **>48a 67f<**

**Witney-La-Roche** **2** ch g Superlative-Ever Reckless (Crever) 4546$^{14}$ 4715$^{14}$ **>51f<**

**Wixim (USA)** **3** ch c Diesis-River Lullaby (USA) (Riverman (USA)) 472$^{2}$ (705) (952) 1441$^{3}$ **>110f<**

**Wizard King** **5** b h Shaadi (USA)-Broomstick Cottage (Habitat) **1995:** 4497a$^{3}$ **1996:** 3083$^{5}$ (3263) (3517) (3822) 4051$^{2}$ 4378$^{2}$ (4649a) (5065a) **>119f<**

**Wobble** **2** ch g Kris-Horseshoe Reef (Mill Reef (USA)) 2413$^{5}$ 4383$^{6}$ 4601$^{8}$ 4814$^{5}$ **>63f<**

**Wolf Cleugh (IRE)** **3** b f Last Tycoon-Santa Roseanna (Caracol (FR)) 1855$^{6}$ 2510$^{5}$ **>64f<**

**Wolf Mountain** **2** ch c Selkirk (USA)-Cubby Hole (Town And Country) 1897$^{2}$ 2878$^{3}$ 4488$^{9}$ (4619) **>94f<**

**Wollstonecraft (IRE)** **3** b f Danehill (USA)-Ivory Thread (USA) (Sir Ivor) 2298$^{6}$ 4074$^{7}$ 4219$^{2}$ 4592$^{2}$ 4791$^{17}$ 4995$^{6}$ **>80f<**

**Wolver Murphy (IRE)** **4** b f Persian Heights-Wolverstar (Wolverlife) **1995:** 4512$^{12}$

**Woman of Wit (IRE)** **2** b br f Petorius-Laughing Matter (Lochnager) 643$^{2}$ **>50f<**

**Wonderboy (IRE)** **2** ch c Arazi (USA)-Alsaaybah (USA) (Diesis) 4516$^{14}$ **>48f<**

**Wonderful Day** **5** b m Niniski (USA)-Zipperti Do (Precocious) 124$^{2}$ 184$^{3}$ 1102$^{8}$ 1861$^{9}$ **>75a 74f<**

**Woodborough (USA)** **3** ch c Woodman (USA)-Performing Arts (The Minstrel (CAN)) 727$^{5}$ 1129$^{5}$ 1483$^{3}$ 2072$^{4}$ 3562a$^{4}$ **>120f<**

**Woodbury Lad (USA)** **3** c Woodman (USA)-Habibti (Habitat) 672$^{7}$ 1994$^{2}$ 2150$^{2}$ 2432$^{3}$ 4997$^{2}$ **>61a 81f<**

**Wooderine (USA)** **2** ch f Woodman (USA)-Exuberine (FR) (Be My Guest (USA)) 683$^{5}$ **>42f<**

**Woodetto (IRE)** **2** b c Maledetto (IRE)-Wood Kay (IRE) (Treasure Kay) 1849$^{8}$ 2161$^{2}$ 2429$^{4}$ 2625$^{5}$ **>65f<**

**Woodfighter (IRE)** **3** gr c Ballad Rock-Cumbrian Melody (Petong) 1753a$^{3}$ **>84f<**

**Woodland Dove** **2** ch f Weldnaas (USA)-Jove's Voodoo (USA) (Northern Jove (CAN)) 2795$^{10}$ 3954$^{11}$ 4988$^{12}$ **>7a 18f<**

**Woodland Nymph** **2** gr f Norton Challenger-Royal Meeting (Dara Monarch) 4699$^{2}$

**Woodlands Electric** **6** b g Rich Charlie-Hallowed

(Wolver Hollow) **1995:** 4447$^{11}$ **1996:** 44$^{9}$ 2561$^{7}$ 2791$^{8}$ 3097$^{5}$ **>3a 20f<**

**Woodlands Energy 5** b m Risk Me (FR)-Hallowed (Wolver Hollow) 2556$^{13}$ 2716$^{12}$ 2906$^{7}$ **>25f<**

**Woodlands Lad Too 4** b g Risk Me (FR)-Hallowed (Wolver Hollow) 43$^{9}$ **>12f<**

**Wood Leopard (USA) 4** b c Woodman (USA)-Thorough (Thatch (USA)) 4026a$^{7}$ **>80f<**

**Wood Magic 3** b g Shaadi (USA)-Majenica (USA) (Majestic Light (USA)) 574$^{7}$ 3691$^{4}$ 4162a$^{7}$ 4313$^{4}$ **>78+a 109f<**

**Woodrising 4** b f Nomination-Bodham (Bustino) 1977$^{12}$ **>37a 70f<**

**Woodsia 2** b f Woodman (USA)-Aquaba (USA) (Damascus (USA)) 3756$^{3}$ 4104$^{2}$ 4608$^{10}$ **>77f<**

**Woods of Cisterna (IRE) 2** 4859a$^{7}$

**Woolverstone Hall (IRE) 4** b f Roi Danzig (USA)-Silver Mantle (Bustino) **1995:** 4351$^{5}$ 4521$^{9}$ **1996:** 42$^{8}$ 107$^{13}$ 179$^{2}$ 244$^{7}$ 387$^{2}$ 487$^{7}$ 834$^{8}$ 1517$^{6}$ **>40a 50f<**

**Wordsmith (IRE) 6** b g Cyrano de Bergerac-Cordon (Morston (FR)) 1468$^{8}$ 3808$^{12}$ **>57da 43f<**

**World Express (IRE) 6** b g Jareer (USA)-Eight Mile Rock (Dominion) 546$^{13}$ 1347$^{3}$ (1511) 1981$^{5}$ 2547$^{6}$ **>6a 65f<**

**World Premier 3** b c Shareef Dancer (USA)-Abuzz (Absalom) 681$^{3}$ 926$^{8}$ 1151$^{3}$ 2039$^{9}$ 2337$^{4}$ 4181$^{5}$ 4444$^{22}$ 4823$^{10}$ **>103df<**

**Worldwide Elsie (USA) 3** b f Java Gold (USA)-Tender Camilla (Prince Tenderfoot (USA)) **1995:** (4373) **1996:** 444$^{17}$ 1172$^{4}$ 1601$^{6}$ 1796$^{6}$ 2170$^{10}$ 2400$^{5}$ **>82a 80?f<**

**Wot No Fax 3** ch g Sharrood (USA)-Priors Dean (Monsanto (FR)) (1079) 1817$^{3}$ 2194$^{6}$ 3211$^{8}$ 3594$^{10}$ 4120$^{11}$ **>101f<**

**Wottashambles 5** b or br g Arrasas (USA)-Manawa (Mandamus) (9) 69$^{2}$ 108$^{5}$ 206$^{4}$ 265$^{4}$ 1472$^{2}$ 1874$^{3}$ 2282$^{8}$ 3318$^{6}$ 3514$^{3}$ **>47a 44f<**

**Written Agreement 8** ch g Stanford-Covenant (Good Bond) 2155$^{12}$ 2587$^{11}$ 2989$^{10}$ 3066$^{7}$ 3605$^{9}$ **>10a 26f<**

**Wrn Princess 2** ch f Handsome Sailor-Sovereign Rose (Sharpen Up) 3685$^{10}$ 4061$^{10}$ 4896$^{6}$ **>57f<**

**Wrong Bride 2** b f Reprimand-Ivory Bride (Domynsky) 3129$^{15}$

***Wurftaube (GER)* 3** ch f Acatenango (GER)-Wurfbahn (GER) (Frontal) (2478a) (3913a) (4542a) **>122f<**

**Wybara 3** ch f Nashwan (USA)-Twyla (Habitat) 3505$^{13}$ 4083$^{4}$ 4362$^{4}$ 4752$^{6}$ **>60f<**

**Wyse Folly 3** ch f Colmore Row-Water Folly (Sharpo) 524$^{10}$ 748$^{17}$ **>11f<**

**X**

**Xenophon of Cunaxa (IRE) 3** b g Cyrano de Bergerac-Annais Nin (Dominion) 692$^{11}$ (1192) 1464$^{4}$ 2160$^{3}$ 2858$^{7}$ 4088$^{15}$ **>83df<**

**Y**

**Yaakum 7** b g Glint of Gold-Nawadder (Kris) 2175$^{8}$ 2423$^{11}$ 2779$^{6}$ 2871$^{3}$ **>54a 34f<**

**Yabint El Sultan 2** ch f Safawan-Dalby Dancer (Bustiki) 4825$^{14}$ 4976$^{12}$ **>56f<**

**Yacht 4** ch g Warning-Bireme (Grundy) 1875$^{6}$ **>70a 76f<**

**Yalaietanee 2** b c Sadler's Wells (USA)-Vaigly Star (Star Appeal) 3407$^{4}$ (3757) **>92+f<**

**Yalta (IRE) 3** b c Soviet Star (USA)-Gay Hellene (Ela-Mana-Mou) 2579$^{2}$ (2996) 3594$^{3}$ **>92f<**

**Ya Malak 5** b g Fairy King (USA)-La Tuerta (Hot Spark) 507$^{5}$ 927$^{5}$ 1616$^{5}$ 2003$^{5}$ 2115$^{17}$ 2698$^{3}$ 3047$^{5}$ 4304$^{7}$ 4518$^{6}$ **>94f<**

**Yamamoto (FR) 3** b c Kendor (FR)-Yamuna (Green Dancer (USA)) 192a$^{2}$ 289a$^{2}$ **>65f<**

**Ya Marhaba 3** b g Efisio-Ichnusa (Bay Express) **1995:** 4429$^{10}$ **1996:** 539$^{8}$ 2235$^{9}$ 2914$^{2}$ 3292$^{4}$ 4989$^{5}$ **>31a 36f<**

**Yam-Sing 2** b g Aragon-Pushoff (USA) (Sauce Boat (USA)) 3994$^{15}$ 4451$^{9}$ 4578$^{11}$ **>57f<**

**Yamuna (USA) 3** b f Forty Niner (USA)-Nimble Feet (USA) (Danzig (USA)) 2918$^{4}$ (3472) 3945$^{3}$ 4218$^{9}$ **>102f<**

**Yanavanavano (IRE) 2** b c Maledetto (IRE)-Dublin Millennium (Dalsaan) 706$^{13}$ 865$^{8}$ **>37f<**

**Yangtze (IRE) 2** b c River Falls-Sister Dympna (Grundy) 815$^{7}$ 2224$^{9}$ 2783$^{11}$ **>55f<**

**Yarob (IRE) 3** ch c Unfuwain (USA)-Azyaa (Kris) 681$^{8}$ 960$^{4}$ 1427$^{6}$ 1817$^{2}$ 2724$^{16}$ 3594$^{13}$ **>104df<**

**Yashmak (USA) 2** b f Danzig (USA)-Slightly Dangerous (USA) (Roberto (USA)) (2302) 2997$^{2}$ 4661a$^{2}$ **>107f<**

**Yaverland (IRE) 4** b c Astronef-Lautreamont (Auction Ring (USA)) 871$^{5}$ 1145$^{19}$ 1841$^{12}$ 4095$^{3}$ **>56a 67f<**

**Yavlensky (IRE) 2** b c Caerleon (USA)-Schwanensee (USA) (Mr Leader (USA)) 4038a$^{9}$ 4253$^{5}$ (5031a) **>66f<**

**Yeast 4** b g Salse (USA)-Orient (Bay Express) (472) (876) 1051$^{2}$ (2053) 2502$^{10}$ (3072) 4028a$^{8}$ (4520) 4568$^{34}$ **>114f<**

**Yeath (IRE) 4** ch g Exhibitioner-Grain of Sand (Sandford Lad) 1048$^{9}$ 3586$^{8}$ 4053$^{8}$ **>49f<**

**Yellow Dragon (IRE) 3** b g Kefaah (USA)-Veldt (High Top) 274$^{6}$ 555$^{6}$ 760$^{5}$ 1047$^{R}$ 1448$^{5}$ 1641$^{15}$ (1970) 2086$^{7}$ 2322$^{8}$ 2594$^{13}$ 2941$^{11}$ 3611$^{8}$ 4107$^{4}$ 4815$^{14}$ **>54a 34f<**

**Yeoman Oliver 3** b g Precocious-Impala Lass (Kampala) **1995:** 4429$^{6}$ 4511$^{6}$ **1996:** 58$^{2}$ 123$^{2}$ 156$^{3}$ 239$^{8}$ (355) 382$^{2}$ 595$^{6}$ 754$^{6}$ 1042$^{4}$ (1490) 1780$^{2}$ 2749$^{10}$ 3063$^{12}$ (3626) 3951$^{5}$ 4799$^{4}$ 4898$^{2}$ 5010$^{7}$ **>70a 74f<**

**Yet Again 4** ch g Weldnaas (USA)-Brightelmstone (Prince Regent (FR)) 760$^{8}$ 968$^{13}$ 1338$^{7}$ 1468$^{10}$ 1691$^{3}$ 2056$^{15}$ (2189) 2409$^{12}$ 2488$^{6}$ 5053$^{15}$ **>47a 57f<**

**Yezza (IRE) 3** b f Distinctly North (USA)-Small Paradise (Habat) 355$^{9}$ 550$^{7}$ 701$^{7}$ 873$^{5}$ 1042$^{12}$ 3334$^{13}$ 3525$^{4}$ 4186$^{17}$ 4263$^{12}$ 4785$^{5}$ **>23a 54f<**

**Yipsilanti 3** ch c Master Willie-Reel Foyle (USA) (Irish River (FR)) 2996$^{7}$ **>62f< (DEAD)**

**Yo Kiri-B 5** b m Night Shift (USA)-Briar Creek (Busted) **1995:** 4379$^{4}$ 4435$^{6}$ 4450$^{3}$ **1996:** 121$^{9}$ 205$^{3}$ 244$^{3}$ (399) 530$^{2}$ 2308$^{2}$ 2403$^{3}$ 3139$^{2}$ 3313$^{8}$ 4778$^{4}$ **>60a 62f<**

**Yom Jameel (IRE) 3** b c Caerleon (USA)-Topping Girl (Sea Hawk II) 684$^{10}$ (847) 1120$^{2}$ 1817$^{4}$ (3669) 3934$^{8}$ **>112df<**

**Yorkie George 2** b c Efisio-Petonica (IRE) (Petoski) 3994$^{12}$ (4469) (4878) 5043$^{3}$ **>93f<**

**Yorkshire (IRE) 2** ch c Generous (IRE)-Ausherra (USA) (Diesis) (4508) **>97+f<**

**Yosna (FR) 2** b f Sicyos (USA)-Tidouna (FR) (Kaldoun (FR)) 3029a$^{2}$ **>57f<**

**Youdontsay 4** ch f Most Welcome-Fabulous Luba (Luthier) 1652$^{4}$ 2114$^{26}$ (3146) 3432$^{20}$ 3827$^{2}$ 4119$^{8}$ 4198$^{21}$ 4772$^{12}$ **>86f<**

**Yougo 4** b g Good Times (ITY)-Young Wilkie (Callernish) **1995:** 4384$^{5}$ 4442$^{3}$ 4489$^{7}$ **1996:** (47) 208$^{3}$ 283$^{2}$ 339$^{3}$ **>78a 79f< (DEAD)**

**Young Annabel (USA) 3** ch f Cahill Road (USA)-Only for Eve (USA) (Barachois (CAN)) 526$^{6}$ 678$^{13}$ 942$^{9}$ (2937) 3172$^{5}$ 3603$^{7}$ 3985$^{13}$ **>69a 66f<**

**Young Ben (IRE) 4** ch g Fayruz-Jive (Ahonoora) **1995:** 4430$^{9}$ **1996:** 347$^{6}$ 387$^{8}$ 607$^{13}$ 1702$^{9}$ 2481$^{13}$ 2933$^{3}$ 3100$^{6}$ 3294$^{3}$ 3342$^{7}$ 4075$^{3}$ 4229$^{5}$ 4805$^{20}$ **>24a 40f<**

**Young Benson 4** b g Zalazl (USA)-Impala Lass (Kampala) **1995:** 4514$^{7}$ **1996:** 45$^{6}$ 99$^{5}$ 297$^{3}$ 402$^{10}$ 598$^{10}$ (734) (839) 1085$^{3}$ 2306$^{8}$ 4573$^{11}$ **>70da 67f<**

**Young Bigwig (IRE) 2** b c Anita's Prince-Humble Mission (Shack (USA)) 699$^{4}$ (895) 1362$^{2}$ 2063$^{2}$ 2879$^{2}$ (3128) 3843$^{5}$ 4189$^{3}$ **>69a 96f<**

**Young Buster (IRE) 8** b h Teenoso (USA)-Bustara (Busted) 535a$^{14}$ **>16a 116f<**

**Young Butt 3** ch c Bold Owl-Cymbal (Ribero) 519$^{5}$ 983$^{13}$ (1337) 1447$^{3}$ 1955$^{7}$ **>65a 75f<**

**Young Duke (IRE) 8** gr g Double Schwartz-Princess Pamela (Dragonara Palace (USA)) (2229) (2858) 4054$^{D}$ 4308$^{3}$ **>72a 80f<**

**Young Ern 6** b h Efisio-Stardyn (Star Appeal) **1995:** 4523a$^{12}$ **1996:** (818) 1582a$^{3}$ 2037$^{4}$ 3573a$^{7}$ **>119f<**

**Young Frederick (IRE) 3** ch g Polish Patriot (USA)-Notre Histoire (Habitat) **1995:** 4408$^{7}$ 4518$^{5}$ **1996:** 81$^{3}$ 157$^{3}$ 387$^{5}$ 2425$^{10}$ 2966$^{10}$ **>62a 29f<**

**Young Mazaad (IRE) 3** b c Mazaad-Lucky Charm (IRE) (Pennine Walk) 408$^{2}$ 467$^{4}$ 488$^{4}$ 669$^{4}$ 782$^{2}$ 856$^{2}$ 1301$^{2}$ (1518) 1677$^{2}$ 2283$^{2}$ 2312$^{8}$ **>72a 77f<**

**Young Precedent 2** b c Polish Precedent (USA)-Guyum (Rousillon (USA)) 4891$^{4}$ **>58f<**

**Young Rose 4** b f Aragon-Primrose Way (Young Generation) 2367$^{13}$ 2785$^{11}$ 2996$^{11}$ 3584$^{8}$ 4833$^{16}$ **>12a 37f<**

**Young Saffy 3** ch g Safawan-Miss Pisces (Salmon Leap (USA)) 4042$^{13}$ **>43f<**

**Your Most Welcome 5** b m Most Welcome-Blues Player (Jaazeiro (USA)) 66$^{6}$ (106) 189$^{7}$ 301$^{10}$ (319) 4307$^{15}$ (4597) 4793$^{12}$ 4967$^{7}$ 4993$^{5}$ **>63a 65f<**

**Yoxall Lodge 6** b h Aragon-Opal Fancy (Kibenka) 2058$^{2}$ 2426$^{7}$ 2581$^{17}$ 4186$^{19}$ **>44a 64f<**

**Yubralee (USA) 4** ch g Zilzal (USA)-Kentucky Lill (USA) (Raise A Native) 216$^{8}$ 1816$^{8}$ **>69a 79f<**

**Yukon Hope (USA) 3** b f Forty Niner (USA)-Sahara Forest (Green Desert (USA)) 3162$^{3}$ 3446$^{4}$ 3949$^{2}$ 4124$^{6}$ 4591$^{2}$ 4813$^{4}$ **>77f<**

**Yuppy Girl (IRE) 3** ch f Salt Dome (USA)-Sloane Ranger (Sharpen Up) 399$^{4}$ 530$^{3}$ 660$^{5}$ 2123$^{7}$ 2587$^{17}$ 3048$^{2}$ 3619$^{7}$ 3849$^{5}$ 4080$^{10}$ 4455$^{15}$ 4882$^{4}$ **>56a 56f<**

**Yxenery (IRE) 2** b f Sillery (USA)-Polyxena (FR) (Pretendre) 3566a$^{3}$ **>86f<**

**Z**

**Zaahir (IRE) 2** b c Marju (IRE)-Abhaaj (Kris) 4962$^{3}$ **>81+f<**

**Zaaleff (USA) 4** ch c Zilzal (USA)-Continual (USA) (Damascus (USA)) 577$^{14}$ 753$^{19}$ 898$^{4}$ 1031$^{5}$ 1173$^{3}$ 1457$^{12}$ 1821$^{2}$ 2058$^{8}$ 2489$^{4}$ 3043$^{8}$ 3109$^{9}$ **>57a 54f<**

**Zabadi (IRE) 4** b g Shahrastani (USA)-Zerzaya (Beldale Flutter (USA)) 726$^{8}$ **>93f<**

**Zacaroon 5** b m Last Tycoon-Samaza (USA) (Arctic Tern (USA)) **1995:** 4415$^{8}$ 4532$^{9}$ **1996:** 521$^{12}$ 3608$^{8}$ 3766$^{4}$ 4337$^{12}$ 4800$^{12}$ **>38a 57f<**

**Zadok 4** ch g Exodal (USA)-Glenfinlass (Lomond (USA)) **1995:** 4363$^{10}$ 4463$^{8}$ **>28a 58f<**

**Zafarelli 2** gr g Nishapour (FR)-Voltigeuse (USA) (Filiberto (USA)) 4970$^{16}$ **>21f<**

**Zaforum 3** b c Deploy-Beau's Delight (USA) (Lypheor) **1995:** 4562a$^{8}$ **1996:** 671$^{6}$ 1076$^{3}$ 1791$^{16}$ 2054$^{13}$ 3781$^{5}$ (4548) 4965$^{3}$ **>105f<**

**Zafzala (IRE) 3** b f Kahyasi-Zerzaya (Beldale Flutter (USA)) 1255a$^{2}$ 1567a$^{6}$ 2465a$^{2}$ (3021a) 4292a$^{5}$ 4654a$^{3}$ 4849a$^{4}$ **>117f<**

**Zagreb (USA) 3** b c Theatrical-Sophonisbe (Wollow) (2473a) 4662a$^{13}$ **>126+f<**

**Zagros (IRE) 2** b c Persian Heights-Hana Marie (Formidable (USA)) 1537$^{12}$ **>38f<**

**Zahid (USA) 5** ch g Storm Cat (USA)-Time An' Care (USA) (Twin Time (USA)) 189$^{2}$ 305$^{2}$ (353) (384) 424$^{3}$ 553$^{2}$ 670$^{13}$ **>73a 65df<**

**Zahran (IRE) 5** b h Groom Dancer (USA)-Welsh

Berry (USA) (Sir Ivor) *200[3] 253[3] 308[8] 412[11] 501[3] 636[9]* 983[4] 1302[2] 1414[3] 1502[5] 1838[6] 2058[6] 2183[2] 2409[4] 2574[13] 2896[8] 3000[6] *3435[7] 3645[6]* 3808[8] 4812[4] *4989[3]* **>48a 39f<**

**Za-Im 2** b c Green Desert (USA)-Al Bahathri (USA) (Blushing Groom (FR)) 4475[5] (4825) **>99f<**

**Zaima (IRE) 2** b f Green Desert (USA)-Usaylah (Siberian Express (USA)) 2892[5] 3206[4] 4123[4] (4440) 4814[3] **>78f<**

**Zain Dancer 4** ch c Nabeel Dancer (USA)-Trojan Lady (USA) (Irish River (FR)) *115[6] 480[14]* 718[10] 1609[2] 2391[2] 2521[3] 2630[4] 2962[6] 3151[3] 3995[14] **>49a 62f<**

**Zajira (IRE) 6** b m Ela-Mana-Mou-Awsaaf (USA) (Naskra (USA)) 2775[6] 3037[17] **>53f<**

**Zajko (USA) 6** b g Nureyev (USA)-Hope For All (USA) (Secretariat (USA)) *967[12]* 1190[9] 2526[6] 3805[10] 4463[3] 4682[20] 4901[W] **>78f<**

**Zalamalec (USA) 3** ch f Septieme Ciel (USA)-Zolinana **1995:** 4499a[3] **>88f<**

**Zalament 4** b f Zalazl (USA)-Key to Enchantment (Key To Content (USA)) **1995:** *4506[9] 4543[8]* **1996:** *47[8]* **>17a 65df<**

**Zalotti (IRE) 3** ch f Polish Patriot (USA)-Honest Penny (USA) (Honest Pleasure (USA)) *(3350)* 3693[16] 4215[11] **>75f<**

**Zalotto (IRE) 2** b g Polish Patriot (USA)-Honest Penny (USA) (Honest Pleasure (USA)) 3987[11] **>37f<**

**Zamalek (USA) 4** b g Northern Baby (CAN)-Chellingoua (USA) (Sharpen Up) 1078[10] 1330[9] 1792[13] 2127[10] 3944[13] *4107[6] 4373[14]* ***>46a 40f<***

**Zamhareer (USA) 5** b g Lear Fan (USA)-Awenita (Rarity) *1044[5]* (1343) (1529) 2148[6] 2697[12] 3855[12] 4302[10] **>60df<**

**Zamindar (USA) 2** b c Gone West (USA)-Zaizafon (USA) (The Minstrel (CAN)) (3390a) 3750a[2] 4294a[3] **>110f<**

**Zanabay 2** b f Unfuwain (USA)-Chrisanthy (So Blessed) 729[7] 2714[4] 2904[7] 3795[4] 4103[5] **>59f<**

**Zanzara (IRE) 5** ch m Efisio-Slick Chick (Shiny Tenth) *236[9]* **>49a 64f<**

**Zaralaska 5** ch g Shernazar-Eskimo Spring (USA) (Riverman (USA)) 4465[17] 4872[8] **>101f<**

**Zarannda (IRE) 3** b f Last Tycoon-Zarna (Shernazar) 3391a[2] 3745a[6] (4417a) 4857a[4] **>116f<**

**Zaretski 2** b c Pursuit of Love-Tolstoya (Northfields (USA)) 841[10] 2009[3] 2302[4] 3214[2] 4100[4] 4519[11] **>71f<**

**Zarma (FR) 4** ch f Machiavellian (USA)-Zartota (USA) (Assert) **1995:** 4498a[3] **1996:** 2840a[2] **>106f<**

**Zatopek 4** b or br g Reprimand-Executive Lady (Night Shift (USA)) 470[3] 649[8] 1522[9] 1983[5] *2749[8] 3630[2] 3955[6] 4080[7]* **>55a 70f<**

**Zdenka 3** b f Dominion-Short And Sharp (Sharpen Up) 1119[13] 1485[9] 2196[4] 2540[5] 2743[10] 3139[9] 3456[13] 4082[15] 4898[5] **>53f<**

**Zelaya (IRE) 3** b f Shaadi (USA)-Zizania (Ahonoora) *5001[6]* **>50a 68f<**

**Zelda Zonk 4** b f Law Society (USA)-Massive Powder (Caerleon (USA)) 888[3] (1092) 1192[5] 1625[13] (1876) 2134[4] 2437[3] 2907[3] 3167[2] **>80f<**

**Zeliba 4** br f Doyoun-Zia (USA) (Shareef Dancer (USA)) *406[12] 1011[7]* 1302[8] 1682[3] 2192[2] 2587[7] (2906) *3086[5] (3303)* 3664[3] 3979[12] 4203[4] 4426[8] 4612[2] 4794[11] 4910[6] **>24?a 48f<**

**Zelzelah (USA) 3** b f Timeless Moment (USA)-Allevition (USA) (Alleged (USA)) 1111[5] **>87f<** **(DEAD)**

**Zermatt (IRE) 6** b h Sadler's Wells (USA)-Chamonis (USA) (Affirmed (USA)) 650[5] 817[6] 968[4] 1066[2] (1440) 1793[13] 2377[10] 2603[6] 2883[6] **>80f<**

**Zero Problemo (IRE) 3** 2109a[4] 2668a[5] 3746a[3] 4290a[3] 4656a[4] **>115f<**

**Zest (USA) 2** gr ro f Zilzal (USA)-Toveris (Homing) 4962[8] **>54f<**

**Zesti 4** br g Charmer-Lutine Royal (Formidable (USA)) *47[2] 125[3] 1488[5] 1967[8] 5053[3]* ***>37a 45f<***

**Zibeth 2** b f Rainbow Quest (USA)-Tiger Flower (Sadler's Wells (USA)) 4705[9] **>46f<**

**Zidac 4** b or br g Statoblest-Sule Skerry (Scottish Rifle) *604[2] (817)* (1047) 4489[14] **>63a 80f<**

**Ziggy's Dancer (USA) 5** b h Ziggy's Boy (USA)-My Shy Dancer (USA) (Northjet) **1995:** *(4517)* **1996:** *507[4]* 711[6] 814[8] 1016[3] 1113[6] 1430[11] 2220[5] 2292[2] 2698[4] 2889[10] 3085[4] 3296[3] 3622[9] 3932[4] 4101[2] 4314[13] 4554[4] 4772[10] 4811[3] **>82a 87f<**

**Ziggy's Viola (IRE) 2** b f Roi Danzig (USA)-Olivia Jane (IRE) (Ela-Mana-Mou) 4618[13] 4748[6] *4985[2]* **>57a f<**

**Zigse 2** b g Emarati (USA)-Primrose Way (Young Generation) 4250[9] 4458[2] **>60f<**

**Zilclare (IRE) 3** ch f Zilzal (USA)-Clara Bow (USA) (Coastal (USA)) 550[12] 4309[3] (4499) 4819[10] **>82f<**

**Zimiri 2** ch c Keen-Annabrianna (Night Shift (USA)) 4050[10] **>42f<**

**Zimmy 3** ch g Zalazl (USA)-Zealous (Hard Fought) 447[11]

**Zingaro (IRE) 2** b c Mujtahid (USA)-Zia (USA) (Shareef Dancer (USA)) 4200[5] 4494[7] **>63f<**

**Zinzari (FR) 2** ch c Arctic Tern (USA)-Model Girl (FR) (Lyphard (USA)) 5041[5] **>70f<**

**Zippersup (USA) 2** b c Alwuhush (USA)-Sunny Sara (USA) (Affirmed (USA)) *4954a[7]* **>95a f<**

**Zorba 2** b c Shareef Dancer (USA)-Zabelina (USA) (Diesis) 800[9] *1489[10] 3099[3]* 3880[3] 3998[8] 4501[3] 4764[3] 5006[2] **>2a 65f<**

**Zorro 2** gr c Touch of Grey-Snow Huntress (Shirley Heights) 4715[16] 4891[10] **>50f<**

**Zuboon (USA) 5** ch g The Minstrel (CAN)-Won't She Tell (USA) (Banner Sport (USA)) 961[8] **>71f<**

**Zugudi 2** b c Night Shift (USA)-Overdrive (Shirley Heights) 2009[4] 2580[8] (2916) 4049[13] 4488[15] 4614[8] **>74f<**

**Zuno Flyer (USA) 4** br g Lyphard (USA)-Triple Tipple (USA) (Raise A Cup (USA)) **1995:** *4357[7]* **1996:** *105[9] 145[3] 216[4] 274[4] 318[4] 351[2] 393[7] 485[5] 745[5]* 3980[4] 4548[6] **>61a 66f<**

**Zuno Princess (IRE) 3** br f Distinctly North (USA)-Flash Donna (USA) (Well Decorated (USA)) *10[8] 307[5] 488[8]* **>37a 36f<**

**Zurs (IRE) 3** b c Tirol-Needy (High Top) *1142[9]* 3513[3] 3839[2] 3999[3] 4254[4] **>84df<**

**Zydecho Queen 2** b f Then Again-Royal Resort (King of Spain) 2519[6] 3080[12] 3769[10] **>24f<**

**Zygo (USA) 4** b c Diesis-La Papagena (Habitat) 577[3] 1192[2] 1843[2] 2053[25] 3440[4] **>86f<**

## RACEFORM RATINGS

The Handicappers continually monitor the overall level of the Ratings and all two-year-old Ratings are likely to rise by a uniform amount before the start of the 1997 Flat season.

# REVIEW OF THE YEAR

*by Richard Onslow*

The 1996 Flat season will be remembered above all for one incredible feat. On Saturday, 28th September, at Ascot's Festival of Racing, Frankie Dettori delighted his legion of followers by winning all seven races, costing the bookmakers £18 million at a conservative estimate and earning the sport priceless publicity. No jockey had ever ridden all the winners on a seven-race card even at a minor meeting, let alone one of the most competitive and prestigious of the season. It was the greatest feat of jockeyship since Sir Gordon Richards rode twelve consecutive winners in 1933, comprising the last at Nottingham on 3rd October, all six at Chepstow the following day and the first five at Chepstow the next.

**HE'SA TOPPA THE POPSA**

Dettori lost his chance of retaining the championship, when he fractured his left elbow after Shawanni reared with him in the paddock at Newbury on 13th June. He missed Royal Ascot and did not return to the saddle until 9th August, riding his next winner on Altamura at Salisbury five days later. Dettori's absence cleared the way for Pat Eddery to secure his eleventh jockeys' title, allowing Eddery the satisfaction of equalling Lester Piggott's total.

*Frankie very much, Frankie very very very much*

The irony of the close-run contest for the trainers' championship between Henry Cecil and Saeed bin Suroor, of Sheikh Mohammed's Godolphin operation, lay in the drama of the previous autumn. In the belief that he had been misled over the condition of Mark of Esteem, the Sheikh removed all 40 horses he had in Cecil's Warren Place stable. And it was none other than Mark of Esteem who was principally responsible for preventing Cecil from finishing at the top of the list for an eleventh time.

Six days after returning from his winter's sojourn in Dubai, Mark of Esteem struck the first heavy blow for Godolphin by winning the 2000 Guineas in a pulsating finish from Even Top and Bijou d'Inde, with the top two-year-old of 1995, Alhaarth, only fourth. Twenty-four hours later Cecil counter-attacked successfully when Bosra Sham put an end to ten days of acute anxiety for him by landing the 1000 Guineas. On the last Thursday of April Bosra Sham had bruised a foot, and although she had cantered on the Saturday there were lingering doubts as to whether she would be able to do herself justice. At 530,000 guineas Bosra Sham was the most expensive yearling sold in Britain in 1994, and is the first horse with a top price-tag to have won an English classic since Sayajirao (28,000 guineas) was successful in the St Leger of 1947.

By the time the Goodwood meeting was in full swing at the outset of August, Cecil had gone through the seven-digit barrier for win and place prizemoney, but a month later Saeed bin Suroor was ahead. At the end of September bin Suroor consolidated his advantage in devastating style on "Dettori Day" at the Ascot Festival by winning the Queen Elizabeth II Stakes with Mark of Esteem and three other races, bringing his tally to £1,622,068 as against Cecil's £1,493,525.

*Henry Cecil proves Godolphin-friendly*

**BOSRA SHAM BRIDGES THE GULF**

In the middle of September the pendulum swung again when Cecil accomplished a feat that must be amongst his finest, by winning the Dubai Champion Stakes with Bosra Sham, who took the measure of the Godolphin candidate, Halling, with positively majestic authority. Bosra Sham had never been an easy subject to train, and once again she had been nursing a bruised foot a matter of days before running. Her difficulties arose from her having lost much of the wall of one foot, and the sole growing faster than the rest. Following that triumph on the part of Bosra Sham, Cecil went to the top with £1,868,609 and a lead of £50,778 over bin Suroor.

The pair of them, though, had not quite finished trading punches in the rarefied atmosphere of Group One level. For the last such event of the season, the Racing Post Trophy at Doncaster, bin Suroor saddled both Medaaly and Asas, while Cecil relied upon Besiege. The relatively unfancied Medaaly came out best, earning £97,489 which put bin Suroor £31,835 ahead. That clinched it. Medaaly, who had been supplemented at a cost of £15,000, provided jockey Gary Hind with his most important success to date.

Three other trainers to enjoy particularly well-deserved success in 1996 were William Haggas, Sir Mark Prescott and David Barron. Haggas showed that he is not only more than capable of handling a top-class horse, but doing so in adverse circumstances. He had intended to send Shaamit to the York May Meeting for the Dante Stakes until an overreach on the near-fore prevented the colt from running, and his trainer was left with the daunting task of bringing him to peak form for the Derby without his having a preliminary outing. An indication that Haggas might be on the verge of achieving his objective was forthcoming on the Saturday before the Derby, when Shaamit accelerated impressively in a mixed gallop over a mile with Paul Kelleway's pair Glory of Dancer, who had won the Dante, and Lear White.

A month before Shaamit fulfilled the promise of that gallop in the Derby, Haggas had reached a lesser landmark in his career when Yeast, owned by his father, won the Victoria Cup at Ascot, thereby giving his son the distinction of having won on every Flat course in Britain. A few weeks later Yeast went on to better things by giving Haggas his first success at Royal Ascot by landing the Royal Hunt Cup.

After twenty-five years of developing the ability of handicappers, and winning other races by the shrewd placing of horses of limited ability at minor meetings, Sir Mark Prescott stepped firmly into the top league in 1996. In August he obtained his first success in a Group One when Pivotal won the Nunthorpe Stakes at York, having won the Group Two King's Stand Stakes with the same horse at Royal Ascot two months earlier. Pivotal had been running a temperature in the spring, so there was no time for him to work his way through handicaps before going to the Royal Meeting for his first race of the season.

*Pivotal blasts to victory*

Between Royal Ascot and York Sir Mark had won the Group Two Nassau Stakes with Last Second at Goodwood, then within a week of Pivotal's splendid performance at York, he had won two Group Three races, the Prestige Stakes at Goodwood with Red Camellia and Sandown's Solario Stakes with Brave Act. In the autumn came another success at championship level when Last Second won the Sun Chariot Stakes (Group Two) at Newmarket. Last Second has a delicate constitution, which places strict limits on the amount of racing she can take. With the meticulous planning that is typical of him, Sir Mark sat down with her owner Prince Faisal Salman at the start of the season and selected just four objectives for her. She did not come to herself in time to contest the 1000 Guineas, was beaten only a neck in the Coronation Stakes at Ascot and achieved the other two. The greatest of Last Second's assets is her explosive, but brief, burst of speed, which George Duffield uses like a precision instrument.

**NO MORE BARRON NIGHTS**

To David Barron belongs the credit of winning three of the most competitive sprint handicaps of the season. Coastal Bluff won the Stewards' Cup in emphatic style, and followed up equally convincingly in the Ayr Gold Cup, although not without having giving Barron serious cause for concern. While turned out one day shortly after the Stewards' Cup, Coastal Bluff put a leg through a fence, taking off some skin. The leg blew up, and the horse did no serious work until he had a gallop at Thirsk a fortnight before Ayr. Coastal Bluff was bought for only 2,700 guineas as a yearling to run with a highly regarded individual who turned out to be useless. Barron's other notable success was with the outsider Musical Season in the Portland Handicap at Doncaster.

Jockeys who were in the news, for a variety of reasons, included Willie Carson, Walter Swinburn, Kieren Fallon, Richard Quinn and Alex Greaves. Willie Carson received severe injuries when kicked in the stomach by Meshhed and hurled 15ft across the paddock at Newbury on 20th September. As likely as not the life of the 53-year-old former champion was saved by the body-protector he was wearing. Inevitably he was out of the saddle for the remainder of the season, but with his usual resilience insisted that he will continue riding.

Having been left with horrific head injuries and multiple fractures after he had been thrown against the rails at Sha Tin, Hong Kong on 11th February, Walter Swinburn was still a long way from ready to ride at the outset of the season. By late June, though, he was able to ride work regularly, and on 12th August he returned to the racecourse, winning on Talathath at Windsor. His rehabilitation was made fully complete when he scored an emotional victory aboard Pilsudski in the Breeders' Cup Turf.

On August 6th, Kieren Fallon reached his first century when riding Jambo at Nottingham, and a few days later came the announcement that he will be first jockey to Henry Cecil in 1997.

The consistently good riding of Richard Quinn, stable jockey to Paul Cole, was one of the features of the season. After bringing off a treble at Brighton on 18th August he was only 13 winners behind Pat Eddery, and in October it became known that Quinn will be retained by Prince Fahd Salman, most of whose horses are with Cole, in 1997. Five years ago Quinn finished fourth in the 2000 Guineas on the Prince's Generous, but shortly afterwards the owner took first claim on Alan Munro, who won the Derby on Generous.

A little piece of racing history was made when Alex Greaves became the first woman to have a ride in the Derby. Her mount Portuguese Lil, a rare filly in the premier Classic, was trained by her husband, David Nicholls, and the combination finished last.

## FORTY DAYS IN THE WILDERNESS FOR WEAVER

Jockeys made the headlines for the wrong reasons, too. The interpretation of the guidelines regarding the use of the whip was once again a point of contention, and Frankie Dettori was hit by a ban after winning both the 2000 Guineas and the St Leger. Jason Weaver was another to incur the Stewards' wrath, serving a total of forty-two days' suspension for a variety of riding offences. On 16th October, the twenty-one jockeys due to ride in the second race at Haydock Park refused en masse to do so, claiming that heavy rain had made the course unsafe, even though the Stewards had passed the track fit for racing after the first event had been run.

The Turf season opened on an unexpected note when Royston ffrench rode his first winner, on the outsider Haya Ya Kefaah. The 20-year-old son of a Telford welder, the promising ffrench is apprenticed to Luca Cumani, who was also responsible for the early careers of Frankie Dettori and Jason Weaver.

Roving Minstrel made a bold attempt to win the Lincoln for the second year in succession, but the task of conceding 7lb to Stone Ridge, stylishly ridden by Dane O'Neill, proved beyond him. O'Neill, from Co. Cork, enjoyed considerable success as a junior showjumper in Ireland, and has been with Richard Hannon for five years. He held off the challenge of another Irishman, Fergal Lynch, to be the Turf season's leading apprentice.

*Glory of Dancer won the Dante*

After Mark of Esteem and Bosra Sham had won their respective Guineas, then came the public trials for the Derby and the Oaks, and so did the defections. On the face of things, the two most informative rehearsals for the Derby were the Dante and the Michael Seely Memorial, both at York. In the Dante, Glory of Dancer made a good job of beating Dushyantor. Glory of Dancer was trained in Italy in 1995 and only joined Paul Kelleway, who backed him at 75/1 for the Derby, on 2nd January. On the strength of his success in the Dante, Glory of Dancer became favourite for the Derby - temporarily.

The unraced Dr Massini went to post for the Glasgow Stakes with a reputation for being very much out of the ordinary and, as far as most observers were concerned, lived up to it. Dr Massini thrived on his work over the next couple of weeks and, on the strength of an impressive gallop, was promoted to favourite for the Blue Riband in early June.

In late May came the news that Mark of Esteem would not contest the Derby. He had been running a temperature and had missed too much work to make his preparation feasible. At the same time it was announced that Mick's Love, first of the Godolphin horses to win on returning from Dubai, would also miss the Epsom showpiece as he had a problem with his off-fore joint.

A few days later, Michael Stoute announced that Dr Massini was lame on his near-fore and highly unlikely to run. As his trainer feared, the position proved hopeless and that colt too had to be withdrawn, easing the way for Shaamit.

**TRIAL AND TRIAL AGAIN**

By contrast to those for the Derby, the rehearsals for the Oaks proved singularly informative. At Newmarket, Pricket, a sister to 1988 winner Diminuendo, won the Pretty Polly most convincingly for Godolphin. While in Dubai, she had proved rather flat-footed, and was obviously happy to be back on grass. Henry Cecil showed his hand for the Oaks at Lingfield, where he sent out Lady Carla to make all the running over the extended mile and three of the Oaks Trial. At Epsom, Pricket proved no match for Lady Carla, who beat the Godolphin filly resoundingly into second place. Few winners can have afforded Henry Cecil more satisfaction. Pricket was one of the forty horses Sheikh Mohammed removed from his yard.

Andre Fabre won the Coronation Cup for a fifth time when Swain beat Singspiel by a neck. Thus the French maestro equalled the record for the race set by Sir Noel Murless.

In the Queen's Birthday Honours list, Jack Berry received the MBE and John Dunlop the OBE. Both trainers earned their awards by their tireless work raising funds for charity.

Some of the prestige that the Gold Cup enjoyed up until World War II was returned to Royal Ascot's Championship for stayers when Classic Cliche became the first Classic winner to be successful in it since Ocean Swell back in 1945. Double Trigger, who had made all the running twelve months earlier, tried to make forcing tactics pay off again, but was unable to match the finishing speed of Classic Cliche. The time was almost three seconds slower than in 1995 and Jason Weaver was much criticised for not setting a more testing pace on Double Trigger. In reply, Weaver pointed out that he could not have gone any faster on ground with appreciably more cut in it than there had been the previous season.

*Bijou d'Inde outbattles Ashkalani*

In the St James's Palace Stakes, Double Trigger's stablemate Bijou d'Inde proved a great deal more at home at Ascot than he had been when running into the Dip in the 2000 Guineas. As Ashkalani took the lead off Bijou d'Inde in almost effortless style a furlong out, he looked set fair to become the Aga Khan's first winner at the Meeting since Dihistan in 1996, but Bijou d'Inde fought like an ocelot, as he clawed back the lead inch by inch until he had secured the verdict.

**COLE MINOR STRIKES RICH SEAM**

Paul Cole, who enjoys training juveniles more than most, had saddled the winner of every two-year-old race at the Meeting except the Queen Mary Stakes until making good the deficiency in no uncertain manner by supplying the first two in Dance Parade and Dame Laura. Somewhat similarly, it was against the backdrop of the season's most glamorous meeting that Godolphin produced its first ever juvenile winner, Shamikh, in the Chesham Stakes, which was being run over seven furlongs for the first time.

Willie Carson won the Cork and Orrery Stakes for the fifth time, on Atraf, following Parsimony (1972), Swingtime (1975), Dafayna (1985) and Danehill (1989). For Atraf's trainer David Morley though, it was a first success in a Pattern race at the fixture. Sylvain Guillot kept his unbeaten record in Britain intact by winning the Ribblesdale Stakes on Tulipa. On the only previous occasion, the 25-year-old Frenchman had ridden on this side of La Manche, he won the Champion Stakes on Dernier Empereur in 1994.

Kevin Darley and Fergal Lynch also rode their first winners at the Royal Meeting, Darley on Emerging Market in the Wokingham, and Lynch on Tykeyvor in the Bessborough.

North Song, winner of the Britannia, was both owned and trained by John Gosden. It was in no small part out of sentiment that Gosden bought him, because he was from the first crop of Anshan, with whom he won the Free Handicap in 1990, but he was unable to sell the horse on after he lost his action and became a "wobbler".

*Dane O'Neill pillaged the Apprentices' Championship*

The week after he had broken the ice at Royal Ascot, Fergal Lynch drew level with Dane O'Neill in the apprentices' table when winning on U-No-Harry at Lingfield. Lynch is apprenticed to Reg Hollinshead, with whom Walter Swinburn, Kevin Darley and Willie Ryan also spent the formative periods of their careers.

The success of Celeric, ridden by Willie Carson in the Northumberland Plate, was very much a family affair. Celeric is trained by David Morley for his brother Jake and brother-in-law Christopher Spence, the latter having bred the horse.

When Halling won the Eclipse Stakes for Godolphin for the second year running, he was back in his element as he was obtaining his eleventh consecutive success on grass. On other surfaces, he has proved less effective, as he failed in the Dubai World Cup On Sand and the Breeders' Cup Classic on Dirt.

*Halling confirmed himself a champion*

There was another family success in the July Cup at Newmarket, as the winner was Anabaa, trained by Criquette Head, ridden by her brother Freddie and carrying the colours of her mother. Anabaa is lucky to be alive, let alone a top-class sprinter. Early in his two-year-old days, injury to his spinal chord disorientated his co-ordination and he would have been put down but for the intercession of Criquette's father Alec, who was made a gift to him by Maktoum Al Maktoum.

Once again the Strutt & Parker maiden, on the first day of the Newmarket July Meeting, produced a potential star, as the winner was Bahhare, whose half-brother Bahri was successful in the Queen Elizabeth II Stakes. In 1995 the Strutt & Parker had been won by Alhaarth, by a neck from Mark of Esteem.

## RICH GROUND PERCS UP BETHELL

After training for twenty years, James Bethell obtained his first success in a Group race with Rich Ground in the July Stakes. Bred by the former Barnstaple trainer John Hill, Rich Ground cost only 8,400 guineas at Doncaster Sales, and is owned in partnership by June Vickers, of Wakefield, and Bethell. At 40/1, he was the longest-priced winner of the of the oldest two-year-old race in the world since its foundation in 1786.

Carranita emphasised that she is one of the biggest bargains on the scene by winning the Manchester-Singapore Stakes at York. That was her third success at Listed level and thirteenth in all. Having cost her trainer Bryn

Palling just 800 Guineas at Doncaster's breeze-up sale she had brought her earnings to almost £100,000.

Richard Hannon had four runners in the Weatherbys Super Sprint at Newbury, which he won for the third time in five years with Miss Stamper. Two days earlier Miss Stamper had been badly lame behind, but massage on a machine, recently acquired by her trainer, achieved the desired effect.

In late July, Michael Hills, who had won the Derby on Shaamit, appealed against a three-day suspension for careless riding on Polinesso at Doncaster. As a result of the penalty being reduced from three days to two he was able to take the mount on Pentire in the King George VI and Queen Elizabeth Diamond Stakes. Beaten a neck by the Derby winner Lammtarra in that race twelve months previously, Pentire duly went one better, being far more suited by underfoot conditions than he had been on the softened ground on which he had run behind Halling in the Eclipse.

Bred by the Earl of Halifax, Pentire is out of a half-sister to the Derby winner Shirley Heights, and carries the colours of Mollers Racing, a trust that finances the racing of a few horses in memory of R. B. "Budgie" Moller, who died in 1980, and his brother Eric, who died in 1988. Their fortune derived from shipping interests in the Far East. It was for Eric Moller that Geoff Wragg, the trainer of Pentire, turned out the 1983 Derby winner Teenoso, who also won the King George. Shortly after he had won at Ascot Pentire was sold to Japan, thus depriving British breeders of another stallion of immense potential.

*Pentire, set to stand in Japan, won the King George*

At Goodwood, Mollers Racing, Geoff Wragg and Michael Hills shared yet another triumph at the highest level when First Island followed up his success in the Prince of Wales's Stakes at Royal Ascot by winning the Sussex Stakes. The remarkable improvement made by First Island reflects enormous credit on Geoff Wragg. Twelve months earlier the colt had been rated 20lb below Pentire and had won just a maiden at the Goodwood May Meeting and a minor event at Doncaster 1995.

Michael Blanshard did well to win the King George Stakes with the highly-strung Rambling Bear. At Ascot the preliminaries had imposed too much on the horse's nerves, so that he had already lost the Cork and Orrery Stakes by the time he reached the start. Rambling Bear is owned by Michael and Sarah Hill, from Hampshire, who bought him through Dan Abbott's marketing agency.

Freequent maintained a family tradition when successful in the Tote Gold Trophy at his first attempt at a mile and a half. His dam Free Guest won the Extel Handicap at the meeting in 1984, and returned to land the Nassau Stakes the following year.

We were again reminded that size is not everything when Thrilling Day won the Oak Tree Stakes. This filly, who stands only 14.3 hands, had already won the Nell Gwyn Stakes at Newmarket in the spring.

**CARMINE FEELS THE NOISE**

Carmine Lake had her revenge on Connemara, to whom she was third at Chester in May, by beating her a neck in the Molecomb Stakes. After having been backed as though defeat was out of the question at Chester, Carmine Lake pulled a muscle when slipping on the bend, and had only come right three weeks before turning the tables.

Another to go to Goodwood a fresh horse was Grey Shot, who won a thrilling race for the Cup from Lear White. After Grey Shot had been beaten in Germany he was found to have a slightly dislocated vertebra, and was turned out on the Littleton Stud of his owner Jeff Smith in the middle of the summer.

Chris Thornton reached a notable landmark when Society Girl landed a claimer at Hamilton Park, as she was his 500th winner. Following the death of Sam Hall in July 1977, Thornton took over Middleham's Spigot Lodge Stable, and obtained his first success with Sioux and Sioux at Edinburgh later that month. Like Sioux and Sioux, Society Girl is owned by Guy Reed.

Halling gave another encore in Group One company by beating First Island in the Juddmonte International Stakes at York. After justifying hot favouritism he returned to a prolonged ovation, greatly appreciated by Frankie Dettori, who had obtained his first major success since resuming riding ten days earlier.

Putting up a pound overweight, instead of claiming his 3lb allowance, never seemed at all likely to prevent Fergal Lynch from winning the Ebor Handicap on Clerkenwell, furnishing Michael Stoute with a third success in the race, after Shaftesbury in 1980 and Deposki in 1991. Clerkenwell carried the colours of Sheikh Mohammed, who had bought him for $230,000 as a foal.

## KEY CHANGE HITS PERFECT PITCH

Irish champion jockey Johnny Murtagh was having his first ride on the Knavesmire when winning the Yorkshire Oaks on Key Change, thereby reaping the rewards of no little privation. Murtagh had had to lose 4lb the previous day and another 2lb in the morning. Key Change was also a first winner at York for her trainer John Oxx.

As a result of Ed Dunlop having taught him to curb his impetuosity, Iktamal was able to rise to the top flight of sprinters with remarkable rapidity. A little more than a year after he had opened his account by winning a maiden race in a field of four at Redcar, he was admirably held up by Willie Ryan before taking the lead inside the final furlong to win the Group One Haydock Sprint Cup. Dunlop had earlier saddled a Classic winner in his second full season with a licence when Ta Rib won the Poule d'Essai des Pouliches, while the other French fillies' classic, the Prix de Diane, was won by Sil Sila, trained at Lambourn by the former jump jockey Bryan Smart.

*Iktamal never stopped improving*

John Gosden won his first English classic when Shantou fulfilled the promise of his pedigree by snatching the St Leger in the last few strides. He is by Alleged, second in the St Leger of 1977, out of Shaima, by Shareef Dancer out of Oh so Sharp, winner of the Leger - as well as the 1000 Guineas and the Oaks - in 1985. Shantou is not without his idiosyncrasies. He declines to go out with the rest of Gosden's string, and has to take his exercise on Newmarket Heath in company with a hack and one other companion.

Bahhare consolidated his reputation by winning the Champagne Stakes. His time was a second faster than the previous two-year-old record set by Chebs Lad in 1967.

Henry Cecil tightened his stranglehold on the May Hill Stakes, which was introduced to the meeting in 1976. He was winning it for a tenth time when Reams of Verse beat Dame Laura.

Doubts as to whether Classic Cliche might have been fortunate to prevail in the Gold Cup necessarily arose after Double Trigger had beaten Celeric comprehensively in the Doncaster Cup, following 84 days' absence from the course. Subsequently his trainer Mark Johnston revealed that Double Trigger had not been able to show his true form at Ascot, as he had developed a foot problem a fortnight beforehand and lost a plate in running.

At the Ayr Western Meeting, Key to My Heart won the Doonside Cup on his third attempt, having been third in 1993 and runner-up in 1994. He was unable to participate in 1995, as he was off the course throughout the season after fracturing a leg on the gallops. On his being sent to the Equine Research Station of the Animal Health Trust at Newmarket, Ian Wright secured his off-fore leg with eight screws. They were removed after four months, and he completed his rehabilitation with another six months in his box. Key to My Heart is trained by Sally Hall, whose uncle Sam Hall won the Doonside Cup three times. On the opening day, Brave Montgomerie became the first Scottish-trained horse to win at the meeting for more than ten years. His handler, Linda Perratt, has the famous Cree Lodge Stable, across the road from the Ayr course.

Mellottie, one of the most popular horses in the North during recent years, retired after recording his twentieth success by winning at Pontefract in late September. The high-water mark of his career was reached when he won the Cambridgeshire in 1991. He is by Meldrum out of Lottie Lehmann, the first winner under Rules trained by Mary Reveley.

## FFRENCH FFINDS FFEET

Both legs of Newmarket's Autumn Double were won by horses trained by former top jumping jockeys. Jeremy Glover won the Cambridgeshire with Clifton Fox, who went on to add the November Handicap, while the Cesarewitch fell to Inchcailloch, trained by Jeff King and partnered by Royston ffrench. Glover was winning the Cambridgeshire for a fourth time, a twentieth-century record in the race, but King was obtaining his most important training success to date.

Barry Hills had his horses in top form during the autumn. When Elegant Warning won at Doncaster on 26th October, he was winning his fifteenth race in sixteen days. Events that he won during that period included the Dewhurst Stakes with In Command, who enabled him to maintain his record of having won at least one pattern race in every season since their introduction in 1971. Only Henry Cecil can match that achievement.

In Command did not appear to be an outstanding winner of the Dewhurst, although his victims in a blanket finish included the Middle Park winner, Bahamian Bounty. More highly regarded as a classic prospect is the Peter Chapple-Hyam-trained Revoque, unbeaten in four starts including two Group Ones at Longchamp. Reams of Verse earned Group One glory too, in Ascot's Fillies' Mile, while the Cheveley Park Stakes was won by Pas De Reponse, trained by Criquette Head. Redcar's Two-Year-Old Trophy, in which the weights are dependent on prices paid for the runners as yearlings, was won by Proud Native, who had cost IR£6,000. By collecting a first prize of £57,417 he took his earnings to £96,154. He is trained by Alan Jarvis for the Australian Leon Fust, who has business dealings in Russia.

## ARC OF DISTINCTION

In the Arc de Triomphe, Shaamit, Pentire and the runaway Irish Derby winner Zagreb all finished out of the frame behind the outstanding Helissio, but Pilsudski seemingly ran above himself in finishing second. Late in the month, he disproved that theory when he was Britain's sole winner at the Breeders' Cup in Toronto. Mark of Esteem flopped in the Mile, which was won by Da Hoss, trained by Michael Dickinson, best remembered for saddling the first five in the 1983 Cheltenham Gold Cup.

The Queen enjoyed her 600th success when Tempting Prospect won the Whatcombe Conditions Stakes at Newbury. Among the races Her Majesty had won earlier in the season were the Geoffrey Freer Stakes with Phantom Gold, making her final appearance while in foal to Cadeaux Genereux, the Moet & Chandon Silver Magnum at Epsom with Arabian Story, ridden by Luis Urbano, the Spanish amateur champion, and a round of the Shadwell Stud Apprentice Series with Step Aloft, ridden by 21-year-old Aimee Cook, daughter of former Royal jockey Paul Cook.

The doyen of the Newmarket trainers Harry Thomson Jones, who first took out a licence in 1951, retired at the age of 71. Among the achievements of Tom Jones was to send out two St Leger winners, while several top jockeys including Greville Starkey and Richard Hills were apprenticed to him. Guy Harwood, who won the King George, 2000 Guineas and Arc with Dancing Brave, also retired, handing his Sussex stable over to his daughter Amanda Perrett. Bill Elsey, responsible for winning the Oaks with Pia (1967) and St Leger with Peleid (1973), will not be renewing his licence either. Nor will Matt McCormack, whose finest achievement was to win the St James's Palace Stakes with Horage in 1983, while Brian Rouse, who won the 1000 Guineas on Quick as Lightning in 1980 and many important handicaps, announced his retirement in April.

*Tom Jones will now have time to mow the green green grass of home*

Lavinia, Duchess of Norfolk, who managed the Arundel stable during the many years it was a private establishment, died at the age of 79 in December 1995. She was one of the best judges of racing in the country and owned and bred the 1986 St Leger winner Moon Madness. Simon Weinstock was also knowledgeable and enthusiastic. He ran horses in partnership with his father Lord Weinstock, and was only 44 when he tragically died in May.

The former trainer Eric Cousins was 74 when he drowned while swimming off a Barbados beach in January. A great handicap specialist, he won the Ayr Gold Cup three times, the Kempton Jubilee in four consecutive seasons, and the Lincoln twice.

Joe Sime, the outstanding lightweight of his generation and long time Cock o' the North, was 73 when he died in October. Always in demand to ride for the gambling stables in the big handicaps, he won the Lincoln and the Cesarewitch three times apiece, and the Ebor no fewer than four times.

After an interval of six years, the Aga Khan had a winner under Jockey Club Rules when Mandilak was successful in the Ranworth Maiden Stakes at Yarmouth. The Aga had withdrawn from British racing as a protest against dope testing procedures, after the disqualification of Aliysa in the Oaks of 1989.

# 1996 SPEED FIGURES

## THREE YEAR-OLDS AND UPWARDS - Sand

Able Choice (IRE) 38 (10f,Lin,Std,Feb 20)
Abtaal 42 (7f,Lin,Std,Jan 25)
Access Adventurer (IRE) 57 (10f,Lin,Std,Jan 23)
African-Pard (IRE) 45 (9½f,Wol,Std,May 25)
Agent 48 (8½f,Wol,Std,Nov 11)
Ajdar 33 (13f,Lin,Std,Feb 15)
Aljaz 31 (5f,Wol,Std,Aug 9)
Allez Cyrano (IRE) 35 (7f,Wol,Std,Feb 28)
Allinson's Mate (IRE) 43 (6f,Sou,Std,Feb 16)
All On 40 (12f,Wol,Std,Oct 5)
Allstars Express 55 (10f,Lin,Std,Nov 7)
Allstars Rocket 48 (8½f,Wol,Std,Oct 19)
Almuhtaram 51 (12f,Lin,Std,Oct 28)
Always Grace 33 (6f,Wol,Std,Mar 15)
Amusing Aside (IRE) 42 (8½f,Wol,Std,Spt 7)
Anak-Ku 35 (8f,Lin,Std,Jan 27)
Anastina 39 (8f,Sou,Std,Mar 1)
Angus McCoatup (IRE) 44 (8½f,Wol,Std,Spt 7)
Anita's Contessa (IRE) 40 (6f,Wol,St,Jun 28)
Anjou 34 (16f,Lin,Std,Feb 24)
Another Batchworth 42 (5f,Lin,Std,Nov 7)
Ansal Boy 35 (8f,Lin,Std,Feb 20)
Anzio (IRE) 30 (7f,Lin,Std,Jan 20)
Apollo Red 41 (7f,Lin,Std,Feb 24)
Appealing Skier (USA) 80 (6f,Fst,Oct 26)
Araboybill 32 (12f,Wol,Std,Jan 17)
Arcady 34 (12f,Wol,Std,Oct 5)
Arzani (USA) 49 (10f,Lin,Std,Nov 7)
Ashgore 64 (7f,Wol,Std,Jan 3)
Ashover 31 (11f,Sou,Std,Jan 22)
At the Savoy (IRE) 38 (6f,Wol,Std,May 2)
Autumn Cover 31 (7f,Lin,Std,Nov 7)
Awasha (IRE) 30 (5f,Lin,Std,Feb 8)
Awesome Power 43 (10f,Lin,Std,Spt 10)
Awesome Venture 61 (7f,Sou,Std,May 13)

Backhander (IRE) 30 (6f,Wol,Std,Apr 27)
Backview 52 (15f,Wol,Std,May 11)
Bakers Daughter 37 (8f,Lin,Std,Feb 20)
Ballymac Girl 30 (16f,Wol,Std,Jan 17)
Ballynakelly 54 (12f,Lin,Std,Jan 6)
Banzhaf (USA) 38 (8f,Lin,Std,Feb 8)
Bardon Hill Boy (IRE) 61 (10f,Lin,Std,Feb 20)
Barrack Yard 42 (7f,Sou,Std,Jly 27)
Barrel of Hope 36 (8f,Sou,Std,Jan 12)
Bartok (IRE) 42 (10f,Lin,Std,Mar 2)
Basood (USA) 38 (8½f,Wol,Std,Spt 7)
Beau Bruno 47 (7f,Wol,Std,Jun 8)
Beauman 50 (9½f,Wol,Std,Jan 3)
Beaumont (IRE) 48 (12f,Wol,Std,Jan 31)
Belinda Blue 32 (5f,Wol,Std,May 25)
Benfleet 52 (16f,Lin,Std,Jan 23)
Benjamins Law 47 (8f,Sou,Std,Jan 22)
Bentico 55 (7f,Wol,Std,Oct 5)
Berge (IRE) 57 (7f,Sou,Std,Aug 16)
Bernard Seven (IRE) 47 (10f,Lin,Std,Jan 23)
Best Kept Secret 34 (6f,Wol,Std,Jan 10)
Best of All (IRE) 36 (7f,Wol,Std,Nov 11)
Biscay 32 (6f,Wol,Std,Jly 26)
Bit of Bother (IRE) 32 (8f,Sou,Std,Apr 24)
Blue Flyer (IRE) 42 (8f,Lin,Std,Feb 8)
Boffy (IRE) 40 (6f,Wol,Std,Jan 31)
Bold Aristocrat (IRE) 44 (6f,Wol,Std,Oct 5)
Bold Street (IRE) 42 (6f,Wol,Std,Oct 19)
Boundless Moment (USA) 85 (6f,Fst,Oct 26)
Bubble Wings (FR) 30 (8½f,Wol,Std,Apr 2)

Cabcharge Blue 34 (8f,Sou,Std,Jan 29)
Calder King 43 (8f,Sou,Std,Feb 26)
Call Me 34 (7f,Sou,Std,Apr 29)
Canary Falcon 49 (8f,Lin,Std,Feb 6)
Can Can Charlie 45 (10f,Lin,Std,Nov 7)
Canton Venture 47 (12f,Wol,Std,May 2)
Capote Belle (USA) 82 (6f,Fst,Oct 26)
Captain Marmalade 32 (13f,Lin,Std,Feb 1)
Carol's Dream (USA) 46 (10f,Lin,Std,Mar 29)
Carrolls Marc (IRE) 43 (12f,Lin,Std,Jan 25)
Cashmere Lady 55 (8½f,Wol,Std,Mar 15)
Catherine's Choice 48 (8f,Sou,Std,Aug 16)
Celestial Choir 55 (9½f,Wol,Std,Jan 31)
Certain Way (IRE) 31 (8½f,Wol,Std,Jan 10)
Chadleigh Lane (USA) 46 (9½f,Wol,Std,Apr 27)
Chadwell Hall 46 (5f,Wol,Std,Jan 3)
Chakalak 45 (16f,Lin,Std,May 25)
Charlie Bigtime 35 (12f,Wol,Std,May 2)
Chatham Island 30 (12f,Wol,Std,Mar 6)
Cheeky Chappy 42 (6f,Wol,Std,Nov 2)
Chevalier (USA) 52 (12f,Wol,Std,Jly 6)
Chewit 58 (6f,Lin,Std,Jan 9)
Chilly Lad 34 (10f,Lin,Std,Nov 7)
China Castle 49 (9½f,Wol,Std,Oct 5)
Chris's Lad 34 (16f,Lin,Std,Aug 10)
Claque 55 (12f,Wol,Std,Jly 6)
Classic Flyer (IRE) 48 (9½f,Wol,Std,Spt 7)
Clear Mandate (USA) 64 (9f,Fst,Oct 26)
Coh Sho No 34 (13f,Lin,Std,Oct 28)
Coleridge 48 (16f,Lin,Std,Jan 13)
Comanche Companion 40 (8f,Sou,Std,Apr 29)
Comedy River 39 (10f,Lin,Std,Spt 10)
Cool Fire 43 (9½f,Wol,Std,Spt 7)
Cretan Gift 68 (6f,Wol,Std,Jun 22)
Criollito (ARG) 75 (6f,Fst,Oct 26)
Crystal Heights (FR) 43 (7f,Lin,Std,Jan 6)
Cuango (IRE) 56 (16f,Lin,Std,Jan 13)
Cuban Nights (USA) 49 (12f,Wol,Std,Mar 30)

Daawe (USA) 56 (5f,Sou,Std,May 27)
Dahiyah (USA) 46 (5f,Lin,Std,Feb 22)
Dancing Cavalier 32 (8f,Sou,Std,Jan 22)
Dancing Lawyer 58 (8f,Lin,Std,Jan 30)
Dancing Sioux 58 (7f,Sou,Std,May 13)
David James' Girl 45 (7f,Sou,Std,Jun 20)
Deadline Time (IRE) 51 (9½f,Wol,Std,Jly 26)
Deeply Vale (IRE) 54 (6f,Wol,Std,Mar 6)
Delrob 33 (6f,Sou,Std,Aug 16)
Desert Invader (IRE) 64 (7f,Sou,Std,Jly 27)
Desert Zone (USA) 47 (8f,Sou,Std,Nov 4)
Dieci Anno (IRE) 30 (6f,Wol,Std,Oct 19)
Different (ARG) 81 (9f,Fst,Oct 26)
Digpast (IRE) 58 (8f,Lin,Std,Feb 6)
Disco Boy 36 (6f,Wol,Std,Apr 2)
Dissentor (IRE) 39 (6f,Sou,Std,Jan 12)
Distinct Beauty (IRE) 43 (8f,Sou,Std,May 13)
Doctor Bravious (IRE) 33 (8½f,Wol,Std,Jan 3)
Doddington Flyer 40 (13f,Lin,Std,Jan 11)
Domak Amaam (IRE) 35 (6f,Wol,Std,Jly 26)
Dombey 36 (9½f,Wol,Std,Mar 16)
Dome Patrol 30 (8½f,Wol,Std,Jly 26)
Domino Flyer 51 (8f,Sou,Std,Nov 4)
Don't Drop Bombs (USA) 35 (8f,Lin,Std,Feb 6)
Don't Get Caught (IRE) 33 (8f,Lin,St,Feb 13)
Double-O-Seven 41 (8f,Lin,Std,Feb 8)
Dragonjoy 39 (7f,Wol,Std,Oct 5)
Dream Carrier (IRE) 38 (8f,Lin,Std,Feb 6)
Duke Valentino 65 (8f,Lin,Std,May 10)
Dummer Golf Time 36 (6f,Wol,Std,Jan 24)
Duveen (IRE) 31 (12f,Lin,Std,Jan 6)
Dvorak (IRE) 32 (16f,Lin,Std,Jan 2)

Eagle Canyon (IRE) 45 (8f,Sou,Std,May 9)
Easy Choice (USA) 49 (10f,Lin,Std,Feb 13)
Efficacy 30 (6f,Wol,Std,Apr 13)
Elton Ledger (IRE) 55 (7f,Sou,Std,Jly 27)
El Volador 49 (12f,Lin,Std,Jan 13)
Encore M'Lady (IRE) 43 (6f,Sou,Std,Jan 22)
Errant 40 (10f,Lin,Std,Mar 27)
Ertlon 56 (8f,Lin,Std,May 10)
Ethbaat (USA) 57 (8½f,Wol,Std,Jly 26)
Etterby Park (USA) 40 (12f,Wol,Std,Jly 6)
Everset (FR) 51 (7f,Wol,Std,Jan 24)
Exalted (IRE) 41 (9½f,Wol,Std,Spt 7)
Expansive Runner (USA) 32 (12f,Wol,Std,Oct 5)
Explosive Power 60 (9½f,Wol,Std,Mar 16)

Faez 31 (8½f,Wol,Std,Jan 10)
Failed To Hit 39 (9½f,Wol,Std,Aug 9)
Far Ahead 44 (11f,Sou,Std,Jan 8)
Farmost 48 (9½f,Wol,Std,Aug 31)
Father Dan (IRE) 54 (10f,Lin,Std,Nov 7)
Featherstone Lane 53 (5f,Sou,Std,Feb 7)
Field of Vision (IRE) 53 (10f,Lin,Std,Feb 20)
First Gold 33 (7f,Sou,Std,Jan 19)
First Maite 50 (6f,Sou,Std,Feb 16)
Flirty Gertie 50 (7f,Sou,Std,Jan 19)
Foist 50 (6f,Sou,Std,Apr 9)
Formidable Liz 31 (7f,Sou,Std,Jly 22)
Fort Knox (IRE) 38 (8f,Lin,Std,Mar 14)
Forzair 35 (8f,Sou,Std,Jan 12)
Four of Spades 56 (8f,Lin,Std,Feb 1)
Freckles Kelly 36 (5f,Wol,Std,May 25)
Fresh Fruit Daily 43 (8f,Lin,Std,Jan 25)
Friendly Brave (USA) 32 (5f,Wol,Std,Feb 21)
Friendly Lover (USA) 81 (6f,Fst,Oct 26)
Frontman (IRE) 32 (6f,Sou,Std,Apr 24)

Galapino 38 (9½f,Wol,Std,Feb 21)
General Haven 34 (10f,Lin,Std,Jly 12)
General Shirley (IRE) 30 (10f,Lin,Std,Feb 27)
Giftbox (USA) 36 (8f,Sou,Std,Aug 16)
Glow Forum 56 (12f,Wol,Std,Oct 19)
Gold Blade 50 (12f,Lin,Std,Jan 20)
Golden Pound (USA) 59 (8½f,Wol,Std,Jan 17)
Golden Touch (USA) 52 (9½f,Wol,Std,Nov 11)
Grand Selection (IRE) 36 (9½f,Wol,Std,Feb 28)
Great Bear 32 (8f,Sou,Std,Jan 8)
Greek Night Out (IRE) 33 (16f,Wol,Std,Jly 26)
Greenspan (IRE) 39 (12f,Wol,Std,Apr 2)
Greenwich Again 38 (10f,Lin,Std,Mar 27)
Guest Alliance (IRE) 33 (16f,Lin,Std,Feb 13)
Guy's Gamble 31 (7f,Sou,Std,Jan 8)

Halebid 45 (9½f,Wol,Std,Jly 15)
Half Tone 51 (5f,Lin,Std,Feb 22)
Halliard 36 (8f,Lin,Std,Feb 20)
Hal's Pal 70 (9½f,Wol,Std,Aug 17)
Hamlet (IRE) 36 (8f,Sou,Std,Mar 18)
Hand of Straw (IRE) 38 (8f,Lin,Std,Jan 18)
Hannah's Usher 49 (6f,Wol,Std,Mar 30)
Hareb (USA) 33 (10f,Lin,Std,Jly 27)
Harry 40 (12f,Lin,Std,Jan 18)
Hatta Sunshine (USA) 37 (8f,Lin,Std,Mar 14)
Hawaii Storm (FR) 39 (7f,Lin,Std,Jan 30)
Hawwam 34 (8f,Sou,Std,Jan 5)
Heathyards Lady (USA) 55 (9½ f,Wol,Std,Aug 31)
Heighth of Fame 56 (12f,Wol,Std,Spt 7)
Herr Trigger 44 (10f,Lin,Std,Mar 23)
Hever Golf Express 34 (6f,Wol,Std,Jan 31)
High Patriarch (IRE) 54 (15f,Wol,Std,Jan 3)
High Premium 56 (7f,Wol,Std,Jun 8)
Hill Farm Dancer 49 (12f,Wol,Std,Nov 11)
Hillzah (USA) 51 (15f,Wol,Std,May 11)
Honestly 37 (7f,Wol,Std,Jan 17)
Honour And Glory (USA) 93 (6f,Fst,Oct 26)
Hoofprints (IRE) 42 (13f,Lin,Std,Oct 28)
Hornpipe 44 (9½f,Wol,Std,May 25)
Houghton Venture (USA) 42 (9½ f,Wol,Std,Mar 30)
How's Yer Father 38 (6f,Wol,Std,Nov 2)

Ikhtiraa (USA) 46 (16f,Lin,Std,Feb 13)
Iktamal (USA) 88 (6f,Fst,Oct 26)
Ilandra (IRE) 32 (10f,Lin,Std,Jan 25)
Imposing Time 51 (6f,Wol,Std,Oct 19)
I'm Your Lady 51 (7f,Wol,Std,Spt 7)
Inn At the Top 36 (14f,Sou,Std,Aug 16)
In the Money (IRE) 48 (12f,Wol,Std,Jly 6)
Intiaash (IRE) 63 (6f,Wol,Std,May 2)
Invocation 40 (7f,Lin,Std,Feb 10)
Iota 39 (16f,Wol,Std,Apr 13)
Irie Mon (IRE) 31 (8f,Sou,Std,Apr 1)
Iron N Gold 37 (13f,Lin,Std,Jan 11)
Ism 45 (7f,Sou,Std,Jly 27)
Itsinthepost 42 (6f,Wol,Std,Spt 7)

Jaazim 30 (5f,Lin,Std,Feb 22)
Jalmaid 31 (8f,Sou,Std,Feb 19)
Jaraab 61 (15f,Wol,Std,Apr 27)
Jess C's Whirl (USA) 63 (6f,Fst,Oct 26)
Jewel Princess (USA) 87 (9f,Fst,Oct 26)
Jigsaw Boy 39 (7f,Wol,Std,Nov 2)
Johnnie the Joker 48 (9½f,Wol,Std,Jly 6)
Johns Act (USA) 41 (12f,Wol,Std,Feb 21)
Jolto 38 (7f,Sou,Std,Aug 16)
Just Harry 41 (9½f,Wol,Std,Spt 7)

Kaafih Homm (IRE) 41 (10f,Lin,Std,Jan 2)
Kalar 56 (5f,Lin,Std,Feb 22)
Karinska 48 (8f,Sou,Std,Jan 5)
Keston Pond (IRE) 50 (6f,Sou,Std,Jun 20)
Kind of Light 39 (6f,Sou,Std,Feb 2)
Kingchip Boy 56 (8f,Sou,Std,Apr 29)
Kingdom Princess 31 (7f,Sou,Std,Feb 7)
King of Tunes (FR) 52 (10f,Lin,Std,Jan 23)
King Parrot (IRE) 30 (7f,Lin,Std,Jan 23)
King Rambo 44 (5f,Wol,Std,Jan 31)
King Rat (IRE) 56 (7f,Wol,Std,Oct 5)
Kings Harmony (IRE) 46 (7f,Lin,Std,Nov 7)
Kintwyn 42 (10f,Lin,Std,Feb 8)
Kira 52 (6f,Wol,Std,Mar 15)
Klipspinger 44 (6f,Wol,Std,Jun 8)
Komiamaite 41 (8f,Sou,Std,Jan 15)
Komlucky 30 (7f,Wol,Std,Jly 6)
Komreyev Dancer 57 (9½f,Wol,Std,Jan 31)
Krystal Max (IRE) 36 (5f,Lin,Std,Jan 6)
Kung Frode 35 (5f,Sou,Std,Jun 14)
Kymin (IRE) 33 (16f,Lin,Std,Jan 23)

Labudd (USA) 40 (8f,Lin,Std,Jan 2)
Lady Dignity (IRE) 43 (9½f,Wol,Std,Oct 5)
Lady Sheriff 41 (5f,Wol,Std,May 2)
Lakota Brave (USA) 92 (6f,Fst,Oct 26)
Lancashire Legend 37 (7f,Lin,Std,Nov 7)
Langfuhr (CAN) 86 (6f,Fst,Oct 26)
Last Roundup 33 (8½f,Wol,Std,Apr 2)
La Tansani (IRE) 43 (8f,Sou,Std,Jly 22)
Law Dancer (IRE) 43 (9½f,Wol,Std,Apr 27)
Lear Dancer (USA) 43 (15f,Wol,Std,Jan 3)
Le Bam Bam 36 (8f,Sou,Std,Jun 20)
Legal Issue (IRE) 48 (8f,Sou,Std,Jan 22)
Leigh Crofter 55 (6f,Sou,Std,Feb 16)
Le Sport 43 (6f,Wol,Std,Mar 2)
Lidhama (USA) 35 (12f,Wol,Std,Jun 22)
Lift Boy (USA) 47 (5f,Lin,Std,Feb 22)
Limerick Princess (IRE) 34 (6f,Wol,Std,May 2)
Lit de Justice (USA) 100 (6f,Fst,Oct 26)
Little Ibnr 46 (6f,Wol,Std,May 2)
Little Saboteur 38 (5f,Wol,Std,May 25)
Live Project (IRE) 52 (8½f,Wol,Std,Jan 10)
Lloc 31 (5f,Wol,Std,Jly 6)
Lochon 33 (6f,Wol,Std,Mar 6)
Loch Style 33 (7f,Wol,Std,Nov 11)
Locorotondo (IRE) 40 (12f,Wol,Std,May 25)
Loki (IRE) 38 (12f,Lin,Std,Nov 7)
Lord Carson (USA) 93 (6f,Fst,Oct 26)
Lord Sky 51 (6f,Wol,Std,Mar 15)
Love And Kisses 33 (14f,Sou,Std,Aug 16)
Loveyoumillions (IRE) 45 (6f,Lin,Std,Feb 24)

Mac's Taxi 32 (8f,Lin,Std,Feb 3)
Mad Militant (IRE) 56 (12f,Wol,Std,Nov 2)
Magic Junction (USA) 69 (12f,Wol,Std,Jan 17)
Magic Role 36 (13f,Lin,Std,Oct 28)
Maiteamia 43 (6f,Sou,Std,Apr 24)
Make a Note (USA) 59 (12f,Wol,Std,Jan 17)
Manabar 41 (8f,Lin,Std,Feb 13)
Manful 36 (12f,Lin,Std,Oct 28)
Mansur (IRE) 64 (9½f,Wol,Std,Oct 5)
Maple Bay (IRE) 70 (8f,Sou,Std,Feb 5)
Marino Street 30 (6f,Wol,Std,Jan 3)
Marjorie Rose (IRE) 43 (6f,Wol,Std,Spt 7)
Mask Flower (USA) 30 (6f,Sou,Std,Apr 29)
Masnun (USA) 38 (10f,Lin,Std,Jan 27)
Master Beveled 39 (8f,Sou,Std,Feb 2)
Master Millfield (IRE) 53 (9½f,Wol,Std,Nov 11)
Matthias Mystique 36 (13f,Lin,Std,Oct 28)
Maybank (IRE) 47 (7f,Sou,Std,May 9)
Medland (IRE) 32 (8½f,Wol,Std,Aug 31)
Meldorf 33 (8f,Lin,Std,Feb 8)
Menoo Hal Batal (USA) 49 (9½f,Wol,Std,Aug 9)
Mentalasanythin 51 (12f,Wol,Std,Jan 31)
Mezzoramio 30 (8f,Sou,Std,Feb 23)
Mighty Keen 51 (8½f,Wol,Std,Nov 11)
Mighty Phantom (USA) 32 (16f,Lin,Std,Aug 17)
Milngavie (IRE) 34 (16f,Lin,Std,May 25)
Milos 49 (6f,Wol,Std,Mar 30)
Mirani (IRE) 30 (7f,Wol,Std,Jly 11)
Miroswaki (USA) 51 (13f,Lin,Std,Jan 13)
Mischief Star 38 (16f,Lin,Std,Aug 29)
Miss Haversham 37 (10f,Lin,Std,Aug 17)
Miss Offset 34 (7f,Sou,Std,Apr 24)
Miss Pickpocket (IRE) 35 (6f,Wol,Std,Jan 3)
Mister 31 (5f,Wol,Std,Apr 27)
Mister Aspecto (IRE) 33 (10f,Lin,Std,Mar 2)
Mister Fire Eyes (IRE) 62 (9½f,Wol,Std,Feb 28)
Mister Rm 49 (8½f,Wol,Std,Jun 28)
Mizyan (IRE) 40 (16f,Lin,Std,Jan 23)
Monis (IRE) 36 (7f,Sou,Std,May 9)
Montecristo 31 (10f,Lin,Std,Feb 17)
Montone (IRE) 52 (10f,Lin,Std,Nov 7)
Move With Edes 37 (7f,Wol,Std,Aug 17)
Mr Bean 35 (12f,Wol,Std,Nov 2)
Mr Frosty 32 (8f,Lin,Std,Feb 1)
Mr Nevermind (IRE) 51 (7f,Lin,Std,Nov 7)
Mr Teigh 58 (9½f,Wol,Std,Jun 8)
Mr Towser 49 (12f,Wol,Std,Jan 17)
Mustn't Grumble (IRE) 47 (6f,Wol,Std,May 2)
My Cherrywell 42 (5f,Sou,Std,May 9)
My Flag (USA) 68 (9f,Fst,Oct 26)
My Gallery (IRE) 48 (9½f,Wol,Std,Spt 7)
Myjinka 35 (8f,Lin,Std,Feb 20)
Mystical Maid 30 (8½f,Wol,Std,Jly 11)
Mystic Tempo (USA) 38 (6f,Wol,Std,Jan 3)
Myttons Mistake 37 (7f,Wol,Std,Jan 17)

Napier Star 42 (6f,Wol,Std,Oct 5)
Nashaat (USA) 56 (7f,Sou,Std,Feb 23)
Naval Hunter (USA) 38 (8f,Sou,Std,Mar 18)
Need You Badly 39 (5f,Sou,Std,Jly 27)
Neuwest (USA) 50 (8f,Lin,Std,Mar 2)
Never So Rite (IRE) 30 (12f,Lin,Std,Jan 4)
New Albion (USA) 55 (8f,Lin,Std,Feb 20)
Newbridge Boy 32 (12f,Wol,Std,Jly 15)
Nicola's Princess 40 (8½f,Wol,Std,Spt 7)
Nigel's Lad (IRE) 34 (10f,Lin,Std,Jan 23)
Night Harmony (IRE) 35 (5f,Wol,Std,Oct 19)
Night Time 31 (8½f,Wol,Std,Jan 17)
Ninety-Five 42 (5f,Sou,Std,May 9)
Niteowl Raider (IRE) 34 (6f,Sou,Std,Apr 9)
Noble Canonire 39 (9½f,Wol,Std,Apr 27)
No Monkey Nuts 39 (6f,Wol,Std,Aug 31)
Nordan Raider 51 (6f,Sou,Std,Feb 16)
Nordic Sun (IRE) 38 (12f,Wol,Std,Feb 14)
Nordinex (IRE) 55 (8f,Lin,Std,Feb 20)
North Ardar 41 (8f,Sou,Std,Spt 9)
Northern Celadon (IRE) 41 (9½f,Wol,Std,Apr 27)
Northern Fan (IRE) 59 (8½f,Wol,Std,May 11)
Northern Trial (USA) 36 (12f,Lin,Std,Jan 23)
Northern Union (CAN) 58 (12f,Wol,Std,Feb 21)
Nose No Bounds (IRE) 32 (10f,Lin,Std,Jly 12)
No Speeches (IRE) 41 (12f,Lin,Std,Jan 13)
No Submission (USA) 36 (8½f,Wol,Std,Mar 15)
Noufari (FR) 49 (15f,Wol,Std,Apr 27)

Oberon's Dart (IRE) 49 (6f,Wol,Std,Aug 31)
Ocean Park 63 (8½f,Wol,Std,Jan 17)
Old Hush Wing (IRE) 32 (8½f,Wol,Std,Spt 7)
Old Provence 49 (12f,Wol,Std,Jan 17)
Old School House 37 (16f,Lin,Std,Aug 17)
One Off the Rail (USA) 49 (12f,Lin,Std,Feb 27)
Oozlem (IRE) 37 (8f,Lin,Std,Feb 3)
Opera Buff (IRE) 77 (12f,Wol,Std,Jan 17)
Orange Place (IRE) 32 (7f,Lin,Std,Feb 27)
Our Eddie 30 (10f,Lin,Std,Aug 10)
Our Main Man 41 (10f,Lin,Std,Nov 7)
Our Robert 30 (7f,Sou,Std,Jan 19)
Our Shadee (USA) 36 (6f,Sou,Std,May 9)
Our Tom 41 (11f,Sou,Std,Jan 8)

Pageboy 54 (6f,Wol,Std,Spt 7)
Palacegate Jack (IRE) 49 (5f,Sou,Std,Spt 9)
Palacegate Touch 59 (6f,Wol,Std,May 2)
Paradise Navy 50 (16f,Lin,Std,Aug 10)
Patsy Grimes 35 (7f,Lin,Std,Jan 6)
Paying Dues (USA) 97 (6f,Fst,Oct 26)
Pc's Cruiser (IRE) 36 (8f,Sou,Std,Aug 16)
Pearl Anniversary (IRE) 33 (12f,Wol,Std,Spt 7)
Pearl d'Azur (USA) 56 (6f,Wol,Std,Jly 26)
Peggy Spencer 53 (7f,Sou,Std,Jan 8)
Pengamon 54 (8f,Lin,Std,Mar 2)
Penmar 46 (9½f,Wol,Std,May 25)
People Direct 46 (7f,Wol,Std,Spt 7)
Perfect Brave 60 (6f,Sou,Std,Apr 9)
Perilous Plight 45 (7f,Lin,Std,Jan 25)
Perpetual Light 45 (8f,Sou,Std,Jun 20)
Persian Conquest (IRE) 48 (12f,Lin,Std,Nov 7)
Petoskin 41 (8f,Lin,Std,Mar 2)
Pharly Dancer 58 (12f,Wol,Std,Nov 2)
Philistar 35 (9½f,Wol,Std,Jly 26)
Pine Essence (USA) 31 (8f,Sou,Std,Mar 18)
Pine Ridge Lad (IRE) 69 (8f,Sou,Std,Feb 5)
Pistols At Dawn (USA) 31 (11f,Sou,Std,Jan 12)
Polar Champ 60 (9½f,Wol,Std,Aug 9)
Portend 43 (6f,Wol,Std,Jun 22)
Precedency 44 (14f,Sou,Std,Aug 16)
Premier Dance 51 (12f,Wol,Std,May 25)
Present Situation 38 (7f,Wol,Std,Mar 30)
Prima Silk 50 (7f,Sou,Std,Aug 16)
Primula Bairn 44 (5f,Wol,Std,Jan 31)
Prince Danzig (IRE) 65 (12f,Wol,Std,Jan 17)
Princely Gait 53 (12f,Wol,Std,Nov 2)
Princely Sound 38 (5f,Lin,Std,Feb 24)
Princess Efisio 40 (7f,Sou,Std,Jly 22)
Prizefighter 36 (8f,Lin,Std,Jan 2)
Progression 45 (10f,Lin,Std,Jan 23)
Proud Image 40 (12f,Lin,Std,Nov 7)
Prudent Princess 38 (8f,Sou,Std,May 13)
Pursuance (IRE) 36 (5f,Wol,Std,Jan 3)

Q Factor 43 (8f,Sou,Std,Feb 5)
Quality (IRE) 37 (10f,Lin,Std,Feb 13)
Queen of All Birds (IRE) 57 (8f,Lin,Std,Mar

2)
Queens Check 46 (5f,Sou,Std,Jly 27)
Quiet Arch (IRE) 33 (8f,Sou,Std,Aug 16)
Quinzii Martin 44 (8f,Sou,Std,Jun 20)
Quivira 34 (9½f,Wol,Std,Jan 31)

Rainbow Top 62 (10f,Lin,Std,Feb 13)
Rakis (IRE) 61 (7f,Lin,Std,Jan 25)
Rambo's Hall 60 (11f,Sou,Std,Jan 8)
Rambo Waltzer 56 (8f,Sou,Std,Jan 5)
Ramsey Hope 49 (5f,Lin,Std,Nov 7)
Real Madrid 31 (10f,Lin,Std,Jan 25)
Red Phantom (IRE) 43 (12f,Wol,Std,May 25)
Red Spectacle (IRE) 37 (13f,Lin,Std,Jan 11)
Rennyholme 42 (5f,Wol,Std,Mar 30)
Renown 41 (10f,Lin,Std,Jan 23)
Restate (IRE) 39 (8½f,Wol,Std,Jan 17)
Rival Bid (USA) 46 (10f,Lin,Std,Jan 4)
River Keen (IRE) 54 (12f,Wol,Std,Mar 6)
Roar on Tour 46 (8f,Sou,Std,Jly 1)
Robellion 51 (10f,Lin,Std,Feb 1)
Robo Magic (USA) 41 (6f,Lin,Std,Feb 13)
Rocky Waters (USA) 39 (8½f,Wol,Std,Jly 6)
Roman Reel (USA) 55 (8f,Lin,Std,Feb 6)
Royal Circus 32 (12f,Lin,Std,Jan 20)
Royal Print (IRE) 30 (12f,Lin,Std,Jan 25)
Runs in the Family 34 (5f,Sou,Std,Jly 27)

Sailormaite 57 (7f,Wol,Std,Jan 3)
Saltando (IRE) 31 (8f,Sou,Std,Jun 20)
Sandmoor Denim 41 (9½f,Wol,Std,May 11)
Sand Star 44 (8f,Lin,Std,Mar 2)
Sapphire Son (IRE) 38 (8f,Sou,Std,Jun 20)
Sarasi 55 (8½f,Wol,Std,Jan 10)
Sarum 37 (8f,Lin,Std,Mar 14)
Sassiver (USA) 34 (12f,Lin,Std,Jan 25)
Scathebury 32 (8½f,Wol,Std,Mar 30)
School Boy 37 (8½f,Wol,Std,Nov 11)
Sea-Deer 65 (6f,Wol,Std,Aug 31)
Sea Devil 39 (6f,Sou,Std,Feb 5)
Sea God 44 (8f,Sou,Std,Jan 26)
Sea Spouse 37 (7f,Sou,Std,Jun 6)
Second Colours (USA) 52 (8f,Lin,Std,Jan 25)
Secret Aly (CAN) 58 (10f,Lin,Std,Feb 20)
Secretary of State 40 (10f,Lin,Std,Jan 4)
Secret Spring (FR) 61 (8f,Lin,Std,Feb 3)
Sense of Priority 50 (6f,Wol,Std,Jan 10)
Serena's Song (USA) 84 (9f,Fst,Oct 26)
Serious Hurry 32 (5f,Lin,Std,Feb 22)
Serious Sensation 65 (9½f,Wol,Std,Aug 17)
Seventeens Lucky 45 (12f,Lin,Std,Jan 13)
Shaarid (USA) 42 (13f,Lin,Std,Jan 2)
Shadow Jury 42 (5f,Wol,Std,Jan 10)
Shahik (USA) 52 (9½f,Wol,Std,Nov 11)
Shakiyr (FR) 50 (16f,Wol,Std,Jan 17)
Sharp Command 33 (12f,Wol,Std,Nov 11)
Sharpical 38 (10f,Lin,Std,May 25)
Sharp 'n Smart 42 (7f,Lin,Std,Feb 10)
Sheraz (IRE) 38 (8f,Sou,Std,Jun 6)
Sheriff 44 (16f,Lin,Std,Feb 13)
She Said No 31 (10f,Lin,Std,Nov 7)
Shinerolla 52 (7f,Wol,Std,Feb 28)
Shirley Sue 41 (12f,Sou,Std,Jly 27)
Shirley Venture 33 (13f,Lin,Std,Oct 28)
Silk Cottage 44 (5f,Wol,Std,Jun 28)
Silktail (IRE) 33 (10f,Lin,Std,Feb 27)
Silver Harrow 35 (8½f,Wol,Std,Spt 7)
Sing With the Band 60 (6f,Wol,Std,Aug 31)
Sir Norman Holt (IRE) 54 (16f,Lin,Std,Jan 18)
Sir Tasker 46 (6f,Wol,Std,Jan 10)
Sir Thomas Beecham 40 (16f,Lin,Std,Feb 13)
Sis Garden 40 (7f,Wol,Std,Spt 7)
Slievenamon 31 (8½f,Wol,Std,Oct 19)
Slip Jig (IRE) 38 (7f,Lin,Std,Nov 7)
Smithereens 34 (7f,Lin,Std,Nov 7)
Smooth Asset (IRE) 30 (6f,Wol,Std,Oct 19)
Snake Plissken (IRE) 44 (8f,Sou,Std,Jan 15)
Soaking 42 (7f,Lin,Std,Feb 3)
So Amazing 66 (8f,Sou,Std,Jan 26)
So Intrepid (IRE) 47 (6f,Wol,Std,Mar 15)
Sommersby (IRE) 33 (9½f,Wol,Std,Aug 31)
Sondos 40 (6f,Wol,Std,Apr 2)
Sooty Tern 36 (8f,Lin,Std,May 10)
Sounds Legal 41 (8½f,Wol,Std,Nov 2)
Sound the Trumpet (IRE) 37 (5f,Wol,Std,Mar 30)
Souperficial 43 (5f,Sou,Std,Jly 27)
South Eastern Fred 68 (10f,Lin,Std,Jan 23)
Soviet Shore 36 (10f,Lin,Std,Mar 29)
Speedy Classic (USA) 50 (7f,Lin,Std,Aug 29)
Spencer's Revenge 53 (8f,Lin,Std,Jan 30)
Spender 37 (6f,Lin,Std,Mar 2)
Splicing 50 (6f,Wol,Std,May 2)
Square Deal (FR) 44 (7f,Sou,Std,Jan 19)
Stackattack (IRE) 43 (6f,Wol,Std,Jly 26)
Stalled (IRE) 48 (16f,Lin,Std,Jan 13)
Stand Tall 56 (6f,Wol,Std,Jun 22)
Star Rage (IRE) 51 (15f,Wol,Std,Apr 27)
Star Talent (USA) 41 (7f,Lin,Std,Jan 11)
Statajack (IRE) 32 (10f,Lin,Std,Mar 2)
State Approval 45 (12f,Wol,Std,Aug 9)
Statistician 35 (7f,Wol,Std,Nov 11)
Step On Degas 32 (5f,Lin,Std,Nov 7)
Stevie's Wonder (IRE) 39 (12f,Wol,Std,Jly 6)
Sualtach (IRE) 32 (8½f,Wol,Std,Jun 22)
Super Benz 55 (7f,Lin,Std,Feb 24)
Super High 60 (9½f,Wol,Std,Jun 8)
Superoo 35 (7f,Lin,Std,Jan 20)
Super Rocky 51 (5f,Lin,Std,Feb 22)
Sweet Mate 40 (7f,Sou,Std,Feb 5)
Sweet Nature (IRE) 30 (6f,Wol,Std,May 2)
Sweet Supposin (IRE) 53 (9½f,Wol,Std,Oct 5)
Sycamore Lodge (IRE) 42 (8f,Sou,Std,Apr 29)

Tafahhus 38 (5f,Sou,Std,Feb 7)
Takhlid (USA) 30 (8½f,Wol,Std,Aug 9)
Tame Deer 44 (7f,Sou,Std,Aug 16)
Tartan Gem (IRE) 48 (12f,Lin,Std,Jan 23)
Tathmin 37 (9½f,Wol,Std,Aug 9)
Tatika 57 (8f,Sou,Std,Feb 16)
Taufan Boy 35 (9½f,Wol,Std,Jly 6)
Tea Party (USA) 61 (9½f,Wol,Std,Oct 5)
Tee-Emm 32 (5f,Wol,Std,Apr 27)
Tenor 51 (5f,Lin,Std,Feb 22)
Thai Morning 63 (8½f,Wol,Std,Oct 19)
Thaleros 44 (8f,Sou,Std,Apr 1)
Theatre Magic 47 (9½f,Wol,Std,Oct 5)
The Frisky Farmer 33 (6f,Sou,Std,Apr 9)
The Great Flood 38 (7f,Wol,Std,Spt 7)
The Institute Boy 51 (5f,Lin,Std,Feb 22)
Three Arch Bridge 51 (9½f,Wol,Std,Jun 8)
Timeless 34 (8f,Lin,Std,Mar 14)
Todd (USA) 36 (10f,Lin,Std,Feb 1)
Top Secret (USA) 67 (9f,Fst,Oct 26)
Tormount (USA) 35 (8f,Lin,Std,Jan 27)
Total Rach (IRE) 32 (10f,Lin,Std,Jan 4)
Tragic Hero 31 (8f,Lin,Std,Feb 6)
Tribal Peace (IRE) 40 (10f,Lin,Std,Jan 23)
Troubadour Song 58 (12f,Wol,Std,Oct 19)
Tudor Falcon 31 (8f,Sou,Std,May 9)
Tuigamala 39 (8f,Lin,Std,Feb 29)
Twin Creeks 45 (8½f,Wol,Std,Oct 19)
Two To Tango (IRE) 46 (8½f,Wol,Std,Nov 2)

Ultimate Warrior 47 (10f,Lin,Std,Jan 25)
Ultra Barley 39 (7f,Lin,Std,Jan 9)
Ultra Beet 32 (6f,Wol,Std,Aug 9)
Undawaterscubadiva 32 (7f,Sou,Std,May 13)

Vax New Way 43 (6f,Wol,Std,Jly 11)
Victim of Love 36 (7f,Wol,Std,Apr 2)
Victory Team (IRE) 59 (8f,Lin,Std,Mar 29)

Waikiki Beach (USA) 53 (8f,Lin,Std,May 10)
Walk the Beat 51 (6f,Wol,Std,Oct 5)
Wardara 56 (6f,Sou,Std,Jun 20)
Warhurst (IRE) 43 (8½f,Wol,Std,Jan 10)
Warm Spell 31 (12f,Lin,Std,Jan 6)
Wasblest 39 (5f,Wol,Std,Apr 27)
Weeheby (USA) 38 (12f,Wol,Std,Oct 5)
Weetman's Weigh (IRE) 37 (6f,Sou,Std,Jan 19)
Well Arranged (IRE) 43 (15f,Wol,Std,May 11)
Well Drawn 33 (8f,Lin,Std,Jan 11)
Welsh Emblem (IRE) 35 (9½f,Wol,Std,Aug 9)
Wentbridge Lad (IRE) 39 (9½f,Wol,Std,Jun 8)
Wet Patch (IRE) 40 (10f,Lin,Std,Apr 4)
What A Fuss 53 (9½f,Wol,Std,Aug 9)
What a Nightmare (IRE) 30 (7f,Sou,Std,Feb 23)
Whatever's Right (IRE) 42 (7f,Lin,Std,Jly 27)
White Sorrel 44 (7f,Sou,Std,Jan 8)
Wildfire (SWI) 36 (10f,Lin,Std,Jan 23)
Wild Palm 47 (8f,Sou,Std,Aug 16)
Wild Strawberry 57 (16f,Lin,Std,Jan 13)
Wonderful Day 47 (12f,Wol,Std,Jan 31)
Woodbury Lad (USA) 30 (7f,Lin,Std,Nov 7)
Wottashambles 33 (13f,Lin,Std,Jan 11)

Yeoman Oliver 41 (8f,Sou,Std,May 27)
Yo Kiri-B 41 (6f,Wol,Std,Jun 28)
Yougo 49 (16f,Lin,Std,Feb 24)
Young Annabel (USA) 41 (7f,Sou,Std,Jly 22)
Young Benson 52 (7f,Wol,Std,Apr 27)
Your Most Welcome 40 (10f,Lin,Std,Feb 22)

Zaaleff (USA) 34 (12f,Wol,Std,May 2)
Zahid (USA) 42 (9½f,Wol,Std,Mar 16)
Zahran (IRE) 37 (8f,Lin,Std,Feb 3)
Zidac 37 (11f,Sou,Std,Apr 9)

## Turf

A-Aasem 45 (10f,Lei,G,Aug 12)
Abalene 34 (12f,Bev,GF,Jly 5)
Abeyr 88 (8f,Asc,GF,Spt 28)
Abir 43 (7f,Yar,GF,Aug 15)
Able Sheriff 43 (5f,Ayr,GF,Spt 19)
Above the Cut (USA) 38 (8f,Sal,GF,Jun 27)
Absolutelystunning 36 (10f,Don,G,Oct 25)
Absolute Magic 63 (7f,Yar,G,Oct 30)
Absolute Ruler (IRE) 33 (8f,Not,G,Oct 24)
Absolute Utopia (USA) 51 (8½f,Eps,GF,Spt 24)
Abtaal 37 (10f,Not,GS,Aug 25)
Access Adventurer (IRE) 62 (10f,Eps,GF,Jun 9)
Accondy (IRE) 46 (7½f,Bev,GF,Jun 12)
Acharne 73 (12f,Eps,G,Jun 8)
A Chef Too Far 40 (12f,Asc,GF,Jun 20)
Achilles Heel 45 (12f,Eps,G,Jun 8)
Acquittal (IRE) 31 (8f,Red,F,Jly 18)
Action Jackson 49 (10f,Not,GF,Jly 26)
Adilov 35 (11½f,Lin,G,Oct 4)
Admirals Flame (IRE) 63 (8f,Wnd,S,Aug 24)
Admirals Secret (USA) 46 (12f,Pon,GF,Jly 19)
Admiral's Well (IRE) 80 (22f,Asc,GF,Jun 21)
Advance East 52 (10f,Pon,GF,Aug 8)
Aerleon Jane 65 (8f,Asc,GF,Spt 28)
Aeroking (USA) 43 (8f,Nwm,G,Jly 9)
Aethra (USA) 48 (10½f,Hay,GS,May 6)
Afarka (IRE) 32 (16f,Cur,GS,Oct 5)
Affidavit (USA) 61 (15½f,Lon,S,May 19)
African-Pard (IRE) 44 (7f,San,GF,Jly 17)
Again Together 36 (8f,Bri,F,Jun 17)
Agent 41 (8f,Not,S,Oct 31)
Agnella (IRE) 39 (6f,Nwm,G,Nov 2)
Agwa 52 (6f,Bri,F,Apr 12)
Ahkaam (USA) 55 (10f,Leo,S,Apr 20)
Ailesbury Hill (USA) 43 (10f,Wnd,GF,Jly 22)
Ailleacht (USA) 75 (5f,Leo,G,Spt 14)
Aim For Stardom 34 (8f,War,GS,Apr 13)

Air Commodore (IRE) 51 (8f,Nwb,GF,Spt 21)
Air Quest 65 (11f,Nwb,G,Apr 19)
Air Wing 43 (6f,Chs,G,May 8)
Ajdar 47 (12f,Bri,F,Apr 12)
Akalim 36 (5f,Bev,GF,Jly 6)
Akhiyar (IRE) 31 (10f,Leo,S,Oct 28)
Akhla (USA) 42 (10f,Nwm,GF,Jun 8)
Akil (IRE) 73 (7f,Nwb,G,Aug 17)
Akiymann (USA) 52 (12f,Hay,G,Jly 5)
Alabang 48 (10f,Nwc,F,Jun 28)
Al Abraq (IRE) 60 (8f,Asc,GF,Jun 18)
Alaflak (IRE) 64 (10f,Asc,GF,Aug 2)
Alambar (IRE) 48 (10f,Yar,GF,Aug 15)
Alamein (USA) 64 (7f,San,GF,Jly 5)
Albaha (USA) 68 (6f,Lei,GS,May 27)
Albert The Bear 59 (7f,Lin,GF,Jly 13)
Aldaneh 40 (10f,Nwb,GF,Jun 27)
Aldevonie 31 (8f,War,F,May 6)
Alessandra 66 (12½f,Dea,G,Aug 10)
Alessia 36 (8½f,Eps,G,Jun 7)
Alfredo Alfredo (USA) 36 (8f,War,GF,Jly 5)
Alhaarth (IRE) 77 (12f,Eps,G,Jun 8)
Alhawa (USA) 58 (8f,San,G,Aug 30)
Alicia (IRE) 51 (10f,Don,G,Oct 25)
Ali-Royal (IRE) 81 (7f,Yor,GF,Aug 22)
Alisura 36 (11½f,Yar,GF,Jly 4)
Alkateb 68 (10f,Asc,G,Oct 12)
Allez Cyrano (IRE) 50 (8f,War,GS,Apr 13)
Allinson's Mate (IRE) 50 (7f,Cat,G,Oct 19)
All Stand 31 (7f,Goo,GS,May 22)
Allstars Express 45 (11½f,Lin,G,Oct 4)
Allstars Rocket 41 (9f,Nwm,G,Nov 1)
Allwight Then (IRE) 50 (5f,Bri,F,Apr 22)
Almapa 36 (5f,Lin,GF,May 18)
Almasi (IRE) 56 (6f,Lei,G,Jun 15)
Almaty (IRE) 75 (5f,Asc,GF,Jun 21)
Al Mohaajir (USA) 83 (10f,Cur,G,Jun 8)
Almond Rock 78 (8f,Rip,GS,Aug 26)
Almuhimm (USA) 73 (7f,Nwc,F,Jun 29)
Almuhtaram 55 (11f,Red,F,Jly 17)
Almushtarak (IRE) 66 (7f,Kem,GF,Jun 1)
Al Nufooth (IRE) 41 (6f,Goo,GS,May 22)
Alphabet Soup (USA) 92 (10f,Fst,Oct 26)
Alpine Hideaway (IRE) 46 (7f,Lei,GF,Oct 14)
Alpine Panther (IRE) 36 (7f,Fol,GF,Apr 16)
Alpine Twist (USA) 58 (5f,War,GS,Apr 13)
Alrayyih (USA) 38 (7f,Kem,G,Spt 6)
Alreeh (IRE) 47 (10f,Nwb,GF,Jun 27)
Al Reet (IRE) 57 (8f,Don,S,Mar 23)
Alsahah (IRE) 38 (12f,Nwm,GF,Aug 10)
Alsahib (USA) 52 (8f,Asc,G,Oct 12)
Al's Alibi 47 (12f,Nwb,GS,Apr 20)
Al Shadeedah (USA) 57 (10f,Yar,GF,Spt 18)
Al Shafa 68 (10f,Nwm,G,Jly 10)
Altamura (USA) 69 (12f,Asc,G,Oct 12)
Alwarqa 39 (17f,Pon,G,Oct 7)
Always Aloof (USA) 72 (15½f,Lon,S,May 19)
Always Earnest (USA) 73 (20f,Lon,S,Oct 5)
Always Grace 41 (7f,Yar,GF,Aug 22)
Alzabella (IRE) 72 (12f,Nwm,GF,Jly 20)
Alzeus (IRE) 44 (8f,Sal,GF,May 2)
Amadour (IRE) 46 (12f,Bri,G,Oct 2)
A Magicman (FR) 79 (7f,Lon,S,Oct 20)
Amaniy (USA) 33 (6f,Kem,GF,May 6)
Amazing Bay 61 (5f,Nwb,GF,Spt 20)
Ambassador (USA) 64 (14f,Yor,G,Aug 21)
Ambassadori (USA) 36 (10f,Nwm,GF,Jun 21)
Amber Fort 62 (7f,Nwm,G,Oct 19)
Ambidextrous (IRE) 38 (12f,Edi,GF,Aug 29)
Ameer Alfayaafi (IRE) 35 (10f,Lei,GF,Oct 15)
America's Cup (IRE) 63 (6f,Cur,G,Jun 30)
Amfortas (IRE) 79 (12f,Asc,GF,Jun 21)
Amiarge 40 (18f,Not,G,Oct 9)
Amlah (USA) 52 (10f,Eps,GF,Jun 9)
Amrak Ajeeb (IRE) 98 (8f,Asc,G,Spt 29)
Amron 44 (6f,Ayr,G,May 31)
Amusing Aside (IRE) 30 (10½f,Hay,G,Jly 6)
Anabaa (USA) 87 (6½f,Dea,GS,Aug 11)
Anak-Ku 48 (8f,Edi,GS,Jly 22)
Anastina 50 (7f,Nwb,GF,Spt 20)
Anchor Clever 62 (16f,Yor,G,Aug 20)
Anchorena 48 (10f,Bev,GF,Apr 25)
Ancient Quest 32 (12f,Nwm,G,May 17)
Androiad (USA) 77 (10f,Lon,G,Jun 23)
Angaar (IRE) 58 (7f,Lei,G,Jly 24)
Angel Chimes 41 (7f,Nwm,GF,May 3)
Anglesey Sea View 52 (16½f,Don,GF,Aug 1)
Angus-G 73 (10f,Don,GF,Spt 14)
Angus McCoatup (IRE) 31 (7f,Lei,GF,Oct 14)
Anita's Contessa (IRE) 32 (6f,Sal,GF,May 2)
Annaba (IRE) 77 (12½f,Lon,S,Oct 5)
Annecy (USA) 49 (10½f,Hay,GS,May 25)
Ann's Pearl (IRE) 60 (5f,Bat,GF,May 11)
Annus Mirabilis (FR) 93 (12f,Asc,GF,Jun 21)
Anonym (IRE) 54 (8f,Nwm,G,Oct 19)
Another Batchworth 50 (5f,Red,GF,Oct 17)
Another Nightmare (IRE) 42 (6f,Hay,GF,Spt 7)
Another Quarter (IRE) 32 (10f,Nwm,GF,Jun 28)
Another Sky-Lark (IRE) 51 (6f,Cur,G,Jun 30)
Another Time 63 (9f,Nwm,GF,Oct 5)
Ansellman 67 (5f,Nwm,G,Oct 19)
Anthelia 50 (10f,Nwb,GF,Jun 13)
Antiguan Jane 37 (10f,San,G,Apr 26)
Antonias Melody 46 (6f,Nwm,GF,Jun 1)
Anzio (IRE) 76 (6f,Asc,GF,Jun 21)
Anziyan (USA) 42 (8f,Lon,GF,Apr 21)
Apache Len (USA) 43 (8f,Asc,G,Oct 12)
Apollono 63 (10f,Nwm,GF,Jly 19)
Apollo Red 49 (7f,Lin,GF,May 11)
April The Eighth 60 (8f,Don,GF,Spt 14)
Aquado 45 (6f,Cat,GF,Jun 7)
Arabian Design 31 (8½f,Bev,GF,Jun 6)
Arabian Story 85 (12f,Nwm,GF,Oct 17)
Araboybill 42 (10f,Bri,F,May 9)
Arabride 66 (8f,San,G,Aug 31)
Arbatax (IRE) 68 (12f,Lon,G,May 5)
Arcady 34 (16f,Cat,G,Oct 18)
Arcatura 41 (10f,Not,GF,Jly 26)
Arch Enemy (IRE) 32 (6f,Sal,G,May 5)
Arc of The Diver (IRE) 38 (12f,Pon,G,Oct 7)
Arctic Fancy (USA) 61 (13f,Nwb,GF,Jly 20)
Arctic Starry (FR) 62 (5f,Dea,G,Aug 24)
Arctic Thunder (USA) 64 (12f,Eps,G,Jun 7)
Arctiid (USA) 62 (10½f,Yor,G,Jly 13)
Arel (FR) 56 (12f,Lon,G,Jun 23)
Argyle Cavalier (IRE) 34 (16f,Asc,GF,Jly 26)
Arian Spirit (IRE) 49 (18f,Pon,G,Oct 21)
Arietta's Way (IRE) 41 (12f,Lei,GF,Jun 3)
Arktikos (IRE) 34 (14f,Yar,F,Jly 23)
Arnhem 67 (14f,Goo,GF,Aug 1)
Arterxerxes 49 (7f,Red,GF,Jly 11)
Artful Dane (IRE) 62 (8f,Nwm,G,Oct 19)
Artic Bay 60 (11½f,Lin,G,Oct 4)
Artic Courier 68 (12f,Eps,G,Jun 8)
Ashanti Dancer (IRE) 30 (7f,Kem,GF,Jun 1)
Ashbal (USA) 67 (10f,Cur,G,Jun 8)
Ashby Hill (IRE) 51 (8f,Goo,GF,Spt 13)
Ashgore 63 (7½f,Bev,GF,Apr 12)
Ashjar (USA) 68 (7f,Lin,GF,Aug 4)
Ashkalani (IRE) 78 (8f,Asc,GF,Jun 18)
Ashover 40 (12f,Pon,G,Oct 7)
Askern 58 (11f,Ham,GF,Aug 3)
Asmara (USA) 51 (10f,Cur,S,Oct 19)
Assessor (IRE) 68 (15½f,Lon,S,May 19)
Asterita 76 (12f,Asc,G,Oct 12)
Asterix 36 (8f,Chp,GF,Jly 2)
Astor Place (IRE) 68 (10½f,Yor,GF,May 16)
Astrac (IRE) 76 (6f,Asc,GF,Jun 21)
Astral Invader (IRE) 41 (8f,Lin,GF,Aug 17)
Astral Weeks (IRE) 42 (11f,Ham,GS,Apr 3)
Athenry 65 (15f,Nwm,GF,Jly 11)
Atherton Green (IRE) 31 (14f,Not,GF,Jun 19)
Atlantic Mist 43 (11½f,San,GS,May 28)
Atlantic Storm 41 (7f,Bri,F,Jly 16)
At Liberty (IRE) 70 (12f,Nwm,GF,Apr 17)
Atraf 73 (6f,Nwm,GF,Jun 1)
Attarikh (IRE) 54 (8f,Chp,GF,Jly 6)
Atticus (USA) 82 (10f,Fst,Oct 26)
Attune (FR) 74 (8f,Dea,G,Aug 15)
Aude la Belle (FR) 30 (16f,Kem,G,Apr 6)
Augustan 48 (12f,Chp,GF,Jly 25)
Aunty Jane 49 (7f,Chs,G,May 8)
Autumn Affair 60 (8f,Yor,GF,Aug 22)
Autumn Cover 64 (8f,Asc,G,Spt 29)
Averring (USA) 81 (10½f,Cha,G,Jun 9)
Averti (IRE) 66 (6f,Hay,G,Jly 5)
A Votre Sante (USA) 68 (10½f,Cha,G,Jun 9)
Awaamir 60 (8f,Asc,G,Oct 11)
Awad (USA) 79 (12f,G,Oct 26)
Awasha (IRE) 45 (5f,Lin,G,May 25)
Awesome Venture 43 (8f,Red,F,Spt 27)
Axford (USA) 50 (8f,Kem,GF,May 6)
Aylesbury (IRE) 50 (7f,Cur,S,Apr 13)
Ayunli 60 (12f,Ham,GS,Spt 30)
Azizzi 67 (7f,Kem,GF,Apr 29)
Azwah (USA) 31 (6f,Sal,G,Aug 15)

Baba Au Rhum (IRE) 40 (8f,Not,G,Oct 24)
Babinda 57 (12f,Nwb,G,Aug 16)
Babsy Babe 66 (6f,Hay,G,Jly 6)
Backdrop (IRE) 65 (16f,Nwc,F,Jun 29)
Backgammon 66 (12f,Eps,G,Jun 7)
Backview 38 (12f,Chs,GF,Jun 26)
Backwoods 37 (16f,Cat,G,Oct 18)
Bag of Tricks (IRE) 44 (12f,Bri,G,May 30)
Bagshot 50 (7f,Bri,F,Apr 12)
Bahamian Knight (CAN) 64 (12f,Goo,GF,Jly 30)
Bahamian Sunshine (USA) 78 (22f,Asc,GF,Jun 21)
Baileys First (IRE) 41 (6f,Ayr,G,Aug 10)
Baileys Sunset (IRE) 44 (6f,Bat,G,May 20)
Baize 57 (6f,Kem,GF,May 6)
Bajan (IRE) 33 (10f,San,G,Aug 31)
Bajan Rose 70 (6f,Yor,G,Oct 12)
Bakers Daughter 41 (8f,Bat,F,Jun 29)
Bakers' Gate (USA) 39 (8f,Rip,G,Apr 10)
Bakheta 50 (10f,Nwb,GF,Jun 27)
Balalaika 77 (12f,Nwm,GF,Jly 20)
Balance of Power 57 (8f,Bri,GF,Aug 28)
Bal Harbour 79 (12f,Don,GF,Spt 13)
Balladur (USA) 54 (8f,Nwc,F,Jun 29)
Ballard Lady (IRE) 33 (6f,Ayr,G,Aug 10)
Ballet High (IRE) 47 (13½f,Chs,G,Spt 25)
Ball Gown 72 (10f,Nwm,GS,Aug 24)
Ballpoint 51 (11½f,Yar,G,Spt 17)
Ballynakelly 66 (18f,Nwm,G,Oct 19)
Baloustar (USA) 40 (7f,Nwm,GF,Apr 17)
Bandit Girl 38 (8f,Lei,G,Aug 12)
Band on the Run 69 (8f,Nwb,GS,Apr 20)
Bang in Trouble (IRE) 43 (14f,Hay,S,Oct 5)
Bangles 55 (5f,Lei,GF,Aug 19)
Banzhaf (USA) 49 (7f,Lin,GF,Jly 13)
Barato 53 (6f,Red,F,Spt 28)
Barbaroja 70 (8f,Don,S,Mar 23)
Barbason 32 (10f,Bri,G,Oct 2)
Bardon Hill Boy (IRE) 76 (12½f,Nwc,F,Jun 29)
Barford Sovereign 56 (16f,Kem,GS,May 25)
Bargash 50 (7f,Cat,GS,Mar 27)
Bark'n'bite 33 (18f,Not,G,Oct 9)
Baron Hrabovsky 39 (8f,Goo,GF,Spt 25)
Barranak (IRE) 60 (5f,Rip,G,Aug 17)
Barrel of Hope 69 (6f,Hay,S,Oct 6)
Barricade (USA) 63 (8f,Lon,G,May 12)
Bashaayeash (IRE) 78 (6f,Dea,G,Aug 25)
Bashful Brave 52 (6f,Bri,F,Apr 12)
Basood (USA) 35 (12f,Bri,G,Oct 2)
Bataleur 42 (6f,Ham,GS,Spt 30)
Bathilde (IRE) 61 (10½f,Yor,GF,May 15)
Batoutoftheblue 30 (12f,Nwm,GF,Aug 3)
Battleship Bruce 56 (8f,Not,G,Apr 2)
Battle Spark (USA) 44 (8f,Nwm,GF,Jun 1)
Bayin (USA) 59 (6f,Nwc,F,Jun 29)

Bayrak (USA) 49 (12f,Lei,G,Apr 27)
Beano Script 39 (7f,Red,F,Spt 28)
Beau Bruno 32 (7f,Kem,GF,Jun 1)
Beauchamp Jade 84 (14f,Yor,G,Aug 21)
Beauchamp Jazz 82 (8f,Asc,GF,Jun 19)
Beauchamp King 73 (8f,Asc,GF,Jun 18)
Beaumont (IRE) 50 (14½f,Don,G,Oct 25)
Beau Venture (USA) 57 (5f,San,GS,Jly 6)
Bechstein 50 (12f,Hay,S,Oct 6)
Bee Health Boy 53 (6f,Ayr,GF,Spt 21)
Behaviour 73 (8½f,Eps,G,Jun 7)
Beldray Park (IRE) 47 (6f,Fol,GS,Mar 25)
Belfry Green (IRE) 79 (8f,Goo,GF,Jun 7)
Believe Me 75 (8f,Hay,GS,May 25)
Bellara 44 (14f,Sal,G,May 5)
Bella Sedona 38 (12f,Lei,G,Apr 4)
Bellas Gate Boy 38 (11f,Ayr,GF,Spt 19)
Bellator 51 (12f,Chp,S,Oct 22)
Belle's Boy 33 (10f,Not,G,Apr 2)
Bellroi (IRE) 30 (17f,Pon,GF,Aug 18)
Belmarita (IRE) 48 (14f,Yor,G,Spt 4)
Belzao 43 (8f,Not,S,Oct 31)
Benatom (USA) 74 (14f,Goo,GF,Aug 1)
Ben Bowden 33 (8f,Lei,G,Apr 27)
Bend Wavy (IRE) 67 (8f,Wnd,G,May 20)
Beneficial 55 (9f,Nwm,G,Oct 18)
Benfleet 65 (12f,Eps,G,Jun 8)
Ben Gunn 39 (7f,Nwm,G,Nov 2)
Benjamins Law 39 (8f,War,G,May 25)
Bentico 55 (8f,Lei,GF,Oct 14)
Benzoe (IRE) 70 (6f,Thi,GF,Aug 2)
Bequeath 73 (12f,Nwm,G,Jun 29)
Berenice 58 (10f,Yar,G,Spt 17)
Berlin Blue 47 (12f,Rip,G,Jly 8)
Bernard Seven (IRE) 53 (8f,War,F,Jun 24)
Best Kept Secret 44 (6f,Cat,GS,Jly 3)
Best of All (IRE) 58 (7f,Red,GF,May 13)
Better Offer (IRE) 87 (14f,Yor,G,Aug 21)
Be Warned 50 (6f,Goo,G,Jun 14)
Bewitching (USA) 60 (8f,Lin,GF,Jly 13)
Beyond Doubt 54 (12f,Nwm,G,Oct 1)
Beyond Our Reach 34 (8f,Chp,G,Jun 13)
Bijou d'Inde 79 (10½f,Yor,G,Aug 20)
Billy Bushwacker 81 (10f,Don,GF,Spt 14)
Biloela 44 (10f,Bev,GF,Apr 25)
Binary 54 (12½f,Lon,S,Oct 5)
Bin Rosie 83 (7f,Nwb,G,Aug 16)
Bint Salsabil (USA) 74 (10f,Nwm,GF,Aug 9)
Bint Shadayid (USA) 73 (10f,Dea,G,Aug 25)
Birchwood Sun 34 (6f,Crl,GF,May 10)
Biscay 41 (8f,Kem,G,Spt 7)
Bishop of Cashel 83 (8f,Don,GF,Aug 1)
Bit of Bother (IRE) 30 (8f,Not,GF,Apr 8)
Bit on the Side (IRE) 64 (11f,War,GS,Apr 13)
Blackpatch Hill 38 (12f,Don,G,May 25)
Blackwater (USA) 78 (9f,Cha,F,Jun 2)
Blatant Outburst 61 (11½f,Yar,GF,Jly 4)
Blaze Away (USA) 68 (16f,Goo,GF,Spt 14)
Blaze of Oak (USA) 40 (10f,Yar,GF,Spt 18)
Blaze of Song 44 (8f,San,GS,Aug 23)
Blazon of Troy 45 (14f,Not,GF,Jun 10)
Blending Element (IRE) 32 (10f,Cur,GS,May 26)
Blenheim Terrace 48 (12f,Edi,GF,Aug 29)
Blessed Spirit 60 (8f,San,G,Aug 30)
Blessingindisguise 52 (6f,Yor,G,Oct 12)
Blockade (USA) 40 (8f,Sal,GF,Jun 26)
Blomberg (IRE) 82 (9f,Nwm,G,Oct 18)
Blossom Dearie 33 (6f,Sal,G,May 5)
Blue Bomber 51 (6f,Cat,GS,Jly 3)
Blue Duster (USA) 78 (6f,Hay,GF,Spt 7)
Blue Flyer (IRE) 52 (7f,Sal,GF,Aug 22)
Blue Grit 39 (7f,Red,GF,May 27)
Blue Iris 66 (5f,Yor,G,Aug 21)
Blueshaan (IRE) 62 (10f,Dea,G,May 16)
Blue Water (FR) 74 (12½f,Lon,S,Oct 5)
Blue Zulu (IRE) 53 (8f,San,GS,Jly 6)
Blurred (IRE) 58 (10f,Lei,GF,Oct 15)
Blushing Flame (USA) 61 (12f,Lei,G,Jun 15)
Blushing Grenadier (IRE) 45 (6f,Wnd,G,Jly 1)
Bobanlyn (IRE) 53 (12f,Edi,G,Jly 8)
Bob's Ploy 56 (10f,Nwm,GF,Jly 19)
Bold Amusement 59 (12f,Don,G,Oct 26)
Bold Angel 39 (8f,Wnd,GF,Jun 3)
Bold Classic (IRE) 43 (14f,Yar,F,Jly 23)
Bold Effort (FR) 66 (5f,Dea,G,Aug 24)
Bold Elect 36 (14f,Red,F,Jun 22)
Bold Enough 31 (7f,Cat,GF,Spt 21)
Bold Habit 31 (7f,Lin,GF,May 11)
Bold Patriot (IRE) 35 (8f,Ayr,GS,May 8)
Bold Pursuit (IRE) 39 (12f,Rip,G,Apr 10)
Bold Resolution (IRE) 36 (14f,San,F,Jun 15)
Bold Street (IRE) 46 (6f,Hay,G,Jun 7)
Bold Top 42 (10f,Pon,G,Spt 3)
Bolivar (IRE) 59 (16f,Asc,GF,Jly 26)
Bollin Dorothy 35 (6f,Hay,GF,Spt 7)
Bollin Frank 52 (8f,Rip,GS,Aug 26)
Bollin Harry 65 (6f,Pon,GF,Jun 10)
Bollin Jacob 33 (8f,Crl,G,May 30)
Bollin Joanne 76 (6f,Yor,G,Oct 12)
Bolshoi (IRE) 80 (5f,Nwm,G,Oct 19)
Bonanza Peak (USA) 48 (10½f,Yor,G,Oct 10)
Bonarelli (IRE) 50 (8f,Don,GF,Aug 1)
Bon Luck (IRE) 62 (8f,Chp,GF,Jly 6)
Bonne Etoile 37 (10f,Asc,GF,Jly 27)
Born A Lady 34 (8f,Not,GF,Jun 24)
Bosra Sham (USA) 80 (8f,Asc,GF,Spt 28)
Boston Rock (IRE) 42 (8f,Rip,G,Apr 10)
Bouche Bee (USA) 47 (6f,Asc,GF,Jun 20)
Bowcliffe 41 (8f,Edi,GS,May 30)
Bowcliffe Court (IRE) 47 (16f,Cat,G,Jun 1)
Bowcliffe Grange (IRE) 38 (5f,Don,GF,Jly 17)
Bowden Rose 71 (5f,Nwm,G,Oct 19)
Bowled Over 62 (10f,Don,G,Spt 11)
Bowlers Boy 56 (5f,Pon,GF,Spt 26)
Braille (IRE) 51 (12f,Hay,GS,May 6)
Brambles Way 37 (10f,Red,F,Spt 28)
Brandon Court (IRE) 59 (15f,Nwm,GF,Jly 20)
Brandon Magic 66 (8f,Asc,GF,Jun 18)
Brandon Prince (IRE) 43 (15f,War,GS,Apr 13)
Branston Abby (IRE) 83 (6f,Nwm,GF,Jun 1)
Branston Danni 45 (5f,Thi,G,Aug 23)
Brave Edge 73 (5f,Lin,GS,Aug 29)
Brave Patriarch (IRE) 44 (12f,Lei,G,Apr 27)
Braydon Forest 37 (11½f,Wnd,G,Aug 12)
Break the Rules 60 (10f,Don,G,Oct 26)
Brecongill Lad 55 (5f,Bev,GF,Aug 14)
Breezed Well 40 (11½f,Lin,G,Oct 4)
Brief Glimpse (IRE) 64 (6f,Nwm,GF,Jun 1)
Brighstone 32 (8f,Kem,GS,May 25)
Bright Diamond 32 (6f,Sal,G,Aug 15)
Bright Eclipse (USA) 34 (8f,Bri,G,May 30)
Brighton Road (IRE) 44 (7f,San,G,May 27)
Bright Water 71 (10f,Nwm,GF,Oct 17)
Brilliant Red 56 (10f,Nwb,G,Aug 16)
Broadstairs Beauty (IRE) 49 (5f,Nwc,GS,Mar 26)
Broctune Gold 59 (8f,Ayr,GF,Spt 20)
Brodessa 33 (16f,Bev,F,Aug 15)
Bronze Runner 34 (10f,San,G,Aug 31)
Brookhead Lady 30 (6f,Pon,G,Apr 23)
Brother Roy 33 (9f,Nwm,G,Nov 1)
Broughtons Formula 31 (16f,Cat,GF,Spt 21)
Broughton's Pride (IRE) 42 (8f,Edi,GS,Nov 7)
Broughtons Turmoil 64 (7f,Nwm,G,Oct 19)
Brown Eyed Girl 30 (10f,Not,G,Apr 22)
Bubble Wings (FR) 56 (8f,Pon,GF,Jly 9)
Budby 50 (8f,Hay,GF,Spt 7)
Bullfinch 60 (8f,San,G,Apr 27)
Bulsara 42 (10f,Nwc,GF,Jly 27)
Bunty Boo 48 (5f,Sal,G,Aug 14)
Burden Of Proof (IRE) 74 (7f,Cur,S,Apr 13)
Burning (USA) 50 (10f,Kem,G,Apr 8)
Burnt Offering 49 (10f,Eps,G,Jun 7)
Burooj 59 (12f,Nwm,GF,May 3)
Busy Flight 78 (12f,Don,GF,Spt 13)
Caballus (USA) 32 (12f,Goo,GF,Jun 14)
Cabaret (IRE) 68 (8f,Asc,GF,Spt 28)
Cachet Noir (USA) 70 (10½f,Lon,G,May 12)
Cadeau Elegant 31 (6f,Nwm,GF,Jly 19)
Cadeaux Tryst 88 (8f,Asc,GF,Jun 19)
Ca'd'oro 41 (8f,Bat,G,Aug 13)
Calder King 55 (11f,Ayr,GF,Spt 19)
Call Me 46 (10f,Eps,G,Jun 7)
Call Me I'm Blue (IRE) 44 (5f,Thi,GF,Apr 20)
Call My Guest (IRE) 31 (16f,War,F,Jun 10)
Call to the Bar (IRE) 44 (5f,Nwc,G,May 22)
Camille (FR) 49 (9f,Lon,GS,Oct 6)
Camionneur (IRE) 39 (5f,Ayr,GF,Jly 15)
Campaspe 41 (12f,Bev,GF,Spt 18)
Camp David (GER) 72 (20f,Lon,S,Oct 5)
Camp Follower 40 (12f,Lei,G,Jun 15)
Camporese (IRE) 71 (12f,Eps,G,Jun 7)
Canary Falcon 40 (11f,Red,GF,Jly 11)
Candle Smile (USA) 78 (20f,Asc,GF,Jun 18)
Candle Smoke (USA) 52 (16f,Goo,GF,Spt 14)
Candrika 35 (12f,Nwm,GF,Aug 10)
Canon Can (USA) 63 (18f,Nwm,G,Oct 19)
Canovas Heart 54 (5f,Hay,GF,Aug 10)
Cante Chico 37 (10f,Bev,GF,Jly 6)
Canton Venture 57 (11½f,Yar,F,Jly 21)
Canyon Creek (IRE) 49 (8f,Pon,G,Oct 7)
Cape Merino 51 (5f,Bat,G,Apr 30)
Cape Pigeon (USA) 54 (8f,Chp,GF,Spt 12)
Capilano Princess 46 (8f,Don,GF,Aug 1)
Cap Juluca (IRE) 84 (10f,Asc,GF,Jun 18)
Captain Carat 52 (5f,Don,GF,Jly 17)
Captain Horatius (IRE) 72 (10f,Goo,GS,May 23)
Captain's Day 55 (7f,Goo,S,May 23)
Captain's Guest (IRE) 47 (16f,Goo,GF,Spt 26)
Carburton 50 (8f,Nwm,G,Nov 2)
Caribbean Dancer 33 (8f,Thi,GF,May 17)
Caribbean Quest 41 (10f,Nwb,GF,Jun 13)
Caricature (IRE) 59 (8f,San,G,Aug 30)
Carling (FR) 55 (10½f,Lon,GF,Apr 28)
Carlito Brigante 67 (10½f,Yor,G,Jly 13)
Carlton Express (IRE) 32 (10f,Not,G,Apr 22)
Carmarthen Bay 38 (7f,Goo,GF,Spt 26)
Carranita (IRE) 89 (6f,Yor,G,Jly 12)
Carreamia 33 (6f,Red,GF,Oct 8)
Cashmere Lady 49 (8f,Ham,G,Jun 12)
Castan (IRE) 47 (8f,Not,G,Oct 9)
Castel Rosselo 56 (8f,Not,GF,Jun 19)
Castlerea Lad 68 (6f,Goo,GS,May 22)
Castle Secret 42 (18f,Chp,GF,Jly 2)
Castletown Count 38 (10f,Rip,G,Apr 27)
Casual Water (IRE) 62 (12f,Eps,G,Aug 26)
Catch The Blues (IRE) 77 (6f,Hay,GF,Spt 7)
Catch The Lights 60 (8f,Nwm,G,Oct 19)
Catherine's Choice 33 (8f,Don,GS,Mar 21)
Cats Bottom 46 (8f,Goo,GF,Spt 25)
Catumbella (USA) 42 (8f,Don,S,Nov 9)
Cavers Yangous 49 (7f,Red,GF,Aug 25)
Cayman Kai (IRE) 83 (7f,Nwm,GF,Apr 17)
Cd Super Targeting (IRE) 34 (10f,Bat,G,May 31)
Cedez le Passage (FR) 55 (8f,Don,S,Mar 23)
Cee-Jay-Ay 46 (8f,Red,F,Spt 27)
Ceilidh Star (IRE) 52 (12f,Hay,G,Spt 6)
Ceirseach (IRE) 56 (10f,Leo,S,Apr 20)
Celandine 36 (5f,Rip,G,May 19)
Celebration Cake (IRE) 55 (8f,Ayr,GF,Spt 20)
Celeric 85 (14f,Yor,GF,May 15)
Celestial Choir 73 (10f,Pon,GF,Spt 26)
Celestial Key (USA) 75 (7f,Yor,G,Oct 10)
Censor 70 (8f,Goo,GF,Aug 3)
Centre Stalls (IRE) 65 (8f,Kem,G,Spt 6)
Cerdan (USA) 59 (10f,Lin,GF,Aug 4)
Cezanne 93 (10f,Asc,GF,Jun 18)
Chabrol (CAN) 55 (8f,Nwm,GF,Apr 17)
Chadwell Hall 55 (5f,Don,S,Nov 8)
Chairmans Choice 55 (7f,Bri,F,Jun 4)

Chakalak 36 (16½f,Fol,GF,Jun 5)
Chalice 41 (5f,Don,G,May 25)
Chalky Dancer 31 (8f,Lei,GF,Oct 14)
Champagne Grandy 51 (7f,Ayr,GF,Spt 21)
Champagne Prince 56 (10½f,Chs,GS,Aug 30)
Chaposa Springs (USA) 50 (8f,G,Oct 26)
Charisse Dancer 30 (8f,Wnd,S,Aug 24)
Charlie Bigtime 34 (12f,Nwm,GF,Jun 8)
Charlie Chang (IRE) 41 (8f,Goo,GS,May 22)
Charlie Sillett 70 (6f,Goo,GS,May 22)
Charlock (IRE) 35 (8f,Leo,G,Aug 5)
Charlotte Corday 56 (10f,Nwm,G,Jly 10)
Charlton Imp (USA) 39 (8f,Goo,GF,Spt 25)
Charming Admiral (IRE) 40 (14f,San,GS,Aug 23)
Charming Bride 32 (7f,Lei,GF,Oct 15)
Charnwood Forest (IRE) 95 (8f,Asc,GF,Jun 18)
Charnwood Jack (USA) 33 (8f,Nwm,GF,Apr 17)
Charter 44 (10f,San,GS,May 28)
Chatham Island 62 (11½f,Yar,F,Jly 21)
Cheeky Chappy 60 (6f,Cat,GS,Jly 24)
Cheerful Aspect (IRE) 50 (10f,Nwm,G,Oct 1)
Cheerful Groom (IRE) 30 (7f,Don,GF,May 7)
Chemcast 43 (5f,Thi,F,Jun 3)
Chewit 61 (5f,San,GS,Jly 6)
Cheyenne Spirit 80 (6f,Nwm,GF,Jun 1)
Chickawicka (IRE) 76 (7f,Nwm,G,Oct 19)
Chief Bearhart (CAN) 72 (12f,G,Oct 26)
Chief Burundi (USA) 73 (8f,San,GS,May 27)
Chief Contender (IRE) 74 (12f,Sal,G,May 5)
Children's Choice (IRE) 50 (14f,Yar,GF,Aug 15)
China Hand (IRE) 35 (5f,Edi,GS,May 30)
Chinensis (IRE) 60 (8f,Bri,F,Aug 18)
Chirico (USA) 63 (7f,Red,GF,Oct 8)
Chocolate Ice 36 (11½f,Yar,G,Spt 17)
Chris's Lad 56 (16½f,San,G,Aug 30)
Christmas Kiss 54 (7f,Nwm,GF,Apr 17)
Cicerone 51 (8f,Rip,G,May 19)
Cigar (USA) 92 (10f,Fst,Oct 26)
Cim Bom Bom (IRE) 57 (6f,Pon,GF,Jly 9)
Ciracusa (IRE) 46 (12f,Chs,GF,Jun 26)
Circled (USA) 31 (14½f,Don,G,Oct 25)
Circus Star 48 (12f,Hay,G,Spt 27)
Ciserano (IRE) 42 (5f,Bat,G,May 31)
Civil Liberty 60 (10f,Wnd,GF,Aug 19)
Claire's Dancer (IRE) 40 (10f,Asc,GF,Aug 2)
Claireswan (IRE) 38 (18f,Nwm,G,Oct 19)
Clan Ben (IRE) 76 (10½f,Yor,G,Aug 21)
Clan Chief 60 (6f,Goo,G,Spt 14)
Classic Affair (USA) 36 (16f,Not,F,Spt 16)
Classic Ballet (FR) 39 (9f,Kem,G,Apr 6)
Classic Beauty (IRE) 36 (11f,Ham,GF,Aug 14)
Classic Cliche (IRE) 100 (14f,Yor,GF,May 16)
Classic Colleen (IRE) 42 (14f,Yar,F,Jly 23)
Classic Colours (USA) 31 (11f,Red,GF,Aug 25)
Classic Defence (IRE) 53 (10f,Bat,GF,Jly 8)
Classic Eagle 69 (12f,Eps,G,Jun 8)
Classic Find (USA) 57 (12f,Goo,GF,Jun 6)
Classic Flyer (IRE) 49 (10f,Don,G,Spt 11)
Classic Leader 43 (8f,Don,GF,May 7)
Classic Look (IRE) 31 (7f,Chp,GF,Spt 12)
Classic Parisian (IRE) 50 (10½f,Hay,GS,May 6)
Classic Romance 38 (10f,Chp,GF,Jly 2)
Classic Royale (USA) 38 (7f,Nwm,GF,Apr 17)
Classy Chief 52 (10f,Wnd,GF,Aug 19)
Clemente 52 (9f,Kem,G,Apr 6)
Clerkenwell (USA) 75 (14f,Yor,G,Aug 21)
Clever Cliche 72 (10f,Asc,GF,Jun 18)
Cliburnel News (IRE) 45 (12f,Lei,G,Apr 4)
Clifton Fox 79 (9f,Nwm,GF,Oct 5)
Clifton Game 31 (16½f,San,G,Aug 30)
Clincher Club 37 (7½f,Bev,GF,Jly 16)
Clouds Hill (FR) 37 (9f,Kem,GF,May 6)
Clued Up 32 (11½f,Yar,G,Spt 17)
Coachella 36 (10f,Wnd,GF,Jly 15)
Coastal Bluff 84 (6f,Ayr,GF,Spt 21)
Cockney Lad (IRE) 50 (12f,Asc,GF,Jun 19)
Code Red 36 (10f,Kem,GF,Apr 29)
Coh Sho No 34 (12f,Bri,G,Oct 2)
Cointosser (IRE) 49 (8f,Chp,GF,Spt 12)
Coleridge 40 (15f,War,GF,Jly 5)
College Night (IRE) 41 (7f,Bri,F,May 9)
Colosse 35 (12f,Pon,G,Oct 7)
Colt D'Or 30 (12f,Bat,F,Jly 24)
Colway Rake 52 (6f,Red,GF,Jun 11)
Comanche Companion 54 (8f,Goo,GF,Jly 30)
Comedy River 37 (11f,War,F,Oct 8)
Comic Fantasy (AUS) 45 (5f,Thi,G,Aug 12)
Commander Glen (IRE) 51 (8f,Pon,GF,Jun 10)
Committal (IRE) 42 (8f,San,GF,Aug 14)
Commoner (USA) 68 (12f,Nwm,G,Jun 29)
Compass Pointer 31 (14f,Not,S,Oct 31)
Concer Un 85 (8f,Yor,GF,Aug 22)
Confronter 62 (8f,Goo,GF,Jly 30)
Congo Man 46 (10f,San,GF,Spt 18)
Conic Hill (IRE) 33 (10f,Yar,F,Jun 5)
Consordino 63 (9f,Ham,G,Spt 29)
Consort 69 (8f,Asc,G,Oct 12)
Conspicuous (IRE) 68 (10f,Asc,GF,Jun 22)
Contrafire (IRE) 54 (10f,Yar,F,Jun 5)
Cool Edge (IRE) 87 (7f,Nwb,G,Aug 17)
Cool Fire 46 (8f,Lei,G,Apr 27)
Cool Jazz 80 (6f,Nwm,GF,Apr 16)
Corniche Quest (IRE) 42 (7f,Nwm,GF,Aug 23)
Corradini 91 (14f,Yor,G,Aug 21)
Cossack Count 45 (6f,Cur,G,Jun 30)
Couchant (IRE) 34 (10f,Wnd,GF,May 13)
Count Basie 49 (10f,Wnd,GF,Jun 3)
Country Lover 58 (10f,Wnd,GF,May 13)
Courageous Dancer (IRE) 65 (8f,Pon,G,Spt 3)
Courbaril 52 (12f,Bri,F,Apr 12)
Coureur 62 (8f,Goo,GS,May 22)
Course Fishing 30 (10f,Chp,G,Aug 26)
Courting Danger 36 (8f,Don,GS,Mar 21)
Court of Honour (IRE) 96 (14f,Yor,GF,May 16)
Coyote Bluff (IRE) 49 (7½f,Bev,GF,Apr 25)
Crabbie's Pride 40 (10½f,Hay,GS,May 25)
Craigie Boy 33 (6f,Rip,S,Aug 31)
Crazy Chief 60 (10f,Asc,GF,Jly 26)
Crested Knight (IRE) 45 (8f,Goo,GF,Spt 25)
Cretan Gift 59 (6f,Red,GF,Nov 5)
Croagh Patrick 43 (7f,Kem,GF,Apr 29)
Croeso Cynnes 37 (6f,Rip,GS,Aug 26)
Crofters Ceilidh 68 (5f,Nwm,G,Oct 19)
Croft Pool 76 (5f,Nwm,GF,Jun 1)
Crossillion 47 (7½f,Chs,G,May 9)
Cross of Valour 38 (6f,Sal,G,Aug 15)
Cross Talk (IRE) 45 (14f,Cat,GS,Mar 27)
Cross The Border 45 (5f,San,G,Apr 27)
Crowded Avenue 64 (5f,San,F,Jun 15)
Crown Court (USA) 62 (10f,Goo,GF,Aug 2)
Crumpton Hill (IRE) 74 (8f,Asc,GF,Jun 19)
Crystal Falls (IRE) 41 (7f,Nwc,G,Apr 8)
Crystal Heights (FR) 52 (7f,Bri,F,Jly 16)
Cuango (IRE) 45 (14f,Hay,GS,Jun 8)
Cuban Reef 34 (10½f,Yor,G,Spt 5)
Cumbrian Maestro 37 (10½f,Yor,G,Spt 5)
Cumbrian Rhapsody 42 (12f,Rip,GF,Aug 5)
Current Speech (IRE) 43 (10f,Rip,G,May 19)
Curtelace 35 (10f,Pon,G,Apr 17)
Cutthroat Kid (IRE) 50 (16f,Red,F,Jly 18)
Cypress Avenue (IRE) 47 (20f,Goo,GF,Jly 31)
Cyrano's Lad (IRE) 80 (6f,Yor,G,Oct 12)
Cyrillic 37 (8f,Kem,G,Apr 6)
Czarna (IRE) 59 (8f,Asc,GF,Jun 19)

Daawe (USA) 68 (6f,Yor,G,Oct 12)
Dacha (IRE) 75 (12f,Hay,GF,Spt 7)
Dahiyah (USA) 50 (7f,Lin,F,Jun 15)
Da Hoss (USA) 105 (8f,G,Oct 26)
Daily Risk 38 (8f,Not,GF,Apr 8)
Daily Sport Girl 30 (13f,Ham,G,Jun 12)
Daira 37 (10f,Nwm,GF,Oct 4)
Dajraan (IRE) 37 (22f,Asc,GF,Jun 21)
Dalwhinnie 46 (12f,Nwm,G,Nov 1)
Damancher 36 (14f,Cur,G,Jun 30)
Dana Point (IRE) 40 (8f,Not,G,Apr 2)
Dance a Dream 83 (12f,Asc,GF,Jun 21)
Dance Clear (IRE) 40 (7f,Leo,S,Apr 20)
Dance Design (IRE) 74 (8f,Asc,GF,Jun 19)
Dance d'Ore (SWE) 69 (22f,Asc,GF,Jun 21)
Dance King 51 (10f,Nwm,GF,Aug 2)
Dance of Joy 30 (8f,Nwc,G,Apr 8)
Dance On A Cloud (USA) 42 (10f,Nwm,GF,Apr 18)
Dance Sequence (USA) 63 (7f,Nwc,GF,Jly 27)
Dance So Suite 78 (12f,Eps,G,Jun 8)
Dance Star 30 (10f,Don,G,Spt 11)
Dances With Hooves 64 (7½f,Bev,GF,Apr 12)
Dance Treat (USA) 78 (12½f,Lon,S,Oct 5)
Dancing Cavalier 39 (12f,Lei,G,Aug 12)
Dancing Debut 40 (10f,Nwm,GF,Jun 8)
Dancing Destiny 33 (11f,Red,F,Jly 17)
Dancing Heart 54 (7f,Lin,GF,May 11)
Dancing Image 60 (7f,Goo,GF,Aug 2)
Dancing Lawyer 47 (6f,Bat,GF,Aug 8)
Dancing Sioux 36 (7f,Edi,G,Apr 15)
Dande Flyer 46 (5f,Nwm,GF,Jun 28)
Danegold (IRE) 73 (10½f,Hay,G,Jly 6)
Danehill Dancer (IRE) 78 (6½f,Dea,GS,Aug 11)
Danish Rhapsody (IRE) 38 (10f,Nwb,S,Oct 24)
Danjing (IRE) 64 (16½f,San,GS,Jly 6)
Dankeston (USA) 81 (10f,Asc,GF,Jun 18)
Danlora 36 (8f,War,F,Oct 8)
Daraydan (IRE) 77 (16f,Goo,GF,Aug 1)
Darazari (IRE) 64 (12f,Lon,G,Spt 15)
Darcey Bussell 45 (7f,Cat,G,Jun 1)
Dare And Go (USA) 67 (10f,Fst,Oct 26)
Daring Destiny 78 (6f,Yor,G,Jly 12)
Daring Ryde 32 (8f,Lei,GF,Jun 3)
Dark Deed (USA) 53 (6f,Nwm,GF,Aug 2)
Dark Nile (USA) 66 (12f,Lon,G,May 5)
Dark Waters (IRE) 51 (10f,Wnd,GF,Aug 19)
Darling Clover 56 (10f,Bev,GF,Jly 22)
Darling Flame (USA) 78 (8f,Asc,GF,Spt 28)
Darter (IRE) 51 (16½f,San,G,Apr 26)
Daryabad (IRE) 61 (7f,Red,GF,Aug 25)
Dashing Blue 61 (5f,Yor,G,Aug 21)
Dashing Dancer (IRE) 32 (6f,Kem,GF,Jun 26)
Dato Star (IRE) 51 (12f,Don,S,Nov 9)
Daunt 85 (12f,Don,GF,Spt 13)
Daunting Destiny (BEL) 57 (10f,Asc,GF,Jly 26)
Dawalib (USA) 49 (7f,Goo,S,May 23)
Dawawin (USA) 43 (8f,Not,GF,Spt 24)
Dawna 58 (8f,Asc,GF,Jun 22)
Dazzling 32 (10f,Wnd,GF,Aug 3)
Deadline Time (IRE) 52 (11½f,San,GS,May 28)
Deano's Beeno 62 (14½f,Don,G,Oct 25)
Dear Life (USA) 74 (12f,Nwm,GF,Oct 17)
Debutante Days 52 (10f,Bat,F,Jly 18)
Decision Maker (IRE) 35 (8f,Not,G,Apr 2)
Decorated Hero 96 (7f,Asc,GF,Spt 28)
Deed of Love (USA) 54 (8f,Leo,S,Apr 20)
Dee-Lady 47 (10f,Ayr,GF,Spt 20)
Deeply Vale (IRE) 48 (6f,Fol,GF,Apr 16)

Deevee 46 (8f,Nwm,GF,Jun 1)
Defined Feature (IRE) 66 (6f,Nwm,GF,Oct 4)
Definite Article 66 (10f,San,GS,Jly 6)
Degree 30 (8f,Sal,GF,May 2)
Delight of Dawn 49 (10f,San,G,Aug 31)
Delphine 38 (7f,Yar,F,Jun 5)
Delta Soleil (USA) 73 (7f,Nwm,G,Oct 19)
Denbrae (IRE) 58 (6f,Ayr,GF,Spt 21)
Denomination (USA) 40 (8f,San,GS,May 28)
Densben 35 (6f,Hay,G,Spt 27)
Depreciate 40 (6f,Nwm,GF,Jun 1)
De Quest 41 (12f,Eps,G,Jun 8)
Desert Boy (IRE) 78 (12f,Asc,GF,Jun 21)
Desert Calm (IRE) 34 (8f,War,F,Jun 5)
Desert Dunes 52 (12f,Sal,G,May 5)
Desert Fighter 49 (14f,Cat,GS,Mar 27)
Desert Frolic (IRE) 63 (14f,Yor,G,Aug 21)
Desert Green (FR) 67 (8f,Asc,GF,Jun 19)
Desert Invader (IRE) 38 (6f,Ham,GS,Spt 30)
Desert Lynx (IRE) 45 (6f,Nwc,G,May 6)
Desert Shot 91 (10f,Asc,GF,Jun 18)
Desert Tiger 31 (5f,Yor,G,Jun 14)
Desert Zone (USA) 40 (8f,Edi,GS,Nov 7)
Designer Lines 38 (8f,Lin,GF,Aug 17)
Detachment (USA) 42 (8f,War,F,Oct 8)
Devil's Dance (FR) 33 (8f,Not,GS,Apr 12)
Devon Peasant 31 (10f,Lei,G,Apr 27)
Deynawari (IRE) 39 (8f,Leo,S,Apr 20)
Dhulikhel 31 (11f,War,G,Apr 8)
Diamond Beach 52 (8f,Asc,GF,Jun 22)
Diamond Crown (IRE) 39 (10f,Not,GF,Spt 24)
Diamond Cut (FR) 48 (12f,Hay,G,Jly 5)
Diamond Dance (IRE) 38 (10½f,Hay,G,Spt 27)
Diamond Mix (IRE) 63 (10½f,Lon,GF,Apr 28)
Dictation (USA) 45 (6f,Ayr,GF,Spt 21)
Diebiedale 38 (8f,Yar,GF,Spt 19)
Diego 41 (12f,Don,G,Jun 8)
Diet 41 (5f,Ham,GF,May 18)
Diffident (FR) 86 (7f,Don,G,Oct 26)
Digpast (IRE) 33 (10f,Lin,GF,May 18)
Dilazar (USA) 74 (8f,Red,GF,Oct 17)
Diligent Dodger (IRE) 64 (6f,Cur,G,Jun 30)
Diminutive (USA) 54 (10f,Yar,GF,Aug 15)
Diplomatic Jet (USA) 72 (12f,G,Oct 26)
Dirab 40 (16f,Red,F,Jly 18)
Disallowed (IRE) 56 (8f,Lei,GF,Oct 14)
Disc of Gold (USA) 44 (14f,Hay,GS,May 24)
Dismissed (USA) 44 (8½f,Eps,G,Jun 7)
Dispol Diamond 41 (7½f,Bev,GF,May 21)
Dispol Gem 46 (8f,Red,F,Spt 27)
Disputed 37 (6f,Nwm,GF,Jly 19)
Distant Oasis (USA) 54 (8f,Goo,G,Aug 24)
Distinct Beauty (IRE) 32 (8f,War,F,Oct 8)
Divina Luna 67 (8f,Asc,GF,Spt 28)
Divine 48 (10f,Yar,G,Aug 1)
Divine Miss-P 38 (5f,Bev,GF,Apr 12)
Divine Quest 56 (7f,San,GF,Spt 18)
Djais (FR) 67 (22f,Asc,GF,Jun 21)
D'naan (IRE) 30 (10f,Pon,GF,Aug 8)
Docklands Courier 31 (10f,Yar,GF,Jly 4)
Docklands Limo 43 (10f,Not,G,Apr 22)
Doctor Bravious (IRE) 39 (8f,War,GS,Apr 13)
Doctor Green (FR) 46 (11f,Red,F,Jun 21)
Dolliver (USA) 51 (10f,Kem,GF,Apr 29)
Domak Amaam (IRE) 53 (6f,Nwm,GF,Apr 18)
Domappel 65 (12½f,War,F,Jun 10)
Dombey 68 (10½f,Yor,GF,May 14)
Domettes (IRE) 30 (10f,Kem,GF,Aug 7)
Domicksky 31 (5f,Edi,G,Apr 4)
Dominelle 41 (6f,Thi,F,Aug 3)
Domitia (USA) 48 (10f,Bev,GF,Jly 22)
Domulla 62 (6f,Nwm,GF,May 5)
Don Bosio (USA) 65 (7f,Goo,GF,Spt 26)
Don Micheletto 63 (12f,Cha,F,Jun 2)
Donna Viola 87 (8½f,Eps,G,Jun 7)
Don Pepe 50 (6f,Goo,G,Jun 6)
Don't Care (IRE) 61 (6f,Hay,S,Oct 6)
Don't Drop Bombs (USA) 31 (10f,Bri,F,Spt 4)
Dont Forget Curtis (IRE) 40 (11f,Ham,GS,Apr 3)
Don't Get Caught (IRE) 45 (8½f,Eps,GF,Spt 24)
Dont Shoot Fairies 61 (12f,Nwm,GF,Apr 17)
Don't Worry Me (IRE) 49 (5f,Lon,GS,Oct 6)
Don Vito 63 (12f,Asc,GF,Jun 21)
Dormy Three 46 (12f,Kem,GF,Apr 29)
Double Agent 49 (14f,Not,GF,Jun 10)
Double Blue 75 (7f,Nwc,F,Jun 29)
Double Bluff (IRE) 66 (9f,Nwm,GF,Oct 5)
Double Bounce 74 (6f,Nwc,F,Jun 29)
Double Diamond (IRE) 65 (10½f,Yor,GF,May 14)
Double Echo (IRE) 39 (12f,Kem,GF,Jun 12)
Double Eclipse (IRE) 78 (15½f,Lon,S,May 19)
Double Leaf 70 (12f,Eps,G,Jun 8)
Double March 40 (7f,Sal,S,May 22)
Double Matt (IRE) 51 (6f,Don,GF,May 6)
Double Oscar (IRE) 46 (7f,War,F,Jun 10)
Double Quick (IRE) 66 (6f,Cur,G,Jun 30)
Double Rush (IRE) 44 (10f,Bri,F,Aug 18)
Double Splendour (IRE) 80 (6f,Yor,G,Oct 12)
Double Trigger (IRE) 73 (16f,Asc,GF,May 1)
Double Up 41 (10f,Lin,F,Spt 19)
Dovaly 54 (10f,Nwm,GF,Apr 16)
Dovebrace 59 (7f,Nwc,F,Jun 29)
Dragon's Back (IRE) 30 (10f,Goo,GF,Jun 14)
Dramatic Gold (USA) 81 (10f,Fst,Oct 26)
Dramatic Moment 41 (10f,Sal,GF,Jun 27)
Dreams End 66 (12f,Yor,G,Oct 10)
Dr Edgar 47 (10f,Ayr,GF,Jun 22)
Dr Massini (IRE) 80 (10½f,Yor,GF,May 16)
Drummer Hicks 42 (10½f,Hay,G,Jun 7)
Dry Point 34 (6f,Kem,GF,Jun 26)
Dubai College (IRE) 37 (7f,Yar,F,Jun 25)
Duchesse de Berri (USA) 30 (8f,Sal,G,Jun 11)
Duel At Dawn 52 (6f,Nwm,G,Jly 9)
Duello 51 (8f,Goo,GF,Spt 13)
Duke Valentino 40 (8f,Hay,GF,Aug 16)
Dumaani (USA) 74 (8f,G,Oct 26)
Dummer Golf Time 50 (8f,San,GF,Spt 18)
Dune River 41 (7f,Yor,G,Jly 13)
Dungeon Princess (IRE) 37 (8f,Edi,G,Jly 8)
Dunrowan 30 (11f,Red,F,Spt 27)
Durham 49 (16f,Asc,GF,Spt 28)
Dushyantor (USA) 84 (14½f,Don,GF,Spt 14)

Eagle Canyon (IRE) 55 (12f,Hay,G,Spt 27)
Early Peace (IRE) 47 (8f,San,GS,May 28)
Eastern Prophets 66 (5f,Don,S,Nov 8)
Easy Choice (USA) 32 (8f,Lin,GF,Jun 1)
Easy Dollar 74 (6f,Nwm,GF,Apr 16)
Easy Jet (POL) 60 (8f,Bat,F,Jun 29)
Easy Listening (USA) 64 (10f,Bat,GF,May 11)
Easy Option (IRE) 72 (6f,Nwm,G,Oct 19)
Eau de Cologne 45 (12f,Ham,GS,Spt 30)
Eben Naas (USA) 31 (8f,Lei,G,Apr 27)
Edan Heights 57 (10f,Nwm,GF,Aug 10)
Edgar Kirby 40 (8f,Thi,GF,Apr 19)
Edipo Re 57 (14f,Sal,GF,Jun 27)
Editor's Note (USA) 46 (10f,Fst,Oct 26)
Effectual 37 (10f,Wnd,GF,Jun 3)
Efharisto 40 (12f,Asc,GF,Jun 19)
Efizia 40 (10f,Ayr,GF,Jun 22)
Efra 36 (6f,Kem,GF,Apr 29)
Egeo (FR) 63 (10½f,Lon,GF,Apr 21)
Ela Agapi Mou (USA) 33 (12f,Bri,F,Spt 3)
Ela-Aristokrati (IRE) 89 (10f,Eps,G,Jun 8)
Ela Man Howa 38 (16½f,San,G,Aug 30)
El Angelo (USA) 56 (10f,Lon,S,Oct 5)
Elashath (USA) 44 (10f,Nwm,GF,Aug 2)
Ela-Yie-Mou (IRE) 50 (14f,Goo,GF,Aug 1)
El Bardador (IRE) 39 (10f,Yar,GF,Spt 18)
Election Day (IRE) 61 (13f,Nwb,GS,May 18)
Elite Bliss (IRE) 31 (11f,Red,GF,Oct 29)
Elite Force (IRE) 40 (7f,Cat,G,Apr 24)
Elite Hope (USA) 54 (7f,San,GF,Jun 14)
Ellie Ardensky 86 (10f,Asc,GF,Jun 22)
Elly Fleetfoot (IRE) 44 (11½f,Wnd,GF,Jly 22)
Elmi Elmak (IRE) 51 (8f,Hay,GF,Aug 10)
El Opera (IRE) 58 (7f,War,GF,Jly 13)
El Penitente (IRE) 40 (8f,War,F,May 6)
Elpida (USA) 44 (10f,Bri,F,Jun 17)
Elpidos 42 (7½f,Bev,GF,Apr 12)
Elsaleet (USA) 60 (6f,Nwm,GF,Apr 16)
Elshabiba (USA) 42 (8f,Kem,G,Apr 6)
El Volador 46 (14f,Yar,GF,Aug 15)
Embankment (IRE) 59 (7f,Chp,S,Oct 22)
Embryonic (IRE) 67 (16f,Asc,GF,Spt 28)
Emerging Market 85 (6f,Asc,GF,Jun 21)
Emily-Mou (IRE) 51 (8f,Nwm,GF,Jun 1)
Emy Coasting (USA) 40 (6f,Kem,GF,May 6)
Enchanted Guest (IRE) 45 (6f,Nwm,GF,Jun 8)
Encore M'Lady (IRE) 33 (6f,Pon,GF,Jun 17)
Endowment 43 (12f,Don,GF,Spt 13)
English Invader 30 (12f,Yor,G,Jly 12)
Enriched (IRE) 56 (10½f,Yor,G,Oct 10)
En Vacances (IRE) 69 (18f,Nwm,G,Oct 19)
Equerry 64 (8f,Ayr,GF,Spt 20)
Eric's Bett 32 (8½f,Bev,GF,Jly 6)
Errant 38 (10f,Nwm,GF,May 3)
Ertlon 60 (7f,Yar,GF,Spt 18)
Erupt 31 (6f,Kem,G,Apr 6)
Erzadjan (IRE) 58 (16½f,San,G,Apr 26)
Escrito (USA) 46 (10f,Cur,GY,Aug 31)
Eskimo Nel (IRE) 50 (10f,Bev,GF,Apr 25)
Espartero (IRE) 69 (6f,Nwb,GF,Jly 20)
Essayeffsee 57 (10f,Pon,GF,Aug 8)
Essesstee (FR) 42 (12½f,Dea,G,May 16)
Eternity Range (USA) 60 (8f,Lon,G,May 12)
Ethbaat (USA) 49 (10f,Not,GF,Spt 24)
Etterby Park (USA) 48 (16f,Asc,GF,Spt 28)
Euphonic 46 (12f,Goo,G,Aug 25)
Euphyllia 49 (7f,Lei,GF,Oct 15)
Eurobox Boy 39 (7f,Yar,GF,Spt 18)
Euro Sceptic (IRE) 46 (7½f,Bev,G,Aug 24)
Eva Luna (USA) 80 (14½f,Don,G,Spt 11)
Evan 'elp Us 46 (7f,Cat,GS,Mar 27)
Eveningperformance 85 (5f,San,GS,Jly 6)
Even Top (IRE) 77 (8f,Nwm,GF,May 4)
Everglades (IRE) 78 (7f,Nwb,GF,Jly 19)
Everset (FR) 40 (7f,Lei,GF,Oct 15)
Ever so Lyrical 43 (8f,Bat,G,May 20)
Evezio Rufo 39 (10f,Don,G,Oct 26)
Evidence In Chief 39 (12f,Nwm,GF,Oct 3)
Ewar Bold 38 (11f,Nwb,G,Apr 19)
Ewar Sunrise 35 (7f,Yar,F,Jun 5)
Exactly (IRE) 46 (14f,Yor,G,Spt 4)
Exalted (IRE) 61 (10f,Asc,GF,Jly 26)
Executive Design 32 (14f,Hay,GS,May 6)
Exemption 40 (10f,Sal,G,Aug 14)
Expensive Taste 57 (10½f,Yor,G,Jun 15)
Explosive Power 39 (8f,Bri,F,Apr 12)
Express Routing 33 (7f,Sal,G,Jun 11)

Faateq 59 (12½f,Nwc,G,May 23)
Fabillion 56 (14f,Hay,GS,Jun 8)
Fabulous Mtoto 46 (12f,Pon,GF,Jly 19)
Face the Future 34 (6f,Kem,G,Apr 8)
Fag End (IRE) 31 (8½f,Eps,G,Jun 7)
Fahal (USA) 93 (10f,Asc,GF,Jun 18)
Fahim 81 (10½f,Yor,G,Aug 21)
Fahs (USA) 60 (10f,Nwm,GF,Jly 26)
Fairelaine 37 (7f,War,F,Jun 5)
Fairly Sure (IRE) 32 (8f,Lin,GF,Aug 17)
Fairy Knight 57 (12f,Eps,G,Aug 26)
Fairy Prince (IRE) 40 (6f,Crl,F,Aug 5)
Fairy Wind (IRE) 59 (5f,San,G,May 27)
Fairywings 60 (9f,Nwm,GF,Oct 5)
Faith Alone 39 (6f,Nwm,GF,Jun 8)
Fakih (USA) 60 (8f,Asc,GF,May 1)
Falcon's Flame (USA) 30 (8f,Pon,GF,Aug 8)
Fame Again 62 (6f,Nwc,F,Jun 29)
Family Man 40 (8f,Not,GF,Spt 24)

Fanadiyr (IRE) 34 (12½f,Nwc,F,Jun 29)
Fancy Heights 67 (14f,Yor,G,Aug 20)
Fantasy Racing (IRE) 61 (6f,Ayr,G,Aug 10)
Far Ahead 63 (11f,Ham,G,Jly 5)
Farasan (IRE) 73 (10f,Lon,G,Jun 23)
Faraway Lass 64 (6f,Yor,G,Oct 12)
Faraway Waters 60 (12f,Eps,G,Jun 7)
Far Dawn (USA) 45 (12f,Goo,GF,Spt 25)
Farhana 67 (6f,Hay,GS,May 25)
Farmost 56 (7f,Fol,GF,Jun 5)
Farringdon Hill 66 (14f,Yar,GF,Aug 8)
Fasih 34 (9f,Ham,GS,Apr 3)
Fasil (IRE) 62 (12f,Goo,GF,Spt 25)
Fast Forward Fred 34 (12f,Fol,F,Apr 23)
Fastini Gold 35 (7f,Nwb,S,May 29)
Fatefully (USA) 84 (8f,Asc,GF,Spt 28)
Father Dan (IRE) 54 (10f,Not,GF,Spt 24)
Faugeron 36 (14f,Lin,GF,Aug 4)
Fearless Wonder 34 (16f,Cat,GF,Aug 6)
Featherstone Lane 31 (5f,Crl,G,May 30)
Federico (USA) 35 (10f,Lon,S,Oct 5)
Femme Savante 53 (5f,Nwm,GF,Jly 20)
Fern's Governor 51 (10f,Not,GF,Spt 24)
Field of Vision (IRE) 61 (13f,Ham,GF,Aug 14)
Fieldridge 50 (10f,Eps,G,Jun 8)
Fighting Times 57 (10f,Lei,G,Apr 27)
Fijon (IRE) 32 (14f,Not,F,Jly 6)
Fikra (USA) 32 (10f,Yar,G,Aug 1)
Filial (IRE) 48 (8f,San,GF,Jly 25)
Fill the Bill (IRE) 59 (12f,Leo,GF,Jly 20)
Filmore West 46 (10½f,Yor,G,Spt 4)
Fine Detail (IRE) 52 (12f,Nwm,GF,Aug 10)
Finisterre (IRE) 34 (6f,Pon,G,Spt 3)
Finsbury Flyer (IRE) 41 (8f,Chp,GF,Jly 11)
Fionn de Cool (IRE) 62 (8f,Goo,GF,Jly 30)
Firbur 46 (12f,Nwm,GF,Jun 28)
Fire Dome (IRE) 65 (6f,Don,S,Mar 23)
Firefighter 44 (11f,Ham,GF,May 18)
Fire on Ice (IRE) 59 (10f,Nwb,S,May 29)
Firle Phantasy 36 (8f,Not,GF,Jly 26)
First Gold 38 (7f,Red,GF,May 27)
First Island (IRE) 103 (10f,Asc,GF,Jun 18)
First Maite 37 (6f,Rip,GS,Aug 26)
Fitzwilliam (USA) 60 (13f,Nwb,GF,Jly 20)
Flag Fen (USA) 52 (8f,Lin,GF,Aug 4)
Flagstaff (USA) 31 (7f,Bri,F,Jun 17)
Flamanda 35 (10f,Lei,F,Spt 10)
Flamands (IRE) 55 (14f,Nwm,G,Oct 18)
Flame Valley (USA) 68 (10f,Wnd,GF,Aug 3)
Flamingo Paradise 49 (20f,Lon,S,Oct 5)
Flashy's Son 44 (5f,Nwc,G,May 22)
Flemensfirth (USA) 63 (10f,Lon,S,Oct 5)
Flight Master 47 (12f,Bri,F,Aug 6)
Floating Line 65 (14f,Nwm,GF,Oct 4)
Flocheck (USA) 60 (16f,Asc,G,Oct 11)
Florentino (IRE) 51 (10f,Bat,GF,Jly 8)
Florid (USA) 77 (10f,Nwm,GF,Oct 17)
Flyaway Blues 33 (8f,Rip,GF,Jun 20)
Flyfisher (IRE) 55 (11f,Nwb,GS,Apr 20)
Flying Green (FR) 51 (10f,Bat,GF,Jly 8)
Flying Harold 36 (8f,Bri,F,Aug 5)
Flying Legend (USA) 59 (14½f,Don,GF,Spt 14)
Flying North (IRE) 53 (9f,Ham,G,Spt 29)
Flying Pennant (IRE) 40 (8f,Wnd,G,Jly 8)
Foist 31 (8½f,Bev,GF,Spt 18)
Fond Embrace 63 (5f,Lin,GS,Aug 29)
Force of Will (USA) 34 (7f,Cur,GS,Apr 27)
Foreign Relation (IRE) 31 (5f,Rip,G,Aug 17)
Forentia 45 (5f,San,GS,Jly 6)
Forest Boy 46 (8f,Ham,S,May 3)
Forest Buck (USA) 75 (9f,Nwm,G,Oct 18)
Forest Cat (IRE) 76 (7f,Yor,GF,Aug 22)
Forest Fantasy 30 (10f,Rip,S,Aug 31)
Forest Heights 52 (12f,Hay,GF,Aug 9)
Forest Robin 62 (8f,Kem,G,Spt 7)
Forever Noble (IRE) 35 (14f,Hay,G,Spt 28)
Forgie (IRE) 34 (17f,Pon,GF,Aug 18)

Forgotten Empress 33 (12½f,Nwc,F,Jun 29)
Formal Gold (CAN) 80 (10f,Fst,Oct 26)
Formidable Liz 43 (6f,Pon,GF,Aug 18)
Formidable Partner 40 (8f,San,F,Jun 15)
For the Present 61 (5f,Nwc,GF,Jly 27)
Fort Knox (IRE) 50 (7f,Bri,F,Jun 4)
Fort Nottingham (USA) 76 (10½f,Lon,G,May 12)
Fortunes Course (IRE) 30 (18f,Not,G,Oct 9)
Forza Figlio 51 (8f,Goo,G,May 21)
Forzair 43 (12f,Bev,GF,May 10)
Forzara 31 (5f,Edi,GS,Jly 22)
Foundry Lane 63 (14f,Yor,G,Spt 4)
Four of Spades 47 (8f,Red,GF,May 13)
Framed (IRE) 37 (8f,Pon,G,Apr 17)
Freedom Flame 54 (10f,Nwm,G,Jly 10)
Freequent 64 (14f,Goo,G,Aug 24)
Free To Speak (IRE) 45 (9f,Leo,G,Jun 3)
French Ballerina (IRE) 57 (10f,Cur,S,Oct 19)
French Grit (IRE) 65 (5f,Thi,GF,Apr 19)
French Ivy (USA) 62 (16f,Goo,GF,Spt 14)
Fresh Fruit Daily 34 (8f,Not,GF,Spt 24)
Fresh Look (IRE) 32 (10f,Not,GF,Jun 10)
Frezeliere 64 (10f,Asc,GF,Jly 26)
Friendly Brave (USA) 63 (5f,Red,GF,Nov 5)
Frog 50 (10f,Bri,F,Jly 17)
Frontier Flight (USA) 37 (16½f,Don,GF,Aug 1)
Frontman (IRE) 32 (5f,Not,GF,Apr 8)
Frozen Sea (USA) 39 (14f,Lin,GF,Jly 13)
Fujiyama Crest (IRE) 80 (16f,Asc,GF,Spt 28)
Full Throttle 47 (12f,Edi,GF,Aug 29)
Fursan (USA) 44 (13f,Nwb,GF,Jun 27)
Further Flight 59 (14½f,Don,S,Nov 8)
Fyors Gift (IRE) 46 (5f,War,F,Jun 5)

Gabr 88 (7f,Nwm,G,Jun 29)
Gadge 32 (8f,Edi,GS,Nov 7)
Gad Yakoun 36 (6f,Red,GF,Oct 8)
Galapino 48 (11½f,San,GS,May 28)
Galine 67 (5f,Nwm,GF,Jun 28)
Game Ploy (POL) 66 (10f,Nwb,GF,Spt 21)
Gan Saru 34 (16f,Cur,GS,Oct 5)
Garnock Valley 83 (6f,Hay,S,Oct 6)
General Academy (IRE) 57 (10½ f,Lon,GF,Apr 21)
General Alan (FR) 44 (5f,Dea,S,May 26)
General Equation 33 (5f,Cat,GS,Mar 27)
General Glow 38 (10½f,Hay,GF,Aug 16)
General Haven 54 (10f,Lei,GF,Oct 15)
General Macarthur 59 (12f,Yor,GF,Aug 22)
General Monash (USA) 66 (6f,Nwm,GF,Apr 16)
General Mouktar 51 (12f,Sal,GF,Jly 13)
Generosa 66 (13f,Nwb,GF,Jly 20)
Generosus (FR) 52 (10f,Nwm,GF,Apr 16)
Genesis Four 45 (12f,Don,G,Jun 8)
Gentilhomme 39 (12f,Yor,G,Spt 5)
Gentle Irony 49 (8f,Bri,F,Jun 17)
George Bull 51 (12f,Kem,GF,Apr 29)
George Dillingham 46 (12f,Cat,G,Apr 24)
Germano 69 (12f,Asc,GF,Jun 21)
Ger's Royale (IRE) 54 (6f,Cur,S,Oct 19)
Get Away With It (IRE) 47 (12f,Lei,GF,Aug 19)
Get Tough 33 (10f,Goo,GF,Jun 7)
Giftbox (USA) 45 (10f,Lei,GF,Oct 15)
Giggleswick Girl 38 (6f,Fol,GF,Apr 16)
Gilling Dancer (IRE) 36 (8f,Crl,F,Jly 6)
Ginger Fox (USA) 65 (13½f,Chs,G,Spt 25)
Give And Take 36 (12f,Bri,G,Oct 2)
Give Me A Ring (IRE) 68 (8f,Ayr,GF,Spt 20)
Gladys Althorpe (IRE) 50 (8f,Nwm,G,Oct 19)
Glen Garnock (IRE) 31 (5f,Rip,G,Aug 17)
Glen Parker (IRE) 36 (8f,Pon,GF,Aug 8)
Glide Path (USA) 60 (10f,Bat,GF,May 11)
Global Dancer 51 (12f,Eps,G,Jun 8)
Gloriana 52 (10f,Wnd,GF,May 13)
Glorious Aragon 64 (5f,Chs,GS,Aug 31)

Glory of Dancer 87 (10f,San,G,Apr 27)
Glow Forum 39 (12f,Nwm,G,Nov 1)
Glowing Jade 56 (7f,Red,F,Spt 27)
Go Between (FR) 55 (11f,Lon,F,Apr 7)
Go Britannia 59 (10f,Nwm,GF,Aug 10)
Godmersham Park 54 (7f,Lin,F,Spt 19)
Go-Go-Power-Ranger 30 (12f,Bev,GF,May 21)
Go Hever Golf 60 (6f,Nwm,GF,May 4)
Gold Blade 48 (10f,Pon,GF,Jly 9)
Gold Desire 37 (10½f,Yor,G,Spt 5)
Gold Disc (USA) 65 (10f,Don,GF,Spt 14)
Golden Ace (IRE) 40 (8f,Nwb,GS,Apr 20)
Golden Arrow (IRE) 68 (14f,Yor,GF,May 15)
Golden Hadeer 34 (12f,Chp,GF,Jly 25)
Golden Pond (IRE) 54 (8f,Asc,GF,Jun 22)
Golden Pound (USA) 69 (6f,Nwm,GF,Aug 2)
Golden Thunderbolt (FR) 55 (8f,Goo,GF,Jly 30)
Golden Touch (USA) 48 (10f,Nwm,GF,May 3)
Gold Spats (USA) 58 (8f,San,G,Apr 26)
Gone for a Burton (IRE) 64 (10½f,Yor,G,Oct 9)
Gone Savage 64 (5f,Yor,G,Oct 9)
Good Hand (USA) 55 (16½f,Don,GF,Aug 1)
Goodwood Rocket 35 (8f,Lei,G,Apr 27)
Gool Lee Shay (USA) 34 (7½f,Bev,G,Aug 24)
Gooseberry Pie 44 (8f,Bat,G,Aug 13)
Gordi (USA) 63 (16f,Asc,GF,Jun 19)
Goretski (IRE) 68 (5f,Ham,Hy,May 2)
Gothenberg (IRE) 72 (8f,Cur,G,Jun 30)
Go With The Wind 47 (12f,Bev,GF,Jly 5)
Graduated (IRE) 44 (10f,Cur,GY,Aug 31)
Granby Bell 41 (13f,Nwb,S,May 29)
Grand Chapeau (IRE) 39 (5f,Ayr,GF,Spt 19)
Grand du Lac (USA) 56 (8f,Asc,GF,May 1)
Grand Musica 50 (8f,Wnd,G,Aug 12)
Grand Selection (IRE) 66 (10½f,Yor,G,Aug 21)
Grand Splendour 56 (10½f,Yor,G,Oct 10)
Grape Tree Road 80 (10f,Lon,G,Jun 23)
Great Bear 32 (7f,Yar,G,Aug 1)
Great Easeby (IRE) 55 (16f,Goo,GF,Spt 14)
Greatest 47 (8f,Bat,F,Jun 29)
Great Oration (IRE) 44 (17f,Pon,G,Oct 7)
Great Tern 43 (14½f,Don,G,Oct 25)
Greek Night Out (IRE) 31 (16½f,Don,G,Jun 8)
Green Barries 72 (7f,Goo,GF,Aug 2)
Green Bopper (USA) 45 (8f,Nwc,G,Apr 8)
Green Gem (BEL) 43 (8f,Ham,S,May 3)
Green Green Desert (FR) 78 (8f,Goo,GF,Aug 1)
Green Land (BEL) 50 (12f,Pon,GF,Jly 19)
Green Perfume (USA) 93 (8f,Goo,G,May 21)
Greenspan (IRE) 46 (12f,Hay,GS,May 6)
Greenstead (USA) 60 (10f,Nwb,G,Aug 16)
Greenwich Again 41 (12f,Bri,F,Jly 16)
Greycoat Boy 53 (16f,Kem,GS,May 25)
Grey Kingdom 32 (7½f,Bev,GF,Jun 12)
Grey Risk (FR) 73 (8f,Dea,G,Aug 15)
Grey Shot 87 (14f,Yor,GF,May 16)
Grief (IRE) 32 (10f,Cur,GY,Aug 31)
Ground Game 61 (10f,Rip,S,Aug 31)
Guesstimation (USA) 50 (10f,Fol,GF,Jly 15)
Guest Alliance (IRE) 32 (12f,Bri,F,Apr 12)
Gulliver 38 (10½f,Yor,G,Spt 4)
Gumair (USA) 48 (14f,Goo,GF,Aug 1)
Gunboat Diplomacy (FR) 44 (10f,Lon,F,Apr 7)
Gwespyr 49 (5f,Not,GF,Jly 26)
Gymcrak Flyer 50 (8f,Lei,GF,Oct 14)
Gymcrak Gem (IRE) 36 (5f,Thi,GF,Spt 7)
Gymcrak Premiere 61 (8f,Yor,GF,Aug 22)

Habeta (USA) 38 (8f,Pon,GF,Jun 10)
Hadadabble 30 (8f,War,F,Oct 8)
Hagwah (USA) 89 (8½f,Eps,G,Jun 7)

Haido'hart 36 (7½f,Bev,GF,Jun 5)
Halbert 32 (5f,Lin,GF,May 10)
Halcon 59 (12f,Lon,G,May 5)
Haleakala (IRE) 58 (12f,Don,GF,Spt 13)
Halebid 32 (10f,Kem,G,Aug 21)
Half An Inch (IRE) 32 (8f,Bri,F,Jly 17)
Half Tone 36 (5f,San,GF,Aug 14)
Hal Hoo Yaroom 57 (16f,Nwm,GF,Aug 9)
Halliard 51 (5f,Lin,GF,May 18)
Halling (USA) 94 (10½f,Yor,G,Aug 20)
Halmanerror 51 (7f,Red,GF,Aug 25)
Hal's Pal 82 (8f,Asc,G,Spt 29)
Hamilton Silk 30 (11½f,Wnd,GF,Jun 3)
Hamlet (IRE) 53 (11f,Red,GF,May 27)
Hammerstein 87 (8f,Goo,GF,Aug 3)
Ham N'Eggs 36 (12½f,Nwc,F,Jly 29)
Hand Craft (IRE) 57 (10f,Wnd,GF,Jun 10)
Hand of Straw (IRE) 36 (11f,War,F,May 6)
Hannah's Usher 31 (7½f,Bev,GF,Jly 5)
Hannalou (FR) 41 (7½f,Bev,GF,May 21)
Harbet House (FR) 35 (12f,Nwb,S,Oct 26)
Harbour Dues 72 (14f,Yor,G,Aug 21)
Harbour Island 71 (16f,Goo,GF,Spt 14)
Hard to Figure 75 (6f,Asc,GF,Jun 21)
Hardy Dancer 67 (10½f,Chs,G,May 7)
Hareb (USA) 55 (8f,Nwm,GF,Apr 17)
Harghar (USA) 60 (10f,Leo,S,Apr 20)
Harry's Treat 36 (7f,Thi,GF,Apr 20)
Harsh Times 36 (8f,Rip,Hy,Aug 27)
Harvey White (IRE) 58 (10f,Kem,G,Spt 7)
Hasta la Vista 34 (14f,Yor,GF,May 15)
Hattaafeh (IRE) 51 (12f,Kem,GF,Jun 1)
Hawa Al Nasamaat (USA) 59 (6f,Goo,GF,Aug 2)
Hawkish (USA) 39 (10f,Don,GF,Jun 30)
Hawksley Hill (IRE) 76 (8f,Nwm,G,Oct 19)
Hawwam 41 (8f,Nwm,GF,Aug 2)
Hayaain 49 (12f,Kem,GF,Jun 12)
Haya Ya Kefaah 54 (12f,Hay,G,Spt 27)
Haydown (IRE) 36 (10f,San,G,Aug 31)
Hazard a Guess (IRE) 67 (10½f,Yor,G,Jly 13)
Heart 59 (13½f,Chs,G,Spt 25)
Heart Lake 49 (8f,Goo,GF,Jly 31)
Heathyards Lady (USA) 38 (8f,Pon,GF,Jun 10)
Heathyards Magic (IRE) 45 (9f,Ham,GS,Apr 3)
Helen Of Spain 84 (12½f,Dea,G,Aug 25)
Helios 54 (8f,Sal,GF,Aug 22)
Helissio (FR) 81 (10½f,Lon,G,May 12)
Hello Mister 54 (6f,Yor,GF,May 14)
Helmsman (USA) 90 (8f,G,Oct 26)
Helsingor (IRE) 39 (7f,Asc,GF,Jun 19)
Henry Island (IRE) 74 (12f,Don,G,Oct 26)
Henry The Fifth 62 (10f,Dea,G,May 16)
Henry the Hawk 39 (5f,Ham,S,May 9)
Here Comes a Star 64 (5f,Thi,GF,Apr 19)
Herodian (USA) 50 (7f,Hay,GF,Spt 7)
Heron Island (IRE) 67 (14½f,Don,GF,Spt 14)
Heronwater (IRE) 42 (12f,Hay,GS,May 24)
He's a King (USA) 36 (14f,Sal,G,May 5)
He's Got Wings (IRE) 32 (11f,Ayr,GF,Spt 19)
He's My Love (IRE) 30 (7f,Lin,GF,May 10)
Hever Golf Express 50 (6f,Bat,GF,Aug 8)
Hever Golf Lady 48 (10f,Eps,GF,Jun 9)
Hever Golf Rose 76 (6f,Hay,GF,Spt 7)
Hickory Blue 32 (6f,Not,GF,May 24)
Hidden Oasis 72 (8f,Asc,GF,Jun 18)
High Baroque (IRE) 69 (12f,Chs,G,May 7)
Highborn (IRE) 74 (7f,Yor,G,Jly 13)
High Cut 32 (7f,Sal,GF,Aug 15)
High Desire (IRE) 30 (12f,Kem,GF,Jun 12)
High Domain (IRE) 55 (6f,Hay,G,Jun 7)
Highfield Fizz 32 (14f,Red,GF,Oct 8)
Highflying 62 (14f,Hay,GS,Jun 8)
High Hope Henry (USA) 46 (7f,Nwm,GF,Oct 5)
Highland Gift (IRE) 52 (12f,Nwm,GF,Apr 16)
Highland Rhapsody (IRE) 45 (7f,Nwb,GF,Jun 13)
High Note 49 (8f,Not,GF,Jun 10)
High Premium 71 (8f,Nwm,G,Oct 19)
High Priority (IRE) 42 (5f,Lin,GS,Aug 29)
High Pyrenees 30 (16½f,Don,G,May 25)
Highspeed (IRE) 47 (8f,Ayr,G,May 31)
High Summer (USA) 71 (7f,Sal,F,Spt 5)
Hilaala (USA) 62 (8f,Wnd,S,Aug 24)
Hill Farm Dancer 41 (12f,Bat,G,Apr 30)
Hill Silver (USA) 61 (9f,Lon,GS,Oct 6)
Hill Society (IRE) 41 (10f,Cur,GY,Aug 31)
Hillzah (USA) 59 (14f,Cat,GS,Mar 27)
Hi Nod 80 (8f,Yor,GF,Aug 22)
Hinton Rock (IRE) 51 (6f,Goo,GF,Aug 2)
Hippy 56 (7f,Yar,GF,Jly 4)
Hi Rock 41 (8f,Rip,G,May 19)
His Excellence (USA) 71 (10f,Cur,G,Jun 8)
Hismagicmoment (USA) 57 (8f,Nwm,GF,Apr 17)
Hit the Canvas (USA) 31 (21½f,Pon,GF,Apr 29)
Hoh Express 76 (10½f,Yor,G,Aug 21)
Hoh Magic 57 (7f,War,G,Apr 8)
Hoh Majestic (IRE) 35 (6f,Chs,G,May 8)
Hoh Returns (IRE) 54 (6f,Nwm,GF,Jun 1)
Hoist To Heaven (USA) 56 (10½f,Lon,GF,Apr 21)
Holloway Melody 43 (8f,Not,G,Oct 24)
Home Counties (IRE) 35 (12f,Yor,G,Oct 10)
Honest Guest (IRE) 68 (10f,Dea,G,Aug 25)
Honorable Estate (IRE) 42 (7f,Lei,G,Aug 12)
Hoofprints (IRE) 37 (13½f,Red,GF,Oct 17)
Horesti 39 (11½f,Yar,GF,Aug 22)
Hotspur Street 31 (12f,Pon,G,May 24)
Housa Dancer (FR) 51 (8f,Lon,G,May 12)
Housamix (FR) 50 (10f,Lon,F,Apr 7)
House of Dreams 32 (14f,Cat,GS,Mar 27)
House of Riches 65 (12f,Hay,G,Spt 27)
How Long 71 (7f,Yor,GF,Aug 22)
Howqua River 39 (12f,Pon,G,Oct 7)
How's Yer Father 57 (6f,Goo,GS,May 22)
Hugwity 75 (8f,Goo,G,May 21)
Hullbank 53 (16f,Cat,GF,Spt 21)
Hulm (IRE) 41 (7f,Red,F,Aug 9)
Humbel (USA) 77 (10f,Cur,G,Jun 8)
Humourless 70 (10½f,Yor,GF,May 14)
Hunter Field (FR) 66 (8f,Dea,G,Aug 15)
Hunters of Brora (IRE) 61 (8f,Yor,GF,Aug 22)
Hutchies Lady 32 (8f,Edi,GS,May 30)

Iamus 43 (8f,Not,G,Apr 2)
Iberian Dancer (CAN) 37 (9f,Goo,GF,Jly 31)
Iblis (IRE) 34 (8f,Rip,GS,Aug 26)
Identify (IRE) 54 (10f,Cur,GS,May 26)
Idris (IRE) 81 (10f,Cur,GF,Jly 27)
Iktamal (USA) 86 (6f,Hay,GF,Spt 7)
Illuminate 49 (10f,Bat,G,Apr 30)
Il Trastevere (FR) 39 (8f,Kem,GF,May 6)
Imlak (IRE) 31 (12f,Lei,G,Apr 4)
Imperial Prospect (USA) 36 (10f,San,GS,May 28)
Imposing Time 45 (5f,Bri,GF,Aug 28)
Impulsive Air (IRE) 55 (8f,Nwm,G,Oct 19)
I'm Supposin (IRE) 67 (10f,Cur,GF,Aug 17)
I'm Your Lady 53 (6f,Nwm,GF,Jly 19)
In Cahoots 30 (10f,Lei,F,Spt 23)
Inchacooley (IRE) 51 (10f,Cur,S,Oct 19)
Inchcailloch (IRE) 60 (18f,Nwm,G,Oct 19)
Inchyre 59 (12f,Asc,G,Spt 29)
Indiahra 39 (7f,Nwm,G,Nov 2)
Indiana Princess 32 (13½f,Red,GF,Oct 17)
Indian Jockey 58 (8f,Bat,F,Jun 29)
Indian Nectar 36 (10f,Wnd,GF,Jly 22)
Indian Relative 59 (6f,Ayr,GF,Spt 21)
Indian Rhapsody 42 (8f,Nwm,GF,Aug 2)
Indonesian (IRE) 32 (10f,Rip,GF,Jun 20)
Indrapura (IRE) 34 (7f,Lei,GF,Jly 18)
Induna Mkubwa 35 (12f,Hay,G,Spt 6)
Infamous (USA) 64 (10f,Don,G,Spt 11)
Infatuation 55 (10½f,Hay,G,Spt 27)
Influence Pedler 36 (14f,Yar,F,Jun 25)
In Good Faith 31 (10f,Pon,G,Oct 21)
Inn At the Top 42 (14f,Not,GS,Aug 25)
Inner Circle (USA) 50 (7f,Lei,G,Apr 4)
Inquisitor (USA) 84 (10f,Nwb,GF,Spt 21)
Insatiable (IRE) 65 (8f,Asc,GF,Jun 18)
Insider Trader 66 (5f,Chs,GS,Aug 31)
Insiyabi (USA) 54 (8f,Don,GS,Mar 21)
Intendant 39 (8f,Ham,S,May 9)
In The Band 30 (10f,Kem,G,Spt 7)
In the Money (IRE) 47 (12f,Lei,GF,Jun 3)
Intiaash (IRE) 50 (6f,Chp,GS,May 27)
Intidab (USA) 52 (8f,Hay,GF,Aug 10)
Intimation 31 (7f,Sal,GF,Aug 15)
In Tune 31 (7f,Kem,GF,Apr 29)
Invest Wisely 62 (16f,Nwb,GF,Jly 19)
Invigilate 40 (6f,Red,GF,Jun 11)
Invocation 39 (6f,Goo,G,Jun 14)
Inzar (USA) 78 (7f,Nwm,G,Jun 29)
Ionio (USA) 76 (12f,Hay,G,Jly 6)
Iota 45 (14f,Not,GF,Jun 10)
I Recall (IRE) 40 (7f,Nwb,S,May 29)
Irish Sea (USA) 33 (10f,Yar,GF,Spt 18)
Irrepressible (IRE) 35 (8f,Yar,F,Jun 5)
Isitoff 43 (11f,Red,GF,May 27)
Isla Del Rey (USA) 60 (6f,Asc,GF,Jun 20)
Istabraq (IRE) 78 (14f,Hay,GS,Jun 8)
It's Academic 50 (7f,Cat,GS,Jly 4)
It'sthebusiness 41 (11f,War,F,Oct 8)
Ivor's Deed 30 (7½f,Bev,GF,May 11)
Ivor's Flutter 76 (16f,Asc,GF,Spt 28)
Ivory's Grab Hire 41 (6f,Not,GF,Spt 24)
Izza 43 (16f,Nwb,G,Aug 16)

Jaazim 42 (6f,Kem,GF,Jly 10)
Jack Jennings 74 (12f,Eps,G,Jun 8)
Jackson Hill 57 (10f,Sal,G,May 5)
Jagellon (USA) 56 (10f,Nwm,GS,Aug 24)
Jalcanto 43 (16½f,Don,GF,Aug 1)
Jamaican Flight (USA) 42 (11f,Red,F,Jun 21)
Jambo 40 (8f,Not,GF,Aug 7)
Jamrat Jumairah (IRE) 41 (8f,Pon,GF,Aug 8)
Jarah (USA) 70 (8f,Don,GF,Spt 14)
Jareer Do (IRE) 37 (7f,War,F,Jun 5)
Jaseur (USA) 54 (10½f,Hay,GS,May 25)
Java Red (IRE) 39 (8f,Pon,GF,Jun 10)
Jawaal 69 (8f,Nwb,GS,Apr 20)
Jayannpee 82 (6f,Asc,GF,Jun 21)
Jazz King 57 (14f,Goo,GF,Aug 1)
Jelali (IRE) 32 (12½f,War,F,Jun 10)
Jermyn Street (USA) 61 (13f,Nwb,GF,Jly 20)
Jerry Cutrona (IRE) 63 (10f,Nwm,GF,Oct 4)
Jessica's Song 32 (5f,Lin,GF,May 18)
Jezyah (USA) 36 (10f,Yar,GF,Spt 18)
Jigsaw Boy 40 (6f,Sal,GF,May 2)
Jilly Beveled 33 (7f,Nwm,GF,Aug 23)
Jimmy the Skunk (IRE) 51 (7f,Chp,S,Oct 22)
Jiyush 71 (14f,Yor,G,Spt 4)
Jobie 50 (6f,Goo,G,Jun 6)
Johayro 43 (5f,Edi,GF,Aug 29)
Johnnie the Joker 37 (8f,Lei,GF,Oct 14)
John O'Dreams 45 (5f,Rip,GF,Apr 18)
Johns Act (USA) 35 (14f,Not,S,Oct 31)
John-T 48 (8f,Nwb,GF,May 17)
Jolto 35 (8f,San,F,Jun 15)
Jo Maximus 58 (7f,Bri,F,Apr 12)
Jo Mell 68 (7f,Yor,G,Oct 12)
Jucea 58 (5f,San,GS,Jly 6)
Judgement Call 30 (5f,Lin,GF,May 10)
Judicial Field (IRE) 40 (16f,Bev,GF,Apr 12)
Juliasdarkinvader 33 (12f,Goo,GF,Jun 7)
Jumairah Sunset 44 (7f,San,F,Jun 15)
Jundi (IRE) 41 (22f,Asc,GF,Jun 21)
Jungle Patrol (IRE) 34 (7f,Don,GF,May 7)
Junior Ben (IRE) 36 (11½f,Wnd,GF,Jun 3)
Jural 84 (12f,Nwm,GF,Jly 20)
Just Bob 58 (5f,Thi,GF,May 17)
Just Dissident (IRE) 46 (5f,Crl,G,Aug 28)
Just Harry 54 (7f,Lei,GF,Jly 18)
Just Millie (USA) 46 (7f,Yar,G,Oct 30)

Juyush (USA) 76 (12f,Chs,GF,Jun 6)

Kaafih Homm (IRE) 60 (10f,San,G,Aug 31)
Kabcast 30 (5f,Rip,GF,Aug 5)
Kadamann (IRE) 45 (12f,Eps,G,Jun 7)
Kadastrof (FR) 62 (16f,Nwb,GS,Apr 19)
Kahir Almaydan (IRE) 69 (7f,Nwb,GS,Apr 20)
Kaitak (IRE) 54 (12f,Hay,G,Jly 6)
Kalabo (USA) 85 (12f,Don,GF,Spt 13)
Kala Noire 37 (12f,Nwm,GF,Jly 26)
Kalar 41 (5f,Thi,G,Aug 23)
Kala Sunrise 65 (8f,Hay,GS,May 25)
Kalmoss (FR) 74 (9f,Cha,F,Jun 2)
Kalou 37 (12f,Yor,G,Oct 10)
Kamari (USA) 61 (8f,Yor,G,Jly 12)
Kama Simba 32 (10f,Not,GF,Jly 26)
Kamikaze 49 (21½f,Pon,GF,Apr 29)
Kammtarra (USA) 79 (8f,Goo,GF,Aug 3)
Karinska 37 (8f,Thi,GF,May 4)
Karisma (IRE) 47 (12½f,Nwc,G,May 23)
Karlaska 67 (12½f,Dea,G,Aug 10)
Kassani (IRE) 67 (15f,Dea,G,Aug 18)
Kassbaan (USA) 58 (6f,Yor,G,Spt 4)
Kathryn's Pet 45 (12f,Nwm,G,Nov 1)
Katun (FR) 58 (12f,Lon,G,May 5)
Kawanin 36 (12f,Chp,G,Jun 13)
Kayvee 78 (7f,Nwb,G,Aug 17)
Kazimiera (IRE) 53 (8f,Lei,GF,Oct 14)
Keep Battling 40 (10f,Ayr,GF,Jun 22)
Keepers Dawn (IRE) 65 (7f,Nwb,GS,Apr 19)
Keltoi 56 (8f,Nwb,GF,May 17)
Kemo Sabo 49 (8f,Crl,GS,Apr 26)
Kentucky Fall (FR) 32 (8f,San,G,Aug 31)
Kerrier (IRE) 30 (8f,Wnd,G,May 20)
Kerry Ring 47 (7f,San,GS,Aug 23)
Keston Pond (IRE) 63 (7f,Nwc,G,Aug 26)
Ketabi (USA) 32 (8f,Chp,GF,Spt 12)
Kevasingo 45 (10f,Not,GF,Spt 24)
Key Change (IRE) 67 (12f,Yor,G,Aug 21)
Key to My Heart (IRE) 94 (12f,Hay,G,Jly 6)
Khabar 32 (10f,Bri,F,Jly 25)
Khalisa (IRE) 78 (10½f,Cha,G,Jun 9)
Kharizmi (FR) 69 (15f,Lon,S,Oct 5)
Khayrapour (IRE) 33 (8f,Goo,GF,Aug 1)
Ki Chi Saga (USA) 62 (8f,Asc,GF,Jly 27)
Kid Ory 51 (7f,Don,G,May 25)
Kidston Lass (IRE) 47 (10f,Asc,GF,Jly 26)
Kilcoran Bay 47 (14f,Sal,G,May 5)
Kildee Lad 55 (6f,Bat,F,Jun 29)
Kilernan 38 (12f,Edi,G,Apr 4)
Kilvine 56 (8f,San,G,Apr 27)
Kind of Light 63 (6f,Lin,GF,Aug 4)
King Alex 75 (10½f,Yor,GF,May 16)
King Athelstan (USA) 60 (10f,Nwm,GF,Jly 19)
Kingchip Boy 59 (8f,War,G,May 25)
King Curan (USA) 58 (8f,Ham,G,Spt 2)
Kingfisher Brave 37 (10½f,Hay,G,Jly 6)
King Kato 61 (10f,Bat,GS,Spt 30)
King of Peru 59 (7f,Goo,G,May 21)
King of Show (IRE) 43 (5f,Ayr,GF,Jly 15)
King of Sparta 46 (9f,Goo,GF,Aug 1)
King of The East (IRE) 61 (5f,Lin,GS,Aug 29)
King of Tunes (FR) 59 (8f,Goo,GF,Jun 7)
King Parrot (IRE) 47 (8f,Goo,GF,Spt 25)
King Rat (IRE) 63 (7f,Red,GF,Aug 25)
King Rufus 38 (10f,Goo,GF,Jun 7)
King's Academy (IRE) 57 (8f,Red,GF,Aug 25)
Kings Assembly 56 (10f,San,GF,Jun 14)
Kings Cay (IRE) 49 (12f,Crl,F,Jun 26)
Kings Harmony (IRE) 40 (6f,Not,GF,May 24)
King's Theatre (IRE) 80 (10f,Nwb,S,May 29)
Kings Witness (USA) 61 (12f,Hay,G,Jly 6)
Kinlochewe 68 (10f,Wnd,GF,Aug 19)
Kira 53 (5f,Don,GF,Spt 13)
Kiridashi (CAN) 96 (8f,G,Oct 26)
Kirov Lady (IRE) 54 (8f,San,G,Aug 30)
Kissel 35 (8f,Pon,G,Spt 3)
Kiss Me Again (IRE) 42 (8f,Asc,GF,Jun 22)
Kistena (FR) 79 (6f,Dea,G,Aug 25)
Kitty Kitty Cancan 45 (11½f,Wnd,GF,Aug 19)
Knobbleeneeze 58 (7f,Nwb,G,Aug 17)
Knotty Hill 45 (8f,Thi,F,Jun 3)
Koathary (USA) 52 (10f,San,GS,May 27)
Komlucky 43 (7f,Nwm,GF,Aug 23)
Komreyev Dancer 65 (10f,Nwm,GF,Jly 19)
Korambi 65 (12f,Eps,G,Jun 7)
Krayyalei (IRE) 45 (6f,Cur,G,Jun 30)
Kriscliffe 48 (9f,Kem,GF,May 6)
Kristal Breeze 43 (10f,Bri,G,Oct 2)
Kristal's Paradise (IRE) 69 (14f,Yor,G,Jly 13)
Krystal Max (IRE) 40 (6f,Chs,G,May 8)
Kuala Lipis (USA) 58 (10f,Goo,GF,Aug 2)
Kuantan (USA) 49 (7f,Lei,GS,May 28)
Kunucu (IRE) 54 (5f,Nwm,G,Oct 19)
Kutman (USA) 45 (8f,Not,GF,Spt 24)
Kutta 84 (12f,Nwb,S,Oct 26)
Kymin (IRE) 41 (16f,War,F,Jun 10)

Laafee 62 (7f,Nwb,G,Aug 17)
Laazim Afooz 56 (12f,Eps,GF,Spt 24)
Labeed (USA) 41 (15f,War,GF,Jly 5)
La Belle Dominique 35 (5f,Bri,GF,Aug 28)
La Blue (GER) 65 (9f,Lon,GS,Oct 6)
La Brief 37 (14f,Hay,S,Oct 5)
Labudd (USA) 30 (12f,Eps,G,Jly 31)
Lacinia 32 (12f,Leo,GF,Jly 20)
Lacryma Cristi (IRE) 45 (6f,Hay,G,Jly 5)
Lady Bankes (IRE) 42 (10f,Bev,GF,Jly 22)
Lady Carla 84 (12f,Eps,G,Jun 7)
Lady Caroline Lamb (IRE) 47 (5f,War,GS,Apr 13)
Lady Isabell 30 (7f,Bri,F,Jly 16)
Lady Joshua (IRE) 47 (10f,Nwm,G,Jly 10)
Ladykirk 48 (12½f,Nwc,G,May 23)
Lady Lucre (IRE) 33 (10f,Nwm,GF,Jun 8)
Lady of Leisure (USA) 57 (10f,Pon,GF,Spt 26)
Lady Sabina 33 (8f,War,G,May 25)
Lady Sheriff 64 (5f,Hay,GF,Aug 10)
La Fille de Cirque 35 (8f,Not,G,Oct 24)
L'Africain Bleu (FR) 55 (12f,Cha,F,Jun 2)
Lago Di Varano 69 (5f,Nwm,G,Oct 19)
Lakeline Legend (IRE) 59 (12f,Goo,GF,Jly 31)
Lalindi (IRE) 68 (11½f,Lin,F,Jun 22)
Lallans (IRE) 59 (14f,Yor,GF,May 14)
La Mafarr (USA) 31 (7f,Red,F,Spt 28)
L'Ami Louis (USA) 59 (8f,Thi,GF,May 18)
La Modiste 49 (7f,Lin,GF,Jly 13)
La Pellegrina (IRE) 43 (7f,Nwm,GF,Apr 17)
La Petite Fusee 67 (6f,Ayr,GF,Spt 21)
Lap of Luxury 61 (8f,San,G,Aug 31)
Larissa (IRE) 35 (8f,Nwm,GF,Jun 1)
Last Second (IRE) 75 (8f,Asc,GF,Jun 19)
La Suquet 53 (5f,Rip,GF,Apr 18)
Latahaab (USA) 63 (20f,Asc,GF,Jun 20)
La Tansani (IRE) 37 (7f,San,GF,Jly 5)
Latching (IRE) 63 (6f,Asc,GF,Jun 21)
Latin Quarter (USA) 34 (10f,Goo,GF,Spt 14)
L A Touch 42 (6f,Yar,GF,Aug 22)
Latvian 42 (12½f,Nwc,G,May 6)
Laurel Delight 61 (5f,Nwc,GF,Jly 27)
Lavender Della (IRE) 38 (10f,Nwb,GF,Jly 19)
Law Commission 71 (7f,Nwm,G,Oct 19)
Law Dancer (IRE) 49 (10f,Asc,GF,Aug 2)
Layik (IRE) 32 (12f,Leo,GF,Jly 20)
Lay The Blame 43 (7f,Nwc,G,Aug 26)
Lead Him On (USA) 33 (10f,Kem,G,Apr 8)
Leading Princess (IRE) 34 (6f,Ham,GF,Aug 19)
Leading Spirit (IRE) 71 (12f,Kem,GF,Jun 1)
Leap for Joy 75 (6f,Dea,G,Aug 25)
Lear Express (USA) 54 (11½f,Yar,GF,Jly 4)
Lear Jet (USA) 49 (10f,Bat,G,Apr 30)
Lear White (USA) 89 (12f,Asc,GF,Jun 21)
Le Bam Bam 34 (7f,Kem,GF,Apr 29)
Le Destin (FR) 66 (12f,Cha,F,Jun 2)
Ledgendry Line 42 (12½f,Nwc,G,May 23)
Leeds (IRE) 82 (12½f,Dea,G,Aug 25)
Legal Issue (IRE) 56 (7f,Cat,GS,Jly 4)
Legal Right (USA) 63 (10½f,Chs,G,May 7)
Leif the Lucky (USA) 55 (10½f,Hay,G,Jly 6)
Leigh Crofter 31 (6f,Kem,GS,May 25)
Leith Academy (USA) 31 (10f,Wnd,GF,Jly 22)
Le Khoumf (FR) 49 (8f,Rip,G,Apr 10)
Lennox Lewis 75 (6f,Goo,GS,May 22)
Leonato (FR) 68 (13½f,Chs,GS,Aug 31)
Leonila (IRE) 61 (12f,Lon,G,Jun 23)
Leonine (IRE) 53 (8f,Nwm,GF,May 4)
Lepikha (USA) 51 (18f,Pon,G,Oct 21)
Le Sport 32 (7f,Yor,G,Oct 12)
Letluce 48 (7f,Hay,GS,May 6)
Le Triton (USA) 82 (9f,Cha,F,Jun 2)
Lidanna 64 (5f,Asc,GF,Jun 21)
Liefling (USA) 56 (14f,Yor,G,Aug 20)
Lift Boy (USA) 37 (5f,Lin,GF,May 18)
Lila Pedigo (IRE) 35 (10f,Not,GF,Spt 24)
Lillibella 42 (5f,War,F,Jun 5)
Lilli Claire 59 (8½f,Eps,G,Jun 7)
Limerick Princess (IRE) 36 (6f,Cat,G,May 31)
Line Dancer 57 (10f,Dea,G,May 16)
Lionel Edwards (IRE) 38 (6f,Cat,G,May 31)
Lionize (USA) 51 (8f,Nwm,G,Nov 2)
Literary Society (USA) 55 (5f,Nwm,GF,Oct 3)
Little Black Dress (USA) 34 (8f,Sal,GF,May 2)
Little Ibnr 33 (6f,War,GF,Jly 13)
Little Murray 32 (8f,Nwm,GF,Jun 1)
Little Noggins (IRE) 46 (5f,Don,GS,Mar 21)
Lituus (USA) 54 (10f,Eps,G,Jun 7)
Lloc 42 (5f,Fol,GS,Mar 25)
Llyswen 42 (10f,Asc,GF,Jly 26)
Loch Patrick 74 (5f,San,GS,Jly 6)
Locorotondo (IRE) 43 (10f,Pon,G,Apr 17)
Loki (IRE) 57 (12f,Eps,GF,Spt 11)
Lombardic (USA) 65 (12f,Hay,GF,Spt 7)
Lomberto 54 (10f,Nwm,GF,Aug 9)
Lonely Leader (IRE) 49 (7f,Goo,GF,Spt 13)
Longcroft 33 (16f,Bev,GF,Jly 16)
Longwick Lad 55 (5f,Lei,GF,Aug 19)
Lookingforarainbow (IRE) 61 (12f,Nwm,GF,Jun 28)
Look Who's Calling (IRE) 47 (8f,Not,GS,Apr 12)
Lord Advocate 39 (13f,Ham,G,Jun 12)
Lord Hastie (USA) 53 (12f,Hay,G,Spt 27)
Lord High Admiral (CAN) 75 (5f,San,GS,Jly 6)
Lord Jim (IRE) 62 (14f,Sal,GF,Jun 27)
Lord of The Manor 33 (10f,Red,GF,May 13)
Lord Olivier (IRE) 67 (6f,Goo,GS,May 22)
Los Alamos 40 (14f,Cat,G,Oct 19)
Lost Lagoon (USA) 62 (8f,Rip,G,Apr 10)
Lothlorien (USA) 53 (10½f,Hay,GS,May 25)
Lough Erne 73 (6f,Hay,S,Oct 6)
Louis Quatorze (USA) 87 (10f,Fst,Oct 26)
Louis' Queen (IRE) 75 (8½f,Eps,G,Jun 7)
Loup Solitaire (USA) 80 (10½f,Lon,G,May 12)
Love And Kisses 36 (10f,Nwm,G,Jly 10)
Love Bateta (IRE) 43 (11½f,Wnd,GF,Aug 19)
Love Legend 36 (7f,Lin,GF,May 11)
Lovely Prospect 30 (7f,Red,GF,May 13)
Love The Blues 43 (16f,Chs,G,Spt 25)
Loveyoumillions (IRE) 52 (9f,Ham,S,May 3)
Lower Egypt (USA) 55 (8f,Not,GF,Jun 10)
Lubaba (USA) 35 (8f,Not,GF,Apr 30)
Lucayan Prince (USA) 75 (6f,Hay,GF,Spt 7)
Lucky Archer 50 (7f,Nwm,GF,Oct 5)
Lucky Bea 39 (8f,Ayr,GF,Jun 21)
Lucky Coin 50 (14f,Yar,GF,Aug 15)
Lucky Di (USA) 85 (10f,Asc,GF,Jun 18)

Lucky Lionel (USA) 74 (6f,Nwm,G,Oct 19)
Lucky Parkes 68 (5f,Lin,GS,Aug 29)
Lucky Revenge 49 (6f,Lin,GF,Jly 12)
Lunar Mist 40 (7f,Chs,GS,Aug 30)
Luna Wells (IRE) 77 (10½f,Cha,G,Jun 9)
Lunch Party 40 (7f,Thi,GF,May 17)
Luso 91 (9f,Nwm,GF,Apr 17)
Lynton Lad 64 (8f,Don,GS,Mar 22)

Macfarlane 37 (5f,Chs,GF,Jun 6)
Macmorris (USA) 46 (14f,Not,GF,May 24)
Madame Steinlen 35 (10f,Kem,G,Apr 6)
Madly Sharp 76 (7f,Nwm,GF,Oct 4)
Mad Militant (IRE) 40 (12f,Yor,G,Oct 10)
Madrileno (IRE) 42 (10f,Lon,S,Oct 5)
Madrina 31 (5f,War,F,Jun 5)
Maftun (USA) 40 (13f,Ham,G,Jly 5)
Magellan (USA) 74 (7f,Nwb,G,Aug 16)
Magic Carousel 32 (8f,Crl,G,May 30)
Magic Combination (IRE) 32 (16f,Cur,GS,Oct 5)
Magic Mail 49 (5f,San,GF,Jly 17)
Magnificient Style (USA) 60 (10½ f,Yor,GF,May 14)
Mahogany Hall (USA) 75 (10f,Fst,Oct 26)
Mahool (USA) 47 (7f,Red,GF,Aug 25)
Maiden Castle 49 (10f,Don,GF,Spt 13)
Maid For Baileys (IRE) 64 (8½f,Eps,GF,Spt 24)
Maid For The Hills 65 (6f,Nwm,GF,Jun 1)
Maid O'Cannie 38 (6f,Not,GF,Apr 30)
Maiteamia 60 (5f,Ham,Hy,May 2)
Majdak Jereeb (IRE) 34 (11f,War,F,Jun 5)
Major Change 69 (10f,San,GF,Jun 14)
Major Dundee (IRE) 51 (12f,Goo,GF,Spt 25)
Major Quality 63 (5f,Hay,GS,May 6)
Make a Stand 67 (12f,Kem,GF,Jun 26)
Male-Ana-Mou (IRE) 65 (14f,Yor,G,Aug 21)
Malibu Man 45 (5f,Chp,GF,Spt 12)
Mallia 48 (6f,Nwc,F,Jun 29)
Mallooh 34 (10f,Rip,GF,Jly 20)
Mam'selle Bergerac (IRE) 30 (8f,Goo,GF,Spt 25)
Manabar 46 (10f,Nwm,GF,May 3)
Manaloj (USA) 47 (8f,Sal,GF,May 2)
Mancini 56 (10½f,Yor,GF,May 14)
Manderella 33 (6f,Wnd,GF,Jun 10)
Manful 59 (11f,Ayr,GS,May 8)
Manninamix 30 (8f,Lon,G,Jun 1)
Man of Wit (IRE) 33 (7f,Red,F,Aug 9)
Manolo (FR) 42 (5f,Red,GF,Oct 17)
Manoy 32 (8f,Nwc,G,Apr 8)
Mansab (USA) 40 (7f,Fol,F,Apr 23)
Mansur (IRE) 38 (14f,Yar,F,Jly 23)
Manzoni (GER) 54 (10f,Lon,S,Oct 5)
Ma Petite Anglaise 63 (10f,Bri,F,Aug 18)
Maple Bay (IRE) 69 (8f,Pon,G,Spt 3)
Maradata (IRE) 46 (10f,Goo,G,Aug 24)
Maralinga (IRE) 78 (10f,Wnd,GF,Aug 19)
Maraschino 35 (6f,Not,GF,Spt 24)
Marchman 33 (12½f,War,F,Jly 20)
Marigliano (USA) 55 (8f,Nwm,GF,May 5)
Marildo (FR) 58 (10½f,Lon,GF,Apr 28)
Marino Street 41 (5f,Lei,GF,Aug 19)
Maristax 47 (7f,Lin,G,Oct 4)
Marjaana (IRE) 33 (7f,Ayr,GF,Jly 15)
Marjorie Rose (IRE) 41 (5f,Ham,G,Spt 2)
Mark of Esteem (IRE) 85 (8f,Asc,GF,Spt 28)
Marl 67 (8f,Asc,GF,Spt 28)
Marlin (USA) 59 (12f,G,Oct 26)
Marqueta (USA) 38 (7f,Cur,GS,Apr 27)
Marsayas (IRE) 34 (16f,Cat,GF,Spt 21)
Martiniquais (IRE) 78 (9f,Cha,F,Jun 2)
Martinosky 35 (7f,Fol,G,May 29)
Masehaab (IRE) 65 (14f,Goo,G,Aug 24)
Masruf (IRE) 34 (6f,Nwm,GF,Jly 19)
Master Beveled 57 (11f,War,GS,Apr 13)
Master Boots 50 (8f,Nwm,GF,Apr 17)
Master Charter 73 (8f,Asc,GF,Jly 27)
Master Hyde (USA) 31 (12f,Crl,F,Aug 5)
Master M-E-N (IRE) 39 (8f,Sal,F,Spt 5)
Master Millfield (IRE) 55 (6f,Bat,F,Jun 29)
Master of Passion 63 (6f,Asc,GF,Jun 21)
Master Ofthe House 42 (10f,Not,G,Apr 22)
Master Planner 43 (6f,Yor,GF,May 14)
Matam 34 (5f,Don,G,May 25)
Matamoros 42 (10f,San,G,Aug 31)
Matarun (IRE) 74 (12½f,Dea,G,Aug 25)
Matiya (IRE) 81 (10½f,Cha,G,Jun 9)
Mattawan 56 (12f,Hay,GF,Spt 7)
Matthias Mystique 52 (12f,Eps,GF,Spt 24)
Mattimeo (IRE) 47 (12f,Goo,GF,Spt 25)
Maurangi 31 (8f,Lei,GF,Oct 14)
Mawared (IRE) 46 (12f,Lei,GF,Oct 14)
Mawingo (IRE) 57 (10f,Goo,GF,Aug 2)
Mawjud 31 (8f,Not,GS,Aug 25)
Mawwal (USA) 62 (7f,Yar,GF,Jly 4)
May Queen Megan 39 (6f,Lin,GF,Jly 12)
Mazcobar 60 (8f,San,GF,Aug 14)
Mazeed (IRE) 38 (7f,Goo,G,May 21)
Mazilla 46 (10f,Yar,G,Aug 1)
Mazurek 32 (10f,Nwm,GF,Apr 16)
Mbulwa 52 (8f,Yor,G,Jly 12)
Mcgillycuddy Reeks (IRE) 34 (10f,Yar,GF,Spt 18)
Meant to Be 57 (16f,Goo,GF,Spt 14)
Me Cherokee 33 (12f,Ham,GS,Apr 3)
Medaille Militaire 72 (10½f,Yor,GF,May 16)
Medfee 40 (10f,Bat,GS,Spt 30)
Mediate (IRE) 33 (8f,Nwm,GF,Aug 2)
Medieval Lady 60 (8f,Asc,G,Oct 12)
Meghdoot 52 (12f,Nwm,GF,Apr 17)
Meg's Memory (IRE) 32 (10f,Bat,GF,Jly 8)
Meldorf 46 (8f,San,G,Apr 27)
Mellaby (USA) 46 (12f,Yor,G,Jun 15)
Mellors (IRE) 44 (5f,Bri,F,Aug 18)
Mellottie 71 (10f,Pon,GF,Spt 26)
Mels Baby (IRE) 47 (8f,Red,F,Spt 27)
Meltemison 41 (10f,Lin,GF,May 10)
Melt The Clouds (CAN) 48 (10f,Lin,F,Spt 19)
Members Welcome (IRE) 36 (6f,Bat,GF,Aug 8)
Memories Of Silver (USA) 89 (8f,G,Oct 26)
Memphis Beau (IRE) 35 (8f,Bri,G,Oct 2)
Menas Gold 50 (10f,Kem,GS,May 25)
Menoo Hal Batal (USA) 44 (7f,San,G,May 27)
Mentalasanythin 58 (10f,Don,GF,Spt 14)
Mental Pressure 66 (14f,Yor,G,Aug 20)
Meranti 34 (6f,Sal,GF,May 2)
Meribel (IRE) 33 (11½f,Lin,GF,May 11)
Merit (IRE) 74 (20f,Asc,GF,Jun 18)
Merrie le Bow 46 (6f,Yar,GF,Spt 19)
Merrily 45 (5f,Rip,G,Aug 17)
Metal Boys 37 (5f,San,GF,Jun 14)
Met Mech Nich (FR) 69 (12½f,Dea,G,Aug 10)
Mezaan (IRE) 69 (12f,Nwm,GF,May 5)
Meznh (IRE) 46 (7f,San,GS,Aug 23)
Mezzanotte (IRE) 70 (7f,Nwm,G,Oct 19)
Mezzogiorno 71 (12f,Eps,G,Jun 7)
Mezzoramio 37 (7f,Lei,GF,Jly 18)
Mick's Love (IRE) 53 (10f,Nwm,GF,May 3)
Midday Cowboy (USA) 47 (8f,Kem,G,Spt 7)
Middle East 41 (6f,Thi,GF,Jun 18)
Midnight Blue 50 (6f,Ham,GS,Spt 30)
Midnight Escape 76 (5f,Nwm,G,Oct 19)
Midnight Legend 92 (12f,Goo,GF,Aug 2)
Midnight Spell 53 (5f,Don,S,Nov 8)
Midyan Blue (IRE) 73 (14f,Yor,GF,May 15)
Miesque's Son (USA) 83 (6½f,Dea,GS,Aug 11)
Mighty Forum (CAN) 71 (8f,G,Oct 26)
Mighty Phantom (USA) 53 (14f,Yor,G,Spt 4)
Migwar 50 (10f,Kem,G,Apr 8)
Mihriz (IRE) 49 (8f,Asc,GF,Jly 27)
Mijas 34 (6f,Lin,GF,May 18)
Miletrian City 36 (7f,Cat,GF,Jly 25)
Miletrian Refurb (IRE) 38 (6f,Nwc,GS,Mar 26)
Milford Sound 41 (8f,Nwc,F,Jun 29)
Milford Track (IRE) 62 (10f,Lon,G,Jun 23)
Mill Force 36 (8f,Pon,GF,Jly 19)
Millyant 58 (5f,Leo,G,Jun 3)
Milos 47 (7f,Chp,S,Oct 22)
Milton 34 (10f,Chp,GF,Jly 2)
Miltonfield 39 (16f,Cur,GS,Oct 5)
Mim-Lou-and 37 (14f,Not,GF,Jun 10)
Mimosa 47 (8f,Asc,G,Oct 11)
Min Alhawa (USA) 51 (12f,Hay,G,Jly 6)
Mind Games 92 (5f,Asc,GF,Jun 21)
Mindrace 51 (5f,Nwm,GF,Oct 3)
Minds Music (USA) 83 (12f,Don,GF,Spt 13)
Ming Dynasty (IRE) 60 (15f,Dea,G,Aug 18)
Minnisam 32 (11½f,Lin,F,Jly 27)
Minoletti 46 (7f,Nwb,S,Oct 24)
Minster Glory 39 (10½f,Yor,G,Spt 5)
Mirador 48 (20f,Asc,GF,Jun 18)
Mironov 45 (10½f,Yor,GF,May 16)
Miroswaki (USA) 57 (16f,Asc,GF,Spt 28)
Mischief Star 30 (12f,Kem,GF,Jun 12)
Misky Bay 31 (8f,Nwc,G,Apr 8)
Misrule (USA) 45 (8f,Bri,G,Oct 2)
Miss Bigwig 48 (5f,Ayr,GF,Spt 19)
Missel 79 (10f,Nwm,GF,Jly 19)
Miss Haversham 43 (10f,Nwb,GF,Jun 27)
Missile 87 (9f,Nwm,GF,Oct 5)
Missile Toe (IRE) 41 (6f,Yar,F,Jun 13)
Miss Laughter 44 (8f,Chp,G,Jun 13)
Miss Pigalle 30 (7f,Cat,GF,Aug 6)
Miss Prism 31 (14f,Cat,G,Oct 19)
Miss Riviera 67 (7f,Goo,GF,Aug 2)
Miss Tahiti (IRE) 85 (10½f,Cha,G,Jun 9)
Miss Universal (IRE) 68 (8f,Asc,GF,Jun 19)
Miss Waterline 58 (6f,Ayr,GF,Spt 21)
Miss Zanzibar 36 (8f,Red,F,Jly 18)
Mister Aspecto (IRE) 48 (13f,Ham,GF,Aug 14)
Mister Fire Eyes (IRE) 51 (7f,Lin,GF,May 11)
Mister Joel 34 (7f,Lei,G,Jly 24)
Mister Jolson 55 (5f,San,G,Apr 26)
Mister O'Grady (IRE) 49 (10f,Bri,F,Aug 18)
Mister Rm 34 (7f,Nwm,GF,Jun 21)
Mister Westsound 54 (6f,Yor,G,Jun 15)
Mister Woodstick (IRE) 31 (8f,Red,GF,Jun 11)
Mistle Cat (USA) 87 (8f,Asc,GF,Jun 18)
Miswaki Dancer (USA) 45 (12f,Kem,GF,Jun 26)
Mitch (USA) 37 (6f,Cur,G,Jun 30)
Mithraic (IRE) 34 (11f,Edi,GF,Jly 19)
Mizyan (IRE) 51 (15f,War,GF,Jly 13)
Mo-Addab (IRE) 62 (8f,Nwb,S,May 19)
Mock Trial (IRE) 44 (12f,Pon,GF,Jly 19)
Mogin 31 (7f,Bri,GF,Aug 28)
Mohannad (IRE) 42 (10f,Nwm,GF,Apr 16)
Mohawk River (IRE) 55 (11f,Nwb,G,Apr 19)
Moi Canard 30 (7f,War,F,May 6)
Mokuti 62 (8f,Crl,GS,Apr 26)
Moments of Fortune (USA) 86 (8f,Yor,GF,Aug 22)
Monaassib 87 (7f,Nwm,GF,Apr 17)
Monarch 62 (10f,Nwm,GF,Aug 10)
Mondragon 52 (16f,Bev,GF,Apr 12)
Mono Lady (IRE) 31 (8f,Not,S,Oct 31)
Mons 76 (14½f,Don,GF,Spt 14)
Montecristo 48 (12f,Asc,GF,Jun 20)
Montendre 65 (6f,Nwb,GF,Jly 20)
Montjoy (USA) 104 (10f,Asc,GF,Jun 18)
Montone (IRE) 58 (11f,Red,GF,Jly 11)
Montrestar 44 (5f,War,GS,Apr 13)
Montserrat 71 (6f,Hay,S,Oct 6)
Monument 55 (10f,Wnd,GF,Jly 22)
Moody's Cat (IRE) 61 (12f,Eps,G,Jun 7)
Moonax (IRE) 75 (20f,Lon,S,Oct 5)
Moonbi Range (IRE) 33 (8f,Leo,G,Aug 5)
Moonlight Calypso 32 (12f,Edi,GS,Nov 7)
Moonlight Quest 63 (16f,Nwb,GF,Jly 19)
Moon Mischief 46 (10f,Nwm,G,Jly 10)
Moon Strike (FR) 75 (5f,Nwm,GS,Aug 24)
More Risk (IRE) 39 (6f,Cur,G,Jun 30)
More Than You Know (IRE) 52 (10½

f,Yor,G,Jun 15)
Morning Surprise 35 (7f,War,F,Jun 5)
Morocco (IRE) 59 (7f,Lei,GF,Oct 15)
Moscow Mist (IRE) 54 (8f,Asc,G,Spt 29)
Most Wanted (IRE) 36 (10½f,Hay,GS,May 6)
Moujeeb (USA) 32 (5f,Fol,GF,Apr 16)
Mountgate 65 (7f,Nwm,GF,Jun 21)
Mount Pleasant (IRE) 65 (12f,Eps,GF,Spt 24)
Mount Row 64 (12f,Hay,GF,Aug 9)
Mourne Mountains 44 (10f,Wnd,GF,Aug 19)
Mousehole 63 (6f,Yar,F,Jun 12)
Move Smartly (IRE) 41 (7f,Red,GF,May 27)
Move With Edes 52 (7f,Crl,F,Jly 6)
Moving Arrow 84 (10f,Nwm,GF,Jly 19)
Mr Bergerac (IRE) 65 (6f,Yor,G,Oct 12)
Mr Browning (USA) 60 (12f,Goo,GF,Aug 3)
Mr Copyforce 32 (14f,Sal,GF,Aug 1)
Mr Cube (IRE) 42 (7f,Bri,F,May 9)
Mr Martini (IRE) 73 (8f,Asc,GF,Jun 18)
Mr Nevermind (IRE) 54 (8½f,Eps,GF,Spt 24)
Mr Oscar 54 (5f,Nwc,F,Jun 28)
Mr Rough 41 (8f,Bri,F,Apr 12)
Mr Speaker (IRE) 37 (6f,Chp,GF,Jly 6)
Mr Speculator 31 (15f,War,GF,Jly 5)
Mr Teigh 55 (8f,Red,GF,Oct 17)
Mr Wild (USA) 31 (10f,San,GF,Spt 18)
Mt. Sassafras (CAN) 91 (10f,Fst,Oct 26)
Mua-Tab 36 (10f,Nwb,GF,Jly 19)
Mubarhin (USA) 38 (8f,Nwm,GF,Apr 17)
Mubariz (IRE) 37 (8f,Not,GF,Jun 24)
Mubhij (IRE) 68 (5f,San,GS,Jly 6)
Muhandis 45 (7f,Yar,F,Jly 21)
Muhassil (IRE) 33 (8f,Don,GF,May 7)
Mukeed 38 (12f,Nwm,GF,Aug 2)
Mukhlles (USA) 47 (8f,Nwb,GS,Apr 20)
Mullitover 59 (7f,Nwm,GF,Jly 11)
Multicoloured (IRE) 65 (10½f,Yor,G,Oct 10)
Multi Franchise 34 (10f,Bat,GF,Jun 15)
Muncie (IRE) 60 (10½f,Lon,GF,Apr 28)
Murajja (USA) 80 (10f,Nwb,S,May 29)
Murheb 66 (10f,Goo,GF,Aug 2)
Murphy's Gold (IRE) 43 (7½f,Bev,GF,Jun 12)
Murray's Mazda (IRE) 40 (7f,Thi,F,Jun 18)
Muse 38 (16f,Nwb,S,May 19)
Musetta (IRE) 76 (8½f,Eps,G,Jun 7)
Mushahid (USA) 69 (10f,Goo,GF,Aug 2)
Musical Season 61 (6f,Ayr,GF,Spt 21)
Music Gold (IRE) 58 (5f,Wnd,G,May 20)
Musick House (IRE) 41 (7f,Hay,GS,May 6)
Mustahil (IRE) 30 (8f,Wnd,GF,Jun 3)
Mustn't Grumble (IRE) 52 (8f,Lei,GF,Oct 14)
Mutadarra (IRE) 37 (7f,San,GF,Jly 5)
Mutamanni (USA) 43 (7f,Lin,GF,May 11)
Mutanassib (IRE) 46 (10f,Lei,F,Spt 10)
My Best Valentine 73 (7f,Chs,GS,Aug 30)
Mybotye 48 (6f,Pon,GF,Jun 10)
My Branch 60 (8f,Nwm,GF,May 5)
My Cadeaux 54 (6f,Wnd,GF,Jun 3)
My Cherrywell 31 (5f,Ham,G,Spt 29)
My Emma 57 (12f,Lon,G,Spt 15)
Myfontaine 48 (10f,Goo,G,Aug 24)
My Gallery (IRE) 71 (7½f,Chs,GS,Aug 31)
My Godson 45 (7½f,Bev,G,Aug 24)
My Handsome Prince 30 (8f,Pon,G,Apr 17)
My Learned Friend 67 (14f,Yor,G,Aug 21)
My Lewicia (IRE) 64 (8f,Goo,GF,Aug 3)
My Mariam 38 (10f,Don,G,Oct 25)
My Melody Parkes 71 (6f,Nwm,GF,Jun 1)
Myself 78 (7f,Dea,S,May 26)
Mystery Matthias 37 (6f,Lin,GF,Jly 12)
Mystic Dawn 57 (8f,Lei,GF,Oct 14)
Mystic Hill 80 (13f,Nwb,GF,Jly 20)
Mystic Knight 76 (12f,Eps,G,Jun 8)
Mystic Maid (IRE) 32 (5f,Bev,GF,May 10)
Myttons Mistake 48 (6f,Chs,G,May 8)

Naazeq 56 (10½f,Hay,G,Spt 27)
Nabhaan (IRE) 59 (12f,Hay,G,Jly 6)
Nador 64 (12f,Asc,GF,Jun 20)
Nagnagnag (IRE) 85 (8½f,Eps,G,Jun 7)
Naissant 48 (6f,Rip,GS,Aug 26)
Najiya 62 (8f,Asc,GF,Spt 28)
Najm Mubeen (IRE) 68 (10f,Nwm,GF,Oct 4)
Nakami 30 (6f,Sal,GF,Aug 1)
Nakayama Express (IRE) 49 (6f,Cur,G,Jun 30)
Naked Welcome 89 (14f,Yor,G,Aug 21)
Nakhal 31 (8f,Sal,GF,Aug 1)
Name of Our Father (USA) 34 (10f,Pon,G,Oct 21)
Namoodaj 34 (12f,Asc,G,Oct 11)
Namouna (IRE) 37 (10f,Asc,GF,Jly 26)
Nanda 46 (10½f,Hay,GS,May 6)
Naninja (USA) 67 (10f,Lon,S,Spt 22)
Nanshan (IRE) 36 (7f,Yar,F,Jly 21)
Nanton Point (USA) 62 (16f,Nwb,S,May 19)
Napoleon Star (IRE) 35 (7f,Bri,F,May 9)
Nashaat (USA) 63 (7f,Sal,GF,Aug 1)
Nashcash (IRE) 39 (6f,Cur,GS,May 25)
Nash House (IRE) 61 (8f,Nwb,GS,Apr 20)
Nasrudin (USA) 52 (8f,Asc,GF,Jly 27)
National Treasure 40 (12f,Nwm,GF,Aug 10)
Nattier 31 (6f,Crl,F,Jun 13)
Natural Key 48 (5f,Ham,G,Spt 29)
Naughty Pistol (USA) 33 (7f,Cat,G,Oct 19)
Nautical Pet (IRE) 46 (7f,Cur,S,Apr 13)
Naval Gazer (IRE) 47 (12f,Bri,F,Spt 4)
Navigate (USA) 52 (7f,Kem,GF,Jun 1)
Nayil 46 (16f,Cur,GS,Oct 5)
Nec Plus Ultra (FR) 51 (8f,Cha,G,Jun 9)
Ned's Bonanza 47 (5f,Sal,F,Spt 5)
Needle Gun (IRE) 87 (10f,Cur,G,Jun 8)
Need You Badly 32 (5f,San,GF,Jly 5)
Nellie North 38 (6f,Wnd,G,Jly 29)
Nelly's Cousin 40 (10f,Nwm,GF,Jly 26)
Nereus 51 (12f,Kem,G,Spt 7)
Neuwest (USA) 69 (7f,Lin,GF,Aug 4)
Never Think Twice 39 (6f,Lin,GF,Aug 4)
New Albion (USA) 46 (9f,Ham,GF,Jly 12)
Newbridge Boy 34 (10½f,Hay,GS,May 25)
New Century (USA) 69 (7f,Chs,GF,Jun 6)
Newlands Corner 31 (6f,Sal,GF,Aug 22)
Newport Knight 40 (12f,Bat,G,Aug 13)
New York New York (FR) 58 (12f,Lon,G,May 5)
Nigel's Lad (IRE) 54 (9f,Nwm,GF,Oct 5)
Night City 61 (8f,Nwb,GF,Jun 27)
Night Dance 66 (8f,Nwb,GS,Apr 20)
Night Harmony (IRE) 45 (5f,San,GF,Spt 17)
Night of Glass 48 (8f,Yar,GF,Spt 19)
Night Parade (USA) 56 (6f,Nwm,GF,Apr 18)
Night Wink (USA) 66 (8f,Bri,F,Jly 16)
Nijmegen 42 (16f,Rip,G,May 29)
Nijo 81 (9f,Nwm,G,Oct 18)
Nikita's Star (IRE) 43 (12f,Bev,GF,Jly 30)
Niknaks Nephew 56 (10f,Nwb,GF,May 17)
Nilgiri Hills (IRE) 51 (6f,Hay,GS,Jly 4)
Nineacres 51 (5f,Don,S,Nov 8)
Ninety-Five 52 (5f,Edi,GF,Aug 29)
Ninia (USA) 75 (8f,Ayr,GF,Spt 20)
Ninotchka (USA) 71 (12f,Asc,G,Oct 12)
Nkapen Rocks (SPA) 40 (8f,Edi,GS,Jly 22)
No-Aman 54 (10f,Goo,GF,Jun 7)
No Animosity (IRE) 38 (7f,Cur,S,Apr 13)
Nobby Barnes 33 (10½f,Yor,G,Oct 10)
Noble Sprinter (IRE) 67 (10½f,Hay,G,Jly 6)
No Cliches 59 (8f,San,GF,Spt 18)
Noeprob (USA) 48 (8f,Wnd,GF,Jun 3)
No Extras (IRE) 52 (6f,Goo,G,Spt 14)
No Monkey Nuts 45 (6f,Cat,GS,Jly 4)
Nononito (FR) 77 (15½f,Lon,S,May 19)
Non Vintage (IRE) 42 (16f,Nwm,GF,Aug 9)
No Pattern 52 (12f,Kem,GF,May 6)
Nordansk 46 (12f,Kem,GF,Jun 26)
Nordic Breeze (IRE) 39 (8½f,Bev,GF,Jun 5)
Nordinex (IRE) 61 (8f,Goo,GF,Jly 30)
Norsong 39 (12f,Eps,G,Jly 31)
North Ardar 46 (10f,Pon,GF,Jun 10)
North Bear 46 (12f,Don,GF,Jly 31)
Northern Celadon (IRE) 40 (8f,Not,G,Oct 24)
Northern Fleet 62 (16f,Asc,GF,Spt 28)
Northern Grey 40 (8f,Yar,GF,Spt 19)
Northern Judge 46 (7f,Nwm,G,Aug 24)
Northern Law 41 (16f,Nwm,GF,Aug 9)
Northern Spark 39 (9f,Ham,G,Jun 12)
North Reef (IRE) 60 (10f,Lin,GF,Aug 4)
North Song 79 (8f,Yor,GF,Aug 22)
Norwegian Blue (IRE) 56 (6f,Hay,S,Oct 6)
Nose No Bounds (IRE) 49 (11f,Ham,G,Jly 5)
Nosey Native 48 (12f,Pon,GF,Jun 4)
No Sympathy 31 (7f,Bri,F,May 9)
Notcomplainingbut (IRE) 36 (16f,Cur,GS,Oct 5)
Noufari (FR) 58 (16f,Nwc,F,Jun 29)
Noyan 37 (17f,Pon,G,Apr 23)
Nukud (USA) 31 (7f,Cat,GS,Mar 27)
Nunsharpa 50 (7f,Yor,G,Oct 12)
Nuzu (IRE) 47 (12f,Nwb,G,Aug 17)
Nwaamis (USA) 82 (8f,San,G,Apr 26)

Oakbury (IRE) 32 (12f,Lei,GF,Oct 15)
Oatey 47 (5f,Thi,G,Aug 23)
Obelos (USA) 58 (10½f,Yor,G,Oct 9)
Oberons Boy (IRE) 46 (8f,Asc,GF,Jun 18)
Oberon's Dart (IRE) 41 (6f,Yar,G,Aug 1)
Obsessive (USA) 56 (10½f,Yor,GF,May 14)
Occupandiste (IRE) 33 (8f,Lon,GF,Apr 21)
Ocean Grove (IRE) 45 (8f,Ayr,G,Aug 10)
Ocean Park 47 (8f,Asc,GF,May 1)
Ochos Rios (IRE) 48 (7f,Don,G,May 25)
Office Hours 49 (7f,Fol,F,Apr 23)
Oggi 56 (6f,Lei,G,Oct 28)
Old Irish 53 (13f,Nwb,S,May 29)
Old Provence 44 (12f,Nwm,GF,Apr 17)
Old Roma (IRE) 32 (6f,Pon,G,May 24)
Old Rouvel (USA) 78 (22f,Asc,GF,Jun 21)
Old School House 37 (16½f,Don,GF,Aug 1)
Oleana (IRE) 44 (7f,Sal,GF,Jun 26)
Oliviero (FR) 71 (12½f,Dea,G,Aug 25)
Omara (USA) 57 (10f,Yar,GF,Oct 23)
Once More for Luck (IRE) 57 (10f,Nwm,GF,Jly 26)
Onefortheditch (USA) 54 (8f,Lei,GF,Oct 14)
Onefourseven 38 (18f,Pon,G,Oct 21)
One Pound 41 (12½f,War,F,Jun 10)
Ood Dancer (USA) 68 (7f,Lin,GF,Jly 13)
Oops Pettie 69 (10f,Don,G,Spt 11)
Opalette 54 (10f,Wnd,GF,Aug 19)
Opal Jewel 38 (10f,Ayr,G,Aug 10)
Opaque 50 (14f,Not,GF,Apr 30)
Open Affair 40 (8f,Goo,GF,Aug 3)
Opera Buff (IRE) 62 (12f,Nwm,GF,Apr 17)
Options Open 77 (7f,Nwc,F,Jun 29)
Opulent 54 (10f,Yar,GF,Spt 18)
Orange Grouse (IRE) 39 (6f,Cur,S,Oct 19)
Orange Order (IRE) 42 (10f,Kem,GF,Aug 7)
Orange Place (IRE) 63 (7f,Goo,S,May 23)
Orchard Gold 37 (8f,Not,GF,Jly 26)
Orchestra Stall 73 (18f,Nwm,G,Oct 19)
Ordained 35 (10f,Ayr,G,Aug 21)
Oriane 33 (10f,Leo,S,Oct 28)
Oriel Lad 33 (7f,Yar,G,Spt 17)
Orinoco River (USA) 64 (12f,Pon,GF,Jun 4)
Orsay 72 (8f,Goo,GF,Jly 30)
Orthorhombus 33 (7f,Nwm,GF,Apr 17)
Ortolan 58 (7f,Sal,GF,Aug 22)
Oscar Schindler (IRE) 94 (12f,Asc,GF,Jun 21)
Otaiti (IRE) 67 (12½f,Lon,S,Oct 5)
Ottavio Farnese 30 (10f,Bri,G,Oct 2)
Otto E Mezzo 56 (12f,Hay,G,Spt 27)
Our Kris 54 (14f,Sal,GF,Aug 1)
Our Shadee (USA) 43 (8f,Lin,GF,Aug 4)
Out Line 59 (6f,Lin,GF,Jly 12)
Out on a Promise (IRE) 56 (12f,Nwm,GF,Apr 17)
Outstayed Welcome 51 (12f,Chp,GF,Jly 25)

Overbury (IRE) 81 (10f,Nwm,GF,Oct 17)
Overpower 33 (8f,Yar,F,Jun 5)
Overruled (IRE) 50 (14f,Hay,GS,May 24)
Oversman 46 (12f,Chs,G,May 8)
Owdbetts (IRE) 46 (10f,Bat,GF,Jun 15)
Owen Meany (FR) 72 (5f,Dea,G,Aug 24)

Paddy's Rice 48 (7f,War,F,Jun 5)
Pageboy 52 (6f,Ham,GF,Aug 14)
Painted Hall (USA) 37 (10f,Nwb,GF,May 17)
Paint It Black 50 (8f,Chp,GF,Jly 11)
Palacegate Jack (IRE) 63 (5f,San,GF,Spt 17)
Palacegate Touch 61 (5f,San,GF,Spt 17)
Palamon (USA) 46 (12f,Kem,GF,Jly 10)
Palatal (USA) 46 (12f,Lon,G,Spt 15)
Pallium (IRE) 41 (6f,Nwc,GF,Aug 4)
Palo Blanco 64 (6f,Don,G,Jun 8)
Paloma Bay (IRE) 53 (7f,Nwb,GS,Apr 19)
Panata (IRE) 59 (8f,Asc,GF,Spt 28)
Panther (IRE) 60 (5f,Chs,GS,Aug 31)
Paojiunic (IRE) 54 (7f,Kem,G,Spt 6)
Papaha (FR) 48 (7f,Lei,G,Apr 4)
Paper Cloud 43 (12f,Chp,GF,Jly 25)
Papering (IRE) 69 (12f,Asc,G,Oct 12)
Parade Sauvage (FR) 50 (8f,Lon,G,May 12)
Paradise Navy 61 (16f,War,F,Jun 10)
Paradise Waters 57 (12f,Kem,GF,Jun 12)
Paris Babe 42 (7f,Lin,GF,May 11)
Parliament Piece 55 (8f,Red,GF,May 13)
Parrot Jungle (IRE) 64 (8f,Asc,G,Oct 11)
Parsa (USA) 52 (8f,Lei,GF,Oct 14)
Passage Creeping (IRE) 51 (10f,Yar,G,Aug 1)
Passion For Life 83 (6f,Nwm,G,Oct 19)
Pasternak 65 (10½f,Yor,G,Oct 9)
Patch Of Blue 46 (8f,Cha,F,Jun 2)
Pater Noster (USA) 34 (8f,Not,GS,Aug 25)
Pathaze 30 (6f,Ham,GF,Aug 14)
Pat's Splendour 35 (10f,Goo,G,Aug 24)
Patsy Grimes 71 (7f,Yar,GF,Jly 4)
Pay Homage 68 (8f,Goo,G,May 21)
Pc's Cruiser (IRE) 40 (8f,Red,GF,May 13)
Peace Offering (IRE) 57 (10f,Leo,S,Apr 20)
Peace Prize (IRE) 34 (7f,Cur,G,Spt 21)
Pearl Dawn (IRE) 51 (7f,Bri,F,Jly 16)
Pearl d'Azur (USA) 56 (6f,Yor,G,Oct 12)
Pearl Venture 60 (16f,Asc,GF,Spt 28)
Peggy Spencer 43 (7f,Cat,GS,Mar 27)
Pegram (IRE) 34 (8f,Nwm,GF,May 5)
Pegwood (IRE) 38 (7f,Leo,S,Apr 20)
Pengamon 70 (7f,War,G,Apr 8)
Pennine Wind (IRE) 34 (10f,Fol,F,Jun 28)
Penny a Day (IRE) 75 (12f,Don,G,Oct 26)
Penny Drops 46 (8f,Don,G,Mar 21)
Penny Parkes 40 (5f,Edi,G,Jly 1)
Pentire 92 (12f,Asc,GF,Jly 27)
Pepitist 36 (11f,Red,GF,Jly 11)
Peppers (IRE) 52 (9f,Nwm,G,Nov 1)
Pep Talk (USA) 51 (10½f,Yor,G,Oct 10)
Percutant 86 (12½f,Dea,G,Aug 25)
Percy Braithwaite (IRE) 72 (8f,Crl,GS,Apr 26)
Perfect Brave 40 (5f,Thi,GF,May 17)
Perfect Gift 33 (17f,Bat,GF,Aug 8)
Perilous Plight 51 (7f,Bri,F,May 9)
Perpetual Light 31 (9f,Nwm,G,Nov 1)
Perryston View 68 (6f,Nwm,GF,May 4)
Persian Affair (IRE) 33 (9f,Goo,GF,Jun 14)
Persian Butterfly 49 (6f,Wnd,GF,Jun 17)
Persian Conquest (IRE) 31 (10f,Lin,GF,May 18)
Persian Dawn 34 (8f,Asc,G,Oct 11)
Persian Fayre 71 (7f,Nwm,G,Nov 2)
Persian Punch (IRE) 66 (15f,Nwm,GF,Jly 11)
Persian Secret (FR) 37 (8f,Thi,GF,May 18)
Personal Love (USA) 38 (7f,Goo,GF,Spt 26)
Peter Monamy 37 (12f,Goo,GF,Jun 7)
Petite Fantasy 45 (6f,Cur,GS,May 25)
Petit Point (IRE) 50 (6f,Wnd,GF,Jun 10)
Petoskin 46 (11½f,Yar,GF,Oct 23)
Petraco (IRE) 45 (5f,War,G,Apr 8)
Phanan 38 (10f,San,G,Aug 31)
Phantom Gold 87 (12f,Asc,GF,Jun 21)
Phantom Quest 72 (8f,Don,GF,Jly 17)
Pharaoh's Joy 45 (5f,Sal,F,Spt 5)
Pharly Dancer 52 (12f,Hay,G,Jly 5)
Pharmacy 54 (7f,Yor,G,Oct 12)
Phase One (IRE) 40 (10½f,Hay,G,Jun 7)
Philgun 38 (11f,Ham,G,Jly 5)
Philmist 36 (12f,Edi,G,Jly 8)
Philosopher (IRE) 54 (8½f,Eps,GF,Jun 9)
Phone Fee (USA) 40 (5f,Dea,S,May 26)
Phonetic 45 (8f,Kem,GS,May 25)
Pibarnon (FR) 61 (15½f,Lon,S,May 19)
Pickens (USA) 50 (12f,Nwm,GF,Apr 17)
Pike Creek (USA) 64 (12f,Don,GF,Spt 13)
Pilsudski (IRE) 92 (12f,G,Oct 26)
Pine Essence (USA) 30 (8f,Not,G,Apr 2)
Pine Needle 55 (12½f,Nwc,G,May 23)
Pine Ridge Lad (IRE) 58 (7½f,Bev,G,Mar 30)
Pinkerton Polka 35 (8f,Bri,F,Apr 12)
Pinkerton's Pal 71 (8f,Goo,G,May 21)
Pip's Dream 39 (12f,Lei,GF,Jun 3)
Pistol (IRE) 62 (10f,Asc,GF,Aug 2)
Pivotal 88 (5f,Asc,GF,Jun 21)
Place de L'Opera 73 (12f,Nwm,GF,Jly 20)
Playmaker 44 (6f,Thi,GF,Aug 2)
Pleading 71 (6f,Lei,GS,May 27)
Pleasant Surprise 69 (12f,Asc,GF,Jun 20)
Please Suzanne 69 (7f,Lin,GF,Aug 4)
Pleasure Time 36 (5f,Nwm,GF,Jun 28)
Plum First 50 (6f,Red,GF,Jun 11)
Poddington 42 (10f,Yar,G,Oct 30)
Poetry (IRE) 49 (7f,Goo,GS,May 22)
Pointer 45 (6f,Sal,G,Aug 15)
Polar Champ 48 (10f,Lei,F,Spt 10)
Polar Eclipse 65 (8f,Goo,GF,Aug 3)
Polaris Flight (USA) 66 (12f,Cha,F,Jun 2)
Polar Prince (IRE) 73 (7f,Yor,GF,Aug 22)
Polar Prospect 53 (7f,San,GF,Jly 5)
Polar Refrain 41 (6f,Yar,GF,Spt 19)
Poliglote 48 (12f,Lon,S,Oct 20)
Polinesso 66 (8f,Don,GF,Jly 17)
Polish Rhythm (IRE) 34 (10f,Yar,GF,Oct 23)
Polish Spring (IRE) 40 (7f,Nwm,GF,May 3)
Polish Widow 36 (7f,Nwm,GF,Apr 17)
Polly Golightly 51 (5f,Lei,GF,Aug 19)
Polly Peculiar 49 (8f,Red,F,Spt 27)
Polo Kit (IRE) 41 (16f,Goo,GF,Spt 14)
Polska (USA) 66 (8f,Asc,GF,Spt 28)
Poltarf (USA) 65 (12f,Nwb,G,Aug 16)
Polydamas 70 (12f,Yor,GF,May 14)
Pommard (IRE) 42 (8f,Don,GF,Spt 13)
Pomona 57 (8f,Wnd,S,Aug 24)
Poplar Bluff (IRE) 39 (6½f,Dea,GS,Aug 11)
Poppy Carew (IRE) 83 (10f,Nwm,GF,Aug 9)
Portelet 70 (5f,Eps,G,Aug 26)
Portend 72 (6f,Goo,G,Aug 24)
Portuguese Lil 40 (8f,Nwm,GF,May 5)
Posidonas 94 (12f,Asc,GF,Jun 21)
Possessive Artiste 38 (8f,Kem,GS,May 25)
Power Game 48 (8f,Ham,G,Spt 29)
Prague Spring 56 (16f,Bev,GF,Jly 16)
Prancing 80 (8f,Asc,GF,Spt 28)
Precedency 35 (12f,Hay,G,Jly 5)
Precious Girl 33 (5f,Ayr,GS,May 8)
Predappio 64 (10f,Cur,GF,Jly 27)
Premier Censure 30 (7f,Lei,G,Apr 4)
Premier Generation (IRE) 42 (8f,Sal,GF,May 16)
Premier League (IRE) 53 (10f,Wnd,GF,May 13)
Premier Night 42 (8f,Kem,GF,May 6)
Premium Gift 43 (5f,Bev,GF,Aug 14)
Prends Ca (IRE) 70 (6f,Nwm,GF,Oct 4)
Present Arms (USA) 59 (12f,Lei,GF,Oct 14)
Present Generation 50 (8f,Kem,GS,May 25)
Present 'n Correct 32 (5f,Thi,GF,Spt 7)
Present Situation 59 (8f,Lei,GF,Oct 14)
Press On Nicky 43 (7f,Nwb,GF,Spt 20)
Pricket (USA) 72 (12f,Eps,G,Jun 7)
Pride of Brixton 56 (5f,Cat,G,Oct 19)
Pride of Hayling (IRE) 47 (5f,Bri,F,Aug 18)
Pride of Pendle 56 (8f,Ayr,GF,Spt 20)
Prima Cominna 46 (7f,Nwm,GF,Apr 17)
Prima Silk 61 (6f,Lin,GF,Jun 1)
Prima Volta 38 (8f,Wnd,S,Aug 24)
Prime Light 31 (7f,Sal,S,May 22)
Primo Lara 71 (7f,Nwc,F,Jun 29)
Prince Arthur (IRE) 74 (10f,San,G,Apr 27)
Prince Aslia 32 (5f,Hay,G,Apr 6)
Prince Babar 79 (8f,Nwm,G,Nov 2)
Prince Danzig (IRE) 50 (12f,Bri,F,Jun 4)
Prince Kinsky 40 (14f,Not,S,Oct 31)
Princely Hush (IRE) 46 (5f,Lin,GS,Aug 29)
Princely Sound 43 (6f,Chs,G,May 8)
Prince of Andros (USA) 84 (10f,Cur,G,Jun 8)
Prince of India 72 (8f,Asc,GF,Jun 18)
Prince of My Heart 79 (9f,Nwm,GF,Oct 5)
Prince Rudolf (IRE) 36 (8f,Bri,F,Jly 17)
Princess Danielle 49 (10f,Rip,S,Aug 31)
Princess Pamgaddy 37 (8f,Bri,F,Aug 5)
Priolina (IRE) 65 (12f,Asc,GF,Spt 28)
Priory Belle (IRE) 56 (8f,Asc,GF,Jun 19)
Private Song (USA) 66 (12f,Asc,GF,Jun 20)
Prizefighter 52 (8f,Crl,F,Aug 5)
Prize Giving 67 (12f,Asc,GF,Jun 21)
Prize Pupil (IRE) 60 (10f,San,GS,May 27)
Progression 69 (12f,Nwm,GF,Apr 17)
Projection (USA) 70 (7f,Nwm,GF,Apr 17)
Promissory 32 (10f,Nwb,GF,Jly 19)
Promptly (IRE) 40 (6f,Pon,G,Apr 23)
Proper Blue (USA) 68 (10f,Asc,G,Oct 12)
Prospector's Cove 55 (10f,Kem,G,Apr 6)
Prospero 40 (10f,Goo,GF,Spt 14)
Proton 38 (12f,Don,G,Oct 26)
Pro Trader (USA) 52 (8f,Leo,S,Apr 20)
Proud Brigadier (IRE) 37 (8f,Wnd,G,Aug 12)
Proud Image 52 (11f,War,F,Oct 8)
Proud Look 38 (6f,Don,S,Mar 23)
Proud Monk 55 (7f,Nwb,S,Oct 24)
Proud Titania (IRE) 42 (7f,Cur,GS,Apr 27)
Province 32 (8f,Nwm,G,Aug 24)
Prudent Pet 41 (7f,Red,GF,May 13)
Prudent Princess 41 (8f,War,G,May 25)
Prussian Blue (USA) 86 (14f,Yor,G,Aug 21)
Psicossis 38 (12f,Kem,GF,Jun 12)
Puce 56 (12f,Goo,GF,Aug 3)
Punishment 86 (12f,Asc,GF,Jun 21)
Punkah (USA) 47 (10f,Wnd,GF,Jun 17)
Purple Fling 63 (6f,Goo,GS,May 22)
Purple Splash 64 (15f,War,GS,Apr 13)
Pusey Street Boy 30 (8f,War,G,May 25)
Pusey Street Girl 35 (6f,Rip,GF,Jun 20)

Qasida (IRE) 55 (10½f,Yor,G,Aug 21)
Q Factor 60 (8f,Not,GF,Jun 19)
Quakers Field 64 (12f,Goo,GF,Jly 30)
Quality (IRE) 57 (7f,Yar,GF,Aug 22)
Quango 39 (12f,Yor,GF,Aug 22)
Queen Bee 33 (12f,Bri,F,Aug 5)
Queenfisher 47 (8f,Lin,GF,Jly 13)
Queen of All Birds (IRE) 61 (8f,Lin,GF,May 10)
Queen of Shannon (IRE) 38 (8f,Wnd,GF,Aug 3)
Queens Consul (IRE) 72 (8f,Yor,G,Jly 12)
Queen's Insignia (USA) 30 (8f,Not,S,Oct 31)
Quest Again 56 (14f,Not,GF,Jun 10)
Questing Star 32 (10½f,Yor,G,Oct 10)
Questonia 71 (8f,Asc,GF,Spt 28)
Quiet Arch (IRE) 46 (10½f,Yor,G,Oct 10)
Quilling 58 (7f,Red,F,Spt 27)
Quillwork (USA) 30 (12f,Nwm,GF,Oct 3)
Quintus Decimus 34 (8f,Chp,GS,May 27)
Quinze 43 (7f,Bri,F,Jly 16)
Quivira 57 (12f,Nwm,GF,Jun 28)
Quota 56 (10f,San,G,Apr 26)

Raased 33 (9f,Ham,G,Jun 12)

Rabican (IRE) 66 (7f,Nwm,GF,Jly 11)
Racing Brenda 35 (8f,Ham,G,Spt 2)
Racing Hawk (USA) 35 (8f,Wnd,GF,Jun 3)
Radevore 70 (10f,Dea,G,May 16)
Radiant Star 56 (10½f,Yor,GF,May 16)
Raed 48 (8f,Red,GF,Oct 17)
Raffles Rooster 43 (14f,Hay,G,Jly 5)
Ragmar (FR) 68 (10½f,Lon,GF,Apr 21)
Ragsak Jameel (USA) 48 (12f,Lei,GF,Aug 19)
Raheefa (USA) 41 (10f,Goo,GF,Spt 14)
Raheen (USA) 30 (8f,Rip,GF,Apr 18)
Rainbow Blues (IRE) 64 (8f,Cur,GS,May 26)
Rainbow Dancer (FR) 41 (12f,Lon,S,Oct 20)
Rainbow Top 62 (12f,Chs,GF,Jun 6)
Raindeer Quest 35 (10½f,Hay,GF,Aug 16)
Raise A Prince (FR) 54 (10½f,Hay,G,Spt 27)
Raisonnable 51 (8f,Lon,G,May 12)
Raiyoun (IRE) 31 (7f,Cur,G,Spt 21)
Rakis (IRE) 67 (7f,San,GF,Jun 14)
Ralitsa (IRE) 30 (14f,Red,GF,Oct 8)
Rambling Bear 70 (6f,Hay,GF,Spt 7)
Rambold 51 (6f,Lin,GF,Aug 10)
Rambo Waltzer 53 (7½f,Bev,G,Mar 30)
Ramooz (USA) 81 (7f,Asc,GF,Spt 28)
Ramsey Hope 43 (5f,Crl,F,Jun 27)
Random 48 (6f,Goo,GF,Aug 2)
Random Kindness 37 (10f,Pon,GF,Jun 4)
Rasayel (USA) 53 (12f,Edi,GS,Nov 7)
Rash Gift 31 (7f,Lei,GF,Oct 14)
Raven's Roost (IRE) 34 (8f,War,F,Jun 5)
Rawi 34 (6f,Sal,G,May 5)
React 69 (6f,Nwm,GF,Jun 1)
Ready Teddy (IRE) 36 (5f,Edi,GF,Jun 24)
Reaganesque (USA) 37 (12f,Kem,GF,Aug 7)
Real Gem 30 (6f,Chp,GF,Jly 6)
Really A Dream (IRE) 59 (7f,Nwm,GF,Apr 17)
Rebel County (IRE) 73 (8f,Nwm,G,Oct 19)
Record Lover (IRE) 31 (12f,Pon,GF,Aug 18)
Red Admiral 49 (6f,Yar,GF,Jly 4)
Red Carnival (USA) 51 (8f,Asc,G,Oct 11)
Red Five 38 (5f,Ham,GF,May 18)
Red Nymph 69 (6f,Goo,G,Aug 24)
Red Raja 34 (12f,Nwb,GF,Spt 20)
Red Robbo (CAN) 64 (8f,San,G,Apr 26)
Redskin Lady 31 (6f,Sal,GF,Aug 1)
Red Spectacle (IRE) 40 (14f,Red,GF,May 27)
Redstella (USA) 45 (12f,Yor,G,Jun 14)
Red Tie Affair (USA) 38 (10f,Not,GF,Spt 24)
Red Time 35 (7f,Bri,F,May 9)
Red Valerian 48 (10f,Red,F,Aug 10)
Reefa's Mill (IRE) 40 (10f,Lei,G,Apr 27)
Reem Fever (IRE) 30 (7f,Kem,G,Spt 6)
Regal Archive (IRE) 73 (9f,Cha,F,Jun 2)
Regal Eagle 43 (12f,Nwb,GF,Jun 13)
Regal Fanfare (IRE) 41 (6f,Nwm,GF,Jun 1)
Regal Splendour (CAN) 35 (7f,Lei,GF,Oct 14)
Regiment (IRE) 46 (8f,Kem,G,Apr 6)
Rehaab 34 (12f,Bri,F,Spt 4)
Reimei 56 (12f,Nwm,GF,Jun 28)
Reinhardt (IRE) 33 (8f,Sal,GF,Jun 26)
Remaadi Sun 73 (14f,Yor,G,Aug 21)
Remontant (IRE) 35 (10f,Pon,GF,Jun 10)
Renown 52 (12f,Bri,F,Jun 4)
Renzo (IRE) 49 (11f,Red,GF,Nov 5)
Repertory 59 (5f,Hay,G,Apr 6)
Requested 39 (14f,Not,GS,Aug 25)
Rescue Time (IRE) 39 (10f,Leo,S,Apr 20)
Resounder (USA) 52 (7f,Nwm,GF,Oct 4)
Respect A Secret 34 (6f,Red,GF,May 28)
Restructure (IRE) 87 (8f,Asc,GF,Jun 18)
Ret Frem (IRE) 39 (8f,Crl,F,Jun 26)
Reticent 35 (10f,San,GF,Aug 14)
Return To Brighton 41 (8f,Bat,F,Jun 29)
Reverand Thickness 52 (8f,War,GS,Apr 13)
Reveuse de Jour (IRE) 41 (7f,Kem,GF,Apr 29)
Rex Mundi 53 (10f,Red,GF,Nov 5)
Riccarton 33 (8f,Ham,G,Spt 2)
Rich Glow 44 (5f,Nwm,G,Jly 9)
Ring of Vision (IRE) 49 (10f,Nwm,GF,Aug 2)
Rinus Manor (IRE) 37 (5f,Crl,GF,May 10)
Rio Duvida 52 (8½f,Eps,G,Jun 7)
Riparius (USA) 70 (14f,Hay,GS,Jun 8)
Rise Up Singing 37 (7f,Nwm,G,Jun 29)
Rising Colours 54 (7f,Lon,S,Oct 20)
Rising Dough (IRE) 63 (10f,Eps,GF,Jun 9)
Rising Spray 49 (12f,Nwb,GF,Spt 20)
Risky Romeo 44 (8f,War,F,May 6)
Risky Rose 37 (14f,Not,F,Jly 6)
Risky Tu 34 (10f,Bev,GF,Apr 25)
Rival Bid (USA) 58 (10f,Lei,GF,Oct 15)
River Bay (USA) 47 (8f,Lon,GS,Oct 6)
Rivercare (IRE) 41 (11½f,San,GS,May 28)
River Keen (IRE) 70 (12f,Don,G,Oct 26)
River North (IRE) 66 (12f,Nwb,G,Aug 16)
Rivers Magic 44 (8f,Asc,G,Oct 11)
River Tern 42 (5f,Rip,G,Aug 17)
Riyadian 59 (12f,Nwm,GF,May 3)
Road Racer (IRE) 30 (12f,Bev,GF,Spt 18)
Robamaset (IRE) 48 (7f,Lei,GF,Oct 14)
Robellion 54 (6f,Nwm,GF,Aug 2)
Roberto Riva 31 (10½f,Hay,G,Spt 27)
Robingo (IRE) 45 (14f,Hay,GS,May 6)
Robo Magic (USA) 37 (6f,Lin,GF,Jun 1)
Robusta (IRE) 42 (8f,Nwm,GF,Apr 17)
Rockcracker (IRE) 48 (5f,Crl,GF,May 10)
Rock Group 40 (12f,Lei,G,Apr 4)
Rock Symphony 69 (6f,Pon,GF,Jun 10)
Rock The Barney (IRE) 36 (12f,Lei,GS,May 27)
Rockville Pike (IRE) 44 (7f,Lei,G,Apr 4)
Rocky Forum 64 (20f,Asc,GF,Jun 18)
Rocky Oasis (USA) 57 (10f,San,GS,May 28)
Rocky Waters (USA) 44 (8f,Bri,F,Jly 17)
Roderick Hudson 49 (7f,Nwb,G,Aug 17)
Roi de la Mer (IRE) 58 (8f,Not,GF,Jun 19)
Roi du Nord (FR) 45 (10f,Yar,GF,Spt 18)
Roisin Clover 60 (12f,Kem,GF,Apr 29)
Rokeby Bowl 69 (12f,Goo,GF,Aug 2)
Roman Gold (IRE) 52 (10½f,Hay,G,Apr 6)
Roman Reel (USA) 58 (8f,Chp,GF,Jun 30)
Romios (IRE) 78 (12f,Nwm,GF,Oct 17)
Ron's Secret 52 (10f,Wnd,GF,Jun 10)
Rory 56 (10f,Yar,GF,Spt 18)
Roseate Lodge 33 (7f,Cat,GF,Aug 6)
Roseberry Avenue (IRE) 51 (16½ f,San,G,Aug 30)
Rose of Glenn 35 (12f,Lei,GF,Oct 15)
Roses In The Snow (IRE) 67 (12f,Asc,G,Oct 12)
Rossel (USA) 46 (11f,Red,F,Jun 21)
Roufontaine 63 (10f,San,G,Aug 31)
Rouge Rancon (USA) 51 (10½f,Yor,GF,May 15)
Roushan 61 (7f,San,GF,Spt 18)
Roussi (USA) 38 (8f,Rip,G,Apr 10)
Roving Minstrel 85 (8f,Don,S,Mar 23)
Royal Action 50 (8f,Not,GS,Apr 12)
Royal Applause 71 (5f,Asc,GF,Jun 21)
Royal Canaska 61 (8f,Asc,GF,Jun 18)
Royal Ceilidh (IRE) 57 (8f,Nwm,G,Oct 19)
Royal Circus 35 (16f,War,F,Jun 10)
Royal Court (IRE) 78 (12f,Hay,G,Jly 6)
Royal Diversion (IRE) 55 (12f,Nwb,S,Oct 26)
Royal Dome (IRE) 61 (5f,Hay,GF,Aug 10)
Royale Figurine (IRE) 76 (5f,Asc,G,Oct 12)
Royal Expose (USA) 38 (12f,Sal,G,May 5)
Royal Expression 55 (16½f,Don,G,Jun 8)
Royal Jade 50 (7f,Yar,F,Jun 12)
Royal of Legend 30 (8f,Pon,G,Spt 3)
Royal Mark (IRE) 62 (8f,Nwm,GF,May 5)
Royal Philosopher 84 (8f,Nwb,GS,Apr 20)
Royal Result (USA) 65 (8f,Red,GF,Oct 17)
Royal Scimitar (USA) 76 (12f,Hay,G,Jly 6)
Royal Thimble (IRE) 44 (10f,Bat,F,Jly 18)
Royal Vacation 34 (17f,Pon,GF,Aug 18)
Roy Boy 36 (10f,Red,GF,May 28)
Rubbiyati 32 (7f,Fol,G,Jly 3)
Rumba Rhythm (CAN) 43 (7f,Nwm,GF,Jun 21)
Runaway Pete (USA) 48 (16f,War,F,Jun 10)
Running Flame (FR) 39 (12f,Lon,S,Oct 20)
Runs in the Family 36 (6f,Rip,S,Aug 31)
Rupert (FR) 73 (9f,Cha,F,Jun 2)
Rushcutter Bay 70 (5f,Hay,GF,Aug 10)
Rushen Raider 59 (16f,Bev,GF,Aug 14)
Rusk 55 (12f,Hay,G,Spt 27)
Russian Music 80 (8f,Goo,GF,Aug 3)
Russian Rascal (IRE) 41 (8f,Nwc,G,May 23)
Russian Request (IRE) 42 (8f,Nwm,GF,Jun 1)
Russian Revival (USA) 83 (6f,Nwm,G,Oct 19)
Russian Snows (IRE) 74 (12f,Yor,G,Aug 21)
Ruwy 39 (8f,San,G,Aug 31)
Ruznama (USA) 73 (7f,Yor,GF,Aug 22)

Sabaah Elfull 30 (6f,Lei,G,Oct 28)
Sabot 49 (7f,Kem,GF,Apr 29)
Sabrak (IRE) 51 (8f,Ayr,GS,Jly 4)
Sacho (IRE) 53 (10f,Nwm,GF,Apr 16)
Sacrament 72 (9f,Nwm,GF,Apr 17)
Sacred Loch (USA) 36 (10½f,Yor,G,Oct 10)
Sacred Mirror (IRE) 40 (12f,Fol,F,Jun 28)
Saddlehome (USA) 49 (6f,Hay,G,Spt 27)
Sadler's Realm 42 (10f,Ayr,G,Aug 21)
Sadler's Walk 53 (10f,Yar,GF,Spt 18)
Safey Ana (USA) 42 (7f,Yar,GF,Aug 22)
Safio 40 (6f,Ayr,G,Aug 10)
Sagar Pride (IRE) 56 (8f,Lon,G,May 12)
Sagebrush Roller 64 (7f,Nwc,G,Apr 8)
Saheeel (USA) 73 (6f,Nwm,G,Nov 2)
Sahhar 30 (11½f,Yar,GF,Aug 22)
Saifan 69 (8f,Red,F,Aug 10)
Sailormaite 65 (6f,Hay,S,Oct 6)
Saint Express 66 (5f,Nwm,GF,Jly 20)
Sakharov 42 (7f,Red,GF,May 27)
Salaman (FR) 71 (16f,Goo,GF,Spt 14)
Saleemah (USA) 59 (8f,Sal,G,Aug 15)
Sally Slade 62 (5f,Goo,G,Jun 7)
Sally's Twins 32 (12f,Nwb,S,Oct 26)
Salmis 52 (8f,San,G,Aug 30)
Salmon Ladder (USA) 96 (10f,Asc,GF,Jun 22)
Salska 44 (15f,War,GF,Jly 13)
Saltando (IRE) 42 (8f,Nwm,GF,Oct 17)
Salty Girl (IRE) 34 (10f,Red,GF,May 28)
Samara (IRE) 61 (8f,Pon,G,May 24)
Samara Song 34 (8f,Bat,GF,Spt 9)
Samba Sharply 68 (8f,Asc,GF,May 1)
Same Old Wish (USA) 97 (8f,G,Oct 26)
Samim (USA) 45 (10½f,Hay,G,Apr 6)
Samraan (USA) 79 (14½f,Don,GF,Spt 14)
Samsolom 44 (7f,Yar,GF,Aug 22)
Samwar 69 (6f,Goo,G,Aug 24)
Sandabar 50 (7f,Fol,GF,Apr 16)
Sandhill (IRE) 53 (8f,San,GF,Spt 17)
Sandmoor Chambray 68 (8f,Nwm,G,Oct 19)
Sand Star 33 (7f,Sal,GF,May 16)
Sandy Floss (IRE) 54 (8f,Not,GS,Apr 12)
Sangria (USA) 63 (9f,Lon,GS,Oct 6)
Sanmartino (IRE) 76 (16f,Nwm,GF,Oct 5)
Sanoosea (USA) 72 (10½f,Yor,GF,May 16)
Santella Katie 40 (8f,San,GF,Jly 25)
Santillana (USA) 81 (10f,San,G,Apr 27)
Sapphire Son (IRE) 39 (7f,Fol,G,Jly 3)
Sarasota Storm 35 (14f,Yar,GF,Aug 8)
Sarawat 51 (14f,Yor,GF,May 15)
Sardonic 51 (10f,Nwb,GF,Jun 13)
Sarmatian (USA) 43 (10f,Ayr,GS,May 31)
Sarum 34 (7f,Fol,GF,Jun 5)
Saseedo (USA) 72 (7f,Nwm,G,Oct 19)
Sasuru 79 (10½f,Yor,G,Jun 15)
Satin Bell 54 (7f,Nwb,GS,Apr 19)
Satin Lover 62 (14f,Hay,GS,Jun 8)

Sawa-Id 42 (10f,Fol,GF,Aug 16)
Sayeh (IRE) 42 (9f,Goo,GF,Spt 13)
Scaraben 65 (8f,Edi,GS,Nov 7)
Scarlet Plume 65 (8f,Asc,G,Oct 11)
Scathebury 33 (7f,Edi,GF,Aug 29)
Scenic Dancer 32 (11½f,Wnd,GF,Jun 3)
Scenicris (IRE) 51 (8f,Not,S,Oct 31)
Scharnhorst 61 (7f,Fol,F,Apr 23)
Scherma 34 (8f,San,G,Aug 31)
School Boy 48 (7f,Chp,GF,Jly 11)
Scimitar 35 (8f,Bat,GS,Spt 30)
Scissor Ridge 44 (6f,Lei,G,Oct 28)
Scorpius 34 (7½f,Bev,G,Mar 30)
Scottish Bambi 47 (10f,Lin,GF,May 10)
Scottish Park 39 (8f,Rip,G,May 19)
Sea Dane 68 (6f,Nwm,G,Oct 19)
Sea Danzig 49 (7f,Yar,G,Oct 30)
Sea-Deer 74 (5f,Hay,GF,Aug 10)
Sea Devil 32 (7f,Cat,GS,Mar 27)
Sea Freedom 57 (16f,Kem,GS,May 25)
Sea God 32 (10f,Don,GF,Jun 30)
Sea of Stone (USA) 37 (10f,Wnd,GF,Jly 15)
Sea Plane 42 (18f,Nwm,G,Oct 19)
Seasonal Splendour (IRE) 69 (16f,Kem,G,Apr 6)
Sea Spray (IRE) 48 (10½f,Yor,GF,May 14)
Sea Thunder 42 (6f,Pon,GF,Apr 29)
Sea Victor 70 (20f,Goo,GF,Jly 31)
Second Colours (USA) 34 (8½f,Bev,GF,Jly 5)
Secret Aly (CAN) 63 (10f,Yar,GF,Spt 18)
Secret Miss 41 (5f,Lin,GF,May 18)
Secret Pleasure (IRE) 45 (6f,Lin,GF,Jly 12)
Secret Service (IRE) 61 (14f,Yor,G,Spt 4)
Secret Spring (FR) 56 (9f,Nwm,GF,Oct 5)
Secret Voucher 52 (5f,War,GS,Apr 13)
Sedbergh (USA) 32 (14f,Red,GF,Jly 11)
Seeking Fortune (USA) 48 (8f,San,GF,Spt 18)
Seigneurial 71 (7f,Nwm,G,Oct 19)
Seirenes 46 (10f,Don,G,Oct 25)
Sejaal (IRE) 44 (8½f,Eps,GF,Spt 24)
Select Few 67 (8f,San,G,Aug 30)
Self Expression 30 (8f,Pon,G,Apr 17)
Selhurstpark Flyer (IRE) 72 (6f,Eps,G,Jun 8)
Sensation 51 (8f,Cha,F,Jun 2)
Sense of Priority 54 (6f,Cat,GS,Jly 3)
Separate Lives (SWE) 58 (20f,Lon,S,Oct 5)
Serape 33 (6f,Lin,GF,Aug 10)
Serendipity (FR) 70 (8f,Goo,GF,Jly 30)
Serenus (USA) 55 (12f,Eps,GF,Spt 24)
Sergeyev (IRE) 87 (7f,Yor,GF,Aug 22)
Serious 73 (8f,Goo,GF,Jun 7)
Serious Hurry 32 (5f,Ham,G,Jun 12)
Serious Sensation 45 (7f,Lin,G,Oct 4)
Set Adrift 58 (11f,Nwb,G,Apr 19)
Set the Fashion 47 (8f,Not,GF,Jly 26)
Seventeens Lucky 62 (8f,San,GF,Aug 14)
Shaamit (IRE) 82 (12f,Eps,G,Jun 8)
Shaanxi (USA) 80 (8f,Dea,G,Aug 15)
Shabanaz 52 (10f,Pon,G,Spt 3)
Shadirwan (IRE) 72 (20f,Asc,GF,Jun 18)
Shadow Jury 50 (5f,Nwm,G,Jly 9)
Shadow Leader 65 (13f,Nwb,GF,Jly 20)
Shady Girl (IRE) 33 (6f,Thi,GF,Apr 19)
Shaffishayes 55 (10f,Red,GF,Nov 5)
Shaft of Light 47 (12f,Nwm,GF,Oct 17)
Shaha 43 (12f,Goo,GF,Aug 3)
Shahik (USA) 47 (10f,Sal,GS,Oct 2)
Shake the Yoke 76 (8f,Asc,GF,Jun 19)
Shakiyr (FR) 37 (16f,Bev,GF,Apr 12)
Shalateeno 43 (10f,Chp,G,Aug 26)
Shamadara (IRE) 65 (12f,Lon,G,Jun 23)
Shamanic 69 (6f,Eps,G,Jun 8)
Shambo 48 (13½f,Chs,G,May 9)
Shamrock Fair (IRE) 40 (8f,Sal,G,Aug 15)
Shanaladee 59 (14f,Goo,G,Aug 24)
Shanghai Girl 73 (5f,Don,G,Oct 26)
Shantou (USA) 84 (14½f,Don,GF,Spt 14)
Sharaf (IRE) 51 (12f,Hay,GF,Aug 9)
Sharaf Kabeer 69 (12f,Nwm,GF,Oct 4)
Sharkashka (IRE) 48 (12f,Bev,GF,Jly 5)
Sharp Consul (IRE) 65 (10f,Wnd,G,Aug 12)
Sharpical 66 (10f,San,G,Aug 31)
Sharp Imp 39 (7f,Bri,F,Spt 3)
Sharp Monty 41 (6f,Lei,GF,Jun 3)
Sharp 'n' Shady 41 (7f,Yar,G,Oct 30)
Sharp 'n Smart 34 (6f,Fol,GS,Oct 21)
Sharp Pearl 44 (5f,Bri,GF,Aug 28)
Sharp Prospect 41 (7f,Hay,GF,Spt 7)
Sharp Rebuff 59 (8f,Goo,GF,Jun 7)
Sharp Shuffle (IRE) 58 (7f,Kem,G,Spt 6)
Shashi (IRE) 48 (5f,Not,GF,Jly 26)
Shavinsky 34 (8f,Nwm,GF,Jun 1)
Shawanni 52 (8f,Lon,G,May 12)
Shayim (USA) 58 (7f,San,GF,Jun 14)
Sheer Danzig (IRE) 73 (12f,Yor,GF,Aug 22)
Shehab (IRE) 50 (8½f,Bev,GF,Jun 6)
Shemozzle (IRE) 80 (12f,Nwm,GF,Jly 20)
Shenango (IRE) 42 (10f,Wnd,GF,Jun 3)
Sheraka (IRE) 66 (10f,Cur,G,Jun 8)
Sheraz (IRE) 45 (12f,Thi,GF,Apr 20)
Sheriff 30 (16f,Goo,GF,Jun 6)
Sherpas (IRE) 61 (12f,Nwm,GF,Apr 16)
She's My Love 55 (7f,Nwm,G,Oct 19)
She's Simply Great (IRE) 31 (8f,Pon,GF,Jly 9)
Shift Again (IRE) 48 (12f,Kem,GF,Jun 12)
Shikari's Son 63 (6f,Yor,G,Jly 13)
Shinerolla 62 (8f,Don,S,Mar 23)
Shining Cloud 53 (5f,Nwm,GF,Oct 3)
Shining Dancer 52 (16f,Asc,GF,Spt 28)
Shining Example 62 (12f,Kem,GF,Jun 1)
Shirley Sue 48 (16f,Goo,GF,Spt 14)
Shirley Venture 48 (14f,Yar,GF,Aug 8)
Shontaine 45 (7f,Cat,GF,Jly 25)
Shooting Light (IRE) 49 (14f,San,GS,Aug 23)
Show Faith (IRE) 38 (9f,Nwm,GF,Oct 5)
Shu Gaa (IRE) 44 (11f,Red,GF,May 27)
Sicarian 33 (14f,Hay,G,Spt 28)
Side Note 47 (8f,Sal,GF,May 2)
Siege Perilous (IRE) 39 (14f,Not,S,Oct 31)
Siesta Time (USA) 34 (12f,Bri,F,Aug 6)
Sihafi (USA) 42 (7f,Cat,G,Jun 1)
Silca Blanka (IRE) 65 (8½f,Eps,G,Jun 7)
Silent Expression 71 (7f,Lin,GF,Aug 4)
Silently 77 (10f,San,GS,May 27)
Silk Cottage 52 (5f,Ham,GF,Aug 8)
Silk Masque (USA) 53 (7f,Nwb,GS,Apr 19)
Silktail (IRE) 50 (12f,Fol,F,Jun 28)
Sil Sila (IRE) 86 (10½f,Cha,G,Jun 9)
Silverdale Knight 37 (12f,Crl,F,Jun 13)
Silver Dome (USA) 69 (10f,San,G,Apr 27)
Silver Groom (IRE) 53 (10f,Nwm,GF,Jun 28)
Silver Harrow 54 (7f,Lei,GF,Oct 15)
Silver Hunter (USA) 34 (11½f,San,GF,Jun 14)
Silvering (FR) 35 (10f,Lon,S,Oct 5)
Silver Prey (USA) 50 (8f,Nwm,GF,Oct 3)
Silver Showers (USA) 37 (8f,Bat,GF,May 11)
Silver Welcome 39 (7f,Cat,GS,Jly 4)
Silver Wing (USA) 35 (12½f,War,F,May 6)
Silvian Bliss (USA) 53 (8f,Asc,GF,Jun 19)
Silvretta (IRE) 44 (12f,Nwm,G,Nov 1)
Simand 32 (10f,Not,GF,Jly 26)
Singapore Sting (USA) 43 (7f,Nwm,GF,Apr 17)
Singspiel (IRE) 90 (12f,G,Oct 26)
Sing Up 50 (6f,Not,GF,May 24)
Sing With the Band 57 (5f,Hay,GF,Aug 10)
Sinking Sun 47 (10f,Pon,GF,Spt 26)
Sir Arthur Hobbs 39 (8f,Thi,F,Jly 26)
Sir Joey (USA) 72 (6f,Asc,GF,Jun 21)
Sir Silver Sox (USA) 67 (6f,Asc,GF,Jun 21)
Sir Tasker 33 (5f,Not,GF,Apr 22)
Sir Thomas Beecham 37 (15½f,Fol,GF,Apr 16)
Sistar Act 47 (8f,San,GF,Spt 18)
Six for Luck 46 (6f,Ayr,G,Aug 10)
Sizzling 47 (6f,Goo,G,Jun 14)
Sizzling Romp 31 (5f,Yar,GF,Aug 8)
Ski Academy (IRE) 53 (10½f,Yor,G,Jun 15)
Ski For Gold 37 (14f,Not,S,Oct 31)
Ski Iberia (ARG) 53 (9f,Lon,GS,Oct 6)
Skillington (USA) 69 (10f,Pon,GF,Spt 26)
Sky Dome (IRE) 63 (8f,Nwm,G,Nov 2)
Slapy Dam 34 (12f,Pon,G,May 24)
Slayjay (IRE) 56 (6f,Cur,G,Jun 30)
Slicious 57 (10½f,Lon,GF,Apr 28)
Slightly Speedy (IRE) 48 (8f,Asc,GF,Jun 18)
Slip Jig (IRE) 42 (8f,Nwb,GF,May 17)
Smart Alec 83 (9f,Nwm,GF,Apr 17)
Smarter Charter 44 (7½f,Bev,GF,May 11)
Smart Guest 41 (6f,Pon,G,Apr 23)
Smart Play (USA) 65 (12f,Don,GF,Spt 13)
Smilin N Wishin (USA) 53 (11f,Nwb,G,Apr 19)
Smithereens 31 (5f,War,GS,Apr 13)
Smooth Asset (IRE) 46 (8f,Goo,GF,Jly 30)
Smooth Runner (USA) 76 (8f,G,Oct 26)
Snow Falcon 44 (14f,Red,GF,Oct 8)
Snow Princess (IRE) 70 (16f,Nwc,F,Jun 29)
Snowy Mantle 34 (8f,Lei,GF,Oct 14)
Soaked 36 (7f,Kem,GF,Apr 29)
Soaking 40 (8f,Goo,GF,Spt 25)
So Amazing 38 (7½f,Bev,GF,Apr 12)
Soba Up 60 (12f,Chs,GF,Jun 26)
Society Girl 36 (8f,Ham,GF,Aug 14)
Society Magic (USA) 35 (7f,Edi,GF,Spt 23)
So Intrepid (IRE) 63 (6f,Kem,GF,Jun 26)
So Keen 30 (10½f,Hay,GS,May 25)
Solar Crystal (IRE) 69 (10½f,Cha,G,Jun 9)
Solatium (IRE) 47 (17f,Bat,F,Jun 29)
Soldier Cove (USA) 32 (8f,Bri,F,Spt 4)
Soldier Mak 43 (11½f,San,GS,May 28)
Solid Illusion (USA) 30 (10f,Lon,S,Oct 5)
Some Horse (IRE) 40 (8f,Hay,GS,May 25)
Somerton Boy (IRE) 53 (7f,Nwc,F,Jun 29)
Sonderise 42 (6f,Cat,GF,Jun 7)
Sondos 32 (6f,Pon,G,Apr 17)
Song of Tara (IRE) 83 (10f,San,GS,May 28)
Songsheet 49 (5f,Edi,GF,Aug 29)
Son of Sharp Shot (IRE) 82 (12f,Nwm,GF,Oct 17)
Soojama (IRE) 47 (12f,Nwm,GF,Jun 8)
Sooty Tern 57 (8f,Bri,GF,Aug 28)
Sophism (USA) 32 (16f,War,F,Jun 10)
Sorbie Tower (IRE) 76 (8f,Asc,GF,Jun 18)
Sotoboy (IRE) 56 (10f,San,GS,May 27)
Sound Check 35 (8f,Sal,GF,Jun 27)
Sound the Trumpet (IRE) 43 (6f,Lei,GF,Jun 3)
Souperficial 41 (6f,Lei,G,Oct 28)
Source of Light 69 (12f,Eps,G,Jun 7)
Southern Dominion 31 (7f,Lei,GF,Oct 15)
Southern Power (IRE) 79 (20f,Goo,GF,Jly 31)
South Salem (USA) 57 (10f,Don,G,May 25)
South Sea Bubble (IRE) 47 (10½f,Hay,S,Oct 6)
Sovereign Page (USA) 55 (10f,Nwm,GF,May 3)
Sovereigns Court 47 (7f,Nwb,S,Oct 24)
Soviet Bride (IRE) 56 (10f,Bri,F,Aug 18)
Soviet Line (IRE) 91 (8f,San,G,Apr 26)
Spa Lane 33 (14f,Not,GS,Aug 25)
Spandrel 39 (6f,Wnd,G,Jly 29)
Spaniards Close 56 (5f,San,GF,Jun 14)
Spanish Falls 60 (12½f,Lon,S,Oct 5)
Spanish Steps (IRE) 46 (8f,Red,GF,May 13)
Spanish Stripper (USA) 38 (6f,Yar,GF,Spt 19)
Spanish Verdict 55 (8f,Crl,F,Jun 26)
Spartan Heartbeat 62 (16f,Goo,GF,Aug 1)
Special Beat 36 (17f,Bat,F,Jly 24)
Special Dawn (IRE) 60 (10f,Wnd,GF,Jly 15)
Special-K 49 (8f,Yor,G,Jly 12)
Spectacle Jim 36 (7f,Fol,GF,Jun 5)
Spectrum (IRE) 86 (10½f,Yor,G,Aug 20)
Speed On 62 (5f,San,F,Jun 15)

Speed to Lead (IRE) 71 (16f,Goo,GF,Jun 6)
Speedy Classic (USA) 46 (7f,Chp,GF,Spt 12)
Speedy Snaps Pride 43 (7f,Nwm,GF,Aug 23)
Spencer's Revenge 41 (7f,Cat,GS,Mar 27)
Spender 62 (5f,Nwm,G,Jly 9)
Speransella (FR) 68 (8f,Dea,G,Aug 15)
Spillo 73 (12f,Don,GF,Spt 13)
Spinning Mouse 43 (14f,Yar,GF,Aug 15)
Spinning World (USA) 98 (8f,G,Oct 26)
Spirito Libro (USA) 61 (10½f,Yor,G,Jly 13)
Splicing 54 (6f,Hay,G,Jly 6)
Splinter (IRE) 59 (6f,Lin,GF,Aug 4)
Sporting Risk 38 (8f,Not,GF,Jly 26)
Spotted Eagle 50 (6f,Fol,F,Apr 23)
Spout 86 (12f,Asc,G,Oct 12)
Spread The Word 48 (12f,Chp,GF,Jly 25)
Spring Campaign (IRE) 31 (10f,Chp,GF,Jly 2)
Squared Away 39 (8f,Red,F,Spt 27)
Squire Corrie 53 (5f,Yor,G,Oct 9)
Stackattack (IRE) 49 (7f,Cat,G,Oct 19)
St Adele (USA) 35 (11½f,Yar,GF,Jly 4)
Stage Pass 65 (12f,Lon,G,May 5)
Stalled (IRE) 41 (12f,Nwb,GF,Spt 20)
Standown 50 (6f,Lin,F,Jun 25)
Stand Tall 43 (6f,Ham,G,Jun 3)
Star Manager (USA) 73 (8f,Asc,GF,Jun 19)
Star of Gold 59 (8f,Bat,GF,Aug 8)
Star of Zilzal (USA) 70 (10½f,Yor,G,Aug 21)
Star Performer (IRE) 33 (17f,Pon,G,Oct 7)
Star Selection 73 (10f,Kem,G,Apr 8)
Star Talent (USA) 73 (8½f,Eps,GF,Jun 9)
Statajack (IRE) 73 (12f,Nwm,GF,Apr 17)
State Approval 39 (11½f,Yar,G,Spt 17)
Stately Dancer 47 (10½f,Yor,G,Oct 9)
State of Caution 41 (7½f,Bev,GF,Apr 25)
State Theatre (IRE) 43 (16f,Asc,GF,Jly 26)
Statistician 56 (7f,Lei,GF,Oct 15)
Statoyork 42 (6f,Nwm,GF,Apr 16)
Steadfast Elite (IRE) 33 (11f,Edi,GS,May 30)
Steal 'Em 38 (7f,Goo,GF,Aug 2)
Steamroller Stanly 51 (12f,Goo,GF,Spt 13)
Step Aloft 69 (10f,Nwm,G,Oct 1)
Stephensons Rocket 36 (5f,Ham,G,Spt 29)
Step On Degas 46 (5f,War,F,Jun 5)
Sterling Fellow 46 (18f,Pon,G,Oct 21)
St Honorine (IRE) 38 (13½f,Chs,G,Spt 25)
St Mawes (FR) 74 (14½f,Don,GF,Spt 14)
Stolen Kiss (IRE) 63 (5f,Thi,GF,Apr 19)
Stolen Melody 54 (7f,Lin,GF,May 11)
Stompin 68 (16f,War,F,Jun 10)
Stone Ridge (IRE) 85 (8f,Don,S,Mar 23)
Stoney End (USA) 43 (7f,Lin,GF,Jly 13)
Stoppes Brow 61 (7f,Nwm,G,Nov 2)
Stop Play (IRE) 35 (6f,Yar,F,Jun 5)
Storm Bid (USA) 30 (7f,Thi,GF,May 4)
Stormless 42 (11f,Ayr,GF,Spt 19)
Storm Trooper (USA) 78 (9f,Nwm,GF,Apr 18)
Story Line 44 (12f,Nwb,S,Oct 26)
Strategic Choice (USA) 98 (14f,Yor,GF,May 16)
Strategic Ploy 44 (12f,Don,GF,Jly 17)
Strat's Legacy 33 (12f,Eps,GF,Spt 11)
Strazo (IRE) 50 (7f,Sal,GF,Jun 26)
Striffolino 30 (10f,Lin,F,Jun 15)
Struggler 81 (5f,San,G,May 27)
Stuffed 61 (5f,Yor,G,Oct 9)
Stylish Ways (IRE) 62 (6f,Yor,G,Jun 14)
Sualtach (IRE) 54 (7f,Nwm,G,Nov 2)
Subterfuge 57 (12f,Asc,G,Oct 11)
Sue Me (IRE) 47 (7f,Nwb,S,May 29)
Sue's Return 68 (8f,Goo,G,May 21)
Sufuf 33 (8f,Not,GF,Spt 24)
Sugar Mill 65 (12f,Don,G,Oct 26)
Sujud (IRE) 35 (17f,Pon,G,Apr 23)
Summer Beauty 39 (8f,San,GF,Jly 25)
Summerhill Special (IRE) 50 (12f,Kem,GF,May 6)
Summer Spell (USA) 64 (14f,Goo,G,Aug 24)
Sun Ballet (IRE) 39 (10f,Cur,GS,May 26)
Sunday Mail Too (IRE) 31 (5f,Ayr,GF,Jly 21)
Sunley Secure 34 (8f,Sal,GF,Jun 27)
Sunset Reigns (IRE) 73 (6f,Cur,G,Jun 30)
Sunset Wells (USA) 45 (10f,Nwm,G,Jly 10)
Sunshack 38 (12½f,Dea,G,Aug 6)
Supamova (USA) 41 (12f,Chs,GS,Aug 31)
Super Benz 62 (6f,Rip,G,Apr 10)
Superbit 41 (5f,Not,G,Oct 24)
Super High 33 (8f,Asc,GF,May 1)
Superior Force 47 (8f,San,GF,Spt 18)
Super Park 48 (8f,Lin,GF,Aug 17)
Superpride 49 (6f,Red,GF,Jun 11)
Super Rocky 50 (5f,Not,GF,Apr 22)
Super Serenade 47 (8f,Chp,GF,Jly 2)
Supertop 35 (11f,Ayr,GF,Spt 19)
Suplizi (IRE) 38 (13f,Nwb,GS,May 18)
Supreme Commander (FR) 62 (11f,Lon,F,Apr 7)
Supreme Star (USA) 34 (14f,San,GF,Jly 24)
Supreme Thought 44 (5f,Sal,F,Spt 5)
Suranom (IRE) 56 (12f,Chs,GF,Jun 6)
Surprise Mission 64 (5f,Don,GF,Spt 13)
Suvalu (USA) 32 (8½f,Bev,GF,May 10)
Sveltana 61 (10f,Nwm,GF,Jly 19)
Swain (IRE) 89 (12f,G,Oct 26)
Swallows Dream (IRE) 61 (11f,War,GS,Apr 13)
Swan At Whalley 56 (5f,Edi,G,Jly 8)
Sweet Amoret 30 (8f,Yar,GF,Aug 8)
Sweet Magic 57 (5f,Nwm,GF,Jun 1)
Sweet Nature (IRE) 41 (6f,Not,G,Apr 2)
Sweetness Herself 51 (12f,Chp,S,Oct 22)
Sweet Pavlova (USA) 38 (10f,Sal,G,Aug 14)
Sweet Wilhelmina 37 (8f,Bri,G,Oct 2)
Swift Fandango (USA) 72 (8f,Goo,GF,Aug 3)
Swift Maiden 35 (10f,Nwb,S,May 29)
Swynford Dream 70 (5f,Nwm,GF,Oct 3)
Sycamore Lodge (IRE) 55 (7f,Don,GF,May 7)
Sylvan Princess 44 (8f,Bri,F,Aug 5)
Sylvan Sabre (IRE) 32 (11f,Red,GF,Jly 11)
Sylva Paradise (IRE) 66 (6f,Asc,GF,Spt 28)
Symboli Kildare (IRE) 67 (5f,Leo,G,Spt 14)

Ta Awun (USA) 56 (10f,Asc,GF,Jly 26)
Tabriz 42 (8f,Ham,S,May 3)
Tachycardia 36 (6f,Lin,GF,Jly 12)
Tadeo 71 (5f,Asc,G,Oct 12)
Tael of Silver 49 (7f,Nwc,G,Aug 26)
Tafahhus 55 (6f,Bri,F,Apr 12)
Tagula (IRE) 69 (8f,Lon,G,May 12)
Taharqa (IRE) 48 (14f,Hay,G,Spt 28)
Taiki Blizzard (USA) 49 (10f,Fst,Oct 26)
Taipan (IRE) 86 (12f,Goo,GS,May 23)
Takadou (IRE) 65 (5f,Nwm,GF,Jun 1)
Takkatamm (USA) 59 (8½f,Eps,G,Jun 7)
Talathath (FR) 59 (8f,Bri,GF,Aug 28)
Talented Ting (IRE) 44 (10f,Bri,F,Jun 17)
Talloires (USA) 84 (12f,G,Oct 26)
Tamayaz (CAN) 99 (10f,Asc,GF,Jun 18)
Tame Deer 51 (8f,Rip,Hy,Aug 27)
Tamhid (USA) 55 (8f,Thi,GF,May 18)
Tamnia 59 (8f,Nwm,GF,Oct 3)
Tamure (IRE) 56 (12f,Lon,GS,Oct 6)
Taniyar (FR) 48 (12f,Lei,GF,Oct 15)
Tappeto 53 (12f,Kem,GF,Jun 12)
Tarator (USA) 78 (12½f,Dea,G,Aug 25)
Tarawa (IRE) 88 (7f,Nwm,GF,Apr 17)
Tarf (USA) 46 (5f,Eps,GF,Spt 11)
Tarian (USA) 34 (10f,Sal,GF,Jun 27)
Ta Rib (USA) 75 (7f,Nwb,G,Aug 16)
Tarneem (USA) 62 (8f,Nwm,GF,May 5)
Tart 43 (11½f,San,GF,Spt 17)
Tart (FR) 48 (10f,Rip,S,Aug 31)
Tart and a Half 71 (5f,Bat,GF,May 11)
Tartan Gem (IRE) 45 (12f,Don,G,Mar 21)
Tarte Aux Pommes (USA) 45 (10f,Don,GF,Spt 13)
Tasdid 69 (12f,Eps,G,Jun 8)
Tassili (IRE) 36 (10f,Kem,G,Apr 8)
Tatika 59 (8f,San,GF,Aug 14)
Taufan Boy 57 (12f,Chp,S,Oct 22)
Taufan's Melody 74 (12f,Nwb,G,Aug 16)
Tauten (IRE) 45 (8f,Wnd,G,May 20)
Tawaaded (IRE) 61 (7f,Nwm,GF,Apr 17)
Tawafij (USA) 62 (7f,Nwc,F,Jun 29)
Tawkil (USA) 68 (10½f,Yor,G,Aug 21)
Te Amo (IRE) 52 (12f,Lei,GF,Oct 15)
Tea Party (USA) 34 (10f,Nwb,GF,Jly 19)
Tedburrow 74 (5f,Nwm,GF,Jly 20)
Teen Jay 52 (16f,Bev,GF,Jly 16)
Temptress 47 (12f,Nwm,G,Nov 1)
Tenor 46 (5f,Edi,G,Apr 15)
Ten Past Six 69 (10½f,Chs,G,May 7)
Terdad (USA) 41 (8f,Nwc,G,Apr 8)
Tereshkova (USA) 84 (8½f,Eps,G,Jun 7)
Tertium (IRE) 76 (8f,Asc,GF,Jun 19)
Tessajoe 55 (12f,Thi,GF,Apr 20)
Thai Morning 38 (7f,Chp,GF,Spt 12)
Thaleros 37 (8f,Red,GF,May 13)
Thaljanah (IRE) 71 (16f,Nwb,S,May 19)
Thames Side 51 (8f,Goo,GS,May 22)
Thatched (IRE) 37 (10f,Red,GF,Nov 5)
Thatcherella 49 (6f,Chp,GF,Jly 11)
Thatchmaster (IRE) 50 (10f,Goo,G,Aug 24)
That Man Again 64 (5f,San,F,Jun 15)
Thea (USA) 55 (7f,Kem,G,Apr 8)
Theano (IRE) 43 (10f,Cur,G,Jun 29)
Theatreworld (IRE) 36 (16f,Cur,GS,Oct 5)
The Barnsley Belle (IRE) 35 (7f,Red,GF,Oct 8)
The Boozing Brief (USA) 42 (12f,Pon,GF,Jun 4)
The Bower (IRE) 60 (6f,Cur,G,Jun 30)
The Butterwick Kid 31 (18f,Pon,G,Oct 21)
The Dilettanti (USA) 63 (10f,Goo,GF,Aug 2)
The Happy Fox (IRE) 58 (5f,Crl,G,Aug 28)
The Institute Boy 33 (5f,Cat,GF,Aug 6)
The Lad 42 (12f,Chp,GF,Jly 11)
The Legions Pride 31 (12f,Bri,F,Aug 7)
The Little Ferret 36 (12f,Bri,G,May 30)
The Puzzler (IRE) 65 (6f,Nwb,S,Oct 24)
Therhea (IRE) 42 (8f,Yor,GF,May 16)
The Scythian 57 (6f,Yor,G,Oct 12)
The Stager (IRE) 58 (7f,Fol,F,Apr 23)
The Swan 52 (16f,Chs,GS,Aug 30)
The Wad 44 (6f,Chs,GF,Jun 6)
Thordis 46 (6f,Lin,F,Jun 25)
Three Arch Bridge 58 (7½f,Bev,GF,Jun 5)
Three Hills 62 (12f,Don,GF,Spt 13)
Thrilling Day 66 (7f,Goo,GF,Jly 30)
Thunder River (IRE) 37 (7f,Don,GF,May 7)
Thwaab 56 (6f,Ayr,GF,Spt 21)
Tiaphena 30 (16f,Cat,G,Jun 1)
Tiger Lake 37 (12f,Goo,GF,Jun 14)
Tilaal (USA) 61 (8f,Rip,G,Apr 10)
Tiler (IRE) 63 (6f,Red,GF,Nov 5)
Tillyard (IRE) 37 (8f,Sal,G,Jun 11)
Timarida (IRE) 82 (8f,Cur,G,Jun 30)
Time Allowed 76 (12f,Asc,G,Oct 12)
Time for Action (IRE) 75 (12f,Don,GF,Spt 13)
Time For Tea (IRE) 44 (7f,Nwm,G,Jun 29)
Time of Night (USA) 53 (7f,Kem,G,Spt 6)
Times of Times (IRE) 51 (6f,Lin,GF,Aug 4)
Time To Tango 52 (5f,Crl,F,Jly 6)
Tinashaan (IRE) 60 (10f,Nwm,GF,May 4)
Tinker Osmaston 54 (6f,Chp,GS,May 27)
Tinklers Folly 45 (7½f,Bev,F,Aug 15)
Tintara (IRE) 34 (12½f,War,F,May 6)
Tirol Hope (IRE) 51 (7f,Leo,S,Apr 20)
Tissisat (USA) 31 (10f,Pon,GF,Apr 29)
Tissue of Lies (USA) 48 (11f,Ham,GF,Aug 3)
Titchwell Lass 40 (10f,Nwm,GF,Jun 28)
Titus Livius (FR) 75 (6f,Dea,G,Aug 25)
Tiutchev 50 (10½f,Yor,G,Oct 10)
Todd (USA) 33 (10f,Goo,G,Aug 24)
Tomal 40 (8f,Bat,F,Jun 29)

Tonys Gift 57 (15f,War,GF,Jly 13)
Tony's Mist 34 (8f,Chp,G,Jun 13)
Too Hasty 32 (7f,Red,GF,Oct 8)
Top Banana 70 (5f,Nwm,GF,Jun 1)
Top Cees 75 (14f,Yor,G,Aug 21)
Top Glory (FR) 69 (10f,Dea,G,May 16)
Top Royal 30 (14f,Not,GF,Apr 30)
Torch Vert (IRE) 30 (16f,Kem,G,Apr 6)
Tormount (USA) 32 (8f,War,F,Oct 8)
Torremolinos (USA) 44 (10f,San,GF,Spt 18)
Tossup (USA) 32 (8f,Nwm,G,Jly 10)
Total Aloof 47 (5f,Nwm,GF,Jun 28)
Totally Yours (IRE) 32 (12f,Cat,G,Oct 18)
Total Rach (IRE) 37 (8f,Wnd,G,Jly 1)
Totem Dancer 48 (14f,Red,GF,Oct 8)
To the Roof (IRE) 84 (6f,Asc,GF,Jun 21)
Tot Ou Tard (IRE) 62 (10½f,Lon,GF,Apr 28)
Toujours Riviera 59 (8f,Nwm,GF,Oct 17)
Tout A Coup (IRE) 54 (11½f,Chs,G,May 8)
Toy Princess (USA) 67 (14½f,Don,G,Jun 29)
Traceability 53 (8f,Nwm,GF,May 5)
Trade Wind 51 (12f,Hay,G,Jly 5)
Trafalgar Lady (USA) 45 (6f,Nwm,G,Jly 26)
Tragic Hero 51 (14f,Red,F,Jun 22)
Trainglot 54 (18f,Nwm,G,Oct 19)
Tregaron (USA) 81 (8f,Yor,GF,Aug 22)
Tremendisto 35 (14f,Red,GF,May 27)
Tremplin (USA) 61 (8f,Asc,G,Oct 12)
Tria Kemata 41 (10f,Kem,G,Apr 6)
Trick (IRE) 52 (10f,Nwm,G,Oct 1)
Trilby 43 (12f,Yor,G,Oct 10)
Triple Leap 50 (10f,Rip,S,Aug 31)
Trivellino (FR) 48 (12f,Lon,G,May 5)
Trojan Risk 67 (10f,Don,G,Spt 11)
Troon 52 (7f,Nwm,GF,Oct 17)
Tropical Beach 55 (5f,Nwm,GS,Aug 24)
Tropical Dance (USA) 65 (6f,Eps,G,Jun 8)
Troysend 43 (8f,Asc,GF,Jun 18)
Truancy 46 (10½f,Yor,G,Jun 15)
True Bird (IRE) 37 (16f,Bev,GF,Apr 12)
True Flare (USA) 53 (8f,Lon,G,May 12)
True Joy (IRE) 35 (7f,Yar,F,Jun 12)
Truly Generous (FR) 66 (12½f,Lon,S,Oct 5)
Truth Or Dare 68 (10f,Cur,G,Jun 8)
Tsarnista 60 (8f,San,G,Aug 30)
Ttyfran 30 (14f,Not,F,Jly 6)
Tudor Island 61 (14f,Hay,GS,Jun 8)
Tulipa (USA) 63 (12f,Asc,GF,Jun 20)
Tulu 44 (12f,Lei,G,Apr 27)
Tumbleweed Ridge 74 (7f,Nwm,GF,Apr 17)
Tumi (USA) 43 (10½f,Yor,G,Oct 10)
Turgenev (IRE) 54 (14f,Hay,GS,Jun 8)
Turia 39 (12f,Kem,GF,Jun 12)
Turning Wheel (USA) 67 (10f,Wnd,GF,Aug 19)
Turnpole (IRE) 41 (14f,Yor,G,Oct 12)
Tuscan Dawn 63 (5f,Thi,GF,May 17)
Twice as Sharp 70 (6f,Goo,GS,May 22)
Twice Purple (IRE) 43 (6f,Lin,GF,Jun 1)
Twin Creeks 33 (8f,Bri,GF,Aug 28)
Tykeyvor (IRE) 66 (12f,Asc,GF,Jun 19)
Tymeera 38 (6f,Not,G,Apr 2)
Typhoon Eight (IRE) 49 (12f,Nwb,GF,Spt 20)
Typhoon Lad 31 (10f,Bat,GF,Jly 8)

Ultimate Warrior 47 (8f,Goo,GF,Aug 3)
Ultra Beet 41 (6f,Nwc,GF,Aug 4)
Unalloyed (USA) 44 (10f,San,G,Apr 26)
Unchanged 65 (20f,Goo,GF,Jly 31)
Uncharted Waters 45 (12f,Sal,G,Jun 11)
Uncle Doug 49 (17½f,Ayr,GF,Spt 20)
Uncle George 42 (7f,Nwm,G,Aug 24)
Unconditional Love (IRE) 72 (7f,Goo,GF,Aug 2)
Unitus (IRE) 53 (8f,Nwc,F,Jun 29)
U-No-Harry (IRE) 49 (5f,Nwm,GF,Oct 3)
Unreal City (IRE) 60 (8f,Kem,GS,May 25)
Up in Flames (IRE) 59 (8½f,Eps,GF,Jun 9)
Upper Gallery (IRE) 62 (16f,Cat,G,Oct 18)
Upper Mount Clair 52 (17f,Pon,G,Apr 23)
Urgent Request (IRE) 84 (8f,G,Oct 26)
Urgent Swift 52 (10f,Kem,G,Spt 7)
Utmost Zeal (USA) 43 (7f,Cat,G,Oct 19)

Vadsa Honor (FR) 69 (12½f,Dea,G,Aug 10)
Vain Prince 39 (14f,Red,GF,May 27)
Valanour (IRE) 70 (10½f,Lon,GF,Apr 28)
Valedictory 60 (12f,Nwm,GF,Apr 16)
Valley of Gold (FR) 45 (12f,Nwm,GF,May 3)
Vanadium Ore 32 (9f,Red,GF,Oct 8)
Van Gurp 62 (10½f,Yor,GF,May 16)
Vaugrenier (IRE) 54 (12f,Don,G,Mar 21)
Vax New Way 38 (5f,Not,GF,Jly 26)
Velmez 31 (14f,Nwm,GF,Jun 1)
Velvet Jones 44 (8f,Goo,GF,Spt 25)
Vendetta 30 (12f,Kem,GF,Jun 12)
Veni Vidi Vici (IRE) 43 (8f,Kem,G,Spt 7)
Venture Capitalist 91 (5f,San,GS,Jly 6)
Veridian 54 (11½f,Lin,GS,Aug 29)
Verzen (IRE) 76 (7f,Yor,G,Oct 10)
Vetheuil (USA) 85 (8f,Dea,G,Aug 15)
Viardot (IRE) 35 (12f,Bev,GF,Jun 6)
Viaticum (IRE) 56 (10f,Cur,S,Oct 19)
Victorian Style 49 (8f,Sal,G,Aug 15)
Victoria's Secret (IRE) 42 (12f,Chp,GF,Jly 11)
Victory Bound (USA) 39 (8f,Don,GF,May 7)
Victory Team (IRE) 56 (8f,Bri,F,Apr 22)
Village King (IRE) 47 (12f,Rip,G,Jly 8)
Villeggiatura 57 (10½f,Yor,GF,May 14)
Vindaloo 45 (10f,San,G,Aug 31)
Voices in the Sky 32 (12f,Bri,F,Spt 4)
Voila Premiere (IRE) 63 (12f,Yor,G,Oct 10)
Vola Via (USA) 63 (10f,Wnd,G,Aug 12)
Volley (IRE) 61 (6f,Nwm,G,Nov 2)
Volochine (IRE) 87 (8f,G,Oct 26)
Voodoo Rocket 36 (9f,Nwm,G,Nov 1)

Wadada 32 (17f,Bat,F,Jun 29)
Waders Dream (IRE) 41 (7f,Lei,GF,Oct 15)
Wafir (IRE) 60 (10f,Nwc,GF,Jly 27)
Waft (USA) 37 (8f,Not,G,Oct 9)
Wahiba Sands 59 (10f,Nwm,GF,Oct 17)
Waikiki Beach (USA) 51 (7f,Fol,F,Apr 23)
Wakeel (USA) 73 (8f,Asc,GF,Jly 27)
Walk the Beat 47 (5f,Don,S,Nov 8)
Wall Street (USA) 74 (12f,G,Oct 26)
Walworth Lady 41 (12f,Rip,G,Apr 10)
Wandering Star (USA) 62 (8f,San,G,Aug 31)
Wandering Thoughts (IRE) 45 (7f,Cur,G,Spt 21)
Wannaplantatree 50 (16f,Kem,G,Apr 6)
Warbrook 61 (14f,Yor,G,Aug 20)
Wardara 59 (6f,Yar,GF,Aug 22)
Warming Trends 84 (7f,Nwm,G,Oct 19)
Warm Spell 32 (15½f,Fol,F,Apr 23)
Warning Reef 62 (10½f,Yor,GF,May 14)
Warning Star 60 (6f,Yor,G,Jly 12)
Warning Time 52 (6f,Nwm,GF,Apr 16)
Warren Knight 32 (8f,Kem,GS,May 25)
War Shanty 36 (10f,Bat,GS,Spt 30)
Watch Me (IRE) 63 (6f,Asc,GF,Jun 20)
Watch Me Go (IRE) 31 (12f,Bri,G,May 30)
Watch The Fire 40 (6f,Fol,F,Apr 23)
Waterlord (IRE) 31 (8f,Edi,GS,May 30)
Water Poet (IRE) 71 (12½f,Dea,G,Aug 25)
Wavian 68 (5f,Asc,GF,Jun 21)
Wayne County (IRE) 64 (12f,Nwb,GS,Apr 20)
Waypoint 37 (7f,Don,G,Oct 25)
Wedding Gift (FR) 78 (10½f,Cha,G,Jun 9)
Wee Hope (USA) 37 (5f,Don,G,Jun 8)
Weet-A-Minute (IRE) 72 (12f,Hay,G,Jly 6)
Weetman's Weigh (IRE) 52 (6f,Nwm,GF,Apr 18)
Welcome Parade 54 (12f,Kem,G,Aug 21)
Well Arranged (IRE) 35 (14f,Not,G,Apr 22)
Welsh Mill (IRE) 67 (16f,Nwm,GF,Aug 9)
Welsh Mist 64 (6f,Nwm,GF,Apr 16)
Welsh Mountain 34 (6f,Red,F,Spt 28)
Welton Arsenal 75 (8f,Nwb,GS,Apr 20)
Welville 42 (7f,Nwm,GF,Apr 16)
Wentbridge Lad (IRE) 61 (8f,War,G,May 25)
Westcourt Magic 74 (5f,Hay,G,Apr 6)
Westcourt Princess 33 (8½f,Bev,GF,May 10)
Western General 50 (8f,Ham,G,Jun 12)
Western Playboy 32 (10f,Bat,G,May 20)
Western Sal 56 (12f,Nwm,GF,Jun 28)
Western Venture (IRE) 41 (8f,Ham,G,Spt 29)
West Humble 50 (7f,Kem,GF,Apr 29)
Westminster (IRE) 52 (12f,Don,GF,Jly 31)
Wet Patch (IRE) 42 (10f,Bri,F,Jun 17)
Whatever's Right (IRE) 53 (7f,War,F,Jly 20)
Whenby (USA) 66 (10½f,Cha,G,Jun 9)
Whispered Melody 31 (5f,Pon,GF,Spt 26)
Whispering Dawn 51 (8f,Edi,GS,Nov 7)
Whitechapel (USA) 67 (13f,Nwb,GF,Spt 21)
White Claret 36 (12f,Kem,GF,Jun 1)
White Emir 50 (6f,Nwm,G,Jly 9)
White Plains (IRE) 48 (10f,Asc,GF,Jly 26)
White Sea (IRE) 52 (12f,Sal,G,Jun 11)
White Settler 52 (6f,Sal,G,Aug 15)
White Sorrel 44 (7f,Thi,GF,Apr 19)
Whitewater Affair 72 (12½f,Lon,S,Oct 5)
Whittle Rock 49 (6f,Pon,G,Apr 17)
Wickins 50 (8f,Pon,G,Spt 3)
Wight 32 (12f,Don,GF,Spt 13)
Wijara (IRE) 65 (10f,Goo,GS,May 23)
Wilawander 81 (14f,Yor,G,Aug 20)
Wilcuma 81 (10½f,Yor,G,Jly 13)
Wild Palm 60 (7f,Nwm,G,Jun 29)
Wild Rice 83 (7f,Nwm,G,Oct 19)
Wild Rita 69 (12f,Don,G,Oct 26)
Wild Rumour (IRE) 44 (10½f,Yor,GF,May 15)
Wildwood Flower 75 (6f,Goo,G,Aug 24)
Wilfull Lad (IRE) 40 (8f,Sal,GF,May 16)
Will Do 47 (6f,Sal,G,May 5)
Willie Conquer 80 (12f,Nwm,GF,Oct 17)
Willie Miles 34 (6f,Red,GF,May 27)
Willisa 34 (8f,Kem,G,Spt 7)
Willow Dale (IRE) 52 (5f,Wnd,G,May 20)
Will's Way (USA) 77 (10f,Fst,Oct 26)
Willy Star (BEL) 41 (11½f,Wnd,GF,Jly 22)
Windmachine (SWE) 48 (5f,Yor,GF,Aug 22)
Windrush Boy 45 (5f,War,G,Aug 26)
Windrush Holly 35 (6f,Nwm,G,Nov 2)
Windsharp (USA) 81 (12f,G,Oct 26)
Windswept (IRE) 38 (8f,Bat,G,May 20)
Windyedge (USA) 32 (10f,San,GF,Jly 25)
Winnebago 35 (10½f,Hay,G,Spt 27)
Winning Smile (FR) 72 (10f,Lon,S,Spt 22)
Winsome Wooster 44 (6f,Lei,G,Jun 15)
Winston 52 (8f,Nwm,G,Oct 19)
Winter Romance 79 (8f,Hay,GS,May 25)
Winter Scout (USA) 37 (7f,War,F,Jun 5)
Wire Act (USA) 34 (6f,Crl,F,Jun 13)
Wisam 60 (7f,Goo,GF,Aug 2)
Witch of Fife (USA) 35 (10f,Nwb,GF,Jun 13)
With Care 45 (7f,Yor,G,Oct 12)
Witherkay 43 (8f,San,GF,Spt 18)
Witney-de-Bergerac (IRE) 47 (16f,Kem,G,Apr 6)
Wixim (USA) 68 (8f,Kem,GS,May 25)
Wizard King 70 (7f,Chp,G,Aug 26)
Wollstonecraft (IRE) 48 (6f,Nwm,GF,Jun 28)
Wonderful Day 40 (10f,Wnd,GF,May 13)
Woodborough (USA) 69 (6f,Asc,GF,Jun 20)
Woodbury Lad (USA) 31 (7f,Hay,GS,Jly 4)
Wood Leopard (USA) 36 (10f,Cur,GY,Aug 31)
Wood Magic 77 (10½f,Yor,G,Aug 21)
World Express (IRE) 39 (14f,San,GS,May 28)
World Premier 77 (7f,Nwm,GF,Apr 17)
Worldwide Elsie (USA) 46 (7f,Lin,GF,May 18)
Wot No Fax 61 (10f,Goo,GF,Aug 2)
Wybara 33 (13½f,Chs,G,Spt 25)

Xenophon of Cunaxa (IRE) 37 (7f,Nwb,GF,Jly 19)

Yalta (IRE) 56 (8f,San,GF,Jly 25)
Ya Malak 59 (5f,Nwb,GF,Spt 20)
Yamuna (USA) 56 (8f,San,G,Aug 31)
Yarob (IRE) 57 (10f,Eps,GF,Jun 9)
Yeast 95 (8f,Asc,GF,Jly 27)
Yeath (IRE) 31 (7f,Kem,G,Spt 6)
Yeoman Oliver 53 (7f,Chp,S,Oct 22)
Yet Again 31 (11f,War,F,Jun 24)
Yezza (IRE) 31 (8f,Not,GF,Apr 30)
Yom Jameel (IRE) 82 (14f,Yor,G,Aug 20)
Youdontsay 67 (5f,Eps,G,Aug 26)
Young Annabel (USA) 42 (7f,Yar,G,Aug 1)
Young Benson 40 (7f,Thi,GF,Apr 20)
Young Butt 43 (8f,Goo,GS,May 22)
Young Duke (IRE) 58 (7f,Nwb,GF,Jly 19)
Young Ern 84 (8f,Asc,GF,Jun 18)
Young Mazaad (IRE) 49 (7f,Fol,GF,Jun 5)
Your Most Welcome 47 (10f,Red,GF,Nov 5)
Yoxall Lodge 58 (8f,Not,GF,Jun 19)
Yubralee (USA) 43 (10f,Eps,GF,Jun 9)
Yukon Hope (USA) 40 (8f,Pon,G,Oct 7)
Yuppy Girl (IRE) 34 (10f,Not,GF,Jly 26)

Zaaleff (USA) 35 (10f,Not,GF,Jun 10)
Zabadi (IRE) 34 (12f,Nwb,GS,Apr 20)
Zaforum 59 (14f,Goo,G,Aug 24)
Zafzala (IRE) 72 (12½f,Lon,S,Oct 5)
Zagreb (USA) 50 (12f,Lon,GS,Oct 6)
Zahran (IRE) 31 (8f,Bat,G,May 20)
Zain Dancer 42 (8f,Crl,F,Jly 6)
Zajira (IRE) 39 (12f,Don,GF,Jly 17)
Zajko (USA) 63 (8f,Asc,G,Spt 29)
Zalotti (IRE) 30 (5f,San,GF,Spt 17)
Zamalek (USA) 61 (8f,Goo,G,May 21)
Zamhareer (USA) 37 (16f,Rip,G,May 29)
Zaralaska 77 (12f,Don,G,Oct 26)
Zarannda (IRE) 72 (10f,Lon,S,Spt 22)
Zatopek 31 (7f,Fol,GS,Mar 25)
Zelda Zonk 61 (7f,Red,GF,May 13)
Zeliba 30 (18f,Not,G,Oct 9)
Zelzelah (USA) 44 (10½f,Yor,GF,May 15)
Zermatt (IRE) 49 (10f,Bat,GF,May 11)
Zero Problemo (IRE) 46 (10f,Lon,S,Oct 5)
Zidac 62 (10f,Lin,GF,May 10)
Ziggy's Dancer (USA) 73 (5f,Chs,GS,Aug 31)
Zilclare (IRE) 35 (8f,Bri,G,Oct 2)
Zuboon (USA) 32 (14f,Hay,GS,May 6)
Zuno Flyer (USA) 33 (14f,Lin,G,Oct 4)
Zurs (IRE) 39 (7f,Sal,GF,Aug 15)
Zygo (USA) 50 (7f,Kem,G,Apr 8)

## TWO YEAR-OLDS - Sand

Acceptable (USA) 71 (8½f,Fst,Oct 26)
Aficionado (IRE) 30 (8½f,Wol,Std,Nov 11)
Assumpta 30 (5f,Sou,Std,Aug 16)

Boston Harbor (USA) 72 (8½f,Fst,Oct 26)
Burkes Manor 54 (6f,Wol,Std,Oct 19)

Cash Deposit (USA) 62 (8½f,Fst,Oct 26)
Cee-N-K (IRE) 40 (6f,Wol,Std,Nov 2)
Critical Factor (USA) 52 (8½f,Fst,Oct 26)

Davis Rock 33 (6f,Wol,Std,Oct 5)

Falkenham 62 (8½f,Fst,Oct 26)
Fruitana (IRE) 39 (5f,Lin,Std,Nov 7)

Gold Tribute (USA) 62 (8½f,Fst,Oct 26)
Greenwich Fore 38 (8½f,Wol,Std,Nov 11)
Gun Fight (USA) 55 (8½f,Fst,Oct 26)

Hello Dolly (IRE) 33 (8½f,Wol,Std,Nov 11)
Hidden Reserve (USA) 32 (8½f,Fst,Oct 26)
His Honor (USA) 51 (8½f,Fst,Oct 26)

Just Loui 38 (6f,Wol,Std,Oct 19)

Larkwhistle (CAN) 40 (8½f,Fst,Oct 26)
Lightning Bolt (IRE) 34 (6f,Wol,Std,Nov 11)
Love That Jazz (USA) 59 (8½f,Fst,Oct 26)
Lucky Oakwood (USA) 32 (7f,Sou,Std,Jly 27)

Minister's Melody (USA) 44 (8½f,Fst,Oct 26)
Mon Bruce 33 (6f,Wol,Std,Oct 5)
Mystic Quest (IRE) 31 (8½f,Wol,Std,Spt 21)

Ordway (USA) 67 (8½f,Fst,Oct 26)

Pericles 33 (6f,Wol,Std,Spt 7)
Princess of Hearts 32 (8½f,Wol,Std,Oct 19)

Ricasso 33 (6f,Wol,Std,Jly 11)
Robec Girl (IRE) 42 (6f,Wol,Std,Nov 11)
Rudimental 34 (6f,Wol,Std,Jly 11)
Runaway Mary (USA) 39 (8½f,Fst,Oct 26)

Sal's Driver (USA) 30 (8½f,Fst,Oct 26)
Storm Song (USA) 67 (8½f,Fst,Oct 26)

Trailblazer 48 (6f,Wol,Std,Nov 2)

Waiting Game (IRE) 32 (7f,Sou,Std,Spt 9)

Zippersup (USA) 55 (8½f,Fst,Oct 26)

## Turf

Abou Zouz (USA) 71 (6f,Yor,G,Aug 21)
A Breeze 45 (6f,Nwm,GF,Oct 5)
Absolute Glee (USA) 41 (7f,Cur,GS,Oct 5)
Abstone Queen 32 (7f,Cat,G,Oct 19)
Aerleon Pete (IRE) 37 (7f,Lei,GF,Oct 15)
Aficionado (IRE) 50 (6f,Goo,G,Jun 7)
Agony Aunt 44 (8f,Don,G,Oct 25)
Aim Seven 37 (6f,Lin,G,Oct 4)
Air Express (IRE) 75 (7f,Nwm,G,Oct 18)
Air Of Distinction (IRE) 34 (7f,Cur,G,Spt 8)
Ajayib (USA) 30 (8f,Chp,G,Aug 26)
Al Azhar 43 (8f,Don,GF,Spt 12)
Alezal 53 (7f,Yar,GF,Oct 23)
Alikhlas 34 (6f,Hay,GF,Aug 10)
Allied Academy 31 (6f,Lin,G,Oct 4)
All In Leather 33 (7f,Lei,GF,Oct 14)
All Is Fair 35 (7f,Kem,G,Spt 6)
Almi Ad (USA) 45 (8f,Don,G,Oct 25)
Al Muallim (USA) 44 (6f,Cat,G,Oct 18)
Alphabet 37 (7f,Kem,G,Spt 6)
Alpine Time (IRE) 39 (6f,Pon,G,May 24)
Amaryllis (IRE) 37 (7f,Red,GF,Oct 17)
American Whisper 35 (7f,Sal,G,Aug 14)
Amid Albadu (USA) 62 (7f,Lei,GF,Oct 15)
Amyas (IRE) 53 (6f,Nwm,GF,Oct 17)
Andreyev (IRE) 62 (7f,Asc,G,Oct 12)
Anokato 39 (5f,Fol,GF,Spt 27)
Another Night (IRE) 36 (7f,Sal,G,Aug 14)
Apache Star 36 (7f,Lin,GS,Oct 28)
Apprehension 40 (7f,Hay,GF,Spt 7)
Arapi 38 (6f,Lei,G,Oct 28)
Archello (IRE) 37 (6f,Red,F,Spt 28)
Arethusa 57 (6f,Yor,GF,Aug 22)
Arruhan (IRE) 32 (5f,Sal,GF,Jun 26)
Asas 42 (8f,Nwm,G,Oct 1)
Atlantic Desire (IRE) 40 (10f,Lei,GF,Oct 14)
Attitre (FR) 51 (7f,Nwm,GF,Oct 5)
Attitude 43 (7f,Lei,GF,Oct 15)
Attribute 36 (7f,Yar,G,Spt 17)
Aybeegirl 35 (7f,Chs,G,Spt 25)
Azra (IRE) 50 (6f,Leo,GS,Aug 11)

Bachelors Pad 58 (7f,Nwm,GF,Oct 4)
Badlesmere (USA) 31 (8f,Nwb,S,Oct 26)
Bahamian Bounty 72 (7f,Nwm,G,Oct 18)
Bahhare (USA) 62 (7f,Don,GF,Spt 13)
Baked Alaska 52 (6f,Nwm,G,Oct 18)
Bali Paradise (USA) 57 (7f,Nwb,GF,Spt 20)
Balladoole Bajan 41 (6f,Eps,GF,Spt 24)
Ballymote 42 (5f,Edi,GF,Spt 23)
Bally Souza (IRE) 38 (7f,Chs,G,Spt 25)
Bandore (IRE) 31 (7f,San,GF,Jun 14)
Bareeq 35 (7f,Kem,GF,Aug 7)
Baritone 32 (6f,Red,GF,Jun 11)
Barnum Sands 61 (8f,Asc,G,Oct 12)
Barrier King (USA) 37 (5f,Lin,F,Jun 29)
Battle Ground (IRE) 37 (7f,Nwm,GF,Oct 17)
Bayford Thrust 40 (5f,Edi,G,May 20)
Bea's Ruby (IRE) 36 (6f,Lei,G,Oct 28)
Beautiful Fire (IRE) 39 (7f,Cur,G,Spt 21)
Begorrat (IRE) 42 (6f,Nwb,GF,Spt 21)
Beguine (USA) 40 (7f,Nwm,G,Nov 2)
Belgravia 38 (6f,Yor,GF,May 16)
Benny The Dip (USA) 61 (8f,Don,G,Oct 26)
Ben's Ridge 41 (8f,Ayr,G,Aug 21)
Beryllium 50 (7f,Chs,G,Spt 25)
Besiege 59 (8f,Hay,GF,Spt 7)
Beyond Calculation (USA) 41 (6f,Asc,GF,Jly 27)
Bianca Nera 58 (6f,Yor,GF,Aug 22)
Bicton Park 36 (7f,Yar,GF,Oct 23)
Big Ben 50 (5f,Lin,GF,Aug 10)
Bilko 34 (5f,Asc,GF,May 1)
Bint Albaadiya (USA) 34 (6f,Lin,G,Oct 4)
Bintang Timor (USA) 47 (6f,Asc,G,Oct 11)
Bint Baladee 42 (7f,Nwb,S,Oct 26)
Bishops Court 35 (5f,Ham,G,Spt 29)
Blane Water (USA) 46 (6f,Red,GF,Oct 17)
Blooming Amazing 30 (6f,Yor,G,Oct 9)
Blue Goblin (USA) 50 (7f,Asc,G,Oct 11)
Blue Movie 30 (6f,Kem,GS,May 25)
Blue Ridge 44 (6f,Dea,G,Aug 18)
Blue River (IRE) 36 (7f,Nwm,GF,Aug 9)
Blues Queen 48 (6f,Ayr,GF,Spt 21)
Blueygreen 35 (6f,Nwm,GF,Oct 5)
Blushing Desert 31 (6f,Asc,G,Oct 11)
Bold African 45 (5f,Thi,GF,Aug 2)
Bold Catch (USA) 41 (6f,Nwm,GS,Aug 24)
Bold Demand 50 (8f,Don,S,Nov 8)
Bold Oriental (IRE) 40 (8f,Goo,GF,Spt 26)
Bold Spring (IRE) 38 (6f,Eps,G,Aug 26)
Bold Words (CAN) 60 (8f,Nwm,G,Oct 18)
Bolero Boy 62 (6f,Ayr,GF,Spt 21)
Bon Guest (IRE) 31 (6f,Goo,GF,Spt 26)
Bonnie Lassie 30 (7f,Cat,G,Oct 18)
Boojum 54 (7f,Nwb,S,Oct 26)
Brand New Dance 37 (8f,Don,S,Nov 9)
Brandon Jack 59 (7f,Chs,G,Spt 25)
Brave Act 63 (7f,San,G,Aug 30)
Braveheart (IRE) 43 (6f,Chs,GS,Aug 31)
Brave Kris (IRE) 50 (8f,Don,G,Oct 25)
Bride's Reprisal 40 (6f,Goo,GF,Jly 30)
Briska (IRE) 31 (7f,Nwm,G,Oct 1)
Broughtons Error 32 (6f,Nwm,GF,Oct 17)
Burkes Manor 48 (5f,Thi,GF,Aug 2)
Burlington House (USA) 59 (6f,Nwm,GF,Oct 17)
Burundi (IRE) 38 (7f,War,F,Oct 8)
Buzzby 43 (7f,Nwm,G,Jly 10)

Cadeaux Cher 40 (5f,Fol,GF,Spt 27)
Caerfilly Dancer 55 (7f,Nwm,GF,Oct 5)
Calypso Grant (IRE) 58 (8f,Don,G,Oct 25)
Calypso Lady (IRE) 60 (7f,Nwb,GF,Spt 20)
Cambodian (USA) 39 (8f,Cur,S,Oct 19)
Cambridge Ball (IRE) 36 (5f,San,GF,Spt 18)
Canadian Fantasy 31 (6f,Ayr,GF,Jly 15)
Can Can Lady 35 (8f,Pon,GF,Spt 26)
Cape Cross (IRE) 36 (8f,Don,GF,Spt 13)
Captain Collins (IRE) 43 (7f,Kem,G,Spt 6)
Carati 38 (6f,Sal,F,Spt 5)
Caribbean Star 30 (6f,Goo,G,Jun 14)
Carmine Lake (IRE) 57 (6f,Yor,GF,Aug 22)

Caspian Morn 33 (6f,Lin,G,Oct 4)
Castles Burning (USA) 37 (7f,Lin,G,Oct 4)
Catchable 43 (8f,Nwm,GF,Oct 17)
Catechism (USA) 38 (7f,Nwm,G,Oct 1)
Catienus (USA) 70 (8f,Don,S,Nov 8)
Catria (IRE) 43 (7f,Chp,S,Oct 22)
Catwalk 39 (8f,Asc,G,Oct 12)
Caution 41 (6f,Ayr,GF,Spt 19)
Caviar Royale (IRE) 44 (5f,Asc,GF,Jun 21)
Champagne Toast 33 (6f,Kem,G,Aug 21)
Check The Band (USA) 66 (5f,Asc,G,Oct 12)
Cherry Blossom (IRE) 31 (5f,Nwb,GS,Apr 20)
Cheval Roc 35 (6f,Goo,GF,Spt 26)
Chili Concerto 33 (5f,Wnd,G,Jly 29)
China Girl (IRE) 47 (5f,Sal,GF,Aug 22)
China Red (USA) 33 (6f,Hay,GF,Aug 16)
Chivalric (IRE) 42 (7f,Yar,GF,Spt 18)
Chorus Song (USA) 31 (6f,Nwb,G,Aug 16)
Cinema Paradiso 41 (6f,Nwb,GF,Jly 19)
City Gambler 36 (8f,War,F,Oct 8)
Clara Bliss (IRE) 41 (5f,San,GF,Spt 18)
Class Distinction (IRE) 34 (5f,Lin,GF,Jun 1)
Classic Park 43 (5f,Cur,GS,May 25)
Close Relative (IRE) 51 (6f,Goo,G,Jun 7)
Cold Steel 31 (7f,Lei,GF,Oct 15)
Colombia (IRE) 34 (6f,Hay,G,Jly 6)
Commander Jones (IRE) 59 (6f,Lin,G,Oct 4)
Compton Place 70 (6f,Yor,G,Aug 21)
Connemara (IRE) 52 (5f,Goo,GF,Aug 2)
Conon Falls (IRE) 42 (8f,San,G,Aug 30)
Conspiracy 50 (5f,Ayr,GF,Spt 19)
Copperbeech (IRE) 41 (5f,Lin,G,Oct 4)
Coretta (IRE) 44 (7f,Nwm,G,Nov 2)
Corsini 38 (6f,Asc,GF,Spt 28)
Cosmic Prince (IRE) 41 (7f,Bri,G,Oct 2)
Count Roberto (USA) 45 (6f,Pon,G,Oct 7)
Courtship 50 (7f,Nwm,GF,Oct 3)
Cowrie 48 (6f,Nwm,GF,Oct 5)
Craigievar 61 (6f,Not,GS,Oct 31)
Crimson Tide (IRE) 64 (7f,Nwm,G,Oct 19)
Cryhavoc 66 (6f,Nwm,GF,Oct 17)
Crystal Crossing (IRE) 51 (6f,Nwb,GF,Jly 20)
Crystal Hearted 42 (7f,War,F,Oct 8)
Cybertechnology 30 (8f,Yor,G,Oct 9)

Dacoit (USA) 52 (7f,Asc,G,Oct 12)
Dalmeny Dancer 41 (7f,Lin,GF,Jly 13)
Dame D'Harvard (USA) 67 (7f,Dea,G,Aug 24)
Dame Laura (IRE) 54 (5f,Wnd,GF,Jun 3)
Dance Parade (USA) 34 (5f,Asc,GF,Jun 19)
Dances With Dreams 44 (6f,Asc,G,Oct 11)
Dancethenightaway 38 (5f,Nwb,GF,Spt 21)
Dancing Drop 59 (7f,Nwm,GF,Oct 5)
Danehill Prince 41 (5f,San,GF,Spt 18)
Danetime (IRE) 65 (7f,Nwm,G,Oct 19)
Darb Alola (USA) 53 (5f,Lin,GS,Oct 28)
Daring Flight (USA) 41 (6f,Yor,G,Spt 5)
Dark Green (USA) 46 (7f,San,GS,Jly 6)
Dark Mile (USA) 37 (5f,Wnd,GF,Aug 19)
Darnaway 43 (7f,Yar,G,Oct 30)
Davoski 35 (8f,Nwm,GF,Oct 17)
Dawam Allail 39 (6f,Goo,GF,Spt 26)
Daylight Dreams 34 (6f,Yor,GF,Aug 22)
Daylight In Dubai (USA) 52 (6f,Asc,GF,Jun 18)
Dayrella 34 (5f,Lin,G,Oct 4)
Dazzle 67 (6f,Nwm,G,Jly 9)
Deadly Dudley (IRE) 56 (5f,San,G,May 28)
Deep Finesse 60 (6f,Nwm,GF,Oct 3)
Deep Water (USA) 51 (8f,Lei,GF,Oct 15)
Demolition Man 40 (6f,Nwm,GF,Aug 3)
Desert Ease (IRE) 40 (6f,Cur,G,Spt 8)
Desert Horizon 51 (8f,Not,S,Oct 31)
Desert King (IRE) 71 (7f,Nwm,G,Oct 18)
Desert Story (IRE) 62 (7f,Nwb,S,Oct 24)
Dickie Bird (IRE) 45 (7f,Goo,GF,Aug 2)
Dick Turpin (USA) 38 (7f,Nwb,G,Aug 17)
Dissertation (FR) 42 (8f,Lon,G,Spt 15)
Divide And Rule 36 (5f,Rip,GF,Jun 20)
Docklands Carriage (IRE) 34 (6f,Pon,GF,Jly 9)
Doc Ryan's 33 (7f,Yar,GF,Oct 23)
Donna's Dancer (IRE) 41 (5f,Cat,G,Oct 18)
Don Sebastian 47 (5f,Lin,G,Oct 4)
Double Action 46 (5f,Bev,GF,Jun 6)
Double Alleged (USA) 33 (7f,Yar,G,Oct 30)
Double Eight (IRE) 31 (7f,Nwm,G,Nov 2)
Double Espresso (IRE) 44 (8f,Red,GF,Nov 5)
Double Flight 39 (8f,Nwm,G,Oct 18)
Double Gold 42 (7f,Nwb,G,Aug 17)
Double-J (IRE) 36 (6f,Kem,G,Spt 7)
Double Park (FR) 55 (7f,Goo,GF,Aug 3)
Dowry 38 (6f,Lin,G,Oct 4)
Doyella (IRE) 34 (7f,Nwm,G,Nov 2)
Dragonada (USA) 51 (7f,Nwb,S,Oct 26)
Drive Assured 35 (7f,San,GF,Spt 18)
Dust Dancer 32 (7f,Kem,G,Spt 6)

Eager To Please 35 (7f,Lin,G,Oct 4)
Easycall 77 (5f,Asc,G,Oct 12)
Eldorado (IRE) 42 (10f,Nwm,G,Nov 2)
Elegant Warning (IRE) 76 (6f,Don,G,Oct 26)
Ellens Lad (IRE) 41 (5f,Fol,GF,Spt 27)
Elnadim (USA) 57 (6f,Yor,GF,Aug 22)
Elriyadh (USA) 34 (7f,Nwm,GF,Aug 9)
Enchantica 48 (5f,Edi,GS,Nov 7)
Entice (FR) 47 (7f,Nwb,GF,Spt 20)
Entrepreneur 44 (7½f,Chs,G,Spt 25)
Epic Stand 30 (8f,Red,GF,Nov 5)
Epworth 36 (8f,Don,G,Oct 25)
Equal Rights (IRE) 58 (8f,Asc,G,Spt 29)
Erosion (IRE) 42 (6f,Cat,G,Oct 18)
Eshtiaal (USA) 41 (8f,Not,S,Oct 31)
Etna 55 (6f,Nwm,GF,Oct 5)
Etoile (FR) 62 (7f,Nwb,GF,Spt 20)
Eurolink Excaliber (USA) 40 (7½f,Bev,GF,Jly 22)
Eurolink Spartacus 42 (7f,Red,GF,Oct 8)
Exit To Rio (CAN) 52 (7f,Chs,GS,Aug 31)
Express Girl 48 (5f,Cat,G,Oct 18)
Eye Shadow 50 (6f,Nwm,G,Jun 29)

Fahris (IRE) 44 (8f,Pon,G,Oct 21)
Fairy Ring (IRE) 30 (6f,Ham,G,Spt 29)
Fairy Song (IRE) 30 (6f,Cur,GY,Aug 31)
Falak (USA) 63 (7f,Nwm,GF,Oct 4)
Falkenham 63 (7f,San,G,Aug 30)
Fallah 37 (7f,Nwb,G,Aug 17)
Family Tradition (IRE) 41 (8f,Lon,GS,Oct 6)
Fanny's Choice (IRE) 31 (5f,Nwb,GF,Jly 20)
Fan of Vent-Axia 34 (7f,Nwm,G,Jly 10)
Fantastic Fellow (USA) 63 (6f,Nwm,GF,Oct 3)
Farewell My Love (IRE) 38 (6f,Nwb,S,Oct 26)
Farhan (USA) 33 (6f,Don,GF,Spt 14)
Farnese (IRE) 42 (7f,Red,GF,Nov 5)
Fascinating Rhythm 30 (8f,Not,G,Oct 9)
Fatal Baraari 38 (7f,San,GF,Spt 18)
Fatal Sahra (IRE) 39 (7f,Yar,GF,Oct 23)
Fayik 36 (7f,Yar,GF,Oct 23)
Fearless Cavalier 36 (5f,Edi,GS,Nov 7)
Fernanda 65 (7f,Nwm,GF,Oct 5)
Ferny Hill (IRE) 35 (7f,Bri,G,Oct 2)
Figlia 35 (5f,Don,S,Nov 8)
Fig Tree Drive (USA) 33 (6f,Nwb,GF,Jun 27)
Final Trial (IRE) 30 (7f,Lei,GF,Oct 15)
Fine Times 43 (5f,Hay,S,Oct 5)
Flaming West (USA) 40 (7f,Yor,G,Jly 12)
Fletcher 46 (7f,Nwb,GF,Jly 20)
Flirting Around (USA) 43 (8f,Not,S,Oct 31)
Flotilla 33 (8f,War,F,Oct 8)
Flourishing Way 35 (6f,Kem,G,Spt 7)
Fly To The Stars 48 (7f,Red,GF,Nov 5)
Fonzy 30 (5f,Thi,GF,May 18)
Foot Battalion (IRE) 37 (5f,Chs,G,May 7)
Forcing Bid 32 (7f,Edi,GS,Nov 7)
For Old Times Sake 57 (5f,Rip,S,Aug 31)
For Your Eyes Only 57 (5f,Bev,GF,Jun 6)
Foxes Tail 38 (7½f,Bev,F,Aug 15)
Fredrik The Fierce (IRE) 40 (5f,Thi,GF,May 18)
Fruitana (IRE) 35 (5f,Hay,GF,Aug 10)
Fullopep 31 (6f,Cat,G,Oct 18)
Fun Galore (USA) 33 (6f,Nwb,GF,Jun 13)
Furnish 49 (7f,Asc,G,Spt 29)
Further Outlook (USA) 51 (7½f,Bev,GF,Aug 14)
Future Prospect (IRE) 40 (5f,Hay,GS,Jun 8)

Gaelic Storm 38 (5f,San,GF,Spt 17)
Galibis (FR) 36 (8f,Nwm,GF,Oct 17)
Gee Bee Dream 32 (7f,Nwm,G,Oct 1)
General Song (IRE) 41 (6f,Nwb,GF,Spt 21)
General's Star 33 (8f,Ayr,G,Aug 21)
Generous Gift 39 (8f,Thi,GF,Spt 7)
Generous Libra 56 (7f,Nwm,G,Oct 19)
Gentleman's Word (USA) 41 (8f,Nwm,G,Oct 18)
Get The Point 35 (7f,Nwm,G,Oct 1)
Gharib (USA) 37 (7f,Yar,G,Oct 30)
Ghataas 32 (7f,Hay,S,Oct 6)
Ghayyur (USA) 33 (6f,Hay,G,Jly 6)
Gingersnap 40 (7f,Nwm,G,Nov 2)
Gipsy Princess 35 (7f,Cat,G,Oct 19)
Globetrotter (IRE) 30 (7½f,Bev,GF,Spt 18)
Golden Fact (USA) 44 (7f,Nwb,G,Aug 17)
Gonzaga (IRE) 37 (7f,Sal,G,Aug 14)
Goodwood Lass (IRE) 31 (7f,Nwb,G,Aug 17)
Grand Lad (IRE) 65 (5f,Asc,G,Oct 12)
Granny's Pet 59 (5f,San,G,Jly 5)
Grapeshot (USA) 69 (7f,Nwm,GF,Oct 4)
Grate Times 53 (7f,Chs,G,Spt 25)
Great Ovation (IRE) 48 (7f,Yor,G,Oct 10)
Green Card (USA) 38 (7f,Nwm,GF,Oct 3)
Green Jewel 46 (7f,Chs,GS,Aug 31)
Green Lady (IRE) 66 (7f,Dea,G,Aug 24)
Green Power 31 (6f,Nwm,GF,Jun 28)
Greenwich Fore 53 (7f,Lin,G,Oct 4)
Gresatre 33 (7f,Nwm,GF,Oct 17)
Gretel 47 (7f,San,GS,Jly 6)
Groom's Gordon (FR) 39 (7f,Nwm,G,Oct 1)
Gunners Glory 32 (5f,Lin,GF,Aug 10)

Hajat 42 (5f,Lin,G,Oct 4)
Hakkaniyah 36 (6f,Nwb,GF,Jly 20)
Hallmark (IRE) 35 (8f,Nwm,G,Nov 2)
Halowing (USA) 46 (7f,Nwm,GF,Oct 5)
Haltarra (USA) 41 (8f,Nwb,GF,Spt 20)
Handsome Ridge 43 (7f,Don,S,Nov 8)
Hangover Square (IRE) 62 (5f,San,GF,Spt 18)
Happy Go Lucky 37 (8f,Nwm,G,Oct 18)
Happy Valentine 61 (7f,Yar,G,Oct 30)
Harmony Hall 42 (7f,Yar,GF,Oct 23)
Harry Wolton 45 (7f,Yar,GF,Spt 18)
Hattab (IRE) 57 (5f,Nwm,GF,Oct 3)
Hawait (IRE) 40 (6f,Ayr,GF,Spt 21)
Haydn James (USA) 45 (7f,Nwb,G,Aug 17)
Head Girl (IRE) 33 (6f,Yor,G,Aug 21)
Head Over Heels (IRE) 64 (6f,Ayr,GF,Spt 20)
Heart Full of Soul 55 (7f,Nwb,S,Oct 26)
Heart of Armor 30 (8f,Bri,F,Spt 3)
Heart Throb 57 (5f,Lin,G,Oct 4)
Heavenly Miss (IRE) 36 (6f,Nwb,S,Oct 26)
Heggies (IRE) 30 (8f,Nwm,G,Nov 2)
Hello (IRE) 58 (7f,Nwb,GF,Jly 20)
Hen Harrier 36 (7f,Nwm,G,Oct 1)
Herecomestheknight 32 (5f,Sal,G,May 5)
Hibernate (IRE) 37 (8f,Goo,GF,Spt 14)
Hidden Meadow 60 (7f,Nwb,S,Oct 24)
High Intrigue (IRE) 30 (8f,Lei,GF,Oct 15)
High Roller (IRE) 61 (8f,Asc,G,Oct 12)
Hindsight (IRE) 32 (7f,San,GF,Jly 17)
Hoh Flyer (USA) 33 (6f,Kem,G,Aug 21)
Home Alone 46 (7f,Nwm,G,Oct 1)
Homestead 32 (7f,Nwb,G,Aug 17)
Hopesay 49 (6f,Nwb,GF,Spt 21)
Hornbeam 42 (6f,Goo,GF,Aug 1)

Hula Prince (IRE) 50 (6f,Yor,G,Aug 21)
Hurricane State (USA) 64 (6f,Goo,G,Spt 13)
Hyde Park (IRE) 33 (5f,Hay,S,Oct 5)

I Can't Remember 42 (8f,Pon,GF,Spt 26)
Idrica 31 (8f,Don,G,Oct 25)
Iechyd-Da (IRE) 35 (6f,Pon,G,May 24)
Ikatania 40 (8f,Pon,GF,Spt 26)
Ikdam (USA) 38 (6f,Wnd,G,Aug 12)
Imperial Garden (IRE) 40 (5f,Edi,GS,Nov 7)
Imperial President 58 (7f,Nwb,GF,Jly 20)
Impetuous Air 47 (7f,San,GF,Jly 25)
Impulsif (USA) 32 (7f,Bri,G,Oct 2)
Imroz (USA) 52 (6f,Nwm,G,Jly 10)
I'm Still Here 36 (7f,Edi,GS,Nov 7)
In Command (IRE) 76 (7f,Nwm,G,Oct 18)
Indian Blaze 33 (6f,Goo,G,Spt 13)
Indian Brave 46 (6f,Yor,G,Oct 9)
Indian Rocket 67 (6f,Rip,GS,Aug 26)
Indian Spark 44 (6f,Yor,GF,May 15)
Indifferent Guy 36 (8f,San,G,Aug 30)
Indihash (USA) 41 (6f,Nwm,G,Jly 10)
Indiscreet (CAN) 74 (6f,Yor,GF,Aug 22)
Indium 39 (7f,Yar,GF,Oct 23)
In Good Nick 40 (6f,Don,GF,Spt 14)
Injazaat (USA) 40 (6f,Lin,G,Oct 4)
Ink Pot (USA) 31 (8f,Thi,GF,Spt 7)
Intikhab (USA) 41 (6f,Yar,GF,Oct 23)
Invermark 35 (7f,Nwb,G,Aug 17)
Irish Accord (USA) 34 (6f,Pon,G,Spt 3)
Irsal 43 (7f,Yar,GF,Oct 23)
Isle of Corregidor (USA) 31 (6f,Yar,F,Jun 12)
Isle of Man (USA) 39 (6f,Kem,GF,Jly 10)
Italian Symphony (IRE) 37 (7f,Red,GF,Oct 8)
Ivan Luis (FR) 44 (8f,Ham,G,Spt 29)

Jalb (IRE) 36 (6f,Nwm,GF,Aug 3)
Jamrat Samya (IRE) 48 (6f,Nwm,GF,Oct 5)
Janib (USA) 36 (5f,Yor,G,Aug 21)
Janie's Boy 39 (6f,Cat,G,Oct 18)
Jaunty Jack 50 (8f,Not,S,Oct 31)
Jawhari 34 (6f,Nwb,GF,Jly 19)
Jeffrey Anotherred 48 (7f,Nwb,GF,Spt 20)
Jennelle 54 (5f,Lin,GS,Oct 28)
Jhazi 61 (6f,Don,G,Oct 26)
Johan Cruyff 50 (7f,Cur,G,Spt 21)
Johnny Staccato 55 (7f,Nwm,GF,Oct 4)
Joint Venture (IRE) 49 (5f,Lin,GS,Oct 28)
Joyeuse Entree 46 (8f,Lon,G,Spt 15)
Joza 43 (5f,Lin,GS,Oct 28)
Judicial Supremacy 41 (7f,Yar,GF,Oct 23)
Julietta Mia (USA) 42 (8f,Nwm,G,Oct 18)
Junie (IRE) 34 (6f,Goo,GF,Spt 26)
Just Nick 38 (6f,Nwb,S,Oct 26)
Just Visiting 43 (6f,Rip,GS,Aug 26)
Juwwi 54 (6f,Nwm,G,Jly 10)

Kadeena 33 (7f,Cat,G,Oct 18)
Kafaf (USA) 33 (7f,Kem,G,Spt 6)
Kafil (USA) 43 (6f,Nwm,G,Oct 18)
Kahal 72 (7f,Nwm,G,Oct 18)
Kaiser Kache (IRE) 59 (7f,Nwb,S,Oct 26)
Kalimat 39 (6f,Ayr,G,Aug 21)
Kalinka (IRE) 30 (7f,Goo,GF,Spt 25)
Kamin (USA) 39 (7f,Yar,GF,Oct 23)
Kawa-Ib (IRE) 34 (7f,Chp,S,Oct 22)
Keen To Please 34 (5f,Red,F,Spt 28)
Keen Waters 32 (5f,Fol,GF,Spt 27)
Key Largo (IRE) 32 (5f,Fol,S,Nov 11)
Kharir (IRE) 40 (6f,Pon,G,Spt 3)
Khassah 51 (8f,Asc,G,Spt 29)
Kingsinger (IRE) 51 (5f,Cur,GS,May 25)
King Sound 42 (8f,Nwb,GF,Spt 20)
Klondike Charger (USA) 33 (6f,Nwb,GF,Spt 21)
Kumait (USA) 51 (6f,Goo,G,Spt 13)
Kweilo 31 (6f,Nwm,G,Oct 18)

Labeq (IRE) 31 (7f,Don,G,Oct 25)
Lady Diesis (USA) 45 (6f,Nwm,GF,Oct 5)
Lady Godiva 32 (7f,Nwm,G,Oct 1)
Lady Mail (IRE) 37 (8f,Goo,GF,Spt 13)
Lamorna 44 (6f,Yor,G,Aug 21)
Largesse 30 (5f,Bev,GF,Aug 14)
Last Chance 40 (5f,San,GF,Spt 18)
Latin Master (IRE) 30 (6f,Goo,S,May 22)
Lawn Lothario 40 (8f,Ayr,GF,Spt 21)
Leading Note (USA) 43 (8f,Don,S,Nov 9)
Lima 44 (6f,Pon,G,Spt 3)
Little Blue (IRE) 32 (5f,Red,F,Spt 28)
Lochangel 37 (6f,Asc,GF,Spt 28)
Logic 43 (8f,Asc,G,Spt 29)
Logica (IRE) 34 (7f,Lin,GF,Jly 13)
Lonely Heart 34 (7f,Chp,S,Oct 22)
Love Has No Pride (USA) 47 (8f,Nwm,G,Oct 18)
Lucky Oakwood (USA) 42 (6f,Nwm,GF,Oct 5)
Lunar Music 34 (6f,Don,GF,Spt 14)
Lycility (IRE) 49 (7f,San,GF,Jly 25)

Madame Chinnery 46 (8f,Nwm,G,Oct 18)
Maftool 40 (7f,Chs,G,Spt 25)
Magical Times 56 (6f,Nwm,GS,Aug 24)
Magic Blue (IRE) 30 (5f,Hay,GS,Jun 8)
Maid By The Fire (USA) 45 (6f,Bat,G,Aug 13)
Makhbar 37 (6f,Nwm,GF,Jun 21)
Maladerie (IRE) 50 (6f,Goo,G,Jun 7)
Mandilak (USA) 31 (8f,Yar,G,Oct 30)
Man Howa (IRE) 47 (6f,Nwm,GF,Jun 28)
Manikato (USA) 38 (5f,San,GF,Spt 18)
Mantles Prince 45 (6f,Eps,GF,Spt 24)
Mantovani (IRE) 65 (6f,Leo,GS,Aug 11)
Maradi (IRE) 37 (8f,Yar,GF,Spt 19)
Marathon Maid 41 (6f,Pon,G,May 24)
Maraud 39 (7f,San,G,Aug 31)
March Star (IRE) 41 (6f,Nwb,S,May 18)
Mardi Gras (IRE) 44 (7f,Nwb,G,Aug 17)
Marengo 47 (6f,Goo,GF,Aug 3)
Maroulla (IRE) 31 (7f,Nwm,G,Nov 2)
Marsad (IRE) 39 (6f,Kem,GF,Jly 10)
Marsh Marigold 37 (7f,Nwb,S,Oct 26)
Maserati Monk 50 (6f,Bat,G,Aug 13)
Mashhaer (USA) 53 (7f,Nwm,GF,Oct 3)
Masterstroke 36 (6f,Lin,G,Oct 4)
Maylane 42 (7f,Lin,GS,Oct 28)
Medaaly 64 (8f,Don,G,Oct 26)
Meliksah (IRE) 63 (5f,Nwm,GF,Oct 3)
Melleray (IRE) 41 (7f,Cur,GS,Oct 5)
Merciless Cop 54 (7f,Lin,G,Oct 4)
Meshhed (USA) 56 (6f,Nwm,GF,Oct 5)
Michael Venture 53 (8f,Lei,GF,Oct 15)
Midatlantic 36 (7f,Lin,G,Oct 4)
Midnight Shift (IRE) 36 (6f,Nwm,G,Oct 18)
Midnight Watch (USA) 35 (8f,Not,G,Oct 24)
Midyan Queen 34 (5f,Hay,S,Oct 5)
Mile High 44 (6f,Goo,GF,Jly 31)
Millroy (USA) 49 (6f,Yor,GF,Aug 22)
Miss Golden Sands 38 (6f,Nwm,G,Oct 18)
Miss Riviera Rose 32 (6f,Goo,GF,Aug 3)
Miss Sancerre 49 (6f,Nwm,G,Oct 18)
Miss Stamper (IRE) 63 (6f,Ayr,GF,Spt 20)
Mister Pink 51 (7f,Nwb,G,Aug 17)
Mithak (USA) 46 (7f,Nwb,G,Aug 17)
Monza (USA) 51 (7f,Nwb,G,Aug 17)
Moon Flower (IRE) 31 (7f,Cur,GS,Oct 5)
Moonlight Paradise (USA) 70 (7f,Nwm,G,Oct 18)
Moon River (IRE) 34 (8f,Don,S,Nov 9)
Moonshine Girl (USA) 50 (6f,Yor,GF,Aug 22)
Moonshiner (USA) 50 (6f,Yor,G,Oct 9)
More Silver (USA) 47 (7f,Nwm,G,Oct 18)
Mosconi (IRE) 38 (5f,Cur,GS,May 25)
Motet 46 (7f,Yar,GF,Oct 23)
Mount Holly (USA) 30 (7f,Nwc,G,Aug 26)
Mount Kamet 55 (7f,San,G,Aug 30)
Mr Bombastique (IRE) 37 (8f,Yor,G,Oct 10)
Mrs Miniver (USA) 40 (8f,Asc,G,Spt 29)
Much Commended 44 (6f,Red,GF,Oct 17)
Muchea 66 (6f,Nwm,GF,Oct 3)
Mujova (IRE) 38 (6f,Red,GF,Oct 17)
Mukaddar (USA) 53 (7f,Nwm,G,Oct 1)
Multitone 44 (7f,Nwc,GF,Aug 4)
Mumkin 32 (6f,Wnd,GF,Aug 3)
Mungo Park 31 (5f,Don,S,Nov 8)
Musalsal (IRE) 49 (6f,Yor,GF,Aug 22)
Musharak 39 (6f,Asc,G,Oct 11)
Musheer (USA) 50 (7f,Don,GF,Spt 13)
Musical Dancer (USA) 65 (7f,Nwm,GF,Oct 4)
Musical Pursuit 76 (7f,Nwm,G,Oct 18)
My Beloved (IRE) 32 (6f,Bat,F,Jun 29)
Myrmidon 60 (5f,Don,S,Nov 8)
My Valentina 56 (7f,Nwb,GF,Spt 20)

Naked Poser (IRE) 43 (7f,Nwm,G,Oct 1)
Nant Y Gamer (FR) 48 (6f,Cat,GF,Aug 16)
Nariskin (IRE) 46 (6f,Asc,G,Oct 11)
Natalia Bay (IRE) 51 (6f,Nwm,G,Jun 29)
Natural Eight (IRE) 41 (8f,Nwm,GF,Oct 17)
Nawal (FR) 41 (8f,Lon,G,Spt 15)
Nawasib (IRE) 47 (7f,Red,GF,Oct 17)
Nightbird (IRE) 56 (7f,Nwm,G,Oct 1)
Night Mirage (USA) 48 (8f,Don,S,Nov 8)
Night Sceptre (IRE) 34 (7f,Nwm,G,Nov 2)
Nigrasine 55 (6f,Red,GF,Oct 17)
Ninth Chord 41 (7f,Don,S,Nov 8)
Noble Dane (IRE) 34 (7f,Kem,G,Spt 6)
Noble Investment 31 (7f,Nwm,G,Oct 1)
No Horse () 56 (7f,Lei,GF,Oct 15)
Nominator Lad 41 (7f,Chs,GS,Aug 30)
Nomore Mr Niceguy 42 (5f,Don,S,Nov 8)
Nopalea 46 (5f,Lin,G,Oct 4)
Nor-Do-I 41 (6f,Don,S,Nov 8)
Northern Sun 44 (8f,Goo,GF,Spt 26)
Nostalgic Air (USA) 30 (6f,Pon,GF,Jly 9)
Nubile 34 (7f,Nwm,G,Nov 2)

Ocean Ridge (USA) 58 (6f,Nwm,G,Oct 1)
Ocker (IRE) 36 (6f,Cat,GF,Jly 25)
Olivo (IRE) 45 (6f,Nwm,GF,Aug 3)
Olympic Spirit 57 (6f,Ayr,GF,Spt 20)
Omaha City (IRE) 66 (6f,Don,G,Oct 26)
One So Wonderful 45 (7f,Kem,G,Spt 6)
Open Credit 63 (6f,Don,G,Oct 26)
Orontes (USA) 37 (8f,San,G,Aug 30)
Osomental 54 (5f,Lei,G,Jly 24)
Other Club 38 (7f,Nwm,G,Oct 19)
Our Home Land (USA) 40 (6f,Cat,GF,Jly 25)
Our Kevin 35 (7f,Nwm,G,Jly 10)
Our People 54 (8f,Lei,GF,Oct 15)
Outflanker (USA) 38 (8f,Not,S,Oct 31)
Out of Sight (IRE) 37 (6f,Yor,G,Spt 5)
Out West (USA) 45 (7½f,Bev,G,Aug 24)
Ovation 42 (7f,Nwm,GF,Jly 19)
Over To You (USA) 35 (8f,Not,G,Oct 24)

Padauk 37 (7f,Asc,G,Oct 12)
Paddy Lad (IRE) 40 (6f,Cur,GY,Aug 31)
Palaemon 44 (7f,Nwb,S,Oct 26)
Palisade (USA) 50 (7f,Nwm,G,Nov 2)
Papita (IRE) 30 (6f,Goo,GF,Jly 30)
Papua 55 (8f,Don,G,Oct 26)
Parijazz (IRE) 31 (6f,Ayr,GF,Spt 19)
Party Romance (USA) 40 (7f,San,GF,Jly 24)
Pas De Reponse (USA) 63 (6f,Nwm,G,Oct 1)
Peartree House (IRE) 36 (7f,Cat,GF,Aug 6)
Pelham (IRE) 56 (6f,Kem,GF,Aug 7)
Pennys From Heaven 35 (8f,Goo,GF,Spt 25)
Pension Fund 30 (5f,Red,GF,Jly 11)
Percy Isle (IRE) 36 (8f,Chp,S,Oct 22)
Perfect Bliss 34 (6f,Cat,GF,Aug 16)
Perfect Paradigm (IRE) 37 (8f,Chp,S,Oct 22)
Perfect Poppy 42 (8f,Don,S,Nov 9)
Pericles 41 (7f,Chs,G,Spt 25)
Perpetual 37 (5f,Fol,GF,Spt 27)
Petite Danseuse 59 (7f,Nwb,S,Oct 26)
Plaisir d'Amour (IRE) 31 (6f,Red,GF,Oct 8)

Plan For Profit (IRE) 47 (6f,Don,GF,Spt 14)
Polar Flight 61 (8f,Don,S,Nov 9)
Polish Romance (USA) 52 (6f,Nwm,GF,Oct 5)
Polish Warrior (IRE) 62 (5f,San,GF,Spt 18)
Polykala (FR) 54 (7f,Dea,G,Aug 6)
Poteen (USA) 63 (8f,Don,G,Oct 26)
Powder River 39 (7f,San,GF,Jun 14)
Praeditus 32 (6f,Asc,G,Oct 11)
Prairie Falcon (IRE) 34 (7f,Goo,GF,Aug 2)
Premier Bay 47 (6f,Pon,GF,Jly 1)
Prince Dome (IRE) 34 (5f,Thi,G,Aug 12)
Prince of Denial 34 (7f,Lei,GF,Oct 15)
Princess of Hearts 43 (7f,Nwm,GF,Oct 17)
Proud Native (IRE) 58 (6f,Red,GF,Oct 17)
Pun 42 (7½f,Bev,F,Aug 15)
Putra (USA) 58 (7f,San,GF,Jun 14)

Queen Sceptre (IRE) 67 (6f,Ayr,GF,Spt 20)
Queen's Pageant 43 (5f,San,G,May 27)
Quest Express 44 (6f,Nwm,G,Jly 10)
Quibbling 31 (7f,Chp,S,Oct 22)
Quintellina 41 (6f,Nwm,G,Jly 10)
Quws 44 (6f,Cur,G,Jun 30)

Raaha 44 (6f,Nwm,GF,Oct 5)
Racing Heart 30 (7f,Lin,G,Oct 4)
Rainbow Rain (USA) 54 (6f,Nwm,GF,Oct 17)
Raindancing (IRE) 44 (6f,Asc,GF,Jly 27)
Rainwatch 33 (8f,Nwb,GF,Spt 20)
Raphane (USA) 49 (6f,Goo,GF,Aug 1)
Rapier 32 (8f,Bri,F,Spt 3)
Rasmussen (IRE) 37 (8f,Nwm,G,Oct 18)
Raven Master (USA) 52 (7f,Nwb,G,Aug 17)
Real Estate 30 (8f,Nwm,GF,Oct 17)
Reams of Verse (USA) 53 (8f,Asc,G,Spt 29)
Rebecca Sharp 47 (7f,Nwm,G,Nov 2)
Recondite (IRE) 41 (6f,Pon,G,May 24)
Red Camellia 68 (7f,San,GF,Jly 25)
Red Guard 48 (7f,Nwm,GF,Oct 3)
Redwing 45 (7f,Nwc,G,Aug 26)
Referendum (IRE) 53 (7f,Cur,G,Spt 21)
Refuse To Lose 36 (6f,Nwb,GF,Spt 21)
Regal Patrol 34 (7f,San,GF,Jun 14)
Regal Thunder (USA) 40 (7f,Nwm,GF,Oct 3)
Rehearsal (IRE) 30 (7f,Yor,G,Jly 12)
Rejoicing (IRE) 38 (6f,Nwm,GF,Aug 3)
Reliquary (USA) 47 (6f,Yor,G,Oct 12)
Restless Spirit (USA) 37 (6f,Not,S,Oct 31)
Return of Amin 35 (7f,Fol,S,Nov 11)
Revoque (IRE) 69 (7f,Lon,G,Spt 15)
Ricasso 42 (6f,Nwm,GF,Oct 5)
Rich Ground 54 (6f,Nwm,G,Jly 10)
Rich In Love (IRE) 48 (7f,San,GF,Jly 25)
Ricky Ticky Tavie (USA) 59 (7f,Asc,G,Spt 29)
Ride Sally Ride (IRE) 45 (6f,Pon,GF,Jly 1)
Right Tune 40 (7f,Goo,GF,Spt 13)
Rihan (USA) 45 (6f,Nwm,G,Jly 10)
River Foyle (USA) 34 (8f,Thi,GF,Spt 7)
River of Fortune (IRE) 45 (7f,Nwb,S,Oct 26)
River's Source (USA) 39 (7f,Lei,GF,Oct 15)
River Usk 41 (7f,Lei,GF,Oct 15)
Rock To The Top (IRE) 31 (6f,Goo,GF,Spt 26)
Roman Imp (IRE) 45 (6f,Goo,GF,Aug 1)
Rose Carnival 35 (7f,Nwm,G,Oct 1)
Rotor Man (IRE) 36 (6f,Nwm,G,Oct 18)
Royal Amaretto (IRE) 60 (7f,Nwb,S,Oct 24)
Royal Born 39 (6f,Goo,GF,Spt 26)
Royal Crusade (USA) 49 (8f,Nwm,GF,Oct 17)
Royal Orchid (IRE) 35 (7f,War,F,Oct 8)
Rudi's Pet (IRE) 48 (5f,Asc,G,Oct 12)
Rumbustious 48 (7f,Lin,G,Oct 4)
Rum Lad 33 (6f,Pon,GF,Jly 9)
Run Lucy Run 35 (7f,San,G,Aug 31)
Russian Olive 32 (7f,Nwm,G,Nov 2)
Russian Ruler (IRE) 43 (7f,Red,GF,Nov 5)
Ryafan (USA) 48 (7f,Cur,G,Spt 8)

Sabina 45 (6f,Nwb,GF,Spt 21)
Saffron Rose 41 (7f,Lin,G,Oct 4)
Sahara River (USA) 34 (6f,Nwb,G,Aug 16)
Sahm (USA) 52 (7f,Goo,GF,Jly 31)
Saint Who (USA) 30 (6f,Nwm,GF,Oct 5)
Saltimbanco 39 (6f,Lin,G,Oct 4)
Salty Behaviour (IRE) 48 (5f,Fol,S,Nov 11)
Salty Jack (IRE) 43 (7f,Nwb,GF,Spt 20)
Sambac (USA) 54 (7f,Nwm,G,Oct 18)
Samsung Spirit 32 (6f,Yor,G,Jun 14)
Sandbaggedagain 33 (8f,Yor,G,Oct 10)
Sandstone (IRE) 59 (8f,Hay,GF,Spt 7)
Sarabi 39 (5f,Cat,G,Oct 18)
Sarayir (USA) 68 (7f,Nwm,GF,Oct 5)
Saunders Wren 36 (5f,Wnd,G,May 20)
Sausalito Bay 38 (8f,Chp,S,Oct 22)
Scarrots 35 (7½f,Bev,GF,Spt 18)
Scottish Mist (IRE) 35 (5f,Cur,GS,May 25)
Seebe (USA) 59 (6f,Yor,GF,Aug 22)
Sekari 55 (7f,Yar,GF,Oct 23)
Selberry 44 (6f,Yor,G,Oct 9)
Select Choice (IRE) 43 (6f,Yor,G,Aug 21)
Senorita Matilda (USA) 38 (6f,Nwm,G,Jly 10)
Serenity 59 (6f,Nwm,GF,Oct 5)
Shaddad (USA) 41 (6f,Nwm,GF,Aug 3)
Shadow Lead 42 (7f,Yor,G,Aug 20)
Shalaal (USA) 35 (7f,San,GF,Spt 18)
Shall We Go (IRE) 46 (7f,Lin,G,Oct 4)
Shamikh 38 (7f,Asc,GF,Jun 20)
Share Delight (IRE) 31 (6f,Don,S,Nov 8)
Sharkiyah (IRE) 38 (7f,Nwm,G,Nov 2)
Sharp Hat 60 (6f,Don,GF,Spt 14)
Shawaf (USA) 41 (6f,Asc,GF,Jly 27)
Shawm 46 (7f,Yar,G,Oct 30)
Shaya 34 (8f,Don,GF,Spt 13)
Sheer Face 47 (7f,Nwb,G,Aug 17)
Shifting Time 35 (6f,Goo,GF,Aug 3)
Shigeru Summit 70 (7f,Dea,G,Aug 24)
Shii-Take 55 (6f,Asc,GF,Jly 27)
Shock Value (IRE) 61 (7f,Nwm,GF,Oct 4)
Shouk 34 (7f,Nwm,GF,Aug 2)
Shoumatara (USA) 40 (7f,San,GF,Jly 24)
Showboat 46 (7f,Lei,GF,Oct 15)
Showcase 30 (7f,Chs,G,Spt 25)
Silca Key Silca 44 (5f,Fol,GF,Spt 27)
Silca's My Key (IRE) 35 (7f,Nwm,G,Jly 10)
Silk St John 57 (7f,Lin,G,Oct 4)
Silverani (IRE) 60 (8f,Don,S,Nov 9)
Silver Kristal 43 (7f,Nwm,G,Nov 2)
Silver Patriarch (IRE) 43 (10f,Nwm,G,Nov 2)
Silver Secret 33 (7f,Lei,GF,Oct 15)
Silver Widget (USA) 30 (6f,Nwm,GF,Jun 1)
Simple Logic 36 (6f,Nwb,S,May 18)
Sinecure (USA) 42 (8f,Yar,GF,Spt 19)
Sioux 38 (8f,Not,S,Oct 31)
Siyadah (USA) 49 (7f,Nwb,GF,Spt 20)
Skelton Sovereign (IRE) 34 (7½f,Bev,F,Aug 15)
Skyers Flyer (IRE) 35 (5f,Lei,G,Jly 24)
Sleepless 52 (7f,Nwb,GF,Spt 20)
Sleepytime (IRE) 50 (8f,Asc,G,Spt 29)
Slip The Net (IRE) 38 (10f,Bat,G,Spt 30)
Smugurs (IRE) 37 (7f,Chs,G,Spt 25)
Snap Crackle Pop (IRE) 40 (6f,Red,GF,Oct 17)
Snow Partridge (USA) 43 (7f,Asc,GF,Jly 26)
Social Pillar (USA) 43 (7f,Nwm,GF,Oct 3)
Soden (IRE) 36 (7f,Nwb,G,Aug 17)
Solfegietto 41 (6f,Ayr,GF,Spt 20)
Solo Mio (IRE) 41 (8f,Nwb,GF,Spt 20)
Song Mist (IRE) 36 (7f,Nwm,G,Oct 1)
Song of Freedom 43 (7f,Red,GF,Nov 5)
Song of Skye 46 (6f,Ayr,GF,Spt 20)
Sophomore 33 (7f,Don,G,Oct 25)
Sous Le Nez 48 (5f,Fol,S,Nov 11)
Southerly Wind 41 (8f,Pon,GF,Spt 26)
Soviet Lady (IRE) 30 (7½f,Bev,GF,Spt 18)
Soviet State (USA) 49 (6f,Don,S,Nov 8)
Spaniards Inn 41 (6f,Kem,GF,Aug 7)
Spaniard's Mount 47 (7f,Edi,GS,Nov 7)
Spanish Knot (USA) 37 (8f,Lei,GF,Oct 15)
Sparkling Harry 33 (5f,Hay,S,Oct 5)
Speedball (IRE) 55 (6f,Nwb,GF,Spt 21)
Speedboat (USA) 38 (7f,Bri,G,Oct 2)
Sporting Fellow 47 (7f,Lei,GF,Oct 15)
Spring Dance (FR) 33 (8f,Lon,GS,Oct 6)
Spy Knoll 44 (8f,Lei,GF,Oct 15)
Stanton Harcourt (USA) 42 (8f,Goo,GF,Spt 25)
Starborough 60 (7f,Nwb,S,Oct 24)
Star Profile (IRE) 52 (6f,Leo,GS,Aug 11)
State Fair 42 (8f,Asc,G,Spt 29)
Statesman 48 (6f,Kem,GS,May 25)
St Blaine (CAN) 42 (7f,Nwm,G,Nov 2)
St Lawrence (CAN) 31 (8f,Bri,F,Spt 3)
St Lucinda (CAN) 40 (6f,Red,F,Spt 28)
Stone Flower (USA) 60 (6f,Nwm,GF,Oct 17)
Stonehaven (IRE) 38 (7f,Cur,G,Spt 21)
Stories To Tell (USA) 47 (7½f,Bev,GF,Aug 14)
Stride 34 (7f,Nwb,G,Aug 17)
Sturgeon (IRE) 48 (7f,Nwm,G,Jun 29)
Stygian (USA) 41 (6f,Nwm,GF,Oct 5)
Style Dancer (IRE) 37 (6f,Nwm,GF,Oct 17)
Suite Factors 35 (5f,San,GF,Spt 18)
Summer Dance 55 (8f,Don,G,Oct 25)
Summerosa (USA) 34 (7f,Chp,S,Oct 22)
Summerville Wood 42 (7f,Nwm,GF,Oct 17)
Sunbeam Dance (USA) 70 (8f,Don,S,Nov 8)
Superbelle 38 (7f,War,F,Oct 8)
Supercharmer 36 (6f,Yor,G,Aug 21)
Superior Premium 58 (6f,Don,G,Oct 26)
Supply And Demand 49 (8f,Nwm,G,Oct 18)
Supremism 34 (7f,Nwm,G,Jun 29)
Sweeten Up 36 (7f,War,F,Oct 8)
Swino 30 (5f,Hay,GS,Jun 8)
Swiss Coast (IRE) 47 (5f,Thi,GF,Aug 2)
Swiss Law 66 (6f,Yor,GF,Aug 22)
Symonds Inn 43 (8f,Pon,G,Oct 21)

Tal-Y-Llyn (IRE) 43 (6f,Yor,G,Oct 9)
Tarski 41 (7f,San,GF,Jly 24)
Tasik Chini (USA) 38 (7f,Lin,GF,Jly 13)
Taufan Rookie (IRE) 45 (5f,Asc,GF,Jun 21)
Taunt 44 (7f,Nwc,G,Aug 26)
Tayseer (USA) 50 (7f,Red,GF,Nov 5)
Tear White (IRE) 39 (5f,San,GF,Spt 18)
Technicolour (IRE) 34 (7f,Chp,S,Oct 22)
Telemania (IRE) 45 (7f,Nwm,G,Oct 1)
Tempting Prospect 33 (8f,Nwb,S,Oct 26)
Teofilio (IRE) 35 (8f,Yar,GF,Spt 19)
Test The Water (IRE) 55 (7f,Asc,G,Oct 11)
Thahabyah (USA) 40 (6f,Red,F,Spt 28)
The Fly 44 (8f,Don,GF,Spt 12)
The Gay Fox 55 (6f,Nwm,GF,Oct 5)
The In-Laws (IRE) 44 (7f,Cat,G,Oct 19)
The Lambton Worm 42 (6f,Hay,GF,Aug 9)
The West (USA) 70 (7f,Nwm,G,Oct 18)
Thornby Park 41 (8f,Don,G,Oct 25)
Tigrello 44 (6f,Nwm,G,Oct 18)
Time Can Tell 41 (8f,Red,GF,Nov 5)
Tinkerbell 40 (7f,Nwm,G,Oct 1)
Tipsy Creek (USA) 52 (5f,Asc,GF,Jun 20)
Tirage 42 (7f,Lin,G,Oct 4)
Tithcar 30 (6f,Nwm,G,Oct 18)
Toi Toi (IRE) 34 (7f,Chp,S,Oct 22)
Token Gesture (IRE) 41 (7f,Cur,GS,Oct 5)
Tomba 54 (6f,Red,GF,Oct 17)
Tom Tailor (GER) 42 (8f,Nwm,G,Oct 18)
Top of The Form (IRE) 46 (5f,Nwm,GF,Oct 3)
Top of The Wind (IRE) 37 (7f,Nwc,GF,Aug 7)
Tough Act 51 (8f,Nwm,G,Oct 18)
Trailblazer 32 (6f,Ham,G,Spt 29)
Triple Hay 37 (6f,War,F,Oct 8)
True Glory (IRE) 38 (8f,Don,G,Oct 25)
Truly Parched (USA) 39 (7f,Asc,G,Spt 29)
Tumbleweed Pearl 47 (7f,Nwb,S,Oct 26)
Tuscany 53 (6f,Goo,G,Jun 7)
Tycoon Girl (IRE) 38 (6f,Red,GF,Oct 8)

Tycoon Todd (USA) 49 (6f,Yor,G,Spt 5)
Tyrolean Dream (IRE) 33 (7f,Yar,GF,Oct 23)

Ultra Boy 34 (6f,Red,F,Aug 9)
Undercover Agent (IRE) 32 (6f,Nwm,GF,Jly 20)
Under Pressure 40 (5f,Thi,GF,Aug 2)
Union Town (IRE) 49 (7f,Asc,GF,Aug 2)
Unknown Territory (IRE) 31 (6f,Lin,GF,Aug 17)
Unshaken 42 (5f,Fol,GS,Oct 21)
Ursa Major 45 (7f,Asc,G,Spt 29)

Valagalore 34 (8f,Nwm,GF,Oct 17)
Vanishing Trick (USA) 35 (7f,Lei,GF,Oct 14)
Vasari (IRE) 55 (6f,Nwm,G,Nov 2)
Vax Star 59 (5f,San,G,Jly 5)
Veiled Threat (IRE) 37 (8f,Lon,GS,Oct 6)
Velour 41 (7f,Nwm,GF,Jly 19)
Velvet Appeal (IRE) 47 (7f,Cur,G,Spt 8)
Verglas (IRE) 59 (6f,Leo,GS,Aug 11)
Victoria's Dream (IRE) 33 (7f,Nwm,GF,Oct 17)
Victory Dancer 52 (6f,Hay,GF,Aug 9)
Village Pub (FR) 35 (6f,Goo,GF,Spt 26)
Voyagers Quest (USA) 43 (8f,Goo,GF,Spt 25)

Waiting Game (IRE) 49 (8f,Ham,G,Spt 29)
Wasp Ranger (USA) 65 (6f,Yor,GF,Aug 22)
Waterspout (USA) 31 (7f,Chp,GF,Spt 12)
Wellaki (USA) 33 (8f,Chp,S,Oct 22)
Well Warned 44 (6f,Nwm,G,Jly 9)
Western Hour (USA) 42 (7f,Red,GF,Oct 17)
White Hot 43 (7f,Goo,GF,Spt 25)
Wild Sky (IRE) 38 (6f,Don,S,Nov 8)
Will You Dance 48 (7f,Nwb,GF,Spt 20)
Wind Cheetah (USA) 66 (7f,Nwm,G,Oct 18)
Windsor Castle 45 (10f,Lei,GF,Oct 14)
Witching Hour (IRE) 51 (6f,Yor,G,Jun 14)
Wolf Mountain 57 (6f,Yor,G,Oct 9)

Yalaietanee 33 (7f,Nwm,GF,Aug 9)
Yashmak (USA) 62 (7f,San,GF,Jly 25)
Yorkie George 52 (6f,Nwb,S,Oct 26)
Yorkshire (IRE) 41 (8f,Sal,GS,Oct 2)
Young Bigwig (IRE) 43 (6f,Goo,GF,Jly 30)
Yxenery (IRE) 55 (7f,Dea,G,Aug 6)

Za-Im 42 (6f,Nwb,S,Oct 24)
Zaima (IRE) 47 (7f,Red,F,Spt 27)
Zamindar (USA) 63 (6f,Dea,G,Aug 18)
Zaretski 42 (7f,Goo,GF,Aug 2)
Zorba 47 (7f,Edi,GS,Nov 7)
Zugudi 31 (7f,Nwm,G,Oct 1)



## KEY TO RACEREADERS' INITIALS

| | | | | | |
|---|---|---|---|---|---|
| (AA) | Alan Amies | (GB) | Gordon Brown | (NB) | Nicola Bowen |
| (AK) | Anthony Kemp | (GM) | Gary Millard | (NR) | Neville Ring |
| (AR) | Ashley Rumney | (GW) | Graham Wheldon | (O'R) | Tom O'Ryan |
| (CR) | Colin Roberts | (Hn) | John Hanmer | (RL) | Richard Lowther |
| (Dk) | David Dickinson | (IM) | Ivor Markham | (SC) | Steven Clarke |
| (DO) | Darren Owen | (KH) | Keith Hewitt | (SM) | Stephen Mellish |
| (DS) | Desmond Stoneham | (LMc) | Lee McKenzie | (WG) | Walter Glynn |

# RACEFORM STANDARD TIMES

## ASCOT

5f ....60.0 secs
6f ....1m 14.0
7f ....1m 27.2
1m (Rnd) ....1m 40.8
1m (Str) ....1m 41.2
1m 2f ....2m 6.8
1m 4f ....2m 30.0
2m 45y ....3m 27.2
2m 4f ....4m 20.0
2m 6f 34y ....4m 50.0

## AYR

5f ....57.0 secs
6f ....1m 9.8
7f ....1m 24.0
1m ....1m 37.4
1m 2f ....2m 4.6
1m 2f 192y ....2m 15.9
1m 5f 13y ....2m 44.8
1m 7f ....3m 10.7
2m 1f 105y ....3m 42.5

## BATH

5f 11y ....60.5 secs
5f 161y ....1m 9.5
1m 5y ....1m 38.5
1m 2f 46y ....2m 7.5
1m 3f 144y ....2m 26.7
1m 5f 22y ....2m 45.7
2m 1f 34y ....3m 41.0

## BEVERLEY

5f .... 61.5 secs
7f 100y ....1m 32.0
1m 100y ....1m 44.0
1m 1f 207y ....2m 2.5
1m 3f 216y ....2m 32.4
2m 35y ....3m 30.5

## BRIGHTON

5f 59y ....60.0 secs
5f 213y ....1m 7.2
6f 209y ....1m 20.0
7f 214y ....1m 32.2
1m 1f 209y ....1m 58.3
1m 3f 196y ....2m 27.6

## CARLISLE

5f ....60.2 secs
5f 207y (Flat) ....1m 12.5
6f 206y (Flat) ....1m 25.7
7f 214y (Flat) .... 1m 38.6
1m 4f ....2m 31.0
1m 6f 32y ....3m 1.0

## CATTERICK

5f ....57.5 secs
5f 212y ....1m 10.9
7f ....1m 23.6
1m 3f 214y ....2m 31.4
1m 5f 175y ....2m 55.5
1m 7f 177y ....3m 21.5

## CHEPSTOW

5f 16y ....57.0 secs
6f 16y ....1m 9.2
7f 16y ....1m 20.0
1m 14y ....1m 32.5
1m 2f 36y ....2m 5.3
1m 4f 23y ....2m 32.4
2m 49y ....3m 28.0
2m 2f ....3m 50.0

## CHESTER

5f 16y ....60.0 secs
6f 18y ....1m 13.3
7f 2y ....1m 25.2
7f 122y ....1m 32.0
1m 2f 75y ....2m 8.7
1m 3f 79y ....2m 23.6
1m 5f 89y ....2m 50.0
1m 7f 195y ....3m 22.9
2m 2f 117y ....3m 58.0
2m 2f 147y ....4m

## DONCASTER

5f ....58.4 secs
5f 140y ....1m 7.0
6f ....1m 11.0
7f ....1m 23.6
1m (Str) ....1m 37.0
1m (Rnd) ....1m 36.5
1m 2f 60y ....2m 7.0
1m 4f ....2m 30.0
1m 6f 132y ....3m 3.6
2m 110y ....3m 29.0
2m 2f ....3m 52.0

## EPSOM

5f ....54.5 secs
6f ....1m 8.0
7f ....1m 20.3
1m 114y ....1m 42.0
1m 2f 18y ....2m 4.4
1m 4f 10y ....2m 35.0

## FOLKESTONE

5f ....57.6 secs
1m 1f 149y ....1m 57.7
1m 7f 92y ....3m 18.0

| Distance | Time |
|---|---|
| 6f | 1m 10.2 |
| 6f 189y | 1m 21.6 |
| 1m 4f | 2m 31.2 |
| 2m 93y | 3m 31.0 |

## GOODWOOD

| Distance | Time |
|---|---|
| 5f | 56.7 secs |
| 6f | 1m 10.0 |
| 7f | 1m 24.8 |
| 1m | 1m 37.2 |
| 1m 1f | 1m 51.4 |
| 1m 2f | 2m 5.5 |
| 1m 4f | 2m 33.2 |
| 1m 6f | 2m 59.0 |
| 2m | 3m 24.0 |
| 2m 4f | 4m 15.0 |

## HAMILTON

| Distance | Time |
|---|---|
| 5f 4y | 58.3 secs |
| 6f 5y | 1m 10.0 |
| 1m 65y | 1m 44.1 |
| 1m 1f 36y | 1m 54.3 |
| 1m 3f 16y | 2m 19.4 |
| 1m 4f 17y | 2m 32.0 |
| 1m 5f 9y | 2m 45.7 |

## HAYDOCK

| Distance | Time |
|---|---|
| 5f | 59.2 secs |
| 6f | 1m 11.7 |
| 7f 30y | 1m 27.5 |
| 1m 30y | 1m 40.6 |
| 1m 2f 120y | 2m 11.5 |
| 1m 3f 200y | 2m 29.4 |
| 1m 6f | 2m 58.2 |
| 2m 45y | 3m 27.2 |

## KEMPTON

| Distance | Time |
|---|---|
| 5f | 58.2 secs |
| 6f | 1m 11.3 |
| 7f (Rnd) | 1m 24.5 |
| 7f (Jub) | 1m 24.5 |
| 1m (Jub) | 1m 37.2 |
| 1m (Rnd) | 1m 37.2 |
| 1m 1f (Rnd) | 1m 50.6 |
| 1m 2f (Jub) | 2m 3.5 |
| 1m 3f 30y | 2m 18.8 |
| 1m 4f | 2m 30.7 |
| 1m 6f 92y | 3m 3.0 |
| 2m | 3m 24.6 |

## LEICESTER

| Distance | Time |
|---|---|
| 5f 2y | 58.5 secs |
| 5f 218y | 1m 10.0 |
| 7f 9y | 1m 23.0 |
| 1m 8y | 1m 35.0 |
| 1m 1f 218y | 2m 3.7 |
| 1m 3f 183y | 2m 29.0 |

## LINGFIELD

| Distance | Time |
|---|---|
| 5f (Turf) | 57.0 secs |
| 5f (AWT) | 58.0 secs |
| 6f (Turf) | 1m 9.0 |
| 6f (AWT) | 1m 10.6 |
| 7f (Turf) | 1m 21.6 |
| 7f (AWT) | 1m 24.0 |
| 7f 140y (Turf) | 1m 28.8 |
| 1m (AWT) | 1m 37.4 |
| 1m 1f (Turf) | 1m 50.5 |
| 1m 2f (Turf) | 2m 4.7 |
| 1m 2f (AWT) | 2m 4.3 |
| 1m 3f 106y (Turf) | 2m 24.2 |
| 1m 4f (AWT) | 2m 30.0 |
| 1m 5f (AWT) | 2m 43.2 |
| 1m 6f (Turf) | 2m 58.3 |
| 2m (Turf) | 3m 24.0 |
| 2m (AWT) | 3m 22.0 |

## MUSSELBURGH

| Distance | Time |
|---|---|
| 5f | 57.7 secs |
| 7f 15y | 1m 25.5 |
| 1m 16y | 1m 38.6 |
| 1m 3f 32y | 2m 19.7 |
| 1m 4f 31y | 2m 33.0 |
| 1m 7f 16y | 3m 10.5 |

## NEWBURY

| Distance | Time |
|---|---|
| 5f 34y | 60.2 secs |
| 6f 8y | 1m 11.8 |
| 7f (Str) | 1m 24.5 |
| 7f 64y (Rnd) | 1m 28.1 |
| 1m (Str) | 1m 37.0 |
| 1m 7y (Rnd) | 1m 36.0 |
| 1m 1f | 1m 50.3 |
| 1m 2f 6y | 2m 3.8 |
| 1m 3f 5y | 2m 17.2 |
| 1m 4f 5y | 2m 30.0 |
| 1m 5f 61y | 2m 46.5 |
| 2m | 3m 25.0 |

## NEWCASTLE

| Distance | Time |
|---|---|
| 5f | 58.4 secs |
| 6f | 1m 11.5 |
| 7f | 1m 24.5 |
| 1m (Rnd) | 1m 39.0 |
| 1m 3y (Str) | No Time |
| 1m 1f 9y | 1m 52.3 |
| 1m 2f 32y | 2m 6.7 |
| 1m 4f 93y | 2m 37.5 |
| 2m 19y | 3m 25.5 |

## NEWMARKET

| Distance | Time |
|---|---|
| 5f (Rwly) | 58.7 secs |
| 5f (July) | 58.5 secs |
| 6f (Rwly) | 1m 11.8 |
| 6f (July) | 1m 12.0 |
| 7f (Rwly) | 1m 24.5 |
| 7f (July) | 1m 25.0 |
| 1m (Rwly) | 1m 37.3 |
| 1m (July) | 1m 37.2 |
| 1m 1f (Rwly) | 1m 51.0 |
| 1m 2f (Rwly) | 2m 3.6 |
| 1m 2f (July) | 2m 5.0 |
| 1m 4f (Rwly) | 2m 30.5 |
| 1m 4f (July) | 2m 30.0 |
| 1m 6f (Rwly) | 2m 56.0 |
| 1m 6f 175y (July) | 3m 8.5 |
| 2m (Rwly) | 3m 23.3 |
| 2m 24y (July) | 3m 25.5 |
| 2m 2f (Rwly) | 3m 50.4 |

## NOTTINGHAM

5f 13y ........ 58.6 secs
6f 15y ........ 1m 10.5
1m 54y ........ 1m 41.3
1m 1f 213y ........ 2m 2.5
1m 6f 15y ........ 2m 58.5
2m 9y ........ 3m 23.0

## PONTEFRACT

5f ........ 60.8 secs
6f ........ 1m 14.3
1m 4y ........ 1m 41.5
1m 2f 6y ........ 2m 8.3
1m 4f 8y ........ 2m 34.3
2m 1f 22y ........ 3m 39.5
2m 1f 216y ........ 3m 52.0
2m 5f 122y ........ 4m 42.5

## REDCAR

5f ........ 57.5 secs
6f ........ 1m 10.2
7f ........ 1m 23.0
1m ........ 1m 35.7
1m 1f ........ 1m 49.8
1m 2f ........ 2m 3.6
1m 3f ........ 2m 18.0
1m 5f 135y ........ 2m 53.2
1m 6f 19y ........ 2m 59.3
2m 4y ........ 3m 25.0

## RIPON

5f ........ 58.4 secs
6f ........ 1m 10.5
1m ........ 1m 37.7
1m 1f ........ 1m 50.2
1m 2f ........ 2m 3.5
1m 4f 60y ........ 2m 34.0
2m ........ 3m 25.0

## SALISBURY

5f ........ 60.0 secs
6f ........ 1m 13.0
6f 212y ........ 1m 26.0
1m ........ 1m 40.4
1m 1f 209y ........ 2m 5.3
1m 4f ........ 2m 32.6
1m 6f ........ 2m 58.7

## SANDOWN

5f 6y ........ 59.8 secs
7f 16y ........ 1m 28.6
1m 14y ........ 1m 41.2
1m 1f ........ 1m 53.1
1m 2f 7y ........ 2m 6.7
1m 3f 91y ........ 2m 23.4
1m 6f ........ 2m 58.9
2m 78y ........ 3m 32.0

## SOUTHWELL

5f (AWT) ........ 57.0 secs
6f (AWT) ........ 1m 13.5
7f (AWT) ........ 1m 26.8
1m (AWT) ........ 1m 40.0
1m 3f (AWT) ........ 2m 20.0
1m 4f (AWT) ........ 2m 32.5
1m 5f (AWT) ........ 2m 45.0
1m 6f (AWT) ........ 2m 59.0
2m (AWT) ........ 3m 26.0
2m 2f (AWT) ........ 3m 54.0

## THIRSK

5f ........ 58.0 secs
6f ........ 1m 9.7
7f ........ 1m 24.2
1m ........ 1m 36.5
1m 4f ........ 2m 30.0
2m ........ 3m 23.0

## WARWICK

5f ........ 58.0 secs
6f ........ 1m 12.0
7f ........ 1m 24.6
1m ........ 1m 36.4
1m 2f 169y ........ 2m 13.5
1m 4f 115y ........ 2m 38.5
1m 6f 194y ........ 3m 10.0
2m 20y ........ 3m 26.0

## WINDSOR

5f 10y ........ 59.2 secs
5f 217y ........ 1m 10.5
1m 67y ........ 1m 42.2
1m 2f 7y ........ 2m 4.9
1m 3f 135y ........ 2m 24.0

## WOLVERHAMPTON

5f (AWT) ........ 58.7 secs
6f (AWT) ........ 1m 11.4
7f (AWT) ........ 1m 24.7
1m 100y (AWT) ........ 1m 45.0
1m 1f 79y (AWT) ........ 1m 56.0
1m 3f (AWT) ........ 2m 14.0
1m 4f (AWT) ........ 2m 32.5
1m 6f 166y (AWT) ........ 3m 7.4
2m 46y (AWT) ........ 3m 27.0

## YARMOUTH

5f 43y ........ 60.5 secs
6f 3y ........ 1m 10.9
7f 3y ........ 1m 24.2
1m 3y ........ 1m 35.3
1m 2f 21y ........ 2m 4.4
1m 3f 101y ........ 2m 23.0
1m 6f 17y ........ 2m 59.4
2m ........ 3m 23.5
2m 2f 51y ........ 3m 54.6

## YORK

5f ........ 57.7 secs
6f ........ 1m 11.0
6f 214y ........ 1m 23.0
7f 202y ........ 1m 36.8
1m 205y ........ 1m 49.2
1m 2f 85y ........ 2m 9.7
1m 3f 195y ........ 2m 27.8
1m 5f 194y ........ 2m 56.2
1m 7f 195y ........ 3m 21.2

# FLAT RECORD TIMES

## ASCOT

| Distance | Time | Age | Weight | Going | Horse | Date | |
|---|---|---|---|---|---|---|---|
| 5f | 59.1 secs | 3 | 8-8 | Firm | Orient | Jun 21, | 1986 |
| 5f | 59.72 secs | 2 | 8-8 | Firm | Lyric Fantasy (IRE) | Jun 17, | 1992 |
| 6f | 1m 12.53 | 4 | 9-4 | Firm | Shalford (IRE) | Jun 17, | 1992 |
| 6f | 1m 13.63 | 2 | 8-8 | Firm | Minstrella (USA) | Jun 19, | 1986 |
| 7f | 1m 25.94 | 3 | 9-1 | Firm | Prince Ferdinand | Jun 17, | 1992 |
| 7f | 1m 27.25 | 2 | 8-11 | Fast | Celtic Swing | Oct 8 , | 1994 |
| 1m (rnd) | 1m 38.58 | 3 | 9-0 | Good to firm | Ridgewood Pearl | Jun 21, | 1995 |
| 1m (rnd) | 1m 40.92 | 2 | 8-7 | Fast | Untold | Spt 26, | 1985 |
| 1m (str) | 1m 38.07 | 4 | 7-8 | Firm | Colour Sergeant | Jun 17, | 1992 |
| 1m 2f | 2m 2.76 | 4 | 9-3 | Good to firm | First Island (IRE) | Jun 18, | 1996 |
| 1m 4f | 2m 26.95 | 5 | 8-9 | Firm | Stanerra | Jun 17, | 1983 |
| 2m 45y | 3m 25.29 | 3 | 9-3 | Firm | Landowner (IRE) | Jun 17, | 1992 |
| 2m 4f | 4m 15.67 | 5 | 9-0 | Firm | Royal Gait (disq) | Jun 16, | 1988 |
| 2m 6f 34y | 4m 51.32 | 4 | 8-8 | Firm | Otabari | Jun 20, | 1986 |

## AYR

| Distance | Time | Age | Weight | Going | Horse | Date | |
|---|---|---|---|---|---|---|---|
| 5f | 57.2 secs | 4 | 9-5 | Fast | Sir Joey (USA) | Spt 16, | 1993 |
| 5f | 57.62 secs | 2 | 8-6 | Good to firm | Conspiracy | Spt 19, | 1996 |
| 6f | 68.98 secs | 7 | 8-8 | Fast | Sobering Thoughts | Spt 10, | 1993 |
| 6f | 69.73 secs | 2 | 7-10 | Good | Sir Bert | Spt 17, | 1969 |
| 7f | 1m 24.97 | 5 | 7-11 | Firm | Sir Arthur Hobbs | Jun 19, | 1992 |
| 7f | 1m 25.71 | 2 | 9-0 | Fast | Jazeel (USA) | Spt 16, | 1993 |
| 1m | 1m 36.0 | 4 | 7-13 | Firm | Sufi | Spt 16, | 1959 |
| 1m | 1m 39.21 | 2 | 9-0 | Firm | Kribensis | Spt 17, | 1986 |
| 1m 1f | 1m 55.25 | 3 | 7-10 | Firm | Virkon Venture (IRE) | Spt 21, | 1991 |
| 1m 2f | 2m 5.2 | 8 | 10-0 | Fast | Knock Knock | Spt 18, | 1993 |
| 1m 2f 192y | 2m 13.31 | 4 | 9-0 | Good | Azzaam (USA) | Spt 18, | 1991 |
| 1m 5f 13y | 2m 45.81 | 4 | 9-7 | Fast | Eden's Close | Spt 18, | 1993 |
| 1m 7f | 3m 13.16 | 3 | 9-4 | Good | Romany Rye | Spt 19, | 1991 |
| 2m 1f 105y | 3m 45.0 | 4 | 6-13 | Good | Curry | Spt 16, | 1955 |

## BATH

| Distance | Time | Age | Weight | Going | Horse | Date | |
|---|---|---|---|---|---|---|---|
| 5f 11y | 1m 0.1 | 4 | 9-9 | Good to firm | To The Roof (IRE) | May 11, | 1996 |
| 5f 11y | 1m 0.8 | 2 | 8-11 | Fast | Cheyenne Spirit | Aug 9 , | 1994 |
| 5f 161y | 1m 8.1 | 6 | 9-0 | Firm | Madraco | May 22, | 1989 |
| 5f 161y | 1m 10.0 | 2 | 8-13 | Fast | Morocco (IRE) | Jly 22, | 1991 |
| 1m 5y | 1m 38.2 | 4 | 9-9 | Firm | Air Commodore (IRE) | Jly 1 , | 1995 |
| 1m 5y | 1m 40.3 | 2 | 8-12 | Good to firm | Khassah | Spt 9 , | 1996 |
| 1m 2f 46y | 2m 6.6 | 3 | 8-11 | Good to firm | Easy Listening (USA) | May 22, | 1995 |
| 1m 3f 144y | 2m 25.9 | 4 | 9-2 | Firm | Alriffa | May 13, | 1995 |
| 1m 5f 22y | 2m 47.3 | 4 | 10-0 | Firm | Flown | Aug 13, | 1991 |
| 2m 1f 34y | 3m 43.9 | 6 | 7-9 | Fast | Patroclus | Jly 10, | 1991 |

## BEVERLEY

| Distance | Time | Age | Weight | Going | Horse | Date | |
|---|---|---|---|---|---|---|---|
| 5f | 1m 0.3 | 4 | 9-11 | Firm | Eager Deva | Apr 25, | 1991 |
| 5f | 1m 1.3 | 2 | 9-0 | Good to firm | Jhazi | Spt 18, | 1996 |
| 7f 100y | 1m 29.4 | 3 | 7-8 | Firm | Who's Tef (IRE) | Jly 30, | 1991 |
| 7f 100y | 1m 30.9 | 2 | 9-0 | Firm | Majal (IRE) | Jly 30, | 1991 |
| 1m 100y | 1m 42.3 | 3 | 8-4 | Firm | Legal Case | Jun 14, | 1989 |
| 1m 100y | 1m 43.3 | 2 | 9-0 | Firm | Arden | Spt 24, | 1986 |
| 1m 1f 207y | 2m 0.65 | 4 | 11-7 | Good to firm | Ooh Ah Cantona | Jly 8 , | 1995 |
| 1m 3f 216y | 2m 30.6 | 3 | 8-1 | Hard | Coinage | Jun 18, | 1986 |
| 2m 35y | 3m 29.3 | 4 | 9-2 | Good to firm | Rushen Raider | Aug 14, | 1996 |

## BRIGHTON

| Distance | Time | Age | Weight | Going | Horse | Date | |
|---|---|---|---|---|---|---|---|
| 5f 59y | 59.4 secs | 3 | 8-9 | Firm | Play Hever Golf | May 27, | 1993 |
| 5f 59y | 1m 0.1 | 2 | 9-0 | Firm | Bid For Blue | May 6 , | 1993 |
| 5f 213y | 1m 7.5 | 7 | 8-12 | Firm | Agwa | Apr 12, | 1996 |
| 5f 213y | 1m 8.1 | 2 | 8-9 | Firm | Song Mist (IRE) | Jly 16, | 1996 |
| 6f 209y | 1m 19.4 | 4 | 9-3 | Firm | Sawaki | Spt 4 , | 1991 |
| 6f 209y | 1m 19.9 | 2 | 8-11 | Hard | Rain Burst | Spt 15, | 1988 |
| 7f 214y | 1m 30.9 | 5 | 8-12 | Hard | Chase The Door | Jly 26, | 1990 |
| 7f 214y | 1m 32.8 | 2 | 9-7 | Firm | Asian Pete | Oct 3 , | 1989 |
| 1m 1f 209y | 1m 57.2 | 3 | 9-0 | Firm | Get The Message | Apr 30, | 1984 |
| 1m 3f 196y | 2m 25.8 | 4 | 8-2 | Firm | New Zealand | Jly 4 , | 1985 |

## CARLISLE

| Distance | Time | Age | Weight | Going | Horse | Date | |
|---|---|---|---|---|---|---|---|
| 5f | 59.4 secs | 7 | 8-8 | Hard | Serious Hurry | Aug 21, | 1995 |
| 5f | 1m 0.2 | 2 | 8-9 | Hard | Metal Boys | Jun 1 , | 1989 |
| 5f 207y | 1m 11.8 | 6 | 8-13 | Firm | Night Patrol | Aug 27, | 1970 |
| 5f 207y | 1m 12.9 | 2 | 8-9 | Hard | Parfait Amour | Spt 10, | 1991 |
| 6f 206y | 1m 25.4 | 4 | 9-1 | Firm | Move With Edes | Jly 6 , | 1996 |
| 6f 206y | 1m 26.6 | 2 | 9-4 | Hard | Sense Of Priority | Spt 10, | 1991 |
| 7f 214y | 1m 37.3 | 5 | 7-12 | Hard | Thatched (IRE) | Aug 21, | 1995 |
| 7f 214y | 1m 44.6 | 2 | 8-8 | Firm | Blue Garter | Spt 9 , | 1980 |
| 1m 4f | 2m 28.8 | 3 | 8-5 | Firm | Desert Frolic (IRE) | Jun 27, | 1996 |
| 1m 6f 32y | 3m 2.2 | 6 | 8-10 | Firm | Explosive Speed (USA) | May 26, | 1994 |

## CATTERICK

| Distance | Time | Age | Weight | Going | Horse | Date | |
|---|---|---|---|---|---|---|---|
| 5f | 57.1 secs | 4 | 8-7 | Fast | Kabcast | Jly 7 , | 1989 |
| 5f | 57.7 secs | 2 | 9-0 | Fast | Verde Alitalia (IRE) | Spt 21, | 1991 |
| 5f 212y | 1m 10.4 | 3 | 8-8 | Firm | Triad Treble | May 31, | 1984 |
| 5f 212y | 1m 11.4 | 2 | 9-4 | Firm | Captain Nick | Jly 11, | 1978 |
| 7f | 1m 23.0 | 4 | 7-12 | Firm | Royal Ziska | Jun 9 , | 1973 |
| 7f | 1m 24.1 | 2 | 8-11 | Firm | Lindas Fantasy | Spt 18, | 1982 |
| 1m 3f 214y | 2m 34.1 | 5 | 9-10 | Good to firm | Keep Your Distance | Oct 13, | 1995 |
| 1m 5f 175y | 2m 54.8 | 3 | 8-5 | Firm | Geryon | May 31, | 1984 |
| 1m 7f 177y | 3m 20.8 | 4 | 7-11 | Firm | Bean Boy | Jly 8 , | 1982 |

## CHEPSTOW

| Distance | Time | Age | Weight | Going | Horse | Date | |
|---|---|---|---|---|---|---|---|
| 5f 16y | 56.8 secs | 3 | 8-4 | Firm | Torbay Express | Spt 15, | 1979 |
| 5f 16y | 57.6 secs | 2 | 8-11 | Firm | Micro Love | Jly 8 , | 1986 |
| 6f 16y | 1m 8.8 | 4 | 8-6 | Fast | African Rex (FR) | May 12, | 1987 |
| 6f 16y | 1m 9.4 | 2 | 9-0 | Fast | Royal Fi Fi (USA) | Spt 9 , | 1989 |
| 7f 16y | 1m 19.9 | 3 | 9-10 | Firm | Prince Titian | Aug 29, | 1978 |
| 7f 16y | 1m 20.8 | 2 | 9-0 | Good to firm | Royal Amaretto | Spt 12, | 1996 |
| 1m 14y | 1m 31.8 | 6 | 9-6 | Firm | Traditional Miss | Jun 27, | 1981 |
| 1m 14y | 1m 33.1 | 2 | 8-11 | Good to firm | Ski Academy (IRE) | Aug 28, | 1995 |
| 1m 2f 36y | 2m 4.1 | 5 | 8-9 | Hard | Leonidas (USA) | Jly 5 , | 1983 |
| 1m 4f 23y | 2m 31.0 | 7 | 9-6 | Hard | Maintop | Aug 27, | 1984 |
| 2m 49y | 3m 27.7 | 4 | 9-0 | Fast | Wizzard Artist | Jly 1 , | 1989 |
| 2m 2f | 4m 0.2 | 8 | 9-1 | Good to firm | Tamarpour (USA) | Jly 4 , | 1995 |

## CHESTER

| Distance | Time | Age | Weight | Going | Horse | Date | |
|---|---|---|---|---|---|---|---|
| 5f 16y | 59.2 secs | 3 | 10-0 | Firm | Althrey Don | Jly 10, | 1964 |
| 5f 16y | 1m 0.4 | 2 | 8-11 | Firm | Cynara | May 3 , | 1960 |
| 6f 18y | 1m 12.78 | 6 | 9-2 | Good | Stack Rock | Jun 23, | 1993 |

| | | | | | | | |
|---|---|---|---|---|---|---|---|
| 6f 18y | 1m 13.4 | 2 | 9-3 | Good | Stung | Jly 27, | 1968 |
| 7f 2y | 1m 25.27 | 3 | 9-3 | Fast | Mizaaya | May 7 , | 1992 |
| 7f 2y | 1m 26.28 | 2 | 8-4 | Fast | By Hand | Aug 31, | 1991 |
| 7f 122y | 1m 32.0 | 6 | 8-5 | Firm | Cee-Jay-Ay | May 6 , | 1993 |
| 7f 122y | 1m 35.0 | 2 | 9-0 | Firm | Double Value | Spt 1 , | 1972 |
| 1m 2f 75y | 2m 7.98 | 3 | 8-10 | Firm | Beneficial | May 10, | 1993 |
| 1m 3f 79y | 2m 23.71 | 3 | 8-11 | Fast | Braiswick | May 10, | 1989 |
| 1m 4f 66y | 2m 34.21 | 3 | 8-11 | Fast | Old Vic | May 9 , | 1989 |
| 1m 5f 89y | 2m 45.43 | 5 | 8-11 | Firm | Rakaposhi King | May 7 , | 1987 |
| 1m 7f 195y | 3m 24.53 | 7 | 7-11 | Good to firm | Moonlight Quest | Jly 30, | 1995 |
| 2m 2f 147y | 4m 3.35 | 5 | 8-8 | Good to firm | Top Cees | May 10, | 1995 |

# DONCASTER

| Distance | Time | Age | Weight | Going | Horse | Date | |
|---|---|---|---|---|---|---|---|
| 5f | 58.2 secs | 3 | 8-8 | Firm | Sir Gatrick | Spt 10, | 1959 |
| 5f | 58.4 secs | 2 | 9-5 | Firm | Sing Sing | Spt 11, | 1959 |
| 5f 140y | 1m 6.2 | 3 | 9-2 | Good | Welsh Abbot | Spt 12, | 1958 |
| 5f 140y | 1m 8.0 | 2 | 8-10 | Good | Crown Flatts | Oct 25, | 1947 |
| 6f | 1m 9.74 | 3 | 8-9 | Good to firm | Iltimas (USA) | Jly 26, | 1995 |
| 6f | 1m 11.2 | 2 | 8-11 | Firm | Paddy's Sister | Spt 9 , | 1959 |
| 7f | 1m 22.6 | 3 | 9-4 | Hard | Pinolli | Jun 3 , | 1963 |
| 7f | 1m 23.21 | 2 | 8-10 | Good to firm | Bahhare (USA) | Spt 13, | 1996 |
| 1m | 1m 36.71 | 3 | 8-10 | Good to firm | Mushahid (USA) | Jly 17, | 1996 |
| 1m | 1m 38.05 | 2 | 8-10 | Good to firm | Al Azhar | Spt 12, | 1996 |
| 1m (rnd) | 1m 35.34 | 3 | 9-0 | Fast | Gneiss (USA) | May 2 , | 1994 |
| 1m (rnd) | 1m 38.32 | 2 | 9-0 | Firm | Sandy Creek | Oct 28, | 1978 |
| 1m 2f 60y | 2m 5.48 | 3 | 8-8 | Good to firm | Carlito Brigante | Jly 26, | 1995 |
| 1m 2f 60y | 2m 13.47 | 2 | 8-8 | Good | Yard Bird | Nov 6 , | 1981 |
| 1m 4f | 2m 29.72 | 3 | 8-6 | Good to firm | Busy Flight | Spt 13, | 1996 |
| 1m 6f 132y | 3m 2.22 | 3 | 8-3 | Firm | Brier Creek (USA) | Spt 10, | 1992 |
| 2m 110y | 3m 34.44 | 4 | 9-12 | Fast | Farsi | Jun 12, | 1992 |
| 2m 2f | 3m 53.0 | 5 | 9-7 | Good to firm | Double Trigger (IRE) | Spt 12, | 1996 |

# EPSOM

| Distance | Time | Age | Weight | Going | Horse | Date | |
|---|---|---|---|---|---|---|---|
| 5f | 53.6 secs | 4 | 9-5 | Firm | Indigenous | Jun 2 , | 1960 |
| 5f | 55.02 secs | 2 | 8-9 | Good | Prince Aslia | Jun 9 , | 1995 |
| 6f | 1m 7.91 | 5 | 7-7 | Firm | Moor Lane | Jun 7 , | 1973 |
| 6f | 1m 7.85 | 2 | 8-11 | Fast | Showbrook (IRE) | Jun 5 , | 1991 |
| 7f | 1m 20.15 | 4 | 8-7 | Firm | Capistrano | Jun 7 , | 1972 |
| 7f | 1m 22.17 | 2 | 8-9 | Fast | Shamrock Fair (IRE) | Aug 30, | 1994 |
| 1m 114y | 1m 40.75 | 3 | 8-6 | Fast | Sylva Honda | Jun 5 , | 1991 |
| 1m 114y | 1m 42.8 | 2 | 8-5 | Fast | Nightstalker | Aug 30, | 1988 |
| 1m 2f 18y | 2m 3.5 | 5 | 7-13 | Good | Crossbow (unofficial) | Jun 7 , | 1967 |
| 1m 4f 10y | 2m 32.31 | 3 | 9-0 | Firm | Lammtarra (USA) | Jun 10, | 1995 |

# FOLKESTONE

| Distance | Time | Age | Weight | Going | Horse | Date | |
|---|---|---|---|---|---|---|---|
| 5f | 58.7 secs | 6 | 10-0 | Firm | Friendly Brave (USA) | Jun 28, | 1996 |
| 5f | 58.5 secs | 2 | 9-2 | Good to firm | Pivotal | Nov 6 , | 1995 |
| 6f | 1m 10.4 | 3 | 8-9 | Firm | Spotted Eagle | Apr 23, | 1996 |
| 6f | 1m 11.0 | 2 | 7-13 | Hard | Fashion Model | Aug 31, | 1970 |
| 6f 189y | 1m 21.3 | 3 | 8-9 | Firm | Cielamour (USA) | Aug 9 , | 1988 |
| 6f 189y | 1m 23.7 | 2 | 8-11 | Good to firm | Hen Harrier | Jly 3 , | 1996 |
| 1m 1f 149y | 1m 57.8 | 4 | 8-11 | Firm | Lord Raffles | Jun 2 , | 1980 |
| 1m 4f | 2m 33.3 | 4 | 8-8 | Hard | Snow Blizzard | Jun 30, | 1992 |
| 1m 7f 92y | 3m 23.1 | 3 | 9-11 | Firm | Mata Askari | Spt 12, | 1991 |
| 2m 93y | 3m 32.5 | 6 | 7-13 | Firm | North West | Jly 21, | 1981 |

# GOODWOOD

| Distance | Time | Age | Weight | Going | Horse | Date | |
|---|---|---|---|---|---|---|---|
| 5f | 56.25 secs | 4 | 9-5 | Good to firm | Hever Golf Rose | Jly 25, | 1995 |

| | | | | | | | |
|---|---|---|---|---|---|---|---|
| 5f | 57.53 secs | 2 | 8-12 | Fast | Poets Cove | Aug 3 , | 1990 |
| 6f | 1m 9.58 | 4 | 8-3 | Firm | For the Present | Jly 30, | 1994 |
| 6f | 1m 10.08 | 2 | 9-7 | Good to firm | April The Eighth | Jly 25, | 1995 |
| 7f | 1m 23.88 | 3 | 8-7 | Good to firm | Brief Glimpse (IRE) | Jly 25, | 1995 |
| 7f | 1m 25.97 | 2 | 8-11 | Fast | Maroof (USA) | Jly 30, | 1992 |
| 1m | 1m 35.71 | 3 | 8-13 | Firm | Distant View (USA) | Jly 27, | 1994 |
| 1m | 1m 39.44 | 2 | 8-11 | Fast | Seattle Rhyme (USA) | Spt 13, | 1991 |
| 1m 1f | 1m 54.24 | 5 | 8-0 | Firm | Coureur | Jly 28, | 1994 |
| 1m 2f | 2m 4.96 | 3 | 8-6 | Firm | Kartajana | Aug 4 , | 1990 |
| 1m 4f | 2m 31.57 | 3 | 8-10 | Firm | Presenting | Jly 25, | 1995 |
| 1m 6f | 2m 58.8 | 3 | 8-10 | Firm | Secret Waters | Aug 2 , | 1990 |
| 2m | 3m 23.57 | 4 | 9-5 | Firm | Tioman Island | Jly 28, | 1994 |
| 2m 4f | 4m 11.75 | 3 | 7-10 | Firm | Lucky Moon | Aug 2 , | 1990 |

## HAMILTON

| Distance | Time | Age | Weight | Going | Horse | Date | |
|---|---|---|---|---|---|---|---|
| 5f 4y | 58.0 secs | 5 | 8-6 | Firm | Golden Sleigh | Spt 6 , | 1972 |
| 5f 4y | 58.0 secs | 2 | 7-8 | Firm | Fair Dandy | Spt 25, | 1972 |
| 6f 5y | 1m 9.3 | 4 | 8-7 | Firm | Marcus Game | Jly 11, | 1974 |
| 6f 5y | 1m 10.1 | 2 | 7-5 | Hard | Yoohoo | Spt 8 , | 1976 |
| 1m 65y | 1m 42.7 | 6 | 7-7 | Firm | Cranley | Spt 25, | 1972 |
| 1m 65y | 1m 45.8 | 2 | 8-11 | Firm | Hopeful Subject | Spt 24, | 1973 |
| 1m 1f 36y | 1m 54.2 | 3 | 8-2 | Hard | Fairman | Aug 20, | 1976 |
| 1m 3f 16y | 2m 20.5 | 3 | 9-3 | Firm | Wang Feihoong | Jly 21, | 1983 |
| 1m 4f 17y | 2m 32.0 | 4 | 7-4 | Firm | Fine Point | Aug 24, | 1981 |
| 1m 5f 9y | 2m 45.2 | 6 | 9-6 | Firm | Mentalasanythin | Jun 14, | 1995 |

## HAYDOCK

| Distance | Time | Age | Weight | Going | Horse | Date | |
|---|---|---|---|---|---|---|---|
| 5f | 58.9 secs | 3 | 7-5 | Firm | Fish and Chips | Jun 6 , | 1970 |
| 5f | 59.2 secs | 2 | 9-4 | Firm | Money For Nothing | Aug 12, | 1964 |
| 6f | 1m 9.92 | 4 | 9-0 | Good to firm | Iktamal (USA) | Spt 7 , | 1996 |
| 6f | 1m 11.63 | 2 | 8-11 | Good to firm | Tamnia | Jly 8 , | 1995 |
| 7f 30y | 1m 27.21 | 4 | 9-4 | Firm | Indian King | Jun 5 , | 1982 |
| 7f 30y | 1m 29.4 | 2 | 9-0 | Good to firm | Apprehension | Spt 7 , | 1996 |
| 1m 30y | 1m 40.2 | 4 | 8-10 | Good to firm | Moving Arrow | Aug 5 , | 1995 |
| 1m 30y | 1m 40.69 | 2 | 8-12 | Good to firm | Besiege | Spt 7 , | 1996 |
| 1m 2f 120y | 2m 8.53 | 3 | 8-7 | Good to firm | Fahal (USA) | Aug 5 , | 1995 |
| 1m 3f 200y | 2m 26.4 | 5 | 8-2 | Firm | New Member | Jly 4 , | 1970 |
| 1m 6f | 2m 59.9 | 4 | 9-10 | Good | Soloman's Dancer | Aug 6 , | 1994 |
| 2m 45y | 3m 27.09 | 4 | 8-13 | Firm | Prince of Peace | May 26, | 1984 |

## KEMPTON

| Distance | Time | Age | Weight | Going | Horse | Date | |
|---|---|---|---|---|---|---|---|
| 5f | 58.07 secs | 3 | 8-1 | Firm | Silent Majority | Jun 25, | 1986 |
| 5f | 58.3 secs | 2 | 9-7 | Firm | Schweppeshire Lad | Jun 3 , | 1978 |
| 6f | 1m 10.04 | 7 | 7-10 | Firm | Jokist | Apr 6 , | 1990 |
| 6f | 1m 10.8 | 2 | 8-10 | Good | Zabara | Spt 22, | 1951 |
| 7f (rnd) | 1m 23.59 | 3 | 9-2 | Good to firm | Wild Rice | Aug 2 , | 1995 |
| 7f (rnd) | 1m 27.52 | 2 | 8-6 | Good | Duke of Ragusa | Spt 1 , | 1972 |
| 7f (Jub) | 1m 23.79 | 3 | 8-11 | Firm | Swiss Maid | Aug 19, | 1978 |
| 7f (Jub) | 1m 24.78 | 2 | 9-0 | Good to firm | Canons Park | Jun 28, | 1995 |
| 1m (Jub) | 1m 35.39 | 3 | 8-12 | Good to firm | Private Line (USA) | Jun 28, | 1995 |
| 1m (Jub) | 1m 42.5 | 2 | 7-4 | Good | Batanolius | Oct 19, | 1962 |
| 1m (rnd) | 1m 35.81 | 4 | 9-1 | Firm | County Broker | May 23, | 1984 |
| 1m (rnd) | 1m 43.4 | 2 | 7-0 | Good | Fascinating | Nov 3 , | 1956 |
| 1m 1f | 1m 50.56 | 3 | 8-12 | Fast | Sky Conqueror (USA) | Jun 29, | 1988 |
| 1m 2f | 1m 59.53 | 4 | 9-6 | Firm | Batshoof | Apr 6 , | 1990 |
| 1m 3f 30y | 2m 16.2 | 4 | 9-2 | Firm | Shernazar | Spt 6 , | 1985 |
| 1m 4f | 2m 30.18 | 6 | 8-5 | Firm | Going Going | Spt 7 , | 1985 |
| 1m 6f 92y | 3m 7.97 | 6 | 9-5 | Good to firm | Wild Strawberry | Jun 14, | 1995 |
| 2m | 3m 26.53 | 4 | 9-10 | Good to firm | Latahaab (USA) | May 27, | 1995 |

# LEICESTER

| Distance | Time | Age | Weight | Going | Horse | Date | |
|---|---|---|---|---|---|---|---|
| 5f 2y | 58.2 secs | 4 | 9-5 | Fast | Lucky Parkes | Spt 6 , | 1994 |
| 5f 2y | 58.4 secs | 2 | 9-0 | Firm | Cutting Blade | Jun 9 , | 1986 |
| 5f 218y | 1m 9.4 | 3 | 8-12 | Fast | Lakeland Beauty | May 29, | 1990 |
| 5f 218y | 1m 10.1 | 2 | 9-0 | Firm | Thordis | Oct 24, | 1995 |
| 7f 9y | 1m 20.8 | 3 | 8-7 | Firm | Flower Bowl | Jun 9 , | 1986 |
| 7f 9y | 1m 23.2 | 2 | 8-9 | Fast | Mandarina | Spt 6 , | 1994 |
| 1m 8y | 1m 33.8 | 3 | 9-0 | Good to firm | Clifton Fox | May 29, | 1995 |
| 1m 8y | 1m 34.6 | 2 | 8-9 | Firm | Lady Carla | Oct 24, | 1995 |
| 1m 1f 218y | 2m 2.4 | 3 | 8-11 | Firm | Effigy | Nov 4 , | 1985 |
| 1m 1f 218y | 2m 7.2 | 2 | 8-13 | Firm | Hardly Fair | Oct 21, | 1985 |
| 1m 3f 183y | 2m 27.9 | 3 | 8-12 | Firm | Al Widyan (IRE) | Oct 23, | 1995 |

# LINGFIELD

| Distance | Time | Age | Weight | Going | Horse | Date | |
|---|---|---|---|---|---|---|---|
| 5f (Equi) | 58.01 secs | 4 | 8-5 | Standard | Little Saboteur | Feb 20, | 1993 |
| 5f (Equi) | 59.11 secs | 2 | 9-2 | Standard | Fruitana (IRE) | Nov 7 , | 1996 |
| 5f | 56.24 secs | 3 | 9-1 | Fast | Eveningperformance | Jly 25, | 1994 |
| 5f | 57.25 secs | 2 | 8-9 | Fast | Quiz Time | Aug 6 , | 1994 |
| 6f (Equi) | 1m 10.58 | 4 | 9-4 | Standard | J Cheever Loophole | Nov 23, | 1989 |
| 6f (Equi) | 1m 11.65 | 2 | 9-7 | Standard | Time's Arrow (IRE) | Jly 10, | 1992 |
| 6f | 1m 8.2 | 6 | 9-10 | Firm | Al Amead | Jly 2 , | 1986 |
| 6f | 1m 8.6 | 2 | 9-3 | Firm | The Ritz | Jun 11, | 1965 |
| 7f (Equi) | 1m 22.99 | 3 | 9-3 | Standard | Confronter | Jly 18, | 1992 |
| 7f (Equi) | 1m 24.0 | 2 | 8-12 | Standard | Scottish Castle | Nov 2 , | 1990 |
| 7f | 1m 20.2 | 8 | 7-10 | Hard | Polar Jest | Aug 19, | 1955 |
| 7f | 1m 21.34 | 2 | 7-6 | Firm | Mandav | Oct 3 , | 1980 |
| 7f 140y | 1m 26.73 | 3 | 8-6 | Fast | Hiaam (USA) | Jly 11, | 1987 |
| 7f 140y | 1m 29.93 | 2 | 8-12 | Firm | Rather Warm | Nov 7 , | 1978 |
| 1m (Equi) | 1m 36.32 | 5 | 9-5 | Standard | Vanroy | Nov 30, | 1989 |
| 1m (Equi) | 1m 36.5 | 2 | 9-5 | Standard | San Pier Niceto | Nov 30, | 1989 |
| 1m 1f | 1m 52.4 | 4 | 9-2 | Good to firm | Quandary (USA) | Jly 15, | 1995 |
| 1m 2f (Equi) | 2m 2.93 | 4 | 9-3 | Standard | Rapporteur | Nov 2 , | 1990 |
| 1m 2f (Equi) | 2m 7.5 | 2 | 8-11 | Standard | Star Fighter | Nov 26, | 1994 |
| 1m 2f | 2m 5.79 | 3 | 9-3 | Firm | Aromatic | Jly 14, | 1990 |
| 1m 3f 106y | 2m 23.95 | 3 | 8-5 | Firm | Night-Shirt | Jly 14, | 1990 |
| 1m 4f (Equi) | 2m 29.3 | 4 | 8-6 | Standard | Puff Puff | Nov 8 , | 1990 |
| 1m 5f (Equi) | 2m 43.82 | 3 | 8-9 | Standard | Ela Man Howa | Nov 26, | 1994 |
| 1m 6f | 3m 2.7 | 4 | 9-3 | Good to firm | Ballynakelly | Jly 13, | 1996 |
| 2m (Equi) | 3m 20.09 | 3 | 9-0 | Standard | Yenoora (IRE) | Aug 8 , | 1992 |
| 2m | 3m 28.96 | 3 | 9-0 | Firm | Lothian | Spt 20, | 1990 |

# MUSSELBURGH

| Distance | Time | Age | Weight | Going | Horse | Date | |
|---|---|---|---|---|---|---|---|
| 5f | 57.4 secs | 4 | 7-2 | Firm | Palm Court Joe | Jly 4 , | 1977 |
| 5f | 57.5 secs | 2 | 8-2 | Firm | Arasong | May 16, | 1994 |
| 7f 15y | 1m 26.0 | 6 | 9-0 | Firm | Show of Hands | Apr 19, | 1982 |
| 7f 15y | 1m 27.5 | 2 | 9-1 | Fast | Mubdi (USA) | Oct 6 , | 1986 |
| 1m 16y | 1m 38.3 | 4 | 8-13 | Firm | Churchillian | Jly 11, | 1977 |
| 1m 16y | 1m 40.9 | 2 | 8-11 | Fast | Trompe d'Oeil | Oct 6 , | 1986 |
| 1m 3f 32y | 2m 19.7 | 3 | 8-10 | Firm | Old Court | Jly 4 , | 1977 |
| 1m 4f 31y | 2m 32.2 | 5 | 7-9 | Good | Glengrigor | Apr 15, | 1946 |
| 1m 7f 16y | 3m 10.4 | 3 | 8-0 | Good | Cunningham | Spt 21, | 1953 |

# NEWBURY

| Distance | Time | Age | Weight | Going | Horse | Date | |
|---|---|---|---|---|---|---|---|
| 5f 34y | 59.77 secs | 4 | 9-4 | Good to firm | Struggler | Spt 20, | 1996 |
| 5f 34y | 1m 0.59 | 2 | 8-2 | Good to firm | Miss Stamper (IRE) | Jly 20, | 1996 |
| 6f 8y | 1m 10.71 | 5 | 9-3 | Good to firm | Jayannpee | Jly 20, | 1996 |
| 6f 8y | 1m 11.49 | 2 | 8-6 | Good to firm | Crystal Crossing (IRE) | Jly 20, | 1996 |
| 7f | 1m 23.84 | 5 | 9-3 | Good to firm | Celestial Key (USA) | Jun 15, | 1995 |

| | | | | | | | |
|---|---|---|---|---|---|---|---|
| 7f | 1m 24.13 | 2 | 8-13 | Good to firm | Imperial President | Jly 20, | 1996 |
| 7f 64y (rnd) | 1m 26.13 | 4 | 9-12 | Good to firm | Green Perfume (USA) | Jly 19, | 1996 |
| 7f 64y (rnd) | 1m 28.81 | 2 | 8-10 | Fast | Duty Time | Aug 14, | 1993 |
| 1m | 1m 35.76 | 4 | 9-0 | Fast | Emperor Jones (USA) | May 13, | 1994 |
| 1m | 1m 38.96 | 2 | 8-10 | Good to firm | King Sound | Spt 20, | 1996 |
| 1m 7y (rnd) | 1m 34.91 | 3 | 8-9 | Fast | Philidor | May 16, | 1992 |
| 1m 7y (rnd) | 1m 37.29 | 2 | 8-11 | Firm | Master Willie | Oct 1 , | 1979 |
| 1m 1f | 1m 49.65 | 3 | 8-0 | Good to firm | Holtye (IRE) | May 21, | 1995 |
| 1m 2f 6y | 2m 1.29 | 3 | 8-7 | Fast | Wall Street (USA) | Jly 10, | 1996 |
| 1m 3f 5y | 2m 17.51 | 4 | 9-0 | Fast | Hateel | May 19, | 1990 |
| 1m 4f 5y | 2m 29.2 | 4 | 8-9 | Hard | Vidi Vici | Jun 21, | 1951 |
| 1m 5f 61y | 2m 44.9 | 5 | 10-0 | Good to firm | Mystic Hill | Jly 20, | 1996 |
| 2m | 3m 25.42 | 8 | 9-12 | Good to firm | Moonlight Quest | Jly 19, | 1996 |

## NEWCASTLE

| Distance | Time | Age | Weight | Going | Horse | Date | |
|---|---|---|---|---|---|---|---|
| 5f | 58.0 secs | 4 | 9-2 | Fast | Princess Oberon (IRE) | Jly 23, | 1994 |
| 5f | 59.2 secs | 2 | 8-2 | Good | Dunce Cap | Aug 6 , | 1962 |
| 6f | 1m 11.21 | 3 | 9-2 | Good | Tadwin | Jun 30, | 1990 |
| 6f | 1m 12.67 | 2 | 9-0 | Firm | Sundance Kid (USA) | Oct 3 , | 1989 |
| 7f | 1m 23.53 | 3 | 8-5 | Firm | Beaudelaire (USA) | Jly 23, | 1983 |
| 7f | 1m 25.1 | 2 | 9-0 | Good to firm | Multitone | Aug 4 , | 1996 |
| 1m (rnd) | 1m 38.96 | 3 | 8-12 | Firm | Jacamar | Jly 27, | 1989 |
| 1m (rnd) | 1m 39.97 | 2 | 9-0 | Firm | Laxey Bay | Oct 3 , | 1989 |
| 1m 1f 9y | 1m 52.3 | 3 | 6-3 | Good | Ferniehurst | Jun 23, | 1936 |
| 1m 2f 32y | 2m 6.59 | 3 | 8-11 | Fast | Missionary Ridge | Jun 29, | 1990 |
| 1m 4f 93y | 2m 37.3 | 5 | 8-12 | Firm | Retender (USA) | Jun 25, | 1994 |
| 2m 19y | 3m 22.0 | 4 | 7-12 | Good | Nectar II | Jun 23, | 1937 |

## NEWMARKET

| Distance | Time | Age | Weight | Going | Horse | Date | |
|---|---|---|---|---|---|---|---|
| 5f (Rwly) | 56.81 secs | 6 | 9-2 | Fast | Lochsong | Apr 30, | 1994 |
| 5f (Rwly) | 58.78 secs | 2 | 8-13 | Good | Clifton Charlie | Oct 4 , | 1990 |
| 5f (July) | 58.52 secs | 4 | 9-6 | Fast | Ned's Bonanza | Jly 6 , | 1993 |
| 5f (July) | 58.52 secs | 2 | 8-10 | Good | Seductress | Jly 10, | 1990 |
| 6f (Rwly) | 1m 10.25 | 4 | 9-8 | Good to firm | Lake Coniston (IRE) | Apr 18, | 1995 |
| 6f (Rwly) | 1m 10.14 | 2 | 9-0 | Good | Lycius (USA) | Oct 4 , | 1990 |
| 6f (July) | 1m 9.82 | 4 | 9-6 | Good | Cadeaux Genereux | Jly 13, | 1989 |
| 6f (July) | 1m 10.61 | 2 | 8-10 | Fast | Mujtahid (USA) | Jly 11, | 1990 |
| 7f (Rwly) | 1m 22.24 | 4 | 9-5 | Fast | Perfolia (USA) | Oct 18, | 1991 |
| 7f (Rwly) | 1m 23.45 | 2 | 9-0 | Fast | Dr Devious (IRE) | Oct 18, | 1991 |
| 7f (July) | 1m 23.56 | 3 | 8-12 | Good | Inchinor | Jun 26, | 1993 |
| 7f (July) | 1m 24.46 | 2 | 8-11 | Good to firm | Ruznama (USA) | Aug 25, | 1995 |
| 1m (Rwly) | 1m 35.08 | 3 | 9-0 | Fast | Mister Baileys | Apr 30, | 1994 |
| 1m (Rwly) | 1m 36.74 | 2 | 9-0 | Fast | Bold Pursuit (IRE) | Oct 18, | 1991 |
| 1m (July) | 1m 36.8 | 4 | 9-7 | Hard | Pink Flower | Jun 6 , | 1944 |
| 1m (July) | 1m 39.01 | 2 | 8-11 | Good to firm | Traceability | Aug 25, | 1995 |
| 1m 1f (Rwly) | 1m 47.45 | 3 | 8-3 | Firm | Sin Timon | Oct 1 , | 1977 |
| 1m 2f (Rwly) | 2m 1.04 | 3 | 8-10 | Good | Palace Music (USA) | Oct 20, | 1984 |
| 1m 2f (Rwly) | 2m 4.65 | 2 | 9-4 | Good | Highland Chieftain | Nov 2 , | 1985 |
| 1m 2f (July) | 2m 2.31 | 4 | 9-1 | Fast | Vallance | Aug 1 , | 1992 |
| 1m 4f (Rwly) | 2m 27.67 | 3 | 8-5 | Fast | Kiveton Kabooz | Oct 17, | 1991 |
| 1m 4f (July) | 2m 26.7 | 3 | 8-1 | Fast | Desert Team (USA) | Jly 6 , | 1993 |
| 1m 6f (Rwly) | 2m 54.34 | 5 | 8-6 | Fast | Tudor Island | Spt 30, | 1994 |
| 1m 6f 175y (J) | 3m 6.07 | 3 | 8-10 | Fast | Spring to Action | Jly 8 , | 1993 |
| 2m (Rwly) | 3m 21.91 | 4 | 9-0 | Good to firm | Celeric | Oct 5 , | 1996 |
| 2m 24y (July) | 3m 24.32 | 5 | 10-0 | Fast | Jack Button | Aug 5 , | 1994 |

## NOTTINGHAM

| Distance | Time | Age | Weight | Going | Horse | Date | |
|---|---|---|---|---|---|---|---|
| 5f 13y | 58.4 secs | 6 | 8-8 | Good | Minstrel King | Mar 29, | 1960 |
| 5f 13y | 57.9 secs | 2 | 8-9 | Firm | Hoh Magic | May 13, | 1994 |
| 6f 15y | 1m 10.0 | 4 | 9-2 | Firm | Ajanac | Aug 8 , | 1988 |

| | | | | | | | |
|---|---|---|---|---|---|---|---|
| 6f 15y | 1m 11.4 | 2 | 8-11 | Firm | Jameelapi (USA) | Aug 8 , | 1983 |
| 1m 54y | 1m 39.6 | 4 | 8-2 | Fast | Blake's Treasure | Spt 2 , | 1991 |
| 1m 54y | 1m 40.8 | 2 | 9-0 | Fast | King's Loch (IRE) | Spt 3 , | 1991 |
| 1m 1f 213y | 2m 2.3 | 3 | 8-8 | Firm | Ayaabi | Jly 21, | 1984 |
| 1m 1f 213y | 2m 5.6 | 2 | 9-0 | Firm | Al Salite | Oct 28, | 1985 |
| 1m 6f 15y | 2m 57.8 | 3 | 8-10 | Firm | Buster Jo | Oct 1 , | 1985 |
| 2m 9y | 3m 24.0 | 5 | 7-7 | Firm | Fet | Oct 5 , | 1936 |

# PONTEFRACT

| Distance | Time | Age | Weight | Going | Horse | Date | |
|---|---|---|---|---|---|---|---|
| 5f | 1m 1.1 | 5 | 7-7 | Hard | Regal Bingo | Spt 29, | 1971 |
| 5f | 1m 1.4 | 2 | 8-9 | Fast | Breakaway | Aug 6 , | 1987 |
| 6f | 1m 12.6 | 3 | 7-13 | Firm | Merry One | Aug 29, | 1970 |
| 6f | 1m 14.0 | 2 | 9-3 | Firm | Fawzi | Spt 6 , | 1983 |
| 1m 4y | 1m 41.4 | 5 | 8-12 | Firm | Nevison's Lad | May 14, | 1965 |
| 1m 4y | 1m 42.8 | 2 | 9-13 | Firm | Star Spray | Spt 6 , | 1983 |
| 1m 2f 6y | 2m 6.2 | 4 | 7-8 | Hard | Happy Hector | Jly 9 , | 1979 |
| 1m 2f 6y | 2m 13.0 | 2 | 9-0 | Good to firm | Warbrook | Oct 2 , | 1995 |
| 1m 4f 8y | 2m 34.3 | 4 | 8-9 | Hard | Ezra | Jun 23, | 1975 |
| 2m 1f 22y | 3m 42.1 | 3 | 9-2 | Firm | Night Eye (USA) | Spt 6 , | 1983 |
| 2m 1f 216y | 3m 51.1 | 3 | 8-8 | Firm | Kudz (USA) | Spt 9 , | 1986 |
| 2m 5f 122y | 4m 47.8 | 4 | 8-4 | Firm | Physical (USA) | May 14, | 1984 |

# REDCAR

| Distance | Time | Age | Weight | Going | Horse | Date | |
|---|---|---|---|---|---|---|---|
| 5f | 56.5 secs | 3 | 9-7 | Firm | Nazela | Aug 10, | 1990 |
| 5f | 56.9 secs | 2 | 9-0 | Firm | Mister Joel | Oct 24, | 1995 |
| 6f | 1m 8.6 | 3 | 9-2 | Fast | Sizzling Saga (IRE) | Jun 21, | 1991 |
| 6f | 1m 9.5 | 2 | 9-7 | Firm | Times of Times | Oct 24, | 1995 |
| 7f | 1m 21.0 | 3 | 9-1 | Firm | Empty Quarter | Oct 3 , | 1995 |
| 7f | 1m 21.9 | 2 | 8-11 | Firm | Nagwa | Spt 27, | 1975 |
| 1m | 1m 33.1 | 3 | 9-5 | Firm | Night Wink (USA) | Oct 24, | 1995 |
| 1m | 1m 36.7 | 2 | 8-8 | Fast | Carbonate | Spt 15, | 1987 |
| 1m 1f | 1m 48.5 | 5 | 8-12 | Firm | Mellottie | Jly 25, | 1990 |
| 1m 1f | 1m 53.8 | 2 | 9-0 | Good | Double Trigger (IRE) | Spt 25, | 1993 |
| 1m 2f | 2m 1.5 | 5 | 9-3 | Firm | Inaad | May 29, | 1989 |
| 1m 3f | 2m 17.0 | 3 | 8-9 | Firm | Photo Call | Aug 7 , | 1990 |
| 1m 5f 135y | 2m 54.6 | 6 | 9-10 | Firm | Brodessa | Jun 20, | 1992 |
| 1m 6f 19y | 2m 59.9 | 3 | 8-6 | Firm | Trainglot | Jly 25, | 1990 |
| 2m 4y | 3m 24.9 | 3 | 9-3 | Fast | Subsonic (IRE) | Oct 8 , | 1991 |
| 2m 3f | 4m 10.2 | 5 | 7-4 | Fast | Seldom In | Aug 9 , | 1991 |

# RIPON

| Distance | Time | Age | Weight | Going | Horse | Date | |
|---|---|---|---|---|---|---|---|
| 5f | 57.6 secs | 5 | 8-10 | Good | Broadstairs Beauty (IRE) | May 21, | 1995 |
| 5f | 57.8 secs | 2 | 8-8 | Firm | Super Rocky | Aug 5 , | 1991 |
| 6f | 1m 9.8 | 5 | 7-0 | Firm | Quoit | Jly 23, | 1966 |
| 6f | 1m 10.9 | 2 | 8-11 | Good | Kahir Almaydan (IRE) | Aug 28, | 1995 |
| 1m | 1m 37.0 | 4 | 7-10 | Firm | Crown Witness | Aug 25, | 1980 |
| 1m | 1m 41.2 | 2 | 7-2 | Good | Roanstreak | Spt 5 , | 1970 |
| 1m 1f | 1m 50.8 | 4 | 8-3 | Firm | Tarda | Aug 5 , | 1991 |
| 1m 2f | 2m 2.7 | 3 | 9-4 | Firm | Swift Sword | Jly 20, | 1991 |
| 1m 4f 60y | 2m 32.2 | 6 | 8-7 | Firm | Cholo | Spt 27, | 1941 |
| 2m | 3m 26.6 | 5 | 9-12 | Fast | Encore Une Fois (IRE) | Aug 30, | 1994 |
| 2m 1f 203y | 3m 51.3 | 3 | 7-8 | Firm | Beechwood Seeker | Spt 1 , | 1981 |

# SALISBURY

| Distance | Time | Age | Weight | Going | Horse | Date | |
|---|---|---|---|---|---|---|---|
| 5f | 59.4 secs | 3 | 8-11 | Firm | Bellsabanging | May 5 , | 1993 |
| 5f | 59.8 secs | 2 | 8-5 | Good to firm | Tarf (USA) | Aug 17, | 1995 |
| 6f | 1m 11.54 | 4 | 8-7 | Fast | Prince Sky | Jun 25, | 1986 |
| 6f | 1m 12.41 | 2 | 9-1 | Fast | Basma (USA) | Spt 6 , | 1991 |

| | | | | | | | |
|---|---|---|---|---|---|---|---|
| 6f 212y | 1m 24.98 | 3 | 9-7 | Firm | High Summer | Spt 5 , | 1996 |
| 6f 212y | 1m 25.97 | 2 | 9-0 | Firm | More Royal (USA) | Jun 29, | 1995 |
| 1m | 1m 38.94 | 5 | 8-10 | Firm | Weaver Bird | Jun 29, | 1995 |
| 1m | 1m 43.86 | 2 | 9-3 | Firm | Carocrest | Spt 1 , | 1983 |
| 1m 1f 209y | 2m 4.46 | 4 | 7-7 | Fast | Kala Nashan | Jun 25, | 1986 |
| 1m 4f | 2m 32.08 | 3 | 8-9 | Good | Chief Contender (IRE) | May 5 , | 1996 |
| 1m 6f | 2m 58.01 | 4 | 10-0 | Fast | Dancing Affair | Aug 16, | 1984 |

# SANDOWN

| Distance | Time | Age | Weight | Going | Horse | Date | |
|---|---|---|---|---|---|---|---|
| 5f 6y | 58.82 secs | 6 | 8-9 | Good to firm | Palacegate Touch | Spt 17, | 1996 |
| 5f 6y | 59.48 secs | 2 | 9-3 | Firm | Times Time | Jly 22, | 1982 |
| 7f 16y | 1m 26.36 | 3 | 9-0 | Firm | Mawsuff | Jun 14, | 1986 |
| 7f 16y | 1m 27.87 | 2 | 8-12 | Good to firm | Red Camellia | Jly 25, | 1996 |
| 1m 14y | 1m 39.08 | 3 | 8-8 | Firm | Linda's Fantasy | Aug 19, | 1983 |
| 1m 14y | 1m 41.14 | 2 | 8-11 | Fast | Reference Point | Spt 23, | 1986 |
| 1m 1f | 1m 54.01 | 3 | 9-7 | Firm | Al Shafa | Jun 15, | 1996 |
| 1m 1f | 1m 57.62 | 2 | 9-0 | Good to firm | Night Watch (USA) | Aug 30, | 1995 |
| 1m 2f 7y | 2m 2.14 | 4 | 8-11 | Firm | Kalaglow | May 31, | 1982 |
| 1m 3f 91y | 2m 21.61 | 4 | 8-3 | Fast | Aylesfield | Jly 7 , | 1984 |
| 1m 6f | 2m 58.85 | 3 | 9-2 | Fast | Sun of Spring | Aug 11, | 1993 |
| 2m 78y | 3m 29.93 | 6 | 9-2 | Firm | Sadeem (USA) | May 29, | 1989 |

# SOUTHWELL

| Distance | Time | Age | Weight | Going | Horse | Date | |
|---|---|---|---|---|---|---|---|
| 5f | 57.7 secs | 3 | 9-6 | Standard | Case Law | Aug 15, | 1990 |
| 5f | 59.0 secs | 2 | 9-0 | Standard | Muzz (IRE) | Dec 16, | 1993 |
| 6f | 1m 13.3 | 3 | 9-2 | Standard | Rambo Express | Dec 18, | 1990 |
| 6f | 1m 13.9 | 2 | 9-0 | Standard | Superstrike | Jly 31, | 1991 |
| 7f | 1m 26.8 | 5 | 8-4 | Standard | Amenable | Dec 13, | 1990 |
| 7f | 1m 27.0 | 2 | 8-4 | Standard | Rejoice (IRE) | Nov 30, | 1990 |
| 1m | 1m 17.0 | 4 | 9-12 | Standard | Bella Parkes | Mar 3 , | 1995 |
| 1m | 1m 38.0 | 2 | 8-9 | Standard | Alpha Rascal | Nov 13, | 1990 |
| 1m 3f | 2m 21.5 | 4 | 9-7 | Standard | Tempering | Dec 5 , | 1990 |
| 1m 4f | 2m 34.1 | 4 | 9-12 | Standard | Fast Chick | Nov 8 , | 1989 |
| 1m 5f | 2m 52.8 | 4 | 9-9 | Standard | Vishnu (USA) | Jan 1 , | 1994 |
| 1m 6f | 3m 1.6 | 3 | 7-7 | Standard | Qualitair Aviator | Dec 1 , | 1989 |
| 2m | 3m 37.8 | 4 | 9-12 | Standard | Megan's Flight | Dec 6 , | 1989 |
| 2m 2f | 4m 5.3 | 4 | 9-1 | Standard | Ceciliano (USA) | Aug 16, | 1990 |

# THIRSK

| Distance | Time | Age | Weight | Going | Horse | Date | |
|---|---|---|---|---|---|---|---|
| 5f | 56.9 secs | 4 | 8-6 | Firm | Singing Star | Aug 3 , | 1990 |
| 5f | 57.4 secs | 2 | 9-1 | Firm | Nifty Fifty (IRE) | Jly 19, | 1991 |
| 6f | 1m 9.4 | 4 | 10-0 | Firm | Tiler (IRE) | Jly 26, | 1996 |
| 6f | 1m 9.2 | 2 | 9-6 | Good to firm | Westcourt Magic | Aug 25, | 1995 |
| 7f | 1m 22.6 | 5 | 6-11 | Firm | Tuanwun | May 29, | 1970 |
| 7f | 1m 24.6 | 2 | 8-12 | Firm | Man of Harlech | Aug 2 , | 1975 |
| 1m | 1m 34.8 | 4 | 8-13 | Firm | Yearsley | May 5 , | 1990 |
| 1m | 1m 38.5 | 2 | 8-9 | Good to firm | Ivan Luis (FR) | Spt 7 , | 1996 |
| 1m 4f | 2m 30.0 | 4 | 8-2 | Firm | Casting Vote | Aug 1 , | 1964 |
| 2m | 3m 22.3 | 3 | 8-11 | Firm | Tomaschek (USA) | Jly 17, | 1981 |

# WARWICK

| Distance | Time | Age | Weight | Going | Horse | Date | |
|---|---|---|---|---|---|---|---|
| 5f | 57.8 secs | 5 | 9-4 | Fast | Another Episode (IRE) | Aug 29, | 1994 |
| 5f | 58.6 secs | 2 | 8-11 | Firm | Olympic Spirit | Jun 10, | 1996 |
| 6f | 1m 11.8 | 4 | 9-5 | Firm | Pride of Kilmallock | Jly 1 , | 1960 |
| 6f | 1m 12.1 | 2 | 7-7 | Firm | Sum Mede | Jly 14, | 1989 |
| 7f | 1m 23.8 | 6 | 7-12 | Hard | Blackshore | May 19, | 1956 |
| 7f | 1m 24.8 | 2 | 9-4 | Firm | Nocino | Jly 28, | 1979 |
| 1m | 1m 36.0 | 3 | 9-0 | Firm | Academic World (USA) | Aug 25, | 1975 |

| | | | | | | | |
|---|---|---|---|---|---|---|---|
| 1m | 1m 37.5 | 2 | 9-3 | Firm | Perfect Stranger | Oct 14, | 1986 |
| 1m 2f 169y | 2m 13.2 | 3 | 8-8 | Firm | Classic Tale | Jly 7 , | 1987 |
| 1m 4f 115y | 2m 37.2 | 5 | 8-12 | Hard | Noirmont Buoy | Jun 19, | 1967 |
| 1m 6f 194y | 3m 8.9 | 4 | 9-1 | Firm | Chucklestone | Jly 7 , | 1987 |
| 2m 20y | 3m 25.8 | 4 | 9-7 | Fast | Sanamar (disq) | Aug 29, | 1988 |
| 2m 2f 214y | 4m 3.9 | 5 | 9-10 | Fast | Fitzpatrick | Aug 27, | 1984 |

# WINDSOR

| Distance | Time | Age | Weight | Going | Horse | Date | |
|---|---|---|---|---|---|---|---|
| 5f 10y | 59.2 secs | 3 | 9-7 | Fast | La Tuerta | Jly 15, | 1985 |
| 5f 10y | 58.9 secs | 2 | 9-0 | Firm | Strictly Private | Jly 22, | 1974 |
| 5f 217y | 1m 10.1 | 3 | 8-4 | Firm | Sweet Relief | Spt 11, | 1978 |
| 5f 217y | 69.0 secs | 2 | 8-7 | Fast | Options Open | Jly 25, | 1994 |
| 1m 67y | 1m 41.5 | 4 | 7-2 | Firm | Blowing Bubbles | Jly 16, | 1984 |
| 1m 2f 7y | 2m 3.0 | 3 | 9-1 | Firm | Moomba Masquerade | May 19, | 1980 |
| 1m 3f 135y | 2m 21.5 | 3 | 9-2 | Firm | Double Florin (USA) | May 19, | 1980 |

# WOLVERHAMPTON

| Distance | Time | Age | Weight | Going | Horse | Date | |
|---|---|---|---|---|---|---|---|
| 5f | 1m 0.5 | 7 | 8-7 | Standard | Sir Tasker | Jan 4 , | 1995 |
| 5f | 1m 2.3 | 2 | 8-10 | Standard | Imperial Garden (IRE) | Aug 31, | 1996 |
| 6f | 1m 13.2 | 7 | 9-8 | Standard | Sea-Deer | Aug 31, | 1996 |
| 7f | 1m 27.3 | 4 | 10-0 | Standard | Rocketeer | Jan 4 , | 1995 |
| 1m | 2m 38.4 | 5 | 8-13 | Standard | Johns Act (USA) | Mar 8 , | 1995 |
| 1m 100y | 1m 48.6 | 3 | 9-0 | Standard | Contrafire (IRE) | Jan 4 , | 1995 |
| 1m 1f 79y | 1m 59.3 | 12 | 9-6 | Standard | Aitch N'Bee | Jan 4 , | 1995 |
| 1m 4f | 2m 38.4 | 3 | 8-2 | Standard | New Inn | Nov 26, | 1994 |
| 1m 6f 166y | 3m 11.3 | 4 | 8-11 | Standard | Noufari (FR) | Jan 4 , | 1995 |
| 2m 46y | 3m 39.3 | 4 | 9-6 | Standard | Secret Serenade | Jan 18, | 1995 |

# YARMOUTH

| Distance | Time | Age | Weight | Going | Horse | Date | |
|---|---|---|---|---|---|---|---|
| 5f 43y | 1m 0.2 | 3 | 8-11 | Fast | Charm Bird | Spt 15, | 1988 |
| 5f 43y | 1m 0.9 | 2 | 8-8 | Firm | Aberbevine | Jun 14, | 1967 |
| 6f 3y | 1m 10.4 | 4 | 8-4 | Good | Denikin | Jly 4 , | 1951 |
| 6f 3y | 1m 10.4 | 2 | 9-0 | Fast | Lanchester | Aug 15, | 1988 |
| 7f 3y | 1m 22.2 | 3 | 8-7 | Fast | Cielamour (USA) | Spt 15, | 1988 |
| 7f 3y | 1m 22.2 | 2 | 9-0 | Fast | Warrshan (USA) | Spt 14, | 1988 |
| 1m 3y | 1m 34.6 | 3 | 8-11 | Firm | Bonne Etoile | Jun 27, | 1995 |
| 1m 3y | 1m 34.4 | 2 | 8-11 | Fast | Alderney | Spt 14, | 1988 |
| 1m 2f 21y | 2m 4.2 | 3 | 8-1 | Firm | On The Foan | Aug 17, | 1983 |
| 1m 3f 101y | 2m 23.0 | 3 | 8-9 | Firm | Rahil (IRE) | Jly 1 , | 1993 |
| 1m 6f 17y | 2m 57.8 | 3 | 8-2 | Fast | Barakat | Jly 24, | 1990 |
| 2m | 3m 29.2 | 3 | 9-7 | Firm | Sedbergh (USA) | Jun 13, | 1996 |
| 2m 2f 51y | 4m 1.1 | 3 | 9-7 | Good to firm | Jiyush | Spt 19, | 1996 |

# YORK

| Distance | Time | Age | Weight | Going | Horse | Date | |
|---|---|---|---|---|---|---|---|
| 5f | 56.16 secs | 3 | 9-3 | Fast | Dayjur (USA) | Aug 23, | 1990 |
| 5f | 57.39 secs | 2 | 7-8 | Firm | Lyric Fantasy (USA) | Aug 20, | 1992 |
| 6f | 1m 8.82 | 4 | 9-4 | Fast | Shalford (IRE) | May 14, | 1992 |
| 6f | 1m 9.59 | 2 | 9-0 | Good | Indiscreet (CAN) | Aug 22, | 1996 |
| 6f 214y | 1m 21.77 | 3 | 8-4 | Good | Ruznama (USA) | Aug 22, | 1996 |
| 6f 214y | 1m 22.98 | 2 | 8-10 | Fast | Options Open | Aug 16, | 1994 |
| 7f 202y | 1m 34.81 | 4 | 8-10 | Good | Concer Un | Aug 22, | 1996 |
| 7f 202y | 1m 37.43 | 2 | 9-0 | Good | Prince of My Heart | Oct 4 , | 1995 |
| 1m 205y | 1m 48.89 | 6 | 8-4 | Fast | No Comebacks | Jun 10, | 1994 |
| 1m 205y | 1m 52.43 | 2 | 8-1 | Firm | Oral Evidence | Oct 6 , | 1988 |
| 1m 2f 85y | 2m 6.18 | 3 | 9-0 | Firm | Erhaab (USA) | May 11, | 1994 |
| 1m 3f 195y | 2m 25.79 | 3 | 9-0 | Fast | Diminuendo (USA) | Aug 16, | 1988 |
| 1m 5f 194y | 2m 52.77 | 4 | 9-0 | Good to firm | Classic Cliche (IRE) | May 16, | 1996 |
| 1m 7f 195y | 3m 18.49 | 3 | 8-0 | Fast | Dam Busters (USA) | Aug 16, | 1988 |

# Group One Races

**1000 GUINEAS**

**1996** Bosra Sham (USA)
**1995** Harayir (USA)
**1994** Las Meninas (IRE)
**1993** Sayyedati
**1992** Hatoof (USA)
**1991** Shadayid (USA)
**1990** Salsabil
**1989** Musical Bliss (USA)
**1988** Ravinella (USA)
**1987** Miesque (USA)

**2000 GUINEAS**

**1996** Mark of Esteem (IRE)
**1995** Pennekamp (USA)
**1994** Mister Baileys
**1993** Zafonic (USA)
**1992** Rodrigo de Triano (USA)
**1991** Mystiko (USA)
**1990** Tirol
**1989** Nashwan (USA)
**1988** Doyoun
**1987** Don't Forget Me

**DERBY**

**1996** Shaamit (IRE)
**1995** Lammtarra (USA)
**1994** Erhaab (USA)
**1993** Commander in Chief
**1992** Dr Devious (IRE)
**1991** Generous (IRE)
**1990** Quest for Fame
**1989** Nashwan (USA)
**1988** Kahyasi
**1987** Reference Point

**OAKS**

**1996** Lady Carla
**1995** Moonshell (IRE)
**1994** Balanchine (USA)
**1993** Intrepidity
**1992** User Friendly
**1991** Jet Ski Lady (USA)
**1990** Salsabil
**1989** Snow Bride (USA) (Aliysa disq)
**1988** Diminuendo (USA)
**1987** Unite

**CORONATION CUP**

**1996** Swain (IRE)
**1995** Sunshack
**1994** Apple Tree (FR)
**1993** Opera House
**1992** Saddlers' Hall (IRE)
**1991** In the Groove
**1990** In the Wings
**1989** Sheriff's Star
**1988** Triptych (USA)
**1987** Triptych (USA)

**ST JAMES'S PALACE STAKES**

**1996** Bijou d'Inde
**1995** Bahri (USA)
**1994** Grand Lodge (USA)
**1993** Kingmambo (USA)
**1992** Brief Truce (USA)
**1991** Marju (IRE)
**1990** Shavian
**1989** Shaadi (USA)
**1988** Persian Heights
**1987** Half a Year (USA)

**CORONATION STAKES**

**1996** Shake the Yoke
**1995** Ridgewood Pearl
**1994** Kissing Cousin (IRE)
**1993** Gold Splash (USA)
**1992** Marling (IRE)
**1991** Kooyonga (IRE)
**1990** Chimes of Freedom (USA)
**1989** Golden Opinion (USA)
**1988** Magic of Life (USA)
**1987** Milligram

**GOLD CUP**

**1996** Classic Cliche (IRE)
**1995** Double Trigger (IRE)
**1994** Arcadian Heights
**1993** Drum Taps (USA)
**1992** Drum Taps (USA)
**1991** Indian Queen
**1990** Ashal
**1989** Sadeem (USA)
**1988** Sadeem (USA) (Royal Gait disq)
**1987** Paean

**CORAL-ECLIPSE STAKES**

**1996** Halling (USA)
**1995** Halling (USA)
**1994** Ezzoud (IRE)
**1993** Opera House
**1992** Kooyonga (IRE)
**1991** Environment Friend
**1990** Elmaamul (USA)
**1989** Nashwan (USA)
**1988** Mtoto
**1987** Mtoto

**JULY CUP**

**1996** Anabaa (USA)
**1995** Lake Coniston (IRE)
**1994** Owington
**1993** Hamas (IRE)
**1992** Mr Brooks
**1991** Polish Patriot (USA)
**1990** Royal Academy (USA)
**1989** Cadeaux Genereux
**1988** Soviet Star (USA)
**1987** Ajdal (USA)

**KING GEORGE VI & QUEEN ELIZABETH DIAMOND STAKES**

**1996** Pentire
**1995** Lammtarra (USA)
**1994** King's Theatre (IRE)
**1993** Opera House
**1992** St Jovite (USA)
**1991** Generous (IRE)
**1990** Belmez (USA)
**1989** Nashwan (USA)
**1988** Mtoto
**1987** Reference Point

**SUSSEX STAKES**

**1996** First Island (IRE)
**1995** Sayyedati
**1994** Distant View (USA)
**1993** Bigstone (IRE)
**1992** Marling (IRE)
**1991** Second Set (IRE)
**1990** Distant Relative
**1989** Zilzal (USA)
**1988** Warning
**1987** Soviet Star (USA)

**JUDDMONTE INTERNATIONAL STAKES**

**1996** Halling (USA)
**1995** Halling (USA)
**1994** Ezzoud (IRE)
**1993** Ezzoud (IRE)
**1992** Rodrigo de Triano (USA)
**1991** Terimon
**1990** In the Groove
**1989** Ile de Chypre
**1988** Shady Heights (Persian Heights disq)
**1987** Triptych (USA)

**ASTON UPTHORPE YORKSHIRE OAKS**

**1996** Key Change (IRE)
**1995** Pure Grain
**1994** Only Royale (IRE)
**1993** Only Royale (IRE)
**1992** User Friendly
**1991** Magnificent Star (USA)
**1990** Hellenic
**1989** Roseate Tern
**1988** Diminuendo (USA)
**1987** Bint Pasha (USA)

**NUNTHORPE STAKES**

**1996** Pivotal
**1995** So Factual (USA)
**1994** Piccolo (Blue Siren disq)
**1993** Lochsong
**1992** Lyric Fantasy (IRE)
**1991** Sheikh Albadou
**1990** Dayjur (USA)
**1989** Cadeaux Genereux
**1988** Handsome Sailor
**1987** Ajdal (USA)

**HAYDOCK PARK SPRINT CUP**

**1996** Iktamal (USA)
**1995** Cherokee Rose (IRE)
**1994** Lavinia Fontana (IRE)
**1993** Wolfhound (USA)
**1992** Sheikh Albadou
**1991** Polar Falcon (USA)
**1990** Dayjur (USA)
**1989** Danehill (USA)
**1988** Dowsing (USA)
**1987** Ajdal (USA)

**QUEEN ELIZABETH II STAKES**

**1996** Mark of Esteem (IRE)
**1995** Bahri (USA)
**1994** Maroof (USA)
**1993** Bigstone (IRE)
**1992** Lahib (USA)
**1991** Selkirk (USA)
**1990** Markofdistinction
**1989** Zilzal (USA)
**1988** Warning
**1987** Milligram

**PERTEMPS ST LEGER**

**1996** Shantou (USA)
**1995** Classic Cliche (IRE)
**1994** Moonax (IRE)
**1993** Bob's Return (IRE)
**1992** User Friendly
**1991** Toulon
**1990** Snurge
**1989** Michelozzo (USA)
**1988** Minster Son
**1987** Reference Point

**DUBAI CHAMPION STAKES**

**1996** Bosra Sham (USA)
**1995** Spectrum (IRE)
**1994** Dernier Empereur (USA)
**1993** Hatoof (USA)
**1992** Rodrigo de Triano (USA)
**1991** Tel Quel (FR)
**1990** In the Groove
**1989** Legal Case
**1988** Indian Skimmer (USA)
**1987** Triptych (USA)

**LOCKINGE**

**1996** Soviet Line (IRE)
**1995** Soviet Line (IRE)
**1994** Emperor Jones (USA)
**1993** Swing Low
**1992** Selkirk (USA)
**1991** Polar Falcon (USA)
**1990** Safawan
**1989** Most Welcome
**1988** Broken Hearted
**1987** Then Again

# Group Two Races

**DANTE**

**1996** Glory of Dancer
**1995** Classic Cliche (IRE)
**1994** Erhaab (USA)
**1993** Tenby
**1992** Alnasr Alwasheek
**1991** Environment Friend
**1990** Sanglamore (USA)
**1989** Torjoun (USA)
**1988** Red Glow
**1987** Reference Point

**QUEEN ANNE**

**1996** Charnwood Forest (IRE)
**1995** Nicolotte
**1994** Barathea (IRE)
**1993** Alflora (IRE)
**1992** Lahib (USA)
**1991** Sikeston (USA)
**1990** Markofdistinction
**1989** Warning
**1988** Waajib
**1987** Then Again

**YORKSHIRE CUP**

**1996** Classic Cliche (IRE)
**1995** Moonax (IRE)
**1994** Key to My Heart (IRE)
**1993** Assessor (IRE)
**1992** Rock Hopper
**1991** Arzanni
**1990** Braashee
**1989** Mountain Kingdom (USA)
**1988** Moon Madness
**1987** Verd-Antique

**PRINCE OF WALES'S**

**1996** First Island (IRE)
**1995** Muhtarram (USA)
**1994** Muhtarram (USA)
**1993** Placerville (USA)
**1992** Perpendicular
**1991** Stagecraft
**1990** Batshoof
**1989** Two Timing (USA)
**1988** Mtoto
**1987** Mtoto

**SANDOWN MILE**

**1996** Gabr
**1995** Missed Flight
**1994** Penny Drops
**1993** Alhijaz
**1992** Rudimentary (USA)
**1991** In the Groove
**1990** Markofdistinction
**1989** Reprimand
**1988** Soviet Star (USA)
**1987** Vertige (USA)

**RIBBLESDALE**

**1996** Tulipa (USA)
**1995** Phantom Gold
**1994** Bolas
**1993** Thawakib (IRE)
**1992** Armarama
**1991** Third Watch
**1990** Hellenic
**1989** Alydaress (USA)
**1988** Miss Boniface
**1987** Queen Midas

**KING'S STAND**

**1996** Pivotal
**1995** Piccolo
**1994** Lochsong
**1993** Elbio
**1992** Sheikh Albadou
**1991** Elbio
**1990** Dayjur (USA)
**1989** Indian Ridge
**1988** Chilibang
**1987** Bluebird (USA)

**PRINCESS OF WALES**

**1996** Posidonas
**1995** Beauchamp Hero
**1994** Wagon Master (FR)
**1993** Desert Team (USA)
**1992** Saddlers' Hall (IRE)
**1991** Rock Hopper
**1990** Sapience
**1989** Carroll House
**1988** Unfuwain (USA)
**1987** Celestial Storm (USA)

**JOCKEY CLUB STAKES**

**1996** Riyadian
**1995** Only Royale (IRE)
**1994** Silver Wisp (USA)
**1993** Zinaad
**1992** Sapience
**1991** Rock Hopper
**1990** Roseate Tern
**1989** Unfuwain (USA)
**1988** Almaarad
**1987** Phardante (FR)

**HARDWICKE**

**1996** Oscar Schindler (IRE)
**1995** Beauchamp Hero
**1994** Bobzao (IRE)
**1993** Jeune
**1992** Rock Hopper
**1991** Rock Hopper
**1990** Assatis (USA)
**1989** Assatis (USA)
**1988** Almaarad
**1987** Orban (USA)

**KING EDWARD VII**

**1996** Amfortas (IRE)
**1995** Pentire
**1994** Foyer
**1993** Beneficial
**1992** Beyton (USA)
**1991** Saddlers' Hall
**1990** Private Tender
**1989** Cacoethes (USA)
**1988** Sheriff's Star
**1987** Love the Groom (USA)

**GOODWOOD CUP**

**1996** Grey Shot
**1995** Double Trigger (IRE)
**1994** Tioman Island
**1993** Sonus (IRE)
**1992** Further Flight
**1991** Further Flight
**1990** Lucky Moon
**1989** Mazzacano
**1988** Sadeem (USA)
**1987** Sergeyevich

NASSAU

**1996** Last Second (IRE)
**1995** Caramba
**1994** Hawajiss
**1993** Lyphard's Delta (USA)
**1992** Ruby Tiger
**1991** Ruby Tiger
**1990** Kartajana
**1989** Mamaluna (USA)
**1988** Ela Romara
**1987** Nom de Plume (USA)

CHALLENGE STAKES

**1996** Charnwood Forest (IRE)
**1995** Harayir (USA)
**1994** Zieten (USA)
**1993** Catrail (USA)
**1992** Selkirk (USA)
**1991** Mystiko (USA)
**1990** Sally Rous
**1989** Distant Relative
**1988** Salse (USA)
**1987** Asteroid Field (USA)

CELEBRATION MILE STAKES

**1996** Mark of Esteem (IRE)
**1995** Harayir (USA)
**1994** Mehthaaf (USA)
**1993** Swing Low
**1992** Selkirk (USA)
**1991** Bold Russian
**1990** Shavian
**1989** Distant Relative
**1988** Prince Rupert (FR)
**1987** Milligram

SUN CHARIOT

**1996** Last Second (IRE)
**1995** Warning Shadows (IRE)
**1994** La Confederation
**1993** Talented
**1992** Red Slippers (USA)
**1991** Ristna
**1990** Kartajana
**1989** Braiswick
**1988** Indian Skimmer (USA)
**1987** Infamy

GREAT VOLTIGEUR

**1996** Dushyantor (USA)
**1995** Pentire
**1994** Sacrament
**1993** Bob's Return (IRE)
**1992** Bonny Scot (IRE)
**1991** Corrupt (USA)
**1990** Belmez (USA)
**1989** Zalazl (USA)
**1988** Sheriff's Star
**1987** Reference Point

FALMOUTH

**1996** Sensation
**1995** Caramba
**1994** Lemon Souffle
**1993** Niche
**1992** Gussy Marlowe
**1991** Only Yours
**1990** Chimes of Freedom (USA)
**1989** Magic Gleam (USA)
**1988** Inchmurrin
**1987** Sonic Lady (USA)

DIADEM

**1996** Diffident (FR)
**1995** Cool Jazz
**1994** Lake Coniston (IRE)
**1993** Catrail (USA)
**1992** Wolfhound (USA)
**1991** Shalford (IRE)
**1990** Ron's Victory (USA)
**1989** Chummy's Favourite
**1988** Cadeaux Genereux
**1987** Dowsing (USA)

GEOFFREY FREER

**1996** Phantom Gold
**1995** Presenting
**1994** Red Route
**1993** Azzilfi
**1992** Shambo
**1991** Drum Taps (USA)
**1990** Charmer
**1989** Ibn Bey
**1988** Top Class
**1987** Moon Madness

**TEMPLE STAKES**

**1996** Mind Games
**1995** Mind Games
**1994** Lochsong
**1993** Paris House
**1992** Snaadee (USA)
**1991** Elbio
**1990** Dayjur (USA)
**1989** Dancing Dissident (USA)
**1988** Handsome Sailor
**1987** Treasure Kay

# Top Two-Year-Old Races

**MIDDLE PARK STAKES**

**1996** Bahamian Bounty
**1995** Royal Applause
**1994** Fard (IRE)
**1993** First Trump
**1992** Zieten (USA)
**1991** Rodrigo de Triano (USA)
**1990** Lycius (USA)
**1989** Balla Cove
**1988** Mon Tresor
**1987** Gallic League

**FILLIES' MILE**

**1996** Reams of Verse (USA)
**1995** Bosra Sham (USA)
**1994** Aqaarid (USA)
**1993** Fairy Heights (IRE)
**1992** Ivanka (IRE)
**1991** Culture Vulture (USA)
**1990** Shamshir
**1989** Silk Slippers (USA)
**1988** Tessla (USA)
**1987** Diminuendo (USA)

**CHEVELEY PARK STAKES**

**1996** Pas De Reponse (USA)
**1995** Blue Duster (USA)
**1994** Gay Gallanta (USA)
**1993** Prophecy (IRE)
**1992** Sayyedati
**1991** Marling (IRE)
**1990** Capricciosa (IRE)
**1989** Dead Certain
**1988** Pass the Peace
**1987** Ravinella (USA)

**DEWHURST STAKES**

**1996** In Command (IRE)
**1995** Alhaarth (IRE)
**1994** Pennekamp (USA)
**1993** Grand Lodge (USA)
**1992** Zafonic (USA)
**1991** Dr Devious (IRE)
**1990** Generous (IRE)
**1989** Dashing Blade
**1988** Prince of Dance/Scenic
**1987** Abandoned

**RACING POST TROPHY**

**1996** Medaaly
**1995** Beauchamp King
**1994** Celtic Swing
**1993** King's Theatre (IRE)
**1992** Armiger
**1991** Seattle Rhyme (USA)
**1990** Peter Davies (USA)
**1989** Be My Chief (USA)
**1988** Al Hareb (USA)
**1987** Emmson

**COVENTRY STAKES**

**1996** Verglas (IRE)
**1995** Royal Applause
**1994** Sri Pekan (USA)
**1993** Stonehatch (USA)
**1992** Petardia
**1991** Dilum (USA)
**1990** Mac's Imp (USA)
**1989** Rock City
**1988** High Estate
**1987** Always Fair (USA)

**GIMCRACK**

**1996** Abou Zouz (USA)
**1995** Royal Applause
**1994** Chilly Billy
**1993** Turtle Island (IRE)
**1992** Splendent (USA)
**1991** River Falls
**1990** Mujtahid (USA)
**1989** Rock City
**1988** Sharp N' Early
**1987** Reprimand

**QUEEN MARY**

**1996** Dance Parade (USA)
**1995** Blue Duster (USA)
**1994** Gay Gallanta (USA)
**1993** Risky
**1992** Lyric Fantasy (IRE)
**1991** Marling (IRE)
**1990** On Tiptoes
**1989** Dead Certain
**1988** Gloriella
**1987** Princess Athena

**CHERRY HINTON**

**1996** Dazzle
**1995** Applaud (USA)
**1994** Red Carnival (USA)
**1993** Lemon Souffle
**1992** Sayyedati
**1991** Musicale (USA)
**1990** Chicarica (USA)
**1989** Chimes of Freedom (USA)
**1988** Kerrera
**1987** Diminuendo (USA)

**ROYAL LODGE**

**1996** Benny The Dip (USA)
**1995** Mons
**1994** Eltish (USA)
**1993** Mister Baileys
**1992** Desert Secret (IRE)
**1991** Made of Gold (USA)
**1990** Mujaazif (USA)
**1989** Digression (USA)
**1988** High Estate
**1987** Sanquirico (USA)

**SOLARIO**

**1996** Brave Act
**1995** Alhaarth (IRE)
**1994** Lovely Millie (IRE)
**1993** Island Magic
**1992** White Crown (USA)
**1991** Chicmond (IRE)
**1990** Radwell
**1989** Be My Chief (USA)
**1988** High Estate
**1987** Sanquirico (USA)

**NORFOLK**

**1996** Tipsy Creek (USA)
**1995** Lucky Lionel (USA)
**1994** Mind Games
**1993** Turtle Island (IRE)
**1992** Niche
**1991** Magic Ring (IRE)
**1990** Line Engaged (USA)
**1989** Petillante
**1988** Superpower
**1987** Colmore Row

**CHAMPAGNE VINTAGE**

**1996** Putra (USA)
**1995** Alhaarth (IRE)
**1994** Eltish (USA)
**1993** Mister Baileys
**1992** Maroof (USA)
**1991** Dr Devious (IRE)
**1990** Mukaddamah (USA)
**1989** Be My Chief (USA)
**1988** High Estate
**1987** Undercut (USA)

**LOWTHER**

**1996** Bianca Nera
**1995** Dance Sequence (USA)
**1994** Harayir (USA)
**1993** Velvet Moon (IRE)
**1992** Niche
**1991** Culture Vulture (USA)
**1990** Only Yours
**1989** Dead Certain
**1988** Miss Demure
**1987** Ela Romara

**RICHMOND**

**1996** Easycall
**1995** Polaris Flight (USA)
**1994** Sri Pekan (USA)
**1993** First Trump
**1992** Son Pardo
**1991** Dilum (USA)
**1990** Mac's Imp (USA)
**1989** Contract Law (USA)
**1988** Heart of Arabia
**1987** Warning

**MILL REEF**

**1996** Indian Rocket
**1995** Kahir Almaydan (IRE)
**1994** Princely Hush (IRE)
**1993** Polish Laughter (USA)
**1992** Forest Wind (USA)
**1991** Showbrook (IRE)
**1990** Time Gentlemen
**1989** Welney
**1988** Russian Bond (USA)
**1987** Magic of Life (USA)

**FLYING CHILDERS**

**1996** Easycall
**1995** Cayman Kai (IRE)
**1994** Raah Algharb (USA)
**1993** Imperial Bailiwick (IRE)
**1992** Poker Chip
**1991** Paris House
**1990** Distinctly North (USA)
**1989** ABANDONED
**1988** Shuttlecock Corner (USA)
**1987** Gallic League

**CHAMPAGNE STAKES**

**1996** Bahhare (USA)
**1995** Alhaarth (IRE)
**1994** Sri Pekan
**1993** Unblest
**1992** Petardia
**1991** Rodrigo de Triano (USA)
**1990** Bog Trotter (USA)
**1989** ABANDONED
**1988** Prince of Dance
**1987** Warning

# Major Handicaps

**LINCOLN**

**1996** Stone Ridge (IRE)
**1995** Roving Minstrel
**1994** Our Rita
**1993** High Premium
**1992** High Low (USA)
**1991** Amenable
**1990** Evichstar
**1989** Fact Finder
**1988** Cuvee Charlie
**1987** Star of a Gunner

**AYR GOLD CUP**

**1996** Coastal Bluff
**1995** Royale Figurine (IRE)
**1994** Daring Destiny
**1993** Hard to Figure
**1992** Lochsong
**1991** Sarcita
**1990** Final Shot
**1989** Joveworth
**1988** So Careful
**1987** Not So Silly

**EBOR**

**1996** Clerkenwell (USA)
**1995** Sanmartino (IRE)
**1994** Hasten to Add (USA)
**1993** Sarawat
**1992** Quick Ransom
**1991** Deposki
**1990** Further Flight
**1989** Sapience
**1988** Kneller
**1987** Daarkom

**CAMBRIDGESHIRE**

**1996** Clifton Fox
**1995** Cap Juluca (IRE)
**1994** Halling (USA)
**1993** Penny Drops
**1992** Rambo's Hall
**1991** Mellottie
**1990** Risen Moon
**1989** Rambo's Hall
**1988** Quinlan Terry
**1987** Balthus (USA)

**CESAREWITCH**

**1996** Inchcailloch (IRE)
**1995** Old Red (IRE)
**1994** Captain's Guest
**1993** Aahsaylad
**1992** Vintage Crop
**1991** Go South
**1990** Trainglot
**1989** Double Dutch
**1988** Nomadic Way (USA)
**1987** Private Audition

**WOKINGHAM**

**1996** Emerging Market
**1995** Astrac (IRE)
**1994** Venture Capitalist
**1993** Nagida
**1992** Red Rosein
**1991** Amigo Menor
**1990** Knight of Mercy
**1989** Mac's Fighter
**1988** Powder Blue
**1987** Bel Byou

**HONG KONG TROPHY**

**1996** Sheer Danzig (IRE)
**1995** Yoush (IRE)
**1994** Knowth (IRE)
**1993** Smarginato (IRE)
**1992** Fire Top
**1991** You Know the Rules
**1990** Bold Fox
**1989** Unknown Quantity
**1988** Rambo Dancer (CAN)
**1987** Loud Appeal

**STEWARDS' CUP**

**1996** Coastal Bluff
**1995** Shikari's Son
**1994** For the Present
**1993** King's Signet (USA)
**1992** Lochsong
**1991** Notley
**1990** Knight of Mercy
**1989** Very Adjacent
**1988** Rotherfield Greys
**1987** Madraco

**ROYAL HUNT CUP**

**1996** Yeast
**1995** Realities (USA)
**1994** Face North (IRE)
**1993** Imperial Ballet (IRE)
**1992** Colour Sergeant
**1991** Eurolink the Lad
**1990** Pontenuovo
**1989** True Panache (USA)
**1988** Governorship
**1987** Vague Shot

**NORTHUMBERLAND PLATE**

**1996** Celeric
**1995** Bold Gait
**1994** Quick Ransom
**1993** Highflying
**1992** Witness Box (USA)
**1991** Tamarpour (USA)
**1990** Al Maheb (USA)
**1989** Orpheus (USA)
**1988** Stavordale
**1987** Treasure Hunter

**SCHWEPPES GOLDEN MILE**

**1996** Moscow Mist (IRE)
**1995** Khayrapour (IRE)
**1994** Fraam
**1993** Philidor
**1992** Little Bean
**1991** Sky Cloud
**1990** March Bird
**1989** Safawan
**1988** Strike Force
**1987** Waajib

**MAGNET CUP**

**1996** Wilcuma
**1995** Naked Welcome
**1994** Cezanne
**1993** Baron Ferdinand
**1992** Mr Confusion (IRE)
**1991** Halkopous
**1990** Eradicate
**1989** Icona (USA)
**1988** Bashful Boy
**1987** Brave Dancer / Wolsey

# WINNING OWNERS

**(Turf only from 21st March to 11th November)**

| | Owner | Races Won | Stakes £ |
|---|---|---|---|
| 1. | Godolphin | 38 | 1,864,160 |
| 2. | Sheikh Mohammed | 84 | 1,387,092 |
| 3. | Mr Hamdan Al Maktoum | 104 | 1,181,067 |
| 4. | Mr K. Abdulla | 82 | 1,089,712 |
| 5. | Maktoum Al Maktoum | 45 | 801,517 |
| 6. | Mr Wafic Said | 17 | 787,637 |
| 7. | Mollers Racing | 5 | 606,405 |
| 8. | Mr Khalifa Dasmal | 1 | 575,832 |
| 9. | Cheveley Park Stud | 26 | 458,834 |
| 10. | H R H Prince Fahd Salman | 33 | 368,706 |
| 11. | Mr R. E. Sangster | 29 | 333,644 |
| 12. | Mr J. S. Morrison | 1 | 243,977 |
| 13. | Mr P. D. Savill | 19 | 223,915 |
| 14. | Sheikh Ahmed Al Maktoum | 32 | 220,724 |
| 15. | Lucayan Stud | 10 | 207,340 |
| 16. | Mr J. C. Smith | 15 | 171,013 |
| 17. | Mr R. W. Huggins | 10 | 158,904 |
| 18. | Mr M. Arbib | 6 | 157,451 |
| 19. | The Queen | 13 | 154,627 |
| 20. | Mr M. Tabor | 12 | 145,328 |
| 21. | Mr Faisal Salman | 4 | 140,238 |
| 22. | Mr Abdullah Ali | 10 | 135,427 |
| 23. | Mr B. Haggas | 12 | 133,894 |
| 24. | Mr Christopher Spence | 5 | 125,840 |
| 25. | Mr Oliver Lehane | 2 | 122,590 |
| 26. | Mr L. Fust | 6 | 121,901 |
| 27. | Mr S. Brunswick | 1 | 120,726 |
| 28. | Mr B. Schmidt-Bodner | 4 | 115,322 |
| 29. | P and S Partnership | 4 | 112,175 |
| 30. | Mrs D. E. Sharp | 3 | 108,978 |
| 31. | Mr B. H. Voak | 4 | 108,962 |
| 32. | Gen Horse Advertizing SRL | 1 | 107,195 |
| 33. | Mr Guy Reed | 19 | 104,181 |
| 34. | Sultan Al Kabeer | 12 | 103,966 |
| 35. | Lady Clague | 1 | 101,823 |
| 36. | Lord Weinstock/Exors late S Weinstock | 5 | 100,446 |
| 37. | Camelot Racing | 10 | 97,481 |
| 38. | Mr Landon Knight | 3 | 97,320 |
| 39. | Lady Rothschild | 6 | 96,753 |
| 40. | Mrs P. W. Harris | 9 | 96,403 |
| 41. | Easycall Partnership | 5 | 92,802 |
| 42. | Mr E. Penser | 4 | 91,052 |
| 43. | H H Aga Khan | 1 | 90,949 |
| 44. | Mrs A. Head | 1 | 90,588 |
| 45. | Lady Oppenheimer | 5 | 89,341 |
| 46. | Lord Swaythling | 4 | 84,715 |
| 47. | J B R Leisure Ltd | 3 | 82,067 |
| 48. | Mr David Abell | 7 | 81,235 |
| 49. | Mr K. M. Al-Mudhaf | 4 | 80,075 |
| 50. | Mr R. Barnett | 4 | 78,549 |

# WINNING TRAINERS

**(Turf only from 21st March to 11th November)**

| | Trainer | Races Won | Stakes £ |
|---|---|---|---|
| 1. | S bin Suroor | 48 | 1,968,434 |
| 2. | H. R. A. Cecil | 113 | 1,942,474 |
| 3. | M. R. Stoute | 73 | 1,103,935 |
| 4. | J. H. M. Gosden | 73 | 1,085,853 |
| 5. | R. Hannon | 107 | 995,358 |
| 6. | M. Johnston | 92 | 994,246 |
| 7. | J. L. Dunlop | 88 | 990,223 |
| 8. | P. F. I. Cole | 74 | 902,233 |
| 9. | G. Wragg | 25 | 863,797 |
| 10. | W. J. Haggas | 26 | 848,731 |
| 11. | B. W. Hills | 84 | 844,268 |
| 12. | D. R. Loder | 52 | 728,513 |
| 13. | L. M. Cumani | 62 | 692,653 |
| 14. | J. Berry | 96 | 647,927 |
| 15. | P. W. Chapple-Hyam | 51 | 604,217 |
| 16. | Sir Mark Prescott | 51 | 561,784 |
| 17. | C. E. Brittain | 25 | 456,334 |
| 18. | I. A. Balding | 33 | 450,817 |
| 19. | Mrs J. R. Ramsden | 51 | 379,416 |
| 20. | M. R. Channon | 56 | 356,213 |
| 21. | B. Hanbury | 29 | 344,962 |
| 22. | B. J. Meehan | 41 | 336,608 |
| 23. | Miss Gay Kelleway | 35 | 332,330 |
| 24. | J. L. Eyre | 51 | 315,542 |
| 25. | E. A. L. Dunlop | 22 | 313,660 |
| 26. | M. H. Tompkins | 23 | 311,869 |
| 27. | R. Charlton | 31 | 303,404 |
| 28. | D. Morley | 21 | 297,014 |
| 29. | R. Akehurst | 30 | 289,981 |
| 30. | Mrs M. Reveley | 45 | 270,116 |
| 31. | T. D. Barron | 21 | 250,986 |
| 32. | M. Bell | 40 | 250,665 |
| 33. | Lord Huntingdon | 26 | 238,387 |
| 34. | J. R. Fanshawe | 22 | 236,074 |
| 35. | R. W. Armstrong | 12 | 235,905 |
| 36. | Lady Herries | 16 | 235,781 |
| 37. | P. J. Makin | 27 | 235,161 |
| 38. | P. W. Harris | 22 | 228,329 |
| 39. | T. D. Easterby | 29 | 216,313 |
| 40. | P. D. Evans | 35 | 203,597 |
| 41. | R. Hollinshead | 32 | 200,928 |
| 42. | A. P. Jarvis | 16 | 199,131 |
| 43. | A. Fabre,France | 2 | 198,831 |
| 44. | Mme C. Head,France | 3 | 194,125 |
| 45. | H. Candy | 20 | 190,880 |
| 46. | D. Nicholls | 19 | 187,823 |
| 47. | M. W. Easterby | 29 | 182,022 |
| 48. | Mrs J. Cecil | 19 | 180,675 |
| 49. | P. A. Kelleway | 3 | 178,441 |
| 50. | G. Harwood | 19 | 178,096 |

# LEADING FLAT JOCKEYS

(Covering from 21st March to 11th November)

| | Win £ | 1st | 2nd | 3rd | Unpl | Total Mts | Per cent | £1 Level stake |
|---|---|---|---|---|---|---|---|---|
| Pat Eddery | 1,686,092 | 186 | 137 | 97 | 463 | 883 | 21.1 | -100.00 |
| T. Quinn | 972,796 | 149 | 117 | 123 | 491 | 880 | 16.9 | -86.74 |
| K. Fallon | 688,867 | 135 | 140 | 136 | 489 | 900 | 15.0 | -213.58 |
| L. Dettori | 1,900,328 | 114 | 68 | 56 | 298 | 536 | 21.3 | **+15.83** |
| K. Darley | 653,839 | 113 | 120 | 104 | 530 | 867 | 13.0 | -182.32 |
| J. Reid | 821,569 | 112 | 102 | 101 | 490 | 805 | 13.9 | -181.81 |
| J. Weaver | 570,002 | 95 | 92 | 73 | 386 | 646 | 14.7 | -117.87 |
| M. Hills | 1,558,760 | 80 | 54 | 68 | 351 | 553 | 14.5 | -46.60 |
| W. Ryan | 556,655 | 79 | 52 | 43 | 302 | 476 | 16.6 | -53.05 |
| J. Carroll | 325,627 | 73 | 63 | 76 | 496 | 708 | 10.3 | -189.28 |
| Dane O'Neill | 361,177 | 72 | 59 | 43 | 478 | 652 | 11.0 | -105.81 |
| R. Hills | 533,089 | 71 | 61 | 51 | 290 | 473 | 15.0 | -29.74 |
| S. Sanders | 285,905 | 69 | 69 | 56 | 529 | 723 | 9.5 | -237.35 |
| J. Fortune | 332,035 | 68 | 68 | 104 | 433 | 673 | 10.1 | -226.47 |
| R. Cochrane | 454,514 | 63 | 58 | 46 | 316 | 483 | 13.0 | -7.67 |
| T. Sprake | 301,504 | 63 | 63 | 63 | 403 | 592 | 10.6 | -114.99 |
| G. Duffield | 468,985 | 61 | 47 | 57 | 421 | 586 | 10.4 | -235.79 |
| R. Hughes | 303,737 | 61 | 68 | 61 | 360 | 550 | 11.1 | -30.47 |
| G. Carter | 273,909 | 57 | 66 | 63 | 388 | 574 | 9.9 | -129.89 |
| D. Harrison | 374,371 | 56 | 37 | 50 | 375 | 518 | 10.8 | -34.38 |
| F. Lynch | 321,323 | 53 | 50 | 68 | 356 | 527 | 10.1 | -98.23 |
| J. Quinn | 252,774 | 52 | 67 | 66 | 563 | 748 | 7.0 | -265.28 |
| W. Carson | 448,903 | 52 | 54 | 41 | 260 | 407 | 12.8 | -164.72 |
| B. Doyle | 291,919 | 50 | 62 | 72 | 404 | 588 | 8.5 | -119.43 |
| A. Clark | 176,577 | 40 | 37 | 37 | 315 | 429 | 9.3 | -121.26 |
| A. Culhane | 139,275 | 38 | 37 | 29 | 275 | 379 | 10.0 | -18.19 |
| S. Whitworth | 124,772 | 37 | 33 | 29 | 262 | 361 | 10.3 | -136.21 |
| M. Fenton | 176,228 | 37 | 35 | 38 | 341 | 451 | 8.2 | -141.70 |
| S. Drowne | 121,814 | 37 | 39 | 37 | 391 | 504 | 7.3 | -149.28 |
| L. Charnock | 159,477 | 36 | 26 | 31 | 377 | 470 | 7.7 | -53.75 |
| Dean McKeown | 126,370 | 35 | 55 | 58 | 349 | 497 | 7.0 | -267.95 |
| J. F. Egan | 130,880 | 35 | 38 | 55 | 361 | 489 | 7.2 | -186.30 |
| M. Henry | 140,926 | 35 | 46 | 48 | 280 | 409 | 8.6 | -155.71 |
| Paul Eddery | 149,047 | 34 | 41 | 24 | 217 | 316 | 10.8 | -137.71 |
| Martin Dwyer | 137,728 | 32 | 35 | 41 | 229 | 337 | 9.5 | -49.11 |
| P. Robinson | 197,610 | 31 | 28 | 31 | 185 | 275 | 11.3 | **+25.01** |
| O. Urbina | 135,928 | 30 | 28 | 17 | 124 | 199 | 15.1 | -17.87 |
| R. Havlin | 106,331 | 30 | 24 | 26 | 167 | 247 | 12.2 | -39.89 |
| G. Hind | 288,585 | 30 | 44 | 31 | 280 | 385 | 7.8 | -154.21 |
| M. J. Kinane | 784,547 | 29 | 21 | 12 | 104 | 166 | 17.5 | **+15.45** |
| D. R. McCabe | 122,779 | 29 | 27 | 21 | 264 | 341 | 8.5 | -134.22 |
| J. Stack | 123,065 | 27 | 32 | 25 | 217 | 301 | 9.0 | -107.21 |
| M. Roberts | 178,587 | 26 | 32 | 29 | 168 | 255 | 10.2 | -56.73 |
| M. Tebbutt | 129,505 | 26 | 36 | 19 | 241 | 322 | 8.1 | -116.66 |
| W. Woods | 156,481 | 26 | 32 | 30 | 145 | 233 | 11.2 | -83.79 |
| A. McGlone | 82,661 | 22 | 18 | 33 | 251 | 324 | 6.8 | -213.73 |
| C. Rutter | 82,685 | 21 | 23 | 27 | 293 | 364 | 5.8 | -195.80 |
| T. Williams | 75,316 | 21 | 38 | 33 | 306 | 398 | 5.3 | -237.38 |